The New
GROVE®
Dictionary of
OPERA

Volume Two

E-Lom

The New
GROVE®
Dictionary of
OPERA

Edited by

STANLEY SADIE

Managing Editor

CHRISTINA BASHFORD

Volume Two

E-Lom

THE MACMILLAN PRESS LIMITED, LONDON
GROVE'S DICTIONARIES OF MUSIC INC., NEW YORK, NY

The New Grove and *The New Grove Dictionary of Music and Musicians* are registered trademarks in the United States of Macmillan Publishers Limited, London.

Macmillan Publishers Limited, London and its associated companies are the proprietors of the trademarks *Grove's*, *The New Grove*, and *The New Grove Dictionary of Music and Musicians* throughout the world.

The New Grove ® Dictionary of Opera
edited by STANLEY SADIE, in four volumes, 1992

First published 1992 by The Macmillan Press Limited, London. In the United States of America and Canada, The Macmillan Press has appointed Grove's Dictionaries of Music Inc., New York, NY, as sole distributor.

Reprinted with corrections, 1994

Database creation and typesetting by Morton Word Processing Limited, Scarborough, Great Britain

Printed and bound in Hong Kong by China Translation and Printing Services Limited.

British Library Cataloguing in Publication Data

New Grove Dictionary of Opera
  I.Sadie, Stanley
  782.103

ISBN 0-333-48552-1

Library of Congress Cataloging-in-Publication Data

The New Grove dictionary of opera / edited by Stanley Sadie
  p. cm.
  "First published 1992 by the Macmillan Press Limited, London" –
  –T.p. verso
    Includes bibliographical references.
    ISBN 0-935859-92-6: $850.00
    1. Opera – Dictionaries. I Sadie, Stanley
ML102.O6N5 1992   92-36276
782.1'03–dc20   CIP
                                                 MN

ISBN 0-935859-92-6

Contents

General Abbreviations

A	alto, contralto [voice]	bur.	buried
AB	Bachelor of Arts		
ABC	American Broadcasting Company; Australian Broadcasting Commission		
Abt.	Abteilung [section]	c	circa [about]
acc(s).	accompaniment(s); accompanied by	CA	California (USA)
AD	anno Domini	Cambs.	Cambridgeshire (GB)
add, addl	additional	cap.	capacity
add(s), addn(s)	addition(s)	carn.	Carnival
ad lib	ad libitum	cb	contrabass [instrument]
AK	Alaska (USA)	CBC	Canadian Broadcasting Corporation
AL	Alabama (USA)	CBE	Commander of the Order of the British Empire
Alta.	Alberta (Canada)		
AM	Master of Arts	CBS	Columbia Broadcasting System (USA)
a.m.	ante meridiem [before noon]	CBSO	City of Birmingham Symphony Orchestra
Amer.	American	CD	compact disc
AMS	American Musicological Society	cel	celesta
Anh.	Anhang [appendix]	cf	confer [compare]
anon.	anonymous(ly)	CG	Covent Garden, London
appx	appendix	CH	Companion of Honour
AR	Arkansas (USA)	chap.	chapter
arr(s).	arrangement(s); arranged (by/for)	Chin.	Chinese
ASCAP	American Society of Composers, Authors and Publishers	Cie	Compagnie
		cl	clarinet
attrib.	attribution, attributed to	cm	centimetre(s)
Aug	August	cmda	comédie mêlée d'ariettes
aut.	autumn	CNRS	Centre National de la Recherche Scientifique (F)
AZ	Arizona (USA)		
		CO	Colorado (USA)
		Co.	Company; County
		col(s).	column(s)
B	bass [voice]	coll.	collection, collected by
b	bass [instrument]	collab.	collaborator, in collaboration with
b	born	comp.	composer, composed
BA	Bachelor of Arts	conc.	concerto
bap.	baptized	cond.	conductor, conducted by
Bar	baritone [voice]	cont	continuo
bar	baritone [instrument]	contrib(s).	contribution(s)
BBC	British Broadcasting Corporation	Corp.	Corporation
BC	British Columbia (Canada)	CRI	Composers Recordings, Inc. (USA)
BC	before Christ	CSc	Candidate of Historical Sciences
bc	basso continuo	CT	Connecticut (USA)
Bd.	Band [volume]	Ct	countertenor
Berks.	Berkshire (GB)	CUNY	City University of New York
Berwicks.	Berwickshire (GB)	CVO	Commander of the Royal Victorian Order
BFA	Bachelor of Fine Arts	Cz.	Czech
bk	book		
BL	British Library		
BLitt	Bachelor of Letters; Bachelor of Literature		
BM	Bachelor of Music; British Museum	D	Deutsch catalogue [Schubert]
BME, BMEd	Bachelor of Music Education	d	died
BMI	Broadcast Music, Inc. (USA)	d.	denarius, denarii [penny, pence]
BMus	Bachelor of Music	Dan.	Danish
bn	bassoon	db	double bass
Bros.	Brothers	DBE	Dame Commander of the Order of the British Empire
BS, BSc	Bachelor of Science		
Bucks.	Buckinghamshire (GB)	dbn	double bassoon
Bulg.	Bulgarian	DC	District of Columbia (USA)

DE	Delaware (USA)
Dec	December
ded.	dedication, dedicated (to)
Dept	Department
Derbys.	Derbyshire (GB)
DFA	Doctor of Fine Arts
dg	dramma giocoso
dir.	director, directed by
diss.	dissertation
DLitt	Doctor of Letters; Doctor of Literature
DMA	Doctor of Musical Arts
DMus	Doctor of Music
DPhil	Doctor of Philosophy
Dr	Doctor
DSc	Doctor of Science; Doctor of Historical Sciences
E.	east, eastern
EBU	European Broadcasting Union
ed(s).	editor(s); edited (by)
edn(s)	edition(s)
e.g.	exempli gratia [for example]
elec	electric, electronic
EMI	Electrical and Musical Industries
Eng.	English
eng hn	english horn
ENO	English National Opera
ens	ensemble
esp.	especially
etc.	et cetera [and so on]
ex., exx.	example, examples
f	forte
f., ff.	folio, folios
facs.	facsimile
fasc.	fascicle
Feb	February
ff	following pages
ff	fortissimo
fff	fortississimo
fig.	figure [illustration]
FL	Florida (USA)
fl	flute
fl	floruit [he/she flourished]
fp	fortepiano
Fr.	French
frag(s).	fragment(s)
GA	Georgia (USA)
Ger.	German
Gk.	Greek
Glam.	Glamorgan (GB)
glock	glockenspiel
Gloucs.	Gloucestershire (GB)
GmbH	Gesellschaft mit beschränkter Haftung [limited-liability company]
govt.	government
GSM	Guildhall School of Music and Drama, London
gui	guitar
H	Hoboken catalogue [Haydn]
Hants.	Hampshire (GB)
Heb.	Hebrew
Herts.	Hertfordshire (GB)
HI	Hawaii (USA)
HMS	His/Her Majesty's Ship
HMV	His Master's Voice
hn	horn
Hon.	Honorary; Honourable
hpd	harpsichord
HRH	His/Her Royal Highness
Hung.	Hungarian
Hunts.	Huntingdonshire (GB)
Hz	Hertz [cycle(s) per second]
IA	Iowa (USA)
IAML	International Association of Music Libraries
ibid	ibidem [in the same place]
ID	Idaho (USA)
i.e.	id est [that is]
IL	Illinois (USA)
IMS	International Musicological Society
IN	Indiana (USA)
Inc.	Incorporated
inc.	incomplete
incl.	includes, including
inst(s)	instrument(s); instrumental
int	intermezzo
IRCAM	Institut de Recherche et de Coordination Acoustique/Musique (F)
ISAM	Institute for Studies in American Music
ISCM	International Society for Contemporary Music
ISM	Incorporated Society of Musicians (GB)
It.	Italian
Jan	January
Jap.	Japanese
Jb	Jahrbuch [yearbook]
Jg.	Jahrgang [year of publication/volume]
jr	junior
K	Köchel catalogue [Mozart; no. after / is from 6th edn]
kbd	keyboard
KBE	Knight Commander of the Order of the British Empire
KCVO	Knight Commander of the Royal Victorian Order
Kgl	Königlich [royal]
kHz	kilohertz [1000 cycles per second]
km	kilometre(s)
KS	Kansas (USA)
KY	Kentucky (USA)
£	libra, librae [pounds, pounds sterling]
LA	Louisiana (USA)
Lancs.	Lancashire (GB)
Lat.	Latin
Leics.	Leicestershire (GB)
lib(s).	libretto(s)
Lincs.	Lincolnshire (GB)
LittD	Doctor of Letters; Doctor of Literature
LlB	Bachelor of Laws
LlD	Doctor of Laws
LP	long-playing record
LPO	London Philharmonic Orchestra
LSO	London Symphony Orchestra
Ltd	Limited
m	metre(s)
M.	Monsieur
MA	Master of Arts
MA	Massachusetts (USA)
mand	mandolin

mar	marimba		OM	Order of Merit
MBE	Member of the Order of the British Empire		Ont.	Ontario (Canada)
MD	Maryland (USA)		op	opera [genre]
ME	Maine (USA)		op., opp.	opus, opera
Met	Metropolitan Opera, New York		opt.	optional
Mez	mezzo-soprano		OR	Oregon (USA)
mf	mezzo-forte		orch	orchestra, orchestral, orchestration
MFA	Master of Fine Arts		orchd	orchestrated (by)
MI	Michigan (USA)		org	organ
MLitt	Master of Letters; Master of Literature		orig.	original(ly)
Mlle(s)	Mademoiselle(s)		ORTF	Office de Radiodiffusion-Télévision Française
MM	Master of Music		os	opera seria
M.M.	Metronome Maelzel		OUP	Oxford University Press
mm	millimetre(s)		ov(s).	overture(s)
Mme	Madame		Oxon.	Oxfordshire (GB)
MMus	Master of Music			
MN	Minnesota (USA)			
MO	Missouri (USA)		P	Pincherle catalogue [Vivaldi]
mod	modulator		*p*	piano
Mon.	Monmouthshire (GB)		p., pp.	page, pages
movt	movement		PA	Pennsylvania (USA)
MP	Member of Parliament (GB)		p.a.	per annum
mp	mezzo-piano		PBS	Public Broadcasting Service (USA)
MPhil	Master of Philosophy		perc	percussion
Mr	Mister		perf(s).	performance(s); performed (by)
Mrs	Mistress		pf	piano(forte)
MS(S)	manuscript(s); Master of Science		PhD	Doctor of Philosophy
MS	Mississippi (USA)		pic	piccolo
MSc	Master of Science		pl(s).	plate(s); plural
MT	Montana (USA)		p.m.	post meridiem [after noon]
Mt	Mount		PO	Philharmonic Orchestra
MusB, MusBac	Bachelor of Music		Pol.	Polish
MusD, MusDoc	Doctor of Music		pop.	population
MusM	Master of Music		Port.	Portuguese
			posth.	posthumous(ly)
			POW	prisoner of war
N.	north, northern		*pp*	pianissimo
nar	narrator		*ppp*	pianississimo
NBC	National Broadcasting Company (USA)		pr.	printed
NC	North Carolina (USA)		PRO	Public Record Office, London
ND	North Dakota (USA)		prol.	prologue
n.d.	no date (of publication)		PRS	Performing Right Society
NE	Nebraska (USA)		Ps, ps	psalm
NEA	National Endowment for the Arts (USA)		pseud.	pseudonym
NEH	National Endowment for the Humanities (USA)		pt(s)	part(s)
NET	National Educational Television (USA)		pubd	published
NH	New Hampshire (USA)		pubn	publication
NHK	Nippon Hōsō Kyōkai [Japanese national broadcasting system]			
NJ	New Jersey (USA)		qnt	quintet
NM	New Mexico (USA)		qt	quartet
no(s).	number(s)			
Nor.	Norwegian			
Northants.	Northamptonshire (GB)			
Notts.	Nottinghamshire (GB)		/R	(editorial) revision [in signature]
Nov	November		R	photographic reprint
n.p.	no place (of publication)		r	recto
nr	near		RAF	Royal Air Force
NSW	New South Wales (Australia)		RAI	Radio Audizioni Italiane
NV	Nevada (USA)		RAM	Royal Academy of Music, London
NY	New York State (USA)		RCA	Radio Corporation of America
NZ	New Zealand		RCM	Royal College of Music, London
			rec	recorder
			recit(s).	recitative(s)
			red.	reduction, reduced for
ob	opera buffa; oboe		repr.	reprinted
obbl	obbligato		Rev.	Reverend
OBE	Officer of the Order of the British Empire		rev(s).	revision(s); revised (by/for)
OC	Opéra-Comique [company]		RI	Rhode Island (USA)
oc	opéra comique [genre]		RIdIM	Répertoire International d'Iconographie Musicale
Oct	October			
OH	Ohio (USA)		RILM	Répertoire International de Littérature Musicale
OK	Oklahoma (USA)			

RISM	Répertoire International des Sources Musicales	U.	University
RMCM	Royal Manchester College of Music	UCLA	University of California at Los Angeles (USA)
RNCM	Royal Northern College of Music, Manchester	UHF	ultra-high frequency
RO	Radio Orchestra	UK	United Kingdom of Great Britain and Northern Ireland
Rom.	Romanian		
r.p.m.	revolution(s) per minute	Ukr.	Ukrainian
RPO	Royal Philharmonic Orchestra (GB)	unacc.	unaccompanied
RSFSR	Russian Soviet Federated Socialist Republic	unattrib.	unattributed
RSO	Radio Symphony Orchestra	UNESCO	United Nations Educational, Scientific and Cultural Organization
RTE	Radio Telefís Éireann (Ireland)		
RTF	Radiodiffusion-Télévision Française	UNICEF	United Nations International Children's Emergency Fund
Rt Hon.	Right Honourable		
Russ.	Russian	unperf.	unperformed
RV	Ryom catalogue [Vivaldi]	unpubd	unpublished
		US	United States [adjective]
		USA	United States of America
		USSR	Union of Soviet Socialist Republics
S	San, Santa, Santo, São [Saint]; soprano [voice]	UT	Utah (USA)
$	dollar(s)		
S.	south, southern		
s	soprano [instrument]		
s.	solidus, solidi [shilling, shillings]	v, vv	voice, voices
SACEM	Société d'Auteurs, Compositeurs et Editeurs de Musique (F)	*v*	verso
		v., vv.	verse, verses
Sask.	Saskatchewan (Canada)	VA	Virginia (USA)
sax	saxophone	va	viola
SC	South Carolina (USA)	vc	cello
SD	South Dakota (USA)	VHF	very high frequency
Sept	September	vib	vibraphone
ser.	series	viz	videlicet [namely]
Serb.	Serbian	vle	violone
sf, *sfz*	sforzando, sforzato	vn	violin
sing.	singular	vol(s).	volume(s)
SO	Symphony Orchestra	vs	vocal score, piano-vocal score
Sp.	Spanish	VT	Vermont (USA)
Spl	Singspiel		
SPNM	Society for the Promotion of New Music (GB)		
spr.	spring		
sq	square	W.	west, western
sr	senior	WA	Washington (USA)
SS	Saints	Warwicks.	Warwickshire (GB)
Ss	Santissima, Santissimo	WI	Wisconsin (USA)
SSR	Soviet Socialist Republic	Wilts.	Wiltshire (GB)
St	Saint, Sankt, Sint, Szent	wint.	winter
Staffs.	Staffordshire (GB)	WNO	Welsh National Opera
Ste	Sainte	WoO, woo	Werk(e) ohne Opuszahl [work(s) without opus number]
str	string(s)		
sum.	summer	Worcs.	Worcestershire (GB)
SUNY	State University of New York (USA)	WV	West Virginia (USA)
suppl(s).	supplement(s); supplementary	ww	woodwind
Swed.	Swedish	WY	Wyoming (USA)
sym(s).	symphony (symphonies); symphonic		
synth	synthesizer		
		xyl	xylophone
T	tenor [voice]		
t	tenor [instrument]		
timp	timpani	Yorks.	Yorkshire (GB)
TN	Tennessee (USA)		
tpt	trumpet		
Tr	treble [voice]		
tr	treble [instrument]	Z	Zimmerman catalogue [Purcell]
trans.	translation, translated by	zar	zarzuela
transcr.	transcription, transcribed by		
trbn	trombone		
TV	television		
TX	Texas (USA)	*	autograph manuscript

Bibliographical Abbreviations

The bibliographical abbreviations used in this dictionary are listed below. Full bibliographical information is not normally supplied for national biographical dictionaries and general music reference works, or if details may be found elsewhere in this dictionary under the heading 'Dictionaries and guides' or 'Editions' (relevant items are indicated with D or E, respectively). General music periodicals are shown with dates only; for those in existence before 1980 full information may be found in the list forming part of the article 'Periodicals' in *The New Grove Dictionary of Music and Musicians*. Opera periodicals, listed in the present dictionary under the heading 'Periodicals', are shown here with an asterisk and serial number in brackets.

In this list, and throughout the dictionary, italic type is used for periodicals and reference works, and roman type for anthologies of music, series etc.

AcM	*Acta musicologica* (1928/9–)
ADB	*Allgemeine deutsche Biographie* (Leipzig, 1875–1912)
AllacciD	L. Allacci: *Drammaturgia* D
AMe (AMeS)	*Algemene muziekencyclopedie* (and suppl.) (Antwerp and Amsterdam, 1957–63; suppl., 1972)
AMf	*Archiv für Musikforschung* (1936–43)
AMI	L'arte musicale in Italia E
AMw	*Archiv für Musikwissenschaft* (1918/19–)
AMZ	*Allgemeine musikalische Zeitung* (1798/ 9–1882)
AMz	*Allgemeine Musik-Zeitung* (1874–1943)
AnM	*Anuario musical* (1946–)
AnMc	*Analecta musicologica* (some vols. in series Studien zur italienisch-deutschen Musikgeschichte), Veröffentlichungen der Musikabteilung des Deutschen historischen Instituts in Rom (Cologne, 1963–)
Baker6(–8)	*Baker's Biographical Dictionary of Musicians* (New York, 6/1978, 7/1984, 8/1992)
BAMS	*Bulletin of the American Musicological Society* (1936–48)
BDA	*A Biographical Dictionary of Actors, Actresses, Musicians, Dancers, Managers & Other Stage Personnel in London, 1660–1800* D
BeJb	*Beethoven-Jahrbuch* (1953/4–)
BMB	Bibliotheca musica bononiensis E
BMw	*Beiträge zur Musikwissenschaft* (1959–)
BNB	*Biographie nationale [belge]* (Brussels, 1866–86)
BordasD	*Dictionnaire de la musique* (Paris: Bordas, 1970–76)
Bouwsteenen: JVNM	*Bouwsteenen: jaarboek der Vereeniging voor Nederlandsche muziekgeschiedenis* (1869/ 72–1874/81)
BSIM	*Bulletin français de la S[ociété] I[nternationale de] M[usique] [previously Le Mercure musical; also other titles]* (1905–14)
BUCEM	*British Union-Catalogue of Early Music*, ed. E. Schnapper (London, 1957)
BurneyFl	C. Burney: *The Present State of Music in France and Italy* (London, 1771, 2/1773); ed. P. A. Scholes, *Dr. Burney's Musical Tours in Europe* (London, 1959)
BurneyGN	C. Burney: *The Present State of Music in Germany, the Netherlands, and United Provinces* (London, 1773, 2/1775); ed. P. A. Scholes, *Dr. Burney's Musical Tours in Europe* (London, 1959)
BurneyH	C. Burney: *A General History of Music from the Earliest Ages to the Present* (London, 1776–89) [p. nos. refer to edn of 1935]
CBY	*Current Biography Yearbook* (New York, 1940–)
CHM	*Collectanea historiae musicae* (in series Biblioteca historiae musicae cultores) (Florence, 1953–)
CMc	*Current Musicology* (1965–)
CMI	I classici musicali italiani E
ČMm	*Časopis Moravského musea* [Journal of the Moravian Museum] (c1915–)
CMz	*Cercetări di muzicologie* (1969–)
COJ	*Cambridge Opera Journal* [*Great Britain 27]
CroceN	B. Croce: *I teatri di Napoli* D
ČSHS	*Československý hudební slovník* (Prague, 1963–5)
CSPD	*Calendar of State Papers (Domestic)* (London, 1856–1972)
DAB	*Dictionary of American Biography* (New York, 1928–36; 8 suppls., 1944–88)
DAM	*Dansk aarbog for musikforskning* (1961–)
DBF	*Dictionnaire de biographie française* (Paris, 1933–)
DBI	*Dizionario biografico degli italiani* (Rome, 1960–)

DBL	*Dansk biografisk leksikon* (Copenhagen, 1887–1905, 2/1933–)
DBP	*Dicionário biográfico de músicos portuguezes* (Lisbon, 1900–04)
DDT	Denkmäler deutscher Tonkunst E
DEUMM	*Dizionario enciclopedico universale della musica e dei musicisti* (Turin, 1985–8)
DJbM	*Deutsches Jahrbuch der Musikwissenschaft* (1957–)
DMV	Drammaturgia musicale veneta E
DNB	*Dictionary of National Biography* (London, 1885–1901, suppls.)
DTB	Denkmäler der Tonkunst in Bayern E
DTÖ	Denkmäler der Tonkunst in Österreich E
EDM	Das Erbe deutscher Musik E
EIT	*Ezhegodnik imperatorskikh teatrov* (1892–1915)
EitnerQ	R. Eitner: *Biographisch-bibliographisches Quellen-Lexikon* (Leipzig, 1900–04, 2/1959–60)
EitnerS	R. Eitner: *Bibliographie der Musik-Sammelwerke des XVI. und XVII. Jahrhunderts* (Berlin, 1877)
EMC	*Encyclopedia of Music in Canada* (Toronto, 1981)
EMc	*Early Music* (1973–)
EMDC	*Encyclopédie de la musique et dictionnaire du Conservatoire* (Paris, 1920–31)
ERO	Early Romantic Opera E
ES	*Enciclopedia dello spettacolo* D
EwenD	D. Ewen: *American Composers: a Bio-graphical Dictionary* (New York, 1982)
FAM	*Fontes artis musicae* (1954–)
FasquelleE	*Encyclopédie de la musique* (Paris: Fasquelle, 1958–61)
FétisB (FétisBS)	F.-J. Fétis: *Biographie universelle des musiciens* (and suppl.) (Brussels, 2/1860–65; suppl., 1878–80)
FlorimoN	F. Florimo: *La scuola musicale di Napoli e i suoi conservatorii* (Naples, 1880–83)
FO	French Opera in the 17th and 18th Centuries E
GänzlBMT	K. Gänzl: *The British Musical Theatre* D
GerberL	E. L. Gerber: *Historisch-biographisches Lexikon der Tonkünstler* (Leipzig, 1790–92)
GerberNL	E. L. Gerber: *Neues historisch-biographisches Lexikon der Tonkünstler* (Leipzig, 1812–14)
GfMKB	*Gesellschaft für Musikforschung Kongress-bericht* (1950–)
GiacomoC	S. Di Giacomo: *I quattro antichi conservatorii musicali di Napoli* (Milan and Naples, 1924–8)
GMB	*Geschichte der Musik in Beispielen*, ed. A. Schering (Leipzig, 1931)
GOB	German Opera 1770–1800, ed. T. Bauman E
Grove1(–5)	G. Grove, ed.: *A Dictionary of Music and Musicians* (London, 1878–90; 2/1904–10 ed. J. A. Fuller Maitland, 3/1927–8 and 4/1940 ed. H. C. Colles, 5/1954 ed. E. Blom with suppl. 1961, all as *Grove's Dictionary of Music and Musicians*)
Grove6	S. Sadie, ed.: *The New Grove Dictionary of Music and Musicians* (London, 1980)
GroveAM	H. W. Hitchcock and S. Sadie, eds.: *The New Grove Dictionary of American Music* (New York, 1986)
GroveI	S. Sadie, ed.: *The New Grove Dictionary of Musical Instruments* (London, 1984)
GSL	*Grosses Sängerlexikon* D
GV	*Le grandi voci: Dizionario critico-biografico dei cantanti con discografia operistica* D [where two authors are separated by a semi-colon, the second one compiled the discography]
HawkinsH	J. Hawkins: *A General History of the Science and Practice of Music* (London, 1776) [p. nos. refer to edn of 1853]
HayJb	*Haydn-Jahrbuch/Yearbook* (1962–71, 1975–8, 1980–)
HiFi	*High Fidelity* (1951/2–1965)
HiFi/MusAm	*High Fidelity/Musical America* (1965–87)
HJb	*Händel-Jahrbuch* (1928–33, 1955–)
HJbMw	*Hamburger Jahrbuch für Musikwissenschaft* (1975–)
HMT	*Handwörterbuch der musikalischen Terminologie* (Wiesbaden, 1972–)
HMw	Handbuch der Musikwissenschaft, ed. E. Bücken (Potsdam, 1927–) [monograph series]
HMYB	*Hinrichsen's Musical Year Book* (1944–61)
HPM	Harvard Publications in Music E
HR	*Hudební revue* (1908–20)
HRo	*Hudební rozhledy* (1948/9–)
HS	Handel Sources E
HV	*Hudební věda* (1961–)
IIM	*Izvestiya na Instituta za muzika* (1952–)
IMa	Instituta et monumenta E
IMSCR	*International Musicological Society Congress Report* (1930–)
IMusSCR	*International Musical Society Congress Report* (1906–11)
IOB	Italian Opera 1640–1770, ed. H. M. Brown E
IOG	Italian Opera 1810–1840, ed. P. Gossett E
IRASM	*International Review of the Aesthetics and Sociology of Music* (1971–)
IRMAS	*The International Review of Music Aesthetics and Sociology* (1970–71)
IRMO	S. L. Ginzburg: *Istoriya russkoy muzïki v notnïkh obraztsakh* (Moscow, 2/1968–70)
ISAMm	Institute for Studies in American Music, monograph series
JAMS	*Journal of the American Musicological Society* (1949–)
JbMP	*Jahrbuch der Musikbibliothek Peters* (1895–1941)
JbO	*Jahrbuch für Opernforschung* [*Germany 60]
JM	*Journal of Musicology* (1983–)
JMT	*Journal of Music Theory* (1957–)
JRBM	*Journal of Renaissance and Baroque Music* (1946–7)
JRMA	*Journal of the Royal Musical Association* (1987–)
JVNM	see *Bouwsteenen: JVNM*
KJb	*Kirchenmusikalisches Jahrbuch* (1886–1911, 1930–35, 1936/8, 1950–)
KM	*Kwartalnik muzyczny* (1911/13–1913/14, 1928/9–1933, 1948–50)
Kobbé10	G. Kobbé: *Complete Opera Book* (New York and London, 10/1987) D

LaborD	*Diccionario de la música Labor* (Barcelona, 1954)
LaMusicaD	*La musica: dizionario* (Turin, 1968–71)
LaMusicaE	*La musica: enciclopedia storica* (Turin, 1966)
LM	*Lucrări de muziciologie* (1965–)
LoewenbergA	A. Loewenberg: *Annals of Opera 1597–1940* D
LS	*The London Stage, 1660–1800* D
MA	*The Musical Antiquary* (1909/10–1912/13)
MAS	Musical Antiquarian Society [Publications] E
MB	Musica britannica E
MD	*Musica disciplina* (1948–)
ME	*Muzikal'naya entsiklopediya* (Moscow, 1973–82)
Mf	*Die Musikforschung* (1948–)
MGG	*Die Musik in Geschichte und Gegenwart* (Kassel and Basle, 1949–68; suppl., 1973–9, index 1986)
MJb	*Mozart-Jahrbuch des Zentralinstituts für Mozartforschung* (1950–)
ML	*Music and Letters* (1920–)
MLE	Music for London Entertainment, 1660–1800 E
MM	*Modern Music* (1925–46)
MMA	*Miscellanea musicologica* [Australia] (1966–70, 1972, 1975, 1977–)
MMC	*Miscellanea musicologica* [Czechoslovakia] (1956–62, 1965–1971/3, 1975–)
MMg	*Monatshefte für Musikgeschichte* (1869–1905)
MMR	*The Monthly Musical Record* (1871–1960)
MMS	Monumenta musicae svecicae E
MO	*Musical Opinion* (1877/8–)
MQ	*The Musical Quarterly* (1915–)
MR	*The Music Review* (1940–)
MS	*Muzikal'nïy sovremennik* (1915/16–1916/17)
MSD	Musicological Studies and Documents, ed. A. Carapetyan (Rome, 1951–)
MT	*The Musical Times* (1844/5–)
MusAm	*Musical America* (1898–1964, 1987–92)
MZ	*Muzikološki zbornik* (1965–)
NA	*Note d'archivio per la storia musicale* (1924–7, 1930–43)
NAW	*Notable American Women* (Cambridge, MA, 1971; suppl., 1980)
NBJb	*Neues Beethoven-Jahrbuch* (1924–5, 1927, 1930, 1933, 1935, 1937–9, 1942)
NBL	*Norsk biografisk leksikon* (Oslo, 1921–)
NDB	*Neue deutsche Biographie* (Berlin, 1953–)
NicollH	A. Nicoll: *A History of English Drama, 1660–1900* (Cambridge, 1952–9)
NMA	W. A. Mozart: Neue Ausgabe sämtlicher Werke, ed. E. F. Schmid, W. Plath and W. Rehm (Kassel, 1955–91)
NNBW	*Nieuw Nederlandsch biografisch woordenboek* (Leiden, 1911–37)
NÖB	*Neue österreichische Biographie* (Vienna, 1923)
NOHM	*The New Oxford History of Music*, ed. E. Wellesz, J. A. Westrup and G. Abraham (London, 1954–)
NRMI	*Nuova rivista musicale italiana* (1967–)
NZM	*Neue Zeitschrift für Musik* (1834–1943, 1950–74, 1979–)
OC	*Opera in Canada* [*Canada 1]
OHM	*The Oxford History of Music*, ed. W. H. Hadow (Oxford, 1901–5, enlarged 2/ 1929–38)

OM	*Opus musicum* (1969–)
ÖMz	*Österreichische Musikzeitschrift* (1946–)
ON	*Opera News* [*USA 13]
OQ	*The Opera Quarterly* [*USA 28]
OW	*Opernwelt* [*Germany 42]
PAMS	*Papers of the American Musicological Society* (1936–8, 1940–41)
PÄMw	Publikationen älterer praktischer und theoretischer Musikwerke E
PBC	Publicaciones del departamento de música de la Biblioteca de Catalunya E
PEM	*Pipers Enzyklopädie des Musiktheaters* D
PMA	*Proceedings of the Musical Association* (1874/5–1943/4)
PNM	*Perspectives of New Music* (1962/3–)
PRM	*Polski rocznik muzykologiczny* (1935–6)
PRMA	*Proceedings of the Royal Musical Association* (1944/5–1984/5)
PSB	*Polskich słownik biograficzny* (Kraków, 1935)
QRaM	*Quaderni della Rassegna musicale* (1964–72)
Rad JAZU	*Rad Jugoslavenske akademije znanosti i umjetnosti* (Zagreb, 1867–)
RaM	*La rassegna musicale* (1928–43, 1947–62)
RBM	*Revue belge de musicologie* (1946–)
RdM	*Revue de musicologie* (1917/19–1943, 1945–)
RdMc	*Revista de musicología* (1978–)
ReM	*La revue musicale* (1920–40, 1946–)
RHCM	*Revue d'histoire et de critique musicales* (1901); *La revue musicale* (1902–11)
RicordiE	*Enciclopedia della musica* (Milan: Ricordi, 1963–4)
RiemannL 11,12	H. Riemann: *Musik-Lexikon* (Leipzig, 1882, 11/1929 rev. A. Einstein, 12/1959–75 rev. W. Gurlitt, H. H. Eggebrecht and C. Dahlhaus)
RIM	*Rivista italiana di musicologia* (1966–)
RISM	*Répertoire international des sources musicales* (Munich and Duisburg, 1960–; Kassel, 1971–)
RMARC	*R[oyal] M[usical] A[ssociation] Research Chronicle* (1961–)
RMFC	*Recherches sur la musique française classique* (1960–)
RMG	*Russkaya muzikal'naya gazeta* (1894–1917)
RMI	*Rivista musicale italiana* (1894–1932, 1936–43, 1946–55)
RosaM	C. de Rosa, Marchese di Villarosa: *Memorie dei compositori di musica del Regno di Napoli* (Naples, 1840)
RRAM	Recent Researches in American Music E
RRMBE	Recent Researches in the Music of the Baroque Era E
RRMCE	Recent Researches in the Music of the Classical Era E
SBL	*Svenska biografiskt leksikon* (Stockholm, 1918–)
SchmidlD (*SchmidlDS*)	C. Schmidl: *Dizionario universale dei musicisti* (and suppl.) (Milan, 1887–90, 2/1928–9; suppl., 1938)
SCMA	Smith College Music Archives E
SeegerL	H. Seeger: *Musiklexikon* (Leipzig, 1966)
SH	*Slovenská hudba* (1957–71)
SIMG	*Sammelbände der Internationalen Musik-Gesellschaft* (1899/1900–1913/14)

SM	*Studia musicologica Academiae scientiarum hungaricae* (1961–)	*VMw*	*Vierteljahrsschrift für Musikwissenschaft* (1885–94)
SMA	*Studies in Music* (1967–) [Australia]	*VogelB*	E. Vogel: *Bibliothek der gedruckten weltlichen Vocalmusik Italiens, aus den Jahren 1500 bis 1700* (Berlin, 1892); rev., enlarged, by A. Einstein (Hildesheim, 1962); further addns in *AnMc*, nos.4, 5, 9 and 12; further rev. by F. Lesure and C. Sartori as *Bibliografia della musica italiana vocale profana pubblicata dal 1500 al 1700* (Geneva, 1978)
SML	*Schweizer Musiker Lexikon* (Zürich, 1964)		
SMN	*Studia musicologica norvegica* (1968, 1976–)		
SMP	*Słownik muzyków polskich* (Kraków, 1964–7)		
SMw	*Studien zur Musikwissenschaft* (1913–16, 1918–34, 1955–6, 1960–66, 1977–)		
SMz	*Schweizerische Musikzeitung/Revue musicale suisse* (1861–)		
SOI	*Storia dell'opera italiana*, ed. L. Bianconi and G. Pestelli (Turin, 1987–)		
SouthernB	E. Southern: *Biographical Dictionary of Afro-American and African Musicians* (Westport, CT, 1982)	*WaltherML*	J. G. Walther: *Musicalisches Lexicon oder Musicalische Bibliothek* (Leipzig, 1732)
SovM	*Sovetskaya muzïka* (1933–41, 1946–)	WE	The Wellesley Edition E
StiegerO	F. Stieger: *Opernlexikon* D	*WurzbachL*	C. von Wurzbach: *Biographisches Lexikon des Kaiserthums Oesterreich* (Vienna, 1856–91)
STMf	*Svensk tidskrift för musikforskning* (1919–)		
TVNM	*Tijdschrift van de Vereniging voor Nederlandse muziekgeschiedenis* (1885–)	*ZfM*	*Zeitschrift für Musik* (1920–55)
		ZIMG	*Zeitschrift der Internationalen Musik-Gesellschaft* (1899/1900–1913/14)
		ZL	*Zenei lexikon* (Budapest, 1930–31, 2/1965)
VintonD	J. Vinton, ed.: *Dictionary of Contemporary Music* (New York, 1974)	*ZMw*	*Zeitschrift für Musikwissenschaft* (1918/19–1935)

Library Sigla

The system of library sigla in this dictionary follows that used in its publications (Series A) by Répertoire International des Sources Musicales, Kassel, by permission. Below are listed the sigla to be found; a few of them are additional to those in the published RISM lists, but have been established in consultation with the RISM organization. Some original RISM sigla that have now been changed are retained here.

In the dictionary, sigla are always printed in *italic*. In any listing of sources a national sigillum applies without repetition until it is contradicted.

Within each national list below, entries are alphabetized by sigillum, first by capital letters (showing the city or town) and then by lower-case ones (showing the institution or collection).

A: AUSTRIA

Gk(h)	Graz, Hochschule für Musik und Darstellende Kunst und Landesmusikschule
Gmi	——, Musikwissenschaftliches Institut der Universität
HE	Heiligenkreuz, Zisterzienserstift
KR	Kremsmünster, Benediktinerstift
LA	Lambach, Benediktinerstift
LIm	Linz, Oberösterreichisches Landesmuseum
M	Melk an der Donau, Benediktinerstift
Sca	Salzburg, Museum Carolino Augusteum
Sm	——, Mozarteum (Internationale Stiftung Mozarteum)
Ssp	——, St Peter (Erzstift oder Benediktiner-Erzabtei)
Su	——, Universitätsbibliothek
SPL	St Paul, Stift
ST	Stams, Zisterzienserstift
Wdtö	Vienna, Gesellschaft zur Herausgabe von Denkmälern der Tonkunst in Österreich
Wgm	——, Gesellschaft der Musikfreunde
Wm	——, Minoritenkonvent
Wn	——, Österreichische Nationalbibliothek, Musiksammlung
Wst	——, Stadtbibliothek, Musiksammlung

ARG: ARGENTINA

BAc	Buenos Aires, Teatro Colón

AUS: AUSTRALIA

CAnl	Canberra, National Library of Australia
Msl	Melbourne, State Library of Victoria
NLwm	Nedlands, Wigmore Music Library, University of Western Australia
Scm	Sydney, New South Wales State Conservatorium of Music
Sfl	——, Fisher Library, University of Sydney

B: BELGIUM

Aa	Antwerp, Stadsarchief
Aac	——, Archief en Museum voor het Vlaamse Culturleven
Ac	——, Koninklijk Vlaams Muziekconservatorium
Ba	Brussels, Archives de la Ville
Bc	——, Conservatoire Royal de Musique
Bcdm	——, Centre Belge de Documentation Musicale [CeBeDeM]
Bmichotte	——, Michotte private collection
Br	——, Bibliothèque Royale Albert 1er/ Koninklijke Bibliotheek Albert I
Gc	Ghent, Koninklijk Muziekconservatorium
Gu	——, Rijksuniversiteit, Centrale Bibliotheek
Lc	Liège, Conservatoire Royal de Musique
Lg	——, Musée Grétry

BR: BRAZIL

Rem	Rio de Janeiro, Escola Nacional de Música, Universidade do Brasil
Rn	——, Biblioteca Nacional

C: CANADA

HNu	Hamilton, McMaster University, Mills Memorial Library
Lu	London, University of Western Ontario, Lawson Memorial Library
On	Ottawa, National Library of Canada
Qsl	Quebec, Séminaire de Québec
Tp	Toronto, Metropolitan Toronto Library, Music Department
Tu	——, University of Toronto, Edward Johnson Music Library

CH: SWITZERLAND

Bu	Basle, Öffentliche Bibliothek der Universität, Musiksammlung
BEl	Berne, Schweizerische Landesbibliothek
E	Einsiedeln, Kloster
EN	Engelberg, Stift
Gc	Geneva, Conservatoire de Musique
Lmg	Lucerne, Allgemeine Musikalische Gesellschaft

Lz	——, Zentralbibliothek
LAcu	Lausanne, Bibliothèque Cantonale et Universitaire
MONbonynge	Montreux, Richard Bonynge, private collection
N	Neuchâtel, Bibliothèque Publique et Universitaire
Zschmitt	Zürich, Schmitt private collection
Zz	——, Zentralbibliothek

CS: CZECHOSLOVAKIA

Bm	Brno, Ústav Dějin Hudby Moravského Musea, Hudebněhistorické Oddělení
Bu	——, Universitní Knihovna
K	Český Krumlov, Pracoviště Státního Archívu Třeboň, Hudební Sbírka
KRa	Kroměříž, Státní Zámek a Zahrady, Historicko-Umělecké Fondy, Hudební Archív
KU	Kutná Hora, Oblastní Muzeum
Pk	Prague, Archív Státní Konservatoře v Praze
Pnd	——, Archiv Národního Divadla
Pnm	——, Národní Muzeum, Hudební Oddělení
Pr	——, Československý Rozhlas, Hudební Archív Různá Provenience
Pu	——, Národní Knihovna v Praze, Universitní Knihovna

CU: CUBA

Hin	Havana, Instituto Nacional de la Música
Hn	——, Biblioteca Nacional

D: GERMANY

As	Augsburg, Staats- und Stadtbibliothek
Au	——, Universitätsbibliothek
ALa	Altenburg, Historisches Staatsarchiv
AN	Ansbach, Regierungsbibliothek
B	Berlin, Staatsbibliothek Preussischer Kulturbesitz, Musikabteilung
Ba	——, Amerika-Gedenkbibliothek (Berliner Zentralbibliothek); Deutsche Akademie der Künste
Bbb	——, Bote & Bock Archiv
Bdhm	——, Deutsche Hochschule für Musik Hanns Eisler
Bds	——, Deutsche Staatsbibliothek (formerly Königliche Bibliothek; Preussische Staatsbibliothek; Öffentliche Wissenschaftliche Bibliothek), Musikabteilung
Bdso	——, Deutsche Staatsoper
Bhbk	——, Staatliche Hochschule für Bildende Kunst
Bhm	——, Staatliche Hochschule für Musik und Darstellende Kunst
Bko	——, Komische Oper
Bmm	——, Märkisches Museum
Bp	——, Pädagogisches Zentrum
Bsommer	——, Sommer private collection
Bsp	——, Sprachkonvikt
BAs	Bamberg, Staatsbibliothek
BAL	Ballenstedt, Stadtbibliothek
BAR	Bartenstein, Fürszt zu Hohenlohe-Bartensteinsches Archiv [in NEhz]
BB	Benediktbeuern, Pfarrkirche
BMs	Bremen, Staats- und Universitätsbibliothek
BNu	Bonn, Universitätsbibliothek
BS	Brunswick, Öffentliche Bücherei (Stadtarchiv und Stadtbibliothek)
Cl	Coburg, Landesbibliothek
Dl	Dresden, Bibliothek und Museum Löbau [in Dlb]
Dla	——, Staatsarchiv
Dlb	——, Sächsische Landesbibliothek
Ds	——, Staatstheater
DEl	Dessau, Stadtbibliothek (formerly Universitäts- und Landesbibliothek)
Dl	Dillingen an der Donau, Kreis- und Studienbibliothek
DL	Delitzsch, Museum und Bibliothek
DO	Donaueschingen, Fürstlich Fürstenbergische Hofbibliothek
DS	Darmstadt, Hessische Landes- und Hochschulbibliothek
DT	Detmold, Lippische Landesbibliothek
DÜl	Düsseldorf, Landes- und Stadtbibliothek
Es	Eichstätt, Staats- und Seminarbibliothek [in Eu]
Eu	——, Universitätsbibliothek
Ew	——, Benediktinerinnen-Abtei St Walburg
EB	Ebrach, Katholisches Pfarramt
F	Frankfurt am Main, Stadt- und Universitätsbibliothek
FS	Freising, Dombibliothek
Ga	Göttingen, Staatliches Archivlager
Gs	——, Niedersächsische Staats- und Universitätsbibliothek
Hmb	Hamburg, Hamburger Öffentliche Bücherhallen, Musikbibliothek
Hs	——, Staats- und Universitätsbibliothek Carl von Ossietzky
HAmi	Halle an der Saale, Martin-Luther-Universität, Sektion Germanistik und Kulturwissenchaften, Fachbereich Musikwissenschaft (formerly Institut für Musikwissenschaft)
HAu	——, Universitäts- und Landesbibliothek
HG	Havelberg, Prignitz-Museum
HR	Harburg über Donauwörth, Fürstlich Oettingen-Wallerstein'sche Bibliothek [in Au]
HVl	Hanover, Niedersächsische Landesbibliothek
HVs	——, Stadtbibliothek
Ju	Jena, Universitätsbibliothek der Friedrich-Schiller-Universität
Kl	Kassel, Landesbibliothek und Murhardsche Bibliothek der Stadt
KA	Karlsruhe, Badische Landesbibliothek
KIl	Kiel, Schleswig-Holsteinische Landesbibliothek
KNha	Cologne, Historisches Archiv der Stadt Köln
KNu	——, Universitäts- und Stadtbibliothek
Lr	Lüneburg, Ratsbücherei und Stadtarchiv
LEm	Leipzig, Musikbibliothek der Stadt Leipzig
LEmi	——, Sektion Kulturwissenschaften und Germanistik der Karl-Marx-Universität, Wissenschaftsgebiet Musikwissenschaft (formerly Institut für Musikwissenschaft) [in LEu]
LEu	——, Universitätsbibliothek der Karl-Marx-Universität
LÜh	Lübeck, Bibliothek der Hansestadt
Mbm	Munich, Metropolitankapitel [in FS]
Mbn	——, Bayerisches Nationalmuseum
Mbs	——, Bayerische Staatsbibliothek
Mh	——, Staatliche Hochschule für Musik
Mo	——, Opernarchiv
Mth	——, Theatermuseum (Clara-Ziegler-Stiftung)
MEIr	Meiningen, Staatliche Museen mit Reger-Archiv
MGmi	Marburg an der Lahn, Musikwissenschaftliches Institut der Philipps-Universität
MGs	——, Staatsarchiv und Archivschule
MH	Mannheim, Wissenschaftliche Stadtbibliothek und Universitätsbibliothek
MHrm	——, Städtisches Reiss-Museum
MÜp	Münster, Diözesanbibliothek, Bischöfliches Priesterseminar und Santini-Sammlung
MÜs	——, Santini-Bibliothek [in MÜp]
MÜu	——, Universitätsbibliothek
Ngm	Nuremberg, Germanisches National-Museum
Nst	——, Stadtbibliothek
NEhz	Neuenstein, Hohenlohe-Zentralarchiv

OB	Ottobeuren, Benediktiner-Abtei
Rp	Regensburg, Bischöfliche Zentralbibliothek
Rtt	——, Fürst Thurn und Taxis Hofbibliothek
RH	Rheda, Fürst zu Bentheim-Tecklenburgische Bibliothek [in *MÜu*]
ROmi	Rostock, Institut für Musikwissenschaft der Universität
ROu	——, Wilhelm-Pieck-Universität, Universitätsbibliothek
RUl	Rudolstadt, Staatsarchiv
Sl	Stuttgart, Württembergische Landesbibliothek
SHs	Sondershausen, Stadt- und Kreisbibliothek
SHsk	——, Schlosskirche [in *SHs*]
SWl	Schwerin, Wissenschaftliche Allgemeinbibliothek (formerly Mecklenburgische Landesbibliothek)
SWth	——, Mecklenburgisches Staatstheater
Tu	Tübingen, Eberhard-Karls-Universität, Universitätsbibliothek
W	Wolfenbüttel, Herzog-August-Bibliothek
Wa	——, Niedersächsisches Staatsarchiv
WD	Wiesentheid, Musiksammlung des Grafen von Schönborn-Wiesentheid
WEY	Weyarn, Pfarrkirche [in *FS*]
WIbh	Wiesbaden, Breitkopf & Härtel, Verlagsarchiv
WRdn	Weimar, Deutsches Nationaltheater
WRl	——, Staatsarchiv (formerly Landeshauptarchiv)
WRtl	——, Thüringische Landesbibliothek, Musiksammlung [in *WRz*]
WRz	——, Zentralbibliothek der deutschen Klassik
WS	Wasserburg am Inn, Chorarchiv St Jakob, Pfarramt [in *FS*]
WÜsa	Würzburg, Stadtarchiv
ZI	Zittau, Stadt- und Kreisbibliothek

DK: DENMARK

Kk	Copenhagen, Det Kongelige Bibliotek
Kmk	——, Det Kongelige Danske Musikkonservatorium
Km(m)	——, Musikhistorisk Museum
Sa	Sorø, Sorø Akademis Bibliotek

E: SPAIN

Bc	Barcelona, Biblioteca de Cataluña
Bcd	——, Centro de Documentación Musical
Bim	——, Instituto Español de Musicología
Bit	——, Instituto del Teatro (formerly Museo del Arte Escénico)
Boc	——, Biblioteca Orfeó Catalá
Fbaudot	El Ferrol, G. Baudot-Puentes, private collection
La	León, Catedral
Mc	Madrid, Conservatorio Superior de Música
Mcns	——, Congregación de Neustra Señora
Mm	——, Biblioteca Municipal
Mn	——, Biblioteca Nacional
Mp	——, Palacio Real
Msa	——, Sociedad General de Autores de España
SC	Santiago de Compostela, Catedral
Zac	Saragossa, Archivo de Música del Cabildo

EIRE: IRELAND

Dam	Dublin, Royal Irish Academy of Music
Dtc	——, Trinity College

F: FRANCE

A	Avignon, Bibliothèque Municipale Livrée Ceccano (formerly Musée Calvet)

AG	Agen, Archives Départementales
AIXc	Aix-en-Provence, Conservatoire
AIXm	——, Bibliothèque Municipale, Bibliothèque Méjanes
AM	Amiens, Bibliothèque Municipale
BER	Bernay, Bibliothèque Municipale
BO	Bordeaux, Bibliothèque Municipale
BOLbrindejoint	Boulogne, Y. Brindejoint, private collection
CLO	Clermont-de-l'Oise, Bibliothèque
COGbuckley	Cognac, W. Buckley, private collection
COM	Compiègne, Bibliothèque Municipale
Dc	Dijon, Bibliothèque du Conservatoire
Dm	——, Bibliothèque Municipale
Lm	Lille, Bibliothèque Municipale
LYm	Lyons, Bibliothèque Municipale
Mc	Marseilles, Conservatoire de Musique et de Déclamation
MAC	Mâcon, Bibliothèque Municipale
ML	Moulins, Bibliothèque Municipale
MON	Montauban, Bibliothèque Municipale
NAc	Nancy, Conservatoire
NS	Nîmes, Bibliothèque Municipale
Pa	Paris, Bibliothèque de l'Arsenal
Pbourdon	——, M.-M. Bourdon, private collection
Pc	——, Fonds du Conservatoire National de Musique [in *Pn*]
Pcf	——, Comédie-Française, Bibliothèque
Pi	——, Bibliothèque de l'Institut de France
Pim	——, Institut de Musicologie de l'Université
Plambert	——, Lambert private collection
Pm	——, Bibliothèque Mazarine
Pmeyer	——, André Meyer, private collection
Pn	——, Bibliothèque Nationale
Po	——, Bibliothèque-Musée de l'Opéra
Poffenbach	——, P. Comte-Offenbach, private collection
Prt	——, Office de Radiodiffusion-Télévision Française
Psal	——, Editions Salabert
R(m)	Rouen, Bibliothèque Municipale
Sim	Strasbourg, Institut de Musicologie de l'Université
SA	Salins, Bibliothèque Municipale
SMcusset	St-Maud, F. Cusset, private collection
SRPalmeida	St-Rémy-de-Provence, A. de Almeida, private collection
TLm	Toulouse, Bibliothèque Municipale
V	Versailles, Bibliothèque Municipale

GB: GREAT BRITAIN

ABu	Aberystwyth, University College of Wales
ALb	Aldeburgh, Britten-Pears Library
Bu	Birmingham, University of Birmingham, Barber Institute of Fine Arts
BEL	Belton (Lincs.), Belton House
BRu	Bristol, University of Bristol Library
Ccl	Cambridge, Central Library
Cfm	——, Fitzwilliam Museum
Ckc	——, King's College, Rowe Music Library
Cpl	——, Pendlebury Library of Music
Cu	——, University Library
CDp	Cardiff, Public Libraries, Central Library [in *CDu*]
CDu	——, University of Wales College of Cardiff (formerly University College of South Wales and Monmouthshire)
DRc	Durham, Cathedral
En	Edinburgh, National Library of Scotland
Er	——, Reid Music Library, University of Edinburgh
Ge	Glasgow, Euing Music Library
Gm	——, Mitchell Library
Gu	——, University Library
Lam	London, Royal Academy of Music

Lbl	——, British Library (formerly *Lbm*, British Museum)
Lcm	——, Royal College of Music
Lfm	——, Faber Music
Lgc	——, Gresham College (Guildhall Library)
Lkc	——, University of London, King's College
Lmic	——, British Music Information Centre
Lpro	——, Public Record Office
Lu	——, University of London, Music Library
Lue	——, Universal Edition
Lva	——, Victoria and Albert Museum
Lwa	——, Westminster Abbey
LEbc	Leeds, University of Leeds, Brotherton Collection
LVp	Liverpool, Public Libraries, Central Library
Mp	Manchester, Central Public Library, Henry Watson Music Library
NWr	Norwich, Norfolk and Norwich Record Office
Ob	Oxford, Bodleian Library
Ouf	——, University, Faculty of Music
SOp	Southampton, Public Library
T	Tenbury, St Michael's College [dispersed: now principally in *F-Pn*, *V*, *GB-Ob*]
TWmacnutt	Tunbridge Wells, Richard Macnutt, private collection
WC	Winchester, Chapter Library

GR: GREECE

Aels	Athens, Ethniki Lyriki Skini
Akounadis	——, Panayis Kounadis, private collection
Aleotsakos	——, George Leotsakos, private collection
Am	——, Mousseio ke Kendro Meletis Ellinikou Theatrou
An	——, Ethniki Vivliothiki tis Ellados [National Library of Greece]

H: HUNGARY

Bn	Budapest, Országos Széchényi Könyvtára
Bo	——, Állami Operaház

HV: CROATIA

Zu	Zagreb, Nacionalna i Sveučilišna Biblioteka

I: ITALY

Ac	Assisi, Biblioteca Comunale
Af	——, S Francesco [in *Ac*]
AC	Acicatena, Biblioteca Comunale
Baf	Bologna, Accademia Filarmonica
Bas	——, Archivio di Stato
Bc	——, Civico Museo Bibliografico Musicale
Bsf	——, Convento di S Francesco
Bsp	——, Basilica di S Petronio
Bu	——, Biblioteca Universitaria
BAc(n)	Bari, Biblioteca Nazionale (Consorziale)
BAn	——, Biblioteca Nazionale Sagarriga Visconti-Volpi
BGc	Bergamo, Biblioteca Civica Angelo Mai
BGi	——, Civico Istituto Musicale Gaetano Donizetti
BRc	Brescia, Conservatorio di Musica
BRq	——, Biblioteca Queriniana
BZtoggenburg	Bolzano, Count Toggenburg, private collection
CAS	Cascia, Archivio di S Rita
CATc	Catania, Biblioteche Riunite Civica e Antonio Ursino Recupero
CATm	——, Museo Belliniano
CCc	Città di Castello, Biblioteca Comunale
CF	Cividale del Friuli, Archivio Capitolare

CHf	Chioggia, Archivio dei Padri Filippini
CMbc	Casale Monferrato, Biblioteca Civica
CNM	Civitanova-Marche, Biblioteca Comunale
CORc	Correggio, Biblioteca Comunale
CR	Cremona, Biblioteca Statale
Fa	Florence, Ss Annunziata
Fas	——, Archivio di Stato
Fbecherini	——, Becherini private collection
Fc	——, Conservatorio di Musica Luigi Cherubini
Fm	——, Biblioteca Marucelliana
Fn	——, Biblioteca Nazionale Centrale
Folschki	——, Olschki private collection
FAN	Fano, Biblioteca Comunale Federiciana
FEc	Ferrara, Biblioteca Comunale Ariostea
FEd	——, Duomo
FERc	Fermo, Biblioteca Comunale
FERd	——, Duomo
FOc	Forlì, Biblioteca Civica Aurelio Saffi
FZc	Faenza, Biblioteca Comunale
Gi(l)	Genoa, Istituto (Liceo) Musicale Paganini; see *Gl*
Gl	——, Conservatorio di Musica Nicolò Paganini
Gim	——, Istituto Mazziniano
Gu	——, Biblioteca Universitaria
IBborromeo	Isola Bella, Borromeo private archive
IE	Iesi, Biblioteca Comunale
La	Lucca, Archivio di Stato
Li	——, Istituto Musicale Luigi Boccherini (incl. Bottini Collection)
Ls	——, Seminario Arcivescovile
Ll	Livorno, Biblioteca Comunale Labronica Francesco Domenico Guerrazzi
Mb	Milan, Biblioteca Nazionale Braidense
Mc	——, Conservatorio di Musica Giuseppe Verdi
Mcom	——, Biblioteca Comunale
Mr	——, Archivio Storico Ricordi
Ms	——, Biblioteca Teatrale Livia Simoni
Msartori	——, Claudio Sartori, private collection
Mt	——, Biblioteca Trivulziana e Archivio Storico Civico
MAav	Mantua, Accademia Virgiliana di Scienze, Lettere ed Arti
MAC	Macerata, Biblioteca Comunale Mozzi-Borgetti
MC	Monte Cassino, Biblioteca dell'Abbazia
MOa	Modena, Accademia Nazionale di Scienze, Lettere ed Arti
MOe	——, Biblioteca Estense
MOs	——, Archivio di Stato
Na	Naples, Archivio di Stato
Nc	——, Conservatorio di Musica S Pietro a Majella
Nf	——, Biblioteca Oratoriana dei Padri Filippini
Nlp	——, Biblioteca Lucchesi-Palli [in *Nn*]
Nn	——, Biblioteca Nazionale
OS	Ostiglia, Fondazione Greggiati
Pc	Padua, Biblioteca Capitolare
Pca	——, Biblioteca Antoniana, Basilica del Santo
Pci	——, Museo Civico, Biblioteca Civica e Archivio Comunale
Pi(l)	——, Istituto Musicale (Biblioteca del Liceo Musicale); see *Pl*
Pl	——, Istituto Musicale Cesare Pollini
PAc	Parma, Conservatorio di Musica Arrigo Boito
PAi	——, Istituto di Studi Verdiani
PAt	——, Teatro Regio
PAVu	Pavia, Biblioteca Universitaria
PCcon	Piacenza, Conservatorio di Musica Giuseppe Nicolini
PEc	Perugia, Biblioteca Comunale Augusta
PEl	——, Conservatorio di Musica Francesco Morlacchi
PEsp	——, S Pietro
PEA	Pescia, Biblioteca Comunale Carlo Magnani
PESc	Pesaro, Conservatorio di Musica Gioacchino Rossini

PESr	——, Fondazione Rossini
PIv	Pisa, Teatro Verdi
PLa	Palermo, Archivio di Stato
PLcom	——, Biblioteca Comunale
PLcon	——, Conservatorio Vincenzo Bellini
PS	Pistoia, Cattedrale
PSrospigliosi	——, Rospigliosi private collection
Rasc	Rome, Archivio Storico Capitolino
Rc	——, Biblioteca Casanatense
Rdp	——, Archivio Doria-Pamphili
Ria	——, Istituto di Archeologia e Storia dell'Arte
Rli	——, Accademia Nazionale dei Lincei e Corsiniana
Rmalvezzi	——, Malvezzi private collection
Rmassimo	——, Massimo princes, private collection
Rn	——, Biblioteca Nazionale Centrale Vittorio Emanuele III
Rp	——, Biblioteca Pasqualini [in *Rsc*]
Rps	——, Archivio dei Padri Scolopi (Chiesa di S Pantaleo)
Rrai	——, Radiotelevisione Italiana
Rrostirolla	——, Giancarlo Rostirolla, private collection
Rsc	——, Conservatorio di Musica S Cecilia
Rsp	——, Şanto Spirito in Sassia
Rvat	——, Biblioteca Apostolica Vaticana
REm	Reggio Emilia, Biblioteca Municipale
RIM	Rimini, Biblioteca Civica Gambalunga
RVI	Rovigo, Accademia e Biblioteca dei Concordi
Sac	Siena, Accademia Musicale Chigiana
Sc	——, Biblioteca Comunale degli Intronati
SA	Savona, Biblioteca Civica Anton Giulio Barrili
SML	Santa Margherita Ligure, Biblioteca Comunale Francesco Domenico Costa
Tci	Turin, Biblioteca Civica Musicale Andrea della Corte
Tco	——, Conservatorio Statale di Musica Giuseppe Verdi
Tf	——, Accademia Filarmonica
Tmc	——, Museo Civico
Tn	——, Biblioteca Nazionale Universitaria
Tr	——, Biblioteca Reale
TAc	Taranto, Biblioteca Civica Pietro Acclavio
TLp	Torre del Lago, Museo Puccini
TOL	Tolentino, Biblioteca Comunale Filelfica
TRc	Trent, Biblioteca Comunale
TSmt	Trieste, Civico Museo Teatrale di Fondazione Carlo Schmidl
TVco	Treviso, Biblioteca Comunale
UDc	Udine, Biblioteca Comunale Vincenzo Soppi
Vas	Venice, Archivio di Stato
Vc	——, Conservatorio di Musica Benedetto Marcello
Vcg	——, Biblioteca Casa di Goldoni
Vgc	——, Biblioteca e Istituto della Fondazione Giorgio Cini
Vlevi	——, Fondazione Ugo Levi
Vmc	——, Museo Civico Correr
Vnm	——, Biblioteca Nazionale Marciana
Vqs	——, Fondazione Querini-Stampalia
Vs	——, Seminario Patriarcale
Vsm	——, Procuratoria di S Marco
Vt	——, Teatro La Fenice
VEc	Verona, Biblioteca Civica
VEs	——, Seminario Vescovile

J: JAPAN

Tn	Tokyo, Nanki Music Library, Ohki Collection [in Tokyo College of Music Library]

N: NORWAY

Ou	Oslo, Universitetsbiblioteket

NL: THE NETHERLANDS

At	Amsterdam, Toonkunst-Bibliotheek
DHgm	The Hague, Gemeentemuseum
DHk	——, Koninklijke Bibliotheek

NZ: NEW ZEALAND

Wt	Wellington, Alexander Turnbull Library

P: PORTUGAL

Em	Elvas, Biblioteca Municipal
EVc	Évora, Arquivo da Catedral
EVp	——, Biblioteca Pública
La	Lisbon, Palácio Nacional da Ajuda
Lan	——, Arquivo Nacional de Torre do Tombo
Lc	——, Conservatorio Nacional
Ln	——, Biblioteca Nacional
Lt	——, Teatro Nacional de S Carlos
VV	Vila Viçosa, Casa da Bragança, Museu-Biblioteca

PL: POLAND

CZp	Częstochowa, Klasztor OO. Paulinów na Jasnej Górze
Kc	Kraków, Muzeum Narodowe, Biblioteka Czartoryskich
Kj	——, Biblioteka Jagiellońska
Kp	——, Biblioteka Polskiej Akademii Nauk
KA	Katowice, Biblioteka Śląska
LA	Łańcut, Muzeum
Wn	Warsaw, Biblioteka Narodowa
Wtm	——, Biblioteka Warszawskiego Towarzystwa Muzycznego
Wu	——, Biblioteka Uniwersytecka
WRol	Wrocław, Biblioteka Ossolineum Leopoldiensis; see *WRzno*
WRzno	——, Polska Akademia Nauk Zakład Narodowy imienia Ossolińskich

R: ROMANIA

Bc	Bucharest, Biblioteca Centrală de Stat

RU: RUSSIA

KAu	Kaliningrad, Universitetskaya Biblioteka
Mcl	Moscow, Gosudarstvennïy Tsentral'nïy Literaturnïy Arkhiv
Mcm	——, Gosudarstvennïy Tsentral'nïy Muzey Muzïkal'noy Kul'turï imeni M. I. Glinki
Mk	——, Gosudarstvennaya Konservatoriya imeni P. I. Chaykovskogo, Nauchnaya Muzïkal'naya Biblioteka imeni S. I. Taneyeva
Mrg	——, Rossiyskaya Gosudarstvennaya Biblioteka (formerly *Ml*, Lenin Library)
SPan	St Petersburg, Biblioteka Rossiyskoy Akademii Nauk
SPia	——, Gosudarstvennïy Tsentral'nïy Istoricheskiy Arkhiv
SPil	——, Institut Russkoy Literaturï
SPit	——, Gosudarstvennïy Institut Teatra, Muzïki i Kinematografii
SPk	——, Biblioteka Gosudarstvennoy Konservatorii imeni N. A. Rimskogo-Korsakova
SPsc	——, Gosudarstvennaya Ordena Trudovogo Krasnogo Znameni Publichnaya Biblioteka imeni M. E. Saltïkova-Shchedrina
SPtob	——, Tsentral'naya Muzïkal'naya Biblioteka Gosudarstvennogo Akademicheskogo Mariinskogo Teatra Operï i Baleta

S: SWEDEN

L	Lund, Universitetsbiblioteket
Sdt	Stockholm, Drottningholms Teatermuseum
Sic	——, Informationscentral för Svensk Musik
Sk	——, Kungliga Biblioteket
Skma	——, Statens Musiksamlingar (formerly Kungliga Musikaliska Akademiens Bibliotek)
Sm	——, Musikhistoriska Museet [in Skma]
Smf	——, Stiftelsen Musikkulturens Främjande
Ssr	——, Sveriges Radio
St	——, Kungliga Teaterns Bibliotheket [in Skma]
Uu	Uppsala, Universitetsbiblioteket

SF: FINLAND

A	Turku [Åbo], Sibelius Museum Musikvetenskapliga Institutionen vid Åbo Akademi, Bibliotek & Arkiv
Hy	Helsinki, Helsingin Yliopiston Kirjasto

[SLN]: SLOVENIA

Lf	Ljubljana, Knjižnica Frančiskanškega Samostana
Lu	——, Narodna in Univerzitetna Knjižnica

UA: UKRAINE

Kan	Kiev, Tsentral'na Naukova Biblioteka, Akademii Nauk
LV	L'viv, Biblioteka Derzhavnoï Konservatorii imeni N. V. Lysenka

US: UNITED STATES OF AMERICA

AA	Ann Arbor, University of Michigan, Music Library
AUS	Austin, University of Texas
Bm	Boston, University, Mugar Memorial Library
Bp	——, Public Library, Music Department
BApi	Baltimore, Peabody Conservatory of Music; Peabody Institute
BAT	Baton Rouge, Louisiana State University Library
BE	Berkeley, University of California, Music Library
BLl	Bloomington, Indiana University, Lilly Library
BLu	——, Indiana University, School of Music Library
BUu	Buffalo, State University of New York at Buffalo
Chs	Chicago, Chicago Historical Society
Cn	——, Newberry Library
CA	Cambridge, Harvard University Music Libraries
CDs	Concord, New Hampshire State Library
CHH	Chapel Hill, University of North Carolina, Music Library
DN	Denton, North Texas State University, Music Library
Eu	Evanston, Northwestern University Libraries
FAlewis	Farmington (CT), Wilmarth S. Lewis, private collection
G	Gainesville, University of Florida Library, Rare Book Collection
I	Ithaca, Cornell University, Music Library

KBrobbin	Key Biscayne (FL), Leon Robbin, private collection
KC	Kansas City, University of Missouri, Kansas City Conservatory of Music
LAu	Los Angeles, University of California, Walter H. Rubsamen Music Library
LAuc	——, University of California, William Andrews Clark Memorial Library
LOu	Louisville, University, School of Music Library
MAhs	Madison, Wisconsin Historical Society
MED	Medford (MA), Tufts University Library
MSu	Minneapolis, University of Minnesota, Music Library
NH	New Haven (CT), Yale University, School of Music Library
NYcu	New York, Columbia University, Music Library
NYgs	——, G. Schirmer, Inc.
NYj	——, Juilliard School of Music
NYlibin	——, Laurence Libin, private collection
NYp	——, Public Library at Lincoln Center, Library and Museum of the Performing Arts
NYpm	——, Pierpont Morgan Library
NYyellin	——, Victor Yellin, private collection
PHci	Philadelphia, Curtis Institute of Music
PHf	——, Free Library of Philadelphia
PHhs	——, Historical Society of Pennsylvania
PHlc	——, Library Company of Philadelphia
PHu	——, University of Pennsylvania Libraries (Otto E. Albrecht Music Library; Van Pelt Library; Rare Book Collection)
PRu	Princeton, University, Harvey S. Firestone Memorial Library
R	Rochester (NY), University, Eastman School of Music, Sibley Music Library
Su	Seattle, University of Washington, Music Library
SB	Santa Barbara, University of California at Santa Barbara Library
SFp	San Francisco, Public Library, Fine Arts Department, Music Division
SFsc	——, San Francisco State University (formerly State College) Library, Frank V. de Bellis Collection
SLug	St Louis, Washington University, Gaylord Music Library
SM	San Marino (CA), Henry E. Huntington Library and Art Gallery
SPmoldenhauer	Spokane (WA), Hans Moldenhauer, private collection
STu	Stanford, University, Division of Humanities and Social Sciences, Music Library
U	Urbana, University of Illinois, Music Library
Wc	Washington, DC, Library of Congress, Music Division
Ws	——, Folger Shakespeare Library
Wsi	——, Smithsonian Institution, Music Library
WM	Waltham (MA), Brandeis University Library, Music Library, Goldfarb Library
WS	Winston-Salem (NC), Moravian Music Foundation

YU: YUGOSLAVIA

(for libraries in the former republic of Yugoslavia, see also under HV, Croatia; and [SLN], Slovenia)

Bn	Belgrade, Narodna Biblioteka N. R. Srbije

E

Eadie, Noël (*b* Paisley, 10 Dec 1901; *d* London, 11 April 1950). Scottish soprano. She studied in London, making her début in 1926 at Covent Garden as Woglinde. With the British National Opera Company she first sang the Queen of Night (1928), her most famous role, at Edinburgh. In 1930 she sang Sandrina in the British première of *La finta giardiniera* at the London Scala. She appeared in Chicago during the 1931–2 season, then returned to Covent Garden, singing the Queen of Night and Gilda (1931), Rosina and Olympia (1936–7) and one performance of Butterfly (1938), replacing Maggie Teyte at three hours' notice. At Glyndebourne (1935–6) she sang Konstanze and the Queen of Night. There was some reserve in the expression of Eadie's singing, but her well-poised voice was an admirable musical instrument, equable and pure. No other Queen of Night of her generation caused the listener so few qualms; and though there may have been heroines more resourceful scenically in *Entführung*, her Konstanze was surpassingly musical. RICHARD CAPELL, ELIZABETH FORBES

Eaglen, Jane (*b* Lincoln, 4 April 1960). English soprano. She studied at the RNCM, Manchester, making her début in 1984 with the ENO as Lady Ella (*Patience*). Other roles for the ENO have included Donna Elvira, Sinais (*Mose*), Elizabeth I (*Maria Stuarda*), Leonora (*Il trovatore*), Eva, Micaëla, Santuzza, Tosca and Fata Morgana (*Love for Three Oranges*). She made her Covent Garden début in 1986 as Berta in *Il barbiere*, returning as First Lady in *Die Zauberflöte*. For Scottish Opera she has sung Mimì, Fiordiligi and Brünnhilde (*Die Walküre*, 1991). She has also sung Butterfly in Brisbane; Amelia (*Ballo*) and Donna Anna at Bologna; Electra (*Idomeneo*) and Senta at the Vienna Staatsoper; and Mathilde (*Guillaume Tell*) at Geneva. She combines strong dramatic conviction with her powerful, well-controlled and vibrant voice. ELIZABETH FORBES

Eames, Emma (*b* Shanghai, 13 Aug 1865; *d* New York, 13 June 1952). American soprano. After early studies in Boston and with Mathilde Marchesi in Paris, she made a brilliant début at the Opéra on 13 March 1889 as Gounod's Juliet, with Jean de Reszke. In 1890 she created Colombe in Saint-Saëns' *Ascanio*. After two seasons in Paris, she made both her Covent Garden and her Metropolitan débuts in 1891. During the following decade she sang leading roles in Mozart, Wagner, Gounod and Verdi in London and New York, continu-

Emma Eames as Juliet in Gounod's 'Roméo et Juliette'

ing at the Metropolitan until 1909 and notably adding to her repertory the role of Tosca. Her lyric soprano was of singularly pure and beautiful quality, and her technique was masterly. Some, though not all, of her gramophone records reveal considerable fullness and power as well as the expected technical perfection.

E. Eames: *Some Memories and Reflections* (New York, 1927/R 1977 with discography)
J. Dennis and L. Migliorini: 'Emma Eames', *Record Collector*, viii (1953), 77–96 [with discography and commentary]
A. F. R. Lawrence and S. Smolian: 'Emma Eames', *American Record Guide*, xxix (1962), 210–17 [with discography and commentary]
DESMOND SHAWE-TAYLOR

Earle, Roderick (*b* Winchester, 29 Jan 1952). English bass. He studied at Cambridge and in London, and from 1978 to 1981 was engaged by the ENO. He made his Covent Garden début in 1980 as Antonio (*Figaro*) and has subsequently sung Masetto, Schaunard, Hobson (*Peter Grimes*), Theseus (*Midsummer Night's Dream*), Wagner (*Faust*), Count Ribbing (*Ballo*), Pietro (*Simon Boccanegra*), the Police Commissioner (*Rosenkavalier*), Zuniga, Abimelech (*Samson et Dalila*), the Nightwatch-man (*Meistersinger*), Lamoral (*Arabella*), De Retz (*Les Huguenots*) and Leuthold (*Guillaume Tell*). A versatile artist, he has sung Leporello and Giorgio (*I puritani*) with Opera North; the He-Ancient (*Midsummer Marriage*), Fafner and Hunding with the WNO; and Mozart's Figaro with Scottish Opera.

ELIZABETH FORBES

Early Music revival. *See* REVIVAL.

Easton, Florence (Gertrude) (*b* Middlesbrough-on-Tees, 25 Oct 1882; *d* New York, 13 Aug 1955). English soprano. She studied in Paris and London and made her début as the Shepherd in *Tannhäuser* (1903, Newcastle upon Tyne). She toured North America with H. W. Savage's English Grand Opera Company (1905–7); both she and her husband (the American tenor Francis Maclennan) were then engaged at the Berlin Hofoper, 1907–13, and for the following three years at the Hamburg Städtische Oper. She made a few appearances at Covent Garden and at Chicago, and in 1917 began a long and fruitful association with the Metropolitan Opera, which continued without interruption until 1929; her versatility was outstanding, and her pure tone, sound technique and fine musicianship singled her out even in the brilliant assembly of singers collected by Gatti-Casazza. She was the first Lauretta in *Gianni Schicchi* (14 December 1918). She made isolated re-appearances at Covent Garden (Turandot in 1927, Isolde and the *Siegfried* Brünnhilde, with Melchior, in 1932) and gave her farewell performance at the Metropolitan in 1936 as Brünnhilde in *Die Walküre*, receiving an ovation for her still splendid singing and interpretation.

J. Stratton: 'Florence Easton', *Record Collector*, xxi (1973–4), 197–239 [with discography]   DESMOND SHAWE-TAYLOR

Eaton, John C(harles) (*b* Bryn Mawr, PA, 30 March 1935). American composer. He completed his formal musical education in 1959 at Princeton University, where he received composition lessons from Roger Sessions while studying the piano privately. He spent the following 11 years in Rome, devoting himself primarily to composition while supporting himself with grants and awards (including three Prix de Rome and two Guggenheim fellowships) and through concert appearances as both a classical and a jazz pianist. His opera *Heracles*, composed in Rome in 1964, was chosen to open the new Musical Arts Center at the University of Indiana in 1972. Eaton was invited to Indiana in 1970 to assist with performance preparations, which led to his appointment there as professor of composition.

Although Eaton has composed works in all major genres, he has especially favoured opera. His first stage work, the chamber opera *Ma Barker*, completed in 1957 while he was still an undergraduate, was followed by *Heracles*, a large-scale three-act work that summed up the first phase of his stylistic development. Fully chromatic and based on a 12-note row (mainly exploited for harmonic consistency rather than melodic continuity), *Heracles* is nevertheless organized around strong tonal

centres, a feature that has remained a hallmark of the composer's style.

Eaton's next opera, *Myshkin*, was not written until 1971, after his return to the USA. The intervening seven years had brought significant changes in his compositional outlook, which were largely due to two related developments of the mid-1960s: intensive exploration of electronic music resources, especially as applied to 'real-time' performance (Eaton worked closely with Paul Ketoff and Robert Moog on the early design of portable synthesizers); and the adoption of microtonal tuning. He developed these new resources in a series of non-operatic works featuring live electronics variously combined with solo voice, chamber ensemble and full orchestra. His music became increasingly dramatic and virtuoso in conception, acquiring an almost expressionistic intensity by the late 1960s.

Myshkin, conceived for television and based on Dostoyevsky's *The Idiot*, put these new resources to dramatic service. The action is seen through the distorted vision of the title character, whose eye becomes the eye of the camera, and whose fluctuations between moments of rationality and irrationality are mirrored in the association of the former with orchestral music in quarter-tone tuning and the latter with electronic music in sixth-tone tuning. In addition the opera adopts a multiple time frame, within which different tempos are combined to distinguish simultaneously occurring actions, and events are linked by psychological association rather than by narrative logic. Eaton's subsequent operas have largely followed the pattern set in *Myshkin*, developing an ever richer and more flexible musical language in response to the varying dramatic requirements of his librettos. Three operas, *The Lion and Androcles* (1974, Indianapolis), *Danton and Robespierre* (1978, Bloomington) and *The Cry of Clytaemnestra* (1980, Bloomington), appeared in rapid succession, establishing Eaton in the eyes of many as the most original and interesting composer of serious opera in the USA. They were followed by *The Tempest* (1985, Santa Fe), the composer's most richly textured dramatic work to date. Here Eaton calls upon the full range of his considerable technical arsenal, integrating several distinct musical styles to project the diverse levels of a multi-dimensional dramatic structure. In 1989 Eaton completed a new full-length opera, *The Reverend Jim Jones*.

Despite the sizable forces and complexity of language that Eaton favours, his music is above all singers' music. It is firmly focussed on the voice, which always carries the main burden of the musical argument, while the instrumental parts, despite their extremely elaborate and virtuoso surface, remain primarily accompanimental in function, setting the scene and underscoring the dramatic content.

See also CRY OF CLYTAEMNESTRA, THE; DANTON AND ROBESPIERRE; and TEMPEST, THE (ii).

Ma Barker, 1957 (chamber op, 1, A. Gold)
Heracles, 1964 (grand op, 3, M. Fried, after Sophocles: *The Women of Trachis*, and Seneca: *Hercules Oetaeus*), Bloomington, Indiana U. Opera Theater, 15 April 1972
Myshkin, 1971 (television op, 1, P. Creagh, after F. M. Dostoyevsky: *The Idiot*), PBS, 23 April 1973
The Lion and Androcles (children's op, 1, E. Walter and D. Anderson, after Aeneas Silvius's fable), Indianapolis, Public School no. 47, 1 May 1974
Danton and Robespierre (grand op, 3, Creagh), Bloomington, Indiana U. Opera Theater, 21 April 1978

The Cry of Clytaemnestra (chamber op, 1, Creagh, after Aeschylus: *Agamemnon*), Bloomington, Indiana U. Opera Theater, 1 March 1980

The Tempest (grand op, 3, A. Porter, after W. Shakespeare), Santa Fe, 27 July 1985

The Reverend Jim Jones, 1989 (grand op, 3, J. Reston jr)

*

R. H. Kornick: *Recent American Opera: a Production Guide* (New York, 1991), 88–95   ROBERT P. MORGAN

Ebell, Heinrich Carl (*b* Neuruppin, 30 Dec 1775; *d* Oppeln [now Opole, Poland], 12 March 1824). German composer and writer on music. While a law student at the University of Halle he studied music with D. G. Türk. After attending the Berlin court he became music director of the Breslau Opera (1801–3); he then returned to law as an administrator. He was a founder of the Philomusische Gesellschaft (1804–6), for which he wrote several scholarly essays, and he contributed to a number of periodicals, including the *Allgemeine musikalische Zeitung* in Leipzig.

Several of Ebell's operas and Singspiels were given in Berlin or Breslau. His career as a professional musician was short but intensive, resulting in several compositions above a mere amateur standard. His chamber music inclines towards the Biedermeier style of the early 19th century, but his operatic arias more closely follow Classical models.

probably lost, unless otherwise stated

Der Schutzgeist (4), Berlin, 1798
Le déserteur (2), Berlin, *c*1800
Melida, Berlin, 1800
Selico und Berissa (4, F. Kinderling), Berlin, 1800
Anacreon in Jonien, 1800 (3, H. W. Loest), rev. Breslau, Feb 1810
Das Fest der Liebe, Breslau, 1802
Die Gaben des Genius (Spl), Breslau, July 1803
Das Fest im Eichthale (3, after J. C. Bock), Breslau, 1807
Der Nachtwächter (Spl, 1, S. G. Bürde), Breslau, 1808, *D-DS*

StiegerO
C. J. A. Hoffmann: *Die Tonkünstler Schliesens* (Breslau, 1830), 73–87
Schlesische Zeitung für Musik, iii (1835), 55, 61, 71, 78, 85, 92
F. Feldmann: 'Breslaus Musikleben zur Zeit Beethovens aus der Sicht L. A. L. Siebigks', *AMw*, xix–xx (1962–3), 160–71
          HUBERT UNVERRICHT

Eberhard [Eberard], Giustina Maria ['La Todesca'] (*b* Venice; *fl* 1727–45). Italian soprano of German origin. She married a German before 1726. For the 1727 Florence carnival season she sang in operas by Bencini and Vivaldi at the Pergola; she was *virtuosa* to Beatrice Violante, consort to Ferdinando de' Medici. In spring 1727 she sang in Brussels in Antonio Maria Peruzzi's company. During 1730–31 she sang minor roles at Count Anton von Sporck's private theatre in Prague. After her return to Italy, she sang in Treviso and at the S Angelo, Venice (1731–2). She spent the following two years in Breslau and then joined the Bayreuth Hofoper, apparently retiring after 1745. A soprano of limited range (*e'–f''*) who was generally cast in secondary (and often male) roles, she excelled in pathetic and cantabile singing as suited to the unfortunate characters she usually portrayed, such as rejected lovers and political losers.

*

S. Mamy: 'La diaspora dei cantanti veneziani nella prima metà del settecento', *Nuovi studi vivaldiani: edizione e cronologia critica delle opere*, ed. A. Fanna and G. Morelli (Florence, 1988), 591–631   CARLO VITALI (with ULYSSES ROSEMAN JR)

Eberl, Anton (Franz Josef) (*b* Vienna, 13 June 1765; *d* Vienna, 11 March 1807). Austrian composer. He displayed talent early and gave piano recitals at the age of eight. At first he studied law; but sudden bankruptcy left the family unable to pay for the law examination, leading him to study music in earnest. He may have been a pupil of Mozart, who befriended him. Eberl worked mainly as a pianist and teacher. In 1795–6 he made concert tours of Germany with Constanze Mozart and Aloysia Lange. He spent two periods in St Petersburg (1796–9, 1801–2), where he was pianist to the royal family and Kapellmeister. After his return to Vienna his critical acclaim as an instrumental composer rivalled Beethoven's, and, on his death at the age of 41, the *Allgemeine musikalische Zeitung* commented that the early death of a composer was seldom so generally regretted.

Eberl was also highly regarded as a theatre composer. Beginning in 1787, possibly the year of his first studies with Mozart, and probably under the influence of his dramatist brother Ferdinand, Eberl put on in Vienna at least seven dramatic works, some of which may have been composed considerably earlier. The first, *Die Marchande des Modes*, was probably a small work; according to Gerber it drew the praise of Gluck after its first performance, the exact date and venue of which are not recorded. The work is known to have been revived at the Theater in der Leopoldstadt on 27 February 1787. Following this, two more of Eberl's operas were performed in the same theatre: *Graf Balduin von Flandern* (1788) and *Die Hexe Megäre* (3 July 1790). *Die Zigeuner*, performed at the Landstrasse Theater in 1793, may have been inspired by the 'Schauspiel mit Gesang' of the same name by Franz Scherzer, which had created a sensation in 1779. In 1794 Eberl's *Pyramus und Thisbe* was performed first in the Burgtheater and then in the Kärntnertortheater, apparently without success. It is one of only two of his operas known definitely to have been performed in these theatres, the other being his last and most important, *Die Königin der schwarzen Inseln*. Both this and another stage work, *Erwine von Steinheim*, were performed on 23 May 1801, *Die Königin* at the Kärntnertor, *Erwine* at Schikaneder's Freihaus-Theater.

Die Königin, Eberl's only extended opera (and his only surviving one), is a Zauberoper in two acts. The young librettist, Johann Schwaldopler, is said to have based his text on Wieland's *Wintermärchen*. Notwithstanding the seven further performances that it received after its première, it seems to have been a failure. Eberl's music was, according to Gerber, too 'learned' for the general public, though he added that it won the approval of Haydn (for which kindness Eberl dedicated the Piano Sonata op.12 to him). The overture was often performed in concerts, and it was the only part of the opera to be published.

all first performed in Vienna; lost unless otherwise stated

Die Marchande des Modes (Spl, 3), Kärntnertor, ?1780s
Graf Balduin von Flandern (komische Oper, 2), ?, 1788
Die Zigeuner (3, H. F. Möller, ?after F. Scherzer), Landstrasse, 1793
Pyramus und Thisbe (Melodram, 1, Eberl), National Hof (Burg), 7 Dec 1794
Der Tempel der Unsterblichkeit (prol., Reinbeck), 1799
Erwine von Steinheim (Parodie, 3, F. X. Gewey, after A. Blumauer), Freihaus, 23 May 1801
Die Königin der schwarzen Inseln (2, J. Schwaldopler, after C. M. Wieland), Kärntnertor, 23 May 1801, *A-Wn*

GerberNL; NDB (H. Federhofer)

F. J. Ewens: *Anton Eberl: ein Beitrag zur Musikgeschichte in Wien um 1800* (Dresden, 1927)

R.-A. Mooser: *Annales de la musique et des musiciens en Russie au XVIIIe siècle* (Geneva, 1948–51)

R. Haas: 'Anton Eberl', *MJb 1951*, 123–30

O. Rommel: *Die alt-Wiener Volkskomödie: ihre Geschichte vom Barocken Welt-Theater bis zum Tode Nestroys* (Vienna, 1952)

F. Hadamowsky: *Die Wiener Hoftheater (Staatstheater) 1776–1966*, i (Vienna, 1966)

A. DUANE WHITE

Eberlin, Johann Ernst (*b* Jettingen, nr Burgau, Bavaria, bap. 27 March 1702; *d* Salzburg, 19 June 1762). German composer. Educated in Augsburg, he participated as an 11-year-old in school performances of musical plays; in later years, this kind of dramatic music occupied him frequently as a composer. After studying in Salzburg he became fourth cathedral organist in 1726 and by 1749 had risen to the rank of court and cathedral Kapellmeister. He came to be widely honoured and respected.

Eberlin composed virtually all kinds of music for which there was official demand in Salzburg, including many sacred works and instrumental pieces (especially for organ). From 1742 he supplied music for numerous school plays and oratorios performed at the university and at St Peter's – a local theatrical and musical tradition that disappeared soon after his death. Three operas with texts by Metastasio are lost (*Demofoonte*, 1759; *Demetrio*, 1760; *Ipermnestra*, 1761, 1763), but in his Schuldramen, intermezzos and pastoral plays Eberlin showed himself a versatile composer in both serious and comic veins. The music is largely in the reigning Italian style, with secco and accompanied recitatives and extended da capo arias. Simple songs in the style of south German folk music also occur. These works are carefully orchestrated, with occasional instrumental solos. Comic intermezzos are frequent in the school plays, with passages in Salzburg dialect. Melodrama (spoken dialogue with orchestral accompaniment) is occasionally used.

C. Schneider: *Geschichte der Musik in Salzburg* (Salzburg, 1935)

M. Cuvay: 'Beiträge zur Lebensgeschichte des Salzburger Hofkapellmeisters Johann Ernst Eberlin', *Mitteilungen der Gesellschaft für Salzburger Landeskunde*, xcv (1955), 179–88

A. Layer: 'Johann Ernst Eberlin', *Lebensbilder aus dem bayerischen Schwaben*, vi (Munich, 1958), 388–405

M. H. Schmid: *Mozart und die Salzburger Tradition* (Tutzing, 1976)

REINHARD G. PAULY

Ebers, Clara (*b* Karlsruhe, 26 Dec 1902). German soprano. After making her début in 1924 at Karlsruhe, she was engaged in 1926 at Düsseldorf, then in 1928 at Frankfurt, where she created Isabella in the stage première of Egk's *Columbus* (1942), and in 1945 at the Hamburg Staatsoper, where she remained until her retirement in 1965. She sang Countess Almaviva with Glyndebourne at Edinburgh in 1950 and made her Covent Garden début as Violetta in 1951. She sang at the Berlin Städtische Oper and other German theatres in a repertory that included Fiordiligi, Rosina, Elisabeth de Valois, Zerbinetta, Sophie and the Marschallin, which became her finest role. She created the Countess in Klebe's *Figaro lässt sich scheiden* at Hamburg in 1963. A stylish singer of great musicality, she had a flexible, creamy-toned voice.

ELIZABETH FORBES

Ebers, John (*b* London, *c*1785; *d* London, *c*1830). English manager. Born of immigrant German parents, he had a successful bookselling business in London which he apparently also used as a ticket agency. When the Italian Opera at the King's Theatre, Haymarket, failed in 1820, Ebers took on the management with William Ayrton as his musical director. After a promising season in 1821, which introduced *La gazza ladra* and *Il turco in Italia* to London, difficulties arose, partly because of exorbitant demands by some singers. Ayrton resigned and was succeeded by a Signor Petracchi from La Scala. Ebers introduced more new works by Rossini to London; but Benelli, the assistant stage manager, to whom he sublet the theatre, sustained huge losses in 1824 and vanished, leaving the artists, including Rossini, unpaid. After a lawsuit, Ebers, with Pasta as his main attraction, opened another season in 1825. In 1826 he was involved in another lawsuit, which he lost, concerning the pay of the chorus. That season and the next ended prematurely; the rent of the theatre was then greatly increased and this, combined with further artistic difficulties, forced Ebers into bankruptcy, after which he resumed his bookselling business.

Ebers's own account of his regime, *Seven Years of the King's Theatre* (London, 1828), is entertaining and vivid. (A unique, very important grangerized, i.e. extra-illustrated, copy is in the library at the Garrick Club.) It gives his version of the complicated affairs of the opera house, with ample supporting documents. Ebers performed a valuable service to the musical life of London during a time of economic uncertainty, and besides half a dozen operas by Rossini, introduced works by Mercadante, Meyerbeer and Spontini.

ALEC HYATT KING

Ebert, (Anton) Carl [Charles] (*b* Berlin, 20 Feb 1887; *d* Santa Monica, CA, 14 May 1980). German, naturalized American, director and administrator. He began his career as a trainee actor in the Deutsches Theater, Berlin, under the tutelage of Max Reinhardt. He belonged to theatre ensembles in Frankfurt (1915–22) and Berlin (1922–7) before working as Intendant of the Landestheater, Darmstadt (1927–31), where he staged his first opera productions, *Le nozze di Figaro* and *Otello* (1929). In 1931 he moved to the Städtische Oper in Berlin. For the next two years, until Hitler came to power, he was at the forefront of the German Verdi revival. He directed the première of Weill's *Die Bürgschaft* in Berlin, 1932, but with the arrival of the Nazis he moved to Buenos Aires, where he took charge of the Teatro Colón's Wagner repertory (1933–6) with the former music director of the Dresden Opera, Fritz Busch. In 1934, Ebert and Busch collaborated on the opening seasons of the Glyndebourne Festival (*Le nozze di Figaro* and *Così fan tutte*); they laid the foundations for the festival's renowned Mozart style, and in 1938 mounted the first professional performance in England of Verdi's *Macbeth* (the 1865 revision). Ebert was Glyndebourne's first artistic director, serving from 1934 to 1939 and again from 1947 to 1959.

In 1936 Ebert founded the opera and drama school of the Ankara Conservatory, remaining as head of the Department of the Performing Arts there until 1947. He was visiting professor (opera school) at the University of Southern California, Los Angeles, from 1948 to 1954. During this period he directed the première of Stravinsky's *The Rake's Progress* at La Fenice, Venice (1951). He also directed the first productions of Krenek's *Dark Waters* and Antheil's *Volpone*. He returned to the Städtische Oper, Berlin, as Intendant in

1954, remaining until 1961. He was made a CBE in 1960 and was awarded honorary doctorates by the universities of Edinburgh (1954) and Southern California (1955). His work was characterized by a dedication to the spirit of ensemble performance and a detailed and naturalistic approach to operatic acting. His son, Peter Ebert (*b* Frankfurt, 6 April 1918), is an opera director and was director of productions with Scottish Opera, 1965–75, then general administrator, 1977–80.

*

ES
J. Russell: 'The Other Ebert', *Glyndebourne Festival Opera 1959*, 28–32 [programme book]
S. Hughes: *Glyndebourne: a History of the Festival Opera* (London, 1965)
M. Caplet: 'Carl Ebert', *Opera*, xxxi (1980), 645–6
H. Oppenheim and others: 'Carl Ebert, Man of the Theatre', *Glyndebourne Festival Opera 1981*, 112–15 [programme book]
HUGH CANNING

Eberwein, (Franz) Carl (Adalbert) (*b* Weimar, 10 Nov 1786; *d* Weimar, 2 March 1868). German composer, younger brother of the violinist Traugott Eberwein. He joined the ducal orchestra at Weimar in 1803; there he met Goethe, on whose recommendation he studied in Berlin with Zelter (1808–9). He held various posts in Weimar, including that of musical director at Goethe's house (1807) and director of music at the cathedral (1818). Although he had been turned down as court Kapellmeister in 1817, he was appointed ducal music director and director of the opera in 1826, retiring in 1849. Eberwein is important not only as a composer, but also for his influence on Goethe and Weimar musical life. He wrote several songs and some Singspiels to texts by Goethe and music to *Faust* and to *Proserpina*. Best known for his songs and stage works, Eberwein also composed an oratorio, cantatas and instrumental works, and wrote about musical life at Weimar. He married the opera singer Henriette Hässler, who performed many of his songs at the court.

all first performed at the Deutsches Nationaltheater, Weimar
Das Liebhaberkonzert, 24 Feb 1815
Der Graf von Gleichen (romantische Oper, 2), 1 May 1824
Der Teppichhändler (Liederspiel, 1, M. Seidel), 3 Feb 1830
Die Heerschau, oder Der hölzerne Säbel (A. von Kotzebue), 5 June 1844
Des Reichen Sohn aus Bremen (romantische Oper, 5, K. Holm), 11 Oct 1845
Die schöne Ruhlaerin (Liederspiel, 1, J. Eberwein), 23 May 1857
Die Reise zur Hochzeit, ? unperf.

*

ADB (M. Fürstenau); *ES* (W. Boetticher); *MGG* (G. Kraft); *NDB* (H. Heussner)
M. Zeigert: 'Goethe und der Musiker Karl Eberwein', *Berichte des freien deutschen Hochstiftes zu Frankfurt* (Frankfurt, 1836)
W. Bode: *Goethes Schauspieler und Musiker: Erinnerungen von Eberwein und Lobe* (Berlin, 1912)
——: *Die Tonkunst in Goethes Leben* (Berlin, 1912)
H. J. Moser: *Goethe und die Musik* (Leipzig, 1949)
GAYNOR G. JONES

Ebrahim, Omar (*b* Greasbrough, 6 Sept 1956). English baritone. He studied in London, then in 1979 joined the Glyndebourne chorus. In 1980 he sang Schaunard with Glyndebourne Touring Opera. For Opera Factory (1982–90) he has sung Birtwistle's Punch, Filch (*The Beggar's Opera*), Mel (*The Knot Garden*), Mercury (*Calisto*) and Don Giovanni; he also created roles in Birtwistle's *Yan Tan Tethera* and Osborne's *Hell's Angels* (1986). For Kent Opera he sang Hector (*King Priam*); for Scottish Opera, Pennybank Bill (*Mahagonny*), Strephon (*A Midsummer Marriage*),

Orlofsky and Macbeth. For Glyndebourne Touring Opera he sang Serezha in the première of Osborne's *The Electrification of the Soviet Union* in 1987 (repeating it at the 1988 festival) and Donny in Tippett's *New Year* (1990). He sang Cipolla in Stephen Oliver's *Mario and the Magician* at Batignano (1988) and made his Covent Garden début in the British première of Berio's *Un re in ascolto* (1989); he sang Parkhearst in the première of Hans-Jürgen von Bose's *63: Dream Palace* (1990, Munich), and created the Fool in Birtwistle's *Gawain* (1991, Covent Garden). A specialist in contemporary music, he is a powerful actor with an expressive, muscular voice.
ELIZABETH FORBES

Eccles, John (*b* ?London, *c*1668; *d* Hampton Wick, 12 Jan 1735). English composer. Perhaps the most unfortunate victim of the shift of taste from the English to the Italian musical style in the early years of the 18th century, Eccles, colleague and younger contemporary of Henry Purcell, was a talented composer of solo vocal music. On the evidence of his unperformed opera *Semele* (composed 1705–6) he might well have assumed Purcell's mantle and established a tradition of all-sung English opera.

Little is known of Eccles's background and early training; he came from a large family of musicians, some of whom had served in the Royal Musick from shortly after the Restoration. He was appointed Master of the King's Musick in 1700. His first published songs date from 1691; by 1693 he was closely associated with the Theatre Royal, Drury Lane, where in two seasons he composed incidental songs for at least 15 plays, six of which also included music by Purcell, namely Thomas D'Urfey's *The Richmond Heiress* (1693), John Dryden's *Aureng-Zebe* (1694 revival), Dryden's *Love Triumphant* (1694), John Crowne's *The Married Beau* (1694), D'Urfey's *Don Quixote*, Parts 1 and 2 (1694) and Dryden's *The Spanish Fryar* (1694 revival).

Throughout his stage career, Eccles was closely associated with the actress-singer Anne Bracegirdle (known as 'the celebrated virgin'), who sang only his music. The victim of an abduction in December 1692 in which her fellow actor William Mountfort was killed defending her honour, Mrs Bracegirdle returned to the stage in D'Urfey's comedy *The Richmond Heiress* in 1693 in the singing role of Fulvia. The highlight of the show was Eccles's dialogue 'By those pigsneyes that stars do seem', which proved more popular than a similar piece by Purcell in the same play. As Dryden reported, 'Mrs Bracegirdle and Solon [Thomas Doggett] were both mad: the Singing was wonderfully good, And the two whom I nam'd sung better than [those in Purcell's dialogue] whose trade it was ... The rest was woefull stuff, & concluded with Catcalls'. During the rest of the 1693–4 season, Eccles's deceptively simple, highly dramatic songs for Mrs Bracegirdle and the other actor-singers continued to overshadow Purcell's much more sophisticated music for the professional singers. In the second part of D'Urfey's *Don Quixote* trilogy (May 1694), for which the two composers were given equal billing, Eccles's scena 'I burn, I burn' (sung by Mrs Bracegirdle) again eclipsed Purcell's music and came to typify the so-called mad-song genre.

In early 1695 Eccles joined Thomas Betterton, Elizabeth Barry, Mrs Bracegirdle and the other actors who left the Theatre Royal to establish a second London playhouse in Lincoln's Inn Fields. Now in direct competition with Purcell, who remained at Drury Lane until his death in November, Eccles was in effect music director, composing both songs and orchestral music for plays, among them Congreve's masterpieces *Love for Love* (1695) and *The Way of the World* (1700). During the late 1690s his music had grown in stature and substance, and 'Love's but the frailty of the mind', a long, virtuoso declamatory song in *The Way of the World*, is decidedly Purcellian. In spite of the small and cramped stage at Lincoln's Inn Fields, the company attempted larger musical productions under Eccles's direction, the most notable of which were the masque *The Loves of Mars & Venus* (1696), in collaboration with Godfrey Finger to a libretto by Peter Anthony Motteux, a lively, witty comedy (unfortunately the recitatives do not survive), and the semi-opera *Rinaldo and Armida* (J. Dennis; 1698), in which Eccles attempted to relate all the music, even the overture, to the main spoken drama. In 1700 he wrote additional instrumental music for *Dido and Aeneas*, which he probably also arranged, for an adaptation of Shakespeare's *Measure for Measure*; this is the first certain public performance of Purcell's opera.

In 1701 a group of noblemen devised a competition to encourage the development of English opera. They commissioned Congreve to write a libretto for a masque on *The Judgment of Paris*, invited composers to submit settings and chose four finalists: Eccles, Finger, Daniel Purcell and John Weldon. The most experienced theatre composer of the group and a close friend of Congreve's, Eccles was widely tipped to win. But the first prize went to the Oxford outsider, Weldon, with Eccles placed second. During the next few years Italian opera gradually gained popularity in London, finally taking root at Vanbrugh's new theatre in the Haymarket, where Eccles was the first music director. Yet even in the face of the extraordinary success of Giovanni Bononcini's *Camilla*, the first Italian opera heard in London, old-fashioned semi-opera remained popular. One of the most successful was Granville's *The British Enchanters* (1706), for which Eccles wrote the lion's share of the music. This work, which at once recalls Purcell's *King Arthur* and anticipates aspects of Handel's *Rinaldo*, was effectively banned by the Lord Chamberlain's decree, which restricted vocal music and spoken dialogue to different theatres, making proper performances of semi-opera impossible.

Hoping to capitalize on the growing vogue for all-sung, italianate opera, Eccles set Congreve's fine libretto *Semele* (perhaps intended as the inaugural work for Vanbrugh's theatre in 1705–6). But *Semele*, in which Eccles skilfully blended features of the English masque with Italian operatic convention, was delayed and finally abandoned in favour of *Thomyris* (1707), a pasticcio arranged by Johann Christoph Pepusch. Following the lead of Congreve, who angrily gave up the theatre at about this time, Eccles withdrew from the scene, moving to Hampton Wick to fish and compose royal birthday and welcome odes, and even the occasional theatre piece, which he sent up to London by courier.

Although Eccles's music occasionally approached greatness, as in 'Couch'd in the dark and silent grave' (from *Don Quixote*, Part 1) or 'A soldier and a sailor' (from Congreve's *Love for Love*), comparisons with Purcell will always be invidious. And what might have been the salvation of English opera, *Semele*, was later transformed by Handel into an oratorio – one of the monuments of baroque music.

See also JUDGMENT OF PARIS, THE and SEMELE (i).

S. Lincoln: 'Eccles and Congreve: Music and Drama on the Restoration Stage', *Theatre Notebook*, xviii (1963), 7–18
——: 'The First Setting of Congreve's *Semele*', *ML*, xliv (1963), 103–17
——: *John Eccles: the Last of a Tradition* (diss., U. of Oxford, 1963)
C. Price: 'The Critical Decade for English Music Drama, 1700–1710', *Harvard Library Bulletin*, xxvi (1978), 38–76
R. Platt: Introduction to J. Eccles: *The Judgment of Paris*, MLE, C1 (1984)
C. Price: *Henry Purcell and the London Stage* (Cambridge, 1984)

CURTIS PRICE

Echegaray (y Eizaguirre), Miguel (*b* Quintanar de la Ordén, Toledo, 29 Dec 1848; *d* Madrid, 20 Jan 1927). Spanish librettist. He was born during a journey his parents were making from Madrid to Murcia. He grew up in Madrid with his brother, the politician, economist, mathematician, poet and dramatist José Echegaray (*b* Madrid, 19 April 1832; *d* Madrid, 14 or 15 September 1916), who wrote the libretto for the opera *Irene de Otranto* (Emilio Serrano, 1891). Miguel Echegaray demonstrated a precocious talent, and at the age of 16 he wrote a comedy, *Cara y Cruz*, which was produced at the Teatro del Circo. He pursued a successful career in law, philosophy and literature, practising as a lawyer for three years and delivering various radical addresses to the Academia de Jurisprudencia. He acted for some time as his brother's secretary, before turning to the theatre. In all he wrote over 100 comedies and zarzuela librettos, particularly for the major successes of Manuel Fernández Caballero. As an author of light pieces, he excelled in comic verve and a feel for situation and character.

selective list; all zarzuelas

El dúo de la Africana, M. F. Caballero, 1893; *El domingo de Ramos*, T. Bretón, 1895; *La viejecita*, Caballero, 1897; *Gigantes y cabezudos*, Caballero, 1898; *Los estudiantes*, Caballero, 1899; *La diligencia*, Caballero, 1901; *La seña Justa*, Caballero, 1902; *El sombrero de plumas*, Chapí, 1902; *La rabalera*, Vives, 1907; *El paleo de la presidencia*, J. Jiménez, 1908; *El castillo*, M. Nieto and Orteles, 1909; *Juegos malabares*, Vives, 1910; *Agua de noria*, Vives, 1911, *El pretendiente*, Vives, 1913   ANDREW LAMB

Echo et Narcisse ('Echo and Narcissus'). *Drame lyrique* in a prologue and three acts by CHRISTOPH WILLIBALD GLUCK to a libretto by Baron Ludwig Theodor von Tschudi after OVID's *Metamorphoses*; Paris, Opéra, 24 September 1779.

Echo *a nymph, ruler of the woods and waters*	soprano
Narcisse [Narcissus] *a young hunter, son of Cephisus*	tenor
Amour [Cupid]	soprano
Eglé ⎫ *nymphs, friends of Echo*	soprano
Aglaé ⎭	soprano
Cynire *friend of Narcissus*	tenor
Two Water Nymphs	sopranos
Two Wood Nymphs	sopranos

Sylphs, Pleasures and Pains (Cupid's attendants), Zephyrs and followers of Echo and Narcissus

Setting A small valley in Thessalia

Echo et Narcisse was Gluck's last opera. He wrote it for the Académie Royale de Musique in Paris, where it was first performed four months after *Iphigénie en Tauride*.

Unlike that opera, *Echo et Narcisse* was a failure and the Académie dropped it from their repertory after only 12 performances; as a result the disconsolate Gluck left Paris, never to return. The principals in the first performance were Henrietta Beaumesnil (Echo), Etienne Lainez (Narcissus), Mlle Girardin (Cupid), Mlle Gavaudan (Eglé), Mlle Joinville (Aglaé) and Joseph Legros (Cynire).

Gluck revised the opera, but this version was no more successful when it was performed the following year and reached only nine performances. At a third attempt, on 8 June 1781, the reception for *Echo et Narcisse* was more favourable, but there were few revivals in the 18th and 19th centuries and no staged performances of any note in this until those conducted by René Jacobs in 1987. One of these, with a cast including Sophie Boulin and Kurt Streit, was recorded live at the Schwetzingen Festival.

The libretto of the original version of *Echo et Narcisse* has survived, but the score and parts have not. The music of the revision, however, is substantially similar: it entailed only the addition of the Prologue, the alteration of the order of certain scenes and numbers of the original, and the elimination of Cupid from the first two acts (leaving him to appear only in the Prologue and at the conclusion).

PROLOGUE *A grove with the temple of Cupid on one side* After a pastoral overture, with double orchestra and echo effects, an offstage chorus of Pleasures sings of the peace of the grove. The temple doors open to reveal Cupid reclining on a bed of roses. He rises and descends the temple steps with his attendants and tells how Echo and Narcissus fell in love in the grove and how the god Apollo wanted Echo so much for himself that he put a spell on Narcissus to separate them. But Cupid is determined that Narcissus will fall in love again, and sings of his powers (*air*, 'Rien dans la nature n'échappe à mes traits') before joining in the general dancing, during which he sings two more *airs* before returning to the temple.

ACT 1 *A flowery hillside with the altar and temple of Cupid, the nymphs' grotto and Narcissus's fountain* Aglaé, Eglé and a chorus of water nymphs are celebrating: today is the wedding day of Echo and Narcissus. Echo and her followers enter, carrying white doves and flowers which they put on the altar and temple steps. In a duet Echo confesses to Cynire that she has been hiding her feelings: Narcissus is avoiding her. Cynire admits that Narcissus has been hiding from him too and Echo, suspecting Narcissus to be unfaithful, sends Cynire to find him. Echo prays to Cupid to take pity on her and help her (*air*, 'Peut-être d'un injuste effroi').

Eglé tells Echo to join the celebrations. Echo is about to disclose what has happened when she sees Narcissus. He goes to the fountain and leans over it, admiring his own reflection, which Apollo's spell has made him see as a beautiful water goddess; his arioso ('Divinité des eaux') is richly scored, using the echo effects of the overture. Echo calls him, but he does not hear her and leaves.

Knowing she now has a rival, Echo tells Cynire that she is ready to die. The act ends with Echo's brief *air* of anguish ('D'une vie aussi malheureuse') followed by a duet ('L'espoir fuit de mon coeur'); its restless, syncopated rhythms convey her agitation.

ACT 2 *A flowery hillside* (as Act 1) Eglé tells Cynire that one look from Narcissus will bring the dying Echo back to life; Cynire hurries off to find him. Echo enters, pale and forlorn; Eglé, Aglaé and two other nymphs join in an extended quartet to try to persuade her to live ('O chère et tendre amie'). But in a touching recitative Echo says she is near to death; sombre choruses follow ('O mortelles alarmes', with three trombones added to the orchestra), after which Echo bids her attendants a final farewell.

Eglé is still waiting for Cynire when Narcissus enters and begs the water of the fountain to open so that he can be with his beloved reflection (*air*, 'Je ne puis m'ouvrir ta froide demeure'). Cynire tries desperately to tell Narcissus what has happened to Echo. Narcissus sings again of his confused passion ('O combats, ô désordre extrême') before Apollo restores him to his senses in a clap of thunder just in time for Narcissus to hear the nymphs lamenting Echo's death (offstage chorus, 'Dieux qu'implorent ses tristes yeux'; this slow, homophonic processional chorus with interjections from Narcissus and Cynire recalls the sacrificial chorus in Act 3 of *Iphigénie en Aulide* as well as the choruses of mourning from *Orfeo* and *Alceste*). The temple doors open to reveal the dying Echo; Narcissus, his senses restored, runs towards her just as the doors close, and he rushes off into the forest.

ACT 3 *A flowery hillside* (as Act 1) Echo's nymphs come hurrying out of the woods, looking up as if to see where Echo's voice, tenderly imitated by the orchestra, is coming from. This simple but beautiful introduction provides the musical material for Aglaé's *air* with its choral lament ('Chère compagne, en vain de ces sombres forêts'). Narcissus enters followed by Cynire, whom he begs to leave him to his guilt. Cynire's elaborately scored *air* affirming his friendship ('Dissipe ce mortel effroi'), with solos for viola and cello, is followed by a remorseful outburst from Narcissus.

Left alone, Narcissus sings of his suffering and calls to the spirit of Echo to take pity on him ('Beaux lieux, témoins de mon ardeur'). Her voice is heard echoing his; he is just about to stab himself, so that he can join her in death, when the temple doors open: Echo lies there, restored to life, and Cupid leads a quartet of rejoicing ('Quel retour, ô dieux, quel moment!'). The opera ends with a hymn in praise of Cupid ('Le dieu de Paphos et de Gnide') and a ballet.

*   *   *

Echo et Narcisse was a failure at its early performances largely because the audiences and critics expected high drama along the lines of *Alceste*, *Armide* and *Iphigénie en Tauride*. But *Echo et Narcisse* is a different type of work; it belongs to the pastoral tradition, still popular at this date, and a genre to which Gluck frequently returned. Comparisons were (and are still) made with Gluck's more popular dramas because *Echo et Narcisse* contains numbers and scenes similar to those that had made greater impressions before. It is not a weak opera, and there is much fine music in it, but despite Gluck's psychological insights and the score's harmonic and orchestral riches and subtleties, *Echo et Narcisse* may well seem a little too restrained and lacking in contrast, dramatically as well as musically. The second and third acts work well, but the Prologue is no more than an excuse for a *divertissement*, and after it the first act hangs fire. This is partly the fault of the libretto, one of the weakest Gluck set, but it is also due to the predominance of 'pastoral' music, beautiful though much of it is. There really is too much prominent woodwind writing and simple harmony with mellifluous 3rds and 6ths.

Yet *Echo et Narcisse* merits an occasional revival, and given a sensitive production and performance it can succeed, as Gluck knew. He himself put the matter in a nutshell when he said that no theatre is too large for *Iphigénie en Tauride*, but none is too small for *Echo et Narcisse*.   JEREMY HAYES

Eclair, L' ('The Lightning Flash'). *Opéra comique* in three acts by FROMENTAL HALÉVY to a libretto by JULES-HENRI VERNOY DE SAINT-GEORGES and F. A. Eugène de Planard; Paris, Opéra-Comique (Salle de la Bourse), 16 December 1835.

L'éclair was the most successful of Halévy's *opéras comiques*, following hard on the heels of his most successful grand opera *La Juive*. The story supposes that a young naval officer, Lionel (tenor), is blinded by a lightning flash near Boston, where an Englishman, George (tenor), has brought his two cousins, Henriette (soprano) and Mme Darbel (soprano). Of the two sisters Henriette is shy and retiring, while Mme Darbel is a merry widow, hankering for the gay life. Their contrasting characters are neatly presented in the opening duet. George, who constantly reminds us that he went to the University of Oxford, restores Lionel's sight, whereupon Lionel identifies the wrong sister as the one to whom he has given his heart. The threads are untangled so that Lionel and Henriette can be united after all. The music is brisk, witty, and abundant in key changes and sudden shifts. Lionel has some fine music, especially his opening *air* 'Partons, la mer est belle' and in the Act 1 finale where he laments his lost sight.   HUGH MACDONALD

Ecole de la jeunesse, L' [*L'école de la jeunesse, ou Le Barnevelt françois* ('The School of Folly, or The French Barnwell')]. *Comédie mêlée d'ariettes* in three acts by EGIDIO DUNI to a libretto by LOUIS ANSEAUME; Paris, Comédie-Italienne (Hôtel de Bourgogne), 24 January 1765.

L'école de la jeunesse was inspired by George Lillo's domestic tragedy *The London Merchant* (1731) and typifies two trends in the *opéra comique* of the 1760s. The first was the influence on French playwrights of English literature – witness also Sedaine's *Le roi et le fermier* (1762), modelled on Robert Dodsley's play *The King and the Miller of Mansfield*, and A.-A.-H. Poinsinet's *Tom Jones* (1767) – which greatly inspired the liberal philosophies of the Enlightenment. The second was the cultivation of a more forceful dramatic style and the treatment of more serious subject matter, characteristics that led to the evolution of a specific type of *opéra comique*, the *drame lyrique*.

Having set some 15 librettos that were lighthearted and comic in tone, Duni ventured on new ground with *L'école de la jeunesse*. The central character in the opera is Cléon (tenor), an elegant but renegade youth, who has abandoned his fiancée, Sophie (soprano), for the charms of a rich widow named Hortense (soprano). This association causes him to accumulate great debts, and, to appease his creditors, he is forced to steal money from his uncle. In Lillo's version, the fallen hero is condemned to the gallows. Anseaume, however, has Cléon repent and return to his first love.

The work called for an unusually large cast of 16, which enabled Anseaume to construct elaborate stage tableaux, particularly at the close of each act, to which Duni responded with large-scale ensemble movements. Indeed, the concerted writing in *L'école de la jeunesse* (which includes one sextet and two septets) explores new ground for its time in its musical complexity and imaginative juxtaposition of characters. The second act, for example, concludes with a septet in which the participants are arranged into three separate groups and create a play within a play: a song is performed by Le Chanteur (tenor); Hortense and two of her suite interrupt incessantly with appreciative comments; and three male characters (two tenors and a bass) indulge in a hotly disputed game of cards. Smith described this finale as 'one of the most vital ensemble passages in all of Duni's *opéras-comiques*'.

Praised also for its adroit mixture of comic and sombre elements by the *Mercure*, *L'école de la jeunesse* was performed 19 times during 1765 and was revived in 1766 and 1768. A reworking of Anseaume's libretto by Alessio Prati in 1779 met with limited success.
                                                    ELISABETH COOK

Ecume des jours, L' ('The Foam of the Days'). Opera in three acts by EDISON DENISOV to his own libretto, after Boris Vian's novel; Paris, Opéra-Comique (Salle Favart), 15 March 1986.

Following his 1973 song cycle *La vie en rouge*, to words by Vian, Denisov returned to the work of the French jazz musician and existentialist poet for his second opera. The libretto incorporates Vian's novel and some of his poetry, texts from the funeral service (in French) and plainchant. The final children's chorus uses liturgical texts. Denisov's libretto echoes the language of the novel, with its bold linguistic constructions and absurd exaggerations, rather in the spirit of jazz; it also depicts the emptiness in a philosophy of life devoted to total freedom and total egotism. The plot, set in Paris in the 1940s, concerns the thoughts, actions and fate of two pairs of young intellectuals. Colin (tenor) and Chloé (soprano) are enjoying their honeymoon when Chloé develops a strange incurable malady caused by a waterlily lodging in her lungs, obstructing her breathing. Their friends Chick (tenor) and Alise (mezzo-soprano) are drifting apart because Chick spends all their money buying the writings of their philosophy teacher. In the final act, the police try to confiscate the writings and Chick is eliminated, Alise dies trying to burn the philosopher's library while Chloé succumbs to her condition. Colin is left talking to a disillusioned and indifferent Jesus (baritone). Among the linguistic jokes are 'Jean-Sol Partre', the philosophy teacher, and a 'trishop', who conducts the wedding, with 'pederasts of honour' (instead of maids of honour) attending the ceremony. Denisov was faithful to his source in setting the wedding section, but it had to be omitted from the first performance in Paris. The inclusion of jazz instruments (soprano and alto saxophone, drums, piano) and taped recordings of Duke Ellington – playing live in Gelsenkirchen – is in line with the exaggeration of the source material. In scene ix there is a quotation from Wagner's *Tristan und Isolde*. According to the composer the musical heart of the opera is Act 3, towards which the whole treatment and all the musical material points.

Stylistically, Denisov set out to turn those elements of the novel arising from the spirit of jazz back into jazz music. Thus there are certain obvious points of contact with the jazz operas of the 1920s (Krenek and Weill), although the composer does not like this relationship emphasized; he would prefer to be seen – in the deliberate planning of the structure of his scenes – as following in the Mozartian tradition.

Denisov completed *L'écume des jours* in 1981 but it was not a commissioned work and, apart from the performance of the concert suite *Colin et Chloé* (17 October 1983, Moscow), it seemed to have a slim chance of gaining a first performance in Russia. Since its Paris première in 1986 it has been staged in Perm' (1989) as *Pena dney* and in Gelsenkirchen (1991) as *Der Schaum der Tage*.   DETLEF GOJOWY

Eda-Pierre, Christiane (*b* Fort de France, Martinique, 24 March 1932). Martinique soprano. She studied in Paris and made her début in 1958 at Nice as Leïla (*Les pêcheurs de perles*). After singing Pamina at Aix-en-Provence (1959) and Lakmé at the Opéra-Comique (1961), she made her début at the Opéra as Fatima in *Les Indes galantes* (1962). At Wexford she sang Imogene in *Il pirata* (1976). Later she took part in the first performance of Messiaen's *François d'Assise* (1983, Paris). She has also sung in Berlin, Lyons and Orange. A most attractive artist, she excels in coloratura roles such as Lucy, Konstanze, the Queen of Night, Zerbinetta and Catharine Glover (*La jolie fille de Perth*), which she recorded for the BBC.   ELIZABETH FORBES

Edelmann, Jean-Frédéric [Johann Friedrich] (*b* Strasbourg, 5 May 1749; *d* Paris, 17 July 1794). Alsatian composer. He went to Paris in 1774 and became famous as a composer, harpsichordist and pianist. Méhul was among his students. Edelmann's opera, *Ariane dans l'isle de Naxos* (1, P. L. Moline), was first performed at the Paris Opéra on 24 September 1782. The score, dedicated to Mme Desallier D'Argenville, was probably published the same year. According to Lajarte, *Ariane* was staged almost every year until 1801, receiving altogether 46 performances. Although it lacks a real plot, the drama is conveyed by short, pithy phrases: in the first part Theseus's psychological conflict is interspersed with choruses of soldiers urging him to depart from Naxos, and in the second part Ariane's mourning comprises a dialogue with a chorus of nymphs. Edelmann set these two dramatic scenes as short, interwoven recitatives, arias and choruses which express the characters' perturbed feelings through strong chromatic alterations and frequent dynamic changes. The work bears stylistic similarities to the music of Gluck, whose *Orfeo ed Euridice* and *Iphigénie en Aulide* Edelmann arranged for the piano. *Ariane* falls historically into the period after Gluck's departure from Paris and before Salieri's arrival, when the success of Piccinni had reached its peak.

Edelmann also wrote a *scène lyrique*, *La bergère des alpes*, to a libretto by Moline (Paris, Tuileries, 20 July 1781), the ballet *Feu* (1782, Paris) and the *opéra-ballet Diane et l'amour* (1802, Paris). In 1789 Edelmann returned to Strasbourg and became administrator of the Lower Rhine. He died under the guillotine.

*
T. de Lajarte: *Bibliothèque musicale du théâtre de l'Opéra*, i (Paris, 1878), 332
A. Pougin: *Méhul, sa vie, son génie, son caractère* (Paris, 1889)
R. Benton: 'Jean-Frédéric Edelmann, a Musical Victim of the French Revolution', *MQ*, l (1964), 165–87   MICHAEL FEND

Edelmann, Otto (*b* Brunn am Gebirge, nr Vienna, 5 Feb 1917). Austrian bass-baritone. He studied in Vienna with Lierhammer and Graarud, making his début in 1937 at Gera as Mozart's Figaro. From 1938 to 1940 he was engaged at Nuremberg. In 1947 he joined the Vienna Staatsoper, where he made his début as the Hermit (*Der Freischütz*). At the first two postwar Bayreuth Festivals (1951, 1952) he sang Hans Sachs, repeating the role at the Edinburgh Festival (1952) and at his Metropolitan début (1954). He sang Ochs in the first opera performance in the new Salzburg Festspielhaus in 1960. His repertory also included Leporello, Rocco, Amfortas, King Henry (*Lohengrin*), Gurnemanz, Plumkett (*Martha*) and Dulcamara.

HAROLD ROSENTHAL/R

Eder, Helmut (*b* Linz, 26 Dec 1916). Austrian composer. After graduating from the Bruckner-Konservatorium, Linz, in 1948, he studied in Stuttgart and with Orff in Munich. He then taught at the Bruckner-Konservatorium, where he was made professor in 1962; he was later professor of composition at the Salzburg Mozarteum (1967) and worked as a choirmaster and concert organizer. He made a name primarily through his operas, ballets and other stage works. His early music shows the influence of Hindemith and J. N. David but later he experimented with neo-classicism, serialism, *Klangfarben* technique and electronic sounds. In *Der Aufstand* (1976), a work set during the Thirty Years War and centring on the rebel leader Stefan Fadinger, Eder's eclecticism displays itself in the form of musical 'borrowing': German folktunes, a quotation from Bach's *St Matthew Passion* and a Dies Irae in the style of his teacher, Orff, are incorporated into a musical language by turns lyrical and dissonant. The orchestral writing is often dark (there are no violins), and vocally Eder makes a special feature of Sprechgesang and ordinary speech. The spoken role of Fadinger was created by Kurt Schossmann.

Oedipus (H. Weinstock, after Sophocles), Linz, 1960
Der Kardinal, 1962 (E. Brauner), Österreichisches Fernsehen, Linz, 1965
Die weisse Frau, 1968 (K. Kleinschmidt), unperf.
Konjugation 3 (R. Bayr), Österreichisches Fernsehen, 1969
Der Aufstand (G. Fussenegger), Linz, aut. 1976
George Dandin, oder Der betrogene Ehemann, 1978

MONIKA LICHTENFELD

Edgar. *Dramma lirico* in three acts (originally four acts) by GIACOMO PUCCINI to a libretto by FERDINANDO FONTANA after Alfred de Musset's dramatic poem *La coupe et les lèvres*; Milan, Teatro alla Scala, 21 April 1889 (definitive version, Buenos Aires, Teatro de la Opera, 8 July 1905).

Puccini's first full-length opera, commissioned by Ricordi to a libretto by the author of *Le villi*, *Edgar* was first given under Franco Faccio with Gregorio Gabrielesco as Edgar (tenor), Pio Marini as Gualtiero (bass), Antonio Magini-Coletti as Frank (baritone), Aurelia Cataneo-Caruson as Fidelia (soprano) and Romilda Pantaleoni as Tigrana (soprano). It was coolly received and ran for only three performances. Of various revivals projected over the next two years the only one to materialize took place at Puccini's native town, Lucca, where it enjoyed great success. Nonetheless the composer decided to suppress the last act, grafting the sensational denouement on to Act 3, transferring the prelude in shortened form to the beginning of Act 1 and assigning some of Fidelia's music to Tigrana, now a mezzo-soprano, in Act 2. Further modifications followed, including the suppression of the prelude, leading to the definitive version of 1905, first performed in Buenos Aires, conducted by Leopoldo Mugnone with Giovanni Zenatello in the title role.

The opera is set in Flanders in 1302 and Act 1 takes place in a village square. Edgar, asleep outside his house, is awakened by Fidelia, who gives him a sprig of almond blossom (see ex.1). The Moorish Tigrana mocks the

Ex.1 Act 1

Andante un poco mosso

p dolciss.

FIDELIA

Già il man - dor - lo vi - ci - no_____ dei pri - mi fior sior - nò; se so - vra il mio cam - mi - no_____

['Already the almond-tree nearby has decked itself with its first blossom; if as I pass by (I should meet Edgar)']

young man's infatuation with an innocent village maiden and reminds him that he once entertained very different desires. When Fidelia's brother, the love-lorn Frank, arrives Tigrana repulses him with scorn, leaving him to lament his enslavement to a woman so base ('Questo amor, vergogna mia'). The villagers assemble for a church service, during which Tigrana scandalizes the congregation with a cruel, implicitly blasphemous song, 'Tu il cuor mi strazi'. They threaten to attack her, but she is defended by Edgar, who sets fire to his house and declares that he will leave the village for ever with her. Their way is barred by Frank. The two men draw their swords, as Fidelia and her father Gualtiero arrive. All express their dismay in a Ponchiellian *pezzo concertato*, after which Edgar drags Tigrana away with him, having first wounded Frank in a duel.

Act 2 takes place on the terrace of a magnificent palace. Edgar regrets his new life of debauchery and thinks longingly of Fidelia ('O soave vision'), while Tigrana vainly tries to re-awaken his desire for her. A troop of soldiers passes, led by Frank. Ignoring Tigrana's pleas Edgar decides to join his former antagonist and redeem his sins in the service of his country. At the beginning of Act 3 a military funeral is in progress on the battlements of a fortress near Courtray. The soldiers pray for the soul of Edgar, their valiant captain, whom they believe to have fallen in battle. Behind the coffin stand Frank and a monk whose face is concealed beneath his cowl. Also present are Gualtiero and Fidelia, who mourns the death of her only love ('Addio, mio dolce amor'). Frank begins the funeral oration but is interrupted by the monk who reminds the bystanders of Edgar's past misdeeds and so works them up into a fury against his memory. Fidelia defends him as one whose heart is pure and whose sins were merely those of youth ('Nel villaggio d'Edgar'). The people retire shamefacedly. Tigrana enters in deep mourning to pray at Edgar's coffin. In a comic terzetto ('Bella signora, il pianto sciupa gli occhi') Frank and the monk bribe her with the offer of jewels to denounce her lover before the returning crowd as a traitor to his country. The people rush to tear open the coffin, but all they find inside is a suit of armour. The monk uncovers his face to reveal Edgar. He embraces Fidelia and declares that he has been reborn; whereupon Fidelia steals up to her rival and stabs her to the heart.

Edgar was first conceived as a grand opera on a Meyerbeerian scale (though without ballet), including a virtuoso role for a dramatic prima donna in the person of Tigrana, modelled partly on Carmen. In revising the opera Puccini eliminated much that was turgid and uncharacteristic; but he also compounded the faults of the dramatic scheme, reducing it to an unexplained succession of bizarre situations. Nowhere does Wagner's gibe about 'effects without causes' seem more apposite. Musically, however, the level of craftsmanship is remarkably high and the crystallization of a personal style already far advanced. Some of the material is re-elaborated from earlier, non-theatrical works, notably the so-called *Messa di gloria* (1880), the *Preludio* in A for orchestra (1882), an *Adagio* for string quartet (1882), the *Capriccio sinfonico* (1883) and the song *Storiella d'amore* (1883). Among the various recurring themes Tigrana's motif has something of the brutality that would later characterize Scarpia in *Tosca*. Other Puccinian features include successions of parallel chords, added notes (especially the 'frozen' sixth) and a fondness for floating a purely diatonic melody on a pattern of unresolved dissonances (ex.1). Part of the duet for Fidelia and Edgar in the discarded fourth act was used again in *Tosca* ('Amaro sol per te'), where, curiously, the harmonic clashes are milder than in the original context.

Alone of Puccini's operas *Edgar* has never been translated into another language. Puccini himself, ever ready to defend his less fortunate offspring such as *La rondine* and *Suor Angelica*, showed no retrospective affection for this one. On a vocal score sent to his friend Sybil Seligman he defaced the title thus: E Dio ti Gu A Rda da quest'opera ('And may God preserve you from this opera'). However, Toscanini conducted the Act 3 'Requiem' at the composer's funeral in Milan Cathedral on 3 December 1924.   JULIAN BUDDEN

Edgcumbe, Richard. *See* MOUNT EDGCUMBE, RICHARD.

Edinburgh. Capital of Scotland. It was the largest town in Scotland before 1800 and its artistic capital until about 1880. The first opera performance, given at the Tailors Hall in 1729, was of Allan Ramsay's ballad opera *The Gentle Shepherd*. In 1737 the town authorities, who took a dim view of the playhouse generally, closed Ramsay's own theatre. A more successful venture was the Canongate Theatre (1750), where such operas as J. F. Lampe's *The Dragon of Wantley* were sandwiched in between orchestral pieces to circumvent the ban against drama. In 1769 the celebrated castrato G. F. Tenducci included several 'Scotch' songs by Robert Fergusson in his performance of Arne's *Artaxerxes* at the Canongate. The focus of Edinburgh entertainment then moved to the New Town, where Domenico Corri presented *The Wives Revenged* in 1778. For a time Corri was manager of the Theatre Royal, Shakespeare Square (opened 1769, cap. 700), which gave three or four performances a week. *Der Freischütz* had its Edinburgh première there in 1824, while *Oberon* was first heard at Corri's Concert Rooms, Broughton Street, in 1826. Jenny Lind visited the city in 1847, 1848 (singing *Lucia di Lammermoor* and *La sonnambula* at the Theatre Royal), 1856 and 1861. A new Theatre Royal, holding 1800 spectators and with a stage measuring some 11 metres by 20, was built on the site of Corri's Rooms. The smaller Lyceum Theatre, Brougham Place (modern cap. 900), was built in 1883; here Hamish MacCunn's *Jeanie Deans* received its première in 1894. Finally, the King's Theatre (now with 1336 seats) opened in 1906 with performances of *Tannhäuser* and *Pagliacci* by the Carl Rosa Opera Company; a short time later the King's was the venue for the visiting Beecham Opera Company. Among other Edinburgh theatres presenting opera at one time or another between 1793 and 1946 were the Sadler's Wells, the Adelphi and the Queen's.

Although Edinburgh has never had a permanent professional company, operatic activity has been stimulated by individuals associated with the city. The soprano Euphrosyne Parepa (later Parepa-Rosa) was born there in 1836. The resident Austrian Ernst Denhof formed the Denhof Opera Company to present Wagner's *Ring* outside London (1910–13). In 1920 the Edinburgh Grand Opera Society was founded to provide chorus members for touring companies; its director was the former Wagnerian tenor Charles Hedmont, who taught singing in the city in the later years of his life. In April 1929 the Society presented Donald Tovey's long-awaited *Bride of Dionysus* (begun 1907, completed 1918) at the renovated Empire Theatre, Nicolson Street (with scenery and costumes by Charles Ricketts). On alternate nights Barbirolli conducted *La bohème* and *Pagliacci* here, featuring the Edinburgh tenor Joseph Hislop.

The Edinburgh Festival – officially the Edinburgh International Festival of Music, Drama and the Visual Arts – was inaugurated in 1947; it grew from a suggestion by Rudolf Bing that aimed at finding an additional outlet for the Glyndebourne Festival (of which he had been the pre-war manager) when its opera productions were resumed after the war, and the desire to renew cultural contact with other countries. Bing was appointed artistic director at Edinburgh and organized the first three festivals. He was succeeded in turn by Ian Hunter (1950), Robert Ponsonby (1956), the Earl of Harewood (1961), Peter Diamand (1966), John Drummond (1979), Frank Dunlop (1984) and Brian McMaster (1991). The festival usually begins on the second Sunday in August and continues for three weeks.

Opera performances are a main feature each year, and have been given in the King's and Royal Lyceum Theatres (with structural and electrical improvements, and now municipally owned), until 1967 in the Empire Theatre, and more recently at the Playhouse Theatre, Greenside Place, the largest indoor theatre in Europe (its stage is 25 metres wide and 12 deep). Until 1955 they were regularly presented by the Glyndebourne Festival company, except in 1952 when the Hamburg Opera became the first foreign opera company to appear at the festival. Visiting companies have successively presented productions from: Hamburg (1952, 1956, 1968, 1983); Milan (1957, 1982); Stuttgart (1958, 1966); Stockholm (1959, 1974, 1986, 1987, 1988); Belgrade (1962); Naples (1963); Prague (1964, 1970); Holland Festival (1965); Munich (1965); Florence (1969, 1971); Frankfurt (1970); West Berlin (1971, 1975); Düsseldorf (1972, 1976); Palermo (1972); Budapest (1973); Zürich (1978); Cologne (1980, 1981); Dresden (1982); St Louis (1983); Washington (1984); Hartford (1985); Lyons (1985); Leningrad (1986, 1991); Helsinki (1987); Houston (1988); Madrid (1989); and Moscow and Bratislava (1990).

In some years these have alternated with, or been supplemented by, British companies, including a further visit by Glyndebourne (1960), and seasons by the Covent Garden Opera (1961, 1965), the English Opera Group (1962, 1963, 1968, 1973) and Kent Opera (1979). Scottish Opera, formed in 1962, first participated in the festival in 1967, and did so in each year to 1984 except 1969 and 1973. The Edinburgh Festival Opera, an ad hoc ensemble for specific productions, was first formed in 1973 to present *Don Giovanni*, which was repeated in 1974 and followed by *Le nozze di Figaro* in 1975–6 and *Carmen* in 1977. In 1988 the Playhouse was used for the first British performance of John Adams's *Nixon in China*.

Despite the evident demand for an opera house in Edinburgh, and after long years of debate over the proposed building of one at a site in Castle Terrace, the civic authorities decided in 1988 to build a financial centre there instead.

Elayo: 'Opera in Edinburgh', *Weekly Scotsman* (9 Oct 1938)

G. Wark: 'The Years of Opera', *New Saltire*, v/Aug (1962), 19–24

R. Telfer: 'The *Ring* in Scotland 1910–13', *Scottish Opera Magazine* (aut. 1971), 9–15, 22–3

G. Bruce: *Festival in the North* (London, 1975)

M. Turnbull: *Edinburgh Portraits* (Edinburgh, 1987), 31–40, 92–8

NOËL GOODWIN, MICHAEL T. R. B. TURNBULL

Editing. The central dilemma facing the editor of an opera, of any period, is that the act of preparing an edition involves imposing a degree of fixity on an unfixed original: in presenting an opera in a textually concrete form when opera itself, being essentially the product of a particular set of circumstances, social, theatrical and musical, varies textually from performance to performance. The present article outlines the textual problems specific to different periods and the solutions appropriate to them. (It does not treat the more routine aspects of editing, such as notational conventions, that are not specific to opera; for discussion of these see Brown, *The New Grove*, v, 839–48.)

1. The 17th century. 2. The 18th century. 3. The 19th and 20th centuries.

1. THE 17TH CENTURY. On the most general level, the editing of an early opera requires essentially the same kinds of decision-making as the editing of any other kind of early music. Most important, the purpose of the edition, whether practical or scholarly or some compromise between the two, must be determined in advance. Such a decision will affect each subsequent

step of the editing process. If the purpose is purely scholarly, a plain facsimile might be most useful, providing the source is clearly legible. (Two outstanding series of publications of this kind are Italian Opera 1640–1770 and Drammaturgia musicale veneta.) If the edition is intended primarily for performance, additional questions must be answered. Does that performance aim to recreate the past as it was or in some way to reinterpret it for the present? If the latter, under what conditions? Should the editing merely aim to translate old-fashioned notational symbols according to modern practice (to reduce note values, regularize barring, modernize key and time signatures, add bass figures), or should it extend further to the interpretation of unfamiliar practices (realization of the continuo, addition of ornaments), to compensating for obsolete conditions (transpositions to accommodate differences in vocal ranges, in particular the absence of castratos) or reorchestration for modern instruments? Should it take the final step and prescribe interpretation by adding tempo, expression and dynamic marks? Each of these interventions, and the decisions attendant upon them, runs the risk of distorting the original even as it attempts to communicate it.

Next, the sources of the work must be evaluated and a decision taken as to whether they (or the general purpose of the edition) dictate a single-source edition or one that collates a variety of sources. If a collation, it must be determined how best to indicate variants (with footnotes, for example, or with distinctive typography). Here opera presents somewhat greater complexity than most other musical genres. Not only will the sources invariably include musical as well as textual ones, which may require different kinds of editorial decision, but there may be no way of determining the relative authenticity or preferability of any of them. Such uncertainty results from the fact that operas were almost always written to order, for specific performing conditions, with particular singers in mind; once performed, they were considered 'used up' and done with. Accordingly, at least in Italy, operatic scores were rarely published. If an opera was revived in a subsequent season, it invariably required alteration to suit new conditions and performers. Often a new composer was engaged to make the revisions, and the result would be a pasticcio. A single work could theoretically be represented by a different source or group of sources for every revival: the concept of a definitive text is anachronistic and irrelevant.

A modern editor is thus left with the problem of evaluating the surviving sources, deciding on their relative authenticity, priority or proximity to the composer. (The lack of definitive sources and the prevalence of the pasticcio model for revised operas has been taken as licensing editors to invent their own music for passages of text from the libretto that may be missing in the score, to add ritornellos to accommodate stage exigencies, or to incorporate music borrowed from other operas – by the same composer or one of his contemporaries – with the excuse that they are reproducing the 'authentic' attitude and practice if not the actual music that was heard at any single performance. This attitude is manifested most successfully in recent recordings of Cavalli, Cesti and Monteverdi under René Jacobs.) There are some exceptional operas that were published in definitive scores, whose overt purpose was celebratory rather than practical: to glorify a ruling dynasty rather than entertain a public. The early Medici operas in Florence, Monteverdi's Mantuan Orfeo, the Barberini operas in 17th-century Rome and Lully's tragédies en musique for Louis XIV were published to commemorate their patrons and the occasions on which they were performed. But even these scores, though rendered definitive by publication, present problems of realization and interpretation that need to be resolved by the modern editor. The printed Lully editions, for example, often do not include inner string parts, and they rarely conform with other surviving source material.

Monteverdi's first and last operas exemplify the range of problems raised by various kinds of sources; and editions of the two works illustrate the range of available solutions. Orfeo, essentially a court opera, survives in two printed scores (the first from 1609, two years after the performance, the other a reprint from 1614) and a libretto published for the Mantuan performance of 1607 that matches the scores in all important respects save the completely different final scene, which suggests that the score may represent a later version of the opera. An edition must necessarily be based on the published score, since there is no extant music for the final scene as it appears in the libretto. But the score, though itself relatively specific as regards orchestration, leaves many questions unresolved. It offers a number of choices (playing the toccata with or without muted trumpets, singing 'Possente spirto' with or without Monteverdi's suggested ornaments). The editor of a practical edition may make the choice himself (Stevens 1968 transposes the toccata, eliminating the participation of muted trumpets), but a scholarly edition needs to acknowledge all the possibilities. Malipiero, for example, in his edition for the Complete Works, essentially reproduces the 1609 score, with all of its choices and lacunae (though he adds dynamics and tempo marks and, rather modestly, realizes the continuo). His edition can be used as the basis of a performance but is not itself a performing edition. Stevens's, on the other hand, is clearly designed for performance. He makes a number of changes and choices intended to facilitate performance by a standard group of players and singers. He rebars many passages to emphasize proper textual accentuation (although this may diminish the effect of hemiola and restrict the flow of the recitative), modernizes key signatures, offers alternatives for what he regards as obsolete or rare instruments (oboes replace cornetts), realizes the continuo and adds cadential ornaments. In specifying instrumentation where Monteverdi did not, he occasionally distorts Monteverdi's aims by mixing groups of instruments intended to signify different realms (oboes with strings, for instance). Although he explains his editorial decisions in a fairly extensive preface, the original readings are not always clear in the score itself.

Monteverdi's last opera, L'incoronazione di Poppea, presents an altogether different range of editorial problems. Because it was designed for the public theatre, no score was ever published. The two surviving manuscript scores, in Venice and Naples, which clearly represent different revivals, both date from well after the composer's death. The remaining sources comprise a scenario (synopsis) published at the time of the first performance (1643) and a number of librettos, two of them printed (1651, 1656), the rest in manuscript. Because only the scenario and possibly one or two of the manuscript librettos date from the composer's lifetime, establishing an 'authentic' text – that is, the one produced by Monteverdi himself at the first performance – is virtually impossible. The problems of authenticity are dwarfed, however, by the ambiguity of the sources themselves and the numerous variants, both musical and textual, that they offer, rendering the establishment of a definitive (even if unauthentic) text extremely difficult. In the important matter of orchestration, for instance, the scores are much more laconic than that of *Orfeo* – in part because the orchestral practice of public opera was more flexible, and the variety of instruments more limited, than that of court opera.

Two performing editions of *L'incoronazione*, by Leppard (1964) and Curtis (1989), vividly illustrate the differences between an undisguisedly practical edition and one with scholarly intent. Making no attempt to collate the sources, and basing his edition, it would seem, on the Venice score, Leppard's intervention affects the work at every level: he alters the original structure of the opera from three to two acts, cuts, re-arranges and transposes much of the original material (including the entire roles of Otho and Nero, originally written for castratos) and changes and amplifies the original orchestration. In addition to providing an elaborate realization of the continuo line, including glissandos and arpeggios, he enlarges the continuo group by the addition of harps and enriches continuo accompaniments by the addition of strings. The result is a 'realization' (as Leppard calls it) rather than an edition as such, intended less to recover the original than to translate its theatrical effect into modern terms, according to present needs and taste. Its best claim to authenticity is that, like Monteverdi's original opera of 1643, it was designed for a specific set of performance conditions (in this case a standard bipartite Glyndebourne performance of the mid-1960s, when Venetian opera was virtually unknown and the style untrusted).

Pursuing the analogy, however, in the 1990s, increased familarity with Venetian opera has rendered Leppard's realization obsolete, requiring that it be replaced by an edition better suited to the times, one that recovers the original more accurately, such as Curtis's. Representing a compromise between the requirements of scholarship and performance, Curtis's edition collates the sources – both musical and textual – and lists the variants, leaves the continuo unrealized so that a performer is free to improvise, modernizes key and time signatures (but distinguishes clearly between added and original markings), fills out the implied figures, indicates the proportional relationships between metres and modernizes the text. The edition manages to remain faithful to the original sources while providing an adequate basis for a modern performance.

Although later Baroque operas are usually documented by a somewhat richer and more informative array of sources – in particular, composers' autographs and multiple, detailed performing scores often survive – the problems (and solutions) are not much more complex. Indeed, the editorial interventions required by these scores may actually be fewer, since their notational conventions are more like those of today, rendering unnecessary the modernization of key and time signatures or the addition of bass figures. An ideal scholarly edition would evaluate and collate all relevant sources in a readable and accessible manner. Given the state of sophistication of specialist conductors, instrumentalists and singers of this repertory, it is likely that with minimal additions (ornaments,

continuo realizations, tempo markings), clearly distinguished from the original text by means of typography such as italics or small print, such an edition could be rendered adequate for performance purposes.

2. THE 18TH CENTURY. The same considerations apply in the 18th century as in the 17th as regards the use of facsimile scores for purely scholarly purposes, but a prospective editor should understand that any manuscript score of an Italian opera may provide a record of only one staging of the work, in one city for one particular cast. Unless it is an autograph score of the composer it may have no claim to authenticity beyond its existence as a record of a single series of events, and, even if it is, it may not correctly represent what was ever actually performed because the revisions that were normally made in an opera in the course of rehearsal would not necessarily be reflected in it.

Every 18th-century opera, especially an *opera seria*, was designed for a specific cast, and if it was to be revived it would be adjusted (probably by a 'house' musical director rather than the original composer) to suit a new cast, with arias substituted from other works or freshly written, commonly by another composer. The collation of surviving scores of a standard Metastasio setting by a popular composer usually discloses substantial variants, some of them 'authentic' (that is, made or authorized by the composer) and others not; the existence of multiple settings of standard texts meant that the substitution of arias, at a singer's preference, was a simple matter. The central role of the singer, as the chief attraction and the highest paid participant, meant that he or she could import favourite arias at choice, and that many surviving scores are in some degree pasticcios.

Besides the musical sources, printed librettos, intended for sale in the theatre for use during the performance, are important tools for an editor in determining what was sung on any particular occasion, though they too are ultimately undependable as, printed in advance, they may not reflect late changes. The collation of the verbal text between libretto and score is an essential step in determining the relationship between sources and particular performances.

The particular issues facing the editor of an 18th-century opera are perhaps best understood by reference to the works of individual composers. The editor of an opera by Handel will often have an autograph score, a so-called 'conducting score' and one or more different librettos to provide guidance in establishing a text; the annotations of singers' names in the scores and the transposition or replacement of individual numbers may clarify which ones were sung on which occasions. The editor's task may thus involve the examination of archival material, press reports and other non-musical matter as well as actual scores (rarely parts), librettos and contemporary printed editions of the music or excerpts from it (collections of 'favourite songs' were usually published at the time of a production in London and in some other large commercial centres, but were virtually unknown in Italy). Operas revived several times, such as Handel's *Giulio Cesare*, have textual histories of great complexity which can be elucidated only by a study of the full circumstances surrounding each revival. The editor's decision, in producing a performing version, will have to be based on whether the première, a particular revival or an 'ideal' (perhaps the opera as first conceived) is to be replicated and to choose a text accordingly. While a modern editor is of course at liberty to devise his or her own version, which may be a compound of existing ones, it is generally felt that an integral version as approved by the composer on some known occasion makes a more proper choice, even though historical precedent may seem to indicate that a version of an opera may be compiled to suit a particular cast or the exigencies of the circumstances surrounding the production. An editor should, of course, explain the basis of any decisions he makes and options he exercises.

In the case of French opera, with its different priorities and dramatic traditions, and where singing as such was much less important in determining the character of an evening's entertainment than it was in Italian opera, texts tended to be changed less because of new casts than with a view to improving the work. That is the case with several operas by Rameau. *Hippolyte et Aricie* was published in about 1733, the year of its première; some copies of the edition bear the rubric 'Changements conformés à la représentation', and later prints show changes corresponding with the text of the 1742 revival. Manuscript sources too show different versions. *Dardanus* underwent major revision, involving extensive changes to two acts, between its première in 1739 and its revival in 1744. There exist two printed editions and proof copies showing corrections as well as manuscript sources. In such cases editors need to make a careful choice in preparing a performing version – should it be the composer's initial conception, his revised version made in the light of theatrical experience, or his considered alterations after a period in which he has been able to ingest criticism of the work? – while critical, scholarly texts need to show and explicate all alternatives.

A special series of editorial problems is raised by the operas of Gluck that exist in two versions. Until recently nearly all revivals of his *Orfeo ed Euridice* and *Alceste* were based on a compound of his Italian original and his rewritten French setting, following the precedent set by Berlioz in his editions and pursued by other 19th-century editors. In the case of *Orfeo* (that of *Alceste* is more complex as the versions differ more radically), the more concise Italian version requires a castrato and the French a high tenor, and the French version includes additional, highly appealing music. Only in the late 20th century have scholars, and following them performers, become aware of the superior artistic unity of the un-mixed texts, which are available in critical editions.

Editions of Mozart's operas have tended, since the Breitkopf critical edition, to follow his autograph scores in the form they have come down to us. This can be mis-leading. In the case of the early *Mitridate*, the text as printed includes one aria, probably performed at the première, by another composer (Quirino Gasparini). The autograph score of *Idomeneo* contains numbers that were not included in the première, although it is impossible to be entirely sure, in the light of the printed librettos (of which there were two different versions) and rediscovered performing material, precisely what was performed in the opera's initial run. Here the editor for the Neue Mozart-Ausgabe preferred to show in his main text the music that, on the evidence then available, was believed to have been given (or intended to be given) at the première, relegating the remainder to an appendix, as opposed to including every item in its position in the main text. The editor of *Don Giovanni*, similarly, showed as the basis the original Prague text of 1787, giving Mozart's revisions for the 1788 Vienna revival in an appendix, although some of them have long been regarded as obligatory in performance. The editors in such cases have to choose between using as their basis a 'pure' text or one that would be more convenient to the generality of performers. The edition of *Le nozze di Figaro* follows the autograph scrupulously although there is reason to think that the original performed text may have differed from it in certain particulars; it does not include, even in an appendix, some of the variant versions found in secondary source material although there is evidence that some of these were Mozart's own. The score of *Così fan tutte* has also traditionally been reproduced in critical editions from the surviving autograph, but there is evidence that certain cuts in contemporary sources, and widespread in performing material used ever since, emanate from Mozart and may represent his final thoughts on the work after rehearsal, so need to be considered seriously and at least indicated as valid options (perhaps with the traditional 'Vi-' and '-de' indications); no such option is offered in the Neue Mozart-Ausgabe. The importance when preparing a critical edition of studying and evaluating the significance of all contemporary source material, and relating it to the circum-stances of performances that bear the composer's authority or copies that reflect such performances, is paramount.

In all serious Italian opera of the 18th century an editor will need to give guidance as to the interpretation of music written for castrato singers. Until the middle or late 20th century there was a tendency, especially in Germany, to transpose heroic parts down an octave and assign them to baritone singers on grounds of dramatic plausibility, but with a fuller understanding of 18th-century dramaturgy and the relation between vocal and instrumental textures it has become usual to sing them at written pitch. Women's voices are mostly used, as they often were at the time for such roles; the use of the countertenor, though a voice not normally heard in the 18th-century theatre, remains an option.

An editor's responsibility also embraces the area of performing practice, including continuo realization – not normally provided in scholarly editions, and in-creasingly rarely in practical ones as players develop their abilities to play from figured or unfigured basses – and the question of ornamentation. Some scholarly edi-tions, such as the Neue Mozart-Ausgabe, include suggestions for cadenzas and give guidance as to obligatory appoggiaturas in the recitative (less often in the lyrical music), though this is rarely done methodic-ally or consistently, partly because of the areas of doubt as to proper realization. The inclusion of any con-temporary examples of ornamentation of a work or a movement from it (or, on the rare occasions where they exist, authentic ones) would be a valuable adjunct to an edition.

3. THE 19TH AND 20TH CENTURIES. In part, doubtless, as a reflection of the recent upsurge of scholarly interest in 19th-century music, the second half of the 20th century has seen considerable resources and energy invested in the making of 'critical editions' of 19th-century operas. New editions of Rossini, Berlioz, Donizetti, Verdi and Wagner are under way, and many repertory works by these and other composers are now appearing in freshly edited versions. In spite of scepticism in certain quarters, this trend seems bound to continue.

Editors of this repertory rarely encounter the levels of textual uncertainty with which a 17th- or 18th-century specialist will regularly grapple. At least until the later part of the century, and the widespread advent of printed orchestral scores 'approved' by the composer, the primary source is almost invariably the composer's autograph full score, a document likely to take automatic precedence over all others. However, such a source is rarely unproblematic, and on the level of small-scale detail rarely offers the kind of precision and completeness a late 20th-century editor or performer will consider essential. In the case of Italian composers, for example, autographs tended to be constructed in two distinct phases: first a so-called 'skeleton score', comprising the main vocal lines, the instrumental bass and various important instrumental cues; later, often during preliminary rehearsals in the venue of the première, the remaining orchestral parts were added. Such a procedure gives rise to frequent contradictions between layers, and the speed at which the instrumentation was usually completed means that the score often has only sporadic – and frequently contradictory – indications of phrasing and dynamics. Even when dealing with composers such as Berlioz or Wagner, who fashioned their autograph scores with particular care, editorial intervention is necessary in virtually every bar, and some compromise has to be struck between absolute fidelity to the composer and the practicalities of present-day performance.

Sources other than the autograph, though they will nearly always be of secondary importance, often supply vital information. The autograph version of an opera's literary text (especially in stage directions and details of punctuation) will rarely be complete, and must be supplemented by a printed or manuscript libretto. In many cases, secondary sources such as preliminary sketches, manuscript copies, printed vocal scores, sets of parts, prompt books etc. will furnish details of performance lacking in the autograph, and perhaps reflect late changes to the score effected or authorized by the composer.

However, such small-scale details, though they will inevitably occupy much of the editor's time, will in many cases be overshadowed by a more basic textual problem. When dealing with early 19th-century operas, choosing the autograph score as primary source usually carries with it a decision to present as the base text that version of the opera seen at its first public performance (the decision of whether to include passages cut during rehearsals for the première sometimes creates an additional difficulty). Later additions to the score (usually for revivals of the work elsewhere), when these were effected or authorized by the composer, are then relegated to appendices, as is vocal ornamentation supplied by the composer or his contemporaries. In many cases, such a decision will seem eminently sensible: early 19th-century composers were sometimes constrained, by star singers and impresarios, to alter their operas to suit the changed circumstances of a revival, and sometimes did so only to prevent others less qualified from taking on the task. However, in more than a few cases, particularly with those composers working in Italy, there is no evidence that authorial revision was always made reluctantly. When a composer such as Donizetti returned to a score, for example, he typically fashioned it anew for the company available; a work was never, in that sense, 'finished', it was merely set aside, awaiting new revivals and new singers to

stimulate further its dramatic possibilities. The first performance was merely a stage in this development, and to offer it the privilege of a 'main text' inevitably distorts the dynamic state of that text during the composer's lifetime.

Later in the century, partly with the advent of firmer copyright laws and with the emergence of an operatic 'repertory', it became more common for composers consciously to fashion a 'definitive' text, and to distinguish between revisions they wished to be universally applied and those that merely responded to a set of local conditions. However, even in this more stable atmosphere, there are extreme examples in which – either through the untimely death of the author or through his multiple revisions – no basic text can be agreed upon. Notorious problem cases include such staples of the international repertory as *Carmen* (Bizet's autograph includes additional material that he is likely to have cut or altered in the course of rehearsals), *Les contes d'Hoffmann*, *Boris Godunov*, *Don Carlos* and *Manon Lescaut*. The preliminary critical edition of *Don Carlos* (an opera which exists in at least four 'authentic' versions) suggests that the only responsible editorial way forward is to offer an anthology of all the available music, allowing performers to decide for themselves which version they adopt. However, even in such cases, a 'base' text must be chosen, and while this is relatively unproblematic for *Don Carlos*, it is hardly so for some of the other operas mentioned above.

In the later 19th century and the 20th century, improved technology and broader dissemination made it increasingly likely that a printed version of an opera's full score would appear near the time of its première. If proofs of this score were checked and approved by the composer, and especially if he made revisions directly on to the proofs, this printed score might in certain cases supersede the autograph score as the primary source. However, this will not necessarily make an editor's task simpler; unless entire sets of proofs are extant, it is often impossible to determine whether or not discrepancies between the autograph and printed versions are the result of authorial revision. It is significant in this respect that the new Wagner edition has returned (where possible) to the composer's autograph as its base text. As an added complication to operas whose full scores were printed soon after composition, there frequently emerge two textual 'streams', one from revisions and reprintings of the orchestral score, another from various versions of the vocal score; both 'streams' may have a level of authorial approval, but they may differ in important and irreconcilable ways. For a composer such as Puccini, whose autograph scores by no means mark the final stage of composition, and who habitually made or authorized extensive changes to the proofs and to reprintings of orchestral and vocal scores, there seems no possibility of establishing a fully 'authentic' text.

This doubtful note seems a fitting one on which to end. The creation of an opera is usually a collaborative achievement, performers often have great influence on a work's eventual shape, and it is usually presented and revived as a highly public event. This means that opera probably generates a richer variety of texts than any other artistic medium. For an editor, this textual richness will always prove both stimulating and frustrating. Which version of a work to establish as the base text; which aspects of a work to pin down, which to leave to the discretion of these who will revive it; which of its various authors and collaborators to privilege at which times: such questions – and they could easily multiply – will surely continue to admit of various answers, which means that the making of operatic editions will continue to be one of the most excitingly equivocal of musicological pursuits.

*

Besides the items cited below, the reader is referred to the prefatory material to recent critical editions, notably those of works by Berlioz, Donizetti, Haydn, Rossini, Scarlatti, Verdi and Wagner, and scholarly series such as Die Oper.

W. Dean: 'The True Carmen?', MT, cvi (1965), 846–55

G. von Dadelsen, ed.: Editionsrichtlinien musikalischer Denkmäler und Gesamtausgaben (Kassel, 1967)

B. Cagli, P. Gossett and A. Zedda: 'Criteri per l'edizione critica delle opere di Gioachino Rossini', Bollettino del Centro rossiniano di studi, no.1 (Pesaro, 1974), 7–34 [Eng. trans., 35–61]

U. Günther: Preface to Verdi: Don Carlos: edizione integrale [vocal score] (Milan, 1974), pp. v–xliv

J. Glover: 'The Metamorphoses of "Orfeo"', MT, cxvi (1975), 135–9

E. Rosand: 'Francesco Cavalli in Modern Edition', CMc, no.27 (1979), 78–83

W. C. Holmes: Review of recording of Cesti: Orontea, MQ, lxix (1983), 286–9

——: 'La Statira' by Pietro Ottoboni and Alessandro Scarlatti: the Textual Sources, with a Documentary Postscript (New York, 1983)

J. J. McGann: A Critique of Modern Textual Criticism (Chicago, 1983)

C. Massip: 'Rameau et l'édition de ses oeuvres: bref aperçu historique et méthodologique', Jean-Philippe Rameau: Dijon 1983, 145–57

A. Porter: Review of Verdi: Don Carlos, JAMS, xxxv (1983), 360–70

G. Sadler: 'Rameau, Pellegrin and the Opera: the Revisions of "Hippolyte et Aricie" during its First Season', MT, cxxiv (1983), 533–7

P. Gossett: 'Toward a Critical Edition of Macbeth', Verdi's Macbeth: a Sourcebook, ed. A. Porter and D. Rosen (New York, 1984), 199–209

D. Lawton: Review of Verdi: Don Carlos, MQ, lxx (1984), 107–21

F. D'Accone: The History of a Baroque Opera: Alessandro Scarlatti's 'Gli equivoci nel sembiante' (New York, 1985)

A. Hicks: 'Handel: the Manuscripts and the Music', Handel: a Celebration of his Life and Times, ed. J. Simon (London, 1985) [exhibition catalogue], 18–24

J. Whenham and N. Fortune: 'Modern Editions and Performances', Monteverdi: Orfeo, ed. J. Whenham (Cambridge, 1986), 173–82

W. Dean and J. M. Knapp: Handel's Operas, 1704–1726 (Oxford, 1987)

Nuove prospettive nella ricerca verdiana (Parma and Milan, 1987) [essays on vols. of the Verdi edn by M. Chusid, C. Gallico, P. Gossett and U. Günther]

A. Tyson: Mozart: Studies of the Autograph Scores (Cambridge, MA, 1987)

C. Schmidt: 'Newly Identified Manuscript Sources for the Music of Jean-Baptiste Lully', Notes, xliv (1987–8), 7–32

P. Brett: 'Text, Context, and the Early Music Editor', Authenticity and Early Music, ed. N. Kenyon (Oxford, 1989), 83–114

A. Curtis: Preface to Monteverdi: L'incoronazione di Poppea (London, 1989)

G. Dotto: 'Opera, Four Hands: Collaborative Alterations in Puccini's Fanciulla', JAMS, xlii (1989), 604–24

S. Scherr: 'Editing Puccini's Operas: the Case of Manon Lescaut', AcM, lxi (1990), 62–81

D. Rosen: Review of Rossini: L'italiana in Algeri, JAMS, xliv (1991), 502–12

T. Walker: Review of recordings of L'incoronazione di Poppea, Historical Performance, iv (1991), 49–54

ELLEN ROSAND (1), STANLEY SADIE (2), ROGER PARKER (3)

Editions. Complete operas are published in various forms, including 'scholarly' or 'critical' editions, which are designed to present the most authoritative authentic versions of works; facsimile publications, which contain reproductions of sources with or without additional comment; and 'practical' or 'performance' editions, which are usually produced from unstated or secondary sources. (For a fuller discussion see EDITING and PUBLISHING.) This article is concerned primarily with scholarly editions, although some remarks will be made about the practical editions used by performers and students.

Historical editions of a scholarly nature are prepared on the basis of a critical evaluation of the known primary sources and presented in such a way that editorial material can be distinguished from the original. These editions may consist of multi-volume sets, which are commonly 'collected editions', publications consisting of a complete repertory, either the entire works of a single composer (also known as a 'complete edition' or 'Gesamtausgabe') or a series in which the majority of individual volumes present a unified musical repertory often derived from the same or from closely related original sources (also known as 'Denkmäler' or 'monuments').

Complete editions for about 50 composers who have written at least one opera have either been completed or are now in progress. Some of these, such as various Handel, Mozart and Rameau editions, were initiated in the second half of the 19th century; others, like the first Monteverdi and Pergolesi editions, came to fruition at the time of World War II. In more recent years, revisions of some complete editions have been initiated for certain opera composers (e.g. Purcell, 2/1961), and entirely new sets have been started for others, generally under the direction of international committees of scholars (e.g. Mozart, 1955–91; Berlioz, 1967–). Citations for all of these publications can be found in the articles on composers in this dictionary. (For a master list of complete editions begun before 1980, see Grove6, 'Editions, Historical', §2.)

The list that follows gives titles, publication information and the operatic contents of major collected editions that contain at least one complete opera. Many of the publications listed are facsimile series, which are not, strictly speaking, editions of works but are clearly designed for scholarly rather than for practical use. These include such large-scale publishing ventures as section 4 of Bibliotheca musica bononiensis and the Italian and German opera series of Garland Publishing. Some of these publications are devoted entirely to opera (e.g. French Opera in the 17th and 18th Centuries and Early Romantic Opera), while others may be compilations of a variety of musical genres, including opera, emanating from a particular region (e.g. Denkmäler deutscher Tonkunst and the publications of Samfundet til Udgivelse af Dansk Musik). Companion piano-vocal scores have in some cases been published to complement the critical edition (e.g. the Verdi edition jointly published by Ricordi and the University of Chicago, 1983–).

Anthological editions, which contain arias, ensembles, overtures and similar kinds of operatic excerpts are not included (see Grove6 for a comprehensive list of these works published before 1980). Regarding practical editions of complete operas, perhaps the most common, and certainly the most affordable, are the piano-vocal scores published by such firms as G. Schirmer, Boosey & Hawkes, Peters Edition and Ricordi. These skilfully arranged piano reductions facilitate rehearsals and make low-budget productions of the work possible, but it is important to mention that the traditional cuts and changes in the voice parts that have been passed down through each generation of singers by teachers and coaches may not be reproduced in such scores. Well-known cadenzas and alternative versions for specific sections are, however, frequently given in smaller print. Full-size conducting scores of older operas have traditionally been made available for hire by Ricordi, Schott, Boosey & Hawkes, Breitkopf & Härtel, and Durand, who held the original copyrights. Publishers such as Kalmus and Dover sell reproductions of the original materials (with or without parts) once the work has come into public domain. For newly written operas, publishers generally prepare manuscript versions of what is the basis of a printed edition; these may subsequently be published once the work has become stabilized through performance.

The editions in the following list contain at least one complete opera, and some contain excerpts from operas and other staged secular works as well. Where the published title of an opera differs significantly from the form used in this dictionary, the latter is shown in square brackets.

Americana Collection Music Series [facs.] [ACMS], New York Public Library (New York: Broude, 1971, 2/1981)
    Joplin (Treemonisha, no.1, vol.ii)

L'arte musicale in Italia [AMI], ed. L. Torchi (Milan: Ricordi, 1897–?1908), 7 vols.
    C. Monteverdi (Ballo [Maschera] delle ingrate, vi; Combattimento di Tancredi e Clorinda, vi), Peri (Euridice, vi)

The Ballad Opera [facs.], ed. W. H. Rubsamen (New York: Garland, 1974); texts of 171 musical plays in 28 vols.

Bibliotheca musica bononiensis [BMB], section 4: *Musica practica* [facs.], ed. G. Vecchi (Bologna: Forni)
    Ariosti (Coriolano, xix), Bertoni (Orfeo ed Euridice, xv), G. Bononcini (Astarto, xx), Bontempi (Il Paride in musica, cxxvi), G. Caccini (Euridice, iii), Cavalieri (Rappresentatione di Anima, et di Corpo, i), Cherubini (Les deux journées, cxxxiii; Lodoïska, cxxxiv), Gagliano (Dafne, iv; Flora, vii), Landi (Sant'Alessio, xi), D. Mazzocchi (La catena d'Adone, ix), C. Monteverdi (L'incoronazione di Poppea, lxxxi; Orfeo, vi), Peri (Euridice, ii), N. Piccinni (Didon, xvi; Roland, xvi), Luigi Rossi (Il palagio d'Atlante [Il palazzo incantato] [MS], lxxxii), M. Rossi (Erminia sul Giordano, xii), Rossini (La Cenerentola [MS], xcii), Rousseau (Le devin du village, xxxiv), Sacchini (Dardanus, xviia; Oedipe à Colone, xvii), Salieri (Les Danaïdes, xviiia; La grotta di Trofonio, xviiib), Sarti (Giulio Sabino, cxxviii), Spontini (Fernand Cortez, cxxx; Milton, cxxix), Veracini (Adriano in Siria [songs], xiv)

[Les] *chefs-d'oeuvre classiques de l'opéra français* [COCOF], ed. J. B. Weckerlin, V. d'Indy and others (Leipzig: Breitkopf & Härtel, 1880/R1972); orig. edn unnumbered; vocal scores
    Cambert (Les peines et les plaisirs de l'amour, ii; Pomone, iii), Campra (Europe galante, iv; Les fêtes vénitiennes, v; Tancrède, vi), Catel (Les bayadères, vii), Collasse (Ballet des saisons, viii; Thétis et Pélée, ix), A. C. Destouches (Issé, x; Omphale, xi), Grétry (La caravane du Caire, xii; Céphale et Procris, xiii), Lalande et A. C. Destouches (Les élémens, xiv), Le Sueur (Ossian, xv), Lully (Alceste, xvi; Armide, xvii; Atys, xviii; Bellérophon, xix; Cadmus et Hermione, xx; Isis, xxi; Persée, xxii; Phaëton, xxiii; Proserpine, xxiv; Psyché, xxv; Thésée, xxvi), F.-A. D. Philidor (Ernelinde, xxvii), N. Piccinni (Didon, xxviii; Roland, xxix), Rameau (Castor et Pollux, xxx; Dardanus, xxxi; Les fêtes d'Hébé, xxxii; Hippolyte et Aricie, xxxiii; Les Indes galantes, xxxiv; Platée, xxxv; Zoroastre, xxxvi), Sacchini (Chimène, xxxvii; Renaud, xxxviii), Salieri (Les Danaïdes, xxxix; Tarare, xl)

I classici della musica italiana [CdMI], Raccolta Nazionale delle Musiche Italiane, ed. G. D'Annunzio (Milan: Istituto Editoriale Italiano, 1918–20, in *quaderni*; Società Anonima Notari la Santa, 1919–21)
    (vol., quaderno): Cavalieri (Rappresentatione di Anima, et di Corpo, v, 35–6), Cherubini (Les deux journées, vii, 172–3), B. Galuppi (Il filosofo di campagna, xiii, 54–8), C. Monteverdi (Combattimento di Tancredi e Clorinda, xix, 76–9, 224–5), Paisiello (La pazza per amore, xx, 80–81), Pergolesi (Livietta e Tracollo, xxiii, 91–2; La serva padrona, xxiii, 89–90), Peri (Euridice, xxiv, 95–6)

I classici musicali italiani [CMI], Fondazione Eugenio Bravi (Milan, 1941–56)

C. Monteverdi (Orfeo, ix), N. Piccinni (La buona figliuola maritata, vii)

Collezione settecentesca Bettarini [CSB], ed. L. Bettarini (Milan: Casa Editrice Nationalmusic, 1969–)
    Hasse (Dorilla e Balanzone [int], xvi; Larinda e Vanesio [int], vii), Legrenzi (Giustino, xii), Pergolesi (Livietta e Tracollo, xv; La serva padrona, xiv), N. Piccinni (Roland [excerpts], x)

Concentus musicus [CM], Deutsches Historisches Institut, Rome (Cologne: Volk, 1974–)
    Hasse (Ruggiero, i)

Denkmäler der Tonkunst in Österreich [DTÖ], ed. G. Adler (i–lxxxiii), E. Schenk (lxxxiv–cxxv) and O. Wessely (cxxvi–), Gesellschaft zur Herausgabe der Denkmäler der Tonkunst in Österreich, Vienna (variously pubd in Vienna: Artaria, later Universal, then Österreichischer Bundesverlag, and Leipzig: Breitkopf & Härtel, 1894–1959/R1959–66 (i–xcv); Graz: Akademische Druck- und Verlagsanstalt, 1960–)
    (vol., Jg.): Caldara (Dafne, xci), A. Cesti (Il pomo d'oro, vi, Jg.iii/2, and ix, Jg.iv/2), Fux (Costanza e Fortezza, xxxiv–xxxv, Jg.xvii), Gassmann (La contessina, xlii–xliv, Jg.xxi/1), Gluck (L'innocenza giustificata, lxxxii, Jg.xliv; Orfeo ed Euridice, xliva, Jg.xxi/2), C. Monteverdi (Il ritorno d'Ulisse in patria, lvii, Jg.xxix/1), J. B. Schenk (Der Dorfbarbier, lxvi, Jg.xxxiv)

Denkmäler deutscher Tonkunst [DDT], 1st ser., ed. R. Liliencron (1901–11), H. Kretzschmar (1912–18), H. Abert (1927) and A. Schering (1928–31), Königlich Preussischer Regierung Berufene Kommission (1892–1900), Musikgeschichtliche Kommission (1901–60) (Leipzig: Breitkopf & Härtel, 1892–1931; ed. H. J. Moser, Wiesbaden: Breitkopf & Härtel, and Graz: Akademische Druck- und Verlagsanstalt, 2/1957–60)
    G. Benda (Der Jahrmarkt, lxiv), Graun (Montezuma, xv), Holzbauer (Günther von Schwarzburg, viii–ix), Jommelli (Fetonte [2nd setting], xxxii–xxxiii), Keiser (Der hochmüthige ... Croesus [Croesus], xxxvii–xxxviii), C. Pallavicino (La Gierusalemme liberata, lv)

Denkmäler deutscher Tonkunst, 2nd ser.: *Denkmäler der Tonkunst in Bayern* [DTB], ed. A. Sandberger, Gesellschaft zur Herausgabe von Denkmälern der Tonkunst in Bayern (Leipzig: Breitkopf & Härtel (i–xx) and Augsburg: Filser (xxi–xxx), 1900–31; ed. H. Schmid, Gesellschaft für Bayerische Musikgeschichte, Wiesbaden, 2/1962–)
    (vol. in rev. edn, Jg.): J. W. Franck (Die drey Töchter des Cecrops, xxxviii, Jg.xxxvii–xxxviii [=EDM, 2nd ser., ii], Gluck (Le nozze d'Ercole e d'Ebe, xxvi, Jg.xiv/2), Pez (Trajano [excerpts], xxxv, Jg.xxvii–xxviii), Steffani (Alarico il Baltha, xxi, Jg.xi/2, and various excerpts, xxiii, Jg.xii/2; [Briseide: see under Torri]), Torri (Briseide [also attrib. Steffani], xxiii, Jg.xii/2; various excerpts, xxxi, Jg.xix–xx), Traetta (various excerpts, xxv, Jg.xiv/1, and xxix, Jg.xvii)

Denkmäler der Tonkunst in Bayern, new ser. (Wiesbaden: Breitkopf & Härtel, 1967–)
    Hoffmann (Aurora, v), J. Löhner (Die triumphirende Treue, vi)

Denkmäler rheinischer Musik [DRM], Arbeitsgemeinschaft für Rheinische Musikgeschichte (Cologne and Krefeld: Staufen (vol.i), and Düsseldorf: Schwann (ii–), 1951–)
    Steffani (Tassilone, viii)

Dramaturgia musicale veneta [facs.] [DMV], ed. G. Morelli, R. Strohm and T. Walker (Milan: Ricordi, 1983–)
    Andreozzi (Amleto, xxvi), Anfossi (Adriano in Siria, xxiv), Bertoni (Orfeo ed Euridice, xxiii), Cocchi (La maestra, xix), B. Galuppi (L'inimico delle donne, xxi), Giacomelli (Merope, xviii), Lucio (Medoro, iv), C. F. Pollarolo (Ariodante, xiii; Faramondo, ix), A. Sartorio (Orfeo, vi), Vivaldi (Ottone in villa, xii)

Earlier American Music [facs.] [EAM], ed. H. W. Hitchcock (New York: Da Capo Press, 1972–)
    Bray (The Indian Princess, xi)

Early Romantic Opera [ERO], ed. P. Gossett and C. Rosen (New York: Garland, 1978–)
    Auber (Gustave III, xxxi; La muette de Portici, xxx), Cherubini (Démophon, xxxii; Les deux journées, xxxv; Eliza, xxxiv; Lodoïska, xxxiii), Bellini (Beatrice di Tenda, v; I Capuleti e i Montecchi, iii; Norma, iv; Il pirata, i; I puritani, vi; La straniera, ii), Donizetti (Dom Sébastien, xxix; La favorite, xxviii; Les martyrs, xxvii; Parisina, xxv; Roberto Devereux, xxvi), Halévy (La Juive, xxxvi),

Le Sueur (Ossian, xxxvii); Méhul (Ariodant, xxxix; Euphrosine, xxxviii; Joseph, xli; Uthal, xl), Meyerbeer (L'Africaine, xxiv; Il crociato in Egitto, xviii; L'étoile du nord, xxii; Les Huguenots, xx; Le pardon de Ploërmel [Dinorah], xxiii; Le prophète, xxi; Robert le diable, xix), Rossini (Le comte Ory, xvi; Elisabetta, vii; Guillaume Tell, xvii; Maometto II, xi; Moïse et Pharaon, xv; Mosè in Egitto, ix; Otello, viii; Ricciardo e Zoraide, x; Semiramide, xiii; Le siège de Corinthe, xiv; Zelmira, xii), Spontini (Fernand Cortez, xliii; Olimpie, xliv; La vestale, xlii)

Das Erbe deutscher Musik [EDM], 1st ser.: *Reichsdenkmale*, 1935–43 Staatliches Institut für Deutsche Musikforschung, Berlin, from 1953 Musikgeschichtliche Kommission; pubd by different Ger. houses in various separately numbered sub-ser., but vols. are also consecutively numbered regardless of Abt. or publisher
  Oper und Sologesang (Mainz: Schott) [EDM vol., OS vol.]: Hasse (Arminio, xxvii–xxviii, OS iii–iv), Keiser (Masagniello, lxxxix, OS xi), Mattheson (Cleopatra, lxix, OS ix), Meder (Die beständige Argenia, lxviii, OS viii), Telemann (Pimpinone, vi, OS i)

Das Erbe deutscher Musik, 2nd ser.: *Landschaftsdenkmale*, Staatliches Institut für Deutsche Musikforschung (1936–); pubd by various Ger. houses in 10 sub-ser.
  Bayern (Brunswick: Litolff): J. W. Franck (Die drey Töchter des Cecrops, ii [=DTB, Jg.xxxvii–xxxviii])
  Schleswig-Holstein und Hansestädte (Brunswick: Litolff): Kusser (Erindo, iii)

French Opera in the 17th and 18th Centuries [facs.] [FO] (Stuyvesant, NY: Pendragon, 1984–)
  Campra (Le carnaval de Venise, v), A. C. Destouches (Issé, i), Le Sueur (La caverne, ii), Méhul (Mélidore et Phrosine, iv), N. Piccinni (Atys, vii), Rameau (Les paladins, iii)

Georg Friedrich Händels Werke [GFHW], ed. F. Chrysander, Deutsche Händelgesellschaft (Leipzig: Breitkopf & Härtel, 1858–1902/R1965)
  Keiser (Octavia, suppl.vi)

German Opera 1770–1800 [facs.] [GOB], ed. T. Bauman (New York: Garland, 1985–6)
  André (Belmont und Constanze, vi, xviii; Der Töpfer, ix, xxii), G. Benda (Ariadne auf Naxos, iv, xviii; Romeo und Julie, v, xxii; Cannabich (Electra, x, xix), Dittersdorf (Die Liebe im Narrenhaus, xv, xxi), J. A. Hiller (Die Jagd, i, xx), F. L. A. Kunzen (Das Fest der Winzer, xi, xix), W. Müller (Das Sonnenfest der Braminen, xvi, xxii), Neubauer (Fernando und Yariko, ix), Reichardt (Die Geisterinsel, vii, xx; Ino, iv, xx), Salieri (Der Rauchfangkehrer, xiv, xxi), J. Schuster (Der Alchymist, v, xviii), Schweitzer (Alceste, iii, xviii), Süssmayr (Der Spiegel von Arkadien, xvii, xxii), I. Umlauf (Die schöne Schusterinn, xiii, xxii), Vogler (Der Kaufmann von Smyrna, viii, xxi; Lampedo, ix, xxi); Winter (Lenardo und Blandine, x, xxi), E. W. Wolf (Die Dorfdeputierten, ii, xix), Zumsteeg (Die Geisterinsel, xii)

Handel Sources: Materials for the Study of Handel's Borrowing [facs.] [HS], ed. J. H. Roberts (New York: Garland, 1986–)
  G. Bononcini (Xerse, viii), Keiser (Adonis, i; Claudius, iii; La forza della virtù, ii; Janus, i; Nebucadnezar, iii), G. Porta (Numitore, iv), A. Scarlatti (Dafni, vii; Pompeo, vi), Steffani (La lotta d'Hercole, ix)

Harvard Publications in Music [HPM], ed. D. G. Hughes, A. T. Merritt, N. Pirrotta and J. M. Ward (Cambridge, MA: Harvard U. Press, 1967–)
  A. Scarlatti (Eraclea, vi; Griselda, viii; Marco Attilio Regolo, vii; Massimo Puppieno, x; La principessa fedele, ix)

Instituta et monumenta [IMa], 1st ser.: *Monumenta*, Biblioteca Governativa e Civica di Cremona and Scuola di Paleografia Musicale dell'Università di Parma (Cremona: Athenaeum Cremonese, 1954–)
  Vivaldi (La fida ninfa, iii)

Italian Opera 1640–1770 [facs.] [IOB], ed. H. M. Brown (New York: Garland, 1977–84); in 2 ser., of 60 and 37 vols., numbered continuously; libs. in vols.li–lx and xcii–xcvii
  Albinoni (Zenobia, xv), Ariosti (Vespasiano, xxvi), J. C. Bach (Carattaco, lxxxvi), Bernabei (Ascanio, lxvi), Bernasconi (La clemenza di Tito, lxxxviii), A. M. Bononcini (Griselda, xxi), G. Bononcini (Il trionfo di Camilla, xvii), Boretti (Ercole in Tebe, vi), Caldara (L'olimpiade, xxxii), Cavalli (Gli amori d'Apollo e di Dafne, i; Oristeo, lxii; Scipione affricano, v), Cesti (Argia, iii; Dori, lxiii), Cocchi (Li matti per amore, lxxvi), Conti (Don Chisciotte in

Sierra Morena, lxix), Draghi (Leonida in Tegea, lxiv), Feo (Andromaca, xxxi), Fischietti (Il mercato di Malmantile, lxxvii), Freschi (Pompeo Magno in Cilicia, lxv), Fux (Orfeo ed Euridice, xix), B. Galuppi (La diavolessa, xliv; L'olimpiade, xli), F. Gasparini (Bajazet, xxiv), Gassmann (Amore e Psiche, lxxxvii; L'opera seria, lxxxix), Gluck (Semiramide riconosciuta, lxxiv), Graun (Artaserse, xl), P. A. Guglielmi (Lo spirito di contradizione, lxxxv), Handel (Tamerlano, xxvii), Hasse (Alcide al bivio, lxxxi; Siroe, xxxiii; Il trionfo di Clelia, lxxxiii), Holzbauer (Alessandro nell'Indie, lxxix), Jommelli (Armida abbandonata, xci; Demofoonte, xlviii; L'olimpiade, xlvi), Lampugnani (L'amor contadino, lxxxii), Latilla (La finta cameriera [Gismondo], xxxvii), Legrenzi (Totila, ix), Leo (Andromaca, xxxix; Catone in Utica, lxx; L'olimpiade, xxxvi), Logroscino (Il governatore, xlii), Lotti (Alessandro Severo, xx), G. F. de Majo (Adriano in Siria, xlix), F. Mancini (Gl'amanti generosi, xviii), Marazzoli and V. Mazzocchi (Egisto [Chi soffre speri], lxi), J. Melani (Ercole in Tebe, iv), Orlandini (Il marito giocatore, lxviii), C. Pallavicino (L'amazone corsara, xiii), B. Pasquini (Idalma, xi), Perez (Solimano, xlv), Pergolesi (L'olimpiade, xxxiv), Perti (Rosaura, lxvii), N. Piccinni (Catone in Utica, l; Cecchina [La buona figliuola], lxxx), C. F. Pollarolo (Gli inganni felici, xvi), Porpora (Semiramide riconosciuta, xxx), Porsile (Spartaco, xxviii), Provenzale (Lo schiavo di sua moglie, vii), Rinaldo di Capua (Vologeso, xxxviii), Luigi Rossi (Il palazzo incantato, ii), Sacchini (L'eroe cinese, xc), Sarro (Arsace, xxii), Sarti (Didone abbandonata, lxxxiv), A. Sartorio (Adelaide, viii), A. Scarlatti (Telemaco, xxiii), Steffani (Le rivali concordi, xiv), Stradella (Moro per amore, x), Terradellas (Sesostri, xliii), Traetta (Ifigenia in Tauride, xlvii; Ippolito ed Aricia, lxxviii), Vinci (Didone abbandonata, xxix; Li zite 'n galera, xxv), Vivaldi (Griselda, xxxv), Wagenseil (Ariodante, lxxiii), P. A. Ziani (L'innocenza risorta, xii)

Italian Opera 1810–1840 [facs.] [IOG], ed. P. Gossett (New York: Garland, 1985–91); complete in 25 vols., although 58 vols. were originally planned and numbering reflects that intention
  Carafa (Le nozze di Lammermoor, ii), Coccia (Caterina di Guisa, iv), Coppola (La pazza per amore, v; Il postiglione di Longjumeau [excerpts], v); Vincenzo Fioravanti (Il ritorno di Columella [Il ritorno di Pulcinella], vii), Levi (Iginia d'Asti, ix), Marliani (Ildegonda, x), Mayr (Adelasia ed Aleramo and excerpts, xi; Medea in Corinto, xii), Mercadante (L'apoteosi d'Ercole [excerpts], xiv; Il bravo, xxi; Elena da Feltre, xxi; Elisa e Claudio, xiv; Il giuramento, xviii; La vestale, xxii), Meyerbeer (excerpts, xxiii), Morlacchi (Tebaldo e Isolina, xxiv), Nicolai (Il templario and excerpts, xxvi), Nini (Ida della torre, xxvii), G. Pacini (Il barone di Dolsheim and excerpts, xxix; Il corsaro, xxxiv; Furio Camillo [excerpts], xxxvi; Niobe [excerpts], xxxii; Saffo, xxxvi; L'ultimo giorno di Pompei, xxxii), Raimondi (Il ventaglio and excerpts, xl), L. Ricci (Un'avventura di Scaramuccia, xliv; Chiara di Rosembergh and excerpts, xlii), Vaccai (Giulietta e Romeo, xlv; Zadig ed Astartea [excerpts], xlv)

Monumenta musicae svecicae [MMS], 1st ser., Svenska Samfundet för Musikforskning (Stockholm: Almquist & Wiksell (vols.i–vi) and Nordiska (vii), 1958–)
  Vogler (Gustav Adolph, vii)

Monumenta musicae svecicae, 2nd ser., Berwald-Kommittén (Kassel: Bärenreiter, 1966–)
  Berwald (Drottningen av Golconda, xviii; Estrella de Soria, xvii; Jag går i kloster, xix; Modehandlerskan, xx)

Monuments of Music and Music Literature in Facsimile [MMMLF], 1st ser.: *Music* (New York: Broude, 1965–)
  Peri (Euridice, xxviii)

Musica [facs.], Reale Accademia d'Italia (Rome: Accademia d'Italia, 1934–41)
  Bellini (Norma, v), Peri (Euridice, iii)

Musica britannica: a National Collection of Music [MB], ed. A. Lewis, Royal Musical Association (London: Stainer & Bell, 1951–, 2/1954–)
  S. Storace (No Song, No Supper, xvi)

Musical Antiquarian Society [*Publications*] [MAS], Musical Antiquarian Society (London: Chappell, 1841–7)
  H. Purcell (Dido and Aeneas, iv; King Arthur, x)

Music for London Entertainment, 1660–1800 [MLE] (Tunbridge Wells, Kent: Richard Macnutt, 1983–7; London: Stainer & Bell, 1987–)
  ser. C: *English Opera and Masque*, ed. C. Price and S. Sadie: Boyce (The Shepherd's Lottery, iv), J. Clarke, Leveridge and

D. Purcell (The Island Princess, ii), Eccles (The Judgment of Paris, i), John F. Lampe (Pyramus and Thisbe, iii)

    ser. D: *Pantomime, Ballet and Dance*, ed. J. Ward: Dibdin (The Touchstone, i)

    ser. E: *Italian Opera*, ed. L. Lindgren: G. Bononcini (Camilla [Il trionfo di Camilla], i)

Die Oper: kritische Ausgabe von Hauptwerken des Opern-geschichte, ed. H. Becker (Munich: G. Henle, 1975–); critical commentary pubd separately
    F. Gasparini (Bajazet, iii), Keiser (Die grossmüthige Tomyris [Tomyris], i), Salieri (Tarare, ii)

Pamyatniki russkogo muzikal'nogo iskusstva [Monuments of Russian Musical Art] [PRMI], ed. Yu. V. Keldïsh, Institute for Art History (Moscow: State Music Publishers, 1972–)
    Bortnyansky (Sokol [Le faucon], v), Fomin (Yamshchiki na pod-stave, vi), Pashkevich (Skupoy [The Miser], iv), Sokolovsky (Mel'nik – koldun [The Miller who was a Magician], x)

Penn State Music Series [PSMS], ed. D. Stevens, Pennsylvania State U. (University Park, PA (vols.i–), and London (ix–), 1963–)
    Mozart (Bastien und Bastienne, xxiii)

Prime fioriture del melodramma italiano [PFMI], ed. F. Mantica (Rome: Casa Editrice Claudio Monteverdi, 1912–30)
    Cavalieri (Rappresentatione di Anima, et di Corpo, i)

Publicacions del Departament de Música Biblioteca de Catalunya) (from vol.xiv entitled *Publicaciones de la Sección de Música, Biblioteca de Catalunya*) [PBC], Biblioteca de Cataluña, Institut d'Estudis Catalans (from xiv Biblioteca Central, Diputación Provincial de Barcelona) (Barcelona, 1921–36, 1943–75); a recent catalogue gives a different numbering system from that shown on vols., and a later ser. beginning in 1981 contains no operas
    Hidalgo (Celos aun del aire matan, xi), Terradellas (Merope, xiv)

Publikationen älterer praktischer und theoretischer Musikwerke vorzugsweise des XV. und XVI. Jahrhunderts [PÄMw], ed. R. Eitner, Gesellschaft für Musikforschung (Berlin: Bahn, later Liepmannssohn, then Trautwein, from 1883 Leipzig: Breitkopf & Härtel, 1873–1905/R1967)
    (vol., Jg.): G. Caccini (Euridice, x, Jg.ix), Cavalli (Giasone [excerpts], xii, Jg.xi), Cesti (excerpts from Le disgrazie d'Amore, Dori, La magnanimità d'Alessandro, Semirami, xii, Jg.xi), Keiser

(Der lächerliche Printz Jodelet [Jodelet], xviii, Jg.xxi–xxii), Lully (Armide [Acts 1–2], xiv, Jg.xiii–xiv), A. Scarlatti (Gli equivoci in amore [Acts i–ii], xiv, Jg.xiii–xiv), Schürmann (Lodovicus [Ludovicus] Pius [excerpts], xvii, Jg.xi), Orazio Vecchi (L'Amfiparnaso, xxvi, Jg.xxx)

Le pupitre: collection de musique ancienne, ed. F. Lesure (Paris: Heugel, 1967)
    Boismortier (Don Quichote chez la duchesse, xxx), Campra (Les fêtes vénitiennes, xix)

Recent Researches in American Music [RRAM], ed. H. W. Hitch-cock (Madison, WI: A–R Editions, 1977–)
    S. Adler (The Disappointment [music for ballad op by A. Barton], iii–iv), W. Shield (The Poor Soldier, vi)

Recent Researches in the Music of the Baroque Era [RRMBE] (New Haven (i–iv) and Madison, WI (v–): A–R Editions, 1964–)
    Albinoni (Pimpinone, xliii), Cesti (Il pomo d'oro [excerpts], lxii), Peri (Euridice, xxxvi–xxxvii), Telemann (Don Quichotte, lxiv–lxv)

Recent Researches in the Music of the Classical Era [RRMCE] (Madison, WI: A–R Editions, 1975–)
    Hasse (Larinda e Vanesio [int], ix)

Samfundet til Udgivelse af Dansk Musik [Society for the Publication of Danish Music] [SUDM] (Copenhagen: Samfundet, 1872–)
    (ser./vol.): Børresen (Kaddara, 3/iv), Du Puy (Ungdom og galskab [ov.], 3/cv), J. E. Hartmann (Balders død, 1/ix; Fiskerne, 1/xxi), J. P. E. Hartmann (Korsarerne, 1/xvi; Liden Kirsten, 3/ccvii), C. F. E. Horneman (Aladdin, 2/vi, 3/cix), J. Jersild (Alice in Wonderland, 3/cxl), Kuhlau (Røverborgen, 3/ci; William Shakespeare, 1/iii, 3/lvii), F. L. A. Kunzen (Gyrithe, 1/i), Lange-Müller (Middelalderlig, 2/xvi; Tove, 1/xii), C. Nielsen (Maskarade [ov.], 3/xxxvii), L. Nielsen (Isabella [ov.], 3/xxiv), F. Rung (Den trekantede hat, 2/xi), Scalabrini (Koerlighed uden strømper, 2/xxvii), Schierbeck (Fête galante [ov.], 3/lxxiii), A. Tofft (Vifandaka, 3/vi, xv), Weyse (Festen paa Kenilworth, 1/vii)

Smith College Music Archives [SCMA], ed. A. Einstein (North-ampton, MA: Smith College, 1935–/R1965)
    F. Caccini (La liberazione di Ruggiero, vii), Fux (Costanza e For-tezza, ii)

The Wellesley Edition [WE], ed. J. LaRue (Wellesley, MA: Wellesley College, 1950–)
    Cesti (Orontea, xi)

INDEX

The symbol C in the following index indicates that there is at least one published complete edition containing the operatic output of the composer concerned. All other citations refer to the collected edi-tions listed in this article.

Holzbauer **DDT, IOB**	Neubauer **GOB**	Scalabrini **SUDM**
Horneman, C. F. E. **SUDM**	Nicolai **IOG**	Scarlatti, A. **HS, HPM, IOB, PÄMw**
	Nielsen, C. **SUDM**	Schenk, J. B. **DTÖ**
Janáček **C**	Nielsen, L. **SUDM**	Schierbeck **SUDM**
Jersild, J. **SUDM**	Nini **IOG**	Schoenberg **C**
Jommelli **DDT, IOB**		Schubert **C**
Joplin **C, ACMS**	Orlandini **IOB**	Schürmann **PÄMw**
		Schuster, J. **GOB**
Keiser **DDT, EDM, GFHW, HS, PÄMw**	Pacini, G. **IOG**	Schweitzer **GOB**
Kuhlau **SUDM**	Paisiello **CdMI**	Shield **RRAM**
Kunzen, F. L. A. **GOB, SUDM**	Pallavicino, C. **DDT, IOB**	Smetana **C**
Kusser **EDM**	Pashkevich **PRMI**	Sokolovsky **PRMI**
	Pasquini, B. **IOB**	Spontini **BMB, ERO**
Lalande **COCOF**	Perez **IOB**	Steffani **DTB, DRM, HS, IOB**
Lampe, John F. **MLE**	Pergolesi **C, CdMI, CSB, IOB**	Storace, S. **MB**
Lampugnani **IOB**	Peri **AMI, BMB, CdMI, MMMLF, Musica,**	Stradella **IOB**
Landi **BMB**	**RRMBE**	Strauss, J. **C**
Lange-Müller **SUDM**	Perti **IOB**	Sullivan **C**
Latilla **IOB**	Pez **DTB**	Süssmayr **GOB**
Legrenzi **CSB, IOB**	Philidor, F.-A. D. **COCOF**	
Leo **IOB**	Piccinni, N. **BMB, COCOF, CMI, CSB,**	Tchaikovsky **C**
Le Sueur **COCOF, ERO, FO**	**FO, IOB**	Telemann **C, EDM, RRMBE**
Leveridge **MLE**	Pollarolo, C. F. **DMV, IOB**	Terradellas **IOB, PBC**
Levi **IOG**	Porpora **IOB**	Tofft, A. **SUDM**
Liszt **C**	Porsile **IOB**	Torri **DTB**
Logroscino **IOB**	Porta, G. **HS**	Traetta **DTB, IOB**
Löhner, J. **DTB**	Prokofiev **C**	
Lotti **IOB**	Protopopov **PRMI**	Umlauf, I. **GOB**
Lucio **DMV**	Provenzale **IOB**	
Lully **C, COCOF, PÄMw**	Purcell, D. **MLE**	Vaccai **IOG**
	Purcell, H. **C, MAS**	Vecchi, O. **PÄMw**
Majo, G. F. de **IOB**		Veracini **BMB**
Mancini, F. **IOB**	Raimondi **IOG**	Verdi **C**
Marazzoli **IOB**	Rameau **C, COCOF, FO**	Vinci **IOB**
Marliani **IOG**	Reichardt **GOB**	Vivaldi **C, CSB, IMa, IOB**
Mattheson **EDM**	Ricci, L. **IOG**	Vogler **GOB, MMS**
Mayr **IOG**	Rimsky-Korsakov **C**	
Mazzocchi, D. **BMB**	Rinaldo di Capua **IOB**	Wagenseil **IOB**
Mazzocchi, V. **IOB**	Rossi, Luigi **BMB, IOB**	Wagner **C**
Meder **EDM**	Rossi, M. **BMB**	Weber, C. M. von **C**
Méhul **ERO, FO**	Rossini **C, BMB, ERO**	Webern **C**
Melani, J. **IOB**	Rousseau **BMB**	Weyse **SUDM**
Mendelssohn **C**	Rung **SUDM**	Winter **GOB**
Mercadante **IOG**		Wolf, E. W. **GOB**
Meyerbeer **ERO, IOG**	Sacchini **BMB, COCOF, IOB**	Wolf, H. **C**
Monteverdi, C. **C, AMI, BMB, CdMI,**	Salieri **BMB, COCOF, GOB, Oper**	
CMI, DTÖ	Sarro **IOB**	Ziani, P. A. **IOB**
Mozart **C, PSMS**	Sarti **BMB, IOB**	Zumsteeg **GOB**
Müller, W. **GOB**	Sartorio, A. **DMV, IOB**	
Musorgsky **C**		

JULIE WOODWARD

Edmonton. City in Canada, capital of Alberta. Opera was first given in the city by occasional visiting touring companies, such as the San Carlo Opera Company which gave *Lohengrin* in 1922. Edmonton Civic Opera, the first attempt to form a regular opera company, survived from 1935 to 1946. In 1961 the newly formed Alberta Opera Association staged *Il trovatore*; the company performed until 1966. The Edmonton Professional Opera Association, opening in 1963 with *Madama Butterfly*, dropped 'Professional' from its title in 1966 and 'Association' in 1984. This company, whose artistic director since 1965 has been Irving Guttman, puts on four productions a season in the Jubilee Auditorium. Its repertory is basically Italian, with excursions into French, German and Russian opera. Broadened by co-operation with the Vancouver Opera Association under the scheme Opera West, it has featured Beverly Sills in *Lucia di Lammermoor* (1969) and *La fille du régiment* (1977) and Joan Sutherland in *Lucrezia Borgia* (1972), and the Canadian premières of *Attila* (1978) and *I puritani* (1983). ELIZABETH FORBES

Eduardo e Cristina. *Dramma* in two acts by GIOACHINO ROSSINI to a libretto by GIOVANNI SCHMIDT, revised by ANDREA LEONE TOTTOLA and Gherardo Bevilacqua-Aldobrandini, after a libretto originally written for Stefano Pavesi's *Odoardo e Cristina* (1810); Venice, Teatro Benedetto, 24 April 1819.

Rossini assembled this operatic pastiche, to Pavesi's adapted libretto, shortly after completing his opera *Ermione* in Naples in March 1819. The plot concerns the secret marriage of Cristina (soprano) to Eduardo (contralto), a gallant Swedish soldier. There is already a child by the marriage which is endangered by Eduardo's imprisonment by the Swedish king. When Sweden is threatened by foreign forces, Eduardo is released and his rehabilitation begun. Rossini wrote a handful of new numbers for this pastiche, notably a chorus 'Nel misero tuo stato', later recycled as the march prefacing the Countess's 'En proie à la tristesse' in *Le comte Ory*. For the rest, Rossini, in his haste, took over numbers from *Adelaide di Borgogna*, *Ricciardo e Zoraide* and *Ermione*. RICHARD OSBORNE

Education manquée, Une ('A Defective Education'). Operetta in one act by EMMANUEL CHABRIER to a libretto by EUGÈNE LETERRIER and ALBERT VANLOO; Paris, Cercle de la Presse, 1 May 1879 (private performance); Paris, Théâtre des Arts, 9 January 1913 (public performance).

Gontran (soprano), a young gentleman in 18th-century Paris, has just married Hélène (mezzo-soprano).

He asks his old tutor, Pausanias (bass), for advice on how to proceed, as his education has not covered certain facts. Pausanias admits that, while knowledgeable in every other branch of science, he does not know anything about marriage. He goes to find out the facts, but before his return, Gontran and Hélène discover them without assistance.

Why this charming little work had to wait so many years for a public performance remains a total mystery. The subject is treated with the greatest delicacy; the casting of the young man Gontran as a travesty role – an accepted convention of the period – surely removes any cause for offence. Musically, the piece is quite enchanting, in particular the central duet for the two high voices, while the bass has a fine comic number.

ELIZABETH FORBES

Edvina [Martin], (Marie) Louise (Lucienne Juliette) (*b* Montreal, 1880; *d* London, 13 Nov 1948). Canadian soprano. She studied with Jean de Reszke in Paris. She made her début as Marguerite (*Faust*) in 1908 at Covent Garden, where she sang every season until 1914, and again in 1919, 1920 and 1924. She was the first London Louise, Thaïs, Maliella (*I gioielli della Madonna*), Francesca da Rimini (Zandonai) and Fiora (*L'amore dei tre re*). Her repertory also included Tosca, Desdemona and Mélisande. She sang with the Boston Opera (1911–13), appearing also in its Paris season in 1914; in Chicago (1915–17); and once at the Metropolitan (1915) as Tosca. Her last operatic performance was in that role at Covent Garden in 1924. She had a beautiful voice and an attractive stage personality.

H. H. Harvey: 'Marie Louise Edvina', *Gramophone*, xxx (1952–3), 7 [with discography]   HAROLD ROSENTHAL/R

Edward John Eyre. Opera in one act by BARRY CONYNGHAM to poems by Meredith Oakes and extracts from Edward John Eyre's *Journals of Expeditions of Discovery*; Sydney, University of New South Wales, Science Theatre, 1 May 1971.

The text consists of five poems, which were written by Oakes for a song cycle, and a series of interludes based on words from Eyre's journals. The poems are sung by three soloists: the first by the soprano (as the Society Lady), the second by the alto, the third and fourth by the tenor (as Edward John Eyre and as Wylie) and the fifth by all; a bass soloist also participates (as Governor Gawler). The interludes, which are sometimes spoken and sometimes intoned, are presented by the Narrator; the chorus responds to both poems and interludes through sounds and actions.

As the poems are dramatically presented, the story of Eyre's journey unfolds. In 1840–41 the explorer treks by foot some 1500 miles across the deserts of south-west Australia. Shadows of previous explorers and settlers accompany the small party. Although the expedition is beset by the elements, Eyre completes the journey with a single aboriginal companion, Wylie. Eyre learns about the vastness, the loneliness and the epic nature of the Australian landscape; the relationship between explorer and landscape takes on a quasi-mystical character.

A highly imaginative early work, *Edward John Eyre* displays great versatility in its sound coloration, a strong feel for orchestrally generated evocation of place and great beauty in the use of the woodwinds as a solo quintet, with incisive string writing in support of a contributing, rather than dominating, melodically agile vocal line.

THÉRÈSE RADIC

Edwards [Mrs Mozeen; first name unknown] (*fl* 1737–53). English soprano. A pupil or protégée of Kitty Clive, she appeared first as a child in a pantomime at Drury Lane (1737). She had two seasons with Handel: 1740–41 at Lincoln's Inn Fields, where she created the parts of Clomiris in *Imeneo* and Achilles in *Deidamia*, and 1743 when she sang in oratorios. The parts Handel composed for her indicate a flexible light soprano with a compass of *d'* to *b''*. She was very active in London theatres, especially in works by Arne and Samuel Howard, and in pantomimes and songs between acts; she also acted in straight plays. In 1748 she was engaged for the Smock Alley Theatre, Dublin, and sang there until 1752, appearing in Boyce's *Chaplet*, Handel's *Acis and Galatea*, and often as Polly in *The Beggar's Opera*.

WINTON DEAN

Edwards, George. Pseudonym of LOUIS GRUENBERG.

Edwards, Sian (*b* West Chiltington, Sussex, 27 Aug 1959). British conductor. A graduate of the RNCM, she studied conducting with Neeme Järvi and others and, during further training at the Leningrad Conservatory (1983–5), won the first Leeds Conductors' Competition (1984). After her operatic début with Scottish Opera (*Aufstieg und Fall der Stadt Mahagonny*, 1986), she conducted two productions at the Glyndebourne Festival (*La traviata* and Ravel double bill, both 1987) and the première of Turnage's *Greek* at the Munich Biennale (1988). Her first appearance at Covent Garden, with *The Knot Garden* (1988), resulted in a three-year contract with the Royal Opera, which yielded among other interpretations a striking *Rigoletto* (1989). She made her Coliseum début in 1990 with Prokofiev's *The Gambler* and the following year was appointed music director of the ENO with effect from 1993. Her performances, especially of 20th-century opera, have been admired for the discipline of their orchestral playing, which combines precision of ensemble and careful dynamic shaping.

Eeden, Jan [Jean-Baptiste] van den (*b* Ghent, 26 Dec 1842; *d* Mons, 4 April 1917). Belgian composer. He studied at the Ghent and Brussels conservatories. In 1869 he won the Belgian Prix de Rome, using the prize money to visit France, Germany, Italy and Austria; his music thereafter was strongly influenced by Wagner. On his return to Belgium he was one of the first musicians to join Peter Benoit's cause in pressing for a Flemish national music culture and music education. He became director of the music academy at Mons (1878) and was elected to the Belgian Royal Academy (1891). His compositions include three operas. In 1883 Eeden finished a draft score to a three-act *opéra comique*, *Barberine* (E. Robert and E. Picard, after A. de Musset); the work was never completed. The second opera, *Numance* (4, M. Carré and C. Narrey, after M. de Cervantes), was first performed at the French Opera in Antwerp on 1 February 1898. His most successful opera, *Rhéna* (4, Carré, after Ouida [M. L. de la Ramée]; pubd Brussels, 1912), received its première at the Théâtre de la Monnaie, Brussels, on 15 February 1912 and was revived in 1925 and 1930.

BNB (A. Fraikin)   PATRICK PEIRE, HENRI VANHULST

Egerton, Francis (*b* Limerick, 14 July 1930). Irish tenor. At first an engineer, he studied singing in London (with Hervey Alan and Vera Rozsa) and in Naples. He joined the Glyndebourne chorus and sang small roles there from 1961 to 1963, and from 1965 worked with both Scottish Opera (as Missail, Goro and Bardolph) and Sadler's Wells Opera; with the latter he took various character roles after his début as a Shepherd in *Orfeo* (Monteverdi). He joined the Covent Garden Opera in 1972 as a character tenor and made his American début in 1978 at San Francisco as Red Whiskers (*Billy Budd*). His Italian début was at Palermo in 1984 as Pedrillo, and his Parisian début the same year as Prince Guidon (*The Golden Cockerel*, Théâtre du Châtelet). He sang Monsieur Taupe (*Capriccio*) and Bardolph at the 1990 Glyndebourne Festival. A keen sense of comedy is allied to scrupulous musicianship, and he is specially admired in the four character roles in *Les contes d'Hoffmann*, as Wagner's Mime and as Berg's Captain (*Wozzeck*).

NOËL GOODWIN

Eggert, Joachim Georg Nikolas (*b* Gingst, Rügen, 22 Feb 1779; *d* Thomastorp, nr Linköping, 14 April 1813). German composer and conductor active in Sweden. His first lessons were with local musicians, and in 1794 he moved to Stralsund to study; he resumed his training in Brunswick in 1800. In 1802 he was appointed Kapellmeister at the court theatre in Mecklenburg-Schwerin, but he resigned after a few months owing to a legal dispute. He was appointed the *hovkapell* in Stockholm in 1803 and was *kapellmästare* from 1808 to 1812; during this period he introduced Mozart's operas to Swedish audiences, and he had two stage works, both dramas with song, staged in Stockholm (1809, 1812). His musical style is bold and original, with striking orchestration (often using massive percussion and brass forces) and an advanced harmonic language. He advocated the introduction of folk instruments into serious opera to provide local colour.

*

B. Guston: 'Joachim Nikolas Eggert', *STMf*, vii (1925), 18–24
B. van Boer: *The Symphony in Sweden Part II* (New York, 1983)

BERTIL H. VAN BOER

Egisto (i). Opera by Virgilio Mazzocchi and Marco Marazzoli; see *CHI SOFFRE SPERI*.

Egisto (ii) ('Aegisthus'). *Favola dramatica musicale* in a prologue and three acts by FRANCESCO CAVALLI to a libretto by GIOVANNI FAUSTINI; Venice, Teatro S Cassiano, 1643.

This second collaboration between Cavalli and Faustini, like the first, *La virtù de' strali d'Amore* (1642), mixes mythological and human characters in a story involving two intersecting love triangles (one of them is more like a quadrilateral): Lidio (alto), Egisto (tenor), a descendant of Apollo (alto) and Ipparco (tenor) love Clori (soprano); Clori and Climene (soprano), Ipparco's sister, love Lidio. The elaborate pre-history, such as Faustini was to present in printed form in all of his subsequent librettos, is here provided by successive narratives sung by Egisto and Climene in Act 1 scene iii. From them we learn that Egisto and Clori, like Climene and Lidio, were once lovers but that they were kidnapped by pirates and separated. Egisto and Climene ended up prisoners of the same cruel master, from whom they have just escaped. Now they both resolve to find their original lovers, who, meanwhile, have fallen in love with one another, a love sealed onstage in the two previous scenes – and observed by Egisto – by an unusual succession of three lyrical, multi-strophe arias, the final one shared between them. Ipparco, who met Clori while imprisoned by the same pirates, and who is unaware of Egisto's designs, determines to pursue her with the encouragement of his servant Dema (alto).

When Egisto confronts Clori, she pretends not to recognize him, and accuses him of being mad to think they were once lovers. Climene, in her turn, is rejected by Lidio, who claims that he has simply replaced her by a new beloved. Ipparco agrees to vindicate his sister's honour by killing her betrayer, but when he captures Lidio Climene is unable to have him killed and asks him for death instead; this reawakens his love for her, and resolves one of the triangles in Act 3 scene iii. Egisto, in the meantime, has actually gone mad, and his madness, in conjunction with the knowledge that Lidio has reverted to his former love for Climene, moves Clori to return to Egisto, thus resolving the second triangle. Ipparco recognizes Egisto's claim to Clori and gives up his passion for her. Acts 1 and 2 end with groups of allegorical scenes that function as *intermedi* and confirm that the vicissitudes of earthly love are under supernatural control. Volupia [Voluptuousness], Bellezza [Beauty] and Amor [Cupid] (all sopranos) are featured in the first act; in the second Cupid is imprisoned by the wronged Heroides – Semele (soprano), Fedra (soprano), Didone (alto) and Hero (soprano) – and begs Apollo to release him.

A staple of the opera companies that travelled up and down the Italian peninsula in the 17th century, *Egisto* was one of the most successful operas of the time. It is unusually rich in arias for its period, not only for the comic character Dema (who has two in his two solo scenes), but also for the serious lovers, a number of which are particularly designed to be overheard (Lidio's and Clori's in the first two scenes by Egisto; Lidio's in 2.v by Climene). Among the most affective arias are two extended laments, one, comprising six long strophes, of Egisto ('Lasso, io vivo, e non ho vita', 2.i); the other, based on a chromatically descending tetrachord ostinato, of Climene ('Piangete occhi dolenti', 2.vi). The most notable scenes in the opera are Egisto's mad scenes (3.v and ix), whose texts are cast primarily in recitative poetry. They were inserted, according to Faustini's preface to the libretto, to satisfy the singer of the role and perhaps also the impresario. The immediate inspiration was probably the similar scenes in Sacrati's *La finta pazza*, the hit of the 1641 season.

ELLEN ROSAND

Egizziello [Giziello]. Nickname of GIOACCHINO CONTI.

Egk [Mayer], Werner (*b* Auchsesheim, nr Donauwörth, 17 May 1901; *d* Inning, nr Munich, 10 July 1983). German composer. After preliminary studies in Frankfurt, he became a pupil of Orff in Munich, where he first came into contact with the theatre. In 1928, living in Berlin, he absorbed the influences of many of the leading theatrical and musical personalities there. He returned to Munich the following year and worked as a freelance composer for the local radio station. After the success of his first stage opera, *Die Zaubergeige* (1935), he was invited by Heinz Tietjen to become Kapellmeister at the Berlin Staatsoper, a post he retained until 1940. Although he never joined the Nazi party, he succeeded Paul Graener as director of the composer's section of the *Reichsmusikkammer* in 1941. He was director of the Berlin Hochschule für Musik, 1950–53, and in 1968 became president of the German Music Council.

Egk's studies with Orff and his subsequent exposure to the experimental atmosphere prevalent in Berlin in the 1920s can be regarded as the most significant formative influences on a composer whose career was dedicated primarily to the creation of theatre works. His seven operas, all to his own texts, cover a vast range of subjects, from mythology (*Circe*), fairy-tale (*Die Zaubergeige*) and history (*Columbus*) to adaptations of great literary or dramatic works (Ibsen's *Peer Gynt* and Kleist's *Die Verlobung in San Domingo*). Despite this apparent diversity of interests, they seem to be connected by a central theme that explores the ability of the individual to overcome evil and shape his own destiny. Sometimes the choice of dramatic material reflects an acute sensitivity to contemporary political issues. Thus *Peer Gynt*, written during the Nazi era, satirizes an uninhibited lust for power, while *Die Verlobung in San Domingo* manifests a concern for the consequences of racial tension particularly apposite to the early 1960s.

Egk's first opera, *Columbus* (composed 1932), remains his most innovatory in dramatic conception. Originally written for the radio, it was revived in a stage version in 1942. The work presents an unusual mixture of play, oratorio and opera, and its subtitle, *Bericht und Bildnis*, indicates Egk's attempt to recreate in almost documentary terms the initial excitement that surrounded the great explorer's discovery of America. To provide an objective and historically accurate background, quotations from 15th-century Spanish music were incorporated into the score, and they easily merge with the somewhat neutral musical language. Yet the opera failed to make a lasting impression because its stage action is more contemplative than dramatic. In contrast, the more conventional setting of Franz Pocci's naive fairy-tale, *Die Zaubergeige*, achieved instantaneous success and became one of the most performed contemporary operas in Nazi Germany. The story of Kaspar, the farm servant, who is presented with a magic violin which gives him the powers of fame, influence and fortune so long as he renounces the love of women, is treated in a witty and brilliant manner. Its musical

idiom, a basically diatonic language lightly spiced with bitonal harmonies influenced by Stravinsky and punctuated by Bavarian folkdances and rhythms, seemed to conform to Goebbels's vision of a Nazi culture with its 'romanticism of steel'. Yet although the opera's popularity was largely responsible for Egk's meteoric rise to prominence during the 1930s, his relationship with the authorities was by no means easy.

In particular, his next opera, *Peer Gynt* (composed 1937–8), commissioned by the Berlin Staatsoper, had a controversial reception. Both the grotesque portrayal of the Trolls, who in the first production paraded around the stage like Storm Troopers, and the musical style, which sometimes recalls Weill and employs jazz effects, aroused considerable hostility. However, after Hitler had attended a performance of the work and personally congratulated the composer, critical opinion had to be drastically revised. At a subsequent performance in Düsseldorf during the *Reichsmusiktage* of 1939, the opera was temporarily rehabilitated and praised as a fine example of Nordic art.

During World War II Egk received a further commission from Berlin for an opera. Following the pattern adopted by several contemporary German composers (e.g. Strauss in *Die Liebe der Danae* and *Daphne*, and Reutter in *Odysseus*), he fashioned material from the world of classical mythology, setting the story of *Circe* (composed 1945). The work was eventually performed in 1948, but the composer became dissatisfied with its musical and dramatic shape. It was subsequently withdrawn and drastically revised, reappearing under the title of *17 Tage und 4 Minuten* in 1966. In this new version, the opera attempts to make classical figures appear meaningful to a modern audience. Consequently, Egk employed an eclectic style, which includes episodes of popular music, *opera buffa* and lyricism.

After the relative failure of *Circe*, the composer spent more than four years working on his next and most ambitious opera, *Irische Legende* (composed 1951–5), which was first heard at the Salzburg Festival in 1955. The libretto, an amalgam of Yeats's tale *Cathleen*

Scene from Act 3 of the original production of Werner Egk's 'Peer Gynt' at the Staatsoper, Berlin, 24 November 1938, with Käte Heidersbach as Solveig and Matthieu Ahlersmeyer as Peer Gynt; set by Wolf Voelker

O'Shea and his play *The Countess Cathleen*, is primarily concerned with human sacrifice and the rescue of a bartered soul. Its complexity inspired a much more dissonant musical style with insistent percussive ostinatos accompanying the scenes in which the Demons appear. Yet for all its sophistication and effective use of theatrical effects, the work has remained neglected. As a consequence, his final operas, *Der Revisor* (1957), a reworking of Gogol's story notable for its virtuoso ensembles and swift-moving action, and *Die Verlobung in San Domingo* (1963), with its passionate concern for racial tolerance, return to more conventional dramatic representation. Both works demonstrate the strengths and weaknesses of Egk's operatic style. While they are immensely rich in terms of dramatic technique, brilliant characterization and colourful orchestration, the music, for all its cleverness, lacks the distinction and sheer memorability to ensure a permanent place in the repertory.

See also Peer Gynt; Verlobung in san domingo, die; and Zaubergeige, die.

Columbus: Bericht und Bildnis, 1932 (3 pts, Egk), Bavarian Radio, 13 July 1933; stage, Frankfurt, Städtische Bühnen, 13 Jan 1942, vs (Mainz, 1942); rev., Berlin, Städtische Oper, 17 May 1951
Die Zaubergeige (3, Egk and L. Andersen, after F. Pocci), Frankfurt, Städtische Bühnen, 22 May 1935; rev., Stuttgart, Württembergische Staats, 2 May 1954, vs (Mainz, 1935, 2/1954)
Peer Gynt (prol., 3, Egk, after H. Ibsen), Berlin, Staatsoper, 24 Nov 1938, vs (Mainz, 1938)
Circe, 1945 (3, Egk, after P. Calderón de la Barca), Berlin, 18 Dec 1948, vs (Mainz, 1947); rev. 1965, as 17 Tage und 4 Minuten, Stuttgart, 2 June 1966, vs (Mainz, 1966)
Irische Legende, 1951–5 (5 scenes, Egk, after W. B. Yeats), Salzburg, Kleines Festspielhaus, 17 Aug 1955, vs (Mainz, 1955); rev. 1969–70, Augsburg, Stadt, 26 Feb 1975
Der Revisor (5, Egk, after N. Gogol), Schwetzingen, Schloss, 9 May 1957, vs (Mainz, 1957)
Die Verlobung in San Domingo (prol., 2, interlude, Egk, after H. von Kleist), Munich, National, 27 Nov 1963, vs (Mainz, 1963)

*

O. Oster: 'Werner Egk's "Columbus": zum Problem der "Funkoper" ', *ZfM*, Jg.100 (1933), 1233–5
W. Egk: 'Meine Oper "Die Zaubergeige" ', *ZfM*, Jg.102 (1935), 738–40
H. Schmidt-Garre: 'Werner Egk', *ZfM*, Jg.103 (1935), 736–8
'Sonderheft Werner Egk anlässlich der Erstaufführung der Oper "Die Zaubergeige" in Berlin', *Blätter der Staatsoper* [Berlin], xvi/2 (1936)
W. Matthes: 'Werner Egk über seine "Peer Gynt" ', *Signale für die musikalische Welt*, xcvi (1938), 609–10
F. Stege: 'Berliner Musik', *ZfM*, Jg.106 (1939), 47–53
W. Egk: 'Columbus: Bericht und Bildnis', *ZfM*, Jg.108, (1941), 638–9
W. Oehlmann: 'Die Oper – Werner Egks', *ZfM*, Jg.108 (1941), 639–43
R. Kreile: 'W. Egk', *Frankfurter Hefte*, viii (1953), 698–705
E. Laaff: 'Werner Egk', *Melos*, xx (1953), 305–12
K. H. Wörner: 'Egk and Orff: Representatives of Contemporary German Opera', *MR*, xiv (1953), 186–204
W. Egk: ' "Irische Legende" ', *ÖMz*, x (1955), 125–30
H. Pringsheim: 'Columbus von Werner Egk', *SMz*, xcv (1955), 46–8
E. Werba: 'Musik der freien Entscheidung: Werner Egks "Irische Legende" ', *ÖMz*, x (1955), 231–6
W. Egk: 'Oper die zauberhafte Ungeheuerlichkeit', *NZM*, Jg.117 (1956), 132–3
——: ' "Der Revisor" als Oper', *ÖMz*, xiii (1958), 47–9
——: *Musik – Wort – Bild: Texte und Anmerkungen, Betrachtungen und Gedanken* (Munich, 1960)
——: ' "Die Verlobung in San Domingo" ', *NZM*, Jg.124 (1963), 440–45
H. Lohmüller: 'Egks neue Kleist: Oper in München erfolgreich', *Melos*, xxxi (1964), 27–9
K. H. Ruppel: ' "Die Verlobung in San Domingo": Über Egks neue Oper', *OW*, v (1964), 24–5
W. Schuh: 'Werner Egks neue Oper "Die Verlobung in San Domingo" ', *SMz*, civ (1964), 46–8
W. Egk: *Opern, Ballette, Konzertwerke* (Mainz, 1966)

——: 'Zweimal Calderón', *Melos*, xxxiii (1966), 109–13
B. Kohl and E. Nolle, eds.: *Werner Egk: Das Bühnenwerk* (Munich, 1971)
E. Krause: *Werner Egk: Oper und Ballette* (Wilhelmshaven, 1971)
H. Schäfer: 'Meister des Musiktheaters: Werner Egk zum 70. Geburtstag', *Musik und Gesellschaft*, xxi (1971), 324–7
W. Egk: *Die Zeit wartet nicht* (Percha, 1973, 2/1981)   ERIK LEVI

Egressy, Béni [Galambos, Benjámin] (*b* Sajókazinc, 21 April 1814; *d* Pest, 17 July 1851). Hungarian composer and librettist. After working as an actor in Kolozsvár (now Cluj-Napoca, Romania) and studying singing in Milan, he settled in Pest (in about 1840), where he found a job at the National Theatre. While there he wrote the libretto for Ferenc Erkel's first opera, *Bátori Mária* (1840), and also for Erkel's chief works, *Hunyadi László* (1844) and *Bánk bán* (1861); he also translated many French plays and 19 Italian and French opera librettos into Hungarian.

As a composer Egressy was self-taught. From 1842 to 1851 he wrote comedies and popular plays with songs and dances for the National Theatre. These works are distinguished by melodic invention and excellent powers of dramatic description; the music is rooted in the spiritual and secular song traditions of the reformed college of Hungary, the German lied and the Hungarian instrumental style (*verbunkos*). With his songs and dances for the theatre in particular, he soon found wide popularity throughout Hungary.

*

K. Isoz: *Egressy Béni elsö dalmü-szövegkönyvéről* [On Egressy's First Opera Libretto] (Budapest, 1911)   FERENC BÓNIS

Egypt. For discussion of opera in Egypt *see* Cairo.

Ehrenberg [Erenberg], **Vladimir Georgiyevich** (*b* Dec 1874/Jan 1875; *d* Kharkiv, 14 Sept 1923). Russian composer and conductor. As music director of Nikolay Yevreynov's celebrated St Petersburg cabaret 'Krivoye Zerkalo' ('The Fun-House Mirror'), Ehrenberg was responsible for the music to the sensationally successful parody *Vampuka, ili Nevesta afrikanskaya* ('Vampuka, or The African Bride'), first presented in 1909, which reached its 1000th performance in 1927. He also composed a one-act opera, *Svad'ba* ('The Wedding'), after Chekhov's eponymous dramatic sketch; dedicated to Shalyapin, it was first performed by Zimin's Opera Studio in Moscow on 13/26 December 1916. Like the young Stravinsky, Ehrenberg was attracted to the satirical verses of 'Kozma Prutkov' (pseudonym for a trio of Russian poets active in the mid-19th century) and composed an album of 'musical illustrations' to them.

See also Vampuka, ili nevesta afrikanskaya.

*

A. Kugel': *List'ya s dereva* [Leaves from a Tree] (Leningrad, 1926)
P. Gnedich: *Kniga zhizni, vospominaniya* [The Book of My Life, Reminiscences] (Leningrad, 1929)
M. Polyakov, ed.: *Russkaya teatral'naya parodiya XIX-nachala XX veka* (Moscow, 1976)
S. Golub: *Evreinov: the Theatre of Paradox and Transformation* (Ann Arbor, 1984)   RICHARD TARUSKIN

Ehrlich, Abel (*b* Cranz, 3 Sept 1915). Israeli composer of German birth. In 1934 he left Germany for Yugoslavia, where he studied at the Zagreb Academy of Music but was expelled for being a Jew. He finally settled in Israel in 1939, studying at the Jerusalem Academy of Music under Shlomo Rosowsky (a former pupil of Rimsky-Korsakov) until 1944 and becoming increasingly active as a teacher. Among his awards is the

Israeli Prime Minister's Prize (1990). Ehrlich's works to 1950 include over 20 operas, which show post-romantic and European influence. His later operas (after 1960) use 12-note and serial writing, reflecting his participation in courses given by Stockhausen and Pousseur at Darmstadt in 1959. Since the mid-1970s he has concentrated on vocal compositions, including operas, in which the musical structure is reinforced by the linguistic structure of the text, sometimes incorporating graphic ideas. These works highlight Ehrlich's skill as a dramatic composer.

The Split Personality of Music Master Botten op.104 (short op, Ehrlich), Jerusalem, 1959
Immanuele Romano [Heaven and Hell] op.207 (short op, I. Romano), Jerusalem, 1971
Gnithon and Gnithemos [I am a Horse] op.450 (music theatre, Ehrlich, after H. Arps), Tel-Aviv, 1977
Dead Souls op.458 (short op, Ehrlich, after N. Gogol), Tel-Aviv, 1978

Early operas (mostly comic and with pf; libs. by Ehrlich; performed privately unless otherwise stated; performed in Jerusalem unless otherwise stated): The Japanese Kaiser op.1, Tilsit, 1926; Konto Buch op.2, Königsberg, 1931–2; Kleinfrauentag op.4 (with 2 other works), Zagreb, 1934–8; Bertolt am Shabbes op.6, 1939; Die grossen Tage [Moritz is Mobilized] op.7, 1939; Pech hoch zwei op.8, 1940; Welt hierhin op.9, 1940; Richter XIX op.24, 1942; Das heroische Wesen op.29, 1942; Die Entführung in den Sarail [Long Live World Peace] op.43, 1945; Der Aufstand der Wissenschaftler [Nine Years after Hiroshima] op. 55, public perf., 1946; Wohnung gesucht op.57, 1946; Des Bankherrn Traum op.63, 1946; Der Kampf im Rif op.66, 1947; Unter feiner Leuten op.67 (after D. Ranyon: Madam La Gimp), 1947; Stop-gap [The Hole in the Ceiling] op.68, 1947; Through the Looking Glass op.69, 1947; Titbayyesh Sha'ul! [Shame on you Saul!] op.72, 1949; Magister Simone op.75, 1950

*

Y. W. Cohen: *Werden und Entwicklung der Musik in Israel* (Kassel, 1976) [pt ii of rev. edn of M. Brod: *Die Musik Israels*]
——: *Ne'imei Zemirot Yisrael* [The Heirs of the Sweet Psalmist] (Tel-Aviv, 1990)   WILLIAM Y. ELIAS

Ehrling, Sixten (*b* Malmö, 3 April 1918). Swedish conductor. He studied at the Stockholm Royal Academy of Music and joined the music staff at the Swedish Royal Opera, making his conducting début in 1940. After briefly assisting Karl Böhm at the Dresden Staatsoper in 1941, then returning to concert work in Sweden, he became music director of the Royal Opera, 1953–60. There he revived neglected works and introduced new operas, notably Blomdahl's *Aniara* (1959) which he brought to the Edinburgh Festival the same year and to Covent Garden in 1960, both with the Swedish company. His début at the Metropolitan was in 1973 with *Peter Grimes*, and in the next four seasons there he conducted a varied repertory including the *Ring* cycle, Puccini's *Il trittico* and the house's first production of *Bluebeard's Castle*. A careful, perceptive executant, he was active at the Vienna Staatsoper from 1982 and continued to make occasional appearances with the Swedish Royal Opera.   RICHARD BERNAS

Eichner, Adelheid (Maria) (*b* ?Mannheim, 1760–62; *d* Potsdam, 5 April 1787). German singer, daughter of the composer Ernst Eichner. She is believed to have studied in Mannheim with a castrato and in 1777 she became the only female vocalist to hold an appointment in the prince's Kapelle in Potsdam. From 1781 she took all the important roles available to her voice in the Italian Opera at Berlin. According to contemporary accounts her range extended from f' to f''', with a pure high register and an extraordinarily fluent and tasteful execution and delivery. She also composed songs.

                        MARIANNE REISSINGER

Einem, Gottfried von (*b* Berne, 24 Jan 1918). Austrian composer. He was educated in Germany and England and in 1938 became a coach at the Berlin Staatsoper and the Bayreuth Festspielhaus. From 1941 to 1943, he studied composition privately with Blacher. In the following year, the success of his first stage work, the ballet *Prinzessin Turandot*, secured him the post of resident composer and music adviser to the Dresden Staatsoper. After World War II he worked as a music administrator for the Salzburg Festival and from 1960 to 1964 he held a similar position at the Vienna Festival. He taught at the Musikhochschule in Vienna from 1963 to 1972.

Von Einem's reputation was established after the war when his opera *Dantons Tod* received its première at the Salzburg Festival (1947). Unusually for a contemporary opera, the work was praised unanimously by both critics and public and it has remained one of his most durable compositions. Its success can be explained on several levels. The opera's passionate sense of historical commitment struck an immediate resonance in a world that was just beginning to recover from the horrors perpetrated by the Nazis. In addition, Blacher's brilliant libretto, which condenses Büchner's drama from its original 32 scenes to just six, emerges as a compelling theatrical experience in its own right. While the musical language is hardly innovatory and individual phrases might momentarily suggest the influences of Strauss, Stravinsky, Weill or Blacher, these disparate elements seem to be fully absorbed into an individual style that has sufficient rhythmic and harmonic flexibility to encompass the vast range of emotions demanded by the text. Following Büchner's designation of the work as a revolutionary drama, the composer gives a particularly prominent role to the chorus; the virtuoso writing for them in the Tribunal Scene (Part 2 scene ii) represents the musical and dramatic high point of the score. Apart from a few recurring motifs, such as the five powerful brass chords which open and close the opera, there is little evidence of formal thematic development. Although an aura of expressionism surrounds the score, especially in its scenes of violence and in its portrayal of Lucile's madness, the opera is fundamentally dissimilar to Berg's *Wozzeck*, despite the fact that both works share the same playwright.

Expressionism inevitably forms the background to von Einem's second opera, *Der Prozess* (composed 1950–52), also written for Salzburg to a libretto by Blacher. Based upon Franz Kafka's novel about the unsuspecting bank signatory who is placed on trial for an unspecified crime, it is a parable about the individual pitted against a bureaucratic society. The central role of Josef K. is delineated by an incessant recitative-like writing that matches the rise and fall of his increasingly deranged speech. With an orchestral accompaniment that is often harsh and bitingly rhythmic, in the manner of Stravinsky, there are few episodes of genuine lyricism. Indeed, the somewhat abrupt changes of scene remind one more of the silent film rather than a conventional opera. The ambiguities of Kafka's text, which contains a bewildering mixture of fantasy and realism, pose considerable problems in the context of an operatic setting and it is questionable whether the composer's basically tonal language has fully met this challenge.

A gap of almost ten years elapsed before von Einem embarked on his next opera, *Der Zerrissene*, which again employs a libretto by Blacher. The subject matter, derived from a play by the Viennese dramatist Nestroy, inspired a clear departure in both musical and dramatic terms. With its predominantly carefree atmosphere, evidently modelled on the traditions of the Mozartian Singspiel, the score is, if anything, more defiantly diatonic than before. It also offers plenty of opportunities for humorous diversions and the parodistic funeral march, which accompanies the assumed death of the two rivals, is especially amusing. Yet at the same time, von Einem understates the contrast between the comic and serious elements of the plot, with the result that the opera lacks a certain personal involvement. This deficiency was overcome in *Der Besuch der alten Dame* (1970), a setting of the play by Dürrenmatt who also wrote the libretto. The opera is a powerful satire on the corruption engendered by lust for money. It made an immediate impression at its première at the Vienna Staatsoper and soon became one of the most frequently performed new operas of the 1970s. In it, the composer's musical language can be compared to Britten's in that it reached a wide audience and remained resolutely unaffected by the more extreme developments in post-war music. Yet there is nothing remotely derivative in the score. Indeed, it reveals a greater depth of characterization and a tighter control of thematic ideas than before. Moreover, the concise instrumental intermezzos which link the opera's ten scenes are especially effective in charting the constant changes of atmosphere throughout the drama.

After writing *Der Besuch der alten Dame*, von Einem worked again with Blacher for his fifth opera, *Kabale und Liebe* (composed 1975), in which Schiller's drama of 1784 is reduced from its original 42 scenes to just nine. But whereas a similar adaptation enhanced the dramatic impact of Büchner's *Dantons Tod*, in this work the revolutionary effect of the plot is scarcely discernible. The music exhibits the composer's customary technical finesse, but fails to illuminate the tragic love-affair that is thwarted because of class conflict. Consequently the opera received a mixed reception and has rarely been revived since its first performance.

Von Einem's next stage work, *Jesu Hochzeit*, has remained equally neglected, but for very different reasons. The opera was originally commissioned as a companion piece to Britten's church parable *The Prodigal Son* but could not be performed in a consecrated building because its text offended the Catholic Church. Indeed, its première, at the Theater an der Wien, caused a national scandal and was nearly cancelled through organized demonstrations. Opponents of the work were particularly incensed by an episode which featured an erotic encounter between Jesus, representing Life and Love, and a female, Death. Equally controversial was the appearance of the 'pop' singer Mary Magdalene who opens and closes the opera by posing theological riddles directly to the audience. Against this, the musical score is rather austere, with sparse instrumentation and juxtapositions of major- and minor-based tonalities curiously reminiscent of Mahler.

See also Besuch der alten Dame, der; Dantons Tod; and Prozess, der.

Dantons Tod op.6, 1944–6 (2 pts [6 scenes], B. Blacher and von Einem, after G. Büchner), Salzburg, Festspielhaus, 6 Aug 1947, cond. Fricsay, vs (Vienna, 1947), full score (Vienna, 1961)

Der Prozess op.14, 1950–52 (2 pts [9 scenes], Blacher and H. von Cramer, after F. Kafka), Salzburg, Festspielhaus, 17 Aug 1953, cond. Böhm, vs (Mainz, 1953), full score (Wiesbaden, 1969)

Der Zerrissene op.31, 1961–4 (2, Blacher, after J. Nestroy), Hamburg, 17 Sept 1964, cond. Sawallisch, vs (London, 1964)

Der Besuch der alten Dame op.35 (3, F. Dürrenmatt), Vienna, Staatsoper, 23 May 1971, cond. H. Stein (London, 1972)

Kabale und Liebe op.44 (2, Blacher and L. Ingrisch, after F. von Schiller), Vienna, 17 Dec 1976, cond. C. von Dohnányi (London, 1978)

Jesu Hochzeit op.52 (2, Ingrisch), Vienna, Wien, 18 May 1980, cond. D. Shallon, vs (Berlin, 1979)

Prinz Chocolat (5 episodes, Ingrisch), Ossiach, 2 July 1983, unpubd

Tulifant op.75 (3, Ingrisch), Vienna, Ronacher, 30 Oct 1990 (Vienna, 1990)

*

H. Rütz: *Neue Oper: G. von Einem und seine Oper 'Dantons Tod'* (Vienna, 1947)

—— ' "Danton's Death": Music Drama or Music Theatre', *Musicology*, ii/2 (1948), 188

O. Schuh: ' "Danton's Death" and the Problem of Modern Opera', ibid, 177

G. von Einem: ' "Der Prozess" ', *ÖMz*, xviii (1953), 198–200

M. Graf: ' "Der Prozess" von G. von Einem', *ÖMz*, viii (1953), 259–64

W. Reich: 'Der Prozess', *MQ*, xl (1954), 62–76

D. Hajas: ' "Dantons Tod" nach 16 Jahren', *ÖMz*, xviii (1963), 204–8

W. Oehlmann: 'Revolution als Schaustück: Einems "Dantons Tod" ', *Musik im Unterricht*, liv (1963), 151–2

G. von Einem: 'Ein Komponist im Turm', *Melos*, xxvi (1964), 113–17

W. Schuh: 'Gottfried von Einem's "Der Zerrissene" ', *Tempo*, new ser., no.71 (1964–5), 22–4

G. von Einem: 'Die Freiheit des Komponisten', *ÖMz*, xx (1965), 278–81

——: 'Komponist und Gesellschaft', *Schriftenreihe Musik und Gesellschaft*, i (Karlsruhe, 1967)

D. Hartmann: 'Bekenntnisoper unserer Zeit', *ÖMz*, xxii (1967), 594–7

——: *Gottfried von Einem* (Vienna, 1967)

R. Klein: 'Von Einems Dürrenmatt-Oper "Der Besuch der alten Dame" ', *ÖMz*, xxvi (1971), 302–6

F. Saathen: 'Gottfried von Einems Oper abgelauscht: Neues über den "Besuch der alten Dame" ', *Das Opernjournal*, no.6 (1971–2), 7–10

H. H. Stuckenschmidt: 'Von Einem's "Der Besuch der alten Dame" ', *Tempo*, new ser., no.98 (1971–2), 28–30

B. Sonntag: 'Wie sich die alten Dame veränderte Dürrenmatts "Tragische Komödie" und von Einems Oper', *OW* (1972), Feb, 45–7

F. Saathen: 'Committed Opera: Gottfried von Einem's "The Visit of the Old Lady" ', *Tempo*, new ser., no.104 (1973), 22–9

R. Klein: 'Gottfried von Einems Oper "Kabale und Liebe" ', *ÖMz*, xxxi (1976), 633–9

M. Dietrich and W. Greisenegger, eds.: *Pro und Kontra Jesu Hochzeit: Dokumentation eines Opernskandals* (Vienna, 1980)

R. Klein: 'Gottfried von Einems Oper "Jesu Hochzeit" ', *ÖMz*, xxxv (1980), 189–99

F. Saathen: *Einem – Chronik* (Vienna, 1982)   ERIK LEVI

Einstein, Alfred (*b* Munich, 30 Dec 1880; *d* El Cerrito, CA, 13 Feb 1952). American musicologist of German birth. A pupil of Sandberger, he took the doctorate at Munich in 1903. He was active chiefly as a critic (in Munich until 1927, then Berlin), editor and lexicographer (he edited the ninth to eleventh editions of Riemann's *Musik Lexikon*, 1910–29), leaving Germany in 1933, first for London, then Florence and finally settling in the USA, where he taught at several universities. A wide-ranging and extremely prolific music historian, his study, *The Italian Madrigal* (1949), is generally recognized as his finest achievement. He treated opera in his general works (such as his 1917 history, published in English in 1936, and his study of the Romantic era, 1947) and in his work on two particular composers: Gluck, in his short but perceptive study (London, 1936), and Mozart, in the context of his 1937 revision of the Köchel catalogue and his 1945 study, which contains valuable chapters on the mature operas and their place in his development. Einstein also edited Gluck's *L'innocenza giustificata* (DTÖ, lxxxii, Jg.xliv, 1937).

Einstein on the Beach. Opera in four acts and five 'knee plays' (intermezzos) by PHILIP GLASS and ROBERT WILSON to a libretto by Christopher Knowles, Lucinda Childs and Samuel M. Johnson; Avignon Festival, 25 July 1976.

Created between 1974 and 1976, *Einstein* is the longest and most famous of Glass's music-theatre works, the first of three operas each concerning a man who changed the world. It is, however, in many ways unrepresentative, being much more than the usual collaboration between librettist and composer. Glass first became aware of Robert Wilson's stage work in 1973 when he attended a 12-hour production by the latter based on the life and times of Josef Stalin. He was immediately attracted to what he called Wilson's sense of 'theatrical time, space and movement', and the two promptly determined to collaborate on a theatrical work based on the life of a historic figure. Discarding Chaplin, Hitler and Gandhi, they agreed upon Albert Einstein, naming the piece *Einstein on the Beach on Wall Street*. The title was later shortened; neither creator now remembers when or why. The opera is intended as a metaphorical look at Einstein: scientist, humanist, amateur musician – and the man whose theories, for better and for worse, led to the splitting of the atom. Although it is difficult to discern a 'plot' in *Einstein*, the final scene may be interpreted as nuclear holocaust: with its renaissance-pure vocal lines, the blast of amplified instruments, a steady pulse and the hysterical chorus chanting numerals as quickly and frantically as possible, it seemed to many a musical reflection of the anxious, *fin-de-siècle* mood of the late 1970s.

The opera runs for four hours and 40 minutes without an interval (the audience is invited to wander in and out at liberty during performances), and is in four interconnected acts. These are alternated with what Glass and Wilson called 'knee plays' – brief interludes that also provide time for scenery changes. In Wilson's original videotaped production, the first knee play is already in progress when the audience is admitted to the auditorium. After about 15 minutes the chorus enters very slowly and takes its place in the orchestra pit. Thus the audience's perception of time is challenged from the outset, and an allusion is made to one aspect of Einstein's theories. The 'story' of *Einstein* comprises visual images and aural references relating to Albert Einstein, his life and his work. Glass and Wilson used as a 'libretto' a sketchbook of visual themes, before developing a spoken and sung text during the rehearsal period. The text consists of numbers, solfege syllables and some cryptic poems by Christopher Knowles, a young, neurologically-impaired man with whom Wilson had worked (as an instructor of disturbed children). To this were added short texts by choreographer Lucinda Childs and Samuel M. Johnson, an actor who played the Judge in the 'Trial' scenes and the Bus Driver in the finale. References are made to Patricia Hearst, who was on trial for bank robbery during the creation of the opera, to the radio lineup on New York's WABC, to the

Two drawings from Robert Wilson's sketchbook of visual themes for 'Einstein on the Beach' showing the train (above) and the trial (below)

popular song 'Mr Bojangles', to the teen idol David Cassidy and to the Beatles.

Einstein is scored for a 16-strong chamber choir, including soprano and tenor soloists, the Philip Glass Ensemble (two keyboards, three wind players, one soprano), and a solo violinist. In the original production the violinist was dressed as Albert Einstein and placed between the stage and orchestra pit. The music is based on two techniques Glass has been working with since the mid-1960s: additive process and cyclic structures. Additive process involves the expansion and contraction of tiny musical modules; a grouping of five notes might be played several times, followed by a group of six notes, similarly repeated, then by seven notes, and so on (ex.1). Thus a simple figure can maintain the same

Ex.1

general melodic configuration while taking on a very different rhythmic shape. Glass defines rhythmic cycles as the simultaneous repetition of two or more different rhythmic patterns, which, depending on the length of the pattern, will eventually arrive together back at the starting points, making for one complete cycle. An early passage from the 'Train' scene from *Einstein* gives an example of this, three repeats of the upper part being equal to four repeats of the lower part (ex.2). With these

Ex.2

two techniques as the basis of his individual style, Glass had already begun to build a music of increasing richness and appeal. *Einstein* added a new functional harmony that set it aside from the early conceptual works.

Einstein was revived in 1984 at the Brooklyn Academy of Music and, in 1989, Achim Fryer attempted a new visual interpretation of Glass's music for the opera at the Stuttgart State Opera, which was generally judged unsuccessful; it is, however, the Glass/Wilson *Einstein*, that has become one of the more famous operatic collaborations of the century, creating something unique and powerful. The sound recording of *Einstein* (recorded in 1977 and released in 1979) won considerable attention though it necessarily lacked Wilson's visual complement and Glass abridged the music to fit on to four LP discs. The opening scene was cut from 40 minutes to a little more than 20 minutes by reducing the number of repeats.

Einstein on the Beach may be said to represent the apogee of Glass's modernism. As the composer observed in *Music by Philip Glass*:

In its own way, the pre-Einstein music, rigorous and highly reductive, was more 'radical' in its departure from the received tradition of Western music than what I have written since. But as I had been preoccupied at the point with that more radical-sounding music for over ten years, I felt I could add little more to what I had already done. Again, it is surely no coincidence that it was at the moment that I was embarking upon a major shift in my music to large-scale theater works that I began to develop a new, more expressive language for myself.

TIM PAGE

Eipperle, Trude (*b* Stuttgart, 12 Aug 1910). German soprano. She studied in Stuttgart, making her début at Wiesbaden in 1930. After singing in Brunswick, she was engaged at the Staatsoper in Munich (1938–44), at Cologne (1945–51) and at Stuttgart (1951). She sang Pamina and Eva at Covent Garden in 1938 and Zdenka (*Arabella*) at Salzburg in 1942. She took part in the first performance of Braunfels's *Verkündigung* (1948, Cologne) and sang Eva at Bayreuth (1952). Her repertory included Countess Almaviva, Elisabeth, Elsa, the Marschallin and Arabella. Though most admired in German opera, she also sang Desdemona and Butterfly.

ELIZABETH FORBES

Eiríksdóttir, Karólína (*b* Reykjavík, 10 Jan 1951). Icelandic composer. After graduating from the Reykjavík College of Music in 1974, where her composition teacher was Thorkell Sigurbjörnsson, she took two MM degrees at the University of Michigan, in music history and musicology (1976) and composition

(1978) under William Albright and George Wilson. Since then her teaching at the Kópavogur School of Music and the Reykjavík College of Music has complemented her activities as a composer.

The highly distilled, aphoristic style characteristic of her instrumental music, which includes orchestral, chamber and solo works, is powerfully apparent in her only opera, the 'musical dream-play' *Någon har jag sett* ('Someone I Have Seen'). It was commissioned by the Vadstena Academy, which first staged it on 27 July 1988. The libretto, which draws on a 1979 collection of poems by the Swedish writer Marie Louise Ramnefalk, evokes music of immediacy without mawkishness in telling of the transformation of a couple's love when one of them faces imminent death.

MARTIN DREYER

Eisenstein [Eyzenshteyn], **Sergey** (**Mikhaylovich**) (*b* Riga, 23 Jan 1898; *d* Moscow, 10 Feb 1948). Soviet film director. He began as a designer and director in the spoken theatre (Proletkul't Theatre, Moscow, 1920–23), before turning to what he regarded as the more progressive form of cinema. The scores for his films *Alexander Nevsky* (1938) and *Ivan Groznïy* ('Ivan the Terrible', 1942–5) were written by Prokofiev and the latter's *Voyna i mir*('War and Peace') was to have been staged by Eisenstein in 1942, but was postponed.

The production of *Die Walküre* at the Bol'shoy in November 1940 was intended by Stalin as a friendly gesture towards Hitler (the Non-aggression Pact had been signed the previous year), but Eisenstein's conception of the work was avowedly anti-fascist and the production was abruptly terminated. Fricka represented for Eisenstein the 'guardian of all-powerful structures of order', anticipating the future class society, while he saw Wotan as an anarchist who recognized no laws save those of the free instincts. In the juxtaposition of the two he discerned the sources of fascism. The ideals of humanity represented by Brünnhilde could be realized, he believed, only in the Communist era.

The influence of Eisenstein's innovatory 'mimic chorus' – Sieglinde's Act 1 narration enacted in pantomime, the Ride of the Valkyries by a group of extras shadowing the singers, Hunding accompanied by a gang of henchmen – can be seen in the work of various modern producers.

*

'Eisenstein Makes his Debut in Opera: Noted Film Director Discusses his Work on "The Valkyrie"', *Moscow News* (28 Nov 1940)
S. M. Eisenstein: 'Voploshcheniye mifa' [The Embodiment of Myth], *Teatr* (1940), 13–38; Ger. trans. in *Über Kunst und Künstler* (Munich, 1977), 67–111
M. Seton: *Sergei M. Eisenstein* (London, 1952, 2/1978), esp. 399–406
'Iz perepiski S. Prokof'yeva i S. Eyzenshteyna' [From the Correspondence of S. Prokofiev and S. Eisenstein], *SovM* (1961), no.4, pp.105–14
V. Shklovsky: *Eyzenshteyn* (Moscow, 1973)
J. Varna: *Eisenstein* (London, 1973)
V. V. Ivanov: *Ocherki po istorii sovetskoy semiotiki* [Essays on the History of Soviet Semiotics] (Moscow, 1976), esp.75–85
O. Bauer: *Richard Wagner: die Bühnenwerke von der Uraufführung bis heute* (Fribourg, 1982; Eng. trans., 1983)
P. M. de Santi: *La messinscena della Valchiria* (Fiesole, 1984)
J. Leyda and Z. Voynow: *Eisenstein at Work* (London, 1985)
H. J. Schlegel: 'Eisensteins Walküre', *Konkret* (1985), Nov, 68–71
E. Burzawa: '*Die Walküre* von Sergej Eisenstein: Versuch der Rekonstruktion', *Richard Wagner und sein Mittelalter*, ed. U. Müller and U. Müller (Anif, Salzburg, 1989), 299–313
R. Bartlett: 'The Embodiment of Myth: Eizenshtein's Production of *Die Walküre*', *Slavonic and East European Review*, lxx (1992), 53–76
BARRY MILLINGTON

Eisentraut, Madame (*b* c1700; *d* after 1735). German soprano. She is first mentioned as singing in Brunswick in 1717, in G. C. Schürmann's *Telemachus und Calypso*. She is noted in Willers's theatrical register of 8 April 1720: 'there was no opera, because the Eisentraut would not sing for the year for 300 Reichsthalers'; presumably she was in Hamburg from 1717 to 1720, and refused to sing because of the devaluation of money at the time. In 1730 she sang in Telemann's *Das neubeglückte Sachsen* at the Gänsemarkt Opera. After another refusal to appear on 19 November 1731, she disappears from the records until the beginning of 1733, when she sang in operas by Telemann and Keiser. On 22 November 1733 Willers notes that 'an infamous lampoon on the Eisentraut' had been published, which 'very much distressed her'. She last sang at the Gänsemarkt Opera in 1735; there is no record of her thereafter.

P. A. Merbach: 'Das Repertoire der Hamburger Oper 1718–1750', *AMw*, vi (1924), 356–7
K. Zelm: 'Die Sänger der Hamburger Gänsemarkt-Oper', *HJbMw*, iii (1978), 35–73, esp. 51–2   HANS JOACHIM MARX

Eisinger, Irene (*b* Schleswig, 8 Dec 1903). German soprano. She studied in Berlin and made her début at Basle in 1926. Two years later she joined the Kroll Opera in Berlin where she sang Susanna, transferring to the Staatsoper in 1932, shortly after which, as a Jewess, she left Germany to join the German Opera at Prague. Successful guest appearances in Vienna led to an engagement at Salzburg where she sang under Bruno Walter from 1930 to 1933. England became her second home after she established herself as a special favourite at Glyndebourne, where her roles were Despina, Papagena, Blonde and Susanna. In 1940 she sang Polly Peachum in the Glyndebourne production of *The Beggar's Opera* and in 1949 reappeared with the company in *Così fan tutte* in Edinburgh. In the winter season of 1936 at Covent Garden she sang Gretel and Adele with captivating style but diminutive voice. At Cambridge in 1939 she sang Ilia in the then unknown *Idomeneo*. She also appeared in films and operetta. She is remembered principally as Despina in the first recording of *Così* (1935), a light-voiced, charming portrayal which only hints at the skill in coloratura revealed in a few of her rarer discs.   J. B. STEANE

Eisler, Hanns (*b* Leipzig, 6 July 1898; *d* Berlin, 6 Sept 1962). German composer. Although he never completed an opera, he must be considered one of the most important composers for the theatre in the 20th century. He wrote music for 38 plays, including ten by Brecht. After four years of study with Schoenberg, he moved to Berlin in 1925 and became increasingly active in the workers' movement, writing articles critical of the state of modern music and causing a distressing personal quarrel with Schoenberg. His earliest contacts with the theatre date from 1927, when he became music director of the Agitprop group 'Das rote Sprachrohr'. In that same year there were plans for an opera with David Weber (i.e. Robert Gilbert) called *150 Mark* or *Moritz Meyer* but few sketches remain. In 1929 he met the actor Ernst Busch, who subsequently performed the marching songs for which Eisler became internationally famous: *Der rote Wedding*, *Kominternlied* and *Solidaritätslied*. The highly original idiom of the songs is modal-tonal (usually in a minor key), a style which,

combined with sophisticated contrapuntal textures and rhythmic variety, proved endlessly fruitful for his theatre music.

In 1930 the lifelong friendship and collaboration between Eisler and Brecht began. Their major works together before Hitler became chancellor were the *Lehrstücke Die Massnahme* (1930) and *Die Mutter* (1931), and the film *Kuhle Wampe* (1931). During the first years of their exile from Germany, from 1933, their work together was sporadic, but the music written between 1934 and 1936 for Brecht's rather unsatisfactory *Die Rundköpfe und die Spitzköpfe* is magnificent. After periods of work in Europe, the USSR and the USA, Eisler moved to New York in 1938 and then to Hollywood in 1942. In 1943 he began the extensive score for Brecht's *Schweyk im zweiten Weltkrieg*, which received its première only in 1957, a year after Brecht's death.

In 1947 Eisler was called before the Committee on Un-American Activities and expelled from the USA. In 1950 he settled in East Berlin and a year later began work on the libretto to a three-act opera, *Johann Faustus* (libretto published, Berlin, 1952). He had recently seen the *Faust* puppet play and enjoyed it greatly. He bypassed Goethe and examined the position of German intellectuals and their class conflict by setting the opera in the time of Müntzer and the Peasants' Revolt of 1525. It is Faust's bad conscience at his behaviour during the Revolt which leads to his pact with the Devil. Faust finally admits that there can be no true evolution for a betrayer of the people. The musical plan of the three acts was fully thought out and sketches begun. However, such was the controversy over the libretto that a nationwide debate took place, centred around three special sessions at the East Berlin Academy of the Arts. Eisler's most passionate critics accused him of portraying the typical German humanist as a turncoat and subverting Goethe's view of the nucleus of the German people as progressive. Eisler was so disheartened that he lost the will to compose the music. The libretto's merit is now recognized and it is performed as a play (with various solutions as to the music needed for set numbers). The première was at the Landestheater, Tübingen, on 11 April 1974. One can only speculate as to the stature of the work that may have been lost to us.

A. Betz: *Hanns Eisler: Political Musician* (Cambridge, 1982)
A. Dümling: *Lasst euch nicht verführen: Brecht und die Musik* (Munich, 1985)   DAVID BLAKE

Ekaterinburg. YEKATERINBURG.

Elberfeld. One of six towns that merged in 1929 to form the city of WUPPERTAL.

El-Dabh, Halim (**Abdul Messieh**) (*b* Cairo, 4 March 1921). American composer of Egyptian birth. He began composing in 1940, and studied the piano and Western music at the Sulcz Conservatory, Cairo (1941–4), while completing a degree in agricultural engineering at Cairo University. He travelled to the USA in 1950 on a Fulbright fellowship and studied at the University of New Mexico, Albuquerque, at the Berkshire Music Center, Tanglewood, with Copland and Irving Fine, at the New England Conservatory and at Brandeis University. By this time his music had attracted a significant American following, and he took American citizenship in 1961. After a period of teaching music at Haile Selassie University, Addis Ababa (1962–4), he returned to the USA in 1966 as a professor of music and African studies at Howard University, Washington, DC. Since 1969 he has been on the faculty of Kent State University, Ohio, where he directs the Center for the Study of World Musics. A simultaneous creative residency at the Hawthorne School, Washington, DC (1968–74), provided him with the facilities to complete and try out most of his operas.

Virtually all of El-Dabh's music is at least nominally programmatic, drawing inspiration by turns from ancient Egypt, Arabic tradition and that of the West. An admixture of contemporary Western techniques with materials and instruments derived from Africa and the ancient world helps to give his theatrical works the flavour of ritual or public ceremony; this is most clearly exemplified perhaps by the *Sound and Light Music* he composed for the Great Pyramids of Giza. His operas in particular resemble pageants or rituals: *Black Epic* (1968) is a history of the African people in America and *Opera Flies*, a surreal commentary on the Kent State killings of 4 May 1970, was intended as a formal purgative for the afflicted campus. His Hawthorne School operas cannot be considered children's opera in any sense for they are uncompromising in their technical demands, and in the level of musical and dramatic sophistication they display. Like many other expatriate Third World intellectuals, El-Dabh has been something of a voice crying in the wilderness. Most of the operas have received only single productions, at the universities that commissioned them, and some remain unperformed. His opera-like ballet *Clytemnestra*, however, in which the narrators (soprano and bass) appear in concert attire, persists in the repertory of the Martha Graham troupe for whom it was written, and has been frequently performed worldwide.

The Eye of Horus (mono-opera, 1, El-Dabh) Boston, spr. 1967
Black Epic, 1968 (opera-pageant, 1, El-Dabh), unperf.
Prometheus Bound (3, El-Dabh, after R. Lowell), Washington DC, Hawthorne School, aut. 1969
Opera Flies (3, El-Dabh), Washington DC, Hawthorne School, 5 May 1971
Ptahmose and the Magic Spell (trilogy, El-Dabh)
The Osiris Ritual, Washington DC, Hawthorne School, Dec 1972
Aton, the Ankh and the Word, Washington DC, Hawthorne School, Dec 1972
The 12 Hours Trip, unperf.
Drink of Eternity (opera-pageant, El-Dabh), Washington DC, Georgetown University, spr. 1981
The Birds (musical fantasy, El-Dabh, after Aristophanes), 1988

*

A. De Rhen: 'El-Dabh's "Opera Flies"', *HiFi/MusAm*, xxi/9 (1971), MA14
A. Kebede: *Roots of Black Music: the Vocal, Instrumental and Dance Heritage of Africa and Black America* (Englewood Cliffs, NJ, 1982), 120–21
M. Carter: *An Annotated Catalog of Composers of African Heritage* (New York, 1983) ANDREW STILLER (with JUDITH KERMAN)

Elder, Mark (Philip) (*b* Hexham, Northumberland, 2 June 1947). English conductor. He was a boy chorister at Canterbury Cathedral and principal bassoon with the National Youth Orchestra before reading music at Cambridge, where he gained his first conducting experience. He joined the music staff at the Wexford Festival in 1968, and at Glyndebourne and Covent Garden the next year. After two years as a staff conductor for Australian Opera, 1972–4, he returned to London and joined the ENO in 1974, becoming music director in 1979. His first ten years in the latter post brought major development in musical standards, vocal

and orchestral, and an adventurous and sometimes controversial presentation of a wide repertory (see R. Milnes: 'Mark Elder', *Opera*, xl, 1989, 1049–54; incl. interview material). By 1990 Elder had conducted over 30 new productions for the ENO, including the première of David Blake's *Toussaint* (1977) and the first British production of Busoni's *Doktor Faust* (1986). During this time he conducted at Bayreuth (*Die Meistersinger*, 1981), led the ENO tour to Austin, New Orleans and New York (1984), made his Metropolitan début with *Le nozze di Figaro* (1988), and led the ENO to Kiev, Moscow and Leningrad (1990).

His performances combine skilled ensemble, vitality of spirit and dramatic perception. His recordings include *Otello*, *Rigoletto* and *Orpheus in the Underworld*, with *Rusalka*, *Gloriana* and *Rigoletto* on commercial video. He was made a CBE in 1989. He became Principal Guest Conductor of the CBSO in 1992–3, which was his final year with the ENO.

NOËL GOODWIN

Electrification of the Soviet Union, The. Opera in two acts by NIGEL OSBORNE to a libretto by Craig Raine after Boris Pasternak's novel *The Last Summer* and his poem *Spectorsky*; Glyndebourne, 5 October 1987.

Based on two autobiographical works by Pasternak, the opera is about a young poet, Serezha Spectorsky (high baritone), his love for two women – a governess, Anna Arild (soprano), and a prostitute, Sashka (soprano) – his efforts to come to terms as an artist with war and revolution, and his ultimately exclusive concern for his own genius. The opera shuttles backwards and forwards in time between 1916, 1914 and 1920, cutting abruptly between Ousolie, Moscow and trains *en route*.

Though it begins with an electronic buzz and incorporates the pre-recorded sound of looms, as well as several interludes of instrumentally conceived machine music, Osborne's music in this work is much closer than that of his earlier opera, *Hell's Angels*, to what an opera audience might conventionally expect. It includes several songs in which the vocal line is set in tonal harmonies, rather than set against a merely colouristic background, and there is a strong melodic interest – in Anna's lament for her dead husband, for example, Serezha's passionately detailed declaration of love for Sashka's body, and a sentimental ditty for a Ticket Collector (bass). Most prominent of all is the vigorous revolutionary hymn with which Pasternak (high baritone) begins the opera and with which, though he has rejected politically motivated art, he ends it.

GERALD LARNER

Elegy for Young Lovers. Opera in three acts by HANS WERNER HENZE to a libretto by W. H. AUDEN and CHESTER KALLMAN; Schwetzingen, 20 May 1961 (in a German translation by Ludwig Landgraf).

Henze asked Auden and Kallman for an opera libretto in 1958, specifying a scenario that would require 'tender, beautiful noises'. The première at the Schwetzingen Festival was conducted by Heinrich Bender and produced by Henze himself, with a cast that included Eva-Marie Rogner, Ingeborg Bremert, Lilian Benningsen, Friedrich Lenz, Dietrich Fischer-Dieskau and Karl Christian Kohn. The text was heard in its original English at Glyndebourne in 1961, although Act 3 scenes vii and viii were omitted. The cast included Dorothy Dorow, Elisabeth Söderström,

Gregor Mittenhofer *a poet*	baritone
Dr Wilhelm Reischmann *a physician*	bass
Toni Reischmann *his son*	tenor
Carolina Gräfin von Kirch-stetten *Mittenhofer's secretary*	contralto
Elizabeth Zimmer	soprano
Hilda Mack *a widow*	soprano
Josef Mauer *an alpine guide*	speaker
Servants at 'Der Schwarze Adler'	silent

Setting 'Der Schwarze Adler', an inn in the Austrian Alps, 1910

Kerstin Meyer and Thomas Hemsley; John Pritchard was the conductor.

ACT 1: 'The Emergence of the Bridegroom' *The parlour and terrace of 'Der Schwarze Adler'*

1.i ('Forty years past') In a highly expressive, wide-ranging aria, whose mixture of coloratura and Sprechgesang will define her vocal character throughout the opera, Hilda Mack remembers the day in the 1870s when her husband went off to climb the Hammerhorn.

1.ii ('The order of the day') Dr Reischmann watches Carolina sort press cuttings. In a duet they comment on their various obligations to the poet Mittenhofer, for which they receive little thanks though he could hardly do without them.

1.iii ('A scheduled arrival') Reischmann waits for his son Toni, who is difficult and has no enthusiasm for anything.

1.iv ('Appearances and visions') Carolina invites Hilda Mack into the inn, just as Mittenhofer is leaving arm in arm with Elizabeth Zimmer. As Mittenhofer begins the introductions Hilda goes into an extravagant coloratura fantasy; it fascinates the poet, appals Toni and contains a foreshadowing of the death of two young people.

1.v ('Worldly business') Mittenhofer is delighted with his 'research', and then rails at Carolina for mistakes in her typing until she faints. Reischmann rushes in to minister to her.

1.vi ('Help') Mittenhofer searches the inn for money, finds what he wants and disappears to his own quarters.

1.vii ('Unworldly weakness') Carolina remains distraught.

1.viii ('Beauty in death') Josef Mauer reports that a body has been found on the Hammerhorn – a young man, almost certainly Frau Mack's husband.

1.ix ('Who is to tell her?') Carolina and Dr Reischmann agree that Elizabeth must tell Hilda of the discovery.

1.x ('Today's weather') Elizabeth breaks the news to Hilda as carefully as possible. She eventually gets through to the widow in a canonic duet; Toni is impressed by her tact.

1.xi ('A visionary interlude') Toni sings a highly expressive aria in which he remembers his mother, long dead; he remains staring at the spot where Elizabeth had been standing.

1.xii ('Tomorrow: two follies cross') Hilda's emotions suddenly erupt. She joins Toni in a rapturous duet, while he pours out his emerging love for Elizabeth.

ACT 2: 'The Emergence of the Bride'

2.i ('A passion') Elizabeth and Toni express their love in a duet: Toni urges her to leave Mittenhofer. Carolina discovers them, and summons the doctor to help her end their dalliance.

2.ii ('Sensible talk') Reischmann tries to talk Toni round, while Carolina attempts the same with Elizabeth.

2.iii ('Each in his place') In two separate monologues interwoven as a duet, the lovers express their anger at the interference in their affairs.

2.iv ('The Master's time') While Elizabeth asks Toni to take her away, Carolina tells Mittenhofer of the burgeoning affair: he asks Carolina to invite Elizabeth to join him for tea.

2.v ('Personal questions') In an extended monologue Mittenhofer tries to play on Elizabeth's feelings of guilt, while feigning self-pity; she cannot get a word in.

2.vi ('The troubles of others') Elizabeth expresses her distress in a slow aria that flows into an orchestral meditation.

2.vii ('What must be told') Elizabeth tells Toni that she has said nothing to the poet; he says that he will instead.

2.viii ('The wrong time') Toni tells Mittenhofer of his love for Elizabeth: his declaration expands into a large-scale quartet as they are joined by Elizabeth (later replaced by Carolina) and the doctor.

2.ix ('The bird') Frau Mack interrupts with an extrovert aria that spirals ever upwards, and then comforts Elizabeth. Mittenhofer asks Reischmann to give his blessing to the lovers.

2.x ('The young lovers') Surrounded by the protagonists, Mittenhofer introduces his new poem *The Young Lovers* which seems to crystallize all their dilemmas.

2.xi ('The flower') The doctor gives his blessing and Mittenhofer asks the couple to stay a few days until his 60th birthday. He asks them to find an Edelweiss for him on the Hammerhorn.

2.xii ('The vision of tomorrow') After a brief en-

'Elegy for Young Lovers' (Henze): scene from the original production at the Schwetzingen Festival, 1961, with Dietrich Fischer-Dieskau as Gregor Mittenhofer and Eva-Marie Rogner as Hilda Mack

semble, Mauer tells the poet that the following day will be fair enough for the lovers to find the Edelweiss.

2.xiii ('The end of the day') Mittenhofer's rage, previously suppressed, erupts in a fierce declamation in which he attacks all of those around him, wishing the lovers dead. It ends only when Hilda Mack confronts him with her hysterical laughter.

ACT 3: 'Man and Wife'

3.i ('Echoes') Hilda is preparing to leave. Toni and Elizabeth set off up the mountain singing a folksong as Hilda bids them goodbye. They are joined in an ensemble by Mittenhofer practising his verse.

3.ii ('Farewells') Frau Mack leaves, giving Carolina the scarf she has been knitting for 40 years.

3.iii ('Scheduled departures') Hilda and Carolina, Mittenhofer and Dr Reischmann join in an elaborate quartet.

3.iv ('Two to go') Carolina attempts unsuccessfully to calm Mittenhofer. Mauer warns that a blizzard is threatened on the Hammerhorn, but the poet denies that he knows of anyone who is on the mountain.

3.v ('Mad happenings') In a confrontation between Mittenhofer and Carolina her sanity finally cracks: he suggests she go away for a rest.

3.vi ('A change of scene') The action moves outside the inn; the blizzard is portrayed in an extended orchestral interlude of increasing violence. Toni and Elizabeth are seen through the snow, unable to continue.

3.vii ('Man and wife') In a long duet over fragile instrumental lines Toni and Elizabeth imagine themselves married for many years. They reflect on their lives together, their children, their infidelities.

3.viii ('Toni and Elizabeth') The lovers prepare for their deaths, fortified by the truth they have discovered in each other.

3.ix ('Elegy for young lovers') Mittenhofer is preparing to give a public reading of his poetry in Vienna. He dedicates his new poem to 'the memory of a brave and beautiful young couple, Toni and Elizabeth'. The wordless offstage voices of Hilda, Elizabeth, Carolina, Toni and the doctor are heard as he finishes the poem.

*　　*　　*

The 'tender, beautiful noises' that Henze wished to draw from Auden and Kallman's libretto are supplied by a chamber orchestra of single wind and strings with a wide range of tuned and untuned percussion. They are used to create textures of great transparency, while a specific instrumental colour is assigned to each of the protagonists: a flute accompanies Hilda Mack, brass the poet, violin and viola signify the young lovers, an english horn Carolina, a bassoon (later an alto saxophone) Dr Reischmann. The highly structured text is matched in Henze's musical setting by an intricate network of set pieces – arias, recitatives and ensembles – though the boundaries between them are sometimes blurred.   ANDREW CLEMENTS

Elektra ('Electra'). *Tragödie* in one act by RICHARD STRAUSS to a libretto by HUGO VON HOFMANNSTHAL after SOPHOCLES' *Electra*; Dresden, Hofoper, 25 January 1909.

At the age of 17 Strauss had set a chorus from Sophocles' *Electra* for male voices and orchestra; but it was probably not until November 1903, when he saw Max Reinhardt's Berlin production of the tragedy as

Electra *Agamemnon's daughter*	soprano
Chrysothemis *her sister*	soprano
Klytemnästra [Clytemnestra] *their mother, Agamemnon's widow*	mezzo-soprano
Her Confidante and her Trainbearer	sopranos
A Young and an Old Servant	tenor, bass
Orest [Orestes] *son of Agamemnon*	baritone
Orestes' Tutor	bass
Aegisth [Aegisthus] *Clytemnestra's paramour*	tenor
An Overseer	soprano
Five maidservants	contralto, two mezzo-sopranos, two sopranos

Men and women of the household

Setting Ancient Mycenae: the inner courtyard of Agamemnon's palace

'rewritten for the German stage by Hugo von Hofmannsthal', that the notion of a full operatic setting entered his head. Earlier that year, the Reinhardt staging of Oscar Wilde's *Salomé* (with the same leading actress, Gertrud Eysoldt) had similarly fired his imagination, and the composer was already hard at work on what was to be his first great operatic success. Only in 1906, with *Salome* safely launched, did Strauss ask Hofmannsthal for permission to set his *Elektra*. The writer was not only amenable, but excited about the prospective partnership; he accepted that the text would need shortening, and also agreed to write new passages as required. It was upon receiving one of those, in July 1908 – some extra lines for the Recognition scene, which Hofmannsthal supplied exactly as Strauss had prescribed – that the composer declared his new collaborator to be 'the born librettist'.

Yet Strauss had undertaken the piece hesitantly. He feared lest it seem too similar in cut to *Salome*, and wondered whether he ought not instead, for canny commercial contrast, to look for a romantic comedy. (Throughout the composing of *Elektra* he and his writer played with ideas for such a project – something about Casanova's exploits, perhaps, or a mythological fantasy after Calderón – until at last the conception of *Der Rosenkavalier* germinated.) On the question of the awkward similarity, Hofmannsthal's reassurances to Strauss make piquant reading. The only parallels he admitted were the single-act form, the eponymous classical heroines and the fact that Fräulein Eysoldt played them both in Berlin; but anybody else might also remark that each heroine is in the grip of an obsession which fuels the main drama, that after their early arrivals each dominates the action until the end (with climactic solo dances unprecedented in opera), and that both texts trade in morbid psychology and strenuous decadence.

There is good reason to think that Hofmannsthal's *Elektra*, hastily written in mid-1903 to Reinhardt's commission, had taken its inspiration directly from the Reinhardt-Eysoldt *Salome*. He protested that the 'blend of colour in the two subjects' was 'quite different in all essentials' – certainly his fervid penetration into his characters was far removed from Wilde's decadent cartoons (he had been reading Freud and Breuer on hysteria, and Rohde's *Psyche*), and he preferred Shakespearean pentameter to Wilde's poetical prose. Yet the broad theatrical form was much the same; it was ultimately the composer who had to establish the difference in musico-dramatic terms. That he did, so persuasively that the two operas do not seem variations on a single form but fiercely individual tales with some points of abstract resemblance. For the monumental effects of *Elektra* Strauss prescribed a still larger orchestra: eight clarinets, for example, and besides his eight horns a sonorous quartet of Wagner tubas, and also three groups each of violins and violas – with the first six violists required twice to switch instruments and become a fourth violin section. He completed the score on 22 September 1908, at his new villa in Garmisch.

Four months later *Elektra* was introduced in Dresden by the conductor Ernst von Schuch and the director Willi Wirk, who had together given *Salome* its première. Annie Krull, Strauss's first Diemut in *Feuersnot*, sang the first Electra; Chrysothemis and Orestes were Margarethe Siems and Karl Perron, who would later create the Marschallin and the Baron in *Der Rosenkavalier*, and Clytemnestra was the redoubtable Ernestine Schumann-Heink. Premières in all the usual countries followed swiftly (though *Elektra* was initially banned at the New York Metropolitan, and had to be performed elsewhere in Manhattan – in French). As conductor, Strauss shared the first British performances in 1910 with Sir Thomas Beecham.

The opera made a forceful mark everywhere, by no means always favourable. Many hearers found it rebarbative, gross and brutal, and the *Wiener Fremdenblatt* commented sourly, 'Wie schön war die Prinzessin Salome …'. It was a sign of Strauss's commitment to the music drama that his *Elektra* offered no feasible excerpts for concerts or recording (until the advent of LPs), but as a result we can hear scarcely anything now of his earlier interpreters. He judged Salomea Kruszelnicka 'perfect' as both Electra and Salome; a famous Clytemnestra was Anna Bahr-Mildenburg, whose husband Hermann Bahr advised Strauss on *Intermezzo* – but the role is a gift to intelligent dramatic mezzos past their vocal prime, and there have been too many of them to mention. In recent years the Electras of Astrid Varnay, Christel Goltz, the young Gerda Lammers and Birgit Nilsson have left powerful impressions.

In literary fact Electra is a neither a figure of Greek mythology nor of pre-classical epic, but an invention of later poets and dramatists. Like her fabled brother Orestes and (in this version) a younger sister Chrysothemis, she is a child of the Mycenaean king Agamemnon, who went off to the Trojan war and stayed away for ten years. Meanwhile his queen Clytemnestra took a lover, Aegisthus; when the king returned they netted and slew him on the way to his homecoming bath – and prudently sent young Orestes into obscure exile. The guilty pair now rule, and the daughters have become young women, barely tolerated in the royal household: Chrysothemis timorous and self-effacing, Electra recalcitrant and implacably vengeful. The stern heroine of Sophocles' *Electra* grew from an austere silhouette in the *Choephoroe* of Aeschylus, but it is uncertain whether Euripides' more 'modern', psychologically fraught portrait came before or after that of Sophocles. It is often remarked that the Euripides version would seem more apt for Hofmannsthal; perhaps he chose the plainer, less subjective Sophocles as basis so that he could do his own psychological freighting.

Elektra has no prelude, but the opening scene for Clytemnestra's servants is a prologue in effect. As the curtain rises, the orchestra bellows 'Agamemnon!' – or more exactly 'A-ga-MEMMMMM!-(non)' – in unison and very loudly, on the notes of the D minor triad. Though we might not have known what it was saying, had we not read our programme notes, Electra herself will shortly invoke her father to that leitmotif. In Hofmannsthal's original text, nobody uttered the name until much later. Strauss had good Wagnerian reasons for introducing it sooner (the motif is to haunt the score, much as the unspoken name hung over the play text); but his treatment of names is always significant. Here it is striking that whereas 'Elektra' and 'Orest' are voiced again and again as passionate pleas, the names of Clytemnestra and Aegisthus are mentioned only in passing, and poor Chrysothemis is never once named aloud: even in Electra's mouth she is merely 'daughter of my mother', or just 'girl'.

Five maids, watched by overseers, are drawing water from a well at twilight, and wondering aloud whether Electra will arrive as usual to wail for the dead king. She does, wildly, almost before the orchestral 'Agamemnon!' has ceased to reverberate, but on seeing the other women she flings an arm over her face and 'darts back like an animal to its lair'. Four of the maids gossip and gloat over Electra's self-willed bestial condition, and her lofty contempt for them; the fifth and youngest protests that she is uniquely noble and scandalously maltreated – she would love to see the other maids hanged in reparation for the wrongs done to her Princess. (Like Mozart's Barbarina in *Figaro*, Strauss's Fifth Maid has long been a role in which promising young sopranos are tried out.) An outraged Overseer thrusts her off to the servants' quarters for a beating. Electra re-emerges to find herself alone.

Since the initial pronouncement of 'Agamemnon!' the music has been tonally frantic – either harmonized in no clear key at all, or slipping into some friendly key (as with the Fifth Maid) only to veer off again into no-man's-land. Yet after the graphic offstage beating, it subsides firmly upon the original D, as if concluding a first paragraph; and now Electra is properly introduced (like Salome) by a restatement of her opening music, as if a symphonic 'development' were under way. The key declines to a curdled Bb minor, however, and the tempo to a dim, sluggish pulse, as she calls upon her father. She relives his grisly death (the music veers again into wild chromatics), and imagines him returning as a spectre to approve a bloody vengeance on his murderers; then, with her siblings, she will slay the royal horses and hounds to honour him, and will dance gloriously at last over the corpses to show the world that this was a king. Studded with pictorial detail, the music of this extraordinary soliloquy is also a fast-forward preview of the rest of the opera, which will prove to echo the sequence of Electra's imaginings. In fact this is the 'symphonic exposition' proper, where the matching portion of *Salome*, the climactic monologue, was a compendious recall. (Ernest Newman suspected that the *Salome* finale had been composed first, and the rest of the score generated backwards from it.) With the visionary dance it stamps into C major, as the opera itself will do at the end – but now the anxious arrival of Chrysothemis breaks it off.

This is the first of the four confrontations with Electra which supply the greater part of the opera. (Then come the murders, and the fatal triumph-dance: like Salome,

'Elektra' (Richard Strauss): Annie Krull as Electra (right) and Ernestine Schumann-Heink as Clytemnestra (centre) in the original production at the Hofoper, Dresden, 25 January 1909; drawing by W. Gause from the 'Illustrirte Zeitung' (Leipzig, 28 January 1909)

Electra never leaves the stage.) Chrysothemis has come to warn her that their mother and Aegisthus mean to imprison her in a dark tower. Against Electra's stoic defiance her sister pleads her own tearful despair, in mellifluous E♭; all she wants is a quiet, normal life with a decent husband and children. Though the waltz music Strauss gives her is often described as bland and regressive, his intention was surely to present her as a simple, warmhearted, conventional soul – the better to set off the intemperate extremes of everyone else. She gets no comfort from Electra, and the next confrontation is imminent; chromatic heavings and churnings in the orchestra herald Clytemnestra's latest parade of sacrificial victims. Chrysothemis flees in terror, but her sister awaits her mother with baleful purpose.

Raddled, bedecked with luck-charms and supported by a pair of servile intimates, Clytemnestra staggers in. Sleepless nights have driven her to breaking-point (Strauss abandons any key signature while he illustrates her nightmares with monstrous, unheard-of effects), and she is in desperate search of the sacrifice that will give her release. She has long suspected that Electra enjoys clairvoyant powers; now, finding her docile, she sues humbly for advice. Electra agrees that a sacrifice is justly required – at once the music pulls itself together in stark C minor, ready to go into bloodthirsty hunt mode – and she spells it out at length with feral excitement: the un-

clean woman and her paramour must be tracked through the palace corridors by Orestes with the sacred axe. Clytemnestra reels back speechless. But secret news is suddenly brought to her; crowing with hysterical relief, she sweeps out. Her other daughter hurries in with the report that Orestes is dead. A young servant calls for a horse: he must bear an urgent message to Aegisthus.

With her long-nurtured hopes facing ruin, Electra tries to enlist Chrysothemis in matricide. She croons over her sister's nubile body, ripe for marriage and motherhood, and promises to be her selfless handmaiden forever if she will collaborate in the murder. (If not quite a love duet, this is certainly a seduction scene.) At the last moment Chrysothemis takes fright and bolts. Electra curses her, and begins digging alone for the buried axe.

While she scrabbles in the earth a stranger arrives, to strange, sombre chorale-chords. At first he takes her for a wretched servant, but as she bewails her familial lot (the agonized theme echoes the wailing wind of the Inferno in Liszt's *Dante Sonata*) Orestes realizes who she must be. Aged retainers come to kiss their young master's feet. Finally recognition dawns for Electra too, and there is a seismic crash from the orchestra, like a great house falling down. Brother and sister embrace, speechless; the music churns for a long time before reaching haven in soft, glowing A♭. Electra pours out her joy and relief, and her shame at her abject condition. Orestes assures her that he knows what duty he has come to fulfil – but his tutor-companion interrupts them to enjoin prudent silence, and no more delay.

The two men enter the palace. In the long, shuddering suspense, Electra remembers the forgotten axe too late. Clytemnestra's death-cry is heard, and Electra screams to her brother to strike again. Her frightened sister and the first four maids gather anxiously in the forecourt with other servants. The return of Aegisthus is heralded; all but Electra flee in dismay, leaving her to enact an ironical welcome. To light his way she dances around him with a torch, which unnerves him (he shares a querulous, petulant vein with Strauss's Herod – and Electra's mocking waltz presages *Der Rosenkavalier*), but he proceeds into the palace. A moment later he is seen at a window, shrieking in the clutches of his murderers.

Until this moment of grim triumph, a signal omission from Hofmannsthal and Strauss's *ersatz*-classical tragedy has been the antique Chorus. Now, while Chrysothemis and her women return to rejoice, massed voices offstage hail 'Orest!' some 27 times. As the music flings itself into raw, brazen tonality (abrupt modulations screwing the excitement ever higher), the sisters exult together, the younger pleading repeatedly 'Who has ever loved us?' Electra declares that nothing but silence and dance should celebrate their release, and herself begins to tread rapturous maenadic steps. The sister shrinks away in terror, but reappears at the height of the dance to witness Electra's fatal collapse to the earth. The orchestra thunders 'Agamemnon!' in C minor, and gets only a deathly-soft E♭ minor chord for reply. Crying vainly for Orestes, Chrysothemis pounds at the locked palace door. (We may guess why no answer comes: he is already pursued by the Furies.)

* * *

The music of *Elektra* is often diagnosed as marking an 'advanced' point – i.e. on the way to modernist atonality – from which the composer then staged a prudent, inglorious retreat. That bespeaks a prejudice which he never espoused. Though passages in the opera share the queasy harmonic climate of Schoenberg's op.11 no.2 piano piece (1909), Strauss felt no natural urge towards atonality as the Music of the Future. The sporadic 'atonalisms' in *Elektra*, as in his Ophelia songs, were meant to convey the exacerbated spiritual condition of his characters, not to promote some more radical cause. Had Hofmannsthal hit upon the idea for *Der Rosenkavalier* a year or two sooner, Strauss would instead have addressed himself to that just as happily. In fact his anti-tonal devices here are few and simple, though hugely effective. Beyond Orestes' fractured cadences à la Wagner, they involve little more than double tritones (flowing chromatically, often in contrary motion, or else impacted to make dissonant chords), and insistent, cross-grain pedal notes which undermine, rather than underpin, the Romantic harmonies that float over them. The apparent similarities between *Elektra* and, say, Schoenberg's atonal *Erwartung* (also 1909) lie in their violent extremes – of vocal line and histrionic moods, of dynamics and post-Romantic orchestration. Strauss's score, however, absolutely presupposes a secure tonal norm against which to measure its harsh, disorientating dramatic effects for an audience with late Romantic ears.   DAVID MURRAY

Elémens, Les ('The Elements'). *Opéra-ballet* in a prologue and four entrées by ANDRÉ CARDINAL DESTOUCHES and MICHEL-RICHARD DE LALANDE to a libretto by PIERRE-CHARLES ROY; Paris, Tuileries, 31 December 1721.

Destouches composed most of the music in *Les élémens*, the overture and at least nine movements in the prologue and first entrée being Lalande's. Jean Balon choreographed the original production. It was the only stage work by Lalande to appear at the Paris Opéra.

Les élémens typifies the organization and subject matter of the *opéra-ballet*. Its four entrées are musically and dramatically independent, but topically related to one another. The prologue represents chaos, which gives birth to the elements and also to the destiny of Louis XV, symbol of world peace and order. 'Air' depicts the love of Ixion (bass) for Junon [Juno] (soprano), and 'Water' presents shipwrecked Arion (male soprano) in the palace of Neptune (bass). 'Fire' is set in the temple of Vesta, with singing and dancing priestesses and Roman lords. 'Earth' presents Vertumne [Vertumnus] (male soprano), Pomone [Pomona] (soprano), and other earth gods, and Louis himself appeared in the epilogue as the sun. The work contains the usual vocal solos and ensembles, choruses and dance movements, with a greater proportion of vocal music than in typical court ballets of the 17th century.

Although it played only twice at court, *Les élémens* is one of its composers' most often cited dramatic compositions because it was revived at the Opéra on 29 May 1725 and repeated frequently there, in whole or in part, throughout the 18th century. The court production compared in scope to the two previous grand court ballets honouring Louis XV, *L'inconnu* and *Les folies de Cardenio* (1720). The *livret* for court indicates a choir of 28, an orchestra of 32, 11 vocal soloists and 34 dancers, including the aged Louis Pécourt in one of his final roles. Louis XV did not participate at the Opéra, and so several *divertissements* in which he was featured were deleted. Additionally, by mid-century most of Lalande's movements seem to have been withdrawn, for unspecified reasons.

At court *Les élémens* marked the end of several eras: it was Lalande's final stage work, Louis XV's last stage appearance and the final French court ballet. As a public production the *opéra-ballet* looked forward, modified and adjusted as necessary to accommodate changing tastes throughout the 18th century.   BARBARA COEYMAN

Elfrida. *Tragedia per musica* in two acts by GIOVANNI PAISIELLO to a libretto by RANIERI DE' CALZABIGI; Naples, Teatro di S Carlo, 4 November 1792.

The opera is set in 10th-century England. King Eggardo [Edgar] (tenor) sends his friend Adelvolto [Adalbert] (soprano) to ask Orgando (bass), the Duke of Devon, for the hand of his daughter Elfrida (soprano) in marriage. Adalbert falls in love with Elfrida, and instead of escorting her to Edgar marries her himself. To hide his deception he jealously isolates her in his sumptuous castle in the woods, with only the company of her confidante, Evelina (alto). Orgando arrives at the castle in search of his daughter. At the same time Edgar, who has been hunting in the surrounding woods, arrives with Osmondo [Osmund] (soprano) to pay his friend an unexpected visit. Adalbert's deception is uncovered, and he is wounded during a duel with Edgar. Elfrida is urged by her father and Edgar to forget Adalbert, a traitor in their eyes, and to marry Edgar. But, rejecting the throne, wealth and glory for the sake of her love for her husband, she stabs herself when Adalbert dies.

Two ballets, *Adelaide* and *La preciosa ridicola*, were performed at the première. The opera was popular and was given throughout Italy until the end of the 18th century. For the revivals in Bologna (1796) and Parma (1798) it acquired a happy ending. In its depiction of love, magnanimity and sacrifice as real human emotions rather than abstractions, the plot displays Romantic tendencies. The collaboration between Calzabigi and Paisiello resulted in a shared interest in operatic reform. There is a predominance of ensembles – duets, trios and quartets – full of passion and sentiment; their appearance at the end of each act provides a sense of inner coherence. Paisiello advised the singers to avoid excessive embellishments and to concentrate on projecting the drama's meaning.   GORDANA LAZAREVICH

Elgar, Sir Edward (William) (*b* Broadheath, nr Worcester, 2 June 1857; *d* Worcester, 23 Feb 1934). English composer. With wide operatic experience and a keen admiration for Wagner, Elgar nourished the idea of writing an opera himself. Among subjects he considered were *The Forest Lovers* (1900) by William Hewlett; a stage adaptation of his own dramatic cantata *Caractacus* (1901); *Diarmuid and Grania* (1900) by George Moore and W. B. Yeats; *The Wicked World* (1906) by W. S. Gilbert; *Lanval* by Lord Howard de Walden; *Comala* by Reginald Buckley; a story of 8th-century imperial China, and *The Madness of Merlin* by Laurence Binyon; and *The Garden of Allah* by Robert Hichens.

A 1909 sketchbook of Elgar's is headed 'Arden, Opera in three Acts'; there he listed ideas used in the incidental music to Binyon's *Arthur* (1923). In 1929 Elgar approached his friend Bernard Shaw for a libretto. Finally he turned to the Birmingham impresario Barry Jackson (1879–1961) for a text based on Ben Jonson's play, *The Devil is an Ass*. The opera, Elgar's op.89, was to be called *The Spanish Lady*. The choice was the composer's own, and he worked hard at what would have been a traditional number opera with evident relish. Sketches, some using material from as early as 1878, were worked and reworked, but the opera was abandoned finally in 1933, having to give way to the BBC commission for a Third Symphony. Two songs and a suite for string orchestra drawn from the opera were published in 1955–6 by Percy Young, who has also edited the work for the Elgar Complete Edition (xli, 1991).

See also SPANISH LADY, THE.

B. Jackson: 'Elgar's "Spanish Lady"', *ML*, xxiv (1943), 1–15; repr. in *An Elgar Companion*, ed. C. Redwood (Ashbourne, 1982), 209–35

P. M. Young: 'Elgar and The Spanish Lady', *MT*, cxxvii (1986), 272–6   ROBERT ANDERSON

Elias, Rosalind (*b* Lowell, MA, 13 March 1929). American mezzo-soprano. She studied at the New England Conservatory and while still a student appeared as Monteverdi's Poppaea. Further study at the Berkshire Music Center, Tanglewood, was followed by four years with the New England Opera Company, 1948–52. She then studied in Italy with Luigi Ricci and Nazareno de Angelis, sang at La Scala, and the S Carlo, Naples, and joined the Metropolitan in 1954. There she sang over 45 roles in more than 450 performances, and

created roles in two operas by Barber: Erika in *Vanessa* (1958) and Charmian in *Antony and Cleopatra* (1966). She was much admired for her rich tone and clarity of vocal character as Cherubino, Octavian, Olga and Carmen. Her British stage début was with Scottish Opera as Rossini's Cenerentola in 1970, and in 1975 she sang Baba the Turk at Glyndebourne. In the 1980s she directed several operas in the USA, including *Carmen*.
                    NOËL GOODWIN

Eliasson, Sven Olof (*b* Boliden, nr Skelleftea, 4 April 1933). Swedish tenor. He studied singing at the Stockholm Academy and made his operatic début in 1961 at Oslo. In 1965 he joined the Royal Opera in Stockholm where he became principal tenor. He sang in the première of Berwald's *Drottningen av Golconda* (1968) and took the title role in the première of Klebe's *Ein wahrer Held* (Zürich, 1975); other successful roles in 20th-century opera included Palestrina, Mephistopheles in Busoni's *Doktor Faust*, Peter Grimes, Aschenbach, Stravinsky's Oedipus and Tom Rakewell, and Aaron which he sang at Vienna in 1973. He also sang Don Ottavio at Glyndebourne in 1961, Parsifal at Edinburgh in 1976 and Siegmund in Århus in 1983. His recordings include *Il ritorno d'Ulisse in patria* under Harnoncourt. While still one of the busiest and most valued actor-singers in Europe, he became artistic director of the Stora Teatern, Göteborg, in 1983 and General Director of Norwegian National Opera in 1990.
                    J. B. STEANE

Elisa [*Elisa, ou Le voyage aux glaciers du Mont St-Bernard* ('Elisa, or The Journey to the Glaciers of Mount St Bernard')]. *Opéra comique* in two acts by LUIGI CHERUBINI to a libretto by Jacques-Antoine Reveroni de Saint-Cyr; Paris, Théâtre Feydeau, 13 December 1794.

This work typifies the 'rescue opera' genre which, though dating from the mid-18th century, became popular early in the French Revolution. Florindo (tenor) arrives at the monks' hospice near Mount St Bernard in the Swiss Alps to await news of Elisa (soprano), his beloved who has been unable to marry him because her father opposed the union. When the expected letter arrives, it tells Florindo that Elisa has eloped with a friend. After trying to jump to his death he is taken back to the hospice, where Elisa soon arrives in search of him. Her father has died and she is ready to marry Florindo, but before he is informed of this, he is swept away by an avalanche. Fortunately, the monks revive him, and he is reunited with Elisa as the chorus sings a hymn of thanksgiving.

According to extant correspondence, Cherubini composed the opera during the second half of 1793, but problems with theatre management and the censor delayed production by a year. The critics enjoyed the music and scenery but judged the text to be unduly protracted in some scenes. Nevertheless, the piece held the stage in France for some time and was frequently performed in Germany, where it was reviewed enthusiastically (*AMZ*, 5 Jan 1803). The heroine in the original cast was Julie-Angélique Scio, who later created the title role in *Médée*. Though labelled 'opéra' by Cherubini, this work conforms to the *opéra comique* form by virtue of its spoken dialogue; in fact, it demonstrates Cherubini's development of the genre. The musical numbers are no longer pauses in the plot, allowing a character to sing quickly a couple of stanzas expressing his sentiments; they scintillate with action and display a continuity which sometimes makes the spoken dialogue seem like an intrusion. *Elisa* is considered by some to be the most consciously romantic of Cherubini's operas.   STEPHEN C. WILLIS

Elisabetta, regina d'Inghilterra ('Elizabeth, Queen of England'). *Dramma* in two acts by GIOACHINO ROSSINI to a libretto by GIOVANNI SCHMIDT after Carlo Federici's play based on Sophia Lee's novel *The Recess*; Naples, Teatro S Carlo, 4 October 1815.

This was Rossini's first opera for the S Carlo, written for a cast that included Isabella Colbran as Elizabeth, Andrea Nozzari as Leicester and Manuel García as Norfolk. Leicester, Queen Elizabeth's favourite nobleman, has returned in triumph from the Scottish wars. There are, however, hostages in the baggage train, among them Matilde (soprano) whom Leicester (tenor) has secretly married, unaware that she is in reality the daughter of Mary Queen of Scots. Despite the rapturous welcome accorded him by Elizabeth (soprano), Leicester is downcast. Unwisely, he confides the dilemma of his love for Matilde and his loyalty to the Queen to Norfolk (tenor) who stirs up a hornets' nest of emotional intrigue by confiding the facts to the Queen. In the superb Act 1 finale, Leicester and his wife are summoned to a public audience with the Queen who proceeds to heap praises on the bewildered Leicester; she even offers him her hand in marriage in a terrible moment of manic irony before the mask is finally dropped and the traitors are dispatched to the dungeons. Stendhal saw this finale as a grim showcase of primary human emotions: '*jealousy* tormenting Elizabeth to the brink of madness, *despair* growing ever blacker in Leicester, and *love*, unbelievably sad and touching, in his young wife'.

In Act 2 Elizabeth tries to persuade Matilde to renounce her husband; their duet turns into a fine trio with the entry of Leicester. In a beautiful *sotto voce* chorus the people gloomily ponder the fate of Leicester, their hero. Meanwhile, Norfolk has been banished by Elizabeth and, sensing the mood of unease among the people, plots her assassination. In a scene in which the imprisoned Leicester is visited by Norfolk and Elizabeth, who is now resolved to engineer Leicester's escape, the assassination is bungled as Matilde and her brother Enrico [Henry] (mezzo-soprano) intervene. In the final scene, Leicester is retored to favour and the Queen renounces all passions.

This is the first Rossini opera in which all the recitatives are string-accompanied; it is also a work of considerable brilliance and vitality despite extensive borrowings from such relatively unsuccessful pre-Neapolitan works as *Ciro in Babilonia*, *Aureliano in Palmira* and *Sigismondo*. Its overture was re-used by Rossini for *Il barbiere di Siviglia*.   RICHARD OSBORNE

Elisa e Claudio [*Elisa e Claudio, ossia L'amore protetto dall'amicizia* ('Elisa and Claudio, or Love Protected by Friendship')]. *Melodramma semiserio* in two acts by SAVERIO MERCADANTE to a libretto by LUIGI ROMANELLI after Filippo Casari's play *Rosella*; Milan, Teatro alla Scala, 30 October 1821.

Before the opera starts Claudio (tenor), son of Count Arnoldo (bass), has secretly married Elisa (soprano) and has had two children by her. His father, suspecting an amorous attachment but having no idea of its depth, proposes a noble and advantageous marriage with Silvia (soprano), the daughter of the Marquis Tricotazio (bass)

which Claudio persistently refuses. In the end the count, out of patience with his son, confines him to his chamber with the intention of sending him off to travel. After about a year the marquis (no doubt out of patience himself) announces his impending visit to the count with Silvia. With them comes Celso (tenor), a former fellow student of Claudio, who has independently met and fallen in love with Silvia and taken service with the marquis as *valet de chambre* in order to be by her side.

The opera opens brilliantly with the arrival of the marquis and his retinue at the count's villa one day too soon. The confusion and bustle generated by this simple device sets the action off at a pace which never relaxes; the usual intrigues and misunderstandings, shot through with a vein of sentimental romance emanating from Elisa and her children, develop in the classic manner but end happily with the marriage of Silvia and Celso and the acceptance of Elisa as Claudio's wife.

Elisa e Claudio was Mercadante's first great success, and his only comedy to maintain its place alongside the serious works of his later years. 'A Rossinian structure with Cimarosa looking out from one of the windows' said a critic of the first London performance, not without perception; but there is much in the harmonic resourcefulness, inventive part-writing and characteristic use of imitation which reveals Mercadante's hand. The *recitativo secco* originally written for this opera is not printed in any of the surviving editions of the score and modern revivals have used spoken dialogue with satisfactory effect. It is good to have one work by this estimable composer in which spontaneity has not been overlaid by too much thought.   MICHAEL ROSE

Elisi, Filippo (*b* ?Fossombrone, *c*1724; *d c*1775). Italian soprano castrato. He was trained in Bologna, but began his career in Venice, in Cardena's *Creusa* (Ascension 1739); this was followed by appearances in Verona, Padua and a two-year stay in Rome. From 1743 to 1753 he was in 14 different Italian cities, and enjoyed great success in Rome and in Naples, which led to engagements in Madrid and Naples up to 1757. He was in northern Italy in 1758–9, and in London, 1760–62; he retreated to Italy until 1765, but returned to London for five months although his voice was in decline. He followed old pathways, first back to Italy (1766–7) and then to Spain, where he appeared in Cádiz (1769). His last known performances were for Rome in the 1771–2 season. Nothing is known of his death. Elisi was one of those castratos who were admired for vocal qualities and emotive expression rather than coloratura. Thomas Gray wrote in 1761: 'Elisi is finer than anything that has been here in your memory ... We have heard nothing, since I remember Operas, but eternal passages, divisions, and flights of execution. Of these he has absolutely none ... His point is expression'. Elisi was fond of wide melodic leaps, and had an enormous range.
                                     DALE E. MONSON

Elisir d'amore, L' ('The Elixir of Love'). *Melodramma giocoso* in two acts by GAETANO DONIZETTI to a libretto by FELICE ROMANI after EUGÈNE SCRIBE's text for Daniel-François-Esprit Auber's *Le philtre* (1831); Milan, Teatro Cannobiana, 12 May 1832.

L'elisir was composed in the six-week period between the première of *Ugo, conte di Parigi* (13 March 1832) and the time the opera went into rehearsal (about 1 May). That the work was evolving up to the last minute we know, as the censors came to the dress rehearsal to

Nemorino *a simple peasant, in love with ...*		tenor
Adina *a wealthy landowner*		soprano
Belcore *a sergeant*		baritone
Dr Dulcamara *an itinerant medicine man*		bass
Giannetta *a peasant girl*		soprano

Peasants, soldiers of Belcore's platoon

Setting An Italian village in the early 19th century

give their final approval (which normally was given before the rehearsal period began). The first run was a huge success at the Cannobiana, where it was introduced by Sabine Heinefetter (Adina), Giambattista Genero (Nemorino), Henri-Bernard Dabadie (Belcore) and Giuseppe Frezzolini (Dr Dulcamara). Its vogue in southern Italy was launched by its production at the Teatro del Fondo, Naples, in the spring of 1834, when it was given with Fanny Tacchinardi-Persiani (Adina), Lorenzo Salvi (Nemorino), Ambrogi (Belcore) and Lablache (Dulcamara). On 27 September 1835, it was first given at La Scala with Malibran (Adina), Poggi (Nemorino) and Salvatori (Belcore), with Frezzolini repeating his famous impersonation of Dulcamara. *L'elisir* continued its rapid triumphal progress across Italy where, as the musical press of the period shows, it was the most frequently performed opera between 1838 and 1848, a time when one out of every four productions in the country was of a work by Donizetti. It went to Berlin as *Der Liebestrank* in June 1834 and to Vienna, in Italian, on 9 April 1835, with a cast headed by Eugenia Tadolini, and Genero and Frezzolini in the parts they had created, and proved a hardy staple on German-language stages for a number of years.

L'elisir was put on at the Lyceum Theatre in London on 10 December 1836 and the following year it entered the repertory at Her Majesty's. It was given in New York in English in June 1838, but not in its original language until 1844. It was received with delight when introduced to Paris at the 'Italiens' on 17 January 1839, with Persiani, Ivanoff (Nemorino – that role later becoming the property of Mario), Tamburini (Belcore) and Lablache.

A notable revival at La Scala was that of 17 March 1900, when, under Toscanini's baton, *L'elisir* was sung by Regina Pinkert (Adina), Caruso, Magini-Coletti and Federico Carbonetti (Dulcamara). Caruso's great days began with the frantic applause that greeted 'Una furtiva lagrima' that night. The work was never given at Covent Garden during the seasons he appeared there, but it formed a central part of his repertory in New York – he appeared in it during ten of his 17 seasons as a member of the Metropolitan company. There Nemorino was later assumed by Gigli, Schipa, Ferruccio Tagliavini, Gedda, Pavarotti and Domingo. The opera was relatively late in entering the Glyndebourne repertory, first being given there on 24 May 1961 in a production by Franco Zeffirelli with a cast that included Eugenia Ratti, Luigi Alva, Enzo Sordello and Carlo Badioli.

Act 1.i *Outside Adina's farmhouse* There is a prelude, consisting of variations on a theme which is not heard again. While the peasants rest from their labours, one of them, Nemorino, watches the owner of the farm, the beautiful Adina, engrossed in a book. He loves her, but he is able only to sigh (cavatina, 'Quanto è bella'). When Adina laughs aloud at the absurd story she is reading, the others crowd round to discover why. It is

the story of Iseult and of the magician who gave Tristan such a powerful love potion that 'Iseult never left him again', adding that she wished she knew the recipe for such an elixir; her cavatina, 'Della crudele Isotta', consists of *couplets* with a choral refrain. A drumroll announces Sergeant Belcore and his platoon. Belcore glances at the girls and then without hesitation takes a nosegay from the barrel of his musket and presents it to Adina. He likens himself to Paris when he awarded the golden apple to Aphrodite, and has given flowers to Adina in hopes of a favourable response. His cavatina, 'Come Paride vezzoso', is in two stanzas, the second embellished; instead of a cabaletta Donizetti supplies a well-wrought concertato. Nemorino is upset by the sergeant's self-assurance. Belcore reminds Adina that later Aphrodite yielded to Ares, a warrior like himself. When Adina declares that she is in no hurry to make up her mind, Belcore observes that time flies; Adina retorts that some soldiers claim a victory before the battle has even begun.

Nemorino wishes he had the courage to declare his feelings for Adina as openly as Belcore did. When they are left alone he wants to talk, but she is tired of his sighing and tells him to go to see to his ailing uncle. Nemorino assures her he is the worse off; love makes him indifferent to the prospect that his uncle might die and leave his fortune to another heir. Adina tells him that although he is kind and modest, she is capricious and feels nothing for him; ask the gentle breezes why they are always in motion, she tells him – it is the nature of things, and like them she is fickle and inconstant (duet, 'Chiedi all'aura lusinghiera'). He swears he cannot leave her and, when she wonders why, he suggests she ask the river why it goes down to the sea – it responds to an irresistible tendency. As she insists on her capriciousness, and he on his constancy, she mocks the obstinacy of one who would die of love. This two-movement duet is one of the parts of Romani's libretto that has no counterpart in its source, Scribe's French *livret*, and it contributes through the purling melody of the first movement and the spirited rhythm of the second to the aura of pastoral romanticism that colours this beguiling score.

1.ii *The village square* A trumpet call summons the curious villagers. Dr Dulcamara arrives in his gaudy carriage (or, in some productions, descends by balloon) and stands to address the crowd, describing the powers of his medicines that can cure anything from impotence to the infirmities of old age. His 'Udite, udite, o rustici' is one of the great *buffo* arias, a torrent of patter set to a series of unctuous melodies that characterize this irresistible fraud. When he has finished his spiel, Nemorino shyly comes to ask if he sells the elixir of Queen Iseult. Needless to say, Dulcamara claims he has just what Nemorino wants. While he is being profusely thanked, the doctor observes that of all the blockheads he has met none can equal this fellow (duet, 'Obbligato, ah, sì! obbligato!'). After drinking the elixir, Dulcamara explains, the 'patient' must wait until the next day for results (by which time the doctor will be gone and Nemorino will have drunk a bottle of harmless Bordeaux). Dulcamara enters the inn, leaving Nemorino alone to sample his purchase. He is starting to feel its effects when Adina appears, wondering how he can be so cheerful. His gauche nonchalance puzzles and annoys her; but he can think only of what tomorrow will bring. Adina asks if he has followed her advice to find another, wondering if that explains his coldness;

'L'elisir d'amore' (Donizetti): the arrival of Dr Dulcamara (sung by Luigi Lablache) in Act 1 scene ii, with Nemorino sung by Giovanni Mario: lithograph by J. Brandard showing a London production, late 1840s

he assures her that tomorrow his heart will be cured.

Belcore marches in and Adina informs him that she has considered his offer and will marry him in six days' time. While Belcore exults, Nemorino cannot help laughing because he is confident that he will be irresistible to Adina the very next day. Giannetta enters, followed by the soldiers, who tell Belcore that new orders have arrived which require their departure tomorrow morning. Adina agrees to advance the wedding to that very evening. Nemorino is appalled (concertato, 'Adina, credimi'). As persuasively as he can, he begs her to wait just one more day, but Belcore, angered by the intrusion, orders Nemorino away; Adina defends him as a maladroit youth who has a fixation about her. When Adina offers to fetch the notary, Nemorino calls for Dulcamara's help. Everyone except Nemorino looks forward to the celebration. The first finale, launched by Nemorino's 'Adina, credimi', is a minor–major sequence of great tenderness; when Adina takes up this melody it is clear that she is not impervious to Nemorino's plight. The giddy stretta shows Donizetti's fondness for dance-like tunes in triple metre.

ACT 2.i *The interior of Adina's farmhouse* Music is provided by the military band among Belcore's troops. To cap everyone's enjoyment Dulcamara proposes that he and Adina sing a 'barcarolle for two voices' (a musical joke: it is in 2/4 metre rather than the characteristic 6/8). As a senator he urges his love on a lady gondolier, while she refuses him, preferring someone of her own station; their efforts are cheered. When the notary arrives, Adina does not want the ceremony to take place without Nemorino as she is still offended by his indifference. Soon Nemorino appears, downcast, and tells Dulcamara that he needs more elixir in a hurry. Dulcamara prescribes repeating the dosage until the desired results are obtained; he agrees to wait in the inn for one more hour as Nemorino has no money. Belcore is annoyed at Adina's delaying tactics; when Nemorino tells him he needs money right away, Belcore informs him that an enlistment pays a bounty of 20 scudi (duet, 'Venti scudi'). Belcore describes the manly delights of a soldier's life, which Nemorino will endure to win Adina. Handed the enlistment papers, Nemorino duly affixes his 'X'.

2.ii *A rustic courtyard* Giannetta and the village girls gossip about the news that Nemorino's immensely wealthy uncle has died and left him his only heir. Nemorino comes in, having spent all the bounty on elixir. The girls express their interest in him, a response which Nemorino attributes to the potion. Dulcamara is amazed at the spectacle of Nemorino surrounded by attentive young females. Adina comes to inquire about his enlistment, for which she feels responsible. Nemorino is sure that Adina is about to declare her feelings, but his sudden popularity with the girls (which Dulcamara now proudly attributes to his elixir) has aroused her jealousy. This scene evolves into a quartet with female chorus, 'Dell'elisir mirabile', the situation being a bit like a comic equivalent of Parsifal amid the flowermaidens; it vividly sets off the varied responses of the characters, yet fuses them into a propulsive ensemble. Nemorino goes off, the girls tagging after. Dulcamara boasts to Adina about the efficacy of his decoction, and when he mentions Iseult she asks if he has sold the elixir to Nemorino. The doctor describes the pitiable state of hopeless love that reduced Nemorino to enlist to pay for the elixir. Adina now realizes the depth of Nemorino's feelings. As Dulcamara offers to concoct a potion for her (duet, 'Quanto amore'), she tells him she has a better one of her own – a glance, a smile, a tender gesture; his slick patter is set against her gentle musing, which turns sprightly and coquettish in the final Allegro.

Nemorino, reflecting on the tell-tale tear he espied in Adina's eye when the village girls were crowding around him, has realized that she loves him, and he could himself die of love: this is expressed in his *romanza*, 'Una furtiva lagrima', with its haunting bassoon obbligato and its beautifully inflected minor-major melody. When Adina enters, she tells him that she has bought back his enlistment papers and hands them to him; her cantabile, 'Prendi, per me sei libero' with its melody at once suave and highly figured, contrasts markedly with her more brittle earlier music. She is happy that he can remain among his own people. As she turns to go, he asks if she wants to say something more, but she does not: whereupon he gives her back the enlistment papers – if the doctor has duped him, he would prefer to die a soldier. Finally Adina confesses her love for him, and Nemorino swears that Dulcamara has not deceived him. Belcore, surprised to see the lovers arm in arm, takes his dismissal in good spirit. Dulcamara reveals to the crowd the news of Nemorino's inheritance, which neither Adina nor Nemorino had yet heard; he boasts how his wondrous remedy can make people fall in love and even turn paupers into millionaires. Dulcamara drives off, leaving the lovers grateful for his elixir.

* * *

The score of *L'elisir* forms a good example of Donizetti's skill at presenting the conventional forms in ways that appear fresh. For instance, the first three vocal numbers follow each other with a minimum of recitative. Nemorino's introductory cavatina, 'Quanto è bella!', is the middle section of a choral introduction, thereby defining the existing relationship between social group and individual. The transition to Adina's cavatina is accomplished by means of her burst of laughter over the tale she is reading and a few interchanges with the peasants (*recitativo stromentato*) before she launches into a *couplet*-style aria set to contrasting dance-rhythms. The transition to Belcore's aria is the march (borrowed from Donizetti's *Alahor in Granata*, 1826) that brings on his platoon. His cavatina is concluded not by a solo cabaletta but by what develops into a sizable ensemble. Although in the strictest sense the *introduzione* to *L'elisir* consists of just the opening chorus with Nemorino's 'Quanto è bella' in the middle of it, the cumulative impression of the first three numbers is a series of contrasting musical episodes that form a single compound structure, creating a balance with the three successive episodes of the Act 1 finale.

Adina's music following 'Una furtiva lagrima' has undergone some changes over the years. Malibran sang a setting of 'Prendi, per me sei libero' by her husband Charles de Bériot designed to fit her mezzo-soprano range and agile voice. For Tadolini Donizetti wrote an air to use at this point that he subsequently re-used as part of Norina's duet with Don Pasquale. More recently Alberto Zedda found in a Paris library a manuscript of another air that Donizetti intended for this point; this discovery was performed in Bergamo in 1987.

Donizetti's score is a study in shrewd contrasts: from the fairly florid lines of the duet 'Chiedi all'aura' – florid yet always rhetorically tidy – to the bumptious 3/8 stretta of the Act 1 finale, or from the sharply differentiated tones of Nemorino and Belcore in the 'Venti scudi' duet, to the comic irony in the duet for Adina and Dulcamara, 'Quanto amore!', which sets off the potion as charm against the charm of Adina herself. The apparently effortless outpouring of melody arouses wonder, especially as it is never melodiousness for its own sake but always describes some aspect of character; moreover, there are those moments of genuine pathos ('Adina, credimi' and 'Una furtiva lagrima', for instance) that keep this comedy from seeming merely heartless or cruel. Ultimately, the continuing appeal of *L'elisir* lies in the appropriateness of Donizetti's music to this bucolic variant of the 'male Cinderella' myth. Nemorino's good-heartedness and his singleness of purpose win out in spite of potions and unforeseen inheritances.   WILLIAM ASHBROOK

Eliza. Opera in three acts by THOMAS AUGUSTINE ARNE to a libretto by Richard Rolt; London, New Theatre in the Haymarket, 29 May 1754.

Although described as an opera, the work has many of the features of a masque or allegory, but without spoken dialogue. The eponymous heroine, Queen Elizabeth, does not appear. After an overture in Handelian style (one of Arne's best), Britannia (soprano) is discovered in melancholy posture, dismayed at the threatened invasion from Spain. She is encouraged by Liberty (soprano), Peace (soprano), Neptune (bass), the Genius of England (tenor) and shepherds and shepherdesses who unite to rouse her from her lethargy. Peaceful Britons are summoned to take up arms in defence of their country. A war march is heard, during which a sea battle takes place. Victory is proclaimed and the Genius of England sings 'We have fought, we have conquer'd'. Peace is welcomed with the aria 'Happy day'. All join in the finale 'Hail glory, like the morning star'.

The published score (1758) omits recitatives and choruses, but the fortunate survival of the MS of Acts 2 and 3 (now in *US-CA*) supplies much of the missing music. Although the work is old-fashioned in style, Arne's orchestration is very ambitious, employing strings, oboes, bassoons, horns, trumpets and drums, with obbligato parts for flute, piccolo, descant recorder and cello. The most popular extracts were Britannia's song 'My fond shepherds of late', a simple pastoral ballad accompanied by muted strings, and the Genius of England's aria 'When all the Attic fire was fled'.

JOHN A. PARKINSON

Elizabethan Trust Opera Company. Australian company based in SYDNEY, founded in 1956 as the Australian Opera Company, and renamed the Elizabethan Trust Opera Company in 1957 and the Australian Opera in 1970.

Elizza, Elise [Letztergroschen, Elisabeth] (*b* Vienna, 6 Jan 1870; *d* Vienna, 3 June 1926). Austrian soprano. Her teacher in Vienna was Adolf Limley who became her husband. She sang first in operetta, then joined the opera company at Olomouc in 1894. The following year she made her début, as Inès in *L'Africaine*, at the Vienna Staatsoper where she remained as a valued and versatile member of the company until 1919. Her roles there ranged from the Queen of Night to Brünnhilde, though she was probably happiest in the lyric-coloratura repertory, such as Violetta, and the Queen in *Les Huguenots*. She later taught in Vienna, where Lotte Lehmann was among her pupils. A prolific early recording artist, she reveals on records a voice of exceptional beauty with a highly accomplished technique and a sensitive style. J. B. STEANE

Elkins, Margreta [Geater, Margaret] (*b* Brisbane, 16 Oct 1932). Australian mezzo-soprano. Her teachers included Pauline Bindley in Melbourne and Harold Williams in Sydney. She made her début as Carmen (1953, Brisbane) with the Sydney-based National Opera of Australia, followed by Azucena (1954), Suzuki and Siebel. In 1958 she became a resident principal at Covent Garden. She regularly partnered Sutherland in *Norma*, as Adalgisa, and in *Alcina*, as Ruggiero. She returned to Australia with the Sutherland-Williamson company (1965) and eventually became a member of the Australian Opera in 1976. Tall, with a commanding stage presence and a creamy, rounded voice with a soprano extension, she has excelled as Amneris, Octavian, Herodias, Maffio Orsini, Brangäne and Delilah. She was Helen in the first performances of *King Priam* (1962, Coventry and London). ROGER COVELL

Elkus, Jonathan (Britton) (*b* San Francisco, 8 Aug 1931). American composer. He studied composition at the University of California, Berkeley (BA 1953), at Stanford University (MA 1957) and with Milhaud at Mills College (1957). He taught at Lehigh University from 1957 to 1973 and became director of music at Cape Cod Academy in 1979. He has been guest conductor with concert bands throughout the USA.

Of Elkus's seven stage works, those conceived for performance by children, *Tom Sawyer* (1953) and *Treasure Island* (composed 1961), are the best known. *Tom Sawyer* uses Mark Twain's original dialogue almost verbatim. The composer's intent in this musical adaptation is, like Twain's, to 'remind adults of what they once were and how they thought and felt'. The musical style is essentially tonal, evoking the work's period setting through galops and marches; instrumental interludes are highly programmatic, and choral ensembles make use of original onomatopoeic devices. The music of *Treasure Island* is more adventurous; colourful hornpipes are used, but the language is richly chromatic and there is considerable rhythmic intensity.

Tom Sawyer (musical, 1, Elkus, after M. Twain), San Francisco, Everett Jr High School, 22 May 1953, vs (London, 1956)
The Outcasts of Poker Flat (1, R. G. Bander, after B. Harte), Bethlehem, PA, Lehigh U., 16 April 1960
Treasure Island, 1961 (musical, 2, B. M. Snyder, after R. L. Stevenson), San Francisco, 1967, vs (London, 1962)
Medea, 1963 (1, Elkus, after Euripides), Milwaukee, U. of Wisconsin Opera Theatre, 13 Nov 1970
The Mandarin, 1967 (ob, 3, R. F. Goldman, after E. de Queiroz)
Helen in Egypt (1, J. Knight, after H. D.), Milwaukee, U. of Wisconsin Opera Theatre, 13 Nov 1970
A Little Princess (musical, N. D. Watson, after F. H. Burnett), Cambridge, England, Perse School for Girls, 27 March 1981
JAMES P. CASSARO

Ellerton, John Lodge (*b* Cheshire, 11 Jan 1801; *d* London, 3 Jan 1873). English composer. He was born John Lodge, and in 1838 or 1839 adopted the name Ellerton. He was educated at Rugby and Oxford (MA

1828), and studied counterpoint in Rome for two years; during this time he frequently visited Germany. He tried his hand at most genres, including opera, church music, the programme symphony and chamber music; his music is more remarkable for quantity than quality.

Treiermain, 1831 (5, Ellerton, after W. Scott: *The Bridal of Treiermain*), ?unperf., vs *US-Bp**
Domenica (Ellerton), London, Drury Lane, 7 June 1838
Carlo Rosa, 1857 (3), vs *Bp*

Undated operas: Andromacca; Annibale in Capua; Berenice in Armenia; Il carnovale di Venezia; Il marito a vista, *Bp**; Issipile; Lucinda; Il sacrifizio di Epito [listed in *Grove5*]

DNB (L. M. Middleton); *Grove5* (W. H. Husk)
Musical World, ix (1838), 120; xii (1839), 348; li (1873), 181
F. Hueffer, ed.: *Briefwechsel zwischen Wagner und Liszt* (Leipzig, 1887); Eng. trans. (London, 1888), ii, 86–7
NICHOLAS TEMPERLEY

Elleviou, (Pierre-)Jean(-Baptiste-François) (*b* Rennes, 14 June 1769; *d* Paris, 5 May 1842). French tenor. He made his début in 1790 at the Comédie-Italienne, Paris, as a baritone in Monsigny's *Le déserteur*. The following year he made a second début, as a tenor, in Dalayrac's *Philippe et Georgette*. He remained at the Comédie-Italienne until 1801, when he was engaged at the Opéra-Comique. There he created the title roles in Méhul's *Joseph* (1807) and Boieldieu's *Jean de Paris* (1812), as well as many other parts. His wide repertory included operas by Grétry, Cherubini and Isouard, whose Michelangelo he created in 1802. He retired in 1813. Elleviou had an attractive stage presence and a style of acting in which wit and gracefulness were combined.

A. Pougin: *Figures d'opéra comique: Madame Dugazon, Elleviou, les Gavaudan* (Paris, 1875)
H. de Curzon: *Elleviou* (Paris, 1930) ELIZABETH FORBES

Ellis, Brent (*b* Kansas City, MO, 20 June 1946). American baritone. He studied in New York and Rome and made his début in 1967, creating Maerbale in Ginastera's *Bomarzo* in Washington, DC. He first sang with the New York City Opera in 1974, as Monteverdi's Otho. In 1976 he created Morris in Pasatieri's *Washington Square* at Detroit and sang Cortez in the American première of Sessions's *Montezuma* at Boston. In 1977 he sang Zurga for the WNO and Ford at Glyndebourne, where he returned as Don Giovanni, Marcello and Germont. He made his Metropolitan début in 1979 as Silvio; he has sung widely in the USA and in Munich, Vienna and Cologne. His repertory includes Rossini's Figaro, Count Almaviva, Guglielmo, Riccardo (*I puritani*), Belcore, Sherasmin (*Oberon*), Tonio, Alfio, Scarpia, Escamillo, Wozzeck, Kunrad (*Feuersnot*), George Milton (Floyd's *Of Mice and Men*) and Konstantin (Pasatieri's *The Seagull*). A versatile artist, he excels in Verdi, notably as Luna, Iago and Macbeth and as Rigoletto, the role of his Covent Garden début (1988). ELIZABETH FORBES

Ellis [née Elsas], **Mary** (*b* New York, 15 June 1900). British soprano of American birth. She made her début in 1918 at the Metropolitan, where she created the role of the Novice in *Suor Angelica*, and later also sang Lauretta during the first run of performances of *Il trittico*. She sang Giannetta to Caruso's Nemorino and Fyodor to Shalyapin's Boris before appearing in drama on Broadway and rising to fame in the title role of

Friml's *Rose Marie* (1924). She pursued her later career in England, where she appeared in Kern's *Music in the Air* (1933) and opposite Ivor Novello in *Glamorous Night* (1935) and *The Dancing Years* (1939). In his *Arc de Triomphe* (1943) she played Marie Forêt, a role inspired by the life of Mary Garden. She also appeared in London in plays by Coward, Rattigan and O'Neill.

M. Ellis: *Those Dancing Years* (London, 1981)
——: *Moments of Truth* (London, 1986)   GERALD BORDMAN

Ellsworth, Warren (*b* MA, 28 Oct 1951). American tenor. He studied at the Juilliard School and with Elena Nikolaidi and Marlena Malas. After beginning his career with the Houston Grand Opera as a baritone (Almaviva and Malatesta), further training took his voice higher and he returned to Houston in 1979 as Pinkerton and in other tenor roles. The next year he went to Britain to work with Reginald Goodall on Parsifal (a role he recorded in 1982), first making his British début with the WNO as Jeník (*The Bartered Bride*). He followed this with Pinkerton and Parsifal for the WNO, and sang Parsifal for the ENO in 1986, and then Siegmund for his Covent Garden début during the Welsh company's *Ring* cycle that year. He has appeared with Canadian National Opera and various American companies including San Francisco and Los Angeles, at the Vienna Staatsoper and the Deutsche Oper, Berlin, which he joined in 1987; there he sang Siegmund, Florestan and Max (*Der Freischütz*). In 1988 he returned to Covent Garden as Parsifal, a role he repeated at La Scala in 1991. He sang Jim Mahoney (*Aufstieg und Fall der Stadt Mahagonny*) at Florence (1990) and Geneva (1992). His voice is large, musical and supported by resourceful dramatic presence.   NOËL GOODWIN

Elmendorff, Karl (**Eduard Maria**) (*b* Düsseldorf, 25 Oct 1891; *d* Hofheim am Taunus, 21 Oct 1962). German conductor. After first studying philology he became a pupil of Steinbach and Abendroth at the Cologne Conservatory in 1913. His conducting début was at Düsseldorf in 1916, and he held posts in Mainz, Hagen and Aachen. He was first conductor at the Berlin and Munich Staatsopern (1925–32) and in 1927 he made his début at the Bayreuth Festival with *Tristan und Isolde*; he returned there regularly each year until 1942. During this period he became widely renowned for his broad readings of Wagner, whose operas he conducted throughout Europe and in South America. He was appointed Generalmusikdirektor of the Staatstheater at Kassel and of the Hessische Staatstheater at Wiesbaden in 1932, moving to a similar appointment at Mannheim in 1935 and to the Dresden Staatsoper in 1942, in succession to Böhm. There he conducted the première of Joseph Haas's *Die Hochzeit des Jobs* (1944), and in the same year added *Capriccio* to the Dresden Strauss repertory, as well as a brilliant revival of Hermann Goetz's *Der Widerspenstigen Zähmung*, shortly before the wartime destruction of the opera house. He returned to Kassel and Wiesbaden (1948–56), and thereafter toured extensively. His talent extended over a wide repertory in style and period, and he was particularly concerned to foster reciprocal interest in German and Italian opera styles by conducting Wagner in Italy (notably at the Florence Maggio Musicale) and introducing lesser-known Italian operas into Germany; he conducted the German première of Wolf-Ferrari's *La dama*

boba at Berlin and of Malipiero's *Torneo notturno* at Munich.

Elmo, Cloe (*b* Lecce, 9 April 1910; *d* Ankara, 24 May 1962). Italian mezzo-soprano. She studied in Rome, making her début as Santuzza at Cagliari in 1934. She then sang Orpheus in Rome, and from 1936 to 1945 she was leading mezzo-soprano at La Scala, where her roles included Mistress Quickly, Ulrica, Azucena and the Princess (*Adriana Lecouvreur*). Engaged at the Metropolitan in 1947, she sang Mistress Quickly in Toscanini's broadcast performance and recording of *Falstaff*. She returned to La Scala in 1951 and created roles in Rocca's *L'uragano* and in *Proserpina y el extranjero* (1952); she also created Moraima in *Re Hassan* (1939, Venice) and Goneril in Frazzi's *King Lear* (1939, Florence), and sang Signora Susanna in the first staged performance of Malipiero's *Il festino* (1954, Bergamo). She had a naturally beautiful voice and a dynamic stage personality.   HAROLD ROSENTHAL/R

Elms, Lauris (*b* Melbourne, 20 Oct 1931). Australian contralto. Born into a musical family, she studied the violin and singing, appeared with the National Theatre Movement in several major productions and worked with Dominique Modesti in Paris. She began singing for the Covent Garden company on provincial tours in 1957 and joined the resident company soon after, giving strongly characterized performances such as Mrs Sedley in *Peter Grimes* (1957), commemorated in the 1959 recording conducted by the composer. When her husband returned to Australia in 1959, she accompanied him, continuing her career largely through guest appearances with Australian-based companies. She was also noted for her interpretation of Azucena opposite Donald Smith's Manrico for the Australian Opera, and for her partnership with Joan Sutherland in the last of the J. C. Williamson tours (*Semiramide*, 1965).
     ROGER COVELL

El-Shawān, Aziz (*b* Cairo, 6 May 1916). Egyptian composer. He received his education in French schools and graduated with a diploma in commercial studies. He studied music as well, but an injury ended his career as a performer and he turned to composition. In 1956 he visited Moscow and was greatly impressed by Khachaturian and Shostakovich. He returned there in 1967 to study composition with Khachaturian, whose influence played an important role in the development of his style.

'*Antar* (1947–9), in two acts, was composed to a play written totally in verse by the Egyptian poet Aḥmad Shawqi (1869–1932). The events in the play take place in the 6th century, some 50 years before Islam, and concern the warrior and poet 'Antar, who is in love with his cousin, 'Abla, and the many obstacles put in their way. It is written in a very traditional manner and represents the early stages of El-Shawān's compositional style, tending to monody with harmony and counterpoint as embellishments.

El-Shawān's second opera, *Anās El-Wugūd* (1970), is in three acts with libretto by Salama El-Abbassi, after a legend from *The Thousand and One Nights*. Anās El-Wugūd, a handsome, brave and generous poet, falls in love with Zahr El-Ward ('the Flower of the Roses'), the fascinating and lovely daughter of the ruler's wazir. The wazir, who opposes the match, exiles his daughter to the temple of Isis on the island of Philae and orders the death of Anās El-Wugūd. The young man escapes and after many adventures is reunited with Zahr. The opera shows strong influence of Khachaturian, whose style is evident in El-Shawān's later works, with their rhythmically rich melodies and folk elements; many of the themes of his instrumental works have a marked vocal character.   WILLIAM Y. ELIAS

Elsner, Józef (**Antoni Franciszek**) (*b* Grodków, nr Opole, 1 June 1769; *d* Warsaw, 18 April 1854). Polish composer, probably of German descent. He studied in Grotków (1775–81), then in Wrocław (1781–9), where he played in the opera house orchestra. For a short time he studied theology and medicine at Wrocław University. At the same time he began composing, in almost all the genres known at the time. After a brief stay in Vienna and Brno, where he was a violinist in the theatre orchestra, in 1792 he was appointed conductor at the German theatre in Lemberg (now L'viv). There he also founded a music society, for which he organized concerts, and composed his first stage works: incidental music, insertions for operas and ballets by other composers, and his own earliest operas. He also made contact, later kept up in Warsaw, with the playwright and actor Wojciech Bogusławski, the father of Polish national theatre, who from 1795 was director of the Polish theatre in Lemberg. Bogusławski was influential in stimulating Elsner's interest in opera; through him Elsner was increasingly drawn to Polish librettos (several by Bogusławski himself), which from then on formed the chief literary basis of his operas. In 1799 Elsner moved permanently to Warsaw, where until 1824 he was the director of opera at the National Theatre, raising it to new artistic standards. He introduced into the repertory the most outstanding operatic works in Europe at that time, enriched it with his own works and oversaw the performances and training of the singers and players. This was the period of his greatest activity as an opera composer, but he was also engaged in mounting concerts and publishing sheet music (1802–6). After 1810 he reduced his operatic output slightly, becoming involved in organizing the music society as well as in teaching. He taught singing, music theory and composition in a number of Warsaw schools and later in the first Polish conservatory, the Szkoła Główna Muzyki, which he founded. His pupils there included Chopin.

A considerable number of Elsner's works are lost, and of those that survive, many do so only in fragments. The extant operas observe the stylistic conventions of the period, with distinct signs of Viennese Classical influence, apparent even in his earliest operas composed in Lemberg. These were written to German librettos and modelled on Mozart (*Die seltenen Brüder*, *Der verkleidete Sultan*). Elsner composed in various operatic genres, most often in Liederspiels (comedies with an overture and sung insertions in the style of the French vaudeville) and melodramas modelled on the German Singspiel, in which the role of the spoken dialogue is increased to such an extent that the music is limited to an overture and few sung fragments. He also wrote comic operas combining features of Italian *opera buffa* and French *opéra comique*. During his early years in Warsaw he also wrote his only through-composed *opera seria* (*Andromeda*). The plots of these works are based on fairy-tales or biblical, exotic and historical themes and usually address themselves, either directly (*Pospolite ruszenie*, *Żona po drodze*) or allegorically

(*Andromeda*, *Karol Wielki*, *Rzym oswobodzony*), to topical issues, thanks to which Elsner's operas enjoyed considerable success. Manners and moral themes are also dealt with, often in satirical form (*Siedem razy jeden*, *Stary trzpiot*). In the vocal parts Elsner used both coloratura arias with recitative (*Andromeda*), *buffo* arias (*Sułtan Wampum*) and modest and simple strophic songs, which predominate in his later works. He also attempted to characterize by musical means, and his overtures, usually in the form of a sonata allegro, became increasingly strongly connected with the musical material and mood of the opera as a whole. Both in orchestration and in his vocal parts he used colouristic and illustrative effects attained through simple instrumental and technical means, incorporation of polyphonic and imitative elements patterned on Cherubini operas, and polyrhythms modelled on Mozart's *Don Giovanni*. He also used Polish and Ukrainian folk music, and, in operas based on oriental themes, Turkish (janissary) melodies. In *Trybunał niewidzialny* he introduced the waltz into Polish opera.

Elsner stands second only to Kurpiński in the history of early Romantic Polish opera. Although after 1813 he composed fewer operas, they played an important role: under the impact of early Romantic ideology there was a striving towards the creation of a national opera, in which Polish historical events could be represented and Polish folk music drawn upon. As well as using folk melodies Elsner incorporated Polish dance rhythms in his newly composed music and for that he is regarded as the precursor of the national style in Polish opera. Most of the operas written at that time were instrumental in raising national consciousness during the Partitions and played an important role during the November Uprising (1830–31).

Elsner wrote music textbooks including a singing treatise, *Szkoła śpiewu* (Warsaw, 1834, Leipzig, 2/ 1855); an account of his career, *Sumariusz moich utworów z objaśnieniami o czynnościach i działaniach moich jako artysty muzycznego* ('Summary of my Works with Explanations of my Activities as a Musician' [1840–49]; Kraków, 1957); and a number of articles, among them 'Die Oper der Polen' (*AMZ*, xiv, 1812, cols.323–31).

first performed at Warsaw, National Theatre, unless otherwise stated

Die seltenen Brüder, oder Die vier Zauberkugeln [Ibrahim und Abdallah, oder Die seltenen Brüder] (2, Elsner), Lemberg, Bulla's, 22 Feb 1795

Der verkleidete Sultan (3, H. G. Bretschneider), Lemberg, Bulla's, 4 Oct 1796

Amazonki [Herminia, czyli Amazonki] [Herminia, or The Amazons] (heroic-comic op, 2, W. Bogusławski), Lemberg, 26 July 1797, *PL-Wn**, aria in Zbiór pieśni polskich (Warsaw, 1802–3)

Izkahar, król Guaxary [Iskahar, the King of Guaxara], (melodrama, 3, Bogusławski), Lemberg, sum. 1797, aria in Zbiór pieśni polskich [A Collection of Polish Songs] (Warsaw, 1802–3)

Sułtan Wampum, czyli Nieroztropne życzenia [Sultan Wampum, or The Rash Wish] (2, A. Gliński and Bogusławski, after A. von Kotzebue), Lemberg, Bogusławski's, 8 Dec 1797, *Wn*

Sydney i Zuma, czyli Moc kochania czarnej niewiasty [Sydney and Zuma, or The Power of Love of a Black Woman] (melodrama, 3, Bogusławski), Lemberg, Bogusławski's, 9 Sept 1798, aria in Zbiór pieśni polskich (Warsaw, 1802–3)

Mieszkańcy wyspy Kamkatal [The Dwellers on the Isle of Kamkatal] (1, L. Dmuszewski), 27 Jan 1804

Siedem razy jeden [Seven Times One] (Liederspiel, 1, Dmuszewski), 14 Dec 1804, *Wn*, ov. and 6 songs, 1v, pf (Warsaw, 1805)

Stary trzpiot i młody mędrzec [The Old Dolt and the Young Sage] (1, Matuszewski, after F.-B. Hoffman), 15 Feb 1805, *Wn*

Nurzahad, czyli Nieśmiertelność i bogactwa [Nurzahad, or Immortality and Riches] (melodrama, 3, J. Adamczewski, after L. C. Caigniez), 8 Dec 1805, ballet arr. pf, 1 song, 1v, pf, in Wybór pięknych dzieł muzycznych i pieśni polskich (Warsaw, 1805)

Wieszczka Urzella, czyli To co się damom podoba [The Soothsayer Urzella, or What Pleases the Ladies] (3, J. Baudouin de Courtenay, after C.-S. Favart), 7 March 1806, Wn, 2 arias, duet (Warsaw, n.d.)

Sąd Salomona [The Judgment of Solomon] (melodrama, 3, Gliński, after Caigniez), 9 Nov 1806, ballet, Wn* [re-used in Ofiara Abrahama]

Andromeda [Perseusz i Andromeda] (os, 1, L. Osiński), 14 Jan 1807, ov. A-Wgm (Leipzig, 1808), cantata in Muzyka do pieśni wolnomularskich [Music to Freemasonry Songs] (Warsaw, 1811)

Trybunał niewidzialny, czyli Syn występny [The Invisible Tribune, or The Wicked Son] (melodrama, 3, Wrzesiński, after J. G. A. Cuvelier de Trie), 24 April 1807, PL-Wtm*

Pospolite ruszenie, cyzli Bitwa z Kozakami [The Levy in Mass, or The Battle with the Cossacks] (Liederspiel, 2, Dmuszewski), 1 May 1807, 1 chorus, 4vv (Warsaw, 1831)

Mieczysław ślepy [Mieczyslaw the Blind] (melodrama, 3, J. Szymaniecki, after Caigniez: L'illustre aveugle), 1 Nov 1807

Karol Wielki i Witykind [Charlemagne and Wittekind] (lyric drama, 2, T. Łubieńska), 5 Dec 1807, D-Dlb*, ov. (as Charlemagne le Grand et Wytykind) A-Wgm, chorus in Muzyka do pieśni wolnomularskich (Warsaw, 1811)

Szewc i krawcowa [The Cobbler and the Dressmaker] (duodrama, 1, J. Drozdowski), 11 March 1808

Urojenie i rzeczywistość [Fantasy and Reality] (1, Adamczewski), 22 April 1808, F-Pn, PL-Wn*, ov. A-Wgm

Echo w lesie [The Forest Echo] (duodrama, 1, W. Pękalski), 22 April 1808, PL-Wn

Śniadanie trzpiotów [The Dolts' Breakfast] (1, A. Huisson, after A. Creuzé de Lesser and J. F. Roger: Le déjeuner de garçons), 22 April 1808

Żona po drodze [A Wife Met on the Journey] (duodrama, 1, Drozdowski), 28 Oct 1808

Leszek Biały, czyli Czarownica z Łysej Góry [Leszek the White, or The Witch of the Bald Mountain] (2, Dmuszewski, after M. D. Krajewski), 2 Dec 1809, ov. Wn, ov., aria Wtm*, orch pts RU-SPsc, ov. (Leipzig, 1811)

Rzym oswobodzony, czyli Powrót wojowników [Rome Liberated, or The Return of the Warriors] (3, F. Wężyk), 21 Dec 1809

Benefis [A Benefit] (duodrama, 1, Pękalski), 26 Jan 1810

Wyspa małżeńska, czyli Żony przez los wybrane [The Isle of Matrimony, or Wives Chosen by Fate] (melodrama, 3, Dmuszewski, after A. de Pujol and C. Desnoyer), 19 April 1811, PL-Wn*

Korsarz francuski w Portugalii [A French Corsair in Portugal] (melodrama, 3, Dmuszewski, after Caigniez), 26 July 1811

Wąwozy Sierra Morena [The Ravines of the Sierra Morena] (3, Dmuszewski), 31 Jan 1812, A-Wgm, I-Fc

Kabalista [The Cabalist] (2, F. Wężyk), 29 Jan 1813, PL-Wn*

Kochankowie ukryci [The Concealed Lovers] (2, ? J. Krasiński), unperf.

Król Łokietek, czyli Wiśliczanki [King Lokietek, or The Women of Wiślica] (2, Dmuszewski), 3 April 1818, Wn*, Wtm*, orch pts RU-SPV, excerpts (Warsaw, 1818)

Jagiełło w Tenczynie [Jagiello in Tenczyn] (3, A. Chodkiewicz), 1 Jan 1820, PL-Wn*, excerpts (Warsaw, 1820)

Ofiara Abrahama [Abraham's Sacrifice] (melodrama, 4, B. Kudlicz, after Cuvelier de Trie and L. Chandezon), 11 Dec 1821, Kj*, Wn*, ov. CZp, ov. arr. pf (Warsaw, n.d.)

La ritrosia disarmata, c1825 (duodrama, 1, P. Metastasio), unperf.

Powstanie narodu [The Insurrection of the Nation] (1, F. S. Dmochowski), 1 Jan 1831, 3 choruses (Warsaw, 1831)

*

SMP (J. Prosnak)

Z. Jachimecki: Muzyka polska w rozwoju historycznym od czasów najdawniejszych do doby obecnej [The Historical Evolution of Polish Music from the Earliest Times to the Present Day], i/2 (Kraków, 1951), 134–56

W. Bogdany: Melodramat Józefa Elsnera 'Ofiara Abrahama' (diss., U. of Kraków, 1953)

K. Michałowski: Opery polskie (Kraków, 1954)

A. Nowak-Romanowicz: Józef Elsner (Kraków, 1957)

A. Papierzowa: Libretta oper polskich z lat 1800–1830 (Kraków, 1959)

A. Nowak-Romanowicz: 'Muzyka polskiego oświecenia i wczesnego romantyzmu' [The Music of the Polish Enlightenment and Early Romanticism], Z dziejów polskiej kultury muzycznej [From the History of Polish Musical Culture], ii (Kraków, 1966), 9–152

H. Szepietowska: 'Kontakty muzyczne polsko-włoskie w pierwszym 30-leciu XIX wieku/Contatti musicali polacco-italiani nel primo trentennio del XIX secolo', Pagine, iv (1980), 325–34

JERZY MORAWSKI

Elston, Arnold (b New York, 30 Sept 1907; d Vienna, 6 June 1971). American composer of Russian-Lithuanian descent. He studied chiefly with Rubin Goldmark (1928–30) and with Webern (1932–5), then from 1939 taught at various institutions, including the University of Oregon (1941–58) and the University of California, Berkeley (1958–71). He died unexpectedly while travelling. Among the honours he received was a joint award from the American Academy of Arts and Letters and the National Institute of Arts and Letters (1969–70). His music balances a wide range of colour with a sureness of line; rhythmic suppleness is subordinated to larger phrase structure. Besides choral and chamber music Elston composed two operas. Sweeney Agonistes (1948–50), a chamber opera (1 scene, T. S. Eliot), was first performed in a two-piano version on 1 May 1957 in Berkeley, directed by Joseph Kerman; the version with orchestra had its première on 16 January 1967 in Oakland. Sweeney employs classical forms (waltz, rondo and fugue) as well as American elements (ragtime and a crooning singing style). The Love of Don Perlimplin (chamber opera, 1, after F. García Lorca) was first performed on 16 May 1958 in Berkeley; it is a 12-note work containing classical dance forms (sarabandes in the first and third scenes) and employing colour in costume and lighting as a dynamic element to indicate the emotional pitch of a scene. Elston's collection of papers at the University of California at Berkeley also contains an unfinished libretto entitled A Penny for Your Life and correspondence regarding plans for an operatic adaptation of Jacques Audiberti's play Le mal court.

*

A. Elston: 'A Score for Eliot – in the Music Hall', San Francisco Chronicle (28 April 1957)

'A Colloquy for the Composer and Director … on the Loves of Belisa and Perlimplin', San Francisco Chronicle (11 May 1958)

R. Commanday: 'A Concern with Humanity in Elston's "Sweeney"', San Francisco Chronicle (18 Jan 1967)

ANN P. BASART, JUDY TSOU

Elvira, Pablo (b San Juan, 24 Sept 1938). Puerto Rican baritone. He enrolled in the Puerto Rico Conservatory (1960) to study the trumpet and singing; from 1966 when he was a finalist in the Metropolitan Opera auditions he devoted himself exclusively to singing. He taught at the Indiana University School of Music (1966–74), but left to perform in South America, Europe, Israel, Puerto Rico and the USA. He has appeared with the New York City Opera and the Metropolitan, where he made his début as Tonio in 1979. Although he has performed a wide repertory he has had particular success as Figaro (Rossini), Rigoletto, Tonio and Germont. Elvira's work is grounded in solid musicianship and artistic consistency; his voice is characterized by clarity, expressive phrasing and broad dramatic qualities.

DONALD THOMPSON

Elwes [Hahessy], **John Joseph** (b London, 20 Oct 1946). English tenor. He studied in London with George Malcolm at Westminster Cathedral, where he was a chorister, and at the RCM. From the age of 14 he lived with the family of the tenor Gervase Elwes (1866–1921) and later took their name. He made his début in 1968 at the Proms in Vaughan Williams's *Serenade to Music*. He has appeared in operas by Monteverdi, Rameau, Handel, Gluck and Mozart and in many others in concert performances. He sang the title roles in Monteverdi's *Orfeo* and *Il ritorno d'Ulisse in patria*, and Nerone in *L'incoronazione di Poppea*. His recordings of operas by Rameau have been widely acclaimed and include *Les Indes galantes* (1974), *Zaïs* (1977), *Pygmalion* (1981), *Le temple de la gloire* (1982) and *Zoroastre* (1983). Other recordings include Vaughan Williams's *The Pilgrim's Progress* (1972), Monteverdi's *Orfeo* (1974), Cavalli's *Serse* (1985), Vivaldi's *L'incoronazione di Dario* (1986) and Albinoni's *Cleomene* (1988). Since the late 1970s he has lived in France and worked mainly on the Continent. His wide tessitura has made him much sought after in French Baroque opera where an ability to sustain clarity and lyricism in exceptionally high registers is required.   NICHOLAS ANDERSON

Emilia di Liverpool ('Emilia of Liverpool') [*L'eremitaggio di Liverpool* ('The Hermitage of Liverpool')]. *Dramma semiseria* in two acts by GAETANO DONIZETTI to a libretto based on the anonymous one for VITTORIO TRENTO's *Emilia di Laverpaut* after Stefano Scatizzi's play of that name; Naples, Teatro Nuovo, 28 July 1824 (revised version, Naples, Teatro Nuovo, 8 March 1828).

With spoken dialogue, *Emilia di Liverpool* belongs to a genre long popular in Naples, but its currency elsewhere was limited as other Italian theatres expected sung recitatives, and *buffo* roles in Neapolitan dialect were unacceptable. The work is implausibly set in the mountains adjacent to Liverpool, and the plot deals with Emilia (soprano), who does pious work in a hospice to atone for her seduction. Her outraged father, Claudio di Liverpool (baritone), turns up just as her seducer, Federico (tenor), has been spilled offstage by an overturned carriage. Everyone's identity is established piecemeal, and there is about to be a duel between the father and the seducer when Emilia, seeing that he is a reformed character, agrees to marry him. Everything ends happily with Emilia singing an ebullient rondò in Eb (in the 1828 version).

The differences between the 1824 and the 1828 versions are considerable. For 1828, not only was the libretto extensively revised by Giuseppe Checcherini, with four of the characters renamed (the seducer becomes Colonel Villars, and the *buffo* character, originally Don Romualdo, becomes Count Asdrubale); seven numbers of the original were suppressed, three new numbers were added to the first act, and Emilia's aria-finale was borrowed from the score of *Alahor in Granata*.

The apparent incongruity of the title has to be considered in a context where England was a distant land with distinct Romantic overtones. *Emilia* was successfully revived in 1871 at the Nuovo-Nazionale in Naples. More recently, the 1828 version was given in Liverpool in 1957 (with Joan Sutherland) and, in shortened form, broadcast by the BBC. In 1987 the 1824 version was given in concert form, also in Liverpool. Since then, Opera Rara has issued a recording giving both versions of the score.   WILLIAM ASHBROOK

Emmanuel, (Marie François) Maurice (*b* Bar-sur-Aube, 2 May 1862; *d* Paris, 14 Dec 1938). French composer.

In 1869 his family moved to Beaune, and the landscape and monuments of Burgundy instilled in him a love of nature and the visual arts. He was interested in folksong and developed a feeling for the beauty of the liturgy. Both of these factors played an important part in the evolution of his music. He entered the Paris Conservatoire in 1880, where his teachers included Dubois and Delibes; he also studied classics, poetics, philology and art history at the Sorbonne and the Ecole du Louvre. His free approach to rhythm and the introduction of medieval modes into his early works met with strong censure from Delibes; as a result Emmanuel studied privately with the more liberal Ernest Guiraud and so came into close contact with Debussy. In 1896 he was awarded the doctorat ès lettres for his thesis on ancient Greek dance. From 1909 he was lecturer in the history of music at the Paris Conservatoire, where his pupils included Migot and Messiaen. He published important musicological writings, including *Essai sur l'orchestrique grèque* (Paris, 1895; Eng. trans., 1916) and *Pelléas et Mélisande de Claude Debussy* (Paris, 1926, 2/1950).

Emmanuel was unusually self-critical and he destroyed all but 30 of his 73 works. His compositions reflect his strong views on the 'tyranny' of the major scale, the conventional cadence, the dominant 7th and the bar-line. He thought modally and he demonstrated how modality and folksong could be used in 20th-century music. His compositions are remarkable for their virility and concision, and their polymodal and polyrhythmic originality. Among them are the three-act *tragédies lyriques Prométhée enchaîné* op.16 (composed 1916–18) and *Salamine* op.21 (composed 1921–3 and 1927–8). Act 1 of *Prométhée* was first given in a concert performance on 23 March 1919; the work was not heard in full until 23 November 1959 at the Théâtre des Champs-Elysées in Paris. *Salamine* was first performed at the Opéra on 19 June 1929. These works, both to Emmanuel's own librettos based on Aeschylus, reflect his great sympathy with ancient Greek civilization; his knowledge of Greek rhythms and methods enabled him to go beyond Fauré's refined interpretation of ancient beauty, nobility and simplicity to achieve powerful, tautly constructed dramas of considerable intensity. One of his greatest gifts was the creation of balanced, large-scale sections filled with a wealth of detail which is perhaps more remarkable for its harmony and rhythm than for its melody. One of the few genuine independents in French music, he sought to liberate it from all that limited its scope, deriving his material from sources mostly outside the Classical and Romantic traditions. Neither of his operas has received the frequency of performance that they merit artistically, though the prologue to *Prométhée enchaîné* and the overture to *Salamine* have achieved a degree of popularity as separate concert items.

E. Vuillermoz: 'Etudes sur Salamine', *Candide* (27 June 1929)

R. de Souza: 'Maurice Emmanuel et le rythme poétique', *Mercure de France* (1 May 1939)

ReM (1947), no.206 [Emmanuel issue, incl. articles by O. Messiaen and C. Koechlin]

R. Stevenson: 'Maurice Emmanuel: a Belated Apologia', *ML*, xl (1959), 154–65   ROBERT ORLEDGE

Emmert, Johann Joseph (*b* Kitzingen, nr Würzburg, 27 Nov 1732; *d* Würzburg, 20 Feb 1809). German composer. He was a schoolmaster at Schillingsfürst, where he also taught music to the children of the

Hohenlohe family. His Singspiel *Die geopferte Un-schuld* was given there in about 1760. By 1765 he had moved to Würzburg, where in 1773 he became university choirmaster and a school Rektor. At least three of his operas were given in Würzburg: *Semiramis* (Hochfürstliches Theater, 1777), *Tomiris* and *Eberhard* (1780). Two other works, *Esther* and *Judith*, are described sometimes as operas, sometimes as oratorios. The larger part of his output consists of Catholic church music (mostly with German texts) in simple style.

His son, Adam Joseph Emmert (*b* Würzburg, 24 Dec 1765; *d* Vienna, 11 April 1812), was employed by the Salzburg Privy Council and later worked at the Haus-und Hofarchiv in Vienna. His compositions, which show both Classical and Romantic characteristics, include three operas: *Don Silvio von Rosalva* (after C. M. Wieland; Ansbach, Schloss, 1801, pubd Salzburg, 1801); *Der Sturm* (1806, Salzburg); and *Der Schlaftrunk*.

MGG (R. Meuer); *StiegerO*   ELIZABETH ROCHE

Emperor Jones, The. Opera in two acts, with a prologue and an interlude, by LOUIS GRUENBERG to his own libretto after EUGENE O'NEILL; New York, Metropolitan Opera, 7 January 1933.

Gruenberg's adaptation follows the play with few alterations, the most frequent changes being either omission of dialogue or repetition for emphasis. The story is that of an ex-Pullman porter Jones (baritone), who makes himself emperor of a West Indian island by combining an appeal to superstition with a white man's cunning. Jones cynically exploits the natives, or 'bush-niggers' (as he calls them), until they rebel and he is forced to flee. Gruenberg made two important changes from the original play: a chorus acts as a commentator on the events taking place, and Jones kills himself rather than being murdered by the natives.

Throughout the opera the orchestra provides a background of syncopated dissonances to the fast-moving drama. Except for one lyrical, dramatic moment when Jones sings the spiritual 'It's me, O' Lord', the singers recite and shout their words in a Sprechgesang manner. The demands of the title role are great (it was sung by Lawrence Tibbett at the first performance). The subject matter, exploitation of blacks by a black, has limited the performance of this controversial work, and the opera is rarely heard today.   ROBERT F. NISBETT

Empress's Slippers, The. Opera by P. I. Tchaikovsky; see CHEREVICHKI.

Enchantress, The [*Charodeyka*]. Opera in four acts by PYOTR IL'YICH TCHAIKOVSKY to a libretto by Ippolit Vasil'yevich Shpazhinsky after his own eponymous tragedy; St Petersburg, Mariinsky Theatre, 20 October/ 1 November 1887.

Tchaikovsky himself conducted the first performance, with Ivan Mel'nikov as Prince Kurlyatev, Mariya Slavina as the Princess, Fyodor Stravinsky as Mamïrov and Emiliya Pavlovskaya as Nastas'ya. A new libretto was prepared by Sergey Gorodetsky for Soviet consumption; in this form the opera was revived at the Kirov Theatre (formerly Mariinsky), Leningrad, on 22 March 1941; the existing recordings conflate Shpazhinsky's text with Gorodetsky's. (The title translates as *The Enchantress*, not – as commonly given – *The Sorceress*.)

The play on which Tchaikovsky based this opera, with its gratuitous 15th-century setting, belongs to that meretricious brand of costume melodrama that dominated the Russian stage during the culturally backward reign of Alexander III. Its main characters are five (of minor characters there is no end): Prince Nikita Kurlyatev (baritone in the opera), vice-regent of Nizhnïy Novgorod; his wife the Princess (mezzo-soprano); his son Yury (tenor); the puritanical deacon Mamïrov (bass); and the title character Nastas'ya (dramatic soprano), a fun-loving, well-preserved widow who keeps an inn where she goes by the name Kuma ('Everybody's girl-friend'). Disregarding an extravagant abundance of anecdotal byplay, the essential action is as follows. Act 1: Mamïrov brings the Prince to Kuma's inn to put an end to the debaucheries practised there; Kuma charms the vice-regent with her hospitality until, at her suggestion, he humiliates the deacon by forcing him to dance (earlier in the act Yury's hunting party passes by and it is clear that Kuma has eyes for him). Act 2: Infatuated with Kuma, the Prince has been visiting her daily; Mamïrov insinuates the worst and inflames the Princess's jealousy; Yury, learning the reason for his mother's distress, vows to kill Kuma. Act 3: In the first of two major confrontations Kuma is seen resisting the Prince's strenuous advances; in the second, her frankness persuades Yury of her innocence, while her confession of love kindles reciprocal feelings in him and they plan to elope. Act 4: The Princess, disguised as a wayfarer, procures a delayed-action poison from a forest-dwelling wizard, a 'diabolus ex machina' if ever there was one, and administers it to the unsuspecting Kuma who dies in Yury's arms. Act 5: The Prince, in a panic of jealousy, arrives upon the scene, disbelieves the news that Kuma is dead and kills his rival-son; when he learns the truth he loses his mind to the accompaniment of a storm and the wizard's lurid laughter.

Tchaikovsky prevailed upon Shpazhinsky to compress Acts 4 and 5 into a single denouement, so that in the opera all the lethal events occur in the course of the 15-minute finale to Act 4. Despite this maniac conclusion the libretto is extremely wordy, obviously the work of an unmusical dramatist, and resulted in Tchaikovsky's longest opera – though far from his 'biggest' – even with all the numerous post-première abbreviations in place. The composer's lyric genius enabled him somewhat to circumvent the libretto's pitfalls by unifying scenes melodically and pointing them towards long-range musical climaxes, in this way somewhat abating their psychological duration. Thus, while *The Enchantress* is sometimes compared with 'kuchkist' opera, thanks to its setting, its many genre pieces, and the tritonish portrayal of the wizard ('à la Musorgsky'), the comparison is superficial: a truly kuchkist – i.e. declamatory – setting of this particular libretto would have been, if not unthinkable, intolerable.

RICHARD TARUSKIN

Ende-Andriessen, Pelagie. *See* GREEFF-ANDRIESSEN, PELAGIE.

Enderlein, Erik (Emil) (*b* Dresden, 18 Feb 1887; *d* after 1928). German tenor. He sang as a lyric tenor from 1912 to 1917 at the Dresden Hofoper. After a year in Schwerin he moved to Hamburg, where he remained until 1926. His voice had by then become a Heldentenor and in 1925 he sang Walther (*Die Meistersinger*) at Bayreuth. The following year he was engaged at the Städtische Oper, Berlin, and began a series of guest performances at the Vienna Staatsoper. In 1927–8 he sang Parsifal and Siegfried (*Götterdämmerung*) at the open-air theatre in Zoppot.   ELIZABETH FORBES

Endrèze [Kraeckmann], **Arthur** (*b* Chicago, 28 Nov 1893; *d* Chicago, 15 April 1975). American baritone. He studied in Paris with Jean de Reszke and made his début in 1925 at Nice as Don Giovanni. In 1928 he sang Karnac in *Le roi d'Ys* at the Opéra-Comique, then in 1929 he was engaged at the Paris Opéra, making his début as Valentin (*Faust*). He also sang Nevers (*Les Huguenots*), Athanaël (*Thaïs*), Herod (*Hérodiade*), Hamlet, Mercutio, Telramund, Kurwenal, Iago, Amonasro, Germont and Rigoletto. He created Mosca in Sauguet's *La chartreuse de Parme* (1939) and sang Creon in the first Paris performance of Milhaud's *Médée* (1940). At Monte Carlo he sang Nilakantha (*Lakmé*), Scarpia and the Duke of Kilmarnock in Alfano's *L'ultimo lord* (1932) and created Metternich in Honegger and Ibert's *L'aiglon* (1937). In 1946 he made his farewell at the Opéra as Jacob in Méhul's *Joseph*. He had a warm, lyrical voice especially well suited to the French repertory.   ELIZABETH FORBES

Enescu, George [Enesco, Georges] (*b* Liveni-Vîrnav [now George Enescu], Botoşani district, 19 Aug 1881; *d* Paris, 3 or 4 May 1955). Romanian composer. He began to play the violin at the age of four and to compose a year later; he studied at the conservatory of the Gesellschaft der Musikfreunde in Vienna, 1888–94, and at the Paris Conservatoire, 1895–9, where his composition teachers included Fauré and Massenet. His reputation as a violinist, chamber musician and conductor advanced swiftly. He was active chiefly in Paris but also in Bucharest, where he did much to foster Romanian musical life. In 1921 he conducted the performance of *Lohengrin* which inaugurated the Romanian Opera of Bucharest as a state-owned company. In 1920 he was elected president of the Romanian Composers' Society, and did much to encourage a new national school of composition, being considered the guiding spirit of Romanian music even after his death. But he had never ceased to work abroad, as both performer and teacher; it was in Paris, at the Opéra, that his only opera, the *tragédie lyrique Oedipe* (4, E. Fleg, after Sophocles) had its première on 13 March 1936. First sketched in 1910, the work was composed mainly between 1921 and 1931 and is commonly regarded by Enescu's compatriots as a supreme peak in Romanian music. It still, however, awaits the international recognition that it deserves, as one of the great operas of the 20th century.

See also OEDIPE.

*

G. Enescu: *Les souvenirs de Georges Enesco*, ed. B. Gavoty (Paris, 1955; as *Contrepoint dans le miroir*, 1982)

L. Voiculescu: *George Enescu şi opera sa Oedip* (Bucharest, 1956)

F. Foni, N. Missir, M. Voicana and E. Zottoviceanu: *George Enescu* (Bucharest, 1964) [with bibliography, pp.379–434]

B. Kotlyarov: *George Enescu* (Moscow, 1965, enlarged 2/1970; Eng. trans., as *Enesco*, 1984)

O. L. Cosma: *Oedipul enescian* [Enescu's *Oedipe*] (Bucharest, 1967)

E. Ciomac: *Enescu* (Bucharest, 1968)

M. Voicana, ed.: *George Enescu: monografie* (Bucharest, 1971) [with bibliography, pp. 1157–220]

G. Enescu: *Scrisori* [Letters], ed. V. Cosma (Bucharest, 1974–)

P. Bentoiu: *Capodopere enesciene* [Enescu's Masterpieces] (Bucharest, 1984)

M. Roşu, ed.: *Simpozion George Enescu* (Bucharest, 1984)

N. Malcolm: *George Enescu: his Life and Music* (London, 1990)
          VIOREL COSMA, JOHN C. G. WATERHOUSE

Enfant et les sortilèges, L' ('The Child and the Spells'). *Fantaisie lyrique* in one act by MAURICE RAVEL to a libretto by COLETTE; Monte Carlo, 21 March 1925.

The Child	mezzo-soprano
Mother	contralto
The Louis XV Chair [*La Bergère*]	soprano
The Chinese Cup	mezzo-contralto
The Fire/The Princess/The Nightingale	soprano
The Female Cat	mezzo-soprano
The Dragonfly	mezzo-soprano
The Bat	soprano
The Owl	soprano
The Squirrel	mezzo-soprano
A Shepherdess	soprano
A Shepherd	contralto
The Armchair	bass
The Grandfather Clock	baritone
The Teapot (Black Wedgwood)	tenor
The Little Old Man (Arithmetic)/The Frog	tenor ('Trial')
The Tomcat	baritone
A Tree	bass

Settle, Sofa, Ottoman, Wicker Chair, Numbers, Shepherds, Shepherdesses, Frogs, Animals, Trees

Setting An old-fashioned country house and its garden

During World War I Jacques Rouché, the newly appointed director of the Paris Opéra, asked Colette to write the scenario for a fairy ballet, and she accepted with enthusiasm his suggestion of Ravel as collaborator. A copy of her libretto finally reached Ravel in 1918, and the following year he wrote to her, touching on one or two details of what he now envisaged as an opera, but progress was held up by his poor health and by work on the Sonata for violin and cello. At some point the initiative passed from the Paris Opéra to that of Monte Carlo, where Raoul Gunsbourg had mounted a highly successful production of *L'heure espagnole* and was keen to have a sequel. Ravel worked unremittingly on *L'enfant* throughout 1924 and the early months of 1925, and it was ready just in time for the première (five days before it he was writing to Colette, asking her for words to fit a few recently composed bars). The work was conducted by Victor de Sabata, with ballet sequences by the young Balanchine.

After an enthusiastic reception in Monte Carlo, the opera was first given in Paris by the Opéra-Comique on 1 February 1926. Colette wrote that it was 'playing twice a week before a packed but turbulent house … The modernists applaud, and shout down the others, and during the "meeowed" duet there's a fearful uproar'. Performances followed in Brussels ten days later, in Prague and Leipzig in 1927, in Vienna in 1929, in San Francisco in 1930 and at the Paris Opéra in 1939. It reached London in a production at Sadler's Wells in 1965–6, although a series of amateur staged performances had been given by the Oxford University Opera Club in 1958. It was not seen at the Metropolitan until 1981, when it was conducted by Ravel's friend and pupil Manuel Rosenthal, with sets by David Hockney.

'*L'enfant et les sortilèges*' (Ravel): model of the set for scene 1, designed by Alphonse Visconti for the original production at the Opéra, Monte Carlo, 21 March 1925

SCENE 1 *A low-ceilinged room in the house, giving on to the garden; midday* Before the curtain rises, two oboes are heard playing a succession of perfect 4ths and 5ths with apparent aimlessness. As the curtain rises, the audience discerns the relevance of this aimlessness to the predicament of the Child, 'en pleine crise de paresse' in front of his homework. But as might be expected from Ravel, the aimlessness is carefully structured, with the same paragraph returning first at the rise of the curtain, then at the first words of the Child and at the entrance of the Mother. However, Ravel deliberately withholds any firm tonal basis at this juncture.

The Child resists motherly encouragement to apply himself and finally sticks his tongue out at her. She responds by giving him tea with no sugar, bread with no butter and a long period until dinner-time in which to reflect on his behaviour. Alone, the Child indulges in an orgy of destruction and cruelty, smashing cups and torturing his pet Squirrel and Tomcat, to bitonal sounds from the piano. Exhausted, he is about to sink into an Armchair when it moves away from him, 'hobbling like an enormous toad', and launches into a duet in minuet rhythm with the Louis XV Chair. Other objects follow suit and sing of the sufferings they have endured at the hands of the little monster, who has kicked holes in the Armchair, pulled the pendulum out of the Grandfather Clock, spilt the kettle on the Fire and reduced both wallpaper and storybook to tatters. All this allows free rein to Ravel's unparalleled gift for parody, but his increase in dramatic control since *L'heure espagnole* (composed 1907–9) may be seen in the gradual efflorescence of emotion, beginning with the song of the Shepherds and Shepherdesses on the wallpaper, growing through the aria of the storybook Princess (a duet with solo flute in which the previous uneasy bitonality resolves into a modal C minor) and culminating in the Child's brief but heart-stopping monologue ('Toi, le coeur de la rose') in a wholly uninflected E♭ major. Ravel based these 20 bars, according to Manuel Rosenthal, on the 'Air de la table' from Massenet's *Manon*.

In his desolation, the Child gives a kick to his mathematics primer on the floor. Out of it springs a host of Numbers, marshalled by the Little Old Man, who proceeds to spout the traditional problems posed by taps running into reservoirs, even if his grasp of arithmetic ('four and four make eighteen') is not beyond ques-

tion. The ensemble reaches a dizzying climax before the tormentors finally retire, leaving the Child once more exhausted. The moon now comes out, and by its light the black Tomcat in the room and his white mate in the garden sing a duet, not in human language (both Colette and Ravel, as cat-lovers, knew that no cat would thus demean itself) but in a variety of 'miinhous', 'môrnâous' and 'moâous' on the linguistic accuracy of which Ravel lavished the greatest care. As the Tomcat joins his beloved, the careful pastiche begins to take on a new depth, with threateningly irrational glissandos in the brass; and as the bitonality yet again resolves, this time on to bare, widely spaced 5ths on the strings, the scene moves outside into the garden.

SCENE 2 *The garden* In the second half of the opera the denizens of the garden pursue their complaints against the Child: first the Trees whose bark he has cut into with a knife, then the Dragonfly and the Bat whose mates he has killed. The distinction between the normally inanimate trees and their animate successors is simply made by a change of time signature, and the new waltz rhythm takes the music on into the only extended orchestral passage in the opera, the Frogs' Dance. Here, to strains reminiscent of the *Valses nobles et sentimentales* and *La valse*, Ravel cleverly offers the audience a respite from wordplay, as well as setting apart the crucial entry of the Squirrel, whom the Child released during his first fit of temper. The Squirrel is physically unharmed, but now he mourns the lost years of imprisonment in yet another preparation for the true emotional climax of the work. The Child, realizing suddenly the wealth of love between the animals from which he is excluded, utters the talismanic word 'Maman!' to Ravel's favourite descending 4th.

At once, sensing his fear and loneliness, the animals turn on him, but in the mêlée the Squirrel is wounded. The Child for the first time in the opera is able to find a point of entry into the 'paradis de tendresse' and ties up the Squirrel's wounded paw with a ribbon. Overcome with amazement at this loving act, the animals gently lead the Child back to the house as they try to imitate the strange human noise that had been the signal for their fury. Mostly they fail to get the interval right, and it is the full orchestra that sets them straight, resolving the bitonal pressures for the last time and grounding the music in its final tonality for the opera's emotional climax. As the animals begin a fugal hymn to the Child's kindness, a light comes on in the house. The oboes of the opening return, now comfortingly supported by G major harmonies, and with his final cry of 'Maman!' the Child's spiritual journey is at an end.

* * *

Ravel told his friend Hélène Jourdan-Morhange that *L'enfant* contained everything: Massenet, Puccini, Monteverdi and American musical comedy. This, together with his earlier admission that he was 'transported by the idea of having two negroes singing ragtime at the Paris Opéra', has sometimes led critics to miss the profoundly serious feeling at the heart of this vivid and entertaining work. In answer to those who complained that his music was artificial, Ravel said: 'Does it not occur to these people that I may be artificial by nature?' In *L'enfant et les sortilèges* Ravel summons up all the artifices of his transcendent technique to reach both Nature and what is most natural in our childhood selves.

ROGER NICHOLS

Engel, (A.) Lehman (*b* Jackson, MS, 14 Sept 1910; *d* New York, 29 Aug 1982). American composer and conductor. He attended the University of Cincinnati and studied composition at the Cincinnati College of Music, where his one-act opera *Pierrot of the Minute* was produced on 3 April 1929. The libretto (inspired by Ernest Dowson) is pastoral, the music decoratively chromatic in the French manner. Subsequent studies in New York with Goldmark and Sessions imparted a more Germanic character to his work. From the early 1930s he devoted himself to writing incidental music for plays, dance scores for Martha Graham and other choreographers, and various vocal and instrumental pieces.

As a conductor Engel is best known for his work in the musical theatre. In addition to Broadway shows, he conducted the premières of Weill's *Johnny Johnson* (1936), Copland's *The Second Hurricane*(1937) and Menotti's *The Consul* (1950). This activity left a mark on the two one-act operas he composed to librettos by the screenwriter Lewis Allan; both are notable for their theatrical effectiveness rather than any independent musical interest. *Malady of Love* (vs, New York, 1954), a slight but cleverly drawn comedy about a patient who seduces her psychoanalyst, was given on 27 May 1954 at Brander Matthews Theater by the Columbia University Opera Workshop. The jazzy, eclectic score contrasts with that of *The Soldier* (vs, New York, 1956), a dark, expressionist psychodrama based on Roald Dahl's short story about a deranged soldier struggling to readjust to civilian life. Engel's music veers nightmarishly between a dissonant, angular idiom and diatonic, Broadway-like episodes for the soldier's flashbacks. The opera was first given, in concert form, at Carnegie Hall on 25 November 1956. Engel's MSS and papers are at Yale University.

HARRY HASKELL

Engel, Stientje. *See* DEUTEKOM, CRISTINA.

Engelmann, Hans Ulrich (*b* Darmstadt, 8 Sept 1921). German composer. He initially studied architecture and then changed to composition, studying with Fortner, Leibowitz and Krenek. He also read musicology and took the doctorate in 1952 with a study of Bartók. From 1954 to 1961 Engelmann was musical adviser to Gustav Rudolf Sellner at the Darmstadt Landestheater, writing his first operas and much incidental music. Lengthy visits abroad took him to Iceland (1953–4) and Rome (as holder of the Villa Massimo scholarship, 1960 and 1967). He later taught composition in Frankfurt.

Engelmann began composing in an atonal style directly after World War II. He discovered Schoenberg and Webern for himself in 1948, and wrote 12-note and serial music, extending his range to include aleatory and graphic composition from the 1960s. His colourful instrumentation, his feeling for direct musical effect and his partiality for music drama kept his music from becoming over-intellectual. Engelmann's numerous stage works include seven operas, several ballets and many pieces of incidental music and entr'actes for plays. His first was the burlesque chamber opera *Doktor Fausts Höllenfahrt*, composed in 1949. This piece, lasting barely an hour and borrowing from the Italian *commedia dell'arte* tradition, comes into the same category as such similar, simply constructed works as Henze's *Das Wundertheater*. *Der Fall van Damm*, which was commissioned by Westdeutscher Rundfunk, concerns the problem of capital punishment, applied to the case of a man condemned to death in several successive trials; the sentence is finally carried out after innumerable stays of execution. The stage première of 1974 had a mixed reception: the character of the music, with its suggestion of epic narrative and commentary, does not really demand staged performance. Engelmann's next opera, *Ophelia*, was a multi-media drama for female mime with chamber ensemble, chamber chorus and tape, using themes from Shakespeare's *Hamlet*. The music drama *Revue*, commissioned by the Bonn Opera, has almost no plot, yet adheres to traditional theatrical methods and introduces Prospero as the audience's guide.

Doktor Fausts Höllenfahrt op.4, 1949–50 (Kammeroper, 1, Klabund [A. Henschke]), Norddeutscher Rundfunk, 11 Jan 1951
Magog op.16, 1955–6 (A. Müller), unperf.
Operette, 1959 (3, M. Kutter), unperf.
Der verlorene Schatten op.22, 1960 (2, after A. von Chamisso: *Peter Schlemihl*), unperf.
Der Fall van Damm op.30, 1966–7 (Funkoper, 3, Kutter), Westdeutscher Rundfunk, 7 June 1968; stage, Münster, 1974
Ophelia op.36 (multi-media drama, M. Goldschmidt, after W. Shakespeare: *Hamlet*), Hanover, 1 Feb 1969; rev. as Musikationstheater, Berlin, 15 May 1970
Revue op.43 (music drama, 2, W. Swaczynna), Bonn, 24 Oct 1973

*

U. Dibelius: 'Hans Ulrich Engelmann', *Melos*, xxxviii (1971), 382–3
U. Stürzbecher: *Werkstattgespräche mit Komponisten* (Cologne, 1971), 161ff

WULF KONOLD

Engen, Keith [Kieth] (*b* Frazee, MN, 5 April 1925). American bass. He studied at Berkeley and in Vienna. After making his début in 1954 at Graz, he joined the Staatsoper in Munich in 1955; he made his Covent Garden début in 1956 as Sarastro and in 1958 sang King Henry at Bayreuth. He created roles in Hindemith's *Die Harmonie der Welt* (1957, Munich), Orff's *Prometheus* (1968, Stuttgart), Bialas's *Aucassin und Nicolette* (1969, Munich) and Cikker's *The Play of Love and Death* (1969, Munich). His repertory included Don Alfonso, Colline, Zuniga and Monteverdi's Seneca, but he excelled in contemporary parts: the Doctor (*Wozzeck*), Würfl (*Excursions of Mr Brouček*), La Roche (*Capriccio*), Wesener (*Die Soldaten*) and the title role of Krenek's *Karl V*.

ELIZABETH FORBES

England. For discussion of opera in England *see* GREAT BRITAIN, §§1–3.

English Bach Festival. Organization founded by Lina Lalandi in 1963 that has staged several early operas in period performances; *see* LONDON, §II,3.

English Cat, The. A story for singers and instrumentalists in two acts by HANS WERNER HENZE to a text by EDWARD BOND after Honoré de Balzac's *Peines de coeur d'une chatte anglaise*; Schwetzingen, 2 June 1983 (in German translation).

Minette *the cat*	soprano
Babette *her sister (cat)*	mezzo-soprano
Tom *(cat)*	baritone
Lord Puff *President of the RSPR (cat)*	tenor
Arnold *his nephew (cat)*	bass
Louise *member of the RSPR (mouse)*	soprano
Miss Crisp ⎫	soprano
Mrs Gomfit ⎬ *members of the RSPR (cats)*	soprano
Lady Toodle ⎭	mezzo-soprano
Peter *Tom's friend (cat)*/Mr Keen *(cat)*/Counsel for the Defence *(dog)*/Lucian *(fox)*/The Parson *(sheep)*	tenor
Mr Jones *the money-lender (cat)*/Mr Fawn *(cat)*/The Judge *(dog)*	bass-baritone
Mr Plunkett *member of the RSPR (cat)*/Counsel for the Prosecution *(dog)*	bass-baritone

Moon, stars, serenaders, members of the jury (chorus parts played by members of cast)

Henze's third collaboration with Bond after *We Come to the River* (1976) and the full-length ballet *Orpheus* (1979) was the result of a joint commission from the Schwetzingen Festival and the Wurttemberg Staatstheater. In 1977 Henze had seen in Paris a stage version of Balzac's epistolary tale *Peines de coeur d'une chatte anglaise* and quickly perceived its operatic possibilities. He put the idea to Bond who produced his own version of the text, transferring the action to 1890s London and giving it a Brechtian satirical edge, evidently envisaging it as a ballad opera with spoken dialogue and independent musical numbers. The libretto was completed in 1979, and Henze worked on the music from March 1980 until April 1983. Henze himself directed the first staging at Schwetzingen, which was conducted by Dennis Russell Davies; the cast included Inge Nielsen as Minette, Elisabeth Glauser as Babette, Wolfgang Schöne as Tom and Martin Finke as Lord Puff. Davies also conducted the French première at the Opéra-Comique in 1984. The first performance using Bond's original English text took place at Santa Fe on 13 July 1985, conducted by George Manahan.

Although the opera received a number of productions during the late 1980s, especially in 1986 – the year of Henze's 60th birthday, the composer continued to have misgivings about its proportions. Following criticism, he shortened the second act substantially in 1990; he conducted and directed the première of this revision at Montepulciano in July 1990, a production that was taken to London in January 1991.

ACT 1.i *Mrs Halifax's drawing-room* The members of the RSPR, the Royal Society for the Protection of Rats, await the arrival of Minette, the prospective bride of their president-elect Lord Puff. As a pedigree cat he is obliged to marry and continue the line. Though Arnold expresses his misgivings in a *Gassenhauer*, a street song, the RSPR agrees to accept God's will over the suitability of the match. Babette vets Lord Puff as a future

brother-in-law while Arnold's cabaletta reveals his private reasons for opposing the marriage: were there to be any offspring he would be disinherited. Minette finally appears and in a cavatina, 'The world is wide', exemplifies both her empty-headedness and the high, demanding coloratura that characterizes all her vocal writing. The RSPR demonstrates its caring attitude to rats, brandishing the orphan Louise as an example of its solicitude, much to Babette's disdain. She tries to persuade her sister to leave while Arnold and the society contemplate the devil and all his smiling disguises.

1.ii *The roof of Mrs Halifax's house* An appropriately feline orchestral interlude leads to the sounds of offstage serenaders: Tom and Peter are cruising the rooftops; they are warned off by Minette who continues in her aria to comment upon the sadness of the moonlit night. Tom returns on the pretext of apologizing for trespassing, and just happens to mention in his cavatina that he dreamt of a cat called Minette who cured his ills with a kiss: it does the trick, and the couple sing a duet, 'Why does beauty bring desire?', just before they are discovered by a delighted Arnold. Minette tries to pass Tom off as a new member of the RSPR but he runs off as she calls after him. The moon and stars close the scene with a delicate ensemble, 'The moon walks naked through the night'.

1.iii *Mrs Halifax's private chapel* Arnold presents his creditor, Jones, to Lord Puff; disguised as a doctor, Jones diagnoses Puff as ill, certainly too ill to marry. The Parson, Mr Plunkett and Tom (got up as a curate) arrive for the wedding singing a tongue-in-cheek trio about the joys of marriage. Puff will not be deterred, nor will he drink the poison that Jones offers. The bride enters in procession and the service begins, but it is interrupted by Arnold who, in a dramatic scena, cross-questions Minette about her behaviour on the roof; she claims she was just enrolling Tom in the RSPR. In a final ensemble, 'Ah cruel world where innocence is lost', the characters express their varied reactions to the scandal, but Puff recovers from his shock to press ahead with the ceremony, lest his presidency be threatened.

ACT 2.iv *Mrs Halifax's drawing-room* Babette arrives from the country: in a duettino with her sister, she reveals that their family have been evicted from their house in the country and are destitute, while Minette can only observe that she has become both rich and unfeeling. She gives money to her sister who leaves. Minette reveals that she cannot forget Tom, who is heard offstage singing a ballad, 'An emperor made a fine garden'. He appears at the window, dressed as a soldier: he has deserted, and offers himself to Minette as an orphan. In the 'Promise duet' she quickly yields but then reveals that she expects him to surrender to the authorities and face the consequences. Just as he is prostrate at her feet the RSPR arrives in force, denouncing them in the RSPR waltz. Though Puff would rather forgive her, the society demands a divorce. Minette is locked away to lament her fate, 'Ah little bird in the tree'.

2.v *Divorce court* An orchestral interlude moves the action to the court, where a jury of birds proclaims its faith in the jury system, and the Judge (a dog) asserts his even-handedness. Every time the Defence Counsel (Tom in disguise) attempts to cross-examine the prosecution witnesses the Judge merely increases the damages, and his attempts to prove that the marriage was not consummated increase the financial penalties yet more. When the court adjourns, Tom

'The English Cat' (Henze), Act 1 scene iii (Mrs Halifax's private chapel): scene from the original production at the Schwetzingen Festival, 2 June 1983, showing the wedding ceremony including (left to right) Tom, dressed as a curate (Wolfgang Schöne), Minette (Inge Nielsen), Louise, the mouse (Regina Marheimeke)

explains to Minette how he was flogged in prison yet managed to escape and imprison the real Defence Counsel in the robing room. He throws himself at her feet once again just as everyone returns. When Minette begins to offer her own version of events from the witness box the real Defence Counsel appears, still bound and gagged; an ensemble adds to the general confusion. The Judge orders the jury to find Minette guilty, sets the damages and orders Tom to be arrested. Tom laments his fate to the Prosecuting Counsel, who recognizes him as the long-lost son of one Lord Fairport; he has to claim his inheritance before he reaches 21, which as it happens is the next day, otherwise the estate will pass to the RSPR. The Judge (a school chum of Lord Fairport) reverses all his decisions, and a final trio celebrates the potency of Fate, 'Fate's command is written in the stars and moon'.

2.vi *Mrs Halifax's drawing-room* News of the divorce has reached the country, and when Babette arrives from the country this time it is to find Minette tied in a sack, on the orders of Mrs Halifax who intends to have her drowned to put her out of her misery. Tom arrives with news of his inheritance and his distress at Minette's fate is soothed by his discovery of her sister. Minette can only give the happy couple her blessing and Tom and Babette sing a reprise of the Promise Duet. The RSPR arrives on cue, as Tom throws himself at Minette's feet for the final time; the members try in vain to persuade Tom to give his inheritance to the society, and when he leaves with Babette they launch into a revenge ensemble, a quodlibet, 'He's an impostor!'. Left alone Minette contemplates her fate in a large-scale aria and rondo, 'Alone? Then I wait quietly for the odd-job man'.

2.vii *Lincoln's Inn Fields – lawyer's chambers* Tom is about to sign his will in the presence of the Prosecuting Counsel; he sings of fate and freedom, 'Man makes his world and makes himself'. Before he can sign the document he is stabbed in the back by the clerk Lucian; as he falls to the ground the RSPR arrives and the counsel declares Tom intestate because of his 'suicide'. Everyone celebrates the victory in an octet, 'In cases of this sort': truth will prevail, the RSPR

will get its money, more rats will learn to respect their betters, and the lawyers will make a huge profit. Minette's ghost appears as everyone leaves, and sings a duet with the dying Tom, 'Ah Minette, at last we meet in death'; he dies and the ghost departs. The last word is left to the mouse Louise, ransacking her RSPR collecting box, and damning the society's hypocrisy in a scena and final villanelle: 'I have become a mouse again'.

* * *

Despite the structure of Bond's text, Henze's music is through-composed; his scheme was modelled upon Beethoven's Diabelli Variations, and a quotation from the penultimate variation appears in Tom and Minette's final duet. Each act runs continuously, with instrumental interludes separating the scenes, and the dialogue freely set as recitative. The 'numbers', parodies, pastiches and neoclassical reworkings of popular and art-music forms are embedded in this musical fabric. The overriding satirical detachment implied by Bond is mitigated in Henze's treatment, whose music, in the second act in particular, acquires a dark, pessimistic undertow. The music calls for a large chamber orchestra, with a number of exotica used to characterize the leading characters instrumentally: a chamber organ is associated with Lord Puff, Minette has a zither, Arnold a heckelphone.　　　　ANDREW CLEMENTS

English Eccentrics, The. Chamber opera in two acts by MALCOLM WILLIAMSON to a libretto by GEOFFREY DUNN based on Edith Sitwell's book; Aldeburgh, Jubilee Hall, 11 June 1964.

A series of revue impressions of eccentricity, the work avoids too much restlessness by ending each act with a sustained and emotionally affecting example of its subject. In Act 1 it is the inability of the formerly high-living Sarah Whitehead (soprano) to comprehend her financial disaster. Act 2 scene i introduces Beau Brummell (tenor) as an arbiter of fashion and reputation and ends with his solitary, deluded old age in a boarding house in Caen. Each act has one central scene of comic irrepressibility – Romeo Coates (tenor) as a would-be Shakespearean actor, and the charade of Mary Barker as an exotic princess, Caraboo (soprano) – but each also moves towards pathos. The work was commissioned by the English Opera Group.   ROGER COVELL

English Music Theatre Company. Opera company formed in 1975 from the ENGLISH OPERA GROUP.

English National Opera. Company based in London, known as Sadler's Wells Opera until 1974 and resident at the Coliseum since 1968; see LONDON, §II, 1.

English National Opera North. British opera company based in LEEDS, founded in 1977 and renamed Opera North in 1981.

English Opera Group. A company formed in 1947 by Benjamin Britten, John Piper and Eric Crozier, after the success at Glyndebourne the previous summer of Britten's *The Rape of Lucretia*. The company intended to devote itself 'to the creation and performance of new operas ... and to encourage poets and playwrights to tackle the writing of librettos in collaboration with composers'. The group also staged chamber operas by composers from the past, and works by non-British composers. It was responsible for the foundation and artistic direction of the Aldeburgh Festival, and the formation of an Opera Studio in London, which developed into the Opera School, then into the National School of Opera, and finally the London Opera Centre.

The English Opera Group commissioned and produced a number of new works, including Britten's *Albert Herring*, *The Turn of the Screw*, *A Midsummer Night's Dream*, the three church parables, *Owen Wingrave*, and *Death in Venice*; Berkeley's *A Dinner Engagement*, *Ruth* and *Castaway*; Williamson's *English Eccentrics*; Walton's *The Bear*; Birtwistle's *Punch and Judy*; Crosse's *The Grace of Todd*; John Gardner's *The Visitors*; and Thea Musgrave's *The Voice of Ariadne*. In addition it mounted productions of *Idomeneo*, *Acis and Galatea*, *The Beggar's Opera*, *Iolanta* (Tchaikovsky), *Trial by Jury* and *La rondine*, as well as revivals of works by Purcell and Holst. The group performed throughout Europe, made a successful tour of the USSR in 1964, and appeared in Montreal during Expo 1967. Many leading British singers regularly appeared with it, including Janet Baker, Kathleen Ferrier, Heather Harper, Sylvia Fisher, Jennifer Vyvyan, Owen Brannigan, Peter Pears, John Shirley-Quirk and Robert Tear. In 1961 its management and financial responsibility were taken over by Covent Garden. Steuart Bedford and Colin Graham were appointed musical director and director of productions respectively in 1971.

In 1975 the English Opera Group was expanded and re-formed as the English Music Theatre Company with Bedford and Graham continuing as artistic directors of a permanent ensemble company of 24 soloists, a chorus of 24 and an orchestra of 20. The change in name reflected a broadening of repertory to include opera, operetta, musicals and new commissions. It gave regional tours and an annual season at Sadler's Wells Theatre, and performed at festivals, notably at Aldeburgh. It commissioned and presented (1979) Minoru Miki's *Ada* (under the title *An Actor's Revenge*) at the Old Vic, but ceased to function in 1980.   HAROLD ROSENTHAL

English Opera House. Name given to the Lyceum, a London theatre, at various times in the 19th century; see LONDON, §II, 2.

English Touring Opera. Name adopted in 1992 by OPERA 80.

Enna, August (Emil) (*b* Nakskov, 13 May 1859; *d* Copenhagen, 3 Aug 1939). Danish composer of Italian-German descent. At the age of 18, after working at a variety of jobs (including shoemaking, his father's trade), he began seriously to learn to play the violin and the piano; as a composer, he was essentially self-taught. As early as 1880 he had been a music director for dramatic performances, for some of which he also composed the music. He became a member of the town orchestra in Björneborg, Finland, but in 1883 returned to Denmark to become music director of Werner's Theatrical Society, a provincial touring company. By 1884 he had composed his first opera, *Agleia*. He was awarded the Anckerske Legat, which enabled him in 1888–9 to work in Flensburg on what was to become one of his best-known operatic works, *Heksen* ('The Witch'). This was produced in 1892 and was subsequently performed abroad. With *Kleopatra* in 1894, Enna's reputation as an operatic composer was firmly established. He continued to produce operas, as well as operettas, incidental music and other instrumental and vocal works. While his music is not specially profound, it derives inspiration from Wagner and Verdi, as well as from the Danish Romantic tradition. His sensitivity to theatrical nuance, effective orchestration and easy melodic gift earned him considerable success.

En idyl (operetta), 1881
En landsbyhistorie [A Village Tale] (operetta), Copenhagen, Frederiksbergs, 1883
Agleia (2, T. Andersen), 1884
Areta (operetta), 1884
Heksen [The Witch] (4, A. Ipsen, after A. Fitger), Copenhagen, Kongelige, 24 Jan 1892, vs (Copenhagen, 1892)
Kleopatra (3, E. Christiansen, after H. R. Haggard), Copenhagen, Kongelige, 7 Feb 1894, vs (Copenhagen, 1893)
Aucassin og Nicolette (4, S. Michaëlis), Copenhagen, Kongelige, 2 Feb 1896, vs (Copenhagen, 1897)
Den lille pige med svolstikkerne [The Little Match Girl] (1, O. Rode, after H. C. Andersen), Copenhagen, 13 Nov 1897, vs (Copenhagen, 1897)
Lamia (prol., 2, H. Rode, after P. Mariager), Antwerp, 3 Oct 1899
Prinsessen på ærten [The Princess on the Pea] (1, P. A. Rosenberg, after H. C. Andersen), Århus, 15 Sept 1900, vs (Copenhagen, 1902)
Ung elskov [Young Love], 1902 (Rosenberg, after K. Mikszath), Weimar, 6 Dec 1904, vs (Leipzig, 1903)
Nattergalen [The Nightingale] (3, K. Friis-Møller, after H. C. Andersen), Copenhagen, 10 Nov 1912, vs (Copenhagen, n.d.)
Gloria Arsena (4, O. Hansen, after A. Dumas *père*), Copenhagen, 15 April 1917, vs (Copenhagen, 1917)
Komedianter [The Actors], 1917 (prol., 3, Enna and Hansen, after V. Hugo: *L'homme qui rit*), Copenhagen, 8 April 1920, vs (Copenhagen, 1920)
Børnene fra Santa Fe [The Children from Santa Fe] (Enna and Hansen), 1918
Don Juan Marana, 1922 (3, Enna, after Dumas *père*), Copenhagen, 17 April 1925, vs (Copenhagen, 1925)
Afrodites praestinde [Aphrodite's Priestess], 1925
Ghettoens dronning [The Queen of the Ghetto], 1932 (2), *DK-Kk**

*

G. Lynge: *Danske komponister i det tyvende aarhundret begyndelse* (Copenhagen and Århus, 2/1917), 67–85
K. A. Wieth-Knudsen: 'August Enna som dramatisk komponist', *Musik: Tidsskrift för Tonekunst*, iv/June (1920), 79–84
K. Å. Bruun: *Dansk Musiks Historie*, ii (Copenhagen, 1969), 293–6
'Enna, August', *Sohlmans musiklexikon* (Stockholm, 1975)
              WILLIAM H. REYNOLDS

Enschede. City in the Overijssel province in the eastern Netherlands. After the German occupation of the Netherlands in World War II ended, there was considerable operatic activity: the Stichting De Nederlandsche Opera, based in Amsterdam, concentrated its activities in the densely populated western provinces; and in the eastern and northern provinces two small troupes, the Nederlandse Reisopera and the Kameropera Camerata, merged forming Opera Forum, a touring opera company. Founded by Chris Burgers, who remained its general administrator until 1973, it made the newly completed Twentse Schouwburg in Enschede its base, giving up to 200 performances annually and instigating numerous educational projects. Since 1973 there has been no permanent company of soloists; international and Dutch singers are contracted for each production. More recently the ballet troupe was disbanded and the number of performances, especially in Enschede, reduced; in the 1989–90 season, under the general direction of Peter Westerhoud, Opera Forum gave 100 performances of six works (one in concert form) in 30 cities. The Twentse Schouwburg, renovated in 1985, with 898 seats and a balcony, is also the site of the Cristina Deutekom Competition for opera singers.

*

S. A. M. Bottenheim: *Opera in Nederland* (Leiden, 1983)

MICHAEL DAVIDSON

Ensemble. In opera contexts, the German 'das Ensemble' means the singing personnel of an opera house; the term is more often used, however, in the sense of the French 'morceau d'ensemble', a piece sung by more than one member of the cast. Short ensembles for a variety of characters, some in the nature of brief interjections, were frequent in 17th-century Italian and French opera; with reforms to the *opera seria* in the early 18th century reducing the number of characters and the increasingly defined formal structure of the post-Lullian *tragédie en musique*, ensembles became rare in serious genres while remaining important in comic works. Although techniques and styles of comic concerted writing were carried over into serious works, it is in the comic sphere that the ensemble has attracted the richest and most varied treatment.

In all genres the duet is the most common type of ensemble, especially for pairs of lovers, whether united, reconciled, forced to part or placed in some other situation giving rise to strong emotional expression. Larger ensembles are included more freely in various genres from about the middle of the 18th century onwards as composers and librettists begin to recognize and explore their unique and varied dramatic potential, resulting in more adventurous character groupings, vocal textures and formal structures. Traditional ensemble finales likewise grow from short, homophonic choruses for the assembled principals (often marked 'coro') to extensive, multi-sectional movements leading the dramatic intrigue to its climax and resolution. The chain (or *buffo*) finale is first encountered in a 1749 collaboration by Baldassare Galuppi and Goldoni, *L'Arcadia in Brenta*; at the end of the century it is treated with most sophistication in Mozart's operas.

A unique feature of the operatic ensemble is its ability to telescope dramatic events through the simultaneous expression of conflicting emotions, thereby increasing the dramatic momentum of a work and offsetting its contrasting characters more vividly. Such pieces often involve several singers and, designed to maximize confusion and bring matters to a climax, are commonly termed ensembles of confusion or perplexity. Their construction demands skill in achieving a distinct diversity of language and music within a prevailing unity,

techniques also employed in action ensembles that embody development or sudden change in the dramatic intrigue. These similarly raised the status of the ensemble from the second half of the 18th century onwards, in allowing the setting to music of events earlier entrusted to recitative or dialogue. Perhaps the most common type of ensemble, however, is that which creates a tableau in which the characters comment on the state of events reached. One notable example is the quartet 'Mir ist so wunderbar' in Beethoven's *Fidelio*, where to the same music, sung in canon, one person expresses love, another alarm at the developing situation, a third jealousy and a fourth benignity: the action momentarily halts as the emotions of the characters are exposed. Outstanding later examples include the sextet in *Lucia di Lammermoor*, the quartet in *Rigoletto*, the septet in *Les Troyens* and the quintet in *Die Meistersinger*.

See also CHORUS; DUET; FINALE; QUARTET; QUINTET; SEPTET; SEXTET; and TRIO.

*

E. Dent: 'Ensembles and Finales in Eighteenth-Century Italian Opera', *SIMG*, xi (1909–10), 543–69; xii (1910–11), 112–38

C. E. Koch: 'The Dramatic Ensemble Finale in the Opéra Comique of the Eighteenth Century', *AcM*, xxxix/1–2 (1967), 72–83

L. I. Wade: *The Dramatic Functions of the Ensemble in the Operas of Wolfgang Amadeus Mozart* (diss., Louisiana State U., 1969)

D. Heartz: 'The Creation of the Buffo Finale in Italian Opera', *PRMA*, civ (1977–8), 67–78

H. Becker: 'Das Duett in der Oper', *Musik, Edition, Interpretation: Gedenkschrift Günter Henle* (Munich, 1980), 82–99

F. Blanchetti: 'Tipologia musicale dei concertati nell'opera buffa di Giovanni Paisiello', *RIM*, xix (1984), 234–60

J. Platoff: *Music and Drama in the Opera Buffa Finale: Mozart and his Contemporaries in Vienna, 1781–1790* (diss., U. of Pennsylvania, 1984)

E. Cook: *The Operatic Ensemble in France, 1673–1775* (diss., U. of East Anglia, 1989)

ELISABETH COOK

Entführung aus dem Serail, Die ('The Abduction from the Seraglio'). Singspiel in three acts, K384, by WOLFGANG AMADEUS MOZART to a libretto by CHRISTOPH FRIEDRICH BRETZNER (*Belmont und Constanze, oder Die Entführung aus dem Serail*), adapted and enlarged by GOTTLIEB STEPHANIE the Younger; Vienna, Burgtheater, 16 July 1782.

Selim *Pasha*	spoken
Konstanze *a Spanish lady, Belmonte's betrothed*	soprano
Blonde *Konstanze's English maid*	soprano
Belmonte *a Spanish nobleman*	tenor
Pedrillo *servant of Belmonte, now supervisor of the Pasha's gardens*	tenor
Osmin *overseer of the Pasha's country house*	bass
Klaas *a sailor*	spoken
Mute *in Osmin's service*	silent

Chorus of Janissaries, guards

Setting The country palace of Pasha Selim, on the Mediterranean coast in an unidentified part of the Turkish Empire

Dismissed from service with the Archbishop of Salzburg, Mozart must have felt satisfaction in writing to his father on 1 August 1781: 'the day before yesterday Stephanie junior gave me a libretto to compose'. Gottlieb Stephanie, director of the National Singspiel, wanted Bretzner's *Belmont und Constanze* set quickly for the visit in September of the Russian Grand Duke Paul Petrovich. Bretzner was a popular librettist, whose name assured interest (*Belmont und Constanze* had been set in Berlin by Johann André). Yet with the postponement of the royal visit (it eventually took place in November, when Gluck's operas were played), *Die Entführung* might have suffered the fate of *Zaide* had not Stephanie and, no doubt, the singers maintained support for Mozart. Mozart had already composed much of Act 1, and he wrote in detail to his father on 26 September about the arias for Valentin Adamberger (Belmonte), Ludwig Fischer (Osmin) and Catarina Cavalieri (Konstanze).

Since time was available, he urged Stephanie to enlarge Act 1. By adding an aria at the beginning for Belmonte and making Osmin's opening number a duet, Mozart virtually turned Bretzner's opening dialogue, with Osmin's song originally its only music, into a continuous introduction. He established Osmin as a major force with 'Solche hergelauf'ne Laffen' (Mozart sent Stephanie the music for words to be added), and wrote the overture, musically linked with the opening aria. His comments to his father concerning Osmin's and Belmonte's arias, 'Solche hergelauf'ne Laffen' and 'O wie ängstlich', contain some of his most important recorded views on operatic aesthetics (*see* MOZART, WOLFGANG AMADEUS). The Janissary chorus is 'short, lively and written to please the Viennese'; he also admitted that he had 'sacrificed Konstanze's aria ('Ach ich liebte') a little to the flexible throat of Mlle Cavalieri'.

Mozart and Stephanie recast the remaining two acts more extensively. The women and Osmin received one additional aria each ('Martern aller Arten', 'Welche Wonne' and 'O, wie will ich triumphieren'), while Belmonte received two (the second, opening Act 3, often cut in modern performances or nonsensically replaced by the first). They devised a new situation for a long ensemble (finale to Act 2) and a new dénouement: the libretto thus remains essentially Bretzner's (he alone was credited on the original playbill and libretto), but with significant differences. Mozart began setting a quintet which, in Bretzner, covers the whole elopement scene. The loss of such an extended action ensemble is tantalizing; doubtless it was rejected because it could not form a finale. Instead the elopement is in dialogue and reaches a musical climax only after its failure, with Osmin's aria. The enhanced importance of Osmin sharpens the oriental setting and makes him a tangible menace; whether this change resulted from, or merely took advantage of, Fischer's immense range and full deep notes, is impossible to determine.

Mozart finished the score in April 1782. Rehearsals began in June and, despite some delays, an alleged cabal and the difficulty of the music, the first performance was a success. Besides those mentioned above, Johann Ernst Dauer sang Pedrillo and Therese Teyber Blonde. Performances continued until the closure of the National Singspiel early in 1783; the German company at the Kärntnertor revived it (1784–5) with Mozart's sister-in-law Aloysia Lange as Konstanze.

The fame of the new opera spread rapidly. The second production, also in 1782, was in Prague, which at once took Mozart to its heart (the first performance in Czech was not until 1829). *Die Entführung* was the foundation of Mozart's reputation outside Austria. In 1783 there were productions in Warsaw, Bonn (under Neefe, Beethoven possibly assisting), Frankfurt and Leipzig.

Depiction of a reported incident in which Mozart attended (and vociferously criticized) a performance of his 'Die Entführung aus dem Serail' in Berlin (19 May 1789): aquatint by Franz Hegi (1774–1850) presumably after an unknown original (the individual flats of the scenery can clearly be seen)

The first translation (Polish) followed in November, again at Warsaw. In 1784 there were productions in Mannheim, Carlsruhe, Cologne and Salzburg; Dresden, Munich and other German cities followed in 1785. It was given in some 40 centres in Germany and the Austrian Empire, and reached Amsterdam in Mozart's lifetime. The second foreign language used was Dutch (1797, Amsterdam), the third French (1798, Paris, in a version by Gluck's librettist Moline); it was also the first opera ever heard in German in Paris (1801). In Moscow it was given in 1810 in Russian (St Petersburg following in 1816) and in 1820 in German.

The first London performance, in English, was at Covent Garden in 1827, the score arranged by C. Kramer with an altered plot; the setting was moved by the translator, W. Dimond, to a Greek island. Such alterations were standard in 19th-century revivals. In Paris the 1859 revival to a translation by Prosper Pascal reordered several numbers and gave 'Martern aller Arten' to Blonde (no less a Mozartian than Beecham placed this aria in Act 3). Later in this century London also saw it in German and Italian (the title *Il Seraglio* is still often used in English). The American première was in New York in 1860, probably in German. An attempt to produce it in 1840 in Milan came to nothing. The Italian première was not until 1935, in Florence, by which time the 20th-century revival of Mozart was under way; it had already appeared at Glyndebourne.

The background is the territorial and cultural intersection of the Islamic lands and the older Christian civilization of Europe, especially Spain; Belmonte's father is Governor of Oran on the coast of North Africa. A major stimulus for artistic interest in things Turkish was the menacing but in the end unsuccessful siege of Vienna in 1683, but the action evokes an earlier period when piracy was rife and crossing between religions not uncommon; Pasha Selim is a renegade Christian.

The overture is a bubbling Allegro in C major, its 'Turkish' style martial and colourful yet, in Mozart's hands, subject to abrupt changes of mood; a promising crescendo lurches into the dominant minor, anticipating the confusion of the action to come. A slow middle section in C minor brings a foretaste of sentiment, its melody by turns hesitant and passionate, richly clothed in woodwind sound. The Allegro resumes, ending on the dominant.

ACT 1 *A plaza before Selim's palace, near the sea* A major-key version of the middle section of the overture ('Hier soll ich dich denn sehen') forms a short aria by the standards of this opera, but after a hesitating start its lyrical cadences convey Belmonte's ardent desire for reunion with Konstanze. Osmin brings a ladder, and begins picking figs; he sings a moral Volkslied (lied and duet, 'Wer ein Liebchen hat gefunden': 'Whoever finds a lover, let him beware'). When Belmonte speaks Osmin refuses to answer, directing the later verses at him instead: plausible strangers bring danger to lovers. Belmonte now sings, wrenching the tempo to Allegro, but the wrath of the Turk, enraged by mention of Pedrillo, dominates the ensemble. In a furious Presto, the original G minor yielding to D major, he drives Belmonte away.

Pedrillo asks Osmin whether Selim has returned. Still not answering, Osmin fumes about vagabond fops fit only to be hanged ('Solche hergelauf'ne Laffen'). A full binary exit aria, portentous and often contrapuntal, it flies off the handle in the coda to which Mozart added 'Turkish' music for comic effect. Belmonte reveals himself. Pedrillo assures him that Selim will not force love on Konstanze, but they are in great danger and Osmin watches everything. Belmonte's heart is beating with anxiety and ardour ('O wie ängstlich, o wie feurig'); both melody and orchestra are suffused with feeling as well as detailed imitation of the lover's symptoms.

A march (possibly cut by Mozart, but restored by the Neue Mozart-Ausgabe) announces the arrival of the Pasha in a boat with Konstanze; the Janissaries greet them with a vigorous chorus in 'Turkish' style. Selim asks why Konstanze remains sad and promises that her answer will not anger him. In the Adagio of her aria Konstanze relives her past love ('Ach ich liebte, war so glücklich!'); the Allegro compresses the Adagio's melodic outline into a vehement protest; all happiness has fled (the Adagio text and mood return in the middle of the Allegro). Mozart's sacrifice for Cavalieri brings coloratura to an inappropriate text ('Kummer ruht in meinem Schoss': 'sorrow dwells in my heart'), but this emphatic utterance tells us that Konstanze is a considerable character. Selim is angry, but when she leaves he admits that he loves her all the more for her resistance. Pedrillo introduces Belmonte as an Italian-trained architect; Selim approves his entry into the household. But Osmin has other ideas. A vivacious trio in C minor ('Marsch, marsch, marsch! trollt euch fort!'), ending with a faster major section, forms a comic finale; eventually the Europeans force an entry.

ACT 2 *The palace garden, with Osmin's house to one side* Osmin is pursuing Blonde, whom the Pasha has given him as a slave; but she will have none of his Turkish ways; tenderness, not force, wins hearts ('Durch Zärtlichkeit und Schmeicheln'). Her Andante aria is the epitome of Mozartean A major elegance, yet Blonde must glide up to *e'''*. Osmin indignantly orders her to love him, but she merely laughs, and wards off an assault by threatening his eyes with her nails and reminding him that her mistress is the Pasha's favourite (duet, 'Ich gehe, doch rate ich dir'). Osmin warns her not to flirt with Pedrillo; she mocks his low notes with her own (to *ab*). In a lugubrious Andante Osmin declares that the English are mad to allow their women such liberties; Blonde rejoices in her freedom.

At the nadir of her fortunes, Konstanze turns to the most intense style of *opera seria*, obbligato recitative ('Welcher Wechsel herrscht in meiner Seele', and aria, 'Traurigkeit ward mir zum Lose'). In an exquisite Adagio Mozart paints her sighing breaths, her halting steps. The aria, its orchestra enriched by basset-horns, is a sustained lament in G minor, like Ilia's (*Idomeneo*, Act 1) but attaining a new poignancy through its higher tessitura.

Blonde tries to comfort her mistress. Selim threatens not death, which Konstanze welcomes, but every kind of torture. Her aria ('Marten aller Arten': 'Every kind of torture awaits me; I laugh at pain; death will come in the end') picks up Selim's threat, but not before a 60-bar ritornello with obbligato flute, oboe, violin and cello has unfolded a rich motivic tapestry founded on a march rhythm (with trumpets and timpani). The closing words are given more emphasis by a faster tempo. This magnificent piece, coming immediately after another long aria for Konstanze, presents a challenge to the actors and the producer; but as the expression of stubborn resistance to coercion from a woman with no hope of deliverance, it is of immense dramatic power. Selim is baffled; affection and force having failed, he wonders if he can use cunning. (This exit line perhaps prefigured a new intrigue intended for Act 3 but not included.)

Pedrillo tells Blonde of Belmonte's arrival. Blonde's reaction, a rondo with a melody from the flute concerto K314 ('Welche Wonne, welche Lust'), sparkles with unalloyed delight. Pedrillo musters his courage in a martial D major ('Frisch zum Kampfe!'), but a nagging phrase ('Nur ein feiger Tropf verzagt': 'Only a cowardly fool despairs') shows his underlying lack of confidence. He succeeds in getting Osmin drunk (duet, 'Vivat Bacchus'), and sends him to sleep it off so that the lovers can meet. Tears of joy are love's sweetest reward; Belmonte's aria of *galanterie* ('Wenn der Freude Tränen fliessen') is a slow gavotte and then a serenade-like minuet announced by the wind and embellished with wide-ranging passage-work.

The escape is planned before the finale (quartet, 'Ach Belmonte!'). The first mature Mozart ensemble to incorporate dramatic development begins with a lively D major Allegro. Joy gives way to anxiety (Andante, G minor); have the women yielded to blandishment? In a faster tempo, Konstanze expresses hurt, Blonde slaps Pedrillo's face, and the voices come together in mingled relief and regret. The men ask forgiveness (Allegretto); Blonde withholds it, singing in compound time against the simple time of the others (a device Mozart might have picked up from *opéra comique*). But eventually misunderstanding is cleared away and the four join in praise of love.

ACT 3 *The scene of Act 1; Osmin's house to one side. Midnight* Pedrillo and Klaas bring two ladders. Belmonte is assured that all is ready, but they must wait for the guards to finish their rounds. Pedrillo advises him to sing; he himself often sings at night and it will not be noticed. In a long Andante, featuring clarinets and extended coloratura, Belmonte builds his hopes on the power of love ('Ich baue ganz auf deine Stärke').

Pedrillo gives the agreed signal, a romance ('In Mohrenland gefangen war ein Mädchen'). The opera's second lied, this too refers to the dramatic situation. Its haunting melody, to a plucked accompaniment, rests upon harmonic ambiguity and ends unresolved after four verses when Pedrillo sees a light. Belmonte fetches Konstanze; they hurry off as Pedrillo climbs up for Blonde. But the mute has seen them. Suspecting thieves and murderers, the bleary-eyed Osmin sends for the guard and dozes. Blonde and Pedrillo spot him too late; all four Europeans are arrested. In a brilliant rondo ('O, wie will ich triumphieren'), with piccolo but without trumpets or Turkish music, which Mozart keeps in reserve, Osmin anticipates the delight of torturing and killing his enemies, his lowest bass notes (to D) filled with ghoulish relish.

The interior of the palace   Osmin claims credit for the arrest. Selim confronts the lovers. Konstanze admits guilt in his eyes, but pleads loyalty to her first lover. She begs to die if only his life can be spared. Belmonte humbles himself; he is worth a fine ransom; his name is Lostados. Selim recognizes the son of the enemy who chased him from his homeland. He bids them prepare for the punishment Belmonte's father would certainly have meted out, and leaves them under guard. Belmonte movingly laments his folly in bringing Konstanze to her doom; she blames herself for his destruction, but death is the path to an eternal union, symbolized by the serenely extended arabesques doubled in 3rds and 6ths (recitative and duet, 'Welch ein Geschick! O Qual der Seele!').

Selim asks if they are prepared for judgment. Belmonte says they will die calmly, absolving him from blame. Selim, however, bids him take Konstanze and go. He despises Belmonte's father too much to imitate him; clemency will be his revenge. As he takes dignified leave of them, Pedrillo begs freedom for himself and Blonde. Osmin is overruled; does he not value his eyes? In a vaudeville finale, each sings a verse of suitable sentiment, with a moral sung by the ensemble: those who forget kindness are to be despised. Blonde is interrupted by Osmin whose rage boils over into the litany of torture from his Act 1 aria, complete with 'Turkish' percussion. He rushes off; the others draw the further moral that nothing is so hateful as revenge. A brief chorus in praise of the Pasha, in the principal key, C major, brings back the merry 'Turkish' style of the overture.

*   *   *

The viewpoint of *Die Entführung* is decidedly European. Muslim life-style is crudely represented as luxurious but immoral; the Enlightenment, through Blonde, makes tart observations about the social position of women. Selim himself, raised to eminence by ability rather than rank, reflects Enlightenment values; he is not moved to clemency by religion, but contrasts his action with the cruelty of Belmonte's Christian father. This ending adds a new dimension to Bretzner's drama in which, implausibly, Belmonte proves to be Selim's son. It is a pity that, unlike the denouement of *Die Zauberflöte*, this scene was not set to music.

The lavish musical invention of *Die Entführung* perhaps exceeds what the dramatic structure is fit to bear; nor is its design immaculate. Apart from the cluster of arias for Konstanze in Act 2, there is surely one aria too many for Belmonte, and the length of the individual numbers (if not their forms) suggests *opera seria* and contrasts starkly with the speed of the dialogue. Was it length or plenitude of instrumentation which induced Joseph II's famous (but probably apocryphal) comment: 'Too many notes, my dear Mozart'? Such problems cannot be overcome by making alterations, still less by cutting the dialogue, for Mozart carefully controlled the flow between speech and music, running some numbers closely together but separating others. His prodigality of invention, however, is also a cause of the opera's enduring fascination. Even as it endangers the dramatic whole, the music, paradoxically through its creation for a specific group of remarkable singers, turns the actors in this serious comedy into humans a little larger than life but of universal appeal.

JULIAN RUSHTON

Entr'acte (Fr.). INTERLUDE.

Entrée (Fr.). In French Baroque *ballet de cour*, *opéra* and *opéra-ballet*, a term that was applied on two levels.

First, it designated the initial dance for a particular character or characters (generally accompanying their entrance on stage) and by extension the first in a set of dances in a *divertissement*. Since an entrée fulfilled a function, rather than serving any specific choreography, there is considerable variety in metre and length, although most are in a moderate or moderately fast tempo and many are march-like.

Second, the term also designated individual scenes devoted to one set of people in the *ballet de cour*; their dances, as well as the *vers*, illustrated a single subject and, particularly in works after 1620, contrasted with other entrées whose common link was a general theme interpreted with considerable variety. So basic was the entrée as a unit that this type of *ballet de cour* was also known as 'ballet à entrées'. According to Saint-Hubert, the number of entrées varied from about a dozen (in a 'petit ballet') to 30 (in a 'beau ballet'). By Lully's time the number of entrées, even in the longest ballets, was fewer, but some contain up to about a dozen pieces (and others only one). Lully's *Alcidiane* is representative. Its three parts contained a total of 21 entrées for the inhabitants of a mythical island and those who land on it – consisting of such diverse groups as Hatred, the other Passions, pearl fishers, buffoons and soldiers. All had their own music. For the last, for example, there were calls to arms and marches for both sides, a military exercise, charges, a retreat, a battle and a celebration of victory.

The concept of unity within each of the entrées and contrast between them was taken further in the *opéra-ballet*, where the term was a synonym for act – each of which had its own plot and characters and differed sharply from the others. Only a very broad idea, usually indicated by the title, provided any logic to the grouping (e.g. *Les élémens* by Lalande and Destouches consisted of 'L'air', 'L'eau', 'Le feu' and 'La terre', 1721, and *Les Indes galantes* by Rameau consisted of 'Le Turc généreux', 'Les Incas du Pérou' and 'Les fleurs', feste persane', 1735; other entrées were added or substituted at revivals). Each entrée generally had *récitatifs*, airs, choruses (often *choeurs dansés*) and one or more *divertissements*; *ariettes*, duets, other vocal and instrumental pieces may also be included. The entrance and exit of characters marked the division into scenes (as was typical for French theatre).

Finally, in the late 18th century and early 19th 'entrée' was occasionally used for the orchestral introduction of a vocal piece marking the entrance of a principal character and often musically defining him or her (see Castil-Blaze 1821).

*

Saint-Hubert: *La manière de composer et faire réussir les ballets* (Paris, 1641)

L. de Cahusac: 'Entrée', *Encyclopédie, ou Dictionnaire raisonné des sciences, des arts et des métiers*, ed. D. Diderot and others (Paris, 1755)

Castil-Blaze [F.-H.-J. Blaze]: *Dictionnaire de musique moderne* (Paris, 1821, 2/1825)

J. R. Anthony: *French Baroque Music from Beaujoyeulx to Rameau* (London, 1973, 2/1978)   M. ELIZABETH C. BARTLET

Entremés. A form of short Spanish scenic entertainment, usually comic, which flourished in the 17th century and was performed between the acts of a larger, more serious theatrical work (*see* INTERMEZZO). It was popular in character and commonly called for instrumentally accompanied songs and dances, but also attracted literary figures as eminent as Tirso de Molina and Quevedo. The traditional place for the *entremés* in its strict sense was after the first act, though at other points similar forms were introduced – a *jácara* (picaresque interlude) or *baile* (dance scene with poetry and music) after the second act and a *mojiganga* (burlesque) at the end. The term may have originated in the court of Aragón in the 14th century as a song or dance interlude between courses of a meal ('entremet'); it was also current in Catalonia in the 15th century for a popular entertainment, with solo songs, unaccompanied choruses or instrumental music, that enlivened religious or solemn festivities.

*

E. Cotarelo y Mori: *Colección de entremeses, loas, bailes, jácaras y mojigangas desde fines del siglo XVI a mediados del XVIII* (Madrid, 1911)

M. N. Hamilton: *Music in 18th-Century Spain* (Urbana, 1937)
                                         LIONEL SALTER

Envallsson, Carl (*b* Stockholm, 24 Oct 1756; *d* Stockholm, 14 July 1806). Swedish librettist and translator. Following his early education in Stockholm, he was appointed a registrar at the Royal War College. He became associated with Carl Stenborg as early as 1780, translating French *opéras comiques* and German Singspiels into Swedish. These included works such as *Nu är hin lös* (Hiller's *Der Teufel ist los*, 1787) and *Konung Rickard Lejonhjerta* (Grétry's *Richard Coeur-de-lion*, 1791). His own most popular original work was the opera *Kopparslagaren* ('The Coppersmith'), set by J. D. Zander in 1781; it had 58 performances to 1808. He wrote or translated more than 80 texts before losing his eyesight in 1802.

*

F. Dahlgren: *Anteckningar om Stockholms teatrar* (Stockholm, 1866)

J. Flodmark: *Stenborgska skådebanorne* (Stockholm, 1893)

J. Massengale: 'Carl Envallsson', *Gustavian Opera 1772–1809* (Stockholm, 1990)   BERTIL H. VAN BOER

Ephesian Matron, The [*The Ephesian Matron, or The Widow's Tears*]. Afterpiece opera by CHARLES DIBDIN to a libretto by ISAAC BICKERSTAFF after Petronius's *Satyricon*; London, Ranelagh Gardens, 12 May 1769.

The Ephesian Matron is a black comedy which as well as deriving from a tale by Petronius includes in the finale the fable of the man and the lion, which was printed in *The Spectator* of 13 March 1711 after a reference to the Petronius tale. The story concerns a young, despairing widow from Ephesus, the Matron (soprano), who is grieving over the recent death of her husband, whose corpse she is unable to leave. Having resolved to forgo all food, drink and worldly pleasures she awaits her inevitable reunification with her husband in death. Nevertheless, she is quickly wooed and won by a passing soldier, the Centurion (tenor), whose life she then saves using her husband's corpse. She agrees to marry him the next day.

Unlike the more typical English opera of the day, *The Ephesian Matron* contains no spoken dialogue, since it was written not for the theatre but for the pleasure gardens at Ranelagh, where, by law, entertainments containing words had to be all-sung. Ranelagh also lacked a proper stage, which is probably why *The Ephesian Matron* was written as a serenata – a series of scenes (eight in this case), none of which contains any action. The first performance was given as part of a jubilee ridotto. Dibdin himself took the part of the Centurion, with Mrs Sophia Baddely as the Matron, Jonathan Legg as the Father (baritone) and Mrs Thompson as the Maid (soprano). The work was performed at Ranelagh several times in 1769 and a number of times the following summer. In his *Complete History of the English Stage* (1797–1800) Dibdin complained that '*The Ephesian Matron* was performed at Ranelagh, where it was considered as vulgar to listen to music, and therefore the real effect of this piece was never known'. It was, however, occasionally performed at the London theatres over the next nine years; but its macabre subject matter probably prevented a more outstanding success.
                                         IRENA CHOLIJ

Epilogue. Epilogues are rare in opera; even the early operas that have allegorical prologues rarely have balancing epilogues. By its nature, comment on action that has passed is undramatic and unlikely to lend itself to operatic treatment. The neo-classical convention underlying Stravinsky's *The Rake's Progress*, however, and the framework it establishes, explain why an epilogue is particularly apt in that work. The last act of Offenbach's *Les contes d'Hoffmann* is described as an epilogue, though it is not one in the traditional sense in that it and the prologue (or first act) constitute the only 'real' action in the work. The final scene in *Don Giovanni*, where the surviving characters draw the moral, is of the nature of an epilogue; so is the last scene of *Boris Godunov* (1872 version), where the Holy Fool laments the fate of his country, and the last two 'pictures' of Delius's *Fennimore and Gerda* in which Niels reflects on his ordeals and finds comfort.

Epstein, Matthew (*b* New York, 23 Dec 1947). American impresario, opera manager and agent. He began his career with Shaw Concerts Inc. in New York City, and joined Columbia Artists Management Inc. in 1973. He became artistic adviser to the Lyric Opera, Chicago, in 1980, while still at Columbia Artists, and has served as consultant to many other organizations, including the Kennedy Center, Santa Fe Opera, Netherlands Opera and San Francisco Opera (from 1992). He has become known for packaging entire operas to sell to regional presenters, provoking some resentment for his tendency to use more prominent singers as a leverage to hire lesser known artists. Nonetheless he exhibited skill as a director when, from 1982 to 1986, he supervised concert performances of opera at the Carnegie Hall, including a Rossini series with Marilyn Horne (1982–3), a French comic series with Frederica Von Stade (1983–4), a Handel tricentennial series (1984–5) and a Richard Strauss series (1985–6). In 1987 he was named artistic director of opera at the Brooklyn Academy of Music, inaugurating his term with the first American visit of the Welsh National Opera presenting *Falstaff* in a production by Peter Stein. He resigned in 1990 after disputes over finances and artistic autonomy, and in 1991 became General Director of the Welsh National Opera, the first American to run an opera company in Britain.

NANCY MALITZ

Equiluz, Kurt (*b* Vienna, 13 June 1929). Austrian tenor. He became alto soloist with the Vienna Boys' Choir, and studied music at the Academy. In 1950 he joined the State Opera Chorus and soon became a valued comprimario, with Scaramuccio in *Ariadne auf Naxos* a part he made his own, singing it also at Florence and Salzburg. He was admired for his cameos in *Die Meistersinger* (Balthasar Zorn) and as Pedrillo in *Die Entführung*. His distinctive, well-focussed voice can be heard in several small roles on records (including Scaramuccio in the famous recording with Karajan), but the most memorable part of his legacy is probably his singing of the Evangelist in Bach's Passions. He joined the teaching staff at the Vienna Academy in 1982.

J. B. STEANE

Equivoci, Gli ('The Misunderstandings' [*The Comedy of Errors*]). *Opera buffa* in two acts by STEPHEN STORACE to a libretto by LORENZO DA PONTE after WILLIAM SHAKESPEARE's play; Vienna, Burgtheater, 27 December 1786.

Da Ponte, in his memoirs, describes how, having just completed the libretto for *Le nozze di Figaro*, he was approached by Storace to adapt a work by Shakespeare. This was to be Storace's second opera for the Italian company at the Vienna Burgtheater. As Da Ponte spoke no English he used as his source a French translation, *Les méprises* by M. Letourneur, published in 1782. He changed or italianized many of Shakespeare's names and omitted the Abbess and the Courtesan, but gave the shipwrecked Dromio a wife. As in the play there are two pairs of identical twins: two servants, both called Dromio, and two masters, here both called Eufemio (in Shakespeare, Antipholus). At the first performance Eufemio of Syracuse was sung by Vincenzo Calvesi (tenor), Eufemio of Ephesus by Michael Kelly (tenor) and the latter Eufemio's wife Sofronia (Adriana) by the composer's sister Nancy Storace (soprano). The names of the other singers are not known.

The adaptation into an opera is skilful, condensing the original five acts into two and allowing each act to develop into a spirited finale. The opera begins more dramatically than Shakespeare's original. A short overture, in which the second part depicts a storm at sea with thunder and lightning cued into the score, leads into Act 1, in which Eufemio of Syracuse and his servant Dromio (baritone) have been shipwrecked and washed up on the shore of Ephesus. Unfortunately there is a feud between the two cities, and travellers from Syracuse must either pay a large fine or be put to death. Scene ii is at the palace of Solinus, Duke of Ephesus (baritone), where Aegon (Egeon, baritone) is in just such a predicament: he is searching for his twin sons, one of

whom was lost in a storm at sea some 20 years previously. The duke allows him one day to raise the ransom money. The confusion that develops between the two pairs of twins builds up to a finale in which Eufemio of Ephesus noisily demands admission to his own house, where his wife is entertaining the other Eufemio, having mistaken him for her husband. Together with Dromio, Eufemio of Syracuse goes outside to confront the other two in the dark street. As Sofronia and her sister Sostrata (Luciana, soprano) follow them out with a lamp, all is about to be revealed when the wind blows out the light. The town guard is heard approaching, and in the darkness the two sets of twins run off.

In Act 2 the continuing confusion concerns a gold chain which Eufemio of Ephesus has ordered from Angelo the goldsmith (baritone). It is mistakenly given to Eufemio of Syracuse, but Angelo demands the money from the other Eufemio, who refuses to pay for what he has not received. As a result he is arrested. He tries to send Dromio to obtain money for his release, and when the other Dromio (baritone) returns without it he becomes distraught. That evening in the town square Aegon is about to be executed when Sofronia approaches the duke for help over what she considers the irrational behaviour of her husband. Solinus sends the guards to apprehend him, but Eufemio of Ephesus enters in a fury. When the guard returns with Eufemio and Dromio of Syracuse, the two pairs of twins can be seen by everyone and the confusion is explained.

The opera represents a development in Storace's compositional style that is due partly to the excellent libretto and to the composer's ability to express the personalities of each character in the music. Storace was a close friend of Mozart and one can sense Mozart's influence in the melodic lines, the extensive use of ensembles and the imaginative orchestration. Sofronia and her sister have a duet featuring two basset-horns, and there are arias with cello and clarinet obbligatos. Though the vocal writing has a distinctly Viennese flavour, there is still an English quality about the music. Sofronia, for instance, is given a 'Scotch' tune which had also been used by J. C. Bach. The playbills describe the work as 'Ein italienisches Singspiel', but it is all-sung, with recitatives. Though it was a success, it did not enter the regular repertory of the Burgtheater; perhaps two sets of twins caused casting problems.

The opera was produced in 1793 at Leipzig and Prague, and in 1797 at Dresden. A German version was given at Pressburg in 1788. On his return to England, Kelly tried unsuccessfully to encourage Sheridan to produce *Gli equivoci* at Drury Lane. However, Storace re-used some of the music. Some found its way into *La cameriera astuta* (1788), and part of the overture was used for *The Haunted Tower* (1789). He used more of it, especially from the Act 1 finale, in *No Song, No Supper* (1790), and *The Pirates* (1792). As Kelly wrote, 'Storace certainly enriched his English pieces, but I lamented to see his beautiful Italian opera dismantled'. Storace also brought to England the use of large-scale action finales, of which for some years he was the main proponent.

An English translation by Arthur Jacobs had its première at the Camden Festival, London, on 20 February 1974.

RICHARD PLATT

Equivoci nel sembiante, Gli ('Equivocal Appearances'). *Dramma per musica* in three acts by Alessandro Scarlatti (*see* SCARLATTI family, (1)) to a libretto by DOMENICO FILIPPO CONTINI; Rome, Contini's private theatre, February 1679.

Contini's libretto is a neatly constructed Arcadian comedy of amorous intrigue, deceits, misunderstandings and reconciliations. In Act 1 the nymph Lisetta (soprano) intercepts a love letter which her elder sister Clori (soprano) has written to the shepherd Eurillo (tenor), with whom they are both in love. Lisetta alters the letter to make out that it is addressed to 'Aminta' and then, filled with remorse, attempts to comfort the inconsolable Clori. In Act 2 a stranger, Armindo (tenor), taking advantage of the fact that both Clori and Lisetta mistake him for Eurillo (who is later identified as his identical twin), resolves to run away with Clori and arranges to meet her for that purpose at dusk. It is, however, Eurillo and not Armindo who turns up by chance. The scene that follows, during which Lisetta confesses her duplicity, leaves the lovers confused but reassured of each other's constancy. Act 3 brings further complications as Clori, still mistaking Armindo for Eurillo, promises to marry him that very evening. Eurillo overhears part of her conversation with the stranger and, overcome, faints. Clori chances upon him and succeeds in reviving him, but, delirious, he faints a second time. Clori's call for help is answered by Armindo, and the two men recognize each other as long-lost brothers when Armindo, after begging forgiveness for the deceit he has practised on Clori, offers to Lisetta a ring identical to the one which Eurillo offers to Clori. The comedy of errors ends with the two couples singing of their future happiness together.

Gli equivoci calls for only four singers, a single set and accompaniment of strings and continuo, but despite its small scale and intimate première it enjoyed instant and widespread acclaim, establishing the 18-year-old Scarlatti as a promising opera composer. Scandals occasioned by its first performance at the Clementine College on 12 February 1679, when Queen Christina's majordomo was embroiled in a scuffle with those guarding the doors, and by subsequent performances during Lent, which inflamed the anger of Pope Innocent XI, ensured the work's notoriety, and productions followed soon afterwards in several other Italian cities and as far afield as Vienna (13 February 1681, as *L'amor non vuole inganni*). What the early audiences admired most in the music was the tunefulness of the arias and duets, of which there are 48, most of them in a brief da capo form and nearly half of them repeated to a second strophe.

MALCOLM BOYD

Equivoco stravagante, L' ('The Curious Misunderstanding'). *Dramma giocoso* in two acts by GIOACHINO ROSSINI to a libretto by Gaetano Gasbarri; Bologna, Teatro del Corso, 26 October 1811.

For his first full-scale two-act opera, Rossini accepted a libretto that mixes pastoral, burlesque, *buffo* and romantic elements. It was an adventurous undertaking, further enhanced by the work's length (over 300 pages in the 1847 Ricordi vocal score) and by the importance given to ensemble writing as opposed to solo numbers and secco recitatives. Unfortunately, the libretto was sufficiently *risqué* to cause the work to be banned by the Bologna police after its third performance. Hardly shocking to modern taste, the story concerns the young impoverished Ermanno (tenor) and his clandestine love for Ernestina (contralto), the literature-loving daughter of the *nouveau riche* farmer Gamberotto (*buffo bass*). Unhappily for Ermanno, both Gamberotto and his daughter are much taken with a poseur called Buralicchio (*buffo bass*), described in the cast list as 'young, rich and stupid'. To scare off the fop, Ermanno dreams up the idea of telling him that Ernestina is a boy: a castrato and (a problem in 1811) an army deserter. On the strength of these ingenious slanders, and some improbable dramatic developments, Ernestina is eventually arrested, only to be freed by Ermanno who ceases to be her tutor and becomes her husband.

Ernestina was created for Marietta Marcolini, an influential singer in Rossini's apprentice years; the role allows the singer to play the charming *ingénue*, the teasing shrew and the glittering warrior. The opera has no extant overture. The 1847 edition prefaces it, implausibly, with the overture to *Il barbiere di Siviglia*, but if a curtain-raiser is needed the overture to *La cambiale di matrimonio* is as good as any from the pre-1812 period.

RICHARD OSBORNE

Eraclea [*L'Eraclea*] ('Heraclia'). *Dramma per musica* in three acts by Alessandro Scarlatti (*see* SCARLATTI family, (1)) to a libretto by SILVIO STAMPIGLIA; Naples, Teatro S Bartolomeo, 30 January 1700.

The action takes place in Syracuse in 212 BC. Heraclia (soprano) and her daughters Flavia (soprano) and Irene (alto), sentenced to death along with the rest of the family of the late King Hiero, are spared by the intervention of Decio [Decius] (soprano castrato), a Capuan noble in love with Heraclia, and by a pardon brought by Damiro (soprano castrato). Heraclia returns Decius's love, but when the Roman conqueror of Syracuse, Marcello [Marcellus] (soprano castrato), also falls in love with her she is unable to reject him outright for fear of what might become of her daughters and the citizens of Syracuse. The resulting conflicts between head and heart, in which the daughters' love affairs with Damiro and another Syracusan noble, Iliso (tenor), become entangled, are finally resolved when Marcellus learns of the true situation and renounces his claims on Heraclia. Comic scenes, unconnected with the main drama, are enacted by Decius's page, Livio (soprano), and the girls' tutor, Alfeo (bass).

None of the surviving scores of *Eraclea* includes the serious recitatives; only those of the comic scenes are extant. Of the 53 solo arias and duets, all but three are in ternary (da capo or dal segno) form, with accompaniments ranging from basso continuo only to full strings; violins, trumpets and flutes are used as obbligato instruments. Of particular interest is the unusual 'aria a 7', 'Che maestà, che brio' (Act 1), a brief but neatly constructed number, the nearest thing in the opera to an ensemble, to which all the serious characters contribute individual comments or asides.

MALCOLM BOYD

Erb, Karl (*b* Ravensburg, 13 July 1877; *d* Ravensburg, 13 July 1958). German tenor. Entirely self-taught (he was a civil servant until his voice was discovered), he made his début in Kienzl's *Der Evangelimann* at Stuttgart in 1907. From 1908 to 1910 he sang at Lübeck, returning to Stuttgart for the seasons 1910–12. In 1913 he joined the Munich Opera, after a successful guest appearance as Lohengrin. His reputation grew rapidly, and his repertory eventually numbered some 70 parts (including Mozart roles and the tenor leads in *Parsifal*, *Euryanthe*, *Der Corregidor* and *Iphigénie en Aulide*). At the first performance of Pfitzner's *Palestrina* in 1917 he took the title role with great distinction (for illustration *see* PALESTRINA). He left the Munich Opera in 1925 but continued to give guest performances in opera until 1930. In 1927 he and his wife Maria Ivogün sang the principal roles in *Die Entführung* at Covent Garden. His last appearance was as Florestan under Furtwängler in Berlin. He then devoted himself entirely to concert singing, and was a famous Bach Evangelist.

Erb sang and recorded to an advanced age. To fine natural musicianship he added incomparable diction. His voice was soft-grained yet powerful, and from an early age it seems to have had the distinctive nasal quality evident in the records of his middle and later years. Among writers who paid tribute to him were Romain Rolland and Thomas Mann – in the latter's novel *Dr Faustus* Erb may be recognized as the model for Erbe, the 'tenor of almost castrato heights', who in masterly fashion sang the role of the narrator in Leverkühn's oratorio *Apocalipsis cum figuris* under Klemperer in a fictitious concert.

*

M. Müller-Goegler: *Karl Erb: das Leben eines Sängers* (Offenburg, 1948)
PETER BRANSCOMBE

Erbse, Heimo (*b* Rudolstadt, 27 Feb 1924). German composer. He studied in Weimar from 1945 to 1947 and at the Berlin Hochschule für Musik in West Berlin, where he was a composition pupil of Boris Blacher from 1950 to 1952. While still studying he began directing operas in Jena, Meiningen and Sondershausen. Since then he has worked as a freelance composer, living in Baden, near Vienna. Early in his career Erbse concentrated on composing piano, chamber and orchestral music. He achieved wider popularity with his four-act opera *Julietta* (1956–7), which had its première at the Salzburg Festival on 17 August 1959. This work, for which the composer wrote his own libretto, is based on Heinrich von Kleist's story *Die Marquise von O...*. Describing the work as an *opera semiseria*, he brings out both the tragic and the grotesque elements of the plot. His musical language is marked by the Stravinskian agility of early Blacher, which outweighs occasional more lyrical elements. In 1965–6 Erbse wrote a full-length comic opera, *Der Herr in Grau*, to a libretto by Carl Merz.

*

VintonD
K. Kanzog and J. Kreutzer: *Werke Kleists auf dem modernen Musiktheater*, Jahresgabe der Kleist-Gesellschaft 1973/74 (Berlin, 1977)
WULF KONOLD

Erckmann-Chatrian. Name used by two French novelists, dramatists and librettists. Emile Erckmann (*b* Phalsbourg, Meurthe, 20 May 1822; *d* Luneville, Meurthe-et-Moselle, 14 March 1899) and Alexandre Chatrian (*b* Soldatenthal, Meurthe, 18 Dec 1826; *d* Villemomble, Seine, 3 Sept 1890) began writing together in Alsace in 1848. Their collaboration continued to the 1880s and yielded works set in Alsace or on historical subjects inspired by a democratic ideology, which led to suspicions of anti-patriotism against them. In addition to their librettos for comic operas, Erckmann-Chatrian won widespread fame for works on which other writers based opera librettos, such as the novel *Le Juif polonais* (Paris, 1869) and the comedy *L'ami Fritz* (1876, Paris).

LITERARY WORKS ON WHICH OPERAS HAVE BEEN BASED
Les amoureux de Catherine (novel, 1866): H. Maréchal, 1876
Le Juif polonais (novel, 1869): C. Erlanger, 1900; K. Weis, 1901
L'ami Fritz (comedy, 1876): Mascagni, 1891
Les Rantzau (comedy, 1882): Mascagni, 1892

LIBRETTOS
La taverne des Trabans (with J. Barbier), Maréchal, 1881; *Le fou chopine*, A. Sellenick, 1883; *Myrtille* (with M. Drack), P. Lacôme, 1885
LUCA ZOPPELLI

Ercole al Termedonte ('Hercules by the Thermodon'). *Opera seria* in two acts by Niccolò Piccinni (*see* PICCINNI family, (1)) to an anonymous libretto; Naples, Teatro S Carlo, 12 January 1793.

Ippolita [Hippolyte] (soprano), Amazon queen of foreign affairs, is in love with her captive Teseo [Theseus] (soprano castrato), who is ashamed of his love for her. Anticipating the arrival of Hercules (tenor), Orizia (mezzo-soprano), Hippolyte's sister and queen of internal affairs, orders Theseus to be chained. Hercules, Evrando (tenor) and their men overcome the Amazons and enter the city with Hippolyte, defiant, in chains; Hercules threatens to kill her. The women plot to destroy Hercules, while he persuades Theseus to sail away with him. After a peace ceremony, Orizia and some Amazons set fire to his ships, blaming Theseus. When Hippolyte comes to Theseus's defence, Hercules forgoes vengeance and reunites the unhappy lovers.

The opera is nearly through-composed, moving freely between textural options and including extensive programmatic recitative for action. Consistent with current trends, the libretto contains two single-sex duets, many cavatinas (both solo and duo) and an interior action duet and quartet as well as two static ensemble finales, thus reducing the number of exit arias to four. Aria texts are set twice through, sometimes with a contrasting B section (ABAB). Theseus has the only two-tempo rondò, 'Nel partir da queste sponde' (2.v). Piccinni adopted the clear, strong and unadorned vocal style of his younger contemporaries, along with their sparse, repetitious accompaniments, which thicken and give way to tremolos during long crescendos. Horn, clarinet, oboe and bassoon often make up the wind section, with flutes still reserved for special effects, but Piccinni was more inclined than his younger contemporaries to use four and even five string parts and to maintain full orchestral textures in solo vocal accompaniments.
MARITA P. McCLYMONDS

Ercole amante ('Hercules in Love'). Opera in a prologue and five acts by FRANCESCO CAVALLI to a libretto by FRANCESCO BUTI after OVID's *Metamorphoses* (book 9); Paris, Tuileries, Salle des Machines, 7 February 1662.

In the Prologue, Cinzia [Cynthia] (soprano), the Tevere [Tiber] (bass) and the chorus of the rivers proclaim the coming marriage of Louis XIV to the Spanish Infanta Maria Theresa; they compare the French monarch and his bride to Hercules and Beauty (Hebe, the Goddess of Youth). Act 1 represents an Oechalian wood with a vast landscape in the distance. Hercules (bass) complains that Iole (soprano) resists his advances while the world joins Cupid in laughing at him. Venere [Venus] (soprano) and the Three Graces descend in a machine. Venus promises to help Hercules seduce the stubborn Iole. Giunone [Juno] (soprano), riding the clouds on her peacock, angrily vows to foil Venus and Hercules by uniting Iole with Hyllo [Hyllus] (tenor), the son of Hercules and his wife Deianira (soprano).

At Hercules' palace, Iole and Hyllus swear their mutual devotion but are interrupted by a page, who invites Iole to meet Hercules in the garden. Iole despises Hercules because he has murdered her father, Eurytus, for consenting to her marriage to Hyllus. She determines to confront her father's murderer. When she enters the garden, Venus dazzles her with magic, and Iole suddenly finds her hatred for Hercules dissipating. Hercules pledges himself as Iole's husband, but Sonno [Sleep] (silent), at Juno's instruction, overcomes him. Juno then gives Iole a sword. Hyllus and Mercurio [Mercury] (tenor) attempt to save Hercules from Iole's attack. Awakening, the dazed Hercules threatens to kill his son. When Deianira and Iole beg for Hyllus's life, Hercules relents, but banishes the mother and imprisons the son in a tower near the seashore. Hyllus throws himself into the sea and Juno calls on Nettuno [Neptune] (bass) to rescue him. The following scene in the cypress-encircled royal cemetery finds Deianira attempting to creep inside a tomb to die. She observes an approaching funeral procession led by Iole and a chorus of priests. As Iole prays for her father's help in sparing her from marriage to Hercules, an earthquake demolishes a tomb and the ghost of Euryto [Eurytus] (bass) emerges. He vows to save Hyllus, but Deianira reports that he is already dead. Deianira remembers that she possesses the shirt of the centaur Nessus. If she can persuade Hercules to wear it, he will forget all his other loves and return to her.

The ghost of Eurytus calls on Hercules' victims in Hades to join him in demanding the death of the evil king. Meanwhile, in Juno's temple, Hercules and Iole prepare for their wedding. Iole presents the centaur's shirt to the king. As he puts the garment on, it burns him to the bone, causing him an agonizing death. Hyllus reappears to console his grieving mother. Juno descends in her heavenly machine to proclaim that Hercules is not dead; he has been rescued by Zeus and married to Hebe. All rejoice when Hercules and Hebe appear in the heavens and join the chorus of the planets in singing the praises of the Gallic Hercules and his Iberian beauty.

Cardinal Mazarin commissioned Cavalli to compose *Ercole amante* to mark the occasion of the wedding of Louis XIV to Maria Theresa of Spain. Gaspare Vigarani and his sons designed a new theatre and spectacular sets and machines for the production but took two years to complete their work. The unfortunate delay necessitated the substitution of Cavalli's earlier opera *Xerse* for the nuptial celebration. When *Ercole* was finally presented to the king and a pregnant queen, the spectacle was augmented by ballets by Isaac de Benserade and Lully. However, the acoustic of the immense Salle des Machines in the Tuileries and the inattention of the French courtiers resulted in an unenthusiastic and ultimately disastrous reception.

One hears the royal glory of *Ercole amante* in the magnificent choruses and in the enriched orchestration. Larger instrumental forces even accompany many of the arias and duets. With the five-part orchestral scoring, which occasionally suggests the brilliance of brass or winds, Cavalli for the first time enlarged his operatic instrumental group beyond the customary transparent three-part string accompaniment. The greater sonority of the accompaniment for the choruses, which are in four, six or eight voices, emphasizes the heroic text and underscores the grandeur of the choral scenes. Thus choruses, virtually absent in earlier Cavalli operas, are an essential element in his tribute to Louis XIV; the choruses of the rivers in the Prologue, the priests in Act 4 scene vii, and the four-part lament on the death of Hercules in Act 5 are specially noteworthy. What originated as a bow to French taste became a permanent preference for fuller sound. Cavalli continued his fuller orchestration in his next three operas, the Roman trilogy of *Scipione affricano*, *Mutio Scevola* and *Pompeo magno*.

There were no further performances of Cavalli operas in France. In 1671 Molière with Pierre Corneille and Philippe Quinault produced in the *tragédie-ballet Psyché* an imitation of *Ercole amante* and an excuse to revive the original sets; Lully again wrote the ballet score. Thomas Shadwell's *Psyche* (set by Locke), produced in London in 1675, was an imitation of the French work. The opera was revived in London in 1980 and a recording issued in 1981.

MARTHA NOVAK CLINKSCALE

Ercole in Tebe ('Hercules in Thebes'). *Drama per musica* in three acts by GIOVANNI ANTONIO BORETTI to a libretto by AURELIO AURELI after GIOVANNI ANDREA MONIGLIA; Venice, Teatro SS Giovanni e Paolo, 12 December 1670.

Hercules (tenor) returns triumphant to Thebes, but sets out almost immediately to rescue Theseo [Theseus] (tenor) from the Underworld. He once again leaves Pelio [Peleus] (soprano) in charge of his kingdom. Peleus covets Hercules' throne as well as his wife, Megara (soprano); Aristeo [Aristaeus] (soprano), Peleus's co-conspirator, seeks to steal Iole (soprano) away from her betrothed Ilo [Hyllus] (soprano), Hercules' son. In order to protect Iole and Hyllus, Megara tells Peleus in a letter that if he allows the young couple to marry, she will look favourably on his suit in the event that Hercules' expedition proves unsuccessful. Upon Hercules' return and defeat of the conspirators' forces, Peleus uses the letter against Megara, but the hero soon learns of her fidelity, and husband and wife are reunited. The opera ends unhappily for the two traitors, who commit suicide; in an alternative ending, Megara pleads for mercy on Peleus's behalf.

The opera is based on the eponymous libretto of Giovanni Andrea Moniglia set by Jacopo Melani for Florence in 1661. It uses many of the leading conventions of the day, such as the letter scene, the sleep scene and the lament. Boretti incorporated numerous arias and ariosos into the dramatic framework; his recitatives are sensitive to the variety of emotions expressed in the text.

BETH L. GLIXON

Erdélyi, Miklós (*b* Budapest, 9 Feb 1928). Hungarian conductor. He studied at the Liszt Academy of Music, Budapest (1946–50), and made his début with *L'elisir d'amore* in 1947 at the Budapest Comic Opera. From 1951 to 1988 he was conductor at the Budapest Opera, where he introduced to the Hungarian repertory such works as *L'incoronazione di Poppea* and *Die Kluge*. He has toured in Europe and the USA, and in the 1980s became a regular guest with the Finnish National Opera in Helsinki as well as appearing at Turin and elsewhere. He has won many Hungarian awards, including the Kossuth Prize in 1975. He published a biography of Schubert (Budapest, 1963, 2/1979).

PÉTER P. VÁRNAI, NOËL GOODWIN

Erede, Alberto (*b* Genoa, 8 Nov 1908). Italian conductor. He studied in Genoa and at the Verdi Conservatory, Milan, then with Felix Weingartner at Basle and with Fritz Busch at Dresden. After his début he joined Busch on the music staff of the first Glyndebourne Festival (1934), returning each year until 1939 and conducting performances of *Le nozze di Figaro* and *Don Giovanni* there in 1938–9. He was also music director of the Salzburg Opera Guild (1935–8), with whose ensemble he first toured the USA in 1937. In 1939 he conducted the première of Menotti's *The Old Maid and the Thief*, originally a radio opera, for NBC. The war years were spent conducting opera and concerts in Italy.

Erede became a familiar figure in London as music director of the New London Opera Company at the Cambridge Theatre (1946–8), where he conducted over 500 performances. In 1950 he was engaged by Rudolf Bing for the Metropolitan Opera (*La traviata*); he conducted there regularly until 1955, including Kirsten Flagstad's farewell in 1952 (Gluck's *Alceste*), and returned in 1974–5. He was Generalmusikdirektor of the Deutsche Oper am Rhein from 1958 to 1961 – the first Italian in the 20th century to hold such an appointment in Germany – and in 1968 he followed Toscanini and Victor de Sabata as the third Italian to conduct at Bayreuth, in *Lohengrin*. His close ties with West Germany were recognized by the award of the Federal Order of Merit. He has continued to appear widely as a guest conductor, including opera performances at Covent Garden (first with *Il trovatore* in 1953) and the Edinburgh Festival (where he conducted performances by the S Carlo Opera from Naples in 1963). In 1988 he returned to the Rome Opera after a 20-year absence and brought a rare unity of Verdian style to *Simon Boccanegra*. He recorded 14 complete operas, mainly in the 1950s, of which those by Verdi, Puccini and others set new standards of opera performance in the early days of LP records, displaying Erede's characteristic blend of rhythmically firm outline with lively feeling for nuances of shading and melodic expression.

HANSPETER KRELLMANN, NOËL GOODWIN

Eremans [Erremans, Heremance], Mlle (*fl* 1721–43). French soprano. She made her début in the 1721 revival of Destouches' *Issé* as First Hesperides in the prologue and was immediately praised for her light, beautiful and flexible voice. In the 1721 revival of Lully's *Phaëton* she sang Astraea in the prologue to the Saturn of the young Chassé. She sang the title role in three performances of *Armide* (1724), for which she was praised by Mlle Le Rochois, but did not generally take such dramatic roles: her Phaedra in the 1742 revival of Rameau's *Hippolyte et Aricie* was an exception. She created Venus in both Francoeur and Rebel's *Pirame et Thisbé* (1726) and Rameau's *Dardanus* (1739). A frequent understudy and replacement for Mlle Antier, she retired in 1743.

A. Pougin: *Un ténor de l'Opéra: Pierre Jélyotte et les chanteurs de son temps* (Paris, 1905), 51ff   PHILIP WELLER

Erenberg, Vladimir Georgiyevich. *See* EHRENBERG, VLADIMIR GEORGIYEVICH.

Erevan (Russ. Yerevan). Capital of Armenia, southern Caucasus, since 1918. The 19th century saw occasional performances of operetta and appearances by touring opera companies, but local opera began only in 1912 with a private performance of the national opera *Anush* by Tigranyan (first performed privately in Alexandrapol [now Kumayrï]). An opera class organized by the composer A. G. Ter-Ghevondyan at the conservatory in 1932 formed the basis of the Erevan State Opera Theatre, which opened in 1933 with Spendiaryan's opera *Almast*. The first public performance of *Anush* followed in 1935, when the theatre became the

Spendiaryani Anvan Operayi ev Baleti T'atron (Spendiaryan Armenian Theatre of Opera and Ballet). The first opera to have its première in Erevan, Step'anyan's satirical opera *K'adj Nazar* ('Brave Nazar'), opened at the theatre on 3 December 1935; his *Lusabatsin* ('At Dawn'), the first Armenian opera on a contemporary theme, had its première in 1938. A theatre designed by A. I. Tamanyan opened in 1940 in the central city square (originally a closed winter hall of 1500 seats and an open summer hall of 200, with a shared stage, the former now has 1120 seats and the latter is covered to form a separate concert hall). 1945 saw the world première of the grand opera *Arshak II* by Tchukhatjian, an Armenian-born composer who made his career abroad in the last third of the 19th century. Other premières have included Tigranyan's *David-Bek* (1950), Terteryan's *Krakē ōghakum* ('The Ring of Fire', 1967) and Harut'yunyan's *Sayat-Nova* (1969). The repertory is a mixture of Armenian works, Russian and European classics, along with works by Soviet composers of other republics.

*

ME (Dj. O. Sarkisyan; also 'Armyanskiy teatr operï i baleta', G. Sh. Geodakyan)
Teatr operi i baleti Armenii (Moscow, 1939)
G. Tigranov: *Armyanskiy muzikal'nïy teatr*, i (Erevan, 1956)
G. Bernandt: *Slovar' oper vpervïy postavlennïkh ili izdannïkh v dorevolyutsionnoy Rossii i v SSSR 1736–1959* [Dictionary of Operas First Performed or Published in Pre-revolutionary Russia and in the USSR 1736–1959] (Moscow, 1962), 537
G. Tigranov: *Opera i balet Armenii* (Moscow, 1966)
Yu. V. Keldïsh, ed.: *Istoriya muziki narodov SSSR* [History of the Music of the Soviet Peoples], i–v (Moscow, 1970–74)
G. Tigranov: 'Opernoye i baletnoye tvorchestvo', *Muzikal'naya kul'tura Armyanskoy SSR* (Moscow, 1985)
Arkhitektura sovetskogo teatra (Moscow, 1986), 112
GREGORY SALMON

Erfurt. City in eastern Germany, capital of Thuringia. Sacred music predominated until about 1750, when secular musical life began to flourish, not least because of the theatre. Carl Theodor von Dalberg, the electoral governor, 1772–1802, did not succeed in his aim of founding a permanent theatre, although the company of the Weimar Hoftheater performed in Erfurt for several weeks every year. He did bring some notable companies of actors to the city, who also gave Singspiel performances in the Ballhaus, which was extended in 1822. The Stadttheater was opened in 1849, and a hundred years later, the Schauspielhaus. The older theatre now functions mainly as the opera house (704 seats) of the Städtische Bühne of Erfurt. Its Generalmusikdirektor was Ude Nissen, 1959–88, followed by Wolfgang Rögner in 1989. The operas first performed there include Robert Hanell's *Die Spieldose* (1957), K.-R. Griesbach's *Kolumbus* (1958), J. K. Forest's *Die Odyssee der Kiu* (1968) and K. O. Treibmann's *Der Preis* (1980).

*

A. Pick: *Erfurter Theatervorstellungen in der guten alten Zeit* (Hamburg, 1899)
DIETER HÄRTWIG

Erickson, Robert (*b* Marquette, MI, 7 March 1917). American composer. He studied in St Paul with Ernst Krenek at Hamline University (BA 1943, MA 1947). In 1953 he moved to California, where he became a highly influential figure both as a teacher and as doyen of the west-coast avant garde. He taught in San Francisco, notably at the Conservatory (1957–66), serving also as director of the Pacifica Foundation (1954–63), and at the University of California, San Diego. He wrote *The*

Structure of Music: a Listener's Guide (New York, 1955) and *Sound Structure in Music* (Berkeley, 1975), a theory of timbre.

From 12-note beginnings, Erickson quickly moved on to free atonality and non-tonal consonant polyphony as well as indeterminate techniques and notations; drones and microtonal filigree are characteristic of his music. His one opera, the one-act *Cardenitas 68*, to his own libretto, was first performed at the University of California, San Diego, on 5 June 1968; it has been variously characterized as an 'operatic work', a 'theater piece' or a 'monodrama'. The one singing role (soprano) is accompanied by a small ensemble incorporating specially designed percussion instruments of marble, brass rods etc. Such 'bespoke' instrumentation is found in a number of other works by Erickson, and reflects the influence of Harry Partch.

R. Erickson: 'Instruments for Cardenitas', *Source*, iii/1 (1969), 26–9
A. Rich: *Music of Robert Erickson* (CRI SD 494, 1984) [record notes]
R. Reynolds, J. MacKay and R. Erickson: 'On Robert Erickson', *PNM*, xxvi/2 (1988), 44–95 [incl. work-list]   ANDREW STILLER

Ericson, Barbro (*b* Halmstad, 2 April 1930). Swedish mezzo-soprano. She studied in Stockholm, making her début there in 1956 as Eboli with the Royal Opera, of which she was a member for over 20 years. She appeared with the Stockholm company at Covent Garden (1960) as Mary (*Der fliegende Holländer*) and at Expo Montreal (1967) as Ulrica and Baba the Turk. At Bayreuth she sang Venus and Kundry (1964). She made her début at the Metropolitan Opera in 1968 as Fricka. Her repertory included Amneris, Nicklausse, Carmen, Brangäne, Ortrud, Suzuki, Herodias and Leda, which she sang in the Swedish première of Bennett's *The Mines of Sulphur* (1967, Stockholm). Among her later roles were Mistress Quickly, Magdelone (*Maskarade*), Madame de Croissy (*Dialogues des Carmélites*) and Clytemnestra, which she sang at Madrid (1981). A singer of great intensity with an opulent, rich-toned voice, she was an excellent comic actress, as she demonstrated in the première of Ligeti's *Le Grand Macabre* (1978), when she created Mescalina.

ELIZABETH FORBES

Erifile. Libretto by GIOVANNI DE GAMERRA, first set by Antonio Sacchini (1778, London). Operas on the subject were also called *Erifile regina di Lacinto* and *Cleomene*.

Learco, general of Zacinto's army, has destroyed the royal family of Lacinto except for Erifile, whom he wishes to wed to establish himself on the throne he has usurped. The queen's unyielding resistance, Cleomene's invincible love for her and the tyrant's rage at their undaunted fidelity constitute the centre of the drama, which ends with the deposition or assassination of the tyrant and the restoration of Erifile and Cleomene.

The first version, as published by Giuseppe Piatolli in 1784, cites Sacchini's setting for London as the first production. Thus Mysliveček's *Erifile* (1773, Munich), for which neither score nor libretto seems to have survived, was probably not based on De Gamerra's text. In De Gamerra's original text, Erifile is forced to take poison and appears to die at the end of the duet closing Act 2. In Francesco Bianchi's setting (1779, Florence), the first given in Italy, her forced suicide takes place in a newly added multi-section, action-ensemble finale – perhaps the first in an *opera seria* outside the works of

Mattia Verazi, the Mannheim court poet whose radical operas for the opening of La Scala had caused such a furore the previous autumn (Bianchi's Act 1 also ends with an ensemble, a trio, which begins with short exchanges between the participants and incorporates action). The setting omits De Gamerra's ghost scene opening Act 3 – in which Erifile's murdered father, the king, appears demanding revenge – and the staged murder after Erifile's revival in Act 3 – in which Learco is assassinated – both scenes ahead of their time by nearly a decade. Also missing from Italian versions are the many choruses, which appear both independently and within the *introduzione*, in scene complexes concluding each act and in the ghost scene. In settings by Giuseppe Giordani (1783, Genoa) and Carlo Monza (1786, Turin), the poisoning takes place offstage. The last scene of the latter version acquires a fashionable major cavatina for Cleomene, and the repentant tyrant participates in the final chorus with soloists. In 1789 Sarti set the same libretto under the title *Cleomene*, in which Learco becomes Toante, Zacinto becomes Lacinto and Erifile becomes Emirene.

For a list of settings *see* DE GAMERRA, GIOVANNI.

MARITA P. McCLYMONDS

Erinnerungsmotiv (Ger.). REMINISCENCE MOTIF.

Erismena. *Drama per musica* in a prologue and three acts by FRANCESCO CAVALLI to a libretto by AURELIO AURELI; Venice, Teatro S Apollinare, 30 December 1655.

The Preface to the libretto explains that, while on a visit to Armenia, Prince Erimante of Media fell in love with Arminda, sister of King Artamene. Before they could marry, Erimante was summoned home to succeed his father as king. Arminda died giving birth to their child, Erismena. When Erimante learnt of Arminda's death he vowed to live a celibate life, but he abandoned this noble intention when he fell in love with his Iberian slave, Aldimira. Erismena, ignorant of her father's identity, grew up outside the Armenian court. Yet she seemed to have had some connection with it because she met Prince Idraspe of Iberia, who on a visit to Armenia seduced her. Although his original intentions were honourable, he left in search of new conquests. Reaching Media, he assumed the name of Erineo, attained a position at court and fell in love with Aldimira, now King Erimante's favourite. When Erismena discovered that Idraspe had gone to Media, she disguised herself in men's clothes and joined the Armenian army.

As the opera begins, Artamene has laid siege to the city of Tauris, where Erimante (bass) and his court reside. Prince Orimeno of Colchus (soprano), another of Aldimira's admirers, brings his army to Erimante's aid and both defeats and kills Artamene. Erismena (soprano) is wounded in battle and taken prisoner by Orimeno's servant Argippo (baritone). Orimeno brings Erismena to the palace so that her wounds can be tended by the skilled hands of Aldimira (soprano), who, already pleasantly torn between Orimeno and Erineo (alto), is smitten by the handsome soldier. Erimante notices that Erismena resembles a soldier whom he had just dreamt would steal the Armenian crown from his head. Alarmed for his future, he orders Erineo to imprison and poison her. He triumphantly places the captured Armenian crown on Aldimira's head and proclaims her queen regent. To his astonishment, she asks for the freedom of the captured Armenians, particularly the soldier whom she has just met.

While pacing her cell, Erismena bemoans her fate in the aria 'Speranze, voi che siete avvezze a lusingar'. Erineo enters with poison. Erismena grabs the vial; her revulsion mounts to fury as she recognizes that Erineo is Idraspe, and she faints. Erimante enters and, assuming the soldier dead, charges Aldimira to attempt a resuscitation. Aldimira sings the aria 'Vaghe stelle' as she casts a spell. Erismena revives and vows revenge against Erineo, who, she says, has distressed her sister. She swears allegiance to Aldimira if she can achieve vengeance against him. Erimante, angry at Aldimira's demands for the soldier's life, condemns all three of them – Aldimira, Erismena and Erineo – to the dungeon.

Diarte (baritone), the prison guard, urges Erimante to spare Aldimira. The king is on the verge of compliance when the alarm is raised as Orimeno storms the dungeon and releases the prisoners. At last Alcesta (alto), Aldimira's old nurse, tells Aldimira that she is the sister of Idraspe, Prince of Iberia, stolen as an infant by Median pirates. As Erismena, Aldimira and Erineo await their fate, Erismena confesses that she is the Armenian girl whom Idraspe deserted. At her revelation Idraspe begs forgiveness. Erimante returns and, as he glimpses the locket that Erismena wears around her neck, realizes that she is a woman. Her life-story and the portraits of her parents in the locket prove that she is Erimante's own daughter. Alcesta reveals to the company that Idraspe and Aldimira are brother and sister. At this news Idraspe bestows Aldimira on Orimeno.

Erismena was the only libretto that Aureli wrote for Cavalli (though he also completed that of *Eliogabalo*). In the Biblioteca Marciana, Venice, there are two versions of the score: the first (Cod. It. IV. 417) corresponds to the original libretto, the other (Cod. It. IV. 360) is a revised version of 1670. The initial run was from 30 December 1655 to 28 February 1656. For the later production Cavalli altered several voice parts: Idraspe became a soprano, Alcesta a tenor, Orimeno a mezzo-soprano, Diarte an alto and Argippo a contralto. Aldimira's attendant Flerida disappeared altogether. The instrumentation of both Venetian manuscripts reflects the customary accompaniment of continuo with two- or three-part treble strings, a slender sound appropriate for the small Venetian theatres.

Further scores of *Erismena* were known in England during the 17th century and may have caught the attention of Pepys and Evelyn; a 17th-century version, blessed with a stylish English translation, has reappeared in recent years (see White 1966). In the 18th century Burney mentioned seeing an Italian manuscript of *Erismena* in a private collection.

MARTHA NOVAK CLINKSCALE

Erkel, Ferenc (*b* Gyula, Békés county, 7 Nov 1810; *d* Budapest, 15 June 1893). Hungarian composer and conductor, the leading figure in Hungarian 19th-century opera.

1. Life and works to 1861. 2. Later works.

1. LIFE AND WORKS TO 1861. The young Erkel frequently attended the chamber-music evenings held in his home town by the head of the county administration, Albert Rosty, a music lover who had studied in Vienna and on whose recommendation Erkel was eventually engaged

by the National Theatre in Pest as an opera conductor. From 1822 to 1825 he attended the Benedictine Gymnasium in Pozsony (now Bratislava) and took music lessons privately. At that time Pozsony, not far from Vienna and mainly German in culture, was one of the few Hungarian towns outside Pest with a relatively high standard of musical life, giving Erkel the opportunity of attending operas and concerts and hearing the popular Hungarian dance tunes (*verbunkos*) of the violinist János Bihari. Further exposure to specifically Hungarian music was afforded him in Gyula in 1828, when a travelling company performed József Ruzitska's *Béla futása* ('Béla's Escape'), the most popular indigenous Hungarian Singspiel before the appearance of Erkel's own works. About that time he moved to Kolozsvár (now Cluj-Napoca, Romania), the cradle of Hungarian theatre and, to some extent, of Hungarian opera as well; there he taught the piano and gained a reputation as a concert pianist, and, in November 1834, began his long career as an opera conductor. In February 1835 the theatre and opera company moved to Nagyvárad (now Oradea, Romania) and soon after to the capital, where it formed part of the Hungarian theatre company of Buda (forerunner of the National Theatre in Pest). The Buda company gave its first performance on 2 April 1835, and Erkel, acting as its opera conductor, settled in the capital at about that time. When the company was beset by financial difficulties, he was temporarily employed (from November 1836) by the (German) Municipal Theatre of Pest, but in January 1838 he was engaged by the six-month-old Hungarian National Theatre, and from then on his name was inextricably bound up with the history of Hungarian opera.

Erkel composed his first opera, *Bátori Mária*, remarkably quickly considering its advance over earlier experiments in Hungarian opera; from its première in 1840 he was acknowledged as a leading Hungarian composer. Béni Egressy's libretto is based on a play with the same title by András Dugonics (1794), which was very popular with Hungarian touring theatrical troupes. Its plot goes back to Camoëns's epic poem *Os Lusíadas* (1572), the basis of many literary works outside Portugal, but Egressy set it in the Hungarian court in the 12th century. Erkel's style in *Bátori Mária* consists largely of the forms and character types of contemporary Italian and French opera infused with the melodic patterns of the instrumental *verbunkos*, and he attempted to build up the finales as grand, coherent concluding scenes. He uses a large contemporary orchestra, with some effective choruses. The overture, the most lastingly successful part of the opera, was first performed much later (11 November 1841); Erkel subsequently added new arias, and in 1858 he rewrote the opera. Outside Pest it was performed complete only in Pozsony, in a guest performance by the opera company of the National Theatre, conducted by Erkel (1844); a large part of it was given in Kolozsvár. The opera was revived in 1860 but it did not remain in the repertory.

After this initial success Erkel devoted his composing efforts almost exclusively to the stage, and two months later a new libretto was in preparation, again by Egressy and based on a play. The new work, *Hunyadi László* (1844), became the most successful of Erkel's operas in Hungary. From the early 1850s provincial companies began to include it in their repertories; one of them performed a shortened version of it in Vienna in 1856, two others in Zagreb and Bucharest in 1860. However,

Thalberg's attempt to introduce the opera to Paris in 1846 failed, as did Liszt's endeavours to have it performed in Weimar in 1856–7. Liszt listened to the opera repeatedly throughout his life and in 1847 made a piano transcription of the Haltyúdal ('Death Song') and March from it. The blending of Italian and Viennese classical influences with indigenous ones is exemplified by the highly developed recitative and the incorporation of features from popular dances. From the *verbunkos* Erkel made use of the 'Hungarian scale' with its two augmented 2nds, of certain rhythmic patterns (especially the choriamb), of the *bokázó* (a characteristically Hungarian cadential figure) and of the mood of the dance – both heroic and, in the slow, minor-mode first section, deeply mournful, even tragic.

In his perpetual and enthusiastic search for fresh librettos, Erkel was also aiming at a new and native genre, the *népszínmű*, popular plays with musical insertions, resembling the English ballad opera. His close imitation of contemporary Hungarian melodies, sometimes used unaltered, contributed to the immediate and lasting success of these interpolated numbers. Some of the *népszínmű*, in particular *Két pisztoly* ('Two Pistols', 9 March 1844) and *A rab* ('The Prisoner', 2 June 1845) and also *A zsidó* ('The Jew', 27 July 1844) and *Egy szekrény rejtelmei* ('Secrets of a Wardrobe', 28 February 1846), became more quickly known in the provinces – and, in the case of the first two, outside Hungary – than his operas. All four used texts by Ede Szigligeti (1814–78), who was at that time the best writer of the new genre and who worked as a stage director, secretary, dramatist and later dramatic director at the National Theatre. Erkel collaborated on a stage work with another musician for the first time in *Two Pistols*: in Act 1 he wrote only the melodies and entrusted the orchestration to Franz Doppler (under his supervision), perhaps because of lack of time; the music of Acts 2 and 3 was written entirely by him, except for the last number and the overture, which were composed by Doppler. From then onwards Erkel collaborated repeatedly with Franz Doppler and his brother Karl. The overture of *The Prisoner* was also Franz's work. Erkel worked with both of them on the short-lived melodrama *Salvator Rosa* (29 December 1855) and on the occasional opera *Erzsébet* (1857), staged when Emperor Franz Joseph and his wife Elizabeth (in Hungarian, Erzsébet) visited Hungary. Out of the three acts of the opera, only Act 2, written by Erkel himself, is of value. In the first two years the work was performed only nine times, and in 1865–6 (when the emperor and his wife were in Pest) four times; finally there were two performances in 1879, on their silver wedding, with the opera thoroughly rewritten in two acts by Erkel's son Sándor (1846–1900).

After Austria's defeat in the campaign against the Italians (June 1859), the heavy oppression of Hungary was relaxed, reviving in Erkel a hope he had been fostering since the completion of *Hunyadi László* of composing an opera on the censored play *Bánk bán*. In order to complete it as quickly as possible he enlisted the help of his two most talented sons, Gyula (1841–1909) and Sándor. From this time on, his opera scores reveal the increasingly important collaboration of these two, especially Gyula. The première in 1861 of *Bánk bán* was enormously successful, and represents the summit of Erkel's career. The story of the 13th-century revolt against the queen's hated foreign court seemed to have set free repressed passions in the composer. He filled his opera with broad, immediately striking melodies whose new flexibility was a direct result of the influence of folksong. *Bánk bán* is the culmination of Erkel's stylistic procedures in *Bátori Mária* and *Hunyadi László*; in it he not only succeeded in constructing the various numbers in accordance with the formal principles of the *verbunkos*, but also achieved a newly vivid dramatic characterization in the grand scenes (especially in the third act) through his handling of recitative and thematic transformation. In the concentration of both plot and music, there is a tendency towards chamber opera; the instrumental writing is chamber-like, both in solos and in ensembles. Erkel was particularly adept at evoking a pastoral nostalgia in instrumental passages composed in folk style; the cimbalom was used here for the first time in composed music.

2. LATER WORKS. *Bánk bán* was the fruit of long years of organic growth, and Erkel never managed in his later operas to write with such fire and spontaneity. His subsequent stylistic development followed two distinct paths. The first involved a simplification of his musical language and an increased realism that found expression in comic opera peopled with peasants and ordinary townsfolk. In *Sarolta* (1862) and still more in *Névtelen hősök* ('Unknown Heroes', 1880), there are popular revels, a bride's farewell, drum signals, recruiting dances and the billeting of troops; this use of folk customs and the portrayal of rustic life is more commonly associated with the later opera of Kodály, *Székely fonó* ('The Transylvanian Spinning-Room').

After Egressy's death in 1851 Erkel could not find a good librettist for *Sarolta*. Before Erkel worked with Egressy, all his operas had been based on first-rate or well-known dramas and plays. The poor text of *Sarolta* was written by an amateur, József Czanyuga, who invented the plot, setting it in a small Hungarian village in the 12th century; it is humourless and uninteresting. Erkel wrote a fine, *verbunkos*-inspired overture and used the same type of Hungarian music as a basis for the huge finales, a closely knit duet and some good arias, but he could not rescue the unsuitable libretto. He entrusted much of the instrumentation to his eldest son, Gyula, though it was carried out according to his own instructions or under his guidance. This was the last opera in which he had sufficient faith to publish the main parts in his own piano transcription without words (1862). However, it was with this opera that his disappointments began. Of the four principal singers, Kornélia Hollósy quitted the stage and Lajos Bignio left for the Vienna Opera, and the two singers who came to replace them did not understand Hungarian. Erkel had to be satisfied with having them perform only in *Hunyadi László* and *Bánk bán*. Meanwhile one of his children died. Erkel lost all enthusiasm for producing his 'comic' opera, and it disappeared from the repertory in 1863 after six performances. It was performed again in the Opera House in Budapest in 1901, but only four times. In 1970 József Romhányi rewrote the libretto (retaining the same plot) and Viktor Vaszy (1903–79) rewrote the music, making many alterations; this version was produced in Szeged in 1971, conducted by Vaszy, but was not staged in the Budapest Opera House.

Erkel's other opera in this populistic vein, *Unknown Heroes*, is an interesting experiment with a new genre. The librettist was Ede Tóth (1844–76), one of the best and most prolific writers of *népszínmű*, whose three finest works were set by Gyula Erkel. It was perhaps

Gyula who suggested that his father should compose a 'light' opera with borrowed well-known airs akin to the English ballad opera but without spoken dialogue. It is impossible to tell who composed which parts, as most of the opera exists only in fair copies. From the few drafts remaining it seems that Ferenc Erkel wrote the melodies and gave some indication of how they were to be orchestrated. Besides Sándor and especially Gyula, another of Erkel's sons, Elek (1842–93), had a substantial role in the orchestration; at the time he was first conductor of the People's Theatre in Budapest and had a reputation as a composer of *népszínmű* and operetta. The plot looks back to the time of the Hungarian war of independence of 1848–9 and is set in a peaceful small village and (in Act 3) in a Hungarian soldiers' camp. In both vocal and instrumental writing the work represents a culmination of the integration of folklike music into an operatic framework, an achievement foreshadowed to a small degree in Erkel's music for song-plays of 1844–6 and in many parts of *Hunyadi László* and *Bánk bán*. It also includes a truly comic figure, a fine duet for the two leading characters, an accomplished *verbunkos* piece, and a *Takarodó* ('Retreat') for chorus which rapidly became known throughout Hungary. At its première the opera was conducted by Sándor Erkel, then the chief conductor of the National Theatre in Budapest. It was performed only six times there and again in Kolozsvár in 1891; a revival in the Budapest Opera House in 1916 was limited to four performances.

Erkel's second path of later development was in music drama on folk subjects, represented by *Dózsa György* (1867) and *Brankovics György* (1874), in which he and his two sons pursued their stylistic experiments furthest. Both were written on existing historical dramas, each with a tragic hero of strong character whose personal fate culminates in that of his people. *Dózsa György* is based on a play by Mór Jókai (1825–1904), adapted as a libretto by Szigligeti. In 1514 a crusade was begun against the Turks, and about 40 000 peasants and craftsmen assembled to fight against them under the leadership of the bold Dózsa, appointed general by the king. But when they heard that the nobles at home had given their work to their own families, they revolted and a bloody uprising began. Eventually the peasants were defeated and Dózsa was cruelly executed. These tragic events marked the beginning of the rapid decline of the Hungarian nation after 500 years of power, and of its conquest by the Turks, followed by centuries of misery. In Jókai's play Dózsa falls in love with an aristocrat and in order to win her tries to become a king, helped by the peasants' revolt. Erkel could not discard this fictitious love affair, but he grossly (and deliberately) 'misinterpreted' it in his setting and portrayed Dózsa as a true hero. This opera therefore contains sharp contrasts, much more declamatory writing and fewer arias than his others; there are vast crowd scenes, choral recitatives, polyphonic writing and, in Act 5, solo scenes in which Dózsa, already imprisoned, awaits execution and recalls the events of his life. The extreme sentiments and situations elicited a developed chromaticism and harmony not used by Erkel before, with diminished 5ths and chords of five or six superimposed 3rds. Unfortunately, Erkel staged this music drama two months before the coronation of Franz Joseph, in the year of the establishment of the Austro-Hungarian dual monarchy, and at the time it appeared to be a political demonstration against the new era. As a result, it was produced only ten times in 18 months, and never again in full.

Much of the opera survives only in the fair copies of Gyula and Sándor Erkel, though the best parts are undoubtedly their father's work, and the others were either partly written or at least supervised and corrected by him.

Erkel's other folk music drama, *Brankovics György*, has its literary background in the play of the same name by Károly Obernyik (1815–55), from which two opera singers, Lehel Odry and Ferenc Ormai, fabricated a poor prose libretto. Brankovics (1367–1456) was the reigning Prince of Serbia from 1427 to 1456. One of his daughters became the wife of Count Ulrik Cilley, while his granddaughter was for a short time the fiancée of László Hunyadi, the hero of Erkel's opera of 1844. Brankovics sought to guard the independence of Serbia from the two great powers of that time, Turkey and Hungary, which had been fighting each other for a century. His was a bold, clever personality, beset by doubt and self-reproach; the plot therefore offers fine opportunities for vigorous characterization, sharp, tragic conflicts and lively crowd scenes. Serbian and Turkish musical influences appear alongside Hungarian ones. Erkel mainly used a major–minor scale system, although there are also elements derived from the Hungarian scale and amalgams of the church modes, besides the whole-tone scale, offering him an opportunity for fresh melodic and harmonic patterns. The music is mostly continuous in a Wagnerian sense, though with organically arising set numbers and large finales, and the orchestra's role approaches a Wagnerian level of relative importance; nevertheless the work is not wholly derivative, but much more an organic transformation of Erkel's own style. The chromaticism and such harmonic elements as 13th chords and chords constructed of superimposed 5ths show a marked similarity to the style of Liszt; the treatment of folk music foreshadows that of Bartók. It is regrettable that only the manuscript of Act 4 shows approximately what was written by Erkel himself and what (mainly the continuation of orchestration and the fair copies) by his sons Gyula and Sándor. All three preceding acts survive only in the sons' fair copies. In staging his new music drama Erkel was again quite indifferent to current political events, for its Serbian, anti-Turkish viewpoint conflicted with the official friendship of the Austro-Hungarian monarchy with Turkey. The performances attracted increasingly large audiences, and some critics considered the work one of Erkel's best. It was performed in the National Theatre 20 times, then was withdrawn before the war between Russia and Turkey. There were 12 stagings in the Opera House, 1889–1910, and in the winter of 1912–13 a new fair copy was made, but further performances were cancelled on the outbreak of World War I. A new version of the opera was made in 1961 by the librettist József Romhányi and the composer Rezső Kókai (1906–62), who rewrote the music and added new numbers; it was performed in Budapest and Szeged and from 1985 in Debrecen.

The last opera, *István király* ('King Stephen', 1885) is an enigma. The libretto was written by Antal Váradi after the tragedy of the same title by Lajos Dobsa but it is not known who composed the music. The incomplete sketches in Ferenc Erkel's hand mostly conflict with the score, which is in Gyula Erkel's and in part Sándor Erkel's hand. Three years before the première, according to newspapers of the day, Erkel played the best numbers, to the enchantment of his hearers, and Marie Wilt sang two passages accompanied by him. Performance is impossible on the basis of the sketches that survive, and there must have been a version, now lost, between these and the finished score. Erkel, by then 72 years old, had 25–30 piano students at the Academy of Music (where he had to act as director as well) and was still conducting his operas in the National Theatre. Not surprisingly the new opera, intended for the opening of the Budapest Opera House on 27 September 1884, was not ready in time. It should be remembered that Gyula conducted only French and Italian operas, while Sándor was a great admirer of Wagner, from whose influence Erkel tried to preserve the National Theatre and Hungarian opera in general; the French or Italian and Wagnerian influences in the opera may therefore be attributed to the sons, and the dramatically most successful solutions, the most effective passages and the Hungarian stylistic elements to the father. In all probability this is the case in all the operas from *Bánk bán* onwards. Sándor tried to compose an opera in 1865, but finished only two acts, which were later given a single performance. Gyula lived for 16 years after his father's death but never wrote an opera independently. The craftsmanship of his sons was undoubtedly of help to Erkel, but he himself was the composer. *István király* had great success at first; in the year of its première it was performed 13 times and was praised by Liszt, Massenet and Delibes. After Erkel's death, however, it was staged only a few times. In the 1960s the composer and musicologist Jenő Vécsey (1909–66), the head of the Music Department of the National Széchényi Library, began to work on a critical complete edition of Erkel's operas. By the time of his death, however, he had prepared only *Bátori Mária, Sarolta*, Act 2 of *Erzsébet* and Act 1 of *Dózsa György*.

See also BÁNK BÁN and HUNYADI LÁSZLÓ.

unless otherwise stated, performed in Pest (from 1873 Budapest), National Theatre, and MSS in H-Bn; all printed works published in [Buda]Pest

Bátori Mária (2, B. Egressy, after A. Dugonics, after L. V. de Camoëns: *Os Lusíadas*), 8 Aug 1840; rev. version, 1 Feb 1858; march arr. pf (1846), ov. (1860)

Hunyadi László (4, Egressy, after L. Tóth), 27 Jan 1844; rev. version, Budapest, Royal Hungarian Opera, 2 Oct 1885; further rev., M. Radnai, 1935; Death Song arr. pf (1843), ov. and excerpts (1846), La Grange aria (1850), vs (1896)

Erzsébet (3, J. Czanyuga), 6 May 1857, march arr. pf (1857); collab. F. and K. Doppler

Bánk bán (3, Egressy, after J. Katona), 9 March 1861, excerpts arr. pf (1861), vs (1902); orchd with G. and S. Erkel; rev. 1939 by N. Rékai, vs (1957)

Sarolta (comic op, 3, Czanyuga), 26 June 1862, ov. and excerpts (1862); mainly orchd G. Erkel

Dózsa György (folk music drama, 5, later 4, E. Szigligeti, after M. Jókai), 6 April 1867, Hymnusz [Hymn] vs (1865), Rósza végbúcsuja [Rózsa's Farewell] arr. pf (1867); collab. G. and S. Erkel

Brankovics György (folk music drama, 4, L. Odry and F. Ormai, after K. Obernyik), 20 May 1874, excerpts arr. pf (1875); collab. G. and S. Erkel

Névtelen hősök [Unknown Heroes] (comic op, 4, E. Tóth), 30 Nov 1880, Takarodó [Retreat] vs (1882); collab. G., S., E. and L. Erkel

István király [King Stephen] (4, A. Váradi, after L. Dobsa), Budapest, Royal Hungarian Opera, 14 March 1885; mainly by G. Erkel

Arias with pf acc. in Erkel Ferenc áriák, ed. J. Kenessey (1954–5)

*

P. Weil: 'Hunyadi Laszlo', *Der Spiegel* (Pest, 31 Jan 1844)

L. Petrichevich Horváth: 'Hunyadi László dalműről és a magyar zenetanról' [On the Opera *Hunyadi László* and Hungarian Music], *Honderű* (Pest, 17 and 24 Feb and 2 March 1844)

M. Mosonyi: 'Erkel Ferenc Bánk bánja' [Ferenc Erkel's *Bánk bán*], *Zenészeti lapok* (21 and 27 March 1861), 193–6, 201–5

K. Ábrányi: *Erkel Ferenc élete és működése* [Life and Works of Ferenc Erkel] (Budapest, 1895)

B. Fabó, ed.: *Erkel Ferenc emlékkönyv* [Memorial Volume for Ferenc Erkel] (Budapest, 1910)

J. Pukánszky Kádár: *A Nemzeti Színház százéves története* [100 Years of the National Theatre], i (Budapest, 1940)

I. Barna: 'Erkel Ferenc első operái az egykorú sajtó tükrében' [The First Operas of Ferenc Erkel in Reviews by the Contemporary Press], *Zenetudományi tanulmányok*, ed. B. Szabolcsi and D. Bartha, ii (Budapest, 1954), 175–218

J. Maróthy: 'Erkel Ferenc opera-dramaturgiája' [Ferenc Erkel's Opera-Dramaturgy], ibid, 25–174

J. Ujfalussy: 'A "Hunyadi László" és irodalmi előzményei' [*Hunyadi László* and its Literary Antecedents], ibid, 219–30

I. Barna: 'Erkel nagy művei és a kritika' [Erkel's Great Works and Criticism], *Zenetudományi tanulmányok*, ed. B. Szabolcsi and D. Bartha, iv (Budapest, 1955), 211–70

Z. László: *Erkel Ferenc élete képekben* [Ferenc Erkel's Life in Pictures] (Budapest, 1958)

I. Vámosy Nagy and P. Várnai: *Bánk bán az operaszínpadon* [*Bánk bán* on the Operatic Stage] (Budapest, 1960)

J. Maróthy: 'Erkels Weg von der "heroisch-lyrischen" Oper zum kritischen Realismus', *SM*, i (1961), 161–74

L. Somfai: 'Az Erkel-kéziratok problémái' [Problems of the Erkel Manuscripts], *Zenetudományi tanulmányok*, ed. B. Szabolcsi and D. Bartha, ix (Budapest, 1961), 81–158

J. Ujfalussy: 'Erkel Ferenc és szövegkönyvei' [Ferenc Erkel and his Librettos], ibid, 37–44

D. Legány: *A magyar zene krónikája: zenei művelődésünk ezer éve dokumentumokban* [A Chronicle of Hungarian Music: 1000 Years of Music History in Documents] (Budapest, 1962)

G. Staud: 'A Nemzeti Színház műsora 1837–1964' [The Repertory of the National Theatre 1837–1964], *A Nemzeti Színház*, ed. G. Székely (Budapest, 1965), 153–240

D. Legány: 'Erkel Hunyadi Lászlója', *Magyar zene*, i/4 (1970), 97–108

——: *Erkel Ferenc művei és korabeli történetük* [Erkel's Works and their Contemporary History] (Budapest, 1975)

G. Véber: *Ungarische Elemente in der Opernmusik Ferenc Erkels* (Bilthoven, 1976)

A. Németh: *Ferenc Erkel: sein Leben und Wirken* (Budapest, 1979)

——: *Az Erkelek a magyar zenében: az Erkel család szerepe a magyar zenei művelődésben* [The Erkels in Hungarian Music: the Role of the Erkel Family in Hungarian Musical Culture] (Békéscsaba, 1987)

DEZSŐ LEGÁNY

Erkel Theatre. Theatre in BUDAPEST, opened in 1911 as the Népopera (People's Opera); it acquired its present name in 1953.

Erlanger, Camille (*b* Paris, 25 May 1863; *d* Paris, 24 April 1919). French composer. Son of an old-established family from Alsace who wanted him to become a silk merchant, he preferred music as a career and studied first the piano, then composition with Delibes at the Paris Conservatoire. In 1888 he won the Prix de Rome, beating Paul Dukas, and during his stay in Italy he composed the dramatic legend *Saint Julien l'Hospitalier*, based on a story by Flaubert, which was performed at the Conservatoire on his return to Paris in 1894.

His first opera, *Kermaria*, a Breton idyll produced in 1897 by the Opéra-Comique, made little impression. In 1900, however, his next attempt, *Le Juif polonais*, based on the Erckmann-Chatrian novel of 1869, a version of the Alsatian legend on which Sir Henry Irving's favourite play *The Bells* is also based, achieved a popular triumph and remained in the repertory of the Opéra-Comique until 1933; the opera was also performed in Germany, Vienna and St Petersburg.

Le fils de l'étoile, an ambitious five-act musical drama with text by Catulle Mendès, and Erlanger's only work intended for the Paris Opéra, was produced there in 1904. The superb cast included Lucienne Bréval, Albert Alvarez and Jean-François Delmas; possibly for that reason, it was given 26 times in less than ten months, before vanishing from the Opéra for ever. In 1906 Erlanger returned to the Opéra-Comique with *Aphrodite*, adapted from Pierre Louÿs's novel; this became, at least in Paris, where it had more than 180 performances in 20 years, his most popular opera. At the première Mary Garden sang Chrysis, the beautiful courtesan.

Erlanger's later operas were much less successful. *Bacchus triomphant* was first performed in 1909 at Bordeaux and *L'aube rouge* in 1911 at Rouen. *Hannele Mattern*, a five-act *rêve lyrique*, based on a play by Gerhard Hauptmann and composed in 1911, was not seen until 1950, when it was performed at Strasbourg. *La sorcière*, an adaptation of Victorien Sardou's drama, received 25 performances by the Opéra-Comique in 1912–13, but *Forfaiture*, based on Hector Turnbill's film *The Cheat*, was sung only three times when produced by the same company in 1921, after Erlanger's death.

Despite his years of study with Delibes, Erlanger (like a number of other French composers of his generation) found his main inspiration in Germany. He was particularly influenced by Weber, whom he greatly admired, and to a much lesser extent by Wagner. That he had a genuine if minor dramatic talent is well demonstrated by his operas, in which musical means are always subservient to dramatic ends. Though his fine-drawn character sketches and rewardingly singable vocal lines appealed to artists and audiences, his musical idiom and style, rooted as they were in the late 19th century, did not survive comfortably in the Paris of the 1920s and 30s.

See also JUIF POLONAIS, LE.

Kermaria (idylle d'Armorique, 3, P.-B. Gheusi), Paris, OC (Lyrique), 8 Feb 1897 (Paris, 1897)
Le Juif polonais (conte populaire d'Alsace, 3, H. Cain and Gheusi, after Erckmann-Chatrian), Paris, OC (Favart), 11 April 1900 (Paris, 1900)
Le fils de l'étoile (drame musical, 5, C. Mendès), Paris, Opéra, 20 April 1904 (Paris, 1903)
Aphrodite (drame musical, 6, L.-F. de Gramont, after P. Louÿs), Paris, OC (Favart), 27 March 1906 (Paris, 1905)
Bacchus triomphant (poème lyrique, 3, Cain), Bordeaux, Place des Quinquonces, 11 Sept 1909 (Paris and Bordeaux, 1909)
Hannele Mattern, 1911 (rêve lyrique, 5, J. Thorel and Gramont, after G. Hauptmann: *Hanneles Himmelfahrt*), Strasbourg, 28 Jan 1950 (Paris, 1911)
L'aube rouge (drame lyrique, 4, A. Bernède and P. de Choudens), Rouen, Arts, 29 Dec 1911 (Paris, 1912)
La sorcière (drame musical, 4, A. Sardou, after V. Sardou), Paris, OC (Favart), 18 Dec 1912 (Paris, 1912)
Forfaiture (comédie musicale, 5, P. Milliet and A. de Lorde, after H. Turnbill: *The Cheat* [film]), Paris, OC (Favart), 11 Feb 1921

*

C. Mendès: 'Le Juif polonais', *Le journal* (11 April 1900)
A. Bachelet: 'Camille Erlanger', *Monde musical*, v (1919)
L. Vuillemin: 'Camille Erlanger', *Courrier musical*, xxi (1919), 128
G. Courty: 'Il y a vingt ans mourait Camille Erlanger', *L'intransigeant* (8 May 1939)
P.-B. Gheuzi: 'Camille Erlanger', *Petit parisien* (23 May 1939)
P. Landormy: *La musique française de Franck à Debussy* (Paris, 1943)
G. Demombynes: *Histoire de la musique française* (Paris, 1946)
ELIZABETH FORBES

Erlanger, Baron Frédéric d' (*b* Paris, 29 May 1868; *d* London, 23 April 1943). British composer of German-American parentage. He studied in Paris and then, in his early twenties, moved to London, where he worked as a banker and took British nationality. His operas and his other compositions, which include choral, orchestral and chamber music, are distinguished by clarity of form

and elegance of idea. *Inès Mendo* was presented at Covent Garden and privately printed in 1897 under the pseudonym Frédéric Régnal.

Jehan de Saintré (2, J. Barbier and P. Barbier), Aix-les-Bains, 1 Aug 1893
Inès Mendo (3, P. Decourcelle and A. Liorat, after P. Mérimée), CG, 10 July 1897
Tess (4, L. Illica, after T. Hardy), Naples, S Carlo, 10 April 1906
Noël (J. Ferrier and P. Ferrier), Paris, OC (Favart), 28 Dec 1910

Erlebach, Philipp Heinrich (*b* Esens, East Friesland, bap. 25 July 1657; *d* Rudolstadt, Thuringia, 17 April 1714). German composer. He probably received his earliest musical training at the East Friesian court. From 1678 to 1679 he was employed at the court of Count Albert Anton von Schwarzburg-Rudolstadt in Thuringia, and became Kapellmeister in 1681. He not only succeeded in making this small establishment into a main centre of musical activity but also made a considerable name for himself as a composer, especially of church cantatas, though he wrote prolifically in nearly all the forms common at the time. In his last years he was revered above all as a teacher.

Several arias from Erlebach's two principal operas – the otherwise lost *Die Plejades* and *Die siegende Unschuld* – were printed in his two volumes of *Harmonische Freude*, but of his other dramatic works (operas, ballets and incidental music) only librettos survive. In his operatic output a preference for comic mythological subjects (e.g. *Die Plejades*) gave way to a deliberate choice of national, historical subjects, with an emphasis on local colour. This trend is found not only in *Die siegende Unschuld*, based on a medieval German legend, and *Der wahrsagende Wunderbrunnen* but also in smaller-scale ballets and pastorals: in contrast, therefore, to the italianate *opera seria* of the more important German courts, these works contained a pronounced element of popular realism. The da capo aria appears as a mature form, and Erlebach adopted many other devices and techniques customary in operas at the time – for example ostinatos and quasi-ostinatos, contrasting tempos and textures for structural purposes, and the through-composition of individual scenes – in order to avoid the danger of too repetitive and stereotyped a structure. He also involved the orchestra in the interpretation of the text, taking advantage of the specific tone colours of individual instruments. It is important to stress that the two parts of *Harmonische Freude* are essentially collections of operatic arias (some to parodied texts): many writers have treated them simply as collections of songs and have mistakenly referred to Erlebach as the last important German songwriter of the 17th century.

Die Plejades oder Das Siebengestirne (3, F. C. Bressand), 1693, 35 arias in Harmonische Freude musicalischer Freunde, i (Nuremberg, 1697)
Die siegende Unschuld unter dem Beispiele Hunonis, Grafen zu Oldenburg (3), 1702, 25 arias in Harmonische Freude, ii (Nuremberg, 1710)
Die erfreute Schäfer-Gesellschaft, 1702, lost
Der wahrsagende Wunderbrunnen, 1704, lost

*

M. Friedlaender: *Das deutsche Lied im 18. Jahrhundert* (Stuttgart and Berlin, 1902)
O. Kinkeldey: Introduction to DDT, xlvi–xlvii (1914)
B. Baselt: *Der Rudolstädter Hofkapellmeister Philipp Heinrich Erlebach* (diss., U. of Halle, 1963)
——: 'Die Musikaliensammlung der Schwarzburg-Rudolstädtischen Hofkapelle unter Philipp Heinrich Erlebach', *Wissenschaftliche Zeitschrift der Martin-Luther-Universität Halle-Wittenberg* (1963)

'*Erminia sul Giordano*'
(M. Rossi), *final scene in
Act 3, designed by
Francesco Guitti for the
first performance at the
Palazzo Barberini, Rome,
30 January 1633: engrav-
ing from the first edition
of the score (Rome: Paolo
Masotti, 1637)*

P. Gülke: *Musik und Musiker in Rudolstadt* (Rudolstadt, 1963)

R. H. Thomas: *Poetry and Song in the German Baroque* (Oxford, 1963)

R. Brockpähler: *Handbuch zur Geschichte der Barockoper in Deutschland* (Emsdetten, 1964)

K.-H. Wiechers: *Philipp Heinrich Erlebach* (Aurich, 1964)

A. Kappelhoff: 'Der Rudolstädter Hofkapellmeister Philipp Heinrich Erlebach, seine ostfriesische Verwandtschaft und sein Werdegang', *Jb der Gesellschaft für bildende Kunst und vaterländische Altertümer zu Emden*, xlv (1965), 148–73

BERND BASELT

Erlo [Camerlo], Louis (*b* Lyons, 26 April 1929). French director. He studied electrical engineering at the Ecole Nationale Professionnelle at Lyon Martinière (1944–8) and taught himself stagecraft. Shortly after his appointment as stage manager at the Lyons Opéra (1950) he was given the opportunity to stage *Lohengrin*, and the success of this, his first production, led to his becoming a director there (1953). He became head of production in 1969 and in 1973 administrator of the Paris Opéra-Studio as well. By 1956 he had an international reputation, and directed productions in Venice (Rabaud's *Mârouf*, 1956), Buenos Aires, San Francisco and the major European centres. He was appointed director of the Aix-en-Provence Festival from 1981; his productions there have included *Pelléas* and *Don Giovanni* (both 1980), *Les contes d'Hoffmann* (1982) and, with Alain Maratrat, an updated, anarchic staging of Chabrier's *L'étoile* that was highly praised.

Erlo has worked to create a new approach to opera. In his attempt to abolish the idea of repertory and introduce eclectic programmes he has given new emphasis to works by contemporary composers (e.g. Kosma's *Les hussards*, 1969; Ohana's *Autodafé*, 1973; Martinů's *Les trois souhaits*, 1973). He aims to involve the performer as much as possible in the staging and preparation of the production and to offer his actors insight into the characters they portray. Erlo's work at Lyons has been emulated throughout France.

*

J. Astier: 'Profil: Louis Erlo', *Scherzo*, no.24 (1973), 38

A. Artaud: 'L'Opéra-Studio', *Scherzo*, no.37 (1974), 32–3

J. Goury: 'Pleins feux sur l'Opéra de Lyon', *Guide musical-opéra*, no.642 (1974), 12–15; no.643 (1974), 46–7

CHRISTIANE SPIETH-WEISSENBACHER/R

Erminia sul Giordano ('Erminia by the Jordan'). *Dramma musicale* in three acts by MICHELANGELO ROSSI to a libretto by GIULIO ROSPIGLIOSI after TORQUATO TASSO's *Gerusalemme liberata*; Rome, Palazzo Barberini alle Quattro Fontane, 30 January 1633.

The five main characters of the pastoral drama form a chain of unfulfilled desires: the shepherd Selvaggio (alto) loves a shepherdess, Lidia (soprano), who has fallen in love with a crusader who fled to their forest by the River Jordan. The knight is really Erminia (soprano), the Princess of Antioch, who loves the crusader hero Tancredi (tenor). He in turn searches for Clorinda, while the sorceress Armida (soprano) plots to trap Tancredi for herself. Everyone is frustrated and unhappy except Ergasto (baritone), a wise old shepherd and former courtier, who takes Erminia under his protection. After refusals, setbacks and attempted suicides, Lidia agrees to marry Selvaggio, Tancredi agrees to champion Erminia, and pastoral harmony is restored.

The original sets by Andrea Camassei, with stage effects by FRANCESCO GUITTI, are illustrated in five plates included with the published score (Rome, 1637; see illustration). Guitti's stagecraft emphasized the disruptiveness of passion, concentrating on the pagan Armida. She enters in a chariot drawn by dragons that disappears as she steps out, and she causes besieged Jerusalem to emerge in the middle of the forest. She vents her final frustration in an infernal scene with 'horrible' rain, hail and wind, calling forth demons and the Furies against the Christians. She represents the religious conflict in the real world, which threatened the ideal world of the literary pastoral.

The musical setting offers a series of tableaux, with brooding recitative monologues and formal, but harmonically responsive, dialogue framed by lively choral ensembles. Rossi's recitative attempts increased rhythmic naturalness, but his stubborn adherence to full-stop cadences results in a short-winded effect. Harmonically he ventured more widely in recitative than his peers (often using A♭ major, B♭ minor and F minor chords, and ranging to the other extreme of F♯ major, G♯ major and C♯ minor chords). He was also fond of making smooth progressions using the dominant 7th. On the whole, however, his text-setting lacks characterization and melodic tension. The closed pieces are generally simple and brief, with the conventional charm of their time.

Citations of an earlier, unconfirmed performance in 1625 all derive from Félix Clément and Pierre Larousse's *Dictionnaire lyrique* (Paris, 1867–81).

MARGARET MURATA

Ermione ('Hermione'). *Azione tragica* in two acts by GIOACHINO ROSSINI to a libretto by ANDREA LEONE TOTTOLA after JEAN RACINE's *Andromaque*; Naples, Teatro S Carlo, 27 March 1819.

The ultimate dramatic source is EURIPIDES, but the version of it closely followed by Tottola comes from Racine who considerably altered the story. In particular, he allowed Astyanax, Andromache's son by the dead Hector, to survive the Trojan wars and become a pawn in this tug-of-love drama. The opera begins with an overture notable for its inclusion of a choral lament by Trojan prisoners of war. In a dungeon, Andromaca [Andromache] (contralto) is allowed a few moments with her son. She is the prisoner of King Pirro [Pyrrhus] (tenor) whose love for her has threatened his promised marriage with Ermione [Hermione] (soprano). Attalo [Attalus] (tenor) advises marriage with Pyrrhus to secure her own and her son's future, but Fenicio [Phoenicius] (bass) warns that the Greeks will never tolerate such a marriage. Outside the royal palace, Hermione's waiting-women console her; but when Pyrrhus appears she angrily confronts him, the music of both characters oscillating between anger and self-pity. The arrival of Oreste [Orestes] (tenor) gives Hermione fresh hope: he has come from the Greeks to demand the death of Astyanax, but his longstanding infatuation with Hermione gives her the chance to create complications for Pyrrhus and Andromache. Pyrrhus once more declares his love for Andromache while trying to fend off Hermione's growing anger, his manner a mixture of affection, menace and blustering self-importance. Finally, frustrated by Andromache's stubbornness, he agrees to hand Astyanax to the Greeks, at which point Andromache asks for time to reconsider. Welcome as this change of heart is for Pyrrhus, he knows that the 'tigress' Hermione may seek a terrible revenge.

In Act 2 it becomes clear that, however compliant Andromache seems, she will be faithful to Hector's memory; after Pyrrhus has guaranteed Astyanax's safety with a sacred oath she will die by her own hand. In a sequence of interlocked vocal movements, Hermione detonates the final crisis. First, she pleads with Phoenicius to tell Pyrrhus of her love and anguish; and in the slow aria 'Amata l'amai' her hopes burgeon, before a bridal march shatters her mood as Pyrrhus leads Andromache to the altar. Hermione now orders Orestes to murder Pyrrhus. In a state of near-collapse he leaves to do her bidding while Hermione sings a cabaletta of astonishing ferocity. After a brief interlude in which Phoenicius and Pilade [Pylades] (tenor) reflect on Pyrrhus's folly, Hermione reappears, riddled with hatred, love and remorse. With the words 'You are avenged', Orestes presents Hermione with the blood-stained dagger; but in a frantic reversal of mood she denies that it was her voice which gave the order: it was the voice of 'a delirious, love-maddened woman'. Too late, Orestes realizes that he has been duped. Hermione

calls on the Furies to destroy him, but Pylades and his followers carry him to his ship while Hermione falls senseless, still cursing her avenger.

Ermione is one of Rossini's finest serious operas; but despite a superb cast at the Neapolitan première it sank without trace until its revival in Pesaro in 1987 with Montserrat Caballé in the title role. Rossini seems to have been resigned to its failure. When London asked him for an opera in 1824 he considered recasting the piece as *Ugo, re d'Italia*, but nothing came of the project. The autograph manuscript was, however, carefully preserved. As an old man, Rossini remarked: 'It is my little *Guillaume Tell* in Italian; and it will not see the light of day until after my death'.

RICHARD OSBORNE

Ermolenko-Yuzhina, Nataliya. *See* YERMOLENKO-YUZHINA, NATALIYA.

Ermoupolis (Gk.). SYROS.

Ernani. *Dramma lirico* in four parts by GIUSEPPE VERDI to a libretto by FRANCESCO MARIA PIAVE after VICTOR HUGO's play *Hernani*; Venice, Teatro La Fenice, 9 March 1844.

Ernani *the bandit*	tenor
Don Carlo *King of Spain*	baritone
Don Ruy Gomez de Silva *a Spanish grandee*	bass
Elvira *his niece and betrothed*	soprano
Giovanna *her nurse*	soprano
Don Riccardo *the king's equerry*	tenor
Jago *Silva's equerry*	bass

Rebel mountaineers and bandits, knights and members of Silva's household, Elvira's maids-in-waiting, the king's knights, members of the *Lega*, Spanish and German nobles, Spanish and German ladies

Walk-on parts Mountaineers and bandits, electors and nobles of the imperial court, pages of the imperial court, German soldiers, ladies and male and female followers

Setting The Pyrenees, at Aix-la-Chapelle and at Saragossa, in 1519

Verdi's fifth opera was commissioned by the Teatro La Fenice, Venice, and was the first he wrote for a theatre other than La Scala. The Venetian authorities, impressed by the recent reception of *Nabucco* at La Fenice and of *I Lombardi* at La Scala, allowed the young composer to negotiate a sizable fee, and to make various unusual conditions, notably that he would have the right to choose from that season's company the singers for his new opera. A contract was signed in June 1843, and various subjects and librettists were mulled over; Verdi made it clear that he intended to break with the format of his previous two Milanese successes. A subject attributed to Sir Walter Scott and entitled *Cromvello* (or, sometimes, *Allan Cameron*) was initially decided upon, the librettist to be an unknown poet called Francesco Maria Piave; but Verdi became enthusiastic about Victor Hugo's *Hernani* and, in spite of worries that its political plot would create difficulties with the censor, persuaded Piave to switch course.

During autumn 1843 the correspondence between Verdi, Piave and the theatre management makes it clear that the composer took an unusually active interest in shaping the libretto, and intervened on several important points, insisting for example that the role of Ernani be sung by a tenor (rather than by a contralto, as had originally been planned). At least in part, this new concern for the poetic text was necessitated by his working with Piave, who was inexperienced in theatrical matters and occasionally made what Verdi deemed errors in broad dramatic planning. Last-minute alterations to the cast caused Verdi to make various late changes to his score, notably in adding a cantabile for Silva to the Act 1 finale. The première run of performances, whose cast included Carlo Guasco (Ernani), Antonio Superchi (Don Carlo), Antonio Selva (Silva) and Sophie Loewe (Elvira), was an enormous success.

Ernani quickly became immensely popular, and was revived countless times during its early years. In general, Verdi was adamant that no changes be made to the score; but he did allow at least one exception. At the request of Rossini, who was acting on behalf of the tenor Ivanoff, he supplied an aria with chorus for Ernani as an alternative ending to the Act 2 finale. The piece was first performed in Parma on 26 December 1844. Although there is no direct evidence, it is possible that Verdi also sanctioned the addition of a cabaletta for Silva in Act 1. This piece, originally written for the bass Marini as part of an additional aria in *Oberto* (1841–2, Barcelona), was inserted by Marini into performances of *Ernani* at La Scala in the autumn of 1844.

The prelude economically sets forth musical ideas connected with the two main dramatic issues of the opera: first, intoned on solo trumpet and trombone, the theme associated with Ernani's fatal oath to Silva; and then a lyrical theme whose initial rising 6th might plausibly be thought to suggest the love between Ernani and Elvira in its purest state.

ACT 1: 'The Bandit'
    1.i *The Pyrenees; Silva's castle is seen in the distance* A simple opening chorus ('Evviva! beviam!') sets the scene by introducing the boisterous, carefree world of 'mountaineers and bandits'. Their leader Ernani enters to tell of his love for Elvira; all agree to help him steal her away from Don Ruy Gomez de Silva, her guardian and fiancé. Ernani's cavatina is in the conventional double-aria format, but the first movement, 'Come rugiada al cespite', shows an expansion of the usual lyrical period as Ernani dwells on his hatred of Silva. The cabaletta, 'O tu, che l'alma adora', makes prominent use of syncopation to suggest Ernani's impatience for action.
    1.ii *Elvira's richly furnished apartments in Silva's castle* Elvira's cavatina, during which she meditates on her beloved Ernani, repeats the double-aria formal outline of Ernani's, though the entire scene is more expansively developed musically. The Andantino, 'Ernani! ... Ernani involami', has the expanded but still highly schematic form that was becoming common in Verdi's early works and, again characteristically, shows a rigorous control of the soprano's ornamental gestures. A jaunty, Spanish-sounding *tempo di mezzo*, during which Elvira's entourage compliment her on her forthcoming marriage to Silva, leads to a forceful cabaletta, 'Tutto sprezzo che d'Ernani', in which the opening phrase's vocal and expressive range gives some indication of the new demands that Verdi was placing on his

principal interpreters. Elvira and her women sweep out and the stage is taken by a disguised Don Carlo, King of Spain. Carlo, in love with Elvira and outraged that he has been passed over, sends Giovanna, Elvira's nurse, to fetch his beloved. Elvira enters to express outrage at the king's audacity and they settle into one of Verdi's most successful formal vehicles, the so-called 'dissimilar' duet between baritone and soprano. The first movement, as usual, is rapid-fire dialogue with continuity preserved by the orchestra, but this soon gives way to a first statement of fixed positions: Carlo leads off with a lyrical outpouring, 'Da quel di che t'ho veduta'; Elvira counters in the parallel minor with spiky dotted rhythms. The third movement offers a thoroughly Romantic *coup de scène*: Carlo impatiently tries to drag Elvira away, she grabs his knife to defend her honour, and at the peak of the action Ernani himself appears through a secret door. There is a shocked *declamato* from Carlo before Elvira and Ernani launch into the furious stretta of the duet-turned-trio, one that is full (perhaps too full) of syncopations to emphasize the young lovers' defiant energy. The extended cadences of the stretta are immediately followed by the appearance of Elvira's third suitor, the aged Silva, and the start of the Finale Primo. Silva is of course dismayed at the scene that greets him and, after angrily summoning his followers, engages in a sorrowful, chromatically inflected Andante, 'Infelice! e tu credevi'. (This is sometimes followed by the cabaletta 'Infin che un brando vindice'; see above.) But there are more surprises to come and, soon after Silva has finished, emissaries reveal the true identity of the king. The revelation precipitates the central Adagio of the Finale, which begins in utter confusion but gradually finds lyrical voice, notably through the repetition and development of a small cadential motif. As the Adagio ends, Silva kneels to ask the king's forgiveness, which the latter grants, explaining that he is there to canvass support for the forthcoming election of emperor. In an aside the king offers to help Ernani and, openly announcing that the bandit is under royal protection, orders him to leave. Ernani's angry aside, in which he threatens to follow Carlo merely to exact revenge, leads off the stretta of the Finale, which begins in hushed but pointed minor and progresses to the major mode with a simple but highly effective crescendo.

ACT 2: 'The Guest'
    A magnificent hall in Silva's castle After a routine, scene-setting chorus praising Silva and Elvira, there occurs an example of the kind of complex articulated scene Verdi often favoured in the middle of an opera. The number is entitled 'Recitativo e Terzetto' but enfolds within its trio a prolonged duet. As the crowd disperses, Silva grants entry to a 'pilgrim' who has asked for shelter. Elvira appears and Silva introduces her as his future bride, at which the 'pilgrim' (who is of course Ernani) throws off his disguise and offers his own head as a wedding present. The ensuing Andante, 'Oro, quant'oro ogn'avido' – Ernani angry, Elvira miserable, Silva (who has not recognized Ernani) simply confused – is dominated by Ernani, and makes dynamic use of triplet figures. Silva assures his 'guest' of protection and speeds off to arm his castle. As soon as the lovers are alone, Elvira assures Ernani that she had intended to kill herself on the wedding night, and their reconciliation is sealed by a brief Andantino with prominent harp and woodwind, sung mostly in 3rds and 6ths. When Silva returns he is horrified to find them in

Title page of an edition of Verdi's 'Ernani' arranged for piano (Milan: Ricordi, c1880), showing the final scene in Act 4

ACT 3: 'Clemency'

Subterranean vaults containing the tomb of Charlemagne at Aix-la-Chapelle Dark instrumental colours suitable to the setting begin the act. Carlo enters with Riccardo, his equerry. It is the day of the election of the Holy Roman Emperor, and Carlo has heard that conspiracy is afoot. He instructs Riccardo to fire three cannon shots if the election goes in his favour. Left alone 'to converse with the dead', the king bitterly reviews his misspent youth and resolves to rise in stature if he is elected. The aria that illustrates this most important turning point in the drama, 'O de' verd'anni miei', is notable for its extreme change in atmosphere halfway through: from sombre musical recollections of the florid baritone that has characterized the previous acts to a new-found strength and broadness of expression at the words 'e vincitor de' secoli'. Carlo conceals himself in Charlemagne's tomb as the conspirators enter: sombre orchestral colours reassert themselves as the plotters exchange the password and draw lots for the task of assassinating the king. Ernani wins and, with the triplet figures that have been sprinkled through the scene gradually gaining ascendency in the orchestra, all join in a grand chorus, 'Si ridesti il Leon di Castiglia'. In rhythmic stamp, this piece bears a certain relationship to 'Va pensiero' (*Nabucco*) and 'O Signore, dal tetto natio' (*I Lombardi*), but here the rhythmic vitality and consequent spur to action is far more immediate. The three cannon shots sound, and Carlo emerges triumphantly from the tomb as the stage fills with his followers. In a magnificent finale to the act, Carlo forgives the conspirators and even consents to the marriage of Ernani and Elvira; his closing peroration to Charlemagne, 'Oh sommo Carlo', eventually draws everyone into his musical orbit.

ACT 4: 'The Mask'

A terrace in the palace of Don Giovanni of Aragon [Ernani] in Saragossa As is common with Verdi and his contemporaries, the final act is by far the shortest. A chorus and a group of dancers tell us that wedding preparations for Ernani and Elvira are under way. The two lovers emerge for a brief but intense affirmation of their happiness, but are cut short by the sound of a distant horn. Ernani attempts to hide the truth from Elvira by complaining of an old wound and sending her for help. Left alone, he momentarily convinces even himself that the horn was an illusion. But Silva appears to demand the life that is owed him. Elvira returns as Ernani takes the proffered dagger; and so begins the final trio, 'Ferma, crudel, estinguere', justly one of the most celebrated pieces in the score, notable above all for its profusion of melodic ideas. The close of the trio is followed immediately by Silva's repetition of the pact music. In spite of Elvira's protests, Ernani takes the dagger and stabs himself. The lovers have time only for a last, desperate affirmation of love before the hero dies, leaving his bride to faint away as the curtain falls.

* * *

As Verdi himself stated more than once, *Ernani* represents an important change of direction in his early career. His two earlier successes, *Nabucco* and *I Lombardi*, had both been written for La Scala, one of the largest stages in Italy and well suited to the grandiose choral effects of those works. For the more intimate atmosphere of La Fenice, he created an opera that instead concentrated on personal conflict, carefully controlling the complex sequence of actions necessary to bring characters into intense confrontation. This new

each other's arms. He learns that Don Carlo is waiting for Ernani outside the castle; but he will not give up the bandit, wishing for a more personal revenge, and in an angry stretta ushers Ernani into a secret hiding place as the lovers voice their despair.

Carlo's entry heralds a long passage of accompanied recitative. The king asks Silva to reveal Ernani's whereabouts and, on being denied, disarms the old man and orders a search of the castle. During the search Carlo sings 'Lo vedremo, o veglio audace', the first movement of what is formally entitled an 'aria', but in which Silva joins freely. The king's anger manifests itself in a wideranging, highly declamatory line while Silva denies him with obsessively restricted rhythms and pitches. The middle movement, though often lyrical, is packed with stage action: Carlo's followers return, having found nothing in the castle; the king threatens Silva; Elvira 'enters precipitously' and begs for mercy; Carlo takes her as a hostage. The closing cabaletta, 'Vieni meco, sol di rose', is a magnificent dramatic stroke: after all the action and conflict, Verdi ends with a passage of pure baritone lyricism, full of gentle ornaments as the king invites Elvira to join him. The stage clears to leave Silva alone. He releases Ernani from hiding and immediately challenges him to a duel. Ernani refuses, and reveals that the king himself is pursuing Elvira. In order to join forces with Silva in taking revenge on Carlo, Ernani offers the old man a hunting-horn and proposes a deadly pact, suitably emphasized with solemn brass chords: when Silva wishes Ernani to kill himself, he must simply sound the horn. The deal is struck; Ernani joins Silva and his followers in an explosive Prestissimo, 'In arcione, in arcion', to close the act.

format brought about a fresh consideration of the fixed forms of Italian opera, in particular an expansion and enrichment of the solo aria and duet, together with a more flexible approach to the musical sequences that bind together lyrical pieces. Most important, however, was Verdi's gathering sense of a musical drama's larger rhetoric, his increasing control over the dynamics of entire acts rather than merely of entire numbers. In this respect, the third act of *Ernani* sets an imposing standard of coherence, one that is rarely equalled until the operas of the early 1850s.　　　ROGER PARKER

Ernelinde, princesse de Norvège ('Ernelinde, Princess of Norway'). *Tragédie lyrique* in three acts by FRANÇOIS-ANDRÉ DANICAN PHILIDOR to a libretto by Antonine Alexandre Henri Poinsinet after FRANCESCO SILVANI's libretto *La fede tradita, e vendicata*; Paris, Opéra, 24 November 1767 (revised version as *Sandomir, prince de Dannemarck*, Opéra, 24 January 1769; second revised version as *Ernelinde*, Versailles, 11 December 1773; further revised for the Opéra, 8 July 1777).

Rodoald (bass), King of Norway, has killed the brother of Ricimer, King of the Goths (baritone). Sandomir (tenor), Prince of Denmark, is betrothed to Ernelinde (soprano), but helps Ricimer take Rodoald's capital 'Nidrosie' (Trondheim). Ernelinde is discovered amid the sounds of war; Sandomir swears to defend her. Ricimer enters in triumph. He too wants to marry Ernelinde; a furious quarrel ensues. Rodoald forbids Ernelinde to listen to the tyrant's courtship. Ricimer arrests his rival and forces Ernelinde to decide whether her father or her lover will die; nature compels her to save Rodoald. She comes to Sandomir in prison and they resolve to die together. At the altars of Odin and Frigga the lovers are about to cheat Ricimer of his prize when Rodoald bursts in with an army; Ricimer is overthrown and Sandomir will inherit the crowns of Norway, Sweden and Denmark.

Ernelinde marks an epoch in the history of the *tragédie lyrique*. In three acts (until the 1773 version, for which the libretto was revised in five acts by MICHEL-JEAN SEDAINE) and without supernatural elements, it challenged tradition radically by its italianate music while retaining extended ballets and making dramatic use of (sometimes double) chorus. The arias, long by French standards, are direct in style. *Ernelinde* fulfilled an Encyclopedist ideal, reconciling French forms with italianate music. Although some pieces (mainly in the *divertissements*) are plagiarized, the dramatic scenes, including Ernelinde's obbligato recitative, the quarrel duet and the principal arias and choruses, represent the Viking dark ages with considerable dramatic power.

See also RICIMER.　　　JULIAN RUSHTON

'Ernelinde, princesse de Norvège' (Philidor): design by Louis-René Boquet for the costume of Rodoald, King of Norway, sung by Nicolas Gélin in the original production at the Paris Opéra (Académie Royale de Musique), 24 November 1767

Ernesaks, Gustav Gustavovich (*b* Peril, 12 Dec 1908). Estonian composer. He studied composition at the Tallinn conservatory and in 1944 formed the first professional choir of the Tallinn Philharmonic; under his direction it became one of the best Soviet choral groups. Ernesaks is also a talented composer of stage and choral works, songs, and music for the theatre and films. He has contributed articles on opera to *Sovetskaya muzïka*. Ernesaks's style evolved gradually as he perfected his stage technique and operatic language; he created individual roles for both recitative and orchestra. He did not however transcend the limits of his chosen form: traditional, realistic opera, with a succession of musical numbers that use leitmotifs as a structural basis. Choral episodes, in a heroic style or depicting everyday life, are prominent; they are frequently based on folk elements.

Pühajärv [The Sacred Lake] (3, J. Syutiste), Tallinn, 19 July 1946
Tormide rand [The Shore of Storms] (3, J. Smuula), Tallinn, 29 Sept 1949, vs (Moscow, 1950)
Käsi käes [Hand in Hand] (comic op, 3, P. Rummo and K. Merilaas), Tallinn, 14 March 1955; rev. as Mari i Mikhail, Moscow, 1956
Tuleristsed [Baptism of Fire] (3, epilogue, Merilaas and K. Irda), Tallinn, 31 Oct 1957
Kosilased Mulgimaalt [Bridegrooms of Mulgimaa] (comic op, Merilaas), Tartu, 16 May 1960

Ernster, Dezső (*b* Pécs, 23 Nov 1898; *d* Zürich, 15 Feb 1981). Hungarian bass. After studying in Budapest and Vienna he sang at the State Opera at Plauen from 1922 to 1924, making his début as the Landgrave in *Tannhäuser*. He then went from Gera to Düsseldorf and in 1929 appeared in the première of Hindemith's *Neues vom Tage* in Berlin. In the 1931 Bayreuth Festival he sang Titurel in *Parsifal* and was also heard in Vienna, Salzburg and (with the Salzburg Opera Guild) New York. During World War II he was imprisoned in Belsen but survived and was able to start a second career in America, joining the Metropolitan in 1946. He was introduced to Covent Garden in 1949 in

Götterdämmerung and sang at Glyndebourne in 1952, travelling widely till his retirement in 1967. With vocal powers much diminished by his wartime ordeals he remained an impressive artist, pursuing a respected operatic career till the age of 69. His Commendatore in Furtwängler's *Don Giovanni* is preserved on film.

J. B. STEANE

Ernst II, Duke of Saxe-Coburg-Gotha (*b* Coburg, 21 June 1818; *d* Schloss Reinhardsbrunn, nr Friedrichroda, 22 Aug 1893). German composer. He studied with H. C. Breidenstein in Bonn and Reissiger in Dresden. His music includes vocal, chamber and piano works and five operas, the last all composed between 1846 and 1858. *Zaire* (1846), on Voltaire's tragedy, was followed by *Tony, oder Die Vergeltung* (1848) and *Casilda* (1851), which were all given in Coburg. The most successful of his operas was *Santa Chiara*, of which the première was conducted by Liszt at the Hoftheater in Gotha on 2 April 1854. Within five years it had been staged in most large German theatres as well as abroad; more than 60 performances were given at the Paris Opéra. Essentially a grand opera, though through-composed, *Santa Chiara* shows the influence of Bellini and Donizetti on the one hand and of the German lied tradition on the other. Ernst's last opera was the five-act *Diana von Solange* (1858).

See also GOTHA.

PEM
O. Mokrauer-Maine: *Herzog Ernst II. von Sachsen-Coburg-Gotha und die Tonkunst* (Hanover, 1893)
E. Müller: 'Die herzogliche Oper "Santa Chiara"', *Rund um den Friedenstein: Blätter für Thüringer Geschichte und Heimatgeschehen*, iv/11 (1929), 2
H. Bachmann: 'Ernst II. von Sachsen-Coburg und Gotha', *Fränkische Lebensbilder*, v (Würzburg, 1973), 253–81
BARRY MILLINGTON

Eroe cinese, L' ('The Chinese Hero'). Libretto by PIETRO METASTASIO, first set by Giuseppe Bonno (1752, Vienna). The title *Narbale* was used for a later version of this libretto.

During an insurrection which forced the Chinese emperor, Livanio [Li-vang], into exile, his son, Svenvango [Swen-vang], was saved by Leango [Le-ang], who wrapped his own infant son in the royal garments and left him for the mob. Later, as regent, Le-ang raised the royal heir as his own child under the name of Siveno [Si-veng].

ACT 1 Si-veng and Lisinga [Li-sing], a captive Tartar princess, are in love. Li-sing is reminded by her sister, Ulania [U-lan], that Si-veng is not only a commoner but also her enemy: for these reasons, U-lan claims, she will leave Minteo [Min-ti], Si-veng's friend and a mandarin in the Chinese army. Si-veng and Li-sing despair when her father sends word that she must marry the unknown heir to the Chinese throne. With this opportunity for an alliance with the Tartars, Le-ang feels ready to reveal Si-veng's identity; Si-veng, however, announces that the populace call for Le-ang himself as emperor. Le-ang's response leads Li-sing to suspect that Si-veng is indeed the heir.

ACT 2 Since Le-ang will not accept the throne, but insists on revealing the true heir, Si-veng resolves to flee. Le-ang, however, explains all to Si-veng and, bidding him remain silent, departs to explain to Li-sing. Meanwhile, Min-ti is summoned by Alsingo [Al-sing], an old man who, having found Min-ti wrapped as a royal

baby, had raised him in the belief that he was Li-vang's son. Min-ti, now convinced that he is the heir, informs Si-veng, who is thrown into confusion and shows little reaction to Li-sing's delight at Le-ang's revelation.

ACT 3 Si-veng departs to suppress an insurrection; U-lan enters to announce that Min-ti is its leader. Challenged by Le-ang, Min-ti reveals that he is the true heir and has prevented the mob from entering the palace. Le-ang corrects his mistake and, learning from U-lan of Si-veng's mission, Min-ti rushes to his friend's aid. Rumours that Si-veng is dead are then dispelled by his arrival with Min-ti, who has rescued him. Appropriate reunions follow as Si-veng is officially identified as Swen-vang and Min-ti as the son of Le-ang.

* * *

Volume i of Jean Baptiste du Halde's *Description géographique … de l'empire de la Chine* contains references to Li-vang, tenth emperor of the third dynasty, and to his son Swen-vang who was saved by a minister who offered up his own child to a rebellious mob. Volume ii contains a drama, translated from the Chinese of Hi-Him-Siang by Joseph de Prémare, entitled *L'orphelin de la maison de Tchao*. This drama and the references cited from volume i appear to be Metastasio's sources. (The *Description géographique* is available in English under the title *A Description of the Empire of China and Chinese-Tartary*, where Siang's drama appears as *The Little Orphan of the Family of Chau*.) Like *Il rè pastore* of the previous year, *L'eroe cinese* was written for a court performance by a group of 'distinguished young ladies and noblemen' – a tenor (as Le-ang, Alexander in *Il rè pastore*) and four ladies (the two sets of lovers). Although *Il rè pastore* had been very well received, Metastasio was displeased at having to write another work for 'the performing ladies'. Since these ladies had to be fully covered by their costumes, Greek and Roman subjects were excluded and, as none would portray an odious character, Metastasio could not use the contrast of vice and virtue. The number of scenes, characters and arias was also limited, as was the length. *L'eroe cinese*, however, received nearly 20 settings over the next 30 years, drawing the attention of such composers as Cimarosa, Galuppi, Perez and Sacchini. For Madrid (1751), Conforto set *Le cinese*, an early *azione teatrale* by Metastasio, under the title *La festa cinese*; this, with versions of *Siroe* (1752) and *L'eroe cinese* (1754), secured him an appointment to compose operas for the Spanish court.

For a list of settings *see* METASTASIO, PIETRO.
DON NEVILLE

Errichelli [Ericchelli, Enrichelli], **Pasquale** (*b* ? Naples, 1730; *d* after 1775). Italian composer. An organist in Naples, he composed operas for that city and for Rome in the 1750s. Little is known of his activities during the following decade but, in 1771, when Gian Francesco de Majo died after having composed only Act 1 of *Eumene*, Giacomo Insanguine and Errichelli completed the opera.

La serva astuta (ob), Naples, Fiorentini, 1753, collab. G. Cocchi
Il finto turco (ob, A. Palomba), Naples, Fiorentini, wint. 1753, collab. Cocchi
Issipile (os, P. Metastasio), Naples, S Carlo, 18 Dec 1754, *I-Mc, Nc, P-La* (2 copies)
La finta 'mbreana (comedia, 3, G. Bisceglia), Naples, Nuovo, wint. 1756, collab. Logroscino
Solimano (os, A. Migliavacca), Rome, Argentina, 13 Jan 1757, *I-Mc, P-La*, arias *I-Nc*

Siroe (os, Metastasio), Naples, S Carlo, 26 Dec 1758, *La*, ?*S-Skma*, arias *I-Nc*

Eumene [Act 3] (os, A. Zeno), Naples, S Carlo, 20 Jan 1771, *Nc*, *P-La* [Act 1 by Majo, Act 2 by Insanguine]

*

EitnerQ; *RosaM*

R. Bossa: 'Luigi Vanvitelli spettatore teatrale a Napoli', *RIM*, xi (1976), 48–70

DENNIS LIBBY

Ershov, Ivan Vasil'yevich. *See* YERSHOV, IVAN VASIL'YEVICH.

Erwartung ('Expectation'). *Monodram* in one act, op.17, by ARNOLD SCHOENBERG to a libretto by MARIE PAPPENHEIM; Prague, Neues Deutsches Theater, 6 June 1924.

In August 1909, shortly before starting work on *Erwartung*, Schoenberg described in letters to Busoni the ideal towards which he was then striving in his music. He wanted to leave behind him concentration on separate feelings in unreal isolation, along with the associated musical structures controlled by conscious logic, and find a means of expressing the multiplicity of contradictory feelings that can arise simultaneously from the unconscious. He had just asked a young doctor of his acquaintance, Marie Pappenheim, to write an opera libretto for him on a subject of her own choosing. It is clear from the resulting drama that she was familiar with recent psychological and psychoanalytical thought, and that she must have known about Schoenberg's current preoccupations; it may not be irrelevant that her relative Bertha Pappenheim was the 'Anna O.' whose illness had been successfully treated by Josef Breuer and described in his and Freud's *Studien über Hysterie* (1895). She was, however, surprised at Schoenberg's request because, although she had published verse pseudonymously, she had never written for the stage. Doubting her ability to cope with a more conventional libretto she hit on the solution offered by a monologue for a single character.

The work consists of three brief scenes taking only a quarter of the total playing time of nearly half an hour, followed by a long final scene. The first shows a moonlit landscape with a road disappearing into a dark wood. A woman (soprano) enters in search of her lover. She is full of apprehension at the solitude and the darkness that confronts her. A scene change finds her groping her way through the darkest part of the wood, starting with terror at every unaccustomed sound and, where a clearing opens up in the next scene, at every movement in the shadows. In the fourth scene she emerges in a state of exhaustion into more open countryside, her dress torn, her hair dishevelled, and her face and hands scratched. In the distance a shuttered house is visible where, apparently, her lover may have been visiting another woman. She stumbles against something which proves to be his murdered and still bleeding body. From here on the action is purely psychological. After disbelief has given way to horrified certainty her reaction passes through three main phases: an initial outburst of love and grief, paroxysms of jealousy and rage, and finally contemplation of an empty future ending in a dream-like resumption of her search.

A dream-like quality is, however, present throughout the piece, because the woman is constantly obsessed with erotic reminiscence and the longing experienced during her fruitless wait for her lover earlier in the evening, so that she scarcely distinguishes between present and past, or between her dead lover and her living

memories of him. Schoenberg once remarked that the whole work could be interpreted as a nightmare, and on another occasion that it represented in slow motion everything that occurs in a single second of the greatest psychological stress. His score marks the extreme point in his cultivation of what later came to be known as expressionism, which he preferred to call the art of representing inner processes. Having in the previous year abandoned tonality as a central controlling factor he succeeded in juxtaposing and sometimes superimposing in his piano and orchestral pieces of 1909 remoter contrasts than music had hitherto known. Pappenheim's drama required him to pursue this line even further, and in an attempt to capture the uncensored spontaneity appropriate to it he set himself the prodigious task of composing it in a fortnight (in the event it took him 17 days, from 27 August to 12 September, but with a short break when he had to consult Pappenheim by post).

It is perhaps understandable that a work of this nature should be heard more often in the concert hall than in the opera house, but like most stage works it loses by it. Schoenberg was anxious that it should not fall into the hands of a director whose only interest was to turn it into something entirely different from what he had intended. He had had every scenic effect precisely before his eyes while composing and was particularly concerned that the forest should be represented naturalistically; it was essential to make the woman's fear of it evident, and while one might shudder at a conventionalized forest one could not be afraid of it. He always remembered with gratitude the acting as well as the singing of Marie Gutheil-Schoder, who gave the belated first performance under Zemlinsky.

O. W. NEIGHBOUR

Erwin und Elmire (i) ('Erwin and Elmire'). *Schauspiel mit Gesang* in two acts by JOHANN ANDRÉ to a libretto by JOHANN WOLFGANG VON GOETHE after Oliver Goldsmith; Frankfurt, private performance, May 1775; Berlin, Theater in der Behrenstrasse (Döbbelin Company), 17 July 1775.

Goethe based this work, his first libretto, on the ballad of Angelica and Edwin in Goldsmith's *Vicar of Wakefield* (chapter 8). Elmire (soprano) repines over having caused her lover Erwin (tenor) to run away by feigning indifference to him in society. At the suggestion of her tutor Bernardo (tenor), she visits a holy man (actually Erwin in disguise) in a nearby valley. Her confession leads directly to the lovers' reunion. Goethe added a fourth, rather extraneous character at the beginning, Elmire's mother Olimpia (soprano), in whose diatribe against modern manners commentators have heard the voice of his mother, Frau Rat Goethe. More importantly, the central action mirrors a falling out between the poet and Lili Schönemann, to whom the text is dedicated.

André's setting, quite varied for its day in mood and character, achieved wide popularity, especially Erwin's poignant elegy 'Ihr verblühet, süsse Rosen'. André's strophic music to the Romanze 'Das Veilchen' is the first of a host of settings crowned by Mozart's through-composed song K476 (1785).

THOMAS BAUMAN

Erwin und Elmire (ii) ('Erwin and Elmire'). Singspiel in two acts by JOHANN FRIEDRICH REICHARDT to a libretto by JOHANN WOLFGANG VON GOETHE; Berlin, early 1793 (concert performance).

Goethe rewrote his first two librettos during his Italian journey, in 1787–8. He recast both in the spirit of *opera buffa*, 'since I now know the needs of the lyric theatre more exactly', with recitative instead of spoken dialogue. For the revised version of *Erwin und Elmire* he introduced a secondary pair of lovers in place of Elmire's mother and the family friend Bernardo (*see ERWIN UND ELMIRE* (i)). A falling out between this new pair, occasioned by the jealousy of Rosa (soprano) over the attentions shown by Valerio (bass) to the distraught Elmire (soprano), lover of Erwin (tenor), is intertwined with the central problem between the title roles, leading to a scene of double reconciliation at the opera's end. Reichardt's music, which received high praise when it appeared in print in 1791, strives for musical primacy and continuity by using accompanied recitative throughout. His was the only setting of the revised text, and was performed only on the concert stage.

THOMAS BAUMAN

Escalaïs, Léon [Léonce-Antoine] (*b* Cuxac d'Aude, nr Toulouse, 8 Aug 1859; *d* Paris, Nov 1941). French tenor. He studied at the Paris Conservatoire and made his début in 1882 at the Théâtre du Château d'Eau in Duvernoy's *Sardanapale*. The following year he was engaged by the Opéra, where one of his most successful roles was that of Arnold in *Guillaume Tell*. He had a big, heroic voice and was in great demand for such operas as *Il trovatore* and *L'Africaine*, and also *La Juive*, in which he appeared at La Scala. In 1892 he left Paris for Lyons, where he became director, returning to the capital to great acclaim in 1908. He also enjoyed a spectacular success at the French Opera in New Orleans. His powerful voice and ringing high notes are well demonstrated in recordings made in 1905 and 1906, which show a skilled technician, somewhat unimaginative in style and interpretation.   J. B. STEANE

Escherny, François-Louis, Comte d' (*b* Neuchâtel, 23 or 24 Nov 1733; *d* Paris, 15 July 1815). Swiss writer on music. A journey to Italy in the early 1750s was formative in shaping his taste for Italian opera. He then moved to Paris, where he frequented literary-philosophical circles, and in 1763–5 followed Rousseau to Switzerland. Escherny's *Fragments sur la musique* (Paris, 1809), which also appeared as part of a larger work, the *Mélanges de littérature* (Paris, 1811), contains miscellaneous criticism; much of the writing is anecdotal (albeit vivid and picturesque), but his musical acumen cannot be doubted. Like Chastellux he favoured the principles of bel canto singing; he thought that music for the theatre should set this in proper relief.

Escherny allows Gluck a prodigious gift for powerful and awe-inspiring effects of orchestration and harmony in 'le genre sombre et terrible', but denies him that of melody. He claimed to have met Gluck in Vienna as early as 1767, and to have heard him speak of his admiration for Lully's scores, which adumbrated 'le fonds d'une musique pathétique et théâtrale'. Gluck apparently wanted even then to follow French dramaturgical practice and to preserve the declamatory *cantilène française*.   PHILIP WELLER

Esclarmonde. *Opéra romanesque* in four acts by JULES MASSENET to a libretto by Alfred Blau and Louis de Gramont after *Parthenopoeus de Blois*, a medieval *chanson de geste*; Paris, Opéra-Comique (Théâtre Lyrique), 14 May 1889.

The opera was composed in Massenet's middle period, immediately after *Werther*. It was written for the Californian soprano Sibyl Sanderson (1865–1903), with whom he was infatuated; its exploitation of her remarkable range (up to *g'''*) and agility, allied to considerable weight of tone, has made revivals comparatively rare. After a flurry of productions in the 1890s, it has been revived in this century notably for Fanny Heldy (1923, Paris) and Joan Sutherland (1974, San Francisco, in a production later seen at the Metropolitan and Covent Garden in 1976 and 1983 respectively).

The setting is the legendary Middle Ages. The Emperor of Byzantium, Phorcas (bass), abdicates in favour of his daughter Esclarmonde (soprano) and bequeaths her his magic powers; to preserve them she must remain veiled until she comes of age, when she and her throne will be won by the victor in a tournament. Esclarmonde loves the knight Roland de Blois (tenor), whom she has glimpsed from afar, and by magic transports him to an enchanted island where they pursue a passionate but anonymous affair (Roland is allowed neither to see her face nor know her name). When Esclarmonde has a vision of the King of France besieged in Blois by the Saracens, she dispatches Roland, gives him a magic sword, and promises to visit him nightly wherever he may be.

Roland successfully raises the siege, and the king offers him his daughter Bathilde as reward. Roland is unable to explain his refusal of this honour, which arouses the suspicion of the Bishop of Blois (baritone),

Poster by Alfred Choubrac for Massenet's 'Esclarmonde', printed by F. Appel (Paris and Lyons) at the time of the first production at the Opéra-Comique (Théâtre Lyrique), Paris, in 1889

who forces him to admit to the existence of the veiled beauty. When Esclarmonde duly appears, she is exorcised by the Bishop and his inquisitors, and the veil is torn from her face. Before escaping, she reproaches Roland for betraying their secret.

In the final act, Esclarmonde is aroused from a deep sleep by her father in his place of retreat, and forced to forswear her lover in order to save his life, a task made harder by his sudden appearance on the scene and suggestion of an immediate elopement. When she renounces him and vanishes, he longs only for death and determines to find it at a tournament in Byzantium, where of course he wins both Esclarmonde and the Byzantine throne.

*   *   *

Esclarmonde has the reputation of being Massenet's most Wagnerian score, but in spite of some brief passages for heavy brass the Wagnerianism is of subject matter rather than musical treatment: there are dramaturgical echoes of *Tannhäuser*, *Lohengrin* and the *Ring* and, given the common source material, some interesting pre-echoes of *Die Frau ohne Schatten*. The musical motifs, though, however resourcefully developed, are as usual with Massenet of the reminiscence as opposed to the leading variety. The composer's passion for his leading lady resulted in some of his most chromatically tortuous erotic writing – the 'discreet, semi-religious eroticism' that Vincent d'Indy found in Massenet's music here decisively sheds the adjectives. The score's other main strengths are the speed and economy with which much grand-operatic event is dispatched in just over two hours of music, the subtle shape of the melodies and the diaphanous delicacy of the instrumentation.

Esclarmonde demands great imagination from its designer and producer, a challenge hardly met in the 1974 production. The complete recording with Sutherland, though, gives a fair idea of the work's picaresque and Romantic qualities, and an opera in which a woman (like Carmen, Alcina and Armida) sets out to get her man and (unlike those ladies) keeps him is rare enough to be treasurable.

RODNEY MILNES

Esclava, La ('The Slave'). Opera in three acts by JOSÉ MAURI to a libretto by Tomás Juliá; Havana, Teatro Nacional, 6 June 1921.

The opera is set in 1860 at a sugar estate in Camaguey, Cuba. Matilde (soprano), the only daughter of a rich Spaniard who owns the sugar refinery, is in love with her cousin Arturo (tenor), who is interested only in her money. Miguel (baritone), a serious and taciturn field-worker, brings the news that her father has been killed in an accident. Eva (contralto), Matilde's governess, tells Matilde the truth about her birth; she is the granddaughter of a black slave and, as she has not been acknowledged by her father, she is legally a slave. Miguel, who loves her, tells her that he knows everything and promises to save her. Arturo arrives at night and persuades Matilde to give herself to him. The estate-owner's property is to be auctioned to pay off his debts; Matilde is among the slaves. Miguel buys the property, frees Matilde, restores her fortune to her and asks her to be his wife. But she cannot deceive him about her infidelity, and she takes poison. Miguel kills Arturo to avenge Matilde.

La esclava, entered in the Bracale competition in 1917, was awarded an honourable mention and a first performance, conducted by Alfredo Padovani. The

original cast included Ofelia Nieto (Matilde), Rhea Toniolo (Eva), Julian Oliver (Arturo) and Nestor de la Torre (Miguel). It is considered to be one of the best Cuban operas and was revived in 1978–80.

JORGE ANTONIO GONZÁLEZ

Escravo, O. Opera by Carlos Gomes; *see SCHIAVO, LO.*

Esham, Faith (*b* Vanceburg, KY, 6 Aug 1948). American soprano. She began her studies as a lyric mezzo-soprano in Kentucky with Vasile Venettozzi and at the Juilliard School. She was later an apprentice at the Santa Fe Opera. She joined the New York City Opera in 1977 as a mezzo, making her début as Cherubino. Later she sang soprano roles including Baby Doe, Cendrillon, Gilda, Manon, Musetta, Pamina, Gounod's Marguerite and Floyd's Susannah. Her European début in Nancy in 1980 was followed by engagements throughout Europe. In 1984 she appeared as Micaëla in Francesco Rosi's film of *Carmen* and in 1986 made her Metropolitan Opera début as Marzelline. In 1990 she sang Desdemona for the WNO. Her full, lyrical voice and vivid, sympathetic acting have made her particularly successful in French opera.

CORI ELLISON

Eslava (y Elizondo), (Miguel) Hilarión (*b* Burlada, Navarre, 21 Oct 1807; *d* Madrid, 23 July 1878). Spanish composer. He was a choirboy in Pamplona Cathedral and held posts in Burgo de Osma and Seville before becoming *maestro de capilla* at the royal chapel in Madrid in 1847; he also taught at Madrid Conservatory (director, 1866). In the polemical climate surrounding issues of tradition and change in Spain he was a controversial figure. He had taken holy orders in about 1833; having turned to opera less than ten years later, he met with sharp criticism from ecclesiastical authorities. Though impugned as a scholar, Eslava made his mark through his teaching and his manuals on composition as well as through his excursions into opera.

Eslava wrote three *opere serie* (all lost), all to Italian librettos and in the Italian style, within two years, apparently out of financial need. *Il solitario del Monte Selvaggio*, in two acts to a libretto by C. Bassi, was first performed at the Teatro Principal, Cádiz, in June 1841; his second, *La tregua di Ptolomaide*, to a libretto by L. Bertocchi, was given there on 24 May 1842. Lope de Vega's *Lo cierto por lo dudoso* was the source for the two-act *Pietro il crudele*, first performed in Seville in summer 1843. All were well received, and all gave rise to arguments about their 'Spanish nature' (the most trivial being about the 'popular' quality of a clapping chorus in *Il solitario*), yet there is no record of any further performances. Nevertheless, they, together with Eslava's presidency of the society España Musical, formed in 1847 in Madrid specifically to foster national opera, urged others along the thorny path of Spanish operatic development.

*

A. Peña y Goñi: *La ópera española y la música dramática en el siglo XIX* (Madrid, 1881; abridged E. Rincón, as *España desde la ópera a la zarzuela*, 1967), 216ff

J. M. Esperanza y Sola: 'Eslava: su vida y sus obras', *Treinta años de crítica musical* (Madrid, 1906), 5–19, 164–203

G. Chase: 'M. H. Eslava', *MQ*, xxiv (1938), 74–83

A. Gallego: 'Eslava y la cuestión de la ópera nacional', *Bellas artes*, no.47 (1975) [whole issue]

L. Hernández Ascunce: *Estudio bibliográfico de don Hilarión Eslava* (Pamplona, 1978)

C. Gómez Amat: *Historia de la música española*, v: *Siglo XIX* (Madrid, 1984)

JACK SAGE

Esmeralda. Opera in four acts by ALEXANDER SERGEYEVICH DARGOMÏZHSKY, to a libretto by the composer and two assistants after VICTOR HUGO's libretto *Esmeralda* on his own novel *Notre-Dame de Paris*; Moscow, Bol'shoy Theatre, 5/17 December 1847.

The work was composed in 1838–41; the libretto, translated after the setting was made, is an abridgment of that prepared by Hugo himself for Louise Bertin. After a lengthy and frustrating bureaucratic delay caused in part by the hegemony of the Italian Opera troupe in St Petersburg from 1843, Dargomïzhsky's opera was finally performed four years later, away from the capital. Between 1866 and 1948 it lay forgotten in St Petersburg (*RU-SPtob*), but was revived (at first on the radio) in response to the nationalist-antimodernist crackdown instigated by Zhdanov. A revised version in three acts to a new libretto by Z. Shilyayev and E. Kaplan, and with additional music by Viktor Sibirsky, has been in the repertory of the Maliy Theatre, Leningrad (now St Petersburg), since 1958. The original vocal score, with the French text and both Russian ones, was published in 1961; the ballet music from Acts 1 and 2 has been issued in full score (1984).

Hugo's libretto, following the conventions of the Paris Opéra, sets the dramatic intrigue against a luxuriant background of genre painting and choral-cum-choreographic display, with the greatest emphasis on huge act-ending *morceaux d'ensemble*. The inexperienced Russian composer followed suit as far as his technical resources allowed. At the time of the opera's third and last St Petersburg revival (Alexandrinsky Theatre, 1859), Dargomïzhsky, who had by then composed *Rusalka*, made what seems a viable assessment of it in a letter to a friend: 'The music is not much, often insipid, such as one finds in Halévy or Meyerbeer; but in the dramatic scenes there already peeps through that language of truth and power which I have since striven to develop in my Russian music'.

RICHARD TARUSKIN

Espert, Nuria (*b* Barcelona, 11 June 1935). Spanish director. Her first professional engagement as an actress was at the age of 11. In 1959 she founded her own company, which travelled worldwide performing both Spanish and foreign plays. After an outstanding career on the stage she turned to directing. Her first opera production, that of *Butterfly* (Scottish Opera, 1987; Covent Garden, 1988), emphasized the culturally and sexually imperialist behaviour of Pinkerton, as well as the inner moral strength of Butterfly. Her *Rigoletto* for Covent Garden (1988) set the action in high Parisian society of the 19th century, but only hinted at a socially critical perspective. Other productions include *Elektra* at La Monnaie (1988), a traditional *Traviata* for Scottish Opera (1989), and *Carmen* for Covent Garden (1991).

N. Goodwin: 'Nuria Espert: from Drama to Opera', *Opera*, xxxix (1988), 1411–14

H. Matheopoulos: 'From Stage to Stage', *Opera Now* (April 1991), 24–7

BARRY MILLINGTON

Esplá (y Triay), Oscar (*b* Alicante, 5 Aug 1886; *d* Madrid, 6 Jan 1976). Spanish composer. After studies in engineering, he turned to music in 1911 and studied in Meiningen and Munich with Reger in 1912 and in Paris

with Saint-Saëns in 1913. In 1930 he was appointed a professor at the Madrid Conservatory (director, 1936–9), and he was president of the Junta Nacional de Música y Teatros Liricos (1931–4). He later held other teaching and administrative posts.

A cultured and highly accomplished musician who contributed prolifically to all genres, he wrote in a style that owed something to Debussy and to Stravinsky, aiming at simplicity, freshness and harmonic refinement. He was influenced by the folk music of the Spanish Mediterranean coast, developing from it an original scale (C-Db-Eb-E-F-Gb-Ab-Bb). He showed great interest in vocal music and opera, as his writings on Berlioz, Mozart and Verdi show. Though *El pirata cautivo* was his only opera to be performed, he contributed important work for the reconstruction and rehabilitation of Elche's *Misterio*. Esplá conceived opera more in symphonic terms than vocal, placing musical considerations before literary or theatrical aspects. Nevertheless he wrote that it was 'a basic error to conceive opera only as an excuse for singing'.

La bella durmiente (3), Vienna, 1909; rev. as La forêt perdue, 1943 (3, K. Willems)
La balteira (op-ballet, 3, d'I. Lewishon), New York, 1935
Plumes au vent, 1941 (1, Weterings)
El pirata cautivo (1, C. de la Torre), Madrid, 1974
Calixto y Melibeá, 1974 (F. Romero, after F. de Rojas: *La Celestina*)

*

O. Esplá: 'Sobra la ópera', *Polyphonie* (1947), no.1, p.26
K. Willems: *Un grand musicien espagnol, Oscar Esplá* (Amsterdam, 1952)
O. Esplá: 'Significación estética de la ópera', *Atlántida*, ix (1971); repr. in A. Iglesias, ed.: *Escritos de Oscar Esplá*, i (Madrid, 1977)
A. Iglesias: *Oscar Esplá* (Madrid, 1973)
L. Hontanón: 'Sobre la obra escénica de Oscar Esplá', *Revista del Instituto de Estudios Alicantinos*, xxi (1977), 19–25
J. Gómez Brufal: 'Oscar Esplá y el "Misterio" de Elche', ibid, 69–72

GUY BOURLIGUEUX

Espoile, Raúl Hugo (*b* Mercedes, 1889; *d* Buenos Aires, 13 April 1958). Argentine composer. His teachers were Edmundo Pallemaerts in Buenos Aires and Vincent d'Indy in Paris; from 1920 to 1940 he studied Argentine traditional music. He composed two operas, which were performed at the Teatro Colón, Buenos Aires. *Frenos* (*c*1918), a 'lyric poem' in four acts, was first performed on 19 June 1928. Victor Mercante's libretto, based on philosophical abstractions, was not ideal for musical setting. *La ciudad roja* (1930), in three acts, was first performed on 17 July 1936 with Isabel Marengo and Pablo Mirassou in the principal roles, under the direction of Héctor Panizza. The Spanish prose libretto was written by Carlos Schaeffer Gallo, after the play *El candombe federal*. Set in Argentina in 1840, during the dictatorship of Juan Manuel de Rosas, the plot concerns loving rivalry among people belonging to opposing political parties. To achieve the desired atmosphere, Espoile used folk elements in some scenes, or melodic motifs and characteristic rhythms which give unity to the work.

*

E. de la Guardia and R. Herrera: *El arte lírico en el Teatro Colón: con motivo de las bodas de plata (1908–1933)* (Buenos Aires, 1933), 147
J. M. Veniard: *La música nacional argentina: influencia de la música criolla tradicional en la música académica argentina, relevamiento de datos históricos para su estudio* (Buenos Aires, 1986), 104, 105, 114

JUAN MARÍA VENIARD

Essen. City in western Germany, in North Rhine-Westphalia. Until the mid-19th century, dramatic performances took place there in inns, tents and the open air. The city acquired its first stage in 1863 when the director of the Düsseldorf theatre planned to give performances in Essen and the Casino Gesellschaft decided to provide a theatre of the same size as the one in Düsseldorf. The Essen Casino was in use from 1865, and a rival theatre, the Vaudeville-Theater, opened in 1876. In October 1887 a wealthy businessman named Friedrich Grillo offered to build a theatre at his own expense and to bear its running costs while he was alive. The opera house, Theater und Philharmonie Essen, opened on 16 September 1892. There were some notable premières and first German performances in the city before World War II, including Alfred Rahlwes's *Madame Potiphar* (1907), Max Weydert's *Enoch Arden* (1909), Honegger's *Antigone* (1928) and Franz Schmidt's *Notre Dame* (as *Der Glöckner von Notre Dame*, 1915).

After surviving several air raids the theatre was damaged so badly on 26 March 1944 that it could no longer be used. Performances continued in the neighbouring towns of Steele and Werden, on a regular basis in the latter after the war. In summer 1949 it was decided to rebuild the house; the theatre, seating 637, opened on 29 December 1950 with *Die Meistersinger*. Works given there include the premières of Hermann Reutter's *Die Brücke von San Luis Rey* (1954) and Klebe's *Die Ermordung Cäsars* (1959), and the first German performances of Krenek's *Karl V* (1950), Berg's *Lulu* (1953), Nono's *Il prigioniero* (1954) and Martinů's *Mirandolina* (1960). Heinz Wallberg became general musical director in 1975. In the 1980s work began on a new theatre based on plans drawn up in 1959 by the Finnish architect Alvar Aalto. On 25 September 1988 the Aalto-Theater (1125 seats) opened with *Die Meistersinger*.

*

F. Feldens: *75 Jahre Städtische Bühnen: Geschichte des Essener Theaters 1892–1967* (Essen, 1967)   SABINE SONNTAG

Esser, Heinrich (*b* Mannheim, 15 July 1818; *d* Salzburg, 3 June 1872). German composer. He studied the violin with Jakob Heinefetter and harmony with Carl Eschborn in Mannheim. From 1834 he studied composition with F. P. Lachner, in Mannheim until 1837 and then in Munich; in 1839–40 he studied with Simon Sechter in Vienna. He was appointed conductor of male-voice choirs in Mainz in 1841, and in September that year became Kapellmeister of the Mainz theatre. In 1847 he was appointed principal Kapellmeister of the court opera at the Kärntnertortheater in Vienna. From 1859 onwards he had close ties with Richard Wagner through the Schott publishing house. After leaving his post as court Kapellmeister in 1869, he returned to Salzburg.

Esser's three operas were staged between 1840 and 1845. His three-act *Sitas* (Mannheim, 26 December 1840) is based on a story about settlers and Indians near colonial Jamestown; the music for this work is lost. *Thomas Riquiqui, oder Die politische Heirat* op.10 (Frankfurt, 8 March 1843; pubd, Mainz, *c*1843) is a comic opera in three acts, based on a libretto by Carl Gollmick after J.-H. Vernoy de Saint-Georges and Adolphe de Leuven. Set at the end of the French Revolution, the subject is derived from revolutionary themes developed by Eugène Scribe and Mélesville. Esser's final opera, *Die zwei Prinzen* op.15 (Munich, 10 April 1845; vs, Mainz, 1845), in three acts to a libretto by M. G. Friedrich, is about the rivalry between the English

houses of Lancaster and York which led to the Wars of the Roses.   KARL-JOSEF MÜLLER

Esser, Hermin (*b* Rheydt, 1 April 1928). German tenor. He studied in Düsseldorf and made his début in 1954 at Krefeld. He then sang at Gelsenkirchen, Wiesbaden and with the Komische Oper, Berlin. In 1964 he was engaged by the Deutsche Oper am Rhein, Düsseldorf. At Bayreuth (1966–72) he sang Froh, David, Erik, Loge, Siegmund and Tannhäuser. He sang Tristan for Scottish Opera (1973) in Edinburgh and at Sadler's Wells. He appeared at all the principal German theatres and in Vienna, Stockholm, Zürich, Geneva and Chicago. His roles included Jimmy Mahoney (*Aufstieg und Fall der Stadt Mahagonny*) and Parsifal. He returned to Bayreuth to sing Tristan in 1981. A fine actor, he compensated for a certain vocal monotony with strong dramatic ability.   ELIZABETH FORBES

Esswood, Paul (**Lawrence Vincent**) (*b* West Bridgford, Notts., 6 June 1942). English countertenor. He studied at the RCM with Gordon Clinton, making his début in Cavalli's *Erismena* (1968, Berkeley) and first appearing in Europe in 1969 in the title role of Alessandro Scarlatti's *Tigrane* at Basle. He has sung extensively in the USA and Europe in a wide variety of roles (many in Handel operas) ranging from the 17th century to the present. In 1976–7 he took part in the Harnoncourt-Ponnelle Monteverdi cycle at Zürich. In 1978 he created the role of Death in Penderecki's *Paradise Lost* in Chicago, repeating it the next year at La Scala and becoming the first countertenor to appear there. He sang Oberon in Britten's *A Midsummer Night's Dream* (1988, Cologne) and created the title role in Glass's *Akhnaten* at Stuttgart (1984). He sang the title role of *Admeto* at Karlsruhe (1990) and that of *Riccardo Primo* for the English Bach Festival at Covent Garden (1991). Esswood's singing is distinguished by a pure, clearly focussed tone and a well-controlled vibrato. His recordings include *Il ritorno d'Ulisse in patria* and *L'incoronazione di Poppea*; *Dido and Aeneas*; *Rinaldo*, *Serse* and *Il pastor fido*; Charpentier's *David et Jonathas* and Telemann's *Der geduldige Socrates*.

NICHOLAS ANDERSON

Estates Theatre. Opera house in PRAGUE, originally the Nostitzsche Nationaltheater, opened in 1783.

Esterházy. Hungarian family, patrons of opera; *see* ESZTERHÁZA and HAYDN, JOSEPH.

Estes, Simon (**Lamont**) (*b* Centerville, IA, 2 Feb 1938). American bass-baritone. He studied with Charles Kellis at the University of Iowa, and after further training at the Juilliard School sang at the Deutsche Oper, Berlin (début as Ramfis in *Aida*), at Lübeck and at Hamburg. His success at the first Tchaikovsky Vocal Competition in Moscow (1966) led to engagements in both North America and Europe, including the role of Carter Jones in Schuller's *The Visitation* for San Francisco (1967). In 1978 he became the first black male artist to take a major role at Bayreuth when he sang the title role in *Der fliegende Holländer*. Estes made his Metropolitan début in 1982 as the Landgrave in *Tannhäuser*. Among his other roles are Philip II, Wotan (at Berlin and the Metropolitan), Oroveso, Boris, Porgy (including the first Metropolitan performances of Gershwin's work, 1985),

79

the title role in Verdi's *Attila*, the four villains in *Les contes d'Hoffmann* and Gounod's Méphistophélès.

MARTIN BERNHEIMER

Esteve [Estebe] y Grimau, Pablo [Pau] (*b* Barcelona, *c*1734; *d* Madrid, 4 June 1794). Catalan composer. He moved to Madrid by 1760 where he won both popular acclaim as the leading composer of *tonadillas escénicas* and notoriety as a colourful character. Though he was imprisoned for allegedly slandering Madrid aristocracy in his *tonadillas*, his talents were such that he was admitted into the service of the Duke of Osuna as music master. Together with his equally famous collaborator, the playwright Ramón de la Cruz, Esteve soon turned to full-length opera, beginning with *La buena muchacha*, an adaptation in Spanish of Piccinni's *La Cecchina ossia La buona figliuola* (libretto by Goldoni after Richardson's *Pamela*), first performed in the Teatro de la Cruz in Madrid on 11 November 1765. This was followed by a partly re-composed adaptation in Spanish of Giuseppe Scarlatti's *Gli effetti della madre natura* (libretto by Goldoni), performed in the Teatro del Príncipe in Madrid on 12 June 1766 as *Los portentosos efectos de la Naturaleza*. Then on 25 December 1768, again in the Príncipe, he launched his own 'ópera cómico-bufo-dramática', with music and libretto by himself, entitled *Los jardineros de Aranjuez o También de amor los rigores sacan fruto entre las flores*. Esteve's contribution to the development of Spanish zarzuela and opera was remarkable not least for the role he played in the polemic between Italianists and nationalists by forging links between fashionable Italian opera and popular Spanish traditions.

*

J. Subirá: *Historia de la música teatral en España* (Barcelona, 1945)
W. M. Bussey: *French and Italian Influence on the Zarzuela 1700–1770* (Ann Arbor, 1980)
A. Martín Moreno: *Historia de la música española*, iv: *Siglo XVIII* (Madrid, 1985)

JACK SAGE

Estonia. Since the 17th century Estonia has come under both Swedish and Russian rule. It was independent from 1918 to 1940 and again after 1991; from 1940 to 1991 it was a member state of the USSR.

The first recorded performance of opera was J. V. Meder's Singspiel *Die beständige Argemia* in 1680 in Tallinn; in the 18th century Singspiels were presented there by opera troupes from western Europe, notably Carl Christian Agthe's Hundemberg company (active 1776–82 and based in Tallinn) and Mme Tilly's visiting troupe, who also gave *Die Zauberflöte* (*c*1795) and *Don Giovanni* (1797). The Revaler Liebhaber-Theater (founded 1784) in Tallinn presented Singspiels by A. von Kotzebue and others, and in the 19th century traditions of German opera continued to prevail, *Der Freischütz* being particularly popular.

The history of Estonian national opera is closely linked to the establishment as opera houses of its two main theatres, the Teatr Vanemuine in Tartu (1906) and the Teatr Estoniya in Tallinn (1913). Although Estonian operas were given early in the century, 1918 marks the inauguration proper of an Estonian national opera: it was then, after the declaration of independence, that regular opera performances began in the Estonia Theatre. They reached a high artistic level even before World War II, with frequent appearances by guest artists; works by Mozart, Verdi, Wagner, Bizet, Puccini, Borodin and Tchaikovsky were given, as well as original Estonian works.

The first professional Estonian composer was Rudolf Tobias (1873–1918), who graduated from the St Petersburg Conservatory in 1897; he planned an opera based on the Estonian national epic *Kalevipoeg*, but it remained unfinished. The first Estonian opera was composed by Artur Lemba (1885–1963): *Sabina* (1905), to a Russian libretto by A. Fet, later translated into Estonian as *Lembitu tütar* ('Lembitu's Daughter', 1908). Estonian national opera was established by Evald Aav (1900–39); his *Vikerlased* ('The Vikings', 1928), to a libretto by V. Loo, deals with the Estonians' battles with invaders in the 12th century. Lemba's *Kalmuneid* ('The Maiden from the Hill', 1929) and A. Vedro's *Kaupo* (1932) were also given in Tallinn.

Although at the Vanemuine Theatre in Tartu both plays and musical works – operas, light operas and (from 1939) ballets – were staged, the Estonia Theatre in Tallinn was the national opera theatre, where light operas and (from 1922) ballets were also given. In 1944 both opera houses were destroyed by Soviet troops. After the Estonia Theatre reopened in Tallinn in 1947, its productions conformed to the ideological demands of Soviet cultural policy, Russian and Soviet operas being given preference. However, new works by Estonian composers have always had a place, for example Eugen Kapp's *Tasuleegid* ('Flames of Vengeance', 1945), Gustav Ernesaks's *Pühajärv* ('The Holy Lake', 1946) and *Tormide rand* ('The Coast of Storms', 1949), Villem Kapp's *Lembitu* (1961) and Eino Tamberg's *Cyrano de Bergerac* (1976). After the war the Vanemuine Theatre continued to stage both plays and musical works, and a new house opened in 1967.

The most brilliant achievements in Estonian opera in recent years are undoubtedly Eduard Tubin's *Barbara von Tisenhusen* (1968) and *Reigi Õpetaja* ('The Parson of Reigi', 1971), both released by Ondine in Finland in 1992; the former, commissioned by the Estonia Theatre, and based on a short story by the Finnish-Estonian writer Aino Kallas, is a psychological drama set in 16th-century Estonia.

For further information on operatic life in the country's principal centre see TALLINN.

*

E. Rosen: *Rückblicke auf die Pflege der Schauspielkunst in Reval* (Reval, 1910)
A. Kasemets: *Eesti muusika arenemislugu* [A History of Estonian Music] (Tallinn, 1937)
J. Aavik: *Eesti muusika ajalugu* (Stockholm, 1965–9) [with Eng. summary]
H. Olt: *Estonian Music* (Tallinn, 1980)

VARDO RUMESSEN

Esule di Roma, ossia Il proscritto, L' ('The Exile from Rome, or The Proscribed Man'). *Melodramma eroico* in two acts by GAETANO DONIZETTI to a libretto by DOMENICO GILARDONI after Luigi Marchionni's *Il proscritto romano*, itself derived from Louis Charles Caigniez and Debotière's *Androclès ou Le lion reconnaissant*; Naples, Teatro S Carlo, 1 January 1828.

The action takes place in Rome during the reign of Tiberius (AD 14–37). Settimio (tenor) has returned to Rome from exile, although by doing so he risks death; he is determined to see his beloved Argelia (soprano) again. Though the false accusations of her father, Murena (bass), were responsible for his proscription, he will not reveal Murena's guilt as he wants to spare Argelia from discovering she is a perjurer's daughter. When Settimio is discovered in Rome and sentenced to die in the Circus Maximus, Murena's sense of shame drives him mad. One of the lions in the Circus defends Settimio, who had befriended the beast during his Caucasian exile, moving Tiberius to lift Settimio's banishment. He also forgives Murena his treachery, but demotes him from his post as Senator. Argelia and Settimio are happily reunited.

Donizetti's score for *L'esule* is best known for the trio ('Ei stesso! La mia vittima!') that forms the finale to Act 1, notable for the naturalness of the diction and the eloquent interplay of the vocal parts. Donizetti's first generally successful *opera seria*, it comes nine operas before *Anna Bolena* in the composer's canon. It enjoyed a real vogue in the 1830s until it was supplanted by more overtly romantic works, such as *Lucrezia Borgia* and *Lucia di Lammermoor*. Donizetti thought well of this score, revising the part of Settimio for Rubini, for a revival at the S Carlo in December 1828. In July of that year, it had enjoyed a modest success at La Scala, with ten performances, in which Lablache and Winter (who had both sung in the première) were joined by Méric-Lalande as Argelia (originally sung by Adelaide Tosi). Donizetti was involved in further revising the opera when it was given in his honour at Bergamo in the summer of 1840, now with Eugenia Tadolini, the tenor Donzelli and Ignazio Marini as Murena. Recent performances and recordings have shown the work to contain much pleasing music, suggesting that it has been unfairly neglected.   WILLIAM ASHBROOK

Eszterháza [Eszterház]. Country residence in what is now Fertőd, western Hungary, owned by the Esterházy family. It was converted from a relatively modest hunting lodge to a Versailles-like palace by Prince Nikolaus I, Joseph Haydn's employer, in the 1750s and 60s; its opera house opened with Haydn's *opera buffa*

Lo speziale in 1768. Extant plans show that the opera house seated about 400, was equipped with the latest stage machinery and had a moderately-sized raked stage. This building burnt down in November 1779; a new theatre was built immediately, and opened a mere ten months later.

The occasional operatic performances at Eszterháza in its early years were chiefly, but not exclusively, of Haydn's operas. Normally these were given as part of days-long pageants honouring visitors to the palace or other special events. In 1776, however, Prince Nikolaus hired seven new singers and inaugurated a regular season, in which twice-weekly operatic productions alternated with spoken plays and concerts in a nightly round of entertainment.

Between 1776 and 1790, the year of Nikolaus's death, about a hundred different operas were produced (including six by Haydn), each receiving anything from one to more than 50 performances. Haydn was responsible, first as arranger, then as musical director, for about 1200 of these performances. In addition, puppet operas were given in the grotto-like puppet theatre; Haydn wrote the complete music for at least five of these. The troupe of (mostly Italian) singers was usually 10–12 strong; they were supplemented by the princely grenadiers and others from around the estate as supernumeraries. The orchestra was fairly small (no more than 24 players). Pietro Travaglia, disciple of the famous brothers Galliari, served as stage designer from 1771, probably, until his retirement in 1798. P. G. Bader was princely librarian and director of the puppet theatre until his death in 1779, and Nunziato Porta was resident librettist and overseer of the theatre costume shop, 1781–90.

The operatic repertory at Eszterháza was broadly similar to contemporary repertories at other centres of

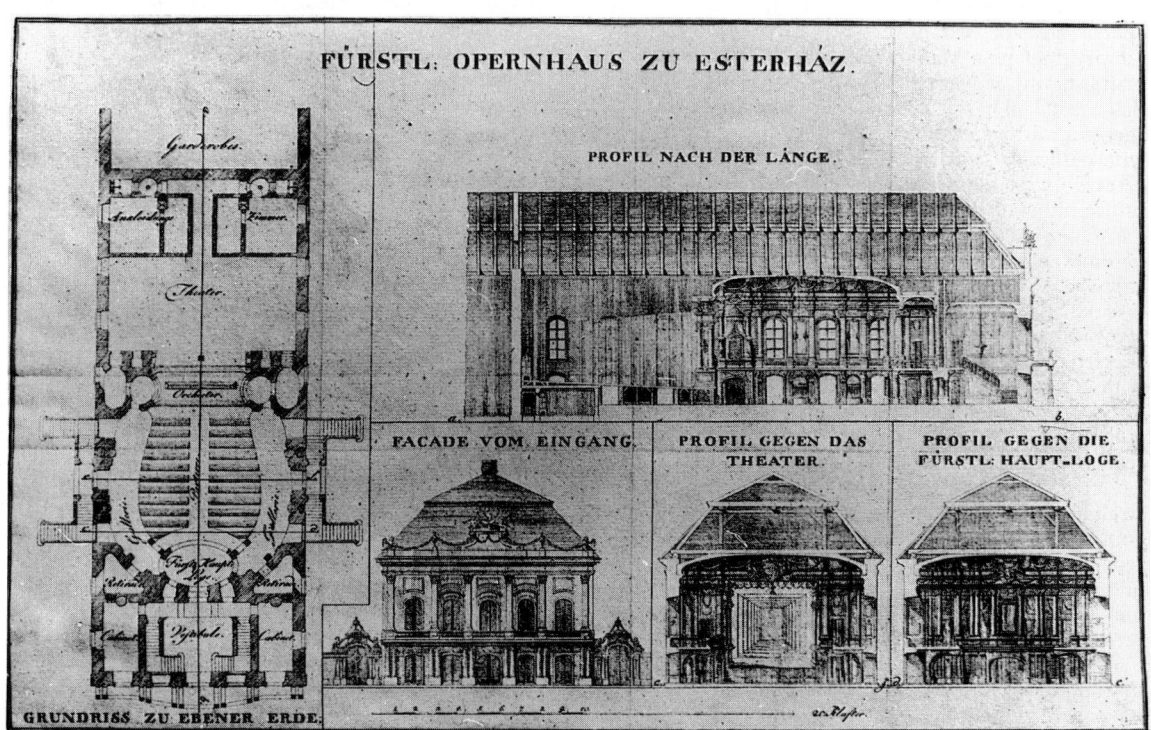

Plan, cross-sections and elevation of the opera house at Eszterháza: engraving from 'Beschreibung des Hochfürstlichen Schlosses Esterház' (Pressburg, 1784)

81

Italian opera in northern Italy and central Europe, especially Vienna, Venice, Turin, Dresden and Prague. The most popular composers were Cimarosa, Anfossi, Paisiello and Sarti. Several operas each by Bianchi, Dittersdorf, Gazzaniga, Guglielmi, Piccinni, Righini, Sacchini, Salieri, Traetta and Zingarelli were also favoured, as well as individual works by Astaritta, Caruso, Luigi Bologna, Fabrizi, Felici and the more renowned Grétry, Gassmann, Martín y Soler and (probably) Gluck. Haydn's *opera seria Armida* (1784) was the single most popular work in the repertory, followed by Luigi Bologna's *L'isola di Calipso abbandonata*, also a mythical story of entrapment and escape.

Other than the six operas by Haydn, none of the works presented at Eszterháza was written for it; most were at least two years old, and a few had been in the repertory more than a dozen years by the time they reached Eszterháza. The older operas were performed mainly at one end or the other of the frenetic period 1776–90, whereas the repertory between about 1782 and 1786 was generally more current. During these middle years the repertory also included a higher proportion of *opere serie*, almost all of which were new. This seems to have been the period when Eszterháza was asserting most strongly its operatic independence from Vienna, which, although its repertory was otherwise closely related to Eszterháza's, did not share the surge of interest in *opera seria*. Over the whole 15-year period, more than half the operas presented at Eszterháza had previously been performed in Vienna. But this proportion does not remain constant throughout the period: from 1778 to 1783, about 80% of the repertory overlaps, falling to less than 30% between 1784 and 1788, and rising again in the last year or two of the prince's life.

Most of the scores used by Haydn to direct these operas are still extant, in the Széchényi National Library, Budapest. Many were produced by the copying establishment of Wenzel Sukowaty in Vienna. Of those that are Italian in origin, some were sent by the prince's agents in various cities and others seem to have arrived with particular singers. It is not clear whether the final choices of repertory were made by Haydn or by the prince, although the latter seems to have preferred *opera buffa* to *opera seria* and to have determined the number of times an opera was performed. Haydn's revisions, still visible in the extant scores, are numerous and fascinating. They range from tiny corrections and transpositions to complete rewritings, and from cuts of short repeated phrases to omissions of whole sections within numbers (Cimarosa's arias were particularly heavily cut).

Haydn's own operas during these years tended to reflect a currently popular genre or subgenre. For example, *Il mondo della luna* (1777) represents the straightforward Goldonian farce; his sentimental comedy *La vera costanza* (1779) appeared in the repertory alongside Anfossi's *La finta giardiniera* and *Metilde ritrovata*; and *Orlando paladino* (1782) and *Armida* respond to the increasing interest in *opera seria*.

After 1790 the opera establishment at Eszterháza was disbanded by Prince Anton Esterházy, who seems to have been uninterested in music. Prince Nikolaus II succeeded Anton in 1794, and although he patronized opera, performances took place at the family castle at Eisenstadt rather than at Eszterháza.

J. Hárich: *Esterházy-Musikgeschichte im Spiegel der zeitgenössischen Textbücher* (Eisenstadt, 1959)

D. Bartha and L. Somfai: *Haydn als Opernkapellmeister* (Budapest, 1960)

J. Hárich: 'Das Repertoire des Opernkapellmeisters Joseph Haydn in Eszterháza (1780–1790)', *HayJb*, i (1962), 9–110

M. Horányi: *The Magnificence of Eszterháza* (London, 1962)

H. C. Robbins Landon: 'Haydn's Marionette Operas and the Repertoire of the Marionette Theatre at Esterház Castle', *HayJb*, i (1962), 111–99

D. Bartha: 'Haydn's Italian Opera Repertory at Eszterháza Palace', *New Looks at Italian Opera: Essays in Honor of Donald J. Grout* (Ithaca, 1968), 172–219

M. McClymonds: 'Haydn and his Contemporaries: "Armida abbandonata"', *Joseph Haydn: Vienna 1982*, 325–32

J. A. Rice: 'Sarti's Giulio Sabino, Haydn's Armida, and the Arrival of Opera Seria at Eszterháza', *HayJb*, xv (1984), 181–98

MARY HUNTER

Etcheverry, (Henri-)Bertrand (*b* Bordeaux, 29 March 1900; *d* Paris, 14 Nov 1960). French bass-baritone. He studied in Paris and made his début in 1932 as Ceprano (*Rigoletto*) at the Opéra, where he sang until the mid-1950s. Among the roles he created there were Tiresias in Enescu's *Oedipe* (1936) and the Prince of Morocco in Hahn's *Le marchand de Venise* (1935); he also sang Bluebeard in the first performance at the Opéra of Dukas' *Ariane et Barbe-bleue*, as well as roles in Egk's *Peer Gynt* and Pfitzner's *Palestrina* in their first productions in France. His repertory at the Opéra included Don Giovanni, Wotan, Boris and Méphistophélès. He first appeared at the Opéra-Comique in 1937 as Golaud, a role he also sang at Covent Garden and La Scala. His roles at the Opéra-Comique included Seneca (*L'incoronazione di Poppea*), Ourrias (*Mireille*) and Nourabad (*Les pêcheurs de perles*).

HAROLD ROSENTHAL/R

Eteocle e Polinice ('Eteocles and Polynices'). *Dramma per musica* in three acts by GIOVANNI LEGRENZI to a libretto by Tebaldo Fattorini; Venice, Teatro S Salvatore, Carnival 1675.

The title heroes of this work are the twin sons of Oedipus. Several other legendary figures appear, including Oedipus as a ghost. In the opera, the tragic end of the Greek legend is averted. The principal action involves the efforts of Polynices (soprano) to have Eteocles (soprano) respect the original pact, according to which the brothers would reign over Thebes in alternate years. There is much love interest: Polynices is betrothed to Argia [Argeia] (soprano); Eteocles falls in love with Deifile [Deipyle] (soprano), whom he captures in battle; Antigona [Antigone] (soprano) attempts to reclaim Tideo's [Tydeus] (alto) love after he has betrayed her for the scornful Deipyle. In addition to eight noble characters, there are four servants. In the end, Polynices accedes to the throne and the couples are appropriately united.

Except for the spectacle of battle, which pervades much of Act 1, the opera has modest stage requirements, contrasting strikingly with the extravagant spectacle of Legrenzi's *La divisione del mondo*, which followed later in the season at the same theatre. There are more than 90 short arias, most of them accompanied only by continuo and in da capo form; many have two strophes. The three revivals of *Eteocle e Polinice* between 1675 and 1684 document its success during Legrenzi's lifetime. A final, posthumous production for Modena in November 1690 was heavily revised, presumably by Antonio Giannettini.

HARRIS S. SAUNDERS

Ethniki Lyriki Skini. National Opera, the principal opera company of Greece; it was founded in 1939 in ATHENS.

Etienne Marcel. Opéra in four acts by CAMILLE SAINT-SAËNS to a libretto by LOUIS GALLET; Lyons, Grand Théâtre, 8 February 1879.

Commissioned in 1877 by Saint-Saëns' friend Aimé Gros for the Grand Théâtre in Lyons, *Etienne Marcel* embraced in its composition both the success of Liszt's performance of *Samson et Dalila* in Weimar and the tragic death of the composer's two sons in 1878. The rebuilding of the Paris Hôtel de Ville after the destruction of the Commune suggested to Gallet and Saint-Saëns a historical drama on the subject of Etienne Marcel, hero of a popular rebellion of 1358 during the regency of the Dauphin Charles.

The libretto is full of complex action, with conspiracies, treachery, secret assignations, crowd scenes, processions, cathedral scenes with organ and some comic elements. In addition, Béatrix (soprano), daughter of Marcel (baritone), is in love with Robert de Loris (tenor), equerry to the Dauphin (contralto). Marcel's gloomy, defiant character has a distinctly heroic ring. He eventually falls foul of an act of treachery and the Dauphin triumphs. The music is vigorous and varied. There is little vocal interest, and a preponderance of basses and baritones, but Saint-Saëns was accomplished enough to copy the better features of grand opera with an abundance of skill if not of imagination. The opera was played in Paris in 1884, but not at the Opéra, and it never became a symbolic work for the city of Paris as its authors hoped.

HUGH MACDONALD

Etoile, L' ('The Star'). Opéra bouffe in three acts by EMMANUEL CHABRIER to a libretto by EUGÈNE LETERRIER and ALBERT VANLOO; Paris, Bouffes-Parisiens, 28 November 1877.

King Ouf I (tenor) entertains his subjects annually with a public execution. This year the choice of victim is Lazuli (mezzo-soprano), a pedlar who struck the king without knowing who he was. However, when Siroco the Astrologer (bass) tells Ouf that his star and that of Lazuli are so intimately bound up that they will both die on the same day, Ouf cancels the execution. Nothing is too good for Lazuli, who even wins the love of the Princess Laoula (soprano). A pompous foreign Ambassador, Hérisson de Porc-Epic (baritone), is meanwhile having trouble with his attractive but unfaithful wife Aloes (mezzo-soprano), and with Tapioca (baritone), his secretary.

Chabrier's score, light as thistle-down, is composed in the best tradition of Offenbachian *opéra bouffe*, with each singer perfectly characterized in his or her music. Princess Laoula has a charming Rose Air, while Lazuli sings gratefully to his star, 'Oh ma petite étoile'. There is a splendid sentimental quartet and a comic duet for Ouf and Siroco, which was always encored at the Bouffes-Parisiens.

ELIZABETH FORBES

Etoile du Nord, L' ('The North Star'). Opéra comique in three acts by GIACOMO MEYERBEER to a libretto by EUGÈNE SCRIBE; Paris, Opéra-Comique (Salle Favart), 16 February 1854.

Tsar Peter the Great (bass) has disguised himself as a carpenter who plays the flute; he has fallen in love with Catherine (soprano), sister of George (tenor), also a carpenter and flautist. George is recruited into the army but Catherine takes his place, telling Peter before she goes that he must distinguish himself in battle before she will consider marrying him. In the second act, set in a military camp, Peter (still disguised) appears as a captain in the same regiment as Catherine, now dressed as a man. He becomes drunk and does not recognize her when she is brought before him for a misdemeanour. She flees before his memory of her is revived. A conspiracy against the tsar brews among the troops. Peter boldly reveals his true identity to them at the end of Act 2, the dramatic highlight of the opera, and urges them to advance intrepidly against the enemy. In the last act Peter longs for Catherine. He learns that she has gone mad and in a successful bid to restore her reason arranges for the village from Act 1 to be reconstructed and earlier scenes to be re-enacted.

L'étoile du Nord grew out of Meyerbeer's earlier German opera, EIN FELDLAGER IN SCHLESIEN. The two plots have virtually nothing in common, though certain elements from *Ein Feldlager* surface in the French work; most important among these are the flute-playing protagonist, the recurrence of the final words of the heroine's mother (associated with the work's most famous melody, given a semitone higher at each appearance) and the military setting of Act 2. A handful of numbers were taken over from *Ein Feldlager*, including Catherine's first-act *ronde*, much of Act 2 (including the Dessauer March, now transplanted to Russia) and the last-act finale featuring virtuoso dialogue between Catherine and two flutes. *L'étoile du Nord* is characterized by a large number of incidental choruses and strophic arias, even by the standards of *opéra comique*; Meyerbeer is particularly successful in imbuing each with distinctive colour and inventive ideas, ranging from the *couplets* sung by Prascovia (soprano), 'En sa demeure', with its choral echoes of the solo line and mildly Slavic flavour, to Catherine's *couplets* 'Ecoutez! écoutez!' in which she re-creates a dialogue between the village innkeeper and herself. The finales of both Act 1 and Act 2 feature the superimposition of elements that are first exposed separately, as in the third act of *Les Huguenots*.

STEVEN HUEBNER

Etranger, L' ('The Stranger'). 'Action musicale' in two acts, op.53, by VINCENT D'INDY to his own libretto; Brussels, Théâtre de la Monnaie, 7 January 1903.

Like D'Indy's *Fervaal*, *L'étranger* has Scandinavian origins, this time in Ibsen's Norwegian drama *Brand* (1866). D'Indy began planning his opera in 1896, completing the score between 1898 and 1900 and the orchestration in summer 1901.

The highly moralistic plot centres on the reclusive Stranger (baritone) who is goodness personified, but who attracts suspicion when he appears in a small fishing community because of the emerald in his cap – a Christian symbol of his charitable works. Only the young Vita (soprano), who is betrothed to the handsome, selfish and arrogant customs officer, André (tenor), is prepared to talk to him. She is strangely attracted to him (and to the all-powerful sea); although twice her age, the Stranger falls in love with her, even though he knows this will lead to disaster.

In Act 2 the Stranger tells Vita he must leave for ever, and gives her his emerald. Left alone, she resolves to belong to no one, and hurls the emerald into the sea. Soon a tempest arises, dooming a boatful of fishermen to certain death. Only the Stranger is prepared to rescue them, and despite his efforts to dissuade her, Vita insists on accompanying him. They manage to reach the boat but, as they do, a huge wave envelops them and they meet their end together as the watching fisherfolk sing the *De profundis*.

There are obvious parallels with Wagner's *Der fliegende Holländer* here, and the score, although only half the length of *Fervaal* and with an orchestra of Mozartian dimensions, again employs leitmotifs. It offers a curious hybrid mixture from folksong and plainchant to the style of the *opéra comique*. There is much of d'Indy himself in the humanitarian and deeply religious Stranger, and he somehow managed through his consummate technique to weld *L'étranger* into a convincing whole, which is remarkable for its lightness of touch, rhythmic flexibility and the audibility of its text. Debussy admired it immensely and paid homage after the première 'to the serene goodwill that hovers over this work, to its deliberate avoidance of all complication, and above all to d'Indy's quiet determination to excel himself'.   ROBERT ORLEDGE

Ettinger, Max (**Markus Wolf**) (*b* Lwów, 27 Dec 1874; *d* Basle, 19 July 1951). German composer. He was a pupil of Thuille and Rheinberger at the Munich Akademie der Tonkunst; after holding conducting posts in Leipzig and Berlin he fled to Ascona in 1933 and remained in Switzerland. His operas were his most significant achievements: *Dolores* received the opera prize of the Emil Hertzka Foundation.

Judith op.28 (3, Ettinger, after F. Hebbel), Nuremberg, 24 Nov 1921
Der eifersüchtige Trinker op.14 (tragische Komödie, 1, F. Freksa), Nuremberg, 7 Feb 1925
Juana op.33 (1, G. Kaiser), Nuremberg, 7 Feb 1925
Clavigo op.34 (Ettinger, after J. W. von Goethe), Leipzig, Stadt, 19 Oct 1926
Frühlings Erwachen op.36 (3, Ettinger, after F. Wedekind), Leipzig, 14 April 1928
Dolores op.40, 1930–31 (Ettinger), unperf.

MGG; StiegerO
E. Jucker: 'Das Werk Max Ettingers', *SMz*, xciii (1953), 501–2
                                          JOHN MORGAN

Ettore [d'Ettore], **Guglielmo** (*b* Sicily, *c*1740; *d* Ludwigsburg, wint. 1771–2). Italian singer. He sang in Hasse's *Achille in Sciro* in Naples in 1759; he later moved to Bologna and in 1761 he was engaged in Munich, remaining in service there to 1771. He appeared in several Italian centres in the 1760s, among them Venice and Verona in 1765, in operas by Sarti, and Turin, where in 1767 he sang in Bertoni's *Tancredi* and Quirino Gasparini's *Mitridate, rè di Ponto*. By then he was a *cavaliere* ('d'Ettore'). He sang the title role in Bernasconi's *La clemenza di Tito* at Munich in 1768 and Admetus in Guglielmi's *Alceste* the next year in Milan. Burney reported that he was the most applauded of the singers in Sacchini's *Scipio in Cartagena* in Padua in 1770; elsewhere he referred to him as reckoned 'the best singer of his kind on the serious opera stage'. Schubart wrote that he had 'never heard anyone sing with the feeling of a d'Ettore' (*Schubart's Leben und Gesinnungen*, Stuttgart, 1791–3, i, p.94). Later that year he sang the title role in Mozart's *Mitridate* in Milan; the young composer had to rewrite one aria four times for him, and Ettore ultimately included an aria by Gasparini (displaying his splendid top *c''*) in place of another of Mozart's. Relations were so strained that

eight years later the mention of Ettore's name evoked unpleasant memories for Mozart. Ettore was engaged at the Württemberg court on 28 January 1771 but died the next winter. His compositions include arias and many vocal duets, in a fluent melodic style.

BurneyFI   HARRISON JAMES WIGNALL

Eugene. American city, in the state of Oregon. The Eugene Opera was founded in 1976 as a community opera company using local, non-professional singers who performed in high school auditoriums. In 1982, under its director James Toland (appointed in 1981), the company took up residence in the 2400-seat Silva Concert Hall of the Hult Center for the Performing Arts, spurring its rapid development into a leading professional company of the Northwest. With three productions a year, the company has featured rising American artists, stage directors and conductors and has established a reputation for building attractive, compact productions of standard operas which have been hired by many other American companies.   NANCY MALITZ

Eugene Onegin. Opera by P. I. Tchaikovsky; *see* YEVGENY ONEGIN.

Eule, Carl Diedrich (*b* 1776; *d* Hamburg, 30 Aug 1827). German conductor and composer. He was the son of Gottlieb Eule, an actor and *buffo* singer (for some years, from 1798, a director of the Hamburg theatre), and succeeded J. F. Hönicke as musical director there in 1809. Eule wrote for Hamburg a number of comic operas, of which *Der Unsichtbare* was the most successful, making the round of the German stages until about 1870. He also wrote a number of concert arias, a string quartet and piano music. According to an account in *AMZ* (December 1821) he was a poor conductor.

all first performed in Hamburg, Theater am Gänsemarkt
Der verliebte Werber (Spl, 2), 10 Sept 1799
Obristleutnant Taps (2), 1803
Fernando (3), 3 April 1807
Der Unsichtbare (Spl, 1, C. Costenoble), 7 July 1809
Der tote Onkel (1, Costenoble), 1810
Der Antiquitätensammler (1, J. André), 1812
Das Amts- und Wirtshaus (operetta, 1, after C. Lebrun), Dec 1822, B-Bc
Giaffar und Zaide (3, G. de Pixérécourt), March 1825; MS in Munich, Staatsoper Archiv

Eumene ('Eumenes'). Libretto by APOSTOLO ZENO, first set by Marc'Antonio Ziani (1697, Venice).

The complex web of relationships that underlie the drama hinges on the conflict between two rivals to the throne of Cappadocia, Artemisia and Laodicea. Artemisia, daughter of King Ariarto [Ariarathes] and rightful successor to the throne, had been left under the guardianship of Laodicea, the king's sister, who usurped the throne and was later recognized as queen by Alexander the Great. The drama begins after the death of Alexander when one of his generals, Eumenes, attempts to restore to the throne Artemisia, the woman he has come to love.

At the beginning of Act 1, a storm disperses Eumenes' navy, whereupon it is destroyed by the fleet of Leonato [Leonnatus], a Macedonian prince in love with Laodicea. Eumenes is captured after being betrayed by Antigene, one of his lieutenants, who is driven by his secret love for Artemisia to remove his rival. In captivity, Eumenes is told by Laodicea that he can save himself only if he persuades Artemisia to surrender.

In the second act, Eumenes is allowed to go to Artemisia, but Aminta, his daughter, is held as a hostage to guarantee his return. Eumenes reveals a certain nobility of character by offering to die so that Artemisia can continue to be free, and by forgiving his betrayer. Antigene tries to save the situation by rescuing Aminta, but Eumenes honours his word and returns to Laodicea, who reveals that she loves him. In soliloquies, Eumenes ponders his fate, and Leonnatus now recognizes Eumenes as his rival.

The test of Eumenes' character continues in Act 3 when Laodicea offers him death as the alternative to accepting her love. Having captured Artemisia, Laodicea increases the pressure on Eumenes by threatening to kill the princess, but he continues to refuse to marry her. At the cusp of the crisis, the jealous Leonnatus attacks the palace of Laodicea; in the ensuing turmoil, he is disarmed by Eumenes and the forces of Artemisia are victorious. In the end, Antigene publicly admits his treachery and leaves; Laodicea is reconciled with Leonnatus and becomes ruler of Lydia; and Artemisia regains the throne of Cappadocia with Eumenes as her consort.

Before the end of the 18th century, *Eumene* was set by more than a dozen composers, primarily for theatres in Italy, but also in Germany, Spain and England. Subsequent versions of *Eumene* commonly simplify the plot through the omission of minor characters (usually Nesso, a confidant of Laodicea, and Aminta), monologues and subsidiary plots (such as Antigene's treachery). Zeno's libretto should not be confused with that of Antonio Salvi.

For a list of settings *see* ZENO, APOSTOLO.   WILLIAM R. BOWEN

Euridice (i). ('Eurydice'). Opera in five scenes by JACOPO PERI, with additions by Giulio Caccini (*see* CACCINI family, (1)), to a libretto by OTTAVIO RINUCCINI after OVID's *Metamorphoses* (book 10); Florence, Palazzo Pitti, 6 October 1600.

La Tragedia [Tragedy]	soprano
Euridice [Eurydice]	soprano
Orfeo [Orpheus]	tenor
Arcetro	alto
Tirsi ⎫ *shepherds*	tenor
Aminta ⎭	tenor
Dafne [Daphne] *messenger*	soprano
Venere [Venus]	soprano
Plutone [Pluto]	bass
Proserpina [Persephone]	soprano
Radamanto [Rhadamanthus]	tenor
Caronte [Charon]	bass

Nymphs and shepherds, shades and deities of hell

Setting Mythological times

Jacopo Corsi, one of Florence's chief patrons of music, sponsored the performance of *Euridice* – the earliest opera for which the complete music survives – as his contribution to the celebrations for Maria de' Medici's wedding to Henri IV of France. The performance took place in Antonio de' Medici's rooms in the Palazzo Pitti, with Peri in the title role and some of the other parts sung (to Caccini's music) by members of Caccini's entourage (Caccini rushed his complete setting of Rinuccini's libretto into print before Peri could do so; *see* EURIDICE (ii)). In the preface, Peri names some of the members of the cast (Francesco Rasi, later Monteverdi's Orpheus, sang Aminta; Daphne was sung by a boy) and also four gentlemen who played instruments behind the scenes: Jacopo Corsi, harpsichord; Grazia Montalvo, chitarrone; Giovan Battista dal Violino, lira grande; and Giovanni Lapi, lute. Other instrumentalists may also have played, since both the prologue and the finale have ritornellos for a single melodic instrument playing in the treble clef (a violin?), and Tirsi's song of celebration is said to have been accompanied by a 'triflauto' (panpipe), which may well have been translated in performance as two recorders. Caccini's contributions at the première consisted of Eurydice's arias, some of those for the shepherds and the nymphs, and the choruses ending Scenes 1, 2 and 4.

SCENE 1 *A meadow* After the Prologue (beginning 'Io che d'alti sospir vaga, e di pianti'), a set of strophic variations in which Tragedy promises to awaken in the hearts of the spectators tender emotions, nymphs and shepherds gather around Eurydice to help her celebrate her impending marriage to Orpheus. When Eurydice leaves with her handmaidens to sing and dance in the woods, the remaining rustic throng sing a chorus of rejoicing, beginning 'Al canto, al ballo', which alternates with solo stanzas sung by various individuals.

SCENE 2 *A meadow* Orpheus invokes nature ('Antri, ch'a miei lamenti') to describe his happiness. His conversation with Arcetro is interrupted by the rustic Tirsi who sings a strophic song in praise of marriage ('Nel pur ardor'). Orpheus has hardly thanked Tirsi, however, when Daphne rushes in, to describe in a moving narrative how Eurydice was bitten by a snake and died (her narrative proper begins 'Per quel vago boschetto'). Stunned, Orpheus sings a lament ('Non piango e non sospiro') and the nymphs and shepherds close the scene with a choral lament with a refrain beginning 'Sospirate, aure celesti'.

SCENE 3 *A meadow* Arcetro describes how he followed Orpheus to the place where Eurydice died, saw him fall on the grass and weep, and then saw a chariot drawn by two white doves descend from the skies. A goddess stepped out of the chariot and raised Orpheus up from the ground. The nymphs and shepherds exclaim at the way fortunes change ('Se de boschi i verdi onori').

SCENE 4 *The gates of hell* Venus leads Orpheus to the gates of hell and encourages him to soften the heart of Pluto with his song. Orpheus sings of his grief ('Funeste piagge, ombrosi orridi campi'). Both Persephone and Charon beg Pluto to listen to Orpheus's pleas. Pluto eventually relents and gives Eurydice back to Orpheus. The shades and deities of hell, singing antiphonally in two choruses, celebrate this unique victory of music over the power of death ('Poi che gl'eterni imperi').

SCENE 5 *A meadow* The nymphs and shepherds worry because they have heard nothing of Orpheus. Aminta arrives to tell them he has seen Eurydice returned from the dead. Eventually Orpheus comes in with Eurydice, and sings of his great joy in a strophic song ('Gioite al canto mio'). The general rejoicing is brought to a close with a danced chorus beginning 'Biond'arcier, che d'alto monte', alternating with an instrumental ritornello and a sung trio.

*   *   *

In *Euridice*, Peri goes further than he had in his *Dafne* (1597) in the devising of ways of writing a drama with continuous music. There are choruses to end each of the five scenes, and several set pieces – Orpheus's invocation of nature, Tirsi's strophic song of celebration and the messenger's moving description of Eurydice's death, all in the second scene, Orpheus's lament before the gates of hell in the fourth and his strophic song of celebration and joy in the fifth. *Euridice* gives a clear impression of Peri's theatrical style and the nature of his contribution to the development of opera, of his special gift for pathetic arioso and his imaginative use of dissonance and striking harmonies.   HOWARD MAYER BROWN

Euridice (ii). Opera in a prologue and five scenes by Giulio Caccini (*see* CACCINI family (1)) to a libretto by OTTAVIO RINUCCINI; Florence, Palazzo Pitti, 5 December 1602.

The first setting of *Euridice* was conceived and produced, in October 1600, as one of the more modest events in a series of entertainments celebrating the marriage of Maria de' Medici to Henri IV of France. Although the music for it was largely composed by Caccini's rival, Jacopo Peri, some of Caccini's own airs and three choruses ('Al canto, al ballo', 'Sospirate, aure celesti' and 'Poi che gl'eterni imperi'), written for members of the cast who were his pupils, were interpolated on that occasion. In order to claim priority in the new *stile rappresentativo*, however, Caccini had his own complete setting of the opera published in January 1601, some weeks before Peri's version appeared in print. Caccini's opera did not receive a complete performance until nearly two years later; apparently eclipsed by the success of Peri's work, it was never repeated.

Caccini used the same Rinuccini libretto – published separately as a wedding souvenir – set by Peri (for characters and plot discussion *see* EURIDICE (i)). In deference to the festive nature of the occasion, Rinuccini modified the original ending in which Eurydice dies a second time and Orpheus, turned misogynist, is torn apart by resentful Thracian women. By simplifying the action and devising a new, happy ending, Rinuccini identifies Eurydice more closely with the newly wed Maria de' Medici. On a symbolic level too, given the poet's statements in the preface to the printed libretto concerning the aims of the new musico-dramatic genre, Eurydice might be seen to represent ancient tragedy herself, whose retrieval for the modern age is accomplished in this new type of union between poetry and music.

In the preface to Caccini's printed score (dedicated to his patron and mentor Giovanni Bardi), the composer articulates his concept of the new recitative style, which he apparently created simultaneously with Peri. While not as sophisticated as Peri's in theory or practice, it shares the same tenets: imitation of speech inflection by the voice; rhythmic flexibility and harmonic freedom between solo voice and basso continuo to convey more effectively the meaning and inherent affections of the text; and 'a certain *sprezzatura*', or studied effortlessness on the part of the performer. Judging by the music, however, Caccini's recitative has a more limited expressive range than Peri's. It employs dissonance, chromatic harmonies and syncopation only sparingly, even in passages of utmost dramatic intensity. At the same time, its more active harmonic rhythm and use of

Title page of Caccini's 'Euridice' (Florence: Giorgio Marescotti, 1600–01); see also PUBLISHING, *fig.1*

melodic sequences (for example, in 'Non piango') reinforce the general impression that Caccini's theatrical style is more lyric than dramatic.

While recitative predominates, Caccini's setting contains one strophic song for Orpheus (justified by its text, 'Gioite al canto mio'), set in a graceful, dance-like style typical of the airs in Caccini's *Le nuove musiche*; and for the seven quatrains of the prologue Caccini provides a single strophe in a declamatory arioso style characteristic of the traditional *arie* for 16th-century strophic poetry. The chorus functions in two ways: interacting with the principal characters to advance the plot (Scenes 3 and 5), and articulating the separation between scenes by commenting reflectively on the preceding action. Musically, these functions are differentiated by, in the first instance, monodic lines in recitative style (assigned simply to 'coro'), and in the second by homophonic strophes for four or five parts (sometimes alternating with solo stanzas). Whether the monodic lines were meant to be performed by a unison chorus of nymphs, shepherds, or both, or by unnamed soloists from their company, it is unlikely that even the homophonic passages involved more than eight or ten singers.

In the fashion typical of the earliest collections of solo song, Caccini's score is without instrumental indications or other embellishment, although the bass line would have been realized by a wide variety of instruments singly or in combination, and the vocalists would certainly have added ornaments to imitate the affections, as advocated by Caccini in his preface to *Le nuove musiche*.   BARBARA R. HANNING

Euripides (*b* ?Athens, *c*485 BC; *d* Aegae [now Vodena], Macedonia, *c*405 BC). Greek dramatist. He is said to have written 92 plays, of which 19 have survived. He had a notable scepticism towards the ancient myths that formed the material of Greek tragedy. His gods impart useful information but inspire scant respect, and in a play such as *Helen* Euripides shows tendencies towards New Comedy. For Euripides human reason is only so far dependable; much depends on chance. The tautest of his plays is the *Iphigeneia in Tauris*, the most terrifying *The Bacchae* with its ruthless portrayal of the god Dionysus. The stories of Iphigenia (in Aulis and Tauris) and Alcestis have been particularly fruitful ground for opera composers, from Lully, Keiser and Campra to the present day, most of all perhaps in the middle and late 18th century (Jommelli, Traetta, Gluck, Piccinni). For many librettists of the 17th and 18th centuries Euripides was filtered through the art of such French dramatists as Corneille (*Médée*, 1634), Racine (*Andromaque*, 1667; *Iphigénie en Aulide*, 1674; *Phèdre*, based on the *Hippolytus*, 1677) and Voltaire (*Oreste*, 1750). More recently the Helen who never went to Troy has appealed to Hofmannsthal and Strauss (*Die ägyptische Helena*), and there have been at least five versions of *The Bacchae* (Wellesz, *Die Bakchantinnen*; Ghedini, *Le baccanti*; Henze, *The Bassarids*; Harry Partch, *Revelation in the Courthouse Park*; Börtz, *Backanterna*; and John Buller, *The Bacchae/Bakxai*).   ROBERT ANDERSON

Europa riconosciuta ('Europa Recognized'). *Dramma per musica* in two acts by ANTONIO SALIERI to a libretto by MATTIA VERAZI; Milan, Teatro alla Scala, 3 August 1778.

After a shipwreck Europa (soprano), Queen of Tyre, her husband Asterio (soprano castrato), King of Crete, and their small son are captured by the wicked Egisto (tenor). Egisto wants to marry Semele (soprano), a princess, but she loves the young warrior Isseo (soprano castrato) and refuses. A sacrificial ceremony is interrupted by a battle in which Isseo slays Egisto. Europa's generous decision to cede the throne of Tyre to Semele and Isseo brings the opera to a joyful conclusion.

In this inaugural opera for La Scala, Salieri and Verazi ignored many of the conventions of Italian serious opera. The chorus is given an important role and action ensembles replace scenes that normally would have been set as recitatives. A character is killed on stage in full view of the audience. Also unconventional is the use of two principal couples requiring two leading castratos (Gasparo Pacchierotti and G. M. Rubinelli) and two prima donnas (Marina Balducci and Franziska Lebrun).

The opera is full of dramatic and violent events. Salieri's music matches the innovatory libretto in its vividness and pathos. The overture, which depicts the shipwreck, is suitably stormy. Asterio's opening cavatina perfectly evokes his desperation with its dialogue of sighing oboes and violins. Equally effective is his big three-tempo aria in G minor in Act 2, 'Del morir l'angoscie adesso', in which the hero, about to be put to death, bids farewell to wife and child. In the ensembles, of which there are several, Salieri effectively differentiated his characters' personalities and skilfully advanced the action.

For illustration *see* MILAN, fig.3.   JOHN A. RICE

Europe galante, L' ('Galant Europe'). *Opéra-ballet* in a prologue and four entrées by ANDRÉ CAMPRA to a libretto by ANTOINE HOUDAR DE LAMOTTE; Paris, Opéra, 24 October 1697.

L'Europe galante is generally considered the first *opéra-ballet*, but its format – an independent intrigue and different characters for each entrée (act) – was not new. Two years earlier, for example, opera habitués observed an identical structure in the *Ballet des saisons* by Pascal Collasse and the Abbé Pic. The originality of *L'Europe galante* and most subsequent *opéras-ballets* lies in the subject matter of the entrées, which, in Louis de Cahusac's happy metaphor, are 'pretty Watteaus, piquant miniatures that demand precision of design, grace of brush stroke and brilliance of colour' (*La danse ancienne et moderne*, 1754). The action does not take place in ancient times, nor is it rooted in allegory and myth. Rather, Campra and Lamotte presented contemporary stereotypes of love as practised in four European nations. Lamotte wrote:

Harem of Sultan Zuliman in Campra's opéra-ballet 'L'Europe galante' (1697): engraving from the libretto in 'Recueil général des opéra', vi (1703)

We have chosen those nations which are most contrasting and which offer the greatest potential for stage treatment: France, Spain, Italy and Turkey. We have followed what is normally considered to be characteristic behaviour of their inhabitants.

The Frenchman is portrayed as fickle, indiscreet and amorous, the Spaniard as faithful and romantic, the Italian as jealous, shrewd and violent. Finally, we have expressed, within the limitations of the stage, the haughtiness and supreme authority of the sultan and the passionate nature of the sultanas.

In 'La France' Silvandre (*haute-contre*), a shepherd, admits to his friend Philène (bass) that Céphise (soprano) is the present object of his desire, not Doris (soprano). He prepares a *fête* to charm Céphise, who remains unmoved by his explanation that 'Doris was my last flirtation; you are my first love'. Doris resolves to hide her anger and to wait until Silvandre's fickleness returns him to her.

In 'L'Espagne' Don Pédro (*haute-contre*) and Don Carlos (bass), two Spanish cavaliers, sing serenades under the balconies of their respective mistresses, Lucile and Léonore, who fail to respond. Each suitor claims to be the most tender and faithful. Surprisingly, neither Lucile nor Léonore ever appears in this entrée.

In 'L'Italie' Octavio (*haute-contre*), a Venetian nobleman and chronic complainer, berates Olympia (soprano) for not returning his love. She correctly surmises that he is alarmed by her acceptance of an invitation to a masked ball. Octavio explains that excessive love causes his jealousy. During the ball Olympia fears for the life of her masked dancing-partner should Octavio identify him as her lover. Later, Octavio, putting away his dagger, pretends to her that he has killed his rival. She is distraught. He confesses his ruse and hopes one day to receive her forgiveness.

'La Turquie' takes place in the harem of Sultan Zuliman (bass) and concerns the rivalry of two sultanas, Zäide (soprano) and Roxane (soprano), for his attention. After Roxane tries to stab her rival Zuliman declares his love for Zäide.

The vocal solo and ensemble music for *L'Europe galante* is of high quality. It ranges from the impressive 'Sommeil qui chaque nuit', a *haute-contre* chaconne air in 'L'Espagne', to the boisterous Bostangi choruses in 'La Turquie'. Each act's *divertissement* includes songs and dances appropriate to the four countries represented.

The first three Paris editions of *L'Europe galante* (1697, 1698 and 1699) appeared anonymously because of Campra's position as *maître de musique* at Notre Dame. The work enjoyed many revivals and was performed, at least in part, until 1775.

JAMES R. ANTHONY

Europeras 1 & 2. Opera in two unrelated parts by JOHN CAGE; Frankfurt, Schauspielhaus, 12 December 1987.

The work is a deliberately randomized phantasmagoria of European opera fragments (Gluck to Puccini), performed with sets, costumes, props, scenery, lighting, movement and scenarios chosen at random and without reference to each other. *Europera 1* lasts for 90 minutes, *Europera 2* for 45. The cast includes singers representing each of 19 different vocal types, plus 12 silent 'assistants' who perform as stagehands, dancers and acrobats.

The many thousands of random choices required to compose the opera were made by means of a computer program designed to simulate the casting of *I Ching* hexagrams. Singers choose their own arias and en-

sembles from specified operas, performing them at their own pitch and tempo but at specified times and for specified durations. The instrumental parts consist of randomly selected 1- to 16-bar snippets drawn from 70 operas in the library of the Metropolitan Opera, played within specified time brackets. Costumes are chosen randomly from a 14-volume, 19th-century encyclopedia of costume; props come from illustrations on random pages of *Webster's International Dictionary of the English Language, Unabridged* (2/1935), as do (somewhat less mechanically) the scenarios, one of which reads in part 'She is bored with most men; he is in love with her. He accepts a preliminary trial hoping to find a way. She persuades him to give her his life. He dies. Now in his dark tomb he goes to her rescue. She awakens his love early in the morning'. There are 12 such scenarios, simultaneous and conflicting, for each of the opera's two parts. The scenery consists of flats whose arrival, departure, position and movement are randomly determined – as are those of the cast. A final element of the collage is a musical 'truckera' of 101 electronically superimposed opera fragments, which intermittently passes through 'like a truck'.

ANDREW STILLER

Euryanthe. *Grosse heroisch-romantische Oper* in three acts, J291, by CARL MARIA VON WEBER to a libretto by HELMINA VON CHEZY after the early French romance *L'histoire du très-noble et chevalereux prince Gérard, comte de Nevers, et de la très-virtueuse et très chaste princesse Euriant de Savoye, sa mye*; Vienna, Kärntnertortheater, 25 October 1823.

King Louis VI	bass
Adolar, Count of Nevers and Rethel	tenor
Lysiart, Count of Forest and Beaujolais	bass
Euryanthe of Savoy	soprano
Eglantine of Puiset	soprano
Rudolf	tenor
Bertha	soprano

Ladies, noblemen, knights and countryfolk

Setting Prémery and Nevers in 1110

On 11 November 1821, as a direct result of the success of *Der Freischütz* some five months earlier, Weber received a letter from the impresario Domenico Barbaia in Vienna, asking him to compose 'an opera in the style of *Der Freischütz*' for the 1822–3 season at the Kärntnertortheater. From the start, though, Weber intended to write a very different kind of opera. He was not alone in thinking that the next stage in the development of German opera should be the replacement of spoken dialogue with continuous music. Some composers with whom Weber was in direct contact had already taken this step; Johann Nepomuk Poissl's *Athalia* (1814) and *Der Wettkampf zu Olympia* (1815), which Weber had staged in Prague and Dresden, and Ignaz von Mosel's *Salem* (1813) and *Cyrus und Astyages* (1818) were examples of through-composed German operas that had achieved a measure of success. But both these composers' operas, with their Classical orientation, were far from the ideal for which Weber was striving. Two other composers who were thinking along lines much closer to Weber's were Spohr and Schubert, who each produced a through-composed German opera (*Jessonda* and *Alfonso und Estrella*) at about the same time as *Euryanthe*. Schubert's efforts were unknown to the other two, but it seems probable that there was even an element of personal rivalry between Weber and Spohr. Weber was certainly determined to show those (including Spohr) who were critical of his 'pandering to popular taste' in *Der Freischütz* that he could successfully conquer the realm of high art.

Weber's first problem was to find a suitable libretto, and it was his failure to do this that marred a potential masterpiece. Having rejected a number of possibilities, he made the mistake of persuading Helmina von Chezy, despite her protestations that she lacked experience, to provide him with a libretto. From a number of suggestions he accepted *Euryanthe* and, after much modification and rewriting of Chezy's drafts, set to work on the music in May 1822; by August 1823 the whole opera, except for the overture, was complete. Its reception in Vienna, with Weber conducting, was initially enthusiastic, but this was probably a tribute more to the composer than to the work. Some voices were raised against the opera even before its première. Schubert, who admired *Der Freischütz*, complained about *Euryanthe*'s 'formlessness' and 'lack of melody' and commented: 'whenever a scrap of tune appears, it is crushed like a mouse in a trap by the weighty orchestration'. Many found the plot confusing and felt that the whole opera was too long. Weber himself sanctioned cuts totalling 172 bars, and after his departure from Vienna the conductor Conradin Kreutzer removed a further 352 bars. Despite these efforts to make the opera more effective, audiences quickly fell off, and it was withdrawn after the 20th performance. Nevertheless, *Euryanthe* was subsequently staged in many theatres and has retained a tenuous place in the operatic repertory despite its irredeemable shortcomings.

The excellence of much of the music in *Euryanthe*, and the many individual moments at which Weber's vivid dramatic gift shines through, have led to various attempts to make new performing versions, but none of these has succeeded.

ACT 1 *King Louis' castle at Prémery* At a celebration of peace the king asks Adolar to sing. Accompanying himself on a 'zither', he sings the romance 'Unter blüh'nden Mandelbäumen' (no.2) in praise of his bride, Euryanthe; pizzicato strings suggest his accompaniment. Everyone joins in Euryanthe's praise in the chorus 'Heil Euryanth'' (no.3) except Lysiart, who in the ensuing recitative wagers his lands against Adolar's that he can prove Euryanthe unfaithful. In a trio with chorus (no.4) Adolar accepts the wager, asserting 'Ich bau' auf Gott und meine Euryanth'' ('I rely on God and my Euryanthe') to a melody which has already been heard in the overture and which recurs later in the opera.

The castle at Nevers Euryanthe sings of her longing for Adolar in the cavatina 'Glöcklein im Thale' (no.5). This leads straight into a recitative as Eglantine, who covertly hates Euryanthe, enters. She attempts to discover the secret of Euryanthe's strange nocturnal behaviour; the orchestral accompaniment is dominated by a chromatic motif representing her deceitfulness, which plays an important part in later numbers. In the aria 'O mein Leid' (no.6) Eglantine asserts that banishment would be preferable to being barred from Euryanthe's confidence; while the orchestra plays the 'ghost' music heard in the overture, Euryanthe reluctantly reveals that the ghost of Adolar's sister Emma appeared to her and told her that, out of grief at

her lover Udo's death in battle, she committed suicide with poison contained in her ring and cannot find rest until the ring has been washed by the tears of an innocent girl in despair. Euryanthe has been nightly praying in Emma's tomb for the repose of her soul and is horrified at having betrayed the secret, but in the duet 'Unter ist mein Stern gegangen' (no.7) Eglantine assures her of her trustworthiness. After Euryanthe has departed, Eglantine, again accompanied by the Deceit motif, vents her rage in the scene and aria 'Bethörte!' (no.8); she plans to denounce Euryanthe to Adolar, whom she secretly loves. She is interrupted by the sound of Lysiart's arrival. Country folk greet Lysiart (no.9), and Euryanthe bids him welcome. His passion for her is awakened. Eglantine plans to ask him for help with her plot.

ACT 2 *The castle at Nevers* Night has fallen and Lysiart, alone, wavers between guilt and desire in the scena and aria 'Wo berg' ich mich?' (no.10); as he resolves to pursue his evil scheme ('So weih' ich mich den Rach' gewalten') his inner turbulence is reflected by rushing strings. (Weber's portrayal of Lysiart here, as a man divided against himself, strongly recalls Spohr's treatment of Faust in his 1813 opera, particularly in the scena 'Blöder Thor!'.) Eglantine, having removed the poison ring from Emma's corpse, comes out of the tomb and, unaware of Lysiart's presence, once more gives way to her jealousy of Euryanthe. She is interrupted by Lysiart, who proposes an alliance and marriage. In the duet 'Komm denn' (no.11) they cement their pact.

The king's hall at Prémery Adolar stills his anxiety and expresses his longing for Euryanthe in the aria 'Wehen mir Lüfte Ruh!' (no.12); the section beginning 'O Seligkeit, dich fass' ich kaum' is set to a melody already heard as the second subject of the overture. Euryanthe hurries in. They express their love for one another in the duet 'Hin nimm die Seele mein' (no.13). After the court has welcomed Euryanthe (no.14), Lysiart advances to claim victory in the wager. At first Adolar expresses his confidence in Euryanthe by singing the melody of 'Ich bau' auf Gott' to the words 'Komm an mein Herz'; but when Lysiart produces Emma's ring and reveals that he knows the secret of the tomb, all are reluctantly convinced of Euryanthe's guilt. Adolar's estates are forfeit and he leads away the distraught Euryanthe to wander in the wilderness.

ACT 3 *A rocky mountain gorge* Adolar plans to kill Euryanthe. Rising 6ths, which form an important melodic feature in the scene, recall the prominent rising 6ths in 'O Seligkeit' and the love duet 'Hin nimm die Seele mein', but here the harmonic context gives them a forlorn quality, underlining Adolar's disillusionment. In the recitative 'Hier weilest du?' (no.15) Euryanthe protests her innocence. Their duet 'Wie liebt' ich dich' is interrupted by the approach of a snake; Euryanthe interposes herself between it and Adolar to protect him, but he rushes off to attack it. Euryanthe waits anxiously ('Schirmende Engelshaar', no.16) until, having slain the snake, Adolar returns and tells Euryanthe that he will abandon her, not kill her. In the scena and cavatina 'So bin ich nun verlassen' (no.17) Euryanthe longs for death, hoping that the flowers by her grave will tell Adolar that 'she did not betray you', but her musing is cut short by the sound of hunting horns. The Huntsmen's Chorus 'Die Thale dampfen' (no.18), in the 'courtly' key of E♭, contrasts effectively with the preced-

'Euryanthe' (Weber): scene from Act 3, with Wilhelmine Schröder-Devrient as Euryanthe and Ignaz Schuster as Adolar in an early production; lithograph (1839)

ing gloomy scene. The king and his hunting party are astonished to discover Euryanthe. In the duet with chorus 'Lasst mich hier' (no.19) Euryanthe, explaining Eglantine's deceit, easily convinces the king of her innocence. At the thought of being reunited with Adolar, Euryanthe gives expression to her joy in the aria with chorus 'Zu ihm! zu ihm!', but as they are about to lead her away she collapses.

An open space in front of the castle at Nevers Country folk are singing a May song as Adolar approaches (no.21). When they recognize him they tell him of Euryanthe's innocence and the treachery of Lysiart and Eglantine. In the solo with chorus 'Vernichte kühn das Werk' (no.22) they pledge their support and implore him to overthrow the traitors. To the sound of a wedding march (no.23), Lysiart and Eglantine approach. The ghost music haunts Eglantine and she falters. Adolar steps forward. In a duet with chorus, 'Trotze nicht!' (no.24), the people curse Lysiart, while he and Adolar confront one another. The king arrives in time to prevent armed conflict. In the finale (no.25) he tells Adolar that Euryanthe's heart is broken. In the ensuing confrontation Eglantine pours scorn on Lysiart, who stabs her to death. Lysiart is led away. To the sound of hunting horns, Euryanthe, now recovered from her collapse, is brought in. A final fragment of the ghost music indicates that, innocent tears having washed the ring, Emma is at rest. A chorus of rejoicing concludes the opera.

*   *   *

From the purely musical point of view, *Euryanthe* is in many ways Weber's masterpiece. Its blending of set pieces with freer sections of recitative and arioso is highly effective. Weber's use of chromaticism, particularly to characterize the evil pair, is masterly, and his employment of musical motif is more subtle than in *Der Freischütz*. The orchestration is vivid and imaginative, contributing much to the overall atmosphere of the opera. Despite the obvious dramatic deficiencies of the work as a whole, its influence on later composers, notably Marschner, Schumann, Liszt and Wagner, was considerable.

CLIVE BROWN

Eva. Opera in three acts, op.50, by JOSEF BOHUSLAV FOERSTER to his own libretto after GABRIELA PREISSOVÁ's play *Gazdina roba* ('The Farm Mistress'); Prague, National Theatre, 1 January 1899.

Eva (soprano), a poor seamstress, and Mánek (tenor), son of a wealthy landlord, are in love despite the social and religious barriers dividing them. Mánek's mother Mešjanovka (contralto), a proud widow, scorns her son's choice and picks a wealthy bride, Maryša, for him. When she sees Mánek dancing with Eva at a country fair, she insults her, telling her that she is a penniless 'pagan' (i.e. Lutheran). Eva, hurt also by Mánek's weak will, decides to break with him. More through compassion than through love she marries a lame furrier, Samko (baritone), who has long been in love with her. In Act 2 it becomes clear that Samko, a bigoted Protestant, has caused the death of their small daughter by refusing to call the doctor, who lives 'in sin', having married a divorced woman. Eva's marriage has since been unhappy and empty. She thinks increasingly of Mánek, and when he, although now married, invites her to a farm in Austria as his '*gazdina*', she leaves with him in the hope that the Austrian authorities will grant him a divorce and allow him to remarry. At a harvest celebration in Act 3, a drunk labourer (bass) turns against Eva, calling her a mere '*roba*' (slut), since she lives unmarried with the landlord. Eva suffers humiliation and has nightmares about her dead daughter. Having learnt that Mánek will not be granted a divorce, she decides to end her life in the waters of the Danube.

Foerster attended the first night of Preissová's play at the Prague National Theatre in 1889 and later wrote: 'The life of the characters, the straightforward action, the dramatic conflict and above all the character of Eva herself, overwhelming in her emotional purity, all called for musical interpretation that must be the emotional fulfilment of everything that words can only hint at but never express'. Jaroslav Kvapil (i) was to have written the libretto, but in 1895 he had still not completed it and Foerster composed a 'Tragická overtura' ('Tragic Overture') based on the themes of the play. In Hamburg he happened to meet an old watchmaker who strongly reminded him of Samko; he immediately wrote Act 1 of the libretto and decided to work alone (1895–7).

Foerster was among the first Czech composers to compose operas on contemporary realistic plays, free of Romantic pathos and an idyllic view of country people. Deeply rooted as he was in the Smetana tradition of idealization, Foerster could not use a libretto in prose, even less one in dialect – though some elements of Moravian-Slovak border dialect eventually found their way into the libretto. For Foerster's operatic aesthetic tended towards lyricism, and stylized poetic expression was for him essential for musical expression that was still melodically, harmonically and structurally rooted in the 19th century. He thus differed in principle from Janáček, who when composing *Jenůfa* at about the same time set a play by Preissová with hardly any changes, used dialect and built directly on the dramatic charge of individual words and sentences.

The score of the opera reflects Foerster's development from his first opera, *Debora*, composed in 1891, to his polyphonic Third Symphony (1894). The cornerstones are the characteristic themes of the four leading characters: Eva, Mánek, Samko and Mešjanovka. Attention is focussed mainly on Eva's destiny; in the melodic, rhythmic and harmonic transformations of her theme Foerster reached the climax of his psychological insight. Her concluding aria, 'Já vidím ráj' ('I see paradise'), achieves a cathartic effect and underlines Foerster's spiritual approach to her drama. In the competition for the best Czech opera in 1897, organized by the Prague National Theatre, *Eva* came third after Kovařovic's *Psohlavci* ('The Dog's-Heads') and Fibich's *Šárka*. The result proved the extent to which Romanticism still dominated public tastes and illustrated the fact that psychological works like *Eva* will always be overshadowed by those that are theatrically more attractive. Nevertheless *Eva* became the most popular of Foerster's six operas; since its première it has been staged more than 40 times in Czech theatres. It was the composer's only opera to be staged abroad – under the title *Marja* in a translation by Johannes Brandt at the Vienna Volksoper (1915).

EVA HERRMANNOVÁ

Evangelatos, Daphne (*b* Athens, 1952). Greek mezzo-soprano. She studied in Athens, Vienna and then Munich, where she was engaged at the Staatsoper (1971–83). She sang Annius (*La clemenza di Tito*) in Edinburgh (1981), Melanto (*Il ritorno d'Ulisse*) in Salzburg (1985) and Clorinde (Campra's *Tancrède*) at Aix-en-Provence (1986). She has also sung in Vienna, Cologne, Hamburg, Frankfurt and Brussels. A stylish artist with a warm, vibrant voice, she has sung many trouser roles: Gluck's Orpheus, Mozart's Sextus, Cherubino, Ramiro (*La finta giardiniera*), Octavian and the Composer (*Ariadne auf Naxos*). Her repertory also includes Fricka, Waltraute, Preziosilla, Olga, Varvara (*Kát'a Kabanová*) and Nancy (*Albert Herring*).

ELIZABETH FORBES

Evans, Anne (*b* London, 20 Aug 1939). English soprano. She studied in London and then in Geneva, where she sang small roles including Countess Ceprano and Wellgunde. In 1968 she joined the Sadler's Wells Opera (later the ENO), making her début as Mimì and singing Countess Almaviva, the Marschallin, Ariadne and Penelope Rich (*Gloriana*). With the WNO (1974–89) she has sung Senta, Chrysothemis, the Empress and the Dyer's Wife (*Die Frau ohne Schatten*), Leonore, Donna Anna and Brünnhilde, the last in a complete *Ring* cycle which was also given at Covent Garden (1986). In 1983 she sang Ortlinde and the Third Norn at Bayreuth, where she returned in 1989 to sing Brünnhilde. She has also sung at San Francisco, San Diego, Düsseldorf and Paris. Her repertory includes Elsa, Eva, Kundry and Elisabeth de Valois. Her strong, clear voice is particularly suited to Strauss and Wagner and she is an excellent actress.

*

R. Milnes: 'Anne Evans', *Opera*, xxxvii (1986), 256–63

ELIZABETH FORBES

Evans, Sir Geraint (Llewellyn) (*b* Cilfynydd, 16 Feb 1922; *d* Aberystwyth, 19 Sept 1992). Welsh baritone. He studied with Theo Hermann in Hamburg and later with Fernando Carpi in Geneva and at the GSM, London. He joined the Covent Garden company in 1948, making his début as the Nightwatchman (*Die Meistersinger*). In his second season he sang Mozart's Figaro (his début role at La Scala in 1960 and at the Vienna Staatsoper a year later). His repertory widened to include Escamillo, Lescaut, Marcello, Papageno, Balstrode, Sharpless, Dulcamara and Bottom (Britten). At Covent Garden he created Mr Flint (*Billy Budd*, 1951), Mountjoy (*Gloriana*, 1953) and Antenor (*Troilus and Cressida*, 1954). He sang at Glyndebourne, 1950–61, in Mozart roles and as Abbate Cospicuo (*Arlecchino*), the Music-Master (*Ariadne auf Naxos*) and Falstaff, the role of his Metropolitan début in 1964. Evans sang regularly at Salzburg from 1962 as Figaro, Leporello and Wozzeck and with the leading American companies, having made his début at San Francisco in 1959 as Beckmesser. He first appeared at the Paris Opéra in 1975 as Leporello. He was knighted in 1969 and in 1973 celebrated the 25th anniversary of his Covent Garden début, as Don Pasquale. In 1984 he made his farewell appearance at Covent Garden, as Dulcamara, and in the same year his autobiography, *A Knight at the Opera*, was published in London. His voice, while not large (his Rigoletto and Scarpia were unsuccessful), was resonant and carefully trained, but it was above all for his resourceful and genial wit that he was admired, notably as Beckmesser and Falstaff and especially in Mozart.

*

GV (G. Baldini; J. P. Kenyon)

L. Dunlop: 'Geraint Evans', *Opera*, xii (1961), 231–6

H. Rosenthal: *Great Singers of Today* (London, 1966)

D. Cairns: *Responses* (London, 1973), 134ff

HAROLD ROSENTHAL/R

Evans [Crozier], Nancy (*b* Liverpool, 19 March 1915). English mezzo-soprano. She studied in Liverpool with John Tobin, then with Maggie Teyte and Eva de Reusz. She made her London stage début in 1938 in Sullivan's *The Rose of Persia*; in 1939 she sang small roles at Covent Garden. Joining the English Opera Group in 1946, she alternated with Ferrier in the title role of Britten's *The Rape of Lucretia* at Glyndebourne. In 1947 she created Nancy in *Albert Herring*, and later sang Polly in Britten's version of *The Beggar's Opera*, Purcell's Dido and Lucinda Woodcock in *Love in a Village*. She travelled with the English Opera Group to the Netherlands, Belgium, Switzerland and Scandinavia. In 1968 she created the Poet and seven other characters in Malcolm Williamson's *The Growing Castle*. Her warm-toned voice and lively personality made her the ideal interpreter of Nancy. She married first Walter Legge, then Eric Crozier.

For illustration *see* ALBERT HERRING.   HAROLD ROSENTHAL/R

Everding, August (*b* Bottrop, 31 Oct 1928). German director and administrator. He studied the piano, philosophy, theology and dramaturgy at the universities of Bonn and Munich. From 1963 to 1973 he was director of the Münchner Kammerspiele while starting his career as an opera director, his work including the première of Searle's *Hamlet* at Hamburg in 1968. From 1973 to 1977 he was resident director at the Hamburg Staatsoper and in 1977 he moved to the Staatsoper in Munich, where he became General Intendant. He has worked regularly in a number of international houses, directing admired stagings of *Der fliegende Holländer* (1969) and *Tristan und Isolde* (1974) at the Bayreuth Festival. At Covent Garden he was responsible for the *Zauberflöte* that was produced in 1979 from the Munich original. He has also directed opera on television. Although he has employed the full panoply of modern stage techniques, Everding's productions are fundamentally traditionalist; his concepts and methods have gradually been discounted and viewed as old-fashioned.

*

N. Ely and S. Jaeger, eds.: *Regie heute: Musiktheater in unserer Zeit* (Berlin, 1984), 89–110   ALAN BLYTH

Evstatieva, Stefka [Kovatcheva, Stefka Evstatieva] (*b* Ruse, 7 May 1947). Bulgarian soprano. She studied at the Sofia Conservatory with Yelena Kiselova, and while a member of the Ruse Opera, 1971–9, made her début as Amelia (*Ballo*) in 1972, and won international competitions in Moscow, Brussels and Sofia, building a repertory of leading roles in Italian, Russian and Bulgarian operas. She joined the National Opera at Sofia in 1978, and began touring in western Europe, appearing at the Vienna Staatsoper, the Deutsche Oper, Berlin, La Scala and the Paris Opéra. She made her British début as Desdemona with the Royal Opera on tour at Manchester in 1981, followed by Donna Elvira and Elisabeth de Valois at Covent Garden. Her American début was as Lisa (*The Queen of Spades*) at Philadelphia in 1983, and she sang Elisabeth de Valois at the Metropolitan the next year. In 1990 she sang Aida in Savonlinna. Her recordings in Bulgaria include *Mefistofele* (Boito), *Prince Igor* and operas by Rimsky-Korsakov and Raichev. Her bright, forward-placed soprano is technically secure and boldly characterized, though her words have not always been clearly projected.   NOËL GOODWIN

Ewart [née Donaldson], **Florence Maud** [Maude; Alden, Sonia] (*b* London, 16 Nov 1864; *d* Melbourne, 8 Nov 1949). Australian composer. She was educated at the Birmingham and Midland Institute and then at the National Training School for Musicians, London. She attended the Hochschule für Musik in Leipzig, distinguishing herself as a violinist and playing in the Gewandhaus Orchestra. Having studied with Adolf Brodsky, she worked for him as a tutor in Leipzig and was a pupil of Joachim in Berlin before returning to Birmingham, where she became established as a performer and conductor. At this time she composed extensively and wrote most of her first opera *Ekkehard*. In 1898 she married Alfred James Ewart, a distinguished botanist, and in 1906 the family settled permanently in Australia. During the next ten years Ewart composed occasional dramatic works, returning to Europe several times to try to have her operas performed and to study composition. She visited the Schola Cantorum, heard Debussy's dramatic music for the first time and between 1924 and 1927 studied with Respighi in Milan.

From 1923 onwards Ewart wrote four operas, of which only excerpts from the first, *The Courtship of Miles Standish*, were staged. Her final opera, *A Game of Chess*, was incomplete at her death. The five completed operas differ in style, particularly in tonality and texture, and reflect the principal changes in operatic composition that had occurred since Wagner. *Ekkehard* makes rudimentary use of leitmotifs, using a superficial thematic structure to outline the principal character's emotional conflict. In *Mateo Falcone* Ewart employed picturesque set pieces to contrast dramatically with the undercurrent of tragedy. *The Courtship of Miles Standish* is an adaptation of Longfellow's poem; the musical setting is essentially lyrical, although abrupt contrasts are incorporated. Tonality and thematic structure are clearly and identifiably linked to the principal dramatic ideas of the opera. American Indian melodies, ostinatos and whole-tone scales are used, and the orchestration recalls Respighi's.

The composers who chiefly influenced Ewart, apart from Wagner and Debussy, were Puccini and Strauss; she did not acquire an identifiably personal style. She combined her names in various ways when signing her works, and also used the pseudonym Sonia Alden. A collection of material relating to her life and works is held at the Grainger Museum in Melbourne.

Ekkehard, ? 1898–1910 (4, Ewart, after J. V. von Scheffel), excerpts, Melbourne, Queen's Hall, 23 Nov 1923
The Courtship of Miles Standish, 1930 (3, Ewart, after H. Longfellow), concert perf., Melbourne, New Conservatorium, May 1931
Mateo Falcone, 1933 (2, Ewart, after P. Mérimée), unperf.
Nala's Wooing, 1933 (after the Mahābharata), unperf.
Pepita's Miracle, c1945 (after A. Bridge), unperf.
A Game of Chess, 1949 (G. Giacosa), inc.

*

M. T. Radic: *Lip* (1978–9) [Women Individual Art Collective pubn]
——: 'Ewart, Florence Maud', *Australian Dictionary of Biography, 1891–1939* (Melbourne, 1981)
F. Patton: 'Rediscovering Our Musical Past: the Works of Mona McBurney and Florence Ewart', *Sounds Australian: Journal of the Australian Music Centre*, xxi/aut. (1989), 10–12

FAYE E. PATTON

Ewen, David (*b* Lwów, 26 Nov 1907; *d* Miami, 28 Dec 1985). American writer on music of Polish birth. He studied at the City College of New York and Columbia University. After working as music editor of *Cue* (1937–8), he was record critic for *Stage* (1938–9), editor of *Musical Facts* (1940–41) and director of a publisher of books on music (1946–9). From 1965 he taught at the University of Miami. He did research in all areas of music, contributed to many music publications and wrote nearly a hundred books; he is particularly noted for his reference works on American music.

Encyclopedia of the Opera (New York, 1955, enlarged 2/1963, ?3/1971 as *New Encyclopedia of the Opera*)
Complete Book of the American Musical Theater (New York, 1958, 2/1970 as *New Complete Book of the American Musical Theater*, 3/1976)
The Story of America's Musical Theater (Philadelphia, 1961, 2/1968)
The Book of European Light Opera (New York, 1962)
Composers for the American Musical Theatre (New York, 1968)
Mainstreams of Music, i: *Opera* (New York, 1972)

PAULA MORGAN

Ewing, Maria (Louise) (*b* Detroit, MI, 27 March 1950). American mezzo-soprano and soprano. She studied at the Cleveland Institute (1968–70) with Eleanor Steber and in later years with Jennie Tourel and O. G. Marzolla. But the decisive encounter of her student days was with James Levine, who informally guided her career; under his direction she made her début in 1973 at the Ravinia Festival. After appearances at Miami, Boston, Cologne, Chicago and Santa Fe, in 1976 she sang Cherubino at Salzburg, then made her Metropolitan début in the same role. She has since sung there as Rosina, Mélisande and Blanche (Poulenc's *Dialogues des Carmélites*), Zerlina, Dorabella, the Composer and Carmen. In Europe her roles have included Cenerentola, Dorabella and Offenbach's La Périchole. She has appeared in Peter Hall's productions at Glyndebourne as Carmen, Dorabella and Poppaea. She made her Covent Garden début as Salome (1988), returning as Carmen (1991). In Los Angeles she has sung Tosca (1989) and Butterfly (1991). A bewitching stage performer, she is able to triumph in roles in the soprano register such as Donna Elvira, for which her agile, warm-toned voice is not really suitable.

RICHARD DYER, ELIZABETH FORBES

Excursions of Mr Brouček, The [*Výlety páně Broučkovy*]. Opera in two parts by LEOŠ JANÁČEK; Prague, National Theatre, 23 April 1920. Part 1, 'Výlet pana Broučka do měsíce' ('The Excursion of Mr Brouček to the Moon') to a libretto by Janáček with František Gellner, Viktor Dyk, F. S. PROCHÁZKA and others after SVATOPLUK ČECH's novel *Pravý výlet pana Broučka do měsíce* ('The True Excursion of Mr Brouček to the Moon'); Part 2, 'Výlet pana Broučka do XV. století' ('The Excursion of Mr Brouček to the 15th Century') to a libretto by F. S. Procházka after Čech's novel *Nový epochální výlet pana Broučka, tentokráte do XV. století* ('The Epoch-making Excursion of Mr Brouček, this time to the 15th Century').

Janáček's interest in Svatopluk Čech's first *Brouček* novel was first evident in 1888, the year of its publication, when he reprinted an extract from it in his musical periodical, *Hudební listy*, but it was not until after Čech's death in 1908 that Janáček seems to have contemplated it as a possible opera subject. He secured the rights to it on 21 March 1908 and immediately began drafting a scenario. Then followed a long and frustrating period in which he failed to find a librettist. Karel Mašek agreed to help, wrote a scene (17 May 1908), but dropped out by the autumn of 1908. Dr Zikmund Janke's primitive Act 1 libretto (16 December 1908) yielded only a couple of suitable lines of a drinking song and he gave up when in January 1909 Janáček proposed far-reaching changes, basically the addition of earth characters to parallel those on the moon (taken by the same singers). Janáček tried many other possible librettists, but in the end had to do most of the work himself. This was a feasible approach for the moon scenes, where

Note Characters appear on earth/on the moon/and [Part 2] in the 15th century. Mr Brouček's Housekeeper, listed in the vocal score, appeared in Part 1, Act 3, which was subsequently suppressed by Janáček.

Mr Brouček ('Mr Beetle') *a landlord*	tenor
Sacristan *of St Vít's Cathedral*/Lunobor/Jan, known as Domšík od zvonu ('from the sign of the bell') *a citizen of 15th-century Prague*	bass-baritone
Málinka *the Sacristan's daughter*/Etherea *Lunobor's daughter*/Kunka *Domšík's daughter*	soprano
Mazal ('Dauber') *a painter*/Blankytný ('Sky-blue') *a moon poet*/Petřík	tenor
Artist at the Vikárka/Oblačný ('Cloudy')/Vacek Bradatý ('Bearded Vacek')	baritone
Artist at the Vikárka/Duhoslav/Vojta od pávů ('Vojta from the Peacocks')	tenor
Artist at the Vikárka/Harfoboj/Miroslav *the goldsmith*	tenor
Artist at the Vikárka/Větroboj/Voice of the Professor	tenor
Würfl *publican at the Vikárka*/Čaroskvoucí ('Magically-shining') *a patron*/Alderman	bass
Young Waiter (*at the Vikárka*)/Child Prodigy/Student	soprano
The Apparition of the Poet (Part 2) (Svatopluk Čech)	tenor
[Mr Brouček's Housekeeper]/Kedruta (Part 2)	contralto
First Taborite (Part 2)	baritone
Second Taborite (Part 2)	tenor
Jan Žižka *the Hussite commander* (Part 2)	silent role

Chorus in Part 1: artists at the Vikárka, Etherea's companions, moon artists

Chorus in Part 2: armed men, children, Hussite people, Prague and Taborite soldiers, priests

Setting Part 1: the Vikárka pub in the castle precincts of Prague towards the end of the 19th century; on the moon
Part 2: the Vikárka pub; Prague, Old Town Square in 1420, and in Domšík's house

Čech's dialogue could be adapted; much less so in the earth scenes, which hardly exist in Čech. Janáček also needed several strophic songs for Act 2. These eventually came from František Gellner in the second half of 1912. Janáček completed two acts by 12 February 1913 and then put the opera aside until the acceptance of *Jenůfa* by Kovařovic in the autumn of 1915 encouraged him to continue. He then had help from both Viktor Dyk and F. S. Procházka enabling him to revise the opera, to fill in the gaps and to compose the third act, an epilogue showing Mr Brouček back at home. He wrote several versions of this, the final one completed in March 1917, by which time Janáček thought of adding a second 'Excursion'.

Čech's first novel (1888) satirically places a philistine Prague landlord 'on the moon', which turns out to be inhabited by over-precious artistic people of the art-for-art's-sake movement; the humour arises from the comic confrontation of these two alien worlds. In Čech's second Brouček novel (1889) Mr Brouček is confronted with the more patriotic circumstances of the Hussite wars of the early 15th century. This was a heroic time in Czech history when the Czechs, defending their own distinctive brand of early Protestantism, beat off Crusader armies drawn from all of Europe. The subject became increasingly relevant as Czech independence (1918) drew nearer: the final dedicatee of the score was T. G. Masaryk, the first president of the new Czechoslovak Republic. This time F. S. Procházka provided a complete libretto, written between 30 April and 28 October 1917. Janáček began composition as soon as he received Act 1 (early May 1917), and completed his work by the end of that year. His epilogue to the first excursion was now redundant and he dropped it in January 1918. Publication and performance, both initiated while the opera was a single 'excursion', were protracted. Universal Edition acquired the rights (and the plates for Acts 1 and 2) from Hudební Matice, but published a vocal score (made by Roman Veselý) only in September 1919. A production under Otakar Ostrčil took place in Prague the next spring, an embittered affair with considerable hostility from the singers despite the simplification of the voice parts. It was Janáček's only original Prague première and the production survived just nine further performances before being taken off in 1921. The only other production in Janáček's lifetime was of the *Moon Excursion* (Part 1) alone, given in Brno in 1926 under František Neumann.

Part 1 'The Excursion of Mr Brouček to the Moon'

ACT 1 *The Vikárka street in Hradčany, Prague; a moonlit night* The prelude is made of a jaunty pentatonic theme in 2/4 which gives way to and then combines with a broadly lyrical theme in 3/2. One of Janáček's objectives was to lighten the satire with 'a whiff of Bohemian love'. He did this by introducing a pair of lovers, Málinka and Mazal, seen after the prelude in the middle of a tiff; she will marry Mr Brouček, she declares, as Mr Brouček, after a heavy evening's beer-drinking, staggers on and is teased by his tenant, Mazal. The atmosphere is filled out by the sounds of songs from the nearby Vikárka pub. The first brief drinking song is Dr Janke's single contribution to the libretto; the second is an attractive waltz, 'Lásko, lásko, čarovný květ' ('Love, love, magical flower'), to words by Viktor Dyk. There are more Vikárka sounds: the Young Waiter chasing after Brouček with a string of sausages for him, the publican Würfl wishing his guests a prompt return. After another scene between the lovers (they end by singing above the lyrical theme from the overture), Brouček contemplates the moon and, over the pentatonic theme of the overture, imagines life to be much happier there. He is mysteriously drawn to the moon – physically, too – and is borne aloft to the fading sounds of earth revels.

A moonscape The ethereal atmosphere in which Brouček is now discovered is depicted by a theme for solo violin. Blankytný approaches leading his winged horse and Brouček takes him for an elaborately dressed version of his earthly counterpart, Mazal. Brouček's claim of owning a three-storey house cuts no ice with his companion, while Blankytný's boast that his name as a poet is known 'throughout the moon' is Brouček's first indication of his new location. This suspicion is confirmed by the arrival of Etherea who, it turns out, needs to be worshipped, like all moon-women, from a kneeling position. Accompanied by her companions, she sings a robust waltz-song, 'Své písně přináším vám' ('I bear my songs to you'). Etherea is immediately attracted to Brouček, and a lively ensemble-finale is woven out of elements of her song,

Costume design by Josef Čapek for the character of Mr Brouček in the 1926 Brno production of Part 1 of 'The Excursions of Mr Brouček' (Janáček)

Brouček's protests and Blankytný's horrified cries at the turn of events. Lunobor, Etherea's father, proposes reading the earth-guest some chapters of his book on moon aesthetics, but his guest has escaped – flying away with Etherea on Blankytný's winged horse Pegasus, to Blankytný's hollow laughs of despair.

ACT 2 *The Cathedral of All Arts* This is the hub of artistic activity on the moon – a central hall with wings going off towards the poets, the painters and the musicians. It is presided over by the patron, Čaroskvoucí, who sings a strophic song about the difficulties of a patron's calling, 'Také prochodil jsem školu' ('I also went through school'), to the adulation of the poets. Etherea and Brouček arrive, pursued by Blankytný and Lunobor, and seek Čaroskvoucí's protection as 'lovers' (as Etherea puts it, to Brouček's dismay). Čaroskvoucí wishes to show his earth-guest the artistic delights of the moon. These include a banquet of flower scents which Brouček is encouraged to sniff to the accompaniment of the moon anthem (a spoof of the Czech national song, including its opening words, 'Domov můj': 'My homeland') sung by the Child Prodigy. Etherea serenades Brouček with another passionate song, 'Již prchám jako vánkem vůně května' ('I'm already fading, like the scent of May in the breeze'). There is a recitation by a moon poet, Oblačný – two verses as melodrama over an orchestral waltz, the third sung. When Brouček falls asleep and is urged once again to 'sniff', he testily declares that his *nose* has had quite enough already. This turns out to be a lapse in etiquette: noses are unmentionable on the moon. He is immediately ostracized by all but Duhoslav, who shows Brouček his latest painting. Brouček remembers his sausages from the Vikárka and eats them, delicately covering his face with his handkerchief. This behaviour Duhoslav takes to be weeping: at last the earth-guest has been affected by some form of art and he calls back the company to witness this miracle. They are quickly disillusioned: Brouček announces that he is eating and proceeds to list the contents of his sausages, which upsets even further the vegetarian moon-beings (a cue for a shocked 'meat' chorus). A finale builds up: love songs from Etherea, cries of anguish from Blankytný, aesthetics from Lunobor, and as Brouček decides to make a get-away on Pegasus, musicians led by Harfoboj celebrate Čaroskvoucí with an exuberant chorus, 'Požehnáni tvoji rtové' ('Blessed be thy lips'). Brouček flies back to earth in an orchestral interlude, a sumptuous development of the lyrical theme from the overture. The musicians' chorus turns into the chorus of artists on earth celebrating Würfl's beer. Würfl's voice is heard, bidding his guests come again soon; the Young Waiter laughs as Brouček is carried home in a barrel. Finally Málinka and Mazal enter and make up their quarrel, ending the first part of the opera in radiant Puccinian octaves.

Part 2 'The Excursion of Mr Brouček to the 15th Century'

ACT 1 *The jewel-chamber of Václav IV; darkness* The tense opening of the prelude with its suggestions of war (off-beat cymbal clashes) gives way to a more expansive section with prominent harp chords as the curtain goes up on the deserted jewel-chamber. The voices of Brouček and his drinking companions at the Vikárka are heard offstage. Würfl bids them goodnight. Brouček loses his way and tumbles into the jewel-chamber; he is amazed by the sight, but manages to find his way out. His place is taken immediately by Svatopluk Čech, who apostrophizes the great day of the Hussite victory.

The Prague Old Town Square; early morning Brouček makes his way through the town, now unfamiliar to him since he has travelled back to 1420. He is outraged by the absence of police and of street lighting. When he calls for help, he is confronted by the Alderman (in 'fancy dress', Brouček decides), who finds Brouček's strange (19th-century) dress and speech suspicious and, with the enthusiastic support of the chorus, arrests him as a spy of the German emperor Sigismund. Offstage strains of the Hussite chorale 'Slyšte rytieři boží' ('Hear, warriors of God') are heard, sung by armed men. Realizing his danger, Brouček gives himself out as a Czech who has returned after many years abroad. He is welcomed by the kind-hearted Domšík, who offers him accommodation in his nearby house. The sound of the Hussite chorale grows, the armed men enter and go into the Týn Church on the Old Town Square, to a triumphant C major peroration of the chorale.

ACT 2 *An inside room in Domšík's house; a late spring morning* After a short prelude, Brouček is discovered, rubbing his eyes in disbelief at his time-travelling. Domšík enters and insists that Brouček get into suitable clothes, and Brouček reluctantly dons bicoloured tights and other oddities. While he completes dressing, the chorale 'Slyšte rytieři' is heard again, indicating the return from church of Domšík's daughter Kunka and her friends. Kunka gives a glowing account of the service and of the sermon by Jan Rokycana, one

of the leading Hussite preachers of the day. Brouček is introduced to the other guests, who soon get embroiled in religious arguments. Their doctrinal quarrels, however, pall into insignificance at Brouček's seeming indifference to the present national peril. An ugly scene is forestalled only by the sudden arrival of Petřík, announcing that the Crusaders have forded the Vltava, and most of the men rush off. Brouček reluctantly takes a halberd as Domšík bids his daughter farewell. The war cries of the fighting men and the clash of arms are heard offstage while Kunka recites the Lord's Prayer. Unable to stand the tension she rushes out with a weapon; Domšík's servant Kedruta continues the prayer, now combining with the sound of the most famous Hussite chorale of all, 'Kdož jste boží bojovnici' ('You, who are warriors of God'), the only chorale Janáček used with its original tune.

Brouček slinks back and gets into his 19th-century clothes, pulling on a hood over the ensemble. He lights up a cigar to the consternation of Kedruta, who sees it as a sign of the devil, and then goes off pursued by her hostile cries of 'Antichrist!' against a final offstage chorale. Kunka returns dejectedly as the curtain falls (Act 3 was to have begun at this point), though the continuous interlude soon gives way to triumphant sounds: offstage trumpet fanfares, a march and cries of triumph first from children and then from the whole chorus.

The Old Town Square; sunset The curtain goes up on a scene of triumph as the armies and people return from their famous victory over Sigismund's forces. Petřík leads the people in a victory chorale ('Dítky, v hromadu se senděme'). The victory procession that goes into the Týn church to give thanks includes the figure of the Hussite general Jan Žižka and his captains. (Janáček later added voice parts welcoming Žižka over the orchestral interlude.)

Attempting to make his escape, Brouček hides from the crowd going into the Týn church, but is discovered by two Taborites (members of an extreme Hussite sect) looking for wounded people. Brouček is treated sympathetically at first and spins an elaborate story of his heroism in the battle. Petřík, coming out of the church and overhearing Brouček in full flood, declares him a liar. The scene is interrupted by the arrival of Kunka, mourning the death of Domšík ('Umřel mi tatíček'). Then the real circumstances of Brouček's 'heroism' are revealed: Petřík describes how he surrendered, in German, to the Crusaders. In his defence, Brouček can only say that he is not a fighter, that he is 'a son of the future'. For his cowardice he is condemned to death and is forced into a beer-barrel to the cries of the hostile crowd and Kedruta's 'Antichrist!'.

An orchestral interlude dissolves this scene (the curtain briefly falls), and Brouček is discovered in the courtyard of the Vikárka. He is stuck in a beer-barrel and his cries have attracted Würfl. Brouček is much relieved to be home. When Würfl asks where he has been, he gives a discreetly edited account of his latest adventure: 'But not a word to anyone!'. The orchestra ends the opera with a brief reminiscence of the victory music, capped by a peal of satirical, scherzando flourishes.

*   *   *

The Excursions of Mr Brouček will always remain a problematic opera. The distinctly patchwork moon excursion comes across with much more theatrical verve than the 15th-century excursion, which has a more unified libretto, but also longueurs quite uncharacteristic of this energetic composer. It is Janáček's only mature opera which needs some local knowledge to understand the intricacies of its plot. It is unique in several other respects. If one discounts the early and unrepresentative *Počátek románu* ('The Beginning of a Romance'), it was his only comic opera, and it was the last opera in which Janáček employed a librettist. Difficulties with the libretto stretched out its period of composition to a decade, the longest time he spent on any work, and during this time his style and his fortunes changed. Halfway through he gave up thoughts of continuing to write operas and abandoned the score; when he took it up again and finished it he stood on the threshold of the great period of his four late operas. An understanding of *Brouček* is crucial to an understanding of Janáček's development as an opera composer.   JOHN TYRRELL

Exoticism. The concept of the exotic in opera – that is, the use of a setting that is alien and accordingly different from accepted local norms in its attitudes, customs and morals – appears first in French dramatic works and in particular *opéra-ballets* of the early 18th century. One of the entrées of Campra's *L'Europe galante* (1697) is set in Turkey; the classic instance of an exotically set work is Rameau's *Les Indes galantes* (1735), set in Turkey, Peru, Persia and north America. The music itself, however, is not coloured by the settings; any passages that seem eccentric in style can readily be paralleled in Rameau's works with conventional classical plots. Nor is there any reflection in the music of such works as the operas or serenatas composed to Metastasio's librettos with a Chinese, Indian or Middle Eastern setting, or (for example) the operas based on Tasso's *Gerusalemme liberata* and set in the Middle East.

In the later 18th century, several comic operas were written with settings in Asia Minor or the Middle East, contrasting Western, Christian attitudes with supposed local, Muslim ones (usually involving cruelty and sensuality); many make use in some degree of certain 'Turkish' musical elements (these are described by Bauman, pp.62–4, in the context of Mozart's *Die Entführung aus dem Serail*, and based on Janissary military music). Some of these characteristic musical patterns are to be found in Weber's *Oberon*.

In the 19th century, exoticism in opera – in the sense of a plot set in a remote or strange culture, and possibly admitting of a populace with a non-Western, non-Christian code of behaviour – has a wider frame of reference, embracing works with an Ossianic origin (such as Méhul's *Uthal*), or works set in remote times or places, for example the Celtic world of ancient Gaul in *Norma*, the Scotland of *La donna del lago* or *Lucia di Lammermoor* (both after Scott), or the legendary world of Chausson's *Le roi Arthus*. Eastern exoticism is found particularly in French opera and refers primarily to the Middle East (an exception is *Les pêcheurs de perles*); the 'paradigmatic plot' (found in *L'Africaine*, David's *La perle du Brésil*, *Aida*, *Lakmé* and *Madama Butterfly*, and to some extent *Samson et Dalila*) is charted by Locke:

Young, tolerant, brave, possibly naive, white-European tenor-hero intrudes, at risk of disloyalty to his own people and colonialist ethic, into mysterious, dark-skinned, colonised territory represented by alluring dancing girls and deeply affectionate, sensitive lyric soprano, incurring wrath of brutal, intransigent tribal chieftain (bass or bass-baritone) and blindly obedient chorus of male savages.

Musically, exotic operas of this period tend to use modal features (such as melodic augmented 2nds) and a style of rhapsodic writing associated with North Africa and the eastern Mediterranean rather than ideas characteristic of music from the true Orient, although by the time of *Madama Butterfly* (1904) and *Turandot* (1926), and indeed *The Mikado* (1885), composers had access to, and made use of, phrases from Japanese and Chinese music. The attitudes they portray (as Locke points out), like those of European exotic art, reflect the colonialist and male-dominated outlook of Western society of the time.

*

L. F. Casamorata: 'Dal colore locale nel melodramma', *Atti dell'Istituto musicale di Firenze* (1877), 33–47

M. Carner: 'The Exotic Element in Puccini', *MQ*, xxii (1936), 45–67

H. Leclerc: '*Les Indes galantes* (1735–1952): les sources de l'opéra-ballet, l'exoticisme orientalisant, les conditions matérielles du spectacle', *Revue d'histoire du théâtre*, v (1953), 259–85

B. Szabolcsi: 'Exoticisms in Mozart', *ML*, xxxvii (1956), 323–32

M. K. Whaples: *Exoticism in Dramatic Music, 1600–1800* (diss., Indiana U., 1958)

M. R. Griffel: *Turkish Opera from Mozart to Cornelius* (diss., Columbia U., 1975)

H. Becker: *Die 'Couleur locale' in der Oper des 19. Jahrhunderts* (Regensburg, 1976)

P. Gradenwitz: 'Félicien David (1810–1876) and French Romantic Orientalism', *MQ*, lxii (1976), 471–506

J. Maehder, ed.: *Esotismo e colore locale nell'opera di Puccini* (Pisa, 1985)

G. Morelli: 'Povero Bajazetto: Osservazioni su alcuni aspetti dell'abbattimento tematico della "paura del turco" nell'opera veneziana del sei-settecento', *Venezia e i Turchi* (Milan, 1985), 280–93

T. Bauman: *W. A. Mozart: Die Entführung aus dem Serail* (Cambridge, 1987)

A. Schmitt: *Der Exotismus in der deutschen Oper zwischen Mozart und Spohr* (Hamburg, 1988)

F. della Seta: ' "O cieli azzurri": Exoticism and Dramatic Discourse in *Aida*', *COJ*, iii (1991), 49–62

R. Locke: 'Constructing the Oriental "Other": Saint-Saëns's *Samson et Dalila*', *COJ*, iii (1991), 261–302

Extraordinary Commissar, The. Opera by V. I. Muradeli; *see* VELIKAYA DRUZHBA.

Extravaganza. A genre of light theatrical entertainment with music, a form of BURLESQUE, popular in England during the 19th century. The term and the genre may be said to have been invented by JAMES ROBINSON PLANCHÉ, who described it as 'the whimsical treatment of a poetical subject' as distinct from 'the broad caricature of a tragedy or a serious opera, which was correctly termed a "Burlesque" '. The first of Planché's dramatic works designated 'extravaganza' was *High, Low, Jack, and the Game* (1833), written for Lucia Vestris's management. The most characteristic and significant extravaganzas were his fairy plays, beginning with *Riquet with the Tuft* (1836).

Extravaganzas tended to be less strongly bound to a model than burlesques and were often based on classical or mythological legends, fairy- or folktales or original stories rather than on serious or tragic subjects. Distinctions between the two genres were often subtle, if not arbitrary; but the best extravaganzas were characterized by more consistent stories rendered more delicately than in burlesque, and in some instances the music tended to be more highly developed.

FREDRIC WOODBRIDGE WILSON

Eybler, Joseph [Josef] **Leopold**, Edler von (*b* Schwechat, nr Vienna, 8 Feb 1765; *d* Vienna, 24 July 1846). Austrian composer. He attended the choir school at St Stephen's, Vienna, and studied composition with Albrechtsberger, 1776–9. He was helped by Haydn as a friend and teacher and also befriended by Mozart, who commissioned him to help coach the singers for the first performance of *Così fan tutte*. On this occasion Eybler experienced the intrigues of the opera house, which, he later confessed, determined him against a career as a theatre composer. He later held ecclesiastical and court posts, in 1804 becoming deputy Hofkapellmeister under Salieri and in 1842 Hofkapellmeister. Eybler's only opera, *Das Zauberschwert* (*A-Wn*), a *romantische Komödie* in three acts to a text by K. F. Hensler, was given at the Theater in der Leopoldstadt (16 February 1802; the overture and selections were published in vocal score). In his final years he received numerous honours and in 1835 was raised to the nobility.

Autobiographical sketch, *AMZ*, xxviii (1826), col.337
R. Haas: 'Josef Leopold Edler von Eybler', *MJb 1952*, 61–4
EVA BADURA-SKODA

Ezio ('Aetius'). Libretto by PIETRO METASTASIO, first set by Nicola Porpora (1728, Venice).

ACT 1 Aetius returns to Rome in triumph after his victory over Attila. The Emperor Valentiniano [Valentinian] III (reigned 425–55), though grateful to his returning general, resents the celebrity being accorded him. To Massimo [Maximus], his confidant, the emperor speaks of Fulvia, Maximus's daughter, whom he loves. Although aware of the love between Fulvia and Aetius, Maximus, instead of enlightening Valentinian, encourages his suit; secretly an enemy of the emperor, Maximus proposes to use this marriage to gain control over the throne. Since Aetius is the throne's protector, Maximus is glad to place enmity between him and the emperor by telling him of Valentinian's intentions towards Fulvia. Informed by her father of his plans, Fulvia is repelled by his proposed treachery against Aetius, Valentinian and herself, but filial duty compels her silence. The emperor offers Aetius the hand of his sister, Onoria [Honoria], in recognition of his military achievements; Aetius asks instead for Fulvia, only to learn from Honoria that Valentinian plans to wed her himself the following day. Honoria, secretly in love with Aetius, is astonished by his violent threats against her brother, and she and Fulvia express their suspicions of each other's affections for Aetius.

ACT 2 Fulvia is horrified to find her father awaiting news of an assassination attempt upon Valentinian. The emperor, however, emerges unharmed, and Fulvia threatens to expose her father when he fails to contradict the accusation of Aetius as author of the plot. She is silenced by Maximus, and her attempt to warn Aetius comes too late to avoid his arrest. Torn between love and duty, Fulvia is advised by Varo [Varus], Prefect of the Praetorian Guard and an old friend of Aetius, that her marriage to Valentinian would provide the only means of saving the young general. While attempting to follow through with this scheme, Fulvia is forced to attend as Aetius is summoned before the emperor. Valentinian, convinced that Fulvia has no feelings for Aetius, attempts to prove the fact, but his plan misfires when Fulvia, unable to maintain deception, defiantly

'Ezio', Act 2 scene xiii (AETIUS: 'Is one of you my judge? Rests my fate with either Caesar or Fulvia?'): engraving from the 'Opere' of Pietro Metastasio (Paris: Hérissant, 1780–82)

confesses her love for Aetius, who is immediately incarcerated.

ACT 3 In the prison yard, Honoria tells Aetius that her brother will release him if he will name the traitor. When he refuses, she begs him relent for the sake of her love for him, but he remains steadfast. Honoria suggests to Valentinian that Aetius will confess only if offered Fulvia's hand. The emperor, however, instructs Varus to kill Aetius should he leave the dungeons unescorted, and then offers Fulvia to Aetius on condition that he confess his guilt. When this condition is refused, Valentinian offers freedom, and soon after Aetius departs, Varus announces to the emperor that his instructions have been carried out. Honoria enters with proof of Aetius's innocence and, upon learning of his execution, condemns her brother, reminding him that Maximus has cause to hate him. To protect her father, Fulvia claims complicity, but repulses Maximus when he attempts to regain her affections. Desperate, Maximus now leads a group of conspirators against the emperor, but is thwarted by the timely arrival of Varus, Aetius (whom Varus has kept in hiding) and their followers. Consent is immediately given to the union of Fulvia and Aetius, whose plea for pardons for Varus and Maximus is granted.

* * *

The deterioration of the relationship between Aetius and Valentinian, which forms the basis of Metastasio's plot, is described in the *De bellis* of Procopius (book 3) and the *Epitoma chronicon* of Prosper Aquitanus (no.1373). Reference is also to be found in Carlo Sigonio's *Historiarum* (book 13). Plot parallels with Thomas Corneille's *Maximian* (1662) suggest that this drama may well have served Metastasio as a more contemporary model. With some 40 settings between 1728 and Mercadante's version for Turin (1827), *Ezio* proved to be as popular as *Antigono* or *La clemenza di Tito*. Within a month of Porpora's Venice première, Auletta's setting opened in Rome. In London, *Ezio* was one of only three Metastasian dramas to be set by Handel, although this version, in spite of having Senesino in the title role, proved unsuccessful at the time. Hasse first set the text for Naples in 1730, but it is the elaborately staged version for Dresden (1755) that has drawn particular attention. *Ezio* was the first Metastasian drama to be set by Jommelli (1741, Bologna), who subsequently produced another three versions. For Sacchini (1771, Naples), the second act was altered to accommodate a quartet. Metastasio approved this change, adding that the resultant reduction in the number of arias for the leading singers would have been unthinkable at the time he wrote the original drama.

For a list of settings *see* METASTASIO, PIETRO.   DON NEVILLE

Ezio ('Aetius'). Opera in three acts by GEORGE FRIDERIC HANDEL to a libretto anonymously adapted from PIETRO METASTASIO's *Ezio*; London, King's Theatre, 15 January 1732.

Ezio, Handel's last opera on a Metastasian libretto, was the first new work produced in the season of 1731–2. Some of the music of the opening scenes was adapted from an abandoned setting of a different libretto on the subject of Titus and Berenice, headed 'Titus l'Empereur' in Handel's autograph. The action of Metastasio's libretto is set in Rome and is based on events in the last years of the rule of the emperor Valentinian III (425–55), mainly as related by Procopius (for fuller information *see* EZIO above). Ezio [Aetius] was sung by the alto castrato Senesino, his fiancée Fulvia

by Anna Strada del Pò (soprano), her father Massimo [Maximus] (a Roman patrician) by Giovanni Battista Pinacci (tenor), the emperor Valentiniano [Valentinian] and his sister Onoria [Honoria] by the contraltos Anna Bagnolesi and Francesca Bertolli respectively, and Varo [Varus], Prefect of the Praetorian Guard, by the bass Antonio Montagnana. The opera received only five performances, the audiences perhaps reacting against the lengthy recitatives (though reduced from Metastasio's original) and the absence of any multi-voice ensembles; in the final number, unusually in vaudeville style, single voices only are heard until the last 14 bars. Handel did not revive *Ezio* and there were no further performances until the production at Göttingen on 30 June 1926, in an arrangement by F. Notholt. The first British revival was by the Handel Opera Society at Sadler's Wells Theatre on 4 November 1977.

The consistent high quality of the arias in *Ezio* fully compensates for the absence of vocal ensembles, and, if the audience is able to understand the confrontations set out in Metastasio's recitatives (e.g. via a translation), the work makes a powerful effect on stage. The characters emerge strongly in the music. Both Aetius and Fulvia display noble defiance and tragic pathos, Fulvia's ringing declaration of fidelity in Act 2 in the aria 'La mia costanza' being a particularly splendid moment. The three arias for the genial Varus – Handel's response to the talents of Montagnana – all transcend what might be expected in a minor role: they include 'Già risonar', Handel's only operatic bass aria with obbligato trumpet, and the well-known 'Nasce al bosco'. Honoria is sketched with a touch of humour, especially in the bagpipe effects of the aria in which she compares herself to a shepherdess ('Quanto mai felice siete'). *Ezio* shows that *opera seria*, even its purest form, can generate excellent musical drama.   ANTHONY HICKS

F

Fabbri, Anna Maria (*b* Bologna; *fl* 1708–23). Italian singer. She appeared in two operas at Florence in autumn 1708 and at Bologna in 1711. She also sang in Naples (1712–13, 1723), Genoa (1715) and often in Venice (1714–17) where she was particularly associated with Vivaldi, taking part in the premières of his *Orlando finto pazzo*, *Arsilda regina di Ponto* and *L'incoronazione di Dario*. She sang male and female roles in roughly equal measure.

She is often identified, probably incorrectly, with the Bolognese contralto Anna Bombaciara, wife of the tenor ANNIBALE PIO FABRI. Bombaciara appeared in four operas by L. A. Predieri at Florence (1718–19), Venice (1720), Milan (1721) and Naples (1722); in 1729 she was expected to accompany her husband to London and was advertised as performing 'a Man's Part exceeding well'.

S. Durante: 'Alcune considerazioni sui cantanti di teatro del primo settecento e la loro formazione', *Antonio Vivaldi: teatro musicale, cultura e società: Venice 1981*, i, 11–63

R. Strohm: 'Vivaldi's Career as an Opera Producer', ibid, ii, 427–81

COLIN TIMMS

Fabbri, Franca (*b* Milan, 28 May 1935). Italian soprano. She studied in Milan, making her début as Violetta at Spoleto in 1963. She sang in all the principal Italian theatres, including La Scala, where she created roles in Bettinelli's *Count Down* (1970), Cortese's *Le notti bianche* (1973) and Nono's *Al gran sole carico d'amore* (1975). She sang in the first performance of Chailly's *L'idiota* at Rome (1970) and in the Italian premières of his *La riva delle Sirti* at Treviso (1971) and of G. F. Malipiero's *Merlino mastro d'organi* at Palermo (1972). Although a specialist in contemporary music, she also sang Fiordiligi, the Queen of Night, Lucia, Gilda, Marguerite de Valois, Musetta and the Governess (*The Turn of the Screw*). A fine actress, she had a flexible, expressive voice.

ELIZABETH FORBES

Fabbri, Guerrina (*b* Ferrara, 21 June 1866; *d* Turin, 21 Feb 1946). Italian contralto. She made her début at Viadana in 1885, and soon became associated with Rossini operas, singing Arsace to Patti's Semiramide in Madrid and appearing in the title roles of *La Cenerentola* and *L'italiana in Algeri* in Rome. She was admired as Gluck's Orpheus, a role she sang in London; she appeared at the Shaftesbury and Drury Lane theatres in 1887 and 1891. She also sang in the USA,

South America and Russia. Growing fat in later years, she turned towards such character roles as Mistress Quickly in *Falstaff* before retiring in 1925. Her recordings are prized examples of the coloratura contralto – fluent, rich and wide-ranging – though perhaps less attractive stylistically.

J. B. STEANE

Fabbri(-Mulder), Inez [Schmidt, Agnes] (*b* Vienna, 26 Jan 1831; *d* San Francisco, 30 Aug 1909). American soprano and impresario of Austrian birth. She studied in Vienna, making her début in the title role of *Lucrezia Borgia* in Kassa (Kaschau), Hungary (now Košice, Slovakia), on 5 October 1847. She was prima donna of the Stadttheater in Hamburg in 1857, and that year was engaged by the impresario Richard Mulder (1822–74), whom she married, to tour the Americas, Canada and the Caribbean islands. Her 25 appearances at the Winter Gardens, New York, in 1860 in a publicity 'war' with Patti secured her international reputation. She returned to Europe in 1862, becoming prima donna of the Frankfurt Stadttheater in 1864. On the outbreak of the Franco-Prussian War, she and Mulder returned to the USA. In 1872, the year after which Fabbri appeared at Covent Garden, they joined forces with another company to present an opera season in New York. In winter 1872–3 Fabbri and Mulder produced 43 operas at the California Theater, San Francisco, and in 1874 they staged the first performance in the city of *Die Zauberflöte*. Fabbri alone produced a remarkable season (1875–6) in which she directed and sang in 60 operas. She retired from the stage in 1880 and undertook several unsuccessful operatic ventures. Her musical memorabilia are in the music library at the University of California at Berkeley.

JOHN A. EMERSON

Fabbrini [Fabrini], **Giuseppe** (*b* ?Siena; *d* Siena, 20 Nov 1708). Italian composer. Presumably a Jesuit, he was alternately organist and *maestro di cappella* of Siena Cathedral, 1671–1708. Dedications and prefaces to the librettos he set show that he taught music and singing at the Collegio Tolomei, Siena, a famous institution open only to the nobility. The writings of Girolamo Gigli, one of the best-known literary figures of the period, contain many references to musical activities at the college during Fabbrini's years there. His operas to librettos by Gigli were all written for the college theatre which opened in 1685. The preface to the libretto of the version of Alessandro Scarlatti's *L'honestà negli amori*

99

performed in the theatre of the Accademia dei Rozzi, Siena, in 1690, for which Fabbrini wrote the prologue, all the intermezzos and some additional pieces, shows that he was a member of the academy with the name 'L'Armonico'. None of his music has survived.

all first performed at Siena, Collegio Tolomei, unless otherwise stated

La Genefieva (G. Gigli), 1 Feb 1685 lib. *US-Wc*
La forza del sangue e della pietà (Gigli), 15 Feb 1686 lib. *Wc*
Lodovico Pio (Gigli), 3 Feb 1687 lib. *Wc*
La fede ne' tradimenti (Gigli), 12 Feb 1689 lib. *Wc*
La forza d'amore (Gigli), 1690, lib. *Wc*, tentatively attrib. Fabbrini by Sonneck
L'Eudossia (Gigli), carn. 1696, lib. *Wc*, tentatively attrib. Fabbrini by Sonneck
Coriolano (?Gigli), carn. 1706, lib. *Wc*, tentatively attrib. Fabbrini by Sonneck

Prologue and addns to A. Scarlatti: L'honestà negli amori (G. F. Bernini), Siena, Accademia dei Rozzi, 24 May 1690, lib. *I-Bc*

*

AllacciD
R. Morrocchi: *La musica in Siena* (Siena, 1886), 101–2
O. G. T. Sonneck: *Library of Congress: Catalogue of Opera Librettos Printed before 1800* (Washington DC, 1914)
FABIO BISOGNI

Fabri, Annibale Pio ['Balino'] (*b* Bologna, 1697; *d* Lisbon, 12 Aug 1760). Italian tenor and composer. A pupil of Pistocchi, he sang female parts in two operas by Caldara at the Ruspoli Palace, Rome (1711), and probably made his public début in 1716 in G. B. Bassani's *Alarico rè dei Goti* at Bologna, followed by five operas at Venice (two of them by Vivaldi). He sang in Rome and Mantua in 1718. By 1720 he was in constant demand all over Italy, singing in Rome (1720–21), Venice (1720–22, 1727–8), Milan (1721, 1728), Genoa (1722), Naples (seven operas in 1722–3, two of them by Vinci), Bologna (1724, in A. Scarlatti's *Marco Attilio Regolo*) and Florence (1725–7, 1729, 1732, 1737). Handel engaged him for two seasons in London (1729–31) and he made a successful début in *Lotario* (Berengario) at the King's Theatre. Handel also composed the parts of Emilio in *Partenope* and Alexander in *Poro* for him, and he sang in *Giulio Cesare, Tolomeo, Scipione, Rinaldo* and *Rodelinda*.

In 1732 Fabri sang in Vienna (Caldara's *Adriano in Siria*) and received the title of virtuoso to the emperor. He appeared in Bologna (1734), Modena and Venice (1735), Genoa (1737 and 1748), Madrid (1738–9), where he enjoyed great success in seven operas (three by Hasse), and Florence (1744–5, in Porpora's *Ezio*). He composed operas for Madrid and Lisbon, including a setting of *Alessandro nell'Indie*. After retiring from the stage he was appointed to the royal chapel at Lisbon.

Fabri was one of the leading singers of his age and did much to raise the status of the tenor voice. Swiney, in recommending him for London (1729), wrote that he 'sings in as good a Taste as any Man in Italy'. Mrs Pendarves described his voice as 'sweet, clear and firm' and called him 'the greatest master of musick that ever sang upon the stage'. The parts Handel composed for him have a compass of nearly two octaves (*B* to *a'*) and require 'great abilities' and 'considerable agility', according to Burney, who declared that 'the merit of this tenor was often sufficient in Italy to supply the want of it in the principal soprano'. Fabri's wife, Anna Bombaciara (Bombaciari, Bombasari), was also a singer. She is often identified with ANNA MARIA FABBRI, although there is some doubt about this.   WINTON DEAN

Fabri [Fabris], **Luca** (*b* ?Fabriano, *c*1740; *d* Naples, 1769). Italian soprano castrato. From 1756 to 1762 he sang mostly female roles in comic opera in Rome, appearing also in Perugia (1756) and Turin (1761). Librettos show that he was in the service of the Prince of Santa Croce. He then probably withdrew for study, reappearing in spring 1764 in *opera seria*, mostly as *secondo uomo* (Padua, Vienna and Venice) and as the female lead at Rome in Carnival 1766. His early death, when he had just reached the top of his profession as *primo uomo* in Turin and Naples, was attributed by Burney to a composer's insisting he sing a note too high for him. This may have been in Piccinni's *Artaserse* (1768) or in Cafaro's *Olimpiade* (1769), the libretto of which describes him as incapacitated. He seems to have been an exquisite cantabile singer, perhaps influenced in this by Guadagni, with whom he sang in Vienna and Venice.   DENNIS LIBBY

Fabris, Jacopo (*b* Venice, 1689; *d* Charlottenborg, nr Copenhagen, 16 Dec 1761). Italian stage designer. He was still in Venice in 1714 (*Iscrizioni veneziane raccolte e illustrate da E. A. Cicognara*, Venice, 1827, ii, 377) but there is evidence that from 28 February 1719 to 1721 he was at Karlsruhe, working as court painter and scene designer to the Margrave Karl Wilhelm of Baden-Durlach. At the invitation of the Count of Ahlefeldt he moved to Hamburg, where from 1724 to 1730 he worked as scene designer for the Opera, producing settings for Handel's *Giulio Cesare* (1725; see HAMBURG, fig.2) and Reinhard Keiser's *Jodelet* and *Mistevojus* (1726). There is no evidence that a planned visit to London was made, though certainly his wife Susanna Geoffreys was English. At Mannheim in 1736 he seems to have known G. A. Pellegrini and Alessandro Galli-Bibiena. From 1740 to 1747 he worked for Frederick the Great in Berlin, collaborating with G. W. Knobelsdorff on the building of the theatre in the castle of Charlottenburg, which opened on 13 December 1741 with *Rodelinda, regina de' langobardi* by C. H. Graun, with sets designed by Fabris, as were the sets for Graun's *Cesare e Cleopatra*, which opened the Unter den Linden opera house on 7 December 1742. Fabris continued to work in the new theatre, designing scenery for works by Graun and Metastasio.

After moving to Copenhagen, he staged musical productions for the Danish court in the theatre at Charlottenborg castle, in a wooden theatre in the city's main square and, from 1748, in the new theatre on Kongens Nytorv. He occasionally assisted the king's architect, Nikolai Eigtved; and he created the whole range of stage settings that Pietro Mingotti required for his performances of Metastasio's *Semiramide riconosciuta, Adriano in Siria, Temistocle, Demofoonte* and *Alessandro nelle Indie*. Fabris earned the title 'Kanzleirat' and was welcomed into the Academy of Arts at Charlottenborg where he taught architecture and perspective.

His treatise *Instruction oder Unterrichtung in den geometrisch-perspectivisch- und architectonischen Lectionen*, in five volumes, was completed in 1760 but remains in manuscript (*DK-Kk*, Thott coll., no.295). A sixth volume is the only one to have been printed (Copenhagen, 1930); its technical subject matter, however, was already lagging behind the evolution of stage technique and scene design as headed by the Bibienas. Yet Fabris did make an influential contribution to the spread of opera staging in the Italian tradition of Torelli and the Bibienas. There is an intense contrast of light and shade in his stage scenes, both in architectural interiors and broad urban exteriors. His few extant scene drawings (Copenhagen, Statens Museum for Kunst and Charlottenborg Academy; Berlin, Kunstbibliothek) testify to an interest in depicting the city which relates to his Venetian origins and the works of Canaletto.

ES (G. Schöne)

T. Krogh: *Jacob Fabris: Instruction in der teatralischen Architectur und Mechanique* (Copenhagen, 1930)

——: *Danske theaterbilleder* (Copenhagen, 1932), 162–79

R. Badenhausen and H. Zielske, eds.: 'Die Anfänge einer Theaterbautheorie in Deutschland im 17. und 18. Jahrhundert', *Bühnenformen, Bühnenräume, Bühnendekorationen: Beiträge zur Entwicklung des Spielorts* (Berlin, 1974), 28–63

M. Mosco: 'Minori del settecento Veneto: Jacopo Fabris', *Arte illustrata*, vii (1974), 82–97   MARINELLA PIGOZZI

Fabritiis, Oliviero (Carlo) de. *See* DE FABRITIIS, OLIVIERO.

Fabrizi, Vincenzo (*b* Naples, 1764; *d* ?after 1812). Italian composer. After starting to compose at the age of 18 or 19, within six years he had written 14 operas and gained an international reputation; he then disappeared from public notices, though Gerber, about 1812, wrote of him as still living. His first stage work – a revision of the Goldoni-Ciampi intermezzo *I tre gobbi rivali* (originally *La favola de' tre gobbi*, 1749, Venice) – was produced in Carnival 1783 during a period when Neapolitan theatres were experimenting with the French fashion of presenting several short comic pieces instead of a full-length opera. This was the third of three short works commissioned by the Teatro dei Fiorentini; as the other two were written by Giacomo Tritto, Prota-Giurleo regarded Fabrizi's contribution as evidence that he was Tritto's pupil. He worked in northern Italy during 1784–5. In 1786 he was in Rome where his comedy *La sposa invisibile* produced loud applause both for its novelty and its expression. As a result he received a three-year appointment as musical director at the Teatro Capranica. His three-act version of the Don Giovanni story, produced in the following year, proved successful throughout Europe.

Gervasoni observed that 'in the space of a few years … [Fabrizi] contributed greatly to the refinement of musical taste'. His extant music, which includes chamber works as well as comic operas, shows him to have been a competent composer, with ensembles distinguished by a solid structural sense and an ability to achieve desired effects with economy of means. In particular his harmony, while essentially simple and diatonic, shows skilful and judicious use of chromatic detail.

There is no evidence that he was related to the composer Paolo Fabrizi (*b* Spoleto, 1809; *d* Naples, 3 March 1869), who studied at Naples under Zingarelli and had seven operas given there, 1830–40, and two later at Spoleto.

opere buffe unless otherwise stated

I tre gobbi rivali (int, after C. Goldoni), Naples, Fiorentini, carn. 1783

La necessità non ha legge, Bologna, Marsigli-Rossi, ?July, 1784; also as Noth hat kein Gesetz

I due castellani burlati (F. Livigni), Bologna, Marsigli-Rossi, aut. 1785; also as I due castellani ossia I due rivali in amore and I due rivali in amore; ?*D-Dlb*, *F-Pc*, *I-Tf*, *P-La*

La sposa invisibile (farsetta a 5), Rome, Capranica, 20 Feb 1786, ?*D-Dlb*, *P-La*

Chi la fà l'aspetti, ossia I puntigli di gelosia (Livigni), Florence, Pallacorda, spr. 1786; also as La moglie capricciosa, I puntigli di gelosia; *I-Bc*, *Fc*

La contessa di Novaluna (G. Bertati), Venice, S Moisè, aut. 1786

L'amore per interese (Bertati), Parma, Ducale, 26 Dec 1786; orig. title La Mirandolina

Il convitato di pietra (G. Lorenzi), Rome, Valle, ?carn. 1787; also as Don Giovanni Tenorio, ossia Il convitato di pietra; *GB-Lbl* (aria, trio, finale), *I-Rmassimo*, *Rsc*

La nobiltà villana, Rome, Capranica, 30 Jan 1787

Gli amanti trappolieri (G. Palomba), Naples, carn./sum. 1787

Il viaggiatore sfortunato in amore (F. Ballani), Rome, Valle, aut. 1787

Il Colombo o La scoperta delle Indie (Mallio), Rome, Capranica, carn. 1788

La tempesta, ossia Da un disordine ne nasce un ordine (M. Mallio), Rome, Capranica, Jan 1788

L'incontro per accidente (G. M. Diodati), Naples, Fondo, spr./sum. 1788; also as Il maestro di cappella, ossia L'incontro per accidente

Il caffè di Barcellona, Barcelona, S Cruz, 1788

Impresario in rovina (dg, A. Piazza), Casale, spr. 1797

ES (U. Prota-Giurleo); *FlorimoN*; *GerberNL*

C. Gervasoni: *Nuova teoria di musica* (Parma, 1812), 129–30
                                        JAMES L. JACKMAN

Facchinelli, Lucia (*b* ?Rome; *fl* 1724–39). Italian soprano. She began her career singing *opera seria* in Venice in 1724, appearing mainly there and in Milan, from 1727 as prima donna, and frequently with the castrato Nicolini, to whom she was well suited: her forte was dramatic expression rather than vocal brilliance or bravura. From 1731 to 1733 she was engaged with Nicolini at Naples, where he died. She thereafter appeared in Venice, Vicenza, Milan, Bologna and Florence up to Carnival 1739, and retired after singing in Spain for a royal wedding.   DENNIS LIBBY

Faccio, Franco [Francesco Antonio] (*b* Verona, 8 March 1840; *d* Monza, 21 July 1891). Italian conductor and composer. Born in humble circumstances, he early manifested a propensity for music and was admitted to the Milan Conservatory in 1855, where he studied composition with Stefano Ronchetti-Montevito. There he struck up a lifelong friendship with Arrigo Boito, two years his junior. Their first collaboration was a patriotic cantata, *Il quattro giugno* (1860), inspired by the death in battle of a fellow pupil; Boito supplied the text and some of the music. The reception of this work at the conservatory, on the heels of the liberation of Lombardy, was so enthusiastic that the next year they produced a sequel, *Le sorelle d'Italia*, a panegyric to nations still under foreign domination. In the patriotic fervour of the times both Boito and Faccio, who were natives of the Veneto (then still in the hands of the Austrians), were received, despite their youth, by the upper echelons of Milanese society, including the famous salon of Countess Maffei. Their precosity, talent and determination to renew the tradition of Italian opera won them such warm support that on the completion of their studies they were awarded 2000 lire each to travel abroad.

Arriving in Paris in the spring of 1862, Faccio and Boito were received, not without irony, by Rossini. Countess Maffei had supplied them with letters of introduction to Verdi. Both were hard at work on operas – Boito on what was to become *Mefistofele*, and Faccio on the three-act *melodramma*, *I profughi fiamminghi*, to a text by Emilio Praga. Faccio was the first to return to Milan, where his work was introduced at La Scala on 11 November 1863 (autograph in *I-Mr*, vocal score published in Milan, 1864). He sought to tap again the euphoric spirit of the times, but this opera achieved only five performances. The reception was cool and there were murmurs of that shibboleth, 'music of the future'. Faccio's friends fêted him with a banquet, however, and it was on this occasion that Boito read his ode *All'arte italiana* that so offended Verdi.

Faccio's second opera, the four-act *Amleto*, to an innovatory libretto by Boito, was first performed at the Teatro Carlo Felice, Genoa, on 30 May 1865 (autograph *Mr*), where its success was contested. There was some resentment of the self-congratulatory iconoclasm of the youthful collaborators, and dismay at the score's paucity of melody. The only section to win general approval was Ophelia's funeral march. In 1866 both Faccio and Boito volunteered to serve under Garibaldi. At the end of their brief duty, Faccio left Italy and for two years honed his skills as an opera conductor in Scandinavia. On the strength of this experience, he was offered a post at the Teatro Carcano on his return to Milan in the autumn of 1868. At this time he was also appointed to teach composition at the conservatory, a post he held for ten years. In 1869 he became Terziani's assistant as conductor at La Scala, succeeding to the full office in 1871.

He won Verdi's approval to conduct the Italian première of *Aida* there (8 February 1872). Henceforth, conducting was to be Faccio's principal activity, particularly after the miserable failure of his remounted *Amleto* at La Scala the year before, a fiasco that caused him to renounce the writing of operas. His tenure as principal conductor at La Scala lasted until his collapse in December 1889. The chief glory of his period there was the première of *Otello* (5 February 1887). Although Verdi's works dominated the repertory during those years, Faccio also conducted the premières of operas by a number of younger Italian composers, notably Ponchielli (*I lituani*, *La Gioconda* and *Il figliuol prodigo*), Catalani (*Dejanice* and *Edmea*) and Puccini (the two-act version of *Le villi* and *Edgar*). He also conducted important performances of *Der Freischütz* and *Lohengrin*, and presented works by Massenet and Bizet. His last task there was the preparation of the first Italian staging of *Die Meistersinger*.

Faccio was also active elsewhere. At Brescia in 1872 he conducted the revised *Forza del destino* to such effect that the survival of the work was assured. At Bologna he made a profound impression with *Don Carlos* in 1878. The following year he conducted a concert there for the local Società del Quartetto; instrumental conducting would soon become second only to his work in the opera house. He led the local premières of *Otello* in Rome, Venice and Bologna, as well as in London (5 July 1889). Shaw remembered this last occasion as one of the finest examples of opera conducting in his experience.

That there were serious problems with Faccio's health became apparent the night he insisted there was no third act to *Die Meistersinger*. To provide him with some relief from the rigours of opera-house routine, Verdi arranged his appointment as director of the Parma Conservatory. He soon proved incapable of coping with even this amount of work, and the faithful Boito accompanied him to Kraft-Ebbing's Sanitorium at Graz. There, his condition was diagnosed as paralysis associated with tertiary syphilis and he spent the brief remainder of his life in an institution at Monza.

See also AMLETO (ii).

T. G. Kaufman: *Verdi and his Contemporaries: a Selected Chronology of Performances with Casts* (New York, 1990)
WILLIAM ASHBROOK

Facco, Giacomo [Jaime, Jayme] (*b* Venice, *c*1680; *d* Madrid, 16 Feb 1753). Italian composer. He provided music in 1710 for a serenata sung at Messina in honour of Philip V and later for a *Dialogo* sung there, and was described as the viceroy's 'virtuoso'. From 1720 he taught the harpsichord to Luis (1707–24), heir to the Spanish throne, and organized chamber concerts for the young prince. He also played the violin and cello in the Spanish royal chapel. In 1721 his two-act Spanish opera, *Amor es todo ymbenzion, o Jupiter y Amphitrión* (2, J. de Cañizares; *E-Bim*), a 'melodrama al estilo ytaliano', was given at the Buen Retiro royal theatre, Madrid, before Philip V and his consort Isabella Farnese; Subirá (1971, pp.90–97), who made a close analysis of the musical score, counted 25 recitatives, 20 arias and two duets. Lacking a plot, the opera consists of a series of disjunct episodes involving classical gods and goddesses, kings of Etolia and Thebes, their attendants and lady opposites, personifications of Night, Dawn, Silence and Forgetfulness and a low-life soldier whose comments in dialect provide comic relief. Constant changes of scene delight the eye. In the same vein, Facco composed a mythological *Festejo* for the queen's birthday in 1722 or 1723. For performances in the palace of the ambassador at Lisbon, his former patron, the Marquis de los Balbases, he composed a serenata for Philip V's birthday and the *loa* and third act of the opera *Amor aumenta el Valor* (collab. J. Nebra and F. Falconi; *Mp*), sung in January 1728 to celebrate the wedding of Facco's pupil, the future Fernando VI, and Maria Bárbara. After a period as music teacher to Prince Charles (later Charles III), 1729–31, he continued as a string player in the royal chapel. Facco's genius was overestimated by his biographer Zanolli, who compared him to Bach; but he was a fine, capable composer fully alive to the developments of his fellow Venetians Albinoni and Vivaldi.

J. Subirá: 'Jaime Facco y su obra musical en Madrid', *AnM*, iii (1948), 109–32

U. Zanolli: *Giacomo Facco Maestro de Reyes: introducción a la vida y la obra del gran músico véneto de 1700* (Mexico City, 1965)

R. Stevenson: *Renaissance and Baroque Musical Sources in the Americas* (Washington DC, 1970), 83, 143, 170

J. Subirá: 'El madrileñizado violinista Don Jaime Facco', *Temas musicales madrileños* (Madrid, 1971), 83–99

E. Casares, ed.: F. Asenjo Barbieri: *Documentos sobre música española y epistolario (Legado Barbieri)* (Madrid, 1988), 148

A. Cetrangolo and G. De Padova: *La serenata vocale tra viceregno e metropoli: Giacomo Facco dalla Sicilia a Madrid* (Padua, 1990)
ROBERT STEVENSON

Fach (Ger., plural *Fächer*). Term for 'voice-category'. Rather more than others, the Germans have systematically distinguished between the various types of singing voice and have stipulated which operatic roles are suitable for each of them. The main categories (soprano, contralto, tenor, baritone, bass) each have their own subdivisions, so that the more dramatic type of soprano, for example, may be said to lie within any one of three *Fächer*: the *jugendliche dramatische Sopran*, the *Zwischenfachsängerin* (or 'in-between type') and the *hochdramatische Sopran* (the 'high' or 'serious' dramatic soprano, as opposed to the first type, the 'youthful' and therefore lighter type). Roles appropriate to each in turn might be Elisabeth in *Tannhäuser*, Aida and Isolde. Once placed within their *Fach*, German singers have traditionally found it relatively difficult to perform outside it, though this has become less so in recent years.

J. B. STEANE

Faenza. City in the Emilia-Romagna, a province of Ravenna. Its early musical history is richly documented. In 1501 the city came under direct papal rule and musical activities focussed increasingly on ecclesiastical and civic functions, which came to include processions of singers and instrumentalists and 'academies' of oratory, poetry and music. The patronage of two Arcadian academies and the intellectual and artistic stimulus provided by Faenza's peripatetic aristocracy made the city a musical centre, and by the middle of the 18th century the opera season was attracting distinguished musicians from many parts of Italy.

The Remoti opened the first theatre in 1674 in a large salon in the Palazzo dei Podestà. By 1723 this was converted to an elaborately furnished and decorated small opera house. Performances of opera and spoken drama increased in frequency over the next century. The opera house soon became inadequate, and a larger one was built in 1788 to designs by the architect Giuseppe Pistocchi, still under the patronage of the Remoti. The present theatre is the result of the periodic expansion and modernization (notably in 1855–70) of this 18th-century structure; in 1903 it was renamed Teatro Comunale Masini after the distinguished tenor from Faenza, Angelo Masini.

The original Teatro dei Remoti had opened on 21 June 1723 with G. M. Buini's *La fede ne' tradimenti*, sung by Luigi Antinori, Maria Giustina Turcotti, Cecilia Bellisani Buini and Maria Negri; the intermezzo was *Il giocatore nelle disgrazie*. The annual celebration of Faenza's patron saint, St Peter (21 June), gave rise to elaborate opera productions and the summer season rapidly eclipsed the traditional carnival season in importance. Operas given included works by Orlandini (1728), Jommelli (1745, 1761), Schiassi (1745), Pergolesi (1749), Galuppi (1753, 1758, 1769), Avossa's *Il ciarlone* (1765) and Traetta (1771), and later Fischietti, Anfossi and others. Operas composed for Faenza include Giuseppe Sarti's *Pompeo in Armenia* (1752) and Giuseppe Giordani's *Caio Ostilio*, commissioned for the opening of the Teatro Comunale (1788).

The upheavals of the French Revolution and Napoleonic era curtailed musical activity. Opera performances at the Teatro Comunale were replaced with spoken drama from 1797 until 1820 when a regular opera season was re-established, but it was often suspended in response to the struggles during the Risorgimento. Musical activity still focussed on opera. Productions followed the traditions established during the 18th century. Rossini's, Donizetti's and Bellini's operas, both serious and comic, favourites in the first few decades of the century, were supplanted by Verdi's from 1843. French and German operas were not performed regularly until the mid-1880s. Many of the leading Italian singers visited the city during the century, among them Sebastiano Ronconi (1842), Giuditta and Ernesta Grisi (1836) and Giuseppina Strepponi (1845–6). Faentine singers included the baritone Antonio Tamburini and Angelo Masini. By the end of the century economic factors had reduced the frequency and scope of opera seasons. Works by Puccini and the *verismo* composers had replaced all but the most popular operas of the previous generation, and composers of French opera such as Bizet, Gounod and Meyerbeer shared the brief seasons with the Italian favourites, while occasionally even Wagner was performed. Singers were predominantly local, with only occasional visits by divas of world fame.

G. Pasolini-Zanelli: *Il teatro di Faenza dal 1788 al 1888* (Faenza, 1888)
A. Messi and A. Calzi: *Faenza nella storia e nell'arte* (Faenza, 1909)
C. Rivalta: *Fasti e glorie del Teatro comunale di Faenza dalla Morichelli (1788) ad Angelo Masini (1883)* (Faenza, 1922)
G. Eive: *Paolo Alberghi and Musical Life in 18th Century Faenza* (diss., U. of California, Berkeley, 1992)

GLORIA EIVE

Faggioli, Michelangelo (*b* Naples, 1666; *d* Naples, 23 Nov 1733). Italian composer. He came from a family of lawyers and in 1687 received the doctorate at the University of Naples in both canon and civil law. He composed, apparently in 1706, the music for the earliest known comic opera in Neapolitan dialect, *La Cilla* (text by F. A. Tullio), which was 'splendidly produced' on 26 December 1707 in the palace of Fabrizio Carafa, Prince of Chiusiano, to celebrate the return of Carafa's son from Spain; the libretto indicates, however, that the work had already been performed in the preceding year. Its novelty was such as to occasion comment in contemporary Neapolitan journals, and Faggioli himself, in his dedicatory letter, shows awareness of having created something new, begging forbearance and protection for it. Further performances held in Carafa's palace in January 1708 attest its success. In this prototype of dialect comic operas all the characters sing in Neapolitan. The plot is a romantic farce set in a village, with comic effects arising from the devices of mistaken identity and transvestite disguise. Some 66 short arias, duets and trios, spaced without any apparent plan, frequently interrupt the action; the exit aria is not yet a standard feature. The music is lost, but Faggioli's style in this genre can be seen in a comic cantata with dialect text for soprano solo and continuo, *Lo Paglietta* (I-Nc), containing two da capo arias in a simple, tuneful melodic style with competent but unadventurous harmony.

M. Scherillo: *L'opera buffa napoletana durante il settecento: storia letteraria* (Naples, 1883, 2/1917), 115
F. Piovano: 'Baldassare Galuppi: note bio-bibliografiche', *RMI*, xiii (1906), 676–726, esp. 678
U. Prota-Giurleo: *Nicola Logroscino: 'il dio dell'opera buffa'* (Naples, 1927), 49
C. Sartori: 'Gli Scarlatti a Napoli', *RMI*, xlvi (1942), 374–90

JAMES L. JACKMAN

Faggioni, Piero (*b* Carrara, 12 Aug 1936). Italian director. He studied at the Accademia Nazionale d'Arte in Rome. After starting his career as an actor he was assistant to Jean Vilar and Luchino Visconti on their opera productions (1963–9). His début as a director was at La Fenice in 1964 with *La bohème*. He now has to his credit more than 100 productions, including *Carmen* at the Edinburgh Festival and *La fanciulla del West* at Covent Garden (1977), *Francesca da Rimini* at the Metropolitan (1984) and a highly-rated *Boris Godunov* at Florence (1987). His stagings, many of which he designs himself, are notable for their painstaking detail and realism. He is also noted for careful direction of his principal singers. He was Principal Guest Producer at Covent Garden, 1989–90.

ALAN BLYTH

Fago, (Francesco) Nicola ['Il Tarantino'] (*b* Taranto, 26 Feb 1677; *d* Naples, 18 Feb 1745). Italian composer and teacher. After studying music in Taranto, he moved to Naples and from July 1693 to August 1695 studied with Provenzale at the Conservatorio S Maria della Pietà dei Turchini. Like Francesco Mancini and Domenico Sarro, he established himself in Neapolitan musical life during the years of Alessandro Scarlatti's absence (1702–8). His first opera, *Radamisto*, was commissioned in 1707 for the wedding festivities of Antonio di Sangro, Prince of S Severo. Between 1709 and 1711 he composed two additional *drammi per musica*, and apparently also two comedies on librettos by Tullio. In 1712 he collaborated with his former student Michele Falco, a composer of comic operas, to produce *Lo Masillo*, a three-act work called 'dramma per musica' on the title page of the libretto, but traditionally considered to be an early *opera buffa*.

Fago's career as a composer of operas was short-lived. Although *La Cassandra indovina* of 1711 was revived for the reopening of the Teatro dei Fiorentini at Naples in 1713, he thereafter abandoned writing for the operatic stage, and dedicated himself completely to sacred music and teaching. He was *maestro* of the Tesoro di S Gennaro (1709–31) and the church S Giacomo degli Spagnuoli (1736–45), and taught as *primo maestro* at the Neapolitan conservatories S Onofrio (1704–8) and S Maria della Pietà dei Turchini (1705–40). Among his students rank the opera composers Falco, Feo, Giuseppe de Majo, Leo, Jommelli, Cafaro and Corbisiero.

Fago's grandson, Pasquale (*b* Naples, *c*1740; *d* before 10 Nov 1794), worked as an organist (1762) and *maestro di cappella* (1766) in Naples. As a composer he adopted the name Pasquale Tarantino (or Tarantini) and wrote a number of fairly successful works, including the comic operas *La caffettiera di garbo* (P. Mililotto; Naples, Nuovo, carn. 1770) and *Il finto sordo* (Mililotto; Naples, Fiorentini, carn. 1771). His musical career, however, was eclipsed by his rise to prominence in government administration.

all performed in Naples

Radamisto (dramma per musica, N. Giuvo), Piedimonte, 1707
Astarto (dramma per musica, A. Zeno and P. Pariati), S Bartolomeo, 24 Dec 1709, 3 arias *I-Nc* [according to Strohm possibly based on a dramma per musica by Albinoni, Venice, 1708]
Le fenzejune abbendurate (commedia per musica, F. A. Tullio), 1710
La Cassandra indovina (dramma per musica, 3, Giuvo), Piedimonte, 26 Oct 1711, *GB-Lbl* (1713 perf.)
La Cianna (commedia per musica, Tullio), 1711
Lo Masillo [Acts 1 and 3] (dramma per musica, 3, N. Orilia), ?Casa del Mattia di Franco, 1712 [Act 2 by M. Falco]

Music in L'Eustachio (1729)

ES (U. Prota-Giurleo); *FlorimoN*; *RosaM*; *StiegerO*
E. Faustini-Fassini: *Nicola Fago 'Il Tarantino' e la sua famiglia* (Taranto, 1931)
A. Della Corte: 'Cori monodici di dieci musicisti per le "Tragedie Cristiane" di Annibale Marchese', *RIM*, i (1966), 190–202; esp. 198
R. Strohm: *Italienische Opernarien des frühen settecento* (Cologne, 1976), ii, 288–96
M. F. Robinson: *Naples and Neapolitan Opera* (Oxford, 1972), 191
G. Hardie: 'Neapolitan Comic Opera, 1707–1750: some Addenda and Corrigenda for *The New Grove*', *JAMS*, xxxvi (1983), 126
C. H. Parsons: *The Mellen Opera Reference Index: Opera Composers and their Works* (Lewiston, NY, 1986)

HANNS-BERTOLD DIETZ

Fagoaga, Isidoro (*b* Vera de Bidasoa, Navarre, 4 April 1895; *d* San Sebastian, May 1976). Spanish tenor. He studied at the Parma Conservatory and in 1920 made his début at Madrid in *Samson et Dalila*, subsequently creating a strong impression in the world première of Guridi's *Amaya* at Bilbao. His first Wagnerian role was Siegmund in *Die Walküre*, in which he made his Italian début at the S Carlo, Naples, in 1921. He sang Parsifal at the Verona Arena and at his South American début in 1925. In that year he became the leading Wagnerian tenor at La Scala, but after the bombing of Bilbao in 1937 refused to sing in Fascist Italy again. In retirement he lectured and wrote several biographies. His recordings are few and flawed, but they show a fine voice and an impassioned style.

E. Arnosi: 'Isidoro Fagoaga', *Record Collector*, xxx (1985), 61–73

J. B. STEANE

Fagottist, Der. Opera by Wenzel Müller; *see* KASPAR DER FAGOTTIST.

Failoni, Sergio (*b* Verona, 18 Dec 1890; *d* Sopron, 25 July 1948). Italian conductor. After studying composition at the Milan Conservatory, he spent two years as Toscanini's assistant. He made his début at Milan in 1921 conducting Rameau's *Platée* and soon developed an international career: in London, Buenos Aires, numerous cities in Europe and the USA and in the great Italian opera houses, including La Scala, 1932–4. From 1928 until his death he was principal conductor at the Budapest Opera House, where he was made a life member. After World War II he was conductor at the Chicago Civic Opera (1946–7) and the Metropolitan Opera, and in 1946 he opened the series of postwar performances at the Verona Arena. In June 1947 he collapsed on the rostrum, and although he recovered he did not conduct again. Failoni has gained an enduring place in the history of opera in Hungary, especially for his performances of Verdi, Wagner and Puccini. He declared Toscanini his ideal, sharing the latter's temperament and sensibility. Although he was an enthusiastic champion of Bartók and Kodály, Failoni's principal merit was to establish firmly an Italian and Wagnerian repertory at the Budapest Opera House.

PÉTER P. VÁRNAI

Faini, Anna Maria (*b* Florence; *fl* 1719–44). Italian contralto. She worked mainly in and around Florence, was a leading performer of comic intermezzos and, with Antonio Lottini, brought the genre to London. Her earliest known appearance was in comic works at Florence in 1719 and 1721, but from 1725 to 1729 she sang principal parts in five *opere serie* there, including trouser roles in the première of Vivaldi's *Atenaide* and in Vinci's *Catone in Utica*.

Her collaboration with Lottini appears to have begun about 1730, when she partnered him in intermezzos in Livorno and Pistoia. They gave similar performances at Florence between 1730 and 1732 and also appeared together in comic operas. In 1735 they performed two pieces at Lucca, which they later brought to London; they were invited to the King's Theatre in the 1736–7 season by the Opera of the Nobility, who hoped by this means to get the better of Handel at Covent Garden. They brought four intermezzos: *Il giocatore* (also known as *Serpilla e Bacocco* and as *Il marito giocatore e la moglie bacchetona*), *Grullo e Moschetta* and

Porsugnacco e Grilletta (all three with music by Orlandini), and Sarro's *L'impresario* (also known as *L'impresario delle (isole) Canarie* and as *Dorina e Nibbio*). Burney described *Il giocatore* as 'the first [work] of the kind which was ever introduced between the acts of an Italian opera in England', but the performers were not a great success. Lottini sang again in London in 1737–8, but Faini disappears from view until 1739, when she performed intermezzos at Florence with Giuseppe Ristorini. Her last known appearances were in two more comic works there in 1744.

BurneyH

R. L. Weaver and N. W. Weaver: *A Chronology of Music in the Florentine Theater, 1590–1750* (Detroit, 1978)

C. E. Troy: *The Comic Intermezzo: a Study in the History of Eighteenth-Century Italian Opera* (Ann Arbor, 1979)

F. Piperno: 'Appunti sulla configurazione sociale e professionale delle "parti buffe" al tempo di Vivaldi', *Antonio Vivaldi: teatro musicale, cultura e società: Venice 1981*, ii, 438–97

A. L. Bellina, B. Brizi and M. G. Pensa: *I libretti vivaldiani: recensione e collazione dei testimoni a stampa* (Florence, 1982)
                                                    COLIN TIMMS

Fair at Sorochintsï, The [*Sorochinskaya yarmarka* ('Sorochintsy Fair')]. Opera, left incomplete, in three acts by MODEST PETROVICH MUSORGSKY to his own libretto (with Arseny Golenishchev-Kutuzov) after the story in NIKOLAY VASIL'YEVICH GOGOL's collection *Evenings on a Farm near Dikanka* (i, 1831); Moscow, Free Theatre, 8/21 October 1913.

Solopy Cherevik	bass
Khivrya *Cherevik's wife*	mezzo-soprano
Parasya *Cherevik's daughter, Khivrya's stepdaughter*	soprano
Kum (Cherevik's 'buddy')	baritone
Grits'ko *a peasant lad*	tenor
Afanasy Ivanovich *son of a village priest*	tenor
A Gypsy	bass
Chernobog *master of the Demons*	bass

Tradespeople, peasants, drivers, Gypsies, Jews, Cossacks, lads and lasses; in 'The Peasant Lad's Dream Vision': Kashchey, Cherv, Topolets, Chuma, Death; Demons, witches, gnomes

Setting Village of Velikiye Sorochintsï, near Poltava in 'Little Russia' (Ukraine)

Musorgsky conceived the opera in 1874; it remained incomplete on his death in 1881. Three numbers appeared in vocal score in 1886, and three were orchestrated by Anatoly Lyadov and published in 1904. Various fragments, edited by Vyacheslav Karatïgin, were performed in concert form with piano and spoken continuity at St Petersburg on 16/29 March 1911 (to commemorate the 30th anniversary of Musorgsky's death); Act 2, completed by Karatïgin, with the Introduction and Fair from Act 1, orchestrated by Lyadov, were given at the Comedia Theatre, St Petersburg, on 17/30 December 1911.

There have been four stage versions. (1): with Musorgsky's completed numbers revised and orchestrated by Lyadov and Karatïgin, incorporating Rimsky-Korsakov's version of *A Night on Bald Mountain* with a little supplementary music by Yury Sergeyevich Sakhnovsky (1866–1930) and the musical

numbers connected by dialogue drawn from Gogol's text; this was the version first performed in Moscow in 1913, under Konstantin Saradzhev (noted above). Later, Sakhnovsky completed the work in continuous music, in which form it was given at the Bol'shoy Theatre, Moscow, under Nikolay Golovanov on 10 January 1925. (2): completed and orchestrated by César Cui, 1915–16, using Golenishchev-Kutuzov's supplementary text; it was published in 1916 and given under Grzegorz Fitelberg at the Theatre of Musical Drama, St Petersburg, on 13/26 October 1917. (3): as a pastiche, by Nikolay Tcherepnin, incorporating items from (1) and (2) with other music by Musorgsky; it was given at the Monte Carlo Opera House on 27 March 1923 and published the same year. (4): edited by Pavel Lamm, completed and orchestrated by Vissarion Shebalin; it was first performed under Grigory Stolyarov at the Nemirovich-Danchenko Musical Theatre, Moscow, on 12 January 1932 (this was a revision of a version prepared by Shebalin in 1930 and given at the Malïy Opera Theatre, Leningrad, 21 December 1931). This, published in Lamm's critical edition of Musorgsky's works (1933), has become the standard performing version and the only one to have been recorded.

The Fair at Sorochintsï is generally regarded as the third and last of the Musorgsky operas in repertory today. Although it was composed alongside *Khovanshchina*, it was started later and was much further from completion at the composer's death. The idea for the opera – originally intended as a vehicle for the great bass Osip Petrov and his wife, the contralto Anna Vorob'yova (as Cherevik and Khivrya) – came to Musorgsky in 1874. After a period of doubt as to a Russian composer's ability to manage Ukrainian speech patterns in recitative, he began composing in July 1876. As was his occasional habit, he worked at the initial stage without a libretto or even a scenario. The first music to be written was the little chorus for girls in Act 1 (fig.26 in the Lamm-Shebalin score), but Musorgsky probably already intended to link that chorus up with one he had written four years earlier for an abandoned group project, MLADA (i): a market scene, it is now the opera's opening number. Also recycled from *Mlada* was the choral ballet in Act 3, itself a recycling of the tone poem *St John's Eve on Bald Mountain* (1867), arbitrarily inserted into the action of the new opera in the guise of a dream vision. (The familiar concert number *A Night on Bald Mountain* is Rimsky-Korsakov's free adaptation, without voices, of the version in *The Fair at Sorochintsï*, the last of its several incarnations in Musorgsky's work.)

A scenario was finally written down (at the Petrovs') in 1877, a year wholly devoted to *The Fair*. Osip Petrov's death in 1878 dashed the composer's original hopes for the piece and slowed work considerably. He left it in fragments. Those for Act 3, to pick the worst case, were decorative 'inserts' only; the whole dénouement and resolution were lacking both in music and in text. Nor do the surviving fragments entirely conform to the scenario, so that even their placement within a reconstruction must remain speculative to some degree (this is undoubtedly why Rimsky-Korsakov never attempted one). The synopsis that follows is based on the Lamm-Shebalin version; the items completed by Musorgsky in vocal score are, besides the Prelude, in Act 1, *a*, *b* and *d*; in Act 2, only *a*; and in Act 3, *b*, *c* and *e*. (Their dates, where known, are given in 'Old Style'.)

Prelude: 'A Warm Day in Little Russia' (orchestrated by Musorgsky).

ACT 1 *a* Market scene with a merry din of traders and the crowd (chorus adapted from *Mlada*); Grits'ko arrives with his companions and Cherevik with Parasya. She happily looks round while he is preoccupied with the sale of his mare and his wheat. The Gypsy attracts the crowd's attention and tells a mysterious story of a red jacket the Devil himself is seeking (the first sketches for the Gypsy were composed by 31 August 1876). Grits'ko flirts with Parasya; Cherevik objects but is mollified when he finds that Grits'ko is the son of an old friend. They go to the tavern to celebrate their meeting.

b Evening. Cherevik and Kum leave the tavern, reeling. They strike up an old song ('Dudu, rududu, rududu', based on a Ukrainian folksong from the Rubets collection of 1872).

c Khivrya enters, scolds Cherevik and forbids Parasya's marriage to Grits'ko; Grits'ko overhears the exchange.

d Grits'ko is disconsolate; he sings 'The Peasant Lad's Dumka', in the style of a melismatic folksong, accompanied by solo wind. (According to the 1877 scenario, this number was meant for Act 3, but all revisers have agreed it fits in best with the existing manuscripts at this point.)

e The Gypsy appears and promises to solve Grits'ko's problem in return for the latter's bullocks.

ACT 2 *a* Khivrya picks a quarrel with Cherevik to get him out of the house (that is, Kum's house, where they are staying) so that she can keep her date with Afanasy Ivanovich, the priest's son. She bustles around the stove preparing food and sings 'Otkoli zh ya Brudeusa vstretila?' ('How in the world did I meet Brudeus?', based on a Ukrainian song taken down from a friend's singing in November 1876; MS dated 10 July 1877). Afanasy Ivanovich arrives; Khivrya plies him with goodies and he makes amorous advances. Their farcical tryst is interrupted by the tumultuous arrival of Kum and Cherevik, with other guests. They are in a panic: the red jacket has been spied, and so has the Devil with a pig's snout. After drinking, courage is restored; Cherevik brazenly invites the red jacket to the house. Kum recounts the tale of the red jacket in all its details (Musorgsky's MS breaks off after a few bars of this narrative).

b Kum finishes the tale; suddenly the window is flung open and a great pig's snout is thrust in. All disperse in great commotion, including the priest's son who runs from his hiding place.

ACT 3.i *a* Cherevik and Kum are running wild and bumping into each other. The Gypsy and peasant lads enter and accuse them of theft. Grits'ko appears and persuades the others to let Kum and Cherevik go if the latter will agree to his marrying Parasya; Cherevik having promised, he and Kum are released. All go home except Grits'ko, who falls asleep under a tree and has a fantastic dream.

b 'The Peasant Lad's Dream Vision' is an elaborate ballet with chorus depicting a Witches' Sabbath ('St John's Eve on Bald Mountain'), presided over by Chernobog (the Devil, in old Slav religion). The chimes of the morning bell and church singing put the demons and witches to flight. Grits'ko awakens and

ponders his dream. (The autograph vocal score of this number, adapted from the *Mlada* music, is dated 10 May 1880.)

3.ii *c* Parasya comes out of Kum's house, missing Grits'ko. The warm sun dispels her melancholy: she sings a merry song and breaks into a hopak. Cherevik spies her and joins in ('Parasya's Dumka': MS dated 3 July 1879; an orchestral score exists, begun by Musorgsky and finished by Rimsky-Korsakov).

d Kum and Grits'ko enter with a group of peasant lads and lasses. Taking advantage of Khivrya's absence, Cherevik blesses his daughter's marriage. When the furious Khivrya returns, the Gypsy suddenly materializes, seizes her, and with the help of the peasant lads carries her off.

e General merriment, ending in a gradual exit (finale, 'Hopak of the merry lads'); whether this general dance (with choral song, indicated with staves and clefs in Musorgsky's piano score but actually written by Shebalin, to a Ukrainian folk text) was intended for this finale, or for that to Act 1, is unclear.

*   *   *

Unlike Musorgsky's serious operas, *The Fair at Sorochintsï* is frankly a number opera, possibly modelled to some degree on Gulak-Artemovsky's popular 'Little Russian' Singspiel *Zaporozhets za Dunayem*. As traditionally befits a peasant comedy, even the dialogue scenes are modelled not on speech but on folktunes (this perhaps having been the composer's way out of his quandary about 'Little Russian recitative' – see ex.1). Nevertheless, Musorgsky's uncanny gift for

Ex.1
(a) Alexander Ivanovich Rubets: *216 Ukranian Folktunes*, no.147

(b) *The Fair at Sorochintsï*, Act 1

Moderato
CHEREVIK
Raz-ve mozh-no s mo-yey doch-koy tak-to ob - ra - shchat'-sya? Da raz-ve è - to_ mozh-no?

GRITS'KO
Ba, da è - to sam So-lo-piy!

Dru - zhi - shche, zdo-ro - vo! Pan Che-re-vik, zdo-ro - vo!

[Cherevik: 'You think it's all right to address my daughter just like that? You think that's all right?' Grits'ko: 'Well it's Solopiy himself! Greetings, old friend! Greetings, Mr Cherevik!']

musical characterization remains as sharply honed as ever: especially droll is the portrayal in Act 2 of Afanasy Ivanovich, the priest's son, through a patchwork of hackneyed ecclesiastical cadences. Presumably in an effort to be discreet, Shebalin supplied the missing scenes in a modest recitative that skilfully parodies Musorgsky's earlier speechsong manner (as in *Marriage*, or the Inn Scene from *Boris Godunov*). That style having been largely superseded in *The Fair*, Shebalin's contribution to the opera came out sounding in an odd way more like Musorgsky than Musorgsky's.

RICHARD TARUSKIN

Fairies, The. Comic opera in three acts by JOHN CHRISTOPHER SMITH to a libretto by DAVID GARRICK or Smith after WILLIAM SHAKESPEARE's *A Midsummer Night's Dream*; London, Theatre Royal, Drury Lane, 3 February 1755.

It has been suggested that Garrick was responsible for the alterations to Shakespeare's text, but he firmly denied it and his prologue suggests that Smith himself was the author. The music survives only in printed score, including the overture, the arias, the final chorus and two symphonies, but omitting the recitatives, dances and other pieces. As in his earlier *Ulysses*, Smith favoured da capo form for the arias, but the music, though assured, is mediocre and unadventurous and the setting is often incompetent. The song texts are by Dryden, Hammond, Lansdowne, Milton and Waller as well as Shakespeare. *The Fairies* was given, 'to very great applause', eight times early in 1755 and twice more in the 1755–6 season; according to the prompter Richard Cross, box-office receipts totalled £1580. Some of the pieces were heard again at Drury Lane in 1763 when George Colman plundered the score for replacements for Charles Burney's *Midsummer Night's Dream* music. The work was given in New York in 1786.

The plot follows Shakespeare's, but the 'rustics' are excluded. The characters are Theseus (tenor) and his betrothed Hippolita (silent); Egeus (bass), his daughter Hermia (soprano), her lover Lysander (alto castrato) and her betrothed Demetrius (tenor; he has no arias), and Helena (soprano), in love with Demetrius; and the king and queen of the fairies, Oberon (baritone) and Titania (soprano), with her servant and Puck (trebles).

The historical significance of *The Fairies* far outweighs its aesthetic merits. It marked Smith's return to the theatre some 20 years after the failure of *Ulysses* in 1733 and was the first in a new series of 'English' operas staged at Drury Lane challenging Italian opera (Smith's *The Tempest* and Thomas Arne's *Eliza* followed). Garrick's (spoken) Prologue is a commentary on the audience's ignorance and prejudice towards English composers:

> Excuse us first, for foolishly supposing,
> Your *countryman* could please you in composing;
> An *op'ra* too! – play'd by an *English* band,
> Wrote in a language which you understand –
> I dare not say, WHO wrote it – I could tell ye,
> To soften matters – Signor *Shakespearelli*.

MICHAEL BURDEN

Fair Theatres. Familiar name for the 'theatres' on the two Fair sites in 17th- and 18th-century Paris, the Foire St Germain and the Foire St Laurent. They became, in 1714, the Opéra-Comique, and merged with the Comédie-Italienne in 1762; see PARIS, §§2(iii) and 3(i).

Fairy Prince, The. Masque in three acts by THOMAS AUGUSTINE ARNE to a libretto by George Colman the elder (*see* COLMAN family, (2)) after BEN JONSON's *Oberon* (1611); London, Covent Garden, 12 November 1771.

Although described as a masque, the work is all-sung. The libretto is little more than an excuse for spectacular scene changes set in and around Windsor, where satyrs and fairies gather to keep watch over the castle and

observe the procession of Knights of the Garter and their installation in St George's Chapel. It concludes with a ceremonial dinner, accompanied by appropriate music. The wood nymphs' music includes the aria 'Let us play and dance and sing', with an extravagant range of well over two octaves. The work was highly successful, with 36 performances in the season, but it was not revived. The published score relegates the dances to an appendix and omits the recitatives and some of the choruses, although it retains the splendid duet and choral finale to Act 1 'Then all the air shall ring', in which the full chorus suddenly enters with shouts of 'God save the king' to splendid effect. In his *English Theatre Music* (2/1986, Appendix F) Roger Fiske proposed a reconstruction of the original order.

JOHN A. PARKINSON

Fairy-Queen, The. Semi-opera in five acts by HENRY PURCELL, anonymously adapted from WILLIAM SHAKESPEARE's *A Midsummer Night's Dream*; London, Queen's Theatre, Dorset Garden, 2 May 1692.

[The Actors]
The Duke (Theseus), Egeus, Helena, Demetrius, Hermia, Lysander, Nick Bottom, Peter Quince, Tom Snout, Francis Flute, Robin Starveling, Snug, Oberon, Titania, Indian Boy, Robin Goodfellow (Puck), fairies

[The Singers]

Drunken Poet	baritone
First Fairy	soprano
Second Fairy	soprano
Night	soprano
Mystery	soprano
Secrecy	countertenor
Sleep	bass
Coridon	bass
Mopsa	soprano/countertenor
Nymph	soprano
Phoebus	tenor
Spring	soprano
Summer	countertenor
Autumn	tenor
Winter	baritone
Juno	soprano
Chinese Man	countertenor
Chinese Woman (Daphne)	soprano
Hymen	baritone

Fairies and attendants

Setting Theseus's palace, a nearby wood, a grotto, a garden of fountains, a Chinese garden

The Fairy-Queen was the third semi-opera Purcell composed for the United Company of the Theatre Royal. It was the most lavish and expensive show of the decade, costing some £3000 to stage. Though the 'Court and Town were wonderfully satisfy'd', it was one of the few semi-operas to lose money. In 1693 Purcell revised and added to the original score, which is probably his finest theatre work; some critics however have condemned it as a desecration of *A Midsummer Night's Dream*. Purcell did not in fact set any of Shakespeare's lines and all the music is in self-contained masques which little affect the play. The author of the new verses and the adapter of the play text is unknown (if indeed they are the work of a single person), but the likeliest candidate is Thomas Betterton, the actor-manager of the United Company who had prepared *Dioclesian* for Purcell in 1690 and who supervised the production of all semi-operas until 1694. (*The Fairy-Queen* adaptation has often been attributed to Elkanah Settle, an error originating in a 1910 biography of the poet.)

The transformation of play into semi-opera is skilfully handled. To make room for Purcell's four substantial masques in Acts 2–5 (a fifth was added to Act 1 for the 1693 version), considerable portions of the lyric poetry were cut, as were the minor characters Hippolyta and Philostrate. Some of the remaining verse was edited, the language being modernized, though not crudely, as has been claimed; rather, passages that would have been obscure to a 1692 audience were adroitly clarified. Purcell and his collaborator decided to eschew the most logical place for music in the original play, the Bergomask of Pyramus and Thisbe in Act 5 (Richard Leveridge and John Frederick Lampe later set it separately as a miniature comic opera). In Shakespeare, Bottom and the other artisans rehearse the Lamentable Comedy in Act 3 and perform it before Theseus and his courtiers in Act 5. In *The Fairy-Queen* rehearsal and performance are neatly compressed into a single scene in Act 3, leaving ample room in the final act for Purcell's Masque of Hymen. This, and all the other masques in the semi-opera, are not directly connected with the plot of the play but are related to it metaphorically: the Masque of Sleep in Act 2 prepares Titania for her dream; the masque in Act 3 is offered to Bottom (in his transfigured state) as a rustic entertainment laced with sexual innuendo; the Masque of Seasons in Act 4 symbolizes the reconciliation of Oberon and Titania; and the Masque of Hymen in Act 5 is a general affirmation of the wedding vows, the Chinese garden setting presumably reflecting Eastern Enlightenment, though the exact meaning is obscure and this may simply be a bit of fashionable *chinoiserie*.

For the second version in 1693, the first scene of the play was cut and replaced by Purcell's brilliantly comic turn of the Drunken Poet who, wandering into the wood, is set upon by fairies, blindfolded and pinched until he confesses to being 'a scu- scu- scu- scu- scurvy, scurvy poet'. Because of the stammering effect, this scene has been taken as a satire on the poet and playwright Thomas D'Urfey, but Settle also suffered the affliction.

Upon Purcell's death in November 1695, the Theatre Royal lost the score of *The Fairy-Queen* and, later desiring to revive the semi-opera, the theatre treasurer placed a newspaper advertisement in October 1701 offering a 20-guinea reward for its safe return. It was not apparently recovered, for in 1703 only one act was performed, and this could have been assembled from printed sources. A partly autograph full score, discovered early this century in the library of the Royal Academy of Music in London, is the most complete and informative of all Purcell's theatre scores, indeed the only autograph of any of his semi-operas. Purcell shared the copying with three scribes but closely supervised their work, even to the extent of inserting almost every accidental himself. The score is a composite of the 1692 and 1693 productions, its only major omission being the Plaint ('Oh let me ever, ever weep') in Act 5, which is inappropriate in this context and may be a later addition.

ACT 1 The opening scene (cut from the 1693 production) closely follows Shakespeare, except that Theseus does not threaten to kill Hermia should she disobey his command to marry Demetrius. After the artisans plan their play to celebrate the anticipated weddings, Titania, attended by fairies, enters with the Indian boy. She asks the fairy choir to entertain him and the opening duet, 'Come, let us leave the town', leads directly to the scene of the Drunken Poet. This autonomous episode comprises a series of rapidly alternating solos in which the fairies torment their victim, whose drunkeness and cries of pain are graphically depicted. Each fairy arietta is followed by a chorus based on the same melody but greatly enriched harmonically and contrapuntally. The pairing of solo and chorus, in which a simple tune is transformed into a highly sophisticated piece, is the dominant form in *The Fairy-Queen*.

ACT 2 Preparing for bed, Titania requests an entertainment to lull her to sleep, and the scene changes 'to a Prospect of Grotto's, Arbors, and delightful Walks ... Between these two Arbors is the great Grott, which is continued by several Arches, to the Farther end of the House'. The masque begins with sprightly music, including the double echo chorus 'May the god of wit inspire' and another fine air and chorus pair, 'Sing while we trip it upon the green'. The fairy revels are cut short by the appearance of Night, Mystery and Secrecy, who sing progressively richer invocations to sleep, including the ravishing countertenor air 'One charming night' with obbligato recorders. The point of sleep is depicted by the long, pregnant rests in the air and chorus 'Hush, no more, be silent', Purcell's characteristically literal setting of the words. When the music is finished, Puck administers the love juice to Titania, while Lysander and Hermia elope.

ACT 3 The confusion between the pairs of mortal lovers unfolds much as in Shakespeare. The artisans rehearse their play, overheard by Puck, who then claps the ass-head on to Bottom. Titania wakes and falls in love with the strange creature, for whom she prepares another fairy masque. 'The Scene changes to a great Wood ... Two great Dragons make a Bridge over the River; their Bodies form two Arches, through which two Swans are seen in the River at a great distance.' The entertainment begins with another solo-chorus pair, 'If love's a sweet passion', which emphasizes a pungent augmented dominant chord heard in various guises throughout the opera. The highlight of the third-act masque is the rustic dialogue of Coridon and Mopsa, 'Now the maids and the men are making of hay'. Purcell first set this in F major for soprano and bass (Mrs Ayliff and John Reading) but a year later recast it in G, with the countertenor Pate replacing the soprano. His performance in drag was presumably intended to broaden the already comic refrain 'No, no, no, no, no; no kissing at all'.

ACT 4 The mortal lovers' confusion is gradually resolved, Puck restores Bottom to his proper form and Oberon wakes Titania and commands a masque to celebrate their reconciliation. While a long, five-section symphony scored for two trumpets, kettledrums and strings is played, the sun rises and 'appears red through the Mist ... it dissipates the Vapours, and is seen in its full Lustre ... In the middle of the Stage is a very large fountain, wherein the Water rises about twelve Foot'. A soprano solo and chorus on a ground bass, 'Now the night is chas'd away', congratulate Oberon on his birthday (there is no mention of the fairy king's birthday in

Shakespeare), and Phoebus 'appears in a Chariot drawn by four Horses'. The god announces the end of winter, and there follows the Masque of the Four Seasons, each represented by a different singer. This scene is rounded off by a repeat of the chorus 'Hail, great parent of us all'.

ACT 5 The Duke finds the pairs of lovers asleep and wakes them with hunting music (not in Purcell's score); he refuses to believe their stories but agrees to the marriages. In a wide departure from Shakespeare, Oberon and Titania reappear and, to convince Theseus that the lovers were telling the truth, invoke Juno to bless the nuptial bed. The goddess enters in a machine drawn by peacocks and sings 'Thrice happy lovers', a two-part aria on a short ground bass which is constantly interrupted by highly decorated recitative. Like the final masques of most semi-operas, this one continues with a hotch-potch of various pieces. The mingling of mortals and fairies in the Chinese garden recalls the revels of a Stuart masque, in which the masquers and the audience met in a fusion of fantasy and reality. In spite of the miscellaneous nature of the final entertainment, the quality of the music remains at the highest level. The famous song for countertenor, 'Thus the gloomy world', is one of Purcell's rare da capo arias, the gentle middle section standing in sharpest contrast to the bravura outer duets for voice and trumpet solo over a walking ground bass. At the centre of the masque is the entry of Hymen, whose torch is rekindled by a pair of sopranos singing 'Turn, turn then thine eyes'.

*　*　*

With its self-contained and largely plotless masques, *The Fairy-Queen* is far removed from true opera. Yet Purcell seems completely at ease with the medium. The music displays a coherence, a harmonic and motivic unity extending even to the instrumental act tunes which is lacking in the other semi-operas. The vocal parts are also much more difficult, perhaps because Purcell was writing for a small nucleus of professional singers (each taking several different roles) rather than for the actor-singers who bore the brunt of the solos in *King Arthur* and the many plays for which he provided music. *The Fairy-Queen* is not a corruption of Shakespeare's play but rather an extended meditation on the spell it casts.

CURTIS PRICE

Fait historique (Fr.). A type of late 18th-century French *opéra* or *opéra comique*, usually in one act, in which the action is based on a heroic event drawn from contemporary French history. *Faits historiques* were often vehicles to extol the valour of enlisted soldiers (rather than generals) or even the common people. An early example is *L'incendie du Havre*, set in vaudevilles to a text by Desfontaines (G. F. Fouques) and performed at the Comédie-Italienne (Salle Favart) in 1786, but the genre became much more popular during the Revolution when it reflected current military, political and social concerns. *Faits historiques*, particularly during the Terror, were the staple repertory of minor theatres and were also performed at the Opéra-Comique (Grétry's *Joseph Barra*, 1794), the Théâtre Feydeau (Méhul's *Le pont de Lodi*, 1797) and even the Opéra (Rochefort's *Toulon soumis*, 1794). As *pièces de circonstance*, they were generally written and rehearsed in haste, and few enjoyed long runs or revivals.

*

M. Albert: *Les théâtres des boulevards (1789–1848)* (Paris, 1902)

S. J. Berard: 'Une curiosité du théâtre à l'époque de la Révolution, les "faits historiques et patriotiques"', *Romantische Zeitschrift für Literaturgeschichte: Cahiers d'histoire et de littérature romanes*, iii (1979), 228–40

M. E. C. Bartlet: 'Revolutionschanson und Hymne im Repertoire der Pariser Oper, 1793–1794', *Die französische Revolution als Bruch des gesellschaftlichen Bewusstseins*, ed. R. Reichardt and R. Koselleck, Ancien Régime, Aufklärung und Revolution, xv (Munich, 1988), 479–507

——: 'The New Repertory at the Opéra during the Reign of Terror: Revolutionary Rhetoric and Operatic Consequences', *Music and the French Revolution*, ed. M. Boyd (Cambridge, 1992), 107–56

M. ELIZABETH C. BARTLET

Fajer, Francisco Javier García. *See* GARCÍA FAJER, FRANCISCO JAVIER.

Falco [de Falco, di Falco, Farco], **Michele** (*b* Naples, ?1688; *d* after 1732). Italian composer. He studied at the Conservatorio di S Onofrio, by differing accounts from 1700 to 1708 or from 1704 to 1712, probably with Nicola Fago. He was *maestro di cappella* and organist of the church of S Geronimo (or S Girolamo). Prota-Giurleo suggested that by 1723 he had taken holy orders, and thenceforth felt it necessary to sign his operatic works anagramatically as 'Cola Melfiche'.

Examination of the librettos he set establishes Falco's place as one of the pioneer figures of Neapolitan *opera buffa*. Unlike most of the others (Riccio, Faggioli, Antonio Orefice and de Mauro), he was a professional musician – one of the first, in fact, to turn attention to the new dramatic form, which appears to have been as much a literary experiment for the enjoyment of dilettantes as a musical one, with works written for production in private houses, seemingly for the novelty of hearing dialect poetry sung. The operas that Falco set, like those of his contemporaries, vary greatly in length, dramaturgical technique and opportunities for musical expression. His first documented work, *Lo Lollo pisciaportelle* (1709), was apparently first performed in the house of its dedicatee (in Sartori's view it may also have been produced at the Fiorentini theatre); it uses only five characters and its plot, in one act, deploys a relatively simple intrigue. His second work, *Lo Masillo*, a collaboration with Fago, was likewise created for private performance, for the governor of the Conservatorio di S Onofrio. By this time, however, the structure of *opera buffa* had moved more towards standardization: Orilia's libretto more closely resembles those of his contemporaries. In particular, he had profited by Tullio's experiments, for this is a full-length work of three acts, with a plot involving eight characters and some 55 short musical numbers. It is uncertain from the libretto whether the arias were intended to be sung da capo; the verse structure in most cases would permit such treatment, but only a few of the numbers are exit arias, a dramaturgical device associated with the musical form in *opera seria*. The work contains an unusual number of ensemble pieces in addition to the finales, another sign of experimentation. Except for a few fragments, all Falco's operatic music has disappeared.

opere buffe unless otherwise stated; all performed in Naples

Lo Lollo pisciaportelle (1, N. Orilia), Casa del Barone Paterno del Gesso, 1709
Lo Masillo [Act 2] (dramma per musica, 3, Orilia), ?Casa del Mattia di Franco, 1712 [Acts 1 and 3 by N. Fago]
Lo mbruoglio d'ammore (A. Piscopo), Fiorentini, 27 Dec 1717
Armida abbandonata (dramma per musica), Real Palazzo, Sala degli Svizzeri; later in S Bartolomeo, 1 Oct 1719

Lo castiello saccheiato (F. Oliva), Fiorentini, Oct 1720, collab. Vinci
Le pazzie d'ammore (F. A. Tullio), Fiorentini, April 1723

ES (U. Prota-Giurleo); *FlorimoN*
M. Scherillo: *L'opera buffa napoletana durante il settecento; storia letteraria* (Naples, 1883, 2/1917), 124–5, 177ff
S. Di Giacomo: *I quattro antichi conservatorii di musicali di Napoli*, i (Palermo, 1924), 80ff, 177
C. Sartori: 'Gli Scarlatti a Napoli', *RMI*, xlvi (1942), 374–90
JAMES L. JACKMAN

Falcon. Term for a type of voice, presumed to have been exemplified by CORNÉLIE FALCON, the dramatic soprano who sang Rachel in the première of *La Juive* (1835) and Valentine in that of *Les Huguenots* (1836). Her voice was exceptionally powerful, dramatic in quality and ample in the middle register. Mainly in France, or in association with the French repertory, 'falcon' has survived as a word which denotes a soprano of this type. Félia Litvinne and her pupil Germaine Lubin, both of whom sang Wagnerian roles such as Isolde and Kundry, would come under this heading. As Falcon herself sang last in 1840, the continued use of the term is of doubtful value, and since her active career covered only six years, terminated by loss of voice in 1838, its application is also a doubtful compliment.

See also SOPRANO, §§4 and 5.   J. B. STEANE

Falcon, (Marie) Cornélie (*b* Paris, 28 Jan 1812; *d* Paris, 25 Feb 1897). French soprano. She studied with Nourrit at the Paris Conservatoire in 1831, winning *premiers prix* for singing and lyric declamation. She made her début at the Opéra as Alice in *Robert le diable* (20 July 1832). Her acting ability and dramatic voice greatly

Cornélie Falcon as Rachel in Halévy's 'La Juive', a role she created at the Paris Opéra, 23 February 1835: portrait by A. Colin

stimulated composers, and roles of the type in which she excelled came to be designated as 'falcon soprano' parts. Her most notable creations were Rachel in *La Juive* (23 February 1835) and Valentine in *Les Huguenots* (29 February 1836); her repertory also included Donna Anna, Julia in *La vestale* and Rossini's French heroines. Her success at the Opéra led to overwork followed by loss of voice. In March 1837 she was forced to abandon a performance of Niedermeyer's *Stradella*, but she soon resumed a busy schedule until October. After a last appearance in *Les Huguenots* (15 January 1838) she twice visited Italy in the hope of recovering her voice. She returned to the Opéra on 14 March 1840 to sing parts of *La Juive* and *Les Huguenots* at a benefit performance, but her voice had been permanently damaged and she retired.

For further illustration *see* ROBERT LE DIABLE.

C. Bouvet: *Cornélie Falcon* (Paris, 1927)   PHILIP ROBINSON

Falcon, Ruth (*b* Residence, LA, 2 Nov 1946). American soprano. She studied at Tulane University and in New York, and made her début in 1974 as Micaëla with the New York City Opera. She sang in Mayr's *Medea in Corinto* at Berne in 1975, then joined the Bayerische Staatsoper; she has also sung in Berlin, Brussels, Houston, Boston, Toronto, Venice, Florence, Strasbourg, Lyons, Toulouse, Aix-en-Provence and at the Paris Opéra. Her repertory includes Countess Almaviva, Electra (*Idomeneo*), Donna Anna, Agathe, Desdemona, Leonora (*Il trovatore* and *La forza del destino*), Amelia (*Il duca d'Alba*), Norma, Julia (*La vestale*), Salome (*Hérodiade*), Anne Boleyn, Elsa and Ariadne. She first sang at Covent Garden in 1987 as the Empress (*Die Frau ohne Schatten*), the role of her Metropolitan début in 1989, and returned to Covent Garden as Chrysothemis in 1988. She has a large, beautiful voice which she uses with skill, but her acting ability is limited.   ELIZABETH FORBES

Falcone. Theatre in GENOA, converted from the ancient Falcon inn in about 1640 and enlarged in 1703.

Falena, La ('The Moth-Woman'). *Leggenda* in three acts by ANTONIO SMAREGLIA to a libretto by Silvio Benco; Venice, Teatro Rossini, 6 September 1897.

The opera is set on a European coast of the Atlantic in the early times of Christianity. King Stellio (tenor) asks Albina (soprano) to become his queen. As they exchange their first kiss at sunset on the seashore, the Falena (mezzo-soprano) emerges from the forest and casts a spell on the king. At night, the evil child of darkness with blazing eyes and black hair receives Stellio in her frightening cave in the forest. She offers him wine and the delirious king abandons himself to the lustful creature. Albina's father, Uberto (baritone), approaches the cave to rescue the king but, at the instigation of the Falena, Stellio kills the old man. At dawn, on the seashore, the Falena slowly wanes and recedes into the forest. Stellio confesses his crime and begs his countrymen to put him to death. As the sun rises, grief-stricken Albina forgives Stellio and dies.

In *La falena* Smareglia created a fascinating musical organism sustained by an all-pervasive symphonic movement. In Act 2, which consists of one extended duet, the evil protagonist and the good king move as hallucinatory figures in a nightmarish atmosphere under the obsessive urge of the music.　　　MATTEO SANSONE

Falewicz, Magdalena (*b* Lublin, 11 Feb 1946). Polish soprano. She studied in Warsaw and made her début in 1973 as Oscar at the Komische Oper, Berlin, where she was engaged until becoming a member of the Staatsoper in 1984. Her repertory includes Countess Almaviva, Susanna and Pamina, Natasha (*War and Peace*), Micaela, Zdenka, Liù, Mimì and Butterfly; she also sang the last role with the WNO (1978) and the ENO (1986). She has sung in Warsaw, Frankfurt and Leipzig and in Dresden, where she created the Countess in Matthus's *Weise von Liebe und Tod des Cornet Christoph Rilke* (1985). A stylish singer, she is also a fine actress.
　　　ELIZABETH FORBES

Falik, Yury Alexandrovich (*b* Odessa, 30 July 1936). Russian composer. He studied at the Leningrad Conservatory, concentrating first on the cello and later on composition, graduating from Boris Arapov's class in 1964. As a composer, teacher at the conservatory and active member of the Composers' Union, Falik has been prominent in the musical life of Leningrad (St Petersburg). His first opera, *Plutni Skapena* ('The Swindles of Scapin'), a three-act *opera buffa* to his own libretto based on Molière's farce, received its première at the Vanemuine Theatre in Tartu, Estonia, in December 1984. In his ironic musical commentary on the action, which takes place in a carnival setting, Falik used modified period conventions and stylization within a colourful, modern musical idiom that includes elements of popular styles. His one-act children's fairy-tale opera *Polly and the Dinosaurs*, to a libretto by C. G. Freund and B. Mahany, had its première in a concert performance in Chicago on 4 March 1990.

M. Galushko: 'Obrashchayas' k Mol'yeru' [Turning to Molièru], *SovM* (1986), no.4, pp.36–40
A. Klimovitsky: 'Yuri Falik's New Opera: The Cheats of Scapin', *Music in the USSR* (1986), Jan–March, 90–91　　LAUREL E. FAY

Fall, Leo(pold) (*b* Olomouc, 2 Feb 1873; *d* Vienna, 16 Sept 1925). Austrian composer. His father, Moritz Fall (1848–1922), was a military bandmaster and composer who from 1882 served in Lemberg (now L'viv), before settling in Berlin, where he founded a café ensemble. Leo received violin lessons from his father and, after schooling in Lemberg, entered the Vienna Conservatory where he studied the violin and piano, as well as harmony and counterpoint with the brothers J. N. and Robert Fuchs. He was briefly a member of the band of the 50th Austrian Infantry Regiment under Franz Lehár senior, playing the violin alongside the young Franz Lehár. Then he moved to Berlin, where he played in his father's orchestra, acted as piano accompanist in cabaret and played the violin in the orchestra of the Reichshallentheater. In 1895 he became an operetta conductor in Hamburg, where he wrote music for various stage pieces. After a further engagement in Cologne he returned to Berlin, composing and conducting at the Zentraltheater and Metropoltheater, the city's leading revue theatres, and composing songs for the cabaret 'Die bösen Buben'. Two attempts at opera composition were unsuccessful, as was his first operetta *Der Rebell* (1905). However, after marrying a daughter of Salomon Jadassohn in 1904, he gave up conducting in 1906 and settled in Vienna to concentrate on operetta composi-

tion. *Der fidele Bauer* (1907), *Die Dollarprinzessin* (1907) and *Die geschiedene Frau* (1908) swiftly established him alongside Lehár and Oscar Straus in the forefront of the new generation of operetta composers and brought him international fame. He visited London several times for productions of his works, composing *The Eternal Waltz* (1911) for the Hippodrome and conducting concerts of his music at the Coliseum. Meanwhile *Der Rebell* had been successfully revised for Berlin as *Der liebe Augustin* (1912), with Fritzi Massary. After a run of lesser successes, including *Die Frau Ministerpräsident* ('The Lady Prime Minister' – set in England), he regained popularity with *Die Kaiserin* (1915), *Die Rose von Stambul* (1916) and *Madame Pompadour* (1922), though a further opera, *Der goldene Vogel*, with Richard Tauber and Elisabeth Rethberg, failed in Dresden. Since 1945 *Madame Pompadour* has entered the repertory of European opera companies, notably the Vienna Volksoper.

Though never achieving the lasting success of Lehár, Fall composed some of the most captivating operetta music of the 20th century. He seemingly pandered much less to popular taste than to his own, and his scores provide rewarding study. He combined a talent for glowing melody with a particular ability for setting rhythmically irregular, conversational texts ('Und der Himmel hängt voller Geigen' from *Der liebe Augustin*, 'Kind, du kannst tanzen wie meine Frau' from *Die geschiedene Frau* and 'Heut' könnt einer sein Glück bei mir machen' from *Madame Pompadour*). Like Lehár, he was unusual in operetta of the time in orchestrating his own works, and could draw from the orchestra a translucent sound, texturally more like chamber music. Of his two brothers, Siegfried (*b* Olomouc, 30 Nov 1877) was a composer of serious music and Richard (*b* Gewitsch, Moravia, 3 April 1882; *d* Auschwitz, 1943 or 1944) a composer of popular songs.

operettas unless otherwise stated; mostly published in vocal score in Berlin or Vienna at time of original production

Paroli [Frau Denise] (opera, 1, L. Fernand), Hamburg, 1902; Irrlicht (opera, Fernand), Mannheim, National, 8 Jan 1905; Der Rebell (3, R. Bernauer and E. Welisch), Vienna, An der Wien, 28 Nov 1905, rev. as Der liebe Augustin, Berlin, Neues, 3 Feb 1912; Der fidele Bauer (3, V. Léon), Mannheim, National, 27 July 1907; Die Dollarprinzessin (3, A. M. Willner and F. Grünbaum), Vienna, An der Wien, 2 Nov 1907; Die geschiedene Frau (3, Léon), Vienna, Carl, 23 Dec 1908; Brüderlein fein (1, J. Wilhelm), Vienna, Hölle, 1 Dec 1909

Der Schrei nach der Ohrfeige, Vienna, 1909; Das Puppenmädel (3, L. Stein and Willner), Vienna, Carl, 4 Nov 1910; Die schöne Risette (3, Willner and R. Bodanzky), Vienna, An der Wien, 19 Nov 1910; Die Sirene (3, Stein and Willner), Vienna, Johann Strauss, 5 Jan 1911; The Eternal Waltz (1, A. Hurgon), London, Hippodrome, 22 Dec 1911; Die Studentengräfin (3, Léon), Berlin, Am Nollendorfplatz, 18 Jan 1913; Der Nachtschnellzug (3, Léon and Stein), Vienna, Johann Strauss, 20 Dec 1913

Die Frau Ministerpräsident [Jung-England] (Bernauer and Welisch), Berlin, Montis Operetten, 14 Feb 1914; Der künstliche Mensch (Willner and R. Oesterreicher), Berlin, des Westens, 2 Oct 1915; Die Kaiserin [Fürstenliebe] (J. Brammer and A. Grünwald), Berlin, Metropol, 15 Oct 1915; Die Rose von Stambul (3, Brammer and Grünwald), Vienna, An der Wien, 2 Dec 1916; Der goldene Vogel (Wilhelm and P. Frank), Dresden, Staatsoper, 21 May 1920

Die spanische Nachtigall (3, R. Schanzer and Welisch), Berlin, Berliner, 18 Nov 1920; Der heilige Ambrosius (1, Willner and A. Rebner), Berlin, 3 Nov 1921; Die Strassensängerin (3, F. Friederichs and A. Neidthardt), Vienna, Apollo, 14 Feb 1922; Madame Pompadour (3, Schanzer and Welisch), Berlin, Berliner, 9 Sept 1922; Der süsse Kavalier (3, Welisch), Berlin, 1923; Jugend im Mai (Schanzer and Welisch), Dresden, Central, 22 Oct 1926; Rosen aus Florida (3, Willner and Reichert), Vienna, An der Wien, 22 Feb 1929, arr. E. W. Korngold

H. Hutten: 'Leo Fall, ein neuer Operettenkomponist', *Musik für Alle* (Berlin, 1908)

F. Lehár, L. Kartousch and H. Marischka: 'Zum Tode Leo Falls', *Die Stunde* [Vienna] (1925)

W. Zimmerli: 'Leo Fall und sein kompositorisches Werk', *Schweizer Musiker-Revue* (1949); repr. as *Leo Fall* (Zürich, 1957)

R. Bernauer: *Das Theater meines Lebens* (Berlin, 1955)

ANDREW LAMB

Falla (y Matheu), Manuel (María) de (los Dolores) (*b* Cádiz, 23 Nov 1876; *d* Alta Gracia, Argentina, 14 Nov 1946). Spanish composer. He spent his youth in Cádiz, where his father was a prosperous businessman. Falla was a shy, withdrawn child, privately educated in a provincial society, where music-lovers relied largely on amateur activity. In the background was the wealth of Andalusian folk music. When his parents moved to Madrid in 1897, he had already been making visits to the capital for piano lessons. He enrolled at the Conservatory and finished the seven-year course in two years.

Madrid offered wider but still limited horizons. Grand opera, symphonic and church music (the glories of the Spanish past being past indeed) all languished. The only genre offering an opening to a young composer anxious to write more than salon pieces was the zarzuela. This form, modest but not disreputable, did not attract Falla. Nonetheless he applied himself and wrote a still uncertain number of zarzuelas, three of them in collaboration with Amadeo Vives. Of these only one, *Los amores de la Inés*, was performed. In these years Falla was stimulated by a theoretical work, Louis Lucas' *L'acoustique nouvelle* (1854), and by the music and personality of the eminent composer and musicologist Felipe Pedrell (1841–1922), who for a short but vital period became Falla's teacher. Pedrell gave him a wider view of Spanish folk music and introduced him to the riches of Spanish polyphony and to the excitements of contemporary music in France and Russia.

In 1904 two competitions were announced in Madrid. One was for composition, including one-act operas, the other was for pianists. Falla entered, and won, both. The rules of the opera competition contained a clause appearing to ensure public performance of the winning work 'in a Madrid theatre'. Falla submitted *La vida breve*. Having scented an opportunity, if he won, to escape to the Paris he longed for, he was bitterly disappointed when no production materialized. Eventually, after touring in France and neighbouring countries as pianist with a mime company, Falla reached Paris in 1907.

He was duly befriended there by Dukas, Debussy, Ravel, and his compatriots Albéniz and the pianist Ricardo Viñes. The score of *La vida breve* proved an invaluable visiting-card. The Four Spanish Pieces for piano and the Three Songs to texts by Gautier were published in 1909 and 1910. Falla earned a modest living (more modest, possibly, than even his frugality required) from teaching, accompanying and translation. Fortunately there was musical nourishment in plenty. The quest for a production of *La vida breve* continued. Reactions in France and elsewhere were friendly but indecisive. At last Nice accepted the work and performed it in 1913. The success stirred the Opéra-Comique in Paris to emulation later the same year. Madrid, belatedly but equally successfully, followed in November 1914.

By that time the outbreak of World War I had forced Falla to return to Madrid, bringing with him the Seven Spanish Folksongs and the soon to be completed *Noches en los jardines de España* for piano and orchestra. Falla's homecoming released in him a spring of creative energy. He wrote at speed the 'gitanería' *El amor brujo* (1916, Madrid) and revised it for concert performance in Madrid in 1916 and 1917; the final revision was staged as a ballet (1925, Paris). The mime-play *El corregidor y la molinera* (based by Martinez Sierra on a story by Alarcón) was expanded and partly rewritten for Dyagilev's Ballets Russes (1919, London), as *El sombrero de tres picos*. This work, a collaboration with the painter Picasso and the choreographer Massine, was as open and extrovert as *El amor brujo* was haunted and claustrophobic and established Falla as an international figure. He also worked on a curious project, a comic opera *Fuego fatuo* ('Will-o'-the-wisp') based on music by Chopin scored by Falla for modest orchestra. Only two of the three acts were orchestrated. Many years later, when the material was found in the archives, a concert suite was prepared from it by Antoni Ros-Marbá (performed at the Granada Festival, 1970).

After the death of his parents in 1919, Falla left Madrid to realize his dream of living in Granada, settling there in 1920 with his sister and faithful companion María del Carmen. In Granada he found new friends, among them his English biographer J. B. Trend and the young poet Federico García Lorca. In 1922 Falla, Lorca and other enthusiasts organized a public competition for *cante hondo*, which was already threatened by commercialism. Ironically, and with the partial exception of the guitar solo *Homenaje: Le tombeau de Claude Debussy* (1921), the *Fantasía baetica* (1919) for piano was the last of Falla's overtly Andalusian compositions. The puppet-opera *El retablo de maese Pedro*, the first work of importance composed in Granada, marked a new development in his music. As a result of his research into folksong and Spanish music, his works had broadened in scope and acquired a more national, less regional, flavour; also he began to exhibit an even greater degree of economy of expression.

In 1926 Falla's attention was drawn to Verdaguer's epic poem in Catalan, *L'Atlàntida*. He decided to use part of it for a choral work, but as the project grew in scope and size it became a 'scenic cantata'. To the end of his days Falla seems to have been undecided whether *Atlántida* (as the title became) was to be staged or not. While his friend, the painter and decorator José María Sert, emphasized the scenic possibilities of *Atlántida*, Falla's Catholicism intensified and his negative attitude towards the stage hardened. He added a codicil to his will which (had it not proved inoperable owing to publishers' contracts) would have prevented the public from seeing any of his ballets and operas performed in theatres. His uneventful life at Granada was interrupted by visits abroad to conduct his music, by increasing ill-health and by winter visits to Majorca in 1933 and 1934. When the political situation deteriorated Falla, opposed equally to military force and to communism, was isolated. The shooting of Lorca in 1936 was a bitter blow. After the Civil War ended in 1939, Falla accepted an invitation to conduct some concerts of Spanish music in Buenos Aires. Carrying the unfinished *Atlántida* with him across the supposed site of the drowned continent, he and his sister left Spain for Argentina. After the exertions of the capital they took refuge in the hills, finally settling at Alta Gracia in the province of Córdoba. For a few more years he worked away at *Atlántida*, lacking the strength to bring the whole into focus. He died in 1946 shortly before his 70th birthday.

The material of *Atlántida*, some of it complete, some complete but not orchestrated, one important section in confusion, was entrusted by the family to Falla's disciple Ernesto Halffter (1905–89), who worked on it for a number of years. Large excerpts from *Atlántida* were finally performed in concert in Barcelona in 1961. A complete staging was given at La Scala in 1962 and productions followed in Berlin and Buenos Aires, but Halffter withdrew the score for revision. After several more years a second, shorter, 'definitive' version was given in concert at the Lucerne Festival in 1976. After further revision an augmented 'definitive' version was heard at the Granada Festival in 1977 and recorded by EMI. The revised edition of the Ricordi vocal score (1962) however reverted to the 'Lucerne' version of 1976.

See also RETABLO DE MAESE PEDRO, EL and VIDA BREVE, LA.

El conde de Villamediana, 1887 (Falla), lost
La Juana y la Petra [La casa de Tócame Roque], c1900 (zar, J. Santero, after D. Ramón de la Cruz), unperf., lost
Limosna de amor, 1901–2 (zar, 1, J. J. Veyán), unperf.
Los amores de la Inés (zar, 1, E. Dugi), Madrid, Cómico, 12 April 1902
El cornetín de órdenes, c1903 (zar, 3), unperf., lost, collab. A. Vives
La cruz de Malta, c1903 (zar), lost, collab. Vives
Prisionero de guerra, c1903–4 (zar), collab. Vives
La vida breve, 1904–5 (lyric drama, 2, C. Fernández Shaw), Nice, Municipal Casino, 1 April 1913
Fuego fatuo, 1918–19 (comic op, 3, G. Martinez Sierra), unperf., suite arr. A. Ros-Marbá
El retablo de maese Pedro, 1919–22 (puppet op, 1, Falla, after M. de Cervantes: *Don Quixote*), concert perf., Seville, S Fernando, 23 March 1923; stage, Paris, home of Princess Edmond de Polignac, 25 June 1923
Atlántida, 1926–46 (cantata escénica, prol., 3 pts, Falla, after J. Verdaguer), inc.; completed by E. Halffter, concert perf. of excerpts, Barcelona, Liceo, 24 Nov 1961; stage, Milan, Scala, 18 June 1962; rev., concert perf., Lucerne, Kunsthaus, 9 Sept 1976

*

J. B. Trend: *Manuel de Falla and Spanish Music* (New York, 1929)
Roland-Manuel: *Manuel de Falla* (Paris, 1930)
A. Sagardia: *Manuel de Falla* (Madrid, 1946)
J. Pahissa: *Manuel de Falla: vida y obra* (Buenos Aires, 1947, 2/1956; Eng. trans., 1954)
J. Jaenisch: *Manuel de Falla und die spanische Musik* (Zürich and Freiburg, 1952)
K. Pahlen: *Manuel de Falla und die Musik in Spanien* (Olten and Freiburg, 1953)
L. Campodonico: *Falla* (Paris, 1959)
R. Arizaga: *Manuel de Falla* (Buenos Aires, 1961)
M. Mila and others: *Manuel de Falla* (Milan, 1962)
F. Sopeña: *Atlántida: introducción a Manuel de Falla* (Madrid, 1962)
Musica d'oggi, v/4–5 (1962) [*Atlántida* issue]
S. Demarquez: *Manuel de Falla* (Paris, 1963; Eng. trans., 1968)
A. Gauthier: *Manuel de Falla: l'homme et son oeuvre* (Paris, 1966)
J. Viniegra: *Manuel de Falla: su vida intime* (Cádiz, 1966)
J. Grunfeld: *Manuel de Falla: Spanien und die neue Musik* (Zürich, 1968)
M. Orozco: *Manuel de Falla: biografía illustrada* (Barcelona, 1968)
G. Fernández Shaw: *Larga historia de 'La vida breve'* (Madrid, 1972)
R. Crichton: *Manuel de Falla: Descriptive Catalogue of his Works* (London, 1976)
——: *Falla* (London, 1982)
A. Gallego: *Catálogo de obras de Manuel de Falla* (Madrid, 1987)
F. Sopeña: *Vida y obra de Falla* (Madrid, 1988)
A. Gallego: *Manuel de Falla y El amor brujo* (Madrid, 1990)
RONALD CRICHTON

Fall of the House of Usher, The (i). Opera by Claude Debussy; *see CHUTE DE LA MAISON USHER, LA.*

Fall of the House of Usher, The (ii). Opera in one act by LARRY SITSKY to a libretto by Gwen Harwood after the story by EDGAR ALLAN POE; Hobart, Tasmania, Theatre Royal, 18 August 1965.

The Narrator (tenor) has been summoned to the house of his friend Roderick Usher (baritone). Roderick, who is on the edge of madness, sits with his fatally ill twin sister, Madeline (soprano); they acknowledge the close and mysterious bond that exists between them. After Madeline apparently dies, Usher and the Narrator witness her entombment. Usher goes mad and the Narrator reads to him; in the background eerie noises resound through the house. Madeline, who has been entombed while still alive, reaches her brother and the two are reunited in death as the house of Usher falls.

Completed in Brisbane in July 1965, *The Fall of the House of Usher* was commissioned for the Hobart Festival of Contemporary Opera and Music. Eight years after its première, on 25 July 1973, it became the first opera to be staged at the Sydney Opera House. The opera's dramatic progression from innocence to evil is equated musically with a progression from singing to semi-spoken delivery. The musical structure is built on ten 12-note rows, half of which are near-clones used to create aspects of Usher's character. *The Fall of the House of Usher* is an instrumentally orientated work with static vocal lines: the musical drama is in the pit and the singers are left with little scope for emotional expression. The work has nevertheless achieved a degree of success not accorded many Australian operas.

The harpsichord part for the overture is Sitsky's *Improvisation for Harpsichord*, composed for the documentary film *Robert Kippel, Junk Sculpture no. 3*. A revised version of the monologue in scene x was composed in Canberra in May 1969. Music for one of the pre-recorded tapes used in the opera was originally composed for the film *Metal Construction*.

THÉRÈSE RADIC

Falmouth Opera Singers. English amateur company founded in 1923 by Maisie and Evelyn RADFORD.

Falsetto (It.; Fr. *fausset*; Ger. *Falsett, Falsettstimme*). The treble range produced by most adult male singers through an artificial technique whereby the vocal chords vibrate only in part. In opera it is chiefly used for special effects, mostly of a comic nature. Moments when the falsetto voice is called upon include Falstaff's imitation, in Verdi's opera, of Mrs Ford's declaration 'Io son di Sir John Falstaff', and it may add to the amusement if the baritone can summon it for an echo-effect in the trio in *Il barbiere di Siviglia*. As a resort for a tenor who cannot produce a full-bodied top note it has long been popularly condemned in Italy, and in other countries the preferred term is normally 'head-voice', though that can mean something different. The terms 'alto' and 'countertenor' also have a different status from falsetto, though it may in practice be difficult to determine at exactly what point a proficient falsettist is entitled to take the more dignified title of 'countertenor'.

J. B. STEANE

Falso canone (It.: 'false canon'). Term used in the discussion of 19th-century Italian opera for a type of ensemble in which the voices enter with the same melodic material, in CANON style; the type originated in the late 18th century and was used by Rossini, Verdi and others.

Falstaff (i) [*Falstaff, ossia Le tre burle* ('Falstaff, or The Three Jokes')]. *Dramma giocoso* in two acts by ANTONIO SALIERI to a libretto by CARLO PROSPERO DEFRANCESCHI after WILLIAM SHAKESPEARE's play *The Merry Wives of Windsor*; Vienna, Kärntnertortheater, 3 January 1799.

One of the first operas to derive its plot from *The Merry Wives of Windsor*, *Falstaff* departs from Shakespeare's play most noticeably in the omission of the young lovers Anne and Fenton. Defranceschi and Salieri focussed their attention on five characters: Mr Ford (tenor) and Mrs Ford (soprano), Mr Slender (baritone) and Mrs Slender (mezzo-soprano), based on Shakespeare's Page and Mistress Page, and Falstaff (bass). The cast is completed by Falstaff's servant Bardolf [Bardolph] (baritone) and Mrs Ford's maid Betty (soprano).

Falstaff contains all the usual ingredients of a late 18th-century *opera buffa*: ensembles predominate over arias; much of the dialogue is set as simple recitative; and there is extensive parody of *seria* style and long, complicated finales. Salieri and his librettist carefully differentiated their characters. Mrs Slender, on reading Falstaff's amorous letter, is outraged; she can think of nothing but revenge and expresses her anger in the quasi-serious 'Vendetta, sì, vendetta!'. Mrs Ford, on the other hand, reacts to her letter, and to the news that Mrs Slender received an identical one, with laughter. The two women express their surprise in the cheerful canonic duet 'La stessa, la stessissima' (used by Beethoven, shortly after the première of Salieri's opera, as the basis for a set of variations). Throughout the opera Mrs Ford is the more carefree and lighthearted.

The women's decision to punish Falstaff leads to an important scene that has no parallel in Shakespeare – and one that must have delighted Viennese audiences – in which Mrs Ford comes to Falstaff disguised as a German girl, speaking in a comic mixture of German and Italian. Falstaff, of course, finds her attractive; she responds to his advances with the pretty aria 'O! die Männer kenn ich schon'. Among the opera's other high points are Falstaff's brilliant *buffo* aria 'Nell'impero di Cupido' and Mr Ford's parody of an *opera seria* rage aria 'Furie che m'agitate'. In spite of its many strengths Salieri's *Falstaff* achieved only moderate success in Vienna and was dropped from the repertory of the court theatres in 1802 after 26 performances.   JOHN A. RICE

Falstaff (ii). *Commedia lirica* in three acts by GIUSEPPE VERDI to a libretto by ARRIGO BOITO after WILLIAM SHAKESPEARE's plays *The Merry Wives of Windsor* and *King Henry IV*; Milan, Teatro alla Scala, 9 February 1893.

Verdi talked intermittently of writing a comic opera during the latter part of his career, but never found a libretto to his taste until, some two years after the success of *Otello* in 1887, his librettist for that opera, Arrigo Boito, suggested a work largely based on Shakespeare's *The Merry Wives of Windsor*. Verdi was immediately enthusiastic about the draft scenario Boito concocted, made relatively few large structural suggestions, and by August 1889 even announced that he was writing a fugue (quite possibly the comic fugue that ends *Falstaff*). Composer and librettist worked closely together during the winter of 1889–90, and by the spring of 1890 the libretto was complete.

The composing of the opera took a considerable time, or rather was carried out in short bursts of activity inter-

Sir John Falstaff	baritone
Fenton	tenor
Dr Caius	tenor
Bardolfo [Bardolph] } *followers of Falstaff*	tenor
Pistola [Pistol] }	bass
Mrs Alice Ford	soprano
Ford *Alice's husband*	baritone
Nannetta *their daughter*	soprano
Mistress Quickly	mezzo-soprano
Mrs Meg Page	mezzo-soprano
Mine Host at the Garter	silent
Robin *Falstaff's page*	silent
Ford's Page	silent

Bourgeoisie and populace, Ford's servants, masquerade of imps, fairies, witches etc.

Setting Windsor, during the reign of Henry IV of England

spersed with long fallow periods. Act 1 was completed – at least in short score – shortly after the libretto was finished, but then Verdi fell into a depression, the deaths of various close friends making him fear he would not live to finish the project. However, the remaining two acts were gradually completed. It seems that, unusually for Verdi, certain scenes were finished out of chronological order (perhaps an indication of the relative independence of individual scenes). By September 1891 the opera was largely complete in short score, and a year later Verdi had finished the orchestration. The première at La Scala, which took place almost to the day six years after *Otello*, was conducted by Edoardo Mascheroni; the cast included Victor Maurel (Falstaff), Antonio Pini-Corsi (Ford), Edoardo Garbin (Fenton), Adelina Stehle (Nannetta) and Giuseppina Pasqua (Mistress Quickly). It was, perhaps inevitably at this stage of Verdi's career, a huge triumph, and was soon seen in the major international opera houses. Verdi made various minor changes to the score (notably recomposing and shortening the final minutes of Act 3 scene i) during these early revivals. *Falstaff* has always retained its place in the international repertory, though it is far less frequently heard than many of the middle-period works.

ACT 1.i *Inside the Garter Inn* An offbeat C major chord and descending arpeggio set in immediate motion a scene (indeed an opera) that is remarkable above all for its sense of rapid change and relentless forward movement. Falstaff, who is busy sealing two letters as the curtain rises, is upbraided by Dr Caius, who accuses him of causing drunken confusion in Caius's house. Falstaff calmly accepts the charge, at which Caius accuses Pistol and Bardolph of getting him drunk and stealing his money. Pistol challenges the doctor to a mock duel and exchanges a furious round of insults with him. But Caius has had enough, and storms out after making a solemn promise never to get drunk with such scoundrels again. This hectic first episode is dominated by two main themes: the arpeggiated idea that opened the opera and a contrasting second theme of more regular tread, appearing as Falstaff replies to Caius's first accusation. The two themes are played out in an overtly developmental manner, with various comic allusions to sonata form, not least in the ineptly contrapuntal 'Amen' intoned by Pistol and Bardolph as Caius leaves and the 'sonata' comes to a close.

After some vain searching for funds, Falstaff lambasts his companions before celebrating his enormous belly in a suitably grandiose climax. Then, in a relatively stable musical episode, the central thread of the drama is first put forth: Falstaff reveals that he has amorous designs on both Alice Ford and Meg Page, the wives of rich townsfolk. But Pistol and Bardolph refuse to deliver his love letters, saying it is beneath their 'honour' to do so. Falstaff sends off his page with the letters and then, in the famous 'Onore' monologue, excoriates the traitors and their highflown ideals. The solo is typical of the opera as a whole, rapidly shifting in mood, full of ironic references, a veritable index of startling orchestral combinations and textures. As C major makes a late, triumphant return, Falstaff takes up a broom and drives his followers from the room.

1.ii *The garden outside Ford's house* A scherzo-like introduction leads in Meg and Mistress Quickly, who meet Alice and Nannetta on the threshold of Alice's house. Meg and Alice discover that Falstaff has sent them identical letters, extracts from which they quote, first to the mournful accompaniment of an english horn, later to a passionately lyrical phrase, undermined at the final cadence by mocking vocal trills. In an elaborate unaccompanied quartet, they pour scorn on the amorous knight and vow to revenge themselves on him. From the other side of the stage appears a male quintet (Fenton, Caius, Bardolph, Pistol and Ford) who, unaware of the ladies, superimpose their own ensemble. As the ladies fade into the background, Bardolph and Pistol warn Ford of Falstaff's designs; Ford vows to keep a close watch. The ladies return and the two groups, at the sight of each other, disperse, leaving Fenton and Nannetta together for the first of their brief love duets, 'Labbra di foco'. One of Boito's early ideas for the drama was to present the young lovers 'as one sprinkles sugar on a tart, to sprinkle the whole comedy with [their] love', and Verdi responded by weaving round them a musical world quite separate from the main body of the score: relaxed and lyrical, shot through with delicate chromaticism and soft orchestral textures. But the spell is soon broken: the ladies return and resolve to send Quickly as their go-between with

Falstaff. Nannetta and Fenton snatch a further few moments; then the men reappear, Ford announcing that he will visit Falstaff in disguise. The finale of the scene involves a masterly superimposition of the women's and men's ensembles. The ladies have the last word: a triumphantly derisive reprise of Falstaff's most passionate epistolary style.

ACT 2.i *The Garter Inn* The opening of the act is extraordinary – even in the context of *Falstaff* – for the extravagant manner in which musical ideas match verbal tags: first as Pistol and Bardolph make elaborate, chest-beating penance before Falstaff; then as Mistress Quickly introduces herself with a low 'Reverenza!'; then as she expresses the amorous states of Alice and Meg with the phrase 'Povera donna!'; and finally as she makes an appointment for Falstaff with the former, 'dalle due alle tre' ('between two and three'). Quickly leaves, and Falstaff has time for a gleeful episode of self-congratulation, 'Va, vecchio John', before 'Mastro Fontana' (Ford in disguise) is shown in. In the ensuing duet, Fontana offers Falstaff money to seduce one Alice Ford (who will thus be made easier for Fontana to conquer); and Falstaff gleefully agrees, saying that he has already arranged an appointment 'between two and three'. The passage carries vague echoes of earlier 19th-century formal practice – perhaps particularly in the cabaletta-like close – but is more usefully seen as a kind of musical prose, in constant flux as the moods of the principals swing to and fro. Highlights include the magnificent orchestral depiction of the money Ford offers Falstaff; Ford's passionate declaration of his feelings for Alice (a hint of the deeply serious tone that will soon break through); and Falstaff's rousing conclusion in 'Te lo cornifico' ('I'll cuckold him for you'). As the knight goes off to pretty himself, Ford is left alone to brood on what he has heard (the impassioned arioso 'È sogno?'). For the first and only time, the opera swings for an extended period into the language of serious opera: with punning horn calls and tortured fragments of the preceding duet (in particular 'dalle due alle tre'), Ford contemplates what he believes is his wife's deception. However, no sooner has Verdi sealed the mono-

1. 'Falstaff' (Verdi): Act 2 scene ii (a room in Ford's house) in the original production at La Scala, Milan (9 February 1893), with sets and costumes by Adolf Hohenstein: engraving from 'L'illustrazione italiana' (19 February 1893)

logue with a stunning orchestral climax than there is yet another stylistic volte-face: to a delicate, trilling violin melody, Falstaff appears, tricked out in his finest clothes; the two men show exaggerated politeness before leaving the scene together to an orchestral reprise of 'Va, vecchio John'. Our knight, the orchestra seems to tell us, is winning the day.

2.ii *A room in Ford's house* A bustling string introduction ushers in Alice and Meg. They are soon joined by Quickly, who gives a detailed narrative of her interview with Falstaff, replete with mocking repetitions of 'dalle due alle tre'. Realizing that the hour of assignation is almost upon them, the women hurry about their preparations, ushering in a large laundry basket; but the busy mood is interrupted by Nannetta, who tearfully reveals that Ford has ordered her to marry old Dr Caius. Alice will have none of this, and assures Nannetta of her support. Preparations then continue, with Alice directing operations and briefly coming to the fore with 'Gaie comari di Windsor!', one of the few, brief moments (at least before the final scene) in which Verdi even hints at a conventional solo aria. Alice then settles down to strum her lute, and is soon joined by Falstaff, who offers elaborate courtship with an ornamented song of Beckmesser-like awkwardness before celebrating his younger, nimbler self in the delightful vignette, 'Quand'ero paggio del Duca di Norfolk'.

However, just as the courtship reaches an intimate stage, Quickly rushes in to announce the imminent arrival of Meg Page. The music dives into a furious Allegro agitato, so beginning the first movement of a conventionally structured but highly complex concertato finale. This first section is in a near-constant state of manic energy: Falstaff hides behind a screen as Meg enters to announce the arrival of an insanely jealous Ford; Ford appears at the head of a band of followers, searches the laundry basket, then rushes off to seek his wife's lover elsewhere; Falstaff is then wedged painfully into the basket and covered with dirty clothes. A brief moment of calm ensues as Nannetta and Fenton meet and slip behind the screen for a few moments together, but very soon the energy is again released as the men reappear to continue their search. The music grinds to a halt as a loud kiss is heard behind the screen: the men are sure they have trapped their quarry, and the realization precipitates the second movement of the concertato, the Andante 'Se t'agguanto!'. In the traditional way, this movement forms a still centre during which all can reflect on their contrasting positions: the men cautiously prepare to pounce; the women vow to keep the game alive; Falstaff emits muffled cries from his suffocating confinement; and Nannetta and Fenton, oblivious to all, rise above the ensemble in lyrically expansive phrases. Eventually the spell is broken. The men overturn the screen, only to find Nannetta and Fenton, the latter angrily rebuked by Ford. But Bardolph seems to see Falstaff outside, and the men rush off again, allowing the women to summon their pages who – with a huge effort – hoist the basket up to the window. The men return just in time to see Falstaff tipped into the river below, and the act closes with a riotous fanfare of triumph.

ACT 3.i *Outside the Garter Inn* As Boito remarked in a letter to Verdi, the problem in finding dramatic form for comic subjects was one of predictability: how to convince the audience that they should stay for the third act when the unravelling of the plot is already clear. In the case of *Falstaff* this problem is acute, as the protagonist's most clamorous punishment has already been inflicted by the close of Act 2. The startlingly original solution Boito and Verdi chose to this problem will be revealed in the second half of this act: but perhaps this first scene suffers slightly, the tempo of the opera winding down, its direction wavering. Falstaff's opening monologue is certainly the most fragmented passage in the opera, occasional reminiscences jostling with a series of violent changes as the knight bemoans his disgrace, calls for wine, and finally revives as the liquor tingles through his body to the accompaniment of a magnificent orchestral trill. The ensuing duet with Quickly repeats some of the motifs of their earlier encounter as Falstaff is again convinced of Alice's affection. A new assignation is made: Falstaff is to await his intended paramour at midnight under Herne's Oak in the Royal Park, disguised as the Black Huntsman. Quickly paints an evocative picture of the supernatural ambience and, as she leads Falstaff into the inn, the evocation is taken up by Alice, who has been observing the scene with Ford, Meg, Nannetta, Fenton and Caius. The scene then plays itself out in a relaxed, French-influenced musical setting, as the plotters decide on their disguises. Quickly overhears Ford and Caius, who are planning Caius's marriage to Nannetta that very night, and privately vows to stop them.

3.ii *Windsor forest* Distant horn-calls introduce Fenton, whose extended solo immediately marks the departure taken in this final scene, which for the most part is structured in discrete units, without the rapid changes that characterize the remainder of the opera. And the delicate, nocturnal ambience serves further to make this final scene self-contained, separate in both formal and timbral terms from the main drama, thus sidestepping the danger of anticlimax that Boito had feared. That the scene begins with Fenton's extended sonnet, 'Dal labbro il canto', is also significant, because the delicate atmosphere established in intervals by the young lovers through the opera now becomes the dominant strain in the music.

Fenton is rudely interrupted by Alice, who provides him with a disguise before they rush off to take their positions. Falstaff appears and solemnly counts the 12 bells of midnight. He is joined by Alice, and a fleeting repetition of their earlier meeting ensues before Meg enters to warn of an approaching pack of witches. As Falstaff throws himself to the ground, fearing death if he sees these supernatural beings, Nannetta begins a delicate invocation that eventually flowers into 'Sul fil d'un soffio etesio', yet another aria suffused with the soft orchestral colours that characterize this scene. A sudden Prestissimo ushers in the rest of the cast, who begin tormenting Falstaff in earnest. Their gleeful chorus, 'Pizzica, pizzica', later adorned with mock religious chanting, is halted only when Bardolph gets carried away and allows his hood to slip. Falstaff immediately recognizes him and bestows on him a generous torrent of abuse. Soon the entire deception is revealed, Falstaff assuming new stature in his philosophical acceptance of what has befallen him.

A gentle minuet introduces Caius and 'The Queen of the Fairies' (whom Caius thinks is Nannetta). They are joined by another couple and both pairs receive Ford's blessing. But with Ford's final words, the deception is revealed: 'The Queen of the Fairies' turns out to be Bardolph in disguise, and the other couple are – of course – Fenton and Nannetta. This time it is Ford's

2. Adolf Hohenstein's design for Falstaff's disguise in Act 3 of the original production of Verdi's opera at La Scala, Milan, 9 February 1893

comic context, it furnishes an important means of filling the musical space with an endless variety of colours. And this is by no means the only level of diversification in the score, for it is clear that Verdi was fully aware of the opera's 'polyphonic' texture and was – on occasion – even prepared to interrupt the drama in order to enhance it. As he said in a letter to Boito discussing Fenton's *sonetto* in Act 3, 'as far as the drama goes we could do without it; but ... the whole piece provides me with a new colour for the musical palette'.

These new aspects, possible only through the medium of comedy, served to stimulate Verdi's creative imagination to new levels of fecundity. In the midst of an increasingly fragmented aesthetic world, he was able to follow the whim of the moment, to gaze back serenely on past achievements and, as he said so many times in letters to Boito, simply to enjoy himself. Few would deny how richly Verdi deserved this final triumph, or how heartening a message *Falstaff* offers. The opera leaves us with a musical image that exactly reflects those famous photographs of Verdi in his last years: an old man, in black hat, with eyes that have lived through a lifetime of struggle, smiling out wisely at the world.

For further illustration *see* MAUREL, VICTOR.   ROGER PARKER

Fancelli, Giuseppe (*b* Florence, 24 Nov 1833; *d* Florence, 23 Dec 1887). Italian tenor. Of humble origins, he made his début in Milan as the Fisherman in *Guillaume Tell*. After engagements in Ancona, Rome and Trieste, he sang Vasco da Gama in Meyerbeer's *L'Africaine* at La Scala (1866) and in the same year made his London début at Covent Garden as Alfredo, later singing Edgardo, Elvino, Ernesto, Raoul and Tonio (*La fille du régiment*). His most important appearance was as Radames in the first Italian performance of *Aida*, at La Scala in 1872. His robust, vibrant voice, with its true intonation and particularly strong upper register, was effective in many roles, but he lacked musical education and his acting ability was severely limited.

ES (R. Celletti)   ELIZABETH FORBES

turn to admit defeat and (the minuet returning) he agrees to accept his daughter's marriage. Falstaff leads off the final ensemble, a comic fugue to the words 'Tutto nel mondo è burla' ('Everything in the world is a joke'). The ironic reference to an academic form, the polyphony and confusion of voices and, most of all, the constant, driving energy of the piece is a fitting end to Verdi's final opera.

*   *   *

Perhaps the most immediately obvious level of difference between *Falstaff* and all Verdi's previous operas lies in the music's tendency to respond in unprecedented detail to the verbal element of the drama. In much of the score, but especially in the great duets and monologues, the listener is bombarded by a stunning diversity of rhythms, orchestral textures, melodic motifs and harmonic devices. Passages that in earlier times would have furnished material for an entire number here crowd in on each other, shouldering themselves unceremoniously to the fore in bewildering succession. And a large number of these fresh ideas spring in a direct and literal way from the words. Such exaggerated literalism would be obtrusive in a tragic opera, in which the need for underlying emotional communication often overrides responses to individual words. But here, in the

Fanciulla del West, La ('The Girl of the West' [*The Girl of the Golden West*]). Opera in three acts by GIACOMO PUCCINI to a libretto by Guelfo Civinini and CARLO ZANGARINI after DAVID BELASCO's play *The Girl of the Golden West*; New York, Metropolitan Opera House, 10 December 1910.

Early in 1907, during his first visit to New York for the Metropolitan premières of *Manon Lescaut* and *Madama Butterfly*, Puccini saw three of Belasco's plays performed on Broadway, among them *The Girl of the Golden West*. He was not enthusiastic. 'I like the ambience of the West', he wrote to Tito Ricordi (ii), 'but in all the "pièces" I've seen I've found only a few scenes here and there. Never a simple thread, all muddle and at times bad taste and old hat'. However, a seed had been sown; and when at the end of May Puccini went to London, his friend Sybil Seligman urged him to consider Belasco's drama, of which she procured him an Italian translation. By July Puccini was firmly decided. He wrote to his publisher asking him to obtain the rights as well as the author's permission to make certain changes to the action (these would amount to transferring the bible-class from the third act to the first and amalgamating Acts 3 and 4, where the setting would be a Californian forest). Of his previous librettists, Giacosa

Minnie	soprano
Jack Rance *sheriff*	baritone
Dick Johnson/Ramerrez *bandit*	tenor
Nick *bartender at the Polka saloon*	tenor
Ashby *Wells Fargo agent*	bass
Sonora	baritone
Trin	tenor
Sid	baritone
Bello	baritone
Harry *miners*	tenor
Joe	tenor
Happy	baritone
Larkens	bass
Billy Jackrabbit *a Red Indian*	bass
Wowkle *his squaw*	mezzo-soprano
Jake Wallace *a travelling camp minstrel*	baritone
José Castro (*mestizo*) *one of Ramerrez's band*	bass
The Pony Express Rider	tenor

Men of the camp and boys of the ridge

Setting A miners' camp at the foot of the Cloudy Mountains, California, during the gold rush, 1849–50

was dead and Illica fully engaged on a libretto about Marie Antoinette (for which Puccini had contracted but which he never set). Tito Ricordi indicated Carlo Zangarini as the ideal collaborator, especially since his mother was American. In August the contracts were signed for what Puccini foretold would prove 'a second *Bohème*, only stronger, bolder and more spacious'. Zangarini completed the libretto in January 1908. Puccini was satisfied with his general scheme but insisted that he take on a partner to polish the details. Zangarini threatened to go to law, but eventually agreed to collaborate with the Livornese poet Guelfo Civinini. By May the first two acts had been reworked to Puccini's satisfaction and he was able to begin composition, but in October a domestic tragedy occurred (*see* PUCCINI, GIACOMO, §4) which caused a hiatus of nine months. Resuming in August 1909, Puccini completed the score a year later. To Sybil Seligman goes the credit for settling on the exact title. The opera was dedicated to the British queen, Alexandra.

In November 1910 Puccini set sail for America for what would be the first world première ever held at the Metropolitan. No expense had been spared. The cast included Emmy Destinn (Minnie), Enrico Caruso (Dick Johnson) and Pasquale Amato (Jack Rance), with Antonio Pini-Corsi, creator of Schaunard in *La bohème*, in the minute role of Happy. The conductor was Toscanini. Belasco himself assisted Tito Ricordi with the production. To all appearances the opera was a triumphant success, the composer receiving 55 curtain calls, but the critics were guarded. The Covent Garden première followed on 29 May 1911, again in Puccini's presence, conducted by Cleofonte Campanini with Emmy Destinn (Minnie), Amadeo Bassi (Johnson) and the Metropolitan's Sonora, Dinh Gilly as Jack Rance. There the reception was less encouraging. *La fanciulla del West* was finally introduced to Italy at the Teatro Costanzi, Rome, on 12 June that year under Toscanini, with Eugenia Burzio (Minnie), Amadeo Bassi (Johnson) and Pasquale Amato (Rance), but it achieved no more than a *succès d'estime*. Although Puccini declared it his best opera to date it failed to enter the general repertory; nor until late in the century was it estimated at its true

worth. However, the tenor solo from Act 3, 'Ch'ella mi creda libero e lontano', is said to have been sung by Italian troops during World War I as an equivalent to the English song 'It's a long way to Tipperary'.

ACT 1 *The Polka saloon, at sunset* A prelude, intended by Puccini to evoke the vast Californian forest, presents two important ideas: the lyrical theme associated with the hero and heroine's first embrace (ex.1) and a modified version of the cake-walk motif

Ex.1 Allegro non troppo

Ex.2 Allegro vibrato

which on its later appearance (ex.2) will connote the bandit Ramerrez. Then the distant voices of the approaching miners are heard. They enter in twos and threes to a hoedown theme, to be welcomed by Nick. Happy, Harry, Bello and Joe sit down to a game of faro with Sid as banker. Jake Wallace regales the company with the nostalgic song 'Che faranno i vecchi miei' (ex.3,

Ex.3
JAKE WALLACE
Andante tranquillo

Che fa - ran - noi vec-chi miei là lon - ta - no, là lon-

- ta - no? che fa - ran - no ___

['What will my old folks be doing there, far away?']

one of the most frequently repeated motifs in the opera), which causes Larkens to break down in tears. All present contribute money for his passage home. Sid is caught cheating and the miners threaten to hang him, but Rance pins a two of spades to his lapel as a mark of shame and has him thrown out of the saloon. Ashby arrives with news of the imminent capture of the bandit Ramerrez. A quarrel breaks out between Rance and Sonora, both in love with Minnie, and Sonora draws a revolver. Trin grabs his arm and diverts the shot. The appearance of Minnie herself to a broad, wide-intervalled theme (ex.4) calms the atmosphere. The

Ex.4 Andante vibrato

miners offer her their modest gifts and settle down to a bible-class, which she takes. The Pony Express Rider arrives with the mail and Ashby interrogates him about one Nina Micheltorena, the bandit's mistress, who is expected to reveal his whereabouts. The men go into the adjoining dance hall leaving Rance alone with Minnie. He declares his love for her and talks of his unhappy background ('Minnie, dalla mia casa'). She, knowing him to be already married, imagines a different picture of domestic bliss based on memories of her own happy childhood ('Laggiù nel Soledad, ero piccina'). Nick returns with a stranger, whose identity is betrayed to the audience by the 'Ramerrez' motif (see ex.2). He gives his name as Johnson. Rance takes an instant dislike to him and orders the men to force him to account for his presence. But Minnie, who remembers once meeting him on the road, vouches for him. A waltz (ex.5) is struck up in the hall, where Minnie and Johnson dance together.

Ex.5

Ashby and a group of men enter from outside dragging in José Castro. Pretending to have deserted Ramerrez's band, Castro promises to lead them to the chief. His real purpose is to draw the miners away from the Polka so that Ramerrez may rob the saloon. When Johnson re-enters Castro manages to whisper to him his plan – a whistle outside will be the signal for him to proceed. The miners prepare to ride away with Castro, leaving Minnie to guard their earnings. She and Johnson express their dawning sympathy for one another in a duet based mainly on a reprise of the waltz melody. The whistle is heard but Johnson takes no action. He accepts Minnie's invitation to visit her later at her mountain hut, then leaves. Nick returns to find Minnie absorbed in the

recollection of Johnson's last words to her – that she has the face of an angel. To echoes of ex.4 the curtain falls.

ACT 2 *Minnie's cabin, later that evening* Wowkle sings to her child a lullaby that develops into a duet with Billy Jackrabbit as both think vaguely of getting married. Minnie enters, orders supper for two and with subdued excitement prepares to receive her visitor. Johnson arrives; Minnie fends off his attempt to embrace her and to a recall of the waltz they begin a decorous conversation, during which Minnie describes her life at the camp ('Oh, se sapeste'). As Wowkle brings the food the orchestra outlines a pentatonic theme (ex.6)

Ex.6

loosely related to the waltz that will frame the love duet, whose central movement is evolved from ex.1, initially twisted into a whole-tone scale. Johnson offers to leave, but a blizzard makes it necessary for him to stay the night. The posse headed by Rance knock at the door. After concealing Johnson behind a curtain Minnie admits them. They are concerned for her safety, Rance tells her, having discovered that Johnson is in fact Ramerrez and is still in the neighbourhood. Minnie sends them away, then rounds angrily on her guest. Remorsefully he makes excuses for his past life, which he now intends to abandon for ever. Minnie can forgive the bandit, but not the man who stole her first kiss under false pretences, and she orders him out of the house. A shot rings out, and he staggers back against the door wounded. Minnie helps him into the attic before Rance arrives, certain that he has found his man. Minnie defies him to search the premises. Thwarted, Rance is about to leave when a drop of blood falls from the ceiling onto his hand. Ignoring Minnie's protests he orders Johnson

Emmy Destinn as Minnie and Pasquale Amato as Jack Rance (Caruso, as Dick Johnson, has collapsed at the table) in Act 2 of the original production of Puccini's 'La fanciulla del West' at the Metropolitan Opera House, New York, 10 December 1910

to come down. Johnson does so and collapses in a faint. Minnie plays her last card. Knowing Rance to be a gambler she challenges him to a game of poker. If he wins, he may take her as his 'wife'; if he loses then Johnson belongs to her. Rance accepts, and is on the point of winning when she pretends to feel faint; as he goes to fetch her a glass of water she takes a new pack of cards from her stocking and lays out a winning hand. He accepts her victory with a bad grace.

ACT 3 *A clearing in the Californian forest at dawn, some time later* Rance and Nick are brooding before a fire; Ashby, Billy Jackrabbit and several miners are sleeping nearby. Nick attempts to console Rance, commending his gallant behaviour in dealing with Minnie. At the sound of distant voices Ashby and the men wake up and joyfully predict the bandit's capture. Rance exults in the prospect of revenge, while Ashby hurries away to join the man-hunt. As the orchestra builds up an impressive action scene recalling previous themes, various miners posted on the look-out describe Johnson's attempts to elude his pursuers. He is brought in tethered to his horse to face an accusing mob. Billy Jackrabbit is ordered to prepare a noose for the lynching, but is secretly bribed by Nick to take his time. Johnson proudly defends himself against the charge of murder. In the few minutes remaining to him he asks only that Minnie never be told of his fate. In the aria 'Ch'ella mi creda libero e lontano', the one self-contained piece in the entire score, he expresses the wish that she may believe him to have gone free to lead a better life in some distant land. Enraged, Rance punches him in the face; but Johnson's words have already caused the men to hesitate. Minnie rides in on horseback to a dissonantly harmonized version of ex.4. When her pleas for mercy prove vain she rushes to Johnson's side, draws a pistol and threatens to shoot both him and herself. During the ensemble that follows opinion among the miners is divided. In the end it is Sonora who sways the balance. Johnson is released, and as he and Minnie ride away to a future of happiness the men bid their beloved 'sister' a sorrowful farewell to the strains of ex.3.

* * *

La fanciulla del West is a remarkable instance of self-renewal on the part of a composer who would seem to have exhausted a vein in which feminine softness predominates. The opera's atmosphere is unyieldingly masculine, at times brutal, the harmonies more astringent than ever before with plentiful use of whole-tone chords and unresolved dissonances, the rhythms vigorous, sometimes syncopated and the lyrical moments comparatively few. The influence of Debussy and the Richard Strauss of *Salome* is clear, though, as always, perfectly integrated within the composer's personal style. The Californian ambience is evoked with the aid of American folktunes and folkdances, either authentic or imitated, with a Red Indian chant to characterize Billy Jackrabbit and his squaw. Minnie is unique among Puccini's heroines – cheerfully authoritative with a touch of the Puritan schoolmarm yet susceptible to tender passion and ready to compromise her strict principles in order to save the life of the man she loves.

Orchestrally *La fanciulla del West* is Puccini's most ambitious undertaking before *Turandot*, his forces including quadruple woodwind, two harps and an assortment of percussion, from all of which he distilled a vast range of instrumental colour from the delicate to the barbaric. Though it has never attained the easy popularity of its three predecessors, the opera has always won the respect of musicians.   JULIAN BUDDEN

Fando (Rais), Urbano (*b* Barcelona, 1855; *d* Porto, Portugal, 1909 or 1911). Spanish composer. He received a musical training as a choirboy of the Merced Church in Barcelona, and then studied further at the Conservatorio del Liceo. He became chorus master at the Teatro del Liceo, conductor at various theatres and during the 1890s composed numerous popular zarzuelas. His major success was with *Lo somni de l'Ignoscencia* (1895), one of several works with Catalan librettos by Conrad Colomer. Later Fando concentrated on conducting for touring zarzuela companies, and it was on one such tour that he died.

all zarzuelas

L'illa tranquilla (Fando), 1894; El princep del Congo (Fando), 1894; Lo somni de l'Ignoscencia (1, C. Colomer), Barcelona, Jardín Español, 5 June 1895; L'amich Motas, 1896; Verdalet, pare i fill del commers de Barcelona (Colomer), Barcelona, Jardín Español, 26 May 1896; Un debut, Barcelona, June 1896; La llissó de dibuix, 1896; Ni él es él ni yo soy yo, Madrid, 1897

*

Enciclopedia universal ilustrada europeo-americana (Barcelona, 1907–30)

R. Alier and others: *El libro de la zarzuela* (Barcelona, 1982, 2/1986 as *Diccionario de la zarzuela*)   ANDREW LAMB

Fane, John, 11th Earl of Westmorland. *See* BURGHERSH.

Fano. Italian city in the Marche region. In 1665, 17 local noblemen, including the architect Giacomo Torelli, asked permission to establish a permanent stage and boxes to let for profit in the hall of the Palazzo del Podestà in the Piazza Maggiore (now the Piazza 20 Settembre); the hall had for some time been used to perform comedies. Torelli designed the new theatre with four rows of 21 boxes each and a gallery, on an irregular U-shaped plan that was later frequently cited in treatises on theatre architecture. The Teatro della Fortuna, as it was named, opened in June 1677. It was managed for the next 12 years by five local nobles, including Torelli, and then passed to the municipality. There were seasons for Carnival and for the July Fair. In 1718–19 Ferdinando Bibiena worked there. The theatre was restored in 1804 by Pietro Ghinelli; it was closed in 1839 because of dilapidation and demolished two years later. Between 1845 and 1863 the municipality built a new theatre on a plan by Luigi Poletti (three rows of 21 boxes each and a gallery, in a horseshoe shape) on the same site. While work was in progress, opera seasons were held in a provisional theatre in the large hall of the Palazzo Malatestiano. The new Fortuna was inaugurated on 24 August 1863 with *Il trovatore* and was in use until 1944, when it sustained war damage. It is in the process of restoration.

*

ES (E. Povoledo)

S. Tomani Amiani: *Del teatro antico Della Fortuna in Fano e della sua riedificazione* (Sanseverino Marche, 1867); repr. in *Guida storica artistica di Fano*, ed. F. Battistelli (Pesaro, 1981)

A. Mabellini: 'La demolizione del palazzo della Ragione di Fano deliberata nel 1841 per la costruzione del nuovo Teatro della Fortuna', *Studia picena*, xiv (1939), 7–18

F. Battistelli: *L'antico e il nuovo Teatro della Fortuna di Fano (1677–1944)* (Fano, 1972)   PAOLO FABBRI

Fantozzi, Maria Marchetti. *See* MARCHETTI FANTOZZI, MARIA.

Faramondo ('Pharamond'). Opera in three acts by GEORGE FRIDERIC HANDEL to a libretto anonymously adapted from APOSTOLO ZENO's *Faramondo* (1699, Venice), as revised for Francesco Gasparini (1720, Rome); London, King's Theatre, 3 January 1738.

Handel composed *Faramondo* between 15 November and 24 December 1737. (He broke off work after completing Act 2 to write the anthem *The Ways of Zion do Mourn* for the funeral of Queen Caroline.) The libretto is based on the early legendary history of France as elaborated at notorious length in La Calprenède's pseudo-historical romance *Pharamond* (1661–70). (Pharamond was supposedly king of the Franks from about 420 to 428.) In the original production the distinguished mezzo-soprano castrato Gaetano Majorano, known as Caffarelli, sang Faramondo; Faramondo's sister Clotilde was sung by Elisabeth du Parc ('La Francesina', soprano), Gustavo, King of the Cimbrians, by Antonio Montagnana (bass), his son Adolfo and his daughter Rosimonda by Margherita Chimenti ('La Droghierina', soprano) and Maria Antonia Marchesini ('La Lucchesina', mezzo-soprano), Gernando, King of the Svevi, by Antonia Merighi (contralto), Gustavo's general Teobaldo by Antonio Lottini (bass), and Childerico, Teobaldo's supposed son, by William Savage. (Childerico's part is written for soprano, but Savage's name is entered against the tenor part of the final chorus. Probably his voice had just broken, and the role – which has no arias – was sung an octave lower than written; much of it seems to have been cut from some performances.)

Faramondo reopened the 1737–8 season at the King's Theatre (interrupted by the death of the queen), to which Handel had returned (sharing the season with Pescetti) after three years at Covent Garden. The opera had an initial run of seven performances and one other on 16 May 1738, near the end of the season. Handel never revived it, and it was not heard again until the production at the Landestheater in Halle on 5 March 1976. The first British revival was at Reading University on 8 May 1981.

The plot, treating the planned vengeance of King Gustavo on Faramondo for the supposed murder of one of his sons, and complicated by multiple deceptions and rivalries in love, is exceptionally tortuous even for a serious opera of this period, and it culminates in a *Trovatore*-like discovery of an exchange of identity long ago between children (which releases Gustavo from his oath of vengeance). The reduction of recitatives to a bare minimum, found in most of Handel's later operas, is taken to an extreme in *Faramondo*, but the result in the theatre is not necessarily incomprehensible, as has been claimed. It may be, however, that new dramatic situations are often established too quickly to allow the arias their full impact, and the characters do not emerge strongly as individuals. The actual quality of the music is hard to fault, lively major-key arias in the new pre-classical manner are mixed effectively with those in Handel's normal contrapuntal style. Several arias are without initial ritornellos, or only short ones, emphasizing the swift-moving nature of the action. The part of Rosimonda is treated with special sympathy, her first and last arias ('Vanne, che più ti miro' and 'Sappi, crudel io t'amo') being particularly moving, as is also the tender duet for Adolfo and Clotilde near the start of Act 3. The finale is unusually extended, beginning as an aria for Faramondo but leading directly into the closing chorus.   ANTHONY HICKS

Farberman, Harold (*b* New York, 2 Nov 1929). American composer. After studying at the Juilliard School he was percussionist and timpanist in the Boston SO for 12 years. His one-act chamber opera *Medea* (libretto by W. Van Lennep), an expressionist work, was first performed in Boston on 26 March 1961. *The Losers*, in two acts, to a libretto by B. Fried (New York, 26 March 1971), on a story about a Californian motor-bike gang, is scored for an ensemble including jazz quartet, a large percussion section and a string trio. It was the first opera commissioned by the American Opera Theater of the Juilliard School after its move to Lincoln Center. Farberman, whose output also includes orchestral and chamber music, was conductor of the Oakland SO, 1971–9, and has appeared widely as a guest conductor.

R. H. Kornick: *Recent American Opera: a Production Guide* (New York, 1991), 96–7

Farinelli [Broschi, Carlo; Farinello] (*b* Andria, Apulia, 24 Jan 1705; *d* Bologna, 15 July 1782). Italian soprano castrato, brother of RICCARDO BROSCHI. He was probably first trained by his father, then by Porpora. He made his début as a singer in Naples in 1720, and developed his operatic career between 1722 and 1724 with productions in Naples and Rome (works mainly by L. A. Predieri and Porpora); by 1723, when he appeared in the title role of Porpora's *Adelaide*, he had become a principal singer, allotted as many virtuoso arias of extended dimensions as any singer in the cast. From 1724 to 1734 he enjoyed extraordinary success in a wide variety of relatively brief engagements all over Europe, singing roles by most of the principal composers of his day. In 1734 Farinelli joined Porpora and Handel's competitors at the Opera of the Nobility in London, staying for three years (with a break and a visit to Paris in 1736). He was then at the height of his powers. Paolo Rolli wrote: 'Farinelli was a revelation to me, for I realized that till I had heard him I had heard only a small part of what human song can achieve whereas I now conceive that I have heard all there is to hear'.

Leaving the public stage in 1737, Farinelli began a remarkable Spanish career, spanning more than two decades in the service of Philip V (whose deep depression was greatly mitigated by Farinelli's singing) and Ferdinand VI. His broad responsibilities included the importation of Hungarian horses, the redirection of the River Tagus, the direction of music at the royal chapel, the redesign of the royal opera house and the production there of a long series of sumptuously staged Italian operas with music by such composers as Corselli, Corradini, Mele, Conforto, Hasse, Galuppi and Jommelli. In 1759 he retired to a luxurious villa near Bologna, writing both poetry and music and singing from time to time, and was visited by such distinguished guests as Padre Martini, Gluck, Mozart, Burney, Casanova, the Electress of Saxony and the Emperor Joseph II. Several 18th-century writers, including Metastasio (with whom he had a substantial correspondence), Mancini, Goudar and Burney, identified Farinelli as a prime influence on the new florid style of vocal composition and performance characteristic of so much *opera seria*, especially after 1730. A few of his compositions survive (*GB-Lbl, I-Bc*).

BurneyFI; *DBI* (A. Zapperi); *ES* (M. Bogianckino and R. Celletti)

Group portrait (c1751) by Jacopo Amigoni showing (left to right) the librettist Pietro Metastasio, the soprano Teresa Castellini, the castrato Farinelli, the artist, and Farinelli's dog and page

G. Sacchi: *Vita del Cavaliere Don Carlo Broschi* (Milan, 1784)

C. Ricci: *Burney, Casanova, e Farinelli in Bologna* (Milan, 1890)

L. Frati: 'Metastasio e Farinelli', *RMI*, xx (1913), 1–32

R. Bouvier: *Farinelli, le chanteur des rois* (Paris, 1946)

R. Freeman: 'Farinello and his Repertory', *Studies in Renaissance and Baroque Music in Honor of Arthur Mendel* (Kassel and Hackensack, 1974), 301–30

F. Boris and G. Cammarota: 'La collezione di Carlo Broschi detto Farinelli', *Accademia Clementina: atti e memorie*, new ser., xxvii (Bologna, 1990), 183–237

C. Vitali: 'Una fonte inedita per la biografia di Farinelli: il carteggio Pepoli presso l'Archivio di Stato di Bologna', ibid, 239–50

ROBERT FREEMAN

Farinelli, Giuseppe [Finco, Giuseppe Francesco] (*b* Este, nr Padua, 7 May 1769; *d* Trieste, 12 Dec 1836). Italian composer. He took the professional name of the castrato Farinelli as a sign of gratitude towards the singer, whose help and protection he had received. After studies in Este and Venice, he entered the Conservatorio della Pietà dei Turchini in Naples in 1785. Among his teachers there were Nicola Sala and Giacomo Tritto. In 1792 his first opera, *Il dottorato di Pulcinella*, was performed at the conservatory with great success, revealing his aptitude for comedy. His first work for the public theatres was *L'uomo indolente*, performed at the Teatro Nuovo in 1795. He lived in Turin from 1810 to 1817 and then in Trieste, where he was *maestro al cembalo* at the Teatro Grande and, after 1819, *maestro di cappella* and organist of the cathedral.

Among the minor masters of *opera buffa* who bridged the 18th and 19th centuries, Farinelli stands out for his rich and easy invention, which very quickly made his success rival that of his older contemporary Cimarosa. He was generally considered to be Cimarosa's successor and cleverest imitator. (His duet 'No, non credo a quel che dite', inserted into *Il matrimonio segreto*, was long thought to be by Cimarosa.) The bulk of his theatrical output, 39 operas (he composed about 60 altogether), was written during the decade 1800–10, the period of his greatest success, before Rossini threw his generation into the shade and probably contributed to the cessation of Farinelli's operatic composition after 1817. A typical practitioner of late 18th-century Neapolitan opera style, he remained largely untouched by Rossini's influence. His greatest successes include *I riti d'Efeso* (1803), *La contadina bizzarra* (1810) and *Ginevra degli Almieri* (1812). His output also included many sacred works.

comic operas unless otherwise stated

Il dottorato di Pulcinella (farsa, G. Lorenzi), Naples, Conservatorio della Pietà dei Turchini, 1792

L'uomo indolente (2, G. Palomba), Naples, Nuovo, 1795

Il nuovo savio della Grecia (2, D. Mantile), Naples, Fondo, Nov 1796

Seldano, duca degli Svedesi (2), Venice, S Benedetto, 5 Nov 1797

Amore e dovere, Rome, Alibert, 1797

Antioco in Egitto (2), Florence, Pallacorda, spr. 1798

L'amor sincero (dg, A. Anelli), Milan, Scala, 29 May 1799

Annetta, o La virtù trionfa (farsa, 1, G. Artusi), Venice, S Samuele, 11 Jan 1800

La bandiera d'ogni vento, ossia L'amante per forza (farsa giocosa, 1, G. M. Foppa), Venice, S Benedetto, 30 Jan 1800

Il conte Rovinazzo (Artusi), Venice, S Giovanni Grisostomo, May 1800

La muta per sempre [La muta per amore], Venice, S Angelo, 15 July 1800

Una cosa strana, o Amor semplice (farsa giocosa, 1, Foppa), Venice, S Luca, 23 Sept 1800

Todero Fabro, Este, Nobile, 1800

Teresa e Claudio (farsa, 2, Foppa), Venice, S Luca, 9 Sept 1801, *F-Pn, GB-Lbl, I-Fc, Nc, US-Wc*, duet (London, ?1810)

Giulietta (dramma semiserio, G. Rossi), Parma, Ducale, carn. 1802; as Le lagrime d'una vedova, Padua, Nuovo, 1802

Il Cid delle Spagne (dramma per musica, S. A. Sografi), Venice, Fenice, 17 Feb 1802

La pulcella di Rab, o Rullo e Dallaton (Sografi), Trieste, Grande, May 1802

Pamela (farsa in musica, 1, Rossi, after C. Goldoni), Venice, S Luca, 22 Sept 1802, *B-Bc, F-Pn, GB-Lbl, I-Bc, Fc*; as Pamela maritata, Cingoli, 1806

Chi la dura la vince (burletta in musica, Rossi, after Goldoni: *La locandiera*), Rome, Valle, 2 Jan 1803, *F-Pn, I-Fc, Nc*; as La locandiera, Padua, 1803; as La locandiera di spirito, Naples, Nuovo, 1803, duet (Paris, 1805)

La caduta della nuova Cartagine (dramma per musica, Sografi), Venice, Fenice, 5 Feb 1803

Un effetto naturale (farsa giocosa, 1, Foppa), Venice, S Benedetto, 18 May 1803

Il ventaglio (farsa comica in musica, Rossi, after Goldoni), Padua, Nuovo, 23 July 1803

I riti d'Efeso (dramma eroico, 2, Rossi), Venice, Fenice, 26 Dec 1803, *F-Pn, I-Fc, Nc*, duet (Paris, ?1820)

Ora senza oro, o siano Le follie amorose (farsa, 1), Rome, Valle, Jan 1804

La tragedia finisce in commedia (farsa, 1, Artusi), Venice, S Moisè, 5 June 1804

Il pranzo inaspettato (farsa, 2, Foppa), Vicenza, Eretenio, 13 Aug 1804

Odoardo e Carlotta (2, L. Buonavoglia), Venice, S Moisè, 12 Dec 1804

L'inganno non dura (2, Palomba), Naples, Fiorentini, 1804

La vergine del sole (dramma per musica, Sografi), Venice, Fenice, 9 Feb 1805

Il finto sordo (farsa in musica, Rossi), Milan, Carcano, 18 April 1805; rev. as L'osteria della posta, ossia Il finto sordo, Padua, spr. 1830 [with one aria by P. Bercanovich]

La locanda dell'amore, Florence, Cocomero, spr. 1805

Stravaganza e puntiglio (farsa, Artusi), Venice, S Moisè, Jan 1806

L'amico dell'uomo, ossia Ser Durando [Il Durando] (farsa giocosa, 1, Foppa), Verona, Filarmonico, spr. 1806

Attila (dramma serio per musica, 2, Rossi), Livorno, Carlo Ludovico, May 1806

Climene (os, 2), Naples, S Carlo, 27 June 1806

Ines de Castro (A. Gasparini), Naples, S Carlo, 11 Oct 1806, collab. S. Pavesi and N. A. Zingarelli [based on Zingarelli work, 1798]

Il testamento, o Seicentomila franchi [I seicentomila franchi] (farsa giocosa, 1, Foppa), Venice, S Moisè, 24 Oct 1806

Calliroe (melodramma eroico, Rossi), Venice, Fenice, 26 Dec 1807

La finta sposa, ossia Il barone burlato (M. Brunetti), Rome, Valle, spr. 1808

Il colpevole salvato dalla colpa (os, L. Prividali), Venice, S Moisè, carn. 1809

L'incognita (farsa giocosa, 2, Foppa), Venice, S Moisè, 3 Oct 1809

L'arrivo inaspettato (B. Mezzanotte), Rome, Valle, carn. 1810

La terza lettera ed il terzo marinello (farsa giocosa, 1, Foppa), Venice, S Moisè, 29 Jan 1810

La contadina bizzarra (melodramma serio, L. Romanelli, after F. Livigni: *La finta principessa*), Milan, Scala, 16 Aug 1810, cavatina (Milan, 1810)

Non precipitare i giudizi, ossia La vera gratitudine (farsa giocosa, 1, Foppa), Venice, S Moisè, 3 Nov 1810

Annibale in Capua (melodramma serio, Romanelli), Milan, Scala, 26 Dec 1810

Amor muto (farsa, 1, Foppa), Venice, S Moisè, 19 Oct 1811

Idomeneo (melodramma eroico, Rossi), Venice, Fenice, 26 Dec 1811

Ginevra degli Almieri (tragicommedia, 3, Foppa), Venice, S Moisè, 8 Dec 1812

Lauso e Lidia (os, L. Andrioli), Turin, Regio, carn. 1813

Il matrimonio per concorso (dg, 2, Foppa, after Goldoni), Venice, S Moisè, 19 April 1813

Partenope (festa teatrale, P. Metastasio), Naples, S Carlo, 15 Aug 1814

Caritea regina di Spagna (os, 2), Naples, S Carlo, 16 Sept 1814

Scipione in Cartagena (os, Andrioli), Turin, Regio, carn. 1815

Vittorina (dg, 2, Foppa, after Goldoni), Venice, S Benedetto, 3 April 1815

Il vero eroismo, ossia Adria serenata (festa teatrale, T. Malipiero), Venice, Fenice, Nov 1815

Zoraide (melodramma eroico, Rossi), Venice, Fenice, 26 Dec 1815

La Chiarina (Anelli), Milan, Scala, 14 June 1816

La donna di Bessarabia (dramma per musica, 1, Foppa), Venice, S Moisè, Jan 1817

*

DEUMM (A. Sommariva); *ES* (C. Sartori); *FlorimoN*

G. C. Bottura: *Storia aneddotica documentata del Teatro comunale di Trieste* (Trieste, 1885), 57ff

A. Boccardi: *Memorie triestine: figure della vita e dell'arte* (Trieste, 1922), 41ff

R. di Benedetto: 'Il dottorato di Pulcinella', *Realtà del mezzogiorno* (Feb–March 1968)   GIOVANNI CARLI BALLOLA

Farkas, Ferenc (*b* Nagykanizsa, 15 Dec 1905). Hungarian composer and teacher. After starting his career as a pianist, he studied with Leó Weiner and Albert Siklós at the Budapest Academy of Music (1922–7). He was co-répétiteur for the chorus at the Municipal Theatre, Budapest, (1927–9); he then studied with Respighi in Rome until 1931. From 1933 to 1935 he wrote film music in Vienna and Copenhagen, then taught composition in Budapest, 1935–41, and from 1941 to 1944 at the conservatory in Kolozsvár (now Cluj-Napoca, Romania), where he became director in 1943. He was director of the music school in Székesfehérvár (1946–8) and professor of composition at the Budapest Academy (1949–75), where his pupils included Ligeti, Kurtág, Vass, Petrovics, Szokolay, Bozay and Durkó. Among his awards are the Liszt Prize (1933), the Erkel Prize (1960) and the Nerder Prize (1979).

Farkas's works include operas and operettas, ballets and Singspiels, pastoral and marionette music, musicals, a dance oratorio and more than 70 film scores. His settings encompass a broad spectrum of subjects, ranging from Eastern fairy-tales to stories from Hungary's historical past. Although his melodies reveal the influence of Bartók and Kodály, the years Farkas spent with Respighi gave him a wider horizon. The influence of Respighi's own teacher, Rimsky-Korsakov, and Stravinsky is evident in the virtuosity of Farkas's instrumental writing and the richness of his orchestral palette; Gesualdo, old Hungarian folk ballads and 12-note music also affected his style. Throughout this multiplicity of sources and forms Farkas has succeeded in defining an individual compositional language. He is a true experimenter, notably in musical synthesis, but his imagination, his technical competence and his taste have assured the coherence of his work.

A bűvös szekrény [The Magic Cupboard], 1938–42 (2, G. Kiszely), Budapest, Royal, 22 April 1942

Fülemüle [Nightingale] (musical play, 3, Á. Szabados, after J. Arany), Budapest, National, 1941

Csínom Palkó, 1949–50 (musical play, A. Dékány), Hungarian Radio, 1950; stage, Budapest, State Opera, 1951; rev. version (Spl, 3), 1960

Búbos vitéz [Hero Búbos] (musical puppet play, 1, Á. Tamási), Budapest, State Puppet Theatre, 1952; rev. version (musical play, 3), Pécs, National, 1975

Zeng az erdő [The Resounding Forest] (operetta, 3, Dékány, G. Baróti and L. Dalos), Miskolc, National, 1952

Vők iskolája [School for Sons-in-law] (operetta, 3, R. Török and E. Innocent-Vincze), Budapest, Municipal Theatre for Operetta, 1958

Vidróczki (radio ballad, Innocent-Vincze), Hungarian Radio, 1959; rev. version (3), 1964

Piroschka (musical comedy, 2, K.-H. Gutheim, after H. Hartung), Kaiserslautern, 1964

A Noszty fiú esete Tóth Marival [The Case of the Noszty-boy with Mary Tóth] (operetta, 3, F. Karinthy, D. Mészöly and P. Zoltán, after K. Mikszáth), Budapest, Municipal Theatre for Operetta, 1971

A holicsi Cupido [Cupido of Holics] (musical play, 1, F. Herczeg and G. Vég), Hungarian Radio, 1978

Egy úr Velencéből [A Gentleman from Venice], 1980 (2, S. Márai), Budapest, State Opera, 4 June 1991   FERENC BÓNIS

Farkas, Katalin (*b* Budapest, 5 Jan 1954). Hungarian soprano. She studied in Budapest and in 1982 joined the Hungarian State Opera. She made her British début in 1985 at Glyndebourne as Zdenka (*Arabella*); in 1986 she took part in Liszt's *Don Sanche* at S Carlo, Naples; and in 1987 she sang Amarillis in Handel's *Il pastor fido* at Göttingen. Her repertory includes Blonde, Marzelline, Rosina, Giannetta (*L'elisir d'amore*), Lola, Frasquita, Sophie (*Werther*) and Zerbinetta. A charming singer, she is equally good in lyrical and coloratura roles.   ELIZABETH FORBES

Farkas, Ödön (*b* Pusztamonostor, nr Szolnok, 27 Jan 1851; *d* Kolozsvár, Transylvania [now Cluj-Napoca, Romania], 11 Sept 1912). Hungarian composer. He initially studied engineering, but in 1875 enrolled at the Royal Hungarian Academy of Music in Budapest to learn composition; he must have received earlier musical training as his first opera, *Bajadér*, was performed privately one month after his matriculation. At its first public performance, in 1876, it was received only as the work of a promising composer. An earlier operetta *Radó és Ilonka* ('Conrad and Helen', 1872) was probably never produced. Farkas finished his studies in 1878 and began teaching at the Kolozsvár Conservatory the following year; from 1880 until his death he was its director. He conducted at the National Theatre in Kolozsvár for one year (1881–2).

Farkas was a versatile composer, at his best in songs; none of his stage works achieved lasting success. His opera *Tündérforrás* ('Fairy Fountain') was produced only in Kolozsvár (1893). *A vezeklők* ('The Penitents') was first performed in Kolozsvár the same year and in Budapest in 1894. The setting, among the Brahmins of Bengal, might have been of interest 20 years earlier, around the time of *Aida* or Goldmark's *Die Königin von Saba*, but such oriental subjects had become old-fashioned and the libretto was poor. Farkas's music follows the declamatory style of Wagner, but uses few leitmotifs. Although the arias, duets and choruses sound well, they are sometimes cloying, and while the orchestral music provides a good background to the scenes, it lacks local colour. The comic opera *Balassa Bálint* (1896), on a Hungarian subject, also had little success, again to some extent because of the libretto. Farkas here broke with Wagner: his music took on a Hungarian idiom, but he was unable to build simple folktunes into large tableaux. His last opera, the one-act *Tetemrehívás* ('Ordeal of the Bier', 1900), was composed on an epic ballad that would have been more suitable for a cantata; it is episodic and has only two main characters. However, with its colourful orchestration and Hungarian motifs developed into arias, choruses and a funeral march, this has proved to be Farkas's best opera. The occasional work *Kuruczvilág* ('The World of the Kurucs'; Budapest, 28 October 1906), based on poems by S. Endrődi about the Rákóczi armies fighting Habsburg oppression at the turn of the 17th century, was first performed when the exiled Prince Rákóczi's ashes were brought home.

Radó és Ilonka [Conrad and Helen], 1872 (operetta), ?unperf.
Bajadér (1, L. Farkas, after J. W. von Goethe: *Der Gott und die Bajadere*), Budapest, 23 Aug 1876
A vezeklők [The Penitents], 1884, (3, J. Dávid and G. Gál), Kolozsvár, 1893, *H-Bn*
Tündérforrás [Fairy Fountain] (1, Gál), Kolozsvár, 1893
Balassa Bálint (comic op, 3, J. Hamvas, after K. Tóth), Budapest, 16 Jan 1896, *Bn*

Tetemrehívás [Ordeal of the Bier] (1, G. Versényi, after J. Arany), Budapest, 5 Oct 1900, *Bn*
Ideiglenes házasság [Temporary Marriage], unperf., lost

*

J. Seprődi: 'Farkas Ödön "Tetemrehívás"-a' ['Ordeal of the Bier' by Ö. Farkas], *Zenevilág*, ii (1902), 285–7
G. Magyarossy: *Huszonöt év* [Twenty-five Years] (Kolozsvár, 1906) [anniversary pubn]
J. Seprődi: 'Farkas Ödön', *Erdélyi hírlap* (30 Nov 1906); repr. in *Seprődi János válogatott zenei írásai és népzene gyűjtése* [Selected Writings and Folk Music Research of J. Seprődi], ed. I. Almási, A. Benkő and I. Lakatos (Bucharest, 1974), 79–81 [Ger. summary, 494–5]
I. Lakatos: 'A kolozsvári magyar zeneélet alapvetője: Farkas Ödön' [The Founder of Hungarian Musical Life at Kolozsvár: Ö. Farkas], *Magyar zenei szemle*, iii (1943), 249–58
J. Benkő: 'Dallamrészletek és dramaturgiai jelentéskörük Farkas Ödön Tetemrehívás című zenedrámájában' [Melodic Patterns and their Dramaturgical Meaning in the Music Drama 'Ordeal of the Bier' by Ö. Farkas], *Zenetudományi Írások*, ed. A. Benkő (Bucharest, 1986), 249–65   DEZSŐ LEGÁNY

Farley, Carole (**Ann**) (*b* Le Mars, IA, 29 Nov 1946). American soprano. She studied with William Shriner at Indiana University and with Marianne Schech at the Hochschule für Musik, Munich. She made her stage début at the Landestheater, Linz, in 1969; in 1971 she sang the title role in the WNO production of Berg's *Lulu*, and she was in the Cologne company, 1972–5. Her American stage début was with the New York City Opera in 1976 in the title role of Offenbach's *La belle Hélène*. For her début at the Metropolitan (1977) she sang Lulu, also appearing in the three-act version staged in Zürich not long after the Paris première (1979). Her repertory of leading roles in 20th-century operas also includes Strauss's *Salome* (1980) and Freihild in *Guntram* (1981); the Maid of Orléans in Phillipe Boesmans's *La passion de Gilles*, which she created for the Monnaie in Brussels (1983); Divara in Alexander Goehr's *Behold the Sun*, which she sang at the British première (1987, BBC broadcast); Jenny in Weill's *Mahagonny* (1987); and Marie in Berg's *Wozzeck* (1989, Buenos Aires). Other important roles in her repertory include Violetta, Donna Anna, Donna Elvira, Mimì and the heroine of Poulenc's opera for solo soprano, *La voix humaine*. Farley is known as an exceptionally versatile singer with a wide range of styles at her command.

                                                 ROBERT FINN

Farncombe, Charles (**Frederick**) (*b* London, 29 July 1919). English conductor. He studied at the Royal School of Church Music and the RAM (1949–51). In 1955, with the assistance of Edward J. Dent, he founded the Handel Opera Society and was its music director for 30 years. With it he conducted many first modern British performances, from *Rinaldo*, *Alcina* and *Deidamia* to *Riccardo primo*, *Rodrigo* and others. He has also directed staged performances of Handel oratorios and performed works by Cavalieri, J. C. Smith, Arne, Haydn and Mozart. Productions by the society were taken to festivals at Göttingen, Halle, Liège and Drottningholm.

Farncombe has conducted on tours in the USA and in Sweden, where he was music director at the Drottningholm Court Theatre, 1970–79, and has appeared at the Stockholm Royal Opera. In 1979 he began an association with the Badisches Staatstheater, Karlsruhe. For the English Bach Festival at Covent Garden in 1981 he conducted the 1754 version of Rameau's *Castor et Pollux*, taking it to Monte Carlo and Paris, and in 1988 the first period-style performance in Britain of Gluck's *Orphée et Eurydice*. His conducting is generally careful over detail, sensitive to tempo and often spirited. He was made a CBE in 1977.

*

R. Milnes: '30 Years of Handel Opera', *Opera*, xxxvi (1985), 1230–37 [with list of productions]
STANLEY SADIE, NOËL GOODWIN

Farnese. Theatre built in PARMA in 1618 on the order of Ranuccio Farnese; inaugurated in 1628, it was active up to the 18th century.

Farneti, Maria (*b* Forlì, 5 Dec 1877; *d* San Varano, nr Forlì, 17 Oct 1955). Italian soprano. She studied at Pesaro, making her début in 1899 at Turin; there she also sang Mascagni's Iris, which became a favourite role. Principally associated with the new *verismo* operas, she appeared in most leading Italian houses. She sang in the first Venice performances of Mascagni's *Le maschere* (1901) and Giordano's *Andrea Chénier*. She toured the USA with a company assembled by Mascagni, and sang regularly in Buenos Aires, where she took the title role in the world première of Mascagni's *Isabeau* (1911). She retired in 1917 but in 1931 made a small number of recordings, the voice still fresh, the style often exquisite.

*

GV (R. Celletti; R. Vegeto)
J. B. STEANE

Farnie, H(enry) B(rougham) (*b* 1836; *d* Paris, 22 Sept 1889). Scottish librettist and translator. At a time when London theatrical managements relied heavily on French importations, he was greatly in demand as a translator of operettas. He supplied the texts for the first English versions produced in London of Offenbach's *Geneviève de Brabant* (1869), *Madame Favart* (1871) and *La fille du tambour-major* (1880); he also translated Gounod's *Roméo et Juliette* for its first British performance in English (1890, Liverpool, Carl Rosa Opera Company). He wrote original librettos for unsuccessful works by Balfe (*The Sleeping Queen*, 1864) and Benedict (*The Bride of Song*, 1864). His translations now seem clumsy and sometimes hastily contrived to fit the music.
ARTHUR JACOBS

Farquhar, David (*b* Cambridge, New Zealand, 5 April 1928). New Zealand composer. He occupies a leading position in the generation of New Zealand composers succeeding Douglas Lilburn. Having graduated in 1948 from Victoria University, Wellington, he studied in England at Cambridge (1949–51) and at the GSM (1951–2) under Benjamin Frankel. He was appointed junior lecturer at Victoria in 1953, becoming professor of music in 1976. He was the founder and first president of the Composers' Association of New Zealand (CANZ) and has played a leading role in the promotion of New Zealand music.

In his student days at Cambridge and in Wellington in the 1950s, Farquhar served an apprenticeship in writing music for live theatre and for radio dramas. The opportunity to branch into opera came with a commission from the New Zealand Opera Company for a family Christmas opera based on Ngaio Marsh's play *A Unicorn for Christmas*, first performed at St James's Theatre, Wellington, on 3 December 1962. Undoubtedly influenced by his early admiration for the vocal works of Britten, the opera confirmed his gifts for vocal writing and sense of theatre and enjoyed wide-spread success, including a royal performance in Auckland on 7 February 1963. A disastrous fire in the New Zealand Opera Company warehouse in 1963 destroyed the entire wardrobe, designed by Desmond Digby. Although broadcast by Radio New Zealand in 1974, the opera has not been staged since.

Thus denied operatic outlets, Farquhar concentrated on writing for the voice. His second music-theatre commission was for a musical, *Oh, Captain Cook*, presented by Downstage in Wellington in 1969. This satirical morality was based on Giraudoux' *Appendix to the Voyages of Captain Cook* and contrasted dubious European morals with natural Tahitian manners. He returned to opera, but on a smaller scale, in 1970 with the one-act chamber opera *Shadow* to a libretto by himself and Edward Hill based on the story by Hans Christian Andersen. In spite of its modest demands, *Shadow* remained unperformed until 1988 (Wellington, Victoria University Memorial Theatre, 19 September). Farquhar's career illustrates the extreme difficulties experienced by composers of opera and theatre music in a country with a sporadic, meagerly funded operatic tradition. Nevertheless, he has provided a landmark with *A Unicorn for Christmas* and, in *Shadow*, an introspective, finely crafted work; both will be seen as affirmations of the spirit of opera in a dormant tradition.

*

M. Lodge: *New Zealand Music Theatre, especially 1920–70* (thesis, Victoria U. of Wellington, 1981)
W. Dart: 'A Unicorn for Christmas, a Right Royal Opera', *Music in New Zealand* (sum. 1988–9), 6–13
J. M. Thomson: *Biographical Dictionary of New Zealand Composers* (Wellington, 1990)
J. M. THOMSON

Farrar, Geraldine (*b* Melrose, MA, 28 Feb 1882; *d* Ridgefield, CT, 11 March 1967). American soprano. She studied in Boston, New York and Paris; soon after her début in *Faust* at the Königliche Opernhaus, Berlin (15 October 1901), she became a pupil of Lilli Lehmann, with whom she was later to sing at Salzburg. After five years in Berlin, Farrar joined the Metropolitan Opera, where she first appeared as Gounod's Juliet in 1906, and soon became one of the leading stars of the company. She remained there without interruption until 1922, when she made her farewell appearance as Leoncavallo's Zazà (22 April). With her personal beauty, clear tone and shapely phrasing she excelled in Mozartian and French roles, as well as in several Puccini characters, among them the heroine in the 1918 première of *Suor Angelica*; she was also the first Goose girl in Humperdinck's *Königskinder* (1910). Among her most popular roles were Butterfly and Carmen. Her seductive voice, with its strongly personal timbre, is well captured on a long series of Victor records.

For illustration *see* KÖNIGSKINDER and SUOR ANGELICA.

*

G. Farrar: *The Story of an American Singer* (New York, 1916, 2/1938 as *Such Sweet Compulsion*, 3/1970 with discography)
W. R. Moran: 'Geraldine Farrar', *Record Collector*, xiii (1960–61), 194–240 [with discography], 279–80; xiv (1961–2), 172–4; xx (1971–2), 163–4
E. Nash: *Always First Class: the Career of Geraldine Farrar* (Washington DC, 1982)
DESMOND SHAWE-TAYLOR

Farrell, Eileen (*b* Willimantic, CT, 13 Feb 1920). American soprano. She studied with Merle Alcock and Eleanor McLellan, and concentrated on concert singing until her belated operatic début in 1956 as Santuzza in

Tampa, Florida. That year she sang Leonora (*Il trovatore*) in San Francisco, returning in 1958 as Cherubini's Medea; Chicago appearances followed, and, in 1960, her much delayed Metropolitan début as Gluck's Alcestis. Her relationship with the Metropolitan management was not easy and she sang there sporadically for only five seasons. Although her voice, temperament and histrionic gifts would have suited the great Wagnerian roles admirably, she sang Brünnhilde and Isolde only in concert performances, notably with the New York PO under Bernstein. She was an intelligent actress; her voice was huge, warm, vibrant and, apart from difficulties at the extreme top in later years, remarkably well controlled.   MARTIN BERNHEIMER

Farrell [née Doyle], **Margaret** [Mrs Kennedy] (*d* London, 23 Jan 1793). Irish contralto. In February 1775 she appeared in Arne's *The Sot*, a piece designed to display the talents of his pupils. Most of her career was spent at Covent Garden, where she made her last appearance in April 1789 as William in Shield's *Rosina*, a part she had created. Since she was tall with a powerful voice she often took male leads, including Macheath, Artaxerxes and roles written for her by the librettist O'Keeffe, such as Patrick in his Irish opera *The Poor Soldier*. She was also an accomplished oratorio performer; Mrs Papendiek remembered her 'contralto voice melodiously sweet' in a Westminster Abbey Handel concert. She sang as Mrs Kennedy from 1779.

*

BDA; *LS*

A. Pasquin [pseud. of J. Williams]: *The Children of Thespis*, iii (London, 1788, 13/1792)
C. Dibdin: *A Complete History of the English Stage*, v (London, 1800)
T. Gilliland: *The Dramatic Mirror*, ii (London, 1808)
J. O'Keeffe: *Recollections* (London, 1826)
Mrs Papendiek: *Court and Private Life in the Time of Queen Charlotte*, ed. V. D. Broughton (London, 1887)
                    OLIVE BALDWIN, THELMA WILSON

Farsa (It.: 'farce'). Term for a type of opera, generally in one act, lasting between 60 and 90 minutes, of a type popular in Venice in the late 18th and early 19th centuries. A typical evening comprised two such pieces and two ballets (one of which was sometimes replaced by a 'gran concertone' or other instrumental work). The centre of production and dissemination was Venice, in particular the Teatro S Moisè, with 106 of the 191 productions documented through printed librettos. Its many precursors aside, the beginnings of the *farsa* repertory may be placed in the early 1790s. Seven new *farse* were given during Carnival 1794, seven more in autumn 1797; production peaked in 1800 with 28 first performances, after which it levelled off to some 15 per year (1801–5), then six (1806–13) and subsequently a maximum of two. The principal librettists were Giulio Artusi, Giuseppe Foppa (76 texts) and Gaetano Rossi (the last, above all, in the context of the *farsa sentimentale*); significant contributions to the musical repertory were made by, among others, Giuseppe Farinelli, Gardi, Generali, Simon Mayr, Giuseppe Mosca, Portogallo, Pucitta, Rossini and Trento.

The internal structure of the *farsa* seems frequently to take as its model the *dramma giocoso per musica*, whose two acts were somehow condensed into one, with a reduction in the number and length of the recitatives and the number of closed-form pieces (especially those involving minor characters); typical, halfway through the

farsa, is the appearance of a concertato piece whose function is largely similar to the ensemble finale in Act 1 of a two-act *dramma giocoso* (generally a moment of particular dramatic tension). Other *farse*, however, are set 'in the manner of the French … with unsung recitative in prose' (F. Bartoli, *Notizie istoriche de' comici italiani*, Padua, 1782), thus embracing the characteristic structure of the French *comédie mêlée d'ariettes*, and still others, at their dramatic climax, adopt an openly 'melodramatic' style in which spoken recitative is accompanied by tremolos and other side effects in the orchestra. As for the texts, sentimental or heroic themes become progressively more common against a basic diet of comic subjects. This apparent inconsistency in dramatic and musical structure is partly due, perhaps, to the openly derivative nature of the vast majority of *farsa* texts: the some 20 librettos whose title-pages bear the description 'farsa originale' are few indeed in comparison with the many derived from earlier *drammi giocosi per musica*, novels, French musical and non-musical theatre and, in particular, Italian theatrical comedies.

Giuseppe Carpani, chief censor and inspector of the Venetian theatres in 1804, associated the introduction of the *farsa* with 'the aim of certain impresarios to fill the theatre with first performances and their hope of later filling them at lower cost'. In this light, it is easy to gauge the importance of earlier operatic and theatrical productions, and literary publications, as a measure of the probable success of the one-act operatic revision. Economic factors are more or less in evidence behind certain other features of the *farsa* tradition: the growing tendency to restage successful works from previous seasons (already by 1801, the fifth year of continuous *farsa* production in Venice, revivals outnumber first performances; *La scelta dello sposo*, by G. L. Buonavoglia and P. C. Guglielmi, was staged on at least 11 separate occasions in Venice between 1805 and 1811, fully anticipating the many Rossini revivals of the following decade); the almost total lack of choruses; the marked reduction in scene changes with respect to contemporary *dramma giocoso per musica*, with a clear preference for single scenes or, at most, one or two simple changes; and the relative absence of stage effects. A further characteristic is 'speed, naturalness, propriety, moderate action', resulting in a greater rapport between actors and audience than in other forms of contemporary musical theatre and more attention to detail, realistic gesture and action.

*

D. Bryant: 'Un sistema di consumo dell'opera italiana nel primo ottocento: il caso della farsa', *IMSCR*, xiv *Bologna 1987*, i, 497–503
M. T. Muraro and D. Bryant, eds.: *I vicini di Mozart: Venice 1987*, ii: *La farsa musicale veneziana*   DAVID BRYANT

Fasch, Johann Friedrich (*b* Buttelstädt, nr Weimar, 15 April 1688; *d* Zerbst, 5 Dec 1758). German composer. He was educated in Leipzig, at the Thomasschule and the university. His first compositions followed the style of his friend Telemann. Although he had no regular instruction in composition, he soon became so well known as a composer that his sovereign in Zeitz commissioned him to write operas for the Naumburg Peter-Paul festivals in 1711 and 1712. During a long tour he studied composition with Graupner and Grünewald at Darmstadt. He then held positions in Bayreuth (1714), in Greiz (until 1721) and as

Kapellmeister to Count Morzin in Prague. In 1722 he reluctantly accepted the position of court Kapellmeister in Zerbst, where he remained for the rest of his life.

Fasch is believed to have written four operas (all lost): *Clomire* (1711, Naumburg and Zeitz), *Lucius Verus* (1711, Zeitz; as *Berenice*, 1739, Zerbst), *Die getreue Dido* (1712, Naumburg) and *Margenis* (after S. von Birken, Carnival, 1715, Bayreuth). His fame as a composer spread far beyond Saxony, though none of his works was published in his lifetime. One of the most important contemporaries of Bach, he composed a large amount of orchestral music, progressive in style and reflecting the transition from the late Baroque idiom to the classicism of Haydn and Mozart. He also wrote much sacred music.

*

BurneyH
J. F. Fasch: 'Lebenslauf', *Historisch-kritische Beyträge*, iii, ed. F. W. Marpurg (Berlin, 1757), 124
——: 'Lebenslauf', *Lebensbeschreibungen*, ed. J. A. Hiller (Leipzig, 1784), 59
B. Engelke: *Johann Friedrich Fasch: sein Leben und seine Tätigkeit als Vokalkomponist* (diss., U. of Halle, 1908)
——: 'Johann Friedrich Fasch, Versuch einer Biographie', *SIMG*, x (1908–9), 263–83
A. Werner: 'Noch einige Bemerkungen zu Fasch', *SIMG*, xi (1909–10), 140
H. R. Jung: Johann Friedrich Fasch', *Musik und Gesellschaft*, viii (1958), 688–91
——: 'Johann Friedrich Fasch in Greiz', *Thüreingische Heimat*, iv (1959)   GOTTFRIED KÜNTZEL

Fassbaender, Brigitte (*b* Berlin, 3 July 1939). German mezzo-soprano. She studied with her father, Willi Domgraf-Fassbänder, at the Nuremberg Conservatory and made her début at the Staatsoper in Munich in 1961 as Nicklausse. After playing Hänsel, Carlotta (*Die schweigsame Frau*) and the various pages and maids of the repertory, she scored a great success in 1964 as Clarice (*La pietra del paragone*). Later her roles included Sextus (*La clemenza di Tito*), Cherubino, Dorabella, Carmen, Eboli, Brangäne and Marina. Her débuts at Covent Garden (1971) and the Metropolitan Opera (1974) were as Octavian, a part in which her dashing looks and her warm, darkly attractive tone have won her particular praise. In 1973 she sang Fricka (*Das Rheingold*) at the Salzburg Easter Festival and in 1976 created Lady Milford in Von Einem's *Kabale und Liebe* in Vienna; she has also appeared in San Francisco, Paris and Japan. Charlotte (*Werther*), Mistress Quickly, Countess Geschwitz (Berg's *Lulu*) and the Nurse (*Die Frau ohne Schatten*) are among the successful roles of her later career. In 1990 she sang Clairon (*Capriccio*) at Glyndebourne, and made her British directing début two years later with *Der ferne Klang* for Opera North.

*

S. Gould: 'Brigitte Fassbaender', *Opera*, xxxii (1981), 789–95
                                           HAROLD ROSENTHAL/R

Fassbender [Mottl-Fassbender], **Zdenka** (*b* Tetschen [now Děčin], 12 Dec 1879; *d* Munich, 14 March 1954). Czech soprano. She studied in Prague with Sophie Loewe-Destinn, making her début at Karlsruhe in 1899 as Rachel (*La Juive*). Her dramatic temperament and voice were eminently suited to the Wagnerian repertory, on which she was encouraged to concentrate by the conductor Felix Mottl (whom she later married). Engaged in 1906 by the Munich Opera, she remained a member of the ensemble until 1932. She was the first Munich Electra and Tosca, and also sang the Marschallin, Leonore and Clytemnestra (*Iphigénie en Aulide*) and roles in operas by Schillings, Pfitzner, Bittner and Schreker. She sang in Beecham's 1910 and 1913 Covent Garden seasons, as Electra and Isolde.

HAROLD ROSENTHAL/R

Fate. Opera by Leoš Janáček; *see* OSUD.

Fate of a Man, The. Opera by I. I. Dzerzhinsky; *see* SUD'BA CHELOVEKA.

Fatinitza. *Operette* in three acts by FRANZ SUPPÉ to a libretto by F. ZELL and RICHARD GENÉE after EUGÈNE SCRIBE's *La Circassienne*; Vienna, Carltheater, 5 January 1876.

During the Crimean War (1853–6) the Russian general Kantschukoff (bass) takes a fancy to a young lady called Fatinitza. In fact Fatinitza is a young lieutenant, Wladimir (mezzo-soprano), who has dressed as a female to enable his girlfriend Lydia (soprano), Kantschukoff's niece, to escape her uncle's watchful eye. While thus disguised, Wladimir is captured and finds himself in a Turkish harem, before Kantschukoff is persuaded that Fatinitza does not exist and that Wladimir and Lydia should marry. Produced with Antonie Link (Wladimir), Hermine Meyerhoff (Lydia) and Wilhelm Knaak (Kantschukoff), the work is noted particularly for the march ensemble 'Vorwärts mit frischem Muth'.

ANDREW LAMB

Faucon, Le ('The Falcon'). *Opéra comique* in three acts by DMITRY STEPANOVICH BORTNYANSKY to a libretto by François-Hermann Lafermière after MICHEL-JEAN SEDAINE; Gatchina Palace, 11/22 October 1786.

The story, adapted from Boccaccio's *Decameron* via Sedaine's libretto for an *opéra comique larmoyant* in one act by Monsigny (1771), is a contrived and sentimental tale of love and sacrifice. An impoverished Spanish nobleman, Don Federigo (tenor), disappointed in love, retreats to his country estate with nothing to his name but his servant and his beloved pet falcon. The widow Elvira (soprano), who has previously rejected him, now visits him and demands the falcon to revive the spirits of her ailing son; Federigo reveals that he has just served the bird to her for dinner, since he had nothing else to offer. Elvira takes this as an earnest of true love, and plights her troth to Federigo on the spot.

Bortnyansky, whose skills as an opera composer had been honed by a ten-year apprenticeship in Italy, managed to turn this bathetic material into a cool, smoothly crafted entertainment, at times genuinely witty (as in the finale of Act 1, where Elvira's maid Marina (soprano) feigns illness to expose a team of quack physicians), at others touching (the lovesick Federigo's *airs*). *Le faucon* was first given by an amateur company of courtiers and ladies; it was successfully revived by the Moscow Chamber Musical Theatre (a subsidiary of the Bol'shoy) in the late 1970s in a production by Boris Pokrovsky, the Bol'shoy's director of production.

RICHARD TARUSKIN

Faull, Ellen (*b* Pittsburgh, PA, 14 Oct 1918). American soprano. After studying at the Curtis Institute and Columbia University, she became a leading singer of the New York City Opera, making her début there in 1947 as Donna Anna. Her performances included roles in the première of Beeson's *Lizzie Borden* (1965), the New York première of Douglas Moore's *Carry Nation* (1968) and the American première of Wolf-Ferrari's *I* *quatro rusteghi* (1951); among her traditional roles were Countess Almaviva, Leonora (*Il trovatore*) and Butterfly. She performed with most of the important American opera companies. Her attractive *lirico spinto* was able to spin out long, limpid phrases in Verdi, yet also to deliver the vehement coloratura of Donna Anna's music with fire and meaning.   THOR ECKERT, JR

Fauré, Gabriel(-Urbain) (*b* Pamiers, Ariège, 12 May 1845; *d* Paris, 4 Nov 1924). French composer. After studying at the Ecole Niedermeyer, Paris, where the professor of piano was Saint-Saëns, a life-long friend, he became assistant organist to Widor at St Sulpice in 1871 and then to Saint-Saëns at the Madeleine in 1874, succeeding him in 1896. Later that year he took over Massenet's composition class at the Paris Conservatoire. To general consternation (he was regarded in academic circles as a dangerous radical) he was appointed director in 1905, proving an excellent teacher and administrator. In spite of increasing deafness he remained in the post until 1920, a central figure in Parisian musical life. His style evolved in a way owing little to fashion or contemporary controversy, pushing tonality to its limits, becoming increasingly economical. Although many of his smaller works became and remained popular, the true worth of his achievement in song, piano and chamber music has only gradually been recognized. Except for *Prométhée* and *Pénélope* he was not attracted to large-scale composition – even the much-loved requiem is small-scale.

Like many other French composers of the time, Fauré was attracted to the theatre, but his fastidiousness made the choice of a libretto difficult. Meanwhile he turned his hand to incidental music: his scores for the tragedy *Caligula* by the elder Dumas (1888, Paris, Odéon) and *Shylock* (a version of *The Merchant of Venice*; 1889, Paris, Odéon) reveal a sure touch. The suite from the music for a London production (1898) of Maeterlinck's *Pelléas et Mélisande* is often played. *Prométhée* (27 August 1900, Béziers) was rather different, but still not an opera. A local magnate had instituted open-air performances, generously planned, of dramas with music on the Greek model. For *Prométhée*, a tragedy by Jean Lorrain and Ferdinand Hérold, Fauré used large vocal and instrumental forces for musical sections alternating with spoken text, moving with ease on a much larger scale than he had previously attempted. Fauré himself made an indoor concert version (at Béziers he had shared the scoring with a military band expert, Charles Eustace). *Pénélope*, a real opera at last, followed at the Monte Carlo Opéra in 1913 (three acts; libretto by René Fauchois; première 4 March). *Masques et bergamasques* (10 April 1919, Monte Carlo) was a one-act divertissement by Fauchois for which Fauré used some of his earlier instrumental pieces and songs (orchestrated for the occasion) along with new pieces; a suite was made from this music. The Paris (Opéra-Comique) production of 1926 remained in the repertory until after World War II.

See also PÉNÉLOPE.

G. Koechlin: *Gabriel Fauré* (Paris, 1927, 2/1945; Eng. trans., 1945)
C. Rostand: *L'oeuvre de Gabriel Fauré* (Paris, 1945)
G. Fauré: *Lettres intimes*, ed. P. Fauré-Fremiet (Paris, 1951) [Fauré's letters to his wife]
J.-M. Nectoux: *Fauré* (Paris, 1972) [with discography and iconography]
R. Orledge: *Gabriel Fauré* (London, 1979)
G. Fauré: *Correspondance*, ed. J.-M. Nectoux (Paris, 1980; Eng. trans., 1984)
R. Crichton: 'Gabriel Fauré', *The Heritage of Music*, ed. M. Raeburn and A. Kendall, iv: *Music in the Twentieth Century* (Oxford and New York, 1989), 19–29   RONALD CRICHTON

Faure, Jean-Baptiste (*b* Moulins, 15 Jan 1830; *d* Paris, 9 Nov 1914). French baritone. He studied at the Paris Conservatoire, making his début in 1852 as Pygmalion (Massé's *Galathée*) at the Opéra-Comique, where he also created Hoël in Meyerbeer's *Le pardon de Ploërmel* (1859). He made his London début at Covent Garden in 1860 as Hoël, and during that season and the next sang Alphonse (*La favorite*), Fernando (*La gazza ladra*), Nevers (*Les Huguenots*) and the title roles in *Don Giovanni* and *Guillaume Tell*. In 1863 he sang Méphistophélès in the first Covent Garden performance of *Faust*. His début at the Paris Opéra was in 1861 as Julien (Poniatowski's *Pierre de Médicis*); there he created Pedro in Massé's *La mule de Pedro* (1863), Nélusko in *L'Africaine* (1865), Posa in *Don Carlos* (1867) and the title role in Thomas' *Hamlet* (1868), also singing Méphistophélès in the first performance at the Opéra of *Faust* (1869). He sang Don Giovanni at the first performance of Mozart's opera given at the newly built Palais Garnier (1875), and then created Charles VII in Mermet's *Jeanne d'Arc* (1876). He retired from the stage in 1886. Although he possessed a fine, resonant, even and extensive voice, Faure was chiefly notable for the innate musicality and stylishness of his singing and for his great gifts as an actor. His voice can be heard on a private cylinder recorded in Milan (*c*1897–9), singing 'Jardins d'Alcazar' from *La favorite*.

For further illustration *see* FAUST (ii).

Jean-Baptiste Faure in the title role of Thomas' 'Hamlet', which he created at the Paris Opéra, 9 March 1868: painting (1877) by Edouard Manet

G. Chouquet: *Histoire de la musique dramatique en France depuis ses origines jusqu'à nos jours* (Paris, 1873)

J.-G. Prod'homme: *L'Opéra (1669–1925)* (Paris, 1925)

S. Wolff: *Un demi-siècle d'Opéra-Comique 1900–1950* (Paris, 1953)

H. Rosenthal: *Two Centuries of Opera at Covent Garden* (London, 1958)

S. Wolff: *L'Opéra au Palais Garnier (1875–1962)* (Paris, 1962)

ELIZABETH FORBES

Fausse esclave, La ('The Pretend Slavegirl'). *Opéra comique* in one act by CHRISTOPH WILLIBALD GLUCK to a libretto after LOUIS ANSEAUME and Pierre-Augustin Lefèvre de Marcouville's *La fausse aventurière* (1757); Vienna, Burgtheater, 8 January 1758.

The Parisian model libretto for this work – the first of Gluck's eight *opéras comiques* for the French theatre in Vienna – included prose, vaudevilles and *airs* parodied from *opere buffe*. These last, and some vaudevilles, Gluck composed anew; prose sections were reworked as vaudevilles, or omitted, not without damage to the plot's coherence. The penniless Agathe (soprano), married secretly to Valère (tenor), fools Valère's miserly father Chrisante (baritone) into approving their union with a teary and fictitious tale of capture by Turkish pirates; as Chrisante signs what he thinks is his contract of marriage to Agathe, the notary reveals himself to be Valère, and the contract to be his own. The lovers' confidant, the gardener Julien, was changed in Vienna to a female role, Lisette (soprano).

While derived from plot archetypes of the *commedia dell'arte*, *La fausse esclave* features a clever and comical central seduction scene. Gluck's music, which survives only in keyboard score, contains elements both French and italianate (including an unacknowledged borrowing from Handel's *Alessandro*), as well as *airs* of folklike allure. The opera's première was noted in the international *Journal encyclopédique*, and two of its *airs nouveaux* were included in the Liège monthly *L'écho*.

BRUCE ALAN BROWN

Faust. Libretto subject, popular in the 19th century. The legend of Faust (or Doctor Faustus), like that of Orpheus or Don Juan, is an old one surviving in several popular sources; it has been extensively drawn upon by opera composers. Its sources fall into two main genres: 'histories', published in folk-books (or chapbooks), and dramatic versions, preserved in puppet plays. The *Historia von Dr. Johann Fausten* published at Frankfurt in 1587 by Johann Spiess seems to have been a source of Marlowe's *Dr. Faustus*, probably first performed in 1594 and printed in 1604 and 1616. Goethe was familiar with both the traditions of the chapbooks and the puppet plays. His *Faust*, in its definitive version, appeared in two instalments, Part I in 1808 and Part II in 1832; although the libretto of Busoni's opera was also affected by the puppet play and by Marlowe, it is fair to say that most Faust operas after 1808 are in some degree influenced by Goethe (possibly in translation: certainly Berlioz and Gounod were indebted to the French translation of Gérard de Nerval, 1828).

In their entirety, the two parts of Goethe's tragedy run to over 12 000 lines, a time dimension impractical even for the spoken theatre. In the history of music, it is the first part, with its many lyrics and its touching love story of Faust and Gretchen (Marguerite), that has served as a primary source of inspiration. But the famous 'Chorus mysticus' concluding Part II has been set by Schumann (1849), Liszt (1857), Mahler (1910) and others – not surprisingly, since Goethe's sonorous verses were themselves inspired by music and hark back to the Easter chorus of Part I (see Sternfeld, 84–9). Part II has influenced not only the oratorio of Schumann and the symphonies of Liszt and Mahler but also the opera librettos of Boito and Busoni.

Among Faust operas, the earliest significant work is that of Spohr (1816), originally performed with spoken dialogue (the recitatives are a later addition). As in all the works discussed here, the librettist's main function was to reduce a modification of Goethe's plot to practicable dimensions by concentrating on the lyrical portions and omitting the discursive or speculative ones. The spoken dialogue, used in the original versions of both Spohr and Gounod, makes, of course, for more rapid progress between the passages, so fitting it better for musical composition. There are no comic characters in Spohr, nor is there any final redemption: Mephistopheles drags Faust to hell, a conclusion reminiscent of the folk legend. The opera, with its clever motivic work, is not without its merits, as Weber noted in a perceptive essay of 1816.

Gounod's *Faust* (1859) was originally conceived, for the Théâtre Lyrique, with spoken dialogue; when it was transferred to the Opéra it was fitted with recitatives and a ballet, in which form it became the most popular of all Faust operas. It has been much criticized (notably by Wagner and Debussy) but sections have won praise (notably from Berlioz). The main objection is that the librettists transformed Faust, a seeker for knowledge (or experience, or power), into an operatic lover; but this merely proves that composer and librettists understood the nature of the genre, and of opera as a business operation, better than their educated and literary critics. (In 1600 Rinuccini had performed similarly radical alterations on the Orpheus legend.) Gounod was not ignorant of Goethe nor of literature generally, and some of the felicitous lyrical passages are closely based on Goethe's dialogue (such as 'Non Monsieur, je ne suis ni demoiselle ni belle'). Like Goethe's Part I, Gounod's opera concludes with the salvation of Marguerite, and in fact the final chorus expands that aspect of the literary model in order to arrive at a proper transfiguration.

Boito was a more literary personality than Gounod; he wrote his own libretto for his *Mefistofele*, which adheres more closely to the outlines of Goethe's drama. He seems to have been intellectually fascinated by the character of Mephistopheles (as his expansion of Iago's role reflects in the libretto he wrote later for Verdi's *Otello*). Boito's conclusion comes closer to that of Goethe's Part II, in that when Faust speaks the crucial words and dies, cherubim cover his corpse with roses and Mephistopheles realizes that heaven has been victorious over hell. But as a lyricist Boito lacked Gounod's gifts, and this may have contributed to the failure of the first version of 1868. Another factor may have been the fidelity to Goethe which extended the time dimension too much. In the 1875 revision, which proved more successful, the composer managed to curtail his material. Still, Boito's respect for his literary model anticipated operas in the decades to come, for instance *Pelléas*, *Salome* and *Wozzeck*.

Busoni, in *Doktor Faust*, followed the plot of Goethe's drama less closely. His very title is reminiscent of the folk legend and of Marlowe. (He had studied both the old puppet play and Marlowe's tragedy, the latter sent to him by Edward J. Dent.) His procedure was not based on ignorance of Goethe, nor of world literature; like Boito, he was an educated intellectual with an international background. But Busoni was concerned about the time dimension of the opera he was to shape. For the same reason his music does not follow the libretto, which like Boito he wrote himself in a descriptive manner; it leaves a good deal to the listener's imagination. As far as the plot goes, the action between Faust and Gretchen takes place before the curtain opens: a radical departure not only from Goethe but also from Gounod and Boito. The main female character is the Duchess of Parma who, at the end of the opera, brings Faust his dead child. When Faust's hour has struck and he dies, both his and the child's corpses lie on the ground. But then a naked youth rises from the ground and steps forth into the night, and Mephistopheles throws Faust's body over his shoulder to carry him off. No salvation for Faust, then, but redemption through a younger generation. A touch of Goethe may be detected here, but Busoni does not employ Goethe's Christian framework; the salvation he achieves is thoroughly humanistic. Mephistopheles carrying off Faust's body reminds us of another puppet play, Stravinsky's *Petrushka*.

An exaggerated respect for a masterpiece of world literature, whether by Goethe, Shakespeare or Dante, may not be the best prescription for a successful opera. But it seems fair to suggest that the folk legend of the wager between Faust and the Devil will not fail to intrigue and tempt composers for years to come.

See also DAMNATION DE FAUST, LA [Berlioz]; DOKTOR FAUST (i) [I. Walter]; DOKTOR FAUST (ii) [Busoni]; DOKTOR FAUSTUS [G. Manzoni]; FAUST (i) [Spohr]; FAUST (ii) [Gounod]; MEFISTOFELE [Boito]; and VOTRE FAUST [Pousseur]. For a list of operas based on Goethe's *Faust, see* GOETHE, JOHANN WOLFGANG VON.

W. Müller (1784, Doktor Faust); I. Walter (1787, Doktor Faust); Hanke (1794, Doktor Fausts Liebgürtel); Lickl (1799, Fausts Leben, Taten und Höllenfahrt); J. Strauss (1815, Faust's Leben und Taten); Spohr (1816); Müller (1817, Dr Fausts Mantel); Bishop and others (1825, Faustus); Béancourt (1827); Saint-Lubin (1829, Le cousin du Docteur Faust); L. Bertin (1831, Fausto); Peellaert (1834); P. D. Hennebert (1835, Fausto); Rietz (1835); L. Gordigiani (1836, Fausto); Berlioz (concert version 1846, staged 1893, La damnation de Faust); F. Füchs (1846, Gutenberg); M. Lutz (1855, Faust and Marguerite); Gounod (1859)

Boito (1868, Mefistofele); Hervé (1869, Le petit Faust); F.-E. Barbier (1869, Faust et Marguerite); F. von Roda (1872); Valente (1875, Fausto); Zöllner (1887); Lutz (1888, Faust Up to Date); Kistler (1905, Faust 1. Teil); A. Brüggemann (1910, Margherita [pt 2 of tetralogy, otherwise unperf.]); Busoni (1925, Doktor Faust); H. Reutter (1936, Dr. Johannes Faust); Engelmann (1951, Dr. Fausts Höllenfahrt); Kupferman (1953, Dr Faustus Lights the Lights); Bentzon (1964, Faust III); J. Berg (comp. 1966, Johannes Doktor Faustus); Pousseur (1969, Votre Faust); Rihm (1977, Faust und Yorick); G. Manzoni (1989, Doktor Faustus)

*

K. J. Simrock, ed.: *Faust: das Volksspiel und das Puppenspiel, nebst einem Anhang über den Ursprung der Faustsage* (Berlin, 1877)

P. Spitta: *Zur Musik* (Berlin, 1892) [incl. 'Die älteste Faust-Oper und Goethes Stellung zur Musik', 199–234]

M. Friedländer, ed.: *Gedichte von Goethe in Kompositionen seiner Zeitgenossen* (Weimar, 1896, 1916)

W. Bode: *Stunden mit Goethe* (Berlin, 1905–21) [incl. K. Eberwein: 'Die Musik zum Goetheschen Faust', viii, 45–55]

E. Newman: 'Faust in Music', *Musical Studies* (London, 1905), 71–100

P. Magnette: *Les traducteurs du 'Faust' de Goethe en musique* (Liège, 1908)

K. W. Kube: *Goethes Faust in französischer Auffassung und Bühnendarstellung* (Berlin, 1931)

Z. Jachimecki: *Od pierwszej do ostatniej muzyki do Fausta* [From the Earliest to the Most Recent Music for Faust] (Kraków, 1932)

G. Bianquis: *Faust à travers quatre siècles* (Paris, 1935)

E. M. Butler: *The Fortunes of Faust* (Cambridge, 1952)

M. Unger: *Der Faustopernplan Beethovens und Goethes* (Regensburg, 1952)

F. W. Sternfeld: *Goethe and Music* (New York, 1954)

C. Dédéyan: *Le thème de Faust dans la littérature européenne* (Paris, 1959)

J. W. Kelly: *The Faust Legend in Music* (Detroit, 1976)

A. Meier: *Faustlibretti* (Frankfurt, 1990)   F. W. STERNFELD

Faust (i). *Romantische Oper* in two acts by LOUIS SPOHR to a libretto by Joseph Carl Bernard; Prague, Estates Theatre, 1 September 1816 (revised version, in three acts, London, Covent Garden, 15 July 1852).

Faust	baritone
Mephistofeles	bass
Wohlhaldt ⎫	tenor
Wagner ⎬ *friends of Faust*	tenor
Kaylinger	baritone
Moor ⎭	bass
Röschen	mezzo-soprano
Franz	tenor
Kunigunde *Count Hugo's fiancée*	soprano
Sir Gulf *a robber knight*	bass
Count Hugo	tenor
A Witch	soprano
Sycorax	soprano

Townspeople, soldiers, demons, imprisoned women, witches, wedding guests

Setting Strasbourg and Aachen in the 16th century

The original version of *Faust* was composed in Vienna between May and mid-September 1813, during Spohr's three-year residence there as orchestral director of the Theater an der Wien. Bernard, a Viennese journalist and author, based his libretto on various versions of the Faust legend (*see* FAUST above), but was not influenced by the recently published first part of Goethe's *Faust*. Disputes between Spohr and the lessee of the theatre, Count Palffy von Erdöd, over the terms of Spohr's contract delayed production of the opera and led to Spohr's resignation. *Faust* received its première three years later in Prague, under Weber's baton, while Spohr was on a concert tour of Italy. When Spohr took up the appointment of opera director at Frankfurt in 1817 he wrote a new recitative and aria, 'Liebe ist die zarte Blüthe' (no.1a) for the baritone Johann Nepomuk Schelbe, who sang Faust in the Frankfurt production. This version of *Faust*, with spoken dialogue linking the musical numbers, was soon performed in other important theatres. From the mid-1820s it became customary to divide the opera into three acts, with Spohr's overture to *Macbeth* (1825) as an introduction to the third act (preceding no.15), and to add the scena and aria 'Ich bin allein' from Spohr's *Der Zweikampf mit der Geliebten* (1811) as an extra aria for Kunigunde (preceding no.14). In 1851 Spohr was approached by Frederick Gye of the Royal Italian Opera in London with a request to set the dialogue to music so that *Faust* could be performed as a grand opera. At first he refused, considering the task impossible, but finally agreed and took the opportunity to revise and shorten much of the dialogue, making several minor changes to the plot. He divided the opera into three acts and composed an

Title page of the vocal score of Spohr's 'Faust' (Leipzig: Peters, 1853)

orchestral prelude to the third act. The new version was taken up by many German theatres during the 1850s. Many of the individual arias and duets were widely popular in the concert hall during the 19th century. 'Liebe ist die zarte Blüthe' is still occasionally heard.

In Bernard's version of the opera Faust is portrayed as a man ruled by his passions. He believes that even though his power is derived from the Devil he can use it for good purposes, and he deludes himself into believing that his will is strong enough to deliver him from the clutches of Mephistofeles. He wavers between his love for the pure Röschen and his lust for the beautiful countess Kunigunde, whom he rescues from the clutches of Sir Gulf. At the wedding feast of Hugo and Kunigunde he seduces Kunigunde by means of a magic potion obtained from the witches on the Blocksberg. He then kills Hugo in a duel. In the final scene Röschen drowns herself, and Faust, deserted by everyone, is dragged off to hell by Mephistofeles' demons.

The overture was described by Spohr as portraying Faust's inner conflict. It introduces an important feature of the opera: the use of short musical motifs which, in Weber's words (in the introduction to his Prague performance), 'hold it together artistically'. The principal motifs, which may be designated the Hell, Love and Faust motifs, form the opening theme of the overture and, together with the Magic Potion motif and various instances of thematic reminiscence, they appear at various key points in the opera. The motifs, nearly always in the accompaniment, make explicit something that would not otherwise be obvious to the audience, or emphasize some connection with an earlier part of the action. For example, the Hell motif appears in the accompaniment to Kunigunde's scena 'Die stille Nacht entweicht', when she asserts that love is powerful enough to vanquish the power of evil; by this means Spohr intimates that her confidence is misplaced. Another

particularly telling appearance of the motif is in the final scene of the opera when Faust defies Mephistofeles with the words 'Doch mein Wille ist mein Schutz' ('But my will is my protection') but sings them to the music of the Hell motif, showing that, contrary to his belief, he is inextricably in the toils of the Devil.

In other respects, too, *Faust* marks an important landmark in the development of German Romantic opera. Spohr's concern to create scene complexes, rather than merely a string of individual numbers, points the way towards the continuity of his later operas. His striking use of chromatic harmony was recognized by Weber, who wrote in his introduction to the Prague première: 'this dark, Romantic spirit-world is ideally matched with the composer's inmost musical character. Owing to this fact the work as a whole is marked by great aptness of colour – grand musical and dramatic effects of charm and tenderness alternating with shatteringly powerful effects in the ensembles and choruses'. CLIVE BROWN

Faust (ii). *Opéra* in five acts by CHARLES-FRANÇOIS GOUNOD to a libretto by JULES BARBIER and MICHEL CARRÉ after Carré's *Faust et Marguerite* and JOHANN WOLFGANG VON GOETHE's *Faust*, Part I (in the French translation by GÉRARD DE NERVAL); Paris, Théâtre Lyrique, 19 March 1859.

Le docteur Faust *a philosopher*	tenor
Méphistophélès	bass
Marguerite	soprano
Valentin *a soldier, Marguerite's brother*	baritone
Wagner *friend of Valentin*	baritone
Siébel *student of Faust*	soprano
Marthe *Marguerite's guardian*	soprano

Young girls, labourers, students, soldiers, burghers, matrons, invisible demons, church choir, witches, queens and courtesans of antiquity, celestial voices

Setting Germany, 16th century

During his tenure of the Prix de Rome, 1839–42, Gounod's interest in *Faust* Part I as an operatic subject was aroused by Nerval's translation of Goethe's play. He attempted a setting of the church scene as early as 1849, but plans for an opera did not materialize until he met the libretto-writing team of Barbier and Carré in 1855. Carré himself had already written *Faust et Marguerite*, a three-act play loosely fashioned after Goethe that was moderately successful at the Gymnase-Dramatique in 1850. It provided the basic scaffolding for Gounod's work, including the idea of enlarged roles for Valentin and Siébel (a minor player in Goethe's *Auerbachs Keller* episode). Some elements from Goethe not included by Carré were also brought into the opera, most notably the death of Valentin, the *Walpurgisnacht*, the prison scene and the apotheosis; Goethe's play, however, is best not taken into account in critical assessments of Gounod's opera as a piece of music theatre.

Gounod finished composing *Faust* in autumn 1858 and it was immediately put into rehearsal at the Théâtre Lyrique. Caroline Carvalho was assigned the role of Marguerite, Emile Balanqué was given Méphistophélès, and Hector Gruyer Faust. Gruyer's inability to cope with the part became painfully clear in dress rehearsals at the end of February 1859, and he was replaced at that late stage by a veteran from the Opéra-Comique roster,

Joseph-Théodore-Désiré Barbot, who went on to give the first performance after having learnt the role in only three weeks. The score that Gounod brought to rehearsals was much longer than the one eventually performed. Several entire numbers were cut before the première: a trio in Act 1 for Siébel, Faust and Wagner; a duet in Act 2 for Marguerite and Valentin; three sets of *couplets* for one of Marguerite's girlfriends (Lise), Valentin and Siébel, as well as a chorus of young girls in Act 4; and a large strophic piece for Marguerite in the last act. The *couplets* for Valentin ('Chaque jour nouvelle affaire') were replaced before the première, by the Soldiers' Chorus, 'Gloire immortelle de nos aïeux', the music of which was taken from Gounod's aborted operatic project *Ivan le terrible*. During the first rehearsal period the church scene was also transferred from its initial spot after Valentin's *couplets* to the end of the fourth act, possibly at the insistence of Carvalho. Gounod tore out of his autograph full score the sections cut before the première, and none of this music was published in his lifetime, save for Siébel's Act 4 *couplets* 'Versez vos chagrins', which appeared as an extract from the opera shortly after the première. The autographs of the trio, duet and Valentin's *couplets*, however, surfaced in public collections during the 1970s.

Faust was a considerable success during its first run at the Théâtre Lyrique in 1859. It was published in June of that year by Antoine Choudens, who helped arrange productions of the work in Strasbourg, Rouen and Bordeaux in 1860. Gounod supplied recitatives to replace the original spoken dialogue for these performances. Productions on many major German stages followed in the next two years; at the Dresden première in August 1861 the work was called *Margarete* for the first time, a symbolic distancing from Goethe's play that has endured on German stages. In the second edition of the vocal score (1860), as well as in several

early productions, the position of the church scene was moved from the end of the fourth act to before the Soldiers' Chorus; the composer himself was non-committal on the placement of the church scene and there is a long record for both solutions. *Faust* had its Italian première at La Scala in November 1862 and was first produced in England (in Italian) at Her Majesty's Theatre in June 1863. At the first English-language production in January 1864 (also at Her Majesty's) Gounod arranged music from the opera's prelude to create a new solo number for Valentin in Act 2, 'Even the bravest heart may swell', to a text by his friend Henry Chorley (the poet Onésime Pradère later supplied the French verse 'Avant de quitter ces lieux'); the composer made this famous addition reluctantly, however, and the number never appeared in a French vocal score in his lifetime. Following the bankruptcy of the Théâtre Lyrique, *Faust* had a lavish production at the Opéra in March 1869 with a ballet and a new set of *couplets* for Méphistophélès supplied by the composer; Christine Nilsson sang Marguerite, Jean-Baptiste Faure was Méphistophélès. It became the most frequently performed opera at that house (new productions followed in 1875, 1893, 1908, 1934, 1956 and 1975) and one of the staples of the international repertory, though since World War II its popularity has waned somewhat.

ACT 1 *Faust's study* Rather than foreshadow later melodies and situations or the opera's principal dramatic argument, the instrumental prelude illustrates Faust's dilemma at the beginning of the work: it alludes both to his erudition, by means of chromatic contrapuntal texture, and to the simple joys of nature, through music tinged with pastoral *couleur locale*. At the outset Faust is deeply depressed by his inability to attain fulfilment through knowledge. In an opening number dominated by measured declamation and rapidly changing textures (an unusual first scene for French opera of the period) he contemplates suicide but is twice stopped short of drinking poison by the sound of an offstage pastoral chorus. He condemns happiness, science and faith, and calls upon Satan for deliverance. Méphistophélès appears (duet, 'Me voici'). Faust confesses that he covets youth above all and launches into an energetic *cabalette* ('A moi les plaisirs'). Méphistophélès agrees to indulge the philosopher in return for eventual service in the nether regions. When Faust hesitates to accept that condition, Méphistophélès conjures up a vision of Marguerite, while love music from the later garden scene is anticipated in the orchestra. Immediately enamoured, Faust signs the parchment and is transformed into a young nobleman. Both sing an ensemble reprise of 'A moi les plaisirs', a semitone higher than at its first appearance, to bring down the curtain.

ACT 2 *Fairgrounds at the town gates; a tavern is seen on the left* The curtain opens to a festive chorus of students, soldiers, burghers, young girls and matrons who sing individually at first and are then contrapuntally combined à la Meyerbeer in a rousing conclusion. The soldier Valentin appears, clutching a medallion given to him by his sister Marguerite; he is about to leave for battle and instructs his friends, including Wagner and Siébel, to look after her. They sit down for a final drink. Méphistophélès suddenly materializes and entertains them with a strophic song about the golden calf (*ronde*, 'Le veau d'or'), the blasphemy rendered more trenchant by a musical parody of hymn style just before the refrain is heard each time. Valentin is incited to violence when Méphistophélès takes the name of his sister lightly, but his sword breaks in mid-air before reaching its target. Confronted with a sinister supernatural power, Valentin and his companions brandish the crossed pommels of their swords before the Devil (chorale, 'De l'enfer qui vient émousser') – a visual echo of the Benediction of the Swords in Meyerbeer's *Les Huguenots*. Méphistophélès, left alone on the stage, is soon joined by Faust and a group of waltzing villagers (waltz and chorus, 'Ainsi que la brise légère'). When Marguerite appears among the villagers, Faust offers her his arm. She modestly rejects his advance and quickly departs, a first appearance for the tragic heroine that is effective because it is understated, brief and set against a background of nonchalant *divertissement*.

ACT 3 *Marguerite's garden* Siébel is in love with Marguerite and leaves a bouquet for her (*couplets*, 'Faites-lui mes aveux'). Faust and Méphistophélès enter; while the latter procures a gift for Marguerite, Faust apostrophizes her home and the protective embrace of nature (*cavatine*, 'Salut! demeure chaste et pure'). Méphistophélès returns and positions a jewel box for the young girl. Marguerite appears, wondering about Faust in a recitative that is confined to a single pitch low in the tessitura, a restrained musical utterance for unaccustomed thoughts. She goes on to sing a large three-part *air*. The initial slow section of this composite set piece is a ballade about the King of Thulé ('Il était un roi de Thulé') with an archaic flavour rendered by modal inflections in the music. In the ensuing section Marguerite comes across the offerings of both suitors; mesmerized by the jewels, she sings a *cabalette* that exudes breathless excitement through effective distribution of the text ('Ah! je ris de me voir'). Dame Marthe, Marguerite's

guardian, tells her that the jewels must be a gift from an admirer. Méphistophélès and Faust join the two women. The former attempts to seduce Marthe, accompanied by music bustling with comic verve, while Faust and Marguerite converse in a more sentimental vein and with more naturalistic declamation (quartet, 'Prenez mon bras'). After both temporarily disappear from view, Méphistophélès casts a spell over the flowers in the garden; the sound of horns beneath shimmering strings evokes an aura of the supernatural. When the two return, Faust woos her directly (duet, 'Laisse-moi, laisse-moi contempler ton visage'), and Marguerite coyly responds by plucking petals of a daisy in the game of 'He loves me, he loves me not'; a rising sequence in 3rds carries the music from F major to B major, a far-reaching modulation that underlines her final 'He loves me'. The music veers flatwards to the incandescent realm of Db major for the central section of the duet ('O nuit d'amour'), containing Marguerite's confession of love. She suddenly breaks away from Faust's embrace and in an agitated *cabalette* ('Partez, partez') begs him to leave. The *cabalette* does not, however, bring the number to a close: Faust continues with a reminiscence of his *cavatine*, and, before running off, Marguerite promises to see him the next day. Faust resolves to abandon his pursuit but is suddenly prevented from doing so by Méphistophélès, who sardonically suggests to the philosopher that he remain to witness Marguerite's soliloquy at her window. She yearns for Faust's quick return, above fragmentation and development (with continually changing instrumental colours) of the melody that will burst forth in complete form and *fortissimo* at the moment Faust emerges from the shadows to take her into his arms.

ACT 4.i *Marguerite's room* Marguerite has given birth to Faust's child; she is ignored by young girls in the street. Saddened that Faust seems to have abandoned her, she sits down to spin and sings. Her *air*, 'Il ne revient pas', compares favourably with the more famous spinning songs by Schubert and Berlioz; particularly evocative is the setting for the refrain 'Il ne revient pas', simply declaimed on the dominant and most often harmonized by a cadential progression using the Neapolitan chord, an apt illustration of her desolation. Siébel, ever faithful, attempts to revive her spirits.

4.ii *A public square* The return of Valentin is heralded by a Soldiers' Chorus ('Gloire immortelle de nos aïeux'), including a noisy stage band. After receiving evasive replies from Siébel to enquiries about his sister, Valentin furiously charges into the house. While he is inside, Méphistophélès and Faust appear. The former satirically plays a lover delivering a strophic serenade beneath Marguerite's window ('Vous qui faites l'endormie'); the effect is made particularly grotesque by the faulty declamation and incisive chromatic turns in the orchestra – in stark contrast with the suave and heartfelt delivery of Faust beneath her window in the previous act. Valentin re-emerges and demands to know who is responsible for Marguerite's fall from innocence. Faust draws his sword while Valentin and Méphistophélès exchange threats (trio, 'Que voulez-vous, messieurs?'); the orchestra unleashes a juggernaut of dotted rhythms that culminate in the duel between Valentin and Faust. Valentin is mortally wounded. As he dies, he lays the blame upon Marguerite and damns her for eternity; the assembled townspeople urge him to display Christian compassion.

2. 'Faust' (Gounod), Act 3 (Marguerite's garden): engraving by Lamy showing the original production at the Théâtre Lyrique, Paris, 19 March 1859

4.iii *A cathedral* Marguerite attempts to pray but organ music, imprecations from Méphistophélès and a liturgical chorus (originally set to the Latin text of the 'Dies irae') combine to oppress her. Formal coherence is achieved largely by two extended periodic solos for each of the principals: Marguerite's 'Seigneur accueillez ma prière' in C major is a counterpoise to Méphistophélès's previous 'Souviens toi du passé' in C minor. She succeeds in completing her prayer but faints when Méphistophélès unleashes a final curse.

ACT 5.i *The Harz Mountains: Walpurgis Night* A chorus of will-o'-the wisps is heard as Méphistophélès and Faust appear. They are soon surrounded by a group of witches who sing music no more terrifying than (and faintly anticipating) Gounod's later Funeral March for a Marionette from the *Jeanne d'Arc* incidental music (chorus, 'Un, deux, et trois'; only in the first edition). Faust wishes to flee but Méphistophélès hastens to carry him off.

5.ii *A decorated cavern peopled with queens and courtesans of antiquity* Faust is surrounded by the most beautiful women in history and momentarily loses his presence of mind in a strophic drinking song ('Doux nectar', only in the first edition; the ballet may be inserted in place of the song). Suddenly Faust sees an image of Marguerite and demands to be taken to her. As Méphistophélès and Faust depart, the mountain closes and the witches return.

5.iii *The interior of a prison* Marguerite has been incarcerated for infanticide, but through the offices of Méphistophélès Faust has obtained the keys to her cell. Diminished 7ths resolving to 6-4 chords create an ecstatic atmosphere when Marguerite awakens to the sound of Faust's voice. They sing a love duet ('Oui c'est toi je t'aime') in which past moments of bliss are recalled musically in the transition between the first set of parallel strophes and the *cabalette* (the latter section, 'Viens! viens! quittons ces lieux!', appeared for the first time in Italian-language editions in 1864 and is absent from most French editions). Faust begs her to flee with

him. Méphistophélès suddenly appears and urges Faust and Marguerite to follow him. Marguerite resists and calls for divine protection, singing the wide-spanning heroic melody 'Anges purs, anges radieux' in an ascending stepwise sequence. The goal of the sequence is the C major of the concluding apotheosis 'Christ est ressuscité!' (recalling the tonality of Marguerite's supplication in the church scene). Faust falls to his knees in prayer as Marguerite's soul rises to heaven.

*   *   *

The case against *Faust* has been made often and vociferously. Buttressed by views of Marguerite as part society débutante, Méphistophélès as tinged with shades of Leporello, and Faust as little more than lovesick, many have not detected the sort of universality in the characters often admired in other 19th-century masterpieces. As a corollary, the transcendental significance apparently demanded by one of the literary sources (Goethe's play) has been considered as sacrificed to bathetic sentimentality, with attendant criticism of the musical style as wanting in dramatic chiaroscuro, merely elegant and sometimes even saccharine.

Standing prominently on the other side of the critical ledger is the sheer effectiveness of many scenes on the stage. In a highly personal adaptation of Goethe's episode of Valentin's death, Gounod draws a clear and theatrically vivid line between the intolerance of Valentin and the Christian morality of the majority. The church tableau brilliantly captures Marguerite's isolation against an impersonal background of archaic organ preluding, chant-like choral writing and gothic set. The ringing down of the Act 3 curtain with Méphistophélès' laughter and a *fortissimo* orchestral statement of a melody heard earlier only softly, and in a fragmented form, was so impressive that the procedure of the act-terminating peroration was taken up by composers such as Ponchielli and Cilea. The concluding apotheosis works well as a spectacular culmination to the musically uplifting 'Anges purs, anges radieux'. Gounod is also successful with the more intimate episodes for Marguerite in Act 3. For example, there is a touching spontaneity in Marguerite's declaimed interruptions in her ballade to wonder about Faust that was new to the French stage in its day and a harbinger of the naturalistic characterization of later figures in French opera such as Massenet's Manon. The ensuing quartet features a wealth of finely wrought detail, both in orchestration (too often overlooked in critiques of the work) and shaping of the melodic line.

Faust became particularly important to the French musical establishment at the end of the century. A work by a winner of the Prix de Rome that could claim to be thoroughly modern and personal in style at its première, and go on to international stages, was a significant enhancement to the musical prestige of a French operatic culture previously dominated by Meyerbeer and the none-too-easily exportable genre of *opéra comique*. Its national value was enhanced because, after some initial assessments as 'Wagnerian', Gounod's compositional voice in *Faust* was heard as important in the definition of a 'French' musical aesthetic.

See also FAUST above.   STEVEN HUEBNER

Fausta. *Melodramma* in two acts by GAETANO DONIZETTI to a libretto by DOMENICO GILARDONI, completed by the composer, after an unidentified source; Naples, Teatro S Carlo, 12 January 1832.

Set during the reign of the Emperor Constantine (306–37), *Fausta* is a variant of the Phaedra story. The second wife of the emperor (baritone), Fausta (soprano), loves her stepson Crispo [Crispus] (tenor), who in turn is enamoured of Beroe (soprano). When the empress declares her love he is horrified and spurns her, a rejection which results in Fausta's false accusation that her stepson had made improper advances to her. Crispus is exiled, but with the connivance of the emperor's enemy, Fausta's father Massimiano [Maximian] (bass), he is condemned to death. Unable to save him, Fausta takes poison and, having confessed her guilt, dies.

As Donizetti's first *opera seria* for Giuseppina Ronzi de Begnis, a singer he preferred to Malibran, *Fausta* contains a remarkable aria-finale in which the Larghetto, with its text almost certainly by the composer, is in the then uncommon scheme of decasyllabic lines and boasts a subtly inflected melody. There was a notable revival at La Fenice, Venice, on 25 December 1833, with Pasta and Donzelli, for whom Donizetti wrote a new duet (later inserted in the Milan score of *Maria Stuarda*). The opera's first 20th-century production was at Rome in 1981, with Raina Kabaivanska as Fausta and Renato Bruson as Constantine (a role originally written for Tamburini).   WILLIAM ASHBROOK

Faustina. *See* BORDONI, FAUSTINA.

Faustini, Giovanni (*b* Venice, 1615; *d* Venice, 19 Dec 1651). Italian librettist and impresario. He was the author of 14 librettos, most of them set to music by Cavalli, and was impresario at the S Cassiano, S Moisè and S Apollinare theatres in Venice. At his death he left several incomplete librettos, which were subsequently finished and performed under the auspices of his brother Marco, who assumed Giovanni's role as impresario.

Except for three mythological works, Faustini's plots are all freely invented variations on one basic pattern. Set in foreign lands, usually African, they involve characters of widely contrasting social levels, often borrowed from the romance tradition – knights errant, maidens in disguise, magicians. Elaborate pseudo-historical backgrounds are provided for them. The action revolves around the romantic misadventures of two pairs of lovers of noble birth, attended by assorted comic servants, who are separated through various complications and coincidences and finally reunited. Many of the devices that help to propel the drama and contribute to the confusion – such as disguise, overheard conversations, misdelivered letters and sleeping potions – were standard comic routines going back through Spanish drama and the pastoral to Roman comedy. Faustini's standard poetic language consists of freely alternating 7- and 11-syllable verses, unrhymed or rhymed irregularly; these are normally set as recitative. They are occasionally interrupted by closed forms (usually strophic), using a single metre or regular rhyme scheme; these are normally set lyrically, in aria style, like the briefer passages of three or four lines used as refrains. In addition to his powers of invention, Faustini is noteworthy for his keen sense of intrigue and superior dramatic craftsmanship, and, in an age of operatic dilettantism, for his commitment (expressed repeatedly in the prefaces to his printed librettos) to libretto writing as a profession. His annual collaborations with Cavalli over a decade helped to define the nature of Venetian opera for the rest of the century.

dm – *drama per musica*

Librettos for Cavalli: *La virtù de' strali d'Amore* (tragicomica musicale), 1642; *Egisto* (favola dramatica musicale), 1643; *Ormindo* (favola regia per musica), 1644; *Doriclea* (dramma musicale), 1645; *Titone* (dm), 1645; *Euripo* (dm), 1649; *Oristeo* (dm), 1651; *Rosinda* (dm), 1651; *Calisto* (dm), 1651; *Eritrea* (drama), 1652; *Elena* (dm, with N. Minato), 1659

Librettos for other composers: *Ersilla* (dm), various comps., 1648; *Eupatra* (dm), P. A. Ziani, 1655; *Medea placata*, comp. 1662; *Alciade* (drama), Ziani, 1667; *Il tiranno humiliato d'Amore, overo Il Meraspe* (dm, with N. Beregan and others), C. Pallavicino, 1667

*

B. Brunelli: 'L'impresario in angustie', *Rivista italiana del dramma*, iii (1941), 311–41

R. Giazotto: 'La guerra dei palchi', NRMI, i (1967), 245–86, 465–508

J. Glover: *The Teatro Sant'Apollinare and the Development of Seventeenth-Century Venetian Opera* (diss., U. of Oxford, 1975)

——: *Cavalli* (London, 1978)

G. Morelli: *Scompiglio e lamento (simmetrie dell'incostanza e incostanza delle simmetrie): 'L'Egisto' di Faustini e Cavalli* (Venice, 1982)

B. Glixon: *Recitative in Seventeenth-Century Venetian Opera: its Dramatic Function and Musical Language* (diss., Rutgers U., 1985)

P. Fabbri: 'Istituti metrici e formali', SOI, vi (1988), 165–233

——: *Il secolo cantante: per una storia del libretto d'opera nel seicento* (Bologna, 1990)

E. Rosand: *Opera in Seventeenth-Century Venice: the Creation of a Genre* (Berkeley, 1990)

B. L. Glixon and J. E. Glixon: 'Marco Faustini and Venetian Opera Production in the 1650s: Recent Archival Discoveries', JM, x (1992–3), 48–73   ELLEN ROSAND

Faustini, Marco (*b* ?Venice; *d* ?Venice, after 1675). Italian impresario, brother of Giovanni Faustini. On the latter's death he took over the contract for the management of the Teatro S Apollinare, Venice, which he ran until 1657, moving from there to the Teatro S Cassiano (1658–60) and finally to the Teatro SS Giovanni e Paolo (1660–68). He used the last-named in particular for productions of his late brother's dramas. His correspondence (in *I-Vas*, Scuola Grande di S Marco, *buste* 188, 194) is an important source of information about theatre practice of the time.

See also VENICE, §2.

C. B. Schmidt: 'An Episode in the History of Venetian Opera: the *Tito* Commission (1665–6)', *JAMS*, xxxi (1978), 442–66

B. L. Glixon and J. E. Glixon: 'Marco Faustini and Venetian Opera Production in the 1650s: Recent Archival Discoveries', *JM*, x (1992–3), 48–73

For further bibliography *see* FAUSTINI, GIOVANNI.

THOMAS WALKER

Favart. Theatre in Paris. The principal home, from 1783, of the Opéra-Comique, it was reconstructed in 1840 and 1898 and known familiarly as the Salle Favart; *see* PARIS, §§3(i), 4(iii) and 5(iii).

Favart [Favard], Charles-Simon (*b* Paris, 13 Nov 1710; *d* Belleville [now in Paris], 12 May 1792). French librettist, playwright, composer and impresario. He was the most highly regarded librettist of *opéra comique* during the mid-18th century, which saw both the Querelle des Bouffons and the gradual replacement in the genre of vaudevilles (popular songs) by newly composed, italianate *ariettes*.

According to his own fragmentary *Mémoires* Favart inherited from his father, a pastrycook, a love of the theatre and of vaudevilles; his mother encouraged his literary studies. He attended a *collège* until the death of his father necessitated his return to the family business, in which he continued even after his first successes at the fairground theatres of the Opéra-Comique. Many of his early pieces (among them several parodies) were written with others, including his mentor Charles-François Panard, whose allegorical satire he imitated. These nevertheless brought him to the attention of noble patrons, including the Marshal de Saxe.

Favart's first masterpiece was *La chercheuse d'esprit* of 1741 (after La Fontaine), which portrayed the awakening to love of young rustic *ingénus*. It was with

Frontispiece to Charles-Simon Favart's 'La chercheuse d'esprit' (1741): engraving from 'Théâtre de M. et Mme Favart', vi (Paris, 1763)

this 'genre galant et comique' (as Favart called it) that he sought to ennoble the tone of *opéra comique*, previously prone to indecency. Without altogether eliminating *double entendre*, Favart emphasized comic naivety of utterance with a transparency of sentiment that looks forward to Rousseau. In 1743 Favart joined with Jean Monnet, the new impresario of the Opéra-Comique, in an effort to reform the spectacle both morally and materially. For a salary of 2000 francs, he agreed to write and adapt pieces, recruit and train new actors and supervise rehearsals; Monnet constructed a fine new theatre at the Foire St Laurent, and engaged Jean-Georges Noverre and François Boucher to create ballets and decors, respectively. In 1743 the Foire St Laurent saw the premières of Favart's *Le siège de Cythère* (a veiled parody of Quinault and Lully's *Armide*) and *Le ballet des Dindons* (a parody of Fuzelier and Rameau's *Les Indes galantes*). During 1745 Marie-Justine Duronceray (as 'Mlle Chantilly') made her début in *Les fêtes publiques*, which celebrated the dauphin's wedding; by the end of the year she and Favart had married. Also during this year the Comédie-Italienne and the Comédie-Française, jealous of the Opéra-Comique's success, suppressed all but pantomime entertainments, and then completely shut down the spectacle. At this point Favart secured employment as director of the theatrical company of Maurice, Marshal de Saxe, commander of French forces in Flanders.

De Saxe told Favart that his troupe entered into his military and political thinking; this manifested itself in the choice of repertory (as in Favart's reworking of *Le siège de Cythère*) and, extraordinarily, in the troupe's performing alternately in allied and enemy camps. In the latter Favart probably met the Genoan diplomat Giacomo Durazzo, who as head of Viennese theatres was later to engage Favart as his theatrical agent. The hardships of war were aggravated for Favart by De Saxe's amorous pursuit of his wife, which provoked her flight to Paris. De Saxe later had her imprisoned in a convent, while Favart fled a trumped-up prosecution for debt. After the marshal's death in 1750 the couple resumed their careers, primarily at the Comédie-Italienne, where Mme Favart had performed briefly in 1749.

The 1750s saw the creation of some of Favart's most genial pieces and his reputation at its height. Parodies such as *Les amours de Bastien et Bastienne* (after Rousseau's *Le devin du village*) and *Raton et Rosette* (after Mondonville's *Titon et l'Aurore*) rivalled their models in popularity. Parisian performances of Italian intermezzos by the 'Bouffon' troupe between 1752 and 1754 prompted Favart (and others) to insert *ariettes* from them into new *opéras comiques*; he also translated several intermezzos, and wrote pasticcios using selections of their *ariettes*. These transitional genres evolved rapidly into the modern form of *opéra comique*.

During this period Favart benefited from the patronage of Mme de Pompadour and the court, especially after 1758, when he became a director of the Comédie-Italienne (which merged with the Opéra-Comique in 1762). Beginning in 1756, Favart composed a number of entertainments for the Marquise de Mauconseil and her palace theatre at Bagatelle. He served briefly as 'Historiographe des Menus-Plaisirs du Roi', and in 1763 was commissioned by the court to write a comedy, *L'Anglais à Bordeaux*, celebrating the end of the Seven Years War. This work earned him a royal pension of 1000 livres, later increased when he was named *compositeur des spectacles de la cour*. (The title first appears in the libretto, dedicated to the dauphine, of *L'amitié à l'épreuve*.)

In 1759 Favart renewed his contacts with Durazzo, who desired his services as a recruiting agent, adapter, censor and supplier of pieces for the French theatre in Vienna (the Burgtheater), and as a window on the Parisian theatrical and literary scene. Their correspondence, of which edited portions have been published, shows Favart assuming much the same urbane tone as Friedrich Grimm in his *Correspondance littéraire*. Favart was originally to have collaborated with Gluck on new works, but did not do so: Durazzo failed to use a ballet scenario Favart had drafted for celebrations of Archduke Joseph's first wedding in 1760, and later there were misunderstandings concerning some of his other works. Favart helped engineer Durazzo's dismissal in 1764, although, before this, he had helped considerably in recruiting for the Viennese company, as he and his wife had at their disposal a vast network of theatrical contacts throughout Europe. He had also supervised the first (Parisian) edition of Gluck's *Orfeo ed Euridice*, thereby greatly enhancing the composer's reputation.

During the latter part of his career Favart attempted to come to terms with the new *comédie mêlée d'ariettes*. His librettos in this genre were not as successful as were his earlier vaudeville comedies, or librettos by more progressive authors such as Sedaine. *Soliman II* (1761), which did achieve wide and lasting success, is really a verse play interspersed with a few musical numbers and with a closing *divertissement*. *Annette et Lubin* (1762, after Marmontel), contains some new music, but many more vaudevilles; in writing the piece Favart had aimed to 'ramener le public à l'ancien goût de l'opéra comique'. *La fée Urgèle* (1765, after Voltaire) and *Les moissonneurs* (1768), both true *comédies mêlées d'ariettes*, were better received, but Favart's 1775 recasting of *Cythère assiégée* as an *opéra-ballet* was neither a success nor an improvement on his version of 1748. After his wife's death in 1772 Favart largely withdrew from active work in the theatre to his home at Belleville.

Favart's fame rests principally on his vaudeville comedies, from *La chercheuse d'esprit* onward. As a parodist he was unrivalled, and gentler than most; the playwright La Noue staged Favart's parody of his own *Mahomet II*, and sent the poet his compliments. Though honoured still as a literary figure, Favart has yet fully to be rediscovered as a musician. He composed many of the *airs* in his *opéras comiques*, mimicking traditional *airs* and *galant* modern melodies with equal ease. But his greatest talent lay in the appropriate choice and retexting of popular tunes (many of which are now untraceable), taking full advantage of their salient musical features.

Despite his discomfort with modern techniques, Favart was a progressive force in French musical theatre. He and his wife pioneered accurate, historical costume before Le Kain at the Comédie-Française. Favart's letters to Durazzo are full of derisive comments on the traditional repertory of the Opéra and news of the triumphs of modern *opéra comique*. Though not entirely able himself to accommodate developments in the new form of the spectacle, he supported its best composers, such as Monsigny, Philidor and Grétry. One of the most important collections of his works is the

Théâtre de M. et Mme Favart, ou Recueil des comédies, parodies et opéras-comiques, published in ten volumes (Paris, 1763–72). Favart's works were enormously popular abroad, in translations and resettings as well as in their original versions.

PCI – *Paris, Comédie-Italienne (Hôtel de Bourgogne)*
PSG – *Paris, Foire St Germain* PSL – *Paris, Foire St Laurent*

oc – *opéra comique* par – *parody*
vaud – *vaudeville*

first performed in Paris unless otherwise stated; composer and title of parodied musical works are in square brackets; composers of other works are unknown unless otherwise stated

OPÉRAS COMIQUES AND PARODIES IN VAUDEVILLES

Polichinelle comte de Paonfier (vaud, with Largillière *fils*, after P. Néricault-Destouches: *Le glorieux*), PSG, 14 March 1732
Les jumelles (oc), PSG, 22 March 1734
Le génie de l'Opéra-Comique (prol.), PSL, 28 June 1735
L'enlèvement précipité (oc), PSL, 29 July 1735
La répétition interrompue (oc, with C.-F. Panard), PSL, 6 Aug 1735 (PSL, 14 March 1757, as La répétition interrompue, ou Le petit-maître malgré lui)
La dragonne (oc, with Panard), PSL, 25 Aug 1736
Le nouveau Parnasse (prol.), PSL, 25 Aug 1736
Le prince nocturne, ou Le Normand dupé, ou La pièce sans titre (oc, with Panard), PSG, 2 Feb 1737
Marianne (with Panard, after P. C. Marivaux: *La vie de Marianne*), PSG, 3 Feb 1737
Le vaudeville (prol., with Panard), PSG, 3 Feb 1737
L'abondance (oc, with A. J. Le Valois d'Orville and T. Laffichard), PSG, 21 March 1737
Le bal bourgeois (oc), PSG, 13 March 1738 (rev., PSL, Aug 1761)
La fête de la Halle (oc with prol., with Carolet and Panard), PSG, 13 March 1738; also as *La Halle galante*
Moulinet premier (par of La Noue: *Mahomet II*), PSG, 15 March 1739
Les réjouissances publiques (ambigu-comique), PSL, 19 Sept 1739
Harmonide (par) [J.-N.-P. Royer: Zaïde], PSL, 1 Oct 1739
Les amours de Gogo (par) [Rameau: La poésie, 1st entrée of Les fêtes d'Hébé], 1739, unperf.
Sansonnet et Tonton (par) [Rameau: La musique, 2nd entrée of Les fêtes d'Hébé], 1739, unperf.
Arlequin Dardanus (par, with Panard and Parmentier) [Rameau: Dardanus], PCI, 14 Jan 1740
Pyrame et Thisbé (par) [Francoeur and Rebel: Pyrame et Thisbé], PSG, 3 March 1740
La servante justifiée (oc, with B. C. Fagan), PSG, 19 March 1740
La barrière du Parnasse (oc), 7 April 1740 (unauthorized rev., PSG, 20 March 1759, as *La parodie au Parnasse*); also as *La muse chansonnière*
Les époux (oc, on a plan by Laffichard), PSL, 1 July 1740
Les jeunes mariés (oc, with Parmentier), PSL, 1 July 1740 (rev., PSG, 15 March 1755)
Les recrues de l'Opéra-Comique (prol.), PSL, 1 July 1740
Les fêtes villageoises (ambigu-comique) [Campra: Les fêtes vénitiennes], PSL, 30 Aug 1740
La joie (oc), PSG, 3 Feb 1741
La chercheuse d'esprit (oc), PSG, 20 Feb 1741
Farinette (par) [Lully: Proserpine], PSG, 9 March 1741 (rev., with M.-J. Sedaine, PCI, 13 Jan 1759, as *Pétrine*)
Le qu'en dira-t-on (oc, with F. C. Boizard de Pontau and Panard), PSL, 22 July 1741
Le bacha d'Alger (oc), PSL, 11 Aug 1741
La fête de Saint-Cloud (oc), PSL, 10 Sept 1741
Les valets (oc, with Le Valois d'Orville), PSL, 21 Sept 1741
Les vendanges d'Argenteuil (oc), PSL, 9 Oct 1741
Le prix de Cythère (oc, with Marquis de Paulmy), PSG, 12 Feb 1742
Hippolyte et Aricie (par, arr. Blaise) [Rameau: Hippolyte et Aricie], PCI, 11 Oct 1742
La fausse duègne, ou Le jaloux corrigé par force (oc, with Parmentier), 1742
Le coq de village (oc), PSG, 31 March 1743
Prologue pour l'ouverture du nouvel Opéra-Comique (prol.), PSL, 8 June 1743
Le pouvoir de l'Amour, ou Le siège de Cythère (par, with Fagan) [Lully: Armide], PSL, 1 July 1743; Brussels, 7 July 1748, as *Cythère assiégée*; (Gluck, Vienna and Schwetzingen, 1759 as *Cythère*; rev., 1775, as opéra-ballet)

L'ambigu de la Folie, ou Le ballet des dindons (prol., 4 entrées) [Rameau: Les Indes galantes], PSL, 31 Aug 1743 (rev., PCI, 26 July 1751, as Les Indes dansantes)

Les bateliers de Saint-Cloud (oc), PSL, 10 Sept 1743

L'astrologue de village (par, with Panard) [Bury: Les caractères de la Folie], PSL, 5 Oct 1743

L'empirique (par of Voltaire: *Mahomet*), PSL, 1743

La coquette sans le savoir (oc, with P. Rousseau de Toulouse), PSG, 23 Feb 1744

Acajou (par of C. Pinot-Duclos: *Acajou et Zirphile*), PSG, 18 March 1744

L'école des amours grivois (oc, with P. Bridard de La Garde and Le Sueur), PSL, 16 July 1744

Le bal de Strasbourg (oc, with La Garde and Le Sueur), PSL, 13 Sept 1744

L'amour au village (oc), PSG, 3 Feb 1745

L'île d'Anticire, ou La Folie médecin de l'esprit (oc), PSG, 3 Feb 1745

Thésée (par, with P. Laujon and Parvi) [Lully: Thésée], PSG, 17 Feb 1745

Les fêtes publiques (oc, with Laujon and Parvi, or La Garde and Le Sueur), PSG, Feb 1745

Les vendanges de Tempé (pantomime), PSL, 28 Aug 1745

Les nymphes de Diane, Brussels, 1 June 1747 (rev. in vaudevilles, PSL, 22 Sept 1755) [written 1741, for PSL]

Fanfale (par, with P.-A. Lefèvre de Marcouville) [Destouches: Omphale], PCI, 8 March 1751

Les amants inquiets (par) [Collasse: Thétis et Pélée], PCI, 9 March 1751

Les amours champêtres (pastorale) [Rameau: Les sauvages, 4th entrée of Les Indes galantes], PCI, 2 Sept 1751

Tircis et Doristée (par) [Lully: Acis et Galatée], PCI, 14 Sept 1751

L'impromptu de la cour de marbre (divertissement comique, with La Garde and Dehesse), 28 Nov 1751

Raton et Rosette, ou La vengeance inutile (par) [Mondonville: Titon et l'Aurore], PCI, 28 March 1753

Les amours de Bastien et Bastienne (par, with M.-J.-B. Favart and Harny de Guerville) [Rousseau: Le devin du village], PCI, 4 Aug 1753

Zéphire et Fleurette (par, with Panard and Laujon) [Rebel and Francoeur: Zélindor], PSG, 23 March 1754 [written 1745]

La fête d'Amour, ou Lucas et Colinette (par, with M.-J.-B. Favart and Chevalier), PCI, 5 Dec 1754

L'amour impromptu (par) [Rameau: La danse, 3rd entrée of Les fêtes d'Hébé], PSL, 10 July 1756

Le mariage par escalade (oc), PSL, 11 Sept 1756

La petite Iphigénie (par, with C.-H. Fusée de Voisenon, after G. de la Touche: Iphigénie en Tauride), PCI, 21 July 1757

Les ensorcelés, ou Jeannot et Jeanette (oc, with M.-J.-B. Favart, J. N. Guérin de Frémicourt and Harny de Guerville), PCI, 1 Sept 1757; also as *La nouvelle surprise de l'amour*

La noce interrompue (par) [Lully: Alceste], PCI, 26 Jan 1758

La soirée des boulevards (ambigu), PCI, 13 Nov 1758

Le retour de l'Opéra-Comique (oc), PSL, 28 June 1759

Le départ de l'Opéra-Comique (compliment de clôture), PSL, 9 Oct 1759

Le procès des ariettes et des vaudevilles (oc, with L. Anseaume, after A. R. Lesage and d'Orneval: Les couplets en procès), PCI, 31 Jan 1760

La ressource des théâtres (prol., ? with Anseaume), PSG, 31 Jan 1760

Supplément de la soirée des boulevards (oc, with Panard and Guérin de Frémicourt), PCI, 10 May 1760

La nouvelle troupe (comédie, with Anseaume and Voisenon), PCI, 9 Aug 1760

L'amour naïf (par, with J. B. Lourdet de Santerre and Chevalier) [Favart and others: Annette et Lubin], Bagatelle, 18 Aug 1762

La fête du château (divertissement), PCI, 25 Sept 1766

La matinée, la soirée, et la nuit des boulevards (ambigu), Fontainebleau, 11 Oct 1776

Les rêveries renouvelées des Grecs (par, with Guérin de Frémicourt) [Gluck: Iphigénie en Tauride], PCI, 26 June 1779

PASTICCIOS AND TRANSLATIONS

Baïocco et Serpilla (intermède, 3) [Orlandini: Il giocatore], Sodi, PCI, 6 March 1753

Le caprice amoureux, ou Ninette à la cour (3 acts) [Ciampi and others: Bertoldo in corte], PCI, 12 Feb 1755; (2 acts), PCI, 12 March 1756

La bohémienne [Rinaldo di Capua: La zingara], PCI, 28 July 1755

Les Chinois [Sellitto: Il cinese rimpatriato] (with Naigeon), PCI, 18 March 1756

OPÉRAS-BALLETS AND BALLETS

Le foire de Bezons (ballet pantomime, with Panard) [partly Rameau: Les Indes galantes], PSL, 11 Sept 1735

L'Amour et l'innocence (ballet pantomime, with J. C. Grandvoinet de Verrière), 4 Oct 1736

Don Quichotte chez la duchesse (ballet comique), Boismortier, 1743

La vallée de Montmorency, ou Les amours villageois (ballet pantomime, rev. of Les vendanges de Tempé), Blaise, 1752

La coquette trompée (comédie lyrique), Dauvergne, 1753

Cythère assiégée (opéra-ballet), Paris, Opéra, 1 Aug 1775; rev. of oc, 1759

COMÉDIES MÊLÉES D'ARIETTES

La fille mal gardée, ou Le pédant amoureux (with M.-J.-B. Favart and Lourdet de Santerre) [Mouret: La Provençale, 5th entrée of Les fêtes de Thalie], Duni, 1758

La fortune au village (with M.-J.-B. Favart and Bertrand) [La Garde: Aeglé], Gibert, 1760

Soliman II, ou Les trois sultanes, Gibert, 1761

Annette et Lubin (with M.-J.-B. Favart and Lourdet de Santerre), Blaise, 1762

La plaideuse, ou Le procès, Duni, 1762

Les fêtes de la paix, Philidor, 1763

Les amours de Gonesse (with S.-R.-N. Chamfort), La Borde, 1765

Isabelle et Gertrude, ou Les sylphes supposés, Blaise, 1765

La fée Urgèle, ou Ce qui plaît aux dames, Duni, 1765

Les moissonneurs, Duni, 1768

L'amant déguisé, ou Le jardinier supposé (with Voisenon), Philidor, 1769

La rosière de Salency, Blaise, Duni, Monsigny, Philidor and G. van Swieten, 1769

L'amitié à l'épreuve (with Voisenon), Grétry, 1770 (rev., 1786, as Les vrais amis, ou L'amitié à l'épreuve)

La belle Arsène, Monsigny, 1773

La vieillesse d'Annette et Lubin (with C.-N.-J. Favart), Jadin, 1791; also as *La vengeance du bailli*

*

J. Monnet: *Supplément au roman comique, ou Mémoires pour servir à la vie de Jean Monnet* (London, 1773); ed. H. d'Alméras, *Mémoires* (Paris, 1909)

A.-P.-C. Favart, ed.: *Mémoires et correspondances littéraires, dramatiques et anecdotiques de C. S. Favart* (Paris, 1808) [with introduction by H.-F. Dumolard]

A. Font: *Favart, l'opéra-comique, et la comédie-vaudeville aux XVIIe et XVIIIe siècles* (Paris, 1894)

G. Cucuel: *Les créateurs de l'opéra-comique français* (Paris, 1914)

R. Haas: *Gluck und Durazzo im Burgtheater* (Vienna, 1925)

A. Iacuzzi: *The European Vogue of Favart: the Diffusion of the Opéra-Comique* (New York, 1932)

F. J. Salvatore: *Favart's Unpublished Plays: the Rise of the Popular Comic Opera* (New York, 1935)

M. Noiray: 'Hippolyte et Castor travestis: Rameau à l'Opéra-comique', *Jean-Philippe Rameau: Dijon 1983*, 109–25

F. Karro: 'De la Querelle des Bouffons à la réforme de Gluck: les lettres du Comte Giacomo Durazzo à Charles-Simon Favart conservées à la Bibliothèque de l'Opéra', *Mitteilungen des österreichischen Staatsarchivs*, xxxviii (1985), 163–96

B. A. Brown: *Gluck and the French Theatre in Vienna* (Oxford, 1991)

BRUCE ALAN BROWN

Favart, Edmée (*b* Paris, 1885; *d* Marseilles, 29 Oct 1941). French soprano. Her parents, both singers, directed a small theatre in Paris, the Casino St Martin, where she made her début at the age of 15. After appearances in Brussels, at the Galeries St-Hubert, she returned to Paris, taking the title role in Fall's *Princesse Dollar* at the Scala. She appeared in other Paris theatres including the Gaîté Lyrique (in a revival of *La fille de Madame Angot*), the Capucines and notably the Femina, where she sang in a revival of Offenbach's *La Grande-Duchesse de Gérolstein*; Hortense Schneider, who attended the dress rehearsal, predicted a brilliant future for Favart. After working as a nurse at the front, she made her début at the Opéra-Comique (20 June 1915) as Mignon, subsequently singing Cherubino,

Despina, Mimì, and Catherine in the première of Levadé's *La rôtisserie de la Reine Pédauque*, with Jean Périer as Abbé Coignard. With Périer she also appeared in a revival of Messager's *Véronique*. Later she created the title roles in Messager's *La petite fonctionnaire* and Hahn's *Ciboulette* (again with Périer, as Duparquet). When she sang Ciboulette, her most famous part, again at the Marigny in 1926, Messager wrote in *Le Figaro*, 'she is so completely inside the role that it is impossible to imagine anyone else taking it on'. She sang the role once more, with the composer conducting, at a performance at the Casino, Deauville, for the unveiling of a monument to the librettist Robert de Flers (4 August 1928); his co-librettist, Francis de Croisset, called her 'muse de l'opérette'. Favart was made a Chevalier of the Légion d'honneur in 1938. Her recordings (for Pathé) include selections from *Ciboulette* and arias by Offenbach.   PATRICK O'CONNOR

Marie-Justine-Benoîte Favart in 'Les amours de Bastien et Bastienne', in which she appeared at the Comédie-Italienne, Paris, 4 August 1753: engraving after C. van Loo

Favart [née Duronceray], **Marie-Justine-Benoîte** ['Mlle Chantilly'] (*b* Avignon, 15 June 1727; *d* Paris, 21 April 1772). French singer and dramatist, wife of Charles-Simon Favart. She made her Paris début at the Opéra-Comique (Foire St Germain) in *Les fêtes publiques* (1745), under the name Mlle Chantilly, and her first great success was in Favart's pantomime *Les vendanges de Tempé*. After her marriage in 1745 she went with Favart to Brussels at the invitation of the Marshal de Saxe, whose persistent advances forced her to flee to Paris in 1747. She made a successful début at the Comédie-Italienne in 1749, but, after a *lettre de cachet* prevented her leaving Paris from October 1749, she was imprisoned in a convent and later taken to a château belonging to the marshal; she could resume her career only on his death. In November 1750 she returned to

the Comédie-Italienne and her later career developed entirely in this theatre.

Favart's singing was received variously by the critics but always acclaimed by the public. She brought about a revolution in theatrical dress by insisting on costumes suitable for the characters she portrayed (a woollen gown and sabots in *Les amours de Bastien et Bastienne*, for example; see illustration) and realistic scenery. She was the inspiration behind many of her husband's female characters, and collaborated with him on numerous works.

Oeuvres de M. et Mme Favart (Paris, 1853)
M. Escudier: *Vie et aventures des cantatrices célèbres* (Paris, 1856)
A. Houssaye: *Princesses de comédie et déesses d'opéra* (Paris, 1858, ?2/1860)
M. Dumoulin: *Favart et Madame Favart: un ménage d'artistes au XVIIIe siècle* (Paris, 1902, ?3/1922)
G. Letainturier-Fradin: *Les amours de Madame Favart* (Paris, 1907)
A. Pougin: *Madame Favart: étude théâtrale* (Paris, 1912)
                                        PAULETTE LETAILLEUR

Favero, Mafalda (*b* Portomaggiore, nr Ferrara, 6 Jan 1903; *d* Milan, 3 Sept 1981). Italian soprano. She studied with Vezzani in Bologna and in 1926 made her début at Cremona, under the name of Maria Bianchi, as Lola (*Cavalleria rusticana*); her 'official' début was at Parma in 1927 as Liù. After singing Elsa and Margherita she was engaged at La Scala, where she made her début as Eva in 1928. She continued to sing there until 1950. A leading singer throughout Italy, she sang Norina, Liù and Zerlina at Covent Garden (1937, 1939) and in 1938 made her only American appearances, at San Francisco and the Metropolitan (where she made her début as Mimì). Her repertory included Carolina (*Il matrimonio segreto*), Susanna, Violetta, Martha, Suzel (*L'amico Fritz*), Zazà and – her most famous role – Puccini's Manon Lescaut. In addition, she created several roles, including the title role in Mascagni's *Pinotta* (1932), Laura in Zandonai's *La farsa amorosa* (1933) and, at La Scala, Gasparina in Wolf-Ferrari's *Il campiello* (1936) and Finea in his *La dama boba* (1939). An attractive singer of vibrant and appealing style, she was considered one of the finest Italian sopranos between the wars.

GV (R. Celletti; R. Vegeto)
I. Buscaglia: *Mafalda Favero, nella vita e nell'arte* (Milan, 1946)
G. Lauri-Volpi: *Voci parallele* (Milan, 1955)
                                        HAROLD ROSENTHAL/R

Favola del figlio cambiato, La ('The Fable of the Changeling Son'). Opera in three acts by GIAN FRANCESCO MALIPIERO to a libretto by Luigi Pirandello, partly from his unfinished *I giganti della montagna*; Brunswick, Landestheater, 13 January 1934.

In keeping with Malipiero's more expansive and euphonious musical style of the 1930s (after the dissonances and stark contrasts of his previous phase), he also showed signs of reverting to more orthodox ideals of dramatic continuity. Yet although in general method *La favola del figlio cambiato* (composed in 1932–3) may be the most 'normal' opera he had written since 1915, it is still by no means wholly conventional in subject matter or musical language.

Pirandello's libretto – most of it written specifically for Malipiero – tells of a Sicilian mother (soprano) who believes that her beautiful child has been stolen by witches and replaced by a misshapen idiot. Undeterred by mocking doubters, she learns from a clairvoyant, Vanna Scoma (contralto), that her little boy is being well looked after in a royal palace and that she must devote herself to bringing up the halfwit instead. The handicapped youngster, growing up convinced that he (now a tenor) is 'the son of a king', becomes the laughing-stock of the village community. But the story takes an unexpected turn when an ailing young Prince (tenor) from a northern land comes to the village to convalesce. The Mother is sure he is her long-lost child, and the Prince plays along with her belief when news arrives that his father the king is dead and that he must return home. Bored with court life, and far preferring the natural human warmth and simplicity of his newfound 'mother', he refuses to go and tells his ministers to take the 'son of a king' back in his place.

The opera's musico-dramatic methods vary somewhat. The first scene – oddly enough the only one whose text was not written for Malipiero in the first place – is stylized in a manner that can be paralleled in the composer's previous operas, with his own librettos. The remaining scenes, however, use a more 'naturalistic' dialogue, such as Malipiero had hitherto usually avoided. It is surely no coincidence that the first scene (where the Mother is in conflict with the doubters) is especially impressive, concentrated and moving, whereas the relatively long last act is the one most open to criticism. The Prince's vocal lines, though hardly Puccinian in the full sense, lend themselves dangerously to a Puccinian style of singing.

The damaging effect of this dichotomy should not, however, be exaggerated. The 1980 production in Palermo, which rescued the opera from its long period in almost complete obscurity after Mussolini had banned it in 1934, showed that the final act, too, can be made to work well. Moreover the short, intermezzo-like second act – set in the village tavern (brothel) and introducing the 'son of a king' – is a spirited invention by any standards. Whatever the Duce may have thought (and his anger seems to have been directed more against the libretto than against the music), *La favola del figlio cambiato* may serve as an excellent introduction to Malipiero for more conventional opera-lovers who might find his earlier, and some of his later, theatre works too perplexing and eccentric.   JOHN C. G. WATERHOUSE

Favola di Orfeo, La ('The Fable of Orpheus'). Chamber opera in one act by ALFREDO CASELLA to a libretto by Corrado Pavolini after Angelo Poliziano's verse drama of the same name; Venice, Teatro Goldoni, 6 September 1932.

Poliziano's version of the ancient legend, unlike those presented in the operas by Monteverdi and Gluck, ends with Orpheus (tenor) being torn to pieces by vengeful maenads. Despite Pavolini's drastic cuts, the outline of the 15th-century original is retained, as are significant parts of its text. In the opera the underworld is revealed to the audience only briefly, through doors which open in response to Orpheus's singing. The total effect is highly stylized, and has been aptly compared to that of a picture on an ancient Greek vase. Musically the work (which was composed quickly in summer 1932) is too uneven to be representative of Casella's best: the finest pages are eloquent examples of his personal brand of neo-classicism, but elsewhere echoes of other composers (Stravinsky, Malipiero) sometimes become disconcertingly overt. Nevertheless, because of its simplicity, this has been much the most often performed of Casella's three operas.   JOHN C. G. WATERHOUSE

Favola in musica (It.: 'tale [presented] in music'). A term used to describe early 17th-century operas and (as 'favola per musica', i.e. 'for music') librettos. The Latin 'fabula' appears in titles of pastoral-mythological entertainments in the 15th century sometimes known as 'hybrid dramas' ('drammi mescidati'), e.g. Poliziano's *La fabula d'Orpheo* (1480) and Niccolò da Coreggio's *La fabula de Caephalo* (1487). The classicizing label was doubtless intended to give respectability to a genre lacking the solid precedents of classical tragedy and comedy. In the 16th century, the Italian equivalent, alone or with a qualifier ('favola pastorale', e.g. Agostino Beccari's *Il sacrificio* (1554); 'favola boschereccia', e.g. Tasso's *Aminta* (1573); 'favola marittima', etc.), is used for plays in the pastoral tradition, again to fill a generic vacuum (Guarini opted for the more loaded 'tragicommedia'). The first opera librettos were often described as 'favole' (e.g. Marco da Gagliano discussing Rinuccini in 1608), placing them squarely in the pastoral tradition, although Alessandro Striggio was the first librettist to use the title in print with his *La favola d'Orfeo* (1607). Monteverdi followed suit, coining 'favola in musica' for the title-page of the score of *Orfeo* (published 1609): the term reflects the aesthetic emphases of the first operas. 'Favola' (and its qualifiers) continues to be applied to librettos in the first half of the century and beyond – Ottavio Tronsarelli's *La catena d'Adone* (D. Mazzocchi, 1626) is a 'favola boschereccia', and Giovanni Faustini's *Ormindo* (Cavalli, 1644) a 'favola regia' – although it fell out of use as operas themselves lost their pastoral-mythological aura.

S. Reiner: 'La vag' Angioletta (and others)', pt i, *AnMc*, no.14 (1974), 26–88

H. W. Kaufmann: 'Music for a *Favola Pastorale* (1554)', *A Musical Offering: Essays in Honor of Martin Bernstein* (New York, 1977), 163–82

N. Pirrotta: *Music and Theatre from Poliziano to Monteverdi* (Cambridge, 1982)   TIM CARTER

Favorita. A name confusingly used for two distinct imperial palaces in Vienna at which theatrical performances were given in the 17th and 18th centuries. Leopold I acquired the Palais Trautson in the Augarten (beyond the Danube Canal, north-east of the city) in 1677. Only one, anonymous opera was performed there, in 1678, and the palace was destroyed during the Turkish siege of 1683; though this 'alte Favorita' was rebuilt, it ceased to be used for theatrical performances. The 'neue Favorita' in the Wieden suburb (now the Theresianum, Favoritenstrasse), also rebuilt after the expulsion of the Turks, became the favourite summer residence of the emperors Leopold I, Joseph I and Charles VI. Opera performances were given both in this palace and in its gardens. *See* VIENNA, §1.

Favorite, La [*La favorita* ('The Favoured One')]. *Opéra* in four acts by GAETANO DONIZETTI to a libretto by ALPHONSE ROYER and GUSTAVE VAËZ, with additions by EUGÈNE SCRIBE, partly based on the plot of *L'ange de Nisida* (derived in some measure from Baculard d'Arnaud: *Le comte de Comminges*), on which the story of Eleonora di Guzman is grafted; Paris, Opéra, 2 December 1840.

The original cast was headed by Rosine Stoltz (Léonor), Gilbert Duprez (Fernand), Paul Barroilhet (Alphonse) in his début and Nicholas Levasseur (Balthazar). The work was last performed at the Opéra,

Alphonse XI (Alfonso XI) *King of Castile*   baritone
Léonor de Guzman (Leonora di
  Gusmann) *his mistress*   mezzo-soprano
Inès (Inez) *her confidante*   soprano
Fernand (Fernando) *a novice*   tenor
Don Gaspar *a king's officer*   tenor
Balthazar (Baldassare) *Superior of a monastery*   bass

Monks, ladies-in-waiting and courtiers

Setting The Monastery of St James of Compostela, the island of León, and the gardens and halls of the Alcazar, about 1340

its 692nd outing, in 1918, and although it disappeared from this repertory, it continued to be given by French provincial theatres. In 1912 *La favorite* was recorded, nearly complete, with a French-language cast, including Ketty Lapeyrette (Léonor) and Henri Albers (Alphonse).

Outside France, the work was best known in its corrupt Italian version. It was first given in Italy at Padua in June 1842, as *Leonora di Guzman*, and at La Scala, in a different translation, in August 1843, as *Elda*, with Marietta Alboni in the title role. Donizetti had nothing to do with either of these productions. The opera had already come out in a German translation, first at Kassel, on 31 May 1841, and in December of that year in Vienna, as *Richard und Mathilde*. It was also a feature of the Italian seasons in Berlin and Vienna in the 1840s.

In London, it was first given in an English translation by Edward Fitzball on 18 October 1843. A company from Brussels introduced the original version there in June 1845. Its first Italian production in London was on 16 February 1847; however, its great popularity, lasting nearly half a century, began in 1848 when the leading roles were first assumed by Grisi and Mario. At Covent Garden, Pauline Lucca, Trebelli, Medea Mei and Scalchi were popular Leonoras.

The opera was introduced to the USA at New Orleans in its original French guise (9 February 1843), and it was in French that the work was first given in New York two years later; it was not sung there in Italian until 1855. Its first Metropolitan production, featuring Mantelli, Cremonini, Ancona and Plançon, was in 1895; ten years later it was revived with Edyth Walker, Caruso and Scotti, after which it had to wait 73 years for another run, when Shirley Verrett and Luciano Pavarotti took the leading roles. The opera survives most hardily in Italy, where it has been particularly associated in the last half-century with Ebe Stignani, Giulietta Simionato and Fiorenza Cossotto. Gianni Poggi and Gianni Raimondi were well received as Fernando, as was Ettore Bastianini's Alfonso. There have been a number of recordings in Italian, including one with a cast headed by Cossotto and Pavarotti.

ACT 1.i *The courtyard of the Monastery of St James of Compostela* There is a restless, brooding overture. As the monks enter the chapel, singing a chorus based on a C major scale, Balthazar asks Fernand why he holds back. The novice confesses that he is obsessed by an unknown woman whom he had seen praying in the chapel; his *air* ('Un ange, une femme inconnue'/'Una vergine, un angiol di Dio') conveys his ardent nature in the subtly varied rhythm of his phrases. Balthazar tries to restore Fernand's thoughts to piety (duo, 'Sais-tu que

devant la tiare'/'Non sai tu che un giusto'), but the young novice remains obdurate and the Superior orders him away.

1.ii *A bosky retreat on the Island of León* Inès and the chorus of ladies enjoy their surroundings (*air and chorus*, 'Rayons dorés'/'Bei raggi lucenti' – borrowed from *Pia de' Tolomei*). Fernand, blindfold, arrives in a small boat and is warmly greeted (*air and chorus*, 'Doux zéphyr, sois-lui fidèle'/'Dolce zeffiro il seconda'). He asks for information, but they teasingly remain silent and then go off as the beautiful Léonor enters (duo, 'Mon idole'/'Ah, mio bene'). Unaware of her status as *maîtresse en titre* to the king, Fernand seeks to learn her identity, but she knows she cannot love the young cavalier without dishonouring him and she hands him a military commission, hoping to assure his future. She leaves him convinced that she loves him, however, even though she is evasive. Alone, he considers the prospects of glorious achievement in battle as a means of winning her favour (*air*, 'Oui, ta voix m'inspire'/'Sì, che un tuo solo accento').

ACT 2 *The gardens of the recently conquered Alcazar* Alphonse meditates on the beauty of the palace so recently conquered from the Moors, won for him by a certain Fernand. Don Gaspar informs him that a papal messenger demands an audience, but the king's thoughts are only of Léonor, as his *air* ('Léonor, viens'/'Vien, Leonora'), at once sensuous and impulsive, shows. She appears, sad and withdrawn (duo, 'Quand j'ai quitté le château de mon père'/'Quando le soglie paterne vareai'), but does not reveal that her affections have changed; instead of concluding with a rapid section, this episode ends with an Andante *a due* ('O mon amour'/'Ah! l'alto ardor'), in which the irony of the situation is reflected in the parallel writing for the voices. The court enters to behold the ballet the king has ordered for the victory celebrations. Don Gaspar reveals to the king that a letter to Léonor from an unknown suitor has been intercepted. She confesses that she loves another, but they are interrupted by the entrance of the furious Balthazar, papal bull of excommunication in hand. He begins the finale, where his denunciation ('Redoutez la fureur d'un Dieu'/'Ah paventa d'un Dio vendicatore') shows that Donizetti remembered the outraged cardinal in Halévy's *La Juive* (which he had heard in Paris in 1835); Balthazar demands that the king renounce his mistress and reinstate his legal consort. When Alphonse angrily refuses, Balthazar delivers an anathema, while the courtiers and Léonor recoil in horror. This extensive finale, largely built on predictable sequences, is unusual in that it makes do without the principal tenor; Fernand does not appear in Act 2.

ACT 3 *The interior of the Alcazar* Fernand has been summoned to court to be ennobled. Don Gaspar enters with the king, discussing what is to be done about Léonor. Alphonse greets Fernand as his benefactor and urges him to ask whatever favour he pleases; Fernand confesses his love for a noblewoman whom he would make his wife. Léonor enters and, when Fernand indicates that she is the lady, the king is cynically amused at this solution to an embarrassing problem. Alphonse's suave aria with *pertichini* ('Pour tant d'amour'/'A tanto amor') is a gem of ironic courtliness. Léonor is left alone to confront her shame and weigh the chances of Fernand's forgiving her when he learns the truth, as she does in a double aria ('O mon Fernand'/'O, mio Fernando'). Léonor entrusts Inès with the delicate task

141

of revealing her situation to Fernand before the ceremony; but her messenger is detained by Don Gaspar and other spiteful courtiers (chorus, 'Déjà dans la chapelle'/'Di già nella cappella').

At the ceremony Fernand shows his usual gallantry; but while the marriage is being solemnized, the contemptuous courtiers denounce him as an opportunist (chorus, 'Quel marché de bassesse'/'Questo è troppo in mia fè!'). Emerging from the chapel, Fernand is outraged when the courtiers, declaring that honour means more than love, refuse his hand. He threatens to fight duels with them all, when Balthazar, learning of Fernand's marriage, reveals that his bride is the king's mistress. Léonor discovers that her message went undelivered; before she can explain, Fernand confronts the king, tears off his orders and breaks his sword, which he casts at the king's feet. Alphonse recognizes Fernand's innate nobility (finale, 'O ciel! de son âme la noble fierté'/'O ciel, di quell'alma il puro candor'); Léonor is beside herself, but at the end Balthazar takes his disillusioned novice back to the monastery.

Rosine Stoltz as Léonor, and Gilbert Duprez as Fernand in Act 4 (the courtyard of the Monastery of St James of Compostela) of Donizetti's 'La favorite' in the original production at the Paris Opéra (Salle Le Peletier), 2 December 1840: lithograph by Desmaisons after Lepaulle, frontispiece to the first edition of the vocal score (Paris: Schlesinger, 1840)

ACT 4 *The courtyard of the Monastery of St James of Compostela* Balthazar, in an *air* of noble simplicity ('Les cieux s'emplissent d'étincelles'/'Splendon più belle in ciel le stelle'), leads the monks and novices in evening prayer. Fernand is about to take his final vows when Balthazar is summoned to a novice, just arrived. Fernand's thoughts return to Léonor, whom he loves in spite of her past. His *romance* ('Ange si pur'/'Spirto gentil') is a fine example of Donizetti's gift for making long structures from simple melodic germs. Balthazar returns and leads Fernand into the chapel for the long-awaited service. The new novice is Léonor, stricken with

a fatal illness but impelled to see Fernand once more. When she understands that he is pronouncing his vows, she makes to leave, but her strength fails. Coming from the chapel, Fernand assists his 'brother' but is outraged when he discovers it is Léonor; he orders her away, but she begs for mercy (Larghetto, 'Fernand, imite la clémence du ciel'/'Pietoso al par del nume'). He is so moved when he understands that she is desperately ill that, in an impassioned duet ('Viens, viens, je cède éperdu'/'Vieni, ah! vieni') he resolves to go away with her. Hearing his forgiveness, she dies in his arms while the monks pray for her soul; Fernand is convinced that tomorrow they will repeat their prayer for him.

* * *

The fourth act of *La favorite* has long been regarded, not least by Toscanini, as one of Donizetti's supreme accomplishments. The score of the opera contains some of his finest music, although it derives from a tangle of sources. The oldest discernible strand goes back to an incomplete Italian *opera semiseria*, *Adelaide*, a good deal of which went into the completed *L'ange de Nisida*, written for the Théâtre de la Renaissance in late 1839 but never performed. Much of the first three acts and all of Act 4 of *La favorite*, except for two solo passages, derive from *L'ange de Nisida*, as the dated autograph testifies. The chief new music is found in the *airs*, which in Donizetti's usual fashion were tailored to the particular vocal aptitudes of his first cast. Léonor's 'O mon Fernand' stands as one of the great monologues of French opera. A critical edition of the original French *La favorite* was used for a production in Bergamo in 1991, but a new Italian version is badly needed to restore to international audiences this noble work in a form consistent with Donizetti's intentions. WILLIAM ASHBROOK

Fay, Etienne (*b* Tours, 1770; *d* Versailles, 6 Dec 1845). French composer and singer. Fay first appeared as a tenor at the Théâtre Louvois in 1791; he joined the company of the Opéra-Comique in 1792 and that of the Théâtre Feydeau in 1797. After 1801 he sang mainly in provincial theatres, but also in the Netherlands and Belgium, where he concluded his career in 1826. His wife, Mlle Rousselois (known as Bachelier), was a singer at the Théâtre Feydeau, and the couple managed the three theatres in Marseilles, 1811–13. Although this venture ended in financial disaster, Fay published a *Plan d'une organisation générale de tous les théâtres de l'Empire* (1813), which contains information on theatrical practice at the time of Napoleon. His *comédie Clémentine* is an ambitious work with substantial numbers, and it is meticulously written. Reviews of Fay's other operas, although sometimes favourable, criticized his heavy orchestration and lack of melody.

all works first performed in Paris

Flora (comédie féerie mêlée d'ariettes, 3, P.-U. Dubuisson), Louvois, 4 Feb 1792, F-Pc*, 1 air (Paris, 1793)

Le projet extravagant (2), Louvois, 11 July 1792

Laure et Zulmé (cmda, 3, Dubuisson), Louvois, 28 Nov 1793, collab. Gebauer and others

L'intérieur d'un ménage républicain (opéra comique en vaudevilles, 1, A.-M.-J. Chastenet de Puységur), OC (Favart), 4 Jan 1794

Les rendez-vous espagnols (oc, 3, A.-J. Coffin Rony), OC (Favart), 10 June 1796

Clémentine, ou La belle-mère (comédie, 1, J. B. C. Vial), Feydeau, 18 Sept 1799 (Paris, 1800)

Emma, ou Le soupçon (3, B.-J. Marsollier des Vivetières), Feydeau, 16 Oct 1799

La famille savoyarde (2, M.-E. Montanclos), Feydeau, 15 Jan 1802

La bonne aventure (cmda, 2, J.-M. Pain), Jeunes-Elèves, 1 April 1802

Julie, ou Le pot de fleurs (comédie mêlée de chants, 1, A. G. Jars), OC (Favart), 12 March 1805, collab. G. Spontini

*

StiegerO
H. Lyonnet: *Dictionnaire des comédiens français* (Paris and Geneva, 1902–8)
V. Combarnous: *L'histoire du Grand-Théâtre de Marseille* (Marseilles, 1927)   MICHEL NOIRAY

Fay, Maude (*b* San Francisco, 18 April 1878; *d* San Francisco, 7 Oct 1964). American soprano. After studying with Orgeni in Dresden she made her début at the Munich Hofoper as Marguerite (1906). Later appearances were in the dramatic repertory, and she was particularly successful in Wagner roles. She sang in Beecham's 1910 season at His Majesty's and in 1914 was heard at Covent Garden as Sieglinde and Elsa, in performances conducted by Nikisch. During World War I she sang at the Metropolitan, but after her marriage her engagements were restricted to the concert hall.

DAVID CUMMINGS

Febiarmonici [Febi Armonici]. One or more touring opera companies working in Italy around the middle of the 17th century. The Febiarmonici ('Musicians of Apollo') are first known for a performance of *La finta pazza*, perhaps by Francesco Sacrati, in Piacenza in May 1644, and they may have performed in Paris in early 1645. The group, also known as (or possibly managed by) the Accademici Discordati, consisted of singers, a number from Rome, musicians, perhaps including Benedetto Ferrari, and stage designers. The head of the group is variously noted as Curzio Manara, an engineer, and Giovan Battista Balbi, a dancer and designer. It was modelled on the touring companies already well established in the spoken theatre and *commedia dell'arte* traditions, working within their own budget and charging admission to performances.

The likely closure of the opera houses in Venice in 1645–7, due to sumptuary legislation on account of the war between Venice and the Turks, encouraged touring. Performances by the Febiarmonici (it is not always clear whether by the same group) are recorded in Florence and Lucca (1645), Bologna and Genoa (1647), Ferrara (1648) and Lucca again (1650; involving Antonio Cesti). In early 1650, the company was brought to Naples by the viceroy, Count d'Oñate, who was anxious to exploit theatrical entertainments as a means of restoring normality after the Masaniello uprising in 1647–8 (*see* NAPLES, §1). *Didone* (Cavalli) was staged in October, and in 1651 the Febiarmonici performed *Egisto* (Cavalli), *Il Nerone, ovvero L'incoronazione di Poppea* (Monteverdi; the Naples manuscript doubtless relates to this performance) and *Giasone* (Cavalli). They also gave the première of Cavalli's *Veremonda* to celebrate the Spanish victory in Catalonia and the queen's birthday in December 1652. The Febiarmonici generally performed Venetian operas, whether or not modified to suit Neapolitan tastes, although from 1653 native librettists and composers were periodically encouraged (full details of repertory are given in Bianconi and Walker, 379–87). With the departure of Count d'Oñate in late 1653, the Febiarmonici transferred to the Teatro S Bartolomeo (from April 1654). Their precarious financial position was exacerbated by the plague of 1656, but performances resumed in 1657, largely of revised Venetian operas, and are recorded through to 1668.

'Febiarmonici' may have become a generic term for opera companies – a separate group is known by the same title in Milan and Turin in 1647–8 – and doubtless the membership of the main group fluctuated. The institution reflects the emergence of important new modes of operatic production fostered by the ostensible shift from 'court' to 'public' opera.

*

G. Baruffaldi: *Notizie istoriche delle accademie letterarie ferraresi* (Ferrara, 1787), 36, 55
U. Prota-Giurleo: *Francesco Cirillo e l'introduzione del melodramma a Napoli* (Grumo Nevano, 1952)
——: *Il teatro di corte del Palazzo reale di Napoli* (Naples, 1952)
L. Bianconi and T. Walker: 'Dalla *Finta pazza* alla *Veremonda*: storie di Febiarmonici', *RIM*, x (1975), 379–454   TIM CARTER

Fedele, Daniele Teofilo. *See* TREU, DANIEL GOTTLOB.

Fedeli [Fedelli], **Giuseppe** [Saggione, Joseph] (*b* ?Venice; *fl* 1680–1733; *d* ?Paris). Italian composer. He was the son of Carlo Fedeli, an instrumentalist at St Mark's, Venice, and was himself appointed as a trombonist there in 1680. He then moved to Paris, where he helped to introduce the double bass into the orchestra of the Opéra. From early 1703 he was working in London; he played in concerts there and later became the leading double bass player in the opera orchestra at the Queen's Theatre, Haymarket. By 1715 he had returned to Paris, where songs and chamber music by him were published.

His only opera was *The Temple of Love*, a pastoral in three acts to a libretto 'English'd from the *Italian*' by Peter Motteux (London, Queen's, 7 March 1706). The heroine was sung by Fedeli's wife, the soprano Maria Gallia, and the hero by the baritone Marcellus Laroon, later famous as an artist. The opera's second couple were the actress-singer Anne Bracegirdle and the tenor Lawrence, while comedy was provided by the bass Cook as a satyr. In October 1706 John Walsh published *Songs In The New Opera, Call'd The Temple of Love Compos'd by Signr: Giuseppe Fedelli Saggione*. These include seven arias for Gallia, the most interesting being the opening 'Charming Roses' and the bird-imitation piece 'Warbling the birds enjoying' with its virtuoso flute part for James Paisible. According to the theatre's prompter, John Downes, the opera had dances 'made and perform'd all by *French* Men'. Only one further performance, on 16 March, is recorded, although Downes remembered that 'it lasted but Six Days, and answer'd not their Expectation'.

*

J. Downes: *Roscius Anglicanus* (London, 1708); ed. J. Milhous and R. D. Hume (London, 1987)
J. Milhous and R. D. Hume: *Vice Chamberlain Coke's Theatrical Papers 1706–1715* (Carbondale, IL, 1982)
                              OLIVE BALDWIN, THELMA WILSON

Fedeli, Ruggiero (*b* Venice, ?*c*1655; *d* Kassel, Jan 1722). Italian composer and singer. The brother of Giuseppe Fedeli, he was active chiefly in Germany. He played the viola in Venetian theatre orchestras in the mid-1660s and at St Mark's, Venice, from January 1669 to January 1674, when he joined the choir as a bass. In April 1677 he was dismissed because of repeated absences. For the next 30 years he held a long succession of appointments at German courts and theatres, but was dismissed from several of these for disobedience. While he remained intermittently active in Venice, he sang in operas at

Bayreuth in 1681 and was recruited in early 1687 for the Saxon court at Dresden by Carlo Pallavicino, who for some years held appointments both as court composer at Dresden and as *maestro di coro* at the Ospedale degli Incurabili, Venice. His prestige was such that the style of his music is bound to have had some influence on Fedeli's. In 1691 Fedeli was hired as composer at the Berlin court chapel. By 1695 he had gone to Hanover and in 1701 he was appointed Kapellmeister at Kassel. He worked at Berlin in 1702, Brunswick in 1703, Wolfenbüttel in 1704 and again at Berlin in 1705. In 1708 he was appointed court composer and conductor at Berlin, but in 1709 he returned to Kassel as Kapellmeister, remaining there until his death.

Fedeli's first dramatic work was a *rappresentatione sacra* entitled *Santa Catterina d'Alessandria* (1675, Venice). Dedicated to Francesco Morosini (who was to become doge in 1688), this three-act work involved ten characters, a chorus of angels and a *ballo* of executioners. The music is lost. Only one significant stage work by Fedeli is extant (*D-LÜh*), the opera *Almira*, produced at Brunswick in 1703. The libretto appears to derive from that by Giulio Pancieri (1691, Venice; music by Giuseppe Boniventi and others). Several of Fedeli's arias seem to have been heard again in Reinhard Keiser's *Almira, Königin von Castilien*, produced at Weissenfels in 1704 (score lost), and his music may have influenced Handel's *Almira* (1705). Fedeli's opera was sung in Italian, though an anonymous German prose translation is interleaved in the libretto (*D-W*). His arias show certain similarities to those of Legrenzi, and a few are in a virtuoso manner.

M. Fürstenau: *Zur Geschichte der Musik und des Theaters am Hofe zu Dresden*, i (Dresden, 1861)

E. J. Luin: 'La famiglia Fedeli', *RMI*, xxxviii (1931), 424–8

W. Dean and J. M. Knapp: *Handel's Operas 1704–1726* (Oxford, 1987), 51–4   ELEANOR SELFRIDGE-FIELD

Fedeltà premiata, La ('Fidelity Rewarded'). *Dramma giocoso* in three acts by JOSEPH HAYDN to a libretto by GIAMBATTISTA LORENZI; Eszterháza, 25 February 1781.

Fillide/Celia *lover of Fileno*	mezzo-soprano
Fileno *lover of Fillide*	tenor
Amaranta *a vain and arrogant woman*	mezzo-soprano
Count Perrucchetto	baritone
Nerina *a nymph, inconstant in love*	soprano
Lindoro *brother of Amaranta, a temple assistant*	tenor
Melibeo *high priest at the temple, in love with Amaranta*	bass
Diana *Roman goddess of the hunt*	soprano

Choruses of nymphs, shepherds, hunters and followers of Diana

Setting Countryside in the land of Cumae, near Naples

In Haydn's opera the nine characters of Lorenzi's original libretto, *L'infedeltà fedele* (set by Cimarosa in 1779), are reduced to eight: the role of Viola, a peasant girl in love with Vuzzachio, is conflated with that of Nerina (Costanza Valdesturla, who also sang the role of Diana); Nerina is no longer the daughter of Melibeo (Antonio Pesci); and Vuzzachio's name is changed to the loftier-sounding Lindoro (Leopold Dichtler). The *parti*

serie, Fileno (Guglielmo Jermoli) and Fillide (Maria Jermoli), and the *parti buffe*, Count Perrucchetto (Benedetto Bianchi) and Amaranta (Teresa Taveggia), remain unchanged. All traces of Neapolitan dialect are removed and the crude jokes of Viola and Vuzzachio are excised. Also omitted are Amaranta's haughty French phrases; she is a more refined character in Haydn's setting. Even the Count and Lindoro are less silly than in the earlier version, in part because several aria texts are entirely new. Despite these changes the basic structure of the original drama remains unchanged; *serio* and *giocoso* still unite to create, in Lorenzi's words, 'a mixed entertainment, discreetly containing elements of both, so that everyone … [might] find a theatrical event corresponding to his taste'.

La fedeltà premiata, written for the inauguration of the enlarged opera house built to replace the one destroyed by fire on 19 November 1779, was Haydn's most successful comic opera, remaining in the repertory until 1785. It was completed in the autumn of 1780, but delays in the construction of the new theatre pushed the opening date into the new year. Haydn's pride in the work is recorded in a letter to Artaria dated 27 May 1781: 'I assure you that no such work has been heard in Paris up to now, nor perhaps in Vienna either'. A second, shorter version, as a 'dramma pastorale giocoso', was first performed on 29 September 1782, with only two of the original seven cast members. The opera subsequently received highly-acclaimed German-language productions at the Kärntnertortheater, Vienna, in 1784, seen by Joseph II and perhaps also Mozart, and at the Erdődy Theatre, Pressburg, 1785–7. The fantastic elements, including the festive hunt for the feast of Diana and her appearance as 'dea ex machina', were spectacularly rendered by Jean-Pierre Ponnelle at the Holland Festival (1970) and again in Zürich (1975). Bernard Haitink conducted the opera at Glyndebourne in 1979, and a condensed (two-act) version was presented at the Stadttheater, Basle, in 1986.

ACT 1.i *Pastoral setting outside the Temple of Diana* After the opening chorus, Amaranta reads an inscription on an altar, giving an outline of the plot: every year two faithful lovers must be sacrificed to the sea monster until a hero offers his own life. Only then will peace return to the land of Cumae. Thus begins the hunt – vividly presented in the overture, subsequently used as the last movement of Symphony no.73, 'La chasse' – for sacrificial victims to be offered to Diana. The characters have ample justification for their coy and felicitous actions, since to be in love without the consent of the devious high priest, Melibeo, means certain disaster. Under Melibeo's protection, Lindoro switches his allegiance from Nerina to the noble Celia. Amaranta is in the process of accepting Melibeo's favour when Count Perrucchetto (literally 'wig-maker') arrives (shouting 'Salva, salva, aiuto'), claiming to have been pursued by thieves. His fright, cowardice and slightly deranged state are readily portrayed in this breathless G minor aria reminiscent of Haydn's *Sturm und Drang* style. Viewing the Count as her entrée to the nobility, Amaranta soon curries his favour, arousing Melibeo's jealousy.

1.ii *A garden* Fileno, heartbroken, laments his lost beloved, whom he presumes dead. Nerina, attracted to him, listens to his tale of woe and consoles him with her own love problems. Neither yet realizes that Celia and Fillide are one and the same person.

1.iii *A pleasant grove* Celia, guarding her sheep, mourns her situation in a short cavatina, 'Placidi ruscelletti'; the babbling brook and idyllic setting are depicted in the lyrical melody of the flute and a rippling accompaniment pattern. Having been lulled to sleep, Celia awakens to find Fileno at her side, but is forced to hide her love since they are observed by Lindoro and Melibeo. Fileno vents his torment. The Count is attracted briefly to Nerina, causing Amaranta to fly into a rage in the B minor 'Vanne, fuggi, traditore', her changes of mood explicit in the oscillation between contrasting themes.

1.iv *An atrium* Melibeo informs Celia that she must either marry Lindoro or go to the sea monster with Fileno. Celia, in soliciting Nerina's aid, expresses her intense suffering in an aria, 'Deh soccorri un infelice'. The difficult, muted horn solo in this piece, probably written for Anton Eckhardt, was later given to the bassoon, perhaps when the music was transposed upwards for soprano. In the finale Celia is nearly forced to accept Lindoro's marriage proposal, when Nerina rushes in unexpectedly, pursued by angry satyrs. Celia is carried away by one of the satyrs, bringing the action to an abrupt end.

ACT 2.i *A lovely country field* Melibeo devises a plan to pair Celia with the Count, thereby gaining Amaranta for himself. He persuades Nerina to seek Fileno's favour, which she easily wins since Fileno wishes to provoke Celia.

2.ii *Mountainous countryside with laurels and cypresses* Heralded by a spirited hunting chorus, all search for a sacrificial offering to Diana. Amaranta is chased by a wild boar which Fileno kills, but Count Perrucchetto claims victory. The Count addresses the not-quite-inert beast in the delightfully comic piece, 'Di questo audace ferro'.

2.iii *A cave* Two back-to-back solo scenes for the *parti serie* form the dramatic climax of Act 2. Fileno's attempt at suicide ('Bastano i pianti') is thwarted when, after carving an account of his fate in a nearby tree trunk, his arrow breaks. Upon finding the message and broken arrow, Celia contemplates her own death in 'Ah come il core', a musically adventurous scene (published separately as a solo cantata in 1782 and analysed in Cramer's *Magazin der Musik*, 1783). Both scenes are sectional, the wide-ranging emotional states of the characters amply served by the flexibility of the music.

2.iv *Outside the cave* Nerina and Melibeo enter, followed by shepherds carrying two white robes and two floral crowns. Jealous of the love vows exchanged by Amaranta and Count Perrucchetto, Melibeo sends him into the cave where Celia has sought refuge. The Count and Celia are then brought forth as the sacrificial couple in the second act finale.

ACT 3.i *A hall* Celia, in a white robe and flanked by shepherds, tries to convince Fileno of her innocence, but throughout their duet he remains indignant and remorseless. They depart in opposite directions as Count Perrucchetto, also clad in white, enters with Melibeo while preparations for the sacrifice continue.

3.ii *Landscape with lake* In a noble deed, worthy of a Metastasian hero, Fileno announces that, rather than see Celia devoured by the sea monster, he will offer himself as the single sacrificial victim. Moved by his devotion, Diana appears amid thunder and lightning to save him. She unites Celia and Fileno, Nerina and Lindoro, and Amaranta and Count Perrucchetto. Melibeo is taken as her victim, for having manipulated events for his own benefit.

*　　*　　*

Despite its convoluted plot and disjointed structure, *La fedeltà premiata* contains some of Haydn's best operatic music and efforts at character definition. The virtues of honesty and fidelity are timeless; their relevance to Haydn, whose affair with the singer Luigia Polzelli was well under way by late 1780, may explain the high level of musical sensitivity shown throughout the score. Haydn derived compositional impetus from Cimarosa's *L'infedeltà fedele*; he owned a copy of this opera and sometimes used it as a springboard for his own invention (Lippmann 1982). The tonal progression of descending 3rds in Haydn's Act 1 finale derives from Cimarosa's setting, although the linking of the *partie serie* in two separate G minor sections (Presto, 2/4) has no counterpart in the earlier version. Similarities in opening melodic gestures probably reflect common practice of the period. In the Act 2 finale Haydn's parody of Gluck's 'Coro di furie' from *Orfeo ed Euridice*, performed at Eszterháza in 1776, was probably meant to please his musically astute patron.

CARYL CLARK

Federici, Vincenzo (*b* Pesaro, 1764; *d* Milan, 26 Sept 1826). Italian composer. His family intended him to study law, but he also studied the harpsichord. At the age of 16 he went to Livorno and then to London, where he gave music lessons and taught himself composition; a set of sonatas by him was published there in 1786. His first opera, *L'olimpiade*, was staged at Turin in 1789. His first known association with the Italian Opera in London was as *maestro al cembalo* for Bianchi's *La villanella rapita* (27 February 1790) at the Little Haymarket Theatre, where his own opera *L'usurpator innocente* (a version of Metastasio's *Demofoonte*) was performed 15 times with a cast including the castrato Luigi Marchesi. He was *maestro al cembalo* at the King's Theatre from 1790 until at least 1800. During that time he contributed to pasticcios and to works by other composers.

In 1802 he settled in Milan, where his *Castore e Polluce* was performed at La Scala in 1803 and 1805; it was also staged at Venice, Turin and Naples. He produced an *opera seria* at La Scala or Turin every Carnival except one until 1809; he also wrote occasional works for La Scala (1803–15). From 1808 he taught at the Milan Conservatory, where he became composition master in 1824 and acting director in 1825.

The highly successful opera *Zaira* (1799, Palermo), often attributed to Vincenzo Federici, is probably by Francesco Federici; the authorship of the *azione lirica* *Pigmalione* (*I-Fc*), by one of the Federicis, remains doubtful.

all opere serie

L'olimpiade (3, P. Metastasio), Turin, Regio, 26 Dec 1789

L'usurpator innocente (2, after Metastasio: *Demofoonte*), London, Little Haymarket, 6 April 1790, excerpts (London, *c*1789)

Castore e Polluce (2, L. Romanelli), Milan, Scala, Jan 1803, *D-Mbs*, *I-Mr*, *Nc*, *US-Wc*, duet (Milan, n.d.)

Oreste in Tauride (2), Milan, Scala, 27 Jan 1804, *I-Mr**

Sofonisba (3, A. Zanetti and G. Zanetti), Turin, Regio, carn. 1805

Idomeneo (2, Romanelli), Milan, Scala, 31 Jan 1806, *Mr**

La conquista delle Indie orientali (3, G. Boggio), Turin, Regio, carn. 1808

Ifigenia in Aulide (2, Romanelli), Milan, Scala, 28 Jan 1809, *Mc*

Federico [Federici], **Gennaro Antonio** [Gennarantonio, Jennaro-Antonio] (*b* ?Naples, *fl* 1726–43; *d* 1743–4). Italian librettist. A lawyer by profession, he worked in Naples where he wrote prose comedies, librettos for sacred and comic operas and the famous intermezzo *La serva padrona* (1733). While it is probably his association with Pergolesi's music in the last-named work that makes Federico known at all today, the vivacity of the libretto, with its implications for the Encyclopedists, played a great part in its initial celebrity. During his career the fashion in Neapolitan comic opera had moved away from a naturalistic representation of lower-class characters, entirely in dialect, and with obvious roots in the *commedia dell'arte*, towards an italianized dialect and an admixture of Italian-speaking non-Neapolitan roles. This demand for a plot involving two social classes, and two sets of theatrical and musical conventions, raised a problem of unity which Federico went some way towards solving in his more convincing works, by linking *seria* and *buffa* roles credibly within the intrigue. Nevertheless, it is most likely the *buffa* arias and ensembles – with their content of folk wisdom, personal characterization, confusion and mockery – and the lively musical settings these inspired, that evoked Charles de Brosses' famous reaction to *Amor vuol sofferenza* (1739): 'Quelle invention! quelle harmonie! quelle excellente plaisanterie musicale!'. Federico's critical reputation rests to a large extent on the freshness of his comedy and his skill in the portrayal of character. Napoli Signorelli, for example, wrote of his expression: 'Sempre è vera, sempre graziosa, sempre naturale, e non mai pulcinellesca'.

commedie per musica unless otherwise stated

Il finto fratello, G. Fischietti, 1730; *La Zita* (commeddeja pe mmuseca), Roberto, 1731 (Sciroli, 1756, as La Zita correvata); *Lo frate nnammorato*, Pergolesi, 1732; *L'Ippolita*, N. Conti, 1733; *La serva padrona* (int), Pergolesi, 1733; *L'Ottavio*, Latilla, 1733; *Gl'ingannati*, Latilla, 1734; *La marina de Chiaja*, 1734; *Il Filippo*, Roberto, 1735 (Sacchini, 1759, as Il copista burlato); *Il Flaminio*, Pergolesi, 1735; *I due baroni*, Sellitto, 1736; *Rosaura*, Sarro, 1736; *Il Gismondo*, Latilla, 1737; *Da un disordine nasce un'ordine*, V. Ciampi, 1737

Il conte, 1738; *La locandiera* (scherzo comico per musica), P. Auletta, 1738; *Inganno per inganno*, Logroscino, 1738; *L'Ortensio*, G. G. Brunetti, 1739; *Amor vuol sofferenza*, Leo, 1739 (Leo and M. Capranica, 1744, as La finta frascatana; Logroscino and A. Ferradini, 1750, as La finta frascatana; Cocchi (rev. C. Goldoni), 1754, as Li matti per amore); *La Beatrice*, Ciampi, 1740; *L'Alidoro*, Leo, 1740 (Capranica, 1748, as L'Aurelio); *L'Alessandro*, Leo, 1741; *La Lionora*, Ciampi and Logroscino, 1742; *Il fantastico*, Leo, 1743 (Leo and Comes, 1748, as Il nuovo D. Chisciotte)

CroceN; ES (E. Battisti)

P. Napoli Signorelli: *Vicende della coltura nelle Due Sicilie* (Naples, 1786), v, 551

M. Scherillo: *L'opera buffa napoletana durante il settecento: storia letteraria* (Naples, 1883, 2/1917), 207–29

C. de Brosses: 'A. M. de Neuilly: Séjour à Naples', *Lettres familières écrites d'Italie en 1739 et 1740* (Paris, 1885), 325–49

C. E. Troy: *The Comic Intermezzo: a Study in the History of Eighteenth-Century Opera* (Ann Arbor, 1979)

GRAHAM HARDIE

Fedora. Opera in three acts by UMBERTO GIORDANO to a libretto by ARTURO COLAUTTI after VICTORIEN SARDOU's play; Milan, Teatro Lirico, 17 November 1898.

Princess Fedora Romazov (soprano) is about to be married to Count Vladimir Andreyevich, captain of the Imperial Guard. Her love for him is symbolized in the Massenet-like theme of the prelude, which forms the first of the opera's two main recurring motifs. However, in the opening scene, at Andreyevich's house in St Petersburg, the servants leave no doubt that he is marrying the princess in order to restore his ruined fortunes. Fedora enters, expecting to meet him ('O grandi gli occhi lucenti'), but when he arrives home it is on a stretcher, fatally wounded. The police chief Grech (bass) interrogates the witnesses: Cirillo (baritone), the coachman who heard two shots fired, the diplomat De Siriex (baritone), who traced bloodstains in the snow to a pavilion where the count's body was found, and the groom, Dmitry (contralto), who remembers the delivery of a letter which was later removed by a visitor. His name was Count Loris Ipanov, who, it turns out, has fled the country. Fedora swears to bring him to justice as Vladimir's murderer.

Act 2 is set in Paris at the house of Fedora, who has succeeded in tracking down her enemy. She has invited him to a party in her house, intending to unmask him. Among her guests are De Siriex and the Countess Olga Sukarov (soprano) who has brought with her a Polish pianist, who claims to be Chopin's nephew. De Siriex teases Olga with a song about Russian women, 'La donna russa è femmina due volte'; she retorts with another about the Parisian male, 'Il parigino è come il vino'. Loris (tenor) enters with Fedora. His friend Borov (baritone) warns him to beware of his hostess; but Loris declares that he is already in love with her. During their flirtation he maintains that she clearly returns his feelings; his aria, 'Amor ti vieta', will furnish the second of the opera's two important motifs. While the Polish pianist plays one of his own nocturnes, Fedora draws from Loris the admission that he has left Russia as a fugitive from justice, having killed a man. He promises to tell her the whole story after the guests have left. De Siriex reads out a telegram reporting an attempt on the tsar's life, whereupon the party disperses. Fedora meanwhile reports Loris's confession to Grech, who accordingly stations his men in the garden with orders to seize the count the moment he leaves the house. Loris reappears. In a long narrative, 'Mia madre, la mia vecchia madre', he tells Fedora how he married a poor young girl, now dead, much against his mother's wishes and installed her in a pavilion in St Petersburg, and how he discovered that she was being visited by a lover, one of whose letters he intercepted. The writer was Vladimir Andreyevich. In it he mentioned his forthcoming marriage to Fedora, adding that it would make no difference to their relationship. To prove it, Loris produces the letter, to the astonishment and humiliation of Fedora, who now insists that Loris remain with her that night. The scene concludes with a love duet, 'Lascia che pianga io solo', the opening of which is recalled in the act that follows.

In Act 3 Loris and Fedora are living happily together in the Bernese Oberland. With them is Olga, who has taken up bicycling. De Siriex arrives with disturbing news. Fedora's report to Grech has reached the ears of the murdered man's father, who has had Loris's brother arrested as an accomplice and then drowned. The shock has caused their mother to die of grief. When De Siriex and Olga have left, Fedora prays that all this may be kept from Loris ('Dio di giustizia'). A postman comes with a letter from Borov recounting the sad events. Fedora confesses her responsibility and begs Loris to forgive her. When he curses her roundly she takes poison and dies in the arms of her remorseful lover.

Ever since seeing a performance of Sardou's play in Naples in 1885, with Sarah Bernhardt in the title role,

Giordano had wanted to make an opera of it. Sardou withheld his permission until after the success of *Andrea Chénier*. The much acclaimed première was conducted by the composer, with Gemma Bellincioni as Fedora, Enrico Caruso as Loris and Delfino Menotti as De Siriex. *Fedora* has proved Giordano's second most popular opera, after *Andrea Chénier*. Famous interpreters of the name part have included Lina Cavalieri, Gilda dalla Rizza, Maria Caniglia and Magda Olivero; notable Loris Ipanovs were Fernando De Lucia, Aureliano Pertile, Beniamino Gigli and Giacinto Prandelli. For a film version made in 1942, Giordano provided some extra music.

In *Fedora* Giordano made abundant use of national idioms. The opening chorus of Act 1 features Russian irregular rhythms; the melody of De Siriex's solo in Act 2 is adapted from a song by the Russian composer Alexander Alyab'yev; and the dance that precedes the exeunt of the guests recalls Glinka's 'Kamarinskaya'. The Polish pianist is introduced by a polonaise, and his own nocturne parodies the style of Chopin. Act 3 opens with a *ranz des vaches* on the horn and later features a folksong-like ditty sung by an offstage treble to the accompaniment of a concertina. Touches of modernity include an electric bell in Act 1 and the appearance in Act 3 of the Countess Olga clad in bloomers and wheeling a bicycle.   JULIAN BUDDEN

Fedra (i) ('Phaedra'). *Dramma per musica* in two acts by GIOVANNI PAISIELLO to a libretto by Luigi Salvioni after CARLO INNOCENZO FRUGONI; Naples, Teatro S Carlo, 1 January 1788.

Ippolito [Hippolytus] (soprano), son of Teseo [Theseus] (tenor), King of Athens, is in love with the Princess Aricia (soprano). Theseus's wife Phaedra (soprano) is preparing to sacrifice Aricia to the gods, but the goddess Diana (soprano), descending in a chariot, prevents this. Phaedra is passionately attracted to her stepson Hippolytus, and following the counsel of her confidant, the unscrupulous Learco [Learchus] (soprano castrato), she tries to seduce Hippolytus while her husband is absent. She is, however, rejected by him. Upon discovering Aricia's love for Hippolytus, Phaedra tries to force her to reject him. Her plans are foiled when Theseus returns safely from the underworld. On Learchus's advice she accuses Hippolytus of having seduced her, causing Theseus to exile his innocent son by sending him out to sea. During a storm a sea monster arises to attack Hippolytus, but Diana again intervenes. Believing Hippolytus dead, Phaedra, guilt-ridden, confesses to Theseus. All is resolved with Hippolytus's appearance in the company of Diana, and nuptial celebrations for him and Aricia follow.

The plot for Salvioni's libretto originated with Euripides. The subject was used by Racine and later by Frugoni, whose treatment of it, with some modifications, became the basis for Salvioni's libretto. The story intermingles royalty and deities – Pluto, Mercury and Tisiphone appear as well as Diana – and it incorporates large choral scenes with priests, priestesses, Furies, huntsmen, fauns and dryads. Choruses are in the French tradition (see, for example, the Furies in 1.x), and ceremonial music and dances add to the large-scale spectacle. The integrated texture of the scene marking Theseus's return from the underworld (2.vi) features a march, the chorus 'Viva l'eroe' and a concluding *ballo* made up of a series of dances. The ceremonial music employs a colourful orchestra including clarinets, horns,

bassoons and percussion. Except for the love duet in Act 2 for Aricia and Hippolytus, there are no ensembles.

GORDANA LAZAREVICH

Fedra (ii) ('Phaedra'). Opera in three acts by ILDEBRANDO PIZZETTI to a libretto by GABRIELE D'ANNUNZIO, a shortened version of his play of the same name; Milan, Teatro alla Scala, 20 March 1915.

Although the broad outline of D'Annunzio's version of the Phaedra story derives from Euripides and Seneca (more than from Racine), he added many significant details of his own. Moreover he clothed the whole in characteristically sumptuous verse, full of elaborate archaisms and recherché phraseology. The story revolves around the uncontrollable passion of Phaedra (mezzo-soprano) for her stepson Ippolito [Hippolytus] (tenor), son of Teseo [Theseus] (baritone) by a previous marriage. Her frustrated longing causes her to rejoice at a false rumour of her husband's death in battle, and then to murder a beautiful slave girl whom Theseus – when he returns home safely after all – brings with him as a present for Hippolytus. In desperation Phaedra kisses her stepson while he is asleep; but he wakes up and fiercely rejects her. In revenge, she convinces Theseus that Hippolytus has tried to rape her. The enraged king calls on the sea god to kill the young man, thus causing Hippolytus to be thrown from his horse and trampled to death near the seashore. As people gather, horrified, around the corpse, Phaedra, who has already taken poison, joins them and only now confesses her guilt. But in D'Annunzio's version she remains defiant to the last,

'*Fedra*' (Pizzetti): finale of Act 1 (the sacrifice of the beautiful slave girl) from the original production at La Scala, Milan, 20 March 1915, with Salomea Krusceniski as Phaedra; from 'L'illustrazione italiana', 28 March 1915

as nobody will be able to oppose her love beyond the grave.

The intricate verbosity of D'Annunzio's text undeniably gives rise to occasional longueurs. Moreover, Pizzetti's orchestral fabric may at times seem rather grey. Yet it fuses linear chromaticism and modality into an evocative, finely wrought and utterly individual synthesis; while the volatile heroine, and her impact on the other characters, are powerfully embodied in the subtly moulded, freely declamatory vocal writing. The chorus plays a more static, contemplative part here than in some of Pizzetti's later operas; but it often contributes intensely to the musical effect, reaching sublime heights of neo-madrigalian expressiveness in the unaccompanied 'Trenodia per Ippolito morto' at the beginning of Act 3. This is a creative response to Renaissance music of comparable stature to Vaughan Williams's exactly contemporary *Fantasia on a Theme by Thomas Tallis*. (Pizzetti composed *Fedra* in 1909–12.)

In Italy the 'Trenodia', like the orchestral prelude to Act 1, has often been performed separately in the concert hall. The work as a whole, although (like all Pizzetti's operas) it has aroused divergent reactions, was much admired and frequently revived right through to the end of the composer's life. Since then it has been neglected, as his reputation abruptly declined (partly for personal and political reasons) after his death. Outside Italy *Fedra* has had relatively few stage productions, mostly in South America. It seems likely that it would have become much more widely known if Pizzetti's relatively weak, self-repeating later operas had not damped people's curiosity about the richly imaginative achievements of his youth. JOHN C. G. WATERHOUSE

Fedra (iii) ('Phaedra'). *Tragedia lirica* in three acts by SYLVANO BUSSOTTI to his own libretto after JEAN RACINE; Rome, Teatro dell'Opera, 19 April 1988. It is a reworking of Bussotti's LE RACINE.

Feen, Die ('The Fairies'). *Grosse romantische Oper* in three acts by Richard Wagner (*see* WAGNER family, (1)) to his own libretto after CARLO GOZZI's *La donna serpente*; Munich, Königliches Hof- und Nationaltheater, 29 June 1888.

The models for Wagner's first completed opera were Weber and Marschner, with whose works the young composer became familiar in his first season as chorus master at Würzburg. He began work on the libretto probably in January or February 1833 and the score was finished on 6 January 1834. An aria for Ada was revised in the spring of 1834. *Die Feen* did not receive its first performance until five years after Wagner's death. It was not staged in Britain until 1969, when it was given by the Midland Music Makers Grand Opera Society at Aston University, Birmingham.

Ada (soprano), half fairy, half mortal, agrees to marry Arindal, King of Tramond (tenor), on condition that he refrain from asking her identity. Unable to curb his curiosity, he asks the forbidden question, whereupon Ada's magic realm disappears from view. Arindal returns to his court. Ada wishes to join him on earth, but a fateful decree obliges her to test him with a series of tribulations. He fails and curses her, only to be told that she is now condemned to be turned to stone for a hundred years. Arindal's despair drives him insane, but following Ada into the underworld he finally restores her to life by singing and playing the lyre. His courage is rewarded with immortality and, renouncing his earthly kingdom, he departs to reign with Ada in fairyland.

The score, by the 20-year-old Wagner, demonstrates a skilful handling of the conventional operatic forms. Particularly worthy of note are Ada's Act 1 cavatina 'Wie muss ich doch beklagen' with its throbbing appoggiatura dissonances, the masterly final ensemble of the same act, the scene and aria for Ada in Act 2 ('Weh' mir, so nah' die fürchterliche Stunde') and that for the distracted Arindal in Act 3 ('Halloh!').

BARRY MILLINGTON

Fée Urgèle, La [*La fée Urgèle, ou Ce qui plaît aux dames* ('Fairy Urgèle, or What Pleases Women')]. *Comédie mêlée d'ariettes* in four acts by EGIDIO DUNI to a libretto by CHARLES-SIMON FAVART after VOLTAIRE's *conte* inspired by Chaucer's *The Wife of Bath's Tale*; Fontainebleau, 26 October 1765.

Favart's libretto is set in 7th-century France. Robert (tenor), a knight, is made the prisoner of a court where women have dominion, and only a successful answer to the question 'What do women most want?' will secure his release. The answer is provided by La Vieille (soprano), an old crone whom Robert is consequently obliged to marry, but his torment gives way to happiness when he discovers that his new bride is really his beloved Marton in disguise. The plot offered opportunities for a lavish medieval *mise-en-scène*: Grimm (*Correspondance littéraire*) estimated that the staging of the court première cost 20 000 livres. Duni responded by including large-scale *divertissements* in each act, a bold move since *opéra comique* had hitherto made scant use of either chorus or dance movements. The work's four-act structure was also unprecedented.

Following its success at court, where Favart's wife was much praised for her performance as La Vieille, *La fée Urgèle* was given at the Comédie-Italienne (Hôtel de Bourgogne) on 4 December 1765. It was staged over a hundred times during the next two decades and inspired further medieval settings by composers including Grétry (*Aucassin et Nicolette*, *Richard Coeur-de-lion*) and Dalayrac (*Sargines*, *Raoul, sire de Créqui*).

ELISABETH COOK

Fegejo, Polisseno. See GOLDONI, CARLO.

Fehling, Jürgen (*b* Lübeck, 1 March 1885; *d* Hamburg, 14 June 1968). German director. After first studying theology, he began directing at the Berlin Schauspielhaus in 1910. A career spanning more than 40 years (mostly in Berlin and lastly in Munich) established him as one of the most important German theatre directors of the century, with especially noted productions of works by Shakespeare, Scribe, Kleist and Sartre. Fehling's two ventures into opera were controversial. His production of *Der fliegende Holländer* at the Berlin Kroll Oper in 1929, conducted by Otto Klemperer, used the severe Dresden version of the score (without the 'Redemption' coda) and was played in modern dress with starkly abstract, highly coloured expressionist sets designed by Ewald Dülberg. Its demythologizing approach was a landmark for modern Wagner production. *Tannhäuser* (Berlin Staatsoper, 1933), also with Klemperer, had medieval costumes and settings, but was shorn of extraneous romantic picture-painting. It was withdrawn under Nazi influence after just three performances.

H. Curjel: *Experiment Krolloper* (Munich, 1975)

MIKE ASHMAN

Feind, Barthold [Aristobulos Eutropius; Wahrmund] (*b* Hamburg, 1678; *d* Hamburg, 15 Oct 1721). German poet and aesthetician. He studied at the universities in Halle and Wittenberg, and received a law degree. His writings show that he was exceedingly well read. In Hamburg, where he divided his career between law and writing, he became entangled in local politics and, particularly through satirical writing in his weekly publication, *Relationes curiosae*, fell foul of the authorities to the extent of being banned from the city and hanged in effigy in 1707; in 1708 a protesting group invaded the opera house during a performance of Graupner's opera *L'amore ammalato*, with a libretto by Feind. An imperial commission restored order to the city and in 1709 exonerated Feind, permitting him to return from Stade where he had worked for a Swedish baron and had developed strong loyalties to the Swedish. He was imprisoned by the Danish in 1717 as he was caught up in the Swedish-Danish war while travelling north of Hamburg. By 1719, however, he had returned to Hamburg, where he became a *Vikarius* at the cathedral.

Feind must be rated with Postel, Bressand and Hunold as an outstanding writer of librettos for the Hamburg Opera in the first decades of the 18th century. He contributed texts for works by both Reinhard Keiser and Graupner, as well as translating Giacomo Rossi's *Rinaldo* as set by Handel. His librettos demonstrate his outspoken concern that opera must be a distinct artistic genre and not simply spoken drama set to music. Feind's aesthetic and practical ideas about opera dramaturgy appear in *Deutsche Gedichte … sammt einer Vorrede … und Gedancken von der Opera* (Stade, 1708), an invaluable primary source for the history of opera aesthetics in 18th-century Germany; it also contains five librettos by Feind.

Feind opposed many of the stereotyped Baroque dramatic conventions, especially those found in French opera. He stressed a belief that individual characterization lies at the heart of opera drama. He insisted that dramatic actions of all kinds were required to stir the emotions of the audience, and he defended his frequent recourse to scenes of violence including murder and suicide: 'Etlichen Weichmühtigen kömmt es cruel vor eine Person auf dem Theatro erstochen zu sehen und dennoch sind bey den grausamsten Executionen alle Märkte Gassen und Richt-Plätze voll' ('Some tender-hearted people think it cruel to see a person stabbed on the stage, and yet there are the most horrible executions filling all the market places, alley-ways and places of execution'). Feind gave one of the clearer contemporary statements about the nature and importance in poetry of the concept of the Affections. His *Deutsche Gedichte* offers a lengthy, pseudo-scientific explanation of the physical nature of emotion current in much of the philosophical writing at the turn of the 18th century and based in part on Descartes' *Les passions de l'âme* (1649).

In essence Feind believed that individual emotions resulted from Man's four temperaments – the sanguine, choleric, phlegmatic and melancholic – which in turn were affected by the acid–alkaline balance of the bodily fluids. Although the concept strikes one today as naive, the great weight given to these ideas by Feind is proof of the aesthetic concerns in the German Baroque for writing poetry and music with an emotional rationale. Few theorists of the early 18th century stated these ideas in as much detail, and the emotionally intense librettos by Feind are classic examples of the results of this philosophy in early 18th-century German opera.

Octavia, R. Keiser, 1705; *Die kleinmüthige Selbst-Mörderin Lucretia, oder Die Staats-Thorheit des Brutus*, Keiser, 1705, as Lucretia; *Masagniello*, Keiser, 1706; *La costanza sforzata/Die bezwungene Bestandigkeit, oder Die listige Rache des Sueno*, Keiser, 1706, as Sueno; *Bellerophon, oder Das in die preussische Krone verwandelte Wagengestirn*, Graupner, 1708; *L'amore ammalato/Die kranckende Liebe, oder Antiochus und Stratonica*, Graupner, 1708; *Der Fall des grossen Richters in Israel, Simson, oder Die abgekühlte Liebesrache der Deborah*, Graupner, 1709; *Desiderius, König der Longobarden*, Keiser, 1709; *Der durch den Fall des grossen Pompejus erhöhete Julius Caesar*, Keiser, 1710, as Julius Caesar; *L'amore verso la patria/Der sterbende Cato* (after M. Noris), Keiser, 1715, as Cato; *Rinaldo* (after G. Rossi), Handel, 1715; *Das römische April-Fest, oder Opera auf die Geburt des kaiserlichen Prinzen Leopold*, Keiser, 1716

*

H. Schröder: *Lexikon der hamburgischen Schriftsteller* (Hamburg, 1851)

G. F. Schmidt: 'Zur Geschichte, Dramaturgie und Statistik der frühdeutschen Oper (1627–1750)', *ZMw*, vi (1923–4), 129–57, 496–530

H. C. Wolff: *Die Barockoper in Hamburg* (Wolfenbüttel, 1957)

G. Flaherty: *Opera in the Development of German Critical Thought* (Princeton, 1978)

S. Leopold: 'Feinds und Keisers Masagniello furioso: eine politische Oper?', *HJbMw*, v (1981), 55–68
GEORGE J. BUELOW

Feinhals, Fritz (*b* Cologne, 4 Dec 1869; *d* Munich, 30 Aug 1940). German baritone. After studies in Italy he made his début in 1895 as Silvio in *Pagliacci* at Essen, where he remained for two seasons. After a year in Mainz, in 1898 he joined the Munich Opera, where he was last heard in 1927. His Covent Garden début as Telramund won high praise in 1898, but he did not sing there again until Van Dyck's German season of 1907 when in addition to Telramund his roles were Hans Sachs, Kurwenal, Wolfram and Wotan (*Die Walküre*). He also appeared in Paris and Vienna, and in 1908–9 at the Metropolitan. There, in addition to the Wagnerian repertory, he sang Amonasro, and Sebastiano in the American première of d'Albert's *Tiefland*. In 1917 he sang in the world première of *Palestrina* at Munich, where he later taught. Though W. J. Henderson of the New York *Sun* wrote of his 'glorious voice', recordings made at about this time (1908) make painful listening. The volume is ample but the tone unsteady, the method providing scant evidence of his Italian training.

J. B. STEANE

Feinstein, Martin (*b* New York, 12 April 1921). American impresario. From 1946 to 1971 he worked for the impresario Sol Hurok, and in 1972 was appointed executive director of the Kennedy Center, Washington, DC. He brought the Bol'shoy Opera, the Paris Opéra, the Deutsche Oper, La Scala and the Vienna Staatsoper to the USA for their first visits, events financed by support from foreign governments. He also organized an international ballet series. In 1979 he assumed the chief executive position at the Washington Opera, and undertook a decade of radical expansion, increasing performances from 16 to 63 per year. His first season won immediate national attention for rarely performed works such as Handel's *Semele*, Argento's *Postcard from Morocco* and Montemezzi's *L'amore dei tre re*. His co-production in 1983 with the Orchestre de Paris of three Mozart-Da Ponte operas, staged by Ponnelle, marked Barenboim's American operatic début. Under Feinstein's leadership the company has toured to Edinburgh (1984), Jerusalem (1985) and Melbourne (1986). In 1986 the company produced the world première of Menotti's *Goya* with Domingo in the title role, and was subsequently acclaimed for exploring the Russian repertory with productions of *Yevgeny Onegin* (1985), *The Tsar's Bride* (1986) and *The Queen of Spades* (1989). In 1992 Feinstein mounted the American première of *The Savage Land* by the Chinese composer Jin Xiang, who was severely punished during the cultural revolution.   NANCY MALITZ

Fel, Marie (*b* Bordeaux, 24 Oct 1713; *d* Chaillot, 2 Feb 1794). French singer. She learnt the Italian style of singing from the Italian singer Mme Van Loo and made her début in 1734 at the Paris Opéra as Venus in the prologue of *Philomèle* by La Coste. She performed at the Concert Spirituel and at the Concerts chez la Reine (where operas given in Paris were previewed or repeated), and frequently performed *cantatilles* (*airs* between the acts of an opera). From 1739 she began to assume leading roles and, with the famous *haute-contre* Pierre de Jélyotte, charmed every opera audience. During her long and brilliant career she performed in over a hundred premières and revivals, including major roles in most of Rameau's works, such as *Castor et Pollux* (Cupid in 1737, Telaira in 1754), *Dardanus* (1739, 1744), *Hippolyte et Aricie* (1742), *Zaïs* (1748), *Platée* (1749) and *Zoroastre* (1749, 1756). Some of her other roles were in works by Lully, Campra, Mouret, Boismortier, Aurore in Mondonville's *Titon et l'Aurore* and Colette in Rousseau's *Le devin du village* (both 1753). In 1757 she appeared with her pupil Sophie Arnould, who replaced her at the Opéra the following year. Her flexibility and clear articulation particularly suited the technically demanding *ariettes*. Grimm, in a letter to Raynal (*Mercure de France*, May 1752), praised her mastery of the Italian style. A singer of sensitivity and intelligence, her many admirers included the librettist Cahusac and the painter Quentin La Tour.

J.-G. Prod'homme: 'Pierre de Jélyotte (1713–1797)', *SIMG*, iii (1901–2), 686–717

——: 'Marie Fel (1713–1794)', *SIMG*, iv (1902–3), 485–518

——: 'A Pastel by La Tour: Marie Fel', *MQ*, ix (1923), 482–507

M. Teneo: 'Marie Fel', *J.-P. Rameau: Naïs*, Oeuvres complètes, xviii (Paris, 1924), p.lxxix

M. Cyr: 'Eighteenth-Century French and Italian Singing: Rameau's Writing for the Voice', *ML*, lxi (1980), 318–37

G. Sadler: 'Rameau's Singers and Players at the Paris Opéra: a Little-known Inventory of 1738', *EMc*, xi (1983), 453–67
                                        MARY CYR

Feldbusch, Eric (*b* Grivegnée, province of Liège, 2 March 1922). Belgian composer. At the Liège conservatory he studied composition with Fernand Quinet; he then embarked on a career as a virtuoso cellist, and also worked as a conductor. In 1963 he was appointed director of the Mons conservatory and from 1974 to 1987 was director of the French section of the Brussels conservatory. His compositional ideas were crystallized in 1951 when he discovered the music of Berg and Carter and had a fruitful meeting with Legley. His works include vocal and instrumental pieces and one opera, *Orestès* op.42; this three-act work, to a libretto by L. Bourgaux after Aeschylus, was first performed in Brussels on 15 August 1969 at Radio Télévision Belge. Feldbusch used a combination of styles in *Orestès*: the vocal parts were composed along Bergian lines, while the orchestral parts range from neo-classicism to atonality.   HENRI VANHULST

Feldhoff, Gerd (*b* Radevormwald, Cologne, 29 Oct 1931). German baritone. He studied in Detmold, making his début in 1959 as Mozart's Figaro at Essen. In 1961 he joined the Deutsche Oper, Berlin, and was still singing with the company in 1990. He has also appeared in Hamburg, Frankfurt, Munich and Vienna and at Bayreuth, where he sang Amfortas (1969). His repertory includes Gunther, Kothner, Kurwenal, Pizarro, Cardinal Borromeo (*Palestrina*), the Music Master (*Ariadne auf Naxos*) and Barak. A forceful actor with an expressive voice, he is particularly successful in the title roles of *Cardillac* and *Wozzeck*.   ELIZABETH FORBES

Feldlager in Schlesien, Ein ('A Camp in Silesia'). Singspiel in three acts by GIACOMO MEYERBEER to a libretto by EUGÈNE SCRIBE, *Le champ de Silésie*, translated by LUDWIG RELLSTAB and Charlotte Birch-Pfeiffer; Berlin, Hofoper, 7 December 1844.

The plot is freely elaborated from an episode during the reign of Frederick the Great. A Count (bass) helps Frederick (speaking role) to escape from hostile Hungarian troops, even though the king has sentenced his son to death for violation of military discipline. The king is actually saved by exchanging clothes with the flute player Conrad (tenor), a member of the count's household who is in love with the gypsy Vielka (soprano). When he is questioned by his enemies at the end of Act 1, Frederick is able to convince them that he is a humble musician by playing the flute. Another attempt to capture Frederick is made in Act 3, and this time it is Vielka who intervenes to save him. *Ein Feldlager* was written for the reopening of the Berlin Hofoper following a fire there in 1843. Meyerbeer asked Scribe to provide the libretto, but, since it was inappropriate for a Frenchman to collaborate on a work written for an important civic occasion in Germany, Meyerbeer turned to the critic Ludwig Rellstab for a translation and kept Scribe's participation a secret. The virtuoso part of Vielka was written for Jenny Lind; local pressure forced Meyerbeer to consent to a première with Leopoldine Tuczek, though Lind took the part several days later. The Swedish soprano gave the first performance in Vienna in 1847, where the work was staged with some modifications as *Vielka*. Meyerbeer and Scribe drew on material from *Ein Feldlager* for their later *opéra comique*, *L'ETOILE DU NORD*.
                                    STEVEN HUEBNER

Feldman, Jill (*b* Los Angeles, 21 April 1952). American soprano. She studied singing privately in San Francisco, and later in Basle, and took a degree in musicology from the University of California at Santa Barbara. She made her American operatic début in 1979 as Music in Monteverdi's *Orfeo*, and the next year made her European début at the Spoleto Festival as Clerio in Cavalli's *Erismena*. In 1984 she sang the title role in a notable revival (concert performance) of Charpentier's *Médée*, directed by William Christie, at the Salle Pleyel, Paris. She has sung throughout Europe, specializing in Baroque roles and touring as a soloist and with ensembles. Her recordings include Rameau's *Anacréon* (1982), Cesti's *Orontea* (1983), Cavalli's *Xerse* (1985) and Charpentier's *Médée* (1984), *Actéon* (1982), *Les arts florissants* (1982) and *Le malade imaginaire* (1990). Feldman's accomplished technique, her fine sense of drama and a vocal range capable of subtle nuances of colour assist her in projecting an authoritative stage presence. Among her operatic roles that of Medea in Charpentier's opera is outstanding for its vivid characterization and subtle interpretation of the text.

NICHOLAS ANDERSON

Feldman, Morton (*b* New York, 12 Jan 1926; *d* Buffalo, NY, 3 Sept 1987). American composer. He began composing at the age of nine and studied with Wallingford Riegger while attending the New York High School for Music and Art. Later he worked in the family coat factory, but continued to study privately with Stefan Wolpe. His earliest known works already dwell on individual, isolated musical events, a trait which was to become his hallmark. By the time he met John Cage in 1950, Feldman's mature style, derived mainly from Varèse (free atonality, music as 'organized sound') and Webern (extremes of pointillism and quietude), was largely formed. He was strongly influenced by the abstract expressionist painters, who presumably inspired him to experiment with graphic scores in which pitch and duration are left indeterminate within broad limits.

From 1950 Feldman was one of the 'New York School' of musicians in the orbit of Cage, adopting from the older composer a characteristic quiescent impersonality of utterance, while Cage was influenced by Feldman's indeterminate notations. From 1967 Feldman used stemless note heads of fixed pitch with free duration and also wrote pieces in conventional notation, using the latter exclusively after 1969. His music of the 1970s and 80s is frequently consonant, even diatonic, without adopting overt tonality, and makes highly effective, if scattered, use of repeating cells. A Guggenheim grant in 1966 had freed him from his factory job, and from 1972 he was professor of music at the State University of New York at Buffalo.

At one hour's duration Feldman's only opera, *Neither* (1977), was by far the longest work he had attempted up to that time. Deliberately undramatic, like all his work, and highly unorthodox, with a plotless, eventless, one-character (soprano) libretto of 16 lines (by Samuel Beckett), *Neither* barely qualifies as an opera, but it does require staging and is clearly intended to be taken as one. To dismiss it as a concert monodrama is to avoid the points Feldman was trying to raise; the similarity of its interior monologue to that of *Erwartung* should especially be noted. The impersonality of the text is emphasized through the use of extremely high tessitura and extremely narrow melodic range, and above all by the glacial slowness of the unfolding 'action'. The work was first performed in Rome at the Teatro dell'Opera on 13 May 1977. Feldman's other Beckett setting, a radio play with some singing entitled *Words and Music* (1987), is far more conventionally dramatic.

H. Skempton: 'Beckett as Librettist', *Music and Musicians*, xxv/9 (1976–7), 5–6

B. Schiffer: 'Rome: Neither', *Music and Musicians*, xxv/12 (1976–7), 49–50

J. Rockwell: 'Opera: Feldman Event', *New York Times* (23 Nov 1978)

J. La Barbara: 'New Music', *HiFi/MusAm*, xxix/2 (1979), MA8–9

W. Zimmerman, ed.: *Morton Feldman Essays* (Kerpen, 1985) [incl. work-list and bibliography]

H. K. Metzger and R. Riehn, eds.: *Morton Feldman* (Munich, 1986) [incl. work-list, bibliography and discography]

ANDREW STILLER

Felici, Alessandro (*b* Florence, 21 Nov 1742; *d* Florence, 21 Aug 1772). Italian composer. He studied first with his father, Bartolomeo, then proceeded to advanced studies with Giuseppe Castrucci in Florence (1756–64) and with Gennaro Manna in Naples (1764–5). He became a teacher at his father's school in 1767 where his pupils included the singer Francesco Porri and Cherubini. He has been confused with the composer Felice Alessandri.

His first work, the *dramma giocoso La serva astuta*, was performed at the Teatro del Cocomero by Giovanni Roffi's Compagnia Toscana. According to the *Gazzetta toscana*, the success of his *Antigono* the following year could not have been greater nor the house fuller. He was chosen to compose a dramatic cantata, *Apollo in Tessaglia*, to inaugurate concerts presented by the Accademia degl'Ingegnosi in 1769. His most successful (and only surviving) opera was *L'amore soldato*, a *dramma giocoso*, given in Venice in 1769 and subsequently in Turin, Parma, Florence, Sassuolo and Leipzig. His music, by comparison with that of his contemporaries Giovanni and Ferdinando Rutini, Moneta and Neri Bondi, is highly expressive, offering presentiments of more romantic styles, especially when portraying melancholy moods.

dg – *dramma giocoso*   dm – *dramma per musica*

La serva astuta (dg, 3), Florence, Cocomero, 5 May 1768; Milan, Ducal, aut. 1769, as La cameriera astuta

L'amante contrastata (dg, 2, G. Lendenesi), Venice, S Moisè, aut. 1768

Antigono (dm, 3, P. Metastasio), Florence, Pergola, 18 Jan 1769

L'amore soldato (dg, 3, N. Tassi), Venice, S Moisè, aut. 1769, *A-Wn, D-Dlb, H-Bn, US-Wc*

Intermezzos to B.-J. Saurin's *Beverley* (tragedia urbana in prosa), 1769; Florence, Tintori, 6 Jan 1782

La donna di spirito (farsa, M. Bernardini), Rome, Capranica, carn. 1770

Doubtful [cited by Jackman]: La lavandaia, Turin, Carignano, aut. 1770; Alessandro nelle Indie (dm, 3, Metastasio), Livorno, S Sebastiano, carn. 1771; Ariana e Teseo (dm, P. Pariati), Florence, Pergola, 29 Jan 1772

*

Grove6 (J. L. Jackman)

M. Fabbri: 'Alessandro Felici: il terzo maestro di Luigi Cherubini', *Musiche italiane rare e vive da Giovanni Gabrieli a Giuseppe Verdi*, Chigiana, xix (1962), 183–94

M. de Angelis: *La felicità in Etruria* (Florence, 1990)

R. Weaver and N. Weaver: *A Chronology of Music in the Florentine Theater, 1751–1800* (Warren, MI, 1993)

ROBERT LAMAR WEAVER

Feller, Carlos (*b* Buenos Aires, 30 July 1925). Argentine bass. He studied in Buenos Aires, making his début in 1946 at the Colón, where he sang for a decade. He made his London début in Cimarosa's *Il maestro di cappella* at Sadler's Wells (1958). For Glyndebourne he sang Don Alfonso, Mozart's Figaro (1959) and Dr Bombasto (*Arlecchino*) at Edinburgh (1960). After appearing in Frankfurt and Brussels, he was engaged at Cologne, where he was still singing in 1991. He made his Metropolitan Opera début as Don Alfonso in 1988. His repertory included Leporello, Mozart's and Rossini's Dr Bartolo, Don Magnifico, Geronimo (*Il matrimonio segreto*), Don Pasquale, Dulcamara, Baculus (*Der Wildschütz*), Nicolai's Falstaff, Lord Tristan (*Martha*) and Varlaam. A superb *basso buffo*, he also sang heavier roles such as Polonius (Szokolay's *Hamlet*), the Doctor (*We Come to the River* and *Wozzeck*) and Schigolch (*Lulu*).

ELIZABETH FORBES

Felsenstein, Walter (*b* Vienna, 30 May 1901; *d* Berlin, 8 Oct 1975). Austrian director. After two terms at a technical college in Graz he studied acting with Ernst Arndt at the Burgtheater, Vienna (1921–3). He made his acting début in Lübeck in 1923, went to Mannheim in 1924 and a year later became dramatic adviser and director in Beuthen, Silesia. In 1927 he was appointed chief opera and drama director at the Stadttheater, Basle; from 1929 to 1932 he worked as an actor in Freiburg, where he was also dramatic adviser and director. He became chief director of the Cologne Opera in 1932 and in 1934 took a similar post in Frankfurt; excluded from the Reichstheaterkammer in 1936, he was able to continue working only by special permission on a freelance basis. From then on his productions (*Der Zigeunerbaron*, Berlin, 1939; *Falstaff*, Aachen, 1941; *Figaro*, Salzburg Festival, 1942) broke away increasingly from conventional ways of producing pure 'singers' opera' as he tried out his own method of dramatically logical, 'realistic' music theatre. During World War II he worked mainly as a drama director (1938–40 in Zürich, 1940–44 at the Schillertheater, Berlin) until he was enlisted (1944–5).

Immediately after the war Felsenstein directed Offenbach's *La vie parisienne* at the Hebbeltheater, Berlin, conceiving it as a programmatic plea for popular music drama based on the traditions of *opéra comique*. In 1947 he was appointed director of the Komische Oper in East Berlin and was able to develop his dramatic and aesthetic concepts of opera consistently and to incorporate them in a long series that subsequently became internationally acclaimed as model productions. He continued to work in the Federal Republic of Germany and abroad, and made operatic and musical films as well as fulfilling assignments in drama teaching. He was chairman of the music-theatre committee of the International Theatre Institute and president of its German Democratic Republic section. He was appointed professor (1959) and vice-president (1962) of the Akademie der Künste (Berlin, GDR) and received numerous national and international awards. His pupils included Götz Friedrich and Joachim Herz.

To Felsenstein 'realistic music theatre' meant using music to create drama so that the phrase became more than a socialist artistic doctrine. Beautiful melody was not an end in itself, nor was the voice an object of ecstasy; indeed, none of the clichés of operatic convention was found in his work. He wrote that music must be exclusively subject to the laws of the theatre, serving solely the dramatic action and its 'historic reality'. Accordingly, all his productions for the Komische Oper aimed to 'make the music and singing on the stage a credible, convincing, authentic and indispensable means of human expression': the singer had to convince the audience that his part could be communicated only in song.

Felsenstein and his assistants had a strong sense of authenticity; texts were sometimes thoroughly re-edited in an attempt to reconstruct the original. The result was a dramatically consistent and precise conception of the production which mediated dialectically between the composer's intentions and the 'associative ability of a contemporary audience'. Not only was the dramatic situation (as expressed in text and music) emphasized, but also the historical, artistic, social and political background.

His Berlin productions, many of which have also been given elsewhere, include *Die Fledermaus* (1947), *Orphée aux enfers* (1948), *Carmen* (1949), *Der Freischütz* (1951), *The Cunning Little Vixen* (1956; for illustration *see* HEINRICH, RUDOLF), Paisiello's *Il barbiere di Siviglia* (1960), *Don Giovanni* (1966), *Fiddler on the Roof* (1971) and *Háry János* (1973). His writings include 'Partnerschaft mit dem Publikum' (*Festschrift 1817–1967 Akademie für Musik und darstellende Kunst in Wien*, Vienna, 1967), *Musiktheater: Beiträge zur Methodik und zu Inszenierungs-Konzeptionen* (with G. Friedrich and J. Herz; ed. S. Stompor, Leipzig, 1970) and many articles in the *Jahrbuch der Komischen Oper* (Berlin, 1960–).

W. Ott and G. Friedrich, eds.: *Die Komische Oper 1947–54* (Berlin, 1954)

R. Münz: *Untersuchungen zum realistischen Musiktheater Walter Felsensteins* (diss., Humboldt U., Berlin, 1964)

G. Friedrich: *Walter Felsenstein: Weg und Werk* (Berlin, 1967)

P. P. Fuchs, ed.: *The Music Theatre of Walter Felsenstein* (New York, 1975) [incl. articles etc. by Felsenstein]

DIETRICH STEINBECK

Femelidi, Volodymyr Olexandrovych (*b* Odessa, 16/29 July 1905; *d* Odessa, 3 Oct 1933). Ukrainian composer. He graduated from the Odessa Music and Drama Institute in 1928. He began composing his only completed opera *Rozlom* ('The Split') the year of his graduation, finishing it in 1929. It was produced in Odessa that same year. The plot describes the revolutionary activities of sailors between July and October 1917, in the city of Kronstadt (Braşov). He began to compose his second opera, *Tsezar' i Kleopatra*, based on G. B. Shaw's play, in 1930, but was not able to finish it before his early death. A new edition of *Rozlom* has been prepared by Myroslav Skoryk.

L. Archimovych: *Shiyachy rozvytku ukraïnskoï radyanskoï opery* [The Paths of Development of Soviet Ukrainian Opera] (Kiev, 1970)

VIRKO BALEY

Fenaroli, Fedele (*b* Lanciano, Abruzzi, 25 April 1730; *d* Naples, 1 Jan 1818). Italian composer and teacher. He studied law and later attended the conservatory of S Maria di Loreto in Naples, of which he became *maestro di cappella* in 1777. From 1807 to 1813 he directed the new conservatory of S Pietro a Majella, with Paisiello and Tritto, and continued teaching until 1817. According to Florimo, the composers Cimarosa, Zingarelli, Giuseppe Nicolini and Carafa were among his pupils; he may also have given private instruction to Saverio Mercadante and Vincenzo Lavigna (see de Napoli). Most of his music is sacred, but two operas (both lost) are known: a *commedia*, *I due sediarii* (P. Metastasio; Carnival 1759, Naples, Fiorentini) and *La disfatta degli Amaleciti* (1780, Chieti). He also contributed an overture and three arias to *Zenobia*, a *dramma per musica* to a libretto by Metastasio, which was performed at the S Carlo, Naples, on 26 December 1767.

*Florimo*N

G. de Napoli: 'Fedele Fenaroli nel secondo centenario della nascita', *Musica d'oggi*, xii (1930), 113–16   SIEGFRIED GMEINWIESER/R

Fenice, La. Theatre in Venice, built in 1792 and until the 1850s one of the principal theatres in the Italian peninsula. It was restored in 1937 and remains the city's chief opera house. *See* VENICE, §§6–10.

Fennimore and Gerda. Opera in 11 pictures by FREDERICK DELIUS to his own libretto after J. P.

Jacobsen's novel *Niels Lyhne*; Frankfurt, Opernhaus, 21 October 1919.

The first two scenes take place at Consul Claudi's house at Fjordby. Two of his nephews, the writer Niels Lyhne (baritone) and the painter Erik Refstrup (tenor), are staying at the house. While Erik is out painting, Niels remains with Fennimore (soprano), the daughter of the house, and declares his love for her. Erik returns when rain threatens, and the young men listen as Fennimore sings to the lute about how she longs for the joys of life. The Second Picture shows Claudi's garden, which descends to the fjord. Erik and Fennimore are sitting in a boat by the landing-stage. They disappear into the dark garden as Niels rows another boat to land. While he ties the boat, Erik and Fennimore return, embrace, and express their mutual passion; it was for Erik that Fennimore had sung.

Three years intervene before the Third Picture, at Erik's house by the Mariager Fjord in summer. Erik has lost interest in his work and is drinking; his marriage to Fennimore has not been a success. He has invited Niels to stay; when he arrives, Fennimore urges him to help Erik. In the Fourth Picture, the same evening, Niels and Erik discuss their work and attitudes to life. Niels is working at a novel, but slowly; Erik feels inspiration has deserted him and his soul is bruised and broken. In the Fifth Picture Erik is taken to the town by his boon companions. Fennimore implores him not to go, but he ignores her. Niels comforts her by telling her of Erik's dashing boyhood; he says he will always be her friend. During the Sixth Picture Fennimore is waiting up for Erik; returning drunk, he abuses Fennimore for not having gone to bed. In the Seventh Picture it is autumn and Fennimore and he are wandering in the forest, among the fallen leaves. They come upon a deserted bird's nest, and the love they have tried to conceal wells up between them. Fennimore laments her decision to marry Erik, but they vow nothing shall part them now. By the Eighth Picture winter has come. Fennimore is anxiously awaiting Niels across the frozen fjord; instead she receives a telegram that Erik is dead, thrown from his cart. The body will soon be returning to the house. In her agony Fennimore cries that Niels must never enter again. The Ninth Picture shows the arrival of Niels. At the news of Erik's death he feels remorse; Fennimore rounds on him and says her love has turned to hate. Niels leaves in bewilderment; Fennimore collapses in the snow as she hears the men bringing Erik's body.

Three more years pass before the Tenth Picture. Niels has returned to the farm where he spent his childhood and found healing for the loss of his friend and of Fennimore; he no longer writes. In the Eleventh Picture he calls on a local councillor, whose four daughters are playing in the garden. The eldest, Gerda (soprano), is teased about her affection for Niels, who comes out of the house and presents her with a book containing an ivy leaf plucked from the tomb of Romeo and Juliet in Verona. Niels asks Gerda to marry him, and she joyously accepts.

Delius's sixth and final opera occupied him mainly during 1909–10. The Danish Jacobsen was an author much admired by Delius, not least because he rejected Christianity and its values. *Niels Lyhne* (1880) was the second of his two novels, both written after Jacobsen had translated Darwin's *Origin of Species* and *The Descent of Man*. Delius selected his scenes from the German translation of *Niels Lyhne*; the English version of the libretto is by Philip Heseltine (Peter Warlock). A 1914 performance of the opera was planned for Cologne; under that stimulus Delius added the two 'Gerda' scenes to a work originally called 'Niels Lyhne'. He wrote to Emil Hertzka of the Universal publishing house concerning the addition in January 1913: '[I] have become convinced that the "Gerda" episode is necessary after all to round off the opera. I have therefore added just 3 short scenes'. This was the origin of the Tenth and Eleventh Pictures; Delius's main concern had been that the Fennimore section ended inconclusively and in gloom.

Delius expounded his aims in *Fennimore and Gerda* both to Hertzka and in an interview for *The Evening News*. The dramatic interest of the libretto was to mount slowly, and the music would clarify matters not elaborated in words so as to avoid longueurs. It would have been wrong to make the libretto artistically complete in itself. His hope was to have achieved 'short, strong emotional impressions given in a series of terse scenes'. There was no reason why opera should not 'become the supreme vehicle for the expression of the finest and subtlest psychological ideas'. By simplifying scenery and reducing the length of intervals Delius wished to make the time-scale of opera less demanding.

Many of the work's 'pictures' are linked by musical interludes, and a separate orchestral 'intermezzo' was devised by Eric Fenby in 1945 from the introductions to the two 'Gerda' scenes. It is the orchestral interludes which provide Delius's main opportunity for scene- and mood-painting, achieved with all the subtlety of his mature orchestral palette. The harmonic asperity of some of the Fennimore scenes is smoothed in the Gerda section, which reverts to Delius's vein of pastoral lyricism with wordless chorus. The more laconic and flat the libretto seems, the more Delius enhances it with the touches of instrumental colour that give the brief episodes their vitality and strength. *Fennimore and Gerda* is his tribute to the Scandinavian culture and countryside he so much admired; it has the most modern setting of his major operas, and it is the least Wagnerian.   ROBERT ANDERSON

Fenton [Beswick], Lavinia (*b* London, 1708; *d* Greenwich, 24 Jan 1760). English actress and singer. She made her acting début in 1726 at the Haymarket Theatre, London, and sprang to fame in 1728 when she created Polly Peachum in *The Beggar's Opera* at Lincoln's Inn Fields Theatre. After she had sung the part more than 60 times she retired, becoming mistress of the third Duke of Bolton, who married her immediately after the death of his wife in 1751 – 23 years after taking her off the stage. Hogarth's contemporary painting of *The Beggar's Opera* shows the duke, in a box on stage, staring lovingly at her. The toast of the town by the age of 20, she combined ingenuous sweetness and youthful charm.

BDA; *DNB*; *LS*
The Life of Lavinia Beswick, alias Fenton (London, 1728)
H. Carey: *Poems on Several Occasions* (London, 1729)
C. E. Pearce: *Polly Peachum* (London, 1913)
      ELIZABETH FORBES, OLIVE BALDWIN, THELMA WILSON

Feo, Francesco (*b* Naples, 1691; *d* Naples, 28 Jan 1761). Italian composer. According to Burney, he was 'one of the greatest Neapolitan masters of his time'.

1. LIFE. Feo received his musical training at the Conservatorio S Maria della Pietà dei Turchini at Naples,

which he entered on 3 September 1704; among his fellow students were Leonardo Leo and Giuseppe de Majo. He first studied with the *secondo maestro*, Andrea Basso, and after 1705 also with Nicola Fago, the then newly appointed *primo maestro*. According to some 19th-century sources, Feo left the conservatory about 1708 to study counterpoint with G. O. Pitoni in Rome, but this claim has not been substantiated. He remained at the Turchini until 1712, and at the conclusion of his studies received the *scrittura* for his first opera, *L'amor tirannico, ossia Zenobia*, successfully presented at the Teatro S Bartolomeo in Naples on 18 January 1713. It was also performed in 1716 in Innsbruck (as *Radamisto*), and apparently as late as 1727 in Prague.

During Carnival 1714 Feo presented *Il martirio di S Caterina*, a *dramma sacro*, and in the following years established himself in Naples as a composer of sacred music with noteworthy works for local churches. He also contributed arias and comic scenes to Neapolitan performances of operas by other composers. In 1719 (according to a surviving libretto) he came forth with *La forza della virtù*, a *commedia per musica*, which was followed by the serious opera *Teuzzone* in 1720. Feo's first true success, however, appears to have been *Siface, re di Numidia*, performed by a star-studded cast (including Nicolini and Marianna Bugarelli) at S Bartolomeo in May 1723. The libretto for *Siface*, based on an older one by Domenico David, was the first attempt at a *dramma per musica* by the then 25-year-old Metastasio, who had just settled in Naples.

Feo's reputation as a church composer and the success of *Siface* led in July 1723 to his appointment as a *maestro* of the Conservatorio di S Onofrio a Capuana, where he joined Ignazio Prota and succeeded Nicola Grillo. During his 16 years of service there he became known as one of the most distinguished Neapolitan teachers of his generation. Among the composers who studied with him at S Onofrio were Nicola Sabatino, Niccolò Jommelli, Gaetano Latilla and his own nephew Gennaro Manna. In 1739 Feo resigned from the conservatory (where Leonardo Leo assumed his position), to succeed Francesco Durante as *primo maestro* of the Conservatorio dei Poveri di Gesù Cristo. There he served for the next four years, assisted by Alfonso Caggi and then by Girolamo Abos. One of his pupils at the Poveri was Giacomo Insanguine 'detto Monopoli'.

Between 1728 and 1741 Feo was at the height of his career and received numerous commissions from outside Naples. He composed six additional and quite successful *opere serie*. Of these only one, *Il Tamese* (1729), was written for Naples; the rest were for theatres in Rome (*Ipermestra*, 1728; *Andromaca*, 1730) and particularly Turin (*Arianna*, 1728; *L'Issipile*, 1733; *Arsace*, 1740). During these years he also wrote much church music, most of his oratorios and the serenatas *Oreste* and *Polinice* (both 1738) for Madrid. After *Arsace*, given at Turin for the reopening of the Teatro Regio on 26 December 1740, he yielded the dramatic field to the younger generation of opera composers represented by Latilla, Jommelli, Terradellas, Abos and Manna.

When the Conservatorio dei Poveri di Gesù Cristo was abolished in 1743 and converted into a seminary, Feo retired from public teaching, although he apparently continued to take private pupils. He also remained active as a composer of sacred music, serving various Neapolitan churches, among them the Annunziata, where he had been appointed *maestro di cappella* in 1726. During his last years he relinquished most of his obligations to Manna.

2. OPERAS. When Feo embarked on his career as an opera composer in 1713, the operatic scene in Naples was dominated by Venetian imports, by Alessandro Scarlatti and by such successful new contenders for public favour as Francesco Mancini, Domenico Sarro and Nicola Porpora. Feo's first opera, *L'amor tirannico*, reflects the situation. He adopted some of Scarlatti's orchestral mannerisms, such as the use of solo violin in the sinfonia and a divided orchestra with specific instrumentation for aria accompaniments, but his compositional approach shows greater affinity with that of Sarro.

Ten years later, with *Siface*, Feo's style was assured, and he helped usher in a new phase of Neapolitan opera in which he pursued a middle ground between the genial, popular Leonardo Vinci and the conservative but inventive Leo. In his mature operas the arias have characteristic opening statements, mellifluous and affecting but never overtly virtuoso vocal lines, smooth harmonic flow and homophonic accompaniments in which the violins duplicate much of the vocal part. In da capo arias the main parts are guided by the modulatory plan of the sonata principle; by 1740 they at times resemble a rudimentary sonata form, with a brief contrasting statement in minor mode articulating the beginning of the secondary tonal area (*Arsace*, Act 1: Mitrane's 'Qual torrente', Statira's 'Non hai difesa'). The middle sections are usually brief and motivically linked with the main part, providing contrast primarily through key change and reduced accompaniment. As a rule, arias are accompanied by strings only or with oboes and violins in unison. Arias scored for horns, oboes and strings provide the chief contrast, though there are also numbers in which wind instruments are used to set momentary dynamic or tutti accents (*Andromaca*, Act 3: Ulysses-Andromache duet 'Quando all' figlio tuo vedrai', the quartet 'Cederai superbo ingrato').

Although *L'Issipile* (1733) was Feo's only other *dramma per musica* to a libretto by Metastasio, his mature operas musically reflect Metastasian ideals. In his comic scenes and intermezzos he early captured the essentials of a straightforward but effective *buffo* style, especially in the bass roles and duets. But his *La forza della virtù*, performed at the Teatro dei Fiorentini in January 1719, remained his only contribution to *commedia per musica*, a field Vinci entered in July of the same year and quickly dominated with a series of successful works.

Feo's style is characterized both by a reliance on contemporary formulae and by forward-looking tendencies: there are the short, immediately repeated phrases, standard harmonic progressions in opening bars, lombardic rhythms, chains of 3rds and of triplet ornamentations, and coloratura writing; but there are also arias with balanced and symmetrical phrase structures that foreshadow elements of the Classical style. Not all his works maintain the same level of quality and inspiration, yet even when stereotyped his music cannot be denied its individual character. The best of his operatic arias indeed deserve Burney's praise for their 'fire, invention, and force in the melody and expression in the words'. His *galant*, early Classical tendencies found sympathetic response and continuation, particularly in the operas of Manna and Gian Francesco de Majo.

See also ANDROMACA (i). For illustration *see* OPERA SERIA, fig.1

L'amor tirannico, ossia Zenobia (dramma per musica, 2, D. Lalli), with the buffo scenes Pincone e Rubina, Naples, S Bartolomeo, 18 Jan 1713, *I-Nc*; as Radamisto (P. de Fleuris, after Lalli), Innsbruck, 1716
La forza della virtù (commedia per musica, F. A. Tullio), Naples, Fiorentini, 22 Jan 1719
Teuzzone (dramma, 3, A. Zeno), with the intermezzo Dalinda e Balbo, Naples, S Bartolomeo, 20 Jan 1720, duet *Rc*
Siface, re di Numidia (dramma, 3, P. Metastasio, after D. David: *La forza della virtù*), with the intermezzo Morano e Rosina (not by Metastasio), Naples, S Bartolomeo, 13 May 1723, *Nc*, arias *D-MÜs*
Don Chisciotte della Mancia (int), Rome, Seminario Romano, carn. 1726
Coriando lo speciale (int), Rome, Seminario Romano, carn. 1726
Ipermestra (os, 3, A. Salvi), Rome, Alibert, Jan 1728, arias in *Bds*, *I-Rc* and *Mc*, sinfonia *D-MÜs*
Arianna [Arianna e Teseo] (os, 3, P. Pariati), Turin, Regio, carn. 1728, arias in *A-Wn*, *F-Pc* and *GB-Lbl*
Il Tamese [Arsilda regina di Ponto] (os, 3, Lalli), with the intermezzo Il vedovo (Senpronio e Arrighetta), Naples, S Bartolomeo, wint. 1729, aria *Lbl*
Andromaca (os, 3, Zeno), Rome, Valle, 5 Feb 1730, *Lbl* (R1977: IOB, xxxi), *US-Wc*, arias *GB-Lbl*
L'Issipile (os, 3, Metastasio), Turin, Regio, 1733 [allegedly not perf.]; Lucca, Pantera, aut. 1735, *I-Nf* (Act 1 only)
Arsace (os, 3, Salvi), Turin, Regio, 26 Dec 1740, *Mc*, *Nf** (Act 2), *US-Wc* [according to Fétis this opera, or a version of it, was perf. Rome, Valle, 1731]
Arias and buffo scenes (Corrado e Lauretta) for Il duello d'amore e di vendetta (pasticcio), Naples, S Bartolomeo, 19 Nov 1715; arias and buffo scenes (Vespetta e Nesso) for G. M. Orlandini: Lucio Papirio, Naples, 1717 [according to Strohm the opera was probably F. Gasparini: Lucio Papirio, Rome, 1714]; intermezzo for L. Leo: Il castello d'Atlante, Naples, 1734

*

BurneyH; *FétisB*; *FlorimoN*; *LoewenbergA*; *RosaM*; *StiegerO*
G. B. Grossi: *I corifei della scuola di Napoli* (Naples, 1820), 216
H. Abert: *Niccolò Jommelli als Opernkomponist* (Halle, 1908), 113
G. Pavan: 'Il Teatro Capranica (1711–1800)', *RMI*, xxix (1922), 425–44
U. Manferrari: *Dizionario universale delle opere melodrammatiche* (Florence, 1954–5)
N. Burt: 'Opera in Arcadia', *MQ*, xli (1955), 154, 157
R. Brockpähler: *Handbuch zur Geschichte der Barockoper in Deutschland* (Emsdetten, 1964), 237
T. Volek and M. Skalická: 'Vivaldis Beziehungen zu den böhmischen Ländern', *AcM*, xxxix (1967), 64–72
R. Strohm: *Italienische Opernarien des frühen settecento* (Cologne, 1976), ii, 160–62
H. E. Smither: *A History of Oratorio*, iii: *The Oratorio in the Classical Era* (Oxford, 1987), 70
D. Libby: 'The Relation of the Score to Performance in Pergolesi's *opere serie* Based on a Study of his *Salustia*', *Studi pergolesiani*, ii (1988), 103–9

HANNS-BERTOLD DIETZ

Feradini, Antonio. See FERRADINI, ANTONIO.

Feramors. Lyric opera in three acts by ANTON GRIGOR'YEVICH RUBINSTEIN to a libretto by Julius Rodenberg after THOMAS MOORE'S *Lalla Rookh*; Dresden, Hoftheater, 24 February 1863.

Moore's poem, about a Kashmiri princess ('Tulip-cheek', soprano in the opera) who loves the poor singer Feramors (tenor) but is betrothed to the Khan of Bukhara – who turns out to be Feramors after all – inspired, in addition to Rubinstein's setting, the almost exactly contemporaneous *opéra comique Lalla Roukh* by Félicien David. The coincidence was unfortunate, because David's work kept Rubinstein's off the Russian stage, except for amateur and school productions, until

1898, some years after the composer's death, by which time even César Cui could afford to praise it faintly. The last production seems to have been in Riga in 1909.

An unpretentious essay in generic orientalism, *Feramors* may be likened to French lyric operas with Eastern settings by Bizet or Delibes. Tchaikovsky, who caught it in Berlin in 1879, wrote to Mme von Meck that 'it comes from the period in which Rubinstein did all his best work, that is 20 years ago', and that 'I love it rather a lot'. Its most popular numbers were the dances of bayadères and Kashmiri brides in Act 1 (much admired by Hanslick) and Lalla Rookh's aria, 'Ich kann nicht ruh'n', in Act 2. There is, of course, an Osmin-like *bouffe* role for a bass (Fadladin, the Grand Vizier of Hindustan), consisting of ungainly chromatic roulades and rapid patter.

RICHARD TARUSKIN

Ferandini, Giovanni Battista. *See* FERRANDINI, GIOVANNI BATTISTA.

Ferdinand III (*b* Graz, 13 July 1608; *d* Vienna, 2 April 1657). Austrian emperor, patron of music and composer. He was the son of Ferdinand II and became king in 1636 and Holy Roman Emperor in 1637. He was, like his father, not only an enthusiastic patron of music but also an admired and respected composer. Under Ferdinand II the long-established Netherlands influence on the music of the Viennese Hofkapelle had come to an abrupt end. From then on the Italians set the tone, and such prominent Italian composers as Bertali and Sances held important posts. Ferdinand III played an active part in the preparation of the great court festivities, especially stage works, which were produced with the utmost magnificence in Vienna and elsewhere in his Habsburg domains; one such occasion was the wedding of his daughter Maria Anna to Philip IV of Spain at Brussels in 1650, when Gioseffo Zamponi's *Ulisse nell'isola di Circe* was given.

Ferdinand's own allegorical *Drama musicum* of 1649 (in *A-Wn*; extracts in Adler, ii) was highly praised by Kircher, who declared (*Musurgia universalis*, 1650) that Ferdinand had 'no equal among sovereigns'. His music reflects the influence of his teacher Giovanni Valentini, but it shows too that he was a composer of some individuality and imagination, and he displays a sure technique.

*

G. Adler: Introduction to *Musikalische Werke der Kaiser Ferdinand III., Leopold I. und Joseph I.* (Vienna, 1892–3)
E. Wellesz: *Der Beginn des musikalishen Barock und die Anfänge der Oper in Wien* (Vienna and Leipzig, 1922); Eng. trans. in E. Wellesz: *Essays on Opera* (London, 1950), 33–45
R. Haas: *Die Wiener Oper* (Vienna, 1926)
——: *Die Musik des Barocks* (Potsdam, 1928), esp. 174–5
H. V. F. Somerset: 'The Habsburg Emperors as Musicians', *ML*, xxx (1949), 204–15
O. Wessely: 'Habsburger Kaiser als Komponisten', *Notring Jb 1959*, p.59
H. Federhofer: 'Musikleben in der Steiermark', *Die Steiermark: Land, Leute, Leistung* (Graz, 1971), 614–60
H. Seifert: *Die Oper am Wiener Kaiserhof im 17. Jahrhundert* (Tutzing, 1985)

JOSEF-HORST LEDERER

Ferencsik, János (*b* Budapest, 18 Jan 1907; *d* Budapest, 12 June 1984). Hungarian conductor. He studied at the National Conservatory in Budapest with Antal Fleischer (conducting) and László Lajtha (composition). He was a répétiteur at the Budapest Opera, 1928–31, and made his début in 1930 conducting a ballet on Rimsky-

Korsakov's *Sheherazade*. His career was based almost entirely in Budapest: at the Opera he was conductor (1931–45), chief conductor (1945–57) and general music director (1957–73, 1978–84). He was also permanent guest conductor at the Vienna Staatsoper from 1948 to 1950 and in 1964. He was president and conductor of the Budapest Philharmonic Society from 1960 to 1966 and chief music director of the Hungarian State Orchestra from 1953 until his death.

Ferencsik's conducting was widely regarded as representing Viennese classicism combined with Hungarian temperament. As an opera conductor he was noted for his precision and his spirited characterization, as well as his command of style. His career of more than 50 years covered an immense repertory, but he was most at home in works by Mozart, Wagner and Puccini, and in those by Hungarian composers such as Erkel, Kodály and Bartók.

P. Várnai: *Ferencsik János* (Budapest, 1972)

F. Bónis: *13 találkozás Ferencsik Jánnossal* [13 Encounters with János Ferencsik] (Budapest, 1984)   PÉTER P. VÁRNAI

Ferenczy, Oto (*b* Brezovica nad Torysou, 30 March 1921). Slovak composer and theorist. He studied music theory at Bratislava University and after working as a music critic joined the staff of the Bratislava Academy (VŠMU), later becoming professor. His one-act comic opera *Nevšedná humoreska* ('An Unusual Humoresque', 1966–7; first staged at the Košice Opera on 25 October 1969) is based on Kurt Goetz's play *Mŕtva teta* ('The Dead Aunt'). Written in a neo-classical style, the opera is notable for its elegance of expression, unsentimental lyricism and intellectual humour. The orchestral part often tends towards the frivolous and farcical. The work moves at a brisk pace, interrupted only by contrasting lyrical sections; a concluding fugue, to words by Ján Smrek, acts as a coda and has a quirky philosophical character. *Nevšedná humoreska* is considered by some to be the best Slovak comic opera to date.

I. Vajda: *Slovenská opera* (Bratislava, 1988), 129–31, 238   IGOR VAJDA

Fernand Cortez, ou La conquête du Mexique ('Hernán Cortez, or The Conquest of Mexico'). *Opéra* in three acts by GASPARE SPONTINI to a libretto by ETIENNE DE JOUY and Joseph Alphonse d'Esmenard; Paris, Opéra, 28 November 1809.

A free version of the historical events of 1520, the opera begins with the revolt of Spanish soldiers in Mexico. Only Cortez (tenor) can control them. He fears for the life of his brother Alvar (tenor) in Mexican captivity, particularly when his lover Amazily (soprano), a niece of Montézuma [Montezuma] (bass), tells him of the violence of the ruling priestly caste. Amazily's brother Télasco (tenor) enters with a retinue of Mexicans and offers Cortez peace if the Spaniards will leave Mexico. By way of reply, Cortez has the whole Spanish fleet sent up in flames. In the second act, Cortez and his army are on the outskirts of Mexico City. He frees his prisoner Télasco, intending to exchange him for Alvar. However, the priests will not release Alvar, and demand the life of the traitress Amazily if he is not to die. Boldly leaping into a lake, Amazily swims to the city to save Alvar, while the Spanish troops prepare to attack. In the third act, Amazily is just in time to prevent the sacrifice of Alvar. As the High Priest (bass) is about

to kill her, the Spaniards force their way into the temple. Télasco unites Amazily with Cortez and all celebrate the reconciliation of the two peoples.

In 1808 Napoleon expressed a wish for an opera on the subject of the conquest of Mexico, as propaganda for his planned Spanish campaign. Esmenard was commissioned to provide a libretto. He had already written an *oeuvre de circonstance* for Le Sueur, *Le triomphe de Trajan* (1807). Subsequently Jouy, the librettist of Spontini's *La vestale*, was co-opted. Spontini's second grand opera aimed to overwhelm the audience, not only with such sensational elements derived from the *mélodrame à grand spectacle* as the appearance of live horses, but also by means of massive ensembles with opposing choruses and sophisticated *da lontano* effects. In this respect, and in the search for historical precision, the work can be seen as a precursor of grand opera, but in the glorification of a military commander Jouy intended to introduce an element of epic into the *tragédie lyrique*. For all the military vigour of the piece, however, Spontini's score, with its wealth of contrasts, also carried conviction in the lyrical emotion of Amazily and the touching prisoners' scenes, thus tending to cancel out the requisite propaganda effect. This is probably why the opera was withdrawn after only 13 performances when first staged, and only a thorough revision (performed at the Paris Opéra on 28 May 1817) helped the work to achieve lasting success. This new version adapted the libretto to political circumstances after the fall of Napoleon, redistributed events between the three acts and so avoided the slackening of suspense felt in the second act of the symmetrically-conceived first version. The contradictions between the neo-classical representation of larger-than-life ruling characters and a melodramatic appeal to the sympathy of the audience were not resolved, however, either in this revision or in two others; in the first of these (Berlin, Königliches Opernhaus, 6 April 1824) further changes to the third act strengthened the progressive *crescendo* form, and in the second (Berlin, Königliches Opernhaus, 26 February 1832) the use of a recurring theme provided a link between the final scene and the first act.

For illustration *see* GRAND OPÉRA, fig.1 and STAGE DESIGN, fig.12.
                                                      ANSELM GERHARD

Fernández, Oscar Lorenzo (*b* Rio de Janeiro, 4 Nov 1897); *d* Rio de Janeiro, 27 Aug 1948). Brazilian composer of Spanish descent. He trained at the Instituto Nacional de Música under Francisco Braga and others, and in 1924 was appointed professor of harmony there. He later founded the Conservatório Brasileiro de Música (1936), which he directed until his death. He was also active as an orchestral conductor. Fernández composed one opera, *Malazarte*, 1933 (Rio de Janeiro, Municipal, 1941). In three acts, it is based on a play of the same title by J. P. Graça Aranha, who himself adapted it into a libretto. The text was translated into Italian for the première. *Malazarte* is specially important in the history of Brazilian opera in that it is clearly a nationalist work, both in subject matter and in musical content; it is considered the first successful Brazilian opera of this sort. The story is based on Iberian-Brazilian folklore and the music relies on popular themes. The characters, who depict specific Brazilian ethnic and cultural traits, are associated with particular folk or popular genres (the choral numbers are all based on folksongs), though without falling into musical exoticism. The last section of the orchestral suite from the opera (1941), 'Batuque' (an Afro-Brazilian folk round dance), won great popularity.

*

L. H. Corrêa de Azevedo: *Relação das óperas de autores brasileiros* (Rio de Janeiro, 1938)

——: *150 anos de música no Brasil (1800–1950)* (Rio de Janeiro, 1956)

G. Béhague: *Music in Latin America: an Introduction* (Englewood Cliffs, NJ, 1979)

J. M. Neves: *Música contemporânea brasileira* (São Paulo, 1981)

Z. Baptista Filho: *A Opera* (Rio de Janeiro, 1987)

GERARD BÉHAGUE

Fernández Caballero, Manuel. *See* CABALLERO, MANUEL FERNÁNDEZ.

Fernández-Guerra, Jorge (*b* Madrid, 17 July 1952). Spanish composer. He studied at the Madrid Conservatory, and from 1970 participated as an actor, musician and composer in the reforming Independent Theatre Movement, composing incidental music for works by Kopit, Brecht, Beckett, Wilde, Smocek, Aeschylus and others. In 1986 he was commissioned by the Ministry of Culture to compose a two-act opera, *Sin Demonio no hay fortuna*, to a libretto by Leopoldo Alas based on the Faust legend. This received its première at the Sala Olimpia, Madrid, on 22 February 1987. According to the composer, the opera illustrates the paradox between dramatic conventions and the requirements of unity of musical language. It is scored for chamber orchestra, and there are four soloists: Fausto and the Croupier (tenors), Margarita (soprano) and Mefistófeles (baritone). Despite the coherence and clarity of the music, the opera's première was not an unqualified success. Both the production and the conducting were unsympathetic, and it was unfortunate that the very subject was similar to those of the Madrid opera season that year. Fernández-Guerra's techniques in this work owe something to *Wozzeck*. He gives a leading role to the orchestra, with interludes and concertante passages, though the orchestral texture is restrained. The vocal line of Fausto resembles speech-song, in contrast to the leaping intervals and rhythmic irregularities of Mefistófeles and the preciosity of Margarita's melodic line; this serves both to convey the different natures of the characters and to underline the lack of communication between them (clear in an extended trio). The composer is at present engaged on a revision of the score for a larger orchestra. *Sin Demonio no hay fortuna* is the most important opera to have been first performed in Madrid since the restoration of democracy. Fernández-Guerra has also written chamber and orchestral works which show him to be a lucid and self-critical composer.

XOÁN M. CARREIRA

Fernández Shaw, Carlos (*b* Cádiz, 23 Sept 1865; *d* Madrid, 7 July 1911). Spanish librettist. He received his initial education in Cádiz, and completed his secondary education in Madrid at the Instituto del Noviciado. He then studied law at the Central University, graduating with distinction in 1885, but after travelling to the USA he decided to abandon law for literature. He first made a name for himself as a poet and reciter, contributed journalism to *La epoca*, *La illustración* and *El correo*, and translated the works of foreign poets. He then began to concentrate on writing for the theatre and was librettist of many highly successful zarzuelas, most notably Chapí's *Las bravías* (1896) and *La revoltosa* (1897). The work with which his name is now most widely associated is Falla's opera *La vida breve* (1913), although this shows a less certain grasp of dramatic pace than his lighter zarzuelas.

selective list; all zarzuelas unless otherwise stated

El cortejo de la Irene, Chapí, 1896; *Las bravías* (with J. López Silva), Chapí, 1896; *La gitanilla* (with L. López Ballesteros), A. Vives and J. Guervós, 1896; *Manolos y patrimentes* (with F. Pérez), J. Jiménez, 1896; *La parranda* C. Zabala, 1896; *La revoltosa* (sainete lírico, with López Silva), Chapí, 1897; *Las castañeras picadas*, J. Valverde Hijo and T. L. Torregrosa, 1898; *La chavala* (with López Silva), Chapí, 1898; *Los hijos del batallón*, Chapí, 1898

Don Lucas del Cigarral (comedía lírica, with T. Luceño), Vives, 1899; *El gatito negro* (with López Silva), Chapí, 1900; *Los buenos mozos* (with López Silva), Chapí, 1900; *Polvorilla* (with F. Iráyzoz), Vives and E. Montesinos, 1900; *La buenaventura* (with López Ballesteros), Vives and Guervós, 1901; *Los timplaos* (with Eusebio), Jiménez, 1901; *La maja de rumbo*, J. Serrano, 1902; *El tio Juan*, Chapí, 1902

El tirador de palomas (with R. Asensio Más), Vives, 1902; *La venta de Don Quijote* (comedía lírica), Chapí, 1902; *La canción del naufrago* (with C. Arniches), E. Morera, 1903; *La puñalada* (mel), Chapí, 1904; *La máscara duende*, Vives, 1905; *Los pícaros celos* (with Arniches), Jiménez, 1905; *El maldito dinero* (with Arniches), Chapí, 1906; *El triunfo de Vénus* (with P. Muñoz Seca), Chapí, 1906

Las tres cosas de Jerez (with Muñoz Seca), Vives, 1907; *Las mil Maravillas*, Chapí, 1908; *Margarita la tornera* (leyenda lírica, after Zorrilla), Chapí, 1909; *Columba* (ópera, with López Ballesteros), Vives, 1910; *El final de Don Álvaro* (ópera), C. del Campo, 1911; *Los juglares* (with Asensio), Jiménez, 1912; *La vida breve* (ópera), Falla, 1913; *Rayo de luna*, Anglada, 1915; *La tragedía del beso* (ópera), del Campo, 1915   ANDREW LAMB

Fernández Shaw (y Iturralde), Guillermo (*b* Madrid, 26 Feb 1893; *d* Madrid, 17 Aug 1965). Spanish librettist. The son of Carlos Fernández Shaw, he pursued his secondary education at the Colegio de la Concepción in Madrid, and then studied law at the Central University. He followed in his father's footsteps as a journalist and poet, and likewise became a prolific zarzuela librettist, writing some 70 librettos, mostly in collaboration with Federico Romero. Together they wrote the librettos for some of the most durable successes between the wars, including *Doña Francisquita* (Vives, 1923), *El caserío* (Guridi, 1926), *La rosa del azafrán* (Guerrero, 1930), *Luisa Fernanda* (Moreno Torroba, 1932) and *La tabernera del puerto* (Sorozábal, 1936). Later he collaborated with his brother Rafael (*b* Madrid, 10 Nov 1905; *d* Madrid, 26 Sept 1967), who devoted himself part-time to libretto writing while pursuing a career in the Banco de España. Guillermo Fernández Shaw visited the French front in 1915 and was later awarded the cross of the Légion d'honneur; in 1963 he was appointed director-general of the Sociedad General de Autores de España.

selective list; all zarzuelas with F. Romero unless otherwise stated

La canción del olvidó, J. Serrano, 1916; *Los fanfarrones*, Eduardo Granados, 1920; *El dictador*, R. Millán, 1923; *Doña Francisquita*, A. Vives, 1923; *La severa [La morería]*, Millán, 1925; *El caserío*, J. Guridi, 1926; *La villana*, Vives, 1927; *Las alondras*, J. Guerrero, 1927; *Los flamencos*, Vives, 1928; *La meiga*, Guridi, 1928; *La rosa del azafrán*, Guerrero, 1930; *Luisa Fernanda*, F. Moreno Torroba, 1932; *Talismán*, Vives, 1932

La chulapona, Moreno Torroba, 1934; *Luna de mayo*, E. Rosillo, 1934; *No me olvides*, P. Sorozábal, 1935; *La tabernera del puerto*, Sorozábal, 1936; *Monte Carmelo*, Moreno Torroba, 1939; *La Rosario, o La Rambla de fin de siglo*, Sorozábal, 1941; *Cuidado con la pintura*, Sorozábal, 1941; *Loza, lozana*, Guerrero, 1942; *Peñamariana*, Guridi, 1944; *Tiene razón, don Sebastián* (with R. Fernández Shaw), Guerrero, 1944

Mambrú se va a la guerra, J. Dotras Vila, 1945; *Un día de primavera* (with R. Fernández Shaw), J. Romo, 1947; *La duquesa del candil* (with R. Fernández Shaw), J. García Leóz, 1949; *A todo colo* (with R. Fernández Shaw), M. Parada, 1950; *El canastillo de fresas* (with R. Fernández Shaw), Guerrero, 1951; *La Lola se vá a los puertos* (with R. Fernández Shaw), A. Barrios, ?1951; *El gaitero de Gijón* (with R. Fernández Shaw), Romo, 1953; *María Manuela* (with R. Fernández Shaw), Moreno Torroba, 1957

ANDREW LAMB

Fernando und Yariko ('Fernando and Yariko'). *Schauspiel mit Gesang* in three acts by FRANZ CHRISTOPH NEUBAUER to a libretto by Karl von Ekhartshausen; Vienna, 1788.

On an island off the American coast, the native woman Yariko (soprano) sees to the needs of several shipwrecked Europeans until they are captured by her brother. She pleads for the lives of the merchant Inkle (tenor), whom she loves, and his servant Pedril (bass). The ungrateful Inkle tries to sell Yariko into slavery, but his plans are foiled by the noble-minded Spaniard Fernando (tenor) despite opposition from his wicked, native-slaughtering father, Admiral Consalvo (bass).

Ekhartshausen's story, obliquely based on Richard Steele's essay on Inkle and Yarico in *The Spectator* (13 March 1711), was first set by Benedikt Schack in 1784 for the Theater in der Leopoldstadt, Vienna. Neubauer's full score was published (Zürich, 1788), a rarity for a German opera in the 18th century. The music is at its best in Neubauer's portrayal of the simple dignity and emotional directness of the heroine.   THOMAS BAUMAN

Ferne Klang, Der ('The Distant Sound'). Opera in three acts by FRANZ SCHREKER to his own libretto; Frankfurt, Oper, 18 August 1912.

After completing the libretto in 1903, Schreker finished the composition of his first staged opera after a performance of the third-act interlude (as *Nachtstück*) in Vienna under Oskar Nedbal in 1909. The première eventually took place in Frankfurt under Ludwig Rottenberg, with Karl Gentner as Fritz and Lisbeth Sellin as Grete. Its considerable success established Schreker as a leading opera composer of the modern school.

ACT 1.i *The modest living-room of the Graumanns' family home* A mysterious prelude introduces music associated with the image of 'the distant sound'. Grete Graumann is talking through the window to her boyfriend Fritz outside. He has told her that he must leave in search of his goal – the 'distant sound' that he hears in his heart, whose source and nature he associates with artistic achievement, fame and fortune. Only when these are his will he return to marry her. Sadly, she resigns herself to his decision and lets him go. A strange old woman engages her in conversation and promises to return, as Grete's mother now enters. The reality of the family's situation becomes clear: old Graumann has taken to drink and run up serious debts. Noises from the nearby inn prove to come from a skittle-game in which he has consistently lost and finally wagered his daughter away. Grete is horrified when the news is brought by staff and customers of the inn in coarsely jocular mood. Apparently promising her mother that she will agree to marry the victor (the Innkeeper), she grasps a momentary opportunity and escapes in search of Fritz.

1.ii *A woodland clearing, with a lake, close to the edge of town* Grete is lost and distraught. She contemplates drowning herself, but experiences involuntary ecstasy as the lake shimmers in the light of the moon and deer come to drink. She drifts into sleep. The strange old

Old Graumann *a retired minor official*		bass
His Wife		mezzo-soprano
Grete Graumann *their daughter*/Greta a 'dancer' [Act 2]/Grete ('Tini') [Act 3]		soprano
Fritz *a young artist*		tenor
Innkeeper of the Tavern 'Zum Schwan'		bass
A Strolling Player		baritone
Dr Vigelius *a shady lawyer*		high bass
An Old Woman		mezzo-soprano/high contralto
Mizi		soprano
Milli	*'dancers'*	mezzo-soprano
Mary		soprano
A Spanish Girl		contralto
The Count *aged 24*		baritone
The Baron *aged 50*	*bons viveurs*	bass
The Chevalier *aged 30–35*		tenor
Rudolf *Fritz's close friend and doctor*		high bass/baritone
The Actor		baritone
First Chorus-member		tenor
Second Chorus-member		bass
The Waitress		mezzo-soprano
An Unsavoury Character		tenor
A Policeman		bass
A Servant		spoken

Guests, male and female staff and servants from the tavern 'Zum Schwan'; girls, dancers of all nationalities, men and women (some masked); theatre personnel, members of the audience, serving girls, cab attendants etc.

Setting Act 1: A small town and nearby woodland (the present)
Act 2: A lavish dance hall and bordello on an island in the Gulf of Venice, ten years later
Act 3: A street tavern in a large city, close to a theatre, then Fritz's study (five years after Act 2)

woman reappears (accompanied by musical material that will be developed in Act 2) and leads the weary Grete away in search of a 'beautiful young sweetheart'. Grete promises to do anything, if she will only not take her back home. They disappear into the darkness.

ACT 2 The Venetian act, with lamp-lit gondolas arriving in the background of a scene depicting the lavish and brilliant Casa di Maschere, opens with a prelude in which are shortly heard siren-like calls of the 'dancers', greeting the arriving male revellers. To these are added an offstage Venetian band, a dreamy love song (women's chorus) and, once the curtain has risen, an onstage Hungarian gypsy orchestra with elaborately notated 'improvised' cimbalom and fiddle music. Schreker indicated that the strands of sung and spoken conversation should emerge indistinctly from the complex textural polyphony. Only gradually does the action come to focus clearly on Grete ('Greta'), now the most beautiful and sought-after hostess of the Casa di Maschere. She is courted by the Count and the Chevalier in a miniature song contest. The Count's gloomy ballad, 'Die glühende Krone' (beginning 'There lived a pale king with a strange crown'), pleases Grete less, however, than the Chevalier's humorous 'Das Blumenmädchen von Sorrent' ('Who doesn't know the sweet little flowergirl of Sorrento?'). The Count's jealousy grows threatening as a boat arrives, bearing the now bearded Fritz, who is pale and distractedly nervous.

FRANZ·SCHRECKER: DER·FERNE·KLANG· III·ACT· 1.

'Der ferne Klang' (Schreker), Act 3 scene i (a street tavern): design by Alfred Roller for the original production at the Frankfurt Oper, 18 August 1912

He is astonished to encounter Grete and confesses that in his bitter recent life, brightened only by partial and hard-won artistic achievement, his thoughts had begun to turn back to her. Grete finds herself torn between the easy seductive manner of her profession and recollection of her old love for him. Fritz, however, is horrified to discover what she has really been doing and storms away, bitterly denouncing her as a whore. Wounded, Grete turns back to the jealous Count, commands the gypsy band to strike up a csárdás, and falls into his arms as the wild dance, accompanied by general confusion, concludes the act.

ACT 3.i *Late evening; the open-air seating of a street tavern with the 'Court Theatre' visible across the street* There is no overture; the first sounds emanate from the theatre in the background (offstage ensemble), where Fritz's opera is being performed. Applause and motifs from *Der ferne Klang* itself (including the opera's actual closing bars) drift towards the tables where Dr Vigelius and the actor are drinking and reminiscing. Grete is helped to a seat by a policeman; deeply moved, she had become ill in the theatre. Now a street prostitute, known as 'Tini', she is accosted by an unsavoury character who claims to have been with her the day before. Dr Vigelius, remembering her, comes to Grete's rescue as the theatre audience streams out, many criticizing the opera's weak ending. Grete sinks into a faint. She comes round, sobbing, recalling her woodland vision that has been revived by Fritz's 'wild music'. As the curtain falls, the implied memory of that music turns into an extended orchestral interlude in which the motivic material of the entire opera is reviewed in a passionate stream of consciousness leading directly into the final scene.

3.ii *Fritz's study, through a window of which is seen a garden in the first light of a spring morning* Fritz, grey-haired and ill, sits at his desk, gazing into the garden. The dawn chorus (realistically notated) has overwhelmed him. All too late he has realized that the secret of the 'distant sound' lay in Nature itself. The sun rises and Rudolf comes to persuade him to rewrite the last act of his opera. He also has news of the woman who had collapsed in the theatre. Fritz begins to suspect who she was and has Rudolf go to find her as he hears the 'distant sound' itself (a series of mysterious arpeggiated chords for offstage celesta and piano), apparently emanating from the garden, and growing in intensity. Dr Vigelius then arrives, but is unable to penetrate Fritz's distracted mood until it becomes clear that he has brought Grete. She enters and they are reconciled, the 'distant sound' now at the peak of its intensity. Ecstatic, Fritz decides that he will rewrite the last act, but he dies in Grete's arms. She cries out as the curtain falls to the already heard Eb minor chords.

*   *   *

Der ferne Klang remained in the German operatic repertory until the 1930s. Its mixture of romantic fantasy with petty bourgeois realism and its richly subtle orchestral and harmonic language initially excited Schreker's contemporaries. It has been suggested that Berg (who prepared the first piano score) was influenced by formal and scenic features of the work in *Wozzeck*, and by the powerful central role of Grete in *Lulu*. While difficult to stage, it has been revived with considerable effect (e.g. 1984, Venice; 1988, Brussels; 1992, Leeds). Until the Hagen Opera recording, under Michael Halasz, in 1989, only extracts were available on commercial recordings. These included the Waldszene und Nächtlicher Reigen (1.ii), recorded by the composer in 1927, with his wife, Maria Schreker, as Grete.

PETER FRANKLIN

Ferni, Carolina (*b* Como, 20 Aug 1839; *d* Milan, 4 June 1926). Italian soprano. She studied the violin in Brussels and Paris, where she also studied singing with Giuditta Pasta. She made her début in 1862 in Turin as Léonor (*La favorite*) and then sang in the principal Italian theatres, including La Scala (1866–8). Agostino Mercuri composed an opera, *Il violino del diavolo*, specially to display her gifts as a singer and violinist. It was first performed in 1878 at Cagli, near Pesaro, with Carolina's husband, Leone Giraldoni, and her sister, the soprano Vincenzina Ferni (*b* Como, 1853; *d* Turin,

1926), also in the cast. In 1881 she sang *Il violino del diavolo* at the Politeama, Rome.   ELIZABETH FORBES

Ferni-Germano, Virginia (*b* Turin, 17 Dec 1849; *d* Turin, 4 Feb 1934). Italian soprano. A cousin of Carolina Ferni, she was a gifted violinist as well as a singer. She made her début as Siébel in *Faust* at a very early age, and then sang in the major European theatres. Her repertory included Mignon, Carmen, both Margherita and Elena in Boito's *Mefistofele* and the title role of Catalani's *Loreley*, which she created at the Teatro Regio, Turin, in 1890.   ELIZABETH FORBES

Feron, Elizabeth (*b* ? London, 1797; *d* London, 1853). English soprano. Her father was a French émigré. She studied with the violinist C. Cobham, who called her the English Catalani, and married the impresario Joseph Glossop in 1812. Her early career was spent mainly in Italy, where she appeared at La Scala, Milan, as Ninetta in *La gazza ladra* (1820), and sang in the premières of Donizetti's *Alfredo il grande* (1823, Naples) and *Alahor in Granata* (1826, Palermo). She left Italy in 1827. Her brief return to London did not fulfil expectations, but she went on to become, with her sister Mme Mangeon, a pioneer of Italian opera in America: she made her American début at the Park Theatre, New York, in the pasticcio *The Cabinet* (1828), also singing Mandane in Arne's *Artaxerxes* and Amenaïde (*Tancredi*) there. She made her final appearances in Italy and at the Princess's Theatre, London (1844). Feron's voice was a coloratura of wide range, brilliant at both ends; she was famous for her 'variations'. However, Cobham had overworked her young voice, and this inevitably shortened her career. Feron was the mother of Augustus Glossop, who took the surname Harris, and grandmother of the impresario Sir Augustus Harris.   D. J. CHEKE

Ferradini [Feradini, Ferrandini], **Antonio** (*b* Naples, ?1718; *d* Prague, 1779). Italian composer. Fétis suggested 1718 as his birthdate. He is first heard of in Carnival 1751, when he and Logroscino provided the new music for a revival in Naples of Leo's *Amor vuol sofferenza* under the title *La finta frascatana*. In 1751–2 he composed operas for the north Italian cities of Lugo and Sinigaglia, and contributed to a pasticcio produced at Forlì. His other brief period of opera production between 1757 and 1760 at more important centres in north central Italy. At Parma in Carnival 1757 he produced his only comic opera, to a libretto by Goldoni, *Il festino*, which is of historical interest as it was written during Goldoni's stay in Parma.

Gerber rated Ferradini very highly as a composer for both the church and the theatre, and also said that he lived for 30 years in Prague (which seems unlikely, as he was producing operas in Italy in the late 1750s). His operas are sometimes confused with those of the better-known Giovanni Battista Ferrandini, as some works bear only a surname.

all opere serie

Ermelinda, Lugo, Fair 1751
Artaserse (pasticcio, P. Metastasio), Forlì, Pubblico, spr. 1752, collab. anon. others
Ezio (Metastasio), Sinigaglia, 10 July 1752
Il festino (dramma giocoso, C. Goldoni), Parma, Reggio, carn. 1757
Solimano (G. A. Migliavacca), Florence, Pergola, carn. 1757
Ricimero (F. Silvani), Parma, carn. 1758, *P-La*
Antigono (Metastasio), Reggio, Fair 1758, *La*
Demofoonte (Metastasio), Milan, Regio Ducal, 26 Dec 1758, *La*
Didone (Metastasio), Lucca, aut. 1760, *La*

Giuseppe riconosciuto, Prague, 1763
Addl nos. in: Leo: La finta frascatana (ob, G. Federico, rev. of Amor vuol sofferenza), Naples, Nuovo, carn. 1750, with N. Logroscino; G. Latilla: L'opera in prova alla moda (dg, 3, G. Fiorini), Lodi, carn. 1752
Miscellaneous excerpts D-Bds, Dlb, GB-Lbl, I-Bc, MOe, PAc
          DENNIS LIBBY, JAMES L. JACKMAN

Ferrandini [Ferandini], **Giovanni Battista** [Johann Baptist; Zaneto] (*b* Venice, *c*1710; *d* Munich, 25 Sept 1791). Italian composer. As a boy he went to Munich, where he later served the elector as a court oboist, chamber composer (from 1732) and director of chamber music (1737). In 1755 he moved to Padua for reasons of health, but continued to compose operas for the court. Leopold and Wolfgang Mozart visited him there in 1771, and the young Mozart performed for him on the harpsichord. He returned to Munich around 1790.

Ferrandini was highly regarded as an opera composer in Munich, where the new Residenztheater, built by Cuvilliés, was opened in 1753 with a production of his *Catone in Utica*; his works were also favourably received elsewhere. His operas, originating in the Venetian tradition, do not show the lightness of the Neapolitan, and reflect the return from French to Italian musical taste at the Munich court. He also wrote solo cantatas, numerous arias (many to texts by Metastasio) and some instrumental works. Among his pupils were the Elector Maximilian III Joseph, his sister Maria Antonia Walpurgis and the tenor Anton Raaff. Ferrandini's daughter Anna Maria Elisabetta was a singer who, among other roles, sang Tamiris in Bernasconi's *Semiramide* at Munich in 1765.

performed at the Munich court unless otherwise stated

Gordio (dramma per musica, A. Perozzo da Perozzi), 22 Oct 1727
Il sacrificio invalido (dramma per musica, Perozzo da Perozzi), Nymphenburg, 10 July 1729
Colloquio pastorale (serenata, Perozzo da Perozzi), Nymphenburg, 6 Aug 1729
Berenice (dramma per musica, L. de Villati), 5 Feb 1730
Scipio nella Spagna (os, A. Zeno), 1732, *A-Wgm*
Ipermestra (os, A. Salvi), 22 Oct 1736
Adriano in Siria (os, P. Metastasio), carn. 1737, *D-Dlb*
Demofoonte (os, Metastasio), 22 Oct 1737
Artaserse (os, 3, A. Pariati ? and Zeno), 22 Oct 1739, *Dlb*, collab. G. Porta
Catone in Utica (os, Metastasio), 12 Oct 1753, *Hs, Dlb*
Le grazie vendicate (serenata, 1, Metastasio), 1753
Diana placata (serenata, 17 Aug 1755; rev. 1758
Demetrio (os, Metastasio), 1758
Talestri (opera drammatica, Maria Antonia Walpurgis), ?1760, *A-Wgm, D-Dlb, Mbs*
L'amor prigionero (componimento drammatico, 1), 1781, *Dlb*
Opera francese, *Dlb*

EitnerQ; StiegerO
F. J. Lipowsky: *Baierisches Musik-Lexikon* (Munich, 1811)
F. M. Rudhart: *Geschichte der Oper am Hofe zu München*, i (Freising, 1865)
E. J. Luin: 'Giovanni Ferrandini e l'apertura del Teatro Residenziale a Monaco nel 1745 [*recte* 1753]', *RMI*, xxxix (1932), 561–6
          ROBERT MÜNSTER

Ferrani [Zanazzio], **Cesira** (*b* Turin, 8 May 1863; *d* Pollone, nr Biella, 4 May 1943). Italian soprano. She studied with Fricci in Turin, where she made her début in 1887 as Micaëla and later sang Gilda. After singing in Venice and Genoa, where she took part in the first performance of Mascagni's *Le maschere* (1891), she created the title role in Puccini's *Manon Lescaut* at Turin (1893), repeating the role in Buenos Aires, Rome and other cities. She sang Suzel (*L'amico Fritz*) at Monte Carlo (1895), then created Mimì in *La bohème* at Turin

Auditorium of the Teatro Obizzi, Ferrara, after its reconstruction in 1660: engraving

(1896). At La Scala she sang Mélisande in the first Milan performance of *Pelléas et Mélisande* (1908). Her repertory included Juliet, Massenet's Sapho and Charlotte, Amelia (*Simon Boccanegra*), Elisabeth (*Tannhäuser*), Elsa and Eva (*Die Meistersinger*). She retired in 1909.   ELIZABETH FORBES

Ferrara. City in the Emilia region of northern Italy. Following Ferrara's devolution to the papacy in 1598, the local Accademia degli Intrepidi provided entertainments in two places: the Teatro degli Intrepidi, or 'di S Lorenzo' (from the name of the neighbouring church, 1604–5, near the present piazza Verdi); and the Teatro della Sala Grande, or 'Grande di Corte', adjoining the ducal palace (1610, between the via Cortevecchia and the via Garibaldi). Designed on classical lines by Giovan Battista Aleotti (though the Intrepidi had a U-shaped plan and a proscenium), and improved from time to time by him and his pupils Francesco Guitti and Alfonso Rivarola ('Il Chenda'), both theatres were used mainly for court celebrations and spectacles. Indeed, for most of the 17th century the city's entertainments consisted of tourneys and spoken drama with musical intermezzos, among them Michelangelo Rossi's *Andromeda* (1638; for illustration *see* GUITTI, FRANCESCO), an *opera-torneo*, and the musical drama *Il pio Enea* (1641, composer unknown). The continuation of such spectacular events probably arose from the need to celebrate with due solemnity the change of papal legate every three years. In 1652 a visit of nobles from the court of Innsbruck was marked by a performance in the Mirogli palace, 'with very surprising machinery', of Mattioli's *Gli sforzi del desiderio* as prologue to a tourney.

A performance of Cavalli's *Egisto* by a touring company in 1648, and a first series of commercial productions in the middle of the century in the Teatro di S Lorenzo (renamed Teatro Obizzi in 1640) prepared the way for the dominance of Venetian-style opera,

beginning with Cavalli's *Giasone* of 1659. The following correspondences of date are significant: in 1660 the Teatro Obizzi was reconstructed by Carlo Pasetti (with five stepped tiers of boxes, access to the stalls and a proscenium in Doric style); in the same year, the Teatro della Sala Grande burnt down; two years later the Teatro Bonacossi (or S Stefano) was built in what is now the via del Turco, and this became the principal house for opera at the end of the 17th century.

The Obizzi burnt down in 1679, and although the Teatro Scroffa, with five tiers of boxes, was built in 1692 (in what is now the corso Porta Reno), opera was performed mainly at the Bonacossi for most of the following century. Notable seasons there included the carnivals of 1737 and 1739, for which Vivaldi provided singers, arrangements of Hasse's operas (*Demetrio, Alessandro nell'Indie, Attalo re di Bitinia*) and the pasticcio *Siroe re di Persia*. Between 1785 and 1798, however, most productions were staged at the Scroffa.

What is now the Teatro Comunale, with four tiers of 23 boxes and a gallery, was first designed by Giuseppe Campana. The building was begun in 1786, but because demolition had taken place without the permission of the papal authorities, work was quickly suspended. When it began again in 1790, violent disagreements occurred between the rival architects, Antonio Foschini from Ferrara and the papal superintendent Cosimo Morelli, who were both asked to improve on the original plan. An outside arbitrating body imposed by the papal legate revised Morelli's plans, and the new 'Teatro Nazionale' opened on 2 September 1798 with Portugal's *Gli Orazi e i Curiazi*. Rossini's importance was recognized early: the première of his *Ciro in Babilonia* took place there in 1812.

Until 1870 the Comunale had two principal seasons of almost equal importance: carnival and the Spring Fair. Opera was also performed at the all-purpose Tosi-Borghi Arena, constructed in 1856 on the site of the old S Lorenzo theatre; originally open-air, the Arena was given a roof the following year, and from the 1870s to

1900 it satisfied a demand for popular entertainment which the more aristocratic Teatro Comunale did not. This situation was to have political implications: the ostentatious productions of the young Gatti-Casazza at the Comunale (1893–8) were followed by a referendum in 1904 and the theatre was refused a municipal subsidy.

In the 20th century opera has not been prominent in Ferrara. Performances have taken place at the Comunale, the Tosi-Borghi (renamed Verdi after its reconstruction in 1912–13) and the Teatro Nuovo in the piazza Trento Trieste (1905–6). The Comunale, which was closed from 1945 to 1964 and reopened after substantial restoration (further work followed in 1987–9), belongs to the Associazione Teatri Emilia Romagna, a regional circuit for touring opera productions. It was designated a 'teatro di tradizione' – one that is only partly funded by the state – in 1967.

*

L. N. Cittadella: *Sul teatro pubblico di Ferrara: lettera* (Ferrara, 1850)

A. Gennari: *Il teatro di Ferrara: cenni storici* (Ferrara, 1883)

P. Antolini: 'Notizie e documenti intorno al Teatro Comunale di Ferrara', *Atti della deputazione ferrarese di storia patria*, ii (1889), 33–83

T. Finotti, G. Pasetti and L. Villani: *Il Teatro Comunale di Ferrara: cento anni di storia (1798–1898)* (Ferrara, 1915) [documentary collection, in *I-FEc*]

C. Savonuzzi: *Il Teatro Comunale della città di Ferrara* (Ferrara, 1965)

A. Cavicchi: 'Inediti nell'epistolario Vivaldi-Bentivoglio', *NRMI*, i (1967), 45–79; suppl. by C. Vitali, *NRMI*, xiv (1980), 404

——: 'Teatro monteverdiano e tradizione teatrale ferrarese', *Claudio Monteverdi e il suo tempo: Venice, Mantua and Cremona 1968*, 139–56

L. Moretti: 'Dopo l'insuccesso di Ferrara: diverbio tra Vivaldi e Antonio Mauro', *Vivaldi veneziano europeo*, ed. F. Degrada (Florence, 1980), 89–99

C. Cavaliere Toschi: 'La magnifica menzogna: proposte per una lettura dell'effimero', *La chiesa di San Giovanni Battista e la cultura ferrarese del seicento* (Milan, 1981), 136–65

C. Molinari: 'Per una storia di alcuni teatri ferraresi', *Teatri storici dell'Emilia Romagna* (Bologna, 1982), 107–26

T. Walker: '"Gli sforzi del desiderio": cronaca ferrarese (1652)', *Studi in onore di Lanfranco Caretti* (Modena, 1987), 45–75

F. Fiocchi: 'L'inaugurazione del Teatro Nazionale di Ferrara', *Ferrara: riflessi di una rivoluzione* (Ferrara, 1989), 119–23

D. Mele: *L'accademia dello Spirito Santo: un'istituzione musicale ferrarese del secolo XVII* (Ferrara, 1990)

ALESSANDRO ROCCATAGLIATI

Ferrarese [Ferraresi, Ferrarese del Bene], **Adriana** [Andreanna, Andriana] (*b* c1760; *d* after 1800). Italian soprano. She studied at the Mendicanti in Venice from 1780 to 1782, and has long been identified with a Francesca Gabrielli, '*detta* la Ferrarese', whom Burney heard at the Ospedaletto in Venice in 1770; Gerber may have been the first to assume that Burney's Gabrielli and Adriana Ferrarese were one and the same, but no solid evidence links them. She eloped with Luigi del Bene in 1783 and appeared at the Teatro Pergola, Florence, on 8 May 1784.

In 1785–6 Ferrarese sang in London, at first in serious opera and then comic (though her roles were in *seria* style), and was generally well received. She returned to Florence, where her roles included Tarchi's Iphigenia and Gluck's Alcestis. In 1788 she settled in Vienna. Her background in *opera seria* made her particularly effective in heroic roles, such as Diana in Martín y Soler's *L'arbore di Diana* (her début role there), Eurilla in Salieri's *La cifra* (1789) and her most famous role, Mozart's Fiordiligi (26 January 1790). Her tenure of 30 months coincided with the peak of Lorenzo da Ponte's

influence; she was dismissed with Da Ponte, with whom she was romantically involved, in early 1791, and continued her career throughout Italy until the late 1790s, after which further records of her performances disappear.

Music written for Ferrarese tends to emphasize *fioriture, cantar di sbalzo* (large leaps) and the low end of her range. She appears to have been unsuited for the comic style; every adaptation of existing music for revivals and new music written for her tends to enhance the serious style at the expense of the comic. Weigl (*Il pazzo per forza*) and Salieri (*La cifra*) in particular met her vocal requirements successfully within roles that made limited demands on her modest acting ability. Her singing won much praise, notably from Count Johann Karl Zinzendorf, who wrote that 'La Ferrarese chanta à merveille' (27 February 1789). The casting of Ferrarese as Susanna for the 1789 revival of *Le nozze di Figaro* met with only qualified enthusiasm from Mozart, who wrote that 'the little aria [K577] I have made for Ferrarese I believe will please, if she is capable of singing it in an artless manner, which I very much doubt' (19 August 1789); he also composed a large-scale rondò in *opera seria* style, K579, to replace 'Deh, vieni, non tardar'. As Fiordiligi in *Così fan tutte* her vain temperament and formidable vocal resources were exploited to perfection by Mozart, creating a rigid *seria* character who is the object of comic intrigue.

*

GerberL

F. C. Petty: *Italian Opera in London, 1760–1800* (Ann Arbor, 1980)

J. Rice: 'Rondò vocali di Salieri e Mozart per Adriana Ferrarese', *I vicini di Mozart: Venice 1987*, 185–209

P. Lewy Gidwitz: *Vocal Profiles of Four Mozart Sopranos* (diss., U. of California, Berkeley, 1991)

PATRICIA LEWY GIDWITZ, JOHN A. RICE

Ferrari [Ferrari 'dalla Tiorba'; Ferrari 'della Tiorba'], **Benedetto** (*b* Reggio Emilia, ?1603 or 1604; *d* Modena, 22 Oct 1681). Italian composer, librettist and impresario. Together with Francesco Manelli he established the tradition of public opera performances at Venice.

1. LIFE. In 1617–18 Ferrari was a member of the choir of the Collegio Germanico, Rome. The few references to him in the college archives for these years suggest that he was still a choirboy, since they record payments made to the rector of the college for clothing him and paying for his journeys to Parma (and once for rescuing his father from prison). By 17 July 1618 he had left the choir, and from 1 January 1619 until 31 March 1623 he was employed as a musician at the Farnese court at Parma. He may also have revisited his native town at this period: a 'Benedetto da Parma' was listed among the singers at Reggio Cathedral in 1618 and 1620. The course of Ferrari's career between 1623 and 1637 is uncertain, though he seems to have been known at the Modenese court. On 8 August 1623 he wrote from the home of his uncle, the governor of Sestola, near Lucca, to Alfonso d'Este, enclosing examples of his compositions for two and five voices (lost); ten years later he dedicated his first book of songs, *Musiche varie* (1633), to Duke Francesco I d'Este.

Between 1637 and 1644 Ferrari was active mainly in Venice, working as both librettist and composer to produce a steady stream of operas for the new commercial theatres. His *Andromeda*, set to music by Manelli and staged in 1637 at the Teatro S Cassiano, was in fact the earliest Venetian opera to which the paying public was admitted, and it was staged, according to the libretto, at the performers' expense. For this production Ferrari also played the theorbo in the orchestra. The success of *Andromeda* prompted Manelli and Ferrari to collaborate again in 1638 to produce the opera *La maga fulminata*. After this their partnership lapsed, at least as far as Venice was concerned. In 1640 and 1641, however, they were both active in a touring company which presented Venetian opera at Bologna: Ferrari's virtuosity as a theorbo player was again noted in 1640, when he played in the Bolognese revival of Manelli's *La Delia*; and in 1641 *La maga fulminata* and *Il pastor regio*, an opera with both text and music by Ferrari, were performed at Bologna.

Little is known for certain of Ferrari's career between 1644 and 1651. It has been suggested that he was employed at Modena during these years. Certainly he wrote the ballet *La vittoria d'Imeneo* for performance there in 1648. Nevertheless, his presence is also noted at other centres. He seems to have been responsible for productions at Genoa in 1645 of *La Delia* and of Cavalli's *Egisto*, and at Milan in 1646 of *La Delia* and *Il pastor regio* (Bianconi 1982). His *Il pastor regio* and *Armida* were revived at Piacenza on 15 April and 22 and 26 May 1646, respectively, and the same city saw a production of his setting of Faustini's *Egisto* on 22 January 1651 (Bianconi and Walker 1975). In 1651 he travelled to Vienna to serve the Emperor Ferdinand III as instrumentalist and director of court festivities. He arrived there on 12 November 1651, having broken his journey at Innsbruck where he was given gifts by Archduke Ferdinand Karl (see letter of 18 November 1651 in *I-La*). His *L'inganno d'Amore*, set to music by Antonio Bertali and given before the imperial electors at the Diet of Regensburg in 1653, effectively marks the introduction of Italian opera into imperial court circles.

Ferrari returned from Vienna to Modena after 31 March 1653 and, according to Tiraboschi, was appointed court choirmaster at Modena on 1 September 1653. At Modena his *Andromeda* was revived for the opening of the Teatro della Spelta in 1656 (Southorn 1988). Apart from renewing his contact with the court at Parma in 1660, he remained at Modena until 1662, when he was dismissed for economic reasons. When, in 1674, Duke Francesco II d'Este began the process of reconstituting the musical establishment at Modena, Ferrari was not immediately given his former position. He applied to be reinstated, sending the duke a long and interesting petition (transcribed by Tiraboschi) in which he refuted charges that he was a dull, old-fashioned composer and gave an account of his career and achievements. In addition to his theorbo playing he drew attention to his skill in performing accompaniments on the spinet. He was reinstated on 1 December 1674 and served as choirmaster, jointly with Giuseppe Paini, until his death.

2. WORKS. The first three librettos that Ferrari wrote for the new Venetian public opera houses do not differ fundamentally from earlier, particularly Roman, models. The story of *Andromeda* was drawn from Greek mythology, while *La maga fulminata* and *Armida* followed in the tradition of the chivalric epic, the latter being based on Tasso's *La Gerusalemme liberata*. In his treatment of these subjects Ferrari allowed opportunities for elaborate stage effects such as the killing of a sea monster in *Andromeda* and conjuration in *La maga fulminata*. At the same time, however, the action was devised to allow for economy through the doubling of roles, as the cast lists for the first two operas show. These early librettos contain few of the subplots, intrigues and comic scenes that were to characterize librettos by Badoaro and Busenello and, indeed, later works by Ferrari himself. In *La maga fulminata*, however, he did introduce the figure of a comic governess, Scarabea (a male role), who was to prove the prototype for many similar characters in later Venetian opera and was in fact borrowed directly (and with humorous acknowledgement) by Giulio Strozzi for his *La Delia* (1639, set by Manelli). Busenello's libretto for *L'incoronazione di Poppea* (set by Monteverdi and possibly Sacrati) includes two such nurses. Among Ferrari's later Venetian operas *Il pastor regio*, written for the modest-sized Teatro S Moisè, Venice, in 1640 (revived at Bologna in 1641) is of particular interest. In his preface to the Venetian libretto he evaluated his own work, saying that he considered himself a good musician rather than a poet and that as such he knew how to write the sort of poetry that was appropriate for musical setting. The Bolognese version of the libretto (reproduced in Della Corte) included, as its final duet, the text 'Pur ti miro, pur ti godo', which also appears, perhaps with Ferrari's music (see Chiarelli, and Curtis), as the final duet in the surviving manuscripts of *L'incoronazione di Poppea* by Monteverdi and possibly Sacrati (1643) and (text only) of Filiberto Laurenzi's *carro musicale Il trionfo della fatica* (1647).

Ferrari appears to have written fewer dramatic works after his departure from Venice. Bianconi and Walker (1975) have, however, added one further opera, perhaps two, to the usual canon. The first is mentioned by Ferrari himself in a letter dated 3 April 1650 (*recte* 1651; in *I-La*), sent from Piacenza to a nobleman at Lucca. He wrote: 'Enone, which you have received from Bologna, was a bad Enone for me, since that gentleman who put me to the drudgery of writing the music made no recognition of this in words, which cost nothing'. This opera may be identified as *Enone abbandonata*, the libretto of which was published at Bologna in 1651, without mention of librettist or composer. The second additional attribution is the setting of *Egisto* mentioned earlier. This is attributed to Ferrari in the chronicle of Benedetto Boselli, who noted its performance at Piacenza in 1651. The libretto for this performance survives, but does not give the composer's name.

Two volumes of Ferrari's verse were published during his lifetime (Milan, 1644; Piacenza, 1651); the first contains six of his librettos.

Edition: B. Ferrari: *Poesie drammatiche* (Milan, 1644, 2/1659) [F]

first performed in Venice unless otherwise stated

L'Armida (Ferrari, after T. Tasso: *La Gerusalemme liberata*), SS Giovanni e Paolo, 1639, lib. in F

Il pastor regio (dramma, Ferrari), S Moisè, lib. ded. 23 Jan 1640, in F

La ninfa avara (favola boschereccia, Ferrari), S Moisè, 1641, lib. in F; perf. with *Proserpina rapita* (intermedio, Ferrari)

La finta savia [parts of Act 3] (dramma, G. Strozzi), SS Giovanni e Paolo, lib. ded. 1 Jan 1643; collab. 3, possibly 5, other composers

Il prencipe giardiniero (Ferrari), SS Giovanni e Paolo, lib. ded. 30 Dec 1643, in F

Egisto (G. B. Faustini), Piacenza, 22 Jan 1651

Enone abbandonata (dramma), ?Bologna, 1651, lib. ded. 9 Feb 1651

Gli amori di Alessandro Magno, e di Rossane (dramma, G. A. Cicognini), Bologna, 1656

L'Erosilda (dramma, C. Vigarani), Modena, Nuovo, 1658, lib. ded. 28 Feb 1658

Other dramatic works: La vittoria d'Imeneo (ballet, Ferrari), Modena, 1648, lib. (Modena, 1648); Dafne in alloro (Ferrari), Vienna, 12 Feb 1652 [introduction to a ballet]; Le ali d'Amore (F. Berni), Parma, ducal garden, 1660 [introduction to a ballet]; La gara degli elementi (Berni), Parma 1660 [introduction to a combattimento a cavallo]

Librettos for other composers: L'Andromeda, F. Manelli, 1637; La maga fulminata (favola), Manelli, 1638; L'inganno d'Amore (drama), A. Bertali, 1653 (Manelli, 1664, as La Licasta)

*

ES (N. Pirrotta); MGG (A. A. Abert)
Letters (MS, I-La, MOs)
B. Boselli: Croniche o diario (MS, I-PCc); see C. Poggiali: Memorie storiche di Piacenza, xi–xii (Piacenza, 1763–6, repr. 1932), and A. Rapetti: 'Il teatro ducale nel palazzo "Gotico" ', Bollettino storico piacentino, xlvi (1951), 45
G. Tiraboschi: 'Ferrari, Benedetto', Biblioteca modenese (Modena, 1781–6), ii, 265–71; vi, 110
N. Pirrotta: 'Tre capitoli su Cesti', La scuola romana (Siena, 1953), 27–79
A. A. Abert: Claudio Monteverdi und das musikalische Drama (Lippstadt, 1954)
W. Osthoff: 'Monteverdi-Funde', AMw, xiv (1957), 266
A. Della Corte: Drammi per musica dal Rinuccini allo Zeno (Turin, 1958)
W. Osthoff: 'Zur Bologneser Aufführung von Monteverdis "Ritorno d'Ulisse" im Jahre 1640', Anzeiger der phil.-hist. Klasse der Österreichischen Akademie der Wissenschaften, xcv (1958), 155–60
——: 'Masque und Musik', Castrum Peregrini, lxv (1964); It. trans., NRMI, i (1967), 16–44
P. Petrobelli: 'L'"Ermiona" di Pio Enea degli Obizzi ed i primi spettacoli d'opera veneziani', Quaderni della RaM, iii (1965), 125–41
——: 'Francesco Manelli: documenti e osservazioni', Chigiana, xxiv (1967), 43–66
T. D. Culley: Jesuits and Music, i: A Study of the Musicians Connected with the German College in Rome during the 17th Century and of their Activities in Northern Europe (Rome, 1970)
I. Mamczarz: 'Francesco Berni, Benedetto Ferrari e l'opera comica veneziana', Venezia e il melodramma nel settecento: Venice 1973, 103–30
A. Chiarelli: 'L'"incoronazione di Poppea" o "Il Nerone": problemi filologici e bibliografici', RIM, ix (1974), 117–51
L. Bianconi and T. Walker: 'Dalla Finta pazza alla Veremonda: storie di Febiarmonici', RIM, x (1975), 379–425
L. Bianconi: Il seicento (Turin, 1982); Eng. trans. as Music in the Seventeenth Century (Cambridge, 1987)
J. Whenham: Duet and Dialogue in the Age of Monteverdi (Ann Arbor, 1982)
A. Magini: 'Le monodie di Benedetto Ferrari e L'incoronazione di Poppea: un rilevamento stilistico comparativo', RIM, xxi (1986), 266–99
I. Mamczarz: Le Théâtre farnese de Parme et le drame musical italien (1618–1732) (Florence, 1988)
J. Southorn: Power and Display in the Seventeenth Century: the Arts and their Patrons in Modena and Ferrara (Cambridge, 1988)
A. Curtis: 'La Poppea Impasticciata or, Who Wrote the Music to "L'Incoronazione"?', JAMS, xlii (1989), 23–54
V. Crowther: 'A Case-Study in the Power of the Purse: the Management of the Ducal "Cappella" in Modena in the Reign of Francesco II d'Este', JRMA, cxv (1990), 207–19
P. Fabbri: Il secolo cantante: per una storia del libretto d'opera nel seicento (Bologna, 1990)
E. Rosand: Opera in Seventeenth-Century Venice: the Creation of a Genre (Berkeley, 1991)
L. Bianconi and T. Walker, eds.: F. Sacrati: La finta pazza (Milan, forthcoming)   JOHN WHENHAM

Ferrari, Francesco (b Cremona, fl ?1624–1677; d ?Fano). Italian composer. He was maestro di cappella of Fano Cathedral, 1636–45, then held the same post at Senigallia, where he was also chamber musician to Cardinal Cesare Facchinetti. His opera L'amorosa libertà (text by C. Barbetta; published libretto in US-Wc) was staged at Senigallia on 10 February 1647. Later he was again maestro at Fano. As the 'moderator della musica' of the Accademia degli Scomposti at Fano he

composed canzonettas, madrigals and short dramatic works, possibly including I due Coralbi (text by C. Amadio, given at S Angelo in Vado, Comunale, on 5 September 1671: see Manferrari). According to Eitner he died about 1683.

*

EitnerQ
G. Radiciotti: Teatro, musica e musicisti in Sinigaglia: notizie e documenti (Tivoli, 1893)
A. Mabellini: 'L'Accademia fanese degli scomposti', Studia picina, iv (Fano, 1928), 51–79
U. Manferrari: Dizionario universale delle opere melodrammatiche (Florence, 1954–5)   THOMAS WALKER

Ferrari, Francesco Gonella di. See GONELLA, FRANCESCO.

Ferrari [Colombari de Montègre], **Gabrielle** [Gabriella] (b Paris, 14 Sept ?1851; d Paris, 4 July 1921). Italian-French composer. She studied first at the conservatories of Naples and Milan, returning to Paris after her marriage to Francesco Ferrari, an Italian correspondent for Le Figaro; there she studied with Théodore Dubois and H. Ketten and was supported as a composer by François Leborne and especially Gounod (after whose death she studied further, at the Leipzig Conservatory). As a concert pianist she received great acclaim in music from Bach to Liszt and for her championship of new Russian music. Her works include five completed operas. Her first success was Le dernier amour, in 1895, but her greatest was Le Cobzar, a drame lyrique on a story of Romanian village life in turn-of-the-century verismo style by Hélène Vacaresco and Paul Milliet. First performed in 1909, and well received, Le Cobzar was the object of much debate and criticism among both pro- and anti-feminist writers when it was revived in Paris in 1912 in a revised two-act version. In it Ferrari used various Romanian folk idioms, including modal melodies, folk dances and arias in the style of the improvisatory doina tradition. It is also noteworthy for its dramatic structure, articulated by a harmonic system of key relationships that involve 3rds, 5ths and tritones, and for its employment of modal mixture and leitmotif.

Sous le masque, Paris, 1874
Le dernier amour (oc, 1, P. Berlier), Paris, Mondaine, 11 June 1895
L'âme en peine, Paris, 1896
Le tartare (tableau musical, H. Vacaresco), Paris, Figaro, 19 June 1906
Le Cobzar (drame lyrique, 1, Vacaresco and P. Milliet), Monte Carlo, 13 Feb 1909; rev. (2), Paris, 1912
Le captif, inc., unperf.
Lorenzo Salvieri, inc., unperf.
Le corregidor, inc., unperf.   MARGARET MONASTRA

Ferrari, Giacomo Gotifredo [Gotifredo Jacopo] (b Rovereto, South Tyrol, bap. 2 April 1763; d London, Dec 1842). Italian composer. The son of a silk merchant, he was intended for the family business but showed great musical talent from an early age. He studied singing and the harpsichord, counterpoint and theory, and before the age of 20 had learnt to play the flute, oboe, violin and double bass. After his father's death (1784) he decided to pursue a musical career. He went to Rome and then to Naples, where he studied counterpoint with Gaetano Latilla; he was befriended by Paisiello, who gave him a few composition lessons. He studied Mozart's operas and many string quartets. His opera Le pescatrici was composed in Naples in 1786 but not performed. In 1787 he went to Paris, where he played accompaniments for the queen, taught singing and was maestro al cembalo to the new Théâtre de Monsieur in the Tuileries. In that capacity he wrote additional music for Bianchi's *La villanella rapita* and for Sarti's *Fra i due litiganti*. In 1791 he composed two operas for the Théâtre-Montansier, *Isabelle de Salisburi*, in collaboration with Bernardo Mengozzi, and *Les événements imprévus* (to a libretto earlier set by Grétry). In 1792 Ferrari moved to London, where he met Haydn and Clementi and quickly became a leading singing teacher. On 14 May 1799 his opera *I due svizzeri* was successfully performed; this was followed by *Il Rinaldo d'Asti* (1802), *L'eroina di Raab* (1814), a vehicle for Catalani, and *Lo sbaglio fortunato* (1817).

Ferrari revisited Rovereto (1799) and Paris (1803), returned to Italy in 1815 and in the 1820s taught in Edinburgh. His memoirs, *Anedotti piacevoli e interessanti occorsi nella vita di Giacomo Gotifredo Ferrari da Rovereto* (London, 1830; ed. S. di Giacomo, Palermo, 1920), are more important than his treatises on singing and theory, as they contain historical information. Besides operas, Ferrari composed ballets, piano concertos, chamber music and songs, which include six Italian ariettas written for Catalani.

Le pescatrici, 1786 (ob, C. Goldoni), unperf.
Isabelle de Salisburi (comédie héroïque et lyrique, 3, P. F. N. Fabre d'Eglantine, after F.-T. Arnaud: *Salisbury*), Paris, Montansier, 20 Aug 1791; collab. B. Mengozzi
Les événements imprévus (3, D'Hale), Paris, Montansier, 5 Dec 1791
I due svizzeri (int, 1), London, Italian, 14 May 1799
Il Rinaldo d'Asti (os, 2), London, 1802
L'eroina di Raab, London, 1814
Lo sbaglio fortunato, London, 1817

E. Zaniboni: *G. G. Ferrari musicista e viaggiatore* (Trent, 1907)
G. Fino: *Giacomo Gotifredo Ferrari: musicista roveretano* (Trent, 1928)   ALFRED LOEWENBERG/PETER PLATT

Ferrari, Serafino (Amedeo) de. *See* DE FERRARI, SERAFINO.

Ferrari-Fontana, Edoardo (*b* Rome, 8 July 1878; *d* Toronto, 4 July 1936). Italian tenor. He turned to singing after starting a career in medicine and then working in the Italian Embassy at Montevideo. After touring South America in operetta he was encouraged by Serafin to study for opera; his début was as Tristan (Turin, 1910), and he soon established himself as the leading Italian Wagnerian tenor of his day. At La Scala he sang Pollione in *Norma* (1912) and the following year appeared as Avito in the première of *L'amore dei tre re*. This he repeated, with Toscanini, at the Metropolitan in 1914, singing with 'a magnificent robust voice with pealing upper tones'. He also appeared in Buenos Aires and was a member of the Boston Company, where he sang Tristan in 1912 (with his wife, Margarete Matzenauer, as Isolde in some performances). From 1926 he taught in Toronto. His few recordings show a voice of fine quality, compact in production, and used with taste and imagination.   J. B. STEANE

Ferrario, Carlo (*b* Milan, 8 Sept 1833; *d* Milan, 12 May 1907). Italian scene painter and stage designer. He went to the Brera academy in Milan in 1852, and joined La Scala the following year as assistant to F. Peroni. From 1859 he taught stagecraft at the academy and, later, courses in the landscape department. At La Scala he designed the premières of Boito's *Mefistofele* (1868), Ponchielli's *La Gioconda* (1876) and Gomes's *Maria Tudor* (1879), as well as new scenes of operas already in the repertory, including *Norma* and *Mosè in Egitto*. After falling out with the La Scala management in 1881, he worked for the Teatro Carcano (where he had painted a curtain in 1872). Without assistance, he created all the scenes there, a stunning achievement that led to commissions from other major theatres, notably the Argentina in Rome (for whom he had designed Gomes's *Salvator Rosa* in 1878) and the S Carlo in Naples, with which he had a long association.

Ferrario accepted Verdi's call to return to La Scala in 1887 to design *Otello*, and was subsequently appointed art director (1889) and director of scene painting (1890). He also supervised the replacement of the stage machinery. He was Verdi's preferred designer and created the first sets for *Falstaff* and a new *Rigoletto*

Set design by Carlo Ferrario for the première of Verdi's revised 'La forza del destino', La Scala, Milan, 27 February 1869, showing the village of Hornachuelos in Act 2 scene i (private collection)

(both 1893). He also designed La Scala's first *Meistersinger* (1899). The most influential Italian scenic artist in the second half of the 19th century, Ferrario continued an unbroken tradition that had begun with the Bibiena family. His style evolved over more than 40 years, adapting to changes in taste and musical form. Although he was regarded as a champion of realism, a strong romanticism pervades his work. He consistently achieved a harmony between what the audience saw on stage and what they heard in the orchestra. His scenic realizations for Verdi are the foundation of the Verdi tradition, and his ideas were carried on by a number of his students and disciples, including Vittorio Rota, Antonio Rovescali and Mario Salas. His sketches are found in the La Scala Museum, the Brera academy, the Ricordi archives and private collections.

For further illustration see MEFISTOFELE and STAGE DESIGN, fig.14.

*

V. Bignami: *Cinquecento bozzetti di scenografia di Carlo Ferrario* (Milan, 1919)
DAVID J. HOUGH

Ferraris, Ina Maria (*b* Turin, 6 May 1882; *d* Milan, 11 Dec 1971). Italian soprano. She studied with Vittorio Vanzo in Milan, gave her first concert in London in 1906 and two years later made her operatic début at Bologna as Philine in *Mignon*. In 1911, at La Scala, she sang Sophie in the first Italian production of *Der Rosenkavalier*. She remained at La Scala for some 20 years, singing light roles, until her retirement in 1934, after which she taught; she was also popular in South America. In 1917, at Monte Carlo, she created the role of Lisette in the première of *La rondine*. On recordings she is best known for her part in some enchanting duets from *Der Rosenkavalier* and *Hänsel und Gretel* with Conchita Supervia, mementos of their association in both operas at La Scala.
J. B. STEANE

Ferrari Trecate, Luigi (*b* Alessandria, Piedmont, 25 Aug 1884; *d* Rome, 17 April 1964). Italian composer. He studied under Mascagni in Pesaro and was director of the Parma Conservatory, 1929–55. His slight, ingratiating talent found its best expression in music for children, ranging from small piano pieces and choruses to operas: the most successful were *Ciottolino* (launched initially as a puppet opera) and *Ghirlino*. These deft little stage pieces, pervaded by the simple, fresh spirit of nursery rhymes and seasoned with occasional 'modernisms' that never go beyond mild postwar Ravel (as, for example, in the 'movimento di Fox' intermezzo from *Ghirlino*), deserved their success. The more ambitious later operas, *L'orso re* and *La capanna dello zio Tom*, stretched his gifts beyond their natural limit.

See also CIOTTOLINO.

Regina Ester (3, A. Montanari), Faenza, Istituto Righi, 1900, destroyed
Galvina (1, G. Forzano), Alessandria, Finzi, 14 May 1904, destroyed
Fiorilla (Forzano), Pesaro, Liceo Musicale, 1904, destroyed
Ciottolino (fiaba musicale, 3 scenes, Forzano), Rome, Piccoli di Podrecca, Palazzo Odescalchi (Sala Verdi), 8 Feb 1922
Pierozzo (poema lirica, 2, Térésah), Alessandria, Municipale, 15 Sept 1922, destroyed
La bella e il mostro (3, F. Salvatori), Milan, Scala, 20 March 1926
Le astuzie di Bertoldo (3, C. Zangarini and O. Lucarini), Genoa, Carlo Felice, 10 Jan 1934/?1930
Ghirlino (3, E. Anceschi), Milan, Scala, 4 Feb 1940
L'orso re, 1943 (favola magica, 3, Anceschi and M. Corradi-Cervi), Milan, Scala, 8 Feb 1950

Buricchio (3, epilogue, Anceschi), Bologna, Comunale, 5 Nov/?Feb 1948
La capanna dello zio Tom (prol., 3, Anceschi, after H. Beecher Stowe), Parma, Regio, 17 Jan 1953
Il ragazzo dei palloncini (teleracconto, L. Deli), RAI, 1959
? Two later operas, unperf.

*

C. Gatti: 'Prime rappresentazioni scaligere: *Ghirlino* di L. Ferrari-Trecate', *L'illustrazione italiana* [Milan], lxvii (1940), 183–4
E. Campogalliani: *Luigi Ferrari Trecate, operista* (Verona, 1955)
JOHN C. G. WATERHOUSE

Ferrata, Giuseppe (*b* Gradoli, nr Rome, 1 Jan 1865; *d* New Orleans, 28 March 1928). American composer of Italian birth. He was a piano pupil of Sgambati and Liszt and after his arrival in the USA in 1892 became a distinguished piano teacher at several American colleges, including Sophie Newcomb College of Tulane University, 1909–28. He composed many songs, piano works, church pieces and chamber music, as well as three operas. *Akrimane*, in four acts and composed in Greenville, South Carolina, in 1895–6, earned him the doctorate of music at the Grand Conservatory of Music of New York University. *Il fuoriuscito*, in one act to a libretto by Luciano Croci, was written in seven months in 1902 for an opera competition in Milan sponsored by the publisher Sonzogno; on the recommendation of the judges, Massenet and Humperdinck, Ferrata won second prize out of 237 contestants. *Il fuoriuscito* was originally entitled *Il bardo dell'Alpe*, then *Il finto giullare*, and was later translated into French by Paul Milliet as a two-act opera, *Le faux jongleur*. Ferrata's third opera was *Nella steppa* (1903; originally *Nadame*, based on Pushkin), about which Victor Herbert wrote: 'I enjoyed your new opera. You have succeeded in catching the atmosphere of the book in a most admirable manner. The work is full of beautiful themes and scenes, and should certainly score a great success' (it was translated into French as *Dans la steppe*). Although *Il fuoriuscito* was announced for performance by Carlo Nicosia's Opera Italiana in New York for the 1916–17 season, neither this nor the other two operas are known to have had public performances.

*

'Opera for the East Side', *New York Times* (30 Nov 1916)
G. F. Bernard: *The Life and Works of Giuseppe Ferrata* (thesis, Eastman School of Music, 1937)
JOHN H. BARON

Ferreira Veiga, José Augusto. See VEIGA, JOSÉ AUGUSTO FERREIRA.

Ferrer, Roberto Sanchez. See SANCHEZ FERRER, ROBERTO.

Ferrero, Lorenzo (*b* Turin, 17 Nov 1951). Italian composer. Initially self-taught, Ferrero worked with Massimo Bruni and Enore Zaffiri before going to Bourges in 1972–3 to do research into electronic resources. In 1974 he began a long-standing collaboration with the Musik-Dia-Licht-Film-Galerie, helping to produce multi-media works; the same year he took a degree at Turin University with a thesis on Cage. Ferrero's electronic research, which focussed on natural overtones, strongly influenced his harmonic language which by the late 1970s had become overtly neo-tonal. An unabashed synthesis of classical traditions and pop has made him the most successful opera composer of his generation in Italy and has also found him enthusiastic audiences in Germany. From 1980 to 1984 he was artistic consultant at the Puccini Festival at Torre del Lago, and in 1991 he became artistic director of the Arena di Verona.

Although the chamber opera *Rimbaud* differs from much of Ferrero's subsequent work in its partial use of a spiky, modernist vocal style and in its alternations of narrative and fantasy, it already shows a typically eclectic stylistic mix. But it was with *Marilyn* that Ferrero made his mark. These 'scenes from the 1950s', with their populist musical idiom and their collage of elements of Marilyn Monroe's private life and of public events (the Korean War, the McCarthy investigations etc.), placed the post-modern aesthetic on the Italian operatic stage in challenging form.

In his collaborations with Marco Ravasini, Ferrero began a game of cat-and-mouse with the conventions of mid-19th-century Italian opera – explicitly anatomized in *La figlia del mago* and gleefully resurrected in *Mare nostro*, where disco and cabaletta are juxtaposed. In direct contrast to the satirical storytelling of *Mare nostro*, *Night* re-asserted Ferrero's links to a more experimental theatre, bringing together a madrigal-like setting of Novalis's evocation of the birth of the son of night with an extended celebration of big-city night-life that Ferrero described as his 'mega-disco'. His works of the late 1980s return to the neo-Romantic fold: carefully crafted narrative librettos by Giuseppe Di Leva set to an increasingly expansive neo-tonal idiom that never forgets its 19th-century precursors.

See also MARILYN.

Rimbaud, ou Le fils du soleil (quasi un melodramma, 3, L.-F. Claude), Avignon, Festival Theatre, 24 July 1978
Marilyn (sceni degli anni '50, 2, F. Bossi and Ferrero), Rome, Opera, 23 Feb 1980
La figlia del mago (children's op, 2, M. Ravasini), Montepulciano, Poliziano, 31 July 1981
Mare nostro (comic op, 2, Ravasini), Alessandria, Comunale, 11 Sept 1985
Night (1, Ferrero, after Novalis [F. L. von Hardenberg]: *Hymnen an die Nacht*), Munich, Marstall, 8 Nov 1985
Salvatore Giuliano (1, G. Di Leva), Rome, Opera, 25 Jan 1986
Charlotte Corday (3, Di Leva), Rome, Opera, 21 Feb 1989
Le bleu-blanc-rouge et le noir (puppet op, A. Burgess adapted by J. P. Carasso), Paris, Centre Georges Pompidou, 11 Dec 1989

*

L. K. Gerhatz: '"Auch die Avantgarde steht in Entwicklungsprozessen … ": Gespräch mit dem italienischen Komponisten Lorenzo Ferrero', *NZM*, Jg. 143 (1982), 4–7
Nascita di un'opera: Salvatore Giuliano (Bologna, 1987)
M. Russo: 'Moderno, post-moderno, neoromanticismo: orientamenti del teatro musicale contemporaneo', *Il verri*, no. 2 (1988), 59–73
E. Simeon: 'Une biographie en forme d'opéra: Rimbaud', *Parade sauvage* (1988) [pubn of Musée-bibliothèque Rimbaud, Charleville-Mézières]
F. Pulcini, ed.: *Charlotte Corday di Lorenzo Ferrero* (Milan, 1989)
DAVID OSMOND-SMITH

Ferretti, Jacopo (*b* Rome, 16 July 1784; *d* Rome, 7 March 1852). Italian librettist. He was born into a cultured middle-class Roman family, and his father introduced him to literature and music. In particular, he was led to appreciate the elegance and clarity of Metastasio, and he began writing verse at an early age. He became fluent in Latin, Greek, French and English, and translated many French plays into Italian.

In 1814 he took up an appointment in the tobacco monopoly, which he held until 1845 (scarcely a suitable environment for an asthmatic whose health was never robust). Six years later he married Teresa Terziani, a fine musician and singer, and their house became a Mecca for visiting poets and musicians. He was an open-hearted and generous man who remained on the most friendly terms with the composers he worked with; Donizetti, in particular, became a firm friend and they corresponded regularly, often in verse of a jocular and witty nature, until 1836.

Ferretti turned his hand to any and every form of literary output – odes for funerals, weddings and other occasions; sonnets; love letters; necrologia; and speeches of welcome (including one for Verdi) – and was in constant demand. He is best remembered for his 70 librettos, over three-quarters of which were written for Rome. His first great success was *La Cenerentola* for Rossini (1817), but his later collaboration with the same composer (*Matilde di Shabran*, 1821) was rather less successful. He wrote five texts for Donizetti; *L'ajo nell'imbarazzo* (1824) and *Il furioso nell'isola di S Domingo* (1833) brought out the best in him, in witty, rapidly moving verse and sympathetic characterization. Some of his most successful librettos came from the mid-1830s, particularly *La casa disabitata* (Lauro Rossi, 1834), *Eran due or sono tre* (Luigi Ricci, 1834) and *La pazza per amore* (Pietro Coppola, 1835).

His best work was in light hearted genres, and he was a master of quick-moving, sparkling verse; in the writing of shorter, five-syllable lines (*quinari*) he was unsurpassed. His serious librettos were, on the whole, less successful, and not so tightly organized, but even his least satisfactory betray a sure-footed theatricality. He was held in great respect by other librettists, and received the rare accolade of a warmly complimentary notice from Felice Romani for the text of *La pazza per amore*. The versatility and spontaneity of his writing mark him out as one of the very few true poets of the Italian romantic opera.

mel – *melodramma*   mele – *melodramma eroico*
melg – *melodramma giocoso*   melss – *melodramma semiserio*

L'inganno dura poco (burletta per musica), C. Jannoni, 1807; *La principessa per ripiego* (dramma giocoso per musica, ? after F. S. Zini: *La vilanella ingentilata*), Morlacchi, 1809; *La Didone* (dramma serio, after P. Metastasio: *Didone abbandonata*), Valentino Fioravanti, 1810; *Baldovino* (dramma serio), Zingarelli, 1811; *Il bello piace a tutti* (melg), Fioravanti, 1811; *Berenice regina d'Armenia* (dramma per musica, after A. Zeno: *Lucio Vero*), Zingarelli, 1811 (C. A. Soliva, 1817, as Berenice in Armenia); *Tito in Langres* (dramma serio), A. Del Fante, 1812

Il voto di Jefte, S. Mayr, 1814, as Il ritorno di Jefte; *Amore assottiglia l'ingegno* (dramma buffo), P. C. Guglielmi, 1814; *Rinaldo d'Asti* (dramma buffo), Coccia, 1816; *La Cenerentola* (dramma giocoso), Rossini, 1817; *Polissena*, F. Rutini, 1817; *Bartolommeo dalla Cavalla* (mel), A. Pauselli, 1817 (C. Conti, 1827, as L'innocente in periglio; P. Lami, 1836; M. Quilici, 1838); *Pulcinella impresario*, Rutini, 1817; *Scipione in Cartagine* (mel serio per musica), Mercadante, 1820; *La festa della riconoscenza* (melg), F. Grazioli, 1821

Matilde di Shabran (melg), Rossini, 1821; *La capricciosa ed il soldato* (melg), Carafa, 1821; *Cesare in Egitto* (mele), G. Pacini, 1821; *Amalia e Palmer* (mel), F. Celli, 1822; *Eufemio di Messina* (mele), Carafa, 1822; *Il corsaro* (melg), Celli, 1822; *Amori ed armi* (after G. Palomba), F. Cianciarelli, 1823; *Zoraide di Grenata* (mele, after B. Merelli), Donizetti, 1824; *L'ajo nell'imbarazzo* (melg), Donizetti, 1824; *Gli amici di Siracusa* (mele), Mercadante, 1824; *L'audacia fortunata* (dramma giocoso per musica), A. Sapienza, 1824 (C. Conti, 1827)

Riccardo l'intrepito (mel per musica), G. Balducci, 1824; *La comunità di Castel Formicolone*, Trento, 1824; *Le civette in apparenza* (mel), L. Gambale, 1826; *La fedeltà fra i boschi*, Grazioli, 1826; *Olivo e Pasquale* (melg), Donizetti, 1827; *La sposa persiana*, Gambale, 1827; *La sciocca per astuzia*, Gambale, 1828; *L'orfanella di Ginevra* (melss), L. Ricci, 1829; *L'eroina del Messico* (mel serio per musica), L. Ricci, 1830; *Il corsaro* (mel romantico), Pacini, 1831

Il nuovo Figaro (melg), L. Ricci, 1832; *Il furioso nell'isola di S Domingo* (mel), Donizetti, 1833; *Torquato Tasso* (mel),

Donizetti, 1833; *Il Cid* (mel serio), L. Savj, 1834; *I due incogniti* (melss), G. Bornacini, 1834; *Eran due or sono tre* (mel), L. Ricci, 1834; *La casa disabitata* (melg), Lauro Rossi, 1834; *Chi dura vince* (mel eroicomico), L. Ricci, 1834; *La pazza per amore* (mel), Coppola, 1835; *Sedecia re di Giuda* (dramma per musica), G. Adrizza, 1835; *Il colonello* (melg), L. Ricci and Federico Ricci, 1835; *Monsieur de Chalumeaux* (mel comico), F. Ricci, 1835 *Giulietta* (mel), Pasquale Guglielmo, 1835; *Il disertore per amore* (mel), L. Ricci and F. Ricci, 1836; *La festa della rosa* (melg), Coppola, 1836; *Salvini e Adelson* (melss), J. Savj, 1839; *Il sogno punitore* (mel), G. Gerli, 1839; *Furio Camillo* (mel tragico), Pacini, 1839; *Contraddizione e puntiglio* (melg), M. Simeoni, 1842; *Paolo e Virginia* (melss), Aspa, 1843 (D. Dugnani, 1857, as *Gli isolani*); *Il folletto* (melg), Coppola, 1843; *Il puntiglio*, A. Brancaccio, 1845; *Gismonda di Mendrisio* (tragedia lirica), L. Badia, 1846; *La figlia di Figaro* (melg), L. Rossi, 1846; *Il cavaliere di S Giorgio*, Lillo, 1846

*

F. Regli: *Dizionario biografico* (Turin, 1860)
A. Cametti: *Jacopo Ferretti* (Milan, 1898)
L. Miragoli: *Il melodramma italiano nell'ottocento* (Rome, 1924)
JOHN BLACK

Ferri, Baldassare [Baldassarre] (*b* Perugia, 9 Dec 1610; *d* Perugia, 18 Nov 1680). Italian soprano castrato. He sang at Orvieto Cathedal (1623–4) before going to Rome to study with Vincenzo Ugolini of Perugia, *maestro* of the Cappella Giulia. In 1625 Prince (later King) Władisław IV of Poland heard him sing in Rome and took him to the Warsaw court, where he took part in performances of *drammi per musica*. In 1643 he was honoured for his singing in Venice and in 1654 he visited Stockholm. Leaving Poland in 1655, Ferri went to Vienna, to the court of Ferdinand III and of his successor Leopold I, who heaped honours on him; in a portrait of the time he is called 'Baldassarre of Perugia, King of Musicians'. He was in London in 1669–70. In 1675 (or 1680) he retired to Perugia. He was praised by his contemporaries, as the 'Phoenix of Swans and of Singers', for his vocal gifts and outstanding musical intelligence.

*

Il pianto de' cigni, in morte della Fenice de' musici, il cav. Baldassarre Ferri (Perugia, 1680)
G. C. Conestabile: *Notizie biografiche di Baldassarre Ferri musico celebratissimo* (Perugia, 1846)
A. Lupattelli: 'Baldassarre Ferri', *Perugia ed i suoi uomini illustri* (Perugia, 1882), 82–4
G. Monaldi: *Cantanti evirati celebri* (Rome, 1919)
K. Targosz-Kretowa: 'Le théâtre d'opéra à la cour de Ladislas IV, roi de Pologne (1635–1648)', *Revue d'histoire du théâtre*, xix (1967), 33–56
GALLIANO CILIBERTI

Ferrier, Kathleen (Mary) (*b* Higher Walton, Lancs., 22 April 1912; *d* London, 8 Oct 1953). English contralto. She studied with J. E. Hutchinson and then Roy Henderson. Established as one of England's leading concert artists, she made her stage début as Lucretia in the première of Britten's *The Rape of Lucretia* at Glyndebourne in 1946. The following year she sang Gluck's Orpheus there. These remained her only operatic roles. Her recordings of *Orfeo ed Euridice* (one, abridged, deriving from the Glyndebourne production, the other from a broadcast from the 1951 Holland Festival) give some idea of the strength and beauty of her interpretation. Covent Garden staged *Orfeo* for her in 1953 with Barbirolli as conductor. She could sing only two of the four scheduled performances before illness forced her to cancel; these were her last public appearances.

Ferrier's warm, ample and beautiful voice was firm through all its range. She used it with increasing expressiveness, overcoming an initial inflexibility.

For illustration see RAPE OF LUCRETIA, THE.

*

N. Cardus, ed.: *Kathleen Ferrier: a Memoir* (London, 1954, 2/1969) [with discography]
W. Ferrier: *The Life of Kathleen Ferrier* (London, 1955)
C. Rigby: *Kathleen Ferrier: a Biography* (London, 1955)
N. Cardus: 'Kathleen Ferrier', *Gramophone Record Review* (1957), 974–5, 1027–8 [with discography by F. F. Clough and G. J. Cuming]
M. Leonard: *Kathleen* (London, 1988)
P. Campion: *Ferrier: a Career Recorded* (London, 1992) [discography]
ALAN BLYTH

Ferroud, Pierre-Octave (*b* Chasselay, nr Lyons, 6 Jan 1900; *d* Debrecen, 17 Aug 1936). French composer. He studied natural sciences at the University of Lyons and the organ with Edouard Commette. From 1920 to 1922 he studied with Guy Ropartz in Strasbourg and later continued his studies with Florent Schmitt. He was active in many aspects of the musical life of Lyons until his untimely death in a car accident (an event which greatly affected his friend Francis Poulenc).

Ferroud's single operatic work *Chirurgie* ('Surgery'), after a story by Chekhov, is a one-act *opéra bouffe* with only two characters, a Sacristan (tenor or Trial; *see* TRIAL (ii)) and a Male Nurse (bass). The Nurse has been left to look after the patients in a provincial hospital while the doctor is away getting married. There is little plot. The verbose Sacristan has acute toothache, and the incompetent Nurse, who smokes a cigar and is shabbily dressed, unsuccessfully attempts to extract his tooth, much to the discomfort of the Sacristan. After the final attempt, the Sacristan feels in his mouth, only to find two teeth in the place of one.

Ferroud's style in the opera successfully combines a biting wit, portrayed through the use of pungent dissonance, with a skilfully varied orchestration in which string glissandos accompany the movements of the stubborn tooth. The work was first performed at the Monte Carlo Opéra on 20 March 1928.

*

L. Aubert: 'P.-O. Ferroud, Marcel Delannoy, Henri Tomasi, E. Bondeville', *Le théâtre lyrique en France* (Paris, 1937–9) [pubn of Poste National/Radio-Paris], iii, 266–74
C. Rostand: *L'oeuvre de Pierre-Octave Ferroud* (Paris, 1958)
RICHARD LANGHAM SMITH

Ferté, Denis Pierre Jean Papillon de la. *See* PAPILLON DE LA FERTÉ, DENIS PIERRE JEAN.

Fervaal. 'Action musicale' in three acts and a prologue, op.40, by VINCENT D'INDY to his own libretto; Brussels, Théâtre de la Monnaie, 12 March 1897.

D'Indy described *Fervaal* as a 'prose poem', and its roots are to be found in his libretto for *Axël* (1878, after Isaïas Tegner) which he transferred from a Swedish setting to his beloved southern France in 1886. The libretto, which focusses on the themes of redemption through death, the power of love and the demise of the Celtic pagan religions, was completed in 1888. D'Indy's score was composed between 1889 and 1893 and orchestrated in 1893–5. It was widely acclaimed as a renaissance in French opera, compelling admiration for its superb technique even from its critics.

The Prologue and Act 1 are set in the Midi at the time of the Saracen invasions. Young Fervaal (tenor), the sole descendant of the chiefs of Cravann, has been brought up under the strict guidance of the druid Arfagard (baritone). During their travels, Fervaal is wounded in a bandit attack but is nursed back to health by Guilhen (mezzo-soprano), the daughter of the Saracen leader who has laid the region waste. Fervaal has been told that he can save his people only through the renunciation of love, and the scene seems set for impending tragedy as Fervaal gives way to human passions. But the hypermoral Arfagard reminds him of his mission, and, although Guilhen is willing to follow him anywhere, Fervaal flees without her, leaving her rejected and swearing revenge on the land of Cravann.

Act 2 is set in Cravann, in the mountains of the Cévennes. The chiefs have assembled to elect a new leader (the Brenn). Arfagard invokes the deity Kaito (contralto), who mysteriously predicts that a new life will be born through death. Fervaal is elected unanimously, but the ensuing religious ceremony is interrupted by the invasion of the Saracen hordes.

Before Act 3 begins, Fervaal's battle against the Saracens has been lost, and already the snow is covering the corpses of his Celtic warriors. He, however, has miraculously survived and he begs Arfagard to sacrifice him to the gods. Then he hears the voice of Guilhen, lost in the mountains. His love is rekindled and, in order to escape from Arfagard, he kills him. But the harsh mountain winds have taken their toll on Guilhen, who dies in his arms. Alone with his grief, it gradually dawns on Fervaal how Kaito's prophecy might be fulfilled. He sees a vision of a new age of Christianity, of a beneficent God and a better life for all. Carrying Guilhen's body, he climbs the mountain towards 'the new Cravann' to the accompaniment of the Christian hymn *Pange lingua*. He sings heroically of the triumph of love over death as he disappears into the clouds surrounding the summit amid the growing light of a symbolic new dawn.

'As far as Wagnerism is concerned', d'Indy told the critic Camille Bellaigue, 'I have lived too close to the orbit of Wagner's star not to have been fatally involved in his revolution'. There are obvious parallels to be drawn between *Tristan und Isolde*, *Parsifal* and *Fervaal*, which uses leitmotifs (12 according to d'Indy), complex chromaticism (especially the augmented 5th) and a distinct tonality for each aspect in the dramatic development (D major for light and triumph, B major for war, and so on). But, for all the similarities and meticulous planning, d'Indy was a strong-willed man of considerable individuality and originality: his vast orchestra (including four saxophones, eight bugles or saxhorns and chromatic pedal timpani) is used economically and imaginatively; he had a better sense of dramatic pacing than Wagner, and more essential humanity; his vocal lines spring naturally from the words, often flowering lyrically into aria-like sections; and, above all, his music remains French – a deeply personal statement of unquestionable integrity. As Debussy wrote in 1903: 'If *Fervaal* still submits to the Wagnerian tradition, it is excused by its morality and its scorn for the grandiloquent hysteria that overwhelms so many Wagnerian heroes'. Dukas (1897) praised especially 'the extraordinary variety and taste of the orchestral effects ... in one of the most brilliant scores ever written', and as late as 1911 d'Indy still refused to change the slightest detail in his opera. '*Fervaal*', he observed, 'is the embodiment of my feelings during the most enthusiastic period of my life'.

ROBERT ORLEDGE

Fesanio, Merindo. *See* PASQUALIGO, BENEDETTO.

Fesca, Friedrich (Ernst) (*b* Magdeburg, 15 Feb 1789; *d* Karlsruhe, 24 May 1826). German composer. After appointments as chamber musician in the Duke of Oldenburg's chapel and solo violinist at the court of West-

phalia in Kassel, he became first violinist in the Grand Duke of Baden's chapel at Karlsruhe (April 1814). Chiefly known in his day as a composer of chamber music, particularly quartets, he wrote two operas: *Cantemire*, in two acts, to a libretto by A. von Dusch (op.19; vocal score published in Bonn, 1820) and *Omar und Leila*, in three acts, to a libretto by L. Robert (op.28; vocal score, Bonn, *c*1825); both were given in Karlsruhe, on 27 April 1820 and 26 February 1824 respectively. They show the influence of early Romantic works such as Spohr's *Faust*, but some elements of *Omar und Leila* are reminiscent of *Die Zauberflöte*.

NDB (H. Heussner)
'Memoir of Friedrich Ernst Fesca', *The Harmonicon*, v (1827), 39
J. F. Rochlitz: *Für Freunde der Tonkunst*, iii (Leipzig, 1830)
F. Pazdírek: *Universal-Handbuch der Musikliteratur* (Vienna, 1904–10)
GAYNOR G. JONES

Festa (Maffei), Francesca (*b* Naples, 1778; *d* St Petersburg, 9/21 Nov 1835). Italian soprano. She studied in Naples with Aprile and in Rome with Pacchierotti, making her début in 1799 at the Teatro Nuovo, Naples. She sang at La Scala between 1805 and 1824, creating Fiorilla in Rossini's *Il turco in Italia* (1814). Her roles included Donna Anna, Cenerentola and Desdemona in Rossini's *Otello*, which she sang at the Teatro S Benedetto, Venice (1818). She also appeared in Paris, Munich and St Petersburg.

ELIZABETH FORBES

Festa teatrale (It.: 'theatrical celebration'). A title applied to a dramatic work. Although attempts have been made to identify them as members of a single, distinct genre, *feste teatrali* fall into two quite distinct classes: operas and serenatas (*see* SERENATA). When divided into acts, as in Marazzoli's *Gli amori di Giasone e d'Issifile* (1642, Venice) and Cesti's *Il pomo d'oro* (1668, Vienna), they belong to the first category; when they are undivided or consist of two parts, as in works written for the Viennese court to librettos supplied by Metastasio, Pariati, Pasquini and others, they belong to the second. What operas and serenatas so labelled have in common is that they are presented on stage (unlike most serenatas described merely as 'drammatico') and celebrate, often with direct allusions, some important public event such as an imperial birthday or wedding.

The first of Metastasio's nine serenatas titled *festa teatrale* by their author was *La contesa de' numi* (1729, Paris, music by Vinci); all the rest except *La pace fra le tre dee* were written for the Viennese court. The last work in the series was Hasse's *Partenope* (1767). No librettist after Metastasio appears to have revived the term.

MICHAEL TALBOT

Festes de l'été, Les ('The Festivities of Summer'). *Opéra-ballet* in a prologue and three *entrées* ('Les jours d'été', 'Les soirées d'été', 'Les nuits d'été') by MICHEL PIGNOLET DE MONTÉCLAIR to a libretto by SIMON-JOSEPH PELLEGRIN (under the pseudonym of Mlle Barbier); Paris, Opéra, 12 June 1716.

Despite criticism of the first *entrée* in the *Mercure*, the work was received warmly at its première. When it was revived three months later a new *entrée* ('La chasse') replaced the first, which was revised and retitled 'Les matinées d'été' to form the second. Various *entrées* were revised in 1725 and 1748, and the work was staged complete in 1752. The theme of summer serves as a pretext for linking charming *divertissements* on the subject of love and constancy, anticipating the plays of Pierre de Marivaux.

JEAN DURON

Festes grecques et romaines, Les ('Greek and Roman Festivities'). *Ballet-héroïque* in a prologue and three (later four) entrées by FRANÇOIS COLLIN DE BLAMONT to a libretto by LOUIS FUZELIER; Paris, Opéra, 13 July 1723 (4th entrée added, Paris, Opéra, 9 Feb 1734).

The Prologue, with Apollo (bass) advising the muses, Clio (soprano), Erato (soprano) and Terpsichore (dancer), is an allegory explaining the approach used in this new genre of 'ballet-héroïque'; in the entrées Fuzelier replaced mythical heroes with historical ones, as had Corneille and Racine in their plays. Of the entrées, *Les jeux olympiques*, *Les Bacchanales*, *Les Saturnales* and *La feste de Diane*, the most admired was the second, depicting the meeting of Cleopatra (soprano) and Antony (bass); the queen's barge arrives to an impressive *marche en rondeau*, including trumpets, *trio de hautbois* and chorus.

Collin de Blamont's most successful 'opera' followed in the tradition of Lalande's three works in which Louis XV had danced (*L'inconnu*, *Les folies de Cardenio*, *Les élémens*) and was intended to celebrate the majority of the young monarch; in the event, the king declined to participate. Revisions to the work were made in 1733.

LIONEL SAWKINS

Festival. A series of performances, held to be of special quality and given for a brief recurrent period in a place attractive to tourists.

1. Survey. 2. List.

1. SURVEY. Modern music festivals are older than festivals devoted wholly or chiefly to opera: in northern Europe they go back to the choral festivals that started in the early 18th century, if not to feasts held in the 1680s on St Cecilia's Day. The earliest opera festival was that at Bayreuth in 1876, held to launch the first complete performance of Wagner's *Der Ring des Nibelungen*. After the second festival launched *Parsifal* (1882), a work designed for exclusive performance there, Bayreuth became an annual fixture. (In our own day, a shorter *Ring* festival has existed since 1975 at Seattle.)

Bayreuth was the model for festivals centred on the work of a single opera composer. There had long been festivals centred on Handel, Haydn, Beethoven and Bach, but the expensiveness of opera meant that a one-composer festival required either a large subsidy or performances of wide appeal. In practice no other festival has for long matched Bayreuth's single-mindedness. Salzburg (launched in 1877) has varied its operatic fare away from Mozart, as has its offshoot Glyndebourne (1934). So has Aldeburgh (1948) away from Benjamin Britten; modest Glastonbury (1914), though remembered for the vogue opera *The Immortal Hour*, likewise gave other work besides Rutland Boughton's. Spoleto (1958) and Montepulciano (1976) have not served mainly as showcases for Menotti's and Henze's operas. Pesaro has lately been able to concentrate on Rossini because so much of his work was both unknown to modern audiences and, when revived, welcome; but although it has enhanced the composer's place in the repertory, undiluted Rossini may not keep it going for a century or more.

The other main type of opera festival is intended to bring forward new or unusual works, or familiar works in innovatory interpretations, without concentrating on one composer or on opera alone. Examples are the Florence Maggio Musicale (1933), a forerunner of Pesaro in the Rossini revival, Aix-en-Provence (1948), Wexford (1951), the Camden and English Bach Festivals in London, Santa Fe in New Mexico, Purchase in New York State, and Savonlinna in Finland, as well as more modest summer ventures scattered through tourist areas.

Elsewhere the term 'festival' may be applied to summer performances not unlike what might be found in the same theatre at other times, as at Munich, or to productions such as those at the Arena di Verona (now emulated in Britain as they long have been in the USA), on a large scale but not otherwise innovatory.

Since attendance at festivals generally involves travel, board and lodging, as well as prices kept high by the costs of a brief season of special quality, it is as a rule more expensive than going to the opera at home. This put paid to Wagner's early notions of a 'people's festival'. Bayreuth became a place of pilgrimage for a mixture of fashionable people on the one hand, and of intellectuals and artists on the other; Gabriel Fauré's and André Messager's trip in 1884 was subsidized by a private lottery. Nowadays a higher national income per head in some countries, and the development of mass tourism, have rubbed the exclusive shine off some festivals; but although business corporations rather than aristocrats may be the chief patrons, audiences at the most expensive festivals such as Salzburg, drawn from the richest parts of Europe, still visibly show off wealth and power. Evening dress, not compulsory but, as at Glyndebourne, recommended, adds to the general expectancy: after all the trouble they have taken, many in the audience seem determined to enjoy themselves, not necessarily thanks to the opera; some, as at Bayreuth first nights, like to boo. Henze at Montepulciano has tried to innovate by enlisting the local population in a continuous 'workshop', but that may be feasible only in a compact small town. Elsewhere, so many tourists now move about the world that – save where local subscribers fill the house – one audience is increasingly like another, whether at ordinary or at festival performances.

*

Grove6 (P. M. Young); *MGG* ('Feste und Festspiele', R. Schall)
D. G. Stoll: *Music Festivals of Europe* (London, 1938)
G. Gavazzeni: *Le feste musicali* (Milan, 1944)
Opera [annual festival issues, 1952–]
D. G. Stoll: *Music Festivals of the World* (Oxford, 1963)
H. W. Heinsheimer: *Best Regards to Aida* (New York, 1968)
K. Pahlen: *Erster europäischer Festspielführer 1978* (Munich, 1978)
C. P. Rabin: *A Guide to Music Festivals in America* (Stockbridge, 1979)
——: *Music Festivals in Europe and Britain* (Stockbridge, 1980)
D. Smith and N. Barton, eds.: *International Guide to Music Festivals* (New York, 1980)
Music Festivals in Europe: including the United States, Canada and Israel (Vienna, 1980) [pubn of the American Music Council, UNESCO]
B. Levin: *Conducted Tour* (London, 1981)

2. LIST. Below are listed many of the festivals at which opera is, or has been, performed. The list is roughly categorized, as follows: A: major festivals in which opera plays a central (or exclusive) part; B: smaller festivals in which opera plays a significant (again, possibly an exclusive) part; C: festivals in which opera generally has some role but may be in abeyance; D: festivals now defunct in which opera played a role.

These categories should not be interpreted too strictly, since the role of opera within a festival will often change from year to year.

The date of foundation is given in parentheses, followed by the time of year at which the festival takes place and a note of any speciality. Fuller information on major festivals (history, premières, artistic policy etc.) may be found in the individual entry on the city where the festival concerned takes place, or on the festival itself.

A: MAJOR FESTIVALS AT WHICH OPERA IS CENTRAL

Aix-en-Provence, France (1948), July–Aug; emphasis on Mozart
Aspen, CO, USA (1949), June–Aug
Bayreuth, Germany (1876), July–Aug; Wagner
Berlin, Germany (1951 – West; 1957 – East), Sept–Oct
Donaufestwochen: see Vienna
Dresden, Germany (1978), May–June
Drottningholm, Sweden (1953), May–Sept; 18th-century opera
Edinburgh, Great Britain (1947), Aug–Sept
Florence, Italy (1933), May–June; Maggio Musicale
Glyndebourne, Great Britain (1934), May–Aug
Holland, Netherlands (1947), June
Maggio Musicale: see Florence
Munich, Germany (1875; annual from 1901), July
Pesaro, Italy (1980), Aug; Rossini
Rome, Italy (1938), July–Aug; Terme di Caracalla
Salzburg, Austria (1877, annual from 1920), July–Aug
    (1966), Easter Week; Easter Festival
Santa Fe, NM, USA (1957), June–Aug
Savonlinna, Finland (1912; annual since 1967), July
Schwetzingen, Germany (1952), April–June
Terme di Caracalla: see Rome
Verona, Italy (1913), July–Aug; mainly Verdi, Puccini
Vienna, Austria (1951), May–June; Donaufestwochen
Zürich, Switzerland (1909), May–July

B: SMALLER FESTIVALS IN WHICH OPERA PLAYS A SIGNIFICANT PART

Academy Summer Opera Festival: see Vadstena
Adelaide, Australia (1960, biennial), March
Albi, France (1974), July–Aug
Aldeburgh, Great Britain (1948), June
American Music Theater Festival: see Philadelphia
Århus, Denmark (1983), Aug–Sept; Wagner
Athens, Greece (1955), July–Sept
Augsburg, Germany (1929), June–July
Bad Ischl, Austria (1961), July–Aug; operetta
Barga, Italy (1967), July
Batignano, Italy (1975), July–Aug; Musica nel Chiostro
Bergamo, Italy (1931–73, 1980), Sept–Oct; Donizetti
Biennale de la Musique, La: see Lyons
Bordeaux, France (1950), May–June; Mai Musical
Bregenz, Austria (1946), July–Aug
Brighton, Great Britain (1967), May
Brno, Czech Republic (1966), Oct
Budapest (1981), March; Spring Festival
Busseto, Italy (1991); Verdi
Buxton, Great Britain (1979), July–Aug
    (1992), April–May; Questfest; musicals
Caramoor, Katonah, NY, USA (1946), June–Aug
Cardiff, Great Britain (1967), Sept–Oct
Carinthian Summer: see Ossiach–Villach
Carpentras, France (1967; staged opera since 1978), July–Aug
Central City, CO, USA (1932), July–Aug
Charleston, SC, USA (1977), June–July; Spoleto USA/Festival of Two Worlds
Cincinnati, OH, USA (1920), June–July; Summer Opera Festival
Colorado Springs, CO, USA (1970), July–Aug
Cooperstown, NY, USA (1975), June–Sept; Glimmerglass Opera Festival
Due Mondi: see Spoleto, Italy
Eisenstadt, Austria (1957), July–Aug; Seefestspiele Mörbisch; operetta
English Bach Festival: see London
Eutin, Germany (1951), July–Aug
Garsington Manor, Great Britain (1989), June; emphasis on Haydn
Glimmerglass Opera Festival: see Cooperstown
Göttingen, Germany (1920), June; Handel

Guelph, Ont., Canada (1968), May
Halle, Germany (1952), June; Handel
Heidenheim, Germany (1964), June–July
Helsinki, Finland (1951), Aug–Sept
Lake George Opera Festival: see Queensbury
Lawrenceville, NJ, USA (1984), June–July; Opera Festival of New Jersey
London, Great Britain (1963), July and occasional; English Bach Festival: period opera esp. French Baroque
    (1986), May–June; London Opera Festival
Lyons, France (1991, biennial), Sept–Oct; La Biennale de la Musique Française
Macerata, Italy (1921), July–Aug
Mai Musical: see Bordeaux
Martina Franca, Italy (1975), July–Aug; Festival della Valle d'Itria
Monte Carlo, Monaco (1970), April–May; Printemps des Arts
Montepulciano, Italy (1976), July–Aug
Montpellier, France (1985), July–Aug
Musica nel Chiostro: see Batignano
Natchez, MS, USA (1991), May, Dec
New Jersey, Opera Festival of: see Lawrenceville
Orange, France (1869), July–Aug
Ossiach-Villach, Austria (1969), July–Aug; Carinthian Summer
Ottawa, Ont., Canada (1971), July
Oviedo, Spain, April–May
Pacific Northwest Festival: see Seattle
Parma, Italy (1989), Sept–Oct; Verdi
Perth, Australia (1953), Feb–March
Philadelphia, PA, USA (1984), March–June; American Music Theater Festival
Prague, Czech Republic (1945), May–June; Prague Spring
Printemps des Arts: see Monte Carlo
Queensbury, NY, USA (1962), July–Aug; Lake George Opera Festival
Questfest: see Buxton
St Louis, MO, USA (1976), May–June
Santander, Spain (1952), July–Aug
Seattle, WA, USA (1975), July–Aug; Pacific Northwest Festival
Seefestspiele Mörbisch: see Eisenstadt
Spoleto, Italy (1958), June–July; Festival dei Due Mondi
Spoleto, USA: see Charleston
Szeged, Hungary (1931), July–Aug; Szegedi Ünnepi Játékok
Torre del Lago, Italy (1930; annual 1952–60, 1971–92; biennial 1960–70), July–Aug; Puccini
Two Worlds: see Charleston
Vadstena, Sweden (1964), July–Aug; Academy Summer Opera Festival
Vaison-la-Romaine, France (1952), July–Aug
Valle d'Itria: see Martina Franca
Wexford, Ireland (1951), Oct–Nov
Wiesbaden, Germany (1896), May
Wildbad, Germany (1989), July–Aug; Rossini
Wolf Trap Farm Park, Vienna, VA, USA (1971), May–Sept
Ystad, Sweden (1978), July

C: FESTIVALS INCLUDING OPERA

Agliè, Italy (1980), July–Aug; chamber opera
Algoma Fall Festival: see Sault Ste-Marie
Almeida International Festival of Contemporary Music: see London
Amiens, France (1988), Sept–Oct; Picardie: Festival des Cathédrales
Århus, Denmark (1965), Sept
    (1978), April–May; contemporary music
Artpark, Lewiston, NY, USA (1974), June–Sept
Arundel, Great Britain (1977; last staged 1985), Aug–Sept
Ash Lawn-Highland, VA, USA (1978), June–Aug
Augsburg, Germany (1951), spring or autumn; Deutsches Mozart Festival (venue varies)
Automne: see Paris
Avignon, France (1946), July–Aug; music theatre
Baden bei Wien, Austria (1906), June–Sept; operetta
Bad Hersfeld, Germany (1960; first staged opera 1980), June–Aug
Bad Kissingen, Germany (1986), June–July; Kissinger Sommer
Banff, Alberta, Canada (1933; present summer-long format 1980)
Bar Harbor, ME (1967; last staged opera late 1970s), July–Aug
Bath, Great Britain (1948), May–June
Bay View, MI, USA (1886), June–Aug
Bear Valley, CA (1969), July–Aug
Belfast, Great Britain (1963), Nov
Belorussian Musical Autumn: see Minsk
Bergen, Norway (1898; annual since 1953), May–June
Berkeley, CA, USA (1990, biennial), June

Bermuda (1976), Jan–Feb

Bloomington, IN, USA (1974), July–Aug; Indiana University School of Music Summer Festival

Blossom Music Center: *see* Cuyahoga Falls

Bodø, Norway (1980), July–Aug; Nordland Musikkfestuke

Bolzano, Italy (1981), Aug

Boonville, MO, USA (1972), Aug; Missouri River Festival of the Arts

Boston, MA, USA (1980, biennial; last staged opera 1985); Early Music Festival

Bournemouth, Great Britain (1991), June

Brevard, NC, USA (1948), June–Aug

Brive, France (1981), July–Aug; Festival de la Vézère

Brühl, Germany (1958), May–Sept; Baroque and early Classical music

Budapest, Hungary (1965), July–Aug; Summer Open-Air Festival

Bumbershoot: *see* Seattle

Cabrillo, CA, USA (1963; last staged opera 1983), July–Aug

Cambridge, Great Britain (1963), July

Camerino, Italy (1983), Sept–Oct; electronic music, music theatre

Canterbury, Great Britain (1984), Oct

Caramoor: *see* Katonah

Carmel, CA, USA (1935), July–Aug; Bach

Castell de Peralada, Spain (1987), July–Aug

Castle Hill, Ipswich, MA, USA (1972; last staged opera 1987), June–Aug

Catania, Sicily, Italy (1989), Sept–Oct; Bellini

Cervantes, Mexico (1972), Oct; Baroque music

Chaise-Dieu, La: *see* Le-Puy-en-Velay

Chautauqua, NY, USA (1874), June–Aug

Cheltenham, Great Britain (1945), July

Chichester, Great Britain (1975), July

Cluj-Napoca, Romania (1966), Oct

College Park, MD, USA (1981), Oct–Nov; Maryland Handel Festival

Constanţa, Romania (1974)

Corfu, Greece (1981), Sept–Oct

Cuyahoga Falls, OH, USA (1985), May–Sept; Blossom Music Center

Davenport, IA, USA (1988), June; Quad City Mozart Festival (venue varies)

December Nights: *see* Moscow

Decorah, IA, USA (1967), July; Nordic Fest

Des Moines Metro Opera, IA, USA (1973), June–July

Deutsches Mozart Festival: *see* Augsburg

Dubrovnik, Croatia (1950), July–Aug

Elora, Ont., Canada (1980; first staged opera 1992), July–Aug; emphasis on choral music

Eureka Springs, AR, USA (1950), May–June; Inspiration Point Fine Arts Colony Opera Festival

Fanfare Festival: *see* Hammond

Fermo, Italy (1987), June–Sept

Firefly Festival for the Performing Arts: *see* South Bend

Flanders, Belgium (1958), April–Nov

Foligno, Italy (1981), Aug–Sept; Baroque music

Gardone Riviera, Italy (1988), July; emphasis on D'Annunzio

Glasgow, Great Britain (1990, biennial), Aug; Early Music Festival

Gmunden, Austria (1987), Aug–Sept

Gorleston St Andrew's Festival: *see* Great Yarmouth

Granada, Spain (1952), June–July

Grant Park, IL, USA (1934; first staged opera 1992), June–Aug

Graz, Austria (1968), Sept–Oct; Steirischer Herbst; operetta (1985), June–July; Styriarte Graz

Great Yarmouth, Great Britain (1969; last staged opera 1981), Nov; Gorleston St Andrew's Festival

Greenwich: *see* London

Gŵyl Gregynog, Great Britain (1988), June–July

Hammond, LA, USA (1986), Oct; Fanfare Festival

Hanover, Germany (1952), July–Aug; Musik und Theater in Herrenhausen; Baroque and Classical music

Harrogate, Great Britain (1927; annual since 1966), Aug

Hartwood, PA, USA (1980), May–Sept

Heidelberg, Germany (1974), July–Aug; Castle Festival; annually includes Romberg: *The Student Prince*

Herrenhausen: *see* Hanover

Homewood, IL, USA (1987), June–July; Starry Nights Summer Concert Series

Hong Kong (1973), Jan–Feb
(1976), Oct–Nov; Asian Arts Festival; Chinese opera

Huddersfield, Great Britain (1977), Nov; Contemporary Music Festival

Húnadagar ('Dog Days'): *see* Reykjavík

Huntington, NY, USA (1966), June–Aug; SummerScape

Ilmajoki, Finland (1974), June; folk opera

Indiana University School of Music Summer Festival: *see* Bloomington

Innsbruck, Austria (1977), Aug; Early Music Festival

Inspiration Point Fine Arts Colony Opera Festival: *see* Eureka Springs

Iraklion, Crete, Greece (1980), Aug; Moussikos Avgoustos Festival; contemporary music

Istanbul, Turkey (1973), June–July

Ivrea, Festival di: *see* Turin

Jerusalem, Israel (1961), May–June; Israel Festival

Joensuu, Finland (1981), June

Karlsruhe, Germany (1978), Feb–March; Handel

Katonah, NY, USA (1946), June–Aug; Caramoor Festival

Kiev, Ukraine, May–June; Kiev Spring

Kissinger Sommer: *see* Bad Kissingen

Lakeside, OH, USA (1873; last staged opera 1979–80), June–Aug

Lappajärvi, Finland (1985), July–Aug

Las Palmas, Canary Islands, Spain (1967), Feb–April

Le-Puy-en-Velay, France (1966; first staged opera 1991), Aug–Sept; La Chaise-Dieu

Lichfield, Great Britain (1982), July

Lille, France (1971), Oct–Nov

Ljubljana, Slovenia (1953), July–Sept

London, Great Britain (1971), June; Greenwich Festival
(1977), June; Spitalfields Festival
(1981–90), June–July; Almeida International Festival of Contemporary Music (now Almeida Opera)

Long Island, NY, USA (1983), early Sept; International Jewish Arts Festival

Los Angeles, CA, USA (1984, triennial), Aug–Sept

Lucca, Italy (1978), July–Aug; Festival Internazionale di Marlia

Ludlow, Great Britain (1959), June–July

Ludwigsburg, Germany (1951), May–Oct

McAllen, TX, USA (1960), Feb; Rio Grande Valley International Music Festival

Madrid, Spain (1985), Sept; Contemporary Music Festival
(1988), April–June; Mozart

Magdeburg, Germany (1962; biennial or triennial), March; Telemann

Malmö, Sweden (1984, triennial), Aug; Baroque music

Malta (1981), June–July

Malvern, Great Britain (1929), May; emphasis on G. B. Shaw and Elgar

Mannheim, Germany (1963, biennial), June

Marlia, Festival Internazionale di: *see* Lucca

Marseilles, France, July–Aug

Maryland Handel Festival: *see* College Park

Matsumoto, Japan (1992), Sept; Saito Kinen Festival

Messina, Sicily, Italy (1973), July–Aug

Miami, FL, USA (1983), Sept–Oct

Midland, MI, USA (1978; last staged opera 1978; last staged operetta 1987), May–June

Minsk, Belarus', Nov; Belorussian Musical Autumn

Missouri River Festival of the Arts: *see* Boonville

Montmartre: *see* Paris

Montignac, France (1983), July–Aug; Périgord Noir; Italian Baroque and Schubert

Moscow, Russia (1981), Dec; December Nights
May; Moscow Stars Art Festival
Dec–Jan; Russian Winter

Mostly Mozart: *see* New York

Moussikos Avgoustos Festival: *see* Iraklion

Musik und Theater in Herrenhausen: *see* Hanover

Naples, Italy, May; Settimane Musicali

Nesbyen, Norway (1989), June

New Brunswick, NJ, USA (1987), June–July; Rutgers SummerFest

Newport, RI, USA (1969), July–Aug

New York, NY, USA (1988, biennial; last staged opera 1988), June; International Festival of the Arts
(1966; last staged opera 1982), July–Aug; Mostly Mozart

Nîmes, France, July

Nordic Fest: *see* Decorah

Nordland Musikkfestuke: *see* Bodø

Norfolk and Norwich, Great Britain (1824), Oct

Nottingham, Great Britain (1971), May–June

Osaka, Japan (1958), April

Oslo, Norway (1983), June; Early Music Festival from 1990
Paris, France (1954; known as the Théâtre des Nations 1957–63), May–June; Festival de Paris
   July–Sept; Festival Estival de Paris
   June–July; Festival de Montmartre
   Sept–Dec; Festival d'Automne
Périgord Noir: *see* Montignac
Perth, Great Britain (1972), May
Perugia, Italy (1937), Sept
Petrus de Dacia Festival: *see* Visby
Picardie: Festival des Cathédrales: *see* Amiens
Plzeň, Czech Republic, Feb
Pompeii, Italy (1986), Aug–Sept
Quad City Mozart Festival: *see* Davenport
Ravenna, Italy (1986), July–Aug
Redlands Bowl, CA, USA (1924), July–Aug
Reykjavík, Iceland (1970, biennial), June
        (biennial), June; Húndadagar ('Dog Days')
Rio Grande Valley International Music Festival: *see* McAllen
Riva del Garda, Italy (1984), July
Round Top, TX, USA (1971; first staged opera planned 1995–6), May–July
Russian Winter: *see* Moscow
Rutgers SummerFest: *see* New Brunswick
Sabbioneta, Italy (1969), July–Sept; music theatre
Saint-Céré, France (1960), July–Aug
Saint-Denis, France (1969), June–July
St Magnus, Kirkwall, Orkney, Great Britain (1977), June
Saito Kinen Festival: *see* Matsumoto
Sakshaug, Norway (1990), June–July; Norwegian music
Salisbury, Great Britain (1973), Sept
San Antonio, TX, USA (1983), June
        (1990, biennial), April–May; Early Music Festival; emphasis on Spanish Colonial style
San Sebastián, Spain (1939), Aug
Santa Barbara, CA, USA (1947), June–Aug; Music Academy of the West Summer Festival
Saratoga Springs, NY, USA (1966; first staged opera 1986), June
Sault Ste-Marie, Ont., Canada (1972), Sept–Oct; Algoma Fall Festival
Savignone, Italy (1976), July–Aug
Seattle, WA, USA (1971), Sept; Bumbershoot
Seoul, Korea (1976; last staged opera 1986), Sept
Settimane Musicali: *see* Naples
Siena, Italy (1939), Aug
Skopje, Macedonia (1972), May
Sofia, Bulgaria, May–June
South Bend, IN, USA (1981), June–Aug; Firefly Festival for the Performing Arts; operetta
Spitalfields Festival: *see* London
Split, Croatia (1954), July–Aug
Starry Nights Summer Concert Series: *see* Homewood
Steirischer Herbst: *see* Graz
Stern Grove, CA, USA (1938), June–Aug
Strasbourg, France (1932), June–July
Styriarte Graz: *see* Graz
Sully, France (1973), June–July
SummerScape: *see* Huntington
Swansea, Great Britain (1948), Sept–Nov
Taormina, Sicily, Italy, July–Sept
Tecklenburg, Germany (1924), May–Sept; operettas, musicals
Tenerife, Canary Islands, Spain (1971), Oct–Nov
Tonsberg, Norway (1991), June–July
Trento, Italy (1986), Oct–Nov; music theatre
Trieste, Italy (1950), June–Aug; operetta
Trondheim, Norway (1981), spring
Turin, Italy (1981), Oct–Dec; Festival di Ivrea
Turku, Finland (1960; last staged opera 1983), Aug
Vale of Glamorgan, Great Britain (1968), Aug; music theatre
Varna, Bulgaria (1926), June–July
Versailles (1992), Sept–Oct; Baroque music
Vichy, France, July–Aug
Visby, Sweden (1929), July–Aug; Petrus de Dacia Festival
Warfield, AR, USA (1986), April–May
Warwick, Great Britain (1980), July
Waterford, Ireland (1959), Sept–Oct; International Festival of Light Opera
Warsaw, Poland (1956), Sept
Weissenburg in Bayern, Germany (1929), July–Aug
Wooster, OH, USA (1979), June–Aug; Light Opera Festival

Würzburg, Germany (1985), Sept
Zagreb, Croatia (1961, biennial), April–May

D: FESTIVALS NOW DEFUNCT OR OPERATICALLY INACTIVE

Camden Festival: *see* London
Cincinnati, OH, USA (1881–4), Feb
Copenhagen, Denmark (1963–90), May; Kongelige Teater: Dance and Opera Festival
Glassboro, NJ, USA (1983–90), July; Hollybush Festival
Glastonbury, Great Britain (1914–26); Rutland Boughton
Hollybush Festival: *see* Glassboro
London, Great Britain (1954), Feb–March; Camden Festival
Lyons, France (1979–89); Berlioz
Montreal, Canada (1939–65), summer
Nantes, France (–1990), June–Aug; Festival Atlantique
Naples, Italy (1948–72)
Paris, France, June–July; Festival du Marais
Purchase, NY, USA (1980–89), July–Aug; PepsiCo Summerfare
Versailles, France (–1990), May–June; 18th-century
        JOHN ROSSELLI (1), SARAH ROBERTS, HILARY FINCH (2)

Festival of Two Worlds. Music festival, founded as the Festival dei Due Mondi by GIAN CARLO MENOTTI in 1958 in SPOLETO. It revolves round opera, and it established its second base in 1977 in CHARLESTON.

Fêtes de l'Amour et de Bacchus, Les ('The Festivities of Cupid and Bacchus'). *Pastorale* in a prologue and three acts by Jean-Baptiste Lully (*see* LULLY family, (1)) to a libretto by PHILIPPE QUINAULT, Isaac de Benserade and the Président de Périgny; Paris, Jeu de Paume de Béquet, *c*10 November 1672.

This was Lully's first opera and was hastily thrown together just after he took charge of the Opéra; it is mainly a pastiche of excerpts from his and Molière's *comédies-ballets La pastorale comique* (1667), *George Dandin* (1668), *Les amants magnifiques* (1670) and *Le bourgeois gentilhomme* (1670). Though it lacks the heroic plot elements found in Lully's *tragédies*, its pastoral plot elements and the nature of its music, dance and spectacle prefigure the features of the *tragédie en musique*. It preceded Lully's first *tragédie* by only five months.
        LOIS ROSOW

Fêtes de l'Hymen et de l'Amour, Les [*Les fêtes de l'Hymen et de l'Amour, ou Les dieux d'Egypte* ('The Festivities of Hymen and Cupid, or The Egyptian Gods')]. *Opéra-ballet* in a prologue and three entrées by JEAN-PHILIPPE RAMEAU to a libretto by LOUIS DE CAHUSAC; Versailles, La Grande Ecurie, 15 March 1747.

Intended to appear as *Les dieux d'Egypte*, this work was adapted for the celebrations surrounding the dauphin's second marriage, to Maria Josepha of Saxony. Its theme was fortuitously appropriate: each of the three entrées, 'Osiris', 'Canope' and 'Aruéris, ou Les Isies', culminates in the marriage of one of the Egyptian gods. In the first, Osiris (*haute-contre*) pacifies a tribe of Amazons and successfully woos the warlike queen Orthésie [Orthesia] (soprano). The second entrée concerns the love of the water god Canope [Canopus] (bass) and Memphis (soprano), a young virgin who is about to be sacrificed to him; at the height of the ceremony, Canopus causes the Nile to overflow and appears on a chariot drawn by crocodiles. He reveals that he is Nilée, the young mortal whom Memphis loves, and thereupon claims her as his bride. The final entrée involves Aruéris [Horus] (*haute-contre*), god of the Arts, who presides over 'les Isies', a competitive festival in honour of his mother Isis. Though diffident of her abilities, Aruéris's beloved Orie (soprano) enters and wins the vocal competition, for which the prize is union with the object of her love – Aruéris himself.

By March 1766 *Les fêtes de l'Hymen* had been performed 106 times at the Opéra or at court; 'Osiris' and 'Aruéris' remained in the repertory until 1772 and 1776 respectively. Nowadays it is unjustly neglected. The plots of the three colourful entrées are simple but dramatically convincing; moreover, the music is consistently inventive and sometimes outstanding, as in the sacrificial scene in 'Canope', with its ten-part chorus as the Nile overflows. Equally fine are the pastoral music in 'Osiris' and the competition songs and dances in 'Aruéris'. In this work Cahusac prided himself on giving a new importance to the supernatural and to the use of spectacular stage machines; those for the overflowing Nile were long admired. The work contains no fewer than seven *ballets figurés*, a symptom of the librettist's growing desire to integrate dance and action.

GRAHAM SADLER

Fêtes de Polymnie, Les ('Polyhymnia's Festivities'). *Opéra-ballet* in a prologue and three entrées by JEAN-PHILIPPE RAMEAU to a libretto by LOUIS DE CAHUSAC; Paris, Opéra, 12 October 1745.

Like Rameau's *Le temple de la Gloire*, this work, the first of at least seven collaborations between Rameau and Cahusac, was commissioned to celebrate the battle of Fontenoy. Despite a first run of 29 performances, the complete work was revived only once, and less successfully, in 1753, though the final entrée was restaged in 1765.

The prologue, 'Le temple de Mémoire', represents a rare return to the panegyric of Lully's prologues. As a tribute to the French victory, the Arts erect a statue of Louis XV, while the Muses extol his glory. Polyhymnia (soprano), muse of lyric poetry, introduces the work's theme: her 'fêtes' (the ensuing entrées) will entertain the victors. 'La fable', based on Greek myth, involves the courtship of Alcide [Alcides] (*haute-contre*) and Hébé [Hebe] (soprano). 'L'histoire' recounts the true story of how the Syrian king Séleucus [Seleucus] (bass) and his son Antiochus (*haute-contre*) discover they both love Stratonice (soprano); the king, finding that Stratonice prefers his son, generously renounces his love. 'La féerie', the first of Rameau's excursions into the world of Middle-Eastern fairy-tale, concerns the love of Argélie (soprano) for Zimès (*haute-contre*), son of her guardian fairy Oriade (soprano). But Zimès has been turned by the wicked fairy Alcine (soprano) into a bloodthirsty brute and can be released from this state only when he feels true love.

Although the opera was criticized for including too many choruses, these contain much of the best music. In particular, the Hymne au Destin (Cahusac was to incorporate hymns in all subsequent librettos) shares with other ensembles in the prologue an elevated, spiritual quality. The work contains a quantity of agreeable *airs* and dances, the latter effectively employed in what was to be another Cahusac hallmark, the *ballet figuré*. At times, however, the music is routine or even clumsy – the result, perhaps, of having to complete four commissioned operas in one year. The most remarkable movement is the overture, the first of Rameau's to break definitively with the Lullian model. The piled-up dissonances of the first section, which recurs when the statue is erected, have the character of a magnificent organ improvisation (Balbastre later arranged it for

organ), while the second would not seem out of place in a contemporary German symphony.   GRAHAM SADLER

Fêtes de Thalie, Les [*Les fêtes, ou Le triomphe de Thalie* ('Festivities, or The Triumph of Thalia')]. *Opéra-ballet* in a prologue and three entrées ('La fille', 'La veuve', 'La femme') by JEAN-JOSEPH MOURET to a libretto by JOSEPH DE LA FONT; Paris, Opéra, 19 August 1714.

The humiliating defeat in the prologue of Melpomène [Melpomene] (soprano), muse of tragedy, by Thalia (soprano), muse of comedy, produced a *succès de scandale* that obliged La Font and Mouret to add a new entrée, 'La critique des fêtes de Thalie' (9 October 1714), emphasizing music and dance rather than comedy and tragedy. In 1715 they substituted 'La veuve coquette' for 'La veuve' and in 1722 added a new entrée, 'La provençale'. With the second edition of the score (1720), the opera's name was changed to *Les fêtes de Thalie*. As in many early *opéras-ballets*, each entrée uses a different comic intrigue involving flesh-and-blood characters in recognizable contemporary settings and costumes. The prologue is set on stage at the Paris Opéra, and 'La fille' in Marseilles. La Font wrote, 'I believe this to be the first Opera where the women are dressed *à la françoise*' (*Avertissement*). Mouret heightened the realism in 'La provençale' by specifying local costumes, local musical instruments and popular meridional tunes sung in Provençal dialect.

In 'La fille' Acaste (bass) brings Cléon (bass) back to Marseilles from ten years' captivity in Algeria. Cléon's wife Bélise (tenor) and daughter Léonore (soprano) have had no news of him. Acaste, in love with Léonore but unaware of her true identity, returns first. Bélise urges Léonore to marry him but she resists and suggests he look elsewhere. Bélise then offers herself. Hoping jealousy will waken love in Léonore, Acaste feigns agreement. Cléon arrives and accuses Bélise of faithlessness. Léonore's jealousy is aroused, she declares her love for Acaste and the entrée ends in the lovers' marriage and the release of Algerian prisoners.

In 'La veuve' Léandre (tenor) ardently woos Isabelle (soprano), a young widow. (The rich financier, Christogon (bass), was added as a second suitor in 'La veuve coquette'.) Léandre arranges a wedding *divertissement* to amuse his beloved, but in spite of encouragement from her confidante Iphise (soprano), and of her seemingly tender feelings for Léandre, Isabelle rejects him: her bereavement is too recent.

The plot of 'La femme' resembles a *Così fan tutte* with the sexual roles reversed. At a masked ball Dorante (bass) becomes infatuated with a charming masked woman, his disguised wife Caliste (soprano). In the hope of seeing her again, he arranges another ball. His valet Zerbin (tenor) tries vainly to dissuade him. Caliste and her confidante, Zerbin's wife Dorine (soprano), arrive masked. Dorante and Zerbin press their attentions, masks are removed and husbands forgiven, for, in the words of Dorante to his wife, 'You are your own rival and need fear no other'.

Les fêtes de Thalie enjoyed four revivals at the Paris Opéra, 1722–54, and single entrées (especially 'La provençale') were performed as *fragments* into the late 1770s. The vocal and instrumental music derives largely from Provençal dances of Mouret's heritage. The vocal *airs* and *ariettes* have melodic elegance and occasionally include instrumental obbligatos. Dances such as those accompanying Melpomène's and Thalia's entrances in the prologue show Mouret's finely developed sense of appropriate musical gesture.   JAMES R. ANTHONY

Fêtes d'Hébé, Les [*Les fêtes d'Hébé, ou Les talents lyriques* ('Hebe's Festivities, or The Lyric Talents')]. *Opéra-ballet* in a prologue and three entrées by JEAN-PHILIPPE RAMEAU to a libretto by Antoine Gautier de Montdorge (with additions by Pierre-Joseph Bernard, Simon-Joseph Pellegrin, Alexandre Le Riche de La Pouplinière and possibly others); Paris, Opéra, 21 May 1739.

Unlike most of Rameau operas, which took time to find favour with the public, *Les fêtes d'Hébé* was an instant and lasting success. After a first run of 71 performances, it was revived in 1747–8, 1756–7 and 1764–5, while individual entrées remained in the Opéra's repertory until 1777. After the believable modern characters of Rameau's first *opéra-ballet*, *Les Indes galantes*, the return to stock classical Greek material in *Les fêtes d'Hébé* may seem retrogressive. In fact, the latter was more in line with current trends, since the vogue for *opéras-ballets* on mythological or legendary subjects had established itself in 1723, with Collin de Blamont's *Les fêtes grecques et romaines*. The theme of the present work is hinted at in the subtitle (in Rameau's day the work was generally known as *Les talens lyriques*) and quickly established in the prologue: the gods' cupbearer Hebe (soprano), tiring of Olympus, persuades her attendants to fly with her to the banks of the Seine, there to celebrate those gifts most cherished on the operatic stage – poetry, music and dance. These 'lyric talents' provide the subject matter of the ensuing entrées.

1RE ENTRÉE ('La poésie')   On the island of Lesbos, the poet Alcée [Alcaeus] (bass) and poetess Sappho (soprano) are in love. As a consequence of the jealous scheming of Thélème [Thelemus] (*haute-contre*), Alcaeus has been banished by Hymas, King of Lesbos (bass). But Hymas is greatly touched by an allegorical entertainment mounted in his honour by Sappho, during which she reveals Thelemus's treachery. The king rescinds the order and the lovers are reunited.

2E ENTRÉE ('La musique')   The Spartan princess Iphise (soprano) is betrothed to Tyrtée [Tyrtaeus] (bass), whose singing produces legendary ethical effects. An oracle reveals that she must marry the warrior who vanquishes the Messenian army, which is already threatening the city. To win Iphise, Tyrtaeus uses the power of his vocal art, inspiring the Spartans to defeat their attackers.

3E ENTRÉE ('La danse')   The shepherdess Eglé (soprano and dancer), the favourite of Terpsichore, muse of dancing, must choose a husband. Her choice falls on an unknown stranger, who later reveals himself as the god Mercure [Mercury] (*haute-contre*). At his request, Terpsichore (dancer) receives Eglé into her court as Nymph of the Dance.

*   *   *

At its first appearance Montdorge's libretto was universally criticized. The second entrée in particular had to be radically revised, with help from the Abbé Pellegrin. The character of Lycurgus (anachronistic by some two centuries) was eliminated, while Tyrtaeus's exhortations of his soldiers and the women's vigil during the battle were reworked. The revision, which involved much new

music, was extensive enough for the result to be described in one libretto as a 'nouvelle entrée'.

While it certainly lacks literary distinction, this libretto served Rameau tolerably well. In each entrée the action is necessarily compressed, yet the chosen situations provide just enough dramatic momentum to maintain interest as far as the all-important *divertissement*. If the first two entrées betray the librettist's inexperience in dramatic pacing, the second was soon to benefit from Pellegrin's surer hand. By now Rameau was at the height of his powers. In many places, indeed, he responded with music far more powerful and dramatic than might have been expected. This is so of 'La poésie', for example, where Sappho's water-pastoral entertainment includes an exhilarating mariners' chorus, 'Ciel, O ciel! le fleuve agite son onde', notable for an agitated accompaniment restricted entirely to rapid unison scales. Similarly, in 'La musique' Tyrtaeus's exhortatory air 'Mortels, pour être heureux' and Iphise's brilliant 'Eclatante trompette' set the tone for a succession of admirably vigorous choruses.

Throughout the work, the ballet music is of an especially high order. This is nowhere more so – or more appropriate – than in 'La danse', an entrée drenched in the wonderfully rich, languorous and often deeply nostalgic pastoral music that is one of the composer's hallmarks. The 'Loure grave' and two sumptuously scored musettes (the second borrowed from the *Pièces de clavecin* of 1724 along with the dionysiac tambourin and 'L'entretien des muses') must surely be among the century's finest ballet music, yet they are only marginally more distinguished than many other dances. The dancing is often convincingly integrated into the plot. The second entrée, for instance, includes an oracular pronouncement in which the divine prediction is acted out in the course of a remarkable six-movement *ballet figuré*. The final entrée includes Rameau's only borrowing from one of his cantatas: the *ariette* 'L'objet qui règne dans mon âme' reworks the last movement of *Le berger fidèle* (1728). The first complete modern revival of *Les fêtes d'Hébé* was at Monte Carlo on 24 January 1914.   GRAHAM SADLER

Fêtes vénitiennes, Les ('Venetian Festivities'). *Opéra-ballet* in a prologue and five (originally three) entrées by ANDRÉ CAMPRA to a libretto by ANTOINE DANCHET; Paris, Opéra, 17 June 1710.

The flexible format of the *opéra-ballet* (an independent intrigue and different characters for each act) allowed for a trial-and-error approach, and between June and October 1710 Campra and Danchet created in all two prologues and seven entrées. Ballard's printed editions are based on the material of the 51st performance, on 10 October 1710, and it is this version that is described here.

1RE ENTRÉE ('Les devins de la place St-Marc')   After the prologue ('Le carnaval dans Venise'), Zélie (soprano), disguised as a gypsy, tests the faithfulness of her lover Léandre (bass), a fickle French cavalier. Telling his fortune, Zélie says there are two who love him and he will find them both in Venice that very day. Léandre looks vainly for the second love. He finally accuses Zélie of deceit. Singing 'I know your thoughts; you can guess mine', she removes her mask.

2E ENTRÉE ('L'amour saltimbanque')   A young French cavalier, Eraste (*haute-contre*), confesses to Filindo (bass), the leader of a circus troupe, that Léonore

175

(soprano) does not respond to his attentions. Filindo allows that her tender years have not prepared her for gestures of love. Léonore's nurse, Nérine (*haute-contre*), tries to poison Léonore's mind against all lovers, but especially against Léandre. Amour (*haute-contre*), himself disguised as a 'barker', extols the pleasures of his wares and observes that faithfulness among lovers is out of fashion. Eraste denies this, and Léonore, over Nérine's protests, consents to marry him.

3E ENTRÉE ('L'opéra, ou Le maître à chanter') Damire (bass), a Neapolitan soldier, is dressed as Boreas for the forthcoming performance of the opera *Le ballet de Flore*, in which his lover, Léontine (soprano), will sing the principal role of Flora. He tells his friend Adolphe (*haute-contre*) that the plan is to abduct Léontine from the stage during a storm *divertissement*. Léontine, dressed as Flora, confesses to her friend Lucile (soprano), dressed as a shepherdess, that she wishes to please her recent admirer, Damire. Léontine's singing teacher (*haute-contre*) cuts short her lesson to tell her that a rash young man, Rodolphe (bass), who has been seen seated near the front of the stage, had previously confided that he loves her. The opera within the opera begins. Under cover of darkness in the *divertissement*, Boreas and his comrades, dressed as the north wind, abduct a willing Léontine.

4E ENTRÉE ('Le bal, ou le maître à danser') Alamir (bass), a Polish prince, has not revealed his identity to his lover, Iphise (soprano). He wants to test her constancy first. He instructs his courtier, Thémir (*haute-contre*), to change clothes with him and to tempt Iphise with riches. Thémir hires a master of music and a master of dance (both *hautes-contres*) to help him prepare a *fête*. Each master demonstrates his skill, Thémir acknowledges each as master of his art. Unmoved by Thémir's offer of wealth, Iphise is offended when Alamir urges her to accept the 'prince' as lover. During the *fête* Alamir, convinced of Iphise's love for him, reveals his true identity. All participate in a lively paean to love.

5E ENTRÉE ('Les sérénades et les joueurs') This entrée takes place at night in a deserted square in front of the Ridotto, a gambling casino. Isabelle (soprano) has decided to spy on her lover, who has deserted her. Lucile (soprano) enters, complaining about a fickle lover. Both women realize that the same man, Léandre (bass), is responsible for their plight. They plot revenge. Léandre exhorts a troupe of musicians to play a serenade to charm Irène (soprano), who appears on the balcony. Ignoring Léandre, she sings 'La farfalla', an Italian aria composed by Campra, which compares the love of Léandre to the flight of a butterfly. Lucile and Isabelle admonish Léandre severely. He retires to the Ridotto to try his luck at gambling.

*   *   *

Les fêtes vénitiennes illustrates the innovative nature of the first period of *opéra-ballet* (1697–1723). As well as recognizable Venetian place names, realistic characters and comic intrigue, it contains a play within a play which, unlike the Italian opera in Campra's LE CARNAVAL DE VENISE (1699), is central to the drama. *Les fêtes vénitiennes* also includes topical references, musical recall for dramatic ends and quotations from well-known operas. Every opera buff would have recognized the tempest from Marais' *Alcyone*, the *sommeil* from Destouches' *Issé* and the 'Entrée des

songes agréables' and 'Entrée des songes funestes' from Lully's *Atys*. *Les fêtes vénitiennes* enjoyed an important place in the repertory of the Opéra during the first half of the 18th century. Its music, lively yet elegant, is ideally suited to its subject matter.   JAMES R. ANTHONY

Fétis, François-Joseph (*b* Mons, nr Liège, 25 March 1784; *d* Brussels, 26 March 1871). Belgian writer and composer. He came from a family of musicians and instrument makers and was probably taught by his father. As a child he played the organ, piano and violin and at the age of nine wrote a violin concerto. He became well acquainted with the music of Mozart and Haydn before leaving for Paris in 1800 to continue his studies at the Conservatoire; there his teachers included Boieldieu, Pradher and J.-B. Rey.

After a period away from Paris, he returned in 1818 and embarked on a career as a composer, teacher and critic. For commercial reasons he wrote several comic operas, of which only *La vieille* (1826) had much success, as well as piano pieces in a popular style. He taught at the Conservatoire from 1821 and was librarian, 1826–30. He contributed articles to daily newspapers (*Le temps*, *Le national*) and in 1827 founded the *Revue musicale*, a weekly journal covering many aspects of music, which he wrote and edited nearly single-handed for six years. In 1833 he became the first director of the Brussels conservatory. He dominated musical life in Belgium, directing concerts and acting as *maître de chapelle* for Léopold I. His most important historical works appeared during the following years, in particular his *Biographie universelle des musiciens*; he continued to contribute to the *Revue et gazette musicale*, the journal which resulted from a merger of the *Gazette musicale de Paris* with his *Revue musicale* in 1835.

With his encyclopedic intellect, Fétis hoped to gather all that was known about the musical past and to supplement it with the fruits of new research. His most important work by far is his *Biographie universelle des musiciens et bibliographie générale de la musique* (Brussels, 1835–44, 2/1860–65; suppl. ed. A. Pougin, 1878–80), an analytical work which for its period contains an amazing amount of information, particularly on contemporaries, though it is plagued by careless errors and has to be used with caution. Fétis is also important for his fundamental view of the structure of music history, explained in the 'Résumé philosophique de l'histoire' that serves as preface to the first edition of the *Biographie universelle*, in which he attempted to show the sequence of musical events as the development of a musical language. His writings also include a *Méthode des méthodes de chant* (Paris, 1869); for this he made an inventory of didactic works in Italian, German and French from which he extracted material for the training of singers.

Fétis's compositions are competent but hardly known today. His comic operas, performed in Paris, were written in the tradition of Grétry but with more concern for elaborate ensembles; the *drame lyrique Marie Stuart* was a failure. Nevertheless, Meyerbeer at the end of his life entrusted Fétis to make final revisions of *L'Africaine* and to supervise its first performance. He wrote incidental music for part of Alexandre Soumet's *Saül*. Huys mentions sketches for an untitled *opéra comique*. The style of work is reactionary, with traces of influence from Haydn and Beethoven, but the compositional

Design attributed to Giacomo Azzolini (school of Galli-Bibiena), probably for Act 1 scene ii (delightful palace of Thetis) of Jommelli's 'Fetonte' in the production at the Teatro Ajuda, Lisbon, June 1769

technique is striking and the inventiveness more lively than might have been expected from this narrow-minded teacher.

performed in Paris; all printed works published in Paris unless otherwise stated

L'école de la jeunesse, 1807 (oc, L. Anseaume), unperf.

L'amant et le mari (oc, 2, C. Etienne and J. F. Roger), OC (Feydeau), 8 June 1820 (1820)

Les soeurs jumelles (oc, 1, F. A. E. de Planard), OC (Feydeau), 5 July 1823, excerpts (1823)

Marie Stuart en Ecosse (drame lyrique, 3, Planard), OC (Feydeau), 30 Aug 1823, *B-Br*

Phidias (2), 1824, unperf., *Br*

Le bourgeois de Reims (oc, 1, J.-H. Vernoy de Saint-Georges and C. Ménissier), OC (Feydeau), 7 June 1825, *Br*

La vieille (oc, 1, A. E. Scribe and G. Delavigne), OC (Feydeau), 14 March 1826 (1826)

Le mannequin de Bergame (opéra bouffe, 1, Planard and E. Duport), OC (Ventadour), 1 March 1832, excerpts (1832)

*

C. Gollmick: *Herr Fétis, Vorstand des Brüsseler Conservatoriums als Mensch, Kritiker, Theoretiker und Componist* (Leipzig and Brussels, 1852)

H. Berlioz: *Mémoires ... 1803–1865* (Paris, 1870, 3/1930–31; Eng. trans., 1969)

R. Wangermée: *François-Joseph Fétis, musicologue et compositeur* (Brussels, 1951)

B. Huys and others: *François-Joseph Fétis et la vie musicale de son temps: 1784–1871* (Brussels, 1972)   ROBERT WANGERMÉE

Fetonte ('Phaethon'). *Opera seria* in three acts by NICCOLÒ JOMMELLI to a libretto by MATTIA VERAZI after OVID's *Metamorphoses*; Ludwigsburg, Schlosstheater, 11 February 1768.

Verazi imbued Ovid's brief account of Phaethon with political and amorous intrigue typical of Italian *opera seria*. Phaethon (soprano castrato), mortal son of Apollo, is in love with his half-sister, Libia [Libya] (soprano). Epafo [Epaphus] (alto castrato), King of Egypt, also claims her hand. Orcane (tenor), King of the Congo, advances his suit with Phaethon's mother, Climene [Clymene] (soprano). In order to win Libia's

hand, Phaethon gains permission to drive the chariot of the sun. But when he loses control of the immortal horses and is in danger of igniting heaven and earth, Zeus strikes him with a thunderbolt, and he falls into the sea. To escape her pursuers, Clymene leaps to her death into the sea. Two other sopranos, Teti/Fortuna [Thetis/Fortune] and Sole/Proteo [Sun/Proteus], participate in the spectacle scenes.

Jommelli's last opera for the Duke of Württemberg, *Fetonte* was written for the newly constructed theatre at Ludwigsburg, specifically designed to accommodate spectacle. Jommelli admitted that the opera was intended chiefly to amaze the audience. Spectacle invades even the sinfonia. The first Allegro serves as an *introduzione* to a scene for Clymene and a priestly chorus of tenors and basses. In the Larghetto they sing and dance an invocation to Thetis, Clymene's mother. The final Allegro di molto accompanies a sudden change of scene: an earthquake destroys the sacred cavern, revealing the beautiful underwater palace of Thetis, where Clymene views a dance of marine deities.

Verazi borrowed several spectacular scenes directly from Quinault's libretto (set by Lully in 1683): from Act 1 scenes iii–v, a marine ballet with chorus, dance and pantomime; from Act 3 scene i, a ballet set in the realm of the Sun; and from Act 3 scenes vi–vii, Phaethon's fatal ride. In Act 1 scene iii, Proteus appears in a conch-shell carriage drawn by sea-horses. At the conclusion of Act 1, the Moors and Egyptians stage a battle followed by a scene of rejoicing; according to archival records, 341 soldiers and 86 horses were involved. Act 3 begins with the French-inspired ballet, featuring in turn the Hours, the Minutes, the Four Seasons, the Years, the Centuries, Justice, Happiness, Dawn, Astraea, Lucifer, Time and Zeus. Although Jommelli provided music for the choruses, the ballet music (now lost) was probably written by another court composer.

Jommelli displayed his skill for musical imagery in the

programmatic sinfonia and in the spectacular finale. Simple recitative has all but disappeared, and traditional formal procedures as well as conventional harmonic usage are abandoned in order to intensify the dramatic effect, as in Libya's aria 'Spargerò d'arame lagrime' (1.vii). Ensembles are treated with a freedom unknown even in *opera buffa*, and the finale moves among the textural options of obbligato recitative, chorus and ensemble with a versatility unequalled before Mozart's late operas. Composed for one of the finest opera establishments in Europe, the virtuoso vocal roles demand a wide range and great flexibility. Jommelli wrote thick, rhythmically complex accompaniments, with independent parts for wind instruments, viola and cello. His musical language has rich, chromatic harmonies and strong dynamic contrasts.

Fetonte represents an early attempt to challenge the dominance of the exit aria in *opera seria*. The number of independent exit arias assigned to the five principals has dropped to a total of seven, most of which are in Act 1. Act 2 has an extraordinary number of ensembles: a duet for Orcane and Clymene (scene ii) and two ensembles with diminishing numbers of personnel. The first of these begins with an aria for Clymene, who exits leaving Epaphus, Orcane, Libya and Phaethon to comment in a quartet. Libya and Phaethon sing a duet and then exit, leaving Epaphus and Orcane to finish the ensemble. In the second, Clymene sings an aria, but, before she exits, Libya and Phaethon join her in a trio; finally, Phaethon departs, and the two women finish the ensemble. Act 3 also has a duet, and the obbligato recitative becomes animated and programmatic as Epaphus, Clymene and a chorus react to Phaethon's fatal ride. As Phaethon plunges into the sea, a multi-sectional, action-ensemble finale begins – the first ever appended to an *opera seria*.

The infusion of spectacle into *opera seria* might be viewed as a last gasp of the Baroque, but at the same time the opera contains several radical departures from Italian dramaturgical conventions: programmatic sinfonia, arias without exits, action ensembles, ballets and choruses incorporated into the drama, a multi-sectional, action-ensemble finale and a tragic ending. The many ensembles and choruses and the flexibility of formal structures foreshadow Venetian works of the 1780s and 90s. The opera had a modern revival at La Scala, Milan, in 1988.　　　　MARITA P. McCLYMONDS

Feudatorio, Il [*Il feudatorio burlato*]. Opera by Giuseppe Sarti; *see* GELOSIE VILLANE, LE.

Feuersbrunst, Die [*Die Feuersbrunst, oder Das abgebrannte Haus* ('The Conflagration, or The House that Burnt Down')]. Singspiel in two acts, probably by JOSEPH HAYDN; Eszterháza, Marionette Theatre, possibly between 1776 and 1778.

The title 'Opera comique Vom abgebrannten Haus' is familiar from Haydn's Entwurf-Katalog, though until the 1950s the work was thought to be lost. Noticing an incident involving the burning-down of a house in the Act 1 finale of an anonymous Singspiel, *Die Feuersbrunst*, preserved in a manuscript copy (*US-NH*), H. C. Robbins Landon made the connection with the work listed in Haydn's catalogue; with Elsa Radant, he reconstructed the spoken dialogue on the basis of the cues in the score, and edited it for publication (London, 1963). The opera's authenticity remains uncertain, however (Preface, *Haydn Werke*, xxiv/3, 1990). Since its

first modern production at the Bregenz Festival (1963), it has been performed several times and has twice been recorded.

The story closely resembles the plots of the typical Viennese 'Hanswurst' farces of a decade or two before the presumed date of Haydn's composition. Hanswurst (bass), a chimney-sweep, eventually manages to win the hand of Colombina (soprano), daughter of Odoardo (tenor), the overseer of the local estate – despite her father's preference for the fop Leander (tenor) and Colombina's own temporary interest in this rich suitor. A ghost and a dragon add to the liveliness of the action, and Hanswurst owes his success to his skill as a quick-change artist (he appears disguised as a soldier, a cavalier, a milliner and a beggar-woman).

The music is simple, lively, touching in some of the slow numbers (no fewer than six begin in minor keys, though two of these end in the major). There is little in the music to suggest contemporaneity with *Il mondo della luna* (1777) or the 'Little Organ' Mass, and Landon's suggested date (based largely on the inclusion in two numbers of clarinets, available in the princely establishment only in 1776–8) seems on stylistic grounds too late. If that is so, then the overture (which includes two movements by Pleyel, who became Haydn's pupil in 1772) and the clarinet parts could be later additions to the score. The preponderance of arias (21 of 26 vocal numbers) may reflect the wishes of the puppeteers.

　　　　　　　　　　　　　　　　PETER BRANSCOMBE

Feuersnot ('Fire-Famine'). *Singgedicht* ('sung poem', or 'lyrical epigram') in one act by RICHARD STRAUSS to a libretto by Ernst von Wolzogen; Dresden, Hofoper, 21 November 1901.

Strauss's second operatic essay was a ribald exercise in snook-cocking. His first opera *Guntram* had suffered a painful fiasco in Munich, his home town, and *Feuersnot* was his jovial revenge. Later he insisted that his target had been Munich's shabby treatment not of himself, but of the great Wagner; in 1901, however, he was already at odds with the Wagnerian loyalists, and Wagnerian gestures are guyed again and again in *Feuersnot*. Understandably, it was four years before Munich took it up (with Strauss to conduct it), and then only because of its success – or *succès de scandale* – in Vienna and Berlin. (Its run in the latter city had been broken off after the seventh performance, by order of the unamused Kaiser, and there was an ensuing furore.) For his librettist Strauss had found another dissident Münchener, Ernst von Wolzogen, newly remembered now as the founder of the Berlin 'Überbrettl' cabaret for which Schoenberg was to compose his downmarket *Brettl-Lieder*. Despite its risqué text, *Feuersnot* boasted distinguished interpreters from the start: in Dresden the cross-grained lovers were Annie Krull and Karl Scheidemantel, destined respectively to be Strauss's original Electra and the first *Rosenkavalier* Faninal, in Vienna Leopold Demuth sang the hero while Mahler conducted, and Berlin fielded Emmy Destinn as the (anti-)heroine. Since then, at least in Bavaria and adjacent regions, the opera has kept a toehold in the repertory.

The action, which Wolzogen adapted from an old Dutch tale, takes place on Midsummer Eve, as in *Die Meistersinger*, but in 12th-century Munich. Kunrad – the first of Strauss's romantic baritones, and like most of them a *persona* of Strauss himself – is an unworldly student of magic, following in the traces of an old

'Feuersnot' (Richard Strauss): scene from the original production at the Hofoper, Dresden, 21 November 1901: engraving from the 'Illustrirte Zeitung' (Leipzig, 5 December 1901)

wizard whom we may suppose to be Wagner; the beautiful Diemut (soprano) is the Burgomaster's daughter, the soul of propriety. Emerging at the solstice from his murky studies, Kunrad is smitten by her, declares himself in passionate arioso, abjures his books in favour of sensual Life, and under the beady eyes of the whole town steals a kiss. Outraged, Diemut rushes home and locks herself in. While the townsfolk go off to the Midsummer bonfire, distantly visible, Kunrad rhapsodizes about fire, magic and love (the musical burden is largely in the orchestra). Overhearing Diemut's plaint from her balcony, he renews his wooing; she seems to relent, and they join in a rapturous duet which Strauss marked to be sung with exaggerated pathos, for Diemut is bent upon revenge. She agrees to hoist Kunrad up to her room in a basket – but leaves him dangling impotently in mid-air, to the raucous glee of the returning burghers.

Wounded, Kunrad pronounces a formidable spell upon the town which holds love in so little respect: all its fires will be extinguished. Amid the instant, comprehensive gloom, he somehow attains the balcony to deliver a lengthy sermon to the appalled townsfolk (about Munich's neglect of his great master, and the creative force of passion against mere bourgeois virtue), and an implied ultimatum: only from a maiden's warm body will the fires spring again. (In the earthy Dutch original, this had a more literal and fundamental sense.) The anxious chorus of burghers soon comes to see what a very good idea it would be for Diemut to surrender to this excellent young man, and they cry to her to relieve their 'Feuersnot'. Indeed she has already drawn Kunrad indoors, and in the darkness their erotic union is now portrayed in an orchestral 'Liebesszene', the first of several in Strauss's operas and the sole familiar extract from this one: in fact, a fervent reprise of the earlier duet. Immediately after the climax there is a long, suppressed gasp, whereupon lights blaze all over the town. Everybody rejoices, in mutual congratulation.

From the composer who had already written *Don Juan*, the bland lines and thick, devoutly Wagnerian textures of *Guntram* had been disappointing. Now he had *Till Eulenspiegel* and *Don Quixote* behind him too.

The spring-heeled orchestra of *Feuersnot* is much happier, lightened by passages for solo wind and strings, the choruses (including a tribe of shameless children) are boldly elaborated in multiple parts, the burghers' cameo roles neatly sketched. Altogether, the score boasts far more assured proportions and variety. Diemut's two songs are in Strauss's melting 3rds-and-6ths vein, along with her *Ariadne*-like trio of friends; Kunrad has his rhetorical moments, though the orchestra speaks too loudly for him, and the invocations of fire, magic and love call up the flickering, chromatic volatility that in *Guntram* Strauss had suppressed.

Yet his score misses the irony presupposed by the nature of the piece. On one hand the music is heartfelt, innocently lusty or conventionally theatrical by turns; on the other, when a comic sting is required, Strauss resorts simply to quoting Wagner and popular Bavarian ditties, or counts upon Wolzogen's bawdy verses and punning references to make their own effect – much as in a college revue. In detail, as time passes and the references grow more obscure, the little opera becomes less funny, especially to non-Bavarians. That *Feuersnot* should be appreciated only by scholars was the last thing Strauss intended: for the sake of the dewily attractive, well-shaped score, there is a strong case for reinventing its text in terms as rudely up to date as need be.   DAVID MURRAY

Feuge, Oskar (*b* Reudnitz, nr Leipzig, 3 July 1861; *d* Dessau, 5 Nov 1913). German tenor. He made his début in 1887 at Mainz, then in 1888 was engaged at Dessau, where he remained until his death. An admired character actor, he sang Lohengrin and Siegmund as well as David and Mime. He was married to the coloratura soprano Emilie Feuge-Gleiss (*b* Rheinpfalz, 1863; *d* Dessau, 1923), who studied in Munich and Leipzig, making her début in 1890 at the Berlin Hofoper. Engaged at Dessau (1893–1922) she sang the Woodbird, a flowermaiden and Freia at Bayreuth (1897–1906). Their daughter, the soprano Elisabeth Feuge (*b* Dessau, 15 Aug 1902; *d* Munich, 4 July 1942), studied with her mother at Dessau, making her début there in 1921. From 1923 until her death she was engaged at the

Staatsoper in Munich, where she sang in the first performance of Jaromír Weinberger's *Milovaný hlas* in 1931. A fine actress with a full, generous-toned voice, Elisabeth Feuge also appeared in Vienna, Dresden, Stuttgart, Amsterdam and Salzburg, where she sang Donna Anna (1934). She took her own life in 1942.

ELIZABETH FORBES

Feustking, Friedrich Christian (*b* Stellau, nr Itzehoe, 1678; *d* Tolk, nr Schleswig, 3 Feb 1739). German librettist. He had a humanistic education, studied theology at Wittenberg and established himself at Hamburg in 1702 as a private teacher and writer. His librettos for the Teater am Gänsemarkt (*Die betrogene Staats-Liebe, oder … Die unglückselige Cleopatra*, Mattheson, 1704; *Der in Krohnen erlangte Glücks-Wechsel, oder Almira, Königin von Castilien*, Handel, 1705, later set by Keiser, 1706; and *Die durch Blut und Mord erlangete Liebe, oder Nero*, Handel, 1705) involved him in a literary quarrel with Barthold Feind and Christian Friedrich Hunold (known as Menantes) who criticized some aspects of rhyme and morals. Both parties issued several pamphlets, until Feustking moved to Tolk to take over a parsonage. His merit as a librettist was in the somewhat unconventional characterization of his heroes, who were allowed to be hesitating and weak, giving way to their feelings in beautifully flowing lyrical arias. The starkly contrasting comic scenes were condemned by Chrysander but appear to be an outgrowth of popular traditions.

H. Schröder: *Lexikon der Hamburgischen Schriftsteller*, ii (Hamburg, 1854), 294–5
F. Chrysander: *G. F. Händel*, i (Leipzig, 1858), 102–3
H. C. Wolff: *Die Barockoper in Hamburg*, i (Wolfenbüttel, 1957)
H. Rupp, ed.: *Deutsches Literatur-Lexikon* (Berne and Munich, 3/1979)

DOROTHEA SCHRÖDER

Février, Henry (*b* Paris, 2 Oct 1875; *d* Paris, 8 July 1957). French composer. He studied composition at the Paris Conservatoire with Massenet and Fauré, and privately with Messager, of whom he later wrote a biography (*André Messager: mon maître, mon ami*, 1948). His early compositions were small-scale, but he later turned almost exclusively to opera composition, beginning with *Le roi aveugle* (1906) which is dedicated to Fauré and already bears certain hallmarks of the style he was to use to good effect in later works. Many of the operas (e.g. *Le roi aveugle*; *L'île désenchantée*, 1925) are set in remote, other-worldly locations, and the redemption of mankind through love is a constant theme, manifested most noticeably in *La damnation de Blanchefleur* (1920). He is probably best known for *Monna Vanna* (1909), and he wrote of the première of this work, and of his musical-dramatic credo, in a chapter of his biography of Messager. Papers in the French Archives Nationales reveal that Février experienced problems in his dealings with Maeterlinck over the casting of this work, similar to those Debussy had over *Pelléas et Mélisande* eight years earlier. Lucien Fugère played a leading role in *Carmosine* (1913), and *Gismonda* (1919, Chicago) opened with Mary Garden in the title role.

In his musical dramas, Février favoured a continuous dramatic flow, uninterrupted by clearly defined arias and choruses. The love duet between the main characters is, however, an exception, and in works such as *Le roi aveugle* takes up what appears to be a disproportionate amount of music. His use of such 'set pieces', plus a limited use of leitmotif, and the nature of his plots, exhibit the influence of Wagner to a high degree, although his contemporaries apparently saw in *Monna Vanna* the influence of Massenet and Italian *verismo*. Besides opera, he also left some incidental music for plays such as *Agnès, dame galante* (1912) and *Aphrodite* (1914). He abandoned composition in the 1930s.

all published in Paris

Le roi aveugle (2, H. le Roux), Paris, OC (Favart), 8 May 1906, vs (1906)
Monna Vanna (drame lyrique, 4, after M. Maeterlinck), Paris, Opéra, 13 Jan 1909, vs (1908)
Carmosine (conte romanesque, 4, H. Cain and L. Payen, after G. Boccaccio and A. de Musset), Paris, Gaîté, 24 Feb 1913, vs (1913)
Gismonda (drame lyrique, 4, Cain and Payen, after V. Sardou), Chicago, Auditorium, 14 Jan 1919, vs (1920)
La damnation de Blanchefleur (miracle, 2, M. Léna), Monte Carlo, Opéra, 13 March 1920, vs (1920)
L'île désenchantée (drame musical, 2, 3 tableaux, M. Star [E. Stern], after E. Schuré), Paris, Opéra, 23 Nov 1925, vs (1925)
Oletta, la fille du corse (drame musical, 3, 4 tableaux, A. Leroy and P. de Choudens), Bordeaux, 28 Oct 1927, vs (1926)
La femme nue (drame lyrique, 4, Payen, after H. Bataille), Monte Carlo, Opéra, 23 March 1929, vs (1929)
Sylvette (opérette, 3, R. Peter and M. Carré), Paris, Trianon Lyrique, 17 Feb 1932, collab. M. Delmas   JOHN WAGSTAFF

Feydeau. Company based in Paris. It was known from its foundation (1789) as the Théâtre de Monsieur until it moved to a purpose-built theatre in the rue Feydeau in 1791; thereafter the name came to be used for both the company and the theatre in which it performed. In 1801 it amalgamated with the Opéra-Comique. *See* PARIS, §4(iv).

Fiamma, La ('The Flame'). *Melodramma* in three acts by OTTORINO RESPIGHI to a libretto by CLAUDIO GUASTALLA, freely based on Hans Wiers-Jenssen's play *Anne Pedersdotter*; Rome, Teatro Reale dell'Opera, 23 January 1934.

Originally set in 16th-century Norway, Wiers-Jenssens's turbulent drama about witchcraft, love and retribution was transferred by Guastalla, at Respighi's request, to Ravenna in the period when it was an outpost of the Byzantine empire. The heroine Silvana (soprano) has become the young second wife of the exarch Basilio (baritone); but she falls in love, Phaedra-like, with her stepson Donello (tenor). Meanwhile the old witch Agnese (mezzo-soprano), whom Silvana has unsuccessfully tried to shelter, reveals – just before dying at the stake – that Silvana's marriage to Basilio was the result of witchcraft by her mother. Realizing for the first time that she may herself have inherited magic powers (the 'flame' of the opera's title), Silvana manages to bewitch her stepson into returning her love. The couple are found together, and Silvana admits that she passionately needs Donello as an escape from the stifling effect of her marriage. On hearing this Basilio drops dead, and Silvana is tried for witchcraft and murder. Finding that even Donello does not wholly believe her innocent, she stops defending herself and is condemned to death.

Guastalla defined *La fiamma* as a 'melodramma', a term usually used to refer to Italian operas of Verdi's time; and the music too (composed during 1931–3) shows signs of reverting to 19th-century traditions. The orchestra, though resourcefully used as one would expect, is more consistently subordinate to the voices than in Respighi's previous large-scale opera *La campana sommersa*. Moreover, the vocal lines do indeed often recall Verdi's, in a way which sometimes seems mannered but can be forcefully dramatic. More recognizably Respighian are the archaic and exotic elements designed to evoke the Byzantine setting: these reach sumptuous climaxes in the choral writing at the end of Act 1 and in parts of the final scene, set in the basilica of S Vitale. As a whole, *La fiamma* may seem less personal than the best parts of *La campana sommersa*; yet it has proved sufficiently effective in its own terms to have become the most widely performed and successful of Respighi's larger operas.

JOHN C. G. WATERHOUSE

Fiasconaro, Gregorio (*b* Palermo, 5 March 1915). South African baritone and producer of Italian birth. He studied in Genoa and with Stracciari in Rome and made his début as Germont in Genoa in 1937. A pilot in the Italian air force during the war, he was interned in Durban, where he settled. In 1949 he began teaching at the University of Cape Town, and he became the first director of the opera school there (1952–80). He produced and often sang in numerous operas for the University of Cape Town Opera Company, and in its London season in 1956–7 he sang the title role in the first British staged performance of Bartók's *Bluebeard's Castle*. Fiasconaro produced for all the arts councils in South Africa, specializing in the works of Verdi and Puccini. As a singer his portrayal of Scarpia was perhaps his most memorable role.

D. Talbot: *For the Love of Singing: 50 Years of Opera at UCT* (Cape Town, 1978)
G. Fiasconaro: *I'd Do it Again* (Cape Town, 1982)   JAMES MAY

Fibich, Zdeněk [Zdenko] (**Antonín Václav**) (*b* Všebořice, Bohemia, 21 Dec 1850; *d* Prague, 15 Oct 1900). Czech composer. He enjoyed a happy childhood at Všebořice and in Libáň, where his father, a forestry official, was transferred in 1857. His education was largely in German (his mother was from a cultured German-speaking Viennese family), but he later attended the second and third forms of a Czech gymnasium in Prague (1863–5). His mother had taught him the piano at home and, encouraged by a local priest, he had written his first composition in 1862. By 1865, when he left Prague, he had written 50 works, mostly piano pieces and songs, but also part of an opera, *Medea*. His training continued in Leipzig (1865–7), initially at the Conservatory. After eight months in Paris (1868–9), where he made a living as a piano teacher and acquired an interest in art and sculpture, his studies ended in Mannheim (1869–70) with the conductor Vinzenz Lachner, who staged Wagner's *Die Meistersinger* during his stay. After his return to Bohemia, he devoted himself to composition, in particular to his first extant opera, *Bukovín* (1870–71).

In 1873 Fibich married Růžena Hanušová and in the autumn took up a school choir-training post in Vilnius. His year there was marred by domestic tragedies, culminating in the death of his wife on their return to Prague. In 1875 Fibich married her sister Betty (1846–1901), a leading contralto at the Provisional Theatre who created several of Smetana's and Fibich's roles. In Prague Fibich earned a living first as deputy conductor and choirmaster at the Provisional Theatre (1875–8), where he had to conduct mostly operettas, and then as choirmaster of the Russian Orthodox

church (1878–81). Thereafter his income came from composition and private teaching except for a year at the end of his life when he was dramaturg at the National Theatre in Prague (1899–1900).

Fibich was a prolific composer in all media except chamber and choral music, achieving considerable distinction in his symphonies and tone poems. Of particular note is his preoccupation with melodrama. From conducting them at the Provisional Theatre he knew the Benda works that had so impressed Mozart, as well as Schumann's declamatory ballads and *Manfred*, and he consciously experimented with the mixing of simultaneous speech and music, first in a series of concert melodramas and finally in his ambitious stage-melodrama trilogy *Hippodamia* (1888–91). *Hippodamia*, which came in the middle of a decade in which he wrote no operas, was an important turning-point in his operatic career. His earlier operas lead logically up to it; those written afterwards can be considered a reaction to it, and take a new direction. Linking both halves of his operatic career is his care and skill with idiomatic word-setting in Czech, unusual for someone with so much German in his background and education; and his penchant, again unusual in Bohemia at the time, for international rather than Czech subjects. Only two of his operas are set in Bohemia. The rest are based mainly on world literature: Schiller, Byron and Shakespeare.

In his teens Fibich attempted four operas. Two, *Medea* and *Loreley*, progressed little further than the first act, but he seems to have completed a serious one-act opera, *Gutta von Guttenfels*, while a comic opera, *Kapellmeister in Venedig*, was performed 'with orchestra' on 6 January 1868. *Loreley* was written to Geibel's text (which he knew from Bruch's setting), but the other librettos were by Fibich himself, and it is surprising in view of his frequently described verbal dexterity that he never again wrote his own librettos and seems not to have taken much initiative in their shaping. *Bukovín*, Fibich's first surviving opera, belongs more with the juvenilia than with the later works. It is still under the influence of early German Romanticism (the librettist was asked for 'something like *Freischütz*' – and obliged), and its word-setting is defective. Fibich never published it, nor was it performed again after its three performances at the Provisional Theatre. For his next opera, Fibich turned to Bendl's and Smetana's librettist Eliška Krásnohorská. The libretto she supplied for *Blaník* (1874–7) took a traditional view of choral and solo ensemble. Its complicated plot, set in 1623, soon after the Battle of the White Mountain, concerns the religious rift in the defeated Czech society, and the notion of the nation's rescue by knights who have taken refuge in the magic mountain of Blaník (the source of messianic legend celebrated in tone poems by both Smetana and Janáček). Fibich's next opera could not have been more different. *Nevěsta messinská* ('The Bride of Messina', 1882–3) is the composer's severest opera, a relentless Schiller tragedy presented in declamatory dialogue which conscientiously avoids set numbers, though Schiller's Greek chorus provides opportunities for some formal ensembles. It was hardly more popular than its predecessors, and despite his evident interest in the theatre (he composed much incidental music for plays) Fibich wrote no more operas for a decade.

When he returned to opera with *Bouře* ('The Tempest', 1893–4), Fibich seemed to have exorcised any

181

serious theoretical leanings urged on him by his last librettist, the Czech aesthetician Otakar Hostinský. He had fallen in love with his pupil Anežka Schulzová, who provided both the librettos, and the more 'operatic' conventions of his last three operas. *The Tempest*, with a libretto by the Czech poet Vrchlický (librettist of *Hippodamia*), also belongs to this group of works in which Fibich's lyrical gifts now flourished freely. It is in *The Tempest*, *Hedy* and *Šárka* that Fibich the sweet-toothed melodist is most evident. Some of the melodic material for these works derives from Fibich's 'love-diary', his collection of 376 short lyrical piano pieces in which he celebrated his relationship with Schulzová. Although there are recurring motifs, there is far less attempt to unify the material over large spans. The works have set numbers, arias, love duets, and (in *Hedy*) even a ballet and a concertato finale. They were all much more successful with the public, particularly *Šárka* with its Czech subject-matter. Fibich's final work, *Pád Arkuna* ('The Fall of Arkona', 1898–9), though also to a libretto by Schulzová, is a more declamatory opera and seemed to indicate a change of direction which was, however, cut short by Fibich's death in his 50th year.

Although earlier in the 20th century Fibich was much promoted by the Prague musicological establishment as Smetana's 'successor', he never quite gained the respect that the Czech public showed for Smetana, or the affection it felt for Dvořák. As the first purely Romantic Czech composer, with a cultural and musical education little different from that of his contemporaries in Germany and Austria, Fibich did not write in a style that sounded obviously 'Czech' to his countrymen, or 'exotic' to foreigners (none of his operas has been staged abroad). This would not have mattered had his own musical personality been stronger, but for all his fine craftsmanship and melodic fervour, the place of his operas in the permanent Czech repertory seems less secure as the centenary of his death approaches.

See also Nevěsta messinská *and* Šárka.

first performed at Prague, National Theatre, and autograph MSS in Prague, Společnost Zdeňka Fibicha (Zdeněk Fibich Society), unless otherwise stated; further MSS in CS-Pnd and Pnm; all printed works published in Prague

Bukovín, 1870–71 (romantic op, 3, K. Sabina), Prague, Provisional, 16 April 1874

Blaník op.50, 1874–7 (3, E. Krásnohorská), Prague, Provisional, 25 Nov 1881, vs *Bm** (1897)

Nevěsta messinská [The Bride of Messina] op.18, 1882–3 (tragic op, 3, O. Hostinský, after F. von Schiller), 28 March 1884, *Pnm**, vs (1884)

Bouře [The Tempest] op.40, 1893–4 (3, J. Vrchlický, after W. Shakespeare), 1 March 1895, vs (1895)

Hedy op.43 (4, A. Schulzová, after Byron: *Don Juan*), 12 Feb 1896, vs (1895)

Šárka op.51 (3, Schulzová), 28 Dec 1897, vs (1897)

Pád Arkuna [The Fall of Arkona] (Schulzová): Helga op.55 (prol.), 1898, vs (1899); Dargun op.60 (3), 9 Nov 1900, vs (1901)

Lost or destroyed: Medea, 1863 (Fibich), frag.; Kapellmeister in Venedig, 1866 (comic op, Fibich), ? Libáň, 6 Jan 1868; Loreley, 1866–7 (romantic op, 3, E. Geibel), frag.; Gutta von Guttenfels, ?1867 (serious opera, 1, Fibich); Litocha, 1871 (J. Kaňka), frag.; Frithjóf, 1874 (P. Lohmann), frag.

*

L. Janáček: 'Hedy Zdeňka Fibicha', *Hlídka*, ii (1897), 601–4; repr. in Rektorys, ii (1952), 306–10

——: České proudy hudební: Šárka [Czech Musical Currents: Šárka], *Hlídka*, iv (1899), 36–41; repr. in Rektorys, ii (1952), 311–18

C. L. Richter [pseud. of A. Schulzová]: *Zdenko Fibich: eine musikalische Silhouette* (Prague, 1900)

Z. Nejedlý: *Zdenko Fibich, zakladatel scénického melodramatu* [Zdenko Fibich, Founder of the Scenic Melodrama] (Prague, 1901)

A. Schulzová: 'Zdenko Fibich: hrstka upomínek a intimních rysů' [Zdenko Fibich: a Handful of Reminiscences and Intimate Traits], *Květy*, xxiv (1902), bk 68, no.6, pp.768–83, bk 69, no.1, pp.67–84; ed. L. Boháček (Prague, 1950); also in Rektorys, ii (1952), 141–99

J. Boleška: 'O Zdeňku Fibichovi: několik vzpomínek na poslední desetiletí jeho života' [Some Reminiscences of the Last Decade of Zdeněk Fibich's Life], *Dalibor*, xxv (1903), 281–2, 289–90, 302–3, 314–15

V. and J. Hornové: *Česká zpěvohra* [Czech Opera] (Prague, 1903), 80–117

O. Hostinský: *Vzpomínky na Fibicha* [Reminiscences of Fibich] (Prague, 1909)

A. Rektorys, ed.: 'Památník Fibichův', *Dalibor/Hudební listy*, xxxii (1910), 315–50 [memorial issue, incl. documentary material and articles, esp. A. Rektorys: 'Fibich dramaturg'; Z. Nejedlý: 'Operní pokusy a plány Z. Fibicha' [Fibich's Operatic Attempts and Plans], and reminiscences by J. B. Foerster, F. A. Šubert and K. Pippich; some material repr. in Rektorys (1951–2)]

Z. Nejedlý: *Česká moderní zpěvohra po Smetanovi* [Modern Czech Opera after Smetana] (Prague, 1911)

V. Brtník: 'Poznámky k libretům Fibichových oper' [Remarks on the Librettos of Fibich's Operas], *Dalibor*, xxxvii (1920–21), 37–9, 51, 59–60, 69–70, 83–5, 99–102, 115–16, 132–4, 145–8

Z. Nejedlý: *Zdeňka Fibicha milostný deník: Nálady, dojmy a upomínky* [Zdeněk Fibich's Erotic Diary: Moods, Impressions and Reminiscences] (Prague, 1925, 2/1948); Eng. summary in G. Abraham: 'An Erotic Diary for Piano', *Slavonic and Romantic Music* (London, 1968), 70–98

M. Očadlík: 'Fibichův Bukovín', *Smetana*, xv (1925), 81–8, 113–24

Listy Hudební matice, v (1925–6), 44–58 [Fibich issue, incl. articles by B. Vomáčka, J. Löwenbach and J. Vogel]

F. Pala: 'Operní odkaz Zdeňka Fibicha' [Fibich's Operatic Heritage], *Národní divadlo*, viii (1930), nos.9–10

J. Hutter and Z. Chalabala, eds.: *České umění dramatické*, ii: *Zpěvohra* [Czech Dramatic Art: Opera] (Prague, 1941), 130–55

R. Newmarch: *The Music of Czechoslovakia* (London, 1942), chap.8

A. Rektorys, ed.: *Zdeněk Fibich: sborník dokumentů a studií o jeho životě a díle* [Zdeněk Fibich: a Collection of Documents and Studies about his Life and Work] (Prague, 1951–2)

A. Hostomská: *Opera: průvodce operní tvorbou* [Opera: a Guide to Operatic Works] (Prague, 1955, enlarged 7/1965), 617–36

J. Jiránek: *Zdeněk Fibich* (Prague, 1963)

J. Hudec: *Fibichovo skladatelské mládí: doba příprav* [Fibich's Compositional Youth: a Time of Preparations] (Prague, 1966)

J. Jiránek: 'Die Bezeihung von Musik und Wort im Schaffen Zdeněk Fibichs', *Music and Word: Brno IV 1969*, 159–69

V. Hudec: *Zdeněk Fibich* (Prague, 1971)

J. Smaczny: 'The Operas and Melodramas of Zdeněk Fibich (1850–1900)', *PRMA*, cix (1982–3), 119–33

L. Šíp: *Česká opera a její tvůrci: průvodce* [Czech Opera and its Creators: a Guide] (Prague, 1983), 104–24

G. Abraham: 'The Operas of Zdeněk Fibich', *19th Century Music*, ix (1985–6), 136–44

J. Tyrrell: *Czech Opera* (Cambridge, 1988)   JOHN TYRRELL

Fidelio [*Leonore, oder Der Triumph der ehelichen Liebe* ('Leonore, or The Triumph of Married Love')]. Opera in two (originally three) acts by LUDWIG VAN BEETHOVEN to a libretto by JOSEPH VON SONNLEITHNER (1805), with revisions by STEPHAN VON BREUNING (1806) and GEORG FRIEDRICH TREITSCHKE (1814), after JEAN-NICOLAS BOUILLY's French libretto *Léonore, ou L'amour conjugal*; Vienna, Theater an der Wien, 20 November 1805 (first version); Theater an der Wien, 29 March 1806 (second version); Kärntnertortheater, 23 May 1814 (final version).

At some time in the early part of 1803 Beethoven moved into an apartment in the Theater an der Wien and began work on his first opera; the libretto was *Vestas Feuer*, by the theatre's director Emanuel Schikaneder. By January 1804 he had abandoned this project and taken up a new libretto, *Léonore, ou*

Florestan *a prisoner* — tenor
Leonore *his wife and assistant to Rocco under*
   the name of Fidelio — soprano
Rocco *gaoler* — bass
Marzelline *his daughter* — soprano
Jaquino *assistant to Rocco* — tenor
Don Pizarro *governor of a state prison* — bass-baritone
Don Fernando *minister and Spanish nobleman* — bass

Soldiers, prisoners, townspeople

Setting A Spanish prison not far from Seville

L'amour conjugal. This drama by J.-N. Bouilly had been set by Pierre Gaveaux in 1798 and was also set in Italian translation by Ferdinando Paer in 1804 and Simon Mayr in 1805. Beethoven worked from a German version translated and enlarged by the Viennese court secretary Joseph von Sonnleithner. The choice was probably influenced both by the recent success in Vienna of another, very similar drama by Bouilly, *Les deux journées*, in a setting by Cherubini, and by the attractiveness of the subject matter, whose themes of undeserved suffering and heroic resolve were very much in Beethoven's mind at about this time.

Composition of the opera continued through much of 1804 and 1805, and last-minute difficulties with the censors delayed the première until 20 November 1805. The principal singers were the soprano Anna Milder as Leonore and the tenor Friedrich Christian Demmer as Florestan. There were only three performances. Vienna was under occupation by French troops, and many of Beethoven's supporters had left the city. The opera was also felt to be too long, and Beethoven was persuaded to abridge and alter it slightly. A revised version in two rather than three acts, with Rocco's aria omitted and other sections shortened and rearranged (see Table 1), was performed on 29 March and 10 April 1806, with Joseph Röckel replacing Demmer as Florestan. To avoid confusion with the operas of Gaveaux and Paer, the theatre had insisted on the title *Fidelio* in the 1805 and 1806 productions; Beethoven himself preferred *Leonore*, and that title appears in the 1806 libretto (which was printed at his own expense) and the vocal score published in 1810. The title *Leonore* is now commonly used to designate the first two versions of the opera. The overtures written for the 1805 and 1806 performances are now known as the *Leonore* no.2 and no.3 respectively. The *Leonore* no.1 overture, earlier thought to have been played in 1805, has recently been shown to date from 1807, when a performance of the opera was planned in Prague.

Although a vocal score of the 1806 version of *Fidelio*, minus the overture and the two finales, appeared in 1810, the opera was not performed again until 1814. When Beethoven was approached about it, following some very successful concerts of his orchestral music, he himself insisted on further revisions. These were undertaken with the help of the poet Georg Friedrich Treitschke. More cuts were made (see Table 1), and nearly every number was changed in some way. This final version was performed on 23 May 1814, with Anna Milder again in the role of Leonore and an Italian tenor named Radichi as Florestan; Pizarro was sung by the baritone Johann Michael Vogl, later a friend and champion of Schubert. There was also a new overture, the fourth, now identified as the *Fidelio* overture, which

however was not ready until the second performance. A vocal score prepared by Ignaz Moscheles appeared in 1814; no full score was published until 1826.

The most famous of 19th-century singers to achieve success with *Fidelio* was Wilhelmine Schröder-Devrient, whose performances as Leonore starting in 1822 exerted a powerful effect on a younger generation of musicians (for illustration *see* SCHRÖDER-DEVRIENT, WILHELMINE). The complicated genesis of the opera was discussed by Otto Jahn, Alexander Thayer and Gustav Nottebohm in the 1860s and 70s, but a revival of the first version was not attempted until 1905, on the centenary of the première. There have been many modern recordings of the final version, perhaps most famously with Jon Vickers in the role of Florestan. The first version has also been recorded.

ACT 1.i *A courtyard of the prison* Marzelline is ironing; Jaquino presses her on the subject of marriage (duet, 'Jetzt, Schätzchen'). She rejects his pleas, for she has fallen in love with Fidelio, her father's new assistant ('O wär ich schon mit dir vereint'). Rocco enters; Leonore, in her disguise as Fidelio, follows, laden with chains and supplies. Rocco takes Fidelio's hard work as a sign of interest in Marzelline (quartet in canon, led by Marzelline, 'Mir ist so wunderbar!'; Fidelio and Jaquino express anxious thoughts). Rocco encourages the romance, but cautions that a successful marriage requires money ('Hat man nicht auch Gold beineben'). Fidelio tests Rocco's trust by asking to accompany him to the subterranean cell where a prisoner is kept who she suspects may be her husband, Florestan ('Gut, Söhnchen, gut').

1.ii [Act 2, 1805 version] *A courtyard of the prison* To the sound of a march, the soldiers enter. Pizarro follows. He reads the dispatches, which include a letter warning of a surprise visit by the minister to question him about prisoners being held without cause. Having imprisoned Florestan for political reasons (only vaguely specified), Pizarro is forced to act. He stations a trumpeter in the tower and resolves to take his revenge at once (aria with chorus, 'Ha! welch ein Augenblick!'). Pizarro calls Rocco aside and attempts, unsuccessfully, to enlist his aid in the murder (duet, 'Jetzt, Alter, jetzt hat es Eile!'). The men leave. Leonore, who has observed them plotting, curses Pizarro and reaffirms her hope and her own resolve (accompanied recitative, 'Abscheulicher! Wo eilst du hin?'; aria in two sections, 'Komm, Hoffnung', 'Ich folg' dem innern Triebe'). Rocco and Marzelline enter, and Leonore (now in her role as Fidelio again) persuades Rocco to allow some of the prisoners out into the open air. They emerge and sing in praise of freedom ('O welche Lust!'); this begins the finale to Act 1. Rocco tells Fidelio that he has obtained permission for the marriage to Marzelline. He will also be permitted to take Fidelio to the cell of the mysterious prisoner, whose grave they must prepare. Jaquino and Marzelline rush in and warn of Pizarro's arrival. Pizarro is enraged by Rocco's presumption in letting the prisoners out, but Rocco deflects the anger by citing the king's name-day and noting that one prisoner has remained inside. The prisoners return to their cells ('Leb wohl, du warmes Sonnenlicht').

ACT 2.i [Act 3, 1805 version] *A subterranean cell* An orchestral introduction depicts the bleakness of the scene. In an accompanied recitative Florestan curses the darkness but accepts God's will ('Gott! welch'

'Fidelio' (Beethoven), Act 2: engraving by H. Merz after a drawing by Moritz von Schwind from an edition of the opera published by Rieter-Biedermann (Winterthur, 1870) to mark the centenary of Beethoven's birth; Von Schwind probably saw the 1822 revival (Vienna) attended by Beethoven

Dunkel hier!'). His two-part aria laments the loss of his happiness as the price of having spoken the truth ('In des Lebens Frühlingstagen') and ends with a vision of rescue by Leonore ('Und spür' ich nicht linde, sanftsäuselnde Luft?'). Leonore enters, but with Rocco to uncover an abandoned cistern that is to serve as Florestan's grave (melodrama and duet, 'Nur hurtig fort, nur frisch gegraben'). When the grave is ready, Florestan stirs. He asks for help and for water. Fidelio comes forward with wine and bread, which Rocco allows Florestan to receive in a communion-like trio ('Euch werde Lohn in bessern Welten'). Rocco gives a signal, and Pizarro enters. The ensuing action takes place in a quartet ('Er sterbe!'): Pizarro reveals his identity to Florestan, who stands defiant; when Pizarro draws his dagger, Leonore steps forward and reveals her own identity at last; as she halts Pizarro with a pistol, the trumpet from the tower signals the arrival of the minister. After Rocco and Pizarro have left the cell, Florestan and Leonore celebrate their reunion (duet, 'O namenlose Freude!').

2.ii *The parade grounds of the prison* This entire scene is set musically as the finale of the act. The townspeople and the prisoners are assembled to greet Don Fernando, who enters accompanied by Pizarro ('Heil sei dem Tag'). Rocco brings in Florestan and Leonore. Don Fernando recognizes his friend, believed dead, and orders Pizarro's arrest. The privilege of unlocking Florestan's chains is given to Leonore ('O Gott! O welch ein Augenblick!'). The opera ends with a chorus in praise of Leonore's bravery ('Wer ein holdes Weib errungen, stimm' in unsern Jubel ein').

*   *   *

Most of the important differences between the 1805 and 1814 versions of *Fidelio* can be accounted for by reference to Bouilly's original libretto, which Sonnleithner followed closely. Bouilly's first act included six musical numbers (nos.1, 2, 5, 10, 11 and the start of 12 in the 1805 *Fidelio*; see Table 1). Dramatically, the only important difference is that Pizarro, who has only a speaking role, tells Rocco merely that a masked man will kill Florestan once the grave is prepared. Bouilly's second act also has six numbers (nos.13, 14, 15, 17 and two sections of 18 in the 1805 *Fidelio*). The dramatic action is similar up to the point of the trumpet signal, though the confrontation that Beethoven was to set as a quartet (no.16) is done here in spoken dialogue. When Pizarro and Rocco leave the cell, Rocco takes the pistol from Leonore, so that she and Florestan are still in doubt about their rescue as they sing their duet. The concluding scene takes place in the cell itself, starting with an offstage chorus demanding vengeance and concluding with the minister's discovery of the truth, all spoken, and a chorus in praise of Leonore.

The only important dramatic change that Sonnleithner introduced in 1805 was to make Pizarro's intentions clear to Rocco already in their first scene together, in the duet 'Jetzt, Alter' (no.10). As in Bouilly, the last act ends in the cell. But Sonnleithner did extend the text at many points to accommodate more musical numbers. In some cases, such as the trio 'Gut, Söhnchen, gut' (no.6) and Pizarro's aria (no.8), he worked from spoken lines in Bouilly. In others he expanded scenes with new material; this is most apparent in the trio 'Ein Mann ist bald genommen' (no.3), the quartet 'Mir ist so wunderbar' (no.4), the duet 'Jetzt, Alter' (no.9) and the Act 2 finale, which is expanded to include a second aria for Pizarro (Bouilly's first act was divided into two acts in 1805). Most of these changes create opportunities for ensemble numbers, which were not a priority in the *opéra comique* conceived by Bouilly and Gaveaux, but which Beethoven no doubt requested.

In its 1806 revision, *Fidelio* was presented in two acts rather than three. There were many small changes in the music, but the important dramatic changes were few. Rocco's aria was omitted, and both the duet 'Um in der Ehe froh zu leben' and the trio 'Ein Mann ist bald genommen' were shifted to a position after Leonore's aria, which now followed the Pizarro-Rocco duet directly. The changes had the positive effect of moving the action more quickly through the opening scene, but the two ensembles that now fell between Leonore's aria and the Act 1 finale slowed the drama again at that point.

The revisions of 1814 went much further. Rocco's aria was restored, but the two offending ensembles before the Act 1 finale were cut. The finale itself was rewritten, eliminating Pizarro's second aria in favour of a second chorus as the prisoners return to their cells. In Act 2 the quartet is interrupted by Jaquino with the news of the minister's arrival. Leonore and Florestan sing their duet knowing they are safe, and the final scene is moved from the darkness of the cell into the light of day. Beethoven also exchanged the position of the first two numbers; the new overture in E major now precedes the duet in A major, whereas the overtures of 1805 and 1806, both in C, had been followed by Marzelline's aria in C minor. Of the many changes in the text, the most important were a new introduction to Leonore's aria

TABLE 1: The Gaveaux and Beethoven versions of *Fidelio* (*Leonore*)

The 1806 and 1814 versions are shown by reference to vocal numbers of the 1805 version

Gaveaux, 1798	Beethoven, 1805	Beethoven, 1806	Beethoven, 1814
Léonore, ou L'amour conjugal (J.-N. Bouilly)	Fidelio (Joseph von Sonnleithner, after Bouilly)	Leonore, oder Der Triumph der ehelichen Liebe (Sonnleithner, rev. Stephan von Breuning)	Fidelio (Sonnleithner, rev. von Breuning, rev. Georg Friedrich Treitschke)
	Overture: Leonore no.2, C	Overture: Leonore no.3, C	Overture: Fidelio, E
ACT 1	ACT 1	ACT 1	ACT 1
Aria (Marceline)	1 Aria (Marzelline) 'O wär ich schon', c/C	1 1805/1	1 1805/2
Duet (Marceline, Jacquino)	2 Duet (Marzelline, Jaquino) 'Jetzt, Schätzchen', A	2 1805/2	2 1805/1
	3 Trio (Marzelline, Jaquino, Rocco) 'Ein Mann ist bald genommen', E♭	3 1805/4	3 1805/4
	4 Quartet (Marzelline, Leonore, Jaquino, Rocco) 'Mir ist so wunderbar', G	4 1805/6	4 1805/5
Aria (Roc) 'Chanson'	5 Aria (Rocco) 'Hat man nicht auch Gold beineben', B♭	5 1805/7	5 1805/6
	6 Trio (Marzelline, Leonore, Rocco) 'Gut, Söhnchen, gut', F	6 1805/8	6 1805/7
	ACT 2	7 1805/9	7 1805/8
	7 March, B♭ (possibly not included)	8 1805/11	8 1805/9
	8 Aria (Pizarro) with chorus 'Ha! welch ein Augenblick', d/D	9 1805/10	9 1805/11 with new recit. 'Abscheulicher! Wo eilst du hin?'
Duet (Marceline, Léonore)	9 Duet (Pizarro, Rocco) 'Jetzt, Alter', A	10 1805/3	
	10 Duet (Marzelline, Leonore) 'Um in der Ehe froh zu leben', C	11 1805/12	
Aria (Léonore) 'Romance'	11 Recit. and Aria (Leonore) 'Ach brich noch nicht ... Komm, Hoffnung', ?E		10 new finale
Aria (Léonore) 'Air' Chorus (prisoners)	12 Finale (Marzelline, Leonore, Rocco, Jaquino, Pizarro, prisoners), B♭		
ACT 2	ACT 3	ACT 2	ACT 2
Recit. and Aria (Florestan) 'Romance'	13 Recit. and Aria (Florestan) 'Gott! welch Dunkel hier ... In des Lebens Frühlingstagen', f/A♭/f	12 1805/13	11 1805/13 with new final section 'Und spür ich nicht linde', F
Duet (Léonore, Roc)	14 Melodrama and Duet (Leonore, Rocco) 'Nur hurtig fort', a	13 1805/14	12 1805/14
Trio (Léonore, Florestan, Roc)	15 Trio (Leonore, Rocco, Florestan) 'Euch werde Lohn', A	14 1805/15	13 1805/15
	16 Quartet (Leonore, Florestan, Rocco, Pizarro) 'Er sterbe!', D	15 1805/16	14 1805/16
Duet (Léonore, Florestan)	17 Recit. and Duet (Leonore, Florestan) 'Ich kann mich noch nicht fassen ... O namenlose Freude', G	16 1805/17	15 1805/17 without recit.
Chorus behind the scenes Chorus 'Finale Choeur général'	18 Finale (Leonore, Marzelline, Rocco, Florestan, Jaquino, Pizarro, Fernando, prisoners, people), c-C	17 1805/18	16 1805/18 but largely rewritten

Note: The evidence of published librettos and Beethoven's sketches shows that 1805/11, 13 and 14 may have been substantially changed in 1806; other movements were revised in 1806 and 1814.

(the accompanied recitative 'Abscheulicher! wo eilst du hin?') and a new concluding section to Florestan's aria, replacing a memory of past happiness with a vision of deliverance by Leonore in the form of an angel ('Und spür' ich nicht linde, sanftsäuselnde Luft?'). At least in the case of Leonore's recitative, the new text may have been inspired by the German translation of Paer's *Leonora* ('Abscheulicher Pizarro! wo gehst du hin?').

Fidelio has two interlocking plots. Leonore, in her real and disguised roles, and Rocco, as father and gaoler, participate in both. The domestic plot involves them in the emotional world of Jaquino and Marzelline. The heroic plot involves them in the deadly confrontation of Pizarro and Florestan. The music of the first scenes, before Pizarro's entrance, is simpler in form and expression than what follows. Marzelline and Rocco sing strophic arias (Jaquino has none). Marzelline and Jaquino have a comic duet, interrupted by a knocking at the gate – a dramatic device foreshadowing the trumpet signal that interrupts the Act 2 quartet. When Fidelio sings, the mood darkens, but the canonic quartet is mysterious rather than complex and the closing trio of scene i (Act 1 in 1805) reaches furthest emotionally when Pizarro is mentioned. After this scene Marzelline and Jaquino effectively disappear from the action, and there is no more music as light as that of the first few numbers (this is not true of the 1805 and 1806 versions).

Pizarro's aria, in a growling D minor and set in sonata form with a coda accompanied by the shocked troops, raises the level of the musical argument. Equally ambitious in its unusual shape, its contrasts and its chromaticism is the following duet, which draws Rocco into the world of Pizarro's conspiracy. Leonore now enters a second time, alone and therefore unconstrained by her disguise. Her scene is distinguished musically from all that has come before: we hear accompanied recitative for the first time, and the aria falls into two large sections in contrasting tempo, with three obbligato horns supporting her heroic resolve. Beethoven duplicates this format in Florestan's solo scene at the beginning of Act 2: accompanied recitative and an aria in two sections in contrasting tempo, this time with a long orchestral introduction to establish the mood. Thus the characters of *Fidelio* are identified and related by the style of their music, with Leonore and Florestan paired at one extreme, Rocco and Marzelline paired at the other, and Pizarro in the middle. Similar hierarchies are present in Mozart's operas, most obviously in *Die Zauberflöte*.

Beethoven planned the tonal structure of the opera with equal care. A great circle-of-5ths progression leads to the C major of the final scene: A minor and A major in the duet 'Nur hurtig fort' and the trio 'Euch werde Lohn'; D major in the quartet 'Er sterbe!'; G major in the duet 'O namenlose Freude!'; and then C major in the finale. It appears there may also be some symbolic significance to his choice of keys for the individual characters. Leonore (E major) and Florestan (F minor/A♭ major) are presented as the extreme poles, four sharps and four flats removed from the key of resolution, as if to emphasize the distance that separates them. Pizarro (aria in D minor/major) and the prisoners (chorus in B♭ major) are placed symmetrically within these extremes.

Some of the musical gestures of *Fidelio* have been ascribed directly to the influence of the earlier settings. Gaveaux had used minor–major contrast in Marzelline's aria, B♭ major for Rocco's aria, 9/8 metre for the Leonore-Marzelline duet (see the 1805 *Fidelio*), a solo horn in Leonore's aria and an imitative, *pianissimo* beginning for the prisoners' chorus. Similarities between Paer's setting and Beethoven's have also been noted, but there is no firm evidence that Beethoven saw or heard Paer's work before its first Viennese performance in 1809. He seems not to have known Mayr's opera.

Less ambiguous is Beethoven's use of his own earlier music. The duet for Leonore and Florestan, 'O namenlose Freude!', is taken from a trio, also in G major and with a similar text, that he had written for the abandoned *Vestas Feuer* in 1803. And for the moment in the Act 2 finale when Leonore unlocks Florestan's chains, 'O Gott! O welch ein Augenblick!', Beethoven reached back to the cantata on the death of Joseph II (WoO 87) that he had composed in Bonn; the borrowed music, also in F major, is from the soprano solo with chorus on the text 'Da stiegen die Menschen ans Licht'. Less obviously, the introduction to the opening chorus of the cantata, where Joseph's death is mourned, is recalled in the gloomy orchestral introduction to Florestan's aria. The symbolic triumph of light over darkness, explicit in the text of the cantata, is implicit in the second act of *Fidelio* in its final form, reflecting the

triumph of reason over hysteria, good over evil, ultimately life over death. One thinks again of *Die Zauberflöte*, though Beethoven had written the cantata a year earlier, in 1790.

Of the many other influences on *Fidelio* that have been proposed, those of Mozart and of post-revolutionary French opera are the most widely acknowledged. The latter repertory is no longer well known, but beginning in 1802 much of it was performed in Vienna. Echoes of Cherubini's *Lodoïska* and *Les deux journées* are easy to hear in *Fidelio*, and the idea of the trumpet signal, anticipated in the overture, may have come from Méhul's *Héléna* (also to a libretto by Bouilly). The musical rhetoric of Cherubini and his French contemporaries, which is quite distinct from Mozart's, is evident throughout *Fidelio* and the other great works of Beethoven's middle period.

Beethoven's preparations for his first opera included the writing out of ensemble passages from *Les deux journées* (known in Vienna as *Der Wasserträger*), from Salieri's *Les Danaides* and from Mozart's *Die Zauberflöte* and *Don Giovanni*. It is tempting to associate the influence of Mozart particularly with the power of Beethoven's large-scale forms, an area in which he clearly surpasses Cherubini. Indeed, Beethoven's musical logic is sometimes so compelling that it transcends even the particulars of the drama that prompted it. This seems true of a movement like 'Mir ist so wunderbar', where the dramatic motivation is much less obvious than in its probable model, the canonic quartet in *Così fan tutte*. More important, however, and more inherently dramatic, are the many movements in sonata form. Beethoven had used sonata form to very powerful effect in his instrumental works, and in Mozart he saw how effectively its essential procedures could be adapted in setting ensemble texts. The parallels are easiest to hear in the most idiosyncratic cases. The duet 'Jetzt, Alter', for example, was probably inspired by the Anna-Ottavio duet that closes the first scene of *Don Giovanni*; in both cases the development section breaks down into accompanied recitative and the recapitulation is given over to an ominous declaration of intent, with the whole process then repeated. Here and elsewhere Beethoven created structures of such musical power that they take on a dramatic life of their own. In this respect he may have missed something in his Mozartian models.

Fidelio has been criticized as two-dimensional in its portrayal of character and as melodramatic in its action. Leonore and Florestan reveal little beyond their primary traits; Pizarro never vacillates. And Rocco, the one character who must choose between his duty and his dignity, is given little musical opportunity to consider his dilemma. Beethoven lacked Mozart's tolerance for human frailty and ambivalence. He formulated the choices in his own life in similarly unambiguous terms.

Let me tell you that my most prized possession, my hearing, has greatly deteriorated...I must withdraw from everything, and my best years will pass away without my being able to achieve all that my talent and strength have commanded me to do! Sad resignation, to which I am forced to have recourse; needless to say, I am resolved to overcome all this, but how will it be possible?

Thus he wrote to a friend in 1801. 'In the springtime of my life my happiness has flown from me' and 'I follow my inner drive; nothing can deter me' – these words of Florestan and Leonore, which echoed his own, are fixed as the divided emotional centres of his opera. And so the reunion, Florestan's loss restored and Leonore's bravery rewarded, must have reconciled symbolically the conflicting emotions in Beethoven himself. Whatever its limitations may be, *Fidelio* endures as a hymn of praise to those virtues of patience and determination that saw Beethoven through his own darkest days.

DOUGLAS JOHNSON

Field, Helen (*b* Awyn, North Wales, 14 May 1951). Welsh soprano. She studied at the RNCM and the RCM, making her début in 1976 with the WNO as Offenbach's Eurydice; during the next decade she sang Musetta, Poppaea, Vixen, Katerina (Martinů's *The Greek Passion*), Marzelline, Mařenka, Tatyana, Micaëla, Jenůfa, Mimì and Desdemona. In 1982 she sang Emma (*Khovanshchina*) at Covent Garden and Britten's Governess in Amsterdam. Her roles for the ENO (1983–90) include Gilda (which she repeated at the Metropolitan in 1984), Jenifer (*The Midsummer Marriage*), Marguerite, Pamina, Violetta, Nedda and Busoni's Helen of Troy/Duchess of Parma. For Opera North she has sung Manon and in 1987 the title role in Strauss's *Daphne* (the first British stage performance). In 1989 she created Jo Ann in Tippett's *New Year* at Houston, repeating the role at Glyndebourne in 1990. She has recorded Mila (Janáček's *Osud*) and Vreli (*A Village Romeo and Juliet*). An excellent actress, she has a bright, flexible voice and sings with impeccable musicianship.

ELIZABETH FORBES

Fielding, Henry (*b* Glastonbury, 22 April 1707; *d* Lisbon, 8 Oct 1754). English playwright, novelist and librettist. Though remembered principally as the author of the novel *Tom Jones* – itself the basis of a popular *opéra comique* by F.-A. D. Philidor, as well as works by Arnold (a pasticcio, 1769), Edward German (1907) and Stephen Oliver (1976) – he was the most prolific and successful playwright in England in the decade following the triumph of Gay's *Beggar's Opera* in 1728. Forced out of business by the Licensing Act of 1737, he turned to fiction and the law. He wrote serious social comedies, irregular topical burlesques and a series of lightweight ballad farces starring Kitty Clive. These works comprise *The Lottery* and *The Mock Doctor* (1732), *Deborah* (1733; lost – probably a jibe at Handel's oratorio), *The Intriguing Chambermaid* (1734), *An Old Man Taught Wisdom* (1735), *Eurydice* (1737) and *Miss Lucy in Town* (1742; possibly a collaboration with Garrick). Cracks at 'Signor Opera' (Senesino) and 'Fairbelly' (Farinelli) are frequent, but two of his works are systematic satires on Italian opera. *Eurydice* is a lively travesty of the form, requiring two star singers (Michael Stoppalaer as Orpheus, Clive as Eurydice). The piece anticipates the tone of Offenbach: Eurydice does not wish to leave the delightful social whirl in Hell and engineers her return. Unfortunately, the music is lost. In *Miss Lucy* the opera director Lord Middlesex is personified as Lord Bawble, and (according to Horace Walpole) Clive mimicked his mistress La Muscovita, while John Beard took off Amorevoli. Fielding was a brilliantly effective satirical critic of opera, both in musical farce and in his journalism (e.g. *The True Patriot*, 31 December 1745).

The Author's Farce (ballad op), 1730; *The Mock Doctor* (ballad op, after Molière), Seedo, 1732; *The Lottery* (ballad farce), 1732; *Deborah* (ballad farce), 1733; *Don Quixote in England* (ballad op), 1734; *The Welsh Opera* (ballad op), 1734; *The Intriguing Chambermaid* (ballad op), 1734; *An Old Man Taught Wisdom,* or *The Virgin Unmask'd* (ballad farce), 1735; *The Miser* (comedy, after Molière), Arne, 1735; *Eurydice* (ballad farce), 1737; *Miss Lucy in Town* (ballad farce), Arne, 1742

*

E. V. Roberts: 'Eighteenth-Century Ballad Opera: the Contribution of Henry Fielding', *Drama Survey*, i (1961–2), 77–85
——: 'Mr. Seedo's London Career and his Work with Henry Fielding', *Philological Quarterly*, xlv (1966), 179–90
L. J. Morrissey: 'Henry Fielding and the Ballad Opera', *Eighteenth-Century Studies*, iv (1970–71), 386–402
E. V. Roberts: 'The Songs and Tunes in Henry Fielding's Ballad Operas', *Essays on the Eighteenth-Century English Stage*, ed. K. Richards and P. Thomson (London, 1972), 29–49
R. D. Hume: *Henry Fielding and the London Theatre, 1728–1737* (Oxford, 1988)
M. C. Battestin and R. Battestin: *Henry Fielding: a Life* (London, 1989)
ROBERT D. HUME

Fierabras. Opera by Franz Schubert; *see* FIERRABRAS.

Fiera di Venezia, La ('The Fair of Venice'). *Commedia per musica* in three acts by ANTONIO SALIERI to a libretto by GIOVANNI GASTONE BOCCHERINI; Vienna, Burgtheater, 29 January 1772.

The action takes place in Venice during the Ascension Fair, and reaches a climax, in the finale of Act 2, during a masked ball. As is common in 18th-century *opera buffa*, the characters represent three levels of society: Duke Ostrogotto (tenor) and his fiancée Calloandra (soprano) represent the nobility; miserly Grifagno (bass), his daughter Falsirena (soprano) and Belfusto (tenor), who is enamoured of Falsirena, represent the bourgeoisie; and the shopkeeper Cristallina (soprano) and her suitor, the innkeeper Rasoio (tenor), represent the urban working class. The breakdown of the normal code of conduct during the festivities allows these characters to mingle, with amusing results.

Falsirena is at the centre of the action, taking advantage of carnival masks and other disguises to pass herself off as an *opera seria* singer, the wife of a French merchant and a German baroness. Among the musical high points of Salieri's score is Calloandra's bravura aria 'Vi sono sposa e amante', with its elaborate concertante parts for solo flute and oboe. Salieri's four-movement overture anticipates the drama, and is, at the same time, linked directly to it. The bustling first movement, with its attractive three-bar phrases, modulates to the dominant and then ends on an open cadence (the dominant of the dominant). The same music returns as the fourth movement, now remaining in the tonic and cadencing there; but instead of ending the music continues with the opera's first vocal number, 'Chi compra? Chi spende?', sung by a chorus of merchants. The overture's second movement is a graceful minuet that reappears in the ballroom scene in Act 2.

Within a few years of its première *La fiera di Venezia* had become popular throughout northern Europe, with performances in Mannheim, Bonn, Warsaw and Dresden before 1775; on the other hand, there were few performances in Italy. By 1785 its popularity had faded among audiences that were growing used to the musical and dramatic richness of works such as Mozart's *Entführung*, Paisiello's *Barbiere di Siviglia* and Salieri's own *Scuola de' gelosi*. When *La fiera di Venezia* was performed in Salzburg in 1785 Leopold Mozart described it as 'full of worn-out commonplace ideas, old-fashioned, its harmony unnatural and empty; only the finales are still tolerable; the subject of the work, as usual, is stupid Italian childishness, past all human understanding'. But Mozart may have had a different opinion. He used a melody from Salieri's ballroom scene as the basis for a set of piano variations (K173c); and the ballroom scene in *Don Giovanni* has musical and dramaturgical echoes of Salieri's masked ball, in which the libretto for the first production calls for a band of musicians on stage.

JOHN A. RICE

Fierrabras [*Fierrabras*]. *Heroisch-romantische Oper* in three acts by FRANZ SCHUBERT to a libretto by Josef Kupelwieser after J. G. G. Büsching and F. H. von der Hagen's story in *Buch der Liebe* (1809) and Friedrich de la Motte Fouqué's *Eginhard und Emma* (1811); Karlsruhe, Grossherzögliches Hoftheater, 9 February 1897 (text revised by O. Neitzel, music revised by FELIX MOTTL).

King Karl [Charlemagne]	bass
Emma *his daughter*	soprano
Eginhard *a young knight*	tenor
Roland *a noble knight*	baritone
Ogier *a noble knight*	tenor
Olivier	
Gui von Burgund	tenors,
Richard von Normandie	basses
Gerard von Mondidier	
Boland *Moorish prince*	bass
Fierrabras *his son*	tenor
Florinda *his daughter*	soprano
Maragond *her companion*	mezzo-soprano
Brutamonte *Moorish army commander*	bass
Moorish captain	spoken

Olivier, Gui von Burgund, Richard von Normandie, Gerard von Mondidier } *noble knights*

Frankish and Moorish knights and soldiers, young women, common people

Setting Charlemagne's castle, the Frankish-Moorish border and Boland's castle, 8th–9th centuries

In 1822, in answer to a request from the Kärntnertortheater management for a German opera for the 1822–3 season, Schubert submitted his recently finished *Alfonso und Estrella*. When this was rejected he turned to the idea of *Fierrabras*. The librettist, brother of his friend Leopold Kupelwieser, was an inexperienced author but as secretary to the theatre he was aware of the requirements of good plays and well placed to write a serious opera that would satisfy the censors. Schubert completed the first two acts in 12 days during May 1823; illness then forced him to put the opera aside and he did not finish the score until early October. Although *Fierrabras* had been advertised it was never performed, and Schubert received no fee. The supplanting of many German singers by Italians, the resignation of Kupelwieser in October 1823 and the failure that month of Weber's *Euryanthe* (also a 'Ritter-romantisch' opera) probably sealed its fate.

After the stage première in 1897, little was heard of *Fierrabras* until recent years, when the opera has had several performances, including a festival production in 1988 at the Theater an der Wien, Vienna, conducted by Claudio Abbado, and later revived at the Staatsoper and recorded.

ACT 1.i *Charlemagne's castle* After a spinning chorus and a duet for Eginhard and Emma, Charlemagne and his victorious army enter to a march and chorus. There follows an extended, grand operatic *scena*, with sections of fine dramatic declamation, first

as Charlemagne, with noble expression, frees the prisoners (at the request of the chivalrous Roland) and then in Roland's vivid description of Fierrabras's valour, 'Am Rand der Ebne', notable for its striking modulations and colourful orchestration. Fierrabras tells Roland, in a short melodrama, that he has recognized in Emma his long-lost love. The two men are left alone when the rest leave to a lengthy repeat of the victory march and chorus. Roland declares his love for Florinda, Fierrabras's sister. United by their secret loves, they swear friendship in a vigorous and concise duet.

1.ii *The castle garden, under Emma's balcony* As darkness falls, Eginhard serenades Emma ('Der Abend sinkt'), describing his fear of losing her; she takes the melody up, now transformed into the major and subtly varied, as she dreams of his victorious return as a hero worthy, in her father's sight, of her hand. She draws him into her rooms. Fierrabras appears; the torment of his love is mirrored in the tonal ambiguity of the introduction to his recitative. The final notes of a motif, heard on his first appearance, dominate his compelling, vocally demanding aria, 'In tiefbewegter Brust'. He realizes the hopelessness of his own love, and when it seems that Emma's father may discover Eginhard's presence he helps Eginhard to escape; but he then finds himself accused of Emma's seduction and is condemned to the dungeon, a drama depicted in a series of ensembles, ending with a quartet and chorus.

ACT 2.i *The Frankish-Moorish borders* The Frankish knights bid their country farewell in an aubade. Eginhard, brooding over his role in Fierrabras's imprisonment, is left behind, and is seized and carried off by a band of Moorish soldiers – though not before he has sounded a horn call for help. They depart; Roland and his companions swiftly return in response to the horn call, and go off to search for Eginhard to music in the style of a hunting chorus.

2.ii *Boland's castle* In a gentle duet ('Weit über Glanz und Erdenschimmer'), marked by its soaring melody, the interweaving of the voices and accompanying woodwind and rich modulations, Florinda dreams of her beloved Roland while her companion Maragond expresses her anxieties. Boland enters and learns from Brutamonte of the approaching emissary. Eginhard, brought in, tells of Fierrabras's defeat, release and conversion to Christianity, and his reimprisonment. A quintet, somewhat Mozartian in manner, ensues, its tone set by Boland's furious opening, 'Verderben denn und Fluch'; more tender expressions of hope come from the sopranos, with cello and viola obbligato. The Frankish delegation arrives, accompanied by Moors praying for peace. Boland unarms the Franks by trickery and swears vengeance; Florinda, as yet unnoticed by Roland, recognizes her beloved. The Romantic horror of the scene, as the knights are sent off to prison to await their deaths, is depicted in the tonal ambiguity and sinister intervals of the opening of the ensuing trio (with double male-voice chorus). Florinda, left alone, gives vent to her fury and her determination to rescue Roland or die with him; her fiery and taxing declamatory aria ('Die Brust, gebeugt von Sorgen') in B minor, a key often associated in Schubert with passion and suffering, modulates rapidly and often violently.

2.iii *A prison tower in the castle* The imprisoned knights sing a patriotic hymn, unaccompanied (and already heard orchestrally in the overture), brief but wide-ranging in its dynamics and tonalities. After Eginhard has explained (in dialogue) his treacherous treatment of Fierrabras, they are disturbed by sounds of an affray. In a melodrama, Florinda fights her way into the dark prison seeking Roland; as she collapses he recognizes her, answering her cry 'Mein Roland!' (in A minor) with an ecstatic 'Florinda!' (in A major). But the Moorish soldiers approach, intent on revenge for her defection. In a melodrama (again with striking modulations) the knights arm themselves with weapons Florinda has found and prepare to defend themselves, serving as cover for Roland and Eginhard's escape to seek help. In the finale, after farewells, Florinda describes his escape bid and recapture, in a colourful melodrama – a brilliant piece of orchestral writing incorporating symphonic development of material from the opening of the ensemble.

ACT 3.i *Charlemagne's castle* Emma's companions attempt to cheer her as she awaits news of the emissary. But the king is incensed when, in dialogue, she admits both her love for Eginhard and their betrayal of Fierrabras: in an effective *scena* he disowns her and then orders Fierrabras's release. His conciliation with the Moor is interrupted by the entry of Eginhard, distraught: he has succeeded in escaping and seeks help for the imprisoned knights (the urgency of his quest is conveyed in the driving rhythms and the dissonances of the ensuing quartet). Charlemagne agrees and places Eginhard in charge, with Fierrabras to help him. In a trio, Fierrabras, who has admitted his love but renounced his suit, looks forward to fulfilment in victory while the lovers sing of union in heaven.

3.ii *The prison tower of Boland's castle and the courtyard below* The knights, hoping that Eginhard will bring about their release, try to raise Florinda's spirits. She responds in a gentle aria with chorus in which major and minor subtly alternate. As the Moors prepare to execute Roland, in full view of the tower, Florinda leads the knights' surrender (in a melodrama to the music of a funeral march). It is now Florinda's turn to confess her secret love to her father and to beg for clemency. She too is rejected: her anguish is depicted in her tortuous melodic line ('Erbarmen fleht zu deinen Füssen die Tochter'), his obduracy in simple rhythmic patterns, latterly rising steadily in pitch. But then (in spoken dialogue) Brutamonte announces the rout of Boland's army and the imminent arrival of Charlemagne and his victorious force. An offstage trumpet heralds his coming, and the Moors are overpowered (in a mere ten bars' music). The opening of Charlemagne's triumphant march is heard again. As peace is restored and universal conciliation achieved, the lovers' unions are blessed by both fathers and Fierrabras wins his place of honour under Charlemagne's standard.

*　　*　　*

In designing *Fierrabras* to represent German grand opera at a time of almost overwhelming enthusiasm in Vienna for Rossini, Schubert largely dispensed with recitative after Act 1. Much of the dialogue, which conveys the plot, is spoken, but for moments of particular dramatic tension Schubert turned to melodrama, often with vivid and colourful orchestral writing and highly dramatic modulations. He called for a large orchestra and some of the longer passages of melodrama are of almost symphonic proportions. Also in keeping with the new concept of Romantic opera the role of the chorus, often subdivided, is varied and dramatically important. Schubert's lyrical, declamatory vocal lines, often given

rich orchestral settings, are striking. The music for the young Frankish lovers, Eginhard and Emma, contrasts with the grander declamation for the other pair of lovers, the Moorish Florinda and Frankish Roland, and of Fierrabras, whose love for Emma is unrequited. His role is disappointing: he does not appear at all in Act 2, and in Act 3 his role is secondary; yet he is at the centre of most of the action or its motivation. Schubert, it seems, attempted to shore up the role by the use of a motif for Fierrabras which permeates much of the music. There are only two true arias in the opera, one each for Fierrabras and Florinda; ensembles, of all kinds, abound. The weaknesses in the plot and the dramatic timing, as well as its length, make this a difficult opera to produce; yet there is much magnificent music in Schubert's score.

For a page of the autograph score of *Fierrabras*, *see* SCHUBERT, FRANZ.

ELIZABETH NORMAN McKAY

Fiery Angel, The [*Ognenniy angel* ('The Flaming Angel')]. Opera in five acts, op.37, by SERGEY PROKOFIEV to his own libretto after the novel (1907) by Valery Bryusov; Venice, Teatro La Fenice, 14 September 1955 (Act 2, abridged, Paris, Opéra, 14 June 1928; concert performance, Paris, Théâtre des Champs-Elysées, 25 November 1954, as *L'ange de feu*).

The full title of Bryusov's erudite novel, which purports to be a translation of a 16th-century manuscript containing a lansquenet's confessions, gives a fair idea both of its content and that of Prokofiev's opera: 'The Fiery Angel; or, a True Story in which is related of the Devil, not once but often appearing in the Image of a Spirit of Light to a Maiden and seducing her to Various and Many Sinful Deeds, of Ungodly Practices of Magic, Alchymy, Astrology, the Cabalistical Sciences and Necromancy, of the Trial of the Said Maiden under the Presidency of His Eminence the Archbishop of Trier, as well as of Encounters and Discourses with the Knight and thrice Doctor Agrippa of Nettesheim, and with Doctor Faustus, composed by an Eyewitness'. As one might expect from a leader of the Russian symbolists, Bryusov's purpose, to quote the penultimate sentence of the novel was 'to cross that sacred edge that divides our world from the dark sphere in which float spirits and demons' so as metaphorically to explore the ambiguities of reality and experience – and, ultimately, of morals. On another level the book is an autobiographical *roman à clef*, motivated by, and describing, a love triangle in which the author was involved at the time of its writing, along with the poet and translator Nina Petrovskaya, and Bryusov's rival for the latter's affections, the great writer Andrey Bely (known, among other things, for his brilliant red hair).

Prokofiev came across Bryusov's novel in America, shortly after finishing *The Love for Three Oranges*. He began sketching a scenario – originally in three acts (11 scenes) that hewed far closer than the final version to the novel's plot – late in 1919. At first composition proceeded slowly owing to the composer's heavy concert schedule, but in March 1922 he retreated to Ettal, in the Bavarian Alps, to devote full time to the opera in a location congruent with its setting. A piano score was completed before the end of the next year. The work is cast in the same declamatory idiom as Prokofiev's earlier opera, *The Gambler*, except that far greater reliance is placed on a conventional network of orchestral leitmotifs. In addition, there are several extended monologues for the main character – the possessed maiden,

*'The Fiery Angel'
(Prokofiev): scene from
the original production at
the Teatro La Fenice,
Venice, 14 September
1955*

Renata – which make an effect comparable with that of a traditional operatic scena, if not an aria. Thus *The Fiery Angel* is not quite so extreme an anti-opera as its predecessor.

Prokofiev revised the work, and orchestrated it with the help of an assistant named Georgy Nikolayevich Gorchakov, pursuant to its acceptance by Bruno Walter for production at the Städtische Oper, Berlin. Delays in the copying of parts prevented performance in the 1927–8 season, and the production was cancelled. When in 1930 the Metropolitan Opera expressed interest in the score, Prokofiev began another revision, for which two additional scenes were planned; but that production too fell through. As Charles Bruck, who conducted the 1954 concert performance, put it, the opera was then 'carefully packed up and consigned to oblivion' in the basement of the Editions Russes de Musique (Koussevitzky's firm) when Prokofiev returned to his Soviet homeland, then the least hospitable venue imaginable for an opera having to do with religious mysticism. That Prokofiev never saw staged the work he considered the magnum opus of his period in emigration was surely his greatest artistic disappointment. (He salvaged some of the music by basing his Third Symphony on the opera's themes, many of which had been originally conceived for various instrumental projects, including a 'white [i.e. diatonic] quartet'; thus the symphony should not be regarded as merely an operatic pastiche.) After the war the score was unearthed by Hans Swarsenski of Boosey & Hawkes, which firm had acquired the Koussevitzky catalogue. Despite periodic revivals following its much publicized Venice première, under Nino Sanzogno, the opera has had difficulty holding the stage. The first Russian production was in the provincial city of Perm in 1987; the Mariinsky Theatre finally staged it in St Petersburg in December 1991, in a joint production with the Royal Opera that opened in London in April 1992. A vocal score with the original Russian text was not available until 1985.

One of the reasons for the opera's continued neglect is its unusual fixation on a single very difficult – and dramatically static – role. Whereas the novel, as a first-person narrative, inevitably centred around Ruprecht (baritone in the opera), the author's surrogate, Prokofiev's libretto overwhelmingly emphasizes Renata (dramatic soprano), the possessed maiden. Her perpetual hysterics dominate every scene but two, making her role one of the longest and (in terms of range and volume) most demanding in opera. The concentration on Renata entailed the sacrifice of a great deal of colourful action (Ruprecht's real-or-imagined attendance at a black mass, his duel with Count Heinrich etc.), resulting in a stagnant quality the composer himself recognized (and which his aborted 1930 revision would have addressed). The two scenes in which Renata does not appear – Ruprecht's visit to Agrippa (*tenor altino*; 2.ii, based on Bryusov's chapter 6) and his encounter with Faust (bass) and Mephistopheles (tenor; 4.ii, based on chapter 11) – are poorly integrated into the libretto and lend the action an episodic quality difficult to overlook in a work of which the literary source is not widely familiar. Finally, Prokofiev's garish music, while often strikingly evocative of Renata's obsessions – e.g. the scene of conjuration (2.i, best known from the scherzo of the Third Symphony), or the last act, in which a whole stageful of nuns are infected with her madness – undeniably overworks the device of ostinato. Though its difficult stage career and its reputation as the composer's most modernistic work have lent *The Fiery Angel* the aura of a *cause célèbre*, familiarity has not always worked to its advantage.   RICHARD TARUSKIN

Fiesque. *Grand opéra* in three acts by EDOUARD LALO to a libretto by Charles Beauquier after FRIEDRICH VON SCHILLER's play *Die Verschwörung des Fiesco zu Genua*; unperformed.

Schiller's early drama is based on the 1547 conspiracy led by Fiesco against the Doria family, doges of Genoa. The librettist, a prominent left-wing politician, may have chosen the subject for its republican message. Lalo composed the opera in 1866–8 and submitted it for a government-sponsored competition. It came third, behind works by Jules Philippot and L. Gustave Canoby. Something of a scandal was created by this judgment, but *Fiesque* was never staged. Lalo eventually dismembered the score and used almost all the music in later works, particularly the Symphony in G minor, the orchestral *Divertissement*, the pantomime *Néron* and the opera *La jacquerie*.

The plot interweaves three conflicts: the Fiesco party, republicans, are entrenched against the ruling Dorias; Léonore (soprano), wife of Fiesque (tenor), is jealous of his involvement with Julie (mezzo-soprano), daughter of Andreas Doria; and Verrina (bass), an old republican fanatic, though a supporter of Fiesque, is deeply distrustful of his ambition. In the final act the Dorias are overthrown; the crowd acclaims Fiesque and Léonore in a triumphal march, but Verrina refuses to allow Fiesque to assume supreme power and throws him into the harbour.

There is much in the score of magnificent quality, especially the ballroom scene in Act 1, the street scene in Act 2, Verrina stirring up the crowd in the same scene, and the trio for Fiesque and the two women in Act 3. The style is predominantly vigorous and foursquare with emphatic rhythms and shows fondness for scherzo rhythms. The vocal writing is assured and effective, and Lalo generated a strong feeling of movement in choral scenes. The vocal score was published by Hartmann in 1872.

HUGH MACDONALD

Fifferi, Lauro. Pseudonym of ANGELO ANELLI.

Figaro [*Figaros Hochzeit*; *Figaro's Wedding*]. Opera by W. A. Mozart; *see* NOZZE DI FIGARO, LE.

Figlia del re, La ('The King's Daughter'). Opera in three acts by ADRIANO LUALDI to his own libretto; Turin, Teatro Regio, 18 March 1922.

Set in ancient India, Lualdi's libretto shows signs of D'Annunzio's influence. Damara (soprano), the daughter of a king who has been slain in battle, has vowed to find her father's body and give him a worthy funeral. To this end, she approaches the victorious enemy leaders Ariuna (tenor) and Svarga (baritone) and brazenly uses her feminine charms. Ariuna, whom she has promised to kill, falls for her instantly and she for him. He helps her to fulfil her duty to her father; but her deep conflict of loyalties is resolved only in death for both of them. Though eclectic and rather uneven, Lualdi's music (composed during 1914–17) has real evocative power, with many modal inflections and touches of exotic colour. Despite the strong postwar reaction against his work owing to the prominent role he had played in Fascist Italy, *La figlia del re* was still being revived in the 1950s.

JOHN C. G. WATERHOUSE

Figliuol prodigo, Il ('The Prodigal Son'). *Melodramma* in four acts by AMILCARE PONCHIELLI to a libretto by Angelo Zanardini after EUGÈNE SCRIBE's libretto *L'enfant prodigue*; Milan, Teatro alla Scala, 26 December 1880.

The action is set in Judaea and Nineveh in biblical times. Azael (tenor), son of Ruben (bass), head of his tribe, kills a panther that has attacked a passing caravan of Assyrians. Two of their number, Amenofi (baritone) and Nefte (mezzo-soprano), given hospitality by Ruben, tempt Azael to go with them to Nineveh. After a struggle with his conscience, he succumbs, much to his father's anger and the distress of Jeftele (soprano), his foster sister and betrothed. In Nineveh he plunges into a life of debauchery, vainly restrained by a remorseful Nefte. Ruben and Jeftele come to Nineveh in search of him. Just as he is about to be initiated into the mysteries of Ilia, Jeftele is discovered in the temple and arrested for sacrilege. Amenofi offers to spare her life if she will yield to his embraces. She refuses. Azael, now repentant, denounces himself as the desecrator, whereupon Jeftele is released and he himself is condemned to death by drowning. Rescued from the Tigris by an unknown hand (possibly Nefte's) he returns home destitute and in rags to be welcomed and forgiven by Ruben and Jeftele.

In this simplified reworking of Scribe's libretto, originally set by Auber, Ponchielli first enters the world of Massenet's *Le roi de Lahore* and Goldmark's *Die Königin von Saba*. Throughout, the concentration is on local colour rather than character. The ambience of Ruben's farm is evoked by austere textures (sometimes two-part only), even rhythms and plain homophonic choruses, aided in Act 4 by a reversion to the pastoral formulae of the mid-century. Common to Acts 1 and 4 is a motif with pentatonic inflexions and a drone bass that is associated with the Passover. By contrast the Nineveh scenes employ a more exotic idiom, by turns languorous and lively. The dances of the Almee in Act 2 develop in a crescendo which neatly parallels the mounting tension of a game of dice in which Azael realizes that he is being cheated by Amenofi. The 'ballabili' of the 'sacred orgy' in Act 3 are no more than an interlude; and Ponchielli authorized their substitution by a chorus printed in an appendix. Inevitably the architectural pinnacle of the score is formed by the grand concertato of Act 3, during which Azael is condemned to death. Cumbersome and slow-moving on stage, *Il figliuol prodigo* might bear revival as an oratorio.

JULIAN BUDDEN

Figner, Medea. *See* MEI-FIGNER, MEDEA.

Figner, Nikolay Nikolayevich (*b* Nikiforovka, nr Kazan', 9/21 Feb 1857; *d* Kiev, 13 Dec 1918). Russian lyric-dramatic tenor. He studied in St Petersburg and Naples, where he made his début in Gounod's *Philémon et Baucis* (1882, Teatro Sannazaro). After further appearances in Italy he sang in Latin America in 1884 and 1886. In April 1887 he sang Raoul (*Les Huguenots*) at the Imperial Opera, St Petersburg. After his Covent Garden début (26 May) as the Duke in *Rigoletto*, he returned to the Imperial Opera, where he became an uncontested star, appearing regularly with his second wife, Medea Mei-Figner, until their divorce in 1904. He took part in the premières of Tchaikovsky's *The Queen of Spades* (1890) and *Iolanta* (1892), and Nápravník's *Dubrovsky* (1895) and *Francesca da Rimini* (1902). From 1910 to 1915 he directed and sang at the Narodnïy Dom opera house. His repertory included Tchaikovsky's Lensky and Andrey Morozov (*Oprichnik*), the Prince in Dargomïzhsky's *Rusalka*,

Nero (Rubinstein), Kuratov in Nápravník's *Nizhniy-Novgoroders*, Grigory (*Boris Godunov*), Don José, Faust, Werther, Arturo (*I puritani*), Fernand (*La favorite*), Enzo (*La Gioconda*), Radames, Vasco da Gama (*L'Africaine*), Lohengrin, Canio and Turiddu. Figner's voice, despite being dry and rather colourless, was extremely expressive; he took enormous pains with diction, acting and costuming, cutting a figure of romantic elegance which held audiences enthralled.

For illustration *see* QUEEN OF SPADES, THE.

GV (R. Celletti; R. Vegeto)

E. Stark: *Peterburgskaya opera i eyo mastera, 1890–1910* (Leningrad, 1940)

A. Favia-Artsay: 'The Fabulous Figners', *Hobbies* (Dec 1954), 22–35

S. Yu. Levik: *Zapiski opernogo pevtsa* [Notes of an Opera Singer] (Moscow, 1955, 2/1962)

M. O. Yankovsky, ed.: *N. N. Figner: vospominaniya, pis'ma, materialii* [Recollections, Letters, Material] (Leningrad, 1968)

M. O. Yankovsky and B. Semeonoff: 'Nikolai N. Figner', *Record Collector*, xxxv (1990), 3–10 [with discography by J. Dennis]

HAROLD BARNES

Filippeschi, Mario (*b* Pisa, 7 June 1907; *d* Florence, 25 Dec 1979). Italian tenor. He began his career as a clarinettist, but after vocal studies he won a prize in a Viennese competition in 1936. His début followed at Colorno the next year, and he obtained engagements in Italy and the Netherlands before the war intervened. After his appearance at La Scala in 1946 he was a mainstay of the major Italian circuit, and also sang at leading theatres in France, Spain and South America. His London début was with a touring company at the Theatre Royal, Drury Lane, in 1958, singing Manrico and Arnold (*Guillaume Tell*). A robust spinto tenor, he was usually eager to exhibit his power above the staff. His records include *Norma* under Serafin with Callas and the title role in *Don Carlos* under Santini with Gobbi and Christoff (both 1954). NOËL GOODWIN

Filleborn, Daniel (*b* Warsaw, 7 Nov 1841; *d* Marcelin, 3 June 1904). Polish tenor. He studied with Quattrini in Warsaw, where he made his début on 3 July 1862 at the Wielki Theatre in Flotow's *Alessandro Stradella*, and in 1863 continued his studies with Francesco Lamperti in Milan. From 1865 he sang all the leading roles in Moniuszko's operas: he was considered one of the finest interpreters of Jontek in *Halka*. His voice was lyrical and mellifluous, but he overstrained it when he transferred to baritone parts. Ill-health forced him to retire, after a final appearance as Don Ottavio on 18 July 1882. IRENA PONIATOWSKA

Fille de Madame Angot, La ['The Daughter of Madame Angot']. *Opéra comique* in three acts by CHARLES LECOCQ to a libretto by CLAIRVILLE, Paul Siraudin and Victor Koning; Brussels, Théâtre des Fantaisies-Parisiennes, 4 December 1872.

La fille de Madame Angot has a particularly strong libretto which features politics and anti-government plots in its first two acts before concentrating on unravelling the love lives of its robustly drawn principal characters in the third. The market-girl Clairette (soprano) is fascinated by the rebel poet Ange-Pitou (tenor) and, rather than wed the kindly wig-maker Pomponnet (tenor), she gets herself imprisoned for singing one of Pitou's libellous songs. She is released by the powerful Mlle Lange (soprano), the mistress of a member of the ruling Directoire, who is actually part of a conspiracy against those in power. Although Lange turns out to be an old friend she too takes a fancy to Pitou and things turn rough, with the two women coming to verbal blows in public before Clairette gives in and returns to Pomponnet.

This libretto inspired Lecocq to write his most celebrated work, from which the Act 3 Quarrelling Duet between the two women ('Ah! C'est donc toi, Madam' Barras'), and the conspirators' chorus and Lange's whirling waltz ('Tournez, tournez') which end the second act, are among the outstanding items, along with a series of solos which gives each of the main characters a chance to shine. Pitou's lilting dilemma, 'Certainement, j'aimais Clairette', Lange's vigorous 'Les soldats d'Augereau', Pomponnet's 'Elle est tellement innocente', Clairette's 'Chanson politique' and the marvellously raucous 'Marchande de marée', delivered by one of the market-women, all go to make a score of exceptional quality.

An enormous success on its Brussels and subsequent Paris productions, *La fille de Madame Angot* has remained one of the most popular of all French *opérettes* of the post-1870 era. It has been regularly revived, and was even admitted to the Opéra-Comique in a celebrated production in 1918. The piece caused a sensation in Britain where, along with Planquette's *Les cloches de Corneville*, it dominated the musical theatre scene for a number of years, appearing in London in a variety of English versions and touring incessantly. Like *Les cloches de Corneville*, it has faded from the current repertory in Britain and in the many other countries in which it was successfully produced in the 19th century. At the first performance Clairette was sung by Pauline Luigini, Mlle Lange by Marie Desclauzas, Ange-Pitou by Mario Widmer and Pomponnet by Alfred Jolly.

KURT GÄNZL

Fille du régiment, La [*La figlia del reggimento*] ('The Daughter of the Regiment'). *Opéra comique* in two acts by GAETANO DONIZETTI to a libretto by JULES-HENRI VERNOY DE SAINT-GEORGES and JEAN-FRANÇOIS-ALFRED BAYARD, later revised to an Italian translation by Calisto Bassi; Opéra-Comique (Salle de la Bourse), 11 February 1840 (revised version, Milan, Teatro alla Scala, 3 October 1840).

Marie (Maria) *a vivandière*	soprano
Tonio *a young Tyrolean*	tenor
La Marquise (La Marchesa) de Berkenfeld [The Marchioness]	mezzo-soprano
Sulpice Pingot (Sulpizio) *a sergeant of the 21st regiment*	bass
Hortensius (Ortensio) *major-domo of the Marchioness*	bass
A Corporal	bass
A Notary	spoken
La Duchesse (La Duchessa) de Crackentorp [The Duchess]	spoken
A Valet	spoken

French soldiers, Tyrolean peasants, wedding guests, servants

Setting The Tyrolean countryside and the chateau of the Marchioness, not long after the battle of Marengo, 1800

The cast of the première consisted of Juliette Bourgeois (who sang in Italy as Borghese, Marie), Marie-Julie Boulanger (the Marchioness), Luigi Henry (Sulpice) and Mécène Marié de L'Isle (Tonio). The work soon established itself at the Opéra-Comique, where it had been given more than 1000 times by 1914. Donizetti prepared an Italian *opera buffa* version, cutting some numbers and adding others, and substituting recitatives for the French spoken dialogue. This version was first performed at La Scala in 1840, with Luigia Abbadia (Maria), Lorenzo Salvi (Tonio) and Raffaele Scalese (Sulpizio). During the 19th century the Italian version proved more popular than the French in England and the USA (except in New Orleans) and many famous singers, including Henriette Sontag, Jenny Lind and

Juliette Bourgeois as Marie, the role she created in the original production of Donizetti's 'La fille du régiment' at the Opéra-Comique, Paris, 11 February 1840

Adelina Patti made their mark as the vivandière. At Covent Garden the work disappeared about 1875, but it was resuscitated happily more than 80 years later with Joan Sutherland as Marie. In Italy during the 1920s Toti Dal Monte was an admired Maria.

La fille first appeared at the Metropolitan, in its original French form, on 6 January 1902 with Sembrich and Charles Gilibert (Sulpice). Later revivals starred Frieda Hempel with Scotti in 1918 and Lily Pons with Baccaloni in 1940, and on 17 February 1972 it returned with Sutherland, Pavarotti and Corena. The Italian version *La figlia del reggimento* served at Hammerstein's Manhattan Opera as a showcase for Tetrazzini, McCormack and Gilibert, introduced on 22 November 1910. In the late 20th century, however, and not just in

the USA, *La fille* began to enjoy increased popularity and can surely be said to have re-entered the repertory after being on its fringes for nearly a century.

ACT 1 *A field in the Tyrolean Alps* The opera is preceded by a sparkling overture which makes prominent use of the melody of the song of the 21st regiment of the French Army ('Chacun le sait'/'Ciascun lo dice'). Women kneel before a wayside shrine, praying for protection from the enemy, whose cannon sound in the distance. The Marchioness is terrified, but her overseer Hortensius tries to calm her. A peasant, Tonio, announces that the French troops have departed, news that is greeted with great relief. The Marchioness comments on the lack of respect for rank and position of the unruly French (*couplets*, 'Pour une femme de mon nom'; not in the Italian version). She retires to wait for Hortensius, whose intent – to find out if they may safely continue their journey – is interrupted by the formidable figure of Sergeant Sulpice of the 21st regiment. Sulpice assures the trembling villagers that his troops have come to restore peace and order. Marie, the pride and joy of the regiment, arrives and is affectionately greeted by Sulpice (duo, 'Au bruit de la guerre'/'Apparvi alla luce'); in this duet the military flavour of the score is established, with brilliant orchestration and a vocal line that imitates bugle calls and drumrolls ('rataplan'). Sulpice reminds her how she was found as an infant on the battlefield and raised by the regiment as their 'daughter'. When he remarks on her recent curious behaviour she explains that she was picking flowers near a precipice when she slipped and fell into the stalwart arms of Tonio, who has lost his heart to her. Sulpice reminds her that she may marry only a member of the regiment.

Troops enter with Tonio as their prisoner, having taken him for a spy. When Marie tells them that Tonio saved her life, they release him, and he explains that he approached the troops only to see the girl he loves. The soldiers decide to toast their daughter's saviour rather than shoot him, and the festivities include Marie's rendition of the 21st's regimental song (*couplets*, 'Chacun le sait'); this infectious tune with its dance-rhythm refrain is, perhaps surprisingly, a self-borrowing from one of Noah's utterances from *Il diluvio universale* (1830). A drum signals a formation, and the soldiers go off, leaving Tonio as Marie's 'prisoner'. He confesses that he loves her; her response, in a solo passage during their charming duo ('De cet aveu si tendre'/'A voti così ardente'), after one of Donizetti's characteristic modulations up a semitone, convinces us of her tender heart. He explains that she has come to occupy his every thought, and she admits that she is not impervious to his presence. Sulpice returns to see Tonio kissing Marie, and reminds her of her promise to marry only within the ranks of the 21st. Tonio departs, determined to win from her other 'fathers' the permission that Sulpice gruffly refuses to grant. Marie, rebellious at his opposition, threatens to join another regiment; Sulpice charges her with ingratitude.

The Marchioness asks permission to return home to her chateau of Berkenfeld. Hearing that name, Sulpice inquires if she had known a certain 'Robert', by whom, it seems, her sister had a child – who turns out to be none other than Marie. The Marchioness is determined to rescue the girl from her unfortunate environment, especially after hearing her command of soldierly oaths. Marie insists on bidding farewell to her comrades before she goes off with her aunt. The soldiers reassemble (chorus, 'Rataplan, rataplan, rataplan!'); with them is Tonio, now in uniform, having joined in order to marry Marie (aria, 'Ah, mes amis, quel jour de fête'/'Amici miei, che allegro giorno'). When the troops consent to give their daughter to Tonio, his joy is unbounded (air, 'Pour mon âme'/'Qual destino, qual favor': the passage is famous for its nine *c″*s). Marie returns to say goodbye (*couplets*, 'Il faut partir'/'Convien partir') and is even more moved when she understands the significance of Tonio's enlistment. Her air, with its english horn obbligato and affecting F minor melody, modulates to the major for the refrain, creating a memorable intensification of feeling. The drums roll, the soldiers in formation salute Marie as, in tears, she departs with her aunt. Marie's air is in effect the slow movement of the finale, which ends in a stretta with a fugato-style interlude.

ACT 2 *A salon in the chateau of Berkenfeld* Several months have elapsed. The Marchioness and the Duchess of Crackentorp discuss the terms of a wedding contract between Marie and the Duchess's son, the Duke Scipion, to be signed that evening. Sulpice appears; wounded three months previously, he has been recuperating at the chateau. The Marchioness tells him of her intentions for Marie, who arrives for a singing lesson (trio, 'Le jour naissait dans la bocage'/'Sorgeva il dì del bosco'); Sulpice induces her to sing the regimental ditty, to the Marchioness's irritation, rather than her 'period' *romance* (adapted from a salon song by Garat). This lesson scene is a moment of high comedy, a musical joke in excellent taste, and one that permits the soprano to indulge herself, legitimately, in a lather of *fioritura*. Alone with him, Marie confesses to Sulpice that she dreads this marriage as she remembers Tonio fondly; as he leaves he reminds her of her duty.

Marie thinks sadly of the meaninglessness of position and money without warm human affection (air, 'Par le rang et par l'opulence'/'Le ricchezze ed il grado fastoso'). She hears a march and is filled with patriotic fervour (cabaletta, 'Salut à la France'/'Salvezza alla Francia'; this at one time served as an unofficial patriotic anthem, and its place in Donizetti's first opera written for a French-language theatre suggests that it is also a personal statement). Her friends of the 21st crowd into the room; among them is Tonio, now an officer. When Hortensius protests at their intrusion, the soldiers carry him off. Marie, Tonio and Sulpice celebrate their reunion (trio, 'Tous les trois réunis'/'Stretti insiem tutti tre'). Tonio tells them that his uncle, the mayor of Laëstrichk, has revealed a secret that assures everyone's happiness and tells the Marchioness that he loves Marie more than life itself; his *romance* ('Pour me rapprocher de Marie'; not in the Italian version), in modified *couplets*, injects once more a needed touch of sincerity into the artificialities of the plot. She remains adamant in her plan for Marie's aristocratic marriage, so Tonio reveals that the Marchioness had no sister and Marie cannot be her niece; she therefore is free to marry whom she pleases. The Marchioness, alone with Sulpice, reveals that in fact she is Marie's mother.

The guests start to arrive. The Marchioness identifies herself to Marie as her mother, and the girl offers to sign the contract. But now Tonio and the regiment burst in, declaring that Marie was a vivandière and the daughter of this regiment; the guests recoil in horror. Marie tells the assemblage that she can never repay her debt to the loyal soldiers; the Marchioness is so moved at her goodness of heart that she impulsively gives her permission to marry Tonio. Everyone bursts into a reprise of 'Salut à la France'.

* * *

The score of *La fille du régiment* is notable for its deft mixture of military tunes, moments of pathos and straightforward sentiment. The plot may be banal, but it is carried out with a good taste everywhere matched by Donizetti's aristocratic elegance of melody and structure; this charming comedy of manners should not be treated as though it were a vulgar farce. Marie's F minor-F major air in the finale to Act 1 stands as one of Donizetti's greatest accomplishments in communicating genuine, deeply felt emotion. Tonio's air to the Marchioness, 'Pour me rapprocher de Marie', shows an equal refinement of sentiment and distinction of melody. The ease and naturalness of Donizetti's setting of the French text is admirable. The exuberance of the regimental song 'Chacun le sait', as surely as the ennui of the singing lesson in Act 2, provide justifiable occasions for coloratura expansiveness. Everywhere in *La fille* is Donizetti's grateful writing for the voice in evidence. If there is one part of the score that shows some diminishing of effect, it is the finale to Act 2, a shortcoming often remedied by the insertion of an aria. For that purpose, Hempel favoured the Adam variations on Mozart, 'Ah! vous dirai-je, maman', and Tetrazzini the waltz from Gounod's *Mireille*; in the context of World War II, however, Lily Pons opted for the *Marseillaise* and carried a flag with the cross of Lorraine. WILLIAM ASHBROOK

Fille du tambour-major, La ('The Drum-Major's Daughter'). *Opéra comique* in three acts and four scenes by JACQUES OFFENBACH to a libretto by Alfred Duru and HENRI CHARLES CHIVOT; Paris, Folies-Dramatiques, 13 December 1879.

Evoking the spirit of Donizetti's *La fille du régiment*, the work is in the more escapist Third Republic operetta style and was the last success Offenbach enjoyed in his lifetime. It starred Juliette Simon-Girard as Stella, and its principal musical numbers include her patriotic song 'Petit français, brave français'. The action takes place in Lombardy in 1806. Lieutenant Robert (baritone) is in charge of a company of French soldiers who have crossed the Alps and joined Napoleon's Italian army against the Austrians. Among his company are Drum-Major Monthabor (baritone), the drummer boy Griolet (tenor) and the regimental vivandière Claudine (soprano). They surround a convent, and all the women flee except for Stella (soprano), daughter of the Duke and Duchess Della Volta. It is love at first sight between her and Robert, but the Duke Della Volta (tenor) arrives to separate them. For financial reasons he intends her to marry the ridiculous Marchese Bambini (baritone). In Act 2 Robert and his company chance to be billeted at the palace of the Duke Della Volta, where Drum-Major Monthabor recognises the Duchess Della Volta (mezzo-soprano) as his ex-wife. Stella, moreover, is really his daughter and, to be with Robert, she enrols in her father's company. When Austrian troops arrive, the company fight them off and, with Stella dressed as a vivandière, they take to the road. Only after various Act 3 complications, culminating in the victorious entry of Napoleon's army into Milan, is Stella finally allowed to marry Robert. ANDREW LAMB

Film. Opera has been presented in film form throughout the 20th century. The present article considers the

1. *Still from Georges Méliès's film 'La damnation du Docteur Faust' (1904) with the director in the role of Méphistophélès (centre)*

history of the filming of opera for presentation primarily in the cinema. (For a discussion of filming techniques, *see* FILMING, VIDEOTAPING; *see also* TELEVISION and VIDEO.)

1. The 'silent' era. 2. The 'sound' era: (i) Before 1970 (ii) Since 1970.

1. THE 'SILENT' ERA. The filming of opera began early in the 20th century and quickly flourished. In 1903 Georges Méliès, the first true *cinéaste*, adapted Berlioz's *Faust* for Pathé (under the title *Faust aux enfers*); its success led to a 'sequel' the following year, a film of Gounod's opera (in 20 scenes, with a running time of 13 minutes) called *La damnation du Docteur Faust*, in which Méliès also took the part of Méphistophélès (fig.1). Among Méliès's many other films of that year was an adaptation of Rossini's *Il barbiere di Siviglia*. Between 1905 and 1910 opera films proliferated. In 1908 a large number of scenes were filmed as illustration for gramophone records: their patrons probably enjoyed better sound reproduction (assuming the good quality and condition of the records and needles used in the cinema) than that of early sound films. According to the German periodical *Kinematograph*, in May of that year Pathé offered scenes from *Pagliacci*, *Otello*, *Die Meistersinger*, *La traviata*, *Lohengrin*, *Manon Lescaut*, *Die Dollarprinzessin* and *Ein Walzertraum*; the same issue also listed *Rigoletto*, *The Bartered Bride*, *Martha*, *Don Giovanni*, *Faust* and *Lucia di Lammermoor*.

Many adaptations went back to the opera's source in a book or play for their material, but these too were often accompanied by music from the score, played by musicians in the cinema: for example, a French film of 1909 (from Pathé) of *Rigoletto* was based on the Hugo original but used Verdi's music. In 1910 a film was made of a Paris Opéra bass singing an aria from *Faust*: a gramophone recording played while the singer performed on the screen. The same year saw films of *Manon* and *Il trovatore* as well as two early versions of

what was to become probably the most frequently filmed of all operas, *Carmen*, the basis of at least 30 films between 1907 and 1990. In 1913 Pathé announced another film of the opera; in 1915 Cecil B. DeMille produced a celebrated *Carmen* with Geraldine Farrar – it was parodied by Chaplin a year later but was also the inspiration for later directors, beginning with Ernst Lubitsch. One of his first feature films was a treatment of *Carmen* based on Mérimée for the German UFA company in 1918 (a peak year in the production of filmed opera), starring Pola Negri and entitled *Gypsy Love* in the USA.

In 1911 there had been a large-scale *Aida*, directed by Oscar Apfel, and a Russian film of *A Life for the Tsar*; between 1912 and 1915 Italian films inspired by *Parsifal* and *Figaro*, and an American version of Prévost's novel *Manon Lescaut* starring the singers Lina Cavalieri and Lucien Muratore; the story of Auber's *La muette de Portici* was the basis of a Universal film of 1916 starring the ballerina Anna Pavlova; and Samuel Goldwyn produced a film of *Thaïs* (1917) with Mary Garden. Mozart was represented in this decade by *Die Zauberflöte* (1911) and a *Figaro* (1919) directed by Max Mack offering, in place of the music, a series of 'lovely, painterly images, a delicate rococo dream'. Among other filmings of Verdi was a *Rigoletto*, using Caruso records. Wagner films included a *Tannhäuser* (1913), *Lohengrin* (1915) and *Der fliegende Holländer* (1918). Versions of Puccini subjects included an Italian *Bohème* (1917, according to some sources based on both the opera and Murger's novel, according to others on the novel alone). The film was intended to be accompanied by Puccini's music, but the composer denied his permission. There was also a German *Butterfly* (starring Lil Dagover) and a *Tosca* in 1918. Offenbach's *Les contes d'Hoffmann* was, in one form or another, to become a frequent film subject: three early treatments date from 1911, 1914 and 1916. There was also a Rossini *Barbiere* in 1917, Meyerbeer's *Le prophète* in 1918, a *Fidelio* and a 'spectacular' *Salome*, both in 1919. *Cavalleria rusticana* was filmed in 1917; there had also been a treatment of the subject in 1912. *Pagliacci* attracted many early film actors: apart from an Italian film of the opera in 1915, there were numerous film impersonations of the tragic clown at this time.

To the obvious problem afflicting silent filmed opera generally – that of missing sound – the Delog company in 1919 offered a radical solution: they presented their film versions of *Der fliegende Holländer*, *Undine*, *Martha* and *Der Waffenschmied* on tour with soloists, orchestra and chorus. A similar principle was employed for the first opera written expressly for the screen, the 1922 German production *Jenseits des Stromes*: a strip of musical notation ran from left to right at the bottom of the image, with an indication to the conductor in the cinema for synchronizing soloists and orchestra.

From Max Reinhardt in 1921 came the 'Kinoweihfestfilm' *Parzifal*. Puccini remained very popular, particularly *La bohème* (an American film in 1921, an Italian reworking of the story with Maria Jacobini in 1922). A 1922 *Don Giovanni* was reported as emphasizing the *buffo* aspects of the opera rather than the demonic-dramatic. In 1923 there was an American version of *Der fliegende Holländer*, in 1925 a series of British shorts called 'Music Masters', which included a one-reel film treating Wagner's life and 'scenes from the operas'. In 1926 Strauss arranged the music of his opera for a film of *Der Rosenkavalier* and conducted the première at the Tivoli cinema, London. Not only were the settings changed to suit the new audiences but even the plot was revamped (battle scenes added, the inn scene replaced by a masked ball, a new ending that reconciled Marschallin and Marschall); Strauss composed a new march for the film score. The director was Robert Wiene, who had made the *Cabinet of Dr Caligari*; the designer was Alfred Roller, who had collaborated in the original stage production of Strauss's opera. In the same year Murger's novel furnished the basis for a film of *La bohème* starring Lillian Gish, John Gilbert and René Adorée, produced by Irving Thalberg and directed by King Vidor, and there was a German version of the subject starring Wilhelm Dieterle. There was also a French *Carmen* and the next year, from Hollywood, *The Loves of Carmen* starring Dolores Del Rio. Also in 1927 there appeared something of a curiosity, a British series of 12 two-reelers called 'Cameo Operas', in which the stories were condensed and which integrated live singers performing in front of the screen. Operettas were filmed in great quantity beginning as early as 1910, especially in Germany (many of the best-known works by Lehár, Johann Strauss, Kalmán, Millöcker, Leo Fall and others), but also in Hollywood: Stroheim's silent version of *Die lustige Witwe* came from MGM in 1925 (there had already been a German version as early as 1913).

2. THE 'SOUND' ERA.

(i) Before 1970. The first sound films of opera employed famous singers to show off the new technical wonder. From 1926 the American company Warner-Vitaphone, for example, produced one-reelers of arias and ensembles with names like Gigli, Martinelli and De Luca. Cameras were enclosed in sound-proof booths (the noiseless camera was yet to be invented) and an orchestra and singers were engaged to make a film and a gramophone recording simultaneously. The projection-

ist had to lower the needle on to a record on a visual cue. The synchronization must often have been rather approximate (in recent years some of these films have been successfully resynchronized by the British Film Institute). There was a film of Friml's *The Vagabond King*, starring Jeanette MacDonald and directed by the German Ludwig Berger, from Paramount in 1930 and Lubitsch's *Die lustige Witwe* with MacDonald and Maurice Chevalier for MGM in 1934 – operetta, with its spoken dialogue, was a close cousin of Hollywood's beloved musical. In the 1930s and early 40s MacDonald, usually with Nelson Eddy as her co-star, appeared in a series of operetta films that were much loved at the time, as well as in features such as *Maytime* and *San Francisco* (both 1936) containing quite well-researched and well-filmed opera sequences. But generally speaking the advent of sound was a greater stimulus to the production of opera films in Europe than in the USA. In 1931 there was an Italian *Fra Diavolo*, freely adapted from Scribe and Auber (two years later there came a memorable parody of the opera with Laurel and Hardy). Also dating from 1931 is G. W. Pabst's screen version of *Die Dreigroschenoper* with Lotte Lenya and Ernst Busch (fig.2). The film's artistic merits are considerable, although the starkness of the action and settings as well as the impact of the musical numbers, significantly cut, were further diluted by Pabst's atmospheric effects. The collaboration ended in lawsuits by Brecht, unsuccessful, and Weill, successful, over the adulteration of their original.

The Bartered Bride (1932), directed by Max Ophüls and starring Jarmila Novotná and Willi Domgraf-Fassbänder, was held in high esteem from its first appearance and is still generally regarded as one of the most successful of all translations of opera to the film medium. Even more than Pabst's *Dreigroschenoper*, it profited from a master director's inimitable, complex visual style. The acoustical perspectives in Ophüls's film were also imaginatively handled: in the director's words, 'All the choruses, solo numbers and orchestral music were recorded outdoors, giving a sense of fresh air to the sound of the film as well' ('all' in this case, of course, not to be understood as a reference to Smetana's original: the film runs only 76 minutes – cuts, transposition of scenes and other alterations being the rule in opera adaptations for the screen until recent years).

In 1934 there appeared a German film of Busoni's *Turandot*, in 1936 a British film of *Pagliacci* with Richard Tauber and *The Last Rose* (based on *Martha*) with Helge Rosvaenge, and in 1939 an Italian *Madama Butterfly* with Maria Cebotari. In France in 1938 Abel Gance directed a film of Charpentier's *Louise*, made under the composer's supervision and starring Grace Moore and Georges Thill. Although in the silent era Geraldine Farrar had appeared as heroine of a number of films for Samuel Goldwyn, Moore was perhaps the first star of opera to be turned into a star of the screen – she had already been featured in a 1930 talkie called *A Lady's Morals* based on the life of Jenny Lind, as well as a number of successful pictures in the years 1934–6. At least in Hollywood, opera in film – i.e. the interpolation of one or more numbers (Flagstad, for example, sang Brünnhilde's battle cry in *The Big Broadcast of 1938*; and, in quite a different vein but probably the best-known of all operatic excerpts in the cinema, an extended scene from *Il trovatore* forms the centrepiece of the Marx Brothers' *A Night at the Opera* from 1935) – would always be preferred to opera as film – film ver-

2. Still from G. W. Pabst's film of Weill's 'Die Dreigroschenoper' (1931) with Ernst Busch as the ballad singer

sions of entire works – which even in the sound era was never really to become commercially viable. Other established singers to have successful Hollywood careers included Pons, Swarthout and Traubel, Kiepura, Melchior, Pinza and Tibbett, who was featured in *Rogue Song*, an adaptation of Lehár's *Zigeunerliebe*, and *The New Moon*, with Grace Moore. Shalyapin played Don Quichotte in a French film directed by Pabst (1933), with an original score by Ibert (more recently, Callas made a non-singing appearance in *Medea*, directed by Pasolini in 1969).

In Italy, not surprisingly the country with the strongest tradition of filmed opera, the director Carmine Gallone made a number of films with Cebotari and Beniamino Gigli in the 1930s, Verdi films with Tito Gobbi (*Rigoletto*, 1946; *La forza del destino*, 1948) and an Italian-Japanese co-production of *Madama Butterfly* (using Japanese actors and Italian singers), shot in Technicolor by Claude Renoir (1954). Gobbi also starred in a *Barbiere* directed by Mario Costa in 1947. A screen version of Menotti's *The Medium* (1951; Prix du Film lyrique, 1952 Cannes festival), filmed in Rome with an American and Italian cast, was directed by the composer himself (he had also been responsible for the original stage production), assisted by Alexander Hammid, and is still widely considered to be among the most successful attempts to put opera on film. It confines sung dialogue to the scenes set in the medium's apartment; in the outdoor scenes, only children's songs or non-vocal music are used (for illustration *see* MEDIUM, THE).

By this time it had become the normal practice to record the voices separately from the shooting of the action; this helped solve the earlier problem of over-reliance on close-ups but opened the way for a new one, that of faulty synchronization. An inevitable adjunct to this was the new fashion for dubbing the voices of well-known singers on to roles played by actors on the screen: in a spectacular (if risible) Italian production of *Aida* (1953) Renata Tebaldi lent her voice to Sophia Loren, and the Wagnerian soprano Martha Mödl could

be heard in a 1953 German film of Nicolai's *Die lustigen Weiber von Windsor*. By 1982 there were extreme cases such as a film of *The Turn of the Screw*, shot in Czechoslovakia with Czech actors by the Czech director Petr Weigl, in which the soundtrack is a pre-recorded studio performance made in London with British and American opera singers.

A number of distinguished Soviet productions were made during the 1950s and 60s: Vera Stroyeva's expressively filmed *Boris Godunov* (1955), which divorces the action from the theatre altogether, relying heavily on exterior scenes, with distant landscape and panning shots as well as close-ups and crowd scenes filmed in the Kremlin itself; Stroyeva's *Khovanshchina* (1959); a *Yevgeny Onegin* (1958; directed by Roman Tikhomirov), notable for its delicate handling of colour; *The Queen of Spades* (1960; also directed by Tikhomirov); and a film of Shostakovich's *Katerina Izmaylova* (1966; directed by Mikhail Sapiro and starring Galina Vishnevskaya).

The most ambitious British production of the postwar period was Michael Powell and Emeric Pressburger's highly stylized *Les contes d'Hoffmann* (1951), with its non-naturalistic designs and expressionistic use of colour (fig.3 overleaf). Reconceiving the work in terms of dance (the same team had made the classic *Red Shoes* a few years earlier), Powell and Pressburger essentially turned Offenbach's opera into a ballet with singing (the leading roles are taken by famous dancers); Beecham conducted. Another all-sung film, Jacques Demy's *Les parapluies de Cherbourg* (1964), was the rare case of an original light opera for the screen; Michel Legrand composed the music. Apart from a biopic, *The Great Caruso* (1951), which became one of the most commercially successful of all films about opera and the highwater mark of Mario Lanza's brief but spectacular career, the only two Hollywood efforts of note during these years were both directed by Otto Preminger: yet another filmed version of *Carmen* (*Carmen Jones*, 1954), this time with an all-black cast, and the lavish *Porgy and Bess* of 1959 (possibly the only opera film to

be shot and exhibited in 70mm), in which, however, spoken dialogue replaced the linking recitatives of Gershwin's opera (André Previn supervised and conducted the music).

Theatrical productions captured or recreated on film represent another line of development. From 1955 the Hungarian-born British director Paul Czinner developed a system of multi-camera coverage of live theatre performances, which he used in documenting two famous Salzburg productions, *Don Giovanni* (1955, with Siepi, conducted by Furtwängler) and *Der Rosenkavalier* (1961, with Schwarzkopf and Jurinac, conducted by Karajan). Karajan himself directed and conducted *Carmen* (with Bumbry and Vickers) in 1967, a studio adaptation of a Salzburg Festival production. The distinction of these three films, however, was limited to the quality of musical performance: none of them used the visual medium to satisfying effect.

The stage director Walter Felsenstein made a number of films based on his celebrated productions for the Komische Oper of Berlin, among them Offenbach's *Hoffmann* (1970) and *Barbe-bleue* and Verdi's *Otello* (1969). More ambitious, but less convincing, was his 1955 film of *Fidelio*, which relied heavily on the use of visual symbols to represent psychological states, for example, waterfall, thunderstorm and falling rocks in Pizarro's vengeance aria and flowery meadows for Florestan's visions of happiness.

(ii) Since 1970. Since World War II opera films, following a general tendency in the film industry, have dwindled in number, and those being made expressly for exhibition in cinemas are gradually disappearing in favour either of studio productions conceived for television broadcast and home video or of television relays of stage performances which are later released on videocassette and laser disc. A pioneering effort in the former category was the BBC's *Der fliegende Holländer* (1976), adapted for the small screen by Brian Large,

who then went on to become a leading filmmaker in the latter category, as the predominating director of live opera (and concerts) for television and video in the following decades. Britten's *Owen Wingrave* (1971) was actually composed for BBC television (as Menotti's *Amahl and the Night Visitors* had been for NBC as early as 1951). Trevor Nunn (with Christopher Swann) reconceived his Glyndebourne staging of *Idomeneo* (1983) for the small screen with striking success.

Other leading directors for the theatre have continued to try their hand occasionally or repeatedly in the medium of film opera. Franco Zeffirelli, whose La Scala production of *La bohème* was recreated on celluloid (with Freni) in 1965, later attempted to employ the wider resources of the cinema (having already established a reputation as a director of non-musical films), leading him – in *La traviata* (1982; fig.4), the name part movingly enacted by Teresa Stratas, and *Otello* (1986), with Domingo – to rely on opulent production values and on flashbacks of his own devising and other glosses on the plots which illustrate what the librettos are wisely content merely to suggest. In both cases, Verdi's opera was heavily cut. The former was something of a commercial success, the latter not. Götz Friedrich has made several films, of varying quality, the best of them perhaps a vividly acted *Salome* (1974, again with a remarkable performance by Stratas; Böhm conducted). These are studio productions, not merely filmed performances of his stagings.

The same is true of Jean-Pierre Ponnelle's many films, which include *Il barbiere di Siviglia* (1972), *Madama Butterfly* (1974), *Le nozze di Figaro* (1976), Monteverdi's *Orfeo* (1978), *La clemenza di Tito* (1980), *Cenerentola* (1981) and *Rigoletto* (1983). Ponnelle, when asked about the essential difference between directing an opera in the theatre and making a film of one, answered that a stage has three walls and is fixed in the direction from the spectator towards the stage, while the camera allows 360° movement. Film allows close-

4. Still from Franco Zeffirelli's film of Verdi's 'La traviata' (1982)

ups as well as a panoramic view: 'The camera lets me show things I can't show on a stage. On the stage I'm tied down [by a different set in each act]. In a film I can move about'. Indeed the exuberant Ponnelle's very fascination with the possibilities of film seems occasionally to have tempted him into exaggeration through overactive camera movement and editing, and excessive reliance on close-up shots with mugging from the singer/actors.

Meanwhile, some distinguished cinema directors have continued to invest their talents and energies in recreating opera on 35mm film for commercial exhibition. The minimalist, avowedly anti-theatrical reconception of

5. Still from Jean-Marie Straub and Danièle Huillet's film of Schoenberg's 'Moses und Aron' (1974)

Schoenberg's *Moses und Aron* by Jean-Marie Straub and Danièle Huillet (1974; fig.5) was hailed by some critics as a refreshingly austere concentration on essentials, a provocative, intellectually demanding reaction against Hollywood–Biblical extravagance, and decried by others as a seemingly interminable study in frustrated expectations. For the musical performance (conducted by Michael Gielen) there was general praise. As with a number of other recent opera films (Joseph Losey's *Don Giovanni*, Francesco Rosi's *Carmen*), this was a co-production with a major recording company.

Ingmar Bergman's film of *Die Zauberflöte* – made in 1975 for Swedish television but also shown successfully in cinemas – begins in a recreation of the Drottningholm Court Theatre and then gradually abandons it for a freer *mise en scène*, with increasing reliance on montage and close-ups, when the action moves into the realms of mind and spirit. The characters and concerns of Mozart's musical fable which had been elemental in the director's earlier works are here given a pure, idealized expression (fig.6 overleaf). Losey's *Don Giovanni* (1979), which removes the action from southern Spain to the Veneto, with its canals and Palladian architecture, derives its fascination in part from the director's exploration of themes running through his other films, such as the relation of master to servant. Hans Jürgen Syberberg's non-realistic, symbol-charged *Parsifal* (1982), far more radically than Bergman's *Zauberflöte* (with its illuminating connections between Sarastro and Amfortas) alludes to and incorporates external elements – from Wagner's life, works and thought, even addressing the problem of Wagner's role in the subsequent development of German culture.

Rosi's *Carmen* (1984) places Bizet's opera in naturalistic settings (it was shot on location in Ronda and Carmona as well as Seville), but uses them in a fastidiously controlled, almost formalized fashion. The

6. Still from Ingmar Bergman's film of Mozart's 'Die Zauberflöte' (1975) with Håkon Hagegård as Papageno

subtle, beautiful visual elements create convincing back-drops for a vivid if conventionally theatrical performance of the opera. It contrasts diametrically with Peter Brook's film of his pared-down, intimate stage version *La tragédie de Carmen* (1983; three films actually, to record performances by different casts). Concentrating almost entirely on the four principal roles, Brook's reworking of the material, notwithstanding the skill and intelligence which informs it, lacks on film as it did on stage the richness and vitality of Bizet's *Carmen*.

By far the most widely seen filmed opera in recent years, it should be added, were excerpts from Mozart operas in Milos Forman's 1984 screen version of Peter Shaffer's play *Amadeus*, staged by the choreographer Twyla Tharp, conducted by Neville Marriner and shot largely in Prague's Tyl Theatre (where *Don Giovanni* was first performed). Other popular films of this time took opera or opera singers as their subject, most notably Fellini's gently satirical *E la nave va* ('And the Ship Sails On', 1982), which is permeated by operatic references and music, but also Jean-Jacques Beineix's witty thriller *Diva* (1981). Once again the general public demonstrated its receptiveness to opera in film.

There have been, and in the 1990s will probably continue to be, however, other examples of full-scale opera films for showing in theatres; but, as indicated earlier, they are few and likely to become fewer still as opera on television and home video continues in its ascendancy, and as rising production costs and the relative un-commerciality of the genre increasingly favour the predominance of videotaped stage productions over new creations for the cinema.

*

W. Freisburger: 'Verfilmte Oper', *Theater im Film* (Emsdetten, 1936), 42–65

L. Bauer: 'Twice Told Tales: Translating Opera into Film', *Theatre Arts*, xxxv/6 (1951), 39–43

C. Gallone: 'Il valore della musica nel film e l'evoluzione dello spettacolo lirico sullo schermo', *Musica e film*, ed. S. Biamonte (Rome, 1959), 203–6

R. Bebb: *Opera and the Cinema* (London, 1969) [pubn of the National Film Theatre]

H. Bertz-Dostal: *Oper im Fernsehen* (Vienna, 1970)

L.-A. Bawden, ed.: *The Oxford Companion to Film* (London, 1976)

J.-P. Ponnelle: 'Bemerkungen zur Opernregie im Fernsehen', *Musik im ZDF* [Zweiten Deutschen Fernsehen] (Mainz, 1976–7), 14–16; Eng. trans. as 'Opera on the Small Screen', *Le nozze di Figaro* (Deutsche Grammophon 072 403/503, 1988) [video notes]

H. Rosenthal and J. Warrack: 'Film Opera', *The Concise Oxford Dictionary of Opera* (London, 2/1979)

J. Batchelor: 'From "Aida" to "Zauberflöte"', *Screen*, xxv/3 (1984), 26–38

H.-K. Jungheinrich, ed.: *Oper – Film – Rockmusik* (Kassel, 1986)

L'avant-scène opéra, no.98 (1987) [*Cinéma et opéra* issue]

A. Garel and M. Salmon: 'Cinéma et opéra', *La revue du cinéma*, no.429 (1987), 55–79

M. Serceau and H. Puiseaux: 'Cinéma et opéra', *La revue du cinéma*, no.430 (1987), 73–83

A. Stanbrook: 'The Sight of Music', *Sight and Sound*, lvi/2 (1987), 132–5

J. Tambling: *Opera, Ideology and Film* (Manchester, 1987)

RICHARD EVIDON

Filming, videotaping. During the 20th century, as viewing opera in the cinema and the home has gained popularity, techniques for producing and recording it on film or videotape have developed, for both financial and artistic reasons; at the same time, broadcasting technology has advanced and interest in distributing opera on video cassettes and laser video discs has rapidly increased.

For more than 50 years, directors have struggled with the technical problems of reducing an essentially theatrical entertainment to a miniature two-dimensional form. Three methods have established themselves: opera designed for television and directed from a television studio; live or recorded relays of theatrical productions from the stage of opera houses; and opera created specially for the cinema and shot on film in the studio, on location or in a combination of both. However, over the last decade, and for economic rather than artistic reasons, there has been a move away from filmed location and studio opera in favour of televised opera from the leading world opera houses. (For a discussion of the history of opera in visual recordings, *see* FILM AND TELEVISION.)

1. Techniques. 2. Videorecording methods: (i) Studio productions (ii) Films (iii) Theatrical productions.

1. TECHNIQUES. The director records images on one of two possible formats: film or videotape. 35mm film is used in the recording of operas in a film studio or in natural locations; because film cartridges have to be changed frequently, it is better suited to the controlled conditions that these settings offer. Costly to buy, film is also expensive to process, since it must be sent to a laboratory before it is edited, optically checked and colour corrected. Videotape is used for recording live or television studio productions. Economical to buy, a single tape can last between one and two hours, and it requires no processing; results can be viewed immediately. Although the softer image quality of film may be preferred, the practical and financial benefits of using videotape have resulted in a favouring of this format for operatic recording, especially given the move towards reproducing live theatrical performances.

The director has at his or her disposal a standard palette of shots from which to create images for television or film. Using various angle and zoom lenses, which have any degree of closeness or wideness, the director chooses between a range of shots: wide angle or full shot, used for scene setting; half-stage or group shots; shots of full figures; and shots that focus on specific parts of the subject (head, waist, from the elbows up etc.). Developing shots are also used: zooming shots, which move closer to or away from the subject; panning shots, which move across to the subject or away from it; shots that follow the subject as it moves; and tracking shots, in which the camera physically moves, laterally on wheels or rails or vertically on a crane arm.

The different shots are joined in a sequence, the pacing of which is determined by the types of shot used and the length that each lasts. Visual interest is created by the frequency of cuts: a quick succession can increase the pace and excitement, while a wide-angle shot may be used to set a mood or relax the pace. Directors often derive the visual pacing from the rhythm of the music itself, as determined by the harmonies, chord structure, orchestration and other factors. In choosing the shots and the pacing of cuts, the director may also be influenced by the opera's period and style, aiming to create a visual style appropriate to the artistic period in which the piece originated or is set. Baroque opera may be recorded in a way that reflects Baroque theatre techniques, exploiting the flat, artificial quality of period scenic design. Furthermore, the formalized musical patterns can affect the structure of the visual pacing; in the 1989 videotaped version of Vivaldi's *Orlando furioso* from the San Francisco Opera, the da capo arias often involved three shots: one for the initial *A* section, a second for the *B* section and a return to the initial shot for the reprise of the *A* section. Later operatic styles might be portrayed with other shooting techniques; for instance, the decaying states of mind of the characters in Strauss's *Elektra* or Berg's *Wozzeck* could be portrayed with harrowing close-up shots, showing manic expressions and physical features in grotesquely realistic detail (as in the Vienna Staatsoper production tapes made in 1982 and 1987 by Österreichischer Rundfunk). The director may choose to introduce or interrupt the opera's action with shots of the audience, the conductor and orchestra, or the backstage of the theatre, in order to place the viewer within the theatrical setting. Non-operatic material may also be included, perhaps to make the opera more accessible to the general public. For instance, the televised version of Houston Grand Opera's *Nixon in China* was hosted by the American reporter Walter Kronkite, who had accompanied President Nixon on the historic visit; Kronkite introduced each scene of the opera with a bird's-eye description of what had actually occurred, illustrated with original news footage.

A visual recording is most frequently based on a single master recording, with an isolated camera (or cameras) providing supporting material. Generally, six cameras are used, although additional cameras may be employed for special perspectives during spectacular scenes; seven cameras were used to videorecord the Metropolitan Opera *Ring*, and ten were used to tape *Aida* at the Roman Arena in Verona. When recording a live performance, the placement of the cameras depends on the shape of the theatre and the nature of the stage production. Generally, four cameras are placed in or near the first row of the stalls, parallel with the front of the stage. The two outer cameras may be used during dialogue and for shooting diagonally across the stage (cross-shooting); the middle cameras may be used during arias. Between one and three further cameras are placed on the central axis further back in the theatre; one, for wide shots, is often placed in a central box and one or two frequently stand at the back of the stalls. In television studio productions or filmed operas, further options involving moveable cameras on tracks or cranes can be employed, which are not possible when a ticket-buying audience must be taken into consideration. However, even during live opera performances, clever onstage camera placement can result in unexpected images: during the Metropolitan *Ring* recording, the fight between Siegfried and the dragon (*Siegfried*, Act 2) was filmed from the dragon's perspective without distracting the audience, through the use of a camera placed strategically behind the dragon so that it was not visible to the audience. Similarly in Act 3 of *Die Walküre* Wotan's Farewell was enhanced by the use of an onstage camera from a lighting tower, which peered down on to Brünnhilde's eyes.

When preparing to record an opera, the director begins as a conductor would, by learning the score – memorizing the music, plot and libretto. His visual interpretation of the score is often translated into a 'story board', a sequence of box drawings which depict the composition of the shots at specific moments. Although this will be adapted, changed and developed as the project progresses, the story board provides the initial framework for the recording. It slowly evolves into a 'shooting script', the written instructions for shooting the chosen images; this script goes through a series of revisions as various ideas or sequences of shots are developed or discarded. These ideas are tested during the camera rehearsals, when the camera operators provide shots as instructed on individual shot sheets prepared from the master script. After each recording the singers, cameramen, audio and lighting technicians and other participants are encouraged to see and hear their work, contributing ideas and refining details of their performances. The preparation culminates in the final taping of the opera.

In preparing for the final taping, the director must ensure that the singers' acting and appearance is suitable for visual recording. Operatic acting style has traditionally been based on a limited number of broad gestures that lack subtlety of movement or facial expression. However, for television and film gestures must be more refined; every movement needs to have a definite meaning and a sense of controlled impetus or focus. Prominent and experienced singers, such as Mirella Freni and Placido Domingo, have developed acting styles for visual recording that are suited to the camera rather than to the gallery and have shown others how to achieve artistic expression on tape by 'speaking with the eyes' as well as singing. The singers are also advised about refining their make-up. In addition, the director may use camera techniques to enhance an artist's appearance. The costumes or scenery may be adapted to make an artist more credible in a role; for instance, very large scenery can make a large singer seem petite and consumptive. Similarly, the director can choose to pull back a shot so as to avoid revealing physical distortions that a singer may make during a technically demanding passage.

After the opera is recorded a period of editing follows. Apart from the principal 'on line' material of the final taping, material from earlier performances can be integrated in order to improve certain sequences, to allow for covering mistakes or to provide extra material for reactions to the principal action. Thus the video director may be selective during editing, using material drawn from more than one take, and can correct any musical mistakes and vocal flaws, as an audio producer does in a sound recording. In certain countries, labour agreements specify that only the final performance may be used in the preparation of the end product; at the Metropolitan Opera, for instance, the last dress rehearsal is used as a camera test run-through, two public performances are used as camera rehearsals and kept as reserves, and a third performance is recorded as the final taping. If material from previous performances is incorporated into the edited recording, extra fees must be paid (to chorus, orchestra and stage hands). In Europe, however, agreements allow previously recorded material to be used in the final product. Following the video edit, the audio (normally recorded on 24 digital tracks) is remixed so that the balance between voices and orchestra and the relationship of picture to sound can be refined.

As the final step, subtitles in the language of the viewing audience must be incorporated, since visual recordings are now usually performed in the work's original language. The goal here is to transmit the subtleties of the text with the minimum number of words. If the opera is not televised live, the subtitles will be added after the editing is completed to ensure exact timing. Since the viewer's eye should not be drawn to more than one place at once, the subtitles must be timed so that they do not last longer than, or 'cross', more than one shot (they should not, for instance, cross a cut from the singer to another character's reaction, since the reaction is often intended as a comment on the action).

Although this process for the visual recording of opera has become standardized, improvements in the available technology and the intended viewing medium continually affect recording techniques. The most significant and wide-reaching development in recent years has been the emergence of High Definition Television (HDTV). Devised in 1964 by engineers at the Japanese state network (NHK), and the subject of 25 years of experimentation, this improved form of television provides a higher quality of picture by increasing the number of lines on the screen from 525 or 625 to 1125 or 1250. The result is an image that is crystal clear and sharp, with great detail of texture, increased richness of colour and deep sense of perspective. Videorecordings for HDTV are made in digital format with 24-track digital sound. The greater width of the 'letterbox quasi cinemascope' screen (ratio 16:9 rather than 4:3) has caused directors to adapt their shooting techniques. Because a larger area is shown, decisions need to be made as to what part of the image will be in sharp focus and which in soft. The breadth of the image also necessitates that close attention be paid to each shot's composition. Close-ups are generally used only for specific reasons since the wider format is better suited to group shots. Because more than one person can be in the frame at the same time fewer cuts are needed and shots can be held longer; thus the painterly aspect of each shot must be precisely determined. The first videorecording of opera in Europe for HDTV was the Bavarian State Opera production of the *Ring*, taped by NHK in 1989 and shown by the BBC in 1990 (for further information see B. Large: 'HDTV: an Eye to the Future', *Opera*, xlii, 1991, pp.1399–402).

2. VIDEORECORDING METHODS.

(i) *Studio productions*. When the influence of television on a mass audience began to be understood during the 1950s, television organizations started to look into the possibilities offered by opera. Directors believed that much of the standard operatic repertory was not suited to the small screen and so avoided scores with lengthy arias and static ensembles; instead, they chose operas with coherent and dramatically effective plots, which could exploit the intimacy of the medium.

It was widely felt that directors were able to make a greater dramatic impact on the viewer by bringing the art-form into the studio. By the 1970s recording normally took place in two or three large studios, with soloists and an 'in-vision' chorus staged and costumed in one or two studios and the conductor, orchestra and 'out-of-vision' chorus in another. The studios were electronically linked so that the orchestral accompaniment was heard by the singers in the drama studios and the soloists' voices were fed to the conductor by way of headphones. The conductor could see the singers on a monitor fitted into his music desk and his image was relayed to the soloists and in-vision chorus by monitors concealed in the scenery, often attached to cameras or suspended above the sets. The system was complicated, but after the sound sources from the studios were mixed in the audio control room, the effect was one of a 'live' performance. For such studio operas the television service became its own opera company, designing scenery and costumes specially for the recording, engaging soloists and orchestra and mounting its own production. The television director was responsible for both the staging of the action and the television presentation. With the use of cranes and mobile cameras he was able to create a sense of spectacle with a flow of movement not possible with fixed camera positions, a limiting factor when televising a public performance from a theatre.

However, such an enterprise was expensive, requiring not only months of preparation but three to four weeks of rehearsal and up to ten days for studio shooting. For this reason, star singers often found it impossible to find time for studio productions and were unwilling to perform for fees a fraction of those they could earn on the international circuit. Some remarkable productions were achieved with the split-studio working method, including the BBC *Billy Budd*, *Peter Grimes* and *Der fliegende Holländer* performances and the NBC abridged Opera Theatre productions of *War and Peace, Dialogues des Carmélites* and *From the House of the Dead*. The heavy cost of this method has, however, gradually eliminated it as a viable option for the visual recording of opera.

(ii) Films. The technique of recording opera on film begins with the preparation of a sound track on which the musical elements have been prerecorded in a sound studio and edited into their final form. The sound track is played back on set during filming; as the artists act out their roles, miming the singing, they match the sound track performance to the best of their ability. Perfect lip-synchronization is difficult to achieve, especially since the sound track may have been made months earlier; however, subtle editing, in which individual frames of the film can be shifted, may help to improve the synchronization between action and sound.

Instead of filming a performance of an opera as such (as in television studio or televised theatre productions), film directors either film an opera or make an opera film; whereas videorecorded opera performances generally attempt to establish a theatrical setting for the viewer, retaining the artificiality of the art form, film directors often use their medium to create a realistic or naturalistic atmosphere and mood in order to draw the viewer into the story's setting. The availability of diverse locations and elaborate costumes are combined with filming techniques that reflect the director's style and personality. In Jean-Pierre Ponnelle's version of *Le nozze di Figaro*, shot in the Pinewood film studios, the director succeeded in capturing the wit and humour of the work without forcing his own personality. The arias and ensembles were prerecorded but the recitatives were shot live, since no singer, however experienced, could be expected to synchronize the delivery of the recitative with an acceptable degree of accuracy. Non-theatrical possibilities are evident in his treatment of 'Porgi, Amor', in which the prerecorded aria serves as a background to the image of the Countess meditating, so that music and image may combine to reveal her emotional state. Franco Zeffirelli uses striking filming techniques to a still greater extent, employing restless, shifting pans and zooms to enhance the drama. In his version of *La traviata*, his choreographic flair and extravagant costumes and decoration enable him to create and exploit excitement in a way that is not possible in stage productions; the entire action is seen as a 'flashback' from Violetta's sickbed, justified by Verdi's re-use of the Act 1 prelude at the opening of the last act. In his film version of *Cavalleria rusticana* Zeffirelli mixed the atmospheric possibilities of film with the inherent theatricality of opera: he established the dramatic context by opening the film with scenes shot on location in Sicily, shown during the prelude; the operatic action was then shot from his stage production at La Scala. Ingmar Bergman also combined film and theatre in his *Die Zauberflöte*. By working within the framework of a Drottningholm-like theatre, built in a studio, he presented Mozart's opera as a period piece within a stylized proscenium arch setting; he gave the film greater depth by using 'before' and 'behind' the curtain scenes. During the overture he focussed the viewer's attention on a little girl in the audience and returned to her image during the opera to remind viewers of their role as spectators in the drama. It is an idea which Ponnelle exploited in his Monteverdi cycle, founded on his original Zürich stage

productions. By placing cameras for *Orfeo* not only in front of the stage but on the stage, and shooting the singers' point of view of conductor, orchestra, audience and auditorium, Ponnelle reminded the viewer of the theatricality of his concept and his respect for Monteverdi's innovatory operatic forms.

Another approach to filming opera may be seen in the work of Peter Weigl, who has used classic gramophone recordings as the source of his sound track and engaged actors as well as singers to play out the drama as visual accompaniment. The evocative effect of this form of music-film is evident in his version of *Yevgeny Onegin*, a visual treatment of Solti's famous recording. Here, and in his version of Britten's *The Turn of the Screw*, film is used to underline the music drama, acting as a counterpoint to the original score.

(iii) Theatrical productions. Whether an opera is to be televised from the Metropolitan Opera, Covent Garden, Vienna or La Scala, the production method is much the same. The television director must translate a production conceived by a stage director into a video production. As always, the video director begins by preparing a story board from the score, although changes will be made after the stage version has been seen. Lighting levels must be adjusted and are sometimes increased by 25%. Costume details and make-up are refined so as to be subtle and credible enough for the close scrutiny of television. In the case of a dated or tired production, scenery and props may need to be refurbished, and colours and surfaces may need adjustment, since red and white are unsuitable for televising, as are glittering or reflecting surfaces. A number of public performances, normally three or four, are selected for the purpose of camera rehearsals and final taping. Camera positions are selected to provide the viewer with a feeling of having the best seat in the house at any given moment. The recording process proceeds as described earlier.

This method of televising opera is now standard, though the risks of recording live productions from open air settings such as those at Verona, Rome (Caracalla) and Aix-en-Provence present special problems. Outdoor performances usually begin at dusk, so initially the lighting directors have to compensate as the natural light fades by slowly increasing the electric lights. The most notable difficulty with recording from outdoor theatres, however, is the acoustics: special provision must be made for capturing and balancing the sound of the soloists and orchestra and ways must be found to combat the noise of wind or storm. In these vast arenas the director may try to bring the atmosphere of the crowds and the unusual location to the viewers; at Verona, for instance, he may choose initially to establish the setting, showing the Roman ruins and the audience of 26000 people before zooming in to the operatic action itself.

In Bayreuth, where all of Wagner's operas have been videotaped, the standard production practice has been adapted. Because only a limited number of performances take place in the Festspielhaus each year, the music dramas can be recorded in the rehearsal weeks preceding the festival, in a closed house. By turning the theatre temporarily into a television studio, not only can Bayreuth's legendary acoustic be preserved but the normally low lighting levels used for Wagner productions can be adjusted without offending a ticket-buying public. The director also has greater freedom with camera placement when large sections of seating can be removed and tracks and towers built, allowing the cameras to achieve effects impossible when audiences are present. The Boulez-Chéreau Bayreuth recording of the *Ring* was spread over two summers; each act could be rehearsed and recorded out of sequence over a three- or four-day period and, after the camera rehearsals and audio tests, the final taping of the act could be recorded continuously, without stops or restarts. After an hour's pause, and before the voices cooled, the act could be repeated. Thus the musical force of a live performance at the Festspielhaus could be preserved in a way that comes close to the experience of actual attendance at a performance there.

For bibliography *see* FILM and TELEVISION.   BRIAN LARGE

Filosofi immaginari, I ('The Imaginary Philosophers'). *Dramma giocoso* in two acts by GIOVANNI PAISIELLO to a libretto by GIOVANNI BERTATI; St Petersburg, Hermitage, 3/14 February 1779.

This work, written for the court of Catherine II and complying with her regulation that operas should last no longer than an hour and a half, is one of Paisiello's most attractive *opere buffe*. The plot concerns a pseudo-learned father, Petronio (bass), and his two daughters – Cassandra (soprano), who is learned and not interested in marriage, and Clarice (soprano), who thinks learning is useless and is interested only in marrying her lover Giuliano (baritone). Disguised as the 'famous philosopher' Argatifontidas, Giuliano tricks Petronio into allowing him to marry Clarice. The libretto includes several discussions between the sisters about their chosen futures. Paisiello's music reflects subtly the differences in personality between the two sisters. Clarice is the more sympathetic figure; she has four arias and they range in tone from the intense lyricism of 'Mi sia guida la mia stella' to the *buffa* patter in 'Una donna letterata'. Cassandra is no buffoon, however; her first aria, like most of Clarice's music, is in the galant manner, and her second is an elevated piece in C major. In general, Paisiello's music is witty and varied. The disguised Giuliano parodies the learned style as he lists the ancient philosophers in 'Per scienza e per dottrina' and, as Catherine II noted, Paisiello 'set coughing to music' in the second-act duet between Petronio and Giuliano.

The opera exists in numerous versions and is also known as *Gli astrologi immaginari*, *I visionari*, and *I letterati immaginari*, as well as in a French translation as *Le philosophe imaginaire* (1780, Paris) and in a German version as *Die eingebildeten Philosophen*.

MARY HUNTER

Filosofo di campagna, Il ('The Homespun Philosopher'). *Dramma giocoso* in three acts by BALDASSARE GALUPPI to a libretto by CARLO GOLDONI; Venice, Teatro S Samuele, 26 October 1754.

Eugenia (soprano), daughter of Don Tritemio (bass, sung by Francesco Carrattoli), confides in the housemaid Lesbina (soprano, sung in the first performance by Clementina Baglioni) that she does not love the man her father has chosen for her to marry, the wealthy farmer Nardo (tenor, sung by Francesco Baglioni), but that she loves Rinaldo (soprano). Lesbina is sympathetic and decides to intervene, but Tritemio later scoffs at her meddling. Rinaldo, a wealthy nobleman, asks Tritemio for Eugenia's hand, but is dismissed. In the countryside Nardo reflects on his steady and peaceful life as a farmer, and ridicules ephemeral city life. Lena (soprano), his niece, approaches and negotiates for her marriage prospects, although she has no suitor. Nardo, a homespun philosopher, mocks her insatiable desire to improve her station and her ill-content with life. In Tritemio's home Eugenia and Rinaldo lament their fate. Lesbina rushes the couple off to hiding when Nardo arrives, and then presents herself to Nardo as Eugenia. Finding him handsome, she schemes further by consenting to marriage in the role of Eugenia. The Act 1 finale combines Tritemio's exits, as he seeks to find his daughter, with Lesbina's well-timed entrances as she poses as Eugenia, completing the marriage arrangements and accepting an engagement ring.

In Act 2 Tritemio sees the ring, which Lesbina has passed to Eugenia. Rinaldo and a notary, Capocchio (tenor), arrive to substantiate Rinaldo's nobility and wealth, but Tritemio is politely obstinate; Eugenia's left hand bears an engagement ring. Rinaldo feels betrayed and bitterly departs. Eugenia is about to disclose all when Lesbina announces a messenger from Nardo's family. After Tritemio leaves the room Eugenia complains to Lesbina, but is consoled that all will end well. Tritemio returns with a large jewel as a gift from Nardo to the bride, which Eugenia in turn gives to Lesbina with the explanation that it will console Lesbina's own lack of a husband. Eugenia, left alone, weeps. Back in the country, Rinaldo visits Nardo and tells him what his gift will be for Nardo's marriage: misery, wounds and death. Nardo asks why he is being so 'generous', and learns of Rinaldo's previous hopes with regard to Eugenia. Nardo suggests that if Rinaldo wants the girl he can take her; it is always better to be reasonable. Rinaldo leaves, and Nardo considers how insane it would be to jeopardize his home, to engage in lawsuits and to risk death just to get a wife. Lesbina, still posing as Eugenia, calls on Nardo, but is surprised when Lena informs Nardo of Lesbina's true identity. Nardo confesses that her position makes no difference to him, and the marriage is on again. Back home, Lesbina completes her intrigue by leading Tritemio to believe that she is in love with him, and he agrees to a double wedding. The finale of Act 2 includes Lesbina's dictation to Capocchio of the double-marriage contract, substituting the names of Nardo and Lesbina, and Rinaldo and Eugenia, when Tritemio is out of earshot. In the meantime Tritemio discovers that Eugenia has eloped.

In Act 3 Rinaldo and Eugenia flee to Nardo's house and seek temporary asylum. Tritemio arrives, looking for his daughter, and Lena tells him that Eugenia is with her fiancé. Tritemio encounters Nardo, is placated and exits. Nardo considers his role as a philosopher and attributes his wisdom to commonsense and experience. With Lesbina they consider her dowry – two able hands, a modest eye, an honest spirit and wit – and he counsels moderation in all things. Meanwhile the notary arrives and the contract is signed. Tritemio discovers, too late, who the marriage partners really are. He is shocked, but recovers enough to agree to his own marriage to Lena. All join in singing praises to Love.

This masterly opera was the most popular of the many collaborations between Galuppi and Goldoni, and was disseminated rapidly throughout Europe (there were 20 separate productions within the first ten years alone), both in its original form and in various altered versions (including one as a two-act intermezzo). It is one of the best examples of the flexibility and clarity of music and poetry in the comic style of the *dramma giocoso*, seen particularly in the comic arias of the two *buffo* male leads and the two large act-ending finales.

For illustration *see* OPERA BUFFA, fig.1.   DALE E. MONSON

Finale (It.; Eng. and Ger. by usage; Fr. *final*). The last part of an opera, or of an act of an opera. The term is usually reserved for a prolonged, continuously composed section, involving several singers and possibly a chorus, but by definition it may be applied to any number that concludes an act. In 17th-century opera there was no uniform pattern for act endings; there are examples of arias, arioso sections, duets or larger ensembles (such as quartets) to conclude operas, and in most French operas there was a concluding divertissement (often, at the end of the opera, with a final chaconne). By the early 18th century it was normal, in serious Italian opera, for the earlier acts to end with an aria for a principal singer or occasionally a duet and for the final act to end with a brief *coro*, or 'chorus', usually in dance rhythm, sung by all the principals in three- or four-part harmony (those who had died in the course of the action would normally reappear).

The concerted finale, essentially an Italian development, dates from the mid-18th century when, in Venice, action began to invade the normally static or reflective ensembles that concluded the first two acts of comic operas, particularly in the collaborations between the librettist Goldoni and the composer Galuppi. The first-act finale of their *Arcadia in Brenta* (1749) has been identified (Heartz 1977–8) as the first opera to a Goldoni text that features a disruptive, surprise entrance within the ensemble. There is action within the second-act finale of Goldoni's *Bertoldo, Bertoldino e Cacasenno*, set by V. Ciampi and given in the carnival season earlier the same year, and a year earlier in that of Antonio Palomba's *L'amore in maschera*, set by Jommelli.

Finales of the 1750s, unlike reflective ensembles of the same period, tend to have little ensemble singing. The texture may thicken to a duet or trio at cadences but the piling up of entrances in ensemble style for a final tutti of five or six does not usually occur until the end. In trio finales the poet will begin with solos, and then sometimes follow a tutti with another set of longer solos after which the composer will reset the textural climax in a textual pattern *abcb'* (an example is Cocchi and Goldoni's *Li matti per amore*, 1754, Act 1). A duo may function as a pair of commentators, sometimes repeating the same material to produce a rondo or refrain effect (as in Piccinni's *La buona figliuola*, 1760, Act 1). Most finales take the form of the so-called 'chain', in which a series of closed, normally unrelated sections follow one another. These may be set in a single tempo and metre, relying on contrasts in musical style and tonality or mode to dramatize the actions and express the reactions of the characters, as well as entrances, emotional responses and any events that need to be reflected in the music (see finales in *Li matti per amore*). Finales in several tempos may be alternately fast and slow, always ending in a fast tempo ('Sì, signora di lassù', in *La buona figliuola*), or they may become steadily faster ('Dove avete la creanza?', in Mozart's *La finta semplice*, 1769). As early as 1755, in Galuppi's *Diavolessa*, the so-called 'shock ensemble', or 'sotto voce ensemble', in which the characters on stage express their alarm or astonishment at a situation, makes an appearance.

During the 1760s the finale in a variety of tempos and metres began to predominate and by the end of the decade each section tends to start with dialogue or action and conclude in a reflective style, often with an accompanying thickening of the texture ('Conoscete eh porporina!', in Gassman's *L'opera seria*, 1769). Tonally, sections tend to move to related keys (the dominant, the dominant of the dominant, the subdominant, the submediant, the parallel minor), for which a change of key signature will often be used. The finale as a whole will, however, normally end in the key in which it began. In early action finales the action may be minimal, merely summarizing what has just transpired or featuring some piece of comic nonsense, but often the plot advances during a first- or second-act finale, usually moving from confrontation to impasse, at which point the act ends, leaving the issues unresolved. The third-act finale, ending the opera, is often a reflective piece for soloists and tutti and may be a simple homophonic *coro* for all the principals. The last finale in *L'opera seria*, 'Noi giuriamo per que' numi', takes the form of a French vaudeville, in which soloists singing the same music to different words alternate with a tutti refrain. As a rule, the serious characters in an *opera buffa* appear only in the last finale, if in any. As the century went on, finales became increasingly long and complex and came to involve all the characters rather than just the three or four principals. A preference developed during the 1780s for finales constructed of a succession of moves between action and reflection, each accompanied by a thickening in texture and each treated as a section ending with a cadence, which was often followed by a change to a new tempo and/or metre; such finales can be found as early as 1775 in Act 1 of Mozart's *La finta giardiniera* and in Act 2 of *Le nozze di Figaro*, 1786.

The chain finale entered *opera seria* in the late 1760s, with Jommelli's *Fetonte*, to a libretto by Verazi (1768, Ludwigsburg). Verazi had already been writing multisectional ensembles with fluctuating numbers of personnel for Mannheim in the early 1760s, for example in Traetta's *Sofonisba* (1762); that does not necessarily imply an action ensemble but simply that more or fewer characters are expressing their emotions at the end than at the beginning. The last act of an *opera seria* makes a better location for an action finale than do the relatively static intermediate act endings; action finales accordingly tend to appear there first. In 1770 the finale to the last act of Verazi and Sacchini's *Calliroe* follows the prototypical comic form, beginning as a trio, expanding to a quintet and adding two further voices in the final tutti. Verazi was also the first to append an action finale to a Metastasio opera, J. C. Bach's *Temistocle* (1772, Mannheim). His operas for the opening of the new La Scala house in 1778–9 contain elaborate finales incorporating chorus. Thereafter, ensembles with some minimal action begin to appear in the works of progressive librettists such as Sertor (in Venice), Serio (Naples) and Moretti (Milan). In finales of the 1780s, two static movements, slow-fast, often follow the action. By the late 1780s, action finales were becoming common. Paisiello's well-known finales for *Pirro* were neither the first nor the only ones produced in 1787. When in 1791 Mozart and Mazzolà appended an action finale to Act 1 of *La clemenza di Tito* they were simply following a current trend. In the 1790s the action finale and the scene complex became the two most common constructions for act finales in *opera seria*.

A peak of development in the history of the chain finale was reached in Vienna during the 1780s and 90s, the period that includes the three *opere buffe* of Mozart and Da Ponte (for a full discussion, see Platoff 1989 and 1991). Viennese finales of this period, by such composers as Salieri, Paisiello, Martín y Soler and Dittersdorf, average some seven or eight sections (as many as 17 in Dittersdorf's *Democrito corretto*, 1787). Most sections begin with action or dialogue and end with a tutti in which the characters express their reactions to the changing situation. Finales always begin and end in the same key; so too do most of the sections within them, though about one quarter modulate, usually to the dominant. Successive movements are mostly in closely related keys, but more distant key changes are used to articulate a particular development in the drama, such as a sudden turn in the action or a change in the characters occupying the stage. Some finales have 'tonal regions', groups of movements clustered around a tonal centre distinct from the principal one and linked with a particular phase in the action or a particular group of characters. The Act 2 finale of *Le nozze di Figaro* (1786), although generally regarded as exceptional in length and structure, is not one of the longest and follows the typical key relationships as outlined above (with a sharp break only where Figaro's entry creates an abrupt change in the nature of the action); its particular key scheme, however, with a first move from E♭ to the dominant B♭, then a shift to G and a series of moves by steps of a fifth back to E♭, is unusual for the tautness it imparts to the structure, while the thematic working within each section is particularly highly wrought.

In the French *tragédie en musique* of the Lully era and thereafter, almost all acts ended with a divertissement, involving dance and choruses as well as solo singing, a tradition maintained throughout the first half of the 18th century. In *opéra comique* of the 1750s and 60s, the earlier acts generally ended with ensembles, usually duets or trios, though quartets also appear (particularly in settings of librettos by Anseaume) as do quintets (such as that by Monsigny in *Le déserteur*, 1769, to a text by Sedaine) and even a septet (Act 2 of Philidor's *Tom Jones*). The finales, virtually all in a single tempo and metre, were not however extensive and were often no longer than a normal *air*; among leading composers, Philidor most consistently wrote finales of over 100 bars. Grétry's *Le magnifique* (1773) contains the first chain finale other than to a final act. The VAUDEVILLE FINAL was favoured for final acts, and particularly for the endings of one-act operas; quartets were also popular where an opera ended with an ensemble number. There are few signs of the incursion of the Italian chain finale though sections with contrasting metre are found in a few works, such as E. Duni's *L'isle des foux* (1760) and *Mazet* (1761). In some finales a 'choeur' is specified; this often implied no more than a homophonic chorus sung by the assembled soloists, though occasionally (for example in Duni's *La fée Urgèle*, 1765) an ensemble (in this case a duet) might be superimposed upon a true chorus; only from the later 1770s was a sufficient chorus available at the Comédie-Italienne for composers to use such facilities with any regularity.

By the 19th century the multi-movement central finale devised by Goldoni for his *drammi giocosi* had become the rule of the entire range of Italian opera, with the result that operatic plots tended to be designed so as to move towards a point of general confrontation somewhere in the middle of the action; the ensemble that follows constitutes the architectural pinnacle of the score. With Rossini and his successors a ground-plan of four movements, evident as early as *Tancredi* (1813), comes into being: a *tempo d'attacco* consisting of dialogue mostly over an orchestral *parlante*; a *pezzo concertato* during which the action freezes while the characters express their reactions to the turn of events in an effusion of lyrical part-writing; a *tempo di mezzo* similar to the first movement and sometimes based on the same material; and a rapid stretta no less static than the *pezzo concertato* to which it forms a structural counterpoise. Classic examples appear in Bellini's *La sonnambula* (1831), Donizetti's *Lucia di Lammermoor* (1835) and Verdi's *Nabucco* (1842). Among early exceptions are Donizetti's *L'esule di Roma* (1828) and Bellini's *Norma* (1831), both of whose central finales are cast as trios. Verdi increasingly tended to dispense with the last two movements, as in *Macbeth* (1847), *Il trovatore* and *La traviata* (1853). The *pezzo concertato* survives as late as *Otello* (1887) and *Falstaff* (1893). On the other hand *Rigoletto* (1851) and *La forza del destino* (1862) avoid the formula altogether. For the definitive version of *La Gioconda* (1876) Ponchielli devised a 'stretta substitute' in the form of an orchestral peroration based on a previous melody, a procedure much exploited by his pupil Puccini.

Outside Italy central ensembles of confrontation, freer in form, are also a common phenomenon, as in Spohr's *Jessonda* (1823), Weber's *Euryanthe* (1823), Tchaikovsky's *Yevgeny Onegin* (1879), Dvořák's *Rusalka* (1901) and Wagner's *Tannhäuser* (1845) and *Götterdämmerung* (1876) – significantly the first drama of *Der Ring des Nibelungen* to be planned; even the tumult that ends Act 2 of *Die Meistersinger* (1868) falls into the same category insofar as it represents the highest point of musical elaboration in the score. In French grand opera and its European derivatives this moment is usually embodied in a ceremony, as in Meyerbeer's *Le prophète* (1849), Wagner's *Lohengrin* (1850), and Verdi's *Don Carlos* (1867) and *Aida* (1871). With the passing of the 'grand' tradition the central finale is often reduced to the equivalent of a curtain line in a play, for example Massenet's 'Elle est d'un autre!' in *Werther* (1892) or Puccini's 'E avanti a lui tremava tutta Roma' in *Tosca* (1900).

By comparison, the 'finale ultimo' remained for a long time musically less important, a notable exception being that of Beethoven's *Fidelio* (1805). With Rossini, in whose operas with rare exceptions the *lieto fine* prevails, it usually takes the form of a commonplace chorus of rejoicing, as in *Tancredi*. *Il barbiere di Siviglia* (1816) reverts to the 18th-century *vaudeville final*. Italian Romantic operas, including some of Rossini's, usually end with an expanded aria for the prima donna – Donizetti's *Anna Bolena* (1830), *Maria Stuarda* (1835) and *Roberto Devereux* (1837), and Bellini's *La straniera* (1829), *Norma* and *Beatrice di Tenda* (1833) – or more rarely the primo uomo – Donizetti's *Torquato Tasso* (1833) and *Lucia di Lammermoor*. From early on, however, Verdi preferred the duet or trio finale, as in *Ernani* (1844), *Rigoletto* and *Aida*, a solution likewise favoured outside Italy, where the prestige of the star singer was less; examples include Gounod's *Faust* (1859), Bizet's *Carmen* (1875), Tchaikovsky's *Yevgeny Onegin* and many others. Rare instances of a *pezzo concertato finale ultimo* appear in Verdi's *Simon Boccanegra* (1857) and

Un ballo in maschera (1859). A number of 19th-century operas follow the tradition inaugurated by Scribe of ending with a spectacular cataclysm, such as a volcanic eruption in Auber's *La muette de Portici* (1828) and Petrella's *Jone* (1858), a massacre in Meyerbeer's *Les Huguenots* (1836) and Verdi's *Les vêpres siciliennes* (1855) or an avalanche in Catalani's *La Wally* (1892) – a list to which the ultimate cataclysm of Wagner's *Götterdämmerung* might perhaps be subjoined.

The diversity of style and dramatic approach in the 20th century, and particularly the pessimistic, sobering temper of many operatic endings, precludes the existence of any established pattern for finales. Quiet, neutral, resigned endings are common, as in such works as *Pelléas et Mélisande* (1902), *Kát'a Kabanová* (1921), *Wozzeck* (1925), *Katerina Izmaylova* (composed 1932), *Mathis der Maler* (1938), *Peter Grimes* (1945), *The Consul* (1950), *The Rake's Progress* (1951; this however has a moralizing epilogue) and *Dialogues des Carmélites* (1957).

*

E. J. Dent: 'Ensembles and Finales in Eighteenth-Century Opera', *SIMG*, xi (1909–10), 543–69; xii (1910–11), 112–38

M. Robinson: *Naples and Neapolitan Opera* (Oxford, 1972)

D. Heartz: 'Vis Comica: Goldoni, Galuppi and *L'Arcadia in Brenta*,' *Venezia e il melodramma nel settecento: Venice 1973–5*, ii, 33–73

——: 'The Creation of the Buffo Finale in Italian Opera', *PRMA*, civ (1977–8), 67–78

J. Platoff: 'Musical and Dramatic Structure in the *Opera Buffa* Finale', *JM*, vii (1989), 191–230

M. McClymonds: '*La clemenza di Tito* and the Action Ensemble Finale in Opera Seria before 1791', *MJb 1991*

J. Platoff: 'Tonal Organization in "Buffo" Finales and the Act II Finale of "Le nozze di Figaro" ', *ML*, lxxii (1991), 387–403

MARITA P. McCLYMONDS, ELISABETH COOK, JULIAN BUDDEN

Finazzi, Filippo (*b* Bergamo, ?1706; *d* Jersbeck [now Segeberg], nr Hamburg, 21 April 1776). Italian soprano castrato and composer. He enjoyed considerable fame in Italy and Germany. His earliest known appearances were in Venice in 1726; he sang in the Italian opera at Breslau, 1728–30, where he contributed arias to the pasticcio *Merope*. By 1732 he had returned to Venice; he was in Bologna in 1735 and by 1739 he was in the service of the Duke of Modena (late librettos describe him as *maestro di cappella*). In the summer of 1743 he joined the opera company of the impresario Pietro Mingotti in Linz, and appears never to have returned to Italy. That October the company moved to Hamburg, where it offered the first extended seasons of new Italian works, both serious and comic. Finazzi was not a regular member after 1744, when he composed for the company and toured with it to Prague and Leipzig. His last known stage appearance was in February 1746 in the title role of his own *Temistocle*. He taught for the next ten years and retired in 1756.

Il matrimonio sconcertato, per forza del Bacco (int, G. Locatelli), Prague, carn. 1744

Adelaide (os, A. Salvi), Leipzig, Easter, 1744, collab. P. Scalabrini

Temistocle (os, P. Metastasio), Hamburg, 16 Feb 1746, 3 arias *D-SWl*

La pace campestre (int), doubtful

Arias in: Merope, 1728; Il tempio di Melpomene su le rive dell'Alstra, 1747

*

E. H. Müller: *Die mingottischen Opernunternehmungen 1732–1756* (diss., U. of Dresden, 1915); rev. as *Angelo und Pietro Mingotti* (Dresden, 1917), 30, pp.cci–ccxviii [incl. thematic catalogue of Finazzi's surviving works]   JAMES L. JACKMAN

Fine, Vivian (*b* Chicago, 28 Sept 1913). American composer. She studied privately with Ruth Crawford-Seeger (1925–30) and Roger Sessions (1934–42), and has held appointments at the Juilliard School (1948), New York University (1945–8) and Bennington College (1964–88). Her first operatic work was a one-act fantasy entitled *A Guide to the Life Expectancy of a Rose* (1956), scored for soprano and tenor soloists and small instrumental ensemble. The libretto, by the composer, consists of a gardening article from a newspaper. The musical style is dissonant, although less so than in some of her earlier works. The work was produced in concert form in New York on 7 February 1956.

Fine's second opera, *The Women in the Garden* (1977), was given its première at the San Francisco Conservatory of Music on 12 February 1978 by the Porta Costa Players. This chamber opera brings together four women artists of the 19th and 20th centuries: Emily Dickinson, Isadora Duncan, Gertrude Stein and Virginia Woolf. The libretto was created by the composer chiefly from their writings. There is little plot as such; each character reveals herself while becoming acquainted with the others as artists and women; in doing so they are drawn together at an emotional, rather than an intellectual, level. According to the composer, 'this is not a feminist work … certain issues come up, but I don't extract them to make political points'. The compositional style is mainly lyrical. As well as introducing jazz music of the 1920s into the score, Fine incorporates musical quotations from Satie's *Véritables préludes flasques, pour un chien* (when Stein is speaking on humanness and dogs) and a few chords from Chopin's Funeral March (when Duncan is reflecting on the death of her children). The opera's most obvious influence may be Satie's *Socrate*.

*

R. Commanday: 'A Plotless "Garden" Gathering of Four Fantastic Personalities', *San Francisco Chronicle* (12 Feb 1978)

——: 'Let the Music do the Talking', *San Francisco Chronicle* (31 March 1982)   JAMES P. CASSARO

Fine, Wendy (*b* Durban, 19 Dec 1943). South African soprano. She studied in Durban and Vienna, making her début as Butterfly at Berne in 1965, then singing in Berlin, Hamburg, Stuttgart, Frankfurt, Munich, Düsseldorf and Cologne. She made her London début as Luise in the British première of Henze's *Der junge Lord*, given by Cologne Opera at Sadler's Wells (1969). At Covent Garden she sang Gutrune, Fiordiligi, Donna Elvira, Musetta, Jenůfa and Tat'yana (1971–7), as well as Marie (*Wozzeck*) at La Scala (1977). Her other roles included Pamina, Mařenka, Desdemona, Sophie and the Marschallin, Jenny (*Mahagonny*), Ophelia (Szokolay's *Hamlet*) and Mary (Martinů's *The Miracles of Mary*). An intelligent and dramatic singer, she has a lyrical, warm-toned voice.   ELIZABETH FORBES

Finger, Gottfried [Godfrey] (*b* ?Olomouc, *c*1660; *d* Mannheim, bur. 31 Aug 1730). Moravian composer. The son of a musician at the Olomouc court, he arrived in London perhaps in 1685 and served in James II's Catholic chapel, opened on Christmas Day 1686. His court appointment was not renewed by William III in 1689, so he embarked on a career in public concerts and in the theatre, writing music for the masque *The Loves of Mars and Venus* (1696, in collaboration with Eccles) and at least eight other productions at Lincoln's Inn

Fields between 1695 and 1697 (when he may have visited Italy), and at least eight more in 1700 and 1701, seven of which were for the rival Drury Lane company. On 3 June 1701 he received the fourth and last prize in the competition to set Congreve's masque *The Judgment of Paris*, whereupon he left England for good, reaching Vienna by early December. He worked subsequently at Breslau, Innsbruck, Neuburg an der Donau, Heidelberg and Mannheim, where his name last appears in the lists of the Hofkapelle in 1723; during this period overtures by him were used in operas by Greber, Heinichen and G. D. Pallavicini. An assessment of Finger's operatic style is hampered by the loss of *The Judgment of Paris* and all his later stage works, though his music for the semi-operas *The Rival Queens, or The Death of Alexander the Great* (after N. Lee; Drury Lane Feb 1701; *GB-Cfm*; collab. D. Purcell) and *The Virgin Prophetess, or The Fate of Troy* (5, E. Settle; Drury Lane, 2 May 1701; *Cfm*, *Lcm*) suggests that the competition of 1701 was not judged entirely on merit. His theatre suites are variable in quality, though some mix traces of Moravian folk music with the Purcellian idiom in an attractive fashion.

See also VIRGIN PROPHETESS, THE.

*

J. Wilson, ed.: *Roger North on Music* (London, 1959)
M. Tilmouth: 'A Calendar of References to Music in Newspapers Published in London and the Provinces (1660–1719)', *RMARC*, no. 1 (1961) [whole issue]
R. Fiske: *English Theatre Music in the Eighteenth Century* (Oxford, 1973, 2/1986)
C. A. Price: *Music in the Restoration Theatre* (Ann Arbor, 1979)
R. Platt: Introduction to J. Eccles: *The Judgment of Paris*, MLE, C1 (1984)

PETER HOLMAN

Fink, Myron S(amuel) (*b* Chicago, 19 April 1932). American composer. Among his teachers were Felix Borowski, Castelnuovo-Tedesco, Bernard Wagenaar at the Juilliard School, and Burrill Phillips at the University of Illinois. After receiving a Woodrow Wilson Memorial Fellowship he studied at Cornell (1954–5) with Robert Palmer, and then in Vienna on a Fullbright scholarship (1955–6). He has taught at Alma College, Hunter College, the Curtis Institute, SUNY, Purchase, and the City University of New York, Graduate Center. Upon retirement he moved to San Diego.

Fink's third opera, *Jeremiah*, concerns a religious fanatic who interjects himself between his son and the son's girlfriend. After Jeremiah seduces the girl, he refuses to repent and instead recounts the biblical story of the sacrifice of Isaac, before killing his son. His fifth opera, *Chinchilla*, captures Manhattan's 1920s nightlife with a combination of jazz syncopations and lyrical vocal lines.

The Boor (1, Fink, after A. P. Chekhov: *The Bear*), St Louis, MO, Jefferson Hotel Ivory Room, 14 Feb 1955
Susanna and the Elders, 1955 (2, D. Moreland)
Jeremiah (4, P. Fink and E. Hawley), Binghamton, NY, Harpur College, 25 May 1962
Judith and Holofernes, 1969–77 (3, Moreland, after J. Giraudoux: *Judith*), concert perf., SUNY, Purchase, Abbott and Caplin Theater, 4 Feb 1978
Chinchilla (3, Moreland), Binghamton, NY, Forum Theater, 18 Jan 1986
The Island of Tomorrow (1, L. Rodgers), New York, 19 June 1986

*

R. H. Kornick: *Recent American Opera: a Production Guide* (New York, 1991), 100–02 [about *Chinchilla*]

BRADLEY H. SHORT

Finke, Fidelio F(riedrich) (*b* Josefstal [now Josefův Důl], Bohemia, 22 Oct 1891; *d* Dresden, 12 June 1968). German composer. After attending the Reichenberg (now Liberec) College of Education, 1906–8, he went to Prague to study the piano with his uncle, Romeo Finke. From 1908 to 1911 he studied composition with Novák at the Prague Conservatory, where he taught from 1915. He held many influential posts in Czech and German musical education, including those of Rector of the Deutsche Akademie für Musik und Darstellende Kunst, Prague (1927–45), Rector of the Staatliche Akademie für Musik und Theater in Dresden (1946–51) and professor of composition at the Mendelssohn Akademie in Leipzig (1951–8). He received many honours for his compositions and his work in education, including the Czechoslovak National Prize in 1928 and, for *Die Jakobsfahrt*, in 1937.

Finke's early music was influenced by the Bohemian style of Dvořák's pupil Novák and above all by Richard Strauss. After 1918 he explored a more experimental range of styles, from expressionism and objectivity to neo-classicism. He encountered dodecaphony, and in the 1950s extended his interests to embrace German and Slavonic folk music.

With *Die Jakobsfahrt* (1936), Finke used the idea of a musical legend initiated by Hans Pfitzner in *Der arme Heinrich* (1895), at the same time moving away from his expressionist phase, which had culminated in this work. He was attracted to the subject not only by the eternal question of guilt, atonement and redemption, but also by the fantastic atmosphere in which mysticism and realism merge. His last opera, *Der Zauberfisch*, is based on the low German fairy-tale *The Fisherman and his Wife*.

Die versunkene Glocke, 1915–18 (4, G. Hauptmann), unpubd, lost
Die Jakobsfahrt (3, Dietzenschmidt [A. Schmidt]), Prague, Neues Deutsches, 17 Oct 1936
Der schlagfertige Liebhaber 2, 1950–54 (comic op, 3, K. Zuchardt), unpubd, vs D-Ba
Der Zauberfisch (Märchen ballade, 2, W. Hübner, after J. L. and W. C. Grimm), Dresden, Staatsoper, 3 June 1960

*

K. M. Komma: 'Schicksal und Schaffen sudetendeutscher Komponisten', *Stifter-Jb*, iii (1953), 83–126
D. Härtwig: 'F. F. Finke: A Entwicklung seines Schaffens', *Sammelbände zur Musikgeschichte der DDR*, ed. A. H. Brockhaus and K. Niemann, i (Berlin, 1969), 237–61
——: *F. F. Finke: Leben und Werk* (Habilitationsschrift, U. of Leipzig, 1970)
——: 'F. F. Finke', *Musiker in unserer Zeit* (Leipzig, 1979), 110

DIETER HÄRTWIG

Finland (Fin. Suomi). Republic in northern Europe, a province of Sweden from the Middle Ages and a Russian Grand Duchy from 1809 until it became independent in 1917. Operas were first performed in Finland in the 1820s by itinerant foreign companies. Travelling the international circuit between Stockholm and St Petersburg, they stopped in the three principal cities in southern Finland – Turku in the south-west, Helsinki, the capital, and Viipuri (now Vyborg) in the south-east. Such visits became relatively frequent; one result was that *Tannhäuser* was heard in Helsinki in 1857, nearly 20 years before being given (in Italian) at Covent Garden.

The first opera performance by Finns – albeit mostly amateurs – seems to have been *Der Freischütz* in Viipuri in 1829. The première in 1852 of *Kung Karls jakt* ('King Charles's Hunt') by Fredrik Pacius in Helsinki is regarded as a milestone. Although the composer was a

German who had become established in Finland (as a highly valued musical educator), it was the first opera written in Finland for Finnish performers. It proved there was potential operatic talent and enthusiasm to be tapped, on however modest a scale.

The second half of the 19th century was a time of vigorous development, accompanied by a great awakening of a national consciousness. A growing demand for literature and drama resulted in the establishment in 1872 of what was to become the National Theatre, and the following year an 'operatic section' was added to the theatre. Its performance of *Lucia di Lammermoor* in Viipuri on 21 November 1873 was another milestone; indeed, the present Finnish National Opera (Suomen Kansallisooppera) regards the date as its birthday. Yet the cultural base of late 19th-century Finland turned out to be too narrow to sustain the operatic section for long, and it foundered after only six years of a somewhat precarious existence. Opera performances, however, continued to be arranged on an ad hoc basis; and in 1911 a new Domestic Opera, forerunner of the present national company, was launched. The first decades of the 20th century also saw the emergence of a number of indigenous operas. They were mainly based on Finnish historical, mythological or folkloristic themes; musically most of them were firmly rooted in a 19th-century nationalist-romantic tradition. Only Aarre Merikanto's *Juha* (1922) was written in a genuinely 20th-century idiom. However, at that time Finnish operatic tastes – largely nurtured by German late-Romantic influences – were still relatively undeveloped. *Juha* was thus felt to be too 'radical', and it remained neglected for decades.

The first notable Finnish opera was Leevi Madetoja's *Pohjalaisia* ('The Ostrobothnians') of 1924. Its not unusual subject is the conflict between a proud local people and alien authority, set against a background of passion and jealousy. Madetoja had a strong feeling for drama, and in *The Ostrobothnians* he skilfully blends elements of regional folk melody with a colourful, boldly impressionistic orchestration. This work was regarded as the 'national opera' until the emergence in 1975 of Joonas Kokkonen's *Viimeiset Kiusaukset* ('The Last Temptations'), and has sustained its position in the Finnish repertory.

One of the most productive Finnish opera composers of the 1930s and 1940s was Tauno Pylkkänen, an inventive if somewhat bland exponent of a kind of Nordic *verismo*. It was only in the 1970s that a generation of opera composers with a strong, highly individual idiom began to emerge: Aulis Sallinen, Kokkonen and Einojuhani Rautavaara. Notable younger composers are Kalevi Aho, who wrote a monologue *Avain* ('The Key', 1979) and Paavo Heininen. The latter's uncompromisingly contemporary yet appealing *Silkkirumpu* ('The Damask Drum', 1984) and his densely written but dramatically highly charged *Veitsi* ('The Knife', 1989) have attracted international attention.

A great impetus to the interest in opera was created in the 1970s by the Savonlinna Opera Festival. One result of this interest has been a growth of amateur operatic societies throughout the country which mount a number of performances – mostly of the standard repertory – each year, their casts often reinforced by professional principals from the National Opera.

Several Finnish singers have made their mark abroad. The earliest was the soprano Aino Ackté, for a number of years a prima donna at the Paris Opéra. In between the wars the sopranos Aune Antti, Lea Piltti and Aulikki

Rautawaara made distinguished careers in Europe. They have been followed since World War II by whole generations of Finnish singers, among them the baritone Tom Krause and the bass Martti Talvela, and later the soprano Karita Mattila, the baritone Jorma Hynninen, and the basses Matti Salminen and Jaakko Ryhänen.

For further information on operatic activity in the country's principal centres *see* HELSINKI and SAVONLINNA.

T.-M. Lehtinen and P. Hako: *Kuninkaasta kuninkaaseen* [From King to King] (Helsinki, 1987)
L. de Gorog and R. de Gorog: 'Stage and Vocal Music in Finland', *From Sibelius to Sallinen* (New York, 1989), 173–93
ERKKI ARNI

Finney, Ross Lee (*b* Wells, MN, 23 Dec 1906). American composer and teacher. His teachers included Boulanger, Sessions and Berg. A member of the Smith College faculty from 1929 to 1948, he achieved further distinction as a teacher after 1949 when he became composer-in-residence at the University of Michigan. He remained there until his retirement in 1971. He has received numerous honours including two Guggenheim fellowships and the Brandeis Creative Arts Award.

Finney's music is characterized by a personal serial technique (the compression of a 'source set' often defines the linear flow of notes) combined with a depth of philosophy influenced by contact with thinkers like Bohr and Oppenheimer. A love for American folk materials informs his music, and the role of memory in communication continues to influence his thinking. Although a mystical and spiritual side has found expression in several pieces, overall it is a rhythmic impetus that energizes his music.

Nun's Priest's Tale (1965) was Finney's first work for musical theatre; it is a compact piece that requires that even concert versions be performed in costume. Finney describes his adaptation of Chaucer's text as a 'secular miracle play' and encourages that as a model for production. The men's chorus is limited to rhythmic speaking; the women's chorus makes hen imitations ('kut-kut') almost exclusively. A familiar folksong, 'Fox went out on a chilly night', frames the action. It is scored for chamber orchestra with a large number of percussion instruments, including such exotica as a dog bark, a cow-bell chain and a slide whistle.

Weep Torn Land (1984) is based on real people and events. It treats three areas of conflict; that between whites and native Americans as witnessed in the Sand Creek Massacre of 1864 (in which 500 Cheyenne were slaughtered by the Colorado Volunteers, attached to the Union Army), that between the North and the South during the American Civil War and that between the children of William Bent. The work is set in the American West (Colorado) and folksong is at its centre. But it has music of wide scope: the massacre, not seen on stage, is represented by taped sounds based on coyote wails, and the musical language is mainly representative of Finney's sophisticated chromaticism mixed with triadic polarization.

Given his fine sense of humour, it is not surprising that Finney's next stage work was a comic opera. *Computer Marriage* (1989) is, in Finney's words, 'nutty'. He has fashioned a wild plot, with the 17th-century astronomer Kepler wound up in a scheme to 'compute' a perfect wife with modern machines. The text is full of clever phrases and fanciful rhymes; the music is cunning in its abandon and frivolity.

Nun's Priest's Tale (1, Finney, after G. Chaucer), Hanover, NH, Aug 1965
Weep Torn Land, 1984 (7 scenes, Finney)
Computer Marriage, 1989 (comic op, 3 acts in 6 scenes, Finney)

P. Cooper: 'The Music of Ross Lee Finney', *MQ*, liii (1967), 1–21
H. Onderdonk: 'Aspects of Tonality in the Music of Ross Lee Finney', *Perspectives on American Composers*, ed. B. Boretz and E. T. Cone (New York, 1971), 248–68
C. Gagne and T. Caras: 'Ross Lee Finney', *Soundpieces: Interviews with American Composers* (Metuchen, NJ, 1982), 179–91
E. Borroff: 'Ross Lee Finney', *Three American Composers* (London, 1986), 101, 251
K. Peacock: 'The Dramatic and Musical Structure of *Weep Torn Land*', *Weep Torn Land, an Opera in Seven Scenes: Sampler* (New York, 1987)
WILLIAM ALBRIGHT

Finnie, Linda (*b* Scotland, 9 May 1952). Scottish mezzo-soprano. She studied in Glasgow, making her début in 1976 with Scottish Opera. In 1978 she sang Ozias in a staged performance of Vivaldi's *Juditha triumphans* at the Bordeaux Festival. Later she sang Larina with the WNO (1980) and Hatred in Gluck's *Armide* at the Spitalfields Festival, London (1982). She has sung Eboli, Brangäne, Amneris and Ulrica with the ENO, and has appeared in Frankfurt, Brussels, Paris, Nice and Amsterdam and at Bayreuth, where she sang Fricka, Siegrune and the Second Norn (1988). Her other roles include the Sorceress (*Dido and Aeneas*), Neris (*Médée*), Waltraute and Herodias (*Salome*). Her voice is not large, but firm and strongly projected.

ELIZABETH FORBES

Finnilä, Birgit (*b* Falkenberg, 24 Jan 1931). Swedish contralto. She studied at Göteborg and in London at the RAM. After some years as a concert singer, she made her stage début in 1967 as Gluck's Orpheus at Göteborg. She appeared at La Scala, the Opéra, in Munich and Geneva and at Salzburg, where she sang Erda in the Easter Festival (1973–4); her repertory included Brangäne and Hedwige (*Guillaume Tell*). She sang the Seashell (*Die ägyptische Helena*) at Carnegie Hall, New York (1979) and made her Metropolitan début in 1981 as Erda, the role that best displayed her deep, resonant voice.

ELIZABETH FORBES

Finnish National Opera. Company based in HELSINKI; tracing its roots to 1914, it gained its present name and status in 1956.

Finnissy, Michael (Peter) (*b* London, 17 March 1946). English composer and pianist. He studied at the RCM, where his teachers included Bernard Stevens and Searle, and later in Italy with Roman Vlad. His early compositions, influenced by his own prodigious keyboard technique, make extravagant virtuoso demands and their notational intricacies led him to be associated, misleadingly, with the 'new complexity' of composers such as Brian Ferneyhough. Finnissy's stylistic roots are however more heterogeneous, with strong affinities with the English experimental tradition of John White and Howard Skempton.

With the puppet entertainment *Mr Punch* (1977) Finnissy began to explore some of the possibilities of small-scale music theatre, while he wrote extensively for dance and for the conventional theatre; these strands of development were finally brought together in the chamber opera *The Undivine Comedy* (1988, Paris), based on Zygmunt Krasinski's drama *Nieboska*

kommedia (1835) but also incorporating material from Hölderlin and De Sade. Finnissy refashioned Krasinki's unambiguously Roman Catholic conclusion in humanist terms, condensing the large cast into five archetypal roles and the disjunct sequence of scenes into two seamless parts. The instrumental textures (obtained from an ensemble of nine players) are predominantly hard-edged, though the score incorporates plainchant, folk material and Middle Eastern vocal techniques in characterizing the roles.

A. Clements: 'Finnissy's Undivine Comedy', *MT*, cxxix (1988), 330–2
ANDREW CLEMENTS

Finscher, Ludwig (*b* Kassel, 14 March 1930). German musicologist. He studied at Göttingen University (PhD 1954) and taught at the universities of Kiel, Saarbrücken, Frankfurt (1968–81) and Heidelberg, where he was appointed professor of musicology in 1981. His interests centre on the Josquin period and the Viennese Classics but he has also worked on a wide range of operas. His contributions to complete works series include editions of *Le nozze di Figaro*, Gluck's *Orfeo ed Euridice* (with A. A. Abert) and *Orphée et Euridice*, as well as Hindemith's *Sancta Susanna* and *Mörder, Hoffnung der Frauen* (both with M. Reissinger). He has written articles on 19th- and 20th-century opera, notably on Auber, Weber and Richard Strauss.

Finta giardiniera, La (i) ('The Pretended Garden-Girl'). *Dramma giocoso* in three acts by PASQUALE ANFOSSI; Rome, Teatro delle Dame, Carnival 1774.

The plot is the same as for Mozart's opera of the same title, as are the texts of the individual numbers with a few minor exceptions (see FINTA GIARDINIERA, LA (ii) for a discussion of the libretto). Anfossi's setting was more immediately successful than Mozart's however, receiving at least 16 productions in the first five years after its première and remaining in the repertory until the end of the 18th century. The pairs of characters fall cleanly into *seria*, *mezzo carattere* and *buffo* types; Anfossi's setting responds to the machinations of the plot, providing a classic example of late 18th-century musical depictions of noble, sentimental and buffoonish characters.

The general means Anfossi uses to depict his characters and situations are, by and large, rather like Mozart's, and indeed there are even some motivic, thematic and formal similarities between the two settings of the same words; Arminda's first aria 'Si promette facilmente' is a case in point. Anfossi's text-setting and phraseology is generally more regular than Mozart's, and his use of the orchestra is considerably less imaginative, employed in a strictly accompanimental and punctuating role. Among the most striking differences between the settings is the scene near the end of the second act where Sandrina, the 'finta giardiniera', finds herself alone and abandoned in the wilderness. Anfossi's touching arias in G major and Bb major at this point do not come close to the intensity of Mozart's through-composed scena, which moves from C minor to A minor. Anfossi's comic gift, however, is evident in the role of the Podestà (Mayor), and in Nardo's mocking aria, 'Con un vezzo all'italiana'.

Anfossi's opera was also performed as *La marchesa giardiniera* (1775, London) and *Die edle Gärtnerin* (1782, Frankfurt).

MARY HUNTER

Finta giardiniera, La (ii) ('The Pretended Garden-Girl'). *Opera buffa* in three acts, K196, by WOLFGANG AMADEUS MOZART; Munich, Salvatortheater, 13 January 1775.

Ramiro *a knight*	soprano castrato
Don Anchise *Mayor (Podestà) of Lagonero*	tenor
Marchioness Violante Onesti *disguised as Sandrina, working in the Mayor's garden*	soprano
Roberto *her servant, disguised as Nardo, a gardener*	baritone
Serpetta *the Mayor's housekeeper*	soprano
Arminda *a Milanese lady, the Mayor's niece*	soprano
Count (Contino) Belfiore	tenor

Setting The Mayor's estate at Lagonero near Milan

No published libretto of *La finta giardiniera* acknowledges its authorship. The attribution 'Calzabigi, revised Coltellini' may derive from confusion with the concurrent production of Tozzi's *Orfeo*. Angermüller has suggested the Roman librettist Giuseppe Petrosellini, but Italian scholars have recently questioned this attribution on stylistic grounds. The first setting, by Anfossi, was given at Rome during Carnival 1774; Mozart's followed within a year.

The Mozarts left Salzburg three weeks before the planned first performance (29 December), which was postponed, Leopold wrote (28 December), to allow more time to learn the music and actions. Three performances took place, the first and third with great success in the old court theatre; the second, in the Redoutensaal, was truncated because one singer was ill. The casting remains uncertain. Rosa Manservisi sang Sandrina and the soprano castrato Tommaso Consoli Ramiro, although the range suits the modern (female) mezzo. Other likely singers include Teresa Manservisi (Arminda or Serpetta), Johann Walleshauser (Belfiore), Augustin Sutor (the Mayor) and Giovanni Rossi (Nardo).

The first revival was as a Singspiel, *Die verstellte Gärtnerin*. Mozart probably helped with the adaptation, which was performed by Johann Böhm's company in Augsburg (1 May 1780). Böhm took it to other German centres including Frankfurt (1782; the first Mozart opera given in North Germany). After 1797 it was not heard until 1891, in Vienna. Until recently, 20th-century revivals necessarily used the German form since no source survived of the Italian first act. Its rediscovery (in time for the Neue Mozart-Ausgabe, 1978) permits revival of the original version (Munich and Salzburg, 1979; several subsequent productions). English performances have been given under the title *Sandrina's Secret*.

ACT 1 *The Mayor's garden* In the *Introduzione* (which replaces a third overture movement) and their first arias the characters develop their initial feelings. Ramiro, spurned by Arminda, finds love a snare; the Mayor compares his love for the garden-maid to a series of musical instruments ('Dentro il mio petto', an aria which had some currency outside the opera). Sandrina (Violante) reminds Nardo (Roberto, pretending to be her cousin) of the background to the story; she is seeking her lover Belfiore who a year ago stabbed her and fled, believing her dead. Her pastoral aria maintains her disguise in front of Ramiro. Nardo is in love with Serpetta, but she intends to marry her master. Arminda clamours for attention until the arrival of her betrothed, who proves to be Belfiore, singing the praises of female beauty. Arminda threatens punishment for any unfaithfulness. Belfiore traces his pedigree to the heroes of Greece and Rome. Serpetta engages in banter with Nardo (each sing a verse of an aria); she adds a sprightly aria of her own.

Hanging Gardens Sandrina bewails her fate in an eloquent cavatina. On learning the name of Arminda's betrothed she faints. In the finale Belfiore recognizes her, but she denies her identity. Nevertheless their behaviour seems compromising. In a brilliantly varied multi-movement 'ensemble of perplexity', Ramiro is pleased, Nardo concerned, Serpetta and Arminda jealous, Sandrina upset, Belfiore bemused and the Mayor vexed by the upset to his household.

ACT 2 *Hall of the Mayor's house* Having dismissed Ramiro, Arminda turns on Belfiore (an aria in a vibrantly emotional G minor). Nardo woos Serpetta in Italian, French and English, but she is too jealous of his 'cousin' to admit to liking him. Sandrina muddles Belfiore still more by giving an eyewitness account of her own death; in his amorous aria in response he accidentally pays court to the Mayor, from whom Sandrina has to repel a further advance. Ramiro appears with a warrant for Belfiore's arrest for killing Violante; the Mayor cannot allow a murderer to marry his niece. Ramiro pleads his cause in the warmest melody of the opera ('Dolce d'amor compagna').

Another room Belfiore is confronted with the accusation. Sandrina defends him: there was no murder, for she is Violante. The others only half-believe her and to Belfiore she denies it again, saying she spoke only to save him. This finally unhinges him (obbligato recitative and aria). Meanwhile we learn that Arminda has had Sandrina abandoned in the wild woods; the men hasten to the rescue, followed by the others. Serpetta's roguish aria leads without a break into the new scene; the music is now continuous to the end of the act.

A dark wood, with rocks and caves Sandrina cries out in fear (Agitato in C minor; 'Crudeli, fermate'; cavatina and recitative). She hides in a cave and in the finale the others appear one by one and pair off in a comedy of mistaken identity revealed when the practical Ramiro brings a light. But the noble lovers find harmony in madness, acting the part of mythological characters amid general consternation.

ACT 3 *A room* The lunatics mistake Nardo for their beloved. He makes his escape, leaving them prey to imaginary disasters (aria and duet). The Mayor complains that he cannot understand what is going on. Arminda is still determined to marry Belfiore; Ramiro gives vent to his feelings in a powerful C minor aria ('Va pure ad altri').

The garden Sandrina and Belfiore are sleeping. They awake restored and take leave of one another in a long recitative and duet, then decide, with ecstatic finality, that they must never part. This news reconciles Arminda with Ramiro; Serpetta, seeing that the Mayor will always sigh for Sandrina, marries Nardo. In a short finale all sing Sandrina's praises.

* * *

La finta giardiniera is Mozart's first mature *opera buffa*, but it is a far cry from the swiftly unfolding, ensemble-driven plots of the Da Ponte operas. Its ancestry lies in Goldoni's librettos, mingling serious emotions with comedy; apart from the finales it consists almost entirely of arias. The *Serva padrona* tradition remains in the Serpetta – Nardo – Mayor intrigue, and the disguised noblewoman, victim of jealousy, descends from Piccinni's *La buona figliuola*. Whereas the Count, who seems decidedly weak in the head, is both comic and pathetic, Ramiro is entirely serious, while Arminda appears to caricature *opera seria*.

The music is almost too elaborate, but it is an astounding achievement for an 18-year-old: richly coloured, distinctive in characterization, alternately good-humoured and searchingly expressive in the arias, and brilliantly inventive in the finales. Characterization includes class distinction. The nobles employ a more developed musical idiom, including obbligato recitative and a greater degree of coloratura, than Ramiro and Arminda (despite the vehemence of their minor-mode arias) and the Mayor. The servants bring a simpler melodic style, largely syllabic word-setting, and lighter orchestration.

The opera contains an almost wilful variety of emotional entanglements but its resolution remains obstinately symmetrical, like that of *Così fan tutte*. Love-ties across class barriers (Arminda – Belfiore; Serpetta or Violante/Sandrina – Mayor) do not work out. The restoration of the aristocrats' wits, and the union of social equals in three couples, symbolize restoration of the order threatened by the aftermath of Belfiore's rash attack on Violante.   JULIAN RUSHTON

Finta pazza, La ('The Pretended Madwoman'). *Drama* in a prologue and three 'azioni' ('protasi', 'epitasi', 'catastrofe') by FRANCESCO SACRATI to a libretto by GIULIO STROZZI; Venice, Teatro Novissimo, 1641 (libretto dedicated 14 January 1641).

The action takes place on the island of Skiros. The Greek ambassadors Ulisse [Ulysses] (alto) and Diomede [Diomedes] (tenor) seek the young Achille [Achilles] (soprano), who, in order to escape the Trojan war, has been hidden by his mother Tetide [Thetis] (tenor) and disguised as a girl in the women's quarters of Licomede [Lycomedes] (bass), king of the island, thereby angering Giunone [Juno] (soprano) and Minerva (soprano). Achilles, secretly in love with Lycomedes' daughter Deidamia (soprano), is impatient to join the warriors preparing to lay siege to Troy. Following the intentions of Giove [Jupiter] (bass) and Vittoria [Victory] (soprano), Ulysses publicly exposes Achilles through a subterfuge. In Act 2 Achilles successfully challenges Ulysses and Diomedes on an issue concerning love and receives an enchanted spear from Vulcano [Vulcan] (bass); Vulcan is reprimanded by Venere [Venus] (soprano), who supports the Trojans. Deidamia's Nurse (tenor) tries to comfort her, but Deidamia is in despair at the thought of Achilles abandoning her for war and tries to dissuade him by pretending to be mad with grief. In Act 3 Deidamia confesses her betrothal to Achilles to her father, who believes she is really mad and has her put in chains. Persevering in her feigned raving, she finally succeeds in touching Achilles' heart, and he asks for her hand in marriage. Amid general rejoicing the warriors embark for Troy, while a chorus of Celestial Minds bears heavenwards the chains which had bound Deidamia, the 'pretended madwoman' of the title.

With the backing of the influential Accademia degli Incogniti (an association of freethinkers of which Strozzi was a member), *La finta pazza* was as successful as the promoters of the Teatro Novissimo had hoped. To overcome competition from other Venetian opera houses, the new building (designed specifically for opera) was endowed with a system of rapid scene changing invented by Giacomo Torelli, who devised a spectacular set (described later by Maiolino Bisaccioni in *Il cannocchiale per la finta pazza*; see DMV, i, Milan,

'La finta pazza' (Sacrati): set designed by Giacomo Torelli for Act 1 scenes i–ii in the production at the Petit Bourbon, Paris, on 14 December 1645; engraving by N. Cochin from 'Feste theatrali per la finta pazza … di Giulio Strozzi' (Paris, 1645)

forthcoming). The leading role was taken by Anna Renzi, brought in from Rome, who was alluring both as singer and as actress, and a young castrato from Pistoia (perhaps Atto Melani) appeared as 'Il Consiglio Improvviso' in the Prologue. The theme of a mad heroine, new to opera (if not to literary and improvised comedy), was used to produce a whirl of contrasting and disconnected emotional situations (Strozzi had tried it in 1627 in *La finta pazza Licori*, left unfinished by Monteverdi). The work's explicit ideology portrays the Venetian Republic as the ideal descendant of Rome, founded as a consequence of the fall of Troy, but it also advocates pretence and dissimulation in love as well as in politics. The tone is lighthearted and saucy, with amusing allusions and moments of hilarious obscenity.

Three years after its Venetian triumph *La finta pazza* (with Cavalli's *Egisto* and other Venetian operas) began touring Italy in productions by companies such as the Febiarmonici and the Discordati. In a considerably reduced version, omitting most of the scenes with gods and goddesses (which were difficult to produce in theatres lacking the necessary machinery), it was performed in Piacenza (May 1644), possibly Lucca (September 1645), Bologna (January–February 1647), Genoa (Carnival 1647), Milan (?1647), Turin (February 1648) and Naples (July 1652). A fuller version was given at Reggio Emilia (March 1648), directed by Sacrati. In Florence a version similar to that of 1644 was produced by the Venetian choreographer G. B. Balbi (February 1645) and then taken at Mazarin's request to Paris (with Torelli as scenographer), where it was given at the Petit Bourbon on 14 December 1645, the first public performance of an opera in France (see illustration).

The score, discovered in 1984 on Isola Bella (*I-IBborromeo*), coincides substantially with the touring version. The Prologue has two orchestral sections which also feature in a manuscript of *L'incoronazione di Poppea* (in *Vnm*). However, since it is impossible to ascertain which parts of the *Finta pazza* score are in fact by Sacrati, comparative attributions of parts of the two operas are not feasible. The first modern performance (Venice, Fenice, 7 July 1987, under Alan Curtis) revealed a lively score with a light recitative which opens into short, intense flourishes of melody, some ostentatious (the arias of gods and goddesses), some languishing (Deidamia's laments), some jocular (the Nurse) and some cheerfully mocking (in the mad scenes).

For further illustration *see* BALBI, GIOVAN BATTISTA.

LORENZO BIANCONI

Finta savia, La ('The Pretended Wise-Woman'). *Drama* in a prologue and three acts, with intermezzos, by FILIBERTO LAURENZI and others to a libretto by GIULIO STROZZI; Venice, Teatro SS Giovanni e Paolo, Carnival 1643.

The music was mainly by Laurenzi, with Act 1 scenes iii–v, x and xii by Tarquinio Merula, Act 1 scene vi by Arcangelo Crivelli (but containing a canzonetta by Laurenzi), Act 2 scenes ii–iii by Crivelli and Act 3 scenes i and vii–ix by BENEDETTO FERRARI; a bifolium bound in between pages 72 and 73 of the libretto contains (in a typeface used in the main text) the texts of two intermezzos by Alessandro Leardini, to be used if intermezzos without dances are required, and a canzonetta by Vincenzo Tozzi which could be substituted for that

by Laurenzi at the end of Act 1 scene vi. Scenery and staging were by Giovanni Burnacini with Pietro Mango and Simonetto Guglielmi.

Since the apportioning of scenes to composers other than Laurenzi seems random, it may be that the original intention was for Laurenzi to set the entire opera, that he was unable to complete it and that others were called in to help at the last minute. There are other hints of last-minute uncertainties. Act 2 scene viii, for example, carries a rubric saying that its position may be changed to Act 2 scene iv in order to make the scene changes simpler; and Strozzi's original intermezzos, related to the main drama and cast in the form of Greek choral odes, required dancers, whereas the substitutes set by Leardini did not.

The plot is set in classical antiquity and forms one of a loosely-related trilogy of librettos by Strozzi covering the period from the fall of Troy (*La finta pazza*, 1641) to the founding of Rome (*Il Romolo e 'l Remo*, 1645). The central character is Aretusa [Arethusa], daughter of Sardanapalo [Sardanapalus], king of Assyria, and the 'pretended wise-woman' of the title. Her feigned wisdom consists in concealing her sensual nature by becoming a pupil of the Cumaean sibyl, then held captive by Proca [Procas], king of Alba Latina. Procas, however, falls in love with Arethusa, as do his two sons Amulio [Amulius] and Numitore [Numitor], the latter of whom causes confusion by claiming to own a magic ring which enables him to change form. Arethusa's nurse, Laverna, who sees through Numitor's trickery, turns the tables on him by encouraging Arethusa to elope with Amulius, whom she represents as Numitor in the guise of his brother. A fourth suitor for Arethusa's hand is Marsio [Marsius], king of Tuscany. In the final judgment scene Arethusa chooses to give herself to Marsius, not as wife but as servant. He, however, gives her as wife to Amulius and takes Amulius's sister Aventina as his own wife. The sibyl is restored to Cumae and Numitor is espoused to Crisilla, daughter of the Cumaean king. Only Procas, who had hoped to father the founders of Rome, is left single at the end of the opera.

A number of scenes, particularly in Act 2, include strophic texts clearly intended as arias. Most are allotted to the two female roles, Arethusa and Aventina, which were sung by Anna Renzi and Anna Valerio, the two star singers from Rome mentioned in the libretto. Act 2 scene x is particularly rich in this respect since it includes five canzonettas sung by Arethusa as she muses on mythological stories, suggested by statues in the sacred garden of the sibyl, of maidens carried off by gods; in the last of these she anticipates the arrival of her own lover who, indeed, carries her away from the rival suitors. The music of these and other arias by Laurenzi were collected by G. B. Verdizotti and published in *Arie a una voce … del Sig. Filiberto Laurenzi … nel dramma della finta savia* (Venice, 1643/4). The remainder of the music is lost.

JOHN WHENHAM

Finta semplice, La ('The Pretended Simpleton'). *Opera buffa* in three acts, K51/46a, by WOLFGANG AMADEUS MOZART to a libretto by CARLO GOLDONI with alterations by MARCO COLTELLINI; Salzburg, Archbishop's Palace, probably 1 May 1769.

La finta semplice was rehearsed in Vienna in 1768 but not performed, because of doubts about its genuineness and other intrigues (indignantly, but not circumstantially, outlined by Leopold). Its only performance in Mozart's lifetime was in Salzburg the next year, with local singers including Maria Magdalena Lipp, Michael Haydn's wife (Rosina). Coltellini's revisions tighten the intrigue and ensure a good third finale.

The three-movement *sinfonia* K45 became the overture, its final cadence elided with the opening *coro*. *La finta semplice* is a comedy of love overcoming obstacles through deceit, its roots in *commedia dell'arte*. Cassandro (bass) and Polidoro (tenor) forbid their sister Giacinta (soprano) to marry Fracasso (tenor) and their maid Ninetta (soprano) to marry his servant Simone (bass). Fracasso's sister Rosina (soprano), the major role whose range of sentiment includes the longest and most serious arias, wins Cassandro's heart by her feigned simplicity (hence the title) and Polidoro's by instructing him in wooing. The brothers' resistance is finally broken by the threat of a duel and the theft of their gold. The lovers succeed in forcing assent to their marriages, and Rosina marries Cassandro.

By Mozart's own standards, rhythmic squareness, lack of ensembles and monotony of key in the long finales may be seen as signs of immaturity. Distinctions of class are not fully reflected in the music. Nevertheless *La finta semplice* shows a complete grasp of the idiom and can stand comparison with contemporary *opera buffa* by such composers as Piccinni.   JULIAN RUSHTON

Finto Stanislao, Il. Opera by Giuseppe Verdi; *see* GIORNO DI REGNO, UN.

Fiocco, Pietro Antonio [Pierre-Antoine] (*b* Venice, *c*1650; *d* Brussels, 3 Sept 1714). Italian composer. The first that is known of him is that his prologue to the opera *Alceste* was performed in Hanover in 1681; but his presence there is not well documented. In 1682 he was in Brussels, where he married. According to Walker, he was master of the ducal chapel there in 1687 and composed a prologue for an (unnamed) opera produced at court that year. From 1694 to 1698 he collaborated with Giovanni Paolo Bombarda in the direction of the Opéra du Quai du Foin. Most of the works performed were by Lully, including *Amadis, Acis et Galatée, Phaëton, Armide* and *Thésée*; Fiocco wrote new prologues for them in honour of the Elector of Bavaria, the imperial representative in the Netherlands. By 1696 he was *lieutenant de la chapelle* at the electoral court chapel; in 1706 he became *maître de chapelle*, succeeding Pietro Torri. His output consists mostly of conventional sacred works with a Venetian flavour, though the surviving prologue and pastorale are in the French style. Two of Fiocco's 14 children were also composers.

Prol. for Alceste (A. Aureli) [music by P. A. Strungk or M. A. Ziani], Hanover, 1681, formerly *D-HVs*
Prols. for revs. of Lully's Amadis, Acis et Galatée, Phaëton, Armide, Thésée, Bellérophon and other operas, all lost
Le retour du printemps (pastorale), Brussels, 1699, *A-Wn*

*

Grove5 (F. Walker)
C. Stellfeld: *Les Fiocco: une famille de musiciens belges aux XVIIe et XVIIIe siècles* (Brussels, 1941)
S. Clercx: *La musique en Belgique: le dix-septième et le dix-huitième siècles* (Brussels, 1950), 181ff   SUZANNE CLERCX-LEJEUNE

Fioravanti, Valentino (*b* Rome, 11 Sept 1764; *d* Capua, 16 June 1837). Italian composer. His musical education was confined to private study, first in Rome and then in Naples (1779). In 1781 he returned to Rome, where he conducted at various theatres and composed his first opera, the intermezzo *Le avventure di Bertoldino*

(1783–4). In 1787 the Teatro del Fondo in Naples commissioned a comic opera, *Gl'inganni fortunati* (1788), which secured his fame.

In Naples Fioravanti was a formidable rival to Paisiello, P. A. Guglielmi and Cimarosa. He toured Italy, writing both comic and serious operas for all the major theatres. His most popular, *Le cantatrici villane*, was written for Naples in 1799 during the revolutionary turmoil. An instant success, it was performed throughout Europe, becoming one of his few works to be revived in the 20th century (1907, Vienna; 1951, Rome).

After the success of *La capricciosa pentita* at La Scala, written for it and put on in 1802, Fioravanti was engaged as director of the S Carlos theatre in Lisbon, a post he retained until 1807 when political strife made life uncomfortable. On his way back to Italy he visited Paris and wrote an opera, *I virtuosi ambulanti* (1807), for the Théâtre Italien. His fame had preceded him with performances of *La capricciosa pentita* in 1805 and *Le cantatrici villane* in 1806, the former famous (according to Castil-Blaze) for introducing the english horn to the French theatre orchestra. In Italy Fioravanti continued to receive contracts for operas until 1816, when his theatrical career declined.

Although remembered for his comic works, Fioravanti wrote an almost equal number of serious ones, borrowing some of his plots, as did many others, from the French theatre and the 'larmoyante' tradition. The most unusual of the melodramas was a trilogy entitled *Adelaide e Comingio* (1812–18, Naples). The blood-and-thunder, Romeo-and-Juliet story, spiced with comic ingredients, was taken by the librettist A. L. Tottola from a popular series of plays by the Revolutionary poet Giacomantonio Gualzetti (1789), derived in turn from a verse drama by François d'Arnaud (1765) and a novel by the infamous Claudine de Tencin (1735). The story was especially popular with the Neapolitans, but only *Adelaide maritata* was ever played outside Naples. This experiment in tragedy was significant for the history of Neapolitan opera, but Fioravanti's greatest gift lay elsewhere, in *opera buffa*. Cimarosa particularly praised his 'parlante' (passages of comic dialogue over orchestral ostinato figures), even though he feared the younger man's undeniable talent and its effect on Neapolitan audiences. Fioravanti's music does not fall into platitudinous forms as readily as does that of some of his contemporaries; the musical language is flexible and lively, and the tempo changes within numbers unpredictable, suiting the situation. His harmonic language is uninventive for its time, but typical of Italian opera innocent of Haydn and Mozart. Comedy is everything, from complicated imbroglios in ensembles to the imitation of barnyard animals (in *La capricciosa pentita*); each dramatic situation receives an appropriate, witty musical treatment. Stendhal in his *Vie de Rossini* (Paris, 1824) paid Fioravanti his greatest compliment; he reported Rossini as believing that the art of *opera buffa* had already reached perfection before he began to compose, and that in the particular comic style known as *nota e parola* there could be no further progress afer Fioravanti.

See also CANTATRICI VILLANE, LE.

cm – *commedia per musica*   dg – *dramma giocoso*
mel – *melodramma*   ob – *opera buffa*

Le avventure di Bertoldino, o sia La dama contadina (intermezzo), Rome, Ornani, carn. 1784, *I-Mr*

Le vicende amorose (ob, 2, G. B. Neri), Naples, Ferdinando, carn. 1784

La fuga avventurata, o sieno I viaggiatori ridicoli (intermezzo), Rome, Pace, carn. 1787

Il rè dei Mori (intermezzo), Rome, Pace, carn. 1787

I tre Orfei (ob, 2), Rome, Pace, aut. 1787

Gl'inganni fortunati (cm, 2, G. Pagliuca), Naples, Fondo, 31 Jan 1788

Il fabbro parigino, ossia La schiava fortunata (farsetta, 2, L. Romanelli), Rome, Capranica, 9 Jan 1789; as Il fabbro, Florence, spr. 1791; as La schiava fortunata, Naples, 1796; Fc, Mr, P-La

Il gentiluomo di Manfredonia (ob, 2), Rome, Capranica, Jan 1789

Il selvaggio di California (ob, 2), Rome, Pallacorda, 27 Dec 1789

Con i matti il savio la perde, ovvero Le pazzie a vicenda (ob), Florence, Pergola, spr. 1791, I-Fc

La famiglia stravagante (ob, G. Petrosellini), Rome, Capranica, 3 Feb 1792; as Gli amanti comici ossia La famiglia in scompiglio, Folignano, carn. 1796; as La famiglia sconcerto, Treviso, 1797

L'alchimista deluso (ob), Rome, Alibert, spr. 1792

L'audacia delusa (cm, 2, A. Fiore), Naples, Fondo, aut. 1793

L'amore immaginario (cm, 2, G. Gasparri), Naples, Nuovo, sum. 1794, Gl, US-Bp

I matrimonio per magia (cm, 1) Naples, Fondo, aut. 1794, I-Nc

L'astuta in amore, ossia Il furbo malaccorta (ob, 2, G. Palomba), Naples, Nuovo, spr. 1795, Fc, Gl, Mc, Mr, Nc, US-Bp (Act 1)

Liretta e Giannino (cm, 2, F. S. Zini), Naples, Fiorentini, 22 Aug 1795, I-Fc, Gl, Nc

La cantatrice bizzara (farsa, 2), Rome, Capranica, 26 Dec 1795

I viaggiatori amanti (ob, P. Mililotti), Rome, Apollo, 25 Jan 1796

I puntigli per equivoco (dg, 2, Gasparri), Naples, Fiorentini, spr. 1796, Fc, Nc, US-Bp

Il furbo contro il furbo (ob, 2, ? Valentino Fioravanti, from A.-R. Lesage: Crispin rival de son maître, 1707), Venice, S Samuele, 29 Dec 1796; rev. as Il ciabattino ringentilito, Vienna, Hof, 10 June 1797; as L'arte contro l'arte, Parma, Ducale, carn. 1798; as Chi la fa, chi la disfa e chi l'imbroglio, Trieste, aut. 1802; as Il ciabattino incivilito, Modena, 1804; as Il ciabattino (lib. rev. A. L. Tottola), Naples, 1822; I-Fc, Gl, Mr, Nc

L'innocente ambizione (ob, 2 Gasparri), Naples, Fiorentini, spr. 1797, Nc

L'amor per interesse (cm, 2, Gasparri), Naples, Fondo, 15 Nov 1797

La fiera di Senigallia (farsa, 2, G. Dolfin), Venice, S Samuele, 10 Dec 1797 [after S. Nasolini: Il medico di Lucca, ? identical with La fiera disturbata, 1808]

L'amore a dispetto (ob, 2, G. Palomba), Naples, Fiorentini, April 1798, Fc, Nc, US-Wc

L'impresario in angustie (ob, 2, G. M. Diodati), Naples, Fiorentini, April 1798

Lo sposo senza moglie (ob, 2, G. Palomba), Naples, Fiorentini, carn. 1799

Le cantatrici villane (cm, 2, G. Palomba), Naples, Fiorentini, Jan 1799; rev. as Le virtuose ridicole (1, G. M. Foppa), Venice, S Moisè, 28 Dec 1801; as Die Sängerinnen auf dem Lande, Munich 1812; A-Wn, D-Bds, Dlb, DS, I-Fc, Mr, Nc; vs (Paris, n.d.)

Cillenio pastore (componimento drammatico, Pagliuca), Naples, Palazzo Reale, carn. 1800

Griselda (3, A. Palomba), Palermo, Sta Cecilia, carn. 1800

I contrasti d'amore (ob, 2), Turin, Carignano, Lent 1800

L'ambizione punita (dramma, 2, G. Palomba), Naples, Fiorentini, spr. 1800, Nc

L'avaro (cm, 2, G. Bertati), Naples, Nuovo, sum. 1800, Nc

Il villano in angustie (dg, 2, F. Cammarano), Naples, Nuovo, spr. 1801, F-Pc, I-Nc, US-Wc

L'inganno cade sopra l'ingannatore (ob), Rome, Valle, aut. 1801; also as Sopra l'ingannator cade l'inganno (Petrosellini), Florence, Risoluti, 26 Dec 1803

Amore e destrezza, ossia I contratempi superati dall'arte (farsa giocosa, 1, Foppa), Venice, S Moisè, 26 Dec 1801

Amore aguzza l'ingegno (farsa giocosa, 1, Foppa), Venice, S Moisè, 3 Feb 1802, I-Fc

La capricciosa pentita (mel giocoso, 2, Romanelli), Milan, Scala, 2 Oct 1802; as La capricciosa ravveduta, Vienna, Kärntnertor, 26 June 1805; as L'orgoglio avvilito, Lisbon, 1806 and London, 1815; as La capricciosa corretta, Turin, carn. 1806; as Capriccio e pentimento, Venice, S Moisè, 4 Dec 1810; as La sposa stravagante, Paris, 1817; A-Wn, Wgm, GB-Lcm, I-Fc, Gl, Mr, Nc, US-Bp, Wc

La trasformazione immaginaria (dg, 2, D. Mantile), Turin, Arti, aut. 1802

L'orgoglio avvilito or La capricciosa corretta (dg, 2), Milan, Scala, Jan 1803 [different from L'orgoglio avvilito, Lisbon, 1806, which is a revision of La capricciosa pentita]

La schiava di due padrone (mel giocoso, 2, Romanelli), Milan, Scala, 15 March 1803 [? partly derived from La schiava fortunata]

La figlia d'un padre (ob, 2), Lisbon, S Carlos, aut. 1803

Il matrimonio per susurro (dg, 2, G. Caravita), Lisbon, S Carlos, aut. 1803; as The Marriage by Noise, London, King's, 24 May 1810

La pulcella di Raab (dramma, 2), Lisbon, S Carlos, carn. 1804

Le astuzie fallaci (dg, 2, Caravita), Lisbon, S Carlos, spr. 1804

Camilla, ossia La forza del giuramento (dramma, 3, Caravita [?Tottola], after G. Carpani), Lisbon, S Carlos, aut. 1804; as Camilla, ossia Il sotterraneo, Chiete, 1815, GB-Lcm, I-Mc, Nc, US-Wc

Le gemelle (dg, 2, Caravita), Lisbon, S Carlos, aut. 1804

La dama soldato (dg, 2, G. Mazzolà, rev. Caravita), Lisbon, S Carlos, 2 Dec 1805, P-La

Sono quattro e paion dieci, ossia Per amor si fa tutto (ob, 2, Caravita), Lisbon, S Carlos, wint. 1805

L'incognito (dg, 2, Caravita), Lisbon, S Carlos, 3 Oct 1806

Il notaro (dg, 2), Lisbon, S Carlos, aut. 1806

Il bello piace a tutti (ob, 1), Naples, Nuovo, 1806; rev. (dg, 2, Ferretti), Dresden, Hof, 1811–12, I-Fc

I virtuosi ambulanti (ob, 2, L. Balocchi, after L.-B. Picard: Les comédiens ambulants), Paris, Italien, 26 Sept 1807; as La virtuosa in puntiglio, London, 1808; as I soggetti di teatro, Florence, 1811, Nc*

I raggiri ciarlataneschi (cm, 2, G. Palomba), Naples, Fiorentini, carn. 1808, Nc

Lo sposo chi più accomoda (cm, G. Palomba), Naples, Fiorentini, sum. 1808

Il giudizio di Paride, ossia I rivali ridicoli (ob, 2, F. Tarducci), Rome, Valle, 28 Dec 1808

La fiera disturbata (ob), Naples, Nuovo, 1808

La bella carbonara (ob, 2, G. Palomba), Naples, Fiorentini, 22 April 1809, Nc, US-Bp

Didone abbandonata (3, P. Metastasio), Rome, Valle, 9 June 1810

Semplicità ed astuzia, ossia La serva ed il parrucchiere (ob, 2, Tottola), Naples, Nuovo, 21 Nov 1810, I-Nc

Nardone e Nanetta (ob, 1, with F. Gardi), Faenza, Remoti, 26 Dec 1810

Amore ed avarizia (burletta per musica, Tottola), Rome, Valle, carn. 1811

Le nozze per puntiglio (ob, 1), Naples, Nuovo, Jan 1811, Mc, Nc

I due sciocchi burlati (ob, 2), Milan, Radegonda, May 1811

Raoul signore di Créqui (mel eroi-comico, 3, Tottola, after Monvel), Naples, Nuovo, aut. 1811, Mc, Nc

Adelaide maritata (mel, 3, Tottola, after G. Gualzetti), Naples, Nuovo, 10 May 1812; as Comingio pittore, Florence, 1813; as Adelaide e Comingio, Parma, 1814; Nc [pt 2 of trilogy Adelaide e Comingio]; possibly also as Adelaide e Commingio romiti (2, Tottola), Naples, Fiorentini, Lent 1813; Fc, Mc, Nc, US-Wc

La foresta di Hermandstad (mel eroi-comico, 3, Tottola), Naples, Nuovo, 1812, I-Nc

Nefte (componimento lirico-tragico, 3, F. Liciense), Naples, S Carlo, 18 April 1813, Nc

L'africano generoso (dramma semiserio per musica, 2, G. Schmidt), Naples, S Carlo, carn. 1814

Gli inganni ed amore (cm, 2, G. Palomba), Naples, Fiorentini, spr. 1814, Nc*

Adelson e Salvini (dramma, 3, Tottola), Naples, Fiorentini, carn. 1816, Nc

Il solitario di Posilippo (dramma, Tottola), Naples, Fiorentini, wint. 1816

La morte d'Adelaide (azione tragi-comica, 3, Tottola, after Gualzetti), Naples, Fiorentini, Lent 1817; also as Comingio eremita [pt 3 of the trilogy Adelaide e Comingio]

La contessa di Fersen (mel, 2, M. Prunetti), Rome, Valle, 14 Oct 1817; as La moglie di due mariti, Milan, Re, 1 Dec 1818; Mr, Nc

Gli amori di Adelaide e Comingio (dramma per musica, 3, Tottola, after Gualzetti), Naples, Fiorentini, Lent 1818 [pt 1 of the trilogy Adelaide e Comingio]

Enrico al Passo della Marno (S. Torelli), Rome, Valle, 9 Sept 1818

L'impresario per amore (farsa, 1), Venice, S Luca, 10 Aug 1819

Paolina e Susetta (dg, 2), Naples, Nuovo, aut. 1819, Nc

La contadina fortunata (ob, 2, Tottola), Rome, Valle, 23 Nov 1820

La donna di genio bizzarro (ob, 2), 1823, Nc

Ogni eccesso è vizioso (dg, 2, Tottola), Naples, Nuovo, carn. 1824, Nc

Music in F. Bianchi: La fedeltà tra le selve, 1789 (4 arias); rev. of D. Cimarosa: I due baroni di Rocca Azzurra, 1802; rev. of G. Paisiello: L'inganno felice, 1804

*

ES (E. Zanetti); FlorimoN; LoewenbergA

G. Roberti: 'L'autobiografia di Valentino Fioravanti', Gazzetta musicale di Milano, l (1895), 371–2

A. Della Corte: L'opera comica italiana del '700, ii (Bari, 1923), 176ff

B. Croce: 'La trilogia di Adelaide e Comingio e il signor Gualzetti', Varietà di storia letteraria e civile (Bari, 1935), 155–63

J. W. Dougherty: Le cantatrici villane (1798) by Valentino Fioravanti: Description and Staging Guidelines (diss., Florida State U., 1985)
                                                          MARVIN TARTAK

Fioravanti, Vincenzo (*b* Rome, 5 April 1799; *d* Naples, 28 March 1877). Italian composer, son of Valentino Fioravanti. His father wanted him to study medicine; without consent, Vincenzo studied composition with Valentino's teacher, Giuseppe Jannacconi. In 1816 he went to Naples and eventually was taught by his father. The first of his 35 operas, *La Pulcinella molinaro*, was performed in Naples in 1819. In 1820 he returned to Rome, sought Donizetti's advice and found success with his second work, *La contadina fortunata* (later *La pastorella rapita*), at the Teatro Valle. After the death of his wife (the marriage had lasted only ten months) he returned to Naples. His next opera, *Robinson Crosuè nell'isola deserta* (1828), was written for the Teatro Nuovo. It was the first of a series of works, mostly *opere buffe*, carrying on his father's tradition, which was not followed by most of his contemporaries. His most popular opera was *Il ritorno di Pulcinella dagli studi di Padova* (1837); it was performed abroad, was constantly adapted by various singers and composers, and was in the repertory for over 80 years. Its success is partly due to the comic scenes that ensue when the hero is thrown into an asylum for crazy musicians.

Soon after his father died (1837), Fioravanti moved to Lanciano in the Abruzzi, where he was *maestro di cappella* at the cathedral, 1839–43. During these years he wrote both sacred and operatic works, but it was between 1843 and 1856, in Naples, that his career reached its zenith. He was director of the music school of the Albergo dei Poveri from 1867, but illness forced him to resign in 1872. He turned to writing graceful, epigrammatic verse. After his death his work was forgotten, but a later reappraisal of his operas by Napoli (1949), Pannain (1952) and others helped to restore his reputation.

La pulcinella molinaro, spaventato dalla fata Serafinetta (ob, 2, F. Cammarano), Naples, S Carlino, carn. 1819

La contadina fortunata (ob, 2, A. L. Tottola), Rome, Valle, 23 Nov 1820; as La pastorella rapita, Rome, Valle, carn. 1822

Robinson Crosuè nell'isola deserta (ob, 3, Tottola, after D. Defoe), Naples, Nuovo, 31 Jan 1828

Colombo alla scoperta delle Indie (2), Naples, Fenice, 14 Feb 1829

La conquista del Messico, Naples, Nuovo, 1829

Il fanatico (farsa), Naples, Fenice, 1830

La portentosa scimmia del Brasile con Pulcinella, ossia La scimmia brasiliana (ob, Tottola), Naples, Nuovo, 27 Feb 1831

Il folletto innamorato (2, P. Giaramicca), Naples, Partenope, 6 Feb 1832

I due disperati per non poter andar in carcere (2, A. Spadetta), Naples, Partenope, 12 June 1832

Il sarcofago scozzese (2, Giaramicca), Naples, Fenice, 5 June 1833

Il cieco del Dolo (2, P. Saladino), Naples, Nuovo, 6 March 1834

Il supposto sposo (ob, A. Passaro), Naples, Fondo, 6 Oct 1834

I due caporali (ob, Saladino), Naples, Nuovo, 22 March 1835

Il ritorno di Pulcinella dagli studi di Padova, ossia Il pazzo per amore (ob, 2, Passaro), Naples, Nuovo, 28 Dec 1837, I-Bsf, vs (Milan, n.d.); as Il ritorno di Columella, ossia Il pazzo per amore, Milan, Re, 17 June 1842, recitatives by Cambiaggio

Un matrimonio in prigione (ob, 1, Passaro), Naples, Nuovo, 15 April 1838

La larva, ovvero Gli spaventi di Pulcinella (ob, A. de Leone and R. d'Ambra), Naples, Nuovo, 19 Jan 1839

I vecchi burlati (ob, ? A. or G. Palomba), Chieti, Fenaroli, carn. 1839

Mille talleri (farsa, 1), Rome, Alibert, 1839

La dama ed il zoccolajo, ossia La trasmigrazione di Pulcinella (ob, Passaro), Naples, Nuovo, 1 Feb 1840

La dama con la maschera di morte (Giaramicca), Naples, Fenice, 8 Jan 1843

Una burla comica, ossia Non tutti pazzi sono all'ospedale (ob, 2, Giaramicca), Naples, Fenice, 16 Feb 1843

La lotteria di Vienna (ob, P. Altavilla), Naples, Nuovo, 25 March 1843

Il notajo d'Ubeda, ossia Le gelosie di Pulcinella (ob, C. Zenobi Caffarecci), Naples, Nuovo, 26 July 1843, Mr; rev. Cambiaggio as Don Procopio, Trieste, Mauroner, 6 Sept 1844, with addl music by G. Mosca, Cambiaggio, Tonassi, Consolini and Mattei

Gli zingari, ossia Gli amori di Pulcinella (ob, M. D'Arienzo), Naples, Nuovo, 30 Jan 1844, Mr

Chi cenerà (ob, 1, Leone and D'Arienzo), Rome, Argentina, carn. 1845; rev. as Un imbarazzo per la padrona e la cameriera (2), Naples, Nuovo, 1848

Una rassegna al campo (ob, N. Tauro), Naples, Fenice, 30 Jan 1845

Il parrucchiere e la crestaja (ob, Leone and G. di Giurdignano), Naples, Nuovo, 14 May 1846

X. Y. Z., ossia Il riconoscimento (ob, Zenobi Caffarecci), Turin, Carignano, Nov 1846

Pulcinella e la fortuna (ob, Spadetta), Naples, Nuovo, 24 Jan 1847

Menella la cianciosa (Giaramicca), Naples, Fenice, 2 April 1847

Amore e disinganno (ob, Giurdignano), Naples, Nuovo, 26 Dec 1847

Il ventaglio (ob), Bologna, Comunale, Feb 1848

Il pirata (Spadetta), Naples, Nuovo, carn. 1849

È lui o non è lui, ossia Quattro la chiedono, il quinto la sposa (ob), Rome, Valle, 14 Feb 1849; as La figlia dell'Fabbro, Venice, S Benedetto, 31 Jan 1850

La Pulcinella e la sua famiglia (ob, Giurdignano), Naples, Nuovo, sum. 1850

Raoul di Créqui (G. Artusi), Naples, Fondo, 20 April 1851

Annella di Porta Capuana (ob, E. Bardare), Naples, Nuovo, 23 June 1854

Jacopo lo scortichino (ob, T. Zampa), Naples, Fenice, Sept 1855

Il signor Pipino (ob, Spadetta), Naples, Nuovo, June 1856

*

FlorimoN; StiegerO

J. Napoli: 'Il tramonto dell'opera buffa', Cento anni del T. San Carlo (Naples, 1949)

G. Pannain: L'ottocento musicale italiano (Milan, 1952)
                        MARVIN TARTAK (work-list with JOHN BLACK)

Fiorè, Andrea Stefano (*b* Milan, 1686; *d* Turin, 6 Oct 1732). Italian composer. He was a child prodigy: the title-page of his *Sinfonie da chiesa* (1699) indicates that he was *musico di camera* of the dedicatee, Vittorio Amedeo II, Duke of Savoy, and a member of the Bolognese Accademia dei Filarmonici. Royal account books show that the duke sent Fiorè, with G. B. Somis, to study in Rome. Several payments for the trip were made between 24 June 1703 and 20 January 1707 although Somis had returned to Turin in 1706. If *Sidonio*, an opera performed during Carnival 1706 in Milan, is Fiorè's work (as Manferrari claimed), then he may have returned from Rome in late 1705. An opera composed for Carnival 1707, *La casta Penelope* (if not also *L'Anfitrione*, also attributed to Fiorè by Manferrari), was well received, and the Duke of Savoy soon thereafter appointed Fiorè his *maestro di cappella*. Until his death in 1732 he was in charge of the 30 to 36 musicians at the Turin court and the singers at the cathedral.

While the Turin Teatro Regio Ducale remained closed (1704–14), Fiorè was at liberty to produce operas elsewhere; three in Vienna (1708–10) and one in Reggio Emilia (1713) imply trips to those cities. For the reopening of the Turin opera house in 1715 Fiorè composed *Il trionfo d'Amore*. Two of his later operas for Turin, *Sesostri* (1717) and *I veri amici* (1728), were written with G. A. Giai, his successor as *maestro* at the Savoy court.

In a letter to Marcello from Turin, on 2 February 1726, Fiorè expressed admiration for Marcello's counterpoint. Quantz, who visited Turin in June 1726 and praised Fiorè's orchestra and its leader Somis, wrote that he regarded Fiorè one of the best Italian composers of church sonatas. Until more scores of his operas come to light, modern judgment of Fiorè's music must be based chiefly on his published trios, a handful of solo cantatas and his surviving choral music.

opere serie unless otherwise stated

La casta Penelope (2, P. Pariati), Milan, Regio Ducal, carn. 1707
La Svanvita (3, Pariati), Milan, Regio Ducal, 26 Dec 1707
Engelberta (5, Pariati and A. Zeno), Milan, Regio Ducal, carn. 1708
Atenaide [Act 1] (3, Zeno), ? Milan, Barcelona or Vienna, Hof, carn. 1709, *A-Wn* [Act 2 by A. Caldara, Act 3 by F. Gasparini]
Ercole in cielo (Pariati), Vienna, Neue Favorita, 1 Oct 1710, *Wn*
Il trionfo di Camilla (3, S. Stampiglia), Reggio Emilia, Pubblico, fiera 1713
Il trionfo d'Amore, ossia La Fillide (favola boschereccia, 2), Turin, Ducale, carn. 1715, ? collab. or by G. A. Giai
Arideno (3), Turin, Ducale, 26 Dec 1715
Merope (3, Zeno), Turin, Carignano, carn. 1716
Teuzzone (3, Bursetti, after Zeno), Turin, Carignano, Sept 1716 [Acts 1 and 2 by G. Casanova]
Sesostri, rè d'Egitto (3, Bursetti, after Pariati), Turin, Carignano, carn. 1717, collab. Giai, *F-Pn*
Il trionfo di Lucilla (3, Zeno: *Lucio Vero*), Turin, Carignano, carn. 1718
Publio Cornelio Scipione (5, A. Piovene), Milan, Regio Ducal, 6 Feb 1718
Il pentimento generoso (3, D. Lalli), Venice, S Angelo, carn. 1719, perf. with La preziosa ridicola (intermezzo); 1 aria *D-SWl*
L'Argippo (pastoral, 3, C. N. Stampa after Lalli: *Il gran mogol*), Milan, Regio Ducal, 27 Aug 1722
Ariodante (3, G. Salvi, after L. Ariosto), Milan, Regio Ducal, 26 Dec 1722, 1 aria *F-Pn*
L'innocenza difesa (F. Silvani), Turin, 1722, perf. with Gildo e Nerina (int), 12 arias *Pc*
Il trionfo della fedeltà (3, Giovanetti), Turin, Ducale, carn. 1723, perf. with Lesbo e Nesa (intermezzo); arias *Pn*
Elena (3, Stampa), Milan, Regio Ducal, Jan 1725
I veri amici (3, Silvani and Lalli, after P. Corneille: *Héraclius empereur d'Orient*), Turin, Ducale, 1728, arias, *A-Wgm, F-Pn* [Act 1 by Giai]
Siroe, rè di Persia (3, P. Metastasio), Turin, Ducale, 26 Dec 1729, 4 arias *Pc*
Arias from unidentified operas in *A-Wgm, D-RH, SWl, GB-Lbl, Ob, T, I-Ac*

Doubtful: Sidonio (3, Pariati), Milan, Regio Ducal, carn. 1706; L'Anfitrione (5, Pariati), Milan, Regio Ducal, carn. 1707; Agrippina, Vienna, Hof, 1709, incl. music by Handel and Caldara; Tito Manlio [Act 1], Milan, Regio Ducal, 1710, *A-Wn*; Zenobia [Act 2], Barcelona, 1711, perf. with Melissa contenta (int), *A-Wn*; Il Pirro [Act 2], Venice or Bologna, 1719, *D-SHsk*

*

P. Breggi: *Serie degli spettacoli rappresentati al Teatro Regio di Torino dal 1688 al 1872* (Turin, 1872)
S. Cordero di Pamparato: *Il Teatro Regio dal 1678 al 1814* (Turin, 1930)
N. Pelicelli: 'Musicisti in Parma', *NA*, x (1933), 314
U. Manferrari: *Dizionario universale delle opere melodrammatiche*, i (Florence, 1954), 389f
M.-T. Bouquet: *Musique et musiciens à Turin de 1648 à 1775* (Turin, 1968, and Paris, 1969), 22, 38, 52ff, 159f
O. E. Deutsch: 'Das Repertoire der Höfischen Oper, der Hof- und der Staatsoper in Wien, Chronologischer Teil', *ÖMz*, xxiv (1969), 369–421
R. Strohm: 'Italienische Opernarien des frühen Settecento (1720–1730)', *AnMc*, no.16 (1976)   SVEN HANSELL

Fiorentina, La. *See* GIGLI, CLARICE.

Fiorentini. Theatre in Naples, opened to opera in 1706; it was the first in Italy to offer regular seasons of comic opera. *See* NAPLES, §§1–2.

Fiorillo, Ignazio (*b* Naples, 11 May 1715; *d* Fritzlar, Hesse, June 1787). Italian composer. He studied with Durante and Leo at the Conservatory of S Maria di Loreto in Naples. He was active as an opera composer in northern Italy, writing operas for Trieste, Venice, Milan and Padua from 1733 to 1745. He then joined a travelling company, with which he toured central and northern Europe for the next four years. Three intermezzos by him were produced in Prague in 1748. The following year he left the company in Brunswick, where his opera *L'olimpiade* was successfully produced. In 1754 he was appointed court conductor there, and in the next eight years he wrote at least five Italian operas and one serenata for Brunswick, all to librettos by Metastasio. From 1762 to 1780 he was employed at the Hessian court in Kassel; he produced only four new operas there but continued to compose church music. Of his 18 or more operas and intermezzos fewer than a third have survived, and other dramatic works (ballet music and pantomimes) have also disappeared. His style was said to be in imitation of Hasse.

opere serie unless otherwise stated

L'egeste (melodramma), Trieste, 1733
Mandane (B. Vitture), Venice, 1736
Partenope nell'Adria (serenata, B. Biancardi), Venice, 1738
Artamene (N. Stampa), Milan, 1739
Il vincitor di se stesso (A. Zaniboni), Venice, S Angelo, aut. 1741, aria *I-Mc*
Volgeso (A. Zeno), Padua, 1742, *D-Dl*, *Wa*
Angelica (P. Metastasio), Venice, 1744, *W*
L'olimpiade (Metastasio), Venice, 1745, *W*
L'amante ingannatore (int), Prague, 1748
Li birbi (int, A. Zanetti), Prague, 1748
Il finto pazzo (int), Prague, 1748
Vecchio pazzo in amore (int), Hamburg, Nicolini, 1748
Astige, re di Medi (dramma per musica, Apolloni), Brunswick, wint. 1749
Demofoonte (Metastasio), Brunswick, 1750, only lib. extant
Didone abbandonata (Metastasio), Brunswick, 1751, *Wa*
Alessandro nell'Indie (Metastasio), Brunswick, 1752
Siface (Metastasio), Brunswick, 1752, *Wa*
Demetrio (Metastasio), Brunswick, 1753, *Wa*, aria *I-PLa*
Ciro riconosciuto (Metastasio), ?Brunswick, 1753, *D-Wa*
Endimione, ?Brunswick, 1754, rev. as Diana ed Endimione, 1763, pt.1, *Kl*, *Wa*
Nitteti (Metastasio), Kassel, ?Brunswick, 1758, rev. 1771, *Wa*
Ipermestra (Metastasio), Brunswick, 1759
Artaserse (Metastasio), ?1750s, Brunswick, rev. Kassel, 1765, pts 2, 3, *Kl*
Andromeda (V. A. Cigna-Santi), Kassel, 1771

*

D. von Apell: *Galerie der vorzüglichsten Tonkünstler ... in Cassel* (Kassel, 1806)   CHAPPELL WHITE (work-list with MARITA P. McCLYMONDS, DON NEVILLE)

Fioritura (It.: 'flowering', 'flourish'; plural *fioriture*). When a composition for the voice contains decorative writing such as scales, arpeggios, trills and *gruppetti* (the groups of notes sometimes known in English as 'turns'), it is described as 'florid' and the decorations themselves will be described collectively as 'fioritura'. It is a more accurate term than 'coloratura', which is frequently used as an alternative.   J. B. STEANE

Firenze (It.). FLORENCE.

Firsova, Yelena Olegovna (*b* Leningrad [now St Petersburg], 21 March 1950). Russian composer. She made

her first efforts at composition at the age of 12, and began formal studies in Moscow in 1966. In 1970 she entered the Moscow Conservatory, where her teachers included Alexander Pirumov (composition) and Yury Kholopov (analysis). While still a student she wrote her first opera, *Pir vo vremya chumï* ('Feast in Time of Plague', 1972), based on a 'little tragedy' by Pushkin. Her graduation in 1975 marked the end of her studies, though her friendship with Edison Denisov has been an important influence on her work. She is married to the composer Dimitry Nikolayevich Smirnov. In 1991 Firsova completed a one-act chamber opera in five scenes, *Solovey i roza* ('The Nightingale and the Rose'), after a story by Oscar Wilde.
STEPHEN JOHNSON

Fischer, Adam (*b* Budapest, 9 Sept 1949). Hungarian conductor. He studied with Hans Swarowsky at the Vienna Academy of Music and made his début at the Helsinki Opera in 1974 conducting *Il trovatore*. He was chief conductor at Helsinki, 1974–7, and music director at Freiburg, 1981–4, and at Kassel from 1987. He has also appeared at Munich and Hamburg (1978), the Vienna Staatsoper (1980), the Paris Opéra (1984), La Scala (1986), and Covent Garden and West Berlin (1989). He conducted the premières of Josef Tal's *Der Sturm* (1987, Berlin) and Wolfgang von Schweinitz's *Patmos* (1990, Munich). His chief merits as a conductor are precision, authenticity and romantic expression, tempered with classical moderation.

His brother Ivan Fischer (*b* Budapest, 20 Jan 1951), who also studied in Vienna, is known chiefly as a concert conductor. He conducted Kent Opera, 1984–9, conducted Yuri Lyubimov's well-known production of *Don Giovanni* in Budapest in 1982, and has appeared in opera in Vienna, Paris and Frankfurt.
PÉTER P. VÁRNAI

Fischer, Anton (*b* Ried, Swabia, bap. 13 Jan 1778; *d* Vienna, 1 Dec 1808). German composer and tenor. After initial study with his brother Matthäus he went to Vienna, joined the chorus of the Josefstadt Theatre and in 1800 went over to Schikaneder's Freihaus-Theater auf der Wieden. Apart from singing small roles he also composed Singspiels for the company and in 1806 became assistant Kapellmeister under Ignaz von Seyfried in the company's new home, the Theater an der Wien. By the time of his early and sudden death he had written a series of once-popular stage works that show a clear ability to meet the current demand for light, melodically pleasing songs and simple ensembles. With his arrangements of Dalayrac's *Les deux petits Savoyards* (Kärntnertor, 1804) and of Grétry's *Les deux avares* (An der Wien, 1805), and especially of the same composer's *Raoul Barbe-bleue* (An der Wien, 1804), he made a valuable contribution to the vogue for *opéra comique* in Vienna.

Not all the Singspiels attributed to Fischer in secondary literature may be accepted as authentic. Of those that are by Fischer, *Swetards Zaubertal* received 41 performances in little over a year, while *Das Hausgesinde*, his greatest triumph, was given 115 times in the Theater an der Wien and staged in many other places, and was followed by two sequels.

Singspiels and first performed at the Theater an der Wien, Vienna, unless otherwise stated

Lunara, Königin des Palmenhains (Zauberoper, 1, J. Waldon), Vienna, Wieden, 20 Sept 1800
Die Entlarvten (komische Oper, 3, E. Schikaneder), 19 March 1803 [sequel to Die Waldmänner]
Die Scheidewand (1, I. F. Castelli), 2 June 1804

Die Verwandlungen (1, J. Baber, after C. A. Sewrin), 9 May 1805
Swetards Zaubertal (komische Zauberoper, 2, Schikaneder), 3 July 1805
Die Festung an der Elbe (3, Castelli), 3 May 1806
Das Singspiel auf dem Dache (1, G. F. Treitschke, after T. M. Dumersan), 5 Feb 1807
Das Hausgesinde, oder Das Kleeblatt (1, F. Koller), 18 Jan 1808
Das Milchmädchen von Bercy (2, Treitschke, after Sewrin), Vienna, Kärntnertor, 5 May 1808
Theseus und Ariadne (romantische Oper, 2, M. Stegmayer), 11 March 1809

*

StiegerO
O. E. Deutsch: 'Das Freihaus-Theater auf der Wieden', *Mitteilungen des Vereines für Geschichte der Stadt Wien*, xvi (Vienna, 1937), 30–73
A. Bauer: *150 Jahre Theater an der Wien* (Vienna, 1952)
PETER BRANSCOMBE

Fischer, Betty (*b* Vienna, 9 Oct 1887; *d* Vienna, 19 Jan 1969). Austrian soprano. She appeared at Viennese variety theatres before being engaged for the Raimundtheater, where she sang in *Die lustige Witwe* and *Eva* before achieving a considerable success in Leo Ascher's *Hoheit tanzt Walzer* (1912). In 1914 she moved to the Theater an der Wien, where for some 20 years she appeared opposite Hubert Marischka, creating the principal soprano roles in such works as Fall's *Die Rose von Stambul* (1916), Lehár's *Die blaue Mazur* (1920), *Frasquita* (1922) and *Die gelbe Jacke* (1923), Kálmán's *Gräfin Mariza* (1924 and *Die Zirkusprinzessin* (1926), and Eysler's *Die gold'ne Meisterin* (1927). Her slim, elegant figure and Viennese charm complemented a natural soprano voice.
ANDREW LAMB

Fischer, Emil (Friedrich August) (*b* Brunswick, 13 June 1838; *d* Hamburg, 11 Aug 1914). American bass of German birth. He studied with his parents (both opera singers) and made his début in Graz as the Sénéschal (a tenor role) in Boieldieu's *Jean de Paris* (1857). He sang baritone roles with the Danzig Opera (1863–70); at some point during the 1870s he began to sing even lower roles. After seasons with the Rotterdam Opera (1875–80) and the Königliche Sächsische Oper, Dresden (1880–85), he made his Metropolitan Opera début in November 1885 and became a mainstay of the company during its German seasons. He sang Hans Sachs in the first American *Meistersinger* (4 January 1886): his was long considered the definitive portrayal. Although renowned for Wagnerian parts (including Wotan, Hagen, King Henry and King Mark), he was equally comfortable in the French and Italian repertory: he sang Boito's Mephistopheles and Verdi's Ramfis; he also sang the High Priest in Goldmark's *Die Königin von Saba* and the title role in Cornelius's *Der Barbier von Bagdad*. After Fischer retired from the Metropolitan in 1898, he taught singing in New York until he returned to Germany shortly before his death.

*

Obituaries: *MusAm*, xx/19 (1914), 27; *New York Times* (4 Sept 1914)
DEE BAILY

Fischer, Ivan. Hungarian conductor, brother of ADAM FISCHER.

Fischer, Jan Frank (*b* Louny, 15 Sept 1921). Czech composer. He studied at the Prague Conservatory (1940–45) and with Jaroslav Řidký (1945–8), and at the same time attended lectures on musicology and comparative literature at the university. He was a committee member of the Přítomnost association for contemporary music (1945–9) and of the Union of Czechoslovak Composers (1953–70).

Fischer is a versatile composer, his work permeated by Stravinskyan neo-classicism and by folksong, notably that of Czech and other Slavonic peoples. There are also elements of jazz. His melodic invention and technical fluency often facilitate the synthesis of highly varied ideas, particularly in the film scores (he has written more than 40, of which several won international prizes). He has worked extensively for the stage and for broadcasting, collaborating with the army arts ensemble and composing much incidental music. In concert works Fischer's style is characterized by lively rhythm and colour, while humour, lightness and wit dominate most of the operas; Romeo, Julie a tma ('Romeo, Juliet and Darkness') is, however, a more serious work.

Ženichové [The Bridegrooms] (comic op, 3, S. K. Macháček), Brno, 13 Oct 1957
Romeo, Julie a tma [Romeo, Juliet and Darkness] (2 pts, J. Otčenášek), Brno, 14 Sept 1962
Oh, Mr Fogg! (chamber op, 2, after J. Verne: Around the World in 80 Days), Brno and Saarbrücken, 27 June 1971
Za'zračné Divadlo [The Miracle-Theatre] (radio op, 1, Fischer and D. Fischerová, after M. de Cervantes), Radio Prague, 1973
Dekameron (6, Fischer and J. Dudek, after Boccaccio), Brno, 1977
Copernicus (2, Fischer and O. Daněk), Prague, 1983

*

ČSHS
I. Jirko: 'Romeo, Julie a tma jako opera', HRo, xv (1962), 775–7
OLDŘICH PUKL

Fischer, (Johann Ignaz [Karl]) Ludwig (b Mainz, 18 Aug 1745; d Berlin, 10 July 1825). German bass. He studied the violin and cello, then singing with Anton Raaff from about 1769, in Mannheim where he became virtuoso da camera at the court in 1772. He moved with the court to Munich (1778), where he married the singer Barbara Strasser (b 1758; d after 1825). From 1780 to 1783 the couple worked in Vienna, where Fischer sang Osmin in the first performance of Die Entführung aus dem Serail, much to the satisfaction of Mozart, who frequently wrote about him in his letters and gave him an introduction for Paris. He then secured his reputation with a tour of Italy and visited Vienna, Prague and Dresden. After serving in Regensburg from 1785 he received a lifelong appointment in Berlin in 1789. Guest appearances in London (1794, 1798), Leipzig (1798), Hamburg (1801–2) and elsewhere added to his fame. He gave up public performance in 1812.

Fischer was regarded as Germany's leading serious bass. His voice, said to range from D to a', was praised by Reichardt as having 'the depth of a cello and the natural height of a tenor'. He also composed. His autobiography, covering up to 1790, is in manuscript in the Berlin Staatsbibliothek. His son (?Anton) Joseph Fischer (b Berlin, 1780; d Mannheim, 1862) was a bass and composer and his daughters Josepha Fischer-Vernier (b 1782) and Wilhelmine (b 1785) were also distinguished singers.

*

J. F. Reichardt: 'Ludwig Fischer', Musikalische Monatsschrift, i (1792), 67–8
H. Theinert: 'Jahrhundertfeier eines deutschen Trinkliedes und Mitteilungen aus dem Leben des Sänger-Komponisten Ludwig Fischer (1745–1825)', Die Musik, ii (1902–3), 262–70
A. Gottron: 'Kleine Beiträge zur Mainzer Musikgeschichte, I: Die Selbstbiographie des Bassisten Ludwig Fischer aus Mainz', Mainzer Almanach (Mainz, 1959)
ROLAND WÜRTZ

Fischer, (Maria) Res [Theresia] (b Berlin, 8 Nov 1896; d Stuttgart, 4 Oct 1974). German contralto. She studied in Berlin (with Lilli Lehmann), Prague and Stuttgart and made her début at Basle in 1927, remaining there until 1935; engagements followed at Frankfurt (1935–41) and Stuttgart (1941–63). Early contact with Felsenstein at Basle and Frankfurt helped to develop her career. She first appeared at Salzburg in 1942 as Marcellina and created there the title role of Orff's Antigonae (1949) and the Grandmother in Das Bergwerk zu Falun (1961); at Bayreuth (1959–61) she sang Mary (Der fliegende Holländer). She scored a great success in Buenos Aires in 1951 as the Kostelnička, Clytemnestra and Ortrud, and with the Stuttgart company in Paris and London. Once a famous Eboli, Amneris and Orpheus (Gluck), she later sang Fricka, Brangäne, Herodias, Gaea (Daphne) and Countess Helfenstein in the German première of Hindemiths' Mathis der Maler (1946). One of the few true German dramatic contraltos of the 1930s and 40s, she became one of the most powerful singing actresses of her day.
HAROLD ROSENTHAL/R

Fischer-Dieskau, Dietrich (b Berlin, 28 May 1925). German baritone. He studied in Berlin with Georg Walter and, after World War II, with Hermann Weissenborn. He made his stage début in 1948 as Posa in Don Carlos, under Tietjen at the Städtische Oper, Berlin, where he then became a leading baritone. In 1949 he began regular appearances at the Vienna Staatsoper and at the Bayerische Staatsoper, Munich, and in 1952 at Salzburg. He sang at Bayreuth (1954–6), as the Herald (Lohengrin), Wolfram, Kothner and Amfortas. In 1961 he created Mittenhofer in Henze's Elegy for Young Lovers at Schwetzingen and in 1978 Reimann's King Lear at Munich. His Covent Garden début was in 1965 as Mandryka in Arabella.

Some of Fischer-Dieskau's most vivid roles, with the dates when he first sang them, were: Wolfram (1949), John the Baptist (Salome, 1952), Don Giovanni (1953), Busoni's Faust (1955), Amfortas (1955), Count Almaviva (1956), Renato (1957), Falstaff (1959), Hindemith's Mathis (1959), Wozzeck (1960), Yevgeny Onegin (1961), Barak (Die Frau ohne Schatten, 1963), Macbeth (1963) and Don Alfonso (1972). He has recorded many of these and in addition, most notably, both Olivier and the Count in Capriccio; Papageno, Kurwenal (for Furtwängler and Carlos Kleiber), the Dutchman, Wotan (in Karajan's Rheingold) and Falstaff (for Bernstein). After much hesitation, he undertook Hans Sachs at the Deutsche Oper, Berlin, under Jochum in the 1975–6 season, and recorded it at the same time. One of the leading singers of his time, an artist distinguished for his full, warm and resonant voice, his cultivated taste and his powerful intellect, he is a noted interpreter of lieder as well as opera. He has sometimes been criticized for giving undue emphasis to specific words and overloading climaxes. Though his Italian is excellent and his Count Almaviva, Don Giovanni, Rodrigo, Iago and Falstaff are appreciable achievements, he is probably at his happiest in German in roles such as the Speaker, Wolfram, Kurwenal, Barak, Mandryka, Mathis and Wozzeck. He published a book of memoirs, Nachklang (Stuttgart, 1988; Eng. trans., as Echoes of a Lifetime, 1989), as well as books on Schubert, Schumann and the lied.

For illustration see ELEGY FOR YOUNG LOVERS.

*

J. Demus and others: Dietrich Fischer-Dieskau (Berlin, 1966)
K. Whitton: Dietrich Fischer-Dieskau: Mastersinger (London, 1981)
ALAN BLYTH

Fischerinnen, Die. Opera by Joseph Haydn; *see* PESCATRICI, LE (ii).

Fischietti [Fischetti], **Domenico** (*b* Naples, ?*c*1725; *d* ?Salzburg, after *c*1810). Italian composer. He studied at the S Onofrio conservatory under Leo and Durante. Florimo listed an opera by him, *Armindo* (Naples, 1742), performed when he was still a student (unless it was in fact by his father). Comic operas by him were given in Naples in 1749 and 1752 and Palermo in 1753. He then settled in Venice and began a collaboration with Goldoni that in the next four years produced four extremely successful comic operas: *Lo speziale* (the first of its three acts was composed by Vincenzo Pallavicini), *La ritornata di Londra*, *Il mercato di Malmantile* and *Il signor dottore*, all of which were widely performed in Italy and elsewhere, remaining popular throughout the 1760s.

Fischietti seems to have been in Prague by 1762, working with the Molinari opera company. He is definitely known to have been part of Bustelli's company, which began working there in 1764. A manuscript (in *D-Dlb*) contains arias by him from several *opere serie* apparently performed there, although three are otherwise unknown (*Zenobia*, 1762; *Olimpiade*, 1763; *Alessandro nell'Indie*, 1764). Whether these were pasticcios or entirely composed by Fischietti is uncertain. Three other operas by him are definitely known to have been performed in Prague in 1763–5. When the Bustelli company began performing in Dresden, Fischietti was also active there. In April 1765 he was engaged as court Kapellmeister (partly because he was prepared to accept a rather low salary). In this post he presented a revised version of *Il mercato di Malmantile* (1766) but composed no new full-scale operas.

Fischietti seems not to have been an effective Kapellmeister and in 1772 his contract was not renewed. He went to Vienna, where the new Archbishop of Salzburg engaged him as Kapellmeister with a three-year contract. Again he seems not to have given entire satisfaction; he was still named in the court calendar as titular Kapellmeister in 1776–83, but Rust was engaged as Kapellmeister in 1777 (remaining only briefly). Fischietti attempted to resume his career as an opera composer in Naples (1775, 1777) and Venice (1778), apparently without much success. In 1779–83 he taught at the Institut der Domsängerknaben in Salzburg. After Gatti's appointment as court Kapellmeister, Fischietti's name disappeared from the court calendar, but according to Villarosa he was still living in Salzburg in 1790, and, according to Florimo, as late as 1810.

Fischietti was a composer of importance only during the brief period in the 1750s when he produced his four famous comic operas. He was one of several composers trained in Naples who found success in Venice during the period of Galuppi's domination of the opera there (Ciampi and Cocchi having preceded him). Although Engländer has analysed his important operas in considerable detail, it still remains to set his work in a larger framework and to ascertain the extent to which he combined such characteristics as can be identified as Venetian and Neapolitan. The popularity of these works lasted until they were outmoded by the more modern style of the younger generation, of Paisiello, Guglielmi and others, a change regretfully acknowledged in La Borde's description (1780) of Fischietti as 'one of those good masters who lived through the change from the former taste, but was too old to change his own. His beautiful music now appears too simple and too bare, but it gives great pleasure to connoisseurs'.

See also MERCATO DI MALMANTILE, IL; SIGNOR DOTTORE, IL; and SPEZIALE, LO (i).

dg – *dramma giocoso* dm – *dramma per musica*

Armindo (commedia per musica), Naples, Fiorentini, wint. 1742
L'abate Collarone (commese chiamma, P. Trinchera), Naples, Pace, carn. 1749; rev. as Le chiajese cantarine, Naples, carn. 1754, addl music by Logroscino and G. Maraucci
Il pazzo per amore, Naples, Fiorentini, carn. 1752
La finta sposa (commedia per musica, after C. Fabbozzi: *La finta cameriera*), Palermo, carn. 1753
Artaserse (dm, P. Metastasio), Piacenza, 1754
Solimano (dm, G. B. Migliavacca), Venice, S Moisè, carn. 1755
Lo speziale [Acts 2 and 3] (dg, 3, C. Goldoni), Venice, S Samuele, carn. 1755, *A-Wn*, *B-Bc*, *F-Pn* [Act 1 by V. Pallavicini]
La ritornata di Londra (dg, Goldoni), Venice, S Samuele, Feb 1756, *A-Wn*, *D-B*, *Bds*, *Dlb*, *LEm*, *I-Fc*
Il mercato di Malmantile (dg, 3, Goldoni), Venice, S Samuele, 26 Dec 1757; rev. Dresden, 1766; *A-Wn*, *D-Dlb*, *Dlb*, *Mbs*, *F-Pc*, *GB-Lcm**, *I-Fc*, *MOe*, *Nc*, *Rdp*, *US-NYp*, Favourite Songs (London, n.d.); as intermezzo, *D-Dlb**
Il signor dottore (dg, 3, Goldoni), Venice, S Moisè, aut. 1758, *A-Wgm*, *Wn*, *D-Dlb*, *HG*, *HR*, *Wa*, *I-MOe*, *Nc*
Semiramide (dm, Metastasio), Padua, Nuovo, June 1759, aria *Rsc*
La fiera di Sinigaglia (dg, Goldoni), Rome, Dame, Jan 1760
Tetide, Vienna, 1760, *F-Pn*
Siface (dm, after Metastasio), Venice, S Angelo, Ascension 1761
Olimpiade (Metastasio), Prague, Nuovo, carn. 1763
La donna di governo (dg, Goldoni), Prague, aut. 1763, *D-Wa*
Vologeso (dm, A. Zeno), Prague, 4 Oct 1764, *A-Wn*
Alessandro nell'Indie (Metastasio), Prague, 1764, 5 arias *D-Dlb*
Nitteti (dm, Metastasio), Prague, 1765; rev. Naples, 1775; *A-Wn*, *I-Nc*
Les métamorphoses de l'amour, ou Le tuteur dupé (intermède), Pfördten, by 1769, *D-Dlb*
L'uccelatrice (intermezzo), by 1769, *A-Wn*
Il bottanico novellista (dg, Goldoni), Treviso, Delfino, spr. 1770
Arianna e Teseo (dm, Pariati), Naples, S Carlo, 4 Jan 1777, *I-Nc*, *P-La*
La molinara (dg, F. Livigni), Venice, S Samuele, carn. 1778
L'isola disabitata (Metastasio), ?1761

Arias: *F-Pn*, *I-BAn*, *Tn*

Doubtful: Zenobia, 1762; Issipile, arias *I-MC*

*

FlorimoN; RosaM
J.-B. de La Borde: *Essai sur la musique ancienne et moderne* (Paris, 1780)
R. Haas: 'Beitrag zur Geschichte der Oper in Prag und Dresden', *Neues Archiv für sächsische Geschichte und Altertumskunde*, xxxvii (1916), 68–96
R. Engländer: 'Domenico Fischietti als Buffokomponist in Dresden', *ZMw*, ii (1919–20), 321–52, 399–422   DENNIS LIBBY/R

Fischietti [Fischetti], **Giovanni** (*b* Naples, 27 March 1692; *d* Naples, 17 Feb 1743). Italian composer, father of Domenico Fischietti. He studied at the conservatory of S Maria di Loreto. From 1724 he was organist at the royal chapel. In 1735 he became assistant to Francesco Mancini at the conservatory, though he did not succeed Mancini on his death in 1737. Nothing is known of his secular career, though Stieger's *Opernlexikon* (Tutzing, 1975–83) lists five operas, all lost.

all opere buffe
La costanza (B. Saddumene), Rome, Capranica, Jan 1729
La somiglianza (Saddumene), Rome, Capranica, 7 Feb 1729
Il finto fratello (G. A. Federico), Naples, Nuovo, aut. 1730
La tresca (3), Naples, Nuovo, 24 Dec 1730
Il baron della Trocciola (T. Mariani), Naples, Fiorentini, carn. 1736

Fišer, Luboš (*b* Prague, 30 Sept 1935). Czech composer. He studied at the Prague Conservatory (1952–6) with Bořkovec and at the Prague Academy of Music (1956–60) with Hlobil and Bořkovec. After graduating he worked with the Vít Nejedlý Military Ensemble. His music for Peter Weigl's film *Bludiště moci* ('Labyrinth of Power') was highly esteemed. For the stage he has composed the opera *Lancelot* (1959–60; 1, E. Bezděková), performed in Prague on 19 May 1961, and the musical *Dobrý voják Švejk* ('The Good Soldier Schweik'; 1962, Prague). Having used tonal, thematic techniques at the outset of his career, he began to be influenced by contemporary developments from the mid-1960s.

MÍLAN KUNA

Fisher, John Abraham (*b* Dunstable or London, 1744; *d* Dublin or London, May or June 1806). English composer and theatre proprietor. He made his début as a violinist at the King's Theatre in London on 25 January 1765, and thereafter frequently played there and at Covent Garden; among the places for which he composed was Sadler's Wells Theatre. On 27 February 1772 he married Elizabeth Powell; as a result he came into a 16th-share in the Covent Garden theatre. For this theatre, where he was also leader of the band from about 1769 to 1778, he wrote music for two masques, two burlesques and about five pantomimes; he also supplied supplementary music for several plays and comic operas. Among his other works are songs, cantatas and some complex and technically demanding violin pieces. In July 1777 he received from Oxford University the degrees of both BMus and DMus. After his wife's death in 1780, Fisher sold his share in the theatre and toured Europe. In autumn 1783 or 1784 he married the soprano Nancy Storace in Vienna. Emperor Joseph II expelled him from the country, however, on hearing that Storace, his favourite singer, had had to endure Fisher's 'very striking way of enforcing his opinion' (Kelly), but Fiske (1975) suspected Joseph II of having ulterior motives. The marriage was never formally dissolved.

Fisher wrote in the *galant* style, with strong melodies and weak orchestration. His first burlesque, *The Court of Alexander* (1770), earned him £82 at his benefit night. *The Golden Pippin* (1773), based on the story of the judgment of Paris, was probably his most popular work. A pasticcio burletta in the customary style of the early 1770s, it mixes original music and recitative with melodies borrowed from English songs and Italian arias. The two masques, *The Druids* (1774) and *The Syrens* (1776), each ran for one season, with journalists damning the former for representing the current vein of managerial bad taste. Each had a strong run despite the 'jumble of monstrous absurdities', and the music received some compliments. After his eviction from Vienna, Fisher went to Dublin, where he indulged his taste for flamboyant dress and virtuoso violin playing.

all first performed in London, Covent Garden

The Court of Alexander (all-sung afterpiece, 2, G. A. Stevens, burlesque on N. Lee: *The Rival Queens*), 5 Jan 1770
The Golden Pippin (burletta, 3, K. O'Hara, burlesque on Ovid: *Metamorphoses*), 6 Feb 1773, vs (London, *c*1773); as afterpiece, 13 Feb 1773
The Druids (masque afterpiece/pantomime, after B. Jonson: *The Haddington Masque*), 19 Nov 1774, vs (London, 1774); masque portions rev. 26 Dec 1774
The Syrens (masque afterpiece, 2, E. Thompson), 26 Feb 1776, ov. pubd in parts (London, 1777)

Addl songs for CG productions of Love in the City (comic op), 1767; Lionel and Clarissa (comic op), 1770, 1777; The Seraglio (comic op), 1776; Love Finds the Way (comic op), 1777; The Tempest (dramatic op), 1779; A Fête (musical entertainment), 1781

*

BDA; *DNB* (L. Middleton); *LS*
M. Kelly: *Reminiscences of the King's Theatre* (London, 1826, 2/1826); ed. R. Fiske (London, 1975)
C. Pohl: *Mozart und Haydn in London* (Vienna, 1867)
M. Maxwell: 'Olympus at Billingsgate: the Burlettas of Kane O'Hara', *Educational Theatre Journal*, xv (1963), 130–35
E. Byrnes: *The English Burletta: 1750–1800* (diss., New York U., 1967)
P. Dircks: 'The Catch on the English Stage', *Theatre Notebook*, xxv (1971), 93–6
——: 'The Eighteenth-Century Burletta: Problems of Research', *Restoration and Eighteenth-Century Theatre Research*, 1st ser., x/2 (1971), 44–52

LINDA V. TROOST

Fisher, Sylvia (Gwendoline Victoria) (*b* Melbourne, 18 April 1910). Australian soprano. She studied at the Melbourne Conservatory, then privately with Adolf Spivakovsky. While a student she made her début (1932) as Hermione in Lully's *Cadmus et Hermione*. She joined the Covent Garden company in 1948, making her début in that year as Leonore. Her many London roles included the Marschallin, Ellen Orford, Mother Marie (*Dialogues des Carmélites*) and Sieglinde. She scored a notable success as the Kostelnička in the first British production of *Jenůfa* (1956), and repeated the role in Chicago in 1959; she also sang Turandot, Brünnhilde (*Die Walküre*) and Isolde, but they were vocally too demanding so she abandoned them. She sang with the English Opera Group from 1963 as Lady Billows (*Albert Herring*), the Female Chorus (*The Rape of Lucretia*) and Mrs Grose (*The Turn of the Screw*); she created the role of Miss Wingrave for the television production in 1971 and repeated it at Covent Garden in 1973. When *Gloriana* was revived at Sadler's Wells in 1966 she made a commanding and dignified Elizabeth I; later she played the role in Brussels, Lisbon and Munich. In 1973 she sang a powerful Kabanicha (*Kát'a Kabanová*) for the ENO.

HAROLD ROSENTHAL/R

Fiske, Roger (*b* Surbiton, 11 Sept 1910; *d* Ambleside, 22 July 1987). English musicologist. He read English at Oxford and then studied at the RCM, London, under Howells and Colles. In 1939 he joined the BBC, where he eventually became producer of music talks for the Third Programme (1953–9). A scholar and musician of wide interests, he wrote successful educational books; his main contribution to scholarship came in his *English Theatre Music in the Eighteenth Century* (London, 1973, 2/1986), a pioneering work in a neglected field, engagingly written and with keen critical perception. He also edited Storace's *No Song, No Supper* (MB, xvi, 1959) and Michael Kelly's *Reminiscences* (London, 1975).

Fitzball [Ball], Edward (*b* Burwell, nr Mildenhall, 1792; *d* Chatham, 27 Oct 1873). English dramatist and librettist. A youthful visit to the Theatre Royal, Norwich, engendered his lifelong passion for the stage. He made his London début with the play *The Innkeeper of Abbeville* (1821–2). From 1828 onwards he wrote for Covent Garden, and from 1830 to 1838 for Vauxhall Gardens. He is best remembered as the author of *The Siege of Rochelle* (set by Balfe) and *Maritana* (Wallace). Fitzball's personal mildness of manner belied his ardently romantic nature. He prefaced his original surname with

'Fitz' (his mother's maiden name) for dramatic effect, and his Transpontine melodramas earned him the nickname 'the Terrible Fitzball'. His facility was inexhaustible, and he revelled in the creation of stage devilry and the lavish use of blue fire. His appeal to composers may be attributed to his professional shrewdness: he calculated for maximum effect and saw his job in terms of entertaining the public. He seems to have worked by having the numbers set as he wrote them, one by one, as he describes in his account of the composing of *Joan of Arc* (*Thirty-five Years*, ii, 122–3):

Balfe took home, piece by piece, the poetry, and, when finished, came again to Twickenham for more, till poem and music were alike complete … of all the composers I ever wrote for, Balfe was the best tempered, and delighted when the slightest opportunity occurred to bestow praise, which is so encouraging to an author, especially a sensitive one like me.

His autobiography, *Thirty-Five Years of a Dramatic Author's Life*, is a chatty and fascinating farrago of theatrical information.

Waverley, or Sixty Years Since (Scottish drama), G. H. Rodwell, 1824; *The Songs of the Birds* (musical drama), Rodwell, 1826; *The Flying Dutchman, or The Phantom Ship* (nautical drama), Rodwell, 1827; *The Bottle Imp* (melodrama, with R. B. Peake), Rodwell, 1828; *The Earthquake, or The Spectre of the Nile* (burletta operatic spectacle), Rodwell, 1828; *The Devil's Elixir, or The Shadowless Man* (musical romance), Rodwell, 1829; *The Night before the Wedding and the Wedding Night* (operatic farce), H. R. Bishop, 1829; *Ninetta, or The Maid of Palaiseau*, Bishop, 1830

Under the Oak, or The London Shepherdess (vaudeville), Bishop, 1830; *Adelaide, or The Royal William* (national and nautical musical burletta), Bishop, 1830; *The Black Vulture, or The Wheel of Death* (musical drama), Rodwell, 1830; *The Sorceress*, Ries, 1831; *The Demon, or The Mystic Branch* (with J. B. Buckstone), Bishop, 1832; *Der Alchymist* (with T. H. Bayly), Bishop, 1832; *The Magic Fan, or The Fillip on the Nose* (vaudeville), Bishop, 1832; *The Bottle of Champagne* (vaudeville), Bishop, 1832; *The Sedan Chair* (operetta), Bishop, 1832; *The Maid of Cashmere* (ballet op), Bishop, 1833

The Soldier's Widow, or The Ruins of the Mill (musical drama), J. Barnett, 1833; *Jonathan Bradford, or The Murder at the Roadside Inn!* (drama), J. Jolly, 1833; *The Lord of the Isles, or The Gathering of the Clans*, Rodwell, 1834; *Paul Clifford* (musical drama), Rodwell and J. Blewitt, 1835; *The Siege of Rochelle* (original op), M. W. Balfe, 1835; *The Bronze Horse, or The Spell of the Cloud King* (operatic drama), Rodwell, 1835; *Quasimodo, or The Gipsy Girl of Notre Dame* (drama), Rodwell, 1836; *The Rose of the Alhambra, or The Enchanted Lute*, J. de Pinna, 1836

The Sexton of Cologne, or The Burgomaster's Daughter (operatic romance), Rodwell, 1836; *Thalaba the Destroyer, or The Burning Sword* (melodrama), Rodwell, 1836; *Joan of Arc* (grand op), Balfe, 1837; *Diadesté, or The Veiled Lady* (opera buffa), Balfe, 1838; *The Maid of Palaiseau*, Bishop, 1838; *The King of the Mist, or The Miller of the Hartz Mountains* (melodrama), G. F. Stansbury, 1839; *Këolanthé, or The Unearthly Bride*, Balfe, 1841; *The Queen of the Thames, or The Anglers, or Uncle Brayling* (operetta), J. L. Hatton, 1842; *Pasqual Bruno* (comic op), Hatton, 1844

Maritana (grand op), V. Wallace, 1845; *The Desert, or The Imann's Daughter* (spectacular op), J. H. Tully, 1847; *The Forest Maiden and the Moorish Page* (musical drama), Tully, 1847; *The Maid of Honour*, Balfe, 1847; *Quentin Durward*, H. R. Laurent, 1848; *The Cadi's Daughter* (operetta), E. J. Nelson, 1851; *Berta, or The Gnome of the Hartzberg*, H. T. Smart, 1855; *Raymond and Agnes* (romantic op), Loder, 1855; *Auld Robin Gray* (burletta), A. Lee, 1858; *Lurline* (grand romantic op), Wallace, 1860; *She Stoops to Conquer*, G. A. Macfarren, 1864; *The Magic Pearl*, T. Pede, 1873

DNB (T. Seccombe); *LoewenbergA*; *NicollH*; *StiegerO*
A. Bunn: *The Stage* (London, 1840)
E. Fitzball: *Thirty-Five Years of a Dramatic Author's Life* (London, 1859)

Obituaries: *The Era* (2 Nov 1873); *Illustrated London News* (8 Nov 1873)
W. A. Barrett: *Balfe: his Life and Work* (London, 1882)
W. Wroth: *The London Pleasure Gardens* (London, 1896), 319
C. Forsyth: *Music and Nationalism* (London, 1911)
E. W. White: *The Rise of English Opera* (London, 1951)
M. Hurd: 'Opera: 1834–1865', *Music in Britain: the Romantic Age, 1800–1914*, ed. N. Temperley (London, 1981), 307–29
E. W. White: *A History of English Opera* (London, 1983)
——: *A Register of First Performances of English Operas and Semi-operas* (London, 1983)
NIGEL BURTON

Fitzthumb, Ignaz. *See* VITZTHUMB, IGNAZ.

Fiume (It.). RIJEKA.

Fiume, Orazio (*b* Monopoli, 16 Jan 1908; *d* Trieste, 21 Dec 1976). Italian composer. He studied at Naples and Palermo, then with Pizzetti at the Accademia di S Cecilia in Rome. Numerous composition prizes included the Belgian Grand Prix International Reine Elisabeth in 1957. He taught at the conservatories of Parma, Milan, Pesaro and Trieste.

His compositions were mainly symphonic, largely tonal but borrowing in moderation from outside that tradition: Fiume was not radically avant-garde but used atonality when he wished. His only opera was *Il tamburo di panno*, based on a 14th-century Japanese noh play. In spite of the exotic source, the composer's musical conservatism is evident in the dramatic organization and in the treatment of voices and orchestra. It was first performed in Rome at the Teatro dell'Opera on 12 April 1962.

DEUMM (R. Zanetti); *ES* (A. M. Bonisconti)
RAFFAELE POZZI

Flagello, Ezio (Domenico) (*b* New York, 28 Jan 1931). American bass. He studied with Friedrich Schorr and John Brownlee at the Manhattan School of Music, making his début as Dulcamara at the Empire State Festival, Ellenville, New York (1955). In 1957 he made his début with the Metropolitan Opera as the Gaoler in *Tosca*. That week, because Fernando Corena was indisposed, he also sang Leporello; he soon became a member of the company, singing an increasingly wide variety of roles. In 1966 he created Enobarbus in Barber's *Antony and Cleopatra* at the inauguration of the new Metropolitan Opera at Lincoln Center. His flexible, dependable technique enabled him to sing *basso cantante* parts, such as Rodolfo in *La sonnambula*, the great Verdi roles (e.g. Philip II), Wagner (e.g. Pogner) and the *buffo* roles of Mozart and Rossini. His jovial, rotund appearance lent a greater degree of individuality to *buffo* roles, and his interpretation of Leporello (which he recorded) was his best-known accomplishment. He retired in 1987.

RICHARD BERNAS

Flagello, Nicolas (Oreste) (*b* New York, 15 March 1928). American composer. He studied with Giannini and Pizzetti, both prolific composers of opera. Between 1950 and 1977 he taught at the Manhattan School of Music. Flagello's best-known operas are *The Sisters* (1958) and *The Judgement of St Francis* (1959). *The Sisters*, first performed in 1961 by the Manhattan School of Music, tells the story of three sisters trapped by their tyrannical father in a New England town in 1820. The libretto, by Dean Mundy, is written in a simple but effective manner which heightens the *verismo* aspects of the drama. *The Judgement of St Francis* has been described as a one-act opera 'in rondo'. The smoothly constructed libretto by Armand Aulicino tells of the events leading up to Francis's decision to devote his life to God. The use of flashback provides an effective way of portraying the drama while allowing the characters to develop. The première was also given by the Manhattan School of Music (18 March 1966). *The Pied Piper of Hamelin* (1970), a one-hour opera with a libretto by Flagello, after Browning's poem, is intended for performance by children.

Flagello's operatic musical language is unabashedly romantic in nature. The influence of Giannini is very evident. Pungent chromaticism is used in a harmonic language that remains strongly tonal.

Mirra op.13, 1953 (3, Flagello, after V. Alfieri)
The Wig op.14, 1953 (1, Flagello, after L. Pirandello)
Rip van Winkle op.22, 1957 (2, C. Fiore)
The Sisters op.25 (1, D. Mundy), New York, Manhattan School of Music, 22 Feb 1961
The Judgement of St Francis op.28 (1, A. Aulicino), Manhattan School of Music, 18 March 1966
The Pied Piper of Hamelin op.62 (1, Flagello, after R. Browning), New York, Manhattan School of Music, 18 April 1970
Beyond the Horizon op.76, 1983 (Flagello, after E. O'Neill)

*

J. W. Freeman: 'Americans Old and New', *ON*, xxv/21 (1960–61), 33
J. Honig: 'Reports: United States', *ON*, xxx/25 (1965–6), 22–3
W. Sargeant: 'Musical Events', *New Yorker* (26 March 1966)
W. Simmons: 'The Judgement of St Francis', *HiFi/MusAm* xxxii/11 (1982), MA40

JAMES P. CASSARO

Flagstad, Kirsten (Malfrid) (*b* Hamar, 12 July 1895; *d* Oslo, 7 Dec 1962). Norwegian soprano. While still a student, she made her début at the National Theatre, Oslo, on 12 December 1913 as Nuri in D'Albert's *Tiefland*; for the next 18 years she sang only in Scandinavia. In 1934 she sang Sieglinde and Gutrune at Bayreuth. Her first appearances at the Metropolitan, as Sieglinde and Isolde in 1935, marked the beginning of her world fame, and her first Brünnhilde performances, in the same season, set the seal on her success. In 1936 and 1937 she sang Isolde, Brünnhilde and Senta at Covent Garden, arousing as much enthusiasm there as in New York. In 1941 Flagstad returned to Norway to join her second husband, who was arrested as a Nazi collaborator after World War II. Although her own wartime record was free from controversy, her return to Nazi-occupied Norway during the war and a certain political naivety in her nature caused her afterwards to be looked at askance in America. During four consecutive Covent Garden seasons, from 1948 to 1951, she repeated all her regular Wagnerian roles, including Kundry and Sieglinde; she made her farewell as Isolde on 30 June 1951. The lasting purity, beauty and power of her tone probably owed much, not only to natural gifts and sound training, but to the enforced repose of the war years and the fact that she had undertaken no heavy roles until middle life. Of her many records, the complete *Tristan und Isolde* with Furtwängler undoubtedly offers the finest memorial to her art. While she was not the most dramatic or magnetic of Wagnerian heroines, no one within living memory surpassed her in sheer beauty and consistency of line and tone.

*

J. Dennis: 'Kirsten Flagstad', *Record Collector*, vii (1952), 173–90 [with discography]
L. Biancolli: *The Flagstad Manuscript* (New York and London, 1953)
E. McArthur: *Flagstad: a Personal Memoir* (New York, 1965)

DESMOND SHAWE-TAYLOR

Flaming Angel, The. Opera by Sergey Prokofiev; *see* FIERY ANGEL, THE.

Flaminio. *Commedia musicale* in three acts by GIOVANNI BATTISTA PERGOLESI to a libretto by GENNARO ANTONIO FEDERICO; Naples, Teatro Nuovo, autumn 1735.

The wealthy Neapolitan Polidoro (tenor) and his sister, Agata (soprano), are staying at a villa near Naples inhabited by a young widow, Giustina (mezzo-soprano), and three other people: Polidoro's secretary Flaminio (soprano), Giustina's nanny Checca (soprano) and Polidoro's servant Vastiano (bass). Flaminio, who has fallen in love with Giustina, is known to everyone as Giulio. Giustina, who reciprocates, is struck by his resemblance to Flaminio, a former suitor whom she rejected before marrying her first husband. Agata, whose betrothed, Ferdinando (tenor), has just arrived at the villa, has fallen in love with Giulio/Flaminio. To further complicate matters, Polidoro wants to marry Giustina. The burgeoning love of Flaminio and Giustina is at the core of this comic opera, which is interlaced with the clowning of Polidoro and the flirting between Checca and Vastiano. In the end Flaminio, assured of Giustina's love, reveals his true identity, Agata goes back to Ferdinando, whom she had unceremoniously rejected, and Checca agrees to marry Vastiano.

Federico, the librettist and the author of *La serva padrona*, imbued his characters with both sentimentalism and realism. The opera includes three Neapolitan dialect parts – Checca, Vastiano and Ferdinando – which add local colour. Neapolitan folk elements are also strongly marked in the music, beginning with

Kirsten Flagstad as Dido in Purcell's 'Dido and Aeneas'

Polidoro's lilting siciliano 'Mentre l'erbetta', to the accompaniment of a chitarrino (a small folk guitar); another example follows in Act 2 scenes xii and xiii, where Polidoro, Vastiano and Checca listen to a band of peasant musicians giving a concert (since neither libretto nor score specifies the type of composition or the scoring, the music was probably improvised on folk instruments).

Slapstick elements deriving from the *commedia dell'arte* are prevalent in the role of Polidoro (especially in Act 3, where he practises his speech for Giustina) and in Checca and Vastiano's burlesque encounters. Polidoro's 'Quando voi vi arrosseggiate' in Act 2 is a sparkling *buffo* aria imitating the mewing of a cat. Checca's incantation 'Benedetto, maledetto', to arouse Polidoro from his feigned faint in Act 3, also belongs to this category. Contrasting with the *commedia dell'arte* buffoonery are the sentimentalism, melancholy and lyrical pathos of Giustina and Flaminio, which make this work a predecessor of Galuppi's sentimental comedies. Pergolesi used *opera seria* conventions, such as large-scale da capo arias, while keeping the ensemble numbers to a minimum. The most famous piece is the Act 3 duet for Checca and Vastiano, 'Per te ho io nel core', a popular piece that was performed as an alternative duet in *La serva padrona* and was appended to a number of other comic operas and intermezzos. It features a charming imitation of a heartbeat: 'ti-pi-ti'.

Flaminio received two Neapolitan revivals in 1737 and 1749. In 1982 it was performed in Venice at the Biennale Musicale, and in 1984 it was recorded by the conductor Marcello Panni. Stravinsky used three numbers from it in his ballet *Pulcinella* (1919).

GORDANA LAZAREVICH

Flanagan, William, (jr) (*b* Detroit, 14 Aug 1923; *d* New York, ?31 Aug 1969). American composer and critic. In 1945 he went to the Eastman School to study under Bernard Rogers and Burrill Phillips. At the Berkshire Music Center in 1947–8 he worked with Barber, Honegger and especially Copland, who became his major influence. He also studied with David Diamond in New York. In the mid-1950s, on the strength of an earlier education in journalism, he became a critic, writing for the *New York Herald Tribune* and for a number of periodicals. He was among the most skilful and caustic verbal commentators on music in the USA.

Flanagan chose his close friend Edward Albee to work on the librettos of both his operas. *Bartleby* (composed 1952–7; 1, J. Hinton and Albee, after H. Melville) was first performed in New York in 24 January 1961, but *The Ice Age*, commissioned by the New York City Opera for their 1966–7 season, was never completed. *Bartleby* is a sombre work with limited dramatic impact; the music, though not tuneful, is melodious. Flanagan excelled particularly in the smaller vocal forms. His vocal works flow with a natural grace attractive to singers and give the impression of having been written with consummate ease; they were in fact produced with an anxiety which, coupled with the increasing stress of being an unappreciated conservative in a time of artistic upheaval, was partly responsible for his early death.

E. Albee: 'William Flanagan', *American Composers Alliance Bulletin*, ix/4 (1961), 12
N. Rorem: '… and his music', ibid, 13–17   NED ROREM

Flanders Opera. Opera association formed between ANTWERP and GHENT in 1982.

Flavio [*Flavio, re di Longobardi* ('Flavio, King of the Lombards')]. Opera in three acts by GEORGE FRIDERIC HANDEL to a libretto by NICOLA FRANCESCO HAYM adapted from MATTEO NORIS's *Il Flavio Cuniberto* (1682, Venice) as revised for Rome (1696); London, King's Theatre, 14 May 1723.

Flavio was Handel's fourth full-length opera composed for the Royal Academy of Music; its eight performances ended the 1722–3 season at the King's Theatre. The cast included Francesca Cuzzoni as Emilia, Margherita Durastanti as Vitige, and the castratos Senesino and Gaetano Berenstadt as Guido and Flavio.

Handel revived *Flavio* at the King's Theatre on 18 April 1732, when the bass Montagnana took over the role of Ugone (originally tenor) and the tenor Pinacci the role of Lotario (originally bass); this reversal of voices actually restored Handel's first plan for the opera, Acts 1 and 2 having been originally written for this combination. Chrysander's edition largely ignores the pre-performance and 1732 versions of the opera, though a few elements of them are included without explanation. *Flavio* received its first modern revival at Göttingen on 2 July 1967, and its first modern British production at Abingdon on 26 August 1969.

ACT 1   The story combines an episode in the legendary history of Lombardy with the central dramatic situation of Corneille's tragicomedy *Le Cid* (1636). The action takes place in a mythical period when Britain is supposed to be under Lombardic rule, and is mainly set in the palace of King Flavio (alto), though the early scenes are in the houses of the king's two counsellors, Ugone (tenor) and Lotario (bass). Lotario's daughter Emilia (soprano) is betrothed to Ugone's son Guido (alto), and Ugone's daughter Teodata (alto) is enjoying a secret affair with her lover Vitige (soprano). The counsellors settle the engagement of Emilia and Guido, and attend court to invite Flavio to the wedding. Ugone presents Teodata to Flavio, who is immediately attracted by her and says he will make her a companion to his queen Ernelinda (who does not appear in the opera). Flavio receives a letter of resignation from the governor of Britain and offers the post to Ugone, much to Lotario's annoyance. He asks Vitige his opinion of Teodata, forcing Vitige to say she does not please him, and, to Vitige's consternation, says he is in love with her. Ugone enters with a red face – the result of a blow from the angry Lotario – and demands that Guido avenge the insult to his honour, despite his love for Lotario's daughter. Guido, not revealing his purpose, gains Emilia's assurance that her love for him will never change.

ACT 2   Flavio receives Teodata, but before he can declare his love Ugone interrupts, still protesting at his injured honour. Teodata assumes that her affair with Vitige has been discovered and (after Flavio has left) confesses it, adding to Ugone's embarassment. Lotario tells Emilia that the wedding is off: if she does not break with Guido, he is no longer her father. Confronted by Guido, she says she will keep her word to him. Flavio asks Vitige to woo Teodata on his behalf. Vitige suggests to her that it will be best if she pretends to respond to the king's advances. Guido challenges Lotario: they draw swords and Lotario is mortally wounded. Emilia finds her dying father and learns from his last words that Guido is his assassin.

ACT 3 Emilia and Ugone appear before Flavio, demanding justice, but the king defers a decision. He receives Teodata and Vitige: Vitige pleads the king's love to Teodata. When she responds favourably (though protesting in asides that she is dissembling), Flavio asks her to become his queen. Teodata appears to accept the offer in earnest, leaving Vitige in despair. Emilia, in mourning, confronts Guido, but when Guido begs her to kill him with the sword that killed her father, she cannot do so. Flavio overhears a scene of recrimination between Vitige and Teodata and learns of their pledged love. Emilia, appearing before Flavio to hear his verdict, is told that Guido has been executed; her reaction makes it plain she still loves him. Flavio insists that she turn to look at her lover's head. She steels herself to do so, and falls into the arms of the living Guido. Flavio ironically 'punishes' Vitige by giving him the hand of Teodata, the woman who 'does not please him', and dispatches Ugone to the governorship of Britain.

* * *

As in his previous opera, *Floridante*, Handel continues to imitate the lighter manner of Bononcini while allowing his own characteristically richer and harmonically bolder style to emerge where appropriate to the dramatic situation. In *Flavio*, the blend of dark tragedy and lighter, satiric comedy is especially subtle, and makes it unique among the operas of the Royal Academy period. (Handel was later to explore a similar vein in *Partenope* and *Serse*, but neither of these encompasses the death of one of the characters.) No deep emotions are touched in the arias of Act 1, though all have musical distinction and the opening duet for Vitige and Teodata is especially charming. A more profound note is struck in Emilia's aria 'Parto, sì' in Act 2, and in her bleak siciliano 'Ma chi punir desio' at the close of the act; Guido's B♭ minor aria 'Amor, nel mio penar' in Act 3 is no less tragic in tone. Yet the music for the other couple – notably the songs of the coquettish Teodata – is no less memorable, and the whole work makes a particularly satisfying evening in the theatre.

ANTHONY HICKS

Fleckno [Flecknoe], **Richard** (*d* ?*c*1676). English composer, poet and theorist. A lutenist, he travelled extensively in the 1640s and 50s, according to his *Ten Years' Travells* (London, 1656). He was a notably unsuccessful poet and playwright (largely self-published) and is now remembered principally as the butt of Marvell's *Fleckno, an English Priest at Rome* (1645) and as a secondary target in Dryden's *Mac Flecknoe* (written ?1676, published 1682).

Fleckno's claim to a place in the history of music rests almost entirely on two operas for which he wrote both words and music: *Ariadne Deserted by Theseus and Found and Courted by Bacchus* (lib. pubd London, 1654) and *The Mariage of Oceanus and Brittania* (lib. pubd London, 1659). There is no record of performance of either, and the music to both is apparently lost. Fleckno's preface to the printed libretto of *Ariadne*, however, makes clear just how radically innovatory a work it was in England: two years before Davenant's *The Siege of Rhodes* he was proffering a defence and an exemplar of italianate all-sung opera. Describing the piece as 'Apted for Recitative Musick', he justifies the form with intelligence and enthusiasm, and

his libretto seems well adapted for effective musical setting. The much longer *Oceanus and Brittania* he calls 'An allegoricall Fiction . . . to be represented in Musick, Dances, and proper Scenes. All Invented, Written, and Composed by Richard Fleckno'. It has many masque-like features but evidently used expository recitative to connect lyrical arias.

*

LS

E. Haun: *But Hark! More Harmony: the Libretti of Restoration Opera in English* (Ypsilanti, MI, 1971)   ROBERT D. HUME

Fledermaus, Die ('The Bat'). *Komische Operette* in three acts by JOHANN STRAUSS to a libretto by Carl Haffner and RICHARD GENÉE, after HENRI MEILHAC and LUDOVIC HALÉVY's *Le réveillon*; Vienna, Theater an der Wien, 5 April 1874.

Gabriel von Eisenstein *a man of private means*	tenor buffo
Rosalinde *his wife*	soprano
Frank *a prison governor*	baritone
Prince Orlofsky	mezzo-soprano
Alfred *his singing teacher*	tenor
Dr Falke *a notary*	light baritone
Dr Blind *a lawyer*	tenor buffo
Adele *Rosalinde's maid*	soprano
Ida *her sister*	soprano
Yvan *the Prince's valet*	speaking role
Frosch *a jailer*	speaking role

Guests and servants of the Prince

Setting A spa town, near a big city

Meilhac and Halévy's vaudeville was first translated for Vienna by Carl Haffner as a straight play. However, the peculiarly French custom of the *réveillon* (a midnight supper party) caused problems, which were solved by the decision to adapt the play as a libretto for Johann Strauss, with the *réveillon* replaced by a Viennese ball. At this point Haffner's translation was handed over for adaptation to Richard Genée, who subsequently claimed not only that he had made a fresh translation from scratch but that he had never even met Haffner.

Two anecdotes attached to the early history of *Die Fledermaus* require comment: the first that the work was composed in 42 nights, and the second that it was such a failure that it had to be taken off after 16 nights. The work was indeed sketched out in six weeks, but six months elapsed from start of composition to production. Moreover, Rosalinde's *csárdás* had already been performed by Marie Geistinger at a charity performance, and her disguise as a Hungarian at Orlofsky's party was a means of enabling her to take it over into the operetta. The work was indeed taken off after 16 performances, but only because of a pre-booked visiting operatic company season, after which it returned. Besides Geistinger, the original cast included Jani Szika as Eisenstein, Ferdinand Lebrecht as Falke, Caroline Charles-Hirsch as Adele and Irma Nittinger as Orlofsky. It was Lebrecht's death of a heart attack on stage at the Theater an der Wien that gave Alexander Girardi, later Strauss's principal stage interpreter, his first Strauss role as Falke in September 1874.

The libretto's French origins originally prevented its production in Paris, and the music was first adapted for France (with interpolations from *Cagliostro in Wien*) to a new libretto as *La tzigane* in 1877, finally being performed in Paris as *La Chauve-Souris* (with Meilhac and Halévy's original character names retained) in 1904. Operatic productions began in Hamburg in March 1894 with Katharina Klafsky as Rosalinde, Heinrich Bötel as Alfred and Ernestine Schumann-Heink as Orlofsky, conducted by Gustav Mahler, and continued at the Hofoper, Vienna, that same year under the composer's direction, subsequent revivals there including one in 1920 with Maria Jeritza (Rosalinde), conducted by Richard Strauss. Other celebrated productions include that at Covent Garden on 14 May 1930 with Willi Wörle (Eisenstein), Lotte Lehmann (Rosalinde), Gerhard Hüsch (Falke), Elisabeth Schumann (Adele) and Maria Olszewska (Orlofsky), conducted by Bruno Walter, and at the Vienna Staatsoper on 31 December 1960, with Eberhard Wächter (Eisenstein), Hilde Güden (Rosalinde), Rita Streich (Adele), Erich Kunz (Frank) and Walter Berry (Orlofsky), conducted by Herbert von Karajan.

ACT 1 *A room in Eisenstein's house* There is a potpourri overture, looking ahead to the third-act prison scene but – like much of the opera – dominated by its waltz. A voice offstage is heard serenading Rosalinde, the lady of the house ('Täubchen, das entflattert ist'). She recognizes the voice as that of her lover, the singing teacher Alfred, whose ringing tenor she finds irresistible. Adele, Rosalinde's maid, has received a letter from her sister Ida, with an invitation to a ball that evening at the villa of the young Russian Prince Orlofsky. She asks her mistress for the evening off 'to visit a sick aunt'. Rosalinde refuses, as her husband is due to start a short prison sentence that evening for assault. When Adele has left the room, Alfred appears and is persuaded to leave only on condition that he can return that evening when Eisenstein has gone to jail.

Eisenstein enters, arguing with his stuttering lawyer Blind ('Nein, mit solchen Advokaten'), his sentence having been increased on appeal; a spirited trio ensues. After Blind has left, Eisenstein's friend Falke arrives and sets about persuading Eisenstein to delay starting his prison sentence in order to accompany him to Orlofsky's party. At the prospect of all the attractive young ladies who promise to be at the party, Eisenstein is soon enough persuaded ('Komm mit mir zum Souper').

When Adele and Rosalinde reappear, Rosalinde, now looking forward to an evening alone with Alfred, tells Adele that she may have the evening off after all. At the prospect of Rosalinde now supposedly being left alone for the evening, she, Eisenstein and Adele, in a delectable trio, each feign a sadness that none of them feels ('So muss allein ich bleiben?'). Eisenstein and Adele leave for their evening commitments, whereupon Alfred reappears. He settles down for an intimate supper with Rosalinde, donning Eisenstein's smoking cap and dressing gown ('Trinke, Liebchen, trinke schnell').

They are interrupted by the arrival of the prison governor, Frank, who has come to collect Eisenstein to start his prison sentence. Discovered alone with a man wearing her husband's smoking cap and dressing gown, Rosalinde protests at the notion that he could be anyone but her husband ('Mein Herr, was dächten Sie von mir?'), and Alfred is forced to go along with the pretence. He reluctantly allows himself to be led off, fortified by a lingering farewell kiss from Rosalinde.

Irma Nittinger as Prince Orlofsky in the original production of Johann Strauss's 'Die Fledermaus' at the Theater an der Wien, 5 April 1874

ACT 2 *At Prince Orlofsky's villa* Orlofsky's guests are all thoroughly enjoying the party ('Ein Souper heut' uns winkt'). Adele, posing as an actress named Olga, is there with her sister Ida, while Falke is in conversation with the Prince. From their conversation it soon emerges that an elaborate charade is in progress, set up by Falke to amuse the young Prince. 'The bat's revenge', he calls it, and he picks out the characters in it for the Prince. Adele is apparently one of them; but then he spots the leading character arriving – Eisenstein, who is introduced as the 'Marquis Renard'. Orlofsky commands his guests to drink. His wealth has left him permanently bored, but he insists that his guests enjoy themselves ('Ich lade gern mir Gäste ein').

Eisenstein soon spots Adele in her mistress's dress, but when he comments on her likeness to his maid he dismisses the suggestion in her famous 'laughing song' ('Mein Herr Marquis'). Next Falke introduces Eisenstein to a guest who has arrived somewhat late. It is Frank, the prison governor, posing as the 'Chevalier Chagrin', and the two struggle to hold a conversation in schoolboy French. Then a masked Hungarian countess arrives, who turns out to be none other than Rosalinde in disguise. Eisenstein has been flirting outrageously with the young ladies at the party, demonstrating his unusual repeater watch, but when he tries the same technique on the supposed Hungarian countess in a charming duet ('Dieser Anstand, so manierlich'), she ends up by pocketing it.

The guests press the Hungarian countess to remove her mask, but Orlofsky defends her, and she proceeds to convince everyone of her credentials by singing a brilliant and fiery Hungarian *csárdás* ('Klänge der Heimat'). Enchanted by her performance, the guests now turn to Falke to urge him to tell them the story of the bat, but it is Eisenstein who triumphantly relates the story of how some years ago, after a fancy-dress ball, he had left Falke to walk home in broad daylight dressed as a bat.

The guests sit down to supper, and Orlofsky proposes a toast to champagne, the king of all wines ('Im Feuerstrom der Reben'). As the wine flows, Falke leads the guests in a declaration of everlasting brotherhood in a slow, gently sentimental waltz ('Brüderlein und Schwesterlein'). All then embark on a fast, swirling waltz, the one already heard in the overture, and generally regarded as 'the' *Fledermaus* waltz ('Ha, welch' ein Fest!'); but, as the clock strikes six in the morning, Eisenstein and Frank both seize their hats and cloaks and rush off.

ACT 3 *The prison governor's office* The voice of Alfred singing in his cell (operatic excerpts, of course) can be heard offstage, despite the efforts of the drunken jailer Frosch to silence him. Frank enters unsteadily, recalling the delights of Orlofsky's party. Then Adele and Ida arrive, asking for the 'Chevalier Chagrin'. She confesses that she is not really an actress, but she believes that the 'Chevalier', as a man of obvious influence, will be able to help her get on the stage, and she proceeds to give him a demonstration of her versatile acting talents ('Spiel' ich die Unschuld vom Lande').

Eisenstein now arrives to start his prison sentence and is surprised to encounter the 'Chevalier Chagrin'. When Eisenstein gives his real identity, Frank points out that he had personally arrested Eisenstein the previous evening and now has him safely under lock and key. Frosch is sent to fetch him. Then Dr Blind arrives, claiming that Eisenstein has summoned him. Anxious to discover who it might be who had been found in his smoking cap and dressing gown in his wife's company, Eisenstein borrows Blind's wig, gown and spectacles. Frosch returns with Alfred, and they are joined shortly afterwards by Rosalinde. Eisenstein, affecting Blind's stutter, questions them about the events of the previous evening, finding it difficult to remain impassive as the details emerge ('Ich stehe voll Zagen'). Eventually, unable to control his moral indignation any longer, Eisenstein reveals his identity, to the music heard at the beginning of the overture.

Rosalinde shows herself equal to the challenge by producing the repeater watch with which the Marquis Renard had the previous evening sought to seduce the Hungarian countess. Now all the other principal characters arrive, and Falke reveals to Eisenstein that the whole affair had been set up by him as the bat's revenge. Eisenstein can do nothing but take it in good heart, and the whole company agree that the blame for any misdemeanours can be laid firmly at the door of King Champagne ('O Fledermaus, O Fledermaus').

*　　*　　*

Just as the wit and originality of Meilhac and Halévy had provided Offenbach with his most enduring successes, so also, in translation, the same writers inspired Johann Strauss to a vitality and sparkle that he achieved in no other of his operettas. The resultant work has, more than any other operetta, transcended its origins to become an acknowledged cornerstone of the operatic repertory.
　　　　　　　　　　　　　　　　　　ANDREW LAMB

Fleischer, Edytha (*b* Falkenstein, 5 April 1898). German soprano. After studying with Lilli Lehmann, she established a reputation in Berlin and Salzburg primarily as a Mozart singer, making her début in 1918 and singing Susanna and Zerlina at Salzburg in 1922. She joined the German touring company which travelled to America in that year. In 1926 she made her Metropolitan début as the First Lady in *Die Zauberflöte* and was soon promoted to Pamina. She created a particularly favourable impression as Marzelline in *Fidelio* and remained with the company for the next ten years. House premières included *Die ägyptische Helena* and *La rondine*, both in 1928, in which she sang, respectively, Aithra and Lisette. Her most frequent role was Hänsel, which she played in the first broadcast from the house, on Christmas Day 1931. From 1936 to 1949 she sang at the Teatro Colón, Buenos Aires, and afterwards retired to teach in Vienna. She made few recordings, and the glimpse of her Gutrune in an early broadcast of *Götterdämmerung* reveals little of an artist whose voice and style were generally much admired.
　　　　　　　　　　　　　　　　　　J. B. STEANE

Fleischer-Edel, Katharina (*b* Mülheim an der Ruhr, 23 Sept 1873; *d* Dresden, 18 July 1928). German soprano. She studied in Dresden, where she made her début at the Hofoper in 1894 as a Bridesmaid in *Der Freischütz*. In 1897 she was engaged at Hamburg, where she remained until her retirement in 1917. In 1904 she sang Elisabeth and Gutrune at Bayreuth, returning in 1906 as Brangäne and Sieglinde and in 1908 as Elsa. She made her Covent Garden début in 1905 as Sieglinde, returning in 1907 as Eva and Elisabeth. Engaged at the Metropolitan in 1906–7, she made guest appearances in Vienna and Berlin.
　　　　　　　　　　　　　　　　　　ELIZABETH FORBES

Fleischmann, (Johann) Friedrich (Anton) (*b* Marktheidenfeld, nr Würzburg, 18 July 1766; *d* Meiningen, 30 Nov 1798). German composer. He studied in Mannheim with G. J. Vogler and Ignaz Holzbauer, and at Würzburg University before becoming private secretary and tutor to the *Regierungspräsident* von Welden's son at Regensburg (1786). From 1789 he was cabinet secretary to Duke Georg I of Saxe-Meiningen, where he exerted a great influence on the court's music.

Fleischmann's earliest known dramatic work is a Singspiel, *Hanns und seine Frau Mama* (C. A. G. von Seckendorff), the text of which, according to Loewenberg, was published in *Neue Beyträge zum deutschen Theater aus Franken* (n.p., 1785); it may not have been performed and is now lost. His principal work, the Singspiel *Die Geisterinsel* (3, F. W. Gotter and F. H. von Einsiedel, after Shakespeare's *Tempest*; *D-Bhm*), was composed in 1796 before the better-known settings of Reichardt and Zumsteeg, and produced without success at Weimar in 1798; the overture later appeared as his op.7 (published in Offenbach, *c*1807). His other compositions include orchestral and chamber works and songs.

*

T. Fleischmann: Biography, *AMZ*, i (1798–9), col.417
E. F. Schmid: *Musik am Hofe der Fürsten von Löwenstein-Wertheim-Rosenberg (1720–1750)* (Würzburg, 1953), 25, 62
　　　　　　　　　　　　　　　　　　KLAUS RÖNNAU

Flensburg. City in north Germany. An independent court theatre was established in 1781, giving the city its first permanent company. Operas were performed in the town hall until a theatre was opened in 1795. The Seyler company visited Flensburg on tour, and in the 19th century a number of other troupes performed as well, sometimes at the open-air Tivoli Theatre. The main theatre was demolished in 1883 and replaced in 1894 by a new building in the neo-classical style (537 seats); it came under civic control in 1934. Artists who have performed there include Gladys Kuchta and Heinz Wallberg.

In 1974 the Flensburg theatre was merged with those of Schleswig and Rendsburg to form the Schleswig-Holstein Landestheater; the opera company is based in Flensburg, while the two smaller towns produce plays. Recent notable productions include Massenet's *Don Quichotte* (1986–7) and Salieri's *Falstaff*. The season runs from September to June.

K. Witt: *Flensburger Theaterleben vom 16. Jahrhundert bis zur Gegenwart* (Flensburg, 1953)
SABINE SONNTAG

Fleta, Miguel (*b* Albalate de Cinca, 28 Dec 1893; *d* La Coruña, 30 May 1938). Spanish tenor. He studied at the Barcelona conservatory and then in Italy with Luisa Pierrich, whom he later married. He made his début in 1919 at Trieste in Zandonai's *Francesca da Rimini*, then sang in Vienna (1920), Rome (1920–21), Monte Carlo (1921), Madrid (1921–2) and Buenos Aires (1922), in *Rigoletto*, *Aida*, *Tosca* and, above all, in *Carmen*. He appeared at the Metropolitan (1923–5) and at La Scala (1924), where he returned to sing Calaf in the first *Turandot* in 1926. His repertory included *Lucia*, *Pagliacci*, *Andrea Chénier* and *Manon*. He had a beautiful tenor voice remarkable for its colour, range, evenness, sensual warmth and ease of inflection and expression. He had also an exuberant and passionate temperament, but lacked taste and style, and failed to care for his voice, so that by 1928 he was already in decline.

His son, Pierre Fleta (*b* 1925), has sung in opera in Barcelona (début 1949) and at the Théâtre de la Monnaie, Brussels.

R. Celletti: 'Miguel Fleta', *Musica e dischi*, no.134 (1957), 66 [discography by R. Vegeto]
J. A. León: 'Miguel Fleta', *Record Collector*, xv (1963–4), 101–8 [with discography]
G. Gualerzi, ed.: 'Tavola rotonda su Miguel Fleta', *Discoteca* (1964), no.41, pp.17–22
A. C. Saiz Valdivielso: *Fleta, memoria de una voz* (Madrid, 1986) [with discography]
RODOLFO CELLETTI

Fleyshman, Veniamin Iosifovich (*b* Bezhetsk, 7/20 July 1913; *d* Krasnoye, Luga district, nr Leningrad [now St Petersburg], 14 Sept 1941). Russian composer. Although he played the violin as a child and tried his hand at composition, he was a schoolteacher before turning to serious studies in music. In 1937 he enrolled at the Leningrad Conservatory, where he studied composition with Shostakovich. As a student, he wrote romances on texts of Goethe and Lermontov and, with the encouragement of his teacher, he embarked in 1939 on the composition of a one-act opera, *Skripka Rotshil'da* ('Rothschild's Violin'), to a libretto of his own based on a story by Anton Chekhov. By June 1941 the opera was substantially complete. At the outbreak of World War II, Fleyshman volunteered for the front; he never returned. In 1943 Shostakovich took upon himself the responsibility of locating, finishing and ensuring the survival of the work of his talented student, and he completed it the following year. It was first performed in concert at the Central House of Composers in Moscow on 20 June 1960, and first staged at the Experimental Chamber Opera Studio of the Leningrad Conservatory on 24 April 1968.

See also SKRIPKA ROTSHIL'DA.

G. Golovinsky: 'S lyubov'yu k cheloveku (ob opere B. Fleyshmana "Skripka Rotshil'da")' [With Love for Man (about Fleyshman's Opera 'Rothschild's Violin')], *SovM* (1962), no.5, pp.28–34
L. D'yachkova: 'Opera V. Fleyshmana "Skripka Rotshil'da"', *Pamyati pogibshikh kompozitorov i muzikovedov 1941–1945: sbornik statey* [In Memory of Composers and Musicologists Who Perished 1941–1945: Collected Essays], i (Moscow, 1985), 70–85
LAUREL E. FAY

Fliegende Holländer, Der ('The Flying Dutchman'). *Romantische Oper* in three acts by Richard Wagner (*see* WAGNER family, (1)) to his own libretto after HEINRICH HEINE's *Aus den Memoiren des Herren von Schnabelewopski*; Dresden, Königliches Sächsisches Hoftheater, 2 January 1843.

Daland *a Norwegian sailor*	bass
Senta *his daughter*	soprano
Erik *a huntsman*	tenor
Mary *Senta's nurse*	contralto
Daland's Steersman	tenor
The Dutchman	bass-baritone

Norwegian sailors, the Dutchman's crew, young women

Setting The Norwegian coast

The supposedly autobiographical inspiration of the *Holländer*, vividly described in *Mein Leben* – according to which the work took shape during the Wagners' stormy sea crossing in July and August 1839 – is in part a fantasy. If any musical sketches were made in the months following the voyage on the *Thetis*, they have not survived. The first numbers to be composed were Senta's Ballad, and the choruses of the Norwegian sailors and Dutchman's crew, some time between 3 May and 26 July 1840. The poem was written in May 1841 and the remainder of the music during the summer, the overture being completed last, in November 1841.

Heine's retelling of the nautical legend provided Wagner with his chief source, but the composer, who identified himself with the persecuted, uprooted, sexually unfulfilled protagonist, introduced what was to become the characteristic theme of redemption by a woman. The purchase of Wagner's original prose scenario in July 1841 by Léon Pillet, the director of the Paris Opéra, led ultimately to a commission not for Wagner (as he had hoped) but for Pierre-Louis Dietsch. Contrary to what is frequently stated, Dietsch's librettists, Paul Foucher and Bénédict-Henry Révoil, based their opera *Le vaisseau fantôme* not primarily on Wagner's scenario but on Captain Marryat's novel *The Phantom Ship*, as well as on Sir Walter Scott's *The Pirate* and tales by Heine, Fenimore Cooper and Wilhelm Hauff (see Millington 1983). However, the appearance of *Le vaisseau fantôme* on the stage at the Opéra in the same month (November 1842) as rehearsals for the *Holländer* began in Dresden was undoubtedly one reason for the 11th-hour changes in Wagner's score. Until just a few weeks before the première, Wagner's opera was set off the Scottish coast, with Daland and Erik named Donald and Georg respectively. Other factors in the change may have been Wagner's desire to reinforce the autobiographical element and to distance himself at the same time from the Scottish setting of Heine.

Wagner originally conceived his work in a single act, the better to ensure its acceptance as a curtain-raiser before a ballet at the Opéra; his later claim that it was in order to focus on the dramatic essentials rather than on 'tiresome operatic accessories' may be retrospective rationalization. By the time he came to write the music, the first consideration no longer applied, his proposal having been rejected by the Opéra. He therefore elaborated the scheme in three acts, but at this stage to be played without a break. Then, some time after the end of October 1842, when he retrieved his score from the Berlin Opera (and possibly acting on advice from that quarter), he recast it in three discrete acts – the form in which it was given in Dresden and subsequently published. Following Cosima Wagner's example when she introduced it at Bayreuth in 1901, the work is now often given, both there and elsewhere, in the single-act version. There is, however, an ideological element in Bayreuth's preference for the version that presents the work most convincingly as an incipient music drama (as Wagner himself viewed it in retrospect), and both versions have some claim to authenticity.

Wagner made revisions to the score, largely in the orchestration, in 1846 and again in 1852. In 1860 (not, as sometimes stated, in 1852) the coda of the overture was remodelled (and the ending of the whole work accordingly), introducing a motif of redemption; the textures of the 1860 revision also reflect Wagner's recent preoccupation with *Tristan*.

The première in Dresden was conducted by Wagner, with Wilhelmine Schröder-Devrient as Senta and Johann Michael Wächter as the Dutchman. The first performance in London was in 1870 (in Italian); it was given there in English in 1876 and in German in 1882. The American première (1876, Philadelphia) was also in Italian; it was first given in New York the following year and at the Metropolitan in 1889. Notable interpreters of the title role have included Anton van Rooy, Friedrich Schorr, Hans Hotter, Hermann Uhde and George London. Senta has been sung by Emmy Destinn, Maria Müller, Astrid Varnay, Anja Silja and Gwyneth Jones.

ACT 1 *A steep, rocky shore* The curtain rises to a continuation of the stormy music of the overture, but now in B♭ minor, in contrast to the overture's D minor/major. Daland's ship has just cast anchor. The cries of the Norwegian sailors ('Johohe! Hallojo!') as they furl the sails allude to their chorus first heard in its entirety in Act 3. The crew is sent to rest and the steersman left on watch. His song, 'Mit Gewitter und Sturm aus fernem Meer' begins confidently, but the phrases of its second stanza are repeatedly interrupted by orchestral comments as he succumbs to slumber. Immediately the storm begins to rage again, and open-5th 'horn calls', string tremolos and a shift of tonality (from B♭ major to B minor) signify the appearance of the Flying Dutchman's ship with its blood-red sails.

The Dutchman's monologue that follows begins with a recitative, 'Die Frist ist um', in which he tells how he is permitted to come on land once every seven years to seek redemption from an as yet unnamed curse. A section in 6/8, marked 'Allegro molto agitato', 'Wie oft in Meeres tiefsten Schlund', projects a powerfully declaimed vocal line against a storm-tossed accompaniment. An earnest entreaty for deliverance is then sung over relentlessly tremolo strings, in a manner criticized

by Berlioz, and the monologue ends with a broadly phrased section, 'Nur eine Hoffnung', in which the Dutchman looks forward to Judgment Day. From their ship's hold, his crew distantly echo his last words.

Daland comes on deck, sees the strange ship, and hails its captain, whom he sees on land. The captain introduces himself simply as 'a Dutchman', going on to give a diplomatically compressed account of his voyaging, 'Durch Sturm und bösen Wind verschlagen'. The regular four-bar phrasing of the latter section, contrasted with the freer phrase structures of 'Die Frist ist um', signify what is to become a characteristic of the score: the 'exterior', public world of Daland, Erik and the Norwegian sailors and maidens is represented by traditional forms and harmonies, while the 'interior', self-absorbed world of the Dutchman and Senta frequently breaks out of the straitjacket of conventionality.

The Dutchman offers Daland vast wealth in exchange for a night's hospitality. Daland, who cannot believe his ears, is no less delighted by the wealthy stranger's interest in his daughter, and in the ensuing duet, 'Wie? Hört' ich recht?', the Dutchman's rugged individuality is entirely submerged by Daland's triteness. Daland's greedy, meretricious character is perfectly conveyed both here and in the duet's continuation, with its jaunty rhythms and elementary harmonic scheme. With the Dutchman preparing to follow Daland to his house, the Norwegian sailors steer the tonality back to B♭ major for a full-chorus reprise of the Steersman's Song.

ACT 2 *A large room in Daland's house* To cover the scene change in the original continuous version, Wagner wrote a passage in which the virile double-dotted rhythms of the sailors are transformed into the humming of the spinning wheels of the opening chorus of the second act, 'Summ und brumm'. The full dramatic effect of that transition is lost when the work is given in three separate acts, though the repetition of music from the end of Act 1 at the beginning of Act 2 has a deleterious effect only when the opera is heard on gramophone records, not in the theatre with an intervening interval. (A similar situation arises between Acts 2 and 3.)

The repetitive figures (both melodic and accompanimental) of the Spinning Chorus evoke not only the ceaseless turning of the wheels, but also the humdrum (if contented) existence of the young women. Urged on by Mary, Daland's housekeeper and Senta's nurse, the women spin in order to please their lovers who are away at sea. Senta is meanwhile reclining reflectively in an armchair, gazing at a picture hanging on the wall of a pale man with a dark beard in black, Spanish dress. She is reproached for her idleness by Mary and mocked in onomatopoeic cascades of laughter by the other women. Senta retaliates by ridiculing the tediousness of the Spinning Chorus, asking Mary to sing instead the ballad of the Flying Dutchman. Mary declines and continues spinning as the other women gather round to hear Senta sing it herself.

Senta's Ballad, 'Johohoe! Johohohoe!', begins with the same bracing open 5ths on tremolo strings that began the overture, and with the 'horn-call' figure of the Dutchman heard first as a pounding bass and then in the vocal line itself. The startling effect of these opening gestures is enhanced, in the version familiar today, by the unprepared drop in tonality from A major to G minor; however, the Ballad was originally in A minor,

'Der fliegende Holländer'
(Wagner), final scene of
Act 3 in the original
production at the
Hoftheater, Dresden, 2
January 1843: engraving
from the 'Illustrirte
Zeitung' (Leipzig, 7
October 1843)

and Wagner transposed it down at a late date (the end of 1842) for Schröder-Devrient. The strophic structure of Senta's Ballad sets it firmly in the early 19th-century operatic tradition of interpolated narrative songs; indeed, there is a direct link with the song sung by Emmy in Marschner's *Der Vampyr*, which Wagner had prepared for performance in Würzburg in 1833. Each of Senta's three turbulent stanzas (in which we learn that the Flying Dutchman's curse was laid on him for a blasphemous oath) is followed by a consolatory refrain featuring the motif associated with redemption; the final refrain is taken by the chorus, but in an abrupt breach of precedent, Senta, 'carried away by a sudden inspiration', bursts into an ecstatic coda expressing her determination to be the instrument of the Flying Dutchman's salvation. Wagner's retrospective account of the genesis of the *Holländer*, representing Senta's Ballad as the 'thematic seed' or conceptual nucleus of the whole work, was designed to depict the opera as an incipient music drama. But although some elements of the Ballad appear elsewhere in the work, and even in some of its central numbers, the use of the various motifs bears little relation to the closely integrated structural organization of post-*Oper und Drama* works such as the *Ring*.

Erik, who is in love with Senta, is horrified to hear her outburst as he enters. He announces that Daland's ship has returned, and the young women busily prepare to welcome their menfolk. Erik detains Senta and launches into a passionate protestation of love, 'Mein Herz voll Treue bis zum Sterben', whose conventionality of utterance and regularity of period scarcely commend themselves to Senta in her present mood. She struggles to get away but is forced to endure another stanza. After an exchange in which Senta alarms Erik by telling of her empathy with the strange seafarer in the picture, the huntsman recounts a dream whose ominous significance he now dimly discerns: 'Auf hohem Felsen'. From several points of view, Erik's Dream Narration represents the most advanced writing in the work. Where in his previous song the regular phrases had frequently forced normally unaccented syllables on to

strong beats, in the Dream Narration the length of phrases is determined by the rhythms of the lines. The lack of melodic interest is an indication of how far Wagner had yet to go to achieve the subtle musico-poetic synthesis of his mature works; nevertheless it is a worthy precursor of the narrations of *Tannhäuser* and *Lohengrin*. As Erik recounts how he dreamt that Senta's father brought home a stranger resembling the seafarer in the picture, Senta, in a mesmeric trance, relives the fantasy, her excited interjections latterly adopting the rising 4th of the Dutchman's motif.

Erik rushes away in despair and Senta muses on the picture. As she croons the 'redemption' refrain of the Ballad, the door opens and her father appears with the Dutchman. Recognizing him as the seafarer in the picture, Senta is spellbound and fails to greet her father. Daland approaches her and introduces the Dutchman in a characteristically breezy, four-square aria, 'Mögst du, mein Kind'.

Daland retires and, after a coda based on themes associated with Daland, the Dutchman and Senta, the long duet that occupies most of the rest of the act begins. Its unconventionality is signified by the opening statements of both characters in turn, each absorbed in his and her own thoughts. The voices eventually come together and there is even a quasi-traditional cadenza. A new plane of reality is signalled by a slight increase in tempo and a shift from E major to E minor. The pair now address each other, and in response to the Dutchman's inquiry, Senta promises obedience to her father's wishes. She goes on to express her desire to bring him redemption, and in an *agitato* section he warns of the fate that would befall her if she failed to keep her vow of constancy. Against an accompaniment of repeated wind chords redolent of a celestial chorus, Senta pledges faithfulness unto death, and the final exultant section of the duet is launched with the singers heard first separately and then together. Although not free of the constraints of traditional opera, the duet is the musical and emotional high point of the work.

Daland re-enters to ask whether the feast of home-coming can be combined with that of a betrothal. Senta reaffirms her vow and the three join in a rapturous trio to bring the act to an end.

ACT 3 *A bay with a rocky shore* Daland's house stands in the foreground, to one side. In the background the Norwegian ship is lit up and the sailors are making merry on the deck, while the Dutch ship nearby is unnaturally dark and silent. According to Wagner's account in *Mein Leben*, the theme of the Norwegian Sailors' Chorus, 'Steuermann! Lass die Wacht!', was suggested to him by the call of the sailors as it echoed round the granite walls of the Norwegian harbour of Sandviken, as the *Thetis* took refuge there on 29 July 1839. After the first strains of the chorus, the men dance on deck, stamping their feet in time with the music. The women bring out baskets of food and drink and call out to the Dutch ship, inviting the crew to participate. Men and women cry out in turn, but a deathly silence is the only response. The lighthearted appeals of sailors and womenfolk, again in alternation, become more earnest, and tension is accumulated in the orchestral texture too. A *forte* and then a *fortissimo* cry are both unanswered, and the Norwegians only half-jestingly recall the legend of the Flying Dutchman and his ghostly crew. Their carousing becomes more manic, and the Dutchman's motif in the orchestra, accompanied by sinister chromatic rumblings, builds to a climax. A storm rises in the vicinity of the Dutch ship, and the crew finally burst into unearthly song, the wind whistling through the rigging. The Norwegian sailors attempt to compete, in a powerful piece of writing for double chorus, but they are eventually subdued.

Senta comes out of the house, followed by Erik, who demands to know why she has changed her allegiance. In a cavatina of conventional cut, 'Willst jenes Tags du nicht dich mehr entsinnen', he reminds her that she had once pledged to be true to him. The Dutchman, who has overheard, makes to return to his ship and releases Senta from her vow to him. She protests her fidelity and the Dutchman, Erik and Senta all voice their emotions in a trio (often needlessly cut).

In a recitative, the Dutchman tells of his terrible fate and how he is saving Senta from the same by releasing her. He boards his ship, and Senta, proclaiming her redeeming fidelity in a final ecstatic outcry, casts herself into the sea. The Dutchman's ship, with all its crew, sinks immediately. The sea rises and falls again, revealing the Dutchman and Senta, transfigured and locked in embrace.

*   *   *

The first work of Wagner's maturity, *Der fliegende Holländer* brings together several ingredients characteristic of the later works, notably the single-minded attention given to the mood and colour of the drama, and the themes of suffering by a Romantic outsider and of redemption by a faithful woman. The initial stages of a tendency towards dissolution of numbers and towards a synthesis of text and music also endorse Wagner's assertion that with the *Holländer* began his career as a true poet.   BARRY MILLINGTON

Fliether, Herbert (*b* Velbert, 29 Oct 1911). German bass-baritone. He studied in Berlin, making his début in 1953 at Essen as Orestes (*Elektra*). In 1957 he joined the Hamburg Staatsoper, remaining there for more than 20 years. He created Field-marshal Dörfling in Henze's *Der Prinz von Homburg* in 1960, a role he sang at the opera's British première, together with Telramund, during the company's visit to Sadlers Wells in 1962; he also appeared as Creon in *Oedipus rex* at La Scala (1963) and the Music Master in *Ariadne auf Naxos* at Edinburgh (1968). In 1961 he sang Pizarro at Glyndebourne, and made his Covent Garden début in 1967 as Wotan (*Die Walküre* and *Siegfried*), replacing Hotter. His repertory included Hans Sachs, Kurwenal, Klingsor, the Grand Inquisitor (*Don Carlos*) and the Foreman (*Jenůfa*). A reliable singer with a firm voice, he was greatly admired in Wagner.   ELIZABETH FORBES

Flitch of Bacon, The. Comic opera afterpiece with dialogue in two acts composed by WILLIAM SHIELD to a libretto by the Rev. Henry Bate (later Sir Henry Bate Dudley); London, Theatre Royal, Haymarket, 17 August 1778.

A disguised couple, accompanied by Captain Wilson (bass), arrives at Dunmow Priory, Essex, to claim the reward for a year and a day of conjugal fidelity. They are Eliza (soprano) and Captain Greville (tenor), who need a blessing on their elopement in order to claim Eliza's marriage portion. At the awarding of the flitch of bacon, Justice Benbow (spoken role) blesses the unknown couple; Eliza then reveals herself to be his daughter. Major Benbow (bass) also blesses the marriage and releases the money, having discovered that the woman Captain Wilson duped him into pursuing has turned out to be his niece. This was Shield's first comic opera and one of the Haymarket's most successful afterpieces. It included five numbers by other composers.   LINDA V. TROOST

Floquet, Etienne Joseph (*b* Aix-en-Provence, 23 Nov 1748; *d* Paris, 10 May 1785). French composer. He studied in the *maîtrise* of St Sauveur at Aix and began his career by writing sacred music. He was in Paris by 1767 and soon gained recognition, having sacred and secular works performed and attracting aristocratic patronage. His first theatrical work, *L'union de l'Amour et des arts*, staged at the Opéra in 1773, is a *ballet-héroïque* with three independent entrées. In a period when tragic opera was languishing it won general approval; Floquet was the first composer to be called on stage after a performance at the Opéra, and the work was given 60 times up to January 1774. The following year Floquet joined the Opéra orchestra, playing the viola; and Gluck began to distract attention from native talent. Floquet's second *ballet-héroïque*, *Azolan*, was performed between *Orphée* and the revival of *Iphigénie en Aulide*. Its comparative failure (it was performed 20 times but never revived) was attributed to Gluckist intrigue: it soon acquired the sobriquet 'désolant'. Nevertheless, Floquet had faithful supporters (self-styled 'Floquetistes') who joined the cabal against Gluck's *La Cythère assiégée* in 1775.

Meanwhile, possibly on the advice of Grimm, Floquet went to Italy. He studied composition with Nicola Sala in Naples and counterpoint with Padre Martini in Bologna. When he returned in 1777, Piccinni was Gluck's established rival, and the Opéra showed little interest in native composers. He composed his first *tragédie*, *Hellé*, to a libretto previously declined by Mondonville, and his first *opéra comique*, *La nouvelle Omphale*; they waited until 1779 and 1782 for performance. *Hellé* had only three performances; Floquet had been offered a greatly increased fee if it was successful. Its failure was attributed to Laguerre's poor performance in the title role, but Floquet was out-

231

stripped in the Italian style by Piccinni and in dramatic strength by Gluck. *La nouvelle Omphale* was well received, as was *Le seigneur bienfaisant*, which deals with the joys and mishaps (righted by the benevolent lord) of ordinary people. Although it was cordially despised by Gluck and his followers, its considerable charms attracted the public and it remained in repertory until 1787.

Floquet determined to try another tragic subject, a revision of Quinault's *Alceste* (*Le triomphe d'Alcide*). Both subject and occasion were unpropitious. Recent resettings of Quinault, by Philidor and Gossec, had failed; Gluck's *Alceste* was well known; and Piccinni had just triumphed with *Didon*. *Alceste* was rehearsed and provisionally accepted by the Opéra committee but it was never performed. Floquet was already in poor health, perhaps as the result of loose living; the disappointment with *Alceste* may have hastened his early death. He left two unfinished operas; one, *Alcindor*, was completed by Dezède and performed in 1787.

Floquet's talents suited the pastoral, the picturesque and sentimental, required of him in *Le seigneur bienfaisant*, rather than tragedy or real comedy. His early works show fashionable interest in Italian music, while remaining within the bounds of French taste. His adoption of an Italian style, fostered by his studies there, was never more than skin-deep. In *Hellé*, his most ambitious and most uneven work, the choruses are reminiscent of an older French style but several of the arias are italianate, particularly the florid piece for Legros (Neptune), with two obbligato clarinets. Of *Alceste* only the opening scenes survive; they suggest that Floquet, perhaps trying to imitate Piccinni, had fallen into prolixity.

first performed at the Paris Opéra unless otherwise stated

L'union de l'Amour et des arts [Bathilde et Chloé; Théodore; La cour d'Amour] (ballet-héroïque, 3, P. R. Lemonnier), 7 Sept 1773 (Paris, ?1773)

Azolan, ou Le serment indiscret (ballet-héroïque, 3, Lemonnier), 22 Nov 1774, Acts 1 and 2 *F-Po*, excerpts pubd

Hellé (tragédie lyrique, 3, Lemonnier and La Boullaye), 5 Jan 1779, *Po*, excerpts pubd

Le seigneur bienfaisant (opéra, 3, M.-A.-J. Rochon de Chabannes), 14 Dec 1780 (Paris, ?1780); rev. (4), 23 Dec 1782 (Paris, 1782)

La nouvelle Omphale (cmda, 3, Beaunoir [A. L. A. Robineau]), Versailles, 22 Nov 1782 (Paris, ?1782)

Grisélidis, 1783 (oc, 3), unperf.

Le triomphe d'Alcide [Alceste], 1783 (tragédie lyrique, 5, P.-A. Razins de Saint-Marc, after P. Quinault), unperf., frags. *Po*

Les françaises, ?1784 (oc, 1, Rochon de Chabannes), unperf.

Alcindor, 1785 (opéra-féerie, 3, Rochon de Chabannes), completed by N. Dezède, perf. 17 April 1787 (Paris, 1787)

La chasse, 1785 (Razins de Saint-Marc), inc.

*

ES (M. Briquet)

De Charnois: 'Nécrologie', *Mercure de France* (6 Aug 1785)

Castil-Blaze: *Théâtre lyriques de Paris: l'Académie impériale de musique de 1645 à 1855*, i (Paris, 1855)

A. Pougin: *Floquet* (Paris, 1863); also in *Revue et gazette musicale de Paris*, xxx (1863), 193, 209, 234, 244, 265

G. le Brisoys Desnoiresterres: *La musique française au XVIIIe siècle: Gluck et Piccinni* (Paris, 1872, 2/1875)

A. Gouirand: *La musique en Provence* (Paris and Marseilles, 1908)

J. G. Prod'homme: *Écrits de musiciens XVe–XVIIIe siècles* (Paris, 1912)

M. Briquet: 'A propos de lettres inédites de Etienne-Joseph Floquet (1748–1785)', *RdM*, xxiii (1939), 1–6, 41–7

——: *E.-J. Floquet* (diss., U. of Paris, 1953)

——: 'L'Alceste de E. J. Floquet', *Mélanges d'histoire et d'esthétique musicales offerts à Paul-Marie Masson*, ii (Paris, 1955), 19–29

J. G. Rushton: *Music and Drama at the Académie Royale de Musique, Paris, 1774–1789* (diss., U. of Oxford, 1970)

JULIAN RUSHTON

Florelle, Odette (*b* Sables d'Olonne, 8 Aug 1898; *d* La Roche-sur-Yon, 28 Sept 1974). French soprano. She began her career at the Théâtre de l'Ambigu and appeared at the Moulin Rouge in *Ça c'est Paris* (1926), then rose to fame as Polly in the French version of G. W. Pabst's film of *Die Dreigroschenoper*. Other film roles followed, notably in Jean Renoir's *Le crime de Monsieur Lange* (with music by Joseph Kosma). Florelle created the title role in Weill's play with music *Marie Galante* (1934), from which she recorded four arias. She retired from the stage during the Occupation, but after the war made occasional film appearances. She had a well-focussed, high soprano voice, with a typically Parisian style of delivery and a vivacious personality, which impresses itself especially strongly in her films.

*

J. Damase: *Les folies du music-hall* (Paris, 1961)

C. Brunschwig, L.-J. Calvet and J.-C. Klein: *100 ans de chanson française* (Paris, 1972)

P. O'Connor: 'Weill à la française', *Kurt Weill Newsletter*, ix/1 (1991), 10–13

PATRICK O'CONNOR

Florence (It. Firenze). Italian city, capital of Tuscany and a cultural and historic centre of the first importance. It has claims to be regarded as the birthplace of opera.

1. The Medici court, academies and palaces, 1595–1647. 2. The Cocomero and Pergola theatres and the dramaturgical academies, 1649–1700. 3. From Francesco and Ferdinando' Medici to the reopening of the Pergola, 1678–1718. 4. Final years of Medici rule (1718–37) and the early regency to 1750. 5. The Compagnia Nazionale Toscana, 1750–65. 6. The reign of Pietro Leopoldo, Grand Duke of Tuscany, 1765–90. 7. From Ferdinando III to the French occupation, 1791–1800. 8. After 1800.

1. THE MEDICI COURT, ACADEMIES AND PALACES, 1595–1647. Opera was created by Florentine academicians, poets and musicians who, inspired by their study of ancient Greek dramatic and music theory and by their own 16th-century theatrical traditions, sought to invent an Italian drama with continuous music. Contributions to the effort were made by the Alterati, Fiorentina and, from 1607, the Elevati academies; two informal *conversazioni*, one the famous Camerata led by Giovanni de' Bardi and the other led by Jacopo Corsi; and the musicians and courtiers of the Medici court. The objectives, aesthetics and historical justification were published in Girolamo Mei's *De modis musicis antiquorum* (in particular book iii, 1571) and Vincenzo Galilei's *Dialogo della musica antica, et della moderna* (1581).

The first operatic prototypes (Emilio de' Cavalieri's *Il Satiro* and *La disperazione di Fileno*, 1590; *Il giuoco della cieca*, 1595; texts by the poet Laura Guidiccioni) established the pastorale as the topic, genus and form of the text, and accompanied solo song, commonly called 'monody', mixed with choruses and ballets as the musical setting. Jacopo Peri and Giulio Caccini more or less simultaneously invented a distinct *stile rappresentativo* employing declamatory rhythm over slow harmonic motion, which Peri called 'recitar cantando'. Peri's *Euridice* (1600; text by Ottavio Rinuccini) is the first wholly extant pastorale (only fragments remain of his earlier *La Dafne*). Caccini's setting of *Euridice* (performed in 1602, though published in 1600) demonstrates the importance of his contribution to the new style.

Use of the new *stile rappresentativo* was restricted in Florence to *intermedi*, *balli*, *veglie*, *mascherate*, *cocchiate* and *balletti a cavallo*, the preferred entertainments that continued the traditions of 16th-century

1. 'La Flora' (Marco da Gagliano), Act 3 scene vi (Amore/Cupid asks Pluto to release Jealousy while Charon, in the background, plies the River Styx): stage design by Alfonso Parigi for the original production at the theatre in the Uffizi Palace, Florence, for the wedding of Odoardo Farnese and Margherita de' Medici in 1628

court theatricals. Weddings or other court occasions called for festival operas, which differed from the smaller genera primarily in duration rather than character. Three notable (and surviving) festival operas were Francesca Caccini's *La liberazione di Ruggiero dall'isola d'Alcina*, a *balletto a cavallo* to a text by Ferdinando Saracinelli (1625), Gagliano's *La Flora* to a text by Andrea Salvadori (1628; fig.1), and *Le nozze degli dei*, a *favola* with music by five 'best composers of the city' to a text by Carlo Coppola (1637; for illustration *see* PARIGI, GIULIO). As a consequence of conditions in the Medici court, the frequency of secular performances declined. Sacred opera, such as Gagliano's *La regina Sant'Orsola* (1624; for illustration *see* PRODUCTION, fig.3), enjoyed a limited vogue through the tradition of religious school drama. Except for such performances, Florence abandoned until mid-century the art form it had created.

2. THE COCOMERO AND PERGOLA THEATRES AND THE DRAMATURGICAL ACADEMIES, 1649–1700. The operatic genera of serious or semi-serious and comic opera, which had evolved from the Florentine pastorale in Rome and then Venice, were not heard in Florence until Sacrati's *La finta pazza* in 1645, followed in the next year by Cavalli's *Egisto*. Two dramaturgical academies were founded partly as a reaction to these performances. The first was an academy of the nobility, the Immobili, established in 1649 under the protection of Cardinal Gian Carlo de' Medici; the second, the Sorgenti (not the Infuocati as is usually stated), whose members were common citizens, was organized some time before or in 1654, obtaining the cardinal's protection in 1657. The construction of two theatres was begun. The earlier was the privately owned, commercially operated Teatro di via del Cocomero, begun in 1650 and opened possibly as early as 1654. The second, the Teatro di via della Pergola, founded in 1652 and opened in 1657 (fig.2), was built largely at the expense of Cardinal de' Medici, the legal owner, for exclusive use by the Immobili, the Accademia dei Nobili and the Medici court.

The inaugural opera for the Pergola was a *dramma civile rusticale* entitled *Il potestà di Colognole* by Jacopo Melani to a text by G. A. Moniglia, mounted on 5 February 1657. It initiated an enduring genre of Tuscan comic opera with distinctive literary and musical characteristics, a genre further defined by the subsequent comic librettos written by Moniglia and set by Melani (or, in the case of *La serva nobile*, by Domenico Anglesi) for the Immobili between 1657 and 1663, and by two later ones, Melani's *Tacere et amare* (Cocomero, 1674) and Lorenzo Cattani's *Il conte di Cutro* (Cocomero, 1682). Only one score, *Il potestà di Colognole*, survives. The Immobili also gave the premières of two *feste teatrali*, both by Moniglia: Cavalli's *L'Hipermestra* (1658; for illustration *see* TACCA, FERDINANDO) and Melani's *Ercole in Tebe* (1661, fig.3) for the wedding of Cosimo de' Medici and Marguerite d'Orléans. On the cardinal's death in 1663, litigation closed the Pergola until 1718 except for occasional noble exercises and the wedding opera of Ferdinando de' Medici and Violante Beatrice of Bavaria, Pagliardi's *Il greco in Troia* (1689; text by Matteo Noris).

The Cocomero was built under a contract between the cardinal and Niccolò Ughi that recognized the latter and his heirs as proprietors of the theatre. The Ughi rented the theatre to a variety of clients: the Medici court, touring companies, and several different academies beginning with the Sorgenti, whose first opera was *Scipione in Cartagine* by Moniglia with music by Melani, the academy's official composer, given on 25 November 1657. Thereafter the academy sponsored imported operas until its last recorded use in 1665 of the Cocomero for the *Intermedio della Cuccagna* (text by

2. Auditorium of the Teatro della Pergola, Florence: engraving (1658) by Silvio degli Alli

the academy member Pietro Susini, with anonymous music).

The Sorgenti constructed a new theatre, probably in the Piazza del Grano, in 1679, but they are not recorded as having performed operas until 1690 when they presented an anonymous *dramma burlesco, Il moccone podestà del Bagno a Ripoli,* followed during the next three years by three anonymous comic operas and one serious opera. After this brief period of activity they apparently disbanded in 1699.

Between 1665 and 1700 the Cocomero was rented first by an academy of 34 cavaliers under the patronage of Carlo de' Medici (*d* 1666), an uncle of Cardinal Gian Carlo, which was the first to use the name of Infuocati. To this noble academy can be assigned, besides prose comedies, Melani's *Tacere et amare* (1674), Alessandro Melani's *Il carceriere di se medesimo* (1681) and possibly Bernardo Pasquini's *Lisimaco* (1690). During the same period travelling troupes of *comici* occasionally rented the theatre to present Venetian or Roman operas; among the latter was a performance in 1670 of Jacopo Melani's *Girello.*

From 1690 until 1693 the Infuocati academy was replaced in the Cocomero by a series of ad hoc academies that changed names and probably membership with each performance (Volante, Innominati, Efimeri and Saggiati, 1690–93). Finally, following several years in which the librettos identify neither the academy nor the theatre, operatic production was reorganized in 1699 under one academy, the Infuocati, but this time composed of citizens rather than nobility. Significantly, the new Infuocati claimed in their 1699 charter that their predecessors were the Sorgenti – not

the 17th-century Infuocati. The new Infuocati consolidated their position in 1704 by obtaining the protection of Ferdinando de' Medici. But the theatre remained the property of the Ughi family until 1763 when it was rebuilt in stone at the expense of the academy, which thereafter claimed proprietorship.

Among several small theatres, two are worthy of note. The Teatro nel Corso de' Tintori was erected in 1676 by the Imperfetti, who performed primarily spoken comedies but undertook a performance of Giuseppe Fabbrini's *La fede ne' tradimenti* in 1697. The second, the Teatro in Borgo Ognissanti (presumably an early form of the theatre rebuilt in 1778), which opened on 18 July 1692 with Alessandro Scarlatti's *La Rosaura di Cipro,* was operated by the Accademici Nascenti. Neither academy was active again, though the theatres continued to be in use over the next century.

3. FROM FRANCESCO AND FERDINANDO DE' MEDICI TO THE REOPENING OF THE PERGOLA, 1678–1718. Francesco Maria (1660–1711, youngest son of Ferdinando II, cardinal in 1686) gathered around him a *conversazione* of young cavaliers to produce operas in his palace, the Casino di S Marco, in 1678. After several productions of operas first performed elsewhere, the *conversazione,* now calling itself an academy, determined to undertake new works by Tuscans, the first being *Sidonio* (9 December 1680) by Giuseppe Giacomini and an unknown composer. There followed two tragic dramas by Moniglia and Cattani: *Quinto Lucrezio proscritto* (1681) and *Gneo Marzio Coriolano* (1686), and a comic opera, *Il conte di Cutro* (1682). Francesco, when appointed cardinal, moved to Rome and thereafter

promoted opera in Florence only on occasional visits and through correspondence with and assistance to his nephew Ferdinando (1663–1713).

In his 16th year Ferdinando de' Medici produced his first opera in the Medici villa at Pratolino. A thoroughly trained and able musician, he rehearsed and directed his operas as the *primo maestro al cembalo*. He most often chose librettos written by native or adopted Tuscan poets: G. F. Apolloni (1), Giacomini (2), G. C. Villifranchi (6), Moniglia (3) and Antonio Salvi (7), in contrast to G. F. Bussani (1), Zeno (3), Noris (3) and Stampiglia (2). Tuscan composers were not so well favoured, though the higher number (5) of anonymous musical settings makes comparison more difficult. He commissioned new or rewritten scores from Cerri (1), Pagliardi (3 – he was in Florence from 1681), Alessandro Melani (?2), G. B. Benini (1), and one pasticcio by Francesco de Castris, Martino Bitti and Alessandro Scarlatti. Foreign composers were Legrenzi (1), A. Scarlatti (6), C. F. Pollarolo (3) and Perti (5). The Tuscans were early favourites, but after 1699, while Salvi remained the most popular librettist, no Tuscans were engaged as composers. During the first three years only pastorales were presented. From 1683 to 1695, comic operas (7) predominated over serious ones (4), but from 1696 until the last in 1710, only serious operas were performed, an indication of Ferdinando's ambition to raise his theatre at Pratolino to an international level. With a few exceptions all librettos and scores were new, but only a small proportion of the scores has survived.

Either Ferdinando or his father, Grand Duke Cosimo III, or both, imposed stringent limitations on the theatres about 1699. In the last decade of the 17th century five Florentine theatres (the Cocomero, Sorgenti, Tintori, Borgo Ognissanti and Casino di S Marco) were engaged in performing operas of one sort or another, and others (the Porta Rossa, Vangelista, Collegio Tolomei, Irresoluti and Casa Fioravanti) prose plays. Abruptly, from 1701 on, the number of operas and plays was reduced. Within the city, only the Infuocati were permitted to present opera.

Ferdinando exerted a powerful influence directly on the bourgeois Infuocati. He supplied his own singers, interceded with other members of the Medici, including the grand duke, to secure their singers, and wrote to other theatres and princely patrons on behalf of the academy to obtain other singers. The composers chosen for the Cocomero – Alessandro Scarlatti, Pollarolo and Perti – often paralleled or repeated the choices for Pratolino. According to a contemporary diarist, Niccolò Susier, his attendance at the Cocomero was 'usual'. After the prince became the protector in 1704, new operas became more numerous; even after Ferdinando's death in 1713 the academy maintained a balance between new operas by exotic composers, new ones by Tuscan residents, and refurbished operas imported from elsewhere. Among the noteworthy premières are Handel's *Vincer se stesso è la maggior vittoria* (1707), Orlandini and Rocco Ceruti's *L'amor generoso* (1708), and Gasparini's *Amor vince l'odio* (1715). The influence

3. 'Ercole in Tebe' (Jacopo Melani), Act 4 scene xix (battle before the walls of Thebes, with Venus (left) and Juno (right) confronting each other above): stage design by Ferdinando Tacca for the original production at the Teatro della Pergola, Florence, for the wedding of Cosimo III de' Medici and Marguerite Louis d'Orléans in 1661

of the prince, who had abandoned comic opera at Pratolino after 1695, is seen also in the fact that only serious operas were performed at the Cocomero until 1717 with one exception, *La serva favorita* (music probably by A. Scarlatti), which had been performed at Pratolino in 1689. Comic contrascenes, on the other hand, were common. Giovanni Battista Fagiuoli, who wrote to Zeno for permission, added the text of contrascenes to Zeno's *Aminta*, set by Albinoni and first performed at the Cocomero in 1703. The first intermezzo, a form which was to become standard over the next few years, was published in 1711: *Barilotto e Slapina*, by Salvi and an unknown composer (possibly Sarro).

The nobility still lacked a theatre of their own. Ferdinando intervened to relieve the bankruptcy of the Immobili, initiated meetings to revive the academy and laid plans for the rebuilding of the Pergola, whose reopening, however, took place only after his death.

4. FINAL YEARS OF MEDICI RULE (1718–37) AND THE EARLY REGENCY TO 1750. The Immobili opened the reconstructed Pergola on 22 June 1718 with the première of Vivaldi's *Scanderbeg* under the protection of Gian Gastone de' Medici, who succeeded Ferdinando. He was not, however, as knowledgeable or dedicated to opera as his brother. Thus responsibility for productions fell more directly on the impresarios, who were at that time normally, but not always, members of the academy. An intimate of Ferdinando and a participant in the production of operas at Pratolino, Luca Casimiro degli Albizzi was the most capable and influential among the various academic impresarios. Among the new works he commissioned were three by Vivaldi and one each by Giovanni Porta and Pescetti. His most frequent *maestro di musica* was G. B. Orlandini, who supplied alterations to scores by others and also new ones of his own including *Ifigenia in Aulide* (1732) and *Temistocle* (1737), and several intermezzos. Francesco Pecori, another distinguished academic impresario, engaged Antonio Predieri for six premières between 1718 and 1720. From Albizzi's last season in 1738 until 1752, the list of premières included scores by Orlandini (2), Giuseppe Scarlatti (2), Domenico Scarlatti (1), Terradellas (1), Lampugnani (1), Michele Fini (2), and Pescetti (5, at the invitation of the impresario Ugolino Grifoni, 1748–50).

In general between 1718 and 1752, anonymous pasticcios predominated (by 54 to 40). Previously performed operas by named composers (12) were a minor portion compared with the 28 new ones, of which only three were Tuscan. The unsystematic season-by-season change of impresarios inevitably imposed mediocrity on much of the theatre's production. The absence of Tuscan composers was due to the character assumed by the Immobili for their theatre (following the preferences exhibited by Ferdinando after 1695) as an internationally famous stage dedicated to serious opera (with occasional comic intermezzos or ballet), albeit in somewhat degraded examples of that repertory.

Following the death of the last Medici grand duke, Gian Gastone, in 1737, the Holy Roman Emperor Francis I, Grand Duke of Tuscany and consort of the Empress Maria Theresa of Austria, ruled Tuscany by a regency (he remained in Vienna) until his own death in 1765. The consequent lack of patronage by a resident grand ducal court and the decline in Tuscany's economy (the general depression afflicting Europe being exacerbated by the unreasonable financial demands of the Viennese imperial government) contributed to a further deterioration in the quality of the operas presented in the Pergola. After 1752 the Immobili sank into a bog of pasticcios and ceased producing operas worthy of notice until the arrival in 1765 of the new grand duke, Pietro Leopoldo, second surviving son of Francis I and Maria Theresa.

The Cocomero, about 1717, changed the character of its offerings by commissioning new works by resident Tuscan composers and reintroducing comic operas after a drought of some 35 years. Premières of operas, intermezzos and other works by Florentines included four (possibly five) by Orlandini, four by Chinzer, one by Chinzer and Gaetano Bracci, two by Carlo Arrigoni, and one by G. N. R. Redi. On the other hand, the premières of operas by foreign composers were notably fewer: one each by Porta, Predieri, Fini, Abos, Schiassi and Giuseppe Scarlatti. The reintroduction of comic opera began with revivals of operas with texts by Moniglia (beginning with *Il potestà di Colognole*) and Villifranchi, all but one with anonymous music and possibly with some of the original music by Melani or Cattani, beginning in 1717 and continuing into the early 1730s. The one exception to the anonymous scores was a setting of Villifranchi's *La serva favorita* by Chinzer in 1726, revived in 1741. The revivals were isolated: neither foreign nor new Tuscan comic operas were performed until 1731 when Vanneschi's *La vanità delusa* and *La commedia in commedia* were presented with music by Chinzer, followed the next year by *La serva padrona* with music by Predieri. *La commedia in commedia*, after it was set by Rinaldo di Capua for Rome in 1738, entered the international repertory.

Neither of the first joint regents, Marc di Craon and Emmanuel de Richecourt, possessed a taste for serious opera, but Craon, ignoring the theatre of the nobility, became the official protector of the Infuocati as the representative of the grand duke in 1738, which apparently increased the frequency of comic operas and introduced for the first time in Florence Neapolitan comic opera with the performance of the pasticcio *Orazio* (by Pergolesi, Latilla and others) in 1740 (repeated in 1742 and 1745).

Craon was most closely associated, however, with the Tuscan company of prose comedians formed as early as 1732 by Domenico Guagni and Gaetano Ciarli in the Coletti theatre. Between 1742 and 1743 five comic operas dedicated to Craon were performed there, four of them imported – two by Latilla and one each by Auletta and Leo – and a fifth by the Florentine G. Lirone. The company of singers moved from the Coletti in May to the Cocomero in June for a staging of a new comic opera. They were joined in the next production in the Cocomero by Pietro and Caterina Brogi Pertici, to whom the theatre was ceded by the regency for the season. During the next eight years from 1742 Guagni and Pertici cooperatively controlled the Cocomero and gave it a decisive turn in favour of comic opera by mounting 18 comic against ten serious operas.

In 1750 Richecourt established the Compagnia Nazionale Toscana headed by Pertici, who was responsible for musical productions and officially the impresario of the Cocomero; it embraced a permanent residency for Guagni and his prose comedians (a few operatic stars continued to be invited season by season to enhance the resident company). The regency at the same time imposed severe restrictions by banning opera in any theatre except the Pergola and Cocomero and prose plays in any theatre except the Cocomero. Moreover, foreign companies (though not opera singers) were forbidden to perform in Florence at any time. Thus until Richecourt left towards the end of the decade, other theatres – the Tintori, Borgo de' Greci, Coletti and Orsanmichele – were opened only for acrobats, magicians, lectures, amateur theatricals and the like, and the distinction between the two opera theatres was clearly maintained, the Pergola as the theatre of serious opera and the Cocomero of comic opera and plays, and, as the national theatre, the more accessible to Tuscan poets and composers.

5. THE COMPAGNIA NAZIONALE TOSCANA, 1750–65. Pertici, as head of the Compagnia Nazionale and at the same time the impresario of the Cocomero (1750–55), had the contractual duty of providing new librettos. Since in the 1740s he had translated a number of French comedies and farces, after 1750 he turned again to French comedy for his sources. While he was impresario, the Cocomero staged seven farces declared to be translations of French stage works, and many of the other farces with unidentified sources were doubtless imitations if not actual translations. The most significant of his farces was *La semplice curiosa*, a translation of C.-S. Favart's *La chercheuse d'esprit* long thought to have been set *alla francese* by Egidio Duni while the composer was in Florence in 1751.

Pertici was also devoted to the plays, intermezzos and comic operas of Goldoni, a preference evidently shared by Guagni, so that the Cocomero became a repertory theatre of Goldoni's works with and without music. In its first year the company presented the burletta *La maestra*, an alteration by Goldoni of Palomba's original libretto, and the première of the comic opera *Buovo d'Antona*, both by unknown composers. Virtually all works were anonymous except two by Galuppi and one by Cocchi, but in any case the company's composers, Niccolò Valenti and Lorenzo Minuti, provided many additions and alterations to almost all scores. During the five years of Pertici's tenure, 12 of Goldoni's comic works for music were staged by the company. Guagni at the same time was performing Goldoni's prose comedies, which reached a high point in the carnival of 1755 when 11 out of 12 comedies offered were by Goldoni, whose works remained highly favoured in the Cocomero afterwards.

Serious dramas were presented only three times between 1750 and 1770, after which they became more frequent. Two of the serious dramas were within the scope of the theatre because the scores were by Florentines (Giovanni Masi's *Muzio Scevola* and Minuti's *Bellerofonte*, both 1760, on texts by Lanfranchi Rossi).

From about 1759 the enforcement of Richecourt's regulations was relaxed (though apparently not rescinded) under the new regency of General Adorno Botta, who permitted the rebuilding and even the construction of new theatres. In 1759 Guagni's company was given permission to perform in a new theatre recently founded by the Accademia degli Arrischiati, the Teatro della Piazza Vecchia di S Maria Novella. (Opera performances did not begin until 1766.) The Coletti or the Teatro di via del Giardino, closed for ten years, was rebuilt and provided with a new entrance that justified its renaming as the Teatro di via S Maria. It opened for Carnival 1761 with a prose comedy with ballets and

began its operatic career in 1763 with *Gli sposi in maschera* (Casorri), with music primarily by Rutini and some arias by J. C. Bach and Galuppi.

The most significant new work by Florentines during this interregnum was the première at the Cocomero in 1765 of G. M. Rutini's *L'olandese in Italia*, a comic opera with a text by Abate Niccolò Tassi. It enjoyed a notable success not only in Italy but also in Lisbon, Prague, Dresden and Lucerne over a period of eight years. Together with *Gli sposi in maschera* it was a cornerstone in the foundation of a new school of Tuscan composers, which, since it flourished during the reign of Grand Duke Pietro Leopoldo (1765–90) and the first decade of his son's, could appropriately be called the Leopoldine school.

6. THE REIGN OF PIETRO LEOPOLDO, GRAND DUKE OF TUSCANY, 1765–90. Florentine opera attained in the last third of the 18th century a vitality exceeding in productive quantity all previous eras. In the last years of Pietro Leopoldo's rule Florence surpassed Milan and Bologna and rivalled Venice, Naples and Rome in the production of new musical dramas, judging by the records kept by the *Indice de' spettacoli teatrali*. And for the first time a Tuscan school of composers and performers took shape which created forms and styles possessing distinctive native character.

At the Pergola pasticcios declined and premières of scores by major composers increased. Composers of new operas included Traetta (the grand duke's favourite), Mysliveček, Francesco Bianchi, Paisiello, Gassmann, Sarti, Gazzaniga, Andreozzi, Anfossi, Cimarosa and others. There were premières of Tuscan operas by G. M. Rutini (1), Alessandro Felici (1), Neri Bondi (1), Brunetti (1) and Cherubini (3). In 1776 Paisiello's *Le due contesse* became the first comic opera to be performed at the Pergola in the 18th century. Thereafter the theatre mounted as many comic as serious operas (sometimes more) and occasionally surpassed the Cocomero in the number of comic operas.

At the Cocomero, which had concentrated for a time on farces and intermezzos, Giovanni Roffi (impresario 1764–9) brought comic and occasionally serious operas back into the repertory. Since the theatre continued to maintain its position as the national theatre, the number of Tuscan works was higher than at the Pergola: Moneta (8), Neri Bondi (6), G. M. Rutini (3), F. Rutini (1), A. Felici (1), G. V. Meucci (1) and Giuseppe Gherardeschi (1), all comic of one genre or another. New comic operas by foreign composers were by Anfossi, Luigi Caruso, Bernardo Ottani, Cimarosa, Tritto and Gazzaniga.

Between 1785 and 1795, while Pietro Andolfati, whose policies were very similar to those of Pertici, was the impresario of the Cocomero, two innovations are noteworthy. The first is the *melodramma* (or in later terminology *melologo*), a form that originated in France in the 1770s and spread to Germany and Italy in the next decade. It was a spoken drama, usually tragic, with illustrative orchestral music called 'musica analoga', and with occasional arias or ensembles; the first was Moneta's *Meleagro* (1785), a tragedy by Camillo Federici. The second innovation was the reduction of musical genera to one act, whether *intermezzo*, *farsa*, *dramma giocoso* or even *dramma per musica*. This fact suggests a change in function in which the musical work was juxtaposed with rather than interposed in a spoken drama. (Ballets, which were the rule before 1785, were

4. Title page and frontispiece (with engraved portrait of Grand Duke Pietro Leopoldo) of the libretto of the comic opera 'Il ratto della sposa' (text by Gaetano Martinelli; music by P. A. Guglielmi), performed at the Teatro Cocomero, spring 1769

abandoned at the Cocomero between 1785 and 1795. Thereafter they were regularly done in the autumn season.)

Three other theatres began the production of opera during this period. The Teatro di via S Maria (formerly the Coletti) initiated in 1768 a summer opera season, not occupied until then by any theatre. Previously performed foreign comedies were staged as well as premières of Tuscan operas and intermezzos, one each by G. M. Rutini and Moneta, two by Bernardo Mengozzi, and six by Neri Bondi, who was *primo maestro al cembalo* at the theatre.

The Teatro della Piazza Vecchia di S Maria Novella, though built in 1759, remained unused except for occasional amateur performances. In 1778, however, farces with music were offered. At this theatre, within its modest output during carnival, Tuscan composers were actually in a majority. The Lucchesan composer Antonio Riccomini directed two of his own works from the keyboard. Neri Bondi provided two comic operas and two farces. The only works by foreign composers were one by Sacchini (a Florentine by birth only), two by Marcello Bernardini and one by Giovanni Valentini.

The third theatre, the Regio Teatro degl'Intrepidi detto della Palla a Corda, was built by a group of nobles and common citizens including at least one Jew, Salomone di Angiolo Finzi, a membership impossible at either the Pergola or the Cocomero, and a union of classes the grand duke consistently favoured in other activities as well. The *Gazzetta toscana* assured its readers that it was the finest theatre of Italy. The theatre opened in 1779 and had a yearly schedule consisting of one or more ballets or intermezzos during carnival, one or two serious operas in the spring, and two to four comic operas with occasional substitutions of serious opera in the autumn. Every year either two or three of its operas were premières of works by eminent foreign

composers such as Sarti, Giuseppe Giordani, Caruso, Andreozzi, Fabrizi and Astarita, while Tuscans were not neglected: Neri Bondi, Moneta, and Brunetti.

Beyond the flourishing of the Leopoldine school, there are other accomplishments of Pietro Leopoldo's reign that should be underlined. The mixing of the noble and bourgeois classes including the Jews formed a broad community to support and finance the arts in general and opera in particular. The tribunal created under Francesco III was converted into a specifically judicial body before which the musicians as a group could sue for fulfilment of their contracts and employment conditions – and did so successfully. The year-round musical seasons, made possible by the founding of concert societies (the Armonici, Ingegnosi, etc.) which supported public concerts in Lent and Advent created a continuous, dependable demand for musicians. On this foundation their number and power increased to such a point that in the 1780s and 90s the musicians themselves clearly had direct influence on the choice of music and the way in which the tasks were distributed among themselves. Finally, the rigid operatic genera (serious opera, burletta and intermezzo) of the mid-century blossomed into a variety of types from farces to melodramas with musical accompaniment to spoken dramas with incidental music, and pantomime ballet, both comic and serious, became an art form equal in sophistication and complexity to the dramatic forms.

7. FROM FERDINANDO III TO THE FRENCH OCCUPATION, 1791–1800. Emperor Joseph II died in February 1790. Pietro Leopoldo succeeded him as Leopoldo II, and Leopoldo's third son, Ferdinando III, became grand duke in 1791. Ferdinando's theatrical policy, a more liberal version of his father's, resulted in the greatest flowering of opera in the city's history. The season took on such an opulence that Florence exceeded all the

capitals of Italy in the production of new musical theatrical works. During carnival six theatres were regularly open with two serious operas at the Pergola and one to four each of intermezzos, comic operas, farces or melodramas at the Cocomero, S Maria, Piazza Vecchia, Borgo Ognissanti and Intrepidi. The Pergola produced a sacred drama and the Armonici sponsored two to four concerts at the Porta Rossa theatre during Lent. In spring the Pergola turned to comic operas, mounting two to four, while the Intrepidi presented two serious operas. The summer belonged exclusively to the S Maria, which usually staged three comic operas during June and July. In autumn two or three serious operas were performed at the Pergola, and at the Cocomero two or four intermezzos or comic operas. The year concluded with a sacred drama during Advent at the Cocomero.

The two principal theatres, the Pergola and the Intrepidi, vied with each other in presenting premières by internationally known composers, the former mounting 23 and the latter 18 during this nine-year period. While the lesser theatres were correspondingly more active in staging works by Tuscans, they still occasionally presented foreign composers. In all Florence saw some 50 premières (compared with 62 in the 25-year reign of Pietro Leopoldo), by Andreozzi, Astarita, Francesco Basili, Curcio, Farinelli, Valentino Fioravanti, Gazzaniga, Gnecco, P. A. Guglielmi, Isola, Isouard, Marinelli, Mosca, Nasolini, Paer, Portugal, Pucitta, Sarti, Scolart, Spontini, Tarchi, Trento and Zingarelli, among others. These premières constituted just under half of the total of 110 musical theatrical works by foreign composers. Tuscan composers gained even more significantly, achieving 57 premières, compared with 51 during the preceding period (and surpassing the number of premières of foreign operas), of works by Moneta, Neri Bondi, Ferdinando Rutini, Riccomini, Francesco Giuliani, Vincenzo Bianciardi (who also wrote five ballet scores), Luigi Barbieri and Antonio Brandi. In fact, a remarkable aspect of the decade is the rise of these national composers and the considerable control they exercised over the theatres from their positions as *maestri al violino* or *cembalo*. However, the French invasions in 1799 and 1800 brought an abrupt end to the development. Those who remained in Florence – Neri Bondi, Moneta, Barbieri, Bianciardi and Giuliani – ceased composing operas while continuing as instrumentalists. Only Ferdinando Rutini, the most productive, survived a few years to compose six more comic operas until 1806, after which he abandoned Florence to take minor church positions near Rome. His attempt to return to the composition of comic operas in Rome in 1816 and 1817 appears to have been unsuccessful.

Under the Napoleonic ruler Elisa Baciocchi, opera in Florence stagnated, becoming once again dependent on foreign resources. Resuscitation would come only with the return of Grand Duke Ferdinando in 1814 after the defeat of Napoleon.

8. AFTER 1800. After the Congress of Vienna of 1815 and the restoration of the house of Lorraine to the grand duchy of Tuscany, the world of music beyond the Alps became increasingly influential with the cultural élite of Florence. The Pergola, which had been designated an 'imperial theatre' from 1810 to 1814 and was managed intermittently by Alessandro Lanari between 1823 and 1862, staged important premières such as those of

Donizetti's *Parisina* (1833), Verdi's *Macbeth* (1847), and Mascagni's *I Rantzau* (1892), and the first Italian performances of *Robert le diable* (1840), *Der Freischütz* (1843) and Meyerbeer's *Dinorah* (1867).

The S Maria was renamed Teatro Alfieri in 1828 after restoration work that included the construction of 96 boxes in five tiers. It was demolished in 1934. The Cocomero was twice restored during the 19th century and in 1859 was renamed after the Florentine poet G. B. Niccolini. Opera and drama ceased to be performed there in 1935. The Teatro Comunale (cap. 2500), originally uncovered, opened in 1852 as the Politeama Fiorentino Vittorio Emanuele II; it was covered over in 1882–3 and modernized after its acquisition by the Comune in 1930, receiving its present name in 1933.

However, the most important events in Florentine musical life before the city was chosen as the provisional capital of the kingdom of Italy (1865–70) concerned the appreciation of instrumental music rather than opera. An influential figure in this area was Abramo Basevi, to whom Wagner sent a letter of praise in 1856 and who wrote a *Studio sulle opere di Giuseppe Verdi* (1859), the first systematic work on the composer. Another member of Basevi's circle was the publisher Giovanni Gualberto Guidi (1817–83), who published a number of scores by Meyerbeer as well as the first modern edition of Peri's *Euridice* (1863). Opera was again staged at the Pergola and the bigger, modern Teatro Pagliano (now Teatro Verdi) in the last years of the century. The most important Florentine musical institution of the 20th century is the Maggio Musicale Fiorentino, the international festival instituted in 1933 by Guido M. Gatti, which takes place annually in May and June and which quickly gained international renown. Vittorio Gui had founded in 1928 one of the first permanent symphony orchestras in Italy, the Orchestrale Fiorentina, later the Orchestra del Maggio, which continues to invite the most celebrated names in the international musical world. Directors of the Maggio Musicale have included Mario Labroca, Francesco Siciliani, Massimo Bogianckino, Roman Vlad, Luciano Berio, Fedele D'Amico and Bruno Bartoletti. Of particular distinction was the directorship of the conductor Riccardo Muti from 1969 to 1981. Important productions have included the first Italian performance of Stravinsky's *Oedipus rex* (1937), the world première of Dallapiccola's *Volo di notte* (1940), Prokofiev's *War and Peace* (1953) and new works by Malipiero, Pizzetti and others. Recent premières include *Il sognatore* by Romano Pezzati (1982) and Bussotti's *L'ispirazione* (1988).

*

ES (F. Ghisi and M. Fabbri)

Indice de' spettacoli teatrali (Milan, 1764, 1767–8, 1770–1800, with slight variations in title)

F. Bartoli: *Notizie istoriche de' comici italiani che fiorirono intorno all'anno MDL. fino a' giorni presenti* (Padua, 1781–2)

P. Andolfati: *Rappresentazioni teatrali di Pietro Andolfati* (Florence, 1791)

A. Ademollo: *I primi fasti del teatro di via della Pergola in Firenze (1657–1661)* (Milan, c1883)

——: *Corilla Olimpica* (Florence, 1887)

A. D'Ancona: *Origini del teatro italiano* (Florence, 1887, 2/1891)

G. Baccini: *Notizie di alcune commedie sacre rappresentati in Firenze nel secolo XVII* (Florence, 1889)

E. Vogel: 'Marco de Gagliano: zur Geschichte des Florentiner Musiklebens von 1570–1650', *VMw*, v (1889), 396–442, 509–68

R. Gandolfi: 'Alcune considerazioni intorno alla riforma melodrammatica', *RMI*, iii (1896), 714–20

G. Pavan: *Saggio di cronistoria teatrale fiorentina: serie cronologica delle opere rappresentate al Teatro degli Immobili in via della Pergola nei secoli XVII e XVIII* (Milan, c1901)

A. Solerti: 'Emilio de' Cavalieri e Laura Guidiccioni Lucchesini', *RMI*, ix (1902), 797–829

——: *Le origini del melodramma* (Turin, 1903)

——: *Gli albori del melodramma* (Milan, 1904)

——: *Musica, ballo e drammatica alla corte medicea dal 1600 al 1637* (Florence, 1905)

R. Gandolfi: 'La cappella musicale della corte di Toscana 1539–1859', *RMI*, xvi (1909), 506–30

Jarro [pseud. of G. Piccini]: *Storia aneddotica dei teatri fiorentini*, i: *Il teatro della Pergola* (Florence, 1912)

O. Sonneck: '*Dafne*, the First Opera', *SIMG*, xv (1913–14), 102–10

U. Morini: *La R. Accademia degli Immobili ed il suo teatro 'La Pergola' (1645–1925)* (Pisa, 1926)

L. Cellesi: 'Documenti per la storia musicale di Firenze', *RMI*, xxxiv (1927), 577–602; xxxv (1928), 553–82

R. Lustig: 'Per la cronistoria dell'antico teatro musicale: il teatro della Villa Medicea di Pratolino', *RMI*, xxxvi (1929), 259–66

H. Martin: 'La "camerata" du Comte Bardi et la musique florentine du XVIe siècle', *RdM*, xi (1932), 61–74, 152–61, 227–34; xvii (1933), 91–100, 141–51

F. Fano: *La camerata fiorentina*, IMi, iv (1934)

F. Ghisi: *Alle fonti della monodia* (Milan, 1940)

——: 'Ballet Entertainments in the Pitti Palace, Florence, 1608–1625', *MQ*, xxxv (1949), 421–36

——: 'An Early Seventeenth Century Manuscript with Unpublished Italian Monodic Music by Peri, Giulio Romano, and Marco da Gagliano', *AcM*, xx (1949), 46–60

N. Fortune: 'Italian Secular Monody from 1600 to 1635', *MQ*, xxxix (1953), 171–95

N. Pirrotta: 'Tragédie et comédie dans la Camerata fiorentina', *Musique et poésie au XVIe siècle: CNRS Paris 1953*, 287–98

——: 'Temperaments and Tendencies in the Florentine Camerata', *MQ*, xl (1954), 169–89; repr. in N. Pirrotta: *Music and Culture in Italy from the Middle Ages to the Baroque* (Cambridge, 1984), 217–34

R. L. Weaver: *Florentine Comic Operas of the Seventeenth Century* (diss., U. of North Carolina, Chapel Hill, 1958)

M. Fabbri: *Alessandro Scarlatti e il principe Ferdinando de' Medici* (Florence, 1961)

——: 'La giovinezza di Luigi Cherubini nella vita musicale fiorentina del suo tempo', *Luigi Cherubini nel II centenario della nascita* (Florence, 1962), 1–46

——: 'Il terzo maestro di Luigi Cherubini: Alessandro Felici', *Musiche italiane rare e vive da Giovanni Gabrieli a Giuseppe Verdi*, Chigiana, xix (1962), 183–94

C. V. Palisca: 'Musical Asides in the Diplomatic Correspondence of Emilio de' Cavalieri', *MQ*, xlix (1963), 339–55

M. Fabbri: 'Nuova luce sull'attività fiorentina di Giacomo Antonio Perti, Bartolomeo Cristofori e Giorgio F. Haendel: valore storico e critico di una "Memoria" di Francesco M. Mannucci', *Chigiana: rassegna annuale di studi musicologici*, xxi (Florence, 1964), 143–90

A. M. Nagler: *Theatre Festivals of the Medici 1539–1637* (New Haven, CT, 1964)

C. V. Palisca: 'The First Performance of "Euridice"', *Queens College Twenty-fifth Anniversary Festschrift (1937–1962)* (Flushing, NY, 1964), 1–24

W. C. Porter: 'Peri and Corsi's *Dafne*: Some New Discoveries and Observations', *JAMS*, xviii (1965), 170–96

F. Ghisi: 'Le musiche per "Il ballo di donne turchi" di Marco Gagliano', *RIM*, i (1966), 20–31

L. Pinzauti: *Il Maggio Musicale Fiorentino* (Florence, 1967)

C. Molinari: *Le nozze degli dei: un saggio sul grande spettacolo italiano nel seicento* (Rome, 1968)

W. C. Holmes: 'Giacinto Andrea Cicognini's and Antonio Cesti's *Orontea* (1649)', *New Looks at Italian Opera: Essays in Honor of Donald J. Grout* (Ithaca, NY, 1968), 108–32

C. V. Palisca: 'The Alterati of Florence, Pioneers in the Theory of Dramatic Music', *ibid*, 9–38

N. Pirrotta: 'Early Opera and Aria', *ibid*, 39–107

R. L. Weaver: 'Opera in Florence: 1646–1731', *Studies in Musicology: Essays in Memory of Glen Haydon* (Chapel Hill, NC, 1969), 60–71

——: '*Il Girello*, a Seventeenth-Century Burlesque Opera', *Memorie e contributi alla musica dal medioevo all'età moderna, offerti a F. Ghisi* (Bologna, 1971), 141–49

C. V. Palisca: 'The "Camerata Fiorentina": a Reappraisal', *Studi musicali*, i (1972), 203–326

F. Hammond: 'Musicians at the Medici Court in the Mid-seventeenth Century', *AnMc*, no.14 (1974), 151–69

L. Bianconi and T. Walker: 'Dalla *Finta pazza* alla *Veremonda*: storie di Febiarmonici', *RIM*, x (1975), 379–454

M. Fabbri and others, eds.: *Spettacolo e musica nella Firenze medicea: documenti e restituzioni*, i: *Il luogo teatrale a Firenze* (Milan, 1975)

J. W. Hill: 'Le relazioni di Antonio Cesti con la corte e i teatri di Firenze', *RIM*, xi (1976), 27–47

E. Strainchamps: 'New Light on the Accademia degli Elevati of Florence', *MQ*, lxii (1976), 507–35

G. Barblan and A. Basso, eds.: *Storia dell'opera* (Turin, 1977)

M. de Angelis: *La musica del Granduca* (Florence, 1978)

P. Roselli, G. C. Romby and O. F. Micali: *I teatri di Firenze* (Florence, 1978)

R. L. Weaver and N. W. Weaver: *A Chronology of Music in the Florentine Theater, 1590–1750: Operas, Prologues, Finales, Intermezzos and Plays with Incidental Music* (Detroit, 1978)

R. Zanetti: *La musica italiana nel settecento* (Milan, 1978)

G. Corti: 'Il tenor la Pergola di Firenze e la stagione d'opera per il carnevale 1726–1727: lettere di Luca Casimiro degli Albizzi a Vivaldi, Porpora ed altri', *RIM*, xv (1980), 182–8

P. Radicchi: *Giovanni Lorenzo Cattani, musicista carrarese al servizio dei Medici* (Pisa, 1980)

M. I. Aliverti: 'Breve storia di un progetto leopoldino (1779–1788)', *Quaderni di teatro*, iii (1981), 21–33

S. Mamone: *Il teatro nella Firenze medicea* (Milan, *c*1981)

M. de Angelis: *Le carte dell'impresario* (Florence, 1982)

W. C. Holmes: 'An Impresario al Teatro la Pergola in Florence: Letters of 1735–36', *Music and Civilization: Essays in Honor of Paul Henry Lang* (New York, 1984), 127–40

M. P. McClymonds: 'Mozart's "La Clemenza di Tito" and Opera Seria in Florence as a Reflection of Leopold II's Musical Taste', *MJb 1984–5*, 61–70

R. L. Weaver: 'Metastasio a Firenze', *Metastasio e il mondo musicale: Venice 1985*, 199–206

L. Bianconi and G. Pestelli, eds.: *SOI* (1987–)

Inaugural Conference for the Ricasoli Collection: Patrons, Politics, Music, and Art in Italy 1738–1859: Louisville 1989 [incl. J. Rice: 'Grand Duke Pietro Leopoldo as Patron of Florentine Music, 1765–1790'; W. C. Holmes: 'Commotion and Confusion at the Pergola with the Advent of the Austrians'; F. Giuntini: 'Giuseppe Maria Orlandini and the *commedia per musica* in Florence at the beginning of the Lorraine Domination'; M. De Angelis: 'After the Medici: Francesco III di Lorena'; G. C. Romby: 'Eighteenth-century Florentine Family Theaters and the Ricasoli Theater at Meleto'; S. Durante: 'A Matter of Taste: Dramatic Pace and Musical Forms in the Reductions of Metastasian Dramas for Florence, ca. 1785']

C. V. Palisca: *The Florentine Camerata: Documentary Studies and Translations* (New Haven, CT, 1989)

M. de Angelis: *La felicità in Etruria* (Florence, 1990)

——: *Melodramma spettacolo e musica nella Firenze dei Lorena (1750–1800)* (Florence, 1991)

R. L. Weaver and N. W. Weaver: *A Chronology of Music in the Florentine Theater, 1751–1800* (Warren, MI, 1993)

ROBERT LAMAR WEAVER (1–7), LEONARDO PINZAUTI (8)

Florentine Opera. American company, founded in 1933 in MILWAUKEE.

Florentinische Tragödie, Eine ('A Florentine Tragedy'). Opera in one act, op.16, by ALEXANDER ZEMLINSKY to his own libretto after OSCAR WILDE's *A Florentine Tragedy*; Stuttgart, Hoftheater, 30 January 1917.

Oscar Wilde's *A Florentine Tragedy* no doubt attracted Zemlinsky for a number of reasons. First, there was the example of *Salome*, which he had first conducted on 23 December 1910. This may have suggested the one-act form and the idea of dispensing with the kind of post-Wagnerian libretto that had marred *Der Traumgörge*. The opera certainly owes something to the claustrophobic chiaroscuro of *Elektra* and *Salome*, though its more immediate models may have been Schreker's *Die Gezeichneten*, Korngold's *Violanta* and Schillings's *Mona Lisa*, one of the principal motifs of which is a precursor of Zemlinsky's 'death' motif. *Eine florentinische Tragödie* also has a personal dimension, for the plot mirrors the tragic events surrounding Mathilde Schoenberg's love affair with the painter Richard Gerstl, who committed suicide in 1908 after she had been persuaded to return to her husband. Zemlinsky composed most of the work in the Bohemian spa of Königswart in the summer of 1915, completing the orchestration in June 1916. The first performance was conducted by Max von Schillings, the parts being created by Rudolf Ritter (Guido), Felix Fleischer (Simone) and Helene Wildbrunn (Bianca).

Zemlinsky made up for the lack of a love scene at the beginning by composing an extended overture. The curtain rises to reveal Guido, the Prince of Florence (tenor), and Bianca (soprano). They start back as her husband Simone (baritone), a merchant, enters. Simone's character is delineated in the opening bars, where he is assigned the first of a series of arioso passages that cumulatively establish his predominance. The motifs assigned to Guido adequately render his youth and erotic energy. There is a certain affinity between the 'love' motif that appears as he praises Bianca's beauty, and the 'ring of marriage' motif in Schoenberg's *Pelleas und Melisande*.

Simone tries to quell his growing suspicions by pretending that Guido has come as a customer, and in two opulent passages shows him his wares: a piece of Lucca damask and a Venetian robe of state. Simone's ariosos set him in clear contrast to Guido and Bianca, whose comments are restricted to parlando. As the dialogue continues, Simone insinuates that Guido has cuckolded men before. After concluding the sale of the robe of state, he offers to place everything in his house at Guido's disposal, and is taken aback when Guido asks for Bianca. Pretending that she is only fit for housework, he asks her to start spinning. His arioso, based on a 'creaking' ostinato bass, is in effect a lugubrious slow waltz. Significantly, Bianca's reluctant answer immediately reverts to parlando. Visibly shaken, Simone launches into two variants of the 'spinning' ostinato, a diatribe against English merchants, and a discussion of Italian politics. Guido's obvious lack of interest in such matters forces Simone once more to reconsider the situation. After he has left the room, Bianca expresses her hatred of him, and wishes him dead. Simone hears this as he returns, and, in an arioso that begins with the 'death' motif, suggests a connection between death and adultery. This, as Schoenberg and Webern noted when they first studied the opera, is one of its principal climaxes, its effect enhanced by the fact that Bianca has just accused her husband of uttering 'a foolish froth of empty words'.

Simone's mood now changes to manic liveliness. This is characterized by an angular horn theme, elements of which bind the ensuing passage into a kind of rondo. After attempting to persuade Guido to play the lute, and then to drink some wine, the jealousy tormenting him proves too much, and again he leaves the stage. Guido and Bianca are now given the only real love scene in the opera. Its effect depends in part on the sweet, almost cloying orchestral textures, on whole-tone configurations and on Bianca's arioso, which Franz Werfel considered to be the most memorable moment of the opera.

As Guido is about to take his leave, Simone hands him his sword. It reminds him of his own weapon, with which he once killed a robber. The insistent repetition of 'sword' and 'death' motifs leads to a majestic B♭ – E♭

ostinato: Simone grimly declares that those who steal from him do so at their peril. The duel begins. As Simone tells Bianca to extinguish the torch there is a fortissimo restatement of the 'death' motif over a D minor-cum-G♯ major chord that refers back to the 'fate' motif in *Pelleas und Melisande*. This signals that Guido is doomed. The duel becomes furious, the excitement being generated by chromatically rising pedals, insistent ostinatos and highly dissonant harmony. Simone finally overpowers his adversary and as he strangles him, sings an expanded version of the 'death' motif. During the duel Bianca has retreated to the door, which she opens to admit the moonlight. She moves towards Simone 'as one dazed with wonder'. They embrace and are reconciled, Bianca at last aware of his strength and he of her beauty.

Eine florentinische Tragödie uses a kind of symphonic structure (the duel, for example, is like a rousing finale), leitmotifs, and what has aptly been called 'musical onomatopoiea' (e.g. the textures that depict the robe of state). Schoenberg was struck by its continuity and powerful climaxes. However, the public and the critics disliked the implausible connubial embrace over Guido's dead body. Yet as Zemlinsky stated in a letter to Alma Mahler, that a life had to be sacrificed to save two other lives was the essential point of this more Viennese than Florentine tragedy.   ALFRED CLAYTON

Floridante. Opera in three acts by GEORGE FRIDERIC HANDEL to a libretto by PAOLO ANTONIO ROLLI based on FRANCESCO SILVANI's *La costanza in trionfo* (1696, Venice, as revised for Livorno, 1706); London, King's Theatre, 9 December 1721.

Floridante was the first new opera of the Royal Academy of Music's third London season. The roles of Floridante and Timante were sung by the castratos Senesino and Berselli, Elmira by the contralto Anastasia Robinson and Rossane by Maddalena Salvai. (Handel first intended Elmira to be sung by the soprano Margherita Durastanti and Rossane by Robinson; he composed Act 1 and most of Act 2 before inverting the voice ranges of these roles.)

Handel first revived the opera on 4 December 1722, when Durastanti took over Rossane and the alto castrato Gaetano Berenstadt Timante. The score was extensively revised, all three arias from the cantata *Crudele tiranno amor* (with altered words) being added to Rossane's part. Handel arranged two further revivals, in 1727 and 1733, and there was a production in Hamburg in 1723. The first of the few modern revivals was directed by Frances and Alan Kitching at the Unicorn Theatre, Abingdon, on 10 May 1962. Chrysander's edition unhelpfully confuses the various versions of the opera, though the first performing version – probably the best – can be reconstructed with fair accuracy.

The libretto seems to be wholly fictional. Silvani gave it a Norwegian setting, but Rolli transfers the action to the Middle East. Oronte (bass) has obtained the throne of Persia by murdering its former king Nino. He supposedly has two daughters, Rossane (soprano) and Elmira (alto); but the latter is the only surviving descendant of Nino, adopted by Oronte as an infant when his own second daughter died. Floridante, Prince of Thrace (alto), gains a naval victory over Tyre, thereby expecting Elmira's hand in fulfillment of a promise by Oronte. Among his prisoners is the Tyrian prince Timante (soprano), disguised under the name of Glicone; he was once betrothed to Rossane, though they have never met. Floridante's return is welcomed by Elmira and Rossane, but he unexpectedly receives orders from Oronte to resign his command to the satrap Coralbo (bass) and leave the country. He obtains an audience with Oronte and seeks an explanation, but gets none and parts sorrowfully from Elmira. Timante reveals his identity to Rossane and is joined by Floridante disguised as a Moorish slave; the two couples plan to escape, but Elmira is summoned by Oronte, who to her horror reveals her true ancestry and declares his love for her. She rejects him as a murderous usurper. The escape is foiled by Oronte and Floridante, still disguised, is captured and threatened with death. Elmira tells Coralbo that she is the last of the race of Nino and gains his sympathy. Oronte orders Floridante to persuade Elmira to accept him; otherwise both she and Floridante will die. Rossane asks Timante to help Floridante escape. Floridante attempts to plead Oronte's cause with Elmira, but she prefers to die. On Oronte's orders she brings a cup of poison to Floridante in prison; she attempts to drink it herself but is stopped by Oronte. Coralbo and Timante intervene, arresting Oronte and proclaiming Elmira as Queen of Persia, under her true name of Elisa. She assumes the throne with Floridante and pardons Oronte at Rossane's pleading. Timante and Rossane are to marry and reign in Tyre.

*   *   *

Faced by the success of Bononcini's operas of the previous season, Handel moved away to some extent from the grand style of *Radamisto* in favour of the older composer's easier, graceful manner. The best numbers are nevertheless those possessing full Handelian expansiveness and harmonic richness, found at the most intense moments of the drama. The final duet of Act 1, 'Ah mia cara', is especially poignant, the Act 2 duet 'Fuor di periglio' haunting and the nocturnal scena for Elmira ('Notte cara') gripping. Floridante has some fine slow arias; the lighter numbers are mainly shared between Rossane and Timante. ANTHONY HICKS

Florimel, or Love's Revenge. Dramatic pastoral in two acts (or 'Interludes', according to most of the contemporary sources) by MAURICE GREENE to a libretto by John Hoadly; Farnham Castle (the episcopal seat of Hoadly's father, then Bishop of Winchester), 1734.

Florimel was the first of five large-scale works (two operas, two oratorios and a masque) on which Greene and Hoadly collaborated. The work was also performed at Winchester in 1737, and in both London and Gloucester (at the Three Choirs Festival) in 1745; later performances took place in 1757, 1768 and 1781, but none was staged. It seems that David Garrick contemplated presenting the piece at Drury Lane (in 1776), but nothing came of the idea. It was first revived at St John's, Smith Square, London, on 8 November 1973.

Both musically and dramatically, *Florimel* is in the tradition of Handel's *Acis and Galatea* (1718). The setting is Arcadia and the subject matter the vicissitudes of rural courtship. There are four characters: Myrtillo (soprano) and Florimel (soprano), shepherd and shepherdess respectively, whose amorous bliss is threatened not only by the mischievous intervention of Cupid (soprano) but also by the activities of a lascivious Satyr (bass). The latter, though he does not appear until the beginning of Act 2, adds both a welcome touch of comic relief and some variety in the vocal scoring which, up to that point, has been entirely treble based. Five

printed librettos and six manuscript scores survive, more than for any other English opera of the period, and these are equally divided between the original version and a later one in which the part of Myrtillo is recast as a countertenor. H. DIACK JOHNSTONE

Florimo, Francesco (*b* S Giorgio Morgeto, Calabria, 12 Oct 1800; *d* Naples, 18 Dec 1888). Italian librarian, musicologist and teacher. A fellow student of Bellini at the Naples Conservatory, he became archivist-librarian there in 1826, also serving as director of vocal concerts and singing teacher. His widely praised *Metodo di canto* (Naples, ?1840; Milan, 1841–3, enlarged 3/?1861) was conservative in tendency, claimed as based on the precepts of the castrato Crescentini, then director of the conservatory's singing school, and intended to restore the 'antico bello' of 'the only true tradition of Italian song', that of Scarlatti, Porpora and Durante, which had been displaced by 'la moda barocca' of the present age. Florimo composed in all genres except the dramatic, but apart from a *Sinfonia funebre in morte di Bellini* (I-Nc*; arr. pf, 4 hands, Milan, 1836), only his songs are of interest.

In his old age Florimo turned to historical writing. His *Cenno storico sulla scuola musicale di Napoli* (Naples, 1869–71) and the supplementary *Cenni storici sul Collegio di musica S. Pietro a Majella in Napoli* (Naples, 1873) were enlarged as *La scuola musicale di Napoli e i suoi conservatorii* (Naples, 1880–83). Florimo's failings as a historian are great, but his collection of unsorted fact, legend and error remains unreplaced and indispensable. Most of his other writings are on Bellini, his close friend. His *Translazione delle ceneri di Vincenzo Bellini* (Naples, 1877; Florimo arranged for the ashes to be moved from Paris to Catania) was reprinted with a biography, anecdotes and letters in *Bellini: memorie e lettere* (Florence, 1882). On the occasion of the first Bayreuth Festival he wrote a short, highly antagonistic pamphlet, *Wagner ed i wagneristi* (Naples, 1876), but after Wagner visited Naples in 1880 and astutely declared to Florimo his predilection for Bellini, Florimo published a longer second version (Ancona, 1883) in which he praised Wagner and criticized only his fanatical followers, advising young Italian composers 'to take from Wagnerism all that agrees with their character, and to keep themselves Italian'.

Florimo was on friendly terms with many figures of his time, including Rossini, Donizetti and Verdi. His view was that Rossini had been the revolutionary who had put an end to the old Neapolitan school, but that his style had been replaced by Bellini's and the Bellinian reform carried on by Donizetti and completed by Verdi in *Don Carlos* and *Aida*. His relations with Mercadante were at times strained during the latter's directorship of the conservatory (1840–70); the praise of Mercadante in the *Cenno storico* was much toned down in the second edition, published after Mercadante's death, and in some cases simply reversed by the addition of 'not'. In 1870–71 Florimo unsuccessfully tried to persuade Verdi to become director and even in extreme old age he continued to live in his beloved conservatory. DENNIS LIBBY

Florinda, La. *See* ANDREINI, VIRGINIA.

Flotow, Friedrich (Adolf Ferdinand), Freiherr von (*b* Toitendorf [Teutendorf] estate, nr Neu-Sanitz,

Mecklenburg-Schwerin, 27 April 1812; d Darmstadt, 24 Jan 1883). German composer. He is best remembered for his romantic comic opera *Martha*, which continues to be staged; the aria 'Ach so fromm' (and in its Italian version as 'M'appari tutt' amor') has become a staple of the tenor aria repertory.

1. LIFE. Flotow was born into one of the oldest aristocratic families of Mecklenburg. Both parents were musical, and he began composing as a child, receiving his first musical instruction from his mother and from Thiem, the local organist. He resisted his parents' wish that he enter the diplomatic service, and in 1828 was taken by his father to Paris, where his musical education was entrusted to Reicha and the Mannheimer Johann Peter Pixis. By the following year he had already been offered the libretto of *Pierre et Cathérine* by Jules-Henri Vernoy De Saint-Georges, who during the ensuing four decades was to provide Flotow with eight further librettos (including that for a ballet, *Lady Harriette, ou La servante de Greenwich*, in 1844, which was to become the basis of *Martha*). The 1830 Revolution caused the composer to return to Mecklenburg, where he completed *Pierre et Cathérine* and had it translated into German by his uncle; as *Peter und Kathinka* it was performed in Ludwigslust, Mecklenburg, in 1835. By 1831 Flotow had already returned to Paris, where he continued composing. During this period he also made the acquaintance of prominent artistic and aristocratic figures there, which helped him towards having Parisian performances of his works, and it was at the *hôtel* of Count Castellane, where aristocratic families ran their own private amateur theatre, that works such as *Rob-Roy* and *Alice* were performed in 1836–7. His first professional performances were of pastiche works to which he contributed, a situation that arose often owing to the tight schedules of theatres whereby portions of a work were given to various composers to write in time for the opening night. The play *Le comte de Charolais* (1836) was such a work, and Flotow gladly accepted the opportunity to write several numbers for it, including a waltz and a hunting chorus. The work was performed at the Théâtre du Palais Royal and served to draw Flotow's abilities to the attention of a wider public.

The first important theatre to mount his works was the Théâtre de la Renaissance with two pastiches: in 1838 *Lady Melvil* (where Flotow's name was not even mentioned; the other composer, Albert Grisar, took all the credit), and in 1839 *L'eau merveilleuse*, for which Flotow wrote much of the music. His first real box office success, however, was *Le naufrage de la Méduse* (later enlarged as *Die Matrosen*), to which he contributed the last two acts, also performed at the Théâtre de la Renaissance (54 times in 1839 alone). In 1840 *La duchesse de Guise* (originally *Le comte de St-Mégrin*) was given an amateur charity performance as *Le duc de Guise* for Polish refugees at the Théâtre Ventadour, and it was there that Flotow met Friedrich Wilhelm Riese, a poet and translator for the Thalia theatre in Hamburg, who was in Paris looking for new vaudeville comedies to translate into German for performances at home. It was Riese, under the pseudonym W. Friedrich, who was to create the librettos for the only two operas which were to bring Flotow lasting fame, *Alessandro Stradella* (1844) and, particularly, *Martha, oder Der Markt zu Richmond* (1847). Flotow's greatest ambition, however, was to make his name as an opera composer in Paris, and his first performance at a major opera house there

(by the Opéra-Comique at the Salle Favart) was in 1843 with the one-act *L'esclave de Camoëns* (later enlarged as *Indra*). He was finally accepted by the Opéra in 1844 with a contribution to the pastiche ballet *Lady Harriette*, the seed of *Martha*. In the meantime *Alessandro Stradella* had been performed in Hamburg in 1844 and within a year was such a success there, and in Berlin, Vienna, Budapest and Prague, that Flotow received a commission to write a new German opera for the Hoftheater in Vienna. He offered Friedrich the *Lady Harriette* plot, and *Martha* was the result. *Martha* was first performed at the Kärntnertortheater in 1847, with immediate success. By 1858 it had already been played across Europe and as far afield as Algiers, San Francisco and Sydney.

In the mid-1840s, still living in Paris, Flotow continued to write French operas, many of which were translated and performed in Germany. The Revolution in Paris caused him to leave France again in 1848, and he returned to Mecklenburg where he had inherited the family estates from his father, who had died the previous year. There he married and had a son; his wife and child died in 1851. In 1850 *Sophie Katharina, oder Die Grossfürstin* was performed in Berlin and he received the Mecklenburg-Schwerin Goldene Verdienstmedaille für Kunst und Wissenschaft in recognition of his achievements. His next moderate success was his second version of *L'esclave de Camoëns*, *Indra*, which had its première in Vienna (1852). As a result of his growing reputation in Vienna, he now moved there, where in 1853 he married his second wife, who bore him three children, only two of whom were to survive into adulthood. In 1855 Flotow was appointed director of the grand-ducal court at Schwerin in Mecklenburg, where he remained until 1862. There he was in charge of the incidental music for the court celebrations, directed performances of opera and ballet at the Hofoper and continued to compose operas for Vienna and Berlin. He achieved modest successes in 1859 with *La veuve Grapin* and incidental music to Shakespeare's *The Winter's Tale*.

In the 1860s Flotow's opera premières were being staged as a matter of course right across Europe. He married for the third time in 1868, having divorced his second wife, and went to live on his new wife's estate in Reichenau in Austria, where he continued to compose. His last success was *L'ombre*, which was performed in Paris in 1870 by the Opéra-Comique. The Franco-Prussian war of 1870 caused a wave of anti-German sentiment in Paris which had a negative effect on Flotow's fortunes there. His *La fleur de Harlem* (completed in 1874), which he may have begun as early as 1866 and which had been accepted by the Opéra-Comique, could now no longer be performed there and had its première in Turin in 1876 as *Il fiore d'Arlem*. In 1873 Flotow finally left Paris and returned to the family estate in Toitendorf, where he resumed work on his most problematic opera; what had started as a French work, the one-act *L'esclave de Camoëns*, in 1843, and been extended to three acts in 1852 as *Indra* with a German text, he now revised and further enlarged to four acts for an Italian première as *Alma l'incantatrice*. Animosities in France having subsided, however, Flotow was able to obtain a performance of the new work in Paris in a French version, as *L'enchanteresse*. In addition, *Indra* was also known at various times as *Zora*, *Die Hexe* and possibly *Griselda*, making a total of seven different names and three different languages used by the composer for this work alone. In 1880 Flotow moved to Darmstadt, where he spent his last years almost blind. He died, as the result of a stroke, at the age of 70.

2. WORKS. The German composers of opera active in the years between Mozart and Wagner (Gluck, J. C. Bach, Haydn, Meyerbeer, Weber) were setting mostly Italian, French or occasionally English librettos; the development of opera in German was slow during this period. Between Weber's death (1826) and Wagner's *Rienzi* its history lay primarily in the hands of Kreutzer, Spohr, Marschner, Lortzing, Nicolai and Flotow. Flotow's musical style is a synthesis of German and French influences. On the German side he may be grouped with Lortzing and Nicolai, with whom he shared a north German musical heritage. These three cheerful, if modest, talents were in turn all influenced by their francophile compatriot Meyerbeer, much of whose cantilena, esprit and orchestration shed its light on their works. But while Meyerbeer is best known for his serious works, these three are remembered today for their comic operas. This Berlin school of composers possessed a profound sense of the stage that German contemporaries such as Schubert, Mendelssohn or Schumann lacked. Flotow's French models can be sought in composers like Boieldieu, Auber and Adam: indeed the comic bandits Malvolino and Barbarino in *Alessandro Stradella* find their musical ancestors in Auber's Giacomo and Beppo (*Fra Diavolo*). Whereas Nicolai combined German Singspiel with *opera buffa*, Flotow was to merge the Singspiel with *opéra comique* to create a kind of French Biedermeier opera, a fusion of styles which had its dramaturgical justification and precedent. Just as Mozart, in *Don Giovanni*, had fused elements of *opera buffa* and *opera seria*, and Beethoven, in *Fidelio*, had combined the Singspiel with an emerging Romantic music drama, so Flotow, in *Martha*, reserved the Singspiel style for his buffoonish and peasant characters (Nancy, Plumkett and the maids of Richmond) and the sustained, bel canto French Romanticism of *opéra comique* for the lovers Martha and Lyonel.

For that reason, Flotow's own description of his works as 'romantic' (*Alessandro Stradella*) or 'romantic comic' (*Martha*) has met with some objection: the former fits rather the description of an *opéra comique*. Meyerbeer referred to *Martha* in his diary as a 'komische Oper (eigentlich semiseria)'. What distinguishes such works as *Alessandro Stradella*, *Martha* or *Indra* (originally *L'esclave de Camoëns*) from *opéras comiques* is that (by contrast, for example, with Lortzing) Flotow omits spoken dialogue and links the numbers with short recitatives, achieving an uninterrupted musical flow. It is perhaps rather the manner of performance of these works that determines which of Singspiel or *opéra comique* is to predominate. In Flotow's two most successful works, *Alessandro Stradella* and *Martha*, a balanced fusion of all stylistic elements is achieved. The former is perhaps the better work, but it was *Martha* that found its way into the hearts of the public. The reason for this lies not only in the quality of the text and the music, but also in the dramatic situations which keep the audience in a state of amused suspense.

Flotow's musical style can be described as consisting of simple harmonies, pithy and gracious rhythms, and short musical forms, among which he often uses dance movements (tarantella, gavotte, mazurka or polka) as the basis for his arias. His melodies are catchy, often italianate, and he is musically most successful when he confines himself to the strophic song with facile melodies. The inclusion of simple folksongs as local colour further adds to the attractiveness of his works, for example the Irish folksong 'The Last Rose of Summer' in *Martha* (which is used to great effect as a leitmotif), or the Hohenfriedberger March and Russian folksong in *Sophie Katharina*. Within the framework of a completely homophonic style, contrapuntal or even motivic writing is only occasionally found and is a little incongruous, such as the moment in the overture to *Martha* where he combines a cheeky motif (symbolizing Martha's flirtations) with Lyonel's heartfelt 'Mag der Himmel Euch vergeben'. In *Die Matrosen* (originally *Le naufrage de la Méduse*) there is a canon to the amusing alliterative text 'O Du, der Du, die, die Dir dienen'. Flotow's instrumentation is well considered and effective, playing host to the melody and thematic material in parlando sections; in the last works an increasing refinement of orchestral technique can be observed. It is perhaps not surprising that his basically lyrical style is least convincing when a plot such as *Indra*'s calls for an exotic Iberian-Indian treatment, a musical exoticism familiar from *L'Africaine*, *Carmen* or *Samson et Dalila*. Here Flotow's French Biedermeier *Spieloper* shows its limitations. At their best, his works are a fascinating Franco-German link in the chain from 18th-century Italian *opera buffa* to Arthur Sullivan in England.

Flotow's librettos are based on works by authors as varied as Kalidasa, Shakespeare, Massinger, Racine, Goldoni, Scott, Dumas and Soulié. A certain emphasis on historical figures is evident: the statesmen Henri III of France (*Le comte de St-Mégrin*) and Peter the Great (*Pierre et Cathérine*); the religious reformer Johann Albrecht of Mecklenburg, the poet Camões (*L'esclave de Camoëns*), and the composers Stradella and Mozart (*Die Musikanten*). Among the mythical subjects are Thetis, Medusa and Rübezahl. Using the pseudonym Marckwort, Flotow himself made excellent translations of some of his French works into German. His most prominent librettists were Salomon Hermann Mosenthal (who wrote the text for Nicolai's *Die lustigen Weiber von Windsor*), Léon Halévy (brother of the composer) and Charlotte Birch-Pfeiffer (who helped Fétis prepare the final version of Scribe's libretto for *L'Africaine*).

A comprehensive survey of Flotow's works today presents almost insurmountable difficulties. At least 14 of them are lost, parts of which were no doubt re-used later. At least eight works are known to have been re-arranged by Flotow. An exact correlation of lost and re-used material is therefore no longer possible. Many of his works also received new titles with each arrangement or even performance, to say nothing of the translations. At least six were written in collaboration with other composers, sometimes, especially the earlier ones, without even mention of Flotow's name. A realistic estimate of the number of Flotow's operas is about 30. Ironically, although he dedicated his life to French opera, and composed mainly French and what might be called Franco-German works, his adopted country never fully returned the compliment. It is perhaps no coincidence that his only lasting successes were two works which, as French as they are in spirit and style (Gustav Kobbé originally classified *Martha* as a French opera), were thoroughly German in their composer, their librettists, their texts and their premières. It may be added that it took *Martha* 11 years to reach Paris and *Alessandro Stradella* 19 years; both were first performed there in Italian. Conversely, the one theatre where almost all his works were performed as a matter of course was the court opera house of Schwerin in Mecklenburg, the land of his birth.

A truer reflection of how disseminated Flotow's operas were can be gained if the performances of his works in such a city as Hamburg are considered. There *Martha* alone had enjoyed 440 performances by 1955 and *Alessandro Stradella* 218 by 1932. Nine other works performed at some time or other in Hamburg never exceeded 16 performances (*Die Matrosen*), and these nine played an average of five performances each. Nonetheless, *Martha* and *Alessandro Stradella* have earned Flotow 15th place among Hamburg's most-played opera composers, just after Beethoven and

Offenbach. During the 19th century Flotow's fame was such that many parodies and potpourris of his works appeared, for example Nestroy's *Martha, oder Die Mischmonder Markt-Mägde-Mietung* in three acts to music by Michael Hebenstreit (1848), Offenbach's one-act *La romance de la rose* (1869) and Johann Strauss's *Quadrilles*, op.46 on themes from *Martha*, and op.122 on themes from *Indra*. Perhaps of interest is that almost every decade of the 20th century has borne witness to the revival of one or another unknown work by Flotow: *Indra* and *Wintermärchen* were still being played until well into the century; in 1922 and 1943 *La veuve Grapin* was revived; in 1925 and 1933 *Zilda* was played, under the title *Fatme*; and in 1934 *L'ombre* and *Rübezahl* were staged. Blacher's opera *Das Zauberbuch von Erzerun* (1942) is based on music by Flotow.

See also ALESSANDRO STRADELLA and MARTHA.

title	genre, acts	libretto	first performance	sources and remarks
Pierre et Cathérine	2	J.-H. Vernoy de Saint-Georges	unperf.	as Peter und Kathinka, Ludwigslust, 1835
Die Bergknappen	2	T. Körner		
Alfred der Grosse	2	Körner		
Rob-Roy [Rob le barbe]	oc, 1	P. Duport and P. J. Desforges, after W. Scott	Royaumont Castle, Sept 1836; Paris, Hôtel Castellane, May 1837	
Sérafine	oc, 2	Desforges, after F. Soulier	Royaumont, 30 Oct 1836	
Alice	oc, 2	H. de Sussy and D. de Laperrière	Paris, Hôtel Castellane, 8 April 1837	
Stradella	pièce lyrique, 1	Duport and P. A. de Forges	Paris, Palais Royal, 1837	
La lettre du préfet	oc, 1	E. Bergounioux	Paris, Salon Gressier, 1837	rev. 1868
Le comte de Saint-Mégrin [La duchesse de Guise]	opéra, 3	F. and C. de la Bouillerie, after A. Dumas *père*: *Henri III et sa cour*	Royaumont, 10 June 1838	rev. version, as Le duc de Guise, Paris, Ventadour, 3 April 1840; as Der Graf von St Mégrin, Schwerin, 24 Feb 1841
Lady Melvil	oc, 3	Saint-Georges and A. de Leuven	Paris, Renaissance, 15 Nov 1838	collab. A. Grisar; rev. Grisar as Le joailler de Saint-James, 1862
L'eau merveilleuse	opéra bouffe, 2	T. M. F. Sauvage	Paris, Renaissance, 30 Jan 1839	collab. Grisar; as Das Wunderwasser, vs (Mainz, n.d.)
Le naufrage de la Méduse	opéra, 3	H. and T. Cogniard	Paris, Renaissance, 31 May 1839	Act 1 by A. Pilati; excerpts (Paris, n.d.); rev., expanded as Die Matrosen (W. Friedrich [F. W. Riese]), Hamburg, 23 Dec 1845, vs (Hamburg, 1845)
L'esclave de Camoëns	oc, 1	Saint-Georges	Paris, OC (Favart), 1 Dec 1843	rev., enlarged as Indra, das Schlangenmädchen (3), Vienna, 18 Dec 1852; as Alma l'incantatrice (4), Paris, Italien, 6 April 1878 [also known as L'enchanteresse, Die Hexe, Zora ? and Griselda]
Alessandro Stradella	romantische Oper, 3	Friedrich	Hamburg, Stadt, 30 Dec 1844	numerous scores pubd
L'âme en peine [Der Förster; Leoline]	opéra, 2	Saint-Georges	Paris, Opéra, 29 June 1846	vs (Paris, n.d.), Ger. vs (Hamburg, ?1847); ? as L'âme jalouse, 1838
Martha, oder Der Markt zu Richmond	romantisch-komische Oper, 4	Friedrich	Vienna, Kärntnertor, 25 Nov 1847	*US-STu**; vs (Vienna, ?1847), full score (Leipzig, 1940)
Sophie Katharina, oder Die Grossfürstin	romantisch-komische Oper, 4	C. Birch-Pfeiffer	Berlin, Hof, 19 Nov 1850	vs (Berlin, 1850)
Rübezahl	romantische Oper, 3	G. H. Gans zu Putlitz	Retzien, 13 Aug 1852 [privately]; Frankfurt, 26 Nov 1853	(Berlin, 1853)
Albin, oder Der Pflegesohn	3	S. H. Mosenthal, after *Les deux savoyards*	Vienna, Kärntnertor, 12 Feb 1856	rev. version, Der Müller von Meran, Gotha, 15 Jan 1860

title	genre, acts	libretto	first performance	sources and remarks
Herzog Johann Albrecht von Mecklenburg, oder Andreas Mylius	3	E. Hobein	Schwerin, 27 May 1857	
Pianella	komische Oper, 1	E. Pohl, after C. Goldoni: *La serva padrona*	Schwerin, 27 Dec 1857	(Paris, 1860)
La veuve Grapin [Madame Bonjour]	opéra comique, 1	de Forges	Paris, Bouffes-Parisiens, 21 Sept 1859	(Paris, ?1859); as Die Witwe Grapin, Vienna, Theater am Franz-Josephs-Kai, 1 June 1861, vs (Berlin, n.d.)
La châtelaine [Der Märchensucher]	2	M. A. Grandjean	Vienna, Karl, Sept 1865	rev. K. Treumann as Das Burgfräulein
Naida [Le vannier]	3	Saint-Georges and L. Halévy	St Petersburg, 11 Dec 1865	(Milan, n.d.)
Zilda, ou La nuit des dupes	oc, 2	Saint-Georges, H. C. Chivot and A. Duru	Paris, OC (Favart), 28 May 1866	vs (Paris, 1866); Ger. trans. as Fatme, vs (Berlin, c1925)
Am Runenstein	2	R. Geneé	Prague, 13 April 1868	(Leipzig, 1868)
Die Musikanten [La jeunesse de Mozart]	komische Oper, 3	Geneé	Mannheim, 19 June 1887	composed ?1869–70; Ger. vs (Leipzig, 1890)
L'ombre	oc, 3	Saint-Georges and de Leuven	Paris, OC (Favart), 7 July 1870	vs (Paris, 1870); as Sein Schatten, Vienna, Wien, 10 Nov 1871 (Berlin and Posen, ?1871)
La fleur de Harlem	3	Saint-Georges and de Leuven, after Dumas *père*: *Le tulipe noir*	unperf.	as Il fiore d'Arlem, Turin
Rosellana	3	A. de Lauzières de Thémines	Vittorio Emanuele, 18 Nov 1876	(Turin, 1876)
Sakuntala	3	C. d'Ormeville, after Kalidasa		inc.

PEM (M. Mäckelmann, R. Didion and P. Cohen)

A. F. Bussensius: *Friedrich von Flotow: eine Biographie* (Kassel, 1855)

E. Hanslick: 'Stradella von Flotow', *Musikalisches und Literarisches*, v: *Der 'Modernen Oper'* (Berlin, 1890), 116–23

R. Svoboda: *Friedrich von Flotow's Leben: von seiner Witwe* (Leipzig, 1892)

B. Bardi-Poswiansky: *Flotow als Opernkomponist* (Königsberg, 1927)

E. J. Dent: 'A Best-Seller in Opera', *ML*, xxii (1941), 139–54 [on *Martha*]

J. S. Weissmann: *Flotow* (London, 1950)

R. Stockhammer: 'Friedrich von Flotows Beziehungen zu Wien', *ÖMz*, xvii (1962), 175–9

W. Hübner: 'Martha, Martha, komm doch wieder', *Musik und Gesellschaft*, xiii (1963), 618

A. Goebel: *Die deutsche Spieloper bei Lortzing, Nicolai und Flotow* (diss., U. of Cologne, 1975)   PETER COHEN

Floyd, Carlisle (Sessions, jr) (*b* Latta, SC, 11 June 1926). American composer. His ancestors on both sides were among the earliest European immigrants to the Carolinas. During his childhood his father, a Methodist minister, was posted to a variety of small South Carolina towns, and the composer has derived much inspiration from this background. Almost all his operas have southern, rural or colonial settings and *The Sojourner and Mollie Sinclair* (1963) has all three.

In 1943 Floyd entered Converse College (Spartanburg, SC), where he studied the piano with Ernst Bacon. When Bacon took a position at Syracuse University, New York, in 1945, Floyd followed him there as his pupil (BM 1946); in 1947 Floyd was appointed to the piano faculty of Florida State University in Talahassee; he remained there for nearly 30 years, eventually becoming professor of composition. Until 1955, however, he was primarily a pianist, returning to Syracuse for a master's degree (1949), then taking private piano lessons with Sidney Foster and Rudolf Firkušný.

While at Syracuse he began to take an interest in composition. Drawing on existing skills as a playwright (as an undergraduate he had won a competition for one-act plays), he wrote his first opera, *Slow Dusk*, to his own libretto, and saw it produced in Syracuse in 1949. A second opera, *The Fugitives*, was produced at Florida State University in 1951, but was withdrawn after a single performance. Floyd's next operatic work, *Susannah*, by contrast, proved a tremendous success. Initially mounted in Talahassee in 1955, it was taken up by the New York City Opera and performed in New York in September 1956 to great acclaim, garnering for its composer a New York Music Critics' Circle Award, a Guggenheim Fellowship and several other awards. The work was chosen to represent American opera at the Brussels World Fair (1958), and has since become a repertory item. It remains the linchpin of Floyd's reputation. Except for *Of Mice and Men* (1969), which has proved to be by far the most successful of his works since *Susannah*, Floyd's other operas have all been commissioned. In 1976, Floyd left his Talahassee post for an equivalent position at the University of Houston in Texas, becoming also co-director of the Houston Opera Studio.

The guiding spirit of Floyd's operas is a studied, almost draconian pragmatism that makes them attractively easy to stage while limiting the heights to which they can aspire. Casts and orchestras are small; plots, action and scenery uncomplicated. No unusual instruments, voices or theatre technologies are required, nor any great virtuosity in the performers. There is little of counterpoint, or of any other musical feature that would demand more than minimal rehearsal time.

Musically, Floyd owes a great deal to Ernst Bacon.

His work is most readily understood as a nostalgic continuation of the populist 'social realism' of the 1930s and 40s, a style of which Bacon was a characteristic exponent. In Floyd's case, this takes the form of an all-purpose substrate of quartal harmonies with numerous parallel 5ths, supporting melodies imitative of various American folk genres; like Virgil Thomson, Floyd can lay claim to this melodic tradition through birth and upbringing. To suit specific dramatic contexts the basic style is fluidly varied, sometimes in the direction of Puccini, sometimes in that of Hindemith. The later operas, starting with *Of Mice and Men*, display greater chromaticism and metric flexibility. *Flower and Hawk* (1972), atypically, features an expanded percussion section, but this monodrama stands apart, too, in not necessarily requiring a staged presentation.

Dramatically, the operas continue the *verismo* tradition. Floyd, who writes his own librettos, has invariably preferred plots that are realistic (in operatic terms) and histrionic, generally involving the activities of ordinary people. Emotional effect relies heavily on the dramaturgy: directions for facial expression and the like are unusually detailed, and emotional climaxes are often expressed by moments of silence or in spoken dialogue.

Perhaps more than any other composer, Floyd embodies a frequent paradox of American opera. Though barely mentioned in surveys of opera, of American music, or of 20th-century music, his works have been more frequently performed on American stages than those of any other living composer, except Menotti. His popularity there reflects his ability to function within, even to exploit, longstanding adverse conditions in American opera production, where new works have been valued above all for conventionality and ease of presentation. Though this situation has altered considerably since about 1983 (in the wake of the success of Philip Glass), *Susannah* and *Of Mice and Men* have continued to hold the stage very strongly.

See also SUSANNAH.

all to librettos by Floyd

Slow Dusk (musical play, 1), Syracuse, U. of Syracuse, 2 May 1949, vs (New York, 1957)

The Fugitives, Talahassee, Florida State U., 1951, withdrawn

Susannah (musical drama, 2), Talahassee, Florida State U., 24 Feb 1955, vs (New York, 1957, 2/1967)

Wuthering Heights (musical drama, prol., 3, after E. Brontë), Santa Fe, 16 July 1958; rev. 1959, vs (New York, 1961)

The Passion of Jonathan Wade (3), New York, City Opera, 11 Oct 1962; rev. version, Houston, Wortham, 18 Jan 1991

The Sojourner and Mollie Sinclair (comic op, 1), Raleigh, NC, East Carolina College, 2 Dec 1963, vs (New York, 1968)

Markheim (1, after R. L. Stevenson), New Orleans, Municipal Auditorium, 31 March 1966, vs (New York, 1968)

Of Mice and Men (musical drama, 3, after J. Steinbeck), Seattle, 22 Jan 1970, vs (New York, 1971)

Flower and Hawk (monodrama, 1), Jacksonville, Civic Auditorium, 16 May 1972, vs (New York, 1977)

Bilby's Doll (3, after E. Forbes: *A Mirror for Witches*), Houston, 29 Feb 1976

Willie Stark (3, after R. P. Warren: *All the King's Men*), Houston, 24 April 1981

*

'Floyd, Carlisle (Sessions, Jr.)', *CBY 1960*

F. J. McDevitt: *The Stage Works of Carlisle Floyd, 1949–72* (diss., Juilliard School, 1975)

W. L. Senter: *The Monodrama 'Flower and Hawk' by Carlisle Floyd* (diss., U. of Texas, Austin, 1980)

R. H. Kornick: *Recent American Opera: a Production Guide* (New York, 1991), 102–8   ANDREW STILLER

Fly. Opera in two acts by BARRY CONYNGHAM to a libretto by Murray Copland; Melbourne, Victorian Arts Centre, State Theatre, 25 August 1984.

In the garden of the Hargrave family's Sydney home in the early years of the 20th century, the daughters, Margaret (mezzo-soprano), and Olive (soprano), discuss their father Lawrence Hargrave, his aviation inventions and his rejection of wealth and fame. The plot gradually lays bare the underlying tensions between Hargrave (tenor) and his socially ambitious wife Maggie (soprano). There are hints that Hargrave's refusal to capitalize on his potentially lucrative kite designs has its origins in his earlier experiences as an explorer.

In the first scene of Act 2 Hargrave recalls these past events. The action takes place on the deck of the steamer *Neva* far up the Fly River, New Guinea, in 1876. The expedition leader, the flamboyant Italian naturalist D'Albertis (baritone), jealous for his own profit and glory, grudges the young engineer Hargrave any credit for the expedition's success. Hargrave, in revulsion, passionately dedicates himself to a lifetime of disinterested research. The second scene returns to the Hargrave's garden in 1915. Mrs Hargrave has mellowed in her attitude to her husband, but when the news arrives that their only son has perished at Gallipoli she is unable to comfort him. He escapes from his unbearable grief, back into his self-appointed 'task'.

Regarded as a substantial addition to Australian music, *Fly* is attractively melodic, accessible and memorably evocative in its use of ostinatos, though generally more lyric than dramatic in style.   THÉRÈSE RADIC

Flying Dutchman, The. Opera by Richard Wagner; *see* FLIEGENDE HOLLÄNDER, DER.

Fodor-Mainvielle [Mainvielle-Fodor], **Joséphine** (*b* Paris, 13 Oct 1789; *d* St Genis-Laval, 14 Aug 1870). French soprano. She studied in St Petersburg with Eliodoro Bianchi and made her début there about 1810 in Valentino Fioravanti's *Le cantatrici villane*. She made her Paris début at the Opéra-Comique in 1814 in Grétry's *La fausse magie* and Berton's *Le concert interrompu*; she also sang numerous roles at the Théâtre Italien. She made her London début in 1816 as Paer's Griselda at the King's Theatre, where her roles included Mozart's Vitellia, Fiordiligi, Countess Almaviva, Zerlina and Susanna.

In 1818 Fodor-Mainvielle sang in the first London performances of Rossini's *Il barbiere di Siviglia* and *Elisabetta, regina d'Inghilterra*. She also took part in the first Paris performances of *La gazza ladra* (1821) and *Elisabetta, regina d'Inghilterra* (1822). She appeared at the Kärntnertortheater, Vienna, as Semiramide, a role she also sang at the Paris première of Rossini's opera (1825), but, not completely recovered from an illness, she lost her voice during the performance. She retired in 1833. Her book *Réflexions et conseils sur l'art du chant* was published in 1857.

*

C. Unger: *Joséphine Mainvielle-Fodor: précis historique sur sa vie* (Paris, *c*1823)

W. C. Smith: *The Italian Opera and Contemporary Ballet in London 1789–1820* (London, 1955)   ELIZABETH FORBES

Foerster, Anton (*b* Osenice, nr Jičín, 20 Dec 1837; *d* Novo Mesto, Slovenia, 17 June 1926). Slovene composer of Czech descent, uncle of J. B. Foerster. He studied law and music in Prague (including work with

Smetana) and was *regens chori* at Senj Cathedral, 1865–7. From 1867 he worked in Ljubljana, holding the post of conductor of the dramatic society (1868–1909) among others. One of the most important Romantic composers in Slovenia during the second half of the 19th century, he strove in his secular compositions to found a national style of Slovene music. The Slovene spirit is particularly evident in his lyrical comic opera *Gorenjski slavček* ('The Nightingale of Upper Krajina'). In three acts, to a libretto by E. F. Züngel after L. Pesjak and given in Ljubljana on 13 December 1896, it was originally composed as an operetta (Ljubljana, 17 April 1872). In this work Foerster tried to compose a national opera with an authentic Slovene melodic idiom, taking as his model Smetana's *Bartered Bride*; *The Nightingale* has become a standard work of the Slovene repertory. Among his other compositions is a five-act opera, *Dom in rod* ('Home and Family', 1920–23), to a libretto by F. Göstl and F. Mohorič; it has not been performed. MANICA ŠPENDAL

Foerster, Josef Bohuslav (*b* Prague, 30 Dec 1859; *d* Vestec, nr Stará Boleslav, 29 May 1951). Czech composer. Born into an established musical family, he studied at the Prague Organ School (1879–82), where his teacher was F. Z. Skuherský; later he worked as a choirmaster and singing teacher. He was acquainted with Smetana and Dvořák and with many other artistic figures. In 1888 he married Berta Lautererová (1869–1936), a soprano at the National Theatre, and in 1893 he moved with her to Hamburg, where she was engaged by the Stadttheater. He worked there as a critic and later as a professor of piano. He became a friend of Mahler, who engaged Lautererová for the Vienna Hofoper in 1901. Foerster himself moved to Vienna in 1903. On the formation of the Czechoslovak Republic in 1918 the couple returned to Prague and Foerster was appointed professor of composition at the conservatory (1919–22) and at the conservatory's master school (1922–31).

Perhaps no Czech composer – with the exception of Smetana – lived in such close contact with the Prague National Theatre as Foerster. As a nine-year-old he saw the laying of its foundation stone, and in 1883 he sang in the chorus of Smetana's *Libuše*. As a reviewer for *Národní listy*, *Dalibor*, *Hudební revue* and other journals he fought in the spirit of Smetana against the influence of commercialism, operettas and Italian *verismo*. He married a member of the National Theatre ensemble, and in the theatre he met Tchaikovsky, who became his lifelong friend. When Foerster died, a senior figure of Czech music, at the age of 91, his funeral started with orations over his coffin in the National Theatre.

Foerster's operas form part of an enormous output, the bulk of which is made up of vocal music; his inclination towards music for voices was the result of his constant and fundamental emphasis on the linking of word and musical sound, and indeed he wrote his own texts for a number of his works. All six of his operas were first staged at the National Theatre. He began composing for the stage in the 1890s, closely following Smetana in dramatic concept and in the structure of declamatory melody; he composed exclusively on rhymed poetic texts. He continued the tradition of Smetana and Dvořák by stylizing Czech folk music and dances (mostly ländler).

In his first opera, *Debora* (1893), Foerster introduced a new theme into Czech opera – the village drama. This tendency culminated shortly afterwards in *Eva*, composed in 1895–7 on the realistic drama by Gabriela Preissová. In this pivotal work the composer developed his own style of dramatic expression, which he used later in works in other genres and which was imitated by others, notably Otakar Ostrčil. Though *Eva* shows the characteristics of a realistic and psychological drama, its highly lyrical and metaphysical emphasis points towards the composer's later development. The Shakespearean opera *Jessika* (1905), which is lighter in mood, represents an evident sideline, though even this work bears the composer's typical touch.

Foerster wrote the librettos of his last three operas himself, using autobiographical elements and expressing his views on the principal questions of human existence. In *Nepřemožení* ('The Invincible Ones', 1918) and *Srdce* ('The Heart', 1923) he depicted the lives of artists who, wounded by life and betrayed by art, reach a recognition of love as an emotional, ethical and moral force. In his entirely subjective and symbolic opera *Bloud* ('The Fool', 1936), inspired indirectly by fables told by Tolstoy, he presented his concept of 'pure love', which is equal only to a belief in God. The characters of the drama symbolize general phenomena of life; music alone, for Foerster the most eloquent interpreter of emotion and belief, becomes the main vehicle for conveying meaning and thought. The melodiousness of Foerster's music, together with his skill in harmony and polyphony, reaches its climax in this work.

Highly cultivated taste is the main feature of Foerster's operas: the composer always worked hard at avoiding cheap effects. He was never a warrior, rather a resigned servant of art who cared about nobility of spirit, human consciousness, love, belief and good nature. It comes as no surprise that his works were often overshadowed by more self-assertive and vigorous operatic compositions. Though much appreciated, his operas are rarely performed: *Eva* is staged occasionally, *Jessika* seldom, and the others are nowadays virtually unknown.

See also EVA.

all first performed at Prague, National Theatre

Debora op.41, 1890–91 (3, J. Kvapil (i), after S. H. Mosenthal), 27 Jan 1893

Eva op.50, 1895–7 (3, Foerster, after G. Preissová: *Gadzina roba* [The Farm Mistress]), 1 Jan 1899

Jessika op.60 (comic op, 3, J. Vrchlický, after W. Shakespeare: *The Merchant of Venice*), 16 April 1905; with addl court scene, 1906

Nepřemožení [The Invincible Ones] op.100, 1906–17 (4, Foerster), 19 Dec 1918

Srdce [The Heart] op.102, 1921–2 (prol., 2, epilogue, Foerster), 15 Nov 1923

Bloud [The Fool] op.158 (7 scenes, Foerster, after L. N. Tolstoy's fables), 28 Feb 1936

A. Geisler: 'Dramatikova cesta' [The Dramatist's Way], *Hudba* (1920), 21

M. Očadlík: 'Jak inscenovat Foerstra' [How to Stage Foerster], *Listy hudební matice* (1927), 16

O. Zich: 'Hudební vývoj J. B. Foerstra' [The Musical Development of J. B. Foerster], *Památník Foerstrův* [Foerster Memorial Album], ed. A. Rektorys (Prague, 1929), 39–60

J. B. Foerster: *Paměti* [Memoirs] (Prague, 1929–47)

H. Doležil: 'Dramatické dílo J. B. Foerstra' [The Dramatic Work of J. B. Foerster], *Národní divadlo* (1934–5), no.6, pp.4–7

J. Hutter: 'Hudební dramatik J. B. Foerster' [The Musical Dramatist J. B. Foerster], *Divadlo* (1939–40), no.11, pp.57–8

M. Očadlík: 'J. B. Foerster a Divadlo' [Foerster and the Theatre], ibid, 59

J. Hutter and Z. Chalabala, eds.: *České umění dramatické*, ii: *Zpěvohra* [Czech Dramatic Art: Opera] (Prague, 1941), 225–67

O. Jeremiáš: 'Foerster dramatik' [The Dramatist Foerster], *Divadlo* (1943–4), 113

J. Plavec, J. Bartoš and P. Pražák, eds.: *J. B. Foerster a jeho životní pouť a tvorba 1859–1949* [Foerster: his Life and Work 1859–1949] (Prague, 1949) [incl. list of works, bibliography, discography]

A. J. Patzáková: 'J. B. Foerster', *HRo*, ii (1949–50), 101–8

J. Plavec: 'Hrát či nehrát Foerstra?' [To Play or Not to Play Foerster?], *HRo*, vii (1954), 942–5

E. Herrmannová: *Realismus oper devadesátých let* [The Opera Realism of the 90s] (diss., U. of Prague, 1957)

M. Očadlík: 'Je Foerstrovo dílo živé?' [Does Foerster's Work Live?], *Divadelní noviny* (1959–60), no.12, p.6

J. Plavec: 'J. B. Foerster a Národní Divadlo' [Foerster and the National Theatre], *Národní divadlo*, xxxv/3 (1959–60), 6–9

F. Pala: *Josef Bohuslav Foerster* (Prague, 1962)

J. Tyrrell: *Czech Opera* (Cambridge, 1988)

OLDŘICH PUKL / EVA HERRMANNOVÁ

Fogel, Johann Christoph. *See* VOGEL, JOHANN CHRISTOPH.

Foignet, Charles Gabriel [Jacques] (*b* Lyons, 1750; *d* Paris, May 1836). French composer and singer. He went to Paris, according to Fétis, in 1779 and taught music; from about 1781 to 1785 he published songs and keyboard arrangements. On 1 November 1788, a *scène* by Foignet was given at the Concert Spirituel. In 1791, when it became a common right in France to open a theatre, he began to compose stage works, initially in collaboration with Louis Victor Simon. These were primarily *opéras comiques* or vaudevilles and enjoyed much success; most are lost.

From 1798 to 1809 Foignet was (with Simon) one of five joint administrators of the Théâtre Montansier, and in 1801 took over the Théâtre des Jeunes-Artistes, rue de Bondy, where he ran a highly regarded troupe with his son François Foignet, who was chief conductor. Almost nothing is known of Foignet after 1807, when most small theatres were closed by Napoleon.

all first performed in Paris

L'apothicaire (2, P. Fabre d'Eglantine), Montansier, 7 July 1790
La force du sang, April 1791, collab. L. V. Simon
L'à-propos de la nature, Montansier, 17 Oct 1791
La boiteuse (1), Montansier, 17 Oct 1791, collab. Simon
Le roi et le pèlerin (3, J. de Lavallée), Montansier, 2 June 1792; arr. in 2 acts as La gageure du pèlerin, perf. date unknown; ov. arr. vn (Paris, 1793)
Le Mont-Alphéa, ou Le français Jatabite (oc, 3, Lebrun-Tossa [J.-A. Brun]), Montansier, 6 Dec 1792, *F-Mc*; 1 aria (Paris, n.d.)
La femme qui sait se taire (1, Lavallée), National, 28 Oct 1793
Le projet de fortune (1, Dumaniant [A.-J. Bourlin]), Cité, 9 Nov 1793
Michel Cervantès (oc, 3, Gamas), Louvois, 24 Dec 1793; 3 arias (Paris, n.d.)
Les petits Montagnards (opéra-bouffon, 3, A. Plancher de Valcour), Cité-Variétés, 17 Jan 1794; Vaudeville (Paris, *c*1794)
La discipline républicaine (fait historique, 1, Plancher de Valcour), OC (Favart), 20 April 1794; lib. (1794)
Les charlatans, ou Le cimetierre (opéra-folie, B.-A. Planterre), Cité-Variétés, 15 Sept 1794
Héléna, ou Les miquelets (drame lyrique, 2, J. A. de R. St-Cyr), Amis de la Patrie, 27 Sept 1794
Le plan d'opéra (opéra-bouffon, 1, Gamas), Cité-Variétes, 27 Oct 1794
Les divertissements de la décade, Cité-Variétés, 1794
Le franc marin, ou La gageure indiscrète (cmda, 2, M. de Pompigny), Amis de la Patrie, 3 Dec 1795
Le gascon tel qu'il est (comédie lyrique, 3, Pompigny), Montansier, 10 July 1797
L'heureuse rencontre, 1797
Les brouilleries (1, Dumaniant), Montansier, 14 Jan 1798
Les prisonniers français en Angleterre (opéra, 2, J.-F. Dognon and Rébory), Montansier, 8 April 1798
L'orage (opéra villageois, 1, Monnet), Montansier, 31 May 1798, *B-Bc*; lib. (Paris, 1798)
L'antipathie (1, P. L. David), Montansier, 11 Dec 1798

Robert le Bossu, ou Les trois soeurs (vaudeville, 1, M.-E. M. de Montaclos), Montansier, 10 Feb 1799
Les jugements précipités (vaudeville, 1), Montansier, 25 March 1799
Le cri de la vengeance, ou Clarisse et Valcour (comédie, 1, Dognon), Montansier, 7 June 1799 [in prose, mixed with arias on the assassination of Radstadt]
Le duel de Bambin (cmda, 1, Dumaniant), Montansier, 20 June 1800
Jacques Rigaud (1, Dumaniant), Montansier, 13 July 1800
Raymond de Toulouse, ou Le retour de la Terre-Sainte (drame lyrique, 3, G. de Pixérécourt), Jeunes-Artistes, 15 Sept 1802, collab. F. Foignet
Cavalo-Dios, ou Le cheval génie bienfaisant (scènes équestres, mêlées de féeries, 2, J. G. A. Cuvelier de Trie and Franconi *fils*), Cirque Olympique, 16 Nov 1808; music arr. J. Navoigille, with new music by Foignet
La fille mendiante (mélodrame, 3, Cuvelier de Trie and L. Corsse [J. B. Labenette]), Ambigu-Comique, 12 Oct 1809
Stanislas Lesczinski, ou Le siège de Dantzick (mélodrame historique, Cuvelier de Trie and E. C. de Boirie), Gaîté, 25 June 1811

Arrs.: La bataille d'Aboukir (Cuvelier de Trie), Cirque Olympique, 7 Sept 1808; Walter le Cruel, ou La géôlière de Mergentheim (pantomime, 3, Cuvelier de Trie), Gaîté, 23 Aug 1809; La main de fer (Cuvelier de Trie), Gaîté, 14 March 1810

FétisB; *MGG* (R. Cotte)
Journal des spectacles (Sept–Nov 1794), 38, 183
N. Brazier: *Chroniques des petits théâtres de Paris* (Paris, 1837, 2/1883)
F. Clément and P. Larousse: *Dictionnaire lyrique, ou Histoire des opéras* (Paris, 1867–81, 3/1905)
A. Pougin: 'Un gentil théâtre lyrique sous la Révolution', *Le ménestrel*, lxxvi (1910), 273, 329
E. C. Van Bellen: *Les origines du mélodrame* (Utrecht, 1927)
M. Noiray: 'Les créations d'opéra à Paris de 1790 à 1794', *Orphée phrygien: les musiques de la Révolution*, ed. J.-R. Julien and J.-C. Klein (Paris, 1989), 193–203
N. Wild: *Dictionnaire des théâtres parisiens au XIXe siècle* (Paris, 1989)
DAVID CHARLTON

Foignet, François (*b* Paris, 17 Feb 1782; *d* Strasbourg, 22 July 1845). French singer and composer, son of Charles Gabriel Foignet. His talents were nurtured in youthful appearances at the Théâtre des Jeunes-Elèves, and his first stage composition was given shortly before his 17th birthday. Between 1801 and 1805, when he and his father ran the Théâtre des Jeunes-Artistes, François made a considerable reputation as a singer and composer. His greatest success was earned while playing in his own *opéra comique La naissance d'Arlequin* (1803), in which he made nine changes of character and costume. This ran for over a hundred performances; August von Kotzebue's remarks on seeing it are quoted by Clément and Larousse. At the time the Foignets' theatre was nicknamed 'Le théâtre lyrique du boulevard'. Foignet's works were not published and the music has not survived.

After Napoleon closed most of the smaller Parisian theatres in 1807 Foignet sought his livelihood as a singer outside Paris, first as a tenor and later as a baritone. In 1818 he was in a troupe in Liège, and the next year he wrote an opera for the theatre at Bruges. In 1822 he sang in the Grand Théâtre, Marseilles. He is afterwards noted as being in Nantes (1824), Lille (1826, 1828), Ghent (1827, 1830) and Rouen (1840). For a time he was regisseur of the theatre at Angoulême.

first performed in Paris unless otherwise stated; music lost

La noce de Lucette (opéra, 1, J. Monnet), Variétés-Montansier, 4 Jan 1799, lib. *F-Pn*
Les gondoliers, ou La soirée vénitienne (1), Montansier, 6 May 1800
Le chat botté, ou Les vingt-quatre heures d'Arlequin (4, opéra-féerie, J.-G.-A. Cuvelier de Trie), Jeunes-Artistes, 19 March 1802, collab. J.-B.-A. Hapdé

Le retour inattendu, ou Le mari revenant (1, Monnet), Jeunes-Artistes, 9 May 1802

Raymond de Toulouse, ou Le retour de la Terre-Sainte (3, R. C. G. de Pixérécourt), Jeunes-Artistes, 15 Sept 1802, collab. C. G. Foignet

Riquet à la houppe (3, pantomime/opéra-féerie), Jeunes-Artistes, 12 Dec 1802

L'oiseau bleu (4, C. de Rougemont), Jeunes-Artistes, 25 March 1803

La naissance d'Arlequin, ou Arlequin dans un oeuf (opéra-féerie, 5, Hapdé), Jeunes-Artistes, 15 July 1803

Arlequin au Maroc, ou La pyramide enchantée (folie-féerie, 3, Hapdé), Jeunes-Artistes, 29 July 1804, lib. Pn

Achille plongé dans le Styx, ou L'oracle de Calchas (scènes allégoriques, Hapdé), Cirque Olympique, 8 June 1811

Barbe-bleue, ou Les enchantements d'Alcine (tableaux, 3, A. Friedelle and Hapdé), Jeux-Gymniques, 16 Dec 1811, lib. Pn, collab. Alexandre

Floreska, ou Les déserts de la Sibérie (tableaux, 3, Hapdé), Jeux-Gymniques, 16 March 1812

La houillère de Beaujonc, ou Les mineurs ensevelis (grand tableau historique, Hapdé and E. T. M. Ourry), Jeux-Gymniques, 24 March 1812

L'heure du supplice, ou Les remords du crime (scène tragi-lyrique), Bruges, 5 Feb 1819

N. Brazier: Chroniques des petits théâtres de Paris (Paris, 1837, 2/1883)

F. Clément and P. Larousse: Dictionnaire lyrique, ou Histoire des opéras (Paris, 1867–81, 3/1905)

L.-H. Lecomte: La Montansier (Paris, 1904)

A. Pougin: 'Un gentil théâtre lyrique sous la Révolution', Le ménestrel, lxxvi (1910), 273, 329

N. Wild: Dictionnaire des théâtres parisiens au XIXe siècle (Paris, 1989)   DAVID CHARLTON

Foire St Germain. Fairground in Paris (near the church of St Germain-des-Prés) where popular theatrical entertainment was staged in the spring; it was one of the two venues used by the Opéra-Comique in the early 18th century. See PARIS, §§2(iii) and 3(i).

Foire St Laurent. Fairground in Paris (located where the Gare de l'Est now stands), used for popular theatrical entertainment in the summer and autumn; like the Foire St Germain, it was used by the Opéra-Comique in the early 18th century. See PARIS, §§2(iii) and 3(i).

Foli [Foley], A(llan) J(ames) (b Cahir, Tipperary, 7 Aug 1835; d Southport, 20 Oct 1899). Irish bass. He studied in Naples with Bisaccia and made his début as Elmiro (Rossini's Otello) at Catania in 1862. After appearances in Milan, Turin and Paris he was engaged for the 1865 season at Her Majesty's Theatre in London, where he sang Saint-Bris (Les Huguenots) and the Second Priest (Die Zauberflöte). He continued to appear in London at Her Majesty's, Drury Lane and Covent Garden until 1887. He sang Daland in the first performance in England of Der fliegende Holländer (1870), and had a repertory of more than 60 roles, including Bertram (Robert le diable), Assur and Oroe in Semiramide, and Rossini's Moses, which he also sang in Russia. He possessed a powerful voice of more than two octaves, from E to f'.   HAROLD ROSENTHAL/R

Foligno. Italian town in Umbria. The earliest documented performances date from the last 30 years of the 17th century. Among works staged at the Teatro Pubblico (built probably in 1675–6) were Arrigoni's La vedova (Carnival 1722), L. A. Predieri's Cesare in Egitto (Carnival 1729) and Sarro's La Partenope (Carnival 1729). In the second half of the 18th century the theatre was renamed Teatro dell'Aquila, and the operas given here include Piccinni's Artaserse (Carnival 1763) and Le finte gemelle (Carnival 1773), Perez's Farnace (Carnival 1763), Paisiello's La frascatana (Carnival 1778), Luigi Caruso's La sposa volubile (Carnival 1790) and Marcello Bernardini's La sposa polacca (Carnival 1800). In the 19th century Rossini, Bellini, Donizetti and Verdi dominated the repertory. The festival 'Segni Barocchi', founded in 1981, takes place annually in August and September; it has put on, among other works, A. M. Abbatini's Il pianto di Rodomonte and Stefano Landi's La morte di Orfeo in their first modern revivals (1982 and 1990, respectively).

GALLIANO CILIBERTI

Fomin, Yevstigney Ipat'yevich (b St Petersburg, 5/16 Aug 1761; d St Petersburg, 16/28 April 1800). Russian composer. The orphaned son of a cannoneer, he was admitted shortly before his sixth birthday to the Foundling School of the Imperial Academy of Fine Arts, a charitable institution set up by Catherine II to foster a new generation of Russian artists. After nine years of general instruction he went on to specialized training in music at the academy, where his teachers included Hermann Raupach, composer of Dobrïye soldati ('The Good Soldiers'), a popular Singspiel of the day. On his graduation with honours in 1782 (as musicians were not eligible for medals, he was awarded 50 rubles), Fomin was sent on a four-year scholarship to Bologna to study with Padre Martini, though he actually worked mainly with Martini's assistant (and, from 1784, successor) Stanislao Mattei. In 1785 he was elected (as 'Eugenio Fomini') to the Accademia Filarmonica. With the possible exception of Maxim Berezovsky, his predecessor in Bologna, no countryman of Fomin's could claim a comparable musical education – or a comparable professional technique – until the institution of the conservatory system in Russia some 80 years later. There is no doubt that he was the finest Russian composer of dramatic music in the 18th century.

On his return to St Petersburg in autumn 1786, Fomin was immediately put to work setting one of the empress's librettos to music: Novogorodskiy bogatir' Boyeslavich ('Boyeslavich, Champion of Novgorod'), after one of the Russian national epics (bïlini) as retold by Chulkov. Fomin completed the work – a 'comic opera compiled from stories, Russian songs and other sources' in five acts with ballet – in about a month; it was performed at the Hermitage the same year. All that survives from it is a set of orchestral parts. A few instrumental excerpts quoted by Dobrokhotov (1968) show an attempt to render the popular scenes in a suitably folklike idiom, but the selection appears somewhat tendentious. The opera ends very much à la française with a choral chaconne.

For whatever reason (there has been much speculation in a documentary vacuum), Fomin's effort evidently failed to please. He did not receive a court appointment until 1797, after the accession of Paul I; nor were his operas performed in the capital during the decade following his début, apocryphal data (originating with V. V. Stasov) to the contrary notwithstanding. Indeed, Fomin's very whereabouts are uncertain in this period. What evidence there is seems to connect him with Gavriil Derzhavin (1743–1816), not only the greatest poet of the period but also a highly placed official, who in the late 1780s served as provincial governor of Tambov in south-central Russia and opened the first municipal theatre there in 1787. It was in Tambov that the libretto of Fomin's next opera, Yamshchiki na podstave ('Postal Coachmen at the Relay Station'; 1787), was published (anonymously) in 1788. A manuscript copy discovered in Derzhavin's archive in 1933 has established the great folksong collector Nikolay Alexandrovich L'vov, Derzhavin's brother-in-law, as the author of the libretto. *Vecherinki, ili Gaday, gaday devitsa, otgadïvay, krasnaya* ('Evening Parties, or Tell my Fortune, Fair Maiden'), of which an anonymous libretto was printed in St Petersburg in 1788, is known to have been performed during the early 1790s as the work of Fomin at the serf theatre on A. R. Vorontsov's estate in Tambov province (the music has been lost). The anacreontic comedy *Klorida i Milon* ('Chloris and Milo'), which Fomin may have set (some sources attribute the music to Alexander Pleshcheyev), is by Vasily Kapnist, another intimate of Derzhavin. Whether the composer spent any time in Tambov during the period of Derzhavin's service there, as Dobrokhotov (1968) has suggested, and whether he led provincial serf orchestras or managed the theatre on Count Sheremet'yev's estate (where his unlucky first opera was revived), are at present open questions.

Towards the beginning of this obscure decade Fomin composed what would eventually prove his most successful opera: *Amerikantsï* ('The Americans'), to a 'heroic' libretto modelled on Sedaine's *Le déserteur* by the later fabulist Ivan Krïlov (1769–1844), then a youth of 19 and a protégé of the poet and dramatist Yakov Knyazhnin. According to the title-page of the holograph score, the opera was written in St Petersburg in 1788, but was rejected by P. A. Soymonov, director of the court theatre, on account of its 'revolting' scene of attempted human sacrifice. It was not performed until very shortly before the composer's death, when it was given a lavish production in the court theatre. (By this time Fomin had found official employment in the Imperial Theatres, as a répétiteur.)

The subject of *The Americans*, drawn from the early period of Spanish conquest in the New World, celebrates the sentimental image of the noble savage. Don Guzman (tenor), a conquistador on a mission with his aide-de-camp Folet (bass) to rescue his sister Elvira (soprano), who has been abducted by Atsem, the leader of the Indians (bass), is captured but spared. When Atsem is captured in return, Don Guzman returns the favour. The action culminates in a peace treaty, at the conclusion of which three mixed couples – Atsem and Elvira, and Don Guzman and Folet each with a sister of Atsem – return in triumph to Spain. Fomin's music is italianate through and through, the Leporello-like role of Folet (who has the lion's share of arias) emerging as particularly vivid. The many ensembles far surpass, in their formal mastery and scope, the work of any Russian contemporary. The success of *The Americans* made Fomin's (posthumous) reputation, and was undoubtedly responsible for the many apocryphal attributions to him, the most conspicuous being that of Sokolovsky's *Mel'nik–koldun, obmanshchik i svat* ('The Miller who was a Wizard, a Cheat and a Matchmaker').

Fomin's theatrical masterpiece, however, was not an opera but the melodrama *Orfey* ('Orpheus'), set to a tragic poem by Knyazhnin as a vehicle for the actor Ivan Dmitrevsky in 1791 (Moscow, 1953). He also wrote choruses for tragedies by Knyazhnin and Vladislav Ozerov. Except for the finale of Act 1, his last opera, the posthumously produced *Zolotoye yabloko* ('The Golden Apple'), to a libretto adapted by one I. Ivanov from the myth of Daphnis and Chloë, has reached posterity in

the same mutilated form as his first: only the orchestral parts survive.

See also YAMSHCHIKI NA PODSTAVE.

Novogorodskiy bogatïr' Boyeslavich [Boyeslavich, Champion of Novgorod] (comic op, 5, Catherine II), St Petersburg, Hermitage, 27 Nov/8 Dec 1786
Yamshchiki na podstave [Postal Coachmen at the Relay Station] (comic op, 1, N. A. L'vov), ?Tambov, Municipal, 1788, *RU-SPtob**, lib. *SPsc**; ed. I. Vetlivtsïna (Moscow, 1977); excerpts in Ginzburg, IRMO
Vecherinki, ili Gaday, gaday devitsa, otgadïvay, krasnaya [Evening Parties, or Tell my Fortune, Fair Maiden] (comic op, 2), estate of A. R. Vorontsov, Tambov province, *c*1790; music lost, lib. (St Petersburg, 1788)
Amerikantsï [The Americans] (comic op, 2, I. A. Krïlov, rev. A. I. Klushin), St Petersburg, Bol'shoy, 8/19 Feb 1800, vs (St Petersburg, 1800); excerpts in Ginzburg, IRMO
Klorida i Milon [Chloris and Milo] (pastoral op, 2, V. Kapnist), St Petersburg, Bol'shoy, 6/18 Nov 1800, music lost
Zolotoye yabloko [The Golden Apple] (2, I. Ivanov), St Petersburg, Bol'shoy, 15/27 April 1803

Doubtful (music lost): Koldun, vorozheya i svakha [The Wizard, the Fortune-Teller and the Matchmaker] (comic op, 3, I. Yukin, after A. Ablesimov), lib. (St Petersburg, 1789); Nevesta pod fatoyu, ili Meshchanskaya svad'ba [The Bride Takes the Veil, or A Middle-Class Wedding] (comic op, 3), lib. (Moscow, 1790); Parisov sud [The Judgment of Paris] ('heroic trifle', 1, L'vov), ? not composed, lib. dated 17 Oct 1796, intended as entr'acte (intermedio) for Kapnist: *Yabeda* [Chicane] (see Keldïsh 1985)

*

A. Finagin: 'Yevstigney Fomin: zhizn' i tvorchestvo' [Life and Works], *Muzïka i muzïkal'nïy bït staroy Rossii: materialy i issledovaniya* (Leningrad, 1927)
A. S. Rabinovich: *Russkaya opera do Glinki* [Russian Opera Before Glinka] (Moscow, 1948)
A. Serov: 'Opera v Rossii i – russkaya opera', *Izbrannïye stat'i*, ed. G. Khubov, i (Moscow and Leningrad, 1950), 202
R.-A. Mooser: *Annales de la musique et des musiciens en Russie au XVIIIme siècle*, ii (Geneva, 1951)
D. Lehmann: *Russlands Oper und Singspiel in der zweiten Hälfte des 18. Jahrhunderts* (Leipzig, 1958)
Yu. Keldïsh: *Russkaya muzïka XVIII veka* [Russian Music of the 18th Century] (Moscow, 1965), chap. 6
G. Fesechko: 'Novïye materialï o kompozitorakh P. A. Skokove i E. I. Fomine', *Muzïkal'noye nasledstvo*, iv, pt.1 (Moscow, 1966), 9–43
B. Dobrokhotov: *Yevstigney Fomin* (Moscow, 1968)
S. L. Ginzburg: IRMO, i, 304–405, 490–91
A. Rudnyova: 'Analiz muzïkal'no-poeticheskoy strofi pesni "Vïsoko sokol letayet"' [An Analysis of the Musical and Poetic Strophe of the Song 'The Hawk Soars Aloft'], *Muzïkal'naya fol'kloristika*, i, ed. A. Banin (Moscow, 1973), 6–34
Yu. Keldïsh: Commentary to *Yamshchiki na podstave*, ed. I. Vetlivtsïna, *Pamyatniki russkogo muzïkal'nogo iskusstva* [Monuments of Russian Art Music], vi (Moscow, 1977)
——: 'K istorii operï "Yamshchiki na podstave"', *Ocherki i issledovaniya po istorii russkoy muziki* (Moscow, 1978), 130–40
——: 'E. I. Fomin', *Istoriya russkoy muziki v desyati tomakh* [The History of Russian Music in Ten Volumes], iii (Moscow, 1985), 84–110
                                                 RICHARD TARUSKIN

Fondo. Theatre in NAPLES (Teatro del Real Fondo di Separazione), opened in 1779 for comic opera; it was renamed the Real Teatro Mercadante in 1871.

Fontaine, Pierre-François-Léonard (*b* Pontoise, 20 Sept 1762; *d* Paris, 10 Oct 1853). French architect and stage designer. He studied at the Ecole des Beaux-Arts, Paris, with Antoine-François Peyre, in whose studio he met Charles Percier (1764–1838). He won a second place in the Prix de Rome for architecture in 1785, and was at the Académie de France in Rome, 1786–92. He joined Percier, who had been asked to take over from Pierre-Adrien Pâris as designer at the Paris Opéra, in December 1792, and they were in partnership there until their resignation in 1796. They returned in 1800 for

Set design by Girolamo Fontana for the prologue to 'La caduta del regno dell'Amazzoni' by Bernardo Pasquini and G. D. De Totis performed at the Palazzo Colonna, Rome, 15 January 1690: engraving

Bernardo Porta's *Les Horaces* and in 1802 for Catel's *Sémiramis*. Under the painter Jacques-Louis David, they did work for the revolutionary *fêtes* (for example, Porta's *Réunion du 10 août*). They also worked for the Théâtre Français, the Vaudeville, Opera Buffa and the Opéra-Comique (for whom they designed Grétry's *Elisca*, 1799, in collaboration with Jean-Thomas Thibault).

In January 1801 Fontaine and Percier were appointed government architects. This official post meant they did less stage designing but were much sought after as architects. They built a theatre at La Malmaison in 1802 (200 seats) and another at St Cloud in 1803. In 1825 Fontaine built a scenery storehouse for the Opéra in the rue Richer, and during Louis-Philippe's reign he restored the hall of the Comédie-Française. He drew up the plans for the rebuilding of the Salle des Machines in the Tuileries in 1832.

Some of Fontaine and Percier's designs have been preserved in Paris in the Ecole des Beaux-Arts, the Musée des Arts Décoratifs and the Opéra library; most are in private collections. His designs, implemented fully in the Revolutionary period, are examples of the neo-classical trend. Fontaine used architectural forms to enlarge the physical space of a scene, while remaining faithful to his three principles of taste – the truthful, the simple and the beautiful.

*

U. Thieme and F. Becker: *Allgemeines Lexikon der bildenden Künstler* (Leipzig, 1932)
P.-F.-L. Fontaine: *Journal* (Paris, 1987)   NICOLE WILD

Fontainebleau. Royal chateau, south of Paris, used for theatrical performances in the 17th and 18th centuries; *see* PARIS, §§1, 2(ii) and 3(ii).

Fontana, Ferdinando (*b* Milan, 30 Jan 1850; *d* Lugano, 12 May 1919). Italian writer and librettist. A violent radical in politics and an adherent of the artistic avant-garde movement known as the 'scapigliatura', he first made his name as a poet and dramatist of subversive tendencies. Through the agency of Ponchielli he was put in touch with the young Puccini, for whom he wrote the librettos of his first two operas, *Le villi* and *Edgar*. After

the failure of the second, their collaboration ceased. Of Fontana's other librettos the most ambitious is *Asrael*, written for Alberto Franchetti, which with its scenes in heaven and hell shows the influence of Boito's *Mefistofele*. One of his more curious beliefs was that a printed opera synopsis should form a work of art in its own right; to this we probably owe the verses which link the two acts of *Le villi* and which were intended to be read by the audience, not declaimed from the stage. Fontana was also the Italian translator of d'Albert's *Tiefland* and of three of Lehár's operettas, including *Die lustige Witwe*. In 1898 he was exiled for having taken part in a political uprising, and he spent the rest of his life in Switzerland.

Le villi (opera ballo), Puccini, 1884; *Anna e Gualberto*, L. Mapelli, 1884; *Flora mirabilis*, Samaras, 1886; *Colomba*, Radeglia, 1887; *Asrael*, Alberto Franchetti, 1888; *Edgar*, Puccini, 1889; *Lionella*, Samaras, 1891; *Il signor di Pourceaugnac*, Alberto Franchetti, 1897; *Sandha* (tragedia indiana), Lattuada, 1924

JULIAN BUDDEN

Fontana, Gabriele (*b* Innsbruck, 11 Feb 1957). Austrian soprano. She studied in Vienna, joining the studio of the Staatsoper in 1980 and singing roles such as Echo (*Ariadne*) and Lauretta. In 1982 she became a member of the Hamburg Staatsoper. At Glyndebourne she has sung Countess Almaviva (1984) and Fiordiligi (1987). Her repertory includes Pamina, Susanna, the Countess (Paisiello's *Don Chisciotte*), Sophie (*Der Rosenkavalier*) and Sophie Scholl (Udo Zimmermann's *Weisse Rose*), which she sang at Hamburg in 1986 and repeated in Vienna in 1987. She sang the title role of Keiser's *Tomyris* at Ludwigshafen (1988) and in the opera's subsequent recording. She has a delightful personality and her fresh, flexible voice is displayed to excellent advantage in Mozart.   ELIZABETH FORBES

Fontana, Giacinto ['Farfallino'] (*b* Perugia; *fl* 1712–35). Italian soprano castrato. He sang in Rome (1712), Fano (1716) and again in Rome (1717), where by 1719 he was singing seconda donna roles, soon rising to prima and beginning a decade-long reign as leading castrato in travesty roles in Roman theatres. He created roles in the late operas of Francesco Gasparini and Alessandro Scarlatti along with those by the younger generation – Sarro, Porpora, Feo and, especially, Vinci. He was prima donna in the inaugural season of the Teatro Argentina (1732), after which his appearances were infrequent; they included Fano and Perugia (1734) and Rome (spring 1735). His stage presence is perhaps hinted at by his nickname, 'Farfallino' ('Little Butterfly'), and this may have been his principal strength, as the music he sang does not suggest extraordinary technical abilities (range approximately e' to a").

DENNIS LIBBY

Fontana, Girolamo [Gerolamo] (b Rome; d Rome, 1714). Italian architect and scene designer. He was descended from a family of architects; his uncle, Carlo Fontana, was renowned for rebuilding the interior of the Teatro di Tordinona in Rome. Girolamo was active predominantly as an architect, while his fame as a scene designer rests on his sets for *La caduta del regno dell'Amazzoni*, a *festa teatrale* by Bernardo Pasquini and De Totis, performed on 15 January 1690 in the Palazzo Colonna to celebrate the marriage of the Habsburg King Carlos II of Spain and Mariana of Pfalz-Neuburg, Countess Palatine. In these stage scenes, recorded in engravings by various artists (see illustration opposite), Fontana displayed a thorough knowledge of Venetian antecedents, but distinguished himself from them by giving prime importance to architectural structures. Filippo Juvarra, a pupil of Carlo Fontana in Rome, picked up some ideas from *La caduta*, suggesting that Girolamo Fontana's staging may have had – at least in Rome – a lasting exemplary effect.

*

La caduta del regno dell'Amazzoni festa teatrale fatta rappresentare in Roma dall'Eccellentissimo Signor Marchese di Coccoglivdo ambasciatore della maestà del re cattolico (Rome, 1690)

C. Molinari: *Le nozze degli dei: un saggio sul grande spettacolo italiano nel seicento* (Rome, 1968), 111–13

MERCEDES VIALE FERRERO

Fontanesi, Francesco (b Reggio Emilia, 4 Oct 1751; d Reggio Emilia, 8 Oct 1795). Italian scene designer. He studied with the stage designer Gaspare Bazzani (1701–80), the perspective and decorative painter Prospero Zanichelli (1698–1772) and then at the Accademia Clementina in Bologna. As a member of the Accademia degli Ipocondriaci of Reggio he was aware of the most recent European advances in science as well as in literature and art, and he wrote theoretical treatises on painting and architecture.

While Fontanesi continued to work successfully in Reggio as a stage designer and decorative painter, there is also evidence for his presence in theatres in Modena (1781, 1787–95), Florence (1786), Rome (1786–7), Venice (1787–92), Vicenza (1789), Brescia and Livorno (1790), Milan (1792–3) and Pisa. He worked at Barga (1794) and Frankfurt (1793) and was invited to the imperial theatre in Vienna and to the Haymarket in London (17 January 1795), an engagement that his early death prevented him from accepting. Pietro Gonzaga, whose scenery Fontanesi had admired at Parma in 1782, encouraged him in December 1792 to go to St Petersburg. He also played a significant part in the controversy over the construction of the new Fenice theatre in Venice, and was responsible for the decoration of the interior of the auditorium, the scenery of the inaugural production and the design of the first curtain.

Characteristic features of Fontanesi's scenery were a simplified and asymmetrical composition of diagonal focus architecture, a restrained perspective and synthetic pictorial definition on the backcloth, sentimental colouration, strongly contrasted light and shade, historical authenticity without pedantry, the avoidance of self-indulgent decoration and the rigorous observation of stylistic norms, a rapid and vigorous line, and close adherence to the content, period and locations of the libretto.

*

ES (E. Povoledo)

'Del Cavaliere Francesco Fontanesi', *Notizie biografiche in con-*

Design for an Egyptian sepulchre by Francesco Fontanesi: pen and wash, early 1790s

tinuazione della biblioteca modenese del cavalier abate Girolamo Tiraboschi, i (Reggio Emilia, 1833), 180

L'arte del settecento emiliano: architettura, scenografia, pittura di paesaggio (Bologna, 1980), 200–03, 259–60

M. Pigozzi: *Disegni di decorazione e di scenografia nelle collezioni pubbliche reggiane* (Reggio Emilia, 1984), 32–9

——: *In forma di festa: apparatori, decoratori, scenografi, impresari in Reggio Emilia* (Reggio Emilia, 1985), 20–22, 60–74

P. Fabbri and R. Verti: *Due secoli di teatro per musica a Reggio Emilia* (Reggio Emilia, 1987), 86

M. Pigozzi, ed.: *Francesco Fontanesi 1751–1795: scenografia e decorazione nella seconda metà del settecento* (Reggio Emilia, 1988)

R. Bossaglia and V. Terraroli, eds.: *Settecento lombardo* (Milan, 1991), 471–2   MARINELLA PIGOZZI

Fontenelle, Bernard le Bovier de (*b* Rouen, 11 Feb 1657; *d* Paris, 9 Jan 1757). French librettist. He was a distinguished man of letters whose operas and pastorales form but a small part of his output. Abandoning a career in law, he later claimed to have joined his uncle Thomas Corneille in writing two librettos for Lully while Quinault was in disgrace. His success in the theatre was limited: he was much criticized for the dryness of his verse and his dependence on spectacle. He achieved greater fame as the secretary to the Académie des Sciences, writing biographies of its illustrious members which show his considerable grasp of scientific and philosophical thought. His career spanned nearly eight decades, and he was able to attend a performance of *Thétis et Pélée* over 60 years after its première.

tragédies en musique unless otherwise stated
Psyché (with T. Corneille), J.-B. Lully, 1678; *Bellérophon* (with Corneille), Lully, 1679; *Thétis et Pélée*, P. Collasse, 1689; *Enée et Lavinie*, Collasse, 1690 (A. Dauvergne, 1758); *Endymion* (pastorale-héroïque), F. Collin de Blamont, 1731

A. Fayol: *Fontenelle* (Paris, 1961)
C. M. Girdlestone: *La tragédie en musique (1673–1750) considérée comme genre littéraire* (Geneva, 1972)   CAROLINE WOOD

Fontenelle, Louisa [Mrs Williamson] (*b* London, 31 Aug 1769; *d* Charleston, SC, Oct 1799). English soprano and actress. She made a successful début as Moggy in Shield's comic opera *The Highland Reel* (1788). Her engagement at Covent Garden lasted only a year, for she performed, as the *European Magazine* put it, with 'rather too much spirits'. She sang in summer seasons at the Haymarket until 1793, working also in the provinces and Scotland. Burns wrote prologues for her on her benefit nights in Dumfries in 1792 and 1793 and a poem in her praise. She joined an English company in Germany and married its manager; they moved to Boston, and on her first appearance there she acted Desdemona and sang Little Pickle in the afterpiece *The Spoiled Child*. After her sudden death in Charleston the theatre there closed for a week.

BDA; LS
'The Highland Reel', *European Magazine*, xiv (1788), 373
The Thespian Magazine, i (1792), 66
The Thespian Dictionary (London, 1802, 2/1805)
J. L. Robertson, ed.: *The Poetical Works of Robert Burns* (Oxford, 1906)   OLIVE BALDWIN, THELMA WILSON

Foppa, Giuseppe Maria (*b* Venice, 12 Aug 1760; *d* Venice, 1845). Italian librettist. He was educated partly at a Jesuit college and became an archivist; later he held several government posts. Foppa was a prolific author: he wrote novels, poetry and plays, and translated many French dramatic works into Italian. In a review of 1797 the *Teatro Moderno Applaudito* called him a third-class dramatist; yet two years later the same journal commented after his *Romilda* that, with experience, Foppa's genius had become 'brilliant and fecund'.

Foppa's father was an amateur violinist, and music-making was important in the household (Galuppi was a close friend). He studied singing with Girolamo Fortuni and harmony with Francesco Bianchi and Carlo Faggi, organist at St Mark's. He was on familiar terms with Ferdinando Bertoni and other Venetian composers. During the 1790s he participated in Venetian musical life, particularly around the four *ospedali*. For the Mendicanti he wrote the texts for several oratorios and cantatas, many of which were set by Mayr.

Foppa's first opera libretto was *Alonso e Cora*, produced during Carnival 1786. By the end of his career in 1819 he had produced over 100 librettos which were set by many of the most important composers of the day, among them Andreozzi, Bianchi, Coccia, Fioravanti, Gardi, Generali, Nasolini, Paer, Portugal, Spontini and Zingarelli. He carried on long and important collaborations with Mayr (12 operas, 1796–1810), Farinelli (14 operas, 1800–17) and Pavesi (11 operas, 1803–19). For Rossini he wrote three *farse* and one *opera seria*.

The librettos are mostly comic. Many are one-act *farse* (*farse giocose*), a genre popular in Venice from the early 1790s to about 1815. He also wrote full-length comic operas, *drammi giocosi* or *eroicomici*. Many of the works he called *commedie* combine spoken dialogue with musical numbers and reflect the influence of *opéra comique*. His one *tragicommedia* and one *operetta di sentimento* demonstrate the influence of the French *larmoyante* genre.

The *drammi giocosi*, all in two acts, begin with a small ensemble (usually a duet), and each act concludes with a large ensemble. Ensembles appear throughout, developing the plot and surpassing the arias in dramatic importance. The *farse* exhibit the same reliance on ensembles; although in one act, they have a large ensemble midway through. Foppa drew his comic material from the *commedia dell'arte*, the French and Neapolitan theatres and Goldoni. The plots almost always revolve around marital or amatory interests and intrigues. He created a wide variety of characters including buffoons, lunatics, impertinent servants and socially climbing merchants and more refined idiosyncratic ones, such as a duchess who loves books more than men and a baron who cannot tolerate any degree of noise. Among his comic artifices are visual gags, pantomime, slapstick, disguises, secret identities and 'magic scenes'. He freely intermingled poetic metres; the more rapid *quinari* and *senari* are used as frequently as the traditional *settenari* and *ottonari*.

Foppa's serious works are mainly *drammi per musica*. He preferred French sources, for example Marmontel (*Alonso e Cora* and *Lauso e Lidia*), Beaumarchais (*Eugenia*) and Corneille (*Euristea*), but also drew from mythology and ancient history as well as adapting some of his own spoken dramas (*Don Gusmano*). He also wrote a handful of dramas that mixed spoken dialogue with music, of which *Dorval e Virginia* is a celebrated example. Based on an episode from the French novel *Paul et Virginie* by Bernardin de Saint-Pierre, Foppa's libretto captured the ideological spirit of the age with its emphasis on the purity and innocence of youth, the wholesomeness of rustic life and the nobility of self-sacrifice.

His style in his early serious operas is relatively conservative. An opening musical number will consist of no more than two or three stanzas for a soloist and chorus. Exit arias of two strophes in *settenari* or *ottonari* remain a prominent feature, and the proportions and variety of verse Foppa employed in his ensembles are relatively modest. By comparison *Giulietta e Romeo*, his only *tragedia per musica*, is a felicitous anomaly: it has a lengthy introduction that includes an opening chorus, solos by the two main characters, a duet and another chorus, swiftly and effectively setting up the basic conflict of the plot. Although the opera has its share of two-strophe arias, other arias employ a mixture of stanza lengths and poetic metres. The Act 1 finale is a lengthy ensemble that uses three types of poetic metre (*senari*, *settenari* and *decasillabi*) grouped into couplets and stanzas of three, four and five lines.

In his later serious works Foppa's style came closer to that of his comic operas. They have fewer arias and exhibit greater variety in the versification of the ensembles. As in his comic operas Foppa used *quinari* and *senari* more frequently, as well as six- and eight-line stanzas. He continued to spurn the tragic endings that were becoming more prevalent on the operatic stage.

In his *Memorie storiche*, published in Venice in 1840 (an appendix followed in 1842), Foppa reaffirmed the classic function of the theatre to educate, and warned against theatrical representations that undermined the morality and good habits of the public. While his admonitions may seem anachronistic against the backdrop of Italian Romanticism, his contributions to the operatic stage remain a testament to the philosophical idealism of a past era.

dg – *dramma giocoso*   dm – *dramma per musica*
f – *farsa*   fg – *farsa giocosa*

Alonso e Cora (dm, after F. Moretti: *Idalide*), F. Bianchi, 1786; *Le villanelle astute* (dg), Bianchi, 1786; *Il Calto* (dm, after Ossian), Bianchi, 1788; *Rinaldo* (dm), P. A. Guglielmi, 1789; *La pianella perduta nelle neve* (f), F. Rutini, 1790; *Amleto* (dm, after Ducis), Andreozzi, 1792; *Eugenia* (dramma prosa e musica, after P.-A. Beaumarchais), Nasolini, 1792; *Aci e Galatea* (dm), Bianchi, 1792; *Dorval e Virginia* (dramma prosa e musica, after Bernardin de Saint-Pierre), Tarchi, 1793 (P. C. Guglielmi, 1795); *Gli innamorati* (dm, after C. Goldoni), Nasolini and Trento, 1793; *Tito e Berenice* (dm), Nasolini, 1793

Gli artigiani (dg, after Goldoni), Anfossi, 1793; *Icilio e Virginia* (dm), Paer, 1793; *Laodicea* (dm), Paer, 1793; *L'impresario delle Smirne* (dg, after Goldoni), Giuseppe Rossi, 1793 (D. Rampini, 1798); *Amore la vince* (dg, after Goldoni), Nasolini, 1793; *Rinaldo d'Aste* (commedia con musica), Portugal, 1794; *Lo spazzacamino principe* (commedia con musica), Portugal, 1794 (G. Nicolini, 1794, as Il principe spazzacamino); *I molinari* (commedia con musica), Paer, 1794 (Nicolini, 1794, as 1 mulinari); *Il matrimonio improvviso, ossia I due sordi* (commedia con musica), Paer, 1794 (Portugal, 1795, as *Lo strattagemma, o siano I due sordi*); *I capricci* (f), Trento, 1794

Una in bene ed una in male (dg), Paer, 1794; *Giulietta e Romeo* (tragedia per musica, after Ducis), N. Zingarelli, 1796; *Un pazzo ne fa cento* (dg, after D. Somigli: *Il conte villano*), Mayr, 1796; *Le nozze de' sanniti* (commedia per musica), F. Gnecco, 1797; *Il secreto* (fg), Mayr, 1797 (F. Rutini, 1802); *Le donne cambiate* (fg, after C. Coffey: *The Devil to Pay*), Portugal, 1797; *L'intrigo della lettera, ossia Il pittore* (fg), Mayr, 1797; *La pianella persa, ossia La veglia dei contadini* (fg), Gardi, 1798; *La maschera fortunata* (fg), Portugal, 1798; *Lauso e Lidia* (dm), Mayr, 1798; *L'equivoco in equivoco* (fg), Portugal, 1798

Fedeltà e amore alla prova (dramma eroicomico), G. Gazzaniga, 1798; *Don Simoncino, ossia Furberia e puntiglio* (fg), M. Bernardini, 1798; *La madre virtuosa* (operetta di sentimento per musica), Portugal, 1798; *Il finto stregone* (fg), Gardi, 1798; *Non irritare le donne, ovvero Il chiamantesi filosofo* (fg), Portugal, 1798; *Il muto per astuzia* (fg), Bernardini, 1799; *La semplice, ovvero La virtù premiata* (dramma eroicomico), Gardi, 1799; *La fata Alcina* (dg, after G. Bertati), P. C. Guglielmi, 1799; *Il maestro di ballo* (f), Paer, 1799; *La principessa filosofa* (f), Gardi, 1799

Gli opposti caratteri (f, after Bertati, with G. Artusi), Nasolini, 1799; *Il contravveleno* (fg, after C. Gozzi), Gardi, 1799; *L'avaro* (fg), Mayr, 1799; *La testa riscaldata* (fg), Paer, 1800; *La bandiera d'ogni vento, ossia L'amante per forza* (fg), G. Farinelli, 1800; *La sonnambula* (fg), Paer, 1800; *La donna ve la fà* (fg), Gardi, 1800; *Il carretto del venditore d'aceto* (fg), Mayr, 1800; *L'impossibile nel possibile* (fg), Trento, 1800; *Il medico a suo dispetto, ossia La muta per amore* (fg), Gardi, 1800; *Ginevra degli Almieri, ossia La peste di Firenze* (tragicommedia), Paer, 1800 (G. Farinelli, 1812)

Una cosa strana (fg), G. Farinelli, 1800; *Il torto immaginario* (fg), Nasolini, 1800; *I matrimoni a forza, ovvero I consulti rabbiosi* (fg), E. Paganini, 1800; *L'equivoco, ovvero Le bizarrie dell'amore* (dg), Mayr, 1800; *L'incantesimo senza magia* (fg), Gardi, 1800 (F. J. Dussek, 1807); *L'imbroglione ed il castiga-matti* (fg), Mayr, 1800; *Poche ma buone, ossia Le donne cambiate* (commedia per musica), Paer, 1800; *Sopra l'ingannator cade l'inganno, ovvero I due granatieri* (fg), Capuzzi, 1801; *La bottega del caffè* (fg, after Goldoni), Gardi, 1801; *Dritto e rovescio, ossia Una delle solite transformazione del mondo* (fg), Gardi, 1801

Le due giornate, ossia Il finto comandante (dramma eroicomico), Mayr, 1801; *Teresa e Claudio* (f), G. Farinelli, 1801; *Non credere alle apparenze, ossia L'amore intraprendente* (f), R. Orgitano, 1801 (F. Orlandi, 1812); *I ripieghi, ossia I gruppi al pettine* (f), F. Grazioli, 1801; *Martino carbonaro, ossia Gli sposi fuggitivi* (fg), Gazzaniga, 1801 (F. Paini, 1814); *Il sedicente filosofo* (fg), G. Mosca, 1801; *Amore e destrezza, ovvero I contratempi superati dall'arte* (fg), Valentino Fioravanti, 1801; *Le virtuose ridicole* (fg, after G. Palomba: *Le cantatrice villane*), Fioravanti, 1801

Il convitato di pietra (f, after Bertati), Gardi, 1802; *Amore aguzza l'ingegno* (fg), Fioravanti, 1802 (P. Celli, 1813); *La rocchetta in equivoco* (fg), Marinelli, 1802; *Le metamorfosi di Pasquale, ossia Tutto è illusione nel mondo* (fg), Spontini, 1802; *I castelli in aria, ossia Gli amanti per accidenti* (fg), Mayr, 1802 (Pavesi, 1803); *Un effetto naturale* (fg), G. Farinelli, 1803; *Sargino, ossia L'allievo dell'amore* (dramma eroicomico), Paer, 1803; *Guerra con tutti, ovvero Danari e ripieghi* (fg), Gardi, 1803; *Un avvertimento ai gelosi* (fg), Pavesi, 1803; *L'amante anonimo* (fg), Gardi, 1803

Il fiore, ossia Il matrimonio per svenimento (fg), Orlandi, 1803; *La forza dei simpatici, ossia Lo stratagemma per amore* (f), Pavesi, 1803; *Camaccio il ricco e Basilio il povero* (f), Dussek, 1804; *Vanità ed accortezza* (fg, after Goldoni: *La sposa sagace*), l. Gerace, 1804; *L'accortezza materna* (fg), Pavesi, 1804; *Un buco nella porta* (fg), Gardi, 1804; *L'amore prodotto dall'odio* (f), Pavesi, 1804; *I due viaggiatori* (dg), Mayr, 1804; *Il pranzo inaspettato* (f), G. Farinelli, 1804; *Amare e non voler essere amante, ossia L'abitatore del bosco* (dramma eroicomico), Pavesi, 1805

La scelta dello sposo (f), P. C. Guglielmi, 1805; *Lo stravagante ed il dissipatore* (dg), F. Basili, 1805; *Questa volta la biscia ha beccato il ciarlatano* (fg), Dussek, 1805; *Orgoglio ed umiliazione, ossia Il fortunato ripiego* (dramma eroicomico), Generali, 1805; *La sorpresa, ossia Il deputato di grosso latino* (fg), Pavesi, 1806; *L'amico dell'uomo, ossia Ser Durando* (fg), G. Farinelli, 1806 (Orlandi, 1808); *Il testamento e seicentomille franchi* (fg), G. Farinelli, 1806; *Amore vince l'inganno* (fg), Pavesi, 1806; *Pan per focaccia* (fg), G. Aloisi, 1806; *La bizzarria d'amore, ossia I due viaggiatori* (dg), Raimondi, 1807

Pandolfo e Baloardo, ossia Le nozze per l'armi antiche (fg), Orlandi, 1807; *Sapersi scegliere un degno sposo, ossia Amor vero e amor interessato* (fg), Pavesi, 1807; *Le metamorfosi* (dramma eroicomico), Lavigna, 1807; *L'uomo benefico* (commedia di sentimento), Orlandi, 1808; *Le lagrime d'una vedova* (fg), Generali, 1808; *Molta paura e nessun male* (fg), Gerace, 1809; *La moglie di tre mariti* (fg), Generali, 1809; *Il ritratto del duca* (fg), Generali, 1809; *L'incognita* (fg), G. Farinelli, 1809; *La verità nella bugia* (fg), Coccia, 1809; *Un perfetto ricambio* (fg), Gerace, 1810

La terza lettera ed il terzo martinello (fg), G. Farinelli, 1810; *Amore non soffre opposizione* (dm), Mayr, 1810; *Amore vince lo sdegno* (dg), Generali, 1810; *Non precipitare i giudizi, ossia La vera graditudine* (fg), Farinelli, 1810; *Una fatale supposizione, ovvero Amore e dovere* (f), Coccia, 1811; *La sciocca per gli altri e l'accorta per se* (dg), Generali, 1811; *Amor muto* (fg), Farinelli, 1811; *L'inganno felice* (f), Rossini, 1812; *La scala di seta* (farsa comica), Rossini, 1812; *Amore e generosità* (fg), Pavesi, 1812; *Isabella, ossia Il più meritato compenso* (f), Generali, 1812

Il signor Bruschino, ossia Il figlio per azzardo (fg), Rossini, 1813; *Rodolfo* (f), Generali, 1813; *Il matrimonio per concorso, ossia*

Avviso al pubblico (dg, after Goldoni), G. Farinelli, 1813; *La donna selvaggia* (dramma eroicomico), Coccia, 1813; *Sigismondo* (dm), Rossini, 1814; *Euristea* (dm, after Corneille: *Timocrate*), Coccia, 1815; *Vittorina* (dg, after Goldoni), Farinelli, 1815; *Claudina in Torino* (dm), Coccia, 1816; *L'avventuriere* (fg), G. Riccardi, 1817; *La donna di Bessarabia* (dm), G. Farinelli, 1817; *I pitocchi fortunati* (commedia per musica), Pavesi, 1819; *Don Gusmano* (dg), Pavesi, 1819; *L'abitator del bosco* (dramma eroicomico), Balbi, 1821

*

E. Masi: *Sulla storia del teatro italiano nel secolo XVIII* (Florence, 1891)

L. Miragoli: *Il melodramma italiano nell'ottocento* (Rome, 1924)

G. Radiciotti: *Gioacchino Rossini*, i (Tivoli, 1927)

R. Angermüller: 'Grundzüge des nachmetastasianischen Librettos', *AnMc*, xxi (1982), 192–235

D. Goldin: 'Aspetti della librettistica italiana fra 1770 e 1830', *AnMc*, xxi (1982), 128–91; repr. in *La vera fenice* (Turin, 1985), 3–72

M. Conati: Introduction to G. Andreozzi: *Amleto*, DMV, xxvi (Milan, 1984)

M. McClymonds: 'The Venetian Role in the Transformation of Italian Opera Seria during the 1790s', *I vicini di Mozart: Venice 1987*, 221–40

S. Kunze: 'Su alcune farse di Giuseppe Foppa musicate da Francesco Gardi', ibid, 479–88

M. McClymonds: '*La morte di Semiramide ossia La vendetta di Nino* and the Restoration of Death and Tragedy to the Italian Operatic Stage in the 1780s and 90s', *IMSCR, xiv Bologna 1987*, iii, 285–92
RONALD SHAHEEN

Forbes, Elizabeth (*b* Camberley, 3 Aug 1924). English writer. A critic of exceptionally wide and international experience, she has contributed reviews and articles to numerous periodicals and newspapers (notably *Opera* and the *Financial Times* in Britain, and also *Opera Canada* and *Opera News*) and is noted for her balanced judgment on the human voice. Her main areas of interest are 19th- and 20th-century opera (French and Scandinavian in particular) and singers, both historical and present-day. She has made singing translations of many operas, from French, German and Swedish, including works by Spontini, Meyerbeer and Berwald. Among her writings are *Mario and Grisi* (London, 1985) and operatic books for a wide readership; she has also contributed extensively to reference works on singers and other operatic topics.

Force of Destiny, The. Opera by Giuseppe Verdi; *see* *FORZA DEL DESTINO, LA.*

Ford, Bruce (Edwin) (*b* Lubbock, TX, 15 Aug 1956). American tenor. He graduated from Houston Opera Studio in 1982, having made his début as L'abate di Chazeuil (*Adriana Lecouvreur*) and sung in the première of Floyd's *Willie Stark* (Houston Grand Opera) and the American première of Glass's *The Madrigal Opera* (Opera Studio) in 1981. Engaged at Wuppertal (1983–5), he sang Belmonte, Dardanus (Gatti's *Scylla*) and Nureddin (Cornelius's *Der Barbier von Bagdad*). He created Peccadillo in P. D. Q. Bach's *The Abduction of Figaro* (by Peter Schickele) for Minnesota Opera (1984) and sang Tamino for the same company in 1985. At Mannheim (1985–7) his roles also included Ferrando, Don Ramiro and Fenton. At Wexford (1986) he sang Argirio (*Tancredi*) and has since become a Rossini specialist, singing Agorante (*Ricciardo e Zoraide*) at Pesaro (1990) and making his Covent Garden début as Almaviva (1991). He also sings James (*La donna del lago*) and Rinaldo (*Armida*). His flexible, lyrical voice is supported by excellent technique and great musicality.
ELIZABETH FORBES

Ford, Clifford (*b* Toronto, 30 May 1947). Canadian composer. He studied composition at the Toronto Conservatory with John Beckwith (1960–64), at Toronto University with Beckwith, John Weinzweig and Gustav Ciamaga (1966–70), at McGill University with István Anhalt and Paul Pedersen (1970–71), and at the Institute of Sonology in Utrecht (1973). He has held teaching positions at McMaster University, Hamilton, Ontario (1974–6), and Dalhousie University, Halifax (1976–80). His only opera, *Hypnos*, a lyric drama to a libretto by Kenneth Peglar, was commissioned by Young Canada Opera Theatre and first performed on 22 August 1972 in Toronto. It is an abstract work, in both music and text; the central character is shown in an illusionary atmosphere controlled by a hypnotist, and the atonal score provides an instrumental soundscape, dominated by a prepared tape through which sounds and characters drift.
RUTH PINCOE

Ford, Ernest (A. Clair) (*b* Warminster, 17 Feb 1858; *d* London, 2 June 1919). English composer. He was a pupil of Arthur Sullivan at the RAM in London (1875) and also spent some time in Paris studying with Lalo. Most of his compositions, which show Sullivan's influence, were for the theatre; they include operas and ballet music. Ford held a professorship of singing at the GSM, where he was in charge of the opera class. He conducted Sullivan's *Ivanhoe* at the Royal English Opera House, Cambridge Circus, and for some years directed the Royal Amateur Orchestral Society.

Daniel O'Rourke (operetta, 3), private perf., Glasgow, Feb 1884

Nydia (duologue, J. H. McCarthy), London, 1889

Joan, or The Brigands of Bluegoria (comic op, R. Martin), London, Opera Comique, 9 June 1890

The Wedding Eve (comic op, W. Yardley), London, Trafalgar Square, 10 Sept 1892, collab. F. Toulmouche and 'Yvolde'

Mr Jericho (operetta, H. Greenbank), London, Savoy, 24 March 1893, songs (London, 1893)

Jane Annie, or The Good Conduct Prize (comic op, 2, J. M. Barrie and A. C. Doyle), London, Savoy, 13 May 1893, vs (London, 1893)

The House of Lords (operetta), London, Lyric, 5 July 1894, collab. G. W. Byng

Forest, Jean Kurt (*b* Darmstadt, 2 April 1909; *d* Berlin, 2 March 1975). German composer. He studied at the Spangenberg Conservatory in Wiesbaden until 1925, and embarked on a career as a violinist. He held posts as Kapellmeister in Neisse (1938) and at the Brunswick Staatstheater (1939–40). After World War II he became adviser on modern choral music to Berlin Radio, where he was chief conductor from 1949. In 1952 he moved to East German Television as chief conductor, becoming a freelance composer in 1955.

Forest was self-taught, and his compositions include orchestral, chamber and occasional works, as well as musicals and film scores. Meetings with Hindemith, Schoenberg and Dessau, and study of their music, influenced Forest's later compositions, and from the 1950s he adopted a dodecaphonic style. In his tonal language he aimed for an effect uniting serious and light elements. His operas, several of which were initially directed by Harry Kupfer, are mainly on historical and political themes and often include attractive illustrative writing, with original sound effects, but are not always dramatically successful.

all librettos by the composer
Die Abenteuer des Don Quijote (after M. de Cervantes), 1940, only frag. survives

Die glückliche Stadt (operetta), 1951
Das leuchtende Ziel (operetta), 1951
Der arme Konrad (after F. Wolf), Berlin, Staatsoper, 1959
Tai Yang erwacht (after Wolf), Halberstadt, 1960
Wie Tiere des Waldes (after Wolf), Stralsund, 1964
Hete (TV op, after H. Sakowski), 1965
Die Passion des Johannes Hörder (after J. R. Becher), Stralsund, 1965
Die Blumen von Hiroshima (after E. Morris), Weimar, 1967
Die Odyssee der Kiu (after Nguyen Dun), Erfurt, 1968
Eine Fahne hab' ich zerrissen (Opera minute, after B. Brecht: *Die Gewehre der Frau Carrar*), 1971
Die Hamlet-Saga (Opera concertant, after F. de Belleforest: *Histoires tragiques*, Saxo Grammaticus: *Historica danica* and W. Shakespeare), Berlin, 1973
Sisyphos und Polyander (Opera minute, with intrada, entr'actes and epilogue, after V. Ivanov), 1974
Tage ohne Krieg (after K. Simonov: *20 Tage ohne Krieg*), 1974, inc.

*

G. Rimkus: 'Der arme Konrad', *Musik und Gesellschaft*, ix (1959), 198–202
H. Schaefer: 'Musikalisches Kammerspiel: "Die Blumen von Hiroshima" ', *Musik und Gesellschaft*, xvii (1967), 682–5
H.-G. Otto: 'Dem Opernkomponisten Jean Kurt Forest zum Sechzigsten', *Musik und Gesellschaft*, xix (1969), 232–6
——: 'Erstrebte Aktualität', *Theater der Zeit*, xxv/2 (1970), 24–7
M. Hansen: 'J. K. Forest', *Musiker in unserer Zeit* (Leipzig, 1979), 217–25, 351–3
K. Klingbeil: 'Streben nach aktivierender Kunst', *Musik und Gesellschaft*, xxxix (1989), 215–16
DIETER HÄRTWIG

Formagliari. Theatre in BOLOGNA, opened in 1636 and burnt down in 1802.

Formes, Karl Johann (*b* Mülheim, 7 Aug 1815; *d* San Francisco, 15 Dec 1889). German bass. He made his début at Cologne in 1842 as Sarastro. Engaged at the Kärntnertortheater, Vienna, he created Plumkett in Flotow's *Martha* (1847). Forced to leave Vienna for political reasons, in 1849 he sang in London for the first time at Drury Lane. He made his Covent Garden début in 1850 as Caspar (*Der Freischütz*) and sang there regularly until 1868. His roles included Bertram (*Robert le diable*), Marcel (*Les Huguenots*), Leporello, Rocco and Peter the Great (*L'étoile du nord*). He took part in the première of the three-act revision of Spohr's *Faust* (1852, London) and the first London performance of Berlioz's *Benvenuto Cellini* (1853), in which he sang the Cardinal. In 1857 he appeared at the New York Academy of Music, returning there for the next 20 years. His voice combined a solid, resonant lower register with considerable flexibility, and he was particularly admired as Caspar.

*

H. Rosenthal: *Two Centuries of Opera at Covent Garden* (London, 1958)
ELIZABETH FORBES

Formichi, Cesare (*b* Rome, 15 April 1883; *d* Rome, 21 July 1949). Italian baritone. After practising law in Rome he studied singing there and made his début at Genoa in 1909, later that year appearing with the Boston Opera Company. He travelled widely in Europe, visiting Russia in 1912, and in 1914 made the first of many appearances in Buenos Aires, where he sang Klingsor in the first performances there of *Parsifal*. For ten years he was principal baritone at Chicago. His début at Covent Garden in 1924 was preceded by his reputation for having 'the biggest voice in the world'. He was last heard there in 1937 when, in addition to singing Iago on the opening night and later appearing, to adverse criticism, as Falstaff, he also acted as impresario, arranging the Italian part of the season. His

powerful voice and dramatic style are well captured on recordings made in the 1920s.
J. B. STEANE

Fornasari, Luciano (*b c*1815; *d* after 1850). Italian bass. Having made his début in 1831 in Milan, he went to America and took part in the first performance in the USA of *L'italiana in Algeri* (1832, New York). He made his London début at Her Majesty's Theatre in 1843 as Donizetti's Belisarius, then sang Malatesta in *Don Pasquale* (1843), Silva in *Ernani* (1845), the title role of *Nabucco* (given as Nino) and Pagano in *I Lombardi* (1846), all first performances in Britain. He created Posa in Costa's *Don Carlos* (1844) and also sang Rossini's Figaro, Assur (*Semiramide*), Fernando (*La gazza ladra*), Antonio (*Linda di Chamounix*), Ernesto (*Il pirata*) and Zampa – a tenor role. He sang in the première of Persiani's *Il fantasma* (1843, Paris). A forceful singer with a handsome presence, he made a particularly fine Don Giovanni.

For illustration *see* DON PASQUALE.
ELIZABETH FORBES

Fornia, Rita [Newman, Regina] (*b* San Francisco, 17 July 1878; *d* Paris, 27 Oct 1922). American mezzo-soprano. Her teachers included Emil Fischer, Sofia Scalchi, Selma Nicklass-Kempner and Jean de Reszke. She did them credit, for, though never rising above secondary status at the Metropolitan, she proved herself to be one of the most useful and adaptable of artists. She made her début at Hamburg in 1901 singing mostly as a coloratura soprano and two years later joined Henry Savage's Opera Company in America as both mezzo and soprano, her roles including Leonora and Azucena in *Il trovatore* and Elisabeth and Venus in *Tannhäuser* (on one occasion she sang the two roles in the same performance). From 1907 to 1922 she sang at the Metropolitan, creating the part of the Abbess in *Suor Angelica* in 1918 and appearing as Eurydice in a concert performance of Monteverdi's *Orfeo* in 1913. Occasionally she stepped into prominence as a substitute but she was usually to be heard in a wide range of small parts. Her few recordings show a pleasing, well-managed voice and a sensitive style.

*

W. R. Moran: 'Rita Fornia', *Record Collector*, x (1955–6), 217–37
J. B. STEANE

Forrest, Hamilton (*b* Chicago, 8 Jan 1901; *d* London, 26 Dec 1963). American composer. Trained by Adolph Weidig at the American Conservatory, Chicago, Forrest won the American Opera Society of Chicago David Bispham Medal in 1926 for his first opera, *Ysdra*. In 1928 Mary Garden became interested in his *Camille* and persuaded Samuel Insull to direct it, putting the resources of the Chicago Civic Opera Company into creating a spectacular 'novelty' production. At Garden's request Forrest's libretto was translated into French, an incongruity, since the cast was to be entirely English-speaking. With its unfamiliar tonality and rhythm *Camille* proved too difficult to prepare for the 1929–30 season and was postponed, having its first performance at the new Civic Opera House on 10 December 1930; the cast included Charles Hackett and Chase Baromeo, and Garden as Marguerite. Criticism was mostly negative for the run of six performances. Forrest went on to write chamber works, songs and theatre music, and in the 1950s composed three one-act operas for Interlochen National Music Camp. He was working on a three-act opera, *Galatea*, at the time of his death.

Ysdra, 1925 (3, Forrest, after L. Ledoux: *Alexander the Great*), unperf.
Camille (prol., 3, Forrest, after A. Dumas *fils*: *La dame aux camélias*), Chicago, Civic Opera House, 10 Dec 1930, *US-Cn**
Don Fortunio (1, Forrest), Interlochen, MI, National Music Camp, 22 July 1952
Daelia (1, Forrest), Interlochen, National Music Camp, 21 July 1954, *Cn**
A Matinée Idyll (1, Forrest), Interlochen, National Music Camp, 17 Aug 1954, *Cn**
Galatea (3, Forrest), inc., *Cn**

DIANA HASKELL

Forrester, Maureen (**Kathleen Stuart**) (*b* Montreal, 25 July 1930). Canadian contralto. After studies with Sally Martin, Frank Rowe and Bernard Diamant, she concentrated on a concert career, appearing only in two minor roles with the Montreal Opera Guild (1953–4). Her first major engagement was as Gluck's Orpheus, in Toronto in 1962. Subsequently she sang, among other roles, Cornelia in *Giulio Cesare* (1966, New York City Opera), La Cieca in *La Gioconda* (1967, San Francisco), Erda (1975, Metropolitan), Madame Flora in Menotti's *The Medium*, Mistress Quickly, Brangäne, Arnalta (*L'incoronazione di Poppea*), Ulrica, Clytemnestra, Mme de Croissy (*Dialogues des Carmélites*) and the Countess (*The Queen of Spades*), which she sang at La Scala in 1990. A character actress of considerable wit, she is a singer of rare tonal opulence with a high standard of musicianship and interpretative imagination. She has been active as a singing teacher.

MARTIN BERNHEIMER

Forsell, (Carl) John [**Johan**] (**Jacob**) (*b* Stockholm, 6 Nov 1868; *d* Stockholm, 30 May 1941). Swedish baritone. He made his début as Rossini's Figaro at the Stockholm Opera in 1896 and sang there regularly until 1911, and as a guest until 1938. In 1909–10 he appeared with success at Covent Garden as Don Giovanni, and at the Metropolitan in numerous roles including Telramund, Amfortas, Germont, Tonio and Prince Yeletsky. He was notable, especially as Don Giovanni, not only for the beauty and skill of his singing, but for the vivacity and zest of his whole dramatic performance – qualities which were still evident as late as 1930, when his fiery and elegant Don Giovanni, in Italian at Salzburg, provided a marked contrast to the sedateness of an otherwise German-speaking cast. From 1924 to 1939 Forsell was director of the Stockholm Opera; from 1924 to 1931 he taught at the Stockholm Conservatory, where his pupils included Jussi Björling and Set Svanholm.

*

C. L. Brunn: 'John Forsell', *Record News* [Toronto], iv (1959–60), 256–63, 292–6 [discography]   DESMOND SHAWE-TAYLOR

Förstel, Gertrude (*b* Leipzig, 21 Dec 1880; *d* Bad Godeberg, 7 June 1950). German soprano. Originally trained in Leipzig as a pianist, she studied singing first in Berlin with Selma Niklass-Kempner, then in Dresden with Aglaja Orgeni. She joined Angelo Neumann's German opera company in Prague, where she sang from 1900 to 1906, mostly in coloratura roles such as that of Amina in *La sonnambula*, the opera of her début. Later, with the Vienna Hofoper from 1906 to 1912, she turned to lyrical roles with a lower tessitura, becoming noted as a Mozart singer and particularly admired for her Pamina and Susanna. In 1911 she sang Sophie in the Viennese

première of *Der Rosenkavalier*. At Bayreuth her roles included the Shepherd Boy in *Tannhäuser* and the Wood Bird in *Siegfried*. She appeared there from 1904 to 1912, in which year she retired from opera, continuing her career in concert work and specializing in Bruckner and Mahler (in Munich she sang in the première of his Eighth Symphony). She later taught in Cologne. Her recordings disclose a delicate voice, pure in timbre and well schooled in scale-work, though one might wish for more colour and energy as well as firmer control of vibrato.

J. B. STEANE

Forster, E(dward) M(organ) (*b* London, 1 Jan 1879; *d* Coventry, 7 June 1970). English writer. Closely associated with Cambridge and the Bloomsbury group, he campaigned actively against censorship. His travels in Europe and India yielded two of his best-known novels, *A Room with a View* (1908) and *A Passage to India* (1924). He borrowed many of his ideas about rhythm and structure in the novel from his knowledge of music, and his lifelong interest in Wagner led him to attempt a leitmotif technique in his own writing. He collaborated with Eric Crozier on the libretto for Britten's *Billy Budd* (1951).

*

P. N. Furbank: *E. M. Forster: a Life* (London, 1977–8)
J. L. DiGaetani: *Richard Wagner and the Modern British Novel* (London, 1978)   ANTHONY PARR

Forti, Anton (*b* Vienna, 8 June 1790; *d* Vienna, 16 June 1859). Austrian baritone. He began his career playing the viola in the orchestra of the Theater an der Wien. In 1808 he was engaged as a singer by Prince Esterházy for his theatre at Eisenstadt. During his three seasons there he sang Dandini in the German-language première of Isouard's *Cendrillon*. From 1813 to 1834 he appeared at the Kärntnertortheater in Vienna. A very stylish singer and actor, he excelled in Mozart roles, especially Don Giovanni, Count Almaviva and Sarastro. In 1814 he sang Pizarro in the first performance of the final version of Beethoven's *Fidelio*, and in 1823 he created Lysiart in the première of Weber's *Euryanthe*. He also sang a number of tenor roles, including Rossini's Otello, Weber's Max and Mozart's Titus.   ELIZABETH FORBES

Forti, Helena (*b* Berlin, 25 April 1884; *d* Vienna, 11 May 1942). German soprano. She studied with Karl Scheidemantel in Dresden and with Theodor Emmerich in Berlin. She sang in Dessau from 1906, making her début as Valentine in *Les Huguenots*, and in Brno and Prague from 1908 to 1911. At the Dresden Hofoper (1911–24) she was successful in dramatic repertory and created Myrtocle in *Die toten Augen* by d'Albert (1916). At Bayreuth in 1914 she sang Sieglinde in the *Ring* cycles conducted by Michael Balling. She made guest appearances in Vienna, Brussels, Amsterdam and Bucharest. From 1917 she was married to the director and Intendant Bruno Iltz (1886–1965).

DAVID CUMMINGS

Fortia de Piles, Alphonse-Toussaint-Joseph-André-Marie-Marseille, Comte de (*b* Marseilles, 18 Aug 1758; *d* Sisteron, Basses Alpes, 18 Feb 1826). French composer of Catalan ancestry. Apparently he studied with the Neapolitan Ligori, a pupil of Francesco Durante. From 1782 instrumental works by him appeared in Paris, and between 1784 and 1786 four operas were produced in Nancy. He left France in 1790, but returned in 1792 to make his living in Paris as a journalist. In 1801 he retired to Sisteron and became a successful writer on philosophical, political and satirical subjects. Some of his writings show him to have been an adherent of Gluck and Méhul.

La fée Urgèle (oc, 4, ?C.-S. Favart), Nancy, 1784, ov. and entr'acte (Paris, n.d.)
Vénus et Adonis (opéra, 1, ?Collet de Messine), Nancy, 1784
Le pouvoir de l'amour (opéra), Nancy, 1785
L'officier français à l'armée (oc, ?J.-F.-H. Collot), Nancy, 1786

*

MGG (M. Briquet)
A. Choron and F. Fayolle: Dictionnaire historique des musiciens (Paris, 1810–11)
A. Jadin: 'Fortia de Piles', Nouvelle biographie générale, xviii (Paris, 1857)   ROGER J. V. COTTE

Fort Lauderdale. American town, in Florida. Opera was first performed there in 1945, in productions brought to the town from elsewhere under the auspices of an Opera Guild; in 1950 the War Memorial Auditorium was opened, providing a suitable location for performances. Seasons were extended to two operas each year in 1967 and to three in 1983. In 1990 Marvin David Levy was appointed artistic director, and in 1991 Fort Lauderdale Opera was established to generate productions of its own; in the first year Le nozze di Figaro, La fille du régiment and The Saint of Bleecker Street were given.

Fortner, Wolfgang (*b* Leipzig, 12 Oct 1907; *d* Heidelberg, 5 Sept 1987). German composer. He studied composition with Hermann Grabner at the Leipzig Conservatory and musicology with Theodor Kroyer at Leipzig University. After graduating in 1931 he taught music theory at the Evangelische Kirchenmusikalische Institut in Heidelberg for 22 years. From 1946 he taught composition at summer courses in Darmstadt where Henze became his most distinguished pupil. In 1954 he was appointed professor of compositon at the Nordwestdeutsche Musik-Akademie in Detmold and three years later moved to a similar position at the Freiburg Hochschule für Musik (1957–73).

With the exception of the youthful school opera Cress ertrinkt (1930), Fortner demonstrated little interest in writing dramatic music while at Heidelberg. Nevertheless, his hard-won mastery of concertante forms proved to be an effective and necessary basis upon which to develop a powerful operatic style. This development coincided with a broadening of idiom which, after 1945, embraced serialism and resulted in an expansion of both harmonic and colouristic elements. All these features are fully realized in his first major opera, Die Bluthochzeit (1957), after García Lorca's play Bodas de sangre (1933). The work follows a tradition established by many 20th-century operas in remaining extraordinarily faithful to the original drama. Indeed, the composer preserves a considerable amount of spoken dialogue to carry the action forward and employs music only at moments of considerable tension. Such an approach might suggest that the score simply fulfils the function of incidental music, but in fact this division of sung and spoken elements deliberately parallels the realistic and mystic levels of the drama. The dichotomy is further underlined by the contrast of 12-note material with Spanish folk elements, particularly in the Wedding Scene. Fortner reserves his most extended writing for the Forest Scene of Act 2, in which the symbolic characters of Moon and Death are introduced to the accompaniment of a wistful canon for two solo violins and throb-bing percussion. Despite Fortner's resisting the temptation to overstate the more dramatic elements of the play – the murder of the two rivals takes place against the simple background of a side drum roll – Die Bluthochzeit came to be regarded as one of the most convincing and theatrically gripping operas of the 1950s.

Fortner's fascination with García Lorca was further explored in another opera, In seinem Garten liebt Don Perlimplin Belisa (1962), conceived for chamber forces. This somewhat elusive play is concerned with the fate of an old bachelor who, having been driven into marriage with a beautiful girl, is betrayed by her. He subsequently assumes the role of her idealized lover, in the process of which he stabs himself and in dying bequeaths his soul to her. Again, the composer barely tampers with the structure of García Lorca's original. However, while the score is naturally dominated by the magical elements of the story (enhanced by luminous orchestration which includes prominent roles for celesta, vibraphone and harpsichord), Fortner also exploits the moments of grotesquery and tragedy. Don Perlimplin is divided into four scenes, each of which has a specific musical form derived from a permutation of the initial 12-note row. The work achieves a high level of integration between text and music which, despite the use of Spanish colouring and baroque-like harpsichord figurations, succeeds in avoiding a direct association with any specific time or place. In contrast to the dreamlike world of Don Perlimplin, the composer's next opera Elisabeth Tudor (1972), commissioned by the Deutsche Oper in Berlin, grapples with the political rivalry between Elizabeth I and Mary, Queen of Scots, during the latter part of the 16th century. It remains his most ambitious dramatic composition, marshalling huge orchestral and choral forces and requiring principal singers with virtuoso vocal techniques. The musical language similarly covers a wide diversity of idioms ranging from strict organized forms to freely improvised sections and from jazz-like street ballads to quotation and collage of English dance music. Yet the opera's ultimate impact is diffused by a multiplicity of scenes which lack clarity by attempting to portray too much historical detail on stage.

See also BLUTHOCHZEIT, DIE.

Cress ertrinkt, 1930 (Schulspiel, 3, A. Zeitler), vs (Mainz, 1931)
Der Wald (1, E. Beck, after F. García Lorca), Hesse Radio, 25 June 1953
Die Bluthochzeit (lyrische Tragödie, 2, Beck, after García Lorca: *Bodas de sangre*), Cologne, Städtische Oper, 8 June 1957, vs (Mainz, 1957)
Corinna (ob, 1, H. Schmidt, after G. de Labrunie de Nerval), Berlin, 3 Oct 1958
In seinem Garten liebt Don Perlimplin Belisa (Kammerspiel, 4 scenes, Beck, after García Lorca: *Amor de Don Perlimplín con Belisa en su jardín*), Schwetzingen, 10 May 1962, vs (Mainz, 1962)
Undine (school op, 1, A. Schäfer), Ober Hammbach, 21 May 1969
Elisabeth Tudor (3 and epilogue, M. Braun), Berlin, Deutsche Oper, 23 Oct 1972, vs (Mainz, 1972)
That Time [Damals] (scenic cantata, 1, S. Beckett), Baden-Baden, 24 April 1977 (Mainz, 1977)

*

W. Fortner: '"Bluthochzeit" nach Federico García Lorca', Melos, xxiv (1957), 71–3
E. Wilde: 'Das Wort zwingt die Musik hinzu: "Die Bluthochzeit", Oper von Wolfgang Fortner in Köln', Theater der Zeit, xii/9 (1957), 54–7
H. Lindlar, ed.: Wolfgang Fortner: eine Monographie (Rodenkirchen, 1960)
E. Beck: 'In seinem Garten liebt Don Perlimplin Belisa', Melos, xxix (1962), 109–11
W. Fortner: 'Wieder ein Lorca?', Melos, xxix (1962), 106–8

K. H. Ruppel: 'W. Fortners neue Oper', *SMz*, cii (1962), 248–50

F. Döhl: 'Oper als lyrisches Kammerspiel', *NZM*, Jg.125 (1964), 183–7

H. H. Stuckenschmidt: 'Grosser königlicher Streit in Fortners "Elisabeth Tudor"', *Melos*, xxxix (1972), 363–6

U. Stürzbecher: *Werkstattgespräche mit Komponisten* (Munich, 1973), 101–11

W. Fortner: 'Die Oper als Tor zu neuen Klangräumen', *Neue Musikzeitung*, iii/2 (1980) [interview]   ERIK LEVI

Förtsch, Johann Philipp (*b* Wertheim am Main, bap. 14 May 1652; *d* Eutin, nr Lübeck, 14 Dec 1732). German composer. After early training in Frankfurt, he studied at Jena and Erfurt (1671–4). He then travelled extensively in Germany and France; he must have continued his musical training, perhaps working with Johann Philipp Krieger. In 1678 Förtsch moved to Hamburg, at first singing with the Ratschor but soon joining the opera as a singer. In 1680 he succeeded Theile as director of the Hofkapelle at Gottorf, the residence of Christian Albrecht of Schleswig-Holstein, returning to Hamburg more than once because of a war with Denmark. Between 1684 and 1690 he became the foremost composer of the Hamburg opera, writing at least 12 works. He then ended his official connection with music to pursue a lengthy and remarkable career as a physician, politican and diplomat.

Förtsch began his brief period with the Hamburg opera just six years after the opening of the theatre, and his operas were almost the only ones heard there during this period. Unfortunately all of them seem to be lost; so also are two MS collections containing 20 arias from seven of them, though excerpts were published by Wolff. From these excerpts one can perceive a strongly personal style, characteristically German in its use of strophic, songlike arias and strong bass lines and in its affective rhythmic and harmonic treatment of the words.

Croesus (L. von Bostel, after N. Minato), Hamburg, 1684

Das unmöglichste Ding (von Bostel, after F. Lope de Vega: *El mayor impossible*), Hamburg, 1684

Alexander in Sidon (Förtsch, after op by M. A. Ziani), Hamburg, 1688

Die heilige Eugenia (C. H. Postel), Hamburg, 1688

Der im Christentum biss in den Tod beständige Märtyrer Polyeuct (H. Elmenhorst), Hamburg, 1688

Das betrübte und erfreute Cimbria (Postel), Hamburg, 1689

Cain und Abel (Postel), Hamburg, 1689

Xerxes in Abydus (after Minato), Hamburg, 1689

Ancile Romanum, das ist Des Römischen Reichs Glücks-Schild (Postel), Hamburg, 1690

Bajazeth und Tamerlan (Postel, after C. Marlowe), Hamburg, 1690

Die grossmächtige Thalestris, oder Letzte Königin der Amazonen (Postel), Hamburg, 1690

Der irrende Ritter Don Quixotte de la Mancia (H. Hinsch, after M. de Cervantes: *Don Quixote*), Hamburg, 1690

20 arias from 7 of the above, formerly *D-Hs*, lost

*

WaltherML

W. Schulze: *Die Quellen der Hamburger Oper* (Hamburg, 1938)

C. Weidemann: *Leben und Wirken des Johann Philipp Förtsch* (Kassel, 1955)

H. C. Wolff: *Die Barockoper in Hamburg* (Wolfenbüttel, 1957)
                    GEORGE J. BUELOW

Fortunati, Gian Francesco (*b* Parma, 27 Feb 1746; *d* Parma, 20 Dec 1821). Italian composer. Following studies in Piacenza and Bologna (with Padre Martini) he returned to Parma, where in 1769 his first opera, *I cacciatori e la vendilatte*, was staged and well received. He succeeded Traetta as *maestro di cappella* there, becoming director of the singing school (1774) and con-

ductor of the orchestra at the ducal theatre (1780–96). He made several journeys to Germany, on the recommendation of Maria Amalia, Duchess of Parma, to superintend performances of his operas, and also composed vocal and instrumental music there. Fortunati's output is of no extraordinary interest; it soon waned in popularity and was dropped from opera repertories. His importance as a teacher was more lasting – among his pupils was Ferdinando Paer.

I cacciatori e la vendilatte (melodramma giocoso), Parma, Ducale, 1769

La notte critica (L. Salvoni, after C. Goldoni), Parma, Ducale, 1771

Le gare degli amanti (melodramma giocoso, Salvoni), Colorno, Real, 1772

Le négociant (opera comica), Berlin, 1772, *D-Bds*

Ipermestra (os, P. Metastasio), Modena, Corte, 1773

L'ospite incomodo (dg), Parma, Colorno, aut. 1778

L'incontro inaspettato o fortunato, Parma, Ducale, 1800

Arias in: Antigono, *I-PAc*; Artaserse, *F-Pn*

*

P. Bettoli: *I nostri fasti musicali* (Parma, 1875), 82

P. E. Ferrari: *Gli spettacoli drammatico-musicali e coreografici in Parma dal 1628 al 1883* (Parma, 1884)

N. Pelicelli: 'Musicisti in Parma nel secolo XVIII', *NA*, xi (1934), 248–81, esp. 274–5

C. Gallico: *Le capitali della musica: Parma* (Milan, 1985)
                    GIAN PAOLO MINARDI

Fortune, George (*b* Boston, 13 Dec 1935). American baritone. He studied in Boston, making his début in 1960 as Nicolai's Ford at Ulm. In 1964 he sang the Count (*Capriccio*) at Glyndebourne, then began a 25-year association with the Deutsche Oper, Berlin, by singing Wolfram (1966). He appeared in the American première of *Boulevard Solitude* at Santa Fe (1967), at La Scala, in Vienna and throughout Germany. His repertory included Handel's Caesar, Count Almaviva, Figaro and Guglielmo, Enrico Ashton, Germont, Amonasro, Posa, Luna, Iago, Tomsky, Silvio, Barnaba, Marcello, Scarpia, Sharpless, Faninal and the Teacher (*Der Besuch der alten Dame*). A good actor, he had a firm, well-projected voice.   ELIZABETH FORBES

Fort Worth. American city in north-east Texas. It grew up around a military post established in 1849. A centre of the oil and cattle industries, Fort Worth has fostered many cultural institutions. In 1878 the Adah Richmond English Opera Troupe, consisting of 40 singers, an orchestra and chorus, presented two evenings of opera at Evans Hall, the first Fort Worth opera house, opened in 1876. The audiences were treated to performances of Planquette's *Les cloches de Corneville* and Offenbach's *La Périchole*. At the turn of the century several music clubs (notably the Harmony Club and the Euterpean Club) sponsored touring companies and occasionally presented their own productions. The companies included the Ellis Grand Opera Company, performing *Carmen* and *Il trovatore* (1916), and the Chicago Opera Company in *Aida*, *Madama Butterfly* and *La bohème* (1919). Early civic productions included Carl Venth's *Fair Betty* and Gounod's *Faust* (1917); many operas by Venth, dean of music at Texas Women's College, were performed during the 1910s and 20s.

In 1946 the Fort Worth Opera Association was formed and presented *La traviata*; it remains the longest continuously operating opera company in the state. It was directed from 1955 to 1982 by Rudolf Kruger, under whom four operas were given each season, but since 1984 three have been given per season, most of them staged at the Tarrant County Convention Center Theater.

Other operatic activity in Fort Worth has been associated with institutions of higher education. Texas Christian University and Texas Wesleyan University have music departments that occasionally give productions, as does the School of Church Music at Southwestern Baptist Theological Seminary. Fort Worth also houses Casa Manana, a theatre specializing in American musicals.

*

L. Spell: *Music in Texas* (Austin, 1936)
L. Sanders: *How Fort Worth Became the TexasMost City* (Fort Worth, 1973)
R. Davis: *Twentieth Century Cultural Life in Texas* (Boston, 1981)
GARY GIBBS

Forza del destino, La ('The Power of Fate' [*The Force of Destiny*]). Opera in four acts by GIUSEPPE VERDI to a libretto by FRANCESCO MARIA PIAVE after Angel de Saavedra, Duke of Rivas's play *Don Alvaro, o La fuerza del sino*, with a scene from FRIEDRICH VON SCHILLER's play *Wallensteins Lager*, translated by Andrea Maffei; St Petersburg, Imperial Theatre, 29 October/10 November 1862 (revised version, with additional text by ANTONIO GHISLANZONI, Milan, Teatro alla Scala, 27 February 1869).

The Marquis of Calatrava	bass
Donna Leonora *his daughter*	soprano
Don Carlo di Vargas *his son*	baritone
Don Alvaro	tenor
Preziosilla *a young gypsy*	mezzo-soprano
The Padre Guardiano	bass
Fra Melitone *a Franciscan*	baritone
Curra *Leonora's maid*	mezzo-soprano
An Alcalde	bass
Mastro Trabuco *a muleteer, then pedlar*	tenor
A Surgeon *(in the Spanish army)*	bass

Muleteers, Spanish and Italian peasants, Spanish and Italian soldiers of various rank, their orderlies, Italian recruits, Franciscan friars, poor mendicants, vivandières

Dancers Peasants, Spanish and Italian vivandières, Spanish and Italian soldiers

Walk-on parts Innkeeper, innkeeper's wife, servants at the inn, muleteers, Spanish and Italian soldiers, drummers, buglers, peasants and children of both nations, a tumbler, pedlars

Setting Spain and Italy, around the middle of the 18th century

After *Un ballo in maschera* (finished in early 1858), Verdi experienced his most serious compositional hiatus to date, repeatedly telling friends that he had ceased to be a composer and that his farmlands at S Agata now took up all his time. The breakthrough to fresh creativity came in late 1860 when the famous tenor Enrico Tamberlik wrote to Verdi offering him a commission from the Imperial Theatre at St Petersburg. Verdi first suggested Victor Hugo's *Ruy Blas*, which initially met with censorship problems and then apparently failed to hold the composer's interest. By the middle of 1861 he had decided on Rivas's *Don Alvaro*, a Spanish romantic melodrama, written under the influence of Hugo. The librettist was again to be Piave, although Verdi approached his friend and former collaborator

Andrea Maffei about using material from Schiller's *Wallensteins Lager* – a move that immediately indicated his intention of writing an opera of wide-ranging dramatic ambience. Serious work began on the opera in August 1861 and by November it was more or less complete (except, as usual, for the orchestration, which Verdi still preferred to complete nearer the time of performance, when he had experienced the singers and the theatrical acoustics at first hand). Verdi left for Russia in late 1861, but the première was postponed owing to the illness of the prima donna. He undertook several lengthy European trips during the first half of 1862 and returned to supervise rehearsals at St Petersburg in September of that year. The first performance, which starred Caroline Barbot (Leonora), Francesco Graziani (Carlo), Enrico Tamberlik (Alvaro) and Constance Nantier-Didiée (Preziosilla), was praised in some journals, but was at best only a moderate success.

It is clear that Verdi was not entirely happy with this or subsequent performances, and by 1863 he was talking of making alterations to the score, notably to the endings of Acts 3 and 4. Various large-scale structural alterations were discussed during the next few years with a view to a Parisian première in the mid-1860s, but pressure of other work caused plans to be shelved. Then in 1868 – after the première of *Don Carlos* at the Opéra – Verdi agreed to a new production of *La forza* at La Scala the following year (for illustration *see* FERRARIO, CARLO). The librettist Antonio Ghislanzoni was drafted to help with modifications (Piave had in 1867 succumbed to a stroke which incapacitated him for the rest of his life); Verdi eventually elected to replace the *preludio* with a full-scale overture, to revise portions of Act 3, make various minor alterations to other passages and, perhaps most important, to replace the bitter catastrophe of the final scene (in which all three principals die) with a scene of religious consolation. The La Scala cast, ably conducted by Angelo Mariani, included Teresa Stolz (Leonora), Luigi Colonnese (Carlo), Mario Tiberini (Alvaro) and Ida Benza (Preziosilla). The performance was a considerable success and *La forza* remained a popular element of the repertory during the later years of the 19th century. There is some evidence that Verdi was actively involved in a cut-down French version of the score, first heard in Antwerp in 1882; but this version seems to have survived only in vocal score and was never sanctioned by Verdi's publisher Ricordi.

The overture (which, as mentioned above, belongs to the 1869 version, though deriving from the shorter *preludio* of 1862) is a potpourri of the score's most memorable tunes. It begins with a solemn three-note unison (usually called the 'fate' motif) and then a driving string theme that proves to be the dominant idea. Subsequent melodies are taken, in order of appearance, from the final-act duet between Alvaro and Carlo, from Leonora's Act 2 aria, 'Madre, pietosa Vergine', and from Leonora's duet with Padre Guardiano (two themes, one associated with Leonora, one with the priest). The overture makes few concessions to classical ideas of balance, though it is given at least a surface impression of greater coherence by continual 'motivic' references to the main theme.

ACT 1 *The Marquis of Calatrava's house in Seville* After twice sounding the three-note unison that began the overture, the scene begins with a restrained string theme, though one whose syncopations and minor inflections hint at troubled undercurrents. The Marquis of Calatrava bids goodnight to his daughter, concerned by her sadness. Leonora can offer only anguished asides. As the Marquis retires, Curra begins preparations for Leonora's elopement. Leonora's indecision is intense, but Curra outlines the bloody consequences for Alvaro if he is now deserted. In the aria 'Me pellegrina ed orfana', which is in two contrasting sections and – as befits its dramatic position – involves no large-scale internal repetitions, Leonora bids a tender farewell to her homeland. The sound of approaching horses heralds Alvaro, who climbs in through a window. He immediately launches a duet, in four movements, conventionally patterned though economical. The first movement, 'Ah, per sempre', is dominated by Alvaro's impetuosity, but when Leonora shows signs of reluctance he settles into a more lyrical second movement ('Pronti destrieri'), which begins as a typical 3/8 wooing piece for romantic tenor but develops unusual vocal power as Alvaro recalls the gods of his native land. The third movement (somewhat revised for 1869) as usual injects new action: Leonora begs that the elopement be postponed another day, protesting her love amid weeping that makes Alvaro suspicious; he accuses her of not loving him; she passionately affirms her feelings – and so to the cabaletta, 'Seguirti fino agl'ultimi', in which the lovers prepare to depart, and which is skilfully structured so that the final, curtailed reprise is preceded and precipitated by the sound of approaching footsteps. A brief recitative, in which Alvaro draws his pistol, is followed by the 'scena-finale', an action movement dominated by the pulsating main theme of the overture, modulating rapidly and purposefully to match events onstage. The Marquis of Calatrava enters. He insults Alvaro, goading him to a duel; Alvaro refuses and throws down his pistol. But the weapon accidentally discharges, fatally wounding the old man, who with his dying breath curses his daughter. Alvaro and Leonora make their escape, thus closing one of the most tightly constructed, economical acts in all Verdi.

ACT 2.i *The village of Hornachuelos and its surroundings* This scene is as expansive and repetitious as the previous one was tight and economical. 18 months have passed. The sprightly opening chorus, 'Holà! Ben giungi, o mulattier', gives way to a peasant dance, both pieces richly imbued with Spanish local colour (the first more a little reminiscent of passages in *Il trovatore*). Supper is announced and a 'student' (in fact Don Carlo, in search of his sister and 'her seducer') says grace. The dance music continues. Leonora enters dressed as a young man, recognizes her brother and immediately retreats. The stage is now taken by Preziosilla, who encourages the young men to join battle against the Germans and sings a rousing canzone, 'Al suon del tamburo', a French-influenced strophic song with refrain which recalls Oscar's music in *Un ballo in maschera*. During the final stages of the song Preziosilla consents to read Carlo's fortune and predicts a miserable future.

A chorus of pilgrims is heard in the distance; their chant forms the basis of a large-scale concertato movement, 'Padre Eterno Signor', which is punctuated by Leonora's desperate cries for divine mercy. As the pilgrims depart, Carlo takes centre stage and treats the company to a narrative ballata, 'Son Pereda, son ricco d'onore': his name is Pereda and he has been helping a friend track down the friend's sister and her lover. The

predictable form and simple rhythm retain something of the comic opera atmosphere, although contrasting internal episodes give hints of tragic undercurrents. But Preziosilla and the others are happy enough, and the scene ends with some elaborate exchanges of 'goodnight' and a lively reprise of the opening chorus and dance tune.

2.ii *A small clearing on the slopes of a steep mountain* Leonora struggles towards the door of a monastery, and in a turbulent recitative recalls her horror at hearing her brother's story at the inn, especially his news that Alvaro, from whom she was separated in flight, has returned to his homeland in South America. She falls on her knees to beg divine forgiveness in the famous 'Madre, pietosa Vergine', which is cast as a minor–major *romanza*, the first part underpinned by an obsessive string motif, the second based on the aspiring melody that had served as climax to the overture.

Leonora rings the monastery bell and, as Melitone (a comic character) departs to find the Padre Guardiano (Father Superior), she sings a further arioso in which the overture's main theme is once again juxtaposed with the aspiring melody. The Padre appears and dismisses Melitone, so beginning one of the opera's grand duets. After a brief scene, the number falls into the conventional four movements, although with the basic difference that Leonora and the Padre have comparatively little interaction: both remain enclosed within their very different views of the world. The first movement, 'Infelice, delusa', is as usual a series of sharply contrasted episodes, as Leonora tells her story and begs for a refuge from life. The second movement, 'Chi può legger nel futuro', offers a brief respite as the two voices come together, but in the third contrast returns. Eventually the Padre agrees to help her, and they join in a final cabaletta, 'Sull'alba il piede all'eremo'.

The great door of the church opens and a long procession of monks files down the sides of the choir. In a solemn ritual, the Padre tells the monks that a hermit is to live in the holy cave, and that no one must invade his seclusion. All join in a curse on any violator, 'Il Cielo fulmini, incenerisca'. The act closes with a quiet, simple hymn, 'La Vergine degli Angeli', before Leonora sets off to her hermitage.

ACT 3.i *In Italy, near Velletri: a wood, at dead of night* A robust orchestral introduction and offstage chorus are hushed as Alvaro comes forward to the strains of a long clarinet solo, which elaborates a theme first heard in the Act 1 love duet. In an arioso punctuated by wisps of clarinet sound, Alvaro explains his noble birth and unhappy childhood. Then, in 'Oh, tu che in seno agli angeli', he asks Leonora (whom he believes dead) to look down on him from heaven. The aria begins in conventionally patterned phrases but soon takes on that 'progressive' form so typical of Verdi's later style.

Offstage noises disrupt Alvaro's pensive mood and he departs to investigate. Moments later he returns with Carlo, having saved him from assassins. The two hurriedly exchange false names and then swear eternal allegiance in a brief, sparsely accompanied duet. Further offstage cries alert them to a renewed enemy attack, and they rush off together.

3.ii *Morning: the quarters of a senior officer of the Spanish army* As the scene changes, the orchestra depicts a battle and a surgeon describes its progress. Although victory is announced, Alvaro is carried on severely wounded. Carlo tries to rally him, promising

'*La forza del destino*' (*Verdi*): *design by Andrey Adamovich Roller for Act 4 scene i (the monastery of Our Lady of the Angels)
in the original production at the Imperial Theatre, St Petersburg, 29 October/10 November 1862*

the Order of Calatrava; but Alvaro reacts violently to the name. The wounded man requests a private interview with Carlo, and in the famous duet 'Solenne in quest'ora' entrusts his new friend with the key to a case wherein lies a packet to be burnt if Alvaro dies. The 'duet', dominated by Alvaro, is reminiscent of a traditional minor–major *romanza*: the opening minor section as the tenor issues his solemn commands, the major emerging as he rejoices that he can now die in peace.

Left alone, Carlo recalls Alvaro's reaction at the name of Calatrava and begins to suspect that he may be Leonora's seducer. He is tempted to break open the packet, but in 'Urna fatale', a cantabile within whose *primo ottocento* conventionality is buried powerful progressive elements, he tells how his honour forbids him from finding the truth. He looks elsewhere in the case and soon finds a portrait of Leonora. Just then the surgeon announces that Alvaro will live and Carlo, knowing he will now be able to wreak his vengeance, breaks into a cabaletta of savage joy, 'Egli è salvo!'

3.iii *A military encampment near Velletri* In the 1862 version the scene progresses from a long choral episode to the quarrel between Alvaro and Carlo, an off-stage duel, and then a double aria for Alvaro; the 1869 version – which defers the choral episode to the end of the act, has the duel onstage and omits Alvaro's aria – has much to commend it, not least that it clarifies the action and shortens one of Verdi's most demanding tenor roles.

The scene opens with a *ronda*, 'Compagni, sostiamo' (new for 1869), a comic-opera style chorus in which a patrol makes a tour of inspection. Alvaro enters, accompanied by the minor-mode version of the clarinet theme that introduced him earlier in the act. Carlo joins him and, after innocently inquiring whether his wounds are healed (we must assume that several days have passed), calls Alvaro by his true name, so precipitating a grand duet. The first movement is the traditional series of contrasting sections: Carlo reveals his own identity,

Alvaro protests his innocence and finally Carlo informs Alvaro that Leonora is still alive. The second movement, 'No, d'un imene il vincolo', is a powerfully 'dissimilar' Andantino, in which Alvaro celebrates the news of his beloved's survival only to be confounded by Carlo's insistence on revenge. This leads swiftly to a closing cabaletta, 'Morte! Ov'io non cada', in which the two swear mutual defiance and begin to fight. But they are separated by a passing patrol; Carlo is dragged off, and Alvaro casts aside his sword, swearing that he will seek refuge in the cloister.

Rolls on the side drum introduce the sequence of choruses and brief solos that will close the act. First comes 'Lorchè pifferi e tamburi', a brief, lively chorus that leads directly into Preziosilla's two-strophe French-influenced song 'Venite all'indovina', in which she offers to tell the soldiers' fortunes. A further brief round of choral celebrations precedes Trabuco's 'A buon mercato', a Jewish pedlar song in which the chorus again joins. The mood darkens with the next episode, in which a group of beggars, their lands destroyed by the war, are followed by a group of miserable conscripts. But some vivandières and Preziosilla soon brighten the atmosphere, leading the conscripts in a tarantella. Melitone enters as the dance is at full tilt and treats the company to an elaborate comic sermon (the passage is taken almost word for word from Maffei's translation of Schiller's *Wallensteins Lager*). The soldiers eventually tire of Melitone and chase him away, leaving Preziosilla to round off the act with the famous 'Rataplan' chorus.

ACT 4.i *Inside the monastery of Our Lady of the Angels, near Hornachuelos* Five years have passed. A crowd of beggars appears, quickly followed by Melitone carrying a cauldron of soup. In a comic-opera *parlante*, Melitone chides the beggars for asking too much, continuing even when the Padre Guardiano advises kindness to the suffering poor. Eventually Melitone's patience runs out: he kicks the pot over and orders the beggars away in the comic cabaletta 'Il resto, a voi prendetevi'. In the subsequent recitative, Melitone mentions to the Padre the strange behaviour of 'Father Raffaele' (who, we soon guess, is none other than Alvaro). The Padre counsels patience in a brief closing duet, 'Del mondo i disinganni', which contrasts his solemn ecclesiastical style with Melitone's frankly comic idiom.

The monastery bell rings loudly; Melitone answers to find Carlo, who dispatches him to seek 'Father Raffaele'. In the ensuing recitative Carlo reiterates his desire to avenge the family honour. Alvaro enters, thus starting a grand duet in which the traditional four movements are still present though radically altered in the light of the dramatic situation. The first movement, 'Col sangue sol cancellasi', offers the usual stark contrasts: Carlo's calls for a duel are underpinned by a martial theme in the orchestra, while Alvaro's offers of peace are more lyrical and subdued. The central Andante, 'Le minacce, i fieri accenti', based on the second theme of the overture, is of the 'dissimilar' type, with Alvaro's opening melody repeated by Carlo with agitated orchestral accompaniment. The movement breaks down as Carlo taunts Alvaro as a half-breed: this is too much, and Alvaro takes up the challenge. Before rushing off to fight, the two offer mutual defiance in a very brief, coda-like cabaletta, 'Ah, segnasti la tua sorte!'

4.ii *A valley amid inaccessible rocks* Strains of the overture's main theme introduce Leonora, pale, worn and in great agitation. Her famous aria, 'Pace, pace, mio Dio!', in which she restates her love for Alvaro and begs God for peace, is like a distant homage to Bellini, whose 'long, long, long melodies' Verdi had so admired. Length indeed is here, as is the simple arpeggiated accompaniment typical of Bellini, but Verdi's line is injected with declamatory asides and harmonic shifts, a perfect expression of the new aesthetic that had overtaken Italian opera. As the aria comes to a close, she takes up food left by Padre Guardiano, but retreats hurriedly as others approach.

In the 1862 version, the opera's final scene reached a bloody conclusion. Alvaro and Carlo enter duelling; Carlo falls mortally wounded; Alvaro summons Leonora. On recognizing each other they sing a brief duet before Carlo calls Leonora to him as he dies, and, vengeful to the last, stabs her fatally. The heroine has a final, intense arioso, 'Vedi destino! io muoio!', before dying in Alvaro's arms. Sounds are heard below, and the monks appear. Padre Guardiano calls Alvaro, but he retreats to the highest point of the mountain and hurls himself into the abyss. For 1869 Verdi decided on a radical change. The opening arioso, which includes the offstage duel up to Alvaro and Leonora's meeting, is largely the same, but there is no duettino for the lovers, merely a continuation of the declamation until Leonora departs to help her brother. Alvaro has time for a brief soliloquy before an offstage scream interrupts him. Leonora, mortally wounded, is led on by Padre Guardiano: furious, dissonant 'death figures' in the orchestra cause a breakdown in the musical flow. But from this arises the final, lyrical trio, 'Non imprecare, umiliati', led off in the minor by Padre Guardiano. At first the two lovers can offer only fragmentary comments, but then the music turns to major, and a new, transfiguring melody arises from the orchestra, over which Alvaro declaims that he is 'redeemed'. Leonora leads off the final section, which concludes the opera with a sense of resolution and lyrical space.

*   *   *

La forza del destino reached something of a low point in the early years of this century, its sprawling action and mixture of comic, tragic and picturesque finding no resonance in a climate dominated by the Wagnerian model. But times have changed, and since the 1930s the opera has become one of the most popular of Verdi's works after the three middle-period masterpieces. This swing of fortune suggests an important shift in our expectations of what constitutes satisfying musical drama, because *La forza* is undoubtedly Verdi's most daring attempt at creating a 'patchwork' drama – or, as he once called it, an 'opera of ideas'. We look in vain for the kind of unifying colours found in *Rigoletto* or *Il trovatore*, and it is surely no accident that Verdi's 1869 revision could so radically change certain sequences in the action, even – as in Act 3 – transferring passages from one part of a scene to another. The opera is, in other words, only loosely linear: a significant precursor of 'native' Russian operas such as *Prince Igor* and *Boris Godunov*.

The presence of certain recurring themes, in particular the main theme of the overture (frequently dubbed a 'destiny' or 'fate' motif) has often been mentioned by commentators and is sometimes advanced as exemplifying the score's 'musical unity'. Perhaps that is so, but one could equally well see these recurring elements as an attempt to give some semblance of musical connectedness to a score that conspicuously lacks the cohesion Verdi so effortlessly achieved in his middle-period works. Nor, of course, are the themes used in anything like a consistent manner. An opera such as this, whose time gaps and scope make necessary a steady sequence of narratives (all the major characters are obliged to explain their past actions to each other), might easily have used a system of recurring motifs on a large scale. Nothing like that is attempted; indeed, in one sense the recurring motifs by their very literalness alert us to the extravagant gaps that are constantly and excitingly thrown up by this most challenging of works.

ROGER PARKER

Forzano, Giovacchino (*b* Borgo San Lorenzo, Florence, 19 Nov 1884; *d* Rome, 18 Oct 1970). Italian playwright, librettist and director. After studying medicine he began his career as a baritone, and then turned to the study of law. Having graduated, he became the editor of several newspapers including *La nazione* in Florence. At the auction of Ouida's effects in 1914 he was called in as literary expert and so made the acquaintance of Puccini, who was interested in acquiring the rights of her novel *The Two Little Wooden Shoes*; though successful, Puccini abandoned the subject, which Forzano later turned into an opera for Mascagni under the title *Lodoletta*. He collaborated with Puccini on *Suor Angelica* and *Gianni Schicchi*, the last two panels of *Il trittico*, having declined *Il tabarro* on the grounds that he preferred to devise his own plots. Of his plays the most successful was *Campo di maggio* (1930) which achieved a number of performances abroad. Again to Puccini he offered an operatic adaptation of his *Sly* (1920), expanded from the prologue to Shakespeare's *The Taming of the Shrew*; but the composer lost interest after seeing the play, and the libretto was eventually set by Wolf-Ferrari. As stage director of La Scala, Forzano mounted Boito's *Nerone* (1924) and Puccini's *Turandot* (1926). His volume of reminiscences, *Come li ho conosciuti* (Turin, 1957), provides revealing sidelights on the composers with whom he had worked.

Notte di leggenda, Franchetti, 1915; *Lodoletta*, Mascagni, 1917; *Suor Angelica*, Puccini, 1918; *Gianni Schicchi*, Puccini, 1918; *Edipo re*, Leoncavallo, 1920; *Il piccolo Marat* (with G. Targioni-Tozzetti), Mascagni, 1921; *Ciottolino*, Ferrari Trecate, 1922; *Glauco*, Franchetti, 1922; *I compagnazzi*, P. Riccitelli, 1923; *Giocondo e il suo re*, Jachino, 1924; *Gli amanti sposi* (with others), Wolf-Ferrari, 1925; *Delitto e castigo*, Pedrollo, 1926; *Sly, ovvero La leggenda del dormiente risvegliato*, Wolf-Ferrari, 1927; *Il re*, Giordano, 1929; *Palla de' mozzi*, G. Marinuzzi (i), 1932

J. W. Klein: 'Giovacchino Forzano, 1884–1970', *Opera*, xxii (1971), 303–8
JULIAN BUDDEN

Fosca. *Opera seria* in four acts by CARLOS GOMES to a libretto by ANTONIO GHISLANZONI after Luigi Capranica's novel *La festa delle Mary*; Milan, Teatro alla Scala, 16 February 1873.

The action takes place in the middle of the 10th century, in Venice and on the Istrian coast. A group of pirates led by Gajolo (tenor) are planning their next adventure: the kidnapping of the rich brides on the day of their wedding, the 'Feast of the Marys'. Fosca (soprano), Gajolo's sister, is passionately in love with Paolo (tenor), who has been captured by the pirates. She declares her love to Paolo who, however, responds that he is engaged to Delia (soprano). Senator Giotta (bass), Paolo's father, arrives to pay the ransom and free his son. While Fosca laments Paolo's departure, Cambro (baritone), Gajolo's Venetian slave who is in love with her, proposes to bring Paolo back on condition that she marry him. In her anger she accepts. On the day of the wedding, in front of the church, the pirates prepare to execute their kidnapping plan. Seeing Paolo and Delia, Fosca attempts to block their way into the church. In the confusion Gajolo is taken prisoner by Venetian soldiers, Cambro kidnaps Delia, and Paolo is once more captured by the pirates. Cambro, who hopes to become the pirates' new leader, continues his intrigues to win Fosca over. In Venice, in front of the senators and the doge, Gajolo offers to save Paolo and Delia in return for his freedom. Fosca urges Delia to take poison and save Paolo's life by her death, but Gajolo arrives in time to free them, regaining his leadership and eliminating Cambro. Fosca then takes the poison and dies asking Paolo and Delia for forgiveness.

The première was a failure because of a quarrel between the defenders of Italian bel canto and the Wagnerian reformers; the latter supposedly comprised all foreigners, including Gomes. A new version, however, achieved considerable success when it was staged at La Scala on 7 February 1878. The most italianate of Gomes's operas, *Fosca* is considered one of his best musical achievements, in terms of both its dramatic structure (supported by a good libretto) and its rich melodic inventiveness. Although the work includes a number of leitmotifs elaborated somewhat in the Wagnerian fashion, its general style and treatment reflect a direct influence from Verdi.
GERARD BÉHAGUE

Foss [Fuchs], Lukas (*b* Berlin, 15 Aug 1922). American composer, conductor and pianist of German parentage. He began to compose at seven and later studied composition with Noël Gallon in Paris (1933–7), with Randall Thompson at the Curtis Institute (from 1937) and with Hindemith at Yale University (1939–40). His other teachers included Koussevitzky and Fritz Reiner for conducting. He has held many appointments as orchestral director and conductor, and was professor of composition and conducting at UCLA (1953–63).

His many awards have included a Guggenheim fellowship (1945), a fellowship at the American Academy in Rome (1950–51) and a Fulbright grant (1950–52).

Foss's three operas, ranging from nine minutes to full length, date from the period 1949–59, when his style evolved from neo-classical and the American folklore tradition, to avant-garde experimentalism. His first and most often-performed opera, *The Jumping Frog of Calaveras County* (1949), is a tall story from the Old West, told mostly in choruses and ensembles. A mysterious Stranger comes to the gold-rush town of Calaveras, hoodwinks the townspeople in a rigged frog-jumping contest, and receives his come-uppance at the end.

Griffelkin (1955), commissioned by NBC Television, is based on the story *The Little Devil's Birthday*, which Foss's mother told him when he was eight, and which inspired one of his first attempts to compose. Foss asked Alastair Reid to supply a libretto based on his mother's story, and composed new music 'for children of my own age, now thirty-three'. The cast consists of adult singers, with an optional children's chorus. Griffelkin, a devil child, receives a birthday present of 24 hours in the world, to work as much mischief as he wants. Armed with a magic elixir that brings inanimate objects to life and turns living things to stone, he arrives in New York City, where he has comical adventures. But the world corrupts him: he falls in love with the blue sky and a little girl, and finally, in desperation, he commits a good deed. For this, he is expelled from Hell, to re-enter the world as a mortal boy, knowing about mother-love, beauty and death. When *Griffelkin* was staged in Karlsruhe in 1972, a programme annotator found in it 'the spirit of the Classical *opera buffa*' and influences of Hindemith, Stravinsky and the Broadway musical. The scoring of the various incidents is witty and picturesque, emphasizing transparent wind sonorities and sometimes alluding slyly to other operas, such as *Falstaff*, *Hänsel und Gretel* and *Der Rosenkavalier*. The Grandmother's aria ('You have learned to bewitch') is based on Mozart's keyboard sonata in C major k545.

Introductions and Good-Byes (1959), commissioned by Menotti for the 1960 Spoleto Festival, is a whimsical attempt to squeeze an entire opera (defined by Foss as 'overture, solos, ensembles; a work which begins, develops, comes to a close') into nine minutes. The libretto consists of pleasantries exchanged at a cocktail party by the host, Mr McC. (baritone), and his guests (nine silent actors, their lines sung from the pit) during their arrivals and departures. A xylophone provides 'Dry-Martini music' in the prelude and epilogue. The text is made up mostly of the fanciful names of the guests (e.g. Miss Addington-Stitch, General Ortega y Guadalupe, Dr Lavender-Gas), which inspire much of the musical imagery.

Around 1980 Foss composed recitatives for the dialogue in Mozart's *Der Schauspieldirektor*, to bring the work closer to what he considers its true nature, an *opera buffa*.

See also JUMPING FROG OF CALAVERAS COUNTY, THE.

The Jumping Frog of Calaveras County (comic op, 1, J. Karsavina, after M. Twain), Bloomington, Indiana U., 18 May 1950
Griffelkin (children's op, 3, A. Reid, after German fairy-tale), NBC Television, 6 Nov 1955; stage, Tanglewood, MA, 6 Aug 1956
Introductions and Good-Byes (nine-minute op, 1, G. C. Menotti), concert perf., New York, 5 May 1960; stage, Spoleto, June 1960

CBY 1966; EwenD; VintonD

L. Kerner: 'The Philharmonic at Cross-Purposes', *Village Voice* (3 Jan 1984), 72

H. Kupferberg: 'Lukas Foss: Newfound Focus for the Composer-Conductor', *Ovation*, v (1984), April, 12–17

L. Francombe: '1985–86 Premieres and Season Highlights', *Symphony*, xxxvi/5 (1985), 45 [première of *Griffelkin* suite]

R. Pace: 'Lukas Foss: Wild Thing', *Ear*, xiii/Dec–Jan (1988–9), 25

L. Kerner: 'Brooklyn Ablaze', *Village Voice* (14 Feb 1989), 84

K. Campbell: 'New Horizons for an Avant-Garde Classicist', *Symphony*, xl/3 (1989), 14–19   DAVID WRIGHT

Foster, Lawrence (Thomas) (*b* Los Angeles, 23 Oct 1941). American conductor. He studied in Los Angeles and attended the Bayreuth Festival master classes, 1961–3, and the Berkshire Music Center, Tanglewood, in 1966 and 1967, winning the Koussevitzky Conducting Prize in his first year there. He conducted opera briefly at Stuttgart in 1964, and began an association with Scottish Opera in 1974. He made his Covent Garden début in 1976, conducting the revised version of Walton's *Troilus and Cressida* in which Janet Baker sang. In 1979 he was appointed chief conductor at Monte Carlo; he was also Generalmusikdirektor of Duisburg, 1981–8. His performances of music in all styles are marked by rhythmic vitality and great structural intelligence.   MICHAEL STEINBERG

Fotek, Jan (*b* Czerwińsk nad Wisłą, 28 Nov 1928). Polish composer. He studied composition with Stanisław Wiechowicz in Kraków and with Szeligowski in Warsaw. Fotek exists on the fringes of postwar Polish music, tangling rarely with the avant-garde techniques of his compatriots (except in early orchestral pieces such as *Epitasis*, 1967). His stage works likewise remain on the margins of Polish operatic composition, although *Leśna królewna* ('The Woodland Princess', 1978) has gained a measure of success because of its effectiveness as an opera-ballet for children.

all unpublished

Morze jedności odnalezionej [The Sea of Recovered Unity] (poetic radio op, 3 pts, B. Ostromęcki), Polish Radio, 1967

Galileusz [Galileo], 1969 (musical drama, 2, M. Konopnicka), unperf.

Vir sapiens dominabitur astris (radio opera-oratorio, Z. Jasińska, after Copernicus, St Francis, Dante Alighieri, Michelangelo, Słowacki, Norwid and others), Polish Radio, 1973

Łyżki i księżyc [The Spoons and the Moon], 1973–6 (opera-burlesque, 3, Fotek, after E. Zegadłowicz), unperf.

Leśna królewna [The Woodland Princess] (opera-ballet, 2 pts, Fotek, after J. Tuwim and A. Oppman), Warsaw, Wielki, 3 June 1978

Człowiek i aniołowie [Man and Angels], 1982 ('misterium sacrum' chamber op), unperf.   ADRIAN THOMAS

Fourestier, Louis (Félix André) (*b* Montpellier, 31 May 1892; *d* Boulogne-Billancourt, 30 Sept 1976). French conductor and composer. He studied at the Montpellier Conservatory and from 1909 at the Paris Conservatoire with Leroux and Gédalge. After winning the Prix de Rome in 1925 he was appointed conductor at the Opéra-Comique (1927–32), and in 1938 he moved to a similar post at the Paris Opéra. He also made tours throughout France and abroad, and in 1946–8 he conducted at the Metropolitan Opera. His début there was with *Lakmé*, followed by *Carmen*, *Manon*, *Louise* and Gounod's *Faust*. From 1945 to 1963 he was professor of conducting at the Paris Conservatoire.   PAUL GRIFFITHS

Fournet, Jean (*b* Rouen, 14 April 1913). French conductor. He studied at the Paris Conservatoire and made his début at Rouen in 1936. His first appointments were there (1938) and in Marseilles (1940), and from 1944 to 1957 he was music director at the Opéra-Comique in Paris. Fournet has toured as a guest conductor in Europe, North and South America, Israel and Japan; he conducted the first performance in Tokyo (1958) of *Pelléas et Mélisande*. He made his début with the Chicago Lyric Opera in 1965, and at the Metropolitan in 1987 with *Samson et Dalila*. Admired for his meticulous and exacting craftsmanship, he has a wide repertory that lays particular emphasis on Berlioz, Debussy and Ravel, and he has been much praised for his performances of *Dialogues des Carmélites* on both sides of the Atlantic. His recording in 1955 at the Opéra-Comique of Rossini's *Il barbiere di Siviglia*, in French with spoken dialogue, was reissued (as a compact disc) in 1988.

CHRISTIANE SPIETH-WEISSENBACHER,
NOËL GOODWIN

Four Saints in Three Acts. 'An opera to be sung' in a prologue and four acts by VIRGIL THOMSON to a libretto by GERTRUDE STEIN with scenario by Maurice Grosser; Wadsworth Atheneum, Hartford, Connecticut, 8 February 1934.

St Settlement	lyric soprano
Commère	mezzo-soprano
Compère	bass
St Teresa I	soprano
St Teresa II	contralto
St Ignatius	baritone
St Chavez	tenor

Choral roles St Plan, St Stephen, St Sara, St Cecilia, St Celestine, St Lawrence, St Jan, St Placide, St Absalon, St Eustace, St Genevieve, St Anne, St Answers

Setting Spain, in the 16th century

Thomson met Stein, a poet and playwright older and more famous than he, in 1926, when they were both living in Paris. By early the following year they were planning an opera. Thomson, whose musical idiom was born of the Baptist hymns of his Kansas City youth by way of Erik Satie, was drawn to Stein, who 'liked rhymes and jingles and ... had no fear of the commonplace'. Her love for artfully constructed verbal edifices using the simplest of means, her contrapuntal interweaving of repeated words and phrases, as well as her childlike abstraction, all defined an inherently musical sensibility. 'She wrote poetry ... very much as a composer works', Thomson recalled. 'She chose a theme and developed it, or rather, she let the words of it develop themselves through the free expansion of sound and sense ... I took my musical freedom, following her poetic freedom, and what came out was a virtually total recall of my Southern Baptist childhood in Missouri.'

The theme Stein and Thomson chose for their first opera was the lives of 16th-century Spanish saints. 'We saw among the religious a parallel to the life we were leading', Thomson wrote, 'in which consecrated artists were practicing their art surrounded by younger artists who were no less consecrated, and who were trying to learn and needing to learn the terrible disciplines of truth and spontaneity, of channeling their skills without loss of inspiration.'

The music was composed between June 1927 and July 1928, but not orchestrated until 1933. Its style was direct and accessible, in the manner of Kurt Weill and other exponents of a folksy leftism in the 1930s but purged of any political subtext. For the première, Thomson's friend, the painter Maurice Grosser, provided a scenario sympathetic to Stein's dreamy poetic abstraction, yet offering some clues as to the significance of this enigmatic work.

The first performance, on 8 February 1934 at the Wadsworth Atheneum in Hartford, Connecticut, was presented not by an established opera company but by an organization called the Friends and Enemies of Modern Music. There was an all-black cast, stage direction and movement by Frederick Ashton and John Houseman and cellophane décor by Florine Stettheimer. The same production was presented that year on Broadway and in Chicago, for a run of more than 60 performances. Despite this success, which established Thomson as an intellectuals' darling, and which vastly augmented Stein's notoriety ('Pigeons on the grass alas' from the third act became a humorist's watchword for vanguard silliness), the opera has never entered the repertory of major opera houses. This is partly because Stein's poetry is something of an acquired taste, and partly because Thomson's *faux-naif* music now seems prescient of minimalism. Its chamber scoring (for an orchestra of about 25, using modest strings) has, however, made it a feasible work for smaller companies. Thomson insisted that the precedent of an all-black cast need not be considered binding, but major productions with white or mixed casts have remained rare, and most companies find it difficult to assemble all-black casts of this size. This synopsis is drawn from Grosser's scenario; it could not be deduced from Stein's words alone. The music throughout is an American patchwork of marches, waltzes, hymns and singsong recitative.

PROLOGUE   A choral introduction to all the saints, some 30 counting the chorus, but concentrating on the four principals (with St Teresa sung by two singers) and including the Commère and Compère.

ACT 1 ('A Pageant, or Sunday School Entertainment') *On the steps of Avila Cathedral*   This consists of seven tableaux focussed on St Teresa II and revealed through a portal by the drawing of a small curtain. The first tableau shows St Teresa II in an early-spring garden, painting Easter eggs and conversing with St Teresa I. In the second scene St Teresa II, holding a dove, is photographed by St Settlement. St Ignatius serenades the seated St Teresa II in the third scene, at the end of which she rises and asks, 'Can women have wishes?' (Stein was an early feminist). St Ignatius offers St Teresa II flowers in the fourth tableau, and in the fifth the two saints admire a model house, a Heavenly Mansion. In the sixth, St Teresa II is shown in 'an attitude of ecstasy'. Finally, she rocks an imaginary child in her arms: 'The act ends with comments, congratulations, and general sociability.'

ACT 2 *A garden party in the country near Barcelona*   The Compère and Commère, dressed in formal attire, observe the action from the side. A Dance of Angels is performed, St Chavez organizes a game and the Compère and Commère share 'a tender scene', observed by the two St Teresas. Everyone peers through a telescope at a vision of the Heavenly Mansion. As all pack to leave, St Ignatius refuses to give back St Teresa I's telescope; St Chavez consoles her, and remains alone on stage after the others depart.

ACT 3 *A monastery garden on the coast near Barcelona*   St Ignatius and his Jesuits mend fishing nets. The two St Teresas and St Settlement discuss monastic life with St Ignatius and see a vision of the Holy Ghost ('Pigeons on the grass alas', etc.). After a military drill St Chavez lectures the men; the women saints enter, doubt the vision, and are reproved by St Ignatius, who predicts the Last Judgment. After a storm passes, the saints file

'Four Saints in Three Acts' (Thomson): Prologue from the original production at Wadsworth Atheneum, Hartford, Connecticut, 8 February 1934

out, chanting and singing hymns about their future heavenly life.

ACT 4 The Compère and Commère argue before the curtain as to whether there should be a fourth act. The curtain rises to reveal the saints in heaven. They remember with pleasure their earthly existence and sing a communion hymn ('When this you see remember me'). The opera ends when the Compère sings, 'Last act', and everyone else shouts, 'Which is a fact'.

* * *

Despite its infrequency of performance, *Four Saints* and Thomson's music in general have risen steadily in prestige, especially since the waning of total serialism among American academic composers after the 1970s. Thomson's style is seen now as an anticipation not just of minimalism, but of the entire movement towards simplicity, accessibility and vernacular inspiration that has defined composition in the 1980s and 90s.

JOHN ROCKWELL

Fowles, Glenys (*b* Perth, 4 Nov ?1947). Australian soprano. After a début as Micaëla with the Western Australian Opera Company she was a prizewinner in the Metropolitan Opera Auditions in 1968 and then made a pert and graceful début with the Australian Opera as Oscar, rapidly becoming one of the company's most favoured young sopranos in both lyric and florid roles. From 1974 to 1981 she maintained a full-time operatic career in the USA, an unusual achievement for an Australian. Her roles with the New York City Opera included Micaëla, Mélisande (successfully essayed at short notice, 1976), Poppaea, Susanna, Mimì and Liù. Among many other North American and European appearances, she has sung Ilia at Glyndebourne and Sophie and Titania for Scottish Opera. As her luminous Juliet demonstrates, she is almost ideally endowed for opera, but her obvious calculation of artifice in voice and manner has sometimes seemed to hinder her communication with an audience. ROGER COVELL

Fox, Carol (*b* Chicago, 15 June 1926; *d* Chicago, 21 July 1981). American impresario. After vocal studies with Giovanni Martinelli, Edith Mason and others in the USA and Italy, she turned to concert management. She resolved to revive opera in Chicago, where no company had been resident since 1947, and her Lyric Theatre of Chicago mounted its first three-week season in November 1954. Its success was assured by engaging Tito Gobbi, Giulietta Simionato and Giuseppe di Stefano, and by including the eagerly awaited American début of Maria Callas in *Norma*. In 1956 Fox assumed full control of the organization, which she renamed the Lyric Opera of Chicago, and within two decades it became a leading American company, with a three-month season of eight productions. Deteriorating health forced her retirement in January 1981.

CBY 1978 * BERNARD JACOBSON

Fra Diavolo [*Fra Diavolo, ou L'hôtellerie de Terracine* ('Fra Diavolo, or The Inn of Terracina')]. *Opéra comique* in three acts by DANIEL-FRANÇOIS-ESPRIT AUBER to a libretto by EUGÈNE SCRIBE; Paris, Opéra-Comique (Salle Ventadour), 28 January 1830.

A group of carabineers sent from Rome to capture the famous bandit Fra Diavolo (tenor) are drinking outside the village inn near Terracina. Their commanding offi-

cer, Lorenzo (tenor), can think of nothing but Zerline (soprano), but she has been commanded by her father to marry Francesco (silent role), a rich farmer's son. The English couple Lord Kokbourg [Cockburn] (tenor) and Lady Pamela (mezzo-soprano) have just been robbed by Fra Diavolo. Soon afterwards, Fra Diavolo himself arrives, disguised as the charming Marquis de San Marco. He listens to Zerline's alarming tales of robbers in the Abruzzi. Lorenzo, having killed several of the bandits, returns the jewellery to the English couple and earns a reward. As Lorenzo promises to capture Fra Diavolo, the robber chief pledges revenge.

In a room at the inn occupied by the English couple, Fra Diavolo and two companions, Giacomo (bass) and Beppo (tenor), have crept in to steal their money. The bandits must pass through Zerline's room, and after she has gone to sleep Fra Diavolo orders his men to murder her and make off with the money of the English couple. But before the deeds are carried out, Lorenzo returns. In the finale of the second act Fra Diavolo, still in the guise of the Marquis, tells Lorenzo that he has had a secret rendezvous; this arouses Lorenzo's and the lord's jealousy.

Back at his mountain hideaway, Fra Diavolo proudly describes the life of a robber chief. He leaves orders that he is to be informed of the departure of the carabineers by the ringing of a church bell. When the drunken brigands Giacomo and Beppo sing part of Zerline's 'toilette' aria from Act 2, she realizes they were present in her room the evening before. Lorenzo arrests the brigands and uncovers the plan. Giacomo is forced to ring the bell, Fra Diavolo falls into the trap and the lovers are united at last.

Fra Diavolo is supposedly based on the life of either Antonio Gargiulo of Calabria, or more probably Michele Pezza, a brigand who ravaged southern Italy around 1800 and was said to unite in his person the qualities of a monk (Fra Angelico) and a criminal. He resisted Napoleon and was hanged in Naples in 1806. Such a character is featured in Christian August Vulpius's novel *Rinaldo Rinaldini, der Räuber-Hauptmann* (1799), and in Cervantes's *Don Quixote*, and appeared in French drama in the adaptation of Le Sueur's *La caverne* by Cuvillier and Franconi, already entitled *Fra Diavolo, chef des brigands dans les Alpes* (performed in Paris in 1808 and in Vienna in 1822 as *Die Räuber in den Abruzzen*). The exact relation to plots like Robin Hood, Schiller's *Die Räuber* and to several 'rescue operas' of the French Revolution should be studied more intensively. But the theme of the charitable rogue, the robber fighting the rich and powerful out of moral conviction, was not one Scribe could use in 1830. Only in the aria 'Je vois marcher sous ma bannière' (in which at the beginning of the third act he expresses a more likable 'philosophy' than he practised on the *air et scène* of Act 2) does the figure of the noble robber emerge in Scribe's version; his villainous deeds and downfall are otherwise treated in a cheerfully ironic vein. The text might have been influenced by Victor Hugo, whose *Hernani*, the tragic counterpart to *Fra Diavolo*, had its première only a month later. (Hugo's father, a general, had taken part in the pursuit of Pezza.) A tragic version of the opera, which was not authorized by Scribe nor by Auber, ending with the death of Fra Diavolo shot by the carabineers in the Act 3 finale, was later abandoned.

Fra Diavolo is considered to be the best of Auber's *opéras comiques*. In contrast to other Romantic composers he presents emotion with a mocking twinkle in his eye, ironically distancing himself from it. Fra Diavolo is a leading role for tenors, and the aria 'Je vois marcher sous ma bannière', with many changes of tempo, is the character's bravura piece. The couplets with refrain in Act 1 and the barcarolles are among the most popular vocal pieces Auber wrote, while the scenes in which the ingenious rhythmic and harmonic effects of the music carry the action forward are typical. Unusually for an *opéra comique* of this period, the climax occurs in the finale of the last act. The most extensive passages, and the richest in their treatment of the action, in order of length, are the finale to Act 1, the introduction (with the nocturne, 'Cher Lorenzo' sung by Zerline and Lorenzo) and the finale to Act 3; the finale to Act 2 is considerably shorter. The two original trios are particularly ironic. Auber omitted the dialogue between the brigands in Act 1 for the performances given in 1858, and replaced it with a trio, 'Vive la joie', from *Les chaperons blancs*, so that there were two consecutive, although very different, trios. The most ingenious of Auber's dramatic techniques is his linking of different pieces by musical quotations throughout the opera. The chromatic motif of the ballad, for instance, is quoted not only in Fra Diavolo's barcarolle, but also in its ritornello at the end, and again in the entr'acte to the third act. The best example of this technique is the finale of Act 3, in which Auber collected quotations of seven themes from earlier scenes.

For the London performance in Italian, Scribe and Auber created a new version of *Fra Diavolo* (1857). The recitatives are new and so too are several numbers: in the introduction to the first act Zerline has a new aria, 'Per te io tremo'. Fra Diavolo's 'O quel piacer', sung before Zerline's 'Je voulais bien/Egliè davver per me un piacer', seems to contradict his original character. At the beginning of the second act, Zerline's 'Quel bonheur je respire' is replaced by the virtuoso aria 'Dès l'enfance les mêmes chaines/Or son sola, alfin respiro' from *Le Serment*, and in Act 3 Auber inserts a tarantella from the Easter chorus 'C'est la grande fête/De' fiori è questa' and the farewell duo 'Il faut partir/Puoi tu partire' from *La neige* just before the finale. This version, inferior to the original with spoken dialogue, is still performed today in Italy.

Fra Diavolo was one of the most frequently performed operas of the 19th century, with more than 900 performances in Paris by 1907. Within two years of its première it had entered the repertory of many opera houses in central and northern Europe, and those of St Petersburg and New York. By 1852 it had made its way to Sydney and Buenos Aires.

HERBERT SCHNEIDER

Fra Gherardo ('Brother Gherardo'). Opera in three acts by ILDEBRANDO PIZZETTI to his own libretto; Milan, Teatro alla Scala, 16 May 1928.

Although the protagonist of this opera (composed in 1926–7) is based on a real person described in the 13th-century chronicle of Fra' Salimbene da Parma, Pizzetti changed his character considerably. Moreover he largely invented the plot, whose main thread concerns the conflicting moralities of politico-religious fanaticism and human love. Having given away his possessions to pursue a quasi-Franciscan ideal of poverty, Gherardo (tenor) is moved to protect and then spend the night with the orphan girl Mariola (soprano). In the morning,

however, thinking of her as a temptress sent by the devil, he abruptly drives her away and goes off with a group of flagellants to expiate his sin. Nine years later, having become a well-known friar, Gherardo returns to Parma to lead an insurrection of the people against the corrupt authorities. But he again meets Mariola, who tells him of the wretchedly deprived life she has led, and of the birth and death of the child of their illicit union. Despite all, she still loves Gherardo, who now sees himself as a father who has murdered his son. Filled with shame, he wants to abandon his mission and seek a new life with Mariola; but she insists that he should fulfil his destiny as a leader of the people, and tries to help him to do so. As a result she is killed and he is condemned to death for heresy and treason. Before being burnt at the stake he proclaims that the one true law is 'to give without asking a reward, and love, love, love'.

Though controversial (not least because of the unsympathetic, weakly vacillating protagonist), this is one of Pizzetti's more theatrically effective stage works, with plentiful spectacle and abundant use of the chorus. Musically, however, it seems more prosaic than his previous operas, and the Musorgsky influence that had been strong in *Dèbora e Jaéle* and *Lo straniero* is less evident. One can sense a certain rapprochement with the 19th-century Italian tradition, though the composer remains true in principle (with some exceptions) to his own subtly moulded declamatory vocal style. There is some charmingly individual pastoral music to set the scene. Nevertheless, the decline towards the disappointingly weak operas of Pizzetti's middle years can already be detected.

JOHN C. G. WATERHOUSE

Fra i due litiganti il terzo gode ('While Two Dispute, the Third Enjoys'). *Dramma giocoso* in two acts by GIUSEPPE SARTI to a libretto after CARLO GOLDONI's *Le nozze*; Milan, Teatro alla Scala, 14 September 1782.

Masotto (tenor), a steward to the quarrelling Count and Countess (soprano) Belfiore, succeeds in winning the hand of the serving-maid Dorina (soprano) after outwitting his two rivals Titta and Mingone (baritone and tenor; they are initially supported by the Count and Countess, respectively). In the end Mingone remains wifeless, while Titta settles for the Countess's maid Livietta (soprano). Many of the characters and some aspects of the story are similar to Mozart's *Le nozze di Figaro*. Masotto and Dorina bear resemblances to Mozart's Figaro and Susanna, although Masotto is a more successful intriguer and Dorina a more passive character than their counterparts. Though closer to stock types, the blustering Count and the jealous Countess resemble the Count and Countess Almaviva. The tone of the work, however, is far lighter and more farcical than that of *Figaro*; only Dorina's plaintive expressions and the Countess's angry outbursts provide moments of greater seriousness. Sarti's music is generally graceful and appealing, but often without much character. Most successful are the ensembles and finales, which at times display considerable textural complexity and rhythmic excitement. Mingone's aria 'Come un agnello' was quoted by Mozart in the Act 2 Finale of *Don Giovanni*.

The opera was among the most successful of the late 18th century, especially in Vienna, where it had received over 60 performances (in both Italian and German) by 1790. *Fra i due litiganti* had appeared in at least 22 other European cities by 1800, with alternative titles including *I pretendenti delusi*, *Im Trüben ist gut fischen* and *Les noces de Dorine, ou Hélène et Francisque*. At an early stage the opera was subjected to an unusual number of aria substitutions and other rearrangements. The version heard in Vienna included arias by Salieri, Storace, Martín y Soler and Anfossi; it was this version, transmitted through Viennese copies, that was heard in many other cities.   JOHN PLATOFF

Framery, Nicolas Etienne (*b* Rouen, 25 March 1745; *d* Paris, 26 Nov 1810). French librettist, critic and composer. While still a student in Paris, he wrote a comedy, *La nouvelle Eve*, to which the censor objected; he then revised it and, as *Nanette et Lucas* with *ariettes* by the Chevalier d'Herbain, it had some success at the Comédie-Italienne in 1764. In 1768 his *La sorcière par hasard*, an *opéra comique* to his own text, was privately performed; its favourable reception may have led to his appointment in the same year as superintendent of music to the Comte d'Artois. The work was later revived with some success at the Comédie-Italienne, and the score was published.

Framery devoted himself to criticism, theoretical works and to writing and adapting librettos. Under the influence of the Encyclopedists, he espoused the cause of Italian music in France, opposing Gluck not as a Piccinnist but as a partisan of Sacchini. He adapted Sacchini's *L'isola d'amore* for the French stage (*La colonie*, 1775), and subsequently tried to persuade the composer to come from London. His adaptation of *L'olympiade* was intended for the Opéra but rejected through Gluckist opposition; with spoken verse dialogue, it was given with success at the Comédie-Italienne in 1777 and formed a rallying-point for the Italian party before Piccinni's first French opera (*Roland*, 1778). Framery adapted other Italian works for various theatres, and (according to Lajarte) assisted with the libretto of Sacchini's first work for the Opéra, *Renaud* (1783). In 1784 he won a competition with a libretto, *Médée*, which he intended for Sacchini. Framery was a critic for the *Mercure de France*, and there published an accusation of plagiarism against Gluck (September 1776) and a eulogy of Sacchini (October 1786). He published a further attack on Gluck in the musical section of the *Encyclopédie méthodique* (vol. i, Paris, 1791), of which he was the editor.

Librettos: *La nouvelle Eve* [Nanette et Lucas, ou La paysanne curieuse] (comédie), Chevalier d'Herbain, 1764; *La sorcière par hasard* (oc), Framery, 1768; *L'indienne* (comédie), Cifolelli, 1770; *Médée*, Framery, 1784–7 [unfinished]; *Alcine*, Count of Lacépède, 1785; *La tourterelle, ou Les enfans dans les bois* (comédie lyrique), A.-F. Gresnick, 1797

Parodies, translations, adaptations: *Nicaise* [F. Bambini], 1767; *Le trompeur trompé* [A. B. Blaise], 1767; *La colonie* [A. Sacchini: *L'isola d'amore*], 1775; *L'olympiade, ou Le triomphe de l'amitié* [Sacchini], 1777; *Le jaloux à l'épreuve* [P. Anfossi: *Il geloso in cimento*], 1779; *L'infante de Zamore* [Paisiello: *La frascatana*], 1780; *Les deux comtesses* [Paisiello], 1781; *Renaud* [Sacchini: *Armida*], 1783; *Le barbier de Séville* [Paisiello], 1784; *Tarare* [Salieri], 1795

*

T. de Lajarte: *Bibliothèque musicale du théâtre de l'Opéra: catalogue historique, chronologique, anecdotique* (Paris, 1878), i, 333

J. Carlez: *Framery, littérateur-musicien* (Caen, 1893)

C. D. Brenner: *A Bibliographic List of Plays in the French Language, 1700–1789* (Berkeley, 1947, 2/1979)

JULIAN RUSHTON

Françaix, Jean (*b* Le Mans, 23 May 1912). French composer. After taking lessons with his father, he went to Paris to complete his training; at the Conservatoire he won a *premier prix* for piano (1932), and studied composition with Boulanger. He composed his first work at the age of six, and this facility for composition remained with him. All his music, which includes dramatic, orchestral, chamber and vocal works, is characterized by a remarkable grace and mastery, the theatre bringing out his verve and his sharp wit. *Le diable boiteux* (1938) is a short work which tells of a demon (tenor, often falsetto) who appears at night in Madrid singing duets with the other characters. There is little plot and the orchestra is small. In *L'apostrophe* (1951) the farcical elements of Balzac are mirrored by Françaix in parodistic set pieces in operetta style with spoken dialogue. Both central characters are cloth-dealers, the Taschereau (baritone) and the Tascherette (soprano). There is a farcical scene with the latter's suitor, the hunchback Carandas (tenor), hidden in a trunk.

The most considerable of Françaix' operas is *La princesse de Clèves* (1965), a modern-day *galanterie* set in the last years of Henry II's reign. The Princess (mezzo-soprano) falls in love with M. de Nemours (tenor) but ultimately renounces this impossible love. There is a substantial part for a narrator who announces the comings and goings of the court while the singers fill in with set pieces, often in the manner of operetta. *La main de gloire* (1951) is more bitingly comic and centres on the figure of M. Gonin (baritone), who sings a ridiculous text and casts spells on those around him, predicting the gallows for Eustache (tenor), whose wife Javotte (mezzo-soprano) has fallen for a handsome soldier, Joseph. Comic duets and trios draw pastiche, 'wrong-note' chords and rhythmic wit from Françaix and there is an extended ballet accompanied by a large choir. After Eustache's execution his hand walks away, hence the title of the work. *Paris à nous deux* (1954) was written for the pupils of the American Conservatoire at Fontainebleau. A biting satire on the fashion for modernist music in postwar France, it concerns an 'arriviste' (tenor) who wishes to succeed in life and is received by a wealthy lady, the Maîtresse de Maison (mezzo-soprano). The simple choral parts take up much of this short work, whose moral is that it is more important to prevent others from arriving than to arrive oneself.

Françaix' style has evolved very little, since he quickly assimilated all that he needed to learn and, more importantly, had an innate gift for invention and for expressing the freshness and wonder of childhood. He was not insensible to the charm of Ravel and Poulenc, nor even to the novelty of *The Rite of Spring*, but such lessons have been integrated into a very individual art, highly polished and classically reserved. He has also made a career as a virtuoso pianist.

Le diable boiteux (chamber op, 1, Françaix, after A.-R. Lesage), Paris, 30 June 1938 [private perf. for the Princess of Polignac]; public perf. Palermo, 22 April 1949

L'apostrophe, 1940 (comédie musicale, 1, after H. de Balzac), Amsterdam, Opera, 1 July 1951

La main de gloire, 1944 (opéra bouffe, 4, after G. de Nerval), Bordeaux, 18 May 1951

Paris à nous deux, ou Le nouveau Rastignac (fantaisie lyrique, 2, P. Kast and Françaix), Fontainebleau, Théâtre Municipal, 7 Aug 1954

La princesse de Clèves (4, Françaix and M. Lanjean, after Mme de Lafayette), Rouen, Arts, 11 Dec 1965

*

M. Lanjean: *Jean Françaix* (Paris, 1961)

ARTHUR HOÉRÉE/RICHARD LANGHAM SMITH

France. The importance of France as an opera-producing nation lies not in the origins of the genre (which was established first in Italy) but in what happened later: for 250 years, France sustained an unbroken tradition of operatic creation. This tradition quickly established a worthy counterbalance to the excellence of 17th-century Italian opera. Owing to the economic and cultural energy of Paris, French opera then became the main focus of opera reform in the 18th century. In the 19th century Paris became the operatic hub of the world, taking in the finest composers and exporting the most influential music and ideas. The 20th century has seen some devolution of Paris's power and a general loss of sense of identity.

The history of opera in France has been nurtured in particular by the following distinctive traits: first, a sense of national identity, manifested (in part) in national support for opera companies; secondly, the French language, with its rhythmic and phonic individuality when set to music; thirdly, the French tradition of spoken theatre in both tragedy and comedy, which always influenced opera; fourthly, the French love of spectacle and entertainment, which influenced the special place allotted to dance in opera, and in allied genres; and lastly, the cultural tendency of the French to welcome ideas and influences from abroad, and to assimilate them.

1. 17th century. 2. 18th century. 3. 19th century. 4. 20th century.

1. 17TH CENTURY. The great Italian *intermedi* (such as the Florentine set of 1589 for the wedding of Ferdinando de' Medici) had their counterparts in France, where Italian innovations were studied. Most celebrated of these proto-operatic events was *Circé, ou Le balet comique de la royne* (1581), staged at Henri III's court for a society wedding. The author, Baltazar de Beaujoyeulx, incorporated a single narrative scheme, as well as music for chorus, for dialogue and for dance. The political background to such displays was turbulent. Religious strife was temporarily quelled by the Edict of Nantes in 1598, but Henri IV was assassinated in 1610 and Catholic power was reasserted at the siege of La Rochelle (1628): this was to have its effect on opera. However, court festivals and ballets (*ballets de cour*, which could also have a single narrative thread) prospered under the new monarch, Louis XIII.

The gradual development in French drama, from a situation of diffuseness (various acting traditions went back to the Middle Ages) to the widespread acceptance of classical convention, was completed about the middle of the 17th century. Coherence of narrative, plus observance of Aristotelian unities of time, place and action became the hallmarks of spoken tragedy, for example in Racine. Opera in France was affected by this; yet, seen as a whole, it was 'based sometimes on tragi-comedy, sometimes tragedy … [using] devices of the machine play and *ballet de cour* as well' (Newman 1979).

After the death of Louis XIII in 1643, leaving his son – the future Louis XIV – as a boy of four, Cardinal Mazarin, as First Minister, pursued an agenda designed to reinforce French links with Italy and the papacy. To this end he organized the performance of six Italian operas between 1645 and 1662, using leading Italian musicians, librettists and designers. These formed the seedbed of indigenous opera by opening French eyes to the innovations of Cavalli's music, Giacomo Torelli's stage designs and the concept of all-sung drama. The

most important works to be staged were Cavalli's *Egisto* (1646), *Xerse* (1660, with ballets by the young Lully) and *Ercole amante* (1662; see below), Luigi Rossi's *Orfeo* (1647) and Carlo Caproli's *Le nozze di Peleo e di Teti* (1654). This last work, which cleverly integrated French *ballet de cour* with an all-sung drama, set the mould whereby important court performances of dramatic music would incorporate sung and danced episodes, called 'divertissements'. This combination of the arts has remained fundamental to French national tradition. Details could also prove influential. The trio 'Dormite, begli occhi' in Rossi's *Orfeo* has been suggested (by James Anthony) as the source for the *sommeil* (sleep scene) tradition in French opera, beginning with the 'Dormez, dormez' trio in Lully's *Les amants magnifiques* (1670). The *sommeil* tradition persisted to 1804, at least, with Le Sueur's *Ossian, ou Les bardes*, Act 4.

The 1650s saw the birth of the three forerunners of French opera, all pastorals, their music now lost: Michel de La Guerre's *Le triomphe de l'Amour* (1655) and the two five-act works by Cambert with texts by Pierre Perrin: the *Pastorale* given at Issy and *Ariane* (both 1659). Perhaps Cambert accepted already that French poetry, especially when cast in the favoured 12-syllable line (Alexandrine), would require a flexible metrical structure when being set as recitative. He may have been influenced by certain predecessors, parts of whose scores survive today, such as Jean de Cambefort and his 1653 *Ballet de la nuit*. By 1671 Cambert was adopting the novel Baroque French recitative notation, with its irregularly mixed time signatures. This imitated the speech-rhythms of French spoken poetry.

In the year 1646 the adolescent Florentine musician Lulli (later naturalized Jean-Baptiste Lully) had arrived in Paris. Originally he was recruited to help the king's cousin Mlle de Montpensier to converse in Italian. She maintained many musicians, however, who must have trained Lully in national styles. In 1652 he entered the service of the king, with whom he enjoyed lasting friendship, and his composing career consequently first responded to royal preference for the dance. Lully's dances were interspersed in Cavalli's festive opera *Ercole amante*, conceived for Louis XIV's wedding. He must have been impressed by its extended tableaux (a sleep scene, a mourning scene or *tombeau*, a Hades scene), but equally warned by the dangers of dramatic diffuseness. *Ercole amante* was long remembered; in 1671 the tragic ballet *Psyché*, by Lully, Molière, Pierre Corneille and Quinault, answered the king's desire to see the 1662 sets and spectacular effects used once more. Lully created 13 ballets with Benserade (1658–81) and ten *comédies-ballets* with Molière (1664–70), which anticipate fully fledged opera in their musico-dramatic resources: recitative, chorus, solo, balletic and instrumental forms are imaginatively combined.

French opera was established permanently through Louis XIV's normal method of granting a monopoly in return for a large sum of money and an annual retainer. The owner of the monopoly then exploited it as a venture at his own risk. Louis' chief minister, Colbert, drew up a form of *lettre patent* for 'Académies d'Opéra' (exploitable in different cities), which was obtained on 28 June 1669 by Pierre Perrin. His and Cambert's pastoral opera *Pomone* was presented under these terms in 1671, with great success. Yet owing to the financial problems in Perrin's establishment, the king decided to offer a fresh opera monopoly to Lully (who compensated Perrin). Thus in 1672 the definitive Académie Royale de Musique was created. It was a privilege, not a building. For this, Lully – still only 40 years of age – imagined a new theatrical genre benefiting from his complete control over its production: *tragédie en musique*. He used Philippe Quinault as his librettist in all but two of the series of 13 such works performed between 1673 and 1686. These, by common consent, were the tablets on which Lully's reputation, and the ground-rules of French lyric theatre, were carved. The Paris home of its Académie Royale de Musique was in the Palais-Royal, and the institution known colloquially as the Opéra.

Lully's *tragédies* formed the first 'classic' repertory in the history of opera; that is, the first body of operas to be (selectively) revived and emulated for a long period after their creation. *Armide* was seen as late as 1781 in Paris. Before mentioning other performances of Lully's works in France, it is pertinent to recall that they were staged in Modena and Rome in the south, Ansbach, Darmstadt and Regensburg to the east, the Netherlands, Hamburg and London (*Cadmus et Hermione*), all before 1700. 'French opera', often synonymous with 'Lully', became by extension a major stylistic force in all music of the mid and high Baroque. Features of this style include the 'French overture'; the French method of bowing and phrasing, with short strokes and tight rhythms; a developed sense of orchestral discipline; the large-scale chaconne form, which could unite singers, players and dancers over a recurring bass; and the various refined dances whose styles (and melodies) were readily exportable in instrumental suites. The fact that Lully's *tragédies* were all published (initially between 1679 and 1720) facilitated their influence. Indeed, from that time forward, the frequent publication of French opera in reliable editions has helped constitute in general the sense of a unified repertory. Of course, each revival of a given work, even by Lully himself, would routinely break with the published 'canonic' text to some degree, to suit the circumstances of performance.

In the great regional cities of France, opera rapidly took its place alongside other forms of theatre; normally the performance would be part of a seasonal presentation, given in a converted indoor tennis-court (*jeu de paume*). The monopoly bought by Lully was tenable, after his death in 1687, by his offspring. The first provincial 'Académie Royale de Musique' was founded at Marseilles (1684), where Pierre Gautier put on his own *Le triomphe de la paix* and *Le jugement du soleil* (1685, 1687) and secured the right to exploit opera in Montpellier and Toulouse. Proximity to the Italian states encouraged the importation of music by Cavalli and others. In 1688 a similar Académie was founded at Rouen, by Bernard Vaultier, and one at Lyons; and in the same year occurred the first known opera performance in Bordeaux. In 1689 Lully's *Atys* was mounted at Rennes for the opening of the Parlement (Rennes being the capital of the province of Brittany) with a new prologue, music by Pascal Collasse, including local colour in its 'Passe-pieds à la manière de Bretagne'. But in this case, too, royal permission was still legally necessary since the opera was all-sung.

However, other forms of opera were quick to take root in France, ones which would not require a costly licence and would be easier to organize through the time-honoured method of travelling troupes. The outcome was works using spoken dialogue, including *opéra comique*, which came to play a crucial role in the operatic history of the country. Again, Paris acted as the guide. Italian improvising players, known in Paris from 1570, had been approved by Louis XIV. This 'Ancien Théâtre Italien', as it is retrospectively called, relied much on music. Pre-existing melodies were often used, whether from the common domain (vaudevilles) or those by Lully and others that became popular (parodies). In this mainly oral culture, with its large collective memory of tunes, the sense of the original words could be taken into account when any melody – to new words – was placed in its new comic context. Irony and wit, topicality and audience participation, all were of the essence. By the time that the Italians were repatriated in 1697 – victim of the censorious atmosphere of Louis' later reign (he died in 1715) – they had accumulated 55 French plays, reproduced in print by Evaristo Gherardi in a *Recueil général de toutes les comédies* ... (1700). Of these, 43, reports James Anthony, 'use music extensively'.

At the same time, of course, there was no shortage of native talent ready to develop musical parody on the stage. As in the provinces, popular theatre in Paris was acted seasonally, at the two main annual fairs (*foires*). The Foire St Laurent ran during August and September, and the Foire St Germain from February to Palm Sunday. Among the publications reproducing popular melodies (many by Lully) that impresarios and others could use as sources, were two by the royal printer, Ballard: *Nouvelles parodies bachiques* (1700) and *La clef des chansonniers* (1717).

2. 18TH CENTURY. This century of opera in France can be thought of as divided in two by the years 1756–63, the period of the Seven Years' War. For example, the years 1752–4 were those of the 'Querelle des Bouffons', or public debate following acquaintance with the latest Italian intermezzos and *opere buffe* on the stage of the Paris Opéra. These performances, by the travelling troupe of Eustachio Bambini, precipitated the growth in France of a modern *opéra comique* consisting of all newly composed music, and the elimination of parody. (The early composers were E. Duni, Philidor, Monsigny, J.-L. Laruette, Gossec and Grétry.) In 1756 the first of a series of permanent theatres in the provinces was inaugurated: the Grand-Théâtre, Lyons. These provided greater stability for regional opera. In 1764 occurred the death of Rameau, and the final passing of the Baroque period in serious and all-sung French operatic genres.

In the first part of the century, the picture nationally was still dominated by seasonal and travelling opera troupes, and by numerous local battles over privileges. The repertory, probably based on music generated in the capital, is difficult to ascertain in detail. In the following anonymous account ('Notice de la vie ... de M. Berton', 1782) the implication is made that newly composed *opéra comique* in itself enabled, or encouraged, regional companies to put down local, permanent roots, i.e. from the 1760s:

Two sizeable troupes then [1746] circulated in the provinces, and performed *grands Opéra*[s]. They disappeared, following the favour accorded to *opéra comique*. Art has perhaps suffered thereby. These troupes were not simply good training schools for the Paris Opéra; because they performed by turns in the principal cities of the kingdom, they inspired emulation there, and also generated the taste for music and [trained] singing ... [*Opéra comique*] performance required neither superior talent, nor voices of undisputed beauty; its arias – excepting several one might perhaps call *grands morceaux* owing to their orchestral accompaniment – are still remote from the nobility and majesty of the *grands airs*, and fine singing, found in heroic opera.

New 'heroic opera' between Lully's demise and Rameau's first opera (*Hippolyte et Aricie*, 1733) meant, predominantly, *tragédies* by Marc-Antoine Charpentier, Collasse, André Campra, Henry Desmarets, André Destouches and Marin Marais. The latter's *Alcyone* (1706) contained a *tempête* that became the model for many later operatic storms in French opera. The tendency, seen in Rossi's *Orfeo* and Cavalli's *Ercole amante*, for opera in France to embrace the musical depiction of physical phenomena, was confirmed by certain celebrated inventions by Lully: his 'frost scene' in *Isis* (1677), for example, which had one issue in Act 3 of Purcell's English opera *King Arthur*. But these episodes should not be dismissed as childish parodies of reality, the 'French trash' mentioned by a critic of Haydn's later oratorio *The Seasons*. The tableaux and ceremonies of French Baroque opera were crucial stages in opera's history in general. This is, first, because they gave the orchestra a privileged position in the creation of stage illusion; and secondly, because the chorus frequently played a part in the 'universal' expression of feelings that became so typical of this art-form. Orchestra and chorus are resources on which opera has continued to rely heavily to the present day.

In the first four decades of the 18th century French opera reached an opposite pole of identity from Italian *opera seria* in matters of aesthetic approach, subject matter, dramaturgy and musical technique. This had at least two related consequences in significant critical literature. One affected the continuing partisan battle between Italian and French styles; the other helped define the role of music within the neo-classical doctrine of imitation. Early key texts in the war of words were François Raguenet's pro-Italian *Paralèle des italiens et des françois, en ce qui regarde la musique et les opéra* (1702; further editions up to 1753; English and German translations in 1709 and 1722); and J. L. Le Cerf de la Viéville's pro-French *Comparaison de la musique italienne et de la musique française* (1704; further editions to 1743). These set the scene for a century of informed and sometimes brilliant critical writing on opera, that took in the polemical periods of the Querelle de Bouffons (mentioned above) and the Gluck–Piccinni controversy of 1777–9. In the related field of aesthetics, French opera became a natural benchmark for writers such as Charles Batteux, Jean-Jacques Rousseau (who himself composed an important operatic *intermède*, *Le devin du village*, 1752) and Denis Diderot.

Jean-Philippe Rameau came to dominate the French lyric stage, reaching an apogee of genuine popularity in the 1750s. Because he took French opera to new heights of intensity within its existing formal and expressive structures (notably including the role of *divertissements*), his are perhaps the most difficult of French operas for us to revive today. Yet Rameau was typical of his time in moving away from tragedy. He composed seven *tragédies* but notably more works in other genres: *opéra-ballet*, *pastorale-héroïque*, *comédie-ballet*.

Indeed, this line of preference – which incidentally proves that audiences of the period did indeed perceive opera as a true form of drama, and not merely a 'concert in costume' – relates to the mid-century crisis of 1752–4. But the real collision of those years was not that of 'France' versus 'Italy'. It was that of Baroque versus pre-Classical musical style; and (allegorically) of the absolute monarchy versus the demands for constitutional government. This is easier to understand if we recall the royal edicts that still bound all opera production, and the extraordinary way that Lully's works for the Sun King remained relevant to the class that could afford to patronize the Opéra itself. From this perspective, the advent of Gluck in Paris can be seen as a political and a musical solution to the tensions in opera, viewed as a social activity. Gluck's arrival in 1774 coincided with the tired end of the reign of Louis XV and the feeling of release and hope attending the accession of Louis XVI, before the events that led to public disillusionment with him and his Austrian consort, Marie Antoinette (who knew Gluck in Vienna, and later patronized Sacchini, Piccinni and Grétry). Almost all quarters could take some satisfaction in the way Gluck united classical themes (*Orfeo*, *Alceste*, *Iphigénie*) with an up-to-date musical style, a sense of moral relevance and profound attention to the achievements of French opera as a branch of drama. Indeed, this sequence of French works (1774–9), forming the climax of Gluck's career, became the seedbed from which Romantic opera grew. In the shorter term Gluck's melody, pathos and orchestral sense were developed in Paris and led to the vital generation of *opéra comique* composers under the Revolution: Méhul, Cherubini, Le Sueur, Gaveaux. In the longer term, Gluck's dramaturgy, his ability to create a sense of dramatic unity encompassing a whole act, became the inspiration for E. T. A. Hoffmann, for Berlioz and for Wagner. Hoffmann felt that 'The music was enkindled not by words but by ideas', that *Iphigénie en Aulide* 'is true musical drama, in which the action moves forward without stopping from one moment to the next'.

At this point, however, it should be recalled that even Gluck's Parisian works were seen at the time as having been prepared for by another genre altogether: *opéra comique*. (Gluck had in fact composed a number of these for Vienna.) A series of writers had continued to refine comedy at the Foires: A. R. Lesage, D'Orneval, A. Piron and the most famous of all, Charles-Simon Favart. The contribution of original music had become a permanent feature, alongside parody. J.-C. Gillier, Jacques Aubert and even Rameau wrote for the early Opéra-Comique, the name adopted by the fair companies. In 1716 a new troupe of Italian players had returned to Paris, acting at the theatre in the Hôtel de Bourgogne. They obtained a royal privilege in 1723, as 'Comédiens Italiens Ordinaires du Roi', but gave French as well as Italian productions. Jean-Joseph Mouret was the house composer, and by 1745 they were (illegally) giving all-sung entertainments, including ballets.

Under the impact of newly composed *opéras comiques* with spoken dialogue, by Duni, Monsigny, Philidor and others, the Crown subsumed the independent company of the Foires in 1762 within the establishment of the Comédiens Italiens, thus assuring the conditions for the rapid, year-round growth of what was in effect a bourgeois opera house (with boxes available for rent) giving French-language works. Within three decades, not least owing to the vision and skill of reforming writers like J. F. Marmontel and M.-J. Sedaine, this genre embraced a vast range of subject matter. Many works eschewed comic characters altogether, and used the chorus with freedom, substituting realistic settings and moral themes for the traditional artificiality of rustic escapism. This repertory long remained staple throughout France, particularly works by Grétry, Dalayrac, Adrien Boieldieu, Isouard and (in the 19th century) Auber.

As we saw earlier, the new *opéra comique* coincided with the construction of purpose-built theatres. These were the first such edifices in France. Jacques-Gabriel Soufflot's design for Lyons, inaugurated in 1756, 'offered a decisive impetus to the subsequent development and independence of the free-standing theatre type' (W. Oechslin, *Macmillan Encyclopedia of Architects*, 1982). In 1765 Brest built the Marine theatre, Rouen a Grand Théâtre (1776), followed by another in Bordeaux (1780; Victor Louis' building is still in use), the visionary design of Claude Nicolas Ledoux for Besançon (inaugurated 1784) and finally Marseilles (inaugurated 1787). Nantes established a permanent company in 1770. Whatever the precise mixture of genres these houses offered the public, the actual repertory – as was to be the case in the coming century – relied totally on what Paris could export.

3. 19TH CENTURY. With the end of the monarchy entered a certain pluralism in French opera, an acceptance of a range of opera from high to low in tone. Literal pluralism was attained in 1791, when new laws declared that anyone could open a theatre and mount any genre of work. In Paris this temporarily gave rise to seven or eight theatres (out of 30 or 40) giving 'opera', from tragedy down to that typically 19th-century genre, *mélodrame*. Parisian pluralism had in fact emerged in the 1780s, to the extent that a new opera company catering for the desire to see modern Italian opera was opened in 1789 (Théâtre de Monsieur, later Feydeau). Popular composers here were Paisiello, Niccolò Piccinni, Cimarosa, Salieri, Anfossi and Sarti.

Napoleon reformed the national structure. On 8 June 1806 he divided France into 25 'theatrical arrondissements' (excepting Lyons, Bordeaux, Marseilles and Rouen), each with a nominated director. In 1807 he cut the number of Paris theatres to eight, reimposed limits to their activity, and re-established the primacy of the Opéra. Thus in the 19th century each type of opera was identified with its own house: Italian opera remained the most fashionable, followed by those works given at the Opéra and Opéra-Comique. The Théâtre Lyrique, staging a mixture of responsible work, opened in 1851, and Offenbach's operetta company (Bouffes-Parisiens) was licensed in 1855.

Napoleon's regional plans underwent much adjustment, but a reflection of the hierarchy in the capital can be seen, for example, in the Rennes constituency after 1824, where two troupes were made obligatory: one for established opera (seasonally organized) and a travelling troupe for plays and vaudeville pieces. Various new regions established permanent theatres, e.g. Strasbourg's Théâtre Municipal (inaugurated in 1825), or even, like Lyons (1831) and Nice (1885), constructed purpose-built opera houses.

19th-century French opera rose to world importance thanks to the country's expansion of wealth, coupled with a judicious balance between state intervention, financial subsidy and individual initiative. But Paris also attracted the most capable dramatists willing to write librettos. Rossini moved to Paris, wrote new works and assisted in the importation of Italian-trained singers. Shortly before the 1830 revolution, with a new directorial committee, the Opéra adopted the latest advances in stagecraft and lighting, which were synthesized by the writer Eugène Scribe and the

composer Meyerbeer into a new, large-scale historical genre: *grand opéra*. *Grand opéra* was also characterized by a pluralistic approach to form, subject, tone and dramatic structure. The way forward had been blazed earlier by the Italian, Spontini, in *La vestale* and *Fernand Cortez*. Meyerbeer himself was from Berlin. After him came Verdi, who created *Les vêpres siciliennes* and *Don Carlos* for Paris and revised other works for the Opéra. The young Richard Wagner also came to learn in Paris, and left his appreciation of *grand opéra* not only in his own stage works, but also in his essays on Auber (concerning *La muette de Portici* and *Gustave III*) and Halévy (on *La reine de Chypre*).

A significant amount of revenue for opera houses came from regularly held balls, as had been the case in Paris before 1789. The social prestige and ritual mystique of 'going to the opera', whether to dance or to attend a stage performance, usually entered fictional writing in a bourgeois imaginative context (e.g. *Madame Bovary*) but in fact a third of the subscribers to boxes at the Paris Opéra and Théâtre Italien before 1848 were of the aristocracy. Against that background the persistent calls for theatrical liberalization in the capital continued until the foundation of the Théâtre Lyrique, and culminated in the legislation of January 1864. This proclaimed that anyone could open a theatre, and that any theatre could show any genre of stage work. By this juncture, in fact, the ancient distinction between all-sung and dialogue opera, and between 'high' and 'low' regions of subject matter, had effectively dissolved. Bizet became the first great French opera composer to see none of his works given on the stage of Paris Opéra. Ironically, the year of his death, 1875, saw the opening of the monumental temple designed by Charles Garnier for this very institution, standing at the centre of the 19th-century nexus of *grands boulevards*.

Bizet's evolution would have been difficult without the example of Gounod, especially *Faust* (Théâtre Lyrique, 1859). Gounod also acted as a subtle influence on the later Berlioz; the latter's *Les Troyens*, published in full score only in 1969, demonstrates the negative side of the Opéra, where those in power denied it a rightful hearing. (His *Benvenuto Cellini* had been briefly seen there in 1838.) Further signs of the company's decadence were revealed when premières of major operas by Saint-Saëns, Massenet, Chabrier, Reyer and Chausson were staged instead in Weimar and Brussels. But the Opéra-Comique ended the century on a curve of high achievement, with works by Delibes, Offenbach (*Les contes d'Hoffmann*), Massenet (*Manon, Werther*), Lalo (*Le roi d'Ys*), Chabrier (*Le roi malgré lui*), Bruneau (*L'attaque du moulin, L'ouragan*), G. Charpentier (*Louise*), and Debussy's *Pelléas et Mélisande* (1902).

Wagner's revision of *Tannhäuser* (1861) for Paris was granted but three performances. Certainly, his general influence on French opera became unavoidable after 1880, both in librettos and musical language. But it is significant that his works did not cause the absolute realignment noted above following earlier guests: Cavalli in the 1660s and Gluck in the 1770s. This was largely because French opera had enough strengths of its own to resist an all-out invasion, for even though many composers as well as literary figures responded to the Wagnerian call, in one way or another, there were immediately contrary voices. The turn of the century revivals of Rameau operas, initiated by Saint-Saëns and d'Indy, were also important in reminding the French of the strength of their operatic heritage and its essential qualities of impressionism, clarity and grace.

By the 1890s Debussy had planned an article entitled 'On the Uselessness of Wagnerism' and his compatriots Chabrier, Chausson and Dukas, although passionate about Wagner's music, all realized that the way forward for French music did not lie in direct imitation. Even Reyer's *Sigurd* (1884), often cited as an example of slavish Wagnerian imitation, has more in common with the *Ring* as regards its plot than its music, of which Reyer was suspicious. Lalo's *Le roi d'Ys*, clearly influenced by Wagner's brass writing and other orchestral effects, is nonetheless thoroughly French in its incorporation of a set piece Breton wedding. Even Chausson, passionately Wagnerian, and dangerously close to a pastiche of the love duet from *Tristan* in his duet between Lancelot and Guinevere in *Le roi Arthus*, consciously avoided Wagnerian harmony in other sections of the work.

Such attitudes, expressed by Debussy as the necessity to be 'post-Wagner' rather than 'after Wagner', prepared the way for what must be the two greatest French operas of the turn of the century: his own *Pelléas et Mélisande* and Dukas's *Ariane et Barbe-bleue*.

Alongside these opposing trends, the mainstream traditions of historical operas, or those on classical themes, was by no means forgotten. Several substantial historical operas requiring enormous casts and luxurious staging date from the turn of the century, and among them may be mentioned operas by Saint-Saëns as well as works by the Hillemachers, Hüe, Leroux, Bruneau and Nouguès.

Although by far the largest amount of operatic activity was centred on the Opéra and the Opéra-Comique during the last 25 years of the 19th century, occasional ventures took place elsewhere, both in other Paris theatres and in the provinces. Apart from some operatic débuts, and partly staged performances in the concert hall of the Conservatoire, several companies mounted productions in the larger theatres normally occupied by non-operatic ventures, among them the short-lived Eden-Théâtre where the riotous Paris premières of Wagner's *Lohengrin* were given in 1887.

The considerable differences between the various French regions naturally resulted in rivalry between the minor houses anxious to score successes with operatic premières. A glance at the list of venues of the French premières of Wagner's operas illustrates the wealth of operatic interest outside Paris (*Lohengrin*, 1881, Nice; *Der fliegende Holländer*, 1893, Lille; *Meistersinger*, 1896, Lyons; *Tristan und Isolde*, 1897, Aix-les-Bains; *Siegfried*, 1900, Rouen; *Rheingold*, 1902, Nice). Particularly important at the end of the century were Lyons, Rouen and Toulouse. In Rouen ambitious programmes of over 20 repertory operas per year were complemented by new productions of contemporary works by such composers as Gounod, Saint-Saëns and Massenet. From the 1890s until the outbreak of war, many lesser-known works, not previously given in Paris, were first performed there, including Albert Cahen's *Le vénitien* (1890), Lenepveu's *Velléda* (1891, previously given in London, 1882), Rubinstein's *Néron* (1894) as well as several operas by Frédéric Le Rey and Isidore de Lara. In 1890 *Lohengrin* ran to 26 performances without a hint of the trouble witnessed by Wagner operas in Paris. The Capitôle in Toulouse was also laying the foundations of its considerable reputation; among other ventures it took over the Eden-Théâtre production of *Lohengrin* in 1891.

4. 20TH CENTURY. A positive aspect of France's independent regional identities was that operatic composers began to show interest in folklore, introducing both local settings and the folk music peculiar to several regions. While this might be seen as an extension of the procedures of Bizet's *Carmen* (1875), it undeniably had a strengthening effect on French opera and was a trait that lasted well into the 20th century. Spanish themes were continued by several composers, most notably Ravel (*L'heure espagnole*, 1911) and Laparra, but many operatic composers began to be drawn to the regions of their own country.

Gounod's *Mireille* (1864) with its Provençal farandoles was followed by Widor's *Nerto* (1924) and Canteloube's *Le mas* (1929); but the most popular region of France for the settings of operas was Brittany. In part because of its heritage of Celtic mythology, particularly popular in the wake of Wagner, several composers were drawn to Arthurian themes, including Chausson (*Le roi Arthus*, 1903), Joncières (*Lancelot*, 1900) and Sylvio Lazzari (*Armor*, 1898). Other composers used the wild coastal settings for more realistic or historical dramas such as Dupont's *La glu* (1910) and Lazzari's *La lépreuse* (1912) and *La tour de feu* (1928). Ropartz's *Le pays* also has a Breton theme, though set in Iceland. Lalo's *Le roi d'Ys* (1888), using popular music of the region, was complemented by other works which also incorporated something of the rich tradition of Breton folksong. Among the composers were Ladmirault, Max d'Ollone and d'Indy (*L'étranger*, 1903). The mythological aspect continued to fascinate composers in the 20th century, a recent example being Bondon's *Ana et l'albatros* (1970).

Other regions to attract opera composers were Corsica (Bachelet's *Le Scemo*, 1914, Büsser's *Columba*, 1921 and Nouguès's *La vendetta*, 1911), the Basque country (Widor's *Les pêcheurs de Saint-Jean*, 1905 and Nouguès' *Chiquiot, le joueur de pelote*, 1909), Normandy (Silver's *Le clos*, 1906), and the Vendée (Silver's *Myriane*, 1913). While all these drew upon local mythology and custom, their incorporation of regional music varied considerably. Regional interest of this kind was at times allied to the naturalist trends initiated by Zola, which in opera gave rise to *vérisme* or French *verismo*. But while some composers were attracted by realistic local colour, or tense love triangles and vendettas in closed communities, others drew more heavily upon folklore – magic trees, sea maidens and denizens of the forest. Occasionally brute realism was juxtaposed with such fantasy.

Allied to themes pertaining to a pre-industrial age were several operas on religious themes, often including miracles, and on occasion juxtaposing realistic with mystical experience. Among such works Hüe's *Le miracle* (1910) and *Dans l'ombre de la cathédrale* (1921) stand out, incorporating extended passages of plainsong chanting, often as a background to passionate dialogue. In a sense Charpentier's *Louise* (1900) and *Julien* (1913), as well as many of the operas of Bruneau, crystallize this blend of regional colour and realism, for besides telling tales of the everyday they take time to evoke Parisian atmosphere and custom in the static tableaux which were at the heart of the French operatic tradition.

While opera felt the pull of realism on one side, it also responded to those trends totally opposed to naturalism, and nowhere more strongly than in settings of Maeterlinck's works. While Février's *Monna Vanna*

(1909) and Nouguès's *La mort de Tintagiles* (1905), in no way approach Debussy's *Pelléas et Mélisande* (1902) or Dukas' *Ariane et Barbe-bleue* (1907) in terms of musical importance, they clearly illuminate the anti-*vériste* trend which gave rise to many fantasy and fairy-tale operas, often reverting to childhood themes.

In the wake of Wagner's Forest Murmurs, operas set in magic woods were particularly common (André Bloch's *Broceliande*, 1925, Savard's *La forêt*, 1910, Silver's *La belle au bois dormant*, 1901 and *Neigilde*, 1909, Aubert's *La forêt bleue*, 1913). Hüe's *Titania* (1903) was also important to this fairy-tale tradition; but Ravel's *L'enfant et les sortilèges* (1925) must rank as the supreme example of childhood-fantasy opera, continuing the traditions of forest and animal noises which several post-Wagnerian composers had attempted.

Also opposed to the realistic movement was the continuing attraction to exotic themes. Delibes' *Lakmé* (1883) was perhaps the most successful of oriental operas, setting a trend for fake exotic music which was taken up by many composers including Massenet (*Thaïs*, 1894), André Bloch (*Maïda*, 1909), Bruneau (*Kérim*, 1887), Dupont (*Antar*, 1921), Mariotte (*Esther*, 1925) and Samuel-Rousseau (*Le Hulla*, 1923 and *Kerkeb*, 1951). It was not until well into the 20th century, in such pieces as Roussel's *Padmâvatî* (1923), that a more genuinely oriental language was incorporated into Western opera.

The foundations of modernism soon solidified after *Pelléas et Mélisande*, during the great Ballets Russes seasons of Dyagilev from 1908, with their epoch-making scores by Ravel, Debussy and Stravinsky. After World War I, partly owing to the attainments of ballet, high points of pure opera became necessarily sporadic, while works in mixed genres proliferated. Ravel's *L'enfant et les sortilèges* (still displaying its share of 'French' descriptivity) is virtually the only operatic survivor today from the 1920s and 30s, even though Milhaud and Honegger were prolific enough. *Padmâvatî* (Roussel, 1923) is an *opéra-ballet*, *Perséphone* (Stravinsky, 1934) a *mélodrame*.

Newer theatres rose to operatic prominence in the capital, especially the Théâtre du Châtelet (1882) and Théâtre des Champs-Elysées (1913). Popular opera after 1919, however, was dealt an unexpected blow: the cinema began to exert serious competition nationally. Its ticket prices were five or six times cheaper than those for *opéra comique*. Faithful theatre audiences still preferred the best of their 19th-century repertory, including late additions by André Messager. The most popular postwar works were Fauré's *Pénélope* (1913) and Samuel-Rousseau's *Le bon roi Dagobert* (1927). Others, less durable, were by Bachelet, Bruneau, Hüe and Milhaud.

In 1940 the Paris Opéra-Comique came under the Opéra's administration. A final decline began, with few premières of note, other than works by Busser and Hahn and Poulenc's *La voix humaine*. In 1972, it was abolished by the Minister of Cultural Affairs to become, as a building, home to visiting companies giving a cross-section of works from Lully to Stockhausen.

A post-1945 crisis of creative direction was all too visible at the Opéra, which gave no world première of a French work between Barraud's *Numance* (1955) and Messaien's *Saint-François d'Assise* (1983). There is some evidence that fewer young composers in France are now interested in writing for the stage than their older colleagues (about 10 per cent as compared with 40 per cent; see Pistone 1987, p.15). But France as a whole is counteracting this crisis by steadily developing a policy of decentralization, which may provide the means for building up audiences for opera throughout the country. Outside Paris there were, in 1991, 13 first-ranking opera houses, four of the second rank and several lesser houses. The first rank (jointly called Réunion des Théâtres Lyriques Municipaux de France, RTLMF) comprises Avignon, Bordeaux, Lyons, Marseilles, Metz, Montpellier, Nancy, Nantes, Nice, Rouen, Strasbourg (Opéra du Rhin), Toulouse and Tours. Some of these have given important new works. Lyons is perhaps the most active in this direction, with premières of Duhamel's *Les travaux d'Hercule* (1981) and Aperghis's *L'écharpe rouge* (1984). Bordeaux, Toulouse (which gave Landowski's *Montségur* in 1985 in the Halle aux Grains) and Rouen (with Prey's *L'homme occis*, 1978) have been innovatory, although normal national planning consists of standard classical works from the European mainstream. Strasbourg (Opéra du Rhin) operates jointly with Mulhouse and Colmar. Recordings, especially those by companies actively devoted to the recording of forgotten French repertory, have brought many of the provincial opera houses to a wider public. Lyons (under John Eliot Gardiner) and Toulouse (under Michel Plasson) have been particularly important in this respect. Also important, although not centred on a particular opera house, has been the work of Les Arts Florissants in reviving and recording French Baroque opera. In particular their lavish production of Lully's *Atys* in various centres in 1987 must rank as the most important revival of French Baroque opera in the 20th century. At the other end of the scale, the Avignon Festival, whose Célestin cloisters were opened to annual productions of opera and music theatre in 1972, has particularly fostered avant-garde and experimental opera, often for chamber orchestra forces, and the works of Maurice Ohana and Claude Prey have proved to be among the most innovatory works performed there.

The four provincial theatres of the second rank are in Dijon, Nîmes, Reims and Toulon. Among the cities where opera is given occasionally are Aix, Angers, Besançon, Boulogne-sur-mer, Calais, Grenoble, Limoges, Orléans, Perpignan, Rennes, Rochefort, St-Etienne, Tourcoing, Troyes and Vichy.

During the last two decades many new composers have come to the fore whose operas are known mainly within France. Apart from those already mentioned above are C. Baillif, A. Clostre, M. Gautherat, M. Levinas, J. Prodromides and G. Reibel. The proliferation of genre titles has continued with examples since 1945 such as *texte musical*, *opéra jazz* and *opéra clinique*. In a grandiose gesture worthy of its monarchical past, the French government inaugurated on 17 March 1990 a completely new home for the Paris Opéra, the Opéra Bastille, administered jointly with the Palais Garnier, which is destined mainly to act as a home for the French national ballet.

In the provinces two events of operatic interest have been the inauguration of a new biennial festival in Lyons (where the opera house is under renovation), devoted to the revival of French works of the 19th and 20th centuries. In northern France a noteworthy event has been the refurbishment of the Théâtre Impérial at Compiègne (Oise), opened in 1991 and to be devoted to French music, particularly opera of the 19th century.

For further information on operatic life in the country's principal centres *see* AIX-EN-PROVENCE; ANGERS; ATELIER DE RECHERCHE ET DE CRÉATION POUR L'ART LYRIQUE; BORDEAUX; CARPENTRAS; COLMAR; COMPIÈGNE; DIJON; LILLE; LYONS; MARSEILLES; METZ; MONTE CARLO; MONTPELLIER; MULHOUSE; NANCY; NANTES; NICE; NÎMES; ORANGE; PARIS; REIMS; RENNES; ROUEN; ST CÉRÉ; STRASBOURG; TOULON; TOURCOING; TOURS; TRAVELLING TROUPES §2; VAISON LA ROMAINE; and VICHY.

*

F. Raguenet: *Paralèle des italiens et des françois, en ce qui regarde la musique et les opéra* (Paris, 1702, 3/c1710); Eng. edn (London, 1709; repr. in *MQ*, xxxii (1946), 411–36)

J. L. Le Cerf de la Viéville: *Comparaison de la musique italienne et de la musique française* (Brussels, 1704–6)

J.-B. Dubos: *Réflexions critiques sur la poësie et sur la peinture* (Paris, 1719; Eng. trans. of 5/1746 as *Critical Reflexions on Poetry, Painting and Music*, 1748)

J.-B. Durey de Noinville: *Histoire du théâtre de l'Opéra de l'Académie de musique en France* (Paris, 1753, 2/1757)

'Notice de la vie … de M. Berton', *Le nécrologe des hommes célèbres de France*, xvii (Paris, 1782), 44–6

J. M. Marmontel: 'Opéra': *Eléments de littérature, Oeuvres complettes*, ix (Paris, 1787), 47–114

Castil-Blaze: *De l'opéra en France* (Paris, 1820)

——: *L'Académie impériale de musique* (Paris, 1855)

E. Campardon: *Les spectacles de la foire* (Paris, 1877)

——: *Les comédiens du roi de la troupe italienne pendant les deux derniers siècles* (Paris, 1880)

C. Nuittier and E. Thoinan: *Les origines de l'opéra français* (Paris, 1886)

H. Prunières: *L'opéra italien en France avant Lulli* (Paris, 1913)

A. R. Oliver: *The Encylopedists as Critics of Music* (New York, 1947)

M. Cooper: *Opéra Comique* (London, 1949)

——: *French Music from the Death of Berlioz to the Death of Fauré* (London, 1951)

A. S. Garlington: 'Le merveilleux and Operatic Reform in 18th-Century French Opera', *MQ*, xlix (1963), 484–97

C. Girdlestone: *La tragédie en musique, considérée comme genre littéraire (1673–1750)* (Geneva, 1972)

J. R. Anthony: *French Baroque Music from Beaujoyeulx to Rameau* (London, 1973, 2/1978, rev. Fr. trans., 1981)

R. M. Isherwood: *Music in the Service of the King: France in the Seventeenth Century* (Ithaca, NY, and London, 1973)

M. M. McGowan: 'The Origins of French Opera', *NOHM*, v (1975), 169–205

P.-M. Masson: 'French Opera from Lully to Rameau', *NOHM*, v (1975), 206–66

J. E. W. Newman: *Jean-Baptiste de Lully and his Tragédies lyriques* (Ann Arbor, 1979)

K. Pendle: *Eugène Scribe and French Opera of the Nineteenth Century* (Ann Arbor, 1979)

W. Dean: 'French Opera', *NOHM*, viii (1982), 26–119

S. Pitou: *The Paris Opéra: an Encyclopedia of Operas, Ballets, Composers and Performers, i: Genesis and Glory, 1671–1715* (Westport, CT, 1983)

R. Fajon: *L'Opéra à Paris du Roi-Soleil à Louis le Bien-aimé* (Geneva, 1984)

W. Weber: 'La musique ancienne in the Waning of the Ancien Régime', *Journal of Modern History*, vi (1984), 58–88

S. Pitou: *The Paris Opéra: an Encyclopedia of Operas, Ballets, Composers and Performers, ii: Rococo and Romantic, 1715–1815* (Westport, CT, 1985)

D. Charlton: *Grétry and the Growth of Opéra-comique* (Cambridge, 1986)

J. Mongrédien: *La musique des lumières au romantisme* (Paris, 1986)

J. Fulcher: *The Nation's Image: French Grand Opera as Politics and Politicized Art* (Cambridge, 1987)

D. Pistone, ed.: *Le théâtre lyrique français 1945–1985* (Paris, 1987)

S. Huebner: 'Opera Audiences in Paris, 1830–1870', *ML*, lxx (1989), 206–25

N. Zaslaw: 'The First Opera in Paris: a Study in the Politics of Art', *Jean-Baptiste Lully and the Music of the French Baroque: Essays in Honor of James R. Anthony* (Cambridge, 1989), 7–24

DAVID CHARLTON (with RICHARD LANGHAM SMITH)

Francesca da Rimini (i) ('Francesca of Rimini'). Opera in a prologue, one act and an epilogue, op.25, by SERGEY VASIL'YEVICH RAKHMANINOV to a libretto by MODEST IL'YICH TCHAIKOVSKY after Canto v of DANTE ALIGHIERI's *Inferno*; Moscow, Bol'shoy Theatre, 11/24 January 1906.

Rakhmaninov began composing his *Francesca da Rimini* in 1900, hard on the heels of a four-act treatment of the same subject by Eduard Nápravník, chief conductor of the Mariinsky Theatre in St Petersburg, and completed it in 1904–5 while occupying the corresponding post at the corresponding Moscow theatre, the Bol'shoy. He conducted the première himself, with Antonina Nezhdanova in the title role and Dmitry Smirnov as Dante, in a double bill with the première of his *Miserly Knight*. Despite a torrid love scene (and though it has found aggressive champions), it is Rakhmaninov's weakest opera, owing in part to a clumsily crafted libretto, in part to the static and disproportionately lengthy prologue and epilogue. These framing scenes are set in the Second Circle of Hell, with Dante (tenor), guided by the shade of Virgil (baritone), accosting the wind-buffeted spirits of Francesca (soprano) and her lover Paolo Malatesta (tenor). The prologue, essentially a grandiose tone poem for orchestra and wordless chorus representing the damned (and inevitably influenced by the famous orchestral fantasia by the librettist's brother), is longer than either of the dramatic scenes.

The first dramatic scene, Modest Tchaikovsky's invention, is a stormy, rather banal scene for the jealous husband, Lanceotto Malatesta (baritone). Intended for Shalyapin (who however did not sing it), it is haunted by Aleko's cavatina in Rakhmaninov's first opera, a Shalyapin speciality. The second scene (composed in Italy in 1900) contains the essential action as related by Dante: Francesca and Paolo, inflamed by reading the romance of Lancelot and Guinevere, succumb to illicit passion. An effective essay in the *verismo* style, it culminates in a perhaps unparalleled 50-bar kiss preceding the lovers' murder by Lanceotto. After that, the lovers' parting words to Dante in the epilogue – 'We read no more that day!' – can hardly fail (though they come straight from the hallowed literary source) to evoke a titter.

RICHARD TARUSKIN

Francesca da Rimini (ii) ('Francesca of Rimini'). Tragic opera in four acts by RICCARDO ZANDONAI to a libretto by Tito Ricordi (ii) (*see* RICORDI family) from the play by GABRIELE D'ANNUNZIO, after DANTE ALIGHIERI's *Inferno*, v:97–142; Turin, Teatro Regio, 19 February 1914.

D'Annunzio's tragedy, written in 1901 for Eleonora Duse and defined by the poet as 'an epic of blood and lust', needed few basic changes to become a libretto, and to some extent he himself assisted with the adaptation. Sections that, although justifiable in the decadent atmosphere of the play, were not essential to the action and would have presented serious musical difficulties were eliminated. What remains is the essence of the story of Francesca, basically as outlined by Dante but with increased sensuality and darker, more amoral overtones.

Act 1 is set in the house of Francesca's family, the Polentani, in Ravenna. Ostasio (baritone) arranges a political marriage for his sister Francesca (soprano) with Giovanni Malatesta, 'lo Sciancato' (the Cripple), known as Gianciotto (baritone). Surrounded by her maids, Francesca is comforted by her sister Samaritana (soprano), and believes her intended husband to be Paolo il Bello (tenor), whom she sees go past and to

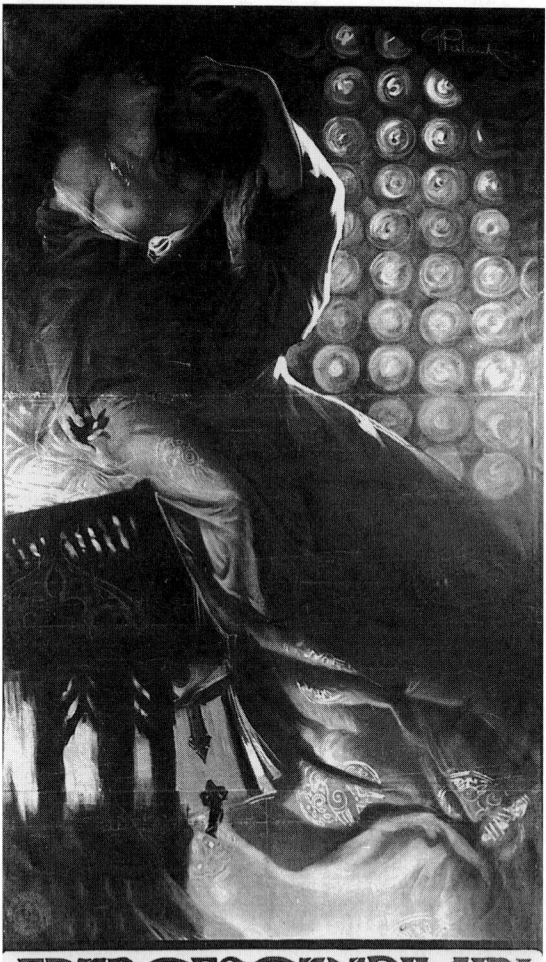

Poster by Giuseppe Palanti for Zandonai's 'Francesca da Rimini' printed at the time of the original production at the Teatro Regio, Turin in 1914

whom she offers a rose; but Paolo is only representing his ungainly and cruel brother in a proxy marriage. In Act 2 Francesca, now Gianciotto's wife, is living in the Malatesta house at Rimini; during a battle Paolo reveals his love to Francesca, to her distress. Act 3 takes place in Francesca's apartments, where her ladies are singing a spring song when the slave Smaragdi (contralto) announces Paolo's arrival; the two are left alone and fall passionately in love, with the encouragement of the love story of Lancelot and Guinevere (as narrated in Canto v of Dante's *Inferno*). Act 4 is in two parts, the first containing the most dramatic moments of the opera: Francesca is spied on by Malatestino (tenor), Paolo and Gianciotto's degenerate brother, who has also fallen under her spell; he discovers her adulterous liaison with Paolo and crudely attempts to blackmail her, and when she rejects him he denounces the lovers to Gianciotto.

In the second part the lovers are together, confident that Gianciotto has departed; but he has in fact set a trap for them, and discovers and kills them.

Francesca da Rimini, considered Zandonai's masterpiece, is not only the most successful of the operas based on the plays of D'Annunzio by the many Italian composers who were inspired by them (others include Franchetti, Pizzetti, G. F. Malipiero, Mascagni, Montemezzi): it is also one of the most original and polished Italian melodramas of the 20th century. Zandonai combines a powerful gift for Italian melody, more nervous and fragmentary than Puccini's, with an exceptional command of orchestration, to some extent influenced by Strauss. *Verismo*-style vocal writing, in the tradition of Mascagni, is on the whole confined to the male voices, especially in Act 2 and the first part of Act 4, the most dramatic points of the opera, which have a degree of rhetorical inflation. The most inspired music, often with a magical effect not to be found in other contemporary composers, is in the evocation of atmosphere (with some careful use of ancient instruments), in the delicate treatment of the female choruses and, in general, in the close fidelity to the natural rise and fall of the words themselves. Particularly effective are the Act 1 finale, where the Paolo theme is developed in a context of great sweetness, and especially Act 3, the finest in the opera, which includes the charming spring song and the ardent love duet between Paolo and Francesca. There are other strongly expressive sections in the music for Francesca and Samaritana in the first and fourth acts. The dominant feeling conveyed by the score, whose harmonic world has some Debussian colouring, is melancholy and oppressed, somewhat distant from the heavy and erotic atmosphere of D'Annunzio's tragedy. Among the most impressive arias are those of Francesca ('Chi ho veduto?' and 'Paolo, datemi pace!') and of Paolo ('Inghirlandata di violette'). But some of the most striking music comes in numbers of a less traditional kind, such as the duets between Francesca and Samaritana and between Paolo and Francesca, and the whole of the first part of Act 4 with Francesca, Gianciotto and Malatestino.   RENATO CHIESA

Franceschini, Giovanni Battista ['Franceschino'] (*b* 1662 or 1672; *d* 6 Aug 1732). Italian tenor. A Florentine, Franceschini was a salaried member of the choir of the Duke of Modena from 1690 until his death. At the same time, he was performing in opera in the principal theatres of northern Italy. The first mention of him is in the libretto for *Il trionfo delle spine* (an oratorio possibly by Barbieri, 1691, Reggio Emilia) as Pietà; between 1694 and 1698 he sang in Bologna, Milan, Reggio and Modena. In 1696 he took the part of Ulysses in Perti's *Penelope la casta* in Rome. In the 1699 and 1700 seasons he was at S Giovanni Grisostomo in second or third male parts. His operatic career continued until the second decade of the 18th century; his last appearance in a libretto was in *Il conte di Altamura* (composer unknown, 1720, Modena). He is often mentioned in the correspondence of L. A. Muratori (see Marri). He was probably a versatile and reliable singer with acting ability, but he was restricted to secondary roles. Marri's suggestion that he also sang falsetto roles is possibly erroneous.

*

F. Marri: 'Muratori, la musica e il melodramma negli anni milanesi (1695–1700)', *Muratoriana*, xvi (1988), 19–124

SERGIO DURANTE

Franceschini, Petronio (*b* Bologna, *c*1650; *d* Venice, *c*18 Dec 1680). Italian composer. He was a brother of the painter M. A. Franceschini. He studied with Lorenzo Perti and in Rome with Giuseppe Corsi. One of the first members of the Bolognese Accademia Filarmonica, he served as its *principe* in 1673, and was a cellist at Bologna Cathedral, 1675–80. Already known for his operas, he was called to Venice by Vincenzo Grimani to compose a work for the Teatro SS Giovanni e Paolo but died before he could complete it. During his brief time in Venice he may have been elected *maestro di cappella* of the Ospedaletto. He was buried in the church of SS Giovanni e Paolo. Franceschini's operas have great rhythmic energy and make much use of the trumpet in dialogue with the voice.

Le gare di Sdegno, d'Amore e di Gelosia (F. M. Bordocchi), prol. and 2 intermedi for Caligula delirante, Bologna, Formagliari, 1674, lost

L'Oronte di Menfi (T. Stanzani), Bologna, Formagliari, 10 Jan 1676, *I-Vnm*

Arsinoe (Stanzani), Bologna, Formagliari, 26 Dec 1676, *Vnm* (2 versions)

Apollo in Tessaglia (Stanzani), Bologna, Formagliari, 27 May 1679, lost

Dionisio, overo La virtù trionfante del vitio [Act 1] (3, M. Noris), Venice, SS Giovanni e Paolo, 12 Jan 1681, *Vc, Vqs* (arias) [Acts 2 and 3 by G. D. Partenio]

*

C. Ivanovich: *Minerva al tavolino* (Venice, 1681, 2/1688)

THOMAS WALKER

Francesina. *See* DUPARC, ELISABETH.

Franchetti, Baron **Alberto** (*b* Turin, 18 Sept 1860; *d* Viareggio, 4 Aug 1942). Italian composer. He studied in Turin and Venice, and later in Dresden with Draeseke and in Munich with Rheinberger. Coming from a noble family of considerable wealth, he was able to dedicate his entire time to composition, to securing the best possible conditions for the premières of his operas, and to the interest in fast cars that he shared with Puccini. The only official position he held in musical life was that of director of the Florence Conservatory (1926–8). No study of his life has yet been published, despite an abundance of material (e.g. his correspondence with Luigi Illica) in Italian libraries. Franchetti's earlier operas were highly acclaimed in their time, and the success of *Asrael* at La Scala (1889) led Verdi to recommend him for the task of composing the commemorative opera for the 400th anniversary of the discovery of America, *Cristoforo Colombo*, commissioned by the city of Genoa.

Franchetti's operas represent an original solution to several aesthetic problems of fin-de-siècle opera composition, although his attempt to blend the tradition of late Italian grand opera on historical subjects with the German influences which he assimilated during his studies now seems somewhat outdated. The eclectic libretto for *Asrael* (1888) by Ferdinando Fontana (the author of the unfortunate librettos for Puccini's first two operas, *Le Villi* and *Edgar*) continued a tradition of Italian operas based on northern fairy-tales begun by Catalani, but its plot appears as a mixture of *Mefistofele* and *Lohengrin*. Nevertheless, the extended crowd scenes in hell (Act 1) and heaven (Acts 1 and 4) succeeded in impressing the public and showed Franchetti's skill in writing effective large-scale scenes. Arguably his finest achievement is *Cristoforo Colombo*, on one of Illica's earliest librettos (1892, Genoa). Although the libretto clearly reveals its models, especi-

ally Meyerbeer's *L'Africaine*, it represents a marked progress towards a new view of musical theatre. The music demonstrates Franchetti's predilection for what was known in contemporary Italian aesthetics as 'sinfonismo'; large symphonic interludes and the complete integration of the soloists' voices into the orchestral texture bear witness to his skill in unifying entire acts through a continuous musical discourse in the orchestra. The second act, with its two ships on stage, presented the moment of discovery, visually through new techniques of staging – under the influence of the Bayreuth *Parsifal*, a revolving backdrop was used – and musically through masterly use of the orchestra; it constitutes what was probably the culmination of Illica and Franchetti's collaboration.

After some indecision about setting Illica's libretto *Tosca* (subsequently given to Puccini), Franchetti had his greatest success with *Germania*, which received its première in 1902 under Toscanini at La Scala. Though much acclaimed by the Italian public of the time, the work suffers from Franchetti's occasional difficulties with individual characterization, but more especially from his naive attempt to create German local colour through the use of folksongs. Although there had been several attempts, by Puccini and others, to write an opera in collaboration with Gabriele D'Annunzio, it was Franchetti who wrote the first based on a play by him, *La figlia di Iorio* (1906, La Scala). But he failed to grasp the pre-rational cruelty of the Abruzzese pagan society depicted in D'Annunzio's drama; the powerful characters seem in ridiculous contrast with the mild pastoral atmosphere evoked throughout by the orchestra. Franchetti's later operas show a marked decline in musical style and underlying dramatic vision; they range from the operetta *Giove a Pompei*, written in collaboration with Giordano on a posthumous libretto by Illica (1921, Rome), to the pre-Fascist opera *Glauco* (1922, Naples), containing some ingredients typical of later propaganda operas on subjects connected with the glory of ancient Rome.

See also ASRAEL; CRISTOFORO COLOMBO; and GERMANIA.

first performed at Milan, La Scala, unless otherwise stated; all printed works published in Milan

Asrael (leggenda, 4, F. Fontana), Reggio Emilia, Municipale, 11 Feb 1888 (1888)

Cristoforo Colombo (dramma lirico, 4, epilogue, L. Illica), Genoa, Carlo Felice, 6 Oct 1892 (1893); rev. version (3, epilogue), 17 Jan 1923, *I-Mr**

Fior d'Alpe (os, 3, L. di Castelnuovo), 15 March 1894 (1894)

Il signor di Pourceaugnac (op comica, 3, Fontana, after Molière), 10 April 1897 (1898)

Germania (dramma lirico, prol., 2, epilogue, Illica), 11 March 1902 (1902)

La figlia di Iorio (tragedia pastorale, 3, G. D'Annunzio), 19 March 1906 (1906)

Notte di leggenda (tragedia lirica, 1, G. Forzano), 14 Jan 1915 (1915)

Giove a Pompei (operetta, 3, Illica and E. Romagnoli), Rome, Pariola, 5 July 1921, unpubd, collab. Giordano

Glauco (os, 3, Forzano), Naples, S Carlo, 8 April 1922 (1922)

Unperf.: Zoroastro, *c*1890 (Fontana); Il finto paggio, 1924 (commedia musicale, Forzano); Il gonfaloniere [? Don Napoleone], 1927 (Forzano)

*

A. Soffredini: 'Cristoforo Colombo di Alberto Franchetti', *Gazzetta musicale di Milano*, xlvii (1892), 651–2

G. Monaldi: 'Rassegna musicale: per l'Asrael', *Nuova antologia*, no.151 (1897), 150–60

I. Valetta: 'Rassegna musicale: Il signor di Pourceaugnac di Alberto Franchetti', *Nuova antologia*, no.160 (1898), 349–53

L. Torchi: 'Germania di Alberto Franchetti', *RMI*, ix (1902), 377–421

A. Lualdi: 'Cristoforo Colombo di A. Franchetti alla Scala', *Serate musicali* (Milan, 1928), 12

L. Tomelleri: 'La figlia di Iorio: D'Annunzio e Franchetti', *RMI*, xliii (1939), 195; repr. in *Gabriele D'Annunzio e la musica* (Milan, 1939)

G. Roncaglia: 'Dimenticato', *La Scala*, no.13 (1950), 59–61

G. Forzano: 'Un musicista ingiustamente dimenticato: A. Franchetti', *Come i ho conosciuti* (Turin, 1957), 33

F. Candida: 'Ottocentista all'indice', *La Scala*, no.136 (1961), 18–21

B. Capobianchi and others: *Ricordi di Alberto Franchetti* (Turin, 1963)

M. Morini: 'L'epopea dell'oceano Atlantico in un'opera sul grande Genovese: Appunti per una cronologia: *Cristoforo Colombo* di Franchetti', *Discoteca alta fedeltà*, xv/143 (1974), 24, 25

J. Maehder: 'Szenische Imagination und Stoffwahl in der italienischen Oper des Fin de siècle', *Zwischen Opera buffa und Melodramma: Perspektiven der Opernforschung I: Bad Homburg 1985–7* [on *Asrael*, *Cristoforo Colombo* and *Germania*]

J. Budden: 'Wagnerian Tendencies in Italian Opera', *Music and Theatre: Essays in Honour of Winton Dean* (Cambridge, 1987), 299–332

J. Maehder: 'The Origins of Italian "Literaturoper": "Guglielmo Ratcliff", "La figlia di Iorio", "Parisina" and "Francesca da Rimini"', *Reading Opera*, ed. A. Groos and R. Parker (Princeton, 1988), 92–128

——: 'Mythologizing the Encounter – Columbus, Motecuzoma, Cortés and the Representation of the "Discovery" on the Opera Stage', *Musical Repercussions of 1492: Encounters in Text and Performance*, ed. C. Robertson (Washington, 1992)

L. Zoppelli: 'Il mito del canto del buon selvaggio nel *Cristoforo Colombo* di Alberto Franchetti', *Opera e libretto*, ed. G. Morelli (Florence, forthcoming)   JÜRGEN MAEHDER

Franchetti, Arnold (*b* Lucca, Italy, 1909). American composer and teacher, son of Alberto Franchetti. The exact date of his birth is unknown. He studied physics at the University of Florence and music at the Mozarteum in Salzburg, where he received the Lehmann Prize for composition. Before moving to the USA in 1947 he taught in Italy, Austria and Sweden.

In 1948 Franchetti joined the composition faculty of the Hartt College of Music, Hartford, Connecticut. A prolific composer of choral works, piano music, chamber music and works for orchestra, band and film, he has composed several short operas, most of which were first performed in Hartford. His three one-act operas *The Princess*, *The Maypole* and *The Game of Cards* form a trilogy, unified by a war theme. Franchetti's operatic style is tonal, showing the influence of Mahler, Strauss and Bartók. Most of his operas are written for full orchestra, often with expanded percussion. Some of the works are for unusual tone colour combinations; for example, *Notturno in La* is scored for a large percussion section and one violin. The work was commissioned by the Cesare Barbieri Center for Italian Studies at Trinity College, Hartford.

Among Franchetti's many awards are the Fromm Award, a Guggenheim Foundation Award and a Koussevitzky Music Foundation grant through the Library of Congress. In 1964 he received the Ditson Award of Columbia University.

The Lion (children's op, 2, R. H. Sanderson and M. Franchetti), New London, CT, Williams Memorial Institute, 16 Dec 1950
The Princess [Tapestry] (1, M. Franchetti), Hartford, CT, Hartt College of Music, 16 March 1952 [pt 1 of trilogy]
The Maypole (1, E. R. Mills), Westport, CT, White Barn, 6 July 1952 [pt 2 of trilogy]
The Game of Cards, 1953 (1, A. Franchetti), concert version, 20 March 1955; stage, Hartt College of Music, 9 May 1956 [pt 3 of trilogy]
The Anachronism (1, Mills), Hartt College of Music, 4 March 1956
The Dowser, 1956 (1, Mills), unperf.
Prelude and Fugue (1, C. Bax), Hartt College of Music, 21 April 1959
Notturno in La, or As a Conductor Dreams (2, L. Berrone, after A. de Musset), Hartford, Trinity College, 20 Oct 1966
The Suncatcher (1, B. Sargeant), U. of Hartford, 8 Feb 1973
Soap Opera (comic op, 1, K. Lombardo), U. of Hartford, 1973
Married Men go to Hell [The Devil Takes a Wife], 1975 (3, E. Willheim, after N. Machiavelli), unperf.
Dracula, 1979 (1, A. Franchetti), unperf.   ELISE K. KIRK

Franchi [de Franchi, de Franchis, de Franco], **Carlo** (*b* ?1743; *d* ?after 1779). Italian composer. He is described as Neapolitan in printed librettos and his music certainly belongs to the Neapolitan school. His first opera, *La vedova capricciosa*, was given at the Teatro Nuovo there in 1765, and his operas continued to be staged until 1779, when *I tre amanti ridicoli* was performed at the Teatro Ducale, Mantua. Franchi's operas had their first performances in principal Italian cities (Rome, Venice, Turin and Naples) and in provincial cities with a strong operatic tradition (Perugia and Mantua). The intermezzo *Il barone di Rocca Antica*, first performed at the Teatro Valle, Rome, was later revived in Florence, Terni, Foligno, Lisbon, Ancona, Passavia, Venice and Dresden. This work marks a fundamental change in the development of Italian *opera buffa* before Rossini. Although it is subtitled 'intermezzi per musica', the work is far removed from the spirit of Pergolesi's intermezzos: the sinfonia is in three parts, the arias are polished and elegant, and secco recitatives are shorter and propelled by lighter, more fluent rhythms.

La vedova capricciosa (commedia, G. Palomba), Naples, Nuovo, carn. 1765
Ifigenia in Aulide (V.A. Cigna-Santi), Rome, Argentina, 3 Feb 1766, *F-Pn*, *I-Rvat* (ov. and arias)
La clemenza di Tito, Rome, Argentina, 1766, aria *Rc* and *Rrostirolla*
Arsace (dramma, ? A. Salvi), Venice, S Benedetto, Jan 1768, *P-La*
La pittrice (int, F. Cerlone), Rome, Pace, carn. 1768
Il gran cidde Rodrigo (dramma, 3, G. Pizzi), Turin, Regio, 26 Dec 1768, *I-Tf*, *P-La*
La contadina fedele (int, 2), Rome, Valle, carn. 1769, *I-Rdp*
Il trionfo della costanza (opera semiseria, D'Oregno), Turin, Carignano, spr. 1769, aria *Tf*
Le astuzie di Rosina e Burlotto (dg), Perugia, Leon d'Oro, carn. 1770
Siroe re di Persia (dramma per musica, 3, P. Metastasio), Rome, Argentina, 13 Feb 1770, *Rdp*, *Rvat*, *P-La*
La pastorella incognita (commedia, P. Mililotti), Naples, Fiorentini, spr. 1770
Il barone di Rocca Antica [Act 1] (int, 2, G. Petrosellini), Rome, Valle, 4 Feb 1771, *D-Dlb*, *Rtt*, *F-Pn*, *I-Fc* [Act 2 by P. Anfossi]; rev. Dresden, 1772 [some sources suggest the Rome version was entirely by Franchi]
La semplice (int, 2), Rome, Valle, 7 Jan 1772, *F-Pn*, *I-Fc*
Farnace (dramma, ? A. M. Lucchini), Rome, Dame, 15 Feb 1772, *F-Pn*, *I-Mc* (ov.), *PAc* (ov. and aria), *PS* (ov.), *Rc* (2 arias)
La finta zingara [cingara] per amore (farsa, 2), Rome, Tordinona, carn. 1774 [probably rev. of Il barone di Rocca Antica]
I tre amanti ridicoli, Mantua, Ducale, carn. 1779

*

O. Landmann: *Die Dresdner italienische Oper zwischen Hasse und Weber: ein Daten- und Quellenverzeichnis für die Jahre 1765–1817* (Dresden, 1976)

B. Brumana and M. Pascale: 'Il teatro musicale a Perugia nel settecento: una cronologia dai libretti', *Esercizi arte musica spettacolo*, vi (1983), 71–134

G. Ciliberti: *Il barone di Rocca Antica ovvero: L'intermezzo sinonimo di opera* (Amelia, 1988) [programme notes]

—: *Il barone di Rocca* (Bongiovanni di Bologna GB 2081/82–2, 1989) [record notes]   GALLIANO CILIBERTI

Franci, Benvenuto (*b* Pienza, Siena, 1 July 1891; *d* Rome, 27 Feb 1985). Italian baritone. He studied in Rome at the S Cecilia Conservatory with Cotogni and Rosati, and made his début there in 1918 at the Teatro Costanzi in Mascagni's *Lodoletta*. In 1919 he appeared at the S Carlo, as Renato, then at leading Italian theatres, including La Scala (1923–36) and the Rome Opera (1928–49). He created roles in operas by Giordano, Zandonai and Boito (Fanuèl in *Nerone*); his German roles included Hans Sachs and Barak. He also sang in Madrid, Barcelona, Buenos Aires and at Covent Garden (1925, 1931 and 1946). He retired in 1953. He had a large and penetrating voice, especially in the middle register, and was remarkable for his vehement singing in many dramatic Verdi roles, particularly Count di Luna, Rigoletto, Don Carlo (*Forza*) and Amonasro, as well as Barnaba in *La Gioconda*, Gérard in *Andrea Chénier* and Scarpia.

GV (R. Celletti; R. Vegeto)   RODOLFO CELLETTI

Franci, Carlo (*b* Buenos Aires, 18 July 1927). Italian conductor and composer, son of Benvenuto Franci. He studied at the Rome Conservatory and in 1952 attended Fernando Previtali's conducting courses at the Accademia di S Cecilia. At first a conductor only of symphonic music, he made his operatic début in 1959, conducting *Hänsel und Gretel* at the Festival of Two Worlds, Spoleto. He then conducted at the leading Italian theatres, at the Vienna Staatsoper and other houses, both in the standard Italian repertory and in important revivals of operas by Rossini, whose *Otello* he took with the Rome Opera to the Metropolitan in 1968, and Spontini (*Fernand Cortez*). He returned to the Metropolitan from 1969 to 1972 and has since conducted widely in Europe and North and South America. His opera *L'imperatore* was produced at Bergamo in 1958.   PIERO RATTALINO, NOËL GOODWIN

Francillo-Kaufmann, Hedwig (*b* Vienna, 30 Sept 1878; *d* Rio de Janeiro, 26 April 1948). Austrian soprano. She studied in Vienna, then with Orgeni in Dresden and with Rosario in Milan. In 1898 she made her début at Stettin, and after some seasons at Wiesbaden and Munich came to Berlin where she sang from 1903 to 1908. The next four years brought her success in Vienna, and in 1911 she appeared there with Caruso in *Rigoletto*. Moving in 1912 to Hamburg, she was again Caruso's partner, but now in *La traviata* and *Pagliacci*. In 1913 under Beecham she sang Zerbinetta in some of the first performances in England of *Ariadne auf Naxos*. She retired in 1927. Her recordings, which include Zerbinetta's aria in the original key, show at best an ample voice, extensive in range and highly accomplished in technique.   J. B. STEANE

Francine, Jean-Nicolas de (*b* 1662; *d* 6 March 1735). French administrator. Former *maître d'hôtel* to the king, and of a Florentine family, he married Lully's daughter Catherine-Madeleine in 1684. Louis XIV appointed him manager of the Opéra (Académie Royale de Musique) by a royal warrant dated 27 June 1687. Francine first went into partnership with three investors (Thouassin, l'Apotre and Montarsy) and then, by letters patent of 30 December 1698, with Hyacinthe de Gauréault Dumont.

Burdened by debts and expenses (the entertainment tax and the payment of pensions and of authors' royalties), the two managers granted their licence first to Pécour and Belleville and then, on 5 October 1704, to Pierre Guyenet, who died in 1712 leaving considerable debts. Francine and Dumont resumed their licence again on 12 December 1712, but under pressure from Guyenet's creditors Francine negotiated with the receivers (Besnier, Chomat, Duchesne and Laval) by a deed dated 24 December of the next year: Francine ceded them his licence and 'the theatre with all its costumes, machinery and scenery', but retained the management of the Opéra. In return, the receivers undertook to settle the debts, pay the salaries and disburse an annual pension of 20 000 livres to Francine and of 12 000 to Dumont. On 13 August 1714 the king appointed Alican de Landivisiau to settle the disputes between Francine and the receivers, and he was joined in December 1715 by the duc d'Antin (who resigned in 1717). The Opéra balls began at this time (1715) under Francine's management. Eventually he was ousted, but after a period of troubles and intrigues the king restored full powers to him on 18 February 1721. On 8 February 1728, pleading 'his great age and his infirmities', Francine finally retired with a pension of 15 000 livres, leaving the management of the Opéra to André Destouches.

Paris, Archives Nationales, ser. AJ[13]1
F-Po, MS Amelot
J. Gourret: *Ces hommes qui ont fait l'Opéra* (Paris, 1984)
                    NICOLE WILD

Franck, César(-Auguste-Jean-Guillaume-Hubert) (*b* Liège, 10 Dec 1822; *d* Paris, 8 Nov 1890). French composer of Belgian birth. His childhood and adolescence were scarred by parental exploitation, and this perhaps contributed to the late maturing of his full creative powers. He entered the Liège Conservatory in 1830 where he rapidly gained *premiers prix* for solfège and piano. Encouraged by his son's success, Franck's father organized a series of concerts in Liège, Brussels and Aachen in 1835. Franck's earliest surviving compositions, trivial showpieces and operatic fantasies *à la mode*, were written in connection with these and subsequent exhibitions. In 1835 the family moved to Paris where Franck took lessons from Pierre-Joseph-Guillaume Zimmermann and Reicha, before enrolling at the Conservatoire in 1837. He was withdrawn from study by his father in April 1842, without having attempted the Prix de Rome, in order to concentrate on a career as a virtuoso; however, following a serious illness, and the poor reception accorded the first performance of his oratorio *Ruth* in 1846, his career declined. He quitted his parents' house and took on work as a teacher and organist. In 1848, despite initial opposition from his father, he married Félicité Saillot Desmousseaux, whose parents were actors at the Comédie-Française. His opera *Le valet de ferme* dates from the early years of his marriage. Unfortunately, Franck was no connoisseur of literature, and this is nowhere more evident than in the execrable libretto for this grim opera set in 18th-century Ireland, which tells of a hired farmhand's affair with his employer's wife. As Franck's recitatives have now been recovered, *Le valet de ferme* should perhaps be considered as a full-scale opera rather than an *opéra comique*, although it is unlikely ever to be revived.

The start of a new phase of Franck's career has been attributed to his appointment, early in 1858, as organist of Ste Clotilde. Here, his after-service extemporizations quickly became a public attraction and formed the basis of his first major work, the *Six pièces*, completed in 1862. Their success was not followed up, however. The ensuing period proved creatively fallow though at this time Franck began to attract a remarkable cluster of pupil-disciples, known as the *bande à Franck*, which included Henri Duparc, Arthur Coquard and Albert Cahen. After succeeding Benoist as professor of organ at the Conservatoire in 1872, he came to teach Vincent d'Indy, who went on to propagate the symphonic ideals of his teacher. From the early 1870s Franck entered a creative phase of tremendous intensity that lasted until his death. He composed oratorios, symphonies and also the ill-fated opera *Hulda*, produced posthumously. *Hulda* can be traced back to a play by Bjørnson about the bloodthirsty tribe of Aslaks in 11th-century Norway. Like *Le valet de ferme*, Franck set it in response to family pressure, and it remains best known for its orchestral set pieces and ballet music, for Franck seems to have had little sympathy for the human emotions displayed in Grandmougin's melodramatic adaptation. In this Meyerbeerian throwback, Hulda (the heroine) is captured by the marauding Aslaks and undergoes all sorts of tribulations as assorted warriors fight for her favours. Each meets a gory death, and Hulda is driven to suicide at the close.

Work on *Ghisèle* occupied him in the late 1880s but he abandoned its orchestration to his pupils. Here, Franck found a slightly superior librettist for another melodramatic tale of the distant past, this time set in the Merovingian court of Neustria where Frédegonde, its regent, holds the Austrian princess, Ghisèle, captive. Franck liked its 6th-century conflict between paganism and Christianity and probably thought it must appeal to the public because it was so crammed with violent dramatic situations and Wagnerian potential. Sadly, he was wrong. However, the failure of his operas cannot be blamed entirely on their absurd and anachronistic librettos; Franck was unable to realize essentially dramatic schemes and his seriousness stood in marked contrast to the superficiality of the Opéra-dominated establishment. As an arranger he produced vocal scores of Philidor's operas *Ernelinde*, *Tom Jones* and *Le bûcheron*, but his finest achievements are represented by his symphonic, chamber and keyboard compositions and by his legacy as a teacher.

See also Hulda.

Stradella, *c*1844 (3, E. Deschamps), unperf., F-Pn*, vs (Paris)
Le valet de ferme, 1851–3 (oc, 3, A. Royer and G. Vaëz), unperf., F-Pn
Hulda, 1882–5 (opéra, 4, epilogue, C. Grandmougin, after B. Bjørnson), Monte Carlo, 4 March 1894; vs arr. Franck (to p.285) and S. Rousseau (from p.285) (Paris, 1894, abridged 2/?1894)
Ghisèle, 1888–90 (drame lyrique, 4, G.-A. Thierry), Monte Carlo, 30 March 1896 (Paris, 1896); Act 1 orchd Franck; Act 2 P. de Bréville, d'Indy and Chausson; Act 3 S. Rousseau; Act 4 A. Coquard

*

G. Derepas: *César Franck: étude sur sa vie, son enseignement, son oeuvre* (Paris, 1897, 2/1904)
C. van den Borren: *L'oeuvre dramatique de César Franck: 'Hulda' et 'Ghiselle'* (Brussels, 1907)
M. Emmanuel: *César Franck* (Paris, 1930)
L. Vallas (trans. H. Foss): *César Franck* (London, 1951)
J. Gallois: *César Franck* (Paris, 1966)
L. Davies: *César Franck and his Circle* (London, 1970)
——: *Franck* (London, 1973)

JOHN TREVITT, ROBERT ORLEDGE

Franck, Johann Wolfgang (*b* Unterschwaningen, Middle Franconia, bap. 17 June 1644; *d* ? *c*1710). German composer. Since his father held an important administrative post at the court of the Margrave of Brandenburg-Ansbach, he would have had a superior education in a Latin school. This is substantiated by his matriculation at Wittenberg University in 1663, although the nature of his studies there is unrecorded, as are details of his musical education. From 1665 at the latest to 1668 he served the Ansbach court in its musical ensemble and also as the tutor of the children of the ruling family. He was away for three years, possibly travelling and studying in Italy. In 1672 he returned to Ansbach as 'Director der Comoedie' and also as household chaplain. His new appointment enabled him to reorganize and rebuild the court orchestra, apparently introducing the French style and discipline of orchestral ensemble playing. As well as writing many sacred and secular vocal works, he wrote music for court plays and a ballet and composed his first operas, *Die errettete Unschuld, oder Andromeda und Perseus* (1675) and *Der verliebte Phöbus* (1678). In January 1679 he fled Ansbach, after being accused of assassinating another court musician. He sought asylum in Hamburg, where he became known primarily as an opera composer.

In 1678 Hamburg became the first city outside Venice to establish a public opera house. In 1679 Franck dominated the repertory with four operas (including a revival of *Andromeda*), and between then and 1686 he introduced at least 17 operas. During this period he served not only as opera Kapellmeister but also as director of music at the Lutheran cathedral. He also wrote many sacred songs, mostly to verses by the Hamburg clergyman Heinrich Elmenhorst. He published collections of arias from four operas, *Aeneas* (1680), *Vespasianus* (1681), *Diocletianus* (1682), and the two-part *Der glückliche Gross-Verzier Cara Mustapha* (1686). His only opera to survive complete, with the recitatives as well as the arias, is *Die drey Töchter des Cecrops* (1680). This was once thought to have been a revival of an Ansbach production of 1679. However, Braun (1983) argues convincingly that the Ansbach performance took place when Franck made a return visit there in 1686. This performance was of a greatly expanded version of the original, and it is of this version that a manuscript score is extant. Franck had left for London by 1690, when he is reported as putting on similar performances, and in subsequent years he joined in consort performances with Robert King, a composer, violinist and concert promoter. Franck composed a number of English songs that appeared in London journals. It is not known when or where he died, although a report in Moller's *Cimbria litterata* (Copenhagen, 1744) suggests that he may have been murdered in Spain.

Franck was a major force in developing the identity of German opera in the later 17th century. His music dominated the Hamburg opera during the period 1679–86 (the theatre was closed in 1685). What survives shows that he emphasized a popular style combining elements from Venetian operas and French music. Arias are of various types. There are strophic songs based on dance rhythms clearly of popular or folk-song character. Others, often strophic, suggest German songs and reflect the spirit and probably at times the actual melodies of chorales. A third kind of aria, usually much longer and with the tempo marking

'Adagio', employs strong affective dissonances and dramatic melodic gestures, with rhetorical outbursts to express tragic or other sad affections. As with Venetian opera arias, Franck often rounds off his arias with brief instrumental postludes picking up the final vocal phrase(s). He seems to have been the first Hamburg opera composer to use the orchestra to accompany some of the arias and to interject short, concerted instrumental passages to highlight a particularly expressive vocal phrase. The several instances of trumpet obbligatos are also noteworthy.

The melodic writing in general has a light, popular tone, but many examples occur of a more complex vocal style, with long melismatic passages that seem more instrumental than vocal in character. The harmonic language, evident from the profusely indicated continuo figures, displays much use of expressive unprepared dissonances and frequent sudden shifts from major to minor chords for rhetorical impact.

See also DREY TÖCHTER DES CECROPS, DIE.

first performed at Hamburg, Theater am Gänsemarkt, unless otherwise stated; music lost unless otherwise stated

Die errettete Unschuld, oder Andromeda und Perseus (after P. Corneille: *Andromède*), Ansbach, 1675
Der verliebte Phöbus, Ansbach, 1678
Don Pedro, oder Die abgestraffte Eyffersuch (Franck, after Molière), 1679
Die macchabaeische Mutter mit ihren sieben Söhnen (H. Elmenhorst), 1679
Pastorelle, Lustschloss, Triesdorff, nr Ansbach, 1679
Die wohl und beständig liebende Michal, oder Der siegende und fliehende David (Elmenhorst), 1679
Die drey Töchter des Cecrops (prol., 5, A. von Königsmark), 1680; rev., Ansbach, ?1686, *D-AN*; ed. in DTB, xxxviii, Jg. xxxvii and xxxviii (1938), and EDM, 2nd ser., *Bayern*, ii (1938)
Aeneas der trojanischen Fürsten Ankunft in Italien (J. P. Förtsch), 1680, arias (Hamburg, 1680)
Alceste (Franck, after Matsen), 1680
Jodelet, oder Sein selbst Gefangener (Matsen), 1680
Charitine, oder Die Goettlich-Geliebte (Elmenhorst), 1681
Hannibal (H. Hinsch, after N. Beregan), 1681
Semele (Förtsch), 1681
Vespasianus (L. von Bostel, after G. C. Corradi), 1681, arias (Hamburg, 1681)
Attila (Bostel), 1682
Diocletianus (Bostel, after M. Noris), 1682, arias (Hamburg, 1682)
Semiramis, oder Die allererste regierende Königin (Hinsch, after P. A. Ziani's opera), 1683; also attrib. N. A. Strungk
Der glückliche Gross-Verzier Cara Mustapha, erster Teil, nebenst der grausigen Belagerung und Bestürmung der Kaiserlichen Residenzstadt Wien; anderer Teil, nebenst dem freulichen Entsatze der Kaiserlichen Residenzstadt Wien (Bostel), 1686, arias from both parts (Hamburg, 1686)

J. Mattheson: *Der musicalische Patriot* (Hamburg, 1728)
A. Werner: 'Die Briefe von Johann Wolfgang Franck, die Hamburger Oper betreffend', *SIMG*, vii (1905–6), 125–8
R. Klages: *Johann Wolfgang Franck: Untersuchungen zu seiner Lebensgeschichte und geistliche Kompositionen* (diss., U. of Hamburg, 1937)
G. F. Schmidt: 'Johann Wolfgang Francks Singspiel "Die drey Töchter Cecrops"' *AMf*, iv (1939), 257–316
H. C. Wolff: *Die Barockoper in Hamburg* (Wolfenbüttel, 1957), esp. i, 213–26; incl. music exx., ii, 24ff
R. Brockpähler: *Handbuch zur Geschichte der Barockoper in Deutschland* (Emsdetten, 1964)
W. Braun: '*Die drey Töchter des Cecrops*: zur Datierung und Lokalisierung von Johann Wolfgang Francks Oper', *AMw*, xl (1983), 102–25
——: '*Cara Mustapha* oder die zweite Eröffnung des Hamburger Schauplatzes', *SMw*, xxxv (1984), 37–64
G. J. Buelow: 'Hamburg Opera during Buxtehude's Lifetime: the Works of Johann Wolfgang Franck', *Church, Stage, and Studio: Music and its Contexts in Seventeenth-Century Germany* (Ann Arbor, 1990), 127–61
GEORGE J. BUELOW

Franckenstein, Clemens (Erwein Heinrich Karl Bonaventura), Freiherr von und zu (*b* Wiesentheid, nr Kitzingen, 14 July 1875; *d* Hechendorf, nr Munich, 19 Aug 1942). German composer, conductor and administrator. The son of an Austrian ambassador, he grew up in the various diplomatic incumbencies filled by his father before receiving a secondary education in Vienna. He studied composition there with the Bruckner pupil Victor Bause (until 1894), then with Ludwig Thuille in Munich at the Bayerische Akademie der Tonkunst (1894–6) and at the Hoch Conservatory in Frankfurt with Ivan Knorr (1896–8). While in Vienna Franckenstein established important connections with major literary and artistic personalities of the day, including Hugo von Hofmannsthal, through whom he was admitted to the Stefan George Kreis, whose members included Arthur Schnitzler, Anton Wildgans, Jakob Wassermann and Oskar F. Mayer; the last two were to become his librettists.

From Frankfurt Franckenstein embarked upon a successful career as a conductor, administrator and composer of opera. His conducting career, which began when he was an itinerant theatre conductor in the USA (1900–01) took him to London, where he was staff conductor with the Moody Manners Opera Company (1902–7). Thereafter he was appointed by Baron von Hülsen as a principal staff conductor at the Wiesbaden Hoftheater, before being appointed, at Richard Strauss's behest, to the Royal Prussian Opera in Berlin. In 1912 he became the last Hofintendant at the Munich Opera, where he introduced Bruno Walter as Generalmusikdirektor and arranged for first performances of new operas by von Klenau, Korngold, Braunfels, Courvoisier, Graener and Pfitzner (*Palestrina*). Rendered inactive during the Räterepublik, Franckenstein resumed his responsibilities, now as Bayerischer Staatsintendant, in 1924 with Hans Knappertsbusch as his musical director; he retired in 1934 as a result of his disapproval of Nazi cultural policy and propaganda.

As an opera composer Franckenstein gained increasing recognition, beginning with his first opera, *Griseldis* (1896–7), first produced at Troppau (now Opava) in 1898, thereafter with *Fortunatus*, then *Rahab*, first performed at Budapest (1909) and *Des Kaisers Dichter Li-Tai-Pe* at the Hamburg Staatsoper (1920). While *Griseldis* (subtitled 'Mysterium') and *Fortunatus* perpetuate the ideals and compositional practices of the post-Wagnerian music drama, the one-act *Rahab*, on a biblical theme, is an example of the large-scale *Jugendstil* symphonic drama, with the kind of exotic and opulent harmonic and orchestral usage encountered in works by Strauss (*Salome*), Schreker and Zemlinsky. In 1901, Franckenstein had in fact written a symphonic poem whose programme is identical with the scenario used by Strauss. *Li-Tai-Pe* (1920) is a *Künstlerdrama* in the tradition of *Die Meistersinger* and *Palestrina* with the famous Chinese poet Li-Tai-Pe as its central figure. Cast in three acts, the work combines motivic usage with the use of extended and recurrent closed forms, and was widely performed on German stages between 1920 and 1933. Franckenstein also wrote a pantomime, *Die Biene* (after Hugo von Hofmannsthal), first performed at Darmstadt in 1916.

The Franckensteiniana collection at the Bavarian State Library of 171 letters to Franckenstein by leading composers, conductors and librettists (including 39 from Richard Strauss and 52 from Hofmannsthal) is a central source for German operatic history of the years 1900–34, in particular on the problem of evolving a suitable version of *Ariadne auf Naxos* between its first Stuttgart and Viennese productions.

MSS in D-Mbs

Griseldis op.6 (3, O. F. Mayer), Troppau, 2 Feb 1898
Fortunatus op.10 (3, after J. Wassermann), unperf., vs (Berlin, 1901), full score (Berlin, c1905)
Rahab op.32 (1, Mayer), Budapest, 4 Dec 1909 (Berlin, 1909)
Des Kaisers Dichter Li-Tai-Pe op.43 (3, R. Lothar), Hamburg, 2 Nov 1920 (Berlin, 1920)

PEM (A. D. McCredie)
W. Zentner: 'Clemens von Franckenstein. Zu seinem 60. Geburtstag am 14. Juli 1935', *ZfM*, cii (1935), 740–43
A. D. McCredie: 'Some Jugendstil Lyric and Dramatic Texts and their Settings', *Miscellanea Musicologica. Adelaide Studies in Musicology*, xiii (1984), 223–32
——: 'Clemens von Franckenstein', *Bayerische Komponisten*, xxvi (Tutzing, 1992)   ANDREW D. McCREDIE

Franc-Nohain [Legrand, Maurice-Etienne] (*b* Corbigny, Nièvre, 25 Oct 1872; *d* Paris, 18 Oct 1934). French poet, novelist and playwright. His greatest success was his one-act play *L'heure espagnole*, given more than a hundred performances after its première at the Théâtre de l'Odéon in 1904 and set as an opera by Ravel. His first publications, including the poems *Flûtes* and the *Chansons des trains et des gares* (both 1899), were admired for their cool ironic quality and their clever use of language. Similar qualities prompted Ravel to approach Franc-Nohain in 1907 for permission to set *L'heure espagnole*, in which he found 'droll lyricism' and 'a mixture of familiar conversation with absurd lyricism'. Franc-Nohain vehemently defended himself against the critic Gaston Garraud, who had called the libretto 'mildly pornographic vaudeville'. Subsequent attempts on Franc-Nohain's part to interest Ravel in a further collaboration came to nothing. His works were also set by Claude Terrasse, Emile Jaques-Dalcroze and Hector Fraggi.   RICHARD LANGHAM SMITH

Francoeur, François [*le cadet*] (*b* Paris, 21 [not 8 or 22] Sept 1698; *d* Paris, 5 Aug 1787). French composer. As an opera composer, director and administrator at the Paris Opéra and the French royal court in the mid-18th century, he collaborated with François Rebel [*le fils*] (*b* Paris, 19 June 1701; *d* Paris, 7 Nov 1775). Francoeur entered the Opéra orchestra in 1710, and Rebel joined in 1714. There the two children acquired the lifelong nickname 'les petits violons'. In 1726 their first opera, *Pirame et Thisbé*, had its première at the Opéra and was a great success. Quantz attended a performance and remarked that one could tell from the music that the composers had been beyond the French borders; the reference was to a trip Rebel and Francoeur had made to Vienna and Prague in 1723.

They continued to write operas in collaboration, and in 1739 both left the violin section to take other positions at the Paris Opéra: Francoeur as *maître de musique*, Rebel as *inspecteur général* (musical director) and, apparently for a short time only, as *batteur de mesure*. In 1741 it was decided that Rebel would hold the positions of *batteur de mesure* and *inspecteur* simultaneously, and that Francoeur, while remaining *maître de musique*, would become co-*inspecteur*. Their appointment as joint *inspecteurs généraux* was confirmed by royal decree in 1743. They thus gained artistic (but not financial) control over the Opéra.

Meanwhile, they acquired a series of court positions (or the rights of succession to those positions) in the Musique de la Chambre du Roi: member of the 24 Violons (Rebel, 1717; Francoeur, 1730), *compositeur* (both in 1727, following the success of *Pirame*), *maître de musique* (Rebel, 1733), and *surintendant* (Rebel, 1733; Francoeur, 1744). In 1745 the court resumed the custom, abandoned several decades earlier, of producing fully staged operas, and responsibility for direction naturally fell to Francoeur and Rebel. They directed operatic productions at Versailles that winter, and at Versailles, Fontainebleau, Choisy and Compiègne throughout the rest of their careers. Rebel sold the succession of his *surintendance* to Bernard de Bury in 1751 but continued to direct court operas nonetheless. Francoeur sold the succession of his first two court appointments in 1756 but continued his duties as *surintendant* until 1776. Both were knighted by the king (Order of Saint-Michel), Rebel in 1760 and Francoeur in 1764.

In December 1753 the *inspecteurs*, apparently weary of the Querelle des Bouffons, asked to retire from the Opéra and received large pensions. Four years later, however, they acquired the royal *privilège* to run the Opéra and became its administrative directors. Despite a thorough reshuffling of the administrative structure, they were unable to control the institution's debt and relinquished the *privilège* in 1767. Rebel returned to the Opéra as *administrateur général* (a position created for him by the king) from 1772 until shortly before his death in 1775.

Many misconceptions surround the sources of the Francoeur-Rebel operas, and these have given rise to persistent misattributions. Scores copied by various professional scribes have been erroneously identified in the Paris Conservatoire catalogue (now in *F-Pn*) as autographs of François Francoeur, while revisions made by François are attributed to his nephew Louis-Joseph. LOUIS-JOSEPH FRANCOEUR, whose handwriting is easily distinguished from François', did not revise his uncle's scores, though he did stamp his signature in them. Between 1777 and 1783 (i.e. after Rebel's death) François Francoeur undertook to revise seven of his works, even though there were no plans for further performances. With the help of professional scribes who wrote in the text, and other verbal material, he made changes in some existing manuscripts and produced several new manuscript 'final editions'. All manuscripts involved in this process bear an autograph statement that 'the score found here conforms to the intentions of the authors'. These late manuscripts do not represent the versions of the operas that were actually performed.

Little is known of the division of labour between Francoeur and Rebel, either as composers or as directors. It was Francoeur who had a royal *privilège* to print his music, and his signature appears in the engraved editions of the operas. Regarding the Fontainebleau productions of 1754, *La gazette de France* reported that 'Rebel and Francoeur ... directed, one the theatre and the other the orchestra'. As for their compositional activities, La Borde complained, 'Each of them used to answer, "That number is by us both"'. Francoeur did attribute the revision of Lully's *Armide* to himself alone in the 1781 'final edition' of that work, although *Le Mercure de France* had attributed it to both of them at the time of performance. Handwriting identification suggests that Francoeur did more composing than Rebel, but that Rebel alone was responsible for revising Lully's *Amadis*.

In a prefatory note to the published score of their first (and most successful) opera, *Pirame et Thisbé*, Rebel and Francoeur wrote that Lully was their 'master and model'. In fact they borrowed from and departed from Lully's style to about the same degree as Campra, Destouches and other French opera composers of the period. From Lully (and his librettist Quinault) came the nature and structure of the libretto for a *tragédie en musique*, and the forms and styles for its various musical genres (overture, recitative, airs, dances, choruses and so on). From their own generation came the occasional italianate writing for strings, contrapuntal and melismatic choruses, ornate instrumental obbligato parts and the da capo *ariette*.

Rebel and Francoeur were not stylistic innovators, they followed the trends of their day. Their works composed after Rameau's *Hippolyte et Aricie* (1733) contain many more contrapuntal textures, rapid arpeggiated figures for strings, florid melismas and rich harmonies than the two *tragédies* from the 1720s; and like most of their French contemporaries, they abandoned the *tragédie en musique* in favour of lighter genres starting in the late 1730s. Their final works, however, seem conservative, since these composers never fully embraced the early Classical style; the 1760 version of *Le Prince de Noisy* consists essentially of Baroque music. Perhaps their most 'modern' moments are the gavottes added to Lully's *Armide* in 1761 (1.iii), influenced by *opera buffa*, and the 'premier air pour les assiriannes' added to *Pirame et Thisbé* in 1759 (1.iv), whose ornate melody evokes the German *galant* style.

One of Francoeur and Rebel's duties as *inspecteurs généraux* of the Opéra in the 1740s was to make revisions, usually minor, in operas that were to be revived. Later it became fashionable to rework old operas thoroughly, bringing them into conformity with the tastes of the Rameau era, both by substituting new dances and other pieces and by revising the remaining original music. Rebel and Francoeur completed several editorial projects of this sort (including a new version of Lully's *Amadis*, not Destouches' *Amadis* as stated elsewhere).

Their non-operatic works include two books of violin sonatas by Francoeur (1720 and *c*1730); two cantatas and several motets (lost) by Rebel; a 'dialogue' sung for the king on his return to Paris in 1744; and two sets of suites compiled by Francoeur from operatic dance pieces by various composers (1766 and 1773).

See also PIRAME ET THISBÉ and SCANDERBERG.

collaborations with Rebel and first performed at the Paris Opéra unless otherwise stated; scores published in Paris; autographs MSS wholly or largely in Francoeur's music hand (and text hand in some cases)

Pirame et Thisbé (tragédie en musique, prol., 5, J.-L.-I. de La Serre, after Ovid), 17 Oct 1726, F-Pn, Po*; (1726)

Tarsis et Zélie (tragédie en musique, prol., 5, La Serre), 19 Oct 1728, Pn*, Po (printed score with perf. annotations by Francoeur); (1728)

Scanderberg (tragédie en musique, prol., 5, A. H. de Lamotte and La Serre), 27 Oct 1735, Pc (pts for Act 1 excerpt), Pn (1 autograph; 1 copy with annotations by Francoeur), Po (incl. autograph passages by Francoeur); (*c*1735)

Le ballet de la Paix (ballet-héroïque, prol., 3, P.-C. Roy), 29 May 1738; Pn*, Po (ov., prol.; 2 sets of pts); (*c*1738; pubd with 2 addl entrées, *c*1739)

Les Augustales (divertissement, 1, Roy), 15 Nov 1744 (*c*1744)

Zélindor, roi des silphes (divertissement, 1, F.-A. P. de Moncrif), Versailles, 17 March 1745; with Le trophée (prol. Moncrif), Paris, 10 Aug 1745, Pn (autograph with later revs.), Po; (1745)

La Félicité (ballet-héroïque, prol., 3, Roy), Versailles, 17 March 1746, lib. Po

Ismène (pastorale-héroïque, 1, Moncrif), Versailles, Petits Cabinets, 20 Dec 1747, Paris, 28 Aug 1750, Pc (pts), Pn (autograph with later revs.; printed score with perf. annotations), Po (1 score with autograph passages and revs. by Francoeur; 1 with pts); (*c*1750–53)

Le Prince de Noisy (ballet-héroïque, 3, C.-A Le Clerc de la Bruère), Versailles, Petits Cabinets, 13 March 1749, Paris, 16 Sept 1760, Pn*, Po (incl. autograph passages by Francoeur); (*c*1760)

Les génies tutélaires (divertissment, 1, Moncrif), 21 Sept 1751, Po (pts)

Prol. and intermèdes for Les fées (comédie, 3, F. C. Dancourt), Fontainebleau, 23 Oct 1753; 2 intermèdes for Le magnifique (comédie, prol., 2, Lamotte), Fontainebleau, 15 Nov 1753; 1 scene in Campra and Desmarets' Iphigénie en Tauride, 1762, Pn, Po; added dance pieces for other operas, Pn

Rev. versions of Lully's Thésée, 1754; Proserpine, 1758, Pn (excerpts), Po; Amadis de Gaule, 1759, Po (printed score of 1684 with autograph perf. annotations by Rebel); Armide, 1761, Pn*, Po (pts), Persée, 1770, collab. A. Dauvergne and B. de Bury

Attrib. Rebel *fils* alone: Pastorale héroïque de la fête des ambassadeurs plénipotentiaires d'Espagne à l'occasion de la naissance de Monseigneur le Dauphin (pastoral, 1, La Serre), Paris, Hôtel de Bouillon, 24 Jan 1730, Pa, Po (pts); Intermèdes for L'amour pour l'amour (comédie, La Chaussée), Versailles, 23 [not 22] Jan 1765

PEM ('François Francœur, François Rebel'; H. Schneider)
Le Mercure de France (Oct 1726, Dec 1735, Jan 1736)
Mémoires pour servir à l'histoire de l'Académie royale de musique vulgairement l'Opéra depuis son établissement en 1669 jusqu'en l'année 1758 (MS Amelot, F-Po rés.516)
J.-B. de La Borde: *Essai sur la musique ancienne et moderne* (Paris, 1780)
L.-F. Beffara: *Dictionnaire de l'Académie royale de musique* (MS, 1783–4, F-Po rés.602)
T. de Lajarte: *Bibliothèque musicale du Théâtre de l'Opéra: catalogue* (Paris, 1878)
L. de La Laurencie: 'Une dynastie de musiciens aux XVIIᵉ et XVIIIᵉ siècles: Les Rebel', *SIMG*, vii (1905–6), 253–307
J.-G. Prod'homme: '"Prise de possession" de l'Opéra en 1753, le neveu de Rameau', *Bulletin de la Société française de musicologie*, no.8 (1921), 102–113
The Maurepas Papers: a Unique Collection of French XVIII Century Historical Documents (New York, 1962)
F. Robert: 'Scanderberg: le héros national albanais dans un opéra de Rebel et Francoeur', *RMFC*, iii (1963), 171–78
M. Benoit: *Musiques de cour: chapelle, chambre, écurie, 1661–1733* (Paris, 1971)
R. Machard: 'Les musiciens en France au temps de Jean-Philippe Rameau d'après les actes du secrétariat de la Maison du Roi', *RMFC*, xi (1971), 7–178
S. Pitou: 'The *Opéra-Ballet* and *Scanderberg* at Fontainebleau in 1763', *Studies on Voltaire and the Eighteenth Century*, no. 129 (1975), 27–66
L. Rosow: *Lully's Armide at the Paris Opéra: a Performance History, 1686–1766* (diss., Brandeis U., 1981)
——: 'From Destouches to Berton: Editorial Responsibility at the Paris Opéra', *JAMS*, xl (1987), 285–309
——: 'How Eighteenth-Century Parisians Heard Lully's Operas: the Case of *Armide*'s Fourth Act', *Jean-Baptiste Lully and the Music of the French Baroque: Essays in Honor of James R. Anthony* (Cambridge, 1989), 213–37
R. Fajon: Preface to *Pirame et Thisbé*, FO, xxxvi (forthcoming)
L. Rosow: Preface to *Scanderberg*, FO, xxxvii (forthcoming)
LOIS ROSOW

Francoeur, Louis-Joseph ['Francoeur neveu'] (*b* Paris, 8 Oct 1738; *d* Paris, 10 March 1804). French composer and opera administrator, nephew of FRANÇOIS FRANCOEUR. From 1745 he was brought up by his uncle. Between 1746 and 1752 he was a page of the Musique de la Chambre, leaving that post to join the Opéra orchestra. In 1754 he bought Luc Marchand's succession to the position of *joueur de luth de la chambre* (which does not necessarily imply that he played this instrument). In 1764 he was raised to assistant *maître de musique* of the Opéra orchestra, and he was first *maître* from 1767 until 1779, when he became director of the orchestra. La Borde praised Francoeur for his reorganization of the Opéra administration and the high standards of performance under his leadership. In 1781 he retired from the Opéra but was re-engaged by 1787 when he was again mentioned as assistant director of the governing committee. The disorders of the French Revolution, however, dealt a heavy blow to Francoeur's career. In 1790 the Opéra became a public utility free of royal ties; Francoeur resigned and tried to organize a new company supported by the king. The Francoeur-Cellerier company, founded in 1792, was short-lived and financially disastrous. On 16 September 1793 he was imprisoned by the revolutionary forces and, though freed less than a year later, found himself without pension and deeply in debt. He was re-engaged at the Opéra, remaining an administrator there until 1799.

Francoeur's few original compositions are of less importance than his revisions of the music of others. The revisions (in *F-Pc*) include Lully's *Amadis* (Act 2 scene i), the aria 'Qu'un beau jour renaisse sans nuage' from François Francoeur's *Scanderberg* and T. Bertin de la Doué's *Ajax* (performed 1770). He was thought to have made late revisions to works of his uncle's, but although he did stamp his signature on revised scores, the difference in their hands makes it clear that the autograph amendments are not by Louis-Joseph. His grasp of compositional technique is evident both in these arrangements and in his theoretical works. Two of his writings are about opera: *Essai historique sur l'établissement de l'Opéra en France, depuis son origine jusqu'à nos jours et diverses notes sur ce théâtre* (*F-Po*), and *L'Opéra avant la Révolution de 1789* (n.d.).

MSS in F-Pc
Les Rémois, ou Les brouilleries villageoises, 1757
L'Aurore et Céphale (ballet-héroïque, 1), Paris, Magasin de Musique de l'Académie, 7 May 1766
Lindor et Ismène, Paris, Opéra, 29 Aug 1766 [1st entrée in Les fêtes lyriques (ballet-héroïque, M. de Bonseval), other 2 entrées by Rameau and P.-M. Berton]
Palémon et Sylvie (pastorale-héroïque)
Chloé et Sylvandre (opéra)

*

L.-C. Lavallière: *Ballets, opéra, et autres ouvrages lyriques* (Paris, 1760)
J.-B. de La Borde: *Essai sur la musique ancienne et moderne*, iii (Paris, 1780), 418ff   MICHELLE FILLION

Frangiossi [Frangiosi, Franciosi], **Catterina** (*b* Reggio Emilia; *fl* 1683–9). Italian singer. Her name appears for the first time in 1683, in the role of Sabina in P. A. Ziani's *Il talamo preservato dalla fedeltà d'Eudossa*, performed in Reggio Emilia, and in 1685 she took part in *Anagilde, over Il Rodrigo*, possibly by C. F. Pollarolo. She was designated 'virtuosa' by Duke Ferdinando Carlo Gonzaga of Mantua, and the title was confirmed on 31 May 1688; as such she sang in G. M. Pagliardi's *Caligula delirante* at Crema in 1689. Although little is known of her career it seems that she had considerable gifts, since she sang with performers such as the Salicola sisters, Barbara Riccioni, Giovanni Buzzoleni, Antonio Cottini and Francesco Ballerini.

P. Besutti: *La corte musicale di Ferdinando Carlo Gonzaga ultimo duca di Mantova: musici, cantanti e teatro d'opera tra il 1665 e il 1707* (Mantua, 1989)   PAOLA BESUTTI

Frank, Ernst (*b* Munich, 7 Feb 1847; *d* Oberdöbling, nr Vienna, 17 Aug 1889). German conductor and composer. He studied composition in Munich with Franz Lachner. In 1866 he became court organist in Munich and répétiteur of the Akademischer Gesangverein. He went to Würzburg in 1868, taking up a post of theatre Kapellmeister, and to the Vienna Opera in 1869 as second chorus master. As court Kapellmeister in Mannheim, 1872–8, he gave a fresh impetus to the town's musical life; premières he directed there included *Der widerspenstigen Zähmung* (1874) and his own completion of *Francesca von Rimini* (1877), operas by his friend Hermann Goetz.

In 1878 Frank went to the Frankfurt Stadttheater, but he resigned in 1879 and worked as a private music teacher. In December 1879 he became Bülow's successor as court Kapellmeister in Hanover and there promoted works by younger composers, including C. V. Stanford, of whose first opera, *The Veiled Prophet of Khorassan*, Frank gave the première in 1881. The onset of a mental illness in 1887 prevented Frank from hearing his own opera *Der Sturm* given in Hanover that year.

Frank was one of the most gifted German conductors of his time, full of imagination and vitality, and with wide-ranging interests. From 1876 he was a close friend of Brahms. He possessed too little creative independence to achieve success as a composer, but his unsentimental lyric gift is evident in his more than 200 songs and vocal duets, and in his opera *Hero*.

MSS in D-Mbs
Adam de la Halle (komische Oper, 2, S. Mosenthal, after P. Heyse), Karlsruhe, Hof, 9 April 1880
Hero (3, F. Vetter, after F. Grillparzer: *Des Meeres und der Liebe Wellen*), Berlin, Hof, 26 Nov 1884, vs (Hanover, 1885)
Der Sturm (musikalisches Märchen, 3, J. V. Widmann, after W. Shakespeare: *The Tempest*), Hanover, Hof, 14 Oct 1887

*

C. V. Stanford: *Pages from an Unwritten Diary* (London, 1914), 189ff
A. Einstein, ed.: 'Briefe von Brahms an Ernst Frank', *ZMw*, iv (1922), 385–416
——: 'Josef Viktor Widmann: Briefe an Ernst Frank', *Österreichische Rundschau*, xx (1924), 415–44
R. Münster: 'Frank, Ernst', *Musik und Musiker am Mittelrhein*, i, ed. H. Unverricht (Mainz, 1974), 55–60   ROBERT MÜNSTER

Frankfurt am Main. German city. It has been a chief trading centre since the 14th century. From 1700 German, French and Italian opera companies often gave guest performances in the city, but the first independent theatre, the Komödienhaus, was built only in 1782, by J. A. Liebhardt. It stood in the Paradeplatz, later the Theaterplatz, and was eventually known as the Schauspielhaus. Renovated and extended several times during the 19th century, it continued in existence until 1901. During its first decade it was leased to private drama and opera companies. A change came in 1792 with the founding of the Frankfurt Nationaltheater, which in practice led to the birth of the Frankfurt opera. A joint-stock company formed by prominent citizens guaranteed financial backing. In the 1830s, however, severe financial crises in Frankfurt left the shareholders unable to make up the theatre's deficit and the 'First Frankfurt Theatre Co. Ltd' was liquidated in 1842. The administration of the theatre, now known as the

Frankfurt Stadttheater, passed to private directors, and for the first time the city itself, rather than its citizens, provided financial support. This period ended in 1855 with the setting up of the second limited company (until 1878), which ensured a more stable and generous basis for the theatre. A new building specially for opera was erected between 1872 and 1880, to plans by the Berlin architect Richard Lucae: this was the neo-classical opera house on the Bockenheimer Anlage, now known as the Alte Oper. It was opened on 20 October 1880, in the presence of Wilhelm I, with *Don Giovanni* conducted by the new musical director, Felix Otto Dessoff.

During World War II all the theatres in Frankfurt were destroyed. After 1945 the Börsensaal (formerly the hall of the corn exchange) was used as a temporary theatre. The first postwar opera performance in the city, a production of *Tosca*, was given here on 29 September 1945. Six years later the opera company moved to its home in the rebuilt Schauspielhaus, with an auditorium accommodating nearly 1400 people. It was opened on 23 December 1951 with *Die Meistersinger*, and was subsequently known as the Grosses Haus. In 1963 the drama and opera companies came under one roof in a modern complex of buildings; the opera company became known as the Frankfurt Opera after 1977, when Michael Gielen was appointed its director. After decades of preliminaries and tedious discussion, the Alte Oper – known for 37 years as 'Germany's finest ruin' – was extensively restored, luxuriously equipped and modernized, and opened as a concert hall and conference centre on 28 August 1981. Six years later, the city's theatrical life suffered a heavy blow when the modern building in the Theaterplatz burnt down, on the night of 11 November 1987. Rebuilding, which took more than three years, gave an opportunity to modernize the stage machinery in line with the latest developments, and to build new rehearsal rooms for the orchestra and for ballet. The ceiling of the auditorium was also improved: a transparent canopy with fibreglass dots simulating a starry sky was installed to provide better acoustics. During restoration the Opera used the drama company's stage.

The tradition of opera in Frankfurt goes back to the late 17th century. The first operatic performance, of Johann Theile's *Adam und Eva*, was given in 1698 by Magister J. Velthen and his 'famous troupe'. During the 18th century, touring companies visited the city: Italian *opera buffa* was very popular, and there are accounts of performances of German Singspiels by the Seyler company towards the end of the 1770s. Frankfurt had its own repertory after the opening of the Komödienhaus in 1782. The central position occupied by the operas of Mozart in the 1780s and 90s is striking; a German version of *La finta giardiniera* was produced in 1782, followed by *Die Entführung* in 1783, the first production in German of *Figaro* in 1788, *Così fan tutte* in 1791, *Die Zauberflöte* in 1793 and *La clemenza di Tito* in 1799.

The founding of the Frankfurt Nationaltheater in 1792 gave the city its own company for the first time. Kunzen, the creator of the Danish national opera *Holger Danske*, was appointed musical director, staying in Frankfurt until 1795; he was followed by Carl Cannabich (1796–1800). Mozart's operas were frequently performed in this period. Under Cannabich, who had been influenced by the magnificence and luxury of Mannheim, the Frankfurt Opera reached the brilliant standards of court opera, thanks partly to the opulent and beautiful neo-classical scenery of the Milanese stage designer Giorgio Fuentes, who worked in Frankfurt until about 1801 or 1802. (His designs were preceded by the equally remarkable work of the Mannheim scene painter Giuseppe Quaglio, who came to Frankfurt in 1782.) Fuentes' superb sets for *La clemenza di Tito* in 1799 were a great sensation (for illustration *see* CLEMENZA DI TITO, LA). Such lavish expenditure had mixed effects on future development, however; the citizens who were financing the theatre clearly felt that too much money had been spent on the scenery. Economy was to be the order of the day, and so Fuentes and Cannabich left, and with them the company's leading singers. Before long, the Opera succeeded in engaging Aloysia Lange, Mozart's sister-in-law and one of the most famous singers of her time.

The Frankfurt Opera flourished again when Louis Spohr was its musical director (from 1817–19). Unfortunately intrigues caused him to leave the city after only two years. His successor Karl Guhr, a conductor highly regarded by Wagner and Berlioz among others, determined the musical fortunes of the house from 1821 to 1847, achieving widely admired artistic standards. The repertory in the first half of the 19th century was dominated by Mozart, Beethoven, Cherubini, Spontini, Weber, whose *Silvana* had its first performance in Frankfurt in 1810, and Rossini; after the 1830s it included works by Bellini, Donizetti and Marschner. In the 1840s works by Lortzing and the young Verdi were added. The first performances of Wagner in Frankfurt were *Tannhäuser* (1853), *Der fliegende Holländer* (1854), and *Lohengrin*, conducted by the composer (1862). A little later the middle-period operas of Verdi were produced in the city: *Il trovatore* in German (1858), *Rigoletto* (1859), *La traviata* (1861) and *Un ballo in maschera* (1872).

After 1880, new artistic perspectives opened up in the new opera house (now the Alte Oper) under its administrator Emil Claar and musical director F. O. Dessoff. This period saw the first performances in Frankfurt of Wagner's *Ring*, *Tristan* and *Die Meistersinger*, as well as *Carmen*, *Aida* and *Otello*. In the long period of Ludwig Rottenberg's musical directorship, 1893–1924, *Falstaff* was performed (1896), the first German performance of *Pelléas et Mélisande* was given (1907), and much attention was aroused by the premières of Franz Schreker's operas – *Der ferne Klang* (1912), *Das Spielwerk und die Prinzessin* (1913, simultaneously with Vienna), *Die Gezeichneten* (1918) and *Der Schatzgräber* (1920). Karl Zeiss's period as administrator, 1917–20, was also a stimulating one, with the operas of Mozart and of modern composers at the heart of the repertory; the first performance of Rudi Stephan's *Die letzten Menschen* and the first German performances of Busoni's *Turandot* and *Arlecchino* were given. The era of Clemens Krauss has been described as the golden age of the Frankfurt Opera. The main emphasis was on Mozart, Wagner and Strauss – with a six-part cycle conducted by the composer in 1927 – and on new works such as Puccini's *Turandot* and *Gianni Schicchi*, Hindemith's *Cardillac*, one-act operas by Krenek and Weill, Krenek's *Jonny spielt auf*, Busoni's *Doktor Faust*, and the first performance of Eugen d'Albert's *Golem* (1926). There were two premières in 1930: Antheil's *Transatlantic* and Schoenberg's *Von heute auf morgen*. After the Nazis' seizure of power in 1933, the administrator Josef Turnau, musical director Hans Wilhelm Steinberg (later William Steinberg), and director

Herbert Graf were immediately dismissed. Other premières given before and during the war include Werner Egk's *Zaubergeige* (1935) and *Columbus* (1942), Carl Orff's *Carmina burana* (1937) and *Die Kluge* (1943), and Hermann Reutter's *Doktor Johannes Faust* (1936) and *Odysseus* (1942). Hans Pfitzner often directed his own works.

Among the happiest periods in the history of the Frankfurt Opera were the nine years when Georg Solti was musical director and Harry Buckwitz administrator (1952–61), with a brilliant company, a distinctive 'Frankfurt style' and superb productions of works by Mozart, Verdi, Strauss and later Wagner. Solti was followed by Lovro von Matačić and Christoph von Dohnányi, who also did notable work in the city. A chapter in itself, and surely one of the most important in the history of the theatre in Frankfurt, was the decade from 1977 to 1987, when Michael Gielen was both musical and opera director and the city was regarded as the centre of modern operatic production. The production team encouraged an avant-garde concept of music drama, with intellectually orientated, sweeping and original interpretations, often showing operatic themes in an entirely new light. Of particular interest were productions by, among others, Ruth Berghaus, Horst Zankl, Hans Neuenfels, Alfred Kirchner and Christoph Nels. Gary Bertini succeeded Gielen in 1987.

At every period leading singers have appeared in Frankfurt. Those engaged as members of the company have included Maria Wilt, Georg Unger (the first Siegfried), Emil Scaria (the first Gurnemanz), Heinrich and Therese Vogl (famous at the end of the last century as Tristan and Isolde), Theodor Wachtel, Selma Kurz, Albert Stritt, Robert vom Scheidt, Franz Völker, Claire Watson, Inge Borkh, Christel Goltz and Sándor Kónya.

The season of the Frankfurt Opera lasts about ten and a half months. The company plays on about 250 evenings, in some 25 works each season, including around five modern operas and five or six *Spielopern*.

*

O. Bacher: *Die Geschichte der Frankfurter Oper im 18. Jahrhundert* (Frankfurt, 1926)

W. Saure: *Die Geschichte der Frankfurt Oper von 1792 bis 1880* (diss., U. of Cologne, 1959)

A. R. Mohr: *Die Frankfurter Oper 1924–1944* (Frankfurt, 1971)

——: *Das Frankfurter Opernhaus 1880–1980* (Frankfurt, 1980)

——: *Zauberwelt: Bühnenbildentwurfe aus zwei Jahrhunderten* (Nördlingen, 1986)

R. Didion and J. Schlichte, eds.: *Thematischer Katalog der Opernsammlung in der Stadt- und Universitätsbibliothek Frankfurt am Main* (Frankfurt, 1990)   GÁBOR HÁLASZ

Franklin, David [Henry Cyril] (*b* London, 17 May 1908; *d* Evesham, Worcs., 22 Oct 1973). English bass. He sang as an amateur and, after a period of study with Jani Strasser, was engaged to sing the Commendatore for the 1936 Glyndebourne season. He sang at Glyndebourne until 1939, and was Banquo in the English première of Verdi's *Macbeth* there (1938). He appeared at Sadler's Wells in 1946 as Sir James Pinchbeck (Cancian) in the first performance in England of *I quattro rusteghi*; from 1947 to 1950 he sang at Covent Garden, where he created Mars in *The Olympians* (1949). His repertory included Rocco, Ochs and Pimen. To these and all his roles he brought a resonant voice, intelligence and a fine sense of theatre. He retired in 1951 but later appeared at Glyndebourne in speaking roles. He wrote a series of articles on 'Style in Singing' for *Opera*, ii (1951) and iii (1952), and an autobiography, *Basso Cantante* (London, 1969).

D. Craig: 'David Franklin', *RCM Magazine*, lxx (1974), 21–3
HAROLD ROSENTHAL/R

Frantz, Ferdinand (*b* Kassel, 8 Feb 1906; *d* Munich, 26 May 1959). German bass-baritone. He studied privately and made his début in 1927 at Kassel as Ortel (*Die Meistersinger*); after engagements in Halle, Chemnitz and Hamburg, in 1943 he was engaged by the Staatsoper in Munich, of which he remained a member until his death. He sang Rocco at the reopening of the Prinzregententheater, Munich, and established himself as leading Heldenbariton, singing Wotan, Hans Sachs, Kurwenal and the Dutchman; such was the range of his voice that he also sang King Mark, Daland, the Landgrave and King Henry (*Lohengrin*) as well as Méphistophélès and Galitsky (*Prince Igor*). He made guest appearances in Vienna, Milan, Paris and London, where he sang Jupiter in the first performance in England of *Die Liebe der Danae* in 1953 (with the Bayerische Staatsoper), and Wotan in 1954. He made his Metropolitan début in 1949 as Wotan, and also appeared there as Pizarro. He had a beautifully schooled voice and sympathetic personality that made him a benign Wotan and a lovable Hans Sachs.

HAROLD ROSENTHAL/R

Franz, Paul [Gautier, François] (*b* Paris, 30 Nov 1876; *d* Paris, 20 April 1950). French tenor. He studied with Louis Delaquerrière in Paris and joined the Opéra in 1909, making his début as Lohengrin, and singing there until his retirement in 1938. He was the first Paris Parsifal in 1914, and his many roles included Aeneas (*Les Troyens*), John the Baptist (*Hérodiade*), Rodrigue (*Le Cid*), Raoul (*Les Huguenots*), Reyer's Sigurd, and Siegmund, Siegfried and Tristan. Franz made his Covent Garden début in 1910 as Samson, returning regularly until 1914. His London roles included Julien (*Louise*), Radames and Otello. He possessed a large, rich voice with an especially fine middle register, as well as a fine stage presence.

HAROLD ROSENTHAL/R

Fränzl, Ferdinand (*b* Schwetzingen, 24 May 1767; *d* Mannheim, 27 Oct 1833). German composer. He first won recognition as a virtuoso violinist during numerous European tours, playing in Vienna, Paris, Switzerland and Italy. He took composition lessons with F. X. Richter and Pleyel in Strasbourg, and with Stanislao Mattei in Bologna. After posts as orchestral leader in Munich, Frankfurt and Offenbach, he resumed concert tours to Vienna, Poland and (until 1806) Russia, where he enjoyed the favour of the tsar. From 1806 he was music director and from 1823 Kapellmeister at the Munich court, where he championed Weber's music.

Die Luftbälle, oder Der Liebhaber à la Montgolfier (Spl, 2, C. Bretzner), Mannheim, 15 April 1787

Adolf und Clara (operetta, 1, after B.-J. Marsollier des Vivetières), Frankfurt, 1800

Der beiden Gefangenen, Mannheim, 1802

Carlo Fioras, oder Die Stumme in der Sierra Morena (3, W. Vogel), Munich, Hof, 16 Oct 1810

Hadrian Barbarossa (3, G. Wohlbrück), Munich, Hof, March 1815

Die Weihe (Festspiel, A. Klebe), Munich, Hof, 12 Oct 1818

Der Fassbinder (Spl, 1), Munich, Hof, 21 Dec 1824

Der Bandit (Spl, 2, after K. Ritter), Mannheim, National, Dec 1835

Der Einsiedler (Spl, 3), unperf.

*

*Stieger*O

R. Würtz: 'Ferdinand Fränzl', *Mannheimer Hefte*, ii (1967), 43–8
ROLAND WÜRTZ

Frascatana, La (i). Opera by Leonardo Leo; *see* AMOR VUOL SOFFERENZA.

Frascatana, La (ii) ('The Girl from Frascati'). *Dramma giocoso* in three acts by GIOVANNI PAISIELLO to a libretto by FILIPPO LIVIGNI; Venice, Teatro S Samuele, autumn 1774.

The story is set at an inn on the outskirts of Rome. Violante (soprano), daughter of a rich gardener from Frascati, is an idealistic young woman who dreams about love. She is upset by the amorous advances of her tutor, Don Fabrizio (bass), and when she meets a young and handsome Roman, Nardone (tenor), they fall in love. The Cavaliere Giocondo (tenor), betrothed to the rich Donna Stella (soprano), also falls in love with Violante. Both the Cavaliere and Nardone confess their love for Violante to Don Fabrizio, who becomes jealous. Complications develop when Lisetta (soprano), the waitress of the inn, falls in love with the Cavaliere. At the same time Donna Stella, furious after being jilted by the Cavaliere, comes to seek revenge. Don Fabrizio schemes to separate Nardone from Violante, but no amount of intrigue can succeed. In the end the Cavaliere returns to Donna Stella, while Nardone and Violante celebrate their happiness.

This extremely popular comic opera was performed as late as 1808 at the Teatro della Pergola, Florence. During the first 30 years after its première it was given on all the major European stages. In French centres such as Versailles, Rouen, Marseilles, Strasbourg and Paris its success was due in part to its transformation by Framery into an *opéra comique* as *L'infante de Zamora*. *La Frascatana* was much in demand in Vienna, where it received 35 performances in two years (1775–7), and it was revived there as late as 1795; Metastasio, in a letter to Saverio Mattei in 1776, commented on its enthusiastic reception at the Burgtheater. In 1783 Nancy Storace sang Violante and Michael Kelly Nardone; three years later both singers would participate in the première of Mozart's *Le nozze di Figaro*. During the opera's performances at Eszterháza Haydn composed new music for Lisetta's 'D'una sposa meschinella'.

GORDANA LAZAREVICH

Fraschini, Gaetano (*b* Pavia, 16 Feb 1816; *d* Naples, 23 May 1887). Italian tenor. He studied in Pavia with Moretti and made his début there in 1837 as Arturo. In 1839 he sang in *Torquato Tasso* at Bergamo and in 1840 in *Marino Faliero* at La Scala. Engaged at the S Carlo, Naples, from 1840 to 1853 he sang in the first performances of Pacini's *Saffo*, *La fidanzata corsa*, *Stella di Napoli*, *La regina di Cipro*, *Merope* and *Romilda di Provenza*. He created Gerardo in *Caterina Cornaro* (1844); other Donizetti operas in which he sang included *Linda di Chamounix*, *Maria di Rohan*, *La favorite*, *Poliuto* and *Lucia di Lammermoor*. He was dubbed the 'tenore della maledizione' because of the force with which he delivered Edgardo's curse in *Lucia*, and was noted as an early *tenore di forza*.

He was chosen by Verdi to create Zamoro in *Alzira* (1845, Naples), Corrado in *Il corsaro* (1848, Trieste), Arrigo in *La battaglia di Legnano* (1849, Rome) and the title role of *Stiffelio* (1850, Trieste). He also appeared in *Oberto*, *Ernani*, *I Lombardi*, *I masnadieri*, *Luisa Miller* and *Il trovatore*. In 1856 he sang in *Les vêpres siciliennes* at Rome, in 1858 in *Simon Boccanegra* at Naples, and he created Riccardo in *Un ballo in maschera* (1859, Rome). It is a commentary on his technique and taste that, after so many forceful roles, he could still be expected to sing with the refinement and elegance necessary for Riccardo's music. He sang in the first London performance of *I due Foscari* at Her Majesty's Theatre (1847), in *La forza del destino* at Madrid (1863), and *La traviata* and *Rigoletto* at the Théâtre Italien, Paris (1864). He made his last appearances as Gennaro in *Lucrezia Borgia* at Rome in 1873 when, though in his late fifties, he still retained the firmness and security of his voice, and then at Florence in *La forza* and *Martha*.

ES (R. Celletti)
G. Monaldi: *Cantanti celebri* (Rome, 1929)   ELIZABETH FORBES

Fraser-Simson, Harold [Simson, Harold Fraser] (*b* London, 15 Aug 1872; *d* Inverness, 19 Jan 1944). British composer. Originally a shipowner, he had songs and partsongs published in the early 1900s and began a series of stage scores. Of these, none outshone *The Maid of the Mountains* (1916), which ran for 1352 performances in London. He also composed incidental music for A. A. Milne's *Toad of Toad Hall* (1929) and settings from Milne's *When we Were Very Young*. Fraser-Simson's songs were often curiously austere for romantic musical plays, but he achieved a noted success with the waltz song 'Love will find a way' (from *The Maid of the Mountains*), whose first eight notes consist of the first four notes of Lehár's *Merry Widow* waltz each played twice.

Bonita (comic opera, 2, W. Peacock), London, Queen's, 22 Sept 1911; The Maid of the Mountains (light opera, 3, F. Lonsdale and H. Graham), Manchester, Prince's, 23 Dec 1916, London, Daly's, 10 Feb 1917; A Southern Maid (musical play, 3, D. C. Calthrop and Graham), Manchester, 24 Dec 1917, London, Daly's, 15 May 1920; Our Peg (musical play, 3, E. Knoblock and Graham), Manchester, Prince's, 24 Dec 1919, rev. as Our Nell (3, L. N. Parker, R. Arkell and Graham), London, Gaiety, 16 April 1924 (collab. I. Novello)
Missy Joe (musical play, 3, J. Clive and Graham), Folkestone, Pleasure Gardens, 4 July 1921; Head Over Heels (musical comedy, 2, S. Hicks, A. Ross and Graham), London, Adelphi, 8 Sept 1923; The Street Singer (musical play, 3, Lonsdale and P. Greenbank), Birmingham, 11 Feb 1924, London, Lyric, 27 June 1924; Betty in Mayfair (musical play, 3, J. H. Turner and Graham), Sunderland, Empire, 26 Oct 1925, London, Adelphi, 11 Nov 1925   ANDREW LAMB

Frasi, Giulia (*b* Milan; *fl* 1742–72). Italian soprano. She studied under G. F. Brivio and later with Burney in London. Engaged for the King's Theatre in 1742, she made her début in the pasticcio *Gianguir* and continued to sing there in opera for many years, appearing in works by Galuppi, Porpora, Lampugnani, Veracini, Terradellas, Paradies, Hasse, Pergolesi, Cocchi and many others. She sometimes played male parts, for example Taxiles (1743) and Cleon (1747–8), both in Handel's *Rossane* (*Alessandro*), and the giant Briareus in the première of Gluck's *La caduta de' giganti* (1746). She sang in the Handel pasticcio *Lucio Vero* in 1747 and his *Admeto* in 1754. She appeared occasionally at other theatres, notably in works by Arne: *Alfred* (New Haymarket, 1753), *Eliza* (Drury Lane, 1756), *Alfred* (Covent Garden, 1759) and *Artaxerxes* (King's, 1769). Handel engaged Frasi for his oratorio season of 1749 and she continued as prima donna in all his later seasons and under his successors until about 1768. She was a great favourite with the public. In her early years, according to Burney, she had 'a sweet and clear voice, and a smooth and chaste style of singing, which, though cold and unimpassioned, pleased natural ears, and escaped the censure of critics'. She benefited greatly from Handel's tuition. The wonderful series of oratorio parts he composed for her, including the two Queens in *Solomon* (1749), the title roles in *Susanna* (1749) and *Theodora* (1750), and Iphis in *Jephtha* (1752), are an indication of his regard for her expressive powers, though they are not technically arduous; their extreme compass is *b* to *a''*.

WINTON DEAN

Frate 'nnamorato, Lo ('The Brother in Love'). *Commedia musicale* in three acts by GIOVANNI BATTISTA PERGOLESI to a libretto by GENNARO ANTONIO FEDERICO; Naples, Teatro dei Fiorentini, 27 September 1732.

Marcaniello (bass) is a rich, elderly proprietor of a house in Capodimonte on the outskirts of Naples. Living with him is Ascanio (tenor), a young man of unknown parentage who has been brought up by Marcaniello. Two sisters, Nena (soprano) and Nina (mezzo-soprano), are objects of Ascanio's love, and his equally tender feelings towards both of them cause him pain and uncertainty. Marcaniello also has designs on the sisters: he wants to marry Nina and sees Nena as a suitable wife for his son, Don Pietro (bass). Marcaniello's daughter Lucrezia (contralto) is in love with Ascanio, but she is the object of amorous advances by Nina and Nena's elderly uncle Carlo (tenor). In a duel with Don Pietro, Ascanio is wounded in the arm, uncovering a birthmark that identifies him as Lucio, the long-lost brother of Nina and Nena. Thus, he is able to marry Lucrezia. Throughout the opera two Neapolitan maids, Vannella (soprano) and Cardella (soprano), contribute burlesque scenes.

This sentimental comedy is permeated with pathos and exudes a mixture of serious and burlesque elements. Federico, the librettist, also wrote two other successful librettos set by Pergolesi: *La serva padrona* and *Flaminio*. The generous use of dialect here reproduces the vivacious and colourful mode of expression exclusive to Naples and captures the character of the Neapolitan populace. Although vestiges of the *commedia dell'arte* stories are traceable in Marcaniello and Carlo, the characters are not stereotypes but are imbued with human qualities. Marcaniello is willing to pursue youth, but he is restrained by his gout-ridden body. Don Pietro is a vain sophist, who pretends to be erudite; in his amorous advances he does not discriminate between noble ladies and rustic maids.

This first comic opera by Pergolesi, then only 22, was received in Naples with enthusiasm and it was repeated there with revisions in 1734 and 1748; but because of its unintelligibility to non-Neapolitan audiences it was not performed outside Naples. Its lyrical, dramatic and comic elements nevertheless clearly show Pergolesi's skill at depicting the essence of the human character in his music. The work also includes Neapolitan folk elements. The opening duet of Act 1 between Vannella and Cardella, 'Passa Ninno da cca rrente', and Vannella's canzona in Act 2, 'Chi disse c'a femmena', are set in a minor key in the lilting 12/8 metre of a siciliano, making harmonic and melodic use of the Neapolitan sixth. Also noteworthy is the quintet at the end of Act 2, 'Deh face piano, piano', in which the combined entries of Vannella and Cardella form a type of refrain.

GORDANA LAZAREVICH

Frau ohne Schatten, Die ('The Woman Without a Shadow'). *Oper* in three acts by RICHARD STRAUSS to a libretto by HUGO VON HOFMANNSTHAL; Vienna, Staatsoper, 10 October 1919.

The Emperor	tenor
The Empress *Keikobad's daughter*	high dramatic soprano
The Nurse *her guardian*	dramatic mezzo-soprano
Barak *a dyer*	bass-baritone
Barak's Wife	high dramatic soprano
The One-Eyed ⎫	high bass
The One-Armed ⎬ *Barak's brothers*	bass
The Hunchback ⎭	high tenor
A Spirit Messenger	high baritone
The Voice of the Falcon	soprano
The Apparition of a Youth	high tenor
The Guardian of the Threshold	soprano/countertenor
A Voice from Above	contralto
Voices of Unborn Children	three sopranos, three contraltos
Voices of Three Nightwatchmen	baritones

Servants of the Empress, other children and beggar-children, Spirit-servants and Spirit-voices

Setting The Emperor's palace, Barak's hut, fantastic caves and landscapes

Soon after the première of their *Rosenkavalier* in 1911, Hofmannsthal suggested to Strauss that they might make an opera out of a fairy-tale by Hauff, to be called *Das steinerne Herz* ('The Heart Turning to Stone'). In the event they first created *Ariadne auf Naxos*, in both its 1912 and 1916 versions; so the fairy-tale piece – now entitled *Die Frau ohne Schatten*, and retaining only threads from Hauff – became their third full operatic collaboration. (*Elektra* had been an independent play before Strauss set it as an opera.) By then much was expected of them, as they knew too well. Hofmannsthal liked to think of *Die Frau ohne Schatten* as 'their' *Zauberflöte*, against *Der Rosenkavalier* as 'their' *Figaro*. The work proceeded slowly, for his mind teemed with so many ideas for it that he had to write a separate prose tale, an *Erzählung*, to accommodate them all. What with their collaboration on the ballet *Josephslegende*, Strauss's new *Alpine Symphony*, the outbreak of war and the reworking of *Ariadne*, it was 1917 before the new opera was completed.

1917 was the year of Apollinaire's surrealist comedy *Les mamelles de Tirésias* – made into an *opéra-bouffe* by Poulenc 27 years later, towards the end of the next great war – with the same philanthropic, regenerative message: 'Make children!' For Apollinaire's heroine, however, non-motherhood is a clause in her New Woman manifesto (her husband has to generate progeny all by himself); Hofmannsthal's young fairy-Empress is barren, 'casts no shadow', because her huntsman-Emperor does nothing but self-absorbedly pursue his game. The librettist chose to give them no scene together until Act 3, when the Emperor is already freezing into stone. Understandably, the composer complained that he found this pair cold and uninspiring. The other childless couple were another matter: the librettist had confessed at the start that he was imagining the dyer's Wife after Strauss's own formidable

Pauline, and Strauss could comfortably identify himself with the decent, much-put-upon Barak.

Unlike *Zauberflöte* or *Tirésias*, *Die Frau ohne Schatten* has no social dimension whatever. As with *Ariadne*, Hofmannsthal's imagination was gripped by 'Two Womanly Types' – one a Peri maid, ethereal to the point of suffocation, the other all-too-human. Beyond their baffled husbands and the ambiguous Nurse, the rest of the numerous cast supply only local colour and celestial commentary; the ethical fable is really concerned with inner, psychic malaises, and the visible 'action' is sketchy. Hofmannsthal aimed nevertheless at an epic-operatic dimension, and to that purpose Strauss enlisted a huge performing apparatus – violas and cellos in double sections like the violins, mostly quadruple winds, extensive percussion (including glass harmonica), an offstage woodwind septet and a dozen extra brass, organ, wind-machine and thunder-machine. Yet he saw that there was no dramatic licence for any communal outcry: even at the triumphal close, the exulting principals are supported only by their invisible Unborn Children, before a rapt diminuendo coda for Spirit-voices. Despite the scale of his forces, Strauss set much of the score in chamber-orchestral terms of pleading delicacy. (Originally, he meant to reserve an *Ariadne*-size band to the Spirit world.) Producers are often led astray by the grandiose scenic descriptions; in fact the life of *Die Frau ohne Schatten* consists in intimate vignettes strung upon a rich orchestral chain, not so unlike Debussy's *Pelléas et Mélisande*.

Maria Jeritza and Karl Aagaard Oestvig sang the first imperial couple. The Barak pair were Richard Mayr and Lotte Lehmann, with Lucie Weidt as the Nurse and Franz Schalk conducting. At almost no time has the opera been staged regularly enough for any singer to establish a famous claim to a role – though Barak's music has been a gift to many mellifluous bass-baritones, and the musico-dramatic rewards of all three soprano roles have been well explored. One exception: though Strauss must have had his Emperor and the Menelaus of his *Ägyptische Helena* in mind when he used later to regret never having learnt to write for tenor, around the start of the 1960s the young American Jess Thomas was in great and justifiable demand as an Emperor *sans pareil*.

ACT 1.i *A roof above the imperial gardens* As in *Elektra*, there is no prelude but the orchestral pronouncement of a sacred name, whose bearer – there Agamemnon, here the Empress's celestial father ('KEIK!-o'Bad', growled thrice in A♭ minor) – will never appear. At daybreak on an imperial terrace where the Nurse skulks, the Spirit Messenger (cousin to the Speaker in *Die Zauberflöte*) arrives on a minatory errand. Though 12 moons have passed since the young Emperor with his falcon brought down the Peri, wandering in the form of a gazelle, and took her to wife, she is all light still; if after three days more she casts no shadow, she must return to Keikobad and the Emperor will turn to stone. The Nurse gloats. Now the Emperor himself passes through, eulogizing his bride-prize (in E♭) 'to the end of time' – for he goes off to hunt every day, and makes love to her every night. Dawn brightens into shimmering F♯ as the Empress enters, still half-dreaming about her husband; then she sees her long-lost Falcon return, weeping and bleeding, to recite the Messenger's warning. Aghast, she pleads for advice from her Nurse, who admits reluctantly that she has often bartered the

1. '*Die Frau ohne Schatten*' (Richard Strauss): *design by Alfred Roller for the costume of the Nurse in the original production at the Staatsoper, Vienna, 10 October 1919*

souls of men, whom she despises, and can help her find a human shadow. As they descend towards the human world an orchestral interlude boils up: much like the *Rheingold* one for Wotan's descent into Nibelheim, down to the raw percussion (here, wooden switch and castanets) that signal their arrivals in the midst of the workaday world.

1.ii *Barak's hut* In the poor dyer Barak's one-room workshop-home, his disabled, dependent brothers are quarrelling again, and his grim young Wife loses patience. Gently, Barak restores temporary peace, and promises her (his music moves from B♭ to Strauss's most heartfelt D♭) that he could also manage to support the children he longs for. Given no reassuring word, he goes wearily off with his dyed skins to market. Amid insidious chromatics Empress and Nurse, disguised, appear as if from nowhere. The Nurse flatters the Wife's beauty, deplores her waste of it on a lowly, aging man, and illustrates the price her shadow could fetch by conjuring up an erotic idyll with slave-girls and an unseen lover (in extreme sharp keys, like the analogous music in *Salome*). The Wife is dazzled and tempted, but then remembers that she has done nothing about dinner, nor the chaste new sleeping arrangements she wants. At a clap of the Nurse's hands the marital bed splits apart, and five fishes spring into the frying-pan – but they wail in childish voices, pleading to be born. When Barak comes home he has to be content with dry bread and a single bed. Outside, nightwatchmen (recalling *Die Meistersinger*) hymn the praises of fruitful married love, providing a grave coda in deep Ab.

ACT 2.i *Barak's hut* Nurse and Empress are now installed as servants in the dyer's house. As soon as he has gone with his brothers to market, the Nurse calls up the seductive idyll again for his Wife, with the lover now in the remembered form of a Youth she secretly fancied. Just in time Barak returns, bringing a rich feast for the family, neighbours and beggars. Amid the long, gluttonous ensemble in D which ensues, the Wife's bitter frustration sounds a dissonant note. An orchestral interlude carries the hearty scene some way further, then declines slowly into G minor ponderings.

2.ii *The Emperor's falconer's cottage, in a forest* Over them, high woodwinds repeat the plangent cry of the Falcon, which has led the Emperor to his falconer's cottage: the Empress sent the bird with a message that she and her Nurse would retreat here for three days. Full of premonitions, he waits now in the shadows. (This is his heroic solo scena.) Soon the women return furtively and slip into the house. He scents the stench of mankind upon them, and is seized by jealousy and grief: must he not kill his gazelle? But he cannot bring himself to that, and the music descends into Eb minor as he beseeches the Falcon to lead him away to lonely despair.

2.iii *Barak's hut* A short interlude leads back to the dyer's home. In sultry heat Barak works doggedly, while his Wife prods him to get off to market and out of the house. The Nurse resolves the impasse by drugging his wine; he slumps, and immediately she revives the apparition of the Youth, now in impassioned voice. At the point of succumbing the Wife abruptly takes fright, rouses her dazed husband ('There's a man in the house!'), rails at him for his lack of understanding, announces that his home is no longer hers and stalks out with the Nurse. Picking up his tools, poor Barak finds someone helping him: 'I, master, your servant!', says the Empress.

2.iv *The falconer's cottage* Asleep in the cottage with the Nurse, the Empress is restless and troubled. She cries out that she has wronged Barak. In a lucid dream she sees the Emperor finding his way into a cavern and towards a bronze door, while invisible men's voices dare him on and the Falcon caws its warning; the door opens, and closes behind him. Keikobad's motto is repeated, and the motif that says 'He turns to stone!' The Empress wakes with a shriek, and bewails her guilt in a monologue that twists painfully from B minor to Eb minor.

2.v *Barak's hut* At midday an uncanny darkness is closing upon Barak's house. Barak feels weighed down and his Wife yearns for escape, while Empress and Nurse voice their contrary sentiments. Then the Wife musters the courage for her declaration of independence. She claims to have betrayed Barak during his absences, though she could not expunge his face from her mind, and now she has found the means of freeing herself: she has sold her shadow, and there will be no children. General horror; as the fire flares up, she seems indeed to cast no shadow. (Urged by the Nurse to seize it, the Empress refuses.) The Nurse conjures a sword into Barak's angry hand – but before he can strike, the unfamiliar vision of him as righteous husband and stern judge stirs his Wife to the core. Ready to die, she confesses that she lied, the bargain was not yet sealed. Over his brothers' protests Barak raises the sword, and suddenly the whole house founders (in Eb minor). The brothers flee, the Baraks sink into the earth and the Nurse sweeps her Empress away, crowing that higher powers are in play.

ACT 3.i *A subterranean vault, divided by a wall* The orchestra suggests cries and whimpers, almost atonal. In a pair of subterranean chambers, unaware of each other, Barak broods and his Wife weeps. She laments her false confession and her failure to see her husband for what he truly was ('Schweigt doch, ihr Stimmen'); Barak reproaches himself for threatening the young creature given into his trust ('Mir anvertraut'), and then their voices combine in a grand duet (Db, in Strauss's maturely ardent vein). Now a voice from above exhorts each in turn to come up: 'The way is free!' The orchestra exults, while clouds cover the scene.

3.ii *A rocky landscape outside a temple* In a setting like that of the Empress's dream, a boat with Nurse and Empress glides towards a rocky terrace, with a bronze portal high above. The fearful Nurse pleads with the Empress to fly with her – she will get her a better shadow; but the Empress hears the trombone summons from beyond the great door, where she expects to find Keikobad and throw herself upon his mercy. Their long, urgent duologue runs on triplet quavers like a frantic scherzo, ever faster until the Empress cuts it off; she has come to love self-rescuing, self-renewing mankind, and rejects the Nurse's contempt for that weak race. She strides up to the door and enters. Abandoned, the Nurse curses men, and when Barak and then the Wife appear seeking each other she cruelly misdirects them. While their unhappy voices continue from different places, the Messenger announces that Keikobad has cast her out; the Nurse let her charge escape her, and must now wander among men forever. The boat carries her swiftly away.

3.iii *Within the temple* Spirits light the Empress's way into the temple. The Guardian of the Threshold urges her to drink from a golden fountain, which will assure her of the Wife's shadow; she refuses, though the ghastly stone form of the Emperor becomes visible in an alcove. In anguish, she still finds the will to refuse again – whereupon her own shadow stretches cleanly across the floor, and her husband rises to greet her. Their raptures call up the chorus of Unborn Children once more, heard through a silvery orchestral haze.

3.iv *A fairy-tale landscape* The Baraks are reunited and the Wife again casts a shadow. The imperial couple join them, and the childish voices too. The rest is rejoicing, lustily led by Barak ('Now will I rejoice, like nobody before!') in a key which Strauss has reserved until now: honest, down-to-earth C major.

* * *

As usual, Strauss projected his score from a full quiver of leitmotifs. More easily labelled and 'heraldic', perhaps, than before – tonally fractured or curdled when he wanted a memorable nickname or motto, but unashamedly 19th-century-Romantic for positive emo-

2. 'Die Frau ohne Schatten' (Richard Strauss): design by Alfred Roller for Act 3 scene iv (a fairy-tale landscape) of the original production at the Staatsoper, Vienna, 10 October 1919

tions; on the other hand he developed them with high authority, especially in the interludes, revelling in advanced polytonal polyphony. That may have been compensation for the constraint he evidently felt when setting Hofmannsthal's newly elevated stage-poetry, which embodied neither a fraught interpersonal drama like *Elektra* nor the conversational fluency of *Rosenkavalier*. The result was a hugely expressive orchestral canvas (including scenic pictures), which carries a few lyrical set-pieces and a great deal of glorified recitative – like the Nurse's florid, crucial role, which boasts scarcely one memorable phrase. Though *Die Frau* suggests a noble new conception of opera, it is never easy to bring it into persuasive theatrical focus.

DAVID MURRAY

Frazzi, Vito (*b* San Secondo Parmense, 1 Aug 1888; *d* Florence, 7 July 1975). Italian composer. He studied in Parma and taught at the Florence Conservatory (1912–58), where for a time he was acting director, and where his pupils included Dallapiccola and Bucchi. He also taught at the Accademia Chigiana, Siena. His most characteristic earlier works reflect his association around 1920 with Pizzetti, whose influence is evident in the method of word-setting and the general approach to music drama revealed in *Re Lear* (a somewhat eccentric adaptation of Shakespeare in which Cordelia appears only as a corpse and an offstage voice). Frazzi was seldom, however, a slavish imitator of Pizzetti: his style shows many individual traits, notably a fondness for patterns derived from a scale of alternating tones and semitones. His rhythms, too, show independent thinking in their sometimes extreme fluidity. The most

important of his stage works is *Don Chisciotte*, in which he broke away from the rather uniform, declamatory style of *Re Lear* towards a far less Pizzettian manner. Among his other operas, *L'ottava moglie di Barbablù* was destroyed by the composer after its première, while *Le nozze di Camaccio*, a semi-autonomous supplement to *Don Chisciotte*, has been published but not, it seems, performed.

See also DON CHISCIOTTE.

Re Lear, 1922–8 (3, G. Papini, after W. Shakespeare), Florence, ?Comunale, 29 April 1939
L'ottava moglie di Barbablù (D. Cincelli), Florence, 1940; destroyed
Don Chisciotte, 1940–50 (6 scenes [performable separately or together], Frazzi, after M. de Cervantes and M. de Unamuno), Florence, Comunale, 28 April 1952
Le nozze di Camaccio (intermezzo al Don Chisciotte), 1953 (1, Frazzi and E. Riccioli, after Cervantes), unperf.
?Il giardino chiuso, unperf.

L. Dallapiccola: 'Musicisti del nostro tempo: Vito Frazzi', *RaM*, x (1937), 220–27 [partly on *Re Lear*]
B. Cicognani: 'Il *Don Chisciotte* di Vito Frazzi', *XV Maggio musicale fiorentino 1952*, 8–10 [programme book]
A. Damerini: 'Il *Don Chisciotte* di Vito Frazzi', *Scena illustrata* [Florence], lxvii/4 (1952), 25
J. C. G. Waterhouse: *The Emergence of Modern Italian Music (up to 1940)* (diss., U. of Oxford, 1968), 632–5
A. Damerini: 'Realtà e sogno nel *Don Chisciotte* di Vito Frazzi', *Chigiana*, no.34 [new ser., no.14] (1981), 329–32
C. Prosperi: 'Vito Frazzi e il *Re Lear*', *Chigiana*, no.34 [new ser., no.14] (1981), 329–32   JOHN C. G. WATERHOUSE

Frederick, Cassandra (*b* c1741; *d* after 1779). ?English mezzo-soprano. She may have been the daughter of a Mrs Frederica who sang in the pasticcio opera

L'incostanza delusa at the New Haymarket Theatre early in 1745. Cassandra was an infant prodigy as a harpsichordist. She studied singing under Paradies, and was engaged by Handel for his oratorio season of 1758, when he adapted five opera arias for her in *The Triumph of Time and Truth*; their compass is *b*♭ to *f*♯". She sang in Arne's *Alfred* (1759), Jommelli's *L'isola disabitata* at the Great Room, Dean Street (1760) and had a benefit in Arne's pasticcio *Love in a Village* in 1775.

WINTON DEAN

Frederick II, King of Prussia [Friedrich II; Frederick the Great] (*b* Berlin, 24 Jan 1712; *d* Potsdam, 17 Aug 1786). German monarch and patron of the arts. His father, Friedrich Wilhelm I, violently opposed his artistic leanings; when Frederick finally acceded to the throne on 31 May 1740 he plunged into social and political reforms, military conquest and the rehabilitation of Prussian arts and letters, all at once. He was determined to bring into his own precincts the same operatic magnificence he had witnessed 12 years earlier at Dresden in a production of Hasse's *Cleofide*. C. H. Graun, who had been attached to his half-clandestine musical establishment since 1735, was immediately dispatched to Italy to employ singers (despite complaints, notably from Mattheson in Hamburg, about Frederick's neglect of German musicians). Other agents, such as Voltaire and Algarotti (both of whom were Frederick's established confidants and correspondents), were commissioned to engage actors and dancers in Paris and more singers from Italy, along with machinists, costumiers and librettists. The royal architect G. W. von Knobelsdorf was ordered to begin work on a monumental opera house, while opera flourished in whatever temporary quarters were available.

The new opera house, whose replica still stands on the avenue Unter den Linden in Berlin, was opened on 7 December 1742. From that date to the outbreak of the Seven Years' War in 1756, the standard season featured two new operas by Graun and an occasional work by Hasse, composers who were the foremost representatives of Italian opera in Germany. Music by J. F. Agricola and Frederick himself was also sometimes performed, and the work of the court librettists G. G. Bottarelli, Giampietro Tagliazucchi and Leopoldo de Villati was supplemented by texts from Metastasio, Zeno and (again) Frederick.

As a composer of consequence Frederick produced mainly instrumental works, but the quality of his dramatic music is surprisingly high. While it emulates the schematism of Graun's style, it nevertheless upholds the ideal of the untrammelled solo voice supported by a judiciously simple, homophonic accompaniment. Arias known to be Frederick's appear in Graun's *Demofoonte* (1746, *D-W*), and *Il giudizio di Paride* (1752) and in a number of pasticcios. He also collaborated with Graun, J. J. Quantz and C. Nichelmann on *Il rè pastore* (1747) and may have contributed to the music of Graun's *Coriolano* (1749). As a librettist too Frederick is not to be disdained. *Montezuma*, for which Frederick wrote the libretto in French (it was translated into Italian by Tagliazucchi), was indeed one of Graun's best works. He also wrote for Graun his *Silla* (1753) and parts of *I fratelli nemici* (1756) and *Merope* (1756), all of which Tagliazucchi translated, and he sketched the plots of Villati's *Coriolano* and Tagliazucchi's *Il tempio d'amore* (Agricola, 1755).

Frederick did not hesitate to become involved in the most fundamental creative work of his artists. Graun was forced from the start to modify his work to please the king. The same was true of the royal librettists and all other participants, even the leading performers such as the sopranos Benedetta Molteni and Giovanna Astrua, the castratos Antonio Uberi (Porporino), Felice Salimbeni and Giovanni Carestini, and the dancer Barbara Campanini (Barbarina).

After the seven-year hiatus of the war none of the Prussian royal cultural enterprises regained their former vitality during Frederick's lifetime. Until his death in 1786 the prematurely aged king allowed the Opera to decline in the hands of J. F. Agricola, C. F. C. Fasch and J. F. Reichardt. Almost all productions were revivals. The atmosphere of decay and rigidity was relieved briefly by the arrival in 1771 of Gertrud Elisabeth Mara as prima donna; it was she who broke down Frederick's prejudice against German singers.

See also BERLIN.

BurneyGN

W. Kothe: *Friedrich der Grosse als Musiker* (Braunsberg, 1869)

G. Thouret: *Friedrich der Grosse als Musikfreund und Musiker* (Leipzig, 1898)

G. Müller: *Friedrich der Grosse: seine Flöten und sein Flötenspiel* (Berlin, 1932)

H. Osthoff: 'Friedrich der Grosse als Komponist', *ZfM*, Jg.103 (1936), 917

A. Yorke-Long: *Music at Court* (London, 1954)

E. E. Helm: *Music at the Court of Frederick the Great* (Norman, 1960)

N. Mitford: *Frederick the Great* (New York, 1970)

H. Becker: 'Friedrich der Grosse und die Musik', *Preussers grosse König*, ed. W. Treue (Freiburg, 1986), 150–61

H. Klüppelholz: 'Die Eroberung Mexikos aus preussischer Sicht, Zum Libretto der Oper "Montezuma" von Friedrich dem Grossen', *Oper als text: romanistische Beiträge zur Libretto-Forschung*, ed. A. Gier (Heidelberg, 1986), 65–94

E. EUGENE HELM

Fredman, Myer (*b* Plymouth, 29 Jan 1932). English conductor. He studied at Dartington Hall (Devon) and at the Opera School (later to become the National School of Opera) in London. In 1959 he joined the music staff of the Glyndebourne Festival Opera; he was the company's chorus master (1962–7) and its first conductor and head of music staff (1971–2). He conducted almost the whole range of works at Glyndebourne, from Mozart and Verdi to Maw's *The Rising of the Moon* and Einem's *Der Besuch der alten Dame*. When Glyndebourne Touring Opera was launched in 1968 he was appointed principal conductor, becoming music director in 1971, and remained in that post until 1974. He was music director of the New Opera Company of Adelaide, Australia (later the State Opera of South Australia) from 1975, and from 1981 to 1992 he was head of opera at the New South Wales Conservatorium of Music (later, after amalgamation with the University of Sydney, the State Conservatorium of Music).

His skill as an operatic conductor was recognized by engagements with the Belgian National Opera (*Ormindo*, 1972), with Polish companies in Łódź and Poznań, with the Hamburg Staatsoper, and with Romanian companies in Bucharest and Cluj. He conducted a new production of *Il barbiere di Siviglia* at the recently opened Sydney Opera House in 1974 and *Death in Venice* there in 1989, as well as the première of *Lawrence Hargrave Flying Alone* by Nigel Butterley at the New South Wales Conservatorium in 1988. In addition, Fredman has conducted opera for the Sadler's Wells company and at the Wexford Festival.

ARTHUR JACOBS, NOËL GOODWIN

Freeman, David (*b* Sydney, 1 May 1952). Australian director. After study at Sydney University (1971–4) he founded Opera Factory in Sydney in 1973, followed by Opera Factory Zürich with Brenton Langbein and Lesley Stephenson in 1976, and Opera Factory London in 1981. Developing rigorous methods of preparation and rehearsal, Opera Factory emphasizes the elements of manufacture and creativity in productions assembled under specific conditions. An impressive roster of innovatory stagings in London includes those of Cavalli's *Calisto*, a conflation of Gluck's two *Iphigénie* operas and the Mozart-Da Ponte trilogy. In conjunction with the London Sinfonietta, with whom the company was associated from 1984 to 1991, a number of 20th-century works have been given, notably the world premières of Nigel Osborne's *Hell's Angels* (for which Freeman also wrote the libretto) and Birtwistle's *Yan Tan Tethera*, as well as Birtwistle's *Punch and Judy*, Tippett's *The Knot Garden*, Ligeti's *Aventures* and *Nouvelles aventures*, Maxwell Davies's *Eight Songs for a Mad King* and Reimann's *Die Gespenstersonate*. Freeman is also an Associate Artist of the ENO, for whom he has directed Monteverdi's *Orfeo* (1981), Glass's *Akhnaten* (1985), Birtwistle's *The Mask of Orpheus* (1986) and *Il ritorno d'Ulisse* (1989).

His highly physical productions require great virtuosity of acting. Those of the classics generally involve a search for the points at which the dynamics of the work can directly engage a contemporary audience. Many have plumbed new depths of emotion while creating humour that borders on the farcical: his *Così*, at once hilarious and psychologically searing in its exploration of sexual relationships, touched a particular chord with audiences of the 1980s.

*

D. Freeman: 'Telling the Story', *Claudio Monteverdi: 'Orfeo'*, ed. J. Whenham (Cambridge, 1986), 156–66

H. Canning: 'Freeman of the Factory', *Classical Music* (1 Aug 1987), 11–13

A. Clements: 'People: 161: David Freeman', *Opera*, xl (1989), 1297–302

BARRY MILLINGTON

Freeman, John (*b* 1666; *d* London, 10 Dec 1736). English tenor/countertenor and composer. In the 1690s he was a leading performer in Purcell's *Dioclesian*, *The Fairy-Queen*, *Don Quixote*, *The Indian Queen* and *Bonduca*. After Purcell's death he sang in new dramatic operas with music by Daniel Purcell, Clarke and Finger until 1700 when he was in Daniel Purcell's *The Grove* and Dryden's *Secular Masque* in *The Pilgrim*. He then left the stage for the choirs of the Chapel Royal, St Paul's Cathedral and Westminster Abbey. His solos, several of which have a trumpet obbligato part, demand a range of *e* to *a'*, with an occasional *b'*. A few songs composed by him were published and the tune of his 'Pretty parrot say' was used in *The Beggar's Opera*.

*

BDA; *LS*

O. Baldwin and T. Wilson: 'Alfred Deller, John Freeman and Mr. Pate', *ML*, l (1969), 103–10

——: 'Who can from Joy Refraine?', *MT*, cxxii (1981), 596–9

OLIVE BALDWIN, THELMA WILSON

Freeman, (Harry) Lawrence (*b* Cleveland, 9 Oct 1869; *d* New York, 21 March 1954). American composer. He was the first black musician to conduct his own works

with a symphony orchestra (1907, Minneapolis) and the first to compose a substantial number of large operatic compositions. Apart from piano studies with Edwin Schonert and Carlos Sobrino, he had little formal training. As a teenager, he organized and performed in a boys' quartet and became organist at the family church. Johann Beck, the founder and conductor of the Cleveland SO, taught him composition and orchestration, and later conducted a few of his early instrumental pieces. A year after moving to Denver in 1892, Freeman composed his first opera, *The Martyr*, subsequently conducting it in Denver, Chicago, Cleveland and at Wilberforce (Ohio) University where he taught (1902–4). It received a concert performance at Carnegie Hall in 1937. He was also active as music director for several musical theatre groups, including the Rufus Rastus Company and the Pekin Theatre Stock Company in Chicago; he moved to New York in 1910 to work with the Red Moon Company. He taught at the Salem School of Music and then established his own institutions, the Freeman School of Music (1911–22) and the Freeman School of Grand Opera (1923). In addition, he helped organize and conduct the Negro Opera Company and the Negro Choral Society and worked as a critic.

Freeman composed over 20 stage works, including operas, musical theatre shows, 'jazz operas' and a children's opera, all with African, oriental, Mexican, western or Indian themes. The operas are made up of individual set pieces and choral segments loosely connected by recitative in a neo-romantic style; folksong-like melodies and simple harmonies predominate. In 1930 he received the Harmon Gold Award for excellence in composition, and excerpts from nine of his operas were performed at Steinway Hall. His wife, Carlotta Freeman, frequently appeared in leading roles in his operas, alongside their son, Valdo (1900–72), who often produced and promoted them. Freeman himself conducted the productions.

librettos written or adapted by the composer

The Martyr (2), Denver, Deutsches, Sept 1893

Nada, 1898, inc., concert perf., Cleveland, 1900; rev. as Zuluki, 1898 (3)

African Kraal (1), Chicago, 30 June 1903

The Octoroon, 1904 (prol., 4, after M. E. Braddon)

Valdo (1 and intermezzo), Cleveland, Weisgerber's Hall, May 1906

The Plantation, 1906–15 (3), New York, 1930

Captain Rufus (musical show), Chicago, 1907, collab. J. Green and A. Anderson

The Tryst (1), New York, Crescent, May 1911

The Prophecy, 1914 (1)

Athalia, 1916 (prol., 3)

Vendetta (3), New York, Lafayette, 12 Nov 1923

American Romance, 1927 (jazz op)

Voodoo (3), WCBS, 20 May 1928; staged, abridged version, New York, 52nd Street

The Flapper (jazz op, 4), Dec 1929

Leah Kleschna, 1930

Uzziah, 1931

Zululand (trilogy, after H. Rider Haggard)
  Nada and The Lily, 1941–4
  Allah, 1947
  Zulu King, 1934

Undated: Dark Canyon; The Wolf (children's op)

*

SouthernB

E. E. Hipsher: *American Opera and its Composers* (Philadelphia, 1927)

J. Mattfeld: *A Handbook of American Operatic Premieres, 1731–1962* (Detroit, 1963)

V. Perlis: Interview with Valdo Freeman, Oral History Project in American Music, Yale U. Library, 1971

E. Southern: *The Music of Black Americans: a History* (New York, 1971, 2/1983)

L. Berry jr: *Biographical Dictionary of Black Musicians and Educators*, i (Guthrie, OK, 1978)

C. Davidson: *Opera by Afro-American Composers: a Critical Survey and Analysis of Selected Works* (diss., Catholic U., 1980)

VIVIAN PERLIS

Freer, Eleanor Everest (*b* Philadelphia, 14 May 1864; *d* Chicago, 13 Dec 1942). American composer. Her father, Cornelius Everest, was an organist, her mother an accomplished singer. She began to play the piano at the age of five, and in her teens sang Josephine in *HMS Pinafore* and tried her hand at composition. She studied singing with Mathilde Marchesi in Paris (1883–6) and composition with Benjamin Godard. While in Europe she sang for Verdi and Liszt. On her return to the USA she taught the piano in Philadelphia and singing at the National Conservatory of Music, New York (1889–91), using the Marchesi method. In 1891 she married, and after seven years in Leipzig moved to Chicago.

Throughout her early career she studied languages and in particular the translation of texts, not only into English. Among the musicians who visited her home during her childhood was the baritone David Bispham, who sang opera roles in English. In 1921, the year of Bispham's death, she established the Opera in Our Language Foundation; a year later the foundation established the David Bispham Memorial Fund and Freer published her first opera, *The Legend of the Piper*. In 1924 the foundation and the fund were merged as the American Opera Society of Chicago, with Freer as the first president. It awarded the David Bispham Memorial Medal for operas with English librettos; 53 awards were made before her death, once to Freer herself. According to her *Recollections* (1929) it was her work with the foundation that prompted her to begin writing operas. Her librettos are mostly set syllabically and in regular metres; the music, while tonal, is rich in seventh chords and decorative chromaticism.

The Legend of the Piper op.28, 1922 (1, Act 1 of J. P. Peabody: *The Piper*), South Bend, IN, 24 Feb 1925, vs (Boston, 1922)

Massimilliano, the Court Jester, or The Love of a Caliban op.30, 1925 (1, E. W. Peattie), Lincoln, NE, Temple, 19 Jan 1926, vs (Chicago, 1925)

The Chilkoot Maiden op.32, 1926 (1, Freer), Skagway, AL, 1927, vs (Milwaukee, 1926)

A Christmas Tale op.35, 1928 (1, B. H. Clark, after M. Bouchor), Houston, 27 Dec 1929, vs (Milwaukee, 1928)

The Masque of Pandora op.36, 1928 (1, Freer, after Longfellow), vs (Milwaukee, 1929)

Preciosa, or The Spanish Student op.37, 1928 (Freer, after H. W. Longfellow), vs (Milwaukee, 1928)

Frithiof op.40 (2, C. Shaw, after E. Tegner: *Frithiofs Saga*), Chicago, Illinois Women's Athletic Club, 11 April 1929, vs (Milwaukee, 1929)

Joan of Arc op.38 (1, Freer), Chicago, Junior Friends of Art, 3 Dec 1929, vs (Milwaukee, 1929)

A Legend of Spain (1, Freer), Milwaukee, 19 June 1931, vs (Milwaukee, 1931)

Little Women op.42 (2, Freer, after L. M. Alcott), Chicago, Musician's Club of Women, 2 April 1934, vs (Chicago, 1934)

The Brownings go to Italy op.43, 1936 (1, G. A. Hawkins-Ambler), Chicago, Arts Club, 11 March 1938, vs (Chicago, 1936)

*

A. G. Foster: *Eleanor Freer, Patriot, and her Colleagues* (Chicago, 1927)

E. E. Freer: *Recollections and Reflections of an American Composer* (Chicago, 1929)   PHYLLIS BRUCE, THOMAS WARBURTON

Freiburg. University city in south-west Germany. It acquired its first permanent theatre in 1770. In 1823 a new one was built in the deconsecrated church of the Augustinian monastery in the Salzstrasse; the first performances here were by private theatrical companies. Regular performances of opera began in the 19th century. In 1886 the city authorities took over the financing of the theatre, and what was then only the second civic theatre in Germany was thus established. In 1910 the theatre in the Bertholdstrasse was opened; it was closed during World War I, damaged in 1917 and reopened in 1920. The building was extensively damaged in 1944, rebuilt, and opened in 1949 with *Die Meistersinger von Nürnberg*. Known as the Städtische Bühnen, it is funded by the city and the *Land* of Baden-Württemberg. The Grosses Haus at Freiburg, with stalls and two circles, accommodates 1064 spectators. In a ten-month season opera, ballet, operetta and musicals occupy up to 170 evenings. The annual repertory includes six to seven operas, one or two being modern works, two or three comic operas and occasionally one Baroque work. Among celebrated figures who have worked at Freiburg are the musical directors Franz Konwitschny (1934–9), Leopold Hager and Marek Janowski, and the administrator Hans-Reinhard Müller (later of the Munich Chamber Theatre). Günther Wich made his conducting début at the Staatstheater in 1952; he became chief opera conductor and remained there until 1959.   GÁBOR HALÁSZ

Freischütz, Der ('The Freeshooter'). *Romantische Oper* in three acts, J277, by CARL MARIA VON WEBER to a libretto by JOHANN FRIEDRICH KIND after Johann August Apel and Friedrich Laun's *Gespensterbuch*; Berlin, Schauspielhaus, 18 June 1821.

Max *an assistant forester*	tenor
Kilian *a wealthy peasant*	baritone
Cuno *a hereditary forester*	bass
Caspar *an assistant forester*	bass
Aennchen *Agathe's relative*	mezzo-soprano
Agathe *Cuno's daughter*	soprano
Samiel *the 'Black Huntsman'*	speaking role
Four bridesmaids	sopranos
Ottokar *a sovereign prince*	baritone
Hermit	bass

Hunters, peasants, spirits, bridesmaids, attendants

Setting Bohemia at the end of the Thirty Years War

Shortly after taking up the post of Kapellmeister of the German opera in Dresden in 1817, Weber revived the idea of writing an opera on the Freischütz story, which he had first considered seven years earlier after reading the tale in Apel and Laun's newly published *Gespensterbuch*. He discussed the project with Kind, a fellow member of the Dresden literary 'Liederkreis', who rapidly produced the draft of a libretto provisionally entitled *Der Probeschuss* ('The Test Shot'). Between the publication of the *Gespensterbuch* and Kind's libretto, the story had been used as the basis of a number of other theatrical pieces. The first treatment of it, by Franz Xaver von Caspar with music by CARL NEUNER (1812, Munich) may have provided certain elements for Kind's libretto. Two versions were also produced in Vienna in 1816, and one of them, *Die Schreckensnacht am Kreuzwege*, by J. A. Gleich with music by Franz de Paul Roser, held the stage until 1828. In 1818 Spohr, with the collaboration of Georg Döring, also began to compose an opera on Apel's tale, but hearing that Weber was working on the same subject he abandoned it in favour of *Zemire und Azor*.

During the composition of *Der Freischütz* Weber made a number of changes to the libretto, the most important of which was the deletion, against Kind's wishes, of the scenes between the Hermit and Agathe which were to have opened the first act. In these the Hermit sees a horrifying vision which he interprets as a warning of danger to Agathe. When Agathe brings him food and tells him of Max's nervousness over the *Probeschuss*, he gives her, for her protection, roses from a tree brought from Palestine.

Weber's work on *Der Freischütz* progressed slowly. His duties in Dresden and his efforts to promote German opera there were burdensome and often frustrating. He was also distracted by other commissions, and his health was increasingly weakened by the progress of tuberculosis. During 1819, however, after he had arranged with the Intendant of the Berlin opera, Count Brühl, that the opera (at that stage known as *Die Jägersbraut*, 'The Hunter's Bride') should have its première in the newly rebuilt Schauspielhaus, he worked more intensively. By 30 November he had completed the first act and was able to promise Brühl that he would finish the opera by March 1820. On 18 June the following year *Der Freischütz* became the first musical piece to be staged in the Schauspielhaus. Its success was immediate and long-lasting. Within a few years it conquered all the major stages of Europe. By 1830 it had been produced in Danish, Swedish, Czech, Russian, English, French, Hungarian, Polish and Dutch, and before 1850 it was staged as far afield as Cape Town, Rio de Janeiro and Sydney. It has long been regarded as one of the seminal works of German Romantic opera.

The C major/minor overture sets the scene for the opera, its two principal tonalities representing the healthy aspects of life as opposed to evil and the dark powers. Horns conjure up a vision of forests and hunting, low clarinets, timpani and especially the sound of the diminished 7th chord, associated with Samiel, presage the dark side of the drama. The Molto vivace is based on Max's 'Doch mich umgarnen finstre Mächte' in Act 1, full of foreboding, and Agathe's exultant 'Süss entzückt entgegen ihm' in Act 2.

ACT 1 *In front of an inn in the Bohemian forest* In a bright, rustic D major chorus (no.1) the peasants congratulate one of their fellows, Kilian, for his victory in a shooting competition. They make fun of the forester Max's failure and accompany Kilian's mocking solo ('Schau der Herr') with laughter in repeated major 2nds. A fight between Max and Kilian is prevented only by the arrival of Cuno and some of his foresters, among whom is Caspar. Kilian explains that they were teasing Max because he had missed all his shots. Caspar (who has made a compact with the Black Huntsman), after giving thanks in an aside to Samiel for his own accuracy, suggests that Max's gun must be bewitched; he mockingly proposes to call on the dark powers for assistance. Cuno intervenes, rebuking Caspar, but warns Max that if he fails in the shooting trial the next day he will not be allowed to marry Agathe. Cuno explains the origins of the shooting trial for whoever is to inherit the chief forester's position. In the trio with chorus 'O! diese

Sonne' (no.2) Max remains despondent, while Cuno admonishes him and Caspar tempts him to rash measures. The trio opens in A minor, and its use of a diminished 7th chord in the third bar hints at the imminence of the dark powers. The ensuing hunting chorus ('Lasst lustig die Hörner erschallen!') turns to a healthy F major. In the dialogue Kilian wishes Max luck and invites him to join the dance. The peasants exit, dancing to a waltz (no.3) which gradually fades and disintegrates, giving way in a highly effective manner to a dramatic scena ('Nein! länger trag' ich nicht die Qualen') as Max is left alone, pondering the abrupt alteration in his success. At one point, as he wonders if Heaven has forsaken him, the diminished 7th is heard and Samiel is seen in the distance. As the music finishes in C minor, Caspar comes out of the inn. He orders wine and insists on Max's drinking several toasts with him; he then sings a coarse drinking song which enrages Max (no.4, 'Hier im ird'schen Jammerthal'); from its initial B minor tonality it modulates to D major, a key which Weber associates with the rustic life, but is wrenched back to B minor to the accompaniment of a shrill piccolo. When Max is about to leave Caspar tells him that he can help him succeed in the trial, and proves the point by giving him his gun to shoot at a distant bird. Max shoots and brings down a massive eagle. Caspar explains that the gun was loaded with a *Freikügel*, a magic bullet that always hits its mark; but it was his last. However, seven more can be cast if Max will meet him in the Wolf's Glen at midnight. After Max has departed, Caspar, who plans to offer him as a victim to Samiel in place of himself, exults in Max's impending damnation and his own triumph in the aria 'Schweig, schweig' (no.5).

1. '*Der Freischütz*' (Weber): designs by Stürmer for the costumes of Samiel (left) and Caspar in the original production at the Schauspielhaus, Berlin, 18 June 1821

2. 'Der Freischütz'
(Weber), Act 2 (the
Wolf's Glen): design
(original presumed lost in
World War II) by Carl
Gropius for the original
production at the
Schauspielhaus, Berlin, 18
June 1821

Act 2 *A room in Cuno's house* Aennchen is fixing a portrait of Cuno's ancestor, which had fallen down and slightly injured Agathe. In the A major duet 'Schelm, halt' fest!' (no.6) the characters of the two young women are nicely established; Aennchen's sprightly phrases show her carefree disposition, while Agathe's slower-moving ones indicate her more serious nature and her concern for Max. Aennchen cheers Agathe in a lively C major arietta in polonaise rhythm, 'Kommt ein schlanker Bursch gegangen' (no.7), and Agathe explains that her brooding was caused by the outcome of her morning visit to the Hermit. Left alone, Agathe sings a recitative and aria in E major, 'Wie nahte mir der Schlummer … Leise, leise' (no.8), not altogether free from the Italian influence about which Weber was so frequently critical but highly effective in painting her character. During this number her uneasiness gives way to joy at the thought of her coming wedding day, when she hears Max's footsteps approaching. Max enters and explains that he must hurry away again to collect a stag which he has shot in the forest near the Wolf's Glen. At the mention of this dreadful place Agathe, in a C minor beginning to the E♭ trio 'Wie? was? Entsetzen!' (no.9), and Aennchen express their horror, while Max exclaims that a hunter cannot be afraid of the forest at night when he has his duty to perform. Samiel's diminished 7th chord is heard as Max exclaims that the bright moonlight will soon be gone. By the end of the trio Aennchen has recovered her usual lightheartedness, oblivious to the concern of the others.

The Wolf's Glen The music of the finale (no.10) begins in F♯ minor with pianissimo string tremolandos and low sustained clarinets and trombones. The subsequent tonalities of the scene are those of the individual notes of the diminished 7th chord which accompanies each of Samiel's appearances. Caspar intones a spell and a chorus of invisible spirits, accompanied by shrieks on the woodwind, answers him with owl-like calls. As a distant clock strikes twelve, Caspar, in a short section of melodrama, calls up Samiel. As the music moves to C minor, Samiel appears and agrees to allow him three more years of life in return for another victim; Caspar suggests that Samiel direct

the seventh bullet at Agathe. The music modulates to E♭ and Max arrives; he is horrified by visions of his dead mother and Agathe, but nevertheless descends. The music returns to C minor and they begin casting the bullets. As they are cast, the music alternates between C minor and A minor with copious use of diminished 7ths. Between each of the seven castings there are supernatural manifestations of mounting horror: flapping nightbirds; a black boar; a hurricane; cracking whips, trampling horses and wheels of fire; a wild hunt; thunder, lightning, hail, meteors and fire; and finally Samiel himself. Caspar and Max fall unconscious and the tonality returns to F♯ minor. As the clock strikes one, calm returns.

Act 3 *A forest* After an entr'acte with horn-calls (no.11), the curtain rises on a hunting party in the forest. Max has made three magnificent shots and has only one magic bullet left; he asks Caspar for more, but is refused. Caspar uses up his last magic bullet so that Max has the only one remaining, the one that belongs to Samiel.

Agathe's room Wearing her wedding dress, Agathe affirms her trust in God in the cavatina 'Und ob die Wolke' (no.12). She has had a bad dream in which she saw herself as a white dove: when Max fired his gun she fell; the dove vanished and she was Agathe again, but a bleeding black bird lay at her feet. Aennchen enters and tries to dispel Agathe's anxiety. In a *romanza* and aria, 'Einst träumte' (no.13), which Weber added to the opera for his first Aennchen, she tells a tale of a cousin who had fearful nightmares which resulted from the sound of the dog rattling its chain (no.13). The bridesmaids arrive and sing a folksong, 'Wir winden dir den Jungfernkranz' (no.14). Aennchen returns; the picture of Cuno's ancestor has again fallen, and the box that Aennchen has brought is found to contain a funeral wreath. Both women are thoroughly shaken, but decide to make a new wreath from roses which the Hermit had given Agathe. To the final chorus of the bridesmaids' song they depart, but the music modulates disturbingly through D minor to A minor, ending with sinister tremolos in the bass. These are answered by a sudden explosion of D major as the orchestral introduction to the rousing Huntsmen's Chorus, 'Was gleicht wohl auf Erden' (no.15), begins.

A 'romantic landscape' Prince Ottokar and his retainers wait for the shooting contest to begin. Cuno requests that it take place before Agathe arrives. The Prince chooses a white dove on a branch as target. As Max takes aim Agathe enters and cries to him to hold fire, since she is the dove. The Hermit touches the bough and the dove flies off to another tree behind which Caspar is hiding. Max shoots; both Agathe and Caspar fall to the ground and the finale (no.16) begins, in C minor, the key of the dark powers. The people think Max has shot Agathe, but she is unhurt. Caspar has been fatally wounded and as Samiel, accompanied by his diminished 7th, appears to him he dies, cursing Heaven and Hell. At this point C major begins to reassert itself. Max makes a full confession, after which, despite the pleas of Cuno, Agathe and the people, the Prince banishes him. However, on the intervention of the Hermit, the Prince agrees that Max be given a year to prove himself, at the end of which the Prince will himself officiate at Max's wedding to Agathe. The opera ends with a hymn of praise for God's mercy in which the triumphant theme from Agathe's aria (no.8), which had also crowned the overture, plays a prominent part.

* * *

Der Freischütz was the culmination of an important phase in Weber's struggle to realize his conception of German opera. His idea of combining the resources of drama, music and the visual aspect of theatre in a unified art work was only partly realized in Der Freischütz; but, owing much to the example of French opera, he moved far beyond the limitations of Singspiel as it was practised by the majority of his German contemporaries. Along with Spohr (Faust, 1813) and Hoffmann (Undine, 1816), who had similar aims, he attempted, with considerable success, to express the essential elements of the drama in his music. Like them, Weber used tonality, musical motif, orchestral colour and various formal and structural devices. Spohr's Faust in particular, which Weber had introduced in Prague in 1816, may have exerted a considerable influence on his use of motif. Weber himself had recognized the effectiveness of Spohr's employment of 'a few melodies, felicitously and aptly devised, [which] weave like delicate threads through the whole, and hold it together artistically' (Prager Zeitung, 1 September 1816). His use of motif in Der Freischütz is less subtle and pervasive than Spohr's, but for precisely that reason, perhaps, it is more effective; while even the alert listener may fail to observe the transformations of Spohr's Hell motif, Samiel's diminished 7th, with its sinister orchestration, is unmistakable. (Spohr, in fact, had used a diminished 7th, strikingly orchestrated, as a motif for supernatural intervention in Zemire und Azor in 1818–19.) Another point of similarity between all three composers was the use of librettos that explored the relationship of the natural and supernatural worlds, a theme which continued to find favour with German Romantic composers. However, while Hoffmann's Undine failed to enter the repertory, and the operas of Spohr (and later those of Marschner) enjoyed only limited success in the long term, Der Freischütz, despite the limitations of its libretto, has held the stage uninterruptedly. This may be attributed largely to Weber's extraordinary ability to judge the effectiveness of his music in the theatre and to his gift for combining musical substance with accessibility. Almost every number of the opera still speaks to its audiences with refreshing vigour and directness.

For further illustration see STAGE DESIGN, fig.13; and WEBER, CARL MARIA VON. CLIVE BROWN

Freitas, Frederico (Guedes) de (b Lisbon, 15 Nov 1902; d Lisbon, 12 Jan 1980). Portuguese composer and conductor. He studied the piano, the violin and composition at the Lisbon Conservatory, graduating in 1925. That year he won a government scholarship to study in several European countries. In 1935 he was appointed conductor of the newly formed Portuguese radio chamber orchestra and in 1940 he founded the Lisbon Choral Society. He continued to combine his career as a composer with that of conducting in Portugal and abroad, with teaching and with research on early Portuguese music. He wrote music of many kinds and all his work shows a melodic talent and mastery of the techniques he used, including polyphony, polytonality and atonality. Freitas was essentially a composer for the theatre, but he wrote only three small-scale operas. His many revues, his operettas and his incidental music for around 20 plays are, however, important contributions to the Portuguese theatre of the 1930s and 40s, when few academic musicians worked in such genres. Little of Freitas's music for the theatre is played now, although some of the songs and concert suites from the ballet are still popular.

operettas unless otherwise stated; all first performances in Lisbon

A flor de S Roque (vaudeville, L. Silva and A. Barbosa), Avenida, 1928

O meu menino (vaudeville), Avenida, 1931

A Senhora da Saúde (2, S. Tavares, A. Amaral and X. Magalhães), Maria Vitória, 1931

Alvorada do amor (V. Rajanto), Ginásio, 1932, collab. A. Melo

De capa e batina (3, L. Ferreira, F. Santos, L. Rodrigues and Magalhães), Politeama, 1933

O Timpanas (3, F. Bermudes), Avenida, 1933

O solar das picoas (3, Ferreira and Santos), Trindade, 1934, collab. W. Pinto

O eremita (op, 1, P. Lemos), 1957

Don João e a máscara (musical scene, 1, A. Patrício), Tivoli, 1960

A igreja do mar (radio op, Lemos), S Carlos, 1960

Fandango, n.d.

*

J. F. Branco: História da música portuguesa (Lisbon, 1959)

Catálogo geral da música portuguesa – repertório contemporâneo (Lisbon, 1978)

J. Almendra: 'Um grande artista que o país perdeu', Canto gregoriano, xciv (1980), 3–18

L. F. Rebelo: História do Teatro de Revista (Lisbon, 1985)

ADRIANA LATINO

Fremstad, Olive [Rundquist, Olivia] (b Stockholm, 14 March 1871; d Irvington-on-Hudson, NY, 21 April 1951). Swedish-American mezzo-soprano and soprano. Of illegitimate birth, she was adopted by an American couple of Scandinavian origin who took her to Minnesota. She studied in New York, and later in Berlin with Lilli Lehmann. During the first decade of her career she appeared in many European operatic centres, including Bayreuth, Vienna, Munich and Covent Garden, where her Wagner roles aroused special attention. On 25 November 1903 she made her Metropolitan début as Sieglinde; she remained there for 11 consecutive seasons, singing both soprano and mezzo roles including the first Salome in the USA. But Wagner, including all three Brünnhildes, Kundry and Isolde (which she sang with both Mahler and Toscanini), formed the backbone of her repertory. Although her few records are clearly unworthy, it is evident from the fascinating account given by her secretary, Mary Watkins Cushing, that her vocal powers were transcendent, and that her vivid temperament made her a difficult colleague as well as an interpreter of genius. Her final performance at the Metropolitan (as Elsa on 23 April 1914) provoked one of the most remarkable demonstrations of affection and admiration in the history of the house.

L. Migliorini and J. Dennis: 'Olive Fremstad', *Record Collector*, vii (1952), 53–65 [with discography]

M. W. Cushing: *The Rainbow Bridge* (New York, 1954); repr. with discography (1977)   DESMOND SHAWE-TAYLOR

French overture. A common type of OVERTURE of the late 17th and early 18th centuries. The opening section is slow and march-like, usually featuring dotted rhythms, *tirate* and frequent suspensions, and it normally ends on the dominant. The second section is quick, usually fugal and often in triple or compound metre. The opening section is generally repeated, and may return in some form after the second section; in earlier examples the second section may also be repeated. Other sections, if any, appear most often as added movements, commonly in dance rhythm, after the two sections described. Later examples show an increasing tendency to hybridize the French overture with other types.

The French overture originated as an expansion of binary dance form. It was established as a standard model by Lully, whose first example appears in the ballet *Alcidiane* (1658) and whose first use of the type in opera came in the overture he composed for a performance of Cavalli's *Xerse* in 1660. It remained the principal type of overture in France, Germany and England for over 50 years and was also used in Italy, but was largely supplanted by the three-movement Italian type before the middle of the 18th century. Leading exponents, besides Lully and his contemporaries, include Rameau, Handel and Telemann; echoes of its manner persist into Mozart's time and beyond. Its slow opening section ending on the dominant represents an important precedent for the slow introductions that gradually became common in italianate overtures after 1760.

H. Prunières: 'Notes sur les origines de l'ouverture française', *SIMG*, xii (1910–11), 565–85

L. de la Laurencie: *L'école française de violon de Lully à Viotti* (Paris, 1922–24)

N. Demuth: *French Opera: its Development to the Revolution* (Horsham, 1963)

J. R. Anthony: *French Baroque Music from Beaujoyeulx to Rameau* (London, 1973, 2/1978)

R. M. Isherwood: *Music in the Service of the King* (Ithaca, NY, 1973)
                                                    STEPHEN C. FISHER

Freni [Fregni], Mirella (*b* Modena, 27 Feb 1935). Italian soprano. She studied with Campogalliani at Bologna and in 1955 made her début at Modena as Micaëla. After a season with the Netherlands Opera, she sang Zerlina at Glyndebourne (1960–61), returning in 1962 as Susanna and Adina. She made her Covent Garden début as Nannetta, and later appeared there as Zerlina, Susanna, Violetta, Mimì, Micaëla, Gounod's Marguerite, and Tatyana (1988). In 1962 she sang Elvira (*I puritani*) at Wexford and first appeared at La Scala as Mimì; subsequent roles included Marie (*La fille du régiment*), Manon and Amelia (*Simon Boccanegra*), which she also sang at Covent Garden during the 1976 Scala visit. She made her Metropolitan début in 1965 as Mimì and her repertory there included Suzel, Gounod's

Juliet, Liù and Tatyana (1989). At Salzburg, where she made her début in 1966 as Micaëla, she took on heavier roles, singing Desdemona (1970), Elisabeth de Valois (1975) and Aida (1979). She later added Manon Lescaut and Butterfly to her repertory, and sang Adriana Lecouvreur at San Francisco (1985), Bologna (1988) and Munich (1990). She sang Lisa (*Queen of Spades*) at La Scala in 1990. The purity, fullness and even focus of her voice have survived the transition from lyric to dramatic soprano, as have her personal charm and magnetism.

R. Jacobson: 'Mirella ritornata', *ON*, xlii/4 (1977–8), 19–23
                                            HAROLD ROSENTHAL/R

Frenkel, Daniil Grigor'yevich (*b* Kiev, 2/15 Sept 1906; *d* Leningrad [now St Petersburg], 9 June 1984). Soviet composer. He studied piano with Y. A. Tkach at the Odessa Conservatory from 1925 and with S. V. Alpers at the Second Leningrad Musical Technical College, 1928–9. Three years later he began lessons in theory and composition with A. P. Gladkovsky, then in 1936 he studied orchestration with M. O. Shteynberg. It was during his period with Gladkovsky that Frenkel produced his first two operas, *Zakon i faraon* and *V ushchel'ye*, both of which apparently remain unperformed. Though he wrote in many forms, opera remained central to Frenkel's output throughout his career. He also held several important theatrical posts. From 1941 to 1944 he was head of music and conductor at the Orenburg regional dramatic theatre, and between 1945 and 1947 he held the same posts at the V. F. Komissarzhevsky Dramatic Theatre, Leningrad. He also directed one of the ensembles of the Soviet Navy for eight years from 1945. Frenkel's music has been praised for its uncomplicated lyricism and feeling for dramatic effect.

Zakon i faraon [Law and the Policeman], 1933 (after O. Henry), unperf.

V ushchel'ye [Into the Ravine], 1934 (after Henry), unperf.

Rassvet [Dawn], Leningrad Conservatory Opera Studio, 1934

Diana i Teodoro [Diana and Teodoro] (M. Lozinsky, after Lope de Vega), 1944

Ugryum-reka [Grim River] (after V. Shishkov), Leningrad, 1950; rev. 1953

Bespridannitsa [The Bride without a Dowry] (4, after Ostrovsky), Leningrad, Malïy, 1956

Dzhordano Bruno [Giordano Bruno], 1966

Smert' Ivana Groznogo [The Death of Ivan the Terrible] (after A. K. Tolstoy), 1970

Sïn Rïbakova [Rïbakov's Son] (after V. M. Gusev), Leningrad, National, Kirov Palace of Culture, 1977   STEPHEN JOHNSON

Freschi, (Giovanni) Domenico (*b* Bassano del Grappa, *c*1630; *d* Vicenza, 2 July 1710). Italian composer. He was already a singer and priest at Vicenza Cathedral when on 24 August 1650 he received a canonry there. On 14 December 1656 he defeated Carlo Grossi to become *maestro di cappella*, a post he held for the rest of his life. He was otherwise mainly active as an opera composer, particularly in Venice (for the Teatro S Angelo), but also for the private theatre of Marco Contarini at Piazzola sul Brenta, near Padua. With the exception of his single-act contribution to *Iphide greca*, Freschi composed his operatic works within a rather brief span of time, between 1677 and 1685; a number were performed throughout the Veneto and in other regions of Italy. *Tullia superba* (1678) has relatively well thought-out melodic writing and makes much use of dotted and anapaestic rhythms, and the arias of

Ermelinda (1682) include interesting rhythmic details; some of the later operas (e.g. *L'incoronatione di Dario*) contain large and demanding da capo arias.

first performed in Venice, S Angelo, unless otherwise stated
dm – *dramma per musica*

Iphide greca [Act 2] (dm, 3, N. Minato), Venice, Saloni, 1671, *I-Vnm* [Act 1 by G. D. Partenio, Act 3 by G. Sartorio]
Helena rapita da Paride (dm, 3, A. Aureli), 1677, *MOe*, *Vnm*, arias *Vqs*, 2 arias ed. in Rosand 1991
Tullia superba (dm, 3, A. Medolago), 29 Jan 1678/9, *MOe*, *Vnm*, arias *Vqs*
Sardanapalo (dm, 3, C. Maderni), 1679; as *L'onor vindicato, o sia L'Armisia gran dinastessa di Tauris*, Reggio Emilia, Commedie, 1681; *MOe*, *Vnm*
La Circe (dm, 3, C. Ivanovich), 23 Jan 1679/80
Berenice vendicativa (dm, 3, ?G. M. Rapparini), Piazzola sul Brenta, 8 Nov 1680, *Vnm*
Il cittadino amante della patria overo, Il Tello (operetta, Rapparini), ? Piazzola sul Brenta, 1680 [lib. printed in lib. of Berenice vendicativa]
Pompeo Magno in Cilicia (dm, 3, Aureli), 22 Jan 1681, *Vnm* (*R*1982: IOB, lxv), arias *Vqs*
Olimpia vendicata (dm, 3, Aureli), 20 Nov 1681, *F-Pn*, *I-Vnm*, arias *Vqs*
Giulio Cesare trionfante (dm, 3, L. Orlandi), 10 Jan 1682, arias *Vqs*
Ermelinda (dm, 3, F. M. Piccioli), Piazzola sul Brenta, 1682, *Vnm*
Silla (dm, 3, A. Rossini), 4 Feb 1683
L'incoronatione di Dario (dm, 3, A. Morselli), 1684, *Vnm*, 1 aria ed. in Worsthorne 1954
Teseo tra le rivali (dm, 3, Aureli), 7 Feb 1685
Gl'amori d'Alidaura (Piccioli), Piazzola sul Brenta, Aug 1685

*

C. Ivanovich: *Minerva al tavolino* (Venice, 1681, 2/1688)
F. M. Piccioli: *L'orologio del piacere* (Piazzola sul Brenta, 1685)
G. Gasparelli: *I musicisti vicentini* (Vicenza, 1880)
S. T. Worsthorne: *Venetian Opera in the Seventeenth Century* (Oxford, 1954)
G. Mantese: *Storia musicale vicentina* (Vicenza, 1956)
M. Viale Ferrero: 'Repliche a Torino di alcuni melodrammi veneziani e loro caratteristiche', *Venezia e il melodramma nel seicento: Venice 1972*, 145–72
L. Bianconi and T. Walker: 'Production, Consumption and Political Function of Seventeenth-Century Opera', *Early Music History*, iv (1984), 211–99
T. Walker: ' "Ubi Lucius": Thoughts on Reading Medoro', *DMV*, iv (1984), pp. cxxxi–clxiv
E. Rosand: *Opera in Seventeenth-Century Venice* (Berkeley, 1991) [incl. 2 arias from *Helena rapita da Paride*, 620–21]

THOMAS WALKER, BETH L. GLIXON

Frešo, Tibor (*b* Spišský Štiavnik, 20 Nov 1918; *d* Piešt'any, 7 July 1967). Slovak composer and conductor. He studied composition with Alexander Moyzes at the Bratislava Academy (1934–9) and went on to study conducting with Bernardino Molinari at the Accademia di S Cecilia (1939–42). He began his conducting career at the Slovak National Theatre in Bratislava (1942–9), was head of the Košice Opera (1949–52) and then chief opera conductor in Bratislava from 1953. His two operas are in a neo-romantic style. *Martin a slnko* ('Martin and the Sun'; Bratislava, 18 Jan 1975), is a children's opera to a libretto by Alexandra Braxatorisová after Branislav Kriška. The story is based on Slovak folk tales and the music draws inspiration from a number of styles, from Classicism to full-blown, especially Russian, Romanticism, from *verismo* to expressionism, and includes some symphonic jazz, all against a background of Slovak folksong. *François Villon* (Bratislava, Slovak National Opera, 14 Feb 1986), to a libretto by Július Gyermek, links a montage of lines from Villon's *Grand Testament* and *Codicille* with a spoken commentary. Some of the songs are delivered with a danced subtext. Central to the opera

are the opposing forces of life and death represented by a Ravelian waltz and an archaic church chorale.

I. Vajda: *Slovenská opera* (Bratislava, 1988), 145–7, 219–22, 239–40
IGOR VAJDA

Fretwell, Elizabeth (*b* Melbourne, 13 Aug 1920). Australian soprano. She trained first as a ballerina, then joined the Melbourne Opera School to study singing in 1947. With the Australian National Theatre Movement (1950–55) she appeared in such leading roles as Donna Anna, Elsa and Desdemona before becoming principal lyric-dramatic soprano at Sadler's Wells. Her Violetta in *La traviata* won much admiration, her Minnie in *La fanciulla del West* still more. In 1961 her Ariadne was praised for its 'stream of golden sound', and her Ellen Orford (*Peter Grimes*) was among the highlights of the company's German tour in 1965. At Covent Garden she appeared in 1965 as Aida and Giorgetta (*Il tabarro*). In 1970 she returned to Australia, where she sang in the opening season of the Sydney Opera House (1973). Her full-bodied tone and direct expression can be heard in recordings of excerpts from operas given at Sadler's Wells. Unfortunately she did not record Gardner's *The Moon and Sixpence*, in which she created Blanche in 1957.
J. B. STEANE

Frey, Paul (*b* Toronto, 1942). Canadian tenor. He studied in Toronto with Louis Quilico. After singing with Canadian Opera, in 1979 he was engaged at Basle, where he sang Idomeneus, Don Ottavio, Titus, Florestan, the Duke, Macduff, Gabriele Adorno, Cavaradossi, Canio, Jeník, Don José, Flamand, Lancelot in the première of Jost Meier's *Der Drache* (1985) and Peter Grimes. He sang Huon (*Oberon*) at Edinburgh (1986), Lohengrin at Bayreuth, Bacchus for his Metropolitan début (1987) and Lohengrin for his Covent Garden début (1988). Other roles include Max, Radames, Aeneas, Walther, Parsifal, the Emperor (*Die Frau ohne Schatten*), Midas (*Die Liebe der Danae*), Apollo (*Daphne*) and Alwa (*Lulu*). He has appeared at Sydney, Munich, Hamburg, Vienna and Cologne, where he sang Siegmund (1990). His voice has developed from lyric to heroic proportions while retaining its tonal beauty.
ELIZABETH FORBES

Freyer, Achim (*b* Berlin, 30 March 1934). German painter, theatre designer and opera director. He studied at the Akademie der Künste in Berlin and made his stage début, designing the sets and costumes for Ruth Berghaus's production of *Il barbiere di Siviglia*, at the Berlin Staatsoper in 1967. He defected to the West in 1973 and made an immediate impression with his striking, painterly and abstract designs for Hans Neugebauer's productions of *Cardillac* (1973) and *Pelléas et Mélisande* (1975) at the Cologne Opera. In 1979, he made his début as director as well as designer with *Iphigénie en Tauride* at the Bavarian State Opera. He staged Philip Glass's *Satyagraha* (1981) and *Akhnaten* (1984, première) at the Stuttgart Opera. His 'pop art' style, evident in his productions of *Die Zauberflöte* for the Hamburg Opera and *Orfeo ed Euridice* for the Deutsche Oper Berlin in 1982, aroused controversy.

*

N. Ely and S. Jaeger, eds.: *Regie heute: Musiktheater in unserer Zeit* (Berlin, 1984), 19–46
HUGH CANNING

Frezzolini [Frezzolini-Poggi], **Erminia** (*b* Orvieto, 27 March 1818; *d* Paris, 5 Nov 1884). Italian soprano. She studied with her father, the bass Giuseppe Frezzolini, and made her début in 1837 in Florence as Beatrice di Tenda. She appeared widely in Italy, notably at La Scala, where she sang Lucrezia Borgia (1840) and created two Verdi roles: Giselda in *I Lombardi* (1843) and the title role of *Giovanna d'Arco* (1845), in which her husband, the tenor Antonio Poggi, sang Charles VII (she had earlier had a stormy engagement to Otto Nicolai). She made her London début at Her Majesty's Theatre in 1842 and sang in North America in 1848, St Petersburg in 1849 and Madrid in 1852–3. She then went to Paris, where in 1857 she sang Gilda and Leonora (*Il trovatore*) at the Théâtre Italien, both first performances in France. In the 1860s she again sang in the USA. Frezzolini was admired for her smooth and expressive legato singing (exploited by Verdi in her *preghiera* in *I Lombardi*); but she was noted too for her power and brilliance, in the modern manner, and she excelled in dramatic roles. ELIZABETH FORBES

Frezzolini, Giuseppe (*b* Orvieto, 9 Nov 1789; *d* Orvieto, 16 March 1861). Italian bass. He studied in Orvieto, making his début in 1819 at Terni in Pavesi's *Ser Marcantonio*. He appeared in Florence, Siena, Modena, Turin, Venice and at La Scala, where in 1827 he sang in the first performance of Mercadante's *Il montamaro*. The same year he created Pasquale in Donizetti's *Olivo e Pasquale* at Rome; he sang in the premières of Donizetti's *Alina, regina di Golconda* (1828, Genoa) and Pacini's *Il talismano* (1829, Milan). In 1832 he created Dulcamara in *L'elisir d'amore* (Teatro della Cannobiana, Milan). In 1840 he sang in the first performance of Mazzucato's *I corsari* at La Scala and, as Mamm' Agata, in the first Viennese performance of Donizetti's *Convenienze ed inconvenienze teatrali*. His repertory included the bass *buffo* parts in operas by Rossini and Luigi Ricci. ELIZABETH FORBES

Friant, Charles (*b* Paris, 1890; *d* Paris, 22 April 1947). French tenor. His father was a principal dancer at the Opéra and he himself sang in the chorus and appeared in the première of D'Indy's *L'étranger* as a boy. He later trained with Sarah Bernhardt and joined her company as an actor, then going to the Conservatoire to study singing in 1910. His operatic début was in the Paris première of Massenet's *Cléopâtre*. From 1920 to 1939 he was a member of the Opéra-Comique, appearing in a wide repertory but enjoying special success in Massenet operas such as *Manon*, *Werther* and *Le jongleur de Notre Dame*. Premières included *Le roi Candaule* by Bruneau and *La Hulla* by Samuel-Rousseau. He also sang at Monte Carlo and La Monnaie, Brussels. His recordings, especially those from *Werther*, are distinctively stylish and expressive. J. B. STEANE

Fribec, Krešimir (*b* Daruvar, 24 May 1908). Croatian composer. He studied music privately in Zagreb with Zlatko Grgošević and held the position of music editor of Radio-Televizija Zagreb from 1943 to 1964. He was a prolific composer, particularly in the fields of opera and ballet. Most of his early music was based on folksong, but between 1955 and 1964 he used 12-note, serial and aleatory procedures. Despite the high quality of many of his instrumental works of this period, Fribec went back to his more conventional and approachable expressionist idiom. His old fluency returned in a large number of works, including operas and ballets, which satisfied his desire to make his music appeal to as large a public as possible.

librettos by the composer

Sluga Jernej [The Servant Jernej], 1951 (opera-oratorio, after I. Cankar and F. Delak), Zagreb, 12 Feb 1952
Romeo i Julija (lyrical scenes, after W. Shakespeare), Zagreb, 1955; rev. 1967
Krvava svadba [Blood Wedding], 1958 (after F. García Lorca)
Maljva, slike s mora [Maljva, Pictures from the Sea], 1959 (after M. Gorky)
Yerma, 1960 (after García Lorca)
Dolazi revizor! [The Inspector General Arrives!], 1965 (after N. V. Gogol)
Dunja u kovčega [Quince in the Chest], 1966 (after M. Begović)
Veliki val [The Great Wave], 1966 (after M. Matić-Halle)
Djeca sunca [The Children of the Sun], 1968 (opera-ballet, after Croatian poets)
Heretik [The Heretic], 1971 (musical drama, after I. Supek)
Usamljenost [Loneliness], 1971 (musico-scenic meditations, after M. Selimović)
Ujak Vanja [Uncle Vanya], 1972 (chamber op, after A. P. Chekhov)
Goran, 1975 (scenic visions of the poet, opera-ballet, after I. Goran-Kovačić's poem)
Kralj Edip [King Oedipus], 1975 (after Sophocles)

Incomplete: Prometej, 1960; Čehovljev humoristicon, 1962; Nova Eva, 1963; Juduška Golovljev, 1964; Adagio melancolico, 1965

B. Sakač: 'Sluga Jernej Krešimira Fribeca', *Muzičke novine* (1 March 1952)
K. Kovačević: *Hrvatski kompozitori i njihova djela* [Croatian Composers and their Works] (Zagreb, 1960), 156–64
J. Andreis: *Music in Croatia* (Zagreb, 1974)
KORALJKA KOS, NIALL O'LOUGHLIN

Friberth [Frieberth, Friebert, Friedberg], **Carl** [Karl] (*b* Wullersdorf, Lower Austria, 7 June 1736; *d* Vienna, 6 Aug 1816). Austrian tenor, librettist and composer, brother of Joseph Frieberth, with whom he is often confused. He sang under Haydn's direction at Eisenstadt and Eszterháza between 1759 and 1776. Many of Haydn's liveliest early roles were written for him; he had an immense range (Frisellino's 'Tra tuoni e lampi' in *Le pescatrici* reaches c'''), and was an accomplished actor. He also wrote the libretto of Haydn's *L'incontro improvviso*, and possibly adapted *Lo speziale*, *Le pescatrici* and *L'infedeltà delusa*. He composed part of a volume of lieder, nine Masses and other sacred vocal music, and was a Kapellmeister in Vienna.

D. Bartha and L. Somfai: *Haydn als Opernkapellmeister: die Haydn-Dokumente der Esterházy-Opernsammlung* (Budapest, 1960)
H. C. Robbins Landon: *Haydn: Chronicle and Works*, ii: *Haydn at Eszterháza* (Bloomington, 1978)
R. V. Karpf: 'Haydn and Carl Frieberth: Marginalien zur Gesangkunst im 18.Jahrhundert', *Joseph Haydn: Vienna, 1982*, 376–86
I. Fuchs and L. Vobruba: 'Studien zur Biographie von Karl Friberth', *SMw*, xxxiv (1983), 21–59
MARY HUNTER

Fricci [Frietsche], **Antonietta** (*b* Vienna, 8 Jan 1840; *d* Trieste, 9 Sept 1912). Austrian soprano. She studied with Marchesi in Vienna and made her début in 1858 at Pisa as Violetta. She sang at Covent Garden from 1862 to 1868, making her début as Valentine (*Les Huguenots*) and also singing Leonora (*Il trovatore*), Alice (*Robert le diable*), Donna Anna, Amelia (*Ballo*), Norma, and Eboli in the first London performance of *Don Carlos* (1867). She was also the first Italian Eboli at Bologna and the first Italian Sélika (*L'Africaine*) at S Carlo (1867). She sang at La Scala from 1865 to 1873 and her wide repertory included Lady Macbeth and

Lucrezia Borgia, the kind of dramatic roles in which she excelled.

ELIZABETH FORBES

Frick, Gottlob (*b* Ölbronn, Württemberg, 28 July 1906). German bass. He studied at the Stuttgart Conservatory and was a chorus member of the Stuttgart Opera (1927–31). He was engaged at Coburg in 1934, making his début as Daland. After periods at Freiburg and Königsberg he was engaged at the Dresden Staatsoper, where he created Caliban in Sutermeister's *Die Zauberinsel* (1942) and the Carpenter in Haas's *Die Hochzeit des Jobs* (1944) and sang Rocco, Nicolai's Falstaff, Prince Gremin, the Peasant (*Die Kluge*) and, especially, the Wagnerian bass roles. He joined the Berlin Städtische Oper in 1950 and the Bavarian and Vienna Staatsopern in 1953. He first sang at Covent Garden in 1951 and appeared there regularly from 1957 to 1967 in the Wagner repertory and as Rocco. He also appeared at Bayreuth, Salzburg (where he took part in the première of Egk's *Irische Legende*), the Metropolitan, La Scala and other leading theatres. Although he officially retired in 1970 he continued to make occasional appearances in Munich and Vienna, and in 1971 sang Gurnemanz at Covent Garden. Frick had a large, dark voice, as rich in its lower reaches as at the top and especially suited to the roles of Hagen, Gurnemanz and Sarastro.

W. Schwinger: 'Gottlob Frick', *Opera*, xvii (1966), 188–93

HAROLD ROSENTHAL/R

Fricker, Peter Racine (*b* London, 5 Sept 1920; *d* Santa Barbara, CA, 1 Feb 1990). English composer. He was educated at St Paul's School, London, and in 1937 entered the RCM, where he studied theory and composition with R. O. Morris. He also attended classes at Morley College, where in 1939 he met Tippett. In 1941 Fricker joined the Royal Air Force and in 1943 was posted to India as an intelligence officer. After World War II he returned to Morley College, where he studied with Mátyás Seiber (1946–8); he continued to work closely with Seiber until the latter's death in 1960. In 1952 he succeeded Tippett as director of Morley College, and from 1955 he also taught composition at the RCM. Fricker wrote two radio operas during this period: *My Brother Died* (1952–4) and *The Death of Vivien* (1955–6). The first, a 75-minute work in three parts, was commissioned by the BBC and was broadcast in 1954; the second has not yet been broadcast. Both works are written in an idiom characteristic of Fricker's language at that time, dissonant, harmonically rich and influenced by Bartók, Berg, Hindemith and Schoenberg. In 1964 he was visiting professor of music at the University of California at Santa Barbara and the following year accepted a full-time appointment as professor of music; he became chairman of the music department in 1970.

IAN KEMP

Fricsay, Ferenc (*b* Budapest, 9 Aug 1914; *d* Basle, 20 Feb 1963). Hungarian conductor. He was a pupil of Kodály and Bartók, of whose music he became an outstanding interpreter, at the Academy of Music in Budapest. After beginning his career at Szeged he first conducted at the Budapest Opera in 1939 and in 1945 became its music director. He replaced the indisposed Klemperer to conduct the première of von Einem's *Dantons Tod* at the 1947 Salzburg Festival, which quickly furthered his international reputation. Thereafter he toured widely in Europe, and was based in Berlin from 1948 to 1952 as music director of the Städtische Oper. His British début was at the 1950 Edinburgh Festival, when he conducted the Glyndebourne Opera in *Le nozze di Figaro*. From 1956 he spent two seasons as music director of the Staatsoper in Munich before returning to Berlin; he inaugurated the rebuilt Deutsche Oper on 24 September 1961, conducting *Don Giovanni*.

Fricsay discarded the use of a baton early in his career, and confounded the adverse critics of this technique by the extreme clarity and precision of his performances. A conductor of dynamic spirit, he stressed vividness of character in familiar classics, and was widely admired as a brilliant exponent of mainstream music of his own time. He made a special study of recording techniques, and made some internationally acclaimed recordings.

F. Herzfeld: *Ferenc Fricsay* (Berlin, 1964) [with complete discography]

A. Werner: 'Fricsay: ein Vergessener unter den Grossen?', *Fonoforum*, xviii (1973), 802–9 [with discography]

NOËL GOODWIN

Frid, Grigory Samuilovich (*b* Petrograd [now St Petersburg], 9/22 Sept 1915). Russian composer. He studied composition with Vissarion Shebalin at the Moscow Conservatory, graduating in 1939 and completing graduate studies there after his war service. From 1947 to 1961 he taught composition at the Moscow Conservatory Secondary School. In 1965 he was one of the founders of the influential Moscow Youth Musical Club of which he remains the leading figure. In his music he has explored serial techniques and other 20th-century compositional methods. His two mono-operas are his best-known works and reflect an interest in the rendering of complex psychological portraits: *Dnevnik Annï Frank* ('The Diary of Anne Frank'), was composed in 1968 and first performed in a concert version in Moscow at the All-Union House of Composers on 17 May 1972, and *Pis'ma Van Goga* ('The Letters of Van Gogh'), was first performed, also in concert at the All-Union House of Composers, on 29 November 1976. In each, the composer builds his libretto as a montage of contrasting episodes, supporting it with succinct yet vivid musical imagery.

S. Shlifshteyn: 'O muzïke Grigoriya Frida', *Izbrannïe stat' i* (Moscow, 1977), 224–32

LAUREL E. FAY

Friderici-Jakowicka [Jakowicka-Friderici], **Teodozja** (*b* Kielce, 18 June 1836; *d* Warsaw, 4 Nov 1889). Polish soprano. She studied with Quattrini and Dobrski in Warsaw and with Lamperti in Milan, and made her début in Warsaw on 21 March 1865 in *La sonnambula*. Her many tours included appearances in Milan (1869–70), Germany (1874–5), Verona (1876), Constantinople and New York. She also performed in Warsaw, Lwów and Poznań every season. She retired from the stage in 1885 and until 1886 directed the singing school at the Wielki Theatre in Warsaw. Her own singing was characterized by technical and dramatic skill, an extensive compass and a large repertory consisting chiefly of the dramatic and coloratura roles in over 40 operas by Bellini, Donizetti, Flotow, Halévy, Meyerbeer, Thomas, Verdi and Moniuszko.

'Teodozja Friderici-Jakowicka', *Echo muzyczne, teatralne i artystydczne*, vi (1889), 547–8

Z. Szweykowski: 'Zapomniana polska śpiewaczka Teodozja Friderici-Jakowicka', *Muzyka*, iii/7–8 (1952), 41–5 [reminiscences]
KATARZYNA MORAWSKA

Fridzeri [Fritzeri, Frizeri, Frizer, Frixer, Frixer di Frizeri], **Alessandro Mario Antonio** (*b* Verona, ?15 Jan 1741; *d* Antwerp, 16 Oct 1825). Italian composer. Although blind from infancy, he learnt to play several instruments and became organist at the Madonna del Monte Berico, Vicenza, at the age of 20. In 1765 he left for a European tour, during which he performed violin pieces by Tartini and others, and received praise for his improvisations; in 1766 he made his Paris début at the Concert Spirituel. He settled in Strasbourg for 18 months and there he composed two operas (*c*1770, both in three acts), which were evidently never performed. By 1771 he was back in Paris where he had two stage works produced: *Le billet du marriage* (private performance) and *Les deux miliciens* (Théâtre Italien). After a tour of the south of France he returned to Paris where he established a printing business. His most successful opera, *Les souliers mordorés*, was performed in Paris in 1776 with great success, and in other countries for the next 20 years. He spent 12 years in Brittany, and when the Revolution broke out resumed his concert touring. He founded a philharmonic academy in Nantes before returning to Paris in 1794. There he became a member of the new Lycée des Arts and founded another philharmonic academy, which was first housed in the Palais Royal and subsequently in the storehouse of the Opéra. There, in 1800, the explosion of an 'infernal machine' destroyed Fridzeri's few belongings. After further travels he settled in Antwerp as a teacher and music merchant.

Though Fridzeri's stage works reflect French influence (in their use of vaudevilles, for example) and his instrumental pieces reveal a knowledge of German music, his style remained primarily Italian. All of the instrumental works, and particularly the opera overtures, show a well-developed sense of form. His stage works, some of which show the influence of Grétry's *comédies-larmoyantes*, are characterized by full vocal ensembles, spontaneous melodies and abrupt modulations.

printed works published in Paris unless otherwise stated

Les deux miliciens, ou L'orpheline villageoise op.2 (comedy with ariettes, 1, L. G. d'Azemar), Paris, Italien, 24 Aug 1771, *F-Pn*; (1771), excerpts pubd separately

Le billet de marriage (oc, 1, Desfontaines [F. G. Fouques]), perf. privately, Paris, 1771

Lucette (oc, 3, E. F. de Lantier), Paris, Italien, 18 Aug 1775

Les souliers mordorés, ou La cordonnière allemande op.4 (comédie lyrique, 2, A. de Ferrières), Paris, Italien, 11 Jan 1776, *D-Rtt*, *F-Pn*; (1776), excerpts pubd separately

Les Thermopyles, unperf.; 1 scene in Recueil d'ariettes, scènes, et duos périodiques op.8 (n.d.), 1 air in Recueil d'airs op.9 (n.d.)

*

MGG (M. Briquet)

U. Manferrari: *Dizionario universale delle opere melodrammatiche* (Florence, 1954–5)
FRÉDÉRIC ROBERT

Friebert [Fribert, Friberth, Frieberth, Friewerth, Frübert, Früheworth], **(Johann) Joseph** (*b* Gnadendorf, Lower Austria, bap. 5 Dec 1724; *d* Passau, 6 Aug 1799). Austrian composer, brother of Carl Friberth, with whom he is often confused. He probably received his early musical training from his father, a schoolmaster and organist. The Benedictines of Melk employed him as tenor at their abbey from the middle of 1743 until

April 1745 with a salary of 30 florins. He left Melk for Vienna to study with Giuseppe Bonno, and entered the service of Joseph Friedrich Wilhelm, Prince of Saxe-Hildburghausen; in the 1750s he established himself as a successful tenor in the Viennese theatres, performing in the premières of Gluck's *Le cinesi* (1754, as Silango) and *La danza* (1755, as Tirsi).

From 1763 until his retirement in 1795 he was music director for the prince-bishops of Passau, where his stage works were performed at the Jesuit College and then, during and after its construction from 1774 to 1783, at the court theatre. His *Das Serail* was given at least as early as 1765 and found its way into the repertory of several troupes. Einstein claimed that a version of the text published in 1779 was the model for J. A. Schachtner's text for Mozart's *Zaide*. Under Friebert's leadership Passau experienced a strong Viennese influence, notably through his introduction of Mozart's operas (*Don Giovanni* and *Figaro*, both in 1789 in German translation, and *Zauberflöte* in 1793).

all Singspiels

Das Serail, oder Die unvermuthete Zusammenkunft in der Sclaverey zwischen Vater, Tochter und Sohn [Der Renegat] (2, F. J. Sebastiani), ?Passau, 1765; lib. (Bolzano, 1779), facs. edn in NMA, II:5/x (1963), Kritischer Bericht, 75–91

Die Würkung der Natur (Schiffner and ?others), Rechnitz-Rohenez [now Burgenland], Batthyány Castle, 1774

Die beste Wahl, oder Das von den Göttern bestimmte Loos [Das Loos der Götter] (J. Nuth and others), Nuremberg, 19 Feb 1778

Adelstan und Röschen (Trauerspiel mit Gesänge, ? B. D. A. Cremeri, after J. F. Schink), Salzburg, 4 Jan 1782

It. operas, first perf. in Passau, 1764–74 (all music lost): Il componimento; Il natale di Giove (P. Metastasio); Dafne vendicata; La Galatea; La Zenobia (Metastasio); Angelica e Medoro

*

W. M. Schmidt: 'Zur Passauer Musikgeschichte', *ZMw*, xiii (1931), 289–308

A. Einstein: 'Die Text-Vorlage zu Mozarts "Zaide"', *AcM*, viii (1936), 30–37

H. Bauer: *Joseph Friebert (1723–1799) und seine Stellung in der Musikgeschichte der Stadt Passau* (diss., U. of Munich, 1952)

K. M. Pisarowitz: 'Joseph (Friebert) und seine Brüder', *Acta mozartiana*, xvii (1970), 74–8

R. N. Freeman: *The Practice of Music at Melk Abbey based upon the Documents, 1681–1826*, Österreichische Akademie der Wissenschaften, philosophisch-historische Klasse, Sitzungsberichte, dxlviii (Vienna, 1989)
ROBERT N. FREEMAN

Friedenstag ('Day of Peace'). *Oper* in one act by RICHARD STRAUSS to a libretto by JOSEPH GREGOR; Munich, Staatsoper, 24 July 1938.

Friedenstag, Strauss's twelfth opera, was his first to a libretto by Gregor – as it was published. The idea, and much of the working-out of the text, came from Stefan Zweig, the author of Strauss's previous opera *Die schweigsame Frau*; but under the anti-semitic Hitler regime he was now *persona non grata*. Though Strauss obstinately insisted that he wanted no partner but Zweig, it would have been impossible to find houseroom anywhere in the country for a new collaboration between the senior German composer and a Jew. (In fact Hugo von Hofmannsthal had been partly Jewish, but no questions were ever raised about the famous operas Strauss had written with him.) Eventually Zweig persuaded the composer to face the facts, and – promising his own private assistance as needed – to take on his close friend Gregor as librettist.

As the new partnership began, Strauss decided that the one-act *1648* (Zweig's original title for *Friedenstag*) should make a double bill with the quite different one-

The Commandant of the besieged town	baritone
Maria *his wife*	soprano
A Sergeant	bass
A Rifleman	tenor
A Corporal	baritone
A Musketeer	bass
An Officer	baritone
A Front-Line Officer	baritone
A Piedmontese	tenor
The Holsteiner *Commandant of the besieging army*	bass
The Burgomaster	tenor
The Prelate	baritone
A Woman of the People	soprano

Soldiers of each Commandant, town officials and women in the deputation, townsfolk

Setting The citadel of a besieged town (perhaps Bamberg): 24 October 1648

act *Daphne* newly proposed by Gregor: for no better reason than that neither was conceived as a self-sufficient operatic evening, unlike *Salome* or *Elektra*. As usual both pieces turned out longer than intended, especially *Daphne*. Their scenarios were developed and completed together in 1935–6, but when Strauss finished the *Friedenstag* score his *Daphne* music was still only sketches. At the time, Strauss owed artistic debts to both his conductor-champions, Clemens Krauss and Karl Böhm; his solution was to give the dedication and the première of *Friedenstag* to Krauss (and his wife Viorica Ursuleac, who sang the first Maria with Hotter's Commandant, Ludwig Weber's Holsteiner and Patzak's Rifleman, directed by Rudolf Hartmann) while reserving *Daphne* and the first integral double bill for Böhm in

Dresden, less than three months later (with Christel Goltz, Marta Fuchs, Matthieu Ahlersmeyer and Kurt Böhme).

Even Böhm thought the double bill intolerably long, and that plan never found favour. The two operas soon went their separate ways, often prefaced with short ballets. After a while *Daphne* faded from the repertory, though 30 years later its 'Green' sentiments began to attract new attention. *Friedenstag* was acclaimed at first by the National Socialists as a lofty expression of their own ideals; in fact it bears a pacifist-liberal 'message' which was unpalatable (and surely brave) in that just-pre-war time, but may now seem all too poster-plain. It is scarcely ever performed.

After three stark, falling tritones register the despair of the beleaguered town, the curtain rises (to a wry military march, somewhere between Mahler and Weill). In the citadel at daybreak, soldiers of the Commandant discuss their plight. A young Piedmontese, who has delivered orders from the Emperor, sings sweetly in his sleep (like Daland's Steersman in *Der fliegende Holländer*, but to words Gregor had noted down in the South Tyrol during World War I), stirring the others to wonder what Peace might be like – they hardly know. A delegation of starving townsfolk arrives, led by their Burgomaster and Prelate, and pleading for surrender. Though the stern, duty-bound Commandant comes to hear them out, his orders are to hold the town at all costs. He sends them away with the promise of a 'signal' to open the town gates. In fact, since the Holsteiners' siege cannot be withstood, the signal will be for his men to blow up the citadel and everyone in it.

As the sun brightens and his anxious wife enters alone, the music changes to post-Wagnerian lyricism. She is appalled by the human desolation around her; with her grim husband, she feels that she is married to the unending war. Finally she has a fervent vision of a

'Friedenstag' (Richard Strauss): design by Ludwig Sievert for the original production at the Staatsoper, Munich, 24 July 1938

time when Peace reigns, the sun bursts forth and her husband smiles. When the unsmiling Commandant discovers her, their militarist-versus-pacifist debate culminates in a duet where they use similar words to declare irreconcilable views (like Strauss's Helen and Menelaus before them). Yet she is ready to die with him, like the loyal soldiers who are setting the fatal fuses.

Cannon-shots seem to presage the final assault. But the 'enemy' forces approach with white banners, and long-silent church bells ring out; far away, peace has been declared. The Holstein commander comes to sue for amity and brotherhood; the Commandant, struggling against his win-or-die instincts, melts at last and embraces him. The communal thanksgiving expands to oratorio (or *Fidelio*) scale, predictably reaching populist C major for a full-throated close.

* * *

Though Gregor praised Strauss's setting of his *Friedenstag* finale in the most abjectly effusive terms, the composer knew better. As work proceeded on their next opera, *Daphne*, he brusquely scrapped Gregor's plan for another static choral peroration in favour of a quite different idea from Clemens Krauss. But *Friedenstag* has other strengths: among them the unexpected, almost miraculous crescendo of village bells – like the burst of homely fire-lights in *Feuersnot*, symbolic of vast communal relief – which precedes that conventional chorus, and which modern theatre electronics could make thrilling. Furthermore, until the entrance of the Commandant's wife Strauss's score is memorably stern (and unmistakably in the astringent vein of other German composers on the protesting 1930s left, far more than anything else he composed). Yet he made professional room for a variety of sharp character-vignettes, which bob upon its long, dour stretches like bubbles amid a relentless flow. The Commandant and his wife get substantial opportunities to realize their psychologies in song, though in distinct operatic modes. In its time, *Friedenstag* was probably a *pièce d'occasion*; but it would be optimistic to expect that there will be no future 'occasion' when it could strike a heartfelt response in an audience.

DAVID MURRAY

Friedrich, Götz (*b* Naumburg, 4 Aug 1930). German director. After studying at the Deutsches Theaterinstitut in Weimar (1949–53) he joined the Komische Oper, Berlin, as assistant to and later collaborator with Felsenstein (1953–72). He also taught dramaturgy in Berlin and, from 1973, in Hamburg, where he was *Oberspielleiter* (1973–7) and *Chefregisseur* (1977–81). He was simultaneously director of productions at Covent Garden (1977–81), before moving back to Berlin, where he became Generalintendant and principal director of the Deutsche Oper in 1981 (*see* BERLIN, §3(ii)), as well as artistic director of the Theater des Westens in 1984.

Particularly notable productions, in a long list staged at many of the leading international houses, include *Fidelio* (1978, Munich), *Lulu* (1981) and *Elektra* (1990) at Covent Garden, and the world première of Berio's *Un re in ascolto* at Salzburg (1984). But the central pillar of Friedrich's work remains his series of Wagner productions. His first *Ring*, at Covent Garden (1974–6), emphasized perceived differences of mode between the four dramas: *Rheingold* as a mystery play viewed ironically through modern eyes, *Walküre* as typical 19th-century psychological theatre, *Siegfried* as black comedy and *Götterdämmerung* as the last stage of a glittering civilization doomed to decline. The purpose of the hydraulic platform on which the action took place was thus not to achieve optical unity but to suggest a space – the stage representing the world – on which an epic drama, open-ended and disparate in its styles, could be unfolded (for illustration *see* PRODUCTION, fig.23 and STAGE DESIGN, fig.26). Adopting Brechtian alienation techniques, Friedrich caused Loge, Alberich and Wotan to address the audience directly, outside the framework of the drama. His second *Ring*, which originated in Berlin (1984–5) before transferring to Tokyo, Washington, DC, and Covent Garden, located the action in a tunnel, inspired by the Washington Metro, but intended to provide a performing space non-specific in chronology and place. The monochrome severity of Peter Sykora's sets, and the images of warlike aggression and destruction, reflected a bleakly pessimistic view of the work as an apocalyptic endgame.

Of Friedrich's productions for Bayreuth – *Tannhäuser* (1972), *Lohengrin* (1978) and *Parsifal* (1982) – the first caused the greatest controversy with its brutal, militaristic representation of Wartburg society and its final chorus with the singers, in everyday clothes, making a clenched-fist salute (abandoned after the first performances).

WRITINGS
Die humanistische Idee der Zauberflöte (Berlin, 1954)
Die Zauberflöte in der Inszenierung Walter Felsensteins an der Komischen Oper Berlin (Berlin, 1958)
Walter Felsenstein: Weg und Werk (Berlin, 1961)
Musiktheater: Ansichten – Einsichten (Berlin, 1986)

*

D. Kranz: *Der Regisseur Götz Friedrich* (Berlin, 1972)
P. Barz: *Götz Friedrich: Abenteuer Musiktheater* (Bonn, 1978)
S. Jaeger, ed.: *Götz Friedrich: Wagner-Regie* (Zürich, 1983)
N. Ely and S. Jaeger, eds.: *Regie heute: Musiktheater in unserer Zeit* (Berlin, 1984), 135–60
J. H. Sutcliffe: 'Götz Friedrich', *Opera*, xxxvi (1985), 28–35
N. Ely: *Richard Wagner: Der Ring des Nibelungen in der Inszenierung von Götz Friedrich: Deutsche Oper Berlin* (Vienna, 1987)
BARRY MILLINGTON

Friedrich, W. [Riese, Friedrich Wilhelm] (*b* Berlin, ?1805; bur. Naples, 15 Nov 1879). German librettist. He went to Hamburg at an early age and remained there until his retirement in the 1850s. He became poet to the Thalia Theatre and, under his pseudonym, W. Friedrich, wrote 98 comedies, which formed the basis of that theatre's repertory for some decades. These were mostly translations and adaptations of English, Italian and French vaudevilles. Among them were works by Eugène Scribe from which Friedrich learnt much about writing opera librettos. In 1840, on one of his frequent visits to Paris to find new material for translation, he met Flotow, who persuaded the highly temperamental poet to write librettos for him. Friedrich provided three exemplary comic opera texts (*Alessandro Stradella*, 1844; *Die Matrosen*, 1845, which was a new libretto for a revised version of Flotow's 1839 opera *Le naufrage de la Méduse*; and *Martha*, 1847), but then the friendship and collaboration dissolved. Neither Kreutzer nor Marschner could subsequently persuade Friedrich to write for them. The success of *Alessandro Stradella* and *Martha* was due in some measure to the happy partnership between Flotow's music and Friedrich's lyrical Biedermeier style.

Die neue Fauchon, oder Muttersegen (Schauspiel mit Gesang), H. Schäffer, 1841; *Farinelli, oder König und Sänger* (Lustspiel), J.

Cornet, 1841; *Lorenz und seine Schwester* (vaudeville), Cornet and E. Stiegmann, 1842; *Zwei Herren und ein Diener* (vaudeville), Stiegmann, 1843; *Eduard von der Vorstadt* (Schauspiel mit Gesang), A. M. Canthal, 1844; *Alessandro Stradella*, Flotow, 1844; *Die Matrosen* (after H. and T. Cogniard): *Le naufrage de la Méduse*), Stiegmann, 1845; *Die weibliche Schildwache* (Liderspiel), Stiegmann, 1845; *Lady Harriet* (vaudeville), Stiegmann, 1846; *Martha*, Flotow, 1847; *Wer isst mit?* (vaudeville), Stiegmann, 1847; *Die Tochter Luzifers* (feerie Oper), Stiegmann, *Guten Morgen, Herr Fischer* (vaudeville), Stiegmann; *Hans und Hanne* (Genrebild), Stiegmann, 1852

*

Jubiläumsschrift des Thalia-Theaters (Hamburg, 1868)
Hamburger Schriftsteller-Lexikon (Hamburg, 1873)
A. Kellner: *Alessandro Stradella* (Leipzig, c1909)   PETER COHEN

Friedrich II. *See* FREDERICK II.

Friedrichs [Christofes], Fritz (*b* Brunswick, 13 Jan 1849; *d* Königslutter, 15 May 1918). German baritone. He was a chorister and a small-part actor in his home town and elsewhere in Germany until 1884, when without special training he sang in opera at Nuremberg. His favourite role was Beckmesser, in which he had a great success at Bayreuth in 1888. In the 1896 festival he appeared as Alberich, and in 1902 as Klingsor. Alberich and Beckmesser were his roles at Covent Garden and the Metropolitan, both in 1900; he also sang Falstaff in *Die lustigen Weiber von Windsor*, reported in Kolodin's history of the house as 'undelightful'. The last 16 years of his life were plagued by mental illness. He made no known operatic recordings.   J. B. STEANE

Friemann, Witold (*b* Konin, 20 Aug 1889; *d* Laski, nr Warsaw, 22 March 1977). Polish composer. He studied at the Warsaw Conservatory, then went to Leipzig in 1910 to study with Reger. For a while he was a professional pianist, then taught at conservatories in Lwów and Katowice. In 1933 he went to Warsaw, where he worked for Polish Radio. From 1946 he was conductor and piano teacher in a home for the blind in Laski, during which period three of his operas were written. Friemann was a Romantic, for whom the main vehicle of expression was lyrical melody. For the last 30 years of his life he was completely isolated from musical circles and the new trends, and continued to write in the same style that he used when he was young. His relatively short and simple operas are saturated with folk material. None has been professionally performed or published.

Giewont, 1927–9 (musical drama, 2, K. Brończyk), inc., *PL-Wn**
Panowie Bracia [Brothers!] op.81, 1939 (Brończyk), unperf.
Polskie misterium ludowe [Polish Folk Mystery Play] op.118 (nativity play, M. Konopnicka), Laski, 1946, *Wn**
Kasia op.193 (fairy op, 1, Friemann), Laski, 1955, *Wn**
Bazyliszek [The Basilisk] op.215, 1958 (3, T. Porayski), unperf.

A. Mitscha: *W. Friemann: życie i twórczość* [W. Friemann: Life and Works] (Katowice, 1980)   ZOFIA CHECHLIŃSKA

Friend, Lionel (*b* London, 13 March 1945). English conductor. He studied piano at the RCM and took the répétiteur course at London Opera Centre before joining the music staff at the WNO in 1968, where he made his conducting début the next year. He joined the Glyndebourne Festival Opera staff in 1969. From 1972 he was second conductor at the Kassel Opera for three seasons, gaining valuable repertory experience before returning to London and, in 1977, becoming a staff conductor for the ENO. His work there has covered a range

of operas from Mozart and Beethoven to Debussy and Britten, and includes the première of David Blake's *The Plumber's Gift* (1989). He has been music director for Nexus Opera since 1981 and for New Sussex Opera since 1989: in 1991 he conducted the first performance in England of Weill's *Lost in the Stars* with the latter company, at the Brighton Festival. His conducting is informed by careful preparation and combines reliable assurance of musical style with concern for the needs of the singers.   NOËL GOODWIN

Frietsche, Antonietta. *See* FRICCI, ANTONIETTA.

Frigel [Frigelius], Per [Pehr] (*b* Kalmar, 2 Sept 1750; *d* Stockholm, 24 Nov 1842). Swedish composer. Educated first in Kalmar, he attended the University of Uppsala (1770–76) before entering government service and also took composition lessons with J. G. Naumann and J. M. Kraus. In 1778 he was elected a member of the Swedish Royal Academy of Music, of which he became secretary in 1796 and later librarian. After 1816 he ceased musical composition. Although his only full-length opera, the three-act *Zoroaster*, (composed in 1788; music lost), remained unperformed, he was a frequent contributor of individual arias and ensembles to comic operas of the late Gustavian period, notably the fairy comedy *Arsène* (1779), for which he arranged music by Monsigny, *Afventyraren, eller Resan till Månens ö* ('The Adventurers, or The Journey to the Isle of the Moon', 1791) and *Eremiten* (1798), all of which are extant (*S-Skma*). He also composed incidental music. In contrast to the more serious style evident in his symphonies and oratorios, his stage music is characterized by a lightness of tone, colourful orchestral textures and lyrical melodies.

*

B. von Beskow: *Pehr Frigel* (Stockholm, 1843, 3/1923)
F. Dahlgren: *Anteckningar om Stockholms teatrar* (Stockholm, 1866)   BERTIL H. VAN BOER

Frigerio, Ezio [Elvezio] (*b* Como, 16 July 1930). Italian painter and designer. He studied architecture at the Milan Polytechnic and soon established a reputation as a painter. He joined Strehler's Piccolo Teatro d'Arte in 1955, initially as a costume designer, and by the 1960s was one of the most active designers in the Italian theatre, noted for his collaboration with Eduardo de Filippo and his continuing association with Strehler. From the late 1960s Frigerio concentrated increasingly on designing for opera, though still working on plays, for television and for the cinema, and later joined the growing number of designers who also direct.

In his work for opera, Frigerio progressively abandoned the functional use of basic elements and painterly style that characterized his theatre work (*Don Pasquale*, 1962, Edinburgh): naturalistically executed, built sets (the sleazy tenements of *Madama Butterfly*, 1987, Scottish Opera), often on a massive scale, like the towering unit set of *Carmen* (1980, Hamburg; see illustration overleaf) or the vastness of his *Tosca* (1976, Cologne), now typify his work, which has provided some of the grandest settings on the contemporary stage. He frequently works in collaboration with the costume designer Franca Squarciapino.

*

ES (F. Mancini)
Il Piccolo Teatro d'Arte: quarant'anni di lavoro teatrale, 1947–1987 (Milan, 1988) [exhibition catalogue]   MARINA HENDERSON

Scene from the 1980 Hamburg Staatsoper production of Bizet's 'Carmen' with sets by Ezio Frigerio

Frigimelica Roberti, Count Girolamo (*b* Padua, 10 Jan 1653; *d* Modena, 30 Nov 1732). Italian librettist and poet. From 1691 to 1720 he was a curator of the public library at Padua, where he was a member and *principe* of the Accademia dei Ricovrati. Family quarrels drove him to spend the rest of his life in Modena. 11 operas to librettos by him were performed in 1694–6 and 1704–8 at the Teatro Grimani di S Giovanni Grisostomo, Venice. He wrote a further libretto, *Il Ciclope*, for Padua, which was first performed at the Teatro Obizzi in spring 1695. All these librettos are in five acts and treat mythological or historical subjects. Some are called tragedies, some (from 1704) tragicomedies; they often include choruses and ballets. Like those of Morselli, Silvani and Zeno they adhere to the predominantly serious, stylistically elevated manner of libretto writing that paid homage to Aristotle and the French classical dramatists.

Ottone, C. F. Pollarolo, 1694; *Irene*, Pollarolo, 1694; *Il pastore di Anfriso*, Pollarolo, 1695; *Il Ciclope*, 1695; *La Rosimonda*, Pollarolo, 1695; *Ercole in cielo*, Pollarolo, 1696; *La fortuna per dote*, Pollarolo, 1704; *Il Dafni*, Pollarolo, 1705; *Il Mitridate Eupatore* (tragedia), A. Scarlatti, 1707; *Il trionfo della libertà* (tragedia), Scarlatti, 1707; *Il selvaggio eroe*, A. Caldara, 1707; *Alessandro in Susa*, L. Mancia, 1708

ES (B. Brunelli)
K. Leich: *Girolamo Frigimelica Robertis Libretti (1694–1708): ein Beitrag insbesondere zur Geschichte des Opernlibrettos in Venedig* (Munich, 1972)
R. S. Freeman: *Opera without Drama: Currents of Change in Italian Opera, 1675–1725* (Ann Arbor, 1981)
H. Saunders: *The Repertoire of a Venetian Opera House (1678–1714): the Teatro Grimani di San Giovanni Grisostomo* (diss., Harvard U., 1985)   KARL LEICH

Friml, (Charles) Rudolf (*b* Prague, 8 Dec 1879; *d* Hollywood, CA, 12 Nov 1972). American composer of Bohemian origin. Friml's parents were supposedly so poor that they stinted on fuel to purchase an old piano for him. Because of his remarkable pianistic talents, neighbours and friends joined in contributing funds to send him to the Prague Conservatory. There his talents were quickly appreciated and he was awarded a scholarship. He studied piano with Joseph Jiránek and composition with Dvořák. He began to compose immediately after graduation, but supported himself by accepting a position as accompanist to the violinist Jan Kubelik with whom he toured Europe and the USA.

On a second American trip in 1904 Friml performed his First Piano Concerto at Carnegie Hall, with the New York SO conducted by Walter Damrosch. Its success led the composer to remain in the USA. Though the next few years proved disappointing, in 1912 he was asked to replace Victor Herbert, who had refused to create a second work for Emma Trentini after an argument with the prima donna. Friml's *The Firefly*, which includes 'Giannina mia', 'Love is like a firefly' and 'Sympathy', earned him instant acclaim and a small fortune. Among the hits that followed were *High Jinks* (1913), recalled for 'Something seems tingle-ingleing', and *Katinka* (1915), remembered for 'Allah's holiday'. During the war years Friml discreetly used the pseudonym Roderick Freeman, although the music for his wartime shows still listed his real name.

After World War I, Friml attempted to break away from his middle-European operetta style and to write more in the idiom of American musical comedy, but shows such as *The Little Whopper* (1919) and *Cinders* (1923) did nothing to enhance his reputation. He enjoyed his biggest successes in the later 1920s when he reverted to the operetta style. *Rose-Marie* (1924), the most lucrative musical of the decade, has left behind at least two standards, 'Indian love call' and the title song. Favourites from *The Vagabond King* (1925) include 'Only a rose', 'Some day' and 'Song of the vagabonds'. *The Three Musketeers* (1928) offered 'Ma belle' and 'March of the musketeers'. In the 1930s tastes changed and the European-influenced operetta was dismissed as passé. This time Friml made no further attempt to alter his basic mannerisms, so when *Luana* (1930) and *Music hath Charms* (1934) both received critical drubbings and quickly folded he retired from stage work, although he continued writing for films.

Along with his contemporary, Sigmund Romberg, Friml was responsible for the last great flowering of American-written, European-style operetta. But whereas Romberg was frequently accused of pilfering themes from the classics and from other popular songwriters, such a charge was never seriously made against Friml. At its best his music seems to have not only more originality than Romberg's but more fervour – a reflection, to those that knew them, of the two men's private personalities. Although Friml's works remained out of favour with many critics until after his death, they never lost their popularity with the general public. A few of his best works have enjoyed revivals, sometimes in the repertory of American opera companies.

operettas except where stated; dates are of first New York performances

The Firefly (comedy-opera, 3, O. Harbach), Lyric, 2 Dec 1912
High Jinks (musical farce, 2, Harbach), Lyric, 10 Dec 1913
Katinka (musical play, Harbach), 44th Street, 23 Dec 1915
You're in Love (Harbach and E. Clark), Casino, 6 Feb 1917
Kitty Darlin' (Harbach and P. G. Wodehouse, after D. Belasco), Casino, 7 Nov 1917
Sometime (3, R. J. Young), Shubert, 4 Oct 1918
Glorianna (after C. C. Cushing: *Widow by Proxy*), Liberty, 28 Oct 1918
Tumble In (Harbach, after M. R. Rinehart and A. Hopwood: *Seven Days*), Selwyn, 24 March 1919
The Little Whopper (Harbach and B. Dudley), Casino, 13 Oct 1919
June Love (musical comedy, Harbach, W. H. Post and B. Hooker), Knickerbocker, 25 April 1921
The Blue Kitten (Harbach and W. C. Duncan, after Y. Mirande and G. Quinson: *Le chasseur de Chez Maxim's*), Selwyn, 13 Jan 1922
Cinders (Clark), Dresden, 3 April 1923
Rose-Marie (musical play, Harbach and O. Hammerstein II), Imperial, 2 Sept 1924, collab. H. Stothart
The Vagabond King (Hooker, Post and R. Janney, after J. H. McCarthy: *If I were King*), Casino, 21 Sept 1925
No Foolin' [Ziegfeld's American Revue of 1926] (Buck and I. Caesar), Globe, 24 June 1926, collab. J. F. Hanley
The Wild Rose (Harbach and Hammerstein), Martin Beck, 20 Oct 1926
The White Eagle (Hooker and Post, after E. M. Royle), Casino, 26 Dec 1927
The Three Musketeers (W. A. McGuire, Wodehouse and C. Grey, after A. Dumas *père*), Lyric, 13 March 1928
Luana (H. E. Rogers and J. K. Brennan, after R. W. Tully: *The Bird of Paradise*), Hammerstein, 17 Sept 1930
Music hath Charms, or Annina (R. Leigh, G. Rosener and J. Shubert), Majestic, 29 Dec 1934

Music in: The Peasant Girl, 1915; Ziegfeld Follies of 1921; Ziegfeld Follies of 1923
GERALD BORDMAN

Frisari, Girolamo (*fl* Venice, 1678–86). Italian librettist. He is referred to as 'dottor' in several sources. Between 1678 and 1681 he wrote three librettos, each for a different Venetian theatre. Although his first work is based on mythology (drawing on Count Francesco Berni's *Il ratto di Cefalo* and Ovid's *Metamorphoses*), his other two are loosely based on history, as was usual for Venetian operas of the time. His first two librettos were for theatres owned by the Grimani brothers, Giovanni Carlo and Vincenzo. Indeed *Aurora in Atene* (which he claims was written in eight days) was dedicated to Antonio Grimani, Giovanni Carlo's son. In 1686 Frisari edited Vincenzo Grimani's first libretto, *Elmiro re di Corinto*, for a production at the Teatro S Giovanni Grisostomo. *Pausania* is apparently the only work of his that was ever restaged (for the provincial theatre of Crema, 1692).

Aurora in Atene, Giannettini, 1678; *Antioco il grande*, Legrenzi, 1681; *Pausania*, Legrenzi, 1681

*

AllacciD
C. Ivanovich: *Minerva al tavolino* (Venice, 1681, 2/1688)
G. Bonlini: *Le glorie della poesia e della musica* (Venice, 1730)

C. Sartori: *I libretti italiani a stampa dalle origini al 1800* (Cuneo, 1990–)
HARRIS S. SAUNDERS

Frischmuth, Johann Christian (*b* Schwabhausen, nr Gotha, 25 Nov 1741; *d* Berlin, 31 July 1790). German composer. He toured with several theatrical troupes as an actor, singer and Kapellmeister, specializing in playing comic old men. In 1775 he was at Münster, from 1775 to 1780 at Gotha and from 1780 with Ackermann's troupe at Hamburg. Having had little success in Hamburg he spent some time without employment in Gotha and Ohrdruf, but from 1782 he was an actor and Kapellmeister for Döbbelin's troupe in Berlin, where his Singspiels *Das Mondenreich* and *Clarisse, oder Das unbekannte Dienstmädchen* had been performed in 1769 and 1775 respectively. After the departure of the music director Johann André (1784) Frischmuth became chief Kapellmeister. When Döbbelin's theatre was reorganized as the Royal National Theatre (1786) Frischmuth was able to retain his position; in 1788 C. B. Wessely was appointed his assistant with equal powers. Of Frischmuth's works only the vocal score of *Clarisse*, dated 1771 (*D-Bds*), and the libretto of *Das Mondenreich* (Schatz Collection, *US-Wc*) are extant; other operas (*Die kranke Frau*, ?1773; *Der Kobold*) are lost.

*

EitnerQ; *MGG* (H. Becker)
C. von Ledebur: *Tonkünstler-Lexicon Berlins* (Berlin, 1861)
GERHARD ALLROGGEN

Frisell, Sonja (*b* Richmond, Surrey, 8 Aug 1937). English director. She studied the piano and acting at the Guildhall School of Music and Drama and began her work in opera in the 1950s under the aegis of Carl Ebert at the Städtische (now Deutsche) Oper, Berlin and at the Glyndebourne Festival. She worked for many years as a staff producer at La Scala, but since the mid-1980s has directed her own productions, principally in North and South America, including *Carmen* (1985) for the Teatro Colón, Buenos Aires, and Verdi's *Don Carlos* (1989) and Musorgsky's *Khovanshchina* (1990) at the Lyric Opera of Chicago. Her 1988 production of *Aida* for the Metropolitan Opera has been televised throughout the world. In Europe she has directed Donizetti's *La favorite* (1977, Bregenz Festival), Vivaldi's *Tito Manlio* (1979, Milan, Scala) and Handel's *Agrippina* (1985, Venice, Fenice). Frisell cites Ebert, the Italian director Giorgio Strehler and the French designer-director Jean-Pierre Ponnelle as the greatest influences on her work and her productions reveal those influences in the monumental, traditionalist pictorialism of her stage effects.
HUGH CANNING

Fritzeri [Frizeri, Frizer, Frixer, Frixer di Frizeri], **Alessandro Mario Antonio**. *See* FRIDZERI, ALESSANDRO MARIO ANTONIO.

Froid de Méreaux, Nicolas-Jean, Le. *See* MÉREAUX, NICOLAS-JEAN LE FROID DE.

Frolov, Markian Petrovich (*b* Bobruysk, 24 Nov/6 Dec 1892; *d* Sverdlovsk [now Yekaterinburg], 30 Oct 1944). Soviet composer and pianist. He studied the piano and theory at the St Petersburg (later Petrograd) Conservatory (1913–19) and at the Kiev Conservatory (1919–21), where he also studied composition with Glier. In 1921 he enrolled at the Petrograd Conservatory, graduating from the piano class in 1924. From 1928 he took an active part in the musical life of Sverdlovsk, where he helped found the conservatory in 1934. He was not a prolific composer and his style was an extension of the traditions of Borodin and Glazunov. In 1939, on a commission from the Buryat Autonomous Republic, Frolov composed the first national Buryat opera, *Enkhe – Bulat-bator* ('Enkhe, the Steel Hero') to a libretto on epic-heroic legends by N. Baldano. The opera received its première at the Bol'shoy Branch Theatre in Moscow at the opening of the Ten-Day Festival of Buryat Culture on 20 October 1940, and has remained the cornerstone of the Buryat operatic repertory.   LAUREL E. FAY

From the House of the Dead [*Z mrtvého domu*]. Opera in three acts by LEOŠ JANÁČEK to his own libretto after FYODOR MIKHAYLOVICH DOSTOYEVSKY's novel *Zapiski iz myortvogo doma* ('Memoirs from the House of the Dead'); Brno, National Theatre, 12 April 1930 (in Osvald Chlubna and Břetislav Bakala's arrangement).

Alexandr Petrovič Gorjančikov	baritone
Aljeja *a young Tartar*	mezzo-soprano
Luka Kuzmič (Filka Morozov)	tenor
Skuratov	tenor
Šiškov	baritone
Prison Governor	bass
Big Prisoner/Nikita	tenor
Small Prisoner	baritone
First Guard	tenor
Second Guard	baritone
Elderly Prisoner	tenor
Voice (*offstage*)	tenor
Cook (*a prisoner*)	baritone
Priest	baritone
Čekunov	bass
Drunk Prisoner	tenor
Šapkin	tenor
Blacksmith (*a prisoner*)	baritone
Prisoner/Kedril	tenor
Prisoner/Don Juan/The Brahmin	bass
Young Prisoner	tenor
Prostitute	mezzo-soprano
Čerevin	tenor

Male chorus: prisoners (taking silent parts in the Act 2 plays); guests, prison guards (silent)

Setting A Russian prison on the River Irtysh, about 1860

Janáček began sketching his final opera in February 1927. He worked directly from his Russian edition of Dostoyevsky's novel, translating into Czech as he went along. He used no libretto, simply brief notes with lists of characters, incidents and page numbers. A first version was complete by 16 or 17 October 1927, a second by 4 January 1928. From March until 20 June 1928, he worked closely with his two copyists (Václav Sedláček and Jaroslav Kulhánek), who together made a fair copy of his autograph which incorporated many changes. By the end of July 1928 Janáček had checked through Acts 1 and 2; Act 3 was on his desk when he died. Apart from any further corrections, doublings and adjustments to the orchestration that Janáček might have made at rehearsals, there is no reason to consider the opera as anything but complete. However, its sometimes

chamber-like orchestration persuaded Janáček's pupils Břetislav Bakala and Osvald Chlubna to revise the opera before its first performance in Brno in 1930. Their work consisted mostly of filling out the orchestration and adding an 'optimistic' ending (an apotheosis of the freedom chorus) to replace Janáček's grim march. The later history of the opera has consisted largely of shedding these accretions. In 1961 Kubelík conducted a version in Munich based mostly on Janáček's original autograph; in 1964 Universal Edition added the original ending as an appendix to their vocal score; and in 1980 Decca released a recording by Charles Mackerras, prepared by Charles Mackerras and John Tyrrell on the basis of the copyists' score.

The overture was originally conceived as a violin concerto titled in successive versions 'Duše' ('Soul') and 'Putování dušičky' ('The Wandering of a Little Soul') and first performed in a realization by Miloš Štědroň and Leoš Faltus in 1988. Its affinity with the opera is suggested by the inclusion of 'chains' in its instrumentation. Janáček's final revision placed it firmly as the separate 'úvod' ('introduction') to the opera, and some of its musical material, for instance the opening motif (ex.1), is employed in the opera. Nevertheless the many

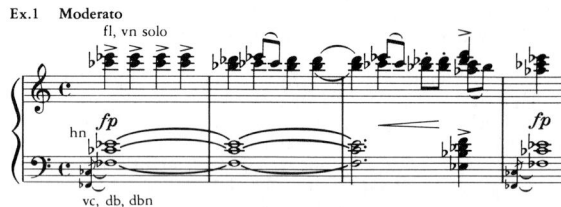

Ex.1 Moderato

passages for solo violin betray its origins. In form it is a rondo; its final *maestoso* episode is a heroic fanfare which suggests the optimistic dimension of Janáček's motto for the opera, 'In every creature a spark of God'.

ACT 1 *A courtyard in a Siberian prison; early morning* The opening motif of the opera (ex.2), with

Ex.2 Moderato

its painful dissonances, is a motto theme that runs through the whole of this act. Prisoners come in from the barracks and wash and argue. They talk of a new prisoner, a gentleman (Alexandr Petrovič Gorjančikov), whose arrival soon follows. His fear and vulnerability is suggested by a high solo violin, heard above ex.2. The Prison Governor interrogates him and on learning that he is a 'political prisoner' orders him to be flogged. Soon ex.2 combines with a new motif and cries of pain off stage.

This music merges into the next episode. The Big Prisoner brings out a captured eagle; the prisoners torment it but admire its defiance in captivity, proclaiming it an 'orel lesů' ('eagle of the forests'). Suddenly the Governor returns with his guards and orders the prisoners off to work. Half of them depart to outdoor

'From the House of the Dead' (Janáček): stage set for Act 2 (with the prisoners' improvised stage) of the original production at the National Theatre, Brno, 12 April 1930

work, singing a 'mournful song' to words quoted by Dostoyevsky, 'Neuvidí oko již' ('My eye will never again see the land of my birth'), punctuated by ex.2.

Skuratov is among those who remain. He sings snatches of a 'cheerful song' (words from Dostoyevsky) and annoys Luka, who picks a quarrel with him. Skuratov recalls his life in Moscow and his previous trade as a cobbler. He breaks into a wild dance, then collapses (a harsh version of ex.2).

Luka, as he sews, recalls his previous imprisonment for vagrancy. He tells how he incited the other prisoners to rebellion and how he killed the officer who came to quell the disturbance. This is a substantial monologue which grows in intensity to the point where Luka describes plunging his knife into the officer (a *fortissimo* version of ex.2). Then follows a dreamy version on two solo violins of the opening motif from the overture. A march-like variant of this theme builds up to an exciting climax, again dominated by ex.2, as Luka describes how he was flogged. Tension is dissolved by a naive question from the Elderly Prisoner. Alexandr Petrovič, who has meanwhile been punished in a similar way, is brought back by the guards, half dead. The long orchestral postlude is built up by a hypnotic peroration on the theme from Skuratov and Luka's quarrel, silenced by a *fortissimo* timpani solo.

ACT 2   *The bank of the river Irtysh with a view of the steppe; a year after Act 1, towards sunset*   The prelude, with an offstage vocalise, evokes the openness of the wide steppe – a contrast to the enclosed prison yard of Act 1. From the outdoor activity it is presumably summer: prisoners are working on a ship – the sounds of metal implements and a saw are specified in the instrumentation.

Alexandr Petrovič asks the Tartar boy Aljeja about his family and offers to teach him to read and write, an offer warmly accepted. With the day's work over (the ship's mast is heard falling), the prisoners throw down their tools. Bells sound from afar, then from the settlement. A colourful march accompanies the arrival of the Governor and Guests, and of the Priest, who blesses the food and the river before going off with the Governor. The prisoners sit down to eat. Skuratov, with the occasional interruption from the Drunk Prisoner, tells how he killed the man his sweetheart Luiza was forced to marry. This is the gentlest and most lyrical of the three major narratives of the opera, a rondo based on a

charming, modally inflected motif. Its end is overwhelmed by the prisoners' excitement at the thought of the 'theatre'.

On an improvised stage the prisoners perform two plays, mostly in mime: 'Kedril [i.e. Leporello] and Don Juan' (who is taken off by devils at the end) and 'The Miller's Beautiful Wife', based on Gogol's tale of a wife hiding various lovers around the room while her husband is absent. The last lover is a 'Brahmin' who turns out to be Don Juan in disguise and who dances off with the Miller's Wife before being consumed by flames.

It grows dark. The Young Prisoner goes off with a Prostitute. A mood of quiet contentment is evoked by offstage folksongs (Luka and chorus). While Alexandr Petrovič and Aljeja are drinking tea the belligerent Small Prisoner, resenting Alexandr Petrovič's 'gentleman-like behaviour', picks a quarrel. He breaks a jug over Aljeja, who falls to the ground. Guards rush in to keep order: the act dies on a sustained side drum roll.

ACT 3.i   *The prison hospital, towards evening*   The gentle prelude ends with a triumphant theme in C major. Aljeja, delirious with fever, is watched over by Alexandr Petrovič. Čekunov waits on both of them to the rage of Luka, dying on an adjacent bed. Šapkin describes how a police officer interrogated him and almost pulled his ears off. Skuratov, now mad, cries for Luiza.

Night falls, suggested by chamber textures and duet-like writing in the orchestra as the prisoners fall asleep. The silence is broken by the Elderly Prisoner's lament that he will never see his children again. Egged on by Čerevin, Šiškov tells the story of Akulka (Akulina), Filka Morozov's sweetheart. Filka refused to marry her, declaring that he had already slept with her. Šiškov has to marry her instead. On his wedding night he beats her and then discovers she is pure. He attempts to take revenge on Filka, who alleges that Šiškov was too drunk to notice her state. Šiškov beats her again, and discovering that she still loves Filka, kills her. This brutal tale, Janáček's longest monologue, is sustained by the virtuoso vignettes (usually in direct speech) of its many characters, and by the tension between the wrongs done to Akulka and the music of utmost tenderness with which she is depicted. It is punctuated both by Čerevin's questions and by the strange choral sighs of the sleeping prisoners. Luka dies as the story ends. An irony added by Janáček is that only now does Šiškov recognize Luka as Filka. Šiškov is almost speechless with rage, but the comment of the Elderly Prisoner that a mother gave birth even to Filka is more true to the humanitarian message of the opera. A Guard calls for Alexandr Petrovič. An automaton-like march leads to scene ii.

3.ii *As Act 1* The Governor, drunk, apologizes to Alexandr Petrovič before the other prisoners and tells him that he is to be released. To a warm-sounding version of ex.2 Alexandr Petrovič's chains are knocked off and he bids farewell to Aljeja, who has run in from the hospital. As Alexandr Petrovič leaves the prisoners release the eagle and celebrate its freedom in a brief chorus; it flies away to the triumphant theme from the prelude to the act. The guards order the prisoners off to work. The automaton scene-change march ends the opera.

*   *   *

This is Janáček's most extraordinary and arguably his greatest opera. There is virtually no plot (the arrival and departure of Alexandr Petrovič provides its slender narrative frame), and except for the tiny part of the Prostitute and the trouser role of Aljeja, there are no women in this opera. There are also no main characters: instead it is a 'collective' opera in which soloists emerge from the chorus and then blend back into anonymity. For all this, it is a compelling stage work, the most powerfully charged of all Janáček's operas, and yet the most tender and compassionate.

For a page from the autograph score, *see* JANÁČEK, LEOŠ, fig.2.

JOHN TYRRELL

Frondoni, Angelo (*b* Pieve Ottoville, Zibello, Parma, 1808 or 1809; *d* Lisbon, 4 June 1891). Italian-Portuguese composer and conductor. He studied at Parma and Milan. His one-act farce *Il carrozzino da vendere* was staged at La Scala in 1833 and *Un terno al lotto*, for *basso buffo* and chorus, at the Teatro Carcano two years later. In 1838, while organist at Soragna (Parma), he was appointed artistic director of the Teatro S Carlos in Lisbon, where he conducted premières of two ballets (1839) and a revival of *Un terno al lotto* (22 March 1841). In 1843 he was dismissed from S Carlos by new management, but his opera *I profughi di Parga* was produced there in 1844. A farce with Portuguese text, *O beijo*, given later in the same year, won immediate popularity. Three more operettas in Portuguese and one in French followed, 1845–9. In 1850 he conducted at the Gymnásio premières of three more, each in one act. Firmly established at Lisbon, he continued to write much successful stage music until 1863. He was artistic director and composer for the newly opened Trindade theatre, 1868–73, and in 1873–4 conducted the S Carlos opera season. He dabbled in literature and wrote a series of choleric pamphlets, one of which (1883) denounced Wagner's *Lohengrin*.

Il carrozzino da vendere (farsa, 1, C. Bassi), Milan, Scala, 29 June 1833, *I-Mr**
Un terno al lotto (scherzo comico, 1, C. Cambiaggio), Milan, Carcano, 24 Aug 1835, *Mr**, vs (Milan, ?1840)
I profughi di Parga (dramma lirico, 3, C. Perini), Lisbon, S Carlos, 29 April 1844
Barbableu, Lisbon, Trindade, 18 July 1868
O evangélio em acção, Lisbon, Gymnásio, 1870
Tres rocas de crystal (ópera cómica, 3), Lisbon, Trindade, 1870
O filho da senhora Angot (ópera burlesca, 3), Lisbon, Prince, 5 May 1875

Operettas (selective list): O beijo (S. Leal), Lisbon, Condes, 26 Nov 1844; O Caçador (Leal), Lisbon, Condes, 25 March 1845; Um bom homen d'outro tempo, Lisbon, Condes, 6 Jan 1846; Mademoiselle de Mérange, Lisbon, Larangeiras, 11 June 1847; Qual dos dois?, Lisbon, Gymnásio, 13 Oct 1849

*

DBP, *StiegerO*   ROBERT STEVENSON

Frugoni, Carlo Innocenzo [Innocenzio] (*b* Genoa, 21 Nov 1692; *d* Parma, 20 Dec 1768). Italian poet and librettist. Born into an aristocratic family, he was actively involved in the Order of the Somaschi until 1731. However, it was his reputation as a poet which led to appointments at the court of the Farnese in Parma in 1725 and, after a brief period in Venice during the War of the Austrian Succession, as court poet to Duke Philipp of Bourbon (in Parma) in 1749. There his work was admired by Guillaume du Tillot, the duke's theatrical director. Du Tillot later arranged Frugoni's successive appointments as secretary of court theatrical productions.

Most of Frugoni's librettos for the court theatre in Parma were reworkings of earlier librettos by others. He also provided Italian translations for French operas performed at the theatre: Francoeur and Rebel's *Zélindor, roi des silphes* (1757), the pasticcio *Gl'Incà del Perù* (1757), Mondonville's *Titon et l'Aurore* (1758) and Rameau's *Castor et Pollux* (1758). Du Tillot's interest in producing a blend of French and Italian opera at Parma coincided with Algarotti's recommendations for the reform of Italian opera as expressed in his *Saggio sopra l'opera in musica* (1755). To Frugoni fell the task of producing Italian 'reform' librettos based on two of Rameau's operas, which Traetta then set to music for production in Parma: *Ippolito ed Aricia* in 1759 (taken from Pellegrin's drama of the same name) and *I tindaridi* of 1760 (an adaptation of P. J. Bernard's earlier French libretto *Castor et Pollux*). In these works Frugoni still adhered closely to the traditional design of an Italian aria opera. Departures lay in the mythological plots, which had long been out of fashion in Italian opera, and the French-inspired choruses, programmatic orchestral music, ballet and spectacle. Although Jommelli's French-inspired operas for Stuttgart in 1755 (*Enea nel Lazio* and *Pelope*) preceded these efforts towards a Franco-Italian synthesis in Italian opera, Frugoni's librettos were the first specifically designed to reform Italian dramaturgical practices. Traetta also set Frugoni's *Le feste d'Imeneo*, a *festa teatrale*, for the wedding of Crown Prince Joseph of Austria and the Infanta Isabella in 1760. In 1769 Frugoni provided a similar vehicle for Gluck, *Le feste d'Apollo*, which incorporated his *Orfeo* (1762, Vienna) as the final act. A complete edition (15 volumes) of Frugoni's works was published in Lucca in 1779–80.

opere serie unless otherwise stated

Il trionfo di Camilla (after S. Stampiglia), Vinci, 1725; I fratelli riconosciuti (after F. Silvani: *La verità nell'inganno*), Capello, 1726; Il Medo, Vinci, 1728 (Leo, 1734; ? F. Poncini Zilioli, 1747; Abos, 1753); Scipione in Cartagine nuova, Giacomelli, 1728; Lucio Papirio dittatore (after A. Zeno), Giacomelli, 1729; Ippolito ed Aricia (after S. J. Pellegrin), Traetta, 1759 (Holzbauer, 1759); I tindaridi [tintaridi], o Castore e Polluce (after P. J. Bernard), Traetta, 1760 (Bianchi, 1779; Vogler, 1787)

*

StiegerO
S. Arteaga: *Le rivoluzioni del teatro musicale italiano*, ii (Bologna, 1785), 168–70
P. E. Ferrari: *Spettacoli drammatico-musicali e coreografici in Parma* (Parma, 1884)

G. Cesari: 'Un tentativo di riforma melodrammatica a Parma', *Il secolo* (1 May 1917)

C. Calcaterra: 'Il Frugoni, compositore e revisore di spettacoli teatrali', *Storia della poesia frugoniana* (Genoa, 1920)

A. Della Corte: 'Musiche italiane e francesi alla corte di Parma', *La stampa* (22 Jan 1929)

A. Yorke-Long: *Music at Court* (London, 1954)

R. Allorto: 'Riformatore agli ordini: C. I. Frugoni', *La scala* (May 1957)

D. Heartz: 'Operatic Reform at Parma: *Ippolito ed Aricia*', *Convegno sul settecento parmense nel 2° centenario della morte di C. I. Frugoni: Parma 1968*, 271–300

G. Massera: 'L'incontro Traetta-Frugoni: riforma o novità?', *I teatri di Parma dal Farnese al Regio*, ed. I. Allodi (Milan, 1969), 117–23

M. Cyr: 'Rameau e Traetta', *NRMI*, xii/2 (1978), 166–82

WENDY N. GIBNEY, MARITA P. McCLYMONDS

Frumerie, (Per) Gunnar (Fredrik) de (*b* Nacka, 20 July 1908; *d* Täby, 9 Sept 1987). Swedish composer. He studied at the Stockholm Conservatory, in Vienna and in Paris. From 1945 he taught the piano at the Stockholm Musikhögskolan, becoming professor in 1962. A man of impulsive and florid temperament, he has absorbed the most varied influences. Compositions from the 1930s show a striving for formal strictness (often following Baroque models), a result of his contact with Parisian neo-classicism. The four-act opera *Singoalla* op.22 (composed 1937–40; E. Byström-Baeckström, after V. Rydberg; Stockholm, Kungliga, 1940), immediately distinguished him as a composer of powerful music drama. It was revived in 1955 with Kerstin Meyer as Singoalla, and recorded in 1985 with Anne Sofie von Otter in the title role. ROLF HAGLUND

Frunze. BISHKEK.

Fry, William Henry (*b* Philadelphia, 19 Aug 1813; *d* Santa Cruz, Virgin Islands, 21 Dec 1864). American composer. One of five sons in a wealthy and well-established Philadelphia family, he demonstrated musical talent at an early age: an overture composed when he was 18 earned him a medal and was given a public performance. Another overture was performed in 1833, while he was studying with Léopold Meignen, at which time Fry heard operas by Auber, Boieldieu, Hérold, Rossini, Mercadante, Halévy and Bellini and began an opera (now lost), *The Bridal of Dunure*. By 1838 he was at work on a three-act opera, *Aurelia the Vestal*, to a libretto by his brother Joseph; it was completed in 1841. Although no performance is known, the surviving scores show evidence of preparation for performance, with rehearsal letters, cuts and corrections, and notes for the copyist.

Fry's next opera, *Leonora*, occupied him from 1841 to 1845. Based on a well-known play by Bulwer-Lytton, it was performed by Arthur Seguin's troupe at Philadelphia in 1845 and again, in a revised version, in December 1846. In 1858, after his return from a sojourn in Europe (as music critic of the *New York Tribune*), *Leonora* was again revived, in a substantially revised four-act version in Italian as *Giulio e Leonora*.

According to his brother Edward, Fry's last opera, *Notre Dame of Paris*, was composed almost in its entirety between 22 January and 21 February 1862. Its gala production at Philadelphia in 1864 was given by 350 performers under the direction of Theodore Thomas (making his début as an opera conductor), as a benefit performance for war wounded, but Fry was unsuccessful in his attempts to interest European impresarios in his operas, despite having them translated into Italian in order to facilitate performances abroad. Fry's operas trace his development from a composer primarily influenced by the melodic style of Bellini and the Italian school to one increasingly influenced by Meyerbeer and French grand opera. In *Aurelia* and the first version of *Leonora* there is much use of elaborate coloratura, as well as paired singing in parallel 3rds or 6ths. After his return from Paris in the mid-1850s, he began to reject this style; revisions in *Leonora* show a more direct and simpler melodic line, coloured by non-harmonic, chromatic auxiliary notes but unencumbered by excessive ornamentation. In *Notre Dame*, too, the lines are simplified, and there are hints of folksong, though Esmeralda's role calls for coloratura. There is more chromaticism in the later works, where it is introduced into a diatonic context for dramatic purposes. While *Aurelia* and *Notre Dame* remain Italian in spirit, they approach the French style by including an optional large-scale ballet. The operas use an orchestration similar to that of Bellini's *Norma*, and each also calls for an onstage military band.

Fry's importance in the history of American opera rests primarily on *Leonora*, the first grand opera by an American composer to be staged in the USA; its production just four years after the American première of *Norma* confirmed the growing acceptance of Italian opera by American audiences and demonstrated that musical alternatives to the English operatic heritage were viable.

MSS at US-PHhs

Aurelia the Vestal [Cristiani ed i pagani], 1838–41 (lyrical tragedy, 3, J. R. Fry), ? unperf.

Leonora (lyrical drama, 3, J. R. Fry, after E. G. Bulwer-Lytton: *The Lady of Lyons*), Philadelphia, Chestnut Street Theatre, 4 June 1845; rev. as Giulio e Leonora (4), New York, Academy of Music, 29 March 1858

Notre Dame of Paris [Esmeralda; Nostra-Donna di Parigi] (lyrical drama, 4, J. R. Fry, after V. Hugo), Philadelphia, American Academy of Music, 4 May 1864

*

DAB (F. L. Gwinner Cole)

W. H. Fry: 'Prefatory Remarks', *Leonora* (Philadelphia, 1846); repr. in Upton (1954) and in *The American Composer Speaks*, ed. G. Chase (Baton Rouge, LA, 1966), 46–52

J. S. Dwight: 'Mr Fry and his Critics', *Dwight's Journal of Music*, iv (1853–4), 140–42

H. C. Lahee: *Grand Opera in America* (Boston, 1902), 63

I. Lowens: 'William Henry Fry: Fighter for American Music', *Musicology*, ii (1948), 162–73

W. T. Upton: *William Henry Fry: American Journalist and Composer-Critic* (New York, 1954)

JOHN GRAZIANO

Fuchs, Anton von (*b* Munich, 29 Jan 1849; *d* Munich, 15 April 1925). German bass-baritone. He studied in Munich and made his début there in 1873 as Liebenau (Lortzing's *Der Waffenschmied*). He remained a member of the Munich Hofoper for more than 20 years, singing a wide repertory that included Papageno, Figaro (both Rossini's and Mozart's), Leporello and Pizarro (*Fidelio*) as well as Alberich, Gunther and other Wagner roles. In 1882 he sang Klingsor in some of the first performances of *Parsifal* at Bayreuth. The following year he also sang Amfortas, Titurel and a Knight of the Grail, returning for Kurwenal in 1889. He acted as stage director both at Bayreuth and in Munich.

ELIZABETH FORBES

Fuchs, Eugen (*b* Nuremberg, 3 Sept 1893; *d* Berlin, 3 March 1971). German baritone. He made his début in

1914 at Nuremberg, remaining there until 1920. After engagements in Saarbrücken, Breslau and Freiburg, in 1930 he joined the Berlin Staatsoper, where he remained a member of the company for over 30 years. At Bayreuth he sang Beckmesser (1933–4 and 1943–4). He appeared at the Paris Opéra (1934–5) and at Covent Garden (1937), where he sang Alberich. From 1956 to 1961, the year he retired, he sang Hans Foltz in *Die Meistersinger* at Bayreuth. A very reliable artist, he had a vast and varied repertory.   ELIZABETH FORBES

Fuchs, Ignacije. *See* LISINSKI, VATROSLAV.

Fuchs, Marta (*b* Stuttgart, 1 Jan 1898; *d* Stuttgart, 22 Sept 1974). German soprano. She studied in Stuttgart, Munich and Milan. She made her début as a mezzo in Aachen in 1928, where she stayed until 1930, and was then engaged by Fritz Busch for the Dresden Staatsoper; among her roles were Octavian, Amneris, Azucena, Eboli and Ortrud. Gradually she assumed dramatic soprano roles, the first being Kundry (1933, Amsterdam; 1933–7, Bayreuth). She became the most important soprano at Bayreuth during the 1930s, succeeding Leider as Brünnhilde (1938–42) and sharing Isolde with her in 1938. She sang at Covent Garden with the Dresden company in 1936 (Donna Anna, the Marschallin and Ariadne), and in Paris (1938) with the Berlin Staatsoper, of which she was also a member. She retired in 1945. Fuchs was at her best in Wagner, especially as Kundry and Brünnhilde. She lacked the agility for Donna Anna and found certain Strauss roles too high.

GV (L. Riemens)   LEO RIEMENS, ELIZABETH FORBES

Fuchs, Robert (*b* Frauenthal, Styria, 15 Feb 1847; *d* Vienna, 19 Feb 1927). Austrian composer. He studied the flute, violin, piano, organ and thoroughbass with his brother-in-law. In 1865 he moved to Vienna and earned a meagre living as a répétiteur and teacher, becoming organist at the Piaristenkirche the following year; he studied composition at the conservatory with Dessoff. In 1875 he was appointed conductor of the orchestral society of the Gesellschaft der Musikfreunde and professor at the conservatory; he was also organist of the Hofkapelle, 1894–1905.

Fuchs taught a generation of musicians that included Mahler, Sibelius, Schreker and Zemlinsky. Brahms thought highly of his work. However, he met with little success as a composer of operas. His first, the three-act *Die Königsbraut* to a libretto by Ignaz Schnitzer, performed and published in Vienna in 1889, is a number opera dominated by song; there is little recitative and practically none in which the orchestra plays an important role. It was not well received by Hanslick. His second, *Die Teufelsglocke*, was given in Leipzig in 1893 but not published.

A. Mayr: *Erinnerungen an Robert Fuchs* (Graz, 1934)
K. Brachtel: 'Robert Fuchs zu seinem 100. Geburtstag', *Neue Musikzeitschrift*, i/4 (1947)
R. Pascall: 'Robert Fuchs', *MT*, cxviii (1977), 115–17
                    R. J. PASCALL

Fuentes, Eduardo Sánchez de. *See* SÁNCHEZ DE FUENTES, EDUARDO.

Fuentes, Giorgio (*b* Milan, 1756; *d* Milan, 1821). Italian stage designer and painter. He studied at the Milan Academy of Fine Arts, then with the scene painter Pietro Gonzaga and was apprenticed to Alessandro Sanquirico at La Scala. He distinguished himself as a painter of decorations. From 1796 to 1805, he was a designer at the National Theatre, Frankfurt, where he created some of the most beautiful settings ever seen there. Goethe was particularly impressed with his new designs for Salieri's *Palmira, regina di Persia* (1797), because 'embedded within them is solid architecture and because they are opulent without being overladen'. Fuentes was invited to Weimar to work with Goethe, but he had no inclination to do so and sent instead Friedrich Beuther, a talented pupil. Fuentes then designed Mozart's *La clemenza di Tito* (1799) and Joseph Weigl's *Der Korsar*. In 1805 he left Frankfurt for Milan, via Paris, where he undertook a commission for Napoleon. He worked at La Scala alone and in collaboration with Pasquale Canna and Giovanni Pedroni. Among the operas he designed were *Odoardo e Carlotta* by Giuseppe Farinelli (1804); *Elisa* by Simon Mayr; *L'italiana in Algeri* by Luigi Mosca (1808; with Pedroni); and *La donna selvaggia* by Carlo Coccia (1813; with Pedroni and Canna).

Fuentes followed the Rococo style but was already influenced by romanticism. A representative neo-classical stage painter, he created settings of imposing grandeur within strict geometric proportions, with strongly contrasting interplay of light and shade, and a controlled use of perspective; such sets are 'destined for action that is more heroic than dramatic'. Some original sketches by Fuentes are in the Städelsches Kunstinstitut in Frankfurt.

For illustration *see* CLEMENZA DI TITO, LA.

ES (F. Hadamowsky and O. Vangelista)   DAVID J. HOUGH

Fuentes (y) Matons, Laureano (*b* Santiago de Cuba, 3 July 1825; *d* Santiago de Cuba, 30 Sept 1898). Cuban composer. A scion of an old-established Cuban musical family, Fuentes Matons won the post of leader of the Santiago de Cuba Cathedral orchestra at the age of 15; at 19 he headed the orchestra in the local Teatro Principal and at 21 he founded the S Cecilia music academy in Santiago. At the opening of the Teatro de la Reina (30 June 1850) he directed the orchestra.

The first travelling Italian opera company brought *Norma* to Santiago in 1839. Fuentes Matons's first stage works were the two zarzuelas *El viejo enamorado* and *Me lo ha dicho la portera*, mounted in 1857 and 1858 respectively by Manuel y Luis Martínez Casado's travelling zarzuela troupe. He continued in the same satirical vein with *Desgracias de un tenor, o El do de pecho*, first performed with such success in 1863 by Baltasar Torrecillas's company that it had to be repeated several times. On 16 May 1875, at the Teatro de la Reina, Rosa Llorens's zarzuela company gave a poorly performed première of Fuentes Matons's biblical opera *La hija de Jefté*; expanded to three acts, renamed *Seila* and with the libretto not very happily translated into Italian by the composer, the opera was successfully mounted at Havana by Adolfo Bracale's company in 1917. Reviews in the *Diario de la Marina* (5 and 7 February), *La lucha* and *El triunfo* (6 February) treated it not as an amiable historical curiosity resurrected through the efforts of the composer's son but as a near masterpiece. Fuentes Matons also composed symphonies and numerous sacred works with orchestra.

zarzuelas first performed in Santiago de Cuba

El viejo enamorado (1, L. Ortega de la Flor), 1857, lib. (Havana, 1858)
Me lo ha dicho la portera (1, J. Martínez and L. Martínez Casado), 1858, lib. (Havana, 1858); aria in Archivo Pablo Hernández Balaguer, Santiago de Cuba Villergas
Desgracias de un tenor, o El do de pecho (1, J. Birelli), 23 Nov 1863
Ismenia (1, E. Aguirreozábal), 1 Jan 1865
Dos máscaras (2, T. Mendoza), 7 May 1866
La hija de Jefté (biblical op, 1, A. Arnao), 16 May 1875; rev. in It. as Seila (3), Havana, Nacional, 5 Feb 1917; MS in Havana, Museo Nacional de la Música, lib. (Santiago de Cuba, 1895) [Sp. and It.]

*

L. Fuentes Matons: *Las artes en Santiago de Cuba* (Santiago de Cuba, 1893)
E. T. Tolón and J. A. González: *Óperas cubanas y sus autores* (Havana, 1943), 67–119
A. Estrada, ed.: *Las artes en Santiago de Cuba: Laureano Fuentes Matons* (Havana, 1981)
R. Stevenson: 'Music', *Handbook of Latin American Studies*, xlviii: *Humanities* (Austin, 1986), 616
ROBERT STEVENSON

Fuertes (y Piqueras), Mariano Soriano. *See* SORIANO FUERTES, MARIANO.

Fuga, Sandro (*b* Mogliano Veneto, 26 Nov 1906). Italian composer. He studied at the Turin Conservatory, where his teachers included Franco Alfano, and initially made his career as a concert pianist. After 1940 he turned to composition and teaching, initially at the Milan Conservatory (1951–2), then at that of Turin, where he was director from 1966 to 1977. As a composer with a discernible predilection for Brahms (Mila) he remained faithful to the Classical-Romantic tradition, evident in the sonata-form principles he retained in much of his chamber music. His works for the theatre, which include *Otto Schnaffs* (1950), a heroic-comic opera to a libretto by his brother Igino, a music critic, reveal a dramatic inventiveness and masterly orchestral writing.

La croce deserta (lauda drammatica, 1, T. Pinelli, after J. P. Jacobsen), Bergamo, Novità, 18 Oct 1950, vs (Milan, 1950)
Otto Schnaffs (op eroicomica, 1, I. Fuga, after G. de Maupassant), Turin, Alfieri, 28 Oct 1950, vs (Milan, 1950)
Confessione (4 scenes, Fuga, after I. Shaw), RAI, Sept 1962; stage, Turin, Nuovo, 6 May 1971, vs (Milan, 1971)
L'imperatore Jones (mimodrama, 7 scenes, after E. O'Neill), Turin, Regio, 2 April 1976
La pesca (op, 1, Fuga, after O'Neill), unperf., unpubd

*

DEUMM (R. Cognazzo); ES (G. Graziosi)
F. Abbiati: 'Al Teatro della Novità "La croce deserta" di Sandro Fuga', *Corriere della sera* (19 Oct 1950)
M. A. Darbesio: 'Deux opéras de Sandro Fuga', *Le diapason*, i (1950), 23–6
G. Pannain: 'Sandro Fuga', *Santa Cecilia*, ix (1960), 8–9
M. Mila: 'Un'opera e un balletto in scena al Nuovo', *La stampa* [Turin] (9 May 1971)
P. Isotta: '"L'imperatore Jones" non canta', *Il giornale* [Milan] (6 April 1976)
S. Fuga: *Sandro Fuga visto da se stesso* (Rome, 1990)
RAFFAELE POZZI

Fugère, Lucien (*b* Paris, 22 July 1848; *d* Paris, 15 Jan 1935). French baritone. He began his career in Parisian cabarets, making his début in 1870 at the *café-concert* Ba-ta-clan. In 1873 he was engaged by the Bouffes-Parisiens and in 1877 by the Opéra-Comique, with whom until 1910, he sang more than 100 roles, over 30 of them in local premières. He created Pandolfe in *Cendrillon* (1899), the Father in *Louise* (1900) and the Devil in *Grisélidis* (1901). He was also famous as Papageno and Figaro, and as Leporello which he sang at Covent Garden in 1897. In 1910 he sang Sancho Panza in the Paris première of Massenet's *Don Quichotte* at the Gaîté-Lyrique; he appeared there regularly until 1913. He returned to the Opéra-Comique in 1919 in Messager's *La basoche*. De Curzon described him as 'a *basse chantante* of easy baritone range, with a ringing clarity in the lower register and a skilful refinement in the upper'. At the age of 85 he sang Dr Bartolo to great acclaim at the Théâtre de la Porte-St-Martin.

ES (F. Lesure and R. Celletti)
H. de Curzon: *Croquis d'artistes* (Paris, 1897)
R. Duhamel: *Lucien Fugère* (Paris, 1929)
V. Girard: 'Lucien Fugère', *Record Collector*, viii (1953), 101–9 [with discography]
HAROLD ROSENTHAL/R

Fugère, Paul (*b* Paris, 25 Jan 1851; *d* c1910). French baritone, brother of Lucien Fugère. A pupil of Péricaud, he made his début in 1877 at the Château-d'Eau in *Le drapeau tricolore* and was an immediate success. He created roles in a number of light operas, including Paillasse in Ganne's *Les saltimbanques* (1899), and roles in Audran's *La poupée* (1896) and Planquette's *Mam'zelle Quat'sous* (1897), but his greatest successes were probably in revivals, as Célestin in Hervé's *Mam'zelle Nitouche* and Larivaudière in Lecocq's *La fille de Madame Angot*. 'A real joker, amusing and sensitive', wrote Laroque, 'he imitated the lion's roar and all the cries of Paris, he seemed to be able to create three voices at once!'

A. Laroque: *Acteurs et actrices de Paris* (Paris, 1898)
R. Traubner: *Operetta* (New York, 1983)
PATRICK O'CONNOR

Fugue. A composition, or a compositional technique, in which imitative counterpoint involving one main theme is the central device of formal extension. It is rare in opera. Although primarily associated with the Baroque period, fugue is not usually found as such in opera of the time outside overtures written in or after the French style, as established by Lully and followed by Purcell, Rameau, Handel and others, where the principal fast section is normally fugal; some ensembles, however, include passages for the voices in fugal style (with harmonic accompaniment), and occasionally a fugal ritornello is to be found. Handel's *Acis and Galatea* (1718), *Semele* (1744) and *Hercules* (1745) contain fugal choruses, but these were not designed for normal stage performance, to which fugue is by its nature unamenable; it is significant that the choral fugue in the opening scene of Saint-Saëns' *Samson et Dalila* (1877) belongs to a work originally conceived as an oratorio. Fugue, or more commonly passages of fugal texture ('fugato'), is often used for special effect: to point a moral, as in the final scene of Mozart's *Don Giovanni* (1787, in fact only a mock fugue) and at the end of Verdi's *Falstaff* (1893); to depict a riot, as in Wagner's *Die Meistersinger* (1868), or a battle, as in Verdi's *Macbeth* (revised version, 1865); or merely to portray a scene of bustling activity, as in Puccini's *Manon Lescaut* (1893) or *Madama Butterfly* (1904); or even for purposes of comic parody, as in the Amen Chorus of Berlioz's *La damnation de Faust* (1846, not in fact a stage work) or as a motif for the Lord Chancellor in Sullivan's *Iolanthe* (1882). There is a 'fuga infernale' in the Brocken scene of Boito's *Mefistofele* (revised version, 1875), and Marie's Bible-reading scene in Berg's *Wozzeck* (1925) takes the form of a fugue on a 12-note subject. The use of fugue or fugato in opera overtures, for example those to Mozart's *Don Giovanni*, *La clemenza di Tito* (1791) and *Die Zauberflöte* (1791), Weber's *Euryanthe* (1823), Smetana's *The Bartered Bride* (1866) and *Die Meistersinger*, has no particular dramatic significance.   JULIAN BUDDEN

Full Moon in March, A. Chamber opera in one act by JOHN HARBISON to his own libretto after W. B. Yeats's dance-play; Cambridge, Massachusetts, Sanders Theater, 30 April 1979.

The mysterious and highly symbolic plot tells of the cold Queen (mezzo-soprano) and the coarse Swineherd (baritone) who dares to woo her. Two Attendants (soprano, tenor) serve as narrators and chorus. The Queen, veiled, awaits the man who best sings of his passion; to him she will give herself in marriage and her throne. A Swineherd comes to sing for her and she warns him that she is 'cruel as the winter of virginity'. He sings, but she interprets his words as insulting and orders his execution. Before he is led away he drops her veil so that he can behold her face. He is led out by the Attendants, who then conceal the Queen behind a curtain. The Attendants comment on the foregoing, then reveal the Queen again (here the singer is replaced by a dancer in the same costume); she holds the head of the Swineherd on a stake; she begins a slow, alluring dance with the head, in the character of an impersonal rite, until the Attendants close the curtain.

In setting Yeats's evocative, complex text, Harbison made no attempt to interpret Yeats's symbolism, but simply responded immediately and naively to the images. The eight players of the accompanying ensemble (flute, oboe, bass clarinet, percussion, violin, viola, cello and prepared piano) produce rhythmically complex patterns with heterophonic textures and gamelan-like percussive timbres that support the opera's ritualistic character. The vocal lines are wide-ranging, often dissonant, but show a careful concern for the rhythms of the English language.   STEVEN LEDBETTER

Fungoni, Papebrochio. Pseudonym of an Italian composer to whom two works, performed in Naples in 1737 and 1738, have been attributed. The first, a sacred opera named *La Teodora* with words by G. Federico (libretto, *GB-Lbl*), was produced in the monastery of S Chiara at the end of Carnival 1737. The second was a comic opera in dialect called *La rosa* (P. Trinchera), presented at the Teatro Nuovo in the autumn of the following year. Since there is no other record of a composer called Fungoni, and since furthermore the comic-opera libretto (*Lbl* and *I-Nc*) refers to him as a native of the Canary Isles (a description well worthy of a character in *opera buffa*), the name is almost certainly fictitious. A much altered version of this opera libretto was produced under the title *Don Paduano* at the Teatro della Pace, Naples, in 1745 with music by Nicola Logroscino. But this does not establish a connection between Logroscino and Fungoni, whose identity remains uncertain.
                    MICHAEL F. ROBINSON

Fuorusciti di Firenze, I ('The Exiles of Florence'). *Opera semiseria* in two acts by FERDINANDO PAER to a libretto by ANGELO ANELLI; Dresden, Hoftheater, 27 November 1802.

In its Gothic setting and 'rescue' plot, *I fuorusciti* exemplifies an important type of turn-of-the-century *opera semiseria*. It also anticipates the later 'exile' and 'outlaw' operas which became common around 1830.

Princess Isabella of Florence (soprano) has been kidnapped by a band of outlaws led by Uberto degli Ardinghelli (bass-baritone), who is holding her in an ancient Tuscan castle. Uberto was exiled from Florence 20 years earlier by his enemy Edoardo de Liggozzi (tenor), now Isabella's husband. Disguised as a shepherd, Edoardo infiltrates Uberto's camp to rescue Isabella but is caught in the act and eventually admits his true identity. Rather than kill him, however, Uberto returns him to Isabella, both out of affection for her and out of respect for the couple's mutual devotion. When Edoardo and Isabella attempt to persuade Uberto to return to Florence with them, Uberto declines, but reveals that he left behind there an infant daughter, who turns out to be Isabella. Light relief is provided by Edoardo's cowardly servant Gianni (bass) and the young peasant girls Cecchina and Lena (sopranos), who are among Uberto's followers.   SCOTT L. BALTHAZAR

Furioso nell'isola di San Domingo, Il ('The Madman on the Island of San Domingo'). *Melodramma* in two acts by GAETANO DONIZETTI to a libretto by JACOPO FERRETTI, based on a play of the same name, after MIGUEL DE CERVANTES' *Don Quixote*, Part I, Chapters 23–7; Rome, Teatro Valle, 2 January 1833.

Cardenio (baritone; originally sung by Giorgio Ronconi), has been driven mad by the thought of his wife's infidelity and has fled to a tropical island. After a long search, he finds that his wife Eleonora (soprano) and brother Ferrando (tenor) are, by coincidence, shipwrecked on the same island. After many misunderstandings, rendered poignant by Cardenio's painful memories, he becomes convinced that Eleonora truly loves him when he sees she would rather die than harm him. His reason restored, they are happily reunited.

Il furioso is sometimes described as an *opera semiseria* because of the presence in the cast of a *buffo* character – Kaidamà, who is a 'natural' defective and therefore a foil to Cardenio's delusions; but he is a figure of pathos rather than fun. It is in fact a Romantic *melodramma* through and through, and is so described in the original libretto. The score contains some finely wrought arias and moving ensembles.

                    WILLIAM ASHBROOK

Furlanetto, Ferruccio (*b* Pordenone, Sicily, 16 May 1949). Italian bass. He made his début in 1974 at Lonigo (Vicenza) as Sparafucile, then sang at Turin, Trieste, Bologna, Venice and Parma. At Aix-en-Provence (1976–7) he sang Dr Grenvil and Cecil (*Roberto Devereux*). He made his American début in 1978 at New Orleans as Zaccaria and sang Alvise at San Francisco (1979). At Glyndebourne (1980–81) his roles were Melibeo (*La fedeltà premiata*) and Don Basilio. He sang Phanuel (*Hérodiade*) and Ernesto (*Parisina*) at Rome; Oberto and Gounod's Méphistophélès at San Diego (1985–8); Mahomet II and Don Giovanni in Paris (1985–6); Philip II, Mozart's Figaro and Leporello at Salzburg (1986–8); Fernando (*La gazza ladra*) at Pesaro (1989); and Leporello at the Metropolitan (1990). His roles have also included Don Alfonso, Assur (*Semiramide*), Mustafà, Don Magnifico, Ramfis and Fiesco. He is a lively actor with a dark-toned voice better suited to Verdi than to Rossini.

                    ELIZABETH FORBES

Fursch-Madi [Fursch-Madier], **Emma** (*b* Bayonne, 1847; *d* Warrenville, NJ, 20 Sept 1894). French soprano. She studied in Paris, making her début there in 1868. After a season with the French Opera Company in New Orleans, she was engaged from 1874 to 1876 at the Paris Opéra, where she sang Marguerite (*Faust*), Valentine (*Les Huguenots*), Donna Elvira and Berthe (*Le prophète*). From 1881 to 1890 she appeared regularly at Covent Garden, making her début as Valentine, then singing Agathe (*Der Freischütz*), Donna Anna, Alice (*Robert le diable*), Aida, Hilda (*Sigurd*), Lucrezia Borgia, Leonora (*Il trovatore*) and Ortrud. In 1883 she sang Laura in the first American performance of *La Gioconda* at the Metropolitan. After touring North America with the National Opera Company, she returned to the Metropolitan in 1893. A very dramatic singer, she had a rich voice and fierce attack.

ELIZABETH FORBES

Fürstin von Granada, Die [*Die Fürstin von Granada, oder Der Zauberblick* ('The Princess of Granada, or The Magic Glance')]. *Grosse Zauberoper* in five acts by JOHANN CHRISTIAN LOBE to a libretto by Lobe and Philip Carl Christian Sondershausen; Weimar, Hoftheater, 28 September 1833.

Die Fürstin von Granada was by far the most successful of Lobe's operas. Its highly acclaimed première was followed by stagings in other major theatres. Unusually for a German opera at this period, not only a vocal score was published but also a full score. The work's popularity owed much to the composer's skilful combination of attractive and characterful music (somewhat influenced by Weber) with striking and colourful stage effects. The plot deals with the attempt of Solabella (soprano), a sorceress (the eponymous Fürstin), to get possession of an enchanted girdle which will strengthen her powers. She uses her magic glance to enslave its owner, Harita (tenor), causing him to break off his engagement to Nadire (soprano); but having obtained the girdle by promising Harita her hand in marriage she discards him. In the end, however, she is frustrated by the intervention of the fairy Zofira (soprano). The opera contains choruses of country folk, fairies and hunters and lavish ballets of giants, dwarfs, elves and fairies. A contemporary review hailed it as an opera 'which achieves everything that the taste of the day demands and, besides that, something better' (*AMZ*, xxxv, 1833, col.711).

CLIVE BROWN

Furtwängler, (Gustav Heinrich Ernst Martin) Wilhelm (*b* Berlin, 25 Jan 1886; *d* Baden-Baden, 30 Nov 1954). German conductor. He was known most of all as a symphonic conductor, especially of Beethoven, Brahms and Bruckner, and as such he was widely regarded as the culmination of the subjective, quasi-mystical German school, the interpretative tradition of Wagner, von Bülow and Nikisch. But opera played an important part in his career. His apprenticeship was the normal one for conductors in Germany: a series of posts in minor, and later major, opera houses; répétiteur at the Breslau Stadttheater (1905–6); then Zürich (1906–7), the Munich court opera under Mottl (1907–9), followed by two years (1909–11) as third conductor at Strasbourg, where Pfitzner was music director. This training led to his first big appointment, at 25, as musical director of the Lübeck Opera (1911–15).

In these four years and the three that followed at Mannheim (1915–18) he emerged as the leading young conductor in Germany. When Nikisch died in 1922,

Furtwängler, aged 36, was appointed to succeed him at both the Berlin Philharmonic and the Leipzig Gewandhaus orchestras. For the next ten years symphonic music absorbed his energies, and he conducted practically no opera. His *Tristan* at the 1931 Bayreuth Festival, however, inaugurated a much more active operatic period. From 1932 until the outbreak of war Furtwängler appeared as guest conductor not only in Germany and in Vienna but also at the Paris Opéra and at Covent Garden. Apart from one *Freischütz* and Pfitzner's *Das Herz*, his repertory in these years was exclusively Wagnerian, including cycles of the *Ring* in Bayreuth (1936, 1937), Berlin (1937) and London (1937, 1938), *Tristan* in Paris (1932–5), *Die Meistersinger* in Berlin, Nuremberg, Paris, Vienna and Salzburg, and *Parsifal* and *Lohengrin* in Bayreuth. In these years he mastered the combination of expressive intensity and command of large-scale tonal architecture which made him one of the supreme Wagner interpreters.

Furtwängler's decision to stay in Germany during most of the Nazi period, though in many ways idealistic and unworldly in motive, aroused fierce antagonism, especially in America, and his return to conducting after the war was delayed for almost two years. From 1948 until his death he conducted a good deal of opera. His repertory now included – in addition to Wagner and Weber – *Die Zauberflöte*, *Don Giovanni*, *Figaro*, *Fidelio* and, for five unforgettable evenings at the Salzburg Festival in 1951, Verdi's *Otello*. From this period come the live recordings (taken from broadcasts) of the *Ring* in Milan and Rome. Furtwängler, though not enthusiastic about recording (which to him was inimical to the essentially exploratory, spontaneous nature of musical re-creation), came to see its advantages for Wagner, and made studio recordings of *Tristan* and *Die Walküre*. Their splendour explains his almost mythic status and his continuing cult among musicians today.

*

H. Keller: 'Wilhelm Furtwängler 1886–1954, an Appreciation', *Opera*, vi (1955), 99–101
H. Smidth Olsen: *Wilhelm Furtwängler: a Discography* (Copenhagen, 1970, 2/1973)
H. -H. Schönzeler: *Furtwängler* (London, 1990)   DAVID CAIRNS

Fusai, Ippolito (*fl* Florence, 1661–96). Italian bass and singing teacher. His first role was Charon in Jacopo Melani's *Ercole in Tebe*, the wedding opera performed at the Teatro della Pergola, Florence, for Marguerite d'Orléans and Cosimo de' Medici (1661). He is listed among the *musici ordinari* of the grand-ducal court in the second half of the 17th century. He sang in the operas mounted by the Grand Prince Ferdinando de' Medici at Pratolino, taking the role of Coridone Bifolco in B. Cerri's *Con la forza d'amore* (1679) and Graticcio in Alessandro Melani's *Il finto chimico* (1686). He also sang in Ferdinando's wedding opera, Pagliardi's *Il greco in Troia* (1689). As a bass, he specialized in comic roles. His fame as a teacher prompted Johann Wilhelm of Bavaria to send his chamber singer, Andrea Fischer, to Florence to study in the 'Scuola del rinomato Fusai', and it may be presumed that his school contributed to the training of the flourishing school of singers patronized by Ferdinando de' Medici.

*

R. L. Weaver and N. W. Weaver: *A Chronology of Music in the Florentine Theater 1590–1750* (Detroit, 1978)
ROBERT LAMAR WEAVER

Fuss, Johann Evangelist. *See* FUSZ, JÁNOS.

Füssl, Karl Heinz (*b* Jablonec, Czechoslovakia, 21 March 1924). Austrian composer and musicologist. He began to compose in 1941 and later studied at the Vienna Akademie für Musik. From 1953 he was a music critic before working as an editor, and has collaborated with H. C. Robbins Landon on editions including Haydn's *Le pescatrici* (Salzburg, 1971) and J. C. Bach's *Temistocle* (Vienna, 1965). He achieved his most important success as a composer with his three-act opera *Dybuk*, performed for the first time in 1970 in Karlsruhe. Based on a 1920s play, the opera deals with the reunion of a young girl with her dead lover, through the agency of the *dybuk* ('demon'). Füssl's compositions employ Schoenberg's 12-note system, lyrical arias and Sprechgesang. Other works include a second opera, *Celestina* (1973–5; 2, H. Lederer, after F. de Rajas; Karlsruhe, 1976), and a ballet.   RUDOLF KLEIN/R

Fusz, János [Fuss, Johann Evangelist] (*b* Tolna, 16 Dec 1777; *d* Buda, 9 March 1819). Hungarian composer. He received his earliest musical instruction in Baja, southern Hungary, then became a church musician and schoolmaster. In the 1790s he entered the service of a rich and highly educated musical amateur, Ignác Végh, as a piano teacher in Vereb (near Pest), where he had his own theatre. From 1801 Fusz gave piano lessons in Pozsony (now Bratislava), where he composed the melodrama *Pyramus és Thisbe*. He then moved to Vienna to study with Albrechtsberger; he won the sympathy of Haydn, who recommended his melodrama to the Theater an der Wien, but the company could not perform it because of the political situation. During a further period in Pozsony (from 1806) he wrote a pantomime for the name-day of the palatine of Hungary, Archduke József, and an opera, *Watwort*, which he later sold to the Theater an der Wien. After returning to Vienna he became a correspondent for the *Allgemeine musikalische Zeitung* in Leipzig. His melodrama *Isaac*, with arias and choruses, to a libretto based on Metastasio, was first produced in Vienna in 1812, and later staged in Buda and Pest (1817), and Pozsony (1818).

In 1813 he was appointed musical director and conductor at the theatre in Pozsony. During his time there he composed the melodrama *Judith*, which he later enlarged as a two-act biblical opera (1814). After losing his best singers, in 1816 he returned to Vienna, where his light opera *Der Käfig* was performed the same year. Until that time he had spent his summers in Vienna, and had met Beethoven about 1815, when both composers were considering setting Treitschke's *Romulus und Remus*; Fusz's work was first performed in Pest in 1816. He then moved to Buda, and despite declining health wrote an unperformed opera, *Das Medaillon* (1817), and a musical satire, *Die Büchse der Pandora* (1818). His last stage work, the patriotic idyll *Jacob und Rachel*, was banned by the censors. All of Fusz's works were written in the Viennese Classical style, and he may therefore be regarded as an important representative of the German tradition in Hungarian music of the early 19th century. No music from his stage works is to be found in Hungarian archives.

Pyramus és Thisbe (melodrama, 1), Pozsony, *c*1801
Watwort, 1806 (3)

Isaac op.17 (melodrama, J. Perinet, after P. Metastasio), Vienna, Leopoldstadter, 22 Aug 1812, ov. (Leipzig, n.d.), arias (Vienna, n.d.)
Judith op.19 (melodrama), Vienna, Leopoldstadter, *c*1813; rev. (biblical op, 2, G. A. Meister), Vienna, An der Wien, 20 April 1814
Der Käfig (operetta, 1, A. von Kotzebue), Vienna, Leopoldstadter, 16 March 1816
Romulus und Remus (3, G. F. Treitschke), Pest, 9 Sept 1816, canon pubd in suppl. to Allgemeine Wiener Musik-Zeitung (4 Sept 1817)
Das Medaillon, 1817, unperf.
Die Büchse der Pandora (musical satire, 2, W. Blum), Vienna, Leopoldstadter, 6 May 1818
Jacob und Rachel (patriotic idyll, 1, Meisel)

*

MGG (A. Orel)
J. K[rüchten]: 'A honnyi mívésznek élet leírása' [Biography of a Native Artist], *Tudományos gyűjtemény* (1818), no.3, pp.122–5
J. Krüchten: 'Fusz János Evangelista emlékezete' [In Remembrance of Johann Evangelist Fusz], *Tudományos gyűjtemény* (1819), no.11, pp.72–88; repr. in D. Legány: *A magyar zene krónikája* (Budapest, 1962), 140–45, 474
——: 'Fusz János Evangelista hangszerzeményei' [The Compositions of J. E. Fusz: a Work-list], *Tudományos gyűjtemény* (1819), no.12, pp.79–89   DEZSŐ LEGÁNY

Fux, Johann Joseph (*b* Hirtenfeld, nr Graz, *c*1660; *d* Vienna, 13 Feb 1741). Austrian composer. The son of Styrian peasants, he entered the Jesuit University in Graz as a *grammatista* (member of the third-year class of secondary school) in May 1680, at the age of about 20; he was admitted to the same level of the imperial Ferdinandeum, a residential school, as *musicus*, in February 1681, but apparently left before completing the required course of study. In 1683 he enrolled at the Jesuit University of Ingolstadt as *logica studiosus pauper*, the preparatory level for a philosophy student, and from autumn 1685 studied law for two years in Ingolstadt (law was not offered at the university in Graz, and this may have been the reason why he originally left the town). He was engaged as organist at the parish church of St Moritz in Ingolstadt on 20 August 1685, a post which he held probably until the end of 1688; during this time he composed some vocal pieces for the church. Details of Fux's life in the years that follow are only to be found in sources written shortly before, and more than 50 years after, his death; according to these, he was in the service of the Hungarian archbishop Cardinal Leopold, Count von Kollonitsch, who at that time resided mainly in Vienna. Emperor Leopold I is said to have heard masses by Fux when visiting the bishop and to have engaged him in spite of the objections of his Italian court musicians. Though it is likely that the composer at some time studied in Italy, such conjectures have not been proved.

Fux married in Vienna on 5 June 1696, at which time he was organist of the Benedictine Schottenkirche. From the beginning of 1698 he was paid as imperial court composer, and one of his first duties was probably the composition of instrumental music for a concert given on 19 March, the name-day of the Emperor's son Joseph I (similar to the works published three years later in his *Concentus musico-instrumentalis* and also dedicated to Joseph). From 1700 he was entrusted with the composition of dramatic music, but nevertheless retained his position as church organist until 1702. He then assumed the additional duties of second Kapellmeister at St Stephen's Cathedral in 1705 and of principal Kapellmeister between 1712 and 1714. Meanwhile he had succeeded M. A. Ziani as imperial vice-*maestro di cappella* after the death of Joseph I in 1711, and became *maestro di cappella* to Joseph's widow, Empress Amalie, probably in 1713. On 16 February 1715 he reached the summit of his career when he was appointed imperial *maestro di cappella* by Charles VI. The height of his fame was marked by the performance of his opera *Costanza e Fortezza* in 1723 during the coronation festivities in Prague, with many princes and noblemen in the audience and foreign musicians taking part.

Fux is known today primarily for his theoretical work, *Gradus ad Parnassum* (1725), which is still the foundation for modern textbooks on counterpoint, but in his time he was also recognized as a composer. Although his principal duty was the production of sacred music, he nevertheless composed the music for 19 Italian secular dramatic works performed at the Viennese court, and for a Latin school drama at Melk monastery (1701). Until 1720 he was mainly entrusted with the composition of music for small-scale works, especially those of the serenata type; three-act operas, of which Fux wrote only three, were usually composed by F. B. Conti or Caldara.

Fux's overtures are of several types, notably the solemn intrada with trumpets and the French, Italian and all hybrid forms. The recitatives are carefully adapted to convey the intended affections, and instrumental accompaniments are used for special emphasis. Each of the operas includes at least one duet or other polyphonic ensemble. Instrumental polyphony, however, is rare in his early operas, but became increasingly important from 1716, especially in *Costanza e Fortezza* (in this case, according to Quantz, perhaps owing to its open-air performance). Fugal arias are also more numerous in his later works; some even have arias with string accompaniment in 'Palestrina' style. Most of Fux's arias, ensembles and choruses are in da capo form, handled with remarkable variety and sometimes incorporating dance elements. The early operas often include set pieces accompanied only by continuo, with a final ritornello for strings. Later he increasingly employed a four-part string orchestra, with two oboes and a bassoon doubling. The use of one or more solo instruments, particularly trumpets, was also common, as was a combination of flute and chalumeau.

In the early operas choruses appear only for short exclamations, and for the final number in the *licenza*. However, in *Le nozze di Aurora*, *Costanza e Fortezza* and *La corona d'Arianna*, choruses abound, mostly homophonic in style and often in dance rhythms; polyphonic settings are rare unlike Fux's oratorio choruses. Ballets occur only in *Angelica vincitrice di Alcina*, *Le nozze di Aurora*, *Costanza e Fortezza*, *La corona d'Arianna* and *Enea negli Elisi*, their music composed by the younger Nicola Matteis except in cases where they were danced to the music of the preceding choruses.

Besides operas, Fux composed 13 oratorios and *componimenti sacri*, more than 80 masses, many other sacred vocal works, church sonatas, partitas, overtures and keyboard works. Of all these, he published only a few instrumental works in 1701 as *Concentus musico-instrumentalis*.

See also Costanza e fortezza. For illustration *see* Galli-bibiena, fig.2; Prague, fig.1; and Vienna, fig.1.

Numbering in Köchel (1872) [κ] and Federhofer (1959) [ε]

Edition: *J. J. Fux: Sämtliche Werke*, v, ed. H. Federhofer and O. Wessely (Graz and Kassel, 1962–) [F]

first given in Vienna, Hofburg, and MSS in A-Wn, unless otherwise stated

Il fato monarchico ε95 (festa teatrale, 1), 16 Feb 1700, lost, pubd lib. A-Wn

L'offendere per amare, ovvero La Telesilla κ302 (dramma per musica, 3, D. Cupeda), 25 June 1702, lost, pubd lib. Wn

La clemenza d'Augusto κ301 (poemetto drammatico, 1, P. A. Bernardoni), 15 Nov 1702, lost, pubd lib. Wn

Julo Ascanio, rè d'Alba κ304 (poemetto drammatico, 1, Bernardoni), 19 March 1708, F v/1 (1962)

Pulcheria κ303 (poemetto drammatico, 1, Bernardoni), Vienna, Favorita, 21 June 1708, F v/2 (1967)

Il mese di Marzo, consacrato a Marte κ306 (componimento per musica, 1, S. Stampiglia), 19 March 1709

Gli ossequi della notte κ305 (componimento per musica, 1, Cupeda), 15 July 1709

La decima fatica d'Ercole, ovvero La sconfitta di Gerione in Spagna κ307 (componimento pastorale-eroico, 1, G. B. Ancioni), Vienna, Favorita, 1 Oct 1710

Dafne in Lauro κ308 (componimento per camera, 1, P. Pariati), Vienna, Favorita, 1 Oct 1714

Orfeo ed Euridice κ309 (componimento da camera per musica, 1, Pariati), Vienna, Favorita, 1 Oct 1715, facs. in IOB, xix (1978)

Teodosio ed Eudossa (os, 3, A. Zeno), Brunswick, 12 Sept 1716, collab. Caldara and Gasparini [after A. S. Fiorè, A. Caldara and F. Gasparini: Atenaide, 1709]; as Teodosio, Hamburg, dedicated 14 Nov 1718, collab. Caldara and Gasparini

Angelica vincitrice di Alcina κ310 (festa teatrale, 3, Pariati), 14 Sept 1716

Diana placata κ311 (festa teatrale per musica, 1, Pariati), 19 Nov 1717

Elisa κ312 (componimento teatrale per musica, 1, Pariati), Vienna, Favorita, 28 Aug 1719 (Amsterdam, c1719)

Psiche κ313 (componimento musicale, 1, Zeno), 19 Nov 1720 (music partly by Caldara), 1 Oct 1722 (completely by Fux)

Le nozze di Aurora κ314 (festa teatrale per musica, 1, Pariati), Vienna, Favorita, 6 Oct 1722

Costanza e Fortezza κ315 (festa teatrale per musica, 3, Pariati), Prague, Hradschin, 28 Aug 1723, ed. in DTÖ, xxxiv–xxxv, Jg.xvii (1910/R1959)

Giunone placata κ316 (festa teatrale per musica, 1, I. Zanelli), 19 Nov 1725

La corona d'Arianna κ317 (festa teatrale per musica, 1, Pariati), Vienna, Favorita, 28 Aug 1726

Enea negli Elisi, ovvero Il tempio dell'Eternità κ318 (festa teatrale, 1, P. Metastasio), Vienna, Favorita, 28 Aug 1731

Overtures in: C. A. Badia: La concordia della Virtù e della Fortuna; G. Bononcini: Proteo sul Reno; M. A. Ziani: Meleagro; A. Lotti: Costantino

*

L. von Köchel: *Johann Josef Fux* (Vienna, 1872) [with thematic catalogue and list of works]

H. Federhofer: 'Unbekannte Kirchenmusik von J. J. Fux', *KJb*, xliii (1959), 1–54

E. Wellesz: Introduction to J. J. Fux: *Costanza e Fortezza*, DTÖ, xxxiv–xxxv, Jg. xvii (1910/R1959)

J. H. van der Meer: *J. J. Fux als Opernkomponist* (Bilthoven, 1961)

E. Wellesz: *Fux* (London, 1965)

O. Wessely: *Pietro Pariatis Libretto zu Johann Joseph Fuxens Costanza e fortezza* (Graz, 1969)

H. Seifert: 'Die Aufführungen der Opern und Serenate mit Musik von Johann Joseph Fux', *SMw*, xxix (1978), 14–27

R. Flotzinger: *Fux-Studien* (Graz, 1985)

H. Seifert: *Die Oper am Wiener Kaiserhof im 17. Jahrhundert* (Tutzing, 1985)

C. Böhm: *Theatralia anlässlich der Krönungen in der österreichischen Linie der Casa d'Austria (1627–1764)* (Vienna, 1986)

H. Seifert: 'Zur neuesten Fux-Forschung: Kritik und Beiträge', *SMw*, xxxviii (1987), 35–52

H. White, ed.: *Johann Joseph Fux and the Music of the Austro-Italian Baroque* (Aldershot, 1992)   HERBERT SEIFERT

Fuzelier [Fuselier, Fusellier, Fusillier, Fuzellier], **Louis** (*b* 1672; *d* Paris, 19 Sept 1752). French dramatist and librettist. He seems to have been well-connected: he was secretary to the Count d'Estampes from 1709 and was twice co-director of the *Mercure de France* (1721–4,

1744–52). He wrote or collaborated on more than 230 stage works, and frequently had performances running concurrently at all the significant theatres in Paris. For instance, during the 12 months from Easter 1725, 15 new works by him (seven wholly his own, eight collaborations) were being given at various Paris theatres, as well as five revivals (two wholly his own, three collaborations).

Though he embraced high culture, Fuzelier was most at home in the informal, unofficial world of the Paris fairs. The bulk of his output consists of vaudevilles, *intermèdes* and operatic parodies written for the fair theatres of St Germain and St Laurent (where he was also probably a stage director). His first known stage work, *Thésée, ou La défaite des Amazones*, was written for the marionettes of Betrand and performed at the Foire St Germain on 11 August 1701. A parody of the Lully–Quinault *Thésée* (1675), it is in three acts, with *intermèdes* for live actors. His second three-act spectacle for Betrand's marionettes, *Le ravissement d'Hélène, ou Le siège et embrasement de Troie*, performed at the Foire St Germain in February 1705, was one of the first to display each character's text upon large placards (*écriteaux*): this was a neat circumvention of the ban on dialogues inflicted on the Théâtres de la Foire by their rivals.

In 1716 Fuzelier began a collaboration with Lesage and Dorneval that lasted 14 years; their best work was collected in the nine-volume *Le Théâtre de la Foire, ou L'opéra-comique*, published between 1721 and 1737. Parodies of operas, tragedies and comedies were among the most popular works in this immense repertory: *Pierrot furieux*, 1717 (parodying Lully's *Roland*); *Arlequin Persée*, 1722 (Lully's *Persée*); *La grand-mère amoureuse*, 1726 (Lully's *Atys*); *Momus exilé*, 1725 (Destouches' *Omphale*) and *Pierrot Tancrède*, 1729 (Campra's *Tancrède*).

At the end of the 1718 season Riccoboni secured the services of Fuzelier for the Comédie-Italienne, where his first unqualified success was *La mode, la meridienne et le may* (21 May 1719). He also wrote several pieces for the Comédie-Française, of which the most popular was the one-act comedy *Momus fabuliste, ou Les noces de Vulcain* (26 September 1719), which was given 63 times. Something of a composer himself, Fuzelier also supplied cantata texts for Campra, Bernier and Courbois; but his most important contributions to French high musical culture are the librettos for 13 works performed at the Opéra. In the *opéras-ballets* of this group he portrayed the regency of Philip of Orleans with a touch of cynicism; they are devoid of sentimentality. *Les âges* (to music by Campra, 1718) gives Fuzelier's view of *opéra-ballet* librettos in its *Avertissement*: 'I have attempted only to weave some playful maxims into a light intrigue which can occasion the use of graceful airs and varied dances. This, it seems to me, should constitute the basis of a ballet [i.e. an *opéra-ballet*]'.

Fuzelier introduced the *ballet héroïque* to the lyric stage via Collin de Blamont's *Les fêtes grecques et romaines* (1723) – a 'completely new type of ballet', according to its preface. But the most important example of the genre is Rameau and Fuzelier's *Les Indes galantes* (1735–6; the two men may well have become acquainted during Rameau's collaboration with Alexis Piron at the Théâtres de la Foire in the 1720s). In the prefaces to his librettos for the Opéra, Fuzelier constantly justified his unusual subject matter and novel stage effects. For his Persian comedy *La reine de Péris* (music by Aubert, 1725) he claimed he consulted works in the 'Oriental Library' of 'M. de Herbelot'; and the earthquake in the second entrée, 'Les Incas du Pérou', of *Les Indes galantes* is supported by references to discussions with 'many esteemed travellers' and with 'the most skilful naturalists'. But he could also make telling use of contemporary writers without drawing attention to so doing: witness the presence of aspects of Louis de la Hontan's *Dialogues curieux entre l'auteur et un sauvage de bon sens* (1703) and of the New World volume of Jean-Frédéric Bernard's *Cérémonies et coutumes religieuses* (1723) in 'Les sauvages', the entrée he added to *Les Indes galantes* in 1736. There they provided a context for Rameau to base a big peace-pipe ensemble on the harpsichord *morceau* he had written a decade before on seeing two native Americans dancing in Paris.

only those performed at the Paris Opéra

Les amours déguisés (opéra-ballet), Bourgeois, 1713; *Arion* (tragédie lyrique), Matho, 1714; *Les âges* (opéra-ballet), Campra, 1718; *Les fêtes grecques et romaines* (ballet héroïque), Collin de Blamont, 1723 (with new entrée, 'La fête de Diane', 1734); *La reine de Péris* (comédie persane), Aubert, 1725; *Les amours des dieux* (ballet héroïque), Mouret, 1727; *Les amours des déesses* (ballet héroïque), J.-B.-M. Quinault, 1729 (with new entrée, 'L'Aurore et Céphale', 1729)

Le caprice d'Érato (divertissement), Collin de Blamont, 1730 (addn to Marais' *Alcyone*); *Les Indes galantes* (ballet héroïque), Rameau, 1735 (with new entrée, 'Les sauvages', 1736); *L'école des amants* (opéra-ballet), Niel, 1744 (with new entrée, 'Les sujets indociles', 1745); *Le carnaval du Parnasse* (ballet héroïque), Mondonville, 1749; *Phaétuse* (fragment), P. Iso, in Les fragments héroïques, 1759; *Apollon, berger d'Admète* (fragment), Grenet, in Les fragments héroïques, 1759

*

ES (G. C. Roscioni) [incl. list of theatre pieces]

Recueil général des opéra, ii, iii (Paris, 1703–46) [incl. Fuzelier's prefaces to operas]

A.-R. Lesage and Dorneval: *Le Théâtre de la Foire, ou L'opéra-comique* (Paris, 1721–37) [incl. 43 pieces by Fuzelier]

Les parodies du nouveau Théâtre italien, ou Recueil de parodies représentées sur le Théâtre de l'Hôtel de Bourgogne (Paris, 1738) [incl. 'Discours à l'occasion d'un discours de M. D.L.M. sur les parodies' by Fuzelier]

F. J. Carmody: *Le répertoire de l'opéra-comique en vaudevilles de 1708 à 1764* (Berkeley, 1933)

D. Trott: 'Louis Fuzelier et le théâtre: vers un état présent', *Revue d'histoire littéraire de la France*, lxxxiii (1983), 604–17

——: 'Pour une histoire des spectacles non-officiels: Louis Fuzelier et le théâtre à Paris en 1725–26', *Revue de la Société d'histoire du théâtre*, xxxvii (1985), 255–75

JAMES R. ANTHONY, ROGER SAVAGE

G

Gabichvadze, Revaz Kondrat'yevich (*b* Tbilisi, 29 May/ 11 June 1913). Georgian composer. He studied at the Tbilisi Conservatory, graduating in 1935, and later taught there. In 1931 he began work as a theatre composer and conductor. Subsequently he was founder-director of the State Light Orchestra (1941–3), a music editor for the radio and (1948–52) secretary to the board of the Georgian Composers' Union. He appeared as a conductor of his own works and contributed articles and reviews to the musical press.

Gabichvadze's work may be divided into two periods: up to the end of the 1950s the works in large forms make extensive use of folk music, are predominantly lyrical and dramatic, and frequently resort to folk and genre episodes. The compositions of the second period are distinguished by a heightening of psychological content and a stylistic renewal involving modern means such as dodecaphony, aleatory writing, electronic music and collage. His first opera, *Nana* (4, Meliva, after A. Arbuzov's *Tanya*), was performed in 1949 at Tbilisi Conservatory and in revised form in 1960 at the Georgian Theatre of Opera and Ballet. His operetta *Strekoza* ('The Dragonfly', after M. Baratashvili's *Merani*) was first performed in Sverdlovsk (now Yekaterinburg) on 31 December 1952. His second opera, *Mi, materi mira* ('We, Mothers of the World'), subtitled *Vosstaniye Niobey* ('The Revolt of Niobe'), was completed in 1966.

K. Ivanov: 'Na estrade kamernaya muzïka' [Chamber Music on Stage], *SovM* (1970), no.9, pp.46–8

YEVGENY MACHAVARIANI

Gabriella di Vergy ('Gabriella of Vergy'). *Tragedia lirica* in two acts by GAETANO DONIZETTI to a libretto by ANDREA LEONE TOTTOLA (first set by Michele Carafa in 1816), composed in 1826, revised (in three acts) about 1838; Naples, Teatro S Carlo, 29 November 1869, in a revision not by Donizetti (1838 version, Belfast, Whitla Hall (Opera Rara), 9 November 1978).

The melodramatic plot derives from Pierre Du Belloy's French tragedy *Gabrielle de Vergy*. Believing her beloved, Raoul, to be dead, Gabriella (soprano) has married Fayel (tenor, 1826; baritone, 1838); but Raoul (alto, 1826; tenor, 1838) turns out to be still alive. Catching the former lovers in a compromising situation, Fayel challenges Raoul to a duel; afterwards Fayel presents Gabriella with an urn containing Raoul's still-

warm heart. She goes mad and dies.

The 1826 *Gabriella* is a landmark in Donizetti's career: he composed this, his first attempt at a tragic ending, for his own purposes, with no performance in view. He later incorporated much of the revision of about 1838 (rediscovered in 1954 in the Stirling Library, University of London) into the score of *Adelia* (1841, Rome).

WILLIAM ASHBROOK

Gabrielli, Caterina (*b* Rome, 12 Nov 1730; *d* Rome, 16 Feb or 16 April 1796). Italian soprano. She was probably a pupil of Porpora in Venice (1744–7) and is said to have made her début at Lucca in 1747 and to have sung in Jommelli's *Didone* at Naples in 1750. After a highly successful concert début at the Burgtheater in Vienna in 1755, she was given a contract there until 1758–9. Metastasio instructed her in the declamatory style and she soon appeared in works by Gluck (*Le cinesi*, *La danza* and *L'innocenza giustificata*, 1755; *Il re pastore*, 1756). In 1758 she was at the Regio Ducal Teatro, Milan; at Padua with the castrato Gaetano Guadagni, one of her most important teachers, she was involved in scandals and had to leave precipitately.

From 1759 Gabrielli often sang in operas by Traetta, creating at Parma the leading roles in his *Ippolito ed Aricia* (1759) and *I tintaridi* (1760). In Vienna, she created the title parts in Gluck's *Tetide* (1760) and Traetta's *Armida* (1761). In Italy again in 1761, she sang in Naples in 1764–5, then retired briefly to live with a young nobleman, but in 1766–7 she again sang in Naples. She then had a three-year engagement at Palermo, and in 1771 was at Milan, where Mozart met her. She was then engaged at St Petersburg (1772–5), probably at Traetta's request, for she again appeared in his operas (*Antigona*, 1772; *Amore e Psiche*, 1773; *Lucio Vero*, 1774). After a season (1775–6) in London, she returned to Italy, singing until 1782 in Naples, Venice, Lucca and Milan. Gabrielli was one of the most eminent and perfect singers of her time. Burney called her 'the most intelligent and best-bred virtuosa' with whom he had ever conversed; to immense technical powers and knowledge she seems to have joined exceptional personal charms. Mozart, however, hearing her after her prime, described her as a 'manufacturer of passage-work and roulades ... who cannot sing' (1778).

Francesca Gabrielli (*b* c1735), probably her sister, often appeared with her as seconda donna.

GERHARD CROLL

321

Gabrielli, Domenico ['Minghin dal violunzel'] (*b* Bologna, 15 April 1651; *d* Bologna, 10 July 1690). Italian composer. A pupil of Franceschini in Bologna and of Legrenzi in Venice, he was admitted to the Accademia Filarmonica in Bologna in 1676 and became its *principe* in 1683; for the academy he composed sacred music and sinfonias. He succeeded Franceschini as cellist at S Petronio in 1681, and from 23 November 1688 until his premature death he served as cellist to the Duke of Modena, who had a high regard for him.

Gabrielli was already acknowledged as a virtuoso cellist and as a composer of vocal music in the 1680s, when he turned to opera; his works were produced in Venice, Bologna, Modena and Turin and were revived elsewhere in Italy. They show an innovatory approach, both in his sensitivity to instrumental colour (notably in arias with instrumental obbligato) and in his tendency to spin out material. In *Flavio Cuniberto* there are no fewer than seven arias with obbligato instruments (theorbo, cello, trumpet and violin); *Maurizio* uses the interesting scoring of theorbo plus violin and has a mandolin obbligato ('Mesti pensieri'). Gabrielli's most expansive aria structures involve changes of tempo and metre (as in 'Prigioniera son io della beltà', with obbligato violin, in *Maurizio*), but his aria forms are varied and include strophic, binary, da capo and ostinato elements. A typical device, also used in *Maurizio*, is the use of contracted forms occasioned by dramatic vocal interjections. Tempos are mostly moderate and melismas brief, limited to intervals of a 2nd or 3rd.

Maurizio, which had a wide circulation (there were revivals in Livorno, Padua and Vicenza in 1691; Rome in 1692, with revisions; Rimini, 1693; and Bologna, 1697), belongs to a type of opera that was popular in the late 17th century in which humorous, even farcical situations arise within the context of a supposedly historical setting. There are no qualms about crudely spectacular effects, such as the appearance of a severed head at the beginning of the opera. The *buffo* character of the servant Leno is typical of the public theatre of the time, while brief appearances of the Sun and Jove seem tailored to a more aristocratic taste. *Carlo il grande* is less unusual in its instrumentation and theatrical effects, and was probably well suited to the more conservative taste of the great Grimani theatre, S Giovanni Grisostomo. Gabrielli's autographs (*I-MOe*) are of particular interest, as they are often related to specific productions and provide evidence of contemporary theatrical practices.

drammi per musica, performed in Venice, unless otherwise stated

Flavio Cuniberto (M. Noris), S Giovanni Grisostomo, 1682, *I-Bc*, *MOe*; doubtful (? by G. D. Partenio)
Il Cleobulo (Neri), Bologna, Aug 1683, lib. (Bologna, 1683)
Il Gige in Lidia (G. B. Neri), Bologna, Formagliari, 1683, *MOe*
Teodora Augusta (A. Morselli), S Salvatore, carn. 1685, lib. (Venice, 1685); rev. Bologna, 1687 [text rev. V. Rapparini, music rev. G. A. Perti], lib. (Bologna, 1687)
Clearco in Negroponte (A. Arcoleo), S Moisè, 1685, *MOe*
Rodoaldo, re d'Italia (dramma da rappresentarsi, T. Stanzani), S Moisè, 1685, *MOe*
Le gare generose tra Cesare e Pompeo (3, R. Cialli), S Salvatore, carn. 1686, *MOe*
Il Maurizio (Morselli), S Salvatore, 26 Dec 1686, lib. (Venice, 1689); rev. Modena, 1689, *MOe*; rev. as Tiberio in Bisanzio, Lucca, 1694
Il Gordiano (Morselli), S Salvatore, 21 Jan 1688, *MOe*
Carlo il grande (Morselli, after L. Ariosto), S Giovanni Grisostomo, Feb 1688, *MOe*

Silvio, re degli Albani (melodramma, P. d'Averara), Turin, 1689, *MOe*

C. Ricci: *I teatri di Bologna* (Bologna, 1888)
M.-T. Bouquet: *Storia del Teatro regio di Torino*, i: *Il teatro di corte dalle origini al 1788* (Turin, 1976)
C. Sartori: 'I recuperi dell'Ufficio ricerche fondi musicali: Domenico Gabrielli, Carlo Pallavicino, Freschi, Legrenzi, Sartorio e Marcantonio Ziani', *NRMI*, xiv (1980), 548–54
H. S. Saunders: *The Repertoire of a Venetian Opera House (1678–1714): the Teatro Grimani di S Giovanni Grisostomo* (diss., Harvard U., 1985)
E. Selfridge-Field: *Pallade veneta: Writings on Music in Venetian Society 1650–1750* (Venice, 1985)
A. Chiarelli: *I codici di musica della raccolta estense: ricostruzione dall'inventario settecentesco* (Florence, 1987)

SERGIO DURANTE

Gabrielli, Count Nicolò [Nicola] (*b* Naples, 21 Feb 1814; *d* Paris, 14 June 1891). Italian composer. His teachers included Carlo Conti and, at the Naples Conservatory, Zingarelli and Donizetti. In about 1835 he began writing for the theatre, and from 1840 to 1854 directed the ballets at the royal theatres in the kingdom of Naples. Summoned by Napoleon III, he lived from 1854 in Paris, where he dedicated himself to composition, writing operas and ballets, some of them for the Opéra. He was successful until the fall of Napoleon III in 1871, after which he stopped composing almost completely. His output included about 20 operas and about 60 ballets.

Fétis acknowledged Gabrielli's gift for dramatic effect, but observed that his ballets, for instance, were written unimaginatively. His melodic lines often have a pleasing dance-like quality, though they are generally weak in substance.

selective list; first performed in Naples unless otherwise stated

I dotti per fanatismo (melodramma buffo, 2), Nuovo, 20 Aug 1835
La lettera perduta (commedia, 1, A. Passaro), Nuovo, 1 Oct 1836
La parola di matrimonio (ob, 1, Passaro), Nuovo, 14 Feb 1837
L'americano in fiera, ossia Farvest Calelas (opera per musica, 2, Passaro), Fondo, 5 Oct 1837
L'affamato senza danaro (farsa, 1), Nuovo, 11 Feb 1839
Il padre della debuttante (commedia buffa, 2, Passaro), Nuovo, 3 Aug 1839
Ester (2), ?1839
La marchesa e il ballerino (farsa, 2), Fondo, 16 Feb 1840
Il bugiardo veritiero (ob, 2, Passaro), Nuovo, 6 Oct 1841
Il condannato di Saragozza (melodramma, 2, Passaro), Nuovo, 2 March 1842
Sara, ovvero La pazza di Scozia (commedia, 2, I. Capecelatro), Palermo, Carolino, 30 March 1843
Il gemello (commedia lirica, 2, A. de Lauzières), Fondo, 21 May 1845
Una passeggiata sul palchetto a vapore (commedia, 1, N. Tauro), Fenice, 9 Nov 1845
Giulia di Tolosa (tragedia lirica, 3, A. Trudi), Fondo, 26 May 1847
Fiorina (melodramma giocoso, 2, A. Salvatore), Nuovo, July 1849 [cited in Manferrari]
Don Grégoire, ou Le précepteur dans l'embarras (oc, 3, T. Sauvage and A. de Leuven, after G. Giraud), Paris, OC (Favart), 17 Dec 1859
Le petit cousin (opérette, H. de Rochefort and C. Deulin), Paris, Bouffes-Parisiens, 17 April 1860
Les mémoires de Fanchette (oc, 1, C.-L.-E. Nuitter and N. Desarbres), Paris, Lyrique, 22 March 1865

FRANCESCO BUSSI (with JOHN BLACK)

Gaburo, Kenneth (Louis) (*b* Somerville, NJ, 5 July 1926). American composer. He studied composition with Bernard Rogers at the Eastman School and with Burrill Phillips at the University of Illinois; he also studied with Goffredo Petrassi at the Accademia di S Cecilia in Rome on a Fulbright scholarship (1954–5).

He has taught at various American universities, and in 1975 founded his own music publishing firm, Lingua Press. Among his many awards are a UNESCO Creative Fellowship (1962), a Guggenheim Fellowship (1967) and a grant from the NEA (1975–6), besides commissions from the Fromm Foundation and the Koussevitzky Foundation. Of Gaburo's two operas designed for the theatre, the first, *The Snow Queen* (3, M. Wilson), was completed in 1952 and staged by the Lake Charles (Louisiana) Little Theater on 5 May. *The Widow* (1, Gaburo, after Herman Melville) received its first performance in Saratoga Springs, New York, on 26 February 1961. His later work has involved the mixture of live, taped and electronically produced sound, often with theatrical elements. Gaburo has explained that his works for the stage have changed from a kind of *verismo* opera (*The Snow Queen*, *The Widow*) through 'music theatre' (*Blur*, 1956, for actors with tape) to stage work (*Lingua*, a four-hour theatre piece in four acts, 1965–9) and to simply 'work' (represented by *Antiphonies VII*, *IX* and *X*, for live musicians and tape, and *The Scratch Project*, a 12-hour theatre work; both 1980–90) 'in which one may only experience a vague sense of place and illusive sign-language'.

In this most recent phase, I have come to embed essential dramaturgy in the implicit fibre of the work, which may not easily be evidenced or explained by its foreground. An observer is asked to question intensely the signs put forth; if, by this invitation, a gradual decoding of those given signs, and a motion to the metaphoric sense-world from which they came can be experienced, the observer will have become an intrinsic part of the work.

JEROME ROSEN

Gabussi [Gabussi-De Bassini], **Rita** (*b* Bologna, *c*1815; *d* Naples, 26 Jan 1891). Italian soprano, sister of Vincenzo Gabussi and wife of ACHILLE DE BASSINI.

Gabussi, Vincenzo (*b* Bologna, 1800; *d* London, 12 Sept 1846). Italian composer. He studied under Stanislao Mattei at the Liceo Musicale in Bologna and became a teacher of singing and the piano. He made his successful début as an opera composer with *I furbi al cimento* (1825, Modena). In the same year he went to London, where he lived for many years, highly regarded as a teacher. His second opera, *Ernani* (1834, Paris), was subjected to spiteful criticism by Bellini, whose *I puritani* followed it at the Théâtre Italien. *Ernani* proved a fiasco, receiving only three performances, and was no threat to Bellini. Also unsuccessful was *Clemenza di Valois* (1841, Venice), which excited its audiences primarily through having caused Rossini to visit Venice. Gabussi's true sphere was that of vocal salon music (his output included more than 30 songs and 100 duets). While amateurish in construction and mediocre in musical and dramatic content, his works reveal a facile and modish melodist.

I furbi al cimento (melodramma comico, 2), Modena, Comunale, 12 Feb 1825
Ernani (dramma serio, 3, G. Rossi, after V. Hugo), Paris, Italien, 25 Nov 1834, excerpts, pf acc. (Paris, n.d.)
Clemenza di Valois (melodramma, 3, Rossi, after E. Scribe: *Gustave III*), Venice, Fenice, 20 Feb 1841, *I-Mr**, vs (Milan, 1841)

GIOVANNI CARLI BALLOLA

Gaci, Pjetër (*b* Shkodër, 27 March 1931). Albanian composer and violinist. He studied at the Jordan Misja college of arts in Tirana (1948–52), and at the Moscow Conservatory, where his teachers were Marina Kazalupova (1952–3) and Abram Il'ich Yampol'sky

(1953–6). Between 1958 and 1967 he was leader of the orchestra at the Opera and Ballet Theatre in Tirana and a violin teacher at Jordan Misja. He then became artistic director at the Tirana Circus, the musical theatre Estrada in Tirana and the Puppet Theatre. Since 1970 he has devoted his time to composition. His first opera, *Përtej mjegullës*('Beyond the Mist'; prol., 3 scenes, S. Kasapi; Tirana, Opera and Ballet Theatre, 27 May 1971), which deals with the struggle against the ancient custom of vendetta in northern Albania, has been praised for its fluent vocal writing and the captivating melodic language of its arias and choruses. Gaci developed these qualities further in *Toka jonë* ('Our Land'; 3, K. Jakova and N. Luca, after Jakova's drama of 1954; Tirana, Opera and Ballet Theatre, 6 June 1981).

S. Kalemi: *Arritjet e artit tonë muzikor: vepra dhe krijues të muzikës Shqiptare* [Achievements of our Musical Art: Creations and Creators of Albanian Music] (Tirana, 1982), 144–7

GEORGE LEOTSAKOS

Gaddes, Richard (*b* Wallsend, nr Newcastle upon Tyne, 23 May 1942). American opera administrator of English birth. He studied at Trinity College of Music, London. He worked in artists' management in London, 1965–9, then emigrated to the USA, where he became artistic administrator of the Santa Fe Opera (until 1978). He founded the Opera Theatre of St Louis in 1975 and served as its general director until 1985. The company mounted productions of *Albert Herring* for WNET and BBC television (1978) and, as part of a six-year Mozart cycle, *Così fan tutte* directed by Jonathan Miller (1982); it also became the first American company to perform at the Edinburgh Festival (1983, with Stephen Paulus's *The Postman Always Rings Twice*). Gaddes has served on the boards of directors of the William Matheus Sullivan Foundation and Opera America. He is a judge for the Metropolitan Opera national auditions and artistic adviser of the Lyric Opera of Boston.

FRANK MERKLING

Gadski, Johanna (*b* Anklam, Prussia, 15 June 1872; *d* Berlin, 22 Feb 1932). German soprano. She studied in Stettin, and made an early début (1889) at the Kroll Opera, Berlin, singing there and elsewhere in Germany for the next five years. In 1895 she began a successful three-year association with the Damrosch Opera Company in the USA, and from 1899 to 1901 was active at Covent Garden and at Bayreuth. Between 1900 and 1917, however, her main centre was the Metropolitan, with whose company (after a previous appearance as Elisabeth in *Tannhäuser* on tour in Philadelphia, on 28 Dec 1899) she made her house début on 6 January 1900 as Senta; she became one of its most valuable Brünnhildes and Isoldes, excelling also in many Verdi roles such as Aida, Leonora (*Il trovatore*) and Amelia. After the USA's declaration of war on Germany, her reputation suffered during the war hysteria of that time. From 1929 until her death (in a car accident) she was active and successful in a Wagnerian touring company in the USA organized at first by Sol Hurok and then by herself. She sang even the heaviest Wagner roles with unfailing beauty of voice and purity of style, and showed the same qualities in her Italian parts. Her powers are well documented in the large number of records which she made between 1903 and 1917.

N. Ridley and L. Migliorini: 'Johanna Gadski', *Record Collector*, xi (1957), 197–231 [with discography], 257–85; xii (1958–60), 36

DESMOND SHAWE-TAYLOR

Gadzhibekov, Uzeir (Abdul Huseyn). *See* HAJIBEYOV, UZEIR.

Gadzhiyev, Dzhevdet. *See* HAJIYEV, JEVDET.

Gaetano [Majer; Kajetan] (*b* Warsaw, 1st half of the 18th century; *d* Warsaw, 1793 or later). Polish composer. He played the violin in the royal orchestra at Warsaw from 1764 and was conductor from 1779 to 1793. He composed and contributed to a number of operas given in Warsaw between about 1779 and 1788. His music in the opera *Żółta szlafmyca* is notable for its use of Polish folk music elements.

all performed in Warsaw

Nie każdy śpi, co chrapi [Not All Sleep who Snore] (int, L. Pierożyński), 1779, lib. (Kraków, 1790)

Bazyli [Basil], 12 Feb 1782 [sequel to Nie każdy śpi]

Żółta szlafmyca, albo Kolęda na Nowy Rok [The Yellow Nightcap, or A Carol for the New Year] (3, F. Zabłocki, after P. Barre and A. de Piis: *Les étrennes de Mercure*), 1 May 1783, lib. (Warsaw, 1783), inc. MS (private collection); incipits in J. Prosnak, *Kultura muzyczna Warszawy XVIII wieku* [Music in Warsaw in the 18th Century] (Kraków, 1955)

Żołnierz czarnoksiężnik, czyli Uczta diabelska [The Soldier-Conjuror, or The Devilish Banquet] (2, Pierożyński, after L. Anseaume), 11 March 1787

Diabla wrzawa, czyli Dwoista przemiana [The Devil's Uproar, or Double Transformation] (3, J. Baudouin, after M.-J. Sedaine), 18 Nov 1787

Les amours de Bastien et Bastienne (int, C.-S. Favart), 7 Sept 1788

Music in: Le couronnement de Roxolane, 1783; Natura mistrzynią [Nature is the Mistress], 1786

*

Z. Raszewski: 'Teatr Narodowy w latach 1779–89', *Teatr Narodowy w dobie Oświecenia* [The National Theatre in the Age of Enlightenment] (Wrocław, 1967)

ALINA NOWAK-ROMANOWICZ

Gaffarello. *See* CAFFARELLI.

Gafforini, Elisabetta (*b* Milan *c*1772; *d* after 1810). Italian mezzo-soprano. She began her career in Venice, where she sang in the premières of *Il cinese in Italia* and *La secchia rapita* by Francesco Bianchi and *La principessa filosofa* by Andreozzi. At La Scala (1802–10) she was admired in the premières of Valentino Fioravanti's *La capricciosa pentita* (1802), Mosca's *L'italiana in Algeri* (1808) and Pavesi's *Ser Marcantonio* (1810). She also sang in operas by Orlandi. She was the leading comic prima donna of her day; her voice and her stage bearing were praised by Stendhal in his volume on Haydn and Metastasio.

DAVID CUMMINGS

Gaggiotti [Gagiotti, Gajotti], **Pellegrino** (*b* Bologna, *fl* 1714–58). Italian tenor. Although he began by singing in *opera seria* (Carasso in an anonymous *Radamisto*, 1714, Modena), he became a leading performer of *opera buffa* in the first half of the 18th century. From 1721 he was a member of the Accademia Filarmonica of Bologna. He sang in G. M. Buini's *Amor non vuol rispetti* in 1724, performed in intermezzos throughout central and northern Italy in company with Anna Maria Faini, Santa Marchesini and others, and from 1737 to 1739 sang with Pietro Mingotti's company at Graz. From 1743 he enlarged his repertory with new *commedie per musica* from Rome, Florence and Naples which he learnt in Venice working with a company of singers that included Filippo Laschi, Anna Querzoli, Grazia Mellini and Maria Paganini. In 1745 he toured with Mellini, Paolo Scalabrini and the Mingotti brothers to Hamburg and Copenhagen, where he was appointed *virtuoso di camera* (1750) to the court and continued to perform in intermezzos until 1758.

*

E. H. Müller: *Angelo und Pietro Mingotti* (Dresden, 1917)
C. E. Troy: *The Comic Intermezzo* (Ann Arbor, 1979)
F. Piperno: 'Buffe e buffi', *RIM*, xviii (1982), 240–84

FRANCO PIPERNO

Gagliano, Marco da (*b* Florence, 1 May 1582; *d* Florence, 25 Feb 1643). Italian composer. He wrote music for court entertainments and religious ceremonies for Medici and Gonzaga patrons, and was among the youngest of the Florentine innovators in the new monodic and representational styles.

A pupil of Luca Bati (*maestro di cappella* at S Lorenzo as well as at Florence Cathedral), Gagliano became Bati's assistant at S Lorenzo in 1602 and his successor at the cathedral in 1608. In 1607 he founded a formal musical academy in Florence, the Accademia degli Elevati, a group of composers, performers and literati that included Jacopo Peri, Giovanni de' Bardi, Ottavio Rinuccini and others; Giulio Caccini may also have been associated with the group, whose patron was Cardinal Ferdinando Gonzaga. The academy flourished at least until 1609 when, according to a letter from Rinuccini to the cardinal in August, internal strife threatened to destroy it. Although the group may have survived this crisis, Gagliano referred to the Elevati and used his academic name 'L'Affannato' ('The Breathless One') on the title-pages of both his 1608 publications and not thereafter.

By 1609 Gagliano's reputation was such that he was given the title *maestro di cappella* at the Medici court. From that time until his death he was involved, as a composer, performer (singing and playing the theorbo and keyboard instruments) and director, in all kinds of musical productions, from lavish occasional spectacles and private entertainments at court – ballets, *intermedi*, operas, oratorios, tournaments, masques, processions, madrigals – to masses, motets and other liturgical works (mostly unpublished) associated with the various religious establishments of Medici Florence (chronicled in Cesare Tinghi's court diary; excerpts in Solerti 1905). Having received holy orders, Gagliano joined the canons of S Lorenzo in 1610 and was elevated to 'protonotary apostolic' in 1615. There is no evidence that he left Florence except to participate in the carnival and wedding festivities in Mantua in spring 1608.

Gagliano's correspondence with the Mantuan court (letters in Vogel 1889, pp.550ff), which began in July 1607, culminated in a six-month sojourn in Mantua, where his setting of Rinuccini's newly revised *Dafne* (originally composed by Peri and Jacopo Corsi and produced in Florence a decade earlier) was performed in January 1608. In a prologue and six scenes, the work is based on Ovid's fable: Daphne (soprano) undergoes metamorphosis into a laurel tree as she flees the amorous god Apollo (tenor). Stylistically *Dafne* adheres to the original Florentine model of courtly pastoral opera, and especially to Peri's conception of recitative. However, Gagliano's continued cultivation of polyphonic genres (he published six books of madrigals between 1602 and 1617), and perhaps his experience as a church organist as well, result in a score that differs from Peri's in its greater control of large-scale harmonic organization.

Other works by Gagliano which qualify as operas by virtue of their poetic coherence and musical continuity are all on texts by Andrea Salvadori: *Lo sposalizio di Medoro et Angelica* and *La Flora* (both in collaboration with Peri), and two dramas on sacred subjects, *La regina Sant'Orsola* and *La istoria di Iudit*. All were performed at the Florentine court; *La Flora* was designed by Alfonso Parigi (*see* FLORENCE, fig.1), *La regina Sant'Orsola* by Giulio Parigi (*see* PRODUCTION, fig.3). The only one to survive with music is *La Flora*, a mythological work in a prologue and five acts that celebrates the nuptials of Margherita de' Medici and Odoardo Farnese, Duke of Parma and Piacenza. Despite its slight subject (the love of Flora and Zephyr, whose tears of joy result in the birth of flowers), it is considerably longer than *Dafne* and reveals Gagliano's predilection for dance choruses, which function here as *intermedi*. The work is also noteworthy for its early introduction into opera of *buffo* elements, in the comic character of Pan.

See also DAFNE.

La Dafne (prol., 6 scenes, O. Rinuccini, after Ovid), Mantua, Feb 1608, collab. F. Gonzaga (Florence, 1608); ed. J. Erber (London, 1978)
Lo sposalizio di Medoro et Angelica (A. Salvadori, after L. Ariosto), Florence, Palazzo Pitti, 25 Sept 1619, collab. J. Peri; rev. as Il Medoro, 1623
La regina Sant'Orsola (sacred drama, Salvadori), Florence, Uffizi, 6 Oct 1624
La istoria di Iudit (sacred drama, Salvadori), Florence, 1626
La Flora, o vero Il natal de' fiori (prol., 5, Salvadori), Florence, Palazzo Pitti, 14 Oct 1628 (Florence, 1628) [role of Chloris by Peri]

*

E. Vogel: 'Marco da Gagliano: zur Geschichte des Florentiner Musiklebens von 1570–1650', *VMw*, v (1889), 396–442, 509–68
A. Solerti: *Musica, ballo e drammatica alla corte medicea dal 1600 al 1637* (Florence, 1905)
A. M. Nagler: *Theatre Festivals of the Medici, 1539–1637* (New Haven, CT, 1964), 118, 131ff, 139ff, 177ff; pls.99–100, 102–7, 110, 113–18
A. T. Cortellazzo: 'Il melodramma di Marco da Gagliano', *Congresso internazionale sul tema Claudio Monteverdi e il suo tempo: Venice, Mantua and Cremona 1968*, 583–98
F. W. Sternfeld: 'The First Printed Opera Libretto', *ML*, lix (1978), 121–38
B. R. Hanning: 'Glorious Apollo: Poetic and Political Themes in the First Opera', *Renaissance Quarterly*, xxxii (1979), 485–513
——: *Of Poetry and Music's Power: Humanism and the Creation of Opera* (Ann Arbor, 1980)
BARBARA R. HANNING

Gail [née Garre], **(Edmée) Sophie** (*b* Paris, 28 Aug 1775; *d* Paris, 24 July 1819). French composer. Her first songs appeared from 1790 in song magazines. At the age of 18 she married the philologist Jean Baptiste Gail; they separated some years later. She then studied singing with Mengozzi, touring successfully in southern France and Spain, and theory with Fétis and, later, F.-L. Perne and Neukomm. She wrote a number of songs and *romances* and five one-act operas. The first, *Les deux jaloux* (27 March 1813), was the most successful. *La sérénade*, the last, contains accomplished music, but its libretto, adapted by Sophie Gay from a comedy by Regnard, was considered scandalous even 50 years later by Félix Clément and Pierre Larousse (*Dictionnaire lyrique*, 1867–9), though they devoted much space to it. Gail sang in London in 1816, and in 1818 toured Germany and Austria with Angelica Catalani. She died prematurely of a chest ailment. She enjoyed a high reputation as both singer and accompanist, and her songs, which cultivate a vein of plaintive, amorous sentiment fashionable in post-Revolutionary France, are original and carefully wrought.

all performed at Paris, Opéra-Comique (Théâtre Feydeau)
Les deux jaloux (oc, 1, C. R. Dufresny and J. B. C. Vial), 27 March 1813
Mademoiselle de Launay à la Bastille (oc, 1, C. de Lesser, R. Villiers and Mme Villiers), 16 Dec 1813
Angéla, ou L'atelier de Jean Cousin (oc, 1, C. Montcloux d'Epinay), 11 June 1814, *F-Pn*, collab. Boieldieu
La méprise (oc, 1, De Lesser), 20 Sept 1814
La sérénade (oc, 1, S. Gay, after J.-F. Regnard), 16 Sept 1818
PHILIP ROBINSON

Gailhard, André(-Charles-Samson) (*b* Paris, 29 June 1885; *d* Paris, 3 July 1966). French composer, son of Pierre Gailhard. A pupil of Massenet and Leroux at the Paris Conservatoire (1905–8), he won the Prix de Rome in 1908 with his cantata *La sirène*. He composed mostly dramatic works, including operas, a ballet-pantomime and an oratorio. Several of these were to texts by Maurice Magre; Gailhard also wrote incidental music to Magre's play *Les deux belles de Cadix* (1923). Throughout his life he remained close to the Conservatoire tradition of his student days, although both *Amaryllis* and *Le sortilège* strongly show the influence of Debussy in their harmonic language and text-setting.

Amaryllis (conte mythologique, 1, Edouard Adenis and Eugène Adenis), Toulouse, Capitole, 25 Jan 1906
La fille du soleil (tragédie lyrique, 3, M. Magre), Béziers, Aréna, 29 Aug 1909 (Paris, 1909)
Le sortilège (conte de fées, 3, Magre), Paris, Opéra, 29 Jan 1913
La bataille (comédie lyrique, 3, C. Farrère), Paris, Gaîté-Lyrique, 1 June 1931
Arlequin (comédie féerique), Paris, 1934

*

ES (E. Haraszti); *StiegerO*   ANNE GIRARDOT, JOHN WAGSTAFF

Gailhard, Pierre [Pedro] (*b* Toulouse, 1 Aug 1848; *d* Paris, 12 Oct 1918). French bass and opera director. He studied in Toulouse and at the Paris Conservatoire. In 1867 he made his début at the Opéra-Comique as Falstaff in Thomas' *Le songe d'une nuit d'été* and in 1871 he was engaged at the Opéra, where he created Richard in Mermet's *Jeanne d'Arc* (1876), Simon in Joncières' *La reine Berthe* (1878) and Guido in Thomas' *Françoise de Rimini* (1882). He appeared regularly at Covent Garden from 1879 to 1883, his roles there including Osmin, Girot (*Le pré aux clercs*) and Gounod's Méphistophélès. His voice was warm and vibrant but also powerful (he was said to be unequalled in vehemence as Saint-Bris in the scene of the Benediction of the Swords in *Les Huguenots*), yet he also had the necessary light touch for comic opera. From 1884 to 1907 he was director of the Opéra, at first jointly, then (from 1899) alone (*see* PARIS, §5(ii)); his regime was distinguished for its Wagner productions. In 1886 he was appointed Chevalier of the Légion d'honneur.

*

ES (E. Haraszti)   HAROLD ROSENTHAL/R

Gaîté. Theatre in Paris, founded in the late 18th century. It became in 1807 one of the four official secondary theatres; it was demolished in 1862 and rebuilt, later becoming prominent under Offenbach. *See* PARIS, §§ 4(vii) and 5(iv).

Gaito, Constantino (*b* Buenos Aires, 3 Aug 1878; *d* Buenos Aires, 14 Dec 1945). Argentine composer and conductor. Born into a musical family, he showed precocious signs of musical ability and was awarded a grant from the Argentine government to study abroad. He attended the S Pietro a Majella Conservatory in Naples, where he studied composition (with Pietro Platania) and the piano, and travelled in Europe, meeting Verdi, Mascagni and Massenet. In 1900 Gaito returned to Buenos Aires, where he co-founded a conservatory and taught at the Conservatorio Nacional de Música. He conducted opera seasons at the Teatro Argentino at La Plata and served for a short time on the board of directors of the Teatro Colón.

Gaito is considered one of Argentina's foremost opera composers; he is also known for, among other works, his ballets and incidental music. His early operas reveal Italian influences, which were a logical product of his background and training. His later works rely on music of a distinctly Argentine character presented within the framework of Italian operatic aesthetics. His opera *Lázaro* (1929) achieves a sense of realism through the incorporation of Argentine folk genres; it is believed to be the first national opera to include a tango. *La sangre de las guitarras* (1932) is one of the most successful and frequently performed works of the Argentine lyric stage. Its central character is a *payador*, a gaucho-singer, who struggles to uphold the ideals of liberty during the Argentine civil war period.

performed in Buenos Aires unless otherwise stated; microfilm copies at US-Wc unless otherwise stated

I Doria (drama lírico, 3, R. Crucinio), La Plata, Argentino, 1902
Shafras (drama lírico, 1, F. Scubla), Politeama, 29 Oct 1907
Caio Petronio, 1911–14 (3, H. Romanelli), Colón, 2 Sept 1919, ARG-BAc*
I paggi di sua Maestà, c1920 (comedia lírica, 1, G. Colelli), unperf., withdrawn, not in US-Wc
Fior di neve (drama lírico, 1, Colelli), Colón, 3 Aug 1922
Ollantay (drama lírico, 3, V. Mercante, after Quechua legend), Colón, 23 July 1926, ARG-BAc
Lázaro (drama lírico, 1, Mercante), Colón, 19 Nov 1929, BAc*
La sangre de las guitarras (drama lírico, 3, V. G. Retta and C. M. Viale, after H. Blomberg), Colón, 17 Aug 1932

*

M. García Acevedo: *La música argentina contemporánea* (Buenos Aires, 1963)
M. Kuss: *Nativistic Strains in Argentine Operas Premiered at the Teatro Colón (1908–1972)* (diss., UCLA, 1976)
R. García Morillo: *Estudios sobre música argentina* (Buenos Aires, 1984)
DEBORAH SCHWARTZ

Gajotti, Pellegrino. *See* GAGGIOTTI, PELLEGRINO.

Gál [Gal], Hans (*b* Brunn, nr Vienna, 5 Aug 1890; *d* Edinburgh, 3 Oct 1987). Austrian composer and musicologist. He lectured at Vienna University, 1919–29, and was then director of the conservatory at Mainz until 1933 and lecturer at Edinburgh University, 1945–65. One of the most gifted disciples of Brahms's friend Eusebius Mandyczewski and of Guido Adler, he grew up under the spell of the Mahler regime at the Vienna Hofoper. He was a prolific composer in a conservative but vital post-Brahms, post-Strauss idiom. Stringently self-critical (among his juvenilia were four Singspiels and a comedy, *Der Fächer*, based on Goldoni, all later destroyed), Gál became the mature composer of four operas, four symphonies, several concertos and much vocal, choral, chamber and piano music. As he was of Jewish descent, his very successful operatic career in Germany ended when the Nazis came to power in 1933. It did not resume in his years of exile after 1938.

Gál's operatic world contains elements of exotic comedy, ironic social commentary, compassion, erotic lyricism, religious awe and fairy-tale. The success at Breslau in 1919 of the comedy *Der Arzt der Sobeide* (set in the *Thousand and One Nights* atmosphere of 16th-century Seville) was followed by a 12-year collaboration with the Viennese dramatist Karl Michael von Levetzow (1872–1945). The planned 1933 Dresden and Hamburg and 1938 Vienna Volksoper premières of their last work, *Die beiden Klaas* (or *Rich Claus and Poor Claus*), a comic and ironic story of poverty outwitting riches, were all stopped by the Nazis. This Singspiel waited 57 years, until May 1990, for its first production, by York Opera in England.

Two earlier Gál-Levetzow collaborations are overdue for revival. *Das Lied der Nacht* is a 'dramatic ballad' set in 12th-century Sicily, with a plot similar to that of *Turandot* but with a surprising denouement. It played in Düsseldorf, Königsberg and Graz after its successful Breslau première in 1926. Better still, however, is *Die heilige Ente*, first given under George Szell in Düsseldorf in April 1923; it not only entered the repertory of many German theatres before 1933 but was also in 1929 the first contemporary opera broadcast by Radio Vienna. This ironic Chinese fable, in which at the whim of the gods a Mandarin finds both wisdom and love, shows melodic power and distinction in the soprano-tenor duets for Princess Li and Kuli Yang, as well as a voluptuous and virtuoso choral and orchestral texture.

Der Arzt der Sobeide op.4 (komische Oper, prol., 2, F. Zoref), Breslau, 1919
Die heilige Ente op.15 (3, K. M. von Levetzow and L. Feld), Düsseldorf, 29 April 1923
Das Lied der Nacht op.23 (dramatische Ballade, 3, Levetzow), Breslau, 24 April 1926
Die beiden Klaas op.42, 1933 (Spl, 3, Levetzow); as Rich Claus and Poor Claus (trans. A. Fox), York, Rowntree, 22 May 1990

*

W. Waldstein: *Hans Gál* (Vienna, 1965)
NEIL MACKAY

Galambos, Benjámin. *See* EGRESSY, BÉNI.

Galán, Cristóbal (*b* ?1630; *d* Madrid, ?24 Sept 1684). Spanish composer. One of the most popular Spanish songwriters of the 17th century – over 100 songs, mostly secular *tonos* and *villancicos*, have survived – Galán was also probably one of the leading composers of spectacular music dramas (zarzuelas) for the court. For some 20 years (c1659–80) he was *maestro de capilla* at the Convent of the Descalzas Reales in Madrid but he clearly set his sights on an appointment as *maestro* at the royal chapel; this move was blocked for some five years until 1680.

Galán's extant songs reveal a talent for catchy tunes and ariosos that owe something to italianate opera as well as to Spanish popular fashion. Behind the deceptive simplicity of the music and text of many of them lie lively sentiments of joie de vivre, wit and sensuality which show more regard for fashionable operatic zarzuela than for 'tasteful' tradition. Fragments of two of his 'fiestas de la zarzuela' have survived (in *E-Mn*): *El labyrinto de Creta* (before 1667, Madrid) and *Lides de amor y desdén* (before 1670, Madrid), with texts by J. B. Diamante.

*

E. Cotarelo y Mori: 'Don Juan Bautista Diamante y sus comedias', *Boletín de la Real Academia*, iii (1916), 272–97, 454–97
M. Agulló y Cobo: 'Documentos para las biografías de músicos de los siglos XVI y XVII', *AnM*, xxiv (1969), 205–25
JACK SAGE

Galatea [*La Galatea*]. *Dramma in musica* in a prologue and three acts by LORETO VITTORI to his own libretto; Naples, Palace of Prince Cariati, February 1644.

In the prologue Nettuno [Neptune] (bass) explains the story. The lovers Aci [Acis] (tenor) and Galatea (soprano) are threatened by the cyclops Polifemo [Polyphemus] (bass), also in love with Galatea. Venere [Venus] (soprano) tells Amore [Cupid] (soprano) to extinguish Polyphemus's passion, but Cupid takes his part and, disguised as Eco [Echo], makes Galatea suspicious of Acis's fidelity. Prompted by the cyclops, the nymph Clori [Chloris] (soprano), whose love has been spurned by Lucindo (soprano), tells Galatea that Acis is unfaithful to her; Galatea accuses Acis, who after a long lament falls unconscious on the shore and is killed by Polyphemus. Galatea, reassured by Venus of Acis's love, bewails his death, accompanied by the chorus, and Giove [Jupiter] (bass) restores him to life transformed into a river. Nymphs, tritons and satyrs join the protagonists in a celebratory chorus.

The opera derives from the Florentine pastoral tradition; recitative, particularly expressive in Galatea's lament, constitutes the most substantial element of the work and passes naturally into *mezz'aria* at moments of great dramatic intensity. Almost every scene contains a closed piece, whether choral or solo, as a light strophic song or in strophic variations. Long choral passages interspersed with solos occur at the end of each act; the chorus of nymphs and satyrs closing Act 2 'may be danced and sung in the Spanish manner'. The 1655 version of the text, dedicated to Cardinal Flavio Chigi, allows for the insertion of some strophes in praise of the Chigi family as well as for some modifications to characters and to the Act 2 finale.

BIANCA MARIA ANTOLINI

Galbán, Ventura. *See* GALVÁN, VENTURA.

Galbert de Campistron, Jean. *See* CAMPISTRON, JEAN GALBERT DE.

Gale, Elizabeth (*b* Sheffield, 8 Nov 1948). English soprano. She studied at the GSM and made her début in 1970 with the English Opera Group as Cupid in *King Arthur*, followed by Flora (*Turn of the Screw*) at the Aldeburgh Festival. After Papagena at Glyndebourne in 1973 she returned there each year until 1986; her roles included Susanna, Zerlina, Drusilla, Titania and Marzelline, which she also sang at Paris (1982) and the Vienna Staatsoper. Her Covent Garden début in 1974 as Jano (*Jenůfa*) led to other roles including Zerlina (which she also sang at Geneva that year), Adele (*Fledermaus*) and Miss Wordsworth (*Albert Herring*). She has sung with the ENO and all the British regional companies, and made her American début at San Diego in 1986 in *La voix humaine*. Her bright, flexible lyric soprano and beguiling personality have led to several video recordings, and her audio recordings include Zerlina under Haitink with the Glyndebourne company (1984).

NOËL GOODWIN

Galeffi, Carlo (*b* Malamocco, Venice, 4 June 1882; *d* Rome, 22 Sept 1961). Italian baritone. A pupil of G. Di Cuomo and E. Sbriscia, he finished his studies with Antonio Cotogni in Rome. He made his début there at the Teatro Adriano in 1904 in *Lucia*. His first great successes were at the S Carlo, Naples, in *Aida* and *Rigoletto* (1909) and he then appeared in Lisbon,

Buenos Aires, Boston and at the Metropolitan. His La Scala début was in 1912 in *Don Carlos*; he sang there for 17 seasons (the last time in 1938). He was also engaged at Chicago (1919–21) and returned to Buenos Aires where he stayed until 1952. Galeffi had a full, smooth voice of extensive range, remarkable for its affecting and moving warmth. His passionate phrasing and dramatically eloquent enunciation made him a first-rate Rigoletto and a fine Verdi interpreter generally (*Nabucco, Traviata, Ballo, Trovatore, Don Carlos*). Other important roles included Tonio and Rossini's Figaro. He took part in the first performances of Mascagni's *Isabeau* (1911) and *Parisina* (1913), Montemezzi's *L'amore dei tre re* (1913) and Boito's *Nerone* (1924).

GV (R. Celletti; R. Vegeto)
A. Marchetti: *Carlo Galeffi: una vita per il canto* (Rome, 1973) [with discography]
R. Celletti: *Carlo Galeffi e La Scala* (Milan, 1977) [with discography]
RODOLFO CELLETTI

Galerati, Caterina (*b* Venice; *fl* 1701–21). Italian soprano. She sang in Florence in 1701–2, Venice in 1703, Naples in 1705–6 and 1710–11 (seven operas, including Porpora's *Flavio Anicio Olibrio*), Vienna in 1709, Genoa in 1712 and Milan in 1718. In 1714–15 she appeared frequently in London, mostly in pasticcios and revivals, playing Goffredo in Handel's *Rinaldo* and possibly replacing Anastasia Robinson as Oriana in his *Amadigi di Gaula*. She was a member of the first Royal Academy for two seasons from 1720, singing in Porta's *Numitore*, Handel's *Radamisto* (first as Tigrane, then as Fraarte), G. Bononcini's *Astarto*, the composite *Muzio Scevola* and two pasticcios. She specialized in male roles; the 12 parts she is known to have sung in London did not include a single woman. Her compass as Tigrane was e' to a''.

WINTON DEAN

Gall, Jeffrey (*b* Cleveland, OH, 19 Sept 1950). American countertenor. He studied with Arthur Burrows and at the Yale School of Music with Blake Stern. He began his career in the early music ensembles Waverly Consort and Pomerium Musices. In 1979 he made his operatic début in *Erismena* at the Brooklyn Academy of Music. He has subsequently sung roles by Britten, Antonio Cesti, Peter Maxwell Davies, Handel, Harbison, Jommelli, Lully, Monteverdi, Mozart, Pergolesi, Purcell, Alessandro Scarlatti, Tippett and Vivaldi. Appearances throughout Europe and the USA preceded his début at the Metropolitan Opera in 1988 as Ptolemy in Handel's *Giulio Cesare*; he was the first countertenor to sing a substantial role there. Other Handel roles include Polinesso and Flavio, which he has recorded.

CORI ELLISON

Gall, Yvonne (*b* Paris, 6 March 1885; *d* Paris, 21 Aug 1972). French soprano. She studied at the Paris Conservatoire and in 1908 was engaged by Messager at the Opéra as Woglinde in the first production there of *Götterdämmerung*. Keeping the French lyric roles such as Marguerite, Manon and Thaïs at the centre of her career, she developed a powerful voice and added more dramatic parts such as Elsa and, in 1923, Isolde to her repertory. At Monte Carlo she sang in the premières of operas by Raoul Gunsbourg, the impresario of the house: *Le vieil aigle* (1909), *Le cantique des cantiques* (1922) and *Lysistrata* (1923). Abroad, she appeared with success in Buenos Aires and in Chicago, where she sang in the first American performance of *L'heure espagnole*. Tosca was the part in which she appeared at La Scala and in her only performances at Covent Garden (1924); Ernest Newman remarked that she presented 'three capable Toscas, a different one in each act'. Her bright, very French soprano is heard in many recordings, notably in one of the first complete operas on record, Gounod's *Roméo et Juliette* (1912).

J. B. STEANE

Gallet, Louis (Marie Alexandre) (*b* Valence, 14 Feb 1835; *d* Paris, 16 Oct 1898). French writer and librettist. For a while he taught in Valence Cathedral choir school, then worked for a printer, writing in his spare time and launching a literary journal. In 1857 he moved to Paris, where his career was in the Assistance Publique, and published treatises on hospital administration. His continuing literary interests are reflected in a long list of novels, memoirs and many librettos, several of which he prepared in collaboration, as was customary at the time. According to his own report it was winning a Ministère des Beaux-Arts competition with the libretto for *La coupe du roi de Thulé*, written in collaboration with Edouard Blau, that persuaded him to devote his talents to the musical theatre. The text was set to music by Eugène-Emile Diaz de la Peña (1873); Bizet started on a setting, and Massenet also composed a version of it. Gallet worked with major composers – Gounod and Massenet – as well as with a good many lesser ones. He was above all associated with Bizet (*Djamileh*, 1872) until the latter's death and then with Saint-Saëns, who set several of his librettos; Saint-Saëns also composed incidental music for his play *Déjanire* (1898) and later made it into an opera (1911). Reminiscences of Bizet, Victor Massé and other composers are found in Gallet's *Notes d'un librettiste* (published with a preface by L. Halévy, Paris, 1891), which, however, contains little that is of more than anecdotal value.

La coupe du roi de Thulé (with E. Blau), Massenet, *c*1866, inc. (Bizet, 1868, inc.; Diaz de la Peña, 1873); *Le Kobold* (with C.-L.-E. Nuitter), Guiraud, 1870; *Djamileh*, Bizet, 1872; *La princesse jaune*, Saint-Saëns, 1872; *Don Rodrigue* (with Blau), Bizet, 1873, inc.; *Beppo*, Conte, 1874, *L'adorable Bel-Boul'*, Massenet, 1874; *La clé d'or* (with O. Feuillet), Gautier, 1877; *Cinq Mars* (with P. Poirson), Gounod, 1877; *Maître Pierre*, Gounod, 1877, inc.; *Le roi de Lahore*, Massenet, 1877; *Etienne Marcel*, Saint-Saëns, 1879; *La fée* (with Feuillet), Hémery, 1880
Le chevalier Jean (with Blau), Joncières, 1885; *Le Cid* (with Blau and A. P. d'Ennery), Massenet, 1885; *La belle au bois dormant*, Cahen, 1886; *Patrie!* (with V. Sardou), Paladilhe, 1886; *Michel Colomb* (with E. Bonnemère), Bourgault-Ducoudray, 1887; *Proserpine*, Saint-Saëns, 1887; *Atala*, Mme de Grandval, 1888; *Esclarmonde* (with L. de Gramont), Massenet, 1889; *Le vénitien*, Cahen, 1890; *Ascanio*, Saint-Saëns, 1890; *Thamara*, Bourgault-Ducoudray, 1891; *Le rêve*, Bruneau, 1891; *Stratonice*, Fournier, 1892; *L'attaque du moulin*, Bruneau, 1893
Thaïs, Massenet, 1894; *Xavière*, Dubois, 1895; *Frédégonde*, Guiraud and Saint-Saëns; 1895; *Photis*, Audran, 1896; *La femme de Claude*, Cahen, 1896; *La Drac*, Hillemacher, 1896; *Moïna*, de Lara, 1897; *Le spahi* (with A. Alexandre), Lambert, 1897; *Jahel* (with S. Arnaud), Coquard, 1900; *Lancelot* (with Blau), Joncières, 1900; *Les guelfes*, Godard, 1902; *Titania* (with A. Corneau), Hüe, 1903; *Déjanire* (adapted by Saint-Saëns), Saint-Saëns, 1911; *Ping-Sin*, Maréchal, 1918   CHRISTOPHER SMITH

Galli, Amintore (*b* Talamello, Rimini, 12 Oct 1845; *d* Rimini, 13 [or ?8] Dec 1919). Italian composer. He studied at the Milan Conservatory, 1862–7, joining Garibaldi during the 1866 war against Austria, along with his fellow-students Marco Praga, Faccio and Boito. In Carnival 1864–5 his *Cesare al Rubicone*, a *gran scena ed aria*, was successfully performed in Rimini, and on graduating he won the composition prize for his secular oratorio to his own text after Moore's *Lalla Rookh*. He then conducted the band in Amelia, Umbria, and was director of the music school in Finale, Emilia, 1871–3. He returned to Milan as music critic of *Il secolo*, published by Sonzogno. He took charge of Sonzogno's music publishing, arranging vocal scores, translating French librettos and replacing spoken dialogue with recitative. He was responsible for a series of cheap editions and took part in Sonzogno's opera competitions (which led to *Cavalleria rusticana* among others works). He also taught at the conservatory (1878–1903) and wrote didactic works. His *Estetica della musica* (Turin, 1900) is written along lines of Kantian idealism, also evident in his historical writings. His *Trattato di contrappunto e fuga* (Milan, 1877) was long used at the Milan Conservatory. He edited several periodicals, including *Il teatro illustrato* (1881–92) and *Musica popolare* (1882–5). He retired from Sonzogno in 1904 and in 1914 returned to Rimini.

He had two operas performed, *Il corno d'oro* (Turin, Balbo, 30 August 1876) and *David* (Milan, Lirico, 12 November 1904), which is in five acts and to his own libretto; both were published by Sonzogno. Three others remained unperformed: *Follia tragica*, *Roma* and *Il risorgimento* (the last two to his own librettos). He also composed sacred, chamber, orchestral and band works.

Galli, Antonio Pietro. *See* COTTINI, ANTONIO.

Galli, Caterina (*b* ?Cremona, *c*1723; *d* Chelsea, 1804). Italian mezzo-soprano. Engaged for the 1742–3 Italian opera season in London, she made her first known appearance at the King's Theatre in Brivio's *Mandane* and sang in Galuppi's *Enrico* and *Sirbace* and Porpora's *Temistocle* (she took male roles in all four operas). In 1745 she was in a pasticcio at the New Haymarket Theatre, but she made her name in Handel's Covent Garden oratorio seasons from 1747 to 1754, scoring a great hit in the first performance of *Judas Maccabaeus* (1747). She was largely trained by Handel, who composed several parts for her. She was re-engaged for the King's Theatre in 1747–8 and appeared in the Handel pasticcios *Lucio Vero* and *Rossane* (*Alessandro*), in which she played Alexander the Great. She also sang there in Arne's *Alfred* (1753).

Galli left England about 1754 and was singing in Genoa in 1757, Naples in 1758–9 (four operas, including Hasse's *Demofoonte* and *Tito Vespasiano*), Venice in 1763 (Sacchini's *Alessandro Severo*) and 1767 (the title role in Traetta's *Armida*). She returned to England in 1773 and appeared in Sacchini's *Lucio Vero* at the King's, where she continued until 1776 in serious and comic operas. She had a compass of *a* to *f♯″* with an occasional *g″*.

WINTON DEAN

Galli, Filippo (*b* Rome, 1783; *d* Paris, 3 June 1853). Italian bass. He made his début in 1801 at Naples as a tenor. On the advice of Paisiello and of Luigi Marchesi, he became a bass, making his second début in Rossini's *La cambiale di matrimonio* at Padua in 1811. The next year he sang Tarabotto in *L'inganno felice* in Venice, the first of eight Rossini premières in which he took part, and made his début at La Scala as Polidoro in Generali's *La vedova stravagante*. During the next 13 years he appeared in over 60 different operas at La Scala, including 26 first performances. In one season (1814) he appeared in three operas by Paer and sang Guglielmo (*Così fan tutte*), the title role of *Don Giovanni*, Dandini in the first performance of Pavesi's *Agatina* and Selim at the première of *Il turco in Italia*.

Elsewhere, Galli sang Mustafà at the première of *L'italiana in Algeri* in Venice (1813), and created the title role of *Maometto II* in Naples (1820); he made his Paris début in 1821 at the Théâtre Italien in *La gazza ladra*. His last Rossini creation was Assur in *Semiramide* at La Fenice (1823). He appeared in London at the King's Theatre from 1827 to 1833, and at the Teatro Carcano, Milan, he sang Henry VIII at the first performance of *Anna Bolena* (1830). He continued to sing, in Mexico and Spain, for another decade, returning to La Scala in 1840 to take the title role in Donizetti's *Marino Faliero*.

The wide range of Galli's magnificent voice and its extreme flexibility are fully demonstrated by the roles that Rossini wrote for him, while his power as an actor can be imagined from Donizetti's Henry VIII.

Stendhal: *Vie de Rossini* (Paris, 1824, 2/1854); ed. H. Prunières (Paris, 1922, 2/1929; Eng. trans., 1956, 2/1970)

G. Radiciotti: *Gioacchino Rossini: vita documentata, opera ed influenza su l'arte* (Tivoli, 1927–9)

F. de Filippis and R. Arnese: *Cronache del Teatro di S Carlo* (Naples, 1961)

H. Weinstock: *Donizetti and the World of Opera in Italy, Paris and Vienna in the First Half of the 19th Century* (New York, 1963)

C. Gatti: *Il Teatro alla Scala nella storia e nell'arte: 1778–1963* (Milan, 1964)

H. Weinstock: *Rossini: a Biography* (New York, 1968)

ELIZABETH FORBES

Gallia, Maria (*fl* 1703–34). Italian soprano. She arrived in London in 1703, perhaps with Margherita de L'Epine, and became a pupil of Haym, making her first stage appearance in her husband Giuseppe Fedeli's *The Temple of Love* at the Queen's Theatre (1706). She sang in Clayton's *Arsinoe* and *Rosamond* (1707), both at Drury Lane, and the pasticcio *Love's Triumph* at the Queen's Theatre (1708). She returned to London as a singing teacher in 1722 and was still alive in 1734. Burney identified Gallia with the 'Sorella della Sig. Margarita' [de L'Epine] who created Clizia in Handel's *Teseo* (1713). The part requires modest skill and a compass of d' to g''.   WINTON DEAN

Galliard, John Ernest [Johann Ernst] (*b* Celle, *c*1687; *d* London, 1749). German composer. An oboist, he went to London in 1706 as court musician to Prince George of Denmark, Queen Anne's consort. As an opera composer he wrote music for *Calypso and Telemachus* (J. Hughes, after F. Fénelon; London, Queen's, 17 May 1712), one of the first 18th-century attempts at pure English opera. The music, consisting mainly of da capo arias but also including some instrumental pieces, is well written and agreeable. No recitative for the opera survives.

After John Rich opened Lincoln's Inn Fields in 1714, Galliard wrote music for his entertainments. His masques *Pan and Syrinx* (14 January 1718) and *Decius and Paulina* (22 March 1718), both with texts by Lewis Theobald, are partly operatic. In 1719 *Circe* (C. Davenant), a full-length opera, was performed seven times beginning on 11 April; only a few songs survive. The music to *Pan and Syrinx* is complete (*GB-Lbl*; see Burney and Fiske), but none for *Decius and Paulina* is

known. His last attempt at a full opera (with Theobald again) was *The Happy Captive* (Little Theatre in the Haymarket, 16 April 1741), but no music for it survives. In the 1720s and 30s Galliard wrote incidental music for many of Rich's pantomimes, a few of which were highly successful. Exactly how a music for these popular entertainments was incorporated into the spectacle is not clear, but the characters did sing individual songs.

Galliard was also known as a musical scholar. He translated Pier Francesco Tosi's *Opinioni de' cantori antichi, e moderni, o sieno Osservazioni sopra il canto figurato* (Bologna, 1723) into English as *Observations on the Florid Song, or Sentiments on the Ancient and Modern Singers* (London, 1742); this book deals indirectly with contemporary opera, both in the text and in the translator's footnotes. Also attributed to him was *A Critical Discourse upon Operas in England*, a survey of operas produced in London from 1705 to 1709. This essay, which was appended to François Raguenet's *A Comparison between the French and Italian Musick and Operas* (English edition, London, 1709), is a rare piece of criticism on works in London that are otherwise not well documented.

See also CALYPSO AND TELEMACHUS.

BurneyH; *HawkinsH*

J. Hughes: Preface, *Calypso and Telemachus* (London, 1712)

S. Johnson: 'John Hughes', *Lives of the English Poets* (London, 1779–81)

J. M. Knapp: 'A Forgotten Chapter in English Eighteenth-Century Opera', *ML*, xlii (1961), 4–16

S. Lincoln: 'J. E. Galliard and *A Critical Discourse*', *MQ*, liii (1967), 347–64

R. Fiske: *English Theatre Music in the Eighteenth Century* (London, 1973, 2/1986)   J. MERRILL KNAPP

Galliari. Italian family of stage designers. Its principal members were the brothers Bernardino (*b* Andorno, nr Biella, 3 Nov 1707; *d* Andorno, 31 March 1794), Fabrizio (*b* Andorno, 28 Sept 1709; *d* Treviglio, June 1790) and Giovanni Antonio (*b* Andorno, 26 March 1714; *d* Milan, 1783). After early tuition from their father, the decorative painter Giovanni Galliari (*b* Andorno, 1672; *d* Andorno, 1722), and further study in Turin and Milan, they worked in northern Italy (and in Innsbruck in 1738) as painters of frescoes and other decoration until, probably towards the end of the 1730s, they became assistants to the theatrical painters Innocente Bellavite, Giovan Domenico Barbieri and Giovanni Battista Medici. When Barbieri died in 1742, Fabrizio and Medici became chief designers at the Regio Ducal Teatro in Milan, and on Medici's retirement a year later Fabrizio was joined by Bernardino and Giovanni Antonio. From then on the stage designs for the Milan opera houses (Regio Ducal, 1742–76; Itinerale, 1776–8; La Scala, after 1778) rested almost exclusively in the hands of the Galliari brothers. Giovanni Antonio settled in Milan, but Fabrizio and Bernardino were also chief stage designers at the Teatro Regio in Turin in 1748 and from 1753 on worked regularly for the Teatro Carignano there and in a number of Italian and foreign opera houses, including Vienna, Berlin and Paris. They retired in the mid-1780s.

The brothers worked together but divided their responsibilities according to their talents. Fabrizio was a creative artist who usually produced the ideas and plans for the sets and carried out the architectural designs. Bernardino, the most talented painter among them,

Design of a rural dance scene by Fabrizio Galliari for an unidentified opera buffa, Teatro Carignano, Turin, 1774: pen, ink and watercolour

produced equally artistic and mature designs, and ideas for curtains, but was mainly concerned with their realization in paint; his work included excellent figures and landscapes. Giovanni Antonio was exclusively an executant. Their work at the Turin and, to a lesser extent, the Milan court theatres was still essentially under the influence of the *opera seria* tradition. The formalized architectural painting of the Bibiena school, passed down from Barbieri and Medici, is to be found in numerous of their early productions of that genre and even remained efficacious when the Galliaris began to develop a style influenced by and in accord with the 'reform' movement of Jommelli, Traetta and above all Gluck, whose *Alceste* they mounted at Vienna in 1767. Here they aimed to overcome the traditional courtly rationalist formalism through sets based on pictorial composition and the re-creation of nature, and through intensified use of landscape and genre motifs and references (albeit superficial) to historical locations and the milieu of the action, like the 'Chinese' sets for Vincenzo Ciampi's *Arsinoe* (1758, ?Turin). Their aim was to represent truth and humanity in opera and in the conflicts it depicts by using the language of middle-class customs and emotions, though in elevated, idealized form. Further scope for this style was provided by *opera buffa*, for which the Galliaris designed exclusively at the Teatro Carignano in Turin (see illustration) and which accounted for well over half their designs for the Milan court theatre. Their stage realism followed operatic structure not simply by reproducing an everyday middle-class environment but by selection and picturesque arrangement.

When the older generation retired in the 1780s Fabrizio's sons and pupils Giovannino (*b* 1746; *d* Treviglio, 1818) and Giuseppino (*b* Andorno, 1742; *d* Milan, 1817) continued their work at the Teatro Regio and Teatro Carignano in Turin. Giuseppino, who closely followed his father's style, also worked as a designer in Geneva (1778) and Marseilles (1787) and apparently retired about 1792. Giovannino turned to academic classicism, worked with his uncle Bernardino for Frederick the Great in 1772 and was still active in Turin in 1798. Bartolomeo Verona (*b* Andorno, 1744; *d*

Berlin, 1813), a son of the brothers' sister Elisabetta, worked for them from about 1762 to 1772 and went with Bernardino and Giovannino to Berlin, where he remained as an influential royal theatrical painter until his death. Gaspare (*b* ?Milan, 1761; *d* Milan, 1823), son of Giovanni Antonio, started his career with the family firm but in 1785 went as stage designer to Parma and elsewhere, including Vienna (1788–94), Venice and Milan. He developed his own style of pictorial classicism with romantic features. Fabrizio Sevesi (*b* Milan, ?1773; *d* Turin, 9 Aug 1837), son of Fabrizio's daughter Ludovica, was the last important designer of the family; he was trained by Giovannino and Giuseppino and succeeded them at the Carignano from 1798 and at the Regio from 1800.

For further illustrations *see* MANZUOLI, GIOVANNI; MILAN, fig.3; OPERA SERIA, fig.4; STAGE DESIGN, fig.7; and TURIN, fig.2.

*

ES (M. Viale)
Numero xxiv invenzioni teatrali di Gaspare Galliari (Milan, 1803)
Serie di decorazioni teatrali inventate dal Capitano Gaspare Galliari e da suoi zii Bernardino e Fabrizio (Milan, 1821)
R. Amerio: 'Il pittore Bartolomeo Verona', *Bollettino della Società piemontese di archeologia e belle arti*, new ser., xii–xiii (1958–9), 173–8
R. Bossaglia: *I fratelli Galliari pittori* (Milan, 1962)
M. Viale Ferrero: *La scenografia del '700 e i fratelli Galliari* (Turin, 1963) [incl. catalogue of stage designs]
A. Griseri: 'I fratelli Galliari pittori', *Burlington Magazine*, cviii (1966), 528–31 [review of Bossaglia 1962 and Viale Ferrero 1963]
M. Viale Ferrero: 'Disegni inediti di Fabrizio Galliari per *L'Europa riconosciuta* – opera inaugurale del Teatro alla Scala di Milano', *Antichità viva*, x/4 (1971), 37
——: *Storia del Teatro regio di Torino*, ed. A. Basso, iii: *La scenografia dalle origini al 1936* (Turin, 1980)
S. Angrisani: *I Galliari: primi scenografi della Scala* (Florence, 1983) [exhibition catalogue]
M. Viale Ferrero: *Scenografi scaligeri tra settecento e ottocento* (Milan, 1988)   MANFRED BOETZKES

Galli-Bibiena [Bibiena, Bibbiena]. Italian family of stage designers and architects. They had a decisive influence on Baroque musical theatre in southern and central Europe. The founder of the family's theatrical activities was Ferdinando Galli-Bibiena (*b* Bologna, 18 Aug 1656; *d* Bologna, 3 Jan 1743), son of the illusionist painter Giovanni Maria Galli (*b* Bibbiena, 1625; *d* Bologna, 1665). Ferdinando studied in Bologna, and from the early 1680s worked as an illusionist painter, architect and stage designer at the court of Ranuccio II in Parma. From 1687, when he was appointed court painter, he became established there and in Piacenza mainly through his work for the stage. He subsequently continued this activity elsewhere in Italy, notably at Bologna (1697–1709). In 1708 he was appointed to the Barcelona court of the Spanish pretender Charles III; when the latter became Emperor Charles VI in 1711 Ferdinando went with him to Vienna as first architect and theatre architect. He returned to Bologna in 1716, having been succeeded by his son Giuseppe, and taught at the Accademia Clementina, working only occasionally as an architect and designer.

Early in his career Ferdinando was confronted with a tradition of stage design bound to the central vanishing-point as a hypostasis of absolute power and he was thus unable to do justice to a musical drama dealing with the real world in a more differential way. Using his experience as an architect and decorative painter, he reformed stage design through the introduction of sophisticated stereometric, illusionistic architectural painting. In its scholarly character this solution matched the rationalism of the middle classes, the new opera public, and through its formal possibilities also satisfied courtly requirements that had previously been met with spectacular machine effects. Ferdinando's first scenic designs, with their accentuated asymmetry, were the first experiments with the 'maniera di veder le scene per angolo' (Sabadini's *Didio Giuliano*, 1687), but still bore traces of the traditional deep stage *all'infinito* and allegorical theatre of machines. However, around 1700 his scenography increasingly emphasized diagonal views and angular perspective, as expounded in his treatise *L'architettura civile* (Parma, 1711; for illustration *see* STAGE DESIGN, fig.6). His style became associated with

the new *opera seria* and was eventually characterized by strong architectonic organization, rationalist principles of construction and 'worm's-eye' perspective which endowed the illusionistic architecture of the stage with a monumental character appropriate to the court spectacle he served, for example at Naples (Alessandro Scarlatti's *Eraclea*, 1700) and Vienna (Fux's *Angelica vincitrice di Alcina*, 1716; for illustration *see* VIENNA, fig.1).

His brother Francesco Galli-Bibiena (*b* Bologna, 12 Dec 1659; *d* Bologna, 20 Jan 1737) studied in Bologna and was active there and elsewhere in Emilia; from about 1682 he worked with Ferdinando in Parma and Piacenza. After his first theatrical works in Genoa in 1689 he was active during the 1690s as a stage designer at many Italian opera houses and foreign courts, including Rome, Reggio Emilia, Bologna and Vienna. From 1726 he taught at the Accademia Clementina in Bologna, where he designed sets for the Teatro Malvezzi. Francesco was also a significant innovator, having experimented with angular perspective in his non-theatrical works as early as 1684. Through his wider sphere of activity, and particularly through his scenery for the operas of Francesco Gasparini, C. F. Pollarolo (fig.1), Scarlatti, Vivaldi, Hasse and Leo, he may have played a greater part than his brother in the propagation of the new style in *opera seria*, having tested it in his designs for the *tragédie lyrique* (Lully's *Thésée* and *Amadis*, 1708–9, Lunéville). By contrast with Ferdinando's technique-orientated works, those of Francesco are masterfully composed and richly ornamented fantasies. The theatres that he designed in Bologna, Vienna, Nancy, Verona and Rome were strongly biased towards courtly performance (for illustrations *see* VERONA, fig.1, and VIENNA, fig.3).

Alessandro Galli-Bibiena (*b* ?Parma, 1686; *d* Mannheim, 5 Aug 1748), a son of Ferdinando, studied with his father and worked as his associate in Spain from 1708 and Vienna from 1711. In 1716 he was appointed architect and stage designer at the Innsbruck

1. *Design by Francesco Galli-Bibiena for C. F. Pollarolo's 'La pace fra Tolomeo e Seleuco' (Act 3 finale) at the Teatro Tordinona, Rome, 1693: engraving by C. A. Buffagnotti*

court; in 1720 he settled with the court at its new Mannheim residence, where he worked until his death. The influence of his father and uncle is specially clear in Alessandro's designs for oratorios, sacred dramas and, later, *opera seria* (C. P. Grua's *Meride* and *La clemenza di Tito*, 1742 and 1748, Mannheim). His *opera seria* sets, with their complex but weightless illusionist architecture and scant decoration, elegantly fulfilled their ostentatious function; in his rustic scenery for pastorales, especially popular at the palatine court (*Crudeltà consuma amore* by Greber and Stricker, 1717, Neuburg), and in the genre scenes for the *commedia dell'arte*, realistic traits also became important. Alessandro designed the provisional opera house in Mannheim (1720) and the opera house in the rebuilt palace (1737–41), his most important work (for illustration *see* MANNHEIM). His brother Giovanni Maria (*b* Piacenza, 19 Jan 1694; *d* Naples, 1777) followed Alessandro to Mannheim about 1722 but went in 1723 to Prague, where he evidently spent most of his life, though he had spells as an architect and stage designer in Rome, Naples and probably Bologna.

A third brother, Giuseppe (*b* Parma, 5 Jan 1695; *d* Berlin, 1757), worked with his father in 1708 in Barcelona and in 1711 in Vienna, succeeding him there in 1716 and becoming principal theatre architect in 1723; he was responsible for the court opera performances under Charles VI in Vienna and at other residences, including Prague (fig.2), and he also worked in Munich, Linz and Graz. After Charles's death (1740) opera productions became fewer and Giuseppe went to Italy, where he worked in Turin, Bologna and Venice. In 1744 he returned to Vienna but gave up his court position there in 1748, having secured an assignment in 1746 to design the interior of the Bayreuth opera house (completed by his son Carlo in 1748; for illustration *see* BAYREUTH, fig.1); in 1747 he went to Dresden, where he rebuilt the Opernhaus am Zwinger (completed in 1750). From 1751 he was occasionally active as a stage designer in Berlin and in 1753 he entered the service of Frederick the Great. Through his association with librettists like Pariati, Zeno and Metastasio and such composers as Caldara, Feo, Jommelli, Hasse and C. H. Graun, Giuseppe's illusionist architecture painting became typical of *opera seria* and established him as the leading stage designer in Europe. He developed the style of his father and uncle in imaginative sets for more than a hundred opera productions, retaining rationalist principles of composition. His sets expanded in amazing diagonal views, conceived primarily as one or more central structures with star-shaped radiating galleries or loges, in which the standard elements of contemporary court architecture were varied, and rich decoration became more pronounced.

A further son of Ferdinando, Antonio (*b* Parma, bap. 1 Jan 1697; *d* Milan, 28 Jan 1774), studied in Bologna and from 1716 occasionally assisted his brother Giuseppe in Vienna, his father in Bologna and Fano, and his uncle in Verona and Rome. From about 1721 he worked with Giuseppe as a stage designer at the Vienna Hofoper, from 1723 as second architect and theatre engineer. Most of his sets were for *opera seria* productions. He succeeded Giuseppe as principal theatre engineer in 1748 but returned to Bologna in 1751; there

2. *Design by Giuseppe Galli-Bibiena for the original production of Fux's festa teatrale 'Costanza e Fortezza' (Act 3 scenes i and ii) in the amphitheatre of Hradschin Castle, Prague, 28 August 1723: engraving*

he designed the Teatro Comunale (1756–63; for illustration *see* BOLOGNA), for which he produced numerous opera sets (including Gluck's *Il trionfo di* *Clelia*, 1763). He was also active in other Italian cities as architect and stage designer. He remained within the family traditions in catering for the requirements of

3. *Design by Giovanni Carlo Sicinivale Galli-Bibiena for Perez's 'La clemenza di Tito' (scene from Act 3, a vast hall with an amphitheatre) at the Casa de Opera, Lisbon, 1755: pen, black ink and grey wash*

4. *Set, probably by Carlo Galli-Bibiena, for the Drottningholm Court Theatre, c1774 (believed to be the only complete surviving set by a member of the Galli-Bibiena family)*

court productions, which in Vienna he developed in his brother's shadow and which he continued to use after his return to Italy. His work was unaffected by the ideals of the emancipated middle classes, and he increasingly became subject to criticism; the Teatro Comunale in Bologna in particular figured in treatises of the Enlightenment as a model of 'bad taste'.

The youngest of Francesco's sons, Giovanni Carlo Sicinivale (*b* ?Bologna, *c*1720; *d* Lisbon, 20 Nov 1760), was educated at the Bologna Accademia Clementina and in the 1740s was active in Bologna and the Emilia region; in 1752 he was appointed architect and stage designer to King José I of Portugal, in whose service he built several opera houses, none of which survives: the Teatro da Casa da India in Lisbon (1752), the theatre at the palace of Salvaterra de Magos (1753), the Opera do Tejo in Lisbon (1755) and the theatre at Ajuda (?1756). For the performances of Perez's *opere serie* he created elegant scenery which simplified the style of his family and attempted greater realism, approaching a bourgeois aesthetic without forsaking court traditions (*Didone abandonnata*, 1753; *La clemenza di Tito*, 1755; fig.3).

Carlo Galli-Bibiena (*b* Vienna, bap. 8 Feb 1721; *d* Florence, 1787), son of Giuseppe, studied in Vienna and worked at Bayreuth from 1746. Up to 1756 he designed sets for the works of Hasse and Bernasconi there and in Erlangen; later he also worked occasionally at Brunswick and after the Seven Years War (1756–63) went to Italy, France, the Netherlands and London. In 1765 Frederick the Great appointed him head stage director at the Berlin Hofoper, but he soon returned to Italy where he worked as an architect and stage designer in Treviso, Naples and Milan. Finally, in 1774, he worked for Gustavus III in Stockholm and Drottningholm (fig.4).

Amelita Galli-Curci as Violetta in Verdi's 'La traviata'

and Catherine the Great in St Petersburg. Carlo never completely relinquished his father's style, but a reduction of illusionism was already evident in his Bayreuth sets, and his work with *opera buffa* further strengthened the trend towards realism, eventually also including neo-classical elements (e.g. Jommelli's *Cerere placata*, 1772, Naples; for illustration *see* JOMMELLI, NICCOLÒ).

See also STAGE DESIGN, §4. For further illustration *see* GRISELDA (ii); LISBON, fig.1; OPERA SERIA, fig.3; and PRAGUE, fig.1.

*

C. Ricci: *I teatri di Bologna nei secoli XVII e XVIII* (Bologna, 1888)

J. Gregor: *Wiener szenische Kunst* (Vienna, 1924)

V. Mariani: *Scenografia italiana* (Florence, 1930)

A. Hyatt Mayor: *The Bibiena Family* (New York, 1945)

J. Gregor, ed.: *Monumenta scenica: Giuseppe Galli da Bibiena* (Vienna, 1954)

F. Hadamowsky: *Die Familie Galli-Bibiena in Wien: ein Leben für das Theater* (Vienna, 1962)

J. Hilmera: ' "Costanza e Fortezza": Giuseppe Galli-Bibiena und das Barocktheater in Böhmen', *Maske und Kothurn*, x (1964), 396–407

K. A. Burnim: 'The Theatrical Career of Giuseppe Galli-Bibiena', *Theatre Survey*, vi (1965), 32–52

A. H. Saxon: 'Giuseppe Galli-Bibiena's "Architetture e prospettive" ', *Maske und Kothurn*, xv (1969), 105–18

M. T. Muraro and E. Povoledo: *Disegni teatrali dei Bibiena* (Venice, 1970) [exhibition catalogue]

M. Monteverdi: *I Bibiena: disegni e incisioni nelle collezioni del Museo teatrale alla Scala* (Milan, 1975) [exhibition catalogue]

G. Ricci: *Dai Parigi ai Bibiena* (Prato, 1979) [exhibition catalogue]

A. Glanz: *Alessandro Galli-Bibiena und sein Bühnenbild für die kurpfälzische Oper (1716–1748): ein Beitrag zur Rezeption der italienischen Theaterarchitekten-Dynastie Bibiena* (Berlin, 1987)

MANFRED BOETZKES

Galli-Curci [née Galli], **Amelita** (*b* Milan, 18 Nov 1882; *d* La Jolla, CA, 26 Nov 1963). Italian soprano of Italian-Spanish parentage. She graduated from the Milan Conservatory in 1903 with a first prize as a pianist; on the advice of Mascagni she also had some vocal lessons there with Carignani and Sara Dufes, but as a singer she was mainly self-taught. She made her début at Trani in southern Italy on 26 December 1906 as Gilda, a role that remained a favourite throughout her career. In 1908 she appeared in Rome with De Luca in the Italian première of Bizet's posthumous *Don Procopio*. During the next eight years she became increasingly successful in the coloratura repertory not only in Italy but in Spain, Egypt and Russia, and in South and Central America.

The great event of Galli-Curci's career was her Chicago début as Gilda on 18 November 1916, which was a spectacular triumph. She remained with the Chicago company for eight consecutive seasons, singing Rosina, Amina, Lucia, Linda di Chamounix, Violetta, Dinorah, Juliet, Manon and Lakmé, as well as an occasional Mimì and Butterfly. Already well known in New York from the visits of the Chicago company, she made her début at the Metropolitan in *La traviata* on 14 November 1921, appearing as a regular member of the company in these and other similar parts until her farewell in *Il barbiere di Siviglia* on 24 January 1930. By that time she had begun to show signs of vocal distress; and, after an operation in 1935 for the removal of a throat tumour, her attempted return to the stage, for a single performance of *La bohème* in Chicago in 1936, was unsuccessful. She was never heard in opera in London. She was married twice: to the artist Luigi Curci (1910, divorced 1920); then, in 1921, to Homer Samuels, her accompanist.

Galli-Curci possessed a limpid timbre of exceptional beauty and an ease in florid singing that sounded natural rather than acquired; her highest register, up to *e'''*, remained pure and free from shrillness. Her style, though devoid of dramatic intensity, had a languorous grace and charm of line capable of conveying both gaiety and pathos. Her numerous Victor records, especially those made before 1925 by the acoustic process, deserved their enormous vogue, being among the best of their kind; during the post-1925 electric period she successfully repeated some of her excellent duet recordings with Schipa and De Luca, but by then her work had begun to be affected by false intonation and other flaws. She remains, along with Caruso, McCormack and Shalyapin, among the supreme gramophone stars of the early period.

*

C. E. Le Massena: *Galli-Curci's Life of Song* (New York, 1945)
A. Favia-Artsay: 'Amelita Galli-Curci', *Record Collector*, iv (1949), 163–79 [with discography by G. Whelan]

DESMOND SHAWE-TAYLOR

Gallignani, Giuseppe (*b* Faenza, 9 Jan 1851; *d* Milan, 14 Dec 1923). Italian composer and teacher. He studied at the Milan Conservatory and then travelled in Europe for ten years, studying and conducting. From 1884 until his death he was *maestro di cappella* at Milan Cathedral. He was director of the Parma Conservatory from 1891 and of the Milan Conservatory from 1897. In both he initiated valuable reforms and improvements, but his outspoken and tactless manner provoked much opposition. He composed six operas, notably *Atala* (1876), *Nestorio* (1888) and the chauvinistic *In alto!* (1921); but he was not very successful in this genre, *Nestorio* receiving only three performances at La Scala. As a composer he was best known for his church music. He was editor of the periodical *Musica sacra*, 1886–94.

Il sindaco cavaliere (ob, 3), Milan, Casa Attendolo Bolognini, 1870
Il grillo del focolare (Gallignani, after C. Dickens: *The Cricket on the Hearth*), Genoa, Sala Sivori, 27 Jan 1873
Atala (E. Praga), Milan, Carcano, 30 March 1876
Nestorio (F. Fulgonio and Gallignani), Milan, Scala, 31 March 1888
Lucia di Settefonti, 1897 (C. Ricci), unperf.
In alto! (Gallignani), Trieste, Politeama Rossetti, 8 Nov 1921

Galli-Marié [née Marié de l'Isle, Marié], **Célestine (-Laurence)** (*b* Paris, Nov 1840; *d* Vence, nr Nice, 22 Sept 1905). French mezzo-soprano. She was the daughter and pupil of Félix Mécène Marié de l'Isle, a singer at the Opéra. After her début in Strasbourg (1859) she sang in Vichy, Toulouse and Lisbon. In 1862 Emile Perrin noticed her success in Rouen in Balfe's *The Bohemian Girl* and engaged her for the Opéra-Comique, where she triumphed as Serpina in a revival of *La serva padrona*.

Galli-Marié was praised for her intelligence, natural acting ability (as both comedian and tragedian), grace and musicianship, and for the warm timbre of her voice, and was excused for the harshness of her upper register and the modest size of her instrument. She created important roles in works by Gevaert, Guiraud, Maillart, Massenet, Offenbach and Paladilhe (who was her lover), but she was most identified with the title roles in *Mignon* (1866) and *Carmen* (1875).

Though Galli-Marié toured within and outside France, she remained principally associated with the Opéra-Comique until 1879. That year she sang in the Italian première of *Carmen* at Naples, and she went on to successes in Spain and England. With her return to that theatre as Carmen in 1883 the work finally achieved the success in Paris it had found elsewhere in

Célestine Galli-Marié as Carmen (in the costume for Act 2), the role she created at the Opéra-Comique, Paris, 3 March 1875: lithograph by Chatin

Europe. She last sang in Paris for a gala performance of *Carmen* (11 December 1890) to raise funds for a Bizet monument.

*

FétisBS
'Galli-Marié', *La grande encyclopédie* (Paris, 1887–91), xviii, 404
A. Soubies and C. Malherbe: *Histoire de l'Opéra-Comique*, ii (Paris, 1892)
H. de Curzon: *Croquis d'artistes* (Paris, 1898), 173–82
C. Pigot: *Georges Bizet et son oeuvre* (Paris, 2/1911)
H. Malherbe: *Carmen* (Paris, 1951)
M. Curtiss: *Bizet and his World* (New York, 1958)

LESLEY A. WRIGHT

Gallini, Giovanni Andrea Battista [John] (*b* Florence, 7 Jan 1728; *d* London, 5 Jan 1805). Italian dancer, choreographer and impresario. He moved to Paris and, according to Antoine de Léris in the *Dictionnaire portatif des théâtres* (1754), was a member of the Académie Royale de Musique company until at least 1754. His first recorded appearance in London was at Covent Garden on 17 December 1757, when he danced in the pantomime ballet *The Judgement of Paris* and in the comic ballet *The Sicilian Peasants*. In autumn 1758 he joined the *corps de ballet* at the King's Theatre, dancing in operas by Cocchi and Perez, and was named director of dances for Cocchi's *Ciro riconosciuto* (3 February 1759). He continued as dance director as well as a performer through the 1762–3 season, providing ballets for J. C. Bach's first London opera, *Orione* (19 February 1763). During 1763–4 he returned to Covent Garden as director of dances and was re-engaged in 1765–6. He did not appear on the London stage after that season.

Gallini achieved popularity as a dancing master and published two treatises on dance. He apparently

335

married one of his pupils, Lady Elizabeth Peregrine Bertie, eldest daughter of the late 3rd Earl of Abingdon. He is said to have been awarded by the pope the Knighthood of the Order of the Golden Spur, and thereafter was styled 'Sir'. He was also proprietor of the Hanover Square Rooms, where J. C. Bach and C. F. Abel gave their subscription concerts from 1775.

Gallini's involvement with London opera began in 1778, when he attempted to purchase the mortgage on the King's Theatre. He became manager temporarily in 1783 and again, after complex litigation, from 1785 until the opera house burnt down on 17 June 1789. During this period the ballet, under the choreographer Jean-Georges Noverre and with such dancers as Charles-Louis Didelot and Marie Madeleine Guimard, became pre-eminent there, in spite of Gallini's dislike of the new *ballet d'action*. Gallini tried to improve the quality of Italian opera in London, engaging Nancy and Stephen Storace and other performers and composers from Vienna. After the destruction of the King's, Gallini had short seasons at Covent Garden and the Little Theatre in the Haymarket, where the main attractions were the singers Luigi Marchesi and Gertrud Elisabeth Mara. After several unsuccessful attempts in the late 1780s to engage Haydn, Gallini (with Salomon) brought him to London in 1791 and commissioned from him *L'anima del filosofo*, which was never performed. He was manager of the rebuilt King's Theatre in the 1791 season, his final season of involvement with London theatre. Despite losses at the opera, Gallini died a wealthy man.

BDA; BurneyH; LS

[W. Allen, T. Luppino and H. Reynell]: *The Case of the Opera-House Disputes Fairly Stated* (London, 1784)

R. B. O'Reilly: *An Authentic Narrative of the Principal Circumstances Relating to the Opera House in the Hay-Market* (London, 1791)

W. Taylor: *A Concise Statement of Transactions and Circumstances Respecting the King's Theatre in the Haymarket* (London, 1791)

R. Ralph: 'Sir John Gallini', *About the House*, v (1979), 30–37

E. Gibson: 'Earl Cowper in Florence and his Correspondence with the Italian Opera in London', *ML*, lxvii (1987), 235–52

C. Price, J. Milhous and R. D. Hume: 'A Plan for the Pantheon Opera House (1790–92)', *COJ*, iii (1991), 213–46

——: 'The Rebuilding of the King's Theatre, Haymarket, 1789–1791', *Theatre Journal*, xl (1991), 421–44

ELIZABETH GIBSON (with CURTIS PRICE)

Gallo, Fortune [Fortunato] **T.** (*b* Torremaggiore, Foggia, 9 May 1878; *d* New York, 28 March 1970). Italian-American impresario. The son of a retired soldier, he went to the USA in 1895, worked as a tout among his fellow immigrants, then used his experience as a school bandsman to become an agent for touring Italian bands. When the coming of ragtime upset the band business, he organized an American tour for an Italian opera company which had been touring California and Central America. This led him in 1913 to start his own touring San Carlo Opera Company, a name taken from an earlier troupe (*see* RUSSELL, HENRY). Until 1951, with a break during the depression (1929–32), it gave many Americans their first experience of opera as both audiences and performers, often through one-night stands in small towns. Though the conductor Carlo Peroni did much to hold it together (from 1916 to 1942), the company was a shifting group of soloists engaged for particular performances; scenery consisted of painted flats, often interchangeable; the chorus was eked out by local amateurs. Almost wholly Italian at first, the San Carlo took on American singers

and other languages; a 1922 *Lohengrin* in Edmonton was sung in four languages. Some artists were on the way up (Alice Gentle, Queena Mario, Manuel Salazar early on, Regina Resnik and David Poleri in the 1940s), others on the way out (Maria Jeritza, 1933); many remained little known in spite of Gallo's trick of giving some of them the surnames of famous singers. His meanness comes through even in his ghosted, fictionalized memoirs. A famous story has him finding the second clarinet doing nothing: 'Why you don't play?' 'There's no part for me at this point in the opera.' 'OK, you play along with the others.'

F. T. Gallo: *Lucky Rooster* (New York, 1967)

C. Bishop: *The San Carlo Opera Company 1913–1955: Grand Opera for Profit* (Santa Monica, CA, 1978)   JOHN ROSSELLI

Gallo [Galli, Galletto], **Giovanni** (*fl* 1726–49). Italian choreographer. He worked primarily in Venice during the second quarter of the 18th century, creating ballets for more than 30 opera productions. Most of his choreography was for two theatres, S Angelo (1726, 1733–4, 1735, 1746), where his work appeared in operas by Vivaldi and Albinoni, among others, and S Giovanni Grisostomo (1731–2; 1746–7, 1748–9), where he choreographed several operas by Hasse. He also was employed for five Ascension seasons at S Samuele (1738, 1740, 1746, 1748, 1749), and for a season each at S Cassiano (1742–3) and S Moisè (1744–5). In 1738 he worked in Milan. He may be the 'Zanetto Galetto' listed as ballet-master for G. M. Ruggieri's *Arrenione* at S Angelo (1708). In *Gli abiti de veneziani* (1754), Giovanni Grevembroch wrote that Gallo, nearly decrepit, was teaching the minuet to the first rank of nobility, and had a school in the Giovanni Grisostomo district.   IRENE ALM

Gallon, Noël (*b* Paris, 11 Sept 1891; *d* Paris, 26 Dec 1966). French composer. He studied at the Paris Conservatoire with Albert Lavignac, Georges Caussade, Lenepveu and Rabaud, whose pupil and friend he became, and in 1910 won the Prix de Rome. He returned to the Conservatoire as a teacher from 1920, becoming director in 1935 of the Concours Général de Musique et de Déclamation, but had more success as a composer, principally of dramatic and orchestral works. Among these are the opera *Paysans et soldats* (5, P. de Sancy; Paris, Gaîté-Lyrique, 19 May 1911) and the *tableau musical La Marseillaise* (Paris, Opéra, 1912). His compositions are marked by elegance and clarity and by a discreet impressionism that veils his contrapuntal skill. His brother Jean Gallon (1878–1959) was a conductor at the Opéra, 1909–14.   ALAIN LOUVIER

Galterio, Lou (*b* New York, 29 Nov 1942). American director and administrator. He studied drama and English at Marquette University, Milwaukee, and worked in spoken theatre before venturing into opera, where he specializes in the comic repertory. His productions for the Opera Theatre of St Louis include *Così fan tutte* (1977), *Le nozze di Figaro* (1981), *Albert Herring* (1976; revived and filmed for television, 1978), *Gianni Schicchi* (1977), *Ariadne auf Naxos* (1979), the American première of *Maddalena* (1982), and *Orfeo ed Euridice* (1983). He has also worked in Santa Fe, directing Nino Rota's *Il cappello di paglia di Firenze* (American première, 1977), *Il barbiere di Siviglia* (1981), *Neues vom Tage* (1981) and *The Nose* (1987), as well as at the Kennedy Center in Washington, where he produced Argento's *Postcard from Morocco* (1980). Galterio made his début at the New York City Opera in 1980 with *La Cenerentola* and at the Chicago Opera Theater in 1984 with *Don Giovanni*. As director of opera production at the Manhattan School (1977–89) he presented several American premières, including Henze's *The English Cat*, Massenet's *Chérubin*, Prokofiev's *Betrothal in a Monastery* and Hindemith's *Sancta Susanna*. Other productions include *L'elisir d'amore* and *La fille du régiment* (1987 and 1990, San Diego), *Rigoletto* (1989, San Juan) and *Madama Butterfly* (1990, Dallas).   FRANK MERKLING

Galuppi, Antonio [Ageo Liteo] (*b* ?Venice; *d* *c*1780). Italian librettist. Son of Baldassare Galuppi, he is mentioned only in the composer's will (16 June 1780), where he is named as recently deceased. For a brief period in the 1760s he was active in Venice, writing the librettos for two of Baldassare's most successful operas, *L'amante di tutte* (1760, which was staged well over 20 times in its first ten years) and *Li tre amanti ridicoli* (1761); he was probably also involved in arranging other comic works for S Moisè. Two librettos for other operas by Baldassare Galuppi, *Il marchese villano* and *Il puntiglio amoroso* (both 1762), have been attributed to Antonio Galuppi but are probably not by him. His poetry and sense of comedy were in the tradition of Goldoni, though less inspired and articulate, more inclined to slapstick, buffoonery and caricature.

DALE E. MONSON

Galuppi, Baldassare (*b* Burano, nr Venice, 18 Oct 1706; *d* Venice, 3 Jan 1785). Italian composer. He was a central figure in the development of the *dramma giocoso* and one of the most important mid-18th-century *opera seria* composers. Known widely as 'Il Buranello', from his birthplace, he was routinely listed in Venetian documents as 'Baldissera'.

1. LIFE. Galuppi's father, a barber, played the violin in small orchestras, which provided entr'acte music for theatres of spoken comedy, and was probably the boy's first music teacher. In his 16th year Baldassare composed *Gli amici rivali* for Chioggia (also performed in Vicenza as *La fede nell'incostanza*, probably by the same troupe), but Caffi reported this as a fiasco, a 'scandal'. The boy went for advice to Marcello, who severely scolded him for attempting something so grand on so little experience and swore him to three years' hard labour, studying counterpoint under Antonio Lotti (first organist at St Mark's) and refraining from operatic composition altogether. Evidence for all this is circumstantial, however; other evidence suggests that Galuppi's studies with Lotti had begun earlier.

If the young composer made this promise, he did not keep it, for two years later he was playing the cembalo in opera houses and writing substitute arias for revivals and pasticcios. By the age of 20 he had established a reputation as a cembalist in Venice and Florence, and was soon engaged in the S Angelo (where Vivaldi reigned), the S Samuele and the S Giovanni Grisostomo theatres, performing and supplying arias. He collaborated with his friend and fellow Lotti pupil, Giovanni Battista Pescetti, writing alternate acts of *Gl'odi delusi del sangue* in 1728 (set earlier by Lotti) and *Dorinda* in 1729. This modest success led to further commissions, and by 1738 his operas were appearing

outside Venice; at the same time his nickname, 'Il Buranello', is first encountered. *Alessandro nell'Indie* was given its première in Mantua at about the same time that *Issipile* graced the stage in Turin (December 1737); the composer was probably present only in Mantua. In 1738 he was in the service of the patrician Michele Bernardo in Venice. Galuppi's music for the festival of S Maria Magdalena in July at the Ospedale dei Mendicanti led to a permanent appointment there on 4 August 1738.

Before 1741 Galuppi's Venetian career remained diverse, but unexceptional. Neapolitan composers were favoured at Venice's most important theatres, and of the native sons only Vivaldi enjoyed any particular favour. In 1741, the year of Vivaldi's death, two serious operas by Galuppi appeared: *Oronte* at the prestigious S Giovanni Grisostomo and *Berenice* at the S Angelo. Galuppi petitioned for nine months' leave and accepted an invitation to travel to London. Permission from the Mendicanti was reluctantly granted, and Galuppi arrived in London in October 1741 and supervised 11 opera productions over the next year and a half, including four original works. Some reported his tenure as less than admirable – Walpole claimed that the 'music displeases everybody' (Fassini, p.168) and Handel, in a letter of 29 December 1741, ridiculed the one serious opera he heard – but in general Galuppi's trip was successful and he was well received. His music was often reprinted for the English public, and two more Galuppi works appeared there soon after he had left. Back in Venice by May 1743, he took up his old professions of cembalist and arranger; not much had changed, and his contract with the Mendicanti was extended for three more years. The spread of comic opera from Naples and Rome had just found its way to Venice, however, and Galuppi began adapting these to northern taste, beginning in 1744 with three Roman works by Latilla and Rinaldo di Capua. His own comic opera in Carnival 1745, *La forza d'amore*, was not particularly successful.

Galuppi's fame began to spread and his fees to climb (as attested by documents from Milan, Madrid, Padua and elsewhere). Angelo Mingotti performed in *Argenide* in Graz (1745), Prague (1746) and Dresden (1746). In 1747 (and probably again in 1748) Galuppi was in Milan for *L'olimpiade*; *Vologeso* received its première in Rome in 1748 and Venice was increasingly enthusiastic. Circumstantial evidence suggests that Galuppi continued to arrange comic operas throughout these years. In May 1748 he was elected vice-*maestro* of the *cappella ducale* of St Mark's. By August he was in Vienna, where *Demetrio* and *Artaserse* were enormously successful, despite Metastasio's criticism that Galuppi's music did not serve the text well; *Demetrio*, performed 19 times over a short period, broke all box-office records. Galuppi left Vienna before the *Artaserse* première and was in Milan for the first performances of *Semiramide riconosciuta*, the second carnival opera of 1749.

The year 1749 marks the beginning of Galuppi's long-term collaboration with the librettist Carlo Goldoni. Over the next eight years a rapid sequence of *drammi giocosi* appeared, beginning with *Arcadia in Brenta* (14 May 1749) and extending through four more works before a year had passed. These operas surged over Europe with unprecedented ease, and by the middle of the next decade Galuppi was the most popular opera composer anywhere. His professional obligations forced his resignation from the Mendicanti in 1751. His *opere serie* continued to command high praise. He wrote his

'L'Arcadia in Brenta' (Galuppi): engraving from Carlo Goldoni's 'Opere teatrale' (Venice: Zatta, 1788–95)

first setting of *Demofoonte* for Madrid in December 1749, to mark the engagement of Maria Antonietta Ferdinanda of Spain to Vittorio Amedeo, heir to the throne of Piedmont, and then supplied the wedding festival music itself, *La vittoria di Imeneo*, for Turin the following June (it was performed more than 20 times; for illustration *see* TURIN, fig.2). A new *Artaserse* opened the Teatro Nuovo in Padua in 1751. By April 1762 Galuppi was unanimously appointed *maestro di coro* of St Mark's, the most important musical position in Venice, and he was later elected *maestro di coro* at the Ospedale degli Incurabili.

In the meantime Galuppi continued to travel, fulfilling commissions for various (mostly serious) operas. Early in 1764 the Venetian ambassador to Vienna conveyed the wishes of the Russian minister to acquire Galuppi's services; the Russian court knew his work and had already staged seven of his operas. By June 1764 the Venetian Senate granted the composer leave to go, and, after securing the welfare of his family, Galuppi travelled to St Petersburg, visiting C. P. E. Bach (in Berlin) and Casanova along the way and arriving on 22 September 1765. For Catherine the Great's court he produced new works (*Ifigenia in Tauride*, possibly a comic work, now lost, and two cantatas), revived *Didone abbandonata* (an enormous success) and *Il rè pastore*, and arranged other operas, as well as providing religious and occasional music. He travelled with the court to Moscow, where comic works were performed (no comic operas were allowed on the St Petersburg stage before 1779). He returned to Venice with many honours and gifts and took up his position at St Mark's in late 1768, after visiting Hasse in Vienna. In summer 1769 *Il rè pastore* was presented in Venice to honour the future monarch, Joseph II.

After this, Galuppi dedicated himself mainly to sacred music, although his operas continued to be performed. Burney reports that the composer was busy all year, playing the organ for Venetian churches and presiding over St Mark's. *La serva per amore*, performed in October 1773, was his last operatic work. In 1782 he conducted performances to honour the pope in Venice

and received a visit from the future Tsar Paul of Russia. By 1784 his health declined, although he continued to compose, completing the Christmas mass for St Mark's a few weeks before his death on 3 January 1785, after a two-month illness. He was buried in the church of S Vitale (exact location unknown), and a month later was honoured by a lavish requiem mass in S Stefano led by Bertoni, his deputy in St Mark's. His wealth was not as extensive as once thought, but his will left inheritances to three sons and the bulk of a sizable estate to his wife, whom he names with tender praise. Seven other children (all daughters) are not mentioned.

Burney offered the most extensive account of Galuppi's personality and appearance from a visit in 1770: 'His character and conversation are natural, intelligent, and agreeable. He is in figure little and thin, but has very much the look of a gentleman'. Galuppi's lifelong dedication to his large family was well known, as Burney reported: 'He has the appearance of a regular family man, and is esteemed at Venice as much for his private character as for his public talents'. To Burney he was witty and charming, referring to his study as the room 'where he *dirtied paper*'. Burney named him the most inspired of all Venetian composers, superior to Piccinni and Sacchini and second only to Jommelli, and said that late in life Galuppi had lost none of the fire of his former years. Hasse, writing to Metastasio, referred to him as a 'most excellent composer' and in a poem Goldoni praised him with the epigram 'What music! What style! What masterworks!'.

2. WORKS. Galuppi was an extraordinarily popular composer of both serious and comic operas. His facile, elegant and flexible melodic style, joined to Goldoni's witty and sometimes poignant poetry, created the central watershed for the dispersion of *drammi giocosi* throughout Europe after 1749; works such as *Il filosofo di campagna* have few peers in that regard. Yet his serious operas were no less important; their performances exceeded his comic operas in number.

Galuppi's music embodies the principal Italian tradition of charming and beautiful melody, clear and lucid accompaniment, and virtuoso or emotive display; as he described it to Burney, good music contained 'vaghezza, chiarezza e buona modulazione'. In the comic works vocal phrases tend to be short, usually of two or four bars, and balanced in relation to each other, with subtle variations in lengths and emphasis to avoid rhythmic monotony. Within the melodic line rhythms are strong and lively, frequently contributing much wit to a comic passage. Galuppi always paid close attention to both the sense and the clarity of the text, emphasizing its emotional or humorous content. His musical ideas were fresh, inventive and sometimes surprising, adding a new dimension to a character or situation.

The principal *opera seria* music throughout Galuppi's career was the da capo aria in five parts, a form already well established in the 1720s. The typical variations of his day – *AABAA*, *AA'BAA'* and *ABCAB* – are all present, as are such other later 18th-century innovations as metre and tempo changes for the *B* text, abbreviated internal ritornellos, 'dal segno' returns to the first or second solo and the expansion of cadential or embellishment sections into larger formal entities. His later operas tend to be more innovative in this regard. Other aria forms often merely shorten the da capo design by eliminating ritornellos and textual repetition. In comic operas the full da capo was reserved for serious roles and comic arias were of simpler design, even including popular song. In the 1750s Galuppi increasingly relied on binary designs; after 1755 the simple *AA* and rounded binary, *ABA'*, were most common, modulating from tonic to dominant and back. The text was often merely repeated, sometimes with shifts of tempo or metre, or both.

While many comic operas of the 1730s and 40s featured small ensembles, credit for the creation of the ensemble finale (or chain finale) is jointly shared by Galuppi and Goldoni. From their first effort of this type (*Arcadia in Brenta*, 1749) musical form, tonality and melody were made the servant of the drama. Goldoni's comic, act-ending text mosaics were matched by Galuppi with short musical sections, either open or closed, in contrasting keys, tempos and metres, through-composed to match the rapid shifts of plot and to reflect the insistent, kaleidoscopic emotions. These were usually organized around a central key; related key areas, new textures and melodies created strong contrast. This model for ensemble finales was widely imitated, by Haydn and Mozart among others.

Galuppi's treatment of the orchestra was praised by Burney and others; the ensemble's interplay with the voice, its sharing of structural motifs, themes and figuration, and its clarity of texture in accompaniment are principal hallmarks. Galuppi, like many other important 18th-century composers, was an exacting orchestral taskmaster; the orchestra of St Mark's was said to lead Italy in its skill.

Galuppi was extremely sensitive to the abilities of his singers, just as Goldoni was to those of his actors. In his comic works Galuppi enjoyed the long cooperation of Francesco Carrattoli, Francesco Baglioni and other Baglionis (particularly Clementina, Francesco's daughter, who sang in at least 16 Galuppi productions, both comic and serious). The serious male roles in comic opera were for high voice, but conceived for women in trouser roles. Galuppi also composed for the finest *opera seria* singers, including Caffarelli, Manzuoli, Gioacchino Conti, Caterina Gabrieli, Guadagni and Amorevoli, and here too he followed the 18th-century

practice of 'tailoring' arias like a suit of clothes. His compositions for Tenducci during that singer's second Italian career attest to this. That a revival of *Didone abbandonata* for Naples in 1770 was refused by the singers (Insanguine rewrote it) probably attests more to Galuppi's sympathy for the original voices than to any outdated musical style, as is sometimes asserted.

See also AMANTE DI TUTTE, L'; ARCADIA IN BRENTA, L'; ARTASERSE (iii); DIAVOLESSA, LA; FILOSOFO DI CAMPAGNA, IL; INIMICO DELLE DONNE, L'; MONDO DELLA LUNA, IL (i); NOZZE, LE; and OLIMPIADE, L' (iv).

LKH – *London, King's Theatre in the Haymarket*
MRD – *Milan, Regio Ducal Teatro*
VA – *Venice, Teatro S Angelo*   VM – *Venice, Teatro S Moisè*
VC – *Venice, Teatro S Cassiano*   VS – *Venice, Teatro S Samuele*

La fede nell'incostanza, ossia Gli amici rivali (favola pastorale, 3, G. Neri), Chioggia, Boegan; Vicenza, delle Grazie, 1722, 1 aria *B-Bc*

Gl'odi delusi dal sangue [Acts 1 and 3] (os, 3, A. M. Lucchini), VA, 4 Feb 1728 [Act 2 by G. B. Pescetti]

Dorinda (pastorale, 3, anon. rev. D. Lalli), VS, 9 June 1729, collab. Pescetti

L'odio placato (os, 3, F. Silvani), VS, 27 Dec 1729

Argenide (os, 3, A. Giusti), VA, 15 Jan 1733

L'ambizione depressa (os, 3, G. Papis), VA, Ascension 1733

La ninfa Apollo (favola pastorale, 3, F. de Lemene with addns by G. Boldini), VS, 30 May 1734

Tamiri (os, 3, B. Vitturi), VA, 17 Nov 1734

Elisa regina di Tiro (os, 3, A. Zeno and P. Pariati), VA, 27 Jan 1736

Ergilda (os, 3, Vitturi), VA, 12 Nov 1736, *Bc*

L'Alvilda (os, 3, Lalli, after Zeno: *L'amor generoso*), VS, 29 May 1737, 1 aria *I-Gl*

Issipile [1st version] (os, 3, P. Metastasio), Turin, Regio, 26 Dec 1737

Alessandro nell'Indie [1st version] (os, 3, Metastasio), Mantua, Nuovo Arciducale, ?Jan 1738, *US-Wc* (for later setting, revival or pasticcio; copy of lost MS, *D-Dlb*)

Adriano in Siria [1st version] (os, 3, Metastasio), Turin, Regio, ?Jan 1740, *B-Bc* (with addns from later productions)

Gustavo I, rè di Svezia (os, 3, C. Goldoni), VS, 25 May 1740, *D-Dlb*

Didone abbandonata [1st version] (os, 3, Metastasio), Modena, Molzo, 26 Dec 1740, *B-Bc* (convoluted MS from different periods), *P-La* (1752, Madrid), *RU-SPtob*, *US-Wc* (?1751)

Oronte rè de' sciti (os, 3, Goldoni), Venice, S Giovanni Grisostomo, 26 Dec 1740

Berenice (os, 3, Vitturi), VA, 27 Jan 1741

Penelope (os, 3, P. A. Rolli), LKH, 12 Dec 1741, Favourite Songs (London, 1741)

Scipione in Cartagine (os, 3, F. Vanneschi), LKH, 2 March 1742, *RU-Mcm*, Favourite Songs (London, *c*1742)

Enrico (os, 3, Vanneschi), LKH, 1 Jan 1743, *B-Br*, Favourite Songs (London, 1743)

Sirbace (os, 3, C. N. Stampa), LKH, 5 April 1743, Favourite Songs (London, 1743)

Arsace (os, 3, A. Salvi), Venice, S Giovanni Grisostomo, 16 Nov 1743

Ricimero [1st version] (os, 3, Silvani), MRD, 26 Dec 1744

La forza d'amore (dg, 3, Panicelli), VC, 30 Jan 1745

Ciro riconosciuto [1st version] (os, 3, Metastasio), MRD, 26 Dec 1745

Il trionfo della continenza (pastorale, 3), LKH, 28 Jan 1746, 1 aria *I-Fc*, Favourite Songs (London, 1746)

Scipione nelle Spagne (os, 3, A. Piovene), VA, Nov 1746, *F-Pn* (2 acts), *RU-Mcm*

Evergete (os, 3, Silvani and Lalli), Rome, Capranica, 2 Jan 1747, Act 1 *P-La*

L'Arminio (os, 3, Salvi), VC, 26 Nov 1747, arias *I-MOe*, *Nc*, *PLcon*, *PS*, *Vc* and *Vnm* (1747, Rome)

L'olimpiade (os, 3, Metastasio), MRD, 26 Dec 1747, *D-Dlb*, *I-Mc* (*R*1978: IOB, xli), Act 1 *Tf* (1758)

Vologeso (os, 3, Zeno), Rome, Argentina, 13 or 14 Feb 1748, *D-B* ('Berenice di Galuppi, 1742')

Demetrio [1st version] (os, 3, Metastasio), Vienna, Burg, 16 or 27 Oct 1748, *A-Wn*, *F-Pc* (2 copies)

Clotilde (os, 3, F. Passarini), VC, Nov 1748 (? with addns)

Semiramide riconosciuta (os, 3, Metastasio), MRD, 25 Jan 1749, *Pc*

Artaserse [1st version] (os, 3, Metastasio), Vienna, Burg, 27 Jan 1749, *A-Wn*, *D-Bds**, *F-Pc*, ov. *I-Rc* (1756, Venice), *TLp* (1757, Lucca)

L'Arcadia in Brenta (dg, 3, Goldoni), VA, 14 May 1749, *B-Bc, I-MOe*

Demofoonte [1st version] (os, 3, Metastasio), Madrid, Buen Retiro, 18 Dec 1749, *Nc*

Alcimena principessa dell'Isole Fortunate, ossia L'amore fortunato ne' suoi disprezzi (os, 3, P. Chiari, after Molière: *La princesse d'Elide*), VC, 26 Dec 1749

Arcifanfano re dei matti (dg, 3, Goldoni), VM, 27 Dec 1749 (? with addns), ov. *MAav* (1759, Venice), arias *Tf*

Il mondo della luna (dg, 3, Goldoni), VM, 29 Jan 1750, *D-Dlb, W, F-Pc, GB-Lbl, Lcm, I-Gl, US-Wc*, Favourite Songs (London, 1760)

Il paese della Cuccagna (dg, 3, Goldoni), VM, 7 May 1750

Il mondo alla roversa, ossia Le donne che comandano (dg, 3, Goldoni), VC, 14 Nov 1750, *A-Wgm, B-Bc* (1752, Venice), *D-Dlb, DS, F-Pc* (1755, Dresden), *GB-Lbl, Lcm, I-MOe, MAav, TLp, Vlevi, US-Wc*

Issipile [2nd version] (os, 3, Metastasio), Bologna, 1750, *D-Dlb, P-La* (1755, Parma), *US-Wc*

Antigona (os, 3, G. Roccaforte), Rome, Dame, 9 Jan 1751, *B-Br, D-Wa* (1754, Brunswick), *GB-Lbl* (as Antigono); as Antigona in Tebe, Naples, 1755, *B-Br*

Dario (os, 3, G. Baldanza), Turin, Regio Ducal, carn. 1751, arias *Rsc*

Lucio Papirio (os, 3, Zeno), Reggio Emilia, Pubblico, Fair 1751

Artaserse [2nd version] (os, 3, Metastasio), Padua, Nuovo, 11 June 1751, 1 aria *MAav*

Il conte Caramella (dg, 3, Goldoni), Venice, aut. 1751, *A-Wn, D-W, Wa, I-Gl, Mr*

Le virtuose ridicole, (dg, 3, Goldoni, after Molière: *Les précieuses ridicules*), VS, carn. 1752, *D-W*

La calamita de' cuori (dg, 3, Goldoni), VS, 26 Dec 1752, *A-Wn, ?D-Bds, W, F-Pc*, Acts 1 and 2 *GB-Lbl, US-Wc*

I bagni d'Abano (dg, 3, Goldoni), VS, 10 Feb 1753, Act 2 *D-W* and *MGmi*; collab. F. Bertoni (? pasticcio)

Sofonisba [1st version] (os, 3, Roccaforte), Rome, Dame, *c*24 Feb 1753

L'eroe cinese (os, 3, Metastasio), Naples, S Carlo, 10 July 1753, *P-La, PL-Wn*

Ricimero re dei goti [2nd version] (os, 3), Naples, S Carlo, 4 Nov 1753, *F-Pc, I-Nc*, Favourite Songs (London, 1755)

Alessandro nelle Indie [2nd version] (os, 3, Metastasio), Naples, S Carlo, 20 Jan 1754, *P-La*

Siroe (os, 3, Metastasio), Rome, Argentina, 10 Feb 1754, *B-Bc, GB-Lbl, Ob, P-La*

Il filosofo di campagna (dg, 3, Goldoni), VS, 26 Oct 1754, *A-Wn, D-Bds, Dlb, SWl, W* (as La serva accorta), *F-Pc, GB-Cfm, Lbl, I-Fc, Mr, Rdp, Sac, Vnm, P-La, US-Bp, Wc*, Favourite Songs (London, 1761); rev. Rome, 1757, as La serva astuta

Il povero superbo (dg, 3, Goldoni, after *La gastarda*), VS, Feb 1755; rev. Brescia, 1755, as La serva astuta

Alessandro nelle Indie [3rd version] (os, 3, Metastasio), VS, Ascension 1755, *D-Mbs* (incl. changes for Munich, 12 Oct 1755)

Attalo (os, 3, ?Silvani or ? A. Papi), Padua, Nuovo, 11 June 1755, *LEmi* (Parma), *F-Pn*

Le nozze (dg, 3, Goldoni), Bologna, Formagliari, 14 Sept 1755, *A-Wn, D-W, ?I-Fc, P-La, US-Wc*; as Le nozze di Dorina, Perugia, 1759, *I-Gl*; (int) Rome, 1760; as O casamente de Lesbina, Lisbon, 1766; rev. Reggio Emilia, 1770 (as Le nozze di Dorina), *P-La, US-Wc*

La diavolessa [L'avventuriera; Li vaghi accidenti fra amore e gelosia] (dg, 3, Goldoni), VS, Nov 1755, *A-Wn* (*R*1978: IOB, xliv), *D-Bds, Wa, GB-Lbl, I-MOe, RU-Mcm, US-Wc*; rev. Leipzig and Prague, 1756

Idomeneo (os), Rome, Argentina, 7 Jan 1756, *P-La*

La cantarina (farsetta, 3, Goldoni), Rome, Capranica, 26 Feb 1756

Ezio (os, 3, Metastasio), MRD, 22 Jan 1757, *La*

Sesostri (os, 3, Pariati), Venice, S Benedetto, 26 Nov 1757, *D-LEmi, P-La* (1759, Venice), *S-Skma* (1760)

Ipermestra (os, 3, Metastasio), MRD, 14 Jan 1758, *P-La* (3 copies, incl. 1761, Pisa)

Adriano in Siria [2nd version] (os, 3, Metastasio), Livorno, spr. 1758, *La* (3 copies, incl. 1759, Naples: *R* in DMV, xx, forthcoming); *D-Dlb* and *P-La* (1760, S Luca); *B-Bc, S-Skma*

Demofoonte [2nd version] (os, 3, Metastasio), Padua, 1758, *B-Bc* (arias autograph), *D-Dlb, I-MOe* (attrib. Caldara), *P-La*; rev. Venice, S Benedetto, 1759, *La*

Ciro riconosciuto [2nd version] (os, 3, Metastasio), Rome, carn. 1759, *F-Pc, P-La*

Melite riconosciuto (os, 3, Roccaforte), Rome, Dame, 13 Jan 1759, *La* (2 copies)

La ritornata di Londra (int, Goldoni), Rome, Valle, *c*19 Feb 1759

La clemenza di Tito (os, 3, Metastasio), Venice, S Salvatore, carn. 1760, *F-Pc, I-CMbc, P-La* (2 copies)

Solimano (os, 3, G. A. Migliavacca), Padua, Nuovo, 11 June 1760, *La* (2 copies)

L'amante di tutte (dg, 3, A. Galuppi), VM, 15 Nov 1760, *A-Wn, B-Bc, D-Dlb* (1770, Dresden), *W* (Act 2), *F-Pc, I-Gl, Mr, MOe, Vc, P-La, US-Wc*

Li tre amanti ridicoli (dg, 3, A. Galuppi), VM, 18 Jan 1761, *A-Wn, D-W, Wa* (1762, Venice), *F-Pn, I-MOe, US-Wc*

Demetrio [2nd version] (os, 3, Metastasio), Padua, June 1761, *P-La*

Il caffè di campagna (dg, 3, Chiari), VM, 18 Nov 1761, *La*

Antigono (os, 3, Metastasio), Venice, S Benedetto, carn. 1762, *La*

Il marchese villano (dg, 3, Chiari), VM, 2 Feb 1762, *A-Wn, B-Bc, I-Nc, P-La*; rev. as La lavandara, Turin, 1770; as La lavandara astuta, Mantua, 1771; as Il matrimonio per inganno, Venice, S Giacomo di Corfù

L'orfana onorata (int), Rome, Valle, carn. 1762, 1 aria *I-TLp*

Il rè pastore (os, 3, Metastasio), Parma, Ducal, spr. 1762, 1 aria *Gl* (1779, Genoa); ?rev. St Petersburg, Sept 1766

Viriate (os, 3, Metastasio: *Siface*), Venice, S Salvatore, 19 May 1762, *P-La*

Il Muzio Scevola (os, 3, C. Lanfranchi Rossi), Padua, Nuovo, June 1762, arias *I-Fc* and *Nc*, ov. *Vc*, Act 2 *P-La*

L'uomo femmina (dg, 3), VM, aut. 1762, *La*

Il puntiglio amoroso (dg, 3, [? C. or G.] Gozzi), VM, 26 Dec 1762, *A-Wn, US-Wc*

Arianna e Teseo [1st version] (os, 3, Pariati), Padua, Nuovo, 12 June 1763, *P-La* (3 copies)

Il re alla caccia (dg, 3, Goldoni), VS, aut. 1763, *F-Pc, I-Nc, Vc, P-La, US-Wc*

Sofonisba [2nd version] (os, 3, M. Verazi), Turin, Regio, carn. 1764, *I-Tf, P-La* (3 copies), *US-Wc*

Cajo Mario (os, 3, Roccaforte), Venice, S Giovanni Grisostomo, 31 May 1764, *P-La*

La partenza e il ritorno de' marinari (dg), VM, 26 Dec 1764, *?D-Bds, Dlb, I-Vc*

Didone abbandonata [2nd version] (os, 3, Metastasio), Naples, 1764, *Nc, P-La* (1765, Venice)

La cameriera spiritosa (dg, 3, Goldoni), MRD, 4 Oct 1766, rev. Prague, ?1768–9, as Il cavaliere della Piuma

Ifigenia in Tauride (os, 3, M. Coltellini), St Petersburg, court, 21 April/2 May 1768, *RU-SPtob, US-Wc*

Arianna e Teseo [2nd version] (os, 3, Pariati), Venice, carn. 1769, *P-La* (2 copies)

Amor lunatico (dg, 3, Chiari), VM, Jan 1770

L'inimico delle donne (dg, 3, G. Bertati), VS, aut. 1771, *B-Bc, P-La* (*R*1986: DMV, xxi)

Gl'intrighi amorosi (dg, 3, G. Petroselini), VS, Jan 1772, *B-Bc*

Motezuma (os, 3, V. A. Cigna-Santi), Venice, S Benedetto, 27 May 1772, *Bc, D-Dlb* (lost; copy in *US-Wc*), *P-La*

La serva per amore (os, 3, F. Livigni), VS, Oct 1773, Act 1 *B-Bc* and *F-Pn**

Dramatic occasional works: L'Adria festosa (serenata, ?2), Naples, 1738; Li amori sfortunati di Ormindo (serenata, ?2, B. Vitturi), Burano, 1738; La vittoria d'Imeneo (festa teatrale, G. Bartoli), Turin, Regio, 7 June 1750, *GB-Lbl* (as Imeneo e Venere); Le nozze di Paride (spettacolo poetico e musicale, Chiari), Venice, S Giovanni Grisostomo, Oct 1756; L'arrivo di Enea nel Lazio (componimento drammatico, 1, V. Alamanni), Florence, Pergola, 15 Nov 1765; La pace tra la Virtù e la Bellezza (componimento drammatico, 1, Metastasio), St Petersburg, court, 28 June 1766

Doubtful: La mascherata (dramma comico, 3, Goldoni), VC, 26 Dec 1750 [? part or all by G. Cocchi]; La finta cameriera (dg, 3, G. Barlocci), Brunswick, 1751, *D-Wa*; Astianatte, 1755; Alceste, *F-Pc*; La fausse coquette, *D-DS*

Revisions: Siroe re di Persia [after L. Vinci] (os, 3, Metastasio), Venice, S Giovanni Grisostomo, carn. 1731, collab. G. B. Pescetti; Ambizione delusa (ob, 3) [after Rinaldo di Capua], carn. 1744

Music in: Alessandro in Persia, 1741; Antigono, 1746; Il villano geloso, 1769

*

BurneyFI

F. Caffi: *Storia della musica sacra nella già cappella ducale di San Marco in Venezia dal 1318 al 1797* (Venice, 1854–5), i, 373–416

P. Molmenti: 'Il Buranello', *Gazzetta musicale di Milano*, i (1899), 59–60

A. Wotquenne: 'Baldassare Galuppi (1706–1785): étude bibliographique sur ses oeuvres dramatiques', *RMI*, vi (1899), 561–79; pubd separately, with addns (Brussels, 1902)

V. G. Cheshikhin: *Istoriya russkoi opery (s 1674–1903g)* (Moscow, 1905), 741–5

F. Piovano: 'Baldassare Galuppi: note bio-bibliografiche', *RMI*, xiii (1906), 676–726; xiv (1907), 333–65; xv (1908), 233–74

G. G. Bernardi: 'L'opera comica veneziana del sec. XVIII', *Atti dell'Accademia virgiliana di Mantova* (1908)

E. J. Dent: 'Ensembles and Finales in 18th Century Italian Opera', *SIMG*, xi (1909–10), 543–69; xii (1910–11), 112–38

A. Della Corte: *L'opera comica italiana nell '700* (Bari, 1923), i, 141–72; ii, 216–46

M. Fuchs: *Die Entwicklung des Finales in der italienischen opera buffa vor Mozart* (diss., U. of Vienna, 1932)

W. Bollert: *Die Buffoopern Baldassare Galuppis* (diss., U. of Berlin, 1935)

——: 'Tre opere di Galuppi, Haydn e Paisiello sul *Mondo della luna* di Goldoni', *Musica d'oggi*, xxi (1939), 265–70

B. Galuppi detto 'Il Buranello': noti e documenti, Chigiana, v (1948)

A. Della Corte: *Baldassare Galuppi: profilo critico* (Siena, 1948)

R.-A. Mooser: *Annales de la musique et des musiciens en Russie au XVIIIme siècle*, ii (Geneva, 1951), 69ff

T. Livanova: *Russkaya muzikal'naya kul'tura XVIII veka v eyo svyazyakhs literatury teatrom i bitom* [Russian Musical Culture of the 18th Century and its Links with Literature, the Theatre and Everyday Life' (Moscow, 1952–3), i, 421, 445; ii, 405–6

W. J. Weichlein: *A Comparative Study of Five Musical Settings of 'La Clemenza di Tito'* (diss., U. of Michigan, 1956), i, chaps. 3, 4

D. Arnold: 'Orphans and Ladies: the Venetian Conservatories (1680–1790)', *PRMA*, lxxxix (1962–3), 31–47

Venezia e il melodramma nel settecento: Venice 1973–5 [incl. D. Heartz: 'Hasse, Galuppi, and Metastasio', i, 309–39; D. Heartz: 'Vis Comica: Goldoni, Galuppi and *L'Arcadia in Brenta*', ii, 33–73; M. F. Robinson: 'Three Versions of Goldoni's *Il filosofo di campagna*', ii, 75–85]

P. Weiss: 'Goldoni poeta d'opere serie per musica', *Studi goldoniani*, iii (1973), 7–40

R. Wiesend: 'Internationales Symposium Venedig und die Oper des 18. Jahrhundert: Venice, 1973', *Mf*, xxvii (1974), 67–8

W. Plath: 'Mozart und Galuppi: Bemerkungen zur Szene "Ah non lasciarmi, no" KV 295a', *Festschrift Walter Senn* (Munich, 1975), 174–8

D. Heartz: 'The Creation of the Buffo Finale in Italian Opera', *PRMA*, civ (1977–8), 67–78

——: 'Goldoni, Don Giovanni and the Dramma Giocoso', *MT*, cxx (1979), 993–8

——: 'Traetta in Vienna: Armida (1761) and Ifigenia in Tauride (1763)', *Studies in Music from the University of Western Ontario*, vii (1982), 65

R. Wiesend: 'Die Arie "Già si sa ch'un empio sei": von Vivaldi oder von Galuppi?', *Bollettino dell'Istituto italiano Antonio Vivaldi*, iv (1983), 76

——: 'Galuppi's erste Oper/Il primo melodramma di Galuppi', *Quaderni di studi galuppiani*, i (1983)

——: 'Il giovane Galuppi e l'opera: materiali per gli anni 1722–41', *NRMI*, xvii (1983), 383–97

——: 'Zum Ensemble in der opera seria', *Colloquium Johann Adolf Hasse und die Musik seiner Zeit: Siena 1983*, AnMc, no.25 (1987), 187–222

——: *Studien zur opera seria von Baldassare Galuppi: Werksituation und Überlieferung–Form und Satztechnik–Inhaltsdarstellung, mit einer Biographie und einem Quellenverzeichnis der Opern* (Tutzing, 1984)

——: 'Ein "einfaches Sekundarierstück ohne individuelle Züge"? Tradition und Erfindung in der Arie "Torna di Tito a lato" ', *MJb* 1984–5, 134–44

Galuppiana 1985: studi e ricerche: Venice 1985

DALE E. MONSON

Galván [Galbán], **Ventura** (*fl* 1762–73). Spanish composer. Famous first as a comic actor, he was also well known as a composer for the lyric stage by 1762; according to Subirá, he was paid 300 reales for three *tonadillas* and some incidental pieces, and 600 reales for the music to the comedy *Riesgo* in that year. He was celebrated as a composer of *sainetes* and zarzuelas.

Galván collaborated with Ramón de la Cruz on various *sainetes* and on the zarzuela *Las foncarraleras* (1772). Four *sainetes* and 20 *tonadillas*, including his famous *Los vagamundos y ciegos fingidos* (ed. in J. Subirá: *La tonadilla escénica*, iii, Madrid, 1930), are in Madrid (*E-Mm*).

J. Subirá: *Tonadillas teatrales inéditas* (Madrid, 1932), 184–5

——: *La tonadilla escénica: sus obras y sus autores* (Barcelona, 1933), 148ff

——: *Temas musicales madrileños* (Madrid, 1970), 269

ELEANOR RUSSELL

Galvani, Giacomo (*b* Bologna, 1 Nov 1825; *d* Venice, 7 May 1889). Italian tenor. After study with Luigi Zamboni (the creator of Rossini's Figaro) he made his début at Spoleto as Carlo in *I masnadieri* (1849). He soon appeared at La Scala, where he was admired in operas by Rossini, Donizetti and Verdi; his art was compared by some to the florid vocal style of Rubini. British appearances took him to Covent Garden (Nemorino, 1852) and Edinburgh (1860). From 1869 he collaborated with the singer Giuseppe Ciampi in a company which toured Russia, and after retiring from the stage he taught in Moscow and Venice.

DAVID CUMMINGS

Galvany, Maria (*b* Granada, 1878; *d* Rio de Janeiro, 2 Nov 1944). Spanish soprano. She studied at the Madrid Conservatory and made her début as Lucia at Cartagena in 1897. Specializing in coloratura roles, she sang with success in Spain and Italy, gaining her greatest popularity in South America. She also toured with a company that performed throughout Europe, including Russia, visiting London in 1909, when she appeared at Drury Lane in *La sonnambula*, *Il barbiere* and *Dinorah*. She retired to Brazil and died there in poverty. Her recordings are memorable for sweetness in the middle range, brilliance in the upper register and the bravura of a stunt-artist in staccato.

J. B. STEANE

Gambill, Robert (*b* Indianapolis, IN, 31 March 1955). American tenor. While studying at Hamburg, he made his début in 1977 at Geneva as the Count of Lerma (*Don Carlos*). Engaged at Wiesbaden from 1981, he sang Tamino, Ernesto, Nicolai's Fenton and Don Ottavio; in 1981 he also created Michael in Stockhausen's *Donnerstag aus Licht* at La Scala. He first sang at Glyndebourne as Rossini's Figaro in 1982, returning in 1985 as Don Ramiro. He has also sung in Frankfurt, Zürich, Hamburg, Venice, Bologna, Santa Fe, Vienna and Aix-en-Provence. His repertory includes Ferrando, Belmonte, Lindoro, Renaud (*Armide*), Iopas (*Les Troyens*), Verdi's Fenton and Wagner's Steersman and David, which he sang at his Metropolitan and Covent Garden débuts respectively in 1990. His lyrical voice is equally effective in Italian, French and German music.

ELIZABETH FORBES

Gambler, The [*Igrok*; *Le joueur*]. Opera in four acts, op.24, by SERGEY PROKOFIEV to his own libretto after the novella (1866) by FYODOR MIKHAYLOVICH DOSTOYEVSKY; Brussels, Théâtre Royal de la Monnaie, 29 April 1929.

Prokofiev's *Gambler* was an early opera to be based on a work by Dostoyevsky, whose novels were in various scenic adaptations enjoying a vogue on the Russian stage at the time of its writing (e.g. *The Idiot* and *The Brothers Karamazov* at the Moscow Arts Theatre). Apart from juvenilia, it was also the composer's first completed opera. He began writing it in 1915, at the invitation of Albert Coates, then the chief conductor for opera at the Mariinsky Theatre, St Petersburg, shortly after returning from his first trip abroad, where he had been tagging along with Dyagilev, Stravinsky and the Ballets Russes. The opera's radical reformist style, which harks back to that of Musorgsky's 'experiment in dramatic music in prose' after Nikolay Gogol's *Marriage* (belatedly given its première in 1908), was undoubtedly motivated not only by Musorgsky's example, but also in reaction to the anti-operatic aesthetics of the Dyagilev circle (as enunciated in various writings by Stravinsky but particularly by Alexandre Benois in his *Reminiscences of the Russian Ballet*). In press interviews he gave in connection with this opera's acceptance for performance by the Mariinsky Theatre during the 1916–17 season, the 25-year-old composer scoffed at every conceivable operatic convention, from the use of rhymed verse for librettos to the unrealistic deployment of the chorus, the casting of voices in combination (ensembles) instead of succession (dialogue), and (it goes without saying) the chopping of the action into 'numbers'. By confining his vocal writing to what he called 'the declamatory style', meaning a melodically heightened recitative in conjunction with a network of leitmotifs (many of them pliable vocal formulae or 'melodic moulds' to which prose dialogue could be accommodated, rather than symphonically developed instrumental motifs of the Wagnerian type), Prokofiev hoped to achieve a 'scenic flexibility' that would rescue opera from its putative impasse and show it to be 'the most vivid and powerful of all the scenic arts'.

Owing to difficulties in casting, the unwillingness of the orchestra, the ineptitude of the director (Nikolay Bogolyubov) and, finally, the political turmoil following the February revolution of 1917, the Mariinsky production (in which the great tenor Ivan Yershov was to have sung Alexey) fell through. Before its cancellation Vsevolod Meyerhold had stepped in to replace Bogolyubov; this was the first of the great director's many aborted collaborations with Prokofiev. Meyerhold hoped to stage *The Gambler* in Moscow in the late 1920s, following Prokofiev's early and very successful Soviet tours. To this end he collaborated with the composer, who was then living in Paris, on a thorough revision of the opera, completed in 1928 (it is this somewhat more lyrical second version that has been published in vocal score, first by Sergey Koussevitzky's Russischer Musikverlag in 1930 and by the Soviet house Muzïka in 1967; the first version, lithographed by the Mariinsky Theatre for in-house use, is now a great rarity). Again the production fell through, this time owing to the opposition of the militantly anti-modernist Russian Association of Proletarian Musicians (RAPM). Prokofiev's interesting published correspondence with Meyerhold on *The Gambler*, although it testifies to a close working relationship marked by mutual respect, does not support the widespread notion that Meyerhold was a formative influence on Prokofiev's operatic aesthetic (they met too late for that; the more radical first version of the opera was completed before they were acquainted).

Following the Brussels première, given in French under Corneil de Thoran, *The Gambler* was not seen again until after Prokofiev's death. Performances in

Naples (1953), Paris (in concert under Charles Bruck, 1956), Darmstadt (1957), Plzeň (1958) and Belgrade (1962) preceded the Russian concert première, by Leningrad radio forces under Gennady Rozhdestvensky, in 1963. In 1974 the opera entered the repertory of the Bol'shoy Theatre, Moscow (with Boris Pokrovsky as director). Both Russian productions have been recorded.

The scenic action faithfully follows the central plot of Dostoyevsky's novella (minus the first three chapters, largely given over to description, and the last two, which are in the nature of an epilogue), while the libretto conserves a fair amount of original dialogue. The setting is the imaginary German spa town of Roulettenburg. Alexey (tenor), in love with Pauline (soprano), is commanded to prove his devotion by pointlessly insulting the Baroness Wurmerhelm (silent role) (Act 1). For this he is impulsively fired from his tutor's position by the General (bass), who is heavily in debt to the Marquis de Grieux (tenor), and has been waiting nervously for news of the death of 'Granny' Babulen'ka (his aunt), which will mean his financial salvation; instead of news, Babulen'ka (mezzo-soprano) herself shows up, to general consternation (Act 2). The old lady proceeds to wipe herself out at the roulette table, whereupon she returns to Russia; the General is ruined and abandoned by Blanche (contralto), his demi-mondaine fiancée (Act 3). The Marquis, with whom Pauline has been having an affair, now abandons her under humiliating circumstances including a pay-off in the form of a transfer to her of some of her stepfather's debts; Alexey runs off to the gaming table to avenge her (Act 4.i). He breaks the bank (4.ii), then returns to Pauline with a fortune; but she, thinking herself bought off a second time, angrily rejects him, leaving him a pathological gambler (4.iii).

In 1931 Prokofiev extracted an orchestral suite from the opera, entitled 'Four Portraits and the Denouement from *The Gambler*'. Since the opera was constructed wholly without detachable numbers, whether vocal or instrumental, the composer (as he related in his autobiography) ripped up a vocal score and 'dealt' it page by page into piles on the floor corresponding to music associated with Alexey, Babulen'ka, the General and Pauline respectively. These then provided the material for the four portraits. The 'Denouement' is an orchestral condensation of the very striking roulette scene (4.ii), in which a musical phrase representing the turning wheel and the bouncing ball acts as a ritornello.

RICHARD TARUSKIN

Gamblers, The [*Igroki*]. Opera by DMITRY SHOSTAKOVICH after the play by NIKOLAY VASIL'YEVICH GOGOL, incomplete; Leningrad, Philharmonic Bol'shoy Hall, 18 September 1978 (concert performance), Moscow, Chamber Music Theatre, 24 January 1990 (stage). Completed in three acts by KRZYSZTOF MEYER; Wuppertal, Opernhaus, 12 June 1983.

Immediately after the completion of his Seventh Symphony (the 'Leningrad') in late December 1941, Shostakovich began work on an operatic setting of Gogol's comedy *The Gamblers*. In his second Gogol project – the first was the opera on the short story *The Nose* completed in 1928 – the composer set the play word for word, without cuts or alterations, an approach reminiscent of Musorgsky's setting of *The Marriage*. Shostakovich worked on the opera throughout 1942. That December he abandoned it, having set slightly less than a third of Gogol's text to approximately 50 minutes of music, concluding that fidelity to Gogol's text would produce an opera of impractical dimensions. In 1975 Shostakovich based the second movement of his last composition, the Sonata for Viola and Piano, on themes from *The Gamblers*. After the composer's death, Gennady Rozhdestvensky resurrected the opera and gave a concert première of the completed portion in 1978; it was staged in Moscow in 1990. In 1980–81, the Polish composer Krzysztof Meyer undertook a completion of the opera. To keep it within manageable limits, he was obliged to make cuts in Gogol's play, but he maintained the flavour of Shostakovich's style, using themes and motifs from the earlier section as unifying devices.

Telling of the cheating of a card-sharper by a number of his intended victims, the opera is unusual in a number of respects: it has no female roles, no conventional love interest and very little stage action, relying for much of its comic effect on social satire and the subtle idiosyncrasies of character and language, ingeniously realized by Shostakovich. The brief instrumental introduction, with its circus-like atmosphere, leads straight into the first scene as Ikharyov (tenor), landowner and card-sharp, arrives with his servant Gavryushka (bass) at the inn of a provincial town and asks the inn's servant, Alexey (bass), about the habits and gambling proclivities of the other guests. Left alone, Ikharyov unpacks and addresses a passionate arioso, 'Kakov vid?' ('What a sight?') to his beloved pack of marked cards, 'Adelaida Ivanovna', invoking her name with reverence. When he leaves to peek at the competition, two of them, Krugel' (tenor) and Shvokhnev (bass), sneak in to pump Gavryushka for information about his master, learning that Ikharyov has recently won 80 000 rubles. To an accompaniment plucked on bass balalaika, Gavryushka fashions a rambling folk lament, 'Provornïye gospoda!' ('Nimble gentlemen'). Ikharyov returns ready for the game, bribing Alexey to substitute a marked pack of cards. Shvokhnev, Krugel' and Uteshitel'ny (baritone) arrive; they make small-talk, including a highly stylized recitative about food, before sitting down to business. The guests, card-sharps themselves, quickly appreciate Ikharyov's unusual talents and invite him to join forces. They all drink to the new friendship, with a fugal toast, and discuss the finer points of their 'art'. Shostakovich's setting of the opera concludes with Uteshitel'ny's story about fleecing the landowner Dergunov and his guests. In the concluding section of Act 1, Ikharyov introduces 'Adelaida Ivanovna' to his admiring new friends.

At the start of Act 2 Ikharyov is impatient to be back in action. Uteshitel'ny introduces Mikhayl Alexandrovich Glov (bass), a rich, incorruptible landowner who has been transacting business in the town. In polite conversation it emerges that, although anxious to return home to his wife and daughter, Glov has been waiting for the payment of 200 000 rubles. He lectures the young men on the evils of gambling. Before his departure, he begs a favour of Uteshitel'ny: to take his inexperienced son, who will remain behind to receive the payment, under his protective wing. Once the elder Glov has left, Uteshitel'ny brings the son, Alexander Mikhaylïch Glov (tenor), to meet his companions. Pouring champagne liberally, they pander to his overweening ambition to become a hussar and persuade him to play cards, using his father's 200 000-ruble promissory note as collateral. In a musical reprise of the Act 1 gambling music, the younger Glov is quickly stripped of the promissory note. When he realizes his predicament, he

pulls a gun and threatens suicide. The gamblers, prudently protecting their investment, restrain him and, with more champagne toasts, give him a rousing send-off to visit his lover.

As Act 3 opens, the gamblers are pondering how to hasten pay-off on the note when a local bureaucrat, Psoy Stakhikh Zamukhrïshkin (baritone), arrives. With a less than subtle approach, Uteshitel'ny tries to bribe him to speed payment on the promissory note, succeeding ultimately in reducing the wait from two weeks to four days. Ikharyov's companions are in despair. They reveal that if they cannot get money immediately, they will forfeit a perfect set-up waiting for them in another town. Ikharyov is in no hurry; he readily agrees to trade his friends his 80 000 rubles in cash for the promissory note worth 200 000 rubles. When the others leave, Ikharyov gloats about his good fortune. The younger Glov bursts in, looking for the others. He reveals to the incredulous Ikharyov that he has participated in a set-up by the others; the promissory note is worthless and both his 'father' and the clerk Zamukhrïshkin were part of the gang. Ikharyov wants to set out in pursuit of the swindlers, but the younger Glov reminds him that he cannot prosecute them for the very crime he himself tried to commit. In disgust, Ikharyov throws 'Adelaida Ivanovna' at the door, scattering the pack.

* * *

The style of *The Gamblers* provides a sharp contrast to the heroism of Shostakovich's Seventh Symphony; crisp rhythms, astringent though fundamentally tonal harmonies, grotesque juxtaposition of instrumental tone colours and, above all, careful attention to the nuances and inflections of the text, are all reminiscent of *The Nose* and Shostakovich's theatre music of the 1920s and early 30s.

LAUREL E. FAY

Gambling. From the early 18th century down to 1814, gambling was an essential source of finance for opera; well into the 20th century it made possible the creation of new operas in a few resort towns.

The *ancien régime* in the Italian and Austrian states oscillated between forbidding games of chance – in

Tombola at a fund-raising ball at the Paris Opéra in 1859 (tombola was tolerated as a mild alternative to harder forms of gambling): engraving from 'L'illustration' (17 December 1859)

practice unenforceable – and tolerating them in the form of a monopoly, usually farmed out or sublet to an impresario who also managed the opera season; the profits were divided between poor relief and the opera. Such monopolies grew up piecemeal with the spread of public opera houses, in whose foyers the gambling took place. Financial need drove even the virtuous-minded Maria Theresa to authorize them in Prague, Trieste and Milan in the 1750s, though she and other rulers suppressed them, again piecemeal, between 1753 and 1788. The upheavals of the French Revolution and the Napoleonic wars led to a craze for gambling, and the newly invented roulette opened it to more people. The Napoleonic kingdoms of Italy and Naples revived the monopoly and used its proceeds in part to meet their rising wartime expenditure, in part to fund lavish seasons at La Scala, Milan, and the S Carlo, Naples, whose pre-eminence in opera and ballet was thereby secured; the seasons were managed by the chief gambling concessionaire, Domenico Barbaia, and his associates. The unpopular monopoly was again suppressed at the fall of Napoleon in 1814, everywhere but in Naples and Palermo; there it was done away with by the 1820 revolutions.

From then on a gambling monopoly used to support ambitious opera seasons endured only in the chief casino towns of Europe: Bagni di Lucca (until 1847), Baden-Baden (at its peak c1850–70) and Monte Carlo (from c1870). Baden-Baden saw the creation of Berlioz's *Béatrice et Bénédict*; Monte Carlo launched operas by Massenet, Franck, Saint-Saëns, Fauré, Messager, Puccini and Ravel.

See also BALOCHINO, CARLO; BARBAIA, DOMENICO; and RICCI, FRANCESCO BENEDETTO.

F. Baser: *Grosse Musiker in Baden-Baden* (Tutzing, 1973)
T. J. Walsh: *Monte Carlo Opera 1879–1909* (Dublin, 1975)
B. Cherubini: *Bagni di Lucca fra cronaca e storia* (Lucca, 1977)
J. Rosselli: 'Governi, appaltatori e giuochi d'azzardo nell'Italia napoleonica', *Rivista storica italiana*, xciii (1981), 346–83

JOHN ROSSELLI

Gamerra, Giovanni de. *See* DE GAMERRA, GIOVANNI.

Ganne, (Gustave) Louis (*b* Buxières-les-Mines, 5 April 1862; *d* Paris, 13/14 July 1923). French composer and conductor. After studying at the Paris Conservatoire, he did his earliest work supplying music for the ballets at the Folies Bergère and the Casino de Paris. A theme from one of these works became popular as the march 'Le père la victoire'. Such pieces were his best-known compositions, but Ganne also turned out successful songs, salon pieces and above all mazurkas while pursuing a career as an orchestral conductor, in several fashionable resorts and, succeeding Olivier Métra, at the head of the Bals de l'Opéra.

His first venture into *opérette* with *Les colles des femmes* (1893) was not encouraging, but a collaboration with Maurice Ordonneau in 1899 produced the colourful circus musical *Les saltimbanques* which, in spite of an unexceptional first run, has survived as a popular favourite throughout France. The Monte Carlo Opera, where Ganne had become a celebrity as the conductor of a series of orchestral concerts under his name, produced his delightful *Hans, le joueur de flûte* (1906), a variant on the *Pied Piper* story, and *Rhodope* (1910), both of which won subsequent Paris performances. Ganne also completed Planquette's last work, *Le para-*

dis de Mahomet (1906), but the difficulties he encountered in trying to secure productions of his works led him to concentrate less on *opérettes* and more on the other areas of his work. *Cocorico* was his only work to be staged subsequently, at the Théâtre Apollo in 1913. A pastiche with a score made up from Ganne's music was produced at the Apollo in 1921 under the title *La belle de Paris*. A composer of pleasant and often catchy light music, most particularly in dance and march rhythms, Ganne has won a continuing place in the musical theatre through his two best-known works.

KURT GÄNZL

Gänsemarkt [Theater am Gänsemarkt]. Familiar name for the theatre built in 1678 in the Gänsemarkt ('goose market') of Hamburg; the first public opera house outside Venice, it closed in 1738 and was demolished in 1763. *See* HAMBURG, §1.

Ganzarolli, Wladimiro (*b* Venice, 9 Jan 1932). Italian bass-baritone. He studied in Venice, making his début in 1958 at the Teatro Nuovo, Milan, as Gounod's Méphistophélès. In 1959 he sang Sandeval (Donizetti's *Le duc de l'Albe*) at Spoleto. At La Scala he sang Bottom in the Italian première of *A Midsummer Night's Dream* (1961), Falstaff, Nevers (*Les Huguenots*), Assur (*Semiramide*), the title roles of Cherubini's *Ali Baba* and Hindemith's *Cardillac*, and Sulpice (*La fille du régiment*). He has appeared throughout Italy, in Vienna and Buenos Aires and at Covent Garden, where he made his début in 1965 as Mozart's Figaro, returning for Guglielmo and Leporello. Other roles included Papageno, Mustafà, Dandini, Don Basilio, Dulcamara, Lunardo (*I quatro rusteghi*), Golaud and Count des Grieux. He made his American début in 1974 at Chicago as Don Pasquale. A fine comic actor, he has been noted for his wide-ranging voice and clarity of diction.

ELIZABETH FORBES

Gänzl, Kurt (Friedrich) [Gallas, Brian Roy] (*b* Wellington, New Zealand, 15 Feb 1946). New Zealand writer. He studied classics in New Zealand and spent one year at the London Opera Centre before taking up writing, primarily on operetta and the musical theatre generally. His breadth of knowledge and his infectious enthusiasm are apparent in his lively books, which include a two-volume study *The British Musical Theatre* (London, 1986), *Gänzl's Book of the Musical Theatre* (with A. Lamb; London, 1988) and *Blackwell's Guide to Musical Theatre on Record* (Oxford, 1990).

Garat, (Dominique) Pierre (Jean) (*b* Bordeaux, 26 April 1762; *d* Paris, 1 March 1823). French tenor and baritone. He studied with Franz Beck at Bordeaux, but developed his technique chiefly by imitating Italian singers after moving to Paris in 1782. He performed frequently at Versailles; sinecures were arranged for him, and Marie-Antoinette twice paid his debts. He left Paris during the Terror and was imprisoned for nine months at Rouen. On his release, he travelled widely, returning to France in 1794. Although obliged to sing professionally, he never adopted a stage career, but he taught at the Conservatoire, 1796–1823. His teaching emphasized interpretation and expression rather than vocal training; his pupils included Mme Branchu, Nourrit *père*, Ponchard and Levasseur. His own voice was soft and sweet, but his three-octave range enabled him to sing arias for tenor, bass and even female voices.

Renowned for his powers of expression and mastery of styles, he was considered the supreme interpreter of Gluck, to whose music he refused to apply his usual brilliant ornamentation. For aesthetic reasons he attempted to suppress the sound 'r' in French speech. Scudo considered him the first French singer to combine French insistence on verbal clarity and expressiveness with fluent italianate vocalization; in this he may be considered to have prepared the way for Rossini's reform of French singing.

ES (R. Celletti)
P. Lafond: *Garat* (Paris, 1900)
B. Miall: *Pierre Garat, Singer and Exquisite* (London, 1913)
H. Radiguer: 'Garat', *EMDC*, I/iii (1921), 1649–50
I. de Fagoaga: *Pierre Garat, le chanteur* (Bayonne, 1944)
PHILIP ROBINSON

Garbin, Edoardo (*b* Padua, 12 March 1865; *d* Brescia, 12 April 1943). Italian tenor. His teachers in Milan were Alberto Selva and Vittorio Orefice. In 1891 he made his début at Vicenza in *La forza del destino*, appearing at La Scala two years later as Fenton in the world première of *Falstaff*. He subsequently married his Nannetta, Adelina Stehle, with whom he then appeared for many years, principally in the Puccini operas. His other important première was that of Leoncavallo's *Zazà* in 1900, also at La Scala, where he remained until 1918. His European successes were not repeated in London where he met with a critical press in 1908. His records show a voice that often bewilders the ear, sometimes ringing, sometimes white in tone, and mixing some rather forced singing with passages of considerable delicacy.

GV (R. Celletti; R. Vegeto)
J. B. STEANE

Garcia, José Maurício Nunes (*b* Rio de Janeiro, 20 or 22 Sept 1767; *d* Rio de Janeiro, 18 April 1830). Brazilian composer (generally known in Brazil as José Maurício). He provided music not only for the royal chapel of Prince Dom João VI but also for the theatre. The prince himself asked for an opera for the birthday of his mother, Queen Mary I, which resulted in *Le due gemelle*, thought until the 1960s to have been meant for a production at the S João theatre but now known to have been produced (on 17 December 1809) at the Teatro Régio. A document dated 3 December 1809 from the royal palace of Santa Cruz indicates that the 'beautiful musical play composed by the Priest José Maurício' needed more rehearsals. The autograph and scores were apparently destroyed in a fire. Earlier he had written the overture *Zemira* (1803) 'with flashes of lightning and thunder', sometimes assumed to be associated with an opera, although there is no evidence that he wrote another besides *Le due gemelle*. Most of Garcia's output consists of sacred music.

GERARD BÉHAGUE

Garcia, José Pablo Moncayo. *See* MONCAYO GARCÍA, JOSÉ PABLO.

Garcia, Manuel (Patricio Rodriguez) (*b* Madrid, 17 March 1805; *d* London, 1 July 1906). Spanish baritone and singing teacher, son of Manuel García. He studied singing with his father, and harmony with Fétis in Paris. He sang in his father's New York season (1825), but retired from the stage in 1829; subsequently he did administrative work in military hospitals in France, where he studied the physiological aspects of the voice.

Garcia's *Mémoire sur la voix humaine*, presented to the Académie des Sciences (Paris, 1840), was the foundation of all subsequent investigations into the voice, and his invention of the laryngoscope (1855) brought him world fame. His *Traité complet de l'art du chant* (1840) remained a standard work for many years. He was a professor at the Paris Conservatoire (1847–50) and at the RAM (1848–95); the latter half of his life was spent in England. His school of singing, a perfection of his father's methods, produced remarkable results as a list of a selection of his pupils makes clear: Jenny Lind, Hans Hermann Nissen, Erminia Frezzolini, Julius Stockhausen, Mathilde Marchesi and Charles Santley. His first wife was the soprano Eugénie Mayer (1815–80); their son was the baritone Gustave Garcia (1837–1925).

A. G. Tapia: *Manuel Garcia: su influencia en la laringologia y en el arte del canto* (Madrid, 1905)
H. Sterling-Mackinlay: *Garcia the Centenarian and his Times* (Edinburgh, 1908)
J. Mattfeld: *A Hundred Years of Grand Opera in New York* (New York, 1927)
J. Levien: *The Garcia Family* (London, 1932, 2/1948 as *Six Sovereigns of Song*)
APRIL FITZLYON

García, Manuel (del Pópulo Vicente Rodríguez) (*b* Seville, 21 Jan 1775; *d* Paris, 10 June 1832). Spanish composer, tenor, director and singing teacher, father of the baritone and noted teacher MANUEL GARCIA. He was baptized Manuel del Pópulo Vicente Rodríguez in the church of S María Magdalena on 23 January 1775, the son of Gerónimo Rodríguez Torrentera (1743–1817) and Mariana Aguilar (1747–1821). The name 'del Pópulo' comes from the Augustinian convent (S María del Pópulo) near the family's home. The name García, long a subject of question, was probably adopted by the grandfather, Diego Rodríguez-García (*d* 1760).

Contrary to rumours of being orphaned or illegitimate which have persisted to the present in biographical studies, García seems to have lived a stable family life with his parents, maternal grandmother and sisters Maria and Rita until he was at least 14, when his name disappears from the parish censuses of S María Magdalena. After musical studies in Seville with Antonio Ripa and Juan Almarcha, García made his début in Cádiz, where he married the singer Manuela Morales in 1797. The next year the couple joined Francisco Ramos's company in Madrid. García's début with the company, in a *tonadilla*, took place on 16 May 1798 in the Teatro de los Caños del Peral. The premières of his own *tonadillas*, *El majo y la maja* and *La declaración*, followed in December 1798 and July 1799.

In 1800–01 García was in Málaga, where he achieved considerable success as a composer and singer. In a letter to the Marquis of Astorga dated 29 November 1800 he expressed an interest in returning to Madrid to promote the cause of Spanish opera. The king's permission was solicited by Astorga in March 1801. Back in Madrid, as well as singing in the capacity of first tenor, García shared directing responsibilities at the Caños del Peral with an actor from Cartagena, Isidoro Maiquez. Opera alternated with theatrical performances, and Maiquez was famous for his interpretation of Shakespeare's Othello, a role with which García later became identified in the guise of Rossini's Otello. Among García's operettas, *El criado fingido* became extremely popular and continued to be performed up to

1832. It was included in a gala for the name-day celebration for Fernando VII on 30 May 1815. Julien Tiersot argued that it was the famous *polo* from this work, 'Cuerpo bueno, alma divina', which inspired the entr'acte to the final act of Bizet's *Carmen*.

While in Madrid, García also sang in oratorios and concerts at the Caños del Peral and composed and directed incidental music for plays. Of note are the choruses with orchestra he composed for performances of Racine's *Athalie* and *Esther* during Lent 1804. In August and September 1804 García, together with Manuela Morales and the singer Joaquina Briones (who later became his second wife), gave performances in Cádiz. In October he returned to the Caños del Peral to sing in the opera *La esclava persiana*. On 28 April 1805 he sang in his monologue opera *El poeta calculista* for the first time. It was a tremendous success: the aria 'Yo que soy contrabandista' gained enduring popularity throughout Europe (31 years later Liszt composed a *Rondeau fantastique* based on it). García's operetta *El cautiverio aparente*, first performed on 19 December 1805, was also enthusiastically received. A second monologue opera, *El preso*, was given on 1 January 1806, but did not attain the same success.

On 2 October 1806 García submitted a request to be named composer to the Teatro del Príncipe in Madrid. His qualifications were substantiated by the composer Blas de Laserna and the violinist Josef Barbieri (*apoderado* of the theatre and grandfather of the composer Francisco Asenjo Barbieri), and his request was granted. However, political problems in the administration prevented him from taking up the post and he left Spain. The last opera he composed in Spain, *Los ripios de maestro Adán*, was performed on 18 January 1807. After brief stays in Valladolid, Burgos, Vitoria, Bayonne and Bordeaux, García and Joaquina Briones settled in Paris. He made his début at the Théâtre de l'Impératrice in Paer's *Griselda* on 11 February 1808. The following year, on 15 March, he presented *El poeta calculista* to the Parisian public with great success.

In 1811 García travelled to Naples where he studied with the tenor Ansani. His *Il califfo di Bagdad* and *Tella e Dallaton, o sia La donzella di Raab* were performed in Naples in 1813 and 1814 respectively, and it was there that in 1815 he created the role of Norfolk in Rossini's *Elisabetta, regina d'Inghilterra*. In 1816 in Rome he sang Almaviva in the première of *Il barbiere di Siviglia* under its original title *Almaviva, ossia L'inutile precauzione*.

Towards the end of 1816 García and his wife returned to Paris to sing at the Théâtre Italien. Paolino in *Il matrimonio segreto* was the role of García's *rentrée* on 16 October. *Il califfo di Bagdad* had its Paris première on 22 May 1817 at the Théâtre Italien. It was performed regularly until García and his wife left the company after a contretemps with the director, Mme Catalani, purportedly resulting from García's receiving more applause than she in a single performance of Portugal's *La morte di Semiramide* on 20 September 1817. He turned to the Opéra-Comique, where his first French opera, *Le prince d'occasion*, was performed on 13 December 1817. In 1818 he travelled to London, appearing at the King's Theatre with great success in *Otello* and *Il barbiere di Siviglia*.

Now in his vocal prime, García returned to Paris the next year and became a sensation in roles such as Almaviva, Otello and Don Giovanni. At the same time he composed prolifically and his operas were given at

Manuel García in the title role of Rossini's 'Otello' at the Théâtre Italien, Paris: lithograph by G. Engelmann (c1821)

the Opéra-Comique, the Théâtre Italien and the Gymnase Dramatique, as well as the Académie Royale. Most notable was *La mort du Tasse* (Opéra, 7 February 1821). While finding fault with the libretto, critics praised the music, in particular the duet 'O moment plein d'attraits!' Within four months the opera appeared in a de luxe full-score edition. In 1824 García returned to London for one more season; he opened a singing academy in Dover Street, and published *Exercises and Method for Singing* (1824). The following October he embarked for New York with his wife and children, Manuel, Maria (later MARIA MALIBRAN) and Pauline (PAULINE VIARDOT). There he directed the first performances of opera in Italian in the USA. As well as Rossini's operas (*Otello*, *Barbiere*, *Cenerentola*, *Tancredi*, *Il turco in Italia*) and his own (*L'amante astuto*, *La figlia dell'aria*), García, at the urging of Lorenzo da Ponte, presented Mozart's *Don Giovanni*. From New York he went in 1827 to Mexico City where he was received with great enthusiasm. After a debate on language which raged for months in the Mexican press, García obligingly translated Rossini's and his own operas into Spanish. *El amante astuto* was chosen for the anniversary celebration on 5 October 1828 of the nation's constitution of 1824.

García had planned to remain in Mexico, but political events forced him to leave and in 1829 he returned to Paris. He won tumultuous applause on his reappearance, as Almaviva, but his voice was in decline and he soon dedicated himself to teaching, for which he seems to have been specially gifted. Among his most successful students, apart from his children, were the tenor Adolphe Nourrit, the Countess (María de las Mercedes Santa Cruz y Montsalvo) Merlin and Henriette Méric-Lalande. Never ceasing to compose, in 1830 García published a delightful collection of Spanish songs dedicated to his 'aficionados'. He continued to perform, and his tremendous energy 'in spite of his white hair' was noted in the *Revue musicale* of March 1831. His last appearance, in August 1831, was in a *buffo* role in a student performance of Count Beramendi's *Le vendemie di Xeres*. His death certificate shows that he died on 10 June the following year (not 2 or 9 June, as stated by Fétis and Richard respectively). He was buried in Père Lachaise cemetery. In his funeral oration Fétis honoured García above all as a composer, remarking that his best works remained unpublished – as is still true today. Among his numerous compositions, of greatest interest are those in a Spanish style where he successfully fused Andalusian and bel canto elements.

Throughout García's career critics commented above all on the remarkable flexibility of his voice. He was also praised for his musicianship, skilful acting and gift of invention. This last led to reproofs for his tendency towards crowd-pleasing ornamentation. The voice was, according to Fétis, a deep tenor. Indeed, it is possible that it was a baritone with a highly developed falsetto which allowed García to tackle the demands of Rossini's *Otello* as well as the fireworks of his own arias. The depth of his voice enabled him to take the title role of *Don Giovanni* which, according to Fétis, he sang with a 'Herculean force'. His expert delivery of recitative, as well as the Andalusian fire of his stage presence, made him ideally suited to dramatic roles such as Otello and Don Giovanni. García's dynamic perfectionism left its impact on three continents and his legacy, in the hands of his children, was carried into the 20th century.

MDCP – *Madrid, Teatro de los Caños del Peral*

El majo y la maja (tonadilla, 1), MDCP, Dec 1798, *E-Mm* (Madrid, 1973)
La declaración (tonadilla, 1, J. Blasco), MDCP, 31 July 1799, *Mm*
El seductor arrepentido (opereta, 1), MDCP, 16 Sept 1802, lib. *Mm*
El reloj de madera (opereta, 1), MDCP, 25 Sept 1802, *Mm*, frag. *F-Pc**
Quien porfía mucho alcanza (opereta, 1), MDCP, 12 Nov 1802, *Pc**, lib., orch pts *E-Mm*
El luto fingido (opereta, 1, ? F. de Paula Martí), MDCP, 30 May 1803, *Mm*
El criado fingido (opereta, 1), MDCP, 2 Feb 1804, *Mm*, frag. *F-Pc**
El padrastro, o Quien a yerro mata a yerro muere (2), MDCP, 21 July 1804, *E-Mm**
El poeta calculista (monologue op, 1), MDCP, 28 April 1805, *F-Pc**, ov. (Paris, ?1806)
El cautiverio aparente (opereta, 1), MDCP, 19 Dec 1805, *E-Mm*, frag. *F-Pc**
El preso (monologue op, 1, M. Bravo), MDCP, 1 Jan 1806, *Pc*, lib., ov. *E-Mm*
Los lacónicos, o La trampa descubierta (opereta, 1, F. Enciso Castrillón), MDCP, 12 Aug 1806, *Mm*, frags. *F-Pc**
Los ripios del maestro Adán (opereta, 1, Enciso Castrillón), Madrid, Príncipe, 18 Jan 1807, *Pc**, *E-Mm*
Il califfo di Bagdad (ob, 2, A. L. Tottola), Naples, Fondo, 30 Sept 1813, *F-Pc**, *I-Nc*
Tella e Dallaton, o sia La donzella di Raab (2, A. Sografi), Naples, S Carlo, 4 Nov 1814, *Nc*
Le prince d'occasion (oc, 3, J. H. F. Lamartellière), Paris, OC (Feydeau), 13 Dec 1817, *F-LYm*, frag. *Pc**
Il fazzoletto (ob, 2), Paris, Italien, 23 March 1820, *Pc*
Le grand lama, ou Sophones, ?1820 (3, E. de Jouy), ?unperf, *Pc**
La mort du Tasse (grand opéra, 3, J. G. A. Cuvelier de Trie and J. Hélitas Demeun), Paris, Opéra, 7 Feb 1821, *Pc* (Paris, 1821)
La meunière (oc, 1, E. Scribe and Mélesville [A.-H.-J. Duveyrier]), Paris, Gymnase Dramatique, 16 May 1821, lib. *US-Wc*

L'amant sans maîtresse, 1821 (R. C. G. de Pixérécourt), unperf.
Florestan, ou Le Conseil des Dix (3, E. J. Debrieu), Paris, Opéra, 26 June 1822, *F-Po**
Les deux contrats de mariage (ob, 2, E. A. de Planard), Paris, OC (Feydeau), 6 March 1824, *Pc**
L'amante astuto (ob, 2, P. Rosich), New York, Park, 17 Dec 1825, *Pc**
Astuzie e prudenza (1), London, 1825, *Pc**
Il lupo d'Ostende, o sia Il inocente salvato dal colpevole (2, Rosich), ?New York, 1825, *Pc**
La figlia dell'aria (1, G. Rossi), New York, Park, 25 April 1826, *Pc**
La buona famiglia (? salon op, 1, ? García), ? New York, 1826, *Pc**
El Abufar, ossia La famiglia araba (3, F. Romani), Mexico City, Provisional, 13 July 1827, Acts 1 and 2 *Pc**
Un ora di matrimonio (ob, 2), Mexico City, Provisional, 1827, *Pc**
Zemira ed Azor (2), Mexico City, ? Provisional, 1827, *Pc**
Acendi (2), Mexico City, Provisional, ?1828, *Pc**
El gitano por amor (2), Mexico City, Provisional, ?1828, *Pc**
Los maridos solteros (2), Mexico City, Provisional, 1828, *Pc**
Semiramis (3, after Voltaire), Mexico City, Provisional, 1828, Acts 1 and 2 *Pc**
Xaira (2, after Voltaire), Mexico City, Provisional, ?1828, *Pc**
Un avvertimento ai gelosi (salon op, 1), 1831, *Pc**
Le cinesi (salon op, 1, Metastasio), private perf., London, ?1831, *Pc**
Il finto sordo (salon op), private perf., London, ?1831, *Pc**
L'isola disabitata (salon op, 1, P. Metastasio), private perf., London, ?1831, *Pc**
I tre gobbi (salon op, 1), London, 1831, *Pc**
I banditi, osia La foresta pericolosa (2), *Pc**
Don Chisciotte (ob, 2, after M. de Cervantes), *Pc**
La gioventù d'Enrico V (2), *Pc**
L'origine des grâces (1), ?unperf.
Le tre sultane (2), *Pc**
El zapatero de Bagdad (2), *Pc**

Doubtful: El preso (opereta, 1), Málaga, 1800; El posadero (opereta, 1), Madrid, 1802; Florinda (opereta, 1), ?Madrid; Sophonisbe (3, Jouy, ? confused with Le grand lama)

*

FétisB
P. Richard: 'Notes biographiques sur Manuel García', *Revue musicale*, xii (1832), 171–4
E. de Olavarría y Ferrari: *Reseña histórica del teatro en México, 1538–1911*, i (Mexico City, 1895)
E. Cotarelo y Mori: *Estudios sobre la historia del arte escénico en España*, iii: *Isidoro Maiquez y el teatro de su tiempo* (Madrid, 1902)
J. Tiersot: 'Bizet and Spanish Music', *MQ*, xiii (1927), 566–81
J. Subirá: *La tonadilla escénica* (Madrid, 1928–30), iii
——: 'El operetista Manuel García', *Revista de la Biblioteca Archivo y Museo Ayuntamiento de Madrid*, i (1935), 179–96
N. Solar-Quintes: 'Manuel García, íntimo: un capítulo para su biografía', *AnM*, ii (1947), 98–104
J. Subirá: 'Dos grandes músicos "desmadrileñizados": Manuel García (padre e hijo)', *Anales del Instituto de estudios madrileños*, iii (1968), 229–38
M. Nelson: *The First Italian Opera Season in New York City: 1825–1826* (diss., U. of North Carolina, Chapel Hill, 1976)
C. de Reparaz: *Maria Malibran, 1808–1836: estudio biográfico* (Madrid, 1976)
J. Radomski: 'Manuel García in Mexico (1827–1828)', *Inter-American Music Review*, xii/1 (1991–2), 119–27
——: *The Life and Works of Manuel del Populo Vicente García* (diss., U. of California, Los Angeles, 1992)   JAMES RADOMSKI

García Fajer, Francisco Javier [Garzia, Francesco Saverio; 'Lo Spagnoletto'] (*b* Nalda, La Rioja, 7 Dec 1730; *d* Saragossa, 26 Feb 1809). Spanish composer. He studied composition with Lorenzo Fago and Giovan Ghalberto Brunetti at the Conservatorio della Pietà dei Turchini in Naples and was *maestro di cappella* in Terni and Saragossa Cathedral (1756–1809). Between 1754 and 1756 four of his operas were given successful first performances and repeated elsewhere (once with the tenor Johann van Beethoven in the role of Dorindo in *La finta schiava*). Three *opere buffe* are apparently lost except for two numbers from *La finta schiava*, in which perfect observance of the vocal requirements of the genre can be discerned. *Pompeo Magno in Armenia* is clearly in the Roman tradition, with all the roles taken by men, Pompeo [Pompey] and Giulia [Julia] being castrato roles and Muzio [Mutius] a tenor. The libretto is clearly in the Metastasian tradition. The vocal writing is virtuoso, while in the instrumental parts the viola is relatively independent of the bass and the use of woodwind is suggestive of dramatic tension. García Fajer also wrote much sacred music and gained considerable fame for his liturgical reforms.

all first performed in Rome

La finta schiava (int, 2), Pace, carn. 1754, 2 arias *GB-Lbl*
Pompeo Magno in Armenia (os, 3, A. Guidi), Dame, carn. 1755, *P-La*
La pupilla (farsetta, 2, A. Lungi), Valle, 1755
Lo scultore deluso (int, 1), Valle, carn. 1756

*

J. J. Carreras-López: *La musica en las catedrales en el siglo XVIII: F. J. García (1730–1809)* (Saragossa, 1883)

XOÁN M. CARREIRA

García Gutiérrez, Antonio (*b* Chiclana, nr Cádiz, 5 Oct 1813; *d* Madrid, 26 June 1884). Spanish playwright. He gave up medicine to devote himself to poetry and the theatre, but spent most of his later life in government service (including a spell in London). From 1872 to 1884 he was director of the Museo Arqueológico in Madrid. He was an enthusiastic admirer of the French Romantic theatre in its more extravagant manifestations, which he developed to excess in his own work. His output covered a wide range of genres, including zarzuelas, but his claim to operatic fame rests on the use of his plays for librettos. *El trovador* (1836), his first triumphant success, was used first by Francisco Porcell (1842, Pamplona; libretto by A. Porcell), then by Francesco Cortesi (1852, Trieste; libretto by A. Lanari) and finally by Verdi (1853, Rome; libretto by Cammarano). *Simon Bocanegra* (1843) was also used by Verdi (1857, Venice; libretto by F. M. Piave); in 1857 Verdi expressed interest in *El tesorero del rey* by García Gutiérrez and Asquerino (though the project came to nothing), and again, in 1870, he sent for a copy of *La venganza catalana*.

*

N. B. Adams: *The Romantic Dramas of García Gutiérrez* (New York, 1922)
Z. Sacks: 'Verdi and Spanish Romantic Drama', *Hispania*, xxvii (1944), 451–65
P. Menarini: 'Dal dramma al melodramma, ii: I tre libretti "spagnoli" di Verdi', *Biblioteca storico giuridica e artistico letteraria: letteratura, musica, teatro*, lxxii (1977), 1–41
D. Puccini: 'Il "Simon Boccanegra" de Antonio García Gutiérrez e l'opera di Giuseppe Verdi', *Studi verdiani*, iii (1985), 120–30

JOHN BLACK

García Lorca, Federico (*b* Fuente Vaqueros, nr Granada, 5 June 1898; *d* Viznar, nr Granada, ?19 Aug 1936). Spanish poet, dramatist and composer. His fascination with Spanish folklore and gypsy flamenco music coloured much of his poetry. After an early training in music, he studied from 1914 at Granada and from 1920 at Madrid University, reading law, philosophy and letters and meeting Turina and others. He met Falla in Granada in 1919, wrote penetratingly about his music (see the editions of Gallego Morell and Eisenberg) and collaborated with him on several occasions. In 1931 he was appointed director of La Barraca, a student travelling theatre, for which he himself wrote incidental music. In the Civil War he was shot, apparently by supporters of Franco for his left-wing sympathies. Many musical works have been based on his writings.

La zapatera prodigiosa (play, 1926): J. J. Castro, 1949; U. Zimmermann, as Die wundersame Schustersfrau, 1982
Amor de don Perlimplín con Belisa en su jardín (play, 1931): V. Rieti, as Don Perlimplin, 1952; W. Fortner, as In seinem Garten liebt Don Perlimplin Belisa, 1962; B. Maderna, as Don Perlimplin, 1962; C. Susa, as The Love of Don Perlimplín, 1984
Bodas de sangre (drama, 1933): Fortner, as Der Wald, radio op (dramatic scene), 1953; J. J. Castro, 1956; Fortner, as Die Bluthochzeit, 1957; Szokolay, as Vérnász, 1964; LeFanu, as Blood Wedding, comp. 1990–92

*

C. Diego: 'El teatro musical de Federico García Lorca', *El imparcial* (1933), April
A. del Hoyo, ed.: *F. García Lorca: Obras completas* (Madrid, 1957, enlarged 2/1963) [with music]
A. Gallego Morell, ed.: *García Lorca: cartas postales, .poemas y dibujos* (Madrid, 1968)
D. Eisenberg: 'Musical Settings of Lorca Texts', *García Lorca Review*, iii (1975)
——: *Textos y documentos lorquianos* (Tallahassee, FL, 1975)

JACK SAGE

García Mansilla, Eduardo (*b* Washington DC, 7 March 1871; *d* Paris, 9 May 1930). Argentine composer. His father was Argentine ambassador to the USA. He received his musical training in Paris (with Massenet) and Vienna, then became a diplomat. Although never a professional musician, he composed over a hundred works. About 1905, when serving at the Russian imperial court, he composed *Ivan*, a *conte lyrique* in one act and three tableaux, to his own French text, based on a traditional Ukrainian legend. The work was dedicated to Tsar Nicholas II, with whom he was on friendly terms, and first performed in the Hermitage, St Petersburg. It was later given at the Teatro Colón in Buenos Aires on 20 July 1915, to great critical acclaim, then in Rome with Schipa in the title role and then at La Scala. The composer consulted Rimsky-Korsakov on the orchestration, as he did with others of his works.

In 1915 he composed *La angelical Manuelita* (subtitled *Escenas nacionales* and described as an 'Argentine opera'). The Spanish text, written by the composer, concerns an imaginary event in Buenos Aires in 1830. Some of the characters represent members of his own family, the leading role being Manuela Rosas, his mother's cousin and daughter of the dictator Juan Manuel de Rosas. Although Argentine stories had already received operatic treatment, García Mansilla's work was the first to bring together an Argentine subject, Spanish language (with local characteristics) and music in the Argentine tradition by a native composer. It was first performed on 5 August 1917 at the Teatro Colón but not well received: the libretto was weak and the music, intended to be simple, was too dull for the public taste. But *La angelical Manuelita* did open the way for the most fertile period in Argentine opera, and the audience that rejected it was soon ready to accept other works in Spanish on Argentine subjects.

*

J. M. Veniard: *Los García, los Mansilla y la música* (Buenos Aires, 1986), 238ff

JUAN MARÍA VENIARD

García Pacheco, Fabián (*b* Escalonilla, Toledo, *c*1725; *d* Madrid, *c*1808). Spanish composer. He was admitted as a *seise* on 23 July 1735 in Toledo Cathedral where he studied with Casellas. In 1756 he was *maestro de capilla* of Soledad church in Madrid and in 1770 at Victoria convent. After making a reputation as a composer of *sainetes*, *tonadillas* and incidental stage music he was commissioned to write the music for Ramón de la Cruz's two-act zarzuela *En casa de nadie no se meta* *nadie, o El buen marido*, staged at the Teatro del Príncipe in Madrid on 28 September 1770 (music in *E-Mm*). In keeping with contemporary Spanish stage practice, the parts of Don Joaquín and Captain Enrique were played by women. It ran until 7 October and was revived for eight performances the next summer.

According to Cotarelo y Mori, García Pacheco also wrote incidental music for José de Cañizares's *Don Juan de Espina en Madrid* (revived in 1765 for a royal marriage) and for two anonymous plays, *Los sueños de José* and *El músico por amor*. His undated *sainete*, *La Arcadia*, consists of a *minué instrumental*, a pastoral duet accompanied by castanets and a vocal quartet (*E-Mm*).

*

J. Subirá: *La musica en la Casa de Alba* (Madrid, 1927), 335ff
——: *Tonadillas teatrales inéditas, libretos y partituras* (Madrid, 1932), 16, 17, 300
E. Cotarelo y Mori: *Historia de la zarzuela* (Madrid, 1934), i, 146–7
A. Palau y Dulcet: *Manual del librero hispanoamericano* (Barcelona and Madrid, 2/1950)
R. Stevenson: *Renaissance and Baroque Musical Sources in the Americas* (Washington DC, 1970), 85, 120, 243

ROBERT STEVENSON

Garcin, Laurent (*b* Neuchâtel; *fl* 1770s). Swiss writer on music. Like Escherny he moved to Paris, where he frequented the literary and intellectual circles of the Encyclopedists and *philosophes*. In 1772 he published his long *Traité du mélodrame*; its immediate occasion was the rebuttal of views expressed in FRANÇOIS-JEAN CHASTELLUX's *Essai*. The *Traité* is a sustained apology for the more complex orchestral style of Bohemian instrumental composers as the musical basis for an effective dramaturgy. He appreciated the obvious plastic beauty of Hasse in individual arias (for instance 'Non ha ragione, ingrato' in *Didone abbandonata*) and admired the inventiveness of motifs in Italian opera, but thought that the hedonistic regularity of a pure singing-based style allowed insufficient contrast to sustain interest and maintain dramatic power. He regarded Philidor's orchestral invention and vivid instrumentation as a model of its kind, and the *Traité* is in this sense a eulogy of Philidor: Garcin made specific bar-by-bar observations on his style with a precision that inspires confidence in his judgment. The standard of criticism is remarkable, considering the early date; and throughout Garcin shows general musical literacy and a keen dramatic imagination.   PHILIP WELLER

Garcisanz, Isabel (*b* Madrid, 29 June 1934). Spanish soprano. She studied in Madrid and in Vienna, where she made her début in 1964 at the Volksoper as Adèle (*Le comte Ory*). At Glyndebourne (1966–70) she sang Ravel's Concepcion, Nerillo (*Ormindo*) and Zaida (*Il turco in Italia*). At Wexford she sang Mab in *La jolie fille de Perth* (1968). With Cologne Opera she sang Vitellia at Sadler's Wells Theatre (1969). She appeared in Paris, at the Opéra du Rhin, Strasbourg, where she created Dara in Georges Delerue's *Médis et Alyssio* (1975), and at Albi, where she sang Florise in Dauvergne's *La coquette trompée* (1976). Her other roles have included Donna Elvira, Countess Almaviva, Fiordiligi, Marzelline, Tatyana and Périchole. She has been admired as an attractive, spirited performer, with a rich-toned and flexible voice.   ELIZABETH FORBES

Gard, Robert (Joseph) (*b* Padstow, Cornwall, 7 March 1927). Australian tenor of English birth. After training

(with Dino Borgioli) and early experience in England, in 1960 he toured Australia, where he has established a strong reputation in traditional character parts, debonair leading roles and cogent interpretations of important 20th-century roles, most for Australian Opera. A superb Quint and Prologue, Albert and Mayor and Male Chorus in Britten's operas, he earned special praise for his Aschenbach, eventually appearing in the film of *Death in Venice* in place of the ailing Pears. Herod and Aegisthus suited his pale, clear, agile voice with its ability to suggest neurotic speed of apprehension. His Don Basilio in *Figaro* was infinitely amusing. Gard's portrayals of Danilo and Eisenstein, Tamino and Don Ottavio, Rakewell and Števa, Loge and even Siegmund, Grosvenor and Le Mesurier (in Meale's *Voss*) have testified to his exceptional versatility.

ROGER COVELL

Garde, Pierre de. *See* LA GARDE, PIERRE DE.

Gardel, Pierre Gabriel (*b* Nancy, 4 Feb 1758; *d* Paris, 18 Oct 1840). French dancer and ballet-master. He made his début as a *danseur noble* in 1774. He was trained by his brother, Maximilien Léopold Philippe Joseph Gardel (*b* Mannheim, 18 Dec 1741; *d* Paris, 11 March 1787), a dancer at the Opéra since 1755 and assistant ballet-master from 1773. The elder Gardel had made a sensation there in 1772 when, asked to replace Gaetano Vestris in Rameau's *Castor et Pollux*, he had removed the traditional mask. In 1783 Maximilien became principal ballet-master and Pierre was appointed his assistant. He became principal ballet-master in 1787 and held the post for more than 40 years. Grimm described him as a worthy successor to Noverre, and Bournonville claimed that 'no one was able to rival' his opera dances, citing the 'wealth of invention' in such works as Le Sueur and Persuis' *Le triomphe de Trajan* (1807) and Salieri's *Les Danaïdes* (1808). He also provided dances for the premières of Salieri's *Tarare* (1787); Grétry's *Aspasie* (1789); Cherubini's *Démophon* (1788), *Anacréon* (1803) and *Les abencérages* (1813); Spontini's *La vestale* (1807) and *Olympie* (1819); and Rossini's *Le siège de Corinthe* (1826) and *Moïse et Pharaon* (1827). Classically educated, Gardel preferred mythological subjects for his ballets. He guided the Opéra ballet through the Reign of Terror, afterwards rebuilding the company to its previous level of almost 200 dancers. By the end of his career (*c*1827), the Romantic ballet style was ready to supplant the neo-classical forms he had so long insisted on retaining.

*

A. Bournonville: *Mit theaterliv* (Copenhagen, 1847–77; Eng. trans., 1979)
M. Tourneux, ed.: *Correspondance littéraire, philosophique et critique par Grimm, Diderot, Raynal, Meister, etc.* (Paris, 1877–82)
J. Chazen-Benneheim: *Dance in the Shadow of the Guillotine* (Carbondale, IL, 1988)   MAUREEN NEEDHAM COSTONIS

Gardelli, Lamberto (*b* Venice, 8 Nov 1915). Swedish conductor and composer of Italian birth. He studied at the Liceo Musicale Rossini in Pesaro, and later in Rome. He worked as an assistant to Tullio Serafin in Rome and in 1944 made his début at the Teatro Reale dell'Opera, Rome, in *La traviata*. From 1946 until 1955 he was resident conductor with the Swedish Royal Opera in Stockholm, where he was chiefly responsible for Italian and modern Scandinavian repertory. He appeared frequently at the Berlin Staatsoper and in Helsinki, and became music director, from 1961, of the Budapest Opera, where he was still conducting into the 1990s. His American début was at Carnegie Hall in 1964 in Bellini's *I Capuleti e i Montecchi*, which led to his first appearance at the Metropolitan Opera in 1966 conducting *Andrea Chénier*. In England Gardelli first conducted at Glyndebourne in 1964 (Verdi's *Macbeth*), returning in 1968 with *Anna Bolena*; his début at Covent Garden (1969) was with Verdi's *Otello*. His long list of recorded operas is particularly noteworthy for *Macbeth*, *I Lombardi*, *Nabucco* and *La forza del destino*, for the first complete recording of Rossini's *Guillaume Tell* (1972), including a rediscovered aria for Jemmy, and for the first recordings, made in Budapest, of Respighi's *La fiamma* (1985), *Belfagor* and *Maria egiziaca* (both 1990). One of the finest Verdi conductors from Italy of his generation, Gardelli shows a high regard for both structure and expression, and has been no less successful with the *verismo* school. His compositions include five operas of which only one has been performed.

Alba novella, 1933 (3, A. Chiodo)
L'etrusco, 1938 (3, R. Cecchini)
Il sogno, 1942 (romantic op, 1, C. Guastalla) [pt 1 of trilogy]
L'impresario delle Americhe, 1959 (chamber op, 1, M. Verdone), Budapest TV, 1982 [pt 2 of trilogy]
Il demone, 1971 (1, Verdone) [pt 3 of trilogy]

ALAN BLYTH, NOËL GOODWIN

Garden, Mary (*b* Aberdeen, 20 Feb 1874; *d* Inverurie, Scotland, 3 Jan 1967). American soprano of Scottish birth. Taken to the USA as a child, she studied singing in Chicago, then in Paris with Trabadelo and Lucien Fugère. Sibyl Sanderson introduced her to Albert Carré,

Mary Garden in the title role of Massenet's 'Manon'

director of the Opéra-Comique, where she made her début in the title role of *Louise* (10 April 1900) after Marthe Rioton had collapsed. Instantly successful, she spent several years building her repertory. Debussy and Carré chose her for Mélisande (1902) despite Maeterlinck's protests. The devoted efforts of Garden, Carré and the conductor Messager pulled *Pelléas* from the near-disaster of the *répétition générale* to full triumph by the end of the season. She sang at Covent Garden, 1902–3. Her Manon, an early Paris and London success, persuaded Massenet to write *Chérubin* for her (1905). Her Chrysis in Camille Erlanger's *Aphrodite* was the Paris opera sensation of 1906–7. Garden's début at Hammerstein's Manhattan Opera House was in the American première of *Thaïs* (25 November 1907). She was hailed as the supreme singing-actress – some critics had reservations about her voice, but none questioned her remarkable gift for tone colouring, subtle phrasing and 'forward' style. With an imported Parisian supporting cast, *Pelléas* (1908) achieved popular success. Her long association with the Chicago Grand Opera began in 1910, with *Pelléas*. In addition to becoming its leading soprano for the next 20 years, she spent the 1921–2 season as its director, and was responsible for the première of Prokofiev's *The Love for Three Oranges* among other things (Prokofiev wrote *The Fiery Angel* for her but she declined to sing it). Though artistically successful her reign was turbulent and financially extravagant.

Essentially a lyric soprano, Garden sang superb coloratura as Violetta (Paris and Brussels), Gounod's Juliet (Paris and London) and Thomas' Ophelia (Opéra). She demonstrated equal accomplishment in heavier roles such as Salome and Carmen, and in spinto roles in Chicago – Tosca, Fiora (*L'amore dei tre re*), in the American premières of Honegger's *Judith* (1927) and Alfano's *Risurrezione* (in French, 1925), and in Massenet's *Werther*, *Sapho* and *Cléopâtre*. She also appropriated the tenor role of Jean in Massenet's *Le jongleur de Notre Dame*, the opera in which she made her last Chicago appearance (1931). Thereafter she sang Carmen in Cleveland (1932) and at the Opéra-Comique in *Risurrezione* (1934).

*

GV (C. Williams, with discography)
E. C. Moore: *Forty Years of Opera in Chicago* (New York, 1930)
O. Thompson: 'Mary Garden', *The American Singer* (New York, 1937), 265–77
M. Garden and L. Biancolli: *Mary Garden's Story* (New York, 1951)
G. Whelan: 'The Recorded Art of Mary Garden', *The Gramophone*, xxix (1951–2), 248–91 [with discography]
R. D. Fletcher: 'The Mary Garden of Record', *Saturday Review* (27 Feb 1954), 47, 49–50, 70
———: 'The Short, Mad Reign of Mary the First', *Panorama* (7 Sept 1963)
H. Cuenod: 'Remembrances of an Enchantress', *High Fidelity*, xiv/7 (1964), 36–8
E. C. Wagenknecht: *Seven Daughters of the Theater* (Norman, OK, 1964), 161–79
R. L. Davis: *Opera in Chicago* (New York, 1966)
H. Pleasants: 'Mary Garden', *The Great Singers* (New York, 1966), 308–13
R. D. Fletcher: '"Our Own" Mary Garden', *Chicago History*, ii/1 (1972), 34–46
D. Shawe-Taylor: 'Mary Garden (1874–1967)', *Opera*, xxxv (1984), 1079–84
RICHARD D. FLETCHER

Gardi, Francesco (*b* ?1760–65; *d* *c*1810). Italian composer. He directed and composed for the women's choir and orchestra of the Venetian conservatory-hospital Poveri Derelitti from about 1787 until 1791. In 1797, and perhaps earlier, he was *maestro di cappella* of the Mendicanti; the libretto for *La semplice* (published 1798) indicates that he belonged to the Accademia Filarmonica of Bologna. For nearly 20 years his settings of comic texts (especially Giuseppe Foppa's one-act farces) were extremely popular in Venice. His several collaborations with the eccentric Count Alessandro Pepoli, who briefly maintained theatres in Venice and Padua and who served Gardi as librettist, impresario and printer, suggest his readiness to participate in movements of experimentation and reform. In 1811 and 1813 the ducal theatre at Parma performed *La pianella perduta*, a revival of Gardi's most popular farce, *La pianella persa*.

VA – *Venice, Teatro S Angelo*
VB – *Venice, Teatro S Benedetto*
VM – *Venice, Teatro S Moisè*
VP – *Venice, Count Pepoli, private theatre*

dg – *dramma giocoso* f – *farsa*
ob – *opera buffa* os – *opera seria*

Enea nel Lazio (os, 2, V. A. Cigna-Santi), Modena, Rangoni, carn. 1786, *I-Tn*
Don Giovanni, o Il nuovo convitato di pietra (dramma tragicomico, 2, after G. Bertati), Venice, S Samuele, 5 Feb 1787, *I-Bc, Mr**
La fata capricciosa (dg, 2, Bertati), VM, carn. 1789
Gernando e Rosimonda (dramma eroico, 2), Treviso, Astori, aut. 1789
Teodolinda (os, 2, D. Boggio), VB, May 1790
Apollo esule, ossia L'amore alla prova (favola, A. Pepoli), VP, 1793
La bella Lauretta (dg, 2, Bertati), VM, Jan 1795, *F-Pc, I-Fc* (2 copies), ov. *Gl, Mr, RU-SPtob*
Tancredi (tragedia per musica, 3, Pepoli, after Voltaire), VP, 26 April 1795
Amor l'astuzia insegna (dg, 2, Bertati), VM, 18 Feb 1797, aria *I-CHf*; rev. as La capricciosa supposta (f, 1, Bertati), Venice, S Luca, 1 Sept 1801
La pianella persa, o sia La veglia de contadini (f, 1, G. Foppa), VM, 15 Jan 1798, *F-Pc, I-Fc, PAc* (2 copies), *RU-SPtob*
Il finto stregone (f, 1, Foppa), VM, 30 Nov 1798, *SPtob*
La principessa filosofa (f, 1, Foppa), VM, carn. 1799
La semplice, ovvero La virtù premiata (dramma eroicomico, 1, Foppa), VM, carn. 1799
Il contravveleno (f, 1, Foppa, after C. Gozzi), VB, 7 Nov 1799
La donna ve la fà (f, 1, Foppa), VM, May 1800, *F-Pc, I-Fc, Gl, Mr, Pl, RU-SPtob*
Il medico a suo dispetto, ossia La muta per amore (f, 1, Foppa), VA, 15 July 1800, *F-Pc, I-Mr, OS* (2 copies), *Pl*
L'incantesimo senza magia (f, 1, Foppa), SM, 9 Dec 1800, *F-Pc, I-Mr*
La bottega del caffè (f, 2, Foppa, after C. Goldoni), VM, 20 April 1801, *Mr*
Diritto e rovescio, ovvero Una della solite trasformazioni nel mondo (f, 2, Foppa), VB, 13 May 1801
Il convitato di pietra (f, 2, Foppa), VB, 27 Jan 1802
Guerra con tutti, ovvero Danari e ripieghi (f, 2, Foppa), VB, 12 Aug 1803
La casa da vendere (f, 2 , G. Piazza, after A. Duval), VA, 4 Jan 1804
Un buco nella porta (f, 1, Foppa), VB, 16 May 1804, *Mr*
Sempre la vince amore (f, 1, G. D. Camagna), VM, spr. 1805, *I-Pl*
La forza d'amore (f, 1), Treviso, Dolfin, 1 May 1805 [according to Stieger]
Nardone e Nannetta (ob, 2, G. Caravita), Lisbon, S Carlos, 7 April 1806

Music in: Pirro, 1794

Doubtful: L'americana (ob), Treviso, Dolfin, sum. 1788, *Mr*; La fata astuta (dg), Padua, Obizzi, carn. 1795 [? same as La fata capricciosa]

*

StiegerO
G. Bustico: 'Alessandro Pepoli', *R. deputazione di storia patria: Nuovo archivio veneto*, xxv (1913), 199–229
B. Brunelli: *I teatri di Padova* (Padua, 1921), 346ff, 359–60
A. Della Corte: *L'opera comica italiana nel '700*, ii (Bari, 1923), 214
G. G. Bernardi: 'Un teatro privato di musica a venezia', *Gazzetta di Venezia* (20 March 1930)
S. Kunze: 'Alcune farse di Foppa musicate da Gardi', *I vicini di Mozart: Venice 1987*, 479–88
SVEN HANSELL

Gardiner, John Eliot (*b* Fontmell Magna, Dorset, 20 April 1943). English conductor. After graduating from Cambridge he studied with Thurston Dart at King's College, London, and in Paris with Nadia Boulanger. While at Cambridge he founded the Monteverdi Choir (1964), with which he made his professional début in London two years later, adding the Monteverdi Orchestra in 1968. He conducted *Die Zauberflöte* for Sadler's Wells Opera in 1969, and Gluck's *Alceste* for the BBC and *Iphigénie en Tauride* at Covent Garden in 1973. His authority in 17th- and 18th-century styles was confirmed by his own editions of Rameau and others, of which he conducted concert performances in the 1970s, and the first ever stage production of *Les boréades* at the Aix-en-Provence Festival in 1982. He was artistic director of the Göttingen Handel Festival from 1981 to 1990, and had an influential period as music director of the Opéra de Lyon from 1983 to 1988. A policy of introducing rare works led to productions at Lyons including Charpentier's *Médée*, Handel's *Tamerlano* and Leclair's *Scylla et Glaucus*, and Gardiner brought to the 1985 Edinburgh Festival Chabrier's *L'étoile* and *Pelléas et Mélisande*. He is a prolific recording artist, winning awards in several countries for the qualities of scholarship, stylistic sensibility and meticulous timing which mark his overall versatility. A cycle of Mozart operas in period-instrument performances and recordings, with the English Baroque Soloists, began in 1989 with *Idomeneo*, and the Gluck repertory was enhanced in 1990 with a first recording of *La rencontre imprévue*. He was made a CBE in 1990.

A. Blyth: 'John Eliot Gardiner', *Opera*, xxxviii (1987), 8–14
ARTHUR JACOBS, NOËL GOODWIN

Gardner, Jake (*b* Oneonta, NY, 14 Nov 1947). American baritone. His first major role was as Valentin (*Faust*) at Houston in 1975 and the following year he took part in a concert performance of Massenet's *Le Cid* in New York. He sang in the premières of Thea Musgrave's *Mary, Queen of Scots* (1977, Edinburgh) and *An Occurrence at Owl Creek Bridge* (1982), and appeared in the American première of Tippett's *The Ice Break* (1979). At Wexford in 1987 he was Valdeburgo in Bellini's *La straniera*, and in 1989 he became principal baritone with the Cologne Opera, where his roles have included Mozart's Nardo (*La finta giardiniera*) and Count Almaviva and Puccini's Lescaut and Marcello. His Glyndebourne début was in 1991, as Guglielmo. Gardner has sung a wide range of roles, from Escamillo in Peter Brook's *Carmen* to the title role in Monteverdi's *Il ritorno d'Ulisse* for Long Beach Opera.

DAVID CUMMINGS

Gardner, John (**Linton**) (*b* Manchester, 2 March 1917). English composer and teacher. He studied at school with Gordon Jacob and at Oxford with Ernest Walker and Thomas Armstrong. He then taught at Repton (1939–40), Morley College (music tutor from 1952, director of music, 1965–9), St Paul's Girls' School (from 1962) and the RAM, retiring in 1975. From 1946 to 1952 he was a répétiteur with the newly formed Covent Garden Opera Company. This operatic experience paid off in his first opera, *The Moon and Sixpence*, commissioned by Sadler's Wells, which demonstrates a forceful, communicative style and an ability to write on a grand scale. *The Visitors*, by contrast, is a Pinteresque domestic comedy. *Bel and the Dragon* is an enterprising work for children very much in the Britten tradition, and *Tobermory* was commissioned for the opening of the Sir Jack Lyons Theatre at the RAM.

See also MOON AND SIXPENCE, THE.

A Nativity Opera op.3, 1949 (2, T. Guthrie and A. V. Coton), unperf., unpubd
The Moon and Sixpence op.32 (3, P. Terry, after W. S. Maugham), London, Sadler's Wells, 24 May 1957, unpubd
Vile Bodies, 1961 (musical, 2, Terry, after E. Waugh; P. Jennings), unperf., unpubd
The Visitors op.111 (chamber op, 3, J. O. Greenwood), Aldeburgh, Jubilee Hall, 7 June 1972, unpubd
Bel and the Dragon op.120 (children's op, T. Kraemer), London, St James' Norlands Church, 15 Dec 1973, vs (London, 1978)
The Entertainment of the Senses op.121 (antimasque, W. H. Auden; conceived as intermission in Gibbons's and Locke's Cupid and Death), concert perf. London, Queen Elizabeth Hall, 2 Feb 1974, unpubd
Tobermory op.137 (1, G. Ewart, after Saki), London, RAM, 26 Oct 1977, unpubd

N. Goodwin: 'John Gardner's Opera "The Moon and Sixpence"', *MT*, xcviii (1957), 250–51
'John Gardner Introduces his New Opera "The Visitors"', *The Listener* (8 June 1972), 769
E. Greenfield: 'Piano forte', *The Guardian* (16 Oct 1972), 8
S. Meares: 'In Recent Times – a Personal Choice', *British Opera in Retrospect* (n.p., 1986) [pubn of the British Music Society], 132

STEPHEN BANFIELD

Gardoni, Italo (*b* Parma, 12 March 1821; *d* Paris, 26 March 1882). Italian tenor. He made his début in 1840 at Viadana in the title role of Donizetti's *Roberto Devereux* and then sang in Turin, Berlin, Milan, Brescia and Paris, first at the Opéra, later at the Théâtre Italien. He made his London début in 1847 at Her Majesty's Theatre, creating Carlo in Verdi's *I masnadieri*. He also sang Pylades (*Iphigénie en Tauride*), Don Ottavio, Tamino, Faust and Florestan. At Covent Garden he made his début in 1855 as Count Ory, then sang Nemorino, Danilowitz in Meyerbeer's *L'étoile du nord* and Corentin in *Dinorah* (1859), both first British performances. He sang regularly in London and Paris until 1874, when he retired. His repertory included Rodrigo (Rossini's *Otello*), Giannetto (*La gazza ladra*), Elvino, Arturo, Fra Diavolo and Alfredo. Versatile both as singer and actor, he had a light but well-focussed voice.

ELIZABETH FORBES

Garducci, Tommaso. *See* GUARDUCCI, TOMMASO.

Gargiulo [Gargiulio], **Terenzio** (*b* Torre Annunziata, nr Naples, 23 Nov 1905; *d* San Sebastiano al Vesuvio, nr Naples, 13 Nov 1972). Italian composer. After studying at the Naples Conservatory he became a concert pianist. From 1928 he also taught at the conservatories of Bari, Parma, Palermo and Naples. His operas, *Il borghese gentiluomo* (1947) and *Maria Antonietta* (1952), resulted from collaboration with the librettist, critic and theatre producer Vittorio Viviani (son of the writer Raffaele Viviani), an outstanding figure in the theatrical and musical world of Naples, where both works were performed. As in his chamber and orchestral music, Gargiulo showed a fondness for folktunes; in theatrical terms he followed the traditions of late 19th-century Neapolitan opera.

RAFFAELE POZZI

Garrard, Don (*b* Vancouver, 31 July 1929). Canadian bass. He studied at Santa Barbara with Lotte Lehmann and later at the Toronto Royal Conservatory. After a period as a principal with the Canadian Opera Company, he undertook further studies in New York and Milan. In 1961 he joined Sadler's Wells Opera in London, with which he sang *basso cantante* roles in over 500 performances as well as appearing with Scottish Opera and the WNO. He took part in the English Opera Group première of Britten's *Curlew River* (1964), made his début at Covent Garden in 1970 as Ferrando (*Il trovatore*) and at Glyndebourne in 1973 in *Der Besuch der alten Dame* (Einem); in 1975 he appeared there as Trulove in *The Rake's Progress*, a role he had recorded under Stravinsky. In Canada he has sung the Grand Inquisitor and Daland (1988–9). His secure technique, warmth of vocal feeling and genial character also brought him engagements elsewhere in Europe and in Israel, North America (notably at Santa Fe) and South Africa.

NOËL GOODWIN

Garrett, Lesley (*b* Thorne, Doncaster, 10 April 1955). English soprano. She studied in London, making her début in 1980 as Alice (*Le comte Ory*) with the ENO, with whom she later sang Despina, Bella (*The Midsummer Marriage*), Papagena, Susanna, Valencienne (*The Merry Widow*), Yum-Yum, Atalanta (*Serse*) and Alsi (*The Making of the Representative for Planet 8*) and in 1991 scored a great success as Janáček's Vixen and provided a conspicuously attractive Adele in *Die Fledermaus*. At Wexford (1980–81) she sang Dorinda (*Orlando*) and Zaide. With the WNO she created Nicola in Metcalf's *The Journey* (1981) and sang Esmeralda (*The Bartered Bride*). For Opera North she sang Sophie (*Werther*) and Susanna, and at Buxton (1981–4) Carolina (*Il matrimonio segreto*) and Hypsipyle (Cavalli's *Giasone*). At Glyndebourne (1984–6) her roles have included Damigella (*L'incoronazione di Poppea*) and Zerlina. She has sung Servilia, Barbarina and the Second Niece (*Peter Grimes*) at Geneva. A most engaging artist, she has a sweet-toned and flexible voice, as well as a delightful personality.

ELIZABETH FORBES

Garrick, David (*b* Hereford, 19 Feb 1717; *d* London, 20 Jan 1779). English actor, manager and playwright. He is remembered primarily as the greatest Shakespearean actor of the mid-18th century and as the vastly influential manager of Drury Lane, from 1747 to his retirement in 1776. But he was also knowledgeable about ballet and opera. In 1749 he married Eva Maria Veigel, who had come to London in March 1746 as prima ballerina for the Haymarket opera. Garrick visited Paris and maintained close contact with his Paris agent, Jean Monnet, who put him in touch with such figures as Noverre, the pyrotechnist Morel Torré, the violinist-composer F. H. Barthélemon (who provided music for Garrick's burletta *Orpheus*) and J. P. de Loutherbourg (who revolutionized stage design at Drury Lane in the 1770s). Garrick's relatively 'naturalistic' acting style made him an important influence on such theatrical and operatic reformers as Algarotti, Diderot and Noverre (*see* PRODUCTION, fig.10). He is said to have taught his acting style to Guadagni, who was to be Gluck's Orpheus (1762).

Garrick's importance to opera, however, lies principally in what he produced as artistic manager at Drury Lane. Early in his long reign he staged Boyce's all-sung afterpiece *The Chaplet* (1749), Arne's *Don Saverio*, an innovatory opera set in the present (1750), and Charles Burney's all-sung burletta, *Robin Hood* (1750). He extended the boundaries of pantomime in both music and ballet in a series of important ventures with Henry Woodward, the best-known of which is *Queen Mab* (1750). His importation of Noverre's *Les fêtes chinoises* (1755) was wrecked by anti-French riots and lost £4000 but proved a significant influence on later pantomime. Garrick staged J. C. Smith's neo-Handelian operas, most notably *The Fairies* (1755). The success of Arne's *Artaxerxes* at Covent Garden in 1762 threw Garrick operatically on the defensive. He struggled for some years to find a counter-attraction to the popular series of comic operas staged by Bickerstaff and various composers at the rival theatre, beginning with *Love in a Village* (1762). With Charles Dibdin and *The Padlock* (1768) he finally found his man. Their relations were frequently strained, however, and Dibdin's view of Garrick in his autobiography *The Professional Life of Mr Dibdin* (1803) is caustic.

English opera of the late 18th century remains understudied, but as it starts to receive attention Garrick will be found to have had a major influence on its development. He was both eclectic and innovatory. His 1770 revival of Dryden and Purcell's *King Arthur* (revised by Arne) is a major landmark in the rediscovery of Purcell. He produced all-sung mainpieces and afterpieces, burlettas, ballad operas, pastiches and sophisticated pantomime-ballets. The near-domination of musical works at Drury Lane and Covent Garden in the last quarter of the 18th century simply extends an artistic policy inaugurated by Garrick and developed by John Beard in the 1750s and 60s.

BDA; LS

K. A. Burnim: *David Garrick, Director* (Pittsburgh, 1961)
D. M. Little and G. M. Kahrl, eds.: *The Letters of David Garrick* (Cambridge, MA, 1963)
D. Heartz: 'From Garrick to Gluck: the Reform of Theatre and Opera in the Mid-Eighteenth Century', *PRMA*, xciv (1967–8), 111–27
R. Fiske: *English Theatre Music in the Eighteenth Century* (London, 1973, 2/1986)
G. W. Stone jr and G. M. Kahrl: *David Garrick: a Critical Biography* (Carbondale, IL, 1979)
H. W. Pedicord and F. L. Bergmann, eds.: *The Plays of David Garrick* (Carbondale, IL, 1980–82)
E. W. White: *A History of English Opera* (London, 1983)
P. T. Dircks: *David Garrick* (Boston, 1985)   ROBERT D. HUME

Garrido (Vargas), Pablo (*b* Valparaíso, 26 March 1905; *d* Santiago, 14 Sept 1982). Chilean composer. He studied humanities and music and after several trips abroad he became a pioneer of jazz in Chile. He published a number of books, worked as a music critic and was a prolific composer, moving from jazz to expressionism and serial techniques. His one-act chamber opera *La sugestión* (1959) was first performed in Santiago in 1961. Scored for soprano, baritone and eight instruments, it was considered an extraordinary step forward in Chilean lyrical theatre. The libretto (of no literary merit) tells of a girl who falls in love with her psychiatrist, but then kills him when she is under hypnotic suggestion. During the 1970s Garrido composed three more operas, of which the last two include electronic music as well as conventional forces.

La sugestión (chamber op, 1, C. R. Cherif), Santiago, Municipal, 18 Oct 1961
Por el camino del alba, 1976 (2, W. Mayorga)
La huella del hombre, 1978 (1, G. Díaz)
En la torre, 1979 (1, M. Arteche)

V. Salas: *La creación musical en Chile, 1900–1951* (Santiago, [1951])
'Crónica', *Revista musical chilena*, no.78 (1961), 88
M. Cánepa: *La opera en Chile (1839–1930)* (Santiago, 1976)
M. Silva: 'Pablo Garrido Vargas (1905–1982)', *Revista musical chilena*, no.158 (1982), 126–7
J. P. González: 'Cronología epistolar de Pablo Garrido', *Revista musical chilena*, no.160 (1983), 4–46
   SAMUEL CLARO-VALDÉS

Garrigues, Malvina. German soprano, wife of LUDWIG SCHNORR VON CAROLSFELD.

Garrison, Jon (*b* Higginsville, MO, 11 Dec 1944). American tenor. He attended the University of New Hampshire and New York University. His Metropolitan Opera début was in 1975 as Rinuccio in *Gianni Schicchi*. Since his 1982 New York City Opera début in Gluck's *Alceste*, he has been a company mainstay, his roles including the Duke of Mantua, Nadir, Don Ottavio, Rodolfo, Ruggero (*La rondine*), Tamino, Tom Rakewell and Nicholas in the première of Reise's *Rasputin* (1988). He has also sung with the opera companies of Cincinnati, Hamburg, Lyons, Miami, Montreal, Pittsburgh, San Diego, Santa Fe and Washington, DC, participated in the première of Stewart Copeland's *Holy Blood, Crescent Moon* in Cleveland in 1989 and the next year sang Skuratov in the American première of *From the House of the Dead* at the New York City Opera. A lyric tenor of sensitivity and solidity, he has also enjoyed an active concert career.

   CORI ELLISON

Garrison [Siemonn], Mabel (*b* Baltimore, MD, 24 April 1886; *d* New York, 20 Aug 1963). American soprano. She studied singing at the Peabody Conservatory with W. E. Heinendahl and Pietro Minetti, and later in New York with Oscar Saenger and Herbert Witherspoon. Using her married name of Siemonn, she made her stage début with the Aborn Opera Company in Boston as Philine in Thomas' *Mignon* in 1912. She joined the Metropolitan Opera two years later, making her official début as Frasquita in *Carmen* (1914). She only attracted real attention, however, when she replaced Raymonde Delaunois at short notice as Urbain in Meyerbeer's *Les Huguenots* in December, and also made a fine impression two years later when she replaced Hempel as the Queen of Night. Her greatest success was as the Queen of Shemakha in *The Golden Cockerel*, covering for Maria Barrientos, in 1918. Among her other roles were Olympia, Gilda, Martha, Rosina, Adina and Lucia, Oscar (*Ballo*) and Mozart's Mme Herz (*Der Schauspieldirektor*).

After her final Lucia at the Metropolitan, in 1921, Garrison performed extensively in Europe for several years. She sang Rosina with the Chicago Civic Opera (1926) and later took part in a Baroque series in Northampton, Massachusetts, which included the American premières of Handel's *Serse* (1928) and *Rodelinda* (1931). Also a recitalist, she was admired for the clarity of her voice and her smooth and elegant style.

A. Favia-Artsay: 'Historical Records: Mabel Garrison', *Hobbies*, lix/8 (1954), 22–3
G. M. Eby: 'The Two Careers of Mabel Garrison', *ON*, xxiii/4 (1958–9), 24–7   PHILIP LIESON MILLER

Garsington Manor. English manor house near Oxford, formerly the home of Lady Ottoline Morrell. Since 1989 it has been the site of the Garsington Opera Festival, which takes place annually in June and concentrates on works by Haydn. Visiting companies, notably Opera 80 and Pimlico Opera, have given covered outdoor performances in the grounds of the house (300 seats), but the festival also maintains its own company, Garsington Opera. The festival is noted for its attractive setting and intimate scale.

Gärtnerplatz [Staatstheater am Gärtnerplatz]. Munich theatre, opened in 1865; see MUNICH, §3(ii).

Garwood, (Miriam) Margaret (*b* Haddonfield, NJ, 22 March 1927). American composer. She studied the piano privately and taught it at the Philadelphia Musical Academy from 1953. She was married to the composer Romeo Cascarino, from whom she learnt orchestration, and began composing about 1962. Her first opera was commissioned by a suburban Philadelphia ensemble in 1965. The modest success of *The Trojan Women* spurred further commissions and Garwood gradually became known as an opera composer.

At this stage she studied composition formally with Miriam Gideon, taking the master's degree at the Philadelphia Musical Academy in 1975; by then she had produced two operas and begun work on a third. Garwood was appointed to the piano faculty of Muhlenberg College (Allentown, Pennsylvania) in 1978, and there wrote *Rappaccini's Daughter*, her best-known composition, completing it in 1983 after nearly a decade of work. In 1984 she left Muhlenberg College to devote all her time to composition.

A slow and cautious composer, Garwood has written little besides her four operas – some songs and chamber music, a widely performed children's ballet and a cantata. Like most successful American opera composers before Philip Glass, she is an extremely conservative musician: her style has at various times been likened to that of Debussy, Delius, Cilea or Richard Strauss but also contains elements of Stravinsky, Berg and even Crumb. She is a particularly skilful and imaginative orchestrator, and the dramatic soundness of her librettos has done much to ensure her the respectful attention of the opera press.

The Trojan Women (1, H. A. Wiley, after Euripides), Chester, PA, P. M. C. Colleges Auditorium, 22 Oct 1967; rev. 1979
The Nightingale and the Rose (1, Garwood, after O. Wilde), Chester, Widener College Alumni Auditorium, 21 Oct 1973
Rappaccini's Daughter (2, Garwood, after N. Hawthorne), Philadelphia, Trocadero, 6 May 1983; rev. 1983
Joringel and the Songflowers (children's op, 1, Garwood, after J. L. and W. C. Grimm), Philadelphia, Shawmont School, 25 Feb 1987

*

D. Webster: '"Trojan Women" on opera program of Chester group', *Philadelphia Inquirer* (9 July 1967)
J. V. R. Bull: 'New Opera Premieres', *Philadelphia Inquirer* (23 Oct 1973)
W. Ashbrook: 'Philadelphia', *Opera*, xxxiv (1983), 1122–3
D. Webster: 'This opera has consumed nearly a decade of her life', *Philadelphia Inquirer* (4 May 1983)
——: 'Story predominates in opera of "Rappaccini's Daughter"', *Philadelphia Inquirer* (7 May 1983)
——: 'Interlude for Opera Composer', *Philadelphia Inquirer* (25 March 1989)
R. H. Kornick: *Recent American Opera: a Production Guide* (New York, 1991)   ANDREW STILLER

Garzia, Francesco Saverio. *See* GARCÍA FAJER, FRANCISCO JAVIER.

Gasdia, Cecilia (*b* Verona, 14 Aug 1960). Italian soprano. In 1981 she won the RAI Maria Callas competition and then sang Giulietta (*I Capuleti e i Montecchi*) in Florence. The following year she took over the title role of *Anna Bolena* at short notice at La Scala and sang Amina (*La sonnambula*) at S Carlo. She has sung throughout Italy, at the Opéra, in Vienna, Madrid, Barcelona, Chicago and Philadelphia and at the Metropolitan where she made her début in 1986 as Gounod's Juliet. Her repertory includes Mrs Ford (Salieri's *Falstaff*), Violetta, Gilda, Hélène (*Jérusalem*), Liù, Lauretta, Mimì, Musetta and Teresa (*Benvenuto Cellini*) as well as many bel canto parts: Rossini's Zelmira, Ermione, Anaïs (*Moïse*) and Corinna (*Il viaggio a Reims*), Donizetti's Argelia (*L'esule di Roma*) and the title role of Bellini's *Beatrice di Tenda*. She has a fine voice with a secure coloratura technique and phrases stylishly.   ELIZABETH FORBES

Gaslini, Giorgio (*b* Milan, 12 Oct 1929). Italian composer. He studied at the Milan Conservatory, where he was a conducting pupil of Votto and Giulini, then worked for the RAI and taught jazz at the conservatories of Milan and Rome. He has written much incidental music, including that for Michelangelo Antonioni's film *La notte*.

Gaslini's originality is marked by an attempt to create a fusion of genres and languages. After his classical training, he turned to jazz and sought to synthesize its oral roots with the language of the European avant garde. He experimented with a combination of jazz and 12-note techniques in his octet *Tempo e relazione* (1957), and in later works tried to assimilate elements from pop music, electronic music and aleatory techniques into his jazz 'total performance'. In the same line is his 'street opera' *Un quarto di vita*, to his own libretto, which uses the avant-garde 'open theatre' experiments of the 1960s. In order to create a total musical experience he brings together different genres and musical languages; his intention was not merely to be eclectic but, as he explained in *Musica totale* (Milan, 1968), to break through the ideological barriers of musical enjoyment in the prevailing political and intellectual climate. *Un quarto di vita* was first performed in Parma in 1968.

*

A. Bassi: *Giorgio Gaslini* (Padua, 1986)
A. Mazzoleni and P. Santi: 'Gaslini, Giorgio', *The New Grove Dictionary of Jazz*, ed. B. Kernfeld (London, 1988)   RAFFAELE POZZI

Gaspari, Giovanni Paolo (*b* Venice, 1712; *d* Munich, 1 March 1775). Italian stage designer, active in Munich. He studied architecture and theories of perspective with his father, Antonio. He first experienced stage design through the work of G. F. Costa, scenic artist at S Giovanni Grisostomo in Venice. In spring 1738 Gaspari was engaged as scenic artist and architect at the court of Margrave Friedrich of Bayreuth, where he remained until 1745. He participated in the renovations and redecoration of the Margrave's theatre in Erlangen, one of the oldest surviving opera houses in southern Germany. After working at the court of Clemens August in Cologne (1745–9), he moved to Munich, where he entered the service of Elector Maximilian III Joseph. In 1751 he supervised the renovations of the St Georg Saal

Design by Giovanni Paolo Gaspari for Gluck's 'Orfeo ed Euridice', performed at the Residenztheater, Munich, in 1773: watercolour and gouache

in the Residenz. He created sets for the court opera there and in the opera house in the Salvatorplatz, among them a production of Galuppi's *Ipermestra* (1751).

During the building of the new court theatre in the Residenz (Cuvilliéstheater) in 1753, Gaspari oversaw the construction and installation of the backstage machinery and technical apparatus (details of his work for this theatre were published in *Ecole bavaroise*, Munich, 1771). The new theatre opened on 12 October 1753 with G. B. Ferrandini's *Catone in Utica*, with sets by Gaspari. During the next 25 years Gaspari designed virtually all the operas performed in the Residenz, among them Bernasconi's *Temistocle* (1754), *Adriano in Siria* (1755), *Didone abbandonata* (1756), *Trionfo della fedeltà* (1761), *Artaserse* (1763), *Semiramide* (1765) and *Demetrio* (1772) and Gluck's *Orfeo ed Euridice* (1773; see illustration). Early in his career Gaspari was greatly influenced by the late Baroque style of the Galli-Bibiena family, but during his first years in Munich he assimilated rococo elements. Many of his designs are in the Graphische Sammlung, Munich.

G. P. Gaspari should not be confused with his brother Pietro Gaspari (*b* Venice, 1720; *d* Venice, 1785), also an architect and painter, who worked alongside him during the construction of the Residenztheater and probably assisted him with *Catone in Utica* in 1753. Shortly thereafter Pietro returned to Venice, where he became a member of the Accademia.

H. Tintelnot: *Barocktheater und Barocke Kunst: die Entwicklungs-geschichte der Fest- und Theaterdekoration in ihrem Verhältnis zur barocken Kunst* (Berlin, 1939)
U. Thieme and F. Becker, eds.: *Lexikon der bildenden Künstler*, xiii (Leipzig, 1947), 229–30
E. Nölle: *Die Theatermaler Gaspari: ein Beitrag zur Geschichte des Bühnenbildes und des Theaterbaus im 18. Jahrhundert* (diss., U. of Munich, 1966)
D. Oenslager: *Stage Design – Four Centuries of Scenic Invention* (New York, 1975)
EVAN BAKER

Gasparini, Domenico Maria Angiolo. *See* ANGIOLINI, GASPARO.

Gasparini, Francesco (*b* Camaiore, nr Lucca, 19 March 1661; *d* Rome, 22 March 1727). Italian composer. He was one of the most important Italian opera composers of the first three decades of the 18th century, the main centres of his operatic activity being Venice (1702–13) and Rome (1714–24). His output includes over 50 full-length operas and over 15 comic intermezzos, as well as oratorios and cantatas throughout his career.

1. LIFE. By 1682 Gasparini was living in Rome, where he was organist at the church of Madonna dei Monti and where he was presumably based throughout the 1680s and 90s. His musical style was moulded by composers in Rome whose principal activities were outside opera; he may have received instruction from Bernardo Pasquini and Corelli, traditionally cited as his teachers. Records of his activities as a performer in the 1680s make clear that he was an accomplished singer, violinist and keyboard player. On 27 June 1684 he was admitted to the Accademia Filarmonica of Bologna as a singer and on 17 May 1685 as a composer (there is no confirmation of Hawkins's claim that he resided in Venice at Legrenzi's house in 1686 and received instruction from him). He became a member of the Accademia di S Cecilia in Rome in 1689 and enjoyed the patronage of Cardinal Benedetto Pamphili, who was protector of the Collegio Clementino.

During the 1680s operatic productions were intermittent in Rome because of papal restrictions. It is not surprising, therefore, that Gasparini's earliest documented involvement with opera was outside Rome: he was *maestro di cappella* at the opera house in Livorno in December 1686 when two works were performed – *Roderico*, which C. F. Pollarolo possibly set as early as 1684 for Brescia, and *Olimpia vendicata*, based on Alessandro Scarlatti's setting for Naples (December 1685). Gasparini wrote new arias for *Roderico* and may have reset the text entirely, as he did for the revival in Rome in 1694; the extent of his editing of *Olimpia vendicata* is less clear. Later, in 1692, he reworked Scarlatti's setting again, also for Rome. Several times in the course of his career Gasparini repeated this pattern of resetting for new cities librettos that he had already set.

For a brief period in the early 1690s, during and shortly after the reign of Pope Alexander VIII (6 October 1689–1 February 1691), a number of music-loving patrons, such as the pope's nephew Cardinal Pietro Ottoboni, Benedetto Pamphili, and the Spanish ambassador (the Duke of Medinaceli), were able to promote public performances of opera in Rome on a more regular basis than during the 1680s. For the 1690 carnival Gasparini wrote *Bellerofonte* for the Collegio Clementino; and in 1692 and 1694 he reset the works he had formerly edited for Livorno. *Aiace*, commissioned for Naples in 1697, probably reflects connections made in Rome, since after the Duke of Medinaceli became viceroy of Naples in 1696 he frequently commissioned operas from composers he had known in Rome. In autumn 1700 Gasparini was in Genoa to supervise the production of his *Gerone tiranno di Siracusa*.

In summer 1701 Gasparini assumed the position of *maestro di coro* at the Ospedale della Pietà in Venice. His residence there lasted until 1713, during which time he wrote 24 operas, all except the first for the Teatro S Cassiano. In working for this theatre he became the leading opera composer in Venice, superseding C. F. Pollarolo, who had dominated Venetian opera in the 1690s. Gasparini's stature was particularly evident between 1706 and 1711, when Pollarolo's steady production of operas for that city lapsed. Composing for the Teatro S Cassiano brought Gasparini together with the leading librettists of his day – Silvani, Zeno and Pariati – whose works distinguish themselves from *seicento* librettos in their clearly motivated plots, extensive recitatives and consistently high moral tone. The comic elements suppressed in these serious dramas were re-introduced through comic intermezzos (first documented on the Venetian stage in 1706); Gasparini thus belongs to the first generation of composers of works in that genre.

Gasparini received six months' leave of absence from the Pietà in 1713 because of ill health (due to gout), and never returned to his post. Already in the summer of 1712 he had settled his family in Città di Castello and he moved there himself in 1713. He claimed the decision to move was motivated by the desire for rest, but he maintained close connections with Roman patrons and frequently travelled to supervise productions of his operas: to Genoa in autumn 1713, Rome for the 1714 carnival, Reggio Emilia in spring 1714 and spring 1715, and Florence for the 1715 carnival (December 1714–March 1715). By 1716 Gasparini had settled again in Rome where he wrote operas for the Teatro Capranica for the 1716 and 1717 carnivals. From 1718 to 1720 he wrote for the new Teatro Alibert and presumably supervised performances there, which sometimes involved adapting his or others' works; his last two works for this theatre marked the first season of its refurbishment. Throughout his Roman years Gasparini was also a teacher of young opera singers.

In July 1716 Gasparini succeeded Caldara as *maestro di cappella* to Prince Francesco Maria Ruspoli, whom he served until May 1718. During these years he lived in a house owned by the prince in Piazza di S Lorenzo in Lucina. In 1718 he was accepted as a member of the Accademia dell'Arcadia in which he used the name Ericreo. This was a rare privilege for a musician and one that he shared with three other composers associated with Rome – Corelli, Pasquini and Alessandro Scarlatti. Scarlatti and Gasparini, close contemporaries, held each other in high esteem, and Scarlatti entrusted his son Domenico to Gasparini for instruction. However, the last phases of their careers as opera composers contrasted strikingly. Scarlatti's last serious operas (1718–22) were produced in Rome rather than his home base, Naples, and reflect the patronage of a small circle of Roman nobles. In the same period, Gasparini was in demand not only in Rome but also in Venice, Milan, Turin and Reggio Emilia.

In the libretto to *Faramondo* of 1720 Gasparini first styled himself 'maestro del principe Borghese', a claim repeated in the librettos for *Nino* (1720), *Zoe* (1721) and the Milan revival of *Astianatte* (1722). His work for the Borghese family was minimal. In lieu of salary, from 1719 until his death he lived rent-free in a house near their palace. In 1723 *Dorinda*, dedicated to Maria Livia Spinola Borghese, may have been performed in this house as a token of his gratitude for her informal patronage, which may have begun as early as 1711. Gasparini may have travelled to Milan for the 1722 carnival to supervise productions of his *Astianatte* and *Flavio Anicio Olibrio*. His last opera, *Tigrena* (1724), was performed in the palace of the Portuguese ambassador to Rome in honour of the birth of a fourth son to João V King of Portugal. On this occasion Gasparini's cast included two of the most famous castratos of his day, Giacinto Fontana (Farfallino) and Carlo Broschi (Farinelli). In February 1725 he became *maestro di cappella* at St John Lateran, but was pensioned off in June 1726.

2. STYLE. In the course of his career Gasparini's style, like that of his contemporaries, became increasingly elaborate. From the outset his active continuo parts revealed his Roman background, distinguishing him from C. F. Pollarolo. Although arias were his central musical focus, Gasparini prided himself on the attention he paid to recitatives; his contemporaries praised him for that. Contrary to Quantz's claim, he was not the inventor of accompanied recitative, though he left impressive examples, for instance in *Bajazet*. At the beginning of his career his arias were usually accompanied by continuo alone, upper melody instruments alternating with the voice; such instruments were used simultaneously only for particularly intense moments or for special effects. By the first decade of the 1700s, however, his arias were usually accompanied by upper melody instruments that often play simultaneously with the voice, either as sonorous support or in a distinctly independent solo role. The standard instrumental forces were four-part strings, two oboes, bassoon and basso continuo, the oboes and bassoon often doubling the violins and continuo. In his serious operas fully-fledged da capo arias predominate, but in his comic works he used more varied forms.

Like those of his contemporaries, Gasparini's works barely outlasted his lifetime, despite his fame. They formed important models for other composers such as Handel, but not for the younger generation. Unlike his contemporaries, however, Gasparini continued to be known after his death, for a treatise, *L'armonico pratico al cimbalo* (Venice, 1708), the most important continuo treatise of his day.

See also AMBLETO and BAJAZET.

drammi per musica in three acts, unless otherwise stated; dates are of first performances unless specified as dedication dates

VC – Venice, Teatro S Cassiano

Roderico (G. B. Bottalino), Livorno, Dec 1686, arias *I-MOe*; rev. Rome, Pace, 25 Jan 1694, arias *D-B*, *F-Pn*, *I-Rvat*

Bellerofonte (G. M. Conti), Rome, Collegio Clementino, carn. 1690, arias *GB-Lbl*, *I-Fc*, *Rvat*

Amor vince lo sdegno, ovvero L'Olimpia placata (A. Aureli), Rome, Capranica, 9 Feb 1692, arias *D-Mbs*, *I-Rvat*; collab. A. Scarlatti

Totila in Roma (M. Noris), Palermo, S Cecilia, 1696

Aiace (P. d'Averara), Naples, S Bartolomeo, ?16 Nov 1697, *D-Dlb*, arias *F-Pc*, *I-Nc*

Gerone tiranno di Siracusa (Aureli), Genoa, Falcone, aut. 1700

Tiberio imperatore d'Oriente (G. D. Pallavicini), Venice, S Angelo, carn. 1702; rev. or new setting as Le vicende d'amor e di fortuna, Venice, S Fantino, carn. 1710

Gli imenei stabiliti dal caso (F. Silvani), VC, 26 Dec 1702

Il più fedel fra i vassalli (Silvani), VC, ded. 3 Feb 1703; as Antioco, London, Haymarket, 12 Dec 1711, songs pubd (London, 1711)

Il miglior d'ogni amore per il peggiore d'ogni odio (Silvani), VC, 7 Nov 1703

La fede tradita e vendicata (Silvani), VC, ded. 5 Jan 1704, *Nc*, 1 aria (London, 1711); rev. with G. Vignola, Naples, S Bartolomeo, carn. 1707; rev. by G. M. Orlandini, Bologna, Marsigli Rossi, August Fair 1712; with arias by Orlandini, G. Bononcini and F. Mancini as Ernelinda, London, Haymarket, 26 Feb 1713; rev. Turin, Carignano, carn. 1719, *D-Hs* (Act 2)

La maschera levata al vizio (Silvani), VC, 4 Nov 1704

Fredegonda (Silvani), VC, ded. 26 Dec 1704

Il principato custodito dalla frode (Silvani), VC, 2 Feb 1705

Alarico, ovvero L'ingratitudine gastigata (Silvani), Palermo, S Cecilia, 1705, collab. Albinoni and others

Antioco (A. Zeno and P. Pariati), VC, week before 14 Nov 1705, *A-Wn*, 2 arias (London, 1711)

Ambleto (Zeno and Pariati), VC, week before 16 Jan 1706, arias *D-Bds*, *GB-Lbl*; rev. Vignola, Naples, S Bartolomeo, 4 Nov 1711; as Hamlet/Ambleto, London, Haymarket, 27 Feb 1712; songs pubd (London, 1712/*R*1986: *Handel Sources*, iv); ed. of orig. lib. by A. Della Corte, *Drammi per musica dal Rinuccini allo Zeno*, ii (Turin, 1958), 263–364

Statira (Zeno and Pariati), VC, 1 Feb 1706, *A-Gk(h)*, arias *D-Bds*; rev. Vignola as Le regine di Macedonia, Naples, S Bartolomeo, 1708

Taican re della Cina (tragedia, 5, U. Rizzi), VC, 4 Jan 1707, 1 aria (London, 1711); perf. with Lisetta e Astrobolo (int), *Rvat* (*R*: DMV, x, forthcoming)

Anfitrione (tragicomedia, prol., 5, Pariati ?and Zeno), VC, 13 Nov 1707, 1 aria (London, 1711); perf. with Erighetta e Don Chilone [Don Chilone] (int, Pariati), arias *GB-Lbl*

L'amor generoso (Zeno), VC, 1 Dec 1707, arias *D-MÜs* [perf. with intermezzos Melissa schernita, Melissa vendicata and Melissa contenta; as Melissa e Serpillo, *Dlb*]; rev. G. de Bottis, Naples, Fiorentini, ded. 30 Dec 1708; rev. S. Lapis, as La fede in cimento, VC, carn. 1730

Flavio Anicio Olibrio (Zeno and Pariati), VC, carn. 1708 [perf. with intermezzos Parpagnacco [Polastrella e Parpagnacco; L'astrologo; Polastrella e Parpagnacco astrologo] (Pariati), Melissa and ?Catulla e Lardone]; rev. Milan, Regio Ducal, carn. 1722, arias *ROu*; ?as Ricimero, Turin, Carignano, carn. 1722

Engelberta [Acts 4–5] (5, Zeno and Pariati), VC, week before 2 Feb 1709, *A-Wn*, *D-B*; arias *GB-Ob* [Acts 1–3 by Albinoni], 1 aria (London, 1711); perf. with La capricciosa e il credulo (int)

Alciade, ovvero L'eroico amore [La violenza d'amore] [Act 1] (opera tragicomica, M. Gasparini), Bergamo, 1709 [Act 2 by C. F. Pollarolo, Act 3 by F. Ballarotti]

Atenaide [Act 3] (Zeno), ?Milan, Barcelona or Vienna, 1709, *A-Wn* [Act 1 by A. S. Fiorè, Act 2 by A. Caldara]; as Teodosio ed Eudossa, Brunswick, 12 Sept 1716, collab. J. Fux and Caldara; as Teodosio, Hamburg, ded. 14 Nov 1718, collab. Fux and Caldara

La principessa fedele (A. Piovene), VC, 10 Nov 1709, arias *D-WD* [perf. with Zamberlucco [Zamberlucco e Palandrana] (int)]; ?as Cunegonda, Mantua, Arciducale, carn. 1718

L'oracolo del fato (componimento per musica da camera, Pariati), ?Vienna, 1709, *A-Wn*; Vienna, Hoftheater, 1 Oct 1719, *A-Wn*

Sesostri re d'Egitto (Pariati), VC, 9 Feb 1710, arias *D-MÜs*, *GB-Lbl*; ?perf. with intermezzos Il nuovo mondo and Tulpiano

La ninfa Apollo (scherzo scenico pastorale, F. de Lemene), VC, 4 March 1710, collab. A. Lotti

L'amor tirannico (5, D. Lalli), VC, aut. 1710, arias *D-WD*

Tamerlano (tragedia, Piovene, after J. Pradon: *Tamerlan, ou La mort de Bajazet*), VC, 24 Jan 1711, arias *B*, *WD*; new setting as Bajazet, Reggio Emilia, Pubblico, Spring Fair 1719, *A-Wn* (*R*1978: IOB, xxiv), *D-MEIr*, ed. M. Ruhnke (Munich, 1981–5); rev. as Bajazette, Venice, S Samuele, Ascension Fair 1723, arias *D-SWl*

Costantino (5, Pariati ?and Zeno), VC, 8 Nov 1711

Merope (Zeno), VC, carn. 1712

Eraclio [Act 2] (P. A. Bernardoni), Rome, Cancelleria, 1712 [Act 1 anon., Act 3 by Pollarolo)

Il comando non inteso ed ubbidito (Silvani), Milan, Regio Ducal, carn. 1713; as Zoe, ovvero Il comando non inteso ed ubbidito, Rome, Pace, carn. 1721

La verità nell'inganno (Silvani), VC, carn. 1713, arias *Dlb*

L'amore politico e generoso della regina Ermengarda, Mantua, spr. 1713, collab. G. M. Capelli

Lucio Papirio (A. Salvi), Rome, Capranica, carn. 1714, arias *B-Bc*, *D-ROu*, *I-Mc*; perf. with Barilotto e Serpina (int)

Eumene (Zeno), Reggio Emilia, Pubblico, [May] Fair 1714; rev. Naples, Reggio Palazzo, 1 Oct 1715, with arias by Leo and others *GB-Lbl*; perf. with intermezzos Mirena and L'alfier fanfarone

Amor vince l'odio, ovvero Timocrate (Salvi), Florence, Cocomero, 11 Feb 1715, aria *I-Rsc*

Il tartaro nella Cina (Salvi), Reggio Emilia, Pubblico, [May] Fair 1715, arias *Bc*, *Rsc*

Ciro (Noris), Rome, Capranica, carn. 1716, arias *GB-Lam*, *I-Bc*, *Rsc*

Vincislao (Zeno), Rome, Capranica, carn. 1716, arias *Bc*; adaptation of F. Mancini's setting (Naples, S Bartolomeo, carn. 1715)

Il gran Cid (J. Alborghetti), Naples, S Bartolomeo, carn. 1717, aria *Bc*

Intermezzi in derisione della setta maomettana (G. Gigli), Rome, Seminario Romano, carn. 1717, lib. pubd (Naples, n.d.)

Pirro (Zeno), Rome, Capranica, carn. 1717, arias *Rsc*

Il trace in catena (Salvi), Rome, Capranica, carn. 1717, arias *F-Pn*, *I-Rsc*, collab. 2 of Gasparini's pupils

Democrito, Turin, Carignano, carn. 1718, aria *GB-Lbl*

Nana francese e Armena [Mirena e Floro] (int), Dresden, Feb 1718, *D-Dlb*

Astianatte (Salvi), Rome, Alibert, carn. 1719, arias *F-Pc*; rev. Milan, Regio Ducal, carn. 1722, *GB-Lbl* (Acts 1–2 only; partial autograph)

Lucio Vero (Zeno), Rome, Alibert, carn. 1719, arias *B-Bc*, *F-Pc*, *GB-Lam*, *Lbl*

Tigranes, Hamburg, 1719, collab. F. Conti and Orlandini

Amore e maestà (Salvi), Rome, Alibert, carn. 1720, arias *D-MÜs*, *F-Pc*

Faramondo (after Zeno), Rome, Alibert, carn. 1720, arias *Pc*

La pace fra Seleuco e Tolomeo (A. Morselli, rev. A. Trabucco), Milan, Regio Ducal, carn. 1720

L'avaro (int, Salvi), Florence, 1720, *I-MC*

Nino [Act 2] (I. Zanelli), Reggio Emilia, Pubblico, May Fair, 1720 (ded. 29 May), arias *F-Pc* [Act 1 by Capelli, Act 3 by A. M. Bononcini]

Dorinda (favola pastorale, ? B. Marcello), Rome, carn. 1723

Silvia (dramma pastorale, E. Bissari), Foligno, carn. 1723

Gli equivoci d'amore e d'innocenza (Salvi), Venice, S Giovanni Grisostomo, aut. 1723

Tigrena (favola pastorale, with intermezzos), Rome, Palazzo De Mello de Castro, 2 Jan 1724

Arias in: Thomyris Queen of Scythia (pasticcio, P. A. Motteux), London, Drury Lane, 1 April 1707; Clotilda, London, Haymarket, 2 March 1709; Nerone fatto Cesare (pasticcio, Noris), Venice, S Angelo, carn. 1715

*

J. M. Knapp: 'Handel's *Tamerlano*: The Creation of an Opera', *MQ*, lvi (1970), 405–30

H. C. Wolff: 'Italian Opera: 1700–1750', *NOHM*, v (1975), 73–162, esp. 93–6

R. Strohm: 'Händel und seine italienischen Operntexte', *HJb* 1975–6, 101–59; rev. and trans. in *Essays on Handel and Italian Opera* (Cambridge, 1985), 34–79

M. Ruhnke: 'Das italienische Rezitativ bei den deutschen Komponisten des Spätbarock', *AnMc*, no.17 (1976), 79–120

R. Strohm: *Italienische Opernarien des frühen Settecento: 1720–1730*, *AnMc*, no.16 (1976)

F. Della Seta and F. Piperno, eds.: *Francesco Gasparini (1661–1727): atti del 1° convegno internazionale: Camaiore 1978*

R. Strohm: 'Ein Opernautograph von Francesco Gasparini?', *HJbMw*, iii (1978), 205–23; trans. in *Essays on Handel and*

Italian Opera (Cambridge, 1985), 106–21

R. L. Weaver and N. Weaver: *A Chronology of Music in the Florentine Theater: 1590–1750* (Detroit, 1978)

R. Strohm: *Die italienische Oper im 18. Jahrhundert* (Wilhelmshaven, 1979)

C. E. Troy: *The Comic Intermezzo: a Study in the History of Eighteenth-Century Italian Opera* (Ann Arbor, 1979)

F. Piperno: 'Francesco Gasparini: le sue abitazioni romane, i suoi allievi coabitanti (1717–1727)', *Esercizi: arte, musica, spettacolo*, iv (1981), 104–15

M. Ruhnke: 'Scena buffa und Intermezzo bei Francesco Gasparini', *Festschrift Heinz Becker* (Laaber, 1982), 58–66

R. Strohm: 'Manoscritti di opere rappresentate a Venezia, 1701–1740', *Informazioni e studi vivaldiani*, iii (1982), 45–51

M. Ruhnke: 'Zum Rezitativ der Opera seria vor Hasse', *Colloquium Johann Adolf Hasse und die Musik seiner Zeit: Siena 1983*, 159–86 [*AnMc*, no.25 (1987)]

R. Strohm: *Essays on Handel and Italian Opera* (Cambridge, 1985)

HARRIS S. SAUNDERS

Gasparini, Quirino (*b* Gandino, nr Bergamo, 1721; *d* Turin, 30 Sept 1778). Italian composer. An abbé, he studied composition with G. A. Fioroni in Milan and with Martini. He lived in Brescia, Venice (as a *maestro di cappella*) and Bologna, where in 1751 he became a member of the Accademia Filarmonica. His opera *Artaserse* (P. Metastasio) was performed at the Regio Ducal Teatro, Milan, on 26 December 1756. After a period as music master to Count D'Aziano of Vercelli, he was *maestro di cappella* of Turin Cathedral, from 1760 until his death.

Gasparini presented his opera *Mitridate re di Ponto* (to the libretto by V. A. Cigna-Santi later set by Mozart in Milan) at the Teatro Regio, Turin, on 31 January 1767 (*F-Pn*, *I-Tf* [lost], *P-La*). A letter dated 2 January 1771 from Leopold Mozart to Martini relates that Mozart's singers (among them the famous Antonia Bernasconi) first wanted to use some arias and the duet 'Se viver non degg'io' from this setting, and in fact an aria of his ('Vado incontro', Act 3) was in the event sung by Guglielmo d'Ettore, as Mithridates, and is included in the standard Mozart text. Later that month the two Mozarts met Gasparini in Turin; references in Leopold's travel notes from 1771 and in two letters from 1778 prove that the relationship was a good one. Gasparini's sacred music was also highly regarded.

F. Raugel: 'Quirino Gasparini', *RdM*, xii (1931), 9–12

M. T. Bouquet: *Musique et musiciens à Turin de 1648 à 1775* (Turin, 1968, and Paris, 1969)

L. F. Tagliavini: 'Quirino Gasparini and Mozart', *New Looks at Italian Opera: Essays in Honor of Donald J. Grout* (Ithaca, 1968), 151–71 [incl. J. S. Mayr's biography of Gasparini]

GIORGIO PESTELLI

Gassier, Edouard (*b* Draguignan, 30 Aug 1820; *d* Havana, 18 Dec 1872). French bass-baritone. He studied in Paris, making his début at the Opéra-Comique in 1845 as Fresque in Auber's *La barcarolle*. He appeared in Italy, Vienna, Spain and at the Théâtre Italien, where he sang Ferrando in the first Paris performance of *Il trovatore* (1854). He made his London début in 1856 at Drury Lane, then at Her Majesty's Theatre he sang Méphistophélès in *Faust* (1863), Falstaff in *Die lustigen Weiber von Windsor* (1864) and Melitone in *La forza del destino* (1867), all British first performances. A versatile singer with good coloratura technique, he also sang Assur (*Semiramide*) and Silva (*Ernani*). He was married to the Spanish soprano Josefa Gassier-Fernandez (*b* Bilbao, 1821; *d* Madrid, 1866), who frequently sang with him. She created Annetta in Federico and Luigi Ricci's *Crispino e*

la comare (1850, Venice) and was heard to best advantage in lyric roles such as Amina, Lucia, Norina, Rosina and Elvira (*Ernani*).
ELIZABETH FORBES

Gassmann, Florian Leopold (*b* Brüx [now Most], 3 May 1729; *d* Vienna, 20 Jan 1774). Bohemian composer. Along with Galuppi and Piccinni he was among the foremost composers of *opera buffa* in the generation before Mozart. He began his musical education in Bohemia, but his choice of a musical career did not meet with paternal approval and he ran away to Italy while still a young boy. He made his way to Venice, where he may have studied with Padre Martini. Gassmann's first opera was a setting of Zeno's *Merope*, performed in Venice in Carnival 1757; his first *opera buffa*, *Gli uccellatori*, followed two years later. In 1763 he was summoned as a ballet composer to Vienna, where in the following year, after the success of his *Olimpiade*, he succeeded Gluck as Theaterkapellmeister. Gassmann returned to Venice early in 1766, during the year of mourning on the death of Franz I. During this sojourn he composed *Achille in Sciro* and met the 15-year-old Antonio Salieri, whom he brought back to Vienna with him as a pupil. *L'amore artigiano*, composed in 1767, became one of Gassmann's two most enduring successes, with performances throughout Italy, Germany and Austria. The other, *La contessina*, was written three years later for a meeting of Joseph II and Frederick the Great at Mährisch-Neustadt. In 1771, a year that saw the composition of both *Il filosofo inamorato* and *Le pescatrici*, Gassmann founded the Tonkünstler-Sozietät, to support retired musicians and their families. On the death of Georg von Reutter in 1772, he was named Hofkapellmeister. His last opera, *La casa di campagna*, was performed in February 1773 and he died in 1774, after months of pain from injuries suffered in a fall from a carriage. His daughters, Maria Anna Fux (*b* Vienna, 1771; *d* Vienna, 27 Aug 1858) and Therese Rosenbaum (*b* Vienna, 1 April 1774; *d* Vienna, 8 Sept 1837), both achieved success as singers; Therese sang the Queen of Night at the first Kärntnertortheater production of *Die Zauberflöte* in 1801.

Gassmann's operas were widely performed and admired, earning praise even from so demanding a critic as Mozart. His output includes both serious and comic operas, but in the latter years of his career he devoted himself almost exclusively to *opera buffa*, for which he was most renowned. In the polemics of operatic Vienna, Gassmann's name was linked with that of Gluck, and his works show some of the characteristics of Gluckian reform; *Amore e Psiche*, written in 1767 to a libretto by Calzabigi's associate Marco Coltellini, was the first clear sign of that allegiance.

Although the characters and situations in his librettos (many by Goldoni) are generally stock types with links to the *commedia dell'arte*, Gassmann's music imbues them with a dramatic vividness that is far from conventional. His choices of tempo and metre, and the melodic and rhythmic design of his themes, all aim to define character and further the drama. In the early operas, Gassmann favoured tuneful, italianate melodies with simple chordal accompaniments, but the orchestra plays an increasingly important role in his later work, contributing rhythmic and melodic figures that help to delineate the dramatic action. The sinfonia of *La casa di campagna* even provides a programmatic sketch of the opera's plot. Gassmann's use of woodwind is especially varied and resourceful, and the ritornellos in the da capo arias of his *opere serie* are often extensive. Particularly in his ensembles, Gassmann turned the relative formal freedom of *opera buffa* to dramatic effect. He often used a multi-sectional ensemble finale, for example, with sudden shifts of tempo, key and metre, to mark the stages in a dramatic crescendo. He lavished particular care on the large-scale planning of these dramatic climaxes; in *L'amore artigiano*, for instance, the finales of all three acts are greatly expanded from Goldoni's original libretto. In his memoirs, Salieri describes his own first attempt at composing an opera, remarking that he followed the procedures he had seen Gassmann employ; in composing the first finale, he claims to have spent three hours sketching the sequence of metres and keys before writing a single note.

See also AMORE ARTIGIANO, L' and NOTTE CRITICA, LA.

Merope (os, 3, A. Zeno), Venice, S Moisè, carn. 1757, ov. and 1 aria, *I-MAav, S-Skma, US-Wc*
Issipile (os, 3, P. Metastasio), Venice, S Moisè, carn. 1758, *A-Wn*, ov. ed. H. C. R. Landon, Diletto musicale, no.28 (1966)
Gli uccellatori (dg, 3, C. Goldoni), Venice, S Moisè, carn. 1759, *Wn, I-Fc, P-La*
Filosofia ed amore (dg, 3, Goldoni), Venice, S Moisè, carn. 1760, *A-Wn, I-Fc*
Catone in Utica (os, 3, Metastasio), Venice, S Samuele, 29 April 1761, 1 aria, *D-Dlb*
Ezio (os, 3, Metastasio), Florence, Pergola, 1761; rev. Rome, Dame, carn. 1770, *A-Wn*
Un pazzo ne fa cento (dg, 3), Venice, S Moisè, aut. 1762, *Wn, DK-Kk*
L'olimpiade (os, 3, Metastasio), Vienna, Kärntnertor, 18 Oct 1764, *A-Wn, I-Nc, US-Wc*
Il trionfo d'amore (azione teatrale, 1, Metastasio), Vienna, Schönbrunn, 25 Jan 1765, *D-Bds*, A-Wn*
Achille in Sciro (os, 3, Metastasio), Venice, S Giovanni Grisostomo, spr. 1766, *Wn, P-La, US-Wc*
Il viaggiatore ridicolo (dg, 3, Goldoni), Vienna, Kärntnertor, 25 May 1766, *A-Wn, CS-K, D-B, Bds, W, DK-Kk, F-Pn, I-Nc*
L'amore artigiano [Die Liebe unter den Handwerksleuten] (ob, 3, Goldoni), Vienna, Burg, 26 April 1767, *A-Wn, CS-K, D-B, Rtt, DK-Kk, H-Bn, I-Fc, Nc, P-La*
Amore e Psiche (os, 3, M. Coltellini), Vienna, Burg, 5 Oct 1767, *A-Wgm, Wn, I-Nc* (*R*1983: IOB, lxxxvii)
La notte critica [Die unruhige Nacht] (ob, 3, Goldoni), Vienna, Burg, 5 Jan 1768, *A-Wgm*, Wn*
L'opera seria (commedia per musica, 3, R. de Calzabigi), Vienna, Burg, 1769, *Wn* (*R*1982: IOB, lxxxix), *P-La*
La contessina [Die junge Gräfin] (ob, 3, Coltellini, after Goldoni), Mährisch-Neustadt, 3 Sept 1770, *A-Wn, B-Bc, CS-K, D-SWl, F-Pn, I-Fc, MOe, Nc, P-La*; ed. in DTÖ, xlii–xliv, Jg.xxi/1 (1914)
Il filosofo inamorato (dg, 3, Coltellini, after Goldoni: *Filosofia ed amore*), Vienna, Burg, 1771, *A-Wn*
Le pescatrici (dg, 3, Goldoni), Vienna, Burg, 1771, *Wn*
Don Quischott von Mancia [Act 3] (commedia, 3, G. B. Lorenzi), Vienna, Burg, 1771 [Acts 1 and 2 by Paisiello]
I rovinati (commedia, 3, G. G. Boccherini), Vienna, Burg, 23 June 1772, *Wn, I-Fc* (inc.)
La casa di campagna (dg, 3, Boccherini), Vienna, Burg, 3 or 13 Feb 1773, *A-Wn*

Contribs. to: B. Galuppi: Il villano geloso; N. Piccinni: Le finte gemelle; P. Anfossi: Lo sposo di tre e marito di nessuna; A. Sacchini: L'isola d'amore

*

BurneyGN; ES (W. Bollert)
[J. Sonnleithner]: 'Biographische Skizze über Florian Leopold Gassmann', *Wiener Theateralmanach für das Jahr 1795*, 31
G. Donath: 'Florian Leopold Gassmann als Opernkomponist', *SMw*, ii (1914), 34–211
F. van Rossum: 'Florian Leopold Gassmann (1729–1774): Zijn opera buffa "La contessina"', *Mens en melodie*, xxvi (1971), 135–8
R. Strohm: 'Gassmann: La contessina', *Die italienische Oper im 18. Jahrhundert* (Wilhelmshaven, 1979), 278–90
JOSHUA KOSMAN

Gast, Peter [Köselitz, Johann Heinrich] (*b* Annaberg, 10 Jan 1854; *d* Annaberg, 15 Aug 1918). German composer. Much of Gast's life was dominated by his friendship with Friedrich Nietzsche, who promoted his operas as the perfect antidote to Wagner. The composer's incidental music for Goethe's *Scherz, List und Rache* of 1880 had the light touch sought by the philosopher, in contrast to Gast's earlier, unfinished Wagnerian-style music drama, *Williram und Siegeher* (1879). His only opera to have gained a wider reputation, *Der Löwe von Venedig*, based on the libretto of Cimarosa's *Il matrimonio segreto* (1792), had to wait from 1883 to 1891, despite Nietzsche's efforts, for its première in the Danzig Stadttheater, under the title *Die heimliche Ehe*. It was revised for the publication of the vocal score (Leipzig, 1901), yet was revived only once, at Chemnitz in 1933. The work anticipated the renewal of interest in 18th-century *opera buffa*, without itself amounting to much more than a string of lyrical melodies. Other unfinished operas of Gast's include *Orpheus und Dionysos* (1881) and *König Wenzel* (1888).

*

PEM (R. Stephan)
C. Fuchs: *Thematikon zu P. Gasts komischer Oper 'Die heimliche Ehe'* (Leipzig, 1890)
E. Wachler: 'Warum ist Peter Gasts "Löwe von Venedig" nicht wieder aufgeführt worden?', *ZfM*, lxxxvi (1929), 159–60
E. Podach: *Gestalten um Nietzsche* (Weimar, 1932), 68–124
F. Tutenberg: 'Peter Gasts "Löwe von Venedig"', *ZfM*, cvii (1940), 76–80
A. Einstein: 'Der "Antipode" Wagners', *Von Schütz bis Hindemith* (Zürich and Stuttgart, 1957), 105–11
F. R. Love: *Nietzsche's Saint Peter: Genesis and Cultivation of an Illusion* (Berlin, 1981)
AMANDA GLAUERT

Gatchina. Town in Russia, some 50 km outside St Petersburg. It was the residence of the Russian crown prince (later tsar) Paul. Two operas were produced in the palace there: *Le faucon*, an *opéra comique* by Bortnyansky to a libretto by François-Hermann Lafermière, Paul's Swiss-born secretary and French tutor (11/22 October 1786); and *Enea nel Lazio* (1799), an *opera seria* by Sarti to a libretto by the court poet Ferdinando Moretti.
RICHARD TARUSKIN

Gatta [Gatto], **Antonio** (*fl* Rome, 1763–71). Italian librettist. He was admitted to the Arcadian Academy during the custodianship of Morei (1743–66), with the Arcadian name Feresio Niceno; in the records he is referred to as '*abate*'. Since membership was not permitted to those under the age of 24, he must have been born before 1743. Gatta's six known librettos, all comic, were set by minor composers.

Vespina serva astuta, Crispi, 1763; L'amante nella caccia, V. Curcio, 1768; Le gare degli amanti, A. Danesi, 1768; Il geloso stravagante, G. B. Cavi, 1769; Domani e carnevale, Curcio, 1769; Il barone in villeggiatura, G. Giorgi, 1771

A. M. Giorgetti Vichi: *Gli Arcadi dal 1690 al 1800: Onomasticon* (Rome, 1977)
BRYAN MARTIN

Gatti, Carlo (*b* Florence, 19 Dec 1876; *d* Milan, 3 March 1965). Italian musicologist. He studied at the Milan Conservatory, with Catalani and others, teaching there from 1898 to 1941, and until 1948 holding the chair of Verdi studies, a position created for him. In 1921 he founded the music section of Teatro del Popolo, Milan, which he directed for more than 30 years. He also served as director at La Scala (1941–4) and was music critic of *L'illustrazione italiana* (1918–48). As a scholar he devoted himself to critical and historical studies of late 19th-century opera: his *Verdi*, in its original 1931 edition, is one of the most comprehensive and fully documented accounts of the composer and his music. He also composed orchestral and vocal music.

Il Teatro alla Scala rinnovato (Milan, 1926)
Verdi (Milan, 1931, 2/1951; part Eng. trans., 1955, as *Verdi: the Man and his Music*)
Verdi nelle immagini (Milan, 1941)
Rivisioni e rivalutazioni verdiane (Turin, 1952)
Catalani: la vita e le opere (Milan, 1953)
Riccardo Wagner: appunti commemorativi (Turin, 1964)
Il Teatro alla Scala nella storia e nell'arte, 1778–1963 (Milan, 1964)

CAROLYN GIANTURCO

Gatti, Gabriella (*b* Rome, 5 July 1916). Italian soprano. She made her début at the Rome Opera in 1934 in Monteverdi's *Orfeo*, and by 1952 had appeared in all the leading Italian theatres. At La Scala she sang in *La damnation de Faust* in the 1946–7 season, at Florence she took part in a revival of *Semiramide* in 1940 and in Rome in the Italian première of *Wozzeck* in 1942. Her voice was lyrical in character and graceful in timbre and expression. She was a notable Mathilde (*Guillaume Tell*, the role of her farewell in Rome) and Desdemona, and her other roles included Helen of Troy (in Boito's *Mefistofele*), Elisabeth (*Tannhäuser*), Mozart's Countess Almaviva and Abigaille (*Nabucco*).

GV (R. Celletti; R. Vegeto)   RODOLFO CELLETTI

Gatti, Guido M(aggiorino) (*b* Chieti, 30 May 1892; *d* Grottaferrata, 10 May 1973). Italian musicologist. He first studied engineering but by the age of 20 was editor of a music journal, *Riforma musicale*, and went on to be editor of several distinguished ones (including *Rassegna musicale* and *Rivista musicale italiana*) as well as important reference works (most notably *La musica: enciclopedia storica* and *La musica: dizionario*, with A. Basso, 1968–71). He was also active as a critic and as an administrator, and was director general of the Teatro di Torino, 1925–31, and organizer of Amfiparnaso, which in its single season put on *Il turco in Italia* with Callas and works by Petrassi, Dallapiccola and Tommasini. He wrote two opera librettos, for Ghedini (*Gringoire*, 1915) and Davico (*La dogaressa*, 1920) and wrote extensively on opera, especially contemporary Italian opera, with studies of Pizzetti (1934) and Pizzetti's *Débora e Jaèle* (1922) and works on Bizet, Rossini, Puccini and the Turin theatre.

Gatti, Luigi (Maria Baldassare) (*b* Castro Lacizzi, ? nr Verona, 11 June 1740; *d* Salzburg, 1 March 1817). Italian composer. He probably received his earliest musical training in Mantua, where his first opera, *Alessandro nell'Indie*, was well received in 1768 and where he later became vice-*maestro* of the church of S Barbara. He also served the Reale Accademia of Mantua, for which he wrote a number of occasional works. In 1783 he became the last Italian Kapellmeister of the Salzburg court and cathedral. Gatti's works in other genres include ballets, cantatas, instrumental pieces, and a large amount of sacred music.

all opere serie

Alessandro nell'Indie (P. Metastasio), Mantua, Ducal, 24 Jan 1768, *P-La*
Nitteti (Metastasio), Mantua, Ducal, spr. 1773, arias *GB-Lbl*, *I-Bc*, *Gl* and *OS*

Armida (G. de Gamerra), Mantua, Ducal, 29 Jan 1775, aria *Mc*
Olimpiade (Metastasio), Salzburg, Hof, 30 Sept 1775, arias *I-Gl*, *OS** and *Tf*, *P-La* (Act 1 only)
Antigono (Metastasio), Milan, Scala, 3 Feb 1781, with some music by Anfossi; *F-Pc*, arias *I-Mc* and *OS**, *P-La* (Act 3 only)
Demofoonte (Metastasio), Mantua, Ducal, 12 May 1787, aria *Rsc*

Arias in: *A-Wgm*, *Sca*, *D-Dlb*, *I-Gl*, *MAav*, *Mc* and *Os*; 1 pubd (London, n.d.)

*

AMZ, vii (1805), col.626
F. J. Lipowsky: *Baierisches Musik-Lexicon* (Munich, 1811), 89
C. Schneider: *Geschichte der Musik in Salzburg* (Salzburg, 1935), 142, 165   SVEN HANSELL

Gatti, Theobaldo [Teobaldo] **di** [Théobalde, Théobal, Théobald] (*b* ?Florence, *c*1650; *d* Paris, 1727). French composer. Facts about his early career are hard to establish: it is to Titon du Tillet that we owe the suggestion of Florence as his birthplace, the information that he died 'at a very advanced age' and the colourful story of his move to France. Apparently attracted by the music of his countryman Lully, he set off for Paris determined to meet him. Lully received him cordially and employed him (from about 1675) in the orchestra of the Académie Royale de Musique, where he played the *basse de violon* for 50 years. He was known in France exclusively by his first name or a French version of it. Titon du Tillet conjectures that di Gatti had his ears continually full of the operas of Lully and others and thereby developed a taste for composing his own. In the event, he produced only two, the first a *pastorale-héroïque*, Coronis (3, C. de Beaugé; 1691, Paris; *F-Pn*, *Po*, also *GB-Cfm* incorrectly attrib. Lully), and the second a *tragédie en musique*, Scylla (prol., 5, J.-F. Duché de Vancy), first performed at the Opéra in September 1701 and revived and published in an altered form later in the same year. Le Cerf de la Viéville refers to *Scylla* as 'well regarded for its fine symphonies'; significantly, it contains an Italian aria. Gatti also published a *Recueil d'airs italiens* (Paris, 1696) and other solo songs and duets.

See also SCYLLA.

*

J.-L. Le Cerf de la Viéville: *Comparaison de la musique italienne et de la musique françoise* (Brussels, 1704–6)
E. Titon du Tillet: *Le Parnasse françois* (Paris, 1732)
M. Barthélémy: 'Theobaldo di Gatti et la tragédie en musique Scylla', *RMFC*, ix (1969), 56–66
J. R. Anthony: *French Baroque Music from Beaujoyeulx to Rameau* (London, 1973, 2/1978)
J. de La Gorce: 'L'Académie royale de musique en 1704, d'après des documents inédits conservés dans les archives notariales', *RdM*, lxv (1979), 160–91
C. Wood: *Jean-Baptiste Lully and his Successors: Music and Drama in the 'tragédie en musique' 1673–1715* (diss., U. of Hull, 1981)
R. Fajon: *L'opéra à Paris du Roi-Soleil à Louis le Bien-aimé* (Geneva, 1984)
W. Weber: '*La musique ancienne* in the Waning of the Ancien Régime', *Journal of Modern History*, lvi (1984), 58–88

CAROLINE WOOD

Gatti-Casazza, Giulio (*b* Udine, 3 Feb 1869; *d* Ferrara, 2 Sept 1940). Italian impresario. He succeeded his father as head of the board of directors of the Teatro Comunale in Ferrara, 1893, and was later director of La Scala, Milan (1898–1908). In conjunction with the young Toscanini, he revitalized La Scala during his tenure; with Toscanini, he was engaged by the Metropolitan Opera, New York in 1908. Until 1910 he shared directorial control with Andreas Dippel and from 1910 to 1935 was sole general manager, the longest tenure in the history of the Metropolitan. The years until Toscanini's resignation (1915) are generally considered the finest in the history of the house.

Gatti-Casazza brought a thorough-going professionalism to the Metropolitan, in terms of singers, staging and design, managing an incredibly large repertory of between 40 and 50 operas in the short season. Under his aegis, the performance of opera in the original language became normal. He introduced, though with little success, American operas and ballets. From Caruso to Flagstad (who appeared first in his final season), Gatti-Casazza's roster included major singers and the Metropolitan became the principal showcase for the designer Josef Urban.

As time wore on, however, a sameness of vision became ever more evident, and the Depression years exposed the financial and artistic shakiness of Gatti-Casazza's cumbersome repertory policies. From 1935 he lived in retirement in Italy. He was married first (1910–28) to the soprano Frances Alda and from 1930 to the ballerina Rosina Galli. His *Memories of the Opera* (New York, 1941; trans. and ed. H. Taubman) cover the years to 1933.

*

O. Thompson: *The American Singer* (New York, 1937), 389–95

PATRICK J. SMITH

Gaubert, Philippe (*b* Cahors, 4 July 1879; *d* Paris, 10 July 1941). French conductor. He studied at the Paris Conservatoire and won the Prix de Rome in 1905. His career as a flautist, and as professor of flute at the Conservatoire from 1919, overshadowed earlier successes as a conductor. From 1920 he was regularly engaged at the Opéra, where his reputation grew chiefly in new works and in the Wagner repertory. He conducted the première of his own three-act *Naïla* there (7 April 1927); he also composed three ballets given there, plus much other music. He gave up regular conducting about 1938 and was made a Commandeur of the Légion d'honneur.

*

D. Sordet: *Douze chefs d'orchestre* (Paris, 1924)

NOËL GOODWIN

Gaudio, Cavalier **Antonio dal** [del] (*b* ?Rome; *fl* 1669–82). Italian composer. According to La Borde he was of Roman origin, but the libretto of his *L'Eudosia* (performed at the inauguration of the Teatro Fedeli, Mantua, 1669, text by di Mileto; music lost) describes him as being from Naples. In 1675, when he wrote the music for *Almerico in Cipro* (text by G. Castelli; scores in *I-Vnm* and, according to its catalogue, *Nc*), performed at the S Moisè, Venice, he was in the service of Prince Gonzaga, Duke of Sabbioneta (presumably Gian Francesco II, Duke of Bozzolo). He also composed *Ulisse in Feaccia* (1681, Venice; text anon., not by Filippo Acciaiuoli; music lost), signing the dedication of the libretto for the Naples performance on 28 January 1682. His only other known works are a duet for two sopranos and continuo and a cantata. *Almerico in Cipro* includes most of the aria types common in Venice in the 1670s but is more than usually stereotyped, repetitive and lacking in invention.

*

C. Ivanovich: *Minerva al tavolino* (Venice, 1681, 2/1688)

J. B. de La Borde: *Essai sur la musique ancienne et moderne* (Paris, 1780)

THOMAS WALKER

Gautier, (Jean-François-)Eugène (*b* Vaugirard, Paris, 27 Feb 1822; *d* Paris, 1 April 1878). French composer and critic. At the Paris Conservatoire he studied the violin with Habeneck and composition with Halévy, winning the Second Prix de Rome in 1842. He played first violin at the Opéra (1838) and the Société des Concerts du Conservatoire (1846), and became assistant conductor at the Opéra-National (1848). His association with opera continued at the Théâtre Italien, where from about 1849 to 1852 he was *chef du chant*. The Opéra-National, later the Théâtre Lyrique, presented most of Gautier's early operas. His most popular work there, the *opéra comique Flore et Zéphire* (1852), had 126 performances as a curtain-raiser. Though some critics found the harmony complicated and the orchestration too rich, Berlioz praised the score's freshness and skilful orchestration, and the elegant and lively style of the melodies. Gautier's greatest success came with another light one-act opera, *Le mariage extravagant* (1857, revived in 1871), presented 175 times by the Opéra-Comique. Its stylish score includes an overture whose orchestral style comes close to that of Auber. The most remarked-upon piece, given an encore at the première, consists of light, catchy *couplets* for the madman Darmancé, a comic bass. Gautier was appointed professor of harmony at the Conservatoire in 1864, and largely gave up writing for the theatre; in 1872 he became professor of music history. As a music critic he occasionally wrote articles for the *Ménestrel*, *Grand journal* and *Constitutionnel*, and from 1874 he wrote regularly for the *Journal officiel*. At his death his writing was described as 'a bit virulent' as well as 'not always kindly nor very scrupulous in questions of scholarship'; he was, however, generally regarded as a skilful composer of *opéras comiques*, with a fine feel for sparkling orchestration, clean phrasing and inherent good taste that always kept his comic effects from becoming vulgar.

first performed in Paris unless otherwise stated; all printed works published in Paris

Le club des arts (?oc), ov. only, Conservatoire, Nov 1843, *F-Pc**

L'anneau de Mariette (oc, 1, L. Jourdain, after Laurencin [P.-D.-A. Chapelle] and E. Cormon [P.-E. Piestre]), Versailles, 12 June 1845; as L'anneau de la marquise, Paris, Spectacles-Concerts, 20 Dec 1848, *Pc** (inc.)

Léona, ou Le parisien en corse, 1847 (?oc), unorchd, *Pc**

Les barricades de 1848 (opéra patriotique, 1, E.-L.-A. Brisebarre and Saint-Yves [E. Déaddé]), Opéra-National, 6 March 1848, collab. A. Pilati

Le marin de la garde (oc, 1, Saint-Yves), Beaumarchais, 21 June 1849, *Pc**, vs (n.d.)

Murdock le bandit (oc, 1, A. de Leuven and an unknown librettist), Opéra-National, 23 Oct 1851, vs (1852)

Flore et Zéphire (oc, 1, de Leuven and C. Deslys), Lyrique, 2 Oct 1852, *Pc**, vs (1853)

Choisy-le-roi (oc, 1, de Leuven and M. Carré), Lyrique, 14 Oct 1852

Le lutin de la vallée (légende, 2, Carré, J. E. Alboize de Pujol and A. Saint-Léon [C.-V.-A. Michel]), Lyrique, 22 Jan 1853, *Po* (? partly autograph)

Le danseur du roi (opéra-ballet, 2, Carré, Alboize and Saint-Léon), Lyrique, 22 Oct 1853, ? collab. Saint-Léon

Schahabaham II (opéra bouffe, 1, de Leuven and Carré), Lyrique, 31 Oct 1854, *Pc*, vs (?1855)

Le mariage extravagant (oc, 1, Cormon, after M.-A.-M. Désaugiers and J.-J.-C. Mourier), OC (Favart), 20 June 1857, *Pc**, vs (1857)

La bacchante (oc, 2, de Leuven and A. de Beauplan [A. Dumas père]), OC (Favart), 4 Nov 1858, *Pc**

Le docteur Mirobolan (oc, 1, Cormon and H. Trianon, after N. de Hauteroche: *Crispin médecin*), OC (Favart), 28 Aug 1860, *Pc**, vs (1861)

Jocrisse (oc, 1, Cormon and Trianon), OC (Favart), 10 Jan 1862, *Pc**, vs (1862)

Le trésor de Pierrot (oc, 2, Cormon and Trianon), OC (Favart), 5 Nov 1864, *Pc**

La clé d'or (comédie lyrique, 3, O. Feuillet and L. Gallet), National Lyrique, 14 Sept 1877, *Pc**, vs (1877)

Bulfarargue (opéra), ?inc., unperf., *Pc**

La pagode (oc), unperf., *Pc*

Romance in La poularde de Caux (opérette, 1, de Leuven and V. Prilleux), Palais-Royal, 17 May 1861, vs (1861), collab. L. Clapisson and others

*

F. Clément and P. Larousse: *Dictionnaire lyrique* (Paris, 1867–81); ed. A. Pougin as *Dictionnaire des opéras* (2/1897, 3/1905)

Obituaries: *L'art musical*, xvii/14 (1878), 111; *Revue et gazette musicale*, xlv/14 (1878), 111

A. Soubies and C. Malherbe: *Histoire de l'Opéra-Comique* (Paris, 1892)

C. Pierre: *Le Conservatoire national de musique et de déclamation: documents historiques et administratifs* (Paris, 1900)

T. J. Walsh: *Second Empire Opera* (London, 1981)

LESLEY A. WRIGHT

Gautier, Pierre [Gaultier de Marseille] (*b* La Ciotat, ?1642; *d* at sea nr Sète, 1696). French composer and director. He probably studied in Paris. In 1682 he was in Marseilles as organist and teacher of the organ, harpsichord and composition. On 8 July 1684 he received permission from Lully to establish an academy of music there: this was Lully's first authorization of an opera house in the provinces. The first performance, on 28 January 1685, was of *Le triomphe de la paix*, with libretto as well as music by Gautier (only the overture survives, in *F-Pn*); it was given successfully several times a week until the beginning of Lent. Later in 1685 Gautier visited Paris to hire new performers. The 1685–6 season met with equal success, with Lully's *Le triomphe de l'amour*, *Phaëton* and *Armide*. On 5 February 1687 Gautier's *Le jugement du soleil* was performed before an audience of over 1000 on the terrace of the home of the superintendent of the galleys to celebrate Louis XIV's successful recovery from an operation. During the summer and autumn of 1687 the company performed *Phaëton* and *Armide* in Avignon with great success. At Marseilles early in 1688 Gautier produced Lully's *Atys*, which he took in June to Avignon, where he also prepared Lully's *Bellérophon* for two performances at the residence of the Marquess of Blauvac. On 4 September of that year, however, he was imprisoned for debt and forced to sell his company's properties in Avignon and Marseilles. Released on 10 September, he left for Lyons, where one of his dancers, Jean-Pierre Leguay, had organized an opera company; he was now engaged as co-manager and conductor. On 16 March 1689 he resigned the post of co-manager but remained as conductor until the company was dissolved in 1692. In 1693 the privilege of giving operas in Marseilles was sublet to his brother Jacques, a sculptor employed as a set designer in Lyons, who became director-in-chief of the academy of music at Marseilles; performances began in January 1694. The company performed at Aix-en-Provence in spring 1695 and at Toulon during the summer. They performed Lully's *Alceste* at Marseilles in 1696 and in May of that year were at Aix, at Avignon in October, at Arles in November and at Montpellier in December. At the end of December Gautier embarked with his brother, some of the company and all his equipment on a return voyage by sea; the ship was lost in a storm.

In his choice of repertory, mostly *tragédies en musique* by Lully, Gautier showed himself a representative of French classicism. He was concerned too with the quality of performance and staging: a number of singers and dancers from Paris, including some from the Académie Royale, followed him to Marseilles. He also paid reasonable salaries to his artists, to the extent of leaving his other debts unpaid. According to Brossard's *Dictionaire de musique* (1703), he wrote 'dans le style et à l'imitation de Lully'. Yet his surviving works are not those of a mere imitator: his published *airs* and dances (for flute, violin and continuo) are spirited and carefully composed; his use of descending melodic patterns is individual, his imitative writing varied, his bass lines expressive, his rhythms lively, and his use of instrumental colour evocative.

*

L. de La Laurencie: 'Un émule de Lully: Pierre Gautier de Marseille', *SIMG*, xiii (1911–12), 39

J. Cheilan-Camboulin: *Un aspect de la vie musicale à Marseille au XVIIIe siècle: cinquante ans d'opéra* (diss., U. of Aix-en-Provence, 1972)

MARCEL FRÉMIOT

Gavazzeni, Gianandrea (*b* Bergamo, 27 July 1909). Italian conductor, composer and writer. He studied at the Accademia di S Cecilia, Rome and with Pizzetti at the Milan Conservatory. His conducting début was in 1940, after his own opera *Paolo e Virginia* had been well received in 1935, but in 1949 he abruptly gave up composition and refused to allow further performances of his works. From 1948 he was associated with La Scala, Milan, where he was artistic director (1965–8) and continued to conduct into the 1990s. He was a perceptive exponent of the *verismo* school both in performance and in print, and his edition of Mascagni's *Le maschere* (with additions to the prologue) was staged at the Florence Maggio Musicale in 1955 and several times revived elsewhere. His British début was at the 1957 Edinburgh Festival in *Il turco in Italia* with the company from La Piccola Scala, and the same year he conducted *La bohème* at the Chicago Lyric Opera. He conducted the Bol'shoy Opera at Moscow in 1964 and appeared at the Glyndebourne Festival in 1965 (*Anna Bolena*) and at the Metropolitan in 1976 (*Il trovatore*). He has recorded several operas by Rossini, Verdi, Mascagni and Puccini, written music criticism for *Il corriere della sera*, and published studies of Bellini, Donizetti, Mascagni, Pizzetti, Musorgsky and Janáček, as well as guides to the operas of Mozart and Wagner (all in Italian).

LEONARDO PINZAUTI, NOËL GOODWIN

Gaveaux [Gavaux, Gaveau], **Pierre** (*b* Béziers, 9 Oct 1760; *d* Charenton, nr Paris, 5 Feb 1825). French singer and composer. He was a choirboy at Béziers Cathedral and studied composition although intended for the clergy. He accepted a post as first tenor at St Séverin, Bordeaux, continuing musical studies under Franz Beck but abandoned his clerical plans and became a conductor and tenor at the Grand Théâtre de Bordeaux. In 1788 he was active in Montpellier and in 1789 went to Paris to sing in the Théâtre de Monsieur. His light and agreeable voice had a fine timbre and he could sing such major roles as Floresky in Cherubini's *Lodoïska* in 1791 and Romeo in Steibelt's *Roméo et Juliette* in 1793. He was, moreover, an excellent musician and an intelligent actor, and was highly valued as a member of the company because of his competence and dynamism. He remained with the company when it moved to the Théâtre Feydeau, where he began his career as a composer of dramatic works with minor *opéras comiques*; these remained fashionable from his *Le paria, ou La chaumière indienne* (1792) to *Le traité nul* (1797). In 1793 Gaveaux founded with his brother Simon (*b* 1759), a répétiteur and prompter at the

Théâtre Feydeau, a music shop in which he published his own works; during the Revolution he wrote a number of patriotic songs.

Gaveaux produced his finest works, *Sophie et Moncars* (1797) and, particularly, *Léonore, ou L'amour conjugal* (1798), during a period in which the nature of the *opéra comique* was becoming diversified. Dalayrac and Cherubini were writing veritable *drames lyriques* on affecting subjects, and the influence of German music was imposing a new style (similar to Singspiel) on the genre; but the traditional form, with its characteristic mixture of airs and spoken dialogue, was retained. *Léonore*, a *fait historique* with a libretto by Bouilly, later provided Beethoven with the subject of *Fidelio*. It enjoyed considerable success; Gaveaux himself sang the part of Florestan and Mme Scio that of Léonore. *Ovinska, ou Les exilés de Sibérie* (1801) and *La rose blanche et la rose rouge* (1809) suffered from mediocre librettos, but *Le bouffe et le tailleur* (1804) and *Monsieur Deschalumeaux* (1806) were more successful and were revived several times during the 19th century.

When the companies of the Théâtres Favart and Feydeau merged in 1801, Gaveaux remained a member, but took only secondary roles as his voice was losing its grace and it was becoming difficult for him to keep up with such rivals as Elleviou or Martin. In 1804 he was appointed a singer in the imperial chapel. He was affected by mental illness and left the stage in 1812. Apparently cured, he resumed his publishing activities, 1813–16. He wrote one more *opéra comique*, but in 1819 retired to a mental asylum.

all opéras comiques, first performed in Paris, OC (Théâtre Feydeau), and published in Paris near the time of their first performance unless otherwise stated

Les deux Suisses, ou Les deux invalides (1, C. A. Demoustier), 6 March 1792, later as L'amour filial, ou La jambe de bois, 10 Aug 1792
Le paria, ou La chaumière indienne (2, Demoustier), 8 Oct 1792
Les deux ermites (1, B. Planterre), 12 April 1793
La famille indigente (1, Planterre), 4 May 1793
La partie carrée (1, L. Hennequin), 26 June 1793, unpubd
Sophronime, ou La reconnaissance (1, Demoustier), 13 Feb 1795
Delmon et Nadine (2, E.-J.-B. Delrieu), 13 June 1795
La gasconnade (1, Leroi), 1795
Le petit matelot, ou Le mariage impromptu (op, 1, C.-A.-G. Pigault-Lebrun), 7 Jan 1796
Lise et Colin (2, E. Hus), 4 Aug 1796
Tout par hasard (1, Monnet), 22 Oct 1796
Céliane (1, J. M. Souriguière de Saint Marc), 31 Dec 1796
Le mannequin vivant ou Le mari de bois (1, R. C. G. de Pixérécourt), 1796, unperf.
Le traité nul (1, B. J. Marsollier des Vivetières), 23 June 1797
Sophie et Moncars, ou L'intrigue portugaise (3, J.-H. Guy), 30 Sept 1797
Léonore, ou L'amour conjugal (fait historique, 2, J.-M. Bouilly), 19 Feb 1798
Le diable couleur de rose, ou Le bonhomme misère (opéra bouffon, 1, G. Lévrier-Champrion), Arts, 23 Oct 1798
Les noms supposés (2, J.-B. Pujoulx), 11 Dec 1798, rev. as Les deux jockeys, 1799
Le locataire (1, C.-A. Sévrin), 26 July 1800
Le trompeur trompé (1, B. Valville), 2 Aug 1800
Ovinska, ou Les exilés de Sibérie (3, Bidon de Villemontez), 20 Dec 1801
Le retour inattendu (1, Valville), 29 March 1802
Un quart d'heure de silence (1, P. Guillet), 1 June 1804
Le bouffe et le tailleur (1, P. Villiers and A Gouffé), 1 June 1804
Avis aux femmes, ou Le mari colère (1, Pixérécourt), 27 Oct 1804
Le mariage inattendu (1), Paris, Montansier, 1804
Trop tôt (1), Montansier, 1804
Le diable en vacances, ou La suite du diable couleur de rose (opéra-féerie, 1, M.-A. Desaugiers and J.-S.-F. Bosquier-Gavaudan), Montansier, 16 Feb 1805

L'Amour à Cythère (2, ballet-pantomime), Opéra, 29 Oct 1805, *F-Po*
Monsieur Deschalumeaux (opéra bouffe, Auguste), 17 Feb 1806
L'échelle de soie (1, F.-A.-E. de Planard), 22 Aug 1808
La rose blanche et la rose rouge (drame lyrique, 3, Pixérécourt), 20 March 1809
L'enfant prodigue (opéra, 3, Riboutté and Souriguière), 23 Nov 1811
Pygmalion (scène lyrique, J.-J. Rousseau), 1816, ?unperf.
Une nuit au bois, ou Le muet de circonstance (1), 10 Feb 1818

1 air in L.-C.-A. Chardiny: L'histoire universelle, 1790

J.-G. Prod'homme: 'Léonore ou L'amour conjugal de Bouilly et Gaveaux', *SIMG*, vii (1905–6), 636–9
W. Dean: 'French Opera', *NOHM*, viii (1982), 26–117

PAULETTE LETAILLEUR

Gavilanes, Los ('The Sparrowhawks'). Zarzuela in three acts by JACINTO GUERRERO to a libretto by JOSÉ RAMOS MARTÍN; Madrid, Teatro de la Zarzuela, 7 December 1923.

Middle-aged Juan (baritone) returns to his home village in Provence after many years making his fortune in Peru. He meets his old love, Adriana (soprano), who married after his departure but is now widowed. He falls in love with her again, but even more with her daughter Rosaura (soprano). This loses him the good-will of the villagers, who liken him to the sparrowhawks that hover above, after their prey. Finally Juan regains the respect of his old friends by leaving Rosaura, so that she is free to marry her young sweetheart Gustavo (tenor).

Los gavilanes remains one of the most frequently performed zarzuelas. Highlights of its richly tuneful score include Juan's greeting to his native village ('¡Mi aldea!') and Gustavo's contemplation of the red rose with which he expresses his love for Rosaura ('Flor roja').

ANDREW LAMB

Gawain. Opera in two acts by HARRISON BIRTWISTLE to a libretto by David Harsent after the anonymous Middle English poem *Sir Gawain and the Green Knight*; London, Covent Garden, 30 May 1991.

King Arthur (tenor) and his court are celebrating the Christmas feast; Morgan le Fay (soprano) and Lady de Hautdesert (mezzo-soprano) are plotting against the court. A Fool (baritone) presents a sequence of riddles, each of which is followed by a knocking at the door. The Green Knight (bass) enters and issues a challenge: he will stand as someone strikes him with an axe, but whoever does so must in a year and a day travel to the Green Chapel to withstand a similar blow. Gawain (baritone), Arthur's nephew, takes up the challenge and decapitates him; the Green Knight departs, carrying his head. In a masque, 'The Turning of the Seasons', under-pinned by a sequence of Marian motets sung by Bishop Baldwin (countertenor) and a chorus, Gawain is pre-pared for his journey.

Act 2 begins with an orchestral depiction of Gawain's journey. He finds shelter in the castle of Bertilak de Hautdesert. Bertilak (bass) offers Gawain another challenge: he will hunt for three mornings and will exchange whatever he captures for what Gawain secures in the castle. This forms a large-scale ritual sequence, articulated by a lullaby (sung by Morgan), the depiction of Bertilak's hunts, and the Lady's attempts to seduce Gawain. Contrary to his bargain, Gawain retains the sash given him by the Lady which may ward off his death. He fulfils his rendezvous with the Green Knight and receives three blows, but he is only grazed – his life has been spared because he has been dishonest for the noblest of motives, the fear of death. The Green Knight is revealed as Bertilak. Gawain returns to Arthur's court but refuses to be regarded as a hero or to tell of his adventures; he is shunned by all except Guinevere (soprano). In a final monologue he reflects on his new self-knowledge and understanding of human frailty, which set him apart from the self-regarding court. Morgan's purpose has been served.

In contrast with Birtwistle's previous large-scale theatre pieces, *Punch and Judy* and *The Mask of Orpheus*, *Gawain* is cast essentially as a linear narrative, even though both its acts are articulated by massive formal schemes in which repetition plays a significant part. Both 'The Turning of the Seasons' in the first act and the hunting episodes in the second use the verse-and-refrain structures that characterize much of Birtwistle's dramatic and instrumental music, and many smaller-scale examples of such patterning are incorporated elsewhere in the score. In vocal terms, however, the opera reveals a much greater expressive freedom and detailed characterization than its predecessors: the ornate, sensuous lines for all three female roles (visually stylized in the 'courtly dances' for Morgan and the Lady in Act 1), the 'heroic' high baritone writing for Gawain and the declamatory power of the Green Knight's utterances. Similarly the orchestral writing includes a collection of melodies, motifs and pitch sets, which symbolize characters and thematic strands; its gestural scale and vividness are likewise unprecedented in Birtwistle's music, though the use of instrumental register and orchestral 'strata' may be traced back to his works of the 1980s and to the orchestral *Earth Dances* (1986) in particular.   ANDREW CLEMENTS

Gay, John (*b* Barnstaple, *c*30 June 1685, bap. 16 Sept 1685; *d* London, 4 Dec 1732). English playwright and poet. As a member of the Scriblerus Club he was a close friend, collaborator and long-time correspondent of Pope and Swift. His importance to the history of opera lies in his invention of the ballad opera, a form that took the London theatre by storm and permanently affected its artistic development. *The Beggar's Opera* had its première at Lincoln's Inn Fields on 29 January 1728 and was performed 62 times during the season – a figure without precedent in the history of the London theatre. Evidence of its success is the appearance of a pirate production at the Little Haymarket as early as June 1728, something that had never happened before in London. The extraordinary success of Gay's opera proved the existence of a large, almost untapped theatre public in London and triggered a boom in new theatres and experimental drama in the following decade.

The Beggar's Opera has often been taken as a harsh attack on both Italian opera and Sir Robert Walpole, but neither seems to be true. Gay had provided the libretto for Handel's *Acis and Galatea* (1718) and, while he mocks the Faustina-Cuzzoni rivalry in Polly and Lucy, he does so without real animus. The Royal Academy of Music was in financial trouble of its own making, and there is no evidence that the success of *The Beggar's Opera* played any significant part in its collapse. The satire on Walpole in Macheath and Peachum is more clever than devastating. Gay's sequel, *Polly*, is by far the more damaging attack on Walpole. It was suppressed before the planned performances in December 1728. In *Polly* he turned Macheath into a West Indian pirate, and the work concludes with his

richly deserved execution. *Polly* is rather lifeless, and Gay probably benefited from its suppression. He rushed a huge edition into print (10 500 copies) and reaped a handsome profit. It was eventually performed in 1779. Modern critics have been inclined to see the suppression of *Polly* as vengeance for *The Beggar's Opera*. Gay responded wittily in *The Rehearsal at Goatham* (unperformed), a farce about an innocent puppet show misinterpreted as personal satire by an audience of country bumpkins.

Gay's last venture into ballad opera, *Achilles* (Covent Garden, 10 February 1733), was a posthumous success but has found few subsequent admirers. Achilles in petticoats has possibilities, but the piece is short on action and only intermittently funny. Gay must be viewed as a clever, minor writer with one stupendous and virtually inexplicable success to his credit. How he got the idea for *The Beggar's Opera* no-one has ever been able satisfactorily to explain: it is one of the most genuinely original works in the history of the theatre, and it is still revived regularly with great success.

See also BALLAD OPERA and BEGGAR'S OPERA, THE.

W. E. Schultz: *Gay's 'Beggar's Opera': its Content, History and Influence* (New Haven, CT, 1923)
W. H. Irving: *John Gay, Favorite of the Wits* (Durham, NC, 1940)
B. H. Bronson: *'The Beggar's Opera': Studies in the Comic* (Berkeley, 1941), 197–231
J. R. Sutherland: '"Polly" among the Pirates', *Modern Language Review*, xxxvii (1942), 291–303
S. M. Armens: *John Gay, Social Critic* (New York, 1954)
J. Preston: 'The Ironic Mode: a Comparison of *Jonathan Wild* and *The Beggar's Opera*', *Essays in Criticism*, xvi (1966), 268–80
I. Kramnick: *Bolingbroke and his Circle* (Cambridge, MA, 1968)
E. V. Roberts, ed.: *John Gay: 'The Beggar's Opera'* (Lincoln, NE, 1969)
R. Fiske: *English Theatre Music in the Eighteenth Century* (London, 1973, 2/1986)
W. A. McIntosh: 'Handel, Walpole, and Gay: the Aims of *The Beggar's Opera*', *Eighteenth-Century Studies*, vii (1974), 415–33
A. Sherbo: 'John Gay: Lightweight or Heavyweight?', *Scriblerian*, viii (1975), 4–8
B. A. Goldgar: *Walpole and the Wits* (Lincoln, NE, 1976)
H. Erskine-Hill: 'The Significance of Gay's Drama', *English Drama: Forms and Development*, ed. M. Axton and R. Williams (Cambridge, 1977), 142–63
C. Kephart: 'An Unnoticed Forerunner of "The Beggar's Opera"', *ML*, lxi (1980), 266–71
P. E. Lewis: 'The Uncertainty Principle in *The Beggar's Opera*', *Durham University Journal*, lxxii (1980), 143–6
L. Lindgren: '*Camilla* and *The Beggar's Opera*', *Philological Quarterly*, lix (1980), 44–61
J. Fuller, ed.: *John Gay: Dramatic Works* (Oxford, 1983)
R. D. Hume: '"The World is all Alike": Satire in *The Beggar's Opera*', *The Rakish Stage: Studies in English Drama, 1660–1800* (Carbondale, IL, 1983), 245–69
——: 'The London Theatre from *The Beggar's Opera* to the Licensing Act', ibid, 270–311
P. Lewis: '"An Irregular Dog": Gay's Alternative Theatre', *Yearbook of English Studies*, xviii (1988), 231–46

ROBERT D. HUME

Gay, Maria (*b* Barcelona, 13 June 1879; *d* New York, 29 July 1943). Spanish mezzo-soprano. Self-taught, she sang in concerts at Brussels in 1902 and soon afterwards at the Théâtre de la Monnaie as Carmen. After study in Paris with Ada Adini she sang at Covent Garden (1906), La Scala (1906–7) and Buenos Aires (1907), always as Carmen. She then sang in St Petersburg, at the Metropolitan in 1908–9, in Madrid and at Chicago, where she appeared virtually without interruption from 1910 until 1927. She was a mainstay of Henry Russell's Boston Opera Company and its short-lived successor

(1909–14, 1915–17), singing such roles as Delilah, Amneris, Azucena and Santuzza. Her merits as a singer were debatable (though her middle and lower registers were rich and resonant), and she owed her fame above all to her realistic Carmen, a portrait inspired by the atmosphere of the Seville gypsy quarter. At first the wife of the composer Juan Gay, she married as her second husband, in 1913, the tenor Giovanni Zenatello.

RODOLFO CELLETTI

Gayarre, Julián (Sebastián) (*b* Valle de Roncal, Pamplona, 9 Jan 1844; *d* Madrid, 2 Jan 1890). Spanish tenor. After studying in Madrid and Milan, he made his début in 1867 as Danieli (*Les vêpres siciliennes*) at Varese. He sang in Parma, Vienna, St Petersburg, Milan, where he created Enzo in *La Gioconda* (1876), and Rome, where he sang Henri in Donizetti's posthumous *Le duc d'Albe* (1882). He made his Covent Garden début in 1877 as Fernand (*La favorite*) and over the next decade sang Don Ottavio, Elvino, Arturo, Edgardo, Gennaro (*Lucrezia Borgia*), Ernani, the Duke, Riccardo (*Un ballo in maschera*), Faust, Raoul, John of Leyden (*Le prophète*), Vasco da Gama, Alim (*Le roi de Lahore*), and Sobinin in the first performance in Britain of *A Life for the Tsar* (1887). He also sang Max, Lohengrin and Tannhäuser, roles much heavier than his usual repertory. In 1889 he collapsed while singing Nadir (*Les pêcheurs des perles*) in Madrid and died a month later. His voice, beautiful in timbre and even in quality throughout its range, was used with great skill and admirable taste.

ELIZABETH FORBES

Gaye [first name unknown] (*fl* 1676–81). French baritone. He created and revived principal *basse-taille* roles in Lully's early *tragédies*: Aegeus (*Thésée*, 1675, revived 1677), Celaenus (*Atys*, 1676), Hierax (*Isis*, 1677) and Jupiter (*Le triomphe de l'amour*, 1681). Durey de Noinville attributes the creation of the title role in *Cadmus et Hermione* (1673) and that of Alcides in *Alceste* (1674) to Gaye, although Parfaict names Beaumavielle in both instances: the casting may have been different for performances at court and in Paris. In *Proserpine* (1680) the role of Pluto was apparently sung at St Germain by Gaye (for illustration *see* COSTUME, fig. 4*b*) and in Paris by Beaumavielle.

*

F. Parfaict and C. Parfaict: *Dictionnaire des théâtres de Paris* (Paris, 1756)
J.-B. Durey de Noinville: *Histoire du théâtre de l'Académie royale de musique en France* (Paris, 1757)
PHILIP WELLER

Gayer [Ashkenasi], **Catherine** (*b* Los Angeles, 11 Feb 1937). American soprano. She studied in Los Angeles and Berlin, where in 1961 she joined the Deutsche Oper, remaining there for 20 years. She sang in the première of Nono's *Intolleranza 60* (1961, Venice), made her Covent Garden début in 1962 as the Queen of Night and sang in the stage première of Milhaud's *Oresteia* (1963, Berlin). She created Nausicaa in Dallapiccola's *Ulisse* (1968, Berlin), which she also sang at La Scala (1970); the title role of Reimann's *Melusine* (1971, Schwetzingen); and Christine in Orr's *Hermiston* (1975) for Scottish Opera, with whom she made her début as Susanna (1968) and later sang the Queen of Shemakha and Hilda Mack (Henze's *Elegy for Young Lovers*). Her repertory included Cherubino, Despina, Rosina, Oscar, Gilda, Mélisande, Aminta (*Die schweigsame Frau*), Zerbinetta, Lulu and Marie in *Die Soldaten*, which she sang in Düsseldorf, Munich, Amsterdam, Edinburgh

and Florence. Her brilliant coloratura technique compensated for any lack of tonal sweetness. She excelled in contemporary music; she created The Woman in Tal's *Versuchung* at Munich, sang Rachel in the German première of Henze's *We Come to the River* (1976) and created Lady Astor in Siebert's *Untergang der Titanic* (1979) in Berlin.
ALAN BLYTH

Gaztambide (y Garbayo), Joaquín (Romualdo) (*b* Tudela, Navarre, 7 Feb 1822; *d* Madrid, 18 March 1870). Spanish composer and conductor. Orphaned at an early age, he became a choirboy at Tudela Cathedral in 1830 and studied there with Rubla. In 1834 he was a pupil of Guelbenzu at Pamplona and in 1842 entered the Madrid Conservatory to study the piano with Pedro Albéniz and composition with Ramón Carnicer. In 1845 the Italian company at the Teatro de la S Cruz in Madrid made him the director of its chorus. In 1846 he went to Paris as conductor of a ballet company, but in 1848 returned to Madrid as director of the Teatro Español, where his first zarzuela, *La mensajera*, had its première in December 1849. This began a series of successes for Gaztambide as a conductor of opera and zarzuela companies in Madrid. For several seasons he conducted operas at the Teatro Real, and he directed the first performance in Spanish of Meyerbeer's *Le prophète*.

In 1862 he was appointed director of the concert society at the Madrid Conservatory, which was later, under Francisco Barbieri, to become the Madrid Concert Society. In 1868 Barbieri appointed him its director, and in that capacity he brought to the Spanish public the most modern works of the time. He was the first to conduct in Spain a work by Wagner, the overture to *Tannhäuser*, which met with great enthusiasm. In 1869 he formed a large zarzuela company and set off on a tour of South America, beginning in Havana. His own work *Catalina* was the first to be presented, but during the performance a popular uprising took place, which caused the suspension of all theatrical spectacles. Badly shaken economically, the company went on to Mexico, where it achieved success. However, Gaztambide fell ill there; in Veracruz he gave his last concert and in January 1870 he embarked for Spain, reaching Cádiz seriously ill. In Madrid he underwent a liver operation, and died a few days later.

Gaztambide composed 44 zarzuelas, of which *Catalina* (1854) was the best and most successful. Also important were *Los magyares* (1857), *El juramento* (1858) and *La conquista de Madrid* (1863). He composed several works in collaboration with Barbieri and others. Javier Gaztambide was his cousin.

all zarzuelas, first performed in Madrid

La mensajera (2, L. Olona), Español, 24 Dec 1849; A última hora (1, J. Olona), Basilios, 29 May 1850; Las señas del archiduque (2, C. Suarez Bravo), Basilios, 8 June 1850; Escenas en Chamberí (1, J. Olona), Variedades, 19 Nov 1850, collab. R. J. M. Hernando, C. D. Oudrid and F. A. Barbieri; La picaresca (2, E. Doncel y Asquerina), Circo, 29 March 1851, collab. Barbieri; Al amánecer (1, M. Pina), Circo, 8 May 1851; Tribulaciones (2, T. R. Rubí), Circo, 14 Sept 1851
Por seguir a una mujer (4, L. Olona), Circo, 24 Dec 1851, collab. Hernando, Barbieri, Oudrid and J. Inzenga; El sueño de una noche de verano (3, P. Escosura), Circo, 21 Feb 1852; El estreno de un artista (1, D. V. de la Vega), Circo, 5 June 1852, vs (Madrid, ?1857); El secreto de la reina (3, L. Olona), Circo, 13 Oct 1852, collab. Hernando and Inzenga, vs (Madrid, 1852); El valle de Andorra (3, L. Olona, after J. H. Vernoy de Saint-Georges), Circo, 5 Nov 1852, vs (Madrid, ?1855); La cotorra (1, L. Olona), Circo, 26 April 1853

Don Simplicio Bobadilla (3, M. Tamayoher-Manos, Circo, 7 May 1853, collab. Hernando, Barbieri and Inzenga; La cisterna encantada (3, Vega), Circo, 17 Nov 1853; El hijo de familia (3, L. Olona), Circo, 24 Dec 1853, collab. Oudrid; Un día de reinado (3, G. Gutierrez and L. Olona), Circo, 11 Feb 1854, collab. Oudrid, Barbieri and Inzenga; Catalina (3, L. Olona, after E. Scribe: *L'étoile du nord*), Circo, 23 Oct 1854, vs (Madrid, ?1860); Estebanillo (3, Vega), Circo, 5 Oct 1855, collab. Oudrid; Los comuneros (3, A. Lopez de Ayala), Circo, 14 Nov 1855

El sargento Federico (4, L. Olona), Circo, 22 Dec 1855, collab. Barbieri; El amor y el almuerzo (1, L. Olona), Circo, 23 March 1856, vs (Madrid, ?1865); Entre dos aguas (3, A. Hurtado), Circo, 4 April 1856, collab. Barbieri; El lancero (1, D. F. Camprodón), Zarzuela, 31 Jan 1857, vs (Madrid, ?1860); Los magyares (4, L. Olona), Zarzuela, 12 April 1857, vs (Madrid, ?1870); Amar sin conocer (3, L. Olona), Zarzuela, 24 April 1858, collab. Barbieri; Casado y soltero (1, L. Olona), Zarzuela, 8 June 1858, vs (Madrid, ?1870)

Un pleito (1, Camprodón), Zarzuela, 22 June 1858, vs (Madrid, ?1865); El juramento (3, L. Olona), Zarzuela, 20 Dec 1858, vs (Madrid, ?1870); La hija del pueblo (2, E. Alvarez), 22 Dec 1859; El diablo las carga (3, Camprodón), Zarzuela, 21 Jan 1860; Una vieja (1, Camprodón), Zarzuela, 11 Dec 1860, vs (Madrid, ?1865); Anarquía conyugal (1, J. Picón), Zarzuela, 17 April 1861; Una niña (1, Camprodón), Zarzuela, 24 April 1861; La edad en la boca (1, N. Serra), Zarzuela, 11 May 1861; Una historia en un mesón (1, Serra), Zarzuela, 5 June 1861

Del palacio a la taberna (3, Camprodón), Zarzuela, 20 Dec 1861; En las astas del toro (1, C. Frontaura), Zarzuela, 30 Aug 1862, vs (Madrid, ?1860); Las hijas de Eva (3, L. M. de Larra), Zarzuela, 8 Oct 1862; Matilde y Malek-Adel (3, Frontaura), Zarzuela, 7 March 1863, collab. Oudrid; La conquista de Madrid (3, L. Olona), Zarzuela, 23 Dec 1863; Antes del baile, en el baile y después del baile (1, Palacio, Alvarez), Zarzuela, 3 June 1864; Los caballeros de la tortuga (3, E. Blasco), Zarzuela, 23 Dec 1867; La varita de virtudes (magia, 3, Larra), Zarzuela, 7 March 1868

*

A. Peña y Goñi: *La ópera española y la música dramática en España en el siglo XIX* (Madrid, 1881; abridged E. Rincón as *España desde la ópera a la zarzuela* (1967), 377, 533ff

'Gaztambide y Garbayo (Joaquín)', *Enciclopedia universal ilustrada europeo-americana*, xxv, 1133–4 (Barcelona, 1907–30)

E. Cotarelo y Mori: *Historia de la zarzuela, o sea el drama lírico* (Madrid, 1934)

A. Fernández-Cid: *Cien años de teatro musical en España (1875–1975)* (Madrid, 1975)

R. Alier and others: *El libro de la zarzuela* (Barcelona, 1982, 2/1986 as *Diccionario de la zarzuela*)
                                        TOMÁS MARCO/R

Gazza ladra, La ('The Thieving Magpie'). *Melodramma* in two acts by GIOACHINO ROSSINI to a libretto by Giovanni Gherardini after *La pie voleuse* (1815) by J. M. T. Badouin d'Aubigny and Louis-Charles Caigniez; Milan, Teatro alla Scala, 31 May 1817.

Musically, *La gazza ladra* is the finest of Rossini's several essays in the *semiseria* that stretch from *L'equivoco stravagante* (1811) to *Matilde di Shabran* (1821). In this instance, the work can be seen to derive in part from the French drama *larmoyant*, in part from the so-called 'rescue' opera. The opera deals with a wide range of social groupings, and conforms to the tradition of the happy ending, the heroine saved from execution at the eleventh hour, even though in the original French play the heroine dies on the gallows.

The story centres on the serving girl, Ninetta (soprano), who works in the house of the wealthy tenant farmer Fabrizio Vingradito (bass) and his wife Lucia (mezzo-soprano). Their son Giannetto (tenor) is about to return from the wars and it is Fabrizio's intention that he should be allowed to marry Ninetta. They have been in love for some time, but it is a match of which Lucia disapproves. She thinks Ninetta unreliable and casual with family possessions. Ninetta sings of her love for Giannetto in her cavatina 'Di piacer mi balza il cor', and

Giannetto is duly welcomed and feasted, with one of Fabrizio's young workers, the gamesome Pippo (contralto) proposing the toast. A pedlar, Isacco (tenor), visits the farm. (His whiningly nasal music makes him an obvious forebear of Verdi's Trabuco in *La forza del destino*.) A vagrant also appears whom Ninetta instantly recognizes as her father, the soldier Fernando Villabella (bass-baritone). He has quarrelled with his commanding officer and has deserted to avoid summary execution. Ninetta's attempt to hide him is compromised by the arrival of an unwanted admirer, the mayor of the village (*podestà*), Gottardo. Outwardly this is a *buffo* role (bass-baritone) but in reality he is a vindictive philanderer well used to manipulating the course of justice: a kind of rural Scarpia. Ninetta urges her father to leave, but to raise the necessary money for him to survive in hiding he asks her to sell a piece of cutlery (it is his own and bears the initials F. V.) and deposit the money in an old chestnut tree nearby. Before either the Mayor or Fernando can be got off the premises, the town clerk, Giorgio (bass), brings news of a deserter on the run. The Mayor has mislaid his glasses, and asks Ninetta to read the description, which she does, altering the details to make it as unlike her father as possible. While the Mayor is weighing the evidence and contemplating the old tramp, a magpie alights in the room and, unobserved, steals a spoon from the table. In due course the spoon is missed by Lucia, and Isacco's testimony that he bought a spoon from Ninetta initialled F. V. is one of several pieces of circumstantial evidence that lead to her arrest for theft. Giannetto is devastated, but the turn of events delights the Mayor, whose advances Ninetta has continued to repulse.

The first scene of Act 2 takes place in the courtyard of the prison where Ninetta is awaiting trial. Thanks to the leniency of the warder Antonio (tenor), she is visited by Giannetto, to whom she protests her innocence. The Mayor appears but is again repulsed. Ninetta, desperate to help her father, decides to enlist the help of Pippo: she takes the gold cross she wears and asks Pippo to sell it and put the money in the old chestnut tree. The deeply affecting recitative and duet for Ninetta and Pippo, 'Deh pensa che domani ... E ben, per mia memoria', is one of the opera's highlights. Meanwhile, Ninetta's father, desperate to know where she is, presents himself at the farmhouse; when he learns of her arrest he resolves to attend the trial. Lucia is also having doubts about Ninetta's guilt (her aria 'A questo seno', which can come either side of the Trial Scene, was usually cut in Rossini's time). In the magnificent Trial Scene Ninetta is found guilty. Fernando intervenes, but to no avail, and he is recognized by the Mayor and arrested as a deserter. The final scene takes place in the village square. The action is resolved partly by an act of clemency granted Fernando by the King, partly by the discovery of the magpie's activities: it has been stealing cutlery and coins and storing them in its nest in the church tower. The discovery is made, though, only after we have witnessed Ninetta's grim march to the scaffold, eerily scored by Rossini in a manner that anticipates Berlioz's orchestrations. However, Ninetta is reprieved, the villagers celebrate, and only the Mayor is left angry and discomfited.

The score of the opera underwent extensive alterations and cutting in subsequent years. Rossini himself pointed the way with revised performing editions, supervised by himself, in Pesaro in 1818 and in Naples, at the Teatro del Fondo in 1819 and the S Carlo in

1820. Of these the 1818 Pesaro revival is perhaps the most significant, with the addition of a cavatina for Fernando, 'Dunque invano i perigli e la morte'. In Paris in 1866 Rossini wrote embellishments and variations for Ninetta's cavatina for use by Giuseppina Vitali and it would appear that in the following year he wrote embellishments and cadenzas for Adelina Patti. In 1941 the opera was revived in Pesaro in an edition by the composer Riccardo Zandonai, which makes substantial changes to the narrative and to the music, including the orchestration; though used for a distinguished revival at the 1959 Wexford Festival, it is a largely spurious version. A definitive critical edition, edited by Alberto Zedda, was published by the Fondazione Rossini, Pesaro, in 1979.   RICHARD OSBORNE

Gazzaniga, Giuseppe (*b* Verona, 5 Oct 1743; *d* Crema, 1 Feb 1818). Italian composer. His father intended him for the priesthood, but he studied music secretly and after his father's death devoted himself to it entirely. In 1760 he went to Venice to study with Porpora, who encouraged Gazzaniga to accompany him to Naples. There Porpora obtained a free place for his young pupil at the Conservatorio di Sant'Onofrio a Capuana for six years. During this time Gazzaniga studied composition and counterpoint with his patron. In 1767 he became a composition pupil of Piccinni, with whom he studied for three years; a year later he made his début with his comic intermezzo *Il barone di Trocchia* in Naples. In 1770 he returned to Venice; there he made friends with Sacchini, whose generous advice was of great benefit to him in his compositions. In the 1770s Gazzaniga wrote operas for various Italian theatres. In 1780 he was again in Naples, where he directed the revival of Jommelli's *Armida abbandonata* at the Teatro S Carlo and in the following year revived his own *Antigono*. His *Il finto cieco*, on a libretto by Da Ponte, was performed at the Burgtheater, Vienna, in 1786 and brought Gazzaniga commissions from Italy, Germany and England; but Da Ponte in his memoirs had little to say in his favour.

Gazzaniga achieved widespread acclaim with his one-act *Don Giovanni, o sia Il convitato di pietra* to a libretto by Bertati (1787, Venice), later also known as *Don Giovanni Tenorio*. The work was performed not only in Italy, but also in Paris (1792), Lisbon (1792) and London (1794). Kunze has recorded no fewer than 32 editions of the libretto up to 1821. Though Bertati's text was decisive in Da Ponte's own *Don Giovanni* for Mozart, it is unclear whether Mozart had studied Gazzaniga's score; his letters say nothing of Gazzaniga's opera, and no Viennese performance of the work is known. Four years after the Venice première Gazzaniga accepted an appointment as *maestro di cappella* at Crema Cathedral, and subsequently composed few dramatic works. Stefano Pavesi was his pupil from 1802, but otherwise almost nothing is known of his final years.

Gazzaniga belongs to the last generation of Italian *buffa* composers whose most brilliant representatives, Paisiello and Cimarosa, provide a link with the comic opera of Rossini. His music typifies the late 18th-century *opera buffa* style. It is less rich in harmony and texture than Paisiello's, but nevertheless closer to the combination of conciseness and judiciously applied sentiment of Paisiello than to the extravagant comic prolixity of Cimarosa. Gazzaniga's style tends to be concise and relatively thin in texture, emphasizing the forward motion of the music as well as the declamation of the text. He seems to have been less tied to symmetrical groups of two and four bars than some of his contemporaries, and interesting rhythmic or melodic details often make up for rather basic harmonies and lean textures. For example, in the final *allegro* section of Maturina's aria 'Se pur degna' in *Don Giovanni*, the repetitions of 'caro, caro' in a variety of tempos give the piece unusual character. His operas contain moments of striking beauty, such as the quartet following the *introduzione* in *L'isola di Alcina*, as well as many numbers that are simply charming. It is notable that in *Don Giovanni* he used the same, rare key (E♭ minor) when the Commendatore dies as when he threatens Don Giovanni. One of the more striking aspects of Gazzaniga's music for his *opere buffe* is its expressive clarity; there is never any doubt about the emotional content or the type of character singing. Though sometimes predictable he often avoided dullness with witty details that enhance the dramatic situation. Gazzaniga was not well educated, but a letter to Simon Mayr shows that he took an interest in older masters as well as in contemporary music, and that he possessed a substantial library.

See also ARGONAUTI IN COLCO, GLI; DON GIOVANNI (i); ISOLA DI ALCINA, L'; and LOCANDA, LA.

Il barone di Trocchia (int, 2, F. Cerlone), Naples, Nuovo, carn. 1768
Calandrano (dg, 3, G. Bertati), Venice, S Samuele, 1771, *A-Wn, D-Dlb, F-Pn*; rev. G. Rust, as L'avaro deluso, Bologna, Formagliari, 1773
La locanda (dg, 3, Bertati), Venice, S Moisè, 1771, *D-Dlb, Rtt, F-Pn, H-Bn, I-MOe, Pi(l), Tf, US-Bp, Wc*
Ezio (3, P. Metastasio), Venice, S Benedetto, Feb 1772, *P-La*
La tomba di Merlino (dg, 3, Bertati), Venice, S Moisè, aut. 1772
L'isola di Alcina (dg, 3, Bertati, after L. Ariosto), Venice, S Moisè, 1772, *A-Wn, D-Dlb, DS, F-Pn, H-Bn, I-Fc, Tf*
Zon Zon [L'inimico delle donne] (dg, 3, Bertati), Milan, Regio Ducal, aut. 1773, *F-Pn, I-Rmassimo*
Armida (os, 3, after T. Tasso: *Gerusalemme liberata*), Rome, Argentina, 1773, arias *Mc, Nc, Rc*
Il matrimonio per inganno (ob), Pavia, 1773
Il ciarlatano in fiera (dg, 3, P. Chiari), Venice, S Moisè, 1774
Perseo ed Andromeda (os, 3, V. A. Cigna-Santi), Florence, Pergola, 15 Sept 1775; ? as Andromeda, Prague, 1781 (private perf.), Brunswick, 1783
L'isola di Calipso (os, G. Pindemonte), Verona, Filarmonica, 1775
Il re di Mamalucchi (dg), Prague, 1775; as Il Mamalucco, Pesaro, Sole, 1776
Gli errori di Telemaco (os, C. L. Rossi), Pisa, Prini, 1776
Il regno dei pazzi, Ferrara, 27 Dec 1777 (private perf. at Count Pinamonte Boncossa's); as Il re dei pazzi (int), Venice, S Giovanni Grisostomo, aut. 1778
La bizzaria degli umori (dg, 2), Bologna, Zagnoni, 1777, *B-Bc, F-Pn, I-Bc*
Il marchese di Verde Antico (int, 2), Rome, Capranica, Jan 1778; collab. F. Piticchio [early version of La vendemmia]
La vendemmia (opera giocosa, 2, Bertati), Florence, Pergola, 12 May 1778, *A-Wn, D-Dlb, Wa, F-Pn, H-Bn, I-Fc*
La finta folletto (int, 2), Rome, Capranica, 29 Dec 1778
Il disertore [Il disertor francese] (dg, 2, F. Casorri, after L. S. Mercier), Florence, Pergola, 5 April 1779, *D-Wa, I-Bc*
Antigono (os, 3, Metastasio), Rome, Argentina, 1779, *Nc*
Il ritorno di Ulisse a Penelope (melodramma, 2, G. A. Moniglia), Rome, Argentina, 1779
La viaggiatrice (dg, 2, F. S. Zini), Naples, Fondo, 1780
Antigono (os, G. Roccaforte), Naples, S Carlo, 1781, *Nc* (inc.)
La stravagante (commedia, 2, Zini), Naples, Fondo, 1781
Amor per oro (dg, 3, C. Arcomeno), Venice, S Samuele, 1782, *US-Wc*
La creduta infedele (commedia, 3, Cerlone), Naples, Fiorentini, 1783
L'intrigo delle mogli (commedia, 2, G. Palomba), Naples, Fondo, 1783
La dama contadina (int, 2), Rome, Capranica, carn. 1784
Il serraglio di Osmano (dg, 2, Bertati), Venice, S Moisè, 27 Dec 1784, *D-DO, Wa, F-Pc, I-Fc*; as La fedeltà di Rosana, Perugia, Pavone, carn. 1786; as Il palazzo di Osmano, Lisbon, 1795

Tullo Ostilio (os, 3, F. Ballani), Rome, Argentina, 1784, *Tf*

La moglie [donna] capricciosa (dg, 2, F. Livigni), Venice, S. Moisè, aut. 1785, *A-Wn, D-Dlb, Wa, F-Pn, H-Bn, I-Fc, Gl*; lib. rev. Giotti (int), Florence, 1791

Il finto cieco (dramma buffo, 2, L. Da Ponte, after M.-A. Legrand: *L'aveugle clairvoyant*), Vienna, Burg, 20 Feb 1786, *F-Pn, I-Fc, US-Bp*

Circe (os, 3, D. Perelli), Venice, S Benedetto, 20 May 1786, *?D-Bds, P-La*

La contessa di Novaluna (dg, 2, Bertati), Venice, S. Moisè, aut. 1786

Le donne fanatiche (dg, 2, Bertati), Venice, S Moisè, aut. 1786

Don Giovanni [Tenorio], o sia Il convitato di pietra (dg, 1, Bertati), Venice, S Moisè, 5 Feb 1787 as pt 2 of G. Valentini and others: Il capriccio drammatico; *A-Wgm, F-Pn, GB-Lbl, I-Bc, Mc, OS, US-Wc*; ed. S. Kunze (Kassel and Basle, 1974)

La Didone (os), Vicenza, Nuovo, sum. 1787

La cameriera di spirito (dg, 2, G. Fiorio), Venice, S Moisè, aut. 1787

L'amore costante [La costanza in amor rende felice] (commedia, 4, Bertati), Venice, S Moisè, 1787, *F-Pn*

Gli Argonauti in Colco (os, 3, S. A. Sografi), Venice, S Samuele, carn. 1790, *D-Mbs, GB-Lbl, US-Wc*

Idomeneo (os, 3, G. Sertor), Padua, Nuovo, 12 June 1790, *D-Mh, US-Wc*

La disfatta dei Mori (os, 3, G. Boggio), Turin, Regio, 1791, *P-La*

La dama soldato (dg, 2, Mazzolà), Venice, S Moisè, 1792

La pastorella nobile (dg), Fortezza di Palma, aut. 1793

La donna astuta (dg, 2), Venice, S Moisè, 1793 [?=rev. version]

Il divorzio senza matrimonio, ossia La donna che non parla (dg, 2, Sertor), Modena, Rangoni, 5 Feb 1794

Fedeltà e amore alla pruova (dramma eroicomico, 1, G. Foppa), Venice, S Moisè, 1798, *F-Pn*

Il marito migliore (dg, 2, T. Menucci di Goro [A. Anelli]), Milan, Scala, 3 Sept 1801; as I due gemelli, Bologna, Comunale, 1807

Martino Carbonaro, o sia Gli sposi fuggitivi (farsa, 1, Foppa), Venice, S Moisè, 1801

Arias in L'ape musicale (commedia, Da Ponte), Vienna, 27 Feb 1789

Doubtful: La Pallacorda (int), Rome, 1770; Le orfane svizzere (dg, Chiari), Novara, 1774; La fedeltà d'amore, 1776; Il marchese carbonaro (ob), Vienna, 1777; Le gelosie villane (ob, T. Grandi), Novara, 1778; Achille in Sciro (os, Metastasio), Palermo, 1780; L'amante per bisogno (dg, C. G. Lanfranchi Rossi), Venice, 1781; L'Orvietano (ob), Rome, 1781; Demofoonte (os, Metastasio), Palermo, 1782; La vivandiera (ob), Berlin, 1786; L'italiana in Londra (ob, G. Petrosellini), Piacenza, 1789; Giasone e Medea (os, G. Palazzi), Venice, 1790; La schiava della China (ob), Ancona, 1790; I due sposi ridicoli (ob), Rome, 1793; Gl'amori in villa (ob), Piacenza, 1793

DEUMM (T. Chini); *FlorimoN*

F. Chrysander: 'Die Oper Don Giovanni von Gazzaniga und von Mozart', *VMw*, iv (1888), 351–435

L. Schiedermair: 'Briefe Teresa Belloc's, Giuseppe Foppa's und Giuseppe Gazzaniga's an Simon Mayr', *SIMG*, viii (1906–7), 615–29

E. J. Dent: *Mozart's Operas* (London, 1913, 2/1947)

H. Abert: *W. A. Mozart* (Leipzig, 1919–21, 3/1955–6)

S. di Giacomo: *Il Conservatorio di Sant'Onofrio a Capuana e quello della Pietà dei Turchini* (Palermo, 1924)

A. Capri: '"Don Giovanni" e "Fidelio"', *RMI*, xvii (1943), 188–211

L. Conrad: *Mozarts Dramaturgie der Oper* (Würzburg, 1943)

A. E. Singer: *A Bibliography of the Don Juan Theme: Versions and Criticism*, West Virginia University Bulletin, 54th ser., no.10–11 (Morgantown, wv, 1954), suppl. (1954–5)

A. Damerini: 'Giuseppe Gazzaniga e Giovanni Simone Mayr', *Immagini esotiche nella musica italiana*, Chigiana, xiv (1957), 57–62

G. Macchia: 'Di alcuni precedenti del "Don Giovanni" di Mozart e Da Ponte', *Studi in onore di Pietro Silva* (Florence, 1957), 169–94

C. Bitter: *Wandlungen in den Inszenierungsreformen des 'Don Giovanni' von 1787–1928: zur Problematik des musikalischen Theaters in Deutschland* (Regensburg, 1961)

G. Macchia: *Vita, avventure e morte di Don Giovanni* (Bari, 1966)

S. Kunze: *Don Giovanni vor Mozart: die Tradition der Don-Giovanni-Opern im italienischen Buffo-Theater des 18. Jahrhunderts* (Munich, 1972)

D. Heartz: 'Goldoni, Don Giovanni and the dramma giocoso', *MT*, cxx (1979), 993–8

S. Sadie: 'Some Operas of 1787', *MT*, cxxii (1981), 474–7

J. Rousset: 'Don Juan dans l'opéra avant Mozart', *L'opéra au XVIIIe siècle: Aix-en-Provence 1982*

W. J. Allanbrook: 'Mozart's Happy Endings: a New Look at the "Convention" of the "lieto fine"', *MJb 1984–5*, 1–5

RUDOLPH ANGERMÜLLER, MARY HUNTER

Gazzaniga, Marietta (*b* Voghera, nr Milan, 1824; *d* Milan, 2 Jan 1884). Italian soprano. She studied in Milan with Mazzucato and made her début at Voghera in the early 1840s. After singing in various Italian opera houses, in 1849 she created the title role of Verdi's *Luisa Miller* at the S Carlo. In 1850 she sang Lina in the first performance of Verdi's *Stiffelio* at Trieste. She first appeared at La Scala in 1851 and sang in North America from 1857 to 1869. Towards the end of her career she became a mezzo-soprano. ELIZABETH FORBES

Gazzetta, La ('The Newspaper'). *Dramma* in two acts by GIOACHINO ROSSINI to a libretto by GIUSEPPE PALOMBA after CARLO GOLDONI's *Il matrimonio per concorso*; Naples, Teatro dei Fiorentini, 26 September 1816.

The ambitious and fantastical Don Pomponio Storione (bass) advertises in the local *gazzetta* for a husband for his flirtatious daughter Lisetta (soprano). In fact, Lisetta has fallen in love with Filippo (baritone) who owns the hotel in which they are staying. Meanwhile, the wealthy and feckless Alberto (tenor) has turned up at the hotel in search of a wife. And to confuse matters still further, a second father, Anselmo (bass), arrives to stay with his daughter Doralice (mezzo-soprano) in whom an old roué called Monsù Traversen (bass) takes a salacious interest. With an itinerant busybody, Madama La Rose (mezzo-soprano), fluttering on the periphery of the action this is just the kind of situation that Rossini liked to exploit with style and brio, from the early *La pietra del paragone* to the later *Il viaggio a Reims*. The score borrows substantially from some of the best numbers in *La pietra del paragone* and *Il turco in Italia* though, interestingly, the overture was newly written and later re-used for the more famous *La Cenerentola*. The opera has a substantial amount of secco recitative and much of the text is in Neapolitan dialect, so it is perhaps best heard in the language of the audience, with a fine *buffo* actor in the role of Don Pomponio. RICHARD OSBORNE

Gdańsk (Ger. Danzig). Polish city on the Baltic coast. Under Polish sovereignty from 1455 to 1793, it subsequently became part of Prussia, then Germany. It was a free city, 1919–39, under German occupation, 1939–45, and was returned to Poland in 1945. Its first operatic productions were *Tragedia o bogaczu i Łazarzu* ('The Tragedy of the Rich Man and Lazarus', 1643), probably by Marcin Gręboszewski, and *Le nozze d'Amore e di Psyche* (1646), by Marco Scacchi, given by the Warsaw court chapel. In 1695 J. V. Meder, leader of the city Kapelle, produced his *Nero*, the first German opera heard in Gdańsk. His second opera, *Die wiederverehligte Coelia*, was given in the nearby town of Schottland in 1698. A German company presented Mozart's *Don Giovanni* and *Die Zauberflöte* (both 1794) in the Old Theatre, and later operas and vaudevilles were performed by touring Polish companies such as the troupes of J. Nowicki, T. Truskolaski and W. Bogusławski.

In 1801 a new municipal theatre, the Danziger, was built, which survived until 1945. It was designed by

K. S. Held, with a capacity of 1000, and German operas and operettas were given there. Gottfried von Weber staged his brother's *Der Freischütz* in 1822 and Marschner directed his own *Der Vampyr* in 1828. The vast repertory of works by Mozart, Auber, Boieldieu, Weber, Lortzing, Spohr and Bellini was enlarged under the direction of Friedrich Genée (1841–55) with operas by Donizetti, Meyerbeer, Verdi and Wagner (*Tannhäuser*, 1853). Subsequent conductors at the Danziger included Richard Genée, Hans von Bülow and Felix Weingartner.

From 1909 operas were also staged in the open-air Waldoper at the nearby sea resort of Zoppot (from 1945 Sopot); Wagner's works were performed almost exclusively from 1922 to 1943 in summer festivals and Zoppot became one of the most celebrated centres for Wagner enthusiasts next to Bayreuth, under its music directors Max von Schillings, Hans Knappertsbusch and Robert Heger. During the insecure interwar period the theatre in Gdańsk continued to be run by Germans, and it was rebuilt in 1935–6. Polish operas were performed occasionally by guest companies from Warsaw (1926) and Poznań (1934).

After World War II, which left the city badly damaged, the Dramatic Studio under Iwo Gall staged occasional performances, beginning with Moniuszko's *Halka* (1949). The Opera Studio at the Gdańsk Philharmonic took over until, in 1953, productions were mounted regularly by the Państwowa Opera Bałtycka (State Baltic Opera). It gave the world premières of Szeligowski's *Krakatuk* (1956) and S. B. Poradowski's *Płomienie* ('Flames', 1966), as well as the Polish premières of *Peter Grimes* (1958) and *The Rake's Progress* (1965). The opera in Sopot was revived in 1960 as Opera Leśna (Forest Opera).

*

O. Rub: *Die dramatische Kunst in Danzig von 1615 bis 1893* (Danzig, 1894)

J. Bolte: *Das Danziger Theater im 16. und 17. Jahrhundert* (Hamburg, 1895)

H. Rauschning: *Geschichte der Musik und Musikpflege in Danzig* (Danzig, 1931)

F. A. Meyer: *Die Zoppoter Waldoper* (Berlin, 1934)

Z. Raszewski: *Z tradycji teatralnych Pomorza, Wielkopolski i Śląska* [The Theatrical Traditions in Pomerania, Great Poland and Silesia] (Wrocław, 1955)

B. M. Jankowski and M. Misiorny: *Muzyka i życie muzyczne na ziemiach zachodnich i północnych 1945–1965* [Music and Musical Life in Western and Northern Poland] (Poznań, 1968)

B. M. Jankowski, ed.: *Państwowa Opera i Filharmonia Bałtycka w Gdańsku* [The State Baltic Opera and Philharmonic in Gdańsk] (Gdańsk, 1971)

B. Zakrzewski-Nikiporczyk: *Życie muzyczne Pomorza w latach 1815–1920* [Musical Life in Pomerania] (Gdańsk, 1982)

KORNEL MICHAŁOWSKI

Gebel [Göbel], **Franz Xaver** (*b* Fürstenau, nr Breslau, 1787; bur. Moscow, 3 May 1843). German composer. He studied with G. J. Vogler and J. G. Albrechtsberger. By 1810 he was in Vienna and had been appointed Kapellmeister at the Leopoldstadt theatre, and in 1812 and 1813 four of his operas were staged there. Of these only *Aschenschlögel* had any success, with 26 performances in its first season; it is a parody of Isouard's *Cendrillon* (1810), which had been performed in Vienna in 1811 as *Aschenbrödel*. Gebel moved to Pest and then Lemberg (now L'viv), where according to Stieger (*Opernlexikon*, 1975–83) he had a fifth opera produced in 1816. The following year he settled in Moscow, where he had a successful career as a teacher

of composition. He also composed orchestral, piano and chamber music.

first performed at Vienna, Leopoldstadt, unless otherwise stated

Rinaldo und Camilla, oder Die Zauberinsel (grosse komische Oper, 3, Hilde), 22 Jan 1812
Aschenschlögel (grosse travestirte Oper, 3, J. Perinet), 11 July 1812
Diamantino, der Ritter im Zauberlande, oder Der Schutzgeist (Zauberoper, 4, Perinet), 19 June 1813
Die travestirte Palmyra (grosse Karikaturoper, 2, Perinet), 21 Aug 1813
Almasine Prinzessin von Tibet (heroische Oper, 3), Lemberg, Oct 1816

Gebel, Georg (*b* Brieg, 25 Oct 1709; *d* Rudolstadt, 24 Sept 1755). German composer. His father, also Georg, was an organist in Breslau. A precocious child, he learnt the harpsichord at the age of three and composed serenades and a German opera at 16. In 1729 he was appointed organist at the Maria Magdalena church and directed performances of a visiting Italian opera company. While in Breslau he also became Kapellmeister at the court of Oels. At 26 he was appointed composer to the Saxon court and harpsichordist to Count Brühl, the court's first minister, initially in Warsaw and subsequently for 12 years in Dresden. In 1750 he became Kapellmeister at the Rudolstadt court. His operas, at least a dozen, are all lost.

selective list; all lost

Serpillo und Melissa, Dresden, *c*1750; Oedipus (J. G. Kloss), Rudolstadt, 1751; Medea (Kloss), Rudolstadt, 1752; Tarquinius Superbus (Kloss), Rudolstadt, 1752; Marcus Antonius (Kloss), Rudolstadt, 1753; Sophonisbe (Kloss), Rudolstadt, 1753

*

J. Mattheson: *Grundlage einer Ehren-Pforte* (Hamburg, 1740); ed. M. Schneider (Berlin, 1910)
F. W. Marpurg: *Historisch-kritische Beyträge zur Aufnahme der Musik*, i (Berlin, 1754), 250
J. A. Hiller: *Lebensbeschreibungen berühmter Musikgelehrten und Tonkünstler* (Leipzig, 1784), 66   GEORGE J. BUELOW

Gebet (Ger: 'prayer'). PREGHIERA.

Gedda [Ustinoff], **Nicolai** (**Harry Gustaf**) (*b* Stockholm, 11 July 1925). Swedish tenor. He studied with Carl Martin Oehman, and at the Stockholm Conservatory. In 1951 he made his début at the Stockholm Opera in the première of Sutermeister's *Der rote Stiefel*; in the following year he sang there as Chapelou in *Le postillon de Lonjumeau*. He made his début at La Scala as Don Ottavio in 1953 and created the Groom in Orff's *Il trionfo di Afrodite*. In 1954 he sang Huon in *Oberon* at the Paris Opéra, and the next year made his Covent Garden début as the Duke in *Rigoletto*. He sang regularly for 22 seasons at the Metropolitan from 1957, the year of his American début (at Pittsburgh as Faust), creating Anatol in Barber's *Vanessa* (1958) and singing Kodana in the first American performance of Menotti's *Le dernier sauvage* (1964). At the 1961 Holland Festival he sang Berlioz's Cellini, a role he repeated at Covent Garden in 1966, 1969 and 1976. A fine linguist, speaking and singing in seven languages, he commanded the range of vocal and idiomatic style for Cellini, Pfitzner's Palestrina, Tchaikovsky's Hermann, Lohengrin, Faust, Riccardo, Pelléas, Pinkerton and Nemorino (which he sang at Covent Garden in 1981).

*

G. Storjohann: 'Nicolai Gedda', *Opera*, xvii (1966), 939–44
J. B. Steane: *The Grand Tradition* (London, 1974), 471ff
          HAROLD ROSENTHAL/R

Gedike, Alexander Fyodorovich (*b* Moscow, 20 Feb/4 March 1877; *d* Moscow, 9 July 1957). Russian composer. He studied the piano at the Moscow conservatory and from 1909 was professor of piano there. He also appeared in Russia and abroad as a concert pianist. Although he had no formal training in composition, he did benefit from advice on music theory from G. Konyus, N. Ladukhin and A. S. Arensky, and was influenced by S. I. Taneyev. His music is notable for its use of polyphony, and he was regarded as the guardian of classical traditions in Russian music.

Gedike wrote four operas, none of which has been performed or published in its entirety. In each, the vocal writing provides the compositional foundation, with an emphasis on melody and folksong as well as choral polyphony. The exact dates of composition of the second and third operas, *U perevoza* ('By the Ferry') and *Zhakeriya* ('Jacquerie'), are unknown but fall within the period 1932–47. The librettos of both, by the composer, are historical and involve revolutionary settings. In *By the Ferry* a personal drama unfolds against the background of the Pugachov Revolt. Gedike incorporated verses by V. A. Zhukovsky and Pushkin into the text. The musical structure follows a rondo form. Two Russian folksongs, 'Uzh tï, Syoma, Semyon' ('Oh! you, Syoma, Simeon') and 'U vorot, vorot' ('By the Gate, the Gate'), are used, developed in the form of variations. These exist independently in a transcription by the composer for voice and instrumental trio. *Jacquerie*, also a response by the composer to revolutionary events in Russia, is set during the peasant uprising in France during the 14th century. Gedike's final opera, *Makbet* op.76, after Shakespeare's *Macbeth*, was written in 1944. When extracts of the work were performed by the State SO in 1947, conducted by the composer, critics remarked on the great expressive power of the music, particularly in Lady Macbeth's sleepwalking scene.

Virineya op.25, 1913–15 (5, Gedike), introduction pubd as Gall'skiy nabeg [The Gallic Raid] (Moscow, 1928)

U perevoza [By the Ferry] op.44 (5, Gedike), 3 choruses (Moscow, 1937), 2 songs (Riga, 1949), duet pubd

Zhakeriya [Jacquerie] op.55 (5, Gedike), ov. (Moscow, 1945)

Makbet op.76, 1944 (5, after W. Shakespeare), extracts, concert perf., 1947

*

B. Levik: 'A. F. Gedike: k 70-letiyu so dnya rozhdeniya' [To Mark the 70th Birthday of Gedike], *SovM* (1947), no.3, pp.12–19

A. F. Gedike: *Sbornik statey i vospominaniy* [Collection of Articles and Reminiscences] (Moscow, 1960)   GALINA GRIGOR'YEVA

Geduldige Socrates, Der ('Patient Socrates'). Comic opera in three acts by GEORG PHILIPP TELEMANN to a libretto by JOHANN ULRICH VON KÖNIG after NICOLÒ MINATO's *La pazienza di Socrate con due moglie*; Hamburg, Theater am Gänsemarkt, 28 January 1721.

Required by Athenian law to take two wives, Socrates (baritone) is plagued by the constant bickering of his shrewish spouses, Xantippe (soprano) and Amitta (soprano). A minor subplot involves a dispute between the conceited playwright Aristophanes (tenor) and Socrates' disciples. The central action of the opera concerns the impending dual marriage of Melito (tenor), an Athenian prince. His father Nicia (bass) has contracted one wedding already, and for the second Melito must decide between two princesses, Rodisette (soprano) and Edronica (soprano). They both love him equally, but Melito feels affection for neither. Another Athenian nobleman, Antippo (alto), is in love with both women, but they reject his advances. Melito eventually comes to love them both as well but is unable to choose between them and decides instead to commit suicide. To prevent the impending disaster, Nicia nullifies Melito's marriage contract, freeing him to marry both Rodisette and Edronica. Rodisette cannot bear the thought of sharing Melito's affection, however, and herself threatens suicide. The situation is resolved when Nicia announces that the Athenian senate has rescinded the double-marriage law. Called upon to decide the outcome, Socrates determines that Melito should marry Rodisette, whereupon Edronica agrees to accept Antippo. Socrates laments that the legislative change has come too late for himself, and counsels men to have patience with their wives.

The two principal plot strands of the opera are differentiated musically. Socrates himself, his wives and his disciples are comic figures and are generally associated with a light *opera buffa* style. Comic high points are the drinking songs of Socrates' foolish disciple Pitho (tenor) and Aristophanes' hilarious parody of an *opera seria* 'rage' aria ('Zum Streit'). The aristocratic characters are exaggerations of stock *opera seria* figures, and their music is cast in the standard aria types of that tradition. Their music is usually of the highest quality and in style is often reminiscent of Handel. *Socrates* is an unusually long work, containing 38 arias (predominantly in da capo form) and 17 ensembles. Variety is achieved through the juxtaposition of serious and comic styles, and especially through Telemann's colourful handling of the orchestra. The choral lament 'Adon ist hin' (Act 3), with its muted trumpets and poignant solo oboe, is an outstanding example. Though the dramatic effectiveness of the opera is hampered by a weak libretto, the strength of Telemann's music ensured its success on the Hamburg stage, where it was repeated as late as 1730.

BRIAN D. STEWART

Gefesselte Phantasie, Die ('Fantasy in Chains'). *Zauberspiel* in two acts by WENZEL MÜLLER to a libretto by FERDINAND RAIMUND; Vienna, Theater in der Leopoldstadt, 8 January 1828.

Queen Hermione (spoken) learns from an oracle that she can save her land from two destructive magic sisters by marrying the son of the king of the neighbouring country. That prince, Amphio (spoken), woos and wins her love under the guise of a poet-shepherd; she vows to give her hand to the winner of a poetic contest, confident of Amphio's victory. However, when the sisters capture Fantasy (soprano) and compel her to inspire the Viennese harpist Nachtigall (tenor), the latter's victory is prevented only by the intercession of Jupiter and Apollo, who release Fantasy so that Amphio may be inspired to win the contest, Hermione's hand and the crown. Of the 17 numbers the most successful are the folksong-like ariettas for Nachtigall and the elegant, witty aria and quodlibet of Fantasy. The second of Raimund's three tragicomic plays, *Die gefesselte Phantasie* did not enjoy the popularity of the farces in his lifetime, and despite frequent revivals it has never held a regular place in the repertory.

PETER BRANSCOMBE

Gehot, Joseph (*b* Brussels, 8 April 1756; *d* USA, *c*1820). South Netherlands composer active in England and the USA. After touring France and Germany he was from about 1780 a violin virtuoso in London, where he published some theatrical pieces for the Royal Grove and the Royal Circus, instrumental pieces and theoretical works. After emigrating to the USA in 1792 he became a violinist in the New Theatre orchestra in Philadelphia under Reinagle.

all performed in London

The Maid's Last Shift, or Any Rather than Fail (burletta), Royal Circus, 1787
The Enraged Musician, Royal Grove, 1789
The Marriage by Stratagem, or The Musical Amateur, Royal Grove, 1789
The Royal Naval Review at Plymouth, Royal Grove, 1789
She Would be a Soldier, Royal Grove, 1789

2 songs in Shield: The Cobbler of Castlebury, LCG, 1779

*

J. R. Parker: 'Musical Reminiscences: Gehot', *The Euterpeiad*, ii (1821–2), 178   ANNE DHU SHAPIRO

Geisha, The. 'Japanese musical play' in two acts by SIDNEY JONES to a libretto by Owen Hall with lyrics by Harry Greenbank and additional numbers composed by Lionel Monckton, James Philp and NAPOLEON LAMBELET; London, Daly's Theatre, 25 April 1896.

In the Japanese Teahouse of Ten Thousand Joys, run by the Chinaman Wun-hi (*buffo*), the geishas welcome visiting English naval officers. Lieutenant Reginald Fairfax (baritone) has a particular interest in the chief geisha, O Mimosa San (soprano), but she is in love with the Japanese Captain Katana (tenor). She is also sought by the pompous Marquis Imari (baritone), though his attentions are readily diverted to a mysterious geisha, Roli Poli – none other than Fairfax's fiancée Molly (soubrette) in disguise. Imari is finally tricked into marrying Juliette (mezzo-soprano), a French interpreter at the teahouse, while Fairfax is reconciled to Molly, leaving O Mimosa San to marry Katana.

Jones's best-known work, it enjoyed immense contemporary success around the world. It achieved more performances in Germany in its day than any native operetta, was featured by Chekhov in his story *The Lady with the Little Dog*, and is still occasionally revived on the Continent. Originally performed with Marie Tempest as O Mimosa San and Hayden Coffin as Fairfax, it contains fine writing in the British comic-opera tradition. Principal numbers include the Sullivanesque opening chorus 'Happy Japan', O Mimosa San's 'The amorous goldfish', her waltz song 'A geisha's life' and her ballad 'The jewel of Asia' (composed by Philp), Fairfax's ballad 'Star of my soul' and Wun-hi's patter song 'Chin-chin-Chinaman'. The ballad 'Love, could I only tell thee!' (composed by J. M. Capel) was also sung by Fairfax in the show for a time.

ANDREW LAMB

Geisler, Paul (*b* Stolp [now Słupsk], Pomerania, 10 Aug 1856; *d* Posen [now Poznań], 3 April 1919). German conductor and composer. He studied with his grandfather, conductor at Marienburg (now Malbork), and for a time with Konstantin Decker. He was répétiteur at Leipzig (1881–2), then joined Angelo Neumann's travelling Wagner company (1882–3) before becoming Kapellmeister in Bremen under Anton Seidl (1883–5). He later worked in Leipzig and Berlin, finally moving to Posen, where he founded a conservatory and conducted. He was made royal Kapellmeister in 1902. Once popular and respected as representative of the New German School, Geisler's music was overshadowed by that of the leading members of the movement and after his death soon fell into neglect. In addition to his operas his

works also include a 'dramatic episode with music', *Wikingertod* and *Reminiscences de l'opéra 'Tannhäuser'* for piano.

MSS in A-Wn

Ingeborg (3, P. Lohmann), Bremen, 30 Nov 1884, vs (Berlin and Posen, 1879)
Die Ritter von Marienburg (3, G. Kleinau), Hamburg, 2 March 1891
Hertha (1, P. Schettler and P. Geisler), Hamburg, 1891
Palm (patriotische Oper, 3, H. Hartig), Lübeck, 10 Jan 1893
Wir siegen, oder Friedericus rex (1, Geisler), Berlin, Des Westens, 3 Jan 1898
Prinzessin Ilse (1, Geisler), Posen, 20 Feb 1898
Warum?, Berlin, 1899

*

*Stieger*O
A. Huch: 'Paul Geisler', *NZM*, Jg.83 (1916), 276–7

Geisterinsel, Die ('The Island of the Spirits'). Libretto in three acts by FRIEDRICH WILHELM GOTTER and Friedrich Hildebrand von Einsiedel after WILLIAM SHAKESPEARE's *The Tempest*. It was first set by Friedrich Fleischmann (1796, Regensburg).

Nine years after arriving on the island and subduing the witch Sycorax, Prospero faces a night of trials: Sycorax will return to join forces with her brutish son Caliban, and Prospero will be powerless to protect his daughter Miranda. A storm gathers; at its height a ship appears in distress and vanishes beneath the waves. After the storm clears Prospero comes upon one of its survivors, young Fernando, who falls instantly in love with Miranda. Elsewhere, several of Fernando's companions encounter Caliban, who enlists them in a plot to kill Prospero. Caliban discovers the lovers, but Prospero's magic protects them from his fury. As night falls Prospero sets Fernando and Miranda counting corals. A deep sleep overtakes him. Sycorax emerges from the ground, but the benign spirit Maja thwarts her attempt on Prospero and pitches her into a flaming ravine. After Prospero awakes, Caliban and his crew mount their assault, but Ariel foils them. Caliban throws himself into the sea. A ship lands, bringing the news that the people of Milan want Prospero to return as their ruler. He bids farewell to his familiar spirits, then breaks his magic staff.

The libretto of *Die Geisterinsel* was fashioned over a five-year period from 1790 to 1795, mostly by the Gotha diplomat and author Gotter. The subject allowed him to use the elements of magic and spectacle then in vogue at Vienna, but he sought to combine them with a Northern concern for seriousness and literary propriety. The result struck contemporaries as mellifluous and well groomed, but lacking in strong emotions and spectacular effects.

Gotter and Einsiedel hoped to offer *Die Geisterinsel* to Mozart, but his untimely death forestalled the plan. It was offered to Dittersdorf, but the major changes he wanted made before he would compose it so displeased the authors that this collaboration also came to naught. Fleischmann was finally given the exclusive right to set it. His music pleased no one, and after Gotter's death the opera achieved fame chiefly through the contemporaneous settings by Johann Friedrich Reichardt (1798, Berlin) and Johann Rudolf Zumsteeg (1798, Stuttgart). Reichardt's music shows how much ground Viennese style had gained in the North in both vocal writing and orchestration, although there is still a heavy emphasis on the male voices. His setting was performed frequently at Berlin well into the 19th century. Zumsteeg's score is even bolder in its intensely wrought harmonic language, and even more wide-ranging in its use of the orchestra; one number is accompanied by a solo mandore, or 'Milanese mandolin'. A fourth setting, by F. W. Haack, was performed at Stettin in 1799.

THOMAS BAUMAN

Geistinger, Marie (*b* Graz, 26 July 1836; *d* Klagenfurt, 28 or 29 Sept 1903). Austrian soprano. Some sources suggest 1833 or 1828 as her year of birth. She performed in Graz as a child and appeared in Munich (1850), Vienna (1852), Berlin (1854–6), Hamburg (1856–7), Riga (1859) and Berlin again (1863–5). She then made her name at the Theater an der Wien in Vienna in the leading roles in Offenbach's *La belle Hélène*, *La Grande-Duchesse de Gérolstein* and *Barbe-bleue*. She became joint manager and created the role of Rosalinde in *Die Fledermaus* (1874) as well as leading roles in Strauss's *Indigo* (1871), *Carneval in Rom* (1873) and *Cagliostro in Wien* (1875). She subsequently sang in Leipzig (1877–80), made major reappearances in Vienna and Berlin and toured America four times (1881, 1891, 1896, 1899), appearing on both coasts. She possessed a full, well-schooled soprano, with an imposing coloratura.

I. Horovitz-Barnay: *Marie Geistinger* (Vienna, 1903)
E. Pirchan: *Marie Geistinger: die Königin der Operette* (Vienna, 1947)
R. Holzer: *Marie Geistinger* (Vienna, 1951) ANDREW LAMB

Geistliche Waldgedicht oder Freudenspiel genant Seelewig, Das. Opera by S. T. Staden; *see* SEELEWIG.

Gélin, Nicolas (*b* Prangey, nr Langres, 15 Nov 1726; *d* after 1779). French bass. He joined the Paris Opéra about 1750, singing Neptune and Polyphemus in the 1752 revival of Lully's *Acis et Galatée*. He then created Borée and Eole in Mondonville's *Titon et l'Aurore* (1753). He took principal roles after the retirement of Chassé in 1757, but faced stiff competition from Larrivée who rose swiftly to prominence after his début in 1755. Though subordinate, Gélin stood his ground, singing Thoas in the last revival of Desmarets and Campra's *Iphigénie en Tauride* in 1762, and creating important roles in Dauvergne's *tragédies lyriques* of the early 1760s. For Gluck he sang Calchas to Larrivée's Agamemnon in the première of *Iphigénie en Aulide* (1774) and the High Priest in *Alceste* (1776); he also created roles for Gossec. He retired in 1779.

PHILIP WELLER

Geliot, Michael (*b* London, 27 Sept 1933). English director. After studying at Cambridge, where he was director of the University Opera Group, he worked at Sadler's Wells (1960–63), Glyndebourne (1960–62), the London Traverse Theatre (1966–8) and the BBC before becoming director of productions at the WNO in 1969. He was later artistic director (1974–8) and principal producer (1978–83) at the WNO, and helped to shape the company into a world-class ensemble, with a challenging repertory which included his production of *Lulu* (first British company performance, 1971). Geliot staged the première of Peter Maxwell Davies's *Taverner* at Covent Garden (1972) and has directed several British premières of other 20th-century works: Henze's *Boulevard Solitude* (1962), Hindemith's *Cardillac* (1970) and Martinů's *The Greek Passion* (1981). He

has also translated a number of operas and plays including *Die Zauberflöte*. ELISABETH INGLES

Gelosie villane, Le ('Peasant Jealousies'). *Dramma giocoso* in three acts by GIUSEPPE SARTI to a libretto by Tommaso Grandi; Venice, Teatro S Samuele, November 1776.

The opera tells of the return of the Marquis (tenor) to his domain and the havoc this causes among the local population. Although the heroine, Giannina (soprano), is already betrothed to Tognino (baritone), she is much attracted by the Marquis's deceitful offer of marriage. This inspires the jealousy of her friends Sandrina (soprano) and Olivetta (soprano). When Tognino points out to the Marquis that Giannina is his fiancée, the Marquis shows his true colours and threatens to beat him. Disguised as Nardo (bass), one of the other villagers, the Marquis makes a secret rendezvous with Giannina, but mistaking him for a commoner the villagers beat him. The opera ends with a trial scene in which the Marquis pardons them all and allows Giannina to marry Tognino. The cast includes two further villagers, Mengone and Cecchino (basses).

The piece is thoroughly satirical, with no characters portrayed sympathetically. The village men are brutish bumpkins, the village women jealous and over-ambitious and the Marquis an arrogant and deceitful snob. Musically, Sarti's finales are the highpoints of the opera; they are lively and varied, with unusual tonal relationships, and demonstrate his imaginative use of the orchestra. Written immediately after Sarti's return to Italy from a long sojourn in Copenhagen, this was one of the most popular *opere buffe* of the late 18th century. Also known as *Il feudatorio* or *Il feudatorio burlato*, it received over 40 productions, and unlike the many comic operas that did not survive the general turn to *opera seria* and *semiseria* in the 1790s *Le gelosie villane* was still being performed almost until the end of the century. MARY HUNTER

Geloso in cimento, Il ('The Jealous Man on Trial'). *Dramma giocoso* in three acts by PASQUALE ANFOSSI to a libretto by GIOVANNI BERTATI after CARLO GOLDONI's play *La vedova scaltra* (1748); Vienna, Burgtheater, 25 May 1774.

Donna Flavia (soprano), a widow, wishes to remarry. Her preferred partner, Don Fabio (tenor), is the eponymous 'geloso'; Donna Flavia wants to cure him of this fault before she commits herself. Fortunately for her, the buffoonish Don Perichetto (bass) and the snobbish Englishman Signor Rosbif (tenor) are also in love with her, and she uses them to goad Don Fabio into behaving better. Donna Flavia's maid Modestina (soprano) tries unsuccessfully to get Signor Rosbif for herself; Donna Flavia's spinster sister Vittorina (mezzo-soprano) remains unattached, and Don Fabio's servant Paterio (bass) provides an earthy foil to the jealous whims of his master. One of many collaborations between Anfossi and Bertati, this opera was extremely popular, achieving over 25 productions in its first five years and surviving in the repertory until the 1790s. Particularly notable is the complex and wide-ranging *introduzione*, which falls into five sections. It resembles a finale in its expressive contrasts, though it lacks the tonal variety requisite in a finale. MARY HUNTER

Gelsenkirchen. City in north-western Germany, in North Rhine-Westphalia. Touring theatrical companies visited the city from 1875 onwards. A local drama company was founded in 1881 and performed in the main room of an inn; after 1908 it staged performances in the Barbarossa Saal, and after 1911 in the town hall. Companies from Essen, Dortmund and Münster brought operatic performances for many years, until the founding of the Stadttheater in 1935 (destroyed in January 1945). After World War II Gelsenkirchen acquired its own opera company. The first Intendant was Hans Meissner (1949–53), who produced eight operas in his first season, including Hindemith's *Mathis der Maler* in the presence of the composer. In 1955 the company moved into the Hans Sachs Haus. Meissner's successor Gustav Deharde staged 50 operatic productions during his five years as director, and built up an able body of singers.

On 3 December 1959 a new theatre built by the architects Ruhnau, Rave and von Hausen opened with Shakespeare's *A Midsummer Night's Dream*. The modern building, in Kennedyplatz, is one of the most original and successful of its kind in Germany, and has three auditoriums; the large hall, with 1044 seats, is used for opera. The first operatic production, *Lohengrin*, was given on 20 December 1959. Major lines of development were determined by the directors Günter Roth (1966–71), who founded the company Musiktheater im Revier; Günter Könemann (1971–7), who helped to raise the reputation of the musical; and Claus Leininger (1977–87), who appointed Uwe Mund as musical director. Leininger engaged Carla Henius to direct a music-theatre workshop, appointed Göran Järvefelt theatrical director and offered an ambitious repertory. Among the well-known singers who began their careers here or have been members of the company are Marilyn Horne, Günter Reich, Ursula Schröder-Feinen, Gerd Nienstedt, Sabine Hass, Günter von Kannen, Livia Budai and Manfred Schenk. First German performances of contemporary operas, including Britten's *Let's Make an Opera* (1951) and Tippett's *The Knot Garden* (1987), have contributed to the company's reputation. In 1988 Ludwig Baum became Intendant and Johannes Kalitzke musical director.

H. Jahn and F. Loskill, eds.: *Musiktheater: Bühnen in Gelsenkirchen* (Gelsenkirchen, 1979)   IMRE FABIAN

Gem, Louis-Adolphe. *See* JAIME, LOUIS-ADOLPHE.

Gemma di Vergy ('Gemma of Vergy'). *Tragedia lirica* in two acts by GAETANO DONIZETTI to a libretto by GIOVANNI EMANUELE BIDERA after ALEXANDRE DUMAS (i)'s play *Charles VII chez ses grands vassaux*; Milan, Teatro alla Scala, 26 December 1834.

In 15th-century France, the Count of Vergy (baritone) arranges the annulment of his marriage to his barren wife, Gemma (soprano), because he needs heirs to inherit his estates. Torn with grief and jealousy, Gemma has a final interview with her husband to try to dissuade him from this action; he is moved by her pleas but the arrival of his new bride Ida (soprano) forces him to order Gemma away. A loyal slave, Tamas (tenor), secretly in love with Gemma, refuses an offer of freedom and avenges her by stabbing the Count at the altar during his marriage to Ida; he returns to confess and stabs himself. Now wanting only the release of death, Gemma thinks despairingly of her abiding love for the Count.

Although Gemma is perhaps vocally the most daunting role Donizetti ever composed for a soprano, being

designed for Giuseppina Ronzi De Begnis, Donizetti's favourite prima donna during the 1830s, the opera retained its popularity in Italy until well into the 1860s. Musically the score has great merits. Gemma's aria-finale – consisting of a prayer of imprecation on her husband's second marriage, succeeded by a change of heart and her resolution to enter a convent, which in turn leads into the eloquent Larghetto 'Un altare ed una benda' and the despairing cabaletta, 'Ah, chi m'accusa' – forms a classic test for a dramatic soprano *d'agilità*. The role of the Saracen Tamas, composed for Domenico Reina, is dramatically effective, and his Allegro giusto in Act 1, 'Mi toglieste a un sole ardente', was long a popular showpiece for tenors; on more than one occasion its libertarian sentiments prompted demonstrations against repression.

In Donizetti's melodramatic *opere serie* the midpoint finales frequently provide the musical climax. That to Act 1 of *Gemma* is unusual because it has two ample slow movements, the first of which is marked Largo and moves from D minor to the parallel major; after a first *tempo di mezzo* the Andante in E major, 'Di' ch'io vada in Palestina', intensifies the emotion. The headlong stretta, in C, is precipitated by the arrival of Ida, Gemma's successor as Countess of Vergy; Gemma's 'Fui tradita' blazes with wrath.

Gemma contains other signs of Donizetti's expanding the conventions to intensify the particular dramatic implications of the plot. For instance, one original touch is the *introduzione*: Guido (bass), the Count's right-hand man, meditates sympathetically on Gemma's plight in a sustained cavatina, set against an agitated choral background as Rolando (comprimario bass), bearer of the royal grant of annulment, and the retainers discuss the current exploits of Joan of Arc.

WILLIAM ASHBROOK

Gencer, Leyla (*b* Istanbul, 10 Oct 1924). Turkish soprano. A pupil of Giannina Arangi-Lombardi in Istanbul, she made her début at Ankara in 1950 as Santuzza, the role she sang for her Italian début at the Arena Flegrea, Naples, in 1953. She sang at La Scala in 1957 as Madame Lidoine in the world première of Poulenc's *Dialogues des Carmélites*. Subsequently she appeared throughout Europe and America but was heard most frequently in Italy. Although her voice was limited in volume and not very even, she was able, thanks to her technique, strong temperament and theatrical intelligence, to tackle with success such dramatic roles as La Gioconda or Aida. Lighter roles such as Gilda and Amina made the best use of her vocal flexibility and impressive soft singing; but her interpretative powers found most scope in the dramatic coloratura repertory, particularly in lesser-known Rossini, Donizetti and Verdi: *Anna Bolena*, *Maria Stuarda*, *Elisabetta, regina d'Inghilterra*, *Lucrezia Borgia*, *Attila*, *I due Foscari* and *La battaglia di Legnano*.

R. Celletti: 'Leyla Gencer', *Opera*, xxiii (1972), 692–6
——: 'Il trono s'addice alla Gencer', *Discoteca*, no. 117 (1972)
F. Cella: *Leyla Gencer* (Venice, 1986) [with discography]
                    RODOLFO CELLETTI

Genée, (Franz Friedrich) Richard (*b* Danzig [Gdańsk], 7 Feb 1823; *d* Baden, nr Vienna, 15 June 1895). German conductor, librettist and composer. He was the son of Friedrich Genée (*b* Königsberg, 1796; *d* Berlin, 1859), conductor at a theatre in Danzig, and, although first intended for the medical profession, took up music, studying with A. Stahlknecht in Berlin. Between 1847 and 1867 he was successively Kapellmeister at theatres at Reval (now Tallinn), Riga, Cologne, Düsseldorf, Danzig, Mainz, Schwerin and Prague. In 1868 he became conductor at the Theater an der Wien, Vienna, and in the following years was increasingly involved with not just the musical but also the literary side of the works produced there. At first concerned with adapting foreign works for production, he became much in demand as a clever writer of operetta librettos. This side of his activities developed particularly through his association with Johann Strauss who, being unfamiliar with writing for the theatre, used Genée not just as lyricist but for the detailed working out of his melodic ideas. Thus Genée's handwriting is to be found extensively in the autograph score of *Die Fledermaus*. Genée's work as librettist reached its height in his collaboration with F. Zell (Camillo Walzel), the latter concerning himself more with the plots and the final elaboration of the librettos of their works while Genée concentrated on the lyrics. They went on to write librettos for Suppé and Millöcker, as well as for Genée's own compositions, often making use of French sources. In 1878 Genée was able to retire from conducting to his villa at Pressbaum, near Vienna. His translations include the librettos of several works by Lecocq, Offenbach and Sullivan.

Genée's own operettas rarely attained more than an ephemeral success, though *Der Seekadett* (1876) and *Nanon, die Wirtin vom goldenen Lamm* (1877) made a considerable hit at the Theater an der Wien and travelled as far afield as America. Both had librettos attributed to Zell, though almost certainly Genée wrote the lyrics, as usual. Genée also wrote many partsongs, among which one for male voices, *Italienischer Salat*, is most amusing in its satire on the older style of Italian operas, being sung to nonsense words. His brother Rudolf (*b* Berlin, 12 Dec 1824; *d* Berlin, 19 Jan 1914) also wrote some librettos.

Polyphem [Ein Abenteuer auf Martinique] (komische Oper, 4, Trautmann), Elbing, 20 Sept 1856

Der Geiger aus Tirol (komische Oper, 3, Rudolf Genée), Danzig, March 1857

Der Liebesring (romantische Oper, 2, H. Schmidt), 1860

Ein Trauerspiel (Operette, 1, Richard Genée), Mainz, 1860

Ein Narrentraum (Karnevalsposse, Richard Genée), Mainz, 1861

Der Musikfeind (Operette, 1, Richard Genée), Berlin, Friedrich-Wilhelmstädtisches, 17 Jan 1862

Der Generalprobe (Operette, 1, Richard Genée), Berlin, 1862

Die Herren von der Livree (Posse, 1, E. Jacobson), Berlin, 1862

Die Talismänner (Karnevalsposse, L. Ullinger), Mainz, March 1863

Rosita (romantische komische Oper, 3, Richard Genée), Mainz, 1 Jan 1864

Der Zopfabschneider (Operette, 1, Richard Genée), Berlin, Handwerker-Verein, 13 April 1866

Der schwarze Prinz (komische Oper, 1, Richard Genée, after A. von Kotzebue: *Don Raundo di Colibrados*), Prague, 14 June 1866

Am Runenstein (romantische Oper, 2, Richard Genée), Prague, 13 April 1868, collab. Flotow

Schwefeles, der Höllenagent (Operette, 1, Richard Genée), Vienna, An der Wien, 24 Nov 1869

Der Hexensabbath (Intermezzo), Vienna, An der Wien, 4 May 11870

Cleopatra [Drei Jahrtausende] (Burleske, 3, J. Steinher), Vienna, Komische Oper, 13 Nov 1875

Luftschlösser (Posse, 3, C. Costa, after W. Mannstädt and A. Weller), Vienna, An der Wien, 11 July 1876

Fliegende Blätter (Quodlibet, Costa), Vienna, An der Wien, 1 Aug 1876

Der Seekadett (komische Operette, 3, F. Zell), Vienna, An der Wien, 24 Oct 1876

Nanon, die Wirtin vom goldenen Lamm (Operette, 3, Zell, after E. G. M. Théaulon and F. V. A. d'Artois), Vienna, An der Wien, 10 March 1877

Im Wunderlande der Pyramiden (Singspiel, 3, Zell and Richard Genée), Vienna, Komische Oper, 25 Dec 1877

Die letzten Mohikaner (Operette, 3, Zell, after J. F. Cooper), Munich, Königliches, 10 Sept 1878

Nisida (komische Operette, 3, M. West and Zell), Vienna, Carl, 9 Oct 1880

Rosina (Operette, 3, Richard Genée), Vienna, An der Wien, 25 Dec 1881

Eine gemachte Frau (Posse, 3, Jacobson), Dresden, Residenz, 6 Jan 1885

Die Zwillinge (Operette, 3, Zell and Richard Genée), Vienna, An der Wien, 14 Feb 1885, collab. L. Roth

Die Piraten (Operette, 3, Zell and Richard Genée), Berlin, Walhalla, 9 Nov 1886

Die Dreizehn (Operette, 3, Zell, after Scribe), Vienna, Carl, 14 Nov 1887

Signora Vendetta (Vaudeville-Operette, H. Herschel), Wiesbaden, 14 June 1892

Rotkäppchen (Vaudeville-Posse, 3, Richard Genée, after H. Meilhac and L. Halévy), Berlin, Thomas, 25 Sept 1892

Die Mädchen-Schule (Vaudeville-Posse, 3, Richard Genée, after A. Bisson), Berlin, Thomas, 25 Sept 1892

Die wachsame Schildwache (Zwischenspiel, 1, Rudolf Genée, after M. de Cervantes), Berlin, Philharmonia, 25 Feb 1893

Freund Felix (Operette, 3, Richard Genée and L. Herrmann, after Herrmann: *Von sieben die Hässlichste*), Berlin, Friedrich-Wilhelmstädtisches, 14 Oct 1893

LIBRETTOS

those for Genée's own compositions are not listed; Operetten unless otherwise stated

Z – *with Zell*

Benjamin, der seinen Vater sucht (Vaudeville), T. Hauptner, 1864; *Die Pilger*, M. Wolf, 1872; *Die Konzertprobe* (Posse, with E. Siebert), Siebert, 1874; *Die Fledermaus* (with C. Haffner), J. Strauss, 1874; *Cagliostro in Wien* (Z), Strauss, 1875; *Fatinitza* (komische Operette, Z), Suppé, 1876; *Die Porträt-Dame* [Die Prophezeiungen des Quiribi] (komische Operette, Z), Wolf, 1876; *Die Fornarina* (komische Operette, Z and West), Zeller, 1878; *Gräfin Dubarry* (komische Operette, Z), Millöcker, 1879; *Boccaccio* (Z), Suppé, 1879; *Capitän Nicoll* [Die Carbonari] (Z and West), Zeller, 1880; *Apajune, der Wassermann* (Z), Millöcker, 1880; *Das Spitzentuch der Königin* (komische Operette, with H. Bohrmann-Riegen [H. Bohrmann and J. Riegen]), Strauss, 1880; *Donna Juanita* (komische Operette, Z), Suppé, 1880; *Die drei Langhälse* (Liederspiel, with E. Pohl), J. Brandl, 1880; *Die Jungfrau von Belleville* (Z), Millöcker, 1881; *Der lustige Krieg* (Operette, Z), Strauss, 1881; *Der Gascogner* (Z), Suppé, 1881; *Der Bettelstudent* (komische Operette, Z), Millöcker, 1882; *Königin Mariette* (Z), I. Brüll, 1883; *Viola* (Z), A. Arensen, 1883; *Eine Nacht in Venedig* (komische Operette, Z), Strauss, 1883; ? *Die Afrikareise* (with M. West and O. F. Berg), Suppé, 1883; *Pfingsten in Florenz* (J. Riegen), A. Czibulka, 1885; *Gasparone* (Z), Millöcker, 1884; *Der Marquis von Rivoli* (with B. Schier), L. Roth, 1884; *Der Jagdjunker der Kaiserin* (komische Operette, Z), Czibulka, 1885; *Der Nachtwandler* (Z), Roth, 1886; *Der Vice-Admiral* (Z), Millöcker, 1886; *Die Musikanten* (Oper), Flotow, 1887; *Rikiki* [Nelly die Blumenhändlerin] (with W. Mannstädt), J. Hellmesberger, 1887; *Der Glücksritter* (with Mannstädt and B. Zappert), Czibulka, 1887; *Ein Deutschmeister* (with Zappert), Ziehrer, 1888; *Die Jagd nach dem Glücke* (with Zappert), Suppé, 1888; *Kapitän Fracassa* (komische Operette, Z), R. Dellinger, 1889; *Die indische Witwe* (Z), G. Geiringer, 1889; *Der Polengraf* (with H. Fritzsche), Roth, 1889; *Polnische Wirtschaft* (with West), H. Zumpe, 1889; *Page Fritz* (with A. Landesberg), A. Strasser and M. von Weinzierl, 1889; *Die Teufelsbrücke* (Oper, with Riegen), T. Tomaschek, 1891; *Der Millionenonkel* (Z), A. Müller jr, 1892; *Der Freiwillige* (with C. Costa), F. Soukup, 1892; *Der Schwiegerpapa* (Z), Weinzierl and A. Zamara, 1893; *Das Mädchen von Mirano* [La stupida] (Z), A. Neumann, 1893; *Die Königin von Gamara* (burleske Operette, with L. Stein), Neumann, 1894; *Die Welfenbraut* (Oper, with M. Füll), Zamara, 1894; *Coeur d'ange* (with H. Regel), R. Mader, 1895

Many translations from French and English

LoewenbergA; *MGG* (F. Hadamowsky) [incl. full list of writings]
R. Holzer: *Die Wiener Vorstadtbühnen: Alexander Girardi und das Theater an der Wien* (Vienna, 1951), 409ff
A. Bauer: *150 Jahre Theater an der Wien* (Vienna, 1952)

ALFRED LOEWENBERG, ANDREW LAMB

Generali, Pietro (*b* Masserano, nr Vercelli, 23 Oct 1773; *d* Novara, 3 Nov 1832). Italian composer. His surname was Mercandetti until his father changed it when, bankrupt, the family moved to Rome. There Generali studied counterpoint with Giovanni Masi, interrupted by four months spent at the Conservatorio di S Pietro a Maiella at Naples. He graduated from the Congregazione di S Cecilia in Rome and began his career as a composer of sacred music, producing his first opera only in 1800 (*Gli amanti ridicoli*). His first great success was *Pamela nubile*, composed for Venice in 1804 and repeated in Vienna in 1805. This was followed by other comic operas and farces which were widely performed in Italy and abroad (*Le lagrime d'una vedova, Adelina, La Cecchina, La vedova delirante, Chi non risica non rosica*). He did not attempt *opere serie* until 1812 with *Attila*, but thereafter produced a considerable number; one of the most successful was *I baccanali di Roma* (1816), which was in demand for many years. In spring 1817, when his popularity began to be obscured by Rossini's successes, he went to Barcelona as director of the opera company at the Teatro de la S Creu. He held the position for about three years, often travelling in Italy and abroad, and contributed one original work (*Gusmano de Valhor*, 1817) and some revivals. From late 1820 to 1823 he was in Naples, composing several operas and teaching; Luigi Ricci was among his pupils.

With the Naples period his activity as an opera composer came virtually to an end. In 1823 he became music director of the Teatro Carolino in Palermo. In spring 1825 he was replaced by Donizetti; he returned to his post the following season, but in 1826 he was charged with being *maestro venerabile* of a masonic lodge and expelled from the kingdom. In poor health and disappointed by the cold reception of his works, he returned to the north of Italy and in 1827 became *maestro di cappella* at Novara Cathedral, a position he held until his death. In his last years he had a few *opere serie* performed, without much success.

Generali composed at least 55 operas as well as sacred works and cantatas. Contemporaries had conflicting opinions of his work. His early comic operas sounded 'moderne' and even 'stravaganti' in their vigorous and brilliant orchestration and a certain unusual harmonic richness. But at the end of his career, like many composers of the same generation, he appeared a pale imitator of Rossini. In 1828 Tommaso Locatelli wrote of *Francesca da Rimini*: 'There prevails a certain carelessness, a certain triviality of style, as if the maestro had been working almost *per otium*' (*Gazzetta di Venezia*). In fact, in spite of their fine melodic qualities and effective delineation of character, his works sometimes lack substance and structural coherence and rarely escape a certain stylistic standardization, partly because of his laziness and his superficial way of composing, which often led him to complete his operas during rehearsals. His use of dramatic orchestral effects anticipates Rossini, but the attribution to Generali of the invention of the orchestral crescendo, as stated on his commemorative tablet in Novara, is superficial.

Gli amanti ridicoli (ob, 2, G. Lorenzi), Rome, Pace, carn. 1800
Le nozze del duca Nottole (ob), Rome, 1801, excerpts *I-Nc*

La villanella in cimento (farsa, 2, L. Romanelli), Rome, Valle, aut. 1802
Le gelosie di Giorgio (farsa, G. Palomba), Bologna, 1802, excerpts *Fc, Gl*; as La caccia di Enrico IV, Venice, S Benedetto, 20 Jan 1810
Pamela nubile (farsa, 1, G. Rossi, after C. Goldoni), Venice, S Benedetto, 12 April 1804, *Fc, Mr*, Nc, Rsc, Vlevi*; as La virtù premiata dall'amore, Vienna, Burg, 20 July 1805
La calzolaia [La calzolaia strasburghese] (farsa, 1, Rossi), Venice, S Benedetto, 10 June 1804, *CNM, Mr*, Nc*
Misantropia e pentimento (farsa, 1, L. Buonavoglia, after A. von Kotzebue), Venice, S Moisè, 15 Jan 1805, *Fc, Mr**
Don Chisciotte (dg, 2, Rossi, after M. de Cervantes), Milan, Scala, 12 May 1805, *Mr**
Orgoglio e umiliazione, ossia Il fortunato ripiego (op semiseria, G. Foppa), Venice, Fenice, 1 Dec 1805
Gli effetti della somiglianza [Gli inganni della somiglianza] (farsa), Venice, ?1805 or later, *Fc**
L'idolo cinese (dg, 2, Lorenzi, rev. Palomba), Naples, Nuovo, carn. 1808, *Mc, Nc**
Lo sposo in bersaglio (dg, 2, G. Gasparri), Florence, Pergola, 8 Sept 1808, *Fc* (?autograph); as Lo sposo in contrasto, Vienna, 1809
Le lagrime d'una vedova (farsa, 1, Foppa, after C. Federici), Venice, S Moisè, 26 Dec 1808, *Fc, Ls, Mc, Mr*, MOe, Nc, Pl, Vnm*
Il ritratto del duca (farsa, Foppa), Venice, S Moisè, 16 Sept 1809, *Mr**
La moglie giudice del marito (farsa, Foppa), Venice, S Moisè, 28 Dec 1809, *Mr**; as La moglie di tre mariti, Venice, S Moisè, 18 Aug 1809
Il matrimonio in contrasto (farsa), Vicenza, before 1810
La villana fortunata (ob), Naples, before 1810
Amore vince lo sdegno (dg, 2, Foppa), Rome, Valle, Feb 1810; as L'amore prodotto dall'odio (L. Prividali), Milan, Scala, 21 Aug 1813, *Mc*
Adelina [Luigina; Luisina] (farsa, 1, Rossi, after S. Gessner), Venice, S Moisè, 15 or 16 Sept 1810, *Bc, CR, Fc, Gl, Ls, Mc, Mr*, MOe, Nc, OS, Pl, PESc, Rsc, Tn*
La Cecchina suonatrice di ghironda [La Cecchina sonatrice] (farsa, 1, Rossi), Venice, S Moisè, 26 Dec 1810, *Mc, Nc, Rsc*
La vedova delirante (ob, 2, J. Ferretti), Rome, Valle, Jan 1811, *Mr*, Nc*; as Bernardino, Barcelona, S Cruz, late 1815; as La donna delirante, Lisbon, S Carlos, 1820
Chi non risica non rosica (dg, 2, Romanelli), first known perf., Milan, Scala, 18 May 1811, *Fc*, excerpts (Milan, 1808)
La sciocca per gli altri e l'accorta per sé (dg, Foppa), Venice, S Moisè, 21 Sept 1811, *Mr**
La vedova stravagante (ob, 2, Romanelli), first known perf., Milan, Scala, 30 March 1812, *Mc*, excerpts (Milan, 1808) [?rev. of La villanella in cimento]
Attila (os, Rossi), Bologna, Comunale, sum. 1812
L'orbo che ci vede, ossia Il medico ciabattino (dg, 2, A. Anelli), Bologna, Corso, Oct 1812, *Fc, Nc*
Isabella, ossia Il più meritato compenso [?Rodolfo] (farsa, 1, Foppa), Venice, S Moisè, 26 Dec 1812, *Mr**
Gaulo e Oitona (os, 2, L. Fidanza), Naples, S Carlo, carn. 1813, *Nc*
Eginardo e Lisbetta (op semiseria, 2), Naples, Fiorentini, 10 June 1813, *Nc**
Bajazet [Bajazetto] (os, 2), Turin, Imperiale [Regio], 26 Dec 1813, excerpts *Tf*, excerpts (Turin, 1814)
Il servo padrone (ob, 2, C. Mazzolà), Turin, Carignano, aut. 1814, *Nc*
La contessa di Colle Erboso, ossia Un pazzo ne fa cento (dg, 2, Foppa), Genoa, S Agostino, Dec 1814, *Ls, MOe, Nc* (with autograph corrections); as La contessa di Colle Ombroso, Milan, Re, carn. 1815; as Tutti matti, Venice, S Giovanni Grisostomo, aut. 1816; as La finta contessa, Livorno, Avvalorati, spr. 1821
L'impostore (op semiseria, 2, Anelli), Milan, Scala, 21 May 1815; as Marctondo, Venice, S Moisè, 1824
I baccanali di Roma [I baccanti; Le baccanti di Roma] (os, 2, Rossi), Venice, Fenice, 14 Jan 1816, *GB-Lbl, I-Fc, Rsc*, vs (Bonn and Cologne, ?1818); rev. as Die Bacchanten, Vienna, An der Wien, 12 June 1820; as I baccanali aboliti, Milan, Re, sum. 1832
Clato (os, 2, A. Lorenzoni), Bologna, Comunale, 4 Jan 1817
Rodrigo di Valenza (os, 2, F. Romani, after W. Shakespeare: *King Lear*), Milan, Scala, 8 March 1817, *Mc*
Gusmano de Valhor (os, ?Peracchi, after Voltaire: *Alzire*), Barcelona, S Creu, 1 Dec 1817
Ebuzio (os), Naples, S Carlo, 9 Sept 1818
La rosa bianca e la rosa rossa, ovvero Il trionfo dell'amicizia (os, 3, Romani), Turin, Regio, 26 Dec 1818

Adelaide di Borgogna (os, 2, Romanelli), Rovigo, Società, 26 April 1819, *Mc*, *Mr**

Il gabbamondo (dg, 2, C. Sterbini), Rome, Valle, 26 Dec 1819

Idomeneo (os, 1, F. Hilbath Romano), Lisbon, S Carlos, 1819

Chiara di Rosembergh, ossia L'eroina tra le figlie (op eroicomica, 2, A. L. Tottola), Naples, Nuovo, Dec 1820, *GB-Lbl*, *I-Fc*, *Mcom*, *Nc*, excerpts (Naples, n.d.)

La testa maravigliosa (os, 2, Tottola), Naples, Nuovo, Lent, 1821, *Fc*, excerpts (Naples, n.d.)

Elena e Olfredo (os, 2, Tottola), Naples, S Carlo, 9 Aug 1821, *Nc** (as Alfredo), excerpts (Naples, n.d.; Milan, 1824)

La sposa indiana (os, 2, G. Schmidt), Naples, S Carlo, 12 Jan 1822, *Nc**

Argene e Alsindo (dramma eroico, 1, Schmidt), Naples, S Carlo, 30 May 1822, *Nc**

Le nozze fra nemici (op semiseria, 2, Tottola), Naples, Nuovo, 20 April 1823, *Nc*

Jefte [Il voto di Jefte] (azione tragico-sacra, 2, ? Foppa, after F. Gnecco), Florence, Pergola, 11 March 1827, *Fc*, *Mr**, *Vt*, excerpts (Milan, 1828–30)

Il divorzio persiano, ossia Il gran bazzarro di Bassora (os, 2, Romani), Trieste, Grande, 31 Jan 1828

Francesca da Rimini (os, P. Pola, after Dante: *Commedia*), Venice, Fenice, 26 Dec 1828, *Vt**, excerpts (Milan, 1829)

Il romito di Provenza (os, 2, Romani), Milan, Scala, 15 Jan 1831, *Mc*, excerpts (Milan, 1831)

Beniowski, ossia Gli esiliati in Siberia (os, 2, Rossi), Venice, Fenice, 17 March 1831, *Fc*, *Vt*, excerpts (Milan, 1831)

La gabbia dei matti (farsa), Novara, spr. 1833

Undated: La donna soldato (farsa), excerpts *Tf*, *Tn*, excerpts (Paris, n.d.); Oro non compra amore, *Mc* (cavatina), *Rsc*.

Arias in: Lo sprezzatore punito, 1816; Otello

Doubtful: La modista raggiratrice (ob, ? after Lorenzi: La scuffiara), Naples, Fiorentini, 1808; Amore ed interesse, ossia L'infermo ad arte (dg, Rossi), Venice, S Moisè, 1810

*

ES (C. Sartori); *FlorimoN*

'Nachrichten: Mayland', *AMZ*, xix (1817), 473

L. Schiedermair: 'Eine Autobiographie Pietro Generalis', *Festschrift … Rochus Freiherrn von Liliencron* (Leipzig, 1910), 250–5

J. Subirá: *La ópera en los teatros de Barcelona: estudio histórico cronológico desde el siglo XVIII al XX*, i (Barcelona, 1946), 72ff

O. Tiby: *Il Real Teatro Carolino e l'ottocento musicale palermitano* (Florence, 1957)

J. Freeman: 'Pietro Generali in Sicily', *MR*, xxxiv (1973), 231–40

A. Galazzo, ed.: *Contributi alla bibliografia di Pietro Generali* (Biella, 1981) [incl. chronology of performance]

ANDREA LANZA

Geneva (Fr. Genève; Ger. Genf). City in western Switzerland. The first theatre to present opera was the Théâtre du Rosimond, a wooden building holding 800, erected in 1766 and destroyed by fire in January 1768. Grétry's *Isabelle et Gertrude* received its première there in December 1766. Opera was performed at the Théâtre de Neuve (cap. 1100), built in 1783, until a new theatre (cap. 1300), also situated at Place Neuve, opened with *Guillaume Tell* on 4 October 1879. Premières of works by Jaques-Dalcroze and Audran were given in the late 19th century, Louis Aubert's *La forêt bleue* in 1913, and Gounod's *Faust* was performed every season between 1879 and 1928. In 1892 Geneva became the first city in French-speaking Europe to hear Massenet's *Werther* after the Vienna première. Ansermet conducted regularly at the theatre between 1915 and his death in 1969, including Fauré's *Pénélope* in 1947 and Frank Martin's *Monsieur de Pourceaugnac* in 1963. Ansermet's Geneva performances of *Pelléas et Mélisande* also contributed to his international renown as an interpreter of Debussy.

The theatre, renamed the Grand Théâtre in 1910, was severely damaged by fire in 1951, and for the following ten years a curtailed programme was given at the Théâtre au Grand Casino. Only the public rooms at the front of the Grand Théâtre survived to be incorporated in the present building (cap. 1500), which opened on 10 December 1962 with *Don Carlos* in the original French, produced by Marcel Lamy. Lamy was succeeded as theatre director in 1965 by Herbert Graf, who raised the Grand Théâtre's international reputation, beginning with *Die Zauberflöte* in settings by Kokoschka, conducted by Ansermet. The repertory under Graf included many unfamiliar and neglected works, notably Bloch's *Macbeth*, Rameau's *Platée*, Honegger's *Antigone*, Chabrier's *L'étoile* and the première of Milhaud's *La mère coupable* (1966). Graf died in 1973 and was succeeded by Jean-Claude Riber, who produced much of the theatre's repertory for the following seven seasons.

The regime of Hugues Gall, which opened in 1980 with a staging of *Don Giovanni* by Maurice Béjart, has been distinguished by imaginative casting and an adventurous staging policy, often with singers and directors on the brink of major careers. Girolamo Arrigo's *Il ritorno di Casanova* was first performed in 1985 and Rolf Liebermann's fifth opera *La forêt* in 1987. Unusual productions during this period included Liebermann's staging of *Parsifal* (1982), his sole venture into opera production in a long career as an administrator, François Rochaix' staging of *Death in Venice* (1983) and Johannes Schaaf's production of *Fidelio* (1989), set in a Middle Eastern internment camp.

The Grand Théâtre operates on the stagione system. The season from September to June consists of eight opera productions (including an operetta every Christmas), each receiving between six and eight performances. There is no permanent ensemble (apart from the chorus and ballet), and no music director. The theatre hires the Orchestre de la Suisse Romande or the Orchestre de Chambre de Lausanne for its productions.

*

R. de Candolle: *Histoire du Théâtre de Genève* (Geneva, 1978)

J.-J. Roth: *Grand Théâtre de Genève: opéras, moments d'exception* (Paris, 1987)

ANDREW CLARK

Geneviève de Brabant ('Geneviève of Brabant'). *Opéra bouffe* in two acts by JACQUES OFFENBACH to a libretto by LOUIS-ADOLPHE JAIME and ETIENNE TRÉFEU; Paris, Théâtre des Bouffes-Parisiens (Salle Choiseul), 19 November 1859 (revised in three acts to a libretto by HECTOR-JONATHAN CRÉMIEUX; Paris, Théâtre des Menus-Plaisirs, 26 December 1867).

A satirical treatment of a medieval legend, the work mixes characters from different historical periods with abandon. It was produced in two significantly different versions, of which the second (1867) is considered definitive and was itself augmented for a production in five acts at the Théâtre de la Gaîté on 25 February 1875. Geneviève (soprano) is neglected by her husband Sifroy (tenor), Duke of Curaçao, who has been rendered sterile by a magic curse. To obtain the post of page, Geneviève's baker lover Drogan (soprano) offers Sifroy a pastry with supposed regenerative powers. Racked with indigestion, Sifroy is summoned by Charles Martel (bass), King of France, to fight the Saracens. Geneviève and Drogan flee into a forest with the nurse Biscotte (mezzo-soprano). The Duke's scheming adviser Golo (*buffo*) usurps the throne, but he is eventually displaced and Geneviève and Sifroy reconciled. The 1867 version is noted for the 'Couplets des deux hommes d'armes', sung in the forest by two armed men. This became known in English as the 'Gendarmes' Duet' and was adapted as the US Marines' Hymn 'From the halls of Montezuma'. Zulma Bouffar sang Drogan in 1867.

ANDREW LAMB

Genoa (It. Genova). City and port in northern Italy. Formerly capital of an independent republic, and part of the French Empire (1805–14), Genoa finally lost its independence when it was annexed to the Kingdom of Sardinia by the Congress of Vienna. Its history of music drama on the Venetian model and its connection with the early development of the commercial public theatre goes back to about 1640. At that time the noble Adorno family, which owned the ancient Falcone inn in Borgo di Prè, where *commedia dell'arte* companies had performed since the end of the 16th century, transformed it into a theatre of the same name, 'oval in shape and with enormous capacity'. The Teatro del Falcone, or Teatro Adorno, was at first managed by its owners. In 1646 it had boxes separated by wooden partitions and lined with fine fabrics. Musical dramas of the time were brought there by professional travelling companies known as the Febi Armonici or Accademici Febiarmonici, associated with the Ferrari-Mannelli group of performers linked with Venetian theatres. Ferrari himself may have lived in Genoa before 1650. Towards 1650, the management of the theatre seems to have been taken up by impresarios, notably Giacomo Ghiglione, the landlord of the inn, and Pietro Francesco Barberini, and from about 1655 to 1666 Pietro Manni, 'il Corso'. Although another theatre with boxes was functioning in Genoa in 1653 (the Teatro di S Domenico), perhaps as the small private theatre of the Spinola family, the dukes of San Pietro, the Falcone remained the only real commercial one, with two fairly regular seasons (in late autumn, often called 'winter', and at Carnival, sometimes continuing into late spring). Throughout the 17th century and beyond, the Falcone was used by *commedia dell'arte* and French and Spanish touring companies as well as for the most famous operas of the time.

Manni's period as impresario saw the appearance of the nobleman Giovanni Andrea Spinola as a librettist and occasional poet, whose success extended beyond the borders of the Genoese republic. In 1655, under the pseudonym Giovanni Aleandro Pisani, he put on *Ariodante* at the Falcone with music by G. M. Costa, with intermezzos *Gli incanti d'Ismeno*. Spinola's name is particularly associated with the Genoese preference for the early Baroque style in opera: in Genoa, unlike Venice, recitative was preferred to arias even in 1688, and Spinola was sometimes asked to write replacement scenes with lengthy recitatives.

In 1677 the Falcone was leased to a group of Genoese noblemen at an annual rent of 50 silver scudi; it was rebuilt and enlarged at their expense with two rows of 16 boxes each, with a third tier 'for the convenience of ordinary people'. In 1677–8 the Falcone was directed by the composer and impresario C. A. Lonati, 'il Gobbo'; at least three operas were performed, including *L'amor stravagante* (a reworking of *Amor per vendetta, ovvero L'Alcasta*, with music by Pasquini for the Roman performance of 1673) and *Amor per destino*, with music elaborated by Lonati himself (a reworking of *Antioco*, staged earlier in Venice). The most important event of those years was the stay in Genoa of Alessandro Stradella (1678–82). This marked perhaps a peak of Roman art and influence there, resulting from marriages between the most important aristocratic families of the two cities. After contributing to the adaptation of *Amor per destino*, Stradella, who became director of the Falcone for a year, prepared three operas: *La forza dell'amor paterno* (1678, a reworking of Sartorio's *Seleuco*, *Le gare dell'amor eroico* (1679, a reworking of Cavalli's *Muzio Scevola*) and *Il Trespolo tutore* (1679, perhaps with the libretto by Villifranchi published in Bologna).

The sale of the Falcone to the Genoese nobleman Eugenio Durazzo in 1680 marked the beginning of the end of Stradella's involvement in the Genoese theatre. Even before he was assassinated (25 February 1682) audiences at the Falcone had enjoyed a Venetian opera by Carlo Pallavicino (*Vespasiano*, 1680), and a few years later Durazzo tended to choose operas from Parma, perhaps because of loans made to the Duke of Parma. Falcone audiences thus became familiar with the grandiose scene designs of Ferdinando and Francesco Galli-Bibiena, the costumes of Gasparo Torelli, the dances of Bernardino Crivelli and the music of Bernardo Sabadini.

In 1702 a new and larger theatre, the S Agostino, was opened by the Genoese nobleman Nicolò Maria Pallavicino, a member of the Arcadian Academy and a well-known patron. It was managed by the Bolognese impresario and costumier Cesare Bonasoli (the works performed were *Flavio Cuniberto*, libretto by Matteo Noris, and *Il sogno trionfante*). Its greater capacity at once challenged the Falcone, which Durazzo hastily refurbished and enlarged in 1703. Serious problems faced the architects both of the S Agostino and of the new Falcone, which had five tiers of projecting and raked boxes and was opened by the impresario Giacomo Maggi in 1705 with *Il più fedel fra i vassalli* (music by Silvani and libretto by Stampiglia, scenery by Francesco Galli-Bibiena) and *Eraclea* (music probably by Bernardo Sabadini, libretto by G. C. Godi). In 1706, however, the Durazzo and Pallavicino families reached an agreement, stipulating alternate years for the activities of the two theatres, which remained in force until the end of the 18th century. Towards 1730 the small Teatro delle Vigne opened, deriving, like the Falcone, from a 17th-century hostelry with an annexe for theatrical entertainments. After 1770 the S Agostino was bought by the Durazzo family, who in 1765 had also acquired a theatre in Sarzana; they later also became proprietors of the Vigne, after its owner's death in 1782.

In 1772 an association of Genoese aristocrats, the Impresa dei Teatri di Genova, was set up, largely financed by the Durazzo family, to exploit local talent, especially in music, scene painting and theatre machinery, and to present opera to a wider audience. At the end of 1790 the S Agostino was rebuilt (six tiers plus the 'gods') and opened with Cimarosa's *Il falegname* with scenery by Pietro Gonzaga. At the same time, a number of small theatres, public and private, came into being in the nearby holiday resorts (Albaro, Sampierdarena, Sestri Ponente and Voltri), while others opened also in towns at the edges of the old republic (Novi and Sarzana) and along the two rivieras (Sanremo, Savona, Rapallo and Chiavari), where *opera buffa* was preferred (Anfossi, Cimarosa, Gnecco, Guglielmi, Paisiello and Sarti were the most popular composers).

Events connected with the Jacobin regime (1797–9) led to the closure and sometimes the destruction of

The new Teatro Carlo Felice, Genoa (designed by the architects Gardella, Reinhart, Rossi & Sibilla), inaugurated on 18 October 1991

many theatres and to the arrival of entertainments inspired by the ideals of revolutionary France. During the period of provisional government (1800–05) the city enjoyed a progressive social and cultural revival, and a lively page of music criticism, aimed at improving the degenerate operatic taste of the Genoese, appeared in the *Gazzetta di Genova*. After Genoa's annexation by France theatres had to observe the dispositions of the *Règlement* proclaimed in Paris in 1807, and the S Agostino, despite structural deficiencies, became the leading theatre, the others being demoted and their repertories diversified. Annexation to the Kingdom of Sardinia again raised the question of a new theatre, for reasons other than those considered in the grandiose plans drawn up and approved by Paris under the Napoleonic regime. After difficulties and delays the new building, designed by the Genoese architect Carlo Barabino and named after the king, Carlo Felice, opened on 7 April 1828 with Bellini's *Bianca e Fernando*. The S Agostino was now doomed to a rapid decline. Composers heard during these years included Pacini, Morlacchi, Mercadante, Donizetti and notably Mayr. The programmes for the early seasons of the Teatro Carlo Felice were intended to satisfy the numerous requests for works by Rossini, who had become undisputed master of the Genoese stage since Carnival 1814, when *Tancredi* was performed at the S Agostino. From the middle of the 19th century, however, Rossini's name was displaced on theatre posters by that of Giuseppe Verdi, whose *Nabucco* was given at the Carlo Felice in April 1843. Verdi's early operas were produced at a time when tastes and habits were changing in Genoa as in the rest of Italy. Bellini and Donizetti figured prominently, but Verdi had no rivals until the coming of Meyerbeer (*Robert le diable* at the Carlo Felice, April 1852).

After the middle of the 19th century Genoa acquired more theatres, not all dedicated to opera but often staging it more or less continuously. Among the most important were the Colombo (1852), the Apollo (1853), the Andrea Doria (1855; rebuilt in 1885 as the Politeama Regina Margherita), the Paganini (1855), the

Gustavo Modena at Sampierdarena (1857) and the Politeama Genovese (1870). It was not until 1880 that Wagner was brought to Genoa, when *Lohengrin* was performed at the Politeama Genovese, but the opera was understood by neither critics nor audience. The historical and political situation of the time had however contributed to making the repertory of local theatres less provincial and opening the way to such composers as Hérold, Gounod and Bizet, and finally to an enthusiastic acceptance of Offenbach, Lecocq and Planquette and a sympathetic reception of Massenet.

With few new Italian operas of acceptable standard towards the 1860s, the Genoese opera repertory had become petrified; and this led to the opening of new cultural frontiers. The *belle époque* saw an almost complete capitulation to Viennese operetta for at least three decades (1870–1900). Although the music of Wagner's most important operas, which reached Genoa between 1900 and 1914, found genuine supporters as well as denigrators, it did not alter the preference for lightweight theatrical entertainment. From 1891, however, theatre posters were dominated by the names of Puccini, Mascagni, Giordano, Cilea and Leoncavallo.

The Carlo Felice was closed to opera during World War I and reopened only in 1921, but without any great novelty in the repertory and, except for occasional Wagner performances, paying little attention to Austrian or German opera: no Mozart, no Beethoven, no Weber. After performances at the Carlo Felice of the last of Mascagni's operas, *Il piccolo Marat* (1923), Puccini's *Turandot* (1927) and Boito's *Nerone* (tepidly received, 1928), the Genoese public, which in the first decades of the 20th century had been anxious for novelty, became less enterprising, and as World War II approached the programmes of the theatres tended increasingly to exclude works outside the central repertory. To a large extent this was the result of 20 years of Fascist rule, during which none of the great European masterpieces of the inter-war period was performed. The time of private impresarios was passing, and the managements of the public theatres were not receptive to the four most representative Italian composers of the generation after Puccini and *verismo* opera (Respighi, Pizzetti, Malipiero and Casella), whose music was not heard at the Teatro Carlo Felice until they had reached the age of 50.

None of the theatres in Genoa survived World War II undamaged. The city was little affected by the glimmerings of a cultural revival in Italy after 1950, although opera was staged after a fashion, occasionally in the rebuilt but narrow Politeama Genovese (1956) but principally in the new Politeama Margherita (1954), where the regular seasons of the Teatro Comunale dell'Opera took place until the long-awaited reopening of the Teatro Carlo Felice on 18 October 1991 with *Il trovatore*. Of the original 19th-century structure surviving the 1943–4 air raids, only a part of the external walls and the wide doric-columned vestibule remain (see illustration). The large auditorium has been designed as a wide, sloping space holding 2000 spectators, with more seats on the side balconies, built to resemble the façades of ancient Genoese palaces with the strongly contrasting colour patterns typical of the older townscape. The high stage-tower solves the problem of shortage of space by means of movable floors and a revolving platform, so that two or three scenes can be prepared simultaneously. The Teatro dell'Opera Giocosa should also be mentioned; this private organization of enthusiasts is dedicated to reviving, studying and encouraging public interest in Italian opera of the 18th and early 19th centuries.

*

ES (C. Bertieri)

Pagano, ed.: *Annuario dei teatri di Genova (1828–1844)* (Genoa, 1844)

Ponthenier, ed.: *Annuario dei teatri di Genova (1844–1855)* (Genoa, 1856–7)

L. T. Belgrano: 'Delle feste e dei giuochi dei genovesi', *Archivio storico italiano*, xv (1872), 417–77; xviii (1873), 112–37

C. Da Prato: *Il Teatro Carlo Felice: relazione storico-esplicativa (1828–1875)* (Genoa, 1875)

A. Neri: *Costumanze e sollazzi* (Genoa, 1883)

A. Brocca: *Il Politeama Genovese: cronistoria dell'anno 1870 al 1895* (Genoa, 1895, 2/1899)

——: *Il Teatro Carlo Felice: cronistoria (1828–1898)* (Genoa, 1898)

P. L. Levati: *Feste e costumi dei genovesi nel secolo XVIII* (Genoa, 1910)

A. Massa: 'Il melodramma in Liguria nel settecento', *Gazzetta di Genova*, xi (1915), 3–5

L. Parodi: 'I direttori d'orchestra del Teatro Carlo Felice', *Gazzetta di Genova*, iv (1920), 9–10

A. Pescio: *Settecento genovese* (n.p., 1922)

G. B. Vallebona: *Il Teatro Carlo Felice: cronistoria* (Genoa, 1928, 2/1935)

S. Rebaudi: 'Il Teatro di Campetto', *Genova*, viii (1942), 27–31

——: 'Il Teatro di S Francesco d'Albaro', *Genova*, viii (1943), 14–18

R. Giazotto: *La musica a Genova nella vita pubblica e privata (secoli XIII–XVIII)* (Genoa, 1951)

A. Schmuckher: *Teatro e spettacolo a Genova e in Liguria* (Genoa, 1963, 2/1976)

G. Piumatti: *Catalogo delle opere dei musicisti liguri del Conservatorio N. Paganini di Genova* (Genoa, 1975)

A. F. Ivaldi: 'Una speculazione edilizia a Genova (1700–1702): l'origine del Teatro di Sant'Agostino', *Critica d'arte*, cl (1976), 69–80

——: 'Un teatrino "qui est près de la Loge des Banquiers"', *Critica d'arte*, cli (1977), 140–50

——: 'L'impresa dei teatri di Genova (1772): per una gestione "sociale" della cultura', *Studi musicali*, vii (1978), 215–36

M. Dolcino and A. F. Ivaldi, eds.: *G. Monleone: storia di un teatro, il Carlo Felice* (Genoa, 1979)

A. F. Ivaldi: 'Un disegno "bibienesco" di una collezione privata genovese', *Antichità viva*, i (1979), 37–9

——: 'Divagazioni sui Durazzo mecenati di "prestigio"', *Atti Società ligure storia patria*, xix (1979), 315–31

——: 'Note in margine all'attività di Ferdinando e Francesco Galli Bibiena a Genova', *Palladio*, i/4 (1979), 97–112

E. Frassoni: *Due secoli di lirica a Genova* (Genoa, 1980)

A. F. Ivaldi: 'Gli Adorno e l'"hostaria"-teatro del Falcone di Genova (1600–1680)', *RIM*, xv (1980), 87–152

——: 'E. Frassoni: due secoli di lirica a Genova', *RIM*, xvi (1981), 287–91

——: 'Scheda per uno scenografo genovese fine settecento: Carlo Alberto Baratta (1754–1815)', *Teatro archivio*, iv (1981), 55–69

M. Bottaro and M. Paternostro: *Storia del teatro a Genova* (Genoa, 1982)

A. F. Ivaldi: 'Una "macchina" funebre nella chiesa dei Padri Somaschi (1683)', *Atti Società ligure storia patria*, new ser., xxii (1982), 227–45

——: 'Spigolature del barocco musicale genovese (musici e cantanti a Genova nel secolo XVII)', *La Berio*, iii (1982), 16–47

L. Sartoris and F. Cosentino: *1841–1861: G. Verdi a Genova* (Genoa, 1983)

F. Dorsi: 'Un intermezzo di N. Jommelli: "Don Falcone"', *NRMI*, iii (1985), 432–56

A. F. Ivaldi: 'Il Diluvio Universale e la "Gazzetta di Genova"', *Teatro Comunale, Genoa 1987*, 23–58 [programme book]

——: 'Théâtre et musique dans la Gazzetta di Genova de 1800 à 1814', *Periodica musica*, iii (1985), 8–18

Il Teatro Carlo Felice di Genova: storia e progetti (Genoa, 1986)

A. F. Ivaldi: 'La famiglia di G. Durazzo: i personaggi decisivi, l'ambiente genovese', *Teatro Comunale, Genoa 1987*, 103–222 [programme book]

A. Schmuckher: *Storia del Teatro Carlo Felice* (Genoa, 1987)

A. F. Ivaldi: 'Il "Nuovo Mondo" e il teatro musicale fra sei e settecento', *Columbus '92*, i (1989), 25–7

——: 'Teatro e società genovese al tempo di Alessandro Stradella', *Chigiana*, new ser., xxxix (1989), 447–574

R. Iovino, I. Mattion and G. Tanasini: *I palcoscenici della lirica* (Genoa, 1990)

ARMANDO FABIO IVALDI

Genovés y Lapetra, Tomás (*b* Saragossa, 29 Dec ?1806; *d* Burgos, 5 April 1861). Spanish composer. He was a choirboy in Saragossa and later moved to Madrid, where he gave singing lessons. Under the influence of Rossini, he set Romani's libretto *Enrico e Clotilde, ossia La rosa bianca e la rosa rossa* (previously set by Mayr). In 1832 he wrote numbers for the zarzuela *El rapto*, to a text by the journalist Mariano José de Larra. Awarded a pension by the Spanish government, in 1834 Genovés went to Italy (residing first at Bologna), where he wrote religious compositions, operas and programmatic orchestral works; Ricordi published his collection of ballads and duets, *Sere d'autunno al Monte Pincio*, praised for their melodic appeal. Genovés's first opera performed in Italy was *Zelma* (1835, Bologna); its agreeable melodies are said to have pleased a public that desired easy amusement. Other operas of his Italian years were *La battaglia di Lepanto* (1836, Rome), *Bianca di Belmonte* (1838, Venice) and *Iginia d'Asti* (1840, Naples). He continued to be influenced by Rossini, but employed musical themes reminiscent of the Spanish zarzuela. *Luisa della Vallière* (1845) brought him modest success when it was performed at La Scala. In 1846 he returned to Madrid, where *Luisa della Vallière* had four performances at the Cruz in February and March. He married the singer Elisa Villó in 1851 and spent his last decade mostly at his retreat in Burgos.

Enrico e Clotilde, ossia La rosa bianca e la rosa rossa (2, F. Romani), Madrid, Cruz, 17 Aug 1831

El rapto (zar, 2, M. J. de Larra), Madrid, Cruz, 16 June 1832, *E-Mm*

Zelma (3, G. Regaldi), Bologna, Comunale, 31 Oct 1835

La battaglia di Lepanto (3, L. Tarantini, after Vicomte d'Arlincourt: *Le Renégat*), Rome, Valle, 14 Oct 1836; ? as Il rinnegato

Bianca di Belmonte (2, Romani), Venice, 1838

Iginia d'Asti (3, G. M. Mariani), Naples, Fondo, 1840

Luisa della Vallière (3, Mariani), Milan, Scala, 1845

StiegerO
B. Saldoni: *Diccionario biográfico-bibliográfico de efemérides de músicos españoles* (Madrid, 1868–81), ii, 231–4; iii, 386–7
A. Peña y Goñi: *La ópera española y la música dramática en España en el siglo XIX* (Madrid, 1881), 158–65
R. Mitjana: 'La musique en Espagne', *EMDC*, I/iv (1920), 2308–9
E. Cotarelo y Mori: *Historia de la zarzuela* (Madrid, 1934), 175–7
J. Subirá: *El teatro del Real Palacio (1849–1851)* (Madrid, 1950), 135–6
C. Gómez Amat: *Historia de la música española*, v: *Siglo XIX* (Madrid, 1983), 111–12   JOHN DOWLING

Genoveva. Opera in four acts by ROBERT SCHUMANN to his own libretto after LUDWIG TIECK's *Leben und Tod der heiligen Genoveva* and Friedrich Hebbel's *Genoveva*; Leipzig, Stadttheater, 25 June 1850.

In 1847 Schumann commissioned the poet Robert Reinick to write a libretto based on Tieck's play (1799), which emphasizes marital fidelity. More than half of the libretto had been completed when Schumann came across Hebbel's play (1842), which centres on highly charged emotion and treachery. Schumann asked Reinick to rewrite the libretto, fusing the two plays. Dissatisfied with the result, he approached Hebbel for help but finally wrote his own libretto based on Reinick's second draft. Reinick refused to acknowledge any part of the finished libretto as his work.

The opera is set in Brabant in the 8th century, when Charles Martel, leader of the Franks, rallied Christian armies from western Europe to check the northward advance of the Moors from Spain into France, which was accomplished by his victory at Tours in 732. In Act 1, Hidulphus, Bishop of Trier (baritone), summons Christian warriors to join the crusade, and Siegfried, Count Palatine (baritone), assembles his army, which marches off to war. Before he leaves, however, Siegfried entrusts his castle, and the care of his new young wife, Genoveva (soprano), to a trusted friend, the young knight Golo (tenor). Alone on the stage, Golo reveals that he is desperately in love with Genoveva. His sorceress foster-mother, Margaretha (soprano), overhears and promises to help him win Genoveva.

In Act 2 Golo presses his love on Genoveva. She rejects him, gently at first, but when this is of no avail against his rising passion, she orders him away as a 'dishonourable bastard'. This reminder of his birth changes Golo's love to a thirst for vengeance. He tricks an elderly steward, Drago (bass), into hiding in Genoveva's chamber. Then he arranges for Margaretha, leading a group of retainers, to burst in at midnight; Golo is with them and immediately kills Drago with his sword. Genoveva seems hopelessly compromised and is imprisoned. In Act 3 Siegfried, returning from his victory over the Moors, is convalescing at Strasbourg after being wounded in battle. Margaretha, disguised as a nurse, is doing all possible to delay his recovery. Golo arrives bringing a letter from the castle's chaplain recounting Genoveva's supposed adultery with Drago, and Siegfried, further incensed by seeing, in Margaretha's magic mirror, pictures which purport to show Drago and Genoveva conversing amorously, orders Golo to return and put Genoveva to death.

Act 4 reveals a rocky wilderness, where, on Golo's orders, Genoveva has been led to be killed by two armed men. Golo appears and gives her a last chance to escape by fleeing with him. This she indignantly refuses, and Golo, not to be seen in the opera again, leaves her to her fate. Genoveva is saved from death at the last second by

a mute youth, Angelo, who has been hiding nearby; and moments later Siegfried hurries in. (Margaretha has been forced to reveal the truth to him by Drago's ghost.) There is a reconciliation, and Siegfried and Genoveva go to their castle, accompanied by a double chorus in which country people singing of the triumph of true love alternate with the hymn of the victorious returning crusaders.

Genoveva lacks the contrasting characterizations, striking dramatic situations and vocal highlights of most successful 19th-century operas. It is the opera of an extremely subjective composer. The music describes the emotions of the watching Schumann – or rather of the two sides of his personality – as he empathizes with the predicaments of the various characters as they appear on stage; it thus tends to be broadly similar for most of them. It is, however, warmly romantic throughout; recitative is replaced by gentle arioso, making the flow of the music continuous; some, admittedly rather tentative, use is made of leitmotifs; and many of the arias are worthy of Schumann the songwriter at his best.

Schumann himself conducted the first two performances. The next production was at Weimar in April 1855, conducted by Liszt, who at once saw the merits and the weaknesses of the work. On 3 April 1855 he wrote, in a letter to Anton Rubinstein, 'I must leave you now to go to rehearse Schumann's *Genoveva* ... Of the operas that have been produced over the last 50 years it is certainly the one I prefer (Wagner excepted – that is understood) – in spite of its lack of dramatic vitality'. Peters published the vocal score in 1851, with the piano part arranged by Clara Schumann, and the full score in 1880. In the late 19th century Novello published a vocal score with English words. More than 80 staged performances of *Genoveva* have taken place, recently at Zwickau (1935, 1976), Florence (1951), Bonn (1956) and Montpellier and Nancy (both 1985). In 1977 EMI issued a complete recording, conducted by Kurt Masur.   BRIAN SCHLOTEL

Gent (Flemish). GHENT.

Gentele, Göran (*b* Stockholm, 20 Sept 1917; *d* Olbia, Sardinia, 18 July 1972). Swedish director and administrator. He studied in Paris and Stockholm. After a short period as an actor, he directed plays at the Stockholm Dramatic Theatre (1946–52). In 1952 he directed a new production of Menotti's *The Consul* at the Royal Opera, Stockholm, and from then until 1963 he directed 16 operas including a controversial *Un ballo in maschera*, which depicted Gustavus III as a homosexual, and the première of Blomdahl's 'space' opera *Aniara*. His original thinking won many admirers. He then succeeded Svanholm as director of the Stockholm Opera, a position he held until 1971 when he went to New York to prepare his first season as Bing's successor as general manager of the Metropolitan Opera; but he died in a car crash a few weeks before the opening.

H. Rosenthal: 'Göran Gentele', *Opera*, xxiii (1972), 786
HAROLD ROSENTHAL/R

Gentil-Bernard. *See* BERNARD, PIERRE-JOSEPH.

Gentili, Serafino (*b* Venice, 1775; *d* Milan, 13 May 1835). Italian tenor. He made his début in 1796 at Ascoli Piceno. From 1800 to 1803 he sang in Naples, and between 1812 and 1828 he appeared frequently at

La Scala. He created Lindoro in Rossini's *L'italiana in Algeri* (1813) at the Teatro S Benedetto, Venice. He also sang in Paris and Dresden. ELIZABETH FORBES

Gentilucci, Armando (*b* Lecce, 8 Oct 1939; *d* Milan, 12 Nov 1989). Italian composer. Brought up in Milan in a family of professional musicians, he entered the Milan Conservatory where he studied with Bruno Bettinelli and Franco Donatoni. From 1964 he taught at the Milan and Bolzano conservatories and, from 1970 until his death, directed the Istituto Musicale of Reggio Emilia. His creative career was divided between composition and criticism: in both he was a major presence in Italian debates over music's social obligations. His only opera, *Moby Dick* (to his own libretto, after H. Melville), was written in the final years of his life to a commission from the Teatro Regio, Turin; he did not live to see it performed. A performance of seven Symphonic Fragments from the opera was given by the RAI orchestra in Milan on 29 March 1990. Long planned, it was a conscious summation of his work of the previous decade, whereby musical structure is based on the gradual unfolding of harmonic resources from an initial fixed field. The large horizons thus suggested are peculiarly appropriate to the seascapes of Melville's novel, as are the impressionistic orchestral textures, which owe something to the example of Debussy and Britten: they underline the tension that Gentilucci established between the 'operatic' narrative of Ahab's whale hunt and the anti-narrative of the ocean's vast indifference to human endeavour. DAVID OSMOND-SMITH

Gentle Shepherd, The. Ballad opera in five acts by Allan Ramsay; Edinburgh, Taylors' Hall, 22 January 1729.

The royalist Sir William Worthy returns to Scotland after the Restoration to be reunited with his son Patie, who has been brought up as a shepherd. Patie fears he will not now be allowed to marry his sweetheart, Peggy, but fortunately she too proves to be of gentle birth.

Ramsay's pastoral comedy, based on two of his earlier poems and containing four songs, was published in 1725. He was a friend of John Gay and, after the success of *The Beggar's Opera*, added 18 further Scottish airs to produce a ballad opera which was first performed by the boys of Haddington Grammar School in 1729 and frequently staged in Edinburgh after 1745. Admired as a beautiful picture of rustic manners, it was much read and frequently republished. London-based Scots performed it a few times at the Little Theatre in the Haymarket in most seasons from 1752 to 1792, and London also saw two shortened and anglicized versions: Theophilus Cibber's 1730 ballad afterpiece *Patie and Peggy* had little success, but an adaptation by Richard Tickell with the music arranged by Thomas Linley (i) did well in the 1780s. In both these versions the role of Patie was sung by a woman, although the tenor Joseph Vernon is also known to have taken it in at least one production. OLIVE BALDWIN, THELMA WILSON

George, Georgina [Lady Oldmixon, Mrs Oldmixon] (*b* ? Oxford, 1768; *d* Philadelphia, 3 Feb 1835). English soprano and actress. A pupil of Philip Hayes, she appeared first in concerts at Oxford. She made her London début in the 1783 Haymarket summer season as Rosetta in *Love in a Village* and was there almost every summer until 1789. She specialized in lively girls and chambermaids and created the role of Wowski in

Samuel Arnold's *Inkle and Yarico* (1787). Despite her good looks and high coloratura, her career at Drury Lane petered out in 1786 and she then appeared mainly in the provinces, Edinburgh and Ireland. When playing Lucy to Mrs Billington's Polly at Crow Street Theatre, Dublin, she surprised and outshone her rival by singing an octave higher in their duet, 'her tones having the effect of the high notes of a sweet and brilliant flute'. She married Sir John Oldmixon in 1788 and later moved with him to the USA. As Mrs Oldmixon she made her American début in Philadelphia in May 1794 as Clorinda in *Robin Hood*. She retired from the stage in 1813.

BDA; LS

A. Pasquin [pseud. of J. Williams]: *The Children of Thespis*, i (London, 1786, 13/1792)

W. T. Parke: *Musical Memoirs* (London, 1830)

W. Dunlap: *A History of the American Theatre* (New York, 1832, 2/1833)

T. J. Walsh: *Opera in Dublin 1705–1797* (Dublin, 1973)
OLIVE BALDWIN, THELMA WILSON

George, Graham (*b* Norwich, 11 April 1912). Canadian composer, theorist and conductor of English origin. He moved to Canada in 1928, becoming a Canadian citizen in 1930. His composition teachers have included Alfred Whitehead in Montreal and Paul Hindemith at Yale University (1952–3). He also studied conducting with Willem van Otterloo in Utrecht (1956). From 1946 until his retirement in 1977, he taught at Queen's University in Kingston, Ontario. He also conducted the Queen's SO (1946–54), and founded and conducted both the Kingston Choral Society (1953–7) and the New SO of Kingston (1954–7).

George's music is in a 20th-century idiom characterized by traditional formal structures and modal harmonies, and influenced by his studies of ethnomusicology and the structural aspects of music. His operas are large-scale works based on historical events with librettos adapted from contemporary writing. He has also composed many choral pieces.

Evangeline (3, P. Roddick and D. Warren), Kingston, Ont., La Salle Hotel, 1 Dec 1948

Way Out (comic op, 2, George), Kingston, Queen's University, 2 Feb 1960

A King for Corsica, 1975 (3, George, after S. Costa, A. Walpole and H. Mann), Kingston, Queen's University, Grant Hall, 23 Jan 1981

Revolt in Upper Canada (4, George), Kingston, Queen's University, Grant Hall, March 1987 (concert perf.); staged Toronto, 1987
RUTH PINCOE

Georges, Alexandre (*b* Arras, 25 Feb 1850; *d* Paris, 18 Jan 1938). French composer. After studying at the Ecole Niedermeyer, he joined the army and then became *maître de chapelle* at the church of Ste Clotilde in Paris, where César Franck was organist. He provided incidental music for two important symbolist plays by Villiers de l'Isle Adam, performed at the Paris Odéon in the 1890s. He also wrote several dramatic oratorios, including *Balthazar*. *Le printemps*, a brief one-act work on a Chinese theme, was followed by his first full-length opera, *Charlotte Corday*. *Miarka*, first given at the Opéra-Comique, was shortened and revived at the Opéra in 1925. It recounts the story of a Romany girl destined, according to the tarot cards, to become a queen. Georges' style, often restlessly chromatic, betrays the influence of Franck, but like many composers of his generation, he introduced local colour into his works by using characteristic regional dances and songs.

Le printemps (oc, 1, C. de Roddez and Montjoyeux), Rouen, Lyrique, 2 May 1890, vs (Paris, 1891)

Charlotte Corday (drame lyrique, 3, A. Silvestre), Paris, Château d'Eau, 16 Feb 1901, vs (Paris, 1901)

Miarka (drame lyrique, 4, J. Richepin), Paris, OC (Favart), 7 Nov 1905, vs (Paris, 1905)

Myrrha (saynète romaine, 1, Silvestre), 13 June 1909, vs (Paris, 1895)

Sangre y sol (drame lyrique, 3, M. Star and H. Cain), Nice, Casino Municipal, 1 March 1912

Unperf.: Fanny Elssler, c1914 (comédie lyrique, 4, A. Bernède and P. de Choudens), F-Pn*; Aucassin et Nicolette (4), Pn*; Le Baz-Volan; La maison du péché (drame lyrique, 4, H. Ferrare, after M. Tinayre), Pn*; Riv-Nah, inc., Pn*

*

D. Boulay: 'Les auteurs de Miarka', Musica, no.38 (1905), 170–71

——: 'Miarka à L'Opéra-Comique', Musica, no.39 (1905), 187–8

H. de Curzon: 'Miarka', Le théâtre, no.169 (1906), 4–11

——: 'Xavier Leroux, Alexandre Georges, Henry Février', Le théâtre lyrique en France (Paris, 1937–9) [pubn of Poste National/Radio-Paris], iii, 124–6

RICHARD LANGHAM SMITH

Georgia. For discussion of Georgian opera see TBILISI.

Georgiadis, Nicholas (b Athens, 14 Sept 1925). British stage designer and painter of Greek birth. After studying architecture in Athens and New York, he won a British Council scholarship to study painting and theatre design at the Slade School, London, 1953–4, and later taught there, 1960–86. Since 1955 he has collaborated frequently with the choreographer Kenneth MacMillan at Sadler's Wells, the Royal Ballet, the Stuttgart Ballet and the Deutsche Oper in Berlin. He also supervised the Dyagilev ballets (sets and costumes) for Herbert Ross's film Nijinsky (1978). His two productions for Covent Garden – Aida (1968) and Les Troyens (1969) – were controversial. In 1971 he designed Cherubini's Médée for Frankfurt Opera, and in 1976 Anna Bolena for the Greek National Opera and Don Giovanni for the Athens Festival. His 1988 La clemenza di Tito, produced by Michael Cacoyannis, was a great success at Aix-en-Provence (see illustration). His designs for Aida were noted for their architectural grandeur and for their use of space, while those for the ballet Manon were

noted for their intense depiction of squalor. The use of colour, however, is the key to their spectacular beauty. Georgiadis is one of the most influential artists in the theatre. In 1984 he was made a CBE.

DAVID J. HOUGH

Gera. City in eastern Germany. Performances of musical drama and school plays date from the mid-17th century. G. H. Stölzel was Kapellmeister and court organist in Gera 1718–19, and many of his operas were performed there in the 18th century. A new theatre was opened in 1822, and productions included Der Freischütz (1822), Fidelio (1857) and Tannhäuser (1866). Since 1919 the city's own opera company has performed in the Jugendstil theatre (670 seats), which opened on 18 October 1902. Contemporary works were particularly encouraged in the 1920s and 30s, and the company still performs music that has been unjustly neglected (for example, the operas of Franz Schreker). Important premières given in Gera include Stölzel's Rosen und Dornen der Liebe (1713), Roderich Mojsisovics's Der Zauberer (1926), Wagner-Régeny's Der nackte König and Moschopulos (both 1928) and Esau und Jakob (1930) and Edmund von Borck's Napoleon (1942). First performances in Germany include Falla's La vida breve (1928) and Respighi's Lucrezia (1940). Theatre performances of all kinds are given, of which musical theatre represents roughly 50%. There are usually two or three opera productions in each season.

DIETER HÄRTWIG

Gérard, Rolf (b Berlin, 9 Aug 1909). British stage designer of German birth. The son of the Italian opera singer Mafalda Salvatini, he was educated in Germany and in Switzerland, where he graduated from Basle University as a physician after studying art and design in Berlin and Paris. He moved to England in 1936. His first opera designs were for Mozart's L'oca del Cairo at Sadler's Wells Opera (1940). During Rudolf Bing's last years at Glyndebourne he designed Carl Ebert's Così fan tutte (1948; it was also given at the Edinburgh Festival), Die Entführung aus dem Serail (1949) and Le nozze di

Set by Nicholas Georgiadis for Mozart's 'La clemenza di Tito' (Aix-en-Provence, 1988)

Rolf Gérard's design for Johann Strauss's 'Die Fledermaus': Ljuba Welitsch (left) as Rosalinde and Patrice Munsel as Adele in a production at the Metropolitan Opera House, New York, in 1950

Figaro (1950). He also designed *Figaro* for Peter Brook at Covent Garden (1950) before leaving for New York.

Although he designed a number of ballets, Gérard made his reputation as Bing's principal designer at the Metropolitan Opera, 1950–70. He designed some 20 new productions, including a revolutionary *Don Carlos* on a grey, velvet-covered set and a colourful and spacious *Die Fledermaus* (see illustration). A successful *Aida* followed in 1951, and Gérard's delicate designs for Alfred Lunt's *Così fan tutte* (1951) could still be seen on the Metropolitan stage in 1975. His work for Tyrone Guthrie's *Carmen* (1952) was also well received.

Gérard enjoyed an unconventional approach, too, and for Peter Brook's *Faust* (1953), for example, he put Méphistophélès in top hat and tails and gave the production a 19th-century setting. Brook returned in 1957 to direct *Yevgeny Onegin* in Gérard's costumes and sets. Gérard's last Metropolitan production was *Orfeo ed Euridice* in 1970. He aimed always to keep the stage uncluttered without sacrificing atmosphere, and to that end he paid particular attention to stage furniture and props.

DAVID J. HOUGH

Gergiyev, Valery (Abissalovich) (*b* Moscow, 2 May 1953). Russian-Ossetian conductor. Brought up in Ordzhonikidze (now Vladikavkaz), North Ossetia, he studied at the Ordzhonikidze Music College and the Leningrad Conservatory. On graduation in 1977 he became assistant conductor to Yury Temirkanov, then artistic director, at the Kirov Theatre, Leningrad (now Mariinsky, St Petersburg). He won second prize in the Herbert von Karajan conducting competition the same year, and was chief conductor of the State SO of Armenia, 1981–5. In 1988 he succeeded Temirkanov as chief conductor and artistic director of the Kirov company. In this position Gergiyev, whose powerful style and concentration show complete identification with the music he performs, has instigated many bold ventures, including festivals of Musorgsky (1989) and Prokofiev (1991) and a partnership with the Royal Opera of London; productions include *Boris Godunov* (Andrey Tarkovsky), *Otello* (Moshinsky), *War and Peace* (Graham Vick) and *The Fiery Angel* (David Freeman).

MARTYN BRABBINS

Gerhard, Roberto (*b* Valls, Catalonia, 25 Sept 1896; *d* Cambridge, 5 Jan 1970). Spanish composer, naturalized British, of Franco-Swiss descent. He studied in Switzerland for a commercial career, but in 1915 went back to Spain as a pupil of Granados and Pedrell. He later went to Vienna to study with Schoenberg, an unusual step for a Spanish composer, moving to Berlin when Schoenberg did in 1924. Gerhard returned in 1929 to Barcelona, where he became closely identified with the heritage and aspirations of Catalonia. After the defeat of the Republicans in 1939 he left Spain and settled in England, at Cambridge, where he remained, taking British nationality in 1960.

Gerhard's single opera, *The Duenna*, was composed in 1945–7 to his own libretto, based on Sheridan. First performed in a BBC broadcast on 23 February 1949, the work was not staged until 21 January 1992 at the Teatro Lírico Nacional, Madrid. This three-act comic opera, set in Seville, centres round the love of two couples: Don Antonio (tenor) and Donna Luisa (soprano), Don Ferdinand (baritone) and Donna Clara (soprano). Luisa is unwillingly betrothed to a man she has never met, while Clara's stepmother plans to sent Clara to a convent, so depriving her of her inheritance. The plot involves much disguise and many misunderstandings, but the opera ends happily with the lovers united. *The Duenna* unfolds as a series of set pieces, clearly related to the song or dance forms of Spanish folk music, and with themes linked to character or situation. Scored for full orchestra, the music is largely tonal, using long-term key relationships to dramatic and often moving effect. The opera represents Gerhard's last extended look at his Spanish inheritance, which thereafter co-existed with the acquired techniques of his maturity. Only its occasional dramatic flaws (which he would undoubtedly have taken steps to correct, had a stage performance been proposed during his lifetime) have prejudiced its inclusion in the repertory.

*

D. Drew: 'Gerhard's "Duenna", and Sheridan's', *Opera*, xlii (1991), 1393–402

SUSAN BRADSHAW

Gerl, Barbara [née Reisinger] (*b* Vienna or ?Pressburg [now Bratislava], 1770; *d* Mannheim, 25 May 1806). Austrian singer and actress. By 1780 she was a member of Georg Wilhelm's troupe, playing in Moravia and Silesia; she is listed in the Gotha *Theater-Kalender* for

1781: 'children's roles, and sings in operettas'. Later she rose from soubrette roles to 'first dancer' and player of queens etc. The company performed in Vienna and provincial Austrian towns in the 1780s. In 1789 she joined Schikaneder's company at Regensburg, making her début as Kalliste in a German version of Guglielmi's *La sposa fedele* (*Robert und Kalliste*), then went with Franz Xaver Gerl (whom she married later that year) to Vienna when Schikaneder became director at the Freihaus-Theater auf der Wieden. Barbara Gerl took the principal female roles in Schikaneder's sequel to Martín y Soler's *Una cosa rara*, *Der Fall ist noch weit seltner*, in *Robert und Kalliste* and in Schikaneder's *Der Stein der Weisen* (1790). She also performed in spoken plays. On 30 September 1791 she achieved her one link with immortality by creating the part of Papagena in *Die Zauberflöte*. She and her husband appear to have left Schikaneder's company in 1793, were at Brünn (Brno), 1794–1801, and from 1802 in Mannheim.

A. Orel: 'Sarastro ... Hr. Gerl/Ein altes Weib ... Mad. Gerl', *MJb 1955*, 66–89
——: 'Neue Gerliana', *MJb 1957*, 212–22

For further bibliography *see* GERL, FRANZ XAVER.

PETER BRANSCOMBE

Gerl [Görl], Franz Xaver (*b* Andorf, Upper Austria, 30 Nov 1764; *d* Mannheim, 9 March 1827). Austrian bass and composer. The son of a village schoolmaster and organist, by 1777 he was an alto chorister at Salzburg, where he must have been a pupil of Leopold Mozart. He was at the Salzburg Gymnasium, 1778–82, and then studied logic and physics at the university. In autumn 1785 he went to Erlangen as a bass, joining the theatrical company of Ludwig Schmidt, who had earlier been at Salzburg. In 1786 he joined G. F. W. Grossmann's company, performing in the Rhineland, and specialized in 'comic roles in comedies and Singspiels'. By 1787 he was a member of Schikaneder's company at Regensburg, making his début in Sarti's *Wenn zwei sich streiten* (*Fra i due litiganti*) and appearing as Osmin in *Die Entführung*. From summer 1789 he was a member of Schikaneder's company at the Freihaus-Theater auf der Wieden, Vienna. On 2 September 1789 he married the soprano Barbara Reisinger. His name first appears as one of the composers of *Der dumme Gärtner aus dem Gebirge* (*Der dumme Anton*), Schikaneder's first new production at his new theatre, on 12 July 1789; it is unlikely that this was Gerl's first theatre score since Schikaneder would hardly have entrusted such an important task to a novice. *Der dumme Anton* proved so successful that it had no fewer than six sequels; Gerl certainly performed in two of these, though he and Schack may not have written all the scores. Between 1789 and 1793 Gerl wrote music for several more plays and Singspiels.

Gerl played a wide variety of parts in plays and operas (including Don Giovanni and Figaro in German) during his Vienna years, though he is most often associated with the role of Sarastro in *Die Zauberflöte*, which he created on 30 September 1791 and continued to sing at least until November 1792 (the 83rd performance, announced by Schikaneder as the 100th). The Gerls appear to have left the Freihaus-Theater in 1793; they were at Brünn (Brno), 1794–1801, and from 1802 Gerl was a member of the Mannheim Hoftheater. Apart from operatic roles he also appeared frequently in plays; he retired in 1826. That year he married Magdalena Deng-

ler (née Reisinger – his first wife's elder sister), the widow of Georg Dengler, director of the Mainz theatre.

Although the paucity of the surviving material and the difficulty of identifying Gerl's contribution to joint scores make it impossible to evaluate him as a composer, the works he wrote were popular in their day. His career as a singer is better documented. When Schröder, the greatest actor-manager of his age, went to Vienna in 1791 he was told not to miss hearing Schack and Gerl at Schikaneder's theatre. At the end of May he heard Wranitzky's *Oberon*, in which both were singing, and thought Gerl's singing of the Oracle 'very good'. Mozart's high regard for his qualities is evident in the aria 'Per questa bella mano' (K612), written for Gerl in March 1791, and above all in Sarastro's music. Mozart's friendly relationship with Gerl is attested by the fact that Gerl was one of the singers who is said, on Mozart's last afternoon, to have joined the dying composer in an impromptu sing-through of the Requiem (the others were Schack and Mozart's brother-in-law Franz Hofer).

See also DUMME GÄRTNER AUS DEM GEBIRGE, DER and STEIN DER WEISEN, DER.

Singspiels, performed in Vienna, Freihaus-Theater auf der Wieden, unless otherwise stated

Der dumme Gärtner aus dem Gebirge, oder Die zween Anton (2, E. Schikaneder), 12 July 1789, vs (Bonn, n.d.), collab. B. Schack [1st 'Anton' Spl]
Jakob und Nannerl, oder Der angenehme Traum (Oper, 3, Schikaneder), 25 July 1789; also attrib. Pecháček, Schack
Die verdeckten Sachen (2, Schikaneder), 26 Sept 1789, vs *I-Fc*, songs A-Wgm, collab. J. G. Lickl and Schack [2nd 'Anton' Spl]
Was macht der Anton im Winter? (2, Schikaneder), 6 Jan 1790, vs *I-Fc*, songs A-Wgm, collab. Schack and others [3rd 'Anton' Spl]
Don Quixotte und Sancho Pansa (3, K. L. Gieseke), 17 April 1790
Der Frühling, oder Der Anton ist noch nicht tot (2, Schikaneder), 18 June 1790, songs Wgm, collab. Schack and others [4th 'Anton' Spl]
Der Stein der Weisen, oder Die Zauberinsel (heroisch-komische Oper, 2, Schikaneder), 11 Sept 1790, *D-B*, vs *I-Fc*, collab. Mozart and Schack
Die Wiener Zeitung (3, Gieseke), 12 Jan 1791, collab. Schack
Anton bei Hofe, oder Das Namensfest (2, Schikaneder), 4 June 1791, collab. Schack and others [5th 'Anton' Spl]
Das Schlaraffenland (2, Gieseke), 23 June 1792, collab. Schack
Der Renegat, oder Anton in der Türkei (2, Schikaneder), 15 Sept 1792, collab. Schack and others [6th 'Anton' Spl]
Der wohltätige Derwisch, oder Die Schellenkappe (3, Schikaneder), 10 Sept 1793, collab. Henneberg, ?W. Müller and Schack; as Die Zaubertrommel, *D-MH*
Graf Balbarone (3, Franzky), Brünn; as Die Maskerade, oder Liebe macht alle Stände gleich, 9 Dec 1797

NDB (K. M. Pisarowitz)
F. L. W. Meyer: *Friedrich Ludwig Schröder: Beitrag zur Kunde des Menschen und des Künstlers* (Hamburg, 1819)
E. Komorzynski: *Emanuel Schikaneder: ein Beitrag zur Geschichte des deutschen Theaters* (Berlin, 1901, 2/1951)
O. E. Deutsch: *Das Freihaus-Theater auf der Wieden* (Vienna, 1937)
E. Komorzynski: *Der Vater der Zauberflöte: Emanuel Schikaneders Leben* (Vienna, 1948)
A. Orel: 'Sarastro ... Hr. Gerl/Ein altes Weib ... Mad. Gerl', *MJb 1955*, 66–89
——: 'Neue Gerliana', *MJb 1957*, 212–22
K. M. Pisarowitz: 'Ein Brief "Sarastros" und sonstige neueste Gerl-Miszellen', *Acta Mozartiana*, x/2 (1963), 38–42

PETER BRANSCOMBE

German, Sir **Edward** [Jones, German Edward] (*b* Whitchurch, Shropshire, 17 Feb 1862; *d* London, 11 Nov 1936). English composer. He grew up in a musical household, acquiring an early enthusiasm for the theatre from performances by itinerant entertainers. In 1880 he entered the RAM, where the violin soon ousted the organ as his principal instrument, and he became increasingly drawn towards composition, studying with Ebenezer Prout. Among his works performed there was the chamber operetta *The Two Poets* (1886; later revised as *The Rival Poets*), subsequently produced at St George's Hall and taken on tour by the students. Encouraged, German considered writing a curtain-raiser for the Carl Rosa company. Nothing materialized, however, and after leaving the RAM he spent a lean period teaching and playing in theatres, including the Savoy. An appointment, engineered by Alberto Randegger, as musical director at the Globe Theatre, and the resultant composition of music for *Richard III* (1889), brought him firmly to the fore. He had a further triumph with music for Henry Irving's production of *Henry VIII* (1892): the dances became extremely popular, exploring a mock archaic 'olde English' style with which the composer became particularly associated. During the 1890s German concentrated on writing music for plays (the impressive music for *Romeo and Juliet*, 1895, especially, demonstrates his operatic potential), symphonic works for leading festivals, songs and light instrumental pieces.

His operatic ambitions persisted, but a proposed opera on a Hungarian subject and approaches to Richard D'Oyly Carte – including a confident offer to write 'something perhaps between Carmen and Faust' for the Royal English Opera House – came to nothing. The rise in German's operatic fortunes began when Carte commissioned him to finish *The Emerald Isle* (1901), left incomplete at Sullivan's death. Following this successful endeavour German wrote his best-known operetta, *Merrie England* (1902), which led many to consider him Sullivan's operatic heir. *A Princess of Kensington* (1903), hampered by a convoluted plot, was, however, less well received. For a time German concentrated on other forms, returning to operetta with *Tom Jones* (1907), arguably his finest achievement in the genre. His final operetta, *Fallen Fairies* (1909), a collaboration with W. S. Gilbert on a variant of the so-called lozenge plot repeatedly rejected by Sullivan, achieved only a *succès d'estime*. Thereafter his output diminished, virtually ceasing after 1922. As a conductor of his own music, however, he remained active until his health declined in the late 1920s. During later years he prepared concert versions of his most popular operettas and produced abridgments for broadcasting. He was knighted in 1928.

German continued the Savoy tradition into the 20th century, maintaining the integrity of British operetta in the face of the increasing popularity of musical comedy. His music may not match Sullivan's for variety and sheer wit; nonetheless, his flair for orchestration is comparable and in vocal writing German generally shows the greater sympathy, his lyrical ballads revealing a romantic warmth that strikes a distinctive note. Ranging beyond the charming, though historically spurious and sometimes mannered, 'olde English' style, German's beautifully crafted, elegant music secures his place among the finest British operetta composers.

See also MERRIE ENGLAND and TOM JONES (ii).

all operettas

The Two Poets (2, W. H. Scott), London, RAM, July 1886, autograph frags. T. Rees collection, Machynlleth, Powys; vs (London, 1901); rev. as The Rival Poets, or The Love Charm, London, St George's Hall, 1901, vs (London, 1900)

The Emerald Isle, or The Caves of Carrig-Cleena (2, B. Hood), London, Savoy, 27 April 1901, autograph, Rees collection; vs (London, 1901) [completion of work by Sullivan]

Merrie England (2, Hood), London, Savoy, 2 April 1902, autograph, Rees collection; vs (London, 1902)

A Princess of Kensington (2, Hood), London, Savoy, 22 Jan 1903, autograph, Rees collection; vs (London, 1903)

Tom Jones (3, A. M. Thompson and R. Courtneidge, after H. Fielding; C. H. Taylor), Manchester, Prince's, 30 March 1907, autograph, D. R. Hulme collection, Aberystwyth; vs (London, 1907)

Fallen Fairies, or The Wicked World (2, W. S. Gilbert), London, Savoy, 15 Dec 1909, *US-NYpm**; vs (London, 1909); temporarily retitled Moon Fairies after initial run

GänzlBMT; *GänzlMT*

'Edward German: a Biographical Sketch', *MT*, xlv (1904), 20–24

S. Mackinlay: *Light Opera* (London, 1926)

W. H. Scott: *Edward German: an Intimate Biography* (London, 1932)

T. F. Dunhill: 'Edward German 1862–1936', *MT*, lxxvii (1936), 1073–7

R. Elkin: 'Edward German', *The Music Masters*, ed. A. L. Bacharach, iii (London, 1952)

E. Irving: *Cue for Music* (London, 1959)

G. Hughes: *Composers of Operetta* (London, 1962)

A. Hyman: *Sullivan and his Satellites* (London, 1978)

R. Traubner: *Operetta: a Theatrical History* (London, 1984)

J. Brown: 'Edward German', *British Music Society Journal*, vii (1985), 11–16

D. Guyver: 'Edward Elgar and Edward German', *Elgar Society Journal*, iv/2 (1985), 15–18; iv/3 (1985), 10–17

B. Rees: *A Musical Peacemaker: the Life and Work of Sir Edward German* (Bourne End, 1986)   DAVID RUSSELL HULME

Germania. *Dramma lirico* in a prologue, two acts, an 'intermezzo sinfonico' and an epilogue by ALBERTO FRANCHETTI to a libretto by LUIGI ILLICA; Milan, Teatro alla Scala, 11 March 1902.

After giving up the *Tosca* libretto to Puccini, Franchetti received a new libretto from Illica, who since their early collaboration on *Cristoforo Colombo* (1892) had been his close friend. The new libretto was in grand opera style, differing astonishingly from Illica's works for Puccini and showing similarities only to *Maria Antonietta* (a libretto Puccini had discarded). The combination of a love triangle among students, who, as members of the secret 'Louisenbund', are working for the liberation of Germany from Napoleon's occupation, with historical events is reminiscent of dramatic models from 19th-century grand opera. The work relies heavily on German local colour. To depict the atmosphere of Germany under the Napoleonic wars, the composer made use of musical quotations from German popular and students' songs; Weber's setting of *Lützows wilde Jagd* by Theodor Körner (who appears as a character in Act 2) is quoted extensively. The battle of Leipzig is represented by a symphonic interlude for large orchestra (including Wagner tubas) with chorus. During the 'intermezzo sinfonico' symbolic projections – described by Illica in his libretto – represent the rebirth of a free Germany, seen through Germanic mythology.

Germania had its première under Toscanini with Caruso as the student Federico, and was to become Franchetti's most successful work. However, despite a variety of Wagnerian techniques of composition, the music does not achieve a stylistic unity of its own; the traditional genre which combines a large historical drama with a love conflict seems to contradict some of Franchetti's more advanced musical techniques.

JÜRGEN MAEHDER

German Reed, Thomas. *See* REED, THOMAS GERMAN.

Germany, Austria. The multiple lines of development that opera followed in German-speaking lands up to the middle of the 19th century reflect not only the absence of a single or dominant tradition of musico-dramatic practice but also a general state of cultural and political decentralization. The pre-eminence gained by Vienna by the end of the 18th century in the cultivation of instrumental music was never equalled by a German operatic centre. Further, even in situations where one can speak of German opera (as opposed to opera in Germany) – notably Hamburg during the first third of the 18th century or North Germany during the last third – opera in the vernacular still depended to some extent on foreign models. Only with Wagner's music dramas (themselves deeply embedded in German instrumental practice, and without successors) did a purely national and indigenous conception of opera obliterate the art form's undertone of foreignness.

1. The beginnings. 2. The 18th century. 3. The early 19th century. 4. 1830–83. 5. 1883–1918. 6. 1919–45. 7. Since 1945.

1. THE BEGINNINGS. A variety of stage representations involving music antedate the arrival of Italian opera on German soil: sacred dramas, Latin school dramas, court entertainments, ballets and plays with music in the popular theatre. Musically, the offerings of the 'englische Comödianten' who came to Germany via Holland and Denmark towards the end of the 16th century never progressed beyond strophic texts set to a single, familiar tune. Similarly, several forms of court-sponsored musical theatre, namely the 'Singballett' and the 'Wirtschaft', made only minimal use of vocal music.

Sacred dramas in either German or Latin maintained a life of their own in schools and religious organizations, but in the course of the 17th century took on more and more features of secular opera, both musical and scenographic. A complementary feature of German-language opera during the century was a preference for biblical themes. The situation at Halle is instructive. Duke August, a strong advocate of German, built a 'Comödienhaus' and set up a little theatre in his residence (with advanced stage machinery) for German plays with songs, which were ample enough musically by 1675 to be called 'Singe-Spiele' and in which stories drawn from the Bible preponderated. In 1664 he also built a theatre for school dramas, and when the German opera productions had to be abandoned in 1680 these took their place on festive court occasions.

For most of the 17th century, operatic activity of any kind in German lands was sporadic and directly dependent on Italian example. The first performances of Italian opera took place at Salzburg in 1614 under Archbishop Marcus Sitticus (who had been brought up at Rome). The first German opera, Heinrich Schütz's *Dafne* (to a libretto adapted from Rinuccini by Martin Opitz) was an occasional piece given in 1627 at Torgau, near Dresden. More important than such isolated initiatives were the first efforts towards a sustained commitment to the cultivation of opera. In 1651 the Munich court had a granary converted to an opera house, initiating a brilliant period of Italian opera, ballet and concerts that ended abruptly with the departure of Elector Maximilian II Emanuel to the Netherlands on his appointment as governor in 1691. The court at Innsbruck under the Habsburg Archduke Ferdinand Karl completed a new theatre, built to modern Venetian standards, in 1654 and installed an Italian opera troupe there in 1659 – the first independent opera house and first permanent operatic company in German-speaking lands.

Wandering troupes of different nationalities offered a variety of musical works at court and civic stages throughout Germany, and by the second half of the 17th century itinerant Italian companies specializing in opera were making their way north of the Alps. But the most characteristic form of opera in Germany were the lavish and varied productions sponsored by courts in order to mark specific festive occasions – a sovereign's birthday or name-day, a wedding, or a state visit of an important dignitary.

The musical or theatrical inclinations of a new ruler often spelt the beginning or end of operatic activity at a German court. At Salzburg, opera performances – a regular part of court life since 1687 – ceased with the death of Archbishop Franz Anton in 1727 and resumed only when Count von Schrattenbach became Archbishop in 1753. Electress Anna Maria Luisa personally supported the regular cultivation of Italian opera at Düsseldorf from 1695 until an economic collapse called a halt in 1713. Three music-loving dukes at Weissenfels promoted German opera (first produced at court in 1680) at a private theatre funded entirely from the court purse from 1684 to 1730. At Hanover Elector Ernst August built three separate theatres between 1678 and 1690 (the last modelled on the Teatro Olimpico at Vicenza); admission to all three was free, and performances were not tied to specific celebrations, but the production of opera under these sanguine conditions ceased with the elector's death in 1698.

New opera houses were built or created by modifying existing structures at several other courts during the second half of the 17th century: Dresden (1667), Darmstadt (1670), Wolfenbüttel (1688), Brunswick (1690) and Düsseldorf (1695). The new Comödienhaus at Dresden seated nearly 2000 and included the most modern lighting and stage machinery. Here Elector Johann Georg III established a standing Italian opera company in 1685. At Vienna, where the earliest court opera celebrated the birthday of Ferdinand II in 1625, entertainments including opera were presented at a variety of locations – the Hoftheater, the Theatersaal der Favorita, an outdoor stage at Laxenburg, and even in private chambers. A new theatre was built at Vienna in 1666–7 for the marriage of Leopold I and Margherita of Spain, celebrated with the most spectacular operatic event of the century, Cesti's *Il pomo d'oro*, performed in two parts on 12 and 14 July 1668 at a cost of 300 000 gulden. When the court left Vienna for various reasons (state visits, coronations, the Turkish siege of 1683 or the plague of 1679–82) it brought operatic resources with it to other cities. A high point of this practice was the coronation of Charles VI at Prague as King of Bohemia in 1723, celebrated with a lavish production of Fux's *Costanza e fortezza*.

Beginning with the arrival of Eleonora Gonzaga at Vienna in 1622, the most important musical posts in the imperial household were filled by Italians. Several other large courts that cultivated Italian opera tended to follow this practice when engaging singers, but talented German composers, who were the mainstay in providing new sacred music for court devotions, often assumed positions of leadership in operatic establishments. While court Kapellmeister at Munich, J. C. Kerll helped inaugurate a new opera house in 1657 with his first opera, *Oronte*. He wrote ten further operas before departing for Vienna in 1673; here operatic affairs were already firmly in Italian hands, and Kerll's creative talents were confined to sacred music (including a Jesuit school drama).

The operas of most Italian composers employed at German courts during the 17th century are for the most part indistinguishable from those that were setting the standard on the peninsula, and which continued to be imported from Italian stages (particularly the works of Cesti). Exception must be made for the operas Agostino Steffani composed for the electoral courts at Munich, Hanover and Düsseldorf between 1681 and 1709. Their unusual contrapuntal density and the abundance of duets and larger ensembles, combined with Steffani's command of Italian vocal suavity (he himself had been a singer at St Mark's), were exemplary for native north German composers who gained prominence around and after the turn of the century. Between 1695 and 1699 Hamburg heard German translation of all six of the operas Steffani composed for Hanover. Two of his texts are based on subjects drawn from German history.

While Germany's large and small courts dominated operatic life throughout the 1600s, publicly supported enterprises in several municipalities took root towards the end of the century. In 1677 a theatre was opened in the Ballhaus at Breslau for the use of wandering troupes, and 42 operas were given between 1725 and 1734 by an Italian company there. At Leipzig, the Dresden court Kapellmeister Strungk embarked on a venture largely funded by his wife and two business associates. He organized an Italian opera company to perform there during the fairs, and in 1693 built a new theatre, the Opernhaus auf dem Brühl. The enterprise received a subvention from the Elector, who regarded it as a conservatory for his own Kapelle and occasionally attended performances, in which university students and choristers participated. Direction passed in 1702 to Telemann, who left in 1705 but continued to supply operas as late as 1719, a year before the enterprise closed down.

Germany's most important civic stage, established at Hamburg in 1678, quickly became the principal centre for German-language opera. Although local diplomats and nobles were involved, the undertaking was essentially civic in nature, with frequent changes of management. A long list of distinguished composers lent their skills, and many were involved in some additional way, as singers (Förtsch, Mattheson), harpsichordists (Mattheson, Handel, Graupner, Kunzen) or Kapellmeister (Theile, Franck, Kusser, Keiser, Mattheson, Telemann). Nearly all the librettists were local figures. At first they concentrated on the kinds of biblical theme typical of earlier German operas, apparently to mollify the angry opposition of church authorities to opera in any form at Hamburg. But by the time Keiser moved there, nearly 20 years later, Italian models had begun to figure prominently; increasingly, texts mixed Italian and German arias. The emphasis fell on an eclectic variety in style and expression, ranging from militantly simple German songs through the pathos of accompanied recitative to the breathtaking virtuosity of the bravura aria.

2. THE 18TH CENTURY. By the time the Hamburg enterprise closed in 1738, travelling companies purveying German, French and Italian repertories had come to play a significant role in German theatrical life. The better German troupes concentrated on spoken offerings, while Italian companies tended to specialize in opera, both serious and comic. The various companies of the Mingotti brothers Pietro and Angelo played before court audiences at Dresden and Copenhagen, plied the fairs at Leipzig and appeared at festive state occasions, such as the crowning of Franz I at Frankfurt. Pietro's wife Caterina Regina's vocal gifts were such that the Dresden court opera hired her away from her husband's troupe.

Italian court opera reached a high point at Dresden during Hasse's years there under Friedrich August II. From 1734 to the beginning of the Seven Years War in 1756 Hasse conducted a new or revised work of his own (usually an *opera seria*) nearly every year, many for Carnival, in productions that became increasingly lavish. The set designer Giuseppe Galli-Bibiena arrived in 1747 and in 1750 supervised renovations to the opera house. But under Friedrich August III, pomp and extravagance became a thing of the past: the Italian opera and comedy were dissolved, as was the ballet.

Allegiance to Italian opera continued unabated at the Viennese court into the reign of Maria Theresa, but other forms of opera and ballet grew considerably in importance during the 18th century. Italian opera and French ballet ministered to an audience drawn largely from the nobility in the small but aristocratic confines of the Burgtheater. The other theatre under direct imperial control, the Kärntnertor, was larger and less exclusive. From 1728 to 1741 private companies to whom the theatre was rented gave Italian comic operas and improvised German plays with intermixed music. Ballet and singing figured prominently in the repertory of the Kurz company, including Haydn's lost operatic farce *Der neue krumme Teufel* of about 1752. That year, incensed by the indecency and bald social criticism in Kurz's offerings, the empress summarily banned all such spectacles.

At the Burgtheater, in addition to opera and ballet, a troupe of French actors was maintained by the court, whose offerings expanded in the 1750s to include the latest *opéras-comiques* from Paris. Gluck arranged and, increasingly, recomposed these works. His so-called 'reform' operas for Vienna, *Orfeo ed Euridice* (1762) and *Alceste* (1767), absorbed something of the unadorned musical style of these works, but also share in important French-derived modifications to serious opera already found in the works of Traetta and Jommelli for Parma, Vienna and Stuttgart. The brilliant international careers of Gluck and also Hasse were duplicated by only a few other central European composers (for example, J. G. Naumann) and always within the system of court-supported serious opera.

At Berlin Italian opera flourished under the despotic control of Frederick the Great upon his accession in 1740. The king's taste was confined to the operas of Hasse and of his emulator C. H. Graun, Frederick's Kapellmeister. No detail concerning a production or even a singer's personal life was too insignificant for the king's attention and control; several of Graun's librettos were based on Frederick's own French prose drafts. After Graun's last opera in 1756 and the rigours of the Seven Years War, the king lost interest in his opera company. Despite a bright moment or two under J. F. Reichardt, the Italian opera dwindled to insignificance by the end of the century, largely replaced by the German theatre in Berlin, which received the strong support of Frederick's successor, Friedrich Wilhelm II.

The political watershed of the war years of 1756 to 1763 also separated the tentative and insignificant stirrings of a new popular form of German opera from a rapid growth and deepening of its artistic and institutional importance everywhere German was spoken during the last third of the century. Although English ballad operas provided sources for many of the earliest, farcically imbued comic operas, notably J. C. Standfuss's *Der Teufel ist los* (1752), after the war the chief textual inspiration came from the idealized rustic innocence of the *opéra comique*. The German comic operas produced at Leipzig, Weimar and later Berlin by the Koch theatrical company from 1767 to 1773 proved irresistible in the simple charm of C. F. Weisse's sentimental, good-hearted plots (fully encapsulated and worked out according to traditional theatrical canons in the works' spoken dialogue) and of the equally engaging musical directness of J. A. Hiller's scores (whose appeal from simplicity was far more an exigency of the limited vocal abilities of the performers at hand than an ideological stance).

Apart from its spread through travelling companies, Italian opera continued to be cultivated throughout the 18th century primarily in court settings. The 'Singspiel', as the new German phenomenon has come to be called, owed its life and lineaments to the German system of private theatrical entrepreneurship, called *Prinzipalshaft*, whereby an impresario (or *Prinzipal*) organized and guided a group of actors at his own risk and profit, sometimes securing a privilege from a court or town council allowing a more or less extensive stay in one place, sometimes wandering from one small centre to the next. Leipzig, where the new genre was born, attracted rival troupes during its commercial fairs; it also drew the kind of middle-class audience that, together with its own population of townspeople and university students, were the true free-market arbiters of the new genre's popularity and economic value to theatrical managers. From then on, no viable troupe could afford to ignore the Singspiel, and a typical repertory and company quickly came to consist of a musical as well as a straight spoken component.

Hiller and Weisse found their more or less direct imitators, but the Singspiel also struck out along several new lines. As German drama came of age, German troupes were increasingly taken into a court environment hitherto dominated by French theatre and Italian opera. The superior musical resources of the court Kapelle and the operatic traditions it represented led to a rapprochement between the Singspiel and Italian opera in the 1770s. There were successful experiments with German-language *opera seria*, initiated by C. M. Wieland's *Alceste* (1773, Weimar), set by Anton Schweitzer. Even such a work as Anton Klein's *Günther von Schwarzburg* (1777, Mannheim), with its subject drawn from Germany history and a powerful score by Ignaz Holzbauer, bears strong witness to the decisive musical role Italian *opera seria* continued to exert in German court cultures, despite the nationalistic polemics that accompanied these new operas. On another front, serious dramatic themes demanding appropriate musical resources turned to account the unique coupling of high dramatic art and improved musical resources represented by court sponsorship of German theatrical companies; the artistic issue of this marriage include the serious operas with spoken dialogue by Georg Benda at Gotha and Joseph Schuster at Dresden, and the German melodrama.

Several cultural centres began shifting musical resources from Italian to German opera during the final decades of the century, prompted by the latter's economic as well as its real or potential artistic attractions. After the dissolution of the expensive *seria* establishment at Dresden, both Italian and German comic opera – first the one, then the other, then both – received court support, although in each case under a private impresario. At Stuttgart *opera seria* formed an essential ingredient in the self-indulgent and ruinous sumptuary ways of Duke Carl Eugen, stirring up such public animosity that the court was forced to move to Ludwigsburg from 1764 to 1767, when economizing measures were finally taken. Italian *opera buffa* and German plays and operas, until then supplied by travelling companies, found a home and court support when a small theatre, the Kleines Schauspielhaus auf der Planie, was built in 1779.

The most idealistic efforts to foster German drama and opera came from Emperor Joseph II at Vienna. His National Theatre for German drama, established in 1776, was supplemented two years later by the National Singspiel. Although it boasted the best resources of any stage in German-speaking lands, the National Singspiel lasted only five seasons and was replaced at the Burgtheater by a court-supported *opera buffa* company. The strongly italianate leanings of the Viennese public, the considerable resources of the court, the virtual absence of *opera seria* (which Joseph refused to subsidize), and the fortuitous presence of such composers as Mozart and Salieri made the Burgtheater the leading stage for *opera buffa* in the 1780s. At the same time, Vienna paralleled other German and Austrian court centres in that German opera continued as a publicly supported alternative to Italian opera. After the fall of the National Singspiel the Kärntnertortheater was let out to private German companies, and after 1785 it was once again taken under court subvention and control for three years.

The situation in Berlin, already mentioned, was similarly characteristic: the Italian opera establishment remained entirely under the financial and artistic control of the court while German opera and theatre retained a significant economic connection with the paying public. In 1784 Friedrich Wilhelm II created the Berlin National Theater as a way of stabilizing and supporting the Döbbelin Company, providing a yearly subvention and use of the Theater in der Gensdarmenmarkt. With its rise under J. J. Engel and A. W. Iffland, the enterprise secured a leading position for Berlin in the cultivation of German opera and drama that continues to this day. At the same time, the repertory of the National Theater came fully under the sway of Italian, Austrian and to a lesser extent French operas in German translation, a situation duplicated on nearly all important stages in northern and southern Germany, and one that persisted throughout the first half of the 19th century.

The most original and decisive point of continuity from the 18th century to the 19th within the sphere of German opera came from the intensive transformations that befell popular operatic traditions in Austria. Philipp Hafner's *Megära, die förchterliche Hexe* (1762; set 1764, composer unknown) served as a point of departure for reconciling the spectacle and indecencies of the mid-century popular theatre with the more refined literary tone and musical resources of *opera buffa* and Singspiel. Three private theatres that fostered such developments opened in the suburban districts of Vienna between 1781 and 1788: the Leopoldstadt, Wieden and Josefstadt. Not since the Hamburg enterprise had a cultural situation been as receptive to a synthesis of traditions, possibilities that were brought to a peak in Mozart's *Die Zauberflöte* (1791).

3. THE EARLY 19TH CENTURY. The situation of opera in Germany and Austria at the turn of the century, despite the political and economic consequences of the Revolutionary and Napoleonic years, remained deeply informed by 18th-century developments. Court theatres retained much of their significance, but now depended on a broadened economic base. Already in 1789 the Italian opera in Berlin had begun charging admission. The rivalry for dominance between German and Italian companies in an era of declining resources is amply attested by Carl Maria von Weber's experiences from 1817 as head of the German opera at Dresden, by then one of two 'departments' of the royal opera. The Italian company at Dresden was finally dismissed in 1832. At smaller courts, as in the preceding century, the enthusiasm of the prince was decisive. Grand Duke Ludwig I at Darmstadt functioned as his own music- and stage-director, more or less compelling attendance from his courtiers by deducting the cost of subscription from their salaries in advance. German opera and particularly Wagner's works flourished under the music- and theatre-loving Duke Ernst II of Saxe-Coburg and Gotha, himself a composer. His opera *Santa Chiara* (1854, with Liszt conducting) was much praised by Meyerbeer, made its way to many other German stages, and received 60 performances in Paris. In 1853 Ernst offered the position of Kapellmeister to Wagner.

Many larger cities took direct control of public stages previously under private management, creating an institution still common in Germany, the Stadttheater. Although a direct counterpart to the Hoftheater, it proved far more responsive to public taste. Travelling companies remained numerous, but were always courting ruin; when they attempted opera, it was normally with resources and on a scale far more modest than either the civic or court theatres.

Although many German composers of operas functioned in traditional roles as Kapellmeister or music director to an operatic establishment, others were often only loosely connected with the theatre. The difficulties composers like Beethoven and Schumann experienced in trying their hand at opera under such circumstances were duplicated endlessly by a whole gamut of lesser musicians. And in general the pressure of successful works from Italy and France was such that very few German or Austrian composers were able to establish themselves at home as theatrical composers. The sensation created by Rossini's *Tancredi* at Vienna in 1816 set a decisive tone for a receptivity to his other works and, later, to those of Donizetti and Bellini. Meyerbeer's grand operas enjoyed equal prestige following a production of *Robert le diable* in a German version at Berlin in 1832, a triumph that also earned the composer the title of court Kapellmeister there.

Stylistically, German opera pursued several lines of development suggested by the state of affairs at the end of the 18th century. The impact of French Revolutionary opera is everywhere apparent in Beethoven's *Fidelio* (1805, rev. 1806, 1814), as is the imprint of *Die Zauberflöte*. E. T. A. Hoffmann was fond of referring to Mozart as the 'inimitable creator of Romantic opera', and in practice Mozart was the only equal of the later masters of Italian and French opera dominating German

repertories before Wagner's ascendancy. The most spectacular success of the era, Weber's *Der Freischütz* (1821), despite its intensive exploration of the supernatural and local colour, is more deeply indebted to the 'Romanticism' Dent has detected in the French 'rescue operas' of the 1790s than to the 'Romantik' that grew out of Austrian magic operas and found expression in Hoffmann's *Undine* (1816). It was this tradition, continued in the operas of Spohr, Marschner and young Wagner, that broke with the 18th-century theatrical ideal still espoused by Beethoven, that the theatre should 'educate and awake noble sentiments'. The triumph of family and social stability came to seem tame next to metaphysical redemption through the sacrifice of a spotless woman. In a more realistic vein, German comic opera deriving from the Singspiel tradition continued in the works of Schenk, Wenzel Müller and later Lortzing, Kreutzer, Flotow and Nicolai.

4. 1830–83. The ideal of German opera, espoused with new fervour by Wagner, Schumann and others of their generation (one of Wagner's earliest essays, written in 1834, is on 'Die deutsche Oper'), remained subject to contradictions, including the greater fecundity of manifestos than of works. There was also the problem that, in order to be properly German, a qualifying work would have to distinguish itself from French and Italian traditions, while in order to be judged properly operatic it would have to measure up to standards created by those traditions. Further, the appeal of German opera was that of a national totem in a nation that did not yet exist as an entity, whose operatic activities were distributed among the court theatres of the various kingdoms, prince bishoprics and electorates (the most important during this period being Dresden, Berlin and Munich, with Vienna some way behind) and the city theatres of the free towns (such as Hamburg). It is a tempting coincidence that the first complete performance of Wagner's *Ring*, in 1876, came just five years after the achievement of German unity under the Prussian king as emperor. Moreover, Wagner's success also resolved the other paradoxes mentioned here, in that it was both manifesto and work at once, and in that it discovered, according to his own view, a foundation for German opera not in the theatre, where the German record was sporadic and ramshackle, but in a sphere where German honour was indisputable: in the concert hall, in the symphonies, and especially the Ninth Symphony, of Beethoven.

Of course, Italy was just as disunited as Germany until very much the same time, but in Italy at least the repertory was homogeneous and national. The case in Germany may be illustrated by the schedule at Würzburg during Wagner's year there in 1833–4, when alongside five German operas (*Fidelio*, two Webers, two Marschners) were performed five by French or French-orientated composers (Hérold, Cherubini, Auber, Meyerbeer) and two by Italians (Rossini, Paer). In Vienna much more Italian music would have been heard, Italians remaining as dominant in the opera there as they had been in Mozart's time, but in Germany there was no rival to the glamour of Paris, and of the new Opéra opened in 1821. It was for Paris, and in French, that Meyerbeer wrote all his mature works (the only exception was a lesser Singspiel, *Ein Feldlager in Schlesien*, written for the opening in 1844 of the new opera house in Berlin, where he was general music director). It was also in Paris that Wagner hoped to make his operatic fortune, when he stayed there in 1839–42.

Wagner's move back from Paris has become a symbol, as it became a cause, of a new age in German opera. Lines of descent remained from Meyerbeer, and from Weber and Marschner, but Wagner's achievement now was new in bringing together grand opera and Romantic opera in *Der fliegende Holländer* (1843), *Tannhäuser* (1845) and *Lohengrin* (1850), the first two of which he presented during his time in Dresden. While there he invited Spontini to conduct *La vestale* in 1844, but there was also the opportunity to build up a more consistent, personal and German pantheon: Gluck, Mozart and Beethoven. Among the other German opera composers of the period, Nicolai died young in 1849, with *Die lustige Weiber von Windsor* (1849) his only work created in German, and Lortzing two years later. Marschner's *Kaiser Adolph von Nassau* was produced in Dresden during Wagner's time there, in 1845, but it was his earlier works, *Der Vampyr* (1828) and *Hans Heiling* (1833), that were repeatedly performed. Schumann's *Genoveva* (1850), prompted by what Wagner was doing in Dresden, was a solitary achievement.

By the middle of the century Wagner's dominance of German opera, even if his radical works all lay ahead, was clear, and for the next four decades the history of German and Austrian opera houses is largely the history of when and where his works were introduced, along with those of the Italians (joined by Verdi from the 1850s, though he never wrote for a German theatre) and Meyerbeer. *Tannhäuser*, for example, reached Schwerin in 1852, Leipzig, Frankfurt and Königsberg in 1853, Rostock in 1854, Munich in 1855, Berlin in 1856, Dessau in 1857 and Stuttgart and Vienna in 1859. After his flight from Dresden in 1849, however, Wagner had no theatre of his own. *Lohengrin* owed its first performance to Liszt at Weimar, as did Cornelius's *Der Barbier von Bagdad* in 1858 (as too did Saint-Saëns' *Samson et Dalila* in 1877; another French visitor was Berlioz, whose *Béatrice et Bénédict* was commissioned for the new theatre at Baden-Baden in 1862). The accession of Ludwig II then made possible the premières in Munich of *Tristan und Isolde* (1865), *Die Meistersinger von Nürnberg* (1868), *Das Rheingold* (1869) and *Die Walküre* (1870), and the king was also the major sponsor of Wagner's purpose-built theatre at Bayreuth, where the complete *Ring* (1876) and *Parsifal* (1882) had their first performances.

Bayreuth was perhaps the realization of the dream of German opera: a place where, as in the Greek theatre that influenced Wagner, the nation could confront its myths. But it became, under his heirs and successors, an exclusively Wagnerian realization, devoted to his works alone (and then only to those from *Der fliegende Holländer* onwards). Even during his lifetime he eclipsed all other German opera composers. Cornelius and Goldmark (*Die Königin von Saba*, 1875, Vienna), who were close to him, escaped from his shadow only by exploiting a vein he did not touch: the oriental. Goetz went in a non-Wagnerian, Mozartian direction in his comedy *Der Widerspänstigen Zähmung* (1874, Mannheim). Brahms, Bruckner and others avoided opera altogether.

Vienna did, however, make a re-entry into operatic history in the 1860s, when the Theater an der Wien became an operetta house, at first importing works by Offenbach, who, like Meyerbeer, had made his artistic home in Paris. He wrote *Der schwarze Corsar* (1872)

for the Viennese theatre, but its greatest success of this period was the younger Johann Strauss's *Die Fledermaus* (1874), followed by his *Eine Nacht in Venedig* (1883) and *Der Zigeunerbaron* (1885). The golden age of Viennese operetta (with such composers as Suppé, Millöcker, Zeller, Heuberger and ultimately Lehár), created for a wealthy bourgeois rather than a courtly audience, thus overlapped with the first Bayreuth festivals, whose aims were similarly, if in a different sense, egalitarian.

5. 1883–1918. Wagner, and Johann Strauss II, continued to overshadow their successors from beyond the grave: perhaps the end of their hegemony can be dated to 1905, the year of the first performances, within three weeks, of Richard Strauss's *Salome* (in Dresden) and Lehár's *Die lustige Witwe* (at the Theater an der Wien). Strauss's work was given in the new Dresden opera house, opened in 1878, which was only one of several coeval with Bayreuth, if designed along less revolutionary lines: there were also new theatres in Frankfurt (1880) and for the court opera in Vienna (1869). The growth of the cities, and the growth of the orchestra to be accommodated in the pit, necessitated change, but change within a period of, at first, creative stagnation. The operas of Wagner's son Siegfried convey the impotence of the period, as does Richard Strauss's first, heavily post-Wagnerian opera *Guntram* (1894). Where success was achieved, as by Kienzl's *Der Evangelimann* (1895), or Pfitzner's *Der arme Heinrich* (1895), or Humperdinck's *Hansel und Gretel* (1893), it was by a return to elements of fairy-tale and folklore that looked back to the age of German opera before Wagner, even though the treatment might be indelibly Wagnerian.

Kienzl and Humperdinck both wrote several more operas without repeating what was for each of them a belated first triumph; taste turned, once again, to France and Italy for a more immediate kind of expressive power. Massenet's *Werther* (1892) was written for the Viennese court opera, while the works of Mascagni, Leoncavallo (whose *Der Roland von Berlin*, 1904, was written for that city) and Puccini swept across the German stages, followed by ephemeral local successors such as Eugen d'Albert's *Tiefland* (1903). At the same time the repertory continued to retract around a corpus of classics. One sign of that lies in the career of the most distinguished opera conductor of the period, Mahler, who, though himself of course a composer, introduced few new works during his terms in Kassel (1883–5), Prague (1885–6), Leipzig (1886–8), Budapest (1881–91), Hamburg (1891–7) and Vienna (1897–1907). Instead his emphasis was on intensive musical preparation and, in collaboration with the designer Alfred Roller during his last Vienna years, on a new simplicity and directness on stage.

One exception to Mahler's eschewing of new works (understandable enough, given what was being written during the two decades after Wagner's death) was Zemlinsky's *Es war einmal* (1900). He also struggled unsuccessfully against Viennese censorship to perform *Salome*, whose première was one of the glories of Schuch's regime in Dresden, a regime which restored the company to the eminence it had known under Weber and Wagner. Strauss too was active as an opera conductor during this period, working in Weimar (1889–94), Munich (1894–8) and Berlin (from 1898), though he retained his connection with Dresden and

Schuch for *Elektra* (1909) and *Der Rosenkavalier* (1911).

These works ensured that the jolt of *Salome*, already widely performed, was repeated. On one level Strauss, like Mozart 120 years earlier, met his Italian contemporaries on their own ground, but *Salome* and *Elektra* could also be interpreted as extensions from late Wagner (and as extensions rather than the prostrate imitations of a Bungert), while *Der Rosenkavalier* was selfconsciously a re-creation of Mozartian sentimental comedy, though with the superbly anachronistic undertow of waltzing carried over from Lehár and the operetta tradition. Embracing, therefore, the great prizes of German opera from the last century and more, these three works enjoyed more success than anything else produced in Germany since the *Ring* (performances of *Parsifal* were a Bayreuth monopoly until 1914).

Conductors associated with Bayreuth helped to build up traditions of Wagner performance in other cities: Levi did so in Munich (1872–1900), as did Mottl in Karlsruhe (1881–1903) and later in Munich (1903–11), and there were Bayreuth satellites too in Rostock, Mannheim and Dessau. At the same time the importance of Wagner in the repertory had an effect on singing, and thereby on the kinds of roles that could be written: for example, the first Salome, Marie Wittich, had sung Isolde, Sieglinde and Kundry at Bayreuth. Big voices and big works, coupled with the demands of an increasingly prosperous urban audience, necessitated big theatres, and the decade or so before World War I saw an acceleration of the building boom, with new theatres in Graz (1899), Munich (Prinzregententheater, 1901), Cologne (1902), Dortmund (1904), Nuremberg (1905), Lübeck (1908), and Kassel and Osnabrück (1909). The greater audience also made possible the creation of second companies, distinct from the court operas, in Vienna (Volksoper, 1898) and in Berlin (Deutsches Opernhaus, 1912), where in 1905 the Komische Oper had opened as an equivalent of the Paris Opéra-Comique (it was here that *Pelléas et Mélisande* had its Berlin première in 1908, the year after it had been introduced to the German stage at Frankfurt).

Perhaps as a result of Strauss, whether he was interpreted as model or antagonist, there was too a new flowering of the repertory. Zemlinsky, working at the Vienna Volksoper, introduced there his *Kleider machen Leute* (1910); his *Eine florentinische Tragödie*, based like *Salome* on Wilde (as was his later *Der Zwerg*), had its first performance in Stuttgart in 1917. Another city of rising importance was Frankfurt, which staged a succession of Schreker premières: *Der ferne Klang* (1912), *Das Spielwerk und die Prinzessin* (1913), *Die Gezeichneten* (1918) and *Der Schatzgräber* (1920), all works combining a post-Straussian opulence and sensuality with an autobiographical projection into the artist hero. The lavishness and the introspection were very much of the period, and Schreker's works enjoyed several years of success throughout Germany and Austria. Pfitzner's more rigorous treatment of the artist's responsibilities in *Palestrina* (1917, Munich) had a longer, slower progress, and neither of Schoenberg's short one-act pieces, *Erwartung* and *Die glückliche Hand*, was performed until 1924, the former being a soprano 'monodrama' which is perhaps the extreme point on a line through the music of Kundry and Electra.

Along with the extrapolation of that line went the return to Mozart, a renascence to which Mahler, Levi and Strauss all contributed, and which had its creative

parallels not only in *Der Rosenkavalier* but also in Wolf-Ferrari's comedies and Busoni's *Die Brautwahl* (1912, Hamburg). Strauss and Busoni both also, against the prevailing trend of the time, wrote operas for smaller forces, respectively *Ariadne auf Naxos* and the double bill of *Arlecchino* and *Turandot* (1917, Zürich). The first performance of *Ariadne*, in its original version, inaugurated the Kleines Haus at Stuttgart, whose construction was itself a sign of renewed concern for small-scale opera. And here too there were of course intimate ties linking architecture, repertory and singers: for example, Claire Dux, a member of Strauss's ensemble in Berlin, was one of a new generation of Mozart singers, her roles including Pamina and Sophie in *Der Rosenkavalier*.

6. 1919–45. German operatic life had not been much affected by the war (except at Bayreuth, where performances ceased in 1914 for a decade), and the changes that came afterwards were at first more administrative than artistic. With the removal of the monarchies, theatres became state institutions and were duly renamed Landestheater or Staatstheater. But many of the same men remained in charge. Strauss moved from Berlin to Vienna (1919–24), where his *Die Frau ohne Schatten* had its première in 1919, though his next four operas – *Intermezzo* (1924), *Die ägyptische Helena* (1928), *Arabella* (1933) and *Die schweigsame Frau* (1935) – were all introduced at Dresden, where the company was directed by Fritz Busch (1922–33) and Karl Böhm (1934–42). Bruno Walter, who had been one of Mahler's assistants in Vienna, was conductor in Munich (1913–22) and then at the Städtische Oper (the old Deutsches Opernhaus) in Berlin (1925–9), while Schillings, who had been conducting in Stuttgart, took charge of the Berlin Staatsoper (until 1925). By now conductors were not usually responsible for stage production, as Mahler had been: key moments in the rise of the professional opera director were the first performances of *Der Rosenkavalier* and *Ariadne auf Naxos*, both staged by Max Reinhardt, who, with Strauss and Hofmannsthal, founded the Salzburg Festival in 1920, giving German opera a second spiritual home (explicitly a Mozart-Strauss residence) to counterbalance Bayreuth. This was the trinity – Mozart, Wagner, Strauss – of German opera, and these were the composers with whom Walter and his colleagues were most concerned during the immediate postwar years.

Busch in Dresden and Kleiber in Berlin (1924–34), however, worked to expand the repertory, partly through revivals (Busch gave the belated German premières of *La forza del destino* and *Macbeth*), partly through new works. Earlier, in Stuttgart, Busch had conducted a double bill of works by the young Hindemith, *Mörder, Hoffnung der Frauen* and *Das Nusch-Nuschi*; Kleiber was a still more zealous advocate of the works of his contemporaries. In 1924 he introduced Krenek's *Der Zwingburg*, and the next year *Wozzeck*; Dresden followed with *Doktor Faust* (1925), Weill's *Der Protagonist* (1926) and Hindemith's *Cardillac* (also 1926). In 1927 Weill's *Royal Palace* was presented at the Berlin Staatsoper, which the same year set up a subsidiary company in the Kroll Theatre for new works and innovatory productions. At another Berlin theatre *Die Dreigroschenoper* had its first performance in 1928, followed by *Happy End* the next year, while the 'Kroll Opera' under Klemperer was presenting works by Schoenberg, Stravinsky (*Oedipus rex*, 1928), Janáček (*From the House of the Dead*, 1931) and Hindemith (*Neues vom Tage*, 1929). When, largely for political reasons, this project was abandoned after four seasons, its work went on at the Städtische Oper, where in 1932 Weill's *Die Bürgschaft* and Schreker's *Der Schmied von Gent* had their first performances. Other companies also took part in this busy period of creative activity, including Leipzig (Krenek's spectacularly successful *Jonny spielt auf*, 1927), Frankfurt (Schoenberg's *Von heute auf morgen*, 1930) and Oldenburg, which gave the second production of *Wozzeck* in 1929 and proved the work to be within the scope of lesser houses. There were also performances of new chamber operas by Weill, Hindemith and Milhaud at Baden-Baden in 1927–9.

The composers responsible for this operatic heyday of the Weimar republic were in the main young men, marked by the war, and marked too by the musical upheaval of the period. Their operas offered new subject matter, from modern life, often with a colouring of jazz or dance-band music; the tone could be sardonic, satirical, swish, almost anything but Romantic. Meanwhile Vienna acted largely as a receiving house for this German repertory, putting on *Cardillac*, *Jonny* and *Wozzeck*, for instance, soon after their northern premières. But then the excitement came to a sudden end with Hitler's accession to power in January 1933. Busch was dismissed two months later; Kleiber left Berlin in December 1934, after conducting the suite from Berg's *Lulu*, which was perhaps the last advanced music to be heard in Germany until 1945.

Many distinguished conductors remained in Germany – Böhm in Dresden, Karajan in Berlin, Jochum in Hamburg, Krauss in Munich – but the repertory of new works was severely constrained. Hindemith's *Mathis der Maler* (1938), concerned with the quandary of the artist in hazardous times, could be given only outside the Nazi domains, in Zürich; two years later the composer followed Schoenberg, Krenek and Weill into American exile. Those who stayed in Germany, and whose works were performed both there and in Vienna after the Anschluss of 1938, included Strauss (*Friedenstag*, 1938, Munich; *Daphne*, 1938, Dresden; *Capriccio*, 1942, Munich), Orff, Egk and Wagner-Régeny.

7. SINCE 1945. The divide of the Nazi years, between those who stayed and those who left, was perpetuated after the war in a different way, between the two republics into which Germany was split, with Austria now taking its own more conservative path, as it had during the Weimar years. Most of Berlin (except for a western sector in which the Städtische Oper, later returning to its original name of Deutsche Oper, reassembled itself) was behind the iron curtain in the German Democratic Republic (GDR), along with Dresden and Leipzig. In the Federal Republic (FRG) were Munich, Hamburg, Frankfurt and Stuttgart. But on both sides a great many of the theatres had been destroyed, necessitating a new round of building. Some of the great houses were reconstructed: the Berlin Staatsoper (1955), the National Theatre in Munich (1963) and finally the Semper theatre in Dresden (1985). Elsewhere, and in a great many of the smaller cities of both German states, new theatres were built during the 1950s and 60s. And although these new theatres generally had to accommodate spoken drama as well as

opera and ballet, handsome state subsidies fertilized a richer and more widely spread operatic culture than had existed before the war.

The great houses – Munich, Dresden, Vienna – returned to their pre-war standards under such conductors as Karajan, Böhm, Solti, Kempe and Keilberth. Karajan also became the dominant figure at the Salzburg Festival. But new additions to the repertory were now going on mostly elsewhere. There was a rediscovery of early opera: Handel at Göttingen (where annual festivals had begun in 1920) and Halle, Telemann at Magdeburg, Mozart at Würzburg (again with a pre-war history, going back to 1921) and Schwetzingen. There was too, in keeping with the architectural programme, an effort to build a new German repertory, though this took different forms in the two republics.

In East Germany the effort to create socialist art caused the composition of opera to be regarded with suspicion: music's theatrical usefulness was less problematic in incidental scores, of which Eisler and Dessau wrote a great number, especially for plays by Brecht, the towering theatrical presence in the new socialist state. The Brecht-Dessau *Die Verurteilung des Lukullus* (1951, Berlin Staatsoper) was one of the few lasting new operas staged during the first two decades of the GDR; works by Alan Bush were also introduced. But the stalemate only affected new pieces: the insistence on dramatic veracity and social-critical value, an insistence that cramped composition, at the same time stimulated a new way of seeing repertory opera, especially in Felsenstein's work at the Komische Oper in Berlin. His productions were widely seen and widely influential, in the FRG as much as in the GDR.

The Felsenstein reform, though touched by his individual thought and charismatic personality, was also another turn of the wheel – of the demand for opera as drama – that had motivated the Kroll experiment and Wagner's construction of his Bayreuth theatre. And at Bayreuth the same impulse was nourished again by Wieland Wagner's productions, radically simplified in setting and movement. It was with his *Parsifal* staging that the festival theatre reopened in 1951; he then staged all the other works in the Bayreuth repertory there. But he had no direct successors. The producers who came to dominate German opera from the 1960s onwards, on both sides of the iron curtain, came rather from East Berlin, and included Friedrich, Herz, Kupfer and Berghaus. Their questioning approach, searching for meanings below and beyond the ostensible drift of the libretto, has resulted in a theatre of challenge and irony, with repercussions well beyond Germany.

Being subversive, though, entails having something to subvert: usually the comforting familiarities of a known work. The great age of 'producer's opera' has therefore existed rather alongside the creation of new works during this period, though here too there has been prodigious activity, in the FRG from the immediate postwar years, and in the GDR since the relative relaxation of artistic policy in the mid-1960s. In part the decentralization of opera, seen as a problem in earlier periods, has been positively beneficial, for putting on a new opera has been a way for a company to draw attention to itself. Also important, in both republics and in Austria, was the arrival of a new generation of composers, stimulated by contact with the music – Schoenberg, Berg, Stravinsky, Bartók – that had been denied a hearing during the Nazi years (and for some time thereafter in the GDR): Henze, Stockhausen, Bernd Alois Zimmermann, Reimann and Klebe in the FRG, Matthus, Kunad and Udo Zimmermann in the GDR, von Einem and Cerha in Austria. At the same time, composers of an earlier generation, such as Blacher and Fortner, could benefit from new materials and new opportunities.

In the FRG the most important houses for new opera were Berlin, Hamburg (especially under Liebermann's regime as Intendant, 1959–73) and Cologne: premières in Berlin included Henze's *König Hirsch* (1956), *Der junge Lord* (1965) and *Das verratene Meer* (1990), Klebe's *Alkmene* (1961), Yun's *Der Traum des Liu-Tung* (1965), Blacher's *Zweihunderttausend Taler* (1969), Fortner's *Elisabeth Tudor* (1972) and Rihm's *Ödipus* (1987), in Hamburg Henze's *Der Prinz von Homburg* (1960), von Einem's *Der Zerrissene* (1964), Penderecki's *Die Teufel von Loudun* (1969) and Kagel's *Staatstheater* (1971), and in Cologne Fortner's *Die Bluthochzeit* (1957) and Zimmermann's *Die Soldaten* (1965). Also at Hamburg a chamber opera group, Opera Stabile, was established in 1973, one of several institutions founded to present new works of a more intimate and often experimental kind, in contrast with the main-stage operas, which tended to be rather conservative, hooked to literary classics and musically extending from Bergian expressionism. The outstanding achievements of the 1960s and 70s were the exceptions: *Die Soldaten*, and the satirically deconstructed *Staatstheater*.

During this same period new opera was neglected in Munich (an exception was Reimann's *Lear*, 1978) and Austria: it had no place at the Bregenz Festival, and little at Salzburg (again an occasional exception: Henze's *Die Bassariden*, 1966, and Penderecki's *Die schwarze Maske*, 1986) and the Vienna repertory was essentially dependent on Salzburg. But in the 1980s this began to change, partly because of more imaginative programming policy, but partly too because of a change in musical atmosphere, whereby composers were no longer so wary of opera as an alien, unalterably conservative enterprise. Especially was this true of younger composers – Rihm, Höller, Udo Zimmermann – who had not lived through the 1950s division between radicalism and traditionalism, and who could take a radical view of a traditional medium: it was to present the works of this generation that the Munich Biennale was founded in 1988. More surprising was the emergence of the leading German radical, Stockhausen, as the composer of an opera cycle *Licht*, the most ambitious adventure in German opera since the *Ring*.

For further information on operatic life in Germany *see* AACHEN; AUGSBURG; BADEN-BADEN; BAYREUTH; BERLIN; BIELEFELD; BONN; BREMEN; BREMERHAVEN; BRUNSWICK (ii); COBURG; COLOGNE; DARMSTADT; DESSAU; DETMOLD; DORTMUND; DRESDEN; DÜSSELDORF; ERFURT; ESSEN; FLENSBURG; FRANKFURT AM MAIN; FREIBURG; GELSENKIRCHEN; GERA; GIESSEN; GOTHA; GÖTTINGEN; HALLE; HAMBURG; HANOVER; HEIDELBERG; HILDESHEIM; HOF; KAISERSLAUTERN; KARLSRUHE; KASSEL; KIEL; KOBLENZ; KÖNIGSBERG; KREFELD; LEIPZIG; LÜBECK; LUDWIGSBURG; LUDWIGSHAFEN; LÜNEBURG; MAGDEBURG; MAINZ; MANNHEIM; MUNICH; MÜNSTER; NUREMBERG; OBERHAUSEN; OLDENBURG; OSNABRÜCK; PASSAU; PFORZHEIM; REGENSBURG; ROSTOCK; SAARBRÜCKEN; SCHWERIN; SCHWETZINGEN; STUTTGART; TRAVELLING TROUPES, §3; TRIER; ULM; WEIMAR; WEISSENFELS; WIESBADEN; WUPPERTAL; WÜRZBURG and ZEITZ. For Austria *see* BADEN BEI WIEN; BAD ISCHL; BREGENZ; GRAZ; INNSBRUCK; KLAGENFURT; KREMSMÜNSTER; LINZ; MELK; OSSIACH; SALZBURG; and VIENNA.

J. F. Reichardt: *Ueber die deutsche comische Oper* (Hamburg, 1774)

W. R. Griepenkerl: *Die Oper der Gegenwart* (Leipzig, 1847)

J. Cornet: *Die Oper in Deutschland und das Theater der Neuzeit* (Hamburg, 1849)

R. Eitner: 'Die deutsche komische Oper', *MMg*, xxiv (1852), 37–92

H. M. Schletterer: *Das deutsche Singspiel von seinen ersten Anfängen bis auf die neueste Zeit* (Augsburg, 1863)

E. Hanslick: *Die moderne Oper* (Berlin, 1875–1900)

L. Schmidt: *Zur Geschichte der deutschen Märchenoper* (Halle, 1895)

H. Kretzschmar: 'Das erste Jahrhundert der deutschen Oper', *SIMG*, iii (1901–2), 270–93

K. M. Klob: *Beiträge zur Geschichte der deutschen komischen Oper* (Berlin, 1903)

E. Istel: *Die Entstehung des deutschen Melodramas* (Berlin and Leipzig, 1906)

G. Calmus: *Die ersten deutschen Singspiele von Standfus und Hiller* (Leipzig, 1908)

M. Ehrenhaus: *Die Operndichtung der deutschen Romantik* (Breslau, 1911)

K. Lüthge: *Die deutsche Spieloper* (Brunswick, 1924)

W. H. Riehl: *Zur Geschichte der romantischen Oper* (Berlin, 1928)

L. Schiedermaier: *Die deutsche Oper* (Leipzig, 1930, 3/1943)

S. Goslich: *Beiträge zur Geschichte der deutschen romantischen Oper* (Leipzig, 1937, rev. 2/1975 as *Die deutsche romantische Oper*)

K. Reiber: *Das Volkstümliche in der deutschen romantischen Oper* (Würzburg, 1942)

E. Hofer: *Die Entwicklung des Musikdramas in der Romantik* (diss., U. of Vienna, 1943)

E. Krenek: 'Opera Between the Wars', *MM*, xx (1943), 102–11

C. Niessen: *Die deutsche Oper der Gegenwart* (Regensburg, 1944)

D. Drew: 'Musical Theatre in the Weimar Republic', *PRMA*, lxxxviii (1961–2), 89–108

A. R. Neumann: 'The Changing Concept of the Singspiel in the Eighteenth Century', *Studies in German Literature*, ed. C. Hammer jr (Baton Rouge, 1963), 63–71

R. Brockpähler: *Handbuch zur Geschichte der Barockoper in Deutschland* (Emsdetten, 1964)

H. H. Stuckenschmidt: *Oper in dieser Zeit* (Hanover, 1964)

E. M. Batley: 'The Inception of Singspiel in 18th-Century Southern Germany', *German Life and Letters*, xix (1965–6), 167–77

J. E. Lindberg: 'Gottsched gegen die Oper', *German Quarterly*, xl (1967), 673–83

E. Padmore: 'German Expressionist Opera', *PRMA*, xcv (1968–9), 41–53

M. Gregor-Dellin: *Die Revolution als Oper* (Munich, 1973)

H.-A. Koch: *Das deutsche Singspiel* (Stuttgart, 1974)

A. S. Garlington jr: 'German Romantic Opera and the Problem of Origins', *MQ*, lxiii (1977), 247–63

J. Warrack: 'German Operatic Ambitions at the Beginning of the 19th Century', *PRMA*, civ (1977–8), 79–88

G. Flaherty: *Opera in the Development of German Critical Thought* (Princeton, 1978)

J. Schläder: *Undine auf dem Musiktheater: zur Entwicklungsgeschichte der deutschen Spieloper* (Bonn, 1979)

K. Achberger: *Literatur als Libretto: das deutsche Opernbuch seit 1945* (Heidelberg, 1980)

P. Heyworth: *Otto Klemperer: his Life and Times*, i: *1883–1933* (Cambridge, 1983)

T. Bauman: *North German Opera in the Age of Goethe* (Cambridge, 1985)

N. Tschulik: *Musiktheater in Deutschland: die Oper im 20. Jahrhundert* (Vienna, 1987)

S. C. Cook: *Opera for a New Republic: the 'Zeitopern' of Krenek, Weill and Hindemith* (Ann Arbor, 1988)

THOMAS BAUMAN (1–3), PAUL GRIFFITHS (4–7)

Gershwin, George [Gershvin, Jacob] (*b* Brooklyn, New York, 26 Sept 1898; *d* Hollywood, CA, 11 July 1937). American composer. He lived most of his life in a songwriter's world. Born to Russian-Jewish immigrants who settled in New York in the 1890s, he began to take piano lessons around the age of 12 and by 1912 had been accepted as a piano pupil by Charles Hambitzer, a musician of talent and taste. Hambitzer recognized 'genius' in Gershwin and sought to open up the world of classical music to him, taking him to concerts and assigning him pieces by such composers as Chopin, Liszt and Debussy. While acquiring skills that were to make him an accomplished and memorable pianist, Gershwin also began with Edward Kilenyi lessons in harmony that continued into the 1920s. At the same time, he was drawn to popular music, admiring especially the songs of Jerome Kern and Irving Berlin. In 1914, a few months short of his 16th birthday, he left high school to work as a song plugger on Tin Pan Alley.

Gershwin received the only professional break he needed four years later, when Max Dreyfus hired him as a staff composer at T. B. Harms, the leading publisher of music for the Broadway stage. Before long, Gershwin composed his first hit song, *Swanee* (1918, lyrics by Irving Caesar; published in 1919), followed by his first full Broadway score, *La La Lucille* (1919), and a contract with the producer George White to compose the music for *George White's Scandals of 1920*, thereafter an annual revue. Throughout the 1920s, a decade in which the Broadway musical theatre flourished creatively and economically, Gershwin was one of its leading lights. Handsome, gregarious, seemingly sure of himself and his talent, he relished the public spotlight and was especially known for presiding at the piano at social gatherings. By the end of 1930, he had composed the scores for 22 complete shows, including successes such as *Lady, be Good!* (1924), *Oh, Kay!* (1926), *Funny Face* (1927) and *Girl Crazy* (1930), as well as collaborating on others with Sigmund Romberg, Herbert Stothart and William Daly.

Having precociously mastered the prevailing types of popular song, from the striding, extroverted one-step to the more contemplative ballad, Gershwin broke new ground by absorbing rhythms and turns of phrase from blues and jazz, African-American styles that began to win a place in the musical life of New York around the time of World War I. From 1924 onwards, his brother Ira Gershwin served as his lyricist and artistic collaborator. Together, within the conventions of the popular song, the brothers discovered an original creative voice. George's responsiveness to black influence brought an enriched musical vocabulary into the Broadway orbit. Ira's lyrics – written, he confided, 'by fitting words mosaically to music already composed' – reflected in their allusive, colloquial urbanity a scholar's eye and an artist's ear and heart. Centred chiefly on romantic love, the Gershwin song combined musical and verbal ingenuity with a capacity for tenderness that crystallized the theatrical sensibility of the time.

While sharpening his gifts as a songwriter, Gershwin also explored other musical challenges. Around 1920 he completed for Kilenyi's harmony class *Lullaby* for string quartet, his earliest instrumental piece not written for piano. As a part of *George White's Scandals of 1922* he composed *Blue Monday* (text by B. G. DeSylva), a 20-minute opera 'ala Afro-American'. Neither proved successful. But Gershwin's first instrumental concert work, *Rhapsody in Blue*, made him famous.

First performed in the Aeolian Hall in New York on 12 February 1924, the *Rhapsody* owed much of its impact to the circumstances of its first performance, at a well-publicized concert organized and conducted by the band-leader Paul Whiteman. The concert was billed as 'An Experiment in Modern Music', and it purported to show that jazz – then considered by most concert musicians and critics a rhythmically vivacious dance music that fostered bad musical habits – was improved when performed in the 'symphonic' arrangements that were the speciality of Whiteman's band. Identified in pre-concert publicity as a 'jazz concerto', the *Rhapsody* was written to demonstrate that jazz-based material need not be confined to short pieces. The concert achieved a sense of occasion. Whiteman had invited many prominent classical musicians and critics, and questions about the destiny of American music were very much in the air, with writers such as Carl Van Vechten and Gilbert Seldes arguing that vernacular idioms could nourish and vitalize the American fine arts of the future. Gershwin's *Rhapsody*, which seemed to confirm their prophecy, won the audience's approval and the critics' attention. It also won renown for its composer. No longer simply another talented American songwriter, he was thereafter recognized as a historical figure – the man who brought 'jazz' into the concert hall.

After the success of the *Rhapsody*, new patterns emerged in Gershwin's composing life. He never lost his touch for writing songs, which he continued to produce for Broadway into the mid-thirties and then for film musicals. His musical comedy satirizing American politics, *Of Thee I Sing* (26 December 1931), won a Pulitzer Prize for his collaborators, Ira Gershwin, George S. Kaufman and Morrie Ryskind. (The Gershwin brothers spent three months in Hollywood in 1930–31; in mid-1936 they moved there from New York City under contract to Radio-Keith-Orpheum (RKO) studios.) But he also devoted considerable time and energy to concert music, studying with a succession of teachers including Wallingford Riegger, Henry Cowell and Joseph Schillinger (1932–6). 'I can't recall a period in George's life', Ira wrote after his brother's death, 'when, despite all his musical creativity, he didn't find time to further his academic studies.' He spent much of the summer of 1925 composing the Concerto in F for piano and orchestra, commissioned by Walter Damrosch and the New York SO. The Preludes for Piano were introduced in December 1926 as part of a recital in which he accompanied the contralto Marguerite d'Alvarez. During much of 1928 Gershwin was occupied with the composition of the tone poem *An American in Paris*. He wrote this work in part during a trip to Europe on which he was welcomed as a musical celebrity, meeting many composers (Prokofiev, Milhaud, Poulenc, Ravel, Walton and Berg) and hearing both *Rhapsody in Blue* and the Concerto in F played in his honour by French musicians. (Except for his composition lessons, Gershwin apparently had little personal contact with American composers outside the musical theatre world; European composers seem to have recognized his gifts more readily than his American contemporaries.) In the summer of 1929 he made his début as a conductor in an open-air concert at Lewisohn Stadium in New York, where before an audience of more than 15 000 he conducted the New York PO in *An American in Paris* and *Rhapsody in Blue*, playing the piano part of the latter himself. In October 1929 he signed a contract to compose a 'Jewish opera', to be called *The Dybbuk*, for the Metropolitan Opera, but he never fulfilled the commission. During his first stay in Hollywood, he composed most of his Second Rhapsody for piano and orchestra, even as he and Ira worked on the songs for the film *Delicious* (released in 1931). Remarkably, Gershwin managed this broadening of his musical activities and interests without sacrificing his popularity.

The idea of writing a full-length opera based on DuBose Heyward's novel *Porgy*, about life among the black inhabitants of 'Catfish Row' in Charleston, South Carolina, first occurred to Gershwin when he read the book in 1926. Heyward's wife Dorothy had later helped him turn *Porgy* into a successful play, and Heyward had been approached by Al Jolson, who hoped to use the story for a musical show in which he would play the lead in blackface. This plan was rejected, however, and in October 1933 Heyward and the Gershwin brothers signed a contract with the Theatre Guild in New York, the same organization that had produced *Porgy* on stage. Gershwin began the score in February 1934, having prepared for this new challenge by including in his Broadway scores of the early 1930s – especially the unsuccessful political satire *Let 'em eat Cake* (1933) – many scenes with continuous music. During much of the summer of 1934 he stayed in South Carolina, composing and absorbing the local atmosphere. A news release from Charleston reported his promise that, if the opera turned out as he hoped, it would 'resemble a combination of the drama and romance of *Carmen* and the beauty of *Meistersinger*'. By early 1935 the composition was finished, and Gershwin spent the next several months orchestrating. Billed as 'an American folk opera', *Porgy and Bess* opened in New York in October 1935, in a Broadway theatre, not an opera house. It ran for only 124 performances, however, and even a subsequent tour failed to earn enough to recoup the original investment; in spite of Gershwin's vaunted record of success, his last and most ambitious work for the stage was at first a financial failure.

Few events in the history of American music were more shocking and unexpected than the death of Gershwin, seemingly still youthful and vigorous and on the threshold of new musical achievements. During the first half of 1937, although he had experienced flashes of discomfort, dizziness and emotional despondency, he continued to work. Inspired by hearing the string quartets of Arnold Schoenberg, his Hollywood neighbour and sometime tennis partner, he thought of writing a quartet himself; and for RKO's *Goldwyn Follies* he planned a ballet, to be called *Swing Symphony*. But on 9 July he fell into a coma. A brain tumour was diagnosed and emergency surgery performed. On the morning of 11 July 1937 he died at the age of 38.

See also PORGY AND BESS.

musical comedies, first performed in New York unless otherwise stated

La La Lucille (F. Jackson; lyrics B. G. DeSylva, A. J. Jackson and I. Caesar), Henry Miller Theatre, 26 May 1919

A Dangerous Maid (C. W. Bell; lyrics A. Francis [I. Gershwin]), Atlantic City, NJ, 21 March 1921

Blue Monday (opera 'ala Afro-American', 1, DeSylva), orchd W. H. Vodery, Globe, 28 Aug 1922; as 135th Street, reorchd F. Grofé, Carnegie Hall (concert perf.), 29 Dec 1925; orig. pt of revue George White's Scandals of 1922

Our Nell (musical comedy, B. Hooker and A. E. Thomas; lyrics Hooker), Nora Bayes Theatre, 4 Dec 1922, collab. W. Daly

Sweet Little Devil (F. Mandel and L. Schwab; lyrics DeSylva), Astor, 21 Jan 1924

Primrose (G. Bolton and G. Grossmith; lyrics D. Carter and I. Gershwin), London, Winter Garden, 11 Sept 1924, vs (London and Sydney, 1924)

Lady, be Good! (Bolton and F. Thompson; lyrics I. Gershwin), Liberty, 1 Dec 1924

Tell me More (Thompson and W. K. Wells; lyrics DeSylva and I. Gershwin), Gaiety, 13 April 1925

Tip-Toes (Bolton and Thompson; lyrics I. Gershwin), Liberty, 28 Dec 1925

Song of the Flame (operetta, O. Hammerstein II and O. Harbach; lyrics Hammerstein and Harbach), 44th Street, 30 Dec 1925, collab. H. Stothart

Oh, Kay! (Bolton and P. G. Wodehouse; lyrics H. Dietz and I. Gershwin), Imperial, 8 Nov 1926

Strike up the Band (G. S. Kaufman; lyrics I. Gershwin), Philadelphia, Shubert, 5 Sept 1927; 2nd version (M. Ryskind, after Kaufman; lyrics I. Gershwin), Times Square, 14 Jan 1930, vs (New York, 1930)

Funny Face (P. G. Smith and Thompson; lyrics I. Gershwin), Alvin, 22 Nov 1927

Rosalie (Bolton and W. A. McGuire; lyrics I. Gershwin and Wodehouse), New Amsterdam, 10 Jan 1928, incl. songs by S. Romberg

Treasure Girl (V. Lawrence and Thompson; lyrics I. Gershwin), Alvin, 8 Nov 1928

Show Girl (McGuire and J. P. McEvoy; lyrics I. Gershwin and G. Kahn), Ziegfeld, 2 July 1929

Girl Crazy (Bolton and J. McGowan; lyrics I. Gershwin), Alvin, 14 Oct 1930, vs (New York, 1954)

Of Thee I Sing (Kaufman and Ryskind; lyrics I. Gershwin), Music Box, 26 Dec 1931, vs (New York, 1932)

Pardon my English (H. Fields; lyrics I. Gershwin), Majestic, 20 Jan 1933

Let 'em eat Cake (Kaufman and Ryskind; lyrics I. Gershwin), Imperial, 21 Oct 1933; sequel to Of Thee I Sing

Porgy and Bess (American folk opera, 3, DuBose Heyward; lyrics I. Gershwin and Heyward, after play by DuBose and Dorothy Heyward: *Porgy*), Alvin, 10 Oct 1935, vs (New York, 1935)

Songs in musical comedies and revues by other composers, 1916–36

*

I. Goldberg: *George Gershwin: a Study in American Music* (New York, 1931, enlarged 2/1958)

I. Kolodin: 'Porgy and Bess: American Opera in the Theatre', *Theatre Arts Monthly*, xix (1935), 853–65

V. Thomson: 'George Gershwin', *MM*, xiii (1935–6), 13–19 [on *Porgy and Bess*]

F. Jacobi: 'The Future of Gershwin', *MM*, xv (1937–8), 3–7

M. Armitage, ed.: *George Gershwin* (New York, 1938)

L. Bernstein: 'A Nice Gershwin Tune', *Atlantic Monthly*, cxcv/4 (1955), 39–42; repr. in *The Joy of Music* (New York, 1959)

E. Jablonski and L. D. Stewart: *The Gershwin Years* (Garden City, NY, 1958, 2/1973)

I. Gershwin: *Lyrics on Several Occasions* (New York, 1959)

W. Mellers: *Music in a New Found Land* (New York, 1966), 392–413

S. Green: *Ring Bells! Sing Songs! Broadway Musicals of the 1930s* (New York, 1971), 17–18, 31–2, 56, 59, 77–8, 90–91, 115–18

R. Crawford: 'It ain't necessarily Soul: Gershwin's *Porgy and Bess* as Symbol', *Yearbook for Inter-American Musical Research*, viii (1972), 17–38

A. Wilder: 'George Gershwin (1898–1937)', *American Popular Song* (New York, 1972), 121–62

R. Kimball and A. Simon: *The Gershwins* (New York, 1973)

C. M. Schwartz: *Gershwin: his Life and Music* (Indianapolis, IN, 1973)

W. D. Shirley: 'Porgy and Bess', *Library of Congress Quarterly Journal*, xxxi (1974), 97–107

R. Crawford: 'Gershwin's Reputation: a Note on *Porgy and Bess*', *MQ*, lxv (1979), 257–64

W. D. Shirley: 'Reconciliation on Catfish Row: Bess, Serena, and the Short Score of *Porgy and Bess*', *Library of Congress Quarterly Journal*, xxxviii (1981), 144–65

S. E. Gilbert: 'Gershwin's Art of Counterpoint', *MQ*, lxx (1984), 423–56

L. Starr: 'Toward a Reevaluation of Gershwin's *Porgy and Bess*', *American Music*, ii/2 (1984), 25–37

A. Porter: 'A Long Pull to Get there', *New Yorker* (25 Feb 1985)

C. Hamm: 'The Theatre Guild Production of *Porgy and Bess*', *JAMS*, xl (1987), 495–532

E. Jablonski: *Gershwin* (New York, 1987)

L'avant-scène opéra, no.103 (1987) [*Porgy and Bess* issue]

H. Alpert: *The Life and Times of Porgy and Bess* (New York and London, 1990)

J. P. Swain: *The Broadway Musical: a Critical and Musical Survey* (New York, 1990), 51–72
RICHARD CRAWFORD

Gershwin, Ira [Gershvin, Israel] (*b* New York, 6 Dec 1896; *d* Beverly Hills, CA, 17 Aug 1983). American lyricist. He submitted light verse to newspapers and periodicals before joining his brother George Gershwin to write songs. His close partnership with his brother extended from 1924 until George's death in 1937. In addition to writing lyrics for more than a dozen of George's Broadway shows and for *Porgy and Bess* (1935), Ira worked with other composers, including Weill (*Lady in the Dark*, 1941, and *The Firebrand of Florence*, 1945), Kern and Arlen. Gershwin's verses are generally humorous and sunny, and make frequent recourse to such slang shortcuts as 'gloom can jump in the riv'.

*

R. Kimball and A. Simon: *The Gershwins* (New York, 1973)
GERALD BORDMAN

Gerster, Etelka (*b* Kassa [now Košice, Slovakia], 25 June 1855; *d* Pontecchio di Bologna, 20 Aug 1920). Hungarian soprano. She studied with Mathilde Marchesi in Vienna, and made her début in 1876 as Gilda (*Rigoletto*) at La Fenice, Venice, where she also sang Ophelia (*Hamlet*). She made her London début at Her Majesty's Theatre in 1877 as Amina (*La sonnambula*) and also sang in *Lucia di Lammermoor*, *I puritani*, *Rigoletto* and *Die Zauberflöte* (as the Queen of Night). The following year she made her New York début as Amina at the Academy of Music, where she appeared in the first American performance of Balfe's *Il talismano* (1878) and also sang Elsa (1881). Her rivalry with Patti was aggravated when they sang together on tour in *Les Huguenots* (Gerster as Marguerite de Valois, Patti as Valentine). Although she had a voice of great brilliance and flexibility, as well as complete security of technique, Gerster was unable to match the elder diva in personality or experience. She retired in 1890.

*

J. H. Mapleson: *The Mapleson Memoirs* (London, 1888); ed. H. Rosenthal (London, 1966)
M. de Castrone Marchesi: *Marchesi and Music* (London, 1897)
ELIZABETH FORBES

Gerster, Ottmar (*b* Braunfels, Hesse, 29 June 1897; *d* Borsdorf, Leipzig, 31 Aug 1969). German composer. He studied composition with Bernhard Sekles and violin with Adolf Rebner at the Hoch Conservatory in Frankfurt, 1913–16. After serving in World War I, he played the viola in the Lenzewski and Witek quartets and was concurrently leader of the Frankfurt SO. From 1927 to 1939 he taught the violin and theory at the Folkwang-Schule in Essen. He was professor of composition at the Weimar Musikhochschule, 1947–52, and at the Leipzig Musikhochschule, 1952–62.

Gerster's early association with workers' choirs and his commitment to the German socialist movement during the 1920s and early 1930s did not seem to hinder his success as an operatic composer during the Third Reich. His first opera, *Madame Liselotte*, heard in Essen only eight months after Hitler came to power, attracted favourable reviews on account of its quasi-nationalist plot which concerns the destiny of a homesick German princess married to the brother of Louis XIV of France. The score demonstrates an easy assimilation of folk and popular idioms spiced with a few palatable modern harmonies. During the following years it was given in over 20 different opera houses. *Enoch Arden*, first performed three years later, proved even more success-

ful and was performed over 500 times in Germany between 1936 and 1944. The plot, based on Tennyson's famous ballad, had previously attracted the attention of Richard Strauss who in 1897 had set the text in the form of a melodrama. It offered the composer considerable dramatic possibilities, with its contrast between the inner psychological torment of the protagonist and the carefree outside world as exemplified in a series of dance tableaux. Gerster binds these diverse elements together through the use of simple and direct leitmotifs, of which the cry of a seagull, characterized by a syncopated rhythmic figure on a falling 2nd, remains the most striking. Such melodic memorability eluded the composer in his next opera *Die Hexe von Passau* (1941), which exposed a certain crudity in its dramatic technique and a poverty of musical invention. However, both this work and *Enoch Arden* have remained in the repertory of several opera houses in Germany. On the other hand, the operas written in the postwar period, *Das verzauberte Ich* (1949) and *Der fröhliche Sünder* (1963), have been overshadowed by the composer's later orchestral and choral compositions.

Madame Liselotte (3, F. Clemens and O. Ginthum), Essen, 21 Oct 1933 (Mainz, 1933)
Enoch Arden: Der Mövenschrei (4 scenes, K. M. von Levetzow, after Tennyson), Düsseldorf, 15 Nov 1936, vs (Mainz, 1936)
Die Hexe von Passau (4 scenes, R. Billinger), Düsseldorf, 11 Oct 1941, vs (Mainz, 1941)
Das verzauberte Ich (heiteres musikalisches Drama, 4, P. Koch, after F. Raimund), Wuppertal, 25 June 1949, vs (Mainz, 1949)
Der fröhliche Sünder, 1959–62 (6 scenes, L. Solowjow and N. Witkowitsch), Weimar, 9 March 1963 (Berlin, 1962)
Madame Legros, 1965–6, inc. (1, Gerster, after H. Mann), Leipzig, 26 April 1970

*

K. Laux: 'Ottmar Gerster', *Musik und Musiker der Gegenwart* (Essen, 1949), 105–15
O. Goldhammer: *Ottmar Gerster* (Berlin, 1953)
K. Laux: *Ottmar Gerster* (Leipzig, 1962)
W. Wolf: 'Ein gewichtiger Beitrag zur neuen Volksoper: das Opernschaffen Ottmar Gersters', *Musik und Gesellschaft*, xv (1965), 653–7
——: *Ottmar Gersters 'Enoch Arden'* (Berlin, 1967)
C. Dahlhaus: 'Politische Implikationen der Operndramaturgie: zu einigen deutschen Oper der dreissiger Jahre', *GfMKB: Bayreuth 1981*, 148–53
H.-G. Klein: 'Viel Konformität und wenig Verweigerung: zur Komposition neuer Opern 1933–44', *Musik und Musikpolitik im faschistischen Deutschland*, ed. H. W. Heister and H.-G. Klein (Frankfurt, 1984), 145–62
ERIK LEVI

Gerusalemme. Opera by Giuseppe Verdi; *see* JÉRUSALEM.

Gervais, Charles-Hubert (*b* Paris, 19 Feb 1671; *d* Paris, 15 Jan 1744). French composer. For most of his life he was in the employ of the Duke of Orléans (later to become Regent of France). A close musical relationship with his patron (whose italianate musical tastes had been nurtured by Marc-Antoine Charpentier) is suggested by the unproved rumours that the duke collaborated with Gervais in the composition of the operas *Penthée* and *Hypermnestre* and other works (*see* PHILIPPE DE BOURBON). As a director of the royal chapel, Gervais wrote a large number of motets, but his talents are best displayed in his four operas.

Méduse appeared in 1697 and, though still heavily indebted to the Lullian style, the work shows early traces of those changes that were to come over French music during the next two decades. The score (issued in MS by Ballard) is only in sketch form, but it indicates a more variegated and colourful orchestral style than is usually found in Lully's music; and unlike the operas of Lully, *Méduse* has moments of tone-painting. These traits are far more pronounced in *Hypermnestre*, first performed at the Opéra in 1716 and revived there in 1728, 1746 and 1765. In its orchestration *Hypermnestre* fore-shadows the stage works of Rameau.

Méduse (tragédie en musique, prol., 5, C. Boyer), Paris, Opéra, 13 Jan 1697, *F-Pn*

Penthée (tragédie en musique, prol., 5, C. A. de la Fare), Paris, Palais Royal, 1705 or 1709, *Pn*

Hypermnestre (tragédie en musique, prol., 5, J. de La Font), Paris, Opéra, 3 Nov 1716 (Paris, 1716) [Act 5 rev. S.-J. Pellegrin, 1717]

Les amoours de Protée (opéra-ballet, prol., 3, La Font), Paris, Opéra, 16 or 23 May 1720 (Paris, 1720)

*

E. Titon du Tillet: *Le Parnasse françois*, suppl.ii (Paris, 1755)

J.-B. de La Borde: *Essai sur la musique ancienne et moderne* (Paris, 1780)

D. E. Tunley: *The Eighteenth-Century French Cantata* (London, 1974)
DAVID TUNLEY

Gerville-Réache, Jeanne (*b* Orthez, 26 March 1882; *d* New York, 5 Jan 1915). French mezzo-soprano. Her studies with Rosine Laborde attracted the attention of both Emma Calvé, a former pupil of Laborde, and the 78-year-old Pauline Viardot who coached her for her début as Gluck's Orpheus at the Opéra-Comique in 1899. She took part in the world première of Erlanger's *Le Juif polonais* and in 1902, as Geneviève, in that of *Pelléas et Mélisande*. She appeared in Brussels and London, and in 1907 was engaged by Oscar Hammerstein I for the new Manhattan Opera Company where she repeated her original role in the American première of *Pelléas* and scored a special success as Delilah, a role she had studied with Saint-Saëns. In 1910 in the first American production of *Elektra* she sang Clytemnestra, a role she promptly renounced. In Chicago she entered the Wagnerian repertory as Fricka and Brangäne. Everything pointed to a brilliant continuation of her career but at the age of 32 she contracted fatal blood-poisoning. By most accounts she had one of the most beautiful voices of the century, with temperament to match – a view borne out by her few recordings, which also show some stylistic faults such as broken phrasing.

*

J. McPherson and W. R. Moran: 'Jeanne Gerville-Réache', *Record Collector*, xxi (1973–4), 53–79
J. B. STEANE

Gesamtkunstwerk (Ger.: 'total work of art'). A term used by Wagner for his notion, formulated in his theoretical essays of 1849–51, of an art form that combined various media within the framework of a drama. Harking back to ancient Greek drama, he suggested that there the basic elements of dance, music and poetry had been ideally combined. Their division into separate genres had diminished their expressive force; only in the total work of art could they regain their original dignity. Similarly, the arts of architecture, sculpture and painting would recover their classical and authentic stature only as constituents of the 'artwork of the future'.

The architect of the theatre of the future would be guided by the law of beauty and the dictates of intelligibility rather than by the demands of social distinctions. Sets would be executed by landscape painters, and the three sister arts would be reunited in the actor of the future, who would be dancer, musician and poet in one. The new work of art would be brought into being not by a single creative artist but by a fellowship of artists, in response to a communal demand. The artist of the future was thus the *Volk*, and the *Gesamtkunstwerk* the product of necessity or historical inevitability. Wagner's concept was concordant with the prevailing radical philosophical outlook of the 1840s: the reuniting of constituent parts in the *Gesamtkunstwerk* mirrored the socialist aim of restoring integrity to a fragmented, divided society. This utopian element, taken with the practical constraints of producing operas, perhaps explains why the theoretical model was not realized in detail in Wagner's music dramas.

The term 'Gesamtkunstwerk' is used in the essay *Das Kunstwerk der Zukunft* (1849) alongside similar terms such as 'das vollendete Kunstwerk der Zukunft' and 'das *allgemeinsame* Drama'. The notion of the reunification of the arts did not originate with Wagner: others who had previously advocated some sort of unification, either in theory or in practice, include G. E. Lessing, Novalis, Tieck, F. W. J. Schelling and Hoffmann.
BARRY MILLINGTON

Gespenst mit der Trommel, Das ('The Ghostly Drummer'). *Deutsches komisches Singspiel* in two acts by CARL DITTERS VON DITTERSDORF to his own libretto, after CARLO GOLDONI's prose comedy *Il conte Caramella*; Oels, Herzogliches Hoftheater, 16 August 1794.

The Count (tenor), thought killed in battle, returns to his home disguised as a pilgrim to discover that his neighbour the Baron (bass) is pressing for the hand and fortune of the Countess (soprano). The Baron has contrived a series of supernatural visitations from a regimental drummer, whom he promises to exorcise if she will agree to marry him. The Count promises to conjure away the 'spirit' himself, and when it next appears he extracts a confession from the drummer, none other than the Baron in disguise.

The best of Dittersdorf's late operas for Oels, the work centres musical interest in its ensembles – the two action finales, filled with compact, contrasting sections; and the sextet with onstage wind band. As in his earlier Viennese operas, Dittersdorf plies a readily apprehensible, tuneful style that avoids extremes.
THOMAS BAUMAN

Gestewitz, Friedrich Christoph (*b* Preischka, nr Meissen, 3 Nov 1753; *d* Dresden, 1 Aug 1805). German composer, pupil and brother-in-law (not son-in-law) of Johann Adam Hiller. In the early 1780s he wrote two German operas, *Der Meyerhof* and *Die Liebe ist sinnreich*, and what may be either a third German opera, or incidental music to Gozzi's play, *Das öffentliche Geheimnis*. (*Pamela nubile* is by Generali, not Gestewitz as Eitner suggested.) Later he became conductor of Bondini's Italian opera company, for which he wrote *L'orfanella americana* (1791) and added a finale to Portugal's *Le donne cambiate* (1799). He also wrote a few sacred and keyboard works.

Der Meyerhof, Leipzig, 20 Sept 1780; 1 song in Hiller's Sammlung der vorzüglichsten Arien, vi (Leipzig, 1780)

Die Liebe ist sinnreich, Dresden, 27 Nov 1781; *B-Bc*, 2 arias in Hiller's Arien und Duetten des deutschen Theaters (Leipzig, 1781)

Das öffentliche Geheimnis (F. W. Gotter, after Gozzi), *c*1780–81; 2 songs in Hiller's Arien und Duetten (Leipzig, 1781)

L'orfanella americana, Dresden, Jan 1791; *D-Dlb*, ov. and ?1 song (Dresden, *c*1791)

Finale to Portugal's Le donne cambiate, Dresden, 2 Oct 1799

Geszty, Sylvia (*b* Budapest, 28 Feb 1934). Hungarian soprano. She studied in Budapest, making her début at the State Opera in 1959. Engaged at the Berlin Staatsoper (1961–70), she sang Gluck's Cupid, Oscar, Susanna, Gilda, Queen of Shemakha and the Queen of Night, which was her début role at Covent Garden (1966) and Salzburg (1967). At Hamburg she sang Olympia, the Fiakermilli and Musetta. Engaged at Stuttgart (1971), she sang Norina and Manon (Henze's *Boulevard Solitude*), which she repeated in Edinburgh (1977). She made her Glyndebourne début (1971) as Zerbinetta, returning for Konstanze (1972), which she sang at Salzburg. In 1973 she made her American début with the New York City Opera, in Los Angeles, as Sophie. Her roles included Donna Anna, Fiordiligi, Paisiello's Rosina and Handel's Alcina. She sang Gismonda in Cimarosa's *Il marito disperato* at Schwetzingen (1976). Her light, silvery voice, effortless coloratura and spirited acting were perfectly suited to Zerbinetta, which she sang in East and West Berlin, Munich, Vienna and Düsseldorf, and also recorded for Kempe.   ALAN BLYTH

Gevaert, François-Auguste (*b* Huysse, nr Oudenaarde, 31 July 1828; *d* Brussels, 24 Dec 1908). Belgian composer and administrator. His first musical studies were with his uncle, an organist. His precocious gifts encouraged his parents to send him in 1841 to the Ghent Conservatory. At the age of 17 he took up a teaching post and began composing cantatas and instrumental music. He persuaded his brother Modest to buy a lithographic printing press so that he could publish his compositions. In 1847 Gevaert was awarded the Belgian Prix de Rome for his cantata *Le roi Lear*. Because of his youth and the political situation in France, his study tour was postponed for two years, during which he wrote two operas, *Hugues de Zomerghem* (1848) and *La comédie à la ville* (1849).

After his Prix de Rome travels (1850–52) Gevaert settled in Paris, where *Georgette, ou Le moulin de Fontenoy* was performed at the Théâtre Lyrique in 1853. Léon Escudier, writing in *France musicale*, praised its orchestration and assured style. The following year *Le billet de Marguerite* had a great success; Berlioz acknowledged Gevaert's skill in *opéra bouffe*, and the work was performed throughout France. In 1858 Gevaert's reputation was consolidated by the première by the Opéra-Comique of the three-act *Quentin Durward*. His stage works are light in character, in keeping with the political and cultural climate of the time; most are vaudevilles in which simple and memorable songs feature prominently.

During the 1860s Gevaert gradually abandoned composition to pursue musicological research. The copying of old opera manuscripts was a lifelong concern of his, and in 1862 he was asked to revise Pergolesi's *La serva padrona* for its revival at the Théâtre Comique. In 1866 he became a member of the Prix de Rome jury, and in February 1867 he was appointed director of music at the Paris Opéra. During his last years in Paris he published *Les gloires de l'Italie*, the fruit of his detailed research into 17th- and 18th-century operas and cantatas.

After Fétis's death Gevaert was appointed director of the Brussels Conservatoire (1871) and master of the Chapelle Royale. His authority, which included the administration of the Théâtre de la Monnaie, extended over the whole of Belgian musical life. Under his strict and efficient guidance the Conservatoire acquired an international reputation, and such artists as Saint-Saëns, Melba and Viardot performed at its concerts, of which Gevaert was conductor. His publications include books on orchestration and music history and editions of early vocal music.

Hugues de Zomerghem (grand opéra, 3, V. Prilleux), Ghent, Grand, 23 March 1848, vs (Ghent, 1848)
La comédie à la ville (opéra bouffe, 1, Prilleux), Ghent, Grand, 5 Jan 1849, vs (Paris, 1853)
Les empiriques (oc, 1, G. Vaëz), 1851, *B-Bc*
Georgette, ou Le moulin de Fontenoy (opéra bouffe, 1, Vaëz and A. Royer), Paris, Lyrique, 27 Nov 1853, vs (Brussels, 1854)
Le billet de Marguerite (oc, 3, A. de Leuven and Brunswick [L. Lhérie]), Paris, Lyrique, 7 Oct 1854, vs (Paris, *c*1854)
Les lavandières de Santarem (oc, 3, A.-P. Dennery and Grangé), Paris, Lyrique, 25 Oct 1855, vs (Paris, *c*1855)
Quentin Durward (oc, 3, E. Cormon and M. Carré, after W. Scott), Paris, OC (Favart), 25 March 1858 (Paris, *c*1858)
Le diable au moulin (oc, 1, Cormon and Carré), Paris, OC (Favart), 13 May 1859, vs (Paris, 1859)
La poularde de Caux (opérette, 1, de Leuven and Prilleux), Paris, Lyrique, 17 May 1861, vs (Paris, 1861), collab. Clapisson, E. Gautier, Poise, A. Bazille and S. Mangeant
Les deux amours (oc, 2, Cormon and A. Achard), Baden-Baden, Maison de la Conversation, 31 July 1861, *Bc*
Le Château Trompette (oc, 3, Cormon and Carré), Paris, OC (Favart), 23 April 1864, vs (Paris, 1864)
Le capitaine Henriot (oc, 3, after V. Sardou and Vaëz), Paris, OC (Favart), 29 Dec 1864, vs (Paris, 1864)

*

F. Dufour: *Le baron François-Auguste Gevaert* (Brussels, 1909)
L. Dubois: 'Notice sur F.-A. Gevaert', *Annuaire de l'Académie royale de Belgique 1930* (Brussels, 1930)
J. Subirá: 'Epistolario de F.-A. Gevaert y J. de Monasterio', *AnM*, xvi (1961), 217–46
J. Hargot: *François-Auguste Gevaert* (diss., Catholic U., Louvain, 1987)   JEAN HARGOT

Gezeichneten, Die ('The Marked Ones'). Opera in three acts by FRANZ SCHREKER to his own libretto; Frankfurt, 25 April 1918.

Italian Renaissance settings became fashionable before World War I, and Schreker's choice of 16th-century Genoa was appropriate to the mixture of aesthetic sensuality and violence with which he had experimented in *Das Spielwerk und Prinzessin* (1913). The extended orchestral overture is suitably opulent (it exists in a much longer concert version as *Vorspiel zu einem Drama*), but *Die Gezeichneten* does more than extend the repertory of symbolic contexts for his musical and dramatic preoccupations: it also explores and confronts critical problems posed by them, both social and psychological. The libretto arose out of a request by Alexander Zemlinsky for a libretto that presented 'for once the tragedy of the ugly man'. Schreker complied but then decided to set it himself.

Alviano Salvago (tenor), a crippled, hunchbacked young nobleman, has decided to give a fantastically designed island park ('Elysium') to the people of Genoa. He has created it as an aesthetic sublimation of the sensual life that his physical appearance denies him in reality. His intention is opposed by Duke Adorno (bass) – who partly doubts the wisdom of the nobility renouncing its property – and Vitelozzo Tamare (baritone), the handsome young count who, with friends, has been enjoying orgies in an underground grotto on the island, for which young Genoese girls have been kidnapped.

The town mayor (the burgher 'Podesta', bass), to whom the island is formally offered, is grateful to Alviano but suspicious of the broader intentions of the nobility. Even his gratitude to Alviano is tempered by concern at the reaction of the straightforward burghers to the erotic statuary and classical fantasy of Elysium, when they attend its festive opening in Act 3. 'I am worried, sir, that you give too much', he comments, 'hungry souls and thirsty eyes revelling in this orgy of colours, scents, sounds and noble forms will return lost and oppressed to the everyday life from which you have alienated them'.

Alviano, whose altruistic decision had been reinforced by partly envious disapproval of Tamare's activities, experiences personally the ambivalent effect of his artistic creation. While fauns and naiads confuse the honest burghers, the one woman he believes to have fallen in love with him is seduced by Tamare in the underground grotto. She is Carlotta Nardi (soprano), the consumptive daughter of the mayor and a talented painter who, in Act 1, persuades the selfconscious and distrustful Alviano to come and sit for her. In the celebrated Act 2 *Atelierszene*, his reserve is melted by her charm as she completes the picture of him greeting the sunrise on the outskirts of the city (a scene she had secretly witnessed). She professes love for him, and his ecstasy provides the expression she had wanted to capture. Carlotta's subsequent seizure, followed by an announced visit from the Duke, permits Alviano no more than a kiss on her forehead and a tentative embrace.

Tamare's Act 3 conquest had been prepared before, however, and Carlotta's interest in Alviano had waned after the completion of her painting. Only when the Duke's police arrive on the island, to arrest him as ringleader of the kidnappers and corrupter of the townsfolk, does the full truth dawn upon Alviano. He leads them to the grotto, where the final scene takes place amid the debris of recent orgies. Tamare and Carlotta are discovered. The former, mockingly unrepentant, is killed by Alviano, who then turns to Carlotta. Her strength drained, she is dying, but longs only for Tamare. Alviano, rejected in the most painful manner, stumbles away madly. A few bars of the dreamlike music with which the overture had opened and to which his awareness of love had dawned in Act 2, are interrupted by a violent cadential victory of D minor over D major.

PETER FRANKLIN

Ghazaryan [Kazaryan], **Yuri** (*b* Tbilisi, 4 Dec 1933). Armenian composer. He studied composition with Grigor Eghiazaryan at the Erevan Conservatory, graduating in 1964. His single, two-act opera *Ernest Hemingway*, composed in 1984 (libretto by G. Chiginova), is based on works by Hemingway; it was first performed in Havana on 17 October 1987. While retaining the background of the American writer's life, the composer builds his operatic structure according to the principle of cinematographic montage. Expressionist in style, the opera features declamatory vocal writing, and scenes of common life taken from Afro-Cuban folklore. Continuous symphonic development leads to the dramatic climax of the opera in the choreographic scene 'The Old Man and the Sea'.

F. Campoamor: 'Hemingway en escena, cantando a la vida', *Bohemia* [Havana], lxxix/42 (1987), 36–8
P. Garcia Albela: 'Yury Kazaryan iz strani muzïkantov i poetov' [Ghazaryan from the Country of Musicians and Poets], *Cuba*, no.4 (1988), 15–23
A. Bayeva: 'Prazdnik opernogo iskusstva v Gavane' [The Festival of Operatic Culture in Havana], *Latinskaya Amerika*, no.5 (1988), 66–71
G. Tigranov: *Armyanskiy muzïkal'nïi teatr* [The Armenian Musical Theatre], iv (Erevan, 1988), 78–86
'Prem'yera v Gavane'/'A Première in Havana', *Muzïka v SSSR* (1989), Oct–Dec, 48

SVETLANA SARKISYAN

Ghedini, Giorgio Federico (*b* Cuneo, 11 July 1892; *d* Nervi, nr Genoa, 25 March 1965). Italian composer. He had piano and organ lessons as a child and in 1905 moved to Turin, where he spent three years as a student of the cello, harmony and counterpoint at the Liceo Musicale. He studied composition privately under Giovanni Cravero and briefly under M. E. Bossi at the Liceo Musicale, Bologna, where he received his diploma in 1911. After a period (1909–20) in which he tried to launch himself as a conductor (acting, among other things, as assistant conductor at the Teatro Regio, Turin) he turned to teaching, first in Turin (where he was in touch with such leaders of the city's musical life as Alfano, Della Corte, Romualdo Giani and G. M. Gatti) and subsequently at the conservatories of Parma (1938–41) and Milan (1941–51, director 1951–62). He was also active as an adviser to the Teatro alla Scala.

Ghedini was slow in making his mark outside a small circle, and began to attract wider notice only in the late 1920s. Nevertheless, there is no shortage of lively inventiveness in some of his early works: the stylistic elements may seldom advance much beyond Pizzetti or mild Ravel, but it is already apparent that timbre was to play a paramount role in Ghedini's best music. By the 1930s his horizons were widening, through an increasing involvement with early Italian music and a growing awareness of his more radical contemporaries. The work which, more than any other, marked his full emergence as a 'modern' composer was the orchestral *Architetture* (1940), a terse, boldly sculptured series of 'edifici sonori' in which Stravinsky's influence is unmistakable.

An important by-product of the experience of *Architetture* was Ghedini's arrival at maturity as an opera composer. *Maria d'Alessandria*, written only four years earlier, had still been too traditional – especially (above all in the effective choral and ensemble scenes) Pizzettian – to seem like a wholly individual statement. And *Re Hassan*, though it marked an enormous step forward in sheer harmonic boldness, had a slightly awkward air, taken as a whole, due partly to the static quality of Ghedini's new musical language, which he had not yet fully mastered. After *Architetture*, however, *Le baccanti* came as a fiercely compelling utterance: although controversial when it was new, this is by far his finest theatre work, even if its oratorio-like stylization perhaps confirms that he was more naturally at ease in more abstract music. Among his lesser operas, *La pulce d'oro* (written as a lightweight contrast immediately after *Re Hassan*) is a spirited if rather uneven comedy that has been relatively often performed; *Billy Budd*, whose stylized libretto (with much spoken narrative) is by no less a writer than Quasimodo, has been overshadowed – even in Italy – by Britten's larger and more powerfully dramatic treatment of the same subject, which appeared two years later; while *Lord Inferno*, though subsequently adapted for the stage with a new title, is better in its original form as an outstandingly effective, much revived radio opera.

See also BACCANTI, LE; LORD INFERNO; MARIA D'ALESSANDRIA; *and* RE HASSAN.

Gringoire, 1915 (G. M. Gatti, after T. F. de Banville), unperf.
L'intrusa, 1921 (R. Giani), unperf.

Maria d'Alessandria (3, C. Meano), Bergamo, Novità, 9 Sept 1937

Re Hassan (3, T. Pinelli), Venice, Fenice, 26 Jan 1939; rev., Naples, S Carlo, 20 May 1961

La pulce d'oro (1, Pinelli), Genoa, Carlo Felice, 15 Feb 1940

Le baccanti, 1941–4 (Pinelli, after Euripides: *The Bacchae*), Milan, Scala, 22 Feb 1948

Billy Budd (1, S. Quasimodo, after H. Melville), Venice, Fenice, 8 Sept 1949

Lord Inferno (radio op, 1, F. Antonicelli, after M. Beerbohm: *The Happy Hypocrite*), RAI, 22 Oct 1952; rev. for stage as L'ipocrita felice, Milan, Piccola Scala, 10 March 1956

*

G. Gavazzeni: 'Lettera da Milano: *Maria d'Alessandria* di Ghedini alla Scala', *RaM*, xii (1939), 175–8

'Lettera da Venezia: *Re Hassan* di Ghedini', *RaM*, xii (1939), 129–32

C. Pinelli: 'Esordio di un operista italiano: *Maria d'Alessandria* di G. F. Ghedini', *RMI*, xliii (1939), 75–96

——: *Re Hassan di Giorgio Ghedini* (Milan, 1942)

G. F. Ghedini: 'Note su *Le baccanti* e su altri lavori', *Agorà* [Turin], ii/1 (1946), 23–5

M. Mila: 'Lettera da Venezia: *Billy Budd* di Ghedini', *RaM*, xix (1949), 223–5

A. Piovesan: 'Premio Italia 1952', *La Scala*, no.38 (1953), 50–51 [on *Lord Inferno*]

M. Mila: 'Il libertino allegorico di Ghedini', *Cronache musicali 1955–9* (Turin, 1959), 176–8 [on *L'ipocrita felice*]

A. M. Bonisconti: 'Il teatro musicale di Giorgio Federico Ghedini', *Musica d'oggi*, new ser., iv (1961), 194–200

A. Parente: '*Re Hassan* di Ghedini al Teatro S. Carlo di Napoli', *Musica d'oggi*, iv (1961), 121–3

G. Ugolini: 'Il teatro di Ghedini', *La Scala*, no.149 (1962), 27–33

G. Salvetti: *Giorgio Ghedini, musicista* (diss., U. of Milan, 1963)

J. C. G. Waterhouse: *The Emergence of Modern Italian Music (up to 1940)* (diss., U. of Oxford, 1968), 717–39

A. Gentilucci: *Guida all'ascolto della musica contemporanea* (Milan, 1969), 170–71

G. Salvetti: 'L' ''antipoetica'' di G. F. Ghedini nella musica italiana tra le due guerre', *Studi musicali*, i (1972), 371–417

P. Santi: 'Ghedini e il suo teatro timbrico', *Ghedini e l'attività musicale in Torino fra le due guerre: Turin 1986*, 15–26

JOHN C. G. WATERHOUSE

Ghent (Fr. Gand; Flemish Gent). City in east Flanders, Belgium. The first communal theatre was built in 1698, when Lully's *Thésée* was performed by a visiting troupe, and from 1706 the town possessed its own lyric company. The theatre burnt down in 1715, and the town in 1736 ceded its rights to the St Sebastian Archer's Guild, who built the St Sebastian Theatre. During the French occupation of 1745–9 Marshal de Saxe arranged for Favart's troupe to play there. The theatre was demolished in 1837, and the Grand Théâtre was built and opened in 1840. It became the Koninklijke Opera (Royal Opera) in 1921; until 1940 most operas presented were sung in French. These included the first performances in French of Puccini's *Il trittico* (1923), Mascagni's *Il piccolo Marat* (1923), Zandonai's *Giulietta e Romeo* (1924) and Albert's *Die toten Augen*. A separate Flemish theatre was opened in 1871, giving some opera and much operetta until 1940. During the German occupation performances at the Royal Opera were given in Flemish; since the early 1960s they have been given in the original language. Vina Bovy enjoyed a successful directorship from 1947 to 1955. She was one of a number of singers such as G.-F. Campenhout (composer of the Belgian national anthem), Jean-Blaise Martin (who gave his name to a type of light baritone), Jean Noté, Albert Alvarez, André Maison, Arnold van Mill and Rita Gorr who started their careers in Ghent before winning international acclaim. In 1982 the company joined with the Koninklijke Opera of Antwerp to form the Opera voor Vlaanderen (Flanders Opera), an alliance that has dissolved and reformed a number of times under various names; it was known from 1988 as De Vlaamsoper, and there was a change in that year from the repertory to the stagione system. In 1990–91 the Royal Opera theatre was renovated.   CHARLES PITT

Gherardeschi, Filippo Maria (*b* Pistoia, 1738; *d* Pisa, 1808). Italian composer. After studying in Bologna with Martini, he held church posts in Tuscany, becoming a *maestro di cappella* in Pisa in about 1766. He was also director of concerts for Grand Duke Leopold of Tuscany. Of his seven operas (all but one performed exclusively in Tuscany) only librettos and scattered arias are extant. Apparently unsuccessful in this form, he seems to have written no operas after 1769, although there are in Pistoia individual arias referring to performances – probably of earlier operas – after that date. Most of his other works are sacred. Gherardeschi's nephew Giuseppe (1759–1824), a *maestro di cappella* in Pistoia, may have written a two-act opera, *Daliso e Delmita* (1782, *I-PS*).

L'amore artigiano (C. Goldoni), Lucca, 1763

Il curioso indiscreto (3, ? G. Petrosellini), Pisa, Pubblico, 1764

I visionari, Pisa, 1765

La contessina (3, Goldoni), Pisa, Pubblico, 1766

L'astuzia felice (dg, 3, ?Goldoni, after Goldoni: *La cameriera spiritosa*), Venice, S Moisè, aut. 1767

I due gobbi, Pisa, Pubblico, carn. 1769

La notte critica (dg, 3, Goldoni), Pisa, Pubblico, carn. 1769

*

*Stieger*O

Obituary, *Magasin encyclopédique* (1809), i, 135

V. Capponi: *Biografia pistoiese o notizie della vita e delle opere di pistoiesi illustri* (Pistoia, 1878)

G. C. Rospigliosi: *Notizie dei maestri ed artisti di musica pistoiese* (Pistoia, 1878)

A. Chiapelli: *Storia del teatro in Pistoia dalle origini alla fine del secolo XVIII* (Pistoia, 1913)   HOWARD BROFSKY

Gherardini [Gherardino, Ghirardini], **Rinaldo** (*b* ? Modena, 1657; *d* 1707 or later). Italian soprano castrato. A petition to the Duke of Modena, probably dating from 1670, stated that Rinaldo Gherardini, 13 years of age, certain of his gifts as a singer and fearing his voice might change, decided to have himself castrated and asked for help towards the expense of the operation; it was then carried out. In 1679 he sang in Parma in F. M. Barzani's *Ottone in Italia*. He went to Bologna, where he was a soprano at S Petronio, 1679–86, and from 1683 a member of the Accademia Filarmonica. On 1 March 1688 he became a virtuoso at the Parma court; remaining at least until 15 January 1707, he took part in many performances until 1697 and was a singer at the cathedral, 1699–1706. From 1687 he also sang in Piacenza, Fabriano, Crema, Rome and Turin. He is mentioned as the composer of a cantata (1685, *I-Bc*) and he signed the dedications of two operas performed in Parma in 1696: *Paride in Ida* (composer unknown) and *Il Mauritio*, which he probably composed.

*

J. Rosselli: 'The Castrati as a Professional Group and a Social Phenomenon, 1550–1850', *AcM*, lx (1988), 143–79

PAOLA BESUTTI

Ghiaurov, Nicolai (*b* Velingrad, 13 Sept 1929). Bulgarian bass. He was a pupil of Brambarov at the Sofia Conservatory and then continued his studies in Leningrad and Moscow. He made his début at Sofia in 1955 as Don Basilio in *Il barbiere*, and in 1958 made the first of many appearances in Italy at the Teatro

Set design by Lorenzo Ghiglia for the original production of Pizzetti's 'Il calzare d'argento', La Scala, Milan, 23 March 1961

Comunale, Bologna, in *Faust*; from 1959 he also sang at La Scala, where his roles have included Boris and Philip II. He made his début at Covent Garden in 1962 (as Padre Guardiano) and at the Metropolitan in 1965 (as Méphistophélès). He first appeared at the Vienna Staatsoper in 1957, as Ramfis, singing regularly there from 1962; his roles have included Ivan Khovansky (1989). At the Opéra he has sung Massenet's Don Quichotte (1974), and he has appeared at the Salzburg Festival, notably as Boris in 1965 and Philip II in 1975. These are among his most notable roles; he sang Boris at the Metropolitan in 1990. He possesses a voice of unusually rich and varied colour allied to an excellent vocal technique and remarkable musicality. A vigorous and painstaking actor, as an interpreter he tends to express the strong and violent emotions rather than the finer and more intimate shades of meaning.

GV (R. Celletti; R. Vegeto)
A. Blyth: 'Nicolai Ghiaurov', *Opera*, xxviii (1977), 941–7
RODOLFO CELLETTI

Ghiglia, Lorenzo (*b* Florence, 26 Nov 1936). Italian stage and costume designer. After studying in Florence he went to Milan, where he won second prize in a competitive exhibition for stage and costume design. One of his first professional commissions was for Giorgio Ferrari's *Cappuccia* at the Bergamo Festival of 1958. He became one of the youngest designers ever to work at La Scala, designing the première of Pizzetti's *Il calzare d'argento* (1961; see illustration) for the director Margherita Wallmann. Other significant early productions were *La bohème* (1961, Palermo), the première of Bruno Gillet's *Il visconte dimezzato* (1961, Monte Carlo), *Attila* (1962, Florence), *Carmen* (1966, Naples) and Petrassi's *Il Cordovano* (1966, Turin). For Houston he designed a *Pagliacci* and a *Rigoletto*, and for Dallas a *Samson et Dalila*, before accepting commissions from Glyndebourne for *Anna Bolena* (1965) and *Dido and Aeneas* (1966). His work, however, has been more readily appreciated in the USA than in Britain.

Ghiglia is not usually concerned with historical or social accuracy, or with period style. His designs tend towards linear simplicity, and he tries to create an en-

vironment, often in a unit set, that allows the director considerable imaginative choice. He has tended to work with a limited number of directors, such as Filippo Crivelli, Franco Enriquez and Mario Missiroli, but on a number of their productions. In his designs for *Le villi* (1972, Florence), *Suor Angelica* (1973, La Scala), Busoni's *Arlecchino* (1975, Florence) and Cherubini's *Médée* (1977, Catania), Ghiglia and the director Roberto Guicciardini readily altered the time and place of setting, mixing realism with fantasy: many critics have felt that the visual charm of this technique was at the expense of other dramatic values.   DAVID J. HOUGH

Ghisi, Federico (*b* Shanghai, 25 Feb 1901; *d* Luserna San Giovanni, nr Turin, 18 July 1975). Italian composer. He spent his early years in China and was taken to Italy in 1908. He studied composition with Carlo Gatti in Milan and Ghedini in Turin, completing his diploma in 1932; he also took a degree in chemistry at the University of Pavia. Later he held teaching posts at the universities of Florence (1937–40) and Pisa (1963–70) and lectured at various American universities. As a musicologist he was concerned not only with Ars Nova and Italian Renaissance and 17th-century music, but also with popular tradition, an interest that underlies his own works for the theatre. *Piramo e Tisbe*, for example, parodies the polyphonic technique of the madrigal to convey humour; the stage pantomimes *Le istorie cinesi di Marco Polo*, which use the scansion typical of Chinese theatre in its original language, are an interesting result of cultural borrowing; the *devozione Sant'Alessio: vita, morte e miracoli* includes anonymous texts and secular musical material from the Middle Ages. Ghisi's music also has affinities with Prokofiev, Falla, Orff and Bartók.

Piramo e Tisbe, 1941–3 (cantare di piazza, 1, after W. Shakespeare: *A Midsummer Night's Dream*), Plauen, Stadt, 5 March 1955
Le istorie cinesi di Marco Polo, 1955 (pantomime sceniche, after Marco Polo: *Il milione* and Chin. popular poems), unperf.
Sant'Alessio: vita, morte e miracoli, 1957 (devozione scenica o per concerto, from anon. medieval texts), RAI, 1963
Il dono dei re magi, 1959 (scena lirica, radiofonica o televisiva, 1, after O. Henry), unperf.
Il vagabondo e la guardia, 1960 (scena popolare, 1, after Henry: *The Cop and the Anthem*), RAI, 1965

DEUMM (C. Terni); Grove6 (C. Gianturco)
G. Hausswald: 'Federico Ghisis *Piramus und Tisbe*', *Das neue Opern Buch* (Berlin, 1957)
A. Damerini: 'Sant'Alessio: vita, morte e miracoli', *La nazione* [Florence] (7 Feb 1963)   RAFFAELE POZZI

Ghislanzoni, Antonio (*b* Lecco, 25 Nov 1824; *d* Caprino Bergamasco, 16 July 1893). Italian librettist. After Boito, he was the most important Italian librettist between 1860 and 1890. He is usually credited with 85 librettos, but this seems to be a considerable overestimate, the correct total being about half that number. He was also a prolific journalist, responsible, on his own count, for more than 2000 articles. Originally intended for the priesthood, he was removed from the seminary at the age of 15 and studied medicine at Pavia instead. In 1846, finding that he had a fine baritone voice, he abandoned his studies and determined on a singing career, which he followed for about eight years. He was fervently patriotic, and in 1848 he founded two republican journals in Milan. He was arrested by the French in Rome and after a brief period of detention in Corsica he returned to the stage, incidentally singing Carlo in Verdi's *Ernani* in Paris in 1851. Three years later he arrived, ill, in Milan, and established himself in literary circles, later editing the *Gazzetta musicale di Milano* and the *Rivista minima*, and contributing to literary and artistic journals. He later made his home in Lecco, for whose theatre he wrote five librettos, but in 1890 retired to Caprino Bergamasco.

Although he began his career as a librettist in 1857, Ghislanzoni is best known for his later work for Verdi. In 1869, the composer, whom he had met 20 years earlier, asked him to help with the revision of *La forza del destino*. The collaboration was successful, so that Ghislanzoni was the obvious choice for *Aida* when a poet was needed to turn a prose text into verse. In the event, Verdi always treated the writer with respect, and also sought his help with the revision of *Don Carlos* in 1872. Ghislanzoni provided a number of first-class librettos for other composers, such as *I promessi sposi* (1869) for Petrella, *Fosca* (1873) and *Salvator Rosa* (1874) for Gomes and *Francesca da Rimini* (1878) for Cagnoni, but his best was probably *I lituani* (1874) for Ponchielli, a noble if rather monochrome work. His sense of dramatic structure was conventional yet secure, and although his work was strongly rooted in traditional forms, he used these with imagination and versatility. His verse was always clear and correct, and he had a gift for the neat and unhackneyed turn of phrase; his librettos are mercifully free from 'librettists' doggerel'. He was in sum a reliable and accomplished literary craftsman. It is easy to see why Verdi found him a congenial collaborator but also clear why it was Boito and not Ghislanzoni who stimulated the composer's last two masterpieces.

dl – *dramma lirico*   mel – *melodramma*   ob – *opera buffa*

Le due fidanzate (mel serio), A. Bauer, 1857; *Il conte di Leicester* (mel), Bauer, 1858; *Maria Tudor* (dramma per musica), Kashperov, 1859; *Marion Delorme* (mel serio), Bottesini, 1862; *Cola di Rienzi* (tragedia lirica), Kashperov, 1863; *La stella di Toledo* (mel), T. Benvenuti, 1864; *I due orsi* (ob), C. Dall'Argine, 1867; *Gli avventurieri* (mel), G. Braga, 1867; *Gli artisti alla fiera* (libretto buffo), Lauro Rossi, 1868; *Valeria* (tragedia lirica), E. Vera, 1869; *I promessi sposi* (mel), Petrella, 1869; *Giovanna di Napoli* (dl), Petrella, 1869; *Un capriccio di donna* (mel serio), Cagnoni, 1870; *Papa Martin* (mel semiserio), Cagnoni, 1871; *Reginella* (mel), Braga, 1871; *Aida*, Verdi, 1871; *Adelinda* (dl), A. Mercuri, 1872; *Caligola*, Braga, 1873; *Fosca* (mel), Gomes, 1873; *Il parlatore eterno* (scherzo comico), Ponchielli, 1873; *I Lituani*

(dl), Ponchielli, 1874; *Salvator Rosa* (dl), Gomes, 1874; *Il duca di Tapigliano* (libretto comico), Cagnoni, 1874; *Atahualpa* (dl), C. E. Pasta, 1875; *Sara* (mel), Luigi Gibelli, 1876; *Gli schiavi di Enna*, N. Ravera, 1877; *Francesca da Rimini* (tragedia lirica), Cagnoni, 1878; *Adelina* (mel serio), L. Sozzi, 1879; *Don Riego* (dl), C. dall'Olio, 1879; *Mora* (mel serio), L. Vicini, 1880; *Edmea* (dl), Catalani, 1886; *Giovanna la pazza*, ? E. Ortiz de Zárate, 1886; *I Doria* (dl), Machado, 1887; *Eduardo Stuart* (mel), C. Pontoglio, 1887; *Carmosina* (dl), Araújo, 1888; *Fiamma*, N. Ravera, 1890 (V. Cicognani, 1892); *Andrea del Sarto* (dl), V. Baravalle, 1890; *Spartaco* (tragedia lirica), Platania, 1891; *Cleopatra*, Morales, 1891; *Celeste* (Idillio), Spetrino, 1891; *Gualtiero Swarten*, A. Gnaga, 1893; *Alda* (dl), L. Romaniello, 1896; *I Mori di Valenza* (dl), Ponchielli, 1914

*

S. Miragoli: *Il melodramma italiano nell'ottocento* (Rome, 1924)
P. Gossett: 'Verdi, Ghislanzoni, and Aida: the Uses of Convention', *Critical Inquiry*, i (1974), 291–334
J. Nicolaisen: *Italian Opera in Transition, 1871–1893* (Ann Arbor, 1980)
J. Budden: *The Operas of Verdi*, iii: *From 'Don Carlos' to 'Falstaff'* (London, 1981)   JOHN BLACK

Ghiuselev, Nikola. *See* GYUZELEV, NIKOLA.

Giacomelli [Jacomelli], Geminiano (*b* Piacenza, *c*1692; *d* Loreto, 25 Jan 1740). Italian composer. In his early years in Parma he studied with Capelli, *maestro di cappella* of the cathedral. The story of his being sent to study with Alessandro Scarlatti in 1724, and afterwards being in the service of Charles VI in Vienna, was doubted by Eitner, and there is little evidence to support either contention: Scarlatti died in 1725, and *Arrenione* and *Catone in Utica*, supposed to have been composed for the Viennese court, are not by Giacomelli.

From 1719 to 1727 Giacomelli was *maestro di cappella* of the court of Parma and the Chiesa della Steccata, serving jointly with his aged teacher Capelli; he held the same position at the church of S Giovanni in Piacenza (1727–32), then returned to his dual position in Parma (1732–7). In 1737 he directed performances of *Cesare in Egitto* in Graz before becoming *maestro di cappella* at the S Casa, Loreto, in 1738.

Giacomelli wrote 19 operas for various Italian cities, almost half of them to librettos by Zeno or Metastasio; his most successful was *Cesare in Egitto* (1735). The set of intermezzos, *Golpone e Birina*, performed in Rome for Carnival 1739 with his *Achille in Aulide* was written by Fini and Zanetti for Venice in 1732, not by Giacomelli. He also composed various sacred works, of which only a few survive. Giacomelli seems to have been highly esteemed by his contemporaries; Marcello published Giacomelli's letter of recommendation in the preface to volume seven of his *Estro poetico-armonico*.

drammi per musica in three acts, lost, unless otherwise stated

Ipermestra (A. Salvi), Parma, Ducale, 1724; Venice, S Giovanni Grisostomo, carn. 1724
Scipione in Cartagine nuova (C. I. Frugoni), Parma, Ducale, spr. 1728, *D-Mbs*
Zidiania, Milan, Regio Ducal, 28 Aug, 1728
Lucio Papirio dittatore (Zeno and Frugoni), Parma, Ducale, spr. 1729
Gianguir (A. Zeno), Venice, S Cassiano, 1729, *B-Bc*
Semiramide riconosciuta (P. Metastasio), Milan, Regio Ducal, Jan 1730
Annibale (F. Vanstryp), Rome, Capranica, Jan 1731, arias *I-IBborromeo*
Epaminonda (? D. Lalli), Venice, S Giovanni Grisostomo, carn., 1732, *Bc*
Rosbale (C. N. Stampa), ?Rome, Argentina, carn. 1732
Alessandro Severo (Zeno), Piacenza, Ducale, aut. 1732
Adriano in Siria (Metastasio), Venice, S Giovanni Grisostomo, carn. 1733, *D-B*

La caccia in Etolia (pasticcio), Vienna, Kärntnertor, 8 April 1733

Merope (Zeno), Venice, S Giovanni Grisostomo, carn. 1734, *A-Wgm*, *B-Bc*

Cesare in Egitto (G. F. Bussani), Milan, Regio Ducal, carn. 1735, *Bc*

Nitocri, regina d'Egitto (Zeno), Rome, Tordinona, carn. 1736

Arsace (Salvi and G. Boldoni), Prato, Pubblico, 1736

Demetrio (Metastasio), Turin, Regio, carn. 1737

La Costanza vincitrice in amore, Parma, Ducale, carn. 1738, ?collab. Genocchi (?Gnocchi)

Achille in Aulide, Rome, Argentina, carn. 1739

Egloga amebea (intermezzo), *A-Wgm*

Arias in La muse lyrique italienne avec des paroles françoises (Paris, 1773) and in *A-Wgm*, *Wn*, *F-Pn*, *D-B*, *Dlb*, *SWl*, *W*, *GB-Lbl*, *Cfm*, *I-Mc*, *Nc*, *S-Uu*

*

N. Pelicelli: 'Musicisti in Parma nel secolo xviii', *NA*, xi (1934), 29–57, esp. 34

C. Anguissola: *Geminiano Giacomelli e Sebastiano Nasolini, musicisti piacentini* (Piacenza, 1935)

A. Yorke-Long: *Music at Court* (London, 1954)

GORDANA LAZAREVICH

Giacomini, Giuseppe (*b* Monselico, Padua, 7 Sept 1940). Italian tenor. He studied at Padua and Milan, making his début in 1967 at Vercelli as Pinkerton. In 1975 he sang at La Scala, the Vienna Staatsoper and the Opéra; he made his Metropolitan début in 1976 as Don Alvaro and his Covent Garden début in 1980 as Dick Johnson. He has appeared throughout Italy and in Munich, Hamburg and Chicago, performing a repertory that includes Edgardo, Pollione, Don José, Chénier, Canio, Turiddu, Manrico, Radames, Rodolfo (*Bohème*), Luigi, Cavaradossi, Calaf and from the late 1980s Verdi's Otello. In 1990 he created Nanni in Tutino's *La lupa* at Livorno. He is noted more for his strong, well-focussed voice than for his dramatic involvement.

ELIZABETH FORBES

Giacomo, Salvatore di. See DI GIACOMO, SALVATORE.

Giacosa, Giuseppe (*b* Colleretto Parella, Ivrea, 21 Oct 1847; *d* Colleretto Parella, 1 Sept 1906). Italian playwright and librettist. After graduating in law at Turin University he joined his father's legal practice until the success of his one-act verse comedy *Una partita a scacchi* (1873) induced him to take up a literary career. He became a member of Boito's circle, specializing at first in stylized period drama. Then followed a number of prose plays in the tradition of the French Théâtre Libre, of which *Tristi amori* (1887) and *Come le foglie* (1900) still hold the stage as worthy examples of intimate bourgeois tragedy. *La comtesse de Chaillant* (1891) was written in French for Sarah Bernhardt. From 1888 to 1894 Giacosa held the chair of literature and dramatic art at the Milan Conservatory. At the time of his death he was editor of the literary periodical *La lettura*. His output also includes a number of prose sketches associated with his native region and entitled *Novelle e paesi valdostani* (1886) and an account of a visit to America in 1891.

Regarded at the turn of the century as Italy's leading playwright, Giacosa is remembered chiefly for his association with Puccini in double harness with the librettist Luigi Illica. The partnership was organized by the publisher Giulio Ricordi in 1894. After Puccini had turned down Giacosa's offer of a Russian subject, Ricordi set the two librettists to work on the text of *La bohème* (1896); it would seem to have been Giacosa's idea to base the character of the heroine on a blend of Murger's Mimì and Francine, so ensuring a total contrast between the two female leads such as eluded Leoncavallo in his treatment of the same subject. The collaboration continued with *Tosca* (1900) and *Madama Butterfly* (1904) with equally successful results. In each case Illica's task was to plan the scenario and draft the dialogue which Giacosa would then put into polished verse. Although he found the work uncongenial and frequently protested against Puccini's ideas he always ended by giving way to them; and his calm, benign presence at their conferences (he was known affectionately as 'the Buddha') did much to smooth their difficulties. In addition to his work for Puccini Giacosa adapted *Una partita a scacchi* for a one-act opera by the Piedmontese composer Pietro Abbà-Cornaglia (1892) and sketched out the text for an oratorio, *Cain*, for Lorenzo Perosi. The plan to write a libretto for Mascagni with Illica never came to fruition.

*

M. Rumor: *Giuseppe Giacosa* (Padua, 1924)

P. Nardi: *Vita e tempo di Giuseppe Giacosa* (Milan, 1949)

A. Barsotti: *Giuseppe Giacosa* (Florence, 1977)

JULIAN BUDDEN

Giai [Giaii, Giaij, Giaj, Giay], **Giovanni Antonio** (*b* Turin, 11 June 1690; *d* Turin, 10 Sept 1764). Italian composer. He was a boy singer in the Cappella degli Innocenti of Turin Cathedral (*c*1700); after studying composition with the *maestro di cappella* of the cathedral, Francesco Fasoli, he may have pursued further studies in Rome. He was generally credited with having composed the opera *Il trionfo d'Amore, o La Fillide* (1715) for the reopening of the Teatro Regio in Turin after the War of the Spanish Succession; this is however now considered to be by A. S. Fiorè, *maestro di cappella* at the court of Vittorio Amedeo II of Savoy, though Giai may have collaborated with him on it, as he did later on *Sesostri, rè d'Egitto* (1717) and *I veri amici* (1728). His own operas were performed over the next 35 years in Turin, Venice, Milan and Rome. The one-act *componimento drammatico*, *Fetonte sulle rive del Po*, was written for the marriage of Vittorio Amedeo and Maria Antonia Ferdinanda of Spain in Madrid (1750).

After Fiorè died in 1732, Giai assumed the duties of *maestro di cappella* and was confirmed in the position by Carlo Emanuele III in a patent of 24 October 1738. In this capacity he directed the instrumental and vocal forces of the court and composed a large amount of church music. Giai held the post until his death and was succeeded by his son, Francesco Saverio.

dm – dramma per musica

Sesostri, rè d'Egitto (dm, 3, Bursetti, after P. Pariati), Turin, Carignano, carn. 1717, *F-Pn*, collab. Fiorè

Artenice (dm, after A. Zeno), Turin, Regio, carn. 1723, addns with others to G. M. Orlandini: Ormisda

Publio Cornelio Scipione (dm, A. Salvi), Turin, 1725

Il Tamerlano (tragedia per musica, 3, A. Piovene), Milan, 1727

I veri amici [Act 1] (os, 3, F. Silvani and D. Lalli, after P. Corneille: *Héraclius empereur d'Orient*), Turin, Ducal, 1728, arias *A-Wgm*, *F-Pn* [Acts 2 and 3 by Fiorè]

Mitridate (dm, 5, Zeno and Lalli), Venice, 1730

Demetrio (P. Metastasio), Rome, 1732, 6 arias in *D-Dlb*, 2 in *GB-Lbl*

Eumene (dm, 3, Zeno), Turin, 1737

Gianguir (dm, 3, Zeno), Venice, 1738

Adriano in Siria (dm, 3, Metastasio), Venice, 1740, *D-Dlb*

Fetonte sulle rive del Po (componimento drammatico, 1, G. M. Baretti), Turin, 1750

Le tre dee riunite, Madrid, 1750

Arias in *D-Dlb*, *KA*, *GB-Cfm*, *I-Fc*, *Vnm*

? Contribs. to Fiorè: Il trionfo d'Amore, o La Fillide, 1715

*

EitnerQ

G. Roberti: La Cappella regia di Torino, 1515–1870 (Turin, 1880)

——: Il Teatro regio di Torino, 1662–1890 (Turin, 1892)

L. Vallas: Un siècle de musique et de théâtre à Lyon, 1688–1789 (Lyons, 1932), 273

M. T. Bouquet: De quelques relations musicales franco-piémontaises (1648–1775) (diss., U. of Paris-Sorbonne, 1967; pt ii pubd as Musique et musiciens à Turin de 1648 à 1775, Turin, 1968)

GORDANA LAZAREVICH

Giani, Nini (b 1904; d Milan, 16 Nov 1972). Italian mezzo-soprano, later soprano. She trained in Milan and made her début as Amneris at the Teatro Adriano, Rome, in 1930. Her successes in the smaller Italian houses led to an engagement at the S Carlo, Naples, in 1934 and at La Scala the following year. She also appeared in Germany, Switzerland and France. Her single Covent Garden season of 1933 was inauspicious; she took part in some poor performances of *Aida* and *Don Carlos* and was criticized for scooping, wobbling and abusing the chest voice. At La Scala she sang in the première of Refice's *Margherita da Cortona* and the first Italian production of *Sadko*, both in 1938. She sang many times at Verona and was popular in South America. Her development towards dramatic soprano was accomplished by way of Santuzza into Tosca and finally Turandot. She retired in 1948, one of the few singers of her time to have recorded no more than a single disc, made as a mezzo-soprano.

J. B. STEANE

Giannettini [Gianettini, Zanettini, Zannettini], **Antonio** (b Fano, 1648; d Munich, bur. 14 July 1721). Italian composer. By 14 January 1674, and possibly by 1672, he was a bass in the choir of St Mark's, Venice. Described as a pupil of Carlo Grossi, he served as organist at the church of SS Giovanni e Paolo from 5 October 1676 until April 1679 and as organist at St Mark's from 25 January 1677. He left St Mark's on 1 May 1686 to become *maestro di cappella* to the Duke of Modena, a post he retained, with interruptions, almost until the end of his life. At Modena he was responsible for the selection and payment of musicians and for organizing musical performances. He was called on to produce oratorios and small occasional works more often than operas. When, during the War of the Spanish Succession, the French occupied Modena in 1702, Duke Rinaldo d'Este fled to Bologna, and Giannettini accompanied him. He soon moved on to Venice with his family, however, and again took up the composition of opera. During this period he is supposed to have returned to Modena twice as opera director. After the war, in February 1707, he resumed his earlier activities at Modena. In 1721 he accompanied his daughter Maria Caterina, a singer at the Bavarian court, to Munich.

Giannettini was among the most talented Italian composers of his generation; his works were fairly popular, and two of his operas circulated in Germany. *Medea in Atene* (1675), his first and most widely performed, shows an unusually large range of gesture and a lively rhythmic style. The vocal writing is smooth but demanding, and there is a particularly effective aria on a chromatic ostinato and considerable use of the *stile concitato*. *Temistocle in bando* (1682) also includes an ostinato aria, as well as a number of motto arias.

Medea in Atene (drama per musica, prol., 3, A. Aureli), Venice, S Moisè, 14 Dec 1675, I-Vnm; as Teseo in Atene, 1688, MOe (arias)

L'Aurora in Atene (drama per musica, 3, G. Frisari), Venice, SS Giovanni e Paolo, 10 Feb 1678, Vqs (arias)

Irene e Costantino (drama per musica, 3, A. Rossini), Venice, S Salvatore, 1681, Vnm, Vqs (arias)

Temistocle in bando (drama per musica, 3, A. Morselli), Venice, S Cassiano, 4 Dec 1682, Vqs (arias)

L'Ermione racquistata [Die wiedergefundene Hermione] (drama per musica, prol., 3, Aureli), Wolfenbüttel, 11 Feb 1686

L'ingresso alla gioventù di Claudio Nerone (drama per musica, 3, G. B. Neri), Modena, Fontanelli, 4 Nov 1692, MOe, Rvat (arias)

Tito Manlio, (M. Noris), Reggio Emilia, Commedie, spr. 1701

Virginio consolo (drama per musica, 3, Noris), Venice, S Angelo, 1704

Artaserse (drama per musica, 3, P. Pariati ?and A. Zeno), Venice, S Angelo, 1705, lib. (Venice, 1705)

*

J. Mattheson: Der musicalische Patriot (Hamburg, 1728)

R. Haas: Die Musik des Barocks (Potsdam, 1928)

E. J. Luin: 'Antonio Giannettini e la musica a Modena alla fine del secolo XVII', Atti e memorie della R. Deputazione di storia patria per le provincie modenesi, 7th ser., vii (1931), 145–230

S. T. Worsthorne: Venetian Opera in the Seventeenth Century (Oxford, 1954)

R. Brockpähler: Handbuch zur Geschichte der Barockoper in Deutschland (Emsdetten, 1964)

THOMAS WALKER/BETH L. GLIXON

Giannina e Bernardone. *Dramma giocoso per musica* in two acts by DOMENICO CIMAROSA to a libretto by FILIPPO LIVIGNI; Venice, Teatro di S Samuele, autumn 1781.

The young and lively peasant girl Giannina (soprano) is married to the wealthy and elderly Bernardone (bass). Insanely jealous, he occasionally locks her in her room and unjustly accuses her of misdemeanours. Suggestions by her brother Masino (tenor), a country tailor happily married to Lauretta (soprano), that women should be treated with love and kindness do not change Bernardone's ways. Giannina is pitied by the Neapolitan Donna Aurora (soprano), her Hungarian uncle Don Orlando (baritone) and her fiancé Capitan Francone (tenor). Playing on Bernardone's jealousy, they make him believe that a letter from Aurora to Francone is from Giannina. Bernardone eventually apologizes, but the angry Giannina plays a joke on him by suggesting that the statue of Cupid resolve their marital differences: as they ask the statue for advice Orlando and Francone, disguised as statues too, scare them by responding cacophonously. In the end all are reconciled, and Aurora and Francone prepare for their wedding.

During its Vienna performances (1784) the opera became a vehicle for the prima donna Luisa Laschi, who sang the role of Giannina with great success (she later created the Countess in Mozart's *Figaro*). The opera acquired at least seven substitute vocal numbers in Vienna, including one by Mysliveček (Aurora's 'Ah non temer ben mio'). For the Naples production in 1785 Cimarosa added more local colour and dialect. In 1790 Haydn composed the substitute aria 'La moglie quanto è buona' for a performance at Eszterháza. The opera was also revived several times between 1870 and 1932.

GORDANA LAZAREVICH

Giannini, Dusolina (b Philadelphia, 19 Dec 1902; d Zürich, 29 June 1986). American soprano. She studied first with her father, the Italian tenor Ferruccio Giannini, then with Marcella Sembrich, and made her operatic début at Hamburg as Aida in 1925. Subsequent engagements took her to Berlin, Vienna and Covent Garden, as well as to Salzburg (1934–6), where she sang Donna Anna under Walter and Alice Ford under Toscanini. In 1938 she created the part of Hester Prynne in *The Scarlet Letter*, an opera by her brother, Vittorio Giannini. Her career at the Metropolitan began with Aida in 1936 and lasted until 1941, during which period she also played Donna Anna, Santuzza and Tosca. After appearing in Chicago (1938–42) and San Francisco (1939–43) she took part in the first season of New York City Opera (1943), as Tosca at the opening, and then Carmen and Santuzza. She retired some 20 years later and devoted herself to teaching. Giannini's voice was a true dramatic soprano, backed by strong temperament and impeccable musicianship. She must be rated a 'freelance' prima donna, who never belonged to any company but made numerous 'star' and guest appearances.

*

W. R. Moran: 'Dusolina Giannini and her Recordings', *Record Collector*, ix (1954), 29–51 [with discography]
L. Rasponi: 'Con principio: Dusolina Giannini', *ON*, xliv/8 (1979–80), 8–13   MAX DE SCHAUENSEE/R

Giannini, Vittorio (*b* Philadelphia, 19 Oct 1903; *d* New York, 28 Nov 1966). American composer. His father and two sisters were opera singers, his mother a violinist. He studied at the Milan conservatory (1914–17) and at the Juilliard School (1925–30). His earliest works, chiefly vocal and chamber music, attracted favourable attention, and in 1932 the American Academy in Rome awarded him the first of three consecutive Rome Prize fellowships. Giannini's sister, Dusolina, was instrumental in having his first opera, *Lucedia*, produced at Munich in 1934; four years later she created Hester Prynne in the Hamburg première of *The Scarlet Letter*. These works, together with three radio operas commissioned by CBS, established Giannini as a leading figure in American opera in the late 1930s. Returning to the USA, he embarked on a distinguished teaching career that included appointments at Juilliard, the Manhattan School and the Curtis Institute. In 1964 he helped found the North Carolina School of the Arts; he served as its first director until his death.

Giannini's outstanding assets as an opera composer were his melodic facility and sound theatrical instincts. His musical language was conservative, not to say reactionary – a euphonious amalgam of Puccinian *verismo* and Wagnerian chromaticism – but he handled the resources of Romantic tonality with freshness and conviction. Both *Lucedia* and *The Taming of the Shrew*, his most popular opera, make extensive use of leitmotifs as a means of musical characterization. Although the thickness of his orchestration sometimes obscures his meticulous prosody, the orchestra is always skilfully integrated into the musico-dramatic fabric. His later operas incorporate greater dissonance and a smattering of 12-note writing, without sacrificing his characteristically italianate lyricism.

Giannini's taste in librettos was similarly conservative. *Lucedia*, the tale of an Indian priest's virgin daughter who is ostracized for falling in love with an adventurer, has overtones of *Norma* and *La vestale*. Several of his operas are based on legends, historical events or literary works. A notable exception is *The Harvest*, commissioned in 1961 by the Ford Foundation as part of a programme to promote American opera. The libretto, by Giannini's long-time collaborator Karl Flaster, is a gritty tale of lust and family strife set in the American South-west at the turn of the century. The subject did not inspire Giannini's best music, and despite a strong cast and

production, the Chicago première was poorly received. In his last operas, *Rehearsal Call* and *The Servant of Two Masters*, he returned to a lighter romantic-*buffo* style. The North Carolina School of the Arts has several of his MSS; the rest are held in a private trust.

Lucedia (3, K. Flaster), Munich, 20 Oct 1934, vs (Berlin, 1934)
Flora (radio op, 3), CBS, 1937
The Scarlet Letter (2, Flaster, after N. Hawthorne), Hamburg, 2 June 1938, vs (Hamburg, 1938)
Beauty and the Beast (radio op, 1, R. Simon), CBS, 1938; stage, Hartford, CT, Hartt School of Music, 14 Feb 1946, vs (New York, 1951)
Blennerhasset (radio op, 1, P. Roll and N. Corwin), CBS, 1939; stage, New York, Institute of Musical Art, 12 April 1940
Casanova (3, Giannini and Simon), ?unperf.
The Taming of the Shrew (3, Giannini and D. Fee, after W. Shakespeare), concert perf., Cincinnati, 31 Jan 1953; televised, NBC, 13 March 1954; stage, New York, City Center, 13 April 1958, vs (New York, 1954)
Christus, 1956 (tetralogy, Flaster), ?unperf.
The Harvest (3, Flaster), Chicago, 25 Nov 1961, vs (New York, 1961)
Rehearsal Call (3, F. Swann and Simon), New York, Juilliard, 15 Feb 1962
The Servant of Two Masters (2, B. Stambler, after C. Goldoni), New York, State Theater, 9 March 1967, vs (New York, 1967)
Edipus (4, ?Giannini, after Sophocles), inc.

R. Parris: 'Vittorio Giannini and the Romantic Tradition', *Juilliard Review*, iv/2 (1957), 32–46
M. de Schauensee: 'The Gianninis', *ON*, xxviii/22 (1963–4), 14–16
M. L. Mark: *The Life and Works of Vittorio Giannini (1903–1966)* (diss., Catholic U. of America, 1970)
A. Simpson and K. W. Flaster: 'A Working Relationship: the Giannini-Flaster Collaboration', *American Music*, vi (1988), 375–408   HARRY HASKELL, WALTER SIMMONS

Gianni Schicchi. Opera in one act by GIACOMO PUCCINI to a libretto by GIOVACCHINO FORZANO after a passage from DANTE ALIGHIERI's narrative poem *Commedia*, part 1: Inferno; New York, Metropolitan Opera House, 14 December 1918 (as no.3 of *Il trittico*).

Gianni Schicchi *(aged 50)*	baritone
Lauretta *his daughter (aged 21)*	soprano
Zita *cousin of Buoso Donati (aged 60)*	contralto
Rinuccio *Zita's nephew (aged 24)*	tenor
Gherardo *Buoso's nephew (aged 40)*	tenor
Nella *Gherardo's wife (aged 34)*	soprano
Gherardino *their son (aged 7)*	contralto
Betto di Signa *Buoso's brother-in-law (of uncertain age)*	bass
Simone *cousin of Buoso (aged 70)*	bass
Marco *Simone's son (aged 45)*	baritone
La Ciesca *Marco's wife (aged 38)*	mezzo-soprano
Maestro Spinelloccio *a doctor*	bass
Ser Amantio di Nicolao *a notary*	baritone
Pinellino *a cobbler*	bass
Guccio *a dyer*	bass

Setting Florence, 1299

Authorities disagree as to whether Puccini or Forzano first had the idea of basing a comedy on a brief passage in Canto 30 of Dante's *Inferno* concerning a sly rogue who cheated the poet's own relatives by marriage out of a substantial inheritance. Forzano submitted his scheme in March 1917 and completed the libretto in June. Puccini began work on it immediately, before laying it aside to finish the second part of *Il trittico*, *Suor Angelica*. The autograph is dated 3 February 1918. The

'Gianni Schicchi' (Puccini): scene from the original production at the Metropolitan Opera House, New York, 14 December 1918

American cast included Giuseppe De Luca (Schicchi), Florence Easton (Lauretta), Giulio Crimi (Rinuccio), Kathleen Howard (Zita) and Adam Didur (Simone); the conductor was Roberto Moranzoni. At the Italian première on 11 January 1919 (Rome, Teatro Costanzi), conducted by Gino Marinuzzi, Carlo Galeffi took the title role with Edoardo de Giovanni (Edward Johnson) as Rinuccio and Gilda dalla Rizza as Lauretta. Of the three operas that make up *Il trittico*, *Gianni Schicchi* won the readiest acceptance on both occasions (at the Metropolitan it was given during several seasons as a curtain raiser to Richard Strauss's *Salome*). Although it later yielded pride of place to *Il tabarro*, it remains nonetheless among the acknowledged masterpieces of Italian comedy.

A bedroom in the house of Buoso Donati Before a large four-poster bed, whose curtains conceal the body of Buoso Donati, recently defunct, Donati's relatives are kneeling in a state of well-simulated grief. The air is filled with their sobs and groans, which give way to anxious whisperings when Betto mentions a rumour that the deceased has left all his property to the Monastery of S Reparata. They turn for guidance to Simone, as he is the oldest member present and a former mayor of Fucecchio. He suggests that they search for the will immediately. All begin frantically emptying drawers and cabinets. The parchment is found by Rinuccio, but before handing it over to Zita as head of the family he makes her promise, should the terms prove satisfactory, to allow his marriage with Lauretta, daughter of Gianni Schicchi. A broad theme, evolving in lyrical sequences, indicates the warmth of Rinuccio's feelings (ex.1).

Ex.1 Allegro
sostenendo

Rinuccio bribes Gherardino to fetch Schicchi and the girl. Meanwhile, as the relatives gather round Zita to read the will, their expressions slowly change from eager anticipation to dismay and finally to fury, as they discover that the rumour was all too well founded. They launch into a tirade against the monks, picturing them pointing the finger of scorn at the impoverished Donati family. If only the will could be changed! But this time Simone cannot help.

Rinuccio suggests that they seek advice from Gianni Schicchi, but by now Zita will not even hear his name mentioned. Gherardino returns to tell them that Schicchi is on his way. Annoyance all round: the man is a mere parvenu, a peasant from the backwoods. Rinuccio springs to his defence in an aria ('Avete torto') which introduces a motif to be associated with Schicchi's cunning (ex.2), and whose concluding section

Ex.2 Moderato

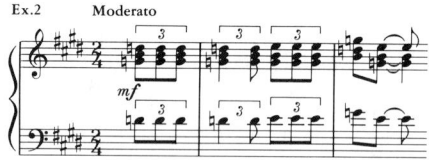

('Firenze è come un albero fiorito'), marked 'to be sung in the manner of a Tuscan *stornello* [folksong]', compares the city to a tree that draws its sustenance from the surrounding countryside. Schicchi arrives with his daughter, astonished to find the family plunged in genuine grief, until he learns that they have been disinherited. A quarrel breaks out between him and Zita, to the chagrin of Lauretta and Rinuccio, who see their hopes of marriage fading (the theme of ex.1 recurs in elegiac vein). Rinuccio begs Schicchi to help them, but in vain, and it is Lauretta who carries the day with her desperate plea, 'O mio babbino caro' – the score's one detachable number, whose opening theme has been anticipated by the orchestra at her first appearance.

After sending his daughter out to the terrace Schicchi proceeds to give his instructions. Buoso's body must be removed and the bed remade. There is a knock at the door and Schicchi slips behind the curtains as Spinelloccio, the doctor, enters and asks after his patient. Imitating Buoso's voice Schicchi declares that he is much recovered and asks him to call again that evening. The doctor leaves, well pleased with the effect of his past ministrations. After a crow of triumph (ex.2) Schicchi unfolds his plan in an aria ('Ah, che zucconi!'). Rinuccio must summon a lawyer and two witnesses; he himself will dress up in Buoso's nightgown and bonnet and dictate a new will leaving everything to the family. Delighted, they discuss the division of the property. There is perfect agreement until they reach the most valuable part of the legacy: the villa, the mule and the mills at Signa. Before the issue can be settled there is a brief alarm as a funeral bell tolls from nearby. They wonder whether news of Buoso's death can have broken, but the tolling turns out to have been for the butler of a wealthy neighbour. Amid general relief they decide to leave the allocation of the coveted items to Schicchi himself, but as they file past him, each handing him an article of clothing, they offer him bribes, all of which he pretends to accept. In a lyrical trio ('Spogliati, bambolino') Zita, Nella and La Ciesca assist him to change clothes. Before retiring behind the curtains he makes them repeat after him the penalty meted out to all who are party to the falsification of a will: namely to have their hands cut off and to be banished from the city. Obediently they chant a mock lament ('Addio Firenze, addio, cielo divino').

Rinuccio arrives with the lawyer, Ser Amantio, and two witnesses, Guccio and Pinellino. The formalities are gone through, amid universal praise for 'Buoso's' generosity. All hold their breath as he reaches the villa, the mule and the mills. These, in succession, are left to 'my dear, devoted and much loved friend, Gianni Schicchi'. The family react with smouldering rage, but, as Schicchi's intermittent chanting of 'Addio, Firenze' reminds them, they are hardly in a position to protest. Only when the lawyer and witnesses have departed do they burst out, rampaging through the house and seizing everything they can lay their hands on, until Schicchi drives them away. The lovers, on the other hand, are perfectly happy, for now that Lauretta is assured of a dowry there can be no obstacle to their marriage – the theme of ex.1 is heard in radiant mood. And Gianni Schicchi feels justified in asking the audience's indulgence, to a recurrence of the motif associated with his cunning (ex.2).

*　　　*　　　*

As early as *La bohème* (1896) Puccini had shown a gift for robust comedy, with which he never failed to leaven his most pathetic plots. In *Gianni Schicchi* this style appears refined and concentrated. Verbal inflection here is as pointed as in Verdi's *Falstaff*; but the organization remains based on recurrent orchestral motifs, mostly sharp and piquant, often lacking precise associations but always sure in their theatrical effect. The harmonic idiom comprises rows of parallel dissonances, as in the scene with Spinelloccio, together with passages of bland, schoolroom diatonicism, as in the reading of the will. Lauretta's aria is sometimes condemned as a concession to popular taste, but its position at the turning point of the action is precisely calculated so as to provide a welcome moment of lyrical repose.　　　JULIAN BUDDEN

Gianturco [née Dooley], **Carolyn** (**Margaret**) (*b* Jersey City, NJ, 15 July 1934). American musicologist. She studied music at Marywood College and, after working

as associate music director of the Turnau Opera Company, Woodstock (1961), taught in the music department at Rutgers University (1963–7). She then went to Oxford where she took the doctorate in 1970 with a dissertation on Stradella's operas. In 1971 she was appointed to teach music history at Pisa University. She has published articles in British and Italian journals on Roman opera in the 17th century and various aspects of Stradella's work, and has edited two symposia on Stradella.

The Operas of Alessandro Stradella (1644–1682) (diss., U. of Oxford, 1970)
Le opere del giovane Mozart (Pisa, 1976; Eng. trans., enlarged, as *Mozart's Early Operas*, 1981)
'Il melodramma a Roma nel seicento', *Storia dell'opera*, ed. A. Basso and G. Barblan (Turin, 1977), i, 183–233
Claudio Monteverdi: stile e struttura (Pisa, 1978)

Giardini, Felice (**de**) [Degiardino, Felice] (*b* Turin, 12 April 1716; *d* Moscow, 8 June 1796). Italian violinist and composer. After studying with Paladini in Milan and with G. B. Somis in Turin, he joined an opera orchestra in Rome while still a youth. Soon after, he moved to the Teatro S Carlo in Naples, where he received a salutary rebuke from Jommelli for his misplaced zeal for embellishment (Burney). Shortly after this incident he settled to a career as a solo violinist, and in 1748 he left Italy to tour Europe. His first public performance in London was at a benefit for the aging Cuzzoni on 27 April 1751, where his reception immediately established him as London's foremost violinist. In 1754 he took over and revitalized the orchestra of the Italian Opera at the King's Theatre, initiating a 'new discipline, and a new style of playing' (Burney). He retained a connection with the Opera for 30 years, sometimes as leader, but also, and less successfully, as impresario for the 1756–7 and 1763–4 seasons.

During this period Giardini composed three complete operas and contributed to numerous pasticcios. He also collaborated with William Mason in 1778 on two dramas for the English stage. In 1784 he returned to Italy, but in 1790 he was back in London, directing the orchestra from the harpsichord at the Little Theatre. He left England for the last time in 1792. Giardini's importance for opera in London lay primarily in his role in improving orchestral standards. Burney observed that 'he had not sufficient force or variety to sustain a whole opera', but his contributions to pasticcios were often enthusiastically applauded. Some surviving arias do indeed add a distinctive melodic piquancy to the bland lyricism of the Italian style.

all first performed in London; some arias published in London

Rosmira (os, 3, S. Stampiglia), King's, 30 April 1757
Enea e Lavinia (os, 3, G. Sertor), King's, 5 May 1764
Il re pastore (os, 3, P. Metastasio), King's, 7 March 1765
Sappho (lyric drama), ?1778

Music in: Cleonice, 1763; Siroe, 1763; Didone, 1775; Astarto, 1776

*

BDA; BurneyH; Grove6 (C. Hogwood, S. McVeigh); RiemannL 12
C. Burney: 'Giardini', *Rees's Cyclopaedia* (London, 1802–19)
F. C. Petty: *Italian Opera in London 1760–1800* (Ann Arbor, 1980)
S. McVeigh: 'Felice Giardini: a Violinist in Late Eighteenth-Century London', *ML*, lxiv (1983), 162–72
——: *The Violinist in London's Concert Life, 1750–1784: Felice Giardini and his Contemporaries* (New York, 1989)
C. Price, J. Milhous and R. D. Hume: *The Impresario's Ten Commandments: Continental Recruitment for Italian Opera in London 1763–4* (London, 1992)　　　SIMON McVEIGH

Giasone ('Jason'). *Drama musicale* in a prologue and three acts by FRANCESCO CAVALLI to a libretto by GIACINTO ANDREA CICOGNINI loosely based on Apollonius's *Argonautica*; Venice, Teatro S Cassiano, 5 January 1648 [=1649].

Apollo	soprano
Amore [Cupid]	soprano
Ercole [Hercules] *an Argonaut*	bass
Besso *Captain of Jason's Guard*	bass
Giasone [Jason] *leader of the Argonauts*	alto
Rosmina *a gardener*	soprano
Medea *Queen of Colchis*	soprano
Egeo [Aegeus] *King of Athens*	tenor
Oreste [Orestes] *Hypsipyle's confidant*	bass
Demo *Aegeus's servant*	tenor
Delfa *Medea's nurse*	alto
Isifile [Hypsipyle] *Queen of Lemnos*	soprano
Alinda *Hypsipyle's lady-in-waiting*	soprano
Volàno *a spirit*	tenor

Gods, winds, spirits, Argonauts, soldiers, sailors

Setting The island of Colchis and the mouth of the River Danube on the Black Sea in mythological times

The only collaboration between Cicognini and Cavalli, *Giasone* became the most frequently performed opera of the entire 17th century. In addition to possible performances in Milan in 1649 and 1650 and Lucca in 1650, published librettos document revivals in 1650 (Florence), 1651 (Bologna), 1652 (Florence), 1655 (Piacenza), 1658 (Vicenza), 1659 (Ferrara and Viterbo), 1660 (Milan and Velletri), 1661 (Naples), 1663 (Perugia), 1665 (Ancona), 1666 (Brescia), 1667 (Naples), 1671 (Rome, as *Il novello Giasone*, edited by Stradella), 1672 (Naples), 1673 (Bologna), 1676 (Rome, as *Il novello Giasone*), 1678 (Reggio), 1685 (Genoa, as *Il trionfo d'Amor delle vendette*) and 1690 (Brescia, as *Medea in Colco*). An unusually large number of these performances are documented by scores (in *A-Wn*, *GB-Ouf*, *I-Fn*, *MOe*, *Nc*, *Rvat* Chigi, *Sc*, *Vnm* and *P-La*). It was also one of the few operas to inspire a play that led an independent existence.

PROLOGUE *A beach with a view of the island of Colchis* In a celestial debate over the outcome of the impending drama, Apollo champions Medea and Cupid supports Hypsipyle as Jason's future wife.

ACT 1.i–ii *A delicious garden with a palace, adjoining the kingdom of Colchis* Hercules and Besso fear that Jason's amorous nightly activities with an unknown princess may make him incapable of stealing the Golden Fleece, an event planned for this very day. Jason shares their concern but nevertheless hopes for a successful outcome.

1.iii Rosmina, a gardener, sings a flirtatious love song ('Per sanar quest'appetito').

1.iv–v *The throne room of Colchis* Medea, who is the unknown princess, expresses her love for Jason. When her former suitor Aegeus arrives, she rejects him, leaving him to bewail his unhappiness.

1.vi–vii [*The nearby countryside*] Orestes, sent by Hypsipyle to search for Jason, meets the stuttering hunchback Demo, from whom he vainly attempts to extract information; the two then retire for liquid refreshment. (Demo's halting delivery of his identifying

song 'Son gobbo, son Demo', which culminates in a hilarious duet with Orestes, is one of the opera's high spots.)

1.viii–xiii [*Medea's apartments*] In a two-strophe aria, Delfa discourses on the problems of fleeting youth and the frustrations of old age ('Voli il tempo, se sà'). She sees Jason approaching and rushes off to warn Medea. Jason, who does not recognize Medea, since he has never seen her face, asks her help in capturing the Golden Fleece. She scolds him for having violated her hospitality by seducing (and fathering twins on) a noblewoman of Colchis (in fact herself), and makes him promise to marry her. He agrees because he is anxious to know his beloved's identity. She teasingly attempts to pass off Delfa as the lady in question but finally identifies herself, to Jason's great joy. The two depart, leaving Delfa to philosophize in a recitative and strophic aria ('Troppo soavi i gusti') on the mores of a society in which girls first prove their capacity as mothers and then get married.

1.xiv *Landscape with tents at the mouth of the Danube, with a view of the Black Sea* Hypsipyle dreams of her betrothed, Jason, father of her twin sons. On awakening, she remembers that she has left her homeland, Lemnos, with Orestes and Alinda to search for him, and wonders when Orestes will return with news.

1.xv *Medea's magic chamber* Medea's incantation, 'Dell'antro magico', invokes the spirits of the underworld to aid Jason in his quest and they assure her that he will be successful.

ACT 2.i–ii *Landscape with tents at the mouth of the Danube, with a view of the Black Sea* Still awaiting Orestes's return with news of Jason, Hypsipyle confides her desperation to Alinda, who, in a three-strophe aria ('Per prova sò'), advises her to find another lover. Hypsipyle rejects her advice and falls asleep, whereupon Orestes, who meanwhile has returned, serenades his sleeping mistress with an aria ('Vaghi labri scoloriti') as prelude to an attempted rape. She awakens just in time, and learns that Jason has fallen in love with another woman; she resolves to travel to Colchis to kill her rival.

2.iii–vi *Courtyard of the castle that houses the Golden Fleece* Encouraged by Medea, who provides him with a magic ring, and accompanied by Besso, Jason enters the castle, overcomes the monsters on guard and captures the Golden Fleece. Hercules reports that the populace is up in arms over its loss and urges Jason to flee to Corinth. Medea insists on joining him, and they set sail on Jason's ship, the *Argo*.

2.vii Demo has overheard their plans and informs Aegeus, who follows them, with Demo, in a small boat, which, however, sinks in a storm.

[2.viii *The caves of Aeolus* Jove, Aeolus, Cupid and a chorus of winds are angered by Jason's success and join forces to sabotage it with a storm. (This scene is not set.)]

2.ix–x *A ruined port at the mouth of the Danube, with a view of the Black Sea* During a love scene of their own, Orestes and Alinda comment on their mistress's unhappy state. They are interrupted by Demo, who has been washed up on the shore and manages to stutter his way through an explanation of what has happened. Orestes departs to inform Hypsipyle of the latest developments.

2.xi–xiv More fortunate than Aegeus's small boat, the *Argo* sails into the port and Jason and Medea disembark with their entourage and set up a temporary camp. Alinda observes them and meets Besso, with whom she immediately falls in love. Their scene, with its multiple puns on music, war and castratos, is one of the most amusing in the opera. Orestes returns to report Hypsipyle's imminent arrival. When she appears and reminds Jason of his vows, he pretends she is a mad-woman he met in Lemnos who thinks that events in other people's lives have happened to her. He goes off with Medea, leaving Hypsipyle to vow revenge.

ACT 3.i–v *A verdant wood* Orestes and Delfa compare notes on their respective employers and find that both love Jason and both are the mothers of twins. Jason and Medea, meanwhile, sing a beautiful lullaby duet before falling asleep ('Dormi, dormi'). This is over-heard by Orestes, who comments lasciviously in an aria ('Non è più bel piacer') on what will happen next. Hypsipyle comes upon the sleeping couple and awakens Jason, who promises to return to her if she will leave without disturbing Medea. But Medea overhears the conversation and extracts Jason's promise that he will have Hypsipyle murdered. Accordingly, Jason instructs Hypsipyle to meet Besso at the nearby valley of Orseno during the night and to ask him whether Jason's orders have been carried out. He tells her that this ques-tion is the password that will entitle her to an audi-ence with him. Besso, on the other hand, is ordered to respond to the question by throwing the questioner into the sea.

3.vi Aegeus arrives at the port and meets Demo, who thinks at first that he is seeing his master's ghost; the two go off together.

3.vii–viii Hypsipyle, rejoicing in the prospect of reunion with Jason, prepares to go to meet Besso but is delayed by Orestes, who urges her to nurse her children first and goes off to collect them.

3.ix–xii *Valley of Orseno* Medea, wishing to ascertain that her rival has been killed, asks Besso if Jason's orders have been carried out; following his in-structions he throws her into the sea. When Hypsipyle arrives and asks the same question, Besso responds an-grily 'Torna a Giason e di/Ch'io solo uccido una persona al dì' ('Tell Jason that I kill only one person a day'), a line that Cavalli enhances by setting it in a jaunty aria style.

3.xiii–xv Aegeus arrives just in time to rescue the drowning Medea, whom he promises to avenge by kill-ing Jason.

3.xvi–xxi *An uninhabited, ruined palace* Jason, meanwhile, having learnt from Besso that his orders were carried out, and overcome with remorse at the pre-sumed death of Hypsipyle, falls asleep. He is about to be stabbed by Aegeus when Hypsipyle grabs the knife and is arrested as a murderer. Seeing that Hypsipyle is alive, Jason accuses Besso of failing to carry out his orders but then is told that Medea died instead. But then Medea appears, explaining that since she was saved by Aegeus she now owes him her affection. She urges Jason to return to Hypsipyle. He protests but is won over after a moving lament by Hypsipyle ('Infelice, che ascolto'). With all the tensions resolved and the proper lovers united, the opera ends with a succession of duets and a final quartet.

[3.xxii Jove, Cupid, a chorus of gods and Zephyr all rejoice in Cupid's – and Hypsipyle's – victory. (This scene is not set.)]

*   *   *

The popularity of *Giasone* helped to make it the symbol of Venetian decadence for the Arcadians. Although Crescimbeni (*La bellezza della volgar poesia*, 1700) called it 'the first and most perfect drama in existence', he blamed it for having opened the floodgates to all kinds of abuses: the mixing of genres, the abandonment of linguistic elegance and purity and, through the in-troduction of arias, the destruction of verisimilitude in drama. Its success in its own time was justified, how-ever. As an opera, *Giasone* represents an ideal meeting of music and drama. In it the definitive separation of aria and recitative was finally achieved; formal distinc-tions were clarified by dramatic function, with recitative reserved primarily for action and commentary and arias for formal songs or moments of intense, reflective feel-ing. Hypsipyle's lament in Act 3 ('Infelice, che ascolto') fuses the two with its affective recitative and aria based on the descending tetrachord ostinato; Delfa's aria at the end of Act 1 illustrates Cavalli's comic style, with its narrow range and strictly syllabic text-setting alterna-ting with exaggerated melismas – the frequent pauses between phrases were presumably for brief dance inter-polations. Most of the operatic conventions of the period are represented, with great musico-dramatic effectiveness: as well as Hypsipyle's lament, a sleep scene (Act 2) and the powerful incantation scene (1.xv), containing Medea's 'Dell'antro magico', with its stark, chordal motion and repetitive *sdrucciolo* rhythm. The libretto, too, is more varied, more individualized and poetically more sophisticated than any other of the period. It stands out for its mixture of comic and serious characters and for the dramatic impact of the poetry itself.
ELLEN ROSAND

Giay, Giovanni Antonio. *See* GIAI, GIOVANNI ANTONIO.

Gibbons, Christopher (*b* Westminster, London, bap. 22 Aug 1615; *d* Westminster, 20 Oct 1676). English composer, son of Orlando Gibbons. Vocal and instru-mental music by him appears, together with music by MATTHEW LOCKE, in the score of the 1659 performance of James Shirley's masque CUPID AND DEATH.

Gibbs, Cecil Armstrong (*b* Great Baddow, Essex, 10 Aug 1889; *d* Chelmsford, 12 May 1960). English composer. He studied history and music at Cambridge, then taught at schools in Sussex. The production of the school play *Crossings* in 1919 caused Boult (its con-ductor) to persuade Gibbs to become a professional composer. He consequently studied at the RCM with Vaughan Williams, Charles Wood and Boult, taking up residence in Danbury, Essex, where he remained until his death except for a period at Windermere during World War II. From 1921 to 1939 he taught at the RCM.

Gibbs published an enormous quantity of utility music for amateurs, but it is for his exquisite songs, especially those to poems by Walter de la Mare, that he is best remembered. With works on a larger scale he was unlucky. His career as a theatre composer faded when *Midsummer Madness* (1924), in which Marie Tempest appeared in the leading role, closed in October 1924 after 115 performances, and his ambitious choral symphony *Odysseus* missed its first performance because of the outbreak of war. Nevertheless, his good tunes, clear characterization of musical numbers and warm harmonic sensibility were well adapted to the lighter operatic stage. *The Blue Peter* (1923) recreated something of the flavour of Dibdin, and *Midsummer Madness*, a modern *fête galante*, was plausibly akin to the pastel wit and charm of Rex Whistler and Claude Lovat Fraser. Gibbs also wrote appositely for children.

The Blue Peter (comic op, 1, A. P. Herbert), London, RCM, 1923, *GB-Lcm*, vs (London, 1925)
Midsummer Madness (comic op, 3, C. Bax), Hammersmith, Lyric, 3 July 1924, vs (London, 1924)
The Sting of Love op.56, 1926 (comic op, 1, L. Gibbs), unperf., *AL*
When One Isn't There op.60, 1927 (children's op, 1, C. W. Emlyn), *AL*, vs (London, 1928)
Twelfth Night op.115, 1946–7 (3, M. Currie, after W. Shakespeare), *AL*
The Great Bell of Burley, ?1949 (children's op, 3, N. Bush), *AL*, vs (London, 1952)
Mr Cornelius, 1952–3 (television operetta, B. Ellis), unperf., MS Boosey & Hawkes   STEPHEN BANFIELD

Gibelli, Lorenzo [Gibellone] (*b* Bologna, 24 Nov 1718; *d* Bologna, 5 Nov 1812). Italian composer. He studied singing and counterpoint and was appointed *maestro di cappella* at several churches in Bologna. In 1749 he became a member of the Accademia Filarmonica, of which he was elected *principe* five times; he was also *maestro al cembalo* of the Teatro Comunale. Gibelli was one of the most celebrated singing teachers of his day. Among his most successful pupils were the castratos Crescentini and Roncaglia and the tenor Babbini; he also gave some lessons to the young Rossini. As well as sacred music, his output includes the pasticcios *Diomeda* (1741, S Giovanni in Persiceto, nr Bologna) and *Gli sponsali di Enea* (1744, Bologna, Formagliari) and the operas *Evergete* (1748, Venice, S Giovanni Grisostomo) and *Demetrio* (1751; libretto by Metastasio), of which only the librettos survive. His intermezzo *Il filosofo Anselmo e Lesbina* (autograph in *I-Bc*) contains graceful arias in the style of Pergolesi.

C. Pancaldi: *Vita di Lorenzo Gibelli, celebre contrappuntista e cantore* (Bologna, 1830)   GIORGIO PESTELLI

Gibert, Paul-César (*b* Versailles, 1717; *d* Paris, 1787). French composer. He studied in Naples, and while there recruited singers for the royal chapel in Paris. On his return to France about 1750, he apparently lived as a teacher of singing and composition, and he also became known as a composer of *opéras comiques*. Of these, *La fortune au village* (1760), *Soliman second, ou Les trois sultanes* (1761) and *Apelle et Campaspe* (1763) are the most notable. *La fortune au village*, performed when the Comédiens Italiens returned to their (remodelled) theatre at the Hôtel de Bourgogne after a summer's absence, was Gibert's first real *comédie mêlée d'ariettes*, in which vaudeville *timbres* had been completely eliminated. It was received favourably by the *Mercure de France* as the work of a 'young musician [he was already 43] of considerable promise and taste'. *Soliman second* was at once a chef d'oeuvre of C.-S. Favart, a high point in the theatrical career of Mme Favart and an important and influential work in the development of the 18th-century 'Turkish' opera, of which Mozart's *Die Entführung aus dem Serail* is the crowning representative. The lack of success of the historical *comédie-héroïque Apelle et Campaspe* was probably occasioned principally by the volatile personality of its librettist, A. A. H. Poinsinet; although Grimm found it 'detestable', Gibert's music is of quite high quality.

After composing three motets, all successfully performed at the Concert Spirituel, Gibert returned to stage works with a serious opera, *Deucalion et Pyrrha*

(1772); after its performance he reportedly received a gold medal worth 300 livres.

Several printed collections, among them *Mélange musical: premier recueil* (Paris, 1775), include *ariettes* from Gibert's *opéras comiques* and dramatic scenes. Despite a pervasive Italian character, Gibert's frequent use of rondeau and *romance* forms, the parallel minor and diminished chords clearly allies him first to Rameau and then more particularly to Grétry. The strong influence of Gluck in the dramatic scenes is not surprising, yet it reveals one of Gibert's major weaknesses as a composer, his tendency towards imitation rather than originality.

unless otherwise stated, first performed in Paris at the Hôtel de Bourgogne by the Comédiens Italiens

Soliman second, ou Les trois sultanes (cmda, 3, C.-S. Favart, after J. F. Marmontel), 9 April 1761 (Paris, n.d.)
La fausse Turque (oc, 1, P.-N. Brunet), Paris, Foire St Laurent, 3 July 1761
Apelle et Campaspe (oc, 2, A. A. H. Poinsinet), Paris, OC (Bourgogne), 21 April 1763 (Paris, n.d.)
Deucalion et Pyrrha (?opéra-ballet, 4, C. H. Watelet), Paris, Vauxhall de la Foire St Germain, 29 April 1772, lost

Parodies: La Sybille [A. Dauvergne: Les fêtes d'Euterpe] (Harny de Guerville), 21 Oct 1758 (Paris, n.d.); Le carnaval d'été, ou Le bal aux boulevards [J. J. Mondonville: Le carnaval du Parnasse] (1, A. J. Labbet de Morambert and A. J. Sticotti), 11 Aug 1759; La fortune au village [P. de La Garde: Aeglé] (1, M.-J.-B. Favart, C.-S. Favart and M. Bertrand), 8 Oct 1760, *F-Po* (Paris, 1761)

Affiches, annonces et avis divers (1758–76)
Mercure de France (1759–87)
J. J. L. de Lalande: *Voyage d'un François en Italie fait dans les années 1765 & 1766*, vii (Paris, 1769), 193
C.-S. Favart: *Mémoires et correspondance littéraires, dramatiques et anecdotiques* (Paris, 1808)
M. Tourneux, ed.: *Correspondance littéraire, philosophique et critique par Grimm, Diderot, Raynal, Meister, etc.* (Paris, 1877–82)   KENT M. SMITH

Gibin, João [Giovanni] (*b* ?1929). Brazilian tenor. He began singing as a baritone; after winning the Metro-Goldwyn-Mayer South American 'Caruso Competition' in 1954, he went to study in Italy and made the change to tenor while at the Scuola della Scala, Milan. His engagements in Italy made him known elsewhere: in 1958 he made débuts at the Vienna Staatsoper and with the Nederlandse Opera, and in 1959 at Covent Garden as Edgardo in some performances of *Lucia di Lammermoor* with Joan Sutherland. He sang leading *spinto* roles at La Scala from 1960, and made his New York début with the City Opera as Radames in 1961. With a dark-toned voice of volume and penetration and a handsome stage presence, he was unsubtle as a singer and usually had more force of character than dramatic conviction.   NOËL GOODWIN

Gibson, Sir Alexander (Drummond) (*b* Motherwell, 11 Feb 1926). Scottish conductor. He studied at the Royal Scottish Academy of Music, Glasgow University and the RCM, and later at Salzburg with Igor Markevich and in Siena with Paul van Kempen. He joined the music staff at Sadler's Wells Opera in 1951, making his professional conducting début there the next year with *The Bartered Bride*. He became a staff conductor at Sadler's Wells 1954–7, then the company's youngest music director, 1957–9. He conducted 26 operas there, including the première of John Gardner's *The Moon and Sixpence* (1957). His Covent Garden début was in 1957 (*Tosca*, with Zinka Milanov, Franco Corelli and Giangiacomo Guelfi). In 1959 he became the Scottish

National Orchestra's first Scottish-born principal conductor, and with it at first helped to found Scottish Opera. He spent 25 years as the company's artistic director, taking charge of planning and casting as well as conducting a wide repertory. This included the first complete performance of Berlioz's *Les Troyens* (1969), Henze's *Elegy for Young Lovers* (1970) and the first German-sung *Ring* cycle in Scotland (1971), as well as the premières of Robin Orr's *Full Circle* (1968), John Purser's *The Undertaker* (1969, Edinburgh) and Iain Hamilton's *The Catiline Conspiracy* (1974, Stirling). He later resumed a freelance career and from 1970 toured in North and South America, conducting opera at Los Angeles, Louisville and elsewhere and returning on occasion to Scottish Opera. A firm orchestral disciplinarian, he has developed a persuasive skill over a broad stylistic range. He was made a CBE in 1967 and knighted in 1977.

C. Wilson: *Scottish Opera: the First Ten Years* (London, 1972)
C. Oliver: *It is a Curious Story: the Tale of Scottish Opera, 1962–1987* (Edinburgh, 1987)   NOËL GOODWIN

Gielen, Michael (*b* Dresden, 20 July 1927). Austrian conductor. He studied in Buenos Aires (where his family emigrated in 1939) and in Vienna, where he was répétiteur, then conductor at the Staatsoper from 1951 to 1960. He was principal conductor at the Royal Opera, Stockholm, from 1960, leaving in 1965 for Cologne, where he conducted the première of Zimmermann's *Die Soldaten* the same year. In 1973 he became principal conductor of the Netherlands Opera, and from 1977 to 1987 was music director at the Frankfurt Opera, engaging avant-garde directors and staging works by Berg, Franz Schreker and others, culminating in a *Ring* cycle directed by Ruth Berghaus. Gielen's performances are marked by a sharp analytic intellect and forceful projection, and he has a high reputation in mastering complex contemporary works. He made the first commercial stereo recording of *Moses und Aron* (1974), and his operatic repertory embraces Mozart, Wagner and Verdi, performed with clarity and brilliance.   WOLFRAM SCHWINGER, NOËL GOODWIN

Gieseke [Giesecke], **Johann Georg Carl Ludwig** [Metzler, Johann Georg] (*b* Augsburg, 1761; *d* Dublin, 5 March 1833). German actor and dramatist. He studied law and later natural science at the University of Göttingen. From 1783 to 1801 he worked on various German and Austrian stages as a minor actor and translator of plays and comic operas. In early 1789 he joined the Theater auf der Wieden in Vienna. His adaptation that year of Sophie Seyler's *Hüon und Amande* as *Oberon, König der Elfen* for Paul Wranitzky became his most successful libretto. Gieseke's later texts for Schikaneder are mostly translations, adaptations, or travesties. In 1796 Schikaneder appointed him theatrical poet to the Theater auf der Wieden.

In 1801 Gieseke left the theatre to pursue his interests in natural science. He spent over seven years in Greenland, and in 1813 was appointed professor of mineralogy at Dublin. On a visit to Vienna in 1818–19 Gieseke purportedly claimed authorship of the bulk of the text to *Die Zauberflöte*, according to the belated testimony of Julius Cornet in 1849. Despite Dent's championship, Gieseke's role in the libretto's creation is today generally considered peripheral. In his

Verzeichnüss Mozart ascribed the text to Schikaneder alone.

Oberon, König der Elfen (romantisches Spl), Wranitzky, 1789; *Die Wiener Zeitung* (Spl), Gerl and Schack, 1791; *Das Schlaraffenland* (Spl), Gerl and Schack, 1792; *Der travestirte Hamlet* (Schauspiel), V. Tuček, 1794; *Idris und Zenide*, Süssmayr, 1795; *Die zwölf schlafenden Jungfrauen* (Schauspiel mit Gesang), Stegmayer, 1796; *Uriels Glöcklein*, Stegmayer, 1796; *Die Belagerung von Cythère*, Gluck, with addns by Hoffmeister, 1796; *Amadis, der fahrende Ritter von Gallien*, G. Stenzerl, 1798; *Agnes Bernauerin* (Burleske), Seyfried, 1798; *Die Pfaueninsel*, Seyfried and Stegmayer, 1799; *Der travestierte Aeneas* (Farce), Seyfried and Stegmayer, 1799; *Aeneas in der Hölle* (Travestie), Stegmayer, 1800; *Die Sonnenjungfrau* (Travestie), Seyfried and Stegmayer, 1801   THOMAS BAUMAN

Giessen. City in central Germany. It had no theatre until the Stadttheater am Berliner Platz (574 seats) opened on 23 July 1907. Regular operatic performances became possible when the theatre acquired a permanent orchestra in 1934; the first operas included Gluck's *Le cadi dupé* and Adam's *La poupée de Nuremberg*. After 1935, when the orchestra was enlarged, the company could perform works on a larger scale. Anton Ludwig, the father of Christa Ludwig, became Intendant in 1943. The theatre suffered bomb damage on 6 December 1944 but was in use again by November 1945 after some provisional repair work. On 18 November 1951 it reopened, fully restored, with *Tannhäuser*. Among the high points in later years have been performances of the works of Menotti, who in 1977 produced *The Consul* and in 1981 *La loca* (European première), having composed the latter in Giessen.   SABINE SONNTAG

Gifford, Helen (**Margaret**) (*b* Melbourne, 5 Sept 1935). Australian composer. She studied music at the University of Melbourne, then trained and worked (until 1974) as a technical librarian. Visits to Europe and India in the 1960s and to Bali in 1971 had a strong influence on her compositions, which include over 50 chamber pieces (some with spoken narration). The greater part of her output is incidental music for the theatre, much of it for the Melbourne Theatre Company, for plays by Brecht, Shakespeare, Sophocles, Stoppard and others. Her three one-act operas were completed with the aid of grants from the Australian Council. *Jo Being* was commissioned by the Victorian Opera Company in 1974, the year that Gifford was composer-in-residence to the Australian Opera. Her music, though apparently using serially derived atonalism, is best described as being free of tonal orientation, with its delicate textures relying on tensions created through percussive and vocal counter-effects.

Jo Being (1, P. Murphy), part perf. Melbourne, 4 June 1978
Regarding Faustus, 1983 (1, Gifford, after C. Marlowe), Adelaide, 12 March 1988
Iphigenia in Exile, 1985 (1, R. Meredith, after Euripides), part perf. Melbourne, ABC FM Radio, 1 Oct 1990

*

H. Gifford: autobiographical chapter in *The Half-Open Door*, ed. P. Grimshaw and L. Strahan (Sydney, 1982), 172–93
J. Murdoch: 'Regarding Faustus', *Arts National*, iii/2 (1985), 70–71
Lord Harewood: 'Festival Drama through Music', *Adelaide Festival Review*, xlviii/March (1988), 16–17
H. Gifford: 'Subliminal Co-ordinates – Drawing Threads', *New Music Articles*, ed. R. Linz., vii (1989), 5–9 [autobiographical article]   THÉRÈSE RADIC

Gigli, Beniamino (*b* Recanati, 20 March 1890; *d* Rome, 30 Nov 1957). Italian tenor. His father, a shoemaker, was the sacristan of Recanati Cathedral where, at the age of seven, Beniamino was admitted to the choir. In Rome, after lessons from Agnese Bonucci, he won a scholarship to the Liceo Musicale; his teachers were Cotogni and Rosati. In 1914 he won an international competition at Parma, and on 14 October that year made a successful début in *La Gioconda* at Rovigo. In 1915 his Faust in Boito's *Mefistofele* was highly appreciated at Bologna under Serafin and at Naples under Mascagni. Spain was the scene of his first successes abroad, in 1917. The climax of his early career was his appearance in the memorial performance of *Mefistofele* at La Scala on 19 November 1918. Gigli sang in South America in 1919–20, and on 26 November 1920 made a brilliant début (again in *Mefistofele*) at the Metropolitan Opera, where he remained as principal tenor for 12 consecutive seasons, singing no fewer than 29 of his total of 56 roles.

In the lyrical and romantic repertory, Gigli was regarded as the legitimate heir of Caruso (Martinelli excelled in the more dramatic and heroic parts). The operas in which he was most often heard were *La bohème*, *La Gioconda*, *L'Africaine*, *Andrea Chénier* and *Mefistofele*. His Covent Garden début was in *Andrea Chénier* on 27 May 1930, with subsequent appearances in 1931, 1938 and 1946. In 1932 he left the Metropolitan, declining to accept a substantial reduction of the salary paid him before the Depression. Thereafter he pursued his career more actively in Italy, elsewhere in Europe, and in South America, returning to the Metropolitan, for five performances only, in 1939. A favourite of Mussolini, Gigli was at first under a cloud after the dictator's fall, but returned to sing in *Tosca* at the Rome Opera in March 1945, and in November 1946 reappeared at Covent Garden in *La bohème*, with his daughter, Rina Gigli, as Mimì. His prestige was at once re-established, and few singers have enjoyed such popular favour as he did in Great Britain up to 1956, when he retired. He continued to appear in opera at Naples and at Rome as late as 1953.

Smoothness, sweetness and fluency were the outstanding marks of Gigli's singing. His style was essentially popular, both in its virtues and its limitations: natural, vital and spontaneous on the one hand, but always liable to faults of taste – to a sentimental style of portamento, for instance, or the breaking of the line by sobs, or ostentatious bids for stage applause 'like a picturesque beggar appealing for alms' (Ernest Newman). He missed refinement in Mozart, and was unequal to the technical demands of 'Il mio tesoro'; in Verdi he was more at home, although notably happier when, as in the second scene of *Un ballo in maschera* or the last act of *Rigoletto*, his grandees had adopted popular disguise; best of all in Puccini and the melodramatic lyricism of *Andrea Chénier* and *La Gioconda*. His mellifluous cantilena in such pieces as Nadir's romance in *Les pêcheurs de perles* was consummately beautiful. Gigli was something less than a great artist; but as a singer pure and simple he was among the greatest.

His many gramophone records offer a complete portrait of his long career; outstandingly successful are the arias from *Les pêcheurs de perles*, *Martha*, *L'elisir d'amore* and *Faust*, duets with De Luca from *La forza del destino* and *Les pêcheurs de perles*, and the complete *Andrea Chénier*.

R. Rosner: *Beniamino Gigli* (Vienna, 1929)

Beniamino Gigli in the title role of Giordano's 'Andrea Chénier'

R. de Rensis: *Il cantatore del popolo: Beniamino Gigli* (Rome, 1933; Ger. trans., 1936)

D. Silvestrini: *Beniamino Gigli* (Bologna, 1937)

A.-M. Cronstrom and G. Cronstrom: 'Beniamino Gigli', *Record Collector*, ix (1954–5), 199–269; xiii (1960–61), 184–8 [with discography]

B. Gigli: *Memorie* (Milan, 1957; Eng. trans., 1957) [with discography by M. Ricaldone]

T. Peel and J. Holohan: 'Beniamino Gigli Discography', *Record Collector*, xxxv (1990), 110–58   DESMOND SHAWE-TAYLOR

Gigli, Clarice ['La Fiorentina'] (*b* Florence; *fl* 1682–90). Italian singer. She was in the service of the Duke of Mantua from 1687. The licence granted her as *virtuosa* by Ferdinando Carlo Gonzaga in 1687 describes her as 'outstanding among virtuoso singers' and specifies an annual salary of 100 *doppie* to be paid 'punctually every year of her life'. This form of employment, among the alternatives she was offered, guaranteed her the greatest liberty, and she was able to live in Florence and travel as she pleased to perform in other theatres. She sang at the Teatro S Giovanni Grisostomo in Venice between 1682 and 1686 in third female roles, and she is probably the 'Florentine' mentioned by the *Mercure galant* as 'one of the good singers' of the 1683 season. She appears in librettos only between 1685 (Carlo Pallavicino's *Vespasiano* at Modena) and 1690, when she sang in Parma in four different productions (Tosi's *L'idea di tutte le perfezioni* and *L'età dell'oro*, and Sabadini's *La gloria d'Amore* and *Il favore degli dei*).

S. Durante: 'Cantanti per Reggio (1696–1717): note sul rapporto di dipendenza', *Civiltà teatrale e settecento emiliano: Reggio Emilia 1985*, (Bologna, 1986), 301–7

E. Selfridge-Field: *Pallade veneta: Writings on Music in Venetian Society, 1650–1750* (Venice, 1985)

P. Besutti: *La corte musicale di Ferdinando Carlo Gonzaga ultimo duca di Mantova: musici, cantanti e teatro d'opera tra il 1665 e il 1707* (Mantua, 1989)   SERGIO DURANTE

Gigli, Gerolamo [Girolamo] (*b* Siena, 14 Oct 1660; *d* Rome, 4 Jan 1722). Italian librettist. He was a member of five academies, but his anti-Della Cruscan sentiments (evident in his *Dizionario cateriniano*, 1717) caused his exile from Siena, the loss of his university chair, expulsion from the Cruscan and Arcadian academies and the public burning of his books in Florence.

As a comedy playwright he moved away from the Spanish style towards an imitation of the French, inserting satire of local events. His tragedies are mainly adaptations from the French. His melodramas almost all have historical subjects, with the addition of comic figures, romantic entanglements, fairy-tale, and biblical and novella motifs. His most eccentric work is *Amore fra gli impossibili* (1693), where the pastoral setting is disturbed by mythological references and the addition of the characters Don Chisciotte and Coriandolo, in an ironic and grotesque atmosphere.

La Genefieva, G. Fabbrini, 1685; *La forza del sangue e della pietà*, Fabbrini, 1686; *Lodovico Pio*, Fabbrini, 1687; *La fede ne' tradimenti*, Fabbrini, 1689 (Griffini, 1691; ? L. Mancia, 1700, as *L'innocenza difesa*; C. F. Pollarolo, 1705; A. Caldara, 1711, as *L'Anagilda*; L. A. Predieri, 1718; Sarro, 1718; C. L. P. Grua, 1721; G. M. Buini, 1723; A. F. Capelli, 1723; G. M. Schiassi, 1732; G. Sarti, 1758, as Anagilda; M. P. Scalabrini, ?1772); *Amore fra gli impossibili, ovvero Don Chisciotte e Coriandolo*, C. Campelli, 1693; *La forza d'amore*, ? Fabbrini, 1695; *Eudossia*, ? Fabbrini, 1696; *Dorina e Grullo* (int for Anagilda), Caldara, 1711; *La Dirindina, o Il maestro di cappella* (farsetta), A. Scarlatti, comp. 1715 (G. B. Martini, 1731); *Intermezzi in derisione della setta maomettana*, F. Gasparini, 1717

*

ES (R. Allorto, B. Brunelli and others)
F. Corsetti: *Vita di G. Gigli senese* (Florence, 1746)
Raccolta di componimenti da teatro (London, 1764)
P. Carmi: *P. J. Martello, A. Zeno, G. Gigli* (Florence, 1906)
T. Favilli: *G. Gigli senese nella vita e nelle opere* (Rocca San Casciano, 1907)
U. Rolandi: 'Librettisti senesi', *La Diana: rassegna d'arte e vita senese*, iii (1928)
W. Binni: 'Il settecento letterario', *Storia della letteratura italiana* (Milan, 1969–70), vi   MARIA GRAZIA ACCORSI

Gilardi, Gilardo (*b* San Fernando, 25 May 1889; *d* Buenos Aires, 16 Jan 1963). Argentine composer. He composed the idyll *Ilse, o Amore di un giorno* (the librettist is unknown), in two acts and three tableaux, in 1919. A youthful work, strongly influenced by Puccini, it was first performed at the Teatro Colón in Buenos Aires on 13 July 1923. Between 1924 and 1929 he composed a lyric drama, *La leyenda del urutaú*, in a prologue and three acts, based on a prose poem of the same name by José Oliva Nogueira (Colón, 25 October 1934). Set at the time of the Spanish conquistadors, it relates a native legend about the origin of a bird with a sad song. Use of the Andean pentatonic scale, other folk music elements and Bolivian dances evoke an indigenous South American atmosphere. An outstanding figure in Argentine musical nationalism, Gilardi also composed orchestral and sacred music and pieces for guitar.   JUAN MARÍA VENIARD

Gilardoni, Domenico (*b* Naples, 1798; *d* Naples, 1831). Italian librettist. Little is known about his background. Dogged by bad luck and ill-health, he died young, having written 20 librettos in five years; the whole of his short career was based in Naples. His first published libretto was for Bellini (*Bianca e Gernando*, 1826), but much of his early work was for the Teatro Nuovo and typically contained long stretches of prose and *buffo*

roles in dialect; collaboration with Donizetti, from *L'esule di Roma* onwards, took him to the royal theatres, the S Carlo and the Fondo. When working with Donizetti he achieved a high level not matched when writing for others, probably due to the influence of the composer, who himself finished *Fausta* after the librettist's death. Although never officially described as a poet of the royal theatres, Gilardoni was widely credited with raising standards there. His most accomplished libretto was *Il paria*, set by Donizetti in 1829; his most frequently performed was certainly *Il ventaglio* (Raimondi, 1831), which demonstrates all too clearly the slack versification that often marred his work.

mel – melodramma

Bianca e Gernando (mel), Bellini, 1826; *Ildegonda* (mel), M. Costa, 1827 (Aspa, 1830, as Il carcere d'Ildegonda); *Gustavo d'Orxa* (mel), A. Curmi, 1827; *Otto mesi in due ore* (mel romantico), Donizetti, 1827; *Il borgomastro di Saardam* (mel giocoso), Donizetti, 1827; *L'esule di Roma* (mel eroico), Donizetti, 1828; *Ulisse in Itaca* (azione per musica), L. Ricci, 1828; *Gianni di Calais* (mel semiserio), Donizetti, 1828 (G. Panizza, 1834); *Il paria* (mel), Donizetti, 1829; *Il giovedi grasso*, Donizetti, 1829
Bannier (mel), Aspa, 1829; *Il contestabile di Chester* (mel romantico), G. Pacini, 1829 [I fidanzati, ossia Il contestabile di Chester] (G. Sangiorgio, 1839; E. Dominguez, 1845, as La dama del castello); *I pazzi per progetto*, Donizetti, 1830; *Il diluvio universale* (azione tragica-sacra), Donizetti, 1830; *Il ventaglio* (commedia per musica), P. Raimondi, 1831; *Edoardo in Iscozia* (dramma per musica), Coccia, 1831; *Francesca di Foix* (mel), Donizetti, 1831; *La romanziera e l'uomo nero*, Donizetti, 1831; *Fausta* (mel, completed Donizetti), Donizetti, 1832; *Ugo d'Erinduro* (mel), G. Moretti, 1833

*

E. Bursotti: *Domenico Gilardoni, autore di dramma per musica* (Naples, c1883)
L. Miragoli: *Il melodramma italiano nell'ottocento* (Rome, 1924)
W. Ashbrook: *Donizetti: le opere* (Turin, 1987)   JOHN BLACK

Gilbert, Anthony (John) (*b* London, 26 July 1934). English composer. He trained as a translator, developing a serious interest in music only at the age of 18. He studied part-time at Trinity College of Music and with Anthony Milner and Alexander Goehr at Morley College, also privately with Mátyás Seiber. Many of his works are for small combinations of instruments, and give clear evidence of an adventurous mind and a keen sense of musical logic based on thematic manipulation.

The opera or 'entertainment' *The Scene Machine*, a one-act work to a libretto by George MacBeth, was designed for an audience of young people and was first staged at Kassel on 4 April 1971 as *Frank Lord Faust*. The English première was given by the New Opera Company at Sadler's Wells, London, on 1 March 1972. The hero of the opera is the folksinger Frank (baritone), who is taken up and exploited by big business, symbolically represented by a woman (mezzo-soprano). When his art becomes degraded, his former fans are incensed. In trying to destroy the system which has corrupted him, they succeed only in destroying Frank. The folksong-like theme with which the opera opens is transformed during the action, undergoing (in the composer's words) 'the same process of corruption and transformation as Frank himself, a sort of musical parallel or illustration of his downfall'. The opera makes some use of electronics.

His radio opera, or song drama, *The Chakravaka-bird*, on poems by Mahadevi, translated by A. K. Ramanujan, received a BBC radio première on 14

January 1981. Commissioned 10 years earlier by the BBC, its inspiration grew out of a visit to India by Gilbert, although Indian musical structures and rhythms are not much used in it.

S. Walsh: '"Time Off" and "The Scene Machine"', *MT*, cxiii (1972), 137–9 [interview]　　　　　　　HUGO COLE

Gilbert, Henry F(ranklin Belknap) (*b* Somerville, MA, 26 Sept 1868; *d* Cambridge, MA, 19 May 1928). American composer. A heart defect and a lack of funds limited his opportunities for the education and foreign training undertaken by many composers among his contemporaries. He played the violin in small orchestras and worked for music publishers. Particularly interested in composing for the stage, he went to Paris in 1901 to hear *Louise* because of its use of street songs. His collection of folksongs, many of them black music and spirituals, served as source material for his compositions. He was unable to complete his opera *Uncle Remus* (begun in 1906), to a libretto by Charles Johnston, because the author of the stories (Joel Chandler Harris) refused him permission. The surviving music ranges from an elaborately worked-out prologue and first-act finale through individual set numbers, with or without text, down to fragmentary pencil sketches, ideas and harmonizations of black melodies. The one-act comedy opera *Fantasy in Delft*, composed 1915–20, was rejected by the Metropolitan Opera and has remained unperformed. To a libretto by Thomas P. Robinson, it concerns 17th-century figures, transferred to vases by Delft potters, who 'come to life on the first Thursday evening following a new moon'. Notes and sketches in the Yale University Music Library are evidence of Gilbert's desire to write an opera about pirates in the Dry Tortugas.

K. M. E. Longyear: *Henry F. Gilbert: his Life and Works* (diss., U. of Rochester, NY, 1968)
K. E. Longyear and R. M. Longyear: 'Henry F. Gilbert's Unfinished "Uncle Remus" Opera', *Yearbook for Inter-American Musical Research*, x (1974), 50–67
A. Nesnow, ed.: *Henry Gilbert Papers* (New Haven, CT, 1983)
　　　　　　　　　　　　　　KATHERINE E. LONGYEAR

Gilbert, Jean [Winterfeld, Max] (*b* Hamburg, 11 Feb 1879; *d* Buenos Aires, 20 Dec 1942). German composer and conductor. As a child he took piano lessons and later studied music in Kiel, Sondershausen and Berlin. He began his professional career in 1897 as a theatre conductor in Bremerhaven, moved to Hamburg in 1898 and, after military service, to Berlin in 1902. He adopted his *nom de plume* for his first operetta, *Das Jungfernstift* (1901). He conducted for a touring circus and at provincial theatres, after which he achieved wide and lasting success with his operetta *Die keusche Susanne* (1910). He then returned to Berlin as conductor at the Thalia-Theater and produced a rapid succession of operettas – he was to compose more than 50 in all – in the lively, commercial style of the Berlin school, among them *Polnische Wirtschaft* (1910), *Autoliebchen* (1912), *Die elfte Muse* (1912), *Puppchen* (1912) and *Die Tangoprinzessin* (1913); most of these achieved wide international currency. His postwar successes included *Die Frau im Hermelin* (1919, Berlin) and *Katja die Tänzerin* (1923, Vienna), but his later operettas, film scores and theatrical management ventures were less successful. In 1933 he emigrated to Buenos Aires, where he became conductor for a radio station. His son Robert

Gilbert (1899–1978) wrote the words for many German films and operettas, including Benatzky's *Im weissen Rössl*, for which he also composed one song; he also adapted numerous American musicals for the German stage.

Operetten, first performed in Berlin, unless otherwise stated

? – place of performance not known

Das Jungfernstift (3, Ritterfeld, after E. Guinot), Hamburg, Centralhallen, 8 Feb 1901; Der Prinzregent (3, H. Forsten), Hamburg, Carl Schulz, 12 Sept 1903; Jou-Jou (Vaudeville, 4, H. Buchholz), Hamburg, Centralhallen, 23 Oct 1903; Onkel Casimir (1, H. Gorden), Düsseldorf, Apollo, 1 Nov 1908; Die keusche Susanne (3, G. Okonkowsky), Magdeburg, Wilhelm, 26 Feb 1910; Die Lieben Ottos (Posse, 3, J. Kren and A. Schönfeld, after L. Xanrof), Thalia, 30 April 1910

Polnische Wirtschaft (Posse, 3, K. Kraatz and Okonkowsky), Thalia, 6 Aug 1910; Die moderne Eva (3, Okonkowsky and Schönfeld), Neues Operetten, 11 Nov 1911; Autoliebchen (Posse, 3, Kren and Schönfeld), Thalia, 16 March 1912; So bummeln wir (Posse, 3, G. Kadelburg), Gross-Berlin, 21 Nov 1912; Puppchen (Posse, 3, J. Ibsen and Kraatz), Thalia, 19 Dec 1912; Die elfte Muse (3, Okonkowsky), Hamburg, Operetten, 23 Dec 1912 (rev. as Die Kinokönigin (Freund), Berlin, Metropol, 8 Sept 1913; as The Cinema Star, London, Shaftesbury, 4 June 1914)

Die Reise um die Erde in vierzig Tagen (Sensationsstück, 4, Freund, after J. Verne), Metropol, 13 Sept 1913; Die Tangoprinzessin (Posse, 3, Kren, Kraatz and Schönfeld), Thalia, 4 Oct 1913; Fräulein Trallala (Posse, 3, Okonkowsky and L. Leipziger), Königsberg, Neues Luisen, 15 Nov 1913; Die Sünden des Lulatsch (burleske Operette, 3, H. Doblin), Chemnitz, Central, 15 March 1914; Wenn der Frühling kommt (Posse, 3, Kren, Okonkowsky and Schönfeld), Thalia, 28 March 1914

Kamrad Männe (Posse, 3, Kren, Okonkowsky and Schönfeld), Thalia, 3 Oct 1914; Woran wir denken (Zeitbild, Arnold and W. Turszinsky), Metropol, 25 Dec 1914; Jung muss man sein (3, Leipziger and E. Urban), Komische Oper, 27 Aug 1915; Drei Paar Schuhe (Posse), Thalia, 10 Sept 1915; Das Fräulein von Amt (3, Okonkowsky and Arnold), Westens, 13 Nov 1915; Der tapfere Ulan (Weihnachtsmärchen, K. Herrmann), Komische Oper, 20 Nov 1915; Arizonda (1, F. Dormann), Vienna, 1 Feb 1916

Blondinchen (3, Kraatz, Kren and Schönfeld), Thalia, 4 March 1916; Die Fahrt ins Glück (3, Arnold and E. Bach), Westens, 2 Sept 1916; Das Vagabundenmädel (Posse, 3, B. Buchbinder, Kren and Schönfeld), Thalia, 2 Dec 1916; Die Dose Sr. Majestät (Spl, L. W. Stein and R. Presber), Komische Oper, 7 March 1917; Der verliebte Herzog [Prinz?] (3, Okonkowsky and Bachwitz), Westens, 1 Sept 1917; Der ersten Liebe goldene Zeit (Spl, 3, L. Kastner), Dresden, Zentral, 8 March 1918

Eheurlaub (Schwank mit Musik, J. Horst and Bachwitz), Breslau, Aug 1918; Zur wilden Hummel (Posse, 3, Kren and E. Ritter), Thalia, 10 March 1919; Die Schönste von allen (3, Okonkowsky), Central, 11 March 1919; Die Frau im Hermelin (3, R. Schanzer and E. Welisch), Westens, 23 Aug 1919; Der Geiger von Lugano (3, Schanzer and Welisch), Thalia, 26 Sept 1920; Onkel Muz (3, B. Decker and R. Pohl), Halle, Apollo, 2 April 1921; Die Braut des Lukullus (3, Schanzer and Welisch), Westens, 26 Aug 1921

Prinzessin Olala (Operette-Vaudeville, R. Bernauer and Schanzer), Berliner, 17 Sept 1921; Die Dame mit dem Regenbogen (3, J. Brammer and G. Beer), Vienna, An der Wien, 25 Aug 1923; Katja die Tänzerin (3, L. Jacobson and R. Oesterreicher), Vienna, Johann-Strauss, 25 Aug 1923; Das Weib in Purpur (3, Jacobson and Oesterreicher), Vienna, Neues Wiener, 21 Dec 1923; Die kleine Sünderin (Operettenschwank, 3, H. Zerlett and W. Prager), Vienna, 1923; Dorine und der Zufall (Lustspiel mit Musik, 3, F. Grunbaum and W. Sterk), Neues Berliner, 1923

Die Geliebte seiner Hoheit, Nollendorfplatz, 1924; Der Gauklerkönig, ?, 1924; Zwei um Eine (Spl), ?, 1924; Uschi (3, L. Kastner and A. Möller), Kommandantenstrasse, March 1925; Annemarie (Okonkowsky and M. Zickel), Schiller, 4 July 1925; Spiel um die Liebe (3, Schanzer and Welisch), Westens, 18 Dec 1925; Der Lebenskünstler (burleske Operette, Kastner and Möller), ?, 1925; In der Johannisnacht (musikalisches Lustspiel), ?, 1926

Eine Nacht in Kairo (3, Hardt-Warden and Jacobson), Dresden, Zentral, 22 Dec 1928; The Red Robe (musical comedy), New York, Shubert, 25 Dec 1928; Hotel Stadt Lemberg (E. Neubach), Hamburg, 1929; Die Männer der Manon, ?, 1929; Das Mädel am Steuer, ?; Die Dame mit dem Regenbogen (J. Brammer and G. Beer), Vienna, An der Wien, 25 Aug 1933

B. Grun: *Kulturgeschichte der Operette* (Munich, 1961, 2/1967)
O. Schneidereit: *Operette von Abraham bis Ziehrer* (Berlin, 1966)
R. Traubner: *Operetta: a Theatrical History* (New York, 1983)
ANDREW LAMB

Gilbert, Sir W(illiam) S(chwenck) (*b* London, 18 Nov 1836; *d* Grim's Dyke, Harrow Weald, 29 May 1911). English dramatist and librettist. The son of a literary father interested in opera, social injustice and abnormal psychology, he used these subjects in his own works. After graduating from King's College, London, he became a journalist while studying for the bar and, as 'Bab', contributed comic verse, prose, illustrations and dramatic criticism chiefly to *Fun*, many of which were published in collections of *Bab Ballads*, 1869–77. Gilbert's legal career was brief, but it provided him with material for future plots and with useful knowledge for coping with the financially haphazard Victorian theatre. His first successful play was a topical extravaganza, *Dulcamara, or The Little Duck and the Great Quack* (1866), a burlesque of Donizetti's *L'elisir d'amore*. Other operatic burlesques followed, and Gilbert was soon recognized as an innovator and reformer.

By 1869 Gilbert, firmly established as a dramatist, was providing 'entertainments' for the German Reeds' Gallery of Illustration. Of these, *Ages Ago*, set by Frederic Clay, was the Reeds' greatest and most often revived success. Between 1870 (*The Palace of Truth*) and 1875 (*Broken Hearts*) Gilbert created four blank-verse fairy plays on themes of truth, love and honour, their tone deepening from whimsicality to bitter satire. By comparison, his 1871 Christmas extravaganza, *Thespis*, with music by Arthur Sullivan, broke no new ground. Their collaboration resumed with *Trial by Jury* (1875), which was immediately recognized as a new kind of work. Thereafter, 'G & S' wrote 12 more Savoy Operas, so named from the theatre their manager, Richard D'Oyly Carte, built in 1881. Of these, *The Mikado* (1885) was the most popular. Critics compared the textual and musical unity of these comic operas to Wagner's; in them Gilbert perfected themes, characters, plot devices and paradoxes initiated in his earlier or concurrent works. His librettos parody melodrama while satirizing both human nature and such contemporary topics as aestheticism (*Patience*), women's education (*Princess Ida*) and the profit motive (*Ruddigore*). The dialogue is formal and often syllogistic, the lyrics metrical tours de force yet regular enough to leave Sullivan a choice of settings. The rhymes are often polysyllabic. Gilbert also directed his own plays and, at the Savoy, controlled costumes and production.

After a financial dispute and subsequent lawsuit, Gilbert left Sullivan and Carte in 1890, turning to lesser musicians with moderate success. The collaboration was temporarily patched up for a lavish, omni-satirical *Utopia (Limited)* in 1893 and an unsuccessful *Grand Duke* in 1896. After this Gilbert wrote relatively little but enjoyed country life. He served as a magistrate, became Deputy Lieutenant for Middlesex and was knighted in 1907. His last libretto, *Fallen Fairies*, set by Edward German, failed, but three months before his death the old dramatist astonished critics with a grimly realistic play, *The Hooligan*, set in a condemned cell.

comic operas, set by Arthur Sullivan, unless otherwise stated
Ages Ago: a Ghost Story (musical legend), F. Clay, 1869; *Thespis, or The Gods Grown Old* (grotesque op), 1871; *Trial by Jury* (dramatic cantata), 1875; *Princess Toto*, Clay, 1876; *The Sorcerer*, 1877, rev. 1884; *HMS Pinafore, or The Lass that Loved a Sailor* (nautical comic op), 1878; *The Pirates of Penzance, or The Slave of Duty* (melo-dramatic op), 1879; *Patience, or Bunthorne's Bride!* (aesthetic op), 1881; *Iolanthe, or The Peer and the Peri* (fairy op), 1882; *Princess Ida, or Castle Adamant* ('respectful operatic per-version of Tennyson's *The Princess*'), 1884

The Mikado, or The Town of Titipu (Japanese op), 1885; *Ruddigore* [orig. *Ruddygore*], or *The Witch's Curse* (supernatural op), 1887; *The Yeomen of the Guard, or The Merryman and his Maid*, 1888; *The Gondoliers, or The King of Barataria*, 1889; *The Mountebanks*, A. Cellier, 1892; *Haste to the Wedding*, G. Grossmith, 1892; *Utopia (Limited), or The Flowers of Progress*, 1893; *His Excellency*, F. O. Carr, 1894; *The Grand Duke, or The Statutory Duel*, 1896; *Fallen Fairies, or The Wicked World*, E. German, 1909

*

*Gänzl*BMT
E. A. Browne: *W. S. Gilbert* (London, 1907)
F. Cellier and C. Bridgeman: *Gilbert, Sullivan and D'Oyly Carte* (London, 1914, 2/1927)
S. Dark and R. Grey: *W. S. Gilbert: his Life and Letters* (London, 1923, 2/1924)
H. Pearson: *Gilbert: his Life and Strife* (London, 1957)
R. Allen: *The First Night Gilbert and Sullivan* (New York, 1958, 2/1975)
——: *W. S. Gilbert: an Anniversary Survey* (Charlottesville, VA, 1963)
J. W. Stedman: *Gilbert Before Sullivan* (Chicago, 1967)
Gilbert and Sullivan: Lawrence 1970
J. B. Jones, ed.: *W. S. Gilbert: a Century of Scholarship and Comment* (New York, 1970)
M. K. Sutton: *W. S. Gilbert* (Boston, 1975)
G. Hayter: *Gilbert and Sullivan* (London, 1987)
JANE W. STEDMAN

Gilfert, Charles H. (*b* ?Prague, 1787; *d* New York, 30 July 1829). American theatre manager and composer. He was in the USA by 1800, when, 'lately arrived from Europe', he played a piano concerto in New York. In 1813 he opened a theatre there; he moved to Charleston, South Carolina, where in 1817 he took over the theatre management and established touring circuits in Virginia and Georgia. In 1825 he moved to Albany, where he managed two theatres, and he returned to New York in 1827.

Gilfert composed several ballad operas: *Rokeby* (1813), *The Spanish Patriots* (1814), *Freedom Ho* (1815), *The Champions of Freedom* (1816) and *Virgin of the Sun* (1823).

*

T. Brown: *History of the American Stage* (New York, 1870)
A. Hornblow: *A History of the Theatre in America* (Philadelphia, 1919)
J. Dorman: *Theatre in the Ante Bellum South* (Chapel Hill, 1967)
J. Hines: *Musical Activity in Norfolk, Virginia, 1680–1973* (diss., U. of North Carolina, 1974)
JAMES R. HINES, BARBARA TURCHIN

Gilibert, Charles (*b* Paris, 29 Nov 1866; *d* New York, 11 Oct 1910). French baritone. He trained at the Paris Conservatoire, made his début at the Opéra-Comique in 1888, and then established himself as a favourite singer of 'character' parts at the Opera in Brussels. In 1894, his first season at Covent Garden, he sang in the premières there of Massenet's *La Navarraise* and reappeared every year until 1909. He joined the Metropolitan in 1900, transferring to the Manhattan in 1906. He was famous for *buffo* roles such as Don Pasquale, Dulcamara in *L'elisir d'amore* and Bartolo in both Mozart and Rossini. The role of the Father in *Louise*, which he sang in both the London and New York premières, was widely considered one of the great portrayals of the time. For many years he was unrivalled as Schaunard in performances of *La bohème* in both cities. His sudden death robbed the operatic stage of one of its most valued artists. The voice itself was of no special beauty, but gramophone records (including two duets with Melba, whom he partnered in a tour of the USA) demonstrate at least something of the stylishness of its use.   J. B. STEANE

Gille, Philippe(-Emile-François) (*b* Paris, 10 Dec 1831; *d* Paris, 19 March 1901). French librettist. After attending the Lycée Charlemagne, Paris, he read law for a while, tried his hand at sculpture, and worked as a clerk in the Préfecture de la Seine before becoming secretary of the Théâtre Lyrique and finally finding congenial employment as an art and music critic, notably on *Le Figaro* from 1869 onwards, and as a prolific librettist. He married the daughter of Victor Massé. Gille collaborated with such experienced librettists as Ludovic Halévy, Adolphe Jaime and H.-J. Crémieux, whose texts were set by composers including Offenbach, Delibes, Dufresne and Massenet. Gondinet is credited with awakening Delibes' interest in Pierre Loti's exotic novel *Le mariage de Loti* (1880), but Gille was soon brought in to help prepare the libretto of the opera, which as *Lakmé* gave the composer a last major success. Though Massenet's *Souvenirs* are not considered a reliable source of information about the origins of his *Manon* it is known that he worked with Meilhac and Gille on the highly successful libretto. Among Gille's other writings is the preface to the autobiography (Paris, 1880) of the singer Gustave-Hippolyte Roger.

Vent du soir, ou L'horrible festin, Offenbach, 1857; *Monsieur de Bonne-Etoile* (oc), Delibes, 1860; *Le carnaval des revues* (with E. Grangé and L. Halévy), Offenbach, 1860; *Le serpent à plumes* (farce, with N. Cham), Delibes, 1864; *Le boeuf Apis* (opéra bouffe, with E. Turpille), Delibes, 1865; *Les bergers* (with H.-J. Crémieux), Offenbach, 1865; *Le sacripant*, Duprato, 1866; *L'écossais de Chatou* (opérette, with A. Jaime), Delibes, 1869; *La cour du roi Pétaud* (opéra bouffe, with Jaime), Delibes, 1869; *Le tour du chien vert* (opérette), Duprato, 1871; *Pierrette et Jacquot* (with J. Noriac), Offenbach, 1876; *Le docteur Ox* (with A. Mortier), Offenbach, 1877; *Jean de Nivelle* (with E. Gondinet), Delibes, 1880; *Lakmé* (with Gondinet), Delibes, 1883; *Manon* (oc, with H. Meilhac), Massenet, 1884; *Rip-Rip* (with Meilhac), Planquette, 1884; *Kassya* (drame lyrique, with Meilhac), Delibes, 1893

*

E. Aynard: 'Notice sur la vie et les oeuvres de M. Philippe Gille', *Recueil de l'Académie des beaux-arts* (6 June 1903)

CHRISTOPHER SMITH

Gillier [Gilliers], Jean-Claude (*b* Paris, 1667; *d* Paris, 30 May 1737). French composer. In 1693 he was appointed *basse de violon* player in the orchestra of the Comédie-Française, a post he held for 30 years. By 1694 he was working for the playwright Regnard and until 1717, when he stopped writing for the Comédie-Française, he collaborated with several authors, notably F.-C. Dancourt, with whom he worked on many productions both for the Comédie-Française and for aristocratic entertainments. Apparently the plays of Regnard and Dancourt, with Gillier's music, together with Molière's dramas, provided the aging Louis XIV with what little entertainment he permitted himself. From 1713 onwards Gillier was involved in the productions of the Théâtres de la foire, working extensively with Lesage and other popular playwrights, including Fuzelier, D'Orneval and Favart; he was concerned with over 70 plays up to 1735. Music by him was also used in several London productions. Despite Gillier's large output, and his long period in the public eye, his career is little documented and his death went largely unremarked. But his collaborators Lesage and D'Orneval

paid enthusiastic tributes to his fame, talents and devotion in the 1722 edition of *Le Theatre de la Foire*.

The tone of Gillier's work at both theatres seems to have been one of cautious innovation. His first commission with Regnard, *La sérénade* (1694), involved simply the overhauling of once-used *airs*; but there was a public demand for music with plays, and instrumental sections were increasingly used. The addition of prologues to old plays gave opportunity for newly composed music, as did the *divertissements* often added after the final acts. The format of the plays written for the fairs was less amenable to new music. The vaudeville, with new words set to a well-known tune, was the staple fare, and it was the musician's job to find a tune appropriate to the new words, possibly to orchestrate it, and to direct its performance. Much of the entertainment lay in the skill with which familiar tunes were adapted to new situations: a *double entendre* could be implied by the choice of a tune whose original first line (or *timbre*) would conflict with the new words. Dialogue songs were effective in this respect. In *La princesse de Carizme* Harlequin and the Prince converse, with alternating lines of the same tune, outside an asylum, while three inmates interrupt, each with his own *timbre*; the effect is of a jigsaw of familiar tunes, made incongruous by juxtaposition.

One of Gillier's main contributions was the introduction of an increasing proportion of new music. As in the plays for the Comédie-Française, there was opportunity for original composition in the *divertissements*, and in the vaudeville finale. His tunes are folklike and easily singable. His orchestration is mainly restricted to strings, though music for special occasions or depicting an exotic situation may demand larger or more varied forces. When *Les musettes de Suresnes* (possibly a revised version of the Dancourt play *Les vendanges de Suresnes*, given at the Comédie-Française in 1695) was given at Lyons in 1710, between 15 and 25 separate parts were required, while the parody of *Télémaque* given in 1715 required eight violins, one contrabass, flute, oboe, bassoon, two horns and harpsichord. This was the most ambitious orchestration yet attempted at the Théâtre de la Foire; Gillier's normal restraint may be attributed more to the restrictions imposed by the Opéra on other theatres than to any lack of imagination.

A son of Gillier, known as Gillier *le fils*, was a bass player in the Comédie-Française orchestra and collaborated with playwrights and the Opéra-Comique in the 1720s and 30s; he may also have been active in London.

Unless otherwise stated, performed in Paris and printed works published there (those for the Théâtres de la Foire in A.-R. Lesage and D'Orneval: 'Le Theatre de la foire', 1721–37, unless otherwise stated)

PSG – Foire St Germain   PSL – Foire St Laurent

Amphion (3), 1696, *F-Pn*
Les plaisirs de l'amour et de Bacchus (idylle), 1697, *Pn*
L'impromptu de Livry (comédie-ballet, F.-C. Dancourt), Livry-le-Château, 12 Aug 1705, airs (1705)
Le divertissement de Sceaux (comédie-ballet, Dancourt), Château de Sceaux, 3 Sept 1705
Circé (tragédie à machines, ? Dancourt), Comédie-Française, 1705 [revival]
Arlequin, roi de Serendib (pièce, 3, A.-R. Lesage), PSG, 3 Feb 1713
L'impromptu de Suresnes (comédie-ballet, prol., 1, Dancourt), Suresnes, 21 May 1713, prol. and divertissements (1718)
Arlequin Thétis (1, Lesage, parody of B. de Fontenelle: *Thétis et Pelée*), PSL, 25 July 1713
Arlequin invisible chez le roi de Chine (pièce, 1, Lesage), PSL, 30 July 1713
Arlequin Mahomet (pièce, 1, Lesage), PSL, 25 Sept 1714
Le tombeau de Nostradamus (oc, 1, Lesage), PSL, 25 Sept 1714

La foire de Guibray (prol. en vaudevilles, Lesage), PSL, 25 ?Sept 1714

Arlequin sultane favorite (oc, 3, J.-F. Letellier), PSG, 3 Feb 1715

Arlequin défenseur d'Homère (oc, 1, L. Fuzelier), PSL, 25 July 1715

Colombine Arlequin et Arlequin Colombine (oc, 1, Lesage), PSL, 25 July 1715

Les eaux de Merlin (oc, prol., 1, Lesage), PSL, 25 July 1715

Le temple du destin (oc, 1, Lesage), PSL, 27 July 1715

La ceinture de Vénus (oc, 2, Lesage), PSG, 1715

Télémaque (1, Lesage, parody of S.-J. Pellegrin: *Télémaque*), PSG, 1715

L'école des amants (oc, 1, Lesage), PSG, 3 Feb 1716

Le tableau du mariage (oc, 1, Lesage), PSG, 3 Feb 1716

Le temple de l'ennui (Lesage and Fuzelier), PSG, 3 Feb 1716

Arlequin traitant (oc, 3, D'Orneval), PSG, 27 March 1716

Le Pharaon (oc, 1, Fuzelier), PSG, 20 Feb 1717

Les animaux raisonnables (1, Fuzelier and M.-A. LeGrand), PSG, 25/27 Feb 1718; collab. J. Aubert

Le monde renversé (oc, 1, Lesage), PSL, 2 April 1718

La querelle des théâtres (Lesage), PSL, July 1718

La princesse de Carizme (oc, 3, Lesage), PSL, July 1718, music also attrib. Lacoste

Les amours de Nanterre (oc, 1, Lesage), PSL, 1718

Les funérailles de la foire (oc, 1, Lesage), PSL, 1718

Le jugement de Paris (Lesage, parody of Pellegrin: *Le jugement de Paris*), PSL, 1718

L'île des Amazones (oc, 1, Lesage), PSL, 1720

La statue merveilleuse (oc, 3, Lesage), PSL, 1720

La forêt de Dodone (oc, 1, Lesage, Fuzelier and D'Orneval), PSG, 3 Feb 1721

Arlequin Endymion (pièce, 1, Fuzelier), PSG, Feb 1721

Le rappel de la foire à la vie (oc, 1 Lesage, Fuzelier, and D'Orneval), PSL, 1 Sept 1721

Pierrot Romulus, ou Le ravisseur poli (oc, 1, Fuzelier), PSG, 3 Feb 1722

Le remouleur d'amour (oc, 1, Fuzelier, Lesage and D'Orneval), PSG, 3 Feb 1722

L'ombre du cocher poète (Fuzelier), 1722

Les dieux à la foire (Fuzelier), 1723

Les trois commères (A. Piron), 1723

Le mariage du caprice et de la folie (oc, 1, Piron), PSL, 16 Aug 1724

L'enchanteur mirliton (Fuzelier), PSL, 21 July 1725

Les enragés (oc, 1, Lesage), PSL, 21 July 1725

Les noces de la folie, ou Le temple de mémoire (oc, 1, Fuzelier), PSL, 21 July 1725

Les pèlerins de la Mecque (oc, 3, Lesage), PSL, 29 July 1726

Les comédiens corsaires (Fuzelier), PSL, 20 Sept 1726

La gran'mère amoureuse (pièce, 3, Fuzelier, parody of P. Quinault: *Atys*), PSG, 1726

L'amante retrouvée (oc, 1, F. de Largillière), PSL, 6 Aug 1727 (1728)

Sancho Pança gouverneur, ou La bagatelle (oc, prol., 2, Thierry), PSL, 28 Aug 1727, unpubd, Pn [?lib. only]

Achmet et Almanzine (oc, 3, Lesage, Fuzelier and D'Orneval), PSL, 30 June 1728

La Pénélope moderne (oc, 2, Fuzelier, Lesage and D'Orneval), PSL, 6 Sept 1728

Les amours de Protée (Fuzelier), 1728

La reine du Barostan (oc, 1, Lesage and D'Orneval), PSG, ?8 Feb 1729

Les couplets en proces (Lesage and D'Orneval), PSG, 18 Feb 1729; rev. as La Basoche du Parnasse (oc, 1), PSL, 6 Sept 1738

Argénie (oc, 3, C.-F. Pannard and F.-C. B. de Pontau), PSG, 26 Feb 1729, unpubd

Le corsaire de Sale (oc, 1, Lesage and D'Orneval), PSL, 20 Aug 1729

Les spectacles malades (Lesage and D'Orneval), PSL, 20 Aug 1729

L'impromptu du Pont-Neuf (oc, 1, Pannard, Lesage and D'Orneval), PSL, 9 Sept 1729, 2 vaudevilles, 'Au jardin de Versailles', 'Plein d'une ardeur extrême', in *Mercure de France* (Sept 1729)

La princesse de Chine (oc, 3, Lesage and D'Orneval), PSL, 1729, music also attrib. Lacoste, excerpt in *Mercure de France* (June 1729)

Le malade par complaisance (oc, 3, Fuzelier, Pontau and Pannard), PSG, 3 Feb 1730

L'Opéra-Comique assiégé (oc, 1, Lesage and D'Orneval), PSG, 26 March 1730

L'industrie (Fuzelier, Lesage and D'Orneval), PSL, 27 June 1730

Les routes du monde (oc, 1, Fuzelier, Lesage and D'Orneval), PSL, 27 June 1730

Zémire et Almazore (oc, 1, Fuzelier, Lesage and D'Orneval),

PSL, 27 June 1730

L'amour marin (oc, 1, Fuzelier, Lesage and D'Orneval), PSL, 5 Sept 1730

L'espérance (oc, 1, Fuzelier), PSL, 5 Sept 1730

L'indifférence (Fuzelier, Lesage and D'Orneval), PSL, 5 Sept 1730

Roger de Sicile, surnommé le roi sans chagrin (oc, 3, Lesage and D'Orneval), PSL, 28 July 1731

La nièce vengée, ou Les petits comédiens (oc, prol., 1, Pannard and B.-C. Fagan), PSL, 27 Aug 1731 (St Laurent, 1750)

L'acte pantomime, ou La comédie sans paroles (Pannard), PSG, 13 Feb 1732

Les désespérées (Lesage), PSL, 7 July 1732

La sauvagesse (oc, 1, Lesage and D'Orneval), PSL, 7 July 1732

Sophie et Sigismund (oc, 1, Lesage and D'Orneval), PSL, 7 July 1732

La reveil de l'Opéra-Comique (D. Carolet), PSL, 18 Aug 1732

La lanterne magique, ou Le Mississippi du diable (oc, 3, Carolet), PSL, 19 Aug 1732 (St Laurent, 1732) [?lib. only]

Le parterre merveilleux (Carolet), PSL, 19 Aug 1732

Le rival de lui-même (oc, 1, Carolet), PSL, 19 Aug 1732

La mère jalouse (oc, 1, Carolet), PSL, 19 Sept 1732

L'allure (oc, 1, Carolet), PSL, 27 Sept 1732 (1732)

La comédie sans hommes (Pannard), 1732

Les mariages du Canada (oc, 1, Lesage), PSL, July 1734

La première représentation (Lesage), PSL, July 1734

La répétition interrompue, ou Le petit-maître malgré lui (oc, 1, C.-S. Favart, Pannard and Fagan), PSL, 6 Aug 1735, rev. PSG, 14 March 1757, vaudeville 'Mars et l'Amour en tous lieux' in *Mercure de France* (Aug 1735); music in *Le Théâtre de Pannard* (Paris, 1763)

La foire de Bezons (ballet-pantomime, 1, Favart), PSL, 11 Sept 1735

Le mari préféré (Lesage), 1736

L'art et la nature (Pontau), 1737

*

Grove6 (M. Hunter; incl. details of works given at Comédie-Française)

F. Parfaict and C. Parfaict: *Histoire générale du théâtre françois depuis son origine jusqu'à présent* (Paris, 1745)

Le théâtre de M. Dancourt (Paris, 1760) [incl. vocal parts of Gillier's music to Dancourt's plays]

E. Campardon: *Les spectacles de la Foire* (Paris, 1877)

G. Becker: 'Aus meiner Bibliothek', *MMg*, ix (1877), 4–7

A. Cucuel: *Les créateurs de l'opéra-comique française* (Paris, 1914)

C. Barnes: *The Théâtre de la Foire (Paris, 1697–1762): its Music and Composers* (diss., U. of Southern California, 1965)

——: 'Vocal Music at the "Théâtres de la Foire" 1697–1762', *RMFC*, viii (1968), 141–60

M. Benoit and N. Dufourcq: 'Documents du Minutier central concernant la musique', *RMFC*, ix (1969), 216–38

MARY HUNTER

Gillis, Don (*b* Cameron, MO, 17 June 1912; *d* Columbia, SC, 10 Jan 1978). American composer. Educated at Texas Christian University and at North Texas State University, he was later chairman of the music department at Southern Methodist University (1967–8), chairman of fine arts and director of media instruction at Dallas Baptist College (1968–72), and composer-in-residence and director of the institute for media arts at the University of South Carolina.

Known for his wit and humour in musical composition, as well as for giving intriguing titles to his works, Gillis composed seven operas (as well as a liturgical drama). Several of these fall into a category between musical comedy and grand opera, and all were written for one purpose: for the audience to enjoy the occasion. They lack the subject matter that gives spice to the genre and instead portray ordinary people doing ordinary things. Often based on American subjects, they include popular and traditional musical source materials employed in Gillis's conservative compositional style. His writings include *A List of American Operas Compiled for the American Opera Workshop of the National Music Camp* (Interlochen, 1959).

all librettos by the composer

The Park Avenue Kids (1), Elkhart, IN, High School, 12 May 1957

Pep Rally (juvenile op, 1), Interlochen, MI, National Music Camp, 15 Aug 1957
The Libretto (1), Dallas, National Opera Convention, 29 Dec 1961
The Legend of Star Valley Junction, 1961–2; scenes perf., New York, Metropolitan Opera Studio, 7 Jan 1969
The Gift of the Magi (1, after O. Henry), Fort Worth, TX, Texas Wesleyan College, 7 Dec 1965
World Première, 1966–7
The Nazarene, 1967–8 (liturgical drama, 1)
Behold the Man, 1973   JAMES P. CASSARO

Gillot, Claude (*b* Langres, 28 April 1673; *d* Paris, 4 May 1722). French painter and designer. The son of an embroiderer, Gillot was attracted by the decorative arts and the theatre. He was at first involved with the Comédie-Italienne but seems to have begun his career in Paris at the Opéra, where he and the younger Jean Berain had 'the conduct of the scenery, machinery and costumes' (according to a letter written by Cronström, 26 June 1712). From about 1697 he was the assistant of Jean Berain the elder. Gillot provided the Académie Royale de Musique with vignettes to illustrate the second edition of Lully's scores for *Amadis* and *Thésée* in 1711. His designs for operatic productions are known principally from a series of engravings showing his 1721 costumes for the *opéra-ballet Les élémens* by Lalande and Destouches. He brought imagination and elegance to his models, reducing the amount of ornamentation; in this he was a precursor of Martin and Boquet.

B. Populus: *Claude Gillot (1673–1722): catalogue de l'oeuvre gravé* (Paris, 1930)
H. J. Poley: *Claude Gillot: Leben und Werk, 1673–1722* (Würzburg, 1938)
R. A. Weigert and C. Hernmarck: *L'art en France et en Suède 1693–1718* (Stockholm, 1964)   JÉRÔME DE LA GORCE

Gilly, Dinh (*b* Algiers, 19 July 1877; *d* London, 19 May 1940). French baritone. After studies in Toulouse and Rome he won a *premier prix* at the Paris Conservatoire in 1902 and made his début on 14 December of that year as Silvio in *Pagliacci* at the Opéra, where he remained until 1908. He sang in Latin America, Spain, Germany and Monte Carlo. From 1909 to 1914 he was a member of the Metropolitan Opera, with which he sang Sonora in the world première of *La fanciulla del West*, Rigoletto, Count di Luna, Amonasro, Lescaut (*Manon*), Albert (*Werther*) and other leading roles. In 1911 he made his Covent Garden début as Amonasro and also sang Jack Rance (in the first London *Fanciulla*), Sharpless, Rigoletto and Athanaël in *Thaïs*. He appeared in several later seasons and was last heard in 1924 as Germont. He was admired as a highly musical and expressive singer, an excellent linguist and a fine actor. He taught in London, where his pupils included John Brownlee. Between 1908 and 1928 he made approximately 40 recordings.

H. H. Harvey: 'Dinh Gilly', *Record Collector*, v (1950), 149–54 [with discography by J. Dennis]   HAROLD BARNES

Gilmore, Gail V. (*b* Washington DC, 21 Sept 1950). American mezzo-soprano. She studied in New Orleans and Bloomington. After an engagement at Krefeld (1975–9), she sang at Wiesbaden, with the New York City Opera and from 1982 at Frankfurt, where her roles included Cassandra (*Les Troyens*), Kundry, Fricka, Octavian and Offenbach's Giulietta. At the Verona Arena (1983–6) she sang Amneris, Carmen and Ulrica. In 1986 she made her Metropolitan début as Kundry and sang the title role of Schoeck's *Penthesilea* at

Düsseldorf. Her repertory includes Gluck's Orpheus, Brangäne, Ortrud, Eboli, the Composer (*Ariadne auf Naxos*) and Begonia (Henze's *Der junge Lord*). She has a warm, vibrant voice, great musical intelligence and a magnificent stage presence.   ELIZABETH FORBES

Gilse, Jan van (*b* Rotterdam, 11 May 1881; *d* Oegstgeest, 8 Sept 1944). Dutch composer and conductor. He studied in Cologne with Wüllner and in Berlin with Humperdinck. He worked as a conductor in Bremen (1905–8), Amsterdam (1908–9) and Utrecht (1917–22) and was a guest conductor with the Concertgebouw Orchestra in Amsterdam. He was co-founder of the Genootschap van Nederlandse Componisten (1911) and the performing rights society BUMA (1913; chairman, 1917–42) and was largely responsible for setting up the Donemus Foundation (1947).

Gilse's music followed the German Romantic tradition of Brahms, Mahler and Richard Strauss. His opera *Thijl* (1938–40; 3, H. Lindt, after C. de Coster: *Thyl Ulenspiegel*) is notable for its broad lyricism, voluptuous orchestration and mainly tonal technique. It was considered the first true national opera in the Netherlands, but apart from the 'mourning music' it was not heard until a concert performance given in 1976; the first complete stage production was at the 1980 Holland Festival (Scheveningen, Circus, 5 June 1980). His early works include another three-act opera, to his own libretto, *Frau Helga von Staveren* (1911–13).

O. Keting: 'From Brigand to Hero of the People: Dutch Opera 1835–1940', *Key Notes*, vi (1977), 4–11
L. Samama: *Zeventig jaar Nederlandse muziek (1915–1985)* (Amsterdam, 1986), 30–31
H. van Dijk: *Jan van Gilse, strijder en idealist* (Buren, 1988)   LEO SAMAMA

Gilson, Paul (*b* Brussels, 15 June 1865; *d* Brussels, 3 April 1942). Belgian composer. Largely self-taught, he was strongly influenced by the *Ring*, which he saw at the Théâtre Royal de la Monnaie in 1883, and by the music of the Five. In 1887 he began studying composition with Gevaert, and two years later he won the Belgian Prix de Rome. His first major work, *La mer* for orchestra (1892), was played in several countries and made his reputation. None of his subsequent works, the most interesting of which were written before 1906, was as successful; among them are several operas and ballets and some incidental music. Gilson was also very active as a teacher. Some of the many composers he trained formed the group known as the 'Synthétistes' in 1925, simultaneously launching the *Revue musicale belge*, of which Gilson became artistic director.

In his *Notes de musique et souvenirs* (1942), Gilson briefly compared different conceptions of opera, and while conceding that 'a new static condition is apparent in Wagnerian drama' (p.207), he gave the Wagnerian style preference and applied its principles to his own operatic composition. Thanks to the quality of its thematic material, *Prinses Zonneschijn* is regarded as his best opera and one of the major Belgian music dramas of the period. The subject is the fairy-tale of the Sleeping Beauty, transformed into a Germanic legend, but by adding episodes which are sometimes naive and improbable the librettist complicated the plot without increasing its dramatic potential. Moreover, as the composer preferred to develop leitmotifs freely, disregarding the special requirements of opera, the work is rather static. Although some features of the writing such as the stereotyped ornamentation of the melodic line are inspired by Wagner, the score bears the mark of Gilson's individual style. Many passages, particularly the preludes and postludes, show his exceptional mastery of orchestration, which enabled him to create music perfectly adapted to the various atmospheres suggested by the libretto. The choruses, in which the composer gave free rein to spontaneous inspiration, are also very successful.

Le démon, 1890 (drame lyrique, 2, L. de Casembroot, after M. Y. Lermontov), Mons, Bourse, 9 April 1893
Prinses Zonneschijn (légende féerique, 4, P. de Mont, after C. Perrault), Antwerp, Vlaamse, 10 Oct 1903; as La princesse Rayon de Soleil, Brussels, Monnaie, 9 Sept 1905
Gens de mer [Zeevolk] (drame lyrique, 2, G. Garnir, after V. Hugo), Antwerp, Vlaamse, 15 Oct 1904; in French, Brussels, Monnaie, 16 Dec 1929
Rooversliefde [I briganti] (drame musical, 1, J. F. Elslanders), Antwerp, Vlaamse, 30 Jan 1910
Thamara (3, L. du Catillon), inc.

*

Revue musicale belge, x (15 June 1935) [special issue]
P. Gilson: Notes de musique et souvenirs (Brussels, 1942)
A. Corbet: 'Paul Gilson: Flemish Composer', ML, xxvii (1946), 71–3
C. van den Borren: Geschiedenis van de muziek in de Nederlanden, ii (Antwerp, 1951), 250ff
G. Brenta: Paul Gilson (Brussels, 1965)   HENRI VANHULST

Gimenez, Eduardo [Giménez, Eduard] (b Mataro, Barcelona, 2 June 1940). Spanish (Catalan) tenor. He studied in Barcelona and Rome, making his début in 1967 at Reggio Emilia as Nemorino. He sang throughout Italy, in Paris, Aix-en-Provence and Barcelona; his roles included Almaviva, Narciso, Don Ramiro, Don Ottavio, Paolino (Il matrimonio segreto), Carlo (Linda di Chamounix) and Leicester (Maria Stuarda). He sang Fadinard (Il cappello di paglia di Firenze) at Brussels; Lysander and the Prince (The Love for Three Oranges) at Florence; Albert Herring at the Piccola Scala. His repertory includes Paisiello's Count Almaviva and Lindoro (Nina); Rossini's Orestes (Ermione), Lindoro (L'italiana in Algeri) and Idreno (Semiramide); Gennaro, Ernesto, Alfredo, Fenton, Iopas (Les Troyens) and Hoffmann. An elegant singer, he has a sweet, flexible voice.   ELIZABETH FORBES

Giménez [Jiménez] (y Bellido), Jerónimo (b Seville, 10 Oct 1854; d Madrid, 19 Feb 1923). Spanish composer and conductor. Accounts of his early life are sketchy and contradictory, but it is known that after taking lessons from his father and from Salvador Viniegra he was appointed a first violinist at the age of 12 in a theatre orchestra (either in Seville or in Cádiz) and that five years later he became conductor of an opera company. He received a grant from the Municipality of Cádiz to study in Paris, where he was a pupil of Alard at the Conservatoire and won premiers prix in harmony and counterpoint in 1877. He then went to Italy, but nothing is known of him until he returned to Spain; in Madrid in 1885, with the backing of Ruperto Chapí, with whom he had collaborated in writing a zarzuela, he became conductor at the Teatro Apolo and then at the Teatro de la Zarzuela, where he gave the first performance in Spain of Bizet's Carmen. His success as a conductor was such that he was appointed director of the publishing house Unión Musical Española and of the Madrid Sociedad de Conciertos, where he gained a reputation for his performances of the German classics

and of works by modern French and Russian composers.

His chief claim to fame, however, was as the composer of over a hundred zarzuelas, mostly in one act (the género chico); about a dozen were written in collaboration with Amadeo Vives. Although his librettos were frequently banal, Giménez's music is distinguished by the charm of its melodic invention and by its colourful orchestration. The habanera from De vuelta al Vivero (1896) became a hit, but soon after his El baile de Luis Alonso (Alonso was a famous Cádiz dancing-master) was an immense triumph, followed up a year later with the even more acclaimed La boda de Luis Alonso. Both these works have remained in the repertory, but Giménez's most famous zarzuela is the passionate La tempranica (1900), which Moreno Torroba later turned into an opera, though this has not matched the appeal of the original version.

See also TEMPRANICA, LA.

all zarzuelas; first performed in Madrid unless otherwise stated

Las niñas desenvueltas (1, E. Arago), 1878, collab. Chapí; A mata caballo (1, G. Valera), Martin, Nov 1886; Cantar de plano (E. Sanchez), Variedades, Dec 1886, collab. C. Espino; El esclavo, 1887; Escuela modelo, 1888; El guía ilustrada (Ruesga and Aranjo), Zarzuela, Dec 1889; La tiple, 1889; Tannhäuser el estanquero (1, E. Gonzalvo), Apolo, 26 April 1890; Tannhäuser cesante (1, Gonzalvo), 1890; Trafalgar (2, J. de Burgos), Barcelona, Principal, Jan 1891; ¡Pero cómo está Madrid!, 1891
La cencerrada (1, G. Perrín and M. Palacios), 1892; El hijo de su excelencia (1, L. Larra and M. Gullón), 1892; El ventorrillo del Chato, 1892; La madre del cordero (1, F. Iráyzoz), Eslava, 1892; La mujer del molinero (1, Iráyzoz), Príncipe Alfonso, 11 March 1893; Cándidita (1, de Burgos), 1893; Los voluntarios (Iráyzoz), Príncipe Alfonso, 1893; Un viaje de los demonios (de Burgos), March 1894; Viento en popa (1, Iráyzoz), 1894; La república de Chamba (1, S. Delgado), Apolo, 1894
La sobrina del sacristán (Ruesga and J. Prieto), 6 June 1895; De vuelta al Vivero (1, Iráyzoz), Jan 1896; El baile de Luis Alonso [El mundo comedia es] (1, de Burgos), Zarzuela, 27 Feb 1896; Manolos y patrimetres (F. Perez and C. Fernández Shaw), Sept 1896; Las mujeres (de Burgos), 1896; La boda de Luis Alonso [La noche del encierro] (1, de Burgos), Zarzuela, 27 Jan 1897; La guardia amarilla (C. Lucio and C. Arniches), Zarzuela, Dec 1897; Aquí va a haber algo gordo [La casa de los escándalos] (R. de la Vega), 1897
Los hombres públicos (de Burgos), Apolo, 17 June 1898; Las figuras de cera (A. Paso and G. Alvarez), Apolo, 15 Sept 1898; Amor engendra desdichas [El guapo y el feo] (de la Vega), Apolo, 13 Jan 1899; Los borrachos (1, Álvarez Quintero), Zarzuela, 3 May 1899; Los garrochistas (Novo), Apolo, 12 Oct 1899, collab. Viniegra; La familia de Sicur (1, de Burgos), Apolo, 16 Dec 1899; Joshé Martin el tamborilero (1, Iráyzoz), Apolo, March 1900; La noche de la tempestad (Iráyzoz), Zarzuela, 9 June 1900; La tempranica (1, J. Romea), Zarzuela, 19 Sept 1900; La Mallorquina (P. Zuniga), Zarzuela, 25 Nov 1900; El sustituto (F. García), Cómico, 6 Dec 1900
El barbero de Sevilla (Perrin and Palacios), Zarzuela, Feb 1901, collab. M. Nieto; Correo interior, 18 June 1901, collab. Nieto and G. Cereceda; Los timplaos (1, E. Blasco and Fernández Shaw), Zarzuela, Nov 1901; Enseñanza libre (1, Perrín and Palacios), Eslava, 14 Dec 1901; El morrongo, Cómico, Nov 1902; La torre del oro (1, Perrín and Palacios), 1902; Maria del Pilar (3, García and G. Briones), 5 Feb 1903; La Camarona (1, Perrín and Palacios), 1903; El general (1, Perrín and Palacios), 1903; La morenita (1, Perrín and Palacios), 1903; La visión de Fray Martin, 1903; Los pícaros celos (1, Arniches and Fernández Shaw), Apolo, 23 June 1904; El húsar de la guardia (1, Perrín and Palacios), Zarzuela, 1 Oct 1904, collab. Vives
Cuadros al fresco, 1904; La sequía, 1904; Los guapos, Moderno, April 1905; Cascabel, Zarzuela, April 1905; El arte de ser bonita (1, Paso and Prieto), Cómico, 7 Sept 1905, collab. Vives; Las granadinas (1, Perrín and Palacios), Cómico, 29 Sept 1905, collab. Vives; El amigo del alma (1, F. Torres and C. Cruselles), Eslava, 16 Nov 1905, collab. Vives; La gitita blanca (1, J. Veyán and J. Capella), Cómico, 23 Dec 1905, Vives; La libertad (Perrín

and Palacios), Price, 30 Dec 1905, collab. Vives; La marcha real (Paso and J. Abati), Zarzuela, 7 Feb 1906, collab. Vives; El golpe de estado (1, Melantuche), Eslava, 3 May 1906, collab. Vives; La Machaquito (1, Larra), Eslava, 29 May 1906, collab. Vives
El guante amarillo (1, Veyán and Capella), Cómico, 5 Oct 1906, collab. Vives; El diablo verde (1, Perrín and Palacios), Zarzuela, 11 Oct 1906, collab. Vives; La venta de la alegría, 1906; La antorcha del himeneo, 1907; Cinematógrafo nacional (1, Perrín and Palacios), Apolo, 1907; El príncipe real, 1907; El palco de la presidencia (M. Echegaray), Apolo, Jan 1908; ABC (1, Perrín and Palacios), Zarzuela, Dec 1908; Los dos rivales, 1908; La eterna revista (J. A. Más and Capella), 1908, collab. Chapí; El grito de independencia, 1908; a Leyenda mora, 1908; El trust de las mujeres, 1908; Pepe el liberal (1, Perrín and Palacios), Cómico, 19 Feb 1909; Las mil y pico de noches (1 Perrín and Palacios), 1909; El patinillo (1, Álvarez Quintero), Apolo, 1909
Los viajes de Gulliver (3, Paso and Abati), Cómico, 21 Feb 1911, collab. Vives; Los julgares (2, Fernández Shaw and R. Asensio), Cómico, 13 Dec 1911; Lirio entre espinas, 1911; La suerte de Isabelita (1, M. Sierra), 1911, collab. Calleja; Las hijas de Venus (F. Palomero), Gran, Nov 1912; Los ángeles mandan, 1912; El coche del diablo, 1912; El cuento del dragón, 1912; Los hombres que son hombres (2, J. Moyrón), Price, Jan 1913; El príncipe Pio (Perrín and Palacios), Gran Via, April 1913; Ovación y oreja, 1913; De España al cielo, Barcelona, Novedades, Feb 1914, collab. J. Padilla; Malagueñas (1), Apolo, Feb 1914; El gran simulacro, 1914; El ojo del gallo, 1914; La pandereta, Apolo, 3 April 1915, collab. V. Lleó; Las castañuelas (Perrín and Palacios), Apolo, Sept 1915; Cine fantomas, 1915; La última opereta, 1915; Ysidrin [Las cuarenta y nueve provincias], 1915
La embajadora (3, Lepina and G. del Toro), 1916; La Eva ideal, 1916; La costilla de Adán (1, Moyrón and del Toro), 2 Aug 1917; Esta noche es nochebuena (J. Ramos Martín), 1917; El Zorro, 1917; Abejas y zánganos (Ramos Martín), 1918; La bella persa, 1918; Tras Tristán (1, Ramos Martín), 1918; El gran Olavide (M. Morcillo and A. Paso jr), Martin, 25 April 1919; La España de la alegría (1, F. Palomero and E. Cordoba), Fuencarra, 27 June 1919, collab. Padilla; Soleares (1, Ramos Martín), Zarzuela, 7 Oct 1919; La cortesana de Osmán, 1920

*

M. Muñoz: *Historia de la zarzuela española y del género chico* (Madrid, 1946)

J. Deleito y Piñuela: *Origen y apogeo del género chico* (Madrid, 1949)

'Chispero': *El Teatro Apolo* (Madrid, 1953)   LIONEL SALTER

Gimenez, Raul (*b* Santa Fe, Argentina, 14 Sept 1950). Argentine tenor. After studying in Buenos Aires, he made his début there in 1980 as Ernesto. At Wexford he sang Filandro in Cimarosa's *Le astuzie femminili* (1984), returning as Lurcanio in *Ariodante*. Having sung in Venice, Bordeaux, Paris, Naples, Pesaro, Frankfurt, Rome, Amsterdam and Geneva, he made his American début at Dallas (1989) and his Covent Garden début (1990) as Ernesto. Although his repertory includes Ferrando, Fenton, Tonie (*La fille du régiment*) and Elvino, his flexible, high-lying and keenly focussed voice is heard to best advantage in Rossini: as Gernando/Carlo (*Armida*), which he sang at Aix-en-Provence in 1988, as Giocondo (*La pietra del paragone*), Florville (*Signor Bruschino*), Rodrigo, Almaviva, Narciso, Count Alberto (*L'occasione fa il ladro*) and Argirio (*Tancredi*). He sang Lynceus in Salieri's *Les Danaïdes* at Ravenna (1990).   ELIZABETH FORBES

Ginastera, Alberto (Evaristo) (*b* Buenos Aires, 11 April 1916; *d* Geneva, 25 June 1983). Argentine composer. He showed precocious gifts and at 12 entered the Williams Conservatory, from which he graduated in 1935 with a gold medal in composition; from then until 1938 he continued his studies at the National Conservatory. His ballet *Panambi*, written while still a student, established his reputation and was awarded

several prizes. In 1941 he was appointed professor of composition at the National Conservatory and obtained the chair of music at the national military academy, but in 1945 he was dismissed from the latter for signing a petition defending civil liberties. He then spent 18 months in the USA, on returning from which he formed a league of composers that became the Argentine section of the ISCM (1948) and became director of the conservatory in La Plata, though four years later he was again deprived of his post by the Perón regime. After the overthrow of Perón he was reinstated; he became successively dean of the faculty of musical arts and sciences at the Catholic University of Argentina and, in 1963 – by which time he had gained international recognition as a composer – director of the newly created Latin American Centre for Advanced Musical Studies at the Instituto Torcuato di Tella in Buenos Aires. There he exerted a decisive influence on younger composers. From 1971 he lived in Geneva, accepting no further full-time academic or official appointments. He was awarded numerous honours in Argentina, Brazil, France and the USA.

Tragic and fantastic elements are prominent in Ginastera's operas, as are all the characteristically expressionistic features. He is reported as saying that 'sex, violence and hallucination are three of the basic elements from which grand opera can be constructed', and these are present in all his three completed operas. These also reveal his determination to achieve structural symmetry and a strict correlation between music and drama. *Don Rodrigo* (1964), commissioned by the city of Buenos Aires, is in three acts, corresponding dramatically to exposition, crisis and denouement: each act is divided into three scenes, with the same internal dramatic sequence. The scenes are separated by instrumental interludes, and each has a specific musical form (rondo, suite, aria etc.). There is a palindromic relation in the sequence of scenes, with the fifth as the central climax, in which Rodrigo violates Florinda. The opera is also unified musically by the use of leitmotifs derived from a 12-note series. At the end of the work there is an impressive and original effect with 25 bells divided into three groups and distributed in different sections of the theatre. The pitches of two groups are derived from a 12-note series, while the third gives a chromatic scale. The resulting aleatory polyphony is heard over a foundation of two chords in the orchestra: one (freely chromatic) played by the strings, the other (from the series) by the brass and woodwinds.

Bomarzo (1967), commissioned by the Opera Society of Washington, was Ginastera's second approach to a subject on which he had written a cantata three years previously. The opera was an extraordinary success in Washington but was denounced by the *Neue Zeitschrift für Musik* as 'Porno in Belcanto', and its scheduled production at the Teatro Colón was banned by the mayor of Buenos Aires. Not until 1972 was this ban lifted, and the composer was then accorded a triumph. Set in 16th-century Italy, the work portrays the sexual neuroses and unhappy fate of Pier Francesco Orsini, Duke of Bomarzo, employing a series of flashbacks in which reality and fantasy are confused. Renaissance musical forms are used to solidify the internal structure, as well as to enhance the elaborate choreographic elements; and unusual vocal and instrumental effects are included, such as the chorus singing on isolated consonants to suggest the whispering of Bomarzo's stone statues. *Beatrix Cenci* (1971), also commissioned by the

Opera Society of Washington, was given at the opening of the Kennedy Center. It too is constructed in a series of separate scenes and makes use of a similar diversity of musical techniques. A fourth opera, *Barabbas*, begun in 1977, was apparently left uncompleted. Ginastera's idioms are contemporary, but the tradition of grand opera is upheld. Penderecki may hover in the pit, but the spirit of Verdi watches in the wings.

See also BEATRIX CENCI; BOMARZO; and DON RODRIGO.

Don Rodrigo op.31 (3, A. Casona), Buenos Aires, Colón, 24 July 1964
Bomarzo op.34 (2, M. Mujica Láinez), Washington DC, Lisner Auditorium, 19 May 1967
Beatrix Cenci op.38 (2, W. Shand and A. Girri), Washington DC, Kennedy Center, 10 Sept 1971
Barabbas, 1977 (after M. de Ghelderode), inc.

PEM (M. Kuss)

*

A. Schering: *Geschichte der Musik in Beispielen* (Leipzig, 1931), 20–21
G. Chase: 'Alberto Ginastera, Argentine Composer', *MQ*, xliii (1957), 439–60
A. Ginastera: 'A propósito de Don Rodrigo', *Buenos Aires musical*, xix/310 (16 July 1964), 1, 3–4
D. Wallace: *Alberto Ginastera: an Analysis of his Style and Technique of Composition* (diss., Northwestern U., 1964)
P. Suárez Urtubey: 'Alberto Ginastera's Don Rodrigo', *Tempo* (1965), no.74, pp.12–18
S. Sontag: 'Marat/Sade/Artaud', *Against Interpretation* (New York, 1966), 163–74
A. Ginastera: 'How and Why I Wrote Bomarzo', *Central Opera Service Bulletin*, ix/5 (1967), 10–13
J. Orrego-Salas: 'Don Rodrigo de Ginastera', *Artes hispánicas*, i/1 (1967), 95–133
P. Suárez Urtubey: *Alberto Ginastera* (Buenos Aires, 1967)
——: 'Ginastera's "Bomarzo"', *Tempo* (1968), no.84, pp.14–21
J. Campos: '"Bomarzo, novelista manierista', *Ínsula* (Madrid, 1971), no.292, p.11
D. W. Foster: 'The Monstrous in Two Argentine Novels', *Américas*, ii/24 (1972), 33–6
A. Borowitz: 'The Cenci Affair', *ON*, xxxvii/19 (1972–3), 11–13
I. Lowens: 'Ginastera's Beatrix Cenci', *Tempo* (1973), no.105, pp.48–53
M. Kuss: *Nativistic Strains in Argentine Operas Premiered at the Teatro Colón (1908–1972)* (Ann Arbor, 1976), 344–72
——: 'Type, Derivation and use of Folk Idioms in Ginastera's Don Rodrigo', *Latin American Music Review*, i/2 (1980), 176–95
F. Spangemacher, ed.: *Alberto Ginastera* (Bonn, 1984) [incl. M. Kuss: 'Symbol und Phantasie in Ginasteras "Bomarzo" (1967)', pp.88–102]
M. Kuss: 'Alberto Ginastera', *Mitteilungen der Paul Sacher Stiftung*, ii (1989), 17–18
GILBERT CHASE, LIONEL SALTER

Ginevra di Scozia ('Ginevra of Scotland'). *Dramma serio eroico* in two acts by SIMON MAYR to a libretto by GAETANO ROSSI after LUDOVICO ARIOSTO's poem *Orlando furioso*; Trieste, Teatro Nuovo, 21 April 1801.

Set in the city of St Andrews, Scotland, the opera centres on a typical Metastasian love-chain. The princess Ginevra (soprano), daughter of the King of Scotland (tenor), loves the Italian knight Ariodante (soprano), who has heroically brought reinforcements from England in time to defeat the attacking Irish army. Ginevra is courted by the king's constable, Polinesso (tenor), who is still loved by Dalinda (soprano). She in turn must fend off Ariodante's brother Lurcanio (soprano). When Ginevra rejects Polinesso, despite her father's efforts to intercede, he plots revenge, persuading Dalinda to impersonate Ginevra and ensuring that Ariodante witnesses their tryst. Presuming himself betrayed by Ginevra, Ariodante attempts to drown himself but survives and returns incognito to defend her against charges of contributing to his death. Meanwhile Dalinda discloses her own role in Polinesso's intrigue after she is rescued from an assassin sent by Polinesso to silence her. Confronted with Dalinda's revelation and defeated by Ariodante in combat, Polinesso finally confesses. Ariodante and Ginevra are reunited and Polinesso is pardoned.

Mayr's *Ginevra* was composed to inaugurate the Teatro Nuovo in Trieste. It belongs to a long tradition of Ariodante operas that had begun with Giacomo Perti's and Antonio Salvi's *Ginevra principessa di Scozia* (1708) and included at least 12 operas by Italian, German and French composers including Handel (1735), Vivaldi (1736), Mayr's teacher Bertoni (1753), Isouard (1798) and Méhul (1799). The plot of Rossi's libretto adheres closely to that of Salvi's original, although the layout of its scenes may owe more to later French versions of the story. The première, with a cast that included the famous castrato Luigi Marchesi and tenor Giacomo Davide, was one of Mayr's great early successes, and the opera held a place in the Italian repertory for 30 years. In its many arias with chorus and secondary characters, the music demonstrates Mayr's skill at constructing asymmetrical, multi-sectional lyric numbers infused with action.　　　SCOTT L. BALTHAZAR

Giocatore, Il. Opera by G. M. Orlandini; *see* MARITO GIOCATORE E LA MOGLIE BACCHETTONA, IL.

Gioconda, La. *Dramma lirico* in four acts by AMILCARE PONCHIELLI to a libretto by Tobia Gorrio (ARRIGO BOITO) after VICTOR HUGO's play *Angélo, tyran de Padoue*; Milan, Teatro alla Scala, 8 April 1876.

La Gioconda *a singer*	soprano
Laura Adorno *a Genoese lady*	mezzo-soprano
Alvise Badoero *a chief of the State Inquisition, husband of Laura*	bass
La Cieca *Gioconda's mother*	contralto
Enzo Grimaldi *a Genoese prince, disguised as a sea captain*	tenor
Barnaba *a ballad singer and spy of the Inquisition*	baritone
Zuàne *a competitor in the Regatta*	bass
A Singer	bass
Isèpo *a public scrivener*	tenor
A Pilot	bass

Regatta spectators, senators, noblemen and women, masks (harlequins, pantaloons, dominoes), populace, sailors, midshipmen, monks, knights, singers

Mute extras: mace-bearers, squires, cut-throats, trumpeters, Dalmatians, Moors, the Grand Chancellor, the Council of Ten, six trainbearers, a boatswain, the victor of the Regatta, a ship's captain, the Doge

Setting Venice in the 17th century

In response to the growing interest shown towards Ponchielli's operas during the early 1870s Ricordi commissioned *La Gioconda* in 1874, entrusting the libretto to Boito, who modelled it strictly on the 'grand opera' style of Scribe (then enjoying a belated vogue in Italy), with massed choral scenes, spectacular historical framework, abundance of contrasts and a central ballet. Taking as his basis a drama that had already served Mercadante, he diminished the importance of Hugo's title role, idealized the heroine and elevated the Venetian spy into a satanic figure conceived in his most lurid vein.

Boito presented the resulting confection under an anagram of his own name which deceived no one. The singers at the première were Maddalena Mariani-Masi (La Gioconda), Maria Biancolini-Rodriguez (Laura), Ormondo Maini (Alvise), Eufemia Barlani-Dini (La Cieca), Julián Gayarre (Enzo) and Gottardo Aldighieri (Barnaba); the conductor was Franco Faccio. The reception was generally cordial. Milan's leading critic, Filippo Filippi, declared that, Verdi apart, only Ponchielli among contemporary Italian composers was capable of producing a work of such importance. Successive revivals, however, were to bring important modifications. For the Venetian première, at the Teatro Rossini on 18 October the same year, Ponchielli added the Furlana to Act 1 and wrote a new cabaletta ('O grido di quest' anima') for the duet between Enzo and Barnaba, as well as a *preghiera* for Laura in Act 2 and a new aria for Alvise in Act 3 (later discarded) that included the lines 'La Morte è il nulla / E vecchia fola il Ciel', which Boito subsequently transferred to Iago's Credo. For the Teatro Apollo, Rome (23 January 1877), Ponchielli wrote a new finale to Act 1, suppressing the reprise of the Furlana, and ended the second act with a duet for Enzo and Gioconda in place of the original naval battle. The definitive version of *La Gioconda* was first given at Genoa on 27 November 1879, although it received critical attention only when it returned to La Scala on 12 February 1880; Ponchielli had recomposed Alvise's aria a second time and made an important alteration to the finale of Act 3, replacing the original stretta with an orchestral peroration of the principal theme of the preceding *pezzo concertato* – a procedure that was considered entirely novel at the time and which was not lost on the composer's best pupil, Puccini. Thereafter the opera entered the Italian repertory, where it has remained ever since. Abroad, it has tended to be confined to theatres such as the New York Metropolitan which can afford the resources that it requires. The 'Danza delle ore' (Dance of the Hours), however, has established itself in the concert hall as an international classic of light music ever since its performance at the Paris Exhibition of 1878.

ACT 1: 'The Lion's Mouth'
The courtyard of the Doge's Palace A reflective prelude establishes two of the opera's motifs: a broad cantilena that will connote the rosary that saves the life of Laura Adorno, and a fidgeting figure (ex.1)

Ex.1

that portrays the villainy of Barnaba. The curtain rises with the Venetians *en fête*, watched cynically by Barnaba. Bells and trumpets announce the Regatta. As the people hurry away to watch it, Barnaba compares the strings of his guitar to the threads of a spider's web, designed to entrap his victims, one of whom now approaches – Gioconda, supporting her blind mother, La Cieca. A terzettino ('Figlia che reggi il tremulo piè') introduces a sinuous phrase sung by La Cieca ('Tu canti agli uomini le tue canzoni') which will recur as a symbol of Gioconda's filial devotion; beneath the upper voices can be heard the Barnaba 'fidget'. Gioconda leaves her mother to her devotions and goes in search of her betrothed, Enzo; Barnaba comes forward and makes advances to her, only to be repulsed with scorn. The crowd returns with the winner of the Regatta. Barnaba

persuades the loser, Zuàne, that his craft was bewitched by La Cieca. The prayers which she seems to be uttering, he says, are evil spells, and he rouses the people to murderous fury against her. Enzo appears; failing to quell the tumult, he goes to rally his sailors in La Cieca's defence.

At that moment Alvise comes out of the palace with Laura, and the crowd falls silent. Ignoring Gioconda's pleas he orders the old woman's arrest and torture. But his wife, noticing La Cieca's rosary, successfully intercedes for her. In her aria 'Voce di donna o d'angelo', La Cieca expresses her gratitude, in token of which she presents Laura with her rosary. Meanwhile Laura and Enzo have recognized one another. Alone with Enzo, Barnaba tells him that he knows his true identity, and that while Enzo loves Gioconda like a brother, the real object of his passion is Laura, for whose sake he has risked his life in coming to Venice, where there is a price on his head. As a state informer he could have Enzo arrested; but instead he has arranged for Laura to meet Enzo that night on his brigantine while Alvise is occupied with his official duties. He thus hopes to further his own cause with Gioconda by demonstrating her idol's treachery. Enzo curses him for his villainy but is overjoyed nonetheless. When he has left, Barnaba calls for the scribe Isèpo and, overheard by Gioconda, dictates a denunciation of Enzo, revealing his plan of elopement. In a monologue after the style of *Rigoletto* ('O monumento'), Barnaba muses on the two faces of Venice – the city of perpetual carnival and the squalid police state. He then deposits the missive in the mouth of the great stone lion and departs. The courtyard fills once more with masqueraders, who dance a Furlana. As the organ sounds from the nearby church, signalizing the Angelus, all fall on their knees in prayer, among them Gioconda, heartbroken at Enzo's betrayal, and La Cieca, who tries vainly to comfort her.

ACT 2: 'The Rosary'
A brigantine It is night. Sailors and midshipmen are making ready to sail. Barnaba arrives in the guise of a fisherman and jokes with the crew, who echo the refrain of his barcarolle ('Pescator, affonda l'esca'). He orders Isèpo to prepare an assault on the brigantine and leaves to fetch Laura. As he waits for her, Enzo apostrophizes the nocturnal scene in the aria 'Cielo e mar', one of the gems of the tenor repertory. Laura arrives, somewhat unnerved by her escort's sinister appearance. In their love duet ('Deh, non turbare') Enzo calms her fears. He goes below to give his orders, and Laura offers up a prayer to the Virgin ('Stella del marinar'). Meanwhile Gioconda has entered unobserved. The two women confront one another in a duet ('L'amo come il fulgor del creato'), each claiming precedence in their love for Enzo. Gioconda is about to stab her rival, when she catches sight of the rosary that Laura is clutching. Recognizing the woman who saved her mother's life, she gives Laura her own mask and thrusts her into a boat which will carry her to safety. Enzo, returning, is dismayed to find Gioconda. Triumphantly she points to where Laura is making her escape, then to a craft on which Alvise can be seen approaching. Barnaba, she says, has betrayed his plan. Enzo sets fire to the brigantine and dives into the sea.

ACT 3: 'The Ca' d'oro'
3.i *A room in Alvise's palace* In a *scena ed aria* ('Sì, morir ella de'!'), Alvise resolves to avenge his

'La Gioconda' (Ponchielli), scenes from the original production at La Scala, Milan, 8 April 1876: engraving from 'L'illustrazione italiana' (28 May 1876)

family's honour by having his wife die by poison. When she enters he ironically compliments her on her beauty and then passes to accusations, which she tries vainly to rebut. He leads her into an adjoining room, where a catafalque is laid out. As a serenade sounds in the distance he gives her a phial of poison, instructing her to drain it before the music has ceased. He leaves and Gioconda enters. She exchanges the poison for a sleeping-draught which will give the appearance of death.

3.ii *A large hall* Alvise is receiving guests, among whom are Enzo and Gioconda. He has devised for their entertainment a spectacular ballet, The Dance of the Hours. At its conclusion Barnaba enters, dragging La Cieca, whom he claims to have discovered casting spells. She protests that she was offering up prayers for the dead; and indeed a distant funeral bell is heard. Barnaba tells Enzo that it tolls for Laura. At this, Enzo flings aside his disguise and reveals himself to Alvise, who orders his arrest. During the huge *pezzo concertato*, which forms the architectural pinnacle of the score, Gioconda promises Barnaba her favours if he will obtain Enzo's release. At the climax of the ensemble Alvise discloses the catafalque on which lies the body of his apparently dead wife.

Act 4: 'The Orfano Canal'
The inner court of a ruined palace on the Isola della Giudecca Gioconda is alone, absorbed in melancholy thoughts. Her friends carry in the sleeping Laura and lay her on a bed. Gioconda begs them to help find her mother, who has disappeared. When they have gone she expresses a longing for death in her grand aria

('Suicidio!'). Enzo arrives, unable to understand why he has been set free. All he wants is to mourn on Laura's tomb. When Gioconda tells him that it is empty, he accuses her of preying on the dead like a hyena. He is about to stab her when Laura's voice is heard. Gioconda explains her deception and indicates the boat which she has got ready for the lovers' escape. Deeply moved, Enzo and Laura bid her farewell in a terzetto ('E così sia! quest'ultimo'). She is about to go in search of La Cieca when Barnaba enters and reminds her of their bargain. Pretending to adorn herself for his delight, she seizes a dagger and kills herself. Barnaba tries to make her understand that he has drowned her mother out of spite; but she no longer hears him.

*   *   *

Apart from Verdi's *Aida*, *La Gioconda* is the only Italian 'grand opera', or 'opera-ballo', to have stayed the course. Its style, in places almost Donizettian, is old-fashioned for the 1870s, but it is fully assured. The score, like that of *Aida*, is articulated in closed numbers embedded in a musical continuum in which conversational, as distinct from arioso, recitative is kept to a minimum and much of the dialogue is carried on to orchestral 'parlanti'. Of the three recurring motifs only the insistent 'fidget' that connotes the sinister Barnaba is purely instrumental. The theme of the rosary is formed from the culminating period of La Cieca's aria; while the undulating strain associated with Gioconda's filial love is taken from her Act 1 terzetto with her mother and the concealed Barnaba. La Cieca is clearly modelled on Meyerbeer's Fidès; otherwise there is little attempt at characterization throughout the opera. Unlike those of Rigoletto, Barnaba's monologue tells us nothing about the man himself. Gioconda herself is less a personality than a succession of moods and attitudes – wilting and forlorn in Act 1, the avenging tigress in Act 2, an almost 'veristic' victim in her great aria in Act 4, from which her descent – in the final scene – to the coquettish language of Violetta in Act 1 of *La traviata* verges on the bathetic.

The opera is sensational rather than truly dramatic, abounding in 'effects without causes' (to borrow Wagner's phrase, re Meyerbeer); but it contains some fine descriptive touches. Night on the lagoon is evoked in Act 2 by an atmospheric prelude and offstage chorus in which one can sense the lapping of water against the hold of the brigantine, and also by the diaphanous scoring that introduces Enzo's aria 'Cielo e mar', notable for its original use of strophic variation. Above all *La Gioconda* demonstrates Ponchielli's skill as a ballet composer. Not only is the Dance of the Hours a classic of light music, forming alone among opera ballets a complete, self-sufficient musical statement; much of the entire score is permeated by dance rhythms which lend extra vitality to the opera's wealth of spontaneous, if not invariably distinguished, lyricism.   JULIAN BUDDEN

Gioia [Gioja], **Gaetano** (*b* Naples, *c*1760; *d* Naples, 30 March 1826). Italian dancer and choreographer. By 1775 he was a principal dancer at the Teatro Regio, Turin. He appeared there regularly up to 1778 and in 1784–9 but also danced in Florence (1776, 1779–80), Lucca (1779), Rome (1781, 1787) and Naples (1783, 1785). He made his choreographic début at Turin in autumn 1789, then worked in Venice and at La Scala, Milan. His first engagement abroad was at Lisbon to stage two new ballets for the opening of the Teatro São Carlos in June 1793; he was then principal choreographer and dancer at the major theatres of Naples (1793, 1795–6), Milan (1793–4), Florence (1798–9), Turin (1799) and Genoa (1800). A period in Vienna from 1800 exposed him to important new stimuli, notably the instrumental music of resident composers, the new lighting techniques and stage effects of the *Zauberopern* and acquaintance with the younger choreographer Salvatore Viganò. Thereafter Gioia and Viganò both worked to advance the use of pantomime in dramatic ballets. Gioia returned to Italy in 1802. His fertile imagination and formidable working pace account for a prodigious output: some 95 different ballets in more than 220 productions.

To an unprecedented degree Gioia's works show the cross-fertilization between opera and pantomime ballet. Several of his early ballets follow a common 18th-century practice of borrowing plots from successful Italian and French operas. At least two, *Nina, o La pazza per amore* (1794) and *Gli Orazi e i Curiazi* (1798), also used music drawn exclusively from their operatic models (Dalayrac and Cimarosa), arranged for orchestra. The scores of most of his ballets, however, were compilations; often containing music from the newest operas, they sometimes had the curious effect of providing an advance local hearing. *I baccanali aboliti*, containing five extracts from Rossini's *Zelmira* (1822, Naples) and four from his *Semiramide* (1823, Venice), had its première at La Scala on 23 August 1823 before either opera was performed there. Among the composers of original scores for Gioia was Pietro Romani.

Gioia's ballets were important models for Italian operas of his and the following generation. In a reversal of earlier trends, his themes were among the first to inspire librettos of vocal works. One of the earliest was Generali's *Cesare in Egitto* (1816, Turin), based on Gioia's most famous choreography (1807, Naples). At least three of Donizetti's operas, *Gabriella di Vergy* (1826), *Otto mesi in due ore* (1827) and *Elisabetta, o Il castello di Kenilworth* (1829), owe their plots to similarly titled ballets by Gioia. In the *coreodramma* the emphasis on pantomime action as opposed to pure dance led to the avoidance both of the closed forms of traditional dance music and of highly virtuoso operatic airs in favour of more dramatic, through-composed pieces; musical recall was exploited for psychological effect. The realistic acting technique of celebrated dancers in Gioia's ballets influenced the expressive art of such outstanding young singers as Pasta and Malibran; and his use of large numbers of dancers and spectacular scenic effects gave audiences a taste for visual extravagance matched only when grand opera conquered Italian stages in the 1850s.

*

K. K. Hansell: 'Il ballo teatrale e l'opera italiana', *SOI*, v (1988), 252–72   KATHLEEN KUZMICK HANSELL

Gioielli della Madonna, I [*Der Schmuck der Madonna*] ('The Jewels of the Madonna'). Opera in three acts by ERMANNO WOLF-FERRARI to a libretto by CARLO ZANGARINI and ENRICO GOLISCIANI; Berlin, Kurfürstenoper, 23 December 1911 (text revised in 1933).

It is unfortunate that this crudely melodramatic opera, in which Wolf-Ferrari strayed a long way from his most natural line of country, has received more attention in the English-speaking world than any of his masterpieces. His immediate reasons for temporarily turning his back on the gracefully updated *opera buffa* style which he had made so distinctively his own were probably partly opportunistic: his earlier operas, from *Cenerentola* to *Il segreto di Susanna*, had proved far more acceptable in Germany than in his native Italy, and it must have seemed reasonable to suppose that his fortunes might be improved south of the Alps by a rapprochement with post-Mascagnian *verismo*. Ironically, the Italians paid even less attention to the new opera than to its comic predecessors, and instead it quickly found markets across the Atlantic and the English Channel.

Set in Naples on the feast-day of the Madonna, the turbulent story dominated by raw jealousy may recall that of *Cavalleria rusticana*. Being spread over three acts, however, the result lacks the concentration as well as the compelling spontaneity of the Mascagnian prototype: by 1911 this kind of opera was already showing its age. The rival males, in this case, are the blacksmith Gennaro (tenor) and Rafaele (baritone), who leads a group of Camorristi (comparable to the Mafia in Sicily). Both men are in love with Gennaro's foster sister Maliella (soprano), who much prefers Rafaele's more adventurous charms. When Gennaro hears about the flamboyant Camorrista's boast that to prove the force of his love he would even steal jewels from the festively decorated statue of the Madonna, he naively decides to get the better of his rival by stealing the jewels himself. This wins him a short-term advantage, in that Maliella does give herself to him (while always having Rafaele in mind). But she then shocks even the Camorristi by sacrilegiously adorning herself with the jewels. Having so profoundly offended the religious sensibilities of the community in which they live, she and Gennaro both, in desperation, commit suicide.

This frankly sensational plot (which is said to have been based, *Pagliacci*-like, on a real event reported in the newspapers) at least has the merit of providing plentiful opportunities for picturesque local colour, which Wolf-Ferrari's music evokes with some zest, making use of at least one real Neapolitan melody. The total effect, however, seems disappointingly thin and vulgar when set alongside the elegance and the psychological insights of his best comic operas. Only in a few passages – notably the profoundly lyrical later part of the duet in Act 1 for Gennaro and his mother Carmela (mezzo-soprano), and the purely orchestral postlude that follows it – does the innermost essence of Wolf-Ferrari's personality come through clearly despite all.

JOHN C. G. WATERHOUSE

Giordani, Giuseppe ['Giordaniello'] (*b* Naples, 19 Dec 1751; *d* Fermo, 4 Jan 1798). Italian composer. A fellow pupil of Zingarelli and Cimarosa at the Conservatorio di S Maria di Loreto, Naples, he studied composition with Fedele Fenaroli. In 1779 he married the singer Emanuela Cosmi ('La Positanella'). From 1774 he was a supernumerary *maestro di cappella* of the Tesoro di S Gennaro, Naples, and from 1789 *maestro di cappella* at Fermo Cathedral. In 1776 he offered to write an opera for the Teatro di S Carlo but was turned down; only three years later his *Epponina* inaugurated the Teatro della Palla a Corda, Florence, and in 1788 his *Caio Ostilio*, with ballets by Martín y Soler, inaugurated the theatre at Faenza. He lacked the talents of such contemporaries as Cimarosa and Paisiello and found it difficult to establish himself in Naples, but his operas were appreciated in other cities, among them Rome, Bologna and Venice. He was also active as a composer of ballet music in Naples in the 1780s and, after his appointment at Fermo, of sacred music, in which he indulged in virtuoso vocal writing. The study of his work has been complicated by questions of attribution arising from the confusion between his name and that of Tommaso Giordani, to whom he was unrelated.

L'astuto in imbroglio (ob), ?Pisa, 1771
Epponina (dramma per musica, P. Giovannini and G. Sertor), Florence, Palla a Corda, aut. 1779
Demetrio (os, P. Metastasio), Modena, Corte, carn. 1780
Erifile (dramma per musica, ? G. De Gamerra), Genoa, S Agostino, 1780, D-Ds, I-PAc
Gl'inganni scambievoli (int), Rome, Valle, carn. 1781
La fiera di Brindisi (ob, G. Palomba), Naples, Fondo, 1781
Lo sposo di tre e marito di nessuna (ob, A. Palomba), Naples, Fondo, 1781; rev. of P. Anfossi and P. A. Guglielmi, 1763
Il convito (farsa per musica, Palomba), Naples, Fondo, carn. 1782
Il ritorno d'Ulisse, Mantua, 1782
L'acomate (dramma per musica), Pisa, Prini, spr. 1783; rev. as Elpinice (os), Bologna, Zagnoni, aut. 1783
Osmano (dramma per musica, Sertor), Venice, S Benedetto, carn. 1784, La
Tito Manlio (dramma per musica, G. Roccaforte), Genoa, S Agostino, carn. 1784
Pizzarro nell'Indie, o sia La distruzione del Perù (dramma per musica, 'N. N.'), Florence, Palla a Corda, spr. 1784
Nitteti (os), Padua, Nuovo, 1784, Pi(l), P-La
La vestale (dramma per musica, ? L. Romanelli), Bologna, Zagnoni, carn. 1785
Ifigenia in Aulide (dramma per musica, ? L. Serio), Rome, Argentina, carn. 1786
Fernando nel Messico (dramma per musica, F. Tarducci), Rome, Argentina, carn. 1786, B-Bc, I-FERd*
L'impegno, ossia Chi la fa l'aspetti (farsetta), Rome, Capranica, carn. 1786
I ripieghi fortunati (farsetta), Rome, 1786
Alciade e Telesia (dramma per musica, 3, E. Manfredi), Bologna, Zagnoni, carn. 1787, FERd*
Il corrivo (ob, 2, G. M. Diodati), Naples, Nuovo, spr. 1787
Orfano cinese, Genoa, 1787
Caio Ostilio (os, Manfredi), Faenza, Comunale, spr. 1788, Fc
Scipione (os), Rovigo, aut. 1788
Li tre fratelli ridicoli (farsa), Rome, Capranica, 1788, Bc
Ariarate (dramma per musica, F. Moretti), Turin, Regio, carn. 1789, P-La
La disfatta di Dario (dramma per musica), Milan, Scala, carn. 1789, F-Pn, I-FERd*, Nc
Cajo Mario (dramma per musica, Roccaforte), Lodi, Nuovo, aut. 1789
Aspasia (dramma per musica, Sertor), Venice, S Benedetto, carn. 1790
Nicomede (os, Manfredi), Genoa, S Agostino, carn. 1790, FERd*
Medonte, re di Epiro (dramma per musica), Rome, Argentina, carn. 1791, FERd*
Don Mitrillo contrastato (ob), Venice, S Cassiano, aut. 1791, FERd*
Atalanta (dramma per musica, C. Oliveri), Turin, Regio, carn. 1792, FERd*
Ines de Castro (dramma per musica), Venice, Fenice, carn. 1793, FERd*, Vnm
Leonilda, Naples
Sedecia, FERd*
Arias and duets in A-Wgm, B-Bc, CH-E, D-SWl, F-Pn, I-Bc, BZtoggenburg, Fc, Gl, Mc, Nc, PEsp, PS, Rc, Rsc, Tf, VEs

*

DEUMM (R. Bossa)
S. Di Giacomo: Maestri di cappella … al Tesoro di S. Gennaro (Naples, 1920)
R. Zanetti: La musica italiana nel settecento (Milan, 1978)
U. Gironacci: 'Il periodo fermano di Giuseppe Giordani 1789–1798', Quaderni dell'Archivio storico arcivescovile di Fermo, i (1986), 105–46
E. Zanetti: 'Di alcuni interrogativi intorno a Caro mio ben', Musica senza aggettivi, ed. A. Ziino (Florence, 1991), 61–9
RENATO BOSSA

Giordani, Tommaso (b Naples, c1730–33; d Dublin, Feb 1806). Italian composer working in the British Isles. All the members of his family were singers, apart from himself and his brother Francesco, a dancer. About 1745, under the management of their father, Giuseppe (unrelated to the composer Giuseppe Giordani known as Giordaniello), the Giordani family formed a small opera troupe and, with a few other singers, travelled across Europe. After performing at Sinigaglia (1747), Graz (1748), Frankfurt (1750), Amsterdam (1752) and Paris (1753), they were invited by John Rich to perform four burlettas in the 1753–4 season at Covent Garden. On 17 December 1753, at the première of the first of these, Gli amanti gelosi (with words by Tommaso's father and music attributed to Cocchi), the singing of Tommaso's sister, Nicolina, caused a sensation; she was nicknamed 'La Spiletta' after her role. The family performed again in London in 1755 and 1756. Tommaso's name is not mentioned, although he composed the music to the burletta La comediante fatta cantatrice, given in January 1756. He may have arranged music and played the harpsichord in the theatre band while the rest of the family was on stage.

The family was in Dublin late in 1764, having been invited to perform at the Smock Alley theatre, and remained in Dublin for three years, during which time Tommaso's career as an opera composer was launched. His first major composing venture in Dublin, however, proved a miscalculation; failing to understand the satirical nature of the work, Giordani mistakenly 'improved' the simple airs of The Beggar's Opera by 'italianizing' them. But his next three comic operas, Don Fulminone, The Enchanter and The Maid of the Mill, all produced between January and March 1765, were better received. The following season Giordani remained at Smock Alley, although the rest of the family transferred to Crow Street. For Smock Alley he composed two operas: Love in Disguise, which was written by a Trinity College student, Henry Lucas (the performance was attended by a crowd of Trinity students); and L'eroe cinese, apparently the first opera seria to be staged in Ireland. Giordani then moved to Crow Street, where his Phyllis at Court was performed in 1767. Charges of plagiarism, however, drove him back to London.

By early 1770 he was very active with the Italian Opera at the King's Theatre. Over the next 13 years he composed the entire music to three operas, collaborated in a pastoral, L'omaggio (1781), and arranged, adapted and added new overtures or airs to a number of Italian pasticcios. He also directed many operas at the King's Theatre and contributed incidental music to plays, including the songs to Sheridan's The Critic at Drury Lane (29 October 1779).

In summer 1783 Giordani returned to Dublin, where he joined the tenor Michael Leoni in a series of concerts at the Rotunda. With Leoni he then rented a theatre in Capel Street, calling it the English Opera House, and put on a season of 'English' operas, with librettos mostly by minor Irish writers and the music by himself. He composed the music for seven staged musical works and adapted music for another half-dozen pieces for an outwardly successful season, which opened, on 18 December, with Gibraltar and The Haunted Castle. Yet the smallish size of the theatre meant that Leoni and Giordani failed to meet their expenses, and the venture ended in bankruptcy in July 1784.

The following season Giordani worked at Smock

Alley under Richard Daly; he moved to Crow Street in 1787 when Smock Alley closed, and became musical director there the following year. (In 1784 he had married one of the daughters of Tate Wilkinson, the manager of the theatre.) Giordani had several successes at both theatres, but seems to have given up composing after writing his comic opera *The Cottage Festival* (1796). The exact date of his death is unknown, but the minutes of the Irish Music Fund (of which he had been president since 1794) record, on 24 February 1806, the payment of five guineas for his funeral. Giordani's gifts as a prolific and versatile composer were sufficient for him to be respected in London and to dominate the Dublin musical scene for many years. He wrote in the prevailing italianate style, with expressive and inventive melodies, his best written with specific singers in mind. He was also a sensitive orchestrator. Generally, though, he was a rather indifferent composer, and was frequently accused of plagiarism.

See also MAID OF THE MILL, THE.

Some music published in Dublin or London shortly after performance

DBCS – *Dublin, Theatre Royal, Crow Street*
DBEOH – *Dublin, English Opera House, Capel Street*
DBSA – *Dublin, Smock Alley*
LCG – *London, Covent Garden* LDL – *London, Drury Lane*
LKH – *London, King's Theatre, Haymarket*
LLH – *London, Little Theatre, Haymarket*

La comediante fatta cantatrice (comic op), LCG, 12 Jan 1756
Don Fulminone, or The Lover with Two Mistresses (comic op), DBSA, 7 Jan 1765
The Enchanter, or Love and Magic (comic op), DBSA, 17 Jan 1765
The Maid of the Mill (comic op, 3, I. Bickerstaff, after S. Richardson, J. Fletcher and W. Rowley), DBSA, 26 March 1765
Love in Disguise (comic op, H. Lucas), DBSA, 24 April 1766
L'eroe cinese (os, 3, P. Metastasio), DBSA, 7 May 1766
Phyllis at Court (comic op, 2, R. Lloyd, after C.-S. Favart), DBCS, 25 Feb 1767
The Elopement (pantomime), LDL, 26 Dec 1767
Il padre e il figlio rivali (comic op), LKH, 6 Feb 1770
Il re pastore (os, 3, Metastasio), LKH, 30 May 1778
Il bacio (comic op, 2, C. F. Badini), LKH, 9 April 1782
Gibraltar (comic op, R. Houlton), DBEOH, 18 Dec 1783
The Haunted Castle (afterpiece, W. C. Oulton), DBEOH, 18 Dec 1783
The Enchantress, or The Happy Island (musical entertainment, A. M. Edwards), DBEOH, 31 Dec 1783
The Happy Disguise (comic op, Oulton), DBEOH, 7 Jan 1784
Genius of Ireland (masque), DBEOH, 9 Feb 1784
The Dying Indian (musical entertainment), DBEOH, 11 March 1784
Orfeo ed Euridice (burlesque op, Houlton), DBEOH, 14 June 1784
The Hypochondriac (afterpiece, Franklin), DBSA, 4 Jan 1785
The Island of Saints, or The Institution of the Shamrock (pantomime, Messink), DBSA, 27 Jan 1785
Calypso, or Love and Enchantment (serio-comic op, Houlton), DBSA, early April 1785
Perseverance, or The Third Time the Best (musical interlude, 2, Oulton), DBCS, 12 March 1789
The Distressed Knight, or The Enchanted Lady (comic op), DBCS, 12 Feb 1791
The Ward of the Castle (comic op, 2, Mrs Burke), LCG, 24 Oct 1793
The Cottage Festival, or A Day in Wales (comic op, L. MacNally), DBCS, 28 Nov 1796

Collaborations: L'omaggio (pastoral, 3), LKH, 5 June 1781, with G. B. Bianchi and V. Rauzzini; The Contract (comic op, 2, R. Houlton), DBSA, 14 May 1782, with P. Cogan and J. A. Stevenson; To Arms, or The British Recruit (musical interlude, 1, T. Hurlstone), LCG, 3 May 1793, with W. Shield and Stevenson

Adaptations (mostly new accs. or new ovs., songs and finales; orig. composer named if substantial part of his music retained): Gli amanti gelosi, DBSA, 23 Nov 1764, most music by B. Galuppi; The Beggar's Opera, DBSA, 2 Jan 1765; J. A. Hasse: Artaserse,

LKH, 25 April 1772, collab. M. Vento; Hasse: Antigono, LKH, 8 March 1774, collab. Vento and T. Traetta; A. Sacchini: Armida, LKH, 8 Nov 1774; G. Paisiello: Le due contesse, LKH, 4 Nov 1777; J. Hook: The Lady of the Manor, DBEOH, 25 March 1784; T. A. Arne: Love in a Village, DBSA, 30 Oct 1784; Shield: Robin Hood, or Sherwood Forest, DBSA, 13 Dec 1784; S. Arnold: Gretna Green, DBSA, 7 Jan 1785; Shield: Fontainbleau, or Our Way in France, DBSA, 29 Jan 1785; Arne, after H. Purcell [Weldon]: The Tempest, DBCS, 26 Nov 1789; Arnold: The Battle of Hexham, DBCS, early Dec 1789; S. Storace: The Haunted Tower, DBCS, 18 Feb 1790; Storace: The Siege of Belgrade, or The Turkish Overthrow, DBCS, 14 Dec 1791

Numerous songs and ovs. in pasticcios and comic operas (many written specially), incl.: Le vicende della sorte (1770); La marchesa giardiniera (1775); La frascatana (1776); Il geloso in cimento (1777); La vera costanza (1778); Alessandro nelle Indie (1779); L'Arcifanfano (1780); Il barone di Torre Forte (1781); Ezio (1781); The Silver Tankard (Arnold, 1781); I viaggiatori felici (1781); Silla (1783); Love in a Village (1791); Inkle and Yarico (1791)

BDA; BurneyH; EitnerQ; LS
ABCdario Musico (London, 1780)
R. Hitchcock: *An Historical View of the Irish Stage, From the Earliest Period down to the Close of the Season 1788, Interspersed with Theatrical Anecdotes, and an Occasional Review of the Irish Dramatic Authors and Actors* (Dublin, 1788)
J. O'Keeffe: *Recollections of the Life of John O'Keeffe* (London, 1826)
W. Hepworth Dixon, ed.: *Lady Morgan's Memoirs: Autobiography, Diaries and Correspondence* (London, 1862)
W. J. Lawrence: 'Tommaso Giordani: an Italian Composer in Ireland', *MA*, ii (1910–11), 99–107
S. Rosenfeld: *Foreign Theatrical Companies in Great Britain in the 17th and 18th Centuries* (London, 1954)
R. Fiske: *English Theatre Music in the Eighteenth Century* (London, 1973, 2/1986)
T. J. Walsh: *Opera in Dublin 1705–1797: the Social Scene* (Dublin, 1973)
IRENA CHOLIJ

Giordano, Umberto (Menotti Maria) (*b* Foggia, 28 Aug 1867; *d* Milan, 12 Nov 1948). Italian composer. The son of a chemist who intended him for the career of a fencing master, he devoted himself to music against his parents' will. In 1882 he was admitted to the Naples Conservatory, where his teachers included Paolo Serrao and Giuseppe Martucci.

While still a student he entered a one-act opera, *Marina*, for the Sonzogno competition of 1889. Although short-listed among the 73 submissions it was awarded only sixth place (the winner being Mascagni with *Cavalleria rusticana*). Nonetheless Sonzogno thought sufficiently well of it to commission from Giordano a full-length opera, *Mala vita* (1892, Rome), based on a novella of low-life in Naples by Salvatore Di Giacomo. With its wealth of local colour and strong story line it proved highly successful in Austria and Germany, where it began a temporary vogue for operas in a Neapolitan setting. In Italy it was found too shocking, and five years later Giordano revised it as *Il voto*, without beneficial results. However, following Ricordi's example with Puccini, Sonzogno provided Giordano with a monthly stipend against the composition of his next opera. This was *Regina Diaz* (1894, Naples), intended for the celebrations of Mercadante's centenary. The subject (essentially that of Donizetti's *Maria di Rohan*) failed to inspire the composer; and the opera was withdrawn after the second performance. As a result, Edoardo Sonzogno decided to withhold Giordano's retainer, but he was persuaded otherwise by Alberto Franchetti, who ceded the libretto of *Andrea Chénier* to his younger colleague.

That same year Giordano settled in Milan, where he married Olga Spatz-Wurms, whose family owned the hotel in which Verdi regularly stayed during his last years – a circumstance which enabled the younger composer to make his acquaintance and receive from him valuable advice. The success of *Andrea Chénier* (1896, Milan) established Giordano in the front rank of the GIOVANE SCUOLA. He then returned to a long-cherished project of an opera based on Sardou's *Fedora*, which was launched at Sonzogno's Teatro Lirico in 1898. This too was destined to remain in the repertory. A third triumph, though more temporary, followed with *Siberia* (1903, Milan), after which Giordano's fortunes declined. *Marcella* (1907, Milan), a story of love and renunciation across the class barrier, failed, as did *Mese Mariano* (1910, Palermo), in which Giordano returned to Di Giacomo; the plot of *Mese Mariano* anticipates to a surprising extent that of Puccini's *Suor Angelica*. Following an old suggestion of Verdi that he write an opera showing Napoleon *en pantoufles* he turned to Sardou's comedy *Madame Sans-Gêne* (1915, New York). Owing to the outbreak of war the première was given in his absence with a cast that included Geraldine Farrar, Giovanni Zenatello and Pasquale Amato; the conductor was Toscanini. But this too made little impression. Together with Franchetti he wrote an operetta, *Giove a Pompei* (1921, Rome), his own contribution having been mostly composed 20 years earlier.

Then came an unexpected success, *La cena delle beffe* (1924, Milan), written to a libretto by Sem Benelli, adapted (with the help of Giovacchino Forzano) from his own gruesome play set in Florence during the reign of Lorenzo the Magnificent. Held by some to be Giordano's dramatic masterpiece, the opera is still occasionally revived. His last work for the stage was the one-act *Il re* (1929, Milan), a lighthearted moralistic fantasy by Forzano composed as a vehicle for the coloratura soprano, Toti Dal Monte. Under Toscanini it enjoyed a certain vogue during the 1930s with Maria Caniglia and Lina Pagliughi as well as Dal Monte. A ballet, *L'astro magico*, remained unperformed, while an opera to a libretto by Forzano on the subject of Rasputin never materialized.

Although he showed no great individuality as a melodist, Giordano handled the late Romantic, emotionally vehement idiom of the *giovane scuola* with ease and fluency, being particularly skilful in weaving into his textures elements of local and historical colour – Neapolitan dance rhythms (*Mala vita*), French Revolutionary songs (*Andrea Chénier* and *Madame Sans-Gêne*), Russian folk music (*Siberia*), 18th-century pastiche (*Chénier*), pseudo-Chopin piano music and Swiss *ranz des vaches* (*Fedora*). Musically his operas are more loosely organized than those of his Italian contemporaries, with sparing use of recurring themes. His largest-scale work is *Siberia*. In his later operas the somewhat crude scoring gives way to a more refined technique, which yields telling results in *La cena delle beffe*, even if the subject could be thought to require a more astringent musical vocabulary. His stage sense is always sure, and his vocal writing unfailingly effective. *Andrea Chénier* owes its place in the repertory to the unusual opportunities it offers to a star tenor.

See also ANDREA CHÉNIER; CENA DELLE BEFFE, LA; FEDORA; MADAME SANS-GÊNE; MALA VITA; RE, IL; and SIBERIA.

Marina, *c*1889 (1, E. Golisciani), unperf.
Mala vita (3, N. Daspuro, after S. Di Giacomo), Rome, Argentina,

21 Feb 1892; rev. as Il voto, Milan, Lirico, 10 Nov 1897
Regina Diaz (2, G. Targioni-Tozzetti and G. Menasci, after Lockroy: *Un duel sous le cardinal de Richelieu*), Naples, Mercadante, 5 March 1894
Andrea Chénier (dramma istorico, 4, L. Illica), Milan, Scala, 28 March 1896
Fedora (3, A. Colautti, after V. Sardou), Milan, Lirico, 17 Nov 1898
Siberia (3, Illica), Milan, Scala, 19 Dec 1903; rev. Milan, Scala, 5 Dec 1927
Marcella (3, L. Stecchetti, H. Cain and J. Adenis), Milan, Lirico, 9 Nov 1907
Mese Mariano (1, Di Giacomo), Palermo, Massimo, 17 March 1910
Madame Sans-Gêne (3, R. Simoni, after Sardou and E. Moreau), New York, Met, 25 Jan 1915
Giove a Pompei (3, Illica and E. Romagnoli), Rome, Pariola, 5 July 1921, collab. A. Franchetti [Giordano's part mostly composed by 1901]
La cena delle beffe (poema drammatico, 4, S. Benelli), Milan, Scala, 20 Dec 1924
Il re (novella, 1, G. Forzano), Milan, Scala, 12 Jan 1929

*

R. Giazotto: *Umberto Giordano* (Milan, 1949)
G. Confalonieri: *Umberto Giordano* (Milan, 1958)
D. Cellamare: *Umberto Giordano* (Rome, 1967)
M. Morini, ed.: *Umberto Giordano* (Milan, 1968)
L'avant-scène opéra, no.121 (1989) [*Andrea Chénier* issue]

JULIAN BUDDEN

Giorgi-Belloc, Teresa. *See* BELLOC-GIORGI, TERESA.

Giorgini, Aristodemo (*b* Naples, 1879; *d* Naples, 19 Jan 1937). Italian tenor. He trained at the Accademia di S Cecilia in Rome and then with Massimo Perelli in Naples. He was one of the first artists to attract attention through his recordings, the first of which appeared in 1904. These were followed in 1905 by a highly successful début at La Scala as Ernesto in *Don Pasquale*. Wisely confining himself to lyric roles, he pursued his career till 1930, travelling widely in Europe and from 1912 to 1914 singing with the Chicago Opera Company. In 1905 at Covent Garden he sang to appreciative houses the roles of Don Ottavio in *Don Giovanni*, the Duke in *Rigoletto* and Rodolfo to Melba's Mimì. On retirement he taught for some years in Naples. His recordings preserve a voice of unusual beauty, touched though not excessively by the quick vibrato popular in Italy at the time; his style, often graceful, also has some of the freedom of its period.

J. B. STEANE

Giorgi-Righetti, Geltrude. *See* RIGHETTI, GELTRUDE.

Giorno di regno, Un ('King for a Day') [*Il finto Stanislao* ('The False Stanislaus')]. *Melodramma giocoso* in two acts by GIUSEPPE VERDI to a libretto by FELICE ROMANI (probably revised by TEMISTOCLE SOLERA) after Alexandre Vincent Pineu-Duval's play *Le faux Stanislas*; Milan, Teatro alla Scala, 5 September 1840.

Verdi's second opera, his only outright comic work until the end of his long career, was written at great speed. It is likely that Bartolomeo Merelli (impresario at La Scala) assigned him the libretto only in late June 1840; Romani's old *melodramma giocoso* (originally set by Adalbert Gyrowetz in 1818 under the title *Il finto Stanislao*) then had to be substantially revised to bring it some way up to date. (Although no direct evidence survives, the reviser was probably Temistocle Solera, who had helped with revisions of Verdi's first opera and seems then to have been a 'house poet' at La Scala.) The opera was a complete fiasco, removed from the stage after only one performance. To judge from contemporary reviews, and from Verdi's later recollections, its failure had as much to do with the performance as with the music. *Un giorno di regno* (which has occasionally reassumed the original title of *Il finto Stanislao*) enjoyed a few revivals in Verdi's lifetime, and has occasionally been staged in modern times.

The action takes place near Brest, in the castle of Kelbar, during the early 18th century. Belfiore (baritone) is an officer posing as King Stanislaus of Poland in order to protect the king from harm. But he is in love with a young widow, the Marchesa del Poggio (mezzosoprano), who is about to marry another. Secondary romantic interest comes from a pair of young lovers, Edoardo (tenor) and Giulietta (soprano); comic scenes are supplied by a pair of *buffo* basses, the Baron Kelbar (Giulietta's father) and La Rocca, the state treasurer (Edoardo's uncle), who wishes to marry Giulietta. After several farcical intrigues, Belfiore uses his disguise to effect the marriage of the young lovers and then reveals his true identity in time to claim the Marchesa as his own.

The opera is curiously uneven and, not surprisingly given the rushed circumstances of its creation, tends to peter out in the second act. It is heavily influenced by Rossini, but there are moments – particularly those passages that were altered from the old Romani libretto – in which we find a more up-to-date, Donizettian conception of sentimental comedy. The opera's most interesting vocal character is the Marchesa, whose role was written for Antonietta Ranieri-Marini, the singer who had earlier created Leonora in Verdi's first opera, *Oberto, conte di San Bonifacio*. The lovelorn tenor Edoardo shows early signs of Verdian robustness (particularly in his Act 1 duet with Belfiore), but later reverts to the lighter, higher style associated with the Rossinian tenor. *Un giorno di regno* must, by and large, be judged an unfortunate interlude in Verdi's progress; but even through the barrier of its alien style there are glimpses of the vital individuality that was to emerge so decisively in his next opera, *Nabucco.*   ROGER PARKER

Giorza, Paolo (*b* Milan, 11 Nov 1832; *d* Seattle, 25 May 1914). Italian composer and conductor. He studied with his father, a baritone and organist, and with La Croix. He worked in Vienna, London and Paris; he also toured in Mexico and visited many cities in the USA as an opera conductor. He was music director at the International Exhibition in Sydney in 1879. He composed a large amount of light music, which was popular, and more than 70 ballets, most of which were produced at La Scala. He also wrote two operas, *Alba Barozzi* (A. Ghislanzoni; pubd, Milan, 1884) and the *opera seria Corrado console di Milano* (3, L. Gualtieri). *Corrado* was given at La Scala on 10 March 1860 but was unsuccessful.

Giorza was considered a reformer of the ballet because of his attempts to make his music, which is often pantomimic and sometimes melodramatic in character, fit the subject by creating a sense of atmosphere.

ES (C. Sartori)   FRANCESCO BUSSI

Giosa, Nicola de. *See* DE GIOSA, NICOLA.

Giotti, Cosimo (*b* Florence, 15 April 1759; *d* Florence, 10 Feb 1830). Italian director and librettist. He wrote spoken tragedies, including *La strage degli innocenti* (1782), performed at the Borgo Ognissanti theatre in Florence, and *Enrico, e Sofia* (1783), given at the Cocomero. About 1784 he became director of prose comedies for the Compagnia Nazionale Toscana, resident at the Cocomero; he was also a poet there with the duty of 'accommodating' librettos. He wrote at least two melodramas, for which Giuseppe Moneta furnished the music, and two comic intermezzos. He then turned to serious opera, with *Ines de Castro*, set to music first by Giordaniello, then by Andreozzi and subsequently, as a pasticcio, by several composers. An ardent patriot and supporter of the Habsburg-Lorraine rule, he wrote *La felicità in Etruria* (which he adjusted to previously composed, anonymous music) in 1799 to celebrate Ferdinando III's restoration to the grand duchy after the first French occupation in that year. An account book of the Accademia degl'Infuocati refers to Giotti in 1791 as 'blind'; Michaud claimed that he was blind from the age of 18. If so, it is the more remarkable that in the last two decades of the 18th century he was an active stage director. He directed the farce *I tre desideri*, with a text by D. Somigli (who was also blind) and music by F. Rutini, at the Borgo Ognissanti in 1794.

La vendetta di Medea (melodrama), Moneta, 1787; *La bella incognita, o siano I tre amanti delusi* (int), Neri Bondi, 1788; *Il sacrifizio d'Ifigenia* (dramma per musica), Moneta, 1789; *La morte di Sansone* (melodrama), Moneta, 1789; *La moglie capricciosa* (int, after F. Livigni), G. Gazzaniga, 1791; *Ines de Castro* (dramma per musica), G. Giordaniello, 1793 (Andreozzi, 1793); *Teseo riconosciuto* (dramma per musica), Spontini, 1798; *La felicità in Etruria* (dramma serio per musica), 8 July 1799; *Il fanatico per la musica* (dg), S. Romani, 1800

Michaud, ed.: *Biographie universelle, ancienne et moderne* (Paris, 2/1856)
M. De Angelis: *Melodramma spettacolo e musica nella Firenze dei Lorena* (Florence, 1991)
R. L. Weaver and N. Weaver: *A Chronology of Music in the Florentine Theater 1751–1800* (Warren, MI, 1993)
                                    ROBERT LAMAR WEAVER

Giovanardi [Zanardi], **Nicolò** ['Lo Zanardino'] (*b* Bologna, 31 July 1661; *d* Bologna, 15 Dec 1729). Italian soprano castrato and composer, son of Vincenzo and Angela Laurenti. A pupil of Agostino Filippucci, he became a member of the Bologna Accademia Filarmonica in 1685. From 1675 to 1688 he spent much of his time as a soprano at S Petronio; evidence from librettos shows that between 1679 and 1687 he also sang in operas by Perti, Tosi and others in Parma and Bologna. In 1688 he entered the Congregazione dell'Oratorio in Bologna, where he became *praefectus musices*, and *maestro di cappella*. According to Penna, 'because of his noble talent he was worthy to serve the Emperor Leopold I as a virtuoso for many years'; in fact he was only in Vienna from May to July 1686. Penna states also that 'in the most celebrated cities in Europe he distinguished himself, both in church and theatre as equal to any musician that lived in that time'.

O. Penna: *Catalogo degli aggregati della Accademia filarmonica di Bologna* (MS, *I-Baf*, 1736/R1971) [sometimes attrib. G. B. Martini]
C. Vitali: 'Giovanni Paolo Colonna, maestro di cappella dell'oratorio filippino in Bologna', *RIM*, xiv (1979), 128–54
                                    CARLO VITALI

Giovane scuola (It.: 'young school'). A term first applied about 1890 to the generation of Italian opera composers born just after the middle of the 19th century, comprising Alfredo Catalani, Smareglia, Leoncavallo, Puccini, Alberto Franchetti, Mascagni, Giordano and Cilea. Later it came to designate more particularly those whose style took as its starting-point the *verismo* of Mascagni's *Cavalleria rusticana* (1890) and was extended to include Alfano, Montemezzi and Zandonai. The works of the 'giovane scuola' are characterized by an emotional rhetoric that owes something both to Massenet and Wagner. Although he claimed quite justifiably to have forged his idiom earlier than Mascagni, Puccini is recognized as one of their number; not, however, Wolf-Ferrari, despite his one foray into *verismo* with *I gioielli della Madonna* (1911).

See ITALY, §3(iv). JULIAN BUDDEN

Giovanna d'Arco ('Joan of Arc'). *Dramma lirico* in a prologue and three acts by GIUSEPPE VERDI to a libretto by TEMISTOCLE SOLERA in part after FRIEDRICH VON SCHILLER's play *Die Jungfrau von Orleans*; Milan, Teatro alla Scala, 15 February 1845.

Carlo VII [Charles VII] *King of France*		tenor
Giacomo *a shepherd in Dom-Rémy*		baritone
Giovanna [Joan of Arc] *his daughter*		soprano
Delil *an officer of the King*		tenor
Talbot *supreme commander of the English army*		bass

King's officers, villagers, people of Reims, French soldiers, English soldiers, blessed spirits, evil spirits, nobles of the realm, heralds, pages, young girls, marshals, deputies, knights and ladies, magistrates, halberdiers, guards of honour

Setting Dom-Rémy, Reims and near Rouen in 1429

There is virtually no evidence, but it seems that Verdi had arranged to write an opera for the 1844–5 Carnival season at La Scala as early as December 1843, and that soon afterwards he suggested to the impresario Merelli that Temistocle Solera be engaged as the librettist. Solera was duly hired, and – with typical exaggeration – made much of the fact that his libretto on the life of Joan of Arc was 'original', owing nothing either to Shakespeare or to Schiller. Verdi's correspondence makes no mention of any changes to the libretto, and we must assume that, as with Solera's earlier *Nabucco* and *I Lombardi*, the composer was willing to set the text more or less as it stood. The score was written during the autumn and winter of 1844–5. Its first performance at La Scala (preceded by a revival of *I Lombardi*) was a great public success, but the standards of production were far below Verdi's expectations and caused a rift between him and Merelli that resulted in Verdi's avoiding premières at La Scala for many years. The cast included Antonio Poggi (King Charles), Filippo Colini (Giacomo) and Erminia Frezzolini in the title role.

The overture is in three movements. The first is stormy and uncertain; the second is an Andante pastorale featuring solo flute, oboe and clarinet (with more than shades of Rossini's *Guillaume Tell* overture); the last returns to the stormy minor but concludes in a triumphant and bellicose major. It is hardly a masterpiece but is worth its occasional concert-hall revival.

PROLOGUE. i *A great hall in Dom-Rémy* The opening scene is a conventional cavatina for the tenor, though

with unusually important choral interventions (Verdi and Solera no doubt wished to sustain their image with the Milanese after *Nabucco* and *I Lombardi*). Even before the tenor enters, the unison chorus decries the sad fate of France in 'Maledetti cui spinge rea voglia', and choral forces are again prominent in the soloist's lyrical movements, particularly in an unusually long *tempo di mezzo*. King Charles, after admitting defeat, narrates a dream ('Sotto una quercia'): as he was lying beneath an oak tree, the Madonna told him to place before her his helmet and sword. On hearing that such an oak exists nearby, he decides to visit it, though insisting that he can no longer be king.

ii *A forest* Giacomo appears for a brief scene, voicing fears that his daughter Giovanna (Joan of Arc) may be in league with the devil. He retires to be replaced by Joan. In a highly ornamented, Bellinian Andante ('Sempre all'alba ed alla sera'), she prays for weapons in the coming battle. As she falls asleep, a chorus of devils (jauntily recommending sins of the flesh) and of angels (promising her glory as the saviour of her country) jostle for her attention. She awakes to find Charles before her, and immediately declares herself ready for battle. They join in a lively, syncopated cabaletta, during which Giacomo sees them together and concludes that his daughter has in some way bewitched the king.

ACT 1.i *A remote place scattered with rocks* The English soldiers have been routed and feel that supernatural forces are against them. Talbot tries unsuccessfully to allay their fears. Giacomo comes on to announce that the woman inspiring the French forces can be their prisoner that evening. In an Andante sostenuto, 'Franco son io', he tells them of his dishonour at the hands of Charles; the ensuing cabaletta, 'So che per via di triboli', explores a father's tender feelings. The usual progression from lachrymose Andante to energetic cabaletta is thus reversed, which allows for a moderate-paced, unusually touching Donizettian cabaletta, quite lacking in characteristic Verdian rhythmic drive.

1.ii *A garden in the court of Reims* Joan of Arc has fulfilled her mission but is unwilling to leave Charles and the court: the demon voices still torment her. She sings of her simple forest home in 'O fatidica foresta', another delightful example of Verdian pastoral, before Charles arrives to initiate an impressive four-movement duet-finale in which he and Joan admit their love for each other. Particularly notable is the Adagio ('T'arretri e palpiti!'), which includes a remarkable range of emotional attitudes as Joan struggles with her conflicting voices and as Charles swings between unease at her behaviour and attempts to calm her with expressions of love.

ACT 2 *A piazza in Reims* A somewhat routine 'Grand triumphal march' introduces the victorious troops, prominent among whom are Charles and Joan. Giacomo looks on, giving vent to his religious zeal in a minor–major *romanza*, 'Speme al vecchio era una figlia', which never seems to find its true point of climax. Then comes the grand central finale of the opera, in which Giacomo denounces his daughter. The most interesting movement is the Andante, 'No! forme d'angelo': unaccompanied duet fragments from Charles and Giacomo are juxtaposed with an extended cantabile for Joan; and even in the grand cadential close Verdi finds room to give rein to her fragile musical persona. The remainder of the number offers high drama as Joan refuses three times to deny Giacomo's accusations of sacrilege; she is turned on by the crowd in the stretta, 'Fuggi, o donna maledetta'.

ACT 3 *Inside a fort in the English camp* Joan of Arc looks on as the English and French do battle, noting with dismay that Charles has been surrounded. Her ardent prayers alert Giacomo to his mistake in accusing her, and they join in a duet of explanation and reconciliation, the most impressive section of which is the slow lyrical movement, 'Amai, ma un solo istante', in which a moving succession of melodic ideas underpins the father's gradual acceptance of his daughter's purity.

Joan rushes to aid the French, and now it is Giacomo's turn to comment on the battle, which with his daughter's help swings decisively against the English. Charles enters victorious, forgives Giacomo, but learns that Joan has been gravely wounded. In the *romanza* 'Quale più fido amico', delicately scored for solo english horn and cello, he bemoans his loss. Joan is brought in to the strains of a funeral march, and has enough strength to salute her father and king and to look forward to a welcome in heaven. She leads off the final ensemble with an elaborately ornamented solo accompanied by obbligato cello before a long-breathed theme for the onlookers carries all before it.

* * *

Giovanna d'Arco is unlikely ever to be a repertory work, but there is nevertheless much to admire. Although the opera was probably intended as a sequel to the grand choral tableau works Verdi and Solera had previously created together, in the end it is dominated by the role of Joan of Arc – Verdi probably being encouraged in this change by the extraordinary skills of his leading soprano, Erminia Frezzolini. And Joan is by no means the typical early Verdian soprano, being entrusted with the kind of delicate ornamentation the youthful composer so rarely saw fit to linger over. The other principals are perhaps less successfully projected, but they are involved in powerfully original ensembles, numbers which again and again make clear that the young Verdi was constantly experimenting with the formal vehicles through which his drama was projected.

ROGER PARKER

Giovanni Gallurese. *Melodramma storico* in three acts by ITALO MONTEMEZZI to a libretto by Francesco D'Angelantonio; Turin, Teatro Vittorio Emanuele, 28 January 1905.

The action takes place in 16th-century Sardinia. Although the bandit Giovanni Gallurese (tenor) is fighting the Spanish rulers, his name arouses terror among the whole population. Giovanni saves Maria (soprano) from an abduction attempt by the Spaniard Rivegas (baritone) and they fall in love, but the bandit does not dare reveal who he is. After the Spaniards have been defeated in battle, Giovanni has to confess his identity to Maria, who at first repulses him, then returns to him. To show his magnanimity Giovanni lets Rivegas go free, but the Spaniard treacherously kills him when he is unarmed and with Maria.

In the libretto, elements of the historical drama are interwoven with the ideals of the Risorgimento and a *verismo* treatment of the Mediterranean setting, but Montemezzi makes little use of *verismo* musical techniques (though there is a song in Sardinian dialect in Act 2). He favours instead a more lyrical and introspec-

tive approach, continuously sustained by the orchestral flow; especially notable are the love duet in the first act and the peroration on liberty in the third. The characteristics of Montemezzi's style are already clearly marked, and the opera was initially a success, largely due to admiration for the composer's orchestral technique, which made his name known. But the opera itself never became established in the repertory.

LUCA ZOPPELLI

Giovannini, Pietro (*fl* Florence, 1779–86). Italian librettist. He wrote two important librettos, the first as traditional as the last was revolutionary. His *Epponina*, apparently written in collaboration with Sertor, was reworked by Giovannini for Sarti and entitled *Giulio Sabino* to become one of the most successful *opere serie* of the late 18th century, enjoying some 20 revivals. In the early 1790s Tarchi and Nasolini reset it. Another reworking, *Tito nelle Gallie*, was less successful. Giovannini's *La vendetta di Nino* with music by Prati (which has been wrongly attributed to Moretti, writer of a libretto on the same subject) initiated the return of death and indeed murder to the Italian operatic stage. In Sografi's reworking of 1791, *La morte di Semiramide*, the matricide became accidental and thus more acceptable. Leopold II of Austria, who had been ruler of Tuscany, and patron of opera in Florence when the opera was first produced in 1786, selected the original version when reintroducing *opera seria* to Vienna in 1791–2.

Epponina (os, with G. Sertor), G. Giordani, 1779; rev. as *Giulio Sabino*, Sarti, 1781 (? Cherubini, 1786; Tarchi, 1790; Nasolini, 1794); rev. as *Tito nelle Gallie*, Anfossi, 1780 (Minoja, 1786)
La vendetta di Nino (melodramma tragico), Prati, 1786 (Bianchi, 1790); rev. S. A. Sografi as *La morte di Semiramide*, Nasolini, 1790 (Borghi, 1791; Trento, 1794)

*

M. McClymonds: '*La morte di Semiramide ossia la vendetta di Nino* and the Restoration of Death and Tragedy to the Italian Operatic Stage in the 1780s and 90s', *IMSCR*, xiv Bologna 1987, 285–92
——: 'The Venetian Role in the Transformation of Italian Opera Seria during the 1790s', *I vicini di Mozart: Venice 1987*, 221–40
J. A. Rice: *Emperor and Impresario: Leopold II and the Transformation of Viennese Musical Theater, 1790–1792* (diss., U. of California, Berkeley, 1987)
C. Questa: *Semiramide redenta* (Urbino, 1989)

MARITA P. McCLYMONDS

Giovo, Nicola. *See* GIUVO, NICOLA.

Giraldoni, Eugenio (*b* Marseilles, 20 May 1871; *d* Helsinki, 23/24 June 1924). Italian baritone. He was the son of the baritone Leone Giraldoni and the soprano and violinist Carolina Ferni (1839–1926). Eugenio was taught by his mother, and he made his début in 1891 as Escamillo at Barcelona. He became well known throughout Italy and in South America and in 1900 was given the role of Scarpia in the world première of *Tosca* at the Costanzi in Rome. He repeated the part later that year at La Scala and in other houses including Covent Garden (1906), but was generally considered to exaggerate the sadism and underplay the refinement of the part. In his single season at the Metropolitan, in 1904, he was also found somewhat coarse in his performances. He nevertheless continued to be in great demand in Europe and South America. He was a widely admired Boris, a part he first sang at Buenos Aires in 1909. He was also Italy's first Yevgeny Onegin in 1900 and Golaud in the Rome première of *Pelléas et Mélisande*. Other roles outside the standard Italian repertory were Hans Sachs, Telramund, Ochs and Rubinstein's Demon. He was considered the best singer of Gérard in *Andrea Chénier* and in 1906 took part in the première of Franchetti's *La figlia di Iorio*. He retired from the stage in 1921 and thereafter taught in Helsinki. His recordings, magnificent in quality of voice, often show him as a colourful stylist too; strangely, they do not include any excerpts from *Tosca*.

GV (E. Gara and R. Celletti; R. Vegeto)   J. B. STEANE

Giraldoni, Leone (*b* Paris, 1824; *d* Moscow, 19 Sept/1 Oct 1897). Italian baritone. He studied in Florence, making his début in 1847 at Lodi. After singing in Florence and, from 1855, at La Scala, he created the title role of *Simon Boccanegra* at La Fenice in 1857 and Renato in *Un ballo in maschera* at the Teatro Apollo, Rome, in 1859. He also sang other Verdi roles, notably Count di Luna (*Il trovatore*). In 1877 he sang Rossini's Figaro at La Scala and in 1878 at Cagli he took part in the first performance of Mercuri's *Il violino del diavolo*, written for his wife, Carolina Ferni, a virtuoso violinist as well as a singer. He created the title role of Donizetti's posthumously produced *Il duca d'Alba* at the Teatro Apollo, Rome (1882), and after his retirement in 1885 taught singing in Moscow. A sensitive artist, he had a rich, high-lying voice.   ELIZABETH FORBES

Girardeau, Isabella (*fl* 1709–12). Italian soprano. Very little is known of her: Burney thought she was an Italian married to a Frenchman and tentatively identified her with one Isabella Calliari. She was a member of the Queen's Theatre company in London from January 1710 (perhaps October 1709) until spring or summer 1712 and sang in six pasticcios, *Almahide, Hydaspe fedele, Pirro e Demetrio, Etearco, Antioco* and *Ambleto*, and in Handel's *Rinaldo*, in which she was the original Almirena. This is an exceptionally modest part for an *opera seria* heroine, and neither elaborate nor taxing (the compass is *d′* to *a″*); moreover much of the material was not new. Girardeau was evidently no great virtuoso; but she could not have lacked power, for in *Ambleto* she had 'a noisy song for trumpets and hautbois obligati' (Burney). She is said to have been a bitter rival of Elisabetta Pilotti-Schiavonetti, Handel's first Armida.   WINTON DEAN

Girardi, Alexander (*b* Graz, 5 Dec 1850; *d* Vienna, 20 April 1918). Austrian comic singer and actor. For over 40 years the favourite of the Vienna theatre, he created roles in more than 50 musical plays, chiefly at the Theater an der Wien, where he was engaged from 1874 to 1896 and again from 1902 to 1905. He inspired many characters in Johann Strauss operettas, including Blasoni (*Cagliostro in Wien*), Don Sancho (*Das Spitzentuch der Königin*), Marchese Sebastiani (*Der lustige Krieg*), Zsupán (*Der Zigeunerbaron*), Kassim Pasha (*Fürstin Ninetta*) and Müller (*Waldmeister*). For Millöcker he created Andredl (*Das verwunschene Schloss*), Plinchard (*Die Jungfrau von Belleville*), Symon Rymanowicz (*Der Bettelstudent*), Benozzo (*Gasparone*), Piffkow (*Der Feldprediger*) and the title role of *Der arme Jonathan*. Zeller wrote Adam (*Der Vogelhändler*) and Martin (*Der Obersteiger*) for him, while Lehár's *Wiener Frauen*, Eysler's *Bruder Straubinger*, Oscar Straus's *Mein junger Herr*, Kálmán's *Der Zigeunerprimas* and Fall's *Der Nachtschnellzug* all contain original Girardi roles.

Alexander Girardi as Adam in Zeller's 'Der Vogelhändler', a role he created at the Theater an der Wien, 10 January 1891: painting (c1891) by Rudolf Hausleithner

A. M. Girardi: *Das Schicksal setzt den Hobel an* (Brunswick, 1942)
F. Hadamowsky and H. Otte: *Die Wiener Operette* (Vienna, 1947)
R. Holzer: *Die Wiener Vorstadtbühnen* (Vienna, 1951)
A. Bauer: *150 Jahre Theater an der Wien* (Vienna, 1952)
B. Grun: *Kulturgeschichte der Operette* (Munich, 1961)
                                               ELIZABETH FORBES

Giraud, Fiorello (*b* Parma, 22 Oct 1868; *d* Parma, 28 March 1928). Italian tenor. The son of the tenor Lodovico Giraud (1846–82), he studied in Parma and made his début as Lohengrin at Vercelli in 1891. His success was rapid and the following year he created Canio (*Pagliacci*) at the Teatro Dal Verme, Milan. Unlike Fernando Valero, who created Turiddu in *Cavalleria rusticana*, Giraud was not invited to sing the part throughout the world, and when engaged at Monte Carlo in 1897 it was only to sing Cassio to Tamagno's Otello. Otherwise, appearances abroad were limited to Spain, Portugal and South America. In Italy his reputation as a Wagnerian tenor grew steadily and in 1907 he sang Siegfried in the première at La Scala of *Götterdämmerung*, under Toscanini. Later in the same season he was also Italy's first Pelléas. Other premières included Tommasini's *Medea* (1906, Trieste) and Stefano Donaudy's *Sperduti nel buio* (1907, Palermo). His few recordings, which include some Wagner but nothing of *Pagliacci*, show a strong, vibrant voice used with imagination and skill, though with a limited upper range.   J. B. STEANE

Giraud [Girault], François-Joseph (*d* after 1788). French composer. His first works are sonatas for cello, published about 1750. In 1752 he joined the orchestra of the Académie Royale de Musique as a cellist and remained there until 1776; he also played occasionally in the orchestra of the Concert Spirituel. His most important work, the ballet *Deucalion et Pyrrha*, contains all the traditional elements of French serious opera in miniature: the sound of a storm during the overture, a denouement consisting of a fight with a monster, and musical writing free of Italian influence. The climax is Deucalion's monologue (scene iv), which is distinguished by a five-part orchestral texture in the first two stanzas. The *comédie-ballet L'opéra de société*, given at the Académie Royale de Musique, shows first the rehearsal of an opera by amateur singers, then the performance of the opera itself, and finally returns to the real-life characters. Such a mixture of genres, compatible with the flexibility of form of the *opéra-ballet*, shows that the Académie was not an institution that shunned humour entirely.

all first performed in Paris

Les hommes (comédie-ballet, 1, G.-F. P. de Saint-Foix), Français, 27 June 1753, vaudeville (Paris, 1753)

Deucalion et Pyrrha (ballet, 1, Saint-Foix), Opéra, 30 Sept 1755, F-Po, 1 duet *Pc*; (Paris, n.d.); collab. P.-M. Berton

L'opéra de société (comédie-ballet, 1, A. Gautier de Mondorge), Opéra, 1 Oct 1762, *Po*

Acante et Cidippe [parody of Rameau: Acanthe et Céphise] (pastorale-héroïque, 1, M.-J. Boutillier), Nicolet, 1764

*

J.-B. de La Borde: *Essai sur la musique ancienne et moderne*, iii (Paris, 1780), 426

C. Pierre: *Histoire du Concert spirituel 1725–1790* (Paris, 1975)

MICHEL NOIRAY

Giraud, Marthe. *See* CARRÉ, MARGUERITE.

Giraudeau, Jean (*b* Toulon, 1 July 1916). French tenor. He studied at Toulon and made his début in 1942 at Montpellier in *Mignon*. In 1947 he sang in the première of Rabaud's *Martine* at Strasbourg and joined both the Opéra and the Opéra-Comique. At the former he created Nicador in Milhaud's *Bolivar* (1950) and sang Tamino, Nicias (*Thaïs*), Shuysky, David (*Die Meistersinger*), Pedrillo, Alfredo, the Duke, Erik, Don Ottavio and the Chevalier (*Dialogues des Carmélites*). At the Opéra-Comique he sang Nadir, Almaviva, Gérald (*Lakmé*), Ferrando, Gonzalve (*L'heure espagnole*), Charles (Bondeville's *Madame Bovary*), Bacchus (*Ariadne auf Naxos*), Pinkerton, the Husband (*Les mamelles de Tirésias*) and Des Grieux (*Manon*). A superb character actor, he had a sweet-toned, lyrical voice. From 1968 until its closure in 1972 he was director of the Opéra-Comique. ELIZABETH FORBES

Girdlestone, Cuthbert M(orton) (*b* Bovey Tracey, 17 Sept 1895; *d* St Cloud, 10 Dec 1975). English writer on music. He studied at the Sorbonne and the Schola Cantorum in Paris, then entered Trinity College, Cambridge. He was a lecturer at Cambridge from 1922, then professor of French in the Newcastle division of the University of Durham, 1926–60. His writing and teaching consistently extolled classical ideals, as his studies of Mistral and Mozart's piano concertos (1939) witness. The neglect of Rameau's music, even in France, and the scant attention it had received from writers led him to write *Jean-Philippe Rameau: his Life and Work* (London, 1957, 2/1969), a standard work; he also wrote a valuable study of French tragic opera texts, *La tragédie en musique (1673–1750) considérée comme genre littéraire* (Paris, 1972). ARTHUR HUTCHINGS

Girelli (Aquilar [Aguilar, Anguilar]), Antonia Maria (*fl* 1752–73). Italian singer. She apparently began as a dancer in 1752 at the Teatro S Samuele, Venice, but was engaged as a singer at the Teatro S Angelo from 1759. In 1760–61 she sang in Prague, in Giuseppe Scarlatti's *Adriano in Siria*. The high points of her career were her performances in the premières of Gluck's operas *Il trionfo di Clelia* (1763, Bologna), in the title role, particularly impressing Dittersdorf, and *Le feste d'Apollo* (1769, Parma), as well as her contribution (as Silvia) to Mozart's *festa teatrale Ascanio in Alba* (1771, Milan), when Leopold and Wolfgang mentioned her as having had to repeat an aria. But in 1772–3, when she appeared in England (in Vento's pasticcio *Sofonisba* and Sacchini's *Il Cid* and *Tamerlano*), Burney found her intonation 'frequently false', though he commented on her 'spirited and nervous style'. A Barbara Girelli, perhaps her sister, sang in Venice in 1763–4, her last performance there being in Pampani's *Demofoonte*.

GERHARD CROLL

Girello [*Il Girello*]. *Dramma musicale burlesco* in a prologue by ALESSANDRO STRADELLA and three acts by Jacopo Melani (*see* MELANI family, (1)) to a libretto by FILIPPO ACCIAIUOLI; Rome, Palazzo Colonna, 4 February 1668.

The gods in Hades, alarmed at the misgovernance of Thebes, decide to take action (Prologue). In Thebes, Ormondo (bass), a king's counsellor, taking advantage of the absence of King Odoardo (bass) and Queen Erminda (soprano), flirts with Pasquella (tenor) and is caught in the act by Girello (bass), who ejects him bodily. Ormondo unjustly exiles Girello in revenge. The gods provide Girello with a magic cloak that makes him appear to be the king and with a root which will, on contact, make the king look like him. Returning to Thebes, false-king Girello discovers the court in an uproar over a love affair between the king's sister Doralba (soprano) and Mustafà (soprano), a slave, whom the king has imprisoned. Girello determines to help the lovers; during the time between his return and his opportunity to convert the true king into the semblance of himself, there occurs a comedy of order and countermand between the true and the false king, much to the distress of the gaoler, Tartaglia (tenor). When the true king appears to be the false one, the former is in danger of being executed by the latter. The gods then restore reality and teach all a lesson about tyranny. The lovers are united when Mustafà is discovered to be a prince in disguise.

One of the four or five most frequently performed operas in the 17th century, *Girello* is an unrecognized masterpiece of the period. In its variety of styles and dramatic representation it surpasses Melani's more famous opera, *Il potestà di Colognole*, and its satire is subtler. An example is the passacaglia lament 'O felice Mustafà/ O Girello in povertà' (Act 1.ii), a comic parody for two males (one rejoicing and the other lamenting) of the century's most revered serious aria form for an operatic heroine. The plot very probably finds its origins in Maria Mancini Colonna's desire to avenge herself against her uncle, Mazarin, and her former youthful sweetheart, Louis XIV; Mazarin prevented the politically unthinkable morganatic match by marrying Maria to Lorenzo Colonna against her wishes. The text is openly critical of the absolute power of monarchs. The great historian of Italian 17th-century literature, Belloni, regarded it as the first Italian comic libretto free of the classical imitations and traditions characteristic of earlier comic librettos by Giovanni Andrea Moniglia and Giulio Rospigliosi.   ROBERT LAMAR WEAVER

Giribaldi, Tomás (*b* Montevideo, 18 Oct 1847; *d* Montevideo, 11 April 1930). Uruguayan composer. A member of a noted musical family, he studied with the cathedral organist Carmelo Calvo, the double bass player Rodolfo Battesini and the band director José Strigelli. His *Parisina*, produced at the Teatro Solís by a visiting Italian company, aroused such enthusiasm that he was awarded a government grant to study at Milan Conservatory. In 1879 he settled in Paysandú, where he wrote his second opera, *Manfredi di Svevia*, again given at the Solís by an Italian company (including Romilda Pantaleoni, Verdi's first Desdemona). His other operas remain unproduced; all four are preserved in the Museo Histórico Nacional, Montevideo. A plaque honouring him as the first Uruguayan opera composer was installed in the Teatro Solís in 1930, and two years later a street behind the Museo de Bellas Artes was named after him.

Parisina (prol., 3, F. Romani), Montevideo, Solís, 14 Sept 1878
Manfredi de Svevia (4, J. E. Ducati), Montevideo, Solís, 18 July 1882
Inés de Castro, 1884 (4), unperf.
Magda, 1905 (2), unperf.

*

S. Salgado: *Breve historia de la música culta en el Uruguay* (Montevideo, 1971)   ROBERT STEVENSON

Girl of the Golden West, The. Opera by Giacomo Puccini; see FANCIULLA DEL WEST, LA.

Girò [Tessieri], Anna (Maddalena) (*b* Mantua, *c*1710; *d* 1748 or later). Italian contralto. Daughter (according to Goldoni) of a wigmaker of French extraction, she went to Venice to study music about 1722 in the company of her elder half-sister Paolina, who remained her guardian and chaperone throughout her career. She made her début in Treviso in 1723 and the following year made her Venetian début. In 1726 she sang for the first time in a Vivaldi opera. Henceforth, until Vivaldi's death in 1741, she became his almost indispensable prima donna. Tongues wagged then as now, but there is no evidence for the common supposition that she became Vivaldi's mistress. She was in demand as a seconda donna and for her role in Hasse's *Dalisa* (1730, Venice) earned the considerable fee of 60 sequins. Her career ended in 1748, the year she married a count from Piacenza. Goldoni and other contemporary commentators found Girò's voice rather weak but praised her appearance and acting ability.

*

C. Goldoni: *Mémoires de M. Goldoni pour servir à l'histoire de sa vie, et à celle de son théâtre* (Paris, 1787)
J. W. Hill: 'Vivaldi's Griselda', *JAMS*, xxxi (1978), 53–82
G. Vio: 'Per un migliore conoscenza di Anna Girò (da documenti d'archivio)', *Informazioni e studi vivaldiani*, ix (1988), 26–45
                    MICHAEL TALBOT

Giró [Jiró], Manuel (*b* Lérida, 5 Sept 1848; *d* Barcelona, 20 Dec 1916). Spanish composer. He studied singing and the organ at the cathedral school in Lérida, then entered the seminary but decided against an ecclesiastical career. After studying harmony privately, he moved in 1870 to Barcelona and in 1874 to Paris, where he stayed for 11 years. A number of his vocal and orchestral pieces were successfully performed there, and a collection of songs, *Tras los montes*, enhanced his reputation. On his return to Barcelona, his opera *Il rinnegato Alonso García*, with an Italian text, had only a single performance because the theatre closed, but the dances continued to be played in concerts. *Nuestra Señora de París* was successful, but *El sombrero de tres picos*, based on Alarcón's popular novella, was not. The libretto of *L'étudiant de Salamanque*, composed for production in Paris, was based on a one-act play by Cervantes. *Florinda* was inspired by the Moors' conquest of Spain.

Giró's operas, inspired by Spanish folktunes and dance rhythms, appeared at a time when Spanish themes were popular in European musical circles (e.g. Bizet's *Carmen* or the gypsy dances in Act 2 of Verdi's *La traviata*), which contributed to the warm reception his works received in Paris, Barcelona and Madrid.

Il rinnegato Alonso García (4, L. Bonnemère and A. de Lauzières), Barcelona, Liceo, 6 June 1885
El sombrero de tres picos (after P. A. de Alarcón), Madrid, Príncipe Alfonso, 1893
Nuestra Señora de París (3, C. Navarro, after V. Hugo), Barcelona, Novedades, 1897, vs (Barcelona, [*c*1910])
L'étudiant de Salamanque (1, after M. de Cervantes: *La cueva de Salamanca*), unperf.
Florinda (3, after Spanish legend), unperf.

*

LaborD
'Giró, Manuel', *Enciclopedia universal ilustrada europeo-americana* (Barcelona, 1925)   JOHN DOWLING

Giroust, François (*b* Paris, 10 April 1737; *d* Versailles, 28 April 1799). French composer. He studied at the choir school of Notre Dame de Paris and had his first composition performed when he was 14. His works were essentially those of a church musician, at least until the French Revolution, but his dramatic music, most of it now lost, is also of some importance. His operas were mainly small-scale works inspired by freemasonry, composed for his lodge, 'Le Patriotisme', of the court of Versailles. They were performed at charity events organized by the freemasons, either on masonic premises or in the theatre of the Hôtel des Chevau-Légers at Versailles. The librettos were written by the master of the lodge, Félix Nogaret, reader to the Comtesse d'Artois, the king's sister-in-law. According to his widow, however, Giroust left many other works of music drama, 'noble and tragic in character', of which we know only a few titles, with texts by other, mainly unknown authors. All that survives of Giroust's operatic works is an overture thought by some to have been intended for the opera *Télèphe*, a remarkable piece, in form similar to that of the overture to Mozart's *Die Zauberflöte*.

Rosemonde (De la Morlière), 1781
Les inquiétudes, ou Les charmes de l'amitié (parodie, 1, F. Nogaret), before 1787
Le renversement du temple de Dagon (scène lyrique, 1, Nogaret), Versailles, Hôtel des Chevau-Légers, before 1789

Undated: Alceste rendue à la lumière (scène lyrique, 1, Nogaret); Le retour de Phaon (scène lyrique, 1, Nogaret), perf. in a masonic ceremony; Télèphe (3), ?ov. *F-Pc*

*

MGG (J. Prim)
M.-F. Giroust de Beaumont-d'Avantois: *Notice historique sur François Giroust* (Versailles, 1799, 2/1804)
E. Genest: *L'opéra-comique connu et inconnu* (Paris, 1925)
R. J. V. Cotte: *La musique maçonnique et ses musiciens* (Braine-le-Comte, Belgium, 1975, 2/1987)   ROGER J. V. COTTE

Gismondi [Resse; Hempson], **Celeste** (*fl* 1725–34). Italian soprano. Acclaimed for her interpretation of intermezzo soubrette roles in Naples between 1725 and 1732, she succeeded Santa Marchesini as partner to the bass Gioacchino Corrado. During that period she created the female roles in all Hasse's intermezzos and in others by Vinci and Sarro. In 1732 she married an Englishman named Hempson who took her to London, where she sang under various names from November 1732 to 1734 in works by Handel. She created the role of Dorinda in *Orlando* and took part in performances of *Alessandro*, the pasticcio *Catone in Utica*, *Tolomeo* and *Deborah* as well as works by Porpora and Giovanni Bononcini.

She had a voice of brilliant quality particularly suited to syllabic declamation but also capable of virtuoso passages; arias written for her often parody the emotional heights of serious roles. Dorinda's music calls for a compass from *b*♭ to *b*♭″.

R. Strohm: 'Händels pasticci', *AnMc*, no.14 (1974), 209–67

F. Piperno: 'Buffe e buffi', *RIM*, xviii (1982), 240–84

——: 'Note sulla diffusione degli intermezzi di J. A. Hasse', *AnMc*, no.25 (1987), 287–303

——: 'L'intermezzo a Napoli negli anni di Pergolesi: Gioacchino Corrado e Celeste Resse', *Studi pergolesiani*, iii (1990)

FRANCO PIPERNO

Gita in campagna, La ('The Trip to the Country'). Opera in one act by MARIO PERAGALLO to a libretto by Alberto Moravia after his story *Andare verso il popolo*; Milan, Teatro alla Scala, 24 March 1954.

The opera is set in the countryside outside Rome, immediately after World War II, where the destruction is still clearly visible. It concerns a couple out on a trip, Mario (tenor) and Ornella (soprano), whose car breaks down and who meet a peasant couple, Leonia (mezzo-soprano) and Alfredo (baritone/bass), who, having survived wartime conditions only by theft, rob them.

In *La gita in campagna*, which is a 'neo-realist' work, Peragallo turns his back on the realist inspiration of his first operas *Ginevra degli Almieri* and *Lo stendardo di San Giorgio*, adopting a language freely inspired by 12-note approaches. As Fedele d'Amico has observed, Peragallo's thematic inventiveness circumvents the use of any anguish-laden language and, while still reflecting the irony of the plot, turns it brilliantly by gestural changes 'into the comic and the good-natured'. Peragallo's musico-dramatic conception displays an optimistic grafting of the problematic linguistic experiments of modern times on to traditional operatic elements.

RAFFAELE POZZI

Giuditta. *Musikalische Komödie* in five scenes by FRANZ LEHÁR to a libretto by Paul Knepler and FRITZ LÖHNER; Vienna, Staatsoper, 20 January 1934.

In a Mediterranean European port, the beautiful Giuditta (soprano) is tired of life with her husband Manuele (baritone). Octavio (tenor), an army captain, passes by, ardently expressing the joys of life ('Freunde, das Leben ist lebenswert!'). Giuditta scents freedom from her dull life and fulfilment of her yearning for love ('In einem Meer von Liebe'), while Octavio is immediately taken by her beauty ('Schönste der Frau'n'). She decides to set sail with him to North Africa, where in Scene 2 they are living together, oblivious to the arrival of Giuditta's friends, the fruit-seller Pierrino (*buffo* tenor) and the fishergirl Anita (soprano) ('Zwei, die sich lieben, vergessen die Welt').

Giuditta and Octavio are blissfully happy ('Schön wie die blaue Sommernacht'), but he knows his regiment will have to move on. In his army camp in Scene 3 the thought of Giuditta haunts him ('Du bist meine Sonne'), but when he tells her he must leave her she vainly pleads with him to desert. In his absence she has, by Scene 4, become a dancer in a North African night club, where her charms prove irresistible to the wealthy customers ('Meine Lippen, sie küssen so heiss'). Octavio, meanwhile, cannot forget her and has finally deserted. He arrives in search of her but can only watch helplessly as she panders to the attentions of her patrons. Years later, in Scene 5, their paths cross again. Now Giuditta is a successful and wealthy dancer, while Octavio is reduced to working as a club pianist. Giuditta assures him that he is the only one she truly loves, but Octavio is by now a broken man.

The most ambitious of Lehár's mature works, *Giuditta* was composed for large orchestra, with Jarmila Novotna in the title role and Richard Tauber as Octavio. A particular favourite of the composer's, with its *Carmen*-like story (distinctly similar to Lehár's own *Frasquita*), it is in many ways the most satisfactory of his later works, its larger-scale plan and the opera-house resources providing a fitting setting for the more ambitious writing that Lehár then favoured. However, rather than serving to bridge the gap between opera and operetta, the work has generally been deemed to fall between the two and has rarely achieved full-scale revivals.

ANDREW LAMB

Giuglini, Antonio (*b* Fano, 1827; *d* Pesaro, 12 Oct 1865). Italian tenor. He studied at Fermo, where he made his début about 1849. After singing in Mantua, Venice, Florence (1850), Rome (1851) and Lucca (1852), he was engaged at the S Carlo, where he appeared in Braga's *Alina* (1853). He sang at the Cannobiana, Milan, in 1855 and first appeared at La Scala in 1856 in the première of Antonio Buzzi's *Sordello*. He made his London début in 1857 at Her Majesty's Theatre as Fernand (*La favorite*). He sang in the first London performances of *Un ballo in maschera* (1861, Lyceum), *Faust* (1863, Her Majesty's), *Die lustigen Weiber von Windsor* and *Mireille* (1864, Her Majesty's). His repertory also included many other Mozart, Bellini, Donizetti, Meyerbeer and Verdi roles. In 1865 he lost his sanity.

J. H. Mapleson: *The Mapleson Memoirs* (London, 1888); ed. H. Rosenthal (London, 1966)

C. Gatti: *Il Teatro alla Scala nella storia e nell'arte: 1778–1963* (Milan, 1964)

ELIZABETH FORBES

Giuliani, Cecilia (*b c*1760; *d* 1792 or later). Italian soprano. She is sometimes identified with a singer named Bianchi, but there is no strong supporting evidence. She seems to have started singing publicly in oratorios in 1778. Seven years later she made her *opera seria* début in Florence in the title role of Tarchi's *Virginia* at the Teatro della Pergola, and she went on to create the role of Semiramide in Prati's *La vendetta di Nino*. Her success in the role may have been an important factor in her sudden rise to prominence as an *opera seria* singer.

Giuliani spent 1788–9 in London, singing works by Sarti, Cimarosa, Cherubini and Tarchi. Back in Florence for Carnival 1791, she created the role of Phaedra in Nasolini's *Teseo a Stige* and revived Prati's *La vendetta di Nino*. Leopold II, assembling an *opera seria* troupe in Vienna, made Giuliani his prima donna, and she made her Viennese début in winter 1791–2 with the operas by Prati and Nasolini that she had sung so successfully in Florence.

J. A. Rice: *Emperor and Impresario: Leopold II and the Transformation of Viennese Musical Theater, 1790–1792* (diss., U. of California, Berkeley, 1987)   JOHN A. RICE

Giulietta e Romeo (i) ('Giulietta and Romeo'). *Opera seria* in three acts by NICCOLÒ ANTONIO ZINGARELLI to a libretto by GIUSEPPE MARIA FOPPA after Luigi da Porto's novella (1530); Milan, Teatro alla Scala, 30 January 1796.

Also known as *Romeo e Giulietta*, the libretto draws upon G. della Corte, Shakespeare and J. F. Ducis. Of the six characters, Romeo, Giulietta, Matilde (her confidante) and Gilberto (mediator between the rival Cappelli and Montecchi) are soprano parts; Everardo Cappello (Giulietta's father) and Teobaldo (Giulietta's unloved suitor and betrothed) are tenors. The opera, typical of Zingarelli's style during the 1790s, centres on effective dramatic situations realized in solo and choral forms of some complexity, such as the finale to Act 1, in which Romeo unintentionally kills Teobaldo in a skirmish between the two rival factions, and the dialogue between Everardo and the chorus (2.xi) when Giulietta is believed to be dead. Also especially noteworthy are some of the solo outbursts of great pathos, which have become justly celebrated, among them Romeo's prayer (2.vi) and 'Ombra adorata' (3.i). The latter became famous not in Zingarelli's original version (found in some sources) but in that created by Girolamo Crescentini, which was soon widely distributed in manuscript and printed form. Crescentini was the first of many great interpreters of that role, among whom were Giuditta Pasta and Maria Malibran. The part of Giulietta was written for Josephina Grassini, who long kept it in her operatic and recital repertory.

The most famous of Zingarelli's operas, it continued to be performed, often reworked and used in pasticcio, until the end of the 1820s in Italy and elsewhere, notably France.   MARIA CARACI VELA

Giulietta e Romeo (ii) ('Giulietta and Romeo'). *Tragedia* in two acts by NICOLA VACCAI to a libretto by by FELICE ROMANI based on an earlier text by Giuseppe Maria Foppa, set by Zingarelli; Milan, Teatro della Cannobiana, 31 October 1825.

The action corresponds to that of Romani's *I Capuleti e i Montecchi* written for Bellini in 1830, though there are differences in the text and the vocal distribution. Tebaldo is a baritone, Capellio a tenor; Romeo, however, is a 'musico' role, as in both Zingarelli and Bellini. In 1835 Vaccai scored the original *secco* recitative for orchestra and re-set certain numbers using verses from the later libretto (for instance Romeo's cabaletta 'La tremenda ultrice spada').

Meanwhile for a performance of *I Capuleti e i Montecchi* given in Bologna in 1832 Maria Malibran as Romeo had substituted for Bellini's ending the penultimate scene of Vaccai's opera, including the aria 'Ah se tu dormi, svegliati'. Her example was regularly followed throughout the 19th century by contraltos and low mezzos who undertook the part. Hence Vaccai's scene appears as an appendix in contemporary vocal scores of Bellini's opera. The opera (Vaccai's most successful, and

the only one to be performed outside Italy) is cast in the standard Rossinian mould that obtained at the time throughout Italy; the style, however, remains rooted in the Neapolitan tradition of Paisiello in which Vaccai had been trained. His music therefore stands nearer to Bellini's, though its emotional charge is much lower and its voice less individual.   JULIAN BUDDEN

Giulietta e Romeo (iii) ('Giulietta and Romeo'). Tragedy in three acts by RICCARDO ZANDONAI to a libretto by ARTURO ROSSATO after novellas by Luigi da Porto and Matteo Bandello; Rome, Teatro Costanzi, 14 February 1922.

The libretto is not based on Shakespeare's play but directly on two of its sources. The first act, which sets the scene, gives special prominence to Tebaldo (baritone) as well as the two lovers (soprano and tenor). Act 2, in the Capulet house, is at first dominated by the women, but in the final section Tebaldo is killed in a duel by Romeo. The first scene of Act 3 is set in Mantua, where Romeo learns of Giulietta's supposed death, and in the second the tragic ending takes place in the chapel of the Capulet house (in this version the lovers die simultaneously).

The opera, second in popularity only to *Francesca da Rimini* among Zandonai's works, is characterized by the *verismo* of the vocal parts and its wealth of melody. Among the most intense arias are those of Giulietta ('Sono la vostra sposa') and Romeo ('Giulietta! son io!'), but musically the most anguished is that of the Cantatore (tenor), 'Done, piansì', which is somewhat Musorgskian in manner. The best-known music from the opera, often heard on its own, is the third-act intermezzo, which describes with great verve Romeo's ride back to Verona.   RENATO CHIESA

Giulini, Carlo Maria (*b* Barletta, 9 May 1914). Italian conductor. He studied the viola and composition at the Accademia di S Cecilia, Rome, and then conducting with Bernardino Molinari. In 1944 he made his conducting début in Rome where, as music director for Italian Radio, he also conducted his first opera in a broadcast performance of *La traviata* in 1948. The next year he began assisting Victor de Sabata at La Scala, and he made his own theatre début with *La traviata* at Bergamo in 1950. A broadcast of Haydn's then little-known *Il mondo della luna* in 1951 brought him to Toscanini's attention, and he began conducting at La Scala in 1952 with Falla's *La vida breve*. When De Sabata reduced his conducting obligations, Giulini became principal conductor from 1953 to 1956, introducing several works new to the Scala repertory, including G. F. Ghedini's edition of *L'incoronazione di Poppea* and *Bluebeard's Castle*. He was also associated with Maria Callas (in *Alceste* and *La traviata*), and with the directors Luchino Visconti and Franco Zeffirelli.

Giulini gained further successes in opera at the Aix-en-Provence and Holland festivals and at the Florence Maggio Musicale, and his American début in Chicago (1955) brought a long association with the Chicago SO. He first appeared in Britain at the 1955 Edinburgh Festival with the Glyndebourne production of *Falstaff*, and established himself there as an outstanding conductor of Italian opera with the Visconti production of *Don Carlos* for the Royal Opera House centenary in 1958. He returned frequently to Covent Garden during the next decade. After *Le nozze de Figaro* in Rome (1968) his dissatisfaction with conditions governing operatic performance led to his total withdrawal from the genre for 14 years, returning only in 1982 with *Falstaff* at Los Angeles (while music director of the Los Angeles PO, 1978–84), in a joint production he also conducted at Covent Garden and Florence, and which was recorded. Since then his limited operatic work has been mainly confined to the studio; he added a vivid *Il trovatore* in 1990 (with Plowright and Domingo) to his early and much praised recordings of *Don Giovanni*, *Le nozze di Figaro*, *Don Carlos* and, later, *Falstaff*.

Giulini has sometimes been compared to Toscanini in his musical integrity and lyrical dynamism, though he usually favoured a more spacious flexibility of tempo and expression. His intense preparation and fastidious sensibility limited his range of repertory but often infused his performances with deep spirituality, especially in choral works. In addition to earlier awards from the Vienna Gesellschaft der Musikfreunde and the International Mahler and Bruckner Societies, he received in 1988 the first Verdi Medal from the London Amici di Verdi and in 1990 the Medal of Honour from the City of Vienna.   ROBERT PHILIP, NOËL GOODWIN

Giulio Cesare in Egitto (i) ('Julius Caesar in Egypt'). *Dramma per musica* in three acts by ANTONIO SARTORIO to a libretto by GIACOMO FRANCESCO BUSSANI; Venice, Teatro S Salvatore, 17 December 1676.

The plot is taken from Roman history of 48–47 BC (*see* JULIUS CAESAR). Julius Caesar (soprano), landing in Egypt after defeating Pompey at the battle of Pharsalia, becomes involved in the quarrels between Cleopatra (soprano) and her brother Tolomeo [Ptolemy] (alto) over the succession to the throne. Ptolemy sends Caesar the head of Pompey by his general Achilla [Achillas] (bass), while Cleopatra gives herself to Caesar. The couple fall in love. Ptolemy tries to kill Caesar but fails. A second strand in the plot concerns Pompey's widow Cornelia (soprano) and their son Sesto [Sextus] (soprano), who want revenge on Ptolemy. Cornelia's machinations fail, and the rash Sextus is no more successful. He is saved only by the intervention of Curio [Curius] (tenor), Caesar's confidant. They are supported by Cleopatra's nurse Rodisbe (tenor) and the page Nireno [Nirenus] (soprano). Ptolemy is deposed by Caesar, and Cleopatra becomes queen. Cornelia agrees to marry Curius.

The background of the drama is the contrast between Caesar, personifying the virtues of a good ruler, and the power-hungry, cruel and lecherous Ptolemy. There are no complicated amorous intrigues or spectacular special effects. Among the best of the 65 or so arias are Caesar's solemnly meditative first aria, 'Alma del gran Pompeo' (1.xi), the lyrical dialogue between Cleopatra and Caesar, 'V'adoro, pupille' (2.iv), and four arias with trumpets which emphasize the majestic mood of the opera. The one score to have survived complete is of the version performed in Naples in 1680; it contains some music not written by Sartorio. The librettos of Antonio Ottoboni and Nicola Haym are based on Bussani's text.   NORBERT DUBOWY

Giulio Cesare in Egitto (ii) [*Giulio Cesare*] ('Julius Caesar in Egypt'). Opera in three acts by GEORGE FRIDERIC HANDEL to a libretto by NICOLA FRANCESCO HAYM adapted from GIACOMO FRANCESCO BUSSANI's *Giulio Cesare in Egitto* (1677, Venice) and a later version of the same libretto (1685, Milan); London, King's Theatre, 20 February 1724.

Romans	
Giulio Cesare [Julius Caesar]	alto castrato
Curio [Curius] *tribune*	bass
Cornelia *widow of Pompey*	contralto
Sesto [Sextus] *son of Pompey*	soprano
Egyptians	
Cleopatra *Queen of Egypt*	soprano
Tolomeo [Ptolemy] *her brother, King of Egypt*	alto castrato
Achilla [Achillas] *general, Ptolemy's adviser*	bass
Nireno [Nirenus] *confidant of Ptolemy and Cleopatra*	alto castrato
Caesar's soldiers, Egyptians	

Setting Egypt, 48–47 BC

Giulio Cesare was Handel's fifth full-length opera for the Royal Academy of Music and received 13 performances on its first run. The unusually splendid cast consisted of the castratos Senesino, Gaetano Berenstadt and Giuseppe Bigonzi (Caesar, Ptolemy and Nirenus), Francesca Cuzzoni (Cleopatra), Margherita Durastanti (Sextus), Anastasia Robinson (Cornelia), Giuseppe Boschi (Achillas) and John Lagarde or Laguerre (Curius). Handel revived it three times at the King's Theatre: on 2 January 1725, 17 January 1730 and 1 February 1732. There were revisions for all of these performances, notably in 1725 when Sextus was recast as a tenor and received three new arias; there was also a new aria for Ptolemy. Two further arias were added during the 1725 run for the soprano Benedetta Sorosina as Nerina – the role of Nirenus converted into Cleopatra's lady-in-waiting. On 21 March 1730 two new arias were added for the benefit performance of Anna Strada del Pò, who took over the role of Cleopatra that season. The popularity of *Giulio Cesare* was also reflected in numerous productions at Hamburg and Brunswick over the period 1725–37, and a concert version was given in Paris in the summer of 1724.

Oskar Hagen's production at Göttingen in 1922 was the first in the 20th century, though using a heavily transformed version of the score which was also followed in the many subsequent revivals. In various versions – though hardly ever any of Handel's own – *Giulio Cesare* has found a place in the repertory of several modern opera houses; it was given at the New York City Opera in 1966 and by the ENO in 1980. Handel's complete score of 1724, with all voices at their correct pitch, was given its first modern revival at the Barber Institute, Birmingham, on 20 January 1977, a precedent that has rarely been followed. Chrysander's edition provides a reasonably accurate view of the 1724 version, but gives inadequate guidance to the later variants. The role of Cleopatra has attracted such singers as Lisa della Casa, Joan Sutherland, Evelyn Lear, Beverly Sills and Montserrat Caballé.

The action is founded on Julius Caesar's visit to Egypt in 48–47 BC; most of the characters are historical, but the details of plot are largely fictional and the character of Caesar seems to be much younger than his historical counterpart (who was 54 when he met Cleopatra). Egypt is under the joint rule of Cleopatra and her younger brother Ptolemy. (*See also* JULIUS CAESAR.)

ACT 1 Caesar enters Egypt in pursuit of his rival Pompey, whom he has defeated at Pharsalia. Attended by the tribune Curius, he crosses the Nile and is acclaimed by the Egyptians. Pompey's wife Cornelia (whom Curius once loved) and her son Sextus beg for a reconciliation. Caesar agrees to embrace Pompey, but at that moment the Egyptian general Achillas appears with a message of welcome from Ptolemy; he presents Caesar with a gift of friendship which, to the horror of the Romans, is revealed to be Pompey's severed head. Caesar warns Achillas that he will punish Ptolemy for this act. Cornelia attempts to kill herself, but Curius intervenes. His offer to marry Cornelia is rejected. Sextus vows to avenge his father's murder.

At the Egyptian court, Cleopatra learns from her attendant Nirenus that Pompey has been murdered on Ptolemy's orders. She resolves to seduce Caesar in a bid to be sole ruler of Egypt, while dismissing Ptolemy as fit only for sexual conquests. Achillas tells Ptolemy that the plan to appease Caesar with Pompey's head was counter-productive; he offers to kill Caesar and win Ptolemy the crown of Egypt if he can have Cornelia as his reward.

At his camp, Caesar reflects on human mortality as he contemplates Pompey's funeral urn. Cleopatra presents herself in disguise: she claims to be Lydia, a noble lady deprived of her fortune by Ptolemy. Caesar and Curius are captivated. Cleopatra and Nirenus observe a further attempt at suicide by Cornelia, this time prevented by Sextus. 'Lydia' tells Cornelia that she serves Cleopatra and engages her help and Sextus's against Ptolemy. Caesar arrives at Ptolemy's palace and warily accepts an offer to be shown the royal apartments. Cornelia and Sextus appear and rail at Ptolemy: Sextus is imprisoned, Cornelia put to tending the seraglio gardens. Achillas makes advances to Cornelia and is rebuffed, leaving mother and son to mourn their fate.

ACT 2 Caesar is led by Nirenus into a garden of cedars leading to a view of the Palace of Pleasure on Mount Parnassus. An instrumental symphony is heard and the scene opens to reveal Cleopatra (still disguised as Lydia) on the throne of Virtue with the Muses as her companions. She takes up the melody of the symphony in a ravishing aria, accompanied by instruments on stage. Caesar runs towards her, but the scene closes and Nirenus assures him that 'Lydia' will welcome him later. In the seraglio garden Cornelia is doing menial tasks. She rejects Achillas's advances. Ptolemy tells Achillas to perform what he promised, but reveals in an aside that Achillas will not get his expected reward. Ptolemy himself then accosts Cornelia, but also gets rebuffed. She again contemplates suicide and is again forestalled by Sextus, who has been released by Nirenus. Cornelia is to appear before Ptolemy, and Nirenus advises Sextus it will be a good opportunity to take his revenge. Cleopatra, in her apartments, feigns sleep as Caesar arrives. Curius arrives with news of a group of conspirators demanding Caesar's death. Cleopatra reveals her true identity and says she will put down the riot, but after assessing the situation advises Caesar to escape. He determines to face the conspirators and leaves the grief-stricken Cleopatra. In the seraglio Ptolemy indicates that Cornelia is to share his bed. Sextus attempts to kill him, but is prevented by Achillas. The latter tells Ptolemy that Caesar has fled and has apparently been drowned; meanwhile Cleopatra is raising troops against Ptolemy. Achillas demands the hand of Cornelia for his pains, but Ptolemy refuses, leaving Achillas to hint at a change of allegiance. Sextus, remorseful at his failure,

attempts to kill himself, but Cornelia gives him courage for a further assault on Ptolemy.

ACT 3 Achillas, at the port of Alexandria, resolves to support Cleopatra. Ptolemy's forces defeat Cleopatra's and Cleopatra is taken prisoner. Caesar emerges from the sea, washed ashore by the waves. He watches as Sextus and Nirenus come upon Achillas, wounded in the battle. He confesses to the murder of Pompey and passes to Sextus a seal which gives command of a troop of warriors. Caesar intervenes, taking the seal and promising to rescue Cornelia and Cleopatra. In the palace Cleopatra is taking leave of her handmaidens, but her sorrow turns to joy as Caesar arrives and drives out Ptolemy's guards. Elsewhere in the palace Cornelia is defending herself with a dagger against Ptolemy's renewed advances. Sextus appears with drawn sword, challenges Ptolemy and kills him. At the harbour Caesar and Cleopatra appear in triumph, and prepare to reward Nirenus and Curius. Cornelia and Sextus bring the news of Ptolemy's death. Cleopatra offers Caesar Ptolemy's crown and sceptre. Caesar returns them to Cleopatra, and she accepts them as 'a tributary queen to Rome's great emperor'. They declare their love, and all look forward to peace and liberty under Rome's protection.

*   *   *

The score of *Giulio Cesare* was by far Handel's most sumptuous to date, not only in its stylistic variety and melodic richness but more specifically in its use of the orchestra, which included two pairs of horns crooked in different keys and a stage band with harp, theorbo and viola da gamba. It is also one of his most dramatically compelling operas, despite the over-frequent suicide attempts and assaults on Cornelia's virtue. The character of Cleopatra in all her 'infinite variety' is painted with special insight and understanding – a tease in Act 1, turning from seduction to despair in Act 2 and returning to triumph in Act 3. Her two arias of grief, 'Se pietà' and 'Piangerò la sorte mia', are among Handel's finest in that vein, while 'V'adoro, pupille', with its ravishing instrumental sonorities, is surely unsurpassed as an exemplar of seductive song. Caesar's role includes some fine accompanied recitative (notably the moving 'Alma del gran Pompeo') and the remarkable aria with solo horn, 'Va tacito'. Ptolemy's viperish character is well caught in his three arias. Cornelia and Sextus may seem to have more music than their position in the drama merits – a consequence of the need to reflect the distinction of the original singers – but this will not be seen to be a defect if the roles are cast from strength. The use of choral ensembles in the opening scene and off-stage for the conspirators in Act 2 is effective and original for its time.

For a page of the autograph score *see* HANDEL, GEORGE FRIDERIC, fig.1.
ANTHONY HICKS

Giulio Sabino ('Julius Sabinus'). *Dramma per musica* in three acts by GIUSEPPE SARTI to a libretto by PIETRO GIOVANNINI; Venice, Teatro S Benedetto, January 1781.

The opera, based on events recounted by Tacitus, Plutarch and Dio Cassius, takes place in Roman Gaul near the end of the reign of Emperor Vespasian (AD 69–79). The Gallic nobleman Julius Sabinus (soprano castrato; first sung by Gasparo Pacchiarotti), declared emperor by his troops but quickly defeated by Vespasian's forces, has hidden for nine years in a chamber beneath the ruins of his castle near Langres.

Luigi Marchesi and Catarina Cavalieri in Sarti's 'Giulio Sabino', Vienna, 1785: engraving (see also OPERA SERIA, *fig.5)*

His faithful wife Epponina (soprano) has kept him alive and borne him two sons. The emperor's son Tito [Titus] (tenor), in command of a Roman garrison nearby, loves Epponina, as does one of his officers, the unscrupulous Annio [Annius] (soprano castrato). Sabinus is at length discovered; Titus throws him into prison, but in the final scene, moved by the conjugal devotion of his adversaries, he decides that clemency for the couple is the wisest course.

With its three acts, exit arias, paucity of ensembles (one duet, one trio and a final homophonic *coro* for the six soloists) and lack of choruses and ballets, *Giulio Sabino* follows closely in the tradition of Metastasian *dramma per musica*. But the libretto's emphasis on conjugal love, as opposed to the amatory intrigues of unmarried couples that predominate in Metastasio's librettos, reflects the same neo-classical values that shaped Beethoven's *Fidelio*. The long and emotionally taut subterranean scene in Act 2, set completely as accompanied recitative, has a dramatic power and a seriousness reminiscent of Gluck, as does the C minor Marcia lugubre that accompanies Sabinus as he walks to his execution in the final act.

Giulio Sabino was one of the most popular *opere serie* of the last quarter of the 18th century, known not only through performances in Italy, Germany, England, Spain, Poland, Austria and Hungary, but also through its publication in full score (Vienna, c1781), unusual for an Italian opera of that period. Salieri's *Prima la musica e poi le parole* (1786) contains a scene that parodies *Giulio Sabino*. The subject had earlier been treated in an opera, *Epponina*, by G. B. Bevilacqua to a libretto by Francesco Fattiboni. Giovannini's text was later reset several times.   JOHN A. RICE

Giunio Bruto ('Junius Brutus'). *Dramma tragico per musica* in two acts by DOMENICO CIMAROSA to a libretto by Eschilo Acanzio [Giovanni Pindemonte]; Verona, Accademia Filarmonica, autumn 1781.

The conquering Roman forces have ousted Tarquin the Proud, a member of the legendary ruling Etruscan family, from Rome. Junius Brutus (tenor) has estab-

lished himself as the first Roman consul. In their rush to leave, the Etruscans have abandoned Tarquin's daughter Tullia (soprano). She has fallen in love with Junius Brutus's son, Tito [Titus] (soprano castrato), and when her father's ambassador Aronte [Arontes] (soprano castrato) arrives in Rome to fetch her she is heartbroken at having to leave her lover. Her confidante Marzia (soprano) also seems to side with the enemy by falling in love with Arontes. Tullia implores Titus to marry her and join Tarquin's forces in order to conquer Rome as their king. Titus is torn between his love for Tullia and his filial obligations to Junius Brutus and his country. The news that the Etruscans are planning a coup reaches Procolo [Proculus] (alto castrato), the Roman magistrate, who denounces both Arontes and Titus. Titus's punishment is swift, as the grief-stricken Junius Brutus orders him to be executed before the Roman populace, showing that the good of Rome must take precedence over personal sentiments.

The opera, given its première in the erudite setting of the academy in Verona, apparently sparked little interest. It had a few revivals, at Genoa (1782), Pisa (1783) and Eszterháza (1788), where it was a failure, despite alterations by Haydn and elaborate stage designs and sets by Pietro Travaglia. It includes three castrato roles, but none for bass. The arias are largely traditional exit arias, with some demanding bravura numbers for Titus and Arontes.   GORDANA LAZAREVICH

Giuochi d'Agrigento, I ('The Games of Agrigento'). *Dramma per musica* in three acts by GIOVANNI PAISIELLO to a libretto by ALESSANDRO PEPOLI; Venice, Teatro La Fenice, 16 May 1792.

After having incurred the wrath of Jupiter, Eraclide (tenor), King of Agrigento in Sicily, is forced to sacrifice his infant son Alceo. Instead of doing so he entrusts his high priest, Cleone (bass), to take the baby to the foot of Mount Etna. Before abandoning Alceo there, Cleone places a necklace round the infant's neck. Alceo is discovered by the husband of the Nurse to Clearco, the recently deceased infant son of the King of Locri in

Calabria. The Nurse secretly substitutes Alceo for Clearco.

The King of Locri's daughter, Aspasia (soprano), and Alceo/Clearco (soprano castrato) are passionately drawn to each other. This causes consistent inner turmoil for Alceo/Clearco who recognizes that these feelings surpass a normal brother-sister relationship. Eraclide, hoping to gain a son-in-law through the marriage of his daughter, Egesta (soprano), arranges for sports to be held at Agrigento, offering to let the winner marry her. As the winner, Alceo/Clearco is uneasy about marrying Egesta, who is also intuitively upset about the prospect. On the death of her father Aspasia searches for her 'brother', the rightful heir to the throne, but she is shipwrecked on the shores of Agrigento. Alceo/Clearco and Aspasia's torments about their mutual passionate feelings are resolved with the arrival of Prince Filosseno (soprano castrato), who delivers a letter from the Nurse in which she reveals Alceo/Clearco's identity. Cleone recognizes the necklace and, with Jupiter's permission, he reveals the rest of the story amid general jubilation. Aspasia and Alceo are therefore free to marry.

The plot develops along an inner plane, depicting the lovers' moral conflicts, without engaging in much external action. The chorus of priests, soldiers and citizens plays an important role, at times projecting a single feeling in unison recitations. Paisiello attempted to integrate large sections in continuous musical numbers, such as the five scenes honouring the winner of the games and the subsequent tempest scene; here the storm is represented by contrasting dynamics. There are few solo arias; most are integrated with the chorus. Aspasia's C minor aria 'Che vi feci avverse stelle' is one of the few numbers in a minor key. The opera is predominantly slow in tempo, and resembles a choral cantata.

This opera was performed at the inauguration of La Fenice, Venice; Gasparo Pacchierotti, the most famous castrato of the late 18th century, sang the role of Alceo. The original Venetian libretto contains etchings of the theatre's façade and of the three leading singers. Two ballets, *Amore e Psiche* and *Divertimento campestre*, choreographed by Onorato Viganò, were performed at the première. GORDANA LAZAREVICH

Giuramento, Il ('The Oath'). *Melodramma* in three acts by SAVERIO MERCADANTE to a libretto by GAETANO ROSSI after VICTOR HUGO's play *Angelo, tyran de Padoue*; Milan, Teatro alla Scala, 11 March 1837.

The subject is the same as that used by Ponchielli for *La Gioconda*, but Rossi handled his material with less imagination than Boito 39 years later and produced a dramatic structure which works, but which has few felicities of language or situation to relieve its sombre and somewhat monotonous complexity.

The action takes place in Sicily (rather than Venice), a good deal of it before the opera begins. Manfredo (bass), Count of Syracuse, has married Bianca (contralto) at the wish of her parents: she is an unwilling bride, being secretly in love with a stranger whom she has not seen for five years and who knows nothing of her except her (presumably maiden) name. Elaisa (soprano), a rich and beautiful French socialite (Ponchielli's Gioconda), arrives in Syracuse: she is searching for a lost benefactress, the daughter of an Aragonese captain who persuaded her father to spare the life of Elaisa's father whom he had captured in

battle. To this girl Elaisa had given a sacred locket and sworn an oath of eternal gratitude, but she has never seen her again. Many hearts in Syracuse have fallen to Elaisa, among them Manfredo's, but to no avail for she herself has lost her heart to a young foreigner, Viscardo (tenor), who rescued her from bandits on her journey across the Apennines and has continued to Syracuse in her company. Unhappily, Viscardo can no more return her feelings than she Manfredo's, for he too is pining for a lost love – the 'bella adorata incognita' of his opening cavatina (which incidentally gives a characteristic idea of Mercadante's best lyrical manner).

During the opera it transpires that Bianca is not only the lost object of Viscardo's affections but also the benefactress for whom Elaisa has been searching. This revelation is precipitated by Brunoro (tenor), a former secretary of Manfredo who, banished because of his amorous advances to Bianca, now wreaks vengeance by setting up a meeting between Bianca and Viscardo and then betraying the two of them to Elaisa. Elaisa's jealous fury is checked by her recognition of the locket hung round Bianca's neck and her realization of Bianca's true identity; for a moment she is torn, but when Manfredo appears as the outraged husband her better nature asserts itself and she protects the lovers.

The rest of the opera is concerned with the fulfilment of Elaisa's oath: Manfredo, persuaded by Brunoro of Bianca's unfaithfulness, announces the death of his wife and imprisons her in the family tomb with intent to murder her; but Elaisa gains his confidence, persuades him to substitute poison for the dagger, and then herself substitutes a strong narcotic for the fatal potion which Manfredo eventually forces Bianca to drink. In the short last act Viscardo, believing Bianca to be dead, bursts upon Elaisa and threatens her too with death; having already decided that suicide is the only way out of her misery, she makes no attempt to explain matters, preferring to die at Viscardo's hand. But as he plunges the dagger into her breast, Bianca enters from an inner chamber, and the opera ends in a scene of remorse and forgiveness. MICHAEL ROSE

Giusti, Girolamo [?Luigi, ?Alvise] (*b* Venice; *fl* 1729–*c*1735). Italian librettist. The preface to *Belmira in Creta*, set to music by Antonio Galeazzi and produced at the Teatro S Moisè, Venice, in 1729, indicates that this was his first libretto and links him with the Accademia dell'Arcadia in Rome. *Belmira* was arranged as a pasticcio by Porpora for London in 1734. Also attributed to Girolamo Giusti is *L'inganno scoperto*, performed at the Teatro S Angelo in 1735. Quadrio (1744) attributed to him the intermezzo *Ginestra e Lichetto* and the opera *Motezuma* (set by Vivaldi, 1733), but later sources contradict this. Confusion has arisen with another Venetian writer named Giusti (Luigi or Alvise), an aristocrat influenced by Zeno. Luigi produced librettos for Galuppi's *Argenide* and possibly Vivaldi's *Motezuma* at the Teatro S Angelo in 1733; in the late 1730s he left Venice to pursue an administrative career in Milan and Mantua, entering the priesthood in 1743 but continuing his administrative work. His reforms in the latter were so successful that he was called to Vienna, where in 1756 he was appointed Regal Councillor for Italy; he died in 1766. The libretto of Anfossi's *Motezuma* of 1776 names Giusti as the author, but it was in fact by Cigna-Santi.

Girolamo and Luigi Giusti may have been the same person; it is notable that Girolamo appears to have stopped writing at about the time Luigi left Venice. Girolamo may have regarded the occupation of a librettist as beneath his dignity (hence the anonymity of his librettos) and may have abandoned the theatre when other opportunities arose.

*

AllacciD
F. S. Quadrio: *Della storia e della ragione d'ogni poesia*, iii (Milan, 1744), 492, 505
E. A. Cicogna: *Delle inscrizioni Veneziane*, iii (Venice, 1830), 158–60, 484, 515   KURT MARKSTROM

Giusti, Luigi [?Alvise]. Italian librettist, possibly identifiable with GIROLAMO GIUSTI.

Giustinelli, Giuseppi (*fl* 1762–9). Italian soprano castrato. Burney wrote that Giustinelli 'had a good voice, and sufficient merit to supply the place of second man on our stage in the serious operas'. He was in the Italian opera company at the King's Theatre, London, for two years, singing in *Orione* (1763), J. C. Bach's first opera in England. In the 1764–5 season he appeared at Drury Lane in two new English operas, M. Arne and Battishill's *Almena* and William Bates's *Pharnaces*. He then visited Lisbon to sing in opera, but after his return to England seems only to have appeared in concerts.

*

BDA; BurneyH; LS
M. C. de Brito: *Opera in Portugal in the Eighteenth Century* (Cambridge, 1989)   OLIVE BALDWIN, THELMA WILSON

Giustino (i) ('Justin'). *Dramma per musica* in three acts by GIOVANNI LEGRENZI to a libretto by NICOLÒ BEREGAN; Venice, Teatro S Salvatore, 12 February 1683.

Giustino was the second and final opera presented at the S Salvatore during Carnival 1683. Such was its success that, according to the *Mercure galant* (March 1683), tickets for the parterre had to be bought two days in advance; it far surpassed *I due cesari*, Legrenzi's first opera of the season. It had a great deal of spectacle and could thus compete with *Il re infante* (Pallavicino, 1683), which was continuing its run at the Teatro S Giovanni Grisostomo. The 11 stage sets displayed magnificent Byzantine architecture and landscaping; the richness of the costumes corresponded to the sumptuousness of the machines. The spectacle included the giant Atlas, an elephant with 20 people mounted upon it, a sea battle in which a vessel is shattered and a land battle in which Vitellio [Vitalian] is mounted on a chariot drawn by two real horses. The plot involves several historical characters: the Eastern Roman Emperor Anastasio [Anastasius], whom Justin succeeded in 518; Ariadne, Anastasius's widow; Amantius, Anastasius's general; and Vitalian, a Scythian general. Although some of the political and military alignments are historical, the many love entanglements are fanciful. The original production involved ten human characters and one ghostly antecedent, as well as seven deities and allegorical characters who appear on spectacular machines. Even if some characters were doubled, the theatre must have added more personnel to the eight singers required for *I due cesari*. Of the 77 arias, 63 are accompanied by continuo alone. The score calls for one trumpet, four- or five-part strings and continuo.

Giustino proved to be Legrenzi's most widely performed work, with 12 productions in Italy between 1683 and 1699 using his music in whole or in part.

Alessandro Scarlatti provided additional music for the first restaging (Naples, Regio Palazzo, 6 Nov 1684), which celebrated the birthday of King Carlos II with a prologue paying homage to the king. The stage designer Gasparo Torelli was probably responsible for productions in Genoa and Bologna, since he signed the dedications of their librettos. Versions of Beregan's libretto were also set by Domenico Scarlatti (1703, Naples), Albinoni (1711, Bologna) and Vivaldi (1724, Rome). Handel used the latter Roman libretto as the basis for his *Giustino* (1737, London).   HARRIS S. SAUNDERS

Giustino (ii) ('Justin'). Opera in three acts by GEORGE FRIDERIC HANDEL to a libretto anonymously adapted from PIETRO PARIATI's *Giustino* (1711, Bologna) as revised for Vivaldi (1724, Rome), after Nicolò Beregan's *Il Giustino* (1683, Venice); London, Covent Garden Theatre, 16 February 1737.

Handel drafted *Giustino* between 14 August and 7 September 1736. He returned to the score after composing *Arminio*, completing the revision and filling-out between 15 and 20 October. *Giustino* was produced as the second new opera of the 1736–7 season, the last in which Handel had to contend with the productions of the rival 'Opera of the Nobility' at the King's Theatre. The libretto is mainly fictional, though most of the characters are historical. Anastasius reigned as Emperor of the East from AD 491 to 518, gaining the position by marrying the widowed empress Ariadne. Justin, of peasant origins, rose through the ranks of the imperial army and was elected emperor on Anastasius's death. Leocasta, Anastasius's sister in the opera, corresponds to Euphemia, the concubine of Justin and later his wife (she is so named in earlier versions of the libretto). Vitalian (described in the libretto as 'tyrant of Asia Minor') led a revolt against Anastasius between 513 and 515; Amansius (general of the imperial army in the opera) was Anastasius's high chamberlain, involved in intrigues connected with the election of his master's successor and executed on Justin's orders.

The roles of Justin and Anastasio [Anastasius] were originally sung by the castratos Domenico Annibali (alto) and Gioacchino Conti ('Gizziello' or 'Egizziello', soprano), Arianna [Ariadne] by Anna Maria Strada del Pò (soprano), Leocasta and Amanzio [Amantius] by the contralto Francesca Bertolli and the mezzo-soprano Maria Rosa Negri, Vitaliano [Vitalian] by John Beard (tenor), his captain Polidarte [Polidartes] by Henry Reinhold (bass), and the goddess Fortune by the young William Savage (perhaps his last appearance as a treble before his voice broke). Reinhold presumably provided the mysterious voice in Act 3. The scenes for the bear and sea-monster in the opera are often supposed to have been the inspiration for *The Dragon of Wantley*, the amusing operatic burlesque by Henry Carey and John Frederick Lampe produced at Covent Garden on 26 October 1737; but as Carey states in the preface to the wordbook that *The Dragon* 'had lain several Years dormant in the Repository' of Drury Lane Theatre, *Giustino* may have provided only the stimulus for its performance. *Giustino* received a total of nine performances during the season and was not revived, though Handel re-used several numbers the following year in his pasticcio *Alessandro Severo* and two arias in the revival of *Semele* in December 1744. After the production at Brunswick in August 1741, in an arrangement by G. C. Schürmann, there were no further performances until the production by the girls of Our

Lady's Convent, Abingdon (directed by Alan and Frances Kitching) on 15 February 1963 and the full-scale revival by the Kitchings at the Abbey Hall, Abingdon, on 21 April 1967. The opera was given at the Komische Oper, Berlin, in 1985, directed by Harry Kupfer.

The action is set in and near Constantinople. The celebrations attending the crowning of Anastasius as emperor by Ariadne are interrupted by Amantius with news of the advance of the rebel forces of Vitalian, who demands Ariadne's hand. Justin, told by the goddess Fortune to join the war against Vitalian, sets off; he meets Leocasta and rescues her from a bear. She invites him to the palace, where he is asked to rescue Ariadne from Vitalian, who has captured her and threatens to expose her to a sea-monster if she rejects his love. The ship carrying Anastasius and Justin is wrecked, but they clamber ashore and Justin, hearing Ariadne's cries as the monster rises from the sea, saves her. They depart; Vitalian discovers the slain monster and, uncertain of Ariadne's fate, resolves to find her. Justin captures him. The jealous Amantius's intrigues lead Anastasius to banish Ariadne and sentence Justin to death. Leocasta helps Justin, but he is found by Vitalian, who makes to kill him, when a mountain splits open, revealing the tomb of Vitalian's father, and a sepulchral voice tells Vitalian that Justin is his brother. The brothers resolve to punish Amantius and as he appears, crowned with laurels, with Anastasius, Ariadne and Leocasta in chains, they enter, take him prisoner and release the others. Anastasius and Ariadne are reconciled, and Justin and Leocasta united.

*   *   *

Beregan's original libretto (set by Legrenzi) was designed as a theatrical extravaganza, and the much altered version set by Handel retains this quality. Narrative continuity is occasionally lacking, partly as a result of the removal of a character (Andronicus, another brother of Vitalian), but the result is effective on stage, the story being exposed in a series of suddenly revealed episodes. Although the characters are not sharply drawn, the music has an engaging vitality, with major keys predominating in the first two acts (Ariadne's D minor lament at the end of Act 1, 'Mio dolce amato sposo', is an apt and moving exception). The use of a true chorus in several scenes (especially those of the vision of Fortune in Act 1 and the embarkation in Act 2) adds variety, as does the appearance of horns and trumpets at appropriate points in the score. (Handel's most original stroke of instrumentation – the recorder consort to set the pastoral mood for Justin's first aria – seems to have been changed to conventional oboe-and-strings scoring before first performance.) Certain details of Handel's final version of the score (in the scenes of the fight with the bear and the overthrow of Amantius) are misrepresented in Chrysander's edition, and careful consideration needs to be given to Handel's last-minute revisions to the start of Act 3, which leave unclear how Vitalian's escape should be staged (the original directions describing his descent from his tower prison are suppressed in the wordbook). Whatever variants are chosen, *Giustino* is lively entertainment.

ANTHONY HICKS

Giuvo [Giovo, Giovio, Juvo], **Nicola** [Nicolò] (*b* Naples, *c*1680; *d* Naples, after 1748). Italian librettist. Born into a humble family, he took minor orders (before 1704) and dedicated himself to a career in letters, initially under the patronage of Nicola Gaetani d'Aragona, Duke of Laurenzano, and his wife Aurora Sanseverino, a member of the Accademia dell'Arcadia and an amateur contralto. In 1711 Giuvo joined the Neapolitan Arcadia under the name of Eupidio Siriano. After Aurora's death in 1726 he appears to have been associated with the noble houses of Carafa di Colobrano and Spinelli di Tarsia, as well as with the cultural circle around the philosopher G. B. Vico, although he continued to perform important legal functions for Nicola (now Prince). After the Bourbon succession to the Neapolitan throne in 1734, he obtained the post of court poet. He was also a member of the Accademia Aletina (founded 1741).

As a librettist, Giuvo cultivated most genres including oratorio, *dramma per musica* and serenata, and he even made a late attempt in the field of *opera buffa*. However, he specialized in occasional pieces, often staged, for weddings or political-dynastic celebrations, mostly commissioned by the Neapolitan gentry – among which the place of honour is held by the libretto for Handel's cantata *Aci, Galatea e Polifemo*.

Il Radamisto (dramma per musica), N. Fago, 1707 (F. Aresti, 1715, as La costanza in cimento, osia Il Radamisto); *L'Agrippina* (dramma per musica), Porpora, 1708; *La Cassandra indovina* (dramma per musica), Fago, 1711; *La Semele* (favola per musica), F. Mancini, 1711; *Le nozze di Teti e di Peleo* (int), Sarro, 1739; *L'amor pittore* (ob), Perez, 1740

*

CroceN

D. Parrino: *Avvisi di Napoli* (1707–13)
Fatto discusso e concordato degli antichi e nuovi giudizi tra S. Severo e Laurenzana (Naples, 1868)
N. Nicolini, ed.: *D. Confuorto: Giornali di Napoli dal 1689 al 1699* (Naples, 1930)
B. de Dominici: *Vite de' pittori, scultori, ed architetti napoletani* (Naples, 1942)
P. Giannantonio: *L'Arcadia napoletana* (Naples, 1962)
F. Nicolini: *Vico storico* (Naples, 1967)
R. Strohm: *Italienische Opernarien des frühen settecento*, AnMc, no.16 (1976)
C. Vitali and A. Furnari: 'Händels Italienreise: neue Dokumente, Hypotesen und Interpretationen', *Göttinger Händel-Beitrage*, ed. H. J. Marx, iv (Kassel, 1991), 41–66

ANTONELLO FURNARI, CARLO VITALI

Gizzi, Domenico (*b* Arpino, *c*1680; *d* Naples, 14 Oct 1758). Italian soprano castrato. He studied with M. T. Angelio, then at the S Onofrio Conservatory, Naples. He was probably the Domenico Gizzio who was singer in the Treasury of S Gennaro, Naples, 1700–07 and 1717–36. In 1706 he was appointed singer of the Neapolitan royal chapel. His reputation reached its height in the 1720s when he sang in several leading Italian opera houses: at the Teatro delle Dame, Rome (1722–4 and 1726), at Reggio Emilia in the first production of Porpora's *Didone abbandonata* (1725), and at the S Giovanni Grisostomo theatre, Venice, in operas by Porpora and Leo (1728 and 1729). He was also a singing teacher; his pupils included Gioacchino Conti ('Gizziello'). He seems to have spent his last years in comparative obscurity.

MICHAEL F. ROBINSON

Gizziello. Nickname of GIOACCHINO CONTI.

Glachant, Antoine-Charles (*b* Paris, 19 May 1770; *d* Versailles, 9 April 1851). French composer. He joined the Théâtre du Délassement-Comique in Paris in 1790 as orchestral leader and conductor, but had left that theatre by 1791. He then embarked on a military career and settled in Arras, where he lived from 1795 to 1823 and from 1830 to 1846; in the intervening period he led the orchestra at the Théâtre-Français in Paris. Glachant was known chiefly as a composer of chamber and orchestral music and the founder of various musical institutions in Arras; he wrote only one opera for the Arras theatre, which suggests a swift loss of interest in the genre.

Pharamond (drame mêlé de choeurs et de chants, 5, P.-A.-L.-P. Plancher de Valcour), Paris, Délassement-Comique, 1790

L'homme à la minute (oc, 2, Valcour), Paris, Délassement-Comique, 1790

Les deux dragons (oc, 1), Arras

Doubtful: Le mannequin vivant, ou Le mari en bois (oc, 1), Paris, Feydeau, 1796

*

Almanach général de tous les spectacles (Paris, 1791), 216, 219

A. de Cardevacque: 'La musique à Arras depuis les temps les plus reculés jusqu'à nos jours', *Mémoires de l'Académie des sciences, lettres et arts d'Arras*, 2nd ser., xvi (1885), 41–177, esp. 137–40

MICHEL NOIRAY

Gladkovsky, Arseny Pavlovich (*b* St Petersburg, 9/21 May 1894; *d* Leningrad [now St Petersburg], 31 July 1945). Russian composer. While studying mathematics at St Petersburg University, he took theory lessons from Vasily Kalafati, with whom he subsequently studied composition at the Petrograd Conservatory (1919–24). From 1918 he lectured and taught music theory in a variety of secondary educational institutions. He was the co-creator, with Yevgeny Prussak, of the three-act 'musico-dramatic chronicle' *Za krasnïy Petrograd: 1919 god* ('For Red Petrograd: the Year 1919'), the first Soviet opera based on a revolutionary topic, which was staged in the Malïy Opera Theatre in Leningrad on 24 April 1925. A populistic work chronicling events in a newsreel fashion to the accompaniment of exaggerated musical stereotyping and mass songs, the opera was roundly criticized by professional musicians and did not hold the stage. Gladkovsky subsequently reworked the material into an opera-oratorio, *Front i til* ('The Front and the Rear'), which had its première at the Malïy Opera Theatre on 7 November 1930 but met with little success.

LAUREL E. FAY

Glanville-Hicks, Peggy (*b* Melbourne, 29 Dec 1912; *d* Sydney, 25 June 1990). Australian composer. Studies with the prolific opera composer-conductor Fritz Hart at the age of 15 led to her enrolling at the RCM in 1932 and to her winning the Carlotta Rowe Scholarship there that year. Over the next five years she studied composition with Vaughan Williams, the piano with Arthur Benjamin and Constant Lambert and conducting with Malcolm Sargent. In 1936 an Octavia travelling scholarship took her to Vienna to work with Egon Wellesz and to Paris to work with Nadia Boulanger. In 1938 she married Stanley Bate and on occasion wrote as Peggy Bate until their divorce in 1949. From 1942 to 1959 she lived in the USA, acquiring American citizenship in 1948. Most of her output was composed in this period, establishing her as an international figure with considerable influence on American musical life. She was active in New York as a music critic and was involved in the commissioning of new works and encouraging young composers.

After her opera *The Transposed Heads* received its première in Louisville, Kentucky, in 1954, it was performed in New York in February 1958 at the Phoenix Theatre and in Sydney in 1970. A recording of the opera (released in 1992) was made in the presence of the composer in 1984. The music assimilates Hindu folk sources into a contemporary Western idiom. *The Glittering Gate* (1959), her next opera, is a short curtain-raiser using electronics, which had its première in New York and was also heard at the Adelaide Festival in 1972. Glanville-Hicks made a further study of oriental music after settling in 1959 in Athens, where she made a comparative investigation into Aegean demotic music and Far Eastern folklorism. The influence of these is present in *Nausicaa* (1961) and the still-unperformed *Sappho* (composed in 1965), which was commissioned by the Ford Foundation for the San Francisco Opera. All her theatre works attempt to revive ancient Greek dramatic forms, musical modes and metres using modern theatrical means. But this creation of a style so divorced from the mainstream has resulted in her work's receiving less attention than it merits. The initial success of the operas has not lasted, and performances have been rare.

See also NAUSICAA and TRANSPOSED HEADS, THE.

Caedmon, 1933 (3 scenes, P. Glanville-Hicks), ?unperf.

The Transposed Heads (6 scenes, Glanville-Hicks, after T. Mann: *Die vertauschten Köpfe*) Louisville, KY, Columbia Auditorium, 3 April 1954, *US-LOu**; vs (New York, 1953)

The Glittering Gate, 1956 (1, Glanville-Hicks, after Lord Dunsany), New York, 15 May 1959 (New York, 1957)

Nausicaa (prol., 3, R. Graves and A. Reid, after Graves: *Homer's Daughter*), Athens, Herodus Atticus, 19 Aug 1961, *AUS-Msl*; (New York, n.d.)

Carlos among the Candles, 1962, unperf.

Sappho, 1965 (3, L. Durrell, after his play), unperf.

*

G. Antheil: 'Peggy Glanville-Hicks', *American Composers Alliance Bulletin*, iv/1 (1954), 2–9

P. Glanville-Hicks: 'At the Source', *ON*, xxvi/6 (1961–2), 8–13 [on *Nausicaa*]

Q. Eaton: *Opera Production: a Handbook* (Minneapolis, 1961–74)

C. Northouse: *Twentieth-Century Opera in England and the U.S.* (Boston, 1976)

D. Hayes: *Peggy Glanville-Hicks: a Bio-Bibliography* (Westport, CT, 1990)

THÉRÈSE RADIC

Gläser [Glaeser], Franz (Joseph) (*b* Obergeorgenthal [now Horní Jiřetín], 19 April 1798; *d* Copenhagen, 29 Aug 1861). Bohemian composer. He studied at the Prague conservatory (from 1813 or 1814) and in 1817 went to Vienna, where for the next 13 years he provided the three popular theatres with a series of mainly unsuccessful scores for farces, parodies and pantomimes: in 1817–18 he wrote ten works for the Theater in der Leopoldstadt, from 1819 until 1827 he provided the Theater in der Josefstadt with some 60 works (including an arrangement of Weber's *Oberon*, 20 March 1827), and from 1827 until 1830 the Theater an der Wien with a further 20. On 3 October 1822 it was Gläser's responsibility as Kapellmeister at the Josefstadt theatre to supervise the performance of Beethoven's music to Meisl's *Die Weihe des Hauses*.

In 1830 Gläser went to Berlin, where his best-known works were written and performed: *Aurora*, *Die Brautschau auf Kronstein* (revised version, 1831), *Andrea* and *Des Adlers Horst* (libretto by Holtei). The last, after its première at the Königstädtisches Theater (29 December 1832), was performed widely and often for half a century; the richness, variety and expressive power of this score show how quickly Gläser matured once he had left behind him the less exacting demands of Vienna's suburban theatres; Wagner conducted *Des Adlers Horst* at Magdeburg and it is one of several now forgotten opera scores that left some mark on his later masterpieces. In 1842 Gläser moved to Copenhagen, was appointed court conductor three years later, and remained there for the rest of his life. Apart from occasional pieces he wrote only three major scores during the Copenhagen years: the operas *Bryllupet ved Como-Søen* ('The Wedding by Lake Como', 1849), *Nøkken* ('The Water-Sprite', 1853) and *Den forgyldate svane* ('The Golden Swan', 1854). Large collections of his works are held by the Kongelige Bibliothek, Copenhagen, the Deutsche Staatsbibliothek, Berlin, and the Gesellschaft der Musikfreunde, Vienna.

selective list; first performed in Vienna unless otherwise stated

Die echte Prima Donna in Hirschau (Posse, 3, F. Wimmer and F. Rosenau), Josefstadt, 6 March 1819

Sküs, Mond und Pagat, oder Tarockerl, der abgewirtschaftete Karten-Fabrikant (Posse, 2, Rosenau), Josefstadt, 29 Jan 1820

Der Tambour, oder Die flamändische Hochzeit (Spl, 1, Rosenau), Josefstadt, 23 March 1820

1722, 1822, 1922 (Zeitgemälde, 3, K. Meisl), Josefstadt, 26 Oct 1822

Timur, der Tartar-Chan, oder Die Cavallerie zu Fuss (Karrikatur-Gemälde, 3, J. A. Gleich), Josefstadt, 30 Nov 1822

Der rasende Roland (Melodram, F. X. Told), Josefstadt, 5 April 1823

Das Gespenst in Krähwinkel (Posse, 2, Meisl), Josefstadt, 11 Dec 1823

Der Brief an sich selbst (komische Oper, 1, Meisl), Josefstadt, 18 Feb 1824

Sauertöpfchen, oder Der Ritter mit der goldenen Gans (romantische Oper, 2, Meisl), Josefstadt, 27 March 1824

Heliodor, Beherrscher der Elemente, oder Das Bild des Glückes (Feenoper, after C. Gozzi), Josefstadt, 11 Feb 1825

Menagerie und optische Zimmerreise in Krähwinkel (Posse, 2, Gleich), Josefstadt, 22 Feb 1825

Sieben Mädchen in Uniform (Vaudeville-Posse, 1, L. Angely), Kärntnertor, 1 July 1825

Die sonderbare Laune, oder Sie sind dennoch verheiratet (komische Oper, 1, G. E. Hofmann), Kärntnertor, 25 July 1825

Claudine von Villa Bella (3, E. Straube, after J. W. von Goethe), Pest, 13 Feb 1826

Monsieur Asurs sauberer Fluch (Parodie, 2, H. Adami and H. Börnstein [Raimund: *Moisasurs Zauberfluch*]), Josefstadt, 27 Oct 1827

Die Brautschau auf Kronstein [Elsbeth] (romantisch-komische Oper, 2, Meisl, after F. von Holbein), An der Wien, 7 May 1828; lib. rev. L. Bartsch, Berlin, Königstädtisches, 8 Jan 1831

Der falsche Virtuos, oder Das Conzert auf der G-Saite (Posse, 2, Meisl), An der Wien, 22 May 1828

Staberl als Physiker (Schwank, 1, K. Carl), An der Wien, 12 Nov 1828

Des Adlers Horst (3, K. von Holtei), Berlin, Königstädtisches, 29 Dec 1832

Aurora (3, Holbein), Berlin, Königstädtisches, 29 March 1836

Der Rattenfänger von Hameln (3, C. Berger), Berlin, Königstädtisches, 15 Oct 1837

Andrea (komische Oper, 3, Berger), Berlin, Königstädtisches, ?1838

Das Auge des Teufels (komische Oper, 2, A. Heinrich, after E. Scribe), Berlin, Königstädtisches, 20 Feb 1840

Bryllupet ved Como-Søen [The Wedding by Lake Como] (3, H. C. Andersen, after A. Manzoni: *I promessi sposi*), Copenhagen, Kongelige, 29 Jan 1849

Nøkken [The Water-Sprite] (1, Andersen), Copenhagen, 12 Feb 1853

Den forgyldate svane [The Golden Swan], Copenhagen, 17 March 1854

*

ADB (A. Fürstenau); *DBL* (T. Krogh); *MGG* (F. Lorenz)

W. Neumann: *Franz Gläser* (Leipzig, 1859)

C. von Wurzbach: 'Gläser, Franz', *Biographisches Lexikon des Kaiserthums Oesterreich*, xiv (Vienna, 1865)

N. Pfeil: *Franz Gläser* (Leipzig, 1870)

F. Hadamowsky: *Das Theater in der Wiener Leopoldstadt* (Vienna, 1934)

A. Bauer: *150 Jahre Theater an der Wien* (Vienna, 1952)

——: *Das Theater in der Josefstadt zu Wien* (Vienna, 1957)

L. Santifaller: 'Gläser, Franz', *Österreichisches Biographisches Lexikon 1815–1950*, i (Graz, 1957)   PETER BRANSCOMBE

Glasgow. The largest city in Scotland, it came to rival Edinburgh as Scotland's artistic capital in about 1880. One of the first operatic stars to appear in the city was Angelica Catalani, in 1808 at the Theatre Royal, Queen Street, which opened in 1805 and burnt down in 1829. The Caledonian Theatre in Dunlop Street, opened in 1823, mounted occasional opera; in 1848 Jenny Lind sang there in *La sonnambula* and *La fille du régiment*. Sims Reeves appeared in *The Bohemian Girl* at the short-lived City Theatre, which opened in 1845 and was destroyed by fire later the same year after a performance of *Der Freischütz*. In 1867 the Royal Colosseum, with 4000 seats, was built in Cowcaddens Street. It was renamed the Theatre Royal in 1869. It burnt down ten years later, but was rebuilt on a slightly smaller scale (3000 seats), only to be struck again by fire in 1895; it reopened later that year. Meanwhile, the Athenaeum School of Music (theatre cap. 816) gave student performances of Gounod's *Mireille* in 1894, followed by Boieldieu's *La dame blanche* in 1895. At least three other theatres were used for opera performances in Glasgow around this period: the Lyceum Theatre, opened in about 1897 (2300 seats, 700 standing places) and burnt down in 1937; the King's Theatre, Bath Street, from 1904 (2216 seats, 185 standing); and the Coliseum, Eglinton Street, from 1905 (2893 seats, 318 standing). The last was used for performances of Wagner's *Ring* in the 1920s, before being converted into a cinema.

From the 1870s Glasgow was an important stop for professional touring companies. Italian groups appeared in 1872 (with Tietjens and Foli) and 1875 (with Albani and Maurel), and in 1877 the Carl Rosa Opera Company made the first of its many visits. The Moody-Manners Company was active in the city from 1900 – its collection of scores is now held by the Mitchell Library – and a few years later the Beecham and British National companies brought works ranging from *Carmen* to *Hugh the Drover* and *The Golden Cockerel*. A decisive step for local operatic activity was the founding in 1905 of the Glasgow Grand Opera Society, meant originally to assist touring companies. In 1934 it gave the British première of *Idomeneo*, and the following year that of *Les Troyens* (in English).

The peak of operatic growth in the city came in 1962, when Alexander Gibson, Richard Telfer and Ainslie Millar helped establish Scottish Opera. They were later joined by Sidney Newman and Robin Orr. The first productions, *Madama Butterfly* and *Pelléas et Mélisande*, were mounted by Denis Arundell at the King's Theatre; then came *Otello* (1963), *Don Giovanni* (1965), *Boris Godunov* (1965) and *Falstaff* (1966). Sharing much of the praise in the early years were the tenor Charles Craig and the bass David Ward. *Die Walküre* was presented in 1966, followed by *Das Rheingold* a year later and *Götterdämmerung* in 1971. In 1974 Scottish Opera obtained a permanent home when it purchased the Theatre Royal. As part of its gala opening in the converted theatre, the company gave *Die Fledermaus* in 1975. Operas by Scottish composers have featured prominently in the repertory, notably Iain Hamilton's *The Catiline Conspiracy* (1974), Robin Orr's *Hermiston* (1975), Thomas Wilson's *Confessions of a Justified Sinner* (1976) and *Mary, Queen of Scots* (1977) by Thea Musgrave. Scottish Opera's activities are continuous throughout the year; the company travels regularly to the north of England as well as around Scotland and abroad. It remains a seedbed for young talent, and through its diversified productions has achieved international recognition.

An opera department was added to the Royal Scottish Academy of Music and Drama (formerly the Athenaeum School) in 1968, and has become one of the academy's outstanding musical features. The Academy moved to new premises in 1987, which include the new Athenaeum Theatre (cap. 344). Among its recent productions is Robin Orr's *On the Razzle* (1988), after the play by Tom Stoppard. The biennial Glasgow International Early Music Festival was established in 1990 and gave the first modern production of Marazzoli's *La vita humana* (1656) that year.

R. Turnbull: 'Old Musical Glasgow', *Old Glasgow Club Transactions*, iii: *1913–18* (Glasgow, 1919), 206–15

G. Wark: 'The Years of Opera', *New Saltire*, v/Aug (1962), 19–24

C. Wilson: *Scottish Opera: the First Ten Years* (London, 1972)

M. H. Hay: *Glasgow Theatre and Music Halls: a Guide* (Glasgow, 1980)

C. Oliver: *It is a Curious Story: the Tale of Scottish Opera, 1962 to 1987* (Edinburgh, 1987)   MICHAEL T. R. B. TURNBULL

Glass, Philip (*b* Baltimore, MD, 31 Jan 1937). American composer.

1. LIFE. He grew up in Baltimore where his father ran a record store; his mother was a teacher and librarian. Glass began violin lessons at the age of six and then studied the flute with Briton Johnson at the Peabody Conservatory (1945–52); he also played the flute in the school band and orchestra. At 14, Glass passed an early-entrance examination into the University of Chicago, where he studied the piano with Marcus Raskin and spent many hours analysing scores. During the summer vacations he studied harmony with Louis Cheslock in Baltimore. Glass took the BA in 1956 and the following year entered the Juilliard School of Music (MS 1962), where his classmates included Peter Schickele and Steve Reich; his principal teachers were William Bergsma and Vincent Persichetti. In summer 1960 he worked at the Aspen Music School with Darius Milhaud and Charles Jones; from 1962 to 1964, he was composer-in-residence for the Pittsburgh public schools.

At this point, Glass had already begun to establish his germinal style which, he later acknowledged, owed much to Milhaud. Several early works were published but the composer has disavowed those written before 1965. He became increasingly dissatisfied with his music and, indeed, with the musical milieu of the time. Acknowledging his colleagues' dedication to serialism, he nevertheless considered serial compositions to be music of the past masquerading as music of the present. In 1964 Glass moved to Europe, where he eventually settled in Paris to study harmony and counterpoint with Boulanger. From Boulanger he acquired a technical mastery of basic compositional skills that he felt he previously lacked. During his second year with Boulanger, Glass was engaged to transcribe a film score by the sitar player Ravi Shankar into Western notation for Parisian studio musicians. As Glass said in *Music by Philip Glass* (1987):

What came to me as a revelation was the use of rhythm in developing an overall structure in music. I would explain the difference between the use of Western and Indian music in the following way: In Western music we divide time – as if you were to take a length of time and slice it the way you slice a loaf of bread. In Indian music (and all the non-Western music with which I'm familiar), you take small units, or 'beats', and string them together to make up larger time values.

Following this new fascination, Glass spent the last part of 1966 and the first months of 1967 in India. On his return to the USA, he worked again with Shankar, who was then a visiting professor at the City College of New York, and with the tablā player Alla Rakha. He also grew close to several other young composers, particularly Reich, Terry Riley and Jon Gibson, who were pursuing similar interests in lower Manhattan; the association with Gibson continued for more than a quarter of a century. In 1968, Glass presented the first concert of his music at the Film-Makers Cinemathique in New York. The same year, he put together the first Philip Glass Ensemble, an aggregate consisting of amplified keyboards, voices, saxophones and flutes (also, on occasion, trumpets and violin) that remained his principal means of musical expression for more than a decade and a key element of his creative life into the 1990s.

During the late 1960s and early 70s Glass composed a number of concert pieces while supporting himself working as a plumber and taxi-driver. His Ensemble gradually built a cult following in the lofts and galleries of Manhattan's nascent Soho district, and he began work as a theatre composer, providing scores for the Mabou Mines company (of which his first wife, JoAnne Akalaitis, was a founder member). With the business acumen he has demonstrated throughout his career, Glass privately produced his first recordings, which disseminated his work to audiences and venturesome radio stations.

Einstein on the Beach, Glass's first opera, created with Robert Wilson, brought the composer fame – and notoriety. It was presented throughout Europe in the summer of 1976, then taken to the Metropolitan Opera House for two sold-out performances in November of that year. Audience response was mixed, but by the early 1980s Glass was a genuinely popular composer in the USA and Europe. Throughout the decade, his Ensemble played as many as 90 concerts every year, in venues ranging from Carnegie Hall to midwestern rock clubs. Glass became an increasingly prolific composer. In addition to five major operas he wrote music for several films, most notably the impressive and widely imitated *Koyaanisqatsi* (1983), and produced scores for several music-theatre works. He created an album of popular songs with Laurie Anderson, David Byrne, Paul Simon and Suzanne Vega, and has written concert works for solo instruments and ensembles, as well as for chorus and orchestra. In 1990, he collaborated with his early mentor Shankar on an album of East-West crossover music.

Even some of Glass's most sympathetic critics have occasionally suggested that he may be producing too much music and that it is not all of the same quality. Glass has, obliquely, acknowledged this. 'My process as a composer is to write a lot of music', he said in 1991, 'I write *through* musical problems and it can sometimes take me several major pieces to fully develop a new idea. This is the only method I have to allow for an organic growth in my musical thinking. And, if you take the long view, the music continues to evolve'.

2. WORKS. Glass's music from the late 1960s is simple in form, melodic content and harmonic language. Names such as *Music in Fifths* and *Music in Similar Motion* (conceived as a sort of teasing homage to Boulanger) are not only titles but apt summations of what happens in the compositions. *Music with Changing Parts* (1970)

and *Music in 12 Parts* (1971–4) were much more ambitious in their scope and provided the first indication that the composer was, seemingly paradoxically, interested in 'epic' music.

Though he loathes the term, Glass is often classified as a 'minimalist' composer. Much of his mature work is based on the extended repetition of brief, melodic fragments interwoven to form an aural tapestry. Particularly in his early works, Glass limited compositional material to a few elements, which were then subjected to a variety of transformational processes. The listener quickly learns not to expect Western musical 'events' such as sforzandos or sudden diminuendos but is, instead, immersed in a sort of sonic weather that twists, turns, surrounds and develops.

Glass has described his first three full-scale operas as a 'portrait trilogy', each concerning a figure who changed the course of history, yet each opera has its own distinctive sound world:

Einstein on the Beach, an opera about a great mathematician who loved music, is for amplified ensemble and small chorus singing a text comprised of numbers (actually the beats of the music) and solfege syllables. *Satyagraha*, a work about one man leading his people to freedom, is a large choral opera with text taken directly from Gandhi's philosophical guidebook in the actual language in which he read it. In *Akhnaten*, my emphasis is orchestral, with choral and solo voices sharing common ground with the orchestra … Should the three operas be performed within a fairly narrow time span (within the same week, for example) I believe their internal connection will become increasingly obvious and provide the audience with a coherent musical and theatrical experience.

A large part of their coherence derives from Glass's attempts to break down the conventional barriers of language between audience and performer by deliberately using only language that cannot be understood: numbers in *Einstein*, Sanskrit in *Satyagraha*, and various extinct languages in *Akhnaten*. Together they may also be said to cover the three major issues of science, politics and religion. Their reception has been mixed: some listeners have been bored, hearing only mindless repetition, while others are transfixed – John Rockwell, for example, declared himself 'profoundly – religiously – moved' by *Einstein*.

Glass's next full-scale opera, *The Making of the Representative for Planet 8* (begun in 1985), is harmonically more dense than its forerunners and has proved less popular with critics. It was preceded by two music-theatre works: *The Photographer* (1982), based on the life of the photographer Eadweard Muybridge, contains no individual sung roles but uses a solo soprano voice and women's chorus instrumentally; *The Civil Wars* (1983) is part of a multi-media epic created by Robert Wilson for the 1984 Olympic Games. Though the complete work is yet to be produced Glass's two-hour 'Rome Section', a non-narrative exploration of time, has been performed as a self-contained unit. Of Glass's two chamber operas *The Juniper Tree* (1985), for small orchestra, chorus and soloists, is a tuneful setting of a tale by the Grimm brothers, created in collaboration with the composer ROBERT MORAN and the author Arthur Yorinks; *The Fall of the House of Usher* (1988), also to a libretto by Yorinks, is a setting of Edgar Allan Poe's famous horror story. Glass's melodrama for actor and small ensemble *1000 Airplanes on the Roof* (1988) derives its title from a description of the sound of an approaching UFO. The staged song cycle *Hydrogen Jukebox* (given at the Spoleto Festival, 1990), for six voices and chamber orchestra, marks a return to non-narrative opera, forming a 'collage' portrait of late 20th-century America.

Glass's work has had a profound effect on the popular music of his age, while his operas continue to attract a mass following in the USA and Europe. Even his detractors – and Glass has inspired considerable controversy over the course of his career – usually credit him with bringing a new and enthusiastic audience to contemporary opera.

See also AKHNATEN; EINSTEIN ON THE BEACH; JUNIPER TREE, THE; MAKING OF THE REPRESENTATIVE FOR PLANET 8, THE; SATYAGRAHA; and VOYAGE, THE.

Einstein on the Beach (4, C. Knowles, S. M. Johnson and L. Childs), Avignon, 25 July 1976, collab. R. Wilson
Madrigal Opera, Amsterdam, Carré, 25 June 1980
Satyagraha (3, P. Glass and C. DeJong, after the *Bhagavad Gita*), Rotterdam, Netherlands Opera, 5 Sept 1980
The Photographer (music-theatre work, 3, Glass and R. Malasch), Amsterdam, Netherlands Opera, 30 May 1982
Akhnaten (3, Glass, S. Goldman, R. Israel and R. Riddell), Stuttgart, Staatsoper, 24 March 1984
The Civil Wars [Rome Section] (music-theatre work, 5, M. di Niscemi and R. Wilson), Rome, Opera, 26 March 1984, collab. R. Wilson
The Juniper Tree (chamber op, prol., 2, A. Yorinks, after J. L. Grimm and W. C. Grimm), Cambridge, MA, American Repertory, 6 Dec 1985, collab. R. Moran
The Fall of the House of Usher (chamber op, 1, Yorinks, after E. A. Poe), Cambridge, MA, American Repertory, 18 May 1988
The Making of the Representative for Planet 8 (3, D. Lessing), Houston, Grand Opera, 8 July 1988
1000 Airplanes on the Roof (science-fiction music drama, 1, Glass, D. H. Hwang and J. Serlin), Vienna, International Airport, Hangar no. 3, 15 July 1988
Hydrogen Jukebox (music-theater work, 2, A. Ginsberg), concert perf, Philadelphia, 22 April 1990; stage, Charleston, SC, 26 May 1990
The Voyage (3, Hwang), New York, Met, 12 Oct 1992

*

R. Palmer and P. Glass: notes, *Einstein on the Beach* (Tomato 4-2901, 1979)
C. DeJong and P. Glass: *Satyagraha, M. K. Ghandhi in South Africa, 1893–1914: the Historical Material and Libretto Comprising the Opera's Book* (New York, 1980)
P. Glass: *Music by Philip Glass* (New York, 1987)
L. Lassetter: 'The Position of Satyagraha in the Operatic Trilogy of Philip Glass', *Opera Journal*, xx/1 (1987), 2–14
T. Page: 'Glass (a Look at Current Activities)', *ON*, lii/June (1987–8), 8–10
M. Blumauer: 'Tausend Flugzeuge unter einem Hirndeckel: Philip-Glass-Uraufführung beim Donaufestival, am Flughafen Wien-Schwechat', *OW*, xxix/Sept (1988), 37–8 [on *1000 Airplanes on the Roof*]
M. Feingold: 'Theater: through Glass, Darkly', *Village Voice* (7 June 1988), 87–8 [on *The Fall of the House of Usher*]
H. Koegler: 'Nach der Abschaffung der Menschen: Einstein on the Beach in Ludwigsburg zum Abschluss der Stuttgarter Philip-Glass-Trilogie', *OW*, xxix/Dec (1988), 46
J. Rockwell: 'Glass at the Crossroads', *Opera*, xxxix (1988), 1275–80
R. Stoeckl: 'Minimalistenmänder unter dem Machandelbaum: Uraufführung einer Märchenoper von Philip Glass und Robert Moran in Würzburg', *OW*, xxix/July (1988), 45–6 [on *The Juniper Tree*]
E. Strickland: 'Usher and Einstein, Pharoahs [sic] and UFOs: an Interview with Philip Glass', *Fanfare*, xi/6 (1988), 65–77
M. Swed: 'Philip Glass's Operas', *MT*, cxxix (1988), 577–9 [on *The Making of the Representative for Planet 8*]
J. Wierzbicki: 'Glass steps closer to convention', *HiFi*, xxxviii (1988), 61–2 [on *Akhnaten*]
R. H. Kornick: *Recent American Opera: a Production Guide* (New York, 1991), 111–27   TIM PAGE

Glaz, Hertha (*b* Vienna, 16 Sept 1908). Austrian contralto. She sang in Breslau from 1931 (making her début as Erda) but with the rise of the Nazis was obliged to leave Germany. She made concert tours of Austria and Scandinavia and appeared at the German Theatre, Prague. After touring the USA with the Salzburg Opera Guild in 1936 she settled in America, singing with the Chicago Opera and in concerts conducted by Otto Klemperer in Los Angeles. At the Metropolitan (1942–56) she sang such character roles as Annina (*Der Rosenkavalier*) and Mary (*Der fliegende Holländer*). She taught in New York from 1956.   DAVID CUMMINGS

Gleason, Frederick G(rant) (*b* Middletown, CT, 17 or 18 Dec 1848; *d* Chicago, 6 Dec 1903). American composer. He studied with Dudley Buck and later (1869–70) at the Leipzig Conservatory and in Berlin and London. He held church posts in New England, but moved in about 1876 to Chicago, where he joined the Hershey School of Musical Art. Like so many of his compatriots, he had to perform many roles: teacher and academic administrator (director of the Chicago Conservatory, 1900–03), editor of periodicals (*Music Bulletin* from 1871, *Music Review* from 1891) and newspaper critic (notably for the *Chicago Tribune*, 1884–9).

Gleason's output comprises works in almost every genre and includes two operas, both to his own librettos. The three-act *Otho Visconti* was composed between 1876 and 1880 but not performed in its entirety until several years after his death (College Theater, Chicago, 4 June 1907), under the direction of Walter Keller; its overture had been given several times by Theodore Thomas. Gleason's second opera, *Montezuma* (1885), was never performed. These works show familiarity with Wagner and employ leitmotif technique.

*
GroveAM
R. Hughes: *Contemporary American Composers* (Boston, 1900), 376
L. C. Elson: *The History of American Music* (New York, 1925), 195
J. T. Howard: *Our American Music: Three Hundred Years of it* (New York, 1931, 3/1946)   STEVEN LEDBETTER

Glebov, Igor. See ASAF'YEV, BORIS VLADIMIROVICH.

Glier, Reyngol'd Moritsevich [Glière, Reinhold] (*b* Kiev, 30 Dec 1874/11 Jan 1875; *d* Moscow, 23 June 1956). Soviet composer. He studied the violin, theory and composition at the Moscow Conservatory until 1900. From 1914 he was director of the Kiev Conservatory; in 1920 he returned to Moscow, where he was a professor of composition until 1941. In 1923 he was invited to Azerbaijan to help in the musical development of the republic. There he composed his opera *Shakh-Senem*, which married elements of the indigenous folk music with the traditionalist Russian Romanticism that had marked his style up to that point. The opera found strong favour with the Soviet musical authorities. In 1936 he turned to Tajik folk sources for his music drama *Gyul'sara*, later recomposed as an opera, in collaboration with a student, Talib Sadïkov. *Leyli i Mejnun*, also inspired by folk material from the eastern Soviet republics, appeared in 1940, two years after Glier's appointment as chairman of the organizing committee of the USSR Composer's Union. *Rashel'*, based on Maupassant's *Mademoiselle Fifi*, marked a return to a conservative Russian idiom. Glier was active as a pianist and conductor but is now best known for his ballets.

See also SHAKH-SENEM.

Zemlya i nebo [Earth and Sky], 1900 (opera-oratorio, after Byron)
Shakh-Senem (3, after Azerbaijani legend), Baku, 17 March 1927, rev. version, Baku, 1934
Gyul'sara (music drama), Tashkent, 24 April 1937; rev. as opera, Moscow, 1949, collab. T. Sadïkov
Leyli i Mejnun, comp. 1940
Rashel', 1942 (after G. de Maupassant)

*
R. Moisenko: *Realist Music* (London, 1949)
I. Belza: *R. M. Glier* (Moscow, 1955, 2/1962)
Obituary, *SovM* (1956), no.8, p.157–8
N. Petrova: *R. M. Glier* (Leningrad, 1962)
S. Krebs: *Soviet Composers and the Development of Soviet Music* (New York, 1970)   STEPHEN JOHNSON

Glimmerglass Opera. Festival company based in COOPERSTOWN.

Glinka, Mikhail Ivanovich (*b* Novospasskoye [now Glinka], nr Yelnya, Smolensk district, 20 May/1 June 1804; *d* Berlin, 3/15 Feb 1857). Russian composer, pre-eminent representative of Romanticism in Russian music and the figure to whom historians trace the existence of a viable national school of Russian art music on the classical Western model.

1. Early years. 2. Official nationalism and the operas: (i) *A Life for the Tsar* (ii) *Ruslan and Lyudmila*. 3. Achievement.

1. EARLY YEARS. Glinka was a member of the petty (untitled) nobility, born to a wealthy and distinguished landowning family of Polish extraction, Russian by virtue of the annexation by Russia of the territories surrounding their estate in 1654. It was his membership in this leisured class that enabled him to become a composer at a time when there was no such recognized profession in Russia. He spent his first 12 years, and received his formative musical impressions, on the rural ancestral lands. Much has been made of the future 'nationalist' composer's early exposure to folk music in its natural habitat. But he received an equally early and far more decisive exposure to Western 'professional' music, thanks to his uncle Afanasy's maintenance of a serf orchestra nearby. In his memoirs Glinka dated his lifelong dedication to music from the day in 1814 or 1815 when he heard some musicians from his uncle's orchestra playing a clarinet quartet by Bernhard Crusell. The Russian music Glinka first came to love was 'Russian songs' (i.e. salon romances) played by a wind octet during supper. It was the style of these 'tender and melancholy' arrangements that he was later to imitate in his operas (particularly in the music for his heroines). His earliest music instruction was from a governess who taught piano and music-reading as one of her routine subjects. In addition one of Afanasy Glinka's violinists taught the rudiments of string playing to the future composer, who also amused himself by playing along with the orchestra on the flageolet.

In 1818 Glinka was sent to St Petersburg to attend the exclusive Boarding School for the Nobility. There he continued his violin and piano instruction (including three lessons with John Field), and began composing. Early testimony to his creative gifts comes from the memoirs of a former school chum, Nikolay Markevich, who loved to listen to Glinka's improvisations at the keyboard, 'which were already exquisite'. His more formal compositions of the period, naturally enough, were variations, of which a chance survivor, noted down in later years by the composer's sister, commands special interest: *Thème de Mozart varié pour pianoforte ou harpe par M. Glinka (composé en l'an 1822) S. P.bourg*, the theme being the glockenspiel accompaniment to the slaves' chorus ('Das klinget so herrlich') from the Act 1 finale of *Die Zauberflöte*.

During the 1820s Glinka divided his time between the capital, where he had landed a civil service sinecure that allowed practically unlimited time for his musical avocation, and Novospasskoye, where he taught himself the rudiments of form and orchestration by rehearsing and conducting the serf orchestra in the classical repertory. His musical university in St Petersburg was the opera house, and he even went so far in his efforts to master the Italian style as to take singing lessons from a local singing master named Belloli. In 1824 Glinka made his first stab at operatic composition, choosing as his subject Sir Walter Scott's poem *Mathilda Rokeby*. Only a few fragmentary sketches survive.

The high point of this provincial dilettante phase was reached during the season of 1828–9, when Count Matvey Vyel'gorsky underwrote the importation of a touring Italian opera company directed by Luigi Zamboni (Rossini's original Figaro) in an attempt to establish a resident company in the Russian capital. The enterprise failed after three seasons, but not before Glinka was exposed to more than a dozen of Rossini's operas. Of greater moment was his decision to apprentice himself to the company's principal coach, the director's son Leopoldo, who schooled him in the forms and conventions of Italian opera, as well as elementary counterpoint ('fugues in two parts without words'). Something over a dozen Italian settings from the period survive.

In 1830 Glinka went abroad for an extended stay. In Milan he became personally acquainted with Bellini and Donizetti and wrote some creditable imitations of their work, publishing in addition a number of instrumental tributes to the Italian opera that included (besides several sets of piano variations) a couple of ambitious concerted compositions: a Divertimento brillante for six instruments on themes from *La sonnambula* and a Serenata for seven on themes from *Anna Bolena* (at whose La Scala première he had 'wallowed in rapture'). Glinka passed the winter of 1833–4 in Berlin, where he studied with Siegfried Dehn, the celebrated music scholar and librarian, and acquired the taste for contrapuntal elaboration so conspicuous in his operatic scores. He returned to Russia shortly before his 30th birthday, the possessor of a fully professional, cosmopolitan technique. (The four notebooks in which Dehn had inscribed Glinka's course of study were passed along to Dargomïzhsky, another leisured gentry youth with a taste for composing music and no local prospects for instruction.) Glinka now turned to the task that made him immortal: composing the first through-composed opera to a Russian text, on a 'national' subject.

2. OFFICIAL NATIONALISM AND THE OPERAS.

(i) A Life for the Tsar. To avoid the misunderstandings that usually becloud discussion of *Zhizn' za tsarya* ('A Life for the Tsar'), the word 'national' must be understood in the proper context. At the time of the opera's composition, 'nationality' (*narodnost'*) was a fairly new concept in Russia, born during the country's brief flicker of 18th-century Enlightenment, and coloured by post-Napoleonic notions of patriotism (the original subtitle of Glinka's first opera was 'patriotic heroic-tragic opera in five acts').

Russian national consciousness was actually an aspect of Westernization. The idea of a national identity transcending social class, vouchsafed by language, customs, religion and history, was one of the many imported concepts Westernized Russia made her own in her ambitious bid for recognition on the world stage; for only a nation can be a nation among nations. It was also the inevitable compensatory product of increased exposure to alien ways.

But any hint of liberalism was thoroughly expunged from the concept by the time of Glinka's maturity, for by the mid-1830s the idea of *narodnost'* had been assimilated to the doctrine of Official Nationality, associated with the reign of Nikolay I. The new dogma had been promulgated in 1833 by a man Glinka knew well: Sergey Uvarov, the former director of the Boarding School for the Nobility, now the tsar's Minister of Popular Enlightenment (Education). It consisted of a trinity of interrelated values to which Russian subjects were expected to subscribe, of which the third was *narodnost'*, subordinated in the new formulation to the older concepts of Orthodoxy and Autocracy. The nation was conceived entirely in dynastic and religious terms, Autocracy being related to Orthodoxy as 'the ultimate link between the power of man and the power of God'. The quoted words are by the poet Vasily Zhukovsky, a close friend and longstanding collaborator of Glinka, on whose novella *Mar'ina Roshcha* ('Mary's Grove') the composer was planning an opera in 1834 – until Zhukovsky himself persuaded his friend to adopt instead the subject of Ivan Susanin, the peasant whose self-sacrifice in the cause of establishing the Romanov dynasty epitomized the official doctrine's ideals. (One might add that the support given this anti-liberal ideology by the Russian intellectual and artistic élite mirrored a general trend in post-Napoleonic Europe, which saw a great rallying of Romantic artists and writers to the cause of reaction.)

Glinka's epoch-making opera was conceived as a celebration of these precepts, reaching its symbolic climax in the Epilogue (to a text by Zhukovsky), a scene of religious veneration of the nation in the person of the tsar. No wonder, then, that the opera became the obligatory season-opener for the Russian Imperial Theatres (by law the personal property of the tsar); and no wonder its libretto had to be superseded under Soviet power by a new one that replaced devotion to the Romanov dynasty with abstract commitment to national liberation (led by the popular militia of Minin and Pozharsky) and to an anachronistically secular concept of the Russian nation. As early as the 1860s the opera had become an embarrassment to the newly liberalized intelligentsia, and even such an ardent disciple of Glinka as Vladimir Stasov could complain that 'no one has ever done a greater *dishonour* to our people than Glinka, who by means of his great music displayed as a Russian hero *for all time* that base groveller Susanin, with his canine loyalty, his hen-like stupidity ['owl-like' in the original Russian] and his readiness to sacrifice his life for a little boy whom, it seems, he has never even seen'.

Thus the use of 'national' musical idioms and quoted folktunes in *A Life for the Tsar* should not be confused with the musical nationalism of a somewhat later time. They are there not for the sake of stylistic novelty or as celebration of Russianness *tout court*, but as carrier of a lofty if blimpish political message. That accounts both for their relative scarcity (something that inevitably

447

bothers those who look for a 'nationalist' in Glinka) and for what is genuinely novel in the opera: to wit, that the folktunes and idioms are not relegated to 'decorative' numbers at the peripheries of the drama (though there are plenty of those), but are heard from the lips of major characters and are made (in Act 4) to bear the full weight of the dramatic crux. Yet even here Glinka observed nice conventions: what made possible such a use of the vernacular style was the fact that all the main characters (Russian ones, that is) are peasants; and what made possible the elevation of a drama about peasants to the station of tragedy was the new concept of *narodnost'*, whereby noble and serf were united (in the words of Prince Kantemir, an early proponent of Enlightenment *à la russe*) by 'the same blood, the same bones, the same flesh'.

In formal and stylistic terms *A Life for the Tsar* was very much an Italian opera, given fancy colours by its pronounced 'bilingualism' – that is, its exploitation of semiotically marked musical idioms (in this case Russian *v* Polish) – and given a cumulative dynamic shape by the use of recalling themes (then considered a 'French' device), one of them reaching monumental proportions in the Epilogue, where it accompanies verses that set forth the opera's ideology in the most blatant terms (*see* LIFE FOR THE TSAR, A).

The truest mark of the opera's italianism is what it demands from its singers; and therein lies a hidden irony. What made production of Glinka's unprecedentedly grandiose Russian opera possible in 1836 (besides the composer's waiver of his honorarium) was a breakthrough the hitherto fairly wobbly Russian opera troupe had made earlier that same year in presenting Rossini's *Semiramide*, with a cast consisting of virtually the same roster of singers that were to create Glinka's work, and in particular with the sensational 19-year-old Anna Vorob'yova in the trouser role of Arsace. She later reproduced the sensation in the corresponding role of Vanya in *A Life for the Tsar*. But the furor over *Semiramide* was what finally aroused a loyal following for Italian opera in the Russian capital, with dire consequences for the native product.

(ii) Ruslan and Lyudmila. One of the earliest victims of that furor was Glinka's second opera, *Ruslan i Lyudmila* ('Ruslan and Lyudmila'), after a mock-epic by Pushkin, first performed in 1842. This astonishingly inventive piece was a 'trilingual' opera, pitting a neutral Italo-Russian idiom against two exotic ones, 'oriental' and 'fantastic', the latter including the precocious use of whole-tone scales. These served as semiotic markers for a quintessentially Romantic triumph of virile heroism over sensuality, symbolized by the knight Ruslan's successful quest to win back his abducted bride by defeating a pair of evil sorcerers. The protagonist of feminizing sensuality was another trouser role for the favourite Vorob'yova – that of the languorous oriental prince Ratmir, Ruslan's unsuccessful rival who is finally disenchanted by the good Nordic sorcerer Finn and becomes the hero's ally.

In *Ruslan*, a riot of motley harmonic and orchestral colour and a virtuosically wrought contrapuntal texture are allied with a remarkably leisurely dramatic rhythm. The combination has always raised problems for the opera's reception: lovers of the Italian style find it too 'German' (i.e. musically heavy and cluttered), while 'opera-as-drama' snobs in the neo-German tradition, beginning with Alexander Serov, the most influential

critic of 19th-century Russia, have always put it down as a musically distinguished farrago. The establishment of a star-studded Italian repertory company in St Petersburg one year after its première quickly rendered debate moot: Glinka's masterpiece was squeezed off the stage by 1848, embittering the composer and leading to a virtual creative block that rendered his final decade operatically barren, although he did create some excellent orchestral works (including the masterly *Kamarinskaya*, hailed by Tchaikovsky as the acorn from which the oak of Russian music grew), and although he received some gratifying recognition abroad (unprecedented for a Russian composer). Some sketches made in 1855 for *Dvumuzhnitsa* ('The Polyandrist'), after a play by Alexander Shakhovskoy, amounted to little. Glinka left Russia for the last time the next year (spitting on the ground, according to his sister's memoirs, and hoping 'never to see this vile country again') and died nine months later in Berlin, where he had gone to consult with Dehn about the possibility of reconciling species counterpoint with Russian church melodies.

3. ACHIEVEMENT. His reputation in conventional historiography notwithstanding, Glinka was a prodigally eclectic composer, natural heir to the full range of operatic styles and conventions practised in his day. The elaborate first-act cavatinas in both his operas, and especially the third act of *A Life for the Tsar* with its multipartite ensembles and its monumental finale, show his mastery of what Budden (*The Operas of Verdi*, i, 1973) has called the 'Code Rossini' – the set of formal moulds that governed the Italian opera of the *primo ottocento* – to the point where, looking back, he could poke fun at his own 'creeping Italianism' (*Ital'yanshchina*). The celebrated Act 1 canon in *Ruslan* ('Kakoye chudnoye mgnoven'ye!': 'What uncanny flash!') is of course a direct emulation of 'Fredda ed immobile' from *Il barbiere di Siviglia*. At the same time, both of Glinka's operas conspicuously exhibit features of the French rescue genre – the genre of Grétry, Méhul and Cherubini, not to mention Beethoven – with its ample choruses, its reminiscence themes and its 'popular' tone. As Berlioz was quick to notice, Glinka's style, especially in *Ruslan*, was heavily tinged besides with 'the influence of Germany' in the prominence accorded the orchestra, the spectacular instrumentation, and the 'beauty of the harmonic fabric'. That the models for his second opera included Mozart (in particular his old favourite, *Die Zauberflöte*) can be readily seen not only from the gaudy glockenspiel and glass-harmonica colours in the magic music but also from the Act 3 finale, in which Finn first intervenes like a Sarastro to break the spells woven by Naina, then stands in as tenor to complete the vocal complement for a concluding quartet ('Teper' Lyudmila ot nas spasen'ya zhdyot': 'Now Lyudmila awaits from us salvation') that reflects something of the serene radiance of 'Bald prangt, den Morgen zu verkünden'. This limpidly scored, loftily diatonic ensemble, too often overlooked in the welter of blinding exotica for which *Ruslan* is justly famed, marks Glinka as Russia's one-and-only 'high classic'.

Thus to look only for a 'nationalist' in him, for all that it grants him an unassailable historiographical niche and assures him a specious immortality, is to imprison him in a cage not of his making. The cage was manufactured, in the first instance, by the committed nationalists of a younger generation, beginning with

Stasov and Balakirev, who claimed his legitimating mantle. Later the insular view of Glinka as father to a national school founded on folklore passed into folklore itself. Reappraisal has begun in Russia, but not yet in the West, where such studies of him as exist still adamantly insist upon his Russianness as sole measure of his worth, where his significance is defined in terms of his 'influence' and where he is still apt to be chided for showing those sides of his talent he himself tended to value most highly.

To complain that Glinka 'could not dispense with Western compositional techniques' is shortsighted. Those techniques were his vehicles, not his impediments; no composer of 'art music' could dispense with them, for they are what define his trade. His greatest significance lay not in having been the first 'truly Russian' composer (if folkishness is the measure, he was hardly that), but in having been the first composer from Russia to establish a European reputation (as witness Berlioz's enthusiastic notice of Glinka's benefit concert in Paris in 1845, and Liszt's even earlier piano transcription – under the title *Tscherkessen-Marsch* – of Chernomor's March from *Ruslan*). Through Glinka Russia did not retreat or withdraw from the West, but rather the opposite. His achievement made it possible for Russian music, and Russian opera in particular, to become a true participant in the classical Western tradition.

See also LIFE FOR THE TSAR, A, and RUSLAN AND LYUDMILA.

Edition: *M. I. Glinka: Polnoye sobraniye sochineniy* [Complete Collection of Works], ed. V. Ya. Shebalin and others (Moscow, 1955–69) [G]

published in St Petersburg unless otherwise stated

title	genre, acts	libretto	first performance	composed	published	remarks	G
Rokeby	opera	W. Scott		1824	Moscow, 1969	sketches for entr'acte only	xvii, 139
Mar'ina Roshcha [Mary's Grove]	opera	V. A. Zhukovsky		1834		sketches; used in Zhizn' za tsarya	
Zhizn' za tsarya [A Life for the Tsar]	'patriotic heroic-tragic opera', 5 (or 4, with epilogue)	Y. F. Rozen, V. Sollogub, N. V. Kukol'nik and Zhukovksy	St Petersburg, Bol'shoy, 27 Nov/9 Dec 1836	1834–6	vs, 1856 or 1857; ov. only, 1858; full score, 1881	ov. arr. pf 4 hands, G v, 106; pt of epilogue arr. solo pf, G vi, 255	xii/a, b, suppl.; vs, xiii
Ruslan i Lyudmila [Ruslan and Lyudmila]	'magic' opera, 5	V. F. Shirkov, with contribs. from N. A. Markevich, Kukol'nik, M. A. Gedeonov and M. I. Glinka, after A. S. Pushkin	St Petersburg, Bol'shoy, 27 Nov/9 Dec 1842	1837–42	vs, 1856; ov. only, 1858; full score, 1881	pt of Finn's ballad and pt of Lyudmila's scena arr. pf, 1852, G vi, 251, 254	xiv/a, b, suppl.; vs, xv
Dvumuzhnitsa [The Polyandrist]	opera	after A. A. Shakhovskoy		1855		sketches, lost	

N. Findeyzen: *Mikhail Ivanovich Glinka: ocherk ego zhizni i muzikal'noy deyatel'nosti* [A Study of his Life and Musical Activity] (Moscow, 1903)

G. Abraham: 'Michael Glinka', *Masters of Russian Music*, ed. M. D. Calvocoressi and G. Abraham (London, 1936), 13–64

B. Asaf'yev: *Glinka* (Moscow, 1947)

E. Kann-Novikova: *M. I. Glinka: novïye materialï i dokumentï* (Moscow and Leningrad, 1950–55)

H. Laroche [G. Larosh]: *Izbrannïye stat'i o Glinke* [Selected Essays on Glinka] (Moscow, 1953)

A. Orlova, ed.: *Glinka v vospominaniyakh sovremennikov* [Glinka in the Reminiscences of his Contemporaries] (Moscow, 1955)

V. Stasov: *Izbrannïye stat'i o M. I. Glinke* [Selected Essays on Glinka] (Moscow, 1955)

R. Mudge, trans.: *M. Glinka: Memoirs* (Norman, OK, 1963)

A. Lyapunova, ed.: *M. I. Glinka: Literaturnïye proizvedeniya i perepiska* [Literary Works and Correspondence] (Moscow, 1973–7)

D. Brown: *Mikhail Glinka: a Biographical and Critical Study* (London, 1974)

R. Taruskin: 'Glinka's Ambiguous Legacy and the Birth Pangs of Russian Opera', *19th Century Music*, i (1977–8), 142–62

——: 'How the Acorn took Root: a Tale of Russia', *19th Century Music*, vi (1982–3), 189–212

A. Rozanov: *M. I. Glinka: chelovek, sobïtiya, vremya* [Glinka: the Man, Events, Time] (Moscow, 1983)

O. Levashova: *Mikhail Ivanovich Glinka* (Moscow, 1987–8)

——: 'M. I. Glinka', *Istoriya russkoy muziki* [The History of Russian Music], v, ed. Yu. Keldïsh and others (Moscow, 1988), 185–284

A. Orlova: *Glinka's Life in Music: a Chronicle* (Ann Arbor, 1988) [trans. of *Letopis' zhizni i tvorchestva M. I. Glinki (1804–43)*, 1978]

A Life for the Tsar

G. Abraham: 'A Life for the Tsar', *On Russian Music* (London, 1939), 1–19

A. Ossovsky: 'Dramaturgiya operï M. I. Glinki "Ivan Susanin"', *M. I. Glinka: issledovaniya i materialï* [Research Essays and Materials] (Leningrad and Moscow, 1950), 7–71

N. Tumanina: 'Otechestvennaya geroiko-tragicheskaya opera Glinki "Ivan Susanin"' [Glinka's Patriotic Heroic-Tragic Opera *Ivan Susanin*], *M. I. Glinka: sbornik materialov i statey* [Collection of Documents and Articles], ed. T. Livanova (Moscow, 1950), 114–74

C. Cui: 'Shestidesyatiletiye "Ivana Susanina" [*recte* "Zhizni za tsarya"]' [The 60th Anniversary of *A Life for the Tsar*], *Izbrannïye stat'i* [Selected Essays], ed. Yu. A. Kremlyov (Leningrad, 1952), 457–9

G. Bernandt, ed.: V. Odoyevsky: *Muzikal'no-literaturnoye naslediye* [Musical and Literary Legacy] (Moscow, 1956), 118–30

N. Riasanovsky: *Nicholas I and Official Nationality in Russia, 1825–1855* (Berkeley and Los Angeles, 1959)

V. Protopopov: *'Ivan Susanin' Glinki* (Moscow, 1961)

B. Yarustovsky: 'Iz istorii operï "Ivan Susanin" – M. I. Glinki', *Ivan Susanin M. I. Glinki* (Moscow, 2/1964), 3–23 [lib.]

T. Livanova and V. Protopopov: *Opernaya kritika v Rossii* [Opera Criticism in Russia], i/1 (Moscow, 1966), 188–220

A. Gozenpud: *Russkiy operniy teatr XIX veka (1836–1856)* [Russian Operatic Theatre in the 19th Century] (Leningrad, 1969), 7–74

A. Lyapunova, ed.: *M. Glinka: Literaturnïye proizvedeniya i perepiska* [Literary Works and Correspondence], i (Moscow, 1973), 29–94, 192–3 [incl. Glinka's original plan and critically edited original lib.]

A. Khomyakov: 'Opera Glinki "Zhizn' za tsarya"' [Glinka's Opera *A Life for the Tsar*; 1844], *SovM* (1980), no.1, pp.91–3

V. Vasina-Grossman: 'K istorii libretto "Ivana Susanina" Glinki' [On the History of the Libretto to Glinka's *Ivan Susanin*], *Stilevïye osobennosti russkoy muzïki XIX–XX vekov* [Stylistic Peculiarities of Russian Music in the 19th and 20th Centuries] (Leningrad, 1983), 17–25

E. Kachanova: *Ivan Susanin M. I. Glinki* (Moscow, 1986)

N. Ugryumov: 'Variatsii na glinkinskuyu temu' [Variations on a Glinkian Theme], *SovM* (1986), no.12, pp.86–97

V. Protopopov and others, eds.: *A. Serov: Stat'i o muzïke* [Articles on Music], iv (Moscow, 1988), 816–92 [incl. 'Opïtï tekhnicheskoy kritiki nad muzïkoyu M. I. Glinki: Rol' odnogo motiva v tseloy opere "Zhizn' za tsarya"', Experiments in Technical Criticism on Glinka's Music: The Role of One Melodic Motif Throughout the Opera *A Life for the Tsar*; orig. pubd 1859]

S. Frolov: 'Glinka: "Ivan Susanin" – "Zhizn' za tsarya"', *SovM* (1989), no.1, pp.83–9

R. Skrïnnikov: 'Sobiratel'nïy obraz' [Collective Image], *SovM* (1989), no.1, pp.89–91

N. Ugryumov: 'Muchenitsa nashego vremeni' [A Martyr of our Time], *SovM* (1989), no.8, pp.78–90

Ruslan and Lyudmila

N. Rimsky-Korsakov: 'Motsart i Glinka', *Muzïkal'nïye stat'i i zametki 1869–1907* [Articles and Notes on Music] (St Petersburg, 1911), 40–43

C. Cui: 'Opernïy sezon v Peterburge: pervoye i vtoroye predstavleniye "Ruslana i Lyudmïlï"' [The Opera Season in Petersburg: the First and Second Performances of *Ruslan*; orig. pubd 1864], *Muzïkal'no-kriticheskiye stat'i* [Critical Articles on Music], i (Petrograd, 1918), 109–14

G. Abraham: 'Ruslan and Lyudmila', *On Russian Music* (London, 1939), 20–42

V. Berkov: *Ruslan i Lyudmila M. Glinki* (Moscow and Leningrad, 1949)

A. Serov: '"Ruslan" i ruslanistï' [orig. 1867], *Izbrannïye stat'i* [Selected Essays], ed. G. N. Khubov, i (Moscow, 1950), 193–253

C. Cui: '"Ruslan i Lyudmila" M. I. Glinki' [orig. 1886], *Izbrannïye stat'i* [Selected Essays], ed. Yu. A. Kremlyov (Leningrad, 1952), 354–61 [incl. thematic analysis of Act 1 introduction]

V. Stasov: 'Muchenitsa nashego vremeni' [A Martyr of our Time; orig. pubd 1859], *Izbrannïye stat'i o M. I. Glinke* [Selected Essays on Glinka], ed. T. Livanova and V. Protopopov (Moscow, 1955), 50–65

V. Odoyevsky: 'Zapiski dlya moyego pravnuka o literature nashego vremeni i o prochem' [Notes for my Great-Grandson on the Literature of our Time, Among Other Things; orig. pubd 1843]; 'Pis'mo k V. V. Stasovu o "Ruslane i Lyudmile" Glinki' [A Letter to Stasov about Glinka's *Ruslan*; orig. pubd 1858], *Muzïkal'no-literaturnoye naslediye* [Musical and Literary Legacy], ed. G. Bernandt (Moscow, 1956), 204–12, 233–7

T. Livanova and V. Protopopov: *Opernaya kritika v Rossii* [Opera Criticism in Russia], i/1 (Moscow, 1966), 262–87

A. Gozenpud: *Russkiy operniy teatr XIX veka (1836–1856)* [Russian Operatic Theatre in the 19th Century] (Leningrad, 1969), 107–76

T. Livanova: *Opernaya kritika v Rossii* [Opera Criticism in Russia], ii (Moscow, 1969), 333–61; iii (Moscow, 1973), 114–33

B. Asaf'yev: 'Slavyanskaya liturgiya Erosu' [The Slavonic Liturgy of Eros], *Simfonicheskiye etyudï* (Leningrad, 1970), 15–34

A. Kandinsky: 'Molodost' operï' [The Youth of Opera], *Pravda* (30 Oct 1972)

A. Lyapunova, ed.: *M. Glinka: Literaturnïye proizvedeniya i perepiska* [Literary Works and Correspondence], i (Moscow, 1973), 95–178, 194–6 [incl. Glinka's plan, lib. drafts, etc.]

M. Aranovsky: 'Dva ocherka o "Ruslane"' [Two Essays on *Ruslan*], *SovM* (1979), no.7, pp.68–84

N. Ugryumov: 'Muchenitsa nashego vremeni' [A Martyr of our Time], *SovM* (1989), no.8, pp.78–90

M. Woodside: 'Leitmotif in Russia: Glinka's Use of the Whole-Tone Scale', *19th Century Music*, xiv (1990–91), 242–51

RICHARD TARUSKIN

Glodeanu, Liviu (*b* Dîrja, Cluj, 6 Aug 1938; *d* Bucharest, 31 March 1978). Romanian composer. He studied at the Cluj Conservatory (1955–7) with Liviu Comes (harmony) and at the Bucharest Conservatory (1957–61) with Marţian Negrea (composition) and Alfred Mendelsohn (orchestration). He began his career as a scientific researcher at the Institute of Folklore in Bucharest, but his main work was with the Filarmonica 'George Enescu' orchestra (1963–78) as musical secretary. His output ranges from orchestral and film music to chamber and choral works and includes two operas based on ancient classical drama, both to his own librettos: the five-scene *Zamolxe* op.23 (1969), after Lucian Blaga, and *Ulysses* op.20*bis*, a one-act ballet-opera versified from Homer's epic by Mihai Ungureanu. *Zamolxe* (published Bucharest, 1972) was broadcast on 8 October 1969, and both works received their stage premières on 25 April 1973 at the Romanian Opera House, Cluj. Glodeanu's highly original melodic and harmonic writing (usually in a modal or folk style) produces intense and dramatic music with strong contrasts. He used recitative and drew on traditional Romanian musical forms (laments, Christmas carols); his imaginative scoring sometimes includes ancient or primitive instruments (pipes, drums, wooden plates).

VIOREL COSMA

Gloria. Opera in three acts by FRANCESCO CILEA to a libretto by ARTURO COLAUTTI; Milan, Teatro alla Scala, 15 April 1907 (revised 1932).

The opera's Capulet-Montague story is set in Siena towards the end of the 14th century. In a public square a truce is being celebrated between the Guelf rulers and the Ghibellines who are laying siege to the city. Gloria De' Bardi (soprano), daughter of the city prior Aquilante (bass), apostrophizes the central fountain as a symbol of peace ('Fonte muta e profonda'). Lionetto De' Ricci (tenor), an exile who has joined the besieging army, demands her hand in marriage. When this is refused he reveals himself as Fortebrando, the celebrated soldier of fortune who commands the imperial forces. In a scuffle, Gloria's brother Folco (baritone) is wounded. Hostilities are resumed and Aquilante is killed. In a villa behind the enemy lines Gloria sadly contemplates the beleaguered city ('O mia cuna fiorita'). Folco, in the guise of an oriental merchant, brings poison which he orders her to pour into Lionetto's wine that night. But Gloria, already in love with her captor, temporizes. When Lionetto arrives she gladly consents to their wedding. During the nuptial ceremony in the Bardi chapel Folco stabs the bridegroom under cover of a fraternal embrace. Gloria stabs herself with Lionetto's dagger and expires on his dead body.

The première was conducted by Toscanini with Salomea Krusceniski (Gloria), Giovanni Zenatello (Lionetto), Pasquale Amato (Folco) and Nazzareno De Angelis (Aquilante). In 1932 Cilea revised and shortened the opera with the librettist Ettore Moschini, changing Folco's name to Bardo and removing a confrontation between him and Lionetto in Act 2. *Gloria* is Cilea's most ambitious opera. With its measured pace and wealth of medieval pageantry it can be seen as a remote descendant of *Lohengrin*. The recurring motifs are handled more flexibly than in his previous works, the harmony is more adventurous (extending to the occasional use of the whole-tone scale) and certain of the ensembles – notably that of the wedding ceremony in Act

3 ('Grazie, Signor, a Te') – are notable for their contrapuntal elaboration.   JULIAN BUDDEN

Gloriana. Opera in three acts, op.53, by BENJAMIN BRITTEN to a libretto by WILLIAM PLOMER; London, Covent Garden, 8 June 1953.

Queen Elizabeth I	soprano
Robert Devereux, Earl of Essex	tenor
Frances, Countess of Essex	mezzo-soprano
Charles Blount, Lord Mountjoy	baritone
Penelope, Lady Rich *sister of Essex*	soprano
Sir Robert Cecil *Secretary of the Council*	baritone
Sir Walter Raleigh *Captain of the Guard*	bass
Henry Cuffe *a satellite of Essex*	baritone
A Lady-in-Waiting	soprano
A Blind Ballad-Singer	bass
The Recorder of Norwich	bass
A Housewife	mezzo-soprano
The Spirit of the Masque	tenor
The Master of Ceremonies	tenor
The City Crier	baritone

Citizens, maids of honour, ladies and gentlemen of the household, courtiers, masquers, old men, men and boys of Essex's following, councillors

Dancers Time, Concord, country girls, rustics, fishermen, morris dancer

Actors Ballad-singer's runner, Sir John Harington, French ambassador, Archbishop of Canterbury, phantom kings and queens, pages

Setting England in the later years of Elizabeth I's reign

Commissioned by the Royal Opera House, Covent Garden, *Gloriana* is 'dedicated by gracious permission to Her Majesty Queen Elizabeth II in honour of whose coronation it was composed'. It is set in the later years of Elizabeth I's reign, and at the time of the première the opera's emphasis on an aging, ungracious monarch was felt in some quarters to be inappropriate; the work has not been extensively revived, though a successful ENO production (1984; later issued on a video recording) vindicated the quality of the work. As William Plomer explained, Lytton Strachey's *Elizabeth and Essex* was the opera's starting-point. Moreover, since this was his first attempt at a libretto and time was very short, the work's genesis was a fraught and turbulent one. Work began in earnest only after royal approval for the project was received in May 1952. Britten began the music in August that year, and the full orchestral score was completed in mid-March 1953. The original cast was led by Joan Cross in the title role and Peter Pears as the Earl of Essex.

The libretto was deliberately heterogeneous – a mixture of prose and verse, archaic and modern English; and the music (especially Act 2.i and Act 2.iii) performs a comparably skilful balancing act between Tudor allusions and Britten's own style, as well as between separate numbers and larger-scale continuity. Above all, *Gloriana* establishes strong, effective contrasts between public and private worlds.

ACT 1.i *At a tournament* Robert Devereux, Earl of Essex, is revealed as hot-blooded and jealous of anyone who might win the Queen's favour. He provokes a fight with the tournament victor, Charles Blount, Lord Mountjoy, and is slightly wounded at the moment when the Queen and her entourage arrive. She expresses her annoyance that her bravest champions should fight among themselves and urges them to attend her at court as friends. Essex and Mountjoy are reconciled and Elizabeth is acclaimed in the 'Green leaves' chorus.

1.ii *The Queen's private rooms in Nonesuch Palace* The Queen discusses the rivalry of Mountjoy and Essex with her chief adviser Sir Robert Cecil. She admires Essex's impulsive arrogance, but Cecil warns her of the political dangers of showing affection for him. He also informs her of the reports that a new Armada may be on the way. Essex is announced and, to distract the Queen from cares of state, sings two lute songs: 'Quick music's best' and, in contrast, 'Happy were he', a brilliant fusion of Britten's style and allusions to Elizabethan lute songs. The poem is by the historical Earl of Essex, and Britten uses a motif from John Wilbye's 'Happy, O happy he'. The Queen is moved, but Essex grows impatient. He wants to go to Ireland to suppress the Tyrone rebellion, and accuses Cecil and Sir Walter Raleigh of intriguing against him. The Queen resists and sends him away. The act ends with a restrained soliloquy in which she prays for power 'that I may rule and protect my people in peace'.

ACT 2.i *Norwich* In the most overtly ceremonial scene in the opera, the Queen visits Norwich. After a welcome from the Recorder of Norwich and some expressions of impatience from Essex, a masque, in celebration of Time and Concord, and comprising six dances and choral pieces, is performed.

2.ii *The garden of Essex's house* Essex's sister Lady Penelope Rich and Mountjoy meet and sing of their love. Essex and his wife Frances enter, the Earl complaining at the way the Queen thwarts his desire to go to Ireland. The couples meet and, in a quartet, imagine themselves gaining increasing power and influence as the Queen ages: only Lady Essex urges caution.

2.iii *The palace of Whitehall* A ball is in progress, dominated by Lady Essex, who has been instructed by her husband to dress with maximum extravagance, even though she is sure that this will annoy the Queen. After a pavane and galliard the Queen enters. She observes Lady Essex in her finery and orders an energetic lavolta, after which, again at her command, the ladies withdraw to change their linen. During the ensuing morris dance the ladies return one by one. Lady Essex, who reappears in plainer clothes, tells Lady Rich that her dress was stolen while she was changing, and when the Queen returns it is clear who appropriated it. Elizabeth looks grotesque: Lady Essex's dress is too small for her, and she soon leaves again, while Essex, Mountjoy and Lady Rich comfort Frances in her humiliation. Essex grows ever more rebellious, but when the Queen returns he is told that he is, after all, to be appointed Lord Deputy in Ireland. He accepts the commission with enthusiasm and leads the Queen in a coranto of celebration.

ACT 3.i *Nonesuch Palace* The Queen's maids discuss Essex's failure to put down the Irish rebellion. Essex appears, demanding to see the Queen. When, despite the maids' protests, a curtain is drawn aside, the Queen is seen in a dressing gown and without a wig. Though sympathetic to Essex, she cannot overlook his failure in Ireland, and his complaints about his enemies at court only make matters worse. After his departure the Queen completes her toilet, and Cecil is admitted, to underline the twin dangers of an Ireland still in revolt and an Essex now making trouble in England. Reluctantly, Elizabeth orders that Essex be kept under guard; he has failed her because she in turn has failed to tame him. As she declares with weary decisiveness, 'it is I who have to rule'.

3.ii *A street in the city of London* A blind ballad-singer regales the crowd with the story of Essex's attempt to foment rebellion. Some of Essex's sympathizers try to persuade others to join them, but the City Crier proclaims the Earl a traitor.

3.iii *The palace of Whitehall* Cecil and the councillors try to persuade the Queen to sign the order condemning Essex to death. At first she refuses and, left alone, laments her indecision. Lady Essex, Lady Rich and Mountjoy are admitted and the two women plead in turn for Essex's life. To the humble Lady Essex the Queen responds kindly, but when Lady Rich insolently attempts to argue that the Earl warrants the Queen's pardon because the Queen needs him, Elizabeth calls for the warrant and signs it. Then the Queen is alone in a timeless void. In a sequence of speeches she recalls her relationship with Essex (the music of the second lute song is heard) and reconciles herself to death. The opera ends with the fading strains of the celebratory 'Green leaves' chorus.

* * *

Britten's imaginative use of allusions to Elizabethan dances and lute songs to create not only local colour but also a sense of ironic distance from the 20th century is one of *Gloriana*'s great strengths. The treatment of the Elizabeth and Essex relationship veers towards the melodramatic, yet there is still a strong sense of two wayward, incompatible temperaments, and the music during the opera's final stages does not shy away from the grandiose, the more firmly to underline the gradual, touching dissolution. Through Plomer's portrayal of the Queen as an 'outsider', Britten was able to transcend irony and create a conclusion of true pathos, worlds away from a conventional operatic death scene and providing a striking counterweight to the opera's earlier emphasis on public ceremonial.

The difficulties Britten experienced with *Gloriana*, and its early reception, may help to explain why Britten failed to compose the much-mooted *King Lear* and moved away to chamber opera. His great achievements in this more intimate medium cannot wholly dispel a sense of regret for what might have been.

ARNOLD WHITTALL

Glösch, Carl Wilhelm (*b* Berlin, 1731/2; *d* Berlin, 21 Oct 1809). German composer. A flautist and keyboard player, he probably studied with J. J. Quantz. In 1765 Princess Ferdinand of Prussia appointed him *maître de musique* of her household; he remained in her service until his death. As well as songs and instrumental pieces he composed a one-act *comédie lyrique*, *L'oracle, ou La fête des vertus et des grâces* (Berlin, 1773), of which only a keyboard reduction survives. His music is craftsmanlike but otherwise unremarkable.

*

Obituary, *AMZ*, xii (1809), 105–6
C. von Ledebur: *Tonkünstler-Lexicon Berlin's* (Berlin, 1861)
C. Sachs: *Musik und Oper am kurbrandenburgischen Hof* (Berlin, 1910)　　　　E. EUGENE HELM

Glossop, Peter (*b* Sheffield, 6 July 1928). English baritone. He studied in Sheffield, making his début in 1949

as Coppélius/Dr Miracle. In 1952 he joined Sadler's Wells chorus and was soon singing principal roles: Gérard, Scarpia, Rossini's Figaro, Zurga, Ramiro (*L'heure espagnole*), Yevgeny Onegin, Rigoletto and Luna. He made his Covent Garden début in 1961 as Demetrius (*A Midsummer Night's Dream*), after singing the part in Edinburgh; later roles at Covent Garden included Renato, Amonasro, Germont, Posa, Iago, Boccanegra, Rigoletto, Nabucco, Marcello, Billy Budd, Escamillo, Choroebus (*Les Troyens*) and John the Baptist. He sang Lescaut in the British première of Henze's *Boulevard Solitude* (1962, Sadler's Wells) and Tarquinius in *The Rape of Lucretia* (English Opera Group, 1963). He made his La Scala début in 1965 as Rigoletto, his Paris and San Francisco débuts in 1966 as Posa. He sang Rigoletto in concert at Newport, Rhode Island, for the Metropolitan in 1967, then made his house début in 1971 as Scarpia, returning as Don Carlo (*Forza*), Falstaff, Mr Redburn (*Billy Budd*), Balstrode (*Peter Grimes*) and Wozzeck. He appeared in Vienna and Salzburg (1970), where he sang Iago for Karajan, later recording the role. His repertory also included Macbeth, Don Carlo (*Ernani*), Tonio and Mandryka, which he sang for the ENO (1980). Although he was not the subtlest of actors, his portrayals were always sung and projected with eager conviction.　　ALAN BLYTH

Glover, Jane (**Alison**) (*b* Helmsley, Yorks., 13 May 1949). English conductor and musicologist. While at Oxford, she conducted *Le nozze di Figaro* with the University Opera Society in 1971. She took the DPhil with a dissertation on Venetian Baroque opera and she produced a valuable study of Cavalli (London, 1978), whose *Rosinda* she edited from the autograph and conducted, and whose *Eritrea* she conducted in her own edition at the 1975 Wexford Festival. She was music director of Glyndebourne Touring Opera, 1981–5, conducting a varied repertory, including *Fidelio* and *A Midsummer Night's Dream*. Her Glyndebourne Festival début was *Don Giovanni* (1982) and was followed by her débuts at Covent Garden (*Die Entführung*, 1988) and with the ENO (*Don Giovanni*, 1989). Her wide travels have included teaching visits to China, where she conducted *Pagliacci* and *Gianni Schicchi* (1987). She was appointed artistic director of the Buxton Festival from 1993. Her performances combine scholarly concern with corresponding character and vitality.

NOËL GOODWIN

Gluck, Alma [Fiersohn, Reba] (*b* Bucharest, 11 May 1884; *d* New York, 27 Oct 1938). American soprano of Romanian birth. She was taken to the USA in infancy and studied singing in New York, making a highly successful début with the Metropolitan Opera at the New Theatre on 16 November 1909 as Sophie in Massenet's *Werther*. She sang for seven seasons between 1909 and 1918 at the Metropolitan, where her roles included Amore and the Spirit in Gluck's *Orfeo* (under Toscanini), Marguerite, Venus, Gilda and Mimì. After a period of further study with Marcella Sembrich, she devoted herself almost wholly to concert singing; in the popular repertory she achieved a success similar to that of John McCormack, rivalling him in purity of tone and line and clarity of enunciation. By her first husband she had a daughter who, as Marcia Davenport, became well known as a novelist and writer on music; her second husband, the violinist Efrem Zimbalist, often played obbligato accompaniments to her recordings.

M. Davenport: *Of Lena Geyer* (New York, 1936) [roman à clef based on Gluck's career]

B. T. Eke: 'Alma Gluck', *Record Collector*, i/8 (1946), 5–10; vi (1951), 33–45, 53 [with discography by H. Chitty]

DESMOND SHAWE-TAYLOR

Gluck, Christoph Willibald Ritter von (*b* Erasbach, nr Berching, Upper Palatinate, 2 July 1714; *d* Vienna, 15 Nov 1787). Bohemian-Austrian composer of Italian and French opera, a leading figure in opera of the second half of the 18th century, and the person chiefly credited with the 'reform' of opera after the age of Metastasian *opera seria*.

1. 1714–46. 2. 1746–61. 3. 1762–73. 4. 1774–87. 5. Opéras comiques. 6. The Italian 'reform' operas. 7. The Paris operas. 8. Historical position, influence.

1. 1714–46. Gluck's interest in music was evident from an early age. He studied the violin, the cello and singing, but his father was opposed to his becoming a professional musician and wanted him to follow his own career as a forester. To escape this, Gluck ran away from home at the age of 13 or 14 and went to Prague, earning his living on the way by singing and playing the jew's harp (as he later told the painter Christian von Mannlich). Although he was involved in a great deal of music-making in the Bohemian capital, and for a time was organist at the Tyn Church, he does not appear to have received any systematic musical education there and was largely self-taught. An early influence must have been the Prague opera house, where Italian opera was popular: Vivaldi, Albinoni and Lolli were among the composers whose works were most often performed there in the first half of the 18th century.

From Prague Gluck went for two years as chamber musician to Prince Lobkowitz in Vienna, where he came under the influence of the Austrians J. J. Fux and the elder Georg Reutter as well as the Italians at the court of Charles VI such as Caldara, Ignazio Conti, Badia and Porsile. Then in 1737 Gluck was engaged by Prince Melzi to play in his orchestra in Milan, where he came into contact with one of the most important figures in Italian music, G. B. Sammartini. There is no evidence that Gluck ever studied with Sammartini, but much of his early music is imbued with the style of the older master, including his first operas, beginning with *Artaserse*, which had its première in Milan in 1741 when the composer was 27; this was a great success and was followed by commissions for seven more operas for Italy as well as collaborations on two pasticcios.

In 1745 Gluck accepted an invitation from the King's Theatre in the Haymarket to write two operas for London. These were received with little enthusiasm, despite the fact that one of them, *La caduta de' giganti*, was a particularly topical patriotic allegory which anticipated the defeat of the Young Pretender, Bonnie Prince Charlie, by the Duke of Cumberland. Music from this and from Gluck's other opera for England, *Artamene*, was published in London, together with six of his trio sonatas. He gave successful concerts in the capital, including two in which he performed on the 'musical glasses', and also met Handel.

2. 1746–61. For the next six years Gluck continued to lead the life of an itinerant musician, operatic commissions and performances taking him to Dresden, Vienna, Hamburg, Copenhagen, Prague, Munich and Naples; during 1747–8 he was working as a musical director with the Mingotti travelling company. In 1752 he settled in Vienna, the city that was to be his base for the rest of his life. He was 38 and had recently made an advantageous marriage to Maria Anna Bergin, a wealthy Viennese merchant's daughter who had important connections with the imperial court. Gluck was appointed Konzertmeister and later Kapellmeister to the Prince of Saxe-Hildburghausen, his duties including directing the prince's orchestra in concerts and performances of oratorios and operas. According to Dittersdorf's autobiography the concerts often included music by Gluck himself, and in 1754 he wrote a one-act opera *Le cinesi* to be performed before the royal family at the Prince of Saxe-Hildburghausen's summer palace at Schlosshof. Its revival in Vienna at the emperor's request led to further commissions including *La danza* and *L'innocenza giustificata*. The words for the arias of the latter were by the imperial poet, Pietro Metastasio, but those for the recitatives were by Count Durazzo, the Intendant of Viennese theatres and an important and influential figure in the city's theatrical and musical life. He was later to be one of the leaders in the movement to reform Italian opera, but in the early 1750s he was instrumental in beginning a new era in the artistic life of Vienna when, together with the imperial chancellor Count Kaunitz, he brought a French drama company to the court. The *opéras comiques* they performed were so popular that similar works were imported from Paris on a regular basis, and Gluck adapted them for the Viennese stage, often replacing the French *airs*, *ariettes* and vaudevilles with his own as well as providing new overtures. The first Viennese *opéra comique* for which Gluck composed all the music was *La fausse esclave*, which was highly successful at its première in 1758. During the next six years he wrote a further seven *opéras comiques*, culminating in his greatest work in the genre, *La rencontre imprévue*, in 1764.

Although the Prince of Saxe-Hildburghausen had disbanded his orchestra in 1761 and Gluck was no longer attached to any patron, besides writing *opéras comiques* he was busy composing ballet music for both of the Viennese theatres, a job he undertook in 1759. Then, in 1761, the year of his collaboration with the choreographer Gasparo Angiolini in a revolutionary *ballet d'action*, *Le festin de pierre, ou Don Juan*, Durazzo's attempts to infuse French spirit into Italian opera were assisted by the arrival in Vienna of Ranieri de' Calzabigi. He was a multi-talented aesthete, poet, librettist, businessman and man of the theatre, a true disciple of Diderot and the French Enlightenment, whom Durazzo saw as an ideal collaborator for Gluck. The partnership was an inspired one, Calzabigi providing the subjects and librettos for three of Gluck's greatest operas.

3. 1762–73. As Gluck later said in an open letter to the *Mercure de France* in February 1773, the idea for the first fruit of their collaboration came entirely from Calzabigi. This was *Orfeo ed Euridice*, the first in the series of three so-called reform operas in which Calzabigi and Gluck reacted against the stylization and conventions of the Baroque *opera seria*. The work was a great success at its first performance in 1762, but, as Calzabigi later acknowledged, that was partly due to the fine interpretation of the role of Orpheus by the alto castrato for whom Gluck had written it – Gaetano Guadagni, one of the greatest singers of the day.

After *Orfeo ed Euridice*, Gluck and Calzabigi wrote *Alceste* (1767), which has a famous dedicatory preface setting out their reform manifesto (see §6 below), and *Paride ed Elena* (1770). In between these three reform operas Gluck fulfilled commissions, composing six new Italian operas including *Il trionfo di Clelia*, *Il Parnaso confuso* and *Telemaco*, and revised two of his earlier ones (*Ezio* and *La vestale*); in all of them his reformist thinking is manifest to a greater or lesser extent.

Gluck was becoming increasingly interested in French opera: he studied the works of Lully and Rameau and even had *Orfeo ed Euridice* published in Paris in 1764, and he must have been somewhat disillusioned at the poor reception accorded to *Paride ed Elena* in Vienna in 1770. So when two years later the attaché to the French Embassy in Vienna, Marie François Louis Gand Leblanc Roullet, showed him the opera libretto which he had based on Racine's tragedy *Iphigénie en Aulide*, Gluck set to work at once. He had never written an opera for Paris before, and having incorporated so many features of French opera into his Italian reform operas, it was logical that his next goal should be the centre of French serious opera or *tragédie lyrique*, the Académie Royale de Musique in Paris.

Gluck and Roullet made careful preparations for their conquest of the Académie Royale de Musique, beginning by publishing open letters to one of its directors in the *Mercure de France* offering *Iphigénie en Aulide* for performance and outlining Gluck's Italian operatic reforms and his intentions in Paris. But when they saw the score of *Iphigénie en Aulide* the directors of the Académie Royale were reluctant to mount a production of the opera unless Gluck undertook to write five more for them, because they feared that the work's boldness and originality would drive all the existing French operas off the stage. As resilient as ever, Gluck enlisted the support of the French dauphine, his former singing pupil in Vienna, Marie Antoinette, and he eventually arrived in Paris towards the end of 1773 to begin rehearsals for *Iphigénie en Aulide*.

4. 1774–87. Judging from contemporary accounts such as the memoirs of Mannlich, the several months of rehearsals for *Iphigénie en Aulide* must have been quite a spectacle, with the irascible 60-year-old composer struggling to reform the bad habits of the singers and players of the Académie Royale to teach them his new opera. However, the première of *Iphigénie en Aulide* in April 1774 was a triumph, but the run of performances was interrupted by the death of Louis XV a month later. All the theatres closed, and during the period of mourning Gluck quickly revised *Orfeo ed Euridice* and made a French version of the opera with a translation of the text by Pierre Louis Moline. Gluck also adapted the role of Orpheus for the *haute-contre* Joseph Legros. At its first performance in August 1774 *Orphée et Euridice* was an even greater success than *Iphigénie en Aulide*, and Gluck dedicated the opera to Marie Antoinette, who awarded him an annual pension of 6000 livres. But Vienna too was vying for Gluck's talents, and when he returned home later that year he was made Hofcompositeur there with a salary of 2000 gulden.

For the next five years Gluck's pattern of work was similar: he composed operas only for France, writing most of each work in Vienna and then travelling to Paris to finish it in close collaboration with his librettists and performers, and to supervise the rehearsals and early performances before returning home. In 1775 Gluck also made a new version of his one-act *opéra comique* *L'arbre enchanté* for a festival at Versailles in honour of Marie Antoinette's brother. Later that year another of Gluck's *opéras comiques*, *Cythère assiégée*, was performed at the Académie Royale in a greatly expanded version in three acts. Illness prevented the composer from attending the rehearsals and performances of the opera, which was not well received.

The following year Gluck took *Alceste* to Paris in a new and substantially altered French version with a translation and adaptation of Calzabigi's libretto by Roullet. After what was initially a mixed reception, Gluck and Roullet made further modifications including the addition of a part for Hercules, but Gluck had to return to Vienna before the new version was ready because his beloved adopted daughter had died, so he left the expansion of the final *divertissement* to Gossec.

In Vienna Gluck worked on settings of two librettos that Quinault had written for Lully, *Armide* and *Roland*. But according to a letter of July–August 1776, he burnt all that he had composed of *Roland* when he heard that the Italian composer Niccolò Piccinni had been invited to Paris by the Neapolitan ambassador as his rival, and furthermore had been given the same libretto to set by the Académie Royale. Opposing factions were quickly set up in Paris with the partisans of the two composers calling themselves the Gluckists and the Piccinnists, but the disputes that ensued were predominantly literary, initially centring on Gluck's opera *Armide*, first performed in September 1777, and Piccinni's *Roland*, given the following January.

The controversy continued with Gluck's last two Paris operas in 1779, as once again the Académie Royale tried to get Gluck and Piccinni into direct competition to compose operas on the same story, albeit with different librettos this time. In the event Gluck's *Iphigénie en Tauride*, with a libretto by Nicolas-François Guillard, was the first to be performed, in May 1779; Piccinni's version had to wait until January 1781. Gluck's was a great public success, unlike his other opera to have its Académie Royale première in 1779, *Echo et Narcisse*, to a libretto by Baron Ludwig Theodor von Tschudi. Gluck had a stroke during the rehearsals for the latter work; that, together with the opera's failure and the continued squabbling and cabals of the opposing factions, resulted in his leaving Paris for the last time in October 1779.

Back in Vienna, Gluck contemplated a German opera and also a setting of Klopstock's *Hermannschlacht*, portions of which he played to Charles Burney but which appear never to have been written down. He did, however, make a German version of *Iphigénie en Tauride* for performance in Vienna in 1781, to a translation of the libretto by Johann Baptist Edler von Alxinger. In 1783 Gluck was invited to London to produce some of his operas at the King's Theatre, but another stroke prevented his going, and he remained in Vienna, where he lived in great style and died in 1787 after defying his doctor and drinking a liqueur.

5. OPÉRAS COMIQUES. Gluck's goals in composing French comic operas changed several times during his decade as musical director of the French theatre in Vienna. Though at first he was required by Durazzo merely to supervise the arrangement of imported Parisian works and contribute replacement *ariettes*, in 1758 he began composing complete original scores in the genre – a task more worthy of his talents, according

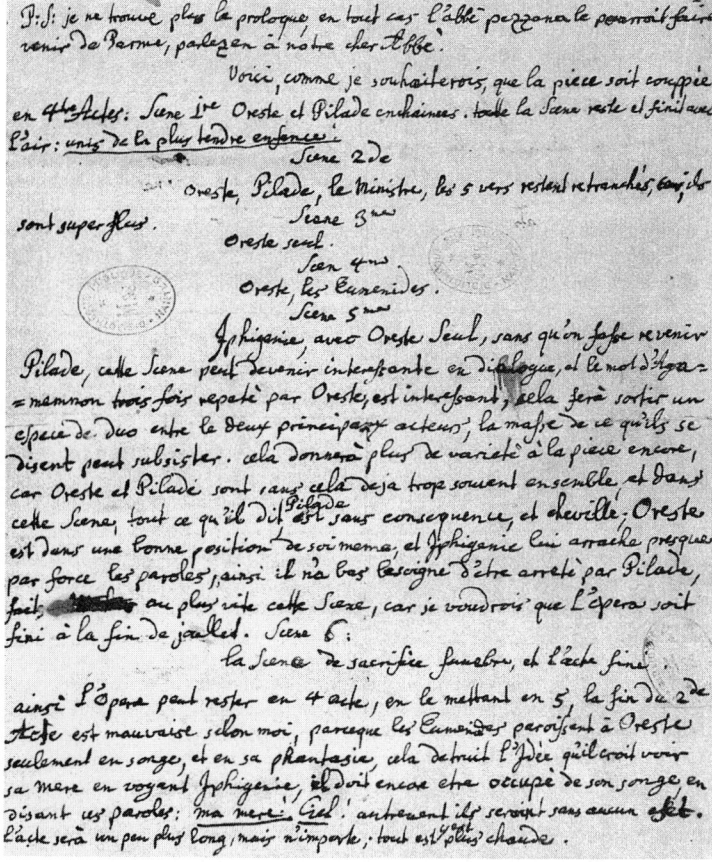

1. Part of an autograph letter (17 June 1778) from Gluck to his librettist N.-F. Guillard containing the composer's proposals for reshaping Act 2 of 'Iphigénie en Tauride' as part of his plan to tighten the dramatic action by condensing the opera from five to four acts

to his later collaborator L. H. Dancourt. Gluck's first *opéras comiques* were seen as curiosities, for though the relatively new genre was popular throughout Europe, few original works were then being written outside Paris. Initially, Gluck's resettings of Parisian texts suffered from court-imposed censorship, and in the pasticcio *Le diable à quatre* (1759) his anonymous 'airs nouveaux' still rubbed shoulders with parodied Italian *ariettes*. But soon his works were competing successfully on the stage of the Viennese Burgtheater with the most recent operas by Duni, Monsigny and Philidor. Gluck did not seriously envisage having his *opéras comiques* staged in Paris – though performances of two of his works in the genre were an incidental result of his visits to the Opéra in the 1770s. This was due in part to the prejudice in France against resettings of operas by living composers; those of Gluck's comic operas that were given in Paris had started as vaudeville comedies. The unavailability in Vienna of original *opéra comique* texts was a serious handicap; *La rencontre imprévue, ou Les pèlerins de la Mecque* (1764), the one work for which a professional librettist (Dancourt) was on hand, was a revision of a 1726 text chosen in consideration of the poet's old-fashioned tastes. Still, in *L'ivrogne corrigé* (1760) Gluck was able to insist on improvements in the Parisian libretto by Louis Anseaume (originally set by J.-L. Laruette) and thereby to create a mock hell scene of impressive musical architecture. Skills developed in writing this comic opera were of much help to Gluck in the composition of *Orfeo ed Euridice* in 1762. Circumstances suggest that as early as 1763 Durazzo was working to bring about a performance of the latter opera at the Paris Opéra.

Critics described Gluck's earliest *opéras comiques* as italianate, and indeed echoes of Pergolesi are to be found in several of them. The multi-sectional act finales in *La rencontre imprévue* likewise have their origin in *opera buffa*. But *Cythère assiégée* of 1759 – Favart's parody of Quinault and Lully's *Armide*, which Gluck was later to reset for Paris – demonstrates his quick mastery of French declamation and musical style. Gluck imitated both the newly composed *ariettes* (with frequent under-appoggiaturas, or *ports-de-voix*, and *inégal* rhythms), and the traditional vaudeville melodies (notably in *L'arbre enchanté* (1759) and *L'ivrogne corrigé*). Yet Gluck remained largely immune to certain Parisian trends in the genre, such as the use of the *romance* and large ensemble numbers. Tonic-accented rhythms characteristic of Gluck's Bohemian homeland are prominent in both *Cythère assiégée* and *L'arbre enchanté*, though they were mostly excised when these operas were brought to Paris in 1775. In other respects, too, Gluck made use in his *opéras comiques* of musical resources unavailable to composers working at the Opéra-Comique in Paris: 'Turkish' music (in *Le cadi dupé* and *La rencontre imprévue*), large choral forces (in *Cythère assiégée*) and italianate coloratura (*La rencontre imprévue*).

The influence of Gluck's *opéras comiques* extended well beyond Vienna. Habsburg connections ensured that his works were well known in Brussels in the Austrian Netherlands, and performances of *Cythère assiégée* at the court of Mannheim in 1759 earned him a large tun 'full of excellent wine' from the elector, according to Burney. Both *Le cadi dupé* and *La rencontre imprévue* circulated widely in German translation, and served as models for Singspiel composers in Austria (e.g. Gluck's protégé Dittersdorf), southern Germany and even northern Germany. *La rencontre imprévue* was translated (by Carl Friberth) as an *opera buffa* and set by Haydn for Eszterháza in 1775. A Viennese revival (in German) in the early 1780s provided much of the inspiration for Mozart's *Die Entführung aus dem Serail*, in which many of the same cast members sang.

Gluck himself was able to re-use much music from his Viennese *opéras comiques* (and ballets) in composing *tragédies lyriques* for Paris. The two genres were in any case rapidly converging – as Philidor implicitly demonstrated in plagiarizing from *Orfeo ed Euridice* in his *opéra comique Le sorcier* of 1764.

6. THE ITALIAN 'REFORM' OPERAS. The most important chapter in Gluck's composing career opens near the start of the 1760s, with the first performance (Burgtheater, Vienna, 1761) of the ballet-pantomime *Don Juan*, based on the Molière play. This première can conveniently be taken as point of departure for a movement initiated by a close group of artistic collaborators – Gluck, Angiolini (choreographer of *Don Juan*), Calzabigi (librettist of the three 'reform' operas, *Orfeo ed Euridice*, *Alceste*, and *Paride ed Elena*) – under the aegis of Count Durazzo. These men were united in their desire to revivify the serious musico-dramatic arts, to free them from the convention-bound complacency in which they seemed to be mired. One might fairly deem this group the Viennese avant garde of the day, the Establishment being represented by the composer Hasse and his longstanding friend and collaborator, the librettist Metastasio, both of whom were also prominent in the city's artistic activities at the time (the latter as court poet).

Since the reforming movement thus launched has tended to be discussed largely in the context of serious opera, it is perhaps worthwhile briefly insisting on its equal importance in the area of serious dance. *Don Juan* had one of the most talked-about premières of the day: it was initially found shocking and disturbing but soon became a popular success. In the longer perspective, it proved to be of the greatest significance in the history of the dance – every bit as significant, indeed, as the première (in the same theatre almost exactly a year later) of *Orfeo ed Euridice* was to prove in the history of opera. In both cases, a work of extraordinary simplicity of outline and directness of dramatic impact came to stand (even if in too summary a fashion) for the starting-point of a whole artistic movement; in both cases, that movement had been fired by the self-same desire for the overhaul of artistic forms that had come to be seen as theatrically inert, and encumbered by moribund traditions. The only real difference is that, while it was the Italian *opera seria* that was seen as the target of reform, in the world of dance it was the high French ballet style, pioneered by Lully and subsequently disseminated throughout Europe.

It is perhaps also necessary to underline the creative importance to the process of operatic reform of Gluck's experience as composer for the dance (in 1759 he had succeeded Starzer as the composer responsible for producing ballet music for the two main Viennese theatres). If, indeed, after the first performance of *Orfeo* his creative energies tended to be directed principally towards works for the lyric theatre, the existence and nature of the ballets *Alessandro* (1764) and *Semiramis*

(1765) nevertheless throw light on Gluck's continuing interest in the dramatic potential of the medium; *Semiramis* (based on the Voltaire play), far shorter and more economical of means than *Don Juan*, is one of the most intensely and sustainedly theatrical of all his scores (as he implicitly acknowledged by later re-using most of it in *Iphigénie en Tauride*). It is noteworthy that both of his principal theatrical duties in the decade preceding the era of reform – as composer of ballet music, and composer and expander of *opéras comiques* – should have thrown up important artistic links with Paris, and at the same time should have directed Gluck (since the mid-1750s under the protection and benevolent, forward-looking gaze of the passionate francophile Durazzo) towards the compression and reduction to theatrical essentials of all his musical techniques. The French musico-theatrical forms, whether of aristocratic or popular descent, had always had as their overall aim a 'continuous' command of theatre, a unity of dramatic purpose ordering the relationship of all component parts. After playing an increasingly significant (albeit tangential) part in the development of the French popular operatic form, and after subsequently aiding in the creation of a new, French-inspired dance-drama form, it is hardly a surprise if in his attempt to do the same for the recalcitrant *opera seria* Gluck should claim principles – set down in words in the preface to the edition of *Alceste* (1769) – which were obviously French-influenced.

The statement of these principles (trans. E. Blom, quoted in Einstein 1936) takes the form of a closely argued attack on the abuses to which *opera seria* had become prey (*mutatis mutandis*, it could serve equally well as the manifesto for the reform of the dance for which both Angiolini and his great rival Jean-Georges Noverre – with whom Gluck was to collaborate on the dances for *Alceste* – claimed the credit):

When I undertook to write the music for *Alceste*, I resolved to divest it entirely of all those abuses, introduced into it either by the mistaken vanity of singers or by the too great complaisance of composers, which have so long disfigured Italian opera and made of the most splendid and beautiful of spectacles the most ridiculous and wearisome. I have striven to restrict music to its true office of serving poetry by means of expression and by following the situations of the story, without interrupting the action or stifling it with a useless superfluity of ornaments; and I believe that it should do this in the same way as telling colours affect a correct and well-ordered drawing, by a well-assorted contrast of light and shade which serves to animate the figures without altering the contours. Thus I did not wish to arrest an actor in the greatest heat of dialogue in order to wait for a tiresome ritornello, nor to hold him up in the middle of a word on a vowel favourable to his voice, nor to make display of the agility of his fine voice in some long-drawn passage, nor to wait while the orchestra gives him time to recover his breath for a cadenza. I did not think it my duty to pass quickly over the second section of an aria of which the words are perhaps the most impassioned and important, in order to repeat regularly four times over those of the first part, and to finish the aria where its sense may perhaps not end for the convenience of the singer who wishes to show that he can capriciously vary a passage in a number of guises; in short, I have sought to abolish all the abuses against which good sense and reason have long cried out in vain.

I have felt that the overture ought to apprise the spectators of the nature of the action that is to be represented and to form, so to speak, its argument; that the concerted instruments should be introduced in proportion to the interest and the intensity of the words, and not leave that sharp contrast between the aria and the recitative in the dialogue, so as not to break a period unreasonably nor wantonly disturb the force and heat of the action.

Furthermore, I believed that my greatest labour should be devoted to seeking a beautiful simplicity, and I have avoided making displays of difficulty at the expense of clearness; nor did I judge it desirable to discover novelties if it was not naturally suggested by the situation and the expression; and there is no rule which I have not thought it right to set aside willingly for the sake of an intended effect.

What Gluck – and Calzabigi, who is thought to have played a crucial part in the formulation of the preface – were clearly aiming for was not the destruction of *opera seria* for its own sake, rather the revitalization of its theatrical potential. Such a manifesto was not new. (The content of Algarotti's *Saggio sopra l'opera in musica* of 1755 prefigures that of the *Alceste* preface so often and so closely as to suggest that it was a text known to members of the Durazzo group.) Nor, in the Age of Enlightenment, was the plea for lucidity, dramatic coherence, and freedom from outmoded display without precedent. As Winton Dean wrote, 'The three Italian reform operas in which Gluck collaborated with Calzabigi were not quite the bolt from the blue they appear in the selective light of historical memory. Rather they crystallized existing tendencies, fortified by the hand of genius' – tendencies already apparent, even if discontinuously so, in the pre-*Orfeo* Gluck himself, and in the *opera seria* composers of the day, Traetta (whose mature works, directly influenced by Rameau's *tragédies lyriques*, were well known to Gluck) and Jommelli foremost among them. The French influence in *Orfeo* is detectable in the expanded importance of the chorus and the ballet movements (forbidden in the Metastasian *opera seria*, even though the greatest of Handel's Italian operas had already broken that rule), the removal of *secco* recitative, and the construction of the acts in massive tableaux. In the end, however, the revolutionary significance of this work lies less in its fully successful grafting together of French and Italian forms and styles, important though that undoubtedly is, than in its purpose in effecting this graft – to achieve for serious opera the same unremitting concentration of musical effect for dramatic purpose that in *Don Juan* had been achieved for serious dance.

There can be little doubt that *Orfeo* was intended to startle. It was written for the name-day of Emperor Franz; its cast-list (three soloists) and duration (little more than an hour) might reasonably have aroused in the uninitiated first-night audience expectations of a *pièce d'occasion* along the lines of, say, Gluck's *Le cinesi* or *La danza*. Instead, the opera strikes hard against traditional *festa teatrale* or pastoral-opera formula. Not immediately: the overture – 'cette incroyable niaiserie', Berlioz was to call it – does not 'apprise the spectators' in the manner prescribed by the *Alceste* preface; this and the conventional *lieto fine* must be seen as concessions to the occasion for which the opera was produced.

There are no others. The start of Act 1 plunges the listener into a world of mourning, evoked by 14 bars of grave C minor orchestral sinfonia and then the solemnly simple choral ensemble, thrice pierced by Orpheus's four-note cry of 'Euridice!' This is all that is needed to summarize the dramatic situation. The close contrast of solo and choral voices may not itself count as a new effect (there are notable parallels in Rameau's *Castor et Pollux* and *Hippolyte et Aricie*), yet in context, and in employment at the very opening, it amounts here to a new operatic invention. Similar points may be made about Gluck's use of the offstage instrumental ensemble during Orpheus's first aria, 'Chiamo il mio ben', the punctuation with repeated choral cries of 'No!' of his pleas to the denizens of Hades, and the picturesque single-strand instrumental elaboration of the heavenly vista unfolding before him in the second scene of Act 2. These are just three examples

among many of simple musical effects sharpened to an unprecedentedly high pitch of dramatic significance by their placing, and by the exact balance achieved between them and the larger dramatic progression: a possible definition of the phrase 'bella simplicità'.

Indeed, the relationship of the parts to the whole was a central concern of Gluck's reformist principles. This accounts for his insistence on the abandonment of formal conventions and stage traditions (such as the strict repetition of da capo sections and the cultivation of vocal bravura *per se*) which might obfuscate that relationship, in order to concentrate on the development of a dramatic subject. Each of the three Viennese reform operas focusses, unwaveringly and with the complete elimination of any Metastasian subplot, on a single dramatic idea. The *tragedia per musica Alceste*, second of the three, is in many ways the fullest demonstration of these principles. This is in spite of the return to passages of *secco* recitative (in apparent contradiction of the opera's preface), the reduced dramatic function of the dance and pantomime movements, and the readmission of confidant roles; in some respects *Alceste* may be said to demonstrate the disadvantages of those principles, being pivoted so completely on the noble, grief-struck defiance of the leading character, and (until the descent of the *deus ex machina* and the *lieto fine*) being occupied so much of the time with mournful or elegiac moods of musical expression. Gluck's and Calzabigi's adaptation from Euripides was ruthless, designed in particular to remove the dramatic contrasts – inadmissible in their new, purified vision of opera – provided by Hercules, a comic as well as heroic figure, and by the treatment of Admetus as a vacillating weakling. The result of such paring down, with Alcestis the essence of heroic courage combined with wifely and maternal tenderness, Admetus a distraught husband, and the god Apollo descending to return Alcestis to life, may indeed have led to the 'bella simplicità' Gluck sought. It also led, in the final act, to an inability to discover any further dramatic impetus in a plot all but resolved the moment Alcestis determines to sacrifice her life for her husband's.

On the other hand, no other serious 18th-century opera creates so monumental a musico-dramatic structure, or sustains it with so complete a reliance on simple tableau formula (the Act 1 scene i alternation with internal repetition of choral and solo episodes provides a typical example); in no other serious 18th-century opera is there so comprehensively demanding a title role. The Vienna *Alceste* remains a 'special case' even among Gluck operas (perhaps its peculiar combination of grandeur and largely unbroken sombreness of atmosphere was in some measure dictated by the *Zeitgeist*: two years before its première the Emperor Franz had died, and the paroxysms of grief, extravagant and long-lasting, suffered by his widow, Maria Theresa, infected the mood of the entire empire). When, nine years later, Gluck came to adapt the work for Paris (as earlier he had done with *Orfeo*), he made the structures much less massively uniform – the interposition of the electrifying choral outcry, 'Dieux, rendez-nous notre roi, notre père!', at the end of the overture may stand as a single example among many of the changes effected (but the Act 3 problem, which the unprepared late introduction of Hercules was intended to address, was never solved). Much was gained by the Paris changes, and a fair amount lost. In the words of Julian Rushton, '*Alceste*, in its original form, is at once Gluck's greatest achievement and his most intolerable ... [it] stands as

2. Autograph score of part of Orpheus's aria 'Ah! La flamme qui me dévore' from Act 2 scene i of Gluck's 'Orphée et Eurydice', revised in 1774 for performance in August at the Académie Royale de Musique, Paris

the purest achievement of Neoclassicism in music drama'.

In the third and last of his collaborations with Calzabigi, *Paride ed Elena*, Gluck attempted to infuse the structural grandeur of *Alceste* (and in particular the greatly increased importance of the choral contributions) with the pastoral intimacy and emotional warmth of *Orfeo*. In this respect, *Paride* may also be said to continue the line of 'erotic' operas – those centrally concerned with the power, sublime and destructive in equal measure, of sexual love – which Gluck had in some respects begun with his 1765 *opera seria Telemaco*, and which he was to conclude with the Paris operas *Armide* and *Echo et Narcisse*. *Paride* is a musically richer work than either of its 'reform' predecessors – more varied in its moods and colour resources (as Gluck himself suggested in the opera's preface), more abundant in its melodic content, with a concentration upon distinctness of vocal characterization that alleviates any threat of monotony in the casting of all four principal roles for soprano (Paris, like Orpheus, having been written for a castrato). It was not a popular success in Vienna; this failure, reflected in the rarity of its subsequent revival, may perhaps be ascribed to the relatively longwinded treatment of the central plot, the wooing by the ardently romantic Trojan Paris of the severe Spartan Helen (Einstein described the libretto as 'shilly-shallying ... prolonged over five acts').

The very existence of *Telemaco* – composed, like the ballet *Sémiramis* and the *serenata teatrale Il Parnaso*

confuso (on a Metastasio libretto), in celebration of the 1765 wedding of the future Emperor Joseph II – indicates that Gluck's concentration on the aims of reform was by no means unbroken. Between the premières of *Orfeo* and *Alceste*, and in addition to the 1765 works mentioned above, he undertook (among other things) settings of two other Metastasio librettos, *Il trionfo di Clelia* (1763) and *La corona* (1765, unperformed). Any charge of backsliding would be inappropriate. As a practical man of the theatre who had reached his position of eminence by fulfilling the commissions of royal and aristocratic patrons, not to mention being one of the most astute businessmen in operatic history, Gluck had learnt to take the temperature of his audiences, actual and potential – and could therefore judge, for instance, that his audience at Bologna (for whom *Il trionfo di Clelia* was written) was unlikely to prove a fruitful testing-ground for any openly intimated notions of reform. Nevertheless, the marks of compositional maturity can be recognized on all the Gluck works of this period; it is indeed arguable that *Telemaco*, which contains many remarkable passages (most of which, characteristically, Gluck was to re-use in his Paris operas), should be added to the list of reform operas. Strictly speaking, it cannot be, for the response to the da capo aria form is uneven, and the recitative varies inconsistently from dry *secco* to dramatically impassioned *accompagnato*; the drama suffers from an ill-shaped and poorly motivated libretto with a profusion of loose threads in the subplots. But the instances of forward-looking musical invention are plentiful (in, for instance, the flexible treatment of ensembles and short ariosos and the contrast of solo and choral voices). The acute, fiery musical characterization of the sorceress Circe makes her a direct ancestress of Gluck's Armide.

7. THE PARIS OPERAS. Force of circumstance may have led Gluck to Paris to complete his operatic career, but in artistic terms Paris can be seen as his inevitable final destination. His years of grounding in *opéra comique* and the ballet and (via Traetta) his response to the French *tragédie lyrique* tradition had already provided the impetus for his overhaul of the *opera seria*; now it was time to confront that tradition on its own territory. On more than one occasion, indeed, Gluck explicitly owned the French influence, and its particular effect on his preparation for Paris. Between them the eight operas that he produced for the Académie Royale de Musique in Paris – the two *Iphigénie* operas; the radical revisions for Paris of the Vienna 'reform' operas *Orfeo* and *Alceste*; the similar revisions of the Vienna *opéras comiques Cythère assiégée* and *L'arbre enchanté*; *Armide*, a new opera on a libretto that Quinault had written for Lully more than 90 years earlier; and the last opera, *Echo et Narcisse* – are all different attempts at the confrontation and revival of that lyric tradition.

The French finale of Gluck's career amounts, in truth, to an act of reform as thoroughgoing as any he had achieved in Vienna. It could be said that the impact he made in Paris, after a difficult initial period marked by open hostility, was more widespread, and its consequences were longer-lasting. There could be no question of any lack of sympathy with the dramatic possibilities of the *tragédie lyrique* form; its potential for long-lined, through-composed, dramatically integrated structures could only have proved thoroughly congenial to his mature tastes and capacities. As he himself declared, describing his period of readying himself for *Iphigénie en Aulide*, 'In looking through the scores of our old operas, despite the trills, cadenzas and other defects with which their *airs* seemed to me to be burdened, I found therein a sufficient number of real beauties to become convinced that the French had their own resources ready to hand (on which I might draw)'. The problem that he faced in Paris, rather, was one of performing standards – solo vocal, choral, instrumental, scenographic – in deep decline. His task was to convert the Paris Opéra from (in Rushton's words) 'a museum into a place of musical novelty and dramatic vitality'; and in successfully accomplishing it he simultaneously brought about the renewal of the *tragédie lyrique* tradition. During the months of rehearsal required before the first night of *Iphigénie en Aulide*, Gluck's demands on his performers were exigent, sometimes abrasive, occasionally furious; he brooked no argument, and dominated every facet of the relationship with his librettists – the subordinate role adopted in the earlier years of *opera seria* and *opéra comique* composition, and the equal partnership with Calzabigi, were things of the past. In Paris, Gluck established the composer as driving force in the creation of any opera.

Each of the *tragédies lyriques* manifests a particular aspect in the renewal of the French tradition. The first *Iphigénie* opera and the Paris *Alceste* can be reckoned formally the most traditional; the construction of the acts by means of tableaux made up of small component units – solo airs, choruses and dance movements – would have been recognizable to Rameau, however

shocking he might have found Gluck's much plainer scoring and melodic style. *Armide*, even if to some extent prepared for by the Paris version of *Orfeo*, with its added ballets and enlarged final *divertissement*, may be deemed the most vital challenge to the traditions of Lully and Rameau: though this opera is weakened by the loose construction of Quinault's libretto, with its fourth act entirely devoted to a subplot episode involving characters of minor importance, the *merveilleux* and dance elements play a larger and more tightly integrated part in its dramaturgy than in any of Gluck's other Paris operas. *Armide* is perhaps the most original and certainly the most underrated of all Gluck's mature works (in retirement he pronounced it 'perhaps the best of all my works'); it is an opera of peculiar, Janus-like character, charged with its own raptly romantic atmosphere, looking back with disciplined reverence to the great French operatic past while for long stretches simultaneously looking forward to the 19th-century ideal of 'continuous' opera. The title role is the most fully rounded and detailed of all Gluck's female portraits; and its shattering final scene – Armide's razing to the ground of her palace in lovetorn fury – provides the single truly climactic close of any Gluck opera.

In all these works, but perhaps most completely in the second *Iphigénie* opera, Gluck's control of means – flexible declamation, expressively economical use of orchestral and vocal colour – and his acute reconciliation of the demands of music and libretto are at their peak of concentrated effectiveness. (The fine quality of all the Paris librettos, apart from the wordy, inexpertly balanced *Echo et Narcisse*, is of crucial significance in the achievement.) All contain large amounts of self-borrowed material; yet their unfailingly exact deployment leads to an appropriately unfailing seamlessness of tone and style. *Iphigénie en Tauride* is full of such recyclings, although, 'Paradoxically, Gluck's most consistent opera is in some senses an anthology of his best ideas over nearly thirty years' (Andrew Porter): no more than a single example – the fact that the music of the second-act *air* 'O malheureuse Iphigénie!', the opera's emotional peak, is almost identical with that of the aria 'Se mai senti' from his *La clemenza di Tito* of 1752 – is needed to demonstrate the point.

The Paris operas, each different in *tinta* and *colorito* (to borrow the Verdian terminology), are also all united by the modernity of their psychological perception, their depth of characterization; to this end Gluck always showed himself ready to undercut or reshape his monumental forms for the purposes of increased dramatic voltage. He is the master of the stripped-bare moment in which a single note or chord, or (in, say, Orestes' 'Le calme rentre dans mon coeur', a passage spiked with the sharpest dramatic irony) a single much-repeated rhythmic pattern, can be made to resonate with the utmost dramatic significance. Even in *Echo et Narcisse*, Gluck's belated return to a pastoral mode of music drama, and the failure that brought to an end his theatrical career, the complexity and subtlety of dramatic perception, realized in music of infinite plastic simplicity, is demonstrated in such passages as Narcissus's wakening from delusion – Einstein deemed his aria 'Beaux lieux, témoins de mon ardeur' 'one of the summits of Gluck's penetration into the human soul'. Such a scene, alongside numerous others from the great *tragédies lyriques*, make it clear that, while Gluck's new vision of opera was unfolded and developed in Vienna, it was in Paris that he achieved its fulfilment.

8. HISTORICAL POSITION, INFLUENCE. Gluck's historical importance rests on his establishment of a new equilibrium between music and drama, his greatness on the power and clarity with which he projected this vision. He simplified both components, but his simplicity is far from artless. It depends to an exceptional degree on consciousness of his own limitations. No composer was ever more adept at turning weaknesses of technique (sketchy counterpoint, occasional thin textures, unadventurous basses) to profitable account. By his choice of subjects he almost turned them into assets: the slenderness of his musical endowment corresponded to the direct impact he sought to convey. His copious self-borrowings and his masterly use of cliché reflect the same economy and self-knowledge. Hence, by only a superficial paradox, his music makes heavy demands on his interpreters; no other great composer's work can sound so impoverished when insensitively performed.

Gluck founded no school, though that was his declared hope. Only a successor with equal powers of discrimination and self-criticism, which the most prominent of his immediate followers, Salieri, scarcely commanded, could have continued his work. But his operas had considerable, if diffused, influence on the subsequent development of the art. His late works re-animated the moribund *tragédie lyrique*, stiffened into immobility since the days of Rameau, and left their mark on Cherubini, Méhul and Spontini, though the most important work of the first two lay in a revitalized *opéra comique*, and Spontini's links were rather with the less concentrated classicism of Piccinni. Mozart, who attended nearly all the rehearsals of the Vienna production of *Iphigénie en Tauride* in 1781, learnt much from Gluck, though his own immeasurably greater creative gifts have obscured the debt. The parallels between *Die Entführung* and *La rencontre imprévue* reach further than the similarity of their plots. Gluck's *Don Juan* ballet left a superficial impression on *Figaro*, whose fandango is related to it, and a deeper one on *Don Giovanni*. *Idomeneo* strikes the same note of classical grandeur and the same blend of *opera seria* and *tragédie lyrique* as Gluck's last operas, of which it is the single worthy successor. Perhaps the most interesting link is to be found in the masonic scenes of *Die Zauberflöte*, where the March of the Priests bears a striking resemblance, in mood and material, to the chorus 'Chaste fille de Latone' in Act 4 of *Iphigénie en Tauride*.

Gluck's more distant heirs, though of course he was not their only forebear, were Wagner and Berlioz. Wagner's enthusiasm, which led him to a not very sensitive rewriting of *Iphigénie en Aulide*, was naturally evoked by the fluid forms of Gluck's later operas, whose subordination of regular musical periods to the forward progress of the drama had no rival, apart from *Euryanthe*, before his own innovations. Berlioz, a fanatical admirer, possessed a deeper spiritual kinship with Gluck. The elevated classicism of *Les Troyens*, appealing directly to the listener's experience of myth, including its literary associations, reproduces much of the mingled detachment and passionate involvement characteristic of the Iphigenia operas. Certain passages in Gluck, such as the repeated note of menace from the horns and the chorus's hollow octave unisons against seething orchestral textures in Alcestis's Act 3 confrontation with the infernal spirits, left echoes in the mature Berlioz. By adapting *Orfeo*, in default of castratos, for the contralto Pauline Viardot, Berlioz showed a finer perception of Gluck's true qualities than Wagner in his dealings with *Iphigénie en Aulide*.

Gluck's stature however is not to be measured by his influence. One of the major issues raised by the controversy between his supporters and those of Piccinni was the relative merit of opera in which the composer accommodates his design to the drama and opera in which he imposes a musical plan based on formal treatment of aria and ensemble. Strauss treated one aspect of that polarity in *Capriccio*, an opera set in Gluck's period. Neither approach is invalid; indeed the history of opera is largely the history of the shifting balance between the two. The compromise struck by Gluck was one of the most satisfying and successful of all, and has placed his greatest works beyond the reach of time.

See also ALCESTE (ii); ARBRE ENCHANTÉ, L'; ARMIDE (ii); CADI DUPÉ, LE; CINESI, LE; CYTHÈRE ASSIÉGÉE; DIABLE À QUATRE, LE; ECHO ET NARCISSE; FAUSSE ESCLAVE, LA; ILE DE MERLIN, L'; IPHIGÉNIE EN AULIDE; IPHIGÉNIE EN TAURIDE (i); IVROGNE CORRIGÉ, L'; ORFEO ED EURIDICE (i); PARIDE ED ELENA; RENCONTRE IMPRÉVUE, LA; and TELEMACO.

Edition: *C. W. Gluck: sämtliche Werke*, ed. R. Gerber, G. Croll and others (Kassel and Basle, 1951–) [G]

title	genre, acts	libretto	first performance	sources; remarks	G
Artaserse	dm, 3	P. Metastasio	Milan, Regio Ducal, 26 Dec 1741	aria *CH-BEl*, aria *GB-Lbl*	
Demetrio [Cleonice]	dm, 3	Metastasio	Venice, S Samuele, 2 May 1742	arias *B-Bc*, arias *CH-BEl*	
Demofoonte	dm, 3	Metastasio	Milan, Regio Ducal, 6 Jan 1743	*B-Bc*, arias *CH-BEl*; vs of Act 1, ed. J. Tiersot (Leipzig, 1914)	
Il Tigrane	dm, 3	C. Goldoni, after F. Silvani: *La virtù trionfante dell'amore, e dell'odio*	Crema, 26 Sept 1743	11 arias *B-Bc*, 1 duet *CH-BEl*	
La Sofonisba	dm, 3	Silvani, with aria texts by Metastasio	Milan, Regio Ducal, 18 Jan 1744	10 arias, 1 duet *BEl*	
Ipermestra	dm, 3	Metastasio	Venice, S Giovanni Grisostomo, 21 Nov 1744	*GB-Lbl*	
Poro	dm, 3	Metastasio: *Alessandro nell'Indie*	Turin, Regio, 26 Dec 1744	sinfonia, 4 arias, 1 duet	
Ippolito	dm, 3	G. G. Corio	Milan, Regio Ducal, 31 Jan 1745	6 arias *B-Bc*, 1 duet	

title	genre, acts	libretto	first performance	sources; remarks	G
La caduta de' giganti	dm, 2	? F. Vanneschi	London, King's, 7 Jan 1746	5 arias, 1 duet (London, [1746])	
Artamene	dm, 3	?Vanneschi, after B. Vitturi	London, King's, 4 March 1746	6 arias (London, 1746)	
Le nozze d'Ercole e d'Ebe	dm, 2		Dresden, Pillnitz Castle (gardens), 29 June 1747	ed. H. Abert, DTB, xxvi, Jg.xiv/2 (1914)	
La Semiramide riconosciuta	dm, 3	Metastasio	Vienna, Burg, 14 May 1748	A-Wn, B-Bc; facs. in IOB, lxxiv (1982)	
La contesa de' numi	festa teatrale, 2	Metastasio	Copenhagen, Charlottenborg, 9 April 1749	Bc	
Ezio [1st version]	dm, 3	Metastasio	Prague, carn. 1750	Bc, GB-Lbl	iii/14
Issipile	dm, 3	Metastasio	Prague, carn. 1752	3 arias CH-BEl	
La clemenza di Tito	dm, 3	Metastasio	Naples, S Carlo, 4 Nov 1752	B-Bc, CH-BEl, D-B, F-Pn	
Le cinesi	azione teatrale, 1	Metastasio	Vienna, Schlosshof, 24 Sept 1754		iii/17
La danza	componimento pastorale, 1	Metastasio	Laxenburg (Vienna), 5 May 1755		iii/18
L'innocenza giustificata	festa teatrale, 1	G. Durazzo and Metastasio	Vienna, Burg, 8 Dec 1755	ed. A. Einstein, DTÖ, lxxxii, Jg.xliv (1937)	
rev. as La vestale			Vienna, Burg, sum. 1768		
Antigono	dm, 3	Metastasio	Rome, Argentina, 9 Feb 1756	B-Bc, CH-BEl, F-Pn	
Il rè pastore	dm, 3	Metastasio	Vienna, Burg, 8 Dec 1756		iii/21
La fausse esclave	oc, 1	after L. Anseaume and P. A. L. de Marcouville: La fausse aventurière	Vienna, Burg, 8 Jan 1758	A-Wn (vs), B-Bc	
L'île de Merlin, ou Le monde renversé	oc, 1	Anseaume, after A. R. Lesage and D'Orneval: Le monde renversé	Vienna, Schönbrunn, 3 Oct 1758		iv/1
Cythère assiégée [1st version]	oc, 1	C.-S. Favart, after Favart and C. B. Fagan: Le pouvoir de l'Amour ou Le siège de Cythère	Vienna, Burg, spr. 1759	A-Wn; rev. as opéra-ballet, 1775	
Le diable à quatre, ou La double métamorphose	oc, 3	M.-J. Sedaine and P. Baurans, after C. Coffey: The Devil to Pay	Laxenburg, 28 May 1759	D-Rtt	iv/3
L'arbre enchanté, ou Le tuteur dupé [1st version]	oc, 1	after J.-J. Vadé: Le poirier	Vienna, Schönbrunn, 3 Oct 1759	A-Wn (vs), B-Bc (vs), F-Po	
L'ivrogne corrigé [Der bekehrte Trunkenbold]	oc, 2	Anseaume and J.-B. Lourdet de Santerre	Vienna, Burg, April 1760		iv/5
Tetide	serenata, 2	G. A. Migliavacca	Vienna, Hofburg, 10 Oct 1760		iii/22
Le cadi dupé	oc, 1	after P.-R. Lemonnier	Vienna, Burg, 8 Dec 1761	A-Wn (vs), B-Bc (vs), D-Rtt; vs arr. F. Krastl and J. N. Fuchs, as Der betrogene Kadi (Leipzig, 1884)	
Orfeo ed Euridice	azione teatrale, 3	R. de' Calzabigi	Vienna, Burg, 5 Oct 1762	(Paris, 1764)	i/1
Il trionfo di Clelia	dm, 3	Metastasio	Bologna, Comunale, 14 May 1763	Bc (2 copies), CH-BEl	
Ezio [2nd version]	dm, 3	Metastasio	Vienna, Burg, 26 Dec 1763	CS-Pnm, D-B	iii/24
La rencontre imprévue	oc, 3	L. H. Dancourt, after Lesage and D'Orneval: Les pèlerins de la Mecque	Vienna, Burg, 7 Jan 1764	Ger. trans. as Die unvermuthete Zusammenkunft (Frankfurt, 1772)	iv/7
Il Parnaso confuso	serenata, 1	Metastasio	Vienna, Schönbrunn, 24 Jan 1765		iii/25
Telemaco, ossia L'isola di Circe	dm, 2	M. Coltellini, after C. S. Capece	Vienna, Burg, 30 Jan 1765		i/2
La corona	azione teatrale, 1	Metastasio	scheduled for 4 Oct 1765 but unperf.		iii/26
Il prologo	prol.	L. O. del Rosso	Florence, Pergola, 22 Feb 1767	ed. P. Graf Waldersee (Leipzig, 1891)	
Alceste	tragedia, 3	Calzabigi, after Euripides	Vienna, Burg, 26 Dec 1767	(Vienna, 1769); rev.	i/3a and b

title	genre, acts	libretto	first performance	sources; remarks	G
Le feste d'Apollo	prol., 3	C. I. Frugoni, Calzabigi, Pagnini and Pezzana	Parma, Corte, 24 Aug 1769	B-Bc, CH-BEl	
Paride ed Elena	dm, 5	Calzabigi	Vienna, Burg, 3 Nov 1770	(Vienna, 1770)	i/4
Iphigénie en Aulide	tragédie, 3	M. F. L. G. L. Roullet, after J. Racine, after Euripides	Paris, Opéra, 19 April 1774	(Paris, 1774)	i/5a and b
Orphée et Eurydice	tragédie opéra, 3	P. L. Moline, after Calzabigi	Paris, Opéra, 2 Aug 1774	(Paris, 1774); rev. of Orfeo ed Euridice, 1762	i/6
L'arbre enchanté [2nd version]		Moline, after Vadé	Versailles, 27 Feb 1775	B-Bc, F-Po	
Cythère assiégée [2nd version]	opéra-ballet, 3	Favart	Paris, Opéra, 1 Aug 1775	(Paris, 1775)	
Alceste	tragédie, 3	Roullet, after Calzabigi	Paris, Opéra, 23 April 1776	(Paris, 1776); rev. of Alceste, 1767	i/7
Armide	drame-héroïque, 5	P. Quinault, after T. Tasso: La Gerusalemme liberata	Paris, Opéra, 23 Sept 1777	(Paris, 1777)	i/8
Iphigénie en Tauride	tragédie, 4	N.-F. Guillard, after G. de La Touche, after Euripides	Paris, Opéra, 18 May 1779	(Paris, 1779)	i/9
Echo et Narcisse	drame lyrique, prol., 3	L. T. von Tschudi, after Ovid: Metamorphoses	Paris, Opéra, 24 Sept 1779; rev., Paris, Opéra, 8 Aug 1780	(Paris, 1780)	i/10
Iphigenie auf Tauris		J. B. E. von Alxinger and Gluck	Vienna, Burg, 23 Oct 1781	Ger. trans. and rev. of Iphigénie en Tauride, 1779	i/11

Music in: La finta schiava (Silvani), Venice, 1744; Tircis et Doristée (Favart), Laxenburg, 1756; La caprice amoureux, ou Ninette à la cour (Favart), Vienna, 1760; Arianna (Migliavacca), Laxenburg, 1762

Doubtful: Arsace (Salvi), Milan, 1743; Enea e Ascanio (componimento per musica), Frankfurt, 1764

CATALOGUES, BIBLIOGRAPHIES, LETTERS

A. Wotquenne: Catalogue thématique des oeuvres de C. W. v. Gluck (New York, 1904; suppl. 1911)

Gluck-Jb, i–iv, ed. H. Abert (Leipzig, 1913–18) [with bibliography by E. H. Müller (von Asow)]

W. Boetticher: 'Über Entwicklung und gegenwärtigen Stand der Gluck-Edition', AcM, xxx (1958), 99–112

C. Hopkinson: A Bibliography of the Printed Works of C. W. von Gluck 1714–1787 (London, 1959, 2/1967) [reviews in Mf, xiii (1960), 227–30; RdM, liii (1967), 195]

H. Müller von Asow and E. H. Müller von Asow, eds.: The Collected Correspondence and Papers of Christoph Willibald Gluck, trans. S. Thomson (London, 1962) [reviews in MT, ciii (1962), 230–31; Mf, xviii (1965), 469–71]

K. Hortschansky: 'Glucks Sendungsbewusstsein, dargestellt an einem unbekannten Gluck-Brief', Mf, xxi (1968), 30–35

H. Hammelmann and M. Rose: 'New Light on Calzabigi and Gluck', MT, cx (1969), 609–11

J. M. Kaplan: 'Eine Ergänzung zu Glucks Korrespondenz', Mf, xxxi (1978), 314–17

P. Howard: Christoph Willibald Gluck: a Guide to Research (New York, 1987)

BIOGRAPHIES, STUDIES OF LIFE AND WORKS

F. J. Riedel: Über die Musik des Ritters Christoph von Gluck (Vienna, 1775)

A. Schmid: Christoph Willibald Ritter von Gluck (Leipzig, 1854)

A. B. Marx: Gluck und die Oper (Berlin, 1863)

G. Desnoiresterres: Gluck et Piccinni: la musique française au XVIIIe siècle 1774–1800 (Paris, 1872, 2/1875)

E. Schuré: 'Gluck, créateur du drame musical', Le drame musical, i (Paris, 1875), 324–43

E. Thoinan: Notes bibliographiques sur la guerre musicale des Gluckistes et des Piccinnistes (Paris, 1878)

A. Reissmann: Gluck: sein Leben und seine Werke (Berlin, 1882)

C. H. Bitter: Die Reform der Oper durch Gluck und R. Wagners Kunstwerk der Zukunft (Brunswick, 1884)

E. Newman: Gluck and the Opera (London, 1895)

J. J. Khevenhüller-Metsch: Aus der Zeit Maria Theresias: Tagebuch (Vienna, Leipzig and Berlin, 1908–72) [1745–73, ed. R. Khevenhüller-Metsch and H. Schlitter; 1774–80, ed. M. Breunlich-Pawlik and H. Wagner]

J. C. von Mannlich: Ein deutscher Maler und Hofmann: Lebenserinnerungen 1741–1822 (Berlin, 1910; Fr. orig., 1948)

J. Tiersot: Gluck (Paris, 1910, 4/1919)

E. J. Dent: 'Italian Opera in the Eighteenth Century and its Influence on the Music of the Classical Period', SIMG, xiv (1912–13), 500–09

A. Heuss: 'Gluck als Musikdramatiker', ZIMG, xv (1913–14), 274–91

F. Vatielli: 'Riflessi della lotta Gluckista in Italia', RMI, xxi (1914), 639–74

E. H. Müller [von Asow]: 'Gluck und die Brüder Mingotti', Gluck-Jb, iii (1917), 1–14

J.-G. Prod'homme: 'Gluck's French Collaborators', MQ, iii (1917), 249–71

W. Vetter: Die Arie bei Gluck (diss., U. of Leipzig, 1920)

G. Cucuel: 'Les opéras de Gluck dans les parodies du XVIIIe siècle', ReM, iii (1922), nos.3–5, pp.210–21; nos.6–8, pp.51–68

W. Vetter: 'Gluck und seine italienischen Zeitgenossen', ZMw, vii (1924–5), 609–46; repr. in idem, Mythos-Melos-Musica, ii (Leipzig, 1961), 220–51

E. Blom: 'A Misjudged Composer', Stepchildren of Music (London, 1925), 57–66

H. Abert: 'Gluck, Mozart und der Rationalismus', Gesammelte Schriften, ed. F. Blume (Halle, 1929), 311–45

——: 'Mozart and Gluck', ML, x (1929), 256–65

J. Tiersot: 'Gluck and the Encyclopaedists', MQ, xvi (1930), 336–57

E. Istel: 'Gluck's Dramaturgy', MQ, xxvii (1931), 227–33

D. F. Tovey: 'Christoph Willibald Gluck (1714–1787) and the Musical Revolution of the Eighteenth Century', The Heritage of Music, ii, ed. H. J. Foss (Oxford, 1934), 69–117; repr. in Essays and Lectures on Music (London, 1949)

M. Cooper: Gluck (London, 1935)

A. Einstein: Gluck (London, 1936; Ger. orig., 1954)

H. J. Moser: Christoph Willibald Gluck: die Leistung, der Mann, das Vermächtnis (Stuttgart, 1940)

R. Gerber: Christoph Willibald Gluck (Potsdam, 1941, 2/1950)

W. Brandl: Christoph Willibald Ritter von Gluck (Wiesbaden, 1948)

J.-G. Prod'homme: Gluck (Paris, 1948, rev. 1985 with preface by J.-M. Fauquet)

R. Tenschert: Christoph Willibald Gluck (Olten and Freiburg, 1951)

R. C. Marek: *The Use of Harmonic Patterns of Similar Sonorities in the Music of Gluck, Mozart, Cherubini and Beethoven* (diss., U. of Rochester, NY, 1957)

A. A. Abert: *Christoph Willibald Gluck* (Munich, 1959)

K. Geiringer: 'Gluck und Haydn', *Festschrift Otto Deutsch zum 80. Geburtstag* (Kassel, 1963), 75–81

P. Howard: *Gluck and the Birth of Modern Opera* (London, 1963)

W. Felix: *Christoph Willibald Gluck* (Leipzig, 1965)

M. Robinson: *Opera Before Mozart* (London, 1966)

D. Heartz: 'From Garrick to Gluck: the Reform of Theatre and Opera in the Mid-Eighteenth Century', *PRMA*, xciv (1967–8), 111–27

E. Winternitz: 'A Homage of Piccinni to Gluck', *Studies in Eighteenth-Century Music: a Tribute to Karl Geiringer* (New York and London, 1970), 397–400

W. Baethge: *Philosophisch-ästhetische Untersuchungen zur Opern-Reform Christoph Willibald Glucks unter Berücksichtigung musik-ästhetischer Aspekte* (diss., U. of Halle, 1971)

G. Croll: 'Gluck und Mozart', *ÖMz*, xxviii (1973), 300–07

K. Hortschansky: *Parodie und Entlehnung im Schaffen Christoph Willibald Glucks*, AnMc, no.13 (1973)

R. Monelle: 'Gluck and the *Festa Teatrale*', *ML*, liv (1973), 308–25

Chigiana, xxix–xxx (1975), 235–592 [Gluck issue; incl. P. Gallarati: 'Metastasio e Gluck: per una collocazione storica della "riforma"', 299–308; K. Hortschansky: 'Gluck e la famiglia degli Absburgo Lorena', 571–83]

P. Gallarati: *Gluck e Mozart* (Turin, 1975)

F. Lesure: *Querelle des Gluckistes et des Piccinnistes* (Geneva, 1984) [facs. of orig. documents]

J. Rushton: 'The Musician Gluck', *MT*, cxxvi (1987), 615–18

Gluck in Wien: Vienna 1987 [incl. B. Junge Gluck – das musikdramatische Umfeld', 21–30; T. Antonicek: 'Glucks Existenz in Wien', 31–41; G. Buschmeier: '"Ezio" in Prag und Wien: Bemerkungen zu den beiden Fassungen von Glucks "Ezio"', 85–8; B. A. Brown: 'Gluck als Hauskomponist für das französische Theater in Wien', 89–99; S. Mauser: 'Musikalische Dramaturgie und Phänomene der Personencharakteristik in Glucks "Orfeo"', 124–30; P. Petrobelli: 'La concezione drammatico-musicale dell'"Alceste" (1767)', 131–8; G. Croll: 'Der "alte Gluck" und Mozart in Wien', 158–65; L. Somfai: 'Die Wiener Gluck-Kopisten – ein Forschungsdesiderat', 178–82]

K. Hortschansky, ed.: *Christoph Willibald Gluck und die Opernreform* (Darmstadt, 1989)

ITALIAN OPERAS TO 1760

M. Fürstenau: 'Die Oper "Ezio" von Gluck', *Berliner Musik-Zeitung Echo*, xix (1869), 157–76

——: 'Das Festspiel "Il Parnaso confuso" von Gluck', *Berliner Musik-Zeitung Echo*, xix (1869), 205–8

——: '*Le nozze d'Ercole e d'Ebe* von Gluck', *MMg*, v (1873), 2–3

F. Piovano: 'Un opéra inconnu de Gluck', *SIMG*, ix (1907–8), 231–81, 448 [on *Tigrane*]

E. Kurth: 'Die Jugendopern Glucks bis *Orfeo*', *SMw*, i (1913), 193–277

M. Arend: 'Glucks erste Oper "Artaxerxes"', *NZM*, Jg.82 (1915), 201–2

W. B. Squire: 'Gluck's London Operas', *MQ*, i (1915), 397–409

M. Arend: 'Das vollständige Textbuch zu Glucks "Tigrane"', *Die Stimme*, x (1915–16), 130–32

W. Vetter: 'Glucks Entwicklung zum Opernreformator', *AMw*, vi (1924), 165–219; repr. in idem, *Mythos-Melos-Musica*, ii (Leipzig, 1961), 180–219

R. Haas: 'Zwei Arien aus Glucks "Poro"', *Mozart-Jb*, iii (1929), 307–30

A. Einstein: 'Gluck's "La vestale"', *MMR*, lxvi (1936), 151–2

W. J. Weichlein: *A Comparative Study of Five Settings of Metastasio's Libretto 'La clemenza di Tito' (1734–1791)* (diss., U. of Michigan, 1956)

K. Hortschansky: 'Gluck und Lampugnani in Italien: zum Pasticcio *Arsace*', *AnMc*, no.3 (1966), 49–64

——: 'Doppelvertonungen in den italienischen Opern Glucks: ein Beitrag zu Glucks Schaffensprozess', *AMw*, xxiv (1967), 54–63, 133–44

——: 'Die Festaufführung fand nicht statt: Bemerkung zu Christoph Willibald Glucks *La corona* (1765)', *NZM*, Jg.129 (1968), 270–74

K. Geiringer: 'Zu Glucks Oper *Il Telemaco*', *GfMkB: Bonn 1970*, 400–02

K. Hortschansky: 'Unbekannte Aufführungsberichte zu Glucks Opern der Jahre 1748 bis 1765', *Jb des Staatlichen Institutes für Musikforschung Preussischer Kulturbesitz 1969* (1970), 19–37

——: '"Arianna" (1762), ein Pasticcio von Gluck', *Mf*, xxiv (1971), 407–11

——: 'Gluck nella *Gazzetta di Milano* 1742–1745', *NRMI*, vi (1972), 512–25

——: 'Unbekanntes aus Glucks "Poro" (1744)', *Mf*, xxvii (1974), 460–4

G. Croll: 'Glucks Debut am Burgtheater: *Semiramide riconosciuta* als Festoper für die Wiedereröffnung des Wiener Burgtheaters 1748', *ÖMz*, xxxi (1976), 194–202

G. Bimberg: 'Dramaturgische Strukturmomente in den "Ezio"-Opern von Händel und Gluck', *Georg Friedrich Händel als Wegbereiter der Wiener Klassik: Halle 1977*, 41–6

J. Joly: *Les fêtes théâtrales de Métastase à la cour de Vienne (1731–1767)* (Clermont-Ferrand, 1978)

R. Strohm: 'Coltellini/Gluck: "Il Telemaco" (1765)', *Die italienische Oper im 18. Jahrhundert* (Wilhelmshaven, 1979), 305–35

M. Loppert: 'Gluck's Chinese Ladies: an Introduction', *MT*, cxxv (1984), 321–5

G. Croll: 'Eine Premiere nach 222 Jahren: zur Aufführung von Metastasio–Glucks "La corona" im Schloss Schönbrunn', *ÖMz*, xlii (1987), 498–503

OPÉRAS-COMIQUES

A. Jullien: 'Les pèlerins de la Mecque', *La cour et l'Opéra sous Louis XVI* (Paris, 1878), 351–9

K. Grunsky: 'Die Pilger von Mekka', *Die Musik*, ix (1912), 169–71

G. Schünemann: 'Das angeblich von Gluck komponierte Schäferspiel *Die Maienkönigin*', *AMz*, xxxix (1912), 465–6

G. Cucuel: *Les créateurs de l'opéra-comique français* (Paris, 1914)

M. Arend: 'Die Ouvertüren zu Glucks *Cythère assiégée*', *ZMw*, iv (1921–2), 94–5

R. Haas: *Gluck und Durazzo im Burgtheater: die opéra-comique in Wien* (Vienna, 1925)

L. Holzer: 'Die komischen Opern Glucks', *SMw*, xiii (1926), 3–37

G. Croll: 'Neue Quellen zu Musik und Theater in Wien 1758 bis 1763: ein erster Bericht', *Festschrift Walter Senn zum 70. Geburtstag* (Munich, 1975), 8–12

H. Wirth: 'Gluck, Haydn und Mozart – drei Entführungs-Opern', *Opernstudien: Anna Amalie Abert zum 65. Geburtstag* (Tutzing, 1975), 25–35

D. Heartz: 'Haydn und Gluck im Burgtheater um 1760: Der neue krumme Teufel, Le diable à quatre, und die Sinfonie "Le soir"', *GfMKB: Bayreuth 1981*, 120–35

B. A. Brown: 'Gluck's *Rencontre imprévue* and its Revisions', *JAMS*, xxxvi (1983), 498–518

——: *Christoph Willibald Gluck and Opéra-Comique in Vienna, 1754–1764* (diss., U. of California, Berkeley, 1986)

——: '"Le Mandarin": an Unknown Gluck Opera?', *MT*, cxxviii (1987), 619–23

——: *Gluck and the French Theatre in Vienna* (Oxford, 1991)

ITALIAN REFORM OPERAS

C. G. A. Winterfeld: *'Alceste' 1674, 1726, 1769, 1776, von Lulli, Händel und Gluck* (Berlin, 1851)

M. Fürstenau: 'Glucks *Orpheus* in München 1773', *MMg*, iv (1872), 218–24

B. Gugler: 'Urform einer Nummer in Glucks *Orpheus*', *Leipziger allgemeine musikalische Zeitung*, xi (1876), 516–24

F. d'Arcais: 'L'*Orfeo* del Gluck', *Nuova antologia di scienze, lettere ed arti*, no.102 (1888), 111–23

H. Welti: 'Gluck und Calsabigi', *VMw*, vii (1891), 26–42

J. Tiersot: 'Etude sur *Orphée* de Gluck', *Le ménestrel*, lxii (1896), 273–385

W. Vetter: 'Stilkritische Bemerkungen zur Arienmelodik in Glucks *Orfeo*', *ZMw*, iv (1921–2), 27–50

H. W. von Walterhausen: *'Orpheus und Euridike': eine operndramaturgische Studie* (Munich, 1923)

H. Abert: 'Glucks *Alkestis* im Stuttgarter Landestheater', *ZMw*, vi (1923–4), 353–61

P. Bruck: 'Glucks *Orpheus*', *AMw*, vii (1925), 436–76

V. Helfert: 'Dosud neznámý dopis Ran. Calsabigiho z r. 1767' [A Hitherto Unknown Letter of Calzabigi from 1767], *Musikologie*, i (1938), 114–22 [letter to W. Kaunitz of 6 March 1767]

R. Müller-Hartmann: 'Wieland's and Gluck's Versions of the *Alkestis*', *Journal of the Warburg Institute*, ii/Oct (1938), 176–7

F. Rühlmann: 'Zur Wiederbelebung Glucks', *Festschrift Fritz Stein* (Brunswick, 1939), 161–82

A. Loewenberg: 'Gluck's *Orfeo* on the Stage with some Notes on other Orpheus Operas', *MQ*, xxvi (1940), 311–39

A. A. Abert: 'Der Geschmackswandel auf der Opernbühne am Alkestis-Stoff dargestellt', *Mf*, vi (1953), 214–35

J. Kerman: *Opera as Drama* (New York, 1956, 2/1989)

H. Rosendorfer: 'Wer hilft dem Ritter Gluck? Über die Bearbeitungen der Oper *Orpheus*', *NZM*, Jg.123 (1962), 449–51

L. Finscher: 'Der verstümmelte Orpheus: über die Urgestalt und die Bearbeitung von Glucks *Orfeo*', *NZM*, Jg.124 (1963), 7–10

——: '"Che farò senza Euridice?" Ein Beitrag zur Gluck-Interpretation', *Festschrift Hans Engel zum 70. Geburtstag* (Kassel, 1964), 96–110

——: 'Gluck und das *lieto fine*: über ein dramaturgisches Problem der heutigen Gluck-Pflege', *Musica*, xviii (1964), 296–301

H. Kaufmann: 'Orpheus zwischen Form und Ausdruck', *ÖMz*, xix (1964), 409–21

F. W. Sternfeld: 'Expression and Revision in Gluck's *Orfeo* and *Alceste*', *Essays Presented to Egon Wellesz* (Oxford, 1966), 114–29

P. Howard: '"Orfeo" and "Orphée"', *MT*, cviii (1967), 892–4

P. Petrobelli: 'L'*Alceste* di Calzabigi e Gluck: l'illuminismo e l'opera', *Quadrivium*, xii/2 (1971), 279–93

F. Degrada: '"Danze di eroi" e "saltarelli di burrattini": vicende dell'*Orfeo* di Gluck', *Il palazzo incantato: studi sulla tradizione del melodramma dal barocco al romanticismo*, i (Fiesole, 1972), 115–31

A. A. Abert: 'Die Bedeutung der opera seria für Gluck und Mozart', *MJb 1971–2*, 68–75

P. Howard: 'Gluck's Two Alcestes: a Comparison', *MT*, cxv (1974), 642–3

M. Loppert: '"Alceste" Reassessed', *Opera*, xxv (1974), 675–80

L'avant-scène opéra, no.23 (1979) [*Orfeo ed Euridice* issue]

P. Gallarati: 'L'*Orfeo ed Euridice* di Gluck: versione viennese del 1762 (Turin, 1979)

G. Paduano: 'La "costanza" di Orfeo: sul lieto fine dell'*Orfeo* di Gluck', *RIM*, xiv (1979), 349–77

P. Howard, ed.: *C. W. von Gluck: 'Orfeo'* (Cambridge, 1981)

L'avant-scène opéra, no.73 (1985) [*Alceste* issue]

FRENCH REFORM OPERAS

J. F. Reichardt: 'Etwas über Gluck und dessen *Armide*', *Berlinische musikalische Zeitung*, i (1805), 109–12

——: 'Etwas über Gluck Iphigenia in Tauris und dessen *Armide*', ibid, ii (1806), 57–60

C.-S. Favart: *Mémoires et correspondance*, ed. A. P. C. Favart and H. F. Dumolard (Paris, 1808)

J. Tiersot: 'L'ultima opera di Gluck: "Eco e Narciso"', *RMI*, ix (1902), 264–96

R. Rolland: 'Le dernier opéra de Gluck: *Echo et Narcisse* (1779)', *RHCM*, iii (1903), 212–15

A. Pougin: '*Armide*', *Le ménestrel*, lxxi (1905), 121–3

C. van Vechten: 'Notes on Gluck's "Armide"', *MQ*, iii (1917), 539–47

R. Sondheimer: 'Gluck in Paris', *ZMw*, v (1922–3), 165–75

G. Kinsky: 'Gluck's Reisen nach Paris', *ZMw*, viii (1925–6), 551–66

L. de La Laurencie: '*Orphée* de Gluck' (Paris, 1934)

A. Gastoué: 'Gossec et Gluck à l'Opéra de Paris: le ballet final de *Iphigénie en Tauride*', *RdM*, xvi (1935), 87–99

H. E. Johnson: *Iphigenia in Tauris as the Subject for French Opera* (diss., Cornell U., 1939)

L. Ronga: 'Dell'*Ifigenia in Aulide* e dello stile gluckiano', *RMI*, lvi (1954), 160–63

M. Hastings: 'Gluck's *Alceste*', *ML*, xxxvi (1955), 41–54

W. Weismann: 'Der deus ex machina in Glucks *Iphigenie in Aulis*', *DJbM*, vii (1962), 7–17

L. Finscher: 'Über die Originalfassung von Glucks *Orphée*', *Jb der Akademie der Wissenschaften in Göttingen 1968* (1969), 21–5

J. Rushton: *Music and Drama at the Académie Royale de Musique (Paris) 1774–1789* (diss., U. of Oxford, 1969)

O. F. Saloman: *Aspects of Gluckian Operatic Thought and Practice in France* (diss., Columbia U., 1970)

J. Rushton: '*Iphigénie en Tauride*: the Operas of Gluck and Piccinni', *ML*, liii (1972), 411–30

C. Dahlhaus: 'Ethos und Pathos in Glucks *Iphigenie auf Tauris*', *Mf*, xxvii (1974), 289–300

A. Stoll and K. Stoll: 'Affekt und Moral: zu Glucks *Iphigenie auf Tauris*', *Mf*, xxviii (1975), 305–11

C. Dahlhaus: 'War Schiller aus Missverständnis "zu Thränen gerührt"? Eine Erwiderung', *Mf*, xxix (1976), 72–3

F. Schneider: 'Texte und Kontexte in Glucks *Iphigenie auf Tauris*: Marginalien zur neuen Übersetzung für die Inszenierung an der Komischen Oper Berlin', *Musik und Gesellschaft*, xxvii (1977), 597–601

M. Noiray: *Gluck's Methods of Composition in his French Operas 'Iphigénie en Aulide', 'Orphée', 'Iphigénie en Tauride'* (diss., U. of Oxford, 1979)

J. Rushton: 'In Defence of the French Alceste', *MT*, cxxii (1981), 738–40

J. Hayes: 'Armide: Gluck's Most French Opera?' *MT*, cxxiii (1982), 408–10

P. Howard: 'Armide: a Forgotten Masterpiece', *Opera*, xxx (1982), 572–6

L'avant-scène opéra, no.62 (1984) [*Iphigénie en Tauride* issue]

C. Dahlhaus: 'Tragödie, tragédie, Reformoper: zur *Iphigenie in Aulis* von Euripides, Racine und Gluck', *Oper als Text: romanistische Beiträge zur Libretto-Forschung*, ed. A. Gier (Heidelberg, 1986), 95–100

G. Buschmeier: *Die Entwicklung von Arie und Szene in der französischen Oper von Gluck bis Spontini* (Tutzing, 1991)

J. Rushton: '"Royal Agamemnon": the Two Versions of Gluck's *Iphigénie en Aulide*', *Music and the French Revolution*, ed. M. Boyd (Cambridge, 1992), 15–36

JEREMY HAYES (1–4, bibliography), BRUCE ALAN BROWN (5), MAX LOPPERT (6, 7), WINTON DEAN (8)

Glückliche Hand, Die ('The Fortunate Hand'). *Drama mit Musik*, op. 18, in one act by ARNOLD SCHOENBERG to his own libretto; Vienna, Volksoper, 14 October 1924.

This work was begun in 1910, but much of the music, including the first and last of the four scenes, was not composed until 1912–13. Like its companion piece, *Erwartung*, it contains only one singing character. It is shorter, lasting only 20 minutes or so, but the action is far more complex, involving two mimed roles, a chorus and elaborate scenic effects synchronized with constantly changing coloured lighting. This last feature was also used by Kandinsky in *Der gelbe Klang*, but Schoenberg did not know about it at the time. His conception coincides with his own most intense period of activity as a painter.

At the beginning the protagonist (baritone) is discovered lying on the ground with a fabulous monster on his back. Through holes in the backcloth can be seen the disembodied faces of a chorus of 12 soloists, six women and six men. Partly singing and partly speaking they ask why he, though endowed with capacity for the spiritual, constantly renews his quest for an earthly happiness which always eludes him. A gust of vulgar music and mocking laughter off stage marks the transition to a different sphere of experience. The man stands up; he is ragged, scarred and bleeding. A young woman (silent) enters. He never looks at her but is aware of her presence and sings of his love. She offers him a goblet, but as he drinks her sympathy fades; a well-dressed gentleman (silent) enters and she goes to him. The man senses what has happened; she returns and kneels for forgiveness, but as he regains his happiness she retreats once more. He does not notice, and is now seen as a self-confident hero entering a rocky landscape indicated precisely but not naturalistically by colours and forms.

In one of two grottos workmen are busy. The man takes over and they show a hostility which does not lessen when he forges with miraculous dexterity a richly ornamented diadem and tosses it to them as a thing of small worth. A wind gets up and rises to a storm expressed by a long crescendo in both the orchestra and the lighting. It seems to emanate from the man himself who manifests ever-increasing pain. Suddenly it stops; the woman comes out of the second grotto with part of her dress torn away. The gentleman appears with the missing piece, throws it towards the man and leaves. The woman returns and picks it up. The man implores her to stay with him, but she escapes and kicks a large rock on to him from a height. The popular music and mocking laughter are heard again, the rock turns into the fabulous beast, the chorus reappears and the work closes where it began, at the point from which it is the man's fate to re-enact the same failures.

The title of the work is ambiguous, containing the ideas of both fortune and fate. Schoenberg ended a discussion of it by emphasizing the element of fate and citing the allusion in the final chorus to the man's efforts to seize what must inevitably slip from his grasp. He admitted to having felt impelled at that time to give expression to a certain pessimism, and indeed the despair of the man in *Die glückliche Hand* is unique in Schoenberg's long sequence of works concerned with spiritual ideals: whereas Moses, for instance, despairs at the impossibility of realizing them, the man, despite the prompting of the framing choruses, fails even to pursue them.

There is an autobiographical background to all this. Two years earlier Schoenberg's wife Mathilde had left him briefly for the painter Richard Gerstl and, although she had been persuaded to return, the situation had remained uneasy. At the same time Schoenberg had become increasingly distressed at the hostile reception of his music. Both these themes are clearly reflected in the symbolic action of the drama, and the music preserves, when expressing the man's plight, noticeably less detachment than in *Erwartung*. Schoenberg's aesthetic intention, however, was that the symbolism should be at least partly submerged in a more abstract conception which he called 'making music with the resources of the stage'. His idea was that movements, forms and colours should combine to produce artistic effects just as the constituent notes of music do. This is clearly difficult to realize, but the first production by Josef Turnau, with Fritz Stiedry conducting and Alfred Jerger as the man, was a considerable success, and Schoenberg was also pleased with another organized by Turnau in Breslau in 1928.

O. W. NEIGHBOUR

Glyndebourne. Opera house near Lewes, the county town of East Sussex, about 100 km south of London. John Christie (1882–1962), whose family owns the estate on which it stands, had the opera house built in 1934 and founded Glyndebourne Festival Opera that year.

Christie initially designed the house, seating 311, for his wife, the soprano Audrey Mildmay. His intention, as announced in 1933, was to open it with *Don Giovanni* or *Die Walküre* and to give the *Ring* and *Parsifal* in due course. The first season, beginning on 28 May 1934 and lasting two weeks, was made up of *Le nozze di Figaro* and *Così fan tutte*, which his wife convinced him would be more appropriate to the scale of the house. Christie was determined to aim for the highest standards, and the exodus of skilled and experienced opera staff from Nazi Germany in the 1930s provided him with the opportunity. He engaged Fritz Busch as musical director, Carl Ebert as head of production and Rudolf Bing as manager. The seclusion of Glyndebourne – not to mention the natural beauty of its surroundings, in gently undulating country (by the South Downs, not far from the sea) – attracted performers of the highest quality and allowed them to develop, during a rehearsal period quite unlike anything that is possible in a traditional opera house in a large city, the sense of ensemble and dedicated purpose that has always distinguished Glyndebourne performances. It can be perceived even as early as the recordings of Mozart operas made in the mid-1930s under Busch.

The house was gradually enlarged in the late 1930s and could seat 537 by 1939, by when the Mozart repertory had been extended to include *Die Entführung*, *Die Zauberflöte* and *Don Giovanni*; although Christie's chief enthusiasms were directed towards German opera, his first extensions of the repertory beyond Mozart were Italian, including *Macbeth* (its professional première in Britain, 1938) and *Don Pasquale*. The casts drew on the finest British singers (with Mildmay herself singing Susanna, Zerlina and Norina) and also artists from Germany and Italy; Mariano Stabile and Salvatore Baccaloni sang in early *Figaro* performances and the 1938 *Don Pasquale*, and Luise Helletsgruber and Willi Domgraf-Fassbänder had appeared in the opening seasons. Christie was coolly disposed towards French opera.

Productions broke off during the war years and restarted in 1946 with the première, given by the English Opera Group with Glyndebourne support rather than by Glyndebourne itself, of Britten's *The Rape of Lucretia*, with Kathleen Ferrier, who sang in Gluck's *Orfeo* the next year, when Britten's *Albert Herring* had its première, again from the English Opera Group. There were however performances by the Glyndebourne company at the Edinburgh Festival most years from 1948 to 1953 (including in 1951 the British professional première of *Idomeneo*). With Moran Caplat as head of administration (1949–81), the festival proper resumed at Glyndebourne in 1950, and during the early 1950s the pattern of festivals, with five or six productions each season, including at least one Mozart opera, was established. Operas are normally given in the original language. The season runs from late in May until early in August. Performances begin at about 5 p.m. and are divided by a 'dinner interval' of about 90 minutes, during which patrons traditionally picnic on the lawns or by the lake (or in a marquee in inclement weather; there are also restaurants). Patrons are expected to wear formal dinner dress; Christie's view was that audiences should be seen to be preparing themselves appropriately to partake in an event over which the artists have taken much trouble.

The house was further enlarged in 1951, to seat 592, and by 1977 a series of further alterations had increased the capacity to 830. In 1951 Busch died; he was succeeded as chief conductor by Vittorio Gui, under whom a Rossini tradition developed, with performances of, among other works, *La Cenerentola* in 1952 and *Le comte Ory* in 1954. Gluck's *Alceste*, given under Gui in 1953, was the first French opera heard there; the first opera by a French composer, *Pelléas et Mélisande*, came nine years later. Ebert retired in 1959 and was succeeded by Günther Rennert, who remained until 1968; John Cox was head of productions, 1972–81, and Peter Hall was artistic director, 1984–90. Gui's successors were John Pritchard, musical director 1964–77, then Bernard Haitink and, from 1989, Andrew Davis. The Royal Philharmonic Orchestra played in 1950–63, to be succeeded by the London Philharmonic, with the Orchestra of the Age of Enlightenment playing for period-instrument performances (initially under Simon Rattle) from 1989. Singers have traditionally been widely recruited, notably from the USA and eastern Europe. The company has occasionally toured abroad, including visits to Scandinavia and Hong Kong; it has made many sound and video recordings. Each year an opera from the repertory is performed in semi-concert fashion at the Proms in the Albert Hall, London.

New Glyndebourne Opera House, due to open in 1994 (site model by the architect Michael Hopkins)

In spite of Christie's early hopes, no Wagner opera has been heard at Glyndebourne, and the house's rather dry acoustic would not favour it. Strauss, however, has been particularly successful there, especially the smaller-scale works such as *Ariadne auf Naxos* (1950, conducted initially by Beecham) and *Capriccio* (1963), as well as *Der Rosenkavalier* (1959) and *Intermezzo* (1974). Verdi's *Macbeth* has remained a favourite, as too has been *Falstaff* (1955). The intimacy of the auditorium has also proved favourable to Janáček. Monteverdi's *L'incoronazione di Poppea* (1962) inaugurated an important and influential series of Italian Baroque opera revivals, including two works by Cavalli, in Raymond Leppard's colourful realizations; Handel's operas, however, have not been explored. Contemporary opera, besides Britten (there was an outstanding *Midsummer Night's Dream* in 1981) and Stravinsky, has been represented by works by Maw (*The Rising of the Moon*, première, 1970), Knussen (a double bill, premières, 1984), Osborne (*The Electrification of the Soviet Union*, 1988; première by the Glyndebourne Touring Opera, 1987) and Tippett (*New Year*, British première, 1990), as well as operas by Henze and von Einem. *Porgy and Bess* was given with great success in 1986. Mozart, however, remains central, partly because his operas lend themselves so ideally to the size of the house and the rehearsal and production circumstances that Glyndebourne can uniquely offer; understandably, many of the Glyndebourne highlights are of Mozart productions, for example the *Don Giovanni* designed by John Piper (1951) and the *Entführung* by Oliver Messel (1956), the very different *Zauberflöte* productions designed by Luzzati (1963) and Hockney (1978; the Peter Sellars *Zauberflöte* of 1990 was less well received) and the remarkable series of Da Ponte operas directed by Peter Hall in the 1970s. An all-Mozart season, including for the first time *La clemenza di Tito*, was given in 1991; but no Mozart opera earlier than *Idomeneo* has been performed at Glyndebourne.

In 1992 work began on the rebuilding of the opera house (capacity 1150), involving its realignment by 180° and its reopening on 28 May 1994 (the 60th anniversary of its first performance) with *Le nozze di Figaro*.

The Glyndebourne Touring Opera was established in 1968, initially under the direction of Myer Fredman, to give Glyndebourne productions, with younger casts, during short seasons in the home house and at other centres in Britain, over a period of four to eight weeks each year; this company, which (unlike the parent company) has received Arts Council support, has occasionally visited Ireland and European cities.

Glyndebourne Festival Programme Book (1952–)
S. Hughes: *Glyndebourne: a History of the Festival Opera* (London, 1965, 2/1981)
W. Blunt: *John Christie of Glyndebourne* (London, 1968)
G. Busch: *Fritz Busch, Dirigent* (Frankfurt, 1970)
R. Bing: *5000 Nights at the Opera* (London, 1972)
J. Higgins: *The Making of an Opera: Don Giovanni at Glyndebourne* (London, 1978)
J. Higgins, ed.: *Glyndebourne: a Celebration* (London, 1984)
                                                    STANLEY SADIE

Glynne, Howell (*b* Swansea, 24 Jan 1906; *d* Toronto, 24 Nov 1969). Welsh bass. He studied with Ben Davies and later with Reinhold von Warlich. In the late 1920s he joined the Carl Rosa Opera Company chorus; his first major role was Sparafucile in 1931. He was the leading bass at Sadler's Wells (1946–51 and 1956–64), singing Mr Crusty (Lunardo) in *I quatro rusteghi* and Fiesco in the first production in England of *Simon Boccanegra*. From 1947 he appeared regularly at Covent Garden where he created Lavatte in *The Olympians* (1949) and was a memorable Ochs. His rich voice and gift for comedy made him an admired King Dodon (*The Golden Cockerel*) and Kecal (*The Bartered Bride*).   HAROLD ROSENTHAL/R

Gmïrya, Boris Romanovich. *See* HMYRYA, BORYS.

Gnecchi, Vittorio (*b* Milan, 17 July 1876; *d* Milan, 5 Feb 1954). Italian composer. He studied with Michele Saladino, Gaetano Coronaro, Serafin and Gatti. His first work for the theatre was a pastoral in two acts, *Virtù d'amore*, privately performed in 1896 at the family home at Verderio, near Como. In the next, the tragedy *Cassandra* (1905), he attempted to recreate the climate of Aeschylus's tragedy, and this involved using material based on Greek modes. The opera gave rise to a violent critical controversy: in 1909 the musicologist Giovanni Tebaldini published two articles (*RMI*, xvi, 400–12, 632–59), in which he maintained, on the basis of a comparative analysis, that there was a similarity so close as to be telepathic between *Cassandra* and Strauss's *Elektra*. In general, however, European critics rejected the idea that *Elektra* (1906–8) had been inspired by the Italian work, attributing the similarities to chance.

Gnecchi's next works – the three-act *La Rosiera* (1927) and *Giuditta* (1953) – confirmed the characteristics of his style, which combines modes and an often dissonant, post-Wagnerian chromatic harmony, creating unusual effects within classically conceived forms.

Virtù d'amore (azione pastorale, 2, M. Rossi Borzotti), Verderio (Como), Villa Gnecchi, 7 Oct 1896
Cassandra (tragedia, prol., 2, L. Illica), Bologna, Comunale, 5 Dec 1905; rev. version, Ferrara, 29 Feb 1909
La Rosiera (3, V. Gnecchi and C. Zangarini, after A. de Musset: *On ne badine pas avec l'amour*), Gera, 12 Feb 1927
Giuditta (3, Illica), Salzburg, 1953 [as oratorio]

*

ES (G. Graziosi)
M. Horwarth: 'Tebaldini, Gnecchi and Strauss', *CMc*, no.10 (1970), 74–91   RAFFAELE POZZI

Gnecco, Francesco (*b* Genoa, *c*1769; *d* Milan, 1810–11). Italian composer. He supposedly studied with Cimarosa. For a while he was *maestro di cappella* of Savona Cathedral, but he was most successful as a composer of comic and serious operas, writing many of his own librettos. His most famous opera, *La prova d'un opera seria*, had a backstage plot; though not the first of this genre, it was the best. Originally in one act with a libretto by Giulio Artusi (1803, Venice) and entitled *La prima prova dell'opera Gli orazi e curiazi*, it was later changed into a two-act work with Gnecco's own libretto (1805, Milan) and was performed until 1860 throughout Europe, with the most famous singers. The plot of the two-act version concerns a rehearsal, not of Cimarosa's *Gli Orazi ed i Curiazi*, but of a non-existent *opera seria*, *Ettore in Trabisonda*, characterized by all the excesses of a style overripe for parody. A number of irrelevant but funny backstage problems add spice to the action: a lesson in instrumentation, a chorus full of mistakes, a soprano mispronouncing her words and so on. To create some tension at the end of the first act Gnecco introduced a picnic in the country for the cast; a storm comes up and the soprano and tenor lovers quarrel. The music is in the best tradition of Paisiello and Cimarosa. Arias are in two tempos, preceded by an introduction highlighting a solo instrument. The few more formal (non-comic) numbers are in da capo form. The ensembles are multipartite and, in what seems to be contemporary practice, appear only in the middle and end of the acts. In keeping with turn-of-the-century *opera buffa* style the vocal lines are principally patter, the orchestra having the connective melodic tissue. Nothing in the music is adventurous or memorable, but the comic backstage shenanigans are first-rate.

Gnecco composed 23 other operas, including *Auretta e Masiello, ossia Il contratempo* (1792, Genoa), *Il nuovo podestà*, later *Le nozze di Lauretta* (1802, Bologna), and *Filandro e Carolina* (1804, Rome). He published chamber works and also wrote sacred music.

Auretta e Masiello, ossia Il contratempo (dg, 2, Gnecco), Genoa, S Agostino, 8 May 1792
La contadina astuta, ossia La finta semplice (dg, 2), Florence, Regio, sum. 1792 or 1793, *I-Fc*
Il nuovo Galateo, San Pier d'Arena, Crosa Larga, 1792

I filosofi in derisione, ossia I filosofi burlati (int), Florence, Intrepidi, carn. 1793
Lo sposo di tre, marito di nessuna (dg, 2, A. Palomba), Milan, Scala, March 1793
L'indolente (dg, 2, G. Palomba), Parma, Corte, carn. 1797
Le nozze de' Sanniti (dramma, 2, G. Foppa), Padua, Nuovo, June 1797, *Gl, Pl*
I due sordi burlati (ob, Foppa), Genoa, Falcone, June 1798
Alessandro nell'Indie (os, 3, P. Metastasio), Livorno, Regio, Oct 1800
Adelaide di Guesclino (os, G. Rossi, after Voltaire), Florence, Pergola, aut. 1800, *Fc*
Il nuovo podestà (ob, 2, G. Caravita), Bologna, Comunale, spr. 1802, *Fc, Rmassimo*; as Le nozze di Lauretta (Gnecco), Rome, Valle, 23 May 1804
La festa riscaldata (ob, 1, Foppa), Florence, Pallacorda, sum. 1802
Il geloso corretto (farsa, G. Artusi), Venice, S Giovanni Grisostomo, 18 April 1803, *OS*
Il finto fratello, Venice, S Giovanni Grisostomo, 25 May 1803
La prima prova dell'opera Gli orazi e curiazi (1, Artusi), Venice, S Giovanni Grisostomo, 8 July 1803, *D-Hs, F-Pn, I-Nc, PS*; rev. as La prova d'un opera seria (2, Gnecco), Milan, Scala, 16 Aug 1805, *D-Mbs, F-Pn, GB-Lbl, I-Fc, Nc, US-Bp*; rev. as L'apertura del nuovo teatro, Naples, Nuovo, aut. 1807, *GB-Lbl, I-Fc, Nc, US-Bp, Wc*
La scena senza scena (ob, Artusi), Venice, S Moisè, 10 Dec 1803
Arsace e Semiramide (os, Rossi, after Voltaire), Venice, Fenice, 31 Jan 1804, *I-Mr**
Filandro e Carolina (ob, 1, Gnecco), Rome, Valle, Oct 1804, *GB-Lbl, I-Fc, Mc*; rev. as Clementina e Roberto, Genoa, Feb 1810, *GB-Lbl, I-Fc*
L'incognito (ob), Vicenza, Eretenio, carn. 1805
L'amore in musica (ob, 2, Gnecco), Bologna, Comunale, 1 April 1805, *Mr**; as Gli amanti filarmonici, Rome, Valle, carn. 1807
Gli ultimi due giorni di carnevale (ob, Artusi), Milan, Scala, 7 April 1806, *Mr**
I bramini (os, S. Scatizzi), Livorno, Avvalorati, aut. 1806
Argete, Naples, S Carlo, Nov 1808
I falsi galantuomini [gentiluomini] (ob, 2, M. Prunetti), Milan, Scala, 16 Aug 1809, *Mc*

*

EitnerQ; MGG (A. Della Corte)
'Biographische Nachrichten von Francesco Gnecco, aus dem Giornale Italiano und aus dem Redattore del Reno im Auszuge mitgetheilt von Chladni', *AMZ*, xiv (1812), 29
MARVIN TARTAK

Gobatti, Stefano (*b* Bergantino, Rovigo, 5 July 1852; *d* Bologna, 17 Dec 1913). Italian composer. He studied in Bologna, with Lauro Rossi in Parma and at the Naples Conservatory. In 1873 his opera *I goti* was staged in Bologna and received with extraordinary acclaim. The city's cultural circles welcomed him as the new musical paragon to rival Verdi, but *I goti* was less enthusiastically received elsewhere in Italy. Verdi called it 'the most monstrous musical miscarriage ever composed'. Two subsequent operas, *Luce* (1875) and *Cordelia* (1881), met with a cold reception even in Bologna; *Masias* (1900) was never performed. Reduced to poverty and entirely forgotten, Gobatti taught singing in primary schools and later entered a monastery.

I goti (tragedia lirica, 4, S. Interdonato), Bologna, Comunale, 30 Nov 1873, vs (Milan, 1874)
Luce (dramma lirico, 5, Interdonato), Bologna, Comunale, 25 Nov 1875, vs (Milan, 1876)
Cordelia (dramma lirico, 5, C. D'Ormeville), Bologna, Comunale, 6 Dec 1881, *I-Bc*
Masias (opera, 3, E. Sanfelice), 1900, unperf.

*

F. Vatielli: 'L'ultima opera di Stefano Gobatti', *La strenna delle colonie scolastiche bolognesi*, xliv (1941)   BRUNO CAGLI

Gobbato, Angelo (Mario Giulio) (*b* Milan, 5 July 1943). Italian bass-baritone and director resident in South Africa. He studied the piano and singing privately while reading science at the University of Cape Town. His singing teachers were Albina Bini, Adelheid Armhold and Frederick Dalberg in Cape Town and, in 1965–6, Carlo Tagliabue and Anna Pistolesi in Milan. He made his début as Kecal (*The Bartered Bride*) in Cape Town in 1965. Gobbato is best known for *buffo* roles such as Dr Bartolo (*Il barbiere*), Don Pasquale and Figaro (*Il barbiere* and *Figaro*); he was awarded the first Nederburg Prize for opera in 1971 for his portrayal of Papageno. He was resident producer at the Nico Malan Opera House in Cape Town, 1976–81, and head of the opera school of the University of Cape Town, 1982–8. In 1989 he was appointed director of opera for the Cape Performing Arts Board. He has directed – mainly from the Italian repertory – for all the arts councils in South Africa.   JAMES MAY

Tito Gobbi in the title role of Verdi's 'Simon Boccanegra'

Gobbi, Tito (*b* Bassano del Grappa, 24 Oct 1913; *d* Rome, 5 March 1984). Italian baritone. He studied in Rome with Giulio Crimi and made his début in 1935 at Gubbio as Rodolfo (*La sonnambula*). In 1937 he appeared at the Teatro Adriano, Rome, as Germont. He sang regularly at the Rome Opera from 1938; his first great success there was as Wozzeck in the Italian première of Berg's opera (1942). He first appeared at La Scala in 1942 as Belcore, the role in which he made his Covent Garden début with the Scala company in 1951. He appeared regularly in London, especially in Verdi roles, including Posa (1958), Boccanegra (see illustration), Iago, Rigoletto and Falstaff. He also sang Don Giovanni, Almaviva, Gianni Schicchi and Scarpia.

Gobbi made his American début as Rossini's Figaro in San Francisco in 1948; from 1954 to 1973 he sang regularly in Chicago in a repertory that included Gérard, Michonnet, Jack Rance and Tonio, and he made his Metropolitan Opera début in 1956 as Scarpia. At Rome he created roles in Rocca's *Monte Ivnor* (1939), Malipiero's *Ecuba* (1941), Persico's *La locandiera* (1941), Lualdi's *Le nozze di Haura* (1943) and Napoli's *Il tesoro* (1958) and at Milan in Ghedini's

L'ipocrita felice (1956). His repertory consisted of almost a hundred roles. Intelligence, musicianship and acting ability, allied to a fine though not large voice, made Gobbi one of the finest singing actors of his generation. He directed several operas, notably *Simon Boccanegra* in Chicago and London, and wrote his autobiography, *Tito Gobbi: My Life* (London, 1979).

GV
D. De Paoli: 'Tito Gobbi', *Opera*, vi (1955), 619–22
A. Natan: 'Gobbi, Tito', *Primo uomo: grosse Sänger der Oper* (Basle, 1963) [with discography]
G. Lauri-Volpi: 'Un grande artista, un amico reale', *Musica e dischi*, no.262 (1968), 49
J. W. Freeman: 'Tito Gobbi Talks', *ON*, xxxvi/17 (1971–2), 14–16
A. Blyth: 'Gobbi: the Singer and the Man', *British Music Yearbook 1975*, 3–21 [with discography by J. B. Steane]
H. Rosenthal: 'Tito Gobbi 1913–84', *Opera*, xxxv (1984), 476–84
                                    HAROLD ROSENTHAL/R

Göbel, Franz Xaver. *See* GEBEL, FRANZ XAVER.

Gockley, David (*b* Philadelphia, 13 July 1943). American administrator. He studied at Brown and Columbia universities and at the New England Conservatory of Music in Boston. He began his career as an opera singer, and taught drama and English. In 1968 he became house manager for Santa Fe Opera and in 1970 assistant to the managing director of Lincoln Center. Later the same year he joined Houston Grand Opera as business manager, and in 1972 became general director there. Gockley has transformed Houston Grand Opera from a small regional company to one of international stature and is widely respected for his support of new works and revivals of classic American musical theatre. He has encouraged contemporary American work, John Adams's *Nixon in China* being one of seven world premières by American composers; other successful productions include *Porgy and Bess*, *Show Boat* and *Hello, Dolly!*. Gockley has helped ensure the company's success by lengthening the season and expanding the budget, as well as by introducing English surtitles and education programmes; the touring Texas Opera Theater is also one of his initiatives.

A. Rich: 'The Gockley Slant', *ON*, xxxviii/17 (1973–4), 10–13
                                    FRANK MERKLING/KAREN CARDELL

Godard, Benjamin (Louis Paul) (*b* Paris, 18 Aug 1849; *d* Cannes, 10 Jan 1895). French composer. He studied with Henri Reber at the Paris Conservatoire and was active as a viola player. Godard's salon music became popular and his *symphonie dramatique Le Tasse*, first performed in 1878, won that year's Prix de la Ville de Paris. He became a professor at the Conservatoire in 1887 and was made a Chevalier of the Légion d'honneur in 1889.

In the 1880s he turned his attention to opera, but with little success. His grand opera *Pedro de Zalamea* (1884) was first performed at Antwerp. From *Jocelyn* (1888) only the Berceuse won favour, and *Dante* (1890) fared little better. After two more operas, both failures, Godard discovered a more congenial formula with the *opéra comique La vivandière*, which enjoyed over 80 performances before 1900 and remained popular until World War I. Its orchestration was completed by Paul Vidal after Godard's death. Godard had a compositional facility comparable to that of Saint-Saëns and a certain melodic gift, but his operas lack substance and dramatic force, despite his attempts to emulate his German contemporaries.

printed works published in Paris unless otherwise stated

Les bijoux de Jeannette, Paris, 1878

Les Guelfes, 1880–82 (grand opéra, 5, L. Gallet), Rouen, Arts, 17 Jan 1902, vs (1898)

Pedro de Zalamea (opéra, 4, L. Détroyat and A. Silvestre, after P. Calderón de la Barca), Antwerp, Royal, 31 Jan 1884, vs (1884)

Jocelyn op.100 (4, V. Capoul and Silvestre, after A. de Lamartine), Brussels, Monnaie, 25 Feb 1888, vs (1888)

Dante op.111 (drame lyrique, 4, E. Blau), Paris, OC (Favart), 13 May 1890, vs (1890)

Jeanne d'Arc op.125 (drame historique, 5, J. Fabre), Paris, Châtelet, Jan 1891, vs (1891)

Ruy Blas, 1891, unperf.

La vivandière (oc, 3, H. Cain), inc., Brussels, Monnaie, 21 March 1893; with orchestration completed by P. A. Vidal, Paris, Favart, 1 April 1895; vs (1895)

*

M. Clerjot: *Benjamin Godard* (Paris, 1902)

M. Clavié: *Benjamin Godard* (Paris, 1906)

C. Le Senne: 'Benjamin Godard (1849–1895)', *EMDC*, I/iii (1921), 1803
JOHN TREVITT, ROBERT ORLEDGE

Goehr, (Peter) Alexander (*b* Berlin, 10 Aug 1932). British composer. The son of the composer and conductor Walter Goehr (1903–60), he was brought to England early in 1933. He was a contemporary of Maxwell Davies and Birtwistle at the RMCM, and with them and others formed the New Music Manchester Group. A year spent in Messiaen's Paris masterclass in 1955–6 broadened the outlook of his essentially Schoenbergian pedigree (his father had been a pupil of Schoenberg) and led to an energetic engagement with the activities of the Darmstadt-based avant garde.

Goehr's first mature compositions, emerging over the next seven years, reflected the characteristic spirit of postwar modernism, though within a wider frame of reference than is usual in the often doctrinaire works of the period. After the composition of the *Little Symphony* (1963), which reconciled Messiaenesque modality and Boulezian *bloc sonore* within the premises of classic serialism, Goehr then explored the potential of this synthesis in all the major genres. Preferring the more immediate 18th- and 19th-century past rather than the earlier stylistic periods favoured by his contemporaries, he made a speciality of sonata, variation and refrain structures in the Piano Trio and in his first opera, *Arden must Die* (2, E. Fried; Hamburg, Staatsoper, 5 March 1967, as *Arden muss sterben*). His experience as a teacher (he was appointed professor of music at Leeds in 1971 and at Cambridge in 1976) as well as acquaintance with the indigenous music of China, Japan, Hungary and Israel gave strength to his composition and roots to his conviction of the need for a humane basis for music-making in a troubled world, a message set before a wider public in his 1987 Reith Lectures.

Many of these preoccupations are bound up in a practical way in Goehr's pioneering work with John Cox and the Music Theatre Ensemble. Collectively entitled *Triptych*, *Naboth's Vineyard* (1968), *Shadowplay* (1970) and *Sonata about Jerusalem* (1971) present a unified evening of experimental theatre, fusing Japanese noh, classical allegory and biblical narrative with a tight, gestural language to illustrate themes that have become central to Goehr's entire dramatic output: oppression, the nature of moral corruption and the desire for Utopia. The exploration of alternative theatrical modes extends to Goehr's most substantial

stage work, the three-act opera *Behold the Sun*, composed during 1981–4 to a libretto by John McGrath and the composer and first performed by the Deutsche Oper am Rhein, Duisburg, on 19 April 1985 as *Die Wiedertäufer*. Envisaging a Baroque dramaturgy for this choral opera on the subject of the 1534 Anabaptist uprising in Münster, Goehr devised a powerful fusion of 18th-century figured-bass method and modern harmonic practice, coinciding with a move towards simpler compositional materials in this and other works. In the 1980s he made a partial return to his earlier serialism, finding new linguistic syntheses in the scena *Eve Dreams in Paradise* (1989), and in the intimate union of words and music in *Sing Ariel* (1990).

See also ARDEN MUST DIE and BEHOLD THE SUN.

*

D. Drew: 'Why must Arden Die?', *The Music of Alexander Goehr*, ed. B. Northcott (London, 1980), 32–9

N. Williams: 'Behold the Sun: the Politics of Musical Production', *Music and the Politics of Culture*, ed. C. Norris (London, 1989), 150–71
NICHOLAS WILLIAMS

Goeke, Leo (*b* Kirksville, MO, 1936). American tenor. Educated at Northeast Missouri State University, the University of Louisiana and the State University of Iowa, he became a member of the Metropolitan Opera Studio and made his début with the parent company in 1971 as Gastone (*La traviata*); he has since sung there in many leading roles, including Don Ottavio, Ferrando (*Così fan tutte*), Tamino, Edgardo, Alfredo, the Duke and Rodolfo. Goeke made his European début in 1973 as Flamand in *Capriccio* (1973) at Glyndebourne, where he also sang Idamantes, Tom Rakewell, Don Ottavio and Tamino. Engaged at Stuttgart, he took part in the first German performance of Philip Glass's *Satyagraha* (1981). His repertory also includes such roles as Belmonte, Massenet's Des Grieux, Pinkerton and Gluck's Admetus, which he sang at Louisville (1982). A lyrical singer, he uses his voice with taste and skill, especially in the Mozart roles that form a large part of his repertory.
ELIZABETH FORBES

Goethe, Johann Wolfgang von (*b* Frankfurt, 28 Aug 1749; *d* Weimar, 22 March 1832). German writer, poet and librettist. Arguably the most powerful and versatile figure in German intellectual history, throughout his long life he cultivated a deep and abiding involvement in a broad range of artistic and scientific endeavours. As a poet, dramatist and theatre director he continually sought to reach beyond the narrow confines of his own culture's operatic horizons and gain a more cosmopolitan familiarity with international currents.

Goethe received the kind of musical training normal for a patrician amateur. His earliest experiences of opera included performances by French and German troupes in the Rhineland specializing in *opéra comique*. As a student at Leipzig he witnessed the triumph of the simple comedies with music by C. F. Weisse and J. A. Hiller. His own early librettos, written at Frankfurt, already move considerably beyond Weisse's dramas in tone, dramatic content and musical structure. *Erwin und Elmire* (1773–5), based on the ballad of Angelica and Edwin in Goldsmith's *The Vicar of Wakefield*, rejects conventional typologies of character and subjects the central love-interest to serious psychological analysis. The rural setting serves as little more than a convenient backdrop. The play includes some of his most memorable lyric poetry, including the Romanze

'Das Veilchen', set in 1785 by Mozart. Like its successor, *Erwin und Elmire* was written for Goethe's friend, the composer Johann André, whose house at Offenbach he frequented at the time. The text was set several more times and enjoyed widespread popularity. Not so *Claudine von Villa Bella* (1775–6), a revolutionary, *Sturm und Drang* work of fraternal strife set against a vivid Spanish backdrop. Technically unruly and dramaturgically demanding, it makes structural use of musical ensembles to a degree unprecedented in German practice. André's setting, completed around 1778, was apparently never performed; in Ignaz von Beecke's setting the drama failed at Vienna in 1780.

After moving to Weimar in 1776, Goethe involved himself with less ambitious operatic projects, several of them occasional pieces conceived in connection with the amateur theatre there. His texts, which vary widely in the degree of musical involvement they require, were set by the likes of Duchess Anna Amalia (*Erwin und Elmire*, *Der Jahrmarktsfest zu Plundersweilern*) and the gifted soprano Corona Schröter (*Die Fischerin*, including the first setting of 'Der Erlkönig'). Goethe's hopes of collaborating with his childhood friend, the composer P. C. Kayser, never bore fruit. *Jery und Bätely*, a story inspired by an incident during Goethe's travels in Switzerland, was destined for Kayser (then resident at Zürich) but was eventually handed over to the courtier Karl Siegmund von Seckendorff, whose music Goethe considered poor.

He also thought little of the Bellomo theatre company, which performed at the Weimar court from 1784 to 1791, and in general grew deeply disenchanted with German theatrical affairs in the course of the 1780s. *Scherz, List und Rache*, written for Kayser during these years (his setting remained incomplete) shows clearly a thoroughgoing aesthetic shift towards *opera buffa*. During his Italian journey of 1786–8 Goethe completely redrafted *Erwin und Elmire* and *Claudine von Villa Bella* in the spirit of his new operatic ideals. He recast the prose dialogue as recitative, restructured and simplified the plots to conform to Italian practice, and rewrote many of the musical numbers. Both new versions were set by J. F. Reichardt, who also composed *Jery und Bätely* (1789; first performed in 1801) and *Lila* (1791), and planned several further operatic projects with Goethe before they fell out over Reichardt's outspoken republican sympathies.

From 1791, under Goethe's direction, the Weimar Hoftheater placed almost exclusive emphasis on Viennese and Italian operatic fare. In Italy Goethe had heard Cimarosa's *L'impresario in angustie*, which so impressed him that he translated it into German and arranged both text and music (including two lieder of his own composition) for Weimar (*see* IMPRESARIO IN ANGUSTIE, L'). Mozart's operas were the undisputed favourites at court: over the 25 years of Goethe's involvement with the theatre they accounted for 280 performances. (Nearly all Viennese operas were given at Weimar with their texts rather ineptly revised by Goethe's brother-in-law C. A. Vulpius.) Goethe specially admired both the text and music of *Die Zauberflöte*, first introduced in early 1794. He began a sequel to it, but Weimar was utterly devoid of compositional talent and Viennese composers like Wranitzky, to whom Goethe offered terms in 1796, feared comparison with Mozart.

Goethe's dramas, alongside his lyric poetry, have proved an inexhaustible source of inspiration for composers of operas, lieder, choral works and symphonies. Along with other facets of Goethe's cultural world, opera figures as an element in many of his works. Hofmannsthal called his *Märchen* (1795) an 'interior opera'; and the musical stage appears as a central, if transfigured, element in his greatest work, *Faust* (*see* FAUST).

LIBRETTOS

Erwin und Elmire, 1st version (Schauspiel mit Gesang), André, 1775 (Vogler, 1781); *Lila* (Liederspiel), Seckendorff, 1777 (Reichardt, comp. 1791, ?unperf.); *Claudine von Villa Bella*, 1st version (Schauspiel mit Gesang), André, 1778, unperf. (Beecke, 1780); *Das Jahrmarktsfest zu Plundersweilern* (Schönbartspiel), Anna Amalia, 1778; *Proserpina* (monodrama), Seckendorff, 1778 (Eberwein, 1814); *Jery und Bätely*, 1st version (Spl), Seckendorff, 1780; *Die Fischerin* (Spl), C. E. W. Schröter, 1782

Scherz, List und Rache (Spl), P. C. Kayser, comp. 1785–6, inc. (Winter, 1790; E. T. A. Hoffmann, 1801; Bruch, 1858; Wellesz, 1928; F. Leinert, 1961); *Claudine von Villa Bella*, 2nd version (Spl), Reichardt, 1789 (Kienlen, 1810; Schubert, begun 1815, inc., 1913; Gläser, 1826); *Jery und Bätely*, 2nd version (Spl), Winter, 1790 (Reichardt, 1801; Bierey, 1803; C. Kreutzer, 1810; A. Adam, 1834; Zopff, comp. *c*1870, unperf.; I. Starck, 1873; Dressel, 1932); *Erwin und Elmire*, 2nd version (Spl), Reichardt, 1793

NOVELS, DRAMAS AND BALLADS

Die Laune des Verliebten (Schäferspiel, 1767): R. Wagner, comp. 1830, inc.; Dressel, 1949

Die Mitschuldigen (drama, 1769): H. Riethmüller, 1957

Satyros (dramatic satire, 1770); Baussnern, 1922; Bořkovec, 1942, as Satyr

Götz von Berlichingen (drama, 1773): Goldmark, 1902

Clavigo (Trauerspiel, 1774): Ettinger, 1926

Die Leiden des jungen Werthers (novel, 1774): R. Kreutzer, 1792, as Charlotte et Werther; Massenet, 1892, as Werther

Faust, 1st version (drama, 1775): I. Walter, 1787, as Doktor Faust

Stella (Schauspiel, 1776): Deshayes, 1791–2, as Zélia and La suite de Zélia; W. Bloch, 1951

Nausikaa (Trauerspiel, 1787): H. Reutter, 1967

Märchen (from *Unterhaltungen deutscher Ausgewanderten*, 1795): Klebe, 1969, as Das Märchen von der schönen Lilie

Wilhelm Meisters Lehrjahre (novel, 1795–6): A. Thomas, 1866, as Mignon

Die Braut von Korinth (ballad, 1797): Chabrier, 1897, as Briséïs

Der Gott und die Bajadere (ballad, 1797): Ö. Farkas, 1876, as Bajadér

Der Zauberlehrling (ballad, 1797): J. Döbber, 1907

Faust, 2nd version, pt 1 (verse drama, 1808): C. E. Horn, H. R. Bishop and T. S. Cooke, 1825, as Faustus; L. Bertin, 1831, as Fausto; Berlioz, 1846, as La damnation de Faust; M. Lutz, 1855, as Faust and Marguerite; Gounod, 1859; Boito, 1868, as Mefistofele; Hervé, 1869, as Le petit Faust; Zöllner, 1887; Kistler, 1905, as Faust 1. Teil; A. Brüggemann, 1910, as Margherita; Busoni, 1925, as Doktor Faust; Bentzon, 1964, as Faust III

*

C. A. H. Burkhardt: *Goethe und der Komponist Ph. Chr. Kayser* (Leipzig, 1879)

W. Wilmanns: 'Ueber Goethe's Erwin und Elmire', *Goethe-Jb*, ii (1881), 146–67

W. Martinsen: *Goethes Singspiele im Verhältnis zu den Weissischen Operetten* (Dresden, 1887)

E. Schmidt: 'Goethes Proserpina', *Vierteljahrschrift für Litteraturgeschichte*, i (1888), 27–52

H. Kling: 'Goethe et Berlioz', *RMI*, xii (1905), 714–32

M. Morris: 'Goethe als Bearbeiter von italienischen Operntexten', *Goethe-Jb*, xxvi (1905), 3–51

H. H. Borcherdt: 'Die Entstehungsgeschichte von "Erwin und Elmire"', *Goethe-Jb*, xxxii (1911), 73–82

E. Bötcher: *Goethes Singspiele 'Erwin und Elmire' und 'Claudine von Villa Bella' und die 'opera buffa'* (Marburg, 1911)

W. Bode: *Die Tonkunst in Goethes Leben* (Berlin, 1912)

A. von Weilen: '"Erwin und Elmire"', *Chronik des Wiener Goethe-Vereins*, xxviii (1915), 18–23

M. Friedländer: 'Goethe und die Musik', *Jb der Goethe-Gesellschaft*, iii (1916), 275–340

E. Blom: 'Goethe's "Magic Flute, part II"', *ML*, xxiii (1924), 234–54

H. John: *Goethe und die Musik* (Langensalza, 1927)

H. von Hofmannsthal: 'Goethes Opern und Singspiele', *Die Berührung der Sphären* (Berlin, 1931), 283–90

W. Krogmann: 'Die persönlichen Beziehungen in Goethes Schauspiel mit Gesang "Claudine von Villa Bella"', *Germanisch-romanische Monatsschrift*, xix (1931), 348–61

V. Junk: 'Zweiter Teil "Faust" und Zweite "Zauberflöte": Betrachtungen zu Goethes musikdramatischer Architektonik', *Neues Mozart-Jb*, ii (1942), 59–77

A. Orel: *Goethe als Operndirektor* (Bregenz, 1949)

A. Henkel: 'Goethes Fortsetzung der "Zauberflöte"', *Zeitschrift für deutsche Philologie*, lxxi (1951–2), 64–9

M. Unger: *Ein Faustopernplan Beethovens und Goethes* (Regensburg, 1952)

M. Treisch: 'Goethes Singspiele in Kompositionen seiner Zeitgenossen', *Wissenschaftliche Zeitschrift der Humboldt-Universität zu Berlin*, Gesellschafts- und sprachwissenschaftliche Reihe, iii (1953–4), 253–70

F. W. Sternfeld: *Goethe and Music* (New York, 1954)

J. Müller-Blattau: 'Der Zauberflöte Zweiter Teil: ein Beitrag zum Thema Goethe und Mozart', *Goethe: neue Folge des Jahrbuchs der Goethe-Gesellschaft*, xviii (1956), 158–79

R. Samuel: 'Goethe and *Die Zauberflöte*', *German Life and Letters*, x (1956–7), 31–7

K. R. Eissler: 'Notes on an Aspect of Goethe's Relationship to Music', *Goethe: a Psychoanalytic Study, 1775–1786* (Detroit, 1963), 1244–65

J. Rosteutscher: 'Mythos und Ethos in Goethes Entwurf der Zauberflöte Zweiter Teil', *Jb des Wiener Goethe-Vereins*, lxvii (1963), 91–100

H.-A. Koch: 'Die Singspiele', *Goethes Dramen: neue Interpretationen*, ed. W. Hinderer (Stuttgart, 1980), 42–64

T. Bauman: *North German Opera in the Age of Goethe* (Cambridge, 1985)

A. Meier: *Faustlibretti: Geschichte des Fauststoffs auf der europäischen Musikbühne* (Frankfurt, 1990)   THOMAS BAUMAN

Goetz, Hermann (Gustav) (*b* Königsberg [now Kaliningrad], 7 Dec 1840; *d* Hottingen, nr Zürich, 3 Dec 1876). German composer. He studied music at the Stern Conservatory in Berlin, Hans von Bülow being among his teachers. In 1863 he moved to Winterthur as a church organist, hoping not only for musical success but also that the Swiss air would cure the tuberculosis contracted in his childhood. Besides playing the organ he began teaching and performed as a concert pianist. In spite of severe depression brought on by his illness, Goetz wrote concertos and chamber works as well as lieder, choral music, a Singspiel, two operas and two symphonies. Of his 24 published works, the chamber music, Symphony no.2 and the two operas reveal the best of a Romantic composer who stands in a direct line of descent from Weber, Marschner, Spohr and middle-period Wagner.

Goetz's first stage work, a Singspiel entitled *Die heiligen drei Königen*, remains unpublished. Written to a libretto by J. V. Widmann for the Winterthur Sonntagskränzchen to perform (with piano accompaniment) on Twelfth Night in 1866, it has a simple, folkloristic story set in a rural community. Ilda, a farmer's daughter, loves Friedrich but is promised by her father to a rich man, Peter. To overcome her opposition, the farmer agrees that she should marry the first man who can restore a smile to her sad face. On Twelfth Night a group of serenading singers arrives at the house, and among them is Friedrich disguised as Balthasar. Neither of the other characters disguised as kings can elicit a smile, but Balthasar/Friedrich succeeds with a love song and wins his bride. The final chorus from *Die heiligen drei Königen* reappears in the finale of his first serious attempt at opera two years later.

In 1868 Goetz began work on his comic opera *Der Widerspänstigen Zähmung* (Widmann, after Shakespeare's *Taming of the Shrew*), after he had rejected Widmann's suggestion of *Parzifal*. It was a

further six years before the Mannheim première, 11 October 1874. In four acts, the work has many ensembles, ranging from duets to a final septet, linked by arias and orchestrally accompanied recitative. It is a natural successor in the field of German comic opera to Nicolai's *Die lustigen Weiber von Windsor* and Cornelius's *Der Barbier von Bagdad*. The opera's success immediately proclaimed its composer's name, from Vienna to London and New York, as one who had turned away from Wagner's concept of opera and drama – Goetz rebutted reports that he had been influenced by *Die Meistersinger* – and remained loyal to the classicism of Mozart, holding strongly to the belief that he must preserve a 'unified, architectural musical form … in achieving the confluence of dramatic and musical development' (Kreuzhage 1916).

Goetz began work on his second mature opera, *Francesca da Rimini*, in 1875 but completed only the first two acts; it was left to his amanuensis Ernst Frank to flesh out the sketches of the overture and the last act after his death. Widmann based his libretto on Silvio Pellico's 1812 adaptation of Dante's text, though Goetz himself was largely responsible for shaping and adapting the work. The original story of Lanceotto Malatesta's jealousy of his wife Francesca because of her love for his brother Paolo provides the basis for the work. The second-act duet for the ill-fated lovers drained the dying composer of his last strength but drew from him the finest music in the opera. First performed in Mannheim on 30 September 1877, *Francesca da Rimini* failed to achieve anything like the success of its predecessor, largely because of its weak and undramatic libretto.

Goetz died four days before his 36th birthday, and by the turn of the century his music was rarely heard. He was overshadowed by the major figures of his day, but his music reveals an extraordinary melodic gift, formal mastery and an expert command of his craft as well as a distinctive style. His Second Symphony (1873) and *Der Widerspänstigen Zähmung* elicited lavish praise from George Bernard Shaw, writing in *The World* (22 November 1893; reprinted in *Music in London*):

You have to go to Mozart's finest quartets and quintets on the one hand, and to *Die Meistersinger* on the other, for work of the quality we find, not here and there, but continuously, in the Symphony and in the opera, two masterpieces which place him securely above all other German composers of the last hundred years, save only Mozart and Beethoven, Weber and Wagner.

That his works have not achieved a place in the repertory despite such praise is to be regretted.

See also WIDERSPÄNSTIGEN ZÄHMUNG, DER.

*

E. Frank: 'Hermann Götz', *Musikalisches Wochenblatt*, vii (1876), 228–399 passim

J. V. Widmann: 'Nekrolog: Hermann Goetz', *NZM*, lxxiii (1877), 41–2

A. Steiner: 'Hermann Goetz', *Neujahrsblatt der Allgemeinen Musikgesellschaft in Zürich*, xcv (1907), 3–39 [whole issue]

E. Kreuzhage: *Hermann Goetz: sein Leben und seine Werke* (Leipzig, 1916)

G. R. Kruse: *Hermann Goetz* (Leipzig, 1920)

E. Radecke: 'Die Berliner Erstaufführung der "Widerspenstigen" von Hermann Goetz', *Jb der Literarischen Vereinigung Winterthur*, xii (1928), 11–33

G. B. Shaw: *Music in London 1890–94* (London, 1932)

G. Puchelt: 'Hermann Goetz (1840–1876)', *SMz*, cxvi (1976), 438–45   CHRISTOPHER FIFIELD

Goetze, Walter W. (*b* Berlin, 17 April 1883; *d* Berlin, 24 March 1961). German composer. He began as a bassoonist in theatre orchestras, became a conductor and song composer, and made a name in the theatre with his music for the revue *Nur nicht drängeln* (1912, Berlin). That led to his first operetta, *Der liebe Pepi* (1913), and some 25 successors. Of these, *Ihre Hoheit, die Tänzerin* (1919) and *Adrienne* (1926) were the most successful. Goetze's works were often based on historical subjects, and in them he sought to retain something of the traditions and standards of classical operetta. Though his works never achieved international success, numbers such as 'Im Rausch des Glücks' (from *Ihre Hoheit, die Tänzerin*) and 'Ein bisschen Talent muss man haben' (from *Adrienne*) have continued to provide rewarding lighter material for German opera singers.   ANDREW LAMB

Goeyvaerts, Karel (August) (*b* Antwerp, 8 June 1923). Belgian composer. He studied composition at the Antwerp Conservatory and, from 1947 to 1951, at the Paris Conservatoire, where his teachers included Milhaud and Messiaen. He was associated with the Institute for Psychoacoustics and Electronic Music in Ghent for 1970 to 1974, when he was appointed producer of new music concerts for Flemish Radio, Brussels, a post he held until 1987. In the 1970s, concurrently with a renewal of interest in his innovatory works of the early 1950s, Goeyvaerts's later compositions began to captivate new audiences with their repetitive and meditative minimalism. He has written for a wide variety of forces, including electronic instruments. His only opera, *Aquarius*, of which the first version is in two parts and was first performed at the Stadsschouwburg Theatre, Rotterdam, on 5 April 1990, was begun in 1983; it is scored for eight sopranos, mixed chorus, five dancers and instrumental ensemble. It is not an opera in the traditional sense: there is no narrative, dramatic tension or solo writing, but instead an emphasis on shared experience. Its subject is the coming astrological age of Aquarius with its promise of universal concord, represented by a diatonicism that discards even the tension of conventional tonality. The minimal movement between keys and in melodic and rhythmic elements, and the use of incantatory repetition, evoke the static nature of everlasting peace. The opera is still being revised: the third version is for eight female and eight male voices, chorus and orchestra.

DIANA VON VOLBORTH-DANYS

Gogol, Nikolay Vasil'yevich (*b* Sorochintsï, Poltava province, 19/31 March 1809; *d* Moscow, 21 Feb/4 March 1852). Russian writer of Ukrainian birth. He has been second only to Pushkin, among Russians, as a literary source for musical dramatization.

An enthusiastic operagoer, Gogol penned a famous welcome to Glinka's *A Life for the Tsar* in 1836: 'What an opera one could make out of our national motifs! Show me a people that has more songs. ... Do we not have the makings of an opera of our own? Glinka's opera is but a beautiful beginning'. Even before Glinka made his operatic début, Gogol had embodied his prescription for 'an opera of our own' in his Ukrainian folktales, collected under the title *Evenings on a Farm near Dikanka* and published in 1831–2 (another collection, *Mirgorod*, followed in 1835). Karlinsky (1976), among others, has shown how operatic many of their plots are; their sources — by no means confined to 'national motifs' (such as the Ukrainian puppet theatre known as the *vertep*, or the contemporary Franco-

Russian vaudeville) – prominently include Weber's *Der Freischütz* and Kauer's *Das Donauweibchen*. The stories also abound in descriptions of folksong and folkdance, sometimes actually specified in text or tune, making them a treasure trove for Russian and Ukrainian composers. (Their ardent pro-Tsarist partisanship was another attraction for musicians working under strict censorship conditions.)

The earliest musical adaptations from these collections were an abortive *Mayskaya noch'* ('May Night') by Alexander Serov (1850–54) and two settings made in the 1860s by the violinist Nikolay Yakovlevich Afanas'yev (1821–98), *Vakula-kuznets* ('Vakula the Smith') after *Noch' pered rozhdestvom* ('Christmas Eve'), and *Taras Bulba*. They were never produced and the manuscripts have perished. Ukrainian regionalists provided the next stage of Gogolian adaptations. The first was *Mayskaya noch'* by Petro Sokal'sky (1876, Kiev). Mykola Lysenko composed a whole series, beginning with *Utoplena* ('The Drowned Maiden', also after *Mayskaya noch'*), on which he embarked in 1871, and continuing with *Rizdv'yana nich* in 1877, after *Noch' pered rozhdestvom*, and *Taras Bulba* (begun in 1880); none achieved performance before 1883. *Noch' pered rozhdestvom* was also adapted, under the name *Tsaritsïnï bashmachki* ('The Empress's Shoes'), as an Offenbachian operetta by the team of Oktavy Mil'chesky (words) and K. Gertman (music).

The Gogolian peasant comedy was established as a major genre of Russian opera through a contest sponsored by the court-backed Russian Musical Society for the best setting of a libretto based on *Noch' pered rozhdestvom*, commissioned in 1866 from the poet Yakov Polonsky for setting by Alexander Serov, who had died in 1871 before composing the score. (The circumstances were significant: the chosen story celebrated Russian hegemony over the Ukraine, and the genre-establishing libretto originated in the highest aristocratic circles; thus the Gogolian folktale opera amounted to an officially sanctioned quasi-political genre.) Tchaikovsky won the contest with *Vakula the Smith* (composed 1874; revised as *Cherevichki* in 1885); among the runners-up were Nikolay Solov'yov and the minor Ukrainian composer and music educator Petro Andriyovich Shtsurovsky (1850–1908). Under the stimulus of the contest, Rimsky-Korsakov (one of the judges) and Musorgsky next turned their attention to the genre, the former with yet another *Mayskaya noch'* (but the only survivor in the repertory) and the latter with *Sorochinskaya yarmarka* ('The Fair at Sorochintsï'), begun in 1874 and left incomplete at his death. After Tchaikovsky's death Rimsky-Korsakov immediately turned to *Noch' pered rozhdestvom*, producing an eponymous opera (1895) that differed radically from his rival's in its treatment of the story. He then turned to *Sorochinskaya yarmarka*, which however did not get beyond a scenario (in two acts) and a single scene of libretto dialogue.

By far the most frequently adapted of Gogol's early stories was *Taras Bulba*, a romantic Cossack adventure tale. In addition to the two already mentioned, its settings include eponymous operas by Konstantin Vil'boa (*c*1861, unfinished), Vasily Vasil'yevich Kühner (1880, St Petersburg), Vladimir Kashperov (1887, Moscow), and Sergey Alexandrovich Trailin (1914, Moscow), in addition to the unperformed but published *Osada Dubno* ('The Siege of Dubno') by Sokal'sky (1878). There were also four settings by non-Russians:

the Argentinian Arturo Berutti (1895, Turin), the Englishman J. D. Davis (1895, Birmingham, as *The Zaporogue Cossacks*), the French composer Marcel Samuel-Rousseau (1919, Paris) and the German Ernst Richter (1935, Stettin). Two early horror stories were also given eponymous operatic settings in pre-revolutionary Russia: *Viy* (1897, Chernigov) by Alexander Leont'yevich Gorelov (1863–after 1937), and *Strashnaya mest'* ('The Terrible Revenge' 1903, Moscow) by Nikolay Razumnikovich Kochetov (1864–1925).

Standing quite apart from the standard Gogolian tradition is Musorgsky's famous verbatim recitative setting (1868) of scenes from the first act of the farce *Zhenit'ba* ('Marriage'). It remained unpublished until 1908 (ed. Rimsky-Korsakov), unperformed until 1909, and thus really belongs to the history of 20th-century opera, on which it has had a certain influence. It was completed by Mikhail Ippolitov-Ivanov in 1931 and by Alexander Tcherepnin in 1935; an independent verbatim setting of the play was made by Grechaninov (1948); more conventional operas on the same subject were composed by Daniel Ruyneman (1930), Alois Jiránek (1945) and Martinů (for television, 1953).

In the 20th century interest has shifted away from the Ukrainian tales, which have reverted in the main to the province of operettists or Ukrainian regionalists such as Alexey Ryabov (*Sorochinskiy yarmarok*, 1936; *Mays'ka nich*, 1937), Mykhaylo Verykivsky (*Viy*, 1946) and, for a latterday example, Vitaly Hubarenko (*Viy*, 1980). A free adaptation of *Sorochinskaya yarmarka* by Iwan Knorr entitled *Dunja* was performed in 1904. Gogol's more ambitious and enigmatic later works, whose wild grotesqueries are susceptible to interpretation as social or moral satire, have attracted such leading Soviet composers as Shostakovich (*The Nose*, 1930; *The Gamblers*, 1978); Yury Butsko (*The Diary of a Madman*, 1971); Alexander Kholminov (*The Overcoat* and *The Carriage*, both 1975); Rodion Shchedrin (*Dead Souls*, 1977); and Moisey Vaynberg (*The Portrait*, 1983). *Revizor* ('The Inspector General'), Gogol's most important play, has given rise to a host of musical adaptations, beginning with a Turkish-language setting by the Armenian composer Tigran Chukhadjian (*Arif*, 1872), and encompassing the work both of Soviet (Dmitry Shvedov, 1934; Georgy Ivanov, 1983), and Western composers (Karel Weis, 1907; Amilcare Zanella, 1940; Werner Egk, 1957; Eugene Zador, 1971; Tibor Sebo-Martinský, 1973). Other 20th-century Westerners who have set librettos derived from Gogol include Karel Moor (*Vij*, 1903), Hilding Rosenberg (*Porträttet*, 1956), Humphrey Searle (*Diary of a Madman*, 1959), Tauno Marttinen (*Päällysviitta*, 1964) and Pierre Ancelin (*Le journal d'un fou*, 1975). Walter Kaufmann, the American composer and ethnomusicologist, wrote two operas based on Gogol: *Die Nase* (1953, performed as *The Research*); and *The Cloak* (1952, performed as *Bashmachkin*).

short stories unless otherwise stated

Sorochinskaya yarmarka [The Fair at Sorochintsï] (1831–2): Musorgsky, 1874–81, perf. 1913; B. K. Dnovsky, before 1903; Knorr, 1904, as Dunja; A. Ryabov, 1936

Mayskaya noch', ili Utoplennitsa [May Night, or The Drowned Maiden] (1831–2): A. Serov, comp. 1850–54; P. P. Sokal'sky, 1876; Rimsky-Korsakov, 1880; Lysenko, 1885, as Utoplena; Ryabov, 1937

Noch' pered rozhdestvom [Christmas Eve] (1831–2): Afanas'yev, comp. 1860s, as Vakula-kuznets; P. A. Shtsurovsky, comp. 1873; K. Gertman, c1875, as Tsaritsïnï bashmachki; Tchaikovsky,

1876, as Kuznets Vakula [Vakula the Smith]; N. F. Solov'yov, 1880, as Vakula kuznets; Lysenko, 1883, as Rizdv'yana nich; Rimsky-Korsakov, 1895; A. Peysin, 1929

Strashnaya mest' [The Terrible Revenge] (1831–2): N. R. Kochetov, 1903

Igroki [The Gamblers] (comic sketch, c1833): Shostakovich, 1942, perf. 1978

Portret [The Portrait] (1833–4): Rosenberg, 1956; Vaynberg, 1983

Nos [The Nose] (1833–5): Shostakovich, 1930; W. Kaufmann, 1953, as The Research

Povest' o tom, kak possorilsya Ivan Ivanovich s Ivanom Nikiforovichem [Tale of how Ivan Ivanovich Quarelled with Ivan Nikiforovich] (1833–5): Banshchikov, 1973, as Opera o tom, kak possorilsya Ivan Ivanovich s Ivanom Nikiforovichem

Viy (1833–5): A. L. Gorelov, 1897; K. Moor, 1903; Verykivsky, 1946; Dobronić, comp. 1947, as Vječnaja pamjat [Eternal Memory]; Hubarenko, 1980

Zapiski sumasshedshego [Diary of a Madman] (1835): Searle, 1959; Butsko, 1971; P. Ancelin, 1975, as Le journal d'un fou; Rajičić, 1981

Taras Bulba (1835): Afanas'yev, comp. 1860s; Vil'boa, comp. c1861; Sokal'sky, 1878, as Osada Dubno [The Siege of Dubno]; V. V. Kühner, 1880; Lysenko, 1880–91, perf. 1924; Kashperov, 1887; Berutti, 1895; J. D. Davis, 1895, as The Zaporogue Cossacks; S. A. Trailin, 1914; Samuel-Rousseau, 1919; E. Richter, 1935

Kolyaska [The Carriage] (1836): Kholminov, 1975

Revizor [The Inspector General] (comedy, 1836): Tchukhatjian, 1872, as Arif; Weis, 1907; D. N. Shvedov, 1934; Zanella, 1940; Egk, 1957; Fribec, comp. 1965; E. Zador, 1971; T. Sebo-Martinský, 1973; G. Ivanov, 1983; Hadjiev, comp. 1989

Shinel' [The Overcoat] (1842): Kaufmann, 1952, as Bashmachkin; Marttinen, 1964, as Päällysviitta; Kholminov, 1975; Rosenfeld, 1978

Myortvïye dushi [Dead Souls] (novel, 1842): Shchedrin, 1977

Zhenit'ba [Marriage] (comedy, 1842): Musorgsky, 1868, perf. 1909; D. Ruyneman, 1930, as Het huwelijk; A. Jiránek, 1945; Grechaninov, 1948; Martinů, 1953

*

G. Abraham: 'Rimsky-Korsakov's Russian Operas', *Studies in Russian Music* (London, 1936), 167–92

A. Gozenpud: 'Gogol' v muzïke', *Literaturnoye nasledstvo*, lviii (Moscow, 1952), 893–924; repr. in *Izbrannïye stat'i* (Leningrad and Moscow, 1971), 28–63

B. Asaf'yev: 'Gogol' v muzïke', *Izbrannïye trudï*, iv (Moscow, 1955), 154–6 [orig. pubd 1927]

G. Tyumeneva: *Gogol' i muzïka* (Moscow, 1966)

L. Keefer: 'Gogol and Music', *Slavic and East European Journal*, xiv (1970), 160–81

S. Karlinsky: *The Sexual Labyrinth of Nikolay Gogol* (Cambridge, MA, 1976)

P. Taylor: *Gogolian Interludes: Gogol's Story 'Christmas Eve' as the Subject of the Operas by Tchaikovsky and Rimsky-Korsakov* (London, 1984)

B. Shteynpress: 'Russkaya literatura v zarubezhnoy opere' [Russian Literature in Foreign Operas], *SovM* (1985), no.6, pp.83–8

RICHARD TARUSKIN

Gokieli, Vano [Ivan] **Rafailovich** (*b* Tbilisi, 9/21 Oct 1899; *d* Tbilisi, 10 July 1972). Georgian composer. He studied at the Leningrad Conservatory, where his teachers included Shcherbachyov, Kushnaryov and Shteynberg. After graduating in 1931, he was music broadcasts editor for Trans-Caucasian and Georgian radio (until 1937). He was President of the Union of Composers of the republic of Georgia, 1938–42, then worked at the Tbilisi Conservatory (1942–5, 1958–72).

His first opera, *Malen'kiy kakhetinets* ('Little Kakhetian'), is based on A. Tsereteli's *Patara kakhi* and was staged in Tbilisi in 1943. *Krasnaya shapochka* ('Little Red Riding Hood') is taken from Charles Perrault's *Contes des temps* and was also first produced at Tbilisi, in 1958.

STEPHEN JOHNSON

Goldberg, Reiner (*b* Crostau, nr Bautzen, 17 Oct 1939). German tenor. He studied in Dresden, making his début in 1966 at the Landestheater as Luigi (*Il tabarro*). In

1973 he joined the Staatsopern of Dresden and Berlin and sang in the première of Ernst Meyer's *Reiter der Nacht* (Berlin). As well as singing in many of the principal theatres of Germany, he has appeared in Vienna, Geneva, Prague, Budapest and Leningrad and at the Paris Opéra. In 1982 he sang Walther at Covent Garden, Erik at the Salzburg Easter Festival and Florestan at the Salzburg Summer Festival. After cancelling his engagement as Siegfried at Bayreuth in 1983, he appeared there in 1987 as Walther and in 1988 as Siegfried (*Götterdämmerung*); in 1984 he sang Tannhäuser at La Scala. His repertory includes Parsifal, Max, Huon (*Oberon*), Bacchus, Faust, Hermann (*The Queen of Spades*), Sergey (*Lady Macbeth of the Mtsensk District*), the Drum Major and the title role of Dessau's *Die Verurteilung des Lukullus*. In 1991 he sang both Siegfrieds at short notice in the Covent Garden *Ring* cycle. He sang Parsifal on the soundtrack of Syberberg's film of the opera. He has a well-focussed voice with a powerful upper register.   ELIZABETH FORBES

Golden Cockerel, The [*Zolotoy petushok* (*Le coq d'or*)]. Dramatized fable (*nebïlitsa v litsakh*) in a prologue, three acts and an epilogue by NIKOLAY ANDREYEVICH RIMSKY-KORSAKOV to a libretto by VLADIMIR NIKOLAYEVICH BEL'SKY after the eponymous imitation folk tale in verse by ALEXANDER SERGEYEVICH PUSHKIN, based in turn on 'The House of the Weathercock' and 'Legend of the Arabian Astrologer' from *The Alhambra* by Washington Irving; Moscow, Solodovnikov Theatre (Sergey Ivanovich Zimin's private opera company), 24 September/7 October 1909.

King Dodon	bass
Prince Guidon	tenor
Prince Afron	baritone
Commander Polkan	bass
Amelfa *royal housekeeper*	contralto
Astrologer	tenore-altino
The Queen of Shemakha	soprano
The Golden Cockerel	soprano

Boyars, guards, footsoldiers, canoneers, servants, the Queen of Shemakha's slave girls and entourage, crowd

Setting The imaginary realm of King Dodon

Rimsky-Korsakov's last opera, incorporating (in Act 2) music originally sketched for abandoned projects on *The Barber of Baghdad* (1895) and *Sten'ka Razin* (1905), was very quickly composed between October 1906 and September 1907. Then began a protracted battle with the censor, which prevented the work from reaching the stage until after the composer's death. The portrayal of a slothful autocrat engaged in idiotic warfare struck too close to home in the wake of the humiliating Russo-Japanese War. The composer, who had suffered indignities during the political disturbances of 1905, did in fact harbour a grudge against the Autocracy, and the censor's sensors were not aroused altogether in vain. Indeed, the autograph full score bore an epigraph, later prudently crossed out, from the role of the Distiller in Rimsky's own *May Night*: 'A fine song, friend! A pity, though, that the head man gets mentioned in it in less than decent words'. The composer refused to alter the libretto, with its reference near the end to 'a new dawn … without the Tsar'. (The cènsor's demands were in any case obtuse, requiring the

elimination of lines from the original, long since published Pushkin text.) The only parts of the opera that were performed during Rimsky's lifetime were the Introduction and Wedding Procession, played at a 'Russian Symphony Concert' (alongside Stravinsky's early vocal suite *The Faun and the Shepherdess*) under the auspices of the Belyayev publishing house in February 1908, and the Queen of Shemakha's Hymn to the Sun, sung in concert the next month by the soprano Nadeshda Zabela. Emil Cooper conducted the first stage performance, the next year; the production was designed by Ivan Bilibin, and Nikolay Speransky sang King Dodon, Aureliya Dobrovol'skaya the Queen of Shemakha.

Though the cartoonish mockery of authority is clear enough in a blanket sort of way, the libretto's symbolism – assuming it exists – has resisted coherent explanation. The *envoi*, 'The fable's false, but contains a hint, a lesson for good young lads!', addressed to the reader by Pushkin and to Rimsky's audience by the Astrologer, remains as teasing in the opera as it had been in the tale.

The Golden Cockerel is the only one of Rimsky-Korsakov's 15 operas to have achieved repertory status beyond Russia. This was Dyagilev's doing. At the prompting of the artist Alexandre Benois, the great impresario staged the opera in Paris and London in 1914 (under the title *Le coq d'or*, which has stuck to it in the West), with the singers seated in rows at the sides

1. '*The Golden Cockerel*' (*Rimsky-Korsakov*): design by Ivan Bilibin for the costume of the Queen of Shemakha in the original production at the Solodovnikov Theatre (Zimin's private opera company), Moscow, 24 September/7 October 1909

2. 'The Golden Cockerel' (Rimsky-Korsakov), Act 3 (the capital): design by Ivan Bilibin for the original production at the Solodovnikov Theatre (Zimin's private opera company), Moscow, 24 September/7 October 1909

of the stage, accompanying the movements of dancers and mimes, who enacted the plot according to the conventions of *ballet d'action* (choreography by Fokin). With colourful sets and costumes by Natal'ya Goncharova in the style of primitive Russian broadside prints (*lubki*), this production delightfully enhanced the cartoonish aspect of the opera (although the composer's enraged widow successfully sought a restraining order through the French courts) and vouchsafed its continuing popularity. (A similar production was mounted at the New York Metropolitan Opera in 1918 with choreography by Adolph Bolm, Pierre Monteux conducting.) It also set an important precedent for Stravinsky, whose opera *The Nightingale*, not to mention such later stage works as *Renard*, *The Wedding* and *Pulcinella*, to a greater or lesser extent embodied the same split between singing and movement. It was an important stage in the modernist dismantling of the *Gesamtkunstwerk*.

PROLOGUE The Astrologer, the opera's framing character and its implied narrator, appears before the curtain to warn the audience that he is about to conjure up a cautionary tale.

ACT 1 *King Dodon's throne room* The king complains that he is tired of warfare but that his neighbours keep on invading. He asks his assembled councillors, including his two sons, how can he avoid engagements in the future. Prince Guidon answers that he should withdraw the army to the capital, because life is more pleasant there than at the frontier. With no army at the border no one will invade. All think this is a marvellous idea until Commander Polkan points out that defending the capital is riskier than defending the frontier. Prince Afron suggests they disband the army and only mobilize it a month before each attack. This idea too is acclaimed until Polkan, whom everyone resents as a killjoy, points out that the enemy is not likely to give a month's notice. Everyone, now baffled, longs for the days when the future could be foretold in beans or in wine-dregs (and begin to argue as to which is the better method). At this point, accompanied by the same music as in the Prologue, the Astrologer appears with a magic Golden Cockerel who, placed on a high perch, can warn of any border disturbance, and can also tell the king when it is safe to 'reign, lying on your side'. Overjoyed, the king promises any reward the Astrologer

can name. The latter says he will claim his reward later, but would like the promise in writing, to make it 'lawful'. The king indignantly refuses ('Lawful? What's that? I never heard of such a thing. My whims and orders – that's the law around here'). Amelfa now brings in the big royal baby's bed, some treats to eat and his pet parrot, who, interpreted by Amelfa, sings his praises. The Cockerel gives reassurance and everyone falls asleep. To judge by his music, the king sees a vision resembling the Queen of Shemakha in his dreams. All at once the Cockerel sounds the alarm. Polkan awakens the king, who mobilizes two armies, placing one of his sons at the head of each. Again the Cockerel sounds the alarm. Now the king must go into battle himself. Grumbling, he dons his rusty armour (which he has grotesquely outgrown) and goes off to battle, his people seeing him off with huzzahs.

ACT 2 *A mountain gorge* Looking in vain for the battle, the king stumbles upon the bodies of his two sons, whose armies have apparently fought each other to total destruction. He spies a tent which, he reasons, must contain the enemy. Before he can attack it out comes the gorgeous Queen of Shemakha, who sings her famous Hymn to the Sun, 'Otvet' mne, zorkoye svetilo' ('Answer me, bright orb'); she then brazenly announces that she has come to subdue King Dodon, not by force of arms but by her voluptuous charms. At her command, Dodon sends Polkan away, removing his only protection from the evil queen's wiles. The rest of the act is given over to the conquest, which begins with the queen's description of her unclothed body, and ends with a wild dance that exhausts the king and makes him her slave. (In his stern performance note, Rimsky-Korsakov directs that the dance should only look strenuous; 'it must not interfere with the singers' breathing'.) Having exacted Dodon's promise to banish Polkan (he goes even further and orders his loyal commander beheaded), the queen 'agrees' to come back with him and become his consort.

ACT 3 *The capital* The crowd is wondering when the army will return. The royal wedding procession approaches; all hail the king and the new queen. Suddenly the Astrologer's music is heard; he materializes and claims his reward – the queen! The king naturally reneges on his promise and has the Astrologer forcibly removed. The Astrologer resists. Dodon strikes him on the head and kills him; at this the sky darkens. The queen laughs it all off, but when the king tries to embrace her she repulses him with taunts. They dismount and begin to ascend the steps to the palace, but the Cockerel swoops down from its perch and pecks the king on the head, killing him. When light returns, both the Cockerel and the Queen of Shemakha have vanished. The terrified crowd laments.

EPILOGUE The Astrologer reappears before the curtain, reminding the audience that what they have seen is only a fairy tale and that the bloody dénouement should therefore not upset them. He leaves with the cryptic assurance that only he and the Queen of Shemakha were real people – 'all the rest were dream, delusion, pale shade, empty air …'.

* * *

The opera opens with a brash trumpet phrase (later to be identified as the Golden Cockerel's cry) which must remind anyone who knows it of the tag with which all the scenes of *The Tale of Tsar Saltan* begin. The trumpet is now muted, yet played fortissimo and doubled, which turns the timbre into a musical cartoon, reminiscent of the garish colours and crude draughtsmanship of *lubki*. That vein of parody is characteristic of the opera throughout. It is a study in calculated tawdriness and triviality – again anticipating Stravinsky, this time the composer of *Petrushka*. The orchestra is full of gaudy sonorities, some of them, like the Astrologer's glockenspiel, functioning as 'leit-timbres'.

Two of the three traditional melodies quoted in the score are of the paltriest sort imaginable. When the Queen of Shemakha forces King Dodon to sing her a love song in Act 2, he does so to the tune of 'Chizhik, chizhik, gde tï bïl?' ('Birdie, birdie, where've you been?'), the Russian equivalent of 'Pat-a-cake' or 'Ring a ring of roses'. The triumphant Wedding Procession in Act 3 reaches its climax with a snatch of 'Svetit mesyats' ('The moon shines brightly'), a veritable roadhouse number. (The remaining folk tune, the aptly named 'Uzh tï, sizen'kiy petun' ('Oh you little grey-blue cock') is associated with Amelfa in Act 1.) The chorus that greets the bridal couple is harmonized in a wicked burlesque of the 'folk harmonizations' that ethnomusicologists like Yevgeniya Linyova, armed with phonographs, had been touting as the 'authentic' Russian idiom of the future. (The chorus proves that Rimsky had seen her work, and that he disapproved of it.) The casting of the eunuch Astrologer as a weird *tenore altino* (for which, according to the composer's performance note, a high tenor with a strong falsetto register may substitute) is the ultimate *lubok* coloration. When he claims the Queen of Shemakha, improbably, for a bride, his voice shoots up to an *e''*.

The Queen of Shemakha's Lakmé-ish coloratura music is a *reductio ad absurdum* of the stereotyped 'oriental' idiom associated with many works by the Five (or 'mighty Kuchka'), and also of the sequence-driven chromaticism (now extended to encompass retrogrades and inversions) long associated with fantastic characters in Rimsky-Korsakov's earlier operas. Even in the act of parody, Rimsky advanced the 'artificial' harmonic idiom in spots to the point of virtual atonality, making *The Golden Cockerel* a *locus classicus* of early modernism (its most direct issue again being early Stravinsky: compare the title characters' music in *The Firebird* or *The Nightingale*). But, as King Dodon says in Act 3, 'to everything there is a limit'. There was a line, firmly

Ex.1 Act 1

(a) Ki-ri-ku-ku! Be-re-gis', bud' na che-ku!
['Cockadoodledoo! Watch out, be on your guard!']

(b)

(c) Pe-tu-shok kri-chit. Vsta-vai-te! Èy, bor-zïkh ko-ney sed-lai-te!
['The cock has cried. Get up! Saddle up the brave steeds!']

drawn in Professor Rimsky-Korsakov's imagination, that he would not and could not cross. 'There you are, decadents, have a feast', he remarked with nervous testiness in a letter to a friend, 'but still and all, pornographic clowns, to decadence I have not descended!'. What kept him 'above' it was precisely the reliance on mechanistic sequences that many analysts and critics now deplore.

Where the fantastic mode had been rigorously segregated in earlier Rimsky-Korsakov from the folkish or diatonic, in *The Golden Cockerel* the two are interwoven to an unprecedented degree, realizing the notion of *nebïlitsa* as embodied in the opera's subtitle – a story in which everything is unreal. The actual cry of the cock, given a 'fantastic' harmonization when it appears as such, also furnishes the background figuration for the saccharine lullaby music in Act 1, and immediately thereafter, for a folkish chorus (ex.1).

RICHARD TARUSKIN

Goldene Kreuz, Das ('The Golden Cross'). *Romantische Oper* in two acts by IGNAZ BRÜLL to a libretto by S. H. Mosenthal, after Mélesville (A.-H.-J. Duveyrier) and Nicolas Brazier's *Catherine*; Berlin, Königliches Opernhaus, 22 December 1875.

To save Nicolas (baritone) from conscription on his wedding day, his sister Christine (soprano) offers to marry anyone who will take his place, giving the recruiting sergeant Bombardon (baritone) a golden cross as pledge. Gontran (tenor), a young nobleman, takes up her offer. Two years later, Nicolas, having volunteered for the army, returns home wounded, his life saved by Gontran, now an officer. Gontran admits losing the golden cross on the battlefield. Bombardon produces it, but he recognizes Gontran as the fallen comrade from whom he had taken it and all ends happily with the wedding of Gontran and Christine.

With Lilli Lehmann as Christine, the opera had a successful run and was widely performed throughout Europe, reaching London on 2 March 1878 in a Carl Rosa production coinciding with the composer's concert tour. An English edition was published by Bote and Bock. Brüll's effortless flow of lyrical melody is here at its best, resulting in a work of considerable power and dramatic effect.   JOHN A. PARKINSON

Golden Pavilion, The. Opera by Toshirō Mayuzumi; *see* KINKAKUJI.

Golden Slippers, The. Opera by P. I. Tchaikovsky; *see* CHEREVICHKI.

Goldenweiser [Gol'denveyzer], **Alexander** (**Borisovich**) (*b* Kishineu, 26 Feb/10 March 1875; *d* Moscow, 26 Nov 1961). Russian composer. At the Moscow Conservatory he studied composition with Arensky, Ippolitov-Ivanov and Taneyev. He first performed publicly in 1896 as a pianist. He played an important role in music education in the USSR, teaching at the Moscow Philharmonic School and the Moscow Conservatory, and helping to found the Central Music School; Kabalevsky was among his pupils. Goldenweiser was on close terms with Tolstoy, and his writings include an article on Tolstoy and music in *Literaturnoye nasledstvo* (1939, nos.37–8). His compositions include three operas, all first performed in Moscow. In 1946 he was made People's Artist of the USSR.

all premières are concert performances

Pir vo vremya chumï [The Feast in the Time of the Plague] op.21, 1942 (1, after A. S. Pushkin), Moscow, Central House of Composers, 1 June 1945

Pevtsï [The Singers] op.22, 1942–4 (1, Yu. Stremin, after I. S. Turgenev), Moscow, House of Actors, 19 Jan 1945

Veshniye vodï [Spring Waters] op.26, 1945–50 (4, Stremin, after Turgenev), Moscow, House of Actors, 4 March 1955

Goldmark, Karl [Carl, Károly] (*b* Keszthely, 18 May 1830; *d* Vienna, 2 Jan 1915). Hungarian composer. The son of a Jewish cantor and notary, Goldmark grew up in Ném
etkeresztúr (now Deutschkreuz, Austria), near Ödenburg (now Sopron, Hungary). Although he never learnt to speak Hungarian, and stated in his memoirs that he considered himself to belong to the world of German culture, he retained a strong affection for his native land. This is reflected in a number of works on Hungarian themes such as the tone poem *Zrinyi* (1903), and in the occasional use of melodic patterns reminiscent of the *verbunkos* repertory. Goldmark received music instruction locally and in 1844 joined his elder brother Josef in Vienna to study the violin; in 1847 he enrolled at the Vienna Conservatory. After a brief involvement in the Hungarian uprising of 1848 he returned to Vienna, and for seven years played the violin in the Carltheater orchestra. This was ill-paid employment, but it allowed him to become intimately acquainted with theatrical routine, something that stood him in good stead when he later embarked on his first opera. Goldmark was largely self-taught as a composer, and, not surprisingly, the critical response to a concert of his works in 1858 was mixed. That year he moved to Budapest and embarked on a serious study of harmony and counterpoint, orchestration and the works of Bach and Beethoven. In 1860 he returned to Vienna, where he taught the piano, conducted a male-voice choir, and composed a number of chamber and orchestral works that gradually established his reputation, including the *Sakuntala* overture (1865). Goldmark formed a number of friendships, notably with Brüll, Rubinstein and Brahms. In the early 1860s he also wrote music reviews for the *Österreichische-konstitutionelle Zeitung*, in which he championed the cause of Wagner. (With Johann Herbeck, Otto Dessoff and others he later signed the *Aufruf* for the first Viennese Wagner society, the Akademische Wagner-Verein, in 1872.) As early as 1861 he was introduced to the music of *Tristan* by Peter Cornelius and Karl Tausig.

Goldmark was made an honorary member of the Gesellschaft der Musikfreunde in 1866. From 1870 until his death he divided his time between Gmunden, where he spent the summer months, and Vienna. Towards the end of his long life he became a respected figure in Viennese musical life, illustrated by Mahler's largely unsuccessful attempts to secure Goldmark's support for his application to the Hofoperntheater in 1897. In 1896 he was awarded the Ritterkreuz of the Order of Leopold. Goldmark's 70th and 80th birthdays were marked by performances of *Die Königin von Saba* and *Götz von Berlichingen* at the Hofoperntheater. In 1910 he was awarded an honorary doctorate by Budapest University and was made a freeman of his birthplace.

Goldmark's most famous, personal and successful work, *Die Königin von Saba*, was inspired by his piano pupil Caroline Bettelheim, who gave the first performances of some of his chamber works. In 1865 Salomon Hermann Mosenthal provided him with a suitable libretto, and in 1869 Goldmark received a grant of 800 gulden from the Hungarian government, enabling him to complete the opera in November 1871. Shortly afterwards he submitted the work to the Hofoperntheater. In 1873, when it seemed about to be rejected, Goldmark wrote a touching letter to Hanslick in its defence. He was persuaded to include part of Act 1, the arrival of the Queen of Sheba, in a Viennese charity concert on 11 January 1874 in which Liszt and Brahms also took part. Despite further intrigues, the première finally took place on 10 March 1875. It was a great success, and performances in many European operatic centres followed, notably in Italy. The opera was rejected by Covent Garden on the grounds that figures from the Old Testament could not appear on an English stage.

In 1877, between *Die Königin von Saba* and his second opera, *Merlin*, of 1886, Goldmark completed his most popular orchestral work, the symphonic poem *Ländliche Hochzeit* op.26. The Arthurian subject matter of *Merlin*, whose libretto was by Mahler's mentor Siegfried Lipiner, may well have been suggested by *Parsifal*. Merlin, the child of a virgin and a devil, is seduced by Viviane at the behest of the Demon, thereby losing his visionary faculties. However, he is able to save Arthur and the Knights of the Round Table in their struggle against the Saxons, though at the cost of his own life. At the end, in a kind of *Liebestod*, Viviane commits suicide in order to redeem him. In the Vienna première on 19 November 1886, conducted by Wilhelm Jahn, the main roles were created by Amalie Materna (Viviane) and Hermann Winkelmann (Merlin). In *Merlin* the influence of the grand-opera model is still very much apparent, especially with regard to the stage effects, the effective employment of crowd scenes and choral ensembles, and the ballet in the second act. As in *Die Königin von Saba*, there are a number of musical reminiscences, though only one real leitmotif, that of the Demon, with which the overture begins. The vocal score of *Merlin* was prepared by Busoni, who also wrote a concert fantasia on themes from the opera.

After *Merlin* Goldmark turned to a subject of a less elevated kind. In 1894 A. M. Willner drew to his attention Dickens's *The Cricket on the Hearth*. The fairy-tale quality of *Das Heimchen am Herd* no doubt owes a debt to the example of Humperdinck's *Hänsel und Gretel*, and its unabashed sentimentality amplifies that of the Dickensian original, with the added twist that Dot is expecting her first child, an unusual operatic feature. However, this is offset by a certain rustic humour, especially the characterization of the aging suitor Tackleton. The music is of deliberate simplicity, with set numbers linked by what virtually amounts to *secco* recitative. One of the rustic choruses quotes the beginning of a well-known German folksong. As Heinrich Schenker remarked, there is nothing particularly English about this opera. The première, conducted by Jahn on 21 March 1896 in Vienna, was a resounding success, the main roles being created by Marie Renard (Dot), Fritz Schrödter (Edward), Irene Abendroth (May), Ellen Forster (Cricket) and Franz von Reichenberg (Tackleton).

The subject matter of Goldmark's next opera, *Die Kriegsgefangene*, which deals with an episode from the Trojan War, may have been prompted by the example of August Bungert's *Odysseus' Heimkehr* of 1896 (although Goldmark had already explored the world of ancient Greece in three concert overtures: *Penthesilea* op.31, 1879, *Der gefesselte Prometheus* op.38, 1889 and *Sappho* op.44, 1893). The première in 1899 was conducted by Mahler; it was only moderately successful. The same is true of Goldmark's last two operas. Goethe's *Götz von Berlichingen* may well have attracted him because the hero was, in Goethe's words, 'someone who fended for himself in a time of anarchy' – an idea Goldmark no doubt found appealing as he contemplated the heady innovations of the Viennese avant garde. The première of this, his most Germanic opera, was given at the Royal Hungarian Opera (1902). His last opera, *Ein Wintermärchen*, an adaptation of *The Winter's Tale*, received a lukewarm response when it was performed in Vienna in 1908.

Max Kalbeck recorded that Goldmark's motto had been: 'Unable to be a pioneer and unwilling to be a fellow traveller, I went my own way'. Certainly he was never in the vanguard of musical progress, yet neither was he ever a slavish disciple of Meyerbeer or Wagner.

See also Heimchen am Herd, das *and* Königin von Saba, die.

first performed at Vienna, Hofoperntheater, unless otherwise stated; MSS in H-Bn

Die Königin von Saba op.27 (4, S. H. Mosenthal, after I Kings 10), 10 March 1875, vs (Bremen, 1876)
Merlin (3, S. Lipiner), 19 Nov 1886, vs (Leipzig, 1886); rev., Frankfurt, 1904
Das Heimchen am Herd (3, A. M. Willner, after C. Dickens: *The Cricket on the Hearth*), 21 March 1896, vs (Vienna, 1896)
Die Kriegsgefangene (2, E. Schlicht [A. Formey]), 17 Jan 1899, vs (Leipzig, n.d.)
Götz von Berlichingen (5, Willner, after J. W. von Goethe), Budapest, Royal Hungarian Opera, 16 Dec 1902, vs (Leipzig, 1902); rev., Frankfurt, 1903
Ein Wintermärchen (3, Willner, after W. Shakespeare: *The Winter's Tale*), 2 Jan 1908, vs (Vienna, 1907)

*

E. Hanslick: 'Die Königin von Saba von K. Goldmark', *Musikalische Stationen* (Berlin, 1880), 298–305

——: 'Merlin von Karl Goldmark', *Musikalisches Skizzenbuch* (Berlin, 1888), 76–85
M. Kalbeck: 'Merlin', *Opernabende*, i (Berlin, 1898), 162–9
——: 'Das Heimchen am Herde', ibid, 169–74
R. Batka: 'Das Heimchen am Herd', *Musikalische Streifzüge* (Florence and Leipzig, 1899), 157–68
E. Hanslick: 'Das Heimchen am Herde von Goldmark', *Am Ende des Jahrhunderts* (Berlin, 1899), 9–17
——: 'Die Kriegsgefangene von Goldmark', *Aus neuer und neuester Zeit* (Berlin, 1900), 1–10
——: 'Die Königin von Saba von Goldmark', ibid, 10–17
O. Keller: *Carl Goldmark* (Leipzig, 1901)
R. Heuberger: 'Das Heimchen am Herd', *Im Foyer: gesammelte Essays* (Leipzig, 1901), 201–7
A. Seidl: 'Karl Goldmark: Heimchen am Herd', *Die Wagner-Nachfolge im Musik-Drama* (Berlin, 1902), 207–13
A. Bettelheim: *Karoline van Gomperz-Bettelheim: ein biographisches Blatt zum 1. Juni 1905* (Vienna, 1905)
R. Batka: *Aus der Opernwelt* (Munich, 1907), 107ff, 185–6
H. Wolf: *Musikalische Kritiken* (Leipzig, 1911), 168, 297–305
R. Louis: *Die deutsche Musik der Gegenwart* (Munich, 3/1912), 58–9
J. Korngold: 'Ein Wintermärchen', *Deutsches Opernschaffen der Gegenwart* (Leipzig and Vienna, 1921), 224–31
——: 'Götz von Berlichingen', ibid, 231–7
K. Goldmark: *Erinnerung aus meinem Leben* (Vienna, 1922, 2/1929)
H. Schwarz: *Ignaz Brüll und sein Freundeskreis* (Vienna, 1922)
M. Kálmán: *Károly Goldmark* (Budapest, 1930)
J. Klempá: *Károly Goldmark* (Budapest, 1930)
L. Koch: *Karl Goldmark* (Budapest, 1930) [with bibliography]
M. Káldor and P. Várnai: *Goldmark Károly élete és müvészete* [Karl Goldmark: Life and Music] (Budapest, 1956)
I. Kecskeméti, ed: *Goldmark Károly: emlékek életemböl* [Karl Goldmark: Memoirs] (Budapest, 1980) [with commentary]
M. Parkai-Eckardt: 'Einflüsse der ungarischen Musik bei Goldmark', *Brahms-Kongress: Vienna 1983*, 427–38

ALFRED CLAYTON

Goldoni, Carlo [Fegejo, Polisseno] (*b* Venice, 25 Feb 1707; *d* Paris, 6 or 7 Feb 1793). Italian playwright and librettist. His best comedies, distinguished by a seemingly effortless dramatic technique and an acute observation of character and manners, place him in the front rank of Italy's dramatic authors. In a career that began slowly but at its peak made uncommon demands on his creative energies (in 1750–51 he promised, and delivered, 16 new comedies), Goldoni also found time to write some 80 librettos, most of them comic, although he also wrote *opere serie*, cantatas and oratorios.

1. LIFE. Goldoni's early years were full of false starts. He evinced a literary bent while still at school but wrote poetry of no special distinction. He studied law at Padua and was admitted to the bar in Venice in 1732. Meanwhile he had written some comic intermezzos (1729/30, 1732) and a *dramma per musica*, which he himself destroyed (1733). Finding his legal profession unprofitable, he attached himself to a *commedia dell'arte* troupe in 1734, furnishing them with spoken tragicomedies and sung intermezzos, the latter set to music by mostly unknown composers and performed between the acts of the spoken plays. It is highly unlikely that Vivaldi set to music *Aristide*, as some believe; this, one of two operatic parodies by Goldoni, was simply another intermezzo, sung inexpertly by the comedians themselves (see Weiss 1984). At the same time he was hired to assist Domenico Lalli, the poet-in-residence at the chief opera house in Venice, S Giovanni Grisostomo; this involved helping to stage *opere serie* and adapting or rewriting their librettos. The experience thus gained in two very different branches of theatre was to stand him in good stead in later years; meanwhile, he appears to have aspired to the dignity of tragic poet *à la* Metastasio, for

the years 1736 to 1741 saw the modestly successful production of five (if not all six) of his serious operas at the S Giovanni Grisostomo.

Financial difficulties put an abrupt end to this early phase of Goldoni's career; in 1743 he left Venice, eventually settling in Tuscany to practise law. When he returned to Venice, in 1748, he was under contract to another *commedia dell'arte* troupe. Abandoning traditional scenarios in favour of wholly written-out comedies, Goldoni at the age of 40 embarked at last on the career that gained him his place in Italian literature. At the same time, he launched upon the long series of *opera buffa* librettos, working at first with Ciampi but soon (from 1749) with Galuppi, in a collaboration that over the next seven years produced some of the century's most successful comic operas. Other composers who availed themselves of his librettos in Venice included Cocchi, Giuseppe Scarlatti, Bertoni and Fischietti. Goldoni worked fast; a comic opera libretto took him four days, as he testified in a letter of 24 July 1762 from Bologna (having just finished *La bella verità*, set by Piccinni – a libretto of peculiar interest, since it deals with the production of an *opera buffa*, making fun of its singers and conventions). Goldoni was then on his way to Paris, where he arrived that August. There he settled permanently, never to return to Italy; his productivity as both playwright and librettist continued for a while but then abated. His last great success was a comedy written in French, *Le bourru bienfaisant*, performed at the Comédie-Française in 1771; but his last stage work, like his first, was a libretto (*Il talismano*, 1778).

2. WORKS. In his various autobiographical writings, Goldoni studiously belittled his librettos; indeed, once he had become famous he invariably signed them with his Arcadian sobriquet, Polisseno Fegejo, as if to distinguish them from the works on which he wished to rest his reputation. To him they were a lucrative sideline. Yet he permitted, and most probably supervised, at least the first collection of his comic librettos, in four volumes, published by Tevernin (Venice, 1753), and very probably approved the ten-volume set (Venice, 1794–5) published by Zatta shortly after his death. At least three other collected editions appeared during his lifetime, not to mention numerous unauthorized versions of single works; of these Goldoni took the trouble to warn readers of his *Mémoires* (Paris, 1787): 'Nota. Les Opéras-Comiques de M. Goldoni ont parcouru plusieurs endroits de l'Italie [he might more correctly have said 'de l'Europe']. L'on y a fait par-tout des changemens au gré des Acteurs et des Compositeurs de musique. Les Imprimeurs les ont pris où ils ont pu les trouver, et il y en a très-peu qui ressemblent aux Originaux.' It was the fate of comic operas, even more than of *opere serie*, to be turned into virtually unrecognizable pasticcios very soon after their first run. If not proud of his librettos, therefore, Goldoni at least was wary lest the numberless corrupt versions circulating be imputed to him; for, being a successful man of the theatre, he was much scrutinized and attacked by literary critics.

Goldoni in fact was no Zeno or Metastasio: his librettos do not stand up as literature. Yet they worked remarkably well in the theatre and were repeatedly set to new music (though not as often as those of his two illustrious predecessors). Indeed, it was through his librettos that Goldoni's work first reached St Petersburg and Moscow, Warsaw, Prague, Brussels, London, Madrid and Barcelona; and Haydn and Mozart were among the many foreign composers who set them to new music.

Goldoni's flair for the living stage prevented any of his productions (whether for the spoken theatre or for the opera house) from ever smacking of literature; they were meant to be seen rather than read. The same genius that produced vignettes of everyday life in the spoken plays provided talented composers with the most variegated materials, drawn mostly from fantasy and rich in spectacle and twists of plot, for the realization of the very different requirements of the *opera buffa*. An opening ensemble (eventually to be termed 'introduzione'), providing a colourful tableau and some inkling of the action to follow, plentiful ensembles sprinkled throughout the rest of the three-act work, a duet between the two principals just before the concluding scene of Act 3: these are some of the hallmarks of the typical Goldoni *opera buffa* libretto. His principal contribution, however, and one recognized as such by his contemporaries (see Gozzi, 427), was the lengthy, action-studded finale, designed for continuous musical setting, that invariably concluded each of the first two acts. It is here that composers learnt to deal musically with one element in opera (action or incident) that had traditionally been beyond their purview, having been relegated until then to recitative.

Before extensive comparative studies have been made of the librettos of less eminent contemporary authors, it is not possible to state categorically that every single aspect of this new, mid-18th-century *opera buffa* type originated with Goldoni. There is no doubt, however, as to the sheer quantity and immense popularity of his librettos. His *Il filosofo di campagna*, set by Galuppi in 1754, and *La buona figliuola*, in the 1760 resetting by Piccinni, were possibly the most influential, certainly the most successful operas of the period. His, it is safe to say, was a pivotal role in the history of the genre; at the very least he helped to give *opera buffa* the shape in which, in the mid-18th century, it gained the ascendancy on the stages of Italy and Europe.

Renewed interest in Goldoni's works on the part of composers in the early 20th century led to operatic settings by, among others, G. F. Malipiero and Wolf-Ferrari.

See also CONTESSINA, LA; MONDO DELLA LUNA, IL and PESCATRICI, LE.

Editions: *Opere complete*, ed. G. Ortolani and others (Venice, 1907–71)

Tutte le opere, ed. G. Ortolani (Milan, 1935–56)

INTERMEZZOS

Il buon vecchio, comp. unknown, Feltre, 1729/30

La cantatrice, comp. unknown, Feltre, 1729/30 (? Apolloni, 1734, as La pelarina)

I sdegni amorosi tra Bettina putta de campielo e Buleghin barcariol venezian, comp. unknown, Milan, ?1733 (Coppola, 1825, as Il gondoliere di Venezia)

La pupilla, Maccari, 1734 (comp. unknown, Florence, 1737; comp. unknown, Bologna, 1756; comp. unknown, Rovigo, 1764; Gialdini, 1896; Mancini, 1908)

La birba, comp. unknown, Venice, 1735 (comp. unknown, Milan, 1743)

L'ippocondriaco, comp. unknown, Venice, 1735

Il filosofo, comp. unknown, Venice, 1735 (comp. unknown, Milan, 1743; comp. unknown, Bologna, 1744)

Aristide, Lotavio Vandini [=Antonio Vivaldi; but see Weiss 1984], 1735

Monsieur Petiton, comp. unknown, Venice, 1736

La bottega da caffè, comp. unknown, Venice, 1736 (comp. unknown, Milan, 1743; comp. unknown, Venice, 1744)

L'amante cabala, comp. unknown, Venice, 1736 (comp. unknown, Venice, 1744)

Lugrezia romana in Costantinopoli, Maccari, 1737 (Trento, 1800)

Il finto pazzo (after T. Mariani: *La contadina astuta*), Pergolesi, Chiarini and ?Latilla, 1741

Il quartiere fortunato, ?Maggiore, ?1744 (S. Cristiani, 1802)

La favola de' tre gobbi, Ciampi, 1749 (Fabrizi, 1783, as I tre gobbi rivali)

Il matrimonio discorde (farsetta), R. Lorenzini, 1756

La cantarina (farsetta), Galuppi, 1756

La vendemmia, Sacchini, 1760

SERIOUS OPERAS

Amalasunta, 1732–3, destroyed by Goldoni

Griselda (after A. Zeno), Vivaldi, 1735

La generosità politica (after D. Lalli: *Pisistrato*), G. Marchi, 1736

Gustavo I re di Svezia, Galuppi, 1740

Oronte re de' sciti, Galuppi, 1741 (Scalabrini, 1742)

Statira, Chiarini, 1741 (Maggiore and others, 1751; Scolari, 1756)

Tigrane (after F. Silvani: *La virtù trionfante dell'amore e dell'odio*), G. Arena, 1741 (Gluck, 1743; Dal Barba, 1744; Lampugnani, 1747; comp. unknown, Venice, 1756; Tozzi, 1762)

Germondo, Traetta, 1776

COMIC OPERAS

La fondazion di Venezia, Maccari, 1736

La contessina, Maccari, 1743 (Lampugnani, 1759; Gherardeschi, 1766; composer unknown, Gorizia, 1766; Gassmann, 1770; Astarita, 1772; Bernardini, 1773; G. Rust, 1774, as Il conte Baccellone; Kürzinger, 1775; Piccinni, 1775; ? Cimarosa, 1778

La scuola moderna o sia La maestra di buon gusto (after A. Palomba: *La maestra*), Cocchi, Fiorini, V. Ciampi and others, 1748

Bertoldo, Bertoldino e Cacasenno, Ciampi, 1749

L'Arcadia in Brenta, Galuppi, 1749 (G. Meneghetti, 1757; Cordeiro, 1764; composer unknown, Cologne, 1771; C. Bosi, 1780)

Il negligente, Ciampi, 1749

Il finto principe, pasticcio, 1749 (? Paisiello, 1768)

Arcifanfano re dei matti, pasticcio, Galuppi and others, 1749 (E. Duni, 1760, as L'isle des foux; Tozzi ?1766–7; Scolari, 1768; Dittersdorf, 1776)

Il mondo della luna, Galuppi, 1750 (Avondano, 1765; Paisiello, 1774, as Il credulo deluso; Astarita, 1775; Haydn, 1777; Paisiello, 1783; Neri Bondi, 1790; Portugal, 1791, as O lunático iludido [O mundo da lua])

Il paese della cuccagna, Galuppi, 1750 (? Mango, 1760; Tozzi, 1771; Astarita, 1777, as L'isola di Bengodi)

Il mondo alla roversa o sia Le donne che comandano, Galuppi, 1750 (? Paisiello, 1764)

La mascherata, Cocchi, 1751

Le donne vendicate, Cocchi, 1751

Il conte Caramella, Galuppi, 1751

Le pescatrici, Bertoni, 1751 (R. Gioanetti, 1754; Haydn, 1770; Gassmann, 1771)

Le virtuose ridicole, Galuppi, 1752 (Geronimo Cordella, 1756; Paisiello, 1765; Ottani, 1769)

I portentosi effetti della madre natura, G. Scarlatti, 1752 (Piccinni, 1761, as Le vicende della sorte)

La calamita de' cuori, Galuppi, 1752 (Salieri, 1774; ?Cimarosa, ?1792)

I bagni d'Abano, pasticcio, Galuppi and F. Bertoni, 1753 (? Paisiello, 1765)

De gustibus non est disputandum, G. Scarlatti, 1754

Il filosofo di campagna, Galuppi, 1754

Li matti per amore (after Federico: *Amor vuol sofferenza*), Cocchi, 1754

Il povero superbo (after Goldoni: *La gastalda*), Galuppi, 1755

Lo speziale, V. Pallavicini and D. Fischietti, 1755 (Haydn, 1768)

Le nozze, Galuppi, 1755 (Cocchi, 1762, as Le nozze di Dorina; Sarti, 1782, as Fra due litiganti il terzo gode)

La cascina, Scolari, 1755 (Brusa, 1758; Brusa and Scolari, 1761, as La quesera)

La diavolessa, Galuppi, 1755 (Bárta, 1772)

La ritornata di Londra, Fischietti, 1756 (Galuppi, 1759, as int)

La buona figliuola, Duni, 1756 (Piccinni, 1760; S. Perillo, 1760)

Il festino, Ferradini, 1757

Il viaggiatore ridicolo, Mazzoni, 1757 (Perillo, 1761; Gassmann, 1766; Scolari, 1770; P. Caramanica, 1771)

L'isola disabitata, G. Scarlatti, 1757

Il mercato di Malmantile, ? G. Scarlatti, 1757 (Fischietti, 1757; Bárta, 1784; Zingarelli, 1792, as Il mercato di Monfregoso)

La conversazione, Scolari, 1758

Il signor dottore, Fischietti, 1758

Buovo d'Antona, Traetta, 1758

Li uccellatori, Gassmann, 1759 (P. A. Guglielmi, 1762, as I cacciatori; Marinelli, 1785)

Il conte Chicchera, Lampugnani, 1759

Filosofia ed amore, Gassmann, 1760 (Gassmann, 1771, as Il filosofo innamorato)

La fiera di Sinigaglia, Fischietti, 1760

Amor contadino, Lampugnani, 1760

L'amore artigiano, Latilla, 1760–61 (Gherardeschi, 1763; Gassmann, 1767; Schuster, 1776; Accorimboni, 1778; ? Neefe, 1779, as Die Liebe unter den Handwerksleuten [see Wirth 1962, p.162])

Amore in caricatura, Ciampi, 1761 (G. Notte, 1763)

La donna di governo, ?pasticcio, Rome, 1761 (Fischietti, 1763; ? Galuppi, 1764)

La buona figliuola maritata, Piccinni, 1761 (Scolari, 1762)

La bella verità, Piccinni, 1762

Il re alla caccia, Galuppi, 1763 (Alessandri, 1769; Ponzo, ?1775)

La finta semplice, S. Perillo, 1764 (Mozart, 1769)

La notte critica, Boroni, 1766 (Piccinni, 1767; Gassmann, 1768; Gherardeschi, 1769; Fortunati, 1771; Lasser, 1790, as Die unruhige Nacht)

La cameriera spiritosa, Galuppi, 1766 (Gherardeschi, 1767, as L'astuzia felice)

Vittorina, Piccinni, 1777

Il talismano, Salieri and Rust, 1779 (Salieri, 1788)

Unperf.: *I volponi*

Doubtful: *Le nozze in campagna*, Sciroli, 1768

*

BurneyH; LoewenbergA

G. Gozzi, ed.: *La gazzetta veneta*, 1760–61; ed. A. Zardo (Florence, 1915)

V. Alfieri: *Vita di Vittorio Alfieri scritta da esso* (London, 1807)

A. G. Spinelli: *Bibliografia goldoniana* (Milan, 1884)

A. Wotquenne: *Alphabetisches Verzeichnis der Stücke in Versen aus den dramatischen Werken von Zeno, Metastasio und Goldoni* (Leipzig, 1905)

A. Della Torre: *Saggio di una bibliografia delle opere intorno a Carlo Goldoni, 1793–1907* (Florence, 1908)

H. C. Chatfield-Taylor: *Goldoni: a Biography* (New York, 1913)

O. G. T. Sonneck: *Miscellaneous Studies in the History of Music* (New York, 1921)

W. C. Holmes: 'Pamela Transformed', *MQ*, xxxviii (1952), 581–94 [on *La buona figliuola*]

V. Branca and N. Mangini, ed.: *Studi goldoniani* (Venice, 1960)

N. Mangini: *Bibliografia goldoniana, 1908–1957* (Venice, 1961) [with sequels in *Studi goldoniani*, 1968–]

G. Ortolani: *La riforma del teatro nel settecento e altri scritti* (Venice, 1962)

H. Wirth: 'Carlo Goldoni und die deutsche Oper', *Hans Albrecht in memoriam* (Kassel, 1962), 160–67

N. Mangini: *La fortuna di Carlo Goldoni e altri saggi goldoniani* (Florence, 1965)

P. Weiss: *Carlo Goldoni, Librettist: the Early Years* (diss., Columbia U., 1970)

——: 'Goldoni poeta d'opere serie per musica', *Studi goldoniani*, iii (1973), 7–40

R. Strohm: *Die italienische Oper im 18. Jahrhundert* (Wilhelmshaven, 1979)

P. Weiss: 'Venetian Commedia dell'Arte "Operas" in the Age of Vivaldi', *MQ*, lxx (1984), 195–217

N. Mangini: 'I teatri veneziani al tempo della collaborazione di Galuppi con Goldoni', *Galuppiana 1985: studi e ricerche: Venice 1985*, 133–42

M. Metzeltin: 'Appunti sulla poetica dei drammi giocosi goldoniani', *Oper als Text: romanistische Beiträge zur Libretto-Forschung*, ed. A. Gier (Heidelberg, 1986), 55–64

A. L. Bellina: Introduction to A. Palomba and G. Cocchi: *La maestra*, DMV, xix (1987), pp.vii–lxiv

T. A. Emery: 'Goldoni's *Pamela* from Play to Libretto', *Italica*, lxiv (1987), 572–82 [on *La buona figliuola*]

D. Heartz: 'The Poet as Stage Designer: Metastasio, Goldoni and Da Ponte', *Mozart's Operas*, ed. T. Bauman (Berkeley, 1990), 89–105

PIERO WEISS

Goldovsky, Boris (*b* Moscow, 7 June 1908). Russian-American conductor and producer. The son of the violinist Lea Luboschutz, he studied the piano with his uncle, Pierre Luboschutz, and attended the Moscow Conservatory. He later studied in Berlin, and attended Ernő Dohnányi's masterclasses in Budapest. In 1930 he moved to the USA and studied conducting with Fritz Reiner at the Curtis Institute of Music. At first antipathetic to opera, Goldovsky became an ardent convert during his early years in America. He has since been an enthusiastic and effective proselytizer, in a variety of capacities: as head of the opera department at the New England Conservatory of Music, Boston (1942–64), and the opera workshop at the Berkshire Music Center at Tanglewood (1946–62); as founder of the New England Opera Theater in 1946; and as director of the Goldovsky Opera Theater, which toured nationwide until 1984. At Tanglewood he presented the American premières of *Peter Grimes*, *Idomeneo* and *Albert Herring*, and in 1955, with his Boston company, he gave the North American première (albeit heavily cut) of Berlioz's *Les Troyens*. For more than 40 years he has been a regular intermission commentator for the Metropolitan Opera's Saturday afternoon broadcasts. His books include *Accents on Opera* (New York, 1953), *Bringing Opera to Life* (New York, 1968), and *My Road to Opera* (Boston, 1979).

For illustration *see* REHEARSAL, fig.3.   PETER G. DAVIS

Goldschmidt, Adalbert von (*b* Vienna, 5 May 1848; *d* Hacking, nr Vienna, 21 Dec 1906). Austrian composer. He gave up a career in banking to write music and poetry, taking composition lessons from F. A. Wolf. Following the success in Berlin and elsewhere of his oratorio *Die sieben Todsünden* (1876), though Hanslick condemned it as an ugly, exaggerated, unoriginal imitation of Wagner, in which the composer had committed 'a hundred thousand deadly sins', he began work on an opera, *Helianthus*, inspired by a watercolour by J. von Führich. He then began his most important work, the opera-oratorio trilogy *Gaea* (completed in 1892). He also wrote a symphonic poem, several songs, chamber and piano works. Both *Gaea* and *Die sieben Todsünden* show the influence of Wagner's music drama. Goldschmidt's salon was an important centre of Viennese musical life; Liszt once played there.

Helianthus (3, A. von Goldschmidt), Leipzig, Stadt, 26 March 1884, vs (Leipzig, 1884)
Gaea (dramatische Tondichtung, 3 parts, Goldschmidt), Berlin, 1893 (concert perf. of part), vs (Vienna, 1912)
Die fromme Helene (komische Oper, F. Gröger), Hamburg, Stadt, 14 Oct 1897

*

StiegerO
E. Hanslick: *Concerte, Componisten und Virtuosen der letzten fünfzehn Jahre 1870–1885* (Berlin, 1877, 4/1896)
R. Hamerling: *Stationen meiner Lebenspilgerschaft* (Hamburg, 1889)
A. von Hanstein: *Musiker- und Dichterbriefe* (Berlin, 1900)
E. Friedegg, ed.: *Briefe an einen Komponisten: musikalische Korrespondenz an Adalbert von Goldschmidt* (Berlin, 1909)
F. Klose: *Meine Lehrjahre bei Bruckner* (Regensburg, 1927)
          GAYNOR G. JONES

Goldschmidt, Berthold (*b* Hamburg, 18 Jan 1903). British composer and conductor of German origin. He studied at the University of Hamburg and at the Friedrich Wilhelm University, Berlin, and from 1922 to 1925 with Schreker at the Berlin Hochschule für Musik. In 1927 he became assistant conductor of the Darmstadt Opera, and while in Darmstadt wrote incidental music for various stage productions. After working as artistic adviser to the Berlin Städtische Oper and as guest conductor with Berlin radio and the Leningrad PO, he emigrated to Britain in 1935. He took British nationality in 1947, the year he conducted the Glyndebourne Opera at the first Edinburgh International Festival.

Goldschmidt's first opera, *Der gewaltige Hahnrei* (1929–30; 3, after F. Crommelynck: *Le cocu magnifique*; 1932, Mannheim), is a setting of a savage farce about sexual jealousy, in which the young husband, Bruno (tenor), has such uncontrollable suspicions of his innocent young wife's fidelity that he eventually drives her to betray him. The vigour of Crommelynck's writing is more than matched by the fierce energy of Goldschmidt's score. After its successful première, *Der gewaltige Hahnrei* was about to be staged at the Berlin Städtische Oper in 1933 when the Nazi takeover intervened. Goldschmidt's composing career was severely disrupted by his enforced emigration, and it was not until 1949 that he began his second opera, *Beatrice Cenci* (3, M. Esslin, after P. B. Shelley: *The Cenci*). This was one of four operas commissioned by the Arts Council as the result of a competition to celebrate the Festival of Britain: none of the four, however, reached a performance at the time; the première of *Beatrice Cenci* was at a concert performance in the Queen Elizabeth Hall, London, on 16 April 1988. Goldschmidt's restrained, classical treatment of a violent story, in which Beatrice (soprano), daughter of the sadistic Count Cenci (baritone), and her stepmother Lucrezia (mezzo-soprano) are hanged for instigating Cenci's assassination, owes much to his commitment to Busoni's aesthetic principles. The opera ends with a chorus that sets Cenci's crimes and the tragedy they provoke in a universal context.

*

P. Banks: 'The Case of "Beatrice Cenci"', *Opera*, xxxix (1988), 426–32
          DERYCK COOKE/DAVID MATTHEWS

Golem. Opera in two parts (Prelude and Legend) by JOHN CASKEN to a libretto by the composer with Pierre Audi; London, Almeida Theatre, 28 June 1989.

The ancient Jewish legend of the Golem describes how a saviour figure is created to protect the innocent when a community is under threat. Casken's treatment of the legend relates its main action in flashback. In the Prelude the Maharal (baritone) remembers in old age how, many years before, he had created a golem. Accompanied by six ghostly madrigalists (the other members of the cast), he relives in his imagination the events that led to the death of his creation, while Ometh (countertenor) reminds the Maharal of his own role in the tragedy. The Legend then tells that story in five scenes. The young Maharal creates the Golem (bass-baritone) from clay on the banks of a river, although Ometh, a wounded, Promethean figure, questions his motives. As the Golem learns to talk and to perform everyday tasks, he comes into contact with the townspeople, with Stoikus (tenor), mourning the loss of his own son, and Miriam (soprano), the Maharal's wife, whom the Golem desires. Ometh arrives and confronts the Maharal: together with the Golem he could drive evil out of the world; the Maharal angrily dismisses him. When the townspeople meet to rise up against their oppression, the Golem unwittingly interrupts them; after being taunted he kills Stoikus. He is briefly united with Ometh, but the Maharal intervenes, only to discover the murder and what his creation has done.

481

Casken's vocal lines and instrumental music (ten players and tape) create a richly coloured web around the story; passages of freely notated counterpoint and folk references serve as points of relaxation and dramatic repose in a highly wrought dramatic scheme. The vocal lines employ deliberate archaisms (as in the use of a madrigal group in the Prelude), and there are well-defined set pieces (such as the extrovert 'Swing your body' in the second scene of the Legend), while the pre-recorded tape both establishes the atmosphere of contemplation when the Maharal creates the Golem and includes specific sounds, such as the wing-flaps of the giant bird that hovers over that creation.

Golem won the first Britten Award for Composition in 1990 and was recorded as part of the award; the American première was at Omaha in 1990, and a second British production toured in 1991.   ANDREW CLEMENTS

Goleminov, Marin (*b* Kyustendil, 28 Sept 1908). Bulgarian composer. In 1930 he graduated from the Sofia Academy of music, then studied in Paris (1931–4), with d'Indy at the Schola Cantorum and Dukas at the Ecole Normale de Musique. He worked as a teacher, violinist and conductor in Bulgaria before leaving for Munich to study composition (1938–9). In 1943 he was offered a post at the Sofia State Academy. His numerous works have their roots in the melody, metre and rhythm of Bulgarian folk music. He has written three operas. *Ivaylo* is in the grand opera style, while in *Thrakiiskite idoli* ('Thracian Idols') a historical subject is used to make a philosophical and ethical point.

Ivaylo (M. Petkanova, after I. Vazov), Sofia, National Opera, 13 Feb 1959
Zakhary Zografat [The Icon-Painter Zakhary] (P. Spasov, after his *Grekhovnata Lyubov na Zografa Zakhary*), Sofia, National Opera, 17 Oct 1972
Trakiiski idoli [Thracian Idols] (S. Dichev), Stara Zagora, Opera, 1981

L. Sagayev: *Balgarsko operno tvorchestvo* [Bulgarian Opera Works] (Sofia, 1959), 150–54
M. Manolova: *Trakiiski idoli na sofiiska tsena* [Thracian Idols on the Sofia Stage], *Puls* (1983)
LADA BRASHOVANOVA, MAGDALENA MANOLOVA

Golisciani, Enrico (*b* Naples, 25 Dec 1848; *d* Naples, 6 Feb 1919). Italian librettist and poet. He was a prolific author; he wrote over 80 librettos between 1871 and the year of his death. His early style was influenced by the melodramatic nature of the works of Hugo and Sardou. Ponchielli's last opera, *Marion Delorme* (1885, Milan), was a setting of Golisciani's libretto, based on the novel by Hugo. After the success of *Cavalleria rusticana* (1890) he was one of the first Neapolitans to exploit the possibilities of *verismo*, notably in P. A. Tasca's setting of *A Santa Lucia* (1892). In the 1890s he also began to introduce local colour, regional characteristics and social realism. His best-known librettos were written for Wolf-Ferrari: *Il segreto di Susanna* (1909, Munich), *I gioielli della Madonna* (with C. Zangarini, 1911, Berlin) and *L'amore medico* (1913, Dresden).

Un matrimonio nella luna, F. Bonamici, 1871; *Rosetta la giardiniera*, G. Avolio, 1872; *Camoens*, P. Musone, 1872; *La fiamma*, V. Magnetta, 1873; *Wallenstein*, Musone, 1873; *Maria Stuarda*, C. Palumbo, 1874; *Naso il montanaro*, L. Caracciolo, 1874; *Il pipistrello*, De Giosa, 1875; *La fata* (operetta), G. Miceli, 1875; *Don Bizzarro e le sue figlie* (operetta), Mugnone, 1875; *Maria e Fernanda*, F. Ferrari, 1875; *Mamma Angot al seraglio di Costantinopoli* (operetta), Mugnone, 1875; *Carlo di Borgogna*, Musone, 1876

Cuor de Marinaio, C. Sessa, 1876; *Griselda*, O. M. Scarano, 1878 (G. Cottrau, 1878); *Lida Wilson*, Bonamici, 1878; *Il conte di S Romano*, De Giosa, 1878; *Gli equivoci*, E. Sarria, 1878; *Gabriella Candiano*, A. Moroder, 1878; *Ginevra di Monreale*, C. Parravano, 1878 (G. Bonavia, 1890); *Il ritratto di perla*, C. Rossi, 1879; *Cleopatra*, Bonamici, 1879; *Un bagno freddo* (operetta), C. De Nardis, 1879; *Il segreto della duchessa*, G. Dell'Orefice, 1879; *Sogno d'amore*, B. C. Bellini, 1880; *I cavalieri di Malta*, A. Nani, 1880

Duca e paggio (operetta), G. Gnarra, 1880; *L'alpigiana*, N. Cassano, 1880; *Il savoiardo* (operetta), V. Galassi, 1880; *Guerra alle donne*, A. Falconi, 1881; *Nella*, F. Frontini, 1881; *Rabagas*, De Giosa, 1882; *Margherita di Borgogna*, Falconi, 1884; *La moglie rapita*, R. Drigo, 1884; *Cordelia de' Neri*, F. Aldieri, 1884; *Re Manfredi*, Sessa, 1884; *Bianca*, P. A. Tasca, 1885; *Marion Delorme*, Ponchielli, 1885; *Una notte a Venezia*, F. Avallone, 1885; *Il testamento dello Zio Saverio* (operetta), Galassi, 1886 (I. De Vita, 1900, as *Amor la vince*)

Etelkà, C. Buongiorno, 1886; *Lockinvar*, R. Kelli, 1887; *Ivanhoe*, A. Ciardi, 1888; *Agnese Visconti*, Nani, 1889; *Gina*, Cilea, 1889; *Bianca di Nevers*, A. Baci, 1889; *Lili* (operetta), R. Martini, 1891; *Erebo*, G. Giannetti, 1891; *Il diavolo zoppo* (operetta), Buongiorno, 1891; *I guanti gialli*, Spinelli, 1891; *Biondino* (operetta), Buongiorno, 1891; *Sara la trovatella*, L. F. Bianco, 1892; *Cimbelino*, Westerhout, 1892; *Vendetta abruzzese*, G. Tanara, 1892; *Il birichino*, Mugnone, 1892; *Colombo a S Domingo*, J. Morales, 1892; *A Santa Lucia*, Tasca, 1892

Teresa Raquin, E. Coop, 1894; *Dea*, P. Ronzi, 1894; *Eros*, N. Massa, 1895; *La sorella di Mark*, Setaccioli, 1896; *La festa della messe*, Buongiorno, 1896; *Wanda*, R. Bacchini, 1896; *La pupilla*, G. Gialdini, 1896; *Max*, G. Menichetti, 1898; *Luigi Rolla*, G. Scognamiglio, 1899; *Atal Kar*, C. Dall'Olio, 1900; *La Moretta*, A. Fimiani, 1900; *Daniella*, M. Marzano, 1901; *La sirena*, Baci, 1903; *Vigile di notte*, T. de Angelis, 1903; *Manuel Garcia*, L. Tarantini, 1904; *Vita brettone*, Mugnone, 1905

Niny-Bily (operetta), M. d'Alessandro, 1906; *Iglesias*, V. Baravalle, 1907; *La borghesina*, Machado, 1909; *Il segreto di Susanna*, Wolf-Ferrari, 1909; *Maritani*, G. Tarantini, 1911; *I gioielli della Madonna*, Wolf-Ferrari, 1911; *Antony*, R. Casalini, 1912; *La Du Barry*, E. Camussi, 1912; *L'amore medico*, Wolf-Ferrari, 1913; *Lulu e Nini* (operetta), Marzano, 1916; *Champagna-Club* (operetta), A. Curci, 1916; *Il candaliere*, Ferrari, 1917; *Donna Rios*, A. Ceccarini, 1920; *Il garafano bianco*, Drigo, 1929
BARBARA REYNOLDS (text), JOHN BLACK (work-list)

Golishev, Efim [Jef] (*b* Kherson, Ukraine, 8/20 Sept 1897; *d* Paris, 25 Sept 1970). Ukrainian composer and painter. A pupil of Leopold Auer, he toured as a violin soloist with the Odessa SO in 1905. In 1909 he went to Berlin, where he studied at the Stern conservatory and won the Reger Prize. He had support from Busoni in his compositional experiments, which in 1915–16 included two operas, one of them being *Cyrano de Bergerac* (after Edmond Rostand); neither was performed, and the manuscripts were lost during World War II. He also wrote music for Pudovkin's film *Igdenbu the Great Hunter*.

Golishev was active as a painter and musician in Berlin dadaist circles, and at the same time studied chemistry and acoustics. Fleeing from Nazi persecution in 1933, he went to Portugal, then Barcelona and finally to France. In 1956 he settled in Brazil, but returned to Paris during his last years.

D. Gojowy: 'Jefim Golyscheff, der unbekannte Vorläufer', *Melos/NZM*, iii (1975), 188–93   DETLEF GOJOWY

Golondrinas, Las ('The Swallows'). *Drama lírico* in three acts by JOSÉ MARIA USANDIZAGA to a libretto by Gregorio Martínez Sierra after his *Teatro del ensueño*; Madrid, Teatro Price, 5 Feb 1914.

Puck (baritone) is the leader of a small troupe of strolling players who are happy in their humble itinerant existence, all but Cecilia (soprano), whose ambition leads her to spurn his ardent declarations of love and, despite the pleas of Lina (soprano), to quit the company she despises in quest of personal fame and riches. The fortunes of the troupe improve, and in Act 2 Puck, Lina and Juanito (tenor) are found at a major Madrid circus performing a mime on the traditional subject of Punchinello, Colombine and Pierrot. By chance, however, Cecilia has been engaged by the same theatre, and though Lina tries to lighten Puck's despondency, confessing her own devoted love for him, he cannot overcome his old infatuation. Cecilia and Lina quarrel, and out of spite Cecilia pretends to reciprocate Puck's ardour; but when he stumbles back into Lina's dressing-room and begs for her pity, it emerges that, having led him on, Cecilia had then scorned and mocked him as a mere clown and he had killed her. On the discovery of her body he is led away and Lina breaks down, crying that she still loves him.

Las golondrinas was written as a zarzuela, and after the composer's death his brother Ramón replaced the original spoken dialogue to convert the work into an opera. Music for the mime in Act 2 is sometimes played separately in orchestral concerts in Spain.

LIONEL SALTER

Goltz, Christel (*b* Dortmund, 8 July 1912). German soprano. She studied with Ornelli-Leeb in Munich and before she was 20 was singing in operetta at the Deutsches Theater. In 1935 she sang Agathe in *Der Freischütz* at Fürth. After a season at Plauen, where she added Santuzza, Eva and Octavian to her repertory, in 1936 she was engaged at Dresden; she remained a member of the company until 1950, creating Juliet in Sutermeister's *Romeo und Julia* and singing Orff's Antigone. In 1947 Goltz sang in Berlin at both the Staatsoper and the Städtische Oper; she then began to appear in Vienna and Munich, as Electra, Salome, Alcestis, the Countess (*Capriccio*), Leonore and Tosca. In 1951 she made her Covent Garden début as Salome and the following year sang Marie in *Wozzeck*, a role she also sang at Salzburg, Vienna and Buenos Aires. At Salzburg she created the title role in Liebermann's *Penelope* in 1954; later that year she made her Metropolitan début as Salome. During the 1957–8 season she sang her first Isolde; at that time her repertory included nearly 120 operas. Goltz had a clear, brilliant voice, three octaves in range, and her acting was intense.

H. Rosenthal: *Sopranos of Today* (London, 1956)
A. Natan: 'Goltz, Christel', *Primadonna: Lob der Stimmen* (Basle, 1962) [with discography]
H. Rosenthal: *Great Singers of Today* (London, 1966)

HAROLD ROSENTHAL/R

Gomes, (Antônio) Carlos (*b* Campinas, 11 July 1836; *d* Belém, 16 Sept 1896). Brazilian composer. The son of a provincial bandmaster, he learnt from his father the rudiments of music and also to play several instruments, and began composing at an early age. In 1859 he went on a concert tour with his brother Sant'Ana Gomes and had considerable success in São Paulo with his verse setting *Hino acadêmico*. He then left for Rio de Janeiro against his father's will and entered the Imperial Conservatory of Music, where he studied composition under the Italian Joaquim Giannini.

The conservatory experience reinforced Gomes's predilection for opera. He soon became acquainted with the works of Rossini, Bellini, Donizetti and Verdi,

whose music exerted a profound influence on him throughout his career. In 1860 two of his cantatas attracted great attention. José Amat, then the musical director of the Opera Lírica Nacional, gave him a copy of the libretto of *A noite do castelo* by Antonio José Fernandes dos Reis, after a poem by Antonio Feliciano de Castilho, which Gomes set to music in three acts and presented with considerable success in September 1861. The work, in the style of early 19th-century Italian opera, deals with a Portuguese crusader, Henrique, believed to have died, who returns from the Holy Land to discover that his fiancée Leonor has married her neighbour Fernando. In a duel Henrique kills Fernando but is himself killed by Count Orlando, Leonor's father. Gomes's second opera, *Joana de Flandres*, in four acts to a libretto by Salvador de Mendonça, was produced successfully in September 1863. A government scholarship gave Gomes the opportunity to go to Italy where he studied with Mazzucato and Lauro Rossi, director of the Milan Conservatory, graduating in composition in 1866. Most of the rest of his life was spent in Italy, and his compositional ideals became so thoroughly italianized that his output has frequently been considered within the history of Italian opera.

Gomes's fame in Italy began with two musical comedies, *Se sa minga* (1867) and *Nella luna* (1868), both to librettos by Antonio Scalvini, which give clear evidence of his ability to write in a popular bel canto style. But it was the triumphal success of his opera-ballet *Il Guarany* at La Scala on 19 March 1870 that brought him international fame. In May of that year, Vittorio Emmanuele II named him Chevalier of the Italian Crown. The opera was produced in Rio de Janeiro the same year on the emperor's birthday (2 December) and in the next few years in some of the principal opera capitals. While in Brazil in 1871 Gomes wrote the operetta *Telégrafo eléctrico* and began *Os mosqueteiros do rei*, which he left unfinished. He returned to Milan, where his next opera, *Fosca* (1873), was produced at La Scala. It did not have a generally good reception, although the critic Giulio Ricordi wrote: 'If after *Il Guarany* Maestro Gomes had my esteem, after *Fosca* he has my whole admiration.' A new version presented at La Scala in 1878, however, had notable success. There followed the triumph of *Salvator Rosa* at the Teatro Carlo Felice, Genoa, in 1874. Gomes is reported to have said that while *Il Guarany* was meant for Brazilians and *Salvator Rosa* for Italians, *Fosca* was meant for the connoisseurs. *Maria Tudor* (1879), after Victor Hugo's drama, was his next opera, presented at La Scala without success on its first performance. Only in 1933 was this opera produced in Rio de Janeiro.

During a visit to Brazil in 1880, Gomes's friend Viscount de Taunay suggested a drama of his own as the theme of his next opera, *Lo schiavo*, begun in 1883 and first performed in Rio de Janeiro in 1889 with great success. Slavery had been abolished in Brazil in 1888, so the subject of the opera had popular appeal despite the alterations to Taunay's work by the librettist. Gomes's last opera, *Condor* (or *Odaléa*), in three acts to a libretto by Mario Canti, had its première at La Scala on 21 February 1891, with little success. The action takes place in the Orient in the 17th-century world of the Tatars. Odaléa, the queen of the Samarcanda country, is loved by Condor, a naïve Siegfried type, who gradually convinces the queen of his love. The people, revolted by this impudence, demand the death of Condor who commits suicide while the city burns. Despite the lack of dramatic interest resulting from the pseudo-legendary and exotic libretto the work reveals a new orientation towards *verismo* from the melodic point of view, with long, fluid phrases anticipating Puccini's style. In 1892, on Columbus day (12 October), the oratorio *Colombo* (called a vocal-symphonic poem by Gomes) was presented in Rio de Janeiro without success. The work comprises four parts on a banal and sentimental text by Albino Falanca (pseudonym of the poet Zanardini) in which Columbus is reduced to the inappropriate figure of an unlucky lover. Later Gomes attempted in vain to transform this work into an opera (though an operatic version was produced in 1936, under the directorship of Heitor Villa-Lobos, for the centenary of Gomes's birth). By the early 1890s the new Brazilian republican government was firmly established and Gomes lost his previous official support. In 1895 he declined nomination for the directorship of the Venice Conservatory, but in 1896 he accepted an appointment to direct the local conservatory at Belém (Pará), where he arrived in April that year; he died a few months later, however.

Gomes's works reveal a strong dramatic sense and his melodic invention a rich lyricism. Within the established patterns of late 19th-century Italian opera he achieved a considerable mastery. In assessing Gomes's position in the panorama of Italian opera, Marcello Conati traced his stylistic development from Verdi and Meyerbeer to the beginning of the 'giovane scuola'. Together with Ponchielli, Gomes is seen as the most significant composer for the 'originality of ideas and the stylistic personality: one cannot fully appreciate in its historical significance the transition phase of Romantic melodrama to the musical theatre, called "naturalist", without making reference necessarily to [Gomes's] work'. While Gomes endeavoured on several occasions to instil a Brazilian feeling in his works, his native orientation has often been overstated. Andrade himself felt that a native feeling pervaded the early works 'in some aspects, such as certain rhythmic traits, a certain abruptness of awkward melodic writing, and certain coincidences with our popular melody'. But he also observed that nationalistic concern was in Gomes's time considered incompatible with the operatic repertory.

See also FOSCA; GUARANY, IL; MARIA TUDOR; SALVATOR ROSA; and SCHIAVO, LO.

most MSS at Centro de Ciencias, Letras e Artes de Campinas, Brazil, and at the Escola Nacional de Música, Rio de Janeiro

A noite do castelo (os, 3, A. J. Fernandes dos Reis), Rio de Janeiro, Lírico Fluminense, 4 Sept 1861, vs (Rio de Janeiro, 1861)
Joana de Flandres (os, 4, S. de Mendonça), Rio de Janeiro, Lírico Fluminense, 15 Sept 1863, vs (Rio de Janeiro, c1864)
Se sa minga (musical comedy, A. Scalvini), Milan, 1867, selections, vs (Milan, c1867)
Nella luna (musical comedy, Scalvini), Milan, 1868
Il Guarany (opera-ballo, 4, Scalvini and C. d'Ormeville, after J. de Alencar), Milan, Scala, 19 March 1870, vs (Milan, 1870)
Telégrafo eléctrico (operetta, França), Rio de Janeiro, 1871
Os mosqueteiros do rei, 1871, inc.
Fosca (os, 4, A. Ghislanzoni, after L. Capranica: *La festa della Marie*), Milan, Scala, 16 Feb 1873, vs (Milan, 1873); rev. Scala, 7 Feb 1878, vs (Milan, c1878)
Salvator Rosa (os, 4, Ghislanzoni), Genoa, Carlo Felice, 21 March 1874, vs (Milan, ?1874)
Maria Tudor (os, 4, E. Praga, after V. Hugo), Milan, Scala, 27 March 1879, vs (Milan, ?1879)
Lo schiavo (os, 4, R. Paravicini, after Viscount de Taunay), Rio de Janeiro, Lírico, 27 Sept 1889, vs (Milan, c1889)
Condor [Odaléa] (os, 3, M. Canti), Milan, Scala, 21 Feb 1891, vs (Milan, 1891)

*

H. P. Vieira: *Carlos Gomes: sua arta e sua obra* (São Paulo, 1934)

Revista brasileira de música, iii (1936) [Gomes centenary issue]
L. H. Corrêa de Azevedo: *Relação das óperas de autores brasileiros* (Rio de Janeiro, 1938)
M. de Andrade: *Carlos Gomes* (Rio de Janeiro, 1939)
G. da Rocha Rinaldi: *Carlos Gomes* (São Paulo, 1955)
S. Ruberti: 'O Guarani' e 'Colombo' de Carlos Gomes: estudo histórico e crítico; análise musical (Rio de Janeiro, 1972)
M. Conati: 'Formazione e affermazione di Gomes nel panorama dell'opera italiana: appunti e considerazioni', *Antonio Carlos Gomes: carteggi italiani*, ed. G. N. Vetro (Milan, 1976), 33–78
J. Bernandes: *Do sonho a conquista* (São Paulo, c1978)
T. G. Kaufman: 'Antonio Carlos Gomes', *Verdi and his Major Contemporaries* (New York, 1990), 47–60   GERARD BÉHAGUE

Gomes (de Araújo júnior), João (*b* Pindamonhangaba, 23 Oct 1868; *d* São Paulo, 19 July 1963). Brazilian composer, son of João Gomes de Araújo. Accompanying his father to Milan in 1884, he studied there with Dominiceti (composition) and Giuseppe Mascardi (piano). In 1893 he became music professor at the São Paulo Escola Modelo do Carmo, subsequently teaching in other nearby schools. Of his three staged operas, the first two were given in São Paulo: *Foscarina* at the Teatro Sant'Ana (1906) and *La boscaiuola* at the Teatro Municipal (1910). *Foscarina* concerns a Spanish nobleman's daughter who unwittingly falls in love with her half-brother. The third, *Dom Casmurro*, was first heard at the Teatro Municipal, Rio de Janeiro (1922). In 1927 Gomes was a founder of the Instituto Musical at São Paulo and later became its director. At his death he left (in addition to much sacred music) the scores of three unproduced operas: *Iugomar* (1911), *Severo Torelli* (1914) and *Anna Garibaldi* (1918).

Foscarina (1, J. Queroz Filho), São Paulo, Sant'Ana, 22 Sept 1906
La boscaiuola (2, F. Fontana, after Viscount de Taunay: *Inocência*), São Paulo, Municipal, 1910
Iugomar, 1911 (3, Fontana), unperf.
Severo Torelli, 1914 (3, H. da Silva), unperf.
Anna Garibaldi, 1918 (1, A. Piccarolo), unperf.
Dom Casmurro (3, Piccarolo, after M. de Assis), Rio de Janeiro, Municipal, 12 Oct 1922

*

L. H. Corrêa de Azevedo: *Relação das óperas de autores brasileiros* (Rio de Janeiro, 1938), 70–72
Enciclopédia da música brasileira (São Paulo, 1977), i, 319
ROBERT STEVENSON

Gomes, Pietro. *See* COMES, PIETRO.

Gomes de Araújo, João (*b* Pindamonhangaba, 5 Aug 1846; *d* São Paulo, 8 Sept 1943). Brazilian composer. After initial studies in his home town, he enrolled in 1861 at the music conservatory of Rio de Janeiro. Returning home in 1863, he joined the clarinettist José Maria Leite to establish a conservatory, organize a band and found an orchestra. In 1884 the favourable reception of his orchestral *Missa de São Benedito*, sung at the consecration of a church in Lorena, São Paulo, caused Emperor Pedro II to send him with his family to Milan where he studied with Cesare Dominiceti.

Edméia (1886), his first opera, did not reach the stage, but *Carmosina* (1888) was given with great success in the emperor's presence at the Teatro Dal Verme, Milan, and repeated in January 1891 at the Teatro São José in São Paulo where, with the exception of 1903–4, he resided from late 1888 until his death. He composed his finest opera, *Maria Petrowna*, the story of a conspiracy to depose Catherine II of Russia, at Milan in 1903, but its première, at the Teatro Municipal, São Paulo, did not take place until January 1929. *Helena* (1908), dealing with events on a coffee plantation, was likewise staged some years after its composition, in 1916. Gomes, meanwhile, had founded the São Paulo Conservatory with Pedro Augusto Gomes Cardim in 1906.

Edméia, 1886 (3, A. Ghislanzoni), unperf.
Carmosina (3, Ghislanzoni), Milan, Dal Verme, 1 May 1888, lib. (Milan, 1888)
Maria Petrowna, 1903 (prol., 2, F. Fontana), São Paulo, Municipal, Jan 1928, vs (Milan, 1929)
Helena, 1908 (1, Bento de Camargo), São Paulo, Municipal, 14 July 1916

*

L. H. Corrêa de Azevedo: *Relação das óperas de autores brasileiros* (Rio de Janeiro, 1938), 49–50
Enciclopédia da música brasileira (São Paulo, 1977), i, 44
ROBERT STEVENSON

Gomez, Jill (*b* New Amsterdam, British Guiana, 21 Sept 1942). British soprano. She studied in London, making her début with Glyndebourne Touring Opera in 1968 as Adina. At Glyndebourne (1969–84) she sang Mélisande, Callisto, Anne Trulove and Helena (*A Midsummer Night's Dream*). She created Flora in Tippett's *The Knot Garden* at Covent Garden (1970), returning for Lisa (*La sonnambula*), Titania and Lauretta. For Scottish Opera she sang Elizabeth Zimmer (*Elegy for Young Lovers*), Anne Trulove, Fiordiligi, Countess Almaviva, Pamina and Leïla (*Les pêcheurs de perles*). With the English Opera Group she created the Countess in Musgrave's *The Voice of Ariadne* (1974) and also sang the Governess (*The Turn of the Screw*) and Ilia. At Wexford she sang Thaïs (1974) and Rosaura in *La vedova scaltra* (1983). For Kent Opera (1977–88) she sang Tatyana, Violetta, Amyntas (*Il rè pastore*) and Donna Anna. She has sung at Frankfurt, Zürich, Vienna, Lyons and Florence, where she took part in *The Fairy-Queen* (1987). She sang Helena at Sadler's Wells in 1990; her roles also include Handel's Cleopatra, Cinna (*Lucio Silla*) and Teresa (*Benvenuto Cellini*). Her voice, bright and expressive, is limited in tonal colour; she is a gifted actress.
ALAN BLYTH

Gomez, Pietro. *See* COMES, PIETRO.

Gomis y Colomer, José Melchor (*b* Onteniente, Valencia, 6 Jan 1791; *d* Paris, 4 Aug 1836). Spanish composer. At the age of seven he was a choirboy in Valencia and at 15 became choirmaster. During the Napoleonic wars he was music director in an artillery regiment (1812). About 1817 a 'melodrama unipersonal' for one voice and orchestra was performed in Valencia; this was probably *Sensibilidad y prudencia, o La aldeana*, which Loreto García introduced in Madrid on 21 June 1821. During the liberal Constitutional Triennium Gomis composed patriotic songs; he was obliged to flee to France in 1823 when Ferdinand VII reassumed absolute power. In Paris and London he taught, wrote songs and choruses with orchestral accompaniment and published *Méthode de solfège et de chant* (Paris, 1826), with introductions by Rossini and Boieldieu. Just before the 1830 July Revolution he composed songs and choruses that contributed to the success of Martínez de la Rosa's drama *Aben Humeya* (19 July 1830, Théâtre de la Porte-St-Martin).

Between 1831 and 1836 Gomis wrote the music for four operas performed at the Opéra-Comique: *Le diable à Seville*, about General Riego's 1820 army rebellion; *Le revenant*, based on 'Wandering Willie's Tale' in Scott's *Redgauntlet*, and much praised for the 'Chanson du sabbat'; *Le portefaix*, his most successful opera; and

Rock le barbu, acclaimed for the purity of its melodies. In 1833 he completed *La révolte du sérail* for the Opéra, but it was not performed. At his death, from tuberculosis of the larynx, he left unfinished *La damnée* and his plans for *Le comte Julien* (a tale of the Moorish invasion of Spain), *Lénore*, *Le favori* and *Botany Bay*. He had begun work on *Le comte Julien* to a text supplied by Scribe, who used the subject again in 1851 for Thalberg's *Florinda*. Louis-Philippe made him a Chevalier of the Légion d'honneur, and Berlioz wrote his obituary.

Le diable à Seville (1, A. Hurtado and H.-A. Cavé), Paris, OC (Ventadour), 29 Jan 1831 (Paris, 1831), *F-Pc**
Le revenant (2, A. de Calvimont, after W. Scott: *Redgauntlet*), Paris, OC (Bourse), 31 Dec 1833 (Paris, 1833)
La révolte du sérail, 1833 (?2, Gomis), unperf.
Le portefaix [Gaspare, ou Le portefaix de Grenade] (3, E. Scribe), Paris, OC (Bourse), 16 June 1835 (Paris, 1835)
Rock le barbu (1, P. Duport and P. Deforges), Paris, OC (Bourse), 13 May 1836
La damnée, inc., *Pc**

*

H. Berlioz: 'Gomis', *Revue et Gazette musicale de Paris* (7 Aug 1836), 275–7
J. Esperanza y Solá: 'Gomis', *Almanaque de la ilustración* (1888), 77–86
J. Dowling: *José Melchor Gomis, compositor romántico* (Madrid, 1973)
JOHN DOWLING

Gondinet, (Pierre-)Edmond(-Julien) (*b* Laurière, Haute-Vienne, 7 March 1828; *d* Neuilly, 19 Nov 1888). French playwright and librettist. He began a career in the civil service, but had been attracted to the theatre from an early age. His first plays, which he signed 'Julien de Laurières', were performed in Montpellier in 1855–6; in 1859 he moved to Paris and ten years later, after considerable success in the theatre, resigned his official post. With a gift for light, satirical comedy, often presented in the form of *comédie-vaudeville*, and for versification, he was associated as a librettist chiefly with Delibes, for whom he wrote *Le roi l'a dit* (1873) and, with Philippe Gille, *Jean de Nivelle* (1880) and *Lakmé* (1883). He also wrote, with Georges Duval, the libretto of *Les voltigeurs de la 32ème*, set by Robert Planquette (1880).

*

F. Gondinet: *Edmond Gondinet, auteur dramatique (1828–88)* (Foix, 1927)
CHRISTOPHER SMITH

Gondoliers, The [*The Gondoliers; or, The King of Barataria*]. Operetta in two acts by ARTHUR SULLIVAN to a libretto by W. S. GILBERT; London, Savoy Theatre, 7 December 1889.

The Gondoliers was the last great collaboration between Sullivan and Gilbert, although they did write two later works. The libretto – one of Gilbert's finest, most balanced and most human – combines the babyswapping of *HMS Pinafore* with a kidnapping recalling the author's claim to have been abducted in infancy by Neapolitan bandits. In the operetta the endangered infant heir to the throne of Barataria is stolen by the Grand Inquisitor, Don Alhambra del Bolero (baritone), and left to be reared by a Venetian gondolier. When the time comes for the prince to succeed to the throne, the Inquisitor seeks out the gondolier's sons, Marco (tenor) and Giuseppe (baritone). Unable to ascertain which should be king, he empowers them to rule jointly for the time being. Forced to leave behind their new brides, Gianetta (soprano) and Tessa (mezzo-soprano), they arrive in Barataria, where they appease republican sympathies by promoting equality throughout the king-

The Gondoliers (Arthur Sullivan), the Act 1 quintet, with (left to right) Frank Wyatt and Rosina Brandram (The Duke and Duchess of Plaza-Toro), W. H. Denny (Don Alhambra del Bolero), Decima Moore (Casilda) and Wallace Brownlow (Luiz), from the original production at the Savoy Theatre, London, 7 December 1889: engraving

dom. Their wives appear and soon they discover that the infant prince was betrothed to Casilda (soprano), daughter of the Duke (baritone) and Duchess (contralto) of Plaza-Toro who have arrived to secure the marriage. Casilda, however, loves Luiz (baritone), the family servant. This awkward situation is resolved when the prince's former nurse reveals that, in time of danger, she had substituted her own baby for the royal one; the boy she had reared, Luiz, is thus the rightful king.

Having cajoled Sullivan back to the Savoy after a particularly bitter artistic estrangement, Gilbert was solicitous of the composer's desire to increase the prominence of the music, permitting it to occupy significantly more of the work's playing time than in their previous full-length pieces. The brilliant and varied score is dominated by dance rhythms. There are the waltz tunes of the opening sequence – virtually 20 minutes of continuous music – and the courtly pastiche of the gavotte, 'I am a courtier', but most striking is the wealth of sparkling Mediterranean measures epitomized by the celebrated 'Dance a cachucha'. Outstanding, not least for its authentic Italian ring, is the duet 'We're called *gondolieri*'; but as well as exotic elements, there is music in the composer's familiar vein. The glee, 'Try we life-long', is related to the pseudo-madrigals of *The Mikado* and *Ruddigore*; 'In enterprise of martial kind' and 'Rising early' are species of patter song, and 'Take a pair of sparkling eyes' maintains a vein of tenor balladry which stretches back to *The Sorcerer* and extends into Sullivan's drawing-room output. For subtle word-setting he is at his best in the ensemble 'Now, Marco dear'.
DAVID RUSSELL HULME

Gonella, Francesco [Ferrari, Francesco Gonella di] (*fl* 1794–1812). Italian librettist. He made an auspicious start to his short career with *Avviso ai maritati*, set by the Maltese-born composer Isouard in 1794; the opera achieved widespread popularity. His most important work, however, was *Lodoiska* (1796) for Simon Mayr. He was one of a number of occasional librettists whose work was grounded in 18th-century practices and who did not contribute to the development of the form. Most of his librettos were published anonymously or with the initials D. F. G. di F. ('Dottore Francesco Gonella di Ferrari', as a result of which he is often indexed under 'Ferrari'), but since they are frequently credited as written 'by the author of *Lodoiska*' or the like, it is possible to assemble a tentative list of his works.

Avviso ai maritati (dramma giocoso per musica), Isouard, 1794 (Mayr, 1798); *Il nipote risuscito* (int), G. Aloisi, 1795; *Lodoiska* (dramma per musica), Mayr, 1796 (L. Caruso, 1797); *Zulima* (dramma per musica), Portugal, 1796; *Il ritorno di Serse* (dramma serio per musica), Portugal, 1797 (Nasolini, 1816); *Oreste* (dramma serio in musica), Moneta, 1798; *Rinaldo e Armida* (dramma serio per musica), G. Mosca, 1799; *Jefte* (dramma sacro per musica), R. Orgitano, 1802; *L'amore vince la parentela* (dramma giocoso per musica), Aloisi, 1808; *Maria Stuarda regina di Scozia* (dramma serio per musica), P. Casella, 1812
JOHN BLACK

Gonsalez [Gonzalez], **Giuseppe** (*fl c*1900–35). Italian impresario. Towards the end of the 19th century, his company was primarily active in touring the Balkans, Asia Minor and Egypt, with Smyrna (now Izmir), Athens, Cairo and Alexandria his favourite stops. During an extended tour of these cities, Giuseppe Anselmi was his leading singer. By 1903–4, he was beginning to head further north, going into Romania and Russia. From 1905 until late 1914 he toured Russia almost exclusively, frequently reaching the Trans-Caucasian region and even Central Asia and Siberia. In 1906 he crossed Siberia all the way to Vladivostok. By now his company had become something of a family affair, and included several brothers, two of whom conducted, and his daughter Ernestina, a soprano. During such a tour, they again reached Vladivostok in late 1914. Blocked by World War I from returning to Italy by the same route, they decided to go down the Chinese coast, stopping in several Chinese cities, Hong Kong, Manila and Singapore before arriving in Batavia in June 1915. By then, Gonsalez had decided against returning home, and went on to Solo, Soerebaya and Semarang. Since some of the singers were homesick, reinforcements were called for – they included the tenor Vittorio Lois, later to become famous. The altered company returned to Batavia, visited Singapore again then Sumatra, Rangoon, Calcutta and Bombay. From there they went to Australia, New Zealand and back to Australia where some of them settled. This particular tour, which lasted for over four years, must surely be one of the most protracted tours in the history of opera.

Gonsalez continued to tour well into the early 1930s, visiting India, Ceylon (now Sri Lanka), Burma and Indonesia in 1924–5, Australia and New Zealand again in 1928, and South Africa (also Mozambique) in 1931.

*

A. Gyger: *Opera for the Antipodes: Opera in Australia 1881–1939* (Sydney, 1990)

TOM KAUFMAN

Gonzaga. Italian family of musical patrons. *See* MANTUA; *see also* MONTEVERDI, CLAUDIO and GAGLIANO, MARCO DA.

Gonzaga, Pietro (*b* Longarone, 25 March 1751; *d* St Petersburg, 25 July/6 Aug 1831). Italian stage designer. He was a pupil of Giuseppe Moretti and Antonio Visentini in Venice. In 1772 he moved to Milan and began working as a stage designer under the Galliari brothers at the Regio Ducal Teatro, and then at the Teatro Interinale and at La Scala, where he was listed among the principal scenographers from 1779, at first for comic operas (Giuseppe Sarti's *Le gelosie villane*, 1779; Cimarosa's *Il falegname*, 1781) and later for all serious productions, including Sarti's *Idalide* (1783), Cherubini's *Ifigenia in Aulide* and Cimarosa's *Olimpiade* (both 1788). Besides working at La Scala and the Cannobiana in Milan, Gonzaga was active in Varese (Teatro Ducale, 1779), Alessandria (Teatro Civico, 1779–82), Genoa (Teatro di S Agostino, 1780–91), Rome (Teatro Alibert, 1781), Mantua (Teatro Regio Ducale, 1784–5), Crema (Teatro Sociale, 1786–9), Monza (Teatro Arciducale, 1787–91), Faenza (Nuovo Teatro, 1788) and Bergamo (Teatro Riccardi, 1791). At the Teatro Ducale in Parma his scenery for Sarti's *Alessandro e Timoteo* (1782), on the occasion of a visit from the future Tsar Paul I and his wife, was particularly successful (see illustration). In Venice he painted a stage curtain and designed the ballets for the inauguration of La Fenice on 16 May 1792. Shortly afterwards (24 June), he was appointed painter-in-chief of the St Petersburg royal theatres by Catherine II; he lived there until his death. During his successful career in Russia he designed many operas and ballets, including Cimarosa's *Il matrimonio segreto*, (1794), Sarti's *Andromeda* (1798), Spontini's *La vestale* (1811) and Cimarosa's *Gli Orazi ed i Curiazi* (1815); he also designed interiors, and was commissioned by Prince Yusupov to plan and provide scenery for the theatre in Arkhangel'sk. He published important theoretical works on the problems of scenography (which he understood as an art concerned with expressing states of mind and dramatic situations). His books include *La musique des yeux et l'optique théatrale* (St Petersburg, 1800) and *Remarques sur la construction des théâtres* (St Petersburg, 1817).

Gonzaga's career fell in a period of transition in theatrical style, and he was fully aware of the crisis faced by traditional typology. He suggested important new models, some of which (the round, classical temple and dark, sepulchral caves) were widely used and imitated. His ability to produce effects of atmosphere and light was greatly admired; new means of lighting (Argand lamps were installed at La Scala in 1788) enabled him to introduce aerial perspective in scenery, on which he made acute observations in his essay *Information à mon chef* (St Petersburg, 1807). An important body of Gonzaga's drawings survives, both in Italy (Fondazione Cini, Venice; Museo Teatrale alla Scala, Milan; Museo Civico, Belluno; Museo Civico, Turin; and private collections) and Russia (Hermitage, St Petersburg).

*

ES (E. Povoledo)

R. Gironi: 'Sulle decorazioni sceniche ed in ispezie su quelle dell' Imp. R. Teatro alla Scala di Milano', *Biblioteca italiana*, liv (1829), 3–23

U. Sofia Moretti: *Pietro Gonzaga: scenografo e architetto veneto* (Milan, 1960)

M. T. Muraro: *Scenografie di Pietro Gonzaga* (Venice, 1967)

Set design by Pietro Gonzaga for a horrible cave representing the mouth of hell in Sarti's 'Alessandro e Timoteo', Teatro Ducale, Parma, 6 April 1782

F. Y. Sïrkina: *P'yetro di Gottardo Gonzaga, 1751–1831: zhizn' i tvorchestvo, sochineniya* [Life, Art and Literary Works] (Moscow, 1974)

M. Korsunova: *P'yetro Gonzaga: eskizï dekoratsiy i rospisey, katalog vïstavki* [Sketches for Stage Designs and Murals, Exhibition Catalogue] (Leningrad, 1980)

E. Tamburini: *Il luogo teatrale nella trattatistica italiana dell' 800* (Rome, 1984), 39–49

Omaggio a Pietro Gonzaga (Longarone, 1986) [exhibition catalogue]
MERCEDES VIALE FERRERO

Gonzales [González], Dalmacio (*b* Olot, 12 May 1945). Catalan tenor. He studied in Barcelona and Salzburg, making his début in 1978 at Barcelona as Ugo (Donizetti's *Parisina*). In 1979 he sang at the Metropolitan, the New York City Opera and at San Francisco. He made his La Scala début in 1981 as Lurcanio in Handel's *Ariodante*. In 1982 he sang Fenton in Verdi's *Falstaff* at Los Angeles and at Covent Garden. He has appeared at Naples, Madrid, Pesaro, Turin, Spoleto, Florence, Aix-en-Provence and Bonn. A specialist in the high, florid roles of Rossini, he has sung Almaviva, Argirio (*Tancredi*), Idreno (*Semiramide*), Ramiro (*La Cenerentola*), Lindoro (*L'italiana in Algeri*), Belfiore (*Il viaggio a Reims*), Uberto/King James (*La donna del lago*) and Rinaldo (*Armida*). His repertory also includes Ferrando, Belmonte, Nemorino, Ernesto and Ford in Salieri's *Falstaff*, which he sang at Parma (1987). His voice is small but well-projected.

ELIZABETH FORBES

Goodall, Sir Reginald (*b* Lincoln, 13 July 1901; *d* Bridge, nr Canterbury, 5 May 1990). English conductor. He studied at the RCM, and during student visits to Munich, Salzburg and Vienna, supporting himself as a piano accompanist, he became deeply influenced by Furtwängler and other leading conductors of the day (notably Knappertsbusch, Kleiber and Krauss). Before 1939 he worked on occasion at Covent Garden as assistant to Albert Coates and, after being invalided from wartime service, joined Sadler's Wells Opera in 1944; he conducted the première of *Peter Grimes* which reopened the theatre on 7 June 1945.

In 1946 Goodall shared with Ansermet the English Opera Group's first production of Britten's *The Rape of Lucretia* at Glyndebourne, and the next year he joined Covent Garden as a staff conductor. After conducting *Manon* in 1947 he spent 15 years conducting repertory performances of *Wozzeck*, *Gloriana*, *Die Meistersinger* and a variety of Italian operas, although these last held little appeal for him. Poor health and the advent of Solti as music director in 1961 meant that Goodall was confined to a répétiteur's functions, to the inestimable benefit of a generation of singers whose talents he brought to fruition.

Goodall reappeared as a conductor in 1968 with much acclaimed performances of *Die Meistersinger* by the Sadler's Wells Opera, sung in English. His depth of understanding in Wagner and sustained sense of involvement were further revealed in succeeding seasons, bringing him to *Parsifal* at Covent Garden (1971) and to a complete *Ring* built up over three seasons at the London Coliseum. The two cycles he conducted there in 1973 were the first sung in English for more than 40 years, and a full recording was made from live performances between 1973 and 1978. The performances were distinguished by Goodall's overall sense of musical flow and architectural unity that meant singers were heard to complement the orchestra, not

fight it. He returned to Covent Garden for single performances of *Das Rheingold* and *Die Walküre* in 1975 and spent three years preparing *Tristan und Isolde* with the WNO at Cardiff (1979). A similar time was spent in preparing *Parsifal* in English with the ENO in 1986. Goodall's last performance was of Act 3 of *Parsifal* at a Henry Wood Promenade concert in 1987. He was made a CBE in 1975 and knighted in 1985.

'Reginald Goodall, 1901–90', *Opera*, xli (1990), 784–93
NOËL GOODWIN

Goodman [Guttmann], Alfred (Grant) (*b* Berlin, 1 March 1920). German composer. After study at the Stern Conservatory and with his father, the music critic Oscar Guttmann, he went to London in 1939 and to New York in 1940, serving in the US Army in World War II. He later worked as an arranger for the dance bands of Benny Goodman and Noro Morales and attended Columbia University, where he studied with Henry Cowell and Otto Luening (BS 1952; MA 1953). In 1961 he moved to Munich, where he worked for Bayerische Rundfunk. Goodman composed and arranged music in various genres. His first opera, the one-act *The Audition*, to a libretto by Elliot Arluck, was first performed at Ohio University in Athens, Ohio, on 27 July 1954. It was revived in a German version by Harry Frohman at Pforzheim in 1968 as *Der Schauspieler* (vs, Mainz, 1968). In 1970 he completed a two-act opera, *Der Läufer*, to a libretto by Marion Alva after the novel *Brot und Spiele* by Siegfried Lenz, and in 1982 he wrote another one-act opera to a libretto by Arluck, *The Lady and the Maid*.
BRADFORD R. DeVOS

Goodman's Fields. Site of a London theatre active in the 1730s and early 40s; *see* LONDON, §II, 2.

Goossens, Sir (Aynsley) Eugene (*b* London, 26 May 1893; *d* Hillingdon, Middlesex, 13 June 1962). English composer and conductor. Both his father and grandfather, of Belgian origin, held the post of principal conductor of the Carl Rosa Opera Company. After studying in Bruges, Liverpool and at the RCM, where Stanford taught him composition, he began his career as a professional violinist; he soon followed in the family footsteps by conducting opera, however, and as assistant to Beecham from 1916 frequently deputized for him on little or no rehearsal. By early 1922 he was conducting the Carl Rosa company at Covent Garden and in 1923 appeared there with the British National Opera Company.

From 1923 until 1947 Goossens spent part of each year in the USA, first conducting the Rochester PO, then (from 1931) the Cincinnati SO. In 1947 he moved to Australia as director of the New South Wales Conservatorium and resident conductor of the Sydney SO. His pioneer work included plans for the Sydney Opera House, which, however, were not to achieve fruition until more than ten years after his death. He returned to England in 1956.

Goossens's compositions are not well known, no doubt partly because of his pre-eminence as a conductor, and may be felt to lack melodic character. Yet they amount to a substantial output, serious, urbane and technically impressive, and until the challenge of performing them is more widely met any overall judgment must remain provisional. Instrumental music predominates, starting from the stylistic premises of musical post-impressionism and developing tougher sinews in the later works; nevertheless, his handling of voices and knowledge of the stage place his two operas among his major achievements. Both were produced between the wars at Covent Garden, conducted by Goossens, and for both Arnold Bennett was librettist. *Judith* op.46 (25 June 1929; vs, London, 1929), which was given a shoddy production, is a melodramatic one-act piece based on the violent Apocrypha story and very much in the mould of Strauss's *Salome*, though there is less to warm to musically. Goossens excels at swift dramatic pacing and a rich, fluent and harmonically sophisticated orchestral fabric, but the music never settles and the vocal writing fails to blossom beyond parlando; nor is the opera helped by Bennett's gauche and unimaginative libretto. *Don Juan de Mañara* op.54 (composed 1935, produced 24 June 1937; vs, London, 1935), is in four acts and came from Bennett's early, un-performed adaptation of a little-known play by Dumas *père*, *Don Juan de Marana*. Dumas in turn had taken his scenario from Mérimée's account of a 17th-century libertine from Seville. Unlike Don Juan Tenorio, this hero is ultimately saved by one of his prospective victims. Goossens, keen to promote opera in English, justifies his extensive use of a parlando vocal style in a foreword to the vocal score, but this must seriously limit the opera's appeal, its theatrical flair and sophisticated orchestral tissue with Spanish colours notwithstanding. Neither opera has been revived.

R. Hull: 'Eugene Goossens', *ML*, xii (1931), 345–53
——: 'Eugene Goossens', *British Music of Our Time*, ed. A. L. Bacharach (Harmondsworth, 1946), 130–36
E. Goossens: *Overture and Beginnings* (London, 1951)
N. Demuth: 'Composers in Isolation: 4, Eugene Goossens', *Musical Trends in the 20th Century* (London, 1952), 290–99
R. Hull: 'Eugene Goossens: a Revaluation – II', *The Chesterian*, xxviii (1954), 99–106
A. Goossens: 'Sir Eugene Goossens (1893–1962) DMus, FRCM', *British Music Society Journal*, iii (1981), 1–10
L. Foreman: 'British Opera Comes of Age: 1916–61', *British Opera in Retrospect* (n.p., 1986) [pubn of the British Music Society], 113
A. Hubble: *The Strange Case of Eugene Goossens and Other Tales from the Opera House* (Sydney, 1988)   STEPHEN BANFIELD

Gordigiani. Italian family of musicians.

(1) **Antonio Gordigiani** (*d* Florence, before 1824). Baritone. He won particular renown for his singing in Rossini's *Aureliano in Palmira*. In 1811 he sang at the Opéra-Comique in Paris. After his retirement, he spent the rest of his life in Florence.

(2) **Giovanni Battista Gordigiani** (*b* Modena, July 1795; *d* Prague, 2 March 1871). Baritone, composer and teacher, son of (1) Antonio Gordigiani. He made his operatic début at the Pergola in Florence in 1817 and sang Dandini (*Cenerentola*) at Pisa later the same year; subsequently, however, he confined himself to singing in concerts. In 1822 he became professor of singing at the Prague Conservatory; the best known of his pupils was the soprano Teresa Stolz. Besides his four operas, he composed church music, as well as a number of canzonettas and a variety of vocal chamber music. In his later years he contributed reports on music in Prague to several musical journals.

Pygmalione (favola, 1), Prague, National, spr. 1845
Consuelo (os, 2, G. B. Gordigiani, after G. Sand), Prague, National, 8 June 1846
Lo scrivano pubblico, Prague, Kaiserliches Schloss, June 1850
Piccolino, unperf.

(3) **Luigi Gordigiani** (*b* Modena, 21 June 1806; *d* Florence, 1 May 1860). Composer, son of (1) Antonio Gordigiani. As a child he lived in several cities, a consequence of his father's peripatetic career. At the age of five, in Paris, he heard compositions by Paer, Crescentini and Zingarelli. At 12 he was admitted to the boys' choir of the Pitti Chapel in Florence. Later he studied the piano with Gava at Brescia and harmony and counterpoint in Florence with Pietro Romani and Disma Ugolini. His first professional appearances were as a pianist. Among his earliest compositions were two cantatas: *Il ratto di Etruria* (1819) and *Comala* (1822). Count Demidoff hired him to accompany performances in his private theatre; when the count died in 1828, Luigi was left a pension and devoted himself thereafter to composition. He is best remembered today for a collection of Tuscan popular songs and for his vocal chamber music, which earned him the nickname 'the Italian Schubert'. After 1836 his principal activity was the composition of works for the public and private stages of the aristocracy in Florence.

L'appuntamento (ob, 1), Florence, Cocomero, spr. 1828; rev. as Le rendez-vous, Florence, private perf., 1830
Fausto (op, 2), Florence, Pergola, 18 Nov 1836
Filippo (op, 2, G. Poniatowski), Prato, private perf., 1840
Gli aragonesi in Napoli (burletta, 2, A. L. Tottola), Florence, Leopoldo, 10 June 1841; rev. as Don Matteo, Florence, Risoluti, carn. 1856–7
I ciarlatani (op, 2), Florence, Leopoldo, 14 Feb 1843
Un eredità in Corsica, ossia La vendetta corsa (os, 3, F. Guidi), Florence, Cocomero, 24 April 1847
L'avventuriero (op, A. de Lauzières), Livorno, Rossini, April 1851, collab. T. Mabellini
Deux mots, ou Une nuit dans la forêt (opéra bouffe, 1, B.-J. Marsollier des Vivetières), Florence, private perf., 1854
Le diable à l'école (opéra bouffe, E. Scribe and F. Bayard), Florence, private perf., 1856

Unperf.: L'assedio di Firenze; Rosmonda; Velleda; Carmelita
WILLIAM ASHBROOK

Gordon, Alexander (*b* Aberdeen, *c*1692; *d* South Carolina, 1754 or 1755). Scottish tenor. A graduate of Aberdeen University, he spent some years in Italy, singing in C. A. Monza's *La principessa fedele* (1716, Messina) and Orlandini's *Lucio Papirio* and Leo's *Sofonisba* (1717–18, Naples). He returned to Britain in 1719 and was a member of the Royal Academy (at the King's Theatre) during its first season (spring 1720), singing in Porta's *Numitore*, Handel's *Radamisto* (Tiridate) and Roseingrave's arrangement of Domenico Scarlatti's *Narciso*. He was back at the King's Theatre in 1723 for the first performances of Ariosti's *Coriolano* and Handel's *Flavio* (Ugone). He then abandoned his singing career to become a scholar, author and antiquary, publishing books on many subjects and becoming secretary to the Society of Antiquaries (1736–41). In 1741 he moved to South Carolina as secretary to the governor. Gordon must have possessed a competent technique to sing the two parts Handel composed for him, which require agile coloratura and a compass from *d* to *a'*. He is said to have taken exception to Handel's accompaniment and threatened to jump on the harpsichord; this drew the reply: 'Oh, let me know when you will do that and I will advertise it; for I am sure more people will come to see you jump than to hear you sing'. Gordon apparently brought back from Naples an MS score of Alessandro Scarlatti's *Tigrane*, now in the Barber Institute at Birmingham, in which the opera is attributed to Scarlatti 'con l'ajuto del Sigr Alessandro Gordoni Inglese'.

C. Morey: 'Alexander Gordon, Scholar and Singer', *ML*, xlvi (1965), 332–5

WINTON DEAN

Gordon, Jeanne (*b* Wallaceburg, Ont., 1884; *d* Macon, MO, 22 Feb 1952). Canadian mezzo-soprano. She studied in Toronto and was 'discovered', by the director of the Brooklyn Opera, singing in a New York cinema. She made her operatic début in Brooklyn as Amneris in 1918, which led to her début as Azucena at the Metropolitan in 1919. Singing in a wide repertory, which included the Wagnerian roles of Fricka and Brangäne, she remained with the company till 1927. The following year she appeared in Monte Carlo as Eboli and Delilah. She retired shortly afterwards and spent the remainder of her life in a mental home. Her fine voice can be heard in a few recordings; she also appeared as Carmen with Giovanni Martinelli in an early film of Act 2, the soundtrack of which survives.

J. B. STEANE

Goring Thomas, Arthur. *See* THOMAS, ARTHUR GORING.

Goritz, Otto (*b* Berlin, 8 June 1873; *d* Hamburg, 11 April 1929). German bass-baritone. He studied with his mother in Bremen and made his début as Matteo in *Fra Diavolo* at Neustrelitz. Engagements followed at Breslau and Hamburg, and in 1903 he began a lasting American career with his début as Klingsor in *Parsifal* at the Metropolitan (the first public staging outside Bayreuth). His other roles there included Papageno, Pizarro, Telramund and Beckmesser; he also took part in several important Metropolitan premières, singing Frank in *Die Fledermaus* (1905), the Fiddler in *Königskinder* (1910) and Ochs in *Der Rosenkavalier* (1913). In 1917 he was dismissed along with the other German members of the company, and in 1919 was prominent in an abortive attempt to open an independent German season at the Lexington Theatre, New York. He later made guest appearances in Berlin and Hamburg. His recordings disclose an expressive style and a voice which was sturdy though not particularly attractive.

J. B. STEANE

Gor'kiy [Gorky]. NIZHNIY NOVGOROD.

Gorr, Rita [Geirnaert, Marguerite] (*b* Zelzaete, 18 Feb 1926). Belgian mezzo-soprano. She studied in Ghent, then at the Brussels Conservatory. In 1949 she made her début in Antwerp as Fricka in *Die Walküre*. Thereafter she sang at the Strasbourg Opera until 1952, the year in which she made her Paris débuts (at the Opéra-Comique as Charlotte and at the Opéra as Magdalene). Her large voice, of rich, metallic timbre, ranging freely over two octaves, was joined to a powerfully dramatic temperament. In Wagner (notably as Fricka and Ortrud) and Verdi (Eboli, Azucena, Ulrica and Amneris) she gave grandly exciting performances; a noble breadth of expression won her special praise in the French repertory – Delilah, Iphigenia (*Iphigénie en Tauride*), Margared (*Le roi d'Ys*), Massenet's Herodias and Charlotte, Cherubini's Medea and Berlioz's Dido. She first sang at Bayreuth in 1958, at La Scala in 1960 and at the Metropolitan in 1962. She made her London début at Covent Garden in 1959 and sang there until 1971. Later roles included Madame de Croissy (*Dialogues des Carmélites*), which she sang at Seattle and Lyons in 1990.

J. Bourgeois: 'Rita Gorr', *Opera*, xii (1961), 637–40

HAROLD ROSENTHAL/R

Gossec, François-Joseph (*b* Vergnies, 17 Jan 1734; *d* Passy, Paris, 16 Feb 1829). South Netherlands composer, active in France. He played a central role in Parisian musical life for more than 50 years. He was born into a Walloon family whose name was variously spelt Gaussé, Gossé, Gossée, Gossei, Gossey or Gossez. In early childhood he displayed remarkable musical talent and reputedly possessed a beautiful voice. From the age of six he sang in local chapel choirs, before becoming a chorister at the Cathedral of Notre Dame in Antwerp in 1742. In 1751 he went to Paris and, with the help of Rameau, became a violinist and bass player in the private orchestra of A.-J.-J. Le Riche de La Pouplinière, *fermier général* of Paris. In 1762 he was made director of the private theatre of Louis-Joseph de Bourbon, Prince of Condé, at Chantilly. His most successful works of this period were the pasticcio *Le tonnelier* (1765), and the *opéras comiques Les pêcheurs* (1766) and *Toinon et Toinette* (1767). Each is set in the countryside, where two lovers have to overcome a series of obstacles before they can marry. The innocent plots are set in a gracious and simple style. While the *ariettes* of *Le tonnelier* are on a modest scale using song-like melodies, the *ariettes* of *Les pêcheurs* and *Toinon et Toinette* are much more operatic. In *Les pêcheurs* Gossec sacrificed the dramatic potential of the plot to prevailing dance-like rhythms, although he achieved great variety of instrumentation. The final ensembles avoid individual musical characterization. In *Toinon* Gossec inserted storm music, with piccolos and thunder effects, to link the two acts. This opera also shows his growing fondness for the dynamic effects which he encountered in the Orchestra de la Pouplinière, under Johann Stamitz. These *opéras comiques* had varied receptions at the Comédie-Italienne. *Les pêcheurs* was the most successful, with more than 160 performances up to 1790. *Toinon* was also performed in the Netherlands, Denmark, Sweden and Germany.

In 1769 Gossec founded the Concert des Amateurs and in 1773 he became co-director of the Concert Spirituel. In the same year his first *tragédie lyrique*, *Sabinus*, was staged at Versailles. Judging from the untidy autography, Gossec may have found his task laborious. In its dramatic and musical layout (a mythological plot in five acts, with accompanied recitatives, rather short arias, extensive choruses, marches and *divertissements*) he clearly emulated Rameau's *tragédies lyriques*. Aside from the conventional, mythological plot, the opera includes the appearance of an allegorical figure, 'Le Génie de la Gaul', who encourages the hero Sabinus by predicting the creation of a French empire. Despite such an effective theme, which clearly foreshadows Gossec's nationalistic interests after the revolution, and equally effective orchestration, the compositional weaknesses cannot be overlooked. His inclination for small musical forms invariably prevented any individual piece from having a lasting impression on the audience. Larger pieces, however, expose the composer's limited ability, with their often triadic melodies, parallel part-writing, rhythmic uniformity and simple harmony. According to Gossec himself, rehearsals for this work began more than a year before the première. Additional clarinets, violins and basses were specially engaged and for the first time trombones were introduced at the Opéra. Although *Sabinus* was revised in a four-act version for the première at the Opéra in February 1774, Gossec's modest success was eclipsed after Gluck's *Iphigénie en Aulide* was first performed on 19 April 1774.

In the following years Gossec, who became an ally of Gluck, composed only pastorals and ballets, one of which, *Les Scythes enchaînés* (1779), was written for incorporation in Gluck's *Iphigénie en Tauride*. Gossec also revised the third act of Gluck's *Alceste* for its Paris performance in 1776. After Gluck had left Paris, Gossec started afresh at the Opéra. Following a fashion for resetting *tragédie lyriques* of Lully and Quinault, Gossec wrote *Thésée* in 1782. He borrowed from his forerunner by copying Aegée's aria, 'Faites grace à mon âge', and adding wind instruments. Gluck's *tragédies lyriques* had a strong influence on *Thésée*. The musical structure is much clearer, Gossec's style is rhythmically and harmonically more inventive, and his use of the full wind section in particular seems much more accomplished. Although *Thésée* is of a higher quality than *Sabinus*, it received only 16 performances and his *Rosine* (1786) was a complete failure.

From 1784 he took on the directorship of the newly founded Ecole Royale de Chant at the Opéra. Together with Méhul and Catel, he was at the forefront of the revolutionary musical activities that characterize the last part of his output for the stage. *L'offrande à la liberté* (1792) dramatizes the battle between the French revolutionaries and their foreign enemies, culminating in a powerful setting of the *Marseillaise*, for every verse of which Gossec chose a different instrumentation. It was performed at the Opéra 143 times up to 1797 and was still used at a national festivity in 1848. *Le triomphe de la République, ou Le camp de Grandpré* (1793) glorifies the victory of the revolutionary troops in the battle at Valmy on 20 September 1792. This *divertissement-lyrique* consists mainly of majestic, hymn-like choruses written in a simple style with homophonic texture which secured *Le Triomphe* a wide audience. It is related to the genre of *tragédie lyrique* by employing a full-scale orchestra, accompanied recitatives and a final ballet with an Entrée des Nations, featuring a dance of 'negroes', a polonaise, an anglaise and a *ranz des vaches*. After 1795 Gossec devoted his energies to teaching at the Paris Conservatoire.

See also PÊCHEURS, LES and TONNELIER, LE.

all printed works published in Paris

PCI – *Paris, Comédie-Italienne*   PO – *Paris, Opéra*

Le périgourdin (int, 1, A. N. Piédefer, Marquis de La Salle d'Offémont), Chantilly, private theatre of the Prince of Conti, 7 June 1761
Le tonnelier (oc, 1, N.-M. Audinot and A. F. Quétant), PCI (Bourgogne), 16 March 1765, collab. Alexandre, Ciapalanti, Kohaut, Philidor, J. Schobert and J. C. Trial
Le faux lord (oc, 3, Parmentier), PCI (Bourgogne), 27 June 1765, incl. La chasse (ballet with songs), excerpts (n.d.)
Les pêcheurs (oc, 1, La Salle d'Offémont), PCI (Bourgogne), 23 April 1766, rev. 7 June 1766, pubd as op.10 (n.d.)
Toinon et Toinette (oc, 2, J. A. J. Desboulmiers), PCI (Bourgogne), 20 June 1767, pubd as op.11 (n.d.)
Le double déguisement (oc, 2, Houbron), PCI (Bourgogne), 28 Sept 1767, excerpts (n.d)
Les agréments d'Hylas et Silvie (pastorale, M.-R.-J. Rochon de Chabannes), Paris, Comédie-Française, 10 Dec 1768, excerpts (n.d.)
Sabinus (tragédie lyrique, 5, M.-P.-G. de Chabanon), Versailles, 4

Dec 1773; rev. (4), PO, 22 Feb 1774, *F-Po* and *Pc* (partly autograph), excerpts (n.d.)
Berthe (opéra, R. T. R. de Pleinchesne), Brussels, Monnaie, 18 Jan 1775; collab. Philidor, I. Vitzthumb and ?H. Botson
Alexis et Daphné (pastorale, 1, Chabanon de Maugris), PO, 26 Sept 1775, *Po**, excerpts (n.d.)
Philémon et Baucis (pastorale, 1, Chabanon de Maugris), PO, 26 Sept 1775, *Po**
La fête de village (int, 1, Desfontaines [F. G. Fouques]), PO, 26 May 1778, *Po* (2 copies, 1 inc. autograph), excerpts (n.d.)
Thésée (tragédie lyrique, 4, E. Morel de Chéfdeville, after P. Quinault), PO, 1 March 1782, *B-Bc*, *F-Pc*, *Po**, airs, arr. pf (n.d.)
Nitrocris (opéra, 3, Morel de Chéfdeville), 1783, unperf., *Po*
Rosine, ou L'épouse abandonnée (3, N. Gersin), PO, 14 July 1786, *Po**, excerpts (n.d.)
Le pied de boeuf (divertissement, 1, Gardel), PO, 17 June 1787, incl. music by Rameau and Grétry
L'offrande à la liberté (scène religieuse, 1, A. S. Boy or J.-M. Girey-Dupré, C. J. Rouget de Lisle and M.-J. de Chénier), PO (Porte-St-Martin), 30 Sept 1792, *Pn* (1792)
Le triomphe de la République, ou Le camp de Grandpré (divertissement-lyrique, 1, Chénier), PO (Porte-St-Martin), 27 Jan 1793, *Po** (1794)
Les sabots et le cerisier (opéra, M.-J. Sedaine and J. Cazotte), Paris, Jeunes-Elèves, 13 Dec 1803

Grove6 (B. S. Brook, D. Campbell and M. H. Cohn); *PEM* (M. Stegemann)
F. M. von Grimm: *Correspondance littéraire, philosophique et critique* (Paris, 1812–14); ed. M. Tourneux (Paris, 1877–82), vii, 57–9
F.-J. Gossec: 'Sur l'introduction des cors, des clarinettes et des trombones dans les orchestres français', *Revue musicale*, v (1829), 217–23
P. Hédouin: *Gossec: sa vie et ses ouvrages* (Valenciennes, 1852)
A. Adam: 'Gossec', *Derniers souvenirs d'un musicien* (Paris, 1859), 143–96
C. Pierre: *Musique des fêtes et cérémonies de la Révolution française* (Paris, 1899)
L. Dufrane: *Gossec: sa vie, ses oeuvres* (Paris, 1927)
T. Tonnard: *François-Joseph Gossec, musicien hennuyer de la Révolution française* (Brussels, 1938)
J.-G. Prod'homme: 'François-Joseph Gossec', *Euterpe* (Paris, 1949), no.8
R. Mortier and H. Hasquin, eds.: *Fêtes et musiques révolutionnaires: Grétry et Gossec* (Brussels, 1990)
E. C. Bartlet: 'Gossec: l'*Offrande à la Liberté* et l'histoire de *La Marseillaise*', *Le tambour et la harpe*, ed. J.-R. Julien and J. Mongrédien (Paris, 1991), 123–46   MICHAEL FEND

Gossett, Philip (*b* New York, 27 Sept 1941). American musicologist. He studied at Columbia and Princeton universities and in 1968 joined the faculty at the University of Chicago. He specializes in 19th-century Italian opera: he is general editor of the collected works of Rossini (Pesaro, 1979–), coordinating editor of the works of Verdi (Chicago and Milan, 1983–) and was co-editor (with Charles Rosen) of the facsimile series *Early Romantic Opera* (New York, 1978–83). In his dissertation (1970) and articles on Rossini he distinguishes authentic sources, points out those aspects of a work which arise from specific performances or operatic conventions and identifies Rossini's borrowings and self-borrowings. He has collaborated with performers in productions of early 19th-century operas and prepared a facsimile edition, with introduction, of *La Cenerentola* (Bologna, 1969). His writings include *The Tragic Finale of Tancredi* (Pesaro, 1977) and *Anna Bolena and the Artistic Maturity of Gaetano Donizetti* (Oxford, 1984).
PAULA MORGAN

Gostič, Josip [Josef] (*b* Stara Luka, 5 March 1900; *d* Belgrade, 25 Dec 1963). Slovene tenor. He studied in Ljubljana, making his début there in 1929. Engaged from 1937 at Zagreb, he also sang in Berlin, Dresden, Prague and Vienna; he created Midas in *Die Liebe der Danae* at Salzburg in 1952, then sang the role at La Scala and the Opéra (1953). In 1953 he made his London début with the Zagreb Opera at the Stoll Theatre in the title role of Gotovac's *Ero the Joker*, his most successful part, and in 1958 he sang Grigory at Covent Garden. His strong, bright-toned voice was also heard to good advantage in Verdi roles including Manrico, Radames and Othello.   ELIZABETH FORBES

Göteborg [Gothenburg]. Second largest city in Sweden. Operatic activity can be traced back to 1783, when Jean-Jacques Rousseau's *Le devin du village* was performed at the old theatre in the Sillgatan near the Crown House. In the same year, the first Swedish performance of Mozart's *Bastien und Bastienne* took place at the same theatre – nearly 30 years before the Royal Opera in Stockholm performed *Die Zauberflöte*. But opera was more the exception than the rule. It was not until the 1830s that the great German, French and Italian works began to be heard in the city, including *Zauberflöte* and *La clemenza di Tito*, Auber's *Fra Diavolo*, Rossini's *Otello* (which has only ever been heard in Göteborg in 1837 and 1862, and never at the Royal Opera in Stockholm), *Norma* and *Lucia di Lammermoor*. The regular performance of opera was encouraged when the Nya Teatern (New Theatre), seating about 900, was built, 1857–9, in the Kungsparken (King's Park) by the architect Bror Carl Malmberg. This theatre is still in use (with seating now reduced to c600) and has one of the most beautiful auditoriums in Sweden. Because of Göteborg's accessibility, many German and Italian companies visited the city, among them a troupe brought by the German singer Emil von Osten that performed works in the 1860s such as *Il trovatore*, *Robert le diable* and *La sonnambula*. Another company was that of Gaudeluis, who brought singers from various opera houses in Europe; the tenor Joseph Tichatschek was engaged several times after his retirement. In 1869 the first Italian company appeared: Achille Lorini's troupe gave the local première of *La traviata*, conducted by Franco Faccio. From 1879 it was known as the Stora Teatern (Grand Theatre); in 1920 it acquired a permanent ensemble and orchestra. Operetta was included to an increasing extent in the repertory, although in 1921 *Der fliegende Holländer* was presented, conducted by Siegfried Wagner at some performances.

Since the 1960s opera has been firmly established in Göteborg. Together with an extremely creative ballet company, the opera division of the Grand Theatre has complemented the work of the national house, the Royal Opera House in Stockholm, with a distinctive repertory of less commonly performed operas by Janáček and such Scandinavian composers as Rangström, Werle and Sallinen. The policy of promoting young directors has resulted in provocative readings, such as Etienne Glaser's of *Don Giovanni* and David Radok's of *Katerina Izmaylova*. Among the conductors who have frequently worked at the theatre are Sixten Ehrling and Nicholas Braithwaite (principal conductor, 1982–4). The Grand Theatre's season runs from September to June, usually with performances six days a week. In 1984 the Lillan (Little Theatre) was created for young people; its mixture of musicals and opera (often in shortened versions) has been well received and is now a permanent feature of the theatre.

J. Svanberg: *Anteckningar om Stora Teatern i Göteborg* (Göteborg, 1894)

A. Fromell: *Stora Teatern i Göteborg 1893–1929* (Göteborg, 1929)

S. Hofsten: 'Opera på Storan under 125 år', *Teatern i Kungsparken: Storan 125 år* (Göteborg, 1984), 46–60   ANDERS WIKLUND

Gotha. German city in the Erfurt district of Thuringia. It became an important cultural centre after being made the seat of the Duchy of Saxe-Gotha in 1247. A permanent Kapelle was established in the 17th century. A few *Singballette* (ballets with some sung numbers) and musical comedies (all lost) were mounted to mark special occasions during the reigns of Ernst the Pious (1640–75) and his son Friedrich I (1675–91). The first true opera was *Die geraubte Proserpina*, performed for the birthday of Friedrich I, 22 April 1683, at the theatre in Schloss Friedenstein. Friedrich I's son, Friedrich II, built up the Hofkapelle, but there was little operatic activity before the arrival of G. H. Stölzel in 1720. His chief duties involved sacred music, but between 1723 and 1744 he composed nine operas for official festivities of the Gotha court, for which only the librettos survive.

Stölzel died in November 1749 and was succeeded by Georg Benda, who composed an *opera seria*, *Xindo riconosciuto*, for the birthday of the Duchess Luise Dorothea, wife of Friedrich III, in 1765, and later that year was sent to Italy at court expense. In 1774 Duke Ernst II brought the theatre company of Abel Seyler to Gotha and a ballroom in the palace was converted into a theatre. Benda's melodramas for this troupe, *Ariadne auf Naxos* and *Medea* (1775), created a sensation throughout Germany. In September 1775 Ernst II established the Gotha Hoftheater out of part of Seyler's troupe, the first German theatre completely under a court's financial and artistic control. A second tier of loges and later a second gallery were added to the theatre in Schloss Friedenstein, increasing its capacity to 300. The townspeople were charged only a nominal price to attend. Seyler's music director, Anton Schweitzer, became Kapellmeister, but important new works came from Benda, notably his serious German operas *Romeo und Julie* and *Walder* (1776). The enterprise closed in 1779.

After a lapse of 25 years musical life at Gotha was reinvigorated during the reign of August I (1804–22), who engaged prominent musicians such as Louis Spohr (Konzertmeister 1805–12) and Andreas Romberg (1815–21), who founded the Gotha Singverein in 1819. After a new division of Thuringian lands in 1826, Duke Ernst I of Coburg-Gotha (reigned 1826–44) organized a new court theatre from members of the Eberwein theatre company. The court shuttled annually between Coburg and Gotha and the theatrical personnel along with it, a practice that continued until 1918. The theatre in Schloss Friedenstein, where the company played during winter, proved too small, so in 1836 Ernst I ordered construction of a new Hoftheater (the present Landestheater), inaugurated in 1840 with Meyerbeer's *Robert le diable*.

German opera, including Wagner's, flourished under the music- and theatre-loving Duke Ernst II (reigned 1844–93), himself a composer. Ernst II's opera *Santa Chiara*, given its première at the Hoftheater in 1854 with Liszt conducting, was much praised by Meyerbeer, made its way to many other German stages and received 60 performances in Paris. In 1853 the position of Kapellmeister was offered to Wagner. Although he refused the post, which involved orchestrating the duke's own operas among other things, Wagner's music was assiduously cultivated at Gotha under Ernst II.

The tradition of a strong commitment to Wagner and to modern German opera continued into the 20th century. Opera remained central to the Gotha Landestheater, organized after Gotha became a free city at the end of World War I, with early performances of the newest German operas by Strauss, Schreker, Hindemith and others. In 1930 the Gotha Landestheater was combined with the Altenburg Landestheater.

*

R. Hodermann: *Geschichte des Gothaischen Hoftheaters, 1775–1779* (Hamburg and Leipzig, 1894)

K. Schmidt, ed.: *Gotha: das Buch einer deutschen Stadt* (Gotha, 1928)

E. W. Böhme: *Die frühdeutsche Oper in Thüringen* (Stadtroda, 1931)

E. Schmidt: *Gotha in heimatkundlichen Schrifttum* (Gotha, 1939)

H. Eichhorn: 'Das Schlosstheater zu Gotha', *Kleine Schriften der Gesellschaft für Theatergeschichte*, xiii (1955), 8–23

H. Engel: *Musik in Thüringen* (Graz, 1966)   THOMAS BAUMAN

Gothenburg. GÖTEBORG.

Gotovac, Jakov (*b* Split, 11 Oct 1895; *d* Zagreb, 16 Oct 1982). Croatian composer. After studies in Split with Dobronić and Hatze, he attended Joseph Marx's composition lectures at the Vienna Akademie (1920). After a short period in Šibenik, from 1923 to 1957 he was a conductor at the Zagreb Opera and the director of several choirs. Gotovac wrote his most important works in the period between the two world wars; he was one of the representatives of the so-called national style, using characteristic elements of folk music in his own idiom and focussing the interest on themes from peasant life. In general his work is homophonic and simple in harmonic structure. After the romantic opera *Morana*, in which the chorus has an important role, Gotovac reached his high point with the comic opera *Ero s onoga svijeta* ('Ero the Joker'), a model of folk verbal humour worked into a structural unity within which he was able to express his own sense of comedy. *Ero* was performed in more than 80 European theatres, and was succeeded by other fine stage works.

Morana (romantic national op, 3, A. Muradbegović), Brno, 29 Nov 1930, vs (Zagreb, 3/1974)

Ero s onoga svijeta [Ero the Joker] (comic op, 3, M. Begović), Zagreb, 2 Nov 1935, vs (Zagreb, 1936)

Kamenik [The Quarry], 1939–44 (3, R. Nikolić, after an idea of M. Fotez), Zagreb, 17 Dec 1946, unpubd

Mila Gojsalića, 1948–52 (historical musical drama, 3, D. Andelinović), Zagreb, 18 May 1952, vs (Zagreb, n.d.)

Đerdan [The Necklace] (musical play, 5 'pictures', Gotovac and C. Jakelić, after D. Šimunović), Zagreb, 29 Nov 1955, unpubd

Stanac (operatic scherzo, 1, M. Držić and V. Rabadan), Zagreb, 6 Dec 1959, vs (Zagreb, 1963)

Dalmaro, 1958 (operatic legend, 1, R. L. Petelinova), Zagreb, 20 Dec 1964, vs (Zagreb, 1970)

Petar Svačić, 1969, finale rev. 1971 (opera-oratorio, Z. Tomičić), unperf.

*

J. Andreis: 'Jakov Gotovac', *Mogućnosti* (1957), nos. 7–8

K. Kovačević: *Hrvatski kompozitori i njihova djela* [Croatian Composers and their Works] (Zagreb, 1960), 164–79

I. Supičić: 'Estetski pogledi u novijoj hrvatskoj muzici: pregled temeljnih gledanja četrnaestorice kompozitora' [Aesthetic Approaches in Contemporary Croatian Music: a Survey of the Basic Views of 14 Composers], *Arti musices*, i (1969), 23–61

J. Andreis: *Music in Croatia* (Zagreb, 1974), 288–97

Jakov Gotovac 1895–1982: spomenica [Jakov Gotovac 1895–1982: Memorial] (Zagreb, 1986) [pubn of the Yugoslavian Academy of Arts and Sciences; with complete list of works]
      KREŠIMIR KOVAČEVIĆ/KORALJKA KOS

Gotter, (Johann) Friedrich Wilhelm (*b* Gotha, 3 Sept 1746; *d* Gotha, 18 March 1797). German poet and librettist. He studied law and pursued a diplomatic career in the service of the Gotha court. He wrote comedies, tragedies, and poetry, translated copiously for the theatre and contributed to German opera and the melodrama. His first comic operas, *Die Dorfgala* and *Der Jahrmarkt*, temper Weisse's sentimental rusticity with a more farcical strain executed with urbane detachment. In 1776 Gotter wrote two serious operas with spoken dialogue, *Walder* and *Romeo und Julie*, for Georg Benda. A year earlier Benda had set Gotter's finest musical text, the melodrama *Medea*. Written for the great tragedienne Sophie Seyler, it surpasses Brandes's *Ariadne auf Naxos* in poetic power and dramatic force. Late in life, Gotter collaborated with Friedrich von Einsiedel on DIE GEISTERINSEL, an operatic adaptation of Shakespeare's *Tempest*. Although dramatically attenuated, its poetry is elegant and mellifluous, and the text enjoyed several settings.

Die Dorfgala (Operette), Schweitzer, 1772; Der Jahrmarkt (komisches Spl), G. Benda, 1775; Medea (musikalisches Drama), Benda, 1775; Walder (Operette), Benda, 1776; Romeo und Julie (Schauspiel mit Gesang), Benda, 1776; Der Holzhauer (komische Oper), Benda, 1778; Das tartarische Gesetz (Schauspiel mit Gesang), J. André, 1779 (Zumsteeg, 1780; Benda, 1787); Pygmalion (Monodrama), Benda, 1779; Die Geisterinsel (Spl, with F. H. von Einsiedel), F. Fleischmann, 1796 (Reichardt, 1798; Zumsteeg, 1798; F. W. Haack, 1799)   THOMAS BAUMAN

Götterdämmerung ('Twilight of the Gods'). Third day of *DER RING DES NIBELUNGEN* in a prologue and three acts by Richard Wagner (*see* WAGNER family, (1)) to his own libretto; Bayreuth, Festspielhaus, 17 August 1876.

Siegfried		tenor
Gunther		bass-baritone
Alberich		bass-baritone
Hagen		bass
Brünnhilde		soprano
Gutrune		soprano
Waltraute		mezzo-soprano
First Norn		contralto
Second Norn		mezzo-soprano
Third Norn		soprano
Woglinde		soprano
Wellgunde	*Rhinemaidens*	soprano
Flosshilde		mezzo-soprano
Vassals, women		

The first draft of *Siegfrieds Tod* (originally spelt *Siegfried's Tod* and later renamed *Götterdämmerung*) is dated (at the end) 20 October 1848. This draft begins in the hall of the Gibichungs, but having been persuaded that too much background knowledge to the story was presupposed, Wagner added a prologue some time before 12 November. He undertook the versification of *Siegfrieds Tod* between 12 and 28 November, but then put it aside, perhaps unsure how to reconcile the diverging strands of the drama: divine myth and heroic tragedy. In the summer of 1850 he made some preliminary musical sketches for the prologue and began a composition draft, which was discontinued after the opening of the leavetaking scene for Siegfried and Brünnhilde. Having then added a preliminary drama, *Der junge Siegfried* (1851), and *Die Walküre* and *Das*

Rheingold (1851–2), Wagner found it necessary to subject *Siegfrieds Tod* to revision: Siegfried had already been replaced as the central figure of the cycle by Wotan; the ending was altered so that the gods and Valhalla are all destroyed by fire; the Norns' scene was completely rewritten; a confrontation between Brünnhilde and the rest of the Valkyries was compressed into the dialogue for Brünnhilde and Waltraute (Act 1 scene iii); and several passages of narrative now rendered superfluous by *Die Walküre* and *Das Rheingold* were removed. The first complete draft of *Götterdämmerung* was begun on 2 October 1869 and finished on 10 April 1872. The second complete draft (short score) was made, as with *Siegfried*, in parallel, between 11 January 1870 and 22 July 1872. The full score was finished in Wahnfried on 21 November 1874.

PROLOGUE *The Valkyrie rock (as at the end of 'Siegfried')* The prologue opens with the two chords heard at the awakening of Brünnhilde (*Siegfried*, Act 3), but now in the darker, mellower tonality of E♭ minor. The Three Norns, daughters of Erda, are weaving the rope of destiny. The First Norn tells how, long ago, Wotan came to drink at the Well of Wisdom, sacrificing an eye as forfeit. He had cut a spear from the trunk of the tree, which had later withered and died. The Second Norn tells how a brave hero broke Wotan's spear in battle; the god then sent heroes from Valhalla to chop down the World Ash. The Third Norn describes how the chopped logs of the World Ash have been piled round Valhalla; one day they will be ignited and the entire hall will be engulfed in flames. Gods and heroes are awaiting that day. As each Norn in turn passes on both rope and narration, the wind and brass intone the theme of the Annunciation of Death (*Walküre*, Act 2 scene iv). The First Norn sees fire burning round the Valkyrie rock and is told that it is Loge fulfilling Wotan's command. A vision of Alberich and the stolen Rhinegold causes the Norns anxiety. To a baleful statement of the Curse motif on the bass trumpet, followed by that of the Twilight of the Gods, the rope breaks.

The Norns descend into the earth and an orchestral interlude evokes sunrise. A pair of themes, exx.1 (a

Ex.1

Ex.2

sturdier form of Siegfried's horn call) and 2 (a new theme associated with Brünnhilde), are worked into a climax as the lovers come out of the cave to which they retired at the end of *Siegfried*. Brünnhilde sends Siegfried off on deeds of glory ('Zu neuen Thaten'), urging him to remember their love. A rapturous duet follows, constructed from exx.1 and 2 and other themes associated with the pair and their love and heroism. The vocal lines continue the new style evolved in Act 3 of *Siegfried*, richly ornamented with figurations and melismas. Siegfried gives Brünnhilde the ring as a token

of his faithfulness; in exchange, she offers him her horse, Grane.

Another orchestral interlude (colourfully scored, with the glockenspiel and triangle adding to the gaiety) depicts Siegfried's Rhine Journey. It begins with a variant of ex.1 and the hero's progress is suggested by the appearance of the Fire motif and those of the Rhine and Rhinemaidens. In its latter stages, the dark-hued diminished triad of the Ring motif initiates a change of mood (and tonality).

ACT 1.i–ii *The hall of the Gibichungs* The action proper begins as Gunther, the chief of the Gibichungs, asks his half-brother Hagen whether his reputation is high: 'Nun hör', Hagen'. The accompanying motif, that of Hagen (ex.3), is a stunted form of the heroic octave

Ex.3

leap of Siegfried's Forging Song (*Siegfried*, Act 1). Hagen replies that it would be higher if Gunther were to find a wife and Gutrune, his sister, a husband. The galloping Valkyrie motif and that of the fire god Loge are heard as Hagen tells them about Brünnhilde lying on a rock encircled by fire. He suggests that Siegfried would win the bride for Gunther if Gutrune had won him first. Hagen reminds them of a potion they have that would make Siegfried forget any other women.

Siegfried's horn is now heard and Hagen calls down to him (scene ii): his 'Heil! Siegfried', with ominous irony, picks out the notes of the Curse motif, sounded simultaneously on a trio of trombones. Such references have become increasingly oblique in the latter part of the *Ring*: a few bars later, the Curse motif sounds again as Siegfried asks whether Hagen knows him – a reminder of what it is that linked their ancestors. Hagen has to tell Siegfried the purpose of the Tarnhelm he is carrying. Gutrune appears, to a tender new motif (ex.4).

Ex.4

She offers Siegfried the drugged potion and he, in a gesture pregnant with irony, drinks to the memory of Brünnhilde and their love. An extended trill symbolically shifts the tonality from the A♭ of Siegfried's memory to the G of Gutrune's presence. Siegfried is immediately drawn to Gutrune and loses no time in offering himself as her husband. He then offers to win Gunther a wife and as he is told about Brünnhilde high on a rock surrounded by fire, it is clear that he has only the faintest recollection of her. (Trills and tremolando strings evoke both the fire and the haziness of his memory.)

Siegfried proposes to use the Tarnhelm to disguise himself as Gunther in order to bring back Brünnhilde. The idea of swearing blood brotherhood brings forth the motifs of the Curse, the Sword (in a fast, energetic variant) and, less expectedly, that of Wotan's Spear: the symbol of the original contracts that have brought such trouble and strife. Siegfried and Gunther swear their oath: 'Blühenden Lebens labendes Blut', with its duetting in 3rds and 6ths, the first of several reactionary structures in the work. Motivic reference slows down here but does not disappear: the menacing presence of Hagen in the background accounts for both the Ring and Curse motifs and for the effective juxtaposition of falling perfect and diminished 5ths (the former associated with heroism, the latter with evil) at 'blüh' im Trank unser Blut!' Siegfried sets off up the river again, followed by Gunther. The dour Hagen sits guarding the palace, contemplating the satisfactory progress of his scheme to win power: 'Hier sitz' ich zur Wacht'. The falling diminished 5th is now irrevocably associated with him, and the falling semitone, which can be traced back ultimately to Alberich's cries of woe in *Das Rheingold*, here attains its most anguished harmonization.

An orchestral interlude meditating on salient themes effects a transition from Hagen sitting malevolently on watch outside the palace to Brünnhilde sitting in innocent contemplation of Siegfried's ring outside the cave. The introduction of Brünnhilde's ex.2, with lighter scoring, dispels some of the oppressive atmosphere, but there remain enough pungent harmonies to suggest that trouble lies ahead.

1.iii *The Valkyrie rock* There is thunder and lightning and Brünnhilde sees her sister Waltraute approach on a winged horse (much use of the galloping Valkyrie motif). In her delight, Brünnhilde fails to notice Waltraute's agitation: has Wotan perhaps forgiven her? Waltraute explains that she has broken Wotan's command in coming, but sadly he is no longer to be feared. She then narrates ('Seit er von dir geschieden'), to a wealth of motivic reference, how Wotan, as the Wanderer, returned to Valhalla with his spear shattered, how he ordered the heroes to pile up logs from the World Ash Tree, how the gods sit there in fear and dread, and how Wotan longs for the ring to be given back to the Rhinemaidens; it is to persuade Brünnhilde to do this that Waltraute has come. Although stunned by this narration (ex.5 with its anguished leaps is

Ex.5

eloquent), Brünnhilde refuses to throw away Siegfried's pledge. The final brief exchange between Brünnhilde and Waltraute is enacted to one of the numerous little congeries of allusive motifs which distinguish the score of *Götterdämmerung* (in the earlier parts of the *Ring*, motivic references are generally more sparing and explicit).

Waltraute departs in a thundercloud which passes to reveal a calm evening sky. But the peace is illusory. The flames leap up again round the rock and Brünnhilde hears Siegfried's horn. She rushes excitedly to the edge of the cliff and is horrified to find a stranger: Siegfried disguised by the Tarnhelm as Gunther. Her rapturous welcome is abruptly terminated with a discord, remembered from Hagen's Watch, but also identifiable as the 'Tristan chord' at correct pitch. The significance of the interpolation of that pivotal chord from Wagner's intervening opera at Brünnhilde's cry 'Verrath!' – the point at which the hero's love (under the influence of a magic potion, be it noted) is perceived to be false – need hardly be laboured. No less notable is the fact that the 'Tristan chord' turns out to be the G♯ minor of the

Tarnhelm motif with the addition of an intensifying diminished 7th (the F). But most extraordinary of all is the fact that the 'Tristan chord' and Tarnhelm motif – both at their original pitch – effect a return to B minor, the key in which the act will end, as it began: a remarkable example of the interaction of local tonal reference with large-scale structural planning. The disguised Siegfried claims Brünnhilde as wife, violently snatches the ring from her finger and forces her into the cave for the night. He places his sword symbolically between them.

ACT 2 *On the shore in front of the Gibichung hall* Hagen, sitting outside the palace in a half-sleep, is visited by his father, Alberich: 'Schläfst du, Hagen, mein Sohn?'. The syncopations of Hagen's Watch reappear here, but in B♭, the key of the Nibelungs. Hagen is urged to acquire the ring, and intends to do so, but will swear faithfulness only to himself. Dawn breaks in a loosely canonic passage scored for eight horns (scene ii) and Siegfried returns, now in his own form once more. Gunther is following with Brünnhilde, he says, and he tells Hagen and Gutrune how he braved the fire and overpowered Brünnhilde. He secretly changed places with Gunther and, using the Tarnhelm's magic, returned in an instant.

Hagen summons his vassals (scene iii) with blasts on his horn; his cries of 'Hoiho!' make frequent use of the ubiquitous falling semitone. The vassals rush in from all directions and are intemperately amused when they find out that Hagen has summoned them not for battle but for celebration. Their chorus in C major, with augmented-triad colouring influenced by Hagen – 'Gross Glück und Heil' – is another example of stylistic regression in *Götterdämmerung*, exciting as it can be in the theatre.

Clashing their weapons together, the vassals hail Gunther and his bride (scene iv), 'Heil dir, Gunther!', the switch to B♭ possibly in recollection of a more celebrated Bridal March in the same key. To a melancholy reminiscence of the galloping Valkyrie motif, Brünnhilde is led forward, her eyes cast down. Gutrune's motif (ex.4) is prominent as she comes out of the hall with Siegfried. The sound of Siegfried's name provokes a violent reaction from Brünnhilde, her mute amazement forcefully depicted in the sustained diminished 7th chord that stops the music in its tracks. It starts up again with the anguished contortions of ex.4 and, less predictably, the Destiny motif from the Annunciation of Death in *Die Walküre*. Has Siegfried forgotten his bride, Brünnhilde asks? She sees the ring on his finger and asks how he got it, as it was seized from her by Gunther. Siegfried states simply that he won it by slaying a dragon. Raging against the gods for allowing Siegfried to betray her, Brünnhilde borrows a broad phrase from the Valhalla motif, in the original key of D♭. Siegfried tells how he won Brünnhilde for Gunther and claims that his sword lay between them during the night. Brünnhilde asserts that Nothung hung on the wall as its master wooed her. Siegfried, pressed by Gunther and the onlookers to declare his innocence, swears on the point of Hagen's spear that he has kept faith with his 'blood-brother': 'Helle Wehr, heilige Waffe!'. His innocently ringing perfect 5ths (both rising and falling) are tellingly offset by Hagen's diminished 5th sounded in the bass. The enraged Brünnhilde swears on the same spear-point that Siegfried has perjured himself. Siegfried calls everyone to the wedding-feast and leads Gutrune into the palace.

Brünnhilde, left alone with Gunther and Hagen, laments Siegfried's treachery (scene v). At first she scorns Hagen's offer to avenge her; the hero would soon make him quake, she says. But then she confides that Siegfried's back would be vulnerable; she gave him no protection there as he would never turn it on an enemy. Gunther bemoans his own disgrace, but initially reacts with horror to Hagen's proposal to strike Siegfried dead (the minatory falling semitones on trombones are combined with the tortured ex.5 on bassoons and double basses). He is persuaded by the promise of obtaining the ring and it is decided to tell Gutrune that Siegfried was killed by a boar while out hunting. The trio of the conspirators is a stylistic regression that runs contrary to Wagner's *Oper und Drama* principles (the libretto for *Götterdämmerung* in fact preceded the theoretical essays), though there is some attempt to integrate the passage by means of motivic reminiscence: the new oath of vengeance principally recalls the oaths sworn on Hagen's spear earlier in the act. Siegfried and Gutrune reappear from the palace and a wedding procession forms. The celebratory C major is chillingly darkened in the final bars by the intervention of the falling semitone on trombones in combination with ex.5 a tritone away from the main key.

ACT 3.i–ii *Wild woodland and rocky valley by the bank of the Rhine* Siegfried's horn call is heard first in the orchestra and then in the distance, supposedly sounded by Siegfried out hunting. It is answered by the horn call of the Gibichungs (an inverted form). The ominous falling semitone and tritone from the end of the previous act are heard, but then the lyrical music of the Rhinemaidens supervenes. They are playing in the river, singing of the lost gold. Siegfried, having lost his way, stumbles on them and they playfully ask him for the ring on his finger; he refuses. Then he relents, but when they tell him of the dangers the curse-laden ring brings he says he will not succumb to threats. The Rhinemaidens abandon the 'fool', leaving Siegfried to meditate on the oddity of women's behaviour.

Hagen's voice and falling semitone are heard, and Siegfried calls the hunting party over (scene ii). He tells them that the only game he has seen was three wild water-birds, who told him he would be murdered that day. Siegfried drinks jovially from a horn, but Gunther can see only Siegfried's blood in his. Siegfried is asked to tell the story of his life, and he begins with his upbringing by the ill-tempered Mime (to the ostinato of the Nibelungs' motif): 'Mime hiess ein mürrischer Zwerg'. The dwarf taught him smithing, but it was his own skills that enabled him to forge Nothung, with which he killed the dragon Fafner (the Sword and Dragon motifs are heard). As yet Siegfried has no trouble in recalling the past. Swirling augmented harmonies conjure the enchantment of the world he is describing. He tells how the taste of the dragon's blood enabled him to understand the song of the woodbird, and the Forest Murmurs are recalled. The bird had warned him of Mime's treachery and he had despatched the scheming dwarf.

Hagen hands him a drugged drink which he says will help him to remember what happened next. The music, recalling the trills of the potion he was given in Act 1, tell us that memories have indeed been stimulated: where the trills previously led to the theme of Gutrune, now they soar into a theme remembered from the prologue duet, closely followed by the Brünnhilde motif,

ex.2. To the appropriate motifs, and in an increasingly ecstatic state as he relives the traumatic but forgotten experience, Siegfried relates how he was led to a high rock surrounded by fire; there he found the sleeping Brünnhilde, whom he awoke with a kiss. The expected C major resolution is thwarted by Gunther's tritonal expression of dismay. Two ravens fly overhead and, as Siegfried looks up, Hagen plunges his spear in his back. Brass instruments thunder out the Curse motif and Hagen's falling semitone; one of Siegfried's heroic motifs is hurled out by the entire orchestra, but it reaches its climax on a discord and finally collapses on to the repeated-note, tattoo figure that is to become the basis of the Funeral March. The themes and radiant C major tonality of Brünnhilde's awakening (*Siegfried*, Act 3) are recalled, and Siegfried dies with Brünnhilde's name on his lips.

Siegfried's Funeral March represents a motivic pageant of his life and ancestry, as his body is carried off by vassals in a solemn procession. Themes associated with the Volsungs and their love are followed by a grand statement of the Sword motif in its original C major (on a trumpet), and by the motifs of Siegfried and his heroism, ending with a triumphant transformation, in E♭, of ex.1.

3.iii *The hall of the Gibichungs* Gutrune comes out of her room into the hall. She thinks she hears Siegfried's horn, but he has not returned. She has seen Brünnhilde walking towards the Rhine, and is anxious. Hagen is heard approaching ('Hoiho!', on falling semitones over ex.5) and Siegfried's corpse is brought in. She accuses Gunther of murdering him, but he blames Hagen, who claims – to the music of the oath-swearing – to have killed him for committing perjury; Hagen steps forward to seize the ring and when Gunther stands in his way, he is murdered by Hagen. Hagen tries again to take the ring, but as he approaches Siegfried, the dead man's hand rises into the air, to the horror of all. The Sword motif, in its other primary key of D major, makes a quietly noble intervention, but gives way to the motif of the Twilight of the Gods.

Brünnhilde enters with calm dignity and tells how Siegfried swore her an eternal oath. Gutrune curses Hagen and prostrates herself over Gunther's body, where she remains, motionless, until the end. Brünnhilde orders logs to be gathered to make a funeral pyre worthy of the hero ('Starke Scheite'). Loge's motif blazes in eager anticipation. She sings of her betrayal by this noblest, most faithful of men. Addressing Wotan in Valhalla, she says that Siegfried's death has atoned for his guilt and has brought her enlightenment through sorrow. This quietly reflective passage is rounded off by a statement, no longer threatening, of the Curse motif and a sublime resolution in D♭, the ultimate goal of the cycle ('Ruhe, ruhe, du Gott!'). She takes Siegfried's ring, promising that it will be returned to the Rhinemaidens, whose carefree music is now heard. She hurls a blazing torch on to the pile of logs, which immediately ignites. Greeting her horse Grane (to recollections of the galloping Valkyrie motif), she mounts it and rides into the flames. The exultant theme sung by Sieglinde in *Die Walküre* on hearing of her future son's destiny ('O hehrstes Wunder') returns now to crown the peroration: Wagner referred to this motif as 'the glorification of Brünnhilde' (ex.6).

The whole building seems to catch fire and the men and women press to the front of the stage in terror. Suddenly the fire dies down and the Rhine bursts its

'Götterdämmerung'
(Wagner), Act 3: Josef
Hoffmann's design for the
final scene in the original
production at Bayreuth,
17 August 1876

Ex.6

banks, flooding the entire space. On the appearance of
the Rhinemaidens, Hagen leaps into the water in pursuit
of the ring. To the sound of the Curse motif, they drag
him down into the depths and hold up the ring in
triumph. The water-level falls again and from the ruins
of the palace, which has collapsed, the men and women
watch a burst of firelight as it rises into the sky. Eventually it illuminates the hall of Valhalla, where gods and
heroes are seen assembled. The Valhalla motif is naturally prominent here, and those of the Rhinemaidens and
the Glorification of Brünnhilde are symbolically
intertwined. To the sound of the motifs of the Twilight
of the Gods and, finally, the Glorification of Brünnhilde in a radiant Db major, Valhalla is engulfed
in flames: the long-awaited end of the gods has come
to pass.

*   *   *

The final opera of the *Ring*, a long evening's
performance in its own right, provides an appropriately
weighty conclusion to the epic cycle. 26 years elapsed
from the time Wagner made his first prose draft for the
work (then called *Siegfrieds Tod*) to the completion of
the full score, with inevitable consequences in terms of
stylistic unity. Retrogressive elements of grand opera
exist side by side with motivic integration representative
of Wagner's most mature style. And yet, the stylistic integrity of *Götterdämmerung* is scarcely compromised,
so skilfully are the disparate elements welded together
and so intense the dramaturgical conviction. The
resources and stamina demanded by the work (from
both singers and orchestra), combined with its sheer
length and theatrical potency, make it one of the most
daunting yet rewarding undertakings in the operatic
repertory.   BARRY MILLINGTON

Göttingen. City in Lower Saxony, north-west Germany.
The first theatre performances (there were only seven)
took place in the Reithalle between 1746 and 1784;
none were given in the next 50 years. In 1834 a subscription system was set up for theatre and opera
performances from November to January, taking place
in the newly built Theatersaal, in Wilhelmsplatz. In
1887 this building was completely destroyed by a fire,
but a new theatre was begun immediately, opening in
1890 with Schiller's *Wilhelm Tell*. In 1920 the city's
own opera ensemble was founded. Theatrical
performances continued up to and during the war: in
1940 Gustav Rudolf Sellner founded a 'Kreis der
Freunde des Stadttheaters'. Performances were restarted
in 1945, but on 2 July 1950 the 50-year-old tradition of
operatic activity in Göttingen (apart from the festival)
came to an end with a performance of *Carmen*: the
theatre was closed for financial reasons.

Göttingen is, however, an important centre for 20th-
century Handel performance. Its Handel Festival was
founded in 1920 by Oskar Hagen, who taught at the
university; the opening production on 26 June was a
revival at the Stadttheater of *Rodelinda*, which had been
forgotten for almost 200 years. From 1931 the festival
has been the responsibility of the Göttinger Händel-
gesellschaft and besides producing Handelian operas
and oratorios devotes much time to chamber music.
Lectures on the works of Handel and other composers
complete the programme. The festival lapsed during
World War II, was resumed in 1946, and has taken
place almost every year since, in June or early July. From
1981 to 1990 John Eliot Gardiner was artistic director,
succeeding Günther Weissenborn, and he gave the
festival international status. In 1991 Nicholas McGegan
took over from Gardiner. Göttingen has had close links
with the Handel Society in Halle, the composer's birthplace, since 1955 when the society was founded.

W. Meyerhoff, ed.: *Festschrift 50 Jahre Göttinger Handel-Festspiele* (Göttingen, 1970)
SABINE SONNTAG

Gottlieb, (Maria) Anna (Josepha Francisca) [Nanette] (*b* Vienna, 29 April 1774; *d* Vienna, 1 Feb 1856). Austrian singer. She was a daughter of two members of the German theatre company of the Nationaltheater. At the age of five she started appearing there in small acting and singing roles. When she was 12 she created Barbarina in Mozart's *Le nozze di Figaro* (1786). In 1789 she was engaged by Emanuel Schikaneder for the Freihaustheater, where Mozart wrote Pamina for her in *Die Zauberflöte* (1791). That role represented the artistic peak of her career (although she was not yet 18).

In 1792 she was engaged at the Leopoldstädter Theater, at that time under the direction of Marinelli. During her 36 years there she gradually moved from a youthful singer to a character actress playing comic old women. Her best years saw her singing in Gluck's *Die Pilgrime von Mekka* (*La rencontre imprévue*) and works by Dalayrac. Her greatest successes were in the roles she created in Singspiels and travesties to words by Perinet and C. F. Hensler (Marinelli's successor at the Leopoldstädter Theater, 1803–17), set by Wenzel Müller and Ferdinand Kauer: in *Das Neusonntagskind* (1793, Perinet and Müller), as Hulda in *Das Donauweibchen* (1798, Hensler and Kauer), a role she performed over a thousand times, as Evakathel in *Evakathel und Schnudi, oder Die Belagerung von Ypsilon* (1804, Parinet and Müller) and in the title role of *Die neue Alceste* (1806, Perinet and Müller). She was absent from the stage in 1808–11 and returned with diminishing success, finally singing mainly secondary roles. She was dismissed without a pension in 1828 and sank into poverty. In 1842 she introduced herself to L. V. Frankl, editor of the *Sonntagsblätter*, as 'the first Pamina' and the last living friend of Mozart; his emotional appeal on her behalf raised enough money to send her to Salzburg for the unveiling of the Mozart monument. She died in the year of Mozart's centenary and, like Mozart, was buried in St Mark's cemetery.

L. A. Frankl: *Erinnerungen* (Prague, 1910)
E. von Kemerzynski: *Pamina: Mozarts letzte Liebe* (Berlin, 1956)
U. Mauthe: *Mozarts 'Pamina' Anna Gottlieb* (Augsburg, 1986)
CLEMENS HÖSLINGER

Gottlieb, Peter (*b* Brno, 18 Sept 1930). French baritone. He was brought up in Rio de Janeiro, where his career began, but since 1962 has been based in Paris. He has sung leading roles in most French opera houses, including Escamillo, Dr Schön (*Lulu*), Malatesta, Don Giovanni, Papageno, Yevgeny Onegin and Britten's Tarquinius. His British début was in 1966 as Albert (*Werther*) at Glyndebourne, where he returned in 1970 to create Major Max von Zastrow in *The Rising of the Moon* (Maw) and Mercury in the Leppard edition of *Calisto* (Cavalli), which he also recorded. A versatile singer with a special interest in contemporary music, he has sung in many premières, among them *L'opéra d'Aran* (Bécaud), *La symphonie pastorale* (Landré), *Egmont* (Meulemans) and *Les liaisons dangereuses* (Prey).
NOËL GOODWIN

Gottschalk, Louis Moreau (*b* New Orleans, 8 May 1829; *d* Tijuca, Brazil, 18 Dec 1869). American composer. At the age of six he began to study the violin, and he later took up the piano. In 1842 he went to Paris, where he eventually became a pupil of Berlioz. Highly successful as a pianist and composer, he travelled widely and visited Cuba three times. Although several of his biographers mention two operas by him, *Isaura di Salerno* op.125 (opera seria, 3, 1859) and *Charles IX* op.52 (supposedly based on Prosper Mérimée's *Chronique du règne de Charles IX*), the only extant operatic music by Gottschalk is a fragment of the latter, 'Final e himno triunfal' (*CU-Hn*; New York, 1969). The opera was composed in Havana, during Gottschalk's last visit to Cuba; for it he used several parts of Felice Romani's libretto *I Capuleti e i Montecchi* (originally written for Bellini). The 'Final e himno triunfal' was performed under Gottschalk's direction at the Teatro de Tacón, Havana, on 17 February 1860 during the music festival that he organized there; the performers included the soprano Josefa Gassier and other members of Max Maretzek's opera company.

L. R. Fors: *Gottschalk* (Havana, 1880)
S. Ramirez: *La Habana artistica* (Havana, 1891)
A. Carpentier: *La música en Cuba* (Havana, 1979)
J. G. Doyle: *Louis Moreau Gottschalk 1829–1869: a Bibliographical Study and Catalog of Works* (Detroit, 1983)
J. A. González: *La composición operística en Cuba* (Havana, 1987)
JORGE ANTONIO GONZÁLEZ

Gounod, Charles-François (*b* Paris, 17 June 1818; *d* St Cloud, 18 Oct 1893). French composer, the leading figure in French opera during the third quarter of the 19th century.

1. LIFE. The son of a painter and a pianist, Gounod showed an early artistic talent, for the visual arts and letters as well as music. Despite pressures from his mother to study law, he decided at the age of 16 to devote himself to music and, after studies with Reicha, Halévy and Le Sueur, he won the Prix de Rome in 1839. During his tenure of the award Gounod fell under the influence of the Dominican preacher Père Lacordaire and completed both an *a cappella* mass in the style of Palestrina and a Requiem; on his return to Paris his musical ambitions continued in the direction of sacred music. In 1843 he became music director of the Missions Etrangères church, a post he held until 1847 when he enrolled formally at the seminary of St Sulpice. At the beginning of the next year, however, Gounod abandoned that vocation and set his sights on the world of opera. He was virtually unknown on the Parisian musical scene, but thanks to the influence of the mezzo-soprano Pauline Viardot, who was favourably impressed by his musical abilities when she first met him in 1849, he received an Opéra commission to set *Sapho*, with Emile Augier as librettist. Most composers had reputations much more firmly established before they wrote for that house. The contract stipulated that Viardot was to assume the title role and the work was to be a two-act curtain raiser.

In the end *Sapho* was cast in three acts and occupied an entire evening on its own. Gounod composed the score during the summer of 1850 at Courtavenel, the country estate of Viardot and her husband, while the singer was on tour. Ivan Turgenev, also a visitor there, pronounced judgment on newly composed passages, and on her return Viardot suggested a number of revisions (although Gounod later claimed in his *Mémoires d'un artiste* that she was entirely satisfied with the work). The office of the censor objected to certain numbers on moral and political grounds but the obstacles were ironed out before the première, which was on 16 April 1851. *Sapho*, however, did not draw well in Paris and a single performance in London on 8 August was a disaster. Nonetheless Gounod's music met with some critical approval and in 1852 he was given another chance at the Opéra when he signed a contract to set Eugène Scribe's *opéra* libretto *La nonne sanglante*. That subject had passed through the hands of several composers before Gounod, among them Berlioz and Verdi. Given the dubious quality of the libretto and the fact that it drew upon dramatic devices and scenic ploys seen often before on the Opéra stage, the odds were against Gounod's new operatic project achieving the much sought-after triumph; *La nonne sanglante* disappeared after 11 performances at the end of 1854.

By that time Gounod had achieved some recognition as the director of a large amateur choral society, the Orphéon de la Ville de Paris. The Opéra administration continued to place great trust in his abilities and some time in late 1855 or early 1856 he was offered a libretto by Henri Trianon and François Hippolyte Leroy to a five-act grand opera, *Ivan le terrible*. Gounod set substantial portions of the work, which centred on a conspiracy against the Russian emperor. But Alphonse Royer, director of the house, cancelled Gounod's project after an attempted assassination of Louis Napoleon at the Opéra in January 1858. Gounod later used music composed for the stillborn piece in *La reine de Saba* and *Mireille* as well as *Faust*. Barbier and Carré completed the libretto for this last work during 1856 and Léon Carvalho, the newly appointed director of the Théâtre Lyrique, readily agreed to produce it. However, when a rival theatre, the Porte-St-Martin, announced its intention at the beginning of 1857 to mount an extravagant spectacle based on the Faust story, Carvalho thought it best to postpone Gounod's opera indefinitely after about half of it had been composed. Gounod promptly turned to the Opéra with the work but Royer also balked because of the Porte-St-Martin production. In consolation for the *Faust* disappointment Carvalho agreed to stage an adaptation by Gounod of Molière's *Le médecin malgré lui*, with Barbier and Carré as librettists. He composed the score in about six months and it was first performed on 15 January 1858. This time the libretto was immune from criticism; to find fault with it was to find fault with a 17th-century classic. The music was also well received, but the work did not achieve the box-office success it merits. Following the première of *Le médecin*, Gounod revised *Sapho* for a new production at the Opéra in the summer of 1858, but this proved to be no more enduring than the original.

Although the Porte-St-Martin Faust spectacle had been postponed until September 1858, Carvalho now changed his mind about Gounod's opera. The composer set to work on it again in April 1858; rehearsals began the following autumn and the première took place on 19 March 1859. Most early reviewers regarded the musical substance of the opera as elevated and serious; Berlioz, for example, noted that the melody of Faust's *cavatine* 'Salut! demeure chaste et pure', now one of the best-loved tunes from French opera, seemed to have been incomprehensible to most of those attending the première. When publishers such as Colombier, Heugel and Escudier rejected *Faust*, Gounod turned to the small firm of Antoine Choudens to publish a vocal score of the work, which appeared in June 1859. *Faust* played a major role in the improvement of Choudens' fortunes after he set out to market it aggressively, arranging productions supervised by the composer first in the

provinces and then in Germany. The operatic public in Paris and elsewhere quickly became accustomed to Gounod's style and *Faust* was soon one of the most popular operas in the international repertory.

While *Faust* was in rehearsal, Gounod and his librettists Barbier and Carré received a commission from Edouard Bénazet to write a two-act *opéra comique* with four soloists, based on La Fontaine's *Philémon et Baucis*, for the summer theatre at Baden-Baden. With an eye towards the obvious taste of Parisian theatre-goers for mythological comedy after the phenomenal success of Offenbach's *Orphée aux enfers* at the Bouffes-Parisiens, Carvalho had the work rerouted to the Théâtre Lyrique for performance during the season of 1859–60; he also arranged for it to be expanded into three acts by the addition of a central tableau which was a close reproduction of Thomas Couture's famous painting *Les romains de la décadence*. In the summer of 1860 Gounod compensated Bénazet with *La colombe*, a two-act work also based on La Fontaine and on a scale originally intended for *Philémon et Baucis*; it was revived in 1866 at the Opéra-Comique. Neither of the La Fontaine operas was at first enthusiastically received, though *Philémon et Baucis* did eventually find favour at the Opéra-Comique for several decades after 1876.

Alphonse Royer was still willing to mount a new work by Gounod at the Opéra, and the subject finally settled upon was the legend of the Queen of Sheba as told by Gérard de Nerval in his *Le voyage en Orient*. *La reine de Saba* was given in February 1862; it was the first operatic première after the *Tannhäuser* fiasco in the previous year. Because of exaggerated rumours of Gounod's friendly association with Wagner as well as certain unconventional circumstances surrounding the production, such as a closed final dress rehearsal and the early engraving of the vocal score, Gounod became an easy target for anti-Wagnerians in the French press. Nor were the fortunes of *La reine de Saba* helped by the fact that the opera's most spectacular scenic *coup*, the explosion of a large furnace in Act 2, was cut shortly before the first performance. Gounod was despondent after the work's failure, noting cynically on one occasion that had Meyerbeer set *La reine de Saba* 'both libretto and music would have been judged excellent'. But in spite of bouts of depression Gounod soon began to contemplate new operatic projects. He briefly considered a *Mignon*, later taken up by Ambroise Thomas, and eventually settled on an adaptation of Frédéric Mistral's recent Provençal epic poem, *Mirèio* or *Mireille*. Invited to Provence by the poet in spring 1863, Gounod visited the site of each tableau in the opera. He composed most of the work on location. A particularly turbulent rehearsal period followed – at one point communication between Gounod and the Carvalhos was effected through an exchange of notarized letters – and important changes continued to be made to *Mireille* during its first run in spring 1864. They did little to prolong its life that year; in 1889, however, a revised three-act version was well received by audiences at the Opéra-Comique.

Though *Mireille* was Gounod's third Parisian failure in succession he continued to be regarded as a leading figure in French music and opera. He turned his attention to *Roméo et Juliette* about a year after the *Mireille* débâcle, returning to Provence to compose the work, but his progress was impeded by a recurrence of the nervous disorder that plagued him at various times in his life. *Roméo* was finally ready for rehearsal in August 1866 and was given at the Théâtre Lyrique during the

Exposition Universelle of 1867. It was Gounod's greatest immediate success; that it fared much better than the Opéra's Exposition offering, Verdi's *Don Carlos*, is a telling indicator of contemporary French taste. Gounod now planned, under the influence of Marcello, a talented female sculptor with whom he was friendly in this period, an opera based on the Francesca da Rimini episode from Dante's *Inferno*; but when renewed depression set in at the beginning of 1868 he abandoned that project and he was even reluctant to supply a ballet for a production of *Faust* at the Opéra, attempting unsuccessfully to delegate the task to Saint-Saëns.

Gounod chose to forgo rehearsals for the new *Faust* at the beginning of 1869 in favour of a therapeutic trip to Rome, which provided the stimulus for the oratorio *La rédemption* as well as an opera based on Corneille's play about Christian martyrs, *Polyeucte*. Royer's successor, Emile Perrin, expressed a willingness to produce not only that work but also *Roméo et Juliette*. These plans went awry in the wake of the Franco-Prussian War of 1870. Fearing a bloody conflict before the capitulation of France, Gounod moved his family to England soon after the outbreak of hostilities. He suspended work on *Polyeucte* partly to compose *Gallia*, a large elegy for his homeland, and partly out of financial necessity; a living was also to be made from smaller compositions destined for the English household market. Friendship with Georgina Weldon, an English soprano who assumed a major role in his business and personal affairs, caused not only an estrangement from his wife Anna but a further delay in the production of *Polyeucte*. Gounod extricated himself from the Weldon household and England quite unexpectedly in 1874, and in retaliation for what she saw as aspersions cast by Gounod upon her reputation Weldon withheld belongings that he had left behind in London, including the nearly complete score of *Polyeucte*. In the summer of 1874 he began to set the work to paper again, only to have the original manuscript sent back to him when he had completed the task.

With the closing of the Théâtre Lyrique in 1870, the Opéra-Comique assumed a major role in sustaining Gounod's works for the stage; *Le médecin malgré lui*, *Roméo et Juliette*, *Mireille* and *Philémon et Baucis* were all produced there before 1876. Carvalho took on the directorship of the house that year and promptly commissioned a new work by Gounod, *Cinq Mars*, to a libretto by Paul Poirson and Louis Gallet after the famous novel of the same name by Alfred de Vigny. It was given a lavish production in April 1877. The first appearance of a new opera by as eminent a figure as Gounod attracted a flurry of attention, but the critical reception was by and large negative. Many noted that Gounod's style appeared to have ossified and even as relatively conservative a critic as Henri Blaze de Bury observed that the 'novelty of yesterday seems outmoded'. *Polyeucte* was finally given at the Opéra in 1878, but it served only to confirm the response accorded to its predecessor, especially in view of Massenet's recent success at that house with *Le roi de Lahore*. Showing remarkable tenacity, Gounod developed an operatic project based on the lives of Abélard and Héloïse, *Maître Pierre*. He wrote and orchestrated nearly half of the score before abandoning it in favour of *Le tribut de Zamora* for the Opéra, a tawdry melodrama that hinged on the recovery of reason by a mad woman. It is not hard to read between the lines of most reviews of the 1881 première the

recommendation to the composer that he give up opera composition. With the exception of major revisions to *Sapho* for a new production in 1884, Gounod did just that: in his last 12 years, before his death in 1893, he did not seriously consider a return to the stage.

2. OPERAS. To most opera lovers today, Gounod is essentially the composer of *Faust* and *Roméo et Juliette* and with good reason, for it would be difficult to defend the critical position that these are not his best works for the stage. The characters in *Faust* are especially well developed: Marguerite is convincingly transformed by Gounod's music from an innocent to a heroine and Méphistophélès is effective as an *opéra comique* type of *basse bouffe* with a villainous streak. Musico-dramatic situations such as the Chorale des Epées, the Church scene and the final trio have not worn thin. *Roméo et Juliette* contains four exquisite soprano-tenor duets, a number almost certainly unprecedented in 19th-century opera and a harbinger of the prominence of love duets in such works as Massenet's *Manon* and *Werther*; to Gounod's great credit each has a distinct musico-dramatic ambience and shape. There are wonderful instances of characterization in the role of Juliet, such as the moment in the Act 2 duet when she gives impassioned musical utterance to her love for Romeo but suddenly reverts to soft-spoken delivery with static accompaniment, warning him with real *pudeur* not to misinterpret her forthrightness as evidence of shallow emotion. Mercutio's Queen Mab ballade is finely wrought, and in the finale of the third act Gounod achieves a dramatic incisiveness all too rare in his work. There are also fine moments in *Mireille*, particularly in the title role where Gounod exhibits his particular talent for feminine characterization; but too great a number of dramatically stagnant numbers and an ineffectively drawn antagonist to the love of the tenor and soprano serve to weaken that work. *Mireille*, however, is a noteworthy contribution to the French lyric stage in another respect: it presents the unsuitability of a love match because of difference in social status entirely within the framework of a rural agrarian society and transforms the daughter of a farmer into a tragic heroine. *Le médecin malgré lui* still deserves to be staged regularly; it is a fine comic opera which in its musical sophistication stands head and shoulders above most of the efforts of Auber and Adam. Gounod's remaining operas are best left for rare revivals as curiosities. The observation of the critic Jacques Hermann about *Polyeucte* can be readily applied to many of his other works: 'one cannot hear a single musical phrase in the opera without ... saying "this is by Gounod", but regardless of the character on stage one can never say: "this is the martyred Christian, this is the sublime spouse, this is the generous lover".'

As Hermann implies, Gounod did develop his own style, one that had considerable influence on younger composers. His melodic writing, in particular, was a breath of fresh air in French opera. It is distinguished not only by rigorous attention to prosody but also by rhythms that are carefully moulded around the expressive nuances of the verse on the local level. His melodies are not generally conceived for purely vocal display; they are largely syllabic and contain relatively plain rhythms with frequent durational accents on weak beats. A representative example of Gounod's craft is his setting of the alexandrine 'Laisse-moi, laisse-moi contempler ton visage' at the beginning of the garden duet

Ex.1

['Let me contemplate your face']

in *Faust* (ex.1). The first three prosodic accents ('moi', 'moi', 'contempler') receive metrically weak durational emphases; at the same time the option for rhetorical stress on the first syllable of each occurrence of 'laisse' is realized through both metrical accent and the rhythmic figure of a dotted quaver followed by a semiquaver. The initial syllable of 'contempler' also falls on a downbeat, but since it cannot be enlisted for expressive effect it is rapidly passed over in favour of durational emphasis on the last syllable. This line of text is immediately repeated with greater stress on the last syllable of 'contempler' and the second syllable of 'visage', giving the impression that Faust sings with greater insistence the second time.

Gounod made more extensive use than previous composers of French opera of a type of 'parlante' texture in which the orchestra emits a slow lyrical melody and the vocal line alternates declamation in speech rhythms with snatches that double the instrumental strain; Massenet was later to draw upon this technique even more frequently. Gounod also enhanced the role of the orchestra in voice-dominated texture, often giving it an independent contrapuntal line that serves especially to bridge rests in the voice part. His harmony has a modernistic veneer for its day, due mainly to a penchant for modulation to the mediant and submediant as well as chromatic movement of voices against pedal notes; but it remains fundamentally conservative in orientation. Gounod did not forsake conventional number opera but his handling of form is rarely stereotypical. Strophic pieces are usually given an interesting structural twist such as a threefold sounding of the refrain or some sort of variation in the second strophe. Ternary *cavatines* are generally more chromatic than strophic numbers and are almost always used to express love. As in other French operas and *opéras comiques*, multi-sectional numbers with two or more strophes or sets of parallel strophes, many related to Italian prototypes, are well represented in Gounod's work. The slow section–transition–*cabalette* design had the most staying power in connection with Gounod's *airs*, though this is clear only when the documentary histories of the works are taken into account. Duets frequently conclude with a *cabalette* but the formal organization before this section is varied; where there is a slow section for both characters, as in the garden duet in *Faust*, it rarely contains ensemble singing. The only one of Gounod's finales with chorus related to the Italian prototype is that of the second act of *Mireille*, though that number is something of a hybrid between Italian concertato–transition–*strette* form and the *opéra comique* patchwork finale consisting of solo numbers followed by *strette*. Gounod did not abandon the convention of a slow concertato in which soloists and assembled masses react to a sudden turn of events with more or less independent contrapuntal lines; a prominent example appears as late as *Polyeucte*.

Gounod's reputation declined precipitously even before he died: what gave the appearance of 'depth' in the Second Empire no longer did by the 1890s. Nonetheless, in his unceasing quest for what he saw as dramatic and spiritual truth, Gounod succeeded in restoring a higher sense of artistic purpose to the French stage, and in strictly musical terms his influence on the course of French music was substantial.

See also FAUST (ii); *MÉDECIN MALGRÉ LUI, LE*; *MIREILLE*; *NONNE SANGLANTE, LA*; *PHILÉMON ET BAUCIS*; *REINE DE SABA, LA*; *ROMÉO ET JULIETTE* (ii); and *SAPHO* (i).

first performed in Paris unless otherwise stated; all published in Paris

title	genre, acts	libretto	first performance	publication details, remarks
Sapho	opéra, 3	E. Augier	Opéra, 16 April 1851	in 2 acts, Opéra, 26 July 1858; in 4 acts, Opéra, 2 April 1884; vs (1860) [3 acts]
La nonne sanglante	opéra, 5	E. Scribe and G. Delavigne, after M. G. Lewis: *The Monk*	Opéra, 18 Oct 1854	vs (1854) [another issue with changes, 1860]
Le médecin malgré lui	opéra comique, 3	J. Barbier and M. Carré, after Molière	Lyrique, 15 Jan 1858	vs (1858)
Faust	opéra, 5	Barbier and Carré, after Carré: *Faust et Marguerite* and J. W. von Goethe: *Faust*	Lyrique, 19 March 1859	with recits., Strasbourg, April 1860; with ballet, Opéra, 3 March 1869; vs (1859 [with spoken dialogue], 2/1860 [with recits.], 3/1861 [several issues with changes], 4/1869); ed. Oeser (1972); full score (1860) [with recits.]; ballet (1869)
Philémon et Baucis	opéra, 3	Barbier and Carré, after J. de La Fontaine	Lyrique, 18 Feb 1860	in 2 acts, OC (Favart), 16 May 1876; vs (1860) [several issues in 3 or 2 acts]; full score (1883 or 1884)

501

title	genre, acts	libretto	first performance	publication details, remarks
La colombe	opéra comique, 2	Barbier and Carré, after La Fontaine: *Le faucon*	Baden-Baden, Stadt, 3 Aug 1860	vs (1860) [several issues with changes]
La reine de Saba	opéra, 5	Barbier and Carré, after G. de Nerval: *Le voyage en Orient*	Opéra, 28 Feb 1862	vs (1862) [earliest issue in 5 acts, several later, with changes, in 4], new edn by H. Busser (c1900); full score (1890s)
Mireille	opéra, 5	Carré, after F. Mistral: *Mirèio*	Lyrique, 19 March 1864	in 4 acts with recits., London, CG, 5 July 1864; in 3 acts with spoken dialogue, Paris, 15 Dec 1864; vs (1864) [several issues with changes, the later ones in 3 acts]; full score (1885 or 1886) [in 3 acts, with another issue c1900 in 5 acts]; new edn by Busser of 5-act version, with Gounod's recits. (c1947)
Roméo et Juliette	opéra, 5	Barbier and Carré, after W. Shakespeare	Lyrique, 27 April 1867	OC (Favart), 20 Jan 1873; with ballet, Opéra, 28 Nov 1888; vs, arr. H. Salomon (1867 [several issues with changes], 2/c1885, arr. A. Bérel [incl. much of 1st edn with addl changes]); full score (1867 or 1868) [several issues with changes, incl. 1888 version]; ballet (c1888)
Cinq Mars	opéra, 4	P. Poirson and L. Gallet, after A. V. de Vigny	OC (Favart), 5 April 1877	with recits., Lyons, 1 Dec 1877; vs (1877) [several issues with changes]; ov., full score (?1880)
Polyeucte	opéra, 5	Barbier and Carré, after P. Corneille	Opéra, 7 Oct 1878	vs (1878) [later issue in 4 acts (?1887)]; ballet, full score (?1890)
Le tribut de Zamora	opéra, 4	A.-P. d'Ennery and J. Brésil	Opéra, 1 April 1881	vs (1881) [several issues with changes]; full score (1881 or 1882)

Unfinished operas: Ivan le terrible (H. Trianon and F. Leroy), begun 1856; George Dandin (Molière), begun 1873; Maître Pierre (Gallet), begun 1877 [on Abélard and Héloïse]

J. J. Debillemont: 'Charles Gounod: étude', *Nouvelle revue de Paris*, ii (1864), 559–68

L. Pagnerre: *Charles Gounod: sa vie et ses oeuvres* (Paris, 1890)

C. Saint-Saëns: *Portraits et souvenirs* (Paris, 1899, 3/1909)

G. Servières: 'La version originale de *Mireille*', *Quinzaine musicale* (1 April 1901)

——: 'La légende de la reine de Saba et l'opéra de Charles Gounod', *Guide musical* (2 Dec 1909)

C. Bellaigue: *Gounod* (Paris, 1910)

J. G. Prod'homme and A. Dandelot: *Gounod (1818–1893): sa vie et ses oeuvres d'après des documents inédits* (Paris, 1911)

A. Pougin: 'Gounod écrivain: III. Gounod épistolaire', *RMI*, xix (1912), 239–85, 637–95; xx (1913), 453–86

A. Soubies and H. de Curzon: *Documents inédits sur le 'Faust' de Gounod* (Paris, 1912)

C. Saint-Saëns: 'Le livret de Faust', *Monde musical* (1914–18); repr. as 'The Manuscript Libretto of Faust', *MT*, lxii (1921), 553–7

R. Northcott: *Gounod's Operas in London* (London, 1918)

P. Landormy: *Le 'Faust' de Gounod: étude et analyse* (Paris, 1922, 2/1944)

M. d'Ollone: 'Gounod et l'opéra-comique', *ReM*, no.140 (1933), 301–8

R. Hahn: 'A propos de la 2000e de Faust', *L'oreille au guet* (Paris, 1937)

R. Hartleb: *Einführung zur Oper Margarethe von Gounod* (Berlin, 1939)

T. Marix-Spire: 'Gounod and his First Interpreter, Pauline Viardot', *MQ*, xxi (1945), 193–211, 299–317

R. Hahn: 'La vraie *Mireille*', *Thèmes variés* (Paris, 1946), 103–11

N. Demuth: *Introduction to the Music of Gounod* (London, 1950)

M. Curtiss: 'Gounod before Faust', *MQ*, xxxviii (1952), 48–67

C. Hopkinson: 'Notes on the Earliest Editions of Gounod's Faust', *Festschrift Otto Erich Deutsch* (Kassel, 1963), 245–9

A. Lebois: 'La reine de Saba ou amour et franc-maçonnerie', *Littératures*, xv (1968), 18–67

J. Harding: *Gounod* (London, 1973)

L'avant-scène opéra, no.2 (1976) [Faust issue]

J.-M. Bailbé: 'Autour de la Reine de Saba: Nerval et Gounod', *Regards sur l'opéra* (Paris, 1976), 113–26

T. J. Walsh: *Second Empire Opera: the Théâtre-Lyrique 1851–1870* (London, 1981)

L'avant-scène opéra, no. 41 (1982) [Roméo et Juliette issue]

S. Huebner: 'Mireille Revisited', *MT*, cxxiv (1983), 737–44

J.-M. Bailbé: 'Polyeucte de Donizetti à Gounod', *Revue d'histoire littéraire de la France*, lxxxv (1985), 799–810

D. Pistone: 'Les critiques de *Faust* de Gounod (1859–1975)', *Revue internationale de musique française*, xvii (1985), 41–56

S. Huebner: *The Operas of Charles Gounod* (Oxford, 1990)

A. Meier: *Faustlibretti: Geschichte des Fauststoffs auf der europäischen Musikbühne* (Frankfurt, 1990)

H. R. Cohen, ed.: *The Original Staging Manuals for Twelve Parisian Operatic Premières/Douze livrets de mise en scène lyrique datant des créations parisiennes* (Stuyvesant, NY, 1991) [incl. production book for *Faust*]

STEVEN HUEBNER

Goupy, Joseph (*b* 1689; *d* London, 1768). Scene designer of French extraction. Variously said to have been born in Nevers or London, he was employed with Pieter Tillemans of Antwerp to paint scenes for Handel's operas at the King's Theatre, London (1724–7); they may have worked on *Tamerlano* and *Giulio Cesare in Egitto* (1724) and *Rodelinda, regina de' longobardi* (1725). Goupy certainly painted new scenes for *Admeto, rè di Tessaglia* and *Riccardo Primo, rè d'Inghilterra* (1727). The elaborate stage directions for Handel's operas were probably not carried out in full as the King's lacked stage space and machinery, but baroque effects were undoubtedly aimed at. In 1736 Goupy was appointed cabinet painter to Frederick, Prince of Wales.

SYBIL ROSENFELD

Governatore, Il ('The Governor'). *Opera buffa* in three acts by NICOLA BONIFACIO LOGROSCINO to a libretto (originally in Neapolitan dialect) by Domenico Canicà; Naples, Teatro Nuovo sopra Toledo, Carnival 1747.

The action takes place in Capua during carnival, permitting a free use of disguises. Don Giulio (soprano castrato), the deaf governor, makes advances to both the cousins Leonora (contralto) and Flavia (soprano); but Leonora loves Crispino (soprano, trouser role) and Flavia loves Leonora's cousin Don Ciccio (bass). With Giulio's encouragement, Don Gianserio (bass) arrives to court the governor's daughter, Rosalba (soprano), even

'*Goyescas*' *(Granados), scene 2 (a lantern-lit tavern) from the original production at the Metropolitan Opera, New York, 28 January 1916, with Flora Perini as Pepa and Giuseppe de Luca as Paquiro (foreground, left of centre); Giovanni Martinelli as Fernando (centre) and Anna Fitziu as Rosario (foreground, right of centre)*

though Rosalba loves Don Celso (contralto, trouser role) and Gianserio has promised to marry Stella (contralto), who has come to Capua disguised as a pilgrim. Leonora finally manoeuvres everyone to the correct partner.

Logroscino's music is competent but routine. The first two acts end with substantial ensembles, though they are all in one tempo. STEPHEN C. FISHER

Goward, Mary Anne (*b* Ipswich, 22 Nov 1805; *d* London, 12 March 1899). English soprano and actress. She made her début in Dublin in November 1823 and sang Rosina and Aennchen (*Der Freischütz*) at the Lyceum Theatre, London, in 1825. In 1826 Weber chose her for the Mermaid in *Oberon* at Covent Garden after two other sopranos had withdrawn from the part. She had difficulty making herself heard but was praised by Weber as 'the most natural singer I ever heard'. Planché described her voice as 'sweet though not very powerful' and commended her competent artistry. After her marriage to the actor Robert Keeley in 1829 she turned to the theatre and became popular, especially in comic roles, under her married name.

J. R. Planché: *Recollections and Reflections*, i (London, 1872)
W. Goodman: *The Keeleys On the Stage and Off* (London, 1895)
A. de Ternant: 'Weber's English "Mermaid"', *The Chesterian*, vii (1926), 232–4 JOHN WARRACK

Goyescas. Opera in one act (three scenes) by ENRIQUE GRANADOS to a libretto by Fernando Periquet; New York, Metropolitan Opera, 28 January 1916.

Goyescas is unique among operas in being based on a piano suite, inspired by the atmosphere and the people of 18th-century Madrid as depicted by the Spanish painter Francisco Goya (1746–1828). It was at the suggestion of the American pianist Ernest Schelling that

Granados transformed the suite into an opera. After creating a dramatic format for the work with Periquet he composed the music, to which Periquet then fitted a libretto.

The setting is Madrid, around 1800. Paquiro (baritone), a bullfighter, is flirting and joking with a group of young people in the Campo de la Florida. His fiancée, Pepa (mezzo-soprano), arrives in her dog-cart ('La calesa') followed by the noblewoman Rosario (soprano), in her sedan chair ('Los requiebros'), who looks for her lover, Fernando (tenor), a captain in the Royal Guard. Paquiro invites her to a dance at a tavern that evening. Fernando arrives in time to announce that he will be taking Rosario himself. Pepa, furious, vows vengeance on Rosario. The second scene is in a lantern-lit tavern. Fernando and Paquiro quarrel and arrange a duel, while the *majas* and *majos* sing and dance a fandango. The final scene is in Rosario's garden, where she sings the delicate aria 'La maja y el ruiseñor' to a nightingale. Fernando joins her for a passionate duet, 'Coloquio en la reja'. A bell tolls, announcing the time for the duel. Paquiro's shadow passes in the background and Fernando leaves, followed by Rosario. The silence is broken by a cry from Fernando. Rosario drags him back to her garden, where he dies in her arms ('El amor y la muerte').

The Paris Opéra planned the première of *Goyescas*, but the outbreak of World War I forced its cancellation. Schelling then arranged for the première to be given at the Metropolitan. The cast included Anna Fitziu (Rosario), Giovanni Martinelli (Fernando), Flora Perini (Pepa) and Giuseppe de Luca (Paquiro). Only an hour in length, *Goyescas* may lack sustained emotional drama, but it has all the freshness and romantic flavour of Granados's music, and the orchestral and choral writing, distinguished by his highly individual harmonic language, are outstanding. Granados, who supervised rehearsals for the première, wrote the famous intermezzo between the first and second scenes overnight (the original being too short) to accommodate a scene change. The opera was the first work performed in Spanish at the Metropolitan, where it received five highly praised performances.

DOUGLAS RIVA

Gozenpud, Abram Akimovich (*b* Kiev, 10/23 June 1908). Soviet musicologist. He is the leading historian of the Russian operatic stage. After a brief teaching career in Kiev and Sverdlovsk (now Yekaterinburg), he became (1953) a senior researcher at the Leningrad Institute of Theatre, Music and Cinematography. From this base he has issued with impressive regularity a series of fundamental expository works, erecting the factological platform that has supported all subsequent work on Russian classical opera from its beginnings to 1941. He was awarded the degree of Doctor of Philology (1962) for his research on musical theatre in Russia as an institution. In addition, he has published literary studies and translations of plays by Shakespeare, Schiller, Hauptmann, Holberg and others into Russian and Ukrainian and has worked as a librettist. His best known opera libretto is *Ukroshcheniye stroptivoy*, an adaptation of *The Taming of the Shrew* for Shebalin (1957).

Opernaya dramaturgiya Chaykovskogo (Kiev, 1940) [in Ukrainian]
N. V. Lisenko i russkaya muzïkal'naya kul'tura (Moscow, 1954)
N. A. Rimsky-Korsakov (Leningrad, 1955)
N. A. Rimsky-Korsakov: temï i idei ego opernogo tvorchestva [Themes and Ideas in his Operatic Works] (Moscow, 1957)
Muzïkal'nïy teatr v Rossii ot istokov do Glinki [Musical Theatre in Russia from its Origins to the Time of Glinka] (Leningrad, 1959)
with V. Obram, ed.: 'A. N. Serov, pis'ma k V. V. i D. V. Stasovïm' [Serov's Letters to V. V. and D. V. Stasov], *Muzïkal'noye nasledstvo*, i–ii/1 (Moscow, 1962–6)
Russkiy sovetskiy opernïy teatr (1917–41) (Leningrad, 1963)
Opernïy slovar' [Dictionary of Opera] (Moscow and Leningrad, 1965)
Russkiy opernïy teatr XIX veka (1836–1856) (Leningrad, 1969)
Dostoyevsky i muzika (Leningrad, 1971)
Izbrannïye stat'i [Selected Articles] (Leningrad, 1971)
Russkiy opernïy teatr XIX veka (1857–1872) (Leningrad, 1971)
Russkiy opernïy teatr XIX veka (1873–1889) (Leningrad, 1973)
Russkiy opernïy teatr i Shalyapin (1890–1904) (Leningrad, 1974)
Russkiy opernïy teatr mezhdu dvukh revolyutsiy (1905–1917) [Russian Operatic Theatre between the Two Revolutions] (Leningrad, 1975)
Rikhard Vagner i russkaya kul'tura: issledovaniye [Wagner and Russian Culture: a Scholarly Investigation] (Leningrad, 1990)
Many articles in *SovM, Muzïkal'naya zhizn'* etc.

RICHARD TARUSKIN

Gozzi, Carlo (*b* Venice, 13 Dec 1720; *d* Venice, 14 April 1806). Italian playwright. Born of a noble family of declining fortune, he was the leading member of the Accademia dei Granelleschi, a learned society devoted to stemming innovation and foreign importations in linguistic usage. He also set himself up against the changes that Goldoni was introducing into Venetian comedy.

Goldoni broke with the age-old Venetian tradition of the *commedia dell'arte*. In his plays stock characters disappeared, masks were no longer worn, and a bourgeois naturalism replaced stereotyped conventions. Though immensely successful, the plays attracted criticism and envy. One of his rivals was Pietro Chiari, a prolific novelist and playwright, who introduced sentimental and extravagant inanities into his comedies. Gozzi despised them both and, in answer to Goldoni's claim that he drew large audiences, declared that he could do the same with any nonsensical tale 'such as grandmothers tell little children'. To prove his point Gozzi

sketched a scenario for the first of his *fiabe* (dramatized fairy tales), *L'amore delle tre melarance*, which he derived from Giambattista Basile's *Pentamerone*, a book of fairy stories in Neapolitan dialect. The play was put on at the Teatro S Samuele, under the direction of Antonio Sacchi, a famous actor-manager of the period. Two of the characters were caricatures of Goldoni and Chiari.

The result was twofold: Goldoni and Chiari, from being bitter rivals, were reconciled; and Gozzi became a successful playwright overnight. During the next four years (1762–6) he wrote another nine *fiabe*, drawing mainly on *The Thousand and One Nights* for his plots. One of them, *Turandot*, was based on a legend of Persian origin, set in China. The *fiabe* met with enthusiastic response; they were twice printed in Venice during Gozzi's lifetime (1772 and 1802) and in 1777 were translated into German. The German Romantics were impressed: Goethe, Schiller, Lessing, the Schlegels and Hoffmann all admired them, and Schiller rewrote *Turandot* as a serious drama. Some of the elements of folklore and fantasy found their way into popular musical plays performed in Vienna, even influencing the libretto of *Die Zauberflöte*.

Gozzi's gift for satire is further seen in his burlesque, mock-heroic poem *La Marfisa bizzarra*, which caricatures the women in Chiari's novels. His lively autobiography, *Memorie inutili*, of particular interest to theatre historians, was translated by John Addington Symonds, who remarked that Gozzi's *fiabe* would make excellent opera librettos; that is in fact what later occurred. In 1911, in Berlin, Max Reinhardt directed a German translation of Gozzi's play *Turandot*. Busoni wrote the incidental music, which he later (1917) developed into his opera of the same title. Puccini's *Turandot* was first performed in 1926. Prokofiev's *The Love for Three Oranges*, the libretto derived by the composer from Gozzi's incomplete scenario for *L'amore delle tre melarance*, was first performed in 1921. Wagner's *Die Feen* was based on yet another of Gozzi's *fiabe*, *La donna serpente*.

L'amore delle tre melarance (fiaba, 1761): Prokofiev, 1921
Il corvo (1761): A. J. Romberg, 1794; J. P. E. Hartmann, 1832
Il re Cervo (1762): Henze, 1956
La donna serpente (fiaba, 1762): Himmel, 1806, as Die Sylphen; Wagner, 1888, as Die Feen; Casella, 1932
Turandot (fiaba, 1762): Blumenröder, 1809; Reissiger, 1835; Vesque von Püttlingen, 1838; H. S. Lövenskjold, 1854; Bazzini, 1867; Busoni, 1917; Puccini, 1926; Zabel, 1928
Il mostro turchino (1764): A. J. Romberg, comp. 1790–93
I pitocchi fortunati (1764): Zumsteeg, 1780, as Das tartarische Gesetz; Benda, 1787, as Das tartarische Gesetz

*

G. Prezzolini, ed.: *C. Gozzi: Memorie inutili* (Bari, 1934; Eng. trans., 1962)
E. J. Dent, ed. and trans.: *The Blue Monster: a Fairy Play by Carlo Gozzi* (Cambridge, 1951)
E. Bentley, ed.: *The Classic Theatre* (New York, 1958)
G. Petronio, ed.: *C. Gozzi: Opere: teatro e polemiche teatrali* (Milan, 1962)
E. Bentley, ed.: *The Genius of the Italian Theatre* (New York, 1964)
R. Taruskin: 'From Fairy Tale to Opera in Four Not-So-Simple Moves', *English National Opera 1991* [programme book]

BARBARA REYNOLDS

Graarud, Gunnar (*b* Holmestrand, nr Oslo, 1 June 1886; *d* Stuttgart, 6 Dec 1960). Norwegian tenor. He was trained in Berlin and made his début in 1919 at Kaiserslautern. After two seasons at Mannheim he joined the Berlin Volksoper, where he sang from 1922 to 1925. In Bayreuth, from 1927 to 1931, he sang Tristan, Siegfried, Siegmund and Parsifal, and at Salzburg he appeared as Aegisthus in *Elektra* and in the title role of *Der Corregidor*. He had a considerable reputation in Scandinavia and sang frequently in Vienna until 1937. His single role at Covent Garden was Herod in *Salome*, under Knappertsbusch (winter 1936); he was described as 'effectively distraught'. On records he is remembered principally for his Tristan in the near-complete recording of the opera, made at Bayreuth in 1928: his clearcut voice serves him well in a sincere performance, sensitively modulated in the quieter passages.   J. B. STEANE

Grabu [Grabue, Grabut, Grebus], **Luis** [Louis, Lewis] (*b* ?Catalonia; *d* after 1693). Spanish composer active in England. Trained in Paris, possibly under Cambert and Lully, he went to London shortly after the Restoration, hoping to capitalize on Charles II's predilection for French music. By 1665 he was composer-in-ordinary for the king's private music and on 24 November 1666 he succeeded the late Nicholas Lanier as Master of the King's Music, the highest position a composer could attain at the English court. His preferments, which included control of a select band of 12 violins, were greatly resented by native musicians, particularly John Banister (whom he ousted from the King's Violins) and Pelham Humfrey, who complained to Pepys (*Diary*, 15 November 1667) that Grabu 'understands nothing, nor can play on any instrument, and so cannot compose'. Attacks on his character and professional competence continued, and in 1674 he was replaced as Master of the Music by Nicholas Staggins, a decision more political than artistic.

In the same year Grabu directed and provided additional music for Robert Cambert's opera *Ariane, ou Le mariage de Bacchus* (libretto by Pierre Perrin), performed in French at the Theatre Royal, Drury Lane, on 30 March 1674. Cambert had arrived in London the year before, having been forced out of the Académie Royale de Musique by Lully. *Ariane* marked the début of the short-lived Royal Academy of Music, set up with the encouragement of Charles II in imitation of the French original. *Ariane* apparently made little impression, in spite of a remarkable 30-day run, yet it was the first all-sung opera to be professionally performed in England (the music is lost).

Grabu's involvement with the semi-royal *Ariane* (which formed part of the celebrations of the marriage of the Duke of York and Mary of Modena) did little to improve his standing at court, and on 31 March 1679 he and his family were issued with passports; Roman Catholics, they prudently withdrew to France during the years following the Popish Plot. Having survived this witch hunt and the far more dangerous Exclusion Crisis of 1680–81, Charles II expressed a desire for a musical celebration of the Restoration and continuation of the Stuart line. Accordingly, he sent the actor-manager Thomas Betterton to Paris 'to endeavour to carry over the Opera', that is, members of the Académie Royale. When this proved impossible, Betterton returned instead with Grabu, who during his years in exile had become immersed in the *tragédie en musique*, and invited him to create 'something at least like an Opera … for his Majesty's diversion'. The result was *Albion and Albanius*, first performed in June 1685 at Dorset Garden Theatre; the libretto, by John Dryden, is a thinly veiled allegory of the Restoration and reign of Charles II. The work was published in full score in 1687; though a *tragédie en musique* in all but language, it is the first full-length opera in English to survive. Grabu also composed songs and instrumental music for several Restoration plays, including Thomas Shadwell's adaptation of *Timon of Athens* and Dryden and Nathaniel Lee's *Oedipus* (both 1678); the latter included the song 'Music for a while' (lost), which Purcell reset in the early 1690s. Shortly before composing *Albion and Albanius*, Grabu contributed a sizable amount of music to Lord Rochester's adaptation of *Valentinian* (1684), including a remarkable dream-sequence ballet.

Grabu's reputation for incompetence is undeserved. He was the victim of sustained character defamation, while later historians, beginning with Sir John Hawkins, have placed too much emphasis on the infamous ballad 'The Raree-Show' (1685), with its refrain 'Prithee learn thrashing of Monsieur Grabu' – not an attack on the composer *per se*, rather a rude comment on the fact that *Albion and Albanius* had put the actors temporarily out of work. Grabu's setting of the English language may pale in comparison with Purcell or even Blow, but the failure of *Albion and Albanius* was due more to circumstances (the death of Charles II shortly before the première and then Monmouth's Rebellion) than to any artistic shortcoming. Grabu's orchestral music does not suffer by comparison with Lully's, and *Albion and Albanius* provided Purcell with models for several features of his major stage works, from the chaconnes of *Dioclesian* and *King Arthur* to long-range tonal planning. Grabu remained in London until 1693, when he was issued with another passport; he then disappears on the Continent.

See also ALBION AND ALBANIUS and ARIANE (i).

E. J. Dent: *Foundations of English Opera* (Cambridge, 1928)

E. Miner, ed.: *The Works of John Dryden*, xv (Berkeley, 1976)

P. Danchin: 'The Foundation of the Royal Academy of Music in 1674 and Pierre Perrin's *Ariane*', *Theatre Survey*, xxv/1 (1984), 53–67

P. Hammond: 'Dryden's *Albion and Albanius*: the Apotheosis of Charles II', *The Court Masque*, ed. D. Lindley (Manchester, 1984), 169–83

C. Price: *Henry Purcell and the London Stage* (Cambridge, 1984)

J. A. Winn: *John Dryden and his World* (New Haven, 1987)

C. Bashford: 'Perrin and Cambert's "Ariane, ou Le mariage de Bacchus" Re-examined', *ML*, lxxii (1991), 1–26

CURTIS PRICE

Gracis, Ettore (*b* La Spezia, 24 Sept 1915; *d* Treviso, 12 April 1992). Italian conductor. He studied at the Parma and Venice conservatories, then at the Accademia Chigiana, Siena. Contemporary music and 17th- and 18th-century works predominated in his career. Between 1951 and 1956 he conducted at the Teatro delle Novità, Bergamo, where he gave the first performances of Luciano Chailly's *Ferrovia sopraelevato*, Flavio Testi's *Il furore di Oreste*, Andrea Mascagni's *Lo starnuto* and Sergio Liberovici's *La panchina*. At the Naples Festival he conducted revivals of 18th-century Italian opera such as Piccinni's *La molinarella* (1960), Rossini's *La gazzetta* (1960) and Cimarosa's *Il matrimonio segreto* (1962), as well as Mozart's *La finta semplice* (1961), *Die Entführung aus dem Serail* (1962) and *Die Zauberflöte* (1963). Gracis also conducted at the Florence Maggio Musicale (1948–50), the Milan Pomeriggi Musicali (1950–59) and the Teatro La Fenice, Venice (from 1959). His recordings include *Don Pasquale* (1965).

CLAUDIO CASINI

Graener, Paul (*b* Berlin, 11 Jan 1872; *d* Salzburg, 13 Nov 1944). German composer and conductor. He was a self-taught musician who received some formal instruction in composition from Albert Becker at the Veit Conservatory in Berlin. Much of his practical experience was gained working as a Kapellmeister in Bremerhaven, Königsberg and Berlin. In 1896 he settled in London, where for a time he became conductor of the orchestra at the Haymarket Theatre. When his contract was terminated after a conflict with the director he remained in England teaching privately and secured a position at the RAM. He returned to the Continent in 1908 and was appointed to teach composition at the Neues Konservatorium in Vienna. From 1910 to 1913 he directed the Salzburg Mozarteum, and he spent the next seven years teaching and composing in several German cities. In 1920 he was elected to the Berlin Akademie der Künste and appointed professor of composition at the Leipzig Conservatory in succession to Reger. He resigned in 1925 to devote his energies to composition. In 1930 he moved to Berlin, where he directed the Stern Conservatory for the next three years and in 1934 held masterclasses in composition at the Akademie der Künste. Goebbels appointed him vice-president of the Reichsmusikkammer in 1933. He replaced Richard Strauss as director of the composers' division in the same organization, 1935–41.

Although Graener attained technical fluency in most areas of composition, a large proportion of his output was devoted to vocal music including numerous lieder and eight substantial operas. His style remained defiantly late Romantic, owing much to the examples of Strauss, Reger and Pfitzner but lacking their individuality. For a time he was attracted to the orchestral timbre and harmonies of French composers, but in his early operas these influences appear only intermittently and usually through the use of parallel augmented triads. The italianate colouring and good humour of *Don Juans letztes Abenteuer* (1914, revised in 1935) and the expressive lyricism of *Schirin und Gertraude* (1920) proved to be immediately attractive to contemporary German audiences, and both operas received numerous performances during the early 1920s. Nevertheless, the composer recognized an inherent dramatic weakness in these works and decided that his future efforts in the genre should be based on established texts of German literature. Accordingly, *Hanneles Himmelfahrt* (1927) was derived from Hauptmann's so-called dream-poem of 1893. The scenario, which is dominated by many episodes of a religious and visionary nature, offered the public a deliberate antidote to the harsh anti-romanticism of the *Zeitoper*. Although the score is primarily lyrical in conception it lacks dramatic impetus in spite of the effective use of a large orchestra and some fine polyphonic choral writing.

The neo-Baroque features of this work are further exploited in Graener's next opera, *Friedemann Bach* (1931), based on Brachvogel's apocryphal novel of the same name. Here the musical argument is framed by a conscious use of such devices as chorale and fugato. Quotations from the music of the Bach family are used to depict the main characters, with the B-A-C-H motif representing Johann Sebastian and a melody ascribed to Wilhelm Friedemann portraying his eldest son. During the 1930s both *Hanneles Himmelfahrt* and *Friedemann Bach* remained in the repertory of German opera houses as a result of the composer's staunch support for the Nazis. In addition, the simple and other-worldly qualities in these operas accorded with the reactionary theories of the new political masters. The Nazis even overlooked the fact that the librettist of *Friedemann Bach* was of Jewish origin.

Graener's pre-eminent position among contemporary German composers was reinforced when the Berlin Staatsoper commissioned a new opera from him for its 1934–5 season. But *Der Prinz von Homburg* turned out to be a severe disappointment: it exposed a fatal flaw in the composer's approach to operatic writing, a failure to recognize that the laws of drama are somewhat different from the conventions of opera. Thus Kleist's play, although subjected to some pruning, is presented in far too literal a manner, with the result that Graener misses the opportunity to develop the drama's inner psychological conflict. Both *Der Prinz von Homburg* and Graener's final opera, *Schwanhild*, first given in Cologne in 1942, were received with respect rather than enthusiasm. Indeed, by the end of the Nazi era the composer's achievement in the field of opera had been almost totally eclipsed by the successes of the younger generation of Egk, Orff and Wagner-Régeny.

Der vierjährige Posten op.1 (Spl, 1, T. Körner), unperf. (London, n.d.)

Das Narrengericht op.38 (Singkomödie, 2, O. Anthes), Halle, 20 Feb 1916, vs (Vienna and Leipzig, 1912)

Don Juans letztes Abenteuer op.42 (3, Anthes), Leipzig, 11 June 1914 (Vienna and Leipzig, 1914); rev., Hamburg, 25 Oct 1935

Theophano op.48 (3, Anthes), Munich, 5 June 1918, vs (Vienna and Leipzig, 1918); rev. as Byzanz, Leipzig, 22 Feb 1922

Schirin und Gertraude op.51 (4, E. Hardt), Dresden, 28 April 1920, vs (Berlin, 1920)

Hanneles Himmelfahrt (2, Graener and G. Gräner, after G. Hauptmann), Dresden, Sächsisches Staats, 17 Jan 1927, vs (Berlin, 1927)

Friedemann Bach op.90 (3, R. Lothar, after A. E. Brachvogel), Schwerin, Mecklenburgisches Staats, 13 Nov 1931, vs (Berlin, 1931)

Der Prinz von Homburg op.100 (4, Graener, after H. von Kleist), Berlin, Staatsoper, 14 March 1935, vs (Berlin, 1934)

Schwanhild (3, Graener, after O. Anthes), Cologne, 4 Jan 1942, vs (Vienna, 1941)

Sieg (3), unperf.

*

PEM (H.-J. Bauer)

G. Gräner: *Paul Graener* (Leipzig, 1922)

F. Stege: 'Paul Graener', *ZfM*, xcix (1932), 9–13

R. Lothar: 'Wie "Friedemann Bach" entstand', *Der Aufstieg*, ii (1933)

P. Grümmer: *Verzeichnis der Werke Paul Graeners* (Berlin, 1937)

E. Krieger: 'Paul Graener, Bauherrntum deutscher Musik', *Musische Besinnlichkeiten* (Düsseldorf, 1939)

H. Killer: 'Paul Graener 70 Jahre alt', *Die Musik*, xxxiv (1941–2), 150–51

E. Schmitz: 'Zum 70. Geburtstag Paul Graeners', *ZfM*, cix (1942), 1–4

H.-G. Klein: 'Ideologisierung von Werken Kleists in Opern aus dem 20. Jahrhundert', *Norddeutsche Beiträge*, i (1978), 44–65

ERIK LEVI

Graf, Herbert (*b* Vienna, 10 April 1904; *d* Geneva, 5 April 1973). American director and administrator. He was the son of the critic Max Graf and studied in Vienna. After appointments in Münster, Breslau and Frankfurt, he was forced to leave Germany and went to the USA, later becoming a naturalized American. In the USA he worked first with the Philadelphia Opera (1934–5) and then at the Metropolitan (1936–60). From 1960 to 1962 he was director of the Zürich Opera and from 1965 until his death of the Grand Théâtre, Geneva. He first worked at Salzburg in 1936 and after World War II was a frequent visitor there. His productions relied on a traditional approach and technique.

Graf taught in the opera department at the Curtis Institute, Philadelphia (1950–60), as well as at several other opera schools, including the Music Academy of the West (Santa Barbara, California) and the International Opera Studio (Zürich), where he especially encouraged young American singers. He wrote three books, *The Opera and its Future in America* (New York, 1941), *Opera for the People* (Minneapolis, 1951) and *Producing Opera for America* (Zürich, 1961).

L. Mansouri: 'Herbert Graf, 1904–1973', *Opera*, xxiv (1973), 702–4   HAROLD ROSENTHAL/R

Graffigna, Achille (*b* San Martino dall'Argine, nr Mantua, 5 May 1816; *d* Padua, 19 July 1896). Italian composer and conductor. He was a pupil of Alessandro Rolla in Milan before becoming director of the episcopal chapel at Cagliari (1834–6). Returning to Lombardy in 1836, he had his first opera première at Lodi that same year. He continued conducting at the Teatro Filarmonico in Verona, the Teatro Imperiale in Odessa (1845), and in Paris, Florence and elsewhere. After 1875 he retired to Padua and taught singing. His regard for Rossini can be seen in his setting of *Il barbiere di Siviglia*, written with Rossini's permission, which was intended as an 'informative study into the spirit, character and colouring of the immortal work of Rossini's' (L. Rognoni: *Rossini*, Parma, 1956, 3/1977).

Un lampo d'infedeltà, Lodi, Sociale, aut. 1836
Ildegonda e Riccardo [Rizzardo] (G. Sapio), Milan, Scala, 3 Dec 1841
I Bonifazi ed i Salinguerra (2, T. Solera: *Oberto, conte di S Bonifacio*, after A. Piazza: *Rocester*), Venice, S Benedetto, 28 March 1842; as Elenora di San Bonifazio, Verona, Filarmonico, 11 March 1843
Mignonè Fanfan (2, D. Perrone), Florence, Leopoldo, June 1844
Gli ultimi giorni di Suli [Sulli] (5), Odessa, Imperiale, carn. 1845
Ester d'Engaddi (3, ? S. Cammarano), Odessa, Imperiale, 9 Feb 1846
Il magnetismo (ob, G. Giacchetti), Milan, S Tadegonda, 24 Feb 1851
I due rivali (farsa, Giacchetti), Mantua, 8 May 1852
Maria di Brabante (os, F. Guidi), Trieste, Mauroner, 16 Oct 1852
L'assedio di Malta (3, L. Scalchi), Padua, Nuovo, 30 July 1853
Gli studenti, ossia Lo zio burlato (ob, L. Zanetti), Milan, Carcano, 7 Feb 1857
Veronica Cibo [Cybo] [La duchessa di San Giuliano] (3, G. Peruzzini and M. M. Marcello), Mantua, Sociale, 13 Feb 1858
Il barbiere di Siviglia (ob, 2, C. Sterbini), Padua, Comunale, 17 May 1879
Il matrimonio segreto (ob, 3, G. Bertati), Florence, Salvini, 8 Sept 1883
La pazza per progetto (operetta), Lucca, Pantera, Jan 1884
La buona figliuola (ob, C. Goldoni), Milan, Filodrammatici, 6 May 1886
I nipoti del borgomastro (ob, C. Marulli), Florence, Arena Nazionale, 20 Dec 1887
La Mandragola (operetta, 3, Marchese Boschi), Turin, Alfieri, 26 May 1888
Il borgomastro (operetta, 3, L. Maresca), Rome, Quirino, 26 Oct 1892, collab. C. Lombardo
La catena d'oro (Marcello), unperf.

Gräfin Mariza ('Countess Mariza'). Operetta in three acts by EMMERICH KÁLMÁN to a libretto by JULIUS BRAMMER and ALFRED GRÜNWALD; Vienna, Theater an der Wien, 28 February 1924.

Count Tassilo Endrödy-Wittenburg (tenor) has had to sell all his possessions to repay his father's debts. To earn a living he takes a job under an assumed name as manager of an estate of the wealthy and independently minded Hungarian Countess Mariza (soprano). She is throwing a party to celebrate her engagement to Baron Koloman Zsupán, and Tassilo's sister Lisa (soubrette soprano) is among the guests. In fact Mariza's fiancé does not exist, and she has merely invented him (using the name of a character from Strauss's *Der Zigeunerbaron*) to keep other suitors at bay. She is accordingly taken aback when someone of that name (tenor or baritone) turns up and claims her as his bride-to-be. Mariza, though, is now falling under Tassilo's spell, while Zsupán is getting on equally well with Lisa, though the closeness of the latter's friendship with Tassilo causes some inevitable misunderstandings and jealousy. When Tassilo's true identity and circumstances are revealed, Mariza still imagines that he is seeking marriage with her for her money. Only when his aunt (spoken) announces that she has bought back all his property is Mariza sufficiently convinced of his genuine love to dismiss him as her estate manager and take him on as husband.

The work was first produced with Hubert Marischka as Tassilo and Betty Fischer as Mariza. Kálmán's music, rich in Hungarian rhythms, contains fine solos for soprano ('Höre ich Zigeunergeigen') and tenor ('Grüss' mir mein Wien' and 'Komm Zigan!'), as well as much more in his most melodic style.   ANDREW LAMB

Graf von Luxemburg, Der ('The Count of Luxembourg'). *Operette* in three acts by FRANZ LEHÁR to a libretto by A. M. WILLNER and Robert Bodanzky; Vienna, Theater an der Wien, 12 November 1909.

The score underwent some changes over the years, and the version currently performed derives from a spectacular production at the Theater des Volkes, Berlin, on 4 March 1937, in which Act 1 was split into two scenes to heighten the portrayal of Parisian street carnival revelries.

The leader of the revelries is René, Count of Luxembourg (tenor) ('Mein Anherr war der Luxemburg'). He has managed to squander most of his inheritance and has been forced to take humble lodgings in the studio of the happy-go-lucky artist Armand Brissard (*buffo* tenor) and his girlfriend Juliette (soprano) ('Wir bummeln durchs Leben'). In their studio René receives a visit from a group of Russians with a proposition for him. Prince Basil Basilowitsch (baritone) has fallen in love with the opera singer Angèle Didier (soprano), but he cannot marry a commoner. Knowing the Count's impecunious situation, they propose that he should marry Angèle and, after three months, divorce her, thereby freeing her for Basil. During the three months René will not set eyes on his bride. René agrees and Angèle arrives apprehensively ('Heut' noch werd' ich Ehefrau'). The marriage duly takes place in the studio with the parties separated from each other's view by an artist's easel. They go their separate ways ('Sie geht links, er geht rechts'), but the feel of each other's hands as they exchange rings and the perfume that Angèle is wearing leave lingering feelings of attraction ('Bist du's lachendes Glück'). In Act 2, on the eve of the divorce, Angèle is acclaimed at a party to mark her retirement from the stage ('Hoch, evoë, Angèle Didier'). René arrives, not knowing she is his wife, but having been attracted to her at the Opéra. He makes his feelings known to her, and her initial protests ('Lieber Freund, man greift nicht nach den Sternen') soon weaken. René begins to suspect something from the feel of her hand and the scent on her glove ('Es duftet nach Trèfle incarnat'). When Basil lets slip that Angèle is already married, the whole story is revealed. Only in Act 3, when one of Basil's former lovers, the Countess Kokozow (mezzo-soprano), comes to claim him, are René and Angèle free to enjoy their marriage together, while Armand finally agrees to marry Juliette ('Mädel fein, Mädel klein').

The work has many points of similarity with *Die lustige Witwe*, whose success it was obviously designed to recapture (which it did to a remarkable degree). Composed in some haste, it shows Lehár at his most fluent and melodic, with beguiling, sensuously orchestrated waltz melodies, if without quite the finished sophistication of its predecessor. The title role was created by Otto Storm, with Annie von Ligeti as Angèle, Bernhard Bötel as Armand, Louise Kartousch as Juliette and Max Pallenberg as Prince Basil.

ANDREW LAMB

Graham, Colin (*b* Hove, Sussex, 22 September 1931). English director. After study at the Royal Academy of Dramatic Art (1951–2) and several years' formative experience as a stage manager, he undertook his first production, the première of Britten's *Noye's Fludde* (Aldeburgh, 1958). This was the start of a close professional relationship with both the composer and his festival (of which Graham became an artistic director in 1968), which resulted in Graham's collaboration on the first performances of the 'church parables', *Curlew River* (1964), *The Burning Fiery Furnace* (1966) and *The Prodigal Son* (1968), as well as *Death in Venice* (English Opera Group, 1973, later staged at Covent Garden and the Metropolitan). In all these productions, and also in those of numerous new operas by other composers (including Walton, Thea Musgrave, Richard Rodney Bennett, Nicholas Maw, Minoru Miki and Stephen Paulus), Graham combined an innate grasp of musical and dramatic processes of many kinds with an impressively direct, economical command of music theatre. He has also written librettos: *Anna Karenina* for Britten (unused), *A Penny for a Song* for Bennett, *The Postman Always Rings Twice* and *The Woodlanders* for Paulus, and *Jōruri* for Miki. His work has been seen in all the most important British operatic theatres; an association with Sadler's Wells, later English National Opera, led to memorable London productions of, among others, Janáček's *From the House of the Dead* (1965), Britten's *Gloriana* (1966) and Prokofiev's *War and Peace* (1972). In recent years he has lived in the USA, and in 1978 was appointed artistic director of Opera Theatre of St Louis.

MAX LOPPERT

Grahn, Lucile [Lucille] (*b* Copenhagen, 30 June 1819; *d* Munich, 4 April 1907). Danish ballerina and choreographer. She was trained by Auguste Bournonville 'after the ideal of Taglioni', and made her début in *La muette de Portici* in Copenhagen in 1834. Excelling in the title role of *La sylphide*, she danced in Hamburg and at the Paris Opéra, then in the 1840s and early 50s in St Petersburg, Milan, London, Berlin, Venice, Rome, Brussels, Darmstadt and Frankfurt. In 1856 she married the tenor Friedrich Young; together they appeared throughout Germany. Unusually for a woman at this time, Grahn was appointed ballet-mistress at the Leipzig opera house, 1858–61. In 1865 she created the choreography for the Bacchanale in Wagner's *Tannhäuser* at its first Munich performance (for illustration *see* DANCE, fig.4), later working as ballet-mistress at the Munich Hoftheater, 1869–75. For the first performance of *Die*

Meistersinger she choreographed the street fight with great care and precision. Though she also contributed to the first performances of *Das Rheingold* and *Die Walküre*, by 1875 Wagner had become dissatisfied with her work.

*

A. Bournonville: *Mit theaterliv* (Copenhagen, 1847–77; Eng. trans., 1979)
E. Newman: *The Life of Richard Wagner* (London, 1933–47)
I. Guest: *The Romantic Ballet in Paris* (London, 1966)
C. von Westernhagen: *Wagner* (Zürich, 1968; Eng. trans., 1979)

MAUREEN NEEDHAM COSTONIS

Gramm [Grambsch], **Donald** (**John**) (*b* Milwaukee, WI, 26 Feb 1927; *d* New York, 2 June 1983). American bass-baritone. After early study with George Graham he made his début, at 17, in *Lucia di Lammermoor* with the 8th Street Theater of Chicago. Further training followed at the Chicago Musical College (1944) and later with Martial Singher at the Music Academy of the West, Santa Barbara. In 1952 he joined the New York City Opera, singing Colline in *La bohème*, and began a long, mutually beneficial relationship with Sarah Caldwell's Opera Company of Boston in 1958. A versatile singer, Gramm sang with every leading opera company in the USA including the Metropolitan (where he first appeared in 1964), and participated in the American premières of works such as Frank Martin's *Der Sturm*, Britten's *Gloriana*, Berg's *Lulu* and Schoenberg's *Moses und Aron*. More traditional roles included Méphistophélès, Falstaff, Figaro and Ochs. His voice was not particularly large, but he used it with uncommon sensitivity to nuance and fidelity to the composer's instructions. An elegant stylist and convincing actor, he ventured into stage direction in 1981 with *Figaro* at Wolf Trap.

MARTIN BERNHEIMER

Gramophone. For a discussion of recorded opera and its performers *see* RECORDING.

Granados (y Campiña), Enrique [Enric] (*b* Lérida, 27 July 1867; *d* at sea, English Channel, 24 March 1916). Spanish (Catalan) composer and pianist. During his lifetime, as now, his reputation was sustained by his piano compositions, and his theatre works did not bring him lasting acclaim. Only since the recent discovery of the scores of the Catalan stage works, which enjoyed widespread local success but never became known outside Barcelona, has it been possible to form a clear and balanced view of his composing career.

1. Life and early works. 2. Involvement with modernism. 3. *Goyescas* and other late works.

1. LIFE AND EARLY WORKS. Granados began to study composition with Felipe Pedrell in 1883; later, after two years' study at the Paris Conservatoire with Charles de Bériot, he embarked on a career as a pianist in Barcelona in 1889 and quickly established a reputation as a fine performer and teacher, founding his own teaching institution, the Academia Granados, in 1901.

Although they contain some of his finest music, Granados's theatre works lack dramatic action, and none has more than three musically significant roles. Granados was essentially a miniaturist who conceived his mature stage works as assemblages of finely wrought cameos that reveal his penchant for ingenious and inventive orchestral effects of a Romantically evocative nature. His collaboration with José Feliu y Codina (1846–97) during his 'nationalist' phase resulted in two works that reflect his increasing interest in traditional Spanish music. The *sainete lírico Ovillejos*, a light-hearted farce set in the time of Goya, was probably inspired by the 1896 celebrations marking the sesquicentenary of the painter's birth. Its lively duos and choruses give maximum opportunity for dancing and lavish visual display, but the music, strongly influenced by the commercialized zarzuela idiom of the day, lacks the originality of the earlier *danzas españolas* (1890–92) for piano. Contrary to popular belief, *Ovillejos* survives complete, and Granados re-used part of it in his last opera, *Goyescas*.

María del Carmen, given its première in the wave of patriotism that followed Spain's disastrous colonial losses in 1898, brought Granados his first big operatic success and is one of his most overtly nationalistic works. Set in a Murcian village, Feliu y Codina's drama on the subject of jealousy is a realistic portrayal of Spanish provincial life, and the music includes at least one identifiable folksong from the region. In the final chorus of Act 2 (based on a *malagueña*) guitars and mandolins are played on stage. Musically, the opera has much in common with *Ovillejos* and is constructed around a series of set numbers linked by recitative, with each act preceded by a short prelude. At the end of the opera an offstage chorus is used to represent the idea of justice, reflecting Granados's increasingly confident exploitation of musical resources as a means of intensifying the dramatic tension. The extent to which the opera was revised after the composer's death cannot be determined since the original score is lost.

2. INVOLVEMENT WITH MODERNISM. Around 1900, Granados's increasing involvement with the emerging Catalan modernist movement led to a stylistic shift away from his earlier overt Hispanicism, and his collaboration with the poet Apeles Mestres (1854–1936), his principal librettist, yielded five works. The historical, legendary and fairy-tale themes that form the bases of Mestres's Catalan librettos are typical of the modernists' search for alternatives to the entrenched Hispanic traditions of the day. Wagner's operas had a profound influence on the modernist movement and, in Catalonia, more than any other region in Spain, a type of Wagnerian opera developed along lines suggested by Pedrell, who wrote several works with specifically Catalan associations. Granados's Catalan operas, *Petrarca* and *Follet*, are constructed around a series of closed numbers linked by longer, more Wagnerian sections of recitative and arioso.

Petrarca (1899–1900) is based on a fictional account of the poet's last day on earth and takes as its central theme his obsessive love for Laura (soprano). In the lengthy soliloquy that opens scene i the brooding Petrarch (bass) angrily bemoans the disarray within Italy and the corrupt papacy, while an ensemble of muted strings interweaving contrapuntally expresses his inner foreboding. The opera is sumptuously orchestrated, but the final scene contains passages of striking spareness which contradict the prevailing image of Granados as a composer of lush, Romantic music.

Follet (1903) is Granados's most meticulously prepared score and his most inspired work of theatre. Its basis in folklore (it was adapted by Mestres from a Breton folktale) is given added colour by the incorporation of genuine Catalan folktunes which, as well as being quoted directly by the main characters, are assimilated into the orchestral texture as fully functional

leitmotifs. Verdian precedents are suggested by the lengthy prelude to Act 3, a musical depiction of a storm presaging the opera's tragic conclusion in which the itinerant bard Follet (tenor) and his jealous rival Arnau (bass) plunge over a cliff as they fight. *Follet* was not performed publicly but received a private concert performance, marred by the singers' inability to cope adequately with the demanding music.

Picarol (1901) and *Gaziel* (1906) belong to a separate tradition of short operettas which aimed to combat the domination of the *género chico*, a short one-act zarzuela performed in continuous rotation with others throughout the evening. In both works short folklike songs and choruses in an overtly popular style are interspersed with spoken dialogue. *Picarol* is a medieval adaptation of Hugo's *Notre-Dame de Paris* and deals with the hopeless love of a court jester, Picarol (baritone), for a princess, Regina (soprano). The work ends with a stirring march, heralding her marriage, which is interspersed with the dying Picarol's lament, the whole exemplifying Granados's love of dramatic contrast. *Gaziel* is a reworking of the Faust legend in which a dedicated poet (tenor) is bewitched by the eponymous female genie. Luring him into a nocturnal garden, Gaziel (soprano) conjures up a vision of a woman, known only as Ella ('She'; soprano), who captivates the poet. The bizarre central scene is dominated by a love duet in the form of a languorous waltz that can be interpreted as a thinly veiled burlesque of the Act 2 duet from *Tristan und Isolde*.

Liliana (1911), almost certainly inspired by the Undine legend, is set in an enchanted forest and tells the tale of the nymph Liliana (soprano), who is courted by Flok, Mik and Puk (tenors), three hapless gnomes who represent nature, wealth and poetry. This curious work blends operetta, ballet and melodrama, but apart from two choruses, for frogs and insects respectively, the only significant vocal material consists of two songs for Liliana containing lengthy symphonic sections.

3. 'GOYESCAS' AND OTHER LATE WORKS. With *Goyescas* (1916) Granados returned to the conventional Hispanicism of his first theatre works, and it is his only opera to have become known outside Spain. One of its main weaknesses is an excess of purely melodic material resulting from the composer's literal adaptation of his earlier piano suite (1909–11), on to which the libretto was grafted, as the basis of the vocal parts. By far the most effective sections are the energetic choruses in the second tableau, which were newly composed. It was after the première that the ship in which Granados was returning home was torpedoed and he drowned while trying, in vain, to save his wife.

The rest of Granados's theatre music consists of two minor works for which little of the original music survives. Fragments adapted from his late song cycle *Canciones amatorias* are all that remain of *La ciguecita de Belén* (1914–15), a children's Nativity opera with accompaniment for piano and woodwind ensemble. Although often erroneously listed as a purely symphonic work, *La leyenda de la fada* includes songs and orchestral interludes. No text survives and the date of the work is unknown, although the existence of some professionally copied parts suggests that a performance had been envisaged. The music of both works recaptures the folklike simplicity of Granados's Catalan operettas.

With the discovery of the scores of the Catalan theatre works it can now be seen that, with the exception of the incidental music to *Miel de la Alcarria* (1895) and *Blancaflor* (1899), Granados's stage works contributed to the turn-of-the century regeneration of native opera within Catalonia and Spain as a whole and that, at their best, they are equal in inspiration to his finest piano compositions.

See also GOYESCAS *and* MARÍA DEL CARMEN.

Los Ovillejos, 1897 (zar, 1, J. Feliu y Codina), unperf., *E-Bcd**; rev. as Ovillejos, 1897–8 (sainete lírico, 2, Feliu y Codina), unperf., *Bcd**
María del Carmen (3, Feliu y Codina), Madrid, Parish, 12 Nov 1898, rev. E. Granados and F. Montserrat i Ayarbe, *Msa*
La leyenda de la fada, *c*1898–1900 (drama líric, 3), unperf., *Bcd** (inc., undated)
Petrarca, 1899–1900 (poema dramàtic, 1, A. Mestres), unperf., *F-Psal**
Picarol (drama líric, 1, Mestres, after V. Hugo: *Notre-Dame de Paris*), Barcelona, Tivoli, 23 Feb 1901, *Psal**
Follet (drama líric, 3, Mestres), Barcelona, Liceu, 4 April 1903 (concert perf.), *E-Bcd**
Gaziel (drama líric, 1, Mestres), Barcelona, Principal, 27 Oct 1906, *F-Psal**
Liliana (poema lírico, 1, Mestres), Barcelona, Palau de Bellas Artes, 9 July 1911, *Psal**
La ciguecita de Belén (children's op, 1, G. Miró), Vallcarca, nr Barcelona, Christmas 1914–15 (private perf.), *E-Bcd** (inc., undated)
Goyescas (3 tableaux, F. Periquet), New York, Met, 28 Jan 1916, facs. of lost autograph *US-NYgs* (entitled Goyesca)

*

J. Pillois: 'Un entretien avec Granados', *BSIM* (15 April 1914), 1–4
F. Periquet: '"Goyescas": How the Opera was Conceived', *Opera News*, vii/12 (1915–16), 4
G. Vernon: 'New York hears its First Spanish Opera', *Opera News*, vii/13 (1915–16), 2–3, 5
J. Van Broekhoven: '"Goyescas" (The Rival Lovers): a Spanish Opera in Three Pictures', *Musical Observer*, xiii/3 (1916), 134–5
W. B. Chase: 'Opera founded on Paintings', *Opera Magazine*, iii/3 (1916), 10–13
E. Granados: 'La opera española moderna: "Goyesca"', *World's Work* (1916), April, 177
E. Newman: 'The Granados of the "Goyescas"', *MT*, lvii (1916), 343–7
F. Periquet: 'La opera española moderna: "Goyesca"', *World's Work* (1916), April, 178–81
Revista musical catalana (15 June 1916) [Granados special issue]
M. Abbado: 'Goyescas', *Rassegna della istruzione artistica*, viii (1938), 116–20
J. R. Longland: 'Granados and the Opera *Goyesca*', *Notes Hispanic*, v (1945), 95–112
J. F. Rafols: *Modernismo y modernistas* (Barcelona, 1949)
C. Wilson: 'The Two Versions of "Goyescas"', *MMR*, lxxxi (1951), 203–5
J. Pahissa: *Sendas y cumbres de la música española* (Buenos Aires, 1955)
A. Fernández-Cid: *Granados* (Madrid, 1956)
F. Curet: *Història del teatre català* (Barcelona, 1967)
W. Sandelewski: 'Spotkanie z córka Enrique Granadosa' [Interview with Granados's Daughter], *Ruch muzyczny* (1977), no.16, pp.7–8
E. Mas-López: 'Apeles Mestres: Poetic Lyricist', *Opera Journal*, xiii (1980), 24–33
X. Aviñoa: *La música i el modernisme* (Barcelona, 1985)
J.-L. Marfany: '"Al damunt dels nostres cants ...": nacionalisme, modernisme i cant coral a la Barcelona del final de segle', *Recerques*, no.19 (1987), 85–113
M. Larrad: 'Los dramas líricos de Enric Granados y Apeles Mestres', *III Congreso nacional de musicología: Granada 1989*
——: *The Catalan Theatre Works of Enrique Granados* (diss., U. of Liverpool, 1992)
MARK LARRAD

Grande-Duchesse de Gérolstein, La ('The Grand-Duchess of Gerolstein'). *Opéra bouffe* in three acts by JACQUES OFFENBACH to a libretto by HENRI MEILHAC and LUDOVIC HALÉVY; Paris, Théâtre des Variétés, 12 April 1867.

The action takes place around 1720 in the mythical Grand-Duchy of Gerolstein. The army commander-in-chief is the blustering General Boum (baritone) ('A cheval sur la discipline'), and the soldiers under his command are very much of interest to the young Grand-Duchess (soprano) ('Ah! que j'aime les militaires!'). In reviewing her troops ('Ah, c'est un fameux régiment') she takes a fancy to a handsome recruit named Fritz (tenor). She promotes him first to the rank of corporal and then, to overcome his friendship with a peasant girl named Wanda (soprano), to that of lieutenant and then captain. Meanwhile the Court Chamberlain, Prince Puck (baritone), is seeking a match for the Grand-Duchess with one Prince Paul (tenor), but she has eyes only for Fritz. When Fritz overhears the General's military plan of campaign, she invites him to take part in discussions. For his contribution he is elevated rapidly to the ranks of general and, finally, commander-in-chief in place of Boum, being invested with the Grand-Duchess's family sabre ('Voici le sabre de mon père'). In Act 2 Fritz returns victorious from battle. The Grand-Duchess now seeks, through indirect references, to declare her love for him ('Dites-lui qu'on l'a remarqué distingué'), but he is too stupid to understand. When he persists in seeking to marry Wanda, the Grand-Duchess joins a conspiracy being hatched by Baron Puck, General Boum and Prince Paul to assassinate Fritz. In Act 3 Baron Grog (baritone), an emissary from Prince Paul, seeks to press the claims of Prince Paul but succeeds only in deflecting the Grand-Duchess's passion to himself. To get Grog to stay at court, the Grand-Duchess agrees to marry Prince Paul, and withdraws the threat to assassinate Fritz, who is allowed to marry Wanda. The Grand-Duchess marks her wedding night with a drinking-song ('Il était un de mes aïeux') based on the ballad of the King of Thule from Goethe's *Faust*. Meanwhile Boum is pacified only by playing a practical joke in which Fritz's wedding night is repeatedly interrupted by serenades, followed by a false call to battle. Fritz is sent to the jealous husband of Boum's mistress and reappears dishevelled, his emblems of command having led him to be mistaken for Boum. Though incensed at this degradation of her former favourite, the Grand-Duchess restores Boum to his original position and, when she discovers Grog is married with four children, reconciles herself to life with Prince Paul.

After the first night, Offenbach cut, moved or replaced several numbers to strengthen the second half of the piece. The work was written for Hortense Schneider as the Grand-Duchess and José Dupuis as Fritz.

For illustration *see* OPERETTA, fig.2.   ANDREW LAMB

Grandi, Margherita [Garde, Marguerite] (*b* Hobart, 4 Oct 1894). Australian mezzo-soprano, later soprano. She studied in London (1912–17) at the RCM and in Paris, from 1919, with Emma Calvé. Engaged (under the name of Djemma Vécla, an anagram of Calvé) as a mezzo-soprano in 1922 at Monte Carlo, she sang Carmen, Charlotte and Boito's Margherita, and created the title role of Massenet's *Amadis*. After further study in Italy with Giannina Russ, she made her soprano début in 1932 under her married name of Grandi at the Teatro Carcano, Milan, as Aida, a role she repeated at Verona (1946). She sang Boito's Helen of Troy at La Scala in 1934. She made her British début in 1939 at

Glyndebourne as Lady Macbeth, but spent the war in Italy, singing Maria in the Italian première of *Friedenstag* at Venice (1940) and Octavia (*L'incoronazione di Poppea*) at Rome (1943). In 1947 she made her London début singing Tosca and Donna Anna at the Cambridge Theatre, then sang Lady Macbeth at Edinburgh. She returned to Edinburgh in 1949 as Amelia (*Un ballo in maschera*) and created Diana in *The Olympians* at Covent Garden, where she also sang Leonora (*Il trovatore*) and, in 1951, made her stage farewell as Tosca. She had a generous, vibrant voice which she was able to colour to great dramatic effect.

HAROLD ROSENTHAL/R

Grandis, Francesco de. *See* DE GRANDIS, FRANCESCO.

Grandis, Renato de. *See* DE GRANDIS, RENATO.

Grand Macabre, Le ('The Grand Macabre'). Opera in two acts by GYÖRGY LIGETI to a libretto by the composer and Michael Meschke after Michel de Ghelderode's play *La balade du Grand Macabre*; Stockholm, Royal Opera, 12 April 1978.

Piet the Pot	high tenor
Amando	mezzo-soprano
Amanda	soprano
Nekrotzar	baritone
Astradamors	bass
Mescalina	mezzo-soprano
Venus	high soprano
Prince Go-Go	treble/soprano/high countertenor
Ruffiak	baritone
Schabiack	baritone
Schabernack	baritone
White Minister	spoken
Black Minister	spoken
Gepopo *Chief of the Secret Police*	soprano

People of Breughelland, spirits, echo of Venus; offstage boys' chorus
Silent: detectives and executioners of the Secret Police, pages and servants of Prince Go-Go's court, Nekrotzar's entourage

Setting Breughelland, an imaginary country

Ligeti's relationship with Sweden, where several of his works had their premières and where he taught from 1961, was confirmed by Göran Gentele's commission for the Royal Opera. At first an *Oedipus* was planned, with Gentele as librettist; then, after his death, Ghelderode's *La balade du Grand Macabre* was suggested by Aliute Meczies, eventually the designer of the first production. Michael Meschke, director of the Stockholm puppet theatre, was given the task of condensing the play (of 'jarryfying' it, to use the composer's term). But Ligeti changed the text again during composition, which began in December 1974 and lasted until 1977. The libretto was originally written in German as *Der grosse Makaber*, but translated into Swedish by Meschke for its première, under the present title.

The plot is simple but all-encompassing, squaring the human compass from sex to politics, inebriation and death, and enabling Ligeti to display all he had achieved during the past quarter century. The scene is set in the kingdom of Breughelland, the kingdom of peasants, monsters and apocalypses glimpsed in that master's paintings. An overture in the form of a short palindrome for 12 motor horns introduces the action, and sets a tone of run-down misuse (there are similar preludes to the second and third scenes). Piet the Pot enters singing the Dies irae: he is the opera's common man, drunk throughout the action. Soon he is joined by a pair of young lovers, 'very beautiful in a Botticellian way', Amando and Amanda (originally called Spermando and Clitoria). They are vocally as well as physically entwined in each other, singing in gasps of Monteverdian embellishment that suggest their excited state. (Ligeti himself has mentioned *Poppea*, *Falstaff* and *The Barber of Seville* as works that lie behind his own, as objects of which he offers distorted snapshots.) But their duet is interrupted by another voice, coming from a tomb. One calling himself Nekrotzar emerges, and declares he has come to announce the end of the world: he is the 'Grand Macabre' of the title. He sends Piet off to the tomb to fetch his props (coat, hat, scythe and trumpet) then rides off, with Piet as his mount, to bring his message of death and destruction. Amando and Amanda meanwhile have taken themselves off to the tomb to complete their lovemaking.

The second scene is concerned largely with a couple whose sexual needs require more encouragement: Astradamors, the astrologer, and Mescalina – he wearing women's underwear over his trousers, she clad entirely in leather and brandishing a whip. Once their activities have culminated in a 'bum kiss', she dispatches her husband to his telescope. He observes, and utters mumbo jumbo, while she falls into a drunken sleep in which she implores Venus to give her a lover more potent than her husband. Nekrotzar then enters on Piet's back and congratulates Astradamors for having prophesied his coming. Mescalina, coming out of her dream, demands a man who is well hung: Nekrotzar offers himself, and in a violent embrace kills her. The act then climaxes in a demonically exultant trio for the three men before they go off to the palace.

The third scene, beginning Act 2, takes place there. The ruler of Breughelland is the boy prince Go-Go, who is beset by warring politicians, the White Minister and the Black Minister (both spoken roles). Gepopo, the Chief of the Secret Police, suddenly arrives with his agents to deliver a warning in nonsense code made the more undecipherable by musical acrobatics. But then the threat is revealed: it is Nekrotzar, who enters during a big orchestral set piece, headed 'Collage', where the ground bass is a disjointed version of that from the finale of the 'Eroica' Symphony (the rhythm is kept as a skeleton, with different pitches). Above this is a gathering mad overlay of cheap dance music and banal fanfares, these eventually taking over and remaining to punctuate Nekrotzar's fuller announcement of the coming doomsday. While there is still some time left, Astradamors and Piet are all for spending it drinking the wine laid out on the palatial table, and Nekrotzar joins them in an alcoholic trio, seemingly believing himself to be drinking human blood already. He then goes off into a distracted reverie, accompanied by music of a fantastic rococo sort, and remembers his satanic destructions of the past. He is, however, recalled to his task by the approach of midnight, and calls down nothingness while the orchestra slowly marches through a sequence of chords, wide-spread, beautiful and ominous. Then, as a canon in the orchestra slowly slips downward, he

511

'Le Grand Macabre' (Ligeti), Act 2: scene from the original production at the Stockholm Royal Opera, 12 April 1978, with Gunilla Slättegård as Prince Go-Go and Britt-Marie Aruhn as Gepopo, Chief of the Secret Police, arriving on roller skates (set and costumes designed by Aliute Meczies)

himself collapses: the end of the world has come, and the only one to die is Death. The curtain descends as another, dense, still, orchestral texture gradually turns into a confused gallop in the brass.

The fourth scene, or Epilogue, has no separate overture but develops straight out of its predecessor, while returning to the setting of the first scene. Astradamors and Piet hover above the ground, believing themselves to be dead; they then float off. Before long all the rest have turned up: Go-Go, Nekrotzar, Mescalina, the Ministers, and finally, emerging from the tomb where they have been settled for two scenes, Amando and Amanda. Have they all really died and been resurrected to find themselves in much the same situation? Or was Nekrotzar merely a powerless charlatan? In the play he is shown up as a fake, but Ligeti leaves the question open, and has his principals sing the amoral moral: 'Fear not to die, good people all! No-one knows when his hour will fall. And when it comes, then let it be … Farewell, till then, live merrily!'. PAUL GRIFFITHS

Grand opéra (Fr.). French opera of the Romantic period, sung throughout, generally in five acts, grandiose in conception and impressively staged.

1. Towards a definition. 2. Antecedents and earliest examples. 3. Meyerbeer and his contemporaries. 4. Influence and legacy.

1. TOWARDS A DEFINITION. A grand style was frequently considered essential for works written for the Paris Opéra. Even in Lully's day contemporaries occasionally referred to *tragédies en musique* as 'grands opéras' (as in the case of his *Cadmus*), although librettists and composers preferred designations underlining the literary genre in lyric setting. In the first half of the 18th century several critics bemoaned the frivolity of many *opéras-ballets* and cited specifically their failure to conform to the grandeur they argued was necessary at this theatre. It was not until the early 19th century, however, that the term 'grand opéra' became current. Castil-Blaze, for example, defined it as sung throughout (in contrast to the *opéra-comique*, which had spoken dialogue) and performed at the Opéra: in his opinion, Gluck, Piccinni and Spontini were the masters of the

genre, which required nobility of subject and of tone. The librettist Jouy concurred, but also argued for an expansion to five acts and for plots drawn from heroic historical events as well as from other more conventional sources. By the 1830s, 'grand opéra' had entered common parlance and was applied to the repertory then dominant – no longer by Gluck and his contemporaries, but by Rossini, Auber, Halévy and, above all, Meyerbeer. While modern scholars usually follow this latter, more restrictive practice, it is worth noting that on the scores and librettos themselves nearly always only 'opéra' (or occasionally 'opéra historique') appears.

The relation of *grand opéra* of the 1830s and later decades to its late 18th- and early 19th-century antecedents will be discussed below. Generally, the later works are sometimes in four acts but more often in five (instead of the three preferred in most works in repertory at the Opéra in the late 18th century and the early 19th); they have plots set in medieval or modern times (rather than taken from classical history and mythology) and which exploit strongly melodramatic and violent situations, with sudden shifts, nearly always ending tragically; they often include major characters from the lower or otherwise disadvantaged classes, portraying them in a heroic light (hitherto a treatment reserved for gods, kings and aristocrats); and they may present controversial themes – religious intolerance or rebellion against oppression, for instance. (Governmental bodies and agents, such as censors, in Paris and elsewhere saw in the genre a possible vehicle for the expression of political and social critique, which required supervision and control; the reactions of contemporary audiences indicate that they too did at times interpret what was being presented on stage in the light of current situations, and not always in the ways that officials and authors intended.)

The forces required to perform a *grand opéra* were enormous: there were many leading characters and secondary roles; the chorus often represented different groups in conflict; the ballet assumed a more extensive role; the orchestra grew in size and variety (with instruments like the ophicleide, triangle, cymbals and bass drum becoming standard members rather than exceptions) and special orchestral effects abound (offstage instruments, muting and so on). The scores contain a wide range of formal types and styles. Virtuoso *italianate airs* with extensive ranges and requiring a formidable technique contrast with relatively simple *romances*. Solo music is often part of larger complexes. Choruses and long ensembles, conceived to advance the drama in as impressive a way as possible, dominate tableaux. Romantic interest in local colour and in pageantry led to a revolution in several aspects of staging – in the style of scenery and costumes, the placement and movement of soloists and chorus, and in techniques of lighting. Spectacle, long a feature of French opera, achieved new heights in *grand opéra*.

2. ANTECEDENTS AND EARLIEST EXAMPLES. Gluck's operas were significant models. Particularly important for his successors were his handling of the chorus, his more thorough integration of spectacle into the drama and his structuring of scenes made up of discrete units (chorus, dances, *airs*) into a cohesive whole (by tonal relationships and repetition of key pieces). During the late *ancien régime* and the Revolution composers built on this heritage, enriching the harmonic vocabulary and using stronger dissonance for dramatic effect, enlarging the scenes and sometimes writing a more symphonic part for it, and increasing the role of the chorus (as in Cherubini's *Démophon*, 1788, and Méhul's *Adrien*, 1799). The Gluckian ideal of balance and classicism began to give way to a more emphatic and dynamic conception. Plots drawn from medieval and modern history, rare in serious operas earlier, became more common; several glorified the heroism of French republicans from the lower classes (for example Louis Jadin's *Le siège de Thionville*, 1793).

During the Consulate and Empire Napoleon sought to have the Opéra serve the state: specific works were commissioned as propaganda; in addition, as the country's 'premier théâtre lyrique', it was to be the showcase for serious and grandiose art. The composer who best met such aesthetic goals was Spontini. His *Fernand Cortez* (1809; fig.1) combines an exotic setting, strong melodramatic turns in the plot, conflict between two races and religions with musical characterizations to match, especially in the choruses, and much pageantry with spectacular tableaux (such as a cavalry charge and the burning of the Aztec temple). This and his other works for the Opéra were the immediate sources for *grand opéra*.

Just before the downfall of Charles X two key works had their premières in Paris, Auber's *La muette de Portici* (libretto by Scribe and Delavigne, 1828) and Rossini's *Guillaume Tell* (libretto by Jouy and Bis, 1829). *La muette de Portici* combines two historical events, the Naples 1647 Revolution and the 1631 eruption of Mt Vesuvius, as the backdrop for a fictional account. The lowly born heroine, seduced by the viceroy's son, is mute and expresses herself through pantomime (a technique more frequently exploited in the repertories of the boulevard theatres). The crowd scenes, the integration of dance into the drama, the construction of huge finales and impressive scenery and stage effects contributed to its success (for illustration *see* DANCE, fig.3, and *MUETTE DE PORTICI, LA*). Like Spontini, Rossini combined italianate vocal lyricism with elements drawn from the French tradition. His last opera, *Guillaume Tell*, exploits local colour deftly in a musical depiction of nature, the grandeur of the Swiss Alps, and the piety and patriotism of its inhabitants (fig.2). The second-act finale, in which each of the three

1. Designs by François-Guillaume Ménageot for the costumes of (left to right) Montezuma, Télasco, Amazily and the Mexican High Priest in the original production of Spontini's 'Fernand Cortez' at the Paris Opéra, 28 November 1809

cantons is given its own character, builds to a climax at the end: a powerful, unifying oath. The chorus often takes centre stage and, significantly, the title character has no independent *air* but rather is presented in dramatically charged duet, trio and ensembles in which he seeks to persuade, to provide leadership, to oppose tyranny. Aspects of both the librettos and the scores of these two operas remain traditional. But their greater length and the degree to which the people in action are prominent in crowd scenes of dramatic importance set them apart from the works of the Empire. Their plots, combining fiction and historical events (reinterpreted to suit the authors' needs, to be sure), though occasionally found earlier, also conform to *grand opéra*.

But what also struck contemporaries as new was their staging: in 1827, recognizing the need for change in this area, the Opéra established a new 'comité de mise en scène' to judge costume and set designs and other aspects of staging from the technical and artistic point of view. Significantly, Ciceri, in charge of the sets, had been sent to Switzerland and to Italy (partly at government expense) so that he could have first-hand experience to create an aura of authenticity (and to see how La Scala handled a volcanic eruption in its version of Pacini's *L'ultimo giorno di Pompei*; see MILAN, fig.5). Further, *La muette* and *Tell* were among the first major productions to benefit from the staging supervision of Solomé, newly hired away from the Comédie-Française (and experienced in boulevard theatre). His *mise-en-scène* booklets for both show that, among several innovations, he forced the chorus to act, to use gesture, to adopt unusual positions (such as kneeling) for dramatic effect and to move often in asymmetrical patterns (*see* PRODUCTION, fig.15). Although some effects (like the erupting volcano) had been used at the Opéra in the previous century, the audience had reason to believe that a new era was beginning. The continuing popularity of both operas for over five decades attests to the 19th-century view of them as *grands opéras*.

3. MEYERBEER AND HIS CONTEMPORARIES. *Robert le diable* (libretto by Scribe and Delavigne, 1831) was the work in which Meyerbeer made his successful début in *grand opéra* at the Opéra. It was followed by three more operas on Scribe librettos that were to dominate the Paris stage for much of the rest of the century: *Les Huguenots* (libretto written in collaboration with Deschamps, 1836), *Le prophète* (1849) and *L'Africaine*

(1865). Other composers working with Scribe made fewer popular contributions but nonetheless significant ones: Halévy in *La Juive* (1835) and Auber in *Gustave III* (1833).

An eminent man of the theatre, Scribe chose themes of great power. *Robert le diable* is somewhat apart in its mixture of medieval legend, superstition, the supernatural and passionate love. Thereafter, he selected historical subjects modified to suit his purposes and often with a possible contemporary application as a background for a story of tragic passion. In *La Juive* religions (Jewish and Christian) clash, and fatherly love (Eléazar and Brogni) cannot save Rachel. Examples of religious strife among Christians in France and in Germany, among other themes, are featured in *Les Huguenots* and *Le prophète*. Opposition to political reform and betrayal of friendship are intertwined in *Gustave III*. In *L'Africaine* the inability of Europeans to understand exotic culture leads to tragedy. Scribe was not a crusading reformer, but rather a practical playwright presenting his audience with material he knew would interest them. His librettos provided no easy solutions to the problems of fanaticism, corruption and hatred. Except in *Robert le diable* (which also had strong ties to the *opéra-féerie* tradition), most of the sympathetic characters are in the end crushed by forces beyond their control. But Scribe's texts, in which strong dramatic situations are starkly presented without extended development, gave his musicians ample scope for intensively emotional settings. Concealment, coincidence and misunderstandings allow for sudden shifts in direction and melodramatic scenes, such as Raoul's rejection of Valentine because of her seeming infidelity in *Les Huguenots*. The final catastrophe is striking theatre – whether Rachel's immolation in *La Juive* (fig.3) or the fate of John and the Anabaptists in *Le prophète*.

Meyerbeer's eclectic style was ideally suited to the emotionalism and variety of situation in Scribe's librettos. With a Germanic approach to harmony and tonal structures, experience in Italian lyricism and a commitment to French traditions of declamation and dramatic stage presentation, he produced rich scores of vast scope. He created huge tableaux so that the music could give support to the text's broad gestures. In *L'Africaine*, for example, most of the first act is one long *morceau d'ensemble* and finale, which comprehends the piety of the Spaniards, Vasco's leadership, their bravery

2. 'Guillaume Tell' (Rossini), Act 3 scene ii (the square at Altdorf): watercolour (probably by Franz Peirot) from a manuscript mise-en-scène (c1840) designed to convey details of the original Paris production of 1829 to provincial (and foreign) theatres intending to stage the opera

3. 'La Juive' (Halévy), final scene of Act 5 (Rachel is about to be hurled into the cauldron) in a production at Covent Garden, London, 25 July 1850: engraving from the 'Illustrated London News' (3 August 1850)

in rescuing African slaves and the consequences. The opposing groups, Europeans and Africans, as well as the leading characters, have individual musical characterizations; and Meyerbeer made excellent use of the orchestra, developing for the Africans traditional 'exotic' gestures in motif and instrumentation more fully than had been done in earlier operas.

Significantly, the isolated *air* has a less important role. Many solo pieces are embedded in larger structures, such as Raimbaut's ballad, 'Jadis régnait en Normandie', which forms part of the introduction of *Robert le diable*. This is an excellent example, too, of Meyerbeer's use of a simple form (here varied strophic) and vocal style (largely syllabic and triadically based) contrasting with the more fully scored choral sections. Long, virtuoso italianate *airs* are generally reserved for the heroine, for example Isabelle's 'En vain j'espère' with chorus in the same opera. The chorus becomes a *personage*, or more often *personages*, in its own right and a vital participant in the action. The variety of the writing for it – from strong unison passages to full homophony to contrapuntal textures – is always closely matched to the dramatic situation (*Les Huguenots* has many striking scenes). The *divertissements* also provided the opportunity for contrast, from relatively simple dances to more complicated pantomime, *airs*, choruses and ensembles linked to form a larger whole. To achieve the grand gestures and the temporal length to correspond to the action on stage, Meyerbeer relied on several devices, including sequence and the repetition of long blocks. As a result, his operas are at times difficult to listen to, but it was never his intention for the music to be heard in isolation. Meyerbeer was, above all, a composer for the theatre, and his contribution can

be judged fairly only in that context.

In their stage sets, designers often sought to represent specific sites rather than generic locations. *Les Huguenots* has the chateau of Chenonceaux in the background (for illustration *see* HUGUENOTS, LES). The fourth act of *Le prophète* is set in the public square and cathedral of Münster (for illustration *see* PROPHÈTE, LE). So elaborate did sets become that, from *Gustave III* onwards, it became common to have a different atelier prepare each act (and sometimes separate scenes within acts) rather than assigning overall responsibility to a single person.

Innovation in *mise-en-scène* remained an admired feature of *grand opéra*. The scene in *Robert le diable* that most impressed the audience was the finale of Act 3 (fig.4). Here, in Ciceri's set – a cloister modelled on a 16th-century monument in Montfort-l'Amaury, bathed in moonlight (an atmosphere of mystery achieved with gas lighting, introduced a few years earlier) – the ghosts of debauched nuns appear as if by magic (technically the new *trappe anglaise* was the means; *see* MACHINERY, fig.11) to dance a bacchanale and entice Robert to violate the tomb of St Rosalie by plucking a magic branch. According to Véron, the idea was that of Duponchel, *metteur-en-scène* (or director), and replaced Scribe's original plan for a traditional Olympus *divertissement*. In any case, the scene is an excellent example of the creative contribution of *metteur-en-scène* and set designer to the success of *grand opéra*. In succeeding works Scribe strove for the unusual in his use of spectacle, and his Opéra collaborators contributed their imaginative realization by employing the advances of the industrial revolution. *Le prophète*, for example, was the first work to use electric lighting which, according to contemporaries, re-created for the skating scene the impression of a winter dawn with startling realism. More generally, the darkening of the house during performance and the lowering of the curtain for changes of scenery helped reinforce theatrical illusion.

4. INFLUENCE AND LEGACY. *Grand opéra* had a significant effect on the culture of 19th-century France. For the aristocracy and the upper bourgeoisie, the Opéra was above all the place to see works of theatrical art and to be seen as leading members of society. Journalists, both left- and right-wing, through their reviews of *grands opéras*, sought to make political statements and social critiques (see Fulcher). Numerous writers found in the genre aesthetic inspiration or at least stimulation for their own works: Stendhal, Honoré de Balzac, George Sand, Théophile Gautier and Gustave Flaubert among them. The broader view of the place of *grand opéra* in French society merits further research.

On a more specific level, the models of French *grand opéra* were crucial for Wagner and Verdi (quite apart from their own works for Paris within the *grand opéra* tradition, Wagner's revised *Tannhäuser*, 1861, and Verdi's *Les vêpres siciliennes*, 1855, and *Don Carlos*, 1867), as well as for Gounod and Saint-Saëns and many of their contemporaries. Wagner's youthful *Rienzi*, a 'grosse tragische Oper', and Verdi's mature extravaganza for Cairo, *Aida*, are obvious examples: both use a melodramatic plot so constructed as to provide ample opportunity for lavish displays; both profited from the tableau approach to dramatic and musical organization; and in both the chorus has an important role. Berlioz adopted and moulded in a highly original way the *grand opéra* form for his greatest opera, *Les Troyens*.

But the influence of *grand opéra* goes far beyond derivative elements. The genre had provided a laboratory for the development of the Romantic orchestra and orchestral textures and effects. Berlioz learnt from this (not only in *Les Troyens*, but also in his dramatic symphonic and choral works), as did Wagner and Verdi even in their later operas (such as *Die Meistersinger von Nürnberg* and *Otello*). The integration in more continuous musical units of disparate ele-

ments is fundamental to Gounod, Massenet and Saint-Saëns. In a sense, strong reactions against certain elements in *grand opéra*, whether by Wagner (who in *Oper und Drama* termed it 'effects without causes') or by the *drame lyrique* composers, are further evidence of the genre's vitality and dominance on the European lyric stage.

The legacy of *grand opéra* goes beyond musical and dramatic features. Its aesthetics, which valued visual display as well as aural satisfaction, resulted in a new importance in the theatrical hierarchy for three people: the set designer, the costumer and the *metteur-en-scène*. They, and the *machiniste* (responsible for the realization of special effects), were consulted in the realization of works – not merely assigned the task of fulfilling as practically as possible the requirements of the authors and theatre administrators – and they were often cited in the librettos just after the names of the author of the text and composer. Huge sums were spent for premières: no longer was it acceptable to use stock costumes and sets with minor adjustments (as was quite frequently done the century before); innovation was expected. In reviews, critics often dwelt on their contribution at length. In short, the modern view, which allows, indeed expects, creativity from the equivalent today of the *metteur-en-scène*, the director, is a heritage, however unwitting, of *grand opéra* (whether in current operatic productions or in cinema or television).

Grand opéra dominated the Parisian stage for over half a century: *Guillaume Tell* and *Les Huguenots* (among others) remained part of the standard repertory there until World War II, and both achieved more than 800 performances at the Opéra. In the 19th century *grand opéra* was exported elsewhere – from New Orleans to Prague, from Havana to St Petersburg. Indeed, for most of Europe, French opera and opera singers were as important as Italian, and far ahead of German and other national traditions. Recent revivals attest to the continuing interest in the genre. Critical editions of Meyerbeer and further research into historical performance aspects, such as staging, would surely encourage a better understanding and appreciation of what for many Romantics was at the summit of the theatrical and music arts.

4. 'Robert le diable' (Meyerbeer), Act 3 finale (the nuns rise from their graves): lithograph after Pierre-Luc-Charles Ciceri's design for the original production at the Paris Opéra, 21 November 1831

5. 'Aida' (Verdi), Act 2 scene ii (one of the city gates of Thebes): engraving showing the first production at the Paris Opéra (Salle Garnier), 22 March 1880

For further illustration see AFRICAINE, L'; GUSTAVE III; JUIVE, LA; and MACHINERY, fig.19.

Castil-Blaze: 'Opéra', Dictionnaire de musique moderne (Paris, 1821, 2/1825)
V. E. de Jouy: 'Essaie sur l'opéra français', Oeuvres complètes, xxii (Paris, 1823), 225–82
L. Véron: Mémoires d'un bourgeois de Paris, iii (Paris, 1854)
Castil-Blaze: L'Académie impériale de musique (Paris, 1856)
T. Gautier: Histoire de l'art dramatique en France (Paris, 1858–9)
J. Moynet: L'envers du théâtre: machines et décorations (Paris, 1873, 3/1888)
M. A. Allévy: La mise en scène en France dans la première moitié du dix-neuvième siècle (Paris, 1928)
W. L. Crosten: French Grand Opera: an Art and a Business (New York, 1948)
H. Becker: 'Die historische Bedeutung der grand opéra', Beiträge zur Geschichte der Musikanschauung im 19. Jahrhundert, ed. W. Salmen (Regensburg, 1965), 151–9
G. Chinn: The Académie Impériale de Musique: a Study of its Administration and Repertory from 1862–1870 (diss., Columbia U., 1969)
K. Pendle: Eugène Scribe and French Opera of the Nineteenth Century (Ann Arbor, 1979)
D. Pistone: 'L'Opéra de Paris au siècle romantique', Revue internationale de musique française, no.4 (1981), 7–56
T. J. Walsh: Second Empire Opera: the Théâtre Lyrique, Paris, 1851 to 1870 (London, 1981)
H. R. Cohen and M. O. Gigou: Cent ans de mise en scène lyrique en France (env. 1830–1930): catalogue descriptif des livrets de mise en scène, des libretti annotés et des partitions annotées dans la Bibliothèque de l'Association de la régie théâtrale (Paris) (New York, 1986)
P. Barbier: A l'Opéra au temps de Rossini et de Balzac, Paris: 1800–1850 (Paris, 1987)
J. F. Fulcher: The Nation's Image: French Grand Opera as Politics and Politicized Art (Cambridge, 1987)
A. Gerhard: 'Die französische "grand opéra" in der Forschung seit 1945', AcM, lix (1987), 220–70
N. Wild: Décors et costumes du XIXe siècle à l'Opéra de Paris (Paris, 1987)
C. Join-Dieterle: Les décors de scène de l'Opéra de Paris à l'époque romantique (Paris, 1988)
M. E. Smith: Music for the Ballet-Pantomime at the Paris Opéra, 1825–1850 (diss., Yale U., 1988)
R. S. Wilberg: The Mise en Scène at the Paris Opéra (1821–1873) (diss., Brigham Young U., 1988)
A. Gerhard: Die Verstädterung der Oper (Stuttgart, 1992)
H. R. Cohen: L'Opéra de Paris à l'époque romantique (Geneva, forthcoming)   M. ELIZABETH C. BARTLET

Granforte, Apollo (b Legnano, nr Verona, 20 July 1886; d Milan, 10 June 1975). Italian baritone. As a young man he emigrated to South America where he studied with Guido Capocci and made his début as Germont in La traviata at the Rosario Theatre in 1913. He returned to Italy during World War I, singing in Rome and Milan. He extended his international reputation through Australian tours with Melba in 1924 and then with an eminent company of Italian singers in 1928. He became a regular member of La Scala in 1935, when he sang in the world première of Mascagni's Nerone. His wide repertory included John the Baptist, the Wanderer, Telramund and Amfortas in Parsifal. After the war he taught at the Ankara Conservatory, then in Prague and finally in Milan where Raffaele Ariè was among his pupils. In the late 1920s it seemed that the HMV record company saw him as Ruffo's successor as Italy's 'star' baritone; but in the 1930s he settled down to a less spectacular career.

A. A. Delicata: 'Apollo Granforte', Record Collector, xii (1958–60), 173–94, 258   J. B. STEANE

Granier, Jeanne (b Paris, 31 March 1852; d Paris, 18 or 19 Dec 1939). French soprano. Discovered and brought to Paris by Offenbach, the young Granier won notice when replacing Louise Théo in the leading role of his La *jolie parfumeuse* (1873). She was given the double title role in Lecocq's *Giroflé-Girofla* (1874) and immediately became one of the biggest musical stars in Paris, a position she retained for more than 20 years, thanks to a notable talent as an actress allied to a light and accurate voice. Among her creations were a series of Lecocq roles, including her greatest, the title role in *Le petit duc*, at the Théâtre de la Renaissance, and parts in works by Planquette, Audran (*La cigale et la fourmi*), Hervé, Messager, Serpette and Lacôme. In her thirties she appeared at the Théâtre des Variétés in many of the great roles of classic *opérette* including Eurydice, Gabrielle (*La vie Parisienne*), the title roles in *La Grande-Duchesse de Gérolstein* and *La belle Hélène*, Boulotte (*Barbe-bleue*) and Périchole.   KURT GÄNZL

Granier [Garnier, Grenier], **Louis** (*b* Toulouse, 1740; *d* Toulouse, 1800). French composer. He studied in Toulouse, and his first important position was in Bordeaux, where he directed the opera. He went to Paris in 1766 and was engaged as a violinist in the Opéra orchestra the same year. His most successful work, the *pastorale-héroïque Théonis* (1767), was written in collaboration with P.-M. Berton and J.-C. Trial, then directors of the Opéra. A review in the *Mercure de France* (November 1767) states that 'the music, ... as graceful, as brilliant as it is new, makes a greater impression each time it is heard, and can only add greatly to the glory of the three composers'. Granier left Paris in 1770 to become music director at the Toulouse theatre. On his return to Paris in 1773, he divided his time between his duties as an orchestral violinist, and composing and arranging ballets and operas. In 1777 he served as an assistant to the director of the Opéra. He reworked three ballets for Noverre and Vestris and wrote additional music for four operas by Campra, Marais and Lully. In 1786 he retired to Toulouse. Granier is chiefly remembered through his association with Berton and Trial; he met them both in Bordeaux, where the latter conducted the orchestra, and he may also have been Trial's composition teacher in Montpellier. In 1773 Granier collaborated with Berton on a new version of Lully's *Bellérophon*.

all performed at the Paris Opéra

Théonis, ou Le toucher (pastorale-héroïque, A.-A.-H. Poinsinet), 11 Oct 1767, collab. P.-M. Berton, J.-C. Trial, *F-Pc, Po* [2nd entrée of Poinsinet: *Fragments nouveaux*]

Revisions: Campra: Tancrède, 1764; Marais: Alcyone, 1771; Lully: Bélléophon, 1773; Lully: Thésée, 1779   MICHAEL BARNARD

Grant, Clifford (Scantlebury) (*b* Sydney, 11 Sept 1930). Australian bass. He studied in Sydney, making his début there in 1951 as Raimondo. In 1966 he joined Sadler's Wells, where his roles included Silva (*Ernani*), Padre Guardiano, Seneca (*L'incoronazione di Poppea*), Sarastro, the Commendatore, Pogner, Hunding, Hagen, Philip II, Count des Grieux and Raleigh (*Gloriana*), which he also sang in Vienna. He made his San Francisco début in 1966 as Lord Walton (*I puritani*), later singing the King (*Aida*), Alidoro, Oroveso, Matteo (*Fra Diavolo*), Trulove, Monterone and Phorcas (*Esclarmonde*), which he also sang at the Metropolitan (1977). At Glyndebourne he sang Neptune (*Il ritorno d'Ulisse*) in 1972. He made his Covent Garden début in 1974 as Mozart's Bartolo. Returning to Sydney in 1976 he sang Nilakantha (*Lakmé*), Pimen, Friar Laurence and a Colonist in Meale's *Voss* (1986). He retired from the stage in 1990, taking the role of Marcel in *Les Huguenots* at Sydney Opera House, in the performance in which Sutherland made her farewell appearance. He had a black-hued voice, strongly projected, suited to both sympathetic and unsympathetic roles.

ALAN BLYTH

Grassi, Cecilia (*b* Naples, *c*1740; *d* ?Italy, after May 1782). Italian soprano, wife of J. C. Bach. Her earliest known appearance was at the Teatro di S Salvatore, Venice, in 1760. She sang in Venice, Bologna, Turin and elsewhere in Italy until 1766 and was then in London as *prima donna seria* for the 1766–7 season. She was back in Italy in 1767 and sang at S Carlo, Naples in 1769. But she returned to London and appeared several times at the King's Theatre (1769–72), performing regularly in the works of, among others, J. C. Bach, including his adaptation of Gluck's *Orfeo* (1770) and *Endimione* (1772). She did not appear in opera again, but was a regular performer in the Bach-Abel concerts. Bach, whom she probably married after her retirement in 1776, wrote many pieces especially for her. Left penniless when he died, she returned to Italy. According to Burney she was 'inanimate on the stage ... but there was a truth of intonation, with a plaintive sweetness of voice, and innocence of expression, that gave great pleasure to all hearers who did not expect or want to be surprised'.

*

BurneyH
C. S. Terry: *John Christian Bach* (London, 1929, 2/1967)
MURRAY R. CHARTERS

Grassini, Josephina [Giuseppina] (**Maria Camilla**) (*b* Varese, 18 April 1773; *d* Milan, 3 Jan 1850). Italian contralto. After studying with Domenico Zucchinetti in Varese and with Antonio Secchi in Milan, she made her début in 1789 at Parma in P. A. Guglielmi's *La pastorella nobile*. In the following year she appeared at La Scala in three comic roles but, realizing that her natural talent was dramatic, during the next decade she sang in Vicenza, Venice, Milan, Naples and Ferrara, creating roles in Zingarelli's *Artaserse* and *Giulietta e Romeo* and in Cimarosa's *Gli Orazi ed i Curiazi*, and singing in Portugal's *Demofoonte*, Bertoni's *Orfeo e Euridice*, Mayr's *Telemaco*, Cimarosa's *Artemisia* and Nasolini's *La morte di Semiramide*.

Grassini made her London début at the King's Theatre in 1804 as Cora in Andreozzi's *La vergine del sole*. She also sang the title roles in Winter's *Il ratto di Proserpina* and *Zaira*, Nasolini's *La morte di Cleopatra* and Fioravanti's *Camilla*. In 1806 she returned to Paris. At the Tuileries she sang in Paer's *Didone abbandonata* and Cherubini's *Pigmalione*, and in 1813 she appeared as Horatia (*Gli Orazi*) at the Théâtre Italien. The following year she returned to London for the season, singing in Pucitta's *Aristodemo*. In 1815 she returned to Italy and sang in Brescia, Padua, Trieste and Florence. She retired to Milan in 1823. Her voice, though narrow in range, was of great power and volume, unusually flexible for its weight and always used with taste and musicality.

*

P. Scudo: 'Josephina Grassini', *Revue des deux mondes* (1 Jan 1852)
A. Pougin: *Un cantatrice 'amie' de Napoléon: Giuseppina Grassini 1773–1850* (Paris, 1920)
A. Gavoty: *La Grassini* (Paris, 1947)
E. Gara: 'Giuseppina Grassini', *La Scala* (1952), nos.29–30
ELIZABETH FORBES

Grau, Maurice (*b* Brno, 1849; *d* Paris, 14 March 1907). American impresario. He went to New York at the age of five; he studied at Columbia University Law School, but in 1872 decided on a career in artist management. He organized many highly successful American tours for musicians, including Jacques Offenbach. In 1873 he formed with Clara Kellogg the English Opera Company. With Henry A. Abbey he gave a special season of 21 operatic performances at the Metropolitan in 1890; John B. Schoeffel joined their partnership and they managed the company from 1891 to 1897. When Abbey died in 1898, Grau formed his own opera company at the Metropolitan which continued in existence until he retired in 1903 and moved to Paris. In addition to his duties in New York, Grau was also managing director at Covent Garden from 1897 to 1900. By understanding and catering to public taste, Grau was the first impresario in America to make money from grand opera. He produced French and Italian works when he sensed the public was weary of German opera, but later met the demand for Wagner. He brought the best singers to the USA, including the De Reszkes, Emma Eames, Nellie Melba, Lillian Nordica and Enrico Caruso. He married the opera singer Marie Durand in 1883.

DAB (E. Mims jr)
Obituaries: *MusAm*, v/3 (1907), 13; *New York Times* (15 March 1907)

DEE BAILY

Graun, Carl [Karl] **Heinrich** (*b* Wahrenbrück, 1703/4; *d* Berlin, 8 Aug 1759). German composer. He was Kapellmeister of the Berlin Opera under Frederick the Great, and he shared with J. A. Hasse the distinction of pre-eminently representing Italian opera in mid-18th-century Germany. Like his brother, the chamber and orchestral composer Johann Gottlieb Graun (*b* Wahrenbrück, 1702–3; *d* Berlin, 27 Oct 1771), he sang at the Dresden Kreuzschule, remaining there until 1721. He was also at the University of Leipzig from 1718, studying composition (and probably string instruments) with J. C. Schmidt, Kapellmeister of the Dresden Opera. But the most potent influence on his early development was his experience, with other Kreuzschule students, in the opera chorus during the establishment of *opera seria* in Dresden under Heinichen and Lotti. It was the Dresden opera that intoxicated the young Prussian Crown Prince Frederick in 1728 and that, after 1731, was the forum for Hasse, Europe's leading composer in the genre. Graun was an avid student: he wrote out Lotti's *Teophano* from memory after three hearings and studied Keiser's scores intensively. A journey to Prague in 1723, as a cellist in a gala performance, acquainted him with Fux's *Costanza e Fortezza*.

Graun's first important post was as a tenor in the Brunswick Opera, where he went in 1725 on the recommendation of the Dresden court poet J. U. König. Even in operas by the Brunswick Kapellmeister, G. C. Schürmann, he was permitted to alter and improvise on his parts. In about 1727 he became vice-Kapellmeister and in 1727 he produced his first opera for Brunswick. He wrote six operas for the Brunswick court; one, *Lo specchio della fedeltà*, was performed for Crown Prince Frederick's marriage to Elisabeth Christine of Brunswick in June 1733.

Frederick had already formed his musical establishment at Ruppin by 1733; Johann Gottlieb Graun had entered his service the previous year, and in 1735 Carl Heinrich followed, moving with the court to Rheinsberg the following year. Since Frederick did not accede to the Prussian throne until 1740, and especially since the king regarded Frederick's musical interests with intense disapproval, Graun's position, like that of the entire princely musical establishment, was at first insecure. He directed the chamber music and sang Italian chamber cantatas (today regarded as among his best works), while Frederick and Franz Benda became his pupils in music theory. It was during the Rheinsberg years that Graun formed the strong friendship with Frederick that was to last for the rest of his life.

When Frederick became king, Graun was appointed Royal Kapellmeister at the high salary of 2000 thalers a year. His first duty, after composing a *Trauerkantate* for the deceased Friedrich Wilhelm I, was to go to Bologna, Rome, Venice, Florence and Naples, between July 1740 and March 1741, to engage singers for the new opera. He returned with five male and three female singers (all of mediocre quality). His first opera for Berlin, *Rodelinda*, was performed on 13 December 1741. It had to be presented on a temporary stage, with extra musicians specially hired. From 1740 to 1742 newly engaged singers, dancers, stage machinists, costumiers and all the apparatus of opera flowed into Berlin while the opera house was under construction; and on 7 December 1742 the Königliches Opernhaus, the famous 'Linden-Opera', was opened with Graun's *Cesare e Cleopatra*.

Graun, as chief composer for the new house, wrote over 20 major operas for Berlin, and the story of his career is inseparable from the history of the Berlin Opera. Furthermore, since political and military activities determined the fortunes of this institution during its founder's lifetime, it is no exaggeration to say that Graun was as distinctively moulded by Frederick the king and military commander as he was by Frederick the musician. The Prussian monarch's musical taste was imposed with ever-increasing strictness on Graun, who was required to write second or third versions of arias the king did not like. A second version of an aria in *Demofoonte* (1746), for instance, was still not to Frederick's taste (this is one of the operas to which Frederick himself contributed, as the composer of three arias). To Graun's embarrassment, Frederick substituted an aria by Hasse, whose music the king fervently admired; the aria became a public favourite. Graun's abandonment, by 1745, of the French overture in favour of the Italian sinfonia was specified by Frederick, as was his adoption of the cavatina as an alternative to the da capo aria in *Montezuma* (of which the libretto was sketched by Frederick himself). Frederick participated in the production of most of the librettos used by Graun, editing them or providing models.

Graun's operas, though totally italianized, show close attention to the value of counterpoint, but remain Neapolitan in their understanding and veneration of the solo voice (including, in particular, the castrato) if bearing signs of the reform tendencies of the Gluck epoch to come. They were most admired for their tender expression of emotion, especially in adagios. Graun was a master in the facile and dependable production of stage works; starting with MS paper on which a copyist had already written the text, he made it a point to write one aria a day, sketched in the morning and finished in the afternoon.

His Berlin operas are, however, too much alike in their adherence to proven formulae. The orchestration is not as colourful as that of his operas for the Brunswick court. The short ballets between acts have little connection with the plot. The arias are heavily laden with coloratura, though his 'chief rule' was that 'one should not make unnatural difficulties without good reason'. In harmony he avoided the 'sharp musical spices' of the younger generation; 'to me', he said, 'seeking new notes in harmony is like seeking new letters in a language'. The musical plan of each opera is little more than an alternation of recitative and aria, with an occasional accompanied recitative, chorus or duet.

Most of Graun's librettos are tragedies, dealing with mythology and legend more than the historical topics favoured by Metastasio. That of *Montezuma* is a noteworthy exception. None of the three librettists in the royal musical establishment during Graun's lifetime – Bottarelli, Villati and Tagliazucchi – were more than mediocre. The libretto of *Montezuma*, written (as were several others of the operas) in French prose by Frederick and translated into Italian verse by Tagliazucchi, is the best that Graun used. Next in quality are those by Metastasio and Zeno, though their adaptation by Frederick's court librettists did nothing to help them. In any case all librettos passed, for better or worse, under the supervision of the king.

The opinions of Graun's contemporaries do not serve his reputation as a composer of opera. Burney was perhaps too harsh in calling him an imitator; but Reichardt, although not noted for his fair opinions, seems to have been close to a reasonable assessment: 'Graun merely worked according to his king's taste. Whatever did not please Frederick was struck out, even if it happened to be the best piece in the opera. Since the king adhered stubbornly to his own unchanging preferences, he could not allow Graun the slightest variety or freedom'. In his church music – especially the Passion *Der Tod Jesu* (today acknowledged his masterpiece), and the *Te Deum* – and in his secular cantatas, Graun was able to express himself in a more individual vein. He also wrote songs and much instrumental music, though here his brother Johann Gottlieb is regarded as the more accomplished.

See also MONTEZUMA (i); for illustration see BERLIN, fig.1.

unless otherwise stated, Italian opere serie first performed at Berlin, Königliches Opernhaus, MSS in D-B or Bds

Sancio und Sinilde (J. U. König, after F. Silvani: *Il miglior d'ogni amore per il peggior d'ogni odio*), Brunswick, 3 Feb 1727
Polydorus (J. S. Müller), Brunswick, sum. 1726/8
Iphigenia in Aulis, 1728 (C. H. Postel), Brunswick, wint. 1731
Scipio Africanus (Fiedeler/Postel), Wolfenbüttel, sum. 1732
Lo specchio della fedeltà [Timareta] (A. Zeno), Salzdahlum, Brunswick, 13 June 1733, only lib. extant
Pharao Tubaetes (J. S. Müller, after Zeno), Brunswick, Feb 1735, D-W
Rodelinda, regina de' langobardi (G. G. Bottarelli, after A. Salvi), Potsdam, Schloss, 13 Dec 1741
Venere e Cupido (prol., Bottarelli), Potsdam, Schloss, 6 Jan 1742
Cesare e Cleopatra (Bottarelli, after P. Corneille: *La mort de Pompée*), 7 Dec 1742
Artaserse (P. Metastasio), 2 Dec 1743
Catone in Utica (Metastasio), 24 Jan 1744
La festa del Imeneo (prol., Bottarelli), 18 July 1744
Alessandro e Poro (Metastasio), 1744
Lucio Papirio (Zeno), 4 Jan 1745
Adriano in Siria (Metastasio), 7 Jan 1746
Demofoonte, re di Tracia (Metastasio), 17 Jan 1746; incl. 3 arias by Frederick II
Cajo Fabricio (Zeno), 2 Dec 1746

Le feste galanti (L. de Villati, after J. F. Duché de Vancy), 6 April 1747
Il re pastore [recit., duet, 2 choruses] (pastorale, 1, Villati), Charlottenburg, 4 Aug 1747, collab. Frederick II, J. J. Quantz and C. Nichelmann
Cinna (Villati, after Corneille), 1 Jan 1748
L'Europa galante (Villati, after A. H. de Lamotte), Schloss Monbijou, 27 March 1748
Ifigenia in Aulide (Villati and Frederick II, after J. Racine), 13 Dec 1748
Angelica e Medoro (Villati, after A. Ariosto), 27 March 1749
Coriolano (Villati and F. Algarotti, after Frederick II), 19 Dec 1749
Fetonte (Villati and Algarotti, after P. Quinault), 29 March 1750; ov. pubd in Raccolta delle più nuove composizioni (Leipzig, 1756) as Sinfonia
Il Mitridate (Villati, ? after Racine), 18 Dec 1750
L'Armida (Villati, after Quinault), 27 March 1751
Britannico (Villati, after Racine), 17 Dec 1751
L'Orfeo (Villati, after M. du Boulair), 27 March 1752
Il giudizio di Paride (pastorale, 1, Villati and Algarotti), Charlottenburg, 25 June 1752, ? 1 aria by Frederick II; ov. pubd (Leipzig, 1757) as Sinfonia
Silla (Frederick II, after Duché de Vancy: *Scylla*, trans. G. Tagliazucchi), 27 March 1753
Semiramide (Tagliazucchi, after Voltaire), 27 March 1754
Montezuma (Frederick II, after Voltaire: *Alzire, ou Les Américains*, trans. Tagliazucchi), 6 Jan 1755; ed. in DDT, xv (1904)
Ezio (Metastasio, rev. ?Tagliazucchi), 1 April 1755
I fratelli nemici (Frederick II, completed and trans. Tagliazucchi after Racine: *La Thébaïde, ou Les frères ennemis*), 9 Jan 1756
La Merope (Frederick II, completed and trans. Tagliazucchi, after Voltaire: *Mérope*), 27 March 1756

Music in: Galatea ed Acide (1748); Il trionfo della fedeltà (1753)

*

BurneyGN
J. F. Agricola: biographical sketch of Graun as introduction to Kirnberger's edn of *Duetti, terzetti, quintetti, sestetti ed alcuni chori* (Berlin and Königsberg, 1773–4); repr. as 'Lebenslauf des Herrn Karl Heinrich Graun' in J. N. Forkel: *Musikalisch-kritische Bibliothek*, iii (Gotha, 1779), 286–99
L. Schneider: *Geschichte des Berliner Opernhauses* (Berlin, 1852)
A. Mayer-Reinach: 'C. H. Graun als Opernkomponist', *SIMG*, i (1899–1900), 446–529
C. Mennicke: 'Zur Biographie der Brüder Graun', *NZM*, lxxi (1904), 129–31
H. Klüppelholz: 'Die Eroberung Mexicos aus preussischer Sicht: zum Libretto der Oper *Montezuma* von Friedrich dem Grossen', *Oper als Text: romanistische Beiträge zur Libretto-Forschung*, ed. A. Gier (Heidelberg, 1986), 65–94   E. EUGENE HELM

Graupner, (Johann) Christoph (*b* Kirchberg, Saxony, 13 Jan 1683; *d* Darmstadt, 10 May 1760). German composer. He received his early musical training in Kirchberg and Reichenbach, then attended the Thomasschule in Leipzig (1696–1704). His teachers there included Kuhnau, for whom he also worked as copyist and amanuensis. After a period at the University of Leipzig he moved in 1706 to Hamburg. In Leipzig he had already made firm and artistically stimulating friendships with G. P. Telemann and Gottfried Grünewald, later to be his vice-Kapellmeister at Darmstadt.

At Hamburg in 1707 Graupner succeeded J. C. Schiefferdecker as harpsichordist of the Gänsemarkt opera company. Between 1707 and 1709 Graupner composed five operas for this theatre and possibly collaborated with Keiser on others. His librettists included Hinrich Hinsch (*Dido, Königin von Carthago*) and Barthold Feind, a jurist, satirist and aesthetician. In 1709, in response to an invitation from Ernst Ludwig, Landgrave of Hessen-Darmstadt, Graupner accepted the position of vice-Kapellmeister to W. C. Briegel, whom he succeeded on the latter's death in 1712. The early years of Graupner's long Darmstadt incumbency were centred on operatic composition; he wrote several new operas, *Berenice und Lucilla* (1710, with text in German and Italian), *Telemach* (1711), *La costanza vince l'inganno* (1715, with overture and ballets by the Landgrave Ernst Ludwig) and possibly *Adone* (1719), as well as a further untitled and unlocated opera listed by Brockpähler for the year 1709. Graupner composed no more operas after 1719, but remained extraordinarily prolific, producing hundreds of cantatas (mostly sacred) and instrumental works. His reputation attracted a number of important composers, including J. F. Fasch, as his pupils.

As an opera composer, Graupner began his career with works in the eclectic north German tradition of Kusser, Keiser, Mattheson and G. C. Schürmann, drawing on the Italian and French styles; *La costanza vince l'inganno* is an entirely Italian setting though including French-style numbers. As early as his Hamburg days, Graupner's operas enjoyed considerable public acclaim, the *Hamburg Relations-Courier* (30 November 1708) reporting of his *Bellerophon* how 'a vast public such as has not been seen for some years attended the performance'. His Hamburg operas sometimes displayed particular skill in the marshalling of large formal structures, for example Act 2 scene i of *Dido, Königin von Carthago*, which is a chaconne over a developed *lamento* bass with music for quartet, individual soloists and duet. In *Antiochus und Stratonica* a scene (Act 1.vi) is cast as a set of variants on the opening march theme, including entrées, dances, choruses, an arioso, an aria and finally a chaconne. The libretto of the opera *Simson* suggests some effective dramatic use of the chorus. Above all, Graupner's Hamburg operas, following Keiser's, were remarkable for the emancipation and development of instrumental motif and the employment of specific obbligato combinations to impart dramatic continuity.

See also DIDO, KÖNIGIN VON CARTHAGO.

HG – Hamburg, Theater am Gänsemarkt

Dido, Königin von Carthago (Spl, 3, H. Hinsch), HG, 1707, *D-Bds**, *US-Wc*

Bellerophon, oder Das in die preussische Krone verwandelte Wagenstirn (B. Feind, after T. Corneille), HG, 28 Nov 1708

L'amore ammalato/Die kränkende Liebe, oder Antiochus und Stratonica (musicalisches Schauspiel, Feind, after L. Assarini and P. Corneille), HG, 1708, *D-Bds**, *US-Wc*; 1 aria by R. Keiser

Il fido amico/Der getreue Freund Hercules und Theseus (Breymann), HG, 1708

Der Fall des grossen Richters in Israel, Simson, oder Die abgekühlte Liebesrache der Deborah (Feind), HG, 1709

Berenice und Lucilla, oder Das tugendhafte Lieben (Osiander, after A. Aureli), Darmstadt, 4 March 1710; see Brockpähler

Telemach (German-Italian), Darmstadt, 16 Feb 1711

La costanza vince l'inganno, Darmstadt, 1715, *D-DS**; revived 1719, *Ga*

Untitled opera, Darmstadt, 1709; see Brockpähler

Arias in Keiser: Der angenehme Betrug, oder Der Carneval in Venedig, 1707, and Die blut-dürstige Rache, oder Heliates und Olympia, 1709; see Wolff

Doubtful: Adone, Darmstadt, 1719; see Brockpähler

Hochfürstliche Hessen-Darmstädter Staats- und Adresskalender auf das Jahr 1781, Anh.19ff

E. Pasqué: 'Geschichte der Musik und des Theaters am Hofe zu Darmstadt', *Die Muse*, ii (1854), 629

F. Noack: 'Die Opern von Christoph Graupner in Darmstadt', *Kongressbericht: Leipzig 1925*, 252–9

H. Kaiser: *Barocktheater in Darmstadt* (Darmstadt, 1951)

H. C. Wolff: *Die Barockoper in Hamburg* (Wolfenbüttel, 1957), 306ff

R. Brockpähler: *Handbuch zur Geschichte der Barockoper in Deutschland* (Emsdetten, 1964)

A. D. McCredie: 'Christoph Graupner as Opera Composer', *MMA*, i (1966), 74–116

——: 'Christoph Graupner's Opern: Hintergründe, Textvorlagen und Musik', *Christoph Graupner, Hofkapellmeister in Darmstadt, 1709–1760*, ed. O. Bill, Beiträge zur mittelrheinischen Musikgeschichte, xxviii (Mainz, 1987), 269–302

ANDREW D. McCREDIE

Graveure, Louis [Douthitt, Wilfried] (*b* London, 18 March 1888; *d* San Francisco, 12 April 1968). English baritone, later tenor, of Belgian extraction. He came to prominence under the name of Graveure through concert work in New York, where his origins were regarded as an interesting mystery. When it was claimed that he was Wilfried Douthitt, the unsuccessful male lead in the first New York production of Cuvillier's operetta *The Lilac Domino*, the singer denied this identity, though it is now accepted as the truth (Graveure being his mother's maiden name). From 1915 his oratorio work and concert tours in the USA and Europe brought him high praise. Then, in 1928, within a week of singing as a baritone, he made a second début, also in concert, as a tenor. An operatic career followed principally in Germany, where he joined the Charlottenburg Opera in Berlin, singing such roles as Lohengrin, Don José and Lyonel in Flotow's *Martha*. He also appeared in German films, and later taught in San Francisco and Los Angeles. His recordings, though variable in quality, generally command interest, especially those of him as baritone.

J. B. STEANE

Gray, Linda Esther (*b* Greenock, 29 May 1948). Scottish soprano. She studied in Glasgow, at the London Opera Centre and with Eva Turner, singing Mařenka and Poppaea in 1970 at Sadler's Wells while still a student. She sang Mimì (1972) for Glyndebourne Touring Opera, then Mozart's First Lady (1973) and Electra (1974) at Glyndebourne. With Scottish Opera, she sang Donna Elvira, Countess Almaviva, Eva and Ariadne; with the WNO, Isolde (1979) and Kundry (1983); with the ENO, Micaëla, Tosca, Leonore, Aida, Isolde and Brünnhilde (*Die Walküre*). She made her Covent Garden début as Gutrune in 1980, returning as Sieglinde in 1982. The possessor of a lovely natural voice and great musical gifts, she prepared Turandot for Scottish Opera in 1984, but withdrew from the performances and suspended her singing career.

ELIZABETH FORBES

Graz. Second largest city in Austria and capital of the province of Styria. Its geographical position and administrative importance, together with a Hofkapelle showing strong Italian influence as early as about 1600, might have marked it out to absorb the new form of opera quite early and disseminate it on the Austrian side of the Alps. One reason this did not occur was that the Archduke Ferdinand became Emperor in 1619 and moved his court to Vienna. Several dramatic performances with music took place in the 17th century. The four works by P. R. Pignatta given between 1688 and 1694 at the castle of the Princes of Eggenberg, for example, may have included true operas. But the first solid evidence that Graz had opera in the modern sense dates from 1728, when the Vienna Hofkapelle performed *La forza dell'amicizia, ovvero Pilade ed Oreste* by Antonio Caldara and Georg Reutter, at a ceremony of homage to Emperor Charles VI. From then on there were increasingly frequent performances of dramatic works, including operas, by touring companies. They were given in temporary wooden structures or in public squares or rented halls.

In spring 1736 Pietro Mingotti built the first opera house in Graz. For ten years he and his brother Angelo staged three performances a week, producing works by Galuppi, Latilla, Pergolesi, Vinci, Giacomelli, Scalabrini, Hasse and others – it is possible that Vivaldi also was active there. Small Italian opera companies, including those of Giuseppe Giordani (1747), Biaggio Barzanti and Gervasio Silani (1749), Angelo Giropodi (1752–3), Francesco Orci (1754), Francesco Crosa (1756–7) and Sanbo Gianvigliord (1760), continued to appear. Librettos were translated into German quite early, and musical adaptations of works by German-speaking composers, particularly those who wrote in the French style, were given, such as *Das Oracul* in 1763–4, J. B. Savio's *Die Zigeuner* in 1766 and K. W. Wratny's *Die drey Sultaninnen* in 1772–4 (the original composers of these works are not known). The theatre passed into civic hands in 1776 with the establishment of the Landschaftstheater, which staged opera as well as Singspiels, drama and ballet. Here the audience could see not only operas by composers now almost forgotten but also the international repertory of the time, from Paisiello, Piccinni, Salieri, Philidor and Grétry to Martín y Soler, Gluck, Dittersdorf and Mozart. (The performances of Mozart given in Graz in 1788 seem to have been particularly significant in introducing his style into Slovenia.)

The theatre's first native director was Franz Eduard Hysel, who held the post from 1813 to 1819, and staged productions not only of Mozart and even Beethoven but also of Rossini in 1816. Like most other locally-born directors before and after him, he was not a success in the post, but he was responsible for the first performances there of Weber, in 1822. The theatre burnt down at Christmas in 1823, but was soon reconstructed. Johann Stöger was the first director (1823–33) to build up a genuine operatic repertory; it gave clear precedence to Italian over French and German opera. Johann Nestroy appeared as a singer at this time, before changing his career and going to Vienna to write comedies (thereafter, Graz was regarded by singers as a springboard to larger theatres).

In the mid-19th century, opera in Graz, and indeed throughout Austria, was rather neglected. But the first Austrian performance of *Tannhäuser*, in Graz on 20 January 1854, was a notable occasion, and since then the city has considered itself particularly Wagnerian. During the period 1854–64 Anton Balvansky built up a new company whose primary aim was light entertainment; it gave the first performances in the city of Offenbach operettas. Eduard Kreibig (1864–76) relegated the old Italian and French operas to the background, produced the entire works of Verdi, and shifted interest to German opera with works by Lortzing, Meyerbeer and Wagner. This repertory reflects a certain division of labour between the opera house and the Thalia-Theater, opened in 1864, which concentrated mainly on the lighter genres of operetta, burlesque and farce. From 1866 to 1870 Kreibig also leased the Thalia-Theater (it was taken over by the city of Graz in 1870 and renamed the Stadttheater). The repertories of the two large theatres did not separate into distinct genres until the 20th century, when the former Land-

schaftstheater devoted itself entirely to drama and the Stadttheater became the opera house.

In 1887 the federal state and the city established joint direction of the two theatres, the preliminary to their later combination into a single economic unit. This development was encouraged by the increase in operatic performances under Heinrich Gottinger (1893–9). In 1898–9 the Stadttheater was partly demolished and rebuilt by the famous Viennese theatre architects Fellner and Helmer. The first Austrian performance of Strauss's *Salome* took place in this building, the present opera house. Strauss's *Intermezzo*, *Die schweigsame Frau*, *Daphne* and *Ariadne auf Naxos* also had their first Austrian performances here, as did works by Weinberger, Pfitzner, Reutter, Britten, Kodály, Orff, Ibert, Dallapiccola, Sutermeister, Prokofiev, Busoni, Henze, Fortner, Krenek, Ligeti and others. Premières have naturally been mainly of works by Austrian composers (Wilhelm Kienzl, Sepp Rosegger, Ludwig Uray, Hanns Holenia, Waldemar Bloch, Franz Mixa and Ivan Eröd). The Graz Opera is the only Austrian company other than the Vienna Staatsoper to play all the year round. Many well-known singers have appeared on its stage, including Emil Scaria, Amalie Materna, Joseph Tichatschek, Josef von Manowarda, Hertha Töpper and Gundula Janowitz. Conductors who have appeared with the Graz Opera include Ernst von Schuch, Carl Muck, Franz Schalk, Karl Böhm and Hans Rosbaud.

The annual autumn festival Steirischer Herbst (founded 1968) gave the first staged performance of Prokofiev's *Maddalena* (1981) and the première of Cerha's *Der Rattenfänger* (1987); the summer festival Styriarte Graz (founded 1985) occasionally presents early operas (Monteverdi's *Combattimento di Tancredi e Clorinda* and Purcell's *Dido and Aeneas* in 1986).

*

R. List: *Oper und Operette in Graz* (Graz, 1966)

K. Fleischmann: 'Das steirische Berufstheater im 18. Jahrhundert', *Theatergeschichte Österreichs*, v/1 (1974)

E. Tarjan: 'Oper und Singspiel in Graz', *Musik in der Steiermark*, ed. R. Flotzinger (Graz, 1980), 275–96

R. Flotzinger: 'Die Anfänge des deutschsprachigen Musiktheaters in Graz zwischen Publikumsnähe und Aufklärung', *Musikološki zbornik XVIII* [Ljubljana] (1982), 23–41

Theater in Graz, Historisches Jb der Stadt Graz, ed. H. Valentinitsch and F. Bouvier, xv (Graz, 1984)

S. Franz: *Vom Thalia-Theater zum Theater am Stadtpark* (diss., U. of Graz, 1989)   RUDOLF FLOTZINGER

Graziani, Francesco (*b* Fermo, 26 April 1828; *d* Fermo, 30 June 1901). Italian baritone, brother of Lodovico Graziani. He made his début in 1851 at Ascoli Piceno in Donizetti's *Gemma di Vergy* and the following season sang at Macerata in Verdi's *I masnadieri*. He appeared at the Théâtre Italien, Paris, from 1853 to 1861 and made his London début at Covent Garden in 1855 as Don Carlo in *Ernani*, continuing to sing there regularly for the next 25 years. Though his repertory was enormous, ranging from Mozart (*Don Giovanni* and *Le nozze di Figaro*), Rossini (*Otello*, *La donna del lago* and *Guillaume Tell*), Donizetti (*Lucia di Lammermoor*, *Linda di Chamounix* and *La favorite*), and Bellini (*La sonnambula* and *I puritani*) to Flotow's *Martha*, Gounod's *Faust*, Meyerbeer's *L'Africaine* and Thomas' *Hamlet*, it was in Verdi roles that he excelled. He was the first Luna in Paris (1854) and in London (1855), and he also sang Germont, Rigoletto and Renato in both capitals. At Dublin in 1859 he sang the title role in the first performance of *Macbeth* in the British Isles. He sang Don Carlo in the première of *La forza del destino* at St Petersburg (1862), Posa in the first London *Don Carlos* (1867) and Amonasro in the first London *Aida* (1876). His final appearance at Covent Garden was in *La traviata* in 1880. He was said to possess one of the finest baritone voices heard in the second half of the 19th century.

H. Chorley: *Thirty Years' Musical Recollections* (London, 1862)
A. Soubies: *Le Théâtre-Italien de 1801 à 1913* (Paris, 1913)
H. Rosenthal: *Two Centuries of Opera at Covent Garden* (London, 1958)
C. Osborne: *The Complete Operas of Verdi* (London, 1969)

ELIZABETH FORBES

Graziani, Lodovico (*b* Fermo, 14 Nov 1820; *d* Fermo, 15 May 1885). Italian tenor. He made his début at Bologna in 1845 and appeared at the Théâtre Italien, Paris, in 1851 as Gennaro (*Lucrezia Borgia*). He sang Alfredo at the first performance of *La traviata* at La Fenice, Venice (1853), and made his début at La Scala in 1855 in Apolloni's *L'ebreo*; he also appeared there as the Duke in *Rigoletto* and as Henri in *Les vêpres siciliennes* (given as *Giovanna di Guzman*). He sang the title role in Donizetti's *Dom Sébastien* at the S Carlo, Naples, in 1856 and returned to La Scala in 1862 for *Un ballo in maschera*. In 1865 he sang in the first Italian performance of Meyerbeer's *L'Africaine* at Bologna.

ELIZABETH FORBES

Great Britain.

1. General. 2. Foreign opera. 3. English opera. 4. Scotland and Wales.

1. GENERAL. Opera does not have deep roots in Britain. Only in the last hundred years, at most, has a flourishing tradition of English-language opera, in the fullest, continental, sense, existed. Most writers have been tempted to treat the earlier history in a teleological fashion: as a series of faltering steps towards the presumed goal, reached perhaps with *Peter Grimes* in 1945. They have singled out the rare examples of all-sung opera in English before 1900 as brave attempts at 'progress', generally followed by a deplorable relapse, which then has to be explained by some combination of prejudices and hostile forces.

Yet this mainstream opera towards which the English are supposed to have been feebly groping was, after all, a problematic and often unsatisfying form, in which music's tendency to run away with the show was a matter for reproach and periodic adjustment. The inventors of opera, and its reformers in each era, set out to tame music – to keep it subservient to drama. They had very limited success. So it should not cause surprise that a nation with a powerful school of drama, where music enjoyed an established but subordinate place, tended to resist encroachments from a form in which it seemed that dramatic truth was so readily sacrificed to musical ends. Foreign opera was welcomed in some circles, and many of its individual features were absorbed into English musical theatre. But an English opera was often felt by critics, probably speaking for the majority of theatregoers, to be a malformed hybrid, aping foreign musical achievements at too great a cost to English theatrical virtues.

English resistance to opera in the 18th century (as Thomas McGeary has shown) was by no means a matter of xenophobic prejudice but was based on a carefully argued intellectual position: that drama, as inherited from ancient Greece, must be rational and intelligible, and must inculcate nobility and virtue. These were sufficient grounds for objecting to coloratura singing, recitative, da capo arias, meaningless repetition of words, interruption of a dramatic plot for purely musical interludes, and artificially contrived happy endings, all of which were part and parcel of Italian *opera seria*. In addition there was a justifiable feeling that all-sung opera and recitative were alien to English language, culture and temperament: 'Throughout the eighteenth century', Roger Fiske has written, 'most Englishmen continued to believe that in opera the plot should be carried forward by means of spoken dialogue. It was a belief that sprang from Restoration practice, and it was scarcely shaken by all-sung entertainments from Italy.'

If we consider the history of English musical theatre from an English point of view, we see it at first identical with the history of the theatre itself, then gradually diverging from 'legitimate' drama as the amount and complexity of music increased. But always the basis of the music was the simple song, chorus or dance, well within the powers of actors and the understanding of auditors, more or less related to the dramatic action but not usually a vehicle for the central matter of plot, character or situation. The music was incidental to the drama. It was not incidental to the total experience in the theatre, any more than a coloratura aria was incidental to an *opera seria*, an entrée to a *tragédie lyrique*, or a symphonic development to a Wagnerian myth. But the drama was free of the shackles of music. It was indeed this freely developed English drama – fundamentally Shakespearean, but with neo-classical modifications – that continental composers in the 19th century would seek to shape into operatic moulds.

'Spoken drama with music' accurately describes not only Elizabethan choirboy plays and Stuart masques; it covers Shakespeare's plays themselves. Their occasional songs and dances were greatly augmented when they were remade in the Restoration period, and the all-sung masques then incorporated into *Macbeth* and *The Tempest* remained an integral part of those plays until the mid-19th century. Similarly in Purcell's semi-operas the music, however potent as an intensifier of feeling and as a symbol of conflicting forces in the play, does not carry the plot and is sung and danced by minor or allegorical characters.

When Italian opera gained a secure foothold in London, after 1710, English entertainments of all kinds continued to grow alongside. The pantomime and the all-sung afterpiece were two such developments, but the momentous event was *The Beggar's Opera* (1728). This was no opera, of course, but a synthesis of music and drama radically different from that of opera and wonderfully suited to English taste and experience. Now the main characters could indeed sing, but in a way that was neither unnatural nor distracting from the progress of the play. By choosing popular tunes of all kinds (including a few from Italian operas) John Gay, in one brilliant stroke, both placed the music within the reach of English actors and tapped a rich source of musical allusion instantly recognizable to his audience.

Gay's success could not be replicated, if only because he had creamed off most of the best-known songs and tied them permanently to their new words. Though *The Beggar's Opera* itself never died, the creative phase of true ballad opera lasted only a decade. The Licensing Act of 1737, however, by confining 'legitimate drama' to Drury Lane and Covent Garden, compelled the 'minor' theatres to incorporate music into their plays, and thus encouraged further development along these lines. Strophic ballads, whether old or new, are still found alongside italianate arias in the burlettas, musical dramas and even 'operas' of 1760–1830. They persist, along with spoken dialogue, through the Romantic period. They are still there in the works of Gilbert and Sullivan, and in the conscious ballad-opera revivals of Vaughan Williams, Holst, Tippett and Bush. A more popular progeny can also be traced, through 19th-century burlesque, melodrama and farce, to modern musical comedy, pantomime and revue.

How much of this vast body of entertainment is to be called 'opera' is entirely a matter of taste or convenience. Composers and playwrights themselves did not use the term with any great consistency; nor have critics and historians. To apply the broadest definition of opera, 'drama expressed through music', is to invite vagueness. To impose the narrowest criterion – that opera must be all-sung – is to reduce English opera between 1762 and 1891 to a mere handful of unsuccessful works. One may argue that what was done in English theatres at that time was not opera but something else with its own values and norms. But for the present purpose an 'English opera' is a work that attempts to apply the methods of mainstream continental opera to a dramatic libretto in English.

No account of English opera can be true or balanced unless it is seen against the native tradition, which at all times has supplied the bulk of musical entertainment in the theatre. Any importing or imitating of mainstream opera was doomed to fail unless it could either accommodate itself to this tradition or command subsidies so large as to be independent of it. English opera has joined the mainstream only as, in the postwar generations, the English – and the Scots and Welsh – have participated in the comprehensive historicism and individual experimentation that now govern the arts in advanced societies.

2. FOREIGN OPERA. Despite the deep-seated, widespread and persistent English hostility to the genre, London, since the early 18th century, has been one of the most important centres in the world for the performance of opera. Although the court supported opera, often substantially, during the 18th century, Britain never had a court opera of the kind that had nurtured the beginnings of the genre and continued to support it in continental capitals until quite recent times. But the landed aristocracy and leading mercantile classes were so numerous, wealthy, urbanized and cosmopolitan that they could successfully pool their resources to support foreign-language opera as an exclusive and semi-private seasonal entertainment of high prestige.

The process began in the first decade of the 18th century, when the leaders of fashion were determined to import Italian opera. It appeared first in translation, then in a mixture of Italian songs with vernacular dialogue (as at Hamburg). In 1710 came the first performance of an opera wholly in Italian (the pasticcio *Almahide*). Next year the success of Handel's *Rinaldo* removed any doubt that foreign-language opera could succeed – with the help of drastically reduced recitatives, and translated librettos made available to patrons as they entered the theatre. The Royal Academy of Music (1719–29), which despite its name was in effect a joint-stock company for the production of operas,

commissioned a series of works from Handel and from Ariosti and Bononcini as well, and paid huge sums to attract the most famous castratos and prima donnas of Europe. Its many successors were generally short-lived and sometimes coexisted in rivalry, but between them they managed to keep an almost unbroken run of Italian operas in production until the 1890s. The principal venue was the larger Haymarket Theatre (successively named Queen's, King's and Her Majesty's) until it was joined by the Theatre Royal, Covent Garden (Royal Italian Opera), in 1847.

Although Italian operas in the theatre never penetrated far below the upper crust of society, arias from them were published for separate use and adapted for English operas, keyboard solos, and even hymns. So they became a truly popular part of the English musical experience and exercised a profound influence, reaching even those large classes of people whose religion or sense of propriety would never have allowed them to enter a theatre.

Handel gave up composing operas in 1741, but London continued to attract a series of distinguished composers such as Gluck, Galuppi, J. C. Bach, Sacchini, Storace and Paisiello. *Opera seria* was the principal type until the 1820s, but increasingly after 1760 relied on pasticcios, in which the music director of the theatre would adapt old arias to a new libretto. *Opera buffa* made slower headway, reaching its height only with the coming of Rossini. Very few new Italian works were produced after 1790: the opera Haydn wrote for London was never performed. The general pattern in the 19th century was for operas to be mounted only after they had succeeded in Italian cities or in Paris. Rare exceptions were Balfe's *Falstaff* (1838) and Verdi's *I masnadieri* (1847). Through much of the Victorian period, both Her Majesty's and Covent Garden restricted themselves to opera in Italian for their main seasons. German, French, Russian and even English operas had to be translated before they could be presented. The Italian opera company often went on a summer tour to several provincial cities.

Seasons of opera in German were occasionally given from 1829 onwards, and in the 1860s French operetta was frequently produced in the original language. A landmark year was 1882, when the *Ring* cycle and other major Wagner operas were given in German, effectively ending the Italian hegemony. For many decades after this the issue of original language versus English translation was debated. Today the two schools of thought are represented in London by Covent Garden and the Coliseum respectively, but the influence of recordings (which allow the listener to peruse a translated text at his leisure), subtitles on film and television, supertitles in the theatre, and the growing pressure for historical authenticity have clearly given the edge to original-language performance, which has come to predominate in the regional companies. Foreign opera, now as always, is for the cognoscenti, but their number is constantly growing. An ever-widening knowledge of operatic history has led, on the one hand, to the revival of operas of almost every style and period, sometimes supported by specialized bodies; and on the other, to an increasing emphasis on originality in both composition and production of modern operas.

In the present century Covent Garden has been the main centre for large-scale productions of the great continental operas. From 1910 until 1939 it was largely dominated by the influence of Thomas Beecham, whose personal fortune helped to save it from financial ruin. Since 1945 it has been a national rather than a commercial house, with an ever-increasing state endowment administered by the Arts Council of Great Britain. Glyndebourne Opera, founded in 1934, has offered more intimate productions on a smaller scale, suited above all to Mozart.

3. ENGLISH OPERA. In the 17th century there were a few instances of operatic incursions on the English stage. It is said that Ben Jonson's masque *Lovers Made Men* (1617) was set in recitative by Nicholas Lanier, but the music is lost, as is Henry Lawes's score for William Davenant's *Siege of Rhodes* (?1658). The latter, usually treated as the first English opera, was cast in that form in order to avoid the Commonwealth ban on plays, and was converted into a spoken play after the Restoration of Charles II in 1660.

This king desired to establish the kind of court opera he had experienced during his exile in France. The semi-operas of Locke are not very far removed in general plan from Lully's *comédies-ballets*, and in 1685 the sole specimen of an English *tragédie lyrique* was performed: *Albion and Albanius*, with a libretto by Dryden and music by Luis Grabu. It was a complete failure. French influence was dominant, also, in two miniature all-sung masterpieces of the era, Blow's *Venus and Adonis* (c1683) and Purcell's *Dido and Aeneas* (c1685), both written for private performance. Many writers have felt it a tragedy that England's greatest dramatic composer, Purcell, lived at a time when the public playhouses offered him no opportunity to develop a true English opera. *King Arthur* and his other great semi-operas gave plenty of scope to his more extrovert sense of theatre, but none to the intensity of feeling with which he could invest a tragic character like Dido.

Semi-operas continued for a time after Purcell's death in 1695, but were doomed by the arrangement finalized in 1710, by which the Lord Chamberlain allowed Italian operas at the Haymarket and plays at Drury Lane (Covent Garden was added by the 1737 Act). This had the effect at first of discouraging mixtures that employed both singers and actors. The masque lingered on for several decades, especially for private or royal occasions. Congreve's masque *The Judgment of Paris*, written for a prize competition in 1701, was set by Eccles, Finger, Daniel Purcell and Weldon as contestants, and later by Sammartini and Arne. It is not known whether Handel's *Acis and Galatea* was staged at Cannons in 1718, but other masques by Pepusch and Galliard certainly were performed with action. Arne's *Comus* (after Milton, 1738) and his remarkably popular *Alfred* (1740), the source of 'Rule, Britannia', have a retrospective flavour that was already beginning to colour English patriotism.

The long Italian dominance was marked by fitful attempts to produce serious English 'answers'. Fully-fledged *opere serie* in English were rare: there were a few at the beginning, led by *Arsinoe* (1705) by Clayton and others; another group in the 1760s, of which only Arne's *Artaxerxes* (1762) enjoyed any success; and a lone effort in 1792, Storace's *Dido, Queen of Carthage*, whose music has not survived. (A large proportion of the music of early English opera is irretrievably lost. Few works were published in full, and many manuscripts were destroyed in fires, especially those at Covent Garden and Drury Lane in 1808–9.)

A strong effort to develop a less derivative style of serious English opera was mounted at two minor theatres (the Little Theatre in the Haymarket and Lincoln's Inn Fields) in 1732–3, with seven full-length works by Lampe, J. C. Smith and Arne. One of the most gifted dramatic composers of the age, Maurice Greene, failed to gain a proper hearing for his works. All-sung afterpieces were occasionally successful throughout the century, as were such burlesques as Lampe's *The Dragon of Wantley* (1737).

A new era began in 1762 with Arne's *Love in a Village*, a succession of 41 songs, mostly borrowed, some new, with spoken dialogue to connect them. Its popularity lasted until the 1840s, during which time it was a model for countless successors. The type has been called 'dialogue opera' (Roger Fiske), but earlier writers used the term 'ballad opera'. As time went on the music gradually became more operatic. Songs were fully orchestrated, and were given introductions or even ritornellos. The Linleys' *The Duenna* (1775) has richly scored arrangements of Scottish and Irish airs as well as arias borrowed from operas by Giordani and Rauzzini. Extended finales were introduced, the first in Arnold's *Maid of the Mill* (1765), one of the best in Storace's *The Pirates* (1792), and one of the most ambitious in Act 2 of Bishop's *Cortez* (1823), depicting a wild scene of human sacrifice interrupted before its consummation. Bishop also sometimes composed italianate 'grand scenas', complete with accompanied recitative, for the leading female singer, and his operas nearly always included at least one glee and some choruses.

From the time of Burney's adaptation of Rousseau's *Le devin du village* as *The Cunning Man* (1766), there was a growing tendency to borrow both plots and music from French operas; after 1790 Germany too became a prime source. Exotic settings and characters also became as popular as aggressively British ones. Harems appeared as early as 1758 in Arne's *Sultan*, a negro in Dibdin's *The Padlock* (1768), West Indians in Arnold's *Inkle and Yarico* (1787) and American Indians in Storace's *The Cherokee* (1794). The same composer's *Haunted Tower* (1789) brought Gothic horror, complete with ghost, to the English stage, along with a clearly Mozartian idiom. In 1802 melodrama was added to the growing multiplicity of genres with Busby's *Tale of Mystery*. This form was distinguished by the extended use of action music, with or without spoken dialogue superimposed.

The first third of the 19th century is usually regarded as a low point in English stage history, for both drama and opera. Wholesale borrowings and adaptations continued, and Bishop, the dominant composer of the time, took freely from the operas of Mozart, Boieldieu, Spohr, Rossini and Meyerbeer. His adaptation of *Don Giovanni* as *The Libertine* (1817) was treated by critics as a revival of Shadwell's play of that name with more or less appropriate music: a reminder of the fact that music remained an essential feature of almost every theatrical production. It was the music director's responsibility to find and adapt suitable music, from whatever source he might think appropriate. Shakespeare's plays were also adorned by Bishop with a miscellany of music in five new productions of 1816–24. In his original operas such as *The Maniac* (1810) and *Clari* (1823), Bishop proved himself a clever imitator of foreign styles and practices as well as earlier English models, and he was particularly skilful in inventing descriptive music. When Weber was commissioned to write an English opera for London (*Oberon*, 1826),

Bishop responded by producing his most elaborate and fully composed opera, *Aladdin*.

In course of time the robust style of the English popular song had gradually paled, as can be seen even in such accomplished operatic 'ballads' as Bishop's 'Come live with me' from the stage piece *The Comedy of Errors* (adapted, 1819) or Horn's 'Cherry ripe' from *Paul Pry* (1826). A trend more noticeable to patriotic critics was the ever increasing tendency to fill the programmes of the 'English' theatres with adaptations of foreign operas. In 1834 a reaction began when S. J. Arnold, the composer's son, reopened the English Opera House at the Lyceum Theatre and began to commission full-length, serious operas from English composers. The enterprise failed after a few years, but it was soon revived and was followed by a series of others, the most important being the Pyne-Harrison company and its successor, the Royal English Opera (1856–64). The precarious nature of these efforts was put down by contemporaries to the absence of patronage by the upper classes, who remained loyal to Italian opera.

The Romantic school of English opera thus instituted was in a sense a continuation of the Bishop era. Spoken dialogue remained, as did the by now sentimental ballad and glee, the arias with occasional recitative, the ensembles and the extended finale. The plots continued to be adapted from continental operas, plays or ballets already known to the public. But new stylistic influences came into the picture: Weber, Meyerbeer, Verdi, Gounod. In Balfe's *The Bohemian Girl* (1843) and Loder's *Raymond and Agnes* (1855) a new order of dramatic intensity and passion could be felt, often triumphing over lyrics of unexampled banality. Romantic nationalism made its English début in the operas of Macfarren, who, beginning with *King Charles II* (1849), resolutely chose English subjects; he even introduced tags from folksongs to give an overtly national colour.

In 1855 a new style of entertainment was started by Thomas and Priscilla German Reed, aimed at those sections of the public who still (with some reason) associated theatres with vice and immorality. They later presented works of both Sullivan and Gilbert, separately, at an early stage in their careers. This experience undoubtedly helped the two men to find a new public for opera in the respectable and sophisticated middle-class family, which in Britain had not previously made a habit of patronizing theatres. Gilbert from the start set himself publicly against the risqué humour of burlesque and French operetta.

The year 1875 saw the founding of both the Carl Rosa touring opera company and Richard D'Oyly Carte's company, which brought about the collaboration of Gilbert and Sullivan in the 'Savoy operas'. This was the most brilliantly successful chapter in the history of English musical theatre and, after *The Beggar's Opera*, the most enduring. The spoken dialogue, strophic ballads, and glee or 'madrigal' (typically one in each opera) were direct products of the native tradition, to which were added many elements of French operetta and the occasional influence of Mendelssohn and Schubert, a result of Sullivan's training at Leipzig. It has often been noted that the biting cerebral wit of Gilbert is perfectly offset by Sullivan's emotionalism. Sullivan's successors, especially Edward German, built successfully on his achievement, but with diminishing intellectual rigour, so that their operettas imperceptibly slide out of the operatic mainstream into the realm of light music.

In serious opera it was difficult for fin-de-siècle composers to ignore Wagner, though Stanford almost managed it, perhaps protected by the walls of academe. Sullivan's one 'grand' opera, *Ivanhoe* (1891), shows Wagnerian influence in superficial ways, as do the operas of Delius (which can only marginally be considered English at all). Two of the most ambitious efforts in English musical history were clearly inspired by the *Ring* cycle, as well as by the Celtic mysticism fashionable at the time: Holbrooke's trilogy, *The Cauldron of Annwn* (1912–29), and Boughton's series of five Arthurian music dramas (1920–45), the latter coupled with an idealistic attempt to found an English Bayreuth at Glastonbury. But the most powerful work of the early 20th century was Ethel Smyth's *The Wreckers* (1906), 'a halfway stage between *Tristan* and *Peter Grimes*' (Burton).

The violent reaction to World War I brought in more radical musical nationalism, reflected in Frederic Austin's realization of *The Beggar's Opera* (1920), new folk operas like Holst's *At the Boar's Head* (1925), parodies of Wagnerian opera like the same composer's *The Perfect Fool* (1923) and radically new word-music combinations like Walton's *Façade* (composed 1923). The turning away from pre-war opulence had more permanent effect, being reinforced by rapid social and economic change. Chamber operas, one-act operas and dramatic pieces with low budgets planned for school, amateur or studio performance have formed a growing proportion of the output of British opera.

In 1931 Sadler's Wells Theatre opened as a 'People's Opera' for the performance of opera in English, and from the first it was an important patron of British composers; the company moved to the Coliseum in 1968 and became the English National Opera in 1974. After closing during the war it reopened in 1945 with the première of Britten's *Peter Grimes*, which ushered in one of the liveliest periods in British opera history, helped, at long last, by official stage subsidy. Britten quickly emerged as the greatest English dramatic composer since Purcell, his success consolidated by the formation of the English Opera Group and his own Aldeburgh Festival. He virtually invented new forms: the opera for child performers, taken up by several composers of the next generation, and the quasi-medieval church play (beginning with *Noyes Fludde*, 1958). Meanwhile Tippett has continued to produce important full-scale operas, whose extraordinary range is illustrated by the contrast between *The Midsummer Marriage* (1955) and *King Priam* (1962). Composers of the next generation include Maxwell Davies, Blake, Goehr and Birtwistle.

The fresh start led by Britten in 1945 rejected what little remained of a living tradition of English opera. Instead, English composers have worked out their styles and methods from fresh principles, often arising out of practicalities. They are better educated than most of their counterparts of earlier generations and, for this reason, more sophisticated in their choice and treatment of the English language, and capable of learned allusions to the musical and literary past. They are cosmopolitan rather than nationalistic. They have claimed and won the right to the total concentration of the listener, as well as the support of the taxpayer, to a degree that would have astonished their predecessors. They know their import as individuals, and their operas tend to carry personal messages about moral or political questions of the day. They are conscious of their place in history, and strive for originality and profundity in ways that may tax an audience's understanding or sympathy. Under these conditions there is not, nor is there likely to be, enough consistent development to make a national school or tradition, but exciting new operas may emerge from time to time.

4. SCOTLAND AND WALES. Opera was scarcely known in Scotland before the late 19th century. In 1877 the Carl Rosa company began visiting Glasgow, where a resident company was founded in 1905. Scottish Opera, also centred in Glasgow, was founded in 1962; Edinburgh still lacks an opera house, though the King's Theatre has housed productions of the Edinburgh Festival since 1947. The first truly Scottish opera was Hamish MacCunn's *Jeanie Deans* (1894), after Scott's *The Heart of Midlothian*, but the works of Learmont Drysdale integrated Scottish traditional music more thoroughly into their scores. More recently Robin Orr and Thea Musgrave have developed Scottish themes in their operas.

The Welsh, though long known as a 'singing people', came still later to the operatic world. No important opera productions are on record in Wales until Welsh National Opera, based at the New Theatre, Cardiff, was founded in 1946. Arwel Hughes's *Serch yw'r doctor* ('Love's the Doctor', after Molière, 1960) appears to have been the first opera with a libretto in Welsh.

For further information on operatic life in Great Britain *see* ABINGDON; ALDEBURGH; BELFAST; BIRMINGHAM; BRIGHTON; BRITISH NATIONAL OPERA COMPANY; BUXTON; CAMBRIDGE; CARDIFF; CARL ROSA OPERA COMPANY; CHELSEA OPERA GROUP; CHELTENHAM; DENHOF OPERA COMPANY; EDINBURGH; ENGLISH OPERA GROUP; GLASGOW; GLYNDEBOURNE; INTIMATE OPERA COMPANY; KENT OPERA; LEEDS; LIVERPOOL; LONDON; MANCHESTER; MOODY-MANNERS COMPANY; NORWICH; OPERA FOR ALL; OPERA RESTOR'D; OXFORD; PHOENIX OPERA; and TRAVELLING TROUPES, §4.

*

BurneyH; LS; NicollH

J. Dennis: *Essay on the Opera's after the Italian Manner, which are About to be Establish'd on the English Stage with Some Reflections on the Damage which they may Bring to the Public* (London, 1706); repr. in J. Dennis: *Critical Works*, ed. E. N. Hooker (London, 1939), i, 382–93

M. Kelly: *Reminiscences* (London, 1826, 2/1826; ed. R. Fiske (London, 1975))

J. Genest: *Some Account of the English Stage* (Bath, 1832)

G. Hogarth: *Memoirs of the Musical Drama* (London, 1838, 2/1851 as *Memoirs of the Opera*)

H. Saxe Wyndham: *Annals of Covent Garden Theatre* (London, 1906)

C. Forsyth: *Music and Nationalism: a Study of English Opera* (London, 1911)

E. J. Dent: *Foundations of English Opera: a Study of Musical Drama in England during the Seventeenth Century* (Cambridge, 1928)

E. M. Gagey: *Ballad Opera* (New York, 1937)

W. C. Smith: *The Italian Opera and Contemporary Ballet in London 1789–1820* (London, 1954)

J. S. Manifold: *The Music in English Drama from Shakespeare to Purcell* (London, 1956)

D. K. Gordon: *Folklore in Modern English Opera* (diss., UCLA, 1959)

I. Lowens: 'St. Evremond, Dryden, and the Theory of Opera', *Criticism*, i (1959), 226–48

P. Hartnoll, ed.: *Shakespeare in Music* (London, 1964)

D. Arundell: *The Story of Sadler's Wells* (London, 1965)

F. Howes: *The English Musical Renaissance* (London, 1966)

N. Temperley: 'The English Romantic Opera', *Victorian Studies*, ix (1966), 293–301

M. Boyd: 'John Hughes on Opera', *ML*, lii (1971), 383–6

R. Fiske: *English Theatre Music in the Eighteenth Century* (London, 1973, 2/1986)

C. A. Price: 'The Critical Decade for English Music Drama, 1700–1710', *Harvard Library Bulletin*, lxxvi (1978), 38–76

N. Burton: 'Opera: 1865–1914', *Music in Britain: the Romantic Age 1800–1914*, ed. N. Temperley (London, 1981), 330–57

B. Carr: 'Theatre Music: 1800–1834', ibid, 288–306

E. W. White: *A History of English Opera* (London, 1983)

C. A. Price: *Henry Purcell and the London Stage* (Cambridge, 1984)

T. N. McGeary: *English Opera Criticism and Aesthetics 1685–1747* (diss., U. of Illinois, 1985)

L. V. Troost: *The Rise of English Comic Opera 1762–1800* (diss., U. of Pennsylvania, 1985)

S. Banfield: 'British Opera in Retrospect', *MT*, cxxvii (1986), 205–7

R. Fawkes: *Welsh National Opera* (London, 1986)

A.-M. H. Forbes: 'Celticism in British Opera: 1878–1938', *MR*, xlvii (1986–7), 176–83

C. Oliver: *It is a Curious Story: the Tale of Scottish Opera* (Edinburgh, 1987)

P. Evans: 'The 20th Century: Britain', *The New Grove History of Opera* (London, 1989), 302–10

N. Temperley: 'Musical Nationalism in English Romantic Opera', *The Lost Chord: Essays on Victorian Music* (Bloomington, IN, 1989), 143–57

R. Platt: 'Theatre Music I [1700–1760]', *Music in Britain: the Eighteenth Century*, ed. H. Diack Johnstone and R. Fiske (Oxford, 1990), 96–158

R. Hoskins: 'Theatre Music II [1760–1800]', ibid, 261–312

NICHOLAS TEMPERLEY

Great Friendship, The. Opera by V. I. Muradeli; *see* VELIKAYA DRUZHBA.

Greber, Jakob (*d* Mannheim, bur. 5 July 1731). German composer. According to the supplement to *A Comparison between the French and Italian Musick and Opera's* (London, 1709; ed. O. Strunk, MQ, xxxii, 1946, p.411), the English version of François Raguenet's *Paralèle des italiens et des françois*, he had studied composition in Italy before arriving in England in the early 18th century. He is first mentioned in connection with the performance of Nicholas Rowe's play *The Fair Penitent* at Lincoln's Inn Fields Theatre on 8 June 1703: the instrumental music was composed by 'Signior Jacomo Greber' and songs were sung by 'the Famous Signiora Francesca Margarita de l'Epine', who was associated with Greber in various musical performances in 1703–4. The association appears to have been more than professional: she was commonly known as 'Greber's Peg'. In 1705 Greber's pastoral *Gli amori di Ergasto* (the first Italian opera given in London in Italian) was given at the opening of the new Queen's Theatre in the Haymarket, though with little success.

In 1707 Greber was Kapellmeister in Innsbruck to Duke Carl Philipp, governor of the Tyrol. Here he produced a *festa teatrale*, *L'allegrezza dell'Eno*, in honour of Elisabeth Christina of Brunswick-Wolfenbüttel: she stayed in Innsbruck on her way to join her husband the Archduke Carl, who had been proclaimed King of Spain by the Grand Alliance. In 1711 the archduke became emperor, and it was probably to celebrate this that Greber made a new setting of *Gli amori di Ergasto*, with a prologue referring to Elisabeth as the emperor's wife. When Duke Carl Philipp succeeded his brother as Elector Palatine in 1717 he took his musicians, including Greber, with him to Neuburg, Heidelberg and finally Mannheim. Greber was closely associated with Gottfried Finger, who like him had been active in London and had served Carl Philipp. Finger composed the overtures for two of Greber's works: *L'allegrezza dell'Eno* and *Crudeltà consuma amore*, the second act of which was written by Augustin Stricker.

See also AMORI DI ERGASTO, GLI.

Gli amori di Ergasto [1st version] (pastoral, prol., 3, after A. Amalateo), London, Queen's, 9 April 1705; lib., with Eng. trans., *GB-Lbl*

L'allegrezza dell'Eno (festa teatrale, G. D. Pallavicini), Innsbruck, 1708 [ov. by Finger]

Gli amori di Ergasto [2nd version], Vienna, 1711, *A-Wn*

Crudeltà consuma amore (3, G. M. Rapparini), Neuburg, 1717 [ov. by Finger; Act 2 by Stricker]

*

LoewenbergA

J. Downes: *Roscius anglicanus* (London, 1708); ed. J. Milhous and R. D. Hume (London, 1987)

G. Salvioli and C. Salvioli: *Bibliografia universale del teatro drammatico italiano* (Venice, 1894–1903)

F. Walter: *Geschichte des Theaters und der Musik am kurpfälzischen Hofe* (Leipzig, 1898)

A. Einstein: 'Italienische Musiker am Hofe der Neuburger Wittelsbacher (1614–1716)', *SIMG*, ix (1907–8), 336–424

A. Nicoll: 'Italian Opera in England: the First Five Years', *Anglia*, xlvi (1922), 257–81

W. Senn: *Musik und Theater am Hof zu Innsbruck* (Innsbruck, 1954)

M. Tilmouth: 'A Calendar of References to Music in Newspapers Published in London and the Provinces (1660–1719)', *RMARC*, no.1 (1961), 1–107

C. Price: 'The Critical Decade for English Music Drama, 1700–1710', *Harvard Library Bulletin*, xxvi (1978), 38–76

H. E. Samuel: 'A German Musician Comes to London in 1704', *MT*, cxxii (1981), 591–3

C. Price: 'English Traditions in Handel's *Rinaldo*', *Handel Tercentenary Collection*, ed. S. Sadie and A. Hicks (London, 1987), 120–37   JACK WESTRUP/CURTIS PRICE

Grebus, Luis. *See* GRABU, LUIS.

Grechaninov, Alexander Tikhonovich (*b* Moscow, 13/ 25 Oct 1864; *d* New York, 4 Jan 1956). Russian composer. After preparatory studies at the Moscow Conservatory with Arensky (harmony and fugue) and Taneyev (form and analysis), he transferred to St Petersburg, where he was one of Rimsky-Korsakov's many pupils. He graduated in 1893. Three years later he moved back to Moscow and became associated with the Moscow Art Theatre, for whose productions of works by Ostrovsky and Alexey Tolstoy he wrote incidental scores. His work as director of a children's chorus at the Berkman music school in Moscow aroused his interest in music for young listeners, an interest reflected in his output for the stage.

Grechaninov's first opera, *Dobrïnya Nikitich*, which concerns the exploits of one of the heroes (bogatyrs) of the Kievan epics, was produced at the Bol'shoy Theatre in 1903. Nine years later his second, *Sestra Beatrisa* ('Sister Beatrice'), inspired by Vera Komissarzhevskaya's portrayal of Maeterlinck's heroine, caused a minor scandal and was taken off the boards at the insistence of the Orthodox Synod.

Grechaninov emigrated from Soviet Russia in 1925, settling first in Paris, later (1939) in the USA. The only opera he produced during his years abroad was *Zhenit'ba* ('Marriage'), a complete, verbatim setting of the same prose comedy by Gogol of which the opening scenes had been set by Musorgsky. Grechaninov's, unlike Ippolitov-Ivanov's, is an independent work, not a completion of Musorgsky's.

Dobrïnya Nikitich op.22, 1895, 1899–1901 (op-bïlina, 3, Grechaninov), Moscow, Bol'shoy, 14/27 Oct 1903, vs (Moscow, 1902)

Sakuntala, 1903 (A. Fyodorov, after Kalidasa), sketches only

Stantsionnïy smotritel' [The Stationmaster], 1906 (Grechaninov, after A. S. Pushkin), sketches only

Sestra Beatrisa [Sister Beatrice] op.50, 1908–10 (op-legend, Grechaninov, after M. Maeterlinck), Moscow, Solodovnikov (Zimin opera company), 12/25 Oct 1912 (St Petersburg, 1912)

Yelochkin son [Dream of a Christmas Tree] op.55, 1911 (children's op, N. Dolomanova and others, vs (St Petersburg, 1912)

Mïshkin teremok [Mousey's Tower] op.92, 1921 (children's op-miniature, 1, V. Popov), vs (Leipzig and Berlin, 1923)

Kot, petukh i lisa [The Cat, the Cock and the Vixen] op. 103, 1919–24 (children's op, 1, Grechaninov, after Afanas'yev)

Zhenit'ba [Marriage] op.180, 1945–6 (comic op, 3, N. V. Gogol), Tanglewood (Berkshire Music Festival), 1 Aug 1948, photocopies of holograph vs *RU-Mcm* and *US-NYp*

*

N. Kashkin: '"Dobrïnya Nikitich" opera A. T. Grechaninova', *Moskovskiy listok* (17/30 Oct 1903)

I. Glebov [B. Asaf'yev]: '"Dobrïnya Nikitich" Grechaninova v Narodnom dome' [Grechaninov's 'Dobrïnya Nikitich' in the People's House], *Khronika zhurnala 'Muzïkal'nïy sovremennik'* [Chronicle of the Journal 'Contemporary Music'], no.2 (1916), 14–16

A. Grechaninov: *My Life* (New York, 1952)

Yu. Alexandrov: *A. T. Grechaninov: Noto-bibliograficheskiy spravochnik* [Grechaninov: a Music-Bibliographic Handbook] (Moscow, 1978)

N. Kinkul'kina: '"Moy bednïy 'Dobrïnya'"': A. T. Grechaninov – A. A. Saninu' ['My Poor "Dobrïnya": Grechaninov to A. A. Sanin'], *SovM* (1990), no.3, pp.82–9   RICHARD TARUSKIN

Grecis, Nicola de. *See* DE GRECIS, NICOLA.

Grécy, Mlle. *See* SCIO, JULIE-ANGÉLIQUE.

Greece. Any student of the history of opera in Greece, a country with limited library and archival resources, is hampered by the destruction of much important material during World War II (not only in Greece itself but in European publishers' archives) and in the earthquake that devastated the Ionian islands in 1953; out of nearly 130 Greek operas known at that time, more than 45 are now lost. Further, much of the research material that has been preserved in private archives is not available for consultation. An important source is the archive of Spyros Motsenigos (1911–70), which is housed at the Greek National Library, Athens.

The earliest opera performance in Greece took place in Corfu in 1733. *Don Crepuscolo* by Nicolaos Mantzaros, given there in 1815, is the first known opera by a Greek composer; other early examples are Ludovico Platonis's *Atreus ke Thyestes* (performed 1817–22 in Zakynthos) and Stephanos Poyagos's *I para Feaxin afixis tou Odysseos*, given in Corfu in 1819 (this may be a kind of ballet). Works of Mantzaros akin to operas were given in Corfu and operas in Lefkas (Leucadia) on festive occasions in 1832 and 1833. The Ionian islands saw a certain amount of operatic composition in the 19th and early 20th centuries, including works by Xyndas, Lambelet, Padovanis, Carrer, Frangiskos Domeneginis (1809–74), Iossif Liveralis (1820–99), Nicolaos Tzannis-Metaxas (1825–1907), Dionyssios Rhodhotheatos (1849–92) and others, and culminating in the work of Samaras and Lavrangas. The stylistic models for the Ionian School were Italian, from Zingarelli and Mercadante to Bellini, Donizetti and Verdi. Several of their operas were inspired not by topics from antiquity but by historical facts and figures from the more recent past, especially the 1821 War of Independence; Italian composers, often resident, including G. B. Ferrari (*Gli ultimi giorni di Suli*, 1859–60) and Rafael Parisini (*Arkadion*, inspired by the Cretan uprising of 1866–7), also drew on such material. Among the few surviving Ionian operas from this period are, besides that of Mantzaros, *O yposifios vouleftis* ('The Parliamentary Candidate', 1867, the first opera to a Greek text) by Xyndas; six operas by Carrer; most of the output of Samaras, whose operas were widely recognized internationally; the operas of Lavrangas, who did much to promote the cause of opera in the country and whose *Ta dyo adelfia* ('The Two Brothers', 1901) can be regarded as the first National School opera; Iossif Mastrekinis's recently discovered *Eleazaros* (1898, a biblical opera in an early Verdian style); and Sakellaridis's only extant opera *Perouze* (1911), which may be seen as an intermediate step between the Ionian group and the central figure of Manolis Kalomiris (1883–1962).

Kalomiris, the leading composer of the National School, was concerned to foster a genuinely Greek idiom as opposed to the italianate one that inevitably pervaded the music of the Ionian composers. He may in some degree have been anticipated by Xyndas and Carrer, and in that sense the seeds of the National School may have been sown on the Ionian opera stage; nonetheless there is a marked difference between the flowing cantilenas of the Ionian operas and the more selfconsciously Greek idiom – drawing on Greek mainland folksong, its intervals (the augmented 2nd in particular) and its rhythms – in Kalomiris's exuberant style, with its sparkling polyphony and powerful dramatic gesture.

The propagation of a truly Greek opera was the more difficult in that native music was regarded in influential circles as inferior to Western music, particularly after the royal marriage in 1889 that increased German influence in the country, and the association of Greek music with liberal politics. Kalomiris was seen to embody this association; his operas ultimately became well known, whereas other composers toiled for years over single operas that either remained unperformed or sank into an unmerited oblivion after a single hearing, such as Dimitri Mitropoulos's *Soeur Béatrice*, after Maeterlinck (Athens, Municipal, 11 May 1920). The stylistic models had become more varied: not only Romantic opera but post-Romantic, impressionist and even neo-classical, German, French, later Italian and Russian. Kalomiris's own musical personality was strong enough for him to override his models. The single opera of Mario Varvoglis (1885–1967), *To apoyema tis agapis* ('The Afternoon of Love', performed 1944), is musically natural and charming though it suffers from a weak libretto. By contrast, Petros Petridis (1892–1977) wrote one of the most dramatically compelling librettos in the Greek repertory for his *Zefyra* (composed 1923–5, revised 1958–64), based on Georgios Drossinis's novel *To mayiko votani tis agapis* ('The Magic Herb of Love'). *Anixiatiko paramythi* ('Spring Fairy-Tale', completed 1953, performed 1976) by the baritone Titos Xirellis (1898–1985) may be seen as an offspring of Kalomiris's operas.

Composers of the next generation tended to be estranged from opera, partly because of the conservative policies of the National Opera, and many of the most gifted settled abroad. The operas of Antoniou, Couroupos and Kounadis, and the music theatre works of Aperghis and Logothetis, are little known in Greece, though since 1980 the Moussikos Avgoustos festival in Iraklion has done much to promote the operas of younger composers (in 1986, for example, it gave a series of six new one-act works). Other notable operas of this generation include two by Mikis Theodorakis (*b* 1925), *Kostas Karyotakis* (1987) and *Medea* (first performed in Bilbao, Arriaga Theatre, 1 October 1991), the former a complex and confused politico-historical allegory of

recent Greek history, in a mixture between a popular song style and a scarcely assimilated neo-classical one; *I fotia* ('The Fire', written 1978, performed 1987) by Yorgos Sicilianos (*b* 1920), a neatly composed atonal work on a weak libretto; *Odyssey* (1984) by Nikos Mamangakis (*b* 1929), a patchwork of atonal polyphony with art and pop songs and ballet; and *I demonismeni* ('The Possessed', after Dostoyevsky) by Haris Vrondos (*b* 1951), a formidably ambitious project completed in 1991. Among the most significant Greek operas of the later 20th century are the delightful works of Koukos (*O Conroy ke i kopies tou*, 'Conroy's Other Selves') and Kounadis (*O Gyrismos*, 'The Return'), the latter a small masterpiece based on a modern approach to the story of Electra.

Some 20 operetta composers, including Samaras and Lavrangas, many of them highly gifted songwriters, also flourished in Greece until about 1940, producing about a thousand scores. The principal topic treated in this repertory, initially the doings of royalty and the establishment, soon became the comedy of manners, sometimes with Greek characters superimposed on French plots; social criticism was never a feature of the Greek genre. The pioneers and the most prolific composers were Sakellaridis and Hadjiapostolou, while significant ones include Kostas Yannidis (a pseudonym for Yannis Constantinidis), Stathis Mastoras, Iossif Ritsiardis and Mimis Katrivanos.

For further information on operatic life in the country's principal centres *see* ATHENS; CORFU; PATRAS; SALONICA; and SYROS.

S. de Viazis: 'Dhyo melodramatike skine en Lefcadi (1832–33)' [Two Opera Scenes in Leucadia (1832–3)], *Panathenaea*, vii/80 (1907), 134–5

T. N. Synadinos: *Istoria tis neoellinikis moussikis, 1824–1919* [History of Modern Greek Music, 1824–1919] (Athens, 1919)

'Melodrama', *Engyklopedikon lexikon eleftheroudaki*, ix (Athens, 1930), 296–7 [inventory of Greek operas]

N. I. Laskaris: *Istoria tou neoellinikou theatrou* [History of Modern Greek Theatre] (Athens, 1938–9)

S. G. Motsenigos: *Neoelliniki moussiki: symvoli i tin historian tis* [Modern Greek Music: a Contribution to its History] (Athens, 1958)

Y. Sideris: 'I. Papaïoannou', *Imera tou ithopoiou* [Actors Day] (1958), 5–30 [programme book]

S. Petras: *Vassiliko theatro, elliniki operetta* [The Royal Theatre and the Greek Operetta] (Athens, 1960)

S. A. Evanghelatos: *Istoria tou theatrou en Kefallinia, 1600–1900* (diss., U. of Athens, 1970)

Y. Karakandas: *Apanda tou lyrikou theatrou* [Everything about Lyric Theatre] (Athens, 1973)

T. Hadjipandazis and L. Maraka: *I athinaiki epitheorissi* [The Athenian Revue] (Athens, 1977)

T. Hadjipandazis: *To komidhyllio* [The Vaudeville] (Athens, 1981)

G. Leotsakos: 'I hamenes ellinikes operes' [Lost Greek Operas], *Epilogos*, i (1992, forthcoming)   GEORGE LEOTSAKOS

Greeff-Andriessen [née Andriessen; Stahmer-Andriessen, Ende-Andriessen], **Pelagie** (*b* Vienna, 20 June 1860; *d* Frankfurt, 17 Dec 1937). German soprano. She studied first with her mother, who taught singing at the Vienna Academy. Originally a mezzo-soprano or contralto, she made her début in operetta at Vienna, then sang in various German cities. In 1882 she joined Angelo Neumann's touring Wagner company, and from 1884 to 1890 was principal dramatic soprano at Leipzig. She continued to oscillate between soprano and mezzo-soprano roles, so that in her single season at Covent Garden in 1892 she was engaged to sing Fricka in *Das Rheingold* but also substituted as the *Walküre* Brünnhilde. At Salzburg in 1891 she had sung Countess

Almaviva in *Figaro*, while at Bayreuth in 1886 her role was Brangäne in *Tristan*. In 1890 she moved to Cologne and from 1893 to 1907 sang in Frankfurt. She added the name of her first and then her second husband to her stage name, and later that of her third, the bass Paul Greeff. She made a few recordings between 1900 and 1907, mostly of Wagnerian excerpts sung with formidable volume and attack, with some expressive contrasts but also a lack of finesse.   J. B. STEANE

Greek. Opera in two acts by MARK-ANTHONY TURNAGE to a libretto by the composer and Jonathan Moore after Steven Berkoff's play *Greek*; Munich, Carl-Orff Saal, 17 June 1988.

Turnage's reworking of the Oedipus myth relocates the story in the East End of London in the late 20th century. Eddy (high baritone), 'spawned in a Tufnell Park that's no more than a stone's throw from the Angel', leaves his working-class family to better himself in the world of free enterprise. He finds that Thatcherite world infected with a 'plague' – greed and self-interest – and maintained as a police state in which minorities are brutally repressed. He argues with a Café Manager (baritone) over croissants, kills him and marries his wife (mezzo-soprano).

Ten years later (Act 2) Eddy has become a successful member of the *nouveaux riches* and is reconciled with his parents, but the plague has persisted; to end it Eddy seeks out a 'Sphinx' on the outskirts of the city, guarded by a pair of punk, man-hating lesbians (soprano and mezzo-soprano). He solves their riddle and returns home in triumph, but his parents (mezzo-soprano and baritone) then reveal that he is adopted ('You're not our son, son'), having been rescued after a wartime accident. The mention of an oil-stained teddy bear brings the realization that Eddy has married his mother, and the opera appears to move towards tragedy. Eddy at first resists the inevitable – 'Why should I tear out my eyes, Greek style – Why should you hang yourself, does it really matter that you're my mum?' – but he does apparently blind himself and is borne away in a funeral *cortège*, only for the myth to be finally subverted: 'Bollocks to all that! I'd rather run all the way back and pull back the sheet, witness gold-bodied wife and climb into her sanctuary … yeah, I wanna climb back inside my Mum, what's wrong with that …?'

Though the forces are small (a singing cast of four taking multiple roles and an orchestra of 17) Turnage matches the rich imagery of Berkoff's prose with music of distinctive variety and power. His language takes elements from several different 20th-century operatic models, including Stravinsky, Puccini, Britten and Henze, inflected with jazz and rock idioms. Act 1 is a sequence of snapshot-like scenes in which the impulse is chiefly rhythmic; the orchestral interludes are as important as the scenes themselves in propelling the action forward. Act 2 is constructed in larger paragraphs, the impulse now lyrical, as the opera moves from stereotypical violence to personal tragedy. Each act has its focal set piece: in Act 1 a riot grows out of one of the interludes, in which the popular song 'The Laughing Policeman' is used to generate an atmosphere of violence and menace; Act 2 reaches its climax with Eddy's arias of self-realization, 'No more, oh no more, will I taste the sweetness of my wife's body', though his final defiant rejection of fate is delivered in speech.

ANDREW CLEMENTS

Greek Passion, The [*Řecké pašije*]. Opera in four acts by BOHUSLAV MARTINŮ to his own libretto with Nikos Kazantzakis after Jonathan Griffin's translation of Kazantzakis's novel *Christ Recrucified*; Zürich, Stadttheater, 9 June 1961.

Grigoris *priest of Lycovrissi*		bass-baritone
The Patriarcheas *an elder*		bass-baritone
Ladas *a miserly elder*		spoken
Michelis *son of the Patriarcheas*		tenor
Kostandis *a café owner*		baritone
Yannakos *a pedlar*		tenor
Manolios *a shepherd*		tenor
Nikolios *a shepherd boy*		soprano
Andonis *a barber*		spoken
Katerina *a young widow*		soprano
Panais [in some versions Panait] *her lover*		tenor
Lenio *engaged to Manolios*		soprano
An Old Woman		contralto
A Voice in the Crowd		baritone
Fotis *priest of the refugees*		bass-baritone
Despinio	} *a refugee*	soprano
An Old Man		bass
A Giant Standard-bearer		silent

Villagers, refugees, children

Setting A mountainous area of Greece in the early 20th century

In late summer 1954 Martinů intended to set an operatic text dealing with Czech or Slovak subject matter, but his encounter with Kazantzakis's novel *Zorba the Greek* in autumn that year diverted him from native subjects. *Zorba* proved unsuitable for operatic adaptation, and Martinů settled instead on the novel *Christ Recrucified*, basing his English libretto on Jonathan Griffin's translation and beginning work late in 1954. He composed most of the music between February 1956 and January 1957 but without reaching a successful conclusion; he returned to the score in February 1958 and completed a final version on 15 January 1959. During the composition of the opera both Kubelík, for Covent Garden, and Karajan, for the Vienna Staatsoper, had shown interest in mounting a production of the work. None was forthcoming, largely because of Martinů's indecision over the final form, in particular the last scene of Act 4 which he had originally intended as a major solo for Katerina; this eventually became the brief valediction followed by a chorus which appears in all productions.

The première of the work did not take place in Martinů's lifetime. The opera was given under Paul Sacher at the Stadttheater in Zürich. Some six productions were staged in Czechoslovakia, including Brno, Prague and Bratislava. These were cut in various ways, but not consistently. Elsewhere on the Continent, *The Greek Passion* has been staged in Linz, Bielefeld, Plauen and Antwerp. The first British production, in a new English version by Brian Large, was given by the WNO at the New Theatre, Cardiff, on 29 April 1981.

Although Martinů went to some lengths to introduce local colour into his score through the use of Greek folksong and Orthodox chant, the musical language of the opera approximates in many ways to that of the cantatas to Czech texts by Miloslav Bureš, composed in the 1950s. The closeness to the Czech style of Martinů's

'The Greek Passion' (Martinů), Act 1 (The village square in Lycovrissi) from the original production at the Stadttheater, Zürich, 9 June 1961

last period goes in tandem with an adaptation of the novel which excludes all but two references to the Turks – a vital element in the original. By focussing on the human issues, without the added political dimension involved in the Turkish presence, Martinů fashioned an opera which is both realist and profoundly touching. The characteristically warm, though boldly original, diatonicism of his later style is apparent throughout *The Greek Passion*, notably in the grand choral statements of the conclusion. He makes use of a small number of recurring motifs which represent both ideas and characters. While many of the most effective moments occur in the large-scale choral contributions of the outer acts, Martinů sustains a considerable degree of dramatic tension in the solo exchanges of the various tableaux into which the opera is divided.

ACT 1 *The village square in Lycovrissi* The act opens with the rejoicing of Easter morning – commemorated by the Orthodox liturgical melody which begins the work – as Grigoris announces the cast for the following year's Passion play. The apostles are chosen from among the village people as are the main characters: Panais is Judas, Katerina is Mary Magdalene and the young shepherd Manolios is Christ. As they contemplate the task of living exemplary lives in preparation for the following year, the sound of psalm singing is heard in the distance. Entering the village is a ragged band of refugees driven from their home by the Turks. Grigoris and the village elders, not wishing any disruption, attempt to repulse them, but Manolios, Katerina and the 'apostles' give them comfort and suggest that they settle nearby on Mt Sarakina.

ACT 2.i–ii *On the outskirts of the village, near Katerina's house* Yannakos worries about the heavy burden of his role as Peter. He is persuaded by the miserly Ladas to swindle the refugees out of their jewellery.

2.iii *Outside the village, at the spring of St Basil* Katerina reveals her love for Manolios, who gently rejects her.

2.iv *On Mt Sarakina* Recognizing their simplicity, goodness and genuine need, Yannakos gives the refugees the money that Ladas had entrusted to him to trade for their goods.

ACT 3.i *In the mountains at night* Manolios is tortured by his human fallibility and Katerina's love for him. In an extended dream sequence he wrestles with his difficulties.

3.ii *The same* Lenio, to whom Manolios is betrothed, asks him why he repulses her; she abandons him to his contemplation.

3.iii *Katerina's house, the same night* Manolios descends to the village to tell Katerina that he can return her love only spiritually. Katerina accepts this unexpected change and becomes a follower.

3.iv *At the roadside in the mountains, some weeks later* Katerina tells Yannakos of her conversion.

3.v *An olive grove on the mountainside* Manolios, growing in stature, preaches of Christ's sacrifice and persuades the villagers to give money to the refugees. Grigoris and the elders plot the downfall of Manolios. The final moments of the act evoke the presence of Christ in the silence of the evening.

ACT 4.i *The village square in Lycovrissi* The villagers celebrate the wedding of Lenio and Nikolios.

531

At the height of the festivities Grigoris denounces the 'apostles' and excommunicates Manolios.

4.ii *The same* In a superbly sustained monologue, Manolios announces his growing awareness of Christ and his intention to fight on behalf of the refugees. Denounced by Grigoris, the 'apostles' declare their support for Manolios. As the refugees approach from Sarakina to demand help, fighting breaks out and Manolios is killed by the Judas figure, Panais. Horrified by what has happened, Katerina speaks for the villagers in an exquisite valediction. Pulling themselves together, the refugees, led by their priest, Fotis, resolve to leave Lycovrissi to find a new home. Martinů had originally planned a concluding scene for Katerina but was persuaded by his publishers to substitute the present concerted end. While flying in the face of his original intentions, the conclusion Martinů provided set the seal on the effective epic qualities sustained through the separate tableaux of the opera.   JAN SMACZNY

Green, Anna (*b* Southampton, 27 Jan 1933). English soprano. She studied in London and made her début in 1961 at Düsseldorf as Amelia (*Ballo*). After singing throughout Germany, she made her Covent Garden début in 1967 as Hecuba (*King Priam*). She sang Brünnhilde in *Ring* cycles at Seattle (1975) and San Diego and for the ENO (1979). She first sang Isolde in 1975 at Bremen, repeating the role in Turin, Berlin and other cities and for the WNO (1979). Her repertory included Donna Anna, Leonore (*Fidelio*), Abigaille, Tosca, Ariadne, Electra, the Marschallin and the Kostelnička, but her strong, bright-toned voice was particularly effective in such modern roles as Marie (*Wozzeck*) and Goneril (*Lear*). She was married to the American tenor-baritone Howard Vandenburg.

ELIZABETH FORBES

Greenawald, Sheri (Kay) (*b* Iowa City, IA, 12 Nov 1947). American soprano. She was a pupil of Charles Matheson, Maria DeVarady, Hans Heinz, and Daniel Ferro, and continued her studies with Audrey Langford in London. She made her début in 1974 in the Manhattan Theater Club's production of Poulenc's *Les mamelles de Tirésias*, a New York première. Her European début, at the Netherlands Opera, was as Susanna in 1980. Among the premières in which she has sung are Floyd's *Bilby's Doll* (1976, Houston), Pasatieri's *Washington Square* (1976, Detroit) and Bernstein's *A Quiet Place* (1983, Houston). Only partly in jest, Greenawald has been described as a 'heroic soubrette'. Her lyric voice is aptly suited to such Mozartian roles as Susanna, Zerlina, and Despina, Norina (*Don Pasquale*) and Sophie (*Werther*), but it also has considerable power and range, suitable for the heavier parts of Ellen Orford, Mimì and Violetta. In 1990 she sang Natasha (*War and Peace*) at Seattle.

For illustration *see* QUIET PLACE, A.   MICHAEL WALSH

Greenberg, Sylvia (*b* Bucharest, *c*1952). Israeli soprano of Romanian birth. She studied in Tel-Aviv and in Zürich, where she made her début in 1977 as the Queen of Night; in 1978 she sang the same role at Glyndebourne. Engaged with the Deutsche Oper, Berlin, from 1980, she has also sung in Hamburg, Munich, Vienna and Cologne and at La Scala. In 1983 she sang the Woodbird at Bayreuth; in 1984 she created Soprano II in Berio's *Un re in ascolto* in Salzburg; and in 1986

she sang Ilia (*Idomeneo*) at Aix-en-Provence. In 1989 she took part in the première of Manzoni's *Doktor Faustus* at La Scala. Her other roles include Olympia, Sophie (*Werther*), Melanto (*Il ritorno d'Ulisse*), Gilda, the Fiakermilli and Zerbinetta, of which the last perfectly displays her brilliant coloratura technique.

ELIZABETH FORBES

Greene, Maurice (*b* London, 12 Aug 1696; *d* London, 1 Dec 1755). English composer. He was organist of St Paul's Cathedral from 1718 and in 1727 succeeded Croft as principal organist and composer of the Chapel Royal; eight years later he became Master of the King's Music as well. As a young man he had been friendly with Handel but the friendship did not last. He is remembered chiefly for his many anthems and for his massive anthology of 16th- and 17th-century English cathedral music, completed and published after his death by his pupil William Boyce.

A founder member of the Fund for the Support of Decayed Musicians and their Families (later the Royal Society of Musicians), Greene was also involved with several London music clubs, at whose concerts his two operas, *Florimel, or Love's Revenge* (1734) and *Phoebe* (1747), and a masque, among other works, were given. Their music is often charming, but cumulatively somewhat enervating in effect, not altogether surprisingly perhaps in view of the essentially undramatic nature of the subject matter. *Florimel* was quite widely performed, though never apparently on the London stage. Both operas are to librettos by John Hoadly (1711–76), a clergyman friend with a passionate interest in the theatre. Hoadly's brother, Benjamin, was Physician in Ordinary to George II and author of *The Suspicious Husband* (1747), one of the most successful comedies of the century.

See also FLORIMEL, OR LOVE'S REVENGE and PHOEBE.

Florimel, or Love's Revenge (dramatic pastoral, 2, J. Hoadly), Farnham Castle, 1734, *GB-Lam*, *Lbl* (incl. autograph addns), *Lcm*, facs. in MLE, C6 (forthcoming)
The Judgment of Hercules (masque, Hoadly), before 1740, music lost
Phoebe, 1747 (pastoral op, 3, Hoadly), first known perf., London, Mr Ogle's Great Room, Dean Street, 16 Jan 1755, *Lbl*, *Ob** (except ov.), facs. in MLE, C6 (forthcoming)

*

H. D. Johnstone: 'Greene's First Opera: "Florimel, or Love's Revenge"', *MT*, cxiv (1973), 1112–13
——: 'Greene's "Phoebe": a Pastoral Opera', *MT*, cxxv (1984), 491–2
H. D. Johnstone: Introductions to M. Greene: *Florimel* and *Phoebe*, MLE, C6 (forthcoming)   H. DIACK JOHNSTONE

Greensboro. American city, in North Carolina. It is the home of the Greensboro Opera Company, founded in 1980 by its artistic director and conductor, Peter Paul Fuchs. The first production was *La traviata*, with June Anderson, in 1981. Since then the company has presented one fully staged opera each autumn and a small production or recital each spring, both accompanied by the Greensboro SO and presented in the 2400-seat War Memorial Auditorium.   DEAN SMITH

Greenwood, Thomas [the elder] (*d* London, 17 Oct 1797). English scene designer. He worked in London, mainly at Drury Lane, from 1772 until his death, first for David Garrick under John French and P. J. de Loutherbourg. After French's death in 1776, he became

Drawing by Thomas Greenwood of a scene for Stephen Storace's 'Lodoiska', 1794 (an engraving after this drawing appeared on the frontispiece of the libretto)

chief resident scene painter, and he was later employed by R. B. Sheridan and J. P. Kemble. When Drury Lane was demolished in 1791 he moved with the company to the King's Theatre, returning to Drury Lane at its reopening in 1794. He also worked during the summer season at Sadler's Wells (1778–95).

He designed scenery for comic operas as well as plays and pantomimes. His first was *The Maid of the Oaks* (Barthélemon; 1774) after designs by Loutherbourg, and he was also scenographer for many of Storace's comic operas including *The Haunted Tower* (1789), *The Siege of Belgrade* (1791; see LONDON, fig.6), *The Pirates* (1792) and *Lodoiska* (1794; see illustration). Four engravings of these scenes were published as frontispieces to texts or scores, and are reproduced in *Theatre Notebook* (xix/2, 1964–5, pls.4 and 5; xx/2, 1965–6, pls.1 and 2). They are all exterior views with a romantic flavour. In addition, two watercolour sketches of Gothic exteriors are in the Victoria and Albert Museum (reproduced in *Theatre Notebook*, xv, 1960–61, p.31). His painting was much admired and he often drew from observation on the spot, particularly at Sadler's Wells, thus introducing a note of realism in his romantic designs.

*

R. C. Kern: 'Two Designs by the Elder Thomas Greenwood', *Theatre Notebook*, xv (1960–61), 31–2
S. Rosenfeld: 'A Transparency by Thomas Greenwood the Elder', *Theatre Notebook*, xix (1964–5), 21–2   SYBIL ROSENFELD

Greevy (Tattan), Bernadette (*b* Dublin, 3 July 1940). Irish mezzo-soprano. She studied in Dublin with Jean Nolan, and in London at the GSM and with Helene Isepp. Her career has been mainly as a recital and concert singer, but she made her operatic début at the 1962 Wexford Festival as Beppe in *L'amico Fritz*, returning there for the title roles in Massenet's *Hérodiade* (1977) and Handel's *Ariodante* (1985). Between 1977 and 1980 she sang Charlotte (*Werther*), Delilah and Gluck's Orpheus at Dublin, and made her Covent Garden début in 1982 as Geneviève (in Debussy's *Pelléas et Mélisande*).

Admired for her rich tonal quality and imaginative verbal colouring, she has given masterclasses, some of them abroad, including China (1985) and New Zealand. Her recordings include Handel's *Ariodante* and *Orlando*.   NOËL GOODWIN

Gregor, Bohumil (*b* Prague, 14 July 1926). Czech conductor. He studied at the Prague Conservatory and made his conducting début at the Prague 5th of May Opera (now the Smetana Theatre) in 1947. He became heir to the Janáček tradition at Brno when working there as assistant to Zdeněk Chalabala, 1949–51, and began to put it into practice as music director at the Ostrava Opera (1958–62) in productions of *Kát'a Kabanová* and *The Excursions of Mr Brouček*. There he also conducted the premières of Trojan's *Kolotoč* ('The Merry-go-round'), Kašlík's *Krakatit* and Pauer's *Manželské kontrapunkty* ('Matrimonial Counterpoints'). He joined the Prague National Theatre as a resident conductor in 1962, and made his British début with the company at the 1964 Edinburgh Festival with *From the House of the Dead*, returning there in 1970 with *Mr Brouček* and *The Cunning Little Vixen*. His performances of *The Makropoulos Case* led to his engagement at the Stockholm Royal Opera (1965–70), and in 1967 he began an association with Netherlands Opera that lasted 20 years, conducting two productions each season. His appearances at the Vienna, Holland, Kiel and other festivals brought him an appointment at the Hamburg Staatsoper (1969–72), where he conducted the première of Kelemen's *Der Belagerungszustand* (1970) as well as Verdi and Czech operas. From 1969 he made several annual visits to the San Francisco Opera conducting *Jenůfa*, *Salome* and *Otello*. He has continued to be active in Prague and elsewhere as a Janáček specialist, in whose operas he has an instinctive feeling for subtleties of tempo and phrasing. He made Czechoslovak recordings of four Janáček operas between 1964 and 1972, as well as other operas of the Czech repertory.

*

B. Gregor: 'V díle Leoše Janáčka není nic samoúčelného' [Nothing Appears by Chance in Leoš Janáček's Work], *HRo*, xxxi (1978), 221–5
V. Pospíšil, ed: Narodni divadlo a jeho předchůdci [The National Theatre and its Predecessors] (Prague, 1988)
ALENA NĚMCOVÁ, NOËL GOODWIN

Gregor, Joseph (*b* Czernowitz [now Chernovtsy, Ukraine], 26 Oct 1888; *d* Vienna, 12 Oct 1960). Austrian theatre historian and librettist. He went to Vienna in 1907, studying German, philosophy and musicology (under Guido Adler) at the university and practical music at the academy. In 1908 he became a private pupil of Robert Fuchs and also studied operatic production at the Vienna Hofoper. In 1910 he became Max Reinhardt's assistant for a production of the second part of Goethe's *Faust* at the Deutsche Theater, Berlin. After war service he was appointed librarian at the Austrian National Library, where he founded a theatre archive in 1922 and a film archive in 1929; he initiated studies in theatre history at Vienna University in 1947. During the last years of his life he was accorded many national and international awards.

Although Gregor left important monographs on the history of Vienna's theatres, on Richard Strauss's operas and on the broad cultural history of theatre and of opera, he is probably best known as the librettist of Richard Strauss's *Friedenstag* (1938), *Daphne* (1938) and *Die Liebe der Danae* (1944). The collaboration began in 1935, after the anti-semitic climate in Nazi Germany had compelled Strauss's librettist Stefan Zweig to break off his fruitful partnership with the composer. In an attempt to mollify the bitterly disappointed Strauss, Zweig proposed that his place be taken by Gregor – intimate knowledge of both his and Hofmannsthal's writing was deemed to be a distinct advantage. But while Strauss strongly admired Gregor's work as a historian, he was unconvinced of his abilities as a librettist. The relationship therefore remained rather one-sided as the reluctant composer continually subjected his new partner's efforts to bitter criticism. Nonetheless, while their three operas did not inspire Strauss's best music, Gregor's librettos are by no means as inferior as has sometimes been suggested. Certainly the characterization in *Friedenstag* – whose scenario was conceived primarily by Zweig – is rather one-dimensional, but in the bucolic drama *Daphne* Gregor produced his most elevated text, which, in the verses depicting Daphne's lament on the death of Leukippos, attains a poetic quality worthy of Hofmannsthal. Yet by the time Strauss and Gregor had completed *Die Liebe der Danae*, the collaboration had declined as the composer increasingly turned to the conductor Clemens Krauss (librettist of his final opera, *Capriccio*) for practical advice. Further operas drafted by Gregor (*Celestina*, *Semiramis* and *Die Rache der Aphrodite*) were summarily rejected by Strauss, although the librettist played a part in shaping the text for his posthumously completed school opera *Des Esels Schatten* (libretto by Hans Adler). Gregor also completed a libretto, *Florian Geyer*, for the composer Hans Ebert, commissioned by Goebbels in 1944 but never staged, and an arrangement of Spohr's *Jessonda* in 1940.

WRITINGS

Das Wiener Barocktheater (Vienna, 1922)

Das Theater in der Wiener Josefstadt (Vienna, 1924)

Wiener szenische Kunst (Vienna, 1924–5)

Mozart-Geist österreichisches Theaters; eine Festrede (Vienna, 1931)

Weltgeschichte des Theaters (Vienna, 1933, 2/1939)

Richard Strauss, der Meister der Oper (Munich, 1939, 3/1952)

Kulturgeschichte der Oper (Vienna, 1941, 2/1944)

Von den Ursprüngen bis zum Ausdruck des Barocktheaters (Munich, 1944)

Geschichte des österreichisches Theaters von seinen Ursprüngen bis zum Ende der ersten Republik (Vienna, 1948)

Clemens Krauss: seine musikalische Sendung (Bad Bocklet, Vienna and Zürich, 1953)

Typen der Regie in der Oper im 20. Jahrhunderts (Vienna, 1956)

Die Theaterregie in der Welt unseres Jahrhunderts (Vienna, 1958)

Librettos: *Friedenstag*, R. Strauss, 1938; *Daphne* (bukolische Tragödie), Strauss, 1938; *Die Liebe der Danae* (heitere Mythologie), Strauss, 1944, rev., with sketch by H. von Hofmannsthal, 1952; *Florian Geyer*, H. Ebert, comp. 1944

*

R. Strauss: 'Betrachtungen zu Joseph Gregors "Weltgeschichte des Theaters"', *Betrachtungen und Erinnerungen*, ed. W. Schuh (Zürich, 1949, 2/1957)

E. Müller von Asow: 'Joseph Gregor in seinen Beziehungen zu Richard Strauss', *Das Antiquariat*, ix (1953), 228–33

R. Strauss: 'Parerga für Joseph Gregor', *Das Antiquariat*, ix (1953), 237–9

R. Tenschert, ed.: *Richard Strauss und Joseph Gregor: Briefwechsel 1934–1949* (Salzburg, 1955)

W. Schuh, ed.: *Richard Strauss – Stefan Zweig: Briefwechsel* (Frankfurt, 1957)

A. B. Brody: *Versuch einer Joseph-Gregor-Bibliographie, 1908–1958* (Berlin, 1958)

H. E. Mutzenbecher: 'Joseph Gregor zum Gedenken', *Internationale Richard-Strauss Gesellschaft: Mitteilungen*, no. 26 (1960), 20–21

H. Fähnrich: 'Richard Strauss über die Verhältnis von Dichtung und Musik: Wort und Ton in seinem Opernschaffen', *Mf*, xiv (1961), 22–35

F. Hadamowsky: 'Joseph Gregor', *Maske und Kothurn*, vii (1961), 365–7

K. Birkin: 'Strauss, Zweig and Gregor: Unpublished Letters', *ML*, lvi (1975), 180–95

G. Brosche: 'Joseph Gregor und die Schüleroper "Des Esels Schatten", mit sechs neu aufgefundenen Briefen in Ergänzung des gedruckten Briefwechsels', *Richard Strauss-Blätter*, new ser., no.3 (1980), 14–24

H. E. Mutzenbecher: 'In memoriam Joseph Gregor: zu seinem 20. Todestag am 12. Oktober 1980', *Richard Strauss-Blätter*, new ser., no.4 (1980), 5–17

K. Birkin: 'The Last Meeting: *Die Liebe der Danae* Reconsidered', *Tempo*, no.153 (1985), 13–19

E. M. Axt: *Musikalisches Form als Dramaturgie: prinzipien eines Spätstils in der Oper 'Friedenstag' von Richard Strauss und Joseph Gregor* (Munich, 1989)
ERIK LEVI

Gregor, József (*b* Rákosliget, 8 Aug 1940). Hungarian bass. He studied with György M. Kerényi and Endre Rösler at the Bartók Conservatory in Budapest (1957–9). After singing in a choir, he joined the Szeged Opera, making his début as Sarastro in 1964. In 1990 he was appointed Intendant of the company. He has been a regular guest at the Budapest Opera, and has also appeared in Belgium, France, Germany, the Netherlands and the USA. With a resonant voice and ebullient personality well suited to *buffo* roles (his speciality), he has received acclaim as Mozart's Osmin and Leporello, and as Don Pasquale and Falstaff; he has also sung in recordings of neglected operas such as Paisiello's *Il barbiere di Siviglia*, Salieri's *Falstaff* and Cimarosa's *Il pittore parigino* (he sang in a performance of the last at Monte Carlo in 1988). Gregor's other roles include Rossini's Moses and Verdi's Attila.
PÉTER P. VÁRNAI

Greindl, Josef (*b* Munich, 23 Dec 1912). German bass. He studied in Munich with Bender and Bahr-Mildenburg, made his début in 1936 at Krefeld as Hunding, sang at Düsseldorf (1938–42), was then engaged by the Berlin Staatsoper, and moved to the Städtische (later Deutsche) Oper in 1949. He first appeared at Bayreuth as Pogner in 1943 and from 1951 to 1970 he sang there regularly in the Wagnerian bass repertory; he also sang Hans Sachs there and at Covent Garden (1963). In 1952 he made his Metropolitan début as King Henry. He appeared as Moses in the first German stage performance of *Moses und Aron* (1959,

Berlin). His repertory included Don Alfonso, Boris, Rocco and David Orth in *Die Bürgschaft*. His rich voice and fine artistry were admired at Salzburg, where he made a magnificent Sarastro and sang in the première of Orff's *Antigonae* (1949).

HAROLD ROSENTHAL/R

Grémont, Henri. Pseudonym of GEORGES HARTMANN.

Grenet, François Lupien (*b* Paris, *c*1700; *d* Lyons, 25 Feb 1753). French composer. His first work, the *divertissement Le triomphe de l'amitié*, was performed at Fontainebleau in 1714. Between then and 1733, the year he became *maître de musique* of the Paris Opéra, he gained a reputation in Paris as a singing teacher; he also held the official administrative post of *conseiller changeur*. *Le triomphe de l'harmonie*, his masterpiece, was first produced at the Opéra on 9 May 1737, and gained him printing privilege for its publication in the same year. Grenet, accused it seems of collaborating with Clérambault and Rameau in the work's composition, left Paris in 1739 for Lyons where he had been invited by the consulate to be the town's official music teacher. About the same time he became director of the Lyons Académie des Beaux-Arts and of the Académie Royale de Musique; he held these posts until his death. In 1745 he dedicated *Apollon berger d'Admette* (described by Grenet on the title-page as a new act added to *Le triomphe de l'harmonie*) to the Lyons consulate. These three stage works, his only compositions printed in his lifetime, are also the only ones to have survived, though we know that he also wrote sacred music.

Le triomphe de l'harmonie (libretto by Lefranc de Pompignan) is styled *ballet-héroïque*. The prologue, representing the descent of Peace, Harmony and Love, is followed by three entrées, 'Orphée', 'Hylas' and 'Amphion', each a self-contained exposition of the legend in question. In layout, as well as in its emphasis on dance and spectacle, *Le triomphe* fits naturally into the mainstream of French *opéra-ballet*. Grenet's music shows a composer of stature: his melodies have a sweep and expansiveness surprising for a French composer, and his harmonic vocabulary is not only rich but also purposeful. Among his ingenious orchestral effects is the evocation of the Styx, with Pluto and his demons, at the beginning of 'Orphée': while low cellos and bassoons churn the thick waters in quavers, the first violins illuminate the scene with flashing scales of demisemiquavers. It is not difficult to see in such music the man Marignan described as 'un homme très vif, plein du génie de son art'.

De Marignan: *Eclaircissements donnés à l'auteur du 'Journal encyclopédique' sur la musique du 'Devin du village'* (Paris, 1781) [the controversy involving Grenet's name and the authorship of *Le devin du village*; A. Pougin, *J.-J. Rousseau musicien* (Paris, 1901), 82–4, cites the relevant parts of Marignan's text]

L. Vallas: *Un siècle de musique et de théâtre à Lyon, 1688–1789* (Lyons, 1932), 231–3 [incl. biographical details of Grenet]

EDWARD HIGGINBOTTOM

Grenser, Johann Friedrich (*b* Dresden, 1758; *d* Stockholm, 17 March 1795). Swedish composer of German birth. The son of the famous Dresden instrument maker Carl Augustin Grenser, he probably received his early musical training from his father and J. G. Naumann. In 1778 he emigrated to Stockholm as first oboist in the *hovkapell*, and in 1783 he changed to first flute. In the latter year he became associated with Carl

Stenborg's theatres, for which, like his colleague J. D. Zander, he provided musical arrangements and original operatic works, such as the perennially popular pasticcios *Tillfälle gör tjufven* ('Coincidence Makes the Thief', 1783) and *Masqueraden* ('The Masquerade', 1788), and the Singspiel *Slädpartiet* ('The Sledging Party', 3, C. G. von Holthusen; Stockholm, 28 March 1790; music lost). His musical style tends towards the simplicity of *opéra comique* and Singspiel, and his orchestration is often fairly heavy, with many rich wind sonorities.

F. Dahlgren: *Anteckningar om Stockholms teatrar* (Stockholm, 1866)

B. van Boer: *The Symphony in Sweden Part II* (New York, 1983)

BERTIL H. VAN BOER

Grenvallet. Pseudonym of ADOLPHE DE LEUVEN.

Grešák, Jozef (*b* Bardejov, 30 Dec 1907; *d* Bratislava, 7 April 1987). Slovak composer. Self-taught in composition, he spent most of his life as a freelance musician, unattached to institutions. His first attempt at opera was *Zlatulienka* ('Coming of Slovaks'), written in 1925 when he was a student at the Teachers' Training College at Spišské Podhradie. On the basis of this he was encouraged by Josef Suk to continue writing. His full-length opera *Neprebudný* ('The Unawakened'), after a story by Martin Kukučin, was originally written in 1951–2. A revised version (1970–81) was given in a concert performance at the Bratislava Festival in 1987. The short opera *S Rozárkou* ('With Rozárka', 1970–73) was based on a story by Vincent Šikula. His most significant opera, *Zuzanka Hraškovie* (Bratislava, 16 January 1974, concert performance), after a ballad by Pavol Országh-Hviezdoslav, has an unusual structure: its tripartite form is framed by an organ prelude and postlude; the music is inventive and shows the influence of east Slovak folksong. Grešák builds his structures by accumulating ideas rather than by developing them.

I. Vajda: *Slovenská Opera* [Slovak Opera] (Bratislava, 1988), 132–4, 230–31

IGOR VAJDA

Gresnick [Gresnich, Gressenich], **Antoine-Frédéric** (*b* Liège, bap. 2 March 1755; *d* Paris, 16 Oct 1799). South Netherlands composer. He was a chorister at St Lambert Cathedral in Liège at the age of nine, and from 1772 to 1779 studied in Naples at the S Onofrio Conservatory, first as a cellist and later as a *maestro di cappella*. He had *opere buffe* performed with success in Turin and Florence in 1779 and 1780; his *Il francese bizzarro* was revived several times in the following years in small towns in the north of Italy. Despite many journeys to Paris and Italy, as well as, probably, Berlin and London, Gresnick apparently settled in Lyons in 1780. On Gresnick's arrival in London in 1786, he was hailed by the press and probably enjoyed the protection of the Prince of Wales. During the production of *Alceste* (1786), he was compared to Haydn and Sacchini but was fiercely attacked by the Italians in London. From 1787 to 1789 he directed the Lyons theatre orchestra, but from then until about 1793 his whereabouts are unknown.

In June 1794, at the height of the Reign of Terror, Gresnick began his Paris career, which was to continue with mixed success. Some of his works saw over a hundred performances at the Théâtre des Amis de la Patrie (previously the Théâtre Louvois). In 1797, after this theatre ceased performances, he devoted himself to concert and salon works, but later wrote many *opéras comiques* using different scenes of Paris. Some achieved considerable fame, while others failed owing to difficult circumstances or even to ill-will: *Le rêve* (1799) was the subject of an obscure intrigue, mentioned by the newspapers after the composer's death; *Léonidas, ou Les Spartiates* (1799) received only three performances at the Opéra because of illness among the actors and a change in the directorship of the theatre; *La forêt de Brama* was never produced. This series of disappointments undermined his strength and may have caused his early death, though he was highly regarded during his lifetime in Paris, London, Berlin, Moscow, and perhaps Stockholm (where several of his works are found).

Gresnick's versatile talent adapted easily to all genres, and his contribution to the *opéra comique* was substantial though not sufficient to distinguish him from the best of his contemporaries. Nevertheless, his works show considerable melodic resource in the tradition of Grétry and Dalayrac, Classical harmony and phrasing, a good dramatic sense, complete mastery of the French and Italian operatic styles, and a refined simplicity. He also contributed to the development of the newly evolved melodrama.

opéras comiques first performed in Paris, and printed works published there, unless otherwise stated

Il francese bizzarro (ob, 2), Turin, Carignano, 1779, only lib. extant
L'ortolana di spirito (ob, 2), Florence, Risoluti, 1780, only lib. extant
Alceste (opéra, 2, C. F. Badini, after P. Metastasio: *Demetrio*), London, King's, 23 Dec 1786, excerpts (London, *c*1787)
Les petits commissionnaires (2, J.-B.-C. Vial), Amis de la Patrie, 12 June 1794, *F-R(m)*
Le savoir faire (2, A. Lebrun-Tossa), Amis de la Patrie, 4 April 1795, *B-Bc*
Le baiser donné et rendu (1, J.-H. Guy), Amis de la Patrie, 16 Feb 1796 (1796)
Les faux mendians (2, Lebrun-Tossa), Amis de la Patrie, 23 Nov 1796 (1797); rev., in 1 act
Eponine et Sabinus (opéra, 2, Vial), Amis de la Patrie, 1796, lost
Les extravagances de la vieillesse (1), Montansier, 1796, lost
Les faux monnayeurs, ou La vengeance (drame lyrique, 3, J.-G.-A. Cuvelier de Trie), Montansier, 1 May 1797, *Ba, F-R(m)*
La tourterelle, ou Les enfans dans le bois (3, N.-E. Framery), Feydeau, 3 Aug 1797, lost
L'heureux procès, ou Alphonse et Léonore (1, C. Le Prévost d'Iray), Feydeau, 29 Nov 1797 (1797)
La grotte des Cévennes (1, Sewrin [C.-A. Bassompierre]), Montansier, 6 Jan 1798, lost, 1 excerpt *B-Lc*
La forêt de Sicile (drame lyrique, 2, R. C. G. de Pixérécourt), Montansier, 23 April 1798 (1798)
Le rêve (1, C.-G. Etienne), Favart, 27 Jan 1799 (1799), lost
Le tuteur original (3, Joigny), Amis-des-arts (Molière), 21 March 1799, lost
Léonidas, ou Les Spartiates (opéra, 1, Pixérécourt), Opéra, 15 Aug 1799, collab. L.-L. de Persuis, *F-Po*
Rencontre sur rencontre (1), Montansier, 1799
La forêt de Brama (opéra, 3, H. Bourdic-Viot), unperf., lost

Spurious: Alessandro nell'Indie; Demetrio; La donna di cattivo umore; L'amour exilé de Cythère; Le petit page, ou La prison d'état

A Choron and F. Fayolle: *Dictionnaire historique des musiciens* (Paris, 1810–11)
A. Pougin: *Gresnick* (Paris, 1862); also in *Revue et gazette musicale de Paris* (1862), 52, 77, 153, 185
E. Gregoir: *Les artistes-musiciens belges au XVIIIe et au XIXe siècle* (Brussels, 1885–90, suppl. 1887)
A. Auda: *La musique et les musiciens de l'ancien pays de Liège* (Brussels, 1930)
R. Vannes: *Dictionnaire des musiciens (compositeurs)* (Brussels, 1947)

C. van den Borren: *Geschiedenis van de muziek in de Nederlanden* (Antwerp, 1948–51)
P. Mercier: 'Recherches récentes concernant … A.-F. Gresnick', *Annales du Congrès de Liège 1968*, i, 225–33
——: *A.-F. Gresnick, compositeur liégeois* (Louvain-la-Neuve, 1980)
PHILIPPE MERCIER

Gresse, André (*b* Lyons, 23 March 1868; *d* Paris, 1937). French bass. The son of Léon Gresse, he studied in Paris, making his début in 1896 at the Opéra-Comique as the Commendatore. During five years there he created Césaire in Massenet's *Sapho* (1897) and the President in Erlanger's *Le Juif polonais* (1900); he also sang Gaveston (*La dame blanche*), Nilakantha (*Lakmé*), Count des Grieux (*Manon*), Nourabad (*Les pêcheurs de perles*) and Colline. In 1901 he was engaged by the Opéra, where he remained for 25 years, singing 60 roles. These included Le Révérend, which he sang at the première of Massenet's *Bacchus* (1909), Ramfis, Méphistophélès, Gesler (*Guillaume Tell*), Leporello, Sparafucile, Friar Laurence (*Roméo et Juliette*), Alphonse (*La favorite*), Varlaam, Osmin, King Mark, Fasolt, Hunding, Wotan, Hagen (*Götterdämmerung* and Reyer's *Sigurd*), Pogner, Don Diègue (*Le Cid*) and Sancho Panza (*Don Quichotte*), which he had created at Monte Carlo in 1910. The very wide range of his powerful voice allowed him to sing many baritone as well as bass roles.
ELIZABETH FORBES

Gresse, Léon(-Pierre-Napoléon) (*b* Charolles, 22 July 1845; *d* Marly-le-Roi, 13 April 1900). French bass. He sang first as an amateur, then obtained engagements at Le Havre and Toulouse. He made his Paris début at the Opéra in 1875 as a Gravedigger (*Hamlet*), then sang Saint-Bris (*Les Huguenots*) and Gesler (*Guillaume Tell*). Engaged in 1878 at the Théâtre de la Monnaie, Brussels, he created Phanuel in *Hérodiade* (1881) and Hagen in Reyer's *Sigurd* (1884), which role he also sang at the Paris première (1885). He remained at the Opéra until his death, singing a wide repertory that included Balthazar (*La favorite*), Brogni (*La Juive*), Sparafucile, Bertram (*Robert le diable*), Don Pedro (*L'Africaine*), Don Diègue (*Le Cid*), the King (*Hamlet*), Friar Laurence (*Roméo et Juliette*) and Lodovico (*Otello*). The first Hunding (1893) and Pogner (1897) in Paris, he created Père Saval in Augusta Holmès's *La montagne noire* (1895). He was succeeded as a principal bass at the Opéra by his son, André Gresse.
ELIZABETH FORBES

Gretchaninov, Alexandr Tikhonovich. *See* GRECHANINOV, ALEXANDER TIKHONOVICH.

Grétry, André-Ernest-Modeste (*b* Liège, 8 Feb 1741; *d* Montmorency, Seine-et-Oise, 24 Sept 1813). Liégeois, later French, composer of Walloon descent. He made decisive contributions to the scope and style of the 18th-century *opéra comique*, and to technical aspects such as musical 'local colour' and the design of overtures. His *opéras comiques* and recitative comedies for the Paris Opéra enjoyed unparalleled success in the 20 years up to the French Revolution. Many of his works were staged abroad, and a number were revived in the early 19th century in Paris: several survived through the middle decades, albeit with updated orchestration.

1. LIFE. Grétry was the second of six children, the son of a professional musician and violinist at the collegiate church of St Denis in Liège. As a boy he entered the choir school of St Denis, where he later learnt the violin.

Because of inexperienced choirmasters, Grétry was sent to H. J. Renkin and Henri Moreau for counterpoint and composition lessons. But a crucial experience was the visit of Crosa and [? Natale] Resta's Italian comic-opera troupe from 1753 to 1755.

After producing a Mass, given at St Denis, and a set of six symphonies given at the house of its provost, Grétry was awarded a place at the Collège Darchis in Rome, a benefaction for Liège boys. He departed in spring 1760. In Rome he studied mainly with Giovanni Casali, producing more church music and six string quartets (later published as op.3a). Eventually he gained a commission for Carnival 1765, when *La vendemmiatrice* was given. (Ginguené said that this followed some months of lessons with Sacchini.) Grétry moved to Geneva in 1766, wrote concertos for Lord Abingdon, and got to know Voltaire and his circle at Ferney. In Geneva Grétry first heard and saw *opéra comique* performed, by a troupe for whom he provided a score (partially extant) in December 1766: *Isabelle et Gertrude*.

The path to success in Paris, where Grétry arrived the following year, was not smooth, but the young composer had the manners and personality to win necessary patronage and support. Backed by the Swedish Count of Creutz, Grétry established a partnership with the well-known writer and critic Jean François Marmontel, who had collaborated with Rameau (1751–3) and Josef Kohaut (*La bergère des alpes*, after his own moral tale). Their sequence of six *opéras comiques* was exceedingly successful, and work together stopped only when Marmontel's projects failed to pass the reading-committees of the Comédie-Italienne.

The impact of these works and *Le tableau parlant* (1769) made Grétry a popular figure, and he became ultimately a quite wealthy and influential man. In 1771 he married Jeanne-Marie Grandon (1746–1807), daughter of a painter, who bore him three daughters; all died young. Lucile Grétry, the second child, wrote two operas, which her father orchestrated and revised. Family life was central to Grétry's existence: his mother came to live with him, and in 1796 he took responsibility for the children of his recently deceased brother. His homespun sense of probity did not hinder a great sense of pride in his own achievements. Grétry's *Mémoires* are essential reading for the detailed account of his operas, his musical and dramatic theories and his unabashed self-projection. In his text *De la vérité* (Paris, 1801) he makes himself into a born republican, though in reality he had been on close terms with the French royal family, as well as other grandees. *Les deux avares* and *L'amitié à l'épreuve* were first given in 1770 during court celebrations of the wedding of the Dauphin and Marie Antoinette; the latter work was dedicated to her. *L'ami de la maison* and *Zémire et Azor* were first given the following year at court, and the latter was dedicated to the king's mistress, Mme du Barry. Marie Antoinette showed a marked liking for Grétry's music, and appointed him as her personal director of music once she had acceded as queen in 1774. The composer's support for Louis XVI is still overt in *Pierre le Grand* (1790).

Grétry's fame spread throughout France, to the Low Countries, Germany, parts of Italy, Austria, Sweden and elsewhere. The Grand-Théâtre in Brussels obtained the rights to new, unpublished works and Grétry made triumphal trips to Liège in 1776 and 1782 to receive official honours. He was made an inspector of the Comédie-Italienne in 1787, and was pensioned by the Opéra and made Royal Censor for Music. His portrait was painted and engraved; he was sculpted by Pajou, Rutxhiel, Stouf and many others (see lists in Brenet 1884 and Lenoir 1989).

The apex of Grétry's career saw *L'épreuve villageoise* and *Richard Coeur-de-lion* (both 1784), together with contemporary successes at the Opéra: *La caravane du Caire* (1783) and *Panurge* (1785). Thereafter the popularity of his new works declined sharply, giving way before those by Dalayrac and, to a lesser extent, by Dezède. Adapting to the changes in taste, Grétry complicated the texture of such works as *Raoul Barbebleue* (1789) and *Guillaume Tell* (1791), with results that found favour. Yet he was also producing slacker work, generally with inferior librettos: but not even the 'republican' *pièces d'occasion* of 1794 lack his stamp. He continued to plan new operas, and in fact both *Lisbeth* (1797) and *Elisca* (1799) had success. The same mental energy was manifested in his programme of writing. *De la vérité* concentrates on philosophical speculation. *Réflexions d'un solitaire* (of which important MS sources have recently come to light) is a fascinating amalgam in which ideas, memories, whimsical thoughts and even dreams set a whole consciousness before us.

Grétry was honoured under the Revolution and the Empire, but declined to contribute to the basic work of the Paris Conservatoire. He had few pupils; Dalayrac was admitted to his study informally.

2. WORKS. Grétry's mission was to create a musical-theatrical language that the French would enjoy, once the path for composed *opéra comique* had been opened up by Duni, Philidor and Monsigny. It therefore had to contain italianate melody, a post-Mannheim symphonic forward impulse and an acute response to the poetry of a text. Grétry was thinking about these criteria as early as December 1767; in a letter to Padre Martini he wrote 'Many [in France] have tried to write music in the Italian taste, but have had no success, since the prosody of the language was incorrect; I believe I have overcome this problem'. Harmony was less important to him; like Rousseau, he placed his faith in the expressive power of melody. In addition, Grétry conceived his art to be entirely at one with the dramatic style and substance of his chosen libretto. Music had to bend faithfully to the character, the incident, the utterance and even the background shown on stage. All these tendencies reveal his art as a true forerunner of Romanticism, as did his belief that he should not tackle the same operatic theme twice (Charlton 1986 and Schneider 1988).

One of Grétry's proposals in the *Mémoires* was for a concealed orchestra and a plain theatre; his was an art that responded minutely to the nuances of words, to the power of irony and to small illustrative details. He was instinctively musical, but had a strong tendency to intellectualize his responses to dramaturgy. The latter are channelled mainly into the foreground of the music, while the orchestral filling remains minimal and the bass functional. Thus the overall balance of Grétry's music is unique: it was tightly fitted to the theatrical practice that was its *raison d'être*.

In keeping with this was Grétry's unshackled approach to musical form. Many pieces avoid regular *ABA* and sonata forms in favour of adaptations that avoid literal repetition. Some early solos and duets use *ABA'B'* form, for example, and Grétry occasionally adopts a loose rondo structure. Other pieces are not classifiable, deriving musical form from the stage situation above a scaffolding of basic tonal modulations.

Grétry entered *opéra comique* when all the resources of Classical opera became applicable to the burgeoning French genre: sonata development; duets and ensembles of every kind; italianate chain finales; new ideas for entr'actes and overtures; and extended choral writing. Grétry absorbed all of them and created memorable results. But he also contributed certain musical innovations: 'local colour', especially medieval imagery for *Aucassin et Nicolette* and *Richard Coeur-de-lion*, and the idea of sophisticated recollection of material, sometimes occurring over the entire span of a work. The most influential example of this was the ninefold use of the *romance* 'Une fièvre brûlante' in *Richard*, where the theme is subjected to systematic variety of treatment, being on one occasion transformed into a sung conversation with new words. Grétry was the first French comic-opera composer to adopt the chain-finale technique for Paris. Because it was against his principles to subordinate a drama to the demands of a stereotyped plan, the form of a Grétry finale is not predictable. He created important examples in *Le magnifique*, *La fausse magie*, *Les fausses apparences* and *L'épreuve villageoise*.

From 1768 to 1775 Grétry's chief collaborator was Marmontel. As a solid Encyclopedist, Marmontel chose themes that were never far from preaching enlightenment, improvement, the need for religious toleration and moral breadth of understanding: hypocrisy existed to be exposed. Of his works for Grétry, only *La fausse magie* is chiefly comic. *Le Huron* derived from a story by Voltaire satirizing French society and the Church. *Silvain* broaches the question of the rights of peasant hunters and poaching restrictions. *Lucile* concerns the daughter of a working man who enters a bourgeois family. *L'ami de la maison* is a social comedy centred on a hypocritical tutor. These librettos gave Grétry the opportunity to depict a wide range of situations and to develop his italianate music for the leisured characters. In *Zémire et Azor* (the story of Beauty and the Beast), where compassion and *sensibilité* are to the fore, Grétry's music found its fullest outlet so far. Marmontel's moral tales furnished other librettists with two works for Grétry: *L'amitié à l'épreuve* and *Les mariages samnites*. Both portrayed dilemmas challenging common moral assumptions by reference to the alien worlds of India and ancient Samnium.

Marmontel's *Mémoires* (1804) proved dismissive of Grétry and *opéra comique*, projecting them as part of a longer-term plan to convert French music to the Italian taste. (Marmontel later became librettist for Piccinni and Cherubini.) The period 1773–9 saw Grétry working with different writers on a range of stage subjects that broke new ground. These works also contained technical advances and further musical developments. *Le magnifique* is remarkable for the functional dramatic role of its overture and entr'actes, as well as for the long 'rose scene' where the Magnifico wins Clémentine's love and the music 'speaks' for Clémentine, who remains silent. In *La rosière de Salency*, *Les mariages samnites* and *La fausse magie* the chorus takes on a new, important role, adding a vital dimension of colour and depth. (At this period, however, the Comédie-Italienne had no permanent established chorus and was still performing on the restricted stage of the Hôtel de Bourgogne.) The first two works extended the genre's historical terms of reference and each included a near-tragic incident. Grétry's scores comprised music of wide scope (with trumpets and clarinets) and also developed the principles of 'functional recollection' of motifs. The three librettos by Thomas d'Hèle (1778–9) emphasized different values: mordant satire, robust characters derived from the English stage, and intelligent methods of incorporating Italian finales. *Le jugement de Midas* burlesques the musical conventions of *tragédie lyrique*, while *Les événemens imprévus* parodies the gestures of *opera buffa*; but both achieve their effect by ingenious integration of music and drama.

After Monsigny was threatened with blindness from constant work, the librettist Michel-Jean Sedaine had to seek a new composer. Partnership with Grétry permitted the continued growth of Sedaine's ambitions and the continued record of his successes. With *Aucassin et Nicolette* and *Richard Coeur-de-lion*, 'gothic' subject matter acted as a catalyst for the coming-of-age of *opéra comique*. No comparable earlier work showed the flexibility and imagination found in Grétry's music. The first version of *Aucassin* faced opposition on account of its strange archaisms and its verse text; *Richard* proved more congenial.

After these, Sedaine worked up *Le comte d'Albert*, a modern parable about the great being rewarded for assisting the humble, and the more original *Raoul Barbe-bleue*, based on the Bluebeard story. The latter broke convention on account of its violent subject and the final murder of Raoul after the rescue of his wife, Isaure. The suspense, gloom and power of the fable were well captured by the music, which found especial success on the German stage. In *Guillaume Tell* a highly-wrought score showed that Grétry could compete with the most recent achievements of Méhul and Cherubini. Indeed, many of Grétry's Sedaine operas incorporated instrumental effects (e.g. muted brass and timpani in *Richard*) and a full complement of wind instruments (piccolo in *Raoul Barbe-bleue* and *Guillaume Tell*). The chorus, particularly after the opening of the new Comédie-Italienne theatre in 1783, formed an essential ingredient of all later works by Grétry, and his choral writing was as original and apt as his vocal ensembles had been.

Grétry's gift for comedy extended widely. In the quartet 'Il a les traits' and Gilotin's slightly imbecilic music in *Le Huron*, he evinced great skills of timing and characterization. The epitome of his simpler comedy was *Les deux avares*, where the physical stage situations are very well captured in music. *Le tableau parlant* crossed *commedia dell'arte* characters with gentle sentiment, while the much later *L'épreuve villageoise* expanded its rustic comedy through clever social irony and worldly-wise characters. In a different league altogether were the spectacular recitative works for the Paris Opéra (1782–5). Essentially, they reproduced techniques of his earlier comedies, but exploited choral and dance episodes to great effect, as, for example, in *La caravane du Caire*. The various temptations to create further large-scale entertainments for the Opéra led to *Amphitryon*, *Aspasie*, *Anacréon chez Polycrate* and *Delphis et Mopsa*. These classical subjects failed to inspire either Grétry or his critics; only *Anacréon* endured, and that for almost 25 years.

Severe problems affected the librettos of *Le prisonnier anglais* and *Le rival confident*; *Cécile et Ermancé* received only one showing and had to be reworked twice, yet gained merely 12 performances; *Basile* was seen twice; *Joseph Barra* four times; *Callias* 14 times;

La rosière républicaine seven times; *Denys le tyran* ten times. Attempts were made to revive *Les mariages samnites* as *Roger et Olivier*, and *La rosière républicaine* as *Le barbier du village*. Of these scores only *Le rival confident* was published, but important musical manuscripts have recently reappeared and will permit further study of this complex period for the first time (Lenoir 1989).

Grétry's operas, which enjoyed such a vogue in France (Charlton 1986 gives statistics), cannot be judged without the contribution of his librettists. Nevertheless, full credit must be given to his own contributions to the planning (partly revealed in his *Réflexions d'un solitaire*), as well as his unrelenting desire to extend the scope of both *opéra comique* and *opéra*. Grétry's very attractive melodic gift was an essential ingredient, and helps justify the occasional revival of his music. With his librettists he brought to life a range of splendidly imagined characters, ranging from bumpkins to monarchs, or from a rebellious female warrior to the murderous Bluebeard. His best scores had wide currency, especially in Germany: it is hard to imagine the evolution of *opéra comique*, and Romantic opera in general, without the part played by his works.

See also AUCASSIN ET NICOLETTE; CARAVANE DU CAIRE, LA; GUILLAUME TELL (i); LUCILE; MARIAGES SAMNITES, LES; RICHARD CŒUR-DE-LION; TABLEAU PARLANT, LE; and ZÉMIRE ET AZOR.

Editions: *A.-E.-M. Grétry: Collection complète des oeuvres*, ed. F. A. Gevaert, E. Fétis, A. Wotquenne and others (Leipzig, 1884–1936) [CC]

First performed and published in Paris unless otherwise stated. Only major revisions are cited (for others, particularly cuts, in works to 1790 see Charlton 1986). Dates in parentheses indicate the publication in Paris of the full score; numerous extracts, particularly instrumental dance suites and solo songs, published in arrangements.

PCI – *Paris, Comédie-Italienne* POC – *Paris, Opéra-Comique*

title	genre, acts	libretto	first performance	sources and remarks	CC
La vendemmiatrice	2 intermezzos	Labbate	Rome, Alberti, carn. 1765	lib. (Rome, 1765)	
Isabelle et Gertrude, ou Les sylphes supposés	cmda, 1	C.-S. Favart, after Voltaire: *Gertrude, ou L'éducation d'une fille*	Geneva, Dec 1766	orch pts (nearly complete) and vocal pts for 4 nos. F-Pn; orig. set by Blaise, 1765	
Les mariages samnites [1st version]	opéra, 1	P. Légier, after J. F. Marmontel	Prince of Conti's chateau, *c*Jan 1768	see also 2nd version, 1776	
Le Huron	cmda, 2	Marmontel, after Voltaire: *L'ingénu*	PCI (Bourgogne), 20 Aug 1768	(1768)	xiv
Le connaisseur	cmda, 3	Marmontel, after his *conte*	unperf.	comp. 1768; lib. destroyed after objections by PCI committee; 8 pieces set [see Marmontel: *Mémoires* (1804, ed. 1891), ii, 330–31, and Grétry (1801–13, ed. 1919–22), ii, 104]	
Lucile	comédie mise en musique, 1	Marmontel, after his *conte L'école des pères*	PCI (Bourgogne), 5 Jan 1769	(1769)	ii
Le tableau parlant	comédie-parade, 1	L. Anseaume	PCI (Bourgogne), 20 Sept 1769	(1769)	ix
Momus sur la terre	prol.	C. H. Watelet	Chateau de la Roche-Guyon, ?1769	cited by Grétry (2/1797) in list of works	
Silvain	cmda, 1	Marmontel, after S. Gessner: *Erast*	PCI (Bourgogne), 19 Feb 1770	(1770)	xxvii
Les filles pourvues	compliment de clôture	Anseaume	PCI (Bourgogne), 31 March 1770	lib. partly pubd in *Mercure de France* (April 1770), 145–9	
Les deux avares	opéra bouffon, 2	C. G. Fenouillot de Falbaire	Fontainebleau, 27 Oct 1770	for marriage celebrations of the dauphin and Marie Antoinette; rev. version, PCI (Bourgogne), 6 Dec 1770 (1771); PCI (Bourgogne), 6 June 1773 (1773)	xx
L'amitié à l'épreuve	cmda, 2	Favart and C.-H. Fusée de Voisenon, after Marmontel	Fontainebleau, 13 Nov 1770	PCI (Bourgogne), 24 Jan 1771 (1772); rev. version (1, Favart alone), Versailles, 29 Dec 1775, PCI, 1 Jan 1776; as Les vrais amis, ou L'amitié à l'épreuve (3), Fontainebleau, 24 Oct 1786, rev. version, PCI, 30 Oct 1786 (1787)	xlii–xliii
L'ami de la maison	cmda, 3	Marmontel, after his *conte moral Le connaisseur*	Fontainebleau, 26 Oct 1771	rev. version, PCI (Bourgogne), 14 May 1772; PCI, 12 Nov 1772 (1773)	xxxviii

title	genre, acts	libretto	first performance	sources and remarks	CC
Zémire et Azor	comédie-ballet mêlée de chants et de danses, 4	Marmontel, after M. Le Prince de Beaumont: *La belle et la bête*	Fontainebleau, 9 Nov 1771	PCI (Bourgogne), 16 Dec 1771 (1772)	xiii
Le magnifique	comédie mise en musique, 3	M.-J. Sedaine, after La Fontaine	PCI (Bourgogne), 4 March 1773	(1773)	xxxi
La rosière de Salency	pastorale, 4	A. F. J. Masson de Pezay	Fontainebleau, 23 Oct 1773	*Pn*; PCI (Bourgogne), 28 Feb 1774; rev. version (3), PCI, 18 June 1774 (1774)	xxx
Céphale et Procris, ou L'amour conjugal	ballet-héroïque, 3	Marmontel, after Ovid: *Metamorphoses* (book 7)	Versailles, 30 Dec 1773	for marriage celebrations of Count of Artois and Marie Thérèse of Savoy; *Pn*; rev. version, Opéra, 2 May 1775, *Po*; (1775); Opéra, 23 May 1777, *Po*	iii–iv
La fausse magie	comédie mêlée de chant, 2	Marmontel	PCI (Bourgogne), 1 Feb 1775	rev. version (1), PCI, 9 Feb 1775 (1775); in 2 acts, PCI, 18 March 1776; PCI, 8 Jan 1778 (?1778) [see Charlton 1986]	xxv
Les mariages samnites [2nd version]	drame lyrique, 3	B. F. de Rosoi, after Marmontel	PCI (Bourgogne), 12 June 1776	lib. new, music partly from 1768 version (see Grétry 2/1797, i, 288); (1776); rev. version, PCI, 22 May 1782; see also parodies: Roger et Olivier, 1792–3, and L'inquisition de Madrid, 1793–4	xxxv
Amour pour amour	3 divertissements	P. Laujon	Versailles, 10 March 1777	added to P. C. N. de La Chaussée's comédie (Paris, 1777)	
Matroco	drame burlesque, 5	Laujon	Prince of Condé's chateau, 3 Nov 1777	incl. vaudeville tunes; rev. version (4), Fontainebleau, 21 Nov 1777; PCI (Bourgogne), 23 Feb 1778; lib. (Paris, 1777, 2/1778)	
Le jugement de Midas	cmda, 3	T. D'Hèle	Mme de Montesson's apartments in the Palais Royal, 28 March 1778	versification partly by Anseaume; rev. version, PCI (Bourgogne), 27 June 1778 (1779)	xvii
Les trois âges de l'opéra [Le génie de l'opéra; Les trois âges de la musique]	prol.	A. M. D. Devismes de Saint-Alphonse	Opéra, 27 April 1778	incl. music by Lully, Rameau, Gluck, and others (see Bartlet, 'A Musician's View', 1989); *Pn*, *Po* (mostly autograph)	xlvi
Les fausses apparences, ou L'amant jaloux	cmda, 3	D'Hèle, after S. Centlivre: *The Wonder, a Woman Keeps a Secret*	Versailles, 20 Nov 1778	versification by F. Levasseur; rev. version, PCI (Bourgogne), 23 Dec 1778 (1779)	xxi
Les statues	opéra féerie, 4	Marmontel, after *The Thousand and One Nights*	unperf.	comp. 1776–8; intended for PCI but only 2 acts set; see Grétry (1801–13, ed. 1919–22), ii, 104	
Les événemens imprévus	cmda, 3	D'Hèle	Versailles, 11 Nov 1779	PCI (Bourgogne), 13 Nov 1779; rev. version, PCI, 12 Oct 1780 (1781)	x
Aucassin et Nicolette, ou Les moeurs du bon vieux tems	comédie mise en musique, 4	Sedaine, after J.-B. de la Curne de Sainte-Palaye, ed.: *Les amours du bon vieux tems*	Versailles, 30 Dec 1779	PCI (Bourgogne), 3 Jan 1780; rev. (3), PCI, 7 Jan 1782 (1783)	xxxii
Andromaque	tragédie lyrique, 3	L. G. Pitra, after Racine	Opéra, 6 June 1780	*Po*; Act 3 rev. version, Opéra, 15 May 1781, *Po*; (1781)	xxxvi–xxxvii
Emilie, ou La belle esclave	comédie lyrique, 1	N.-F. Guillard	Opéra, 22 Feb 1781	added as Act 5 to the ballet pantomime La fête de Mirza; *Po*	xlvii
Colinette à la cour, ou La double épreuve	comédie lyrique, 3	J. B. Lourdet de Santerre, after Favart: *Ninette à la cour*	Opéra, 1 Jan 1782	*Po*; (1782)	xv–xvi
L'embarras des richesses	comédie lyrique, 3	Lourdet de Santerre, after L. J. C. S. d'Allainval: *Le savetier et le financier*	Opéra, 26 Nov 1782	*Po*; (1783)	xi–xii

title	genre, acts	libretto	first performance	sources and remarks	CC
Electre	tragédie lyrique, 3	J. C. Thilorier, after Euripides	unperf.	comp. 1781–2; intended for the Opéra; lib. (Paris, 1808); cited by Grétry (2/1797) in list of works	
Les colonnes d'Alcide	opéra, 1	Pitra	unperf.	comp. 1782; intended for the Opéra; *Po* (inc. score, complete pts)	
Thalie au nouveau théâtre	prol.	Sedaine	PCI (Favart), 28 April 1783	for opening of PCI at Théâtre Favart; mostly vaudevilles; lib. (1783)	
La caravane du Caire	opéra-ballet, 3	E. Morel de Chédeville	Fontainebleau, 30 Oct 1783	rev. version, Opéra, 15 Jan 1784, *Po*; (1784)	xxii–xxiii
Théodore et Paulin	comédie lyrique, 3	Desforges [P. J. B. Choudard]	Versailles, 5 March 1784	frags. *B-Bc*, lib. *F-Pn*; PCI (Favart), 18 March 1784; much rev. as L'épreuve villageoise	
L'épreuve villageoise	opéra bouffon, 2	Desforges	PCI, 24 June 1784	rev. of Théodore et Paulin, 1784 (1784)	vi
Richard Coeur-de-lion	comédie mise en musique, 3	Sedaine, after account in *Bibliothèque universelle des romans*, ii (July 1776) [attrib. A. R. Voyer d'Argenson, Marquis de Paulmy]	PCI (Favart), 21 Oct 1784	rev. (4), Fontainebleau, 25 Oct 1785; PCI, 22 Dec 1785; in 3 acts, PCI, 29 Dec 1785 (1786)	i
Panurge dans l'île des lanternes	comédie lyrique, 3	Morel de Chédeville, after F. Parfaict	Opéra, 25 Jan 1785	*Po*; (1785)	xix, xxiii
Oedipe à Colonne	tragédie lyrique, 3	Guillard, after Sophocles	unperf.	comp. 1785, inc.; intended for the Opéra; Act 1 written but destroyed; set by Sacchini in 1786	
Amphitryon	opéra, 3	Sedaine, after Molière	Versailles, 15 March 1786	rev. version, Opéra, 15 July 1788; *Pn*, *Po*	xxxiii–xxxiv
Les méprises par ressemblance	cmda, 3	J. Patrat, after Plautus: *Menaechmi*	Fontainebleau, 7 Nov 1786	PCI (Favart), 16 Nov 1786; rev. version, PCI, 30 Nov 1786 (1791)	v
Le comte d'Albert	drame mis en musique, 2; 'suite', oc, 1	Sedaine, after J. de La Fontaine: *Le lion et le rat*	Fontainebleau, 13 Nov 1786	perf. with 'suite'; PCI (Favart), 8 Feb 1787 (1787); rev. as Albert et Antoine, ou Le service récompensé, POC (Favart), 7 Dec 1794	xxvi
Le prisonnier anglais	cmda, 3	Desfontaines [F. G. Fouques], after a *cause célèbre*	PCI (Favart), 26 Dec 1787	rev. version, PCI, 18 Feb 1788; as Clarice et Belton, ou Le prisonnier anglais, PCI, 23 March 1793; *B-Br* (Acts 2 and 3, partly autograph), *Lg* (partly autograph)	xlviii–xlix
Le rival confident	comédie mise en musique, 2	N. J. Forgeot	PCI (Favart), 26 June 1788	rev. version, PCI, 6 Oct 1788 (1789)	xlv
Raoul Barbe-bleue	comédie mise en musique, 3	Sedaine, after C. Perrault	PCI (Favart), 2 March 1789	(*c*1790–91)	xviii
Aspasie	opéra, 3	Morel de Chédeville	Opéra, 17 March 1789	*F-Po*	
Pierre le Grand	comédie mêlée de chants, 4	J. N. Bouilly, after Voltaire: *Histoire de Russie sous Pierre le Grand*	PCI (Favart), 13 Jan 1790	rev. (3), PCI, 2 Nov 1790 (1791)	xl
Guillaume Tell	drame mis en musique, 3	Sedaine, after A.-M. Lemierre	PCI (Favart), 9 April 1791	(1794)	xxiv
Cécile et Ermancé, ou Les deux couvents	cmda, 3	C. J. Rouget de Lisle and J.-B.-D. Desprès	PCI (Favart), 16 Jan 1792	*B-Br* (inc.; partly autograph), ov. *F-Pn*; rev. as Le despotisme monacal, PCI, 1 Nov 1792	
Basile, ou A trompeur, trompeur et demi	cmda, 1	Sedaine, after M. de Cervantes: *Don Quixote*	PCI (Favart), 17 Oct 1792	*Br** (inc.), *Lg** (inc.)	
L'officier de fortune	drame, 3	E.-G.-F. de Favières	unperf.	comp. 1792; intended for PCI; *Lg** (inc.); not to be confused with A. Bruni's L'officier de fortune, ou Les deux militaires, 1782	

title	genre, acts	libretto	first performance	sources and remarks	CC
Roger et Olivier	opéra, 3	J. M. Souriguère de Saint-Marc, after L. d'Ussieux: *Roger et Victor de Shabran*	unperf.	comp. 1792–3; intended for POC; *F-Pn**, *Pn* (printed score with autograph adds.), *C-Lu**; mostly parodied on Les mariages samnites, 1776 (see Bartlet 1984)	
Séraphine, ou Absente et présente	comédie mêlée de chant, 3	A. J. Grétry	unperf.	comp. 1792–3; intended for PCI; *B-Lg**; see A. J. Grétry, 28	
L'inquisition de Madrid	drame lyrique, 3	A. J. Grétry	unperf.	comp. 1793–4; intended for PCI; mostly parodied on Les mariages samnites, 1776, with 1 piece from Les deux couvents, 1792; see Froidcourt, 164	
Le congrès des rois	cmda, 3	Desmaillot [A. F. Eve]	POC (Favart), 26 Feb 1794	collab. H.-M. Berton, Blasius, Cherubini, Dalayrac, Deshayes, Devienne, Jadin, Kreutzer, Méhul, Solié, Trial; suspended after second perf., later banned; *F-Pn** (Berton's duo)	
Joseph Barra	fait historique, 1	G. D. T. Levrier Champ-Rion	POC (Favart), 5 June 1794	*B-Br**	
Denys le tyran, maître d'école à Corinthe	opéra, 1	P. S. Maréchal	Opéra, 23 Aug 1794	*F-Pn, Po*	xxviii
La rosière républicaine, ou La fête de la vertu	opéra, 1	Maréchal	Opéra, 2 Sept 1794	orig. entitled La fête de la raison; *B-Br** (1 duo), *F-Pn, Po*	xxix
Callias, ou Nature et patrie	opéra, 1	F.-B. Hoffman	POC (Favart), 19 Sept 1794	*B-Br** (1 air), *F-Mc* (see Bartlet 1987)	
Diogène et Alexandre	opéra, 3	Maréchal	unperf.	comp. 1794; intended for the Opéra; *B-Lg** (Act 1); cited by Grétry (2/1797) in list of works	
Lisbeth	drame lyrique, 3	Favières, after J. P. C. de Florian: *Claudine*	POC (Favart), 10 Jan 1797	(1798)	lxiv
Anacréon chez Polycrate	opéra, 3	J. H. Guy	Opéra, 17 Jan 1797	*F-Po*; (1799)	vii–viii
Le barbier du village, ou Le revenant	oc, 1	A. J. Grétry	Feydeau, 6 May 1797	*B-Br* (inc.); lib. (Paris, 1797); music partly from La rosière républicaine, 1794	
Elisca, ou L'amour maternal	drame lyrique, 3	Favières	POC (Favart), 1 Jan 1799	*Bc* (inc.); rev. (A. J. Grétry) as Elisca, ou L'habitante de Madagascar, PCI, 5 May 1812 (1812)	xxxix
Le casque et les colombes	opéra-ballet, 1	Guillard	Opéra, 7 Nov 1801	to celebrate peace with England; *F-Po*	
Zelmar, ou Les Abencerages [Zelmar, ou L'asile]	drame lyrique, 2	A. J. Grétry	unperf.	comp. 1802; intended for the Opéra; lib. Archives Nationales, Paris; see A. J. Grétry, 28	
Delphis et Mopsa	comédie lyrique, 2	Guy	Opéra, 15 Feb 1803	orig. entitled Le ménage; *Po*	xli

Doubtful: Pygmalion, 1776 (comédie lyrique, 1, Rosoi) [according to Moreau (see Froidcourt, 89) begun by Grétry; later set by Bonesi]

Spurious: Alcindor et Zaïde (opéra, 3, Bouquet *fils*) [cited in *FétisB*; lib. rejected by the Opéra, 1787–8, never set]; Iphigénie en Tauride (opéra, 4, Guillard) [cited in Brenet, 121, but set by Gluck; see Froidcourt, 95]; Les maures d'Espagne [cited in *FétisB*; a confusion with Zelmar, ou Les Abencerages]; Le sage dans sa retraite (comédie, 5, Dalaïnval, after J.-M. Fragoso), The Hague, Français, 19 Sept 1782 [attrib. Grétry in lib.; incl. 3 airs from Les mariages samnites, 1776]; Ziméo (opéra, 3, Lourdet de Santerre) [cited in *FétisB*, but set by J.-P.-E. Martini, 1800]

According to Grétry (1797), he did not set Voltaire's *Le baron d'Otrante* (rejected by the PCI) or *Les deux tonneaux*; libs. written in 1767–8 and pubd in P. A. Caron de Beaumarchais and others, ed.: *Oeuvres complètes de Voltaire*, ix (Kehl, 1785)

Works by Lucile Grétry, orchd and rev. by A.-E.-M. Grétry: Le mariage d'Antonio (cmda, 1, Mme de Beaunoir [A. L. B. Robineau]), PCI, 29 July 1786 (?1786); Toinette et Louis (divertissement, 2, Patrat, after his Le mariage de Toinette, ou La fête bretonne, 1781), PCI, 22 March 1787 [Julien et Colette (oc, 1), parodied on the music of Toinette et Louis, intended for PCI, 1787, was unperf.]

A. D'Origny: *Annales du théâtre italien depuis son origine jusqu'à ce jour* (Paris, 1788)

A.-E.-M. Grétry: *Mémoires, ou Essais sur la musique* (Paris, 1789, enlarged 2/1797)

P. L. Ginguené: 'France', *Encyclopédie méthodique*, i (Paris, 1791), 621

A.-E.-M. Grétry: *De la vérité* (Paris, 1801)

J.-F. de La Harpe: *Lycée ou cours de littérature ancienne et moderne*, xii: *De l'opéra* (Paris, 1801)

——: *Correspondance littéraire* (Paris, 1801–7)

A.-E.-M. Grétry: *Réflexions d'un solitaire* (MS, 1801–13, inc.); ed. L. Solvay and E. Closson (Brussels and Paris, 1919–22)

J.-F. Marmontel: *Mémoires d'un père*, Oeuvres posthumes, i–iv (Paris, 1804); ed. M. Tourneux (Paris, 1891)

A. J. Grétry: *Grétry en famille* (Paris, 1814)

J. N. Bouilly: *Mes récapitulations* (Paris, 1836–7)

F. Van Hulst: *Grétry* (Liège, 1842)

M. Tourneux, ed.: *Correspondance littéraire, philosophique et critique par Grimm, Diderot, Raynal, Meister, etc.* (Paris, 1877–82)

M. Brenet: *Grétry: sa vie et ses oeuvres* (Paris, 1884)

M. Dietz: *Geschichte des musikalischen Dramas in Frankreich während der Revolution* (Vienna, 1885, 2/1886)

H. de Curzon: *Grétry* (Paris, 1907)

P. Long des Clavières: *La jeunesse de Grétry et ses débuts à Paris* (Besançon, 1920)

H. Wichmann: *Grétry und das musikalische Theater in Frankreich* (Halle, 1929)

S. Clercx: *Grétry, 1741–1813* (Brussels, 1944)

A. Vander Linden: 'La première version d'*Elisca* de Grétry', *Académie royale de Belgique: bulletin de la classe des beaux-arts*, xxxv (1953), 135–82

C. D. Brenner: *The Théâtre Italien, its Repertory 1716–1793*, University of California Publications in Modern Philology, lxiii (1961)

G. de Froidcourt, ed.: *La correspondance générale de Grétry* (Brussels, 1962)

R. D. Jobe: *The Operas of André-Ernest-Modeste Grétry* (diss., U. of Michigan, 1965)

C. E. Koch jr: 'The Dramatic Ensemble Finale in the Opéra Comique of the Eighteenth Century', *AcM*, xxxix (1967), 72–83

K. Pendle: 'The Opéras Comiques of Grétry and Marmontel', *MQ*, lxii (1976), 409–34

——: '*Les philosophes* and *opéra comique*: the Case of Grétry's *Lucile*', *MR*, xxxviii (1977), 177–91

P. Culot: *Le jugement de Midas: opéra-comique d'André-Ernest-Modeste Grétry* (Brussels, 1978)

J. B. Kopp: *The 'Drame lyrique': a Study in the Esthetics of Opéra-comique, 1762–1791* (diss., U. of Pennsylvania, 1982)

M. E. C. Bartlet: 'Politics and the Fate of *Roger et Olivier*, a Newly Recovered Opera by Grétry', *JAMS*, xxxvii (1984), 98–138

——: 'Grétry, Marie-Antoinette and *La rosière de Salency*', *PRMA*, cxi (1984–5), 92–120

D. Charlton: *Grétry and the Growth of Opéra-Comique* (Cambridge, 1986)

G. R. Marschall: 'Zum Verhältnis von Text und Musik in der französischen Oper: Bemerkungen zu Grétrys Ansichten über die Umsetzung von Sprache in Musik', *Aufklärungen: Studien zur deutsch-französischen Musikgeschichte im 18. Jahrhundert*, ed. W. Birtel and C.-H. Mahling (Heidelberg, 1986), 55–71

M. E. C. Bartlet: 'Patriotism at the Opéra-Comique during the Revolution: Grétry's *Callias, ou Nature et patrie*', *IMSCR, xiv: Bologna 1987*, iii, 839–52

D. Charlton: ' "L'art dramatico-musical": an Essay', *Music and Theatre: Essays in Honour of Winton Dean* (Cambridge, 1987), 229–62

M. E. C. Bartlet: 'Revolutionschanson und Hymne im Repertoire der Pariser Oper, 1793–1794', *Die französische Revolution als Bruch des gesellschaftlichen Bewusstseins*, ed. R. Reichardt and R. Koselleck (Munich, 1988), 479–507

M. Noiray: 'L'opéra de la Révolution (1790–1794): un "tapage de chien"?', *La Carmagnole des muses*, ed. J.-C. Bonnet (Paris, 1988), 359–79

H. Schneider: 'Tradition und Fortschritt in Grétrys Poetik', *Florilegium Musicologicum: Festschrift H. Federhofer zum 75. Geburtstag* (Tutzing, 1988), 327–74

M. E. C. Bartlet: 'A Musician's View of the French Baroque after the Advent of Gluck: Grétry's *Les trois âges de l'opéra* and its Context', *Jean-Baptiste Lully and the Music of the French Baroque: Essays in Honor of James R. Anthony* (Cambridge, 1989), 291–318

——: 'From *Académie Royale de Musique* to *Opéra National*: the Republican 'Regeneration' of an Institution', *The French Revolution, a Bicentennial Celebration: East Lansing, Michigan 1989*

Y. Lenoir, ed.: *Documents Grétry dans les collections de la Bibliothèque Royale Albert 1er* (Brussels, 1989)

M. Couvreur: 'Le Diable et le Bon Dieu, ou l'incroyable rencontre de Sylvain Maréchal et de Grétry', *Etudes sur le XVIIIe siècle*, xvii (1990), 99–125

P. Vendrix, ed.: *Grétry et l'Europe de l'opéra-comique* (Liège, 1992)

DAVID CHARLTON (text, bibliography),
M. ELIZABETH C. BARTLET (work-list)

Grétry, Lucile [Angélique-Dorothée-Louise] (*b* Paris, 15 July 1772; *d* Paris, March 1790). French composer. She was the second daughter of A.-E.-M. Grétry and was named in the family after the heroine of his second Paris opera. Details of her life emerge from her father's letter to the *Journal de Paris* of 29 July 1786, the day of the première of her *Le mariage d'Antonio* at the Comédie-Italienne (Salle Favart): Lucile received early lessons from her father in counterpoint and declamation, and from Jean-François Tapray (*b* 1738) in harmony. Bouilly's memoirs inform us of her unhappy marriage, as does her father's letter of 12 February 1790 (in Froidcourt). Like her two sisters, she was a youthful victim of tuberculosis.

Le mariage d'Antonio, a *comédie mêlée d'ariettes* (1, Mme de Beaunoir [A. L. B. Robineau]) takes as its point of departure Sedaine's libretto for A.-E.-M. Grétry's *Richard Coeur-de-lion* (1784), in which the young Antonio had acted as Blondel's guide. Blondel now facilitates Antonio's betrothal with gifts from himself, Richard and Marguerite. Lucile composed the vocal parts, the bass, and a harp accompaniment, which her father scored up for orchestra. The *Correspondance littéraire* praised its musical aptness, attractive melody and freshness. The full score was published in Paris in about 1786, and the work was relatively successful, gaining 47 performances up to February 1791. However the *divertissement mêlée d'ariettes Toinette et Louis* (2, J. Patrat), of which the libretto was criticized, had only a single performance (Comédie-Italienne, Favart, 22 March 1787).

A. D'Origny: *Annales du Théâtre Italien depuis son origine jusqu'à ce jour* (Paris, 1788), iii, 264–5, 299–300

A.-E.-M. Grétry: *Mémoires, ou Essais sur la musique* (Paris, 1789, enlarged 2/1797)

J.-N. Bouilly: *Mes récapitulations* (Paris, 1836–7)

M. Tourneux, ed.: *Correspondance littéraire, philosophique et critique par Grimm, Diderot, Raynal, Meister, etc.* (Paris, 1877–82)

M. Brenet: *Grétry, sa vie et ses oeuvres* (Paris, 1884), 190, 194–5

P. Long Des Clavières: *La jeunesse de Grétry et ses débuts à Paris* (Besançon, 1920)

G. de Froidcourt: *La correspondance générale de Grétry* (Brussels, 1962), 131–3, 151

D. Charlton: *Grétry and the Growth of Opéra-Comique* (Cambridge, 1986)

DAVID CHARLTON

Grey, (Constance) Gladys de. See DE GREY, GLADYS.

Grieg, Edvard (**Hagerup**) (*b* Bergen, 15 June 1843; *d* Bergen, 4 Sept 1907). Norwegian composer. He studied composition and the piano at the Leipzig Conservatory, 1858–62. In 1874, partly on Liszt's recommendation, the Norwegian parliament granted him a small annuity; this enabled him to divide most of the rest of his life between composing quietly at home in Norway and undertaking prolonged concert tours as a performer and conductor of his own works. The first significant composer to make the world of nature central to his art, he composed over 140 songs and orchestral, chamber, choral and piano music, most of it strongly Norwegian in mood and character.

Grieg collaborated with the two leading Norwegian poets of his day, Henrik Ibsen and Bjørnstjerne Bjørnson, in producing works for the stage. When in 1874 Ibsen adapted his poem *Peer Gynt* for the theatre, he invited Grieg to compose incidental music; Grieg provided 26 numbers – songs, choruses, entr'actes, melodramas and dances – most of them inseparably tied to stage production, highlighting the romantic episodes and the Norwegian rural scenes (1876, Christiania [now Oslo]). For Bjørnson's play *Sigurd Jorsalfar*, set in 12th-century Norway, Grieg had also written incidental music (1872, Christiania). In 1873 Bjørnson suggested to Grieg that they should collaborate on an opera relating how the baptized Viking warrior Olav Trygvason, King of Norway from 995 to 1000, brought Christianity to his country. On 10 July 1873 he sent Grieg the first three scenes, promising the next by October, and Grieg enthusiastically set to work. But he was never to receive any further libretto. In 1876 he pleaded with Bjørnson for more text, but the latter had lost interest. A final attempt made in 1888 proved to no avail, so Grieg orchestrated and published the fragments, about 30 minutes' music, as *Scenes from Olav Trygvason* op.50; the first concert performance was conducted by the composer in Oslo on 19 October 1889. The three scenes are set in a pagan Viking temple at Trondheim: in the first a High Priestess and worshippers call on Odin and the old Norse gods for help; in the second a prophetess announces that they will meet Olav in the temple, and the chorus of worshippers express hate for him and his new creed; the third consists of ritual dances in honour of the Norse gods. The period is suggested by the strong modal colouring of the score. There have been occasional stage productions of the three scenes (the first was at the National Theatre, Oslo, 8 October 1908), but the pervasive and unrelenting darkness of the music and the setting – the contrast was to have come with the arrival of Olav, in shining armour, in the fourth scene – tell against it.

D. Monrad-Johansen: *Edvard Grieg* (Oslo, 1934, 2/1956; Eng. trans., 1938)
J. Horton: 'Works for the Stage', *Grieg: a Symposium*, ed. G. Abraham (London, 1948), 93–105
——: *Grieg* (London, 1974)
F. Benestad and D. Schjelderup-Ebbe: *Edvard Grieg: mennesket og kunstneren* (Oslo, 1980; Eng. trans., rev., 1988)
B. Schlotel: *Grieg* (London, 1986)   BRIAN SCHLOTEL

Griesbach, Karl-Rudi (*b* Breckerfeld, Westphalia, 14 June 1916). German composer. He studied composition with Philipp Jarnach and conducting with Eugen Körner at the Cologne Hochschule für Musik, from which he graduated in 1941. For a short time after World War II he lived in Hamburg as a composer and pianist. In 1950 he moved to Dresden, where he was active as a music and theatre critic, lecturer and artistic adviser to the Dresden Staatsoper. A successful opera composer, he is also an accomplished librettist and has written on the theory of music drama. His music is directly expressive and clearly structured and shows individuality in the colouring and shaping of themes.

librettos by composer unless otherwise stated
Kolumbus (prol., 4 scenes, epilogue), Erfurt and Neustrelitz, 23 Dec 1958
Die Weibermühle (Spl, 4 scenes, T. Zahn, after J. N. Nestroy: *Talisman*), Weimar, 7 April 1960
Marike Weiden (3), Weimar, Görlitz and Neustrelitz, 7 Oct 1960
Der Schwarze, der Weisse und die Frau (Musiktheaterstück, 4 scenes), Dresden, 8 Dec 1963
Aulus und sein Papagei (3), Dresden-Radebeul, 2 Oct 1982
Florian, 1984 (3)
Noah, 1987 (3)

Belle und Armand, 1988 (2, after G.-S. de Villeneuve: *La belle et la bête*), Dresden

C. Hohlfeld: 'Wieder eine neue Oper: "Kolumbus" von Karl-Rudi Griesbach', *Musik und Gesellschaft*, ix (1959), 80–82
T. Marfordt: 'Noch einmal "Kolumbus": Analyse', ibid, x (1960), 203–8, 278–83
I. Winter: '"Marike Weiden", Karl-Rudi Griesbachs neue Oper', ibid, x (1960), 707–12
H.-J. Schaefer: 'Im Dienste der Oper', ibid, xvi (1966), 391–2

Griffel, Kay (*b* Eldora, IA, 26 Dec 1940). American soprano. She studied in Chicago and with Lotte Lehmann at Santa Barbara, making her début in 1960 at Chicago as Mercédès. After further study in Berlin, she was engaged at Cologne in 1973. She sang Fiordiligi for the WNO (1975) and the ENO (1985). At Glyndebourne she sang Alice Ford (1976). She has appeared at Berlin, Hamburg, Munich, Rome, Florence, Boston and the Metropolitan Opera, where she made her début in 1982 as Electra (*Idomeneo*), later singing Arabella, Countess Almaviva, Tatyana and Rosalinde. Her roles include Donna Elvira, Donna Anna, the Marschallin, Miss Jessel, Elisabeth (*Elegy for Young Lovers*) and Soldier Two's Wife (*We Come to the River*). In 1990 she sang Eva at Wellington, New Zealand. She has a smooth, creamy-toned voice that is ideal for Mozart and Strauss.   ELIZABETH FORBES

Griffini, Giacomo (*fl* 1692–7). Italian composer. He wrote most of his known operas between 1692 and 1697 for Lodi, where in 1697 he became *maestro di cappella* of the Church of Ss Incoronata.

Le fede ne' tradimenti (G. Gigli), Lodi, 1691, mentioned by Gerber; lib. of 1695 perf., *I-Mb* (anon.)
Endimione [last 2 acts] (F. de Lemene), Lodi, 24 Nov 1692, lib. *Bc* [Act 1 by P. Magni]
La Gosmena, Lodi, 1693, mentioned by Gerber
La fortunata sventura di Medoro o La pazzia d'Orlando (G. Giovanalli), Lodi, 1697

Aria in L'Arione, 1694 (see Sartori)

GerberL
C. Sartori: 'Dori e Arione: due opere ignote di A. Scarlatti', *NA*, xviii (1941), 35–42   THOMAS WALKER

Grillparzer, Franz (*b* Vienna, 15 Jan 1791; *d* Vienna, 21 Jan 1872). Austrian dramatist and poet. He studied law in Vienna and worked as a civil servant (1813–56). A series of sketches and works from his student days was followed in 1817 by the première and brilliant success of the fate-tragedy *Die Ahnfrau*. The next few years saw a remarkable series of completed works or sketches that were worked up in later years (including *Melusina*, the only completed libretto of several that Grillparzer projected for Beethoven). Travels to Italy (1819), Germany (1826, to visit Goethe), France and England (1836) and Greece (1843) were events in an otherwise settled existence marked by limited public success for the series of dramas that posterity has recognized to be the supreme achievement in Austrian literature.

Grillparzer's love of and interest in music throughout his life are evident. His favourite early reading was the copy of *Die Zauberflöte* owned by his nurse, who had played a monkey in it and kept the libretto as a prized possession. In his youth he studied music, and he composed songs and a rhapsody for piano. During his early and middle years he was a keen operagoer, and it seems likely that he derived the inspiration for his impressive simultaneous presentation of contrasting dramatic effects (e.g. in the play *Des Meeres und der Liebe Wellen*, 1829) from the ensembles in the Mozart operas he admired so profoundly. Grillparzer first met Beethoven at his uncle Joseph von Sonnleithner's house in 1805, and although Beethoven never set the libretto Grillparzer wrote for him, they continued to meet periodically. *Melusina* was ultimately set to music by Conradin Kreutzer and performed at Berlin (1833) and at the Theater in der Josefstadt, Vienna (1835). Bretón wrote an opera based on the play *Die Jüdin von Toledo* (1900, *Raquel*), Braunfels on *Der Traum ein Leben* (1934–7), Mraczek one on the same play (1909, *Der Traum*), and Max Mikorey on *Der König von Samarkand* (1910). Kaun based an opera on *Sappho* (1917) and Frank one on *Des Meeres und der Liebe Wellen* (1884, *Hero*); Andreas Nezeritis entitled his opera based on the same play *Hero and Leander* (before 1947). Grillparzer made parodistic versions of scenes from *Die Zauberflöte* and *Der Freischütz* for private purposes.

PETER BRANSCOMBE

Grimaldi, Giovanni Francesco ['Il Bolognese'] (*b* Bologna, 1606; *d* Rome, 28 Nov 1680). Italian stage designer and architect. In 1627 he went to Rome and remained there for the rest of his life, except for a brief period in the service of the French court in Paris (1648–51) at the invitation of Cardinal Mazarin, in whose house (now the Bibliothèque Nationale) he painted. He married Elena Luigia Aloisi, a relative of the Carracci family, and it was in their circle that he received his artistic training. Although he was predominantly interested in landscape, his best work was' the pictorial decoration of churches and palaces and the temporary constructions for religious ceremonies and secular celebrations. He designed the Giostra dei Caroselli for the Barberini palace (1656), in honour of Queen Christina.

His most important works for the theatre were the designs for Angelo Cecchini's *La Sincerità trionfante, ovvero L'Erculeo ardire* (1638) and Marco Marazzoli's *La Vita humana, ovvero Il trionfo della pietà* (1656), recorded in a splendid set of engravings.

For illustration *see* CASTELLI, OTTAVIANO and MARAZZOLI, MARCO.

*

L. Pascoli: *Vite de' pittori, scultori ed architetti moderni*, i (Rome 1730), 45–51
P. Bjurström: *Feast and Theatre in Queen Christina's Rome* (Stockholm, 1966)
W. Witzenmann: 'Die römische Barockoper *La vita humana, ovvero Il trionfo della pietà*', *AnMc*, no.15 (1975), 158–201
M. Fagiolo and S. Carandini: *L'effimero barocco: strutture della festa nella Roma del '600* (Rome, 1977–8)   ROSELLA ARIULI

Grimaldi, Nicolo. *See* NICOLINI.

Grimani. Family of Venetian nobles. They were the most powerful and influential dynasty of Venetian theatre proprietors, owning at different times four different theatres. The earliest was SS Giovanni e Paolo, named in Venetian fashion after the parish in which it was situated. It was built by Giovanni Grimani (1603–63) and Antonio Grimani (1605–59) especially for opera and opened its doors in Carnival 1639 with Manelli's *La Delia*. In 1655 the brothers opened a second theatre, S Samuele, which specialized in comedy. Following an interregnum after Antonio's death, during which SS Giovanni e Paolo was managed by the impresario Marco Faustini, his sons Giovanni Carlo

(1648–1714) and Vincenzo (1652/5–1710) took over in 1668. Under the brothers the family's involvement with opera reached its greatest height. In 1677 they built the S Giovanni Grisostomo theatre, which immediately became the premier opera house of Venice, exceeding all its rivals in magnificence. As a result, the prestige of SS Giovanni e Paolo declined; it was inactive during the 18th century, except in Carnival 1715 when S Giovanni Grisostomo was closed, and it was finally sold in a half-ruined state.

Both Giovanni Carlo and Vincenzo took a personal interest in operatic theory and practice. Gian Carlo's house in the parish of S Maria Formosa, furnished in mock-antique style, was the meeting-place of the Accademia degli Animosi, founded by Apostolo Zeno in 1691. This academy, which became a local branch of the Roman Arcadia in 1698, strongly promoted the 'reform' tendencies in opera advocated by such librettists as Domenico David and Zeno; the new principles are clearly evident in five miniature operas performed under the auspices of the Animosi at the turn of the century. (For Vincenzo's work as a librettist, *see* GRIMANI, VINCENZO.)

For some time after Gian Carlo's death, S Giovanni Grisostomo continued to keep its pre-eminent position through the efforts of his sons, among whom Michele (1696–1775) was the leading figure. It maintained its high ticket prices and disdained (except once, in 1734) to admit comic operas or intermezzos. However, economic difficulties caused it to be turned over to spoken comedies in 1751; it was finally sold by the family in 1819. S Samuele, on the other hand, became increasingly hospitable to opera. From 1720 onwards it frequently hosted the annual Ascension opera and after 1748 enjoyed a period of success with works in the comic genre. A financial crisis caused the family to sell it in 1768.

The fourth theatre, S Benedetto, opened in 1755. It filled the void left by the desertion of opera by S Giovanni Grisostomo. In 1766 Michele Grimani ceded it to an association of box-holders, a step which marked the end of his family's century-long ascendancy over the Venetian stage.

*

N. Mangini: *I teatri di Venezia* (Milan, 1974)
M. Talbot: 'Musical Academies in Eighteenth-Century Venice', *NA*, new ser., ii (1984), 21–65
H. S. Saunders: *The Repertoire of a Venetian Opera House (1678–1714): the Teatro Grimani di San Giovanni Grisostomo* (diss., Harvard U., 1989)   MICHAEL TALBOT

Grimani, Vincenzo (*b* Venice, 15 May 1652, or Mantua, 26 May 1655; *d* Naples, 26 Sept 1710). Italian cardinal, diplomat and librettist. His family (*see* GRIMANI) owned several Venetian opera houses. Destined for the church as a younger son, Vincenzo received the lucrative abbey of Lucedio in 1677. As a valuable diplomatic agent serving the Habsburgs, he was rewarded with a cardinal's hat in 1697 and the viceroyalty of Naples in 1708. His private diplomacy led to his being banned from Venice from 1690 to 1698.

His three librettos were issued anonymously for productions at the Teatro S Giovanni Grisostomo. (A fourth work, *Teodosio*, produced at the Teatro S Cassiano in 1699, is incorrectly attributed to him.) The first, *Elmiro re di Corinto*, was set by Carlo Pallavicino (1686). *Orazio* (1688, set by G. F. Tosi) is the earliest example of a Venetian libretto derived from a neo-classical French play (Pierre Corneille's *Horace*); *Agrippina* (1709), the basis for one of Handel's greatest successes, is one of the last examples of 17th-century libretto style. All three share the same *seicento* focus on the lively interaction of clearly defined characters, reflecting Grimani's interest in the *commedia dell'arte*. Arias are numerous and recitative is minimal.

Agrippina's amorality contrasts strikingly with the high-toned seriousness of librettos by Frigimelica Roberti, Zeno, Pariati and Silvani, who dominated Venetian opera at the time. Strohm interprets Grimani's portrayal of Emperor Claudius as a satire of Pope Clement XI, whom Grimani frequently opposed in the course of protecting Habsburg interests at the Papal court.

A. M. Quirini: *Tiara et purpura veneta* (Brescia, 1761), 286–7

G. Moroni: 'Vincenzo Grimani', *Dizionario di erudizione storico-ecclesiastica*, xxxiii (Venice, 1845)

E. Bocchia: 'Documenti teatrali del secolo XVIII: II. Informazione di alcuni comici pretesi dal sig. abate Grimani', *Archivio storico per le provincie parmensi*, new ser., xxii (1922), 209–22

H. C. Wolff: *Agrippina, eine italienische Jugendoper von Georg Friedrich Händel* (Wolfenbüttel, 1943)

——: 'L'opera comica nel XVII sec. a Venezia e l'*Agrippina* di Handel (1709)', *NRMI*, vii (1973), 39–50

R. Strohm: 'Händel in Italia: Nuovi contributi', *RIM*, ix (1974), 152–74

——: 'Händel und seine italienischen Operntexte', *HJb*, xxi–xxii (1975–6), 101–59; rev. and trans. in *Essays on Handel and Italian Opera* (Cambridge, 1985), 34–79

E. Selfridge-Field: 'One Hundred Venetian Arias of the Late *Seicento* in the Bodleian Library', *Notes*, xl (1984), 503–9

H. S. Saunders: *The Repertoire of a Venetian Opera House (1678–1714): the Teatro Grimani di San Giovanni Grisostomo* (diss., Harvard U., 1985)

——: 'Handel's *Agrippina*: The Venetian Perspective', *IMSCR, xiv Bologna 1987*, 251–61

L. Bianconi and G. La Face Bianconi, eds.: *I libretti italiani di Georg Friedrich Händel e la loro fonti* (Florence, 1992–)

HARRIS S. SAUNDERS

Grimm. German brothers renowned for their contribution to the literature of the fairy-tale. Jacob Ludwig Grimm (*b* Hanau, 4 Jan 1785; *d* Berlin, 20 Sept 1863) and Wilhelm Carl (*b* Hanau 24 Feb 1786; *d* Berlin, 16 Dec 1859) both held posts at Göttingen University from 1830, Jacob as a professor of philology and Wilhelm as a librarian; in 1840 they settled in Berlin as members of the Academy of Sciences. In the first edition of their highly popular *Kinder- und Hausmärchen* of 1812 they professed to have gathered their stories straight from the people and to have presented them in unvarnished form. The direct, folklike quality of the tales particularly attracted librettists and composers in the later 19th century; the genre of *Märchenoper*, which emerged in the 1880s, was born out of a concern for the essential simplicity of fairy-tales. Humperdinck's setting of *Hänsel und Gretel* of 1893 is the most famous example of an operatic adaptation of a Grimm fairy-tale; the composer also worked on the Grimm tales *Sneewittchen, Der Wolf und die sieben jungen Geislein* and *Dornröschen*.

The range of the Grimms' scholarly activity might be thought to support the claim that the tales are authentic. Jacob pioneered the systematic study of German language and medieval literature with his *Deutsche Grammatik* (1819–37) and *Deutsche Sagen* (1816–18), and both brothers worked on the monumental *Deutsches Wörterbuch*. Their academic approach to their material has often been contrasted with the more literary one of Achim von Arnim and Clemens Brentano

in the latter's folksong collection, *Des Knaben Wunderhorn* (1805–8). However, as revealed by the many changes in later editions of *Kinder- und Hausmärchen*, the brothers Grimm were also concerned with literary qualities and with making the tales conform to their ideal of a German folk idiom.

Many of the stories in fact show signs of an international origin; *Aschenputtel* and *Dornröschen* were probably taken from Charles Perrault's versions of the Cinderella and Sleeping Beauty stories in his collection *Contes de ma mère l'oye* (1697). Yet the Grimms succeeded in creating a distinct national identity for their tales. They accentuated repetitive and symmetrical patterns which they felt were appropriate to a primitive style of story-telling, and emphasized the fairy-tale's character as a battle between good and evil, making sure that evil was always roundly punished and that good was rewarded. These latter characteristics are reflected in many aspects of German Romantic opera and Wagnerian music drama; indeed Wagner drew on the Grimms' *Märchen von einem, der auszog das Fürchten zulernen* for part of the text of *Siegfried*. Kaun's opera *Der Fremde* (1920), Schoeck's *Vom Fischer un syner Fru* (1930), Orff's *Der Mond* (1939) and *Die Kluge* (1943), and Bresgen's *Der ewige Arzt* (1956), confirm that the fairy-tales have retained their fascination into the 20th century.   AMANDA GLAUERT

Grisar, Albert (*b* Antwerp, 26 Dec 1808; *d* Asnières, 15 June 1869). Belgian composer. A great admirer of Boieldieu and a pianist and amateur singer, he gave up the tradesman's career his family wished him to pursue in order to devote himself temporarily to music; his teacher was Joseph Janssens, a former pupil of Le Sueur. Although in 1829 he briefly resumed his commercial career, in Liverpool, the revolutions in France of 1830 attracted him to Paris, where he studied with Reicha for two years. The great success of his *romance La folle*, composed some years earlier, helped him to gain entry to the Brussels Opéra. His first opera produced there, *Le mariage impossible* (1833), in the style of Boieldieu, was rapturously received. Returning to Paris, he composed a number of popular romances of which thousands of copies were sold. Soon he made his début at the Opéra-Comique in 1836 with *Sarah*, a touching tale but a weak opera. *L'an mil* was worse, but from that point onwards Grisar's sense of comedy became sharper as he entered into the spirit of composers such as Rossini, Donizetti and, as certain arias show, Bellini. His feeling for humour and tempo variation improved, leading him to produce several increasingly amusing scores which, in their dynamic verve, clearly foreshadowed Hervé, Lecocq, Chabrier and even Offenbach.

In 1840 Grisar took up a grant from the Belgian government to study the music of Belgian composers in Italian church archives. However, in Rome, and then in Naples where he studied with Mercadante, he worked further on his compositional technique, immersing himself in the spirit of *opera buffa*. The eight years he remained in Italy yielded positive results. His *Gille ravisseur*, sent back from Naples (though he claimed to have written it in Paris before he left), may be regarded as his first small masterpiece; successfully produced in 1848, the work is remarkable for its intelligence, inspiration, subtlety, humour and sense of theatre. A stream of witty comedies followed, all characterized by variety, elegance and musical resourcefulness. Only one serious work briefly interrupted the flow, *Le carillonneur de Bruges*, produced in 1852 and inspired by a patriotic enthusiasm for the history of the composer's native Flanders; it was a kind of *drame lyrique* in the style of Meyerbeer, but it lacked the necessary breadth and, with a weak libretto, its success was limited.

Grisar was always in financial difficulty and had to work uninterruptedly until his sudden death. He had a mania for beginning pieces of work, and many of the scores he embarked upon never reached the stage. Some of them, nevertheless – *Riquet à la houppe*, *Le parapluie enchanté*, *Rigolo*, *L'âne et le prince* and *Afraja* – seem to have been virtually finished by July 1868. He also collaborated on several works, particularly with his great friend Flotow.

An immediate precursor of Offenbach, Grisar always worked within the confines of French good taste which he inherited from Boieldieu. His comedy is never vulgar or completely burlesque, and the music, of considerable merit, may be compared to that of Ambroise Thomas who, unlike Grisar, has not fallen into oblivion.

opéras comiques, first performed in Paris, unless otherwise stated

Le mariage impossible (2, Mélesville [A.-H.-J. Duveyrier] and Carmouche), Brussels, Monnaie, 4 March 1833, *B-Ba*

Sarah, ou L'orpheline de Glencoe (2, Mélesville), OC (Bourse), 26 April 1836 (Paris, ?1836)

L'an mil (1, Mélesville and P. Foucher), OC (Bourse), 23 June 1837, vs (Paris, ?1840)

La suisse à Trianon (1, J.-H. Vernoy de Saint-Georges and A. de Leuven), Variétés, 8 March 1838

Lady Melvil (3, Saint-Georges and de Leuven), Renaissance, 15 Nov 1838, collab. F. Flotow [9 songs later used in Le joaillier de Saint-James, 1862]

L'eau merveilleuse [Das Wunderwasser] (opéra bouffe, 2, T. M. F. Sauvage), Renaissance, 30 Jan 1839, vs (Paris, ?1839), collab. Flotow

Les travestissemens (1, P. Deslandes), OC (Bourse), 16 Nov 1839, vs (Paris, 1839)

Gille ravisseur (1, Sauvage), OC (Favart), 21 Feb 1848, vs (Paris, ?1848)

Les porcherons (3, Sauvage), OC (Favart), 12 Jan 1850, vs (Paris, ?1850)

Bonsoir, Monsieur Pantalon! (1, de Morvan and J. P. Lockroy), OC (Favart), 19 Feb 1851, vs (Paris, 1851)

Le carillonneur de Bruges (3, Saint-Georges), OC (Favart), 20 Feb 1852, vs (Paris, 1852)

Les amours du diable (opéra féerie, 4, Saint-Georges), Lyrique, 11 March 1853, vs (Paris, 1853)

Le chien du jardinier (1, Lockroy and E. Cormon), OC (Favart), 16 Jan 1855, vs (Paris, 1855)

Voyage autour de ma chambre (1, A. F. Duvert and Lauzanne, after X. de Maistre), OC (Favart), 12 Aug 1859, vs (Paris, 1859)

Le joaillier de Saint-James (3, Saint-Georges and de Leuven), OC (Favart), 17 Feb 1862, vs (Paris, ?1860); incl. 9 songs from Lady Melvil

La chatte merveilleuse (3, P. F. Dumanoir and A. P. Dennery), Lyrique, 18 March 1862, vs (Paris, 1862)

Les bégaiements d'amour (1, C. Deulin and E. de Najac), Lyrique, 8 Dec 1864, vs (?1900)

Les douze innocentes (opéra bouffe, 1, de Najac), Bouffes-Parisiens, 19 Oct 1865, vs (Paris, 1865)

Le procès (1), excerpts in *Journal des demoiselles* (July 1867)

Contribs. to: Flotow and A. Pilati: Le naufrage de la Méduse, 1839; L. Boieldieu and others: L'opéra à la cour, 1840; A. Karr: La Pénélope normande, 1860

Inc.: Riquet à la houppe, Le parapluie enchanté, Rigolo, L'âne et le prince, Afraja, L'oncle Salomon, Le mariage forcé (after Molière), Les contes bleus, Manon Giroux, La reine Mab, La mort du Cosaque

*

Fétis B; Stieger O

A. Pougin: *Albert Grisar* (Paris, 1870)

E. Gregoir: 'Lettres inédites d'Albert Grisar', *Littérature musicale: documents historiques relatifs à l'art et aux artistes-musiciens*, iv (Brussels, 1876), 73–86   PHILIPPE MERCIER

Griselda (i). *Drama* in three acts by ANTONIO MARIA BONONCINI to a libretto by APOSTOLO ZENO; Milan, Regio Ducal Teatro, 26 December 1718.

The plot is based on an old story familiar from the versions in Chaucer's *The Canterbury Tales* and in Boccaccio's *Il decamerone* (on which Zeno drew for his libretto). It was one of the most popular of all 18th-century librettos, being set by some 15 composers in the first two decades of the century and used frequently thereafter. The action unfolds near Palermo in Sicily. King Gualtiero (alto castrato), in order to convince his rebellious nobles that his peasant wife Griselda (soprano) is worthy to be their queen and the mother of their future king, tests her virtue and steadfastness with a series of cruel ordeals. He tells her that their long-lost daughter was killed on his orders, banishes her from the court and announces that he intends to take another wife. This will be Costanza (contralto), who is in fact the missing daughter and in love with Roberto (soprano castrato), younger brother of Corrado, Prince of Puglia (tenor). In the humble cottage to which she has returned Griselda is pursued by Ottone, a Sicilian nobleman (alto castrato), who threatens to kill her infant son Everardo unless she agrees to marry him. Griselda refuses, and after being allowed to return to the palace as a servant to Gualtiero's 'fiancée', she also refuses Gualtiero's order to marry Ottone. This is her last ordeal. Gualtiero reveals his true motive for tormenting her and accepts her again as his queen; Costanza and Roberto are reunited; and Ottone, who confesses to have stirred up the nobles in the hope of winning Griselda, is forgiven.

The 1718 text is so faithful to Zeno's original (Venice, 1701) that only a few aria texts were deleted or altered. Bononcini was a gifted contrapuntist, and his score is superbly wrought. Yet, in spite of its frequent Baroque textural complexities, pre-classical features predominate: for example, two-thirds of the arias are in major keys, two-thirds are vivacious, and only three of the 38 feature the slow, dotted rhythms that indicate pathos.

Prince Maximilian Karl von Löwenstein, the Austrian governor of Milan, to whom the opera was dedicated, died at the première.   MALCOLM BOYD, LOWELL LINDGREN

Griselda (ii) [*La Griselda*]. *Dramma per musica* in three acts by ALESSANDRO SCARLATTI (*see* SCARLATTI family, (1)) to a libretto, possibly by Prince Francesco Maria Ruspoli, after APOSTOLO ZENO; Rome, Teatro Capranica, January 1721.

Griselda (illustration overleaf; for details of the plot *see* GRISELDA (i)) is the last of Scarlatti's operas to survive complete, and musically, if not dramatically, it is a richly satisfying work. The leading roles were taken by castratos: Griselda, Costanza and Roberto by sopranos, Gualtiero and Ottone by altos; Corrado was sung by a tenor. After the conventional three-movement 'Italian' overture the basic musical constituent is the recitative-aria unit, but many of the arias are imposing pieces, accompanied mostly by full strings, often with woodwind support, and there is some prominent writing for two horns, in the embarkation scene in Act 1, the hunting scene in Act 2, and the garden scene in Act 3. Unusually in such a late work, Scarlatti accompanies the recitatives, after the first four bars, with continuo only until the strings return in the final scene to add fervour to Griselda's last and successful plea for Gualtiero's mercy.   MALCOLM BOYD

'Griselda' (A. Scarlatti), Act 1 scene ii: design by Francesco Galli-Bibiena for the original production at the Teatro Capranica, Rome, 1721

Griselda (iii). *Drama* in three acts by GIOVANNI BONONCINI to a libretto by PAOLO ANTONIO ROLLI after APOSTOLO ZENO's libretto (Venice, 1701); London, King's Theatre, 22 February 1722.

Zeno's plot, set by Bononcini's brother Antonio Maria in 1718, (*see* GRISELDA (i)), was retained but his text rewritten. Corrado was eliminated and three characters were renamed: Ottone is now Rambaldo (bass), Costanza is Almirena (soprano) and Roberto is Ernesto (soprano). The success of the work (given 16 performances during a four-month run) was partly attributed to the suitability of Anastasia Robinson for the humble role of Griselda (contralto). Francesco Bernardi, called Senesino, was Gualtiero (mezzo-soprano); he presumably instigated the revival by Handel and Heidegger's company on 22 May 1733, and was probably likewise responsible for the revival of Bononcini's *Astarto* (1720) by the Opera of the Nobility in 1734, since he alone repeated his roles in these revivals.

Astarto and *Griselda* are the only two London operas for which Bononcini published the overture and all the arias. Burney owned a score of *Griselda*, but neither it nor any other score including recitatives is extant. The dulcet arias suit a plot revolving around a gentle shepherdess (rather than a vindictive tyrant), and they were largely responsible for the success of the work. In Richard Steele's *The Conscious Lovers* (1722) Indiana found 'something in that Rural Cottage of *Griselda*, her forlorn Condition, her Poverty, her Solitude, her Resignation, her Innocent Slumbers, and that lulling *Dolce Sogno* that's sung over her; it had an Effect upon me, that – in short I never was so well deceiv'd at any [other Opera]'. Among the tuneful pieces, 'Dolce sogno, deh le porta' and 'Volgendo a me lo sguardo' for Gualtiero and 'Per la gloria d'adorarvi' for Ernesto were apparently the best-known. The last two were reprinted, for example in Richard Neale's *A Pocket Companion for Gentlemen and Ladies*, i (London, 1724) and in *The British Musical Miscellany*, iii–iv (London, 1735), in the latter with English texts.

LOWELL LINDGREN

Griselda (iv). *Dramma per musica* in three acts, RV718, by ANTONIO VIVALDI to a libretto by APOSTOLO ZENO revised by CARLO GOLDONI after Giovanni Boccaccio's *Il decamerone*; Venice, Teatro S Samuele, 18 May 1735.

Griselda dates from near the end of Vivaldi's career and was his only opera produced in Venice during the Ascension Fair. The manager of the Teatro S Samuele, Michele Grimani, engaged the young playwright Goldoni to adapt the libretto. Goldoni left two slightly differing accounts of his first meeting with the composer, during which Vivaldi, initially sceptical of the inexperienced poet, was completely won over when he provided a new aria text on the spot. From Goldoni's evidence it is likely that many of the alterations to Zeno's original text were on Vivaldi's specific instructions. These changes included reducing the total number of scenes and arias (there are 19 arias and a trio in Vivaldi's opera compared with 34 arias and five duets in Zeno's original 1701 libretto) and providing many new aria texts; these often employ similes which offered scope for the kind of pictorial writing familiar from Vivaldi's concertos. Vivaldi set the role of Griselda for a contralto; Gualtiero is a tenor, his confidant Corrado a contralto and the remaining three roles all sopranos. (For details of the plot, *see* GRISELDA (i).)

In *Griselda*, as in many of his other later operas, Vivaldi borrows a number of arias from earlier works, and his musical style frequently comes close to that of his younger contemporaries. The orchestral textures emphasize four-part strings (with the addition of a pair of horns in two arias) and are often built out of repeated short violin figures. Much of the vocal writing displays considerable virtuosity, as in Costanza's 'Agitata da due venti' and Ottone's 'Scocca dardi l'altero suo ciglio' from Act 2. Griselda's arias exploit the energetic, mainly syllabic text-setting typical of Vivaldi's writing for his protégée Anna Girò, whose vocal technique was limited but who was, according to Goldoni, a fine actress. Her soliloquy at the end of Act 1, added by Goldoni, culminates in the fine aria 'Ho il cor già lacero'. Its relentless rhythmic drive, sudden dynamic contrasts and adventurous harmonies vividly portray Griselda's emotional exhaustion, making this aria, together with the fine trio at the end of Act 2, one of the dramatic peaks of the opera. ERIC CROSS

Grisélidis. *Conte lyrique* in a prologue and three acts by JULES MASSENET to a libretto by Armand Sylvestre and Eugène Morand after their own dramatization of the medieval French tale (1891, Comédie-Française); Paris, Opéra-Comique (Salle Favart), 20 November 1901.

The legend of 'patient Grissil', familiar from Boccaccio, Chaucer and Perrault, has been set by more than 25 composers, among them Vivaldi, Piccinni and Scarlatti. The subject matter is hardly calculated to appeal to 20th-century audiences, describing as it does a husband's cruel, cynical test of his wife's constancy and – even worse – her submissive acceptance of his behaviour. Massenet and his librettists make the action more readily acceptable by introducing an extra character, the Devil, to tempt Grisélidis in place of her disguised husband, and by making this a comic role.

The setting is medieval Provence. In the prologue the shepherd Alain (tenor) sings of his love for the shepherdess Grisélidis (soprano); the Marquis de Saluces (baritone), out hunting, is enchanted by her beauty and proposes marriage on the spot. She accepts demurely, to Alain's distress. By the first act, Grisélidis has borne the Marquis a son, Loÿs. As he leaves for the Crusades, his household promises to confine his wife to the castle but, having complete trust in her, he angrily insists she be given her freedom. Were the Devil himself present, he would feel the same. The Devil (bass) promptly appears and, unhappily married himself, describes how he and his wife (mezzo-soprano) take pleasure in deceiving husbands. The Marquis accepts the challenge to Grisélidis's honour, gives the Devil his ring as pledge, and takes tender farewell of his wife and child without, however, warning them of this supernatural intervention.

In the second act the Devil and his wife approach Grisélidis in the guise of a Levantine slave-trader and a Persian houri, and produce the Marquis's ring to substantiate their claim that he has rejected Grisélidis in favour of the supposed slave. Grisélidis meekly but sadly submits. To tempt the obedient wife further, the Devil conjures up a neo-Wagnerian enchanted garden and draws the shepherd Alain into it. The appearance of the child Loÿs strengthens Grisélidis's resolve not to return to her first love, but when her attention is momentarily distracted by Alain's departure, the Devil snatches the child away from her. In the third act the Devil, disguised as an old man, tells Grisélidis that an amorous pirate is holding Loÿs hostage and will release him only in exchange for a kiss. The Marquis returns from the Crusades, and the Devil points out to him his wife rushing in distraction to the seashore, but the Marquis notices his ring on the old man's finger and realizes he is the victim of a fiendish plot. Husband and wife are reunited, the former properly remorseful. They pray at the shrine of St Agnès, and Loÿs is miraculously restored to them to the accompaniment of a heavenly choir.

Grisélidis does not deserve its comparative neglect: on its own terms it is one of Massenet's most successful operas. The action moves swiftly through just over two hours of music, the instrumentation shows the composer at his most economic and delicate, and in no other of his operas are his melodies so unconstrained. The use of reminiscence motif is judiciously calculated. Much of the score's appeal lies in its skilful mixture of comedy and sentiment. The role of the Devil was written for Lucien Fugère, one of Massenet's favourite singers; his music is full of sprightly, dry Gallic wit. Despite the frequent intervention of offstage chorus, the sentiment is kept within reasonable bounds, and the title role is as touching in its delineation as it is vocally rewarding – it was originally sung by Lucienne Bréval, who also created Fauré's Pénélope and Dukas' Ariane. Only a comparatively weak duet for husband and wife in the final act stops *Grisélidis* from being on a level with *Werther* and *Manon* in Massenet's output, and this minor flaw is balanced by the dance music in the enchanted garden and the tenderly nostalgic duet for Grisélidis and her first love, written with rare psychological insight and showing the composer at his best.
For illustration *see* PARIS, fig.21. RODNEY MILNES

Grisi, Giuditta (*b* Milan, 28 July 1805; *d* Robecco d'Oglio, nr Cremona, 1 May 1840). Italian mezzo-soprano. The elder sister of Giulia Grisi and the niece of Josephina Grassini, she studied with her aunt and at the Milan Conservatory. She made her début in Vienna in 1825 in Rossini's *Bianca e Falliero*. After engagements in Florence, Parma and Turin, she sang in Venice for several seasons. It was in Bellini's music above all that she excelled; in 1830 she appeared in *Il pirata* and sang Romeo in the première of *I Capuleti e i Montecchi*, which she also sang at La Scala. During 1832 she appeared in *La straniera* in Venice, London and Paris. In 1833 she sang the title role of *Norma* at Bologna, and the following season sang Romeo and Norma in Madrid. She retired in 1838, after an engagement at the Teatro Valle in Rome. ELIZABETH FORBES

Grisi, Giulia (*b* Milan, 22 May 1811; *d* Berlin, 29 Nov 1869). Italian soprano. She studied in Milan with Marliani and with Giacomelli in Bologna, where she made her début in the 1828–9 season in Rossini's *Zelmira* (Emma) and also sang in his *Torvaldo e Dorliska* and *Il barbiere di Siviglia*, and in Cordella's *Lo sposo di provincia*. After singing at the Pergola, Florence, she made her début at La Scala in the first performance of Strepponi's *Ullà di Bassora*, also creating Adalgisa in *Norma* (1831) and Adelia in Donizetti's *Ugo, conte di Parigi* (1832). She then broke her contract and left Italy, never to sing there again (bar a visit in 1863). Grisi made her Paris début at the Théâtre Italien in the title role of *Semiramide* (1832) and in the next two years sang Desdemona (Rossini's *Otello*), Giulietta (*I Capuleti e i Montecchi*), Anne Boleyn, Ninetta (*La gazza ladra*) and Ellen (*La donna del lago*). In 1834 she made her London début at the King's Theatre as Ninetta, and sang Donna Anna, Pamyre (*Le siège de Corinthe*) and Amina.

From 1835 until 1847 (except for 1842) Grisi alternated between the two capitals. In Paris she created Elvira in *I puritani*, Elena in *Marino Faliero* (both 1835) and Norina in *Don Pasquale* (1843), also singing in Donizetti's *Parisina*, *Roberto Devereux*, *Belisario*, *Maria di Rohan* and *Gemma di Vergy*, in Bellini's *Il pirata* and Verdi's *I due Foscari*. In London she sang the title roles in *Norma* and *Beatrice di Tenda*, Donizetti's *Lucrezia Borgia* and *Fausta* and Rossini's *La Cenerentola*, as well as Carolina and Elisetta (*Il matrimonio segreto*), Giselda (*I Lombardi*), Mozart's Susanna, and Mistress Ford in Balfe's *Falstaff*. Transferring to Covent Garden, she sang Semiramis at the opening of the Royal Italian Opera (1847; see illustration overleaf). Later

T. G. Kaufman: 'Giulia Grisi: a Re-evaluation', *Donizetti Society Journal*, iv (1980), 180–96
'A Chronology of Grisi's Operatic Performances', ibid, 197–223
'Grisi's Repertory', ibid, 224–5
E. Forbes: *Mario and Grisi* (London, 1985)   ELIZABETH FORBES

Grist, Reri (*b* New York, 29 Feb 1932). American soprano. She studied in New York while working in the theatre (she was in the first cast of *West Side Story*, 1957) and made her operatic début in 1959 at Santa Fe as Blonde. She sang the Queen of Night at Cologne (1960) and Zerbinetta at Zürich, where she was engaged from 1961 to 1964. She made her Covent Garden début in 1962 as the Queen of Shemakha, later singing Olympia, Gilda, Susanna and Oscar. At San Francisco (1963–9) she sang Rosina, Despina, Sophie, Burgundian Lady (*Carmina burana*), Adèle and Zerbinetta. She made her Salzburg début as Blonde (1965), returning there as Despina (1972). Having made her Metropolitan début in 1966 as Rosina, she returned as Sophie, Norina and Adina, which she also sang in Vienna (1973). With a light, silvery voice of wide compass and great agility, and an ebullient personality, she excelled as Zerbinetta and Oscar, both of which she recorded, and in the Mozart soubrette roles.   ALAN BLYTH

Griswold, Putnam (*b* Oakland, CA, 23 Dec 1875; *d* New York, 26 Feb 1914). American bass-baritone. He studied with Randegger in London, Emmerich in Berlin, Julius Stockhausen in Frankfurt and Bouhy in Paris. His début was at Covent Garden in 1901, as Leonato in the première of Stanford's *Much Ado about Nothing*. He appeared with the Berlin Opera (1904, 1906–11) and the Munich Opera, and toured the USA as Gurnemanz with Henry W. Savage's Company (1904–5). In 1911 he made his Metropolitan Opera début as Hagen and remained with the company for three seasons. There he sang 72 performances of 12 roles, including Daland, King Mark, Pogner, Wotan and De Guiche in the première of Walter Damrosch's *Cyrano de Bergerac* (1913), until his premature death from appendicitis. In both the USA and Europe he was considered one of the foremost Wagner singers of his time.   CORI ELLISON

Grobe, Donald (**Roth**) (*b* Ottawa, IL, 16 Dec 1929; *d* Berlin, 1 April 1986). American tenor. He studied at Mannes College, New York, and with Martial Singher. He made his début as Borsa (*Rigoletto*) in Chicago in 1952. After engagements at Krefeld-Mönchengladbach and Hanover, in 1960 he joined the Deutsche Oper, Berlin. There he created Wilhelm in *Der junge Lord* (1965) and Arundel in Fortner's *Elisabeth Tudor* (1972), sang Aschenbach in the German première of *Death in Venice* (1974) and took part in the première of Reimann's *Die Gespenstersonate* (1984). He first appeared at the Edinburgh Festival in 1965 with the Munich Staatsoper company as Ferrando; he returned with the Deutsche Oper in 1971 as Oleander (Riemann's *Melusine*) and in 1975 as Alwa. He made his Metropolitan début in 1968 as Froh, created Claude Vallée in Cikker's *The Play of Love and Death* (1969, Munich) and made his Covent Garden début with the Munich company in 1972 as Flamand and Henry Morosus (*Die schweigsame Frau*). His repertory also included Hoffmann, Eisenstein and Tom Rakewell. Although his voice was not outstandingly beautiful, he was a highly intelligent singer and a gifted actor.
HAROLD ROSENTHAL/R

Giulia Grisi in the title role of Rossini's 'Semiramide', which she sang at the opening of the Royal Italian Opera, Covent Garden, in 1847: lithograph from a contemporary sheet music cover

roles included Léonor (*La favorite*), Valentine (*Les Huguenots*), Fidès (*Le prophète*), Alice (*Robert le diable*) and Leonora (*Il trovatore*). Her professional partner in many of these roles, and her lifelong companion, was the tenor Giovanni Mario (she was separated, though not divorced, from the man she had married in 1836). Accompanied by Mario, she visited St Petersburg (1849), New York (1854) and Madrid (1859), before retiring in 1861. Grisi's voice, perfectly placed and even over a range of two octaves, *c'* to *c'''*, easily made the transition from the florid writing of Rossini and Donizetti to the more forceful style of Verdi and Meyerbeer. If she lacked the interpretative genius of Pasta or Malibran, she was an impressive singing actress, magnificent in such roles as Donna Anna, Semiramis and Norma, where her passionate involvement was allowed full scope.

For further illustration *see* DON PASQUALE; LONDON, fig.9; and NORMA.

Castil-Blaze: *L'Opéra-Italien de 1548 à 1856* (Paris, 1856)
T. Gautier: *L'histoire de l'art dramatique en France depuis vingt-cinq ans* (Paris, 1858–9)
H. F. Chorley: *Thirty Years' Musical Recollections* (London, 1862)
B. Lumley: *Reminiscences of the Opera* (London, 1864)
E. Creathorne Clayton: *Queens of Song* (London, 1865)
H. Sutherland Edwards: *The Prima Donna* (London, 1886)
W. Beale: *The Light of Other Days* (London, 1890)
L. Arditi: *My Reminiscences* (London, 1896)
H. Rosenthal: *Two Centuries of Opera at Covent Garden* (London, 1958)

Grob-Prandl, Gertrude (*b* Vienna, 11 Nov 1917). Austrian soprano. She studied with Singer-Burian at the Vienna Musikakademie and in 1939 made her début at the Volksoper as Santuzza in *Cavalleria rusticana*. During the next five years she established a large repertory there, including *Fidelio*, *Tannhäuser*, *Il trovatore* and *Aida*, as well as *Die ägyptische Helena* in performances conducted by Strauss. Her first appearance at the Staatsoper was as Elsa in 1944 and she returned there in 1947 after a period in Zürich. She also sang at Salzburg (First Lady, *Die Zauberflöte*, 1949) and in most leading German houses, with guest appearances in Spain, France and Italy, her roles at La Scala being Isolde and the *Götterdämmerung* Brünnhilde. At Covent Garden she made her début in 1951 singing Turandot in English. In 1950 she sang for the first time at the Colón, Buenos Aires, and in 1953 made her North American début at San Francisco. In those years her ample voice rang out with remarkable freedom and she was at all times an adaptable, conscientious artist. Her Turandot can be heard in an inferior recording; she is probably best represented by excerpts from the Milan *Tristan* of 1951 under Victor De Sabata.   J. B. STEANE

Gronamann, Sybilla. *See* SIBILLA.

Groppo, Antonio (*fl* 1643–67). Italian theatre chronicler. His *Catalogo di tutti drammi per musica* (Venice, *c*1745) lists operas staged in Venice from 1637 to 1745; some copies have hand-written or printed additions up to 1752. Based on earlier works by Ivanovich and Bonlini, Groppo's catalogue goes beyond these in including a list of the Venetian banquet plays. The detailed bibliographic information he gives on the librettos suggests that it was meant to be used as a guide for collectors. It is not known whether the various other catalogues announced in the book were ever printed, but the *Catalogo purgatissimo* (MS in *I-Vnm*, dated 1741, but continuing to 1767), a forerunner of the printed version and in large part copied from Bonlini, contains indexes of intermezzos. He also wrote *Notizie generali de' teatri della città di Venezia* (1766, according to Cicogna), supplemented by an essay of the French theatre historian Nicolas Boindin.

*

E. A. Cicogna: *Saggio di bibliografia veneziana* (Venice, 1848)
P. Ryom: 'Les catalogues de Bonlini et de Groppo', *Informazioni e studi vivaldiani*, ii (1981), 3–30   NORBERT DUBOWY

Grosheim, Georg Christoph (*b* Kassel, 1 July 1764; *d* Kassel, 18 Nov 1841). German composer. The son of a violinist, he was largely self-taught in music. In 1781 or 1782 he entered the Hofkapelle in Kassel as a violist; he was director of music at the city's Hoftheater (1800–02) and was later active as a teacher, writer and publisher.

His surviving published music, which hardly rises above the conventional, includes two operas: *Titania, oder Liebe durch Zauberei* (Singspiel, 2, O. von Weber; perf. Kassel, 1792; vs, Bonn, ?1792) and *Das heilige Kleeblatt* (2; Kassel, Oct 1794; MS score *D-B* and *Dlb*, inc. vs, Bonn, 1798, lib., Kassel, 1793). A third, *Les esclaves d'Alger* (Kassel, 14 Oct 1808), is lost. Grosheim also composed songs and church music. His writings include a biography of the singer Gertrud Elisabeth Mara (1823), and *Über den Verfall der Tonkunst* (Göttingen, 1805), in which he attacked the operatic conditions and conventions of the day.

G. C. Grosheim: *Selbstbiographie* (Kassel, 1819)
H. Kummer: *Beiträge zur Geschichte des Landgräflichen und Kurfürstlichen-Hessen Hoforchesters, der Hofoper und der Musik zu Kassel im Zeitraum von 1760–1822* (diss., U. of Frankfurt, 1922), 47–99
G. Heinrichs: 'Georg Christoph Grosheim', *Lebensbildern aus Kurhessen und Waldeck 1830–1930*, i (Marburg, 1939)
PHILIP ROBINSON

Grossatesta [Grossa Testa, Testagrossa, Testa Grossa, Teste Grosse], **Gaetano** (*b* Modena, *c*1700; *d* Naples, ?1774). Italian dancer, choreographer and impresario. He spent the early part of his career in Venice, where he created ballets for more than 40 operas, 1720–45. His name first appears as a choreographer for the 1720 Ascension season (Orlandini's *Griselda*) at the Teatro S Samuele; here he worked for 11 Ascension seasons (later productions included works by Porpora, Albinoni and Galuppi, and Gluck's *Demetrio* in 1742). He also choreographed at S Giovanni Grisostomo (24 operas, 1722–45, including Porpora's *Siface*, *Meride e Selinunte*, *Rosbale* and *Statira*, and Hasse's *Alessandro nell'Indie* and *Semiramide riconosciuta*) and at S Angelo, S Cassiano, and S Moisè. At the Teatro Falcone in Genoa (1731) and the Regio Ducal Teatro in Milan (1732–3, Lampugnani's *Candace*; 1737–40, works by Bernasconi, Brivio and Leo) he worked with his wife Maria, a Venetian ballerina. While in Milan Goldoni, who knew the couple from Venice, spent an evening at their home; in his *Memoirs* he praised Gaetano as a spirited and learned man, and Maria as an excellent dancer. Letters from the impresario Albizzi in Florence during the 1730s record efforts to hire Grossatesta, his wife and his sister-in-law Francesa Guizzati. In the early 1740s the pair worked at the Teatro Regio in Turin, and at the Teatro degli Obizzi in Padua, with Gaetano employed both as choreographer and principal dancer. From 1745 onwards they directed the ballet company at S Carlo in Naples, where Gaetano was also choreographer for the opera seasons in 1738 (Ristori's *Temistocle*), 1746–9 (works included Hasse's *Lucio Papirio* and *Siroe*, and Jommelli's *Ezio*) and 1752 (Cocchi's *Sesostri, re d'Egitto*). He succeeded Diego Tufarelli as impresario of the theatre in 1753. During his tenure, Grossatesta brought some of the best dancers and choreographers from France and Vienna to Naples. With the exception of a three-year period (1764–7), he continued as impresario at S Carlo until 1774.

*

L. C. degli Albizzi: Letters, 1732–7 (Florence, Palazzo Guicciardini library, A770 and A771)
J. Sasportes: 'La danza 1737–1900', *Il Teatro di San Carlo*, ed. C. M. Roscioni, i (Naples, 1987), 365–96   IRENE ALM

Grossi, Carlo (*b* Vicenza, *c*1634; *d* Venice, 14 May 1688). Italian composer, organist and singer. Several sources refer to him as 'cavalier', but the basis for this is unclear, as is the reference to him as 'dottore' in the second issue of *Nicomede in Bitinia*. Before 1657, he was *maestro di cappella* at the Reggio Emilia cathedral. From 1657 he held positions in Vicenza, where he was *maestro di cappella* of the Accademia Olimpica until 1662. He soon moved to Venice, where he was organist and singing teacher at the church of SS Giovanni e Paolo from September 1664; because of repeated absences, he was dismissed as singing teacher in August 1666 and as organist in May 1667. His absences may have been because he was a bass at St Mark's from 21 February 1666. Grossi twice competed for the position of vice-*maestro di cappella* at St Mark's, losing to Sartorio in

1676 and to Partenio in 1685. In 1676 he succeeded Le-grenzi as *maestro di musica* at the Ospedale dei Derelitti (or Ospedaletto), a position he held until his death. There he enjoyed great esteem, to judge from reports in *Pallade veneta*. In July 1676 he was granted semi-retirement because of ill-health; he continued to draw his salary as a singer. On 16 April 1687 he received a patent as *maestro di cappella* of the Duke of Mantua, but this may have been honorary.

Grossi wrote four operas over the course of nearly two decades (1659–77). The first was for his native city, Vicenza, in 1659. A decade later, after he had settled in Venice, he wrote *Artaxerse, ovvero L'Ormonda costante* for the Teatro SS Giovanni e Paolo. For the 1676–7 season he wrote his last operas for the small Teatro S Moisè. His operatic style resembles that of his more prominent contemporaries in Venice. Like them, he focussed on the solo voice. His rhythmically active continuo lines especially resemble Legrenzi's. Continuo arias predominate. He scores sinfonias and detachable ritornellos for strings with continuo (*Nicomede in Bitinia* calls for a trumpet). The *Mercure galant* reported that his last two operas were well received. Both these operas were enriched with new arias during the course of their runs; another character was added to *Giocasta regina d'Armenia*, and a prologue was added to *Nicomede in Bitinia*.

Romilda (prol., 3, P. P. Bissari), Vicenza, Piazza, carn. 1659, *I-Vnm*

Artaxerse, ovvero L'Ormonda costante (3, A. Aureli), Venice, SS Giovanni e Paolo, carn. 1669, *Vnm*

Giocasta regina d'Armenia (3, G. A. Moniglia, rev. G. Castoreo), Venice, S Moisè, aut. 1676, arias *Vqs*

Nicomede in Bitinia (3, G. M. Giannini), Venice, S Moisè, carn. 1677, *F-Pc, I-Vnm*

*

Mercure galant (Aug 1677)

E. Selfridge-Field: 'Organists at the Church of SS. Giovanni e Paolo', *ML*, l (1969), 393–9

——: 'Addenda to some Baroque Biographies', *JAMS*, xxv (1972), 236–40

Arte e musica all'Ospedaletto (Venice, 1978) [exhibition catalogue]

E. Selfridge-Field: *Pallade veneta: Writings on Music in Venetian Society, 1650–1750* (Venice, 1985)

C. Sartori: *I libretti italiani a stampa dalle origini al 1800* (Cuneo, 1990–)

E. Rosand: *Opera in Seventeenth-Century Venice: the Creation of a Genre* (Berkeley and Los Angeles, 1991)   HARRIS S. SAUNDERS

Grossi, Eleonora (*fl* 1868–71). Italian mezzo-soprano. She sang in London at Covent Garden (1868–9) as Nancy (*Martha*), Urbain (*Les Huguenots*) and Pippo (*La gazza ladra*). She created Amneris in *Aida* at Cairo on 24 December 1871. To judge from these roles, she had a flexible voice of considerable dramatic weight.

ELIZABETH FORBES

Grossi, Giovanni Francesco ['Siface'] (*b* Chiesina Uzzanese, nr Pescia, 12 Feb 1653; *d* nr Ferrara, 29 May 1697). Italian soprano castrato. He achieved early fame and his performance of Syphax in Cavalli's *Scipione af-fricano* in Rome (1671) earned him his nickname. In 1675 he was admitted to the papal chapel, then in 1679 he entered the service of the Duke of Modena, remaining there for the rest of his life. In 1678 he sang Vespasian at the opening of the Teatro S Giovanni Grisostomo, Venice. In the Venetian Carnival of 1679 he sang in Pallavicino's *Nerone*, a report of which in the *Mercure galant* bears witness to his increasing fame; but success seems to have turned his head, and he began to display the arrogant behaviour that marked the rest of

his career. In 1683 he sang in *Il re infante* at Venice; the next year he sang Mithridates in Alessandro Scarlatti's *Pompeo* at Naples, and in 1686 appeared in Florence. In 1687 Grossi went to England to entertain the duke's sister, Maria Beatrice d'Este, now James II's queen. John Evelyn heard him in James II's chapel and at Pepys's house. He brought a standard and quality of singing to England which was remarkable at the time, but would sing only when in the right humour and complained that the climate affected his voice. He soon left again for Modena. Between 1688 and 1697 he sang in Naples, Parma, Bologna, Modena, Milan and Reggio Emilia. He was assassinated after an indiscreet affair with a member of the Marsili family.

*

P. F. Tosi: *Opinioni de' cantori antichi e moderni* (Bologna, 1723; Eng. trans., 1742, 2/1743 as *Observations on the Florid Song*), 102–3

A. Heriot: *The Castrati in Opera* (London, 1956), 129–35

MICHAEL TILMOUTH

Grossman, Ludwik (*b* Turek, nr Kalisz, 6 March 1835; *d* Wiesbaden, 15 July 1915). Polish composer. He was taught the piano by J. Drobniewski and the violin by W. Kopiński while at school in Kalisz. Later he studied in Warsaw with August Freyer and in Berlin (1854–7) with C. F. Rugenhagen, both also teachers of Moniuszko. On his return to Warsaw he was active as pianist, organist, choral conductor and teacher. In 1857 he co-founded a large firm selling keyboard instruments. In 1866 he travelled to Paris, where he worked on his opera *Rybek z Palermo* ('The Fisherman from Palermo'). He paid a second visit to France in 1895, but his life was centred on Warsaw, where he played a central role in the organization of musical life.

Composition was never at the forefront of Gross-man's activities, but his music is well crafted and was occasionally given distinguished seals of approval. *Rybek z Palermo*, to a libretto by Jan Chęciński, was highly praised by Rossini when Grossman showed him the manuscript in Paris. It had its première in Warsaw in 1867. The second (comic) opera, *Duch wójewody* ('The Ghost of Voyvode'), to a libretto by W. L. Anczyc, was given its first performance in Warsaw on 25 October 1875; it was later produced in Vienna to great acclaim (with special admiration from Hanslick), as well as in St Petersburg (1877), Graz, Berne and Berlin (1884). Grossman's other two operas, *Kornet Hamilton* (1867), to a libretto by Anczyc, and *Les sabots de la marquise* (1896), were neither performed nor published.

JIM SAMSON

Grossmann, Gustav Friedrich Wilhelm (*b* Berlin, 30 Nov ?1746 [or 1743 or 1744]; *d* Hanover, 20 May 1796). German actor, manager, dramatist and librettist. While in the Prussian civil service he was offered the chance of standing in for a member of Abel Seyler's company at Gotha in 1774; he remained with the company until 1778, when he established his own company at the Elector of Cologne's theatre at Bonn. From 1784 he directed a second company performing at Mainz and Frankfurt. His last play, *Wer wird sie bekommen?*, was given at Hanover in 1795; in it he lampooned prominent local citizens, and the resulting trouble ended with his imprisonment. He was released owing to ill-health, and died shortly afterwards.

Grossmann adapted Beaumarchais' *Le barbier de Séville* (1776) and Georg Benda wrote music for its production by Seyler's troupe. His volume of *Singspiele nach ausländischen Mustern für die deutsche Bühne* (Frankfurt, 1783) included works that enjoyed considerable popularity in their day: *Adelheid von Veltheim*, set by Joseph Grätz and later Neefe (who became musical director of the company in 1779) was very successful for a number of years and *Nicht mehr als sechs Schüsseln* (Bonn, 1780) was an influential early example of domestic comedy; *Was vermag ein Mädchen nicht?*, a Singspiel set by Neefe in 1789, was also popular. In 1788, the year after his company had given Mozart's *Die Entführung aus dem Serail* at Hanover under B. A. Weber, he mounted one of the earliest productions of *Le nozze di Figaro* at Lübeck and Frankfurt. *Don Giovanni* was also in his company's repertory. Until the disastrous production in Hanover of his last play, Grossmann had enjoyed high regard wherever he performed, though some contemporaries mentioned his restless and sometimes difficult temperament.

*

ADB (J. Kürschner); *ES* (A. M. Nagler)

C. H. Schmid: *Chronologie des deutschen Theaters* (Leipzig, 1775); ed. P. Legband (Berlin, 1902)

K. Goedeke: *Grundriss zur Geschichte der deutschen Dichtung*, iv/1 (Dresden, 2/1891), 254

J. Wolter: *Gustav Friedrich Wilhelm Grossmann: ein Beitrag zur deutschen Litteratur- und Theatergeschichte des 18. Jahrhunderts* (Cologne, 1901)

E. Pies: *Prinzipale: zur Genealogie des deutschsprachigen Berufstheaters vom 17. bis 19. Jahrhundert* (Ratingen, Kastellaun and Düsseldorf, 1973), 145–9   PETER BRANSCOMBE

Grossmith, George (*b* London, 9 Dec 1847; *d* Folkestone, 1 March 1912). English light baritone and composer. He first came to stardom when he created the role of John Wellington Wells in Gilbert and Sullivan's first full-length opera, *The Sorcerer* (1877). He subsequently created Sir Joseph Porter in *HMS Pinafore*, played the Major-General in the London première of *The Pirates of Penzance*, and thereafter created the principal comedy baritone roles in each of the Gilbert and Sullivan works of the next decade: Bunthorne (*Patience*), the Lord Chancellor (*Iolanthe*), King Gama (*Princess Ida*), Ko-Ko (*The Mikado*), Robin/Ruthven (*Ruddigore*) and Jack Point (*The Yeomen of the Guard*) in 1888, before retiring. He was occasionally lured back to the theatre thereafter without much success. He is remembered for the style that, with a limited singing voice and a nervy acting manner, he brought to the comedy roles of the Gilbert and Sullivan canon. His creative versatility showed itself not only in *The Diary of a Nobody*, written with his brother Weedon and published in *Punch* in 1892, but also in the composition of many songs and sketches and a few larger works. The most popular of these were the musical playlets *Cups and Saucers* (1878) and *Mr Guffin's Elopement* (1882), and the most ambitious *Haste to the Wedding* (1892), a musical version of *Un chapeau de paille d'Italie* with words by W. S. Gilbert.

His son, George Grossmith (1874–1935), acted in musical comedy at the Gaiety Theatre and elsewhere, wrote librettos and produced a series of musicals, notably at the Winter Garden Theatre.   KURT GÄNZL

Grosz, Wilhelm [Will; Williams, Hugh] (*b* Vienna, 11 Aug 1894; *d* New York, 9 or 10 Dec 1939). Austrian composer. He studied at the Vienna Academy with Schreker and others, and at Vienna University. After conducting at the opera house in Mannheim (1920–21),

he built up a substantial reputation in Vienna as a pianist and composer of stage and concert music. In 1928 he moved to Berlin, where he devoted himself increasingly to more popular musical forms. In 1933 he became conductor at the Kammerspiele Theater in Vienna, but in 1934, compelled as a Jew to leave Austria, he took refuge in London and became one of the most successful composers of 'Tin Pan Alley' before emigrating to the USA in 1938. In his main work, the one-act *opera buffa Sganarell* op.14 (R. Konta, after Molière; Dessau, 21 Nov 1925), he favoured an opulent, Straussian style, but he was also among the first to introduce jazz elements into concert music.   ANDREW LAMB

Title-page of the score of Salieri's 'La grotta di Trofonio' (Vienna: Artaria, 1786), showing a scene from Act 2

Grotta di Trofonio, La ('Trofonio's Cave'). *Opera comica* in two acts by ANTONIO SALIERI to a libretto by GIOVANNI BATTISTA CASTI; Vienna, Burgtheater, 12 October 1785.

Aristone (bass) tells his two daughters that it is time for them to marry. They have very different personalities, and each loves a man with a similar character to her own. Ofelia (soprano), serious and studious, loves the philosophical Artemidoro (tenor); Dori (soprano), lighthearted and playful, loves the fun-loving Plistene (tenor). Aristone approves of their choices, and all look forward to the weddings. Deep in a forest is a cave with magical properties. Accompanied by slow music in D minor (anticipated by the opening of the overture) the magician Trofonio (bass) sings an incantation to the spirits of the cave (male chorus), who respond but remain unseen. Artemidoro arrives, a volume of Plato in hand, in peaceful thought; when Trofonio invites him to enter the cave Artemidoro, always in search of knowledge, eagerly accepts. Plistene, singing happily, arrives; when Trofonio tells him that his friend is in the cave, he enters in search of him. Artemidoro emerges from another entrance, transformed: full of gaiety, and caring nothing for philosophy, he can only sing 'Evviva la gioia'. Soon Plistene also emerges, surprised that he is now as serious as Artemidoro used to be. The finale of Act 1 begins with Ofelia alone, singing of her pleasure in Artemidoro ('È un piacer col caro amante', with a lyrical clarinet solo); she is shocked when he enters, singing happily. Plistene arrives, deep in thought; Dori thinks he must be pretending. Aristone eagerly announces wedding plans to his daughters, who now begin to have second thoughts. The act ends with a general expression of perplexity.

Aristone tries to persuade his daughters that they can change husbands, but they are not convinced. Plistene and Artemidoro re-enter the cave; when they reappear their original personalities have been restored. Trofonio begins a grand aria rejoicing in his magical power but is interrupted by Ofelia and Dori, whom Trofonio invites into the cave (see illustration); the girls are now transformed, to the astonishment of their lovers. In the finale of Act 2 Aristone calls on Trofonio's help. The spirits of the cave respond, and Trofonio explains the cave's secret. Ofelia and Dori re-enter the cave; when they emerge it is clear that everything is well. All sing of their amazement at the cave's powers and in a final ensemble bid the magician farewell.

The original cast included Nancy Storace (Ofelia), Vincenzo Calvesi (Artemidoro), Celeste Coltellini (Dori) and Francesco Benucci (Trofonio). The symmetrical plot, with its pairs of lovers, may have been in Da Ponte's mind when he wrote Così fan tutte; Salieri's treatment of the two sopranos, with many passages in parallel 3rds, looks forward to Mozart's Fiordiligi and Dorabella. Salieri made effective use of wind instruments: Ofelia's aria 'D'un dolce amor' has elaborate parts for clarinets and bassoons; as Artemidoro wanders meditatively through the woods, oboes and flutes play bird calls; and when the formerly lighthearted Plistene emerges for the first time from Trofonio's cave, english horns and bassoons reflect his new seriousness.

JOHN A. RICE

Grout, Donald J(ay) (b Rock Rapids, IA, 28 Sept 1902; d Skaneateles, NY, 9 March 1987). American musicologist. He studied at Harvard with Davison and Kinkeldey, and then travelled in Europe (working under Gérold, Prod'homme and R. M. Haas) before returning to take the doctorate with a dissertation on early opéra comique. He taught in California and Texas before moving to Cornell University in 1945, where he taught until 1970 with brief breaks to serve as visiting professor, notably at Utrecht and Berkeley. He was twice (1952–4, 1960–62) president of the American Musicological Society and was president (1962–4) of the International Musicological Society. His work as an opera historian began with his dissertation and culminated in his authoritative Short History of Opera; he also published many articles on opera, chiefly on French opera and Alessandro Scarlatti, of whose operas he planned a collected edition, himself editing the initial volume, Ericlea (1974). New Looks at Italian Opera:

Essays in Honor of Donald J. Grout (ed. W. W. Austin) was published in 1968.

The Origins of the 'Opéra comique' (diss., Harvard U., 1939)
A Short History of Opera (New York and London, 1947, 2/1965, rev. W. H. Williams, 3/1988)
A History of Western Music (New York, 1960, 2/1973, rev. C. Palisca, 4/1988)
Mozart in the History of Opera (Washington DC, 1972)
Alessandro Scarlatti: an Introduction to his Operas (Berkeley, 1979)

*

H. M. Brown: 'In Memoriam Donald Jay Grout (1902–1987)', AcM, lix (1987), 217–19

GAYNOR G. JONES

Grovlez, Gabriel (Marie) (b Lille, 4 April 1879; d Paris, 20 Oct 1944). French composer and conductor. He studied at the Paris Conservatoire, where his teachers included Fauré, then toured as an accompanist until he was appointed professor of piano at the Schola Cantorum (1899–1909). He was choirmaster and conductor of the Opéra-Comique (1905–8) and music director at the Théâtre des Arts (1911–13), where he was responsible for revivals of operas by Monteverdi, Lully, Rameau and Gluck. In 1914 he was appointed director of the Opéra, a post he retained for two decades while also conducting opera in Monte Carlo, Lisbon, Cairo, New York and Chicago. His last appointment was as professor of chamber music at the Conservatoire (1939). Grovlez's compositions are cultivated and finely coloured, achieving individuality despite a melodic and harmonic indebtedness to Fauré. His works for the theatre include the operas Coeur de rubis (comp. 1906; fairy-tale, 3, G. Montoya; Nice, Opéra, 1922) and Le marquis de Carabas (comp. 1926; conte lyrique, 3, R. Coolus), and several ballets.

ALAIN LOUVIER

Grua, Carlo Luigi Pietro [Pietragrua, Carlo Luigi] (b Florence, c1665; d Venice, ?29 March 1726). Italian composer, resident in Germany. He joined the electoral Hofkapelle in Dresden in 1691 and, after being appointed vice-Kapellmeister on 20 February 1693, moved to Düsseldorf probably the following year; his Telegono (tragedia in musica, 5, S. B. Pallavicino; MS score in A-Wn) was performed there during Carnival 1697. Court calendars establish his presence in Düsseldorf until 1713. It is possible that he remained longer with the Kapelle, even after the death of Johann Wilhelm in 1716 and the court's removal to Heidelberg and the merger with the Innsbruck Kapelle of the new Elector Carl Philipp in 1718; other members of the family went with the court. He did not acompany the court to Mannheim but was elected maestro di coro at the Pietà, Venice, on 26 February 1719. At least three of his operas were performed in Venice in the early 1720s; the librettos give the composer as 'Carlo Luigi Pietragrua, Florentino'. These works include the tragicommedia pastorale Il pastor fido (5, B. Pasquaglio, after G. B. Guarini) and the dramma per musica La fede ne' tradimenti (3, G. Gigli), both performed at the Teatro S Angelo in 1721, and Romolo e Tazio (3, V. Cassani), a dramma per musica performed at the Teatro S Giovanni Grisostomo in 1722. Among Steffani's literary legacy (in the archive of the Propagande Fide, Rome) are letters from Grua, who knew Steffani from Düsseldorf, which reveal that while in Italy he recruited singers on Steffani's behalf for the Schönborn Kapelle at Würzburg.

EitnerQ; FétisB

M. Fürstenau: *Zur Geschichte der Musik und des Theaters am Hofe zu Dresden*, i (Dresden, 1861), 314–15

J. Loschelder: 'A. Steffani und das Musikleben seiner Zeit', *106. Niederrheinisches Musikfest in Düsseldorf* (Düsseldorf, 1951), 33ff

D. Arnold: 'Orphans and Ladies: the Venetian Conservatoires (1690–1797)', *PRMA*, lxxxix (1962–3), 31–47

ROLAND WÜRTZ (with PAUL CORNEILSON)

Grua, Carlo Pietro [Pietragrua, Carlo] (*b* c1700; *d* Mannheim, 11 April 1773). Italian composer, resident in Germany. It is likely that he was a son of CARLO LUIGI PIETRO GRUA, in which case his birthplace was probably not Milan, as Fétis suggested, but Düsseldorf where Carlo Luigi served as a court musician until at least 1713. The family probably followed the Elector Palatine to Heidelberg in 1718 and to Mannheim about 1720. By 1734 he had been appointed Kapellmeister at the electoral court, a title he held until his death; after Holzbauer's appointment in 1753, however, he devoted his attention exclusively to church music. Grua composed two operas during his tenure at Mannheim: *Meride* (text by G. C. Pasquini; libretto in *US-Wc*), performed on 18 January 1742 for the inauguration of the Hoftheater and in conjunction with the wedding of the future elector, Carl Theodor; and *La clemenza di Tito* (text by Metastasio), performed for the birthday of the electress on 17 January 1748. The music of both works is lost.

His son, Franz Paul (1753–1833), though also primarily a composer of church music (having been a pupil of Padre Martini), wrote an *opera seria*, *Telemaco* (text by Count Serimann, probably after Danchet's *Télémaque*; MS score in *D-Mbs*). This, given at the Residenztheater in Munich during Carnival 1780 (with ballet music by C. J. Toeschi), preceded by one year Mozart's *Idomeneo*.

EitnerQ; FétisB

F. J. Lipowsky: *Baierisches Musiklexikon* (Munich, 1811)

F. Walter: *Geschichte des Theaters und der Musik am kurpfälzischen Hofe* (Leipzig, 1898)

R. Würtz: *Verzeichnis und Ikonographie der kurpfälzischen Hofmusiker zu Mannheim nebst darstellendem Theaterpersonal, 1723–1803* (Wilhelmshaven, 1975)

K.-H. Nagel: 'Die Familie Grua: italienische Musiker in kurpfälzischen Diensten', *Mannheim und Italien: zur Vorgeschichte der Mannheimer*, ed. R. Würtz (Mainz, 1984), 32–40

ROLAND WÜRTZ (with PAUL CORNEILSON)

Gruberová, Edita (*b* Bratislava, 23 Dec 1946). Slovak soprano. She studied at the Bratislava Conservatory, as well as in Prague and Vienna. Her début was in 1968 in Bratislava as Rosina (*Il barbiere*), and two years later she was engaged for the Queen of Night at the Vienna Staatsoper. There she became a regular member of the company in 1972, making a base for a successful international career, especially in coloratura roles. As the Queen of Night she made débuts at Glyndebourne in 1974 and at the Metropolitan Opera in 1977, in which year she first appeared at the Salzburg Festival, as Thibault (*Don Carlos*) under Karajan. Her other major successes have included appearances as Zerbinetta, Gilda, Violetta, Lucia, Konstanze, Manon and Oscar; her Covent Garden début was as Giulietta in *I Capuleti e i Montecchi* (Bellini) in 1984. She sang Donna Anna at La Scala (1987); Marie (*La fille du régiment*, 1987) and Semiramis (1992) at Zürich; and Queen Elizabeth I (*Roberto Devereux*) in Vienna in 1990. A voice of great agility and tonal clarity is combined in her performances

with an engaging stage personality. She has made many recordings and is a *Kammersängerin* of Austria.

NOËL GOODWIN

Gruenberg, Louis [Edwards, George] (*b* nr Brest-Litovsk [now Brest], 22 July/3 Aug 1884; *d* Beverly Hills, CA, 10 June 1964). American composer of Russian origin. He arrived in the USA with his family in 1885 and received his first lessons from his father, later studying at the National Conservatory of Music in New York. In 1905 he went to Berlin for nine months and studied with Friedrich Koch; he returned there in 1908 and became a pupil of Busoni, an association and friendship that continued until the older man's death in 1924, and Busoni's influence can be seen in the juxtaposition of serious and humorous elements in Gruenberg's music. Busoni encouraged him to develop new means of expression and Gruenberg's response was to create an American idiom by using jazz and black spirituals.

During his years in Europe Gruenberg wrote two operas, *The Witch of Brocken* (1912) and *The Bride of the Gods* (1913). The latter was his first serious opera, but he was not satisfied with the work and it was never performed. He returned to the USA in 1914 on the outbreak of World War I and until 1919 tried to establish himself in New York as a composer and concert pianist. Having little success, he turned to the popular stage and collaborated with the violinist Eddy Brown in writing the musical *Roly-Boly Eyes*, which had a successful run of 100 performances. Gruenberg's interest in the popular stage was not new – two operettas, *Signor Formica* (1910) and *Piccadillymädel* (1913), were written during his stay in Europe – but he referred to such works as 'stomach music', that is, music which provided an income, and thus gave him freedom to write 'art music'. In the 1920s, in order to dissociate himself from popular music, he adopted the pseudonym George Edwards, under which he composed two operettas, *Hallo! Tommy!* (c1924) and *Lady X* (1927); both had many performances in Europe.

During the 1920s Gruenberg established a reputation as an innovator, with jazz-inspired vocal and instrumental works, but he returned to opera, completing *Jack and the Beanstalk* in 1930 and *The Emperor Jones* in 1931. Both were well received, with *The Emperor Jones* being hailed as the first important American opera. *Jack and the Beanstalk* was a commission from the Juilliard School as part of a celebration, with a libretto by John Erskine, president of the school. The opera was so successful at its first performance that it moved to the 44th Street Theatre on Broadway for two weeks of performances. *The Emperor Jones*, Gruenberg's finest work, is based on Eugene O'Neill's play. The opera received widespread praise and was awarded the David Bispham Memorial Medal in 1932. First performed by the Metropolitan Opera Company, it had 11 performances during its first two seasons, and was later revived in Chicago (1940), Rome (1950) and Detroit (1979).

From 1933 to 1936 Gruenberg was head of the composition department at the Chicago Musical College, but the demands of teaching made it impossible for him to continue composing, and in 1937 he took his family to California, where he hoped to establish himself as a film composer; he wrote music for nine films between 1940 and 1950 and also had a commission for a radio opera, *Green Mansions* (1937), from the Columbia Broadcasting Company. He tried several experiments in this new medium, using microphone amplification to increase the volume of instruments, and gramophone records to re-create the sounds of the jungle; the jungle girl's voice was represented by the musical saw. The opera was given mixed reviews and has not been repeated.

Gruenberg's next two operas, *Volpone* and *Antony and Cleopatra*, were completed in the 1950s. He considered them to be his finest achievements, but they have never been performed. Both are in three acts and written on a large scale. *Volpone* was begun in 1948 and revised several times, the last in 1958. *Antony and Cleopatra* was started in 1951 and completed in 1956, with a final revision in 1961. In his later years Gruenberg continually revised works because of the frustration he experienced with few performances or lack of recognition. Among his last works were three one-act operas intended for television: *One Night of Cleopatra*, *The Miracle of Flanders* and *The Delicate King*. Although they have never been performed, they deserve further study. Throughout his life Gruenberg maintained an integrity and originality in his music, which also shows craftsmanship of the highest standard.

See also EMPEROR JONES, THE.

Signor Formica, 1910 (operetta, 3, Gruenberg, after E. T. A. Hoffmann)
The Witch of Brocken op.1, 1912 (children's operetta, 3, E. F. Malkowski); (Boston, 1931)
The Bride of the Gods op.2, 1913 (1, F. Busoni, after the Mahābharata), unperf.
Piccadillymädel, 1913 (operetta, 1, T. Grunberg)
The Dumb Wife op.12, 1922 (chamber op, 2, after A. France)
Hallo! Tommy!, c1924 (operetta)
Lady X, 1927 (operetta, 3, L. Herzer); (Vienna, 1927)
Jack and the Beanstalk op.35 (fairy op for the childlike, 3, J. Erskine), New York, Juilliard School, 20 Nov 1931, vs (Boston, 1930)
The Emperor Jones op.36 (2, Gruenberg, after E. O'Neill), New York, Met, 7 Jan 1933 (New York, 1932)
Green Mansions op.39 (radio op, after W. H. Hudson), Columbia Broadcasting Company, 17 Oct 1937
Helena's Husband op.38, 1938 (P. Moeller), unperf.
Volpone op.57, 1948–58 (3, Gruenberg, after B. Jonson), unperf.
Antony and Cleopatra op.68, 1951–61 (3, after W. Shakespeare), unperf.
The Miracle of Flanders op.65, 1954 (television op, 1, after H. de Balzac), unperf.
One Night of Cleopatra op.64, 1954 (television op, 1, Gruenberg, after T. Gautier), unperf.
The Delicate King op.67, 1955 (miniature farce for television, 1, Gruenberg, after A. Dumas *fils*), unperf.

*

A. W. Kramer: 'Louis Gruenberg', *MM*, viii/1 (1930), 3–9
——: 'Emperor Jones, in opera guise, has world premiere', *Musical America*, liii/1 (1933), 3, 5, 20
R. F. Nisbett: 'Louis Gruenberg: a Forgotten Figure of American Music', *CMc*, no.18 (1974), 90–95
——: *Louis Gruenberg: his Life and Work* (diss., Ohio State U., 1979)
——: 'Louis Gruenberg's American Idiom', *American Music*, iii/1 (1985), 25–41
ROBERT F. NISBETT

Grümmer, Elisabeth (*b* Niederjeutz, nr Diedenhofen, Alsace-Lorraine, 31 March 1911; *d* Warendorf, Westphalia, 6 Nov 1986). German soprano. She studied in Aachen and made her début there as the First Flowermaiden in *Parsifal* in 1940, following it with Octavian. From 1942 to 1944 she was first lyric soprano in Duisburg and in 1946 joined the Städtische (later Deutsche) Oper, Berlin, where she sang until 1972. She sang Ellen Orford in the first Berlin performance of *Peter Grimes* and appeared as Agathe, Desdemona, Pamina and Eva. She sang this last role in Dresden and

London and at Bayreuth, where her roles also included Elsa, Freia and Gutrune. In 1952 she appeared with the Hamburg Staatsoper in Edinburgh as Agathe, Pamina and Octavian and in 1953 made her first appearances in Vienna and Salzburg. She also sang at Glyndebourne and the Metropolitan (Elsa, 1967). Grümmer's beautiful voice, aristocratic style and innate musicianship specially suited her to Mozart and Strauss; her Countess Almaviva, Donna Anna, Pamina and Ilia, her Marschallin (New York City Opera, 1967) and Countess Madeleine in *Capriccio* were greatly admired.

*

H. Rosenthal: *Sopranos of Today* (London, 1956)
A. Natan: 'Grümmer, Elisabeth', *Prima donna* (Basle, 1962) [with discography]
H. Rosenthal: *Great Singers of Today* (London, 1966)
HAROLD ROSENTHAL/R

Grün, Friederike (*b* Mannheim, 14 June 1836; *d* Mannheim, Jan 1917). German soprano. She studied in Mannheim, joining the Hofoper chorus there in 1857. She was engaged at Frankfurt (1862), Cologne, Kassel, the Berlin Hofoper (1866) and, after further study in Milan, at Stuttgart (1870); she also made appearances in Vienna. Her repertory included Agathe, Norma, Valentine and Elisabeth, which she sang in the Italian première of *Tannhäuser* at Bologna in 1872. Her last engagement was at Coburg (1875–7). Although her voice was a dramatic soprano, she sang Fricka, a mezzo role, in *Das Rheingold* and *Die Walküre*, and created the Third Norn in the first complete *Ring* at Bayreuth (1876).
ELIZABETH FORBES

Grünbaum, Therese [née Müller] (*b* Vienna, 24 Aug 1791; *d* Berlin, 30 Jan 1876). Austrian soprano. She studied with her father, the composer Wenzel Müller, appearing on the stage while still a child (including the part of Lilli in Kauer's *Das Donauweibchen*). While engaged in Prague, she sang Zerlina in 1807 and later became a famous Donna Anna. For her benefit performance of the title role of Méhul's *Helena* in 1815, Weber composed a special scena and aria. In 1816 she moved to the Kärntnertortheater, Vienna, where in 1819 she sang Desdemona in the first Viennese performance of Rossini's *Otello* and in 1823 created Eglantine in Weber's *Euryanthe*. Later she sang in Munich (1827) and Berlin (1828–30). She had a brilliant, flexible voice with secure technique. Her husband was the tenor Johann Christoff Grünbaum (1785–1870), who sang in Prague, Vienna and Berlin. Their daughter, Caroline Grünbaum (*b* Prague, 18 March 1814; *d* Brunswick, 26 May 1868), had a successful career as a soprano and created Anna in Marschner's *Hans Heiling* in Berlin (1833).
ELIZABETH FORBES

Grünewald [Grunewald], **Gottfried** (*b* Eibau [now Eywau], nr Zittau, Upper Lusatia, 1675; *d* Darmstadt, 19 Dec 1739). German composer and bass. In 1703 he appeared with the Hamburg Opera. The same year his opera *Der ungetreue Schäfer Cardillo* (lost) was given in Leipzig, and in 1704 another opera, *Germanicus* (also lost), was performed there with the composer singing the title role. It was repeated in Hamburg and Naumburg the same year, and another performance is recorded in Leipzig in 1720.

Between 1709 and 1711 he acted as vice-Kapellmeister and chamber singer at the court of

Weissenfels, serving under J. P. Krieger, and from about 1713 he was employed at the court at Darmstadt as vice-Kapellmeister, composing many church cantatas. In 1717 he toured parts of Germany as a soloist on the pantaleon. He was a close friend of Christoph Graupner; Noack conjectured that Graupner wrote the leading role in his opera *Costanza vince l'inganno* for him.

*

MGG (F. Noack)
W. Nagel: 'Gottfried Grünewald', *SIMG*, xii (1910–11), 99–107
A. Schering: *Musikgeschichte Leipzigs, 1650 bis 1725* (Leipzig, 1926)
R. Brockpähler: *Handbuch zur Geschichte der Barockoper in Deutschland* (Emsdetten, 1964)   GEORGE J. BUELOW

Grüning, Wilhelm (*b* Berlin, 2 Nov 1858; *d* Berlin, 2 Dec 1942). German tenor. He studied at the Stern Conservatory, Berlin, and began his career in Danzig. After engagements in Chemnitz, Magdeburg and Düsseldorf he sang at the German Opera in Rotterdam from 1885 to 1887. He appeared with the Damrosch Company in America (1895) and between 1891 and 1897 was heard at Bayreuth as Parsifal, Siegmund, Tannhäuser and Siegfried. At the Berlin Hofoper (1898–1911) he sang in the premières of *Der Pfeifertag* by Schillings and Leoncavallo's abortive *Der Roland von Berlin*. Although most successful as a Heldentenor he was also a noted Mozartian.   DAVID CUMMINGS

Grunn, (John) Homer (*b* Salem, WI, 5 May 1880; *d* Los Angeles, 6 June 1944). American composer. He studied the piano and composition in Chicago and at the Stern Conservatory in Berlin. After teaching at music schools in Chicago (1903–7) and Phoenix (1907–10), he settled in Los Angeles, working as a composer, teacher and performer.

Grunn studied Indian culture during visits to New Mexico and used the Indian melodies he collected in his ballets and in songs and piano pieces, harmonizing them in Romantic style. From the 1920s he also composed operettas and children's operas, most of which were produced locally; his ballets were more widely performed. The operettas poke fun at such topics as feminism (*In Woman's Reign: AD 2024*), Hollywood (*The Mars Diamond*) and religious fakery (*The Isle of Cuckoo*). Grunn's early operatic models were Gilbert and Sullivan, but the music of *The Isle of Cuckoo* (1931) is more sophisticated and reflects the influence of Broadway.

MSS in US-LAu

In Woman's Reign: AD 2024 (operetta, W. H. Howells), Los Angeles, Chickering Hall, 21 April 1924
The Isle of Cuckoo (comic op, C. Roos and J. Roos), Los Angeles, Wilshire Ebell Theatre, 30 April 1931; rev. as Barbecue Isle (operetta, G. C. Turner), Los Angeles, Belasco Theatre, 2 Dec 1937
Dates unknown: The Golden Pheasant (operetta, Roos and Roos); The Magic of Ho-Kum (operetta, Roos and Roos); The Mars Diamond (operetta, M. Stedman); The Return of Spring (children's operetta, Roos and Roos)

*

'Contemporary American Musicians, No.397', *MusAm*, xlii (26 Sept 1925), 17
J. H. Grunn: 'My Journey with Music', *Hazard's Pavilion*, i/3 (1987), 2, 13–28 [excerpts from 1939 typescript]
          CATHERINE PARSONS SMITH

Grünwald, Alfred [Wald, A. G.] (*b* Vienna, 16 Jan 1884; *d* New York, 24 Feb 1951). Austrian librettist. He worked for a theatrical agency before turning to libretto writing. He worked particularly with Brammer and later Löhner on some of the most effective operetta librettos written in Vienna after World War I, successfully adding a modern social slant to the traditional formula. With Brammer he collaborated on Fall's *Die Rose von Stambul* (1916), Straus's *Der letzte Walzer* (1920), Kálmán's *Gräfin Mariza* (1924) and Eysler's *Die gold'ne Meisterin* (1927), and with Löhner on Abraham's *Viktoria und ihr Husar* (1930). With the rise of the Nazis he left Vienna, first for Paris and later for the USA.

operettas unless otherwise stated; written with J. Brammer unless otherwise stated

Fräulein Sherlock Holmes (Posse mit Gesang), G. Criketown, 1907; Die grüne Redoute (Vaudeville-Operette), L. Ascher, 1908; Die lustigen Weiber von Wien, R. Stolz, 1908; Elektra (Parodie-Operette), B. Laszky, 1909; Georgette, Laszky, 1910; Vindobona, du herrliche Stadt (Operette-Burleske), Ascher, 1910, rev. as Hoheit tanzt Walzer, 1912; Das goldene Strumpfband, Ascher, 1911; Die Dame in Rot, R. Winterberg, 1911; Das Damenparadies, R. Fall, 1911
The Dancing Viennese [Eine vom Ballett], Straus, 1912; Die ideale Gattin, Lehár, 1913, rev. as Die Tangokönigin, 1921; Der lachende Ehemann, E. Eysler, 1913; Die schöne Schwedin, Winterberg, 1915; Die Kaiserin [Fürstenliebe], L. Fall, 1916; Die Rose von Stambul, L. Fall, 1916; Bruder Leichtsinn, Ascher, 1917; Dichterliebe (Singspiel), E. Stern, after Mendelssohn, 1919; Der letzte Walzer, Straus, 1920; Das Sperrsechserl [Wiener Gemütlichkeit] (with R. Blum), Stolz, 1920
Die Bajadere, E. Kálmán, 1921; Mädi (with L. Stein), Stolz, 1923; Die Perlen der Cleopatra, Straus, 1923; Gräfin Mariza, Kálmán, 1924; Die Zirkusprinzessin, Kálmán, 1926; Die gold'ne Meisterin, Eysler, 1927; Die Herzogin von Chicago, Kálmán, 1928; Marietta (Komödie mit Musik), Straus, 1929; Das Veilchen vom Montmartre, Kálmán, 1930; Viktoria und ihr Husar (with F. Löhner), Abraham, 1930; Die Blume von Hawaii (with Löhner and E. Földes), Abraham, 1931
Venus in Seide (with L. Herzer), Stolz, 1932; Ball im Savoy (with Löhner), Abraham, 1932; Eine Frau, die weiss, was sie will (Komödie mit Musik), Straus, 1932; Märchen im Grand-Hotel (Lustspiel-Operette, with Löhner), Abraham, 1934; Die verliebte Königin (with Löhner), N. Brodsky, 1934; Dschainah [Das Mädchen aus dem Tanzhaus] (with Löhner), Abraham, 1935; Das Walzerparadies, Straus, 1935; Roxy und ihr Wunderteam (Vaudeville-Operette, with H. Weigel, after L. Zsilagi and D. Keller), Abraham, 1937; Polnische Hochzeit (with Löhner), J. Beer, 1937; Mr Strauss Goes to Boston (musical, with F. Brentano, L. L. Levinson and R. Sour), Stolz, 1945; Božena, Straus, 1952; Arizona Lady (with G. Beer), Kálmán, 1954; Fiesta (with Beer), Cardona, 1955

*

H. Grünwald, G. Markus and others: *Ein Walzer muss es sein: Alfred Grünwald und die Wiener Operette* (Vienna, 1991)
          ANDREW LAMB

Guaccero, Domenico (*b* Palo del Colle, Bari, 11 April 1927; *d* Rome, 24 April 1984). Italian composer. He studied the piano at the Bari Conservatory, taking his diploma in 1948; the following year he graduated in literature at the university. He then studied composition at the S Cecilia Conservatory, Rome, with Barbara Giuranna and Goffredo Petrassi until 1957, and in 1957 and 1959 he attended Darmstadt summer courses. He founded the periodical *Ordini: studi sulla nuova musica* in 1959. The next year he was a founder-member of the group Nuova Consonanza and began teaching at the Pesaro Conservatory; later he taught at the conservatories of L'Aquila, Frosinone and Rome. In 1965 he was one of the founders, with Egisto Macchi, of the Compagnia del Teatro Musicale in Rome.

Guaccero's compositions up to 1957 show the indirect influence of Stravinsky, Hindemith and Bartók through the teachings of Petrassi, and a rather free use of serial techniques. One of his first works was the one-act chamber opera *La farmacista* (1956), after Chekhov. His next theatre work, the chamber opera *Scene del potere* (composed during 1962–8), showed his efforts to forge a personal style through the use of aleatory techniques, graphic notation and spatial separation, which continued to fuel his interest in experimentation and encouraged him towards total theatre. The general conception of the opera, which has some correspondence with Nono's *Intolleranza*, is closely related to the theory and mimo-gestural practice of the musical and theatrical avant gardes of the 1960s. Also from 1968 is the *azione sacra Rappresentazione et esercizio*, in an invented Sardinian-Apulian dialect, based on sources that include St John of the Cross's *Noche oscura* (a text which had inspired Petrassi's cantata of the same name). This opera seeks to create a new reciprocity between actors and audience, typical of the theatrical avant garde of the time.

In *Rot*, composed during 1970–72, the succession of three colours acquires symbolic value as it passes from apocalyptic black at the beginning, through white to the red of new revolutionary vitality, symbolizing the composer's political commitment.

Guaccero resumed a central theme, that of power, in his last work for the theatre, *Novità assoluta* (1972). The action takes the form of a game in which the executants impersonate various powers – military, religious, scientific and judicial. With influences from Beckett to Grotowski's 'poor theatre', from Stravinsky's chamber theatre to the Living Theatre experiments of Julian Beck and Judith Malina, Guaccero's music-theatre project (in which the strong influence of Cage is also perceptible) seeks to overcome the traditional barriers of genres and approach a theatrical totality.

La farmacista (opera da camera, 1, D. Guaccero and E. Pannunzio, after A. P. Chekhov: *Aptekarskaya*), Rome, Conservatory, 19 June 1956

Scene del potere, 1962–8 (opera da camera, 3, Guaccero, F. Nonnis and other sources), Palermo, Biondo, 30 Dec 1968

Rappresentazione et esercizio (azione sacra, 2, after Old and New Testaments and St John of the Cross: *Noche oscura*), Perugia, church of S Filippo Neri, 28 Sept 1968, vs (Milan, 1969)

Rot, 1970–72 (azione coreografica, 1, texts from Cynewulf and T'ien Chien), Rome, Opera, 12 June 1973

Novità assoluta (azione scenica, 1, Guaccero and others), Positano, 30 June 1972

*

P. Dallamano: '*Rappresentazione et esercizio* di Guaccero a Perugia', *Spettatore musicale*, iii/10–11 (1968), 15

G. Zaccaro: 'Intervista con Domenico Guaccero', *Spettatore musicale*, iii/2 (1968), 16–19

T. Geraci: 'Domenico Guaccero compositore e musicologo', *Di Domenico Guaccero: prassi e teoria* (Rome, 1984)

RAFFAELE POZZI

Guadagni, Gaetano (*b* Lodi or Vicenza, 11 Dec 1729; *d* Padua, 11 Oct 1792). Italian alto castrato. He joined the *cappella* of S Antonio in Padua in 1746. At the same time he tried his hand at *opera seria* in Venice, but the price of singing a small number of second leads (two at S Moisè) was his dismissal from S Antonio in 1747–8. He then went to London as the leading singer in Croza's comic opera company, but at once embarked on a period of activity (1749–53) in oratorios by Handel. In 1750 Handel revised for him the parts in *Samson* (Micah) and *Messiah* originally written for Susanna Cibber and wrote for him the part of Didymus in *Theodora*. In London, according to Charles Burney, who claimed to have helped Guadagni study these parts, he was 'more noticed in singing English than Italian'. In April 1754 he was in Paris and at Versailles, but there is no confirmation of Burney's statement that in 1754–5 he retreated to a convent in Lisbon to study with the soprano castrato Gioacchino Conti. In 1755 he was again in London, engaged by Garrick at Drury Lane as Lysander in *The Fairies* by J. C. Smith. Garrick coached him in his own revolutionary style and according to Burney the actor 'took much pleasure in forming him'.

From 1756 to 1761 he played various roles in Italian theatres, including Sammete in Traetta's *Nitteti* (1757, Reggio Emilia), Arbaces in J. C. Bach's *Artaserse* and the title role in *Il Tigrane* by Piccinni (both 1761, Turin). In addition to his 'most beautiful voice' he was admired for his restrained style and the appropriate manner of acting which he adapted to the characters he played; but there was also trouble with impresarios because 'he rarely does his duty'. At Parma, nevertheless, he was increasingly in demand, singing in two important pre-reform operas by Traetta, *Le feste d'Imeneo* in 1760 and *Enea e Lavinia* in 1761.

His connection with the new operatic style of Parma and Vienna soon led him to the even more élite celebratory productions of the 'enlightened' Habsburg dynasty. The leading roles in the new mythological and classical operas were written for him during the first period of the reform: Gluck's Orpheus (1762), Orestes in Traetta's *Ifigenia in Tauride* (1763) and the title role in Gluck's *Telemaco* (1765). Jommelli, Hasse, Gassmann and Gluck also wrote Metastasian roles for him, among the most successful and heroic being those of Horatius in Hasse's *Il trionfo di Clelia*, with which he made his Vienna début (1762), and the title role in Gluck's *Ezio* (revised in 1764). In this remarkable period in Vienna he enjoyed both financial fortune and wide European fame; he was considered an ideal interpreter of Metastasian music drama, and his Orpheus was long legendary.

In 1767–8 he sang in Venice in operas by Mysliveček, Galuppi, Borghi and Guglielmi. For Bertoni he returned to Metastasian roles in *Ezio* (1767) and *Il trionfo de Clelia* (1769, Padua). But his reception was at best tepid; as the Venetian Abate Ortes recorded in 1767, the expressiveness of his style 'gave pleasure' but infinitely less than the bravura of a virtuoso singer such as Anna Lucia de Amicis. In 1768 Guadagni rejoined (until his death) the *cappella* of S Antonio, with freedom of movement and a salary of 400 ducats. In summer 1769 he went to London, beginning the long and contentious final period of his career (1770–84), almost wholly devoted to *Orfeo* and to sacred music. He sang Orpheus in the English premières (1770–71) of the opera arranged as a pasticcio with additions by J. C. Bach and P. A. Guglielmi, and his own reworking of the aria 'Men tiranne'.

His career continued in the Venetian area, but he was in Munich in 1772–5. In 1773 he took the leading role in a new pasticcio of *Orfeo* (with additions by J. C. Bach and himself) which was recorded as a spectacle of extraordinary effect, but lugubrious and difficult, like an oratorio. Two years later Guadagni again sang Orpheus, in a new version by Antonio Tozzi, in a part that made great vocal and dramatic demands.

On his return to Italy he yet again sang Orpheus, in a new version by Bertoni (1776, Venice). That year he retired to Padua, although he performed frequently in private academies up to 1784. The contribution of Guadagni, who was increasingly inclined to mysticism, was another *Orfeo* pasticcio, largely based on the versions of Gluck and Bertoni. He increased the dramatic effect of Act 2 of the originals by inserting two reworkings at strategic points in the action: by adding his own *largo* setting of 'Men tiranne', written in London, and also omitting Gluck's preceding 'Mille pene', he replaced the 'diffused pathos' with which Gluck softened the violence of Orpheus's encounter with the Furies with a more decisive confrontation; and in 'Che puro ciel' (composed for Padua) he emphasized, as Gluck had not, Orpheus's changes of emotion as suggested by the literary text. He also introduced two new characters symbolizing abstract antagonistic forces, Pluto and the Shade, who were assigned conventional *opera seria* music, by J. C. Bach, to contrast with Orpheus's simple humanity. In 1781 Antonio Calegari wrote the last original part for him, that of Deucalion in *Deucalione e Pirra*. About 1785 Guadagni suffered a stroke which deprived him of speech and made it almost impossible for him to sing.

Guadagni favoured a syllabic style (to which he readily applied his stupendous *messa di voce*, or simple extemporary solo passages interspersed with suggestive pauses); but he was not averse to energetic displays of agility. His technical and stylistic abilities were, however, generally used according to their dramatic relevance. Burney's description of his voice at a fairly early stage is substantially reliable ('a full and well toned counter-tenor'); but his idea that he changed his register from contralto to soprano is unlikely, although it developed an upward extension to *f"* or *g"*.

*

BurneyGN; *BurneyH*

S. Arteaga: *Le rivoluzioni del teatro italiano dalla sua origine fino al presente* (Venice, 1784)
M. Fürstenau: 'Gluck's Orpheus in München 1773', *MMg*, iv (1872), 218–24
R. Haas: *Gluck und Durazzo in Burgtheater* (Vienna, 1925)
L. Finscher: 'Che farò senza Euridice?: ein Beitrag zur Gluck-Interpretation', *Festschrift Hans Engel* (Kassel, 1964), 96–110
D. Heartz: 'From Garrick to Gluck: the Reform of the Theatre and Opera in the Mid-Eighteenth Century', *PRMA*, xciv (1967–8), 111–27
P. Petrobelli: 'La scuola di Tartini in Germania e la sua influenza', *AnMc*, no.5 (1968), 1–17
D. Heartz: 'Orfeo ed Euridice: Some Criticism, Revisions and Stage-Realizations during Gluck's Lifetime', *Chigiana*, xxix–xxx (1973), 383–94
P. Cattelan: 'La musica della "omnigena religio": accademie musicali a Padova nel secondo settecento', *AcM*, lix (1987), 152–87
——: 'Altri Orfei di Gaetano Guadagni: dai pasticci al nuovo Orfeo di Bertoni', preface to the facs. of the score of F. Bertoni's *Orfeo ed Euridice*, DMV, xxiii (Milan, 1989)   P. CATTELAN

Guadagno, Anton (*b* Castellammare del Golfo, 2 May 1925). Italian conductor. He studied at the Palermo Conservatory, at the Accademia di S Cecilia, Rome, and at the Salzburg Mozarteum, where he won a first prize for conducting in 1948. He began his career in South America, and had a long association with the international opera seasons in Mexico City. His début in the USA was at a Carnegie Hall concert in New York in 1952, and as assistant conductor at the Metropolitan (1958–9) he appeared in *Un ballo in maschera*. He has been active in the theatre and the concert hall, including periods as music director of the Philadelphia Lyric Opera and conductor of the Cincinnati Summer Opera. He also regularly conducted Italian repertory at the Vienna Staatsoper for some years, and in 1965 was appointed Cavaliere by the Italian government for his services to Italian opera. He first appeared in London at

a concert performance of *Andrea Chénier* at the Theatre Royal, Drury Lane in 1970 and made his Covent Garden début the following year with *Un ballo in maschera*. His performances are admired for dramatic thrust and incisive clarity, and after *Aida* at Verona (which was recorded) he received the 1981 Verdi d'Oro award. His recordings include *Le villi*; his sensitivity as an accompanist has made him a sought-after conductor for recital recordings by leading singers including Caballé, Domingo, Milnes and Tebaldi.

BERNARD JACOBSON, NOËL GOODWIN

Guadalajara. Second largest city in Mexico, capital of the province of Jalisco. Opera performances have been given since the middle of the 19th century at the Teatro Degollado. Sometimes these visits were by companies engaged for Mexico City, which went on brief tours after the season in the capital, and at other times by companies on extended tours of the entire country. These seasons usually lasted four to six weeks and included as many as 18 operas. Angela Peralta, a Mexican soprano later turned impresario, visited Guadalajara in 1866, 1881 and 1882. Luisa Tetrazzini sang there in 1903, as did Maria Gay and Giovanni Zenatello in 1918. The theatre is still used for opera performances, frequently in conjunction with seasons at the Bellas Artes in Mexico City or the Teatro Floridi in Monterrey. Placido Domingo has sung there on several occasions.

*

A. Hidalgo: *El Teatro Degollado 1866–1896* (Guadalajara, 1966)
C. Diaz Du Pond: *15 Temporadas de Opera en el Teatro Degollado* (Guadalajara, 1987)
J. O. Sosa and M. Escobedo: *Dos Siglos de Opera en Mexico* (Mexico City, 1988)   TOM KAUFMAN

Gualandi, Antonio. *See* CAMPIOLI.

Gualandi, Margherita. *See* CAMPIOLI.

Guarany, Il [*O Guarani* ('The Guaraní')]. *Opera-ballo* in four acts by CARLOS GOMES to a libretto by Antonio Scalvini and CARLO D'ORMEVILLE after José de Alencar's novel; Milan, Teatro alla Scala, 19 March 1870.

The action takes place near Rio de Janeiro in 1560. A group of hunters approaches the castle of Don Antonio de Mariz (bass), a Portuguese nobleman; among them are Don Alvaro (tenor) and the Spanish adventurer Gonzales (baritone), both in love with Don Antonio's daughter, Cecilia (soprano). Peri (tenor), son of the chief of the Guaraní tribe, appears, and Don Antonio thanks him for saving his daughter's life by rescuing her from the Aymoré Indians. Cecilia enters and her father announces that Don Alvaro will be her husband; she answers that she is ready to obey but intimates that she does not love Alvaro. With two of his companions, Gonzales plots against Don Antonio. Peri, who has heard them, warns Cecilia of the plot. As they part, they declare their mutual love.

In the Grotto of the Savage at night, Peri hears the three adventurers conspire to attack the castle. Only Cecilia will be spared, as Gonzales plans to abduct her. As he becomes aware of Peri's presence, Gonzales pretends to renounce his project.

In her bedroom, Cecilia sings the ballad 'C'era una volta un principe', accompanying herself on a guitar, then falls asleep. Gonzales enters her room through a window. She wakes up and repulses him. Peri intervenes by firing an arrow through the window; Gonzales fires his gun, waking everyone in the castle. Don Antonio arrives and requests an explanation for Gonzales's presence. Peri appears in the window and points to Gonzales as the leader of the traitors. Suddenly, a tremendous noise from outside terrifies everyone; the castle is surrounded by Aymoré Indians. All swear loyalty in the defence of the castle.

The next day in the Aymoré camp, Cecilia is prisoner. The Aymoré chief Cacico (baritone or bass) tells her that she can be his queen. A group of warriors brings in Peri, also taken prisoner. The chief recognizes him as a friend of the Portuguese and orders the ritual preceding the death of the enemy. Peri reveals to Cecilia that he has taken a poison that will kill the Aymoré when they devour his body. They exchange vows of love. The chief returns, but before he can give the deadly blow the Portuguese invade the camp, kill him and overpower the tribe. Peri takes an antidote to the poison.

Gonzales's new plans are overheard by Don Antonio who decides to destroy his castle since he cannot overcome both Gonzales and the Aymoré. Peri offers his help but Don Antonio refuses. Peri then proposes to save Cecilia but Don Antonio hesitates since Peri is not a Christian. Peri asks to be baptized and Don Antonio performs the sacrament. Cecilia enters and her father tells her that Peri will take her to her relatives in Rio de Janeiro. In despair, she faints. Don Antonio bids them farewell. Gonzales and his group come after them, but Don Antonio lights several powder barrels, causing his own death and that of the traitors, while Cecilia and Peri escape.

The triumphal success of the première brought Gomes international fame. *Il Guarany* was produced in almost all European capitals in the next few years. Verdi heard it in Ferrara in 1872 and referred to it in a letter as the work of a 'truly musical genius'. This success was due to the opera's effective melodic content, its dramatic construction, and the choice of libretto. Its Indian hero, Romantic stylization of indigenous dances, and picturesque story made the work all the more appealing to European audiences. The final version of the overture, written in 1871, has become virtually a second national anthem in Brazil. Its first theme, which takes on an epic character in the context of the whole opera, functions as a leitmotif and is a typically Romantic idealization of indigenous music. The natural flow of arias and duets, the timing and sequence of scenes and the striking contrasts in the staging reveal Gomes's technical competence, and the work shows imaginative traits within the limits of its style.　　　GERARD BÉHAGUE

Guardasoni, Domenico (*b* ?Modena, *c*1731; *d* Vienna, 13 or 14 June 1806). Italian impresario, tenor and opera producer. In May 1764 he sang in the première of Boroni's *Sofonisba* at the Teatro S Salvatore, Venice, and on 4 October 1764 he sang in Prague in the opening performance by the Bustelli company. In 1772–3 he was with the Vienna opera, in summer 1773 with the Bustelli company in Dresden and Leipzig, and in December 1773 he was the leading male singer in the Joseph Kurz company at Warsaw. In 1776 he returned to Bustelli's company. He acted as the impresario for the première in Prague of *Don Giovanni* (1787) and soon after took over the direction of the company. In June 1788 he presented *Don Giovanni* in Leipzig and in 1789 took the company to Warsaw. He returned to Prague in July 1791 to help prepare the celebrations for the coronation of Leopold II and commissioned from Mozart the

coronation opera *La clemenza di Tito*. Guardasoni attempted to counter the declining interest in Italian opera with frequent presentations of Mozart's operas, German Singspiels in Italian translation and Italian opera in Czech translation; through his efforts the era of Italian opera reached its peak in Leipzig in 1794 and in Prague in 1807.

O. Teuber: *Geschichte des Prager Theatres*, i–ii (Prague, 1883–5)

P. Nettl: *Mozart in Böhmen* (Prague, 1938)

M. Rulikowski and B. Król: *Warszawski teatr Sułkowskich dokumenty z lat 1774–1785* [The Warsaw Sułkowski Theatre: Documents from the Years 1774–1785] (Wrocław, 1957)

T. Volek: 'Über den Ursprung von Mozarts Oper "La clemenza di Tito"', *MJb 1959*, 274–86

O. E. Deutsch, ed.: *Mozart: die Dokumente seines Lebens* (Kassel, 1961; Eng. trans., 1965, 2/1966 as *Mozart: a Documentary Biography*)

T. Volek: 'Repertoir Nosticovského divadla v Praze z let 1794, 1796–8', [The Repertory of the Nostitz Theatre in Prague, 1794 and 1796–8], *MMC*, no.16 (1961), 3–190

F. Kneidl: 'Libreta italské opery v Praze v 18. století', *Strahovská knihovna* [Librettos of the Italian Opera in Prague in the 18th Century], iv (1969), 186–215　　　TOMISLAV VOLEK

Guarducci [Garducci], Tommaso (*b* Montefiascone, *c*1720; *d* after 1770). Italian soprano castrato. He studied with Bernacchi and began his theatrical career in Italy about 1745. In 1750 he was engaged by Farinelli for the Spanish court, where he sang for the rest of his career, and from 1752 was in the service of the Viennese court, where he sang with Caterina Gabrielli in the première of Gluck's *L'innocenza giustificata* (1755). He also sang in Lisbon, in Italy (where he appeared in Traetta's *Alessandro nell'Indie*, 1762, Reggio Emilia) and for two seasons (1766–8) at the King's Theatre, London, singing in the première of J. C. Bach's *Carattaco*. Among his last engagements was a highly successful appearance in Rome in Piccinni's *Didone abbandonata* in 1770, the year of his retirement. According to Burney, Guarducci 'was tall and awkward in figure, inanimate as an actor, and in countenance ill-favoured and morbid', but he made up for these defects by a highly polished and correct use of his voice, which was 'clear, sweet, and flexible'. 'Guarducci was the plainest and most simple singer of the first class, I ever heard'.

BurneyFI; *BurneyH*

M. Kelly: *Reminiscences* (London, 1826, 2/1826)

F. Haböck: *Die Kastraten und ihre Gesangskunst* (Stuttgart, 1927)　　　GERHARD CROLL

Guarini, (Giovanni) Battista (*b* Ferrara, late 1538; *d* Venice, 7 Oct 1612). Italian poet and playwright. In 1564 he was a member of the Accademia degli Eterei in Padua, and in 1567 he entered the service of Alfonso II d'Este, Duke of Ferrara, whom he served as courtier, diplomat and poet. His uneasy relationship with the duke led to estrangement from Ferrara from 1588 to 1595, and he moved from court to court (Turin, 1588; Mantua, 1592–3) in search of employment. On the death of Alfonso II in late 1597, he again led a peripatetic existence (Florence, 1598–1601; Urbino, 1602–4), spending his last years largely in Rome.

The 1580s and 90s were dominated by attempts to stage his pastoral play *Il pastor fido* (completed by 1585). Although Guarini took his model from Tasso's *Aminta* (1573), he produced a much more complex work staking grandiose claims for the pastoral tragicomedy as a viable and theoretically acceptable dramatic genre. The result aroused considerable academic controversy. The performance history is hazy until the staging in Mantua in November 1598: most agree that it was staged in some manner in Turin in 1585, but plans for performance in Mantua (1584), Ferrara (1584–5), Florence (1589) and Mantua again (1592) never came to fruition, and details of performances in Ferrara (1595), Crema (1596) and Ronciglione (1596) remain obscure. Music was used in the *intermedi*, and also in at least one scene of the play itself, the 'Giuoco della cieca' (Act 3 scene ii): Guarini reports a setting by the Ferrarese composer Luzzasco Luzzaschi; in 1592 music was to have been provided by Giaches de Wert and Francesco Rovigo; and a version survives by G. G. Gastoldi (1598, ?Mantua). Its combination of dance, music and dramatic action established important precedents for early 17th-century court entertainments.

Guarini provided other court entertainments for Ferrara, Florence (the *Dialogo fra Giunone e Minerva* with music by Cavalieri in 1600) and Mantua, while *Il pastor fido* remained a quarry for texts set repeatedly in madrigals, monodies and, later, cantatas. The 'Giuoco della cieca' was the basis for a pastoral entertainment (now lost), with music by Cavalieri and verse by Laura Guidiccioni, staged in Florence in October 1595 (it was one predecessor of the first Florentine operas), and Guarini's verse provided several models for the early opera librettos of Ottavio Rinuccini. Antonio Bertali's *Il ciro crescente* (1661, Vienna) was first staged as intermezzos for *Il pastor fido*, and at least four operas were based directly on the play: by Handel (libretto by G. Rossi, 1712, London), C. L. P. Grua (B. Pasqualigo, 1721, Venice), possibly Salvatore Apolloni (1739, Venice) and Salieri (Da Ponte, 1789, Vienna).

Guarini's defence of the pastoral (in his *Compendio della poesia tragicomica*, 1601) provided a significant impetus for the formation of a poetics of opera in the 17th century. Moreover, the play and its many translations (including the splendid English version by Sir Richard Fanshawe of 1647) established a vogue for pastoral subjects, particularly in Germany. Busenello cited *Il pastor fido* to justify the intrigues in his *Gli amori d'Apollo e di Dafne* (1640); Metastasio owes a clear debt to Guarini (see Pennacchietti 1915); and in 1707 C. F. Hunold called the play 'a source for all opera'.

V. Rossi: *Battista Guarini ed il Pastor fido* (Turin, 1886)
G. Brognoligo, ed.: *G. B. Guarini: Il pastor fido, e il Compendio della poesia tragicomica* (Bari, 1914)
B. Pennacchietti: 'Studi Metastasiani', *Studi di letteratura italiana*, xi (1915), 155–202
A. Hartmann jr: 'Battista Guarini and Il Pastor Fido', *MQ*, xxxix (1953), 415–25
B. Hathaway: *The Age of Criticism: the Late Renaissance in Italy* (Ithaca, NY, 1962)
I. Fenlon: *Music and Patronage in Sixteenth-Century Mantua*, i (Cambridge, 1980)
E. T. Harris: *Handel and the Pastoral Tradition* (London, 1980)
P. Fabbri and A. Pompilio, eds.: *Guarini e la musica* (Florence, forthcoming)   TIM CARTER

Guarnieri, Adriano (*b* Sustinente, nr Mantua, 10 Sept 1947). Italian composer. He completed his musical education with Giacomo Manzoni at the Bologna Conservatory. At first strongly rooted in the more radical tendencies of the late 1960s and early 70s, he evolved a distinctive style in which multiple highly expressive melodic lines coalesce into a contrapuntal magma. This

he put to particularly striking use in his *Trionfo della notte*, a one-act opera in four 'pictures' based on fragments from Pasolini's collection of poems *Religione del mio tempo*. Guarnieri tends to divest Pasolini's almost cinematic meditation on the Roman night – boys searching for erotic adventure, prostitutes, the physical immediacy of working-class life – of concrete detail. Yet he projects it into intertwining vocal lines for two sopranos, tenor and chorus that reactivate the erotic and affective intensity of Pasolini's poetry beyond the specificity of the visual. It is in keeping with this process that Guarnieri abstains entirely from stage directions (beyond indications of the relatively rare occasions when the singers perform on stage, rather than off): it is the director's task to create, by whatever visual means he chooses, a counterpoint to the score. The opera was first performed at the Teatro delle Celebrazioni, Bologna, on 3 February 1987; an edition, by S. Camerini, was sponsored by the theatre to accompany the production.

Guarnieri's second opera, *Medea* (1991), is based on a libretto by Pier'Alli after Euripides, Seneca and Pasolini. The action alternates between stage and film (the latter constituting the base for an autonomous film version). In this work Guarnieri develops in more violently dramatic form the idiom established in *Trionfo della notte*, articulating fragments from Medea's monologues within a fierce, magmatic counterpoint of three sopranos, an actress and instruments.

DAVID OSMOND-SMITH

Guarnieri, Antonio (*b* Venice, 1 Feb 1880; *d* Milan, 25 Nov 1952). Italian conductor and composer. After studying privately in Venice, taking lessons in composition and the organ with M. E. Bossi, he made his conducting début at Siena in 1904; he quickly gained a wide reputation in Italian theatres, and was considered by some to have a greater natural talent than Toscanini. Guarnieri was engaged by the Vienna Hofoper in 1912 on a seven-year contract but he left after a year because of disputes over conditions. In the 1914–15 season at Florence, he conducted the Italian première of *Parsifal*, confirming his reputation as a Wagnerian. He made his La Scala début with *Lohengrin* in 1922; the next year he conducted the première of Respighi's *Belfagor*, and his later seasons embraced a wide repertory including Debussy, Casella and Pizzetti. In 1934 Gui invited him to conduct at the Florence Maggio Musicale, where he also conducted the première of Casella's *Il deserto tentato* (1937); he gave the Italian premières of Bloch's *Macbeth* (1938, Naples) and Lully's *Armide* (1950, Florence). Until 1946 he held a postgraduate course for conductors at the Accademia Chigiana, Siena, where he conducted revivals of Vivaldi's oratorio *Juditha triumphans* and Alessandro Scarlatti's *Il trionfo dell'onore*.

During his last years Guarneri was often in poor health, but he retained the hypnotic power and technical mastery which drew sound quality of great sensual beauty from the orchestra. He had a sharp tongue, and was sarcastic towards other conductors and composers. His operas *Giuditta* (1913) and *Hannele* are in the late Italian *verismo* style with some influence from French impressionism but without any marked originality.

LEONARDO PINZAUTI

Guarnieri, (Mozart) Camargo (*b* Tietê, São Paulo, 1 Feb 1907). Brazilian composer of Italian descent. He studied the piano, composition and conducting before meeting Mário de Andrade, his mentor, who directed him towards folk and popular music, and so to composition in the nationalist aesthetic. He held a teaching appointment in São Paulo from 1927, began to conduct in 1935, visited Paris in 1938, and had performances of his works in the USA in 1942, 1944 and 1946–7. On his return to Brazil, he became the permanent conductor of the orchestra of the Departamento de Cultura de São Paulo. In 1960 he was appointed director of the São Paulo Conservatory and in 1964 teacher of composition and conducting at the Santos Conservatory.

As a composer Guarnieri occupies a paramount position within the Brazilian national school. In over half a century of intense activity, he has been one of the most prolific and creative Brazilian composers, writing in all the major genres with a consistent and sustained concern for national musical expression. He took a firm stand in 1950 against atonality and serialism. His obvious feeling for vocal music and his strong lyricism is especially clear from the almost 200 songs written between 1928 and 1980. His one-act comic opera, *Pedro Malasarte*, written in 1932 and produced 20 years later (Rio de Janeiro, Teatro Municipal, May 1952), is to a libretto by Andrade. Another Brazilian poet, Gianfrancesco Guarnieri, provided the libretto for the one-act lyric tragedy *Um homem só*, composed in 1960 and performed in Rio de Janeiro in 1962 with moderate success.

See also PEDRO MALASARTE.

M. de Andrade: *Música, doce música* (São Paulo, 1963)
GERARD BÉHAGUE

Guasco, Carlo (*b* Solero, Alessandria, 13 March 1813; *d* Solero, 13 Dec 1876). Italian tenor. He made his début in 1836 at La Scala as the Fisherman in *Guillaume Tell*, which was billed as 'Vallace' for reasons of censorship. In 1841 he took part in the first performance of Federico Ricci's *Corrado d'Altamura* at La Scala. He created the Count de Chalais in Donizetti's *Maria di Rohan* in Vienna (1843); Oronte in Verdi's *I Lombardi* at La Scala (1843); the title role of *Ernani* at La Fenice (1844); and Foresto in *Attila* at La Fenice (1846). At Bergamo he sang Donizetti's Crispus (*Fausta*) and Percy (*Anna Bolena*). He retired in 1853. He had a very powerful voice, but could use it with some sensitivity.

For illustration see MARIA DI ROHAN.   ELIZABETH FORBES

Guastalla, Claudio (*b* Rome, 7 Nov 1880; *d* ?Rome, 1948). Italian librettist. A contributor to literary and musical journals, he was caught up in the fashion for medievalism in the early 20th century. He much admired the high-flown style of D'Annunzio, which he tried to imitate. Ottorino Respighi set five of his 15 librettos: *Belfagor* (1923, Milan), *La campana sommersa* (1927, Hamburg), *Maria Egiziaca* (1932: concert performance, New York, 16 March; stage, Venice, 10 August), *La fiamma* (1934, Rome) and *Lucrezia* (completed by E. Respighi and performed in 1937, Milan). *La grazia*, written in collaboration with Grazia Deledda, was set to music by V. Michetti (1923, Rome), *Odette* by M. Marangolo (1929, Brescia) and *Gli Orazi* by E. Porrino (1941, Milan).

BARBARA REYNOLDS

Guatemala City. Capital of Guatemala. Opera performances were given at the Teatro Carrera as early as 1859, when *Ernani* was performed. Unlike other Central American cities dependent on touring companies, Guatemala City had opera seasons that usually lasted from late autumn to early spring, given by a specially engaged company. These seasons were fairly regular events and occasionally featured well-known singers. Carolina De Cepeda sang there in 1870–71, Carlo Bulterini in 1876, Adelaide Bianchi-Montaldo in 1880–81, Gino Martinez-Patti in 1889–90 and Olimpia Boronat in 1890–91. These full seasons ended in 1893, after which touring companies under such impresarios as Augusto Azzali, Mario Lambardi and, in 1928, Adolfo Bracale visited the city.

R. Vasquez: *Historia de la musica en Guatemala* (Guatemala City, 1950)
TOM KAUFMAN

Gubarenko, Vitaly Sergeyevich. See HUBARENKO, VITALY SERHIYOVYCH.

Gubbio. Italian city in Umbria. The first documented operatic performance was of Alessandro Scarlatti's *Aldimiro* on 16 May 1687; it was conducted by Carlo Clerici, the *maestro di cappella* at the cathedral, and probably presented by an academy. Other academy productions followed, including J. A. Hasse's *Don Tabarano* (Carnival 1747), before the Teatro dei Nobili, known as Teatro della Fama, opened in the middle of the 18th century. Among the operas performed there were Rinaldo da Capua's *Il bravo burlato* (Carnival 1754), Galuppi's *L'amante di tutte* (May-June 1761), *Li tre amanti ridicoli* (Carnival 1765) and *Il marchese villano* (Carnival 1768), P. A. Guglielmi's *La sposa fedele* (Carnival 1770), Anfossi's *L'incognita perseguitata* (spring 1774), G. B. Bevilacqua's *L'amor prigioniero* (May 1784) and Marcello Bernardini's *Il conte di bell'umore* (spring 1788).

For several years the Gubbio Festival has been mounted in collaboration with New York University. Mozart's *Der Schauspieldirektor* was given in 1990, and his *Lo sposo deluso* and Cimarosa's *Le donne rivali* (both to the same libretto) in 1991.   GALLIANO CILIBERTI

Gudehus, Heinrich (*b* Altenhagen, nr Celle, 30 March 1845; *d* Dresden, 9 Oct 1909). German tenor. He studied with Malvina Schnorr von Carolsfeld at Brunswick and with Gustav Engel in Berlin, where he made his début in 1871 as Nadori in Spohr's *Jessonda*. After further study, he reappeared at Riga (1875) as Raoul in *Les Huguenots*. From 1880 to 1890 he was engaged at Dresden, making his début there as Lohengrin. He sang Parsifal at the second performance of Wagner's opera at Bayreuth (1882), returning there as Tristan (1886) and Walther (1888). In 1884 he appeared at Covent Garden, singing Walther, Max (*Der Freischütz*), Tannhäuser and Tristan, and sang at the Albert Hall in the first concert performance in England of *Parsifal*. He made his New York début at the Metropolitan in 1890 as Tannhäuser, also singing Raoul, Lohengrin, John of Leyden (*Le prophète*), Florestan, Walther, Siegfried, Siegmund and Tristan. On his return to Europe he was engaged at the Berlin Hofoper, remaining there until his retirement in 1896. One of the second generation of Wagnerian heroic tenors, he was also much admired in the dramatic French repertory.

W. H. Seltsam: *Metropolitan Opera Annals* (New York, 1949)

I. Kolodin: *The Story of the Metropolitan Opera 1883–1950* (New York, 1951)

H. Rosenthal: *Two Centuries of Opera at Covent Garden* (London, 1958)

G. Skelton: *Wagner at Bayreuth* (London, 1965)

ELIZABETH FORBES

Gueden, Hilde (*b* Vienna, 15 Sept 1917; *d* Klosterneuburg, 17 Sept 1988). Austrian soprano. She studied at the Vienna Conservatory and first appeared at the Volksoper in 1935 in Stolz's operetta *Servus servus*. She then went to Zürich, making her operatic début there in 1939 as Cherubino. In 1941 she was engaged at the Staatsoper in Munich. At Strauss's suggestion she sang Sophie in *Der Rosenkavalier*, first in German and then in Italian (1942, Rome). She sang Zerlina at Salzburg in 1946 and was then engaged at the Vienna Staatsoper, where she sang until 1973. She made her London début at Covent Garden with the Vienna company in 1947, returning in 1956 as Gilda, the role of her Metropolitan début in 1951. In nine seasons at the Metropolitan she sang Susanna, Zdenka, Mimì, Micaëla and Anne Trulove in the American première of *The Rake's Progress* (1953). In 1954 at Salzburg she sang Zerbinetta, displaying a newly acquired coloratura technique. She scored further successes as Aminta (1959, Salzburg) and in the title role of *Daphne* (1964, Vienna). Gueden's vocal and dramatic abilities made her a much sought-after artist in modern works including Britten's *The Rape of Lucretia* and Blacher's *Romeo und Julia*, in both of which she sang at Salzburg.

GV (R. Celletti; R. Vegato)

H. Rosenthal: *Sopranos of Today* (London, 1956)

H. Liversidge: 'Hilde Gueden', *Gramophone Record Review*, no.58 (1958), 809–13 [with discography by F. F. Clough and G. G. Cuming]

H. Rosenthal: *Great Singers of Today* (London, 1966)

HAROLD ROSENTHAL/R

Guédon de Presles [first name unknown] (*b* early 18th century; *d* *c*1754). French composer and singer, possibly the sister or daughter of Honoré-Claude Guédon de Presles. She worked at the Paris court theatre as a singer, actress and composer under the name 'Mlle Guédon'. From 1748, when she appeared in the entrée *La vue* from Mouret's *Le triomphe des sens*, she sang many secondary roles at the Théâtre de la Reine. More notable operas in which she appeared were Collasse's *Thétis et Pélée*, Mouret's *Les amours de dieux* and Campra's *Tancrède* (all 1748), and Lully's *Bellérophon* (1749). Her name also appears in details of three opera performances in the dauphine's salon: Lully's *Armide* in 1749 and Campra's *Hésione* and Lully's *Phaëton* (both 1750). Other performances in which she sang included Campra's *L'Europe galante* (1750–52), *Les élémens* by Lalande and Destouches and Lully's *Roland* (both 1751), and lastly *Iphigénie en Tauride* by Campra and Destouches (1753). NICHOLAS ANDERSON

Guelfi, Giangiacomo (*b* Rome, 21 Dec 1924). Italian baritone. Among his teachers was Titta Ruffo, with whom he was sometimes compared. He made his début at Spoleto as Rigoletto in 1950, and within two years appeared at La Scala in the role of the visitor in J. J. Castro's *Proserpina y el extranjero*. Though he returned regularly, and was heard in other novelties such as Napoli's *Mas'aniello* (1953) and Mortari's *La figlia del diavolo* (1954), it was not until 1964 that he fully made his mark there, with Birgit Nilsson, in *Macbeth*. Meanwhile, a broadcast of *I due foscari* under Giulini in 1951 and performances of the opera at Venice in 1957 had shown him to be a Verdi baritone of great resource. In 1954 he sang Gérard in *Andrea Chénier* at Drury Lane, London, and in 1970 made two appearances at the Metropolitan, in *Tosca* and *La fanciulla del West*. He also sang in Vienna, Berlin, Chicago and Dallas. In the 1970s he was increasingly criticized for over-emphatic singing and exaggerated histrionics. Recordings expose the limitations of his art and probably do less than justice to the voice which, as Lauri-Volpi wrote (*Voci parallele*, Milan, 1955), was without competitors in his time for power and sheer abundance. J. B. STEANE

Guelph. Canadian city, in Ontario. Murdo Mackinnon and Nicholas Goldschmidt founded an annual spring festival there in 1968. The festival is held in May, and one opera is normally performed with local and international singers. Britten's 'church parables' dominated the early years, though the repertory has included Gluck, Mozart, Schenk, Argento and Maxwell Davies, as well as new Canadian works (Derek Healey's *Seabird Island*, 1977, and Charles Wilson's *Psycho Red*, 1978). Other premières include Menotti's children's opera *Chip and his Dog* (1979) and John Beckwith's *Crazy to Kill* (1989), a detective chamber opera to a libretto by James Reaney using popular forms from the 1930s.

Guercoeur. *Tragédie en musique* in three acts, op.12, by ALBÉRIC MAGNARD to his own libretto; Paris, Opéra, 24 April 1931.

Magnard composed his second opera during the years 1897–1901 and published its vocal score in 1904. Act 3 was given in a concert performance at the Conservatory in Nancy on 23 February 1908, and Act 1 at the Concerts Colonne in Paris on 18 December 1910. The full scores of these two acts were incinerated when German troops burnt down Magnard's house in 1914, but they were reconstructed from memory by his close friend Joseph Guy Ropartz for the 1931 première.

An agnostic, Magnard here devised his own myth and eschatology. In Paradise, ruled by the goddess Truth (soprano), Guercoeur (baritone), the deceased democratic leader of a free city in medieval times, remains dissatisfied, still yearning for the love of his wife Giselle (mezzo-soprano), of his companion-in-arms Heurtal (tenor) and of the people he led to freedom. The goddess Suffering (contralto) returns him to earth, where he discovers Giselle guiltily cohabiting with Heurtal, who has made himself a dictator, manipulating and enslaving the people by demagoguery. Guercoeur forgives the faithless Giselle, but is lynched by Heurtal's supporters and returns to Paradise sadder and wiser, aware that his achievement was one transient symbol among those that inspire future generations to seek love and liberty and thus aid the development of the human race.

In the opera Magnard was influenced by the historical and philosophical writings of Renan and Clémence Royer, and by his own pessimistic liberalism. Acts 1 and 3, set in a heaven inhabited by personified virtues, have a grave, static quality that evokes Baroque oratorio, although the musical language is manifestly indebted to *Parsifal*. The human world of Act 2 is however delineated with almost Berliozian passion and vigour. The various scene changes are accomplished by substantial interludes in Magnard's thrusting symphonic style, and the scene between Guercoeur and Giselle has a lyric warmth and nobility that places it among the composer's greatest music. In 1988 a complete recording starring José van Dam as Guercoeur demonstrated that in its idealism this oddly compelling work, however rare its appearances on stage, is no mere curiosity.

MALCOLM MACDONALD

Guerrero (y Torres), Jacinto (*b* Ajofrín, Toledo, 16 Aug 1895; *d* Madrid, 15 Sept 1951). Spanish composer. He was a choirboy at Toledo Cathedral, then studied at the Madrid Conservatory with Benito Laparro and Conrado del Campo. He joined the orchestra of the Teatro Apolo as a violinist and was later its conductor. His early compositions included a symphonic poem and religious music, but his future path in popular music was determined by the huge success of a song, *Himno a Toledo*. *La alsaciana* (1921) established him in the field of the zarzuela, and was followed by many more. *Los gavilanes* (1923) was performed simultaneously at five theatres in Barcelona and has remained one of the most performed of all zarzuelas, along with *La montería* (1922), *El huésped del sevillano* (1926) and *La rosa del azafrán* (1930). He later composed music for films and revues; his stage works number about 200 in all. His broad, rich melodies have kept him to the fore among 20th-century zarzuela composers. Guerrero also organized travelling zarzuela companies to perform in Spain and abroad, and he was at one time president of the Sociedad General de Autores de España.

See also GAVILANES, LOS.

selective list of zarzuelas

El camino de Santiago (1, A. Díaz Enrich and M. Díaz Enrich), Madrid, Martín, 14 Feb 1919, collab. E. Fuentes; La hora del reparto (1, P. Muñoz Seca and P. Pérez Fernández), Madrid, Apolo, 1920/21; La alsaciana (1, J. Ramos Martín), Barcelona, Tivoli, 12 Nov 1921; El rey nuevo (Muñoz Seca and Pérez Fernández), Madrid, Apolo, 9 May 1922; La montería (2, Ramos Martín), Saragossa, Circo, 24 Nov 1922; Los gavilanes (3, Ramos Martín), Madrid, Zarzuela, 7 Dec 1923

Don Quintín el Amargao (2, A. Estremera), Madrid, Apolo, Nov 1924; El huésped del sevillano (2, J. I. Luca de Tena and E. Reoyo, after M. de Cervantes: La ilustre fregona), Madrid, Apolo, 3 Dec 1926; Martierra (Fernández Catá), 1928; La rosa del azafrán (2, F. Romero and G. Fernández Shaw), Madrid, Calderón, 14 March 1930; La fama del tartanero (2, M. de Góngora and L. Manzano), Valladolid, Lope de Vega, 1931

El ama (L. Fernández Ardavín), Madrid, Ideal, 1931; La canción del Ebro (E. Calonge and Reoyo), Madrid, Coliseum, 1941; Loza lozana (Romero, G. Fernández Shaw and R. Fernández Shaw), Madrid, Coliseum, 1942; Tiene razón don Sebastián (G. Fernández Shaw and R. Fernández Shaw), Saragossa, Principal, 1944; El canastillo de fresas (G. Fernández Shaw and R. Fernández Shaw), Madrid, Albéniz, 16 Nov 1951

*

'Guerrero y Torres (Jacinto)', *Enciclopedia universal ilustrada europeo-americana* (Barcelona, 1907–30), xxvii; appx v (1931); suppl. 1949–52 (1955)

A. Fernández-Cid: *Cien años de teatro musical en España (1875–1975)* (Madrid, 1975)

J. Arnau and C. M. Gomez: *Historia de la zarzuela* (Madrid, 1979)

R. Alier and others: *El libro de la zarzuela* (Barcelona, 1982, 2/1986 as *Diccionario de la zarzuela*)

ANDREW LAMB

Guerrini, Guido (*b* Faenza, 12 Sept 1890; *d* Rome, 14 June 1965). Italian composer. He attended the Liceo Musicale in Bologna, where he studied composition with Luigi Torchi and Busoni. After service in World War I he became a teacher. He was director of the conservatories of Florence (1928–47) and Bologna (1947–9) and of S Cecilia in Rome (1950–60). He encouraged the interest of young people in music by founding Agimus (Associazione Musicale Giovanile). In

1964–5 he was President of the Accademia Nazionale di S Cecilia. His first work for the theatre was the one-act opera *Zalebi*, which has never been performed. His development as a theatre composer emerged in the three-act *I nemici* (1929), the three-act burlesque opera *La vigna* (1935), the 'legend' *L'arcangelo* (1949) and the three-act *Enea* (1953). They show in particular a sense of drama and a liking for spectacle and comic effect (the model for the last seems to be Verdi's *Falstaff*) in Italian tradition. On the other hand his operas show chromatic and orchestral harmonic writing that is also evident in his symphonic poems, in which the influence of Strauss is discernible.

Zalebi, 1915 (G. Campajola), unperf., unpubd
I nemici (dramma, 3, Guerrini), Bologna, Comunale, 19 Jan 1929
La vigna (opera burlesca, 3, Guerrini and A. Testoni, after A. F. Grassini), Rome, Opera, 7 March 1935
L'arcangelo [L'isola di finale] (leggenda drammatica, Guerrini, after V. Hugo: La légende des siècles), Bologna, Comunale, 26 Nov 1949
Enea (mito, 3, A. Angeli, after Virgil), Rome, Opera, 11 Feb 1953

*

M. Saint-Cyr: 'Guido Guerrini', *Rassegna dorica*, iii (1931–2), 147–50

M. Rinaldi: 'Guido Guerrini', *Rassegna musicale delle edizione Curci*, viii (1955)

J. C. G. Waterhouse: *The Emergence of Modern Italian Music (up to 1940)* (diss., U. of Oxford, 1968), 710ff
RAFFAELE POZZI

Guéymard, Louis (*b* Chapponay, 17 Aug 1822; *d* Corbeil, nr Paris, July 1880). French tenor. He made his début at the Paris Opéra in 1848 in the title role of *Robert le diable*, which he also sang at the 500th performance of Meyerbeer's opera (1867). In 1849 he created Jonas in *Le prophète* and the following year sang John of Leyden, the title role. He created Rodolphe in Gounod's *La nonne sanglante* (1854), Henri in Verdi's *Les vêpres siciliennes* (1855) and Adoniram in Gounod's *La reine de Saba* (1862). His repertory included Raoul (*Les Huguenots*), Arnold (*Guillaume Tell*), Edgardo, Manrico and Eléazar (*La Juive*), which he also sang at Covent Garden in 1852. After leaving the Opéra he sang with the French Opera Company in New Orleans (1873–4). He was married to the soprano Pauline Guéymard-Lauters.
ELIZABETH FORBES

Guéymard-Lauters [née Lauters], **Pauline** (*b* Brussels, 1 Dec 1834; *d* 1876 or later). Belgian soprano. She made her début in 1854 at the Théâtre Lyrique, Paris. From 1861 to 1876 she was engaged at the Paris Opéra, making her début there as Valentine (*Les Huguenots*). She created Balkis in Gounod's *La reine de Saba* (1862); Alda in Mermet's *Roland à Roncevaux* (1864); Eboli in Verdi's *Don Carlos* (1867) and the Queen in Thomas' *Hamlet*. Her roles also included Leonora (*Il trovatore*), Donna Anna, Gluck's Alcestis, Fidès (*Le prophète*) and Léonor (*La favorite*). She was married to the tenor Louis Guéymard.
ELIZABETH FORBES

Guglielmi. Italian family of musicians.

(1) Pietro [Pier, Piero] **Alessandro Guglielmi** (*b* Massa, 9 Dec 1728; *d* Rome, 19 Nov 1804). Composer. He was one of the most important figures in late 18th-century opera.

1. Life. 2. Reputation. 3. Works.

1. LIFE. Contemporary reports, not yet verified by archival research, state that Guglielmi learnt the keyboard and counterpoint from his uncle, that his father,

Jacopo Guglielmi (*maestro di cappella* to the Duke of Massa), taught him to play the viola and the bassoon, and that he later played the viola in his father's theatre orchestra (but this cannot be true, since Jacopo is thought to have died in 1731). According to Nerici, he also studied with Giacomo Puccini (1712–81). Under the patronage of the Duchess of Massa he was sent to the S Maria di Loreto conservatory in Naples (in 1746, according to Gervasoni); he is alleged to have composed a *farsetta* (otherwise unknown) at the age of 17. He became a pupil of Francesco Durante and by 1750 was serving as *primo maestrino*. He probably left the conservatory in 1754.

Guglielmi's earliest known opera was a dialect comedy, *Lo solachianello 'mbroglione*, for the Teatro dei Fiorentini performed in winter 1757. Until 1763, when he received his first commission for an *opera seria* from the Teatro Argentina in Rome, he apparently lived in Naples, writing several comic operas each year for theatres there and in Rome. To judge from performance records, he spent the next four years in northern Italy, probably mostly in Venice. Villarosa's claim that he taught at the Ospedaletto conservatory there is implausible. In autumn 1767 he and Felice Alessandri were engaged to go to London to share the post of composer and music director of the King's Theatre, where he made his début on 27 October, conducting the pasticcio *Tigrane*. Early biographers' reports that he spent part of the 1760s as *maestro di cappella* first at the Dresden court and then at Brunswick have not been substantiated. He left London for good in 1772, though he seems to have made at least one shorter trip back to Italy before that date. Between 1772 and 1776 he produced new operas in Venice, Rome, Turin and Milan. By autumn 1776 he had returned to Naples, where he remained until 1793, writing two to five operas, both serious and comic, almost every year. According to Sartori, in 1777 he was elected a member of the newly founded Nobile Accademia di Musica. On 3 March 1793 he succeeded Boroni as *maestro di cappella* at St Peter's in Rome; in July 1797 he also assumed those duties at S Lorenzo Lucina. Although much of his church music dates from this late period, he continued to write for theatres until the year before his death. He belonged to the Accademia di S Cecilia in Rome and the Institut National des Sciences et des Arts; in 1799 he was inscribed a member of the arts and sciences section of the Istituto Nazionale created in Naples during the Parthenopean Republic.

2. REPUTATION. Accurate judgments about Guglielmi are hampered by a lack of modern research as well as by conflicting contemporary accounts. He both attracted the friendship and patronage of influential people and inspired bitter personal enmity. The picture that emerges is of a difficult but fearless personality, manifesting itself as early as his schooldays, when, after a brief period of application, he lost himself in the urban dissipations of Naples. When a competition was announced for the best student fugue in eight real parts, no one considered him a possible contender, and his behaviour became so disruptive that he was excluded from classes. Stung by this rebuke, he produced, after more than 30 hours' uninterrupted work, a composition instantly recognized as far superior to any other entry. In later years, when a star soprano wished to embellish her part with the customary improvised *fioriture*, he remarked 'Madam, you do the singing, and I'll do the composing'. Returning to Naples in 1776, after 13 years' absence, he found the comic stage in the hands of Paisiello and Cimarosa, whose popularity he immediately challenged. Although Paisiello in particular is said to have responded with fury, going to the extent of hiring claques to disrupt the performances of new Guglielmi operas, such active spite cannot have lasted long, as Paisiello was in Russia between 1776 and 1784. According to a common anecdote, the three composers resolved their quarrel on the king's order and under the management of his minister, the Prince of Severo; this must have taken place between 1784 and 1787, not around 1780 as is often said. Similarly, the pact that the three allegedly made not to accept less than 600 ducats for new opera commissions must belong to the same period (although the account books of the Teatro S Carlo, extant throughout 1786, show that lesser sums were paid them there).

19th-century biographers censured Guglielmi severely for his domestic conduct. He was married, probably some time before 1763, to a singer known variously as Maria Leli or Lelia Acchiapati (or Acchiappati). Under the latter name she sang in Milan in 1769 and was with her husband in London, first singing in 1770 as seconda donna; under the former name she had an unsuccessful season in Naples in 1777–8 as prima donna at the Teatro S Carlo, after which she disappeared from public notice. Guglielmi was said to have had eight sons by her, the youngest born in 1782, whom he completely abandoned to be reared and educated by a family friend in Naples (but such an arrangement was probably the only practicable one, given the professionally peripatetic life of both mother and father). Although Guglielmi and his wife seem to have been separated during the 1780s, the family was reunited in Rome in 1793. Guglielmi also had the reputation of a fearsome duellist and of a tireless amorist, said late in life to have ruined himself financially in pursuit of the singer Oliva, but his papal appointment in Rome may cast some doubt on the truth of such reports.

Burney wrote of Guglielmi's English visit that he 'never had great success here', but Petty's statistics show that while Guglielmi was in England, only Piccinni's *La buona figliuola* was more popular than Guglielmi's *I viaggiatori ridicoli tornati in Italia*. Burney also wrote that Guglielmi's lack of success seemed 'to have been fairly proportioned to the abilities he manifested, though he has since composed better and more successfully in Italy … [he] had some Neapolitan fire, and brought over the new and fashionable musical phrases from Italy, but he wrote too fast and with little invention or selection of passages'. (On the other hand Burney also found *I viaggiatori ridicoli* 'exceedingly pretty'.) Ferrari expressed a similar opinion in stronger terms: 'Guglielmi was knowledgeable about dramatic music, but lazy, stingy, and without self-respect. He used to write completely two or three numbers for each opera, and then he had the voice parts of the arias and the ensembles orchestrated by his students or by copyists'. Ferrari, who went to Naples in 1784, was a pupil and close friend of Paisiello and thus not unbiased. Such 'laziness' was then common practice among popular composers, and the success of an opera often turned on the beauty and originality of a few pieces in it; a widely told anecdote relates how Guglielmi himself once turned indifference to acclaim by the substitution of a single trio.

La Borde was particularly impressed by the originality

of Guglielmi's work and, while somewhat doubtful about his adoption 'of the licences of the modern style', felt that his composition was always 'correct' and its popular success 'approved by the schoolmen'. Gervasoni was 'stunned' by his musical learning, and described his style as 'truly harmonious, pure, natural', that highest term of later 18th-century praise, and 'pleasing'. An obituary probably written by his son (2) Pietro Carlo (now in *F-Pi*) notes that competition with Paisiello and Cimarosa helped him realize his compositional potential. The elegance, clarity, vivacity, grace and originality of his music are particularly commended. He was considered by most to be the equal of Cimarosa and Paisiello; the esteem in which he was held may be judged by the frequency of his commissions to write the important festive operas celebrating the royal name days and other occasions of public rejoicing in Naples. He composed more than a dozen comic operas that were international successes, some of which remained in the repertory for 30 years. These include *Il ratto della sposa*, *La sposa fedele*, *L'impresa d'opera*, *La villanella ingentilita*, *La Quakera spiritosa*, *Le vicende d'amore*, *La virtuosa di Mergellina*, *La pastorella nobile*, *La bella pescatrice* and *La serva innamorata*, as well as the two oratorios often mounted in secularized stagings, the *azione sacra Debora e Sisara* (Naples, S Carlo, 13 Feb 1788) and the *tragedia sacra La morte di Oloferne* (Rome, Palazzo Colonna, 22 April 1791). *Debora e Sisara* was almost universally regarded as one of the most sublime works of the late 18th century. Later even Stendhal, not an admirer, admitted Rossini's debt to Guglielmi. The wide distribution of complete surviving manuscripts attests to his popularity.

3. WORKS. Modern appreciation of Guglielmi's work has lagged behind that of some contemporaries. Although historians mention him mostly for his comic works, his *opere serie* command as much admiration as do those by other Italian composers of the time. Written over almost two generations, they kept abreast of changing fashions and were even innovatory. Guglielmi introduced in them expanded ensembles, especially the duet and trio that by 1765 had become fixtures at the end of the first and second acts in his *opere serie*.

A striking characteristic of these operas is a special kind of aria containing a long-phrased, wide-arched, mainly conjunct melodic line in long note values over a rhythmically active accompaniment (a vocal counterpart of the period's so-called 'singing allegro' instrumental style), producing an effect of great beauty and dignity, often within a contrastingly tense dramatic situation. In these works the arias still derived mainly from da capo forms, but the da capo repetition was now often written out in varied form. Simple da capo forms (text *aba*; music *ABA'*) still occasionally appeared, but less often as the century progressed, and apparently for the sake of formal variety and musical brevity. More common was the written-out 'grand' da capo (text *aabaa*; music *AA'BA''A'''*, *ABCA'B'* or some other variation) or, increasingly, a truncated version of it, with the repeat either written out or not (text *aaba*; music *AA'BA''*, *AA'BA'''*, *ABCB'* etc). Scenas with arias or ensembles preceded by accompanied recitative occupied an increasing proportion of each act, especially those portions leading up to act endings or scene changes, allowing an increasing degree of organization of the act as a large-scale musical unit with carefully placed climaxes achieved as much by musical as by dra-

matic means. Increasingly, as in *opera buffa*, this climax occurred with the ensemble finale, forcing changes in the traditional structure of the Metastasian libretto. By the time of *La morte di Cleopatra* (1796) the traditional dramaturgy of Guglielmi's early *opere serie* had been replaced by a more international form incorporating features from French opera and anticipating Romantic works of the 19th century: two-act construction, prominent structural use of the chorus (men for the first act, women for the second), frequent interior ensemble numbers, a shorter text and simplified action, and a freer flow between recitatives and set numbers: this was no longer a drama of moral reflection but one of rapidly moving sentiment and passion. It is not yet possible to determine how much of this shift Guglielmi pioneered, but he certainly participated in it.

To comic opera Guglielmi brought a superior talent, while following the formal fashions of the time. During the 1760s and 70s, three-act works predominated, thereafter two-act ones, and he experimented with the French taste, new to Italy, for combining two one-act *farsette* into one programme. Over more than 40 years, when he was writing *opere buffe*, he constantly used a larger number of ensembles in each act, displaying great skill in the handling of many voices at the act endings, where the action may comprise several scenes and an increasing number of characters. Thus *La sposa fedele* (1767, Venice) is constructed as follows (r = recitative; A = aria; D = duet; E = ensemble, F = finale, both with number of voices; / = scene change):

Act 1: E3 r A / A r A r / r A r / r A r A r A r A r F2, 3, 4/
Act 2: r A r A r A / r D r A r A r A r / r F2, 2, 5 /
Act 3: r A r A r / r D r Coro F /

La lanterna di Diogene (1794, Naples production), on the other hand, appears thus:

Act 1: E4 r A r E3 r A r D / r A r A r E5 r A F3, 3, 4, 5, 7/
Act 2: r E3 r A r D r / D r A r A r E4 / r A D A r / F2, 2, 7/

Here the ratio of arias to ensemble numbers changed from approximately 3:1 to nearly 1:1, and the convention of the exit aria to close a scene became decreasingly rigid. Guglielmi's early ensembles tended to be of the 'chain' variety, a series of musically more or less discrete pieces, each with separate expressive effect; by the late 1770s, this plan gave way to a great degree of internal organization, with complex cross-cutting and cross-referring of internal formal relationships.

By the 1770s Guglielmi had completely abandoned the da capo aria form in his comic works; instead the basic aria type had become the so-called 'whole repeat' form, in which both stanzas of text are sung and then repeated to varied or different music with the key scheme (in its simplest form) I–V–V–I, the return to the tonic occurring some time after the text repetition starts (although the dominant and subdominant were the favoured contrasting key areas, Guglielmi was also fond of the mediant and minor dominant keys). This basic pattern allowed endless structural variety in the individual arias, depending on the length, poetic complexity and expressive requirements of the texts. He sometimes treated the two sections of the text in composite fashion, with different metres, tempos and even keys for the two musical divisions, sharply articulating the two halves of the text. More often his treatment was a sophisticated 'instrumental' one, in which the seams between the textual sections were minimized in the music, as between the end of the first statement of the text and the beginning of its repetition: textual shapes were often subordinated to musical ones, especially in the later works. Hence musical forms range from the most obvious *ABA'B'*, through *ABCB'* and the more complicated *ABCA'B'CC* to arias (usually accompanying stage action) that are virtually through-composed. Another frequent type of variation was to truncate one or more of the repeated varied sections in the second half of the aria. Through-composed and less symmetrical closed forms became increasingly frequent towards the end of the century. The cavatina, in either composite or simple *AA'* form, appeared frequently in these operas, and during the 1770s Guglielmi began to use rondo forms.

His melodic style, as many 18th-century critics noted, is concise. In his *opere buffe*, at least, he tended to work in short phrases, almost always two or four bars long, and very often immediately repeated, either exactly or sequentially. This characteristic seems to be more pronounced in the earlier music than in the later, but to a modern ear, even a later piece like *La Quakera spiritosa* (1783) can seem numbingly regular.

In the course of his *opera buffa* writing Guglielmi moved from the customary 'Italian' three-movement sinfonia, through, in the late 1770s, a one-movement 'French' type involving a good deal of imitative counterpoint at the opening, to a one-movement 'Austrian' one in his late works – an Allegro preceded by a slow introduction. Contrasting key and thematic areas are clearly defined in all of these; developmental central sections, when included at all, are rudimentary. His orchestration was competent but perhaps the most conservative feature of his works, both serious and comic; however, he showed an interest in orchestral innovation by endorsing Marescalchi's redisposition of the Teatro S Carlo orchestra in spring 1786.

See also ALCESTE (iii); *BELLA PESCATRICE, LA*; *PASTORELLA NOBILE, LA*; *RATTO DELLA SPOSA, IL*; *SPIRITO DI CONTRADIZIONE, LO*; and *SPOSA FEDELE, LA*.

LKH – *London, King's Theatre in the Haymarket*
NC – *Naples, Teatro di S Carlo*
NFI – *Naples, Teatro dei Fiorentini*
NFO – *Naples, Teatro del Fondo*
NN – *Naples, Teatro Nuovo*
VB – *Venice, Teatro S Benedetto*
VM – *Venice, Teatro S Moisè*

Lo solachianiello 'mbroglione (dg, D. Pignataro), NFI, wint. 1757
Il filosofo burlato (commedia per musica), NFI, wint. 1758
La ricca locandiera (int, ? A. Palomba), Rome, Capranica, carn. 1759, arias US-NYp
I capricci di una vedova [not I capricci d'una marchesa] (dg), NFI, spr. 1759
La moglie imperiosa (commedia per musica, 3, ? A. Villani), NFI, aut. 1759
I due soldati (dg, A. Palomba), NN, wint. 1760
L'Ottavio (commedia per musica, 3, G. Federico), NN, wint. 1760
Il finto cieco (dg, P. Trinchera), NFI, sum. 1761
I cacciatori (farsetta, after C. Goldoni: *Li uccellatori*), Rome, Tordinona, 30 Jan 1762, *I-Af*, *Bc*, *Fc*, *PAc*; ? also as Gli uccellatori, *D-Dlb*, songs (London, c1770–72)
La donna di tutti i caratteri (commedia per musica, A. Palomba), NFI, aut. 1762
Don Ambrogio (?int), NFI, wint. 1762
Tito Manlio (os, 3, G. Roccaforte), Rome, Argentina, 8 Jan 1763, *I-Rmassimo*, *P-La*
La francese brillante (commedia per musica, 3, P. Mililotti), NFI, sum. 1763
Lo sposo di tre e marito di nessuna (commedia per musica, 3, A. Palomba), NN, aut. 1763, *A-Wn*, *I-Bc*, collab. Anfossi
L'olimpiade (os, 3, P. Metastasio), NC, 4 Nov 1763, *P-La*; Venice, 1766, Act 1 [?new version] by Guglielmi, Act 2 by A. G. Pampani, Act 3 by F. Brusa
Le contadine bizzarre (farsetta), Rome, Capranica, 1763

Siroe re di Persia (os, 3, Metastasio), Florence, Pergola, 5 Sept 1764, *La*
Li rivali placati (dg, 3, G. Martinelli), VM, aut. 1764, *A-Wn*, *D-Dlb*, *Rtt*, *F-Pn*, *I-MOe*, *US-Wc*
Farnace (os, ? A. M. Lucchini), Rome, Argentina, 4 Feb 1765, *I-Rdp*
Tamerlano (os, 3, A. Piovene), Venice, S Salvatore, Ascension 1765, *P-La*
L'impresa d'opera (dg, 3, B. Cavalieri), Milan, Regio Ducal, aut. 1765 *D-Dlb*, *H-Bn*, *I-Fc*, *Tf* (Acts 2 and 3), *P-La*; also as Il teatro in scena; L'impresario dell'opera; ? Gli amori teatrali, *F-Pn*
Il ratto della sposa (dg, 3, G. Martinelli), VM, aut. 1765, *A-Wn*, *B-Bc*, *D-Dlb*, *Hs*, *F-Pn*, *H-Bn*, *I-MOe*, *P-La*; also as La sposa rapita, Il vecchio deluso; rev. London, 1768
Adriano in Siria (os, 3, Metastasio), VB, 26 Dec 1765, *La*
Lo spirito di contradizione (dg, 3, Martinelli), VM, carn. 1766, *A-Wn*
Sesostri (os, 3, P. Pariati), Venice, S Salvatore, 7 May 1766, *P-La*; rev. (Bottarelli), LKH, 1768; also as Le feste d'Iside
Demofoonte (os, 3, Metastasio), Treviso, Onigo, 8 Oct 1766, *La*
La sposa fedele (dg, 3, P. Chiari), VM, carn. 1767, *A-KR*, *Wn*, *D-Dlb*, *Wa*, *F-Pn*, *GB-Lbl*, *I-Gl*, *MOe*, *P-La*, Favourite Songs (London, n.d.); also perf. Berlin, 1777, as Robert und Kalliste, oder Der Triumph der Treue, *B-Bc*, *D-Bds*, *DO*, *F-Pn*, *US-Bp*, abridged vs (Berlin and Leipzig, 1777); also as La Rosinella, ossia La sposa fedele; La fedeltà in amore; La sposa costante; La costanza di Rosinella [possibly 1st perf. Cremona, 1765]
Antigono (os, 3, Metastasio), Milan, Regio Ducal, Jan 1767, *F-Pn*, *I-Nc*, *P-La*, *US-Wc*
Il re pastore (os, 3, Metastasio), VB, Ascension 1767 [not Turin, 1765, a pasticcio], *F-Pn*, *P-La*
Ifigenia in Aulide (os, G. Bottarelli), LKH, 16 Jan 1768, Favourite Songs (London, 1768)
I viaggiatori ridicoli tornati in Italia (dg, Bottarelli, after Goldoni), LKH, 24 May 1768, Favourite Songs (London, 1768)
Alceste (os, 3, R. de' Calzabigi, rev. G. Parini), Milan, Regio Ducal, 26 Dec 1768, *F-Pn*, *P-La*
Ruggiero (os, 5, C. Mazzolà, after L. Ariosto), Venice, S Salvatore, 3 May 1769, *P-La*; also as Bradamante e Ruggiero, *D-Mbs*
Ezio (os, 3, Metastasio), LKH, 13 Jan 1770, Favourite Songs (London, 1770), ?collab. others; Rome, Argentina, 3 Jan 1774 [mostly new], *F-Pn*
Il disertore (dg, 3, C. F. Badini, after M.-J. Sedaine), LKH, 19 May 1770, Favourite Songs (London, 1770)
L'amante che spende (dg, N. Tassi), VM, aut. 1770, cavatina *I-OS* (perf. 1771)
Le pazzie di Orlando (dg, 3, Badini, after Ariosto), LKH, 23 Feb 1771, *D-Bds*, *DS*, *F-Pn*, *GB-Lbl*, Favourite Songs (London, 1771); also as Orlando paladino; Orlando furioso
Il carnovale di Venezia, o sia La virtuosa (dg, Badini), LKH, 14 Jan 1772, Favourite Songs (London, 1772)
L'assemblea (dg, 2, Bottarelli, after Goldoni: *La conversazione*), LKH, 24 March 1772
Demetrio (os, 3, Bottarelli, after Metastasio), LKH, 3 June 1772
Mirandolina (dg, 3, G. Bertati), VM, carn. 1773, *D-Dlb*
La contadina superba, over Il giocatore burlato (int), Rome, Valle, carn. 1774, *B-Bc*, *D-Dlb*, *P-La*; also as Il giocatore burlato
Tamas Kouli-Kan nell'Indie (os, 3, V. A. Cigna-Santi), Florence, Pergola, 16 Sept 1774, *I-Fc*, *?PAc*
Gl'intrighi di Don Facilone (int, 2), Rome, Valle, carn. 1775, *D-Dlb*, *I-MOe* (perf. 1776), *P-La*
Merope (os, 3, Zeno), Turin, Regio, carn. 1775, *La*
Vologeso (os, 3, Zeno: *Lucio Vero*), Milan, Regio Ducal, 26 Dec 1775, *F-Pn*, *P-La* (Acts 2 and 3)
La Semiramide riconosciuta (os, 3, Metastasio), NC, 12 Aug 1776, *F-Pn*, *?I-Mc*, *Nc*
Il matrimonio in contrasto (commedia per musica, 3, G. Palomba), NFI, sum. 1776, *F-Pn*, *I-Fc*, *Nc*, *Rdp* (inc.)
Artaserse (os, 3, Metastasio), Rome, Argentina, 29 Jan 1777, *P-La* [possibly 1st perf. Pistoia, Risvegliati, sum. ?1775]
Ricimero (os, after F. Silvani: *La fede tradita e vendicata*), NC, 30 May 1777, *F-Pn*, *I-Nc*, *P-La*
I fuorusciti (commedia per musica, ?G. Palomba), NFI, wint. 1777, cavatina *I-Mc* and *Nc* [not trans. as Die beyden Flüchtlinge, by Paisiello]
Il raggiratore di poca fortuna (dg, G. Palomba), NFI, 1 Aug 1779, *F-Pn*, *?I-Mc*, *Tf*, *US-Wc*
La villanella ingentilita (commedia per musica, 3, F. S. Zini), NFI, 8 Nov 1779, *F-Pn*; also as I due fratelli sciocchi, I fratelli sciocchi, Li fratelli Pappamosca, I due fratelli Pappamosca, La finta principessa [not as La villanella incivilità; La contadina fortunata]

Narcisso (int, ? G. Palomba), Naples, Accademia di Dame e Cavalieri, 19 Dec 1779, *D-B*, *Bds*

La dama avventuriera (commedia per musica, 3, G. Palomba), NFI, spr. 1780

La serva padrona (dg, ? after G. Federico), NFI, aut. 1780

Le nozze in commedia (dg, 3, G. Palomba), NFI, Jan 1781; also as Il medico burlato, *F-Pn*, *I-Rmassimo*

Diana amante (serenata, Metastasio: *Endimione*, rev. L. Serio), Naples, Accademia di Dame e Cavalieri, 28 Sept 1781

I Mietitori (commedia per musica, 3, Zini), NFI, 20 Oct 1781, *Rmassimo*

La semplice ad arte (commedia per musica, 2, G. Palomba), NFI, 12 May 1782, *Mc*, *Rmassimo*

La Quakera spiritosa (commedia per musica, 2, G. Palomba), NFI, sum. 1783, *F-Pn*, *H-Bn*, ?*I-Mc*, *Tf*, *Rmassimo* [possibly 1st perf. Monza, Arciducale, spr. ?1782]

La donna amante di tutti, e fedele a nessuno (commedia per musica, 3, G. Palomba), NFO, aut. 1783

Le vicende d'amore (int, 2, ? G. B. Neri), Rome, Valle, carn. 1784, *A-Wn*, *D-Dlb*, *Rtt*, *W*, *Wa*, *H-Bn*, *I-BZtoggenburg*, *US-Wc*; also as Der verliebte Zwist, *H-Bn*

I finti amori (commedia per musica, not G. Bertati), NFI, sum. 1784, *I-Nc*; also as L'impostore punito, *F-Pn* (1776, Parma), *I-Gl*, *Rmassimo*, *P-La*

La finta zingara (farsa, 1, G. B. Lorenzi), NFI, 10 Jan 1785, *F-Pn*, *I-Mr*, *Rdp*, *P-La*; also as La finta zinghera, ossia Il solachianello; Il solachianello [not the same as in 1757]

Le sventure fortunate (farsa, ? Lorenzi), NFI, 10 Jan 1785, *I-Mc*, *P-La*

La virtuosa in Mergellina (dg, 3, Zini), NN, sum. 1785, *D-Dlb*, *F-Pn*, *GB-Lbl*, *I-BRq*, *Fc*, *Gl*, *Mc*, ?*Mr*, *P-La*, *US-Wc*; also as Adalinda; La virtuosa bizzarra; Chi la dura la vince, ossia La finta cantatrice

Enea e Lavinia (os, 3, V. de Stefano or G. Sertor), NC, 4 Nov 1785, *D-Mbs*, *F-Pn* (perf. 1788), *I-Nc*

L'inganno amoroso (commedia per musica, 3, G. Palomba), NN, 12 June 1786, *B-Bc*, *I-Gl*, *Nc*, *P-La*, *US-Wc*; also as Le due gemelli, *F-Pn*; Gli equivoci nati da somiglianza, Rome, 1787, excerpts *I-Mc*; Le nozze disturbate; L'equivoco amoroso, ossia Le due gemelle; Le due finte gemelle; Le due equivoci per somiglianza; Die Zwillingsbrüder

Le astuzie villane (commedia per musica, 3, G. Palomba), NFI, sum. 1786, *F-Pn*, *I-Rmassimo*

Lo scoprimento inaspettato (dg, 3, Stefano), NN, carn. 1787 [rev. from La coerede fortunata because of censorship]

Laconte (os, G. Pagliuca), NC, 30 May 1787, *F-Pn* (inc.), *I-Nc*, *US-Bp* (as Laocoonte)

La pastorella nobile (commedia per musica, 2, Zini), NFO, 15 or 19 April 1788, *B-Bc*, *D-Dlb*, *Wa* (perf. 1793), *F-Pn*, *I-Bc*, *CR*, *Fc*, *Gl*, *Mr*, *MOe*, *Nc*, *Rmassimo*, *US-Wc*; excerpts (Vienna, n.d.); also as L'erede di Belprato; Die Schöne auf dem Lande; Das adelige Landmädchen; Die adelische Schäferin

Arsace (os, 3, after G. De Gamerra: *Il Medonte re d'Epiro*), VB, 26 Dec 1788, rondò *I-Fc*

Rinaldo (os, 2, G. Foppa, after T. Tasso), VB, 28 Jan 1789, *F-Pn*, *P-La*; also as Armida

Ademira (os, 3, F. Moretti), NC, 30 May 1789, *F-Pn*, *I-Nc*

Gl'inganni delusi (commedia per musica, 2, G. Palomba), NFO, 13 June 1789, *Rmassimo*

La bella pescatrice (commedia per musica, 2, Zini), NN, Oct 1789, *B-Bc*; *D-B*, *Bds*, *Dlb*, *DO*, *DS*, *Mbs*, *SW*, *Wa*; *F-Pn*; *I-Fc*, *MC*, *Mr*, *Nc*, *Rmassimo*; *US-Bp*, *Wc*; ov. and arias (Vienna, n.d.); also as La villanella incivilità, La pescatrice

Alessandro nell'Indie (os, 3, Metastasio), NC, 4 Nov 1789, *B-Bc*, *F-Pn*, *I-Nc*, *US-Wc*

La serva innamorata (dg, 2, G. Palomba), NFI, ? July 1790, *D-B*, *F-Pn*, *I-Fc* (as La serva bizzarra), *Mr*, *P-La*, *US-LOu*; rev. as La giardiniera innamorata, Vienna, court, 1791, *Wc*

L'azzardo (commedia per musica, 2), NFO, 9 Oct 1790, *I-Nc*

Le false apparenze (commedia per musica, G. Palomba), NFI, spr. 1791, *Rmassimo*

La sposa contrastata (commedia per musica, 2, Zini), NFO, aut. 1791, *F-Pn*

Il poeta di campagna (commedia per musica, 2, Zini), NN, spr. 1792, *I-CR*, *Rmassimo*, *Vnm*, *US-Wc*; also as Lo sciocco poeta di campagna, *I-Fc*

Amor tra le vendemmie (commedia per musica, 2, G. Palomba), NN, aut. 1792, *F-Pn*, *US-Bp*

La lanterna di Diogene (dg, 2, N. Liprandi [A. Anelli], after Palomba), Venice, S Samuele, aut. 1793; rev. (Palomba), NFI,

?aut. 1794, *B-Bc*, *D-Dlb*, *E-Bc*, *F-Pn*, *I-Fc*, *I-Mr*, *Pl* (perf. Padua, 1810), *US-Wc*

Gli amanti della dote (farsa, 1, Zini: L'ultima che si perde è la speranza), Lisbon, S Carlos, carn. 1794

Admeto (?os, G. Palomba), NFO, 5 Oct 1794, *F-Pn*

La pupilla scaltra (dg, 2), VB, 8 Jan 1795, *I-Rmassimo*

Il trionfo di Camilla (os, 2, ? after S. Stampiglia), NC, 30 May 1795, *Fc*, *Li*, *Nc*, *Rmassimo*, *F-Pn*

La Griselda (os, G. Sertor), Florence, 1796

La morte di Cleopatra (os, 2, S. A. Sografi), NC, 22 June 1796, *F-Pn*, *I-Fc*, *Nc*, *Rmassimo*

L'amore in villa (dg, 2, G. Petroselllini), Rome, Casa di Sforza Cesarini, 1797

Ippolito (os), NC, 4 Nov 1798

Siface e Sofonisba (os, 2, A. L. Tottola), NC, 30 May 1802, *Nc*

MS operas attrib. Guglielmi: Le cantatrici villane, pubd duet *US-NYp*; La conte, *F-Pn*; La donna bizzarre, *Nc*; La donna re la fa, aria *Nc*, excerpts *PAc*; I due baroni, arias *Gl* (perf. Genoa, 1799 and 1804); Il giovatore; Mario in Numidia, aria *I-Mc*; ? Morte di Cesare, aria *Nc*, *Pl*, *Rsc*; Pirro, aria *Gl*, *Rsc* (perf. Genoa, 1790 and 1794); La serva astuta ed amorosa, *Fc*; La scelta dello sposo (farsa), *B-Lc*, *D-Hs*; Sposo in Periglio, aria *I-Mc*

Music in: Traetta: Armida, NC, 1763; 2 arias and 2 finales in Paisiello: Madama l'umorista, Modena, 1765; Tigrane, LKH, 1767, songs (London, 1767); Siface, LKH, 1767; Amintas, London, CG, 1769; arias in Gluck: Orfeo ed Euridice, LKH, 1770, *B-Bc*; L'olimpiade, LKH, 1770; arias in Paisiello: La disfatta di Dario, NC, 1777, *F-Pn*, *I-Nc*; Il sacrificio di Jefte, NFO, 1790 [probably a pasticcio]; choruses in L. Ruspoli: L'Ajace, Rome, Palazzo Ruspoli, 1801

Doubtful or false attributions: Scipione nella Spagna, Venice, 1746, by Galuppi; Der Lohn weiblicher Sittsamkeit, Hanover, 1755; La donna scaltra (int), Florence, Pallacorda, carn. ?1765; La pace tra gli amici, Brescia, 1766; Il matrimonio, Novara, 1770; La virtuosa, London, 1770; Il giuoco di picchetto, Coblenz, 1772 = Jommelli: La conversazione; La frascatana, Bologna, 1773; La locanda (Bertati), Casale, 1776; La virtuosa alla moda, Naples, 1780, *I-Gl*, ? by L. Caruso; La vendammio (burletta), Naples, 1780, *Gl*, *Rmassimo*; Didone, Venice, 1785; La clemenza di Tito, Turin, 1785; L'impostore punito, Milan, 1785, *F-Pn*; Li cinque pretendenti, ? Genoa, 1790; Die Freundschaft auf der Probe = Grétry: L'amitié à l'épreuve; La schiava riconosciuta, Fano, 1797 = ? Il raggiratore di poca fortuna; La donna fanatica, Madrid, 1798 = ? P. C. Guglielmi: La sposa bisbetica; La sposa di stravagante temperamento, Venice, 1798 = P. C. Guglielmi: La sposa bisbetica; Amore in caricatura, *Pn*; Gli amanti teatrali, *Pn*; Il regno delle amazoni, *Pn*; La muta per amore (? G. Foppa), Faenza, 1804, ? by P. C. Guglielmi; La statua matematica (? Bertati), Ravenna, 1799, ? by P. C. Guglielmi; Il matrimonio villano, *Pn*; La guerra aperta, *Pn*, *US-Bp* (Act 2), ? by F. Ruggi

(2) Pietro Carlo Guglielmi [Guglielmini] (*b* London, 11 July 1772; *d* Naples, 21 Feb 1817). Composer, eldest son of (1) Pietro Alessandro Guglielmi. About 1782 he is thought to have entered his father's conservatory in Naples, S Maria di Loreto, where he studied singing, the keyboard and composition. By 1794 he was apparently in Madrid, where his first opera was produced (Gervasoni's account of a successful early *opera seria* performed under patronage at the Teatro S Carlo in Naples in 1783 is now generally discounted); in 1795 he was in Lisbon and, by December, in Florence. By 1797 he had returned to settle in Naples for several years, with theatrical commissions taking him to Rome, Palermo and, briefly in 1805, to Pavia and Venice. By 1808 he had begun to travel again, returning to Lisbon and, by spring 1809, settling for a time in London, where he wrote operas and taught. He returned to Naples by the spring of 1811 and then, within two years, to his ancestral home in Massa. In 1816 he was made *maestro di cappella onorario* at the court of the Archduchess Maria Beatrice d'Este. He continued to produce operas occasionally until his death.

Like his father, Guglielmi produced mainly comic

operas, but he lacked much of his father's musical intelligence and originality. Even contemporary biographers dismissed him as a pale imitation, but his works were popular, as their number and their frequent revivals testify. His melodic invention is competent but unmemorable. Harmonic treatment is 'correct' for the period but unadventurous, and he had little of his father's flair for complex and exciting ensemble textures. His rhythmic treatment inclines to be foursquare, with monotonously regular phrasing. His most impressive work was probably the oratorio ('dramma sacro') *La distruzione di Gerusalemme* (1803, Naples), which exhibited more harmonic colour and a more carefully worked-out structure than his comic pieces customarily did.

opere buffe unless otherwise stated

NFI – *Naples, Teatro dei Fiorentini*
NN – *Naples, Teatro Nuovo*

Dorval e Virginia (op semiseria, 4, G. M. Foppa), Lisbon, S Carlos, 13 May 1795; as Paolo e Virginia (De Gamerra), Vienna, Kärntnertor, 2 March 1800; *I-Fc, Mr, Nc*

Griselda (os, 3, G. Sertor), Florence, Pergola, 27 Dec 1795, *Fc*

La sposa bisbetica (farsa, 2), Rome, Valle, carn. 1797, *Fc, Mr, Nc*

L'inganno per amore (2, F. Cammarano), NN, sum. 1797; as Lo sposalizio villano, Florence, Pergola, spr. 1799

Chi la dura la vince (2, D. Piccinni), NN, sum. 1798

I tre rivali (2), NN, sum. 1798

La fata Alcina (dg, 2, Foppa, after Bertati: *L'isola Alcina*), Rome, Alibert, carn. 1799; as Alcina, Venice, S Benedetto, June 1800

I raggiri amorosi (burletta, 2), Rome, Valle, spr. 1799, *F-Pn, I-Mr, US-Wc*; also as Il matrimonio villano [Il feudatorio]

I due gemelli (2), Rome, Valle, aut. 1799, *Wc*

Gli amanti in cimento (2, G. Palomba), NFI, carn. 1800, *I-Nc*; rev. as farsa, Venice, S Benedetto, 8 May 1804

Due nozze e un sol marito (2), Florence, Infuocati, aut. 1800, *F-Pn, I-Mr*

La fiera (2, Palomba), NFI, carn. 1801, *Nc, US-Bp*; also as La cantatrice di spirito, Genoa, 1807; as L'isola incantata, NN, 1813

Le convenienze teatrali (2, ? Palomba), Palermo, S Cecilia, 30 May 1801, *B-Bc, D-Mbs, I-Bc, Mr, Nc, US-SFsc*

La serva bizzarra (2, G. Palomba), Rome, spr. 1803, *I-Bc, Fc, US-Bp, Wc*; as Amor finto, amor vero, amor deluso, Trieste, 1813; also as Cameriera astuta, I raggiri della serva, La serva raggiratrice

La distruzione di Gerusalemme (dramma sacro, 2, ? Sografi), Naples, Fondo, Lent 1803, *GB-Lbl, Lcm, I-Af, Li, Nc, PAc, US-Wc*; also as Il Sedecia, Florence, 1807; as Semira, Barcelona, S Cruz, 16 Sept 1816

Asteria e Teseo (op semiseria, 2), Naples, S Carlo, 13 Aug 1803, *I-Nc*

Il naufragio fortunato (2, G. Palomba), NFI, 1804, *Fc, Nc, US-Bp*

L'equivoco fra gli sposi (2, G. Palomba), NFI, 1804, *I-Fc, Mc, Nc*; as Tre sposi per una, Vienna, Kärntnertor, 19 Jan 1805

Ines de Castro (os, 2, F. Tarducci), Rome, Argentina, 2 Jan 1805

La fedeltà nelle selve [La villanella rapita] (2, Bertati), Pavia, Quattro Cavalieri, carn. 1805

La scelta dello sposo (farsetta, 1, Foppa), Venice, S Moisè, 24 April 1805, *B-Lc, D-Mbs, GB-Lbl, Lcm, I-Fc, Gl, Mr, US-Wc*; as I concorrenti alle nozze, Palermo, 1821; also as Li tre pretendenti, I tre pretendenti delusi

La donna di spirito (farsa, 1, G. Artusi), Padua, Nuovo, July 1805

La vedova contrastata (burletta, 2, Tarducci), Rome, Apollo, 28 Dec 1805, *I-Mr*; as La vedova capricciosa, Paris, Italien, 1810; also as La vedova in contrasto, La scelta del matrimonio, La contessa bizzarra, La contessina contrastata, La donna di genio volubile

Amor tutto vince (2, G. Palomba), NFI, 1805, *Fc, PAc, US-Wc*; as La donna di più caratteri, Bologna, 1806; as Don Papirio, Bassano, 1811; Da un Locanda all'altra

La Pamela casada (after G. Rossi: *La Pamela maritata*), Madrid, Príncipe, 5 Feb 1806

La sposa del Tirolo (2, Palomba), NFI, spr. 1806, *I-Nc, US-Bp*

Il matrimonio in contrasto (G. Ceccherini), Naples, 1806

La guerra aperta, ossia Astuzia contro astuzia (2, B. Mezzanotte), Rome, Valle, carn. 1807, *D-Dlb, I-Fc, Mr, PAc*; as La scommessa, London, 1809, *US-Bp*

Amori e gelosie tra congiunti (2, G. Palomba), NFI, spr. 1807, *I-Nc*

Il trionfo di Davidde (dramma sacro, 2, G. Caravita), Lisbon, S Carlos, Lent 1808

Sidagero (os, S. Buonaiuti), London, King's, 20 June 1809, excerpt *GB-Lbl*

Romeo e Giulietta (os, Buonaiuti), London, King's, 20 Feb 1810, excerpt *Lbl*

Atalida (pasticcio, Buonaiuti), London, King's, 20 March 1810

Le nozze in campagna (2, Palomba), NN, spr. 1811, *A-Wn, I-Mr, Nc*

Oro non compra amor (2, A. Anelli), Senigallia, Condominale, Aug 1811; as Un vero amore non ha riguardi, ossia La villanella fortunata, Rome, Argentina, 1812; as Il pretendente burlato, Paris, Italien, 24 April 1819

Le due simili in una (2, Palomba), NN, 1811, *Nc*

Amalia e Carlo, ovvero L'arrivo della sposa (op semiseria, 3, A. L. Tottola), NN, 1812, *Nc*

L'isola di Calipso (os, 2, L. Romanelli), Milan, Scala, 23 Jan 1813, excerpt *GB-Lbl*

La presunzione corretta (2, L. Prividali), Milan, Scala, 19 April 1813, *I-Mc*

Ernesto e Palmira (2, Romanelli), Milan, Scala, 18 Sept 1813, *Mc*

La moglie giudice del marito, Milan, Re, sum. 1814

Amore assottiglia l'ingegno, ossia Il tutore indiscreto (dramma buffo, J. Ferretti), Rome, Valle, 26 Dec 1814

Amore y innocencia, Madrid, Cruz, 20 July 1815

L'amore e dispetto (Palomba), Naples, Palazzo Maddeloni, 1816

Paolo e Virginia (os, 3, G. M. Diodati), NFI, 2 Jan 1817, *Nc, Mc* [? = Dorval e Virginia, 1795, rev. 1800]

Il biglietto d'alloggio, Crema, Jan 1817

Doubtful: La caccia d'Enrico IV (farsa), Pisa, *Fc*

(3) Giacomo Guglielmi (*b* Massa, 16 Aug 1782; *d* ?Naples, after 1820). Tenor, son of (1) Pietro Alessandro Guglielmi. He studied with Ferdinando Mazzanti and Piccinni's nephew. After his début at the Teatro Argentina, Rome, he sang, mostly in comic opera, at Parma, Naples, Florence, Bologna and Venice. He then went to Amsterdam and in 1809 to Paris for two years. By 1812 he had returned to Naples, to sing leading roles; he sang there again in 1819–20 and is thought to have died soon afterwards. He created the role of Don Ramiro in *La Cenerentola* (1817, Rome). Fétis judged his voice to be 'pleasant, but of weak power; he sang with more taste than spirit'.

BurneyH; *CroceN*; *FétisB*; *FlorimoN*; *PEM* (S. Leopold, F. Lippmann); *RicordiE* (C. Sartori); *RosaM*

J.-B. de La Borde: *Essai sur la musique ancienne et moderne* (Paris, 1780), iii, 193–4

J. Le Breton: 'Notice sur P. Guglielmi', *Magasin encyclopédique* (Paris, 1806), vi, 98

A. Choron and F. Fayolle: *Dictionnaire historique des musiciens* (Paris, 1810–11)

C. Gervasoni: *Nuova teoria di musica* (Parma, 1812), 41, 160ff

G. B. G. Grossi: *Le belle arti: opusculi storici musicali* (Naples, 1820), i, 33–4

G. Orloff: *Essai sur l'histoire de la musique en Italie, depuis les temps les plus anciens jusqu'à nos jours* (Paris, 1822), ii, 133ff

Stendhal: *Vie de Rossini* (Paris, 1824), 21, 95, 308

G. G. Ferrari: *Aneddoti piacevoli e interessanti* (London, 1830); ed. S. di Giacomo (Palermo, 1920), 147ff

L. Nerici: *Storia della musica in Lucca* (Lucca, 1879), 165

C. Riccio: 'Cenno storico delle accademie fiorite nella età di Napoleone', *Archivio storico per le province napoletana* (Naples, 1880), v, 133

M. Scherillo: *L'opera buffa napoletana durante il settecento: storia letteraria* (Naples, 1883, 2/1917), 451–2

G. Bustico: 'La giovinezza di Pier Alessandro Guglielmi', *Iride* (Genoa, 1897), i

——: *Pier Alessandro Guglielmi: appunti biografici* (Massa, 1898)

——: 'Un musicista poco noto del settecento: Pier Alessandro Guglielmi', *Rivista teatrale italiana*, i (1901), 246

F. Piovano: 'Elenco cronologico delle opere (1757–1802) di Pietro Guglielmi (1727–1804)', *RMI*, xii (1905), 407–47

S. Di Giacomo: 'Paisiello e i suoi contemporanei', *Musica e musicisti* (1905), 762–8; repr. in *Napoli: figure e paesi* (Naples, 1909) and *Opere*, ii (Milan, 1946)

G. Bustico: 'Pietro Metastasio e Pier Alessandro Guglielmi', *Rivista teatrale italiana*, vii (1908), 257

F. Piovano: 'Notizie storico-bibliografiche sulle opere di Pietro Carlo Guglielmi (Guglielmini) con appendice su Pietro Guglielmi', *RMI*, xvi (1909), 243–70, 475–505, 785–820; xvii (1910), 59–90, 376–414, 554–89, 827–77

A. Della Corte: *L'opera comica italiana nel settecento* (Bari, 1923)

G. de Saint-Foix: 'Les maîtres de l'opéra bouffe dans la musique de chambre, à Londres', *RMI*, xxxi (1924), 507–26

G. Bustico: *Un musicista massese: Pier Alessandro Guglielmi* (Barga, 1926)

——: 'Pier Alessandro Guglielmi nel II centenario della sua nascita', *Bolletino bibliografico musicale*, iii/3 (1928), 1

C. F. Terry: *J. C. Bach* (London, 1929, 2/1967), 110ff, 120, 143

K. Geiringer: 'Die *Orlando*-Opern von Pietro Alessandro Guglielmi', *Musicae scientiae collectanea: Festschrift Karl Gustav Fellerer* (Cologne, 1973), 141–6

M. Donà: 'Dagli archivi milanesi: lettere di Ranieri de' Calzabigi e di Antonia Bernasconi', *AnMc*, no.14 (1974), 268–300

M. Robinson: 'Two London Versions of *The Deserter*', *IMSCR*, xii *Berkeley 1977*, 239–45

S. Giampaoli: *Musica e teatro alla corte di Massa: I Guglielmi* (Massa Carrara, 1978)

F. C. Petty: *Italian Opera in London, 1760–1800* (Ann Arbor, 1980)

R. Candiani: 'L' "Alceste" da Vienna a Milano', *Giornale storico della letteratura italiana*, clxi, fasc.514 (1988), 227–40

MARY HUNTER, JAMES L. JACKMAN

Guglielmini, Pietro Carlo. *See* GUGLIELMI family, (2).

Guglielmo Ratcliff ('William Ratcliff'). *Tragedia* in four scenes by PIETRO MASCAGNI to a text based on Andrea Maffei's Italian translation of HEINRICH HEINE's novel *William Ratcliff*; Milan, Teatro alla Scala, 16 February 1895.

Mascagni was captivated by *William Ratcliff* during his first year at the Milan Conservatory (1882), and he decided to set to music the words of Maffei's Italian translation virtually as they stood; this is accordingly one of the earliest Italian examples of the *Literaturoper* genre. He wrote part of the opera rapidly, but finished it only in 1894; the stupendous success of *Cavalleria rusticana* was an influential factor in his completing a work that looked back to the principles of the SCAPIGLIATURA movement in vogue between 1870 and 1890. *Ratcliff* is a story of spirits and crimes set in northern Scotland in 1820.

In his castle MacGregor (bass) blesses the betrothal of his daughter Maria [Mary] (soprano) and Count Douglas (baritone). Meanwhile William Ratcliff (tenor) waits for an opportunity to kill Douglas in a duel, as he has done to Mary's two earlier fiancés. But he comes off worse, escaping only with his life. Meanwhile the nurse, Margherita [Margaret] (mezzo-soprano), tells Mary of the unhappy love between William's father, killed by the jealous MacGregor, and her mother, who died of a broken heart as a result. Ratcliff bursts in, obsessed by the ghosts of the two former lovers, and kills Mary in his delirium; he then kills MacGregor and, finally, himself.

It is difficult to ignore the model of *Cavalleria* in the orchestral introduction, in which Margaret's song is inserted as a 'programme'. *Ratcliff* offers several inspired and original melodies, but in a musical context that is often exaggerated and supported by an over-complicated dramatic structure. The opera was already dated at the time of its première and soon disappeared from the repertory, in spite of the composer's fondness for it.

MICHELE GIRARDI

Guhr, Karl (Wilhelm Ferdinand) (*b* Militsch, 30 Oct 1787; *d* Frankfurt, 22 July 1848). German conductor and composer. He studied in Breslau with Schnabel and Janitschek, then held conducting appointments in Nuremberg, Wiesbaden, Kassel and Frankfurt (1821–48). In Nuremberg 'he brought fire and life into everything' and there and in Kassel he raised mediocre companies to a new state of excellence. On his arrival in Frankfurt (1 March 1821) he immediately restored the standards that had dropped in the wake of Spohr's resignation two years previously: he was said to 'understand with virtuosity how to play the orchestra', which played like men awakening from sleep. Spontini described him as the leading music director in Germany, and Wagner, who admired his *Die Zauberflöte* in *Mein Leben*, also praised him as 'of high standing, secure, strong and despotic' (*Über das Dirigieren*). Berlioz was impressed by his *Fidelio*, and left a lively personal account of Guhr in his *Mémoires*, saying that 'everything about him suggests musical intelligence and purpose'. His operas include a setting in German of Spontini's *La vestale* text (reviewed at length, with music examples, in *AMZ*).

Das Gespenst (4, A. von Kotzebue), Nuremberg, 1808; as Deodata, Kassel, Hof, 28 July 1815

Feodora (1, Kotzebue), Nuremberg, 1811

Die Vestalin (3, E. van Jouy, trans. J. von Seyfried), Kassel, Hof, 3 June 1814

König Siegmar (3, F. Rochlitz), Kassel, Hof, 8 May 1818; rev. version, Frankfurt, Dec 1823

Aladin, oder Die Wunderlampe (3, K. Gollmick), Frankfurt, National, 1830

*

StiegerO

AMZ, xi (1809), col. 411; xvi (1814), 641ff, 662ff; xxiii (1821), 275

C. Gollmick: *Karl Guhr: Nekrolog* (Frankfurt, 1848)

JOHN WARRACK

Gui, Vittorio (*b* Rome, 14 Sept 1885; *d* Florence, 17 Oct 1975). Italian conductor and composer. He studied in Rome at the Liceo di S Cecilia and at the university. At the Teatro Adriano in Rome in 1907, he was called on at short notice to take over the conducting of *La Gioconda*, with a success that led to engagements in Naples and Turin. On Toscanini's invitation, Gui opened the 1923–4 season at La Scala with *Salome*. In 1928 he formed the Orchestra Stabile of Florence, the organization of which developed in 1933 into the Maggio Musicale festival. There he conducted such then rare operas as Verdi's *Luisa Miller*, Spontini's *La vestale*, Cherubini's *Médée* and Gluck's *Armide*. Bruno Walter invited him to Salzburg in 1933 as the festival's first Italian guest conductor. Gui was a leading figure in the Rossini revival, and his 1952 performances of *Le comte Ory* at Florence initiated a new international success for that opera, as had his 1925 performances of *L'italiana in Algeri* in Turin (with Supervia). He continued to conduct after his 86th birthday, but withdrew from the reopening of the Teatro Regio, Turin, in 1973, having revived *L'occasione fa il ladro* in that city the previous year.

Gui appears never to have conducted in North America but gained a special following in Britain, where he won high praise for the warmth, buoyancy and attack of his performances. At Covent Garden, at that time under Beecham's direction, he first conducted *Rigoletto*, *Tosca* and *La bohème* in 1938. He returned there after the war only for a famous *Norma* with Callas in 1952, having meanwhile appeared with the Glyndebourne Festival Opera at the Edinburgh Festival (first in *Così fan tutte*, 1948). At Glyndebourne itself he conducted from 1952 (*La Cenerentola*, *Macbeth*, *Così*) every season until 1964. His recordings include Glyndebourne's 1953 *La Cenerentola*, the 1955 *Figaro* and *Le comte Ory*, and the 1962 *Il barbiere di Siviglia*.

In Italy Gui also won some regard as a composer, although his creative career was virtually over by the mid-1920s. *David* (with a libretto by Gui and Corrado Cozza based on the Bible and published in 1906) may never have been performed, but the three-act fairy opera *La fata Malerba* (given at the Teatro di Torino, Turin, on 15 May 1927) became his most widely successful composition. Written in about 1921 to a libretto by Fausto Salvatori, this whimsical tale about a rebellious child who is temporarily changed into a deformed monster has charm despite its lack of originality: the eclectic music makes use of folksongs of various nationalities, and the second act (set in a fairy-tale palace) features a fragment from a 16th-century lute piece. The pervading nursery-rhyme-like simplicity suggests parallels with Humperdinck and Ferrari Trecate, yet the poignancy also found in Gui's best songs is apparent, for example, in Masetto's lament when he finds that even his own mother fails to recognize him.

Gui made arrangements of Mozart's *Idomeneo* and Gluck's *Alceste* (in which he conflated the French and Italian versions). He was a prolific writer of articles (some of which were collected as *Battute d'aspetto*), and he wrote Italian singing versions of the librettos of Purcell's *Dido and Aeneas*, Stravinsky's *Perséphone* and other works. He received Portuguese and Swedish, as well as Italian, state honours.

WRITINGS

Nerone di Arrigo Boito (Milan, 1924)

Battute d'aspetto (Florence, 1944) [collected essays]

'Mozart in Italy', *Opera Annual*, ii (1955–6), 19–21

*

G. M. Gatti: 'Vittorio Gui', *Critica musicale*, iii (1920), 133–9; rev. in G. M. Gatti: *Musicisti moderni d'Italia e di fuori* (Bologna, 2/1925), 65–72; Eng. version in *MT*, lxii (1921), 685–7

G. Pannain: 'Vittorio Gui', *Piano forte*, viii (Turin, 1927), 241–6 [mainly about *La fata Malerba*]

R. Paoli: 'Vittorio Gui', *Opera*, iii (1952), 403–6

U. Bonafini: 'Vittorio Gui tra musica e poesia', *Discoteca alta fedeltà*, no.156 (1975), 14–15 [with discography by M. Vicentini]

G. Christie: 'Vittorio Gui, 1885–1975: an Appreciation', *Opera*, xxvi (1975), 1125–7

ARTHUR JACOBS, JOHN C. G. WATERHOUSE

Guicciardi, Francesco (*b* Modena; *fl* 1705–24). Italian tenor. His earliest known appearance was in the title role of Giannettini's *Artaserse* at Venice in 1705. From 1707 to 1710 he sang in five operas at Florence and the Pratolino, including Handel's *Vincer se stesso è la maggior vittoria* (*Rodrigo*); he played the substantial role of Giuliano which, as Dean observes, demands a fine technique and a compass of *d* to *a'*. He appeared in Orlandini's *L'odio e l'amore* at Genoa in 1709 and in two operas by Fiorè at Turin in 1715–16. Between 1716 and 1723, throughout which period he was described as a 'virtuoso' of the Duke of Modena, he sang in eight operas at Venice, including new works by C. F.

Pollarolo, Antonio Pollarolo, Lotti, Porta and Leo. In July 1719 Handel tried to engage him for the Royal Academy of Music in London; in 1724 he was in Naples.

*

W. Dean and J. M. Knapp: *Handel's Operas 1704–1726* (Oxford, 1987), 669

COLIN TIMMS

Guichard, Henry, Sieur d'Hérapine (*fl* 1670–early 18th century). French architect and librettist. He was the son-in-law of the architect Le Vau and *intendant et ordonnateur des bâtiments* to the Duke of Orléans. In 1670 he built a theatre for the productions of Perrin and Cambert's Académies d'Opéra at the Jeu de Paume de la Bouteille in Paris. In 1671 he wrote the libretto for *Les amours de Diane et d'Endymion*, a pastoral opera with music by Jean Granouilhet Sablières, and helped organize the production at Versailles (13 November). The work was revived at St Germain-en-Laye in February 1672 as *Le triomphe de l'amour*. By then, Guichard and Sablières believed they had obtained Perrin's privilege to produce operas – Guichard himself owned some of the rights – but when Louis XIV granted a monopoly to Lully in March 1672, there followed a long lawsuit between Guichard and Lully, which turned to scandal when the singer Marie Aubry became involved. In 1674 Guichard obtained a privilege to found an 'académie royale des spectacles' for the organization of carousels, tourneys, firework displays etc., with, however, a prohibition on 'the singing of any piece of music'. He also tried to join forces with the stage designer Carlo Vigarani. But his continuing lawsuit with Lully was prejudicial to him and prevented the registration of his privilege in 1678. He therefore left for Madrid in 1679 with a company of 40 performers to establish a musical academy at the court. On his return from Spain he lived in Valence, then retired to Grenoble.

Guichard may have written the text of a ballet set to music by Sablières in 1679 on the occasion of the peace treaty with Spain, and he certainly wrote the libretto of the opera *Ulysse*, with music by J.-F. Rebel, performed in 1703.

*

C. Nuitter and E. Thoinan: *Les origines de l'opéra français* (Paris, 1886)

L. de La Laurencie: *Les créateurs de l'opéra français* (Paris, 1921)

S. Pitou: *The Paris Opéra: an Encyclopedia of Operas, Ballets, Composers, and Performers*, i: *Genesis and Glory, 1671–1715* (Westport, CT, 1983)

MARCELLE BENOIT, CHRISTINA BASHFORD

Guidi, Francesco (*fl* 1841–60). Italian librettist. He first came to notice for his translation of Meyerbeer's *Les Huguenots* (as *Gli Anglicani*) in 1841. By then he had been married for some years to Isabella Lanari, sister of the impresario Alessandro Lanari. She managed Lanari's costume department; Guidi continued to work for the firm both as a translator (notably of Weber's *Der Freischütz* and Halévy's *La reine de Chypre*) and as a librettist in his own right. In 1846 he was appointed poet of the Royal Theatres in Turin, though he went on working for Lanari, and after the mid-1850s his work appeared in many other theatres.

Guidi was a careful and conscientious librettist, judicious and consistent, though breaking no new ground. One of his most successful librettos was *Il conte di Lavagna* for Mabellini (1843), and he worked for important composers such as Giovanni Pacini (*Ester d'Engaddi*, 1848, and *La regina di Cipro*, 1846), as well as many now forgotten. He added informative prefaces to his texts acknowledging his sources, which covered a wide field of European literature.

Vannina d'Ornano (tragedia lirica), Campana, 1842; *Il conte di Lavagna* (tragedia lirica), Mabellini, 1843; *Bonifazio de' Geremei* (tragedia lirica), Poniatowski, 1843; *Luisa di Francia* (melodramma), Campana, 1844; *I veneziani a Costantinopoli* (melodramma storico), Mabellini, 1844; *Ippolita degl'Azzi* (dramma lirico), G. M. Sborgi, 1845; *La regina di Cipro* (dramma lirico), G. Pacini, 1846; *Maria di Francia* (dramma tragico), Mabellini, 1846

Il birraio di Preston (melodramma giocoso), L. Ricci, 1847; *Luisa di Monfort* (with F. Meucci), M. Bergson, 1847; *Un eredità in Corsica* (melodramma), L. Gordigiani, 1847 (Usiglio, 1864, as *L'eredità in Corsica*); *Enrico Howard* (dramma lirico), Basevi, 1847; *Esmeralda* (dramma lirico), Poniatowski, 1847; *La tirolese* (dramma lirico), G. Magazzari, 1847 (Zajc, 1855); *Tancreda* (dramma lirico), Peri, 1847

La bocca degl'abbati (tragedia lirica), L. A. Ronzi, 1848; *Ester d'Engaddi* (dramma tragico), G. Pacini, 1848; *Il gladiatore* (tragedia lirica), P. Bona, 1849; *Piero de' Medici*, G. Roberti, 1849; *L'alcade di Zalamea* (melodramma semiserio), G. L. Bazzoni, 1850; *Leoni* (dramma lirico), G. Litta, 1850; *Alberico da Romano* (dramma lirico), T. Ramarini, 1851; *Maria di Brabante*, Graffigna, 1852

La maschera (melodramma giocoso), Dominiceti, 1854; *Il nuovo Tartufo* [Don Griffone] (commedia lirica), C. A. Gambini, 1854; *Una burla per correzione* (melodramma giocoso), F. Chiaromonte, 1855; *Leonora de' Medici* (melodramma tragico), G. Briccialdi, 1855; *Le figlie di Don Liborio* (melodramma giocoso), Cagnoni, 1856; *Lida di Carcano* (dramma lirico), Taddei, 1857; *La torre di Nesle*, O. Giannoni, 1857; *I tre rivali*, F. Luvini, 1857

Il vecchio della montagna (tragedia lirica), Cagnoni, 1860; *La savoiarda* (dramma lirico), Ponchielli, 1861; *Roderico re dei goti*, Ponchielli, 1863; *La vergine di Kermo* (melodramma romantico), Cagnoni, Pedrotti, Mazzucato, Cortesi, Ponchielli, G. Pacini and others, 1870; *Roderigo di Spagna* (dramma lirico), M. Bavagnoli, 1878; *La rosa di Perona*, T. Guidi-Lionetti, 1881; *Il Profugo*, G. Gnarro, 1883; *Tusnelda*, G. Del Bono, 1910   JOHN BLACK

Guido et Ginevra [*Guido et Ginevra, ou La peste de Florence* ('Guido and Ginevra, or The Plague of Florence')]. *Opéra* in five acts by FROMENTAL HALÉVY to a libretto by EUGÈNE SCRIBE; Paris, Opéra, 5 March 1838 (revised in four acts, Paris, Opéra, 23 October 1840).

The libretto is based on an episode in the history of Florence as told by Louis-Charles Delécluze. Ginevra (soprano), daughter of Cosimo dei Medici (bass), collapses during her marriage to the Duke of Ferrara (bass). She has been poisoned by a magic veil but is assumed to be a victim of the plague then ravaging Florence, so she is buried in the Medici vault. Later she awakes, but everywhere she goes in the plague-ridden city she is shunned, until a young sculptor, Guido (tenor), gives her shelter. Eventually Cosimo is persuaded to approve his daughter's marriage to Guido.

Scribe included in his libretto an effective contrast between Guido's village background, seen in the first and last acts, and the noisy pleasure-seeking Florentine court. A further contrast is provided by the constant threat of the plague hanging over the city. Ginevra's sepulchral appearance in Act 3 makes a striking scene, as does her reunion with Guido in the snow-covered street in Act 4. The best moments in the score are perhaps Guido's lament over Ginevra's supposedly dead body in Act 2 and the final trio for Cosimo and the two lovers. Halévy introduced a melophone in the orchestration of the ballet in Act 2.   HUGH MACDONALD

Guilbert de Pixérécourt, René Charles. *See* PIXÉRÉCOURT, RENÉ CHARLES GUILBERT DE.

Guillard, Nicolas-François (*b* Chartres, 16 Jan 1752; *d* Paris, 26 Dec 1814). French librettist. In 1771 he gained access to Parisian literary circles through an epistle on the exile of the Duke of Choiseuil. Sociable, modest, and perhaps rather indolent, he wrote little apart from librettos, but he received a government pension in recognition of his work, and he was on the Opéra's Comité de Lecture.

Guillard was probably the best French librettist of his generation, but he never surpassed his first opera, *Iphigénie en Tauride*, which he wrote about 1777. Gluck, for whom Guillard intended it, at first showed little interest and it was offered through an intermediary (Roullet) to Gossec. Gluck's change of mind caused justifiable chagrin to the other composer. Gluck took a hand in shaping what is sometimes considered the best libretto he ever had; he instructed Guillard to recast its five acts into four so that the crazed Orestes could mistake Iphigenia for the ghost of his murdered mother, demanded verses for existing music ('O malheureuse Iphigénie'), and made changes in the denouement. Even without Gluck's intervention, however, Guillard's work was superior in structure and as poetry to the libretto on the same subject offered to Piccinni, by Alphonse du Congé Dubreuil.

Much of Guillard's work was adaptation rather than original creation. He was Sacchini's principal French librettist, adapting Pierre Corneille's play *Le Cid* (as *Chimène*), and skilfully blending the two versions of *Dardanus* previously set by Rameau. His librettos are marred by uncertainty in handling the endings of stories. His most widely performed work, *Oedipe à Colone*, ends fatuously in reconciliation, and the stark tragedy of *Les Horaces* is weakened because Camille is not murdered. This libretto was revised for Bernardo Porta in 1800; the new version represents the duel of Horatius and Curiatius as an action ballet. *Electre*, on the other hand, is an unmitigated tragedy.

Guillard showed ingenuity in effecting necessary compressions and in conforming to the operatic convention of showing, rather than describing, important events. He could write neat, sometimes elegant verses, and he was enterprising in choice of subjects, twice using the otherwise neglected Corneille as a source, and taking an English play for Sacchini's last opera (*Arvire et Evelina*). He turned his hand to works suitable for the revolutionary 1790s. His largest original work is the biblical epic *La mort d'Adam*, written for Le Sueur about 1799 but not performed for ten years.

Iphigénie en Tauride (tragédie lyrique, after G. de la Touche), C. W. Gluck, 1779; *Emilie, ou La belle esclave* (acte de ballet), A.-E.-M. Grétry, 1781 [as Act 5 to *La fête de Mirza*, arr. Gossec]; *Electre* (tragédie, after Voltaire: *Oreste*), J.-B. Lemoyne, 1782; *Chimène* (tragédie, after P. Corneille: *Le Cid*), A. Sacchini, 1783; *Dardanus* (tragédie, after C.-A. Le Clerc de la Bruère), Sacchini, 1784; *Oedipe à Colone* (opéra, after Sophocles), Grétry, comp. 1785 [Act 1 only] (Sacchini, 1786); *Les Horaces* (tragédie lyrique, after P. Corneille: *Horace*), A. Salieri, 1786 (B. Porta, 1800)

Arvire et Evelina (tragédie lyrique, after W. Mason: *Caractacus*), Sacchini and J.-B. Rey, 1788; *Louis IX en Egypte* (opéra, with F. Andrieux), Lemoyne, 1790; *Elfride* (drame héroïque), Lemoyne, 1792; *Miltiade à Marathon* (opéra), Lemoyne, 1793; *La casque et les colombes* (opéra-ballet), Grétry, 1801; *Proserpine* (tragédie lyrique, after P. Quinault), G. Paisiello, 1803; *La mort d'Adam* (tragédie lyrique et religieuse, after F. G. Klopstock), J.-F. Le Sueur, 1809

*

J.-F. Le Sueur: *Lettre en réponse à Guillard* (Paris, 1801)
F. Pillet: 'Guillard (Nicolas-François)', *Biographie universelle*, ed. L. G. Michaud (Paris, 1843–65)

E. Desnues: 'Guillard (Nicolas-François)', *Nouvelle biographie générale*, ed. J. C. F. Hoefer (Paris, 1852–66)

A. Jullien: *Le cour et l'Opéra sous Louis XVI* (Paris, 1878)

P. Howard: *Gluck and the Birth of Modern Opera* (London, 1963)

P. Smith: *The Tenth Muse: a Historical Study of the Opera Libretto* (London, 1971)

J. Rushton: '"Iphigénie en Tauride": the Operas of Gluck and Piccinni', *ML*, liii (1972), 411–30

——: 'Salieri's *Les Horaces*: a Study of an Operatic Failure', *MR*, xxxvii (1976), 266–82   JULIAN RUSHTON

Guillaume Tell (i) ('William Tell'). *Drame mis en musique* in three acts by ANDRÉ-ERNEST-MODESTE GRÉTRY to a libretto by MICHEL-JEAN SEDAINE after Antoine-Marin Lemierre's play *Guillaume Tell*; Paris, Comédie-Italienne (Salle Favart), 9 April 1791.

The overture is mimed, and portrays sunrise over a Swiss valley, with Tell's young son on a rock playing the *ranz des vaches* on a pipe. (This is performed by the clarinet, heard against the sound of a 'corne'.) An angry Allegro presages the effects of Austrian tyranny.

Tell (tenor) wakens his daughter Marie (soprano), who is to be married this day to Melktal *fils* (tenor). The bridegroom arrives: he explains that his father, chief of their canton, has been detained by Guesler (bass), the local Austrian commander. Tell and his wife (soprano) are joined by villagers; a folksong is performed ('Noisette, noisette'). The meal commences. As all leave for church news arrives that Melktal *père* (bass) has refused to salute Guesler's cap and, for punishment, has had his eyes put out. Tell seizes his bow and the party breaks up. A soldier pursues a girl on to the stage, but she is rescued by Mme Tell who drives him off with a knife.

Act 2 opens to show a square in a market town. Guesler's cap is seen on a pike; armed troops oblige citizens to acknowledge it. Tell has refused to do so and has been arrested. His family and the people appeal for him to Guesler, but in vain. The chained Tell is brought in and ordered to shoot an apple from his son's head at 50 paces. He does; but Guesler finds a hidden second arrow intended for himself, had the trial failed. Troops descend on the people and Tell is dragged off for execution. Swiss women mock the inaction of their men, who then break out in revolt.

An entr'acte depicts a storm breaking over the boat taking Tell to prison; he escapes. Lightning reveals his son watching from a rock. Soldiers are everywhere; the revolt has begun. Soon Tell summons his compatriots with a horn-call; he sings of his unquenchable thirst for vengeance. Melktal *père* arrives, escorted by armed Swiss. As they wait for torches to signal the readiness of more distant patriots ('A Roncevaux'), the women express their willingness to die for freedom. Combat ensues. Guesler's castle is set ablaze. Melktal *fils* fights Guesler, who is shot by Tell. The Austrians are routed; a final chorus urges posterity, also, to sacrifice everything for liberty.

The opera is remarkable for the power and consistency of its style; Grétry's writing emphasized the Revolutionary taste for advanced harmony, dynamic strength and a prominent role for the chorus, whose energy is unabated. Long ensemble sections articulate the action. Grétry took trouble over the 'Swiss' local colour, and unified the message of the work by the musical application of a recurrent motif suggesting Austrian oppression. *Guillaume Tell* had 82 performances and was rearranged in 1828–9 to vie with Rossini's opera of the same name.   DAVID CHARLTON

Guillaume Tell (ii) [*Guglielmo Tell* ('William Tell')]. *Opéra* in four acts by GIOACHINO ROSSINI to a libretto by ETIENNE DE JOUY and HIPPOLYTE-LOUIS-FLORENT BIS, assisted by Armand Marrast and Adolphe Crémieux, based on FRIEDRICH VON SCHILLER's play *Wilhelm Tell*; Paris, Opéra, 3 August 1829.

Arnold Melcthal	*Swiss*	tenor
Guillaume Tell [William Tell]	*conspirators*	baritone
Walter Furst		bass
Mathilde *Princess of the House of Habsburg*		soprano
Melcthal *Arnold's father*		bass
Gesler *Governor of the cantons of Schwyz and Uri*		bass
Rodolphe *commander of Gesler's archers*		tenor
Leuthold *a herdsman*		baritone
Ruodi *a fisherman*		tenor
Hedwige *Tell's wife*		mezzo-soprano
Jemmy *Tell's son*		soprano
A Huntsman		baritone

Chorus of peasants of the cantons of Uri, Schwyz and Unterwalden; knights, pages, and ladies of the train of Mathilde; hunters, soldiers, and guards of Gesler; three brides and their bridegrooms

Setting Switzerland in the 13th century, near Altdorf in the canton of Uri

Guillaume Tell, Rossini's last opera, is the new *grand opéra* he had been contracted to write under the terms of the agreement with the French government drawn up in 1824 at the time of his arrival as a resident in Paris. A number of texts were considered for the project, including two by Scribe, one of which later became Auber's *Gustave III* and Verdi's *Un ballo in maschera*, the other Halévy's *La Juive*. The choice of Schiller's *Wilhelm Tell* (1804) was both adventurous and shrewd. Whether or not Rossini intended this to be his last opera, it brings together elements of his art he had successfully developed over the previous 17 years. Schiller's original play engages themes in which the mature Rossini showed a special interest: among them, the political ideals of a conservative people who seek independence with peace, and the psychology of paternal relations. It also enabled Rossini to exploit further an underlying interest in the related genres of folk music, pastoral, and the picturesque. The libretto, drafted by Étienne de Jouy, was revised by H.-L.-F. Bis, Armand Marrast, Adolphe Crémieux (who helped shape the Act 2 finale) and, most importantly, by Rossini himself.

The publication rights to the opera were acquired, well in advance of the première, by Eugène Troupenas. As a result, a generally accurate contemporary edition of the opera was quickly available as a basis for editions in Mainz, Vienna, Naples, Milan and elsewhere. Troupenas's edition is not, however, entirely reliable since the promptness of publication involved a start to the process of engraving while the opera was still in rehearsal. Significant changes to both music and text were made by Rossini and his collaborators during rehearsals and immediately following the first performances. Few of these changes were incorporated into the Troupenas edition; some, absent from the autograph manuscript, appear only in the theatre's own parts. Apart from altering the scale and proportions of the opera, the modifications affect our perception of the character of Arnold and the role of the men of Schwyz. Any theatre production needs to take into account the full range of available options. (These have been clearly set out in M. Elizabeth C. Bartlet's critical edition of *Guillaume Tell*.)

The première of the opera was conducted by François-Antoine Habeneck with Henri-Bernard Dabadie in the title role, Adolphe Nourrit as Arnold, Laure Cinti-Damoreau as Mathilde, Alex Prévost as Gesler and Nicolas Levasseur as Walter Furst. Rossini left Paris within a fortnight of the opening but on his return to the city he prepared an abridged edition of the opera, first seen in 1831. This reduces the work to three acts, with a new finale based partly on the concluding section of the famous overture. During the 1830s it was not uncommon for the Paris Opéra to stage Act 2 by itself, but the most significant French revival of the period came on 17 April 1837 when a revised version of the three-act abridgement was staged with Gilbert Duprez as Arnold. Though Rossini personally disliked the sound of the new *tenore di forza*, the emergence of Duprez was a phenomenon that did much to ensure the work's continuation in the repertory. In 1856 the four-act version was restored to the Paris stage. In February 1868, in Rossini's presence, the Opéra celebrated the work's 500th performance, and it remained an integral part of the Parisian stage repertory until 1932. (During some of the centenary performances in Paris in 1929, the role of Arnold was sung by James Joyce's protégé John O'Sullivan.)

Foreign-language versions of the opera, often adaptations or much truncated, appeared in Europe and the USA in the early 1830s. The first New York performance took place, in English, in 1831. London did not see the original French *Guillaume Tell* until it

Henri-Bernard Dabadie in the title role of Rossini's 'Guillaume Tell', which he created at the Paris Opéra, 3 August 1829: portrait (1836) by François-Gabriel Lépaulle

was staged at Covent Garden in 1845. Previous English productions included *Hofer, the Tell of the Tyrol*, adapted by J. R. Planché and arranged by Henry Bishop, at the Drury Lane Theatre in 1830 and the Italian *Guglielmo Tell* at Her Majesty's Theatre in 1839. Though Rossini supervised an adaptation of the opera, *Rodolfo di Sterlinga*, created in Bologna in 1840 partly as a vehicle for the tenor Nichola Ivanoff, he appears to have had no hand in the various Italian versions of the score. The first Italian staging, to a translation-cum-adaptation by Luigi Balocchi, was in Lucca on 17 September 1831 with Duprez as Arnold. Subsequent Italian revivals used Calisto Bassi's fuller and more reliable version, or a conflation of Bassi and Balocchi. It is a sad fact, however, that what major revivals there have been outside France over the years have tended to be of the italianized *Guglielmo Tell*.

La Scala, which had staged a carnival season adaptation in 1837, first staged *Guglielmo Tell* in 1845. Toscanini conducted performances there in 1899, and in the early years of this century Francesco Tamagno was heard as Arnold. His immediate successor in the role was Giacomo Lauri-Volpi who sang it frequently in Italy and the USA. In 1972 at the Florence Maggio Musicale, Riccardo Muti conducted an uncut version of *Guglielmo Tell* with Norman Mittelmann as Tell, Nicolai Gedda as Arnold and Eva Marton as Mathilde; and he later led a further uncut revival, using a revised Italian translation by Paolo Cattelan, at La Scala in 1988 with Giorgio Zancanaro as Tell, Chris Merritt as Arnold and Cheryl Studer as Mathilde. In 1990, in their first staging of the opera since 1889, Covent Garden mounted a beautifully considered and eminently naturalistic French-language production by John Cox, with Gregory Yurisich as Tell, Chris Merritt as Arnold and Lella Cuberli as Mathilde. The opera has been recorded, complete and in French, only once: a distinguished set conducted by Lamberto Gardelli with Gabriel Bacquier as Tell, Nicolai Gedda as Arnold and Montserrat Caballé as Mathilde. Of the various Italian-language recordings, the finest is Riccardo Chailly's version with Sherrill Milnes as Tell, Luciano Pavarotti as Arnold (a role he declined to sing on stage) and Mirella Freni as Mathilde.

The opera is prefaced by a four-movement overture, programmatic in intention and formally different from anything Rossini had previously devised. The opening colloquy for five solo cellos is a rare inspiration, evoking, Berlioz suggests, 'the calm of profound solitude, the solemn silence of nature when the elements and human passions are at rest'. The pastoral scene that follows the storm is also memorable. The use of a traditional Swiss herdsman's melody, a *ranz des vaches*, gives Rossini material for one of the finest of his many english horn solos; it is a melody that undergoes a number of transformations during the course of the opera, giving it something of the character of a leitmotif.

ACT 1 *On the shores of Lake Lucerne* As the curtain rises a triple wedding celebration is to hand while Ruodi the fisherman sings a love song. To William Tell the prospect of festivities is marred by fear of the Austrian regime which, since the loss of influence of the Holy Roman Empire in the region, has become increasingly repressive. Local Swiss customs have been a particular target of the Austrians; but in the three forest cantons of Uri, Schwyz and Unterwalden resistance to the

Austrians is growing, something typified by the decision of a revered elder, Melcthal, to officiate personally at the wedding ceremony. Unfortunately his son Arnold, who has served with Austrians, has fallen in love with the Austrian princess, Mathilde. When Tell puts to Arnold the urgency and justice of the Swiss cause (duet, 'Où vas-tu ... Ah! Mathilde, idole de mon âme!'), Arnold's private dilemma is eloquently addressed as orchestrally accompanied dialogue gives way to the lyrical 'Ah! Mathilde', the pitch wrenched up from Gb to Ab as Arnold's anguish becomes increasingly palpable. After Melcthal has blessed the couples, festivities resume with dancing and an archery competition won by Tell's young son Jemmy. But the idyll is not to last. A local herdsman Leuthold has killed an Austrian soldier who was attempting to rape his daughter. With the Austrians in pursuit, he asks to be rowed to safety; but with dangerous waters and a storm brewing the response is muted until Tell volunteers as ferryman. Thwarted by Leuthold's escape and by the people's loyalty to Tell, the Austrians prepare to sack the village while the Austrian Governor's henchman Rodolphe (tenor) takes old Melcthal hostage. It makes a gripping end to an opening act in which Rossini is far more expansive than Schiller. In particular, Rossini seems concerned to establish the communal life of the Swiss people as a key factor in the evolving drama. Central to this strategy is the inclusion in Acts 1 and 3 of a considerable amount of colourful and expertly written choral and dance music. It is often cut in performance; but, far from being extraneous to the drama, it is crucial to it.

ACT 2 *The Rütli Heights overlooking Lake Lucerne and the nearby Cantons* A hunting chorus is answered by an evening song of Swiss folk working in the hills and fields. Mathilde has glimpsed Arnold and sings of her love for him in 'Sombre forêt', an exquisite strophic aria in the French style, finely orchestrated (the quiet drum roll prefacing each stanza is one of the opera's most affecting instrumental gestures). Their reunion persuades Arnold that he must win military glory with the Austrian army so as to become worthy of Mathilde in the eyes of the world (duet, 'Oui, vous l'arrachez à mon âme'). Tell and Walter have seen the lovers together but their mission is to persuade Arnold to join the anti-Austrian confederates. In the trio 'Quand l'Helvétie est un champ de supplices', the appeal to Arnold is reinforced by the revelation that the Austrians have murdered his father, Melcthal. This is one of Rossini's finest creations, a superbly structured ensemble rich in telling musical and psychological detail; it also marks a significant departure from Schiller's play where old Melcthal is blinded, not murdered, and where Tell, the simple man of action, declines to be involved in the various meetings on Rütli Heights. The men of Unterwalden, Uri and Schwyz now begin to appear, crossing woods, mountains and water to gather for the swearing of an oath of allegiance. Rossini characterizes each group separately, with the good faith of these so-called rebels reflected in the idyllic music he writes for the men of Schwyz. As forces – military and musical – grandly mass, the confederates ask Tell for guidance. At the great oath-swearing ('Jurons, jurons par nos dangers') the trumpets sound; but there is no melodramatic denouement. Day breaks over the mountains, the drum again quietly rolls, and the cry 'Aux armes!' is repeated three times before the orchestra adds a torrential 16-bar coda. ('Ah, it is sublime',

remarks Berlioz in his essay on the opera, 'let us take breath'.)

ACT 3.i *A secluded chapel in the gardens of the Altdorf palace* In this scene, subjected to various revisions and emendations by Rossini, Mathilde comes face to face with Arnold, her now bereaved lover. He has no option but to renounce her, and in 'Sur la rive étrangère' she bids him farewell.

3.ii *The Square at Altdorf* Gesler has ordered enforced festivities to mark one hundred years of Austrian rule. Sensing public hostility, he demands that the people pay homage to his hat. The dances that follow are vividly characterized by Rossini; in particular we sense the festering resentment of the local women who are forced to cavort with the salacious Austrians in the 'Soldiers' Dance'. Tell refuses to pay homage to Gesler; but he is recognized as the man who saved Leuthold and is promptly arrested. He tells his son, Jemmy, to carry the signal for the start of the Swiss revolt, but Jemmy is also arrested. With both Tell and Jemmy in his grasp, Gesler dreams up his sadistic ploy to test Tell's nerve and marksmanship by ordering that Tell shoot an arrow through an apple placed on Jemmy's head. Tell is defiant and appalled – 'Ah! tu n'as pas d'enfant' – and in the great aria 'Sois immobile' he addresses Jemmy before finally drawing his bow. The aria stands at the heart of the opera and is one of the most personal of all Rossini's musical utterances. A solo cello is used at the outset, as it might be in a Bach Passion, but the major-minor oscillations and the lie of the line itself are fashioned in Rossini's own way. Verdi was to follow some of Rossini's cues when he came to portray another grieving father, Rigoletto. Tell hits the apple, but he is re-arrested when he confesses that a second bolt was intended for Gesler. Mathilde now intervenes. She demands that Gesler release Jemmy into her care; she also vows to effect Tell's release. But Gesler has other ideas and, amid growing civil unrest, Tell is despatched to the dangerously infested dungeons of the fortress at Küssnacht.

ACT 4.i *Melcthal's house* Returning to the family home, Arnold plans revenge for his father's murder. He also recognizes that, with Tell's capture, he is now the man who must lead the uprising. Berlioz thought Arnold's aria here, 'Asil héréditaire', the finest thing in the score, a filial lament of great finish and beauty. It is also very powerful. As Arnold is joined by men from the cantons, he reveals Tell's and old Melcthal's cache of arms in a violent cabaletta that looks ahead to the more declamatory writing for the tenor voice that Donizetti and Verdi would shortly develop.

4.ii *A rocky shore by Lake Lucerne* Mathilde and Jemmy join Hedwige, Tell's wife, who is desperate for news of her husband. Mathilde is prepared to offer herself as hostage for Tell's safe return. Jemmy lights the beacon to signal the uprising. Tell braves the storm in an Austrian boat. He lands and wastes no time in hunting down and shooting Gesler. Meanwhile, Altdorf has been freed. The confederates gather, the skies clear and the mountain landscape is seen again in all its majesty. Moved by the scene before him, Arnold addresses his dead father in lines that are not in Schiller: 'Ah, father why are you not here in this moment of joy for all Helvetia?'. The tribute over, Rossini's hymn to nature and liberty steals forth, the *ranz des vaches* entering softly on the horns with a numinous beauty that Wagner would later match but not surpass.

* * *

Schiller's *Wilhelm Tell* is neither revolutionary nor tragic. Susanne Langer has described it as 'a species of serious heroic comedy'. As such, *Guillaume Tell* is heir to a tradition which Rossini closely embraced in his *opere serie* of the years 1813–23. Langer writes of Schiller's Tell:

Tell appears as an exemplary personage in the beginning of the play, as citizen, husband, father, friend and patriot; when an extreme political and social crisis develops, he rises to the occasion, overcomes the enemy, frees his country, and returns to the peace, dignity and harmonious joy of his home. The balance of life is restored. As a personage he is impressive; as a personality he is very simple ... Such are the serious products of comic art; they are also its rarer examples. The natural vein of comedy is humorous – so much so that 'comic' has become synonymous with 'funny'.

By 1829, Rossini had become a master of the comic style in both its aspects: comedy as humour and comedy as a vehicle for expressing vitality, continuity and harmony in human affairs, however strong the potential for disorder in those affairs may be.

For further illustration *see* GRAND OPÉRA, fig.2.

RICHARD OSBORNE

Guiraud, Ernest (*b* New Orleans, 23 June 1837; *d* Paris, 6 May 1892). French composer. He studied first with his father, the composer Jean-Baptiste-Louis Guiraud, who had won the Prix de Rome in 1827 (in competition with Berlioz). At 15 he set the libretto *Le roi David*, which they had found on a trip to Paris; his opera, *David*, was a resounding success in New Orleans (April 1853). In December of the same year he entered Marmontel's piano class at the Paris Conservatoire, where later he also studied composition with Halévy. Guiraud capped his student career with a first prize in piano (1858) and the Prix de Rome (1859). He was a close friend of Saint-Saëns, Paladilhe and Dubois, and he and Bizet renewed their lifelong friendship in Rome and travelled together in the summer of 1860. In 1876 Guiraud returned to the Conservatoire, to teach harmony and accompaniment, and (from 1880) composition. A kind, devoted, observant teacher, he probably helped mould the talents of Dukas, Debussy and others.

Guiraud made his Paris début with *Sylvie* (1864, Opéra-Comique), originally an 'envoi de Rome'. Though critics thought the score pretty and spirited, like most curtain-raisers, it disappeared from the repertory after its initial run. In 1870 his one-act *opéra-ballet Le Kobold*, supposedly written in only 18 days, briefly graced the stage of the Opéra-Comique, but the onset of the Franco-Prussian War soon closed all theatres. Guiraud chose to volunteer for the infantry.

Despite its old-fashioned plot, Pougin preferred *Mme Turlupin* (1872), Guiraud's next *opéra comique*, to the full-length *Piccolino* (1876), which most agree represents the peak of Guiraud's operatic career – though after a long run by the Opéra-Comique, it was dropped from their repertory. Its most successful number, an appealing *sorrentino* (sung by Galli-Marié), was said to have been improvised in a few hours during rehearsals. For the ballet Guiraud incorporated 'Carnaval', the most effective, brilliant movement of his first orchestral suite (*c*1871), and already a favourite piece at Pasdeloup's Concerts Populaires. Guiraud's last two works for the stage were not successful; *Galante aventure* (1882) received only 15 performances, and the more ambitious and modern opera *Frédégonde*, completed by Saint-Saëns and partly orchestrated by

Dukas, was coldly received at its first performances in 1895.

Ironically, the success that Guiraud sought in the theatre came only through his association with others. He wrote the recitatives for *Carmen* in the summer and early autumn of 1875, after Bizet's death (he also arranged the second suite from *L'Arlésienne*, 1880, and may have been involved in the preparation of other Bizet works published in the 1880s). By 1881, also after the death of the composer, he had completed and orchestrated Offenbach's most ambitious opera, *Les contes d'Hoffmann*.

In 1891 Guiraud succeeded Delibes at the Institut, and agreed to complete the orchestration of Delibes' five-act opera *Kassya*, but his own death interrupted this task. The size of Guiraud's output was probably limited by his inability to put his own work before his concern for that of his friends and his students. In any case, the charming melodies, rhythmic verve and elegant orchestration praised by his contemporaries do not now seem exceptionally original.

David (3, after A. Soumet and F. Mallefille: *Le roi David*), New Orleans, Théâtre d'Orléans, 14 April 1853
Gli avventurieri, 1861 (melodramma giocoso, 1), unperf., *F-Pc**
Sylvie (oc, 1, J. Adenis and J. Rostaing), Paris, OC (Favart), 11 May 1864 (Paris, 1864)
La coupe du roi de Thulé, 1868–9 (opéra, 3, L. Gallet and E. Blau), unperf.
En prison, ?*c*1859 (oc, 1, T. Chaigneau and C. Boverat), Paris, Lyrique, 5 March 1869
Le Kobold (opéra-ballet, 1, Gallet and C. Nuitter), Paris, OC (Favart), 26 July 1870, *Pc** (inc.), ov. (Paris, n.d.)
Madame Turlupin (oc, 2, E. Cormon and C. Grandvallet), Paris, Athénée, 23 Nov 1872, *Pc** (inc.), vs (Paris, 1873)
Piccolino (oc, 3, V. Sardou and Nuitter, after Sardou), Paris, OC (Favart), 11 April 1876 (Paris, n.d.), vs (Paris, 1876)
Le feu (opéra, E. Gondinet), inc.; int perf. 9 March 1879, Danse persane *Pc**
Galante aventure (oc, 3, L. Davyl and A. Silvestre), Paris, OC (Favart), 23 March 1882, vs (Paris, 1882)
Frédégonde (drame lyrique, 5, Gallet, after A. Thierry: *Les récits des temps mérovingiens*), inc.; Acts 1–3 orchd P. Dukas, Acts 4 and 5 and ballet in Act 3 comp. by Saint-Saëns, Paris, Opéra, 18 Dec 1895, *Po**, vs (Paris, 1895)

Music in: Le baron Frick [no.3 Romance de Phébus] (opérette, 1, E. Depré and Clairville), Paris, 1885, collab. Joncières and others

*

A. Pougin: Obituary, *Le ménestrel*, lviii/19 (1892), 148
A. Soubies and C. Malherbe: *Histoire de l'Opéra-Comique: la seconde Salle Favart*, ii: *1860–1887* (Paris, 1893)
G. Vapereau: *Dictionnaire universel des contemporains*, (Paris, 6/1893)
A. Jullien: *Musiciens d'aujourd'hui*, 2nd ser. (Paris, 1894), 290–310
H. Imbert: 'Ernest Guiraud', *Médaillons contemporains* (Paris, 1903), 285–94
P. Landormy and J. Loisel: 'Institut de France: Guiraud', *EMDC*, II/vi (Paris, 1931), 3528–9
J. S. Kendall: 'The Friend of Chopin, and Some Other New Orleans Musical Celebrities', *Louisiana Historical Quarterly* (1948), Oct, 856–76
T. J. Walsh: *Second Empire Opera* (London, 1981)
G. Favre: *Compositeurs méconnus* (Paris, 1983), 13–60
D. Weilbaecher: *Ernest Guiraud: a Biography and Catalogue of Works* (diss., Louisiana State U., 1990)   LESLEY A. WRIGHT

Guiraudon, Julia (*b* 2 Dec 1873; *d* after 1914). French soprano. Her entire career was pursued in France, mostly at the Opéra-Comique. In 1897 she sang Mimì in the French première of *La bohème*, the Farewell being among her five recordings. She created the title role of Messager's *La basoche* and of Massenet's *Cendrillon*, the librettist of which, Henri Caine, was her husband. She also took part in the première of Erlanger's *Le Juif* *polonais*, and, at Monte Carlo, of Massenet's *Roma* (1912) and Fernand Labori's *Yato* (1913). Other roles included Louise, Mignon and Susanna. Her recordings show a lyric voice of exceptional purity used with imagination and an exquisite sense of style.

J. B. STEANE

Guirlande, La [*La guirlande, ou Les fleurs enchantées* ('The Garland, or The Enchanted Flowers')]. *Acte de ballet* by JEAN-PHILIPPE RAMEAU to a libretto by JEAN FRANÇOIS MARMONTEL; Paris, Opéra, 21 September 1751.

A slender plot indulges in thinly-veiled symbolism: Myrtil (*haute-contre*) and Zélide (soprano) exchange enchanted garlands that will stay fresh as long as the lovers remain faithful. But after a flirtation Myrtil's garland wilts embarrassingly. When Zélide discovers it on Cupid's altar, she unselfishly substitutes her own, which leads to a quarrel and eventual reconciliation. The various conflicts of sentiment are sensitively handled, and the music is characterized throughout by extreme delicacy of decorative detail. The work is, indeed, little inferior to that of Rameau's better-known miniature masterpiece, *Pigmalion*.

GRAHAM SADLER

Guitti, Francesco (*b* Ferrara, 1605; *d* Ferrara, *c*1645). Italian architect and designer. A pupil of Giambattista Aleotti, he devoted himself almost entirely to stage design in the then fashionable form of spectacle known as *opera-torneo*, in which he distinguished himself by inventing stage machines, illusionist devices and original landscape settings (e.g. in M. Rossi's *Erminia sul Giordano*, 1633, Rome; Antonio Goretti's *La discordia superata*, 1635, Ferrara). He reportedly devised distinguished productions at Ferrara (1626, 1631, 1635, 1638; see illustration), at Parma, where he also worked with a large team in the Teatro Farnese on the festivities

for the marriage of Odoardo Farnese and Margherita de' Medici (1628), and in Rome, where with Andrea Sacchi and others he planned the *giostra-torneo, Corsa del Saracino*, in Piazza Navona in 1634. As an architect he designed temporary theatres in the Sala della Racchetta and the Bevilacqua palace in Ferrara and in the courtyard of S Pietro Martire, Parma; he is also credited with being the first to provide a separate enclosure for musicians in front of the proscenium, which was to become the normal position for theatre orchestras.

For further illustration *see* ERMINIA SUL GIORDANO.

*

ES (E. Povoledo)
E. Povoledo: 'Macchine e ingegni del teatro Farnese', *Prospettive*, xix (1959)
I. Lavin: 'Lettres de Parme (1618, 1627–28) et débuts du théâtre baroque', *Les lieux théâtrales à la Renaissance*, ed. J. Jaquot (Paris, 1968)
A. Cavicchi: 'Teatro Monteverdiano e tradizione teatrale ferrarese', *Claudio Monteverdi e il suo tempo: Venice 1968*, 139–56
C. Molinari: *Le nozze degli dei: un saggio sul grande spettacolo italiano del seicento* (Rome, 1968)
D. Lenzi: 'Teatri ed anfiteatri a Bologna nei secoli XVI e XVII', *Barocco romano e barocco italiano, il teatro, l'effimero, l'allegoria*, ed. M. Fagiolo and M. L. Madonna (Rome, 1977)
M. Fagiolo dell'Arco and S. Carandini, eds.: *L'effimero Barocco: strutture della festa nella Roma del '600* (Rome, 1978)

ANGELA PAMPOLINI

Gulak-Artemovsky [Artemovsky, Hulak-Artemovsky], **Semyon** [Simeon] **Stepanovich** (*b* Gulakovshchina, nr Gorodishche [now in Ukraine], 4/16 Feb 1813; *d* Moscow, 5/17 April 1873). Russian baritone and composer of Ukrainian birth. The son of a priest, he was at first educated for his father's calling. At the Kiev district divinity school, where he was sent at the age of 11, his outstanding soprano voice caught the ear of the Metropolitan of Kiev, who had the boy enrolled in the

Set design by Francesco Guitti for Michelangelo Rossi's opera-torneo 'Andromeda', performed at Ferrara in 1638: engraving showing a seascape with the carriage of Neptune and Amphitrite (a separate enclosure for musicians can be seen in front of the proscenium)

episcopal choir at St Sophia's Cathedral. From there he was transferred in 1830 to the choir of St Michael's monastery, the seat of the Kiev vicariate; eight years later Glinka, the newly appointed head of the court chapel choir on a recruiting mission to the Ukraine, heard Gulak-Artemovsky sing and invited him to St Petersburg with an eye to training him for an operatic career.

At first Glinka taught the raw provincial youth himself – both to cultivate his voice and manner and to pronounce Russian properly; later, instruction in French and Italian was added to his training. In 1839 he was sent abroad for finishing touches in bel canto, which he received at first in Paris, then in Florence (from Pietro Romani). He made his operatic début (as Filippo in Bellini's *Beatrice di Tenda*) with the Florence Opera at the Teatro della Pergola in January 1841. After singing there for a season, he returned to St Petersburg in January 1842.

His début in the Russian capital followed in June, as Enrico Ashton in *Lucia di Lammermoor*. He remained a leading soloist of the Russian opera company until 1864, specializing in bel canto roles sung in Russian, and was one of the few Russian singers to appear as well with the Italian troupe in St Petersburg (singing in Italian); his most historic achievement as a singer was the creation (alternately with Osip Petrov) of Ruslan in the original production of Glinka's *Ruslan i Lyudmila* (1842). (A complete list of his roles is given by Kaufman.) After his retirement from the St Petersburg stage (1863) he sang in Moscow for a season as soloist at the Bol'shoy Theatre.

Gulak-Artemovsky began composing in the 1850s, starting with a spate of 'Little Russian' folksong arrangements, some of them organized into larger theatrical entertainments such as a seven-part *divertissement* portraying a Ukrainian village wedding (*Ukrainskaya svad'ba*, 1851). He also wrote plays and vaudevilles: one of the latter, *Noch' nakanune Ivanova dnya* ('St John's Eve', 1852), contains a chorus, a mazurka and some couplets of his own composition. His creative career culminated in a comic opera with spoken dialogue, *Zaporozhets za Dunayem* ('A Cossack beyond the Danube'), for which he composed both the music and the text (1861–2) and in which he also created the title role (Ivan Karas) at its première (Mariinsky Theatre, 14/26 April 1863).

Not a trained composer, Gulak-Artemovsky had a small range, limited for the most part to folklike songs and dances in strophic or ritornello forms, simply harmonized. His theatrical works were orchestrated by others, chiefly Konstantin Lyadov (father of the composer Anatoly Lyadov), a staff conductor for the Russian opera. Notwithstanding these limitations, his single opera is a significant work, being the first of its kind on a Ukrainian national subject. Adapted to a libretto in the Ukrainian language (and with both music and words heavily revised by others), it became in Soviet times a cornerstone of the operatic repertory in the composer's native region, with many productions in other parts of the USSR as well.

See also ZAPOROZHETS ZA DUNAYEM.

*

N. Findeyzen: 'Pis'ma iz zagranitsï russkogo pevtsa Mikhaylova-Ostroumova (1839–1841)' [Letters from Abroad by the Russian Singer Mikhaylov Ostroumov], *Muzikal'naya starina*, ii (1903), 160–70

G. Bernandt and I. Yampol'sky: 'S. S. Gulak-Artemovsky i ego russkiye svyazï' [Gulak-Artemovsky and his Russian Connections], *Iz istorii russko-ukrainskikh muzikal'nïkh svyazey*, ed. T. I. Karïsheva (Moscow, 1956), 71–99

A. A. Gozenpud: *Russkiy operniy teatr XIX veka 1857–72* [The Russian Opera Theatre of the 19th Century, 1857–72] (Leningrad, 1971), chap.2

L. Kaufman: *S. S. Gulak-Artemovsky* (Moscow, 1973)

RICHARD TARUSKIN

Gulbranson, Ellen (*b* Stockholm, 4 March 1863; *d* Oslo, 2 Jan 1947). Swedish soprano. She studied with Mathilde Marchesi in Paris, and also with Marchesi's daughter Blanche, who successfully transformed her from a mezzo-soprano into a dramatic soprano. She made her début in Stockholm in 1889 as Amneris and sang Brünnhilde and Ortrud there in 1898. She was a leading figure among the second generation of Bayreuth singers, whose fame was largely, but not wholly, confined to the Wagner festivals there. In 1896, 20 years after the opening of Bayreuth, she shared the role of Brünnhilde with Lilli Lehmann, but thenceforward remained its sole exponent until 1914, appearing also as Kundry during five seasons. Her Covent Garden Brünnhilde in 1900 made no great mark in the proximity of Ternina and Nordica; but when she returned in 1907 to sing in two *Ring* cycles under Richter, she was found to have greatly improved. Gulbranson's few Edison and Pathé recordings, made by the obsolete 'hill-and-dale' system, are so rare as to be virtually unknown.   DESMOND SHAWE-TAYLOR

Gulin, Angeles (*b* Ribadavia, 18 Feb 1943). Spanish soprano. At an early age she accompanied her father to Montevideo, where she made her début at the Teatro Sodre in 1963 as the Queen of Night. After returning to Europe she first sang Amelia (*Simon Boccanegra*) at Düsseldorf in 1965, followed by Santuzza and Abigaille. In 1968 she won first prize at the Verdi Competition at Busseto, a success which brought her leading roles in Italy and elsewhere, one of them in the first 20th-century production of Verdi's *Stiffelio* (1968, Parma). Her American début was in 1969 as Marta (*Tiefland*) with the American Opera Society, her Covent Garden début in 1975 as Amelia (*Ballo*). After changing from coloratura to dramatic soprano roles she was notably successful for singing of generous emotional scope.

NOËL GOODWIN

Gulyás, Dénes (*b* Budapest, 31 March 1954). Hungarian tenor. He studied at the Budapest Conservatory and Liszt Academy (1973–8), and first appeared at the Erkel Theatre in 1978, as Rinuccio and Alfredo; subsequent roles there have included Rodolfo and Pinkerton. In 1978 he also made his début in Vienna; his career was fully launched three years later when he won the Pavarotti Competition. Since then, he has performed at Philadelphia, San Francisco (as Ferrando, 1986), the Metropolitan Opera (début as the Italian Singer in *Der Rosenkavalier*, 1985), Covent Garden, Montreal and the major European centres. His roles include Don Ottavio, Massenet's Des Grieux, Verdi's Duke, Rossini's Almaviva, Gounod's Romeo, and Prince Andrey in *Khovanshchina*; he has recorded *Gianni Schicchi*, *László Hunyadi*, *La damnation de Faust* and Paisiello's *Il barbiere di Siviglia*, and has directed *Roméo et Juliette* for Budapest Opera (1988) and an open-air production of *Pagliacci*. Gulyás is an outstanding actor and musician, endowed with a flexible yet powerful voice that is strikingly vigorous in its upper register.   PÉTER P. VÁRNAI

Gundry, Inglis (*b* London, 8 May 1905). English composer. He studied law at Balliol College, Oxford (1923–7), and at the Middle Temple (1927–9), but his interests were elsewhere, and he took a post as librarian at Mill Hill School (1932–5) and wrote a novel (1934). In 1935 he turned to music, studying at the RCM with Vaughan Williams, Gordon Jacob and R. O. Morris until 1938. He won the 1936 Cobbett Prize and in the following year completed his first opera, *Naaman: the Leprosy of War*. Opera remained his chief interest: besides many contributions to the genre he published two essays, *Opera in a Nutshell* (London, 1945) and *The Nature of Opera as a Composite Art* (London, 1947). He joined the Royal Navy in 1941, and from 1946 lectured to the Workers' Educational Association and to the extramural departments of London and Cambridge universities.

librettos by the composer

The Return of Odysseus, 1938 (3, after Homer), London, Parry Memorial (RCM), 25 May 1940 (Act 1 only)
The Partisans (2 scenes), London, St Pancras Town Hall, 28 May 1946, vs (London, 1948)
Avon, London, Scala, 11 April 1949
The Tinners of Cornwall (3, after A. K. Jenkins: *The Cornish Miner*), London, Rudolf Steiner Hall, 30 Sept 1953
The Logan Rock (comic op, 3, after W. Bottrell), Porthcurno, Minack, 15 Aug 1956
The Prince of Coxcombs (comic op, 3, after J. Vanbrugh: *The Relapse*), London, Morley College, 3 Feb 1965
The Three Wise Men (1), Kings Langley parish church, 7 Jan 1967
The Prisoner Paul (chamber op, 2), London, St Paul's, Covent Garden, 16 Oct 1970
A Will of her Own, 1971–3 (comic chamber op, 4 scenes, after G. Findler: *Legends of the Lake*), London, Essex Hall, 31 May 1985

Unperf.: Naaman: the Leprosy of War, 1936–7 (1); The Horses of the Dawn, 1950–53 (school op, prol., 1, after Euripides: *Rhesus* and Homer: *Odyssey*); The Rubicon, 1981–3 (serious op, 5); Lindisfarne, 1984–6 (3); Claudia's Dream, 1986–9 (3)

P. Crossley-Holland: 'The Music of Inglis Gundry', *HMYB*, iv–v (1947–8), 138–42

Gunlöd. Opera in three acts by PETER CORNELIUS (i) to his own libretto after the Edda; Weimar, Grossherzogliches Hoftheater, 6 May 1891.

In this setting of a Norse tale Cornelius came spiritually close to Wagner's *Ring*, though musically the work is more akin to song than to music drama. The king of the gods, Odin (tenor), battles for immortal power, which resides in mead made from the blood of the poet Kwasir. The giant Suttung (bass) killed Kwasir and seeks, like Alberich in the *Ring*, to appropriate such power to himself. The mead is guarded in Suttung's cave by Gunlöd (mezzo-soprano), who has resolved to obey Kwasir's wishes and keep it for Odin alone. Such loyalty is tested by her love for Bölwerk, a stranger who serves Suttung, hoping to gain the mead as his reward. Gnomes soon reveal, however, that he is Odin in disguise. In Act 2 Odin departs with the mead for Walhalla, leaving Gunlöd to face the anger of Suttung's kindred, gathered to celebrate his marriage to Gunlöd. In revenge for her giving away the mead, in Act 3 Suttung drags her off to the gates of Helheim. But her sacrifice for Odin allows Gunlöd to join him in Walhalla, as eternal guardian of the mead.

Having begun work on *Gunlöd* in 1866, Cornelius left it unfinished at his death in 1874. None of the music was orchestrated, though nearly all of the first act and a good portion of the third exists in piano reduction. All he left of the third are Suttung's two ironic wedding songs. Karl Hoffbauer completed and published a version of the opera in 1879; this was reorchestrated by Lassen and performed in Weimar on 6 May 1891. Max Hasse produced a vocal score from the original manuscript in 1894 and subsequently asked Waldemar von Baussnern to complete a version for the collected edition; this was first performed in Cologne on 15 December 1906.   AMANDA GLAUERT

Gunsbourg, Raoul (*b* Bucharest, 25 Dec 1859; *d* Monte Carlo, 31 May 1955). French composer and impresario of Romanian birth. He studied medicine in Bucharest and then played small parts in the French theatre company there. In 1881 he was managing the first theatre for French *opéra comique* to be established in Moscow, and the following year he established another one in St Petersburg. He was director of the Grand Théâtre, Lille (1888–9), and of the Nice Opéra (1889–91), where in 1891 he mounted Berlioz's *La prise de Troie* for the first time in France. From 1893 to 1951 he was director of the Monte Carlo Opéra, where during his regime there were many important premières including *Le jongleur de Notre-Dame*, *Don Quichotte*, *Pénélope*, *La rondine*, *L'enfant et les sortilèges*, *Judith* (Honegger) and *L'aiglon* (Honegger-Ibert).

Gunsbourg composed six operas, most of them to his own librettos, but, as he had had no formal music instruction, they were all orchestrated by the conductor Léon Jehin. His first effort, *Le vieil aigle* (1909), based on a story by Gorky, was the most successful: after its première at Monte Carlo it was produced at the Paris Opéra and the Théâtre de la Monnaie, Brussels, with Fyodor Shalyapin as the protagonist, Khan Aswab, in all three places. *Ivan le terrible* (1910), his first full-length opera, was not very successful, and his other four works were all presented at his own opera house. *Satan* (1920) was a lengthy 'philosophical music drama' on which Gunsbourg had worked for nearly 20 years; Lucien Muratore took the title role, assuming a different disguise in each act: the Serpent, the Stranger, the Scribe, the Vandal, the Black Knight, the Shadow and the Traveller. *Lysistrata* (1923), based on Aristophanes' comedy, and obviously too daring for the Monte Carlo audience, marked the end of Gunsbourg's career as an opera composer, although in 1946 he contributed two episodes ('Marguerite de Valois' and 'Catherine de Cleves') to *Les dames galantes de Brantôme*, his own five-scene adaptation of *Les vies des dames galantes* (1583) by Pierre de Bourdeilles. Gunsbourg had a facility for writing tuneful, undemanding theatre music, and a fine sense of dramatic effectiveness.

librettos by the composer unless otherwise stated

Le vieil aigle (drame lyrique, 1, after M. Gorky), Monte Carlo, 13 Feb 1909
Ivan le terrible (drame lyrique, 3, after A. Tolstoy), Brussels, Monnaie, 26 Oct 1910
Venise (3), Monte Carlo, 8 March 1913
Manole (3, J. Lahovary), Monte Carlo, 17 March 1918
Satan (philosophical musical drama, prol., 7, epilogue), Monte Carlo, 20 March 1920
Lysistrata (musical comedy, 3, after Aristophanes), Monte Carlo, 20 Feb 1923
Les dames galantes de Brantôme [2 scenes] (5, after P. de

Bourdeilles: *Les vies des dames galantes*), Monte Carlo, 12 Feb 1946 [2 scenes by M. Thiriet, 1 by H. Tomasi]

T. J. Walsh: *Monte Carlo Opera 1879–1909* (Dublin, 1975)
——: *Monte Carlo Opera 1910–1951* (Kilkenny, 1986)
HAROLD ROSENTHAL/ELIZABETH FORBES

Günstling, Der [*Der Günstling, oder Die letzten Tage des grossen Herrn Fabiano* ('The Favourite, or The Last Days of the Great Signor Fabiano')]. Opera in three acts by RUDOLF WAGNER-RÉGENY to a libretto by CASPAR NEHER after VICTOR HUGO's play *Marie Tudor*; Dresden, Staatsoper, 20 February 1935.

The action takes place in London in 1553. Fabiano Fabiani (tenor) has risen to power as the lover of Queen Mary Tudor (soprano). The minister Simon Renard (bass) is seeking an opportunity to overthrow the favourite and keeps watch on him. He thus knows of Fabiani's nocturnal visits to Jane (soprano), the fiancée and foster-daughter of Gil the craftsman (baritone), and sees Fabiani murder the father of a previous mistress by night. Fabiani forces Gil, on his way home from work, to help him dispose of the corpse; the situation opens Gil's eyes to the fact that Jane has been seduced by Fabiani. Renard approaches Gil, intending to use the craftsman's desire for revenge for his own ends.

In Act 2 Fabiani feels that the time has come for him to win the throne. He promises eternal loyalty to the queen, but Renard accuses the favourite of murder, perjury and infidelity. He has induced Gil to denounce Fabiani to the queen for incitement to murder, but in accordance with the law both men are condemned to death. In the final act the queen asks the council to pardon Fabiani, but in vain. She begs Renard to let Fabiani escape in Gil's clothing, but Renard helps Gil himself to escape (as he had promised) and has Fabiani executed. The queen realizes that her plan has failed and hears the favourite curse her with his last words.

The success of *Der Günstling*, two years after Hitler's rise to power, was enormous. Fritz Busch had left his post as conductor in Dresden, and Karl Böhm had taken his place. Weill had fled from Germany but his librettist and designer Caspar Neher was still in the country, and Wagner-Régeny, then aged 30, could begin a productive partnership with him. It is wrong to suggest that *Der Günstling* was an opera with a message of resistance to the Third Reich, a claim frequently made in East Germany and one that the composer himself made no attempt to correct. (In fact, revivals throughout Europe coincided with the spread of the Third Reich's dominance: it was performed in Graz, Brno, Bratislava, Ljubljana and Brussels.)

In East Germany *Der Günstling* was performed more often than any other modern opera. Some hundred staged productions, as well as recordings, radio and television, kept it in the public eye. During the 1980s the conductor Gerd Puls, a former pupil of Wagner-Régeny's, revised the libretto of the third act in line with the intentions of Hugo and Büchner (who had translated and adapted the play). Puls also adapted the music to provide a more convincing denouement.

The action of *Der Günstling* is reminiscent of a Romantic opera, as simple as a picture-book and completely without irony. In the early 1930s Wagner-Régeny was setting himself against the operatic grandiloquence of past and present (including that of *Der Rosenkavalier*) and hoping that a purged, reformed operatic genre of Bauhaus-like simplicity would emerge if he ventured to embrace Gluck and Handel. Indeed the neo-Baroque, neo-classical musical style of *Der Günstling* suggests echoes of the Handel revival. Wagner-Régeny also used conventional vocal characterization, with a lyric soprano for Jane, a dramatic soprano for the powerful queen, a bass for the upright minister and a tenor for the Italian seducer. Opera had become clear and simple again after the excesses of Strauss and Schreker. Wagner-Régeny's first full-length opera fell back on the sometimes bourgeois virtues of German opera and could therefore be accepted within the cultural policy of the Third Reich. However, the composer never actually succumbed to the ideals of that policy as did, for instance, Werner Egk, and in the two operas he later wrote under the totalitarian East German regime he distanced himself even more clearly from the authorities.
TILO MEDEK

Günter, Horst (*b* Leipzig, 23 May 1913). German baritone. He studied in Bologna, Innsbruck and Berlin. After engagements at Schwerin (1941–4), Göttingen and Wiesbaden, in 1950 he joined the Hamburg Staatsoper, where he continued to sing until 1968, taking part in the 1954 concert performance of *Moses und Aron*. He also appeared at Vienna, Berlin and Munich, where he sang in Frank Martin's *Le vin herbé* (1962). His finest roles were Papageno and Mozart's and Rossini's Figaro, parts which admirably displayed his considerable talent for comedy, as well as his keenly focussed, flexible voice.
ELIZABETH FORBES

Günther, Julius (*b* Göteborg, 1 March 1818; *d* Stockholm, 22 March 1904). Swedish tenor. He studied in Stockholm, where he made his début in 1838 as Fra Diavolo and where he was chief lyric tenor at the Royal Opera until 1856. He also sang in Hamburg and Copenhagen. He studied further in Paris with Manuel García the younger (1846–7) and toured with Jenny Lind during the 1840s. After his retirement from the stage he taught in Stockholm, where his pupils included John Forsell and Ellen Gulbranson.
ELIZABETH FORBES

Günther, Mizzi (*b* Warnsdorf, Bohemia, 8 Feb 1879; *d* Vienna, 18 March 1961). Bohemian soprano. She made her career in operetta, starting at Hermannstadt (Sibiu) in 1897 and achieving her first great success as O Mimosa San in Sidney Jones's *The Geisha* at Vienna in 1901. In 1905 she sang the title role in the première of Lehár's *Die lustige Witwe* at the Theater an der Wien, and in 1907 had a comparable triumph in the première of Leo Fall's *Die Dollarprinzessin*. The following year she sang in the Viennese première of his *Der fidele Bauer* and in 1912 in the première of Kálmán's *Der kleine König*. She remained popular in Vienna for many years and also sang in Russia, France and England. Her few early recordings, which include excerpts from *Die lustige Witwe*, suggest a lively personality and a voice of pleasant quality used without much care for phrasing.

For illustration *see* LUSTIGE WITWE, DIE.
J. B. STEANE

Günther von Schwarzburg. Singspiel in three acts by IGNAZ HOLZBAUER to a libretto by Anton Klein; Mannheim, Hoftheater, 5 January 1777.

Based in part on an episode from German history, *Günther von Schwarzburg* is set in 1349 and focusses on Karl (tenor), King of Bohemia, and his rival Günther (tenor), who struggle for control of the Holy Roman

Empire. With the support of the Count Palatine Rudolf II (bass) of the Wittelsbach house, Günther is crowned in Frankfurt. Karl loves Anna (soprano), the countess palatine and daughter of Rudolf, but Asberta (soprano), the dowager queen and mother of Karl, is more intent on gaining the empire for her son. She tries through a variety of intrigues to destroy Günther, finally poisoning him and taking her own life. Anna and Karl are united as the chorus mourns the fallen hero, Günther.

The opera, written for a distinguished cast featuring Anton Raaff in the title role, Franziska Danzi as Anna, Ludwig Fischer as Rudolf, Barbara Strasser as Asberta and Franz Hartig as Karl, was one of the first attempts to revive German serious opera. The commission to Klein and Holzbauer to write a German opera for Mannheim followed the successful performances of Wieland and Schweitzer's *Alceste* there in 1775. A local advocate of the German language, Klein set out to create a drama that would rival Italian *opera seria*. Though updated to reflect some of the reforms advocated by Algarotti, Calzabigi and Wieland, the text remains within the bounds of Metastasian principles in its basic content. The plot has many of the characteristics of *Sturm und Drang* drama of the period.

Mozart, who heard the revival in November 1777, was impressed by what he called the 'fire in Holzbauer's music'. From the outset the music, similar in form and style to that of the operas of Holzbauer's Italian contemporaries, was praised more highly than the text. Elegant melodies alternate with passages of dramatic intensity, although sometimes the colourful orchestral accompaniment detracts from the vocal line. The first German opera to be published in full score (Mannheim, 1777), it was the crowning achievement of Holzbauer's career.

PAUL CORNEILSON

Guntram. Opera in three acts by RICHARD STRAUSS to his own libretto; Weimar, Grossherzogliches Hoftheater, 10 May 1894.

The successful première of this first Strauss opera proved to be a false dawn. He had greatly hoped for a première not in provincial Weimar, where he was serving as Kapellmeister to the Grand Duke of Saxe-Weimar-Eisenach, but in his native city of Munich. When at last *Guntram* was performed there – just once, on 16 November 1895 – its reception was so discouraging as to curdle his operatic ambitions for several years. His dramaturgy was flat and clumsy: in effect, as the Munich critic Oskar Merz wrote, *Guntram* amounted to 'a psychological event in one act, with two preceding acts'. It would be almost a quarter-century before Strauss dared again to write his own libretto (for *Intermezzo*). Yet Merz praised the 'undoubted nobility and purity' of his artistic intentions, and was no less impressed than dismayed by his profligate orchestral genius. Furthermore, in the soprano role of Freihild his wife Pauline made as great an impression as in Weimar, where on the day of the première he had announced their engagement.

In a medieval German land, Freihild is the unhappy wife of the grasping tyrant Duke Robert (baritone), who thwarts all her charitable projects. The knightly minstrel Guntram (tenor – an exceedingly long, taxing role), a member of a high-minded, pacific Christian brotherhood, comes by in time to dissuade her from drowning herself. Invited to the court, Guntram angers the duke by singing a paean to peace and to generous rulers, and then urges rebellion. Robert attacks the singer, who

slays him. While awaiting sentence in prison, Guntram agonizes over his true motives; but against the judgment of Friedhold, an elder of the brotherhood (and like Wagner's Gurnemanz a bass), that by their rules his violent act was an absolute sin, he declares that God speaks to him only through himself, and only his own choice can make atonement. When Freihild arrives to rescue him, he realizes that the mainspring of his deed was not a pure ideal of liberation but his love for her. His expiatory choice is to renounce both the rule-bound brotherhood and his adored lady: he will rediscover his true self in solitude, while Freihild, left to rule benevolently over her peasants, will inspire him from afar.

Guntram was very much a product of the Wagnerian circle over which the formidable widow Cosima presided, and into which young Strauss was welcomed for a time. Like the diction of his libretto, the music is studded with hand-me-down Wagnerisms. In retrospect many pre-echoes of the mature Strauss can be discerned, but they are only musical fingerprints, lending character to passing moments (especially Freihild's) without lubricating the stiff progress of the drama. There is some irony in the fact that the one real 'psychological event' Merz found in the opera – the guilty hero's decision to choose his own form of expiation, instead of surrendering to the judgment of his peers – was just what Strauss's Wagnerite peers saw as his 'subjective', Nietzschean betrayal of the true faith. The composer preserved a defiant affection for his 'prentice-work, as composers do. Not only did he quote it lavishly among 'The Hero's Works of Peace' in *Ein Heldenleben*, a few years later, but in 1940 he took some trouble to abridge and reduce the over-egged score, in the hope of making it viable: in vain.

DAVID MURRAY

Gura, Eugen (*b* Pressern, Bohemia, 8 Nov 1842; *d* Aufkirchen, 26 Aug 1906). German bass-baritone. He studied with Joseph Herger in Munich, making his début there in 1865 in Lortzing's *Der Waffenschmied*. In 1867 he was engaged at Breslau, and in 1870 at Leipzig, where he first appeared as Wolfram (*Tannhäuser*). He sang both Donner and Gunther in the first complete performance of the *Ring* at Bayreuth (1876), returning there to sing Amfortas, King Mark (1886) and Hans Sachs (1889). From 1876 to 1882 he was engaged at Hamburg, where he sang Wotan in *Das Rheingold* and *Die Walküre* (1878). He made his London début at Drury Lane in *Der fliegende Holländer* (1882) and sang Hans Sachs and King Mark in the first performances in England of *Die Meistersinger* and *Tristan und Isolde*, also appearing as Lysiart in Weber's *Euryanthe*. From 1882 until his retirement in 1896, he was engaged at the Hofoper, Munich. His repertory included Iago, Falstaff and Leporello. The wide range of his voice encompassed both bass and baritone roles.

E. Gura: *Erinnerungen aus meinem Leben* (Leipzig, 1905)
H. Wagner: *200 Jahre Münchner Theaterchronik 1750–1950* (Munich, 1958)
G. Skelton: *Wagner at Bayreuth* (London, 1965)

ELIZABETH FORBES

Gura, Hermann (*b* Breslau, 5 April 1870; *d* Bad Wiessee, 13 Sept 1944). German baritone and director, son of Eugen Gura. He studied in Munich and made his début in Weimar in 1890 as the Dutchman. After engagements in Riga (1890–91), at the Kroll Opera, Berlin (1891–2), Aachen (1892–3), Zürich (1893–4), Basle

(1894–5) and Munich (1895–6), he joined the Schwerin Hoftheater, remaining there until 1908. In 1911 he was appointed director of the Berlin Komische Oper and in 1913 was responsible for the staging of *Der Rosenkavalier* at its first London performance and of other operas during Beecham's Covent Garden season. During the 1920s he was a director at the Helsinki Opera, then taught singing in Berlin. HAROLD ROSENTHAL/R

Gurecký [Guretzky, Kuretzky], **Václav Matyáš** (*b* Přerov, bap. 4 Aug 1705; *d* Olomouc, end of July 1743). Czech composer. He received his education at Piarist schools and later taught in Kroměříž. By 1729 he was presumably already employed by the Olomouc bishop, Cardinal Wolfgang von Schrattenbach (1711–38), who enabled him to study composition with Caldara in Vienna. In 1736 he left the Schrattenbach orchestra and took the post of musical director of Olomouc Cathedral. He was a prolific composer of operas, oratorios, church and instrumental music, but most of his works are now lost. From the librettos (now in Ljubljana) we know that he composed the operas *Antioco* (Kroměříž, 31 October 1729) and *Griselda* (Kroměříž, 31 October 1730) for the bishop's orchestra, both to texts by Zeno.

V. Helfert: *Hudební barok na českých zámcích* [The Musical Baroque in Czech Castles] (Prague, 1916), 198–9

J. Sehnal: 'Počátky opery na Moravě' [The Beginnings of Opera in Moravia], *Acta Universitatis Palackianae* (Olomouc, 1973)

JIŘÍ SEHNAL

Guridi (Bidaola), Jesús (*b* Vitoria, 25 Sept 1886; *d* Madrid, 7 April 1961). Spanish (Basque) composer. Born into a family of professional musicians, he early showed signs of musical talent. He studied the piano, violin and harmony, started to compose before he was in his teens, and eagerly assimilated the performances and discussions of the 'Cuartito' musical circle which met nightly in Bilbao. Concerts of his early compositions attracted the attention of the Count de Zubiría, who paid for him to go to Paris in 1904 to study at the Schola Cantorum, where d'Indy and Grovlez were among his teachers, and then to Brussels and Cologne. After his return to Bilbao he was appointed organist at the Basilica de Santiago, where he remained for 20 years, gaining a reputation as a brilliant improviser; in 1912 he became conductor of the Bilbao Choral Society, with which for 15 years he gave numerous large-scale works throughout Spain. In 1927 he became professor of organ and composition at the newly founded Biscay Conservatory, and in 1944 transferred to a similar post at the Madrid Conservatory, of which he became director a dozen years later.

Local patriotism led him to write a number of orchestral and choral compositions based on Basque themes, and some of his stage works likewise reflect his profound love of his native region. The first of these, the sentimental idyll *Mirentxu* (1910), quotes various folktunes and is written in the Basque tongue. Its great success led to performances (in Spanish) in other cities and it was twice revised with a new libretto; on the last occasion, in 1947, it was converted from its mixed form of musical numbers linked by dialogue into a true opera. *Amaya* (1920), based on a novel about the Navarrese shrine of San Miguel, was much praised for its dramatic power but was slow to make its way until the composer conducted a triumphant performance of it, with Hina Spani in the title role, in Buenos Aires on 19 August

1930. Meanwhile Guridi had composed two zarzuelas, *El caserío* and *La meiga*, on Basque and Galician subjects respectively. The former, his most famous work, was an immense success both financially and artistically, and is still considered one of the masterpieces of the zarzuela repertory. Later stage works were never again to win such acclaim, though *Peñamariana*, a highly original score about the performance of a medieval mystery play in a Salamancan village, was enthusiastically received in ten cities. Guridi's cultivated musical tastes and his technique (in particular his orchestral finesse) set him in a completely different class from earlier zarzuela writers.

See also CASERÍO, EL.

Mirentxu (idilio lírico vasco, 2, A. Echave), Bilbao, Campos Elíseos, 31 May 1910; rev. (F. Romero and G. Fernández Shaw), Bilbao, Feb 1934; as op (J. M. de Arozamena), San Sebastián, Gran Kursaal, 24 Nov 1947

Amaya (drama lírico, 3, epilogue, J. M. Arroita Jáuregui), Bilbao, Coliseo Albia, 23 May 1920

El caserío (zarzuela vasca, 3, Romero and Fernández Shaw), Madrid, Zarzuela, 11 Nov 1926

La meiga (zarzuela gallega, 3, Romero and Fernández Shaw), Madrid, Zarzuela, 28 Dec 1928

La cautiva (zarzuela, 2, L. F. de Sevilla and A. Carreño), Madrid, Calderón, 10 Feb 1931

Mandolinata (zarzuela, 3, A. C. de la Vega), Madrid, Calderón, 17 Nov 1934

Mari-Eli (zarzuela vasca, 2, E. Garay and C. Arniches), Madrid, Fontalba, 11 April 1936

Nacimiento (zarzuela, 3, V. Espinós and Arozamena), San Sebastián, Victoria Eugenia, 3 Jan 1938; collab. Moreno Torroba and F. Cotarelo

La bengala (sainete lírico, 1, L. Tejedor and J. Huecas), Zaragoza, Argensola, 12 Jan 1939

Déjame soñar [Chicas de oficina] (sainete, 1, Tejedor and Huecas), Bilbao, Arriaga, 27 May 1943

Peñamariana (retablo popular, 3, Romero and Fernández Shaw), Madrid, Madrid, 16 Nov 1944

Acuarelas vascas (estampas líricas, J. Echevarría and J. L. Albéniz), Bilbao, Ayala, 22 Dec 1948

La condesa de la aguja y el dedal (zarzuela, 2, A. Torrado and Arozamena), Madrid, Madrid, 5 April 1950

A. Sagardia: *Jesús Guridi* (Bilbao, n.d.)

A. Valverde: *Con fondo de chistu* (San Sebastián, 1965)

J. M. de Arozamena: *Jesús Guridi* (Madrid, 1967)

LIONEL SALTER

Gurlitt, Manfred (*b* Berlin, 6 Sept 1890; *d* Tokyo, 29 April 1973). German composer and conductor. He studied composition in Berlin with Humperdinck and Kaun. In 1908 he was appointed chorus répétiteur at the Berlin Hofoper, and in 1911 he became an assistant at Bayreuth and Kapellmeister at the municipal theatres of Essen and Augsburg. In 1914 he took a post as principal Kapellmeister and opera director in Bremen; he returned to Berlin in 1924 as Generalmusikdirektor and guest conductor at the Staatsoper. In 1939 he settled in Japan, where he did much to make German opera known, notably, from 1953, with his own company.

Die Heilige (dramatische Legende, 3, after C. Hauptmann), Bremen, Stadt, 27 Jan 1920

Wozzeck (musikalische Tragödie, 18 scenes, epil., after G. Büchner), Bremen, Stadt, 22 April 1926, vs (Vienna and New York, 1926)

Soldaten (3, Gurlitt, after R. Lenz), Düsseldorf, Nov 1930, vs (Vienna and Leipzig, 1931)

Nana (4, M. Brod, after E. Zola), Dortmund, 1933, vs (Vienna and Leipzig, 1933)

Nächtlicher Spuk, 1937

Warum? (Gurlitt), 1940

Nordische Ballade (after S. Lagerlöf), 1944

Wir schreiten aus (Gurlitt), 1958

'*Gustaf Wasa*' (*J. G. Naumann*), *Act 3: design by Louis-Jean Desprez for the original production at the Royal Opera House, Stockholm, 19 January 1786*

Gustafson, Nancy (*b* Evanston, IL, 27 June 1956). American soprano. She studied at Northwestern University and made her début in 1983 at San Francisco as Woglinde and Helmwige, later singing Freia, Musetta, Antonia (*Les contes d'Hoffmann*) and Electra (*Idomeneo*). Having sung Donna Elvira in 1986 with Glyndebourne in Hong Kong, in 1988 she sang Kát'a Kabanová at Glyndebourne and also made her Covent Garden début as Freia. She has appeared at Chicago, Santa Fe, Munich, Brussels, Hamburg, and with the ENO and Scottish Opera. Her roles include Marguerite, Alice Ford, Leïla, Violetta and the Foreign Princess (*Rusalka*). In 1990 she made her Metropolitan début as Musetta and sang Eva at La Scala and Amelia (*Simon Boccanegra*) at La Monnaie. An extremely effective actress, she has a strong, vibrant voice.

ELIZABETH FORBES

Gustaf Wasa. *Tragédie lyrique* in three acts by JOHANN GOTTLIEB NAUMANN to a libretto by JOHAN HENRIK KELLGREN based on a draft by GUSTAVUS III; Stockholm, Royal Opera, 19 January 1786.

The opera concerns the war for independence waged by the Swedish king Gustaf Eriksson Wasa against the Danes in the 16th century. The wives and children of the enslaved Swedish nobility have been imprisoned by Danish King Christiern (tenor). Cecilia af Eka (soprano) expresses her hope that her son, Gustaf Wasa (tenor), will free them and Sweden from the Danish yoke. Christiern's boasting of his ruthless suppression of the Swedes is interrupted by the news that a rebel army is approaching and that Gustaf has besieged Stockholm. Christiern takes hostage the son of Christina Gyllenstjerna (soprano), wife of a defeated Swedish rebel, and sends her with his admiral Severin Norrby

(bass) as an emissary to the Swedish camp. Norrby, shaken by his ruler's cruelty, vows to help her. They present Christiern's demands to Gustaf; he refuses them, placing Sweden above the welfare of the hostages, and prepares his troops for battle. Norrby reports to Christiern that Gustaf Wasa has refused his terms, adding that he finds the Swedish resolve too strong; enraged, Christiern orders him imprisoned. Later, as Christiern is haunted by the ghosts of the great Swedish heros of the past whom he has murdered, Gustaf attacks and the Danes are swiftly defeated; Christiern flees but Norrby, who was captured in the battle, is pardoned. The opera ends with Gustaf Wasa's coronation.

Gustavus III planned *Gustaf Wasa* as a propaganda event to be used in his war against Denmark and Russia. It was an immediate success and throughout the next several years was used to inspire confidence in Gustavus's leadership. It is closely related to Gluck's *tragédies lyriques*, with large-scale scenic effects and elaborate sets and action on stage. Considered by Naumann to be his best work, the opera has a mixture of styles. His orchestration is skilful, with heavy woodwind textures giving the music a dark, emotional colour. He also adopts a folk style in several scenes; Gustaf's aria 'Ädla skuggor' ('Noble shades') was the de facto Swedish national anthem for over a century.

BERTIL H. VAN BOER

Gustave III [*Gustave III, ou Le bal masqué* ('Gustavus III, or The Masked Ball')]. *Opéra historique* in five acts by DANIEL-FRANÇOIS-ESPRIT AUBER to a libretto by EUGÈNE SCRIBE; Paris, Opéra, 27 February 1833.

The opera is based on the assassination of Gustavus III, King of Sweden, during a masked ball in Stockholm. The plot is familiar today chiefly through Somma and

'Gustave III' (Auber), Act 3 (the place of execution near Stockholm): design by Pierre-Luc-Charles Ciceri for the original production at the Paris Opéra (Salle le Peletier), 27 February 1833

Verdi's *Un ballo in maschera* (1859). Gustavus (tenor) is in love with Amélie (soprano), the wife of Count Ankastrom (bass), who has warned the king of a conspiracy against him. The king visits the fortune-teller Arvedson (mezzo-soprano) incognito and overhears her advising Amélie to renounce her guilty love for him. When his own fortune is told, he learns that the next man to give him his hand will kill him. Ankastrom enters and shakes his hand. Gustavus follows Amélie to the place of execution, where she hopes to pick a herb to cure her of her adulterous love. Ankastrom, who suspects nothing, urges the king to flee. Ankastrom agrees to accompany the veiled lady back to the city. Gustavus leaves and the conspirators rush in, to find only Ankastrom. Amélie's veil slips aside, and Ankastrom realizes that his wife is the king's mistress. He joins the conspirators, who draw lots to decide who is to murder Gustavus. The king has decided to send Ankastrom to Finland, and a masked ball is held before he leaves. Two warnings fail to deter Gustavus from attending. A page innocently tells the conspirators what disguise the king is wearing, and Ankastrom shoots him.

Following the production of *Robert le diable*, particular emphasis was placed on the sets and effects, especially in the ballroom scene, when about 300 people were on stage and more than a hundred danced the sensational galop. Auber had to finish the last three acts after rehearsals of *Gustave III* had begun, and although the opera has a logical conception in its entirety, the individual numbers are of mixed quality. But the opera was performed 168 times in Paris (after the end of April 1834 they were partial performances only), and it was also successful in England and Germany. As late as 1877 it was performed in Vienna as *Die Ballnacht*. The opera had considerable influence on Verdi's *Un ballo in maschera*: *Gustave III* contains Auber's most developed 'parlante' scene, similar to those that Verdi introduced in his operas after *Macbeth*.

For further illustration *see* CAMBON, CHARLES-ANTOINE.

HERBERT SCHNEIDER

Gustavus III [Gustaf Adolph, King of Sweden] (*b* Stockholm, 24 Jan 1746; *d* Stockholm, 29 March 1792). Swedish patron and librettist. Son of the music-loving Queen Lovisa Ulrika and the German-born King Adolph Frederick, he was trained in the fine arts from an early age. In his youth he was sent to Paris to be educated; while there he began to write paraphrases of *opéras comiques* by Favart and *tragédies lyriques* by Racine, Marmontel, Quinault and others. In 1771 his father died suddenly and he returned home to become king. An autocrat at heart, he chafed under the restrictions imposed upon him by Sweden's powerful nobility, and in March 1772 he staged a coup which gave him absolute authority. One of his first aims was to create a Swedish national opera. He drafted an opera plot which, set to music by F. A. B. Uttini as *Thetis och Pelée*, became the first Swedish grand opera. It was first performed in January 1773 with immense success. Over the next decade Gustavus personally oversaw the development of Swedish opera, gathering around him a group of native writers to put his prose texts and outlines into verse. He established a court theatre and gave financial support to private theatres, one of which was run by Carl Stenborg, a leading theatrical figure in Stockholm. He encouraged the composers J. G. Naumann, J. M. Kraus and G. J. Vogler, the ballet-masters Louis Gallodier, Frederico Terrade and Anton Bournonville and the set designer Louis-Jean Desprez. He also built the Royal Opera (1782), which contained the most advanced stage machinery in Europe. Among his own works are a wide variety of sketches, prose drafts and librettos for operas and plays with music including Kraus's *Proserpin* and *Aeneas i Cartago*, Naumann's *Gustaf Wasa*, Vogler's *Gustav Adolf och Ebba Brahe*, Åhlström's *Frigga*, C. F. Müller's *Drottning Christina* and Haeffner's *Electra*.

The war with Russia (1787–90) and a restive nobility made numerous enemies for Gustavus, many of whom were satirized in a small Singspiel by Kraus, *Födelsedagen* ('The Birthday'), given in 1790. A conspiracy among the nobility led to the king being shot at a masked ball at the Stockholm opera house on 16 March

1792, an event that formed the basis for two 19th-century operas, Auber's *Gustave III* and Verdi's *Un ballo in maschera*. After his death, the active musical establishment in Stockholm went into decline.

F. Dahlgren: *Anteckningar om Stockholms teatrar* (Stockholm, 1866)

O. Levertin: *Gustaf III som dramatisk författare* (Stockholm, 1911)

A. Beijer: *Drottningholms slottsteater på Lovisa Ulrikas och Gustaf III:s tid* (Stockholm, 1981)

E. Lönnroth: *Den stora rollen* (Stockholm, 1986)

B. H. van Boer: 'Gustavian Opera: an Overview', *Gustavian Opera 1771–1809* (Stockholm, 1990)   BERTIL H. VAN BOER

Gute Freund, Der. Opera by Ethel Smyth; *see* BOATSWAIN'S MATE, THE.

Gutheil-Schoder, Marie (*b* Weimar, 16 Feb 1874; *d* Bad Ilmenau, Thuringia, 4 Oct 1935). German soprano. She studied in Weimar, where she made her début in 1891. After an apprenticeship in secondary roles, she had a notable success in 1895 as Carmen. She was then engaged by Mahler for the Vienna Staatsoper where, in spite of being dubbed 'the singer without a voice', she remained as one of the most admired artists from 1900 to 1926. During this time she became most closely associated with the operas of Mozart, and of Richard Strauss who coached her in Electra and Octavian for the Viennese premières of *Elektra* and *Der Rosenkavalier*; she also appeared as Salome. At Salzburg she sang Susanna in *Le nozze di Figaro*, and at Covent Garden, in a single appearance under Beecham in 1913, Octavian. She gained additional respect among musicians for her support of some avant-garde composers, especially Schoenberg, whose *Erwartung* she sang at its première in Prague in 1924. On retirement as a singer she taught and directed at Vienna and Salzburg. Her few recordings, made in 1902, reveal very little about her. The admiration of other artists, such as Bruno Walter and Lotte Lehmann, tells far more, as does the faith reposed in her by Mahler and Strauss. Her singing was famous for its subtlety and refinement; and about the voice, Erwin Stein wrote that it was 'the perfect instrument of a great artist'.   J. B. STEANE

Guthrie, Frederick [Frank] (*b* Pocatello, ID, 31 March 1924). American bass. He studied in Los Angeles with Glynn Ross and Hugo Strelitzer. His first engagements, beginning in 1950, were with small American opera companies. In 1953 he went to Vienna as a Fulbright scholar, where he studied with Elisabeth Rado and sang in *Oedipus rex* under Karajan. He was a member of the Vienna Staatsoper (1954–8), then sang with the Frankfurt Opera as a guest artist in Munich, Rome and Trieste. In 1956 he sang Sarastro at Glyndebourne and three years later repeated the role in Aix-en-Provence. Among other roles were the Commendatore (1969, Interlaken), Daland (1972, Seattle), a Dignitary in the première of Marcel Rubin's *Kleider machen Leute* (1973, Vienna) and the Man in Armour (*Die Zauberflöte*; 1979, Vienna). His was a bass voice of notable depth and clarity.   CORI ELLISON

Guthrie, Tyrone (*b* Tunbridge Wells, 2 July 1900; *d* Newbliss, Ireland, 15 May 1971). English producer. Originally an actor, he directed at the Old Vic in London (1933–4; 1937; 1953–7) and was an administrator for the Old Vic/Sadler's Wells (1939–45). He was a founder of the Shakespeare Festival at Stratford,

Ontario, where he directed from 1953 to 1957, and in 1963 he established the Guthrie Theatre in Minneapolis. His first operatic staging was *Peter Grimes* for Covent Garden in 1947, but his most significant achievements in opera took place at the Metropolitan during the early years of Rudolf Bing's administration, when Bing engaged numerous directors from the worlds of theatre and film in the hope of giving opera production in New York a more contemporary flavour. Bing first called upon Guthrie in 1952 to stage *Carmen* with Risë Stevens and Richard Tucker; the production was widely considered to be boldly realistic and startlingly innovatory at the time. Guthrie subsequently returned to the Metropolitan to direct *La traviata* with Renata Tebaldi (1957) and *Peter Grimes* with Jon Vickers (1967).   PETER G. DAVIS

Gutiérrez (y) Espinosa, Felipe (*b* San Juan, Puerto Rico, 26 May 1825; *d* San Juan, 27 Nov 1899). Puerto Rican composer. He was mainly self-educated in music, though he received instruction from his father and acknowledged the influence of the organist Domingo Delgado. In 1845 he became a musician with the Spanish forces in Puerto Rico. In 1871 he established a free music school, the Academia de Música de Puerto Rico, which operated from 1872 until 1874. He was a founder-member of the Ateneo Puertorriqueño in 1876 and taught music theory there. He served as *maestro de capilla* at San Juan Cathedral from 1858 until 1898, when government support for the church ended following the surrender of Puerto Rico to the USA. He died in poverty, subsisting as a school janitor and finally on a small pension.

Gutiérrez was a central figure in the musical life of 19th-century Puerto Rico. As a conductor at the San Juan Municipal Theatre during the third quarter of the century he absorbed the Italian and Spanish styles of lyric theatre brought to the island by visiting companies and cultivated locally. His melodious and carefully wrought compositions include church, orchestral, chamber and theatre music. His three known operas are *Gaurionex* (libretto by Alejandro Tapia y Rivera), *El bearnés* (libretto by Antonio Biaggi) and *Macías* (probably on his own libretto). His only known zarzuela is *El amor de un pescador* (libretto by Carlos M. Navarro y Almanso). Of these four only *Macías* is extant; it received its première in San Juan on 19 August 1977, more than a century after its composition.

See also MACÍAS.

PEM (M. Kuss)

B. Dueño Colón: 'Felipe Gutiérrez y Espinosa, maestro-compositor', *Música y músicos portorriqueños*, ed. F. Callejo (San Juan, 1915, 2/1971, ed. A. Veray)

R. Stevenson: *A Guide to Caribbean Music History* (Lima, 1975); repr. as 'Caribbean Music History: a Selective Annotated Bibliography with Musical Supplement', *Inter-American Music Review*, iv (1981–2), 37ff

T. Marco: '*Macías* de Gutiérrez Espinosa: estreno actual de una ópera romántica', *Arriba* [Madrid] (1 Sept 1977); repr. in *Inter-American Music Review*, i (1978–9), 96–7

D. Thompson: 'Musical archaeology, fine talent bring *Macías* to life', *San Juan Star* (7 June 1978); repr. in *Inter-American Music Review*, i (1978–9), 98–9

G. Batista: *Felipe Gutiérrez y Espinosa y el ambiente musical en el San Juan de su época* (thesis, Centro de Estudios Avanzados de Puerto Rico y el Caribe, 1982)

N. de Frontera: *A Study of Selected Nineteenth Century Puerto Rican Composers and their Musical Output* (diss., New York U., 1988)   DONALD THOMPSON

'Gwendoline' (Chabrier), Act 3, the death of Gwendoline and Harald, in the first Paris production (Opéra, 27 December 1893): engraving from 'L'illustration' (30 December 1893)

Guyenet, Pierre (*d* Paris, 20/30 Aug 1712). French administrator. He was granted the licence of the Opéra (Académie Royale de Musique) by a deed signed on 5 October 1704, when the current managers, Jean-Nicolas de Francine and Hyacinthe de Gauréault Dumont, became overwhelmed by debt. In exchange the new manager undertook to pay salaries, pensions, the entertainment tax and all the debts of the Opéra. He was also to pay an annual pension of 75 000 livres to Francine and one of 25 000 livres to Dumont. Despite his financial experience, Guyenet failed. In eight years he burdened the Opéra with debt, leaving liabilities in the region of 400 000 livres. He ruined his family and his own health. Hounded by his creditors, he took refuge in his theatre at the Palais-Royal and died there. On his death his creditors, represented by their delegates, the receivers, negotiated with Francine and Dumont.

*

F-Po, MS Amelot
J. Gourret: *Ces hommes qui ont fait l'Opéra* (Paris, 1984)
NICOLE WILD

Guy-Ropartz, Joseph. *See* ROPARTZ, JOSEPH GUY.

Gwendoline. Opera in three acts by EMMANUEL CHABRIER to a libretto by Catulle Mendès; Brussels, Théâtre de la Monnaie, 10 April 1886.

Armel (tenor), chief of a settlement on the coast of Britain in Saxon times, and the other men set off to fish. Gwendoline (soprano), Armel's daughter, and the women sing as they spin. Cries are heard as the Saxons rush in pursued by Danish pirates. Harald (baritone), the Danish leader, threatens to kill Armel, but Gwendoline runs between them to save her father. Harald is struck by her beauty. Dismissing everyone else, he tries to express his love for her. When the Danish warriors return they find their bloodthirsty leader seated at the spinning-wheel. This scene, written in Chabrier's most delicate style, is the finest in the score, much of which is over-inflated.

Harald has obtained Armel's permission to marry Gwendoline. The marriage blessing ceremony builds up to an effective, Donizetti-style finale. Armel orders the Saxons to kill the Danes, using their own weapons, dur-ing the wedding festivities. He gives his daughter a knife with which to kill Harald. She tries to warn Harald of danger, but he refuses to listen and the lovers embark on a passionate duet, interrupted by cries from the Danes as the Saxons attack them. Harald, mortally wounded, leans against a tree. Flames from the burning Danish ships redden the sky as Gwendoline, stabbing herself with her father's knife, dies in Harald's arms. Both text and music are appropriately and consciously Wagnerian in this last scene. ELIZABETH FORBES

Gye, Frederick (*b* London, 1809; *d* Dytchley, 4 Dec 1878). English theatre manager. He was educated mainly in Germany and originally helped his father manage the Vauxhall Gardens. He was associated with the Jullien Promenade Concerts at Covent Garden (1843–4) and became acting manager of the Theatre Royal, Drury Lane (1847). In 1848 he became business manager to Edward Delafield (director of the Royal Italian Opera, Covent Garden, 1848–9), and the next year obtained the lease of Covent Garden, initially for seven years though he remained there until 1877. At Covent Garden he introduced many operas to London, including the first performances in England of *Rigoletto* (1853), *Il trovatore* (1855), *Don Carlos* (1867), *Aida* (1876), *Lohengrin* (1875) and *Tannhäuser* (1876), with artists including Patti, Albani, Pauline Lucca, Tamberlik, Faure and Maurel. He was succeeded by his son Ernest Gye, who married Albani.

*

H. Rosenthal: *Two Centuries of Opera at Covent Garden* (London, 1958)
HAROLD ROSENTHAL/R

Gyrowetz, Adalbert [Jírovec, Voytěch Matyáš] (*b* Česke Budějovice, 19 or 20 Feb 1763; *d* Vienna, 19 March 1850). Bohemian composer and conductor. He studied the piano, the violin and composition with his choirmaster father and wrote his first full-scale works (church compositions and wind serenades) while still a schoolboy. After studying philosophy and law in Prague, he became secretary to Count Franz von Fünfkirchen; he also played in his orchestra. Intent on furthering his musical career, in 1784–5 Gyrowetz travelled to Vienna, where he met Mozart who took a friendly interest in his work. Shortly afterwards he became secretary and music master to the family of Prince Ruspoli, with whom he travelled widely in Italy. He studied with Nicola Sala in Naples, and went to Paris in 1789. The revolutionary atmosphere soon prompted him to move to London, where he remained for three years. His stay coincided with Haydn's first London visit, and Gyrowetz's writings are full of his admiration for the older composer, on whose style he had modelled his own work. Gyrowetz considered his time in London the happiest period of his life. A number of his instrumental works were published there, and he also became involved, for the first time, with a major operatic project. Unfortunately *Semiramis*, the opera he was commissioned to write for the London Pantheon, came to nothing; he claimed that it was destroyed when a fire gutted the theatre in 1792, but it now seems that the opera was not completed nor (as he claims) rehearsed (see Price). Leaving England shortly thereafter, Gyrowetz visited his native Bohemia before returning permanently to Vienna in 1793.

In 1804 he became a Kapellmeister and composer to the Viennese Hoftheater, and his energies were transferred from orchestral to stage music. His contract required him to compose at least one opera and one ballet each year as well as to conduct rehearsals and supervise performances. He secured his first operatic success with *Agnes Sorel* (1806), an *opera seria* which achieved 124 performances in Vienna over the next decade, and was widely performed throughout Europe for some 30 years. His greatest success was the Singspiel *Der Augenarzt* (1811), and other stage works include *Il finto Stanislao* (to a libretto later used by Verdi in *Un giorno di regno*) and the first operatic treatment of Hans Sachs.

Gyrowetz's music was very well received, certainly until the mid-1820s, when changes of fashion caused its popularity to wane. The Viennese nevertheless continued to regard him with personal affection, although increasingly as a kind of musical anachronism. Despite his friendship with Beethoven (at whose funeral in 1827 he was a pallbearer), he found himself able to assimilate the techniques only of Beethoven's early period. His style remained so firmly based on the music of Haydn that some of his manuscripts were wrongly ascribed to that composer. He also admired the music of his court theatre colleagues, Weigl and Salieri. He maintained a strong association with the Czech nationalist movement, although there was little opportunity for the exploitation of national colour in the music he was required to write for the court theatre.

Gyrowetz retired from the court theatre in 1831 and subsequently appeared little in society, although the public's regard for him was shown in 1844 when a benefit concert of his music was given in the Musikvereinsaal. His last years were dogged by financial hardship, and he was helped by younger musicians, notably Meyerbeer. Much of his music was directed at the salon audience of Vienna and as a result suffers from a certain triviality, but nevertheless shows fine qualities of balance, considerable skill in orchestration and an attractive melodic simplicity. He entirely outlived his stylistic period, and in his lifetime his music ceased to be taken seriously. A comment from his memoirs wryly sums up the situation: 'What a peculiar feeling it is to remain alive and yet realize that one is already spiritually dead'.

See also AUGENARZT, DER.

publication dates refer to vocal scores published in Vienna; principal MS collections: A-Wgm, Wn

WK – *Vienna, Kärntnertortheater*
WW – *Vienna, Theater an der Wien*

Semiramis (P. Metastasio), 1791, ?inc., destroyed except for ov. (Augsburg, n.d.)
Selico (Spl, 2, Hummel), WK, 15 Oct 1804 (?1804)
Mirana, die Königin der Amazonen (melodrama, 3, F. I. von Holbein), WW, 27 May 1806 (?1806)
Agnes Sorel (os, 3, J. von Sonnleithner), WW, 4 Dec 1806 (1806)
Ida, die Büssende (5, Holbein), WW, 26 Feb 1807
Die Junggesellen-Wirtschaft (Spl, 1, J. G. von Treitschke), WK, 18 June 1807
Emericke (komische Oper, 2, Sonnleithner), WK, 11 Dec 1807
Die Pagen des Herzogs von Vendôme (komische Oper, 1, Sonnleithner), WK, 5 Aug 1808
Der Sammtrock (Operette, 1, after A. von Kotzebue), WK, 24 Nov 1809 (1809)
Der betrogene Betrüger (Operette, 1, after Valville), WK, 17 Feb 1810
Das zugemauerte Fenster (Spl, 1, after Kotzebue), WK, 18 Dec 1810
Der Augenarzt (Spl, 2, J. E. Veith), WK, 1 Oct 1811 (1811)
Federica ed Adolfo (os, 2, G. Rossi), WK, 6 April 1812
Das Winterquartier in America (Spl, 1), WK, 30 Oct 1812
Fünf und zwei (Spl, I. F. Castelli), WK, 20 March 1813, collab. Mosel, Seyfried and others
Robert, oder Die Prüfung (Spl, 2, L. Huber), WK, 15 July 1815
Helene (2, G. von Hofmann), WK, 16 Feb 1816
Der Gemahl von ungefähr (1), WK, 26 Sept 1816
Die beiden Eremiten (1)
Montag, Dienstag, Mittwoch (Posse, 3), WW, 23 May 1817, collab. Kinsky and Seyfried
Die beiden Savoyarden, c1817
Il finto Stanislao (ob, F. Romani), Milan, Scala, 5 Aug 1818
Aladin (1), WK, 7 Feb 1819
Das Ständchen (Spl, 1), WK, 7 Feb 1823
Des Kaisers Genesung, ? WK, 1 May 1826
Der blinde Harfner (1), WK, 19 Dec 1827
Der Geburtstag (Spl, 1), WK, 11 Feb 1828
Der dreizehnte Mantel (Spl, 1, after E. Scribe), WK, 12 Jan 1829
Felix und Adele (romantische Oper, 3, J. von Weissenthurn), WK, 10 Aug 1831
Hans Sachs im vorgerückten Alter (romantisch-komische Spl, 2), Dresden, 1833

*

PEM (R. Fischer-Wildhagen)
E. T. A. Hoffmann: review of *Der Augenarzt*, AMZ, xiv (1812), 855–64; Eng. trans., *E. T. A. Hoffmann's Musical Writings*, ed. D. P. Charlton (Cambridge, 1989), 293–6
M. Schletterer: *Das deutsche Singspiel von seinen ersten Anfängen bis auf die neueste Zeit* (Leipzig, 1879)
K. Mey: 'Adalbert Gyrowetz und seine neu aufgefundene "Hans Sachs"- Oper', *Die Musik*, ii (1902–3), 290–303
A. Einstein, ed.: *Lebensläufe deutscher Musiker*, iii–iv: A. Gyrowetz (Leipzig, 1915)
F. Bartoš, ed. and trans.: *Vlastní životopis Vojtěcha Jírovce* [Gyrowetz's autobiography] (Prague, 1940)
E. Doernberg: 'Adalbert Gyrowetz', ML, xliv (1963), 21–30
C. Price: 'Italian Opera and Arson in Eighteenth-Century London', *JAMS*, xlii (1989), 55–107, esp. 71–3   ADRIENNE SIMPSON

Gyurkovics, Mária (*b* Budapest, 19 June 1915; *d* Budapest, 28 Oct 1973). Hungarian soprano. She studied under Imre Molnár at the Budapest Academy of Music, making a successful Budapest Opera début in 1937 as Gilda. She soon became the theatre's leading coloratura soprano, admired for her warmth of voice, virtuoso technique and fine lyric feeling. She took the principal roles of the coloratura repertory (notably Konstanze, the Queen of Night, Lucia, Rosina, Oscar, Lakmé and Norina), as well as Sophie and Flotow's Martha; at the end of her career, her portrayal of Miss Wordsworth (*Albert Herring*) revealed to Hungarian audiences her gift for comedy. Her most important international appearances were at Berlin and Dresden (1951), Moscow, Leningrad and Tallinn (1953), and Vienna (1957).   PÉTER P. VÁRNAI

Gyuzelev [Ghiuselev], **Nikola** (*b* Pavlikeni, 17 Aug 1936). Bulgarian bass. He studied at Sofia and joined the Bulgarian National Opera in 1960, making his début as Timur. In 1965 he toured France, Germany and Italy with the company and made his Metropolitan début as Ramfis. He has sung in most major European theatres, including La Scala, the Paris Opéra, the Vienna Staatsoper and Covent Garden, where he made his début in 1976 as Pagano (*I Lombardi*). His repertory includes Boris, Dosifey, Borodin's Galitsky (which he sang at Covent Garden in 1990), Don Giovanni, Rossini's Don Basilio, Oroveso, Henry VIII (*Anna Bolena*), Gounod's and Boito's Mephistopheles and the four villains in *Les contes d'Hoffmann*. His rich, dark-toned voice is most effective in Verdi, notably as Philip II, Attila, Silva and Fiesco.

ELIZABETH FORBES

H

Haack [Haacke, Haak, Haake], **Friedrich Wilhelm** (*b* Potsdam, 1760; *d* Stettin [now Szcezecin, Poland], 1827). German composer. Apparently a violin pupil of Franz Benda, he began his professional career in the private orchestra of the crown prince of Prussia at Potsdam, and later held posts as organist at Stargard (from 1779) and Stettin (from 1790), where he led a renowned amateur music group. After 1800 Haack was a theatre Kapellmeister and Kantor at Stettin. His opera *Die Geisterinsel*, written in 1799 (lost), was the fourth to use Gotter's libretto based on Shakespeare's *The Tempest*. The *Allgemeine musikalische Zeitung* (ii, 1799–1800, col.135) remarks that 'the richness, fullness and elaboration of the harmony, especially in solemn and sublime passages, are supposed to distinguish this composition greatly'. Haack also wrote other vocal works and various instrumental pieces.

THOMAS BAUMAN, E. EUGENE HELM

Haag, Den (Dutch). HAGUE, THE.

Haas, Joseph (*b* Maihingen, 19 March 1879; *d* Munich, 30 March 1960). German composer. He was a pupil of Reger in Munich (from 1904) and in Leipzig (1907), where he also studied the organ with Karl Straube. In 1911 he was appointed teacher of composition at the Stuttgart Conservatory and ten years later returned to Munich to take over the composition class and the Catholic church music department at the Akademie der Tonkunst. From 1945 to 1950 he served as president of the Munich Musikhochschule, and did much to rebuild musical life in the city after the war.

The writer of numerous liturgical compositions as well as intimate chamber and piano works, Haas earned a reputation as a miniaturist. In the 1930s, however, he enjoyed considerable success with his folk oratorios *Die heilige Elisabeth* (1931), *Christnacht* (1932) and *Das Lebensbuch Gottes* (1934), and these works, together with the earlier Christmas fairy-play *Die Bergkönigin* (1927), gave him the confidence to tackle a full-length opera. From 1934 to 1937 he collaborated with his publisher Ludwig Andersen on fashioning operatic material from Ortner's drama of 1929 about the woodcarver Tobias Wunderlich and his pious devotion to the altar figure of the Holy Barbara. After its first performance, in Kassel in 1937, *Tobias Wunderlich* aroused a good deal of controversy. Some critics claimed that the work, as defending the purity of the artist against the un-scrupulous influence of trade and commerce, represented the finest German opera since Pfitzner's *Palestrina*. On the other hand, the Rosenberg wing of the Nazi party lambasted the composer for introducing episodes of Catholic mysticism on the operatic stage. These attacks initially precluded the work's production elsewhere in Germany, although by the beginning of the war it had gained general acceptance. At the same time, the conservative musical idiom – which juxtaposes south-German folk elements with Gregorian, psalmodic and liturgical melodies, yet which owes much to the traditional techniques of the through-composed post-Wagnerian *Volksoper* – met with little criticism. A similar otherworldliness characterizes the comic opera *Die Hochzeit des Jobs* (1944), in which Haas once again strongly identifies with the main character, an endearing simpleton who eventually marries his loved one in spite of the wicked machinations of the Lord Mayor. Both *Tobias Wunderlich* and *Die Hochzeit des Jobs* were revived in German opera houses during the 1950s but, like most of Haas's other compositions, have fallen into almost complete neglect since the composer's death.

Die Bergkönigin op.70 (Weihnachtsmärchen, 3, F. Rodenstock), Munich, Rezidenz, 18 Nov 1927, vs (Augsburg, 1927)
Tobias Wunderlich op.90 (3, H. H. Ortner and L. Andersen), Kassel, Staats, 24 Nov 1937, vs (Mainz, 1937)
Die Hochzeit des Jobs op.93 (komische Oper, 4, Andersen), Dresden, Staatsoper, 2 July 1944, vs (Mainz, 1943)

*

PEM (E. Voss)
K. Laux: *Joseph Haas* (Mainz, 1931, 2/1954)
M. Gebhard, O. Jochum and H. Lang, eds.: *Festgabe Joseph Haas: Beiträge von seinen Schülern, Mitarbeiten und Freunden, nebst einem Verzeichnis seiner Werke: zum 60. Geburtstag am 19.3.1939* (Mainz, 1939) [incl. bibliography]
H. Vogl-Eich: 'Tobias Wunderlich: eine Betrachtung', *Mitteilungsblatt der Joseph Haas-Gesellschaft* (1961), no.33, pp.1–7
J. Haas: *Reden und Aufsätze* (Mainz, 1964)
K. G. Fellerer: 'Ludwig Strecker und Joseph Haas in der Arbeit an "Tobias Wunderlich"', *Festschrift für einen Verleger: Ludwig Strecker* (Mainz, 1973), 191–202
ERIK LEVI

Haas, Pavel (*b* Brno, 21 June 1899; *d* Oświęcim, 17 Oct 1944). Czech composer. He studied composition at the Brno Conservatory in Janáček's masterclass (1920–22) and then worked as a private music teacher. During World War II he was interned in the Terezín concentration camp; he died in a gas chamber. His mature style had been developed in the brilliant Piano Suite (1935) and in the opera *Šarlatán* ('The Charlatan'), which was composed between 1934 and 1937; it was performed in Brno on 2 April 1938. Whereas other pupils of Janáček became imitators or else abandoned their teacher's style, Haas succeeded in assimilating Janáček's methods within his own idiom, combining concise, expressive motifs with remarkably inventive harmonic and rhythmic textures. His music was also influenced by Moravian folksong and Jewish chant, by jazz rhythms to some extent, and by the instrumentation of Stravinsky and Honegger. *The Charlatan* is a tragi-comic opera in three acts to Haas's own libretto, after Josef Winckler's novel *Doktor Eisenbart*. Its modern style is melodic and accessible.

*

L. Peduzzi: *Pavel Haas a jeho tvorba za okupace* [Pavel Haas and his Work during the Occupation] (diss., U. of Brno, 1963)
——: 'Haasův *Šarlatán*' [Haas: *The Charlatan*], OM (1986), 293–300   LUBOMÍR PEDUZZI

Hába, Alois (*b* Vizovice, 21 June 1893; *d* Prague, 18 Nov 1973). Czech (Moravian) composer. He was a pupil of Novák and Schreker, although Schoenberg and Busoni also influenced his development in semitonal and microtonal composition. He studied in Prague, Vienna and Berlin and then worked in Prague, where he created his own school of composition at the conservatory. At the instigation of Edward Dent he began to work with the ISCM where, as an honorary member and influential official, he supported Czech and other Slavonic composers. Although he composed in the semitone system, he is best known for his microtonal works. Folk music was important in Hába's musical development; he had a keen ear for microtonal deviations in the folk music performed by his father's band (in which he played the violin and double bass). Drawing also on his studies of Arab music, he constructed his own system (theorized in his *Neue Harmonielehre des diatonischen, chromatischen, Viertel-, Drittel-, Sechstel- und Zwölftel-Tonsystems*, Leipzig, 1927). His Moravian background is clearly perceptible in his works.

Hába wrote three operas. The first, *Matka* ('The Mother') op.35, a quarter-tone opera in ten scenes to his own libretto, draws on events from his time in Moravia. Composed in 1927–9, it was first performed in Munich at the Staatstheater am Gärtnerplatz (in German) on 17 May 1931 under Hermann Scherchen; it was first given in Czech in Prague on 23 May 1947 at the Grand Opera of the Fifth of May (now Smetanovo Divadlo) under Karel Ančerl. His second opera, composed in the semitone system, was *Nová země* ('New Land') op.47, in three acts to a libretto by Ferdinand Pujman based on Fedor Gladkov's novel of the same name. It was composed between 1934 and 1936 but has never been performed. His third opera, composed between 1937 and 1940, also remains unperformed: *Přijd' království tvé* ('Thy Kingdom Come') op.50, sometimes known as *Nezaměstnaní* ('The Unemployed'), is a musical drama in seven scenes in the sixth-tone system, using as libretto an adaptation by Pujman of Hába's own text.

See also MATKA.

*

J. Vysloužil: '*Matka* před Florencií' [*Matka* before Florence], *Hudební rozhledy*, xvii (1964), 556–7
——: 'Hába's Idea of Quarter-tone Music', HV, v (1968), 466–72
——: 'A Note on Alois Hába', MT, cxiv (1973), 590–92
——: *Alois Hába: život a dílo* (Prague, 1974)   JIŘÍ VYSLOUŽIL

Hába, Karel (*b* Vizovice, 21 May 1898; *d* Prague, 21 Nov 1972). Czech (Moravian) composer, brother of

Alois Hába. He studied at the teacher's training institute of Příbor, later completing his studies at the Prague Conservatory, where he attended violin masterclasses and Vítězslav Novák's composition classes. From 1925 to 1927 he participated in courses in quarter-tone music given by his brother Alois, and performed quarter-tone music throughout Europe on the violin and the viola. Between 1929 and 1950 Hába worked for Prague Radio, from 1936 as head of music education. From 1951 he lectured on music education in Prague. He was made a member of the Czech Academy of Sciences and Arts in 1940.

Of Hába's four operas only his first, *Jánošík* op.17, in four acts to a libretto by Antonín Klášterský, was performed at the National Theatre, Prague (23 February 1934), and received wide recognition. The opera's story is based on historic folktales about Juro Jánošík (1688–1713), 'the Slovak Robin Hood', providing moral and biblical justification for the actions of the hero and his band of outlaws. In genre the work is akin to the kind of symphonic opera represented by Novák's *Lucerna* and *Dědův odkaz*. Hába followed his teacher's style harmonically and contrapuntally, but was also influenced by Schoenberg and by the operatic works of his brother. *Jánošík* makes use of Moravian and Slovak rhythmic and melodic idioms and contains quotations from Slovak songs associated with the Jánošík tradition, 'Hej, hore háj' and 'Pime, chlavci, pime víno' ('Let's drink, lads').

Jánošík op.17, 1932 (4, A. Klášterský), Prague, National, 23 Feb 1934
Stará historie [An Old Story] op.20, Prague Radio, 25 Sept 1940
Smolíček op.33 (children's radio op, V. Čtvrtek), Prague Radio, 28 Sept 1950
Kalibův zločin [Kaliba's Crime], 1960   JIŘÍ VYSLOUŽIL

Habeneck, François-Antoine (*b* Mézières, 22 Jan 1781; *d* Paris, 8 Feb 1849). French conductor. He studied the violin with his father and later in Pierre Baillot's class at the Paris Conservatoire, where he won a *premier prix* for the violin in 1804. In the same year he joined the orchestra of the Opéra-Comique, but moved almost at once to that of the Opéra. When Rodolphe Kreutzer was promoted to director of the Opéra in 1817 Habeneck succeeded him as principal violin. From 1821 to 1824 he was director of the Opéra, from 1824 to 1831 he shared with Henri Valentino the title of *premier chef* there, and from 1831 to 1846 he fulfilled that function alone. Thus he was conductor of the Paris Opéra during one of its most brilliant periods, conducting the first performances of Rossini's *Guillaume Tell*, Meyerbeer's *Robert le diable* and *Les Huguenots*, Halévy's *La Juive*, Berlioz's *Benvenuto Cellini* and many others. He raised the standard of orchestral playing there to a level prompting Henry Chorley, writing of the orchestra in 1836, to describe it as 'a machine in perfect order, and under the guidance of experience and intellect – for these are thoroughly personified in M. Habeneck'. His most lasting achievements were the introduction of Beethoven's music to France and the founding of the Société des Concerts du Conservatoire; the orchestra of the society quickly attained the same high standard as that of the Opéra and was admired and emulated throughout Europe.

Habeneck generally conducted with a bow and from a first violin part. Wagner admired his efficiency and the command he had over his forces. Berlioz, as a representative of the new type of baton conductor, was more critical, particularly over performances of his Requiem in 1837 and *Benvenuto Cellini* in 1838, though he should perhaps have given the conductor more credit for his audacious undertaking of the *Symphonie fantastique* in 1830. Habeneck's influence and standing in Paris music was unrivalled during the last 20 years of his life. He taught the violin at the Conservatoire from 1808 to 1816 and from 1825 to 1848, and also composed, mainly for the violin.

P. Smith: 'Habeneck (François-Antoine)', *Revue et gazette musicale*, xvi (1849), 50 [obituary]
——: 'Habeneck', *Illustrated London News* (17 Feb 1849)
R. Wagner: *Über das Dirigieren* (Leipzig, 1869; Eng. trans., 1887)
A. Carse: *The Orchestra from Beethoven to Berlioz* (Cambridge, 1948)
H. C. Schonberg: *The Great Conductors* (New York, 1967)
H. Berlioz: *Mémoires* (Paris, 1870; Eng. trans., ed. D. Cairns, 1969)
HUGH MACDONALD

Habich, Eduard (*b* Kassel, 3 Sept 1880; *d* Berlin, 15 March 1960). German baritone. He studied in Frankfurt and made his début in 1904 at Koblenz. After engagements in Posen, Halle and Düsseldorf, in 1910 he joined the Berlin Hofoper (later Staatsoper), of which he remained a member until 1930. He appeared at Bayreuth for the first time in 1911 as Alberich, a part he sang at every festival there until 1931; he was also heard as Klingsor and Kurwenal. He sang at Covent Garden each season from 1924 to 1936 and again in 1938, his roles including Telramund, Alberich, Beckmesser, Klingsor, Falke (*Die Fledermaus*) and Faninal. He sang in Chicago, 1930–31, and at the Metropolitan, 1935–7.

HAROLD ROSENTHAL/R

Hackett, Charles (*b* Worcester, MA, 4 Nov 1889; *d* New York, 1 Jan 1942). American tenor. On the recommendation of Lillian Nordica he studied at the New England Conservatory with Arthur J. Hubbard, and later with Vincenzo Lombardi in Florence. In 1914 he made his début in Genoa as Wilhelm Meister, which also served for his La Scala début (1916). He appeared at the Paris Opéra in *Maria di Rohan* in 1917, returning as the Duke and Romeo in 1922. After a season in Buenos Aires (1917–18) he made his Metropolitan début in 1919 as Almaviva; there he later sang Lindoro (*L'italiana in Algeri*), Rodolfo, Pinkerton, Romeo and Alfredo. At Monte Carlo (1922–3) he sang Cavaradossi and Des Grieux (*Manon*). He was closely identified with the Chicago Opera (1922–35) and took part in the première of Cadman's *A Witch of Salem* in 1926. In the same year, he appeared at Covent Garden as Almaviva, Fenton, and Romeo in Melba's farewell performance. He continued to sing until 1939. Hackett made a number of records, including duets with Barrientos and Ponselle; they document a secure technique and a certain elegance, though there is also a sense of routine about them. That sense is completely dispelled by the sweep and finesse of his style in a recording of a Metropolitan Opera broadcast of Gounod's *Roméo et Juliette* from 1935.

L. F. Holdridge: 'Charles Hackett', *Record Collector*, xxii (1974–5), 173–214
RICHARD DYER, ELIZABETH FORBES

Hacquart [Haccart], **Carolus** [Carel] (*b* Bruges, 1640; *d* ? shortly after 1700). Netherlands composer. He settled in Amsterdam about 1670, but moved to The Hague in about 1675 or shortly after. Very little is known of his later whereabouts or when and where he died. He composed motets, ensemble sonatas and a set of viol sonatas, and is known to have provided the music for the first 'Dutch opera', in reality a *zangspel* (light theatre play with a mixture of spoken texts and songs), *De triomfeerende min* (published 1680). It was written by Dirk Buysero on the occasion of the Peace of Nijmegen (1678), but probably never performed. The libretto combines pastoral and allegorical elements. Hacquart's music consists of four-part choruses, a number of arias for solo voices and three duets; there are occasional references to instrumental interludes.

P. Andriessen: *Carel Hacquart (1640–1701?): een biografische bijdrage* (Brussels, 1974)
RUDOLF A. RASCH

Hader [von Hadersberg], **Clementin**. *See* CLEMENTIN.

Hadjiapostolou, Nikolaos [Nikos] (*b* Athens, or nr Athens, ? May 1879; *d* Athens, 9 Aug 1941). Greek composer and bass. He studied at the Lottner Conservatory, Athens, with Karl Boehmer (*c*1899–1905) and sang with Lavrangas's Elliniko Melodrama company (*c*1905–15). After writing music for revues, in 1916 he began writing operettas, between one and three a year for more than 20 years, staged by Athenian companies. A cultured, self-disciplined musician, he owed his great popularity to the hundreds of songs he composed; mostly written for, or incorporated into, his operettas, they often have an irresistible dramatic impact and vary from simple strophic forms to more complex opera-like scenes. Although the plots of some of his works are based on French plays, they are adapted to Greece, with heroes that are usually simple and kind-hearted working-class Athenians, maintaining their national and class identity in ultimately peaceful confrontations with wealthy city dwellers. His best-known operetta, *I apahides ton Athinon* (1921), was made into a film in 1930 and successfully revived in 1985 by the National Lyric Theatre in Athens. Many of his scores were destroyed in a fire in 1968.

selective list of operettas, all first performed in Athens

Moderna kamariera [Modern Chambermaid] (3, N. Paraskevopoulos, after G.-L.-J.-M. Feydeau), Papaioannou, 14 July 1916, vs, orch pts *GR-Am**
Erotika gymnassia [Manoeuvres in Love] (3, Paraskevopoulos, after *Amour et Preston*), Dionyssia, 12 April 1917, vs *Am*
Panourgiae arlekinou [The Guiles of Harlequin], 1917
I bebeka [Baby Doll] (V. Vekiarellis), Kendrikon, 1 June 1918
I erotevmenoi, i I erotevmenoi mylonades [People in Love, or Millers in Love] (A. Nikas), Alhambra, 12 Aug 1919
Kontessina [The Countess] (after Fracarolli), Kendrikon, 30 June 1920
Sta triandafylla [Among the Roses] (3, Paraskevopoulos, after *Emprunte-moi ta femme*), Panellinion, 19 Aug 1920, vs *Am*
I apahides ton Athinon [The Athenean Apaches] (3, Y. Prineas), Alhambra, 17 Aug 1921, vs, orch pts *Am*, *Aels**, vs *Akounadis*
To proto fili [The First Kiss] (3), Alhambra, 25 April 1922, vs, orch pts *Am*
To koritsi tis yitonias [The Girl of the Neighbourhood] (3, Z. Thanos), Alhambra, 11 July 1922, vs *Aels*
Pos pernoun i pandremenoi [Married Life] (3, Thanos), Alhambra, 1923, vs, orch pts *Am*
Ta dichtya tis agapis [Love's Nets] (Thanos), Alhambra, 1923
O Adam ke i Eva [Adam and Eve], Alhambra, 13 Aug 1923
I gyneka tou dromou [The Tramp] (dramatic operetta, 3), Alhambra, 21 May 1924, vs *Aels*, *Akounadis*
Boemiki agapi [Bohemian Love] (3, O. Karavias), Panellinion, 1926, vs *Aels*
Palia ke nea hronia [Times Old and Modern], Kendrikon, 1927
I proti agapi [First Love] (prol., 2, epilogue), Panellinion, 18 May 1928 or 1929, vs *Aels*; perhaps as Palies agapes [Old Loves], 1930 or earlier

I vlamissa [The Tomboy], Panellinion, 17 Sept 1929

Yola (operetta-revue, 2), Mondial, 14 Oct 1931, vs *Aels*

O maharayas [The Maharajah], Athenaeon, 20 Aug 1932

Blue-blue, Olympia, 13 Oct 1933; ?rev. as I fakirides ton Athinon [The Fakirs of Athens], Mikado or Makedo, 16 July 1937

O vassilias tou halva [The King of the Nugget] (2, A. Sakellarios), Kotopouli, 7 Dec 1934

I piratae [The Pirates], Athenaeon, 22 June 1935

O babas ekpedevetae [Daddy's Education] (3, Hadjiapostolou, after S. Melas), Casino, 5 June 1936

To trellokoritso [The Crazy Girl], Mondial, 13 July 1937 or 1938

I kardia tou patera [Father's Heart] (2, after Cormon and Granger: *Le vieux Martin*), Ideal, 8 Nov 1939, vs, orch pts *Am*

Gremismeni folia [Destroyed Nest] (dramatic operetta, 2, after A. Bisson: *L'inconnue*), vs *Akounadis*

San i kardia pona [A Heart in Travail] (2, ?Hadjiapostolou)

*

H. Halikias: 'Ellines moussourghoi: Nikolaos Hadjiapostolou', *Radiotileorassis* [Athens] (5–11 Aug 1973), 92–3

G. Karakandas: *Apanda tou lyrikou theatrou* [Everything about Lyric Theatre] (Athens, 1973), 712–20

E.-A. Delveroudi: *Apahides tou Athinon – Nikos Hadjiapostolou* (Athens, 1985) [programme notes for the 1985 revival]

GEORGE LEOTSAKOS

Hadjiev, Parashkev (*b* Sofia, 27 April 1912; *d* 28 April 1992). Bulgarian composer. He was taught initially by his parents, both leading lights in the early years of Bulgarian opera (his father was a conductor, and his mother a singer); he then studied composition with Josef Suk (1932–3) before entering the State Musical Academy in Sofia (1933) as a pupil of Vladigerov, on whose recommendation he took lessons with Joseph Marx in Vienna before completing his studies at the Berlin Hochschule für Musik (1938–40). In 1940 Hadjiev became a lecturer at the Sofia Academy. He was one of the most prolific Bulgarian opera composers, and one of the most frequently staged. His spontaneously emotional side and inborn theatrical sense are evident in both dramatic and humorous contexts, and he has proved able to communicate effectively with children. For his librettos he has drawn on foreign as well as Bulgarian literature and on fairy-tales. The individuality of his musical language results above all from his characteristic melodies, built on elements of Bulgarian folk music. Artistic simplicity, accessibility, knowledge of how to write for the human voice and a rich harmonic palette are dominant features. *Lud gidiya* ('The Madcap'), generally regarded as the best example of Bulgarian comic opera, has also been performed abroad.

first performed at Sofia, National Opera, unless otherwise stated

Imalo edno vreme [Once upon a Time] (4, P. Spasov), Sofia, State Musical, 11 April 1957

Lud gidiya [The Madcap] (comic op, 3, I. Genov), 15 Nov 1959

Albena (5 scenes, P. Filchev), Varna, Opera House, 2 Nov 1962

Yulska nosht [July Night] (2 pts, Genov and P. Hadjiev, after Genov: *Septemvriyska balada*), Varna, National Opera, 15 July 1964

Milionerat [The Millionaire] (comic op, 3, Spasov and S. Donev), Sofia, State Musical, 14 March 1965

Maistori [The Masters] (2 pts, Hadjiev, after R. Stoyanov), 9 Oct 1966

Ritsaryat [The Knight] (comic op, 4 scenes, Spasov), Varna, National Opera, 25 Feb 1969

Zlatnata yabalka [The Golden Apple] (children's op, 5 scenes, Genov), 28 Jan 1972

Sluzhbogontsi [Careerists] (musical, 5 scenes, B. Banov, after I. Vazov), 30 Sept 1972

Leto 893 [The Year 893] (9 scenes, Ruse, National Opera, 26 March 1973

Syrano de Bergerac (musical, 5 scenes, Banov, after E. Rostand), Sofia, State Musical, 9 March 1974

Zar Midas ima magazeshki uschi [King Midas has Asses' Ears] (comic op, 2 pts, Genov), Sofia, State Musical, 15 May 1976

Maria Desislava (7 scenes, K. Zidarov), Ruse, National Opera, 24 March 1978

Ioannis rex (2 pts, R. Radkov), Pleven, National Opera, 26 Jan 1981

Paradoxi [Paradoxes] (trilogy, each 1 act, P. Raykov, after O. Henry), Ruse, Opera House, 9 Jan 1982 [Razvod (Divorce), Kradetsat (The Thief), Podaratsite (The Presents)]

Az, Klavdiy [I, Claudius] (7 scenes, Raykov), 16 Feb 1984

Zvezda bez ime [A Star without a Name] (2 pts, O. Stamboliev), 26 Nov 1985

Mnimiyat bolen [The Hypochondriac] (2 pts, Banov, after Molière: *Le malade imaginaire*), Plovdiv, National Opera, 17 March 1987

Babinata pitka [Granny's Loaf] (children's op, 6 scenes, V. Mirchovski), Blagoevgrad, 24 Dec 1989

Joan Kukuzel, 1989 (4 scenes, Mirchovski), 8 Feb 1992

Revizor [The Inspector General], 1989 (Banov, after N. V. Gogol), unperf.

Over 100 radio operettas for children

MAGDALENA MANOLOVA

Hadley, Henry (Kimball) (*b* Somerville, MA, 20 Dec 1871; *d* New York, 7 Sept 1937). American conductor and composer. The date of his death is sometimes given incorrectly as 6 September 1937. Both his parents were musicians, and George Whitefield Chadwick, who had a summer home near the family, was his first composition teacher and remained his lifelong colleague. Hadley went twice to Europe to study, including counterpoint with Mandyczewski and composition with Ludwig Thuille. Having conducted for two years in Germany, in 1907 he went to the Mainz Stadttheater, where his first opera, *Safié*, was produced. He made his living mainly from conducting, notably the Seattle SO, the newly formed San Francisco Orchestra and the Metropolitan Opera. He was appointed associate conductor of the New York Philharmonic Society in 1920, then in 1929 helped form the Manhattan SO. He founded the National Association of American Composers and Conductors in 1933 and the Berkshire Symphonic Music Festival the following year. His highly successful conducting career took him to all parts of the USA as well as to Europe, South America and the Far East.

Hadley's operas exhibit his penchant for the music of Wagner and Strauss, the orchestral accompaniment tending to dominate the voices. His music is highly chromatic with an effusion of 7th chords. Much of *Cleopatra's Night* is written in a declamatory style, lyricism emerging as the heroine reads a love message on a papyrus attached to an arrow that is shot to her. In addition to the operas he wrote operettas and the music for three plays for the Bohemian Club of San Francisco, of which he was a member. He was elected to the American Academy of Arts and Letters and was awarded the David Bispham Medal.

Happy Jack, 1897 (operetta, S. F. Batchelder)

Nancy Brown (operetta, F. Ranken), New York, 1903

Safié op.63 (1, E. Oxenford, after a Persian legend), Mainz, Stadt, 4 April 1909

The Pearl Girl op.73 (operetta, W. J. Hurlburt)

The Atonement of Pan (music drama, J. Redding), Sonoma County, CA, 10 Aug 1912

Azora, the Daughter of Montezuma op.80 (3, D. Stevens), Chicago, Auditorium, 26 Dec 1917

Bianca op.79 (1, G. Stewart, after C. Goldoni: *La locandiera*), New York, Park, 18 Oct 1918

Cleopatra's Night op.90 (2, A. L. Pollock, after T. Gautier), New York, Met, 31 Jan 1920

Semper virens op.97 (music drama, Redding), Sonoma County, CA, 1923

The Fire Prince (operetta, Stevens), Schenectady, NY, 1924

A Night in Old Paris (1, F. Truesdell, after G. McDonough), private perf. New York, Dec 1924; NBC Radio, 20 Jan 1930

The Legend of Hani (music drama, J. Cravens), Sonoma County, CA, 29 July 1933

*

J. C. Canfield: *Henry Kimball Hadley: his Life and Works (1871–1937)* (diss., Florida State U., 1960)

THOMAS WARBURTON

Hadley, Jerry (*b* Princeton, IL, 16 June 1952). American tenor. After vocal studies at the University of Illinois and with Thomas Lo Monaco in New York, he made his début as Lyonel in *Martha* in 1978 in Sarasota. Several seasons at the New York City Opera, beginning in 1979 (as Arturo in *Lucia di Lammermoor*), established him as a leading lyric tenor: his roles included Des Grieux (*Manon*), Pinkerton, Tom Rakewell, Werther and Gounod's Faust. His European début in Vienna as Nemorino in 1982 was followed by appearances in Berlin, Geneva, Glyndebourne, Hamburg, London and Munich. He made his Metropolitan Opera début as Des Grieux in 1987. He sang Rodolfo at Covent Garden in 1990. His lyrical, italianate voice and dramatic immediacy make him a fine interpreter of the Mozart, French lyric and Italian repertories. CORI ELLISON

Haeffner, Johann Christian Friedrich (*b* Oberschönau, Thuringia, 2 March 1759; *d* Uppsala, 28 May 1833). German composer active in Sweden. The son of a schoolmaster and church organist in Klein-Schmalkalden, he received his earliest musical education from his father. As a student at Leipzig University he became acquainted with J. A. Hiller, from whom he learnt the Singspiel tradition. From 1778 to 1780 he was musical director of theatre troupes in Frankfurt and Hamburg. In 1780 he was appointed organist at the German Church (St Gertrude) in Stockholm, and held that post until his dismissal in 1793. In autumn 1781 he began to teach singing at the Royal Theatre and also acted as musical director of Carl Stenborg's theatre; he was made assistant director of the Royal Theatre in 1782 for J. G. Naumann's production of *Cora och Alonzo* and was given a formal contract as a teacher of singing in 1783. In 1792 he was appointed interim successor to J. M. Kraus as *Hovkapellmästare*, a position he held until he was forcibly removed in 1808 and sent to Uppsala, where he became *director musices* at the university. His last formal appointment was as organist at the cathedral there in 1826.

Haeffner's often stormy relationship with his subordinates in Stockholm led to considerable controversy. Unlike his articulate predecessor Kraus, he spoke Swedish poorly and his conducting style was often uninspired and pedantic. He was considered authoritarian and unable to get along with either colleagues or superiors, and his departure for Uppsala was greeted by the court orchestra with relief. As a composer, however, he demonstrated considerable knowledge of both the Singspiel tradition of Hiller and the heroic French style of Gluck. His best work, the three-act opera *Electra*, is filled with colourful orchestration and shows a conscious attempt to bring out an emotional text. The music is heavily influenced by the German *Sturm und Drang*, and in his other stage works (which include incidental music) there is well-crafted and often harmonically advanced writing. As a teacher, he helped to train more than three generations of Swedish opera singers.

all first performed in Stockholm

Electra (3, A. F. Ristell, after N. F. Guillard), Drottningholm, 22 July 1787, *S-St*

Alcides inträde i världen [Alcide's Entrance into the World] (1, A. N. Clewberg-Edelcrantz), Royal, 11 Nov 1793, *Skma, St, Uu*

Epilogue to R. Kreutzer: Lodoiska (1, C. Lindegren), Royal, 2 Nov 1795, *St*

Renaud (lyric tragedy, 3, N. B. Sparrschöld, after Leboeuf and others, after T. Tasso), Royal, 29 Jan 1801, *St, Uu*

*

F. Dahlgren: *Anteckningar om Stockholms teatrar* (Stockholm, 1866)

BERTIL H. VAN BOER

Haefliger, Ernst (*b* Davos, 6 July 1919). Swiss tenor. He studied at Zürich and Geneva, and in Vienna with Patzak. He made his début in 1949 at Salzburg, creating Tiresias in Orff's *Antigonae*. While engaged at the Städtische, later Deutsche Oper, Berlin (1952–74), he sang Belmonte at Glyndebourne (1956), Idamantes at Salzburg (1961) and Tamino in Chicago (1966). He created roles in Blacher's *Zwischenfälle bei einer Notlandung* (1966, Hamburg) and *Zweihunderttausend Taler* (1969, Berlin). His repertory included Ferrando, Don Ottavio, Pelléas, Jeník, Busoni's Calaf, Froh and Palestrina, his most striking characterization. His voice was notable for its clarity and focus rather than its tonal quality. He recorded several of his Mozart roles with Fricsay and also Florestan in *Fidelio*, which he never sang on stage. ALAN BLYTH

Haentjes, Werner (*b* Bocholt am Niederrhein, 16 Dec 1923). German composer. He studied at the Musikhochschule in Cologne, and attended the Darmstadt summer courses given by Fortner and Leibowitz (1947–50). During this period he was conductor at the Stadttheater of Bielefeld and Heidelberg; since 1949 he has worked as a freelance composer in Cologne. His freely tonal, essentially contrapuntal music is highly individual but non-experimental. In 1958 the cultural circle of the Confederation of German Industry awarded him its composition prize; his television opera *Leonce und Lena* was commissioned by Westdeutsche Rundfunk.

Leonce und Lena (television op, 3, after G. Büchner), Cologne, 1962

Nichts Neues aus Perugia (chamber op, 2, Haentjes and H. Reinhold, after Boccaccio), Cologne, 1964

Gesucht werden Tote (chamber op, 1, M. Thomas), Cologne, 1966

HANSPETER KRELLMANN

Hafgren [Hafgren-Waag, Hafgren-Dinkela], **Lilly** (*b* Stockholm, 7 Oct 1884; *d* Berlin, 27 Feb 1965). Swedish soprano. She trained first as a pianist and was advised by Siegfried Wagner to take up singing. Her studies in Frankfurt and Milan being completed, she was invited to Bayreuth, where in 1908 she made her début as Freia in *Das Rheingold*. Further roles there were Elsa in *Lohengrin* and Eva in *Die Meistersinger*, in which role she reappeared at the festival in 1924. From 1908 to 1912 she was with the opera at Mannheim, after which there followed six years at the court opera in Berlin. Her large repertory now ranged from Brünnhilde and Isolde to Pamina and Countess Almaviva, Tosca, Carmen and Charlotte in *Werther*. She sang the Empress in the Berlin première of *Die Frau ohne Schatten* and the title role in that of *Ariadne auf Naxos*. She travelled widely in Europe, appearing at La Scala as Brünnhilde in the seasons of 1925, 1926 and 1930. Her operatic career continued in Dresden until 1934, and she was also a noted recitalist. For a time she appeared under the name of Hafgren-Waag after her first marriage and Hafgren-

Dinkela after her second. Her voice on records is bright in tone, conveying a strong sense of dramatic commitment.

J. B. STEANE

Hafner, Philipp (*b* Vienna, 27 Sept 1735; *d* Vienna, 30 July 1764). German playwright. He served as a secretary in the Viennese municipal court during his short life, and wrote a series of successful plays that developed a distinctively Viennese brand of written comedy out of local improvisatory traditions. His lone musical text, the three-act Zauberlustspiel *Megära, die förchterliche Hexe* (1764, composer unknown), achieved such spectacular popularity that it earned Hafner a sinecure as court poet. Various musical adaptations of his plays, notably by Wenzel Müller, remained a mainstay of Viennese suburban theatres well into the next century.

THOMAS BAUMAN

Hagegård, Håkon (*b* Karlstad, 25 Nov 1945). Swedish baritone. He studied in Stockholm, making his début at the Royal Opera in 1968 as Papageno, the role he later sang in Ingmar Bergman's film of *Die Zauberflöte* (1975). He first appeared at Glyndebourne as the Count in *Capriccio* (1973), returning as Count Almaviva and Guglielmo. After his Metropolitan début as Malatesta (1978) he sang Rossini's Figaro, Eisenstein and Wolfram, the role of his Covent Garden début in 1987. He has sung with Scottish Opera, at La Scala and Drottningholm, and in Paris, Copenhagen, Hamburg, Geneva, Zürich, Santa Fe, San Francisco and Chicago. Among his other roles are Don Giovanni, Pacuvio (*La pietra del paragone*), Yevgeny Onegin, Posa, Rigoletto and Pelléas. In 1991 he sang Beaumarchais in the première at the Metropolitan of Corigliano's *The Ghosts of Versailles*. With the years his light, lyrical voice has grown more powerful, without losing its beauty of tone or flexibility.

Håkon's cousin, Erland Hagegård (*b* Brunskog, 27 Feb 1944), also a baritone, made his début in 1968 at the Vienna Volksoper. He has sung at Frankfurt, the Vienna Staatsoper and in Stockholm. His repertory includes Escamillo, Valentin, Albert (*Werther*) and Germont as well as Don Giovanni and Onegin.

ELIZABETH FORBES

Hageman, Richard (*b* Leeuwarden, 9 July 1882; *d* Beverly Hills, CA, 6 March 1966). American composer and conductor of Dutch birth. When he was 16 he was appointed coach to the Netherlands Opera Company, and in 1899 he became conductor. In 1906 he travelled to New York as accompanist to Yvette Guilbert. He conducted at the Metropolitan Opera (1908–22), the Chicago Civic Opera (1922–3) and the Los Angeles Grand Opera (1925), and was head of the opera department at the Curtis Institute in Philadelphia. From 1938 he worked at the Paramount studios in Hollywood. In 1931 Hageman wrote the opera *Caponsacchi*, for which he received the David Bispham Memorial Medal. It was first performed at Freiburg as *Tragödie in Arezzo* (18 February 1932) and staged at the Metropolitan on 4 February 1937. The 'concert drama' *The Crucible* was performed in Los Angeles in 1943. Hageman's music was conservative in style, and he lacked the ability to turn flowing melody into telling drama. He also wrote orchestral pieces, film music and many art songs.

PHILIP LIESON MILLER

Hager, Leopold (*b* Salzburg, 6 Oct 1935). Austrian conductor. He studied at the Salzburg Mozarteum and made his début in 1958 with *L'italiana in Algeri* at Mainz, where he was principal conductor until 1962, followed by appointments at Linz and Cologne. He was music director at Freiburg, 1965–9, and principal conductor of the Salzburg Mozarteum Orchestra, 1969–81. During this time he appeared frequently in opera at Salzburg, Munich, Stuttgart and Cologne. His first engagement at the Vienna Staatsoper was for *Fidelio* (1973), followed by débuts at the Metropolitan (1976) and Covent Garden (1978) with *Le nozze di Figaro*, and at the Teatro Colón (1977) with *Tristan und Isolde*. His recordings include all the early Mozart operas; his performances combine elegance and vitality.

NOËL GOODWIN

Häggander, Mari Anne (*b* Trökörna, 23 Oct 1951). Swedish soprano. She studied in Göteborg, and made her début in 1977 at Stockholm, then sang Elisabeth de Valois at Savonlinna (1979), Hero (*Béatrice et Bénédict*) at Buxton (1980) and Eva and a flowermaiden at Bayreuth (1981). She has also sung in Berlin, Hamburg, Oslo and Vienna and in New York, where she made her Metropolitan début as Eva (1985); in Brussels she sang in the première of André Laporte's *Das Schloss* (1986). Her repertory includes Pamina, Cherubino, Countess Almaviva, Fiordiligi, Tatyana, Freia, Sieglinde, Elsa, which she sang at San Francisco in 1989, Mme Lidoine, Mimì and the Marschallin. She has a smooth-toned voice and sings with great intelligence.

ELIZABETH FORBES

Hague, The (Dutch: Den Haag, 's-Gravenhage). City and seat of government in the Netherlands. After the Treaty of Utrecht in 1579 William of Orange made The Hague his seat of government; because of the presence of the diplomatic corps opera was constantly in demand, particularly French works. In 1681 the city council approved a proposal to stage French opera in a small building on the Casuaristraat. There, until 1804, spectators could enjoy the latest operatic and theatrical works from Paris. Frequently the operas were short pieces given before or after the plays; the orchestra numbered some 20 members. In the same period German, Italian and Flemish troupes appeared in a hall on the Assendelftstraat. In 1795 the court fled the Napoleonic armies, but during the brief reign of Louis Napoléon opera flourished again. A former royal palace on the Korte Voorhout was renovated in 1804 to provide suitable theatrical amenities for the city. This lovely theatre, the Koninklijke Schouwburg (extensively renovated in 1863), is still used for theatrical productions.

After the return of the Staathouder, the Koninklijke Franse Opera (Royal French Opera), financed by the royal house and the municipality, became the most stable opera company in the country during the 19th century. Some productions were sent to other cities, usually Amsterdam and Utrecht, and occasionally there were joint productions with the French opera company in Amsterdam. In 1874 the Gebouw voor Kunsten en Wetenschappen, on the Zwarteweg, was opened. During the latter half of the 19th century interest in the German repertory steadily increased. The Residentie-Orkest, founded by the conductor Henri Viotta (also founder of the Wagner Society in Amsterdam), gave its first concerts in 1903. Eight years later Richard Strauss conducted his *Feuersnot, Salome, Elektra* and *Rosen-kavalier* in one season in The Hague.

At the end of World War I the Royal French Opera was disbanded. The Nationale Opera, soon superseded by the Co-opera-tie, staged their productions in the Gebouw voor Kunsten en Wetenschappen. In the 1920s The Hague saw several premières of works by Dutch and Belgian composers. *Beatrijs* (1925), by the Dutch composer Willem Landré (1874–1948), reached the Paris Opéra. Just before World War II, there was an exceptionally attractive season in Scheveningen, the city's seaside resort: *Pelléas et Mélisande* was conducted by Ansermet and *Figaro* by Carl Schuricht. In 1939 the Royal Conservatory inaugurated an opera division.

After the war Dutch operatic activity concentrated on the newly founded Stichting de Nederlandsche Opera and the Holland Festival, both based in Amsterdam. The Gebouw voor Kunsten en Wetenschappen was destroyed by fire in 1964. Two years later the 1600-seat Circustheater in Scheveningen was renovated to provide better accommodation for the new national company based in Amsterdam, the Nederlandse Operastichting, which used the theatre for many of its rehearsals. Most productions were first staged in The Hague before progressing to other Dutch cities. Under the intendancy (1971–86) of Hans de Roo there were several premières of Dutch works in the Circustheater: *Dorian Gray* (Hans Kox, 1974), *Axel* (Jan van Vlijmen and Reinbert de Leeuw, 1977), *Winter Cruise* (Hans Henkemans, 1979) and the post-Romantic *Thijl* (Jan van Gilse, 1980). Maderna's *Satyricon* was first given there in 1973. *Dummies* by Otto Ketting had its première in the Kurzaal in 1974, and the one-act *Mirrors of the Truth* by Ian McQueen and *The Telltale Heart* by Daniel Kessner in the HOT-Theater in 1982. Since the opening of Amsterdam's Muziektheater in 1986 there have been only occasional productions by the Netherlands Opera staged in The Hague's AT-en-T Danstheater (the base of the Netherlands Dans Theater), opened in 1987 and seating 1001.

J. Fransen: *Les comédiens français en Hollande au 17e et au 18e siècles* (Paris, 1925)
G. A. Gillhoff: *The Royal Dutch Theatre at The Hague 1804–1876* (The Hague, 1938)
S. A. M. Bottenheim: *De opera in Nederland* (Amsterdam, 1946, 2/1983)
E. Reeser: *Een eeuw nederlandse muziek, 1815–1915* (Amsterdam, 1950, 2/1986)
T. Coleman, ed.: *Een noodzakelijke luxe* (Zutphen, 1986)
MICHAEL DAVIDSON

Hahn, Reynaldo (*b* Caracas, 9 Aug 1874; *d* Paris, 28 Jan 1947). French composer and conductor of Venezuelan birth. His family, originally from Hamburg, moved to France when he was three. One of his most famous and popular *mélodies*, 'Si mes vers avaient des ailes', written when he was 14, was taken up by numerous opera singers; it was recorded as early as 1901 by Marie Tempest and later by Melba and Calvé. He studied composition with Massenet, whose influence can be discerned in much of his early music, but his interest in Rameau can also be heard in the ballets *Le bal de Béatrice d'Esté* and *La fête chez Thérèse*, and Debussy's *Pelléas et Mélisande* cannot be ignored when his *mélodies* or more serious stage works are considered. His first opera, *L'île du rêve*, had only a critical success, but *La Carmélite*, in which Calvé took the part of Louise de la Vallière, favourite of Louis XIV, was received with enthusiasm.

Hahn wrote incidental music for several stage productions starring Sarah Bernhardt, including Racine's *Esther* and Hugo's *Méduse*. A commission from Dyagilev, *Le dieu bleu*, with a scenario by Cocteau, was a failure despite having Nijinsky in the title role. His operas *Nausicaa*, given at Monte Carlo with a cast including Marcel Journet and Robert Couzinou, and *La colombe de Bouddha*, given at Cannes in 1921, were completely overshadowed by the popularity of his *opérettes Ciboulette* and *Mozart. Ciboulette*, with its references to Murger's *La vie de bohème*, the waltzes of Métra and a libretto that was at once a parody and a celebration of the age of Offenbach, was Hahn's greatest success. His devotion to the music of Mozart did not stop him from composing *Mozart*, a pastiche of the composer's early works to fit beside Hahn's own arias written for Yvonne Printemps, who played the young Mozart *en travestie*. Subsequent *opérettes* did not achieve the same measure of popularity, although *O mon bel inconnu* contains what is probably Hahn's most infectious tune, the title song, a trio for three sopranos. His only major creation for the Paris Opéra, *Le marchand de Venise*, shows the influence of Verdi, and was successful enough to have several revivals. Reviewing the first performance, Irving Schwerké wrote, 'His orchestra, in point of its regard for voice and verb, is a model of deference. Everything seems singable, nary a syllable is covered by harmonic folderols or swamped in any of those amazing innovations of which the epoch has made such a fetish'. His music for a French *Much Ado about Nothing* failed to impress and his last opera, *Le oui des jeunes filles*, produced at the Opéra-Comique after his death, was given only 11 times and seems never to have been revived.

As a conductor Hahn specialized in Mozart's operas (*Don Giovanni* at Salzburg in 1906 with Lilli Lehmann and Maggie Teyte) and was for a time the musical director of the opera companies at Cannes and Biarritz. After World War II he became director of the Opéra in Paris and conducted several Mozart performances as well as a revival of Méhul's *Joseph*. He became chief music critic of *Le Figaro* in 1933 and was a fastidious, ironic but dedicated reviewer. His lectures on singing were gathered in his first book, *Du chant* (Paris, 1920, 2/1957; Eng. trans., as *On Singers and Singing*, London, 1990), and like his reviews and diaries provide a splendidly focussed view of music in Paris and *belle époque* society in general.

The two decades after Hahn's death saw an almost total eclipse of his music with the exception of *Ciboulette*, which has never passed from the repertory in France. However, since 1970 a new interest in his music has led to numerous performances, including revivals of *Le marchand de Venise* and *Mozart* and the first complete recording of *Ciboulette*.

See also CIBOULETTE and MARCHAND DE VENISE, LE.

first performed in Paris unless otherwise stated

L'île du rêve (idylle Polynésienne, 3, A. Alexandre and G. Hartmann, after P. Loti), OC (Favart), 23 March 1898
La Carmélite (comédie musicale, 4, C. Mendès), OC (Favart), 16 Dec 1902
La pastorale de Noël (Christmas mystery, 3, La Tourasse and de Taurines), Arts, 23 Dec 1908
Miousic (opérette, 3, P. Ferrier), Olympia, 22 March 1914, incl. music by Saint-Saëns, Lecocq, Messager and others
Nausicaa (oc, 3, R. Fauchois), Monte Carlo, 10 April 1919

Fête triomphale (3, St Georges de Bouhélier), Opéra, 14 July 1919

La colombe de Bouddha (conte lyrique, 1, A. Alexandre), Cannes, 21 March 1921

Ciboulette (opérette, 3, R. de Flers and F. de Croisset), Variétés, 7 April 1923

Mozart (comédie musicale, 3, S. Guitry), Edouard VII, 2 Dec 1925

La reine de Scheba (scène lyrique, 1, E. Fleg), Châtelet, 6 March 1926

Une revue (comédie musicale, 1, M. Donnay and H. Duvernois), Porte-St-Martin, 28 Oct 1926

Le temps d'aimer (comédie musicale, 3, P. Wolff, Duvernois and H. Delorme), Michodière, 7 Nov 1926

Brummel (opérette, 3, Rip and R. Dieudonne), Folies Wagram, 16 Jan 1931

O mon bel inconnu (comédie musicale, 3, Guitry), Bouffes-Parisiens, 5 Oct 1933

Le marchand de Venise (3, M. Zamacoïs, after W. Shakespeare), Opéra, 25 March 1935

Malvina (opérette, Donnay and Duvernois), Gaîté-Lyrique, 23 March 1935

Beaucoup de bruit pour rien (comédie musicale, 4, J. Sarment, after Shakespeare), Madeleine, March 1936

Le oui des jeunes filles (comédie lyrique, 3, Fauchois, after Moratin), orchd Büsser, OC (Favart), 21 June 1949

*

ES (J. A. Le Monnier)

M. Proust: *Lettres à Reynaldo Hahn* (Paris, 1956)

A. Morrison: 'Reynaldo Hahn', *Recorded Sound* (1966), no.21, p.11 [with discography by H. M. Barnes and V. Girard]

D. Benahan: *Reynaldo Hahn: su vida y su obra* (Caracas, 1973)

B. Gavoty: *Reynaldo Hahn* (Paris, 1976)

J. Harding: *Folies de Paris* (London, 1979)   PATRICK O'CONNOR

Haibel [Haibl, Heibel], **(Johann Petrus) Jakob** [Jacob] (*b* Graz, 20 July 1762; *d* Djakovar [now Ðakovo], 27 [?24 or 25] March 1826). Austrian composer and singer. He joined Schikaneder's company at the Freihaus-Theater auf der Wieden in or around 1789, acted and sang tenor roles and, from the mid-1790s, supplied the theatre with Singspiels and incidental music. After the death of his first wife in 1806 he left Vienna and went to Djakovar, Slavonia, as choirmaster at the cathedral. On 7 January 1807 he married Sophie Weber, thereby becoming Mozart's posthumous brother-in-law.

Haibel's first score for Schikaneder, the ballet *Le nozze disturbate*, was given no fewer than 39 times in 1795, the year of its première. His greatest success was *Der Tyroler Wastel* of 1796, to an 'opera' libretto by Schikaneder; it was given 66 times that year and 118 times in all at the Freihaus-Theater, and was also staged in innumerable other theatres. None of Haibel's other original scores even remotely equalled its success, though in 1809 the 'musical quodlibet' *Rochus Pumpernickel* began its triumphant progress: 136 performances in the Theater an der Wien between 1809 and 1843, productions in numerous Austrian and German theatres, and at least three sequels. It is not known what direct part Haibel (then a distant provincial choirmaster) took in preparing the work.

See also TYROLER WASTEL, DER.

first performed in Vienna and music lost unless otherwise stated

WJ – *Theater in der Josefstadt*
WL – *Theater in der Leopoldstadt*
WW – *Theater an der Wien*
WWD – *Freihaus-Theater auf der Wieden*

Le nozze disturbate, oder Die unterbrochene Hochzeit (ballet-pantomime, 4, G. B. Checchi), WWD, 18 May 1795, excerpt ed. G. Cappi, *Musikalisches Wochenblatt*, iii/32 (1809)

Der Einzug in das Feindesquartier, *c*1795 (Spl)

Der Tyroler Wastel (komische Oper, 3, E. Schikaneder), WWD, 14 May 1796, *D-Mbs*, ov., songs (Vienna, *c*1796), vs (Vienna, 1969)

Östreichs treue Brüder, oder Die Scharfschützen in Tirol, oder Der Landsturm (Spl, 2, Schikaneder), WWD, 25 Oct 1796 [pt 2 of Der Tyroler Wastel]

Das medizinische Konsilium (komische Oper, 2, Schikaneder), WWD, 4 March 1797

Tsching! Tsching! Tsching! (Spl, 3, Schikaneder), WW, 6 Feb 1802

Die Entstehung des Arlequins und der Arlequinette (pantomime, 2, F. Kees), WL, 1 July 1805

Der Müllertomerl, oder Die Bergmännchen (Operette, 3, after Schikaneder), WL, 25 July 1807

Rochus Pumpernickel (Quodlibet, 3, M. Stegmayer, after Molière: *Monsieur de Pourceaugnac*), WW, 28 Jan 1809, *A-Wn*, vs (Bonn, n.d.) and (Vienna, n.d.), collab. I. von Seyfried

Plays with songs: Das Jägermädchen [Act 3] (3, M. Stegmayer), WWD, 25 Sept 1798, collab. Seyfried and J. Henneberg; Astaroth der Verführer, oder Der Gürtel und die Harfe, pt 1: Ritter und Harfner (2, Perinet), WWD, 13 April 1799; Der Papagei und die Gans, oder Die zisalpinischen Perücken (3, Schikaneder), WWD, 25 May 1799; Alle neun und ins Zentrum (3, Perinet), WW, 19 Feb 1803; Das Scheibenschiessen, oder Die ausgespielten Bräute (3, Perinet), WL, 19 March 1804; Der kleine Cesar, oder Die Familie auf dem Gebirge (3, Perinet), WL, 25 July 1804; Der Hungerturm, oder Edelsinn und Barbarey der Vorzeit (3, J. A. Gleich), WL, 7 Nov 1805; Waldram von Hartenstein, oder Die Berghöhle (3, Gleich), WJ, 2 Aug 1814; Hanswurst, Doctor nolens volens (W. C. Mylius, after Molière: *Le médecin malgré lui*), WW, 22 May 1841, entr'acte music *Wn*

Music in Die Liebe macht kurzen Prozess, oder Die Heirat auf gewisse Art, WW, 24 July 1802

*

ADB (J. Kürschner)

J. Haibel: Autobiographical sketch (MS, *A-Wgm*)

I. F. Castelli: *Memoiren meines Lebens*, i (Munich, 1913)

O. E. Deutsch: 'Das Freihaus-Theater auf der Wieden', *Mitteilungen des Vereines für Geschichte der Stadt Wien*, xvi (1937), 30–73   PETER BRANSCOMBE

Haile, Eugen David (*b* Ulm, 21 Feb 1873; *d* Woodstock, NY, 14 Aug 1933). American composer of German birth. He studied at the Stuttgart Conservatory before going to the USA in 1903 as accompanist to Ludwig Hess. He also gave concerts with his wife, the singer Elise Haile, though later he was hampered by illness that prevented him from walking. In 1914 an Eugen Haile Society was formed in New York to promote his music. His first opera, *The Happy Ending* (3, Haile), which had its première at the Shubert Theatre on 21 August 1916, uses *Sprechgesang* throughout. The more conventional *Harald's Dream* (3 scenes, Haile) was produced *al fresco* in Woodstock on 13 June 1933, shortly before his death. Another opera, *Viola d'amore* (2, H. von Wolzogen), remains unperformed. Haile favoured Romantic texts, allowing the words to be heard clearly amid a musical texture influenced by Wagnerian chromaticism and restless modulation. A collection of his manuscripts comprising autograph full scores, vocal scores and papers can be found in the New York Public Library.

MICHAEL MECKNA

Haiti. For discussion of opera in Haiti *see* PORT-AU-PRINCE.

Haitink, Bernard (Johann Herman) (*b* Amsterdam, 4 March 1929). Dutch conductor. His boyhood violin training, both privately and at the Amsterdam Conservatory, as well as frequent attendance at concerts, contributed to his early success. In 1955 he was appointed principal conductor of the Netherlands Radio Philharmonic, an orchestra he had earlier played in, and in 1961 he became the youngest ever principal conductor of the Concertgebouw Orchestra. Opera conducting came much later. Though he had always disliked opera house politics, he was won over by the relaxed but intensive atmosphere of Glyndebourne

Festival Opera. His début there came in 1972 with *Die Entführung*, and was followed by *Die Zauberflöte* in 1973 and by Stravinsky's *The Rake's Progress* in 1975, an outstandingly successful production with sets by David Hockney. In 1977 he was appointed music director, succeeding John Pritchard, and over the following years conducted a wide range of repertory from Mozart and Haydn (*La fedeltà premiata*) to Prokofiev (*The Love for Three Oranges*) and Britten (*A Midsummer Night's Dream* and *Albert Herring*). He made his début at Covent Garden in 1977, conducting *Don Giovanni*, which he also directed at Glyndebourne. Ten years later, having conducted eight different operas, including new productions of *Lohengrin*, *Parsifal* and *Jenůfa*, he was appointed music director of the Royal Opera. A new *Ring* cycle was the house's principal project, and though Götz Friedrich's production was criticized, Haitink's broad, direct treatment of the score was widely praised. So too was his reading of Borodin's *Prince Igor* in 1990, another new production. His principal opera recordings have been those based on Glyndebourne productions, including Mozart's three Da Ponte operas, and those he has recorded in Munich with the Bavarian RO, including the *Ring* cycle. As in his concert work his greatest strength as an opera conductor lies in his patient concentration and unswerving determination to serve the composer's intentions, with personal mannerism reduced to a minimum.

*

A. Blyth: 'Bernard Haitink', *Opera*, xxxii (1987), 561–7
S. Mundy: *Bernard Haitink, a Working Life* (London, 1987)

EDWARD GREENFIELD

Haizinger [Haitzinger], **Anton** (*b* Wilfersdorft, Lower Austria, 14 March 1796; *d* Karlsruhe, 31 Dec 1869). Austrian tenor. He was engaged at the Theater an der Wien as *primo tenore* in 1821, making his début as Gianetto (*La gazza ladra*); he then sang Don Ottavio, Lindoro (*L'italiana in Algeri*) and Florestan (1822). Among parts written for him was that of Adolar in *Euryanthe*; Benedict described his performance in the première. He made successful visits to Prague, Pressburg (now Bratislava), Frankfurt, Mannheim, Stuttgart and Karlsruhe, where he settled in 1826. He sang in Paris (1829–30) and with the German opera company at Covent Garden (as Tamino, Florestan and Max) in 1832–3; Mount-Edgcumbe considered his voice 'very beautiful', although Chorley found it 'throaty and disagreeable'. In 1835 he visited St Petersburg and in 1841 revisited London. He established a school of dramatic singing in Karlsruhe with his wife and in 1843 published a teaching manual.

One of the finest German tenors of his generation, Haizinger contributed much to the success of *Fidelio* and of Weber's operas, especially as a partner to Wilhelmine Schröder-Devrient. The dramatist P. A. Wolff wrote to F. W. Gubitz (31 January 1826): 'To hear Haitzinger is something extraordinary ... he has not made much progress as an actor; but one forgives him everything when one considers his moving voice, his expressive delivery, his admirable technique'.

*

ES (R. Celletti)
J. Benedict: *Weber* (London, 1881)
L. Eisenberg: *Grosses biographisches Lexicon der deutschen Bühne im XIX. Jahrhundert* (Leipzig, 1903)

Hajibeyov [Gadzhibekov], **Uzeir** (**Abdul Huseyn**) (*b* Agjabedï, nr Shusha, 5/17 Sept 1885; *d* Baku, 23 Nov 1948). Azerbaijani composer. He was the founder of modern art music in Azerbaijan and of a national school of composers. His interest in his native folk music began at an early age, and by his mid-teens he was playing and singing it professionally. From 1905 he lived in Baku, where he taught and published social criticism. In 1907 he wrote *Leyli i Mejnun*, the first opera of the eastern Islamic world; in this and in his other completed operas the solo singers improvise within the limits of the indigenous *mugam* style. He went to Moscow in 1911 to study at the conservatory and also took private lessons. In 1913 he wrote a musical comedy, *Arshin mal alan* ('The Travelling Salesman'), in which he attacked the contemporary values of his homeland; numbers from this work are accepted as folk music in Azerbaijan. Hajibeyov returned to Baku in 1914, and after the October Revolution took an important role in official arts and education programmes. He edited, with Mahomayev, the first collection of Azerbaijani folksongs (1927), founded the first orchestra of Azerbaijani folk instruments (1931) and established the State Choir (1936); in 1938 he was appointed permanent director of the Baku Conservatory, which he had helped to found, and became a National Artist of the USSR.

Hajibeyov's most highly acclaimed work is the opera *Kyor-ogli* (1937), in which he achieved a fusion of Western formal principles with native melodic elements. Using music with a strongly national colouring, it tells of the rebel peasant leader and *ashug* musician Kyoroglï, depicting him as the embodiment of his people's struggle for freedom. The opera won a USSR State Prize for Hajibeyov in 1941 and has remained an important model for succeeding generations of Azerbaijani composers.

His brother Zulfugar Hajibeyov (1884–1950) was also a composer and wrote one of the earliest Azerbaijani operas, *Ashug Garib* (four acts, to his own libretto), given at the Tagiyev Theatre, Baku, on 13 May 1916. Based on a local legend about a wandering singer and drawing on regional folk music, it has held its place in the repertory.

selective list; first performed in Baku, with librettos by the composer, unless otherwise stated

Leyli i Mejnun (after Fizuli), 12/25 Jan 1908
Sheykh Sanan, 1909
Muzh i zhena [Man and Woman] (musical comedy), 1910
Ne ta, tak eta [Not that One, Then this One] (musical comedy), 1910
Rustam i Zokhrab (after Firdousi), 1910
Asli i Kerem, 1912
Shakh Abbas i Khurshid Banu, 1912
Arshin mal alan [The Travelling Salesman] (musical comedy), 14/27 Nov 1913
Garun i Leyla, 1915, unperf.
Kyor-ogli [Blind Man's Son] (M. Ordubadï), Moscow, 30 April 1937
Firuza, inc.

*

Arshin mal alan (Baku, 1938) [coll. of articles]
Opera 'Kyor-ogli' (Baku, 1938) [coll. of articles]
E. Abasova: *Opera 'Leyli i Meinun' Uzeira Hajibeyova* (Baku, 1961)
I. Abezgauz: 'Melodicheskiy stil' Uz. Gadzhibekova v opere "Kyor-ogli" ', *Uchyonïye zapiski Azerbaydzhanskoy gosudarstvennoy konservatorii* (1968), no.5, pp.3–48

YURY GABAY/STEPHEN JOHNSON

Hajiyev, (**Akhmet**) **Jevdet** (**Ismail**) [Gadzhiyev, Dzhevdet] (*b* Nukha [now Seki], 5/18 June 1917). Azerbaijani composer. He studied at the Azerbaijan State Conservatory (1935–8) and at the same time composed the first examples of the symphonic poem in Azerbaijan. In 1938 he entered the Moscow Conservatory, where he was a pupil of Alexandrov and Vasilenko. In 1945 he and Kara Karayev completed the heroic-patriotic opera *Veten* ('Fatherland'; I. Idayatzade and M. Ragim), which was performed in Baku on 4 May that year; it won a State Prize in 1946. After World War II Hajiyev returned to Moscow Conservatory for further composition studies with Shostakovich (1945–7). He was artistic director of the Baku PO (1947–8) and from 1947 on the staff of the Azerbaijan State Conservatory (rector 1957–69). Characteristic of his style are monumental forms, programmatic development, an expressive astringent polyphony and frequent recourse to the *mugam* improvisatory techniques of Azerbaijani folk music, the last giving his work its distinctive national colouring.

S. Kasimova: 'Opera *Veten* K. Karayeva i Dzh. Gadzhiyeva', *Uchyonïye zapiski Azerbaydzhanskoy gosudarstvennoy konservatorii* (1969), no.6, pp.27–53   YURY GABAY

Halasz, László (*b* Debrecen, 6 June 1905). American conductor of Hungarian birth. He studied at the Liszt Academy in Budapest with Bartók, Kodály and Ernő Dohnányi, and began his career as a répétiteur and assistant conductor at the Budapest State Opera (1928–9), the German Theatre in Prague (1929–31) and at Salzburg (1929–36). His conducting début was in a performance of Kienzl's *Der Evangelimann* at the Vienna Volksoper in 1933. He made his American début in 1937 conducting *Tristan und Isolde* at the St Louis Grand Opera and was music director there, 1938–42. In 1943 he became the first artistic and musical director of the New York City Opera, directing the inaugural performance (*Tosca*) on 21 February 1944. He spent seven fruitful but controversial years in that post until he was dismissed in 1951. From 1955 to 1958 he served as music director of the German wing at the Liceo, Barcelona. He appeared as a guest conductor in Baltimore, Chicago, Frankfurt, Montreal, Philadelphia, Rio de Janeiro and Washington, DC, in addition to maintaining an active concert career.

CORI ELLISON

Hale, Robert (*b* San Antonio, TX, 22 Aug 1943). American bass-baritone. He studied in Boston, making his début in 1966 with the Goldovsky Opera. In 1967 he joined the New York City Opera, where he sang Mozart's Figaro and Count Almaviva, Don Giovanni, Raimondo, Henry VIII (*Anna Bolena*), Oroveso, Giorgio (*I puritani*) and the Father (*Louise*). At San Diego (1978) he sang Claudius (*Hamlet*), and at Buenos Aires (1980) the four Hoffmann villains. Meanwhile, after singing the Dutchman in Stuttgart (1978), he began to take on heavier roles: Pizarro, Iago, Mephistopheles (Gounod and Boito), Scarpia and Escamillo, which he sang in Germany and at Zürich and Lisbon. He made his Covent Garden début (1988) as John the Baptist and his La Scala (1989) and Metropolitan (1990) débuts as the Dutchman. His imposing presence, great dramatic ability and strong, expressive voice make him a superb Wotan, a role he has sung at Berlin, Vienna, Geneva, Cologne and San Francisco. In 1990 he sang Pizarro at Salzburg.

ELIZABETH FORBES

Hales, Thomas. *See* D'HÈLE, THOMAS.

Halévy, (Jacques-François-)Fromental (-Elie) [Fromentin(-Elias)] (*b* Paris, 27 May 1799; *d* Nice, 17 March 1862). French composer. He was, with Meyerbeer and Auber, one of the leading composers of French opera in the period between 1830 and 1860, although only two of his 40 operas, *La Juive* and *L'éclair*, survived in the repertory into the 20th century.

His parents were Jewish, his father coming from Germany and his mother from eastern France. In 1810 Halévy entered the Paris Conservatoire where he became a pupil of Cherubini for composition. This was an important step since Cherubini showed great interest and confidence in Halévy and was able to guide his career with all his considerable influence. Halévy acknowledged a profound debt to his teacher; his brother Léon wrote: 'The teaching and friendship of Cherubini implanted in Halévy his love of great art and confirmed his instinctive repugnance to everything vulgar or shoddy'. He was also briefly a pupil of H.-M. Berton (for harmony) and Méhul. He won the Prix de Rome in 1819.

After a stay in Italy, where he composed a number of works, including the finale of an Italian opera *Marco Curzio*, he visited Vienna, where he met Beethoven. After returning to Paris he began his career as a composer for the stage, at first without making his mark, but eventually with success and public honour. He was a tireless composer of operas and led a full life as teacher and administrator as well. From 1826 to 1829 he was *chef du chant* at the Théâtre Italien, and from 1829 to 1845 he held the same post at the Opéra, the period of his greatest successes there. In 1836 he was elected to the Institut and in 1854 he became its permanent secretary, a position of considerable eminence in the field of arts and letters.

Halévy's first few operas, *Les bohémiennes*, *Les deux pavillons*, *Erostrate* and *Pygmalion*, were not produced, although *Pygmalion* was rehearsed in 1827. By that time *L'artisan* had played at the Opéra-Comique, where it enjoyed only moderate success, though it was important in being the first of Halévy's many collaborations with Vernoy de Saint-Georges, one of the ablest and most sought-after librettists of the day. The post at the Théâtre Italien brought him into contact with Maria Malibran, for whom he wrote *Clari*, an opera to an Italian text, in 1828. But his true success was with *Le dilettante d'Avignon*, played at the Opéra-Comique in 1829 and retained for many years in the repertory. Part of its success lay in Léon Halévy's skill in turning a libretto by F.-B. Hoffman into a topical satire on Italian librettos; Léon remained a faithful collaborator to the end of his life.

Having moved to the Opéra as *chef du chant*, Halévy had his ballet on Prévost's *Manon Lescaut* played there in 1830 and another ballet, *La tentation*, two years later. He also wrote four more *opéras comiques* – one of them, *Ludovic*, being the completion of an unfinished opera by Hérold – before attempting his first serious grand opera, *La Juive*. This became the greatest success of his life and the work on which his fame has rested. It received a spectacular première at the Opéra on 23 February 1835, took an instant hold on the public and became, with Meyerbeer's operas, one of the central pieces in the French repertory. Excepting the ballet *Manon Lescaut*, it was his first collaboration with Scribe (to be followed by many more) and it epitomized the type of grand opera which is associated with Véron's directorship of the Opéra. It preceded Meyerbeer's equally successful *Les Huguenots* by more than a year.

In the same year, Halévy won yet another success at the Opéra-Comique, with *L'éclair*. These two successes gave him a commanding position in the principal opera houses of Paris and unquestioned entrée to both for the rest of his life. *Guido et Ginevra* followed in 1838, to another Scribe text. The main tenor role (Guido) was sung by Duprez following his earlier success as Eléazar in *La Juive*. *Le drapier* (1840), also by Scribe, provided a mélange of the tragic and the burlesque. Two more grand operas, *La reine de Chypre* (1841) and *Charles VI* (1843), may be considered among Halévy's most successful achievements.

Le lazzarone (1844) is more nearly an *opéra comique* than a grand opera, although it was played at the Opéra. *Le Juif errant* (1852) suffers from the confinement of the far-reaching fantasy of Eugène Sue's immensely popular novel to the stage. In 1850 Halévy set an Italian translation of a Scribe libretto on Shakespeare's *The Tempest* for Her Majesty's Theatre, London; the result is uncomfortably bizarre. Despite the fact that his later works offered little that was different from the well-proven style of earlier years – or perhaps because of it – public interest in Halévy's music remained keen. *La magicienne* (1858), to another Saint-Georges libretto, treats the world of spectres and spirits with notable success, but was never revived.

Halévy's principal comic operas after *L'éclair* were *Le shérif* (1839), based on a story by Balzac, *Le guitarrero* (1841), in which a Portuguese princess marries a street guitarist, *Les mousquetaires de la reine* (1846), set amid the siege of La Rochelle, *Le val d'Andorre* (1848), set in the Pyrenees, and *Jaguarita l'Indienne* (1855), which stimulated French taste for Indian, Ceylonese and Indonesian locations.

Halévy's music is fluent and professional. The style, like Meyerbeer's, owed much to Italian music and also to Boieldieu and Auber. His works display most of the mannerisms associated with 19th-century grand opera, both French and Italian: block choruses without counterpoint, triple metres, dotted rhythms, large ensembles built out of a single dramatic moment, and a fondness for local colour, especially in *divertissements* and ballets. His harmony can be chromatic when required and he was fond of the German 6th. He had a fair gift for melody but it was impaired by monotonous phrase lengths and by a lack of concern for word stress that allowed him to let a musical pattern override the natural stresses of speech. He also lapsed too readily into repetitiousness, using self-contained four- and eight-bar units to extend the musical structure; this feature was common to Meyerbeer, Donizetti, Verdi and many contemporaries. Halévy owed many of his most powerful moments to his librettists; the successive revelations in *La Juive* perfectly exemplify Scribe's (and Halévy's) craft in contriving scenes wherein surprise and shock can generate big choral movements based on simple musical motifs, with the accumulation of voices and instruments creating a vast stage tableau.

As an orchestrator Halévy earned the praise of Berlioz and was considered an innovator, especially in his use of chromatic brass. He introduced the melophone in *Guido et Ginevra* and a whole family of saxhorns and saxtubas in *Le Juif errant*. He should be recognized as a skilled writer for woodwind, which he always handled with imagination. The pair of english horns for Eléazar's 'Rachel, quand du seigneur' in *La Juive* is a famous effect, and his use of the organ at the beginning of the

same opera, with the *Te Deum* sung off stage, is strikingly bold – an interesting anticipation of the opening of *Die Meistersinger* perhaps.

Wagner held Halévy's work in high esteem, especially *La Juive* and *La reine de Chypre*. He described him as 'frank and honest; no sly, deliberate swindler like Meyerbeer'. He drew attention to Halévy's sense of historical period, achieved without recourse to mock-antique devices: 'For my part,' he wrote, 'I have never heard dramatic music which has transported me so completely to a particular historical epoch'. Berlioz admired certain parts of what he nonetheless called 'cette misérable *Juive*' and liked *Le shérif* and *Le val d'Andorre*. His view was that Halévy's gifts were better suited to lighter genres, and it is clear that tripping rhythms, regular phrase lengths and brisk orchestration came easily to his pen. Halévy would not have wished to be found wanting in any genre and he spread his talents widely; yet they were not sufficient to ensure immortality, and even *La Juive*, though it appears in the record catalogues, has now vanished from the stage.

Halévy left a small and varied literary output which reveals his wide reading and his enquiring historical sense; he wrote on the beginnings of French opera, for example. He had the gifts of tact and social judgment, and he enjoyed his sustained success. He led an active social life, especially after his marriage in 1842 to Léonie Rodrigues, who was both rich and extravagant; their daughter married Bizet. Yet his well-balanced exterior harboured, according to Sainte-Beuve, 'an intimate sadness, a hidden wound', although he added that 'Halévy was too rich, too complex a nature, too open and communicative, too well organized in every sense, too susceptible to the pleasures of social and family life; he was a man with too many strings to his bow ever for any length of time to be profoundly unhappy'.

See also CHARLES VI; ECLAIR, L'; GUIDO ET GINEVRA; JUIVE, LA; and REINE DE CHYPRE, LA.

first performed and published in Paris unless otherwise stated

Les bohémiennes, 1819–20, unperf., lost
Marco Curzio, 1822, unperf. [finale only]
Les deux pavillons, ou Le jaloux et le méfiant, *c*1824 (oc, J. B. C. Vial), unperf.
Pygmalion, *c*1824 (opéra, 1, Patin and Arnoult), unperf.
Erostrate, *c*1825 (opéra, 3, Arnoult and L. Halévy), inc.
L'artisan (oc, 1, J.-H. Vernoy de Saint-Georges), OC (Feydeau), 30 Jan 1827 (1827)
Le roi et le batelier (oc, 1, Saint-Georges), OC (Feydeau), 8 Nov 1827, collab. L. Rifaut
Clari (op semiseria, 3, P. Giannone), Italien, 9 Dec 1828, vs (*c*1830)
Le dilettante d'Avignon (oc, 1, F.-B. Hoffman and L. Halévy), OC (Ventadour), 7 Nov 1829 (Paris and London, 1829)
Attendre et courir (oc, 1, Fulgence and Henri), OC (Ventadour), 28 May 1830, collab. H. de Ruolz
La langue musicale (oc, 1, Saint-Yves), OC (Ventadour), 11 Dec 1830 (1830)
La tentation (opéra-ballet, 5, Cavé and J. Coralli), Opéra, 20 June 1832, collab. C. Gide, excerpts (1832)
Yella, 1832 (oc, 2, Moreau and P. Duport), unperf.
Les souvenirs de Lafleur (oc, 1, P. Carmouche and C. de Courcy), OC (Bourse), 4 March 1833, vs (1834)
Ludovic (oc, 2, Saint-Georges), OC (Bourse), 16 May 1833, excerpts pubd [completion of opera by Hérold]
La Juive (opéra, 5, E. Scribe), Opéra, 23 Feb 1835 (Paris, 1836/ R1980: ERO, xxxvi)
L'éclair (oc, 3, Saint-Georges and F. A. Eugène de Planard), OC (Bourse), 16 Dec 1835 (1836)
Guido et Ginevra, ou La peste de Florence (opéra, 5, Scribe), Opéra, 5 March 1838 (1838); rev. in 4 acts, Opéra, 23 Oct 1840
Les treize (oc, 3, Scribe and Duport), OC (Bourse), 15 April 1839, vs (1839)

Le shérif (oc, 3, Scribe, after H. de Balzac), OC (Bourse), 2 Sept 1839 (1839)
Le drapier (opéra, 3, Scribe), Opéra, 6 Jan 1840
Le guitarrero (oc, 3, Scribe), OC (Favart), 21 Jan 1841 (1841)
La reine de Chypre (opéra, 5, Saint-Georges), Opéra, 22 Dec 1841
Charles VI (opéra, 5, C. Delavigne and G. Delavigne), Opéra, 15 March 1843, vs (1841), full score (c1855)
Le lazzarone, ou Le bien vient en dormant (opéra, 2, Saint-Georges), Opéra, 23 March 1844, vs (?1844)
Les mousquetaires de la reine (oc, 3, Saint-Georges), OC (Favart), 3 Feb 1846 (1846)
Les premiers pas (scène-prologue, A. Royer and G. Vaëz), Opéra-National, 15 Nov 1847, collab. Adam, Auber and Carafa
Le val d'Andorre (oc, 3, Saint-Georges), OC (Favart), 11 Nov 1848 (1848)
La fée aux roses (oc, 3, Scribe and Saint-Georges), OC (Favart), 1 Oct 1849 (1849)
La tempestà (opéra italien, 3, Giannone and Scribe, after W. Shakespeare), London, Her Majesty's, 8 June 1850, vs (?1850)
La dame de pique (oc, 3, Scribe), OC (Favart), 28 Dec 1850 (1850)
Le Juif errant (opéra, 5, Scribe and Saint-Georges, after E. Sue), Opéra, 23 April 1852, vs (1852)
Le nabab (oc, 3, Scribe and Saint-Georges), OC (Favart), 1 Sept 1853 (1853)
Jaguarita l'Indienne (oc, 3, Saint-Georges and A. de Leuven), Lyrique, 14 May 1855, vs (1855)
L'inconsolable (oc, 1), Lyrique, 13 June 1855 [perf. under pseud. Alberti]
Valentine d'Aubigny (oc, 3, J. Barbier and M. Carré), OC (Favart), 26 April 1856, vs (?1856)
La magicienne (opéra, 5, Saint-Georges), Opéra, 17 March 1858, vs (1858)
Noé (opéra, 3, Saint-Georges), Karlsruhe, 5 April 1885, inc., completed by Bizet as Le déluge (1886)
Vanina d'Ornano (opéra, 3, L. Halévy), inc.

*

H. Berlioz: notices of Halévy's operas in Le rénovateur (1 March 1835) [La Juive], (22 Dec 1835) [L'éclair]; in Revue et gazette musicale de Paris (11 March 1838) [Guido et Ginevra]; in Journal des débats (18 April 1839) [Les treize], (5 Sept 1839) [Le shérif], (9 Jan 1840) [Le drapier], (24 Jan 1841) [Le guitarrero], (26 Dec 1841) [La reine de Chypre], (3 April 1844) [Le lazzarone], (14 Nov 1848) [Le val d'Andorre], (4 Oct 1849) [La fée aux roses], (1 Jan 1851) [La dame de pique], (4 Sept 1853) [Le nabab], (19 May 1855) [Jaguarita l'Indienne], (24 March 1858) [La magicienne]; notices on La Juive and Le val d'Andorre repr. in Berlioz: Les musiciens et la musique, ed. A. Hallays (Paris, 1903)
R. Wagner: 'Bericht über eine neue Pariser Oper: La reine de Chypre von Halévy', Dresdener Abend-Zeitung (26–9 Jan 1842); Eng. trans. in Wagner: Prose Works, ed. W. A. Ellis, vii (London, 1898), 205–22
——: 'Halévy et La reine de Chypre', Revue et gazette musicale de Paris, ix (1842), 75, 100, 179, 187; Eng. trans. in Wagner: Prose Works, ed. W. A. Ellis, viii (London, 1899), 175–200
C. Saint-Saëns: Ecole buissonnière: notes et souvenirs (Paris, 1913)
M. Curtiss: 'Fromental Halévy', MQ, xxxix (1953), 196–214
J. W. Klein: 'Jacques Fromental Halévy (1799–1862)', MR, xxiii (1962), 13–19
H. C. Wolff: 'Halévy als Kunst- und Musikschriftsteller', Musicae scientiae collectanea: Festschrift Karl Gustav Fellerer (Cologne, 1973), 697–706
J. W. Klein: 'Halévy's La Juive', MT, cxiv (1973), 140–41
K. Pendle: Eugène Scribe and French Opera of the Nineteenth Century (Ann Arbor, 1979)
L'avant-scène opéra, no.100 (1987) [La Juive issue]
H. R. Cohen, ed.: The Original Staging Manuals for Twelve Parisian Operatic Premières/Douze livrets de mise en scène lyrique datant des créations parisiennes (Stuyvesant, NY, 1991) [incl. production book for La Juive] HUGH MACDONALD

Halévy, Ludovic (b Paris, 1 Jan 1834; d Paris, 8 May 1908). French librettist. He belonged to a distinguished Jewish family; his uncle was the composer Fromental Halévy, and his father, Léon, was respected in literary circles. On leaving the renowned Lycée Louis-le-Grand in Paris he had little difficulty, despite an unimpressive academic record, in obtaining civil service appointments. Plainly he had both ability and the benefits of patronage. His interests, however, lay in the theatre. Initially he adopted the pseudonym Jules Servières, and later, in 1858, when working with Crémieux on the libretto for Orphée aux enfers (with which Offenbach was to have such a significant success), he is said to have insisted that the credit and the royalties should go to his collaborator; at a time when his prospects in colonial administration were especially promising, he was afraid his reputation might be blighted by association with opéra comique. Both as a playwright and as a librettist Halévy generally worked with collaborators. However, it was his association with Henri Meilhac that proved decisive; after the triumph of La belle Hélène in 1864 they went on to provide Offenbach with some of his most brilliant librettos. In 1865 Halévy abandoned his career in the public service and worked with Meilhac until the latter's death in 1897.

It was a partnership of contrasting personalities, with Meilhac the more ebullient and fanciful, and Halévy the more staid and craftsmanlike. Their achievement lay to a considerable extent in exploiting to the full the existing forms of opéra comique, with its combination of music and speech, its transparently artificial plot and its topicality, which often found expression in irreverent parody. Pace is essential in their librettos, and opportunities are regularly created for brilliant displays of costume and scenery. Situations are contrived for concerted numbers, especially at the ends of acts, and solos and ensembles are both energetic and varied. The versification of the lyrics is deft, rhyme and vocabulary are amusing, and sentiments are expressed clearly. The spoken dialogues are crisp and laconic, sometimes colloquial and never pompous except in jest. With these means Halévy and Meilhac mocked everything they observed around them in a Second Empire society that took itself too seriously: the government, the military, the Church, money-making, fast living of every sort, and even foreigners. Although the satiric element in these librettos has been stressed by some, the mode is generally festive (or carnivalesque), with the criticism offered as humorous impertinence rather than subversive challenge. It was not the serious side of La belle Hélène or La Grande-Duchesse de Gérolstein that made so great an impression at the time; they were criticized not for satirizing the age but for reflecting it all too accurately.

Carmen, written for Bizet, who was married to Geneviève Halévy (the daughter of Fromental and the cousin of Ludovic), is perhaps the most famous product of the Halévy-Meilhac collaboration, but not a very typical one, even though it was cast in the form of an opéra comique. There is some justice in the complaint that the remarkable style of Mérimée's original narrative is lost. Halévy also wrote novels (La famille Cardinal of 1883 was the source for A. Willemetz and P. Brach's libretto of the opera Les petites Cardinal by Honegger in collaboration with Ibert, 1938). His eminence as a literary figure was recognized when he was elected to the Académie Française in 1884.

Entrez, messieurs, mesdames (prol., with F.-J. Méry), Offenbach, 1855; Une pleine eau (opérette), J. Costé and Comte d'Osmond, 1855; Madame Papillon (bouffe musicale), Offenbach, 1855; Bata-clan (chinoiserie musicale), Offenbach, 1855; Le Docteur Miracle (opérette, with L. Battu), Bizet, 1857 (Lecocq, 1857); L'opéra aux fenêtres, L. G. C. Gastinel, 1857; Orphée aux enfers (opéra bouffe, with H.-J. Crémieux), Offenbach, 1858; Polichinelle dans le monde (opérette, with W. Busnach), attrib. Offenbach, 1859

Voici le jour (opérette), J. Ward, 1859; *Le carnaval des revues* (with
E. Grangé and P.-E.-F. Gille), Offenbach, 1860; *Un mari sans le
savoir*, Saint-Rémy, 1860; *La chanson de Fortunio* (oc, with
Crémieux), Offenbach, 1861; *Le pont des soupirs* (opéra bouffe,
with Crémieux), Offenbach, 1861; *M. Choufleuri restera chez lui
le ...* (opéra bouffe, ?with Crémieux and E. de l'Epine), Offenbach
and Saint-Rémy, 1861; *Les eaux d'Ems* (opérette, with
Crémieux), Delibes, 1861
La baronne de San Francisco (opérette, with Crémieux), L. H. J.
Caspers, 1861; *Le roman comique* (opéra bouffe, with
Crémieux), Offenbach, 1861; *Une fin de bail* (oc, with Crémieux
[collab. as P. d'Arcy]), P. J. A. Varney, 1862; *Jacqueline* (opérette,
with Crémieux [collab. as P. d'Arcy]), Offenbach, 1862; *La belle
Hélène* (opéra bouffe, with H. Meilhac), Offenbach, 1864;
Barbe-bleue (opéra bouffe, with Meilhac), Offenbach, 1866; *La
vie parisienne* (opéra bouffe, with Meilhac), Offenbach, 1866
La Grande-Duchesse de Gérolstein (opéra bouffe, with Meilhac),
Offenbach, 1867; *Le château à Toto* (opéra bouffe, with
Meilhac), Offenbach, 1868; *La Périchole* (opéra bouffe, with
Meilhac), Offenbach, 1868; *La diva* (opéra bouffe, with
Meilhac), Offenbach, 1869; *Les brigands* (opéra bouffe, with
Meilhac), Offenbach, 1869; *Pomme d'api* (oc, with Busnach),
Offenbach, 1873; *Tricoche et Cacolet* (with Meilhac), Suppé,
1873
Madame l'archiduc (oc, with Meilhac and A. Millaud), Offenbach,
1874; *Carmen* (with Meilhac, after P. Mérimée), Bizet, 1875; *La
boulangère a des écus* (opéra bouffe, with Meilhac), Offenbach,
1875; *La créole* (oc, with Meilhac and Millaud), Offenbach,
1875; *Le petit duc* (oc, with Meilhac), Lecocq, 1878; *La petite
mademoiselle* (oc, with Meilhac), Lecocq, 1879; *Janot* (oc, with
Meilhac), Lecocq, 1881; *La roussotte* (oc, with Meilhac and Millaud), M. Boullard, Lecocq and Hervé, 1881

*

E. C. Hansen: *Ludovic Halévy: a Study of Frivolity and Fatalism in
Nineteenth-Century France* (Lanham, MD, 1987)

CHRISTOPHER SMITH

Halifax. City in Canada, capital of Nova Scotia. Its
establishment as a British settlement and military base in
1749 meant that there was an active musical life from an
early stage. Opera was first heard there in 1790, when
The Duenna, by the Linleys, was given; this was
followed by Shield's *Rosina* (1794), Dibdin's *The
Waterman* and *Love in the City*, Storace's *No Song, No
Supper* and Samuel Arnold's *The Surrender of Calais*
(1805) and *The Review* (1806). Grétry's *Richard
Coeur-de-lion* was also produced, in 1798 at the
Theatre Royal. Years later, the Academy of Music, an
auditorium opened in 1877, gave light operas such as
The Mikado (1887) and *Martha* (1896); it was
demolished in 1929. To mark the bicentenary of the city
in 1949, the Nova Scotia Opera Association was formed
by Mariss Vētra, director of the opera course at the
Halifax Conservatory. The first production was of *Don
Giovanni*, and during the seven years of the associa-
tion's existence *Le nozze di Figaro*, *Orfeo ed Euridice*,
Cavalleria rusticana, *Rigoletto*, *Faust* and Trevor
Jones's *The Broken Ring* (1953, the première) were
performed, most of them at the Capitol Theatre. Since
1958 the Canadian Opera Company (from Toronto)
has visited Halifax on tour. The première of Dennis
Farrell's *The Birthday of the Infanta* was given at
Dalhousie University in 1979.

*

H. Kallmann: *A History of Music in Canada 1534–1914* (Toronto,
1960)   ELIZABETH FORBES

Halka. Opera in four (originally two) acts by STANISŁAW
MONIUSZKO to a libretto by Włodzimierz Wolski after a
story from Kazimierz Wójcicki's *Stary gawędy i obrazy*
('Legends and Pictures'); concert performance, Vilnius,
1 January 1848 (staged Vilnius, 18 February 1854);
standard, revised version, Warsaw, Wielki Theatre, 1
January 1858.

Stolnik *a nobleman*	bass
Dziemba *Stolnik's steward*	bass
Janusz *a young nobleman*	baritone
Zofia *Stolnik's daughter*	soprano
Halka *a peasant girl*	soprano
Jontek *a mountaineer*	tenor
Piper	baritone
Villager	tenor

Stolnik's guests, villagers

Setting Southern Poland in the late 18th century

Moniuszko met the poet Włodzimierz Wolski during a
visit to Warsaw in September 1846. He read Wolski's
poem *Halska*, based on a story by Kazimierz Wójcicki,
and asked the poet to prepare a libretto on the theme of
the poem. The original two-act version of the opera was
completed in Vilnius in May 1847 but was rejected by
the Wielki Theatre in Warsaw, probably because its
theme of class conflict was considered politically inflammatory. The first, concert, performance was
organized by the composer and given with amateur
singers and players.

In 1856 Moniuszko made several changes and additions to the opera, making Jontek a tenor rather than a
baritone role and adding the duet for Jontek and Janusz
(Act 2 of the standard version) and the Highlander
Dances (Act 3 of the standard version). When the Wielki
Theatre finally agreed in July 1857 to stage *Halka*, the
composer expanded the work to its present four-act version, subdividing each of the original acts into two. The
further additions were as follows: Act 1, Stolnik's
polonaise aria and a concluding orchestral mazurka;
Act 2, an orchestral prelude and Halka's opening aria;
Act 3, an orchestral prelude; Act 4, an orchestral pre-
lude and Jontek's opening aria. Wolski again provided
the text for the new material. The première of this, the
standard version of *Halka*, took place at the Wielki
Theatre to immediate acclaim with Wilhelm Troszel as
Stolnik, Jan Stysiński as Dziemba, Aloizy Żółkowski as
Janusz, Cornelia Quattrini as Zofia, Paulina Rivoli as
Halka and Julian Dobrski as Jontek. The director was
Leopold Matuszyński and the conductor, Jan Quattrini.
The popularity of *Halka* was such that it was given 36
times in its first year and 500 times by 1900. Productions in Polish theatres outside Warsaw were first
performed in 1866, Kraków; 1873, Poznań; 1877,
Łódź; 1899, Bydgoszcz; 1920, Bytom; 1920, Katowice;
1945, Wrocław; and 1949, Gdańsk. It was given in
Prague (conducted by Smetana) in 1868, in Moscow in
1869 and in St Petersburg in 1870, and more recently in
cities including Vienna in 1926, Chicago in 1934, Berlin
in 1936, Helsinki in 1936, Jerusalem in 1942 and
Budapest in 1949.

ACT 1 *The drawing-room of Stolnik's manor house,
near Kraków* The overture introduces several of the
themes used in the opera. The introductory Andante
presents the theme associated with Halka's sorrow and
culminates in a *largo* passage which returns in the final
act just before her suicide. The main body of the movement (*agitato*) has a two-part structure with concluding
Presto, akin to many Rossini overtures. Of the three
themes in the exposition, the second appears in the
noblemen's drinking chorus in Act 1 and the third
accompanies Halka's pleas to Jontek in Act 2. The
bridge between exposition and recapitulation introduces

Characters from an early production of Moniuszko's 'Halka'

a theme from Jontek's G minor aria in Act 2 and the theme associated with Janusz's guilt.

The curtain rises on a betrothal party in Stolnik's manor house. Stolnik's daughter Zofia has become engaged to a young nobleman, Janusz, and the guests wish the couple happiness and long life in a colourful choral polonaise. As the guests move to another room, Janusz and Zofia are left with Stolnik. In a terzetto they ask his blessing on their engagement but are interrupted by a distant voice, which Janusz recognizes as that of Halka, a village girl whom he has seduced and abandoned; she sings a simple Krakovian folksong. Although an ensemble, the terzetto has musical affinities with the typical cavatina-cabaletta designs of early 19th-century Italian opera. Janusz is left alone to give vent to his conflicting emotions, fear of the consequences of Halka's arrival and guilt over his treatment of her. This short strophic romance is his only solo item in the opera. Halka enters singing her folksong, as yet unaware of Janusz's betrayal. She questions him about his intentions, but he answers evasively and arranges a further meeting, fearing that they will be discovered. The folksong leads into a multi-sectional duet of considerable formal complexity and dramatic power. The opening Allegro depicts Halka's rapturous greeting and Janusz's evasive response in an extended ternary movement. This leads to an arioso section in which Janusz expresses his remorse through one of the opera's several recurring themes. A *largo* section in a chromatic C major is an expression of tenderness which culminates in affirmations of mutual love in the final cabaletta. The layout of the entire sequence and its skilful dramatic pacing are reminiscent of an extended scena in Rossini or Donizetti. In the last scene, we return to the festivities of the betrothal party, as Stolnik and the guests drink the health of the young couple. The noblemen's drinking chorus, possibly inspired by some of the choruses in *Der Freischütz*, was the final number of the original Act 1. Stolnik's rather conventional polonaise aria and the lively concluding mazurka were added when Moniuszko revised the work in 1857.

ACT 2 *The garden of Stolnik's manor house* The prelude prefigures much of the early part of the act, referring to Halka's 'sorrow' theme, to the main theme of her opening aria, to the festivities continuing inside

the manor house and to Jontek's aria. Throughout the act the music is continuous. Halka has returned to the garden of the manor house, haunted by a sense of Janusz's presence within. Her G minor aria was described by Bülow as 'a little masterpiece, full of warmth and tenderness'. It is really a double aria, with the opening cavatina enclosing a nostalgic middle section in the major and the cabaletta leading directly into the next number. Jontek, a mountaineer from Halka's village – himself in love with Halka – appears and warns her of Janusz's deceit, begging her to return to the village. His G minor aria following Halka's recitative is of a folk-bravura character, with *krakowiak* rhythms which are especially strong in the second section.

One of the main dramatic scenes of the opera, the finale begins with a brief impassioned orchestral prelude, followed by three extended ensemble numbers. The first is a duet between Halka and Jontek (repeated with chorus), in which the third overture theme is heard: Halka, in distress, knocks at the door of the manor house. Janusz appears and reprimands Jontek for disturbing the celebrations. As Halka faints Jontek turns on Janusz and in a powerful multi-sectional duet accuses him of deserting her. (This number was added for the Warsaw première.) Halka recovers and names Janusz as the father of her child. In the final sextet with chorus a crowd gathers, but Janusz persuades them that she is mad. His steward Dziemba is ordered to drive the intruders away.

ACT 3 *Halka's village in the Tatra mountains* The first part of the prelude was added for the Warsaw première and consists mainly of elaborations of Halka's folksong. The original prelude follows, a brief movement in which we hear the bells ringing for Vespers. The entire act is really an extended scenic tableau in the manner of French grand opera; there is no significant dramatic action. In the opening chorus the villagers come out from Vespers and discuss the forthcoming wedding of Janusz. The music alternates a solemn style appropriate to the occasion with lively dance-based sections anticipating the festivities. Next follow the Highlander Dances; this ballet, added for the revised version of 1856, is the centrepiece of the act. The dances are based on the distinctive folk music of the Tatra highlands of southern Poland, which had already become familiar on the operatic stage in Warsaw through Jan Stefani's *Cud mniemnany* ('The Supposed Miracle') of 1794, a Singspiel enormously popular with Polish audiences in the early 19th century. In a duet with chorus, Jontek and Halka arrive and relate the events at the manor house to a sympathetic crowd. An alternation of solos rather than a true duet, this movement contains some of the most foursquare and conventional material in the opera, and is curiously at odds with the vitality of the preceding dances. In the finale, a villager spots a black crow, regarded as a bad omen. To Halka's distress, a wedding procession is heard in the distance. A semi-fugal chorus, with interjections from Jontek, Halka and the Villager, brings the act to a close.

ACT 4 *The square in front of the village church* A piper is playing a cheerful melody in the village square. Jontek asks for a dumka (lament), and sings of his grief over Halka. The slow mazurka (*kujawiak*) rhythms of this lament are the foundation for some of the most expressive and beautiful solo vocal writing in *Halka*. The wedding procession arrives; as it passes Zofia sees Halka's distress and innocently questions her. Halka tries to explain her predicament, but the wedding procession then enters the church. The chorus is based on a Polish folksong, and it gives way to a Rossinian quintet accompanied by chorus and a trio for Stolnik, Janusz and Zofia, before resuming as the procession enters the church. There is a short duettino in which Jontek once more tries to convince Halka of Janusz's deceit, while she still proclaims her love for him. As the choir sings Halka resolves to set fire to the church, but relents as she hears the music. She laments her child, who died of starvation, but still declares her love for Janusz. This is an effective scena, powerfully alternating the choral hymn with Halka's increasingly demented dramatic recitatives and her poignant *preghiera*, an italianate cavatina notable for its solo cello accompaniment. Halka now resolves in a cantilena to kill herself and commends her soul to God. She rushes to the edge of a precipice and hurls herself over before Jontek can stop her. As the wedding procession emerges from the church Jontek confronts Janusz with news of her death. In some ways the opera ends ambivalently. Despite the tragedy, the final section is an affirmative D major chorus, as the villagers are forced by Dziemba to sing in praise of the Lord and Lady. It is difficult to be sure if this is an ironic play on different levels of meaning or simply a response to the censor.

*   *   *

In Poland *Halka* is as popular today as it was over a hundred years ago. It is regularly performed at the Wielki Theatre, Warsaw, and can also be heard periodically at opera houses in the provinces. Clearly this reception transcends issues of musical quality. The work has become for many a powerful national symbol, and its lively dance movements and tuneful arias have acquired something of the popularity and even the status of a folk art. Historically it may be regarded as the first Polish 'grand opera', comparable in a way to Glinka's *A Life for the Tsar* and Smetana's *Dalibor*. Yet, unlike those works, *Halka* has remained a product for home consumption only. Its characteristic blend of conservative italianate melodic idioms and Polish national dance rhythms at times results in music of lively charm, but also courts mediocrity, allowing the well-tried formula to act as a substitute for genuine creative vitality.

JIM SAMSON

Hall, Janice (*b* San Francisco, 28 Sept 1953). American soprano. In 1977 she took several parts in Cavalli's *Egisto* with the Wolf Trap Opera Company and sang Zerlina at San Diego. For the New York City Opera (1978–81) she sang Servilia (*La clemenza di Tito*) and Anne Page (*Die lustigen Weiber von Windsor*). Engaged at the Cologne Opera from 1982, she has also appeared in Washington, DC, Houston, Santa Fe, Tel-Aviv, Drottningholm, Venice and Salzburg, where she sang Fortune in Henze's version of Monteverdi's *Il ritorno d'Ulisse in patria* (1985). Her repertory includes Callisto, Poppaea (*Agrippina*), Dalinda (*Ariodante*), Pamina, Elisetta (*Il matrimonio segreto*), Rosina, Norina, Oscar, Nannetta, Violetta and Lauretta. In 1989 she sang Fanny (*La cambiale di matrimonio*) and Marianna (*Signor Bruschino*) at Schwetzingen. She is a most musical singer and has a charming voice.

ELIZABETH FORBES

Hall, Sir Peter (Reginald Frederick) (*b* Bury St Edmunds, 22 Nov 1930). English director. He was educated at Cambridge and directed his first West End play, the English-language première of *Waiting for Godot*, in 1955. He was director of the Royal Shakespeare Company (1960–68), and of the National Theatre (1973–88). In 1969 he was made joint director (with Colin Davis) of the Royal Opera, an appointment due to take effect from September 1971; but he resigned in the summer of 1971 before officially taking up the post. He was artistic director of Glyndebourne Festival Opera from 1984 to 1990. He was made a CBE in 1963, and knighted in 1977.

His first opera production was the première of John Gardner's *The Moon and Sixpence* (1957, Sadler's Wells), but the first to catch the public eye was the British stage première of *Moses und Aron* (1965, Covent Garden), in which the presence of a cow and, until quite late in rehearsals, a camel, not to mention four seminaked virgins, ensured that the production received plenty of publicity in the popular press. Neither the Schoenberg nor his fine productions for the Royal Opera of *Die Zauberflöte* (1966) and *Tristan und Isolde* (1971) were easy to revive for technical reasons, but his popular staging of *Yevgeny Onegin* (1971) remained in the repertory for 18 years.

His first Glyndebourne production was *La Calisto* (1970), which led to *Il ritorno d'Ulisse in patria* (1972) and *L'incoronazione di Poppea* (1984), all three in very free realizations by Raymond Leppard, which nevertheless did much to make early Venetian opera accessible to a lay audience. The role of Poppaea was one of several sung in Hall's productions by his then wife, Maria Ewing. His most valuable work at Glyndebourne, however, where he enjoyed his most consistent success in opera, was centred on his outstanding Mozart-Da Ponte productions: *Figaro* (1973), *Don Giovanni* (1977) and *Così fan tutte* (1978). His Britten productions – *A Midsummer Night's Dream* (1981) and *Albert Herring* (1985) – were also much admired. A projected Verdi cycle faltered after only three productions, and his reworking of the Mozart triptych was brought to a premature end by his sudden resignation as artistic director.

His work outside the UK has found less favour. Success has eluded him at the Metropolitan in New York (*Macbeth, Carmen*), and his semi-naturalistic *Ring* at Bayreuth (1983) was savaged by the European press but appreciated by the public. His most notable American production has been *Salome* (1986, Los Angeles), designed, like so many of his successes, by John Bury, with whom he has enjoyed a most fruitful partnership. He has also been closely associated with Michael Tippett, staging the premières of *The Knot Garden* (1970, Covent Garden) and *New Year* (1989, Houston).

Hall's generally representational approach to opera is based on fidelity to the text (his Mozart triptych was given without cuts) and sobriety almost to a fault – his *Così fan tutte* was thought by many not to be funny enough. His adherence to the original stage directions (for example, at the end of Act 1 of *Don Giovanni*) seemed particularly daring, and caught more than one Mozart specialist on the hop. His scrupulously faithful productions emerge from, as he puts it, joint discovery of the work during a long rehearsal period, which sometimes makes his singers impatient; the productions, however, have often brought startling revelations in their wake, none more so than *Fidelio* (1979, Glyndebourne), whose roots in French *opéra comique* were exposed greatly to the advantage of the dramaturgy of a work traditionally subjected to heavily romantic and needlessly epic interpretations.

For illustration *see* BURY, JOHN.

H. Rosenthal: 'Midsummer Reflections on *The Knot Garden*', *Opera*, xxi (1970), 1090–93 [interview]
J. Higgins: *The Making of an Opera: Don Giovanni at Glyndebourne* (London, 1978)
M. Loppert: 'Travelling from Z-A', *Opera*, xxxv (1984), 596–603, 715–21 [interview]   RODNEY MILNES

Hallam, Isabella. *See* MATTOCKS, ISABELLA.

Halle. City in eastern Germany, on the Saale river. In the second half of the 17th century it was the residence of Duke August of Saxony; as administrator of the archbishopric of Magdeburg, he made it his seat from 1638. The court was the scene of considerable activity in the field of early German opera. *Die Hochzeit der Thetis* and *Charimunda* by Philipp Stolle (musical director of the Hofoper, 1654–60) were first performed in 1654 and 1658 respectively. David Pohle also worked in Halle, from 1660 onwards, and had many of his operas (now lost) first performed there, as did J. P. Krieger (1677–80). Singspiels with solo and choral interludes and opera-ballets on pastoral or mythological themes were the favoured types of theatrical entertainment in this period. Opera flourished again under the university music director Daniel Gottlob Türk, who included concert performances of opera and Singspiel in public concerts from 1780 onwards. In the early 19th century the Weimar court theatre company gave guest performances of operas by Cherubini, Mozart, Paer and Wranitzky (1811–14). Subsequent touring groups included the court theatre company of the Duke of Anhalt-Bernburg (1842–4), which for a while numbered among its members Albert Lortzing as conductor, and Richard Wagner's brother Albert.

The Stadttheater, an imposing building designed by Heinrich Seeling, was opened on 9 October 1886 with Schiller's dramas *Wallensteins Lager* and *Piccolomini*. The opera company saw its first heyday under Max Richards (1897–1915), who replaced the town band by an orchestra especially for the theatre. In 1910 *The Ring* was performed in its original Bayreuth version, as well

as *Die Meistersinger* in the Munich festival version. Graener's *Narrengericht* had its première in 1916. After World War I, works by Richard Strauss, Pfitzner, Schreker and Schoeck (*Das Wandbild*, first performed 1921) were heard for the first time in Halle. Musical directors included Erich Band (1924), Johannes Schüler (1932), Bruno Vondenhoff (1933) and Richard Kraus (1937). The theatre suffered war damage in March 1945 and was reopened as the Theater des Friedens (843 seats) with a production of *Fidelio* on 31 March 1951. It was renovated in 1968 as the Landestheater Halle. The singers Irmgard Arnold and Anny Schlemm and the designer Rudolf Heinrich were among the company at this time. In 1950 Horst-Tanu Margraf took over the opera's musical administration and, together with the director Heinz Rückert (1951–5) and the dramatist Waltraud Lewin (1961–74), started the annual Handel festivals held at the beginning of June since 1952, mounting the operas of Handel (born in Halle in 1685) in newly edited versions. With this emphasis, the theatre joined the revival movement that had begun in Göttingen in the 1920s, and had indeed made its mark in Halle earlier, with productions of *Orlando* (1922), *Rodelinda* (1925), *Giulio Cesare* (1929), *Ottone* (1935), *Tamerlano* (1939) and *Agrippina* (1943; the first performance in Germany, in the adaptation by H. C. Wolff). The Landestheater, which is also used for plays, now stages three or four opera productions a season, one of which is usually a Handel opera. Margraf was succeeded by Thomas Sanderling, Volker Rohde (1976–9) and Christian Kluttig (1979–90). The opera company also performs in the Goethe Theatre at Bad Lauchstädt and in studio theatres.

W. Serauky: *Musikgeschichte der Stadt Halle* (Halle and Berlin, 1935–43)
——: 'Halles Opernpflege in der Vergangenheit', *50 Jahre Stadttheater Halle* (Halle, 1936)
K. Sasse, W. Serauky and W. Siegmund-Schultze: *Halle als Musikstadt* (Halle, 1954)
W. Siegmund-Schultze: 'Report from Halle: the Handel Opera Renaissance', *CMc* (1968), no.7, pp.68–74   DIETER HÄRTWIG

Hallén, (Johannes) Andreas (*b* Göteborg, 22 Dec 1846; *d* Stockholm, 11 March 1925). Swedish composer. Between 1866 and 1871 he studied in Leipzig with Reinecke, in Munich with Rheinberger and in Dresden with Julius Rietz. Back in Sweden he was conductor of the Filharmoniska Sällskapet (1885–95) and at the Royal Opera (1892–7), as well as founder and conductor of the Sydsvenska Filharmoniska Sällskapet (1902–7); from 1909 to 1919 he taught composition at the Stockholm Conservatory.

Hallén was an accomplished composer. His earlier works show traces of Schumann and of Swedish folk music but his style soon moved towards that of Liszt and Wagner; he argued energetically in favour of the ideals of Wagnerian music drama, with which he was deeply sympathetic. His operas, which are conceived with undeniable dramatic skill, use Wagnerian models: historical topics, leitmotifs and a richly scored orchestral sound.

MSS in S-Skma
Harald der Wiking (3, H. Herrig), Leipzig, 16 Oct 1881, vs (Berlin, 1883); Swed. trans. as Harald Viking, Stockholm, 18 Feb 1894
Häxfällan (2, F. Hedberg), Stockholm, Royal, 16 March 1896; rev. as Valborgsmässan (3, rev. E. von Enzberg), Stockholm, 15 March 1902
Waldemarsskatten [Waldemar's Treasure] (4, A. Klinckowström), Stockholm, 8 April 1899, vs (Stockholm, c1900)

SBL (A. Halén)

T. Norlind: 'Andreas Hallén', *Ur nutidens musikliv*, iii (1922), 1–7

M. Pergament: 'Andreas Hallén: Wagnerianen', *Svenska tonsättare* (Stockholm, 1943), 58–61   AXEL HELMER

Hallin, Margareta (*b* Karlskoga, 20 Feb 1931). Swedish soprano. She studied at the Royal College of Music, Stockholm, and became a member of the Royal Opera there in 1956. In 1957 and 1960 she appeared at Glyndebourne as the Queen of Night; her repertory at that time included Gilda, Violetta, Konstanze, Zerbinetta and Handel's Alcina. In 1959 she created the Blind Poetess in Blomdahl's *Aniara*, repeating the role at Edinburgh the same year and at Covent Garden in 1960. She sang Anne Trulove in the Swedish première of *The Rake's Progress* (1961) and created Thérèse in Lars Johan Werle's *Drömmen om Thérèse* (1964), and took part in the première of Hans Gefors's *Christina* (1986), all in Stockholm. While retaining the vocal agility of a coloratura soprano, she undertook parts of a more dramatic nature: Leonora (*Il trovatore*), Aida, Elisabeth de Valois (*Don Carlos*), Mathilde (*Guillaume Tell*) and Donna Anna, as well as the four heroines of *Les contes d'Hoffmann*. In 1973 she sang the Queen Mother in G. J. Vogler's *Gustaf Adolf och Ebba Brahe* at Drottningholm, where she also sang Clytemnestra in Haeffner's *Electra* (1991).   ELIZABETH FORBES

Hallstein, Ingeborg (*b* Munich, 23 May 1937). German soprano. She made her début in 1956 at Passau as Musetta and in 1959 became a member of the Staatsoper in Munich. In 1960 she sang Rosina in *La finta semplice* at Salzburg; in 1962 she sang the Queen of Night at the Theater an der Wien, Vienna, and at Covent Garden. She sang in all the major cities of Europe and created Autonoe in Henze's *The Bassarids* (1966, Salzburg). Her repertory included Konstanze, Fiordiligi, Susanna, Norina, Marie (*Zar und Zimmermann*), Aennchen (*Der Freischütz*), Violetta, Gilda, Nedda, Sophie and Zerbinetta, the role which best displayed her brilliant coloratura technique. Since 1981 she has been professor of singing at the Musikhochschule in Würzburg.   ELIZABETH FORBES

Hallström, Ivar Christian (*b* Stockholm, 5 June 1826; *d* Stockholm, 11 April 1901). Swedish composer. Trained as a pianist, he was self-taught as a composer. He studied law in Uppsala and was appointed librarian to Prince Oscar (later King Oscar II). His connection with the court aroused envy in the musical establishment (see Lindgren), but he won considerable success among wider audiences with his operas and his songs, which account for the bulk of his output. He was the only prominent opera composer in Sweden in the 19th century.

After contributing a duet to Prince Gustaf's *Hvita frun på Drottningholm* (1847), Hallström made his operatic début with a romantic operetta, *Hertig Magnus och sjöjungfrun* (1867). This was the first of the five works on which he collaborated with the librettist Frans Hedberg to produce the most successful operatic works in 19th-century Sweden. Their next opera, *Den bergtagna* (1874), was performed 84 times up to 1909 and succeeded Naumann's *Gustaf Wasa* (1786) as the Swedish national opera. In it the heroine, rebelling against a planned marriage, falls victim to a stranger revealed to be the Mountain King. Hallström's dramatic gifts are fully revealed in this opera. He was accused of

being eclectic, but was able through his use of melody to establish characters and their relationships; this may reflect his study of Wagner. The combination of a strong French influence, especially of Gounod, and his striking gift for writing in a folk style led him to a personal dramatic and musical language that is exceptional in Swedish Romantic music. His colourful orchestration and the exquisite use of chromaticism in his melodies create impressive moments that are reminiscent of Wagner and Verdi. The dance tune from Act 3 of *Hertig Magnus* was recorded as a folktune in Sweden in the 1960s; this shows how natural was his imitation of folk music.

In *Vikingarne* (1877) the musical style is more refined and varied. The work is set in Normandy during the ravages of the Vikings, and Hallström used his almost impressionistic orchestration to portray the French while giving the Vikings harsh Nordic music. Folklike music is less in evidence here, and there is some influence of Wagner's *Tristan*, especially in the music highlighting the love between the Viking Rolf and the Norman queen Isaura. The melodic writing has a depth and intensity never before heard in Swedish opera, and the love duet in Act 2 in particular shows Hallström at the height of his powers.

When in 1881 Hedberg left the Royal Opera, where he had worked both as librettist and director, the collaboration stopped. In Hallström's subsequent operas decline is perceptible: the librettos are on a lower level, and the music becomes rhetorical and superficial. But in his unperformed late opera *Liten Karin* (1897), again to a libretto by Hedberg, Hallström showed that his creative powers were still at a high level. In this story of the mentally weak King Erik XIV of Sweden and his young queen Karin Månsdotter, he provides a touching portrait of the conflict between power and love.

Hallström's operas have been revived after nearly 80 years' neglect: in 1986 *Den bergtagna* was given at Umeå by Norrlandsoperan, who also performed it at the York Festival in 1988; the performance was televised in the same year. *Hertig Magnus och sjöjungfrun* was performed by the International Vadstena Academy in 1988 and broadcast by Swedish television in 1990.

first performed at Stockholm, Royal Opera, unless otherwise stated; vocal scores published in Stockholm; autograph MSS (both full scores and vocal scores) in S-Skma unless otherwise stated

Hertig Magnus och sjöjungfrun [Duke Magnus and the Mermaid] (romantic operetta, 3, F. Hedberg), 28 Jan 1867

Den förtrollande katten [The Enchanted Cat] (fairy play, 3, rev. Hedberg), 20 April 1869

Mjölnarvargen (operetta, 1, after E. Cormon and M. Carré: *Le diable au moulin*), 18 Feb 1871, vs (1871)

Den bergtagna [The Bride of the Mountain King] (romantic op, 3, Hedberg), 20 May 1874, vs (1874)

Vikingarne [The Vikings] (romantic op, 3, Hedberg), 6 June 1877

Silverringen [The Silver Ring], 1870 (operetta, 1, after J. Barbier and I. Battu), 13 Dec 1880

Rolf Krake [Act 1] (Old Norse impromptu operetta, 2, E. Forsberg), 1880, vs (1880) [Act 2 by V. Svedbom]

Nero, 1882, lost

Jaguarita l'Indienne (oc, 3, J.-H. Vernoy de Saint-Georges and A. de Leuven), unperf. (1883)

Neaga (4, Carmen Sylva [pseud. of Elisabeth, Queen of Romania]), 24 Feb 1885

Aristoteles (operetta, 1, after P. Aurène and A. Daudet), 1886

Per Svinaherde [Peter the Swineherd] (fairy play, 3, H. Christiernson), 29 Dec 1887

Granadas dotter [The Daughter of Granada], 1888 (romantic operetta, 3, Christiernson), 26 Nov 1892, vs (1892)

Liten Karin (4, Hedberg), unperf. (1897)

Hin Ondes snaror (fairy play, prol., 3, Christiernson), Göteborg, Stora, 7 March 1900

*

SBL (A. Helmer)
A. Lindgren: 'Ivar Hallström', *Svensk musiktidning*, xv (1884), 114–15
'Ivar Hallström', *Svensk musiktidning*, xii (1892), 153
Obituary, *Svensk musiktidning*, xxi (1901), 57
M. Tegen: 'Tre svenska vikingaoperor', *STMf*, xliii (1960), 12–75
——: 'Ivar Hallström – vår meste operakompositör', *Operan 200 år* (Stockholm, 1973), 69–73   ANDERS WIKLUND

Halmen, Pet(re) (*b* Talmaciu, Romania, 14 Nov 1943). German designer and director. After studying in Berlin he worked in Kiel and Düsseldorf, where he was much influenced by Heinrich Wendel. He then began a fruitful association with Jean-Pierre Ponnelle, designing costumes for many of his productions. Critics and audiences acclaimed their Monteverdi cycle in Zürich in 1975. There followed challenging interpretations of *Idomeneo*, *Lucio Silla*, *Die Entführung aus dem Serail* and *Mitridate, rè di Ponto* as well as the première of Aribert Reimann's *Lear* (1978, Munich), an extravagant staging of Wagner's *Das Liebesverbot* in 1983, an elegant *Lulu* in 1985 and the première of Reimann's *Troades* in 1986.

Halmen had already designed an exotic *Aida* for Götz Friedrich (1982, Berlin) and another for Nicolas Joel (1983, Chicago) when his and Ponnelle's 1984 Covent Garden production caused a furore. More controversy attended their *art déco Parsifal* (1988, San Francisco). Halmen has designed productions, including two *Ring* cycles, for many other international opera houses. In 1986 he began to design and direct only his own productions: *Lohengrin* (1987, Düsseldorf), Paer's *Achille* (1988, Lugo and Bologna), *Aida* (1989, Düsseldorf), *La straniera* for the Spoleto Festival, USA (1989), and *Nabucco* for the Munich Festival (1990). In 1991 he designed *Parsifal* for Mainz and a Mozart triple bill for the Salzburg Landestheater's tour of Japan.

Halmen built his reputation as a costume designer. His aesthetic views acknowledge (without depending heavily on) the surrealistic influence of Magritte in particular. He is as much at home with the standard repertory as with the most realistic 20th-century works, but in his own productions he has never allowed design to upstage other theatrical elements.

For illustration *see* COSTUME, fig.24 and REIMANN, ARIBERT.
                                        DAVID J. HOUGH

Hamal, Henri (*b* Liège, 20 July 1744; *d* Liège, 17 Sept 1820). South Netherlands composer, nephew of Jean-Noël Hamal. A chorister at Liège Cathedral, he studied in Rome from the age of 19, and in Naples. In 1769 he returned to Liège, where he became deputy director of music at the cathedral. He composed two works for the stage: a comedy 'en prose mêlée de chant et de danse', *Le triomphe du sentiment* (3, J. Bernars; Liège, 28 Jan 1775; *B-Lc*), and the *opéra lyrique Pygmalion* (1, J.-J. Rousseau; Liège, ?1781; *Lc*). A large proportion of Hamal's work consists of sacred choral music.
                                        MONIQUE DE SMET

Hamal, Jean-Noël (*b* Liège, 23 Dec 1709; *d* Liège, 26 Nov 1778). South Netherlands composer. He was a choirboy at the cathedral of St Lambert in Liège, where he studied with Canon Henri Dupont; from 1728 to 1731 he was in Rome at the Liège College, where he was a pupil of Giuseppe Amadori and wrote mainly church

music. Returning to Liège, he took a post at the cathedral and became director of music in 1738. After a second trip to Italy in 1749–50, during which he met Jommelli at Rome and Durante at Naples, he composed four burlesque operas to librettos in the liégeois dialect. These works, especially their vocal characteristics, are in the Neapolitan tradition but without its exaggerated bel canto style.

all opéras burlesques, first performed in Liège, and all in B-Lc

Li voègge di Chôfontaine (3, S. de Harlez, de Cartier, J.-J. de Fabry and P.-G. de Vivario), Hôtel de Ville, 23 Jan 1757 (Act 1, concert perf.), 16 Feb (Act 2), 25 Feb (Act 3)
Li liegeoi ègagï (2, Fabry), Hôtel de Ville, 14 April 1757
Li fiess di Hoûte-si-ploû (3, Vivario), Hôtel de Ville, 8 Dec 1757
Les hypocontes (3, Harlez), Ecole des Jésuites, 17 Feb 1758

*

H. Hamal: *Annales de la musique et du théâtre à Liège de 1738 à 1806* (MS, *B-Lu*); ed. M. Barthélémy (Liège, 1989)
C. Bellaigue: 'Un opéra-comique wallon du XVIIIe siècle: *Le voyage de Chaudfontaine*', *Revue des deux mondes*, lxv (1921), 458–68
A. Auda: *La musique et les musiciens de l'ancien pays de Liège* (Brussels, 1930)
M. de Smet: *Jean-Noël Hamal (1709–1778), chanoine impérial et directeur de la musique de la cathédrale Saint-Lambert de Liège: vie et oeuvre* (Brussels, 1959)   PHILIPPE GILSON

Hamari, Julia (*b* Budapest, 21 Nov 1942). Hungarian mezzo-soprano. She studied in Budapest at the Liszt Academy and in 1964 won a prize that enabled her to continue her studies in Stuttgart. Although her career developed mainly in the concert hall – she became renowned as a contralto soloist, notably in Bach, and a lieder singer – she also sang a successful Carmen at Stuttgart, and was a member of the Deutsche Oper am Rhein in the 1970s; among her other roles have been Fatima (*Oberon*), Cornelia (*Giulio Cesare*) and Gluck's Orpheus, all of which she recorded. Her British operatic début was at Glyndebourne in 1979 as Celia in Haydn's *La fedeltà premiata*, and she first appeared at the Metropolitan Opera as Rosina (*Il barbiere*) in 1984. Hamari's singing is distinguished by ease and smoothness of technique, fullness of tone and musicality of interpretation.
                                        NOËL GOODWIN

Hamburg. City in Germany, a port on the Elbe about 90 km from the river's mouth. It is noted as the first German city to have a public opera house.

1. To 1740.   2. After 1740.

1. To 1740. Since the Middle Ages an imperial city-state and a member of the Hanseatic League, Hamburg developed into a prosperous commercial and cosmopolitan centre. It was saved from the destruction of various wars in the 17th century by its impregnable defensive battlements and a determined policy of neutrality. By 1680 the city had a population of about 70 000; much of its growth resulted from the influx of foreigners escaping religious and political upheavals elsewhere in Europe.

A notable event in the city's music history occurred on 2 January 1678 with the opening of the first public opera house outside Venice. Although operas had previously been performed sporadically in some German aristocratic settings, nowhere else had opera been attempted as a commercial enterprise dependent on public enthusiasm and financial support. The establishment of opera in Hamburg was the achievement of Gerhard Schott, a Hamburg patrician and lawyer, Peter Lütjen, also a lawyer, and Johann Adam Reincken, the famous organist at St Catherine's church. Schott probably had the encouragement, if not the financial assistance, of Duke Christian Albrecht of Schleswig-Gottdorf, a lover of opera who lived in exile in Hamburg from 1673 to 1679. His court composer, Johann Theile, came with him and became the first composer to write operas for the new theatre.

Schott engaged the Italian architect Girolamo Sartorio to build an opera house on rented land in the Gänsemarkt immediately adjacent to the location of the modern Hamburg Staatsoper. Sartorio would later build opera houses also in Amsterdam and Leipzig. His Hamburg theatre was unusually spacious for its time, seating approximately 2000 persons in a parterre, four levels of boxes and a gallery. The stage area was about 24 metres deep and 12 wide, with the proscenium some 10 metres high. There were also boxes on either side of the proscenium arch. The stage had elaborate machinery and no fewer than 15 sliding side wings.

Performances began in January and the season ran throughout the year except for the usual closures during Lent, other major church holidays and summer. They took place two or three times a week on Monday, Wednesday and Thursday afternoons, and could last from four to six hours. Eight to ten operas were staged in a typical year, with from two to ten premières; the total number of yearly performances could fluctuate from as few as 65 to over a hundred. As the only accessible public opera house in Northern Europe where one could learn about the most innovative and modern musical compositions, Hamburg no doubt attracted not only royalty, aristocrats, politicians, upper-class businessmen and professionals, but also many performing musicians and composers. Even after other commercial opera houses opened in Hanover (1689), Brunswick (1690) and Leipzig (1693), Hamburg remained the most important centre in Northern Europe until it faltered and finally closed in 1738.

The Hamburg theatre had opened in 1678 with Theile's *Der erschaffene, gefallene und auffgerichtete Mensch* (*Adam und Eva*). This work, like many others staged during the early years, was based on a biblical subject and reflects an attempt to pacify church officials, especially ministers of the Pietist movement, who attacked opera and all stage entertainments as the evil work of 'dark forces'. For a while opera was the focus of heated attacks from the pulpits of the city's churches and provoked almost an avalanche of pamphlets and other writings condemning the singers, composers, librettists, and the director of the theatre. Later, as the controversy waned, composers turned largely to myth and history for the subjects of their librettos, many of which were translations or adaptations of texts originally by French and Italian writers. The Hamburg opera also turned to a number of distinguished native poets to create librettos, including Lucas von Bostel, Christian Postel, Heinrich Elmenhorst, Hinrich Hinsch, Christian Hunold ('Menantes'), Barthold Feind, Friedrich Christian Bressand and Johann Ulrich von König. During the first decade composers for the Gänsemarkt theatre included, in addition to Theile, Nicolaus Adam Strungk, Johann Philipp Förtsch and Johann Wolfgang Franck. None of their scores survives, but several collections of arias from Franck's operas exist which show that his style, although strongly influenced by Venetian opera, included marked German elements of both the secular and the sacred lied and even the spirit, if not actual quotation, of chorale tunes.

The first Hamburg opera to survive complete is J. G.

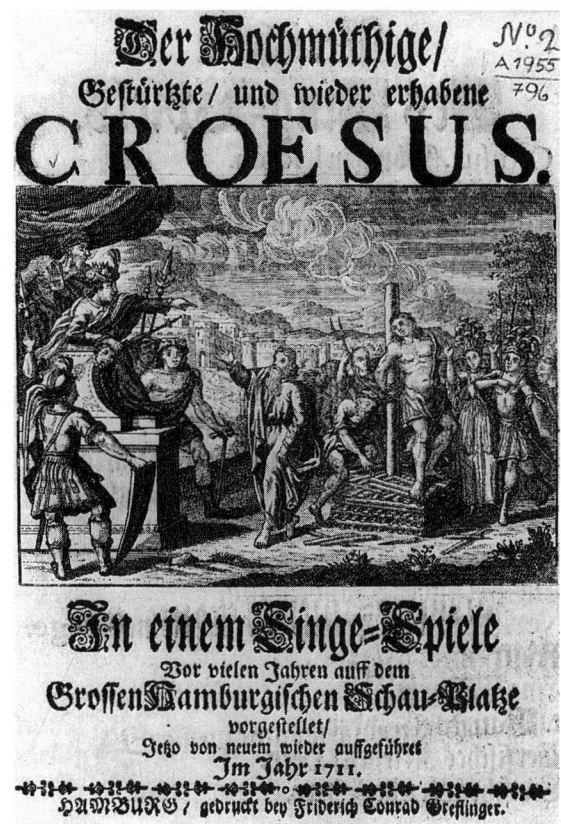

1. *Title-page of the libretto of Reinhard Keiser's opera 'Croesus', first performed at the Theater am Gänsemarkt, Hamburg, in 1711*

Conradi's *Die schöne und getreue Ariadne* (1691). Like the operas of Johann Sigismund Kusser, it reveals the influence of French opera, especially Lully, whose *Acis et Galatée* was performed in Hamburg in 1689. However, the pinnacle of musical achievement in the 61-year history of Hamburg's opera was reached in the numerous works by Reinhard Keiser. He arrived in the city around 1695, and until the 1730s presented at least 60 operas and other dramatic works. Of these all but 17 have been lost. Keiser's contemporary and friend, Johann Mattheson, praised him as 'the greatest opera composer of the world' (*Grundlage einer Ehren-Pforte*), and Keiser's operas were frequently extolled for their remarkable melodic originality and the dramatic handling of orchestral instruments.

Keiser directed the opera in Hamburg from 1703 to 1706, the very period when the young Handel came to the city and found work playing in the opera orchestra. Handel composed four operas for Hamburg, including *Almira*, the only one to survive. Keiser's influence was one of the principal musical experiences forming the young composer's future career and he often availed himself later of Keiser's melodies as a basis for his own compositions.

In 1721 Georg Philipp Telemann produced his *Der geduldige Socrates*, the first of his 20 or so operas written for Hamburg. He was the last gifted German composer to contribute to Hamburg's illustrious operatic history in the early 18th century. During the final decade, 1728–38, financial problems multiplied and the affluent merchant-class society sought their entertainment increasingly in the spoken theatre. Even attempts to introduce purely Italian operas failed, and after 61 years Hamburg's first period of opera came to an end. The theatre was used variously for plays and visiting Italian opera troupes until it was demolished in 1763.

2. AFTER 1740. In the decades between 1738 and 1771 opera in Hamburg took second place to spoken drama. Operatic life was dominated by visiting Italian companies, particularly those directed by Angelo and Pietro Mingotti in the Reithaus from 1748 onwards. Gluck visited Hamburg as Kapellmeister of the Mingotti company in 1748. In 1765 Konrad Ernst Ackermann had a new theatre constructed to replace the demolished opera house; it held 1600 people and was opened on 31 July 1765. Known at first as the Ackermannsches Komödienhaus, it was renamed the Deutsches Theater in 1797. At the end of the 18th century the works of Mozart, Dittersdorf and Salieri were particularly popular.

The theatre was renamed again more than once in the early 19th century: it became the Hamburgisches Stadt-Theater in 1809 and the Hamburgisches Deutsches Stadt-Theater in 1811. The old building was replaced in 1825 with a new one (cap. 2260) designed by Karl Friedrich Schinkel. This Neues Stadt-Theater in the Dammtorstrasse was opened on 3 May 1827 with Goethe's *Egmont*. It still served as a place for shows by conjurors and variety artists as well as for performances of spoken drama, musical drama and dance. Compared with the size of the auditorium, the stage of the new theatre was rather modest, in order 'to keep the expense of scenery and lighting moderate'. Even in its first decade, 1827–36, the Theater am Dammtor staged 11 local premières, with Rossini, Bellini and Donizetti occupying a central place in the repertory. Later it also produced the operas of Wagner, while composers such as Marschner and Kreutzer conducted their own works. In 1844 Wagner conducted *Rienzi* in its second production after the Dresden première. The following year Hamburg saw its first performance of an opera by Verdi (*Nabucco*) here. Meanwhile the Thalia-Theater, opened in 1842, was devoted primarily to light entertainment.

The Theater am Dammtor underwent alterations in 1873, and three years later a rival house, the Altona Stadttheater, opened and began presenting the same repertory. After years of economic crisis, a noticeable recovery took place following the appointment of the Intendant Bernhard Pohl (known as Pollini) in 1874. In 1891 Gustav Mahler became the conductor; his tenure concluded in 1897 with a production of *Fidelio*. The Pollini era ended with his death in the same year. Arthur Nikisch, who made his Hamburg début with a production of *Tannhäuser*, appeared regularly as conductor from 1901. Eugen d'Albert and Gustave Charpentier also conducted their own works. In 1904 Richard Strauss made his first guest appearance in the city as conductor of *Die Feuersnot*. The operas of Siegfried Wagner held a special position in Hamburg; *Der Kobold*, *Bruder Lustig* and *Sternengebot* had their premières there in 1904, 1905 and 1908 respectively. The guest appearances of Enrico Caruso between 1906 and 1913 were regarded as sensational, and the conductors Otto Klemperer (1910–12) and Egon Pollak (1917–31) ensured high musical standards. Among singers closely connected with the house were Elisabeth Schumann and Lotte Lehmann.

In 1927–8 the repertory contained 57 works, including contemporary operas by Wolf-Ferrari, Pizzetti, Weinberger and Krenek. Operas having their premières in Hamburg included Busoni's *Die Brautwahl* (1912), Korngold's *Die tote Stadt* (1920) and *Das Wunder der Heliane* (1927), and Respighi's *La campana sommersa* (1927). Bruno Walter made his first guest appearance in the city in 1929 as conductor of Verdi's *Otello*; Karl Böhm was appointed Generalmusikdirektor in 1931 and remained in the post for three years.

After the Nazis seized power many fine artists of Jewish origin were obliged to leave the theatre. The new rulers renamed it again in 1933 as the Hamburgisches Staatstheater, and then in 1934 as the Hamburgische Staatsoper. In 1934 Eugen Jochum became musical director of the house, which developed a scenic style of 'magic realism' independent of prevailing political tendencies, shaped by the work of the chief dramatic director Oscar Fritz Schuh and the designer Wilhelm Reinking. Their ideal was 'the equal integration of music, words and movement in space as a total image of a higher reality'. It was counterbalanced by the work of the designer Caspar Neher. In August 1943 the auditorium was destroyed in an air raid, and performances subsequently took place in the Thalia-Theater.

2. *Design by Jacopo Fabris for the port of Alexandria in a production of Handel's 'Giulio Cesare in Egitto' at the Theater am Gänsemarkt, Hamburg, in 1725*

3. Enthusiastic reception of a concert given by Jenny Lind in the Neues Stadt-Theater, Hamburg, 1845 ('We are lucky! We are delighted! The Lind has turned our heads'): anonymous lithograph

Wir sind beglückt! wir sind entzückt! die Lind hat uns den Kopf verrückt.

At the end of the war a provisional auditorium was constructed in front of the surviving stage structure, and the company resumed performances on 9 January 1946. Meanwhile many opera productions were also presented in the larger Schauspielhaus. After the provisional auditorium was enlarged, opera was given there exclusively between 1949 and 1954. The auditorium was then demolished and, during the construction of a new building at the same location, the company moved to the Theater am Besinbinderhof for the 1954–5 season. On 15 October 1955 the rebuilt opera house, with 1675 seats, opened with *Die Zauberflöte*. The productions of Günther Rennert, the first postwar director, had great influence on the style of the house; he was succeeded by Heinz Tietjen (1956–9). Leopold Ludwig served as Generalmusikdirektor from 1951 to 1970.

The years during which Rolf Liebermann was Intendant, 1959–73, were marked by a consistent attention to contemporary opera, winning international renown and recognition for the Hamburg Staatsoper. Among the major premières of these years were Krenek's *Pallas Athene weint* (1955), Henze's *Der Prinz von Homburg* (1960), Stravinsky's *The Flood* (1963), Gottfried von Einem's *Der Zerrissene* (1964), Antonio Bibalo's *Das Lächeln am Fusse der Leiter* (1965), Schuller's *The Visitation* (1966), Humphrey Searle's *Hamlet* (1968), Menotti's *Help, Help, the Globolinks!* (1968), Lars Johan Werle's *Resan* (1969), Penderecki's *The Devils of Loudun* (1969) and Mauricio Kagel's *Staatstheater* (1971).

Liebermann's successor, August Everding, was director of the theatre from 1973 to 1977. Horst Stein was Generalmusikdirektor (1972–9) and Götz Friedrich principal dramatic director (1973–7); John Neumeier became chief choreographer and ballet director at the beginning of the 1973–4 season. The conductor Christoph von Dohnányi took over from Everding in 1977 and under him a number of influential directors worked at the Staatsoper, including Adolf Dresen, Achim Freyer and Herbert Wernicke. Dohnányi left in 1984, and his successor Kurt Horres stayed for hardly a season. Since 1973 the studio and experimental theatre 'Opera

stabile', directed by the chief Dramaturg Peter Dannenberg, has acquired an outstanding reputation, staging premières of works by Wolfgang Rihm, Udo Zimmermann, Josef Tal and others.

After the resignation of Horres in 1985, Liebermann returned to the scene of his great successes, as an interim director. Since 1988 the conductor Gerd Albrecht (as Generalmusikdirektor) and Peter Ruzicka (Intendant) have been running the Staatsoper, and under them it has been able to consolidate itself and win a high artistic reputation after years of vicissitudes. The season runs from the end of August to early July.

*

E. O. Lindner: *Die erste stehende deutsche Oper* (Berlin, 1855)

J. Sittard: *Geschichte des Musik- und Concertwesens in Hamburg* (Altona and Leipzig, 1890)

W. Kleefeld: 'Das Orchester der Hamburger Oper 1678–1738', *SIMG*, i (1899–1900), 219–89

W. Schulze: *Die Quellen der Hamburger Oper 1678–1738* (Hamburg, 1936)

H. C. Wolff: *Die Barockoper in Hamburg* (Wolfenbüttel, 1957)

I. Scharberth: *Musiktheater mit Rolf Liebermann* (Hamburg, 1975)

300 Jahre Oper in Hamburg (Hamburg, 1977)

G. J. Buelow: 'Opera in Hamburg 300 Years Ago', *MT*, cxix (1978), 26–8

H. J. Marx: 'Geschichte der Hamburger Barock Oper: ein Forschungsbericht', *HJbMw*, iii (1978), 7–34

J. Wenzel: *Geschichte der Hamburger Oper (1678–1978)* (Hamburg, 1978)

K. Zelm: 'Die Sänger der Hamburger Gänsemarkt-Oper', *HJbMw*, iii (1978), 35–73

S. Leopold: 'Feinds und Keisers Masagniello furioso: eine politische Oper?', *HJbMw*, v (1981), 55–68

H. J. Marx: 'Politische und wirtschaftliche Voraussetzungen der Hamburger Barockoper', *HJbMw*, v (1981), 81–8

M. Ruhnke: 'Telemanns Hamburger Opern und ihre italienischen und französische Vorbilder', *HJbMw*, v (1981), 9–27

M. W. Busch and P. Dannenberg, eds.: *Die Hamburgische Staatsoper* (Zürich, 1988)

G. J. Buelow: 'Hamburg Opera during Buxtehude's Lifetime: the Works of Johann Wolfgang Franck', *Church, Stage, and Studio: Music and its Contexts in Seventeenth-Century Germany*, ed. P. Walker (Ann Arbor, 1989), 127–41

GEORGE J. BUELOW (1), IMRE FABIAN (2)

Hamerik [Hammerich], **Asger** (*b* Frederiksberg, nr Copenhagen, 8 April 1843; *d* Frederiksberg, 13 July

1923). Danish composer. He studied music from an early age, and became a piano pupil and conducting student of Bülow in Berlin in 1862. At the outbreak of hostilities between Germany and Denmark in 1864 he left Berlin and, declining Wagner's invitation to Munich, went to Paris, where he became associated with Berlioz. (He later claimed to have been Berlioz's only pupil and it appears that he enjoyed a privileged relationship, being much encouraged and helped by him.) On 6 May 1865 excerpts from his first opera, *Tovelille*, were given in a concert performance at the Salle Pleyel. In December 1866 he set aside work on his second opera, *Hjalmar och Ingeborg*, to assist Berlioz with the preparation of the Viennese performance of *La damnation de Faust*. He completed his opera in Paris at the end of 1868 and, after Berlioz's death in 1869, returned to Copenhagen, where he performed substantial extracts from his first two operas in a concert given at the end of that year. Excerpts from *Tovelille* were performed the following year in Milan, where his third opera, *La vendetta*, in five scenes, was given a successful first performance on 23 December 1870. In 1871 he proceeded to Vienna, where he composed his last opera, *Den rejsende* ('The Traveller'), a comic opera in one act. It was reportedly accepted for performance in Vienna and elsewhere, but these undertakings apparently came to nothing when Hamerik left Vienna to become director of the conservatory of the Peabody Institute in Baltimore. He held this post and conducted the orchestra there for 27 years (1871–98), before returning to Copenhagen in 1900.

Tovelille op.12, 1863–5 (5, Hamerik), excerpts, concert perf., Paris, Salle Pleyel, 6 May 1865, vs (Copenhagen, *c*1865)
Hjalmar och Ingeborg op.18, 1866–8 (5, L. Josephsson), excerpts, concert perf., Copenhagen, Casino, 1869, *DK-Kk*
La vendetta op.20 (1, Hamerik), Milan, 23 Dec 1870, vs (Milan, 1871); as Die Blutrache, vs (Offenbach am Main, 1871)
Den rejsende [The Traveller] op.21 (comic op, 1, Hamerik), unperf., vs (Vienna, 1871)

*

DBL (E. Abrahamsen)
G. Lynge: *Danske komponister i det 20. aarhundredes begyndelse* (Århus, Copenhagen and Christiania, 2/1917)
K. Ribers: 'Asger Hamerik: in memoriam', *Musik*, vii (1923), 108–10, 117–21, 132–7
JOHN BERGSAGEL

Hamerik, Ebbe (*b* Copenhagen, 5 Sept 1898; *d* in the Kattegat, 11 Aug 1951). Danish composer, son of Asger Hamerik. He was taught theory and orchestration by his father, and then studied conducting with Frank van der Stucken. After a remarkable début as a conductor in 1919, he was appointed deputy chief conductor at the Kongelige Teater, Copenhagen, the same year. Dissatisfied with the lack of stimulating work in the theatre, however, he resumed his studies abroad in 1922 and returned to Copenhagen only in 1927 as conductor of the Musikforeningen. By this time he had also made a name for himself as a composer; his first opera, *Stepan*, had its première in Mainz in 1925. After the dissolution of the Musikforeningen (1931) Hamerik continued to conduct in Denmark and in Austria and Germany. In 1939 he volunteered for service in the Finnish Winter War. After his return to Denmark in spring 1940, he had his greatest operatic success to date when he conducted the first performance of *Marie Grubbe* at the Kongelige Teater. From 1943 he concentrated on composition; he frequently found inspiration during solitary sea voyages, a passion which resulted in his death by drowning.

Opera and the symphony were the two spheres in which Hamerik made his most substantial contribution to Danish music: he was the most important opera composer of his generation, and even though his success in Denmark was limited – two of his operas were given their premières abroad (*Stepan* and *Leonardo da Vinci*) and his last, *Drømmerne* (1949), was not produced until 23 years after his death – he remained preoccupied with the form throughout his life. He ranged from a Danish national style of simple lyricism, as in *Marie Grubbe*, to the polytonal music drama of *Drømmerne*, where the text is spoken by actors and the orchestra has an illustrative function in preludes and interludes.

Stepan (3, F. Nygaard), Mainz, Stadt, March 1925
Leonardo da Vinci, 1930–32 (4, M. Moretti and C. Muzzi), Antwerp, Royal Flemish Opera, March 1939
Marie Grubbe (2, Nygaard, after J. P. Jacobsen: *Fru Marie Grubbe*), Copenhagen, Kongelige, 17 May 1940
Rejsekammeraten (9 scenes, K. Nielsen, after H. C. Andersen: *The Travelling Companion*), Copenhagen, Kongelige, 5 Jan 1946
Drømmerne [Dreams], 1949 (11 scenes, Hamerik, after K. Blixen), Danish Radio, 26 Aug 1974; stage, Århus, Jutland Opera, 9 Sept 1974

*

G. Lehrmann: 'Stepan', *Dansk musiktidsskrift*, i (1925–6), 133–8
F. Nygaard: *Den virkelige Marie Grubbe* (Copenhagen, 1940)
V. Kappel: 'Ebbe Hameriks opera *Rejsekammeraten*', *Dansk musiktidsskrift*, xxi (1946), 47–50
J. Hye-Knudsen: 'Ebbe Hamerik', *Dansk musiktidsskrift*, xxvi (1951), 191–4
NIELS MARTIN JENSEN

Hamilton, David (Peter) (*b* New York, 18 Jan 1935). American critic. He worked as music and record librarian at Princeton University (1960–65) and music editor at W. W. Norton (1967–74), becoming in 1969 the New York music correspondent for the *Financial Times* (to 1974) and a contributing editor of *High Fidelity* (to 1984). As a critic and writer he is particularly concerned with 19th- and 20th-century music, and his broad knowledge of the recorded literature has led to a special interest in discography. In 1981 he became co-producer of the Metropolitan Opera Historic Broadcast Recording series. He is the editor of *The Metropolitan Opera Encyclopedia* (New York and London, 1987).
PAULA MORGAN

Hamilton, Iain (Ellis) (*b* Glasgow, 6 June 1922). Scottish composer. After seven years in engineering, he won a scholarship to the RAM in 1947. Between 1951 and 1961 he taught at Morley College and at London University. He moved to the USA in 1961, later becoming professor at Duke University, Durham, North Carolina, a post he held until 1981.

Hamilton's early reputation was based on his concert works. It was not until 1974, when *The Catiline Conspiracy* was given its première by Scottish Opera, that his all-round abilities as librettist and dramatic composer were widely recognized. Hamilton deals briskly and cogently with a complex plot involving intrigue and corruption in high places. *Pharsalia*, the radio opera *Tamburlaine* and *The Royal Hunt of the Sun* are similarly concerned with the uses and misuses of power and with conflicts between personal and public interest; Hamilton's lean and vigorous contrapuntal style is well suited to the illustration of such themes.

In *Anna Karenina* both plot and music take another direction. Here, as the composer has written, 'one thing matters above all else – love. It is born, rejoiced in, suffered through, betrayed, and finally lost'. *Anna Karenina* adopts the traditions and forms of 19th-century Romantic opera, the idiom being expansive, lyrical and largely tonal. This new approachability finds a parallel in many of his later concert works.

Lancelot brought a partial return to the manner and idiom of the earlier operas. Hamilton follows Malory in concentrating on human and political issues rather than on the magical or mystical aspects of Arthurian legend, the great love of Lancelot and Guinevere providing only one strand in the dramatic tissue. As in *The Catiline Conspiracy*, the plots and counter-plots of the main characters are aptly delineated in an active and purposeful score.

See also ANNA KARENINA; CATILINE CONSPIRACY, THE; and ROYAL HUNT OF THE SUN, THE.

all to librettos by the composer

Agamemnon, 1967–9, 1987, 1989 (dramatic narrative, 1, after Aeschylus), unperf.

The Royal Hunt of the Sun, 1968 (3, after P. Shaffer), London, Coliseum, 2 Feb 1977, vs (Bryn Mawr, PA, 1978)

Pharsalia (dramatic commentary, 1, after Lucan), Edinburgh, Freemason's Hall, 27 Aug 1969

The Catiline Conspiracy (2, after B. Jonson), Stirling, MacRobert Centre, 16 March 1974, vs (Bryn Mawr, 1975)

Tamburlaine (lyric drama for radio, 24 scenes, after C. Marlowe), BBC, 14 March 1977; also 2-act stage version

Anna Karenina, 1978 (3, after L. N. Tolstoy), London, Coliseum, 7 May 1981, vs (Bryn Mawr, 1979)

Dick Whittington, 1980–81 (lyric comedy, 2, after E. Tracey), unperf.

Raleigh's Dream (prol., 8 scenes), Durham, NC, Duke U., 3 June 1984

Lancelot (2, after T. Malory), Arundel Castle, 24 Aug 1985

*

A. Besch: 'The Catiline Conspiracy', *MT*, cxv (1974), 210–11

A. Jacobs: 'The Catiline Conspiracy', *Opera*, xxv (1974), 382–6

I. Hamilton: 'The Royal Hunt of the Sun', *MT*, cxviii (1977), 23–5

N. Goodwin: 'Hamilton's "Anna Karenina"', *Opera*, xxxii (1981), 457–62

I. Hamilton: 'Anna Karenina: an Operatic Version', *MT*, cxxii (1981), 295–7
HUGO COLE

Hamlet. *Opéra* in five acts by AMBROISE THOMAS to a libretto by MICHEL CARRÉ and JULES BARBIER after WILLIAM SHAKESPEARE; Paris, Opéra, 9 March 1868.

Carré and Barbier (who also wrote the libretto for Gounod's *Faust*) have been greatly blamed for the distortions of Shakespeare in their text for *Hamlet* but, apart from the ending, they managed to condense a very long play into a reasonable opera libretto.

The coronation of Gertrude (mezzo-soprano), queen and consort of Claudius, King of Denmark (bass), is taking place at the castle of Elsinore. Prince Hamlet (baritone) expresses his sadness at the death of his father and the hasty remarriage of his mother. He sings a love duet, 'Doute de la lumière', with Ophélie [Ophelia] (soprano). Together with her father Polonius (bass), Ophelia bids farewell to her brother Laerte [Laertes] (tenor), who is leaving Denmark. On the ramparts Hamlet sees the Ghost of his father (bass), who relates how he was murdered by his brother Claudius. Hamlet swears to avenge his father.

In Act 2 Ophelia complains that Hamlet no longer loves her. She asks the queen's permission to enter a convent, but Gertrude, already worried by her son's strange behaviour, refuses the request. Claudius tries in vain to calm his wife's fears. Hamlet proposes to divert the court with a play put on by a troupe of strolling actors. After a chorus and a drinking song, the play, about the murder of King Gonzago as he lay sleeping, is mimed to Hamlet's commentary. Claudius pales, reveal-

ing his guilt, and Hamlet is overcome with rage; the act ends with a magnificent septet.

Act 3 starts with Hamlet's monologue, based on 'To be or not to be'. Hamlet hides behind a tapestry as Claudius attempts unsuccessfully to pray. He is joined by Polonius and their conversation proves Hamlet's suspicions to be correct. Shattered to discover that Polonius knew of the plot, Hamlet violently repulses Ophelia and her love for him. The act ends with a long duet (based largely on Shakespeare's Closet Scene) between Gertrude and Hamlet, who finally draws a dagger with which to kill his mother, but is stopped by the Ghost.

A *ballet-divertissement* (obligatory at the Opéra) 'La fête du printemps' begins Act 4, followed by Ophelia's mad scene ('A vos jeux ... Partagez-vous mes fleurs ... Et maintenant écoutez ma chanson') and her subsequent suicide by drowning.

In Act 5, after a curtailed version of the gravediggers' scene, events depart radically from Shakespeare. On learning of the death of Ophelia, Hamlet sings 'Comme une pâle fleur éclose au souffle de la tombe'. A funeral march heralds the arrival of Ophelia's coffin, followed by a chorus of young girls. Prompted by a final visit from the Ghost, Hamlet kills Claudius and is acclaimed king: 'Vive le roi Hamlet'.

In Paris, at least, a *Hamlet* with a comparatively happy ending did not worry either the critics or the public, who flocked to hear the great baritone Jean-Baptiste Faure in the title role. The hundredth performance at the Opéra, scheduled for 28 November 1873 at the Salle Le Peletier, did not take place until four months later at the Salle Ventadour, as the Salle Le Peletier burnt down on the morning of that date. Meanwhile, on 19 June 1869, *Hamlet* was produced with considerable success at Covent Garden, London, where Christine Nilsson repeated the triumph she had scored as Ophelia in the Paris première. Other famous singers of Ophelia included Calvé, Albani, Melba and Garden.

The mad scene, much on the lines laid down by Donizetti in *Lucia di Lammermoor*, is in several sections. Ophelia asks the courtiers if she can join in their games; imagining that she is married to Hamlet, she fears that he will be faithless. In a waltz movement she distributes flowers before singing the ballad 'Pâle et blonde, dort sous l'eau profonde', about the Wilis, spirits who lead faithless lovers to a watery grave. (Its melody is hummed by an invisible chorus after Ophelia's death.)

Although it was undoubtedly the mad scene that ensured the opera's popularity during the 19th century, it is mainly as a superb vehicle for a baritone that *Hamlet* has survived since then. Faure was succeeded in the title role by singers such as Maurel, Lassalle, Renaud, Ruffo, Battistini and Singher. More recently Sherrill Milnes and Thomas Allen have sung in noteworthy revivals. Hamlet's music is much more dramatic than that of the other characters; everything he sings is consistent with Shakespeare's Hamlet, apart from the drinking song; even that can be seen, like his madness, as part of the camouflage put on to deceive Claudius.

Another well-drawn character is Gertrude. Her second-act arioso, 'Dans son regard plus sombre', was considered by several contemporary critics as the finest solo number in the score, while her third-act duet with Hamlet is the opera's dramatic and musical centre, as the Closet Scene is the heart of Shakespeare's play. Though Laertes, Claudius, Polonius and the others are

'Hamlet' (Thomas), Act 2 scene ii: lithograph by A. Lamy after Charles-Antoine Cambon's design for the original production at the Paris Opéra (Salle Le Peletier), 9 March 1868

more conventional in their musical characterization, Thomas' skill in atmospheric scene-painting is frequently at its most vivid in this work. The Ghost's appearance on the ramparts, accompanied by eerie writing for the brass, is most effective, as also is the melodrama of the mimed play about Gonzago. The ballet music for 'La fête du printemps' is less interesting and overlong, but the scene of Ophelia's funeral procession is very impressive.

For further illustration see FAURE, JEAN-BAPTISTE; NILSSON, CHRISTINE; and REHEARSAL, fig.2.   ELIZABETH FORBES

Hamlin, George (*b* Elgin, IL, 20 Sept 1869; *d* New York, 20 Jan 1923). American tenor. He was well known as a lieder and oratorio singer when Victor Herbert invited him to take over the role of Paul Merrill in *Natoma*, a part created by John McCormack. His successful début in Philadelphia (15 December 1911) led to his assumption of other roles, notably Turiddu in *Cavalleria rusticana*, Gennaro in Wolf-Ferrari's *I gioielli della Madonna* and Edward Plummer in Goldmark's *Das Heimchen am Herd*. He remained with the Chicago Opera until 1917. Moving to New York in that year, he joined with Albert Reiss and David Bispham in forming the Society of American Singers for the production of opera in English. He also became active as a teacher. His daughter Anna, a pupil of Sembrich, sang with the Chicago Civic Opera (1926–8) and had a long and distinguished career as a teacher.

A. M. Hamlin: *Father was a Tenor* (Hicksville, NY, 1978)
                                          PHILIP LIESON MILLER

Hamlisch, Marvin (*b* New York, 2 June 1944). American composer. He won a scholarship to the Juilliard School when he was seven and later studied music at Queens College. Subsequently he composed film music and wrote material for cabaret entertainers before turning to the lyric stage. He won praise for his first Broadway score, *A Chorus Line* (1975), a dramatization of auditions by (mostly) young aspirants for roles in a musical chorus line: the length of its run set new records. There followed the film *The Sting* (1975), which draws on rags by Joplin. His second successful musical was *They're Playing our Song* (1979). His pleasant score for the failed *Smile* (1986) may have been underrated. Hamlisch's music combines traditional forms and styles with more modern idioms, including soft rock. Such songs as 'One' and 'What I did for love', from *Chorus Line*, enjoyed widespread popularity.

Hamm, Charles (Edward) (*b* Charlottesville, VA, 21 April 1925). American musicologist. He studied at the University of Virginia and at Princeton University, and taught at Princeton, the Cincinnati Conservatory, Tulane University and the University of Illinois at Urbana-Champaign. In 1976 he was appointed professor of music at Dartmouth College, Hanover, New Hampshire. Besides Dufay and music of the Renaissance, his main areas of study have been American and popular music, and opera. His book *Opera* (Boston, 1966) discusses the basic concepts and techniques, while *Yesterdays: Popular Song in America* (New York, 1979) and *Music in the New World* (New York, 1983) also look at opera. Hamm has composed several short operas, mainly to his own librettos. These include *The Secret Life of Walter Mitty* (after James Thurber), given in Athens, Ohio, in 1953, and *The Box*, performed in New Orleans in 1961.

The Secret Life of Walter Mitty (Hamm, after J. Thurber), Athens, Ohio University, 30 July 1953
One-act operas: The Monkey's Paw, Cincinnati, Conservatory of Music, 2 May 1952; The Cask of Amontillado, Cincinnati, Conservatory of Music, 1 March 1953; A Scent of Sarsaparilla, San Francisco, 5 Sept 1954; The Salesgirl, Bristol, Virginia Intermont College, 1 March 1955; The Box, New Orleans, Tulane University, 4 Feb 1961   PAULA MORGAN

Hammerich, Asger. *See* HAMERIK, ASGER.

Hammerstein, Oscar, I (*b* Stettin [now Szczecin, Poland], 8 May 1846; *d* New York, 1 Aug 1919). American impresario. He studied harmony and counterpoint, and also learnt to play the piano, flute and violin. While still in his teens he ran away to Hamburg, and later to New York, where he worked in a cigar factory. He began to speculate in real estate and, as his fortunes increased, built theatres in which he presented a variety of productions. He composed intermezzos, a ballet and the operettas *The Kohinoor* (1893) and *Santa Maria* (1896), none of which achieved any success. In 1906 he founded the Manhattan Opera Company, which opened with Bellini's *I puritani* on 3 December in the newly built Manhattan Opera House. The company challenged the entrenched Metropolitan Opera in presenting the standard Italian repertory as well as contemporary works, and gave the American premières of four operas by Massenet, Giordano's *Siberia*, Charpentier's *Louise*, and *Elektra* and *Pelléas et Mélisande*. Singers who performed with the company included Melba, Bonci, Nordica, Tetrazzini, Garden, Calvé, McCormack, Zenatello and Renaud. In April 1910 Hammerstein sold his interests in the company to the Metropolitan for $1 200 000, and promised not to produce opera in New York, Boston, Philadelphia or Chicago for the next decade.

V. Sheean: *Oscar Hammerstein I: the Life and Exploits of an Impresario* (New York, 1956)
J. F. Cone: *Oscar Hammerstein's Manhattan Opera Company* (Norman, OK, 1966)   JOHN FREDERICK CONE

Hammerstein, Oscar (Greeley Clendenning), II (*b* New York, 12 July 1895; *d* Doylestown, PA, 23 Aug 1960). American librettist, lyricist and impresario, grandson of Oscar Hammerstein I. He wrote lyrics for collegiate shows while at Columbia University, but began his professional career by attempting to write a serious drama. When this failed he turned his hand to musical comedy and wrote *Always You* in 1920. That same year the librettist Otto Harbach became his mentor and the pair worked together on a series of shows: *Wildflower*, *Rose-Marie*, *Sunny*, *Song of the Flame* and *The Desert Song*. In 1927 he collaborated with Kern on what may be considered his masterpiece, *Show Boat*. The musical was a landmark in that it was the first major work of its kind to employ a colourful segment of the American past for its background and to use largely American musical idioms. It was to serve as the prototype for the 'musical play' – the singularly American type of operetta that was popularized by Hammerstein and RICHARD RODGERS. It was also the first work that Hammerstein directed himself.

Other notable musicals of the 1920s were *The New Moon* – the last operetta in the older European style to enjoy a long New York run – and *Sweet Adeline*. Hammerstein's only major success in the 1930s was *Music in the Air*, though songs from *Very Warm for May* remain popular, despite the failure of the production. With Rodgers, in the 1940s and 50s, he created some of the most successful and masterly works in the genre: *Oklahoma!*, *Carousel*, *South Pacific*, *The King and I* and *The Sound of Music*. Hammerstein's works are notable for their succinct dialogue and taut construction, as well as the excellence of their lyrics. If these are sometimes excessively sentimental, they more often display a simplicity and poetic freshness rare in the musical theatre. With Rodgers, Hammerstein produced all his own shows from *South Pacific* onwards, as well as a revival of *Show Boat* and a staging of Berlin's *Annie Get Your Gun* (1946). Many of his most successful works were later filmed, and he also wrote some original screenplays and lyrics for Hollywood.

musicals unless otherwise stated; book and lyrics by Hammerstein, unless otherwise stated

†*– book with* ‡*– lyrics with*

Always You, H. Stothart, 1920; *Tickle Me* (†‡ O. Harbach and F. Mandel), Stothart, 1920; *Jimmie* (†‡ Harbach and Mandel), Stothart, 1920; *Daffy Dill* († G. Bolton), Stothart, 1922; *Queen o' Hearts* († Mandel); ‡ S. Mitchell), L. Gensler and D. Wilkinson, 1922; *Wildflower* (†‡ Harbach), V. Youmans and Stothart, 1923; *Mary Jane McKane* (†‡ W. C. Duncan), Youmans and Stothart, 1923; *Rose-Marie* (operetta, †‡ Harbach), R. Friml and Stothart, 1924; *Sunny* (†‡ Harbach), Kern, 1925; *Song of the Flame* (operetta, †‡ Harbach), G. Gershwin and Stothart, 1925
The Wild Rose (†‡ Harbach), Friml, 1926; *The Desert Song* (operetta, † Harbach and Mandel; ‡ Harbach), S. Romberg, 1926; *Golden Dawn* (†‡ Harbach), E. Kalman and Stothart, 1927; *Show Boat*, Kern, 1927; *Good Boy* († Harbach and H. Myers; ‡ B. Kalmar), Kalmar, H. Ruby and Stothart, 1928; *The New Moon* († Mandel and L. Schwab), Romberg, 1928; *Rainbow* (†‡ L. Stallings), Youmans, 1928; *Sweet Adeline*, Kern, 1929; *Ballyhoo* (†‡ H. Ruskin and L. K. Brill), L. Alter, 1930; *The Gang's All Here* (†‡ R. Crouse, M. Ryskind, O. Murphy and R. A. Simon), Gensler and R. Whiting, 1931
Free for All (†‡ Schwab), Whiting, 1931; *East Wind* († Mandel), Romberg, 1931; *Music in the Air*, Kern, 1932; *May Wine* († Mandel), Romberg, 1935; *Very Warm for May*, Kern, 1939; *Sunny River*, Romberg, 1941; *Oklahoma!*, Rodgers, 1943; *Carmen Jones*, after Bizet, 1943; *Carousel*, Rodgers, 1945; *Allegro*, Rodgers, 1947; *South Pacific* († J. Logan), Rodgers, 1949; *The King and I*, Rodgers, 1951; *Me and Juliet*, Rodgers, 1953; *Pipe Dream*, Rodgers, 1955; *Flower Drum Song* († J. Fields), Rodgers, 1958; *The Sound of Music* († H. Lindsay and Crouse), Rodgers, 1959

D. Taylor: *Some Enchanted Evenings* (New York, 1952)
S. Green: *The Story of Rodgers and Hammerstein* (New York, 1963)
H. Fordin: *Getting to Know Him: a Biography of Oscar Hammerstein II* (New York, 1977)   GERALD BORDMAN

Hammes, Karl (*b* Zeil, 25 March 1896; *d* Warsaw, 10 Sept 1939). German baritone. He made his début in 1925 at Cologne, then moved to Berlin; in 1927 he sang Amfortas, and Gunther at Bayreuth. From 1929 to 1935 he was a member of the Vienna Staatsoper, scoring a special success in the title role of *Švanda the Bagpiper*. He also sang in Bittner's *Der Musikant* and *Das Veilchen*. At Salzburg his roles included Don Giovanni, Figaro and Guglielmo. During World War I he had served in the German air force; he rejoined in 1939 and was killed in a raid on Warsaw. His beautifully produced, lyrical voice, ideal in music such as Wolfram's, is well preserved on records.   J. B. STEANE

Hammond, Arthur (*b* Sheffield, 9 Dec 1904; *d* London, 12 Nov 1991). English conductor. He first studied engineering, then conducting (with Henry Wood), and began his career as a coach with the British National Opera Company. In 1927 he joined the Carl Rosa company as chorus master, making his conducting début at Glasgow (*Un ballo in maschera*) in 1928, in which year he became principal conductor; the works he conducted with the company included a *Ring* cycle. In 1933 he became Albert Coates's assistant, first on a Metropolitan tour in the USA and then at Covent Garden, where he made his début in 1936 (*Madama Butterfly*). He was principal conductor of the Dublin Opera (1936–47), then returned to the Carl Rosa company as musical director (1948–57, 1960), later conducting in Israel (1963–5) and in Detroit, where he taught before taking a post at the RNCM (1969) and moving to Covent Garden as consultant (1973–88). Among the premières he conducted are Holbrooke's *Bronwen* (1929) and two operas by George Lloyd, *Iernin* (1934) and *John Socman* (1951). Hammond was particularly authoritative in the field of French 19th-century opera and prepared editions of several works, including *Benvenuto Cellini* and *Les contes d'Hoffmann*, that helped restore them to the repertory in authentic form.

Hammond, Dame Joan (**Hood**) (*b* Christchurch, 24 May 1912). Australian soprano of New Zealand birth. She studied in Sydney where in 1928 she made her début as Giovanna (*Rigoletto*), then sang Venus and Helmwige (1935). After further study in Vienna, London and Florence, she was engaged at the Vienna Volksoper in 1938 to sing Nedda, Martha and Konstanze; in 1939 she sang Mimì and Violetta at the Staatsoper. Engaged by the Carl Rosa company (1942–5), she sang Butterfly, Tosca, Violetta, Marguerite and the Marschallin. In 1947 she returned to Vienna, then made her Covent Garden début in 1948 as Leonora (*Il trovatore*), returning as Mimì, Beethoven's Leonore and Aida. She made her American début with the New York City Center Opera in 1949, and sang Elisabeth de Valois (1951) and Rusalka (1959) at Sadler's Wells, Tatyana and Fevroniya (*The Invisible City of Kitezh*) in Russian in Barcelona, Aida and Tatyana in Leningrad and Moscow (1957), and Desdemona and Tosca (1957) and Salome (1960) in Australia for the Elizabethan Theatre Trust. Her roles included Pamina, Donna Anna and Elvira, Agathe, Elisabeth, Elsa, Norma and Turandot. Her record of 'O my beloved father' sold over a million copies and won a golden disc in 1969. She had a strong, vibrant voice and a warm stage personality. *A Voice, a Life*, her autobiography, was published in 1970. She was made a DBE in 1974.

GV (R. Celletti and C. Williams; C. Williams)　　ALAN BLYTH

Hammond-Stroud, Derek (*b* London, 10 Jan 1926). English baritone. From 1948 he studied for two years at Trinity College, and then in Europe with Elena Gerhardt and Gerhard Hüsch. His first significant operatic role was Pluto in the first British production of Haydn's *Orfeo*, a concert performance put on by the Impresario Society at the St Pancras Festival in 1955. His stage début, at the same festival, was as Publius (*La clemenza di Tito*) in 1957. After joining the Sadler's Wells company in 1961, he built up an impressive gallery of finely detailed *buffo* portraits – Rossini's Dr Bartolo, Papageno, Melitone and many Sullivan and Offenbach roles – in which pointed enunciation and intelligent musicianship completed the vivid impact. A new dimension was lent his strong, well-focussed baritone with appearances as Beckmesser (1968) and Alberich (*Götterdämmerung*, 1971) in the company's historic English-language Wagner performances under Reginald Goodall. He made his début both at Covent Garden in 1971 and at the Metropolitan in 1977 as Faninal in *Der Rosenkavalier*, and his roles at the Coliseum have included Rigoletto, Sharpless and Napoleon (*War and Peace*). He has also appeared at Glyndebourne, San Diego and Houston. His recordings include Alberich in the complete *Ring* cycle and Faninal.

A. Blyth: 'Derek Hammond-Stroud', *Opera*, xxxvi (1985), 1359–64
MAX LOPPERT

Hampe, Michael (**Hermann**) (*b* Heidelberg, 3 June 1935). German director. He studied at the universities of Vienna, Munich and Heidelberg. He was a director at the Stadttheater, Berne (1961–4), deputy director of the Schauspielhaus, Zürich (1965–70), and director of the Nationaltheater, Mannheim (1972–5). Since 1975 he has been Intendant of the Cologne Opera, where he has produced a wide range of works. He has also worked with success at the Salzburg and Edinburgh festivals, at the Maggio Musicale in Florence, and at Covent Garden, where he directed *Andrea Chénier* (1984), *Il barbiere di Siviglia* (1985) and *La Cenerentola* (1990). His style is predominantly traditional, with a special gift for witty but never farcical treatment of comedies.
ALAN BLYTH

Hampson, Thomas (*b* Elkhart, IN, 28 June 1955). American baritone. He studied in Los Angeles and Santa Barbara. Engaged at Düsseldorf (1981–4), he sang the Herald (*Lohengrin*), Harlequin (*Ariadne*), Belcore and Nanni (Haydn's *L'infedeltà delusa*). He sang Henze's Prince of Homburg at Darmstadt, Guglielmo at St Louis (1982), Malatesta at Santa Fe (1983) and Count Almaviva at Aix-en-Provence (1985). At Zürich (1985–9) his roles have included Massenet's Lescaut, Handel's Julius Caesar, Marcello, Don Giovanni and Rossini's Figaro. He made his Metropolitan début in 1986 as Count Almaviva, returning as Guglielmo, both of which he has also sung in Salzburg (1988–90). He has appeared regularly at Los Angeles, Cologne, Hamburg and Vienna. A charismatic actor, he has a grainy, flexible voice perfectly suited to Mozart.　ELIZABETH FORBES

Handbill. *See* PLAYBILL.

Handel [Händel, Hendel], **George Frideric** [Georg Friedrich] (*b* Halle, 23 Feb 1685; *d* London, 14 April 1759). English composer of German birth. Though he was widely acknowledged as one of the greatest composers of his age, his reputation from his death to the early 20th century rested largely on the popularity of a small number of orchestral works and oratorios, *Messiah* in particular. In fact he contributed to every musical genre current in his time, both vocal and instrumental. His operas were until recently the most neglected of his works, being in a format which became regarded as obsolete almost within his lifetime. Yet the composition of operas, mainly on Italian librettos, dominated his activities for over 35 years; they were modelled (like much else in his music) on both German and Italian precedents, modified to satisfy his own artistic preferences and to suit the English contexts in which most of them were produced; and they are the finest (though not the most typical) of their kind. Handel was always by inclination a composer for the theatre, and maintained a commitment to dramatic music (albeit without action) in his English oratorios, at first produced alongside his Italian operas and later his exclusive preoccupation.

1. Halle. 2. Hamburg. 3. Italy. 4. Hanover, Düsseldorf and London. 5. Cannons. 6. The Royal Academy of Music. 7. The Second Academy. 8. Opera at Covent Garden. 9. From opera to oratorio. 10. Oratorios and musical dramas. 11. Revivals. 12. Handel as an opera composer.

1. HALLE. He was the son of Georg Händel (1622–97), a barber-surgeon in the service of the Duke of Saxe-Weissenfels, and his second wife Dorothea Taust (1651–1730), daughter of a pastor. Though some documentation of Handel's life in Halle survives, the only substantial account of his early years appears in John Mainwaring's anonymously published *Memoirs* (1760), which seems to derive its information from Handel himself, perhaps recorded near the end of his life through intermediaries. Though its chronology is unreliable, many of the incidents it mentions have been confirmed by later research and it is probably as accurate as reminiscence allows. The boy's early interest in music was at first frowned upon by his father; he was denied access to musical instruments and encouraged to study for the law. According to Mainwaring, Handel practised secretly on a clavichord in the attic. The Duke of Saxe-Weissenfels, having heard him playing the organ when he was about nine, persuaded his father to give him a musical education under Friedrich Zachow, organist at the Liebfrauenkirche at Halle, who gave him excellent tuition both on organ and harpsichord as well as in composition.

His first musical appointment was as organist at the Calvinist Cathedral of Halle, taken up in 1702 – he had matriculated at the University of Halle, where he may briefly have studied civil law – but the appointment was not renewed after the probationary year. A taste for a career as an opera composer may first have been stimulated on a visit to Berlin; opera there 'was in a flourishing condition' and Handel is said to have met both Giovanni Bononcini and Attilio Ariosti. This visit, assigned to 1698 by Mainwaring, is otherwise undocumented and its date is problematical (Ariosti was not at Berlin until 1702), but there is no reason to doubt it, or its importance in widening the young composer's horizons. In summer 1703 Handel left Halle; his new life was to be spent in the great opera centres of Europe, beginning in Hamburg.

2. HAMBURG. The advantage of Hamburg to an aspiring and independent-minded theatre composer was that it contained the only regular opera company in Germany operating outside the courts. Since 1696 it had been dominated by the energetic and influential figure of Reinhard Keiser. Handel went to the opera house in 1703 as a second violinist, later playing continuo harpsichord. He also took the opportunity to gain additional income by giving private lessons. He soon became friends with the composer, singer and theorist Johann Mattheson, and it is Mattheson's later writings (his *Grundlage einer Ehren-Pforte* of 1740 and his

annotated translation of Mainwaring) which provide much information on this period of Handel's life.

Opportunities for Handel arose in 1704 at the opera house. Keiser, being (in Mainwaring's words) 'a man of gaiety and expence, involved himself in debts, which forced him to abscond'. In fact he moved temporarily to Weissenfels, leaving the management of the opera house to his partner Drüsicke. This allowed the younger composers a chance to display their talents, and occasioned some friendly rivalry. At a performance of Mattheson's new opera *Cleopatra* on 5 December 1704 Handel refused to give up his place at the harpsichord to Mattheson after the latter had finished singing the role of Antony, and the two men fought an ineffectual duel.

Handel got the chance to compose his first opera because (again according to Mainwaring) 'Keiser, from his unhappy situation, could no longer supply the Manager, who therefore applied to Handel, and furnished him with a drama to set'. The drama was F. C. Feustking's *Der in Krohnen erlangte Glücks-Wechsel, oder Almira, Königin von Castilien* (usually known as *Almira*) – a challenging choice, since it was a libretto that had been prepared for Keiser himself and which he had already set to music; only his enforced move prevented its performance in Hamburg. (At Weissenfels on 30 July 1704 Keiser produced a much revised version of *Almira*; his original setting was never performed.) Handel's version, opening on 8 January, proved very successful, with about 20 performances, and was followed immediately (on 25 February) by the less successful *Nero* (again on a Feustking libretto), the music of which is lost. Handel remained in Hamburg until the summer of 1706, but his activities as a composer seem to have been cut off with the return of Keiser in August 1705. At some point he composed *Der beglückte Florindo* and *Die verwandelte Daphne*, a sequence of operas to be performed on successive nights; both are lost. Presumably they were composed before he left Hamburg, but they were not produced until January 1708, when he appears to have been in Italy, though it is just possible he might have returned to supervise their production.

Keiser's influence on *Almira* and the whole of Handel's subsequent operatic output can hardly be exaggerated. Not only did Handel incorporate fragments of musical material from several of Keiser's operas in his own works almost throughout his life – the earliest such 'borrowings' appear definitively in Handel's first compositions for Italy in 1707 – but he also absorbed from Keiser the eclectic mix of national styles apparent in so much of his music. Though he was soon to refine and consolidate the specifically Italian elements in his music in Italy itself, he never relinquished French forms for overtures and dance music, and his use of orchestral colour, particularly the occasional instrumental doubling of the voice *colla parte*, was derived from German models. Less happy was his adoption in *Almira* of Keiser's tendency to write for voice in quasi-instrumental style, but this was a fault which the next stage of his career was quick to remove.

3. ITALY. Mainwaring relates that 'the Prince of Tuscany' (i.e. Ferdinando de' Medici, heir to Grand Duke Cosimo III), while visiting Hamburg, sought Handel out and met him several times, showing him examples of the latest Italian music and assuring him 'that there needed nothing but a journey to Italy to reconcile him to the style and taste which prevailed

there'. Handel seems to have been wary of accepting a specific invitation from the Prince (whose motives for cultivating young men were often mixed) and resolved 'to go to Italy on his own bottom, as soon as he could make a purse for that occasion'. Nevertheless, he seems to have followed Ferdinando to Florence in the second half of 1706, though the date of this journey remains uncertain; he may have composed some chamber cantatas in Florence at this time. By the beginning of 1707 he had reached Rome and already made the acquaintance of two important ecclesiastical patrons, the cardinals Carlo Colonna and Benedetto Pamphili, and probably also Cardinal Pietro Ottoboni at whose concerts, says Mainwaring, Handel 'was desired to furnish his quota' of compositions. It was probably from Colonna that he obtained commissions to write several of his early church compositions, performed in the celebrations of the feast of Our Lady of Mount Carmel on 16 May 1707. By then Handel had received from Pamphili his first major Italian libretto to set – not an opera, because a papal ban forbade public operatic performances in Rome, but the allegorical oratorio *Il trionfo del tempo e del disinganno*. Also in May, Handel joined the household of his most important secular patron in Rome, the Marquess (later Prince) Francesco Maria Ruspoli. Working partly at the Bonelli Palace in Rome and partly on Ruspoli's country estate at Vignanello, and collaborating with such excellent musicians as the soprano Margherita Durastanti, Handel settled to the regular provision of chamber cantatas for Ruspoli's weekly assemblies, also producing church compositions and large-scale cantatas for special occasions.

His first opera commission, for Florence, presumably came from Ferdinando de' Medici, but the score seems to have been composed in Rome and revised in Florence for the performance around November 1707 at the Cocomero theatre under the title *Vincer se stesso è la maggior vittoria*; the more familiar title (used by Mainwaring) is *Rodrigo*. The opera shows the benefits of his Italian studies, largely avoiding the occasional vocal difficulties and harmonic quirks apparent in *Il trionfo del tempo* and showing touches of a new elegance in several arias (but *Il trionfo* remains in some ways the more characterful work). The lengthy recitatives show confidence in handling the Italian language.

It is in connection with *Rodrigo* that Mainwaring brings in the name of a singer, Vittoria, coyly hinting at an affair with the composer that began in Florence and was later resumed in Venice. The reference seems to be to the soprano Vittoria Tarquini, who, Mainwaring implies, turned her attention to Handel after a liaison with the bisexual Ferdinando. The fact that she is not listed in the cast of *Rodrigo* casts doubt on Mainwaring's story, but in 1710 the Electress Sophia, discussing Handel's appointment to the Hanover court, mentions gossip that Handel had been the lover of Vittoria ('amant de la Victoria'). No other evidence of a sexual attachment is known for the rest of his life, though an early annotator of Mainwaring hints at occasional discreet affairs with women, adding that 'his amours were rather of short duration, always with[in] the pale of his own profession'.

Handel may have spent the winter of 1707–8 at Venice, but the documentary record resumes in Rome, where, working once more for Ruspoli, he composed the dazzling score of his second oratorio *La resurrezione* in time for performance at the Bonelli palace on Easter Sunday (8 April) 1708. A specially designed set was prepared for the performance, with a backdrop illustrating scenes from the story, and the massive orchestra (at least 45 players) was led by Arcangelo Corelli. This unacted work illustrates Handel's dramatic flair more strikingly than any previous composition, not only in its characterizations (the blustering Lucifer, the grief-stricken yet resolute Mary Magdalene) but also in such effects as the Angel's interruption of the overture with a trumpet aria of great brilliance. His next major work was the dramatic cantata *Aci, Galatea e Polifemo*, written on a visit to Naples in June 1708, and almost certainly commissioned by the Duchess of Laurenzano for the wedding of her niece to the Duke of Alvito.

After the Naples interlude Handel's movements are uncertain, though further excursions to Florence and Venice are likely. He was in Venice at the end of 1709, when his second Italian opera, the satirical comedy *Agrippina*, opened the carnival season at the S Giovanni Grisostomo theatre on 26 December with enormous success. This was the season most popular with visitors, and Handel's triumph before the international audience at once established a worldwide reputation and provided him with influential contacts. Among the latter were probably Prince Ernst Georg of Hanover, brother of the elector (the future George I of England), and the Duke of Manchester (the English ambassador), both of whom may have issued invitations for Handel to visit their respective countries. Much of the music of *Agrippina* was drawn from works Handel had composed earlier in Italy (with a little admixture of material from Keiser) and shows an assured mastery of the Italian idiom, the music more certainly reflecting character and dramatic context than in *Rodrigo*.

4. HANOVER, DÜSSELDORF AND LONDON. It is likely that Handel had several options open to him when the run of *Agrippina* closed near the end of February 1710. He journeyed north, passing through Innsbruck in March, where he was received by Prince Carl von Neuburg, Governor of the Tyrol, to whom he had been recommended, but he did not take up an offer of assistance and continued to Hanover where he was appointed Kapellmeister to the electoral court on 16 June at a salary of 1000 thaler. The Electress Sophia reported that the electoral prince and princess (the future King George II of England and Queen Caroline) were delighted with his harpsichord playing. The Hanoverian appointment made generous allowance for travel, and by July Handel had moved on to Düsseldorf, where he was received for several weeks by the Elector Palatine and the electress Anna Maria de' Medici (Ferdinando's sister) before travelling to London in the early autumn. A few compositions can be assigned to this period, the most important being the splendid dramatic cantata *Apollo e Dafne*, apparently begun in Italy but not completed until 1710 (it may have been a substitute for the opera which the Electress Sophia believed Handel had been asked to write for Düsseldorf).

Italian-style opera had been introduced to London in 1705 and had gained popularity with the production (in English) of Nicola Haym's arrangement of Giovanni Bononcini's *Camilla* at Drury Lane on 30 March 1706. There followed three seasons of experiment and controversy among London theatre managers, in which attempts to establish a new genre of all-sung opera in English were swiftly suppressed by the more urgent public demand for real Italian music sung by Italian singers (especially the castratos). The Queen's (later King's) Theatre in the Haymarket, built by John Vanbrugh, became London's opera house. However, up to the time of Handel's arrival in the autumn of 1710, the Italian operas produced in London had all been arrangements of earlier works or pasticcios. It fell to Handel to compose the first Italian opera specifically designed for London, using the all-Italian company engaged by the manager Aaron Hill for the 1710–11 season. (A little of Handel's music had reached London before him: most of the overture to *Rodrigo* had been used as act tunes in a revival of Jonson's *The Alchemist* in January 1710.) The new opera, *Rinaldo*, opened on 24 February 1711, by which time Handel had already made a mark with 'a Dialogue in Italian, in Her Majesty's praise' (apparently no longer extant) performed at St James's Palace on Queen Anne's birthday, 6 February.

Giacomo Rossi wrote the libretto of *Rinaldo* but the scenario had been designed by Hill himself to 'afford the Musick scope to vary and display its Excellence and fill the Eye with more delightful Prospects' than had been the case with earlier Italian operas in London. The combination of an elaborate series of scenic effects with music of great passion and brilliance made *Rinaldo* the sensation of the season, with 15 performances, despite mockery from Addison and Steele in the *Spectator*. The harpsichord improvisations provided for in Armida's aria 'Vo far guerra' gave Handel opportunity to display his prowess as performer as well as composer. After the end of the season (2 June), he returned to Hanover, stopping at Düsseldorf on the way, and visited his family in Halle in November. He was not in England for the 1711–12 London season (though *Rinaldo* was revived in January 1712), but a reference to his study of English in a letter of July 1711 makes it clear that he intended to return. Mainwaring assigns to this period at Hanover the set of 12 chamber duets found collected in several manuscript copies, but some are earlier in origin. 'Towards the end of the year 1712, he obtained leave of the Elector to make a second visit to England, on condition that he engaged to return within a reasonable time' (Mainwaring).

On his return to London Handel (according to Hawkins) stayed at the town house of 'Mr Andrews, of Barn Elms', but he soon moved to the more luxurious and stimulating environment of Burlington House in Piccadilly, where the young Earl of Burlington exercised a wide range of artistic patronage. Handel seems to have stayed there about three years (1713–16). A new opera, *Il pastor fido*, opened on 22 November 1712, but its unsensational pastoral style proved disappointing after *Rinaldo*, and Handel swiftly returned to heroic gesture and magical effects with the more successful *Teseo* (10 January 1713) and a revival of *Rinaldo* (6 May). A further opera, *Silla*, was written for private performance in June before the newly appointed French ambassador, but despite the existence of a printed wordbook it is not clear whether the work was actually given. There were no Handel operas in the season of 1713–14, and he composed only one more for the rest of the decade – *Amadigi* (25 May 1715), which, like *Teseo*, was based on a French libretto and was again of magical-heroic character. However, Handel was not absent from the opera house in the 1715–16 and 1716–17 seasons (the last in London before 1720), since additional arias for revivals of *Rinaldo* and *Amadigi* belong to this period, and Handel also provided three new arias for the castrato Bernacchi in the 1716

revival of *Pirro e Demetrio*, which he may have directed.

As in Italy, Handel was anxious to show that his compositional skills extended beyond opera. He wrote several English compositions for the church, presumably intended for the Chapel Royal in St James's Palace; his first public church compositions were the *Te Deum* and *Jubilate* composed in 1713. He also seems to have composed the Ode for Queen Anne's Birthday for the appropriate day (6 February) in 1713, but the queen's poor health may have prevented the performance.

At the beginning of June 1713 Handel was summarily dismissed from his Hanover post. The reasons probably relate to his involvement in the celebration of the Treaty of Utrecht (which was against Hanoverian interests); Handel may also have indiscreetly dropped a hint that he would prefer to remain in England. The Hanoverian representative in London, C. F. Kreienberg, expressed anxiety at the breach for the surprising reason that Handel had been useful in supplying reports on Queen Anne's failing health obtained through his friendship with John Arbuthnot, her physician. But matters were smoothed over and he was assured that he could enter Queen Anne's service and continue to serve when the elector became king. On 28 December 1713 the queen granted him an annual pension of £200, and when George succeeded to the crown on 1 August 1714 he kept his word: Handel's arrears of salary from Hanover were paid and his new *Te Deum* was sung in the king's presence on 26 September 1714. Other musical activities in these years are hinted at by the existence of compositions of the period, including two substantial Italian cantatas (one referring to the Spanish Succession) of about 1711–12, perhaps given as court entertainments (they survive only as fragments), chamber cantatas that hint at private musical evenings, and keyboard music, of which he published eight suites through Christopher Smith, by then his chief copyist and business assistant. Handel may have met Smith (originally J. C. Schmidt of Ansbach) on a visit to Germany in 1716, but this journey cannot be confirmed. The most important non-operatic vocal work of this time was the setting of B. H. Brockes's Passion oratorio, of uncertain date (no later than early 1717, possibly three years earlier); its first known performance was in Hamburg Cathedral on 23 March 1719, with settings of the same text by Keiser, Telemann and Mattheson. The best-known work of this time is the Water Music, an orchestral suite first played on 17 July 1717 to accompany a trip on the River Thames made by the king and his entourage. Mainwaring's story that it helped to heal Handel's relations with the king in 1714 cannot be true, but Mainwaring may have confused the 1714 affair with a second period of difficulty in 1717, when a rift developed between the king and his son the Prince of Wales; the water trip (avoided by the Prince and Princess Caroline) was a political event, the first of a series arranged to allow the king to be more visible to his subjects. Handel's provision of music may have indicated that, despite his good standing with the younger members of the royal family, his first loyalty was to the king.

5. CANNONS. In summer 1717 Handel began a brief but fruitful period in the service of James Brydges, Earl of Carnarvon and later Duke of Chandos, based mainly at Cannons, Brydges's newly built mansion near Edgware. His presence at dinner there is recorded in August 1717; by the following summer he had completed eleven

'Chandos' anthems and a large-scale *Te Deum*, all performed in the local parish church of St Lawrence, Whitchurch. Of greater significance for later activities were two dramatic works, the masque *Acis and Galatea*, composed in spring 1718, and the oratorio *Esther*, probably composed shortly afterwards. The first (unconnected with the Naples cantata) was modelled on the English masques by Pepusch and others produced at Drury Lane and Lincoln's Inn Fields in 1715–18 as a modest (and moderately successful) counterblast to the Italian opera; but it comprehensively transcends them with its profound evocation of tragedy in a pastoral setting, leavened by touches of grotesque humour in the characterization of the giant Polyphemus. *Esther*, based on Racine's biblical drama, is a less polished work, recycling substantial portions of music from the Brockes Passion, but it is not without dramatic power. The revivals of both these works in 1732 inspired the series of English oratorios and secular musical dramas that were to crown Handel's achievement.

6. THE ROYAL ACADEMY OF MUSIC. On 20 February 1719 Handel wrote to his brother-in-law Michael Michaëlsen to apologize for not having visited the family at Halle since the death of Michaëlsen's wife (Handel's sister) the previous summer; he had been detained, he said, 'par des affaires indispensables, et d'ou, j'ose dire, ma fortune depend'. These urgent affairs were the establishment of the Royal Academy of Music, an organization designed to put Italian opera in London on a secure footing. It was founded as a joint stock company, financed by subscription and incorporated by Letters Patent. The directors were elected by the subscribers (who were entitled to one vote per £200 subscribed) and, like the subscribers themselves, were drawn from the nobility and landed gentry, many of whom had been on the Grand Tour and had personal knowledge of opera in Italy; some were also good amateur musicians. Their interest in the venture was therefore not merely formal, nor specifically financial. Though the original proposal for the founding of the Academy offered the optimistic forecast that 'the Undertakers will be Gainers at least five and twenty percent upon Twenty percent of their Stock', the subscribers (who received only one dividend payment in the nine seasons of the Academy's operation) cannot have harboured such illusions after the first couple of seasons. They subscribed partly from a genuine desire to see first-class opera in London and partly because subscribing was an appropriate way of exercising the artistic patronage expected from persons of their rank in society.

In May 1719 the king authorized an annual bounty of £1000 to the Academy and ordered its legal incorporation. On 14 May Handel was commissioned by the Lord Chamberlain to visit the Continent and contract 'with such Singer or Singers ... fit to perform on the English Stage', mentioning Senesino in particular. Handel seems not to have returned to Italy, however, but instead went to Dresden, probably taking in Düsseldorf and Halle on the way. He was there by July and stayed on until September, when an illustrious opera company (including Senesino and Handel's old colleague Durastanti) was assembled for a lavish production of Lotti's *Teofane* to celebrate a royal marriage. Four of the singers (Senesino, Durastanti, Berselli and Boschi) were later engaged for the Academy, though only Durastanti came for the short first season. On 30 November the directors recommended that Handel (apparently still abroad) be appointed as 'Master of the Orchester with a Sallary'; the duties and the salary are not known. At the same meeting it was agreed to approach Bononcini 'to know his Terms for composing & performing in the Orchester'.

The first season of the Academy opened belatedly at the King's Theatre on 2 April 1720 with Giovanni Porta's *Numitore*. This seems to have been a stop-gap: Handel's *Radamisto*, produced on 27 April, made a much greater impression and the première was marked by the first public appearance together of King George I and the Prince of Wales since their reconciliation earlier in the month. Handel's dedication of the opera to the king acknowledged this indication of royal favour. An arrangement by Thomas Roseingrave of Domenico Scarlatti's *Narciso* was the only other opera of the season. By the autumn the Academy was in full operation. Bononcini had been engaged, and the Academy's first full-length season opened with his *Astarto* on 19 November 1720, with Senesino making his London début in the title role. For the rest of the decade Handel's activities were closely bound to the fortunes of the Academy, which gave seven more seasons, the last closing in June 1728. As a composer, however, especially in the early years, he did not have the wholly dominant position that posterity accords him, and some of the directors and singers (who ranked in importance above composers) seem always to have been hostile to him. In the 1720–21 season he provided no complete new opera, though he wrote new music for the extensively revised version of *Radamisto* produced on 28 December 1720 and for the third act of *Muzio Scevola* (15 April 1721, the other acts being by the Academy's cellist Filippo Amadei and Bononcini). *Floridante* (9 December 1721) was his only new opera of the following season, the main successes of which were Bononcini's *Crispo* and *Griselda*.

Political events gave Handel the opportunity to take a more prominent role in subsequent seasons. The exposure in May and June 1722 of the Jacobite conspiracies involving Francis Atterbury, Dean of Westminster, put all Catholics under suspicion and made it more difficult for the directors to support Bononcini. His close friend Paolo Rolli, who had provided most of the librettos for the Academy operas and acted as its secretary, also lost his position. As a result Handel gained more opportunity for composition as well as a more congenial librettist in Nicola Haym. His position was not affected by the arrival in the autumn of 1723 of a third composer, Attilio Ariosti, who made some impact with *Coriolano*, produced on 19 February 1723, but always remained a secondary figure. The most important event of the 1722–3 season as far as the public were concerned was the arrival of the soprano Francesca Cuzzoni, a worthy match to Senesino, and it was Handel's new opera *Ottone* in which she made her début on 12 January 1723. Handel was then sufficiently confident of his status to take her to task in rehearsals for refusing to sing her first aria ('Falsa immagine'), though he had composed the opera before her arrival and must soon have become aware that he had not done justice to her capabilities. The three new arias added to *Ottone* for Cuzzoni's benefit performance on 26 March could well have been a peace offering. There is no reason to suppose that Handel was always imperious with his singers: the role of Matilda in *Ottone* gave trouble to the contralto Anastasia Robinson, and was

1. *Autograph score of part of Act 2 scene viii of Handel's 'Giulio Cesare in Egitto', composed in 1723. Queen Cleopatra is threatened by a revolt led by her brother Ptolemy, and in his aria 'Al lampo dell'armi' Julius Caesar vows to defend her. Handel increases the dramatic effect by extending the repeated first section of the aria with a threatening chorus of conspirators. As the only singers available were those who sang the solo parts in the opera, Handel uses their voices to form an offstage chorus ('Voci di congiurati'), and enters their names in abbreviated form: 'Durast' (Margherita Durastanti), 'Sin' (Senesino, who played Caesar), 'Rob' (Anastasia Robinson), 'Bern' (Gaetano Berenstadt), 'Big' (Giuseppe Bigonzi), 'Bos' (Giuseppe Boschi) and 'La Gard' (John Lagarde).*

substantially reworked before performance in response to her diplomatically expressed requests. The season ended with a second new Handel opera, *Flavio* (14 May 1723), its lighter, satirical tone making a contrast to preceding Academy operas and perhaps reflecting a particular preference of the composer.

In the 1723–4 season Bononcini was again allowed two new operas (*Farnace* and *Calfurnia*); they were the last before *Astianatte* (6 May 1727), his final contribution to the London stage. They were quite outshone, however, by Handel's *Giulio Cesare in Egitto* (20 February 1724). This deservedly made a sensational effect with its sumptuous scoring and melodic richness, and gave Senesino and Cuzzoni (as Caesar and Cleopatra) roles that fully stretched their vocal and dramatic talents. Two comparably great though very different masterpieces dominated the next season. *Tamerlano*, which opened the season on 31 October 1724, and *Rodelinda* (13 February 1725) are comparatively restrained in instrumentation, but possess a taut dramatic power to which it is hard to find a parallel in opera of this period; and *Rodelinda* is as well endowed with melody as *Giulio Cesare*. These three operas marked the artistic peak of the Academy's operations. By spring 1725 the directors, ever anxious for new sensations, had determined to obtain the services of a second great soprano, Faustina Bordoni, and thereby sowed the seeds of dissension which were ultimately to

prove disastrous to the Academy. The loss of Haym as librettist and the return of Rolli was an additional hindrance to Handel. The 1725–6 season hung fire until Faustina finally appeared in Handel's *Alessandro* on 5 May 1726, the time meanwhile having been filled in by a pasticcio (*Elisa*), revivals and Handel's hastily prepared *Scipione* (12 March 1726). The choice of subject for *Alessandro* (Alexander the Great's simultaneous wooing of the princesses Roxana and Lisaura), and Handel's ingenious equalization of Cuzzoni's and Faustina's music, amusingly but unwisely pointed up the rivalry between the two prima donnas.

The 1726–7 season began late because of the absence of Senesino and opened with Ariosti's *Lucio Vero* on 7 January 1727. Handel's only new work was *Admeto* (31 January 1727); it proved the finest of the Cuzzoni-Faustina operas, the contrasting styles of the two singers being made a significant element of the characterization. The sopranos themselves, no doubt egged on by their supporters, nevertheless became increasingly hostile and finally came to blows on the stage during a performance of Bononcini's *Astianatte* on 6 June. The incident caused great offence to the Princess of Wales, who was present, and brought the season to an abrupt end.

There were some directors who were prepared to resolve the matter by not renewing Cuzzoni's contract for the following season, but eventually the same company (apart from the contralto Anna Dotti) was re-engaged, perhaps to make sure there was an opera season to celebrate the accession of the new king, George II (George I had died on 11 June). The first of Handel's three new operas, *Riccardo primo* (11 November 1727), had been intended for the previous season, but its British subject proved particularly apt for the celebration of the new king's coronation. All the operas in the rest of the season were Handel's, including two new works: *Siroe* (17 February 1728), the first opera with a libretto by Metastasio to be heard in London, and *Tolomeo* (30 April 1728). By this time the directors and subscribers, riven by dissension and annoyed by the frequent calls for extra cash to meet the financial demands of the singers, were wearying of the whole venture. The production of John Gay's *Beggar's Opera* at Lincoln's Inn Fields on 29 January 1728, which included the Academy's troubles among its objects of satire, helped to devalue opera as a fit object for aristocratic support. Some subscribers indicated to the opera house manager J. J. Heidegger a willingness to carry on, but they were not enough to secure a season, and Heidegger fell back on masquerades to keep the theatre in use during winter 1728–9. At an ill-attended meeting on 18 January 1729 the directors effectively wound up the Academy as an active body and resolved (as the Earl of Egmont noted) 'to permit Hydeger and Hendle to carry on operas without disturbance for 5 years'. Within ten days Handel set off for Italy to engage new singers for the following season.

Despite his involvement with opera Handel found time for some other musical activities in the 1720s. Services at the Chapel Royal gave opportunities for the composition of church music, and the splendour of the anthems for the coronation service of George II and Queen Caroline on 11 October 1727 shows how much Handel welcomed the chance to use the massed forces denied him in the opera house. His work in this field was recognized by his honorary appointment as Composer of Music for His Majesty's Chapel Royal on 25 February 1723. He became the music master to the royal princesses, and, particularly in 1724–5, wrote several solo and trio sonatas which, with other earlier works, were later published as his opp.1 and 2. In August 1723 he took a lease on a new house in Brook Street (now no.25), where he lived for the rest of his life, and he made plain his commitment to England as his adopted country by becoming a naturalized British subject in February 1727.

7. THE SECOND ACADEMY. Between February and July 1729 Handel was in continental Europe in search of new singers. After visiting Venice, Bologna and Rome he went on to Germany to see his mother at Halle for the last time (she died in December 1730) and took in Hamburg on his way back. He succeeded in engaging a full company of seven singers, all but one (the aging castrato Bernacchi) new to London; they included the soprano Anna Strada del Pò, to remain his leading female singer for the next eight years. The first season under the new arrangements, much dependent on the support of the king, opened on 2 December 1729 with *Lotario*, newly composed but in the heroic style typical of the Academy period. This was followed (after a revival of *Giulio Cesare*) by the attractively satirical *Partenope*, suggesting a departure from tradition. But neither opera was well liked. The pasticcio *Ormisda* was more successful: it was the first of a number of such works compiled or arranged from the works of other companies (usually those of the new 'Neapolitan' school) which Handel was to offer over the next seven years in addition to his own compositions. For the ensuing season Handel had little choice but to re-engage Senesino, Bernacchi having proved a poor substitute. He opened with a revival of *Scipione* on 3 November 1730. *Poro* (2 February 1731) was the only new opera and was well received. Handel strengthened his company for the following season with two newcomers to London, the tenor Pinacci and the excellent bass Antonio Montagnana, but his first new opera, *Ezio* (Handel's last on a Metastasio text), was taken off after only five performances. *Sosarme*, the second new work, fared better.

During the run of *Sosarme*, on 23 February 1732, Bernard Gates, Master of the Children of the Chapel Royal, gave the first of three private performances of the Cannons oratorio *Esther* at the Crown and Anchor Tavern in the Strand, beginning a long series of inter-related events which eventually led Handel away from operatic composition and established English oratorio and unstaged musical drama as his main form of composition. The *Esther* revival stimulated the first public performance of the piece in London, by an unnamed group, on 20 April. This was without Handel's authority, and he responded by producing a newly enlarged version of the work at the King's Theatre on 2 May 1732, sung in English but using most of his Italian singers with English reinforcements. Though Gates's performance had been staged, this presentation in a public theatre had to be given without action because of the Bishop of London's intervention. On 15 May an unauthorized performance of Handel's other dramatic work for Cannons, *Acis and Galatea*, took place at the Little Theatre in the Haymarket, and Handel again responded on 10 June with a new version of the same work – a combination of the Naples cantata *Aci, Galatea e Polifemo* with the Cannons masque and other music, sung in a mixture of English and Italian and presented as a serenata. In the space of six weeks two musical forms new to London – oratorio and serenata – had found a place in the city's theatrical entertainment, but only as an occasional alternative to opera.

The season of 1732–3 led to further developments and a crisis. The new works were the remarkable *Orlando* (27 January 1733) and a second English oratorio, *Deborah* (17 March 1733). Handel's attempt to charge double prices for the latter was however resented. Senesino's relations with Handel deteriorated – he may have been unhappy with the unusually difficult and irregular role of Orlando, and with having to sing in English again in *Deborah* – and Handel dismissed him. Meanwhile a group of the nobility and gentry, headed by Frederick, Prince of Wales, were moving to undermine Handel's position as the sole provider of Italian opera in London. Their motives are not easy to determine but were undoubtedly wider than personal hostility to the composer. Handel's position as the effective controller of opera performances, with no body of aristocratic directors to govern him, appeared presumptuous in an age when musicians were regarded as servants; and the fact that he owed this position primarily to the king allowed him to be seen as a symbol of the corrupt Whig government, making him a natural focus of hostility for the new opposition groups cultivating Frederick as a future 'patriot king'. In June a subscription was begun to form a new opera company (the so-called Opera of the Nobility), the directors of which

2. Autograph score of the opening scene of Act 2 of Handel's 'Poro', composed December 1730 and January 1731, showing the composer's meticulous inclusion of the stage directions of Metastasio's libretto. The directions at the bottom of the page describe the encounter between the Indian King Porus and the Macedonian general Alexander at a bridge over the River Hydaspes: 'The Indians attack the Macedonians in the flank but are swiftly put to flight and Timagenes disappears in the crowd. Only Porus and Alexander remain; they join in combat, Alexander forcing Porus to retreat behind the scene. At the first attack of the Indians, Gandartes, with a troupe of pioneers, mounts the bridge and causes it to be broken at both ends, close by the banks, then, throwing his sword and helmet into the river, Gandartes himself jumps into the river, followed by the pioneers'.

immediately engaged Senesino and other members of Handel's company (Strada excepted) to sing for them the following season under the direction of Nicola Porpora.

The attacks on Handel had the beneficial effect of galvanizing his supporters and generating (especially after the performances of *Acis and Galatea* and the English oratorios) a wider recognition of his stature as a musician. He was invited to receive the honorary degree of Doctor of Music at the revival of the 'Publick Act' (the degree-giving ceremony) at Oxford in summer 1733 and to provide music for the occasion. He did not in the event accept the degree but gave a series of concerts of mainly English works including the first performance of a new oratorio, *Athalia*.

By the autumn Handel had managed to assemble a new opera company – Heidegger may have done the negotiations – which included his old colleague Margherita Durastanti and a fine new castrato, Giovanni Carestini. He opened on 30 October 1733 with the pasticcio *Semiramide* and continued with a revival of *Ottone* and two other pasticcios; but his

audiences were thin, and four opera nights in December passed without a performance being given. The rival opera company opened its operations with Porpora's *Arianna in Nasso* at Lincoln's Inn Fields on 29 December, beginning four years of operatic warfare. Handel seems to have held his own in this first season of rivalry. Carestini swiftly gained admirers, and Handel's new opera *Arianna in Creta*, which opened on 26 January 1734, showed off his talents to the full. For the marriage of the Princess of Wales to the Prince of Orange in March Handel produced *Parnasso in festa* (his only full-scale Italian serenata), the music of which was partly new and partly adapted from *Athalia*. Some of the new music was included in a much-altered revival of *Il pastor fido* which opened on 18 May 1734 and had a very successful run, extending the season into July.

8. OPERA AT COVENT GARDEN. Handel's five-year agreement with Heidegger ended in 1734 and the Nobility Opera took over at the King's Theatre. Fortunately another venue had become available: John Rich had opened his new theatre at Covent Garden on 7

December 1732 and saw advantage in offering Handel two opera nights a week as an alternative to the repertory of spoken plays. In the season of 1734–5 both opera companies gave of their best. The Nobility had managed to engage Farinelli, the greatest castrato of the age, as their leading singer and opened their season at the King's Theatre with Hasse's *Artaserse* on 29 October 1734, following with a much-mangled version of Handel's own *Ottone*. Handel could also offer an extra attraction at Covent Garden, the French dancer Marie Sallé and her company, for whom Handel provided newly written ballets in all the operas of the season. He opened on 9 November with a further revival of *Il pastor fido*, to which a new prologue featuring Sallé as the muse Terpsichore was added. The new works were *Ariodante* (8 January 1735) and *Alcina* (16 April 1735) – two of his greatest operas, rivalling those of the Academy's mid-1720s period. Their productions were separated by a Lenten season in which Handel performed *Athalia* and his two earlier oratorios, adding the further attraction of organ concertos – a new form of composition – in the intervals: thus in this one season Handel displayed the full range of his musical genius, both as performer (in the organ concertos) and as composer. Italian and English music for solo voices, Italian and English choral music, orchestral music in the dances and concertos were all represented, and there were even examples of English church music in the Coronation Anthems incorporated into *Esther* and *Deborah*. It was not enough, however, to secure adequate financial returns, and Handel declined to attempt a further challenge to the Nobility Opera (again with Farinelli) in the following season. Instead he produced a brilliant setting of Dryden's ode *Alexander's Feast* at Covent Garden on 19 February 1736, filling out the evening with new concertos and an Italian cantata. Revivals of *Acis and Galatea* and *Esther* followed. The wedding of the Prince of Wales on 27 April gave Handel an excuse for a short, celebratory opera season consisting of a revival of *Ariodante* (in which Gioacchino Conti, a new castrato, was allowed to include non-Handelian arias from his previous continental repertory) and eight performances of the newly composed *Atalanta* (12 May 1736) – light in mood, as befitted the occasion, but not at all shallow; Frederick ostentatiously refused to attend the first night.

By the autumn some sort of rapprochement seems to have taken place. The Nobility Opera were once more at the King's Theatre (for what was to be their last season), but Handel was also able to offer a full season of opera and other works at Covent Garden, with the prince and princess making a point of attending the opening production (a revival of *Alcina* on 6 November 1736). Handel produced three new operas – *Arminio* (12 January 1737), *Giustino* (16 February) and *Berenice* – as well as a substantially rewritten version of his first Italian oratorio, renamed *Il trionfo del tempo e della verità*, and an adaptation of Leonardo Vinci's *Didone abbandonata* (13 April 1737). The operas, all based on old-fashioned librettos with recitatives ruthlessly cut, display a level of musical invention lower than that in *Alexander's Feast* or even (with the help of some borrowings from Telemann) for the new music of *Il trionfo del tempo*. Opera seemed no longer to be Handel's prime interest, though he was wary of abandoning it altogether. A crisis of confidence is suggested by a sudden deterioration in Handel's health in April 1737, marked by the temporary paralysis of his right hand. In September he visited Aix-la-Chapelle (Aachen) where the vapour-baths effected a complete cure.

3. Revival of Handel's 'Il pastor fido' (directed by R. Peterson) at Drottningholm in 1969

9. FROM OPERA TO ORATORIO. By November 1737 Handel was back in London composing a new opera, *Faramondo*. The demise of the Nobility Opera enabled him to return to the King's Theatre, where he shared musical activities with the composers Pescetti and Veracini in a season organized by Heidegger. This opened with a pasticcio on 29 October 1737 but the death of Queen Caroline on 20 November closed the theatre until the new year. It reopened with *Faramondo* on 3 January 1738, Handel's reappearance after his illness receiving acclaim along with the London début of the castrato Caffarelli. (In the closed period Handel had composed an expansive anthem for the queen's funeral.) Handel next prepared *Alessandro Severo* (25 February), a pasticcio drawing mainly on the operas of the previous season, and composed *Serse* (15 April), based on a largely comic Venetian libretto. The latter, the finest of his late operas (and one over which he took much trouble), received only five performances. Any financial difficulties which Handel might have met during the season were cleared by a benefit concert at the King's on 28 March, under the title 'An Oratorio'; it contained church music and excerpts from oratorio and reportedly earned him about £1000. He was now on the way to becoming a revered public figure, though perhaps on account more of his recent English choral works than of his operas. In May 1738 a marble statue of him by Louis Roubiliac was commissioned for the pleasure gardens at Vauxhall; it shows the composer informally posed and playing the lyre to suggest an identification with the god Apollo – a unique honour for a living composer. Two months earlier the full score of *Alexander's Feast* (shown in the statue) was published: seven members of the royal family headed the lengthy subscription list. This was also the time when Handel first became involved in charitable work with his contribution to the establishment of the Fund for the Support of Decayed Musicians (now the Royal Society of Musicians).

Heidegger attempted to arrange a further opera season at the King's, but on 25 July announced that he had failed to obtain the requisite number of subscribers and 'could not agree with the Singers th'I offer'd One Thousand Guineas to One of them'. Handel turned resolutely to oratorio, beginning *Saul* the following day; he immediately went on to compose the biblical oratorio *Israel in Egypt*, but meanwhile he drafted *Imeneo* (a 'wedding opera', like *Atalanta*), probably on hearing of the betrothal of Princess Mary to Prince Frederick of Hesse. (It was not performed until November 1740, no connection being made with the princess's marriage in May that year.) *Saul* opened a season of oratorio and ode at the King's on 16 January 1739, concluding on 19 April. Handel may have intended to perform *Imeneo* in a short post-Easter season, but instead he produced the semi-pasticcio *Giove in Argo* on 1 and 5 May; it drew some numbers from *Imeneo* and was described as a 'Dramatical Composition', presumably indicating that it was not fully staged. The new oratorios created a good impression, but audiences who hankered after Italian opera were not appeased by their massive choruses and rich orchestration; the mainly choral *Israel in Egypt* proved particularly difficult to swallow and its second performance was advertised as 'shortned and Intermix'd with Songs' (i.e. Italian arias).

Hints of a new move to revive Italian opera, and of a new rival for Handel, occurred at Covent Garden in April and May 1739, when Pescetti's serenata *Angelica e Medoro* was performed four times by a company almost certainly financed by Charles Sackville, Earl of Middlesex and heir to the Duke of Dorset (his mistress, known as La Muscovita, was one of the singers). He had just returned from an extended stay in Italy and became the leading light of a new 'opera party'. By May he had obtained a modest subscription for operas the following season. However, both he and Handel seem to have been anxious not to begin another operatic war. The King's Theatre remained dark; Handel moved to Rich's old theatre at Lincoln's Inn Fields, giving English works at the end of 1739 and in Lent 1740. There were new works, a setting of Dryden's *A Song for St Cecilia's Day* and *L'Allegro, il Penseroso ed il Moderato*, a perfect expression of the moods suggested by the imagery of Milton's poetry. Most of the 'Grand Concertos' (composed in September and October 1739 and published in April 1740) were first heard at these concerts. Meanwhile Middlesex offered his season of Italian works (mainly in a light pastoral vein) at the Little Theatre in the Haymarket, opening on 1 December.

Middlesex was not active the following season, a circumstance which seems to have led Handel (perhaps unwisely) to present himself once more as the nation's operatic provider. He made a continental journey in summer 1740 (the only known detail of which is his playing of the organ in Haarlem on 9 September), when he presumably engaged the two Italians who joined his company for the winter season, the castrato G. B. Andreoni and the soprano Maria Monza. *Imeneo* was finally completed for performance but given only twice, apparently because of the illness of Francesina (Elisabeth Duparc). Handel's last opera, *Deidamia*, in which Monza appeared for the first time, opened on 10 January 1741, but after its second performance Handel continued his season with *L'Allegro* with several new numbers sung in Italian by Andreoni. After the third and last performance of *Deidamia*, on 10 February, Handel returned to English works sung partly in Italian. The wide gaps between performances hint at a boycott of Handel, but the reference in a published letter of 4 April 1741 to 'a *faux pas* made but not meant' suggests that the gaffe was a social one, perhaps connected with Handel's renewed (and to some, arrogant) return to operatic promotion.

10. ORATORIOS AND MUSICAL DRAMAS. Whether Handel specifically decided to forsake Italian opera at this moment is unclear; but such a decision had almost certainly been taken by the time he had completed his next venture – a series of oratorios and other concert works given in Dublin between December 1741 and June 1742. Before leaving London he had composed the oratorio *Messiah* and drafted *Samson*. Just before his departure Handel also saw the first production (the pasticcio *Alessandro in Persia*) of a new, full, season promoted by Middlesex at the King's; he later reported to Charles Jennens (a shade patronizingly) that it made him 'very merry all along my journey'. The first performance of *Messiah* on 13 April formed the climax to Handel's Dublin season. As his final farewell to Italian opera Handel had performed a concert version of *Imeneo* on 24 March, with Susannah Cibber as Tirinto. The success of the Dublin season gave Handel the confidence to face London again purely as a composer of English concert works, performed under his sole control, and allowing him (with the use of a chorus) a far wider range of musical expression than was possible in opera at that time.

In Lent 1743 Handel offered oratorio performances at Covent Garden, setting a pattern he was generally to follow for the rest of his life. The revised and completed *Samson* was especially well received, but London still contained hostile elements. Horace Walpole's remark that 'Handel has set up an Oratorio against the Operas, and succeeds' shows that the opera supporters still regarded Handel as a potential rival, and there was a particular difficulty over the London première of *Messiah*, which drew pietistic objections to the singing of scriptural words in a theatre. In summer 1743 Lord Middlesex, hoping to restore the flagging fortunes of his opera enterprise (and perhaps genuinely wanting to banish old enmities), made Handel what seem to have been very fair terms to compose new operas or revise old ones. Handel, immersed in setting an English operatic text (Congreve's *Semele*) for concert performance, refused, apparently breaking a promise and again causing aristocratic offence; his copyist and business manager Christopher Smith wondered 'how the Quality will take it that He can compose for himself and not for them when they offered him more than ever He had in His life'. Handel did however allow Middlesex's company to revive his *Alessandro* under the title *Rossane*. *Semele* appeared with a new oratorio *Joseph and his Brethren* in Handel's next season, but 'the opera party' (as Mrs Delany specifically called them) were still annoyed, particularly by *Semele*, which despite its English text and its presentation 'after the manner of an Oratorio' (i.e. unstaged) they saw as encroaching on their territory. The unabashed sensuousness of a score depicting both wittily and tragically the fate of one of Jupiter's paramours must also have taken aback those who (on the strength of *Samson* and *Messiah*) were now looking to oratorio for spiritual uplift, and *Joseph* proved generally more acceptable.

Handel ignored the implications of his 1744 season. He composed a new oratorio that summer (*Belshazzar*) but also reasserted his interest in secular drama with *Hercules*, like *Semele* on a classical subject. Moreover, he took advantage of the fact that the opera company, racked by financial problems and legal actions, was not able to present a season in 1744–5. He therefore returned to the King's Theatre and offered a subscription series of 24 oratorio-style concerts on Saturdays throughout that winter. This venture once again annoyed the opera party, or a faction of them, and a section of society led by Lady Brown, the wife of the British resident in Venice, boycotted the performances. A dignified newspaper announcement by Handel, offering subscribers their money back, had the effect of rallying his supporters and 16 of the promised 24 concerts were eventually given; *Hercules* (performed on 5 January 1745) was seen by some as 'an English Opera', and therefore meriting the same objections as *Semele*; Jennens observed that 'for want of the top Italian voices, Action, Dresses, Scenes & Dances … [it] had scarce half a house the first night, much less than half the second'.

Handel thereafter kept to the safer formula of Lenten oratorio seasons at Covent Garden, though the '45 Jacobite rebellion upset London entertainments in 1746, and in February that year he gave only three performances of his 'New Occasional Oratorio', a patriotic piece incorporating excerpts from *Israel in Egypt*. An oratorio celebrating victory over the rebels was by then already being planned, though the decisive battle of Culloden (16 April 1746) came too late for it to be given in Lent. The new piece was *Judas Maccabaeus*,

dedicated to the Duke of Cumberland, leader of the triumphant Hanoverian forces. Handel performed it during the Lent season of 1747. Generally jubilant in style, it was well received and the season seems to have marked the end of all opposition to Handel. (Middlesex had restarted Italian opera at the King's, and on 13 November 1747 produced *Lucio Vero*, an all-Handel pasticcio, now probably in tribute to the composer rather than in rivalry.) Handel presented two new oratorios, *Joshua* and *Alexander Balus*, in his 1748 season, the latter having operatic leanings in its sympathetic narration of the doomed love of Cleopatra for the Syrian king Alexander. In 1749 the new works were *Solomon* and *Susanna*, marked by a new richness of style and depth of feeling; and in 1750 *Theodora* showed a more specifically spiritual profundity, continued the following year in *Jephtha*, the composition of which was interrupted by the composer's encroaching blindness. The possibility of a new theatrical venture opened at the start of 1750 with *Alceste*, a play by Thomas Smollett intended to include substantial musical interludes. These Handel provided, in splendid French-influenced style, for a projected production at Covent Garden; but the work was never performed and Handel adapted the music for the 'musical interlude' *The Choice of Hercules*, first given on 1 March 1751.

Handel continued to supervise oratorio seasons until just before his death in April 1759. With the help of the younger Christopher Smith he was able to compose some additions to revived works and even, in 1757, to create *The Triumph of Time and Truth*, a new English version of the oratorio originally composed in 1707 and rewritten in 1737. On a personal level his reputation was enhanced during these last years by charitable acts, notably the annual benefit performances of *Messiah* from 1750 onwards at the chapel of the Foundling Hospital; they helped raise that work to the special place in English music which it has never relinquished.

11. REVIVALS. During Handel's lifetime many of his operas for London were given performances in Hamburg and Brunswick, invariably with alterations and additions by local composers (including Keiser, Telemann and Mattheson in Hamburg); the last seems to have been that of *Berenice* (1743, Brunswick). *Agrippina* was also revived in Hamburg (1718), and one of his London operas was performed in Italy (*Rinaldo*, with additions by Leo; 1718, Naples). In London itself the only revival apart from *Alessandro* (as *Rossane*) in 1743, 1747 and 1748, was that of *Admeto* on 12 March 1754 at the King's Theatre, under Vanneschi's management. That was the last revival of any Handel opera before the 20th century, not counting Samuel Arnold's production at the King's Theatre on 1 March 1787 of what purported to be *Giulio Cesare* (in fact a pasticcio from several operas compiled to please George III) or the reduced, one-act version of *Almira* produced to celebrate the bicentenary of the Hamburg opera in 1878 (repeated in 1879 and 1885). Yet the operas were never quite forgotten; music from them continued to be heard in recitals and in interpolations in the oratorios. Handel himself rarely used his operatic music in his oratorios but versions of operatic arias, with new-dubbed English texts, began to appear in the oratorios during the period of the composer's blindness and the practice was extended in the decade after his death. Arias from *Ezio* and *Orlando* added to *Israel in Egypt* in 1765 remained there well into the Victorian era. Between 1868 and

4. Revival of Handel's 'Giustino' (directed by Harry Kupfer) at the Komische Oper, Berlin, 1984

1885 Friedrich Chrysander published full scores of all the operas in his Händel-Gesellschaft edition, but by then their *opera seria* format, their modest orchestration and their use of high voices for the leading male roles were so far from prevailing operatic ideals that no attempt was made to perform them.

The 20th-century revival of the operas began in Göttingen in 1920 with Oskar Hagen's production of *Rodelinda*, soon followed by *Ottone* (as *Otto und Theophano*), *Giulio Cesare* (*Julius Cäsar*) and *Serse* (*Xerxes*). Strictly speaking, these were arrangements. Hagen dealt with problematic elements by removing them: librettos were translated and partly rewritten, arias were transposed, shortened and dovetailed into the recitatives, the male roles were allocated to tenors and basses and new orchestration was provided. His approach characterized the vast majority of German revivals in the following years (as most of the arrangements were unpublished their form cannot be precisely described). The first revival at Halle was that of *Orlando* in 1922, but it was not until the inauguration of the annual Handel festival in 1952 that Halle became the main centre of German Handel opera revival. By then the scores were being treated less freely, though high voices in male roles were still taboo, and the orchestration was frequently retouched. Examples of the style can be heard in the recordings of the Halle productions of *Radamisto* (1955) and *Poro* (1958). Though the sound of Hagen's productions and those of his successors was remote from anything Handel could have imagined, their purpose was nevertheless well intended: Hagen recognized the quality of the music and the dramatic impact of at least some of it, and wanted it to be judged in its rightful place, the theatre; the results were ponderous and suppressed many of the elements that give life to the music, but the performances, always fully professional, sincerely attempted to bring out neglected aspects of Handel's genius.

The revival in Britain, largely independent of the German movement, was stimulated by stage productions of the English musical dramas and dramatic oratorios – particularly at Cambridge, where *Semele* was staged by the University Musical Society in 1925. An amateur element often characterized these British productions, but they were generally far more respectful of Handel's scoring for both voices and orchestra and, though cuts were common, the structure of the operas was seldom violated. The first British revival of an Italian Handel opera (sung in English, as were most 20th-century British productions) was that of *Giulio Cesare* by the London Festival Opera Company at the Scala Theatre in 1930. There were only two further staged opera revivals before World War II (*Rinaldo* in 1933 by a school music department, *Serse* in 1935), to which a staged *Hercules* by Alan and Frances Kitching in 1939 must be added as prophetic of later ventures. In 1955 the Handel Opera Society was founded with Anthony Lewis as chairman and Charles Farncombe as conductor. Their first production was *Deidamia* at St Pancras Town Hall, chosen with the encouragement of Edward Dent, who provided the English translation. The society was constituted as an amateur choral society and during most of its 30-year period of operation it gave equal prominence to operas and to the dramatic oratorios, the amateur chorus being used in conjunction with professional soloists and orchestra. From 1959 to its closure in 1985 it gave an annual season, usually of two Handel productions at Sadler's Wells Theatre; it staged 18 Handel operas. Another centre of the Handel opera revival in Britain was the University of Birmingham, where the enthusiasm of Professor Anthony Lewis, with Brian Trowell as director, led to six Handel revivals between 1959 and 1968, including distinguished performances of *Tamerlano* (1962), *Ariodante* (1964), *Orlando* (1966) and *Admeto* (1968); Ivor Keys, Lewis's successor, included four further Handel operas (among them a truly complete *Giulio Cesare* in 1977) in an ensuing series. The remarkable productions by Unicorn Opera in Abingdon, initially amateur, were also launched in 1959 (with *Orlando*) and continued until 1975, the last production (*Lotario*) being given in Henley-on-Thames. They were organized by Alan Kitching (as translator and director) and, initially, Frances Kitching (as conductor); the stagings were mostly given in the Unicorn Theatre in Abingdon Abbey. Awareness of Handel's operas in Britain was also significantly increased by BBC broadcasts, from *Rodelinda* as early as 1928, through occasional performances directed by Arnold Goldsborough in 1948–64 to *Amadigi* under Roger Norrington in 1985.

By 1990 virtually all of Handel's operas had been revived and productions of the better-known works in Europe were no longer uncommon. It is clear from the performances at Halle and Göttingen in the 1980s that the German prejudice against high voices in male roles had largely vanished, the alto voice parts usually being allocated to countertenors. The movement for historically aware performances of early music had the effect of suppressing the inclination to tamper with Handel's scores, though theatre managements continued to find their length (usually about three hours of music, or four hours in the theatre) unacceptable. Handel's operas have not escaped 'concept' productions, such as Peter Sellars's *Orlando* (1982, Boston), in which the libretto was re-treated as a science-fiction fantasy; attempts have also been made to present the operas in 'authentic' stagings, with sets modelled on 18th-century originals and with Baroque gesture and movement. But, broadly speaking, the period of pioneering has passed, and Handel's operas should now expect to have a modest place in the repertory and receive treatment no less respectful than that accorded to works of other periods.

12. HANDEL AS AN OPERA COMPOSER. Throughout the 36 years in which Italian opera was his major preoccupation Handel adhered closely to the standard form of the period, determined by the priority given to solo singing and to stage presentation in which sets were changed in view of the audience and the curtain not lowered until the end of the evening. Solo arias, invariably in da capo form (though often with a shortened return to the main section), therefore dominate the operas, and scenes are generally constructed to begin with a number of characters on stage, each of whom sings an aria and leaves. The final scene usually ends with a *coro* sung by the soloists; ensembles are otherwise rare and largely confined to scenes of public rejoicing; only 'Dall'orror' in Act 3 of *Alcina* touches the profundity of the choruses in the English choral works.

Handel's operas thus appear at a first glance very like those of his contemporaries; what sets them apart is the excellence of the music and its ability to express with immediate conviction the emotional states of the characters in the context of the drama. The latter

quality, though already apparent in the prison scene of *Almira* (1705), is only intermittently present in the earlier operas (before 1720), in which the arias often hold the attention by musical interest alone. This is good enough for works which are comic or use magical effects to propel the plot, as *Agrippina* (1709) and *Rinaldo* (1711) particularly demonstrate; the wholly serious *Rodrigo* (1707) is less successful. Much of the music of this period is worked out from ideas first found in the cantatas and other works of Handel's Italian period, and in *Agrippina* the characteristic harmonic quirks of this period are often attractively retained. The harmony of the first London operas is smoother, but the orchestration is richer, with its new use of bassoon tone colour; the extravagance of four trumpets in *Rinaldo* was not repeated.

The operas of the Academy period are generally more serious in tone (the enjoyable exception is *Flavio* (1723), though *Giulio Cesare* (1724) is not without touches of wit), arias are more expansive and musical expression is more consistently allied to drama. *Giulio Cesare* is all-encompassing; the deft characterization of Cleopatra's 'infinite variety', the sumptuous orchestration and the emotional power of so much of the music have rightly earned it a high reputation, though its odd structure, with secondary characters commanding the final scenes of the first two acts (a circumstance dictated by the status of the original singers), presents problems in a modern context. *Tamerlano* (1724) and *Rodelinda* (1725) have less highly coloured scores but maintain dramatic force throughout, the tenor roles for Borosini (Bajazet in *Tamerlano*, Grimoaldo in *Rodelinda*) being especially striking. The later Academy operas, with the exception of the subtle and tender *Admeto* (1727), are slightly lesser achievements; the rivalry between the leading sopranos Cuzzoni and Faustina and the need to balance their parts proved more an inhibition than a stimulant to Handel's inspiration.

In the 1730s, when Handel was free to choose a wider range of librettos, a comic and fantastic note returns in

5. Revival of Handel's 'Teseo' (directed by Nicholas McGegan) at the Boston Early Music Festival, June 1985

Partenope (1730), *Orlando* (1733) and *Alcina* (1735), and the influence of the newer pre-classical manner developed by Vinci and Leo is often present, most notably in 'Sta nell'Ircana' in *Alcina*, but never exactly imitated; Handel's bass lines and harmonies always have more movement than is typical for the style. The mid-1730s operas attain a greatness comparable with the peak of the previous decade, with the *scena*, a potent element in many Handel operas, reaching new heights in the mad scene of *Orlando* and the end of Act 2 of *Alcina*. (For their full impact these works require the orchestral forces known to have been employed by Handel at the time: they include a band of over 30 strings – divided approximately 12.8.6.4.2 – with four bassoons and two harpsichords in addition to the stipulated winds.) Hints of new directions in opera are suggested in the later 1730s, but none, sadly, was followed up. A move to a synthesis with the French operatic style adumbrated in the sequences of dances and choruses in the operas of 1734–5 did not extend beyond that season. The romantic *Ariodante* (1735) also pointed to a more intimate, less artificial style, as did *Atalanta* (1736), but Handel turned back to older heroic librettos in 1737 and 1738 with what seems to be diminished musical inspiration (especially in comparison with the English choral works to which he was then giving attention); *Giustino* (1737) nevertheless has much to commend it. *Serse* (1738), a wholly successful comic opera deepened by moments of real anguish, indicated yet another line of development, but by then external circumstances were drawing Handel away from opera, and his final efforts in the genre, though by no means negligible, are comparatively slight.

Handel's personal attitude to opera has at all times to be deduced from external evidence. His surviving correspondence is sparse, and, with the tantalizingly brief exception of his comments to Jennens on the oratorio *Belshazzar* in 1744, not concerned with artistic matters. What does survive is the unique archive of his composition autographs, nearly all in the British Library. Many are extant in near-complete form; only the autographs of *Amadigi* and *Admeto* (and the early Hamburg operas) are wholly lost. These are supplemented by the collection (mainly at Hamburg) of Handel's working copies or 'conducting scores' which, taken with contemporary MS copies, printed word-books and (for the London operas) the selections of songs published by Walsh and others, allow the often complex textual history of the operas to be determined in great detail. Several of the autographs display a remarkable degree of pre-performance revision, usually far more than would seem necessary to accommodate last-minute changes of cast or other such exigencies. The revisions attest to a striving for high artistic ideals which while including dramatic truth were perhaps more concerned with purely musical values. Alterations made for revivals occasionally show the same concerns (for example in the second version of *Radamisto*), but more frequently the addition or substitution of new music to suit new singers, with compensating cuts, impairs the integrity of the original and suggests a lessening of the composer's interest after the initial process of creation. It will be possible to draw firmer conclusions when all the operas are published in full critical editions, a process that the Hallische Händel-Ausgabe has only just begun. Meanwhile the addition of Handel's operas in reasonably authentic form to the performing repertory allows modern audiences to gain a fuller and hence more truthful perspective on a composer whose popularity has for too long been based on a narrow selection of his output; and to draw their own conclusion that, in the hands of a great composer, early *opera seria* has its own values and validity.

See also ACIS AND GALATEA; ADMETO; AGRIPPINA; ALCINA; ALESSANDRO; ALESSANDRO SEVERO (ii); ALMIRA; AMADIGI DI GAULA; ARIANNA IN CRETA; ARIODANTE; ARMINIO; ATALANTA; BERENICE; DEIDAMIA; EZIO; FARAMONDO; FLAVIO; FLORIDANTE; GIULIO CESARE IN EGITTO (ii); GIUSTINO (ii); HERCULES; IMENEO; LOTARIO; MUZIO SCEVOLA; ORESTE; ORLANDO (ii); OTTONE; PARTENOPE; PASTOR FIDO, IL; PORO; RADAMISTO; RICCARDO PRIMO; RINALDO; RODELINDA; RODRIGO; SCIPIONE; SEMELE (ii); SERSE; SILLA; SIROE (i); SOSARME; TAMERLANO; TESEO; and TOLOMEO.

Editions: *G. F. Händels Werke: Ausgabe der Deutschen Händelgesellschaft*, ed. F. W. Chrysander, i–xlviii, l–xcvi, suppls.i–vi (Leipzig and Bergedorf bei Hamburg, 1858–94, 1902) [HG]
Hallische Händel-Ausgabe im Auftrage der Georg Friedrich Händel-Gesellschaft, ed. M. Schneider, R. Steglich and others (Kassel, 1955–) [HHA] [vols. in progress are given in square brackets]

HWV [Händel Werke Verzeichnis] refers to the numeration of works in the *Händel-Handbuch*, i–iii. For a complete list of early editions, see Smith (1960).

MS sources cited include only major MS collections, important isolated MSS and available sources containing autograph material; for more detailed source information see the *Händel-Handbuch*, i–iii, and Baselt, *Verzeichnis* (1986). [R] added to *GB-Lbl* distinguishes the Royal Music Library collection (see Squire 1927) from that of the Department of Manuscripts (see Hughes-Hughes 1906–9 and Willetts 1970). MS full scores of the operas from *Rinaldo* to *Arianna* (except *Silla*), and *Acis and Galatea*, also exist in the Earl of Malmesbury's private collection (on microfilm at the Hampshire Record Office, Winchester).

operas in three acts unless otherwise stated

HG – *Hamburg, Theater am Gänsemarkt*   LCG – *London, Covent Garden*   LKH – *London, King's/Queen's Theatre in the Haymarket*
LLF – *London, Lincoln's Inn Fields*   LLH – *London, Little Theatre in the Haymarket*
‡ – *printed libretto extant (facs. in Harris 1989)*
* – *autograph, wholly or primarily in Handel's hand*   † – *includes performing score, or other MSS with autograph annotations*

HWV	title	libretto	première (perfs. under composer)	sources	remarks	HG	HHA
1	Almira [Der in Krohnen erlangte Glücks-Wechsel, oder Almira, Königin von Castilien]	F. C. Feustking, after G. Pancieri	HG, 8 Jan 1705 (*c*20)‡	D-B	some music lost	lv	[ii/1]

HWV	title	libretto	première (perfs. under composer)	sources	remarks	HG	HHA
2	Nero [Die durch Blut und Mord erlangete Liebe]	Feustking	HG, 25 Feb 1705 (?3)‡		music lost		
5	Rodrigo [Vincer se stesso è la maggior vittoria]	adapted from F. Silvani: *Il duello d'Amore e di Vendetta*	Florence, Cocomero, cNov 1707‡	A-Wm, GB-BENcoke, Cfm, Lbl[R]*, Mp	some music lost	lvi	[ii/2]
3, 4	Der beglückte Florindo; Die verwandelte Daphne	H. Hinsch	HG, Jan 1708‡	Mp (frag.), ?Lbl [R]	written as one opera but perf. separately; music almost all lost		
6	Agrippina	V. Grimani	Venice, S Giovanni Grisostomo, 26 Dec 1709 (?27)‡	A-Wn, GB-BENcoke, Cfm*, Lbl[R]*, Lbl, Mp	1 aria in Songs in … Etearco (London, 1711); ov. and 1 aria in Songs in … Antiochus (London, 1712); 1 aria in Songs in … Hamlet (London, 1712)	lvii	[ii/3]
7a, 7b	Rinaldo	G. Rossi, based on scenario by A. Hill after T. Tasso: *La Gerusalemme liberata*	LKH, 24 Feb 1711 (15)‡ LKH, 23 Jan 1712 (9) LKH, 6 May 1713 (2) LKH, 30 Dec 1714 (11) LKH, 5 Jan 1717 (10)‡ LKH, 6 April 1731 (6)‡	D-Hs†, GB-BENcoke, Cfm*, Lbl[R]*, Lbl, Lcm, Mp	rev., 4/5 new arias rev., many addns from other operas	lviii (2 edns)	[ii/4]
8a, 8b, 8c	Il pastor fido	Rossi, after B. Guarini	LKH, 22 Nov 1712 (7)‡ LKH, 18 May 1734 (13)‡ LCG, 9 Nov 1734 (5)‡	D-Hs†, GB-BENcoke, Cfm*, Lbl[R]*†, Lbl, Lcm, Mp, US-Wc	? 1 aria added during run rev., many addns incl. choruses from other works and 2 new arias further rev., ballet, prol. (Terpsicore) dances and 2 arias added	lix, lxxxiv	[ii/5] [ii/31]
9	Teseo	5 acts, N. F. Haym, after P. Quinault: *Thésée*	LKH, 10 Jan 1713 (13)‡	GB-BENcoke, Cfm, Lbl[R]*, Lbl, Mp, Ob	last perf. incl. addns (?2 new arias)	lx	[ii/6]
10	Silla	Rossi	?LKH, 2 June 1713 (?1)‡	BENcoke, Cfm*, Lbl[R]*, Lbl, Mp	misattrib. G. Bononcini in GB-Lbl Add.5334	lxi	[ii/7]
11	Amadigi di Gaula	after A. H. de Lamotte: *Amadis de Grèce*	LKH, 25 May 1715 (6)‡ LKH, 16 Feb 1716 (6) LKH, 16 Feb 1717 (5)	D-Hs†, GB-BENcoke, Cfm*, Lbl[R]*, Lbl, Lcm, Mp, Ob, US-Wc	main autograph lost; arias added during run 5th perf. (20 June) incl. 2 new syms. 3rd perf. incl. un-identified 'new scene'	lxii	ii/8
12a, 12b	Radamisto	adapted from D. Lalli: *L'amor tirannico, o Zenobia*, as rev. for Florence, 1712	LKH, 27 April 1720 (10)‡ LKH, 28 Dec 1720 (7)‡ LKH, 25 Nov 1721 (4) LKH, Jan-Feb 1728 (c5)‡	D-Bds*, Hs†, GB-BENcoke, Cfm*, Lbl[R]*, Lbl, Lcm, Mp	rev., 13 new items further revs., 1 aria added	lxiii	[ii/9]

HWV	title	libretto	première (perfs. under composer)	sources	remarks	HG	HHA
13	Muzio Scevola	P. A. Rolli, after Livy, as rev. for Vienna, 1710	LKH, 15 April 1721 (10)‡	D-Hs†, GB-BENcoke, Cfm, Lbl[R]*, Lbl, Mp, J-Tn	only Act 3 by Handel; Act 1, F. Amadei; Act 2, G. Bononcini	lxiv	[ii/10]
			LKH, 7 Nov 1722 (3)		rev. and shortened		
14	Floridante	Rolli, adapted from Silvani: *La costanza in trionfo*, ? as rev. for Livorno, 1706	LKH, 9 Dec 1721 (15)‡	D-Hs†, GB-Cfm, Lbl[R]*, Mp, Ob		lxv	[ii/11]
			LKH, 4 Dec 1722 (7)		5 arias added, 2 new		
			LKH, 29 April 1727 (2)		shortened, 2 new arias (MS lib. amendments Lbl)		
			LKH, 3 March 1733 (7)‡		1727 version rev. and shortened		
15	Ottone, re di Germania	Haym, adapted from S. B. Pallavicino: *Teofane*	LKH, 12 Jan 1723 (14)‡	D-Hs†, GB-BENcoke, Cfm*, DRc, Lbl[R]*, Lbl, Ob†	last 3 perfs. with 4 new arias	lxvi	[ii/12]
			LKH, 11 Dec 1723 (6)				
			LKH, 8 Feb 1726 (9)‡		rev., 5 new arias		
			LKH, 11 April 1727 (2)				
			LKH, 13 Nov 1733 (4)‡		rev., 3 arias and new duet added		
16	Flavio, re di Longobardi	Haym, adapted from M. Noris: *Flavio Cuniberto*, as rev. for Rome, 1696	LKH, 14 May 1723 (8)‡	D-Hs†, GB-BENcoke, Cfm, Lbl[R]*, Lbl, Mp*		lxvii	[ii/13]
			LKH, 18 April 1732 (4)‡		much rev.		
17	Giulio Cesare in Egitto	Haym, adapted from G. F. Bussani	LKH, 20 Feb 1724 (13)‡	D-Hs†, GB-BENcoke, Cfm†, Lbl[R]*, Lbl, Mp		lxviii	[ii/14]
			LKH, 2 Jan 1725 (10)‡		rev., 4 new arias; 2 more added during run		
			LKH, 17 Jan 1730 (11)‡		further revs., 2 new arias added during run (MS lib. amendments Lbl, King's 442)		
			LKH, 1 Feb 1732 (4)‡				
18	Tamerlano	Haym, adapted from A. Piovene and rev. version: Il Bajazete, 1719, after J. Pradon: *Tamerlan*	LKH, 31 Oct 1724 (12)‡	D-Hs†, GB-BENcoke, Lbl[R]*, Lbl, Mp		lxix	[ii/15]
			LKH, 13 Nov 1731 (3)‡		shortened, but 1 new aria		
19	Rodelinda, regina de' Longobardi	Haym, adapted from A. Salvi, after P. Corneille: *Pertharite, roi des Lombards*	LKH, 13 Feb 1725 (14)‡	D-Hs†, GB-BENcoke, Cfm*, Lbl[R]*, Lbl, Mp		lxx	[ii/16]
			LKH, 18 Dec 1725 (8)		4 new arias and new duet (MS lib. amendments Lbl)		
			LKH, 4 May 1731 (8)		2 arias and duet added from other operas		
20	Scipione	Rolli, adapted from Salvi: *Publio Cornelio Scipione*	LKH, 12 March 1726 (13)‡	D-Hs†, GB-BENcoke, Cfm†, Lbl[R]*, Lbl, Mp		lxxi	[ii/17]
			LKH, 3 Nov 1730 (6)‡		rev. with 14 added items incl. 2 new arias		

HWV	title	libretto	première (perfs. under composer)	sources	remarks	HG	HHA
21	Alessandro	Rolli, adapted from O. Mauro: *La superbia d'Alessandro*	LKH, 5 May 1726 (13)‡	*D-Hs*†, *GB-BENcoke*, *Cfm*, *Lbl[R]**, *Lbl*, *Mp*	new aria added during run	lxxii	[ii/18]
			LKH, 26 Dec 1727 (over 3)				
			LKH, 25 Nov 1732 (6)‡		shortened		
					revived as Rossane, LKH, 1743‡, 1744, 1747, 1748‡, probably with Handel's co-operation		
22	Admeto, re di Tessaglia	adapted from A. Aureli: *Antigona delusa da Alceste*, as rev. Mauro for Hanover, 1681	LKH, 31 Jan 1727 (19)‡	*BENcoke*, *Cfm*, *Lbl[R]**, *Lbl*, *Mp*	main autograph and perf. scores lost; new aria added during run	lxxiii	[ii/19]
			LKH, 30 Sept 1727 (6)				
			LKH, 25 May 1728 (3)‡		new aria		
			LKH, 7 Dec 1731 (6)‡		rev., 6 arias added, 3 new		
23	Riccardo primo, re d'Inghilterra	Rolli, adapted from F. Briani: *Isacio tiranno*	LKH, 11 Nov 1727 (11)‡	*D-Hs*, *GB-BENcoke*, *Cfm**, *Lbl[R]**, *Lbl*, *Mp*, *Ob*		lxxiv	[ii/20]
A²	[Genserico/Olibrio]	after N. Beregan: *Genserico*, as rev. for Hamburg, 1693		*Cfm**, *Lbl[R]**	only pt of Act 1 drafted; music mostly used in Siroe and Tolomeo		
24	Siroe, re di Persia	Haym, adapted from P. Metastasio, as rev. for Naples, 1727	LKH, 17 Feb 1728 (18)‡	*B-Bc*, *D-Hs*†, *GB-BENcoke*, *Cfm*, *Lbl[R]**, *Lbl*, *Mp*		lxxv	[ii/21]
25	Tolomeo, re di Egitto	Haym, adapted from C. S. Capece: *Tolomeo e Alessandro*	LKH, 30 April 1728 (7)‡	*D-Hs*†, *GB-BENcoke*, *Cfm*, *Lbl[R]**, *Lcm*, *Mp*		lxxvi	[ii/22]
			LKH, 19 May 1730 (7)‡		much rev. with 12 addl items		
			LKH, 2 Jan 1733 (4)‡		6 further addns		
26	Lotario	adapted from Salvi: *Adelaide*, as rev. for Venice, 1729	LKH, 2 Dec 1729 (10)‡	*D-Hs*†, *GB-BENcoke*, *Cfm**, *Lbl[R]**, *Lbl*, *Mp*		lxxvii	[ii/23]
27	Partenope	adapted from Stampiglia, as rev. for Venice, 1707	LKH, 24 Feb 1730 (7)‡	*D-Hs*†, *GB-BENcoke*, *Cfm**, *Lbl[R]**, *Mp*		lxxviii	[ii/24]
			LKH, 12 Dec 1730 (7)‡		rev., new aria		
			LCG, 29 Jan 1737 (4)‡		shortened and re-arranged		
28	Poro, re dell'Indie	adapted from Metastasio: *Alessandro nell'Indie*	LKH, 2 Feb 1731 (16)‡	*D-Hs*†, *GB-BENcoke*, *Cfm**, *Lbl[R]**, *Mp*		lxxix	[ii/25]
			LKH, 23 Nov 1731 (4)‡		rev., 3 arias added		
			LCG, 8 Dec 1736 (4)‡		rev., 6 arias added (1 by L. Vinci, 2 by G. A. Ristori)		
A⁵	[Tito]	after J. Racine: *Bérénice*		*Lbl[R]**	only Act 1 scenes i–iii composed, entitled Titus l'Empereur; music partly used in Ezio		

HWV	title	libretto	première (perfs. under composer)	sources	remarks	HG	HHA
29	Ezio	adapted from Metastasio	LKH, 15 Jan 1732 (5)‡	D-Hs†, GB-Cfm, Lbl[R]*, Mp		lxxx	[ii/26]
30	Sosarme, re di Media	adapted from Salvi: Dionisio rè di Portogallo	LKH, 15 Feb 1732 (11)‡	D-Hs†, GB-BENcoke, Cfm, Lbl[R]*, Mp		lxxxi	[ii/27]
			LKH, 27 April 1734 (3)		shortened, but 4 arias added		
31	Orlando	adapted from Capece, after L. Ariosto: Orlando furioso	LKH, 27 Jan 1733 (10)‡	D-Hs, GB-BENcoke, Cfm, Lbl[R]*, Lbl, Mp		lxxxii	ii/28
32	Arianna in Creta	adapted from P. Pariati: Teseo in Creta, as rev. for Naples, 1721, and Rome, 1729	LKH, 26 Jan 1734 (16)‡	D-Hs†, GB-BENcoke, Cfm*, Lbl[R]*, Mp		lxxxiii	[ii/29]
			LCG, 27 Nov 1734 (5)‡		rev., with 2 arias, 1 new, and ballet		
A11	Oreste	adapted from G. Barlocci	LCG, 18 Dec 1734 (3)‡	D-Hs, GB-Mp	pasticcio, music by Handel incl. new recits. and ballet	xlviii, 102 (ov.)	ii/ suppl.1
33	Ariodante	adapted from Salvi: Ginevra, principessa di Scozia, after Ariosto: Orlando furioso	LCG, 8 Jan 1735 (11)‡	D-Hs†, GB-BENcoke, Cfm*, Lbl[R]*, Lbl, Mp	incl. ballet music	lxxxv	[ii/32]
			LCG, 5 May 1736 (2)		dances omitted; 7 arias added (none by Handel)		
34	Alcina	adapted from L'isola di Alcina, 1728, after Ariosto: Orlando furioso	LCG, 16 April 1735 (18)‡	D-Hs†, GB-BENcoke, Cfm*, Lbl[R]*, Lbl, Mp	incl. ballet music	lxxxvi	[ii/33]
			LCG, 6 Nov 1736 (3)‡		dances omitted		
			LCG, 10 June 1737 (2)				
35	Atalanta	adapted from B. Valeriano: La caccia in Etolia	LCG, 12 May 1736 (8)‡	D-Hs, GB-BENcoke, Cfm, Lbl[R]*, Mp		lxxxvii	[ii/34]
			LCG, 20 Nov 1736 (2)				
36	Arminio	adapted from Salvi	LCG, 12 Jan 1737 (6)‡	D-Hs†, GB-BENcoke, Cfm*, Lbl[R]*, Mp		lxxxviii	[ii/35]
37	Giustino	adapted from Beregan, as rev. Pariati for Rome, 1724	LCG, 16 Feb 1737 (9)‡	D-Hs†, GB-Cfm*, Lbl[R]*, Mp		lxxxix	[ii/36]
38	Berenice	adapted from Salvi: Berenice, regina d'Egitto	LCG, 18 May 1737 (4)‡	D-Hs†, GB-Cfm*, Lbl[R]*, Mp		xc	[ii/37]
39	Faramondo	adapted from A. Zeno, as rev. for Rome, 1720	LKH, 3 Jan 1738 (8)‡	D-Hs†, GB-Cfm*, Ckc, Lbl[R]*, Mp		xci	[ii/38]
A13	Alessandro Severo	adapted from Zeno, as rev. for Milan, 1723	LKH, 25 Feb 1738 (6)‡	D-Hs, GB-Cfm*, Lbl[R], Lbl	pasticcio, music by Handel, incl. new ov. and recits.	xlviii, 104 (ov.)	
40	Serse	adapted from N. Minato, as rev. Stampiglia for Rome, 1694	LKH, 15 April 1738 (5) ‡	D-Hs, GB-BENcoke, Cfm*, Lbl[R]*, Mp		xcii	ii/39
A14	Giove in Argo [Jupiter in Argos]	adapted from A. M. Lucchini	LKH, 1 May 1739 (2)‡	BENcoke, Cfm*, Lbl[R]*, Mp	pasticcio semi-staged; new recits., 5 arias and final chorus		
41	Imeneo	adapted from Stampiglia	LLF, 22 Nov 1740 (2)‡	D-Hs†, GB-BENcoke, Cfm*, Lbl[R]*, Lbl, Mp	drafted Sept 1738, rev. for perf. Oct 1740	xciii	[ii/40]
			Dublin, New Music Hall, 24 March 1742 (2)‡		concert perf.; cuts, but 2 arias and 2 duets added		

HWV	title	libretto	première (perfs. under composer)	sources	remarks	HG	HHA
42	Deidamia	Rolli	LLF, 10 Jan 1741 (2)‡ LLH, 10 Feb 1741 (1)	D-Hs†, GB-Cfm*, Lbl[R]*, Lbl, Mp		xciv	[ii/41]

MASQUES, MUSICAL DRAMAS

HWV	title	libretto	première (perfs. under composer)	sources	remarks	HG	HHA
49a, 49b	Acis and Galatea	1 act (later 2 and 3), J. Gay and others, after Ovid: Metamorphoses, xiii	Cannons, Edgware, sum. 1718; LKH, 10 June 1732 (4)‡, 5 Dec 1732 (4); Oxford, Christ Church, 11 July 1733 (1)‡; LKH, 7 May 1734 (1); LCG, 24 March 1736 (2); LLF, 13 Dec 1739 (2)‡, 28 Feb 1741 (2); Dublin, New Music Hall, 20 Jan 1742 (2)	Cannons version: D-Hs, GB-BENcoke, DRc, Lbl[R]*, Lbl, Mp, Ob, US-Wc; later versions: GB-BENcoke, Cfm*, DRc, Lbl[R]†, Lbl†, US-Wc	composed May 1718 (see Rogers 1973), rev. for perfs. 1732–6 (as serenata) with added It. airs from cantata Sorge il dì (Aci, Galatea e Polifemo) and elsewhere	iii, liii	i/9
58	Semele	3 acts, W. Congreve, rev. with addns from his poems and from A. Pope: Summer, or Alexis	LCG, 10 Feb 1744 (4)‡; LKH, 1 Dec 1744 (2)‡	D-Hs†, GB-BENcoke, Cfm*, Lbl[R]*, Mp, US-Wc	MS lib. in US-SM†, 6 airs added for Dec 1744, some in It.	vii	[i/19]
60	Hercules	3 acts, T. Broughton, after Sophocles: Trachiniae and Ovid: Meta-morphoses, ix	LKH, 5 Jan 1745 (2)‡; LCG, 24 Feb 1749 (2)‡, 21 Feb 1752 (2)‡	D-Hs†, GB-BENcoke, Cfm, Lbl[R]*, Mp		iv	[i/22]

ARRANGEMENTS OF OPERAS BY OTHER COMPOSERS (NOT IN HG OR HHA); ALL IN THREE ACTS

HWV	title	libretto	première (perfs. under composer)	sources	remarks
A¹	Elpidia	adapted from Zeno: Li rivali generosi	LKH, 11 May 1725 (10)‡, 30 Nov 1725 (5)	GB-Lbl†	pasticcio mainly from L. Vinci: Ifigenia in Tauride and La Rosmira fedele, and G. F. Orlandini: Berenice, Venice, 1725; perf. Nov 1725 with revs.
A³	Ormisda	adapted from Zeno	LKH, 4 April 1730 (14)‡, 24 Nov 1730 (5)	D-Hs, GB-BENcoke, Lbl†	pasticcio with arias by Vinci, J. A. Hasse, Orlandini and others; 12 'new songs' announced from 21 April; 2 different sets of lib. amendments extant
A⁴	Venceslao	adapted from Zeno	LKH, 12 Jan 1731 (4)‡	D-Hs†	pasticcio with arias by Vinci, Hasse, N. Porpora and others
A⁶	Lucio Papirio	Zeno, rev. C. I. Frugoni	LKH, 23 May 1732 (4)‡	Hs†, GB-Lam	by G. Giacomelli, Parma, 1729, slightly adapted
A⁷	Catone	Metastasio	LKH, 4 Nov 1732 (5)‡	D-Hs†, GB-Lam†	mostly by L. Leo, Venice, 1729, with arias by other composers
A⁸	Semiramide	Metastasio	LKH, 30 Oct 1733 (4)‡	D-Hs†, GB-Cfm†	mostly by Vinci, with arias by other composers
A⁹	Cajo Fabricio	Zeno	LKH, 4 Dec 1733 (4)‡	D-Hs†	mostly by Hasse, Rome, 1732, with arias by other composers
A¹⁰	Arbace	Metastasio: Artaserse	LKH, 8 Jan 1734 (8)‡	Hs†	mostly by Vinci, with arias by other composers
A¹²	Didone	Metastasio	LKH, 13 April 1737 (3)‡	GB-Lbl†, US-Cn†	mostly by Vinci, Rome, 1726

BASIC BIBLIOGRAPHIES

HJb (1928–33, 1955–)

K. Sasse: *Händel-Bibliographie* (Leipzig, 1963; suppl., 1967)

W. C. Smith: *A Handelian's Notebook* (London, 1965)

Händel-Handbuch, i–iv (Leipzig, 1978–85) [i: S. Flesch: *Lebens-und Schaffensdaten* and B. Baselt: *Thematisch-systematisches Verzeichnis*; ii–iii: Baselt: *Verzeichnis*; iv: *Dokumente zu Leben und Schaffen*, trans. and rev. from O. E. Deutsch, *Handel: a Documentary Biography*, London, 1955]

Göttinger Händel-Beiträge, ed. H. J. Marx (Kassel, 1984–91) [incl. current bibliography] [*GHB*]

M. A. Parker-Hale: *G. F. Handel: a Guide to Research* (New York, 1988)

CATALOGUES, DESCRIPTIONS OF SOURCES

J. A. Fuller Maitland and A. H. Mann: *Catalogue of the Music in the Fitzwilliam Museum, Cambridge* (London, 1893)

A. Hughes-Hughes: *Catalogue of Manuscript Music in the British Museum* (London, 1906–9)

R. A. Streatfeild: 'The Granville Collection of Handel Manuscripts', *MA*, ii (1910–11), 208–24

Sotheby, Wilkinson and Hodge Sale Catalogue of the Collection of the Earl of Aylesford 13 May 1918 (London, 1918)

N. Flower: *Catalogue of a Handel Collection formed by Newman Flower* (Sevenoaks, 1920)

W. B. Squire: *Catalogue of the King's Music Library*, i: *The Handel Manuscripts* (London, 1927)

F. Zobeley: 'Werke Händels in der Gräfl. von Schönbornschen Musikbibliothek', *HJb 1931*, 98–116

E. H. Fellowes: *The Catalogue of Manuscripts in the Library of St. Michael's College Tenbury* (Paris, 1934) [MSS now in *GB-Ob*]

J. M. Coopersmith: 'Handelian Lacunae: a Project', *MQ*, xxi (1935), 224–9

——: 'Some Adventures in Handel Research', *PAMS 1937*, 11–23

W. C. Smith: 'Recently Discovered Handel Manuscripts', *MT*, lxxviii (1937), 312–15

J. M. Coopersmith: 'Concert of Unpublished Music by Georg Friedrich Händel: Program Notes', *PAMS 1939*, 213–25

——: 'The First *Gesamtausgabe*: Dr. Arnold's Edition of Handel's Works', *Notes*, iv (1946–7), 277–88, 439–49

P. Hirsch: 'Dr Arnold's Handel Edition (1787–1797)', *MR*, viii (1947), 106–16

W. C. Smith: *Handel: a Descriptive Catalogue of the Early Editions* (London, 1960, 2/1970)

A. H. King: *Handel and his Autographs* (London, 1967)

P. J. Willetts: *Handlist of Music Manuscripts Acquired* [by *GB-Lbl*] *1908–67* (London, 1970)

Catalogue of Rare Books and Notes (Tokyo, 1970) [Ohki Collection, Nanki Music Library]

H. D. Clausen: *Händels Direktionspartituren ('Handexemplare')* (Hamburg, 1972)

A. D. Walker: *George Frideric Handel: the Newman Flower Collection in the Henry Watson Music Library* (Manchester, 1972)

J. M. Knapp: 'The Hall Handel Collection', *Princeton University Library Chronicle*, xxxvi (1974), 3–18

D. Burrows: *A Handlist of the Paper Characteristics of Handel's English Autographs* (typescript, 1982)

J. Milhous and R. D. Hume: *Vice-Chamberlain Coke's Theatrical Papers 1706–1715* (Carbondale, IL, 1982)

D. Burrows: 'Paper Studies and Handel's Autographs: a Preliminary Report', *GHB*, i (1984), 103–15

C. Timms: 'Handelian and other Librettos in Birmingham Central Library', *ML*, lxv (1984), 141–67

[G. Coke]: *The Gerald Coke Collection* (Bentley, 1985) [exhibition catalogue]

W. Dean: 'Handel's Early London Copyists', *Bach, Handel, Scarlatti: Tercentenary Essays*, ed. P. Williams (Cambridge, 1985), 75–97; repr. in *Essays on Opera* (Oxford, 1990), 8–21

H. J. Marx, ed.: *Händel und Hamburg: Ausstellung anlässich des 300. Geburtstages von Georg Friedrich Händel* (Hamburg, 1985) [exhibition catalogue]

J. Simon, ed.: *Handel: a Celebration of his Life and Times* (London, 1985) [exhibition catalogue]

B. Baselt: *Verzeichnis der Werke Georg Friedrich Händels: Kleine Ausgabe* (Leipzig, 1986)

T. Crawford: 'Lord Danby's Lute Book: a New Source of Handel's Hamburg Music', *GHB*, ii (1986), 19–50

K. Watanabe: 'Die Händel-Handschriften der Ohki-Bibliothek in Tokyo', ibid, 234–52

J. H. Roberts, ed.: *Handel Sources: Materials for the Study of Handel's Borrowing* (New York, 1986)

E. T. Harris, ed.: *The Librettos of Handel's Operas* (New York, 1989)

L. Bianconi and G. La Face Bianconi, eds.: *I libretti italiani di Georg Friedrich Händel e le loro fonti* (Florence, 1992–)

BIOGRAPHIES, BIOGRAPHICAL SOURCES

BurneyH; HawkinsH

J. Mattheson: *Grundlage einer Ehren-Pforte* (Hamburg, 1740); ed. M. Schneider (Berlin, 1910)

[J. Mainwaring]: *Memoirs of the Life of the Late George Frederic Handel* (London, 1760)

J. Mattheson: *Georg Friedrich Händels Lebensbeschreibung* (Hamburg, 1761)

C. Burney: *An Account of the Musical Performances in Westminster Abbey and the Pantheon May 26th, 27th, 29th; and June the 3rd and 5th, 1784: in Commemoration of Handel* (London, 1785)

[W. Coxe]: *Anecdotes of George Frederick Handel and John Christopher Smith* (London, 1799)

V. Schoelcher: *The Life of Handel* (London, 1857)

F. Chrysander: *G. F. Händel* (Leipzig, 1858–67); index, S. Flesch (Leipzig, 1967)

M. Delany: *Autobiography and Correspondence of Mary Granville, Mrs Delany* (London, 1861–2)

R. A. Streatfeild: *Handel* (London, 1909, 2/1910)

R. Rolland: *Haendel* (Paris, 1910, 2/1974; Eng. trans., 1916)

N. Flower: *George Frederic Handel: his Personality and his Times* (London, 1923, 3/1959, with bibliography by W. C. Smith)

H. Leichtentritt: *Händel* (Stuttgart, 1924)

W. C. Smith: 'George III, Handel and Mainwaring', *MT*, lxv (1924), 789–97

J. Müller-Blattau: *Georg Friedrich Händel* (Potsdam, 1933)

E. J. Dent: *Handel* (London, 1934)

P. M. Young: *Handel* (London, 1946, 3/1975)

W. C. Smith: *Concerning Handel, his Life and Works* (London, 1948)

——: 'Handeliana', *ML*, xxxi (1950), 125–32; xxxiv (1953), 11–24

W. Siegmund-Schultze: *Georg Friedrich Händel: Leben und Werk* (Leipzig, 1954, 4/1980)

O. E. Deutsch: *Handel, a Documentary Biography* (London, 1955); rev. Ger. trans., in *Händel-Handbuch*, iv (Leipzig, 1985)

W. Serauky: *Georg Friedrich Händel: sein Leben, sein Werk* (Kassel, 1956–8) [only iii–v pubd]

B. Matthews: 'Unpublished Letters Concerning Handel', *ML*, xl (1959), 261–8; see also 406–7

K. Sasse: 'Opera Register from 1712 to 1734 (Colman-Register)', *HJb 1959*, 199–223

B. Matthews: 'Handel: more Unpublished Letters', *ML*, xlii (1961), 127–31; see also 395–6

W. Rackwitz and H. Steffens: *George Frideric Handel: a Biography in Pictures* (Leipzig, 1962)

S. Sadie: *Handel* (London, 1962)

J. Gress: 'Händel in Dresden (1719)', *HJb 1963*, 135–49

M. Fabbri: 'Nuova luce sull'attività fiorentina di Giacomo Antonio Perti, Bartolomeo Cristofori e Giorgio F. Haendel', *Chigiana*, xxi (1964), 143–90

P. H. Lang: *George Frideric Handel* (New York, 1966)

U. Kirkendale: 'The Ruspoli Documents on Handel', *JAMS*, xx (1967), 222–73, 517–18

W. Dean: 'Charles Jennens's Marginalia to Mainwaring's Life of Handel', *ML*, liii (1972), 160–64; repr. in *Essays on Opera* (Oxford, 1990), 74–7

R. Strohm: 'Händel in Italia: nuovi contributi', *RIM*, ix (1974), 152–74

W. Siegmund-Schultze and K. Sasse, ed.: *Georg Friedrich Haendel: Beiträge zu seiner Biographie aus dem 18. Jahrhundert* (Leipzig, 1977, 2/1984)

C. Hogwood: *Handel* (London, 1984, 2/1988) [with chronological table by A. Hicks]

J. Keates: *Handel: the Man and his Music* (London, 1985)

W. Rackwitz: *Georg Friedrich Händel: Lebensbeschreibung in Bildern* (Leipzig, 1986)

OPERAS: GENERAL

G. G. Gervinus: *Händel und Shakespeare: zur Asthetik der Tonkunst* (Leipzig, 1868)

G. A. Macfarren: 'The Accompaniment of Recitative', *MT*, xv (1872), 687–9

F. Volbach: *Die Praxis der Händel-Aufführung* (Charlottenburg, 1900)

S. Taylor: *The Indebtedness of Handel to Works by other Composers* (Cambridge, 1906)

M. Seiffert: 'Händels Verhältnis zu Tonwerken älterer deutscher Meister', *JbMP 1907*, 41–57

P. Robinson: *Handel and his Orbit* (London, 1908)

M. Seiffert: 'G. Ph. Telemanns *Musique de table* als Quelle für Händel', *Bulletin de la Société 'Union Musicologique'*, iv (1924), 1–28

E. J. Dent: 'Englische Einflüsse bei Händel', *HJb 1929*, 1–12; Eng. trans., *MMR*, lxi (1931), 225–8

H. Leichtentritt: 'Handel's Harmonic Art', *MQ*, xxi (1935), 208–23

W. F. H. Blandford: 'Handel's Horn and Trombone Parts', *MT*, lxxx (1939), 697–9, 746–7, 794

G. Abraham, ed.: *Handel: a Symposium* (London, 1954)

J. S. and M. V. Hall: 'Handel's Graces', *HJb 1957*, 25–43

W. Siegmund-Schultze: 'Das Siciliano bei Händel', *HJb 1957*, 44–73

A. Lewis: 'Handel and the Aria', *PRMA*, lxxxv (1958–9), 95–107

Händel-Ehrung der Deutschen Demokratischen Republik: Halle 1959

W. Siegmund-Schultze: 'Zu Händels Schaffensmethode', *HJb 1961–2*, 69–136

J. A. Westrup: 'The Cadence in Baroque Recitative', *Natalicia musicologica Knud Jeppesen* (Copenhagen, 1962), 243–52

W. Siegmund-Schultze: *Georg Friedrich Händel, Thema mit 20 Variationen* (Halle, 1965)

W. Dean: 'Handel and Keiser: Further Borrowings', *CMc*, no.9 (1969), 73–80

W. Meyerhoff, ed.: *50 Jahre Göttinger Händel-Festspiele* (Kassel, 1970)

H. C. Wolff: 'Händel und Frankreich', *Festschrift der Händel-Festspiele* (Göttingen, 1973), 19–27

A. Hicks: 'Handel's Early Musical Development', *PRMA*, ciii (1976–7), 80–89

W. Dean: 'The Performance of Recitative in Late Baroque Opera', *ML*, lviii (1977), 389–402; repr. in *Essays on Opera* (Oxford, 1990), 78–90

D. R. B. Kimbell: 'Aspekte von Händels Umarbeitungen und Revisionen eigener Werke', *HJb 1977*, 45–67

E. T. Harris: *Handel and the Pastoral Tradition* (Oxford, 1980)

J. H. Roberts: 'Handel's Borrowings from Telemann: an Inventory', *GHB*, i (1984), 147–71

P. Brainard: 'Aria and Ritornello: New Aspects of the Comparison Handel/Bach', *Bach, Handel, Scarlatti: Tercentenary Essays*, ed. P. Williams (Cambridge, 1985), 21–33

D. Burrows: 'Handel's London Theatre Orchestra', *EMc*, xiii (1985), 349–57

W. Dean: 'Handel and Alessandro Scarlatti', *Händel e gli Scarlatti a Roma: Rome 1985*, 1–14

J. H. Roberts: 'Händel's Borrowings from Keiser', *GHB*, ii (1986), 51–76

S. Sadie and A. Hicks, eds.: *Handel Tercentenary Collection* (London, 1987)

P. J. Rogers: *Continuo Realization in Handel's Vocal Music* (Ann Arbor, 1989)

OPERAS: PARTICULAR

R. A. Streatfeild: 'Handel, Rolli, and Italian Opera in London in the Eighteenth Century', *MQ*, iii (1917), 428–45

I. Leux: 'Über die "verschollene" Händel-Oper "Hermann von Balcke"', *AMw*, viii (1926), 441–51

R. Steglich: 'Die neue Händel-Opern-Bewegung', *HJb 1928*, 71–158

E. J. Dent: 'Handel on the Stage', *ML*, xvi (1935), 174–87

W. Schulze: *Die Quellen der Hamburger Oper (1678–1738)* (Hamburg, 1938)

J. Eisenschmidt: *Die szenische Darstellung der Opern Händels auf der Londoner Bühne seiner Zeit* (Wolfenbüttel, 1940–41)

E. Dahnk-Baroffio: 'Zu den Libretti der Händelzeit', *Festschrift der Händel-Festspiele* (Göttingen, 1953), 15–20

R. Gerber: 'Von Wesen der Händel-Oper', *Festschrift der Händel-Festspiele* (Göttingen, 1953), 5–15

R. Brockpähler: *Handbuch zur Geschichte der Barockoper in Deutschland* (Emsdetten, 1954)

W. Serauky: 'Das Ballett in G. F. Händels Opern', *HJb 1956*, 91–112

H. C. Wolff: *Die Händel-Oper auf der modernen Bühne* (Leipzig, 1957)

J. M. Knapp: 'Handel, the Royal Academy of Music, and its First Opera Season in London (1720)', *MQ*, xlv (1959), 145–67

W. Serauky: 'Händel und die Oper seiner Zeit', *HJb 1959*, 27–44

B. Trowell: 'Handel as a Man of the Theatre', *PRMA*, lxxxviii (1961–2), 17–30

P. Tinel: 'Haendel, réformateur de l'opéra et dramaturge de l'oratorio', *Bulletin de l'Académie royale de Belgique: classe des beaux-arts*, xlvi (1964), 78–103

J. M. Knapp: 'Probleme bei der Edition von Händels Opern', *HJb 1967–8*, 113–23

D. R. B. Kimbell: *A Critical Study of Handel's Early Operas* (diss., U. of Oxford, 1968)

E. Dahnk-Baroffio: 'Die Völkerwanderungsopern und Händels "Olibrio"', *Festschrift der Händel-Festspiele* (Göttingen, 1969), 29–43

W. Dean: *Handel and the Opera Seria* (Berkeley and Los Angeles, 1969)

P. Gülke: 'Zur Einrichtung Händelscher Opernpartituren', *HJb 1969–70*, 87–122

J. M. Knapp and E. Dahnk-Baroffio: 'Titus l'Empereur', *Festschrift der Händel-Festspiele* (Göttingen, 1970), 27–31

W. Dean: 'A French Traveller's View of Handel's Operas', *ML*, lv (1974), 172–8; repr. in *Essays on Opera* (Oxford, 1990), 38–44

R. Strohm: 'Händels Pasticci', *AnMc*, no.14 (1974), 208–67; Eng. trans. in *Essays on Handel and Italian Opera* (Cambridge, 1985), 164–211

B. Baselt: 'Zum Parodieverfahren in Händels frühen Opern', *HJb 1975–6*, 19–39

W. Dean: 'Twenty Years of Handel Opera', *Opera*, xxvi (1975), 924–30

R. Strohm: 'Händel und seine italienischen Operntexte', *HJb 1975*, 101–59; Eng. trans. in *Essays on Handel and Italian Opera* (Cambridge, 1985), 34–79

B. Baselt: 'Händel auf dem Wege nach Italien', *G. F. Händel und seine italienischen Zeitgenossen: Halle 1978*, 10–21

W. Dean: 'Die Ausführung des Rezitativs in den Opern der Händel-Zeit', *G. F. Händel und seine italienischen Zeitgenossen: Halle 1978*, 94–115

S. Stompor: 'Die deutschen Aufführungen von Opern Händels in der ersten Hälfte des 18. Jahrhunderts', *HJb 1978*, 31–89

R. Strohm: 'Francesco Gasparini: le sue opere tarde e Georg Friedrich Händel', *Francesco Gasparini (1661–1727): Camaiore 1978*, 71–83

A. Kitching: *Handel at the Unicorn* (n.p., 1981)

W. Dean: 'Händels kompositorische Entwicklung in den Opern der Jahr 1724/25', *HJb 1982*, 23–34

B. Baselt: 'Wiederentdeckung von Fragmenten aus Händels verschollenen Hamburger Opern', *HJb 1983*, 7–24

W. Dean: 'The Recovery of Handel's Operas', *Music in Eighteenth-Century England: Essays in Memory of Charles Cudworth* (Cambridge, 1983), 103–13

J. Milhous and R. D. Hume: 'New Light on Handel and the Royal Academy of Music in 1720', *Theatre Journal*, xxxv (1983), 149–67

E. Gibson: 'Owen Swiney and the Italian Opera in London', *MT*, cxxv (1984), 82–6

J. Milhous and R. D. Hume: 'Handel's Opera Finances in 1732–33', *MT*, cxxv (1984), 86–9

T. Best: 'Handel's Overtures for Keyboard', *MT*, cxxvi (1985), 88–90

G. Bimberg: *Dramaturgie der Händel-Opern* (Halle, 1985)

R. Strohm: *Essays on Handel and Italian Opera* (Cambridge, 1985)

G. J. Buelow: 'Handel's Borrowing Techniques: some Fundamental Questions derived from a Study of *Agrippina* (Venice, 1709)', *GHB*, ii (1986), 105–28

R. D. Hume: 'Handel and Opera Management in London in the 1730s', *ML*, lxvii (1986), 347–62

H. Meynell: *The Art of Handel's Operas* (New York, 1986)

W. Dean and J. M. Knapp: *Handel's Operas 1704–1726* (Oxford, 1987)

E. Gibson: 'The Royal Academy of Music (1719–28) and its Directors', *Handel Tercentenary Collection*, ed. S. Sadie and A. Hicks (London, 1987), 136–64

L. Lindgren: 'The Staging of Handel's Operas in London', ibid, 93–119

J. H. Roberts: 'Handel and Charles Jennens's Italian Opera Manuscripts', *Music and Theatre: Essays in Honour of Winton Dean* (Cambridge, 1987), 159–202

C. Taylor: 'Handel's Disengagement from the Italian Opera', *Handel Tercentenary Collection*, ed. S. Sadie and A. Hicks (London, 1987), 165–81

E. Gibson: *The Royal Academy of Music 1719–1728* (New York, 1989)

W. Dean: *Essays on Opera* (Oxford, 1990)

F.-J. Fasse: 'Instrumentale Einleitungen in Händels späten Opern', *GHB*, iv (1991), 194–207

OPERAS: INDIVIDUAL

Mainly English-language and recent studies are listed; for more extensive bibliographies, see Sasse (1963 and suppl. 1967), and the entries for each work in *Händel-Handbuch*, i and iii.

Admeto

G. Ellinger: 'Handels *Admet* und seine Quelle', *VMw*, i (1885), 201–24

B. Baselt: 'Zur Gestaltung des Alceste-Stoffes in Händels Oper *Admeto*', *Georg Friedrich Händel im Verständnis des 19. Jahrhunderts: Halle 1983*, 74

Agrippina

H. C. Wolff: '*Agrippina*: eine italienische Jugendoper Händels' (Wolfenbüttel, 1943)

H. F. Redlich: 'Handel's *Agrippina* (1709): Problems of a Practical Edition', *MR*, xii (1951), 15–23

Teatro Malibran, Venice 1985 [programme book for *Agrippina*]

H. S. Saunders: 'Handel's *Agrippina*: the Venetian Perspective', *GHB*, iii (1989), 87–98

Alcina

L'avant-scène opéra, no.130 (1990) [*Alcina* issue]

Alessandro

W. Dean: 'Zur Oper *Alessandro* von Georg Friedrich Händel', *Concerto*, ii/3 (1985), 47–51

R. King: *The Composition and Reception of Handel's 'Alessandro' (1726)* (diss., Stanford U., 1991)

Almira

R. F. C. Fenton: '*Almira* (Hamburg, 1705): the Birth of G. F. Handel's Genius for Characterisation', *HJb 1987*, 109–31

J. H. Roberts: 'Keiser and Handel at the Handel Opera', *HJb 1990*, 63–88

W. Braun: 'Der "*Almira*"-Stoff in den Vertonungen von Ruggiero Fedeli, Reinhard Keiser und Georg Friedrich Händel', *HJb 1990*, 139–46

D. Schröder: 'Zu Entstehung und Aufführungsgeschichte von Händels Oper "*Almira*"', *HJb 1990*, 147–54

Amadigi di Gaula

W. Dean: 'Handel's *Amadigi*', *MT*, cix (1968), 324–7

D. R. B. Kimbell: 'The "*Amadis*" Operas of Destouches and Handel', *ML*, xlix (1968), 329–46

W. Dean: 'Vocal Embellishment in a Handel Aria', *Studies in Eighteenth-Century Music: a Tribute to Karl Geiringer* (London, 1970), 151–9; repr. in *Essays on Opera* (Oxford, 1990), 22–9

——: 'The Musical Sources for Handel's *Teseo* and *Amadigi*', *Slavonic and Western Music: Essays for Gerald Abraham* (Ann Arbor and Oxford, 1985), 63–80

——: 'A New Source for Handel's *Amadigi*', *ML*, lxxii (1991), 27–37

Arianna in Creta

E. Dahnk-Baroffio: 'Das Libretto der Oper "*Ariadne*"', *Göttinger Händel-Opern Festspiele* (Göttingen, 1946), 16

Ariodante

E. Dahnk-Baroffio: 'Zur Stoffgeschichte des *Ariodante*', *HJb 1960*, 151–61

Atalanta

W. Dean: 'Handel's Wedding Opera', *MT*, cxi (1970), 705–7

Ezio

G. Bimberg: 'Dramaturgische Strukturmomente in den "*Ezio*"-Opern von Händel und Gluck', *Georg Friedrich Händel als Wegbereiter der Wiener Klassik: Halle 1977*, 41–6

R. Strohm: 'Handel, Metastasio, Racine: the Case of "*Ezio*"', *MT*, cxviii (1977), 901–3

——: 'Handel's *Ezio*', *Essays on Handel and Italian Opera* (Cambridge, 1985), 225–31

Flavio

E. Dahnk-Baroffio: 'Zum Textbuch von Händels *Flavio*', *Festschrift der Händel-Festspiele* (Göttingen, 1967), 37–40

J. M. Knapp: 'Händels Oper *Flavio*', *Festschrift der Händel-Festspiele* (Göttingen, 1967), 25–33

W. Dean: 'A Handel Tragicomedy', *MT*, cx (1969), 819–22

Floridante

H. D. Clausen: 'Die Entstehung der Oper *Floridante*', *GHB*, iv (1991), 108–33

Giove in Argo [Jupiter in Argos]

J. M. Coopersmith: 'The Libretto of Handel's *Jupiter in Argos*', *ML*, xvii (1936), 289–96

B. Baselt: 'Georg Friedrich Händels Pasticcio *Jupiter in Argos* und seine quellenmässige Überlieferung', *Festschrift Martin Ruhnke zum 65. Geburtstag* (Neuhausen-Stuttgart, 1986), 19–30

Giulio Cesare in Egitto

W. Dean: 'Handel's *Giulio Cesare*', *MT*, civ (1963), 402–4

J. M. Knapp: 'Handel's *Giulio Cesare in Egitto*', *Studies in Music History: Essays for Oliver Strunk* (Princeton, 1968), 389–403

C. Monson: '*Giulio Cesare in Egitto* from Sartorio (1677) to Handel (1724)', *ML*, lxvi (1985), 313–43

L'avant-scène opéra, no.97 (1987) [*Giulio Cesare* issue]

Giustino

E. Prout: 'Graun's *Passion Oratorio* and Handel's Knowledge of it', *MMR*, xxiv (1894), 97–9, 121–3

R. Strohm: 'Vivaldi's and Handel's Settings of *Giustino*', *Music and Theatre: Essays in Honour of Winton Dean* (Cambridge, 1987), 131–58

R. Bossard: 'Von San Luca nach Covent Garden: die Wege des *Giustino* zu Händel', *GHB*, iv (1991), 146–73

Imeneo

C. Hill: *Handel's "Imeneo": a Pre-Edition Study* (Armidale, Australia, 1988)

Muzio Scevola

W. Siegmund-Schultze: 'Händels "Muzio Scevola"', *Festschrift der Händel-Festspiele* (Halle, 1965), 27–35

Oreste

B. Baselt: 'Dramaturgische und szenische Aspekte der Coventgarden Opern Händels, dargestellt an der Oper *Oreste* (1734)', *Symposium-Bericht: Karlsruhe 1986–7*, 133–42

——: 'Zum Libretto von Händels Oper *Oreste*', *HJb 1988*, 7–55

Orlando

S. Flesch: 'Händels "Orlando"', *Festschrift der Händel-Festspiele* (Halle, 1961), 42

E. T. Harris: 'Eighteenth-Century *Orlando*: Hero, Satyr and Fool', *Opera & Vivaldi*, ed. M. Collins and E. K. Kirk (Austin, TX, 1984), 105–28

R. Strohm: 'Comic Traditions in Handel's *Orlando*', *Essays on Handel and Italian Opera* (Cambridge, 1985), 249–69

Teatro La Fenice 1985 [programme book for *Orlando*]

W. Feinstein: 'Dorinda as Ariostean Narrator in Handel's *Orlando*', *Italica*, lxiv (1987), 561–71

Ottone

C. Spitz: 'Die Opern *Ottone* von G. F. Händel (London, 1722) und *Teofane* von A. Lotti (Dresden, 1719): ein Stilvergleich', *Festschrift zum 50. Geburtstag Adolf Sandberger* (Munich, 1918), 265–71

W. Dean: 'Handel's *Ottone*', *MT*, cxii (1971), 955–8

J. M. Knapp: 'The Autograph Manuscripts of Handel's "Ottone"', *Festskrift Jens Peter Larsen* (Copenhagen, 1972), 167–80

W. Dean: 'The Genesis and Early History of *Ottone*', *GHB*, ii (1986), 129–40

Il pastor fido

D. Chisholm: 'The English Origins of Handel's *Pastor Fido*', *MT*, cxv (1974), 650–54

Poro

G. Bimberg: 'Die Figurenkonzeption in Händels Oper *Poro, re dell'Indie*', *Probleme der Handelschen Oper: Halle 1982*, 82–93

G. Cummings: 'The London Performances of Handel's Opera *Poro*', ibid, 62–81

R. Strohm: 'Metastasios *Alessandro nell'Indie* und seine frühesten Vertonungen', ibid, 40–61; Eng. trans. in *Essays on Handel and Italian Opera* (Cambridge, 1985), 232–48

G. Cummings: 'Reminiscence and Recall in Three Early Settings of Metastasio's *Alessandro nell'Indie*', *PRMA*, cix (1982–3), 80–104

Radamisto

W. Gwacharija: 'Die historischen Grundlagen von G. F. Händels Oper *Radamisto*', *G. F. Händel und seine italienischen Zeitgenossen: Halle 1979*, 59–65

W. Dean: 'Mattheson's Arrangement of Handel's *Radamisto* for the Hamburg Opera', *New Mattheson Studies*, ed. G. J. Buelow and H. J. Marx (Cambridge, 1985), 169–78; repr. in *Essays on Opera* (Oxford, 1990), 30–37

J. Milhous and R. D. Hume: 'A Prompt Copy of Handel's *Radamisto*', *MT*, cxxvii (1986), 316–21

Riccardo primo

W. Dean: 'Handel's *Riccardo primo*', *MT*, cv (1964), 498–500

E. Dahnk-Baroffio: 'Händels "Riccardo primo" in Deutschland', *50 Jahre Göttinger Händel-Festspiele*, ed. W. Meyerhoff (Kassel, 1970), 150–66

R. Gerlach and E. Dahnk-Baroffio: 'Über Georg Friedrich Händels Oper Riccardo I', *Festschrift der Händel-Festspiele* (Göttingen, 1970), 75–88

J. M. Knapp: 'The Autograph of Handel's *Riccardo primo*', *Studies in Renaissance and Baroque Music in Honor of Arthur Mendel* (Kassel and Hackensack, NJ, 1974), 331–58

A. McCredie: 'The Early Reception of Handel's London Operas on the German Stage – the Case of *Riccardo Primo*', *GHB*, iii (1989), 124–38

Rinaldo

R. Kubik: *Händels Rinaldo: Geschichte, Werk, Wirkung* (Stuttgart, 1982)

L'avant-scène opéra, no.72 (1985) [*Rinaldo* issue]

C. Price: 'English Traditions in Handel's *Rinaldo*', *Handel Tercentenary Collection*, ed. S. Sadie and A. Hicks (London, 1987), 120–37

Teatro Municipale Valli Reggio Emilia 1985 [programme book for *Rinaldo*]

Rodelinda

E. Dahnk-Baroffio: 'Nicola Hayms Anteil an Händels *Rodelinde*-Libretto', *Mf*, vii (1954), 295–300

Rodrigo [Vincer se stesso è la maggior vittoria]

J. M. Knapp: 'Handel's First Italian Opera: "Vincer se stesso è la maggior vittoria" or "Rodrigo"', *ML*, lxii (1981), 12–29; see also 385–6

A. Hicks: 'The Late Additions to Handel's Oratorios and the Role of the younger Smith', *Music in Eighteenth-Century England: Essays in Memory of Charles Cudworth* (Cambridge, 1983), 147–69 [refers to lost *Rodrigo* arias]

Scipione

W. Dean: 'Handel's *Scipione*', *MT*, cviii (1967), 902–4

Serse

H. S. Powers: 'Il Serse trasformato', *MQ*, xlvii (1961), 481–92; xlviii (1962), 73–92

Silla

J. M. Knapp: 'The Libretto of Handel's "Silla"', *ML*, l (1969), 68–75

D. Chisholm: 'Handel's *Lucio Cornelio Silla*: its Problems and Context', *EMc*, xiv (1986), 64–70

Siroe

S. Flesch: 'Einige Bemerkungen zu Händels Oper *Siroe*', *Festschrift der Halle Festspiele 1952–62* (1962), 35–44

Sosarme

W. Dean: 'Handel's *Sosarme*, a Puzzle Opera', *Essays on Opera and English Music in Honour of Sir Jack Westrup* (Oxford, 1975), 115–47; repr. in *Essays on Opera* (Oxford, 1990), 45–73

Tamerlano

J. M. Knapp: 'Handel's *Tamerlano*: the Creation of an Opera', *MQ*, lvi (1970), 405–30

T. Best: 'New Light on the Manuscript Copies of *Tamerlano*', *GHB*, iv (1991), 134–45

Teseo

D. R. B. Kimbell: 'The Libretto of Handel's *Teseo*', *ML*, xliv (1963), 371–9

W. Dean: 'The Musical Sources for Handel's *Teseo* and *Amadigi*', *Slavonic and Western Music: Essays for Gerald Abraham* (Ann Arbor and Oxford, 1985), 63–80

MASQUES AND MUSICAL DRAMAS

W. B. Squire: 'Handel's *Semele*', *MT*, lxvi (1925), 137–9

W. Dean: *Handel's Dramatic Oratorios and Masques* (London, 1959)

W. Rackwitz: 'Die Herakles-Gestalt bei Händel', *Händel-Ehrung der Deutschen Demokratischen Republik: Leipzig 1959*, 51

E. Dahnk-Baroffio: 'Zu Aci e Galatea', *Göttinger Händeltage 1966*, 41

W. Dean: 'Masque into Opera' [*Acis and Galatea*], *MT*, cviii (1967), 605–6

B. Trowell: 'Congreve and the 1744 Semele Libretto', *MT*, cxi (1970), 993–4

W. Dean: 'How Should Handel's Oratorios be Staged?', *Musical Newsletter*, i/4 (1971), 11–15

A. Hicks: 'Ravishing Semele', *MT*, cxiv (1973), 275–80; see also 696

P. Rogers: 'Dating *Acis and Galatea*', *MT*, cxiv (1973), 792

A. Lewis: 'Some Notes on Editing Handel's "Semele"', *Essays on Opera and English Music in Honour of Sir Jack Westrup* (Oxford, 1975), 79–83

W. Windzus: *Georg Friedrich Händel – Aci, Galatea e Polifemo, Cantata von 1708; Acis and Galatea, Masque von 1718 ... Serenata von 1732: Kritischer Bericht im Rahmen der Hallische Händel-Ausgabe* (Hamburg, 1977)

B. Trowell: '*Acis, Galatea and Polyphemus*: a "serenata a tre voci"?', *Music and Theatre: Essays in Honour of Winton Dean* (Cambridge, 1987), 31–93   ANTHONY HICKS

Handel Opera Society. Organization founded in London in 1955 (renamed Handel Opera in 1980) to give stage performances of the dramatic works; it ceased in 1985. *See* LONDON, §II, 1.

Handlung für Musik (Ger.: 'action in music'). Term used by Wagner to describe the libretto for *Lohengrin*; it has occasionally been used since.

Handt, Herbert (*b* Philadelphia, 26 May 1926). American tenor and conductor. While studying at the Juilliard School he sang in the NBC chorus under Toscanini, and continued his studies at the Vienna Academy with Julius Patzak and Hans Swarowsky. His début as a tenor was at the Vienna Staatsoper as Rinuccio in *Gianni Schicchi* (1949), and he soon acquired a reputation as a specialist in contemporary music; he created roles in Malipiero's *Venere prigionera* (1957, Florence) and Menotti's *Maria Golovin* (1958, Brussels), and appeared in the first Italian or French productions (sometimes both) of works by Berg (*Wozzeck*), Busoni (*Turandot*), Britten (*Midsummer Night's Dream*), Menotti (*Martin's Lie*) and Henze. He made his conducting début at Rome in 1960, and devoted time to conducting performances of little-known Italian works by Francesco Barsanti, Boccherini, Francesco Geminiani and Rossini, often preparing the performing editions; he was associated with the Rossini Foundation in Pesaro for many years. He made his home in Lucca, where he formed the Associazione Musicale Lucchese. He also directed the Opera School of Chicago and instituted the first spring season of the Chicago Opera Theatre (1974). His early recordings include *Idomeneo* (1950), for which he was much praised as Arbaces, Haydn's Orpheus in *Orfeo ed Euridice* with Swarowsky (also 1950), Sextus in the first complete *Giulio Cesare* (Handel) also with Swarowsky (1952), and the original-cast recording of *Maria Golovin*.

WILLIAM WEAVER, NOËL GOODWIN

Hanke [Hancke], Karl (*b* Rosswald, Moravia [now Rudoltice], 1750; *d* Flensburg, 10 June 1803). German composer. In his youth he was in the famous Rosswald court orchestra, which he led in 1776–8, and some time between 1772 and 1775 was a pupil of Gluck at Vienna (as shown by the dedication in the vocal score of his Singspiel *Robert und Hannchen*). Later, after visiting Italy, he was successively musical director at theatres in Brno, Warsaw, Hamburg (from 1783) and Schleswig (from 1786). In 1792 he settled in Flensburg, where as *Stadtmusikant* he played a leading role in the city's musical life. Hanke's comprehensive output (first catalogued by Gerber) is that of a skilled, versatile composer of *Gebrauchsmusik*. His most successful work was *Robert und Hannchen* (or *Der Wunsch mancher Mädchen*, as it was first produced in Warsaw); most of his other works, including ballets, incidental music and vocal and instrumental pieces, are apparently lost.

Cassandra abbandonata (int), Rosswald, before 1781, lost
Der Wunsch mancher Mädchen (Spl, 2, C. Plümicke), Warsaw, 1781, *B-Bc*; vs, as Robert und Hannchen (Hamburg, 1786)
Xaphire (romantisches Oper, A. B. C. d'Arien), Hamburg, 1786, lost
Doktor Fausts Liebgürtel, comp. by 1786 (Spl, 2, d'Arien, after J.-J. Rousseau and W. C. S. Mylius), Flensburg, 1794, lost
Hüon und Amande (romantisches Spl, 5, S. Seyler, after C. M. Wieland: *Oberon*), Schleswig, Hof, 1789, lost

*

GerberNL
A. Einstein: 'Ein Schüler Gluck's', *AcM*, x (1938), 48–50
H. P. Detlefsen: *Musikgeschichte der Stadt Flensburg bis zum Jahre 1850* (Kassel and Basle, 1961)   KLAUS RÖNNAU

Hann, Georg (*b* Vienna, 30 Jan 1897; *d* Munich, 9 Dec 1950). Austrian bass. After study with Theodor Lierhammer in Vienna, he joined the Staatsoper in Munich in 1927. There he sang a wide variety of roles ranging from the deep bass of Sarastro to dramatic baritone parts such as Scarpia and Tonio. In 1942 he created La Roche in *Capriccio*. He also appeared at the Salzburg festivals of 1931, 1946 and 1947, and was a guest artist in Vienna and Berlin. At Covent Garden he sang in *Salome* in 1924 and reappeared there, with the Vienna Staatsoper, in 1947 as Leporello and Pizarro. His strong personality, vivid characterization and tendency to roughness and exaggeration are evident in many recordings, some of them taken from wartime broadcasts; among the best is his Daland in *Der fliegende Holländer*.
     J. B. STEANE

Hannan, Eilene (*b* Melbourne, 4 Nov 1946). Australian soprano. She studied in Australia and London, making her début in 1971 with Australian Opera as Barbarina. She sang Natasha (*War and Peace*) at the opening of the Sydney Opera House (1973) and also sang Zerlina, Cherubino, Mimì, Leïla, Janáček's Vixen, Blanche (*Dialogues des Carmélites*) and Santuzza. In 1977 she made her British début at Glyndebourne as the Vixen and sang Salome (*Hérodiade*) at Wexford. With the ENO (1978–87) she has sung Pamina, Susanna, Lauretta, Marzelline, Natasha, Mélisande, Poppaea, Rusalka, the Governess (*The Turn of the Screw*), Kát'a, the Duchess of Parma/Helen of Troy (*Doktor Faust*), Pauline (*Toussaint l'ouverture*) and Míla (*Osud*); her roles for Opera North include Tatyana. She made her Covent Garden début in 1987 as Nice Caroline (Sallinen's *The King Goes Forth to France*). Turning to heavier roles, she sang Venus (*Tannhäuser*) at Melbourne (1989) and the Marschallin at Sydney (1991). She has a beautiful voice and great musicality.
     ELIZABETH FORBES

Hannay, Roger (Durham) (*b* Plattsburgh, NY, 22 Sept 1930). American composer. He studied at Syracuse University, Boston University, the Eastman School of Music (PhD 1956), the Berkshire Music Center and the Princeton Seminar for Advanced Studies (1960). His teachers included Bernard Rogers and Howard Hanson. Since 1966 he has taught at the University of North Carolina at Chapel Hill, where he founded the UNC New Music Ensemble and the electronic studio. He has composed more than 120 works, his style evolving from dissonant tonality, through the use of 12-note methods, to recomposition and quotation in multi-media theatre works and, by the 1980s, to a new lyricism within a neo-Romantic harmonic context, culminating in his

Symphony no.5. Hannay has written three operas. Both the comic opera *Two Tickets to Omaha* (1960) and the *opera seria The Fortune of St Macabre* (1963) are in one act, with set arias, recitatives and ensembles. *The Journey of Edith Wharton* (1982) is a setting of Russell Graves's play, *E*. An 'opera-biographica' in two acts, it portrays personal and professional relationships in the life of Edith Wharton, centring on her husband, his sister, Henry James and Morton Fullerton, Wharton's lover. The music for each of the 32 scenes is composed in a style that Hannay considers relevant to the subject at hand: Act 1 contains a *verismo* art song, pavane and foxtrot, besides quotation and recomposition (scene iv uses music from Gounod's *Faust*), while Act 2 includes a military march, tango, ballad, waltz and barcarolle. *Scenes from a Literary Life* is a radically condensed version of *The Journey of Edith Wharton*, with new transitional music.

Two Tickets to Omaha (comic op, 1, J. Lamb), Moorhead, MN, Concordia College Opera Theatre, 1960
The Fortune of St Macabre (os, 1, R. Bonnard), Concordia College Opera Theatre, 1963
The Journey of Edith Wharton, 1982 (opera-biographica, prol., 2, epilogue, after R. Graves: *E*), Chapel Hill, U. of North Carolina Opera Workshop, 1988 [excerpts]; rev. in 1 act as Scenes from a Literary Life, 1990, unperf.   WILLIAM DUCKWORTH

Hanover (Ger. Hannover). City in Germany, capital of Lower Saxony. The first operatic performance there was of Cesti's *Orontea*, produced in the Kleines Schlosstheater in the Guelphs' ducal castle, the Leineschloss, in 1678. In the ensuing years the dukes preferred to visit the opera in Venice rather than put on their own, but as such trips were vastly expensive the princes urged Duke Ernst August to have an opera house built in Hanover. The Hanover and the Brunswick sides of the Guelph family (descended from Duke Heinrich der Löwe) competed to be the first to build a theatre. Hanover just won: the Grosses Schlosstheater in the Leineschloss was finished in 1689, less than a year before the Brunswick theatre, and the Hanoverian Guelph, Duke Ernst August, boldly commissioned an opera about Heinrich der Löwe for its opening. Agostino Steffani was summoned from Munich and appointed court Kapellmeister. On 30 January 1689 his *Henrico Leone* opened the theatre (cap. 1300), which was regarded as one of the finest of its time. Steffani wrote at least eight Italian operas for Hanover over the next few years; performances were also given at the Gartentheater in Herrenhausen (the oldest surviving theatre in palace grounds in Germany, built 1689–91). Some of the operas were performed elsewhere, in German translation, notably in Hamburg. However, when Ernst August died in 1698 and his son Georg Ludwig (George I of England) left Hanover, the opera closed.

In the late 18th century a revival of operatic activity was brought about by itinerant companies. Singspiels were brought by Seyler's company in 1769 and, from 1773, F. L. Schröder of Hamburg staged operas and Singspiels by Johann Beckmann, Friedrich Fleischer, Hiller, Grétry, Paisiello and Georg Benda. Gustav Grossmann's company first staged operas in Hanover in 1787, performing over 92 works during the next decade in German, French and Italian.

Soon after the formation of the Kingdom of Hanover in 1815, a permanent company was formed (1818). Heinrich Marschner's *Hans Heiling* and *Der Vampyr* were well received, and in 1831 Marschner was appointed Kapellmeister. Despite several successful seasons at the Schlosstheater, however, problems arose: the auditorium could not be heated, and the seating arrangement meant that in the event of fire the audience would have had to pass through the whole castle to escape.

When, in 1837, Hanover gained full independence from its joint sovereignty with Great Britain, plans were made to rebuild the Schlosstheater. In 1843, however, King Ernst August commissioned a new building from the court architect, G. Laves: the new Hoftheater in the Georgstrasse opened in September 1852, under his successor, Georg V. During his reign opera flourished; artists such as Albert Niemann and Hans von Bülow were engaged, and Gounod conducted his *Faust* in 1862 with great success. In 1866, however, when Hanover became a province of Prussia, the city lost its operatic independence and was governed from Berlin.

Dependence on Berlin ended in 1921. The Hoftheater became the Städtisches Opernhaus and Rudolf Krasselt, who was appointed Generalmusikdirektor in 1924 and later became administrator, built up a strong company, engaging soloists such as Tiana Lemnitz and Peter Anders. He was especially interested in the works of Wolf-Ferrari and conducted the premières of nine of his 13 operas. After falling out of favour with the Nazi party he was removed from his post in 1943. The opera house was bombed in July that year but the Baroque building at Herrenhausen remained undamaged and within a few weeks the hall and gallery were converted into a temporary theatre. After a short break performances resumed in 1945. In 1950, after only 11 months of rebuilding, the opera house in the Georgstrasse reopened as the Landestheater with *Der Rosenkavalier*. The administrator was Kurt Ehrhardt and the Musikdirektor Franz Konwitschny. In 1952, to celebrate its centenary, the theatre gave the world première of Henze's *Boulevard Solitude*. Ehrhardt and his successors Reinhard Lehmann, Günter Roth and (since 1980) Hans-Peter Lehmann have been advocates of ensemble theatre. Among the artists to have begun their international careers in Hanover are Helen Donath, Bernd Weikl, Christa Ludwig, Franz Crass, Deborah Polaski and Waltraud Meier.

In 1970 the Landestheater was renamed the Niedersächsisches Staatstheater. Its personnel comprises the Staatstheater company, whose home is the historic Ballhof, and the Staatsoper company. Both organizations are financed by the *Land* of Lower Saxony and the city of Hanover. The Staatsoper is a repertory company which stages 35 operas each season including six new productions. The German premières of *Owen Wingrave* and von Einem's *Jesu Hochzeit* were given there. Operas are staged throughout the year except for six weeks of holiday and two of preliminary rehearsal. Each season a number of gala evenings are held; guest artists have included Grace Bumbry, Maria Chiara, Gwyneth Jones, Mara Zampieri, José Carreras, Siegfried Jerusalem and Sherrill Milnes. The building was renovated in 1984–5: the auditorium (cap. 1207) is modern in style but with classical elements relating it to the external façade. In 1989 the combined companies numbered 830 including an orchestra of 111, a chorus of 63, 45 soloists and 43 dancers. The Staatsoper has an active education department which holds children's festivals and performs children's operas.

In 1989 the tercentenary of opera in Hanover was celebrated with a revival of the opera which opened the

Schlosstheater, Steffani's *Henrico Leone*, directed by Herbert Wernicke. That year Zimmermann's *Die Soldaten* was also staged and a competition for young singers was inaugurated.

G. Fischer: *Musik in Hannover* (Hanover, 1903)
H. Sievers: *Die Musik in Hannover* (Hanover, 1961)
S. Hammer: *Das Opernhaus in Hannover* (Hanover, 1985)
——: *Oper in Hannover* (Hanover, 1989)   SABINE SONNTAG

Hänsel und Gretel ('Hänsel and Gretel'). *Märchenspiel* in three acts ('Bilder') by ENGELBERT HUMPERDINCK to a libretto by ADELHEID WETTE after a fairy-tale by the Brothers GRIMM, Jacob Ludwig and Wilhelm Carl; Weimar, Hoftheater, 23 December 1893.

Gretel	soprano
Hänsel *her brother*	mezzo-soprano
Gertrud *their mother*	mezzo-soprano
Peter *a broom-maker, their father*	baritone
Sandman	soprano
Dew Fairy	soprano
Witch	mezzo-soprano

14 angels, children

Setting The woods of the Ilsenstein

In April 1890 Humperdinck was asked by his sister, Adelheid Wette, to set to music four folksongs from the Grimm fairy-tale *Hänsel und Gretel* for performance by her children. The work might have rested there; but at the time Humperdinck was seeking the text for a comic opera, and his family persuaded him that the songs might be extended into a small Singspiel. The piece was performed privately in this version in the Wettes' house; the delighted response encouraged Humperdinck to turn the material into a fully-fledged opera, even though he had doubts about the fairy-tale being suited to such treatment.

On receiving the completed score in October 1893, Richard Strauss declared the opera a masterpiece. The première was due to be conducted by Hermann Levi in Munich, on 14 December 1893; but the illness of Hanna Borchers (Gretel) caused a postponement and the honour of conducting the first performance fell to Strauss in Weimar. Pauline de Ahna was to have sung Hänsel, but she too was ill and Fräulein Schubert sang Hänsel in her place, while Schubert's part of Gretel was taken over at short notice by Marie Kayser. Ferdinand Wiedey sang Peter and Hermine Finck the Witch. The overture could not be performed as the parts had not arrived; any shortcomings in the première, however, were compensated for by the speed and success with which the opera was taken up by other theatres, aided by the *Hänsel und Gretel* touring company founded by Georg Richard Kruse in 1894. The emperor praised the work at its Berlin première, conducted by Weingartner on 13 October 1894. Two outstanding individual performances were given within the first year, by Hedwig Schako as Gretel in the Frankfurt première and by Ernestine Schumann-Heink as the Witch in Hamburg with Mahler.

The progress of *Hänsel und Gretel* abroad was equally impressive. The London première took place as early as 1894: Arditi conducted the opera in English at Daly's Theatre, with Marie Elba as Hänsel and Jeanne Douste as Gretel. The American première, at the Metropolitan in 1905, was conducted by Alfred Hertz. *Hänsel und*

Gretel was the first opera to be broadcast complete from Covent Garden, in January 1923. In 1954 the first recording of the opera was made, Karajan conducting, with Elisabeth Grümmer as Hänsel and Elisabeth Schwarzkopf as Gretel. In Germany, performances of *Hänsel und Gretel* have remained popularly associated with Christmas.

Humperdinck referred to the overture as 'Children's Life'; it sums up much of the poetic and musical content of the work. Exuberant dances are balanced by the hymnlike sounds of the 'Evening Prayer'; its phrases spread in extending arches, suggesting the divine providence that will protect the children in their adventures. As this theme combines polyphonically with the folklike dances, the music becomes more rumbustious – but, as Humperdinck said, such is the way with children and their games.

ACT 1 *In the broom-maker's house* The curtain rises to show the children at more serious business, Hänsel making brooms and Gretel knitting stockings. Gretel sings a folksong, 'Suse, liebe Suse', to accompany her work; Hänsel takes over, though a slight interruption of the gentle flow suggests that their minds are not wholly on their business. Hänsel then breaks the thread more decisively by throwing down his work and complaining of hunger. Even Gretel's reference to providence, to a phrase of the Evening Prayer, cannot silence his cries. A dance provides the diversion needed; Gretel makes a game of sweeping all Hänsel's grumbling out of the house ('Griesgram hinaus'). The reappearance of the gentle accompaniment of 'Suse, liebe Suse' at the close of the song confirms that peace has returned. Gretel is even able to show Hänsel some milk that a neighbour has given them for the family's supper. The children's delighted expectation is reflected in the new variations woven from the 'Suse' folksong; but one fragment from the original persists, reminding Gretel of the work they should be doing. It seems the reminder may prove effective until Hänsel mentions the word 'dancing', when thoughts of work vanish and the 'Suse' motif is swept into the dance-song 'Brüderchen komm tanz mit mir'. Unlike 'Suse, liebe Suse' (or the later 'Ein Männlein steht im Walde'), this is not a quoted folksong though it is equally successful in evoking a children's world. The variations stray more and more from the opening as the children are led further and further into their game. The momentum of the dance is halted only by the dramatic entry of Gertrud. As the children attempt to explain why they have done so little work, the forgotten 'Suse' fragment slips back, punctuated by ominous signs of the mother's anger. Gertrud knocks over the precious milk and in despair chases the children out to pick strawberries. Her solitary lament, 'Da liegt nun der gute Topf', is accompanied by last sorrowful echoes of the 'Suse' motif.

The distant sounds of the broom-maker's song, 'Ral-la-la-la, ral-la-la-la', begin in the minor key as a slightly humorous lament for the poor man in his hunger, but a lilting major version soon follows. At first Gertrud puts such energy down to drinking, but as Peter produces food from his basket the mood of lamentation is forgotten. Even Gertrud's account of the spilt milk fails to damp their spirits and dance fragments continue to punctuate their dialogue. At the height of their jubilance Peter pauses to inquire about the children. When Gertrud reveals that they have been sent into the forest,

the rhythms change in character, and Peter warns of the Witch's Ride. At first the music remains spirited, but as Peter settles into his Witch's Ballad it grows in intensity. Finally convinced of the children's real danger in the forest, Gertrud hurries out of the house with Peter to seek them.

ACT 2 *In the wood* As the prelude develops the music of the Witch's Ride from folksong to orchestral tone-painting, it seems that Peter has hardly exaggerated the terrors of the gingerbread Witch. With a gradual calming of the Bacchanalian dance figures, the curtain rises on the more peaceful forest scene of Gretel making a garland of roseships and Hänsel picking strawberries. They sing a cheerful folksong, 'Ein Männlein steht im Walde', to a spare orchestral accompaniment. After the heavy rhythms of the Witch's Ride the children's innocent pleasures are suggested by the weaving of delicate melodic fragments. When a cuckoo picks up their falling interval of a 3rd, they echo its call and absorb it further into their melodies. They also make a game of mimicking his stealing habits with their strawberries, only to find to their horror that they have eaten every one.

From this point the melodic lines and orchestral texture take on a more opaque quality, as if the wood were darkening around them. From the sudden silence as Hänsel admits he has lost their way, a more mysterious and sustained melodic line emerges, one first heard as a background to the Witch's Ride. It is repeated in shorter note values and chromatically distorted versions as the children's fear of the forest grows. Mists rise, and their imaginations succeed in turning the cuckoo's call into a portent of doom and even in invoking the rhythms of the Witch's Ride. When the mists clear, all that is revealed is the Sandman, a small grey figure with a sack on his back. The heavier sonorities vanish, leaving harmonics from harp and strings to accompany his simple song, 'Der kleine Sandmann bin ich'. As though to indicate that the peaceful sleep the Sandman brings, as he sprinkles his sand on to the children's eyes, is real, his song is carried over into an expansive chorale-like melody. The children respond by singing their Evening Prayer, its reassuring triadic shapes purging their minds of all horrors. The earlier mysterious shape is incorporated into the polyphonic sequences that grow from the Prayer, which is now connected with heavenly mysteries, as in a 'Dream Pantomime' a ladder reaches down from heaven and 14 angels are seen to surround the sleeping children. The symphonic proportions of this ballet-pantomime more than balance the excesses of the Witch's Ride and leave one in no doubt that good will triumph in the coming battle between evil and innocence.

ACT 3 *The gingerbread house* The spiky motif for the gingerbread house which begins the third act promises a rude awakening for the children. Its staccato rhythms foreshadow the character of the Witch herself, but the prelude soon weaves them into a smoother texture, as though seeking to prolong the mood of the ballet-pantomime. When the Dew Fairy enters to awaken the children, he sings his own version of the Sandman's song, 'Der kleine Taumann heiss' ich', followed by a melody from the overture closely associated with the Evening Prayer. The suspended melodic lines of Gretel's first words show her still hovering on the borders of sleep; then she wakes Hänsel and a more everyday world returns, as the two children mimic

*'Hänsel und Gretel'
(Humperdinck): wood
engraving after A. Zick
(1894) showing the
closing scene of Act 2*

birdsong. Hänsel, however, soon refers back to the music of the Prayer, and Gretel joins him in relating their dream of the 14 angels.

The polyphonic lines of the ballet-pantomime prove so pervasive that they seem to overflow into the moment when the morning mists clear to reveal the gingerbread house, making it seem part of the same dream-imagery, except that barcarolle rhythms now convey a more sensual character. As the children express their delight in the sweets making up the house, a new staccato figure is heard, offering a more obvious contrast to the Prayer. The combination of these two figures creates an irresistible momentum. The children ignore the warnings of the gingerbread house's spiky motif in the orchestra and they remain unaware of the Witch creeping up on them and throwing a noose round Hänsel's neck until the staccato rhythms of her laughter break out from the whole orchestra.

From this point the barcarolle rhythms seem like an ensnaring web, with the Witch singing many new variations to prolong the flow. Although she entices the children with words of endearment, their responses show that they recognize her true nature. Indeed, when Hänsel slips his halter and tries to escape with Gretel, the melodic façade drops and she fixes them with a spell. She shuts Hänsel in a cage, intending to fatten him up, and sends Gretel indoors to set the table: Gretel is already plump enough for cooking. The Witch's power might seem frightening, except that the constant return to the barcarolle rhythms makes her culinary preparations seem like a reckless game. At one point her excitement grows so great that it spills over into a return of the Witch's Ride, 'Hurr hopp hopp'. The children await their moment. As the oven burns hotter and the Witch's excitement continues to rise, Gretel breaks her spell and frees her brother; when the Witch tells her to look into the oven she feigns stupidity and asks the witch to demonstrate, and the two of them bundle her into the oven. They express their feelings in the Gingerbread Waltz, 'Nun ist die Hexe tot', their own version of the barcarolle figures. The explosion of the Witch's oven heralds a further transformation: the gingerbread figures surrounding the house are revealed as dead children, waiting for the touch of Hänsel and Gretel to bring them back to life. As their subdued song 'O rühre mich an' changes into a dance (the sign of returning life), more of the opera's themes become woven into the fabric, as in the overture. 'Ral-la-la-la' heralds the arrival of Peter and Gertrud, closely followed by the dance-song from the first act. The reappearance of the Evening Prayer confirms its place in the children's triumph.

＊ ＊ ＊

Critics have often debated as to whether the richness of the musical material of *Hänsel und Gretel* and the elaboration of its development are not too much for a simple, traditional fairy story. Yet despite the Wagnerian range of colours and textures that Humperdinck drew from the orchestra, he succeeded in keeping the melodic and rhythmic foundations of his music simple. By indulging in seemingly endless polyphonic variations on his folk melodies, Humperdinck actually remained close in spirit to the carefree sensuousness of children. It was this uninhibited exploitation of Wagnerian musical techniques, without the complexities or philosophical undertones of music drama, that so attracted audiences at the time. Yet perhaps the opera's most enduring quality is its melodic appeal, which ties the music directly to folksong and gives reality to Humperdinck's claim of having recreated *Märchenoper*. AMANDA GLAUERT

Hans Heiling. *Grosse romantische Oper* in a prologue and three acts by HEINRICH AUGUST MARSCHNER to a libretto by EDUARD DEVRIENT after legends about the Hans Heiling Cliffs in Bohemia; Berlin, Hofoper, 24 May 1833.

According to various legends, the outcroppings of rock on the cliffs cut by the River Eger (now Ohře) near Karlsbad (now Karlovy Vary) in western Bohemia were once members of a wedding procession that was turned to stone by Hans Heiling, king of the gnomes or earth spirits. Although Devrient does not say specifically in his memoirs which legends he studied for the *Hans Heiling* libretto, one likely source was the first published work on the subject, C. H. Spiess's *Hans Heiling, vierter und letzter Regent der Erd-, Luft-, und Wassergeister, ein Volksmärchen des 10. Jahrhunderts* (Leipzig, 1798),

The Queen of the Gnomes	soprano
Hans Heiling *her son*	baritone
Anna *his bride*	soprano
Gertrude *her mother*	contralto
Conrad *a baronial hunter*	tenor
Niklas *another hunter*	speaking role
Stephan *the village blacksmith*	bass

Gnomes, peasants, wedding guests, musicians and hunters

Setting The cavernous underground realm of the gnomes; later the village and surrounding woodlands immediately above it

---

which included in a prologue several legends Spiess had collected. Since Spiess's time, many other writers have created works on the same theme. These stories fall into three groups.

In the first group Heiling is a spooky prince of the dwarfs (sometimes a dwarf himself), a troll, or a sovereign of the gnomes. Best known is *Die Heilingszwerge*, by the Grimm brothers, in which Hans Heiling, here an old troll, lives in an ancient house that appears once a century at the foot of the cliffs that bear his name. Tired from picking berries, a woman appears at the house and asks for hospitality. Heiling grants it, then disappears to hunt for his dwarfs. The house vanishes and the woman is unable to go back to her village for a hundred years.

In the second group Heiling is a youth who looks into the Eger to be greeted by a beautiful water nymph who promises to teach him many things if only he will remain unmarried. But when the unfortunate Hans falls in love with a girl and prepares to marry her, he is met at the altar by the nymph, who wreaks revenge by turning the whole wedding party into stone.

In the third group Heiling is a man of ill repute who tries to win the heart of a girl betrothed to a virtuous young journeyman carpenter. While the youth is gone, Heiling presses the father for his daughter's hand and is eventually successful; but when the youth returns wealthy the father relents and allows the lovers to reunite. Enraged, Heiling calls on the devil to turn the wedding party into stone in exchange for his soul. Included in this group is Theodor Körner's *Hans Heiling Felsen, eine böhmische Volkssage*.

Like Heine in *Die verzauberte Zwergenhochzeit* (1834), Devrient combined elements from all three groups with some new material of his own. His Heiling is ruler over the gnomes but not actually one of them; his dominion is limited to the Lower World. Nor is anyone turned to stone here, although this appears to be an important feature of the legends. What sets Devrient's libretto apart from other treatments of the subject, however, is his character development, particularly that of Heiling. Though a supernatural monarch, benevolent and respected, he succumbs to the temptations of men and falls in love with Anna, a mortal girl who appears to return his love. But when she jilts Heiling in favour of an ordinary man, he promises vengeance, and it is only the intercession of his mother that prevents him from unleashing the fury of the subterranean hordes on the wedding party. Thus Heiling displays a dual nature: he is at once tyrannical yet magnanimous, mortally weak yet supernaturally strong – in short, both villain and hero.

Devrient first offered his work to Mendelssohn, who however could not warm to the character of Heiling and

regarded such subjects, in the *Freischütz* mould, as out of fashion. Marschner, however, saw in the libretto great possibilities for developing his concept of German opera, and he began work on the music in 1831. The thunderous applause that greeted the Berlin première soon spread throughout Europe, and the work has remained in the repertory of German and Czech houses ever since. Important revivals took place in Prague in 1889 and 1938, in Dresden in 1923 and in Berlin in 1929. For the landmark Dresden performances Pfitzner invented a way of making Heiling's magic book, with pages that turn progressively faster (plans for its manufacture were published in 1930). Among several modern British productions, two have attempted to modernize the story by transplanting the action to a Swiss bank (1972, Oxford) and a psychiatric ward (1983, Wexford). C. F. Peters published the full score, which was favourably reviewed by Philipp Spitta, in 1892.

PROLOGUE *A cavern under the earth* Accompanied by a relentless, almost Baroque walking-bass pattern set in a chromatically rich harmonic context that by this time had become one of Marschner's trademarks, a chorus of gnomes are mining gold and diamonds. Hans Heiling, their king, declares that he has fallen in love with Anna and will forsake his subterranean kingdom for life on earth with her. A poor country girl, Anna has been cajoled by her mother to consent to an engagement with this rich stranger whom she respects but does not love. Because Heiling must give up his reign if he decides to live above ground, his mother and the other gnomes entreat him not to go, but in vain. Mother and son part; to accommodate a complex scene change, the overture, cast in Weberian sonata-allegro form with the recapitulation modified to serve as an entr'acte, is played next.

ACT 1.i *A room in a building above the underground realm* Heiling arises from beneath the earth, closing forever the entrance to the gnomes' realm. Met by Anna and Gertrude, he gives Anna a golden chain; adorning herself, she imagines how she will be the envy of her friends. She asks Heiling to accompany her to a festival, but he, naturally serious and even bad-tempered, refuses. Anna gets over her disappointment, however, when she sees the pages in his magic book turning automatically. But the commotion begins to terrify her, and Heiling, angered that she has meddled with his belongings, pushes her away. She entreats him to destroy the frightening book, and finally he casts this last vestige of his power into the fireplace. Thunder is heard. Anna thanks him for destroying the fearful book but begins to grow distrustful of him. After what seems to have been a whirlwind courtship, Heiling and Anna are already beginning to react to traits in each other that they find distasteful. Only Heiling's grand tripartite aria 'An jenem Tag' (with an italianate middle section resembling a siciliana) interrupts the ensemble texture to allow him to express his undying love for Anna – a point to emphasize since the balance of the opera is devoted to the destruction of their love.

1.ii *The village fairgrounds* Peasants celebrate the Feast of St Florian with a rousing march and chorus. Heiling has agreed to accompany Anna to the festival after all, provided she does not dance; but the young men of the village badger her until she consents, thereby breaking her word to Heiling. The youths are jealous of the taciturn older man who has won the hand of the fairest maid in the village. Conrad, who has loved Anna since childhood, chides Heiling mercilessly in his allegorical strophic lied with laughing choral refrain, 'Ein sprödes, allerliebstes Kind'. Heiling leaves in despair. For this scene, designed to provide comic relief and develop intrigue, Marschner abandoned much of the extended ensemble writing of the earlier scenes in favour of a simpler style reminiscent of folk music. The opening march and chorus are essentially free of the chromatic harmony and rapid modulation of the earlier sections. The same may be said of Conrad's lied, although here the device also serves a psychological purpose, because Conrad uses it to arouse Heiling's jealousy much as Caspar does in Max (Der Freischütz) and Iago in Otello. The development of intrigue, which requires a rapid, impassioned interchange of ideas, is carried out in spoken dialogue unencumbered by music.

ACT 2.i A forest Anna has lost all affection for Heiling, whom she now fears; she loves only Conrad. In the aria 'Sonnst du verfallen', upon whose melody Wagner based his 'Todesverkündigung' leitmotif (Die Walküre), the Queen, who suddenly appears with her gnomes, reveals to Anna the origin of her betrothed and urges her to give him back to his heartbroken mother and her realm. When the gnomes have gone, Anna asks Conrad to help her against the possible revenge of the gnome king. He consents and takes her home.

2.ii A hut in the forest The sound effects of a storm outside are multiplied by means of the spoken voice over the orchestra in an ominous Melodram und Lied ('Ein geiziger, hartherziger Mann') in which Gertrude expresses fear that her daughter is lost; but Conrad brings her inside to safety. Heiling enters with jewels to adorn the bride, but Anna falls back from him in fear. As he leaves he lunges at his rival with a dagger, wounding him.

ACT 3.i A ravine in the mountains Heiling realizes that he has sacrificed his supernatural powers for life on earth but has gained nothing. He decides to return to the land of the gnomes.

3.ii A churchyard To contrast with the heavy drama that has just transpired, Marschner returns to his diatonic folk style to provide a satisfactory conclusion. Having recovered from his wound, Conrad prepares to marry Anna, but Heiling reappears to take revenge on him. Conrad draws his sword, but it mysteriously shatters. Meanwhile, the Queen materializes, begs her son to forgive and forget, and leads him into the kingdom beneath the earth. The peasants breathe a sigh of relief, while Anna and Conrad sing of their love.

* * *

While the earlier Der Vampyr could be described at least architectonically as modelled on Der Freischütz, in its first scene (Act 1.i) Marschner begins to pull away from that mould into one that is musico-dramatically more integrated – one that presages Wagner's Der fliegende Holländer – by casting practically everything in ensemble. The four individually numbered sections (an inheritance from Singspiel) have so many subsections whose music is only tangentially related that they might best be termed 'ensemble complexes'. This kind of construction grew naturally out of the need Devrient imposed on Marschner to reinforce the personality transformations he had written into the parts of Anna and Heiling.

A. DEAN PALMER

Hanslick, Eduard (b Prague, 11 Sept 1825; d Baden, nr Vienna, 6 Aug 1904). German critic and aesthetician. His Jewish mother taught him French and a love of the theatre; from his father, a Catholic musician and librarian, he acquired a taste for books and music, and soon made progress in piano playing and composing. At 18 he began to study with Tomášek and read law at Prague University, where he met the philosopher Zimmermann and the music historian Ambros. In his earliest articles, for the Prague journal Ost und West, Hanslick emulated the subjective Jean-Paulian style of Schumann, who invited him to Dresden. There Hanslick also renewed an acquaintance with Wagner. In 1846 he moved to Vienna for a final year of legal studies, and wrote for the Wiener Musikzeitung and other journals.

After graduating in 1849 he entered government service, first in Klagenfurt and then in Vienna. In 1854 he published his famous monograph Vom Musikalisch-Schönen, which so impressed the Vienna University authorities that they appointed him to an honorary readership. His lectures on music appreciation, then a novel concept, were well attended and influential; they became a regular feature of his work. By 1861 he had advanced to a paid associate professorship, which together with his earnings as a critic enabled him to retire from the civil service. In 1870 he became a full professor of music history and aesthetics. He retired from that post in 1875, and in 1876 he began his happy marriage with the young singer Sophie Wohlmuth. In his later years he enjoyed unequalled eminence throughout the German-speaking world and beyond.

Despite his renown, Hanslick was far from universally revered. As a critic, he avowedly spoke for his time and class: 'For my heart, [music] really begins with Mozart and culminates in Beethoven, Schumann and Brahms' (Aus meinem Leben, ii, 307). But at least he could see his subject in historical and social perspective, and he readily conceded that the future might well belong to music that lay outside his own frame of reference. Within it, his ideals were orderliness and formal perfection. Even melody, his other main desideratum ('ohne Melodie keine Musik, ohne gesungene Melodie keine Oper'; Aus dem Tagebuch eines Musikers, 179), was admired less for its continuity of flow than for its regularity of pattern. Thus the prelude to Tristan was chided for its lack of contrast or repose (Aus dem Concertsaal, 327). Not only Wagner but Verdi (Otello) lacked melody in this sense (Musikalisches und Literarisches, 72).

Hanslick's reviews, characterized by the integrity, liveliness and clarity that he admired in music, dealt with works rather than performances. They were often carefully planned round some central theme or aspect (such as the history of the instrument or genre concerned) and regularly entailed extra-musical research (such as studying Shakespeare before discussing Verdi's Otello). Hanslick was always concerned with practical music-making, and his experience as pianist, composer and adjudicator, together with his wide circle of musical acquaintance (including a friendship with Brahms), render his writings an exemplary source of information as well as criticism. Even his detractors could admire his grasp and style. He, conversely, duly acknowledged the genius and achievements of his adversaries, notably Wagner and Liszt. But he felt strongly that they and their followers had forced music far beyond its proper bounds, for example in the Ride of the Valkyries (Aus dem Concertsaal, 281). Wagner also lacked verisimilitude, insofar as his operas presented mythological characters and not real people; his main failing was succinctly defined as 'the subjection of music to words' (*Aus meinem Leben*, ii, 228). For Hanslick, music in all contexts always had to be an end in itself, never the means to the end of poetic or dramatic expression. Thus opera was first of all music, not drama. Wagner had broken the rules, and was duly condemned. He rejected all such jurisdiction; in the first draft of *Die Meistersinger* Beckmesser was named 'Hanslich'.

Personal antipathies played a prominent part in this *cause célèbre*. Wagner's political and social stance, and his anti-Semitism, defied the cultured society and human values for which Hanslick spoke. As the latter conceded (*Aus meinem Leben*, ii, 236, 242), *Vom Musikalisch-Schönen* had begun as a polemic against Wagner. But it is not thereby invalidated, and its main thesis – that the value of music lies in its formal relations and not its expressiveness – has an assured place in the history of aesthetics and criticism.

Hanslick's emphasis on autonomy and structure prepared the ground for such analysts as Schenker and Réti. His acknowledgment of the symbolic function of music found fruitful development in the theories of Susanne Langer, and his critical praxis directly affected the course of music history by implanting and nurturing the seeds of reaction against Wagner.

Vom Musikalisch-Schönen: ein Beitrag zur Revision der Ästhetik der Tonkunst (Leipzig, 1854; Eng. trans., 1891, 1986) [most edns rev. and enlarged]
with W. Lübke: *Wilhelm Lübke und Eduard Hanslick über Richard Wagner* (Berlin, 1869)
Geschichte des Concertwesens in Wien, i (Vienna, 1869); ii: *Aus dem Concertsaal: Kritiken und Schilderungen aus den letzten 20 Jahren des Wiener Musiklebens, 1848–1868* (1870, 2/1896)
Die moderne Oper, i: *Kritiken und Studien* (Berlin, 1875, 2/1876, 3/1911); ii: *Musikalische Stationen* (1880, 6/1911); iii: *Aus dem Opernleben der Gegenwart* (1884, 4/1911); iv: *Musikalisches Skizzenbuch* (1888, 3/1911); v: *Musikalisches und Literarisches* (1889, 3/1911); vi: *Aus dem Tagebuch eines Musikers* (1892, 3/1911); vii: *Fünf Jahre Musik (1891–1895)* (1896, 3/1911); viii: *Am Ende des Jahrhunderts (1895–1899)* (1899, 3/1911); ix: *Aus neuer und neuester Zeit* (1900, 3/1911)
Operncyclus im Foyer des K. K. Opernhauses in Wien (Munich, 1880)
Aus meinem Leben (Berlin, 1894, 4/1911)
H. Pleasants, ed.: *Eduard Hanslick: Vienna's Golden Years of Music 1850–1900* (New York, 1950, 2/1963 as *Eduard Hanslick: Music Criticisms 1846–99*) [selected writings]

*

F. P. Laurencin d'Armond: *Eduard Hanslicks Lehre vom Musikalisch-Schönen: eine Abwehr* (Leipzig, 1859)
F. Stade: *Vom Musikalisch-Schönen mit Bezug auf Dr. Eduard Hanslick's gleichnamige Schrift* (Leipzig, 1870, 2/1904)
O. Hostinský: *Das Musikalisch-Schöne und das Gesamtkunstwerk vom Standpunkte der formalen Ästhetik* (Leipzig, 1877)
R. Hirschfeld: *Das kritische Verfahren Eduard Hanslicks* (Vienna, 1885)
P. Schneider: *Über das Darstellungsvermögen der Musik: eine Untersuchung von Eduard Hanslicks Buch Vom Musikalisch-Schönen* (Leipzig, 1892)
R. Schäfke: *Eduard Hanslick und die Musikästhetik* (Leipzig, 1922)
S. Deas: *In Defence of Hanslick* (London, 1940)
M. Mila: 'Verdi e Hanslick', *RaM*, xxi (1951), 212–24
A. Della Corte: 'Le critiche di Eduard Hanslick alle opere di Richard Wagner', *RaM*, xxix (1959), 12–26
——: *La critica musicale e i critici* (Turin, 1961)
E. Fubini: *L'estetica musicale dal settecento a oggi* (Turin, 1964)
H. Ullrich: 'Musikkritik und -Kritiken im Wiener Vormärz', *ÖMz*, xxvi (1971), 353–65
W. Abegg: *Musikästhetik und Musikkritik bei Eduard Hanslick* (Regensburg, 1974)
E. Sams: 'Eduard Hanslick, 1825–1904: the Perfect Anti-Wagnerite', *MT*, cxvi (1975), 867–8
H. Grimm: 'Die Musikanschauungen Franz Grillparzers und Eduard Hanslicks: Geistesverwandtschaft und Distanz', *Beiträge zur Musikwissenschaft*, xxiv (1982), 17–30
H. Lenneberg: 'Il Bismarck della critica musicale: the Memoirs of Eduard Hanslick', *OQ*, ii (1984), 29–36
G. Payzant: 'Eduard Hanslick on the Role of the Performer', *Opuscula aesthetica nostra*, ed. C. Cloutier and C. Seerveld (1984), 73–80
C. Dahlhaus: 'Studien zur romantischen Musikaesthetik', *AMw*, xlii (1985), 157–65
G. Payzant, ed.: E. Hanslick: *On the Musically Beautiful* (Indianopolis, IN, 1986)   ERIC SAMS

Hanson, Howard (Harold) (*b* Wahoo, NE, 28 Oct 1896; *d* Rochester, NY, 26 Feb 1981). American composer. Following studies at Northwestern University, in 1924 he became director of the Eastman School of Music in Rochester, New York, a post he held for 40 years. He founded the Institute of American Music at Eastman in 1964 and was noted for his long dedication to the cause of American music. A prolific composer, he wrote only one opera, *Merry Mount* op.31 (1933), which won the David Bispham Medal. The opera, in three acts of six scenes, has a libretto by Richard L. Stokes based on Nathaniel Hawthorne's 'The Maypole of Merry Mount'. The story, of witchcraft and sexual obsession among Puritan settlers in 17th-century New England, derives from a historical episode involving a Puritan belief that a Saturnalian maypole invented by the devil had been built in 1625 near what is now Quincy, Massachusetts. The opera's main character, Wrestling Bradford (baritone), is a fanatical Puritan clergyman obsessed by demonic dreams that ultimately lead to his immolation with his lover Lady Marigold Sandys (soprano) in a church consumed by flames. Hanson felt that a parallel to *Merry Mount* was Musorgsky's *Boris Godunov* with its lone tormented protagonist and prominent use of the chorus. *Merry Mount* employs elaborate ballets and a large orchestra that features a wind machine and oriental percussion effects. Its harmonic colours are rich, often modal, with reminiscences of Debussy, Puccini and Strauss. A concert version of the opera was performed by the Chicago SO at Ann Arbor, Michigan, on 20 May 1933 but it was first staged by the Metropolitan, who commissioned it, on 10 February 1934. The première, conducted by Tullio Serafin with a cast of 18 including Lawrence Tibbett as Bradford, was a success and drew 50 curtain calls though the opera did not remain in the repertory. In 1937 Hanson fashioned an orchestral suite from portions of the music, and in 1964 the opera was revived at San Antonio, Texas, with Beverly Sills and Brian Sullivan in the principal roles.

*

E. E. Hipsher: *American Opera and its Composers* (Philadelphia, 1927, 2/1934), 241–4
'*Merry Mount*: New Opera described by Dr Hanson', *Musical Courier* (5 March 1932)
R. T. Watanabe: *Music of Howard Hanson* (Rochester, NY, 1966)
                                                                    ELISE K. KIRK

Hans Sachs. *Komische Oper* in three acts by ALBERT LORTZING to a libretto by Philipp Reger with the composer and Philipp J. Düringer after Johann Ludwig Ferdinand Deinhardstein's play; Leipzig, Stadttheater, 23 June 1840 (revised version, Mannheim, Nationaltheater, 25 May 1845).

The action takes place in Nuremberg in 1517. Hans Sachs (bass), a master cobbler and Mastersinger, has heard that Kaiser Maximilian (bass) admires his songs. Lortzing establishes Sachs as a serious and dignified figure in a scena and aria which incorporates a short section of melodrama. In sharp contrast to Sachs is the comic character of Eoban (tenor), an Augsburg city councillor who is Sachs's rival for the hand of Kunigunde (soprano), daughter of the goldsmith Steffen (bass). Another important comic character is Sachs's apprentice Görg (tenor), betrothed to Kunigunde's friend Kordula (soprano). Eoban tells Steffen, who is puffed up with pride after being elected burgomaster of Augsburg, about Sachs's love for Kunigunde, and Steffen expresses his opposition to the match.

Act 2 opens with a singing competition in which the citizens acclaim Sachs as victor; but the judges have been bribed and award the prize to Eoban, despite the obvious deficiencies of his composition and performance. Sachs determines to leave the city and sings a simple folklike farewell. He takes leave of Kunigunde, but Steffen interrupts their embrace and orders Sachs out of the city. In Act 3 news arrives that the Kaiser is due in the city and that he wishes to honour the author of a poem which has been found by one of his courtiers. Eoban claims the poem as his, but in fact it is Sachs's, which Görg had appropriated and passed off as his own to impress Kordula. Görg confesses his theft of the poem, Eoban is ridiculed, Sachs is honoured and the lovers are reunited.

The music of the opera, written with Lortzing's usual fluency, contains effective ensembles and many attractive folksong-like numbers, including dances. There is however a degree of unresolved tension between the serious and comic elements in Sachs's character in particular, and this may account for the opera's relative lack of success at the time. Comparison of Lortzing's *Hans Sachs* with Wagner's treatment of the same story in *Die Meistersinger* is interesting. In Lortzing's opera Sachs is both the revered master and the romantic lover struggling to overcome adversity; Wagner divided these elements between Sachs and Walther.

CLIVE BROWN

Hanssens, Charles-Louis(-Joseph) [*l'aîné*] (*b* Ghent, 4 May 1777; *d* Brussels, 6 May 1852). South Netherlands conductor and composer. He was taught the violin by Wauthier, first violin at the Ghent theatre, and composition by Verheym, choirmaster at the cathedral. After over a year in Paris studying harmony with Berton he returned to Ghent and completed his studies. He began his career in 1802 as conductor of a theatre for amateurs in Ghent, the Théâtre de Rhétorique; soon he left to conduct a French company performing in Amsterdam, Utrecht and Rotterdam. In 1804 he went to Antwerp as conductor of the theatre, but returned to Ghent, where he was conductor of the theatre until 1825. In that year he succeeded Charles Borremans at the Théâtre de la Monnaie in Brussels. In 1827 King William of the Netherlands chose Hanssens as his musical director and later in the same year he became inspector at the school of music (forerunner of the conservatory). During the Revolution in 1831 he fell under suspicion and was arrested. On being released he remained in obscurity until 1835 when he returned to direct the orchestra at the Monnaie. He was dismissed in 1838 but took over a third time in 1840, at the same time taking a financial interest in the theatre: this speculation was a failure and he spent the last years of his life in poverty. Of his four operas, *Alcibiade* (1829, Brussels), to a libretto by Scribe, shows the influence of Spontini.

His son Charles-Louis Hanssens (*b* Ghent, 12 July 1802; *d* Brussels, 8 April 1871), a cellist, worked as a conductor at the National Theatre in Amsterdam before becoming assistant conductor at the Monnaie in Brussels in the mid-1820s. In 1834 he went to Paris, where he worked at the Théâtre Ventadour until it went bankrupt; he then went to The Hague and to Ghent. From 1848 to 1869 he was conductor at the Monnaie in Brussels. As a composer he was, Fétis noted, not strikingly original; his skilful orchestral writing however drew praise. Hanssens apparently wrote several operas, including *Le siège de Calais* (4, E. Wacken; Brussels, Monnaie, 20 March 1861). Other attributions – *Néron* (5, A. Soumet; 1830, Brussels), *Agneessens* (G. Vaez; 1849, Brussels) and *Marie de Brabant* (unperformed) – remain doubtful.

Les dots (oc), Ghent, 1804
Le solitaire de Formentara (2, after A. von Kotzebue), Ghent, 1807, B-Bc
La partie de trictrac, ou La belle-mère (oc, 2), Ghent, 1812
Alcibiade (grand opéra, 2, E. Scribe), Brussels, Monnaie, 30 Oct 1829, Bc

FétisB
L. de Burbure: *Notice sur Ch. L. Hanssens* (Brussels, 1872)
E. Grégoir: *Les artistes-musiciens belges au XVIIIme et au XIXme siècle* (Brussels, 1885)
L. Bärwolf: *C.-L. Hanssens: sa vie et ses oeuvres* (Brussels, 1894)

Hanuš, Jan (*b* Prague, 2 May 1915). Czech composer. He studied composition with Jeremiáš, at first privately (1932–40) and later at the Prague Conservatory (1940), where he also studied conducting. From 1934 he worked in publishing and, as director of Panton (1963–70), played an important part in the commissions concerned with the complete editions of Dvořák and Fibich. In addition he was widely active in Czech musical life, serving on various committees and as the holder of several posts in the Union of Czechoslovak Composers. A versatile and prolific composer, Hanuš has written in almost all genres; his compositional style grew out of the Czech national musical tradition, especially Dvořák, and he was deeply influenced by Jeremiáš. In the course of his development, however, he expanded and enriched his style by assimilating new methods, including those of electronic music. He is endowed with a rich melodic invention, a feeling for broad and often adventurous formal designs and an unerring grasp of the techniques of composition and orchestration. His dramatic works (five operas and three ballets) have been regularly and successfully performed in the Czech lands and elsewhere, especially Germany.

Plameny ('Flames'), composed towards the end of World War II, is an artistic reflection of the events of the time but with a vision of victory. Its story of the priest-soldier unfolds in two interconnected spheres – at the front and behind the lines, in the realm of daily activity and in a series of dream-like sequences. The terrible conditions of war and the subjugation of the nation transform the hero from a passive lover of peace into a politically enlightened warrior. This bold dramaturgical conception is effected by means of sharp contrasts, conveyed through a neo-Romantic musical language. Hanuš uses closed musical numbers, through-composed dialogue and speech. *Sluha dvou pánů* ('The Servant of Two Masters') is a neo-classical *opera buffa* in the spirit of Rossini. Here the emphasis is on the voice, with shapely melodic lines, uncomplicated harmonies and restrained orchestration. The experimental opera

Pochodeň Prométheova ('Prometheus's torch') is a synthetic, modern *Gesamtkunstwerk* in which the mythological subject is expressed through dance and pantomime, while a parallel science-fiction element is expressed operatically. The chorus has the same function as that in Greek tragedy. Hanuš draws on electronic music and *musique concrète*, tonal and polytonal systems of composition and a stylization of jazz. His next opera, *Pohádka jedné noci* ('The Story of One Night'), subtitled 'an opera about genies, viziers, jugglers and the true love of Hasan and Laila', is a richly fantastic piece. Quirky humour and a dream-like atmosphere are conveyed with all the kaleidoscopic colours of an oriental fairy-tale. His most recent operatic work is a good-humoured burlesque, *Spor o bohyni* ('A Dispute over the Goddess'), written for Czech television.

Plameny [Flames] op.14, 1944 (Spl-rhapsody, 2, J. Pokorný), Plzeň, Tyl, 8 Dec 1956
Sluha dvou pánů [The Servant of Two Masters] op.42 (ob, 5, Pokorný, after C. Goldoni), Plzeň, Tyl, 18 April 1959
Pocodeň Prométheova [Prometheus's Torch] op.54, 1961–3 (3, Pokorný, after Aeschylus), Prague, National, 30 April 1965
Pohádka jedné noci [The Story of One Night] op.62, 1961–8 (Pokorný, after *The Thousand and One Nights*)
Spor o bohyni [A Dispute over the Goddess] op.105, 1983–4 (television op, 1, Hanuš, J. F. Fischer and A. Moskalyk, after Aristophanes), Czech Television, 13 July 1986

ČSHS
A. Hořejš: 'O Hanušových "Plamenech" ', *Divadlo*, viii (1957), 161–5
V. Pospíšil: 'Hanušovy *Plameny* na plzeňské scéně' [Hanuš's *Plameny* on the Plzeň Stage], *HRo*, x (1957), 14–16
L. Šip: *Česká opera a její tvůrci* [Czech Opera and its Creators] (Prague, 1983), 269–78
K. Mlejnek: 'Jan Hanuš – tvorba z let 1980–1985' [Jan Hanuš – Works, 1980–85], *HRo*, xxxix (1986), 178–82
HELENA HAVLÍKOVÁ

Happy End. Comedy with music in three acts by KURT WEILL to a book by Elisabeth Hauptmann (as Dorothy Lane) and lyrics by BERTOLT BRECHT; Berlin, Theater am Schiffbauerdamm, 2 September 1929.

Bill Cracker's dance hall in Chicago is the headquarters of a bunch of criminals led by one Dr Nakamura. The local Salvation Army attempts without success to reform the gangsters. Then one of their number, Lilian Holliday, falls victim to Bill's charms and whisky, and scandalizes her colleagues with her singing of the 'Matrosen-Tango'. Rejected and then reinstated by the Army, she succeeds, especially through the passionate song 'Surabaya Johnny', in winning over Bill and, in due course, his gangster colleagues and even the mysterious Lady in Grey, ruler of the underworld.

The work was a successor to the Brecht-Weill *Die Dreigroschenoper*, its original cast featuring Carola Neher as Lilian, Oskar Homolka as Bill, Peter Lorre as Dr Nakamura and Helene Weigel as the Lady in Grey. Theo Mackeben was the conductor. The work was originally unsuccessful and was virtually forgotten until Lotte Lenya recorded the 'Bilbao Song', 'Matrosen-Tango' and 'Surabaya Johnny' in 1955 and the entire score in 1960. In its story of redemption of villains by a Salvation Army girl, the comedy has striking parallels with Gustave Kerker's *The Belle of New York* and, most particularly, Frank Loesser's *Guys and Dolls*.

ANDREW LAMB

Hara, Kazuko (*b* Tokyo, 10 Feb 1935). Japanese composer. She studied with Tomojirō Ikenouchi, and later with Dutilleux in Paris (1962) and with Alexander Tcherepnin. She also studied singing and Gregorian chant at the Venice Conservatory (1963), an experience that greatly expanded her creative horizons. She made her début as an opera composer in 1981 with a chamber opera, *Shārokku Hōmuzu no jikenbo* ('The Casebook of Sherlock Holmes'). Her second opera, *Iwai-uta ga nagareru yoru ni* ('On the Merry Night', 1984), an anti-war drama describing the downfall of a rich and traditional family, was a sensational success in Tokyo, establishing her name and winning a Giraud Opera Prize as well as a prize for its libretto. She wrote six more operas in quick succession. *Chieko-shō* ('A Selection for Chieko', an early work, revised 1984) describes the mutual devotion of the poet-sculptor Kōtarō and his wife Chieko, and her death. *Sute-hime* ('Princess Sute', 1986), for which Hara received another Giraud Opera Prize, is the story of a medieval woman who survives a life among thieves and of the awakening of her womanhood as a mother. *Sonezaki shinjū* ('A Love Suicide at Sonezaki', 1987) is her version of a well-known puppet play by Chikamatsu. *Nōshi o koete* ('Beyond Brain Death', 1988) created another sensation for its topical subject matter of organ transplants as well as its expressionistic music; it won a Ministry of Education Prize at the National Art Festival. *Yosakoi-bushi kien* ('The History of Yosakoi-bushi') narrates the tragic love of a Buddhist priest and a beautiful girl, while *Iwanaga-hime* ('Princess Iwanaga'), commissioned by the city of Amagasaki, is based on another classic by Chikamatsu.

Hara is particularly skilled at depicting character in her music, which is spare, never romantic and always well controlled, creating tension with minimal material. Her melodies are usually simple and expressive, the rhythms pulsating and effective, and each note is placed with care.

first performed in Tokyo unless otherwise stated

Chieko-shō [A Selection for Chieko], 1978 (radio op, 4, Maeda), NHK Radio, 22 Sept 1985
Shārokku Hōmuzu no jikenbo: kokuhaku [The Casebook of Sherlock Holmes: the Confession] (chamber op, 2, J. Maeda, after A. C. Doyle), Mozart Salon, 5 March 1981
Iwai-uta ga nagareru yoru ni [On the Merry Night] (2, Hara, after I. Kikumura), Sunshine, 5 Oct 1984
Sute-hime: shita o kamikitta onna [Princess Sute: the Woman who Bit off her Tongue] (2, Hara, after S. Muroo), Shinjuku Bunka Centre, 21 May 1986
Sonezaki shinjū [A Love Suicide at Sonezaki] (1, Hara, after M. Chikamatsu), Metropolitan Festival Hall, 8 Dec 1987
Nōshi o koete [Beyond Brain Death] (chamber op, 1, Hara, after S. Fujimura), Komaba Emināsu, 9 March 1988
Yosakoi-bushi kien [The History of Yosakoi-bushi] (2, Hara, after F. Tosa), Shinjuku Bunka Centre, 19 May 1990
Iwanaga-hime [Princess Iwanaga] (2, B. Yoshida, after Chikamatsu), Amagasaki, Amagasaki shi Arukaikku Hall, 12 Oct 1990
MASAKATA KANAZAWA

Harapi, Tonin (*b* Shkodër, 4 June 1928; *d* Tirana, 30 July 1992). Albanian composer. Encouraged in music as a child by Prenkë Jakova, he studied in Moscow with M. I. Chulaki (1959–61), and at the conservatory in Tirana with Andrea Zadeja (1961–4). His opera *Zgjimi* ('The Awakening'), on a libretto by Mirosh Markaj, was first performed in Tirana at the Theatre of Opera and Ballet on 15 February 1976. Based on the play *Kosta Bardhi's Mill* by Naum Prifti, it explores different aspects of war as experienced by the miller, Kosta, and the other inhabitants of his village. The music is constructed on a system of motifs with which tonal conflict is developed. The village scenes use material based on folksong.

Harapi's last opera, *Mira e Muysit* ('Mira, Daughter of Muysi'), completed in 1990, is based on the 12th- or 13th-century poem about a girl who dresses up as a man in order to fight for her family honour.

S. Kalemi: *Arritjet e artit tonë muzikor* [The Arrival of our Musical Art] (Tirana, 1982)
J. Emerson: *Albania: the Search for the Eagle's Song* (Studley, Warwicks., 1990)   JUNE EMERSON

Harbison, John (*b* Orange, NJ, 20 Dec 1938). American composer. He studied at Harvard College (BA 1960) with Piston, at the Berlin Hochschule für Musik (1961) with Boris Blacher and at Princeton University (MFA 1963) with Sessions and Earl Kim. Since 1969 he has taught at the Massachusetts Institute of Technology in Boston, with periods of leave as composer-in-residence at Reed College and with the Pittsburgh SO and the Los Angeles PO. His honours include a Kennedy Center Friedheim Award (1980), the 1987 Pulitzer Prize for his cantata *The Flight into Egypt* and a five-year MacArthur Fellowship, awarded in 1989. Harbison's output includes a substantial number of chamber and orchestral works, but large vocal compositions predominate. Most are choral works, but he has also set a large body of poetry for solo voice, usually with chamber ensembles of varying size and type. Though not conceived for the stage, these works may be seen from their style of word-setting as being allied to the characteristic mode of expression in his two operas.

Harbison does not generally use techniques of Romantic mimesis in his operas but creates a somewhat abstracted style, using motifs and thematic networks, often with a continuous but irregular pulse, to shape the expressive effect. His first opera, *A Winter's Tale*, was composed in 1974 and first performed on 20 August 1979 at the San Francisco Opera. On 30 April that year his other opera, *A Full Moon in March*, received its première in Boston, at the Sanders Theater. Both works are composed to his own librettos, and are cast in a ritualistic mode, the former by means of 'dumbshows' that project significant parts of the plot wordlessly through instrumental music and pantomime, the latter by means of dance (a dancer actually replaces the principal female character halfway through). Both employ singing narrators as a distancing device, though in *A Winter's Tale* the narrator, Time, functions also as a messenger within the action. The formalized, hieratical quality of the stage action contrasts with the assertive vocal style of the principal characters (though the second half of *A Winter's Tale*, which consists of a series of reconciliations, effectively moderates and broadens this approach). Harbison is a great admirer of Stravinsky; his own operas share many elements of the formalistic approach (though scarcely the musical style) of *Oedipus rex* and of the smaller works with dance and song like *Renard*.

See also FULL MOON IN MARCH, A and WINTER'S TALE, A.

EwenD
L. Schwartz: 'Hard-won Directness', *Atlantic Monthly*, ccliii/3 (1984), 116–20
J. Tassel: 'A Homecoming for John Harbison', *Boston Globe Magazine* (26 Feb 1984)
R. H. Kornick: *Recent American Opera: a Production Guide* (New York, 1991), 132–7   STEVEN LEDBETTER

Hardouin [first name unknown] (*b* Brittany; *fl* *c*1694–1718). French baritone (*basse-taille*). Having first sung in various cathedrals, he was recruited for the Paris Opéra in about 1694 to replace Moreau in the principal roles, the latter having retired in 1693. The ascent of Thévenard was so forceful, however, that Hardouin was relegated to secondary roles from Destouches' *Issé* (1697) onwards. He nonetheless sang Lully's Celaenus (*Atys*) and Collasse's Neptune (*Thétis et Pélée*) with success when both works were revived in 1699, as well as Lully's Polyphemus (*Acis et Galatée*, 1718 revival).   PHILIP WELLER

Harewood, 7th Earl of [Lascelles, George Henry Hubert] (*b* London, 7 Feb 1923). English administrator and writer. Educated at Eton and Cambridge, he began writing opera criticism for the *New Statesman* and *Ballet and Opera* in 1948; in 1950 he founded the periodical *Opera*, which he edited until 1953. The following year he brought out a revised edition of *Kobbé's Complete Opera Book* (further revised and enlarged editions, 9/1976 and, with much new material, 10/1987). He was a director of the Royal Opera House, Covent Garden (1951–3, 1969–72) and an administrative assistant there (1953–60), and was also a director of the Edinburgh Festival (1951–5). Managing director of Sadler's Wells (later English National) Opera from 1972 to 1985, he held the same post at English National Opera North (1978–81) and was a member of the board of Australian Opera (1968–76). His musical tastes show a particular leaning to Slavonic music and the operas of Verdi; his years as the head of the ENO were marked by their imaginative artistic policy, manifested in the company's enterprising choice of repertory and performers. His memoirs, *The Tongs and the Bones*, were published in London in 1981.

HAROLD ROSENTHAL/R

Hargreaves, Francisco (*b* Buenos Aires, 31 Dec 1849; *d* Buenos Aires, 30 Dec 1900). Argentine composer. He was a pupil at the Royal Conservatory, Florencia (1872–6), and while still a student his one-act operetta *La gatta bianca*, based on a French libretto, was given its première at Vilá, near Florencia, and was later performed in Buenos Aires. When he returned home he produced orchestral works and also piano pieces which won him fame among his contemporaries and were his only works to be published. He composed five further theatrical works, but only two were performed: *Los estudiantes de Bolonia* (1879) and *Una noche en Loreto* (1890); another work, *Il vampiro* (1876), was known only through concert versions of some of the numbers.

Hargreaves was a pioneer of opera writing in Argentina and a member of the first group of Argentine composers to cultivate a national type of music. In his operas, however, he was not tempted by nationalist themes, and only one was set in Argentina: the *juguete-cómico-musical* (a variant on zarzuela) *Una noche en Loreto*, which has only a few musical numbers, and only one with a trace of nationalism. His other operas are italianate and were composed to Italian words. He considered *Psyche*, with a mythological libretto by Carlos Francisco Scotti, composed at the end of the century, to be his best work.

La gatta bianca (opereta, 1, after Mélesville [A.-H.-J. Duveyrier] and E. Scribe: *La chatte métamorphosée en femme*), Vilá, Sept 1875
Los estudiantes de Bolonia (2), Buenos Aires, Victoria, 1879
Una noche en Loreto (juguete-cómico-musical, 1, A. Menchaca), Buenos Aires, Onrubia, 1890

Unperf: L'assedio di Livorno; Psyche (opera mitológica, 4, C. F. Scotti); Il vampiro (melodrama fantástico, 3), 1876

*

V. Gesualdo: *Historia de la música en la Argentina* (Buenos Aires, 1960), ii, 426–41

J. M. Veniard: *La música nacional argentina: influencia de la música criolla tradicional en la música académica argentina, relevamiento de datos históricos para su estudio* (Buenos Aires, 1986)

CARLOS SUFFERN

Harling, William Franke (*b* London, 18 Jan 1887; *d* Sierra Madre, CA, 22 Nov 1958). American composer. He was trained as an organist, violinist and choir director and in 1909–10 was organist and choir director at the US Military Academy, after holding a similar post in Brussels (1907–8). His first opera, *Alda*, was produced in Boston in 1908, but is now lost. *The Sunken Bell* (1914) was never completed, but the first act survives in manuscript and bears the inscription 'Bruxelles – June 10 – 1914 W. F. H.'. *A Light from St Agnes*, the best known of his operas and the only one to be published in full, associates jazz idioms with one of the main characters; it was first performed by the Chicago Civic Opera Company (1925). For this work the American Opera Society awarded Harling the David Bispham Memorial Medal. *Deep River* (1926) is described as 'a native opera with jazz'. His output also includes the two operettas *Double-Crossed* (for boys' voices) and *Honey*, as well as music for several films among which is the song 'Beyond the Blue Horizon'.

Alda, Boston, 1908, lost
The Sunken Bell, 1914 (after G. Hauptman), inc., MS Act 1, Gavilan College, Gilroy, CA
Double-Crossed (operetta, 2, R. F. Allen), vs (Boston, 1925)
A Light from St Agnes (lyric drama, 1, M. M. Fiske), Chicago, Auditorium, 26 Dec 1925, vs (New York, 1925)
Deep River (3, L. Stallings), Philadelphia, Shubert, 24 Sept 1926, MS, Gavilan College; excerpts, vs (New York, 1926)
Honey, *c*1930 (operetta, S. Coslow), 4 songs (New York, 1930)

THOMAS WARBURTON

Harmonie der Welt, Die ('The Harmony of the World'). Opera in five acts by PAUL HINDEMITH to his own libretto; Munich, Prinzregententheater, 11 August 1957.

Based on the life of the astronomer Johannes Kepler (1571–1630) and set against the background of the Thirty Years War, the opera describes in a series of scenes, far apart in time and place, the astronomer's search for universal harmony, deriving its title from Kepler's own book, *De harmonia mundi*. Kepler (baritone) is shown in encounters with the emperors Rudolf II and Ferdinand II (combined role, bass) and the warlord Wallenstein (tenor), for all of whom he worked; and with less powerful figures such as the astrologer Tansur (bass); Hizler, the priest who denied him holy communion (bass); and his sceptical pupil Grüsser (tenor), eventually one of Wallenstein's assassins. Others playing a significant part in his life are his superstitious mother Katharina (contralto), his second wife Susanna (soprano), and young Susanna, his daughter (soprano). On his deathbed Kepler realizes that his efforts have been in vain: 'The great harmony is death. To effect it, we must die. In life it has no place'. The opera ends with an extended visionary scene (musically a passacaglia), in which the main characters reappear as the planets they embodied in their life on earth: the emperors (Sun), Kepler (Earth), Wallenstein (Jupiter), Grüsser (Mars), Hizler (Mercury), Tansur (Saturn), Susanna (Venus), Katharina (Moon) and finally the chorus as the Milky Way. They proclaim that the planets are themselves only a part of the sublime order and have no knowledge of its ultimate origin and aim, but Kepler and Susanna, in their humble search for world harmony, 'dreaming, sensing, believing, praying', had raised themselves high above the fallible ways of mankind.

The wide range of this opera and its division into many separate scenes, some of them played simultaneously, prevent the emergence of a clear dramatic structure and allow little scope for the development of individual character. Hindemith sought to overcome these difficulties by making each episode dramatically self-contained (the unstable Emperor Rudolf's physical attack on Kepler; Susanna's intervention in Hizler's rejection of him from the communion table; the trial of Katharina, accused of witchcraft; Kepler and Wallenstein seen against the background of a ball in the latter's sumptuous palace etc.).

There is, however, a unifying factor in the music itself. In his book *Unterweisung im Tonsatz* (Mainz, 1937–70; Eng. trans., 1941) Hindemith rearranged the notes of the chromatic scale in 'a tonal planetary system', comparing the relationship between note and 'parent' note with that of the planets surrounding the sun, the sun's power diminishing as the distance increases. His belief that conscious awareness of these tonal relationships adds meaning to the words to which they apply governed his compositional method in *Die Harmonie der Welt*. It also clearly played a part in his choice of an astronomer (Kepler) as its hero and the identification of the main characters with their planetary counterparts. The opera can consequently be regarded as an expression not only of his musical beliefs, but also of his convictions concerning the individual's role in a fallible world: the search for perfection, though never attained, must always continue. A basically philosophical work of this kind is not easily absorbed under theatrical conditions, hence the cool reception it received at its first performance and its virtual neglect by opera houses ever since. It is nonetheless an important and imposing work representing all that Hindemith, after many years of reflection, believed and strove for.

For illustration *see* LIGHTING, fig.13.   GEOFFREY SKELTON

Harms, Johann Oswald (*b* Hamburg, bap. 30 April 1643; *d* ?Brunswick, 1708). German stage designer and painter. He was a pupil of the Hamburg painter Ellerbrock and from the mid-1660s studied panel and mural painting in Rome in the circle of Salvator Rosa and Pietro da Cortona. A stay in Venice from about 1669 made him familiar with the artistically and technically most advanced forms of opera production and stage design. He probably saw sets and machines designed by Gaspare Mauro, Francesco Santurini and Ippolito Mazzarini, and in Vienna, where he moved about 1672, the work of Ludovico Ottavio Burnacini. On his return to Germany Harms worked first as a painter of panels and murals, but from the time of his appointment as the chief theatrical designer to the Dresden court (1677), most of his work was done in the theatre, in the operatic centres of north and central Germany (about 50 works): Dresden (1677–81), Eisenberg (1681–6), Weissenfels (1681–6), Hanover (1684 and later), Wolfenbüttel (1686–90 and later), Brunswick (1691–8) and Hamburg (1695–1705).

Design by Harms for a market scene in Kusser's 'Cleopatra', first performed in Brunswick, 1690: pen and ink drawing with colour wash, showing five scenery flats for the right-hand side of the stage

Harms was the most important designer for the German Baroque operatic stage. His sets for numerous first performances of operas by Kusser, Steffani, Krieger, Keiser, the young Handel and others do astonishing justice to the formal restraint, emotional strength and lyrical atmosphere of these works. Stage design was still largely dominated by architectonic formalism, but the principles of Harms's work primarily concerned painting. His designs for the stage benefited, in particular, from his experience as a muralist; he united the middle-class realism typical of art in Hamburg with the bold, expansive compositional techniques of Italian mural painting. His artistic achievement advanced beyond his Venetian and Viennese models: the realism of his urban and rural settings, especially those for Kusser's *Cleopatra* (1690, Brunswick; see illustration) and Keiser's *Störtebecker und Jödge Michaels* (1701, Hamburg), anticipate the principle of the imitation of nature that was a cornerstone of later theories of design for middle-class theatre in Germany.

For further illustration *see* STAGE DESIGN, fig.5.

*

ES (H. Richter)

Ballet von Zusammenkunft und Wirckung derer VII. Planeten auf Ihr Churf. Durchl. zu Sachsen grossem Theatro gehalten den 3 Februarii 1678 (Dresden, 1678) [with 9 engravings]

Opera-Ballett von dem Judicto Paridis und der Helenae Raub (Dresden, 1679) [with 8 engravings]

J. Mattheson: *Der musicalische Patriot* (Hamburg, 1728), 182

A. F. Harms: *Tables historiques et chronologiques des plus fameux peintres anciens et modernes* (Brunswick, 1742), no.xxxi

H. Tintelnot: 'J. O. Harms: ein norddeutscher Maler des Barock', *Zeitschrift des Deutschen Vereins für Kunstwissenschaft*, viii (1941), 245

H. C. Wolff: *Die Barockoper in Hamburg* (Wolfenbüttel, 1957), 347, 359ff

H. Richter: *J. O. Harms: ein deutscher Theaterdekorateur des Barock* (Emsdetten, 1963)

——: 'Der erste deutsche Bühnenbilder', *275 Jahre Theater in Braunschweig* (Brunswick, 1965), 34   MANFRED BOETZKES

Harnoncourt, Nikolaus (*b* Berlin, 6 Dec 1929). Austrian conductor. He was brought up in Graz and studied the cello, playing in the Vienna SO from 1952 to 1969. In 1953 he formed the Vienna Concentus Musicus to perform early music (playing the viola da gamba in it as well as the cello). In 1971 he conducted Monteverdi's *Il ritorno d'Ulisse* at the Vienna Festival; this was followed by other performances of Baroque and Classical operas, among them a Monteverdi cycle of three works, given in a production by Jean-Pierre Ponnelle first at Zürich (1975–9) and later at the Edinburgh Festival and elsewhere, though the period style aimed at in the musical realization was not reflected in the staging. Harnoncourt also conducted works by Rameau (making in 1972 the first complete recording of *Castor et Pollux*) and especially Mozart, whose mature operas he came to perform with a modern orchestra. Several of these he also recorded in the 1980s and early 90s, notably *Idomeneo*, *Don Giovanni* and *Die Zauberflöte*, in performances remarkable for their clear textures, incisive accents and strong characterization of detail.   STANLEY SADIE

Harper, Edward (James) (*b* Taunton, 17 March 1941). English composer. After reading music at Oxford (1959–63), he studied composition at the RCM with Gordon Jacob (1963–4) and in Milan with Franco Donatoni (1968). Since 1964 he has taught at Edinburgh University, becoming a Reader in 1989.

Harper's earlier instrumental works, notably the orchestral *Bartók Games* (1972), evidence a thorough absorption of aleatory procedures. Similar techniques resurfaced in the chamber opera *Fanny Robin* (1, Harper and R. Savage; Edinburgh, George Square Theatre, 5 Feb 1975). Based on episodes from Thomas Hardy's *Far from the Madding Crowd* which describe a servant girl courted and subsequently spurned by a handsome sergeant of dragoons, it contains often dense instrumental textures — with note-clusters prominent in the spoken 'dialogue' sections — that set into bold relief quotations of the folk ballad 'I'm seventeen come Sunday' and a metrical psalm.

The juxtaposition of tonal and atonal elements is also a feature of Harper's second opera, *Hedda Gabler* (prol., 3, Harper; Glasgow, Theatre Royal, 5 June 1985), commissioned by the BBC for Scottish Opera; but here the stylistic confrontation is mediated through the retention of the major triad as a point of referential focus in the absence of straightforward tonal functionality. In passages of tautly controlled motivic argument, the music succeeds in communicating

Hedda's impulsiveness and desperation, although the libretto at times underplays the irony and ambiguity of Ibsen's original drama. In *The Mellstock Quire* (1, R. Savage; Edinburgh, George Square Theatre, 10 Feb 1988) Harper, returning for inspiration to Hardy (*Under the Greenwood Tree*), presents Fancy Day's encounters with her rival suitors alongside the village controversy over the dismissal of the church musicians. Although a lighter work than its predecessor, with its sharply etched comic characterization, it elicits some of Harper's most fluent and expansive vocal writing to date.

E. Harper: 'An Ibsen Opera', *MT*, cxxvi (1985), 334–7
CHARLES A. WILSON

Harper, Elizabeth. English soprano; *see* BANNISTER family, (2).

Harper, Heather (Mary) (*b* Belfast, 8 May 1930). British soprano. She studied in London and made her début in 1954 as Lady Macbeth with the Oxford University Opera Club. She sang First Lady (*Die Zauberflöte*) in 1957 at Glyndebourne, returning as Anne Trulove in 1963. With the New Opera Company she created Lucie Manette in Benjamin's *A Tale of Two Cities* (1957) and sang the Woman in the British stage première of *Erwartung* (1960). Her Covent Garden début was as Helena (*A Midsummer Night's Dream*) in 1962, and she returned as Ellen Orford, Micaëla, Blanche (*Dialogues des Carmélites*), Gutrune, Eva, Antonia, Mrs Coyle (*Owen Wingrave*), which she had created on television (1971), Arabella and Nadia in the première of Tippett's *Ice Break* (1977). At Bayreuth (1967–8) she sang Elsa and in Buenos Aires (1969–72) Arabella, Donna Elvira, Marguerite and Vitellia (*La clemenza di Tito*). She was highly praised as the Governess (*The Turn of the Screw*) with the English Opera Group (1972), although Ellen Orford was her most sympathetic role, admirably suited to her firm, well-projected voice and eloquent enunciation. She retired from opera in 1984, but sang Nadia in a concert performance of *The Ice Break* at the 1990 Promenade concerts in London.
ALAN BLYTH

Harrell, Mack (*b* Celeste, TX, 8 Oct 1909; *d* Dallas, 29 Jan 1960). American baritone. He studied at the Juilliard School and in 1939 won the Metropolitan Opera Auditions of the Air and made his début with the company as Biterolf in *Tannhäuser*. He continued to appear at the Metropolitan until 1958, singing a wide repertory that included Masetto, Papageno, Köthner, Amfortas, John the Baptist, Captain Balstrode (*Peter Grimes*) and Nick Shadow, his best-known role, which he sang in the American première of *The Rake's Progress* in 1953. He appeared with New York City Opera, making his début in 1944 as Germont, and in Chicago and San Francisco; his repertory also included Escamillo, Marcello, Valentin, Luna, Golaud and Wozzeck, which he recorded. He taught at the Juilliard School from 1945 to 1956. Harrell possessed a sturdy lyric baritone of remarkable beauty and was a considerable musician and artist, but perhaps the most notable aspect of his singing was the directness of its human appeal. The cellist Lynn Harrell is his son.
RICHARD DYER, ELIZABETH FORBES

Harrhy, Eiddwen (Mair) (*b* Trowbridge, Wilts., 14 April 1949). Welsh soprano. She studied at the RMCM,

winning the Imperial League of Opera Prize and then the Miriam Licette Prize, which led to further studies in London and Paris. She made her début in 1974 as Ilia with Oxford University Opera Club, then singing Wellgunde (*Das Rheingold*) at Covent Garden and Creusa (*Medea in Corinto*) at Wexford. For Kent Opera she sang Rose (*Ruddigore*) and the title role of *Iphigénie en Tauride*; for the WNO she created Oriane in Mathias's *The Servants* (1980) and sang Poppaea, Gilda, Asteria (*Tamerlano*) and Marie (*Wozzeck*). Her roles for the ENO have included Butterfly, Mimì, Pamina and Marian Singleton in the première of David Blake's *The Plumber's Gift* (1989). For Opera North she has sung Fiordiligi, Octavian, Adalgisa, Kát'a and Hecuba (*King Priam*) in 1991. She made her first appearance in the USA in 1986 at Los Angeles as Morgana (*Alcina*) and has also performed at La Scala and the Teatro Colón. Her strong, clear voice with its well-controlled vibrato is equally effective in Baroque, Classical and 20th-century music. Her recordings include *The Fairy-Queen*, *Alcina*, *Ercole amante*, *La princesse de Navarre*, *L'assedio di Calais* and *Ugo, conte di Parigi*.
NICHOLAS ANDERSON, ELIZABETH FORBES

Harries, Kathryn (*b* Hampton Court, 15 Feb 1951). British soprano. She studied in London, making her début in 1983 as a flowermaiden with the WNO, for whom she has also sung Adalgisa, Leonore, Sieglinde, Gutrune and the Composer. At Buxton (1983) she sang Sylvia in Gounod's *La colombe*. Her roles for the ENO (1983–90) have included Irene (*Rienzi*), Female Chorus (*The Rape of Lucretia*), Eva, Donna Anna (*The Stone Guest*) and Kát'a. She created the title role in Harper's *Hedda Gabler* (1985) for Scottish Opera, later singing Senta, Dido (*Les Troyens*), a role she also sang at Lyons, and Bartók's Judith (1990). For Opera North (1986–8) she sang Donna Elvira and Hanna Glawari (*The Merry Widow*). She made her Metropolitan début in 1986 as Kundry, returning as Gutrune. Having sung Sieglinde in the WNO *Ring* cycle at Covent Garden (1986), she made her Royal Opera début as the Protagonist in *Un re in ascolto* in 1989, when she also sang Dukas' *Ariane et Barbe-bleu* at Amsterdam. She has a handsome appearance and a rich, flexible voice especially strong in the middle register.
ELIZABETH FORBES

Harriet, the Woman called 'Moses'. Opera in two acts by THEA MUSGRAVE to her own libretto; Norfolk, Virginia, 1 March 1985.

The libretto is based on the true story of Harriet Tubman, an escaped slave who led more than 300 of her people to freedom, surviving to fight in the American Civil War. Harriet (soprano), having found refuge in the North with the Quaker Mr Garrett (bass), recalls in dreams her life as a slave. On the death of her kindly Master (baritone), she runs away to escape the attentions of his drunken son Preston (tenor) and the cruelty of the Overseer (tenor). In Act 2, Harriet returns to the South many times to help other slaves escape. A reward of $40 000 is put on her head. She is torn between her desire to stay in the North with her lover Josiah (tenor) and the urge to fulfil her mission. She returns South to rescue her mother Rit (mezzo-soprano), her father Ben (bass), and her brother Benjie (tenor). They make for the Canadian frontier, pursued by Preston. As they cross, Josiah is killed shielding Harriet from Preston's shot. Harriet and the freed slaves affirm their determination to fight together for liberty, peace and harmony.

Musgrave makes free use of the idioms of popular music, notably in hymns and spirituals with quasi-improvisatory embellishments and in a love duet which would hardly be out of place in a Broadway musical. The chorus plays a vital role throughout the opera, while the orchestra remains for the most part discreetly supportive, except in the escape scenes at the beginning of Act 2, which are played in pantomime. Minor characters are conceived in conventional terms, and the forces of evil are hardly given a hearing in the music. But Harriet, her mother Rit and the long-suffering slaves are vividly and passionately portrayed.   HUGO COLE

Harris, Sir Augustus (Henry Glossop) (*b* Paris, 1852; *d* Folkestone, 22 June 1896). English impresario. He was the son of Augustus Harris, stage manager at Covent Garden from 1853 to 1873, and grandson of the soprano Elizabeth Feron. With his brother Charles he accompanied the Mapleson company on tour as stage manager and producer. As manager of Drury Lane (1879–94) he gave seasons by a German company under Richter in 1882 and by the Carl Rosa company from 1883. In 1887 he presented an important Italian season, the success of which led in 1888 to his taking over Covent Garden, which he managed until his death with great artistic and financial success. Eventually performances were given there in the original languages (previously they had all been in Italian) and Covent Garden was renamed the Royal Opera, instead of the Royal Italian Opera. Harris did much to popularize Wagner, giving *Ring* cycles at Covent Garden in 1892, conducted by Mahler.

H. Rosenthal: *Two Centuries of Opera at Covent Garden* (London, 1958), 222–73
——, ed.: *The Mapleson Memoirs* (London, 1966)
HAROLD ROSENTHAL/R

Harris, Ross Talbot (*b* Amberley, North Canterbury, 1 Aug 1945). New Zealand composer. He succeeded Douglas Lilburn as director of the Victoria University of Wellington electronic music studio in 1980. Besides working in this medium he has written many instrumental and vocal works and also for television, stage and film. Harris wrote his first opera, *The Clockmaker* (1979), in the Baroque manner. *Waituhi* ('The Life of the Village', 1984) is an innovatory setting of a libretto based on the novel *Whanau*, by the leading Maori writer Witi Ihimaera. It aroused intense interest as the first collaboration of its kind between a Maori writer and a European composer. (Earlier attempts to synthesize the two cultures had begun with the romantic opera *Tapu*, 1903, by Alfred Hill.) In a period of racial ferment and a Maori renaissance in the arts, *Waituhi* addressed issues such as land disputes, the drift of young Maori away from the village to the city and the loss of traditional values, combined with a central love theme involving rivalries and jealousies. Harris uses the traditional operatic framework of arias, duets, ensemble pieces and choruses, interspersing them with *haka*, *poi*, action song and *waiata* (traditional Maori song). In their second collaboration Harris and Ihimaera produced *Tanz der Schwäne* (composed 1989), the story of a German Jewish immigrant woman who arrives in New Zealand after World War II and encounters parochial small-town hostility. The work is for six singers and chamber orchestra, and the soprano soloist sings in German in

moments of passion or despair. This contrasts with the bleak environment in which she finds herself.

The Clockmaker (chamber op, 1, A. Kiernander), 1979
Waituhi [The Life of the Village] (4, W. Ihimaera), Christchurch, State Opera, 8 Sept 1984
Tanz der Schwäne, 1989 (chamber op, 3, Ihimaera), unperf.

P. Walls: Review of 'Waituhi', *Music News* [National Music Council of New Zealand] (1984), Sept, 8–9
E. Kerr: 'A Multi-Coloured Canvas', *New Zealand Listener* (6 Oct 1984)
J. Commons: 'A New Maori Opera', *Opera*, xxxv (1984), 1258–60
——: 'Maori Opera's Topical Themes', *Opera Australia*, no.83 (1985), 15
J. M. Thomson: *Biographical Dictionary of New Zealand Composers* (Wellington, 1990)   J. M. THOMSON

Harrison, Lou (*b* Portland, OR, 14 May 1917). American composer. He studied with Henry Cowell in San Francisco (1934–5) and with Schoenberg in Los Angeles. During World War II he organized recitals of percussion music, alone and with John Cage, while working as a florist, record clerk, veterinarian, poet, dancer, dance critic, music copyist and playwright. In 1943 he moved to New York, where he wrote for *View*, *Modern Music*, *Listen* and the *New York Herald Tribune*, and conducted, in 1947, the first complete performance of Ives's Third Symphony. Shortly thereafter he left to teach in Portland and then at Black Mountain College, eventually settling in California.

In 1954 the second of two Guggenheim fellowships took him to Rome, where his opera *Rapunzel* (composed 1952; after W. Morris) was performed in concert with Leontyne Price in the title role; it was first staged at the Cabrillo Music Festival in 1959. This work, for three singers and 20 conventional instruments, is based on a tone row; it won a 20th-century masterpiece award conferred by Stravinsky. In 1961–2 Harrison travelled to the Far East on a Rockefeller Grant, which enabled him to study Korean court music and Chinese classical music in Taiwan. He was senior scholar at the East-West Center of the University of Hawaii in 1963, and in 1965 spent a year in Oaxaca, Mexico. There he began his *Music Primer* (finished in 1971), which provides valuable insight into his approach to composition. He began teaching at San Jose State University in 1967 and was visiting professor at Stanford University, the University of California at Berkeley and the University of Southern California. In 1973 he was elected to the American Institute of Arts and Letters. He joined the faculty of Mills College in 1980, and in 1983 was Senior Fulbright Scholar to four universities in New Zealand.

Harrison's lifelong obsession with pitch relations, in particular with just intonation, and his interest in the music of other cultures have led him to include non-Western or folk instruments in a number of works. He has also constructed or adapted a wide range of other instruments. One of the earliest was the 'tack piano', an upright piano with thumb tacks or drawing pins driven into the hammers to create a metallic, percussive quality. His opera *Young Caeser* (14 scenes, R. Gordon; Pasadena, CA, 5 Nov 1971), uses such unconventional instruments exclusively, and is based on the simplest of diatonic ragas. Written originally for puppets, it tells the story of a youthful homosexual love affair of Julius Caesar. Harrison's large output also includes many ballets and other stage pieces. Though demonstrating a wild variety of means, his works show him as a melodist above all. Rhythm has a significant place in his work, though it is likely to be four-square, using an ostinato or drone; counterpoint and harmony are unimportant.

See also YOUNG CAESER.   NED ROREM

Harrison, Tony [Anthony] (*b* Leeds, 30 April 1937). English librettist and translator. He studied at Leeds University and worked first as an English lecturer. His first collection of poetry, *The Loiners*, appeared in 1972. Harrison's verse translations for the National Theatre led to collaborations with Harrison Birtwistle. The first was the music-theatre piece *Bow Down* (1977), based on the ballad *The Two Sisters*, and the second, the 'mechanical pastoral' *Yan Tan Tethera* (1986), which was derived from a northern English folktale collected by K. M. Briggs. Harrison's rhymed-couplet translation of Smetana's *The Bartered Bride* was first sung at the Metropolitan Opera in 1978, and he provided the libretto for *Medea: a Sex-War Opera*, commissioned from Jacob Druckman by the Metropolitan in 1985. That text is a vivid reworking of Euripides' tragedy, into which Harrison introduces literary and operatic references to other versions of the legend. The result is a historical continuum that brings the action up to the present day.

*
T. Harrison: *Theatre Works 1973–1985* (Harmondsworth, 1986)
ANDREW CLEMENTS

Harrison, William (*b* London, 15 June 1813; *d* London, 9 Nov 1868). English tenor and impresario. He studied at the RAM and made his début at Covent Garden in 1839 in the première of Rooke's *Henrique*. During Bunn's seasons at Drury Lane in the 1840s he sang the leading tenor roles in the first performances of *The Bohemian Girl*, *Maritana* and Benedict's *Brides of Venice* and *The Crusaders*. In collaboration with LOUISA PYNE he established the Pyne-Harrison Opera Company in 1854 in New York; after a successful American tour they opened at the Lyceum Theatre in 1857 and ran for eight seasons at Drury Lane and Covent Garden. During that period he produced and sang in 15 new operas, including six by Balfe, as well as English versions of Italian and French operas.

For illustration see BALFE, MICHAEL WILLIAM, and PYNE, LOUISA.

Harriss, Charles (**Albert Edwin**) (*b* London, midnight 16–17 Dec 1862; *d* Ottawa, 31 July 1929). Canadian composer of English birth. He studied at St Michael's College, Tenbury, and worked as an organist in Ottawa and in Montreal from 1883 to 1894, when his interests shifted to composition and touring as a concert organist. He founded the McGill Conservatorium in Montreal in 1904 and directed it until 1907. His marriage to a wealthy widow in 1897 enabled him to organize music festivals, concert and lecture tours and gala performances in Canada and other parts of the British Empire, and to have nearly all of his compositions, mostly large choral works and songs in Romantic style, published. He composed two stage works, the opera *Torquil: a Scandinavian Dramatic Legend* (E. Oxenford; Toronto, 22 May 1900; vs, 1896) and the operetta *The Admiral* (1902). The music of *Torquil*, in spite of its subtitle, shows mainly German Romantic influences. It could be sung by choral societies, and the composer stipulated that it 'must be given without Costume or Action'.

*
EMC (N. Turbide)   HELMUT KALLMAN

Harsányi, Tibor (*b* Magyarkanisza, 27 June 1898; *d* Paris, 19 Sept 1954). French composer of Hungarian descent. He received guidance from Bartók, in whose circle he moved, but owed his technical training to Kodály, with whom he studied at the Budapest Academy of Music. After making concert tours, he worked in the Netherlands (from 1920) as a pianist, conductor and composer, and in 1924 moved to Paris, where he also taught composition.

Harsányi's compositions comprise dramatic, vocal and instrumental works, which may be divided into two periods. The first (1920–27) exhibits a certain Romanticism, though some works have a more aggressive style, largely influenced by Hungarian folk music. In his second period Harsányi approached neo-classicism; his style became plainer and more austere, although there are moments of dazzling orchestration. Of his dramatic works, the short opera *Les invités* (1928; 1, J.-V. Pellerin) was performed with great success in Paris in 1937. This slightly surreal domestic comedy centres on a nameless couple in their late 30s (baritone and mezzo-soprano), their maid (soprano) and a bald man (baritone) who doubles as a dentist and a huge hat. The hat is meant to represent the woman's fantasy life, in which the dentist plays a part, while a typewriter, behind which the maid undresses, triggers off that of the man. The opera includes ironic set pieces, such as a foxtrot and a blues. *Illusions, ou L'histoire d'un miracle* (opéra radiophonique, 2, P. Brive, after E. T. A. Hoffmann; Radio France, 1949) won the 1948 Italia Prize.

*
E. Vuillermoz: 'Les invités', *Candide* [Paris] (1937), July
ARTHUR HOÉRÉE

Harsdörffer, Georg Philipp (*b* Nuremberg, 1 Nov 1607; *d* Nuremberg, 22 Sept 1658). German poet and librettist. Having received a broad classical education at home and at the university in Altdorf, he embarked on a European tour that took him from England to Italy; his experiences in Strasbourg, Rome, Venice and Padua, as well as his contact with the Accademia degli Intronati in Siena, helped shape his ideas on music and literature. He settled finally in his native city in 1634, where in 1655 he was elected to the city council.

Harsdörffer campaigned strongly for the purification of the German language. In 1644 he helped to found the Pegnesische Blumenorden, a literary society that met regularly in Nuremberg and was modelled on humanist societies in Renaissance Italy and on the German academy, the Fruchtbringende Gesellschaft. He provided poetry for the society which he collected in his musically most important work, the *Frawenzimmer Gesprächspiele* (8 vols., Nuremberg, 1641–57). It contains literary works and texts for music; several are translations or imitations of various types of foreign work with which he became acquainted on his travels. The fourth volume contains the text of the oldest surviving German opera, *Seelewig*, set to music by S. T. Staden (1644, Nuremberg). Other music in the collection includes four strophic songs each dedicated to a season, an equestrian ballet and incidental music to plays.

See also SEELEWIG.

*
F. van Ingen: 'Bericht über die *Seelewig*-Aufführung in Utrecht', *Inszenierung und Regie barocker Dramen* (Hamburg, 1976), 69–73
P. Keller: *Die Oper 'Seelewig' von Sigmund Theophil Staden und Georg Philipp Harsdörffer* (Berne and Stuttgart, 1977)
J. Leighton: 'Die Wolfenbütteler Auufführung von Harsdörffers und

Stadens *Seelewig* im Jahre 1654', *Wolfenbütteler Beiträge 1978*, 115–28

G. Dünnhaupt: *Bibliographisches Handbuch der deutschen Barockliteratur* (Stuttgart, 1980–81)

H. J. Bauer: *Barockoper in Bayreuth* (Laaber, 1982)

I. Boettcher: 'Der Nürnberger Georg Philip Harsdörffer', *Deutsche Dichter des 17. Jahrhunderts* (Berlin, 1984)

M. R. Wade: '*Seelewig*: the Earliest Extant German Opera and its Antecedent', *Daphnis*, xiv (1985), 559–78

S. R. Huff: 'The Early German Libretto: some Reconsiderations based on Harsdörffer's "Seelewig"', *ML*, lxix (1988), 345–55

M. R. Wade: *The German Baroque Pastoral 'Singspiel'* (Berne, 1990)

J. P. Aikin: 'Narcissus and Echo: a Mythological Subtext in Harsdörffer's Operatic Allegory "Seelewig"', *ML*, lxxii (1991), 359–71   JOHN H. BARON, MARA R. WADE

Harshaw, Margaret (*b* Philadelphia, 12 May 1909). American mezzo-soprano, later soprano. She studied at the Juilliard School with Anna Schoen-René. After winning the Metropolitan Opera Auditions of the Air in 1942, she made her Metropolitan début as the Second Norn in *Götterdämmerung* and in subsequent seasons sang such roles as Azucena, Amneris and Mistress Quickly. At San Francisco (1944–7) her roles included Ulrica, Brangäne and Debussy's Geneviève. During the 1950–51 season she changed to soprano parts, succeeding Helen Traubel in the heroic Wagnerian repertory (Isolde, Senta, Kundry and Brünnhilde), and remaining with the Metropolitan until the close of the 1963–4 season. During this period she also fulfilled engagements at Covent Garden (1953–6), Glyndebourne (appearing as Donna Anna in 1954) and elsewhere. She was a convincing actress and possessed a good, though by no means great, Wagnerian voice; her tone was evenly produced over a wide range. She later taught at Bloomington, Indiana, and became one of the finest singing teachers in the USA.

H. Rosenthal: *Great Singers of Today* (London, 1966)
                    MAX DE SCHAUENSEE/R

Hart, Fritz (Bennicke) (*b* Greenwich, 11 Feb 1874; *d* Honolulu, 9 July 1949). English composer and conductor. As a child he studied with his mother, a pianist, and sang in his father's choirs in London. At 10 he became a chorister at Westminster Abbey, remaining there until his voice broke at 13. In 1893 he entered the RCM, where he came under the influence of Stanford, though he did not study composition. His close friends there included Holst and Coleridge-Taylor, and later Vaughan Williams and Ireland. After graduating in 1896 Hart toured for 18 months as an actor with a dramatic company, experience which prompted his first work for the stage, incidental music for *Julius Caesar*. During this tour, he made his début as a conductor at Eastbourne, with his own music for *Romeo and Juliet*. From 1898 to 1909 he was a music director for the touring companies of the Savoy Opera and George Edwardes. In 1908 he was offered a 12-month engagement conducting the new Comic Opera Company in Australia that was subsequently extended to four years. He emigrated to Australia in 1909.

In 1913 Hart took over the lecturing duties of his friend George Marshall-Hall at the Albert Street Conservatorium of Music in Melbourne and a year later became director. Nellie Melba, who felt herself in harmony with Hart's views on the worth of English music, founded a school of singing at the Conservatorium. Hart defined the characteristics of English music as 'directness of utterance, a certain large

simplicity of structure, a deliberate avoidance of hysteria, and an emotional restraint which scorns to tear passion to tatters' (*Art in Australia*, 1 November 1922). All these traits are found in his own music, which has also been described as 'lyrical, often fragile, introspective and melodic, with a strong English feeling for song' (T. Roberts, in B. Hyams: 'Fritz Hart's *Dedication* at Long Last Scheduled', *c*1974, *AUS-Msl*, Hart Archive).

Late in 1913 Hart and Alfred Hill founded the Australian Opera League, whose first production was Hart's first opera, *Pierrette*, which received its première on .3 August 1914. Hart composed 22 operas, 18 of them while he was in Melbourne, and they reveal the influence of Melba and her school and of the poet laureate of the Celtic revival, George William Russell ('A. E.'), whom Hart met in England in 1920. From that time, Hart became increasingly interested in the revival and rediscovery of his own Cornish origins (he had been reared on Celtic folktales and folksong), and these interests influenced the shaping and subject matter of his subsequent librettos. Melba and the women of her school supported the production of four other operas, all given at the Playhouse, Melbourne, between 1917 and 1929: *Ruth and Naomi*, *Malvolio*, *Deirdre in Exile* and *The Woman who Laughed at Faery*. After Melba's death the school provided assistance for the production of *St George and the Dragon* at St Kevin's Hall (1931). *Even Unto Bethlehem* was first produced in Honolulu on 20 December 1943, after Hart had left Australia. All these operas were successful, but revivals since Hart's death have been rare.

Hart was made a fellow of the RCM in 1924. He became permanent conductor of the Melbourne SO in 1928, and from 1932 was joint conductor, with Bernard Heinze, when it amalgamated with the University Conservatorium Orchestra. From 1931 he was guest conductor of the Honolulu SO, becoming permanent conductor in 1937, when he also became the first professor of music at the University of Hawaii. He continued to compose, paint and write: his musical output includes over 500 songs and he left over 300 paintings and 23 unpublished novels. The Hart Archive is housed in the Latrobe manuscript section at the State Library of Victoria.

MP – *Melbourne, Playhouse*

Malvolio op.14, 1913 (comic op, 3, after W. Shakespeare: *Twelfth Night*), Act 1 only, MP, 5 Dec 1919
Pierrette op.13 (comic op, 1, Hart), Sydney, Repertory, 3 Aug 1914
The Land of Heart's Desire op.18, 1914 (1, after W. B. Yeats)
Riders to the Sea op.19, 1915 (1, after J. M. Synge)
Deirdre of the Sorrows op.21, 1916 (3, after Synge)
Ruth and Naomi op.24 (7 scenes, Hart, after the Bible), MP, 7 July 1917
The Fantastics op.35, 1918 (romantic comic op, 3, after E. Rostand)
The Travelling Man op.41, 1920 (1, after I. A. Gregory)
The King op.43, 1921 (5, after S. Philips)
Esther op.57, 1923 (2, Hart, after the Bible)
The Woman who Laughed at Faery op.58, 1924 (fantastic comic op, 1, Hart), MP, 25 Sept 1929
Deirdre in Exile op.66 (1, Hart), MP, 22 Sept 1926
The Forced Marriage op.79, 1928 (4, after Molière)
St George and the Dragon op.99 (1, after Cornish mummers' play), Melbourne, St Kevin's Hall, 10 July 1931
The Nativity op.105, 1931 (prol., 3 scenes)
The Dead Heat, 1931 (1, operetta)
The Fiancées, 1931 (1, operetta)
Isolt of the White Hands op.106, 1933 (4, E. A. Robinson)
St Francis of Assisi op.117, 1937 (1, Hart)
Even unto Bethlehem op.155 (nativity play, 4 scenes, Hart), Honolulu, Academy of Arts, 20 Dec 1943

The Swineherd, the Toad and the Princess op.156, 1944 (5, Hart)
The Vengeance of Faery op.164, 1947 (3, Hart)   THÉRÈSE RADIC

Hartford. American city, capital of Connecticut. Located between New York and Boston, Hartford has frequently been host to touring opera companies, including the Metropolitan. In 1934 the Wadsworth Atheneum presented the première of Virgil Thomson's *Four Saints in Three Acts*. Hartford is the home of the Connecticut Opera Company, a professional regional company, and the Hartt Opera Theater, a collegiate department of the Hartt School of Music.

Connecticut Opera was founded in 1941 by Frank Pandolfi, who presided over the company until his death in 1975. Singers who appeared with the company during this period include Richard Tucker, Lily Pons, Leonard Warren, Joan Sutherland and Beverly Sills. The company mounts its productions – usually four a season, with two or three performances each – in the Horace Bushnell Memorial Hall (cap. 2800). In 1981 the company gave four performances of *Aida* in the Hartford Civic Center coliseum (cap. 11 000); with a cast of a thousand, it was promoted as one of the largest indoor opera productions in the western hemisphere and was repeated in 1991 for the company's 50th anniversary. The company's educational programme, Opera Express, plays to more than 25 000 schoolchildren each year. George Osborne was appointed general director in 1980.

Hartt Opera Theater, founded in 1942 by Elemer Nagy and Moshe Paranov, was one of the first undergraduate opera training programmes in the country. It has presented a number of world premières (Schuman's *The Mighty Casey*, 1953; Siegmeister's *Miranda and the Dark Young Man*, 1956) and American premières (Egk's *Peer Gynt*, 1966). In 1943 Hartt presented one of the first televised operas, Offenbach's *Le mariage aux lanternes*, broadcast by WRGB in Schenectady, New York. Since 1963 its productions have been given in the school's Millard Auditorium (cap. 430). Adelaide Bishop was appointed artistic director in 1982.

*

F. H. Johnson: *Musical Memories of Hartford* (Hartford, 1931)
STEVEN P. METCALF

Hartig, Franz Christian (*b* Heldenbergen, 31 Jan 1750; *d* ?Munich, 1819). German tenor. At the age of 18 he was appointed musical director of St Catherine's in Oppenheim am Rhein, then became a member of Marchand's troupe in Frankfurt. He is said to have made his début as early as 1772 at the Mannheim court, where he had tuition from Anton Raaff. From 1777 he sang in the new Mannheim Nationaltheater (managed by Marchand) as well as the Hoftheater, his roles including Karl in Holzbauer's *Günther von Schwarzburg* (1777); his singing was praised by Mozart (letter of 18 December 1778). He moved with the court to Munich and shared leading parts with the aging Raaff in both Italian opera and Singspiel (1778–89); he sang Belmonte in the first Munich performance of *Die Entführung* (1785). He made several guest appearances in Mannheim and also, in 1795 and 1797, in Frankfurt.

Hartig's daughter Johanna (*b* 1779), after a spectacular début in Grétry's *Zémire et Azor* (1794), went to Stuttgart as leading soprano in 1797 and sang at the Mannheim Nationaltheater, 1799–1801.
ROLAND WÜRTZ

Hartmann, Carl (*b* Solingen, 2 May 1895; *d* Munich, 30 May 1969). German tenor. In 1921 he began vocal study with Senff in Düsseldorf. He made his début in *Tannhäuser* in 1928 at the Wuppertal-Elberfeld Stadttheater. Two years later he toured the USA with Johanna Gadski's German opera company. In 1931 he sang in Berlin and subsequently in Austria, France, Italy and Switzerland. His Metropolitan Opera début, as Siegfried, took place in 1937, and he remained a stalwart of the company's Wagnerian wing until 1940. He sang Tristan at Bayreuth in 1938. After World War II Hartmann retired. A handful of recordings he made for Homochord and Parlophone (including popular music) hint at the powerful voice that made him one of the leading Wagnerian tenors of his generation.
CORI ELLISON

Hartmann, Emil [Wilhelm Emilius Zinn] (*b* Copenhagen, 21 Feb 1836; *d* Copenhagen, 18 July 1898). Danish composer, son of Johan Peter Emilius Hartmann. He was taught music theory and the organ by his father and studied briefly in Leipzig. Although he was by profession a church musician, he wrote a great deal for the theatre. His early stage works of the 1860s and 70s failed to equal the success of his first ballet, *Fjeldstuen* ('The Mountain Cottage', 1859), but his later compositions of this kind made a much stronger impression. Nevertheless it was his instrumental music, including symphonies, concertos and arrangements of Scandinavian folksongs and dances, that established his reputation.

first performed in Copenhagen unless otherwise stated
En nat mellem fjeldene [A Night in the Mountains] op.3 (Sangstykke, J. C. Hostrup), excerpts, 11 April 1863, vs (Copenhagen, n.d.)
Elverpigen [The Elf Girl] op.4 (3, T. Overskou), excerpts, 5 Nov 1867, vs (Copenhagen, n.d.)
Korsikaneren [The Corsican] (Sangspil, 2, A. Hertz), 7 April 1872, DK-Kk*
Ragnhild [Runic Spell] (1, J. Lehmann, after H. Hertz); trans. E. Klingenfeld as Runenzauber, Hamburg, 15 Oct 1896; Dan. orig., Copenhagen, Kgl, 27 Dec 1896; ov. (Leipzig, 1896), vs (Leipzig, 1896)
Det store lod [The Big Prize], 1897 (2, A. Ipsen, after Hertz), vs Kk

*

DBL (E. Abrahamsen)
T. Overskou: *Den danske Skueplads*, vii (Copenhagen, 1876), 148–9, 429–40, 707
W. Niemann: *Die Musik Skandinaviens* (Leipzig, 1906)
JOHN BERGSAGEL

Hartmann, (Jean-François-Romain-)Georges [Grémont, Henri] (*b* Paris, 15 May 1843; *d* Paris, May 1900). French librettist. He sometimes used the pseudonym Henri Grémont. Far less a man of the theatre than many of the French librettists of the period, and considerably less prolific, he nonetheless made a significant contribution to the development of opera by furthering the trend for taking themes from 'fine' literature, especially by contemporary authors. As well as fashioning an emotional libretto after Goethe's *Werther* for Massenet (in collaboration with Milliet and Blau), he turned to Flaubert's *Trois contes* (published in 1877) for *Hérodiade* and to Longfellow for *Evangéline*. With André Alexandre he found exoticism and decadence in Pierre Loti's novel *Madame Chrysanthème* (1888) for the setting by Messager and, with Loti and Alexandre, collaborated on the libretto of *L'île du rêve*, a 'Polynesian idyll' set to music by Reynaldo Hahn.

Hérodiade (with P. Milliet), Massenet, 1881; *Werther* (with Milliet and E. Blau), Massenet, 1892; *Mazeppa* (with C. Grandmougin), Comtesse de Grandval, 1892; *Madame Chrysanthème* (with A. Alexandre), Messager, 1893; *Evangéline* (légende acadienne, with L. de Grammont and Alexandre), Leroux, 1895; *L'île du rêve* (idylle polynésienne, with Alexandre and Loti), Hahn, 1898; *Muguette* (oc, with M. Carré), E. Missa, 1903

CHRISTOPHER SMITH

Hartmann, Johann Ernst [Joseph] (*b* Gross Glogau, Silesia [now Głogów, Poland], 24 Dec 1726; *d* Copenhagen, 21 Oct 1793). Danish composer of German origin. It is assumed that he had his musical training in the Jesuit College in Gross Glogau. In 1754 he joined the orchestra of the Prince-Bishop of Breslau, which was disbanded in 1757. In 1761 he was at the Rudolstadt court, but in the same year moved to the ducal court at Plön in Holstein, where he was made Konzertmeister. With the death of the duke, this duchy passed to the Danish crown in October 1761, and in 1762 the Plön band was called to Copenhagen to play in the theatre orchestra for Sarti's Italian opera company until 1764. Hartmann was taken to Copenhagen again in 1766, settling permanently as a member of the royal chapel. The conductorship of the orchestra being vacant and the 'virtuoso extraordinary' J. H. Freithoff sick, Hartmann became in effect the leader and acting conductor. He succeeded Freithoff as first court violinist in 1767 and was appointed first concert master in 1768.

Hartmann's duties included composing, but most of his music was lost in a fire that destroyed Christiansborg Palace in 1794. Besides two published instrumental works several manuscripts survive, including six trio sonatas, a violin concerto, two Passion cantatas and a cantata in honour of the crown prince, later King Frederik VI. His most significant works, however, are the Singspiels he began to compose after the age of 50, which, being composed for the royal theatre, escaped the palace fire. In particular, the two he wrote as birthday pieces for Christian VII to texts by the eminent writer Johannes Ewald, *Balders død* ('The Death of Balder'; Copenhagen, 30 Jan 1779; vs, Copenhagen, 1876; full score, Copenhagen, 1980) and *Fiskerne* ('The Fishermen'; Copenhagen, 31 Jan 1780), are important for the way in which he found an original musical expression for the incipient Romanticism of Ewald's plays. These works, the first one drawn from Norse mythology, the second based on a contemporary event demonstrating the natural nobility of humble people, are considered to have laid the foundation for Danish Romantic opera.

Balders død is a remarkably successful attempt at realizing the atmosphere of Nordic mythology, not only in its arias, ensembles and impressive choruses, but also by an imaginative disposition of sound, at times involving an offstage chorus and a backstage orchestra of 18 in addition to the one in the pit. In *Fiskerne*, on the other hand, in addition to arias and ensembles, Hartmann uses simple songs, revealing the influence of folksong or of medieval Danish ballads, as a way of depicting the peasant milieu of the fishing village. The well-known 'Liden Gunver' may, in fact, be an actual folksong.

The texts for which Hartmann wrote his other stage music did not provide him with anything like the same inspiration. His Singspiels *Hyrdinden paa Alperne* ('The Shepherdess in the Alps'; Copenhagen, 30 Jan 1783) and *Den blinde i Palmyra* ('The Blind Man in Palmyra'; *c*1785, unperf.) both have texts translated from the French (Marmontel and Desfontaines respectively) and

fall back into a more traditional French style. For *Gorm den Gamle* ('Gorm the Ancient, 1785'), a heroic drama on a subject from ancient Danish history, he wrote an overture, two entr'actes and three songs in Act 2, one of which was adopted as the Faeroese national song.

*

V. C. Ravn: Introduction to *Balders død* (Copenhagen, 1876) [vocal score]

C. Thrane: *Fra hofviolonernes tid* (Copenhagen, 1908)

T. Krogh: *Zur Geschichte des dänischen Singspiels im 18. Jahrhundert* (Copenhagen, 1924)

——: *Danske teaterbilleder fra det 18de aarhundrede* (Copenhagen, 1932)

J. Mulvad: 'Om kildeproblemer i dansk syngespilrepertoire med særligt henblik på *Fiskerne*', *DAM*, vii (1973–6), 141–89

N. Schiørring: *Musikkens historie i Danmark*, ii (Copenhagen, 1978)

J. Mulvad, ed.: Introduction to *Balders død* (Copenhagen, 1980) [full score]
JOHN BERGSAGEL

Hartmann, Johan Peter Emilius (*b* Copenhagen, 14 May 1805; *d* Copenhagen, 10 March 1900). Danish composer, father of Emil Hartmann. He was taught music theory and the organ, piano and violin by his father. He began to compose as a child, and at the age of 15 played the violin in public. He read law at the University of Copenhagen, graduating in 1828. From 1828 until 1870 he held an appointment in a government department, but also pursued a full career as a composer, organist, conductor and educator. On the foundation of the Copenhagen Conservatory (1867) he was appointed a joint director with N. W. Gade and the conductor H. S. Paulli. Throughout his life he was respected as one of his country's leading musicians, but whereas his son-in-law Gade achieved an international reputation through his association with Mendelssohn and the Leipzig circle and came to represent Danish music to the outside world, Hartmann never attracted the attention he deserved outside Denmark.

In 1836 he travelled through Germany, Switzerland, Austria and France, with Marschner on the first part of the journey, and met Spontini, Chopin, Rossini, Cherubini, Paer and Spohr; in 1839 he met Mendelssohn and Schumann in Leipzig. Schumann had already reviewed Hartmann's music in the *Neue Zeitschrift für Musik*, including a lengthy consideration of his opera *Ravnen*. Hartmann's friendship with Liszt, whom he met in Hamburg in 1841 and accompanied to Copenhagen, resulted in a German performance of his operatic masterpiece *Liden Kirsten* (1846) in Weimar in 1856.

The music Hartmann encountered in the great European centres in the 1830s and 40s seems not to have tempted him to imitation in any marked degree. On the contrary, it was during these years that he became more intensely Danish and, more particularly, 'Old Norse'. This characteristic aspect of Scandinavian Romanticism was already evident in the melodrama he wrote on Oehlenschläger's poem *Guldhornene* (1832), which was followed by other works in which the ancient sources of Scandinavian culture were brought to life with increasing power; these include his incidental music to Oehlenschläger's dramas, and his ballets for August Bournonville. With these works, and others such as *Liden Kirsten* (in which he evoked the atmosphere of the medieval Danish ballads), numerous hymns and biblical and national songs, Hartmann not only satisfied Danish national feelings but also gave encouragement (acknowledged by Grieg) to the growing sense of self-awareness in Scandinavia as a whole in the 19th century.

Ravnen, eller Broderprøven [The Raven, or The Brothers' Test] op.12 (3, H. C. Andersen, after C. Gozzi), Copenhagen, 29 Oct 1832, vs (Copenhagen and Leipzig, 1839); rev. version (4), Copenhagen, 1865
Korsarerne [The Corsairs] op.16 (3, H. Hertz), Copenhagen, 1835, vs (Copenhagen, 1883)
Liden Kirsten [Little Christine] op.44 (1, Andersen), Copenhagen, 12 May 1846, vs (Copenhagen, 1846); rev. version (2), Copenhagen, 1858, vs (Copenhagen, n.d.)
Kong Saul [King Saul], c1865 (Andersen), inc.

*

C. Thrane: Danske komponister (Copenhagen, 1875)
E. Grieg: 'J. P. E. Hartmann', Musikbladet (14 May 1885)
A. Hammerich: J. P. E. Hartmann: biografiske essays (Copenhagen, 1916) [incl. autobiographical frag.; enlarged from article in SIMG, ii (1900–01)]
W. Behrend: J. P. E. Hartmann (Copenhagen, 1918)
R. Hove: J. P. E. Hartmann (Copenhagen, 1934)
V. Bitsch: J. P. E. Hartmann (Hellerup, 1955)
S. Sørensen: 'En dansk guldalder-opera: den musikalske karakteristik i Hartmanns "Liden Kirsten"', Dansk musiktidsskrift, xlii (1967), 122–9   JOHN BERGSAGEL

Hartmann, Karl Amadeus (b Munich, 2 Aug 1905; d Munich, 5 Dec 1963). German composer. He studied with Joseph Haas at the Munich Academy from 1924 to 1927 and later became a pupil of Hermann Scherchen. After the Nazis came to power he withdrew into a kind of self-imposed exile and refused to allow his compositions to be performed in Germany. During World War II he embarked on further studies with Webern (1941–2). From 1945 until his death he was engaged in the rebuilding of German musical life and founded the Musica Viva Concerts in Munich to promote contemporary music.

Although Hartmann's posthumous reputation rests almost entirely on the eight symphonies he wrote between 1936 and 1962, he was strongly attracted to the medium of opera. Throughout his career he contemplated setting texts by such authors as Hauptmann, Giraudoux, Lope de Vega and Zuckmayer, but was able to complete only two stage works. The first of these, Wachsfigurenkabinett, one of his earliest compositions (1929–30), was written at the invitation of the Bavarian State Opera Studio, but financial stringencies prevented its public performance. It comprises five short operas, each exploring a different mode of expression, from morality and biting social criticism to literary cabaret, jazz cantata and parody. The musical style is strongly anti-Romantic and follows the techniques employed in similar operas by Hindemith, Toch and Krenek. A few years later, in 1934, under very different circumstances, he began work on his second opera, Simplicius Simplicissimus, the composition of which occupied him intermittently for the next 20 years. Given his spiritual isolation during the Nazi era, it is easy to understand how the composer perceived uncanny parallels with his own situation in Grimmelshausen's novel about the simple, almost Parsifal-like shepherd boy who wanders through Germany witnessing the devastation and social degradation perpetrated during the Thirty Years War. The original version of this chamber opera, although completed in the 1930s, did not receive its première until after World War II, in a broadcast performance by Bavarian Radio in 1948. However, largely through the suggestion of Rolf Liebermann, it was extensively revised in 1956 to accommodate larger instrumental forces and allow for considerable structural alterations.

Although commentators have suggested that it is modelled on Stravinsky's The Soldier's Tale in the employment of such closed forms as the lied, march, dance and chorale, and in the prominent role allotted to a narrator, the musical idiom of Simplicius Simplicissimus is strongly influenced by the expressionism of the Second Viennese School.

See also SIMPLICIUS SIMPLICISSIMUS.

Wachsfigurenkabinett, 1929–30 (Komisch-phantastische Kammerspieloper, E. Bormann), Munich, 29 May 1988 (Mainz, 1988)
  Die Witwe von Ephesus
  Chaplin – Ford – Trott [reconstructed by W. Hiller]
  Der Mann, der vom Tode auferstand [reconstructed by G. Bialas and H. W. Henze]
  Leben und Sterben des heiligen Teufels
  Fürwahr …?! [reconstructed by Henze]
Simplicius Simplicissimus: drei Szenen aus seiner Jugend, 1934–5 (Kammeroper, 3 scenes, H. Scherchen, W. Petzet and Hartmann, after H. Grimmelshausen: Der abenteuerliche Simplicissimus), Munich, Bavarian Radio, 2 April 1948 [as Des Simplicius Simplicissimus Jugend]; stage, Cologne, Stadt, 20 Oct 1949, vs (Heidelberg, 1949); rev. 1955, Mannheim, National, 9 July 1957 (Mainz, 1960)

*

H. Schmidt-Garre: 'K. A. Hartmanns Kammeroper "Des Simplicius Simplicissimus Jugend"', Melos, xviii (1951), 117–18
G. A. Trumpff: 'Zwei neue Opernfassungen', Musica, xi (1957), 576 [on Simplicius Simplicissimus]
K. A. Hartmann: 'Zu meinem "Simplicius Simplicissimus"', Kleine Schriften, ed. E. Thomas (Mainz, 1965), 49–52
A. D. McCredie: 'Karl Amadeus Hartmann (1905–1963)', MMA, vii (1975), 142–87
H.-W. Heister: 'Politische Expressivität – musikalische Humanität: zum Werk Karl Amadeus Hartmanns', Philosophische Akademie der Künste: Junges Ensemble für Musik Theater (Berlin, 1978), 31–4
D. Stern: 'Zu Hartmanns "Simplicius Simplicissimus"', ibid, 28
A. D. McCredie: 'The Role of Sources and Antecedents in the Compositional Process of Karl Amadeus Hartmann', MMA, x (1979), 166–212   ERIK LEVI

Hartmann, Rudolf (b Ingolstadt, 11 Oct 1900; d Munich, 26 Aug 1988). German director. He studied in Munich and Bamberg, then joined the municipal theatre of Altenberg as resident director (1924). After engagements in Nuremberg (1928–34) and with the Berlin Staatsoper (1934–8), he was invited by Clemens Krauss to become chief director of the Bayerische Staatsoper in Munich, where he remained until Goebbels ordered the closure of all theatres in Germany in 1944. It was during this period that he formed his personal and professional association with the aging Richard Strauss. He directed the premières of Friedenstag (1938) and Capriccio (1942) at Munich. He was also responsible for the abortive first production of Die Liebe der Danae, which had its dress rehearsal at the Salzburg Festival on 16 August 1944 but whose first night was cancelled when the theatres closed days later. The opera was eventually staged by Hartmann in Munich in 1952. This was the year he was appointed Staatsintendant of the Bayerische Staatsoper, where he took charge of the great German works and consolidated Munich's status as the Strauss city after World War II by restaging most of his operas there. He had directed Die Meistersinger von Nürnberg at the first postwar Bayreuth Festival (1951) in a traditional production which contrasted starkly with Wieland Wagner's 'new Bayreuth style' and he was never invited back. After 1952, he set about establishing Munich as a rival to Bayreuth as a centre of Wagner production. In 1967 he was succeeded in Munich by Günther Rennert and he embarked on a late freelance career, directing Strauss's *Die Frau ohne Schatten* (1967) in controversial designs by Josef Svoboda and a romantic production of *Die Meistersinger von Nürnberg* (1968) at Covent Garden, where earlier triumphs had included *Elektra* (1953), a *Ring* cycle (1954) and a legendary *Arabella* with Lisa della Casa and Dietrich Fischer-Dieskau (1965). Apart from the Covent Garden *Frau ohne Schatten*, his work was notable for his fidelity to the composer's and librettist's conception. He was a devotee of the German ensemble system with house casts and meticulously prepared new productions.

HUGH CANNING

Harut'yunyan, Alexander Grigor (*b* Erevan, 28 Sept 1920). Armenian composer. In 1941 he graduated from the Erevan Conservatory, where he later taught composition. He continued his studies in Moscow at the House of Armenian Culture (1946–8) and in 1954 was appointed artistic director of the Armenian PO. He was made a People's Artist of the USSR in 1970. The predominantly lyrical character of his work arises from peasant music, while the improvisations of the *ashughner* (folk minstrels) have fundamentally influenced his style. His opera *Sayat'-Nova* (A. Khandjyan; 1969, Erevan), based on the life of a prominent 18th-century *ashugh*, represents the culmination of his preoccupation with *ashugh* music. In it the synthesis of improvisation and songstyle with other elements forms the backbone of the work and set the tone for his later musical vocabulary. His other work for the stage is the musical comedy *Medsapativ muratskanner* ('Honourable Beggars', 1972).

SVETLANA SARKISYAN

Harwood, Elizabeth (Jean) (*b* Kettering, 27 May 1938; *d* Fryerning, Essex, 21 June 1990). English soprano. After studying in Manchester, in 1960 she won the Kathleen Ferrier Memorial Prize and made her début as Second Boy (*Die Zauberflöte*) at Glyndebourne, where she later sang Fiordiligi, Countess Almaviva and the Marschallin. In 1961 she joined Sadler's Wells, where her roles included Susanna, Konstanze, Adèle (*Le comte Ory*), Zerbinetta and Massenet's Manon. In 1963 she toured Australia, singing Lucia, Adina and Amina. She made her Covent Garden début in 1967 as the Fiakermilli, returning for Marzelline, Gilda, Bella (*The Midsummer Marriage*), Norina, Donna Elvira and Teresa (*Benvenuto Cellini*). For Scottish Opera (1967–74) she sang Fiordiligi, Sophie and Lucia. After Karajan heard her at Aix-en-Provence, in 1970 she was invited to Salzburg, where she sang Konstanze, Fiordiligi, Countess Almaviva and Donna Elvira. She also appeared at La Scala (1972) and the Metropolitan (1975). Her voice, capable of brilliant coloratura and lyrical warmth, was used with elegance, and she had a charming stage presence. She recorded Hanna Glawari and Musetta for Karajan.

M. Kennedy: 'Elizabeth Harwood – an Appreciation', *Opera*, xli (1990), 932–3
ALAN BLYTH

Háry János [*Háry János kalandozásai Nagyabonytul a Burgváráig* ('János Háry: his Adventures from Nagyabony to the Vienna Burg')]. Singspiel in a prologue, four adventures (five at the first three performances) and an epilogue by ZOLTÁN KODÁLY to a libretto by Béla Paulini and Zsolt Harsányi after János Garay's comic epic *Az obsitos* ('The Veteran'); Budapest, Royal Hungarian Opera House, 16 October 1926.

János Háry (baritone), an old veteran, boasts in the village inn of the heroic deeds of his youth: how he rescued Maria Luisa (mezzo-soprano), the daughter of Kaiser Franz (baritone), at the Russian-Austrian border and was taken by her to the Vienna Burg, how he was nominated a general and alone won a battle against Napoleon (baritone), and how he conquered the heart of the Emperor's Wife (soprano) and could have married her, had he not remained true to his bride Örzse (mezzo-soprano) and to his native village Nagyabony.

For Kodály, *Háry János* symbolized the poetic power of folklore to transcend political frustration. The main musical objective of the Singspiel was to bring genuine folksong on to the operatic stage. Kodály also used 19th-century *verbunkos* (Hungarian dance pieces) in the Intermezzo; other illustrative orchestral numbers are of his own invention. These movements were arranged into the suite that secured world-wide renown for the work's instrumental music.

TIBOR TALLIÁN

Häser, Charlotte (*b* Leipzig, 26 June 1784; *d* Rome, 1 May 1871). German singer. She studied with her father, the composer and Kapellmeister Johann Georg Häser. After success as a concert singer she appeared on stage in Dresden from 1803. She was one of the first German singers to make a reputation in Italy, being acclaimed as 'la divina Tedesca'. Returning to Germany she was admired by Spohr and E. T. A. Hoffmann, who dedicated a chapter to her in his *Fantastische Erzählungen*. She achieved some success in men's roles, notably as Tamino, and was praised for her simple, unaffected style. After her marriage to Giuseppe Vera she returned to Italy in 1814. She was the mother of the composer Edoardo Vera.

DAVID CUMMINGS

Hass, Sabine (*b* Brunswick, 8 April 1949). German soprano. She studied in Berlin and Munich and made her début in 1970 at Stuttgart. Since 1976 she has sung regularly in Munich and Vienna, and has also appeared at Bregenz, Salzburg, Florence, Naples, Turin, San Diego and Barcelona. In 1983 she sang Elsa at La Scala, and in 1985 made her Metropolitan début in the same role. Her repertory includes Senta, Sieglinde, Isolde, Gutrune, Isabella (*Das Liebesverbot*), Agathe, Reiza and Leonore. She has a bright, vibrant voice, and is heard to particular advantage in works by Richard Strauss: as Freihild, Diemut, Chrysothemis, Ariadne, the Empress, Aithra, the Commandant's Wife (*Friedenstag*) and Danae, which she sang at Munich in 1988.

ELIZABETH FORBES

Hassall, Christopher (Vernon) (*b* London, 24 March 1912; *d* in a train, 25 April 1963, bur. Canterbury). English librettist and translator. After an early career as an actor he became famous as a lyricist for Ivor Novello's shows, including *Glamorous Night* (1935) and *The Dancing Years* (1939). He composed the music for his own play *Christ's Comet*, produced at the Canterbury Festival in 1938. Having provided librettos for Antony Hopkins (*The Man from Tuscany*, 1951) and Franz Reizenstein (*Anna Kraus*, 1952), he did the same for Walton's *Troilus and Cressida* (1954); although this was not an easy collaboration, his libretto was described by Ernest Newman as 'the best poetic opera text since Hofmannsthal'. Later he was Bliss's librettist for *Tobias and the Angel* (1960).

His literary resourcefulness and theatrical expertise, combined with a technical knowledge of music, led to commissions to translate a number of operas and operettas, including *Bluebeard's Castle* (1957), Lehár's *The Merry Widow* (1958), Dvořák's *Rusalka* (1959), and *Die Fledermaus* (1959), all for Sadler's Wells Opera; the Strauss achieved the unusual distinction of being printed in the Eulenburg miniature full score (1968).   ARTHUR JACOBS

Hasse, Johann Adolf (*b* Bergedorf, nr Hamburg, bap. 25 March 1699; *d* Venice, 16 Dec 1783). German composer. For nearly half a century, his *opere serie* were performed in the leading Italian and German opera houses. He delighted singers and audiences with the classical restraint and lyrical beauty of his music and became known as 'il caro Sassone'. Although he was slow to recognize all the requirements of the Metastasian drama, he gradually made Metastasio's philosophy his own and became one of the poet's favourite composers: between 1743 and 1771 Hasse was usually the first composer to set the librettist's texts.

1. Early years: Germany, Naples and Venice. 2. The first Dresden period, 1730–33. 3. Dresden and Venice, 1734–44. 4. Hasse and Metastasio. 5. The final Dresden period, 1744–63. 6. Last years. 7. Musical style and reputation.

1. EARLY YEARS: GERMANY, NAPLES AND VENICE. Hasse belonged to a dynasty of church musicians active in Lübeck and Bergedorf (today a suburb of Hamburg). In 1718 he joined the Hamburg Opera and in 1719 became court singer in Brunswick thanks to Johann Ulrich von König, who later produced German translations of Hasse's operas in Dresden. König's son Friedrich August functioned as the impresario at the Dresden court and signed decrees naming Hasse Oberkapellmeister on 7 January 1750 and Supremus Musices Rector for life on 19 January 1764. In Brunswick he sang in operas by Schürmann, F. B. Conti and Caldara, as well as his own opera *Antioco*, performed during the summer fair of 1721.

Hasse seems to have left Germany in 1722; according to testimony in his secret marriage contract of June 1730, he had spent several months in Venice, Bologna, Florence and Rome before living for six or seven years in Naples (where he converted to Roman Catholicism) and then for six months in Venice. His first work for Naples, the serenata *Antonio e Cleopatra*, was given privately in autumn 1725. Sung by Carlo Broschi (Farinelli) and Vittoria Tesi, its success earned him commissions from the S Bartolomeo opera house. Quantz, who visited Hasse in 1725, reported that Alessandro Scarlatti had befriended him and was giving him lessons. Arias from Scarlatti's *Griselda* reworked by Hasse (*I-Mc*) demonstrate his study of Scarlatti's music.

Sesostrate, given on 13 May 1726 and revived with minor changes on 28 August, was the first of Hasse's seven serious operas in six years for S Bartolomeo. His rapid emergence as one of the busiest opera composers in Naples has few parallels in 18th-century music. The intermezzos he wrote for the *buffo* singers Gioacchino Corrado and Celeste Resse were popular in Naples and were sung by other comedians throughout Italy and Germany as well as in revisions Hasse made for Cosimo and Margherita Ermini in Dresden. A full-length *opera buffa*, *La sorella amante*, his only work of the kind, was performed in spring 1729 at either the Teatro Nuovo or the Toledo theatre in Naples. The autograph score, curiously, shows alterations in the handwriting of Hasse's later years. Almost nothing is known about two

serenatas for Naples, *Semele, o sia La richiesta fatale* (1726) and *Enea in Caonia* (1727).

Hasse's earliest documented visit to Venice was at Carnival 1730, when his *Artaserse* was given at S Giovanni Grisostomo. The libretto, nominally by Metastasio, had been extensively altered by Giovanni Boldini or perhaps Domenico Lalli. Farinelli, who performed in several of Hasse's operas, was particularly pleased with his *Artaserse* arias: he sang them in his London début on 27 October 1734 in a pasticcio, and performed two every evening for Philip V during his decade of service with the king (1737–46).

2. THE FIRST DRESDEN PERIOD, 1730–33. The libretto of *Artaserse* for Carnival 1730 identifies Hasse as 'Maestro sopranumerario della Real Cappella di Napoli'. But the librettos of *Dalisa* (Venice, May 1730), *Arminio* (Milan, August 1730) and *Ezio* (Naples, autumn 1730) identify him as 'Primo maestro di cappella di S. M. Re Augusto di Polonia ed Elettore di Sassonia'. Evidently he was appointed Kapellmeister at Dresden some time after the carnival season but before Ascension and before his marriage to the soprano Faustina Bordoni on or shortly after 24 June. But he did not set foot in Dresden until July 1731.

In early 1731 Hasse visited Vienna, where his oratorio *Daniello* was performed at the Habsburg court. During a longer visit in 1733–4 he gave Maria Theresa music lessons. It is clear from many public and private performances of his music, especially in the 1760s, that he came to be her favourite composer; arguably he was court Kapellmeister in all but name.

On 7 or 8 July 1731, immediately after their arrival in Dresden, Faustina made her début before the Saxon crown prince. Hasse conducted sacred works in the court chapel on 15 August, but the main event of the year was the première of *Cleofide* on 13 September. Based on Metastasio's *Alessandro nell'Indie*, the text had been substantially altered for Hasse by Michelangelo Boccardi; half the aria texts were not Metastasio's. Moreover, the music for many arias was taken from Hasse's earlier operas. Among other changes, Boccardi introduced an *ombra* scene in Act 2 reminiscent of the ghost scene that had been added for *Artaserse*. The première of *Cleofide* may have been attended by J. S. Bach, who gave an organ recital in the Sophienkirche the next day. C. P. E. Bach told Forkel in 1775 that his father and Hasse had been well acquainted.

On 7 October 1731 Hasse directed at Dresden his cantata *La gloria sassonia* in honour of the crown prince's birthday. The next day he left with Faustina for the premières of his next operas, *Catone in Utica* at Turin in December and *Cajo Fabricio* in Rome in January. The libretto of *Catone* shows that 11 of the arias did not belong to Metastasio's original text; of *Cajo Fabricio* only four aria texts were from Zeno's original. Probably earlier arias were used; but Hasse's productivity was nevertheless enormous. He soon supplied two operas for Venice: *Demetrio* (all new) for S Giovanni Grisostomo and *Euristeo* (a pasticcio) for S Samuele. Faustina did not sing in the Turin and Rome operas (Mennicke conjectured that she was pregnant), but she did appear in *Demetrio* and in Giacomelli's *Epaminonda* during Carnival.

In autumn 1732 Hasse again visited Naples. His opera *Issipile*, given at S Bartolomeo on 1 October, celebrated the birthday of Emperor Charles VI. With

Spain's recovery of the city in 1734, Hasse's influence diminished. Except for a much altered performance of *Cajo Fabricio* in 1733 and one of *Alessandro nell'Indie* (*Cleofide*) in 1736 (under Giuseppe de Majo, who provided a prologue), he had no works performed in Naples until *La clemenza di Tito* (*Tito Vespasiano*) in November 1738. Interest in his music returned only with the marriage in May 1738 of the Saxon princess Maria Amalia to the Bourbon king, Carlo; a dozen of his operas were staged at S Carlo during her reign. But even after the royal couple left Naples in 1759, Hasse's popularity continued: six more of his operas were produced there before *Ruggiero*, his last, in 1772.

Late in 1732 Hasse was again in Venice. Then on 2 May 1733, at the Teatro Malvezzi, Bologna, his *Siroe* was produced in an exceptionally grand manner; it was repeated 25 times up to 21 June. Hasse officiated at the harpsichord in 19 performances and was well paid, with 1260 lire and lodging. The opera was revived in more than a dozen cities before 1763, when Hasse conducted a revised version at Dresden. His patron Friedrich August I died on 1 February 1733, and, observing a year of mourning, the court let Hasse remain abroad. It was probably in 1733 that he began writing his many solo motets, oratorios and choral works for the Ospedale degli Incurabili, Venice; over 40 solo motets, in an operatic style, survive.

Hasse's *Euristeo* (1732, Venice) was dedicated to the English nation, and his *Demetrio* honoured the Earl of Middlesex. He may have been invited to London (as Burney reported). On 4 December 1733 Handel directed *Cajus Fabricius* in London: 19 of its arias were taken from Hasse's *Cajo Fabricio*, two each from *Ulderica* and *Tigrane* (both 1729) and only five from other composers' operas. Handel's respect for Hasse is further shown by the 49 arias from 15 different Hasse operas he used in seven of his London pasticcios of 1730–34.

3. DRESDEN AND VENICE, 1734–44. Hasse was in Dresden from 3 February until 5 November 1734, but wrote no new opera. When the Elector of Saxony (also King of Poland) took his court to Warsaw in November 1734, Hasse was again free to visit Italy. The court remained in Poland for a year and a half, but Hasse did not return to Dresden until early 1737. In Pesaro he directed his new setting of *Tito Vespasiano* (a modified version of Metastasio's *La clemenza di Tito*) to inaugurate the Teatro Pubblico on 24 September 1735; Faustina was in the cast. On 4 November 1736 Hasse's *Alessandro nell'Indie* (*Cleofide*) was staged at S Giovanni Grisostomo, Venice. Its libretto is the first to name Hasse *maestro di cappella* of the Incurabili in Venice (even though he had probably composed for the institution intermittently since 1730).

When at Dresden between February 1737 and autumn 1738, Hasse composed five operas to texts by S. B. Pallavicino, the Italian court poet, and prepared a revision of *Tito Vespasiano* (*La clemenza di Tito*, 17 January 1738). For *Alfonso* (11 May 1738), celebrating the marriage of Princess Maria Amalia with Carlo, King of the Two Sicilies, the court opera house was rebuilt and a revised version of Hasse's intermezzo *Lucilla e Pandolfo* given between the acts. After the Saxon court's removal to Warsaw in September 1738, Hasse returned to Venice, where Faustina sang in several operas including his *Viriate*, based on Metastasio's *Siface*. He was extremely popular in Venice: the French traveller

Charles de Brosses declared 'le Saxon est aujourd'hui l'homme fêté'.

Hasse's next and longest stay in Dresden was between early 1740 and January 1744. *Demetrio*, given there on 8 February 1740, was probably very different from the version performed almost simultaneously at the Teatro S Angelo, Venice (as *Cleonice*), though the latter was dedicated to the Saxon crown prince Friedrich Christian, then in Venice. A revised setting of *Artaserse* was given on 9 September 1740 on the prince's return; it resembled the 1730 version but had 12 new arias, five of them for Faustina. *Numa Pompilio*, Hasse's last opera of 1741 and his last to a Pallavicino text, was performed on 7 October in a small theatre at Hubertusburg, near Dresden. An intermezzo, *Pimpinella e Marcantonio*, was given between the acts of the opera and also appears within the fifth and sixth scenes of Act 2 (an old-fashioned usage). It was Hasse's first new intermezzo for over a decade; this and *Rimario e Grilantea*, possibly performed with *Numa Pompilio* on 3 November 1741, were Hasse's last two comic works. He evidently came to share the opinion Faustina later voiced to Vogler (in October 1775) when she bade him never to compose an *opera buffa* because it could only hurt the sublime style of singing.

4. HASSE AND METASTASIO. Hasse's appreciation of Metastasio's art developed only gradually. The roles of Francesco Algarotti and perhaps Frederick the Great in bringing Hasse to respect Metastasio's poetry were crucial. The king entered Dresden on 18 January 1742 to sign a treaty and that evening ordered a performance of Hasse's new opera, *Lucio Papirio*. Frederick later revealed his enthusiasm for the opera in letters to Algarotti, who, in Dresden between 1742 and 1747, seems to have influenced the city's cultural circles towards a heightened interest in classical principles. In 1742 Algarotti altered for Hasse Metastasio's *Didone abbandonata* for performance on 7 October at the Hubertusburg theatre: the burning of Carthage which concludes the original was replaced by a lengthy recitative and aria. The neo-classical restraint of Algarotti's substitution must have seemed an improvement on Metastasio's youthful libretto: as late as 1757 Hasse asked Algarotti to send him the score of the closing scene (now in *I-Bc*) so that he could give it to Padre Martini.

In 1743 and 1744 Hasse was asked to set two new Metastasian texts; he was thus obliged to set them without changes. These were *Antigono*, for the Dresden court, and *Ipermestra*, for the Vienna court. Hasse's friendship with Metastasio blossomed at this time, as the poet wrote on 9 March 1744:

never until now had I happened to see him in all his glory, but always detached from his many personal relationships in such a way that he was like an aria without instruments; but now I see him as a father, husband and friend, qualities which make an admirable union in him with those solid bases of ability and good behaviour, for which I will cherish him so many years...

The friendship deepened. Within a dozen years Hasse had set all but four of the texts Metastasio had written before *Antigono* (*Temistocle* was the only one of those that he never set). The altered Metastasian librettos that Hasse had earlier prepared were reset with great fidelity to the poet's original intentions: *Demofoonte* (1758), *La clemenza di Tito* (1759), *Artaserse* (1760) and *Siroe* (1763); and as Metastasio wrote new *opera seria* and *festa teatrale* texts during the 1760s Hasse was generally the first to set them. Following *Ruggiero* (1771), their last collaboration, Burney remarked:

This poet and musician are the *two halves* of what, like Plato's *Androgyne*, once constituted a *whole*; for as they are equally possessed of the same characteristic marks of true genius, taste, and judgement; so propriety, consistency, clearness, and precision, are alike the inseparable companions of both…[Hasse] may without injury to his brethren, be allowed to be as superior to all other lyric composers, as Metastasio is to all other lyric poets.

5. THE FINAL DRESDEN PERIOD, 1744–63. Except for a performance of *Semiramide riconosciuta* at Venice on 26 December 1744 (possibly also a month earlier at Naples), no new operas by Hasse were given in Italy during his next stay there, which lasted about a year until late summer 1745. *Lo starnuto d'Ercole*, a pasticcio, was performed with life-size puppets in the garden of the Labia palace, Venice, in autumn 1745. There is evidence that the Nicolini troupe, which toured Germany and Bohemia in the 1740s, performed some of Hasse's intermezzos with puppets.

The most significant event of Hasse's subsequent period in Dresden, from autumn 1745 until spring or summer 1746, was the visit of Frederick the Great after the battle of Kesselsdorf. He heard a Hasse *Te Deum* in the Kreuzkirche on 19 December 1745 and ordered a performance of Hasse's opera *Arminio* (the first to a libretto by the court poet, G. C. Pasquini). Frederick's enthusiasm for Hasse's operas was undoubtedly matched by interest in his flute music, and Hasse probably wrote at least some of his many flute sonatas, trios and concertos for the king. The Dresden opera house was closed from December 1745 until January 1747, but several operas, including Hasse's *La clemenza di Tito*, were given in a temporary wooden theatre by the Mingotti troupe.

After visits to Venice and Munich, Hasse returned to Dresden to stage *La spartana generosa* (14 June 1747) for the double wedding of the Elector of Bavaria Maximilian III Joseph and his sister Maria Antonia Walpurgis to the Saxon princess Maria Anna and her brother Friedrich Christian. Soon afterwards, Maria Antonia engaged Porpora as her vocal tutor; he came to Dresden in February 1748, was named Kapellmeister on 13 April and remained until 1 January 1752. His appointment undoubtedly prompted Hasse's promotion to Oberkapellmeister in 1750. For the marriage, also in 1747, of the Saxon princess Maria Josepha to the dauphin of France, Hasse prepared a reworked *Semiramide riconosciuta* (the score in *I-Vc* shows extensive revisions in his hand). This union no doubt explains Hasse's visit to Paris in summer 1750. His *Didone abbandonata* was given, perhaps with the intermezzo *Pimpinella e Marcantonio*, at Versailles on 28 August 1753. The numerous manuscript copies of Hasse's operas handsomely bound with the emblem of the Menus Plaisirs du Roi (in *F-Pn*) attest to Maria Josepha's admiration for him.

While the Saxon court was again in Warsaw from May 1748 until early 1749 Hasse directed revised versions of his *Demofoonte* and *Leucippo* in Venice. When he returned to Dresden, his serenata *Il natal di Giove* was given at Hubertusburg (August or October 1749); he also set Metastasio's *Attilio Regolo*, a libretto written in 1740 but, because of the Emperor Charles VI's death that year, never set. In a famous letter to Hasse of 20 October 1749 Metastasio described each character and

offered advice about the use of the orchestra. For example:

a brief symphony seems necessary to me to give the consul and the senators time to take their seats and in order that Regulus may arrive without haste and take time to reflect…it is necessary that the instruments anticipate him, assist him, and support him until he is seated…Although [in recitatives] there are places…which could be suitably accompanied by the violins, it seems to me unwise to make this ornamental procedure too familiar, and I should be pleased if, particularly in the third act, there were no instruments used until the last scene…

Since Hasse generally did as Metastasio recommended, especially in using *recitativo accompagnato* with discretion, the letter may have been written mainly for the benefit of interested connoisseurs at the Dresden court. In 1748 Metastasio had arbitrated in a dispute between Faustina and Regina Mingotti, suggesting at Hasse's bidding that, although Faustina played the role of a princess (in *Demofoonte*), she should yield rank to Mingotti on stage while disguised as a handmaiden.

The highlight of the 1751 Carnival in Dresden was the singing of Felice Salimbeni, a celebrated castrato lured away from the Berlin court, in a revised version of Hasse's *Leucippo* and a setting of *Ciro riconosciuto*. The latter saw the last operatic performances both of Faustina, who retired from the stage, and of Salimbeni, who died of consumption in August.

Among the operas of the mid-1750s, *Solimano* (Carnival 1753) and a substantially revised *Ezio* (Carnival 1755) were imposing spectacles with hundreds of extras for crowd scenes and an array of animals including horses, mules, elephants and camels. For the production on 6 February 1754 of Hasse's *Artemisia*, acting space outside the theatre was illuminated by thousands of candles and lamps. The librettist of *Solimano* (and *Artemisia*), G. A. Migliavacca, displeased Hasse, who set and then cut much recitative, as can be seen from the holograph score (*I-Mc*). Except for Coltellini's tragic intermezzo *Piramo e Tisbe* (1768), Hasse was never to set texts by any poet but Metastasio.

Hasse's new operas for the autumn and carnival seasons of 1755–6, *Il re pastore* and *L'Olimpiade*, were of conventional dimensions. Then the Seven Years War closed the Dresden theatre, and from September 1756 to January 1762 the Saxon court resided in Warsaw. In fact, a revival in 1763 of *Siroe* was the only opera Hasse ever again directed in Dresden. Thenceforth he composed new works for the court in Warsaw, for S Carlo, Naples, and, above all, for Empress Maria Theresa in Vienna.

Between 1757 and mid-1760 Hasse lived in Italy, at first in Venice, as documented in letters from Metastasio and Algarotti, and thereafter in Naples, where he first of all supervised the production of a new setting of *Demofoonte* (autumn 1758). His conducting there was reported by P. J. Grosley de Troyes, so Fürstenau's claim that Hasse composed *Il sogno di Scipione* for a Warsaw performance in October seems mistaken. Revised versions of *La clemenza di Tito* (20 January 1759) and *Artaserse* (20 January 1760) and a new *Achille in Sciro* (4 November 1759) were also staged at S Carlo. Hasse may also have visited Warsaw to supervise productions of his operas; 11 were staged there between August 1759 and Carnival 1763. The autograph scores for *Zenobia* and *Siroe* (*I-Mc*), specifically designated for Warsaw, imply that he visited Poland at least in autumn

Autograph score of Hasse's 'Artaserse' (Act 2 scene v), as revised for the performance at the Teatro S Carlo, Naples, 20 January 1760

1761 for *Zenobia* and from October 1762 to Carnival 1763 for *Il re pastore* and *Siroe*.

From autumn 1760 to summer 1762 Hasse lived in Vienna. First he set Metastasio's *festa teatrale Alcide al bivio* for the wedding of the Archduke Joseph. Its première in the Grosser Redoutensaal (8 October 1760) was presumably staged, but a revival 'was sung seated with the parts held in the hands by the singers and without costumes', according to a letter of 28 February 1761 from Francesco Maria Hasse, the composer's son, to Abate G. M. Ortes in Venice (*I-Vmc*). Other new works included settings of Metastasian *complimenti*, sacred works for the children of Maria Theresa and cantata texts for professional singers. Larger works staged at the Vienna court in 1761–2 were *Il re pastore*, *Zenobia* and the new *Il trionfo di Clelia*, given on 27 April 1762 to celebrate the birth of a child to Archduchess Isabella, consort of Joseph.

When hostilities ceased, the Elector of Saxony returned to Dresden on 2 April 1763; Hasse too returned, to find the court's library of sacred music burnt, his home destroyed and the opera house devastated. Nevertheless, a production of his *Siroe* was mounted for the elector's name day (3 August). When Friedrich August II died on 5 October, the new elector, Friedrich Christian, decreed that expensive musical events would not be allowed. Hasse and Faustina were paid 12 000 thalers (two years' salary) and were preparing to leave when Friedrich Christian died of smallpox. Hasse's Requiem in C had been performed on 22 November for Friedrich August II; now exequies for his son delayed Hasse's departure until 20 February 1764. He was paid 1000 thalers for performances in November and December 1763 but given no pension.

6. LAST YEARS. Hasse returned to Vienna, where on 24 April 1764 his setting of Metastasio's *festa teatrale Egeria* was produced at court for the coronation of Joseph II. Another work commissioned by the Vienna court, though performed at Innsbruck, for the wedding of Archduke Leopold on 6 August 1765, was *Romolo*

ed *Ersilia*. The death of the Emperor Franz I on 18 August caused the cancellation of further entertainments. A revised version of *L'Olimpiade* was performed at Turin in Carnival 1766, but by August Hasse was again in Vienna, where his *festa teatrale Partenope* was given in 1767 to mark the engagement of Archduchess Maria Josepha to Ferdinand IV. Mozart heard it, according to a letter from his father (29 September 1767). Like most of Hasse's theatrical works for Vienna in the 1760s, it was successfully repeated in Naples.

Possibly Hasse's best opera is the tragic intermezzo *Piramo e Tisbe* (1768), a chamber work for three singers with fine duets and much *recitativo accompagnato*. The vocal parts are demanding, although, remarkably, the work was given by amateur singers (including the librettist Coltellini); it was revived with the same cast in September 1770. Maria Theresa rewarded Hasse for the latter performance and bade him compose a further opera in 1771. He had intended to retire from opera with *Piramo e Tisbe* but reluctantly agreed to set Metastasio's *Ruggiero* for the marriage in Milan of Archduke Ferdinand to Maria Beatrice d'Este. On 3 May 1769 Hasse had written to Ortes: 'for almost a year I have not attended the theatre, in which strange ideas hold sway'. Despite their awareness of public expectations and of the modern qualities *Piramo e Tisbe* had already demonstrated, Hasse and Metastasio created a very conservative work with none of the dances and choruses that are so prominent in Mozart's *Ascanio in Alba*, the companion piece in Milan. Mozart, however, was delighted with Hasse's opera and wrote to his sister (2 November): 'There is a performance of Hasse's opera today, but as Papa is not going out, I cannot be there. Fortunately, I know nearly all the arias by heart, so I can see and hear it at home in my head'.

In August and September 1773 Burney visited Vienna and interviewed Hasse. He reported:

Party runs as high among poets, musicians and their adherents, at Vienna as elsewhere. Metastasio and Hasse, may be said, to be at the head of one of the principal sects; and Calsabigi and Gluck of another. The first, regarding all innovations as quackery, adhere to the ancient form of the musical drama, in which the poet and musician claim equal attention from an audience; the bard in the recitatives and narrative parts; and the composer in the airs, duos and choruses. The second party depend more on theatrical effects, propriety of character, simplicity of diction, and of musical execution, than on, what they style flowery description, superfluous similes, sententious and cold morality, on one side, with tiresome symphonies, and long divisions, on the other.

Having always been one of the most popular composers, Hasse was probably not happy to find himself rejected by progressive factions. After hearing a reportedly well-received performance of his oratorio *S Elena al Calvario* by the Tonkünstler Sozietät, he left Vienna to retire to Venice. He spent his last decade composing sacred music, revising earlier works and teaching.

Hasse had invested money in the Incurabili, but it became insolvent in 1777; this was probably the Venetian bankruptcy in which (according to the *Musikalischer Almanach für Deutschland* of 1784) Hasse lost much of his wealth. On 4 November 1781 Faustina died, after a long illness. On 20 September 1782 Hasse made his will (*I-Vas*), in which he wrote: 'As regards my musical papers, if the Lord God grant me yet a little time on earth, I will put them in better order'. He died 15 months later after suffering severe arthritis. He was virtually forgotten in Venice until F. S. Kandler financed a gravestone in S Marcuola, where Hasse is buried, and wrote a biography in 1820.

7. MUSICAL STYLE AND REPUTATION. The German-born Hasse's central place in Italian opera represents one of the most intriguing chapters in 18th-century musical history. The popularity of his operas in Naples, Venice and Dresden recommended him to all other operatic capitals. When in the 1760s he became an important influence at the Vienna court, the excellence of his achievements seemed to find its ultimate recognition. His music served several generations of singers as a touchstone for their abilities.

Melody is certainly the most important element of Hasse's music. Clear contrapuntal textures and transparent orchestration support it with elegance. Hasse's abridged da capo arias, and especially his through-composed arias and duets (as in *Piramo e Tisbe*), recall his settings for solo voice of liturgical texts, such as Marian antiphons, that do not easily permit the repetition of music after contrasting passages with different texts. That Hasse was able to set medieval Latin poetry with irregular verse lines as though it conformed to the rules of 18th-century Italian prosody was no small achievement; the sacred works taught him how to compose without relying on the da capo form to ensure structural balance and clarity. Towards the end of his career his arias grew longer and more complicated rhythmically, but never less lyrical.

Hasse chose the keys for his arias with great care. The sinfonia is usually in the same key as those arias and passages within recitatives that deal with the central issue or action of the drama. D major often appears in this role. Other keys identify the real or pretended mental state of the characters. C and B♭, for instance, express aristocratic decorum – the former often with trumpets, the latter with flutes – while E♭ represents the nobility of sentiment appropriate to protestations of virtue. Simple, honest feelings (whether good or evil) and behaviour usually associated with the non-aristocrat are presented in F and G, while A major expresses sensuous love and E major intense anguish. In *Piramo e Tisbe* Hasse even turned to B major for the lovers' painful death. Arias rarely begin in minor keys;

the minor mode functions chiefly in the *B* section of a da capo aria, but its choice there seems to determine the major key selected for the aria as a whole. G, D and A minor generally express sadness, but C and F minor add fear and even notions of the supernatural (as in *Artaserse*, 1730, and *Cleofide*, 1731).

After his death, Hasse's operas were quickly forgotten. His sacred music was performed only sporadically in Berlin, Leipzig and Vienna; it was only in Dresden that his liturgical works were given regularly well into the 20th century. In 1774, G. B. Mancini claimed that Hasse was 'padre della musica'; only now is his mastery of musical invention being rediscovered.

The autograph scores of his operas, to which he referred in his will, went to the Milan Conservatory; the *Allgemeine musikalische Zeitung* reported their acquisition on 23 July 1817. Manuscript copies survive with corrections in Hasse's hand (*D-Dlb*). The largest group of letters are the 97 to G. M. Ortes (*I-Vmc*); others too are extant (*A- Wn, D-Dla, I-Moe, Rsc*).

See also ALCIDE AL BIVIO; ARTASERSE (ii); ATTILIO REGOLO; CLEOFIDE; PIRAMO E TISBE; RUGGIERO; SIROE (ii); and TRIONFO DI CLELIA, IL.

opere serie in three acts unless otherwise stated

Antioco (B. Feind, after A. Zeno and P. Pariati), Brunswick, Hof, 11 Aug 1721, 6 arias *D-SWl*

Antonio e Cleopatra (serenata, 2, F. Ricciardi), C. Carmignano estate, nr Naples, Sept 1725, *A-Wn*

Il Sesostrate (A. Carasale, after Pariati), Naples, S Bartolomeo, 13 May 1726, rev. 28 Aug 1726, *A-Wgm*, arias *D-MÜs, I-Nc, US-Wc*

La Semele, o sia La richiesta fatale (serenata, 2, Ricciardi), Naples, aut. 1726, *A-Wgm*

L'Astarto (Zeno and Pariati), Naples, S Bartolomeo, Dec 1726, *I-MC*

Gerone tiranno di Siracusa (after A. Aureli), Naples, S Bartolomeo, 19 Nov 1727, *A-Wn, I-Mc** (Acts 2 and 3), *MC*, arias *Nc*

Enea in Caonia (serenata, 2, L. M. Stampiglia), Naples, 1727, *Nc*

Attalo, re di Bitinia (F. Silvani), Naples, S Bartolomeo, May 1728, *D-Dlb* (sinfonia), *I-MC, Vnm*

L'Ulderica, Naples, S Bartolomeo, 29 Jan 1729, arias and duets *A-Wn, D-Dlb, Hs, MÜs, GB-Lbl, I-Mc, MC, Nc, Rc*

La sorella amante [Lavinia] (commedia per musica, ?2, B. Saddumene), Naples, Nuovo or Toledo, spr. 1729, *D-Dlb**

Tigrane (Silvani), Naples, S Bartolomeo, 4 Nov 1729; rev. A. Palella, Naples, S Carlo, 4 Nov 1745; *A-Wgm*, 11 arias, duet *D-MEIr, GB-CDp* (without recits.), *Lam, T, I-Mc**

Artaserse (P. Metastasio, rev. G. Boldoni or D. Lalli), Venice, S Giovanni Grisostomo, Feb 1730, *D-MÜs, D-Cfm, Lam, Lbl* (2 copies, incl. 1734 pasticcio), *I-Mc* (Act 1), *Nc* (without recits.), *Vnm, US-Wc*; rev. Dresden, Hof, 9 Sept 1740, *A-Wn, D-B, Dlb* (2 copies, incl. vs), *Hs* (without recits.), *SWl* (sinfonia, 25 arias, parts), *F-Pc* (inc.), *US-NH, Wc*; rev. Naples, S Carlo, 20 Jan 1760, *D-Dlb, F-Pc, I-Mc, Nc, P-La* (2 copies), *US-Wc*; *A-Wgm, Wn, B-Bc, D-LEm, LEmi, GB-Lbl, I-MC* (Acts 1 and 3), *US-NH*

Dalisa (Lalli, after N. Minato), Venice, S Samuele, May 1730, arias and duets *A-Wn, D-Dlb, Mbs, MÜs, Rtt, F-Pc, GB-Ob, I-MC*

Arminio [1st version] (A. Salvi), Milan, Regio Ducal, 28 Aug 1730, arias *A-Wn, B-Bc, D-Dlb, Mbs, MÜs, F-Pn, GB-Lbl, Ob, I-MC*

Ezio (Metastasio), Naples, S Bartolomeo, aut. 1730, *GB-Lbl*; rev. Dresden, Hof, 20 Jan 1755, *B-Br, D-Dlb, US-Wc; A-Wn, B-Bc* (2 copies, incl. vs), *D-As* (2 copies), *B* (without recits.; 2 copies, incl. vs), *Dl* (without recits.), *LEmi, WER* (vs), *WRz, F-Pc* (without recits.), *GB-Lbl, I-Mc* (?1755)

Cleofide [Alessandro nell'Indie] (M. Boccardi, after Metastasio), Dresden, Hof, 13 Sept 1731, *D-B* (2 copies, 1 without recits.), *Dlb* (2 copies, incl. vs), *LEm, Mbs* (without recits.), *F-Pc*; rev. Venice, S Giovanni Grisostomo, 4 Nov 1736, *GB-Lbl*; rev. Venice, carn. 1738 and carn. 1743, *B-Bc, D-HAmi, Rtt* (sinfonia parts), *F-Pc* (without recits.), *GB-CDp*, arias of 1738 *I-Vnm*

Catone in Utica (Metastasio), Turin, Regio, 26 Dec 1731, arias *D-Dlb, Mbs, MÜs, F-Pc, Pn, GB-Lbl, I-Mc, MC*

Cajo Fabricio (after Zeno), Rome, Capranica, 12 Jan 1732, *D-MÜs, F-Pc, US-Cn*; rev. Naples, S Bartolomeo, wint. 1733; rev.

Dresden, Hof, 8 July 1734, ?*A-Wgm*, *D-Dlb*; as Pirro, Jaromeritz, Schloss Questenberg, aut. 1734, *I-Mc**; rev. Berlin, Hof, Sept 1766, *D-B*; *B-Bc*, *Br*, *D-B* (addl sinfonia), *Hs* (1733 London pasticcio), *I-Vc** (after 1740), *US-Wc*

Demetrio (Metastasio), Venice, S Giovanni Grisostomo, Jan 1732, *I-Vnm*; as Cleonice, Vienna, ?court, Feb 1734; as Demetrio, Venice, S Cassiano, carn. 1737; as Demetrio, Dresden, Hof, 8 Feb 1740, *B-Bc*, *D-Dlb*, *LEmi*; as Cleonice, Venice, S Angelo, 1740; as Demetrio, Venice, S Giovanni Grisostomo, carn. 1747; *A-Wn* (1739 Reggio pasticcio), *D-B* (sinfonia), *Dlb* (vs, parts), *F- Pc*

Euristeo (Lalli, after Zeno), Venice, S Samuele, May 1732 [pasticcio], *B-Bc*, *D-Dlb* (with sinfonia), *F-Pc* (1733, Warsaw)

Issipile (Metastasio), Naples, S Bartolomeo, 1 Oct 1732, 14 arias *D-MÜs*; rev. Leo, Naples, S Carlo, 19 Dec 1742; rev. Cafaro, Naples, S Carlo, 26 Dec 1763; *A-Wgm* (Acts 1 and 2), *I-Mc* (Act 1), *MC*, *Tco* (inc.)

Siroe re di Persia (Metastasio), Bologna, Malvezzi, 2 May 1733, *A-Wn*, *D-Dlb*, *F-Pc*, *GB-Lbl* (without recits.); rev. Naples, S Carlo, 4 Nov 1747; rev. Dresden, Hof, carn. 1763, *D-B*, *Dlb*, *A-Wn* (R1977: IOB, xxxiii), *B-Bc* (2 copies), *D-B* (1763, Warsaw), *Dlb* (sinfonia score and parts), *GB-Cfm* (14 arias), *Lbl*, *Lcm* (7 arias), *I-Mc** (1762, Warsaw), *Nc* (recits.), *Vnm*, *S-Skma* (without recits.), *US-Wc* (1763)

Sei tu, Lidippe, ò il sole (serenata, 1), Dresden, 4 Aug 1734, *D-Dlb*

Tito Vespasiano [La clemenza di Tito] (Metastasio), Pesaro, Pubblico, 24 Sept 1735, 3 arias *A-Wn*; rev. Dresden, Hof, 17 Jan 1738, *B-Bc*, *Br*, *D-Dlb*, *DS*, *US-AA*; rev. Naples, S Carlo, 20 Jan 1759, *D-Dlb*, *I-Mc* (?2 copies, incl. autograph), *Nc* (2 inc. copies); *B-Bc* (3 copies), *D-B* (2 copies and addl sinfonia), *Hs*, *LEmi*, *Mbs* (1742, Berlin), *SWl* (sinfonia, 25 arias, parts), *F-Pc*, *GB-Lcm* (2 copies), *I-Mc*, *Nc* (1737), *PLcon*, *Rc* (2 copies), *P-La* (2 copies), *RU-SPtob*; *S-Skma* (without recits.), *US-Cn* (dated 1743), *Wc*

Senocrita (5, S. B. Pallavicino), Dresden, Hof, 27 Feb 1737, *B-Bc*, *Br*, *D-B*, *Dlb*, *HAmi*, *LEm* (without recits.), *Mbs*, *SWl*, *GB-Ob*, *S-Skma*, *US-NH*

Atalanta (Pallavicino), Dresden, Hof, 26 July 1737, *D-B* (16 arias), *Dlb* (1750), *LEm*, *LEmi*, *I-Mc**

Asteria (favola pastorale, Pallavicino), Dresden, Hof, 3 Aug 1737, *B-Bc*, *D-B* (20 arias, addl sinfonia), *Dlb*, *DS*, *Mbs*, *F-Pc*

Irene (Pallavicino), Dresden, Hof, 8 Feb 1738, *D-B* (without recits.) (1738, no sinfonia), *Dlb* (1738, with sinfonia score and parts), *LEmi*, *US-Wc* (without recits.)

Alfonso (5, Pallavicino), Dresden, Hof, 11 May 1738, *B-Bc*, *D-Dlb* (score and parts), *DS*, *LEmi*, *MEIr*, *US-Bp*

Viriate (Lalli, after Metastasio: *Siface*), Venice: S Giovanni Grisostomo, carn. 1739, *I-Mc*

Numa Pompilio (Pallavicino), Hubertusburg, nr Dresden, 7 Oct 1741, *B-Bc*, *D-B* (incl. int Pimpinella e Marcantonio), *Dlb* (4 copies: 1741, 1743, vs and full scores), *SWl* (sinfonia, 17 arias), *I-Mc* (autograph Acts 1 and 2), *PLcon* (incl. int Pimpinella e Marcantonio), *US-AA* (without recits.; 3 copies, 2 inc.)

Lucio Papirio (Zeno), Dresden, Hof, 18 Jan 1742, *D-Dlb* (score, parts, addl sinfonia), *LEmi* (2 copies); rev. G. de Majo, Naples, S Carlo, 4 Nov 1746; rev. Hasse or Graun, Berlin, Hof, 24 Jan 1766, *B-Bc*, *D-B* (incl. undated score, vs)

Asilio d'amore (festa teatrale, 1, Metastasio), Naples, ?court, July 1742, *B-Bc*, *D-Dlb* (2 copies, addl sinfonia), *HAmi*, *LEmi*, *F-Pc*, *I-Mc**, *Nc*

Didone abbandonata (Metastasio, rev. Algarotti), Hubertusburg, 7 Oct 1742, *D-Dlb*; rev. N. Logroscino, Naples, S Carlo, 20 Jan 1744; rev. Berlin, Hof, 29 Dec 1752, *DS*; rev. Versailles, court, 28 Aug 1753, *F-Pn**; *A-Wn*, *B-Bc*, *D-B* (without recits.; 3 copies, incl. vs, full score with parts), *LEm* (3 copies, incl. vs), *SWl*, *F-Pc*, *GB-CDp*, *Lcm*, *Ouf* (5 arias), *I-Mc* (score, addl sinfonia), *Nc*, *Rc* (inc.), *Vc* (without recits.; Dresden), *S-Uu* (vs, without recits.), *US-Wc*

Endimione (festa teatrale, 2, Metastasio), ? Naples, July 1743, *D-Dlb*

Antigono (Metastasio), Hubertusburg, 10 Oct 1743, and Dresden, Hof, 20 Jan 1744; rev. Palella, Naples, S Carlo, 19 Dec 1744; rev. as Alessandro, re d'Epiro, 1753; *A-Wn*, *B-Bc* (score, addl sinfonia), *Lc*, *D-B* (without recits.), *Dlb* (score, parts, vs), *LEmi*, *F-Pc* (vs), *GB-Lbl* (Dresden), *Ouf* (arias), *I-FERc*, *Mc* (arias), *US-R*, *Wc*

Ipermestra (Metastasio), Vienna, court, 8 Jan 1744, *A-Wgm*, *Wn*, *D-Dlb*, *I-Mc*; rev. Palella, Naples, S Carlo, 20 Jan 1746; rev. Hubertusburg, 7 Oct 1751, *D-B* (score, addl sinfonia), *Dlb* (2 copies), *LEm* (Act 2), *LEmi*, *ROu*, *F-Pc*; *A-Wn* (vs), *B-Bc* (full score, vs), *F-Pc* (without recits.; 2 copies: 1757, n.d.), *I-Mc**, *S-*

Skma (score, addl sinfonia)

Semiramide riconosciuta (Metastasio), Naples, S Carlo, 4 Nov 1744 and/or Venice, S Giovanni Grisostomo, 26 Dec 1744; rev. Dresden, Hof, 11 Jan 1747, *B-Bc*, *D-Dlb* (score, parts, addl sinfonia), *GB-Lbl*; rev. Warsaw, Imperial, 7 Oct 1760; *B-Bc* (2 copies), *Br*, *D-B* (without recits.; 2 copies), *LEmi*, *W*, *F-Pc* (without recits.; 2 copies), *I-Bc*, *Vc**, *S-Skma* (without recits.; addl sinfonia), *US-Wc*

Arminio [2nd version] (G. C. Pasquini), Dresden, Hof, 7 Oct 1745, *D-Dlb*, *W*, *I-Mc*, *Nc*; rev. Dresden, Hof, 8 Jan 1753, *D-Dlb*; *B-Bc*, *Br*, *D-B* (2 copies: 1747, n.d., addl sinfonia), *HAmi*, *LEmi*, *Mbs*, *F-Pc*, *GB-CDp*, *I-Mc* (score, parts for Act 1), *S-Skma* (3 copies, addl sinfonia), *US-Wc*; ed. in EDM, 1st ser., xxvii–xxviii (1957–66)

La spartana generosa, ovvero Archidamia (Pasquini), Dresden, Hof, 14 June 1747, *B-Bc*, *D-B* (sinfonia parts), *Dlb*, *Hs*, *LEmi*, *SWl* (sinfonia, 22 arias, duet, parts), *F-Pc* (without recits.)

Leucippo (favola pastorale, Pasquini), Hubertusburg, 7 Oct 1747, *D-Dlb*, *GB-Lbl* (without recits.); rev. Venice, S Samuele, May 1749; rev. Dresden, Zwinger, 7 Jan 1751, *D-B* (without recits.; 2 copies, incl. vs); rev. Berlin, Hof, 7 Jan 1765; *A-Wgm*, *B-Bc* (2 copies), *D-B* (without recits.; 2 copies, 1 with autograph corrections, sinfonia parts), *Dlb* (2 vs), *LEmi*, *MÜs*, *W*, *SWl*, *I-Mc**, *Nc*, *Vc* (sinfonia), *S-Skma*, *St*, *US-BE*, *Cn**, *Wc*

Demofoonte (Metastasio), Dresden, Hof, 9 Feb 1748, *B-Br*, *D-Dlb* (without recits.) (2 copies), *I-Nc*; rev. Venice, S Giovanni Grisostomo, carn. 1749; *Vc* (inc.), *Vnm*; rev. Naples, S Carlo, 4 Nov 1758, *D-Dlb* (addl sinfonia parts), *F-Pc*, *I-Mc* (Acts 1 and 3), *Vc* (Acts 1 and 2); *B-Bc* (3 copies), *D-B* (2 copies), *HAmi*, *LEm* (without recits.), *WRz*, *F-Pc* (without recits.; 4 copies, incl. 1 ?1748, Dresden), *GB-Lbl* (without recits.; ?1748), *Lcm*, *I-Mc**, *Vc*, *US-Wc* (2 copies)

Il natal di Giove (serenata, 1, Metastasio), Hubertusburg, 3 Aug or 7 Oct 1749, *B-Bc*, *Br* (1756), *D-B* (1749, addl sinfonia parts), *Dlb* (2 copies 1749), *LEmi*, *Mbs* (1750), *F-Pc* (1750), *I-Mc**

Attilio Regolo (Metastasio), Dresden, Hof, 12 Jan 1750, *A-Wn*, *B-Bc* (2 copies), *Br*, *D-B* (2 copies, addl sinfonia), *Dl* (2 copies 1750, incl. vs, parts), *LEmi*, *RH* (arias), *W*, *F-Pc*, *I-Mc**, *S-Skma* (Act 2, addl sinfonia), *US-R*, *Wc* (1750)

Ciro riconosciuto (Metastasio), Dresden, Hof, 20 Jan 1751, *A-Wgm*, *Wn*, *B-Bc*, *Br*, *D-B* (without recits.; 2 copies 1751, addl sinfonia), *BS*, *Dlb* (1751 score, parts, addl sinfonia), *LEmi*, *Mbs*, *RH* (sinfonia), *Sl* (1752, Stuttgart), *F-Pn*, *GB-CDp*, *GB-Lbl* (inc. full score, sinfonia), *I-Mc**, *S-Skma* (score, addl sinfonia), *US-R*, *U*, *Wc* (sinfonia)

Adriano in Siria (Metastasio), Dresden, Hof, 17 Jan 1752, *A-Wn* (Act 1), *B-Bc* (3 copies, incl. vs), *D-B*, *BD* (without recits.), *Dl* (without recits.; 2 copies), *Mbs* (2 copies, incl. vs), *ROu*, *I-Mc**, *I-MOe* (1762), *S-Skma* (without recits.), *Uu*, *US-Wc*

Solimano (G. A. Migliavacca), Dresden, Hof, 5 Feb 1753, *F-Pc*, *GB-Lbl* (without recits.); rev. Dresden, Hof, 7 Jan 1754; *B-Bc* (2 copies), *Br*, *D-B* (2 copies, incl. vs, parts, addl sinfonia), *BD* (vs), *Dlb* (2 copies, parts), *DS* (without recits.), *HAmi*, *LEm* (2 copies, incl. vs), *Mbs* (2 copies, incl. vs), *ROu* (without recits.), *F-Pc* (2 copies), *I-Mc**, *S-Skma* (without recits.; incl. vs)

L'eroe cinese (Metastasio), Hubertusburg, 7 Oct 1753; rev. ?Hasse, Potsdam, 18 July 1773, arias *GB-Lbl*; *B-Bc*, *Br*, *D-B*, *Bs*, *Dlb* (2 copies, incl. vs, parts, addl sinfonia), *LEmi*, *F-Pc*, *I-Mc**, *US-Wc* (vs)

Artemisia (Migliavacca), Dresden, Hof, 6 Feb 1754; *B-Bc*, *Br*, *D-B* (without recits.) (3 copies, incl. 1754, ?1786, Berlin, addl sinfonia parts), *LEmi*, *I-Mc**, *S-Skma*, *US-AA* (without recits.)

Il re pastore (Metastasio), Hubertusburg, Hof, 7 Oct 1755, *D-Dlb*; rev. Warsaw, Imperial, 7 Oct 1762, or Vienna, 1760, *Dlb* (parts); *A-Wgm*, *B-Bc* (3 copies, incl. vs, addl sinfonia), *Br*, *D-B* (2 copies, 2 addl sinfonia), *Bs*, *BD* (parts), *HAmi*, *LEm* (without recits.) (2 copies), *ROu*, *F-Pc* (2 copies, incl. vs), *GB-Lcm*, *I-Mc**, *S-Skma* (vs), *US-NYp* (vs), *Wc*

L'Olimpiade (Metastasio), Dresden, Hof, 16 Feb 1756, *A-Wn*, *D-B*, *Dlb*; rev. Warsaw, Imperial, carn. 1766; rev. Turin, Regio, 26 Dec 1766; *A-Wgm*, *Wn* (inc.), *B-Bc* (3 copies), *Br*, *D-Dlb* (1762, Warsaw, parts), *HAmi*, *LEm* (without recits.; 2 copies, incl. vs), *F-Pc* (2 copies, incl. vs), *Pn* (1765 revival), *GB-Lbl*, *I-Mc**, *Tn*, vs *US-Bp*

Nitteti (Metastasio), Venice, S Benedetto, Jan 1758, *D-Dlb*, *F-Pc*, *I-Vnm* (Acts 1 and 3); rev. Vienna, ?court, 1762, *F-Pc*; *A-Wgm*, *B-Bc* (3 copies, incl. 2 vs), *D-B* (1759, Warsaw), *Dlb*, *LEmi*, *Mbs*

Il sogno di Scipione (azione teatrale, 1, Metastasio), ? Warsaw, 7 Oct 1758, lost or possibly never composed [Fürstenau]

Achille in Sciro (Metastasio), Naples, S Carlo, 4 Nov 1759, *D-Dlb*, *F-Pc*, *GB-Lcm*, *I-Mc**, *P-La* (2 copies)

Alcide al bivio (festa teatrale, 1, Metastasio), Vienna, Redoutensaal, 8 Oct 1760 (Leipzig, 1763; without recits.); *A-Wgm*, *Wn* (3 copies), *B-Bc* (3 copies, incl. 2 vs), *Br*, *D-B* (score, parts, addl sinfonia), *Dlb* (score, parts), *DS*, *HAmi*, *LEm* (sinfonia), *GB-Lbl*, *I-Mc* (*R*1983: IOB, lxxxi [part autograph]), *MOe*, *Nc* (1770), *PAc*, *Tn*, *P-La*, *US-CA*, *Wc*

Zenobia (Metastasio), Vienna, ?court, carn. 1761, *B-Bc,*, *D-B* (parts), *Dlb** (1761, Vienna), *LEmi*, *F-Pc*, *I-Mc** (1761, Warsaw), *Nc*

Il trionfo di Clelia (Metastasio), Vienna, Burg, 27 April 1762, *D-B*, *Hs*, *Sl*, *I-MOe*; rev. G. de Majo, Naples, S Carlo, 20 Jan 1763, *P-La* (2 copies); *A-Wgm*, *Wn* (2 copies), *B-Bc* (vs), *D-Dlb**, *LEmi*, *F-Pc* (2 copies), *I-Fc*, *Mc** (*R*1981: IOB, xvi), *PAc*, *US-Bp*

Egeria (festa teatrale, 1, Metastasio), Vienna, Burg, 24 April 1764; *A-Wgm*, *Wn* (2 copies), *B-Bc* (2 copies, incl. vs), *D-Dlb*, *F-Pc*, *I-Mc**, *MOe*, *Nc*, *US-Wc* (Act 2)

Romolo ed Ersilia (Metastasio), Innsbruck, 6 Aug 1765, *A-Wgm*, *Wn* (score, parts), *B-Bc* (2 copies, incl. vs, addl sinfonia), *F-Pc*, *GB-Lbl*, *P-La* (1766, Naples), *US-AA* (vs, without recits.)

Partenope (festa teatrale, 2, Metastasio), Vienna, Burg, 9 Sept 1767, *A-Wn*, *B-Bc*, *I-Nc*; rev. Berlin, Sans-Souci, 18 July 1775; *B-Bc* (vs), *D-Dlb*, *I-Mc**

Piramo e Tisbe (int tragico, 2, M. Coltellini), Vienna, Burg, Nov 1768; rev. Vienna, Laxenburg, Sept 1770, *A-Wn* (2 copies), *B-Bc* (4 copies, incl. 1 Ger.), *Br*, *Lc*, *D-B* (2 copies: 1771, Berlin; parts, addl sinfonia), *Dlb* 2 copies, addl sinfonia, *DS* (1769, addl sinfonia), *Mbs*, *WRz* (parts), *F-Pc*, *GB-Lbl* (1769), *I-Mc* (3 copies, incl. autograph), *MC* (Act 2), *Nc* (2 copies, 1 inc.), *PLcon* (2 copies), *S-Skma*, *US-Cn*, *Wc* (2 copies, incl. vs)

Il Ruggiero, ovvero L'eroica gratitudine (Metastasio, after L. Ariosto: *Orlando furioso*), Milan, Regio Ducal, 16 Oct 1771, *A-Wn*, *D-B* (sinfonia), *Dlb*, *GB-Lbl* (without recits.), *I-Mc**, *Nc*, *P-La*, *US-Wc*; ed. in Concentus musicus, i (Cologne, 1973)

Numerous arias, mainly performed in pasticcios, published in 18th-century anthologies

INTERMEZZOS

Miride e Damari (2), perf. with Il Sesostrate, Naples, S Bartolomeo, 13 May 1726; *A-Wgm* (?inc.), *US-Wc*

Larinda e Vanesio [L'artigiano gentiluomo, L'artigiano galantuomo, Il bottegaro gentiluomo] (3, A. Salvi and/or Carasale, after Molière: *Le bourgeois gentilhomme*), perf. with Astarto, Naples, S Bartolomeo, Dec 1726; rev. Dresden, court, 8 July 1734; ? rev. Venice, S Angelo, carn. 1739; *B-Bc*, *D-Dlb*, *MÜs*, *I-MC*, *Rc*; ed. in Collezione Settecentesca Bettarini, vii (Milan, 1973), and in RRMCE ix (Madison, WI, 1979)

Grilletta e Porsugnacco [Monsieur de Porsugnacco] (3, after Molière: *Monsieur de Pourceaugnac*), perf. with Albinoni's L'incostanza schernita, Venice, S Samuele, May 1727; ? rev. Naples, S Bartolomeo, 19 Nov 1727; rev. Dresden, court, 4 Aug 1747; *B-Bc*, *D-Dlb*, *MÜs*, *I-Mc*, *Rc*

Carlotta e Pantaleone [La finta tedesca] (3), perf. with Attalo, re di Bitinia, Naples, S Bartolomeo, May 1728; ? rev. Naples, S Bartolomeo, carn. 1734; rev. Potsdam, 1749; arias and duet *D-MÜs*, *I-Nc*

Scintilla e Don Tabarano [La contadina, Don Tabarrano, Der in sich selbst verliebte Narcissus] (2, Saddumene), perf. with P. Scarlatti's Il Clitarco, Naples, S Bartolomeo, aut. 1728; ? rev. Venice, S Angelo, aut. 1731; rev. Dresden, 26 July 1737; ? rev. Dresden, 1745 and ?11 Jan 1747; *A-Wn*, *B-Bc*, *D-B* (?autograph), *Dlb*, *Hs* (inc.), *MÜs*, *SWl*, *W*, *F-Pc* (?pasticcio), *I-Bc*, *Fc*, *MC*, *PAc*, *Rc*, *US-Wc*

Merlina e Galoppo [La fantesca, Il capitano Galoppo] (3, Saddumene), perf. with L'Ulderica, Naples, S Bartolomeo, 29 Jan 1729; ? rev. Venice, S Angelo, aut. 1741; rev. Dresden, 1749; *A-Wn*, *D-MÜs* (?inc.), *Hs*, *WRI*, *I-MC*, *Nc*, *PLcon*

Dorilla e Balanzone [La serva scaltra, La moglie a forza] (3), perf. with Tigrane, Naples, S Bartolomeo, 4 Nov 1729; rev. Venice, 1732; *A-Wgm*, *D-MÜs*, *GB-Lam*, *Rc*, *US-Wc*; ed. in Collezione Settecentesca Bettarini, xvi (Milan, 1985)

Lucilla e Pandolfo [Il tutore], perf. with Ezio, Naples, S Bartolomeo, aut. 1730; perf. with Alfonso, rev. Dresden, May 1738; ? rev. Venice, 1739; rev. Dresden, 1755; *B-Bc*, *D-Dlb*, *Mbs*, *WRI*, *GB-Cfm*, *Lcm*, *I-MC*

Arrighetta e Cespuglio [La donna accorta] (2), Naples, c1730, ?lost

Pimpinella e Marcantonio (1), perf. with Numa Pompilio, Hubertusburg, 7 Oct 1741; ? rev. Dresden, 14 Jan 1743; ? rev. Versailles, 28 Aug 1753; *B-Bc*, *D-B*, *Dlb* (Act 1), *I-Nc* (duet), *PLcon* (Act 3), *US-AA* (2 copies)

Rimario e Grilantea, 1739 or 3 Nov 1741; *B-Bc*, *D-Dlb* (2 copies, incl. vs)

Doubtful works: Cipollina e Moscatello [Il bevitore], St Petersburg, 1746, Dresden, 1747, Potsdam, 1749; Drusilla e Strambone [La vedova ingegnosa, ovvero Il medico ignorante], Hamburg, 1743, Venice, 1746, Prague, 1747, Dresden, 1747, Hamburg, 1772; Il giocatore, Dresden, 1746, Frankfurt, 1755

*

BurneyFI; BurneyGN; BurneyH; GerberL

J. A. Scheibe: *Critischer Musikus* (Leipzig, 2/1745), 148, 315

F. W. Marpurg: *Historisch-kritische Beyträge zur Aufnahme der Musik* (Berlin, 1754–6), i, 228; ii, 475

P. J. Grosley de Troyes: *Nouveaux mémoires, ou Observations sur l'Italie* (London, 1764; Eng. trans., 1769), ii, 54; iii, 60, 95

J. A. Hiller: *Anweisung zum musikalisch-richtigen Gesange* (Leipzig, 1774)

G. J. Vogler: *Betrachtungen der Mannheimer Tonschule*, i (Mannheim, 1778), 159ff, 306–7

J. A. Hiller: *Über Alt und Neu in der Musik* (Leipzig, 1787), 11

J. A. Hasse and J. A. Hiller: *Beyträge zur wahren Kirchenmusik* (Leipzig, 2/1791)

F. S. Kandler: *Cenni storico-critici intorno alla vita ed alle opere del cel. Gio. Adolfo Hasse detto il Sassone* (Venice, 1820)

M. Fürstenau: *Zur Geschichte der Musik und des Theaters am Hofe zu Dresden* (Dresden, 1861–2), ii, 173, 204ff, 375ff

G. M. Urbani de Gheltof: *La 'nuova Sirena' e il 'caro Sassone': note biografiche* (Venice, 1890)

H. Kretzschmar: 'Aus Deutschlands italienischer Zeit', *JbMP 1901*, 47–61

M. Seiffert: 'Zur Biographie J. A. Hasse's', *SIMG*, vii (1905–6), 129–31

C. Mennicke: *Hasse und die Brüder Graun als Symphoniker nebst Biographien und thematischen Katalogen* (Leipzig, 1906)

B. Zeller: *Das Recitativo accompagnato in den Opern J. A. Hasses* (Halle, 1911)

O. G. T. Sonneck: 'Die drei Fassungen des Hasse'schen Artaserse', *SIMG*, xiv (1912–13), 226–42

R. Gerber: *Der Operntypus J. A. Hasse und seine textlichen Grundlagen* (Leipzig, 1925)

M. Högg: *Die Gesangskunst der Faustina Hasse und das Sängerinnenwesen ihrer Zeit in Deutschland* (Königsbrück, 1931)

R. Engländer: 'Dresdner Musikleben und Dresdener Instrumentalpflege in der Zeit zwischen Hasse und Weber', *ZMw*, xiv (1931–2), 410–20

A. Yorke-Long: *Music at Court* (London, 1954)

W. Vetter: 'Italiens Musik im Lichte von Dichtung und bildender Kunst', *DJbM*, viii (1964), 91–3

U. Prota-Giurleo: 'Notizie biografiche intorno ad alcuni musicisti d'oltralpe a Napoli nel Settecento', *AnMc*, no.2 (1965), 124–34

S. Hansell: 'Sacred Music at the Incurabili in Venice at the Time of J. A. Hasse', *JAMS*, xxiii (1970), 282–301, 505–21

O. Landmann: *Quellenstudien zum intermezzo comico per musica und zu seiner Geschichte in Dresden* (diss., U. of Rostock, 1972)

K. Hortschansky: Preface to *Ruggiero*, Concentus musicus, i (Cologne, 1973)

K.-H. Viertel: 'Neue Dokumente zu Leben und Werk J. A. Hasses', *AnMc*, no.12 (1973), 209–23

D. Heartz: 'Raaff's Last Aria: a Mozartian Idyll in the Spirit of Hasse', *MQ*, lx (1974), 517–43

F. L. Millner: 'Hasse and London's Opera of the Nobility', *MR*, xxxv (1974), 240–46

R. Strohm: 'Handels Pasticci', *AnMc*, no.14 (1974), 208–67

F. Degrada: 'Aspetti gluckiani nell'ultimo Hasse', *Chigiana*, xxix–xxx (1975), 309–29

D. Heartz: 'Hasse, Galuppi and Metastasio', *Venezia e il melodramma nel settecento: Venice 1973–5*, i, 309–39

R. Strohm: 'Hasse, Scarlatti, Rolli', *AnMc*, no.15 (1975), 220–57

——: *Italienische Opernarien des frühen Settecento (1720–1730)*, *AnMc*, no.16 (1976)

R. Monelle: 'Recitative and Dramaturgy in the Dramma per Musica', *ML*, lix (1978), 245–67

F. L. Millner: *The Operas of Johann Adolf Hasse* (Ann Arbor, 1979)

R. Strohm: *Die italienische Oper im 18. Jahrhundert* (Wilhelmshaven, 1979), 113, 198

C. E. Troy: *The Comic Intermezzo: a Study in the History of 18th-Century Italian Opera* (Ann Arbor, 1979)

G. Cummings: 'Reminiscence and Recall in Three Early Settings of Metastasio's *Alessandro nell' Indie*', *PRMA*, cix (1982–3), 80–104

F. Lippmann, ed.: *Colloquium Johann Adolf Hasse und die Musik seiner Zeit: Siena 1983, AnMc,* no.25 (1987)
H. Lühning: '*Titus*'-Vertonungen im 18. *Jahrhundert: Untersuchungen zur Tradition der Opera seria von Hasse bis Mozart, AnMc,* no.20 (1983) [whole issue]
F. Lippmann: 'Motivische Arbeit bei Hasse', *AnMc,* no.22 (1984), 197–208
R. Strohm: *Essays on Handel and Italian Opera* (Cambridge, 1985)
M. T. Muraro, ed.: *Metastasio e il mondo musicale* (Florence, 1986) [incl. J. Joly: 'Il fragore delle armi nella Nitteti', 99–132; K. Hortschansky: 'Die Rolle des Sängers im Demofoonte', 207–34; S. Mamy: 'Les révisions pour Giovanni Carestini du rôle de Timante dans le *Demofoonte* de J. A. Hasse (Venise 1749)', 235–74; D. Heartz: 'Metastasio "maestro dei maestri di cappella drammatici"', 315–38] SVEN HANSELL

Hasselmans, Louis (*b* Paris, 15 July 1878; *d* S Juan, Puerto Rico, 27 Dec 1957). French conductor. After study at the Paris Conservatoire he played the cello in the Capet Quartet (1893–1909). He made his début as a conductor in 1905 and worked at the Opéra-Comique, 1909–11. His North American début was in Montreal in 1911 and he conducted at the Chicago Opera Association, 1918–19. He was in Paris until 1922; that year he conducted *Faust* at the Metropolitan, and in the next 14 years he directed 378 performances of 14 French operas in New York, including the local premières of *Pelléas et Mélisande* (1925), *L'heure espagnole* (1925) and Massenet's *Don Quichotte* (1926).
DAVID CUMMINGS

Hatrík, Juraj (*b* Orkucany, 1 May 1941). Slovak composer. He studied with Moyzes in Bratislava. A feature of most of his theatre works is that the instrumentalists take part in the action. *Adamove deti* ('Adam's Children'; 1973–4, revised 1989–90) is an allegorical morality play consisting of seven staged madrigals. *Šťastný princ* ('The Happy Prince'), with a Slovak and English text after Oscar Wilde's tale, was first performed at the Piešťany summer music festival on 14 July 1981. More significant are his children's operas. *Janko Polienko*, written in 1976 but given its first (concert) performance only at the New Composition Weeks in Bratislava on 13 February 1987, is scored for two children's choirs and two soloists. The music, distinguished by a refined simplicity, makes use of nursery rhymes and folktunes; structurally the opera is a rondo. *Mechúrik Koščúrik s kamarátmi* ('Mechúrik Koščúrik and his Friends', 1980), to a text by Milan Rúfus, is a Singspiel for speaker and children's voices with chamber ensemble. Each character has his own instrument (generally a folk instrument) and individual melody. The director Marián Chudovský made this into a television film (1983–4), in which the three-part form was filled out with a prose prologue and epilogue.

I. Vajda: *Slovenská opera* (Bratislava, 1988), 182–5, 224, 242
IGOR VAJDA

Hatto, Jeanne (*b* St Armour, 30 Jan 1879; *d* Paris, March 1958). French soprano. She studied in Lyons and at the Paris Conservatoire. Her début at the Opéra was as Brunehild in Reyer's *Sigurd* (1899). Her powerful voice and commanding stage presence made her a favourite in the dramatic repertory: Elisabeth, Sieglinde, Marguerite, Rameau's Telaira (*Castor et Pollux*) and Diana (*Hippolyte et Aricie*), Donna Elvira and Salammbô in the opera by Reyer. She sang in the premières of Saint-Saëns' *Les barbares* and Leroux' *Astarté* at the Opéra (1901), and at Brussels in 1903 took part

in the posthumous première of Chausson's *Le roi Arthus*.
DAVID CUMMINGS

Hatton, John Liptrot (*b* Liverpool, 12 Oct 1809; *d* Margate, 20 Sept 1886). English composer. At 16 he was organist at three churches. He also gained experience as an actor and singer. In 1832 he moved to London, and began to compose piano pieces and songs. In 1842 he was engaged to direct the chorus at Drury Lane Theatre, where his first stage piece was performed. During this season he became friendly with the singer Staudigl, who encouraged him to write the opera *Pasqual Bruno* for Vienna (1844). One song from this work, 'Revenge', was published in England and became very popular. The *London Review* reported that his opera *Rose* 'deserves a hearty welcome after the loose scrambling productions which have of late cast ridicule on the very name of English Opera' (3 December 1864).

Hatton worked in Vienna, the USA and Stuttgart, as well as London. For most of his life he was engaged in performing, both as a pianist and as a comic singer. He was the inventor, or at least one of the earliest exponents, of a kind of popular one-man show, in which he spoke, played the piano and sang to his own accompaniment. From 1853 to 1859 he was musical director at the Princess's Theatre under Charles Kean's management, and during this period he composed and arranged incidental music for Shakespeare plays. He also wrote much vocal music.

The Queen of the Thames, or The Anglers [Uncle Grayling] (operetta, 1, E. Fitzball), London, Drury Lane, 25 Feb 1842, vs (London, 1843)
Pasqual Bruno (Fitzball, after A. Dumas (i)), Vienna, Kärntnertor, 2 March 1844, 1 song (London, 1844)
Rose, or Love's Ransom (3, H. S. Edwards), London, CG, 26 Nov 1864, vs (London, 1865)

DNB (J. A. Fuller Maitland)
W. Spark: 'John Liphot Hatton' [*sic*], *Musical Memories* (London, 1888), 309ff NICHOLAS TEMPERLEY

Hatze, Josip (*b* Split, 21 March 1879; *d* Split, 30 Jan 1959). Croatian composer. He graduated in 1902 from the Liceo Musicale in Pesaro after studying composition with Mascagni, then became a music teacher and choral conductor. Together with his contemporaries Blagoje Bersa (1873–1934) and Dora Pejačević (1885–1923), he was one of the founders of modern Croatian music; he brought fresh nuances and international experience to the Romantic tradition in Croatia, which at the turn of the century was rather conservative. The Mediterranean tradition in which he grew up and was educated gave a characteristic flavour to his compositions, which are mostly vocal with a rich, highly personal melodic style of the bel canto type. For the musical stage he left two important works: *Povratak* ('The Return'; 1, S. Tucić; Zagreb, 21 March 1911) is a musical drama in the style of the Italian *verismo*; in his lyric folk opera, *Adel i Mara* ('Adel and Mara'; B. Radica, after N. Bartulović and L. Botić; Ljubljana, 30 November 1932) Hatze tried to distinguish within the music two separate worlds – the old Dalmatian and the oriental – which clash symbolically in the tragic forbidden love of a Croatian girl and a Turkish nobleman. By the use of stylized folk elements he succeeded in creating local colour in this predominantly lyrical work. The first performance of *Povratak* in 1911, the year in which Blagoje Bersa's *Der Eisenhammer* was also first performed, as *Oganj*, in Zagreb, marked an important point in Croatian operatic history.

K. Kovačević: *Hrvatski kompozitori i njihova djela* [Croatian Composers and Their Works] (Zagreb, 1960), 180–84

J. Andreis: *Music in Croatia* (Zagreb, 1974)

——: 'Luka Botić dva puta na opernoj pozornici' [Luka Botić Twice on the Operatic Stage], *Zvuk* (1979), no.3, pp.5–18

Josip Hatze, hrvatski skladatelj [Josip Hatze, a Croatian Composer] (Zagreb, 1982) [pubn of the Music Information Centre; studies in Croatian and Eng. by K. Kovačević, S. Tuksar, M. Janaček-Buljan, A. Tomašek, K. Kos, B. Perić-Kempf, L. Županović, N. Roje, J. Bezić]   KORALJKA KOS

Haubenstock-Ramati, Roman (*b* Kraków, 27 Feb 1919). Austrian composer of Polish origin. He studied at the Kraków Conservatory (1934–8), where his composition teacher was Artur Malawski, and at the Lwów Academy of Music (1938–41) with Józef Koffler. From 1947 to 1950 he was director of music for Kraków Radio, secretary of the Polish section of the ISCM and editor of *Ruch muzyczny*. He emigrated to Israel in 1950, teaching at the Academy of Music in Tel-Aviv, and on his return to Europe seven years later immersed himself in the avant-garde movement; in 1959 he organized the first exhibition of graphic scores at Donaueschingen.

In his own works of the 1950s Haubenstock-Ramati attempted to find solutions to the problems of form that preoccupied the post-Webern serial movement, exploring in particular the possibilities of sound mobiles and collages, and the ways in which they might be juxtaposed with fully determined structures. In his two-act opera *Amerika* (1962–4), to his own libretto based on Max Brod's adaptation of Franz Kafka's novel (Berlin, Deutsche Oper, 8 October 1966), the possibilities of using such mobiles to create a multi-dimensional musical and dramatic space were most exhaustively explored. A sequence of 25 segments (two groups of 14 and 11), together with an epilogue, depicts the discovery of the New World by the 'hero' Karl Rossmann (lyric tenor), in a treatment that emphasizes simultaneity over linear chronology. Haubenstock-Ramati later experimented with music-theatre, particularly in the one-act 'anti-opéra' *La Comédie*, after Samuel Beckett (St Paul-de-Vence, Alpes Maritimes, 21 July 1969).

W. Burde: 'Amerika', *NZM*, xxvii (1966), 438–41
                                          ANDREW CLEMENTS

Haubiel [Pratt], Charles Trowbridge (*b* Delta, OH, 30 Jan 1892; *d* Los Angeles, 26 Aug 1978). American composer. From 1909 to 1913 he studied in Europe with Rudolf Ganz (piano) and Alexander von Fielitz (theory). After teaching in Oklahoma City at Kingfisher College and the Musical Arts Institute (1913–17), he returned to New York in 1919 to study with Rosario Scalero (composition) and Modest Altschuler (orchestration). From 1920 to 1930 he taught the piano at the Institute of Musical Art, and from 1923 to 1947 taught composition and theory at New York University. In 1935 he founded the Composers Press. He moved to California in the 1960s.

Haubiel's stage works are principally in the categories of operetta or children's operas; he also wrote one comic opera (*Brigands Preferred*) and several works described as folk operas. A prolific composer in all genres, Haubiel described himself in 1949 as a 'pure classicist'; he attributed the rejection of his earlier 'revolutionary tendencies' to his training under Scalero. He was also a skilful contrapuntist; his music is characterized by a synthesis of Romantic, Classical and impressionistic elements, combining a diatonic vocabulary with flowing and graceful melodic lines and colouristic 20th-century harmonies.

Brigands Preferred, 1929–46 (comic op, M. Leonard)
The Witch's Curse, 1940 (fairy-tale op)
The Birthday Cake, c1942, (operetta, H. Flexner), ? unperf.
Sunday Costs Five Pesos (Mexican folk op, J. Niggli), Charlotte, NC, 6 Nov 1950; rev. as Berta, 1954
The Enchanted Princess, c1955 (fairy-tale op), ? unperf.
Adventure on Sunbonnet Hill, c1971 (children's operetta, K. H. Bratton), ? unperf.

J. T. Howard: *Our Contemporary Composers* (New York, 1941)
D. Ewen: *American Composers Today* (New York, 1949)
Obituary, *Bill Board* (9 Sept 1978), 70   KATHERINE K. PRESTON

Hauer, Josef Matthias (*b* Wiener Neustadt, 19 March 1883; *d* Vienna, 22 Sept 1959). Austrian composer. He began his career as a teacher in elementary schools and was active as a conductor and instrumentalist. He taught himself theory and composition and in 1919 developed a system of 12-note composition similar to Schoenberg's, though his insistence on his own priority in discovering serialism prevented any cooperation with Schoenberg. During the following years he composed prolifically in almost all genres. He wrote two operas: *Salambo* op.60, composed in 1929 (7 scenes, after G. Flaubert), which received an incomplete concert performance under Klemperer in Berlin in 1930, and the Singspiel *Die schwarze Spinne* op.62, composed in 1932 (H. Schlesinger, after J. Gotthelf; Vienna, Theater an der Wien, 23 May 1966). Hauer was awarded the Vienna Artists' Prize in 1927 and from 1930 received a state honorarium. In the 1930s, however, his music was pronounced decadent, and he composed his later works, all in 12-note technique, in retirement. His many writings include *Zwölftontechnik* (Vienna, 1926, 2/1953).

After World War II there was renewed interest in Hauer and in 1955 he received a major Austrian State Prize. His artistic remoteness, prolix musical philosophy and whimsically ascetic way of life surrounded him with legend during his lifetime.   MONIKA LICHTENFELD

Haug, Hans (*b* Basle, 27 July 1900; *d* Lausanne, 15 Sept 1967). Swiss composer. He studied at the Basle Conservatory and with Courvoisier in Munich. Returning to Switzerland, he was appointed musical director at Grandson and Solothurn and choirmaster and assistant conductor at the Basle Stadttheater (1928–34). Later he worked as a teacher and a conductor in Switzerland and abroad. As a composer he had most success with his operas and with various radio operas and operettas. Many drew on mythology or legend, as in *Madrisa*, a mountain legend of a fairy girl marrying a shepherd, or on well-known sources such as Molière or Goldoni. In *Le miroir d'Agrippine* Nero is pursued by the reflections of his depravity after murdering his mother Agrippina, and in *Le souper de Venise* the heroine falls victim to her jealous lover; but many of the works are lighthearted, with atmospheric and evocative orchestration. He also wrote ballets, some with sung roles, film scores and much other vocal and instrumental music. Avoiding contrapuntal and tonal complication, his music was deliberately popular in appeal.

autographs in CH-LAcu

Don Juan in der Fremde [Don Juan à l'étranger] (komische Oper, 2, D. Müller), Basle, 1930

Madrisa (Volksoper, 3, J. Jegerlehner), Basle, 15 Jan 1934, vs (Basle, 1934)

Tartuffe (komische Oper, 2, after Molière), Basle, 24 May 1937, vs (Basle, n.d.)

Liederlig Kleeblatt (opérette, 3, E. Beurmann, after J. N. Nestroy: *Lumpazivagabundus*, in Swiss-Ger. dialect), Zürich, 1938, vs (Basle, 1938)

Gilberte de Courgenay, 1940 (opérette militaire, R. B. Mäglin), vs (Basle, 1940)

Annely us der Linde (opérette populaire, 3, Haug and A. Roesler, in Swiss-Ger. dialect), Basle, 1940, vs (Basle, n.d.)

Barbara, 1942 (opérette, 3, Ger. text by G. Hartung and K. E. Heine, after G. Sand: *La petite Fadette*), vs (Basle, 1942)

Leute von der Strasse, 1944 (opérette, E. Hegetschweiler); (Basle, n.d.)

La mère Michel (opérette, 3, W. Aguet), broadcast, Lausanne, 1945

Der unsterbliche Kranke (oc, 3, B. Diebold, after Molière: *Le malade imaginaire*), Zürich, 1946, vs (Basle, n.d.)

Leucosia (jeu radiophonique, M. Budry, after Homer: *Odyssey*), Radio Lausanne, 1949

Le premier chapeau (fantaisie radiophonique, Budry), Radio Lausanne, 1951 [described as Récit du temps de la Création]

La colombe égarée [Die verirrte Taube] (opéra radiophonique, D. Anet), Radio Basle, 1951

Orfée (opéra-ballet, Anet, after Ovid and Poliziano), broadcast, RTF, Paris, 24 Sept 1954; stage, Lausanne, 12 June 1955 (Basle, 1955)

Le miroir d'Agrippine [Der Spiegel der Agrippina], 1953–4 (opéra, 3, F. Tschudi, after H. Müller-Einigen)

Les fous [Die Narren], 1957 (oc, Budry after C. Goldoni: *Arcifanfano, re dei matti*), Radio Geneva, Nov 1959

Le souper de Venise (opéra, 1, P. Sabatier), Radio Suisse Romande, 1966

Le gardien vigilant (opérette radiophonique, 1, G. H. Blanc, after M. de Cervantes), Radio Lausanne, 1966

Undated: L'îlot des sirènes (opérette radiophonique, Budry)

J.-L. Matthey and L.-D. Perret, eds.: *Hans Haug Werkverzeichnis* (Lausanne, 1971)
                                                                    FRITZ MUGGLER

Haugland, Aage (*b* Copenhagen, 1 Feb 1944). Danish bass. He was a soloist with the Copenhagen Boys' Choir and later studied music and medicine at the university there; he made his début with the Norwegian Opera in 1968 in Martinů's *Comedy on the Bridge*. In 1973 he became a member of the Danish Royal Opera, with which he has a permanent contract as First Bass. His British début was in 1975 as Hunding at Covent Garden, and he sang Hagen with the ENO the same year; in 1979 he made his American début at St Louis as Boris, then sang Ochs at the Metropolitan Opera, where he has since taken several other roles, including Wozzeck in 1990. He sang King Henry in *Lohengrin* for his début at La Scala in 1981, and Hagen at Bayreuth in 1983. His big, warm and evenly produced voice has also been heard to advantage as Klingsor, Rocco, Fafner, Gremin, Prince Ivan Khovansky and King Mark.
                                                                    NOËL GOODWIN

Hauk, Minnie [Hauk, Amalia Mignon] (*b* New York, 16 Nov 1851; *d* Triebschen, nr Lucerne, 6 Feb 1929). American soprano, later mezzo-soprano. She studied in New Orleans and New York, making her début in Brooklyn, at the age of 14, as Amina in *La sonnambula* (13 October 1866); the next month she made her New York début as Prascovia in *L'étoile du nord*. On 15 November 1867 she sang Juliet in the American première of Gounod's *Roméo et Juliette*. She studied further with Maurice Strakosch in Paris, singing there in spring 1869 and making her London début at Covent Garden on 26 October. After appearances in Italian opera in Paris, Moscow and St Petersburg (1869–70),

and in German opera in Vienna and Berlin (1870–77), where she was a principal singer during the first season of the Komische Oper (1874–5) and was acclaimed as Katharine in Götz's *Der Widerspänstigen Zähmung* (1876), she sang in Brussels and London (1878), then alternately in the USA and London until 1881. She was the first American Carmen (1878, New York) and Manon (1885). In 1890–91 she appeared at the Metropolitan Opera and then organized her own company, with which she gave the Chicago première of *Cavalleria rusticana*. She made her last appearance at Philadelphia in 1893 as Sélika (*L'Africaine*). Hauk's voice became a mezzo-soprano of great force and richness. Her vast repertory included about a hundred parts; Carmen alone she sang some 500 times, in four languages.

M. Hauk: *Memories of a Singer*, ed. E. B. Hitchcock (London, 1925)
O. Thompson: *The American Singer* (New York, 1937), 93ff
                                                                    H. WILEY HITCHCOCK

Haunted Manor, The [*Straszny dwór*]. Opera in four acts by STANISŁAW MONIUSZKO to a libretto by Jan Chęciński after a story from Kazimierz Wójcicki's *Stary gawędy i obrazy* ('Legends and Pictures'); Warsaw, Wielki Theatre, 28 September 1865.

Zbigniew } Stefan } *soldiers*		bass tenor
Maciej *their retainer*		baritone
Marta *their housekeeper*		soprano
Czesnikowa *their aunt*		mezzo-soprano
Miecznik *a nobleman*		baritone
Jadwiga } Hanna } *Miecznik's daughters*		soprano soprano
Grzes *a country lad*		tenor
Old Woman		contralto
Damazy		tenor
Skołuba *Miecznik's steward*		bass

Soldiers, country folk, Miecznik's guests, hunters, musicians

Setting Poland in the mid-18th century

Moniuszko's intention to compose the opera was first announced in a Warsaw newspaper, *Kurier Wileński*, on 25 January 1861. The libretto was completed in December 1861 and the composer began work during a visit to Paris early in 1862. In the course of its composition there was a major insurrection in the Russian sector of Poland (January 1863), and in its aftermath censorship was severe. The libretto of *The Haunted Manor* was submitted to the Russian censor early in 1864 and much of its patriotic sentiment removed. Moniuszko orchestrated the work in the second half of 1864, and rehearsals began in January 1865. The cast of the première included Adolf Kozieradski (Miecznik), Bronisława Dowiakowska-Klimowiczowa (Hanna), Josefa Hess (Jadwiga), Julian Dobrski (Stefan), Wilhelm Troszel (Zbigniew) and Honorata Majeranowska (Czesnikowa). The director was Jan Matuszyński and Moniuszko himself conducted. The work was so successful and caused such excitement on its first production that the Russian censor banned it after three performances. It was not staged again during the composer's lifetime, and not again in Warsaw until 1914. The opera was given in Lwów and Kraków in 1877; in Łódź in 1905; in Poznán in 1909; and in

Katowice in 1923. Outside Poland, the opera was heard in Prague and Kiev in 1891 and Vienna in 1892.

ACT 1 *An army camp* The *Intrada* is an arch-like movement, using the theme of Miecznik's song in Act 4. The central melody, over shimmering strings, is derived from Stefan's aria in Act 3. In the Prologue, soldiers are having a last drink before dispersing to their homes. Zbigniew and his brother Stefan vow never to marry but to devote themselves to their country. This is a stirring soldiers' chorus in several sections – the first (in triple time) led by Zbigniew, the second (a march) led by Stefan, the third a song with refrain, the fourth a rousing, dotted-rhythm song from Maciej and the fifth a return to the march-like second section.

The home of Zbigniew and Stefan Marta and the servants prepare for the return of Zbigniew and Stefan. There are traditional welcoming gifts of bread and salt. This is a female chorus, led by Marta, whose main theme (as she sings of future happiness) foreshadows the music of the two brothers in subsequent scenes. The brothers arrive home. As they notice the arrival of Czesnikowa's carriage they confirm their resolve to remain single. A lively, madrigalesque trio, sung by the brothers and Maciej, is introduced by oboe and clarinet solos; there is a obbligato cello line in the da capo. Czesnikowa then tells the brothers of the marriages she has arranged for them and is alarmed to hear of their vow to remain single. They tell her of their intention to visit Miecznik at Kalinów. Czesnikowa's opening music, reminiscent of Offenbach, leads into a trio based on two alternating ideas – a *krakowiak*, with characteristic off-beat accents, and a contrasting 6/8 theme. The italianate finale that follows is in three sections. In the first, aware that Miecznik has two beautiful daughters, Czesnikowa tries to dissuade the brothers from visiting Kalinów, telling them that the manor is haunted. The crowd gradually assembles to listen to her tale. The second section is the tale itself, a dramatic arioso with interjections from the other characters and the chorus. As the brothers are not deterred, Czesnika sets off for Kalinów ahead of them; the final section is a lengthy ensemble, with some lively antiphonal writing between ensemble and chorus.

ACT 2 *Miecznik's manor* It is New Year's eve. The act opens with a spinning chorus for Jadwiga and Hanna's companions, with solo episodes for the two sisters and a pictorial 'spinning' motif in the accompaniment. The music alternates a slow mazurka (*kujawiak*) rhythm and a rapid polka rhythm. Jadwiga then sings a folklike *dumka*, a strophic song with an impassioned chromatic coda. The women are joined by Damazy, a suitor to Hanna. As he dances and sings a duet with Hanna, Miecznik arrives. The musical characterization stresses Hanna's lack of interest in the foolish Damazy. The dance, which has a distinct French flavour, is a traditional minuet. The women engage in traditional fortune-telling games, dropping melted wax into water in the belief that it will form the shapes of the men they will marry. The fortune-telling episode falls into three main sections; first, a duet for Hanna and Jadwiga with choral accompaniment; second, a mainly choral section representing the fortune-telling, with pizzicato violas depicting the drips of wax; and third, a cabaletta-like conclusion for the quartet of soloists and chorus. Miecznik then sings a stirring polonaise aria of intense patriotic fervour, describing the kind of son-in-law he would like (it was this aria which provoked the

demonstrations that ultimately caused the opera to be banned). At the end Czesnikowa tries to blacken the names of her nephews, accusing them of cowardice. In the finale Czesnikowa is interrupted by the huntsmen. As the brothers arrive, Damazy plots with Skołuba, the steward, to frighten them away, while the sisters resolve to test their courage. Until this point the act has been in the nature of a scenic tableau. The finale, however, is an extensive dramatic scene, comprising a huntsmen's chorus (reminiscent of *Der Freischütz*), Miecznik's arioso, a sextet for the main characters and a final ensemble in which the soloists are joined by the male chorus (huntsmen) and female chorus (spinners).

ACT 3 *Miecznik's manor* Skołuba terrifies Maciej with stories of the haunted manor. When Maciej relates these to the brothers they are merely amused. Skołuba's aria, doubled in the bass section of the orchestra, has a dark-hued accompaniment and 'ghostly' woodwind effects. Stefan thinks of Hanna, reminisces about his childhood and recognizes the conflict between his love and his vow to remain single. This is an emotionally powerful and wide-ranging polonaise aria. Zbigniew and Stefan then confess their love for Jadwiga and Hanna respectively in a semi-strophic italianate duet. The quartet that follows is a paired ensemble (as in *Rigoletto*), in which the sisters hide behind two portraits to test Zbigniew and Stefan but are discovered by them and chased. Damazy is found hiding behind the clock. In the first section of the finale, the brothers accuse Damazy of mocking them; he in turn attacks the manor and the household. After a brief, atmospheric quartet, Zbigniew and Stefan resolve in a cabaletta to leave Kalinów before they become inextricably embroiled in the situation.

ACT 4 *Miecznik's manor* Hanna, in an impressive coloratura aria with solo violin accompaniment, heavily indebted to Italian models, describes her disappointment at Stefan's imminent departure. Stefan explains to her that he must leave because of the conflict between his love and his vow. The couple sing a bipartite duet, the second part a varied repetition of the first. A recitative and an ensemble follow in which Miecznik expresses his anger at his guests' proposed departure but then Maciej relates Damazy's account of the manor. The dialogue is interrupted by the beginning of the *kulig* ('festivities'). The *kulig*, comprising a choral *krakowiak* and an orchestral mazurka, is followed by an explanation scene, in which Miecznik calls Damazy to account and unveils the mystery of the haunted manor. The brothers make their proposals to Jadwiga and Hanna and taunt Czesnikowa for her plotting, and the betrothals of the two couples are celebrated.

*   *   *

Although it proved much less successful than *Halka*, *The Haunted Manor* has strong claims to be considered Moniuszko's masterpiece. Chęciński provided a lively and challenging libretto, full of comic situations, affording opportunities for skilful musical characterization and dramatic ensembles. The composer met the challenge with a score whose balance of native and cosmopolitan elements is more satisfactory than in his other mature operas. The large cast is well balanced vocally and the musical idiom, while derivative of both Italian and French models, is tuneful and harmonically assured. The work has a similar place in Polish opera to that held by Smetana's *The Bartered Bride* in Czech opera. It is arguably the one opera by Moniuszko, indeed the one 19th-century Polish opera, that might be exported with success.   JIM SAMSON

Haunted Tower, The. Mainpiece dialogue opera in three acts by STEPHEN STORACE to a libretto by JAMES COBB; London, Drury Lane, 24 November 1789.

The Haunted Tower was Storace's first full-length English opera. It proved to be one of his most successful and profitable works, and stayed in the Drury Lane repertory for more than 30 years. At the première Storace's sister Nancy made her début in English opera as Adela (soprano). She was joined by her friend and colleague Michael Kelly, along with John Bannister and Anna Maria Crouch as their partners. These partnerships, established with *The Haunted Tower*, lasted for the rest of Storace's career.

James Cobb's libretto is a tale of false identities and disguises in a fashionably Gothic setting. In obedience to her father, Lady Elinor de Courcy (soprano) arrives at Dover with her retinue to marry Edward (baritone), son of the newly titled and despotic Baron of Oakland. The latter, originally a ploughman, had bought his title when the previous baron had been wrongly punished for a crime and his son and heir could not be found. That son is Lord William (tenor), who loves Lady Elinor and, under the name Sir Palamede, has concealed himself on her ship from France to plead his own case.

Lady Elinor, having heard unpleasant stories about the baron and his son, presents herself at the baron's castle disguised as her own maid and accompanied by Lord William in the guise of a jester. She represents herself as an advance party in order to see how auspicious the planned alliance might be. Meanwhile, Edward wants only a quiet, working man's life married to Adela, whom he persuades to disguise herself as his official prospective bride in the hope that the baron will approve their marriage, which would take place before the real Lady Elinor arrived. Lady Elinor allows the disguise to stand; it is exposed only when her brother arrives unexpectedly. When Lord William finally obtains proof of his title, he dons his father's armour to regain the castle by force. He is mistaken for his father's ghost by the servants, who use the 'haunted' tower as their regular drinking place. The 'baron' returns humbled whence he came; the couples are united.

In the tradition of English operas of the 18th century, the action takes place almost entirely in the spoken sections. Cobb and Storace had yet to try the effect of action ensembles on an English audience, as they did in their later collaborations. The music in *The Haunted Tower* therefore has little dramatic function, and the choruses and finales are short descriptive and reflective ensembles. Storace adapted the overture from his own overture to *Gli equivoci* (1786), adding a fast introduction to the section that portrays a thunderstorm at sea while the curtain rises. He also adapted other music, including numbers from Italian, French and English operas, plus a few folktunes and instrumental melodies. Each borrowed piece is identified on the vocal score (no orchestral score or set of parts survives). Some orchestration is also indicated, including a carillon, offstage horns and various obbligato wind instruments. The most popular of the songs in print was 'Whither my love', sung originally by Nancy Storace and adapted from Giovanni Paisiello's 'La rachelina molinara' in *L'amor contrastato* (1788). Lord William's 'Spirit of my sainted sire', a virtuoso showpiece for Kelly, was also published in several editions. There is a notable

character duet, 'Begone I discharge you', sung by Adela and Lady Elinor, both in their disguises and neither able to keep entirely in character. The complete vocal score of *The Haunted Tower* ran to five editions before the end of the century.   JANE GIRDHAM

Hauser, Franz [František] (*b* Krasowitz [now Krasovice], nr Prague, 12 Jan 1794; *d* Freiburg, 14 Aug 1870). Bohemian baritone. Having studied with Tomášek in Prague, he sang first there (1817–21, making his début as Sarastro), then in Kassel (1821–5), Dresden (1825–6), Frankfurt (1826–9) and Vienna (1829). In 1832 he visited London and also sang in Leipzig; he was in Berlin in 1835 and Breslau in 1836, and made many guest appearances throughout Germany. On his retirement from the stage in 1837 he settled in Vienna as a teacher, and in 1846 he was appointed director of the newly founded Musikschule in Munich. On its reorganization after Wagner's arrival he retired in 1864. According to Fétis his style was pure though his acting was considered cold; but he pleased Weber and was praised as Figaro, Bertram, William Tell and Spohr's Faust. His *Gesanglehre für Lehrende und Lernende* (Leipzig, 1866) had a wide circulation.

Hauser's son Moritz (*b* Dresden, 28 Aug 1826; *d* Königsberg [now Kaliningrad], 31 May 1857) studied with Mendelssohn and Hauptmann in Leipzig and was music director at Königsberg. He wrote an opera, *Der Erbe von Hohenegk* (1855, Leipzig). Franz's younger son Joseph (*b* Frankfurt am Main, 29 Sept 1828; *d* after 1869) was a baritone who sang at Karlsruhe for almost 40 years with a repertory of more than 130 roles. Wagner wanted him to sing Kurwenal in 1865 and Alberich in 1869, but he was refused leave of absence from Karlsruhe to do so. He was, however, noted in Wagner roles, including Hans Sachs.

A. Schöne, ed.: *Briefe von Moritz Hauptmann an Franz Hauser* (Leipzig, 1871)
E. Hanslick: 'Aus dem Leben und der Correspondenz von Franz Hauser', *Suite* (Vienna and Teschen, 1884), 1–37
L. Eisenberg: *Grosses biographisches Lexicon der deutschen Bühne im XIX. Jahrhundert* (Leipzig, 1903)   JOHN WARRACK

Haute-contre (Fr.). The highest and most favoured of the three male voices intermediate between the *dessus* (soprano) and *basse* in Baroque and Classical French opera, with a range *c–d"*, notated in the alto clef. (Throughout this period, pitch in France was as much as a whole tone lower than that now used.) These three voices (the others were *taille* or *haute-taille*, later *ténor*, and *basse-taille*, later *baryton*) corresponded to the three *parties intermédaires* of the string orchestra, played by violas. Brossard (1703) described the *haute-contre* as 'the voice closest to and above the *taille*'. Rouseau's antipathy to French opera must be taken into account in evaluating his view of the *haute-contre* (*Dictionnaire de musique*, 1768) as 'not natural' and 'always sour and rarely in tune'.

Scholars have been divided as to whether the *haute-contre* was a falsettist or a true high tenor who might occasionally employ falsetto, but the latter view is now generally accepted, not only on the basis of musicological research (as late as 1844, Berlioz equated the term with 'very high tenor' in his *Grand traité d'instrumentation*) but in the light of experience of modern performance with orchestras using period instruments in appropriate numbers, playing at the lower pitches employed in late 17th- and early 18th-century

France. Lully assigned the principal male role in eight of his 14 operas to the *haute-contre* – *Atys*, *Psyché* (Cupid), *Bellérophon*, *Persée*, *Phaëton*, *Amadis*, *Armide* (Renaud) and *Acis et Galatée*. These roles, and those in the operas of the *préramiste* composers and of Rameau himself, go too low for a falsettist to be audible; at the other end of the range, the solos that include sustained notes in the range b'–d'', in roles frequently portraying warriors and other heroic figures, often accompanied by full orchestra and chorus, present considerable problems of balance for falsettists.

The most demanding roles for *haute-contre* were written to exploit the talents of a very small number of outstanding singers, notably Pierre de Jélyotte (1713–97) for whom Rameau wrote most of his principal *haute-contre* title roles, including those of *Dardanus*, *Platée*, *Zaïs*, *Pigmalion*, *Zoroastre* and *Castor et Pollux* (1754 version; Castor). The power of Jélyotte's voice was attested to by Dufort de Cheverny (quoted in Pougin 1905): '[his] singing in *Pigmalion* covered the chorus and in *Zoroastre* all Paris ran to hear, in the middle of the thunder, "Ciel! Thémire expire dans mes bras!"'. François Poirier, a younger contemporary of Jélyotte, would appear to have excelled him at the top of the range; the Duke of Luynes reported him singing up to e'' and described his voice as 'parfaitement belle'. In the unusually demanding duo for two *haute-contres*, 'Charmant amour' in Rameau's *La princesse de Navarre* (1745), Poirier sang the upper part (a–d'') and Jélyotte the lower ($f\sharp$–c''). In opera performances at court, Marc-François Bêche (*b* 1729) was the most appreciated *haute-contre* besides Jélyotte and Poirier. Of the next generation, the most notable was Joseph Legros (1739–93), for whom the *haute-contre* roles in Gluck's French operas were written (including the revision of that of Orpheus, previously for castrato).

In the French Baroque opera chorus, women singers again contributed only to the *dessus*, all other parts including the *haute-contre* being assigned to male voices. *Haute-contre* chorus parts, coming between the *dessus* and the *taille* (although often overlapping the latter), were of more restricted range than those for soloists, except when the normal four-part texture gave way to the three-part *petit choeur* of *haut-dessus*, *bas-dessus* and *haute-contre*, the last of which then functioned as the harmonic bass, doubled by the *basse-continue*, and ranged more widely.

The revival of many operas of the French Baroque, especially those of Rameau, has stimulated renewed interest in the *haute-contre* voice. High tenors who have become distinguished exponents of *haute-contre* roles include Bruce Brewer, Michael Goldthorpe, John Elwes, Howard Crook, Guy de Mey and Gilles Ragon.

*

A. Pougin: *Un ténor de l'opéra au XVIII siècle: Pierre Jélyotte et les chanteurs de son temps* (Paris, 1905)

N. Dufourcq, ed.: *La musique à la cour de Louis XIV et de Louis XV d'après les mémoires de Sourches et Luynes (1681–1758)* (Paris, 1970)

N. Zaslaw: 'The Enigma of the Haute-Contre', *MT*, cxv (1974), 939–41

M. Cyr: 'On Performing 18th-century *haute-contre* Roles', *MT*, cxviii (1977), 291–5

G. Sadler: 'Rameau's singers and players at the Paris Opéra', *EMc*, xi (1983), 453–67

L. Sawkins: 'New Sources for Rameau's *Pigmalion* and other works', *EMc*, xi (1983), 490–96

L. Rosow: 'Performing a Choral Dialogue by Lully', *EMc*, xv (1987), 325–35
                                                                    LIONEL SAWKINS

Havana (Sp. *La Habana*). Capital of Cuba. According to the *Diario de la Habana* of 19 December 1815, the first opera sung in the city, on 12 October 1776 in the first theatre there, the brand new Teatro Coliseo, was *Didone abbandonata* (composer not named). Grétry's *Zémire et Azor* was sung in Spanish in 1791, but in 1800 a French company from New Orleans gave the same work in French, along with operas by J.-F. Edelmann, Grétry, Monsigny and Gossec. The Teatro Coliseo was renamed the Principal in 1803. Two works by Dalayrac and Cimarosa were given in Spanish in 1804, then during the 1811–12 season nine 'new' operas, including Blas de Laserna's *La Isabela*, Manuel García's *El poeta calculista*, Méhul's *Une folie*, Gaveaux's *Le petit matelot*, Pucitta's *Adolfo e Chiara* and Salieri's *La scuola de' gelosi*, were sung in Spanish by a company from Madrid. *Don Giovanni* was sung for the first time in the Americas at the Teatro Principal on 3 November 1818. Later that month local audiences heard their first Rossini opera, *Tancredi*. Spontini's *La vestale*, Mozart's *La clemenza di Tito* and Rossini's *La pietra del paragone* were the novelties of 1821. The first Mercadante opera heard in Cuba was *Elisa e Claudio* in 1828; Meyerbeer's first was *Il crociato in Egitto* in 1830. The 1832 season concluded in the year of García's death with his *L'amante astuto* – also the last opera to feature the Spanish-born prima donna Mariana Galino, who had ruled the Havana stage since her advent in 1809.

The first Italian touring company contracted for Havana arrived in 1833 and the following year gave Bellini's *Il pirata* and *La straniera*. *Anna Bolena*, first given in 1835, inaugurated a series of local Donizetti premières in 1839–40. On 11 October 1844 the Teatro Principal was damaged by a cyclone and in December 1846 it closed. Meanwhile the Teatro Tacón had opened on 28 February 1838. Seating 2287 (with standing room for another 700), it presented plays until 6 May 1839, when *Norma* was given, followed by ten more Italian operas that season. A French opera and ballet company included *La fille du régiment* among its novelties in 1843. *Ernani*, which opened the seasons of 1846–8, introduced Verdi to Cuban audiences.

The first world première at the Tacón took place on 31 January 1848, when Bottesini's *Cristoforo Colombo* was sung for the bass player's benefit, under his own direction. The next, on 4 February 1848, was the two-act *Gulnara* by Bottesini's colleague Arditi. The most prolific Cuban opera composer was Eduardo Sánchez de Fuentes, with five premières in Havana to his credit. His most important contemporary was José Mauri, whose *La esclava* (with a setting in Camagüey in 1860) was first performed in 1921 at the Teatro Nacional (as the Tacón was renamed from 1915).

That theatre had passed from owner to owner early in the century. Newly rebuilt, it was inaugurated in 1915 under visiting impresarios; the first opera given there was *Aida*, under Serafin, followed by *Otello*. The impresario Bracale took over in 1916; his company included Galli-Curci and Lazaro, and Caruso sang for him in 1920. A new, large theatre, the Teatro Auditorium, was opened in 1929; it became the centre of operatic activity in Havana (the Nacional was adapted as a cinema), saw the revival of operas by the Cuban composer Gaspar Villate (notably *Baltasar*, 1939) and was the site of performances by such visiting artists as Del Monaco, Milanov, Tebaldi and de los Angeles. In 1959, at the revolution, it became the Teatro Amadeo

Roldán; three years later it was burnt down. The Teatro Nacional Lírico was then established, at the former theatre, now the Gran Teatro de la Habana (the main theatre was called the Teatro García Lorca, the smaller auditorium the Sala Ernesto Lecuona).

To celebrate the 25th anniversary of the founding of the Teatro Nacional Lírico, the national opera company, five operas were mounted during the first Festival Internacional de Arte Lírico de Habana, 17–31 October 1987. The opening work, at the Teatro García Lorca, was Yuri Ghazaryan's *Ernest Hemingway* (libretto by Grigori Chiguinov). The one Cuban opera was Sánchez de Fuentes's *El caminante*. *Cecilia Valdés* (1932), one of the 40 zarzuelas by Gonzalo Roig (1890–1970) and one of the most famous Cuban works of that genre (Faro, 1988), and Lehár's *Die lustige Witwe* (in Spanish) completed the festival. The management did much in the 1980s to promote female directors, among them Elena Herreva, Corina Campos, Ana Menéndez and Maria Elena Ortega.

S. Ramírez: *La Habana artística* (Havana, 1891)
E. Tolón and J. A. González: *Operas cubanas y sus autores* (Havana, 1943)
A. Carpentier: *La música en Cuba* (Mexico City, 1946, 2/1979)
J. A. González: 'Fue en Cuba donde se estrenó, en América, la ópera "Don Juan" de Mozart', *Revista de música*, i/2 (1960), 100
E. Tolón and J. A. González: *Historia del teatro en La Habana* (Santa Clara, 1961)
R. Stevenson: *A Guide to Caribbean Music History* (Lima, 1975)
——: 'Caribbean Music History: a Selective Annotated Bibliography with Musical Supplement', *Inter-American Music Review*, iv/1 (1981–2), 50, 75
J. A. González: *La composición operística en Cuba* (Havana, 1986)
L. Bacalis Zoila, ed.: *Exposición sobre teatro dramático musical: bibliografía* (Havana, 1987)
A. Báeva: 'Festival de ópera en La Habana', *América latina* [Moscow], viii (1988), 70–74
A. J. Faro: 'Cuba: First Opera Festival', *Opera*, xxxix (1988), 80–82
ROBERT STEVENSON

Havana Opera Company. Name for a series of travelling Italian opera companies based in Havana, Cuba, 1833–50. The earliest version of the troupe was run by Francesco Brichta; that of 1843 was assembled by the Cuban businessman Marti y Torrens and made a historic, extended tour of the USA. Later versions took more than a hundred performers on each tour. *See* TRAVELLING TROUPES, §5(iv).

Hawes, William (*b* London, 21 June 1785; *d* London, 18 Feb 1846). English musician. He was a violinist for a time in the Covent Garden orchestra, and was appointed Master of the Choristers at St Paul's Cathedral in 1812 and Master of the Children of the Chapel Royal in 1817, holding the latter two posts until his death. He ran a publishing business in the Strand and for many years was conductor of the Madrigal Society and organist of the Lutheran Chapel of the Savoy. After 1804 his connection with the stage, for which he produced a long series of adaptations of continental operas with musical interpolations of his own, occupied ever more of his time. In 1824 he was appointed musical director of the English Opera House (Lyceum) where many of those adaptations were staged, among them Weber's *Der Freischütz* (1824) and *Preciosa* (1825), Mozart's *Così fan tutte* (1828) and *Don Giovanni* (1830), and Hérold's *Le pré aux clercs* (1833). Hawes also wrote several original operettas, among them *Broken Promises* (1825) and *The Irish Girl* (1830), songs for various plays, a requiem and a monody on the death of Princess Charlotte (1817). BERNARR RAINBOW

Hawkins, Osie (*b* Phenix City, AL, 16 Aug 1913). American baritone. He studied in Atlanta and with Friedrich Schorr in New York. He made his Metropolitan Opera début in 1942 as Donner, and sang with the company until 1962 as Amfortas, Telramund, Wotan, Kurwenal and Gunther; he also took minor roles in Italian operas. Guest appearances took him to the Central City Opera, Colorado, and the Cincinnati Summer Opera. From 1963 to 1978 he was executive stage manager at the Metropolitan Opera.

DAVID CUMMINGS

Hayashi, Hikaru (*b* Tokyo, 22 Oct 1931). Japanese composer. A pupil of Hisatada Otaka and Tomojirō Ikenouchi, he won the Otaka Prize in 1956. His first opera, *Hadaka no ōsama* ('The Emperor's New Clothes', 1955), was written for radio and was followed by two television operas, of which one, *Amanjaku to Uriko-hime* ('Amanjaku and Princess Uriko', 1958), has often been performed in a stage version; these three early operas are based on folktales. *Esugata nyōbō* ('The Beautiful Wife', 1961) is a more ambitious work with a commendable treatment of the Japanese text. In 1975 Hayashi became the music director of a small-scale opera group, Konnyaku-za, for which he has written a series of chamber operas with piano accompaniment, including *Okonjōruri* (1975), *Hakuboku no wa* ('The Caucasian Chalk Circle', 1978), and *Sero-hiki no Gōshu* ('Gorsh the Cellist', 1986). The music of these chamber operas, as well as that of many of his other works, is basically diatonic and lyrical in a popular vein. He is best known for his choral works, which, like his songs, often reflect his pacifist beliefs. He has also been active as a music critic for a major Japanese newspaper and has written books on music.

Hadaka no ōsama [The Emperor's New Clothes] (radio op, 1, after H. C. Andersen), NHK, 1955
Amanjaku to Uriko-hime [Amanjaku and Princess Uriko] (television op, 1, I. Wakabayashi, after Japanese folktale), NHK, 1958; stage, Tokyo, 1959; vs (Tokyo, 1978)
Urashima (television op, 1, after Japanese folktale), NHK, 1959
Esugata nyōbō [The Beautiful Wife] (2, after S. Yashiro), Osaka, Sankei Hall, 10 May 1961
Okonjōruri (chamber op, 1), Tokyo, Chūō Hall, 12 Nov 1975
Ukare-no-Hyōroku hataori-uta [Merry Hyōroku Weaving Song], (chamber op, 2, Wakabayashi), Tokyo, Chūō Hall, 4 Feb 1977
Bekkanko-oni (chamber op), Tokyo, Chūō Hall, 3 Feb 1978
Hakuboku no wa [The Caucasian Chalk Circle] (chamber op, 2, T. Hirowatari, after B. Brecht), Tokyo, Arakawa Kumin Hall, 27 May 1978
Tsurutomi (2), Miyazaki, 1979
Nezumi-tachi no densetsu [Legend of Mice] (chamber op), Tokyo, Nakano Bunka Centre, 12 Sept 1980
Chūta no kūsō [Fantasy of Chūta], (ob, Hirowatari, after T. Ozawa), Tokyo, Chūō Hall, 31 Jan 1981
Sero-hiki no Gōshu [Gorsh the Cellist] (chamber op, after K. Miyazawa), Tokyo, 1986
Shiroi kemono no densetsu [Legend of a White Beast] (chamber op), Tokyo, Toshi Centre Hall, 21 Feb 1987
MASAKATA KANAZAWA

Hayashi, Yasuko (*b* Kanagawa, 19 July 1948). Japanese soprano. She studied in Tokyo and Milan, making her début in 1972 at La Scala as Butterfly. In 1973 she sang Ninetta (*La gazza ladra*) in Rome and the title role of *Maria Stuarda* in Chicago; the following year she took the title role of *Luisa Miller* at Aix-en-Provence and made her Covent Garden début as Donna Anna. She has sung throughout Italy and in Barcelona, Tokyo and

Dresden. Her repertory includes Fiordiligi, Sinais (*Mosè in Egitto*), Adina, Violetta, Leonora (*Il trovatore*), Desdemona, Mimì, Manon Lescaut, Liù and Anne Trulove; she also sings Norma, but her exquisite portrait of Butterfly remains her finest achievement.

ELIZABETH FORBES

Haydn, (Franz) Joseph (*b* Rohrau, Lower Austria, 31 March 1732; *d* Vienna, 31 May 1809). Austrian composer. He was more or less deeply involved in operatic direction and composition for much of his career, from the early and penurious years of his first independence in Vienna after his dismissal from St Stephen's choir school at 17 or 18 to the abortive opera on the subject of Orpheus and Eurydice that he wrote in London in 1791. The bulk of Haydn's theatrical activity dates from the years 1762 to 1790, during which he was responsible for directing operatic performances for his employer, Prince Nikolaus Esterházy, which involved selecting and editing as well as composing and conducting opera. The years of his most intensive theatrical activity were 1780 to 1789, a decade during which no fewer than 1034 performances of 73 operas were given (*see* ESZTERHÁZA).

1. Up to 1766. 2. 1766–79. 3. 1779–91. 4. Insertion arias and ensembles. 5. Haydn and opera.

1. UP TO 1766. Though his early biographers differ about the date, Haydn's first work for the stage seems to have been his setting of Kurz-Bernardon's *Der (neue) krumme Teufel*. According to Griesinger, Haydn was at the time 'about 19 years of age'; Dies has him a year or two older. Both writers give a similar account of the incident: Haydn serenaded Kurz's wife and was promptly invited in by the famous actor-manager and asked whether he would write the music for his latest comedy. When faced with the challenge of depicting Bernardon escaping from drowning by swimming to safety, Haydn needed a graphic demonstration from Kurz before satisfying him as to his abilities; he was thereupon given the commission, which brought him 25 ducats. The libretto – and that only for the later revision or revival of about 1752 – does survive, but there is no trace of the music despite the fact that the work was quite popular in its day. The 38 numbers include 32 arias, a duet, a trio, three choruses, and an extended sequence with two recitatives and a further duet. Haydn has also been plausibly suggested as the composer of some of the *Teutsche Comedie Arien* (DTÖ, lxiv and cxxi); there is however no firm evidence that he wrote further music for the German stage until the Singspiels and marionette operas of the 1770s, long after his appointment in 1761 as vice-Kapellmeister to Prince Esterházy (he succeeded to the post of full Kapellmeister in 1766, after Werner's death). If we discount the lost and doubtful *Genovefens vierter Theil* of summer 1777 (Haydn's setting of which is attested by an entry in the 1805 *Haydn-Verzeichnis* and thrown into question by Haydn's entry in his list of librettos) and the likewise lost *Hexenschabbas* (?1773), *Dido* (1776) and *Die bestrafte Rachbegierde* (1779), we are left with part of one indisputably authentic German Singspiel by Haydn, *Philemon und Baucis*, and two further not-quite-complete Singspiel scores of disputed authenticity. These are *Die Feuersbrunst* (composed *c*1775–8), which is probably identical with the 'Opera comique Vom abgebrannten Haus' (mentioned in Haydn's draft catalogue, *c*1773–9), and the dialect comedy with music *Die reisende Ceres* (?*c*1770), which

its editor Eva Badura-Skoda suggests may be identical with the otherwise unexplained entry *Die Erlösung* in the libretto list. Though the music of the latter is tuneful and pleasing it hardly bears the stamp of Haydn (and the fact that five of its nine numbers are ensembles, an unusually high proportion for Haydn, might be held to argue against his authorship). *Die Feuersbrunst*, however, with its preponderance of colourful arias and its well-drawn characters, especially Wurstl and Colombine, can lay stronger claim to authenticity.

Haydn's first operatic setting in Italian was the *festa teatrale Acide* of 1762. The original libretto survives (in *H-Bn*), but of Haydn's score we have only the sinfonia, three arias, an accompanied recitative and a quartet finale. The only item that is reasonably familiar is the aria 'Tergi i vezzosi rai', originally composed for Thetis (soprano) but rewritten 12 years later for Neptune (bass); from that revival there also survive three other fragments, but the work remains at best an interesting hulk. In the years leading to the composition of the earliest comic opera by Haydn that survives virtually complete, *La canterina* of 1766, he wrote five further settings of Italian comedies, of most of which little or nothing survives. That he did actually write them is made clear by the survival of four arias and fragments of two others in autograph for 'Marchese' ('La marchesa Nespola') and of fragments from another, untitled, comic opera of at latest 1762.

2. 1766–79. When Haydn composed the two-part intermezzo *La canterina* in 1766 he was already a successful composer. The story, about a young singer outwitting her older teacher, drew from Haydn music of brightness and charm, spiced with witty parodistic touches; the second finale is a fairly extensive ensemble in three sections. Two years later he wrote *Lo speziale* for the opening of the new opera house at Eszterháza. Although Goldoni's three-act libretto was reduced by removal of the two *parti serie*, the strong comic situations drew skilful and spirited music from Haydn, most obviously in his imitation of a constipated man, or in conventional held notes and wide intervals to convey physical distances and heights, more subtly in the depiction of love, jealousy and the use of disguise. Unfortunately much of the score for Act 3 is lost; apart from a brief finale a mock-Turkish aria survives that vividly illustrates the composer's response to the exotic-ridiculous situation and words. It is a D major Allegretto in 2/4 metre, with semi-nonsense words, in which a disguised (and unsuccessful) suitor tries to banish his elderly rival to Constantinople. For the only time in the score, a bassoon is introduced into what is – not coincidentally – the shortest and most memorable number in this *dramma giocoso*. Thus early in his operatic career Haydn displays the strengths and weaknesses of his contribution to the genre – imaginative responses to particular stimuli have to be set against numbers that, however beautiful their music, outstay their welcome. Haydn's own awareness of the problem is suggested by the often extensive cuts he marked; yet he continued to write leisurely ritornellos even for numbers that cry out for a rapid verbal response to the situation reached in the preceding recitative. And he was content to accept and maintain the convention of a brief, dramatically inconsequential (even bathetic) third act.

Although about a quarter of the autograph of *Le pescatrici* is lost, probably destroyed in the fire of 1779 that burnt down the princely opera house, enough survives for us to be able to state with confidence that it is Haydn's most important opera up to this point (though the first surviving page of the manuscript is dated 1769, most of the work was probably written the following year, in which it was first performed). Like *Lo speziale*, it is based on a Goldoni libretto, but unlike Haydn's setting of that work the two *parti serie* are kept; the result is a full-length opera, including a fairly extensive third act (which alone survives in its entirety), and with a comparatively large number of ensembles: nine in the surviving autograph, as against 15 solos. The scoring is varied by the inclusion of a pair of english horns in Lesbina's cavatina and in a sextet in Act 1; one or two flutes occasionally either replace or are added to the oboes which, with a pair of horns, are the staple apart from the strings (a bassoon is specified in three numbers). The finales of the first two acts alternate slow and fast sections; that for Act 3 moves from a common-time Allegro di molto to a brief 6/8 Presto.

With *L'infedeltà delusa* (1773), the major series of stage works begins. The story is simple, concerning the confusions in the love of four of the five characters (the fifth is the father of the seconda donna). Despite the success of the work when first staged at Eszterháza, and its repeat performance for the famous visit of Maria Theresa in September of the same year, it was revived only once more in Haydn's lifetime; since the 1950s however it has been quite frequently performed (and recorded at least four times). It has some delightful arias, two for the disguised Vespina being especially notable, but its only extended ensemble is perversely an opening quintet. There is an angry duet for the brother and sister in the middle of Act 1, but despite three pairings of lovers there is no love duet – indeed, apart from the rather brief two-tempo finales the score consists solely of recitatives and arias, some of them anything but dramatic. To take one instance, when (in 2.vii) Nanni is anxious to find out his sister's further plans, she says she has no time to tell him now – and proceeds to sing a lovely six-minute-long aria ('Ho teso la rete') without even then putting him properly in the picture.

Next in chronological order come *Philemon und Baucis* which, with its lost prologue *Der Götterrath*, was performed on 2 September 1773, and the lost *Hexenschabbas* ('Witches' Sabbath'), probably of the same year. *L'incontro improvviso*, first performed at the castle theatre at Eszterháza on 29 August 1775, is an attractive but dramatically tame version of the half-century-old French play *Les pèlerins de la Mecque*, familiar from Gluck's *opéra comique* of 1764, *La rencontre imprévue*, and close in its story to the best-known of all oriental escape operas, *Die Entführung aus dem Serail*. The overture, with its exotic local colour, arouses expectations that Haydn does not consistently satisfy. If the fault is at least in part that of Carl Friberth, Haydn's house librettist, for not sharpening the dramatic situations, the composer certainly seized the lyrical opportunity provided by some of the short canzonettas and arias, not to mention the glorious terzet for the three ladies in Act 1, with horns, english horns and muted violins, though as so often in his stage works he lets it go on too long (one brief authentic cut – 25 bars out of a 242-bar Andantino – indicates his recognition of the problem but hardly amounts to a solution to it). Clarinos and timpani as well as the Turkish percussion instruments enrich the sonorities. It is difficult to escape the feeling that Haydn was too content simply to

set what was put before him, rather than exert a firm, perceptive influence on the course and the tempo of the action; the first finale is dramatically inept, though the second, in G major, into which a love duet in E major leads directly, is a strong, extended movement of considerable character in three asymmetrical sections, and Friberth provided a third act which, though quite brief, is not supererogatory.

Either side of *L'incontro improvviso* Haydn was occupied with the writing of marionette operas, of which little music survives: *Hexenschabbas* and *Dido* are lost, while the 'Opera comique Vom abgebrannten Haus' (?c1773–9) is probably identical with *Die Feuersbrunst*, which is variously described as a Singspiel and a marionette opera. With the next Italian opera we are back on firm ground: *Il mondo della luna* was performed at Eszterháza on 3 August 1777 (possibly earlier) and has proved one of the more popular of Haydn's stage works in modern times. Given its superior musical setting of a Goldoni libretto and the popularity of the topic in the 17th and 18th centuries (dramatic versions include Aphra Behn's *The World on the Moon* and Riccoboni's *Arlequin Empereur dans la lune*), it is surprising that Haydn's opera seems to have had just one performance in his lifetime, the more so as he expended greater care on revisions to this score than on almost any other of his operatic works. In the choice of contrasting keys, as in the imaginative use of woodwind instruments, balletic interludes and accompanied recitatives, Haydn shows a new mastery; there are individual arias of great charm, and occasionally of dramatic aptness, while the finales, especially the lengthy one to Act 2 with its five sections in increasingly rapid tempos, show a new awareness of large-scale structures. However, the obviousness of the outcome of the plot, the commodious and unhurried sequence of solo numbers, and the artificiality of the characterization all suggest that Haydn was too readily inclined to set unquestioningly the conventional and often vapid librettos that were proposed, denying himself the irregularities and even the humour that are memorable characteristics of the best of his instrumental music.

La vera costanza was first performed at Eszterháza on 25 April 1779, but the performance material and Haydn's score seem to have perished in the fire that destroyed the opera house that November; Haydn had to recompose much of it from memory for the revival in April 1785. (Haydn later stated that this work was originally commissioned by Joseph II for production in Vienna, but his memory seems to have let him down; it was Anfossi's setting that was staged in the Burgtheater on 13 January 1777.) Following the 1785 staging at Eszterháza the opera was given in a German adaptation in various centres, including Vienna, and a French adaptation, *Laurette*, was staged and also published in Paris in 1791. Once again the problem lies in the first place with the libretto, by Francesco Puttini, and Haydn's readiness to set it uncritically. There is here too a series of fine arias, including an impressively bellicose one for the Count in Act 1, and the first two finales show a new awareness of the claims of lyrical expansion and dramatic tension. That for the first act, in G major and 633 bars long, includes contrasting ensemble sections in mainly rapid tempos and striking duet passages first for the noble lovers, then for the Count and his secret wife, the virtuous fisherwoman Rosina. The second, in D major, again includes a duet for the Count and his wife, now with a spoken interjection by their young son; it is even longer (651 bars), but in one fewer section, than that to the first act. By contrast the conclusion to Act 3, which like the earlier ones employs all seven soloists, is finished almost before it has started; it is a mere 48 bars. Seldom has Haydn so unwittingly and poignantly pointed up the difference between a heightened theatrical response, such as he brings to the first two finales, and the arid conventionality of that to the last act.

3. 1779–91. The two versions of *La vera costanza* are separated by the six years that witness Haydn's most intensive preoccupation with operatic composition. The first of the four operas written in rapid succession was *L'isola disabitata*, an *azione teatrale* in two parts to a text by Metastasio – Haydn's first and last setting of a book by the century's most famous librettist – that was given on the prince's name-day, 6 December 1779. One can make a strong case for this as Haydn's most compact and satisfying operatic score. The economy of the action – just four characters, sisters stranded on a desert island, the husband of the older one and his companion, who falls in love with the younger when the rescue mission is finally possible – is matched by Haydn's composition: a small orchestra (one flute, two oboes, one bassoon, two horns and strings, with timpani in the finale), and a complete avoidance of *recitativo secco*. The accompanied recitatives are often of considerable length and the arias (almost all of them exit arias) are unusually brief (two for each sister and the companion, just one for the tenor hero); the only ensemble is the extended quartet finale. The absence of duets and trios points to the old-fashioned tradition in which Haydn was happy to work. Though the lack of action would militate against the success of the opera on the modern stage, the score has proved its musical appeal in recordings. The finale is most striking, with especially effective solo writing for flute, violin, bassoon and cello (one instrument for each of the characters); it is the only number with more than one tempo, and Haydn must have been reluctant to make in it the cuts he introduced in 1802.

Some 14 months later *La fedeltà premiata* was given for the first time, on 25 February 1781, as the opening production in the rebuilt opera house. The new *dramma giocoso* was to prove one of Haydn's most successful works; a new edition of the libretto was required in 1782 (when the adjective *pastorale* was added to the description), by which time there were five changes to the original cast. One sign of the work's comparative popularity is that it was revived each season until 1784, enjoying in all 36 performances at Eszterháza; it was also given in German (as *Die belohnte Treue*) by the Schikaneder-Kumpf troupe at the Kärntnertortheater in Vienna in 1784 and received at least eight performances at Pressburg in the following three years, as well as stagings at Ofen, Pest and Graz. Haydn's own high regard for the work is clear from his letter to Artaria of 27 May 1781, and his perception of its earning power is reflected in his re-use of its overture in Symphony no.73 ('La chasse') as well as in numerous publications of vocal numbers from the opera. Act 1 of *La fedeltà premiata* opens with a terzet and chorus and closes with Haydn's most extensive ensemble, a finale of 822 bars, yet all the other numbers are recitatives and arias. Indeed, apart from a duet for the lovers (not a love duet) in Act 3, and another fine extended finale to Act 2, there is no number employing more than one voice except for the brief and conventional *coro* at the end of the work. Further disadvantages for the modern opera lover are the shallowness and inconsistency of some of the characterization and the bewilderingly naive plot. On the other hand some of the arias contain superbly inventive touches, such as the bars leading to the recapitulation in Fileno's 'Se da' begli occhi tuoi'. Celia's scena and aria later in Act 2, 'Ombra del caro bene', is a splendid achievement, and the serious scenes are set off by the comedy of the cowardly Count Perrucchetto, who Papageno-like accepts credit for the killing of a dangerous beast.

Following the curious mixture of classical myth and modern social comedy in *La fedeltà premiata*, Haydn turned decisively in his last two operas for Eszterháza to the genre of heroic drama. In *Orlando paladino*, first performed on the prince's name-day in 1782, the serious action is leavened, as in the Viennese popular theatre tradition, by the comic, at times mock-heroic, antics of Orlando's servant Pasquale and his amorous pursuit of the shepherdess Eurilla. On the heroic plane the librettist (Nunziato Porta) and the composer display an Orlando who is by no means to be taken wholly seriously, an enchantress, Alcina, who shows farcical touches, and in Rodomonte a braggadocio in whom Haydn's irony is also revealed. This leaves only the loving couple Angelica and Medoro to uphold the serious action. Haydn's response to the mixed comic and serious situations is a score full of riches, though as usual there is no relief from (admittedly superb) recitatives and arias between a brief opening ensemble and the extended finale to Act 1, apart from a short sinfonia to mark the appearance of Alcina. Act 2 has a contrasting pair of duets, but Act 3 is one of those brief and rather inconsequential appendages despite the shortcomings of which, the opera succeeds; its stage life, once the series of 21 performances at Eszterháza from 1782 until 1784 had come to an end, proved more extensive and longer lasting than that of any of Haydn's other operas – the work was given in at least 24 theatres up to 1814. Page after page of the score reveals Haydn's attention to felicitous detail, in harmonic daring, unexpected touches of orchestration (including whistling from Pasquale in his first-act cavatina 'La mia bella diceva di no') and considerable melodic variety. On the other hand there are numbers in which, despite competence and charm, it is difficult to escape the thought that Haydn might more appropriately have written into this score, rather than that of the D major Horn Concerto HVIId/3, 'in Schlaff geschrieben'.

Though Haydn remained director of Prince Nikolaus's opera performances for a further six and a half years, until the prince's death, the production of the *dramma eroico Armida* on 26 February 1784 was the last of a new Haydn opera at Eszterháza. The chief glory of the work, which consistently maintains its serious tone, lies in the sequence of connected numbers in the third act, normally the weakest part of a Haydn opera score. The dramatic relevance of the overture, which points ahead to the last act, is not followed by anything of comparable originality in Act 1, which apart from its closing duet for Armida and Rinaldo is merely a sequence of recitatives and arias; Act 2 is similarly structured, though there is a greater sense of musical continuity in the middle scenes, and the act ends with a trio (in which Ubaldo attempts to persuade Rinaldo to put his knightly duty above love for Armida). One may argue that the predominance of arias is justified by the emphasis on the characters' individual predicaments,

Design attributed to Pietro Travaglia for the costume of Armida, the title role of Haydn's opera, first performed at Eszterháza, 26 February 1784: pen and watercolour

though the participation of all six characters at the close of Act 3 draws attention to the earlier lack of ensembles. Be that as it may, the sequence of imaginatively scored, highly expressive and dramatic numbers that make up the central scene of Act 3, set in the enchanted forest – some 25 minutes of unbroken accompanied recitative, orchestral mood-painting, aria, arioso and pantomime – ranks among Haydn's grandest achievements as an opera composer. *Armida* was the most popular of Haydn's operas with his prince, being given no fewer than 54 times until 1788; indeed, no stage work was as often performed at Eszterháza. It was also staged in the following years at Pressburg, Pest, Vienna (a concert performance in 1797 at the Theater auf der Wieden) and Turin.

Haydn's career as opera composer ended on an unhappy note. During the first months of his first London sojourn he composed for Gallini's newly rebuilt King's Theatre, Haymarket, the opera *L'anima del filosofo, ossia Orfeo ed Euridice*. According to Dies's report (14 January 1806) the first rehearsal was halted by sheriffs' men acting for king and parliament, as Gallini had not been granted permission to give theatrical performances. The score (entitled by Haydn simply *L'anima del filosofo*, presumably a reference to King Creonte's portentous moralizings) may not have been quite completed; the work was not performed in its entirety (though excerpts were published and performed in

the composer's lifetime) until a production at Florence in 1951; it had been recorded the year before.

The music is of uneven quality; or rather, the appropriateness of Haydn's musical response to parts of Carlo Badini's libretto is at times open to question. The sequence covering Orpheus's second loss of Eurydice is shallow and perfunctory, and passages in some of the arias are brilliant in too generalized a manner (Haydn was composing for the famous tenor Giacomo Davidde and the German soprano Rosa Lops). However, the series of choruses, most notably in the last act, ending with the Bacchae drowning in a storm while Orpheus's body is borne off to the island of Lesbos, is of outstanding quality, and there are expressive recitatives as well as noble arias. The dying Eurydice's cavatina 'Del mio coro' in Act 2, with english horns, horns and strings, and Orpheus's lengthy scena and aria when he discovers that she is dead – where the music moves from conventional responses to a poignant Allegro con spirito in F minor, 'In un mar d'acerbe pene' – are striking examples. Had Haydn not been deprived of its production he might in the course of rehearsals have tautened the structure, though the nature of the libretto poses problems that would have taxed the greatest of opera composers, including its division in at least four acts (in letters Haydn refers to its being in five), its uneasy swing between dynastic concerns and timeless tragedy, not to mention dramatic inanities in the handling of such incidents as Eurydice's death by snake-bite, and indeed the heroine's second death.

4. INSERTION ARIAS AND ENSEMBLES. Apart from some 20 arias that Haydn wrote for insertion into operas by other composers that he was preparing for production in Prince Nikolaus's theatre, he also revised a similar number of arias and ensembles in these works. Though little of this revised material has been published, most of it survives and has been studied and described (Bartha and Somfai 1960). Practically none of the operas for which Haydn's autograph revisions survive is even on the fringes of the specialist repertory. However, a brief study of the insertion arias is justified both by their inherent quality and by the fact that they have been published, and many of them have been recorded. Apart from an incomplete aria written before 1762 these vocal pieces date from the period of Haydn's most intensive preoccupation with the theatre, between the late 1770s and 1790. In only two cases – Traetta's *Ifigenia in Tauride* (June–July 1786) and Cimarosa's *I due supposti conti* (January–February 1789) – did Haydn's work extend both to new composition and revision, and in only one – the pasticcio *Circe, ossia L'isola incantata* (June–July 1789) – did Haydn write more than a single piece of music for insertion; in this case he wrote two arias and a terzet, as well as revising another, anonymous aria.

In no case can we readily reconstruct the circumstances or context for Haydn's insertion arias, which means that we are likely to hear and judge them by very much the same standards as we bring to the non-operatic works such as the cantatas *Miseri noi, misera patria* (1786) and *Berenice, che fai* (1795) or the Petrarch sonnet *Solo e pensoso* (1798). The arias cover as wide a musical range as they do a chronological spread, of about 35 years. Several of them were either definitely or probably written for Luigia Polzelli, Haydn's mistress, who seems to have had a light soprano voice of restricted range. Typically hers are soubrette arias, either with a tender or playful slow introduction and a sparkling Allegro concluding section in 6/8 metre (as in 'Son pietosa, son bonina', from *Circe*; of this type, though not written for Polzelli, is 'Va adagio, signorina' for Guglielmi's *La quacquera spiritosa* of 1787), or numbers in one slow tempo, such as 'Chi vive amante' (for Bianchi's *Alessandro nell'Indie*, 1787) or 'Sono Alcina' (for Gazzaniga's *L'isola di Alcina*, 1786). Technically more demanding is the splendid C major 'D'una sposa meschinella' for Paisiello's *La Frascatana* (1777), an aria with prominent oboe obbligato, wide intervals, and the considerable dramatic tension proper for an unhappy heroine; its leisurely, elegiac slow introduction makes a brief and striking reappearance. In similar vein, and again in two tempos, is 'Infelice sventurata', composed in 1789 for Cimarosa's *I due supposti conti*.

All the arias so far mentioned – indeed, this is true of roughly two-thirds of the corpus – are for soprano. Though there are only two for bass, both of them delightful, there are five tenor arias, including a powerful scena and F minor aria ('Qual destra omicida') for Traetta's *Ifigenia in Tauride* (1786) and an elegant slow number ('Se tu mi sprezzi, ingrata') for Sarti's *I finti eredi* (1788); but the most interesting of these is a scena for the comic character Pedrillo in Act 2 of the pasticcio *Circe*, as he seeks entry to a mysterious castle and is put off by various apparitions. Apart from the soprano aria 'Son pietosa, son bonina', there is from this pasticcio a male-voice terzet, 'Lavatevi presto' (not 'Levatevi', as sometimes stated), in which, at considerable length and again in two tempos, Haydn sets a text about the preparations for a jolly meal; this number might almost be thought to prefigure Rossini, though the minor-key opening of the final Vivace assai, when a noise frightens the characters, introduces a more serious note.

5. HAYDN AND OPERA. Though posterity has largely ignored Haydn's operas, at least in comparison with his symphonies, concertos, string quartets, keyboard pieces and choral works, the importance of this area of his output has only in recent years begun to be recognized. Thanks to the work of scholars and publishers we are now in a better position than any previous generation to evaluate and appreciate Haydn's operatic achievement. Time will tell whether the publication of all Haydn's stage scores in the Joseph Haydn Institute's complete edition will lead to more frequent and widespread productions, or whether these works are destined to remain a minority interest, best suited to transmission through performances in concert-hall and broadcasting or recording studio. Since World War II there has been a marked growth of interest in his operas, reflected in the comparative frequency with which they have been staged and broadcast in many countries, and especially perhaps in the availability of high-quality recordings of most of them.

Opinion varies widely about the merits of Haydn's operas, but that neither extreme view can any longer be maintained. Opera houses have on the whole had limited success with them, owing probably in roughly equal measure to the expense and technical and musical problems of staging them, and to lukewarm public support. They do not transfer readily to a larger modern theatre where intimacy and familiarity with the operatic conventions of the composer's day are inevitably lacking.

With our limited practical experience of the operas of Haydn's contemporaries – Paisiello and Anfossi, Gazzaniga and Bianchi, Naumann and Martín y Soler, to name some of those for whose works Haydn wrote insertion arias – we perforce find ourselves making comparisons with Gluck, and above all, of course, with Mozart. Such comparisons, if inevitable, are less than fair. For one thing, Haydn's mature style was established, and seven-eighths of his stage scores had been written, before Mozart wrote *Die Entführung aus dem Serail* (and *Armida*, Haydn's last operatic score for Eszterháza, was composed more than two years before *Le nozze di Figaro*); for another, Haydn himself was well aware of the restricted appeal outside Eszterháza of the operas written for that establishment. He wrote to the head of the commissariat in Prague, Franz Roth, in December 1787:

You request an *opera buffa* of me; with the greatest pleasure, if you have the desire to possess some vocal composition of mine all for yourself. But if it is to be performed in the theatre in Prague, I cannot oblige you on this occasion, because all my operas are too closely tied to our personnel (at Eszterháza in Hungary), and moreover would never produce the effect that I calculated according to local conditions.

He went on to say that his response would have been quite different had he been commissioned to write a new opera for Prague – except that he would be in direct competition with 'the great Mozart'. His warmth and generosity of spirit then break through in a revealing passage:

For if I were able to impress upon the soul of every music-lover, and even more, of the potentates, the incomparable works of Mozart – so profound and so full of musical intelligence – with so great a feeling and understanding as I bring to them, then the nations would vie with one another to possess such a jewel within their walls. ... Forgive me for straying from the path; I love the man too much.

This letter, along with a lighthearted passage in one written some two years later, bears moving testimony to an evaluation of Mozart's works that most present-day opera lovers would consider justifies the continuing adulation of the stage works of the one and the comparative neglect of those of the other. Haydn had obtained a score of *Le nozze di Figaro* in July 1789, with a view to producing it in the princely theatre; two other scores obtained at the same time were given within a few months, but despite the immediate commissioning of estimates for sets and costumes, and the copying of the orchestral parts in 1790, the production did not take place: Princess Maria Elisabeth Esterházy died on 25 February 1790, and her husband followed her to the grave on 28 September. The reference to Mozart's opera conveys tantalizingly Haydn's hopes for some joy in the bleak and lonely atmosphere to which he had reluctantly returned from a sojourn in Vienna. On 9 February 1790 he told his young friend Marianne von Genzinger of the misery of his first days back at Eszterháza: 'I could sleep little, even my dreams pursued me, then, just as I dreamed I was hearing the opera le Nozze di Figaro most splendidly performed, the wretched North wind woke me up and almost blew my nightcap off my head'.

Haydn's operas leave one in no doubt, of course, that they are the product of a composer of the very highest quality. They are scored with ingenuity, and at times with richness; the themes are often strikingly melodious; every now and then there occurs an aria or scene of memorable wit or beauty. But of the sovereign mastery of drama, pace and psychological insight that we too easily take for granted in the very greatest of stage composers, there is scarcely a sign. The faults – as we see it – lie in Haydn's apparently uncritical acceptance of the librettos put before him, his preparedness to set very long scenes of dry recitative, the leisureliness of the musical structures (lengthy orchestral ritornellos, and verbal and musical repetitions, which Haydn himself occasionally later shortened), the rather rare occurrence, and occasionally odd placement, of concerted numbers, and the short, dramatically inconsequential third acts even in some of the best of the operas. The elegant princely court for which Haydn was writing evidently relished the unhurried sequence of individually beautiful musical numbers; late 20th-century ears and minds have been conditioned to expect stronger contrasts and greater structural coherence. This is probably why his arias written for insertion into the works of his con-

temporaries, and numerous isolated numbers in his own stage scores, can strike the listener as more immediately appealing, and more memorable, than much of the music in its context. In other words, the first master dramatist among symphonists and string quartet writers of the Classical period reveals limited feeling for the ebb and flow of dramatic action and symphonic build-up in his works written for the stage. The level of dramatic interest in even the most successful of his operas, then, is inconsistent, although none of them lacks music of beauty and power.

See also Anima del filosofo, l'; Armida (v); Canterina, la; Fedeltà premiata, la; Feuersbrunst, die; Incontro improvviso, l'; Infedeltà delusa, l'; Isola disabitata, l' (ii); Mondo della luna, il (ii); Orlando paladino; Pescatrici, le (ii); Philemon und baucis; Speziale, lo (ii); and Vera costanza, la (ii).

Edition: *J. Haydn: Werke*, ed. J. Haydn-Institut, Cologne, directed J. P. Larsen (1958–61) and G. Feder (1962–) (Munich, 1958–) [HW]
Catalogue: A. van Hoboken: *Joseph Haydn: Thematisch-bibliographisches Werkverzeichnis* (Mainz, 1957–78) [H]

H	title	genre, acts	libretto	composition date	edition	première, remarks, Haydn autographs
XXIXb:1a	Der krumme Teufel	Spl	J. F. von Kurz [Kurz-Bernardon]	?1751		1st known perf. Vienna, 29 May 1753; lost or = Der neue krumme Teufel; lib. cited by Haydn
XXIXb:1b	Der neue krumme Teufel [Asmodeus, der krumme Teufel]	Spl, 2	Kurz	[?1752]	lib. in HW xxiv/2	music lost; incl. Il vecchio ingannato (int) [? not by Haydn] and Arlequin, der neue Abgott Ram in America (pantomimic Singspiel)
XXVIII:1	Acide	festa teatrale, 1	G. A. Migliavacca	1762	HW xxv/1	Eisenstadt, 11 Jan 1763, frags. in D-B, F-Pn (ov.), Po and H-Bn; lib. Bn
	[2nd version]			[1774]	HW xxv/1	Eszterháza, 25 Sept 1774
XXX:1	Marchese [La marchesa Nespola]	comedia		1763	HW xxv/1	frag. Bn; dialogues lost
XXIVb:1	[Untitled]	?ob or ?It. comedy		?1762		? = Il dottore, ?c1761–5; aria Costretta a piangere and recit. in HW xxv/1
ii, 448	Il dottore	comedia		?c1761–5		lost; cited in Haydn's *Entwurf-Katalog*, c1765
ii, 448	La vedova	comedia		?c1761–5		lost; in *Entwurf-Katalog*
ii, 448	Il scanarello	comedia		?c1761–5		lost; in *Entwurf-Katalog*
XXVIII:2	La canterina	int in musica, 2		1766	HW xxv/2	?Eisenstadt, before 11 Sept [? July] 1766; Pressburg, 16 Feb 1767; lib. from int in Piccinni: L'Origille, 1760, text of nos.2 and 3 from A. Zeno: Lucio Vero, 1700; Bn
XXVIII:3	Lo speziale [Der Apotheker]	dg, 3	C. Goldoni, ?rev. C. Friberth	[1768]	HW xxv/3	Eszterháza, aut. 1768; Act 3 inc.; Bn
XXVIII:4	Le pescatrici [Die Fischerinnen]	dg, 3	Goldoni, ?rev. Friberth	1769–70	HW xxv/4	Eszterháza, 16 Sept 1770; Bn (Acts 1 and 2 inc.)
XXVIII:5	L'infedeltà delusa [Liebe macht erfinderisch; Untreue lohnt sich nicht; Deceit Outwitted]	burletta per musica, 2	M. Coltellini, ?rev. Friberth	[1773]	HW xxv/5	Eszterháza, 26 July 1773; Bn, D-B (ov. frag.)
XXIXa:1,1a; XXIXb:2	Philemon und Baucis, oder Jupiters Reise auf die Erde	Spl/ marionette op, 1	G. K. Pfeffel	[1773]	HW xxiv/1	Eszterháza, 2 Sept 1773; frag. B; supposed ov. and frag. of prelude extant, drama extant in rev. version
XXIXa:2	Hexenschabbas	marionette op		?1773		lost; mentioned in Dies (1810)
XXVIII:6	L'incontro improvviso [Die unverhoffte Zusammenkunft; Unverhofftes Begegnen]	dg, 3	Friberth, after L. H. Dancourt: *La rencontre imprévue*	[1775]	HW xxv/6 (I, II)	Eszterháza, 29 Aug 1775; B (ov. frag.), RU-SPsc

H	title	genre, acts	libretto	composition date	edition	première, remarks, Haydn autographs
XXIXa:3	Dido	Spl/ marionette op, 3	P. G. Bader	[1776]	lib. in HW xxiv/2	Eszterháza, ?March 1776, aut. 1778; ?1 aria extant, lib. cited by Haydn
XXIXa:4	Opera comique Vom abgebrannten Haus			?c1773–9		lost or = Die Feuersbrunst, ?1775–8; in Entwurf-Katalog
XXIXb:A	Die Feuersbrunst	Spl/ marionette op, 2		?1775–8	HW xxiv/3	?Eszterháza, 1776–8; dialogues lost; part of ov. by I. J. Pleyel
XXVIII:7	Il mondo della luna [Die Welt auf dem Monde]	dg, 3	Goldoni	[1777]	HW xxv/7 (I, II, III)	1st known perf. Eszterháza, 3 Aug 1777 [possibly July]; frags. in D-B, F-Po, H-Bn and PL-Kj
XXIXb:3	Die bestrafte Rachbegierde	Spl/ marionette op, 3	Bader	?1779	lib. in HW xxiv/2	Eszterháza, 1779; music lost
XXVIII:8	La vera costanza	dg, 3	F. Puttini	by 1779 [?April– Nov 1778]	sketches HW xxv/8, 356	Eszterháza, 25 April 1779; music lost where not incl. in 2nd version
	[2nd version]; also as Der flatterhafte Liebhaber, oder Der Sieg der Beständigkeit; Die wahre Beständigkeit; List und Liebe; Laurette]			1785	HW xxv/8	Count Errico's Act 2 scene = that in Anfossi's 1775 setting; F-Pn (partly in copyists' hands)
XXVIII:9	L'isola disabitata [Die wüste Insel]	azione teatrale, 2 pts	P. Metastasio	1779	vs (Vienna and Leipzig, 1909)	Eszterháza, 6 Dec 1779; finale rev. 1802; frag. PL-Kj
XXVIII:10	La fedeltà premiata [Die belohnte Treue]	dg, 3	G. Lorenzi: L'infedeltà fedele	1780	HW xxv/10 (I, II)	Eszterháza, 25 Feb 1781; D-B (Act 1 finale), frag. H-Bn, I-Tn (copy rev. by Haydn)
XXVIII:11	Orlando paladino [Der Ritter Roland]	dramma eroicomico, 3	N. Porta, after L. Ariosto	1782	HW xxv/11 (I, II)	Eszterháza, 6 Dec 1782; D-B (Act 3), frag. GB-Lbl (Acts 1 and 2)
XXVIII:12	Armida	dramma eroico, 3	Porta, after T. Tasso: Gerusalemme liberata	1783	HW xxv/12	Eszterháza, 26 Feb 1784; Lcm, frag. US-CA
XXVIII:13	L'anima del filosofo, ossia Orfeo ed Euridice	dramma per musica, 4/5	C. F. Badini	1791	HW xxv/13	Florence, 9 May 1951; frag. D-B

Contribs. to operas by other composers performed at Eszterháza: Paisiello: La Frascatana, 1777; Anfossi: Il geloso in cimento, ?1778/1785; Anfossi: La Metilde ritrovata [L'incognita perseguitata], 1779; Salieri: La scuola de' gelosi, 1780; Anfossi: Il matrimonio per inganno, 1785; Gazzaniga: L'isola di Alcina, 1786; Traetta: Ifigenia in Tauride, 1786; Bianchi: Il disertore, 1787; Guglielmi: La quacquera spiritosa, 1787; Bianchi: Alessandro nell'Indie, 1787; Sarti: I finti eredi, 1788; Cimarosa: I due supposti conti, 1789; Circe, ossia L'isola incantata [pasticcio], 1789; Gassmann: L'amore artigiano, supposti 1790; Cimarosa: L'impresario in angustie, 1790; Cimarosa: Giannina e Bernardone, 1790

SELECTED DOUBTFUL AND SPURIOUS WORKS

H	title	genre, acts	librettist	remarks
XXIXa:5	Genovefens vierter Theil	Spl/marionette op, 3	J. K. von Pauersbach	perf. Eszterháza, sum. 1777; music lost; by various composers according to Haydn's list of librettos, by Haydn according to J. Elssler: Haydn-Verzeichnis, 1805 [catalogue supervised by Haydn]; lib. in HW xxiv/2
XXIXb:F	Die reisende Ceres	Spl	P. M. Lindemayr	music inc. (Vienna, c1982)
XXXII:2	Der Freybrief	Spl, 1	? G. E. Lüderwald	pasticcio perf. Meiningen, 1789, with Haydn's music, ? arr. Fridolin Weber; several versions, all lost
XXXII:3	Alessandro il grande	os, 3		pasticcio arr. J. Schellinger from works by Haydn and others
XXXII:4	Der Äpfeldieb	Spl, 1	C. F. Bretzner	music by [?M.] Jast [Jost]; perf. Hamburg, 1791, with addns by Haydn
i, 576–8	Die [Das] Ochsenmenuette	Spl, 1	G. E. von Hoffmann	pasticcio arr. I. von Seyfried from Haydn's works; perf. Vienna, 1823 (Mainz, 1927)
	Das Teebrett	comedy	E. Fischer	music from L'incontro improvviso, L'infedeltà delusa and Orlando paladino (Berlin, 1914)
	Finale: … sey voll edlen Stolzes		author unknown	MS D-LEm (not a Haydn autograph)

BASIC RESOURCES

A. van Hoboken: *Joseph Haydn: Thematisch-bibliographisches Werkverzeichnis* (Mainz, 1957–78)

H. C. R. Landon, ed.: *The Collected Correspondence and London Notebooks of Joseph Haydn* (London, 1959)

D. Bartha and L. Somfai: *Haydn als Opernkapellmeister: die Haydn-Dokumente der Esterházy-Opernsammlung* (Budapest, 1960)

M. Horányi: *The Magnificence of Eszterháza* (London, 1962)

V. Gotwals, ed.: *Joseph Haydn: Eighteenth-Century Gentleman and Genius* (Madison, WI, 1963, 2/1968 as *Haydn: Two Contemporary Portraits*) [trans. of biographies by G. A. Griesinger (1809) and A. C. Dies (1810)]

D. Bartha, ed.: *Joseph Haydn: Gesammelte Briefe und Aufzeichnungen: unter Benützung der Quellensammlung von H. C. Robbins Landon* (Kassel, 1965)

Haydn Studies: Proceedings of the International Haydn Conference: Washington 1975 [incl. 9 contributions on opera]

H. C. R. Landon: *Haydn: Chronicle and Works*, 5 vols. (London, 1976–80)

U. Tank: *Studien zur Esterházyschen Hofmusik von etwa 1620 bis 1790* (Regensburg, 1981)

Joseph Haydn: Vienna 1982 [incl. 18 contributions on Haydn's stage works]; review by C. Clark, *JM*, vi (1988), 245–57

G. Mraz, G. Mraz and G. Schlag, eds.: *Joseph Haydn in seiner Zeit* (Eisenstadt, 1982) [exhibition catalogue]

H. C. R. Landon and D. Wyn Jones: *Haydn: his Life and Music* (London, 1988)

L. Somfai: 'Haydn at the Esterházy Court', *Man and Music: the Classical Era*, ed. N. Zaslaw (London, 1989), 268–92

OPERAS: GENERAL

PEM (G. Feder)

L. Wendschuh: *Über Joseph Haydn's Opern* (Halle, 1896)

R. Haas: 'Teutsche Comedie Arien', *ZMw*, iii (1920–21), 405–15

H. Botstiber: 'Haydn und Luigia Polzelli', *MQ*, xviii (1932), 208–15

K. Geiringer: 'Haydn as an Opera Composer', *PRMA*, lxvi (1939–40), 23–32

H. Wirth: *Joseph Haydn als Dramatiker: sein Bühnenschaffen als Beitrag zur Geschichte der deutschen Oper* (Wolfenbüttel and Berlin, 1940)

J. Harich: *Esterházy-Musikgeschichte im Spiegel der zeitgenössischen Textbücher* (Eisenstadt, 1959)

G. Lawner: *Form and Drama in the Operas of Joseph Haydn* (diss., U. of Chicago, 1959)

J. Harich: 'Das Repertoire des Opernkapellmeisters Joseph Haydn in Eszterháza (1780–1790)', *HayJb*, i (1962), 9–110

H. C. R. Landon: 'Haydn's Marionette Operas and the Repertoire of the Marionette Theatre at Esterház Castle', *HayJb*, i (1962), 111–99

D. Bartha: 'Haydn the Opera Conductor', *MR*, xxiv (1963), 313–21

——: 'Haydn's Italian Opera Repertory at Eszterháza Palace', *New Looks at Italian Opera: Essays in Honor of Donald J. Grout* (Ithaca, NY, 1968), 172–219

G. Feder: 'Einige Thesen zu dem Thema: Haydn als Dramatiker', *Haydn-Studien*, ii (1969–70), 126–31

——: 'Ein Kolloquium über Haydns Opern', *Haydn-Studien*, ii (1969–70), 113–31 [incl. catalogue of roles in Haydn's operas]

E. Badura-Skoda: '"Teutsche Comoedie-Arien" und Joseph Haydn', *Der junge Haydn: Internationale Arbeitstagung des Instituts für Aufführungspraxis: Graz 1970*, 59–72

J. Harich: 'Das Opernensemble zu Eszterháza im Jahr 1780', *HayJb*, vii (1970), 5–46

H. C. R. Landon: 'The Operas of Haydn', *NOHM*, vii (1973), 172–99

E. Badura-Skoda: 'The Influence of the Viennese Popular Comedy on Haydn and Mozart', *PRMA*, c (1973–4), 185–99

——: 'Reflections on Haydn Opera Problems', *Haydn Studies: Washington 1975*, 27–31

G. Feder: 'Opera seria, opera buffa und opera semiseria bei Haydn', *Opernstudien: Anna Amalie Abert zum 65. Geburtstag* (Tutzing, 1975), 37–55

——: 'A Special Feature of Neapolitan Opera Tradition in Haydn's Vocal Works', *Haydn Studies: Washington 1975*, 367–71

——: 'A Survey of Haydn's Operas', ibid, 253–5

K. Geiringer: 'The *Comedia la Marchesa Nespola*: some Documentary Problems', ibid, 53–4

J. Kolk: '"Sturm und Drang" and Haydn's Opera', ibid, 440–45

E. Kanduth: 'Die italienischen Libretti der Opern Joseph Haydns', *Joseph Haydn und die Literatur seiner Zeit*, ed. H. Zeman (Eisenstadt, 1976), 61–96

E. Badura-Skoda: 'Zur Salzburger Erstaufführung von Joseph Haydns Singspiel "Die reisende Ceres"', *ÖMz*, xxxii (1977), 317–24

H. C. R. Landon: *Haydn at Eszterháza 1766–1790* (London, 1978) [vol.ii of *Haydn: Chronicle and Works*]

A. P. Brown: 'Tommaso Traetta and the Genesis of a Haydn Aria', *Chigiana*, xxxvi (1979), 101–42 [on H XXIVa 10]

G. Feder: 'Haydns Opern und ihre Ausgaben', *Musik – Edition – Interpretation: Gedenkschrift Günter Henle* (Munich, 1980), 165–79

G. Borsa: 'Neu aufgefundene, gedruckte Librettos für Eszterháza in der Zeit von Haydn (1766–1790)', *Magyar könyvszemle*, xcvii (Budapest, 1981), 229–34

A. A. Abert: 'Haydn und Gluck auf der Opernbühne', *Joseph Haydn: Vienna 1982*, 296–302

E. Badura-Skoda: 'Haydns Opern: Anmerkungen zu aufführungspraktischen Problemen der Gegenwart', *ÖMz*, xxxvii (1982), 162–7

H. Belitska-Scholtz: 'Die Theaterpflege der Fürsten Esterházy, *Joseph Haydn in seiner Zeit*, ed. G. Mraz, G. Mraz and G. Schlag (Eisenstadt, 1982) [exhibition catalogue], 240–48

P. Branscombe: 'Hanswurst redivivus: Haydn's Connections with the "Volkstheater" Tradition', *Joseph Haydn: Vienna 1982*, 369–75

G. Feder: 'Bemerkungen zu Haydns Opern', *ÖMz*, xxxvii (1982), 154–61

——: 'Haydn und das Libretto', *FUSA: Journal für Kenner & Liebhaber von Kunst – Literatur – Musik*, x (Cologne, 1982), 9–20

M. K. Hunter: *Haydn's Aria Forms: a Study of the Arias in the Operas Written at Eszterháza, 1766–1783* (Ann Arbor, 1982)

R. V. Karpf: 'Haydn und Carl Friberth: Marginalien zur Gesangskunst im 18. Jahrhundert', *Joseph Haydn: Vienna 1982*, 361–9

G. Lazarevich: 'Haydn and the Italian Comic Intermezzo Tradition', *Joseph Haydn: Vienna 1982*, 376–86

H. Schneider: 'Vaudeville-Finali in Haydns Opern und ihre Vorgeschichte', *Joseph Haydn: Vienna 1982*, 302–14

K.-H. Viertel: 'Joseph Haydn und das Musiktheater', *Musik und Gesellschaft*, xxxii (1982), 141–5

F. Lippmann: 'Haydns opere serie: Tendenzen und Affinitäten', *Studi musicali*, xii (1983), 301–31

N. Rossi: 'Joseph Haydn and Opera', *OQ*, i (1983), 54–78

M. K. Hunter: 'Haydn's Sonata-Form Arias', *CMc*, nos.37–8 (1984), 19–32

D. Altenburg: 'Haydn und die Tradition der italienischen Oper: Bemerkungen zum Opernrepertoire am Esterházyschen Hofe', *Joseph Haydn: Tradition und Rezeption*, Kölner Beiträge zur Musikforschung, cxliv (Regensburg, 1985), 77–99

F. Lippmann: 'Haydn und die Opera buffa: Vergleiche mit italienischen Werken gleichen Textes', *Joseph Haydn: Tradition und Rezeption*, Kölner Beiträge zur Musikforschung, cxliv (Regensburg, 1985), 113–40; It. trans. in *NRMI*, xvii (1983), 223–46

G. Feder and G. Thomas: 'Dokumente zur Ausstattung von *Lo speziale*, *L'infedeltà delusa*, *La fedeltà premiata*, *Armida* und anderen Opern Haydns', *Haydn-Studien*, vi (1986–8), 88–115

G. Thomas: 'Haydns deutsche Singspiele', *Haydn-Studien*, vi (1986–8), 1–63

G. Feder: 'Haydn und Hasse', *AnMc*, no.25 (1987), 305–27

M. K. Hunter: 'Text, Music and Drama in Haydn's Italian Opera Arias: Four Case Studies', *JM*, vii (1989), 29–57

C. Clark: *The Opera Buffa Finales of Joseph Haydn* (diss., Cornell U., 1991)

P. Debly: *Joseph Haydn and the Dramma Giocoso* (diss., U. of Victoria, British Columbia, in preparation)

INDIVIDUAL OPERAS
Acide

D. Heartz: 'Haydn's *Acide e Galatea* and the Imperial Wedding Operas of 1760 by Hasse and Gluck', *Joseph Haydn: Vienna 1982*, 332–40

G. Thomas: 'Anmerkungen zum Libretto von Haydns Festa teatrale "Acide"', *Haydn-Studien*, v (1982–5), 118–24

K. Geiringer and G. Thomas: Preface and critical commentary, J. Haydn: Werke, xxv/1 (1985)

L'anima del filosofo (Orfeo ed Euridice)

G. Pugliese: 'Florence', *Opera*, ii (1951), 448–56, esp. 455–6 [review of première]

H. Wirth: Preface and critical commentary, J. Haydn: Werke, xxv/13 (1974)

S. Leopold: 'Haydn und die Tradition der Orpheus-Opern', Musica, xxxvi (1982), 131–5

C. Price: 'Italian Opera and Arson in Late Eighteenth-Century London', JAMS, xxxxii (1989), 55–107

Armida

W. Pfannkuch: Preface, J. Haydn: Werke, xxv/12 (1965)

A. Basso: 'La rappresentazione a Torino (1804) dell' "Armida" di Haydn', Quadrivium, xiv (1973), 235–47

G. Staud: 'Haydns "Armida" oder die unerschlossenen Quellen der Theaterforschung', Maske und Kothurn (Vienna, 1982), 87–104

J. A. Rice: 'Sarti's Giulio Sabino, Haydn's Armida, and the Arrival of Opera Seria at Eszterháza, HayJb, xv (1984), 181–98

La canterina

D. Bartha: Preface and critical commentary, J. Haydn: Werke, xxv/2 (1959)

G. Allroggen: 'Piccinnis "Origille"', AnMc, no.15 (1975), 258–97

F. Lippmann: 'Haydn e l'opera buffa: tre confronti con opere italiane coeve sullo stesso testo', NRMI, xvii (1983), 223–46

G. Allroggen: 'La canterina in den Vertonungen von Nicolà Piccinni und Joseph Haydn', Joseph Haydn: Tradition und Rezeption, Kölner Beiträge zur Musikforschung, cxliv (Regensburg, 1985), 100–12

G. Feder: Preface to N. Piccinni: La canterina, Concentus musicus, viii (Laaber, 1989)

La fedeltà premiata

G. Thomas: Preface and critical commentary, J. Haydn: Werke, xxv/10 (1968)

——: 'Zu "Il mondo della luna" und "La fedeltà premiata": Fassungen und Pasticcios', Haydn-Studien, ii (1969–70), 122–6

A. Porter: 'Haydn and "La fedeltà premiata"', MT, cxii (1971), 331–5

H. C. R. Landon: 'A New Authentic Source for La Fedeltà Premiata by Haydn', Soundings, ii (1971–2), 6–17; Ger. version in Beiträge zur Musikdokumentation: Franz Grasberger zum 60. Geburtstag (Tutzing, 1975), 213–32

E. Smith: 'Haydn and La fedeltà premiata', MT, cxx (1979), 567–70

F. Lippmann: 'Haydns "La fedeltà premiata" und Cimarosas "L'infedeltà fedele"', Haydn-Studien, v (1982–5), 1–15

——: 'Haydn e l'opera buffa: tre confronti con opere italiane coeve sullo stesso testo', NRMI, xvii (1983), 223–46

Die Feuersbrunst

H. C. R. Landon: Preface to score (London, 1963)

H. Geyer-Kiefl: 'Joseph Haydns vis comica: die beiden Opernproduktionen der Wiener Festwochen', ÖMz, xxxvii (1982), 225–32

G. Thomas: Preface and critical commentary, J. Haydn: Werke, xxiv/3 (1990)

L'incontro improvviso

H. Wirth: Preface and critical commentary, J. Haydn: Werke, xxv/6 (1962–3)

A. Porter: 'L'incontro improvviso', MT, cvii (1966), 202–6

K. M. Smith: Three Eighteenth-Century Turkish Operas: Gluck's 'La rencontre imprévue', Haydn's 'L'incontro improvviso' and Mozart's 'Die Entführung aus dem Serail' (MA thesis, U. of Wisconsin, 1972)

H. Wirth: 'Gluck, Haydn, Mozart: drei Entführungsopern', Opernstudien: Anna Amalie Abert zum 65. Geburtstag (Tutzing, 1975), 25–35

L'infedeltà delusa

H. C. R. Landon: 'Some Notes on Haydn's Opera "L'infedeltà delusa"', MT, cii (1961), 356–7; Ger. version in ÖMz, xvi (1961), 481–4

D. Bartha and J. Vécsey: Preface and critical commentary, J. Haydn: Werke, xxv/5 (1964)

L'isola disabitata

H. C. R. Landon and A. Boustead: Preface to score (privately printed, 1976)

Il mondo della luna

W. Bollert: 'Tre opere di Galuppi, Haydn e Paisiello sul Mondo della luna di Goldoni', Musica d'oggi, xxi (1939), 265–70

G. Thomas: 'Zu "Il mondo della luna" und "La fedeltà premiata": Fassungen und Pasticcios', Haydn-Studien, ii (1969–70), 122–6

——: 'Observations on Il mondo della luna', Haydn Studies: Washington 1975, 144–7

——: Preface and critical commentary, J. Haydn: Werke, xxv/7 (1979–82)

F. Lippmann: 'Haydn e l'opera buffa: tre confronti con opere italiane coeve sullo stesso testo', NRMI, xvii (1983), 223–46

M. Brago: 'Haydn, Goldoni and Il mondo della luna', Journal of Eighteenth-Century Studies, xvii (1984), 308–32

G. Thomas: 'Zur Frage der Fassungen in Haydns Il mondo della luna', AnMc, no.22 (1984), 405–25

Orlando paladino

A. van Hoboken: 'Nunziato Porta und der Text von Joseph Haydns Oper "Orlando Paladino"', Symbolae historiae musicae: Hellmut Federhofer zum 60. Geburtstag (Mainz, 1971), 170–79

K. Geiringer: 'From Guglielmi to Haydn: the Transformation of an Opera', IMSCR, xi Copenhagen 1972, i, 391–5

——: Preface and critical commentary, J. Haydn: Werke, xxv/11 (1972–3)

H. Geyer-Kiefl: 'Guglielmis Le pazzie d'Orlando', Joseph Haydn: Vienna 1982, 403–15

——: 'Joseph Haydns vis comica: die beiden Opernproduktionen der Wiener Festwochen', ÖMz, xxxvii (1982), 225–32

L'avant-scène opéra, no.42 (1982) [Orlando paladino issue]

B. A. Brown: 'Le pazzie d'Orlando, Orlando Paladino and the Uses of Parody', Italica, lxiv (1987), 583–605

Le pescatrici

D. Bartha and I. Becker-Glauch: Preface and critical commentary, J. Haydn: Werke, xxv/4 (1972)

S. Leopold: '"Le pescatrici" – Goldoni, Haydn, Gassmann', Joseph Haydn: Vienna 1982, 341–9

G. Thomas: 'Kostüme und Requisiten für die Uraufführung von Haydns "Le pescatrici"', Haydn-Studien, v (1982–5), 64–71

Philemon und Baucis

J. Müller-Blattau: 'Zu Haydns Philemon und Baucis', Haydn-Studien, ii (1969–70), 66–9

J. Braun: Preface and critical commentary, J. Haydn: Werke, xxiv/1 (1971)

Lo speziale

H. Wirth: Preface and critical commentary, J. Haydn: Werke, xxv/3 (1959)

La vera costanza

H. Walter: 'On the History of the Composition and the Performance of La vera costanza', Haydn Studies: Washington 1975, 154–7

——: Preface and critical commentary, J. Haydn: Werke, xxv/8 (1976)

E. Badura-Skoda: 'Zur Entstehungsgeschichte von Haydns Oper La vera costanza', ÖMz, xxxvi (1982), 487–90

——: 'Zur Entstehung von Haydns Oper La vera costanza', Joseph Haydn: Vienna 1982, 243–55

E. Melkus: 'Haydn als Dramatiker am Beispiel der Oper La vera costanza', Joseph Haydn: Vienna 1982, 256–76

M. K. Hunter: 'Pamela: the Offspring of Richardson's Heroine in Eighteenth-Century Opera', Music and Literature, ed. W. J. Rempel and U. Rempel (Winnipeg, 1985), 61–76

PETER BRANSCOMBE (with CARYL CLARK)

Haydn, (Johann) Michael (*b* Rohrau, Lower Austria, 13 Sept 1737; *d* Salzburg, 10 Aug 1806). Austrian composer, younger brother of Joseph Haydn. His early career was much like Joseph's. He moved to Vienna when only about eight years old to become a chorister at St Stephen's Cathedral. He was educated by the Jesuits, studied Fux's music and treatises, and probably witnessed the improvised musical comedies put on by Prehauser and Kurz-Bernardon at the Kärntnertortheater. After his voice broke he underwent several years of hardship until in 1757 he joined the orchestra of the Bishop of Grosswardein in Hungary (now Oradea, Romania); he was appointed Kapellmeister there in 1760. In 1762 he was offered an attractive position as Konzertmeister to Sigismund Schrattenbach, Archbishop of Salzburg, which he took up the following year.

Haydn remained in Salzburg for the rest of his life and achieved a considerable reputation throughout Europe as a composer of sacred music. He was less active in the field of dramatic music. Unlike the young Mozart, he was never commissioned to write for the Italian opera establishment kept by Schrattenbach. He did write oratorios, cantatas, *serenate teatrali* and pantomimes under Schrattenbach and later his successor, Hieronymus Colloredo. Some of these works were for use in the archbishop's residence, but others, along with Haydn's first three German operas, were performed as part of the major theatrical event held each year in the Aula academy of the Benedictine university at Salzburg. This was the 'Finalcomödie' that concluded the academic year, a five-act spoken drama in Latin to which various kinds of music and dance were added.

The librettos of Haydn's German operas and the Latin plays they accompanied were written by Father Florian Reichssiegel (1735–93). (According to his early biographers, Haydn was particularly discriminating in the texts that he set.) *Die Hochzeit auf der Alm*, given in 1768 along with Reichssiegel's *Pietas conjugalis in Sigismundo et Maria* and later performed separately in the Theatersaal at the residence, was one of his more successful efforts at opera. It mixes classical personages and country folk in its two brief acts, which are all in verse. The instrumental numbers – sinfonia, two-movement entr'acte and orchestral finale – almost engulf the vocal numbers (two arias in Act 1, a duet and a quintet in Act 2). Haydn's arias have a lied-like charm, but the duet borders on a symphonic minuet, and the extensive quintet is wholly instrumental in style and form, perhaps something Leopold Mozart had in mind when he declared that Haydn had 'no genius for theatrical music'. On the other hand, Leopold reported high praise for Haydn's incidental music to Voltaire's tragedy *Zaïre*, first given at court on 30 September 1777. Archbishop Colloredo declared that he did not think Haydn capable of such music, which is attuned very closely to the course of the drama.

Rebekah als Braut (Spl, F. Reichssiegel), 10 April 1766, *H-Bn**
Die Hochzeit auf der Alm (dramatisches Schäfergedicht, 2, Reichssiegel), 6 May 1768, *D-Mbs**, pts *A-Ssp*, vs (Salzburg and Stuttgart, 1959)
Die Wahrheit der Natur (Spl, Reichssiegel), 7 July 1769, *H-Bn**
Der Bassgeiger zu Wörgl (Spl), c1775–7, *A-SPL*
Der englische Patriot (Spl), c1779, *H-Bn**
Andromeda e Perseo (os, G. B. Varesco), 14 March 1788, *Bn**, *I-Fc*, sinfonia in DM, clxxxv (1968)
Die Ährenleserin (Spl, 1, C. F. Weisse), 2 July 1788, *D-Mbs*

*

C. von Wurzbach: *Joseph Haydn und sein Bruder Michael* (Vienna, 1861)
C. Schneider: *Geschichte der Musik in Salzburg* (Salzburg, 1935)
H. Jancik: *Michael Haydn: ein vergessener Meister* (Vienna, 1952)
ÖMz, xxvii/1 (1972) [M. Haydn issue]
M. H. Schmid: *Mozart und die Salzburger Tradition* (Tutzing, 1976)
G. Croll and K. Vössing: *Johann Michael Haydn: sein Leben, sein Schaffen, seine Zeit* (Vienna, 1987)   THOMAS BAUMAN

Hayes, Catherine (*b* Limerick, 25 Oct 1825; *d* London, 11 Aug 1861). Irish soprano. She studied in Paris with the younger Manuel García and Milan with Giorgio Ronconi, then made her début at Marseilles (10 May 1845) as Elvira (*I puritani*). Her performance in *Linda di Chamounix* at La Scala later that year established her supremacy in Italian opera, and she appeared in works by Mercadante, Rossini and Verdi throughout Italy and in Vienna. She made her London début in *Linda di Chamounix* at Covent Garden (10 April 1849), where she also sang Lucia, then toured America, Australia and India before giving an immensely successful season in Ireland (1857). She is said to have been 'a true soprano, with more than an average share of the middle voice' (*Musical World*, 17 August 1861).

Haym, Nicola Francesco (*b* Rome, 6 July 1678; *d* London, 31 July 1729). Italian composer, poet and theatre manager. According to his obituary in *The Weekly Medley* (9 August 1729), he was 'deservedly famous for divinely touching the *Violoncello*', manifested 'Genius for Musick as a Composer, ... devoted several Hours daily to the *Belles-Lettres*' and 'was Secretary for many Years to the Royal Academy of Musick in this City, in which Employment he distinguish'd himself by his indefatigable Industry and the general Satisfaction he gave to all the Directors'. His 'uncommon Modesty, Candour, Affability and all the amiable Virtues of Life' undoubtedly contributed much to his operatic activities as continuo cellist, stage manager and adapter of librettos and scores written by others.

From 1694 to 1700 he was employed by Cardinal Pietro Ottoboni in Rome as a performer and composer and by the Seminario Romano as a teacher of the cello. He may have played in the orchestra at the Teatro Capranica, which staged the first two operas he later adapted for London, Alessandro Scarlatti's *Pirro e Demetrio* (1694) and Giovanni Bononcini's *Il trionfo di Camilla* (1698). In 1701 he arrived in London (with the violinist Nicola Cosimi) to serve as master of chamber music to Wriothesley Russell, second Duke of Bedford (*d* 1711). When italianate operas were introduced in 1705 at Drury Lane and the Queen's Theatre, he was continuo cellist and manager for his wife, the singer Joanna Maria (*d* 1724), Baroness Linchenham (sometimes wrongly spelt Lindelheim). In addition, he created the two most successful adaptations of the decade, *Camilla* (1706) and *Pyrrhus and Demetrius* (1708). They are the only works praised in 'A Critical Discourse on Opera's and Musick in England' (1709), and they certainly served to help Haym gain future commissions. They also show how rapidly he adjusted to changing conditions. He was able to retain Bononcini's overture and arias for *Camilla*; but singers undoubtedly demanded many revisions in *Pyrrhus and Demetrius*, so he retained only 14 of Scarlatti's arias, composed an overture and 21 arias himself and inserted 19 from other sources, mainly 'suitcase arias' (carried around by travelling performers to sing in any opera) of the two castratos.

During his second decade in London, when operas began to be performed entirely in Italian (rather than wholly or partly in English), Haym probably adapted both text and music for many of the pasticcios that featured suitcase arias. He certainly reworked *Etearco*, *Dorinda*, *Creso* and *Lucio Vero*, and perhaps at least four more whose adapter is unknown: *Almahide* (1710), *Ernelinda* (1713), *Arminio* (1714) and *Vincislao* (1717). No source attributes the music of an aria in any of these works to Haym, whose adaptive hand in fact began to turn to texts during this decade: he supplied Handel with *Teseo* (1713) and perhaps *Amadigi* (1715) and *Radamisto* (1720). He may also have provided Ariosti with *Tito Manlio* (1717), which, unlike all the other texts that Haym prepared for the London stage, has no known predecessor, and thus may be a new creation. The only original text attributed to him is 'La cagion de' miei tormenti', a cantata set by Jakob Greber (in *GB-Cfm*, MS 44), dated 1704.

During his final decade in London, for six seasons (from autumn 1722 until spring 1728), Haym was Secretary of the Royal Academy of Music, working as stage manager for all productions. He adapted texts for

Handel (*Ottone, Flavio, Giulio Cesare in Egitto, Tamerlano, Rodelinda, Siroe, Tolomeo* and perhaps the pasticcio *Elpidia*), Ariosti (*Caio Marzio Coriolano, Vespasiano, Artaserse* and perhaps *Aquilio consolo, Dario, Elisa, Lucio Vero* and *Teuzzone*), and Bononcini (*Calfurnia* and *Astianatte*). He is listed as one of two continuo cellists in the plans (drawn up about 15 February 1720) for the orchestra of the Royal Academy of Music, so he could normally have filled such a post from the time of the first opera produced in London (Thomas Clayton's *Arsinoe* of 1705) until the end of the Academy in 1728. His position as stage manager, however, probably prevented him from playing in the orchestra.

Haym's adaptations reflect the shrewdly practical approach to his task that the Modenese diplomat Giuseppe Riva described in letters written to Lodovico Antonio Muratori in 1725–6. After saying that Haym was a perfect idiot in the realm of *belles-lettres*, Riva explained how a libretto for London had to be written to a certain formula for the singers in the company and how any libretto from Italy had to be 'reformed, or rather deformed, in order to encounter favour: they must have few lines of recitative and many arias, and this is why some of the best operas of Apostolo [Zeno] will never be done and why the two most beautiful by Metastasio, *Didone* and *Siroe*, will suffer the same fate'. Paolo Antonio Rolli, who was Secretary of the Royal Academy in the years 1720 to 1722, had been a fellow student with Metastasio in Rome. In comparison with Haym, he strove to maintain some poetic artifice in his adaptations, which he disparagingly termed 'dramatic skeletons'. Poetic artifice is best displayed in long recitatives, and they were of little or no interest to the English, who came to hear dazzling singers and affecting music. As a result, Haym's 'skeletons' advance the plot rapidly, and focus on melodramatic incidents. They thus pleased his audiences, singers and composers (with the possible exception of Bononcini), and remain stageworthy today.

When he died, Haym was helping Handel and Heidegger plan a new academy of music and it is possible that he had already done some editing of three texts (*Partenope, Ormisda* and *Venceslao*) that were produced in 1730–31. If we include these three, the number of operatic texts that Haym might have adapted in London is 35, but only 19 of them are certainly by him. His work with *belles-lettres* extended, however, far beyond opera librettos. In other publications he drew and described hundreds of ancient medals belonging to 18 British collectors, edited three Italian literary works and compiled a valuable bibliography of Italian books. All of these projects were partly based on his own magnificent collections of books, prints, coins and paintings.

Just before his death, he had finished *A General History of Musick*, which John Lockman was translating into English. According to its table of contents (reprinted in Hawkins), volume two (books III–VI) treated the introduction of operas, their subsequent spread and their reception in England from 1700 to 1728. If these books are ever found, they should provide us with many insights into Baroque opera.

only the London works for which Haym is known to have adapted music as well as text are listed

Camilla [G. Bononcini: Il trionfo di Camilla], Drury Lane, 30 March 1706, partial score *GB-Lcm* (*R*1990: MLE, E/ii); ov. and 52 arias (London, 1706)

Pyrrhus and Demetrius [A. Scarlatti: Pirro e Demetrio], Queen's, 14 Dec 1708, ov. and 54 arias (London, 1709)

Etearco [G. Bononcini: Etearco], Queen's, 10 Jan 1711, ov. and 36 arias (London, 1711)

Dorinda [C. F. Pollarolo: La fede riconosciuta], Queen's, 10 Dec 1712

Creso, re di Lidia [G. Polani: Creso tolto a le fiamme], Queen's, 27 Jan 1714, ov. and 24 arias (London, 1714)

Lucio Vero, imperatore di Roma [T. Albinoni: Lucio Vero], King's, 26 Feb 1715

BDA; BurneyH; HawkinsH; LS

A Critical Discourse on Opera's and Musick in England (London, 1709) [pubd with F. Raguenet: *A Comparison between the French and Italian Musick and Opera's*, pp.62–86]

E. Sola: 'Curiosità storico-artistico-letterarie tratte dal carteggio dell'inviato estense Giuseppe Riva con Lodovico Antonio Muratori', *Atti e memorie della R. Deputazione di storia patria per le provincie modenesi e parmensi*, 3rd ser., iv (1887), 197–392

S. Fassini: *Il melodramma italiano a Londra nella prima metà del Settecento* (Turin, 1914)

G. S. Thomson: *The Russells in Bloomsbury, 1669–1771* (London, 1940)

E. Dahnk-Baroffio: 'Nicola Hayms Anteil an Händels Rodelinde-Libretto', *Mf*, vii (1954), 295–300

K. Sasse, ed.: 'Opera Register from 1712 to 1734 (Colman-Register)', *HJb* 1959, 199–223

D. R. B. Kimbell: 'The Libretto of Handel's *Teseo*', *ML*, xliv (1963), 371–9

S. Rosenfeld: 'An Opera House Account Book', *Theatre Notebook*, xvi (1964–5), 83–8

G. E. Dorris: *Paolo Rolli and the Italian Circle in London, 1715–1744* (The Hague, 1967)

D. R. B. Kimbell: 'The "Amadis" Operas of Destouches and Handel', *ML*, xlix (1968), 329–46

J. M. Knapp: 'Handel's *Tamerlano*: the Creation of an Opera', *MQ*, lvi (1970), 405–30

C. A. Price: 'The Critical Decade for English Music Drama, 1700–1710', *Harvard Library Bulletin*, xxvi (1978), 38–76

L. Lindgren: '*Camilla* and *The Beggar's Opera*', *Philological Quarterly*, lix (1980), 44–61

J. Milhous and R. D. Hume, eds.: *Vice Chamberlain Coke's Theatrical Papers, 1706–1715* (Carbondale, IL, 1982)

C. Monson: '*Giulio Cesare in Egitto*: from Sartorio (1677) to Handel (1724)', *ML*, lxvi (1985), 313–43

R. Strohm: *Essays on Handel and Italian Opera* (Cambridge, 1985)

W. Dean: 'The Genesis and Early History of *Ottone*', *Göttinger Händel Beiträge*, ii (1986), 129–40

W. Dean and J. M. Knapp: *Handel's Operas, 1704–1726* (Oxford, 1987)

L. Lindgren: 'The Accomplishments of the Learned and Ingenious Nicola Francesco Haym (1678–1729)', *Studi musicali*, xvi (1987), 247–380

E. Gibson: *The Royal Academy of Music (1719–1728): the Institution and its Directors* (New York and London, 1989)

E. Harris, ed.: *The Librettos of Handel's Operas: a Collection of Seventy-One Librettos Documenting Handel's Operatic Career* (New York, 1989)

LOWELL LINDGREN

Haymarket Theatre. A name variously used for a succession of London theatres on two different sites in the Haymarket – the King's (or Queen's) Theatre in the Haymarket (later Her or His Majesty's), on the west side, which was the principal Italian opera house in London for more than a century, and the Little (or New) Theatre (later Theatre Royal), on the east. *See* LONDON, §II, 2.

Haymon, Cynthia (*b* Jacksonville, FL, 6 Sept 1958). American soprano. She studied in New York and in 1984 became an apprentice at Santa Fe, where she took part in the American première of *We Come to the River* and later sang Diana (*Orphée aux enfers*) and Xanthe (*Die Liebe der Danae*). In 1985 she created the title role in Musgrave's *Harriet, the Woman called 'Moses'* for Virginia Opera. She made her European début at Glyndebourne in 1986 as Gershwin's Bess, returning in

1989 as Gluck's Eurydice. She sang Liù with the Royal Opera in South Korea, Japan and at Covent Garden (1987), where she also sang Mimì. She has sung Micaëla and Susanna at Seattle and has appeared at Brussels, Hamburg and Munich. An attractive artist with a charming appearance, she has a warm and vibrant voice.   ELIZABETH FORBES

Haywood, Lorna (Marie) (*b* Birmingham, 29 Jan 1939). English soprano. She studied at the RCM and the Juilliard School; while a student she sang the title role in the first New York performance of *Kát'a Kabanová* (1964). She made her Covent Garden début in 1966 as the First Lady (*Die Zauberflöte*), and first sang with Sadler's Wells Opera, later the ENO, at the Coliseum as Micaëla in 1970. She appeared widely in the USA, in Chicago, Dallas, Fort Worth, Lake George, St Paul and San Diego, where she sang the title role of Menotti's *The Saint of Bleecker Street* (1976). Her repertory included Pamina, Countess Almaviva, Mařenka, Butterfly, Tosca, Musetta, Mimì, Nedda and Hanna Glawari. The strength and clarity of her warm-toned voice and her intense dramatic involvement were especially convincing in Janáček's operas – *Jenůfa*, which she sang at Covent Garden (1972), for Opera North (1980) and in Prague; *The Makropulos Affair*; *Kát'a Kabanová*, the opera with which she was most closely identified; and *The Excursions of Mr Brouček*, in which she sang Málinka, Etherea and Kunka at the ENO (1978).

ELIZABETH FORBES

Head, Michael (Dewar) (*b* Eastbourne, 28 Jan 1900; *d* Cape Town, 24 Aug 1976). English composer. He abandoned studies in mechanical engineering and went to the RAM (1919–25), where he studied composition with Corder and was later appointed professor of piano. He toured widely as a recitalist and was a singularly persuasive interpreter of his own music. As a composer he is known almost exclusively for his vocal music, which is melodically simple, harmonically conservative and fastidiously crafted. In 1931 he wrote a one-act chamber opera, *The Bidder's Opera*, to a libretto by Mary Dunn, followed some years later by two children's operas with spoken dialogue, *The Bachelor Mouse* (1954) and *Through Train* (1956), to librettos by his sister Nancy Bush. More important are three one-act 'light operas' (librettos again by his sister), two for the Intimate Opera Company, *Key Money* (1960) and *Day Return* (1967), both performed at the Mercury Theatre in April 1970, and one, *After the Wedding* (1969), for the Opera Workshop, which presented it at the RAM in 1972. The music is a continuous web of thematic units, with conversational vocal lines that blossom into brief passages of arioso. Harmonically, the style is somewhat more advanced and aggressive than that of his songs.

MICHAEL HURD

Head voice (Fr. *voix de tête*; Ger. *Kopfstimme*; It. *voce di testa*). A term widely used to denote quiet ('soft') singing in the upper range, or register, of the voice. The singer aims the sound high in the face (or 'mask') and may experience it as in the head itself, the opposite of the CHEST VOICE. In practice, what seems like a simple piece of nomenclature can describe very different things, particularly in tenors and baritones, where reference to an 'exquisite head voice' may mean nothing more than a pleasant FALSETTO. A singer trained soundly in the Italian school will regard the *voce di testa* as a method

of placement, the tone itself being as consistent as possible with the voice at a *forte*.   J. B. STEANE

Healey, Derek (*b* Wargrave, 2 May 1936). English composer. He studied composition at Durham University with Howells and in Italy with Petrassi, Boris Porena and Berio. In 1969 he moved to Canada where he taught at several universities before emigrating to the USA in 1979 to teach at the University of Oregon; he returned to Britain in 1988. His musical style embraces several different influences; beginning as a neo-classicist, he later absorbed the techniques of the Second Viennese School and post-Webern serialists, studied electronic music and developed an interest in ethnic music, particularly Appalachian shape-note hymns and Canadian Inuit and West Coast Indian music. These stylistic aspects are evident in his largest work *Seabird Island*, a two-act opera to a libretto by Norman Newton based on a Tsimshian (West Coast Indian) legend; the work was commissioned by the Edward Johnson Music Foundation and first performed at the Guelph Spring Festival on 7 May 1977. Newton describes his libretto as 'the story of a girl who gives up a socially valuable life for an illusion which eventually destroys her'; the plot involves a Prince (bass-baritone), Shaman (tenor), King (bass), Queen (mezzo-soprano), Princess and her Maid (both sopranos). Healey's music is advanced, encompassing atonal melodic lines, tone clusters and aleatory and prepared tape passages. The influence of Indian singing is evident in some of the decorative vocal writing and in the choice of some of the percussion instruments. He also wrote a children's opera, *Mr Punch* (1969).

*

M. Schulman: 'Country of Residence: an Influence on Healey's Music', *Music Scene*, no.274 (1973), 4

J. Beckwith and K. MacMillan, eds.: *Contemporary Canadian Composers* (Toronto, 1975), 94–6

K. Keiser: 'Derek Healey's New Opera Based on Indian Legend', *Fugue*, i/7 (1977), 7–8, 28–9

F. R. C. Clarke: 'They Went to Canada', *British Opera in Retrospect* (n.p., 1986) [pubn of the British Music Society], 99–101

R. H. Kornick: *Recent American Opera: a Production Guide* (New York, 1991), 137–9   F. R. C. CLARKE

Heartz, Daniel (*b* Exeter, NH, 5 Oct 1928). American musicologist. He studied at the University of New Hampshire and at Harvard University (PhD 1957) and has taught at the universities of Chicago (1957–60) and California at Berkeley (from 1960). Heartz combines precise scholarship with a breadth of knowledge that makes him equally expert in the 16th and 18th centuries and he has a formidable grasp of social and political history. His interests include Gluck, opera reform and Mozart. His work on the genesis and antecedents of *Idomeneo*, of which he prepared an edition in 1972, led him towards new views on opera reform and the change of musical style during the late 18th century. He is the author of *Mozart's Operas* (Berkeley, 1990).

PHILIP BRETT

Hebenstreit, Michael (*b c*1812; *d* after 1850). Austrian composer. Although very little is known about his life, he was one of the most talented and successful purveyors of music for Viennese suburban theatres in the 1830s and 40s. He wrote a few works for the Theater an der Wien, for a time under the same management as the Theater in der Leopoldstadt (known after 1847 as the Carltheater), but was mainly associated with the latter. The first of his 75 scores for farces, Singspiels and parodies for the Leopoldstadt theatre was to Schickh's *Das Zauberdiadem*, first performed on 6 February 1836. He provided the music for a number of works by Carl Haffner, including *Die Wiener Stubenmädchen* (1840), and for lesser works by Friedrich Kaiser, including the *Charakterbild Das Armband* (1842) and *Mönch und Soldat* (1849); but he is best remembered for his scores to ten of Nestroy's plays. These include the unsuccessful *Martha* parody (1848); the very popular *Die schlimmen Buben in der Schule*, performed 110 times between 1847 and 1862; *Judith und Holofernes* (1849), a brilliant parody of Hebbel's drama *Judith*; *Die Freiheit in Krähwinkel*, performed 36 times during the Revolution of 1848; *Liebesgeschichten und Heiratssachen* (1843) and *Karrikaturen-Charivari mit Heiratszweck*, which was Hebenstreit's last work for the theatre, performed on 1 April 1850. Apart from these works, his scores for J. Fenzl's pantomime *Harlekin als Adept* (1837) and Friedrich Hopp's *Doktor Fausts Hauskäppchen* (1840, revived at the Theater in der Josefstadt in 1855) enjoyed considerable popularity. In 1850 his name disappeared from the repertory lists and theatre almanacs.

References to a J. Hebenstreit and to a W. Hebenstreit in the Leopoldstadt Theatre's repertory lists almost certainly refer to Michael Hebenstreit.

WC – *Vienna, Carltheater*
WL – *Vienna, Theater in der Leopoldstadt*
WW – *Vienna, Theater an der Wien*

Das Zauberdiadem (Zauberspiel, 2, J. Schickh), WL, 6 Feb 1836; Henri (Posse, 2, Schickh), WL, 1 Sept 1836; Mathilde und Knauserl, oder Die Wucherschätze (Zauberspiel, 2, Schickh), WL, 15 March 1837; Nur Eine löst den Zauberspruch, oder Wer ist glücklich? (Zauberposse, 3, W. Turteltaub), WL, 29 April 1837; Die Abenteuer am Brunnen, oder Das Portrait (Posse, 2, W. Brabbée), WL, 18 Sept 1837; Musiker und Friseur, oder Zwei Söhne auf ein Mal (Zauberposse, 2, D. F. Reiberstorffer), WL, 28 Oct 1837

Der Kobold (Zauberspiel, 2, F. X. Told), WL, 17 April 1838; Der magische Stockzahn, oder Hirngrillerls Wanderung in das Reich der Gegenfüssler (Zauberspiel, 2, Told), WL, 26 May 1838; Das unzertrennliche Kleeblatt, oder Armut, Reichtum und Weisheit (Zauberspiel, 2, A. Blankowsky), WL, 21 June 1838; Die Verwechslung der Bindbänder am Annatag (Posse, 1, K. Meisl), WL, 25 July 1838; Die beiden Übellaunigen, oder Die ästhetische Familie (Posse, 2), WL, 22 Nov 1838

Lady, Fee und Holzdieb, oder Die Wette gilt ein Mädchen (Posse, 3, K. Haffner), WL, 26 Dec 1838, collab. A. Müller; Der Sylvesterball, oder Millionär und Nachtwächter (Posse, 2, ? after W. A. Gerle and H. Zschokke), WL, 31 Dec 1838; Der bezähmte Weiberfeind, oder Mutter und Tochter in einem Alter (Posse, 2, A. Blankowsky), WL, 23 Jan 1839; Die Tochter der Berge, oder Der Vogelfänger und das reisende Genie (Zaubermärchen, 3, Haffner), WL, 16 March 1839

Der 1. Mai, oder Die magische Kunsthütte im Prater (Posse, 2, F. Kaiser and Alexander), WL, 1 May 1839; Die gespenstige Mühle, oder Der Student als Neusonntagskind (Posse, 2, Kaiser and Alexander), WL, 22 May 1839; Der Schneider und seine Tochter, oder Der Schwager aus Amerika (Posse, 3, Haffner), WL, 5 June 1839; Der Bader Igel, oder das Fest zu Neubrunn (Posse, 3, Brabbée), WL, 19 July 1839; Der Schuss vor dem Duelle, oder Staberls List und Lügen (Posse, 3, Kaiser), WL, 25 Jan 1840

Doktor Fausts Hauskäppchen (Zauberposse, 3, F. Hopp), WL, 5 Feb 1840; Dienstbotenwirtschaft, oder Schatulle und Uhr (Posse, 2, Kaiser), WW, 26 March 1840; Pelzpalatin und Kachelofen (Posse, 3, Hopp), WW, 7 May 1840; Der Haderlumpenhändler, oder Die Zinspfändung (Posse, 2), WL, 26 June 1840; Die Wiener Stubenmädchen, oder Der Ball in der Schusterwerkstatt (Posse, 2, Haffner), WL, 4 July 1840; Die Familienverwirrung, oder Wem gehört die Tochter? (Posse, 3, Brabbée), WW, 4 Aug 1840

Alles will jetzt zum Theater, oder Das Feuerwerk im Prater (Posse, 3, Hopp), WL, 5 Aug 1840; Hyronimus Bitterklee, oder Die doppelten Bräutigame (Posse, 2, Blum), WL, 22 Aug 1840; Die Müllermeisterin, oder Die Folgen einer Erbschaft (Posse, 3, Schickh), WL, 18 Sept 1840; Lichtschirm, Dampfkessel und Federkiel, oder Die unerwartete Gefangenschaft (Posse, 2), WW, 28 Nov 1840; Der Tod und der Wunderdoktor (Märchen, 3, Haffner), WL, 19 April 1841

List und Zufall, oder Der Bauchredner aus dem Stegreif (Posse, 3, J. Landner), WL, 5 May 1841; Die Bahn des Glückes (Posse, 3, A. Wimmer), WL, 6 Aug 1841; Der Millionär und der Hochmütige, oder Liebe und Geld kann viel in der Welt (Posse, 2, Brabbée), WL, 17 Sept 1841; Das schwarze Mandl, oder Die Reise durch Luft, Feuer, Erde und Wasser (Posse, 2, Schickh), WL, 19 Nov 1841; Die reiche Bäckerfamilie, oder Liebesbrief und Wechselbrief (Posse, 2, Kaiser), WW, 24 Feb 1842

Der Kirchtag in Lainz, oder Helf, was helfen kann (Posse, 2), WL, 9 April 1842; Der Fassbinder (Posse, 3, Haffner), WW, 13 May 1842; Die Europäer in Afrika (Spektakelstück, 4, Carl), WW, 17 June 1842; Bürger und Soldat (Posse, 2, Kaiser), WL, 25 July 1842; Hütte, Haus und Palast (Posse, 3, Blum), WW, 29 Oct 1842; Der Zauberspiegel (Zauberspiel, 2, A. Hesse), WL, 5 Jan 1843; Das Posthaus zu Sèvres (Posse, 4, C. Birch-Pfeiffer), WW, 25 Jan 1843

Der verkaufte Schlaf (Volksmärchen, 3, Haffner), WW, 7 March 1843; Liebesgeschichten und Heiratssachen (Posse, 3, J. Nestroy), WW, 23 March 1843; Die Abenteuer in den beiden Posthäusern (Posse, 3, Blum), WL, 6 April 1843; Müller und Schiffmeister (Posse, 3, Kaiser), WL, 20 May 1843; Er kennt sich nicht aus, oder Der ist die und die ist der (Posse, 2, Haffner), WL, 24 July 1843; Drei Bälle in Wien (Posse, 3, Blum), WL, 16 Oct 1843; Der unschuldige Schuldige, oder Sebastian Wutzelberger (Posse, 2, Hopp), WL, 8 June 1844

Allopathie, Homöopathie, Sympathie und Antipathie, oder Der Doktor aus dem Stegreif (Posse, 3, Blum), WW, 21 June 1844; Der letzte Mensch, oder Die Sternenjungfrau (Märchen, 3, Haffner), WL, 3 Aug 1844; Ein Loch im Plafond (Posse, 3, E. Liebold), WL, 12 July 1845; Die schlimmen Buben in der Schule (Posse, 1, Nestroy), WC, 10 Dec 1847; Martha, oder Die Mischmonder Markt-Mägde-Mietung (Parodie, 3, Nestroy), WC, 25 Jan 1848; Die lieben Anverwandten (Posse, 5, Nestroy), WC, 21 May 1848

Freiheit in Krähwinkel (Posse, 3, Nestroy), WC, 1 July 1848; Der Zauberdrache (Posse, 2, J. B. Lang), WC, 18 Nov 1848; Lady und Schneider (Posse, 2, Nestroy), WC, 6 Feb 1849; Judith und Holofernes (Parodie, Nestroy), WC, 13 March 1849; Merkwürdig (Posse, 3), WC, 30 May 1849, collab. A. M. Storch; Das Kirchweihfest zu St Anna im Böhmerwalde (Volksstück, 3, Kaiser), WC, 23 June 1849; Höllenangst (Posse, 3, Nestroy), WC, 17 Nov 1849; 'Sie sollen ihn nicht haben!', oder Der holländische Bauer (Posse, 2, Nestroy), WC, 12 Jan 1850; Karrikaturen-Charivari mit Heiratszweck (Posse, 3, Nestroy), WC, 1 April 1850

F. Hadamowsky: *Das Theater in der Wiener Leopoldstadt*, Kataloge der Theatersammlung der Nationalbibliothek in Wien, iii (Vienna, 1934)

A. Bauer: *150 Jahre Theater an der Wien* (Zürich, 1952)

PETER BRANSCOMBE

Hedges, Anthony (John) (*b* Bicester, 5 March 1931). English composer. He read music at Keble College, Oxford, where he was awarded a postgraduate scholarship in composition (1949–56). In 1957 he joined the staff of the Royal Scottish Academy of Music and in 1963 moved to Hull University. His one opera, *Shadows in the Sun* op.61 (2, J. Hawkins), was first performed at Hull University on 17 March 1977. The work was designed for young people with little previous experience of opera, bringing together professional and non-professional forces, with a children's chorus playing a vital part in the action. The small orchestra consists mainly of wind instruments. The plot concerns a television camera crew, assembled at a stone circle to make a commercial, who are transported back to Roman Britain at the time of Caractacus. Hedges's music is expertly written in a direct and accessible style.

HUGO COLE

Hedmont, Charles [Hedmondt, Emanuel Christian] (*b* ?Ontario, 24 Oct 1857; *d* London, 25 April 1940). Canadian tenor. He studied in Montreal and Leipzig, then made his début in Berlin. He sang at the Leipzig Opera (1882–9), notably as Max, Don Ottavio, Belmonte, Tamino and Idomeneus; he also sang in the première of Mahler's completed version of Weber's *Die drei Pintos* in 1888. He toured the USA and from 1891 lived in England, singing with the Carl Rosa and Quinlan companies. He sang Lohengrin in 1891 at Covent Garden and in 1895 presented his own season of opera there, during which he sang Lohengrin, Tannhäuser and Siegmund. He was Loge in the 1908 English *Ring*.   HAROLD ROSENTHAL/R

Heermann, Gottlob Ephraim (*b* Leschwitz, 1727; *d* Weimar, 11 Feb 1815). German librettist. His entire life was spent in the service of the ducal court at Weimar. He achieved popularity in the 1770s as a close follower of Weisse's manner with his librettos for the Weimar Kapellmeister, Ernst Wilhelm Wolf. Two of his texts, *Die treuen Köhler* and *Der Abend im Walde*, are based tangentially on local historical events.

Das Rosenfest (Operette), E. W. Wolf, 1770; *Die Dorfdeputierten* (komische Oper), Wolf, 1772 (Schubaur, 1783); *Die treuen Köhler* (Operette), Wolf, 1772 (Knecht, 1786; Schubaur, 1786); *Der Abend im Walde* (Operette), Wolf, 1773; *Der Schulze im Dorfe* (komische Oper), Dieter, 1779; *Don Quixotte, oder Der irrende Ritter von der traurigen Gestalt* (Spl), F. Dunkel, 1799
                                                THOMAS BAUMAN

Heger, Robert (*b* Strasbourg, 19 Aug 1886; *d* Munich, 14 Jan 1978). German conductor and composer. He studied composition at Strasbourg, Zürich and Munich (under Max von Schillings) and subsequently became an opera conductor in Strasbourg (1907), Ulm (1908), Barmen (1909), Vienna (Volksoper, 1911), Nuremberg (1913), Munich (1920) and from 1925 at the Vienna Staatsoper. In 1933, he moved to Berlin where he conducted at the Staatsoper and also directed the Staatstheater in Kassel and the Zoppot (now Sopot, Poland) Waldoper. After the war, he remained in Berlin at the Städtische Oper before returning to Munich in 1950, where he became a principal conductor at the Bavarian Staatsoper.

Heger's reputation as a conductor, enhanced by his numerous appearances at Covent Garden (from 1925 to 1933, and in 1953 for the British première of Strauss's *Capriccio* with the Bavarian Staatsoper) and his famous recording of an abridged *Rosenkavalier* with Lotte Lehmann and Elisabeth Schumann, has tended to overshadow his achievements as a composer. Of his five operas, *Der Bettler namenlos* remained the most successful: it was produced in several German opera houses in the 1930s and revived by the composer in Munich in 1967. Like the majority of Heger's other compositions, it emanates from the late Romantic tradition of Strauss, Reger and Pfitzner and is notable for a sensitive approach to vocal writing and a virtuoso handling of orchestral sonority. *Der verlorene Sohn*, which was given by Karl Böhm at the Dresden Staatsoper, failed to make so strong an impression, although its conservative musical language met with the approval of the Nazi authorities. Nevertheless in 1939 Heger received a commission for a further opera from the Berlin Staatsoper. He was unlucky enough to select as his subject matter the relationship between Lady Hamilton and Admiral Nelson. Inevitably such material could not be performed in Germany during the war. When it was eventually heard in Nuremberg for the first time in 1951, *Lady Hamilton* aroused a mixed response and its musical style seemed outmoded.

Ein Fest auf Haderslev op.17 (3, Heger, after Storm), Nuremberg, 12 Nov 1919 (Munich, n.d.); rev. Klagenfurt, 1943
Der Bettler namenlos op.22 (3, Heger), Munich, Nationaltheater, 8 April 1932, vs (Vienna, 1931)
Der verlorene Sohn op.25 (2, Heger), Dresden, Staatsoper, 31 March 1936, vs (Vienna, 1935); rev., Kassel, May 1942
Lady Hamilton op.27, 1942 (3, Heger), Nuremberg, 11 Feb 1951, vs (Vienna, 1941)
Das ewige Reich op.29; rev. as *Tragödie der Zweitracht* op.46 (3), 1972, unperf.

*

F. Beck: 'R. Heger zum 50. Geburtstag', *Die Musik*, xxviii (1936), 828–30
K. Laux: 'Robert Heger: "Der verlorene Sohn"', *Die Musik*, xxviii (1936), 609–10
E. Kroll: 'Robert Heger', *Neue Musikzeitschrift*, iv (1950), 194–5
J. Herrmann: 'Robert Heger 70 Jahre', *Musica*, x (1956), 547–8
L. Schrott: 'Ein Meister als Paladin Hans Pfitzners', *Mitteilungen der Hans-Pfitzner-Gesellschaft*, xvii (1966), 9–11
W. Zentner: 'Dirigent und Komponist: Robert Heger fünfundachtzig Jahre', *Musica*, xxv (1971), 339   ERIK LEVI

Heidegger, John Jacob [Johann Jakob] (*b* Zürich, 19 June 1666; *d* Richmond, Surrey, 5 Sept 1749). Swiss impresario active in London. He was the son of a professor of theology from Nuremberg. He married in 1688 and had four children, all of whom died before their parents (Heidegger's wife died in 1747). Leaving Switzerland as the result of an unfortunate love affair, he travelled in Europe, reaching London perhaps as early as 1696 and certainly by 1707. He remained in England until his death but was apparently not naturalized. According to the *Scots Magazine* he served for a time in Queen Anne's Life Guards. He soon acquired a reputation as a man of taste and business acumen, and played a considerable part in the establishment of Italian opera in London.

Heidegger was involved with the production of opera at the Queen's Theatre in the Haymarket as early as the 1707–8 season. At this date he was not manager of the house but was involved in its business affairs. He selected arias for the pasticcios *Tomiri* (produced at Drury Lane on 1 April 1707) and *Clotilda* (Queen's Theatre, 2 March 1709). The anonymous *A Critical Discourse upon Opera's in England* (1709) attributes these two operas to Heidegger, referring to him facetiously as the 'Swiss Count whose Earldom lies in the Land of the Moon'. He was assistant manager of the opera house by 1711 and succeeded to its management in January 1713 when Owen Swiney ran off to Italy. *The Tatler*, 14 January 1710, reported: 'You must needs know that such a Creature as Count Hideacre has been able to get 2 or 3000 guineas an Opera subscribed', evidence of Heidegger's success in establishing himself and Italian opera in London's social and musical circles. Between 1710 and 1715 his name was associated with a number of operas produced at the Queen's Theatre (from 1714 the King's Theatre): *Almahide* (10 January 1710), *Antioco* (12 December 1711), *Ercole* (3 May 1712), *Ernelinda* (26 February 1713), *Creso* (27 January 1714), *Arminio* (4 March 1714), *Lucio Vero* (26 February 1715) and Handel's *Amadigi* (25 May 1715). Although Heidegger signed the dedication of the libretto of *Amadigi*, this was in his capacity as theatre manager; there is no evidence of his authorship of the text, which was probably prepared by either Giacomo

Rossi or Nicola Haym. John Vanbrugh let the King's Theatre to Heidegger for £400 per annum from Michaelmas 1716 and he remained in joint or sole control of the theatre until at least 1745. A cashbook which survives for the 1716–17 season under Heidegger's management shows that he was given a benefit on 30 March 1717 at which he received £141 14s. 9d.

There was no Italian opera in London between 1717 and 1719, but Heidegger was active in the arrangements for the foundation of the Royal Academy of Music which was incorporated in 1719 with Heidegger as a director and Handel as a principal composer. The Academy began its first season in spring 1720 and it flourished until the end of the 1726–7 season, when factions supporting the rival sopranos Faustina Bordoni and Francesca Cuzzoni disrupted a performance on 6 June 1727. The near-riot inspired a satirical pamphlet entitled *The Contre Temps; or, Rival Queans*, in which Heidegger appeared as 'High-Priest to the Academy of Discord'. Although the Academy offered operas in 1727–8, dissension within the company and its directors brought the venture to a close. In January 1729 Heidegger and Handel were granted permission by the defunct Academy to use its scenery and costumes for five years, and their new opera venture opened on 2 December 1729 with Handel's *Lotario*. Even with George II contributing £1000 a year to this undertaking there were difficulties which were compounded by the formation in 1733–4 of the rival Opera of the Nobility. On 6 July 1734 Handel's agreement with Heidegger expired and the pair gave up the enterprise. Heidegger let the King's Theatre to the Opera of the Nobility in 1734, and when that undertaking failed in 1737 he engaged Handel as musical director for one season at a fee of £1000. On the failure of an attempt to raise public subscriptions for the opera in the summer of 1738 Heidegger let the theatre to Handel for oratorios, and from 1741 to Charles Sackville, Lord Middlesex, for operas.

Opera was not Heidegger's most profitable concern. He arranged many public and private festivities, including the illumination of Westminster Hall for the coronation of George II in October 1727, and from at least as early as 1711 organized masquerades at the opera house. These continued for more than 30 years and brought Heidegger both wealth and notoriety in abundance. The masquerades were attacked by moralists, including the Bishop of London in a celebrated sermon on 6 January 1724. Attempts were made to suppress them by act of parliament and royal proclamation, and a Middlesex grand jury censured Heidegger as 'the principal promoter of vice and immorality'. Perhaps in consequence the masquerades remained popular and gave rise to lively pamphlet warfare. Heidegger figured in satires by John Hughes, Fielding, Pope and others, and in caricatures by Hogarth (*The Bad Taste of the Town*, 1724, *see* LONDON, fig.4; and *Masquerade Ticket*, 1727). Heidegger's ugliness was frequently alluded to. Pope, in the first book of *The Dunciad*, wrote 'And lo! her bird (a monster of a fowl, Something betwixt a Heideggre and owl)'.

Heidegger's income in some years is said to have amounted to £5000, but he spent freely on charity as well as gambling and helped indigent Swiss immigrants. The *General Advertiser* wrote on his death: 'Of him, it may be truly said, what one Hand received from the Rich, the other gave to the Poor'. He left a natural daughter, Elizabeth Pappet, who became licensee of the

King's Theatre and married Captain (later Vice-Admiral) Peter Denis on 2 September 1750. Heidegger's house, no. 4 Maids of Honour Row in Richmond, was decorated with views (which still survive) of Italy, Switzerland and China executed by Antonio Jolli, a scene painter at the King's Theatre from 1744 to 1748.

Portraits of Heidegger include a drawing by Marcellus Laroon showing him at the harpsichord for a gathering at Montagu House (1736); a mezzotint engraving by John Faber after Jean Baptiste Van Loo (1749); two anonymous engravings entitled 'Hei! Degeror, o!' (1724) and 'Heidegger in a rage' (c1740); and an engraving by Joseph Goupy after a sketch by Marco Ricci, showing Cuzzoni and Farinelli standing in front of a seated Heidegger; (1730; *see* LONDON, fig.3).

BDA

A Critical Discourse upon Opera's in England (London, 1709) [pubd with F. Raguenet: *A Comparison between the French and Italian Musick and Opera's*, pp.62–86]

T. Vetter: *Johann Jakob Heidegger, ein Mitarbeiter G. F. Händels* (Zürich, 1902)

E. Croft-Murray: 'The Painted Hall in Heidegger's House at Richmond', *Burlington Magazine*, lxxviii (1941), 105–12, 155–9

O. E. Deutsch: *Handel: a Documentary Biography* (London, 1955)

J. Milhous and R. D. Hume, eds.: *Vice Chamberlain Coke's Theatrical Papers, 1705–1715* (Carbondale, IL, 1982)

E. Gibson: *The Royal Academy of Music (1719–28): the Institution and its Directors* (New York, 1989)

ELIZABETH GIBSON, WINTON DEAN

Heidelberg. German city in Baden-Württemberg, on the Neckar. Its castle theatre, built by Elector Heinrich V in 1616, was one of the first independent theatres in Germany. An Italian opera was given there in 1687, but six years later the castle was partially destroyed during the War of the Palatine Succession. It was almost 150 years before a temporary theatre was opened in the inn Zum Prinzen Max, and in 1853 an imposing municipal theatre was built in the Theaterstrasse. This building remained unharmed through both world wars, but has been renovated several times, in 1924–5, in the 1950s, in 1978 and in 1990. Now the Theater der Stadt Heidelberg, with stalls and two circles, it has a total capacity of 619 seats. The regular season lasts about ten months, during which there are about 115 opera performances from a repertory of seven or eight works, usually including a modern opera, one from the pre-Mozartian period and at least three *Spielopern*. There is also an annual Castle Festival, which always includes a performance of *The Student Prince*. The city funds the theatre, with assistance from the Land of Baden-Württemberg. Artists who worked in the city early in their careers include the outstanding chorus master Walter Hagen-Groll (later of the Deutsche Oper, the Vienna Staatsoper and the Salzburg Festival) and the conductor Peter Schneider.

L. Fehrle-Burger: *Die Welt der Oper in den Schlossgärten von Heidelberg und Schwetzingen* (Karlsruhe, 1977)

GÁBOR HALÁSZ

Heiden, Bernhard (*b* Frankfurt, 24 Aug 1910). American composer of German birth. He studied composition with Hindemith at the Berlin Hochschule für Musik and in 1935 moved to the USA; later he studied musicology with Grout at Cornell University. Between 1946 and 1981 he taught at Indiana University. His only opera, *The Darkened City* (1961–2), to a libretto by Robert Glynn Kelly, was first performed at Bloomington on 23 February 1963. The plot, which is reminiscent of a medieval miracle play, has two central themes: the effect of crisis on individuals and a miraculous return from the dead. It is set in a small 14th-century English city that is also a pilgrims' shrine. Lazurus, a city councillor, dies of the plague, but is later resurrected (Act 2). Lazurus's widow is courted by a variety of suitors, a situation similar to Penelope's plight in Monteverdi's *Il ritorno d'Ulisse in patria*. Eventually she meets her resurrected husband, who has become fervently religious. This transformation leads to the Act 3 confrontation between the zealot Lazurus and the city's pragmatic mayor. At the end, Lazurus is struck down again, and the light in the shrine dies out.

The opera is characterized by the use of 12-note motifs, the structural use of silence and timbre, and conciseness of form. There is some use of Gregorian chant; leitmotif is employed to portray characters and situations; and there is symbolic use of key relationships. The vocal lines are chromatic and ensemble scenes are kept to a minimum. The influence of Hindemith is apparent throughout. Because of the libretto's rather static quality the opera demands inventive staging to be truly effective.

*

Anderson2; *Baker7*; *VintonD*

P. Nettl: 'Bernhard Heiden: the Darkened City', *SMz*, ciii/2 (1963), 94–5

A. S. Yama: 'The Darkened City: a Lyrical Opera', *Opera Journal*, xii/4 (1979), 29–36   JAMES P. CASSARO

Heidersbach, Käthe (*b* Breslau [now Wrocław], 30 Oct 1897; *d* Kyrkhult, Sweden, 3 March 1979). German soprano, naturalized Swede. She trained first as a pianist and in 1918 began to study singing in Berlin. Her début at Detmold in 1922 led to a four-year engagement in her home town, and then from 1927 to 1944 she appeared regularly at the Berlin Staatsoper. At Bayreuth (1928–40), her principal roles were Elsa, Freia, Gutrune and Eva, the last two of which she sang, making a charming impression, at Covent Garden in 1934. Her repertory was wide, and included Luisa Miller which she sang at the Kroll Opera in 1929. She married a Swedish singer, Nils Källe, and from 1945 lived in Sweden. In recordings her voice has a maidenly gentleness, somewhat lacking in colour and emotional energy.

J. B. STEANE

Heilbronn, Marie (*b* Antwerp, 1851; *d* Nice, 31 March 1886). Belgian soprano. She studied in Paris and made her début in 1867 at the Opéra-Comique, as Alice in the first performance of Massenet's *La grand'tante*. In 1870 she appeared at La Monnaie as Violetta, the role of her début at Covent Garden in 1874. She returned in 1879 as Ophelia (*Hamlet*). The same year she appeared at the Paris Opéra as Marguerite and in 1880 she sang Zerlina and Ophelia there. At Monte Carlo in 1883 she sang Susanna, Philine (*Mignon*), Marguerite, Massé's Galatea and Rose in Maillart's *Dragons de Villars*. In 1884 she created the title role of Massenet's *Manon* at the Opéra-Comique. She was immensely gifted and very attractive in appearance, but her private life intruded upon her career.

For illustration *see* MANON.   ELIZABETH FORBES

Heimchen am Herd, Das ('The Cricket on the Hearth'). Opera in three acts by KARL GOLDMARK to a libretto by A. M. WILLNER after CHARLES DICKENS's story; Vienna, Hofoperntheater, 21 March 1896.

The opera is set in England at the beginning of the 19th century. May (soprano), a doll-maker, was betrothed to Edward (tenor), who has gone away to sea; now she is to marry Tackleton (bass), owner of the doll factory. The postilion John (baritone) arrives with an old sailor who, in the second act, reveals his identity only to Dot (soprano), John's wife. Jealous, John contemplates suicide, but the Cricket (soprano) intervenes in a dream sequence to tell him that Dot is expecting their first child. Act 3 begins with the stranger singing a sea shanty to May and disclosing that he is Edward. They leave in Tackleton's carriage to be married, while their friends detain the latter. Dot admits to John that she is pregnant, and everything ends happily, for all except Tackleton. Stylistically *Das Heimchen* marks a departure from Goldmark's earlier operas, with set numbers linked by *secco* recitative. The music is deliberately simple, alluding to folk music in the dances and choruses that accompany Tackleton's discomfiture.

ALFRED CLAYTON

Heimkehr aus der Fremde, Die ('The Homecoming from Abroad' [*Son and Stranger*]). Liederspiel in one act, op.89, by FELIX MENDELSSOHN to a libretto by Karl Klingemann; private performance, Berlin, 26 December 1829 (first public performance, Leipzig, 10 April 1851).

Mendelssohn composed the opera during his first visit to England, in 1829, to celebrate his parents' silver wedding anniversary. Dramatically the work is unsophisticated; the music, though limited in scope, is beautifully crafted and contains some finely conceived moments.

The plot centres on the attempt of an unscrupulous but amusing rogue, Kauz (baritone), to impersonate Hermann (tenor), son of a local magistrate, Schulz (bass). Hermann has been away serving as a soldier and his mother (contralto) and sweetheart Lisbeth (soprano) have been longing for his return. Everyone except Lisbeth fails to recognize him when he arrives unexpectedly. Kauz, disguised as the nightwatchman, disrupts Hermann's serenading of Lisbeth, but in turn Hermann, also disguised as the nightwatchman, likewise interrupts Kauz and drives him away. The following day, at the celebration of the magistrate's 50th year in office, Kauz announces himself as his son, only to be confounded when the real Hermann steps forward; after this denouement everything is speedily brought to a happy conclusion.

The opera consists of an overture, an entr'acte and 13 vocal numbers. Mendelssohn's deft command of orchestral colour is evident throughout the work and his ability to create charming effects with the simplest of means is impressive. The opera is formally unpretentious; the finale is brief and straightforward, the ensembles are uncomplicated and all seven solo numbers except one (the mother's Romanze, no.1) are entitled 'Lied'. But the basically strophic forms of the solos are subtly varied; they contain many delightful details and are skilfully designed to enhance atmosphere and to build up the individuality of the characters. The entr'acte (no.11), which beautifully portrays the transition from night to day, concludes with a reminiscence of the charming overture.   CLIVE BROWN

Heine, Heinrich [Harry] (*b* Düsseldorf, 13 Dec 1797; *d* Paris, 17 Feb 1856). German poet and writer. He studied law at Bonn, Göttingen and Berlin, and his first book of poems (1822) was published while he was a student. In 1825 he was baptized into the Protestant church (changing his name from Harry to Heinrich), took a doctorate in law, and continued the journeys begun the previous year. In 1827 he published *Buch der Lieder*, the volume on which his fame and his reputation as a musical poet are mainly based. He moved to Paris in 1831 and, apart from brief visits to Germany and the Pyrenees, remained there for the rest of his life, interpreting German life and art to the French, and vice versa. His last years were a period of growing immobility and pain, caused by a paralytic illness, but they also witnessed a remarkable outpouring of verse. The vast majority of musical settings of Heine are of the early and short lyrics, but he also had important connections with opera and ballet: Wagner derived the story of *Der fliegende Holländer* from *Aus den Memoiren des Herren von Schnabelewopski* (from vol.1 of *Der Salon*, 1834–40); *Tannhäuser* too perhaps owes something to Heine's long poem *Der Tannhäuser* (1836); and *Deutschland ist noch ein kleines Kind* (1840) with its lively evocation of young Siegfried may well have been familiar to Wagner. The Gautier-Adam ballet *Giselle* and Taglioni's *Satanella* are based on Heine texts. For London Heine wrote an (unset) scenario, *Die Göttin Diana*; and Andreae, Cui, Dopper, Leroux and Mascagni all based operas on Heine's early play *William Ratcliff*.

PETER BRANSCOMBE

Heinefetter, Sabine (*b* Mainz, 19 Aug 1809; *d* Illenau, 18 Nov 1872). German soprano. She made her début in 1824 at Frankfurt in Ritter's *Der Mandarin*. Spohr heard her there, and at his urging she signed a contract for life with the Kassel opera; but in 1829 she went to Paris, where she studied with Banderali and Giovanni Tadolini and sang at the Théâtre Italien. She also appeared in Dresden, Berlin, Vienna, Milan, where she created Adina in *L'elisir d'amore* (1832), and Danzig, where she sang Alaide in *La straniera* (1833). Her last appearance was in Marseilles in 1846. Her sister, Clara Stöckl-Heinefetter (*b* Mainz, 7 Sept 1813; *d* Vienna, 23 Feb 1857), who was a more dramatic soprano, studied in Vienna, making her début there in 1831 as Agathe (Sabine sang Aennchen) at the Kärntnertortheater. She was engaged there for many years, singing roles that included Smeton, Lucrezia Borgia, Zayda (*Dom Sébastien*), Donna Anna, Alice and Jessonda. She made her London début in 1840 at the St James's Theatre, returning in 1842 to Covent Garden when she sang Agathe, Donna Anna, Susanna, Pamina, Leonore (*Fidelio*), Norma and Valentine in the British première of *Les Huguenots*; she was praised for her 'exquisite sweetness of tone'. She retired in 1850.

CHARLES JAHANT, ELIZABETH FORBES

Heinichen, Johann David (*b* Krössuln, nr Weissenfels, 17 April 1683; *d* Dresden, 16 July 1729). German composer. He studied at the Leipzig Thomasschule, taking harpsichord and organ lessons from Johann Kuhnau. In 1702 he entered Leipzig University as a law student, moving to Weissenfels in 1706 to practise as an advocate. Attracted by the musical life of the court there, he wrote music for court occasions and came into contact with other musicians, including Reinhard Keiser, the leading Hamburg opera composer. In 1709 Heinichen returned to Leipzig at the request of the manager of the opera house. During this period he was appointed composer to the court of Zeitz and opera composer to the court of Naumburg; he also wrote the

first version of a thoroughbass treatise, which in its final version (1728) established him at the forefront of Baroque theorists.

In 1710 Heinichen gave up his successful career in Leipzig to travel to Venice to learn Italian operatic style at first hand. In 1712 he went to Rome and remained in Italy, mainly in Venice, until 1716; in 1717 he was engaged as Kapellmeister to the court at Dresden, a post he retained for the rest of his life. For the court theatre he wrote only one opera, *Flavio Crispo*, which was never performed. For reasons that remain obscure, the Italian opera company at court was dissolved by order of the king when quarrels broke out between the composer and the singers Senesino and Berselli. The score, extant in Dresden, breaks off without explanation near the end of the final act, as if the composer gave it up at the time of these disagreements. Although opera no longer had any significance in Heinichen's career, he wrote a vast amount of music, both secular and sacred.

Heinichen's musical style proves his own credo that music should be composed in a style mixing the national idioms of German, French and Italian music. As such, his music is somewhat more *galant* or pre-Classical in character than reminiscent of the contrapuntal complexity associated with north German Baroque composers. His operas show obvious connections with Venetian practice of the early 18th century, and little remains of the greater musical-dramatic scope of earlier German opera composers such as Keiser.

Der Karneval in Venedig, oder Der angenehme Betrug, ?Weissenfels, 1705, 1 aria *D-SWl*
Hercules, ?Leipzig, *c*1709, 11 arias *SWl*
Olimpia vendicata (? A. Aureli, after L. Ariosto), Naumburg, 1709
Paris und Helene, oder Der glückliche Liebeswechsel, Naumburg, 1710, *B**
Le passioni per troppo amore (3, M. Noris), Venice, S Angelo, carn. 1713, *Dlb**
Mario (G. Braccioli), Venice, S Angelo, 1713, *Dlb**; as Calpurnia, oder Die römische Grossmut, Hamburg, 1716
L'amicizia in terzo, overo Il Dionigio [Act 3] (G. M. Rapparini), Neuburg an der Donau, 1718 [Act 1 by 'Cavaliere Messa', Act 2 by A. R. Stricker, ov. and ballet music by G. Finger]
Flavio Crispo, 1720, unperf., *Dlb**

MGG (G. Hausswald); *StiegerO*; *WaltherML*
G. Seibel: *Das Leben des königl. polnischen und kurfürstl. sächs. Hofkapellmeisters Johann David Heinichen* (Leipzig, 1913)
R. Tanner: *Heinichen als dramatischer Komponist* (Leipzig, 1916)
G. J. Buelow: 'The *Loci Topici* and Affect in Late Baroque Music: Heinichen's Practical Demonstration', *MR*, xxvii (1966), 161–76
GEORGE J. BUELOW

Heininen, Paavo (Johannes) (*b* Helsinki, 13 Jan 1938). Finnish composer. He studied music privately before attending the Sibelius Academy, Helsinki, from 1956 to 1960. Postgraduate studies followed in Cologne with Bernd Alois Zimmermann, at the Juilliard School with Vincent Persichetti and Eduard Steuermann, and in Warsaw with Lutosławski. In the mid-1960s Heininen taught at the Turku Music College and in 1966 was appointed to teach theory and composition at the Sibelius Academy, where his pupils have included most of the younger generation of leading Finnish composers.

From the beginning of his career in the late 1950s Heininen adopted atonality and serialism as his mode of expression. His early works were received with uncomprehending hostility by musical establishment and audiences alike. Nevertheless, with a few exceptions, he has continued to follow an avant-garde line, and his music has gradually become more widely accepted. A musician of formidable and uncompromising intellect, Heininen now occupies a highly respected position in Finnish musical life.

By the early 1980s Heininen's compositions included several large-scale symphonies, two concertos and various chamber works, as well as a number of vocal pieces that paved the way for his first opera, *Silkkirumpu* ('The Damask Drum', 1984), based on a 14th-century noh play by Motokiyo Zeami. The scenes are connected by orchestral and choral interludes, and the music has a vividness and an immediacy that have helped to establish the work in the Finnish National Opera's repertory. Heininen's second opera, *Veitsi* ('The Knife', 1989), was commissioned for the Savonlinna Opera Festival as part of the city's 350th anniversary celebrations. Though concerned with an essentially personal tragedy in a low-life setting, the opera is conceived on a grand scale and involves many peripheral characters.

See also Silkkirumpu and Veitsi.

S. Heikinheimo: 'The Damask Drum', *Nordic Sounds* (1984), no.2, pp.8–9
J. Kaipainen: 'Paavo Heininen, Composer, Cosmopolitan, Controversialist', *Finnish Music Quarterly* (1986), no.2, pp.31–43
P. Heininen: 'The Music of *The Knife*', *Finnish Music Quarterly* (1989), no.2, pp.21–6
A. Jacobs: 'Savonlinna: Three Knives', *Opera* (1989), festival issue, 59–60
J. Kaipainen: notes, *Silkkirumpu* (Finlandia FACD 106, 1989)
K. Ketting: 'Suicide in Savonlinna', *Nordic Sounds* (Sept 1989), 5–6
V. Meri: 'From *The Death of a Poet* to *The Knife*: Verse into Drama', *Finnish Music Quarterly* (1989), no.2, pp.16–21
ERKKI ARNI

Heinisch, József [Joseph] (*b* before 1800; *d* Pest, 7 Nov 1840). Hungarian composer, probably of Austrian origin. About 1812 he entered the service of the Transylvanian Count Farkas Bethlen as a music teacher.

From 1824 to 1830 he was a theatre conductor in Kolozsvár (now Cluj-Napoca, Romania), and from 1830 to 1836 was active in Kassa (now Košice, Slovakia). It was here that the first performance of his only opera, the Singspiel *Mátyás királynak választása* ('The Election of Matthew as King'; 2, after L. Szentjóbi Szabó) was given, in 1830; the work was composed in collaboration with another Hungarian, György Arnold. The Hungarian Theatre in Pest, the centre of opera in Hungary until 1884, was opened on 22 August 1837 with an overture by Heinisch, and on the same day he conducted the first opera performance there, Rossini's *Il barbiere di Siviglia*.

Heinisch was one of the pioneers of opera in Hungary, and his compositions and arrangements contributed significantly to the enlargement of the theatre repertory. He composed mainly in the international opera style of his time but could also express himself in the Hungarian instrumental (*verbunkos*) style. Although possessing little originality, he was a forerunner of Ferenc Erkel, the 'father of Hungarian opera'. His works include three ballets, a pantomime comedy, incidental music and arrangements of earlier Hungarian operatic music.
FERENC BÓNIS

Heink, Ernestine. *See* SCHUMANN-HEINK, ERNESTINE.

Heinrich, Rudolf (*b* Halle, 10 Feb 1926; *d* London, 1 Dec 1975). German stage designer. He studied painting for nearly two years before becoming an assistant designer in Leipzig (1948–50). He then designed a dozen Handel operas in Halle, joining the Berlin Komische Oper in 1953 to become Felsenstein's chief designer. After 1961 he worked internationally, using Munich as his base. For Felsenstein Heinrich designed *Carmen*, *The Cunning Little Vixen* (a sensation in Paris in 1956, as was *Les contes d'Hoffmann* in 1958),

Scene from Walter Felsenstein's 1956 production of 'The Cunning Little Vixen' (Janáček) for the Komische Oper, Berlin, with sets and costumes designed by Rudolf Heinrich

Otello, *La traviata* and *A Midsummer Night's Dream*. These productions were notable examples of 'realistisches Musiktheater'. For the Metropolitan he designed *Salome* (1965), *Elektra* (1966), *Tosca* (1968) and *Werther* (1971), and staged as well as designed *Der Freischütz* (1971). He designed and produced the first American *Lulu* for Santa Fe (1963), and designed also in Boston (*Boris Godunov*), Salzburg (*Figaro*, 1966) and Vienna (*Moses und Aron*, 1972; *Lohengrin*, 1974). When his untimely death occurred at the age of 49, two months after that of his mentor Felsenstein, Heinrich was lighting the set for his production of *Salome* for the ENO. He was also working on designs for *Tosca* (Hamburg) and the première of Josef Tal's *Die Versuchung* (Munich), both with Götz Friedrich. His later work departed from his earlier stylized realism, and, while still a music-theatre unity, revealed a greater political commitment. This is seen especially in his designs for Wagner's *Ring*, a project begun in Leipzig in 1973 with Joachim Herz, and complete except for *Götterdämmerung*.   DAVID J. HOUGH

Heise, Peter (Arnold) (*b* Copenhagen, 11 Feb 1830; *d* Tårbaek, nr Copenhagen, 12 Sept 1879). Danish composer. After graduating in 1847 he studied theory, then became a private pupil of Moritz Hauptmann in Leipzig (1852–3). In 1854 he became conductor of the Studentersangforening and in December 1857 music teacher at the academy in Sorø and organist at the church there. In 1865 he returned to Copenhagen, where a secure financial position (due to his marriage to a wealthy merchant's daughter) allowed him to concentrate on composition and teach only a select group of private pupils.

Heise's chief importance is as a composer of vocal music, although his output includes a few important instrumental works too, and his more than 300 songs secured him a position as the leading Danish song composer of his generation. He was increasingly involved in composition for the stage from the late 1860s. From this period date the Singspiel *Paschaens datter* ('The Pasha's Daughter'; 3, H. Hertz; 30 Sept 1869; *DK-Kk**; 5 songs, Copenhagen, 1869) and some incidental and ballet music, leading up to his principal work as a dramatic composer, the tragic opera *Drot og marsk* ('King and Marshal'; 4, C. Richardt; 25 Sept 1878; *Kk**; vs, Copenhagen, 1879), finished a few years before his premature death. All were first performed at the Royal Theatre, Copenhagen. Editions of five songs from each of the operas are in volume four of *Peter Heise: sange med klaver* (Copenhagen, 1990).

See also DROT OG MARSK.

*
G. Hetsch: 'Peter Heise og Henrik Hertz', *Aarbog for musik*, i (1922), 23–42
——: *Peter Heise* (Copenhagen, 1926)
——, ed.: *Breve fra Peter Heise* (Copenhagen, 1930)
K. Aa. Bruun: *Dansk musiks historie*, ii (Copenhagen, 1969), 160ff
N. Schiørring: *Musikkens historie i Danmark*, iii (Copenhagen, 1978), 43ff
D. Fog: *Heise-Katalog: Verzeichnis der gedruckten Kompositionen von Peter Heise* (Copenhagen, 1991)   NIELS MARTIN JENSEN

Heldenbariton. German term, meaning 'heroic baritone'. In the German opera houses a true *Heldenbariton* is a prize possession: a singer with exciting power at command and a brightly resonant quality serving well for roles such as Telramund in *Lohengrin* and the Count di Luna in *Il trovatore* ('hero-voices' being required for both despite the fact that both are villains). In his prime, Dietrich Fischer-Dieskau had the qualities of this voice type, which could also be found in singers of other nationalities such as the American Leonard Warren and, pre-eminent among Italians of the century, Titta Ruffo.

See also BARITONE.   J. B. STEANE

Heldentenor. German term, meaning 'heroic tenor'. It is now virtually inseparable from the Wagnerian repertory: the successful singer of Tannhäuser, Tristan and Siegfried is counted a *Heldentenor* almost by definition. The type is also a rarity, and when an able specimen appears he is likely to find himself so much in demand for these strenuous tenor roles in Wagner that he is effectively monopolized by them. That was the case with the most famous *Heldentenor* of the century, Lauritz Melchior (1890–1973), who occasionally elsewhere sang Otello, Florestan and Canio, but whose appearances with the Metropolitan numbered almost 500 performances, all of them in Wagner. It can be argued that a redefinition might be useful, distinguishing the *Heldentenor* voice from the TENORE ROBUSTO. The *robusto*, like the *Heldentenor*, has a voice of great power and has the stamina to sustain a long and demanding role, but he should also have the type of tenor voice that can combine this with a brilliance in the upper register, putting the role of Manrico in *Il trovatore* within his scope, and perhaps even Arnold in Rossini's *Guillaume Tell*. The supreme example of this type is Francesco Tamagno, the original Otello. There is then another type, more baritonal or broad of tone, less happy in roles with a high tessitura. An example here is Jon Vickers, whose repertory, with Otello, Aeneas, Grimes, Siegmund and Tristan at its centre, might then represent the more internationally based concept of the *Heldentenor*. The part of Siegfried, with its slightly higher tessitura (at least in the third opera of the *Ring* cycle), would better suit the correspondingly widened view of the *robusto*.

See also TENOR.   J. B. STEANE

Heldy, Fanny [Deceuninck, Marguerite Virginia Emma Clémentine] (*b* Ath, nr Liège, 29 Feb 1888; *d* Paris, 13 Dec 1973). French soprano of Belgian birth. After studies at the Liège Conservatory she made her début as Elena in Gunsbourg's *Ivan le Terrible* in 1910 at La Monnaie, remaining there until 1912. At Monte Carlo (1914–18) she sang Mimì, Elvira (*Ernani*), Salome (*Hérodiade*), Gounod's Marguerite and Boito's Margherita. Her début at the Opéra-Comique was as Violetta in 1917; she sang there for two decades as Rosina, Butterfly, Manon, Olympia, Antonia and Giulietta, and Tosca. At the Opéra, where she made her début in 1920 as Juliet, she also sang Nedda, Elsa, Ophelia, Esclarmonde and Thaïs, and created Portia in Hahn's *Le marchand de Venise* (1935). Toscanini chose her for Mélisande and Louise at La Scala in 1923, and she sang Manon at Covent Garden in 1926. Returning to Monte Carlo she sang Nelly Harfield in Gunsbourg's *Venise* (1928), Freddie in Alfano's *L'ultimo Lord* (1932), the Duc de Reichstadt in the première of *L'Aiglon* (1937) and Carmen and Octavian (1939). Ravel's Concepcion she made her own; her Violetta had both brilliance and pathos. Despite a metallic quality to her voice, she was the leading singing actress of her day.

*
GV (R. Celletti; R. Vegeto)   ANDRÉ TUBEUF, ELIZABETH FORBES

Hèle, Thomas d'. *See* D'HÈLE, THOMAS.

Hélène ('Helen'). *Poème lyrique* in one act by CAMILLE SAÏNT-SAËNS to his own libretto; Monte Carlo, 18 February 1904.

Saint-Saëns was among the many critics of Offenbach's *La belle Hélène* who objected to the operetta's lax moral tone and its trivialization of the ancient world. In his own treatment of the story of Paris and Helen he aspired to a more serious and exalted level, even though the opera displays the triumph of Eros and celebrates sexual passion more strongly than any other of Saint-Saëns' operas. *Hélène* was the first of his operas composed for the theatre at Monte Carlo then under the enterprising direction of Raoul Gunsbourg. It is also the first for which he wrote his own libretto, in strongly poetic rhyming verse. Melba sang the title role, and it shared a double bill with Massenet's veristic *La Navarraise*. Apart from the two principal characters, the opera has scenes for Vénus [Venus] (soprano), who tries to persuade Helen (soprano) to abandon Menelaus for love, and for Pallas (contralto), who warns her of the dreadful events that will ensue if she abandons Sparta for Troy. Helen heeds the words of Venus, not Pallas, and sets sail with Pâris [Paris] (tenor) in an ecstatic embrace.

HUGH MACDONALD

Hell, Theodor. *See* WINKLER, CARL GOTTFRIED THEODOR.

Helletsgruber, Luise (*b* Vienna, *c*1898; *d* nr Vienna, 5 Jan 1967). Austrian soprano. She studied in Vienna and in 1922 made her début as the Shepherd Boy in *Tannhäuser* at the Staatsoper, where she appeared regularly throughout the next 20 years. Her lyrical voice and charming stage presence were well suited to such roles as Marguerite and Micaëla in French opera, Eva and Elsa in Wagner, and Liù in *Turandot*. She also specialized in Mozart, appearing at Salzburg (1928–37) and at Glyndebourne (1934–8), where she sang Cherubino, Dorabella, Elvira and the First Lady in *Die Zauberflöte*; of these, the first three can be heard in complete recordings of the operas by the Glyndebourne casts of those years under Fritz Busch. Deficiencies of technique showed up in recitals, but there was charm and flair as well as a vibrant and unmistakably personal quality of voice.

J. B. STEANE

Hellmann, Maximilian Joseph (*b* *c*1703; *d* Vienna, 20 March 1763). Austrian composer. Pantaleon Hebenstreit trained him as a virtuoso on the cimbalom (or pantaleon) in Dresden, and his reputation rests mainly on his accomplishments as a performer. He was court cimbalist in Vienna from 1724 until his death. Only five of his compositions survive, including the oratorio *Abigaile* (1734). His four secular dramatic works were written for the name-days of archduchesses Maria Anna and Maria Theresa. Typical of the Viennese *festa di camera*, they were presented against a simple backdrop symbolizing the congratulatory message of the libretto. They are scored for two solo voices, strings and continuo; the da capo arias emphasize vocal virtuosity and *L'adolescenza coronata dal senno* and *Il premio dell'onore* each contain one aria featuring the cimbalom in a solo role. The works are notable for the involvement of the newly appointed court poet, Giovanni Pasquini, as librettist, and the appearance of the best singers at court in their performances, including the castrato Felice Salimbeni.

all feste di camera in one act to librettos by G. C. Pasquini; first performed in Vienna, Hofburg; scores in A-Wn

L'adolescenza coronata dal senno, 26 July 1733
La Maestà condotta al tempio dell'onore dal consiglio, 15 Oct 1733
La Virtù guida della fortuna, 15 Oct 1734
Il premio dell'onore, 26 July 1737

*

F. Hadamowsky: 'Barocktheater am Wiener Kaiserhof; mit einem Spielplan (1625–1740)', *Jb der Gesellschaft für Wiener Theaterforschung* (1951–2), 7–117; pubd separately (Vienna, 1955)
A. Bauer: *Opern und Operetten in Wien: Verzeichnis ihrer Erst-aufführungen in der Zeit von 1629 bis zur Gegenwart* (Graz, 1955)

RUDOLF SCHNITZLER

Hellmesberger, Georg (*b* Vienna, 27 Jan 1830; *d* Hanover, 12 Nov 1852). Austrian composer. He was taught the violin and music theory by his father Georg Hellmesberger (1800–73), with whom he and his elder brother Joseph made a concert tour to London in 1847. In 1850 he was appointed Hofkonzertmeister in Hanover, with the responsibility of directing vaudeville and ballet music at the court theatre. His compositions (largely unpublished) include symphonies, chamber music, violin pieces and songs, as well as nine operas, most of which remain unperformed.

Die Favoritin, Graz, 1847
Die Bürgschaft, 1848 (3, K. von Biedenfeld, after F. von Schiller), Hanover, 1851
Der Tag der Verlobung (3, O. Prechtler), Olomouc, March 1849
Les deux reines [Die beiden Königinnen, oder Die Begegnung in Helsingör] op.100 (oc, 2, J. G. Seidl, after Soulié and Arnould), Hanover, 28 April 1851

Unperf.: Fiesco, 1848–9 (4, T. Herzenskron, after Schiller); La rose de Péronne, 1849 (oc, 3, A. de Leuven and A. d'Ennery); Il matrimonio segreto (2, G. Bertati, lib. also in Ger. trans.); Palma, oder Die Reise nach Griechenland (2); Der treue Arzt (4, after E. Scribe)

*

MGG (A. Orel); *StiegerO*
R. M. Prosl: *Die Hellmesberger* (Vienna, 1947)

RICHARD EVIDON

Hellmesberger, Joseph [Pepi] (*b* Vienna, 9 April 1855; *d* Vienna, 26 April 1907). Austrian composer. He was taught the violin by his father Joseph Hellmesberger (1828–93), and at the age of eight was a soloist in a conservatory concert. By 1878 he was a solo violinist of the Hofkapelle and Hofoper, and in 1880 two of his operettas, *Kapitän Ahlström* and *Der Graf von Gleichen und seine beiden Frauen*, were performed successfully at a café theatre in the Prater. But his first engagement as a theatre conductor in 1881, at Franz Jauner's new Ring-Theater, ended abruptly on 8 December of that year with a fire that destroyed the theatre and took hundreds of lives, and from which he barely escaped.

His fortunes having suddenly declined, in the autumn of 1882 Hellmesberger accepted the post of Kapellmeister at the impoverished Carltheater, while continuing to compose operettas and concentrating on his career as a violinist. He was appointed Konzertmeister and ballet music director of the Hofoper in 1884, was made vice-Hofkapellmeister in 1889 and the following year succeeded Richter as Hofkapellmeister. When Mahler decided not to renew his candidacy for the Philharmonic conductorship (1901), Hellmesberger was elected by the players. He was re-elected in 1902 and 1903, but Mahler gradually limited his conducting at the opera.

The discovery of his liaison with a married dancer (a member of the Hofoper) led Hellmesberger to resign from the Philharmonic, and he later also resigned as Hofkapellmeister and from the Hofkapelle. He was saved from ruin by the great success of his operetta *Das Veilchenmädel*, produced at the Carltheater in 1904 and soon afterwards throughout Europe; the success was repeated in November of that year with *Wien bei Nacht*. He was Hofkapellmeister in Stuttgart in 1904–5 but returned to Vienna, where he composed further operettas and accepted work conducting mediocre orchestras.

operettas, first performed in Vienna, unless otherwise stated

Kapitän Ahlström (2, A. Hofmann), Ronacher-Theater im Prater, 15 May 1880

Der Graf von Gleichen und seine beiden Frauen (3, A. Just), Ronacher, 31 July 1880

Der Rattenfänger von Hameln (Märchenkomödie, 3, C. A. Görner), Ring, 13 April 1881

Fata Morgana (ballet-op, 4, H. S. Mosenthal), Hofoper, 30 March 1886

Der schöne Kurfürst (3, Bohrmann-Riegen), Munich, Gärtnerplatz, 15 May 1886

Rikiki [Nelly, die Blumenhändlerin], Carl, 28 Sept 1887

Das Orakel (3, I. Schnitzer), An der Wien, 30 Nov 1889

Der bleiche Gast (3, V. Léon and H. von Waldberg), Hamburg, 6 Sept 1890, collab. A. Zamara

Vater Radetsky (Festspiel, S. Schlesinger), Hofoper, 24 April 1892

Die Doppelhochzeit (vaudeville, 3, Léon and Waldberg), Josefstadt, 21 Sept 1895

20 000 Meilen unterm Meer (Ausstattungsstück, 4, C. E. Julius), Jantsch, 18 Nov 1900

Das Veilchenmädel (3, L. Krenn and C. Lindau), Carl, 27 Feb 1904

Wien bei Nacht (Burleske, 1, Lindau and J. Wilhelm), Danzers Orpheum, 28 Oct 1904

Die drei Engel (3, Lindau and F. Antony), Venedig in Wien, 4 May 1906

Mutzi (3, Wilhelm and R. Pohl), Carl, 15 Sept 1906

Der Triumph des Weibes (3, A. Neidhardt), Danzers Orpheum, 16 Nov 1906

Eine von Moulin Rouge (Burleske, 1, Krenn), Danzers Orpheum, 22 Dec 1906

Letzter Fasching (3, L. Windhopp), Graz, Stadt, 11 Feb 1909; arr. and ed. L. Prechtel

Der Veilchenkavalier (1, Krenn), Ronacher, 16 April 1911; arr. and ed. from posth. works

E. Hanslick: 'Müller und Hellmesberger', *Geschichte des Concertwesens in Wien*, ii: *Aus dem Concertsaal* (Vienna, 1870), 50–53

R. M. Prosl: *Die Hellmesberger* (Vienna, 1947)

J. Freyenfels: 'Mahler und der "fesche Pepi" – eine Konfrontation und ihre Elemente', *NZM*, Jg.132 (1971), 178–83

H.-L. de La Grange: *Mahler*, i (New York, 1973), 31, 619–20

RICHARD EVIDON

Helm, Anny (*b* Vienna, 20 July 1903). Austrian soprano. Her teachers were Marie Gutheil-Schoder and Gertrude Förstel in Vienna and Ernst Grenzebach in Berlin. She made her début at Magdeburg in 1924, joining the Berlin Staatsoper in 1927. She was an admired singer at Bayreuth, where from 1927 to 1931 her roles included Brangäne and Venus. In 1933 she married Giuseppe Sbisà, director of the Trieste Opera, and under the name of Anny Helm-Sbisà continued her career, mainly in Italy. She sang La Gioconda at Verona in 1934 and Brünnhilde (*Die Walküre*) during the 1934–5 season at La Scala. Her only appearances at Covent Garden were in 1939, when she sang Venus and was described as 'Germanic'. Although her power and range were sufficient for her to encompass such roles as Turandot and Isolde, she is most widely remembered now as the Brangäne of the near-complete recording of *Tristan und Isolde* made at the Bayreuth Festival of 1928, a part she sings with incisive tone and a keen sense of drama.

J. B. STEANE

Helm, Everett (**Burton**) (*b* Minneapolis, 17 July 1913). American composer. He was educated at Harvard, and in Europe (1936–8), where he studied composition with Ralph Vaughan Williams in London and Gian Francesco Malipiero in Italy. He held several teaching positions in the USA before moving to Europe in 1950. His first opera, *Adam and Eve* (Wiesbaden, Hessisches Staatstheater, 28 Oct 1951), is an adaptation of a medieval mystery play and makes use of plainsong melodies. Helm's most significant opera is *The Siege of Tottenburg*, a three-act radio opera commissioned by Süddeutscher Rundfunk and broadcast in November 1956. Simple folklike melodies form the basis of this work, accompanied by some imaginative atonal orchestral writing which obscures neither the clarity of the text nor the direct appeal of the vocal lines. Another work, the Singspiel *500 Dragon Thalers* (composed in 1956), has not been performed.

H. G. Bonte: 'Neue Musik im Rundfunk: Funkoper und Fernsehoper', *Melos*, xxiii (1956), 360–61

Helm, Hans (*b* Passau, 12 April 1934). German baritone. He studied in Munich and Krefeld, and made his début in 1957 at Graz as Andrey Shchelkalov (*Boris Godunov*). A member of the Vienna Staatsoper for 30 years, he sang Stolzius (*Die Soldaten*) and Yevgeny Onegin at Kassel (1968–9); Count Almaviva at Glyndebourne and Covent Garden (1976); Don Fernando at La Scala (1978) and in Washington (1979); Harlequin (*Ariadne auf Naxos*) at Salzburg (1981); and Count Peter Homonay (*Der Zigeunerbaron*) at Bregenz (1982). He created Lopakhin in Kelterborn's *Der Kirschgarten* at Zürich (1984). A singer of great height and authority, he had a vast repertory including Agamemnon (Gluck's *Iphigénie en Aulide*), Malatesta, Melot, Silvio, Faninal, Dominik (*Arabella*), the Count (*Capriccio*), Ashby (*La fanciulla del West*), Count Luna (*Palestrina*) and Frank (*Die tote Stadt*).

ELIZABETH FORBES

Helm-Sbisà, Anny. *See* HELM, ANNY.

Help, Help, the Globolinks! Opera in one act by GIAN CARLO MENOTTI to his own libretto; Hamburg, Staatsoper, 21 December 1968 (as *Hilfe, Hilfe, die Globolinks!*); Santa Fe, 1 August 1969.

The Globolinks are beings from another planet who invade earth and are 'sinister but with a touch of humor'. The 70-minute opera (commissioned by the Staatsoper) 'for children and those who like children' is in four scenes preceded by a Prologue of electronic tape music representing the invasion of the Globolinks in the form of a ballet. In the first scene the invasion causes a bus full of schoolchildren to break down. 14-year-old Emily (soprano) plays her violin. The Globolinks are allergic to music; they are always accompanied by tape music, whereas the rest of the score is tonal, strongly marked by sliding first-inversion triads. The second scene is in the office of Dr Stone (baritone), dean of St Paul's School. Dr Stone wonders 'Where, where can the children be?'. Madame Euterpova (soprano), the music teacher, accuses him of not liking music and not singing. She resigns because the children have not practised their instruments. The Globolinks come and turn Dr Stone's voice into electronic Globolink sounds. Madame Euterpova teaches Dr Stone's voice to sing 'la'. The scene ends with an ensemble of teachers in B♭ with Dr Stone stuck on the leading note. The third scene returns to the bus, where the teachers arrive playing instruments. But Emily is no longer there and inexplicably Dr Stone begins to fly away. The final scene is in 'The Forest of Steel'. Emily plays her violin until she falls asleep. The Globolinks try to play the violin but always drop it. Dr Stone flies in, and then away to the land of the Globolinks.   BRUCE ARCHIBALD

Helsinki (Swed. Helsingfors). Capital of Finland. Opera performances were occasionally given in Helsinki by visiting companies from the 1820s, and a local amateur society gave the première of Pacius's *Kung Karls Jakt* ('King Charles's Hunt') in 1852. In 1873 an 'operatic section' was added to the recently founded National Theatre. This bold effort petered out after only six years, however, mainly because of small resources and a narrow cultural base. In 1911 a new part-time company, Domestic Opera, was launched and put on a permanent footing in 1914 as the Suomalainen Ooppera (Finnish Opera). Two years after Finland had gained her independence, the company secured a small theatre, the Aleksanterinteatteri (built 1879, cap.544), and opened with *Aida* on 19 January 1919. This building remains the home of the National Opera and Ballet until a new 1385-seat opera house is completed in the early 1990s.

Since 1956 the company has been called Suomen Kansallisoopera (Finnish National Opera); it is a semi-official institution supported in part by public funding. Besides presenting a comprehensive standard repertory, the company has always encouraged native opera. Notable premières have included Leevi Madetoja's *Pohjalaisia* ('The Ostrobothnians', 1924), Joonas Kokkonen's *Viimeiset kiusaukset* ('The Last Temptations', 1975), Aulis Sallinen's *Punainen viiva* ('The Red Line', 1978), Paavo Heininen's *Silkkirumpu* ('The Damask Drum', 1984) and Einojuhani Rautavaara's *Vincent* (1990). In the 1970s and 80s the Finnish National Opera made several highly successful tours abroad, visiting, perhaps most notably, the Metropolitan Opera in 1983.   ERKKI ARNI

Heming, Percy (*b* Bristol, 6 Sept 1883; *d* London, 11 Jan 1956). English baritone. He studied at the RAM and in Dresden and joined the Beecham Opera Company in 1915, making his début as Mercutio (*Roméo et Juliette*). In 1919 he was the first to sing Amfortas in English; and he added Scarpia, Ford, the Dark Fiddler (*A Village Romeo and Juliet*) and the Emir in De Lara's *Naïl* to his repertory. In 1920 he toured the USA as Macheath, returning to England in 1922 to join the British National Opera Company. He made guest appearances with Sadler's Wells Opera (1933–5); his last operatic appearances were as Scarpia at Sadler's Wells in 1940 and as Sharpless at the New Theatre, London, in 1942. Between 1937 and 1948 he held administrative and advisory posts at Covent Garden. Heming's voice was of a beautiful quality: his musical and dramatic feeling for words was always in evidence, and his diction was exemplary.   HAROLD ROSENTHAL/R

Hemmings, Peter (**William**) (*b* Enfield, Middx, 10 April 1934). British administrator. He was a Cambridge choral scholar and became president of the University Opera Group. After taking a degree in classics he was repertory and planning manager of Sadler's Wells Opera (1959–65), general manager of the New Opera Company (1957–65) and the first general administrator

of Scottish Opera (1962–77). In the latter post he was responsible, with Alexander Gibson, for the swift rise of the company to become a major force in British opera, and he persuaded many leading singers and producers to work in Scotland. He also organized the company's move to the renovated Theatre Royal in Glasgow in 1975. In 1977 he became general manager of Australian Opera but gave up the post after two years in Sydney because of policy differences. He was managing director of the LSO from 1979 to 1984, when he was appointed general director of the Los Angeles Music Center Opera Association, another organization which he helped to create. From its opening in October 1986, the company quickly established an international reputation, with singers, conductors and producers of a high quality. Hemmings's energetic combination of organizational acumen and musical knowledge have made him an administrator of the highest ability.   ALAN BLYTH

Frieda Hempel as Gilda in Verdi's 'Rigoletto'

Hempel, Frieda (*b* Leipzig, 26 June 1885; *d* Berlin, 7 Oct 1955). German soprano, later naturalized American. She studied in Leipzig and Berlin, after which her early career was centred at the Berlin Königliche Oper (début on 22 August 1905 as Mrs Ford in *Die lustigen Weiber von Windsor*). She was first heard at Covent Garden in 1907 in a double bill as Mozart's Bastienne and Humperdinck's Gretel, then as Eva and Mrs Ford. Her fine schooling and purity of tone immediately marked her out, but her big London success came during Beecham's Drury Lane season of 1914, when she sang the Queen of Night (perhaps her most famous part) and the Marschallin, a role she had introduced to Berlin in 1911 and to New York in 1913. Her Metropolitan début on 27 December 1912, as Marguerite de Valois in a brilliantly cast *Les Huguenots*, began a period of seven years with that company, during which she settled in New York. She sang Eva and Euryanthe there under Toscanini, besides many of the lighter Verdi, Rossini and Donizetti parts, in which she was regarded as the natural successor of Sembrich. After a farewell Metropolitan appearance, in *Crispino e la comare*, on 10 February 1919, she devoted herself mainly to a concert career.

GV (R. Celletti, with discography)
F. Hempel: *Mein Leben dem Gesang* (Berlin, 1955)
P. H. Reed, G. T. Keating and B. F. Stone: 'The Recorded Art of Frieda Hempel', *Record Collector*, x (1955–6), 53–71 [with discography]   DESMOND SHAWE-TAYLOR

Hempson, Celeste. *See* GISMONDI, CELESTE.

Hemsley, Thomas (*b* Coalville, Leics., 12 April 1927). English baritone. He studied privately and made his début in 1951 as Purcell's Aeneas at the Mermaid Theatre, London. In 1953 he sang Hercules (Gluck's *Alceste*) at Glyndebourne, returning as Masetto, the Music-Master (*Ariadne auf Naxos*), Don Fernando and Dr Reischmann in the British première of Henze's *Elegy for Young Lovers* (1961). Engaged at Aachen (1953–6), the Deutsche Oper am Rhein (1957–63) and Zürich (1963–7), he sang more than a hundred roles, including Guglielmo, the Speaker, Germont and Marcello. He created Demetrius (*A Midsummer Night's Dream*) with the English Opera Group at Aldeburgh (1960). He sang Beckmesser at Bayreuth (1968–70) and made his Covent Garden début in 1970 creating Mangus in *The Knot Garden*. For Scottish Opera he sang Dr Malatesta and Balstrode and created Caesar in Hamilton's *The Catiline Conspiracy* (1974). His roles for the WNO (1977–85) included Rossini's Dr Bartolo, Dr Kolenatý (*The Makropulos Affair*) and Don Alfonso. For Kent Opera he sang Falstaff in 1980 and also directed *Il ritorno d'Ulisse in patria* in 1989. He had a flexible voice, incisive enunciation and a keen dramatic sense.

ALAN BLYTH

Henderson, Roy (Galbraith) (*b* Edinburgh, 4 July 1899). Scottish baritone. He studied at the RAM and made his Covent Garden début in 1928 as Donner, later singing Köthner and the Herald (*Lohengrin*). In 1934 he sang Count Almaviva in the opening performance of *Le nozze di Figaro* at Glyndebourne, returning there until 1939 as Papageno, Masetto and Guglielmo and also singing Peachum in *The Beggar's Opera* on tour and in London (1940). Though his voice was not intrinsically very beautiful, he used it with intelligence and charm. A gifted teacher, he numbered Ferrier among his pupils. He took part in the Glyndebourne Mozart recordings as Count Almaviva and Masetto.

ALAN BLYTH

Hendricks, Barbara (*b* Stephens, AR, 20 Nov 1948). American soprano. She studied at the Juilliard School and with Jennie Tourel. In 1974 she made her début in San Francisco as Erisbe in Cavalli's *Ormindo*, then sang the title role of *Calisto* at Glyndebourne and Jeanne in Egk's *Die Verlobung in San Domingo* at the St Paul

Opera Summer Festival. The following year she sang the title role in *The Cunning Little Vixen* at Santa Fe, Nannetta (*Falstaff*) at Boston, and has since appeared at the Aix-en-Provence, Orange, Schwetzingen and Salzburg festivals. She made her Paris Opéra début as Gounod's Juliet in 1982 and the same year sang Nannetta in Los Angeles and at Covent Garden. In 1985 she sang Liù at Bonn, and in 1986 she made her Metropolitan début as Sophie. During that year she also sang Leïla in Nice and Gilda at the Deutsche Oper, Berlin. Her light, well-focussed voice is suitable for both soubrette and lyric roles, and her repertory includes Susanna, her début role at La Scala in 1987, Pamina and Ilia, as well as Antonia, which she sang at Parma in 1988.

ELIZABETH FORBES

Henneberg, Johann Baptist (*b* Vienna, 6 Dec 1768; *d* Vienna, 26 Nov 1822). Austrian composer. An organist in Vienna, he had joined Schikaneder's company at the Freihaus-Theater (later the Theater an der Wien) as Kapellmeister and composer by 1790. He supervised rehearsals of *Die Zauberflöte* while Mozart was in Prague and conducted the opera from the third performance. From 1797 he had an able co-director in Seyfried. In addition to works he wrote himself, he arranged the piano scores of Süssmayr's *Der Spiegel von Arkadien* (1794), Winter and Mederitsch's *Babylons Pyramiden* (1797) and Winter's *Das Labyrinth* (1798). For the Theater an der Wien he wrote no new operas and resigned as Kapellmeister in 1802. In 1804 he left Vienna and settled near the Hungarian border; he became organist to the Esterházys at Eisenstadt and in 1811 Kapellmeister. Later he returned to Vienna and became court organist. He had the reputation of being a good, careful conductor. Henneburg's output was modest by the standards of the time, and much of it is lost, but he was clearly a skilful composer of tuneful, un-demanding theatre music. His most successful work was his setting of Schikaneder's *Die Waldmänner*, a comic opera given nearly a hundred times in the Freihaus-Theater auf der Wieden after its première on 14 October 1793. Apart from his stage works he also wrote sacred and secular vocal works and instrumental pieces.

librettos by E. Schikaneder and first performed at the Freihaus-Theater auf der Wieden, Vienna, unless otherwise stated

Der redliche Landmann (Familienszene mit Musik, 5), 24 April 1792
Johanna von Weimar (Ritterschauspiel, 5), 7 July 1792
Die Eisenkönigin (Zauberoper, 3), 12 Jan 1793
Der wohltätige Derwisch, oder Die Schellenkappe (Zauberoper, 3), 10 Sept 1793, collab. Gerl, ? W. Müller and Schack; as Die Zaubertrommel, *D-MH*
Die Waldmänner (komische Oper, 3), 14 Oct 1793
Der Scherenschleifer (carnival op, 2), 24 Jan 1795
Das Jägermädchen (ländliches Gemälde mit Gesang, 3, M. Stegmayer), 25 Sept 1798, collab. I. Seyfried and J. Haibel
Konrad Langbart von Friedburg, oder Der Burggeist (Ritterschauspiel, 3), 23 Feb 1799
Mina und Peru, oder Die Königspflicht (heroisch-komisches Spl, 2), 30 April 1799, collab. Seyfried
Holga die Göttin des Kristallengebirges (Spl, 3), 1 Feb 1800, collab. Seyfried
Die Gigantin (grosse Oper), unperf.

ADB (E. Komorzynski); *StiegerO*; *WurzbachL*
E. Komorzynski: *Emanuel Schikaneder: ein Beitrag zur Geschichte des deutschen Theaters* (Berlin, 1901, 2/1951)
O. E. Deutsch: 'Das Freihaus-Theater auf der Wieden', *Mitteilungen des Vereines für Geschichte der Stadt Wien*, xvi (1937), 30–73
E. Komorzynski: 'Johann Baptist Henneberg, Schikaneders Kapellmeister (1768–1822)', *MJb 1955*, 243–5

K. Honolka: *Papageno: Emanuel Schikaneder, der grosse Theatermann der Mozart-Zeit* (Salzburg and Vienna, 1984; Eng. trans., 1990)
PETER BRANSCOMBE

Henry [Henri], Monsieur (*fl* 1813–49). French baritone. He sang for more than 35 years with the Opéra-Comique, appearing in the premières of Boieldieu's *Le nouveau seigneur de village* (1813) and *La fête du village voisin* (1816); Hérold's *La clochette* (1817) and *Marie* (1826); Auber's *Leicester* (1823), *Le maçon* (1825), *Fra Diavolo* (1830), *Les diamants de la couronne* (1841) and *Le duc d'Olonne* (1842); Adam's *Le postillon de Lonjumeau* (1836) and *Cagliostro* (1844). He created Sulpice in *La fille du régiment* (1840), John Bred in Monpou's *Lambert Simnel* (1843) and Aboul-y-far in Thomas' *Le Caïd* (1849). In 1841 he sang Williams in the first performance by the Opéra-Comique of *Richard Coeur-de-lion*. A stylish and versatile singing actor, he excelled in comedy, but his most famous role was Gaveston, the villainous steward in *La dame blanche*, which he created in 1825 and was still singing 700 performances later in 1849.

ELIZABETH FORBES

Henry VIII. *Opéra* in four acts by CAMILLE SAINT-SAËNS to a libretto by Léonce Détroyat and Armand Silvestre; Paris, Opéra, 5 March 1883.

Vaucorbeil, director of the Opéra from 1880, was well disposed towards Saint-Saëns and passed on to him a libretto originally intended for Gounod. Although more inclined to treat a topic from French history, Saint-Saëns immersed himself in the subject and obtained a theme from the Royal Library at Buckingham Palace to use as a main motif. The opera was composed in 1881–2. Originally based on Calderón's play *La cisma in Inglaterra*, the libretto was much modified to concentrate on Henry VIII's renunciation of Rome, his rejection of Catherine of Aragon and his marriage to Anne Boleyn. Plans for a comic character and for the death of Anne Boleyn were scrapped. The interaction of Henry's political ambitions and his defiance of Rome with the jealousy of the two queens makes fine operatic material, with a series of confrontations, especially in the Act 2 Richmond scene. Anne's former lover Don Gomez, the Spanish ambassador, takes the main tenor role. The needs of grand opera are served by a lengthy *divertissement* in Act 2, including an 'Idylle écossaise' and a 'Pas des Highlanders', and a majestic session of the Synod in which Henry arouses the people's fervent support for his breach with Rome. The baritone role of Henry ranges from tenderness and suspicion to defiance and menace, while the two female roles, Catherine and Anne (soprano and mezzo-soprano) are well contrasted; Catherine, who dies at the end of the opera guarding the secret of Anne and Don Gomez, is a finely drawn character, rising nobly above the intrigue and suspicion that consume the others. The finale to Act 1 is particularly fine, with a build-up of conflicting tensions against the solemn tread of a funeral march for the beheaded Duke of Buckingham; and the last meeting of Catherine and Anne, though poor history, makes excellent opera.

Despite Saint-Saëns' care for authenticity of period and place, the music's strongest impression is of a tightly constructed score with vocal and orchestral resources skilfully deployed, especially in the confrontation scenes. After *Samson et Dalila* this was his most successful opera, widely performed in the composer's lifetime, often in a reduced three-act version that simply omitted Act 3; Saint-Saëns refused to make the reductions the Opéra demanded.

HUGH MACDONALD

Henschel, Sir (Isidor) George [Georg] (*b* Breslau [now Wrocław], 18 Feb 1850; *d* Aviemore, Scotland, 10 Sept 1934). English composer and baritone of German birth. In 1862 he made his début as a pianist in Berlin and in 1866 as a bass in Hirschberg. His teachers at the Leipzig Conservatory (1867–70) included Moscheles (piano), Reinecke and Richter (theory) and Franz Götze (singing). While in Leipzig he sang Hans Sachs in a concert performance of *Die Meistersinger*. After further composition and vocal studies in Berlin, in 1875 he sang in a *St Matthew Passion* under Brahms, with whom he became closely acquainted. Two years later he moved to England, where he met his future wife, the American soprano Lillian Bailey. They travelled to Massachusetts in 1881 for their wedding and while in Boston he was engaged as the first conductor of the new Boston SO. After three seasons in Boston, Henschel settled in England, where he continued to appear as a singer until his retirement in April 1914, in which year he was knighted.

Henschel composed three works for the stage. Nothing seems to have come of his first opera, *Friedrich der Schöne*. At the end of his last season with the Boston SO, he collaborated with the American writer William Dean Howells on a comic opera conceived in the style of Gilbert and Sullivan and planned for production in the USA and England. He composed *The Sea-Change, or Love's Stowaway* in May and June 1884 and completed the full score while sailing back to England. The work was to be performed at the Bijou Theatre in Boston in November, but the death of the impresario brought the production to a halt. A concert performance given in Boston on 27 January 1885, possibly to attract backers for a production, received generally favourable reaction, though one reviewer thought the music more suitable for a cantata performed by the Handel and Haydn Society. Sullivan's influence shows in a mock-Handelian number, and a march with 'a flavor of *Lohengrin* about it' is set in counterpoint to 'Yankee Doodle'. The action takes place aboard the steamer Mesopotamia, two days out from Boston. The opera finally received a broadcast performance on the BBC in 1929.

Henschel's serious three-act opera, *Nubia*, was composed in 1898–9 to a libretto by Max Kalbeck based on a novel by Richard Voss. The story, set in the Sabine hills of Italy, concerns a fatal love triangle between an Italian peasant girl, a German painter and a rival suitor. The work was first performed in Dresden on 9 November 1899. Most of the critics described it as 'aristocratic music' that remained uninvolved with the drama; there were also complaints of thinness and lack of variety in the scoring. Two days after the first performance, one of the singers became ill and Henschel himself (in his only operatic appearance) sang the role of Fra Giròlamo.

STEVEN LEDBETTER

Hensel, Heinrich (*b* Neustadt, 29 Oct 1874; *d* Hamburg, 23 Feb 1935). German tenor. He studied in Vienna and Frankfurt and made his début at Freiburg in 1897, remaining a member of the ensemble there until 1900. After engagements at Frankfurt, where he created the Prince in Humperdinck's *Dornröschen* (1902), and Wiesbaden, he became the leading Heldentenor at the Hamburg Opera (1912–29). He was chosen by Siegfried

Wagner to create the tenor lead in *Banadietrich* (1910, Karlsruhe) and to sing Parsifal at Bayreuth, where he also sang Loge (1911–12). During the 1911–12 season he visited the USA, singing Siegmund, Siegfried and Lohengrin at the Metropolitan and Siegmund in Chicago. He appeared at Covent Garden from 1911 to 1914 in the Wagner repertory, and sang Parsifal in the first staged London production in 1914.

HAROLD ROSENTHAL/R

Hensler [Henseler], **Karl Friedrich** [Hennseler, Albert Friedrich] (*b* Vaihingen, Württemberg, bap. 1 Feb 1759; *d* Vienna, 24 Nov 1825). German librettist and director. A doctor's son, he studied theology at Tübingen University before moving in 1784 to Vienna, where he spent the rest of his life. He became a freemason. Marinelli engaged him as a house poet at the Theater in der Leopoldstadt, and between 1785 and 1803 Hensler turned out about 100 plays, farces, Singspiels and librettos. He succeeded Marinelli as director in 1803, and remained there until 1816. In 1818 he was at the Theater an der Wien, then in Pressburg (Bratislava) and Baden, near Vienna; back in Vienna, he helped finance the building of the Theater in der Josefstadt and became director on its inauguration in 1822.

Together with Schikaneder and Perinet, Hensler was among the most successful of late 18th-century dramatists in Vienna. He aimed above all to establish a truly popular genre of Viennese theatre with a repertory of high quality. His early dramas show the influence of bourgeois comedy and of Kotzebue in particular; later he took up the *Zauberspiel* ('magic play'). Wenzel Müller and Ferdinand Kauer, house composers at the Theater in der Leopoldstadt, set several of his librettos: among the most successful were Müller's heroic-comic opera *Das Sonnenfest der Braminen* (1790), which probably prepared the ground for Schikaneder's libretto for Mozart's *Die Zauberflöte*, and Kauer's *Das Donauweibchen* (1798). As a theatre director, notably at the Theater in der Leopoldstadt, Hensler earned a reputation for high-mindedness and generosity and managed to attract the best popular Viennese writers of the day. His tenure at the Theater in der Josefstadt coincided with that theatre's most flourishing period.

ES (O. Rommel); *MGG* (E. Badura-Skoda)

Henze, Hans Werner (*b* Gütersloh, 1 July 1926). German composer. His early enthusiasms were divided between music and the plastic arts, though he was determined from an early age to follow a musical career. After overcoming parental resistance he was allowed to study the piano and percussion at a school for orchestral musicians in Brunswick while a pupil at the high school in Bielefeld. He began to compose at the age of 12, before he had received any formal training. Even when he was in his early teens his natural instincts led him towards modernism in literature and music, towards the very writers, composers and artists condemned as decadent and proscribed by the Nazis: he felt the cultural barrenness of the Third Reich profoundly.

In 1944 he was conscripted into the German army, serving in Poland and Magdeburg before being seconded to a propaganda-film unit. Throughout this period he continued to compose covertly, though opportunities to hear new music were scant: one of the few fruitful encounters at that time was with the music of Kurt Weill. At the end of World War II Henze was briefly a British prisoner of war; on his return to civilian life he found work as a répétiteur at the Bielefeld Stadttheater. In the spring of 1946 he resumed his musical education, studying at the Evangelische Kirchenmusikalische Institut in Heidelberg with Wolfgang Fortner. His first acknowledged compositions, predominantly instrumental pieces, date from his two years' study with Fortner, which combined a rigorous grounding in harmony and counterpoint with a survey of contemporary compositional methods. From 1947 Henze attended the Darmstadt summer school, where he was quick to embrace the 12-note techniques propagated by René Leibowitz. In his prodigious output of the late 1940s and early 50s there is a gleeful integration of a heterogeneous collection of idioms from jazz through neo-classical pastiche to serialism.

In his first full-scale opera, *Boulevard Solitude* (1952) – an updating of the Manon story – Henze was able to combine these disparate idioms. In a dramatic scheme combining dance, drama, cinematic and 19th-century operatic conventions he demonstrated how an eclectic stylistic palette could nevertheless be derived from a single 12-note series. *Boulevard Solitude*'s adroit use of received forms – arias, ensembles, recitatives – and confident handling of style brought Henze considerable success. Together with the other dramatic products of his twenties – six ballets, the opera for actors after Cervantes *Das Wundertheater* (1949) and the two radio operas *Ein Landarzt* and *Das Ende einer Welt* – it brought a plethora of commissions and considerable critical acclaim. At the same time it estranged him from many of his European contemporaries, who detected in this 'synthetic thinking' and willingness to use such outmoded vehicles as ballet and opera an evasion of the consequences and imperatives of post-Webern serialism.

By 1953, however, Henze felt himself cut off from more than just his musical contemporaries: his mistrust of Germany and of postwar German society, fostered by his experiences during the 1930s and 40s, led him to move in the spring of that year to Italy, where he settled on Forio d'Ischia in the Bay of Naples. He celebrated his escape with the completion of his second full-length opera, *König Hirsch*. As if to emphasize his break with his native culture, in this massive score, playing for over five hours in its original version, Henze also abandoned the strict discipline of serialism and explored a much freer, more luxuriant expressive world that was to mark a decisive turning-point in his development and whose instinctive, lyrical flow set him still further apart from most of his European peers of the 1950s.

Over the next decade Henze's output was to be dominated by his operas, with groups of smaller works, vocal, instrumental and orchestral, clustered around each of them. The four operatic works that followed *König Hirsch* (first given in 1956 in a severely shortened version; Henze prepared his own abridgement in 1963, as *Il re cervo*) each represented a different approach to the problems of inventing and sustaining an operatic form. In *Der Prinz von Homburg* (1960), to a libretto by Ingeborg Bachmann, the model was explicitly that of 19th-century Italian opera, of Verdi in particular. In *Elegy for Young Lovers* (1961) he specified to his librettists Auden and Kallman that the scenario should include the opportunity for 'tender, beautiful noises'; its sequence of compact, highly wrought scenes was to be accompanied by a chamber orchestra used with great discrimination and restraint. A second collaboration with Bachmann, *Der junge Lord* (1965), was an attempt to write an *opera buffa*, very much indebted to the spirit of Rossini and Bellini and with a classical economy of means, while *The Bassarids* (1966), again with Auden and Kallman, confronted the problems of symphonic drama head on, even to the extent of articulating the work as the four movements of a symphony.

Henze left Naples to live near Rome in 1961, and from the early 1960s began to teach at the Salzburg Mozarteum. The première of *The Bassarids* at the Salzburg Festival in 1966 brought the composer his greatest success to date, but nevertheless he was aware that it represented a point of no return in his development. During the second half of the 1960s he subjected both his musical and political beliefs to intense scrutiny, and in a series of concert works began to strip away the inessentials from his style. The explicitly *engagé* works of the late 1960s and early 70s, typified by the 'oratorio volgare e militare' *Das Floss der 'Medusa'* (1968), would not embrace anything as bourgeois as conventional opera. Henze's main dramatic output of that period was directed towards smaller-scale music theatre: *El Cimarrón* (1970), based on Esteban Montejo's *The Biography of a Runaway Slave*, the 'show for 17' *Der langierige Weg in die Wohnung Natascha Ungeheuer* (1971) and the vaudeville *La cubana* (1974).

When he did return to the opera house, with *We Come to the River* (1976), commissioned by Covent Garden, his approach to Edward Bond's heavy allegory was far more indebted to the experience and the polyglot musical expression of the political works than to any of his earlier operas. *We Come to the River* has been

arguably the least successful of all Henze's stage works, and his subsequent development has signalled a measured return to the line abandoned after *The Bassarids* and a recovery of the sense of lyricism deliberately submerged for almost a decade. In *The English Cat* (1983) elements of the earlier political didacticism remain, not least in Bond's satirical treatment of Balzac's short story; yet Henze's treatment combines the closed vocal forms into through-composed acts in which the neo-classical pastiche of the early scenes progressively gives way to music that is much darker and expressionistically hard-edged. *Das verratene Meer* (1990) carries the reorientation a stage further, with designated numbers embedded in a through-composed scheme, and a musical language that uses a serial organization in an idiom that reveals a clear debt to Berg. The scoring of *Das verratene Meer* is also indebted to a preceding project in which Henze made his own transcription and orchestration of Monteverdi's *Il ritorno d'Ulisse* (1985, Salzburg). In this and other projects, such as the reworking of Paisiello's *Don Chisciotte* (1976, Montepulciano) as well as in his stewardship of the Montepulciano Cantiere since 1986, and of the Munich Biennale which he founded in 1988, Henze appears to have struck perhaps the truest balance between his activities as a creative musician of enormous but sometimes undisciplined gifts and those of a political activist, as complementary rather than integrated preoccupations.

See also BASSARIDS, THE; BOULEVARD SOLITUDE; ELEGY FOR YOUNG LOVERS; ENGLISH CAT, THE; JUNGE LORD, DER; KÖNIG HIRSCH; PRINZ VON HOMBURG, DER; VERRATENE MEER, DAS; and WE COME TO THE RIVER.

		printed scores are published in Mainz		
title	genre, acts	libretto	première; remarks	publications
Das Wundertheater	Oper für Schauspieler, 1	after M. de Cervantes, trans. A. Graf von Schack	Heidelberg, Stadt, 7 May 1949; rev. for singers, Frankfurt, Kammerspiel, 30 Nov 1965	vs 1949, vs 1965 (rev. version)
Ein Landarzt	radio op	after F. Kafka	Nordwestdeutscher Rundfunk, 19 Nov 1951; staged, Cologne, Kammerspiele, 27 May 1953; rev. for stage, Frankfurt, Kammerspiel, 30 Nov 1965	vs 1965
Boulevard Solitude	lyrisches Drama, 7 scenes	G. Weil, scenario by W. Jockisch	Hanover, Landes, 17 Feb 1952	vs 1952
Das Ende einer Welt	radio op, prol., 2, epilogue	W. Hildesheimer	Nordwestdeuscher Rundfunk, 4 Dec 1953; rev. for stage, Frankfurt, Kammerspiel, 30 Nov 1965	vs 1965
König Hirsch	op, 3	H. von Cramer, after C. Gozzi	Berlin, Städtische Oper, 23 Sept 1956 [heavily cut]; rev. as Il re cervo, or The Errantries of Truth, Kassel, Staats, 10 March 1963; orig. version, Stuttgart, Staatsoper, 5 May 1985 [complete]	vs 1956, vs 1964
Der Prinz von Homburg	op, 3	I. Bachmann, after H. von Kleist: *Prinz Friedrich von Homburg*	Hamburg, Staatsoper, 22 May 1960	vs 1960
Elegy for Young Lovers	op, 3	W. H. Auden and C. Kallman	Schwetzingen, Schloss, 20 May 1961	1961
Der junge Lord	komische Oper, 2	Bachmann, after W. Hauff	Berlin, Deutsche Oper, 7 April 1965	vs 1965
The Bassarids	opera seria with intermezzo, 1	Auden and Kallman, after Euripides	Salzburg, 6 Aug 1966	vs 1966
We Come to the River	actions for music	E. Bond	London, CG, 12 July 1976	1976
Pollicino	Märchen für Musik	G. Di Leva, after Collodi, J. L. and W. C. Grimm, and C. Perrault	Montepulciano, Poliziano, 2 Aug 1980	vs 1980

title	genre, acts	libretto	première; remarks	publications
The English Cat	story for singers and instrumentalists, 2	Bond, after H. de Balzac	Schwetzingen, Schloss, 2 June 1983	vs 1983
Das verratene Meer	Musikdrama, 2	H.-U. Treichel, after Y. Mishima: *Gogo no eiko*	Berlin, Deutsche Oper, 5 May 1990	

Music theatre: Moralities (3 scenic cantatas, Auden, after Aesop), Cincinnati, 18 May 1968, vs (1967); El Cimarrón (recital for four musicians, M. Barnet, after E. Montejo: *The Biography of a Runaway Slave*), Aldeburgh, 1970 (1972); Der langwierige Weg in die Wohnung der Natascha Ungeheur ('show for 17', G. Salvatore), Rome, RAI, 17 May 1971; La cubana, oder Ein Leben für die Kunst (vaudeville, 5 scenes, H. M. Enzensberger, after Barnet), New York, NET Opera, 4 March 1974, vs (1984)

Arrangements and transcriptions: Don Chisciotte (arr. of Paisiello), Montepulciano, 1 Aug 1976; Il ritorno d'Ulisse in patria (transcr. of Monteverdi), Salzburg, 16 Aug 1985

WRITINGS

'Mein *König Hirsch*', Melos, xxiii (1956), 241–4

'On Writing *Elegy for Young Lovers*', Opera, xii (1961), 433–4

Essays (Mainz, 1964)

'Meine Musik auf dem Theater', ÖMz, xxi (1966), 369–73

Musik und Politik: Schriften und Gespräche 1966–1975, ed. J. Brockmeier (Munich, 1976 [incl. *Essays*, 1964]; Eng. trans., rev., as *Music and Politics*, 1982; enlarged as *Musik und Politik: Schriften und Gespräche 1955–1984*, 1984)

'Musiktheater und Wirklichkeit', Beiträge zur Musikwissenschaft, xix (1977), 284–92

'*Pollicino*: an Opera for Children', MT, cxxi (1980), 766–8

Schriften und Gespräche 1955–1979 (Berlin, 1981)

'Kurzbericht über die Enstehung meiner Oper *Die englische Katze*', Schwetzingen Festival 1983 [programme book]

Die englische Katze: Arbeitstagebuch 1979–82 (Frankfurt, 1988)

ed.: *Neues Musiktheater. Almanach zur erste Münchener Biennale* (Munich, 1988)

INTERVIEWS

G.-W. Baruch: 'Hans Werner Henze am Tyrrhenischen Meer: süditalienischer Dialog', Melos, xxiii (1956), 70–73

A. Blyth: 'Henze's New Opera', Opera, xvii (1966), 608–10 [on *The Bassarids*]

P. Heyworth: 'I can imagine a future …', The Observer (20 Aug 1970)

H. Lück: 'Der lange Weg zur Musik der Revolution', Neue Musikzeitung, xx (1971), 3–4

H. K. Jungheinrich: '4 Stunden auf Henzes neuem Weg', Melos, xxxix (1972), 207–13

U. Stürzbecher: 'Hans Werner Henze', Werkstattgespräche mit Komponisten (Cologne, 1972), 106–20

P. Griffiths: '*The Bassarids*: Hans Werner Henze talks to Paul Griffiths', MT, cxv (1974), 831–2

P. Heyworth: Interview, The Observer (6 Oct 1974)

R. Stephan: 'Hans Werner Henze', Die Reihe, iv (1958), 32–7; Eng. trans. in Die Reihe, iv (1960), 29–35

H. Pauli: 'Hans Werner Henze's Italian Music', The Score (1959), no.25, pp.26–37

D. de la Motte: *Hans Werner Henze: Der Prinz von Homburg* (Mainz, 1960)

J. Warrack: 'Two New Operas in Germany', Opera, xi (1960), 457–61

W. H. Auden and C. Kallman: 'Genesis of a Libretto', in libretto of *Elegy for Young Lovers* (Mainz, 1961)

A. Porter: '*Elegy for Young Lovers*', MT, cii (1961), 418–19

Melos, xxxii/2 (1965) [Henze issue]

ÖMz, xxi (1966), 369–82 [articles on *The Bassarids*]

A. Whittall: 'Henze: Tradition and the Music of the Future', MO, xc (1967), 446–7

K. Geitel: *Hans Werner Henze* (Berlin, 1968)

S. Walsh: 'Henze and Fascism', The Listener (29 Feb 1968)

A. Porter: 'Henze's *Young Lord*', MT, cx (1969), 1028–30

P. Heyworth: 'Henze and the Revolution', Music and Musicians, xix/1 (1969–70), 36–40

S. Walsh: 'Henze's *Il re cervo*', The Listener (18 Jan 1973)

W. H. Auden and C. Kallman: 'Euripides for Today', MT, cxv (1974), 833–4

R. Henderson: 'Henze's Progress: from *Boulevard Solitude* to *The Bassarids*', Opera, xxv (1974), 851–7

R. Blackford: 'The Road to *The River*', Music and Musicians, xxiv/2 (1975–6), 20–24

W. Burde: 'Tradition und Revolution in Henzes musikalischen Theater' Melos/NZM, ii (1976), 271–5

R. Henderson: 'Hans Werner Henze', MT, cxvii (1976), 566–8

H. Keller: 'Drowning in the River', Opera, xxvii (1976), 817–21

K. Schultz, ed.: *Hans Werner Henze: eine Auswahl* (Bonn, 1976)

K. Stevens: '*The Raft of the Medusa*', Music and Musicians, xxv/2 (1976–7), 24–6

A. Porter: 'Crossing the River', Music of Three Seasons: 1974–1977 (New York, 1978), 451–7

E. H. Flammer: *Politische engagierte Musik als kompositorisches Problem, dargestellt am Beispiel von Luigi Nono und Hans Werner Henze* (Baden-Baden, 1981)

E. Restagno, ed.: *Henze* (Turin, 1986)

D. Rexroth, ed.: *Der Komponist Hans Werner Henze* (Mainz, 1986)

P. Petersen: *Hans Werner Henze: ein politischer Musiker* (Hamburg, 1988) [12 lectures]

A. Porter: 'Melodious Cats', Musical Events: a Chronicle 1983–1986 (New York, 1989), 350–52

A. Clements: 'Hans across the Ocean', Opera, xli (1990), 928–31

ANDREW CLEMENTS

Heppner, Ben (*b* Murrayville, 14 Jan 1956). Canadian tenor. He studied at the University of British Columbia. During the mid-1980s he sang lyrical Mozart, Rossini and Donizetti roles in Toronto. In 1987 he went back to study as a dramatic tenor and in 1988 he sang Bacchus at Melbourne, the Prince (*Rusalka*) at Philadelphia, Zinovy (*Lady Macbeth of the Mtsensk District*) at Toronto and Walther von der Vogelweide in Chicago. He went on to sing Lohengrin in Stockholm and San Francisco (1989); Walther von Stolzing at Seattle, La Scala and Covent Garden, Bacchus at Santa Fe and Frankfurt, and Florestan at Cologne (1990); and the Prince in Vienna, Laca (*Jenůfa*) at Brussels and Erik in Geneva (1991). He has a powerful heroic voice with a solid middle register and ringing top notes, and an impressive stage presence. ELIZABETH FORBES

Herbain, Chevalier d' (*b* Paris, *c*1730–34; *d* Paris, 1769). French composer. He composed three operas while on military duty in Italy: an intermezzo *Il geloso* (performed in Rome in 1751 and later given at the Teatro del Cocomero, Florence, and at Bastia in Corsica), *Il trionfo del Giglio* and *Lavinia*. Extracts from *Lavinia*, published soon after his return to Paris, consist of bravura arias and a duet in typical *opera seria* style. In 1756 his *Iphis et Célime* (sometimes incorrectly listed as *Célimène*) was performed at the Paris Opéra. Two works in a lighter vein were *Les deux talents* (1763) and *Nanette et Lucas* (1764), revealing a pleasantly lyrical style appropriate to *opéra comique*.

Il geloso (int), Rome, 1751

Il trionfo del Giglio (3), Bastia, Pubblico, 1751

Lavinia (3), Bastia, Pubblico, *c*1753, extracts (Paris, n.d.)

Iphis et Célime, ou Le temple de l'Indifférence détruit par l'Amour (opéra-ballet, 1, Chennevières), Paris, Opéra, 28 Sept 1756 (Paris, n.d.)

Les deux talents (oc, 2, Bastide), Paris, Comédie-Italienne, 11 Aug 1763
Nanette et Lucas, ou La paysanne curieuse (oc, 1, N. E. Framery), Paris, Comédie-Italienne, 14 June 1764 (Paris, n.d.)

DAVID TUNLEY

Herbert, Victor (August) (*b* Dublin, 1 Feb 1859; *d* New York, 26 May 1924). American composer, the most talented and successful American composer of operettas.

1. LIFE. His father died when he was an infant; his mother remarried a German and the family settled in Stuttgart. He retained a lasting pride in his Irish (Protestant) heritage, which is reflected in many of his operettas. After studying the cello privately, he entered the Stuttgart Conservatory; he later spent a year in the orchestra of Eduard Strauss, in Vienna: a formative experience for his later work in operetta. In 1881 he returned to Stuttgart to join the court orchestra. There he met his future wife Therese Foerster (1861–1927), a soprano in the court opera; they moved to the USA when she was hired by the Metropolitan Opera to sing the title role in the American première of *Aida* (in German), and he was appointed principal cellist in the orchestra.

Herbert was active in the city's musical life as a soloist, a member of the New York String Quartet and assistant conductor to Anton Seidl during the 1888 summer season. He joined the faculty of the National Conservatory of Music, produced a number of concert works and in 1893 became director of a celebrated band. He composed his first operetta *Prince Ananias* in 1894 for a popular troupe, the Bostonians. By the turn of the century Herbert had achieved considerable success as an operetta composer (*The Serenade*, 1897; *The Fortune Teller*, 1898), but he withdrew from the theatre to concentrate on his work as conductor of the Pittsburgh SO (1898–1904). A disagreement with the management led to his resignation, whereupon he founded the Victor Herbert Orchestra, which he conducted on tours and at summer resorts for most of the rest of his life in programmes of light orchestral music.

Before leaving Pittsburgh, Herbert returned to the theatre with *Babes in Toyland* (1903), the first of a series of works that made him one of the best-known figures in American music. It was followed by *Mlle Modiste* (1905) and *The Red Mill* (1906), both successes. After an extended search for a serious libretto, he composed *Natoma*, produced in Philadelphia by the Philadelphia-Chicago Opera Company on 25 February 1911; a splendid cast included John McCormack and Mary Garden. The company kept the work in its repertory for three years. *Madeleine*, a lighter work in one act, was produced at the Metropolitan Opera in 1914. Even while composing his two operas, Herbert was working on more operettas, including two of his finest, *Naughty Marietta* (1910) and *Sweethearts* (1913). His longstanding wish to compose an Irish operetta was gratified with the production of *Eileen* (originally *Hearts of Erin*) in 1917, which boasts a solid libretto and a rich score. He had also composed one of the earliest original orchestral scores for a full-length film, *The Fall of a Nation* (1916; the music was rediscovered in the Library of Congress and recorded in 1987).

By the end of World War I, musical styles in the popular theatre had changed. Herbert wrote several 'musical comedies' with simpler songs and less elaborate ensembles, but his heart remained with the sentimental European-style operetta.

2. STAGE WORKS. Herbert was prolific and occasionally composed as many as four shows simultaneously; he wrote well over 50 scores for the stage, in addition to numbers for the Ziegfeld Follies and elaborate skits for private entertainments. Though he had as thorough a grounding in composition as any American composer of his day, he never lost his popular touch. Among his most successful shows, with first runs on Broadway of 100 performances or more and lengthy tours, were *Babes in Toyland*, *Mlle Modiste*, *The Red Mill*, *Naughty Marietta* and *Sweethearts*. Other strong scores are those for *The Serenade*, *The Fortune Teller*, *Cyrano de Bergerac* (1899), *The Singing Girl* (1899), *The Enchantress* (1911), *The Madcap Duchess* (1913), *The Only Girl* (1914) and *Eileen*.

Some of Herbert's operettas were written for actors, others for trained singers. The operettas composed for stars such as Alice Nielson (*The Fortune Teller*), Fritzi Scheff (*Mlle Modiste*) or Emma Trentini (*Naughty Marietta*) placed great demands on the chorus and orchestra as well as the principals. These tended to reflect the Viennese tradition, although Herbert was also perfectly capable of imitating Gilbert and Sullivan, as the quintet 'Cleopatra's Wedding Day' from *The Wizard of the Nile* shows. Many of his songs achieved remarkable popularity, and some of the waltz songs have irresistible charm, such as 'I'm falling in love with someone' from *Naughty Marietta* or 'I have a dream' from *The Enchantress*. 'Kiss me again' from *Mlle Modiste* demonstrates Herbert's stringent vocal requirements as well as his love of lush harmonies using augmented 7th chords and chains of secondary dominants.

In his operettas Herbert used a larger orchestra than Sullivan's, often employing a harp and more varied percussion instruments to colourful effect. Except when short of time he did his own orchestration, and his handling of the orchestra consistently attracted praise from critics. Revivals generally used updated orchestration, heavy with saxophones and far from his own string-dominated sonorities. Most of his works were criticized in his own day for the triviality or weakness of their librettos and for the conventionality of the lyrics. A few revivals with heavily rewritten texts took place in the 1980s, possibly the harbinger of a wider reconsideration of his art.

Herbert naturally wanted to compose a serious opera. The announcement that he had signed a contract with Oscar Hammerstein I for a grand opera (the impresario had offered $1000 for a libretto; *Musical America*, 13 April 1907, p.6) triggered wide speculation and enthusiasm. The choice of libretto and the progress of the composition and production were also followed eagerly by the press, raising expectations that could hardly be satisfied with even the most glorious of successes. Though *Natoma* was produced with great care and a superb cast, the première enjoyed only a *succès d'estime*, mainly because of the weakness of Joseph Redding's book and the use of French, Irish and Italian singers in what was proclaimed as an American opera (it is set on the California coast in the 1820s and concerns the love of Paul, an American naval officer, for the Indian princess Natoma). An ardent admirer of Wagner, Herbert wrote a score that effectively used leitmotif construction in a continuing orchestral counterpoint with colourful and melodious set pieces. Herbert's second opera, *Madeleine*, is a slight one-act comedy based on a French play about an operatic prima donna. At the première, it was paired with *Pagliacci*, with Caruso in the principal part, and functioned as little more than a curtain-raiser. The style is 'conversational' throughout, with constant motivic commentary from the orchestra. The one real set piece, Madeleine's pensive reflections ('A perfect day'), was added at the last moment on the insistence of Frances Alda, who refused to sing otherwise. Herbert handles Madeleine's mercurial changes of mood with great flexibility and characterizes each of her admirers in a different way. Apart from a short, recurrent theme associated with her mother's portrait, which closes the opera to touching effect, the score is almost entirely through-composed. The work was dropped from the repertory of the Metropolitan after half a dozen performances, though Schirmer published it in full score, an unprecedented distinction for an American opera.

comic operas unless otherwise stated; published in vocal score in New York, in the year of first performance unless otherwise stated; most MSS in US-Wc

Prince Ananias (2, F. Neilson), New York, Broadway, 20 Nov 1894 (1895)

The Wizard of the Nile (3, H. B. Smith), Wilkes Barre, PA, 26 Sept 1895, New York, Casino, 4 Nov 1895

The Gold Bug (musical blend, 2, G. MacDonough), New York, Casino, 21 Sept 1896, excerpts (1895)

The Serenade (3, Smith), Cleveland, 17 Feb 1897, New York, Knickerbocker, 16 March 1897

The Idol's Eye (3, Smith), Troy, NY, 20 Sept 1897, New York, Broadway, 25 Oct 1897

The Fortune Teller (3, Smith), Toronto, 14 Sept 1898, New York, Wallack's, 26 Sept 1898

Cyrano de Bergerac (3, S. Reed, after E. Rostand; lyrics Smith), Montreal, 11 Sept 1899, New York, Knickerbocker, 18 Sept 1899

The Singing Girl (3, S. Stange; lyrics Smith), Montreal, 2 Oct 1899, New York, Casino, 23 Oct 1899

The Ameer (extravaganza, 3, F. Ranken; lyrics K. La Shelle), Scranton, PA, 9 Oct 1899, New York, Wallack's, 4 Dec 1899

The Viceroy (3, Smith), San Francisco, 12 Feb 1900, New York, Knickerbocker, 9 April 1900

Babes in Toyland (extravaganza, 3, MacDonough), Chicago, 17 June 1903, New York, Majestic, 13 Oct 1903

Babette (3, Smith), Washington DC, 9 Nov 1903, New York, Broadway, 16 Nov 1903

It Happened in Nordland (musical extravaganza, 2, MacDonough), Harrisburg, PA, 21 Nov 1904, New York, Lew Fields, 5 Dec 1904 (1905)

Miss Dolly Dollars (musical comedy, 2, Smith), Rochester, NY, 30 Aug 1905, New York, 4 Sept 1905

Wonderland [Alice and the Eight Princesses] (musical extravaganza, 3, MacDonough), Buffalo, NY, 14 Sept 1905, New York, Majestic, 24 Oct 1905

Mlle Modiste (2, H. Blossom), Trenton, NJ, 7 Oct 1905, New York, Knickerbocker, 25 Dec 1905

The Red Mill (musical comedy, 2, Blossom), Buffalo, NY, 3 Sept 1906, New York, Knickerbocker, 24 Sept 1906

Dream City (2, E. Smith), New York, 25 Dec 1906 (1907)

The Magic Knight [Night] (operatic burlesque, 1, E. Smith), New York, 25 Dec 1906 (1907)

The Tattooed Man (2, A. N. C. Fowler; lyrics H. B. Smith), Baltimore, 11 Feb 1907, New York, Criterion, 18 Feb 1907

Miss Camille (operatic burlesque, G. V. Hobart), New York, 14 April 1907, excerpts (1907)

The Song Birds (operatic outburst, Hobart), New York, 13 May 1907, excerpts (1907)

Algeria (musical play, MacDonough), Atlantic City, NJ, 24 Aug 1908, New York, Broadway, 31 Aug 1908; rev. as The Rose of Algeria, 1909

Little Nemo (musical play, 3, H. B. Smith, after comic strip by Winsor McKay), Philadelphia, 28 Sept 1908, New York, New Amsterdam, 20 Oct 1908

The Prima Donna (3, Blossom), Chicago, 5 Oct 1908, New York, Knickerbocker, 30 Nov 1908

Old Dutch (musical comedy, 2, E. Smith; lyrics Hobart), Wilkes Barre, PA, 6 Nov 1909, New York, Herald Square, 22 Nov 1909

Naughty Marietta (2, R. J. Young), Syracuse, NY, 24 Oct 1910, New York, New York Theatre, 7 Nov 1910

When Sweet Sixteen (song play, 2, Hobart), Springfield, MA, 5 Dec 1910, New York, Daly's, 14 Sept 1911

Natoma (op, 3, J. D. Redding), Philadelphia, 25 Feb 1911 (1913)

Mlle. Rosita (3, J. Herbert; lyrics H. B. Smith), Boston, 27 March 1911; as The Duchess, New York, Lyric, 16 Oct 1911

The Enchantress (2, F. de Gresac; lyrics H. B. Smith), Washington DC, 9 Oct 1911, New York, New York Theatre, 19 Oct 1911

The Lady of the Slipper (musical comedy, 3, A. Caldwell and L. McCarty; lyrics J. O'Dea), Philadelphia, 8 Oct 1912, New York, Globe, 28 Oct 1912

Sweethearts (2, H. B. Smith and De Gresac; lyrics R. B. Smith), Baltimore, 24 March 1913, New York, New Amsterdam, 8 Sept 1913

The Madcap Duchess (2, D. Stevens, after J. H. McCarthy), Rochester, NY, 13 Oct 1913, New York, Globe, 11 Nov 1913

Madeleine (lyric op, 1, G. Stewart, after A. Decourcelle and L. Thibaut: *Je dine chez ma mère*), New York, Met, 24 Jan 1914, full score and vs (1913)

The Debutante (musical comedy, 2, H. B. Smith; lyrics R. B. Smith), Atlantic City, NJ, 21 Sept 1914, New York, Knickerbocker, 7 Dec 1914

The Only Girl (musical farcical comedy, 3, Blossom, after L. Fulda), Atlantic City, NJ, 1 Oct 1914, New York, 39th Street, 2 Nov 1914

The Princess Pat (3, Blossom), Atlantic City, NJ, 23 Aug 1915, New York, 29 Sept 1915

Hearts of Erin (3, Blossom), Cleveland, 1 Jan 1917; as Eileen, New York, Shubert, 19 March 1917

Her Regiment (musical play, 3, W. Le Baron), Springfield, MA, 22 Oct 1917, New York, Broadhurst, 12 Nov 1917

The Velvet Lady (musical comedy, 3, Blossom), Philadelphia, 23 Dec 1918, New York, New Amsterdam, 3 Feb 1919

Angel Face (musical play, 3, H. B. Smith; lyrics R. B. Smith), Chicago, 8 June 1919, New York, Knickerbocker, 29 Dec 1919 (1920)

My Golden Girl (musical comedy, 2, F. A. Kummer), Stamford, CT, 19 Dec 1919, New York, Nora Bayes, 2 Feb 1920, excerpts (1920)

Oui Madame (musical play, 2, G. M. Wright; lyrics R. B. Smith), Philadelphia, 22 March 1920, excerpts (1920)

The Girl in the Spotlight (musical play, 2, R. Bruce), Stamford, CT, 7 July 1920, New York, Knickerbocker, 12 July 1920, excerpts (1920)

Orange Blossoms (comedy with music, 3, De Gresac; lyrics B. G. de Sylva), Philadelphia, 4 Sept 1922, New York, Fulton, 19 Sept 1922

The Dream Girl (musical play, 3, Young; lyrics H. Atteridge), New Haven, CT, 22 April 1924, New York, Ambassador, 20 Aug 1924, excerpts (1924)

Other music for revues, incl.: The Century Girl, New York, 1916, collab. I. Berlin, excerpts (1916); scores for stage works (Seven Little Widows, The House that Jack Built, The Lavender Lady, Hula-Lula, The Garden of Eden and unidentified material) in Wc.

*

GroveAM (E. N. Waters, H. Wiley Hitchcock)

H. B. Smith: *First Nights and First Editions* (Boston, 1931)

C. L. Purdy: *Victor Herbert – American Music Master* (New York, 1944)

E. N. Waters: *Victor Herbert: a Life in Music* (New York, 1955) [incl. lists of compositions and recordings]

G. Bordman: *American Musical Theatre: a Chronicle* (New York, 1978, 2/1986)

A. G. Debus: 'The Early Victor Herbert', *Music of Victor Herbert* (Smithsonian Collection DMP30366, 1979) [record notes]

C. Hamm: *Yesterdays: Popular Song in America* (New York, 1979)

F. S. Roffman: record notes, *Naughty Marietta* (Smithsonian Collection N026, 1981)

EDWARD N. WATERS/H. WILEY HITCHCOCK, STEVEN LEDBETTER

Herbert (Seligman), Walter (*b* Frankfurt, 18 Feb 1902; *d* San Diego, CA, 14 Sept 1975). American conductor and administrator of German birth. He studied composition with Schoenberg in Vienna before gaining practical experience as a conductor in Germany and Switzerland and at the Vienna Volksoper. In 1938, just before the Anschluss, he left Austria for the USA, and became an American citizen in 1944. He was director of Opera in English, San Francisco, and in 1943 became the first general director of the New Orleans Opera. He founded the Houston Grand Opera in 1955, directing it until 1972, and served as music director of Opera/South in Jackson, Mississippi. As general director and conductor from 1969 of the San Diego Opera (founded under his leadership in 1965), he was responsible for the American première of Henze's *Der junge Lord* in 1967 and the world première of Alva Henderson's *Medea* in 1972.   FRANK MERKLING

Hercegovina. Region in southern Europe, formerly in Yugoslavia. For discussion of operatic activity *see* SARAJEVO.

Hercigonja, Nikola (*b* Vinkovci, 19 Feb 1911). Croatian composer. He studied at the Academy of Music in Zagreb with Bersa and Odak, and in 1942 became a member of the National Liberation Theatre. From 1950 he was a professor at the Academy of Music in Belgrade. His theatre music has been inspired by Musorgsky and Janáček and by folk music. He has tended to favour the scenic oratorio as a form in which to attempt to represent people's struggles, but there are four other stage works in varying genres. *Vječni Žid u Zagrebu* ('The Eternal Jew in Zagreb') satirizes Croatian political life of the 19th century with trivial music, a clash of different styles and the use of well-known melodies in caricatures. *Planetarijom* ('Planetarium'), scored for a large ensemble including reciting choir and organ, evokes the suffering of people over the centuries: apocalyptic visions and grotesque fantasy are conveyed by music of great intensity. *Stav'te pamet na komediju* ('Let's do a Comedy'), by contrast, is in the style of a madrigal comedy, with a pantomime on the stage accompanied by choir, soloists and orchestra.

Vječni Žid u Zagrebu [The Eternal Jew in Zagreb], 1940–42 (musical burlesque, 3, after A. Šenoa), unperf.
Mali Hans [Small Hans], 1942–59 (children's radio op, 2, after O. Wilde: *The Faithful Friend*), unperf.
Planetarijom [Planetarium], 1958–60 (stage musical vision, 8 pts, after M. Krleža: *Balade Petrice Kerempuha* [The Ballads of Petrice Kerempuh], pt 3), Radio Belgrade, 28 July 1965
Stav'te pamet na komediju [Let's do a Comedy], 1962–4 (opera-ballet, 3, after M. Držić: *Dundo Maroje*, and Dalmatian poetry), Radio Belgrade, 1967; rev. for Belgrade television, 1974

*

V. Peričić: *Muzički stvaraoci u Srbiji* [Musical Creators in Serbia] (Belgrade, 1969)
B. Radović: *Muzičko-scensko delo Nikole Hercigonje* [The Musical-Scenic Work of Nikola Hercigonja] (thesis, U. of Art, Belgrade, 1988)   ROKSANDA PEJOVIĆ

Hercules. Musical drama in three acts by GEORGE FRIDERIC HANDEL to a libretto by Thomas Broughton after SOPHOCLES' *Trachiniae* and OVID's *Metamorphoses*; London, King's Theatre, 5 January 1745 (concert performance).

Hercules is not an opera, nor (as it has sometimes been called) an oratorio. The original description was 'musical drama'. It was not intended for staging, though like many of Handel's biblical oratorios it shows signs of being conceived in visual terms and has several times been given on the stage. During the 1740s Handel was occupied principally with oratorios, many of which aspire to the nature of Greek tragedy in their treatment, and with *Semele* (1744) and *Hercules* he moved into the

realms of Greek tragedy itself. The London public, however, was not receptive to it; the moral and uplifting element that was a part of the appeal of the biblical oratorios was lacking. *Hercules* had only two performances initially; it was revived for a further two each in 1749 and 1752, with damaging cuts. The original cast included Henry Reinhold in the title role, Miss Robinson as Dejanira, Elisabeth Duparc ('La Francesina') as Iole, John Beard as Hyllus and Susanna Cibber as Lichas (her popularity explains the size of what is really a minor role, which Handel in fact omitted in revivals). The work remained one of Handel's less popular, with only occasional performances in the later 18th century and the 19th. Its first staging was at Münster in 1925, revived later with ballet, a huge chorus and electric amplification; in Britain, it was staged in Merstham, Surrey, in 1939 and by the Handel Opera Society in London in 1956. It has never secured the place in an opera-house repertory that its musical quality and its dramatic vigour would justify.

The version of the myth adopted by the Rev. Thomas Broughton, prebendary of Salisbury, is ingeniously adjusted from the Sophocles original by drawing also on Ovid: by presenting Iole and Hercules as innocent, the focus is firmly placed on Dejanira's furious jealousy, with its tragic consequences.

ACT 1 In Hercules' palace in Trachis, the herald Lichas (alto) comments on the hero's prolonged absence. Hercules' wife Dejanira (mezzo-soprano) laments and fears that he will not return ('The world, when day's career is run'). Their son Hyllus (tenor) reports in a dramatic recitative that his consultation of the oracle provoked flames and quaking of the earth, with a prediction of Hercules' death; he resolves to seek his father ('Where congeal'd the northern streams'). The chorus applauds his 'filial piety'. But now Lichas reports that Hercules is approaching, having conquered Oechalia, and bringing the princess Iole as captive. Iole (soprano) and her attendant virgins are led in, mourning their loss of liberty. A pompous march heralds the arrival of Hercules (bass). After Iole has bewailed the death of her father at Hercules' hands, the hero himself sings of finishing his labours ('The god of battle quits the bloody field'). The chorus celebrates.

ACT 2 Iole laments her fate as a princess, as opposed to a 'maid ordain'd to dwell in humble cell'. Dejanira enters: 'It must be so!', she exclaims, believing that Hercules has betrayed her with the beautiful, sorrowing Iole. Iole denies it, and the chorus offers a solemn disquisition on 'Jealousy! infernal pest, tyrant of the human breast'. Hyllus, attracted to Iole, expresses his feelings to her. Now Dejanira reproaches Hercules, to which he responds with a boastful military song (with oboes, 'Alcides' name in latest story'). Dejanira responds with an enraged, taunting outburst ('Resign thy club and lion's spoils'), sneering at him for succumbing to 'Venus and her whining boy'. He denies her charges and she calls on the gods ('Cease, ruler of the day, to rise': this item was never in fact performed under Handel). She now sends Hercules, through Lichas, the robe given her by Nessus, whom Hercules long ago killed, which Nessus said would 'revive th' expiring flame of love'. When Iole comes to her, she dissembles, apologizing for her suspicions (duet, 'Joys of freedom'). The chorus celebrate the apparent happy outcome in gavotte rhythm ('Love and Hymen').

ACT 3 An intense, violent French overture makes it clear that all is not well. Lichas announces that Hercules has fallen, 'inglorious, by a woman's hand': the robe, poisoned, has fatally torn and burnt his flesh. The chorus mourn ('Tyrants now no more shall dread'). Hercules expresses his agonies in a furious recitative and air ('Oh Jove! what land is this'). Hyllus arrives to witness his father's death and to build him a funeral pyre. Dejanira is tortured by her guilt and visions of the Furies in what is in effect a mad scene, compounded of recitative and airs ('Where shall I fly!'). A Priest (bass) tells Dejanira that an eagle has borne Hercules' 'part immortal' to Olympus, to join the gods. Iole and Hyllus rejoice in their now mutual love, and the chorus sings in Hercules' praise.

* * *

The strength of *Hercules* lies in its vivid characterization, equally in the fierce jealousy and bitter remorse of Dejanira (her mad scene recalls not only Purcell but also Handel's own *Orlando*) and the touchingly gentle and innocent Iole; Handel's insights into a wide range of female emotion are, as always, remarkable. The men are more ordinary, though the portrait of Hercules as bluff extrovert has an unexpected touch of humour which in no way lessens the force of his ultimate fate. Handel's use of the chorus, both as the people of Trachis and (Greek chorus-style) as external commentators on the situation, is characteristic of his works not intended for the stage, and it poses difficulties in staging, particularly as the static, often fugal forms that he uses do not lend themselves to theatrical realization. But *Hercules* is more a drama of personal psychology than – like the biblical oratorios – of the fates of nations, and it is for this that its revival on the stage is above all justified.

STANLEY SADIE

Herder, Johann Gottfried (*b* Mohrungen, East Prussia, 25 Aug 1744; *d* Weimar, 18 Dec 1803). German writer. Familiar from his earliest years with the Protestant songbooks, he was fond of music all his life. In his Königsberg student days he became acquainted with Kant and Hamann, who introduced him to the theory of the common roots of music and language. After securing a post as teacher (and later as preacher) at Riga, in 1769 he undertook a journey by sea to France, meeting leading Parisian men of letters. In Germany he met Lessing, Claudius and (at Strasbourg in 1770) the young Goethe. From 1771 until 1776 he was at Bückeburg, the court of Count Wilhelm of Schaumburg-Lippe, where his collaboration with J. C. F. Bach produced a series of important cantatas, oratorios and 'dramas for music'. In 1776 he moved to Weimar, where he collaborated with the court Kapellmeister E. W. Wolf on several festal cantatas. A journey to Italy in the company of Dalberg in 1788 gave him little satisfaction, and he spent the rest of his life prematurely old and out of sympathy with the spirit both of the excesses of the *Sturm und Drang* and also of rarefied Weimar classicism.

Important as were many of Herder's literary writings, he was still more significant for the ideas he introduced, especially to Goethe. He played a large role in the development of the studies of history, language, theology, philosophy and sociology. Though he never worked out in detail his views on music, they are based on a wide knowledge of both the theory and practice of earlier generations and of his contemporaries. The essays on Shakespeare and on the songs of ancient peoples that were included in the manifesto *Von*

deutscher Art und Kunst (1773) were of epoch-making importance. He wrote various essays on music, including 'Über die Oper' and 'Tanz und Melodrama'. While despising much in contemporary German opera, he nevertheless conceived of a unified theatrical work in which poetry, music, action, décor and dance would become one. Gluck was the opera composer against whose achievements he measured all others, but Gluck did not accept Herder's invitation to set his *Brutus, ein Drama zur Musik* (1774; it was actually set by J. C. F. Bach, who also composed his *Philoktetes, Scenen mit Gesang*, for both of which the music is lost). Other sketches and fragments intended for musical setting are *Aeon und Aeonis, eine Allegorie* (1801), *Ariadne-Libera* (1802), *Der entfesselte Prometheus* (1802) and *Admetus Haus, der Tausch des Schicksals* (1803). In all these works Herder reveals a deep commitment to ancient history and myth, and a willingness to experiment with verse forms in the interest of 'a composite lyric structure in which poetry, music, action and decor are one'.

*

R. Haym: *Herder nach seinem Leben und seinen Werken* (Berlin, 1877–85, 2/1954)

B. Suphan, ed.: *J. G. Herder: Sämmtliche Werke* (Berlin, 1877–1913)

H. Günther: *J. G. Herders Stellung zur Musik* (diss., U. of Leipzig, 1903)

E. Purdie, ed.: *J. G. Herder: Von deutscher Art und Kunst* (Oxford, 1924)

W. Nufer: *Herders Ideen zur Verbindung von Poesie, Musik und Tanz* (Berlin, 1929)

A. Gillies: *Herder* (Oxford, 1945)

E. Keyser, ed.: *Im Geiste Herders: gesammelte Aufsätze zum 150. Todestag* (Litzingen, 1953)

R. T. Clark: *Herder: his Life and Thought* (Berkeley, 1955)

F. E. Kirby: 'Herder and Opera', *JAMS*, xv (1962), 316–29

PETER BRANSCOMBE

Herincx, Raimund [Raymond] (**Frederick**) (*b* London, 23 Aug 1927). English bass-baritone. He studied in Belgium and Milan, making his début in 1957 as Boito's Mefistofele for the WNO, with whom he later sang Germont, Scarpia, Pizarro and Nabucco. For Sadler's Wells (1957–67) he sang Count Almaviva, Jack Rance, Nick Shadow, Messenger/Creon (*Oedipus rex*), Baron Prus (*The Makropulos Affair*) and Agénor (Williamson's *The Violins of St Jacques*). He created Segura in *Our Man in Havana* (1963). He made his Covent Garden début in 1968 as King Fisher (*The Midsummer Marriage*), which he also sang with the WNO in Lisbon, Adelaide and San Francisco (American première, 1983); later he sang Donner, Rangoni, Escamillo and Alfio and created Faber in *The Knot Garden* (1970), White Abbot in *Taverner* (1972), which he also sang in Boston (American première, 1986), and the Governor in *We Come to the River* (1976). He sang Wotan for the ENO (1974–7) and in Seattle (1977–81) and made his Metropolitan début in 1977 as Mathisen (*Le prophète*). He sang Mr Redburn (*Billy Budd*) at San Francisco (1978), Telramund at Barcelona (1979) and the Hoffmann villains for Opera North (1983). He was particularly successful at portraying villainy and anger.

ALAN BLYTH

Herklots, Carl Alexander (*b* Dulzen, East Prussia, 19 Jan 1759; *d* Berlin, 23 March 1830). German librettist. After studying law at Königsberg he moved to Berlin in 1790 where he took up a position connected with the Prussian Supreme Court. He developed close ties with the court theatre, for which he wrote prologues, celebratory poems, and nearly 70 translations of French and Italian opera texts. His original librettos and adaptations for local composers are varied, skilful works blending Northern poetic virtues with a sense of latitude for significant musical elaboration. In the 1820s he prepared two librettos for Spontini, both based on fairy-tales.

Die böse Frau (komisches Original-Spl), Bierey, 1792 (I. Walter, 1794); *Das Opfer der Treue* (Vorspiel), B. A. Weber, 1793; *Die Geisterbeschwörung* (komisches Spl), C. A. Cartellieri, 1793; *Der Mädchenmarkt* (komisches Spl), Kospoth, 1793 (Bierey, 1794; Dittersdorf, 1797); *Schwarz und weiss* (Spl), 1793; *Elternfreude* (Vorspiel), Weber, 1793; *Pygmalion, oder die Reformation der Liebe* (lyrisches Drama), 1794; *Die Insel der Alcina*, A. Bianchi, 1794; *Friedensfeyer* (Vorspiel), Weber, 1795

Der Theaterprinzipal (lyrische Posse), Weber, 1796; *Das Inkognito* (Spl), J. A. Gürrlich, 1797; *Hero* (lyrisches Monodrama), Weber, 1800; *Mudarra* (Spl), Weber, 1800; *Frohsinn und Schwärmerei* (Liederspiel), Himmel, 1801; *Sulmalle* (lyrisches Duodrama mit Chören), Weber, 1802; *Dichterlaunen*, Niccolò Mussini, 1803; *Der Onkel*, J. P. S. Schmidt, 1804; *Asträas Wiederkehr* (Schauspiel), Weber, 1814; *Nurmahal, oder Das Rosenfest von Kaschmir* (lyrisches Drama), Spontini, 1822; *Alcidor* (Zauberoper mit Ballett), Spontini, 1825   THOMAS BAUMAN

Herlea, Nicolae (*b* Bucharest, 28 Aug 1927). Romanian baritone. He studied at the Bucharest Conservatory and made his début at Bucharest in 1950 as Silvio (*Pagliacci*). He joined the Romanian Opera in 1951 and thereafter toured widely, making appearances at La Scala, Salzburg, Covent Garden (as Rossini's Figaro, 1960), the Metropolitan (from 1964) and the Bol'shoy. His repertory is mostly Italian, including Tonio, Rigoletto and Count di Luna. The varied nuances and ample vibrato of his voice have led to his being considered the leading Romanian baritone.   VIOREL COSMA

Her Majesty's Theatre. The name of the King's Theatre, London, after the accession of Queen Victoria (1837). It became known as His Majesty's on her death (1901) but became Her Majesty's once more at the accession of Elizabeth II. *See* LONDON, §II, 2.

Hermann, Roland (*b* Bochum, 17 Sept 1936). German baritone. He studied with Paul Lohmann and Flaminio Contini. After making his operatic début in Trier (1967, as Mozart's Count Almaviva), he became a member of the Zürich Opera. As a guest artist he has appeared in Buenos Aires (as John the Baptist and Wolfram), Berlin, Paris, Hamburg and Milan (from 1986). One of the most admired baritones of his generation, he sings a wide repertory including Amfortas, Beckmesser, Mandryka and Busoni's Faust, as well as roles in operas by Kelterborn, Schoeck, Zemlinsky, Rameau, Janáček and Krenek. In 1989 he sang the title role in a BBC radio production of Henze's *Der Prinz von Homburg* and created the Master in Höller's *Der Meister und Margarita* for the Opéra.   DAVID CUMMINGS

Hermopolis. SYROS.

Hernando (y Palomar), Rafael (José María) (*b* Madrid, 31 May 1822; *d* Madrid, 10 July 1888). Spanish composer. From 1837 to 1843 he studied with Carnicer, Pedro Albéniz and Saldoni at the Madrid Conservatory (where he later taught). During the next five years he took lessons with Filippo Galli, the younger Manuel García and others at the Paris Conservatoire, where in 1848 he completed the opera *Romilda*. Unable to get it performed in Paris, he returned to Madrid that same year, thenceforth dedicating himself to smaller theatrical genres, variously called 'sainete', 'zarzuela' and 'opereta'. Thanks to Peral, the librettist of *Romilda*, he was invited to add a number to Oudrid's zarzuela *El ensayo de una ópera* (1848), the success of which led Peral to collaborate with him again in the one-act *Palo de ciego* (1849). His greatest triumphs were the zarzuelas *Colegiales y soldados* (1849) and *El duende* (1849), whose première was followed by a 126-night run. In the 1850s he composed five more zarzuelas and collaborated in another five. Hernando blamed the commercial failure of his last zarzuelas on his quarrels with Gaztambide, Oudrid and Barbieri; he attributed his 'exclusion' from the theatre to their opposition (preface to *Colegiales y soldados*, 1872). Thereafter he composed religious works and music for state occasions and dedicated himself to other aspects of music. His *Petición de subvención para el teatro lírico nacional* in support of opera was published in Madrid in 1881.

zarzuelas etc.; all first performed in Madrid; printed works are vocal scores published in Madrid

Palo de ciego (1, J. del Peral), 15 Feb 1849 (1851); *Colegiales y soldados* (2, M. Pina and F. Lumbreras), Instituto, 21 March 1849 (1872); *El duende* (2, L. Olona), Variedades, 6 June 1849, (1849); *Bertoldo y comparsa* (2, G. Romero y Larrañaga), Basilios, 23 May 1850; *Escenas en Chamberí* (1, J. Olona), Circo, 19 Nov 1850, collab. Barbieri, Gaztambide and Oudrid; *Segunda parte de El duende* (2, L. Olona), Circo, 18 Feb 1851; *El confitero de Madrid* (2, L. Olona), Circo, 7 Nov 1851, collab. Inzenga

Por seguir a una mujer (4, L. Olona), Circo, 24 Dec 1851, collab. Barbieri, Gaztambide, Inzenga and Oudrid; *El novio pasado por agua* (3, M. Bretón de los Herreros), Circo, 20 March 1852; *El secreto de la reina* (3, L. Olona), Circo, 13 Oct 1852 (1852), collab. Gaztambide and Inzenga; *Don Simplicio Bobadilla* (3, M. and V. Tamayo y Baus), Circo, 7 May 1853, collab. F. A. Barbieri, Gaztambide and Inzenga; *Cosas de Don Juan* (3, Bretón de los Herreros), Circo, 9 Sept 1854 (1854); *El tambor* (1, E. Alvarez), Conservatorio, 28 April 1860

Unperf.: *Romilda* (opera, 4, Peral), 1848; *Una noche en el serrallo* (2), 1856; *El alcázar* (1, J. Ruiz del Cerro), 1858; *Don Juan de Peralta* (3, J. Morán), 1862; *Aurora* (3)

*

J. Parada y Barreto: *Diccionario técnico, histórico y biográfico de la música* (Madrid, 1866)

B. Saldoni: *Diccionario biográfico-bibliográfico de efemérides de musicos españoles* (Barcelona, 1867)

A. Peña y Goñi: *La ópera española y la música dramática en España en el siglo XIX* (Madrid, 1881; abridged E. Rincón, as *España desde la ópera a la zarzuela*, 1967), 324ff

A. L. Salvans: 'Necrología: D. Rafael Hernando y Palomar', *Ilustración musical hispano-americana*, i/13 (1887–8), 103

E. Cotarelo y Mori: *Historia de la zarzuela, o sea el drama lírico* (Madrid, 1934)

M. Muñoz: *Historia de la zarzuela y el género chico* (Madrid, 1946), 24ff

J. Subirá: *Historia de la música española* (Barcelona, 1953)

F. Sopeña Ibáñez: *Historia crítica del Conservatorio de Madrid* (Madrid, 1967), 226, 237, 259   ROBERT STEVENSON

Hérodiade ('Herodias'). *Opéra* in four acts by JULES MASSENET to a libretto by Paul Milliet and Henri Grémont [GEORGES HARTMANN] based on the story by Gustave Flaubert (1877); Brussels, Théâtre de la Monnaie, 19 December 1881 (revised version, Paris, Théâtre Italien, 1 February 1884).

Following the success in France and Italy of *Le roi de Lahore*, Massenet's publisher Georges Hartmann suggested Flaubert's *conte* as the source of his next opera, and he was one of the writers credited with the libretto (Angelo Zanardini was responsible only for the Italian translation, the original plan being for simultaneous premières at the Paris Opéra and La Scala). The score was finished in the summer of 1881 but the new

Salomé [Salome]	soprano
Hérodiade [Herodias]	mezzo-soprano
Jean [John the Baptist]	tenor
Hérode [Herod]	baritone
Phanuel *Chaldean astrologer*	bass
Vitellius *Roman Proconsul*	baritone
High Priest	baritone

Merchants, Romans, Priests, Levites, Pharisees, Sadducees, Galileans, Samaritans, Ethiopians, Nubians and others

Setting Jerusalem, in the reign of Herod Antipas

director at the Opéra, Auguste Vaucorbeil, found the plot incoherent and rejected it. The opera was not performed at the Palais Garnier until 1921. In his unreliable *Mes souvenirs* Massenet describes a chance meeting in the street with the director of the Théâtre de la Monnaie, Brussels, who begged for the privilege of presenting the première; more prosaic negotiations were doubtless put in hand by Hartmann. The Monnaie gave the piece a lavish staging, which earned the composer the Ordre de Léopold, and the work ran for 55 performances. The Italian première followed two months later at La Scala on 23 February 1882.

The most significant revival was that at the Théâtre Italien in Paris on 1 February 1884. The cast included Victor Maurel (who also directed) as Herod, Jean de Reszke as the Baptist and Edouard de Reszke as Phanuel, and Massenet took the opportunity to change the original three-act, five-scene format of the Brussels première into the four acts detailed below, to expand the role of Phanuel for the bass de Reszke brother (the first scene of Act 3 was added for him), and slightly to rearrange the running order of the remaining scenes. The dramaturgy is marginally tauter, but even the most fervent admirer of Massenet has to admit that Vaucorbeil had a point: dramatic coherence is not *Hérodiade*'s strongest suit. Nevertheless, it was staged frequently on both sides of the Atlantic up to the turn of the century (reaching London in 1904 under the title of *Salomé*) and has never quite lapsed from the repertory. One reason for this is that its five leading roles are rewarding to star singers (Emma Calvé sang both Salome and Herodias), and most recently it has been a vehicle for Montserrat Caballé and José Carreras.

ACT 1 *A courtyard in Herod's palace* A caravan of merchants and their slaves greet Jerusalem and the end of their journey. Phanuel quells a dispute between Judeans and Samaritans and upbraids the people for failing to make common cause against a greater enemy, the Romans. He prophesies imminent revolt ('Le monde est inquiet'). Salome enters. Phanuel knows her to be the daughter of Herodias, but she does not, and while searching for the mother who abandoned her as a child she has fallen under the spell of John the Baptist ('Il est doux, il est bon'). They leave. Herod enters in search of Salome, swiftly followed by Herodias, who tells her husband of the Baptist's insults and insists that he avenge her honour by having him executed ('Ne me refuse pas'), reminding him that she abandoned her family and her child for him. He demurs for political reasons. The Baptist enters with cries of 'Jézabel', and they flee before his wrath. Salome returns and in a three-part duet with the Baptist expresses chaste love for him ('Ce que je

veux') but is politely but firmly rejected. The Baptist, mindful of his mission, encourages her to concentrate instead on the new dawn about to break ('Aime-moi donc alors, mais comme on aime en songe').

ACT 2 *Herod's apartments* Herod sings of his obsession for Salome ('Vision fugitive'). Phanuel accuses him of neglecting political considerations in favour of private passion, but Herod remains confident of using the Baptist's popularity to help drive out the Romans and then in turn dealing with such religious agitators. The scene changes to a square in Jerusalem. Herod incites his subjects to revolutionary frenzy, but Roman cohorts are already at the gates of the city. Vitellius enters and quells the people with an angry glance. In Tiberius's name he grants the crowd's demands for religious freedom. A group of Canaanites led by Salome and the Baptist enters, proclaiming the superiority of spiritual power over temporal.

ACT 3 *Phanuel's house* The Chaldean tries to fathom the significance of the Baptist – is he human or divine ('Dors, ô cité perverse ... Astres étincelants')? Herodias asks him the identity of the girl who has stolen her husband's love, and he prompts her to recall her abandoned daughter ('Si Dieu l'avait voulu') before telling her that rival and child are one. She refuses to believe him and storms out. The scene changes to the temple, in whose vaults the Baptist has been imprisoned. Salome recalls happier days ('Charmes des jours passés'). Herod enters stealthily, planning to release the Baptist as an act of defiance against Vitellius, but soon forgets the plan when he discovers Salome. His ardent advances are haughtily rejected, and Herod threatens to have them both put to death. The High Priest summons the people to prayer. The priests demand that Vitellius sentence John, hailed as the new Messiah, to death, and after a brief trial death by crucifixion is confirmed (but in the event not carried out). When Salome offers to share the Baptist's fate, Herod's fury is redoubled.

ACT 4 *An underground vault* John prepares for death ('Adieu donc, vains objets'). When Salome appears, he admits his love ('Que je puis respirer') but forbids her to join him in death. The scene changes to a room in the palace. Roman soldiers celebrate the subjugation of Judaea. Vitellius, Herod and Herodias enter, and after a suite of dances Salome begs for mercy for the Baptist. Herodias feels faint stirrings of maternal emotion when Salome sings of the mother who abandoned her. The executioner enters, his sword dripping with the Baptist's blood. Salome draws a dagger and hurls herself at Herodias but, when the latter exclaims 'Grâce, je suis ta mère', turns the blade upon herself.

* * *

Hérodiade is the best of Massenet's three attempts at traditional *grand opéra*: there is an energy, a masculine thrust that those who know only the later works might find surprising. The musical motifs attached to the various characters are fresh and apposite, and used for much more than purposes of reminiscence: they develop, and there are subtle interconnections between them – the Salome theme, for instance, and one of Herod's or, more properly, Salome-as-desired-by-Herod. The shape of the musical gestures in arioso had a palpable influence on the early Italian *veristi*.

Hérodiade is also the first of his operas in which Massenet's word-setting reaches maturity. Regular phrases are broken up with purposeful mis-stresses and *enjambements* that add their own rhythmic counterpoint (see especially Salome's 'Il est doux' and Herod's 'Vision fugitive'). The instrumentation is heavily perfumed, with pseudo-orientalisms delicately sketched in; Tchaikovsky must have had the second-act ballet at the back of his mind when he wrote the 'Danse arabe' in *The Nutcracker*. (There is also a curious anticipation of Sardou and Puccini when Phanuel comes across Herod lying in a drugged stupor and remarks 'Voilà l'homme qui fait trembler tout un empire'.)

Despite the well-oiled skill of the public scenes, the strength of the work lies in more familiar Massenet territory: erotic obsession. The musical portrait of Herod, his lustful slaverings vividly suggested by copious use of saxophone, is a powerful one, and that of the hag-ridden Herodias, gradually coming to accept that her husband's affections have been stolen by her daughter, is scarcely less compelling (a modern-dress staging of *Hérodiade* could be quite disturbing). Both are worthy of Flaubert, to whose fine story the depth of Oscar Wilde's debt can scarcely be overstressed. If the Baptist and Salome are more conventionally drawn, their duets are beautifully crafted and exude the 'discreet, semi-religious eroticism' for which the composer is famous.

One reason for the opera's dramaturgical incoherence – and an example of the eroticism verging on the indiscreet – is the 'heavy-breathing' identification of the Baptist with Christ. The Priests demand his death because he has proclaimed himself the Messiah; crucifixion is the first sentence passed on him; in his prison aria he addresses a *père* who is plainly Jehovah, not Zachariah. This lends the Baptist-Salome relationship a heady sex-and-religion charge that, even so heavily veiled, must have seemed shocking in 1881.

RODNEY MILNES

Heroic Warriors, The. Opera by A. P. Borodin; *see* BOGATĪRI.

Hérold, (Louis Joseph) Ferdinand (*b* Paris, 28 Jan 1791; *d* Paris, 19 Jan 1833). French composer. Primarily an opera composer, he wrote some of the most enduring masterpieces in the genre of *opéra comique*.

1. LIFE. Hérold's father, François-Joseph Hérold, was a piano teacher who died when Ferdinand was only 11. In 1806, at the age of 15, the son entered the Paris Conservatoire, where he studied piano with his godfather Louis Adam (father of the composer Adolphe Adam), violin with Rodolphe Kreutzer and composition with Méhul. In 1812 Hérold won the Prix de Rome with his cantata *Mademoiselle de la Vallière* which was sung at the prize-giving concert by the soprano Mme Branchu. He stayed only one year in Rome, then travelled on to Naples where his first opera, *La gioventù di Enrico quinto*, was performed at the Teatro del Fondo on 5 January 1815, with the tenor Manuel García in the title role. Hérold then went to Vienna, where he heard operas by Weigl and Salieri as well as Mozart's *Don Giovanni*, *Le nozze di Figaro* and *Die Zauberflöte*. He also met Salieri, but was too shy to present his letter of introduction to Beethoven.

Back in Paris he obtained a post as *maestro di cembalo* at the Théâtre Italien. In 1816 he was invited by Boieldieu to collaborate on *Charles de France* for the Opéra-Comique; Hérold wrote the second act, which was well received. A one-act piece, *Corinne au capitole*,

intended for the Opéra, was abandoned, but in January 1817 Hérold scored his first popular success with *Les rosières*, which achieved 44 performances. He began another project for the Opéra, *La lampe merveilleuse*, but, as a work on the subject of Aladdin had already been commissioned by that establishment, *La lampe* became *La clochette, ou Le diable page* and was produced by the Opéra-Comique in October 1817.

The initial impetus of Hérold's career as a composer then appeared to falter and in the next three years none of the works he wrote was successful. In 1821 he was sent by the Théâtre Italien to Italy to search for new singers, in particular a soprano and a high bass; he returned having engaged Giuditta Pasta and Filippo Galli. He also brought back with him the score of Rossini's *Mosè*, which was given at the Théâtre Italien in 1822. Hérold, already suffering from the tuberculosis that had killed his father, was too ill to attend the performance he had prepared.

The following year, his health temporarily restored, Hérold achieved a fair success at the Opéra-Comique with *Le muletier* and at last made a modest début at the Opéra with the one-act *Lasthénie*; he collaborated with Auber on *Vendôme en Espagne*, which was followed by another *pièce d'occasion*, *Le roi René*; this was performed in August 1824 to celebrate the birthday of Louis XVIII and in November 1826 for that of Charles X. Meanwhile Hérold was working on one of his finest and most popular works, *Marie*; produced by the Opéra-Comique in August 1826, it achieved 100 performances in less than a year.

Hérold then left the Théâtre Italien and in November 1826 he became principal singing coach at the Opéra, where during the next three years he wrote five successful ballets, including *La fille mal gardée* (1828). Three minor and unsuccessful works for the Opéra-Comique were followed, in 1831, by *Zampa*, Hérold's most powerful stage work. Owing to dire financial troubles and consequent managerial changes, the theatre was forced to close several times during this period; nonetheless, *Zampa* received 56 performances in 15 months; then Chollet, the tenor for whom Hérold had written the title role, moved to the Théâtre de la Monnaie in Brussels for two seasons (making his début as Zampa) and the work could not be revived in Paris until 1835, after the composer's death.

Le Pré aux clercs, Hérold's last completed and finest work, was first performed by the Opéra-Comique on 15 December 1832, evoking unparalleled approval from the audience who, at the final curtain, called again and again for the composer. Hérold, already gravely ill, had fainted and could not appear. Five weeks later he died. *Ludovic*, left half-finished at his death, was completed by Halévy and performed in 1833. Meanwhile, at the Opéra-Comique *Le Pré aux clercs* was continuing its triumphant course; the 1482nd performance, preceded by the first act of *Zampa*, celebrated the centenary of Hérold's birth in January 1891.

2. WORKS. Hérold was influenced above all by two other French composers: first by Méhul, who was his teacher and became his surrogate father after the early death of F.-J. Hérold; second by Boieldieu, who, though only just over five years his senior, generously helped Hérold to establish himself in Paris. *La gioventù di Enrico quinto*, adapted by Hérold himself from the play by A. V. Pineux-Duval, then translated into Italian, pays patent tribute to Méhul; so does *Les rosières*, dedicated to his

teacher; but by 1817 Hérold had collaborated on *Charles de France* with Boieldieu, and in *La clochette*, which is dedicated to him, Boieldieu's influence has become paramount. *La clochette* marked a considerable development in the richness and originality of Hérold's orchestration, and in his skill in character drawing.

Like Boieldieu and many other composers before him, Hérold had great difficulty in obtaining suitable librettos. Not until *Le muletier* (1823) did he find a subject, originating in a story by Boccaccio, that offered him a briskly amusing text (considered slightly improper at the time). The charming score reveals for the first time the great potential of Hérold as a dramatic composer. Four months later he finally achieved his declared objective of writing for the Opéra: *Lasthénie*, a cold, unfunny comedy, has some delightful numbers, which the strong cast that included both Adolphe Nourrit and his father Louis no doubt displayed to their best advantage.

After two official commissions and a fiasco (*Le lapin blanc*) that had only one performance, Hérold arrived at the first of the three operas on which his reputation rests: *Marie* (1826). His contemporaries thought this touching love story utterly delightful; they considered the text both interesting and in good taste, and Hérold's music full of novel ideas expressed with 'exquisite tenderness' and 'graceful elegance'. Once again the freshness of the scoring was singled out for special praise. It is particularly ironic that Hérold, having finally discovered a truly individual and popular operatic style, should spend the next three years composing ballet music for the Opéra.

On returning to the Opéra-Comique he notched up three more semi-failures; the first of these, *L'illusion* (1829), suffered from a poor text ending with a suicide, a sure recipe for disaster at the Comique; it was prefaced by an overture based on the theme of Mozart's 'Voi che sapete', which earned praise. *L'auberge d'Auray* (1830), the third, has a certain interest as a vehicle for the talents of the actress Harriet Smithson, who later became the wife of Berlioz.

Zampa, ou La fiancée de marbre (1831), the second of Hérold's trio of major works, is more powerfully dramatic than any of his previous operas. The subject matter of Mélesville's text, in which a statue takes revenge on a seducer, evokes the Don Juan legend, but is treated in romantic, Byronic fashion. The work was strong stuff for the Opéra-Comique, a number of whose patrons considered that *Zampa* rightly belonged at the Opéra; it was several decades before *Carmen* would become the most popular *opéra comique* ever written.

Although the Comique was going through a financial crisis in 1832, the new management was assured of success with the triumphant launch of *Le Pré aux clercs*. In the third and finest of his major operas Hérold balanced the musical and dramatic aspects of the work in an ideal manner. For once he had an excellent text, derived by Eugène de Planard from Mérimée's novel *Chronique du règne de Charles IX* (far better than the libretto on a similar subject provided by Scribe for Meyerbeer's *Les Huguenots*); the characters are superbly drawn in their music. *Le Pré aux clercs*, like Boieldieu's masterpiece, *La dame blanche*, is a perfect specimen of *opéra comique* from the first half of the 19th century.

See also Pré aux clercs, le and Zampa.

first performed in Paris unless otherwise stated; printed works published in Paris

La gioventù di Enrico quinto (oc, 2, Hérold, after A. V. Pineux-Duval), Naples, Fondo, 5 Jan 1815, vs (c1890)

Charles de France, ou Amour et gloire [Act 2] (oc, 2, E. de Rancé, M. E. G. M. Théaulon de Lambert and F. V. A. d'Artois de Bournonville), OC (Feydeau), 18 June 1816, vs (1816) [Act 1 by A. Boieldieu]

Les rosières (oc, 3, Théaulon de Lambert), OC (Feydeau), 27 Jan 1817 (1817)

La clochette, ou Le diable page (opéra féerie, 3, Théaulon de Lambert), OC (Feydeau), 18 Oct 1817 (1817)

Le premier venu, ou Six lieus de chemin (oc, 3, J. B. C. Vial and F. A. E. de Planard), OC (Feydeau), 28 Sept 1818 (1818)

Ovide en exil, 1818 (R. C. G. de Pixérécourt), unperf.

Les troqueurs (oc, 1, F. V. A. d'Artois and L. C. A. d'Artois, after J.-J. Vadé, after J. de la Fontaine), OC (Feydeau), 18 Feb 1819 (1819)

L'amour platonique (oc, 1, A. Rousseau), comp. 1819, unperf., *F-Pn*

L'auteur mort et vivant (oc, 1, Planard), OC (Feydeau), 18 Dec 1820 (1820)

Le muletier (oc, 1, P. de Kock, after La Fontaine, after Boccaccio), OC (Feydeau), 12 May 1823 (1823)

Lasthénie (opéra, 1, M. de Chaillou), Opéra, 8 Sept 1823 (c1824)

Vendôme en Espagne (opéra, 3, E. Mennechet and A.-J.-S. d'Empis), Opéra, 5 Dec 1823, collab. Auber

Le roi René, ou La Provence au XVe siècle (oc, 2, Belle and C.-A. Sewrin), OC (Feydeau), 24 Aug 1824

Le lapin blanc (oc, 1, Mélesville [A.-H.-J. Duveyrier] and P. Carmouche), OC (Feydeau), 21 May 1825, *Pn*

Marie (oc, 3, Planard), OC (Feydeau), 12 Aug 1826 (?1826)

L'illusion (oc, 1, J.-H. Vernoy de Saint-Georges and C. Ménissier), OC (Ventadour), 18 July 1829 (?1829)

Emmeline (oc, 3, Planard), OC (Ventadour), 28 Nov 1829 (c1830)

L'auberge d'Auray (oc, 1, C. F. J. B. Moreau and J.-B. V. d'Epagny), OC (Ventadour), 11 May 1830 (1830), collab. Carafa

Zampa, ou La fiancée de marbre (oc, 3, Mélesville), OC (Ventadour), 3 May 1831 (1831)

La marquise de Brinvilliers (drame lyrique, 3, E. Scribe and Castil-Blaze [F.-H.-J. Blaze]), OC (Ventadour), 31 Oct 1831 (1831), collab. Auber, Batton, H.-M. Berton, Blangini, A. Boieldieu, Carafa, Cherubini and Paer (1831)

La médecine sans médecin (oc, 1, Scribe and J. F. A. Bayard), OC (De la Bourse), 15 Oct 1832 (?1832)

Le Pré aux clercs (oc, 3, Planard, after P. Mérimée), OC (De la Bourse), 15 Dec 1832 (?1833)

Ludovic (oc, 2, Saint-Georges), OC (De la Bourse), 16 May 1833 (1833); completed by F. Halévy after Hérold's death

*

H. Berlioz: 'De la partition de *Zampa*', *Journal des débats* (27 Sept 1835)

A. Adam: *E. H. Méhul, L. J. F. Hérold: Biographien* (Kassel, 1855)

——: 'Hérold', *Souvenirs d'un musicien ... précédés de notes biographiques* (Paris, 1857)

F. Clément and P. Larousse: *Dictionnaire lyrique* (Paris, 1867–81, 2/1897, 3/1905 ed. A. Pougin as *Dictionnaire des opéras*)

F. Clément: *Les musiciens célèbres depuis le seizième siècle jusqu'à nos jours* (Paris, 1868, 4/1887)

B. J. B. Jouvin: *Hérold: sa vie et ses oeuvres* (Paris, 1868)

A. Pougin: 'La jeunesse d'Hérold', *Revue et gazette musicale*, xlvii (1880), 138–321 passim

O. Fouqué: *Histoire du Théâtre-Ventadour 1829–1879* (Paris, 1881)

M. Berthelot: *Ferdinand Hérold* (Paris, 1882)

A. Pougin: *Hérold* (Paris, 1906)

E. Hérold: 'Souvenirs inédits de Ferdinand Hérold: un musicien français a Vienne', *BSIM*, vii (1910), 100–111, 156–170

J. Chantavoine: *Cent opéras célèbres* (Paris, 1948)

ELIZABETH FORBES

Herold, Vilhelm Kristoffer (*b* Hasle, Bornholm, 19 March 1865; *d* Copenhagen, 15 Dec 1937). Danish tenor. He studied in Denmark and Paris and made his début at the Kongelige Teater, Copenhagen, as Gounod's Faust in February 1893; later that year he appeared at the World Exhibition in Chicago. He sang at the Stockholm Opera (1901–3, 1907–9) and made his Covent Garden début in 1904 as Lohengrin, his most famous role; his voice was said to resemble that of Jean de Reszke in sweetness and beauty of timbre. In Denmark his Canio (*Pagliacci*) was equally esteemed. He returned to Covent Garden in 1907 as Walther and also sang in Berlin, Dresden and other German cities, but continued to sing in Copenhagen until he retired in 1915. He was director of the Kongelige Opera, Copenhagen, 1922–4, after which he taught (Melchior was among his pupils). He was made a *Kammersänger* in 1901.

LEO RIEMENS

Herrmann, Bernard (*b* New York, 29 June 1911; *d* Los Angeles, 24 Dec 1975). American composer. A violinist and songwriter as a child, he studied composition with Percy Grainger, Philip James and Bernard Wagenaar. His conducting and composing skills were put to professional use in concerts and the theatre, but it was through radio that Herrmann, via Orson Welles, found a route to composing for films, the medium in which he achieved his greatest fame, creating 40 scores between 1941 and 1966. He spent the last ten years of his life in England, conducting and composing, and continuing to write occasional film scores.

Herrmann's most frequently heard 'operatic' composition is undoubtedly the fragments of *Salammbô*, in the style of Massenet, which he devised as plot-serving pastiche for the film *Citizen Kane* (1941). Of his real operatic works, the first to be heard were two short television operas, *A Christmas Carol* (1954) and *A Child is Born* (1955), but his most important work is *Wuthering Heights*, an opera based on Emily Brontë's novel, composed between 1943 and 1951, though not staged until 1982. The work concentrates on the relationship between Heathcliff and Catherine, with few other characters and only an offstage chorus. It exhibits Herrmann's skill in evocation of atmosphere, character and emotion, his fertility of melodic and textural invention, and his orchestral mastery. He also composed one stage musical, *The King of Schnorrers*, which played for just under four weeks in 1970 at the Goodspeed Opera House in East Haddam, Connecticut.

Wuthering Heights, 1943–51 (prol., 4, L. Fletcher, after E. Brontë), Portland, OR, 6 Nov 1982, vs (London, 1965)
A Christmas Carol (television op, M. Anderson, after C. Dickens), CBS, 23 Dec 1954, vs (New York, 1955)
A Child is Born (television op, after S. V. Benét), CBS, 25 Dec 1955
The King of Schnorrers (musical, P. A. Mayer, after I. Zangwill; lyrics D. Lampert), East Haddam, CT, Goodspeed Opera House, 17 April 1970

*

EwenD
E. Johnson: *Bernard Herrmann: Hollywood's Music-Dramatist* (Rickmansworth, 1977)
F. Kinkaid: 'Scaling the Heights', *ON*, xlvii/5 (1982–3), 16–19
R. Downer: 'Portland Opera: Herrmann "Wuthering Heights" [première]', *Hi Fi/Mus Am*, xxxiii/3 (1983), MA27
S. E. St John: *A Study of the Opera 'Wuthering Heights' by Bernard Herrmann* (diss., U. of Oregon, 1985)
S. C. Smith: *A Heart at Fire's Center: the Life and Music of Bernard Herrmann* (Berkeley, CA, 1991)

JON ALAN CONRAD

Herrmann, Josef (*b* Darmstadt, 20 April 1903; *d* Hildesheim, 19 Nov 1955). German baritone. He studied at Darmstadt and made his début in 1925 at Kaiserslauten. Over the next decade he established himself as a reliable artist with a resourceful style and wide repertory, singing successively at Stettin, Königsberg and Nuremberg. Throughout the war years he was principal baritone at Dresden, singing not only Wagner but also Italian roles such as Iago and Scarpia, and in the première of Sutermeister's *Die Zauberinsel* (1942).

Highlights in his career were his Wozzeck at Salzburg and appearances at La Scala (1950) as The Wanderer and Gunther in performances conducted by Furtwängler and with Flagstad as Brünnhilde. Recordings of these and other roles preserve the fine, manly quality of his voice and the excellent diction that was a noted feature of his stage work.

J. B. STEANE

Herrmann, Karl-Ernst (*b* Neukirch, Upper Lusatia, 1936). German director and designer. He studied design and scenography with Rudi Wagner and with Willi Schmidt at the Hochschule für Bildende Kunst in Berlin. He began designing for the theatre in Ulm (1961) and in 1969 encountered the director Peter Stein in Bremen, beginning a long association with him with a sensational production of Brecht's early play *Im Dickicht der Städte*. After working with Stein at the Berlin Schaubühne, Herrmann left in 1978 to work as a freelance opera and theatre designer. His first major opera production was *Das Rheingold* (directed by Stein), the first part of the Paris Opéra *Ring* of 1976 (which proceeded only as far as *Die Walküre*, directed by Klaus-Michael Grüber, before the cycle was abandoned). In 1978 Herrmann designed *Così fan tutte* for Luc Bondy at the Théâtre de la Monnaie, Brussels, which has since been the centre of his activities. There he made his début as the director as well as the designer of an opera, in Mozart's *La clemenza di Tito*. The success of that production led to a cycle of Mozart operas (*Don Giovanni*, *Die Entführung aus dem Serail*, *La finta giardiniera*, *Die Zauberflöte* and *Le nozze di Figaro*), which has been hailed as one of the most original in the 1980s and early 1990s. He has also directed *La traviata* and Gluck's *Orfeo ed Euridice* there (for illustration *see* STAGE DESIGN, fig.28). Herrmann's work, in close conjunction with his wife, Ursel Herrmann, and Geoffrey Layton, is characterized by a strong neo-classical visual vocabulary and the creation of a temporary ensemble of actor-singers. His productions have formed the keystone of Gérard Mortier's régime at La Monnaie. Significantly, Mortier imported his Brussels versions of *La clemenza di Tito* and *La finta giardiniera* for his inaugural Salzburg Festival in 1992.

HUGH CANNING

Herrmann, Theo (*b* Vienna, 26 Jan 1902; *d* Hamburg, 18 Feb 1977). Austrian bass. He made his début at Zagreb in 1922 and for the next five years sang in Prague. From 1927 to 1934 he was at Darmstadt and thereafter at Hamburg, where he remained till 1961. His first British appearance was during the visit of the Dresden Opera to Covent Garden in 1936, when he sang Leporello. In 1948 he sang in *Rigoletto* and *Il barbiere di Siviglia* at the Cambridge Theatre in London, and in 1952 appeared with the Hamburg Opera at the Edinburgh Festival, in *Fidelio*, *Mathis der Maler* and *Der Rosenkavalier*. At Salzburg (1942–3) he sang Waldner in *Arabella*. He made frequent guest appearances in Vienna, and on retirement from Hamburg continued to sing in opera at Augsburg. In lieder recordings his voice is firmly placed, capable of gentleness and expressively used.

J. B. STEANE

Hersee, Rose (*b* London, 1845; *d* London, 26 Nov 1924). English soprano. She studied with her father, Henry Hersee. After singing small roles, including the Mermaid in *Oberon*, with Mapleson's company at Her Majesty's and Drury Lane in the 1860s, she toured the USA with the Parepa-Rosa company from 1865 to

1871. She then joined the new Carl Rosa Opera Company, singing Susanna in its opening performance of *Le nozze di Figaro* at the Princess's Theatre, London, in 1875. She subsequently toured Australia, where in 1879 she sang the title role in *Carmen* every night for three weeks in the opera's first production in that country. In 1884 she appeared in a season of opera in English at Covent Garden, singing in the first London performance of *Der Rattenfänger von Hameln* (in a translation by her father).   HAROLD ROSENTHAL/R

Hertz, Alfred (*b* Frankfurt, 15 July 1872; *d* San Francisco, 17 April 1942). American conductor of German birth. He was educated at the Hoch Conservatory in Frankfurt, after which he held posts in Halle (1891–2), Altenburg (1892–5) and Barmen-Elberfeld (1895–9). In 1899 he conducted concerts in London, then went to the Breslau Opera for three years. In 1902 he moved to the Metropolitan Opera, making his début with *Lohengrin* and staying until 1915 as principal conductor of German opera. There, on Christmas Eve 1903, he conducted the first *Parsifal* outside Bayreuth (to the displeasure of Cosima Wagner – Hertz never again appeared in a German theatre); he also conducted during his tenure the American premières of *Salome* and *Der Rosenkavalier*, as well as the world premières of Humperdinck's *Königskinder* and of all the American works brought out during his time there. After disagreements with Gatti-Casazza over artistic policy, Hertz turned his attention to concert and radio work. He was married to the Austrian lieder singer Lilly Dorn. His diverting autobiography appeared posthumously in the *San Francisco Chronicle* in 30 instalments, between 3 May and 14 July 1942.   MICHAEL STEINBERG

Hertz, Michał (*b* Warsaw, 28 Sept 1844; *d* Warsaw, 8 Jan 1918). Polish composer. He studied composition at the Warsaw Music Institute with Adam Minchejmer, and in Berlin, and conducting with Hans Richter and Hans von Bülow in Munich. Between 1870 and 1872 he conducted at the Polish Theatre in Poznań, then became professor of piano at the Stern Conservatory in Berlin. From 1878 he lived in Warsaw, taking an active part in the city's musical life. He taught at various institutions and for over 20 years was assistant director of the Warsaw Music Society. As a conductor he appeared with the Wielki Theatre orchestra and he was an accompanist and répétiteur at the Warsaw Opera. To a large extent he was responsible for staging Wagner's works in Warsaw at that time.

Hertz composed two operas: *Gwarkowie* ('The Miners'; 4, F. Schober, after T. Körner: *Die Bergknappen*; vs of Act 1 *PL-Wtm*, excerpts, Warsaw, *c*1880), which was performed in Warsaw at the Wielki Theatre on 19 November 1880, and *Bogna, córka wygnańca* ('Bogna, the Exile's Daughter'; 4, M. Radziszewski), which was written about 1890 (vs, Leipzig, 1900).   ZOFIA CHECHLIŃSKA

Hervé [Ronger, Louis Auguste Joseph Florimond] (*b* Houdain, 30 June 1825; *d* Paris, 3 Nov 1892). French composer, singer and manager. The father of the French *opérette*, Hervé began his career as organist of the chapel of the lunatic asylum of Bicêtre where his first stage work, a musical version of Scribe and Saintine's *L'ours et la pacha*, was played by the inmates. He continued to work as an organist at Bicêtre, and later the prestigious parish church of St Eustache, while pursuing a career as an actor and vocalist in Paris theatres. In 1848 his *Don Quichotte et Sancho Pança* was staged by Adolphe Adam at the Théâtre Montmartre, with the tall, thin author appearing as Don Quichotte. Hervé subsequently became *chef d'orchestre* at the Odéon and then at the Palais-Royal where two of his short pieces were staged, but it was the five-act burlesque *Les folies dramatiques* which attracted the attention of the powerful Duc de Morny and resulted in Hervé being permitted to operate, from 1854, his own small theatre, the Folies-Concertantes, later renamed the Folies-Nouvelles. At this venue, Hervé produced a stream of novel short shows subtitled with such descriptions as *bouffonerie-opérette* or *folie-opérette*, including dozens of his own but also the works of other composers such as Delibes and Offenbach, in whose early work *Oyayaye* Hervé appeared in the feminine title role.

Ill-health eventually obliged Hervé, worn out by the multiple roles of manager, writer, composer and performer, to give up his theatre, and he spent some time travelling and working abroad before returning to Paris where he took engagements as musical director at the Eldorado and the Délassements-Comiques. Offenbach and his librettists had by then put the *opéra bouffe*, which Hervé had initiated, on a different level with the production of their earliest full-length works, but although Hervé now produced several smaller pieces, revues and the music for the Cogniard brothers' *féerie*, *La biche au bois*, it was 1866 before his first three-act burlesque *Les chevaliers de la table ronde* was produced at the Bouffes-Parisiens. His outstanding works followed over the next few years: *L'oeil crevé* (1867), *Chilpéric* (1868), *Le petit Faust* and *Les Turcs* (both 1869), all examples of the frenetically crazy burlesque style which Hervé the writer and composer employed with a disarming naturalness and played with enormous style and success. *Chilpéric*, a flamboyant burlesque of medieval heroic France, with vivacious music, shot through with comedy and parody, has many high spots, among them the King's celebrated 'Chanson du jambon', sung while trying not to fall off his horse, the Princess's bolero, 'À la Sierra Morena' and a first-act finale, sung by a chorus of druids, sheltering under gaily-coloured modern umbrellas, all of which became favourites.

The stagings of *Chilpéric* and *Le petit Faust*, with the composer starring, caused a sensation in London and Hervé remained there to lay the foundations of the newly active British musical theatre, with his music for *Aladdin the Second* (1870) at the Gaiety, and a contribution to Boucicault's grandiose *féerie*, *Babil and Bijou* (1872), at Covent Garden.

As the vogue for extravagant burlesque passed, Hervé found another outlet for his talents composing the music for a series of *comédie-opérettes* in which Anna Judic starred at the Théâtre des Variétés. *La femme à papa* (1879), *Lili* (1882) and *La cosaque* (1884) all featured the star to fine advantage, but it was the delicious musical comedy, *Mam'zelle Nitouche* (1883), which proved the pick of the group and which, more in line with 20th-century tastes, has remained the one representative of Hervé's work in the modern repertory. In this, Hervé drew upon his own early experiences, working for the church and the stage, with a story of the convent girl who discovers that her music master, Célestin, leads a double life as Floridor, a composer of *opérettes*.

An extraordinary example of a polyvalent man of the

theatre, Hervé, by his originality and spirit, provided much of the base from which not only French but worldwide light musical theatre would develop during the second half of the 19th century. His burlesque texts were dazzling and daring in their comedy, his music, often underrated, brilliantly suited their style, and the works which he produced in the late 1860s remain among the most appreciable of the comic musical stage.

first performed in Paris, with librettos by the composer, unless otherwise stated; many published in vocal score in Paris shortly after first performance

pantomimes, revues etc. excluded

PBP – *Bouffes Parisiens*
PFC – *Théâtre des Folies-Concertantes*
PFN – *Théâtre des Folies-Nouvelles*
PV – *Théâtre des Variétés*

L'ours et le pacha (vaudeville-opérette, 1, E. Scribe and Saintine [J. X. Boniface]), Bicêtre, March 1842
Don Quichotte et Sancho Pança (tableau grotesque, 1, after M. de Cervantes: *Don Quixote*), Opéra, 5 March 1848
Les gardes françaises (oc, 1), Odéon, 16 Dec 1849
Les parisiens en voyage, 1849 (vaudeville-opérette, 1, J. Méry, G. de Nerval and P. Bocage) [rehearsed at Odéon but unperf.]
Passiflor et cactus (opéra bouffe, 1), Palais-Royal, 6 May 1851
L'enseignement mutuel (vaudeville-opérette, 1, T. Barrière and A. Decourcelle), 1852
Roméo et Mariette (parodie-opérette, 1, P. Dumanoir), Palais-Royal, 1852
Les folies dramatiques (vaudeville-opérette, 1, P. Dumanoir and Clairville), Palais-Royal, 2 March 1853
Prologue d'ouverture (fantaisie, 1, C. Bridault), PFC, 8 Feb 1854
La perle d'Alsace (pastorale-opérette, 1), PFC, 24 Feb 1854
L'anglais incompris (scène comique), PFC, 30 March 1854
Le compositeur toqué (bouffonerie musicale, 1), PFC, 11 April 1854
Amour, poésie et turlupinade! (bouffonnerie musicale, 1), PFC, 20 June 1854
Les folies nouvelles (prologue, T. de Banville), PFN, 21 Oct 1854
La fine fleur de l'Andalousie (excentricité musicale, 1), PFN, 21 Oct 1854
La caravane de l'amour (saynète, 1, de Banville), PFN, 10 Dec 1854
La belle créature (pochade-opérette, 1, Bridault), PFN, 8 Jan 1855
Vadé au cabaret (saynète, 1, H. de Kock), PFN, 20 Jan 1855
L'intrigue espagnole, ou La sérénade à coups de bâton (folie-opérette, 1), PFN, 24 Jan 1855
Le Sergent Laramé (croquis militaire, Durandeau), PFN, 3 Feb 1855
Fanfare (scène villageoise, 1, de Banville), PFN, 29 March 1855
La soeur de Pierrot (mimodrame, 1, Mercier and Legrand), PFN, 7 April 1855
Un drame en 1779 (folie musicale, 1), PFN, 21 April 1855
Latrouillat et Truffaldini (saynète-opérette, J. Petit and E. Blum), PFN, 10 May 1855
Latrouillat et Truffaldini, ou Les inconvénients d'une vendetta infiniment trop prolongée (saynète, Petit and Blum), PFN, 28 May 1855
Un ténor très léger (opéra de grand route, 1, R. Lordereau), PFN, 27 July 1855
Le testament de Polichinelle (opérette, 1, A. Montjoye), PFN, 17 Nov 1855
Un trio d'enfoncés (épisode de la vie commerciale, 1), PFN, 27 Dec 1855
Le chevrier blanc (conte-pantomime, 1, Mercier and Legrand), PFN, 27 Dec 1855
Fifi et Nini (à-propos carnavalesque, 1, A. Monnier), PFN, 15 Jan 1856
Le prince infortuné (cascade pantomimique), PFN, 15 Jan 1856
Agamemnon, ou Le chameau à deux bosses (tragédie étrange, 1), PFN, 24 April 1856
Toinette et son carabinier (croquis musicale, 1, M. Delaporte), PFN, 15 Sept 1856
Femme à vendre (opéra bouffe, 1, P. de Kock), PFN, 4 Oct 1856
La dent de sagesse (1, E. Martin), PFN, 25 April 1857
Le pommier ensorcelé (1, F. Morin), PFN, 28 April 1857
Brin d'amour (1, A. Lafont), PFN, 23 Sept 1857
Phosphorus (opéra bouffe, 1), PFN, 21 Nov 1857
Vadé au cabaret (1, H. de Kock), PFN, 1857
Le voiturier (1), Deburau, 3 Sept 1858
Simple histoire (1), Deburau, 10 Oct 1858

Les noces de Bigaro (parodie, 1), Délassements-Comiques, 24 Dec 1858
La belle espagnole (1), Deburau, 1858
L'alchimiste (opérette, 1), Deburau, 1859
La belle Nini (folie-vaudeville), Palais-Royal, 28 Jan 1860
Entre deux vins (pochade musicale), Eldorado, 1860
Le hussard persécuté, ou Le fourré des taillis (1, Blum), Délassements-Comiques, 30 May 1862; rev. version (2), Palais-Royal, 1873
La fanfare de St Cloud (vaudeville-opérette, 1, Blum and P. Siraudin), Délassements-Comiques, 30 May 1862
Le retour d'Ulysse (opéra bouffe, 1, E. Montagne), Délassements-Comiques, 21 Aug 1862
Les toréadors de Grenade (vaudeville, 1), Palais-Royal, 15 June 1863
Les Troyens en Champagne (parodie, 1), Palais-Royal, 30 Dec 1863, collab. J. Renard
Le joueur de flûte (1, J. Moinaux), PV, 16 April 1864
La liberté des théâtres (pièce musicale, 5, Clairville), PV, 10 Aug 1864
Moldave et Circassienne (pochade musicale), Eldorado, 1864
Une fantasia (1, C. Nuitter and N. Désarbres), PV, 12 Nov 1865
La biche au bois (féerie, 5, Cogniard brothers), Porte St Martin, 1865
Les chevaliers de la table ronde (3, H. Chivot and A. Duru), PBP, 17 Nov 1866
Les métamorphoses de Tartempion (opéra bouffe, 1, L. Quantin), Eldorado, 1866
La nouvelle biche au bois, Porte St Martin, 15 June 1867, collab. J. J. Debillemont and A. Artus
Le pédicure (trilogie micomico-lyrique, H. Bedeau), Eldorado, 14 July 1867
L'écho des nations (cantate, F. Straus), Eldorado, 15 Aug 1867
L'oeil crevé (opéra bouffe, 3), Folies-Dramatiques, 12 Oct 1867
L'enfant de la troupe (saynète, Beaumaire and Blondelet), Eldorado, Dec 1867
Clodoche et Normande (saynète, 1), Eldorado, 1867
Le gardien du sérail (scène comique), PV, 8 March 1868
Trombolino (opéra bouffe, 1, P. Renard and C. de Saint-Piat), Eldorado, 9 May 1868
Chilpéric (opéra bouffe, 3), Folies-Dramatiques, 24 Oct 1868; rev. version (Hervé and P. Février), PV, 2 Nov 1895
Le roi Amatibou (vaudeville, 4, E. Labiche and E. Cottinet), Palais-Royal, 27 Nov 1868
Chilméric (opérette-parodie, 1, Renard and Saint-Piat), Eldorado, 10 Dec 1868
Juliette et Dupiton (saynète bouffe), Comédie Parisien, 1868
N'i ni c'est fini (vaudeville, 1, Taratte), Molière, 1868
Deux portières pour un cordon (pochade, 1), Palais-Royal, 19 March 1869, collab. Lecocq, Legouix and G. Maurice
Faust passementier (parodie, 1), Eldorado, 4 April 1869
Le petit Faust (opéra bouffe, 4, A. Jaime and H. Crémieux), Folies-Dramatiques, 23 April 1869
Une Giboule d'amoureux (1, Lefebvre), Grand Comédie Parisien, 8 Aug 1869
Les Turcs (opéra bouffe, Jaime and Crémieux), Folies-Dramatiques, 23 Dec 1869
Aladdin the Second, or A New Light on an Old Lamp (operatic extravaganza, 5 scenes, A. Thompson), London, Gaiety, 23 Dec 1870; as Le nouvel Aladin, PFN, 23 Dec 1871
Les contes de fées (féerie, 4, O. François and E. Bloch), Délassements-Comiques, 5 March 1871, collab. Graziani and Raspail
Le trône d'Ecosse (opéra bouffe, 3, Jaime and Crémieux), PV, 17 Nov 1871
Babil and Bijou or The Lost Regalia (fantastic music drama, 5, D. Boucicault and J. R. Planché), London, CG, 29 Aug 1872, collab. Clay, J. Rivière and J.-J. de Billement
La veuve du Malabar (opéra bouffe, Crémieux and A. Delacour), PV, 26 April 1873
La France et la chanson (scène lyrique, H. Bideau), Eldorado, 28 Feb 1874
La noce à Briochet (vaudeville-opérette, A. Hermil), Délassements-Comiques, 26 April 1874
Alice de Nevers (opéra bouffe, 4), Folies-Dramatiques, 22 April 1875
La belle poule (opéra bouffe, 3, Crémieux and A. de Saint-Albin), Folies-Dramatiques, 30 Dec 1875
Estelle et Némorin (opéra bouffe, 3, A. de Hallais), Menus-Plaisirs, 2 Sept 1876

Niniche (vaudeville, 3, A. Hennequin, A. Millaud and M. Boullard), PV, 15 Feb 1878

La marquise des rues (opéra bouffe, 3, Siraudin and G. Hirsch), PBP, 23 Feb 1879

Les Sphinx (divertissement), Folies-Bergère, 29 April 1879

Panurge (opéra bouffe, 3, Clairville and O. Gastineau), PBP, 10 Sept 1879

La femme à papa (comédie-opérette, 3, Hennequin and Millaud), 3 Dec 1879

Le voyage en Amérique (opéra bouffe, 4, M. Boucheron and H. Raymond), Nouveautés, 16 Sept 1880

La mère des compagnons (opéra bouffe, 3, Chivot and Duru), Folies-Dramatiques, 15 Dec 1880

La roussotte (vaudeville-opérette, 3, H. Meilhac, L. Halévy and Millaud), PV, 26 or 28 Jan 1881, collab. Lecocq and M. Boullard

Les deux roses (3, Clairville, J. Grangé and V. Bernard), Folies-Dramatiques, 20 Oct 1881

Lili (comédie-opérette-vaudeville, 3, Hennequin and Millaud), PV, 11 Jan 1882

Mam'zelle Nitouche (vaudeville-opérette, 3, Meilhac and Millaud), PV, 26 Jan 1883

Le vertigo (opéra bouffe, 3, H. Crisafulli and H. Bocage), Renaissance, 29 Sept 1883

Espagne et Tyrol (saynète, Gardel and Hervé), ?1883

La cosaque (comédie-vaudeville, 3, Meilhac and Millaud), PV, 1 Feb 1884

La nuit aux soufflets (2, D'Ennery and P. Ferrier), Nouveautés, 18 Sept 1884

Mam'zelle Gavroche (comédie-opérette, 3, E. Gondinet, Blum and Saint-Albin), PV, 24 Jan 1885

Frivoli (comedy-operetta, 3, W. B. Kingston), London, Drury Lane, 29 June 1886

Fla-Fla (vaudeville, 3, Hirsch and Siraudin), Menus-Plaisirs, 4 July or September 1886

La noce à Nini (vaudeville-opérette, 3, E. de Najac and Millaud), ?19 March 1887

Les bagatelles de la porte (1, L. Real), Menus-Plaisirs, 14 Aug 1890

Bacchanale (3, G. Bertel and J. Lecocq), Menus-Plaisirs, 22 Oct 1892

La cabinet Piperlin (3, Raymond and Burani), Athénée Comique, 17 Sept 1897

Les aventures [amoureuses] de Télémaque (1, Gardel and Hervé), Scala, 9 March 1900

*

StiegerO

L. H. Lecomte: *Histoire des théâtres de Paris: les Folies Nouvelles* (Paris, 1909)

L. Schneider: *Les maîtres de l'opérette française; Hervé, Charles Lecocq* (Paris, 1924)

C. Beaumont Wicks: *The Parisian Stage* (Alabama, 1950–79)

I. Guest: *The Empire Ballet* (London, 1962)

R. Traubner: *Operetta: a Theatrical History* (New York, 1983)

KURT GÄNZL (text), ANDREW LAMB (work-list)

Herz, Das ('The Heart'). *Drama für Musik* in three acts, op.39, by HANS PFITZNER to a libretto by Hans Mahner-Mons; Berlin, Staatsoper, and Munich, Nationaltheater, 12 November 1931.

Pfitzner's last opera is set in southern Germany in about 1700. Dr Daniel Athanasius (baritone) invokes the power of black magic to restore life to the duke's son (spoken) for one year, at the price of a human heart. After the year goes by, the celebrated doctor is horrified to discover that the forfeit heart is that of his wife Helge (soprano). He is condemned for sorcery but rejects the offered reprieve should he again restore the boy to life and is redeemed by his adamant desire to atone. A glowing heart returns to the astral body of Helge, who leads Athanasius into a heavenly vision; after it fades the executioners find that their victim, the doctor, is already dead.

PETER FRANKLIN

Herz, Joachim (*b* Dresden, 15 June 1924). German director. He was educated at the Kreuzschule, Dresden (1934–42), and studied the piano, clarinet and theory privately. He then attended the Musikhochschule in Dresden (1945–50) and the Humboldt University, Berlin (1949–51), where he studied musicology. From 1953 to 1956 he assisted Felsenstein at the Komische Oper, Berlin, returning, after appointments in Cologne (1956–7) and Leipzig (1957–77), as Intendant (1976–81). He was principal director of productions at Dresden from 1985 to 1990.

Herz's first important production was of Richard Mohaupt's *Die Bremer Stadtmusikanten* at the Dresden Staatstheater (1950), with students of the Musikhochschule and Palucca School; the choreographer was Ruth Berghaus. The first of his productions at the Komische Oper was of Joseph Haas's *Die Hochzeit des Jobs* (1953) and at the Dresden Staatsoper of *Albert Herring* (1955). His *Meistersinger* (his first Wagner production) opened the new opera house at Leipzig in 1960; his *Fliegender Holländer* in 1963 was the first work to be produced at the Bol'shoy by a foreigner; his *Katerina Izmaylova* at Leipzig in 1965 was the first performance of the work in East Germany; and his *Freischütz* opened the restored Semper Oper in Dresden in 1985. For a large part of his career his work was scarcely known outside East Germany, but his *Guillaume Tell* at the Colón in 1966 initiated a series of productions there, and his *Ring* (Leipzig, 1973–6) was influential in the establishment of the new wave of socially critical stagings of Wagner: several of its ideas (for example the setting of Act 2 of *Walküre* inside Valhalla) became commonplaces in subsequent productions, as did the highlighting of class divisions and other forms of oppression and alienation perceived by Herz and his Leipzig collective as stemming from capitalist production relations.

His first production in Great Britain was of *Salome* for the ENO in 1975, in which the princess expired 'having attained her fulfilment' rather than being crushed by the soldiers' shields. Further productions there were a powerfully theatrical *Fidelio* (1980) that emphasized the contemporaneity of the work's revolutionary aspirations, and a *Parsifal* (1986) that not only turned traditional notions of seduction on their heads in the magic garden scene, but also offered a radical reappraisal of the role of Kundry (who participated actively in the final Grail ceremony) and of womankind generally. Herz has also staged *Madama Butterfly*, restoring some of the original music (1978) and *Forza del destino* (1981) for the WNO. His production of *Lulu* at the Komische Oper in 1980 was the first staging of this opera in the former East Berlin.

WRITINGS

ed. S. Stompor: *Joachim Herz über Musiktheater* (Berlin, 1974)

——: *Musiktheater: Beiträge zur Methodik und zu Inszenierungskonzeptionen* (Leipzig, 1976) [writings by Herz and Felsenstein]

'Und Figaro lässt sich scheiden': *Oper als Idee und Interpretation* (Munich, 1985)

Theater: Kunst des erfüllten Augenblicks (Berlin, 1989)

*

H.-J. Irmer and W. Stein: *Joachim Herz: Regisseur im Musiktheater* (Berlin, 1977)

U. Müller and U. Müller, eds.: *Opern und Opernfiguren: Festschrift für Joachim Herz* (Anif, Salzburg, 1989) [incl. list of productions]

I. Kobán, ed.: *Joachim Herz: Interviews* (Berlin, 1990)

BARRY MILLINGTON

Hesch, Wilhelm [Heš, Vilém] (*b* Elbeteinitz [now Týnec nad Labem], Bohemia, 3 July 1860; *d* Vienna, 4 July 1908). Bohemian bass. He studied in Prague and in 1880 made his début at Brno in *The Bartered Bride*. In 1882 he joined the National Theatre in Prague, singing there with great success for 12 years and afterwards as an honoured guest. He was with the Hamburg Opera for two seasons and then moved to the Vienna Hofoper, where he remained as principal bass until the end of his career. There he sang 60 roles, being particularly admired for his Sarastro and Osmin in Mozart, Landgrave and King Henry in Wagner, Rocco in *Fidelio* and Kecal in *The Bartered Bride*. He took part in many first Viennese performances, including those of *La bohème*, *Yevgeny Onegin* and *Louise*. An essential member of the great ensemble formed under Mahler, he was valued as much for his acting as for his singing. His dark, sturdy voice can be heard in a large number of recordings, which show something of the liveliness as well as the authority of his portrayals.

*

B. Benoni: 'Za přítelem' [Tribute to a Friend], *Dalibor*, xxx (1908), 117–19 [obituary]
V. J. Novotný: 'Za Vilémem Hešem', *HR*, i (1908), 122–3 [obituary]
C. Norton-Welsh: 'Wilhelm Hesch', *Record Collector*, xxxiii (1988), 135–50   J. B. STEANE

Hesse, Ernst Christian (*b* Grossgottern, Thuringia, 14 April 1676; *d* Darmstadt, 16 May 1762). German composer. An excellent viola da gamba player, he first served the Landgrave Ernst Ludwig of Hesse-Darmstadt in Giessen and Darmstadt; after touring extensively as a virtuoso he became Kapelldirektor in 1707. In 1708 he went to Mantua with Prince Philipp, Ernst Ludwig's brother, to study Italian operatic style under the prince's Kapellmeister, Vivaldi. After a short spell in Darmstadt, where Johann Christoph Graupner had recently taken charge of the musical establishment, Hesse visited Dresden and Vienna, before securing a permanent position in Darmstadt (1710). He resigned his post as Kapelldirektor in 1714 but was given a military appointment. In about 1712 his Italian opera *La fedeltà coronata* (*D-DS*) was performed. It includes arias according to 'Lombard' taste, expressive recitatives and an important ensemble. His only other extant compositions are a divertimento and two chamber works.

*

E. Pasqué: 'Geschichte der Musik und des Theaters am Hofe zu Darmstadt', *Die Muse*, ii (1854), 629
H. Kaiser: *Barocktheater in Darmstadt* (Darmstadt, 1951)
E. Noack: *Musikgeschichte Darmstadts* (Mainz, 1967)
ELISABETH NOACK

Hesse, Ruth (*b* Wuppertal, 18 Sept 1936). German mezzo-soprano. She studied at Hamburg and Milan, making her début in 1958 at Lübeck. Engaged in 1962 at the Deutsche Oper, Berlin, she sang there for 26 years. In 1963 she took part in the first staged performance of Milhaud's *Oresteia* music and in 1965 created Frau von Hufnagel in *Der junge Lord*. She sang at Bayreuth (1963–5) and from 1966 at the Vienna Staatsoper, where her roles included Ortrud, Brangäne and Eboli. She made her Covent Garden début in 1969 as the Nurse (*Die Frau ohne Schatten*), a role she sang at Salzburg (1974), San Francisco (1976) and Buenos Aires (1979). Her repertory included Carmen, Mistress Quickly, Fricka, Herodias and Clytemnestra, which she sang in Florence and Washington, as well as Berlin and Vienna. A singer of great intensity, she had a rich and vibrant voice, particularly strong in the lower register.
ELIZABETH FORBES

Heuberger, Richard (**Franz Joseph**) (*b* Graz, 18 June 1850; *d* Vienna, 28 Oct 1914). Austrian composer. He

gave up an engineering career in 1876 to devote himself to music, studying in Graz with W. A. Rémy. Moving to Vienna, he became director of the Academischer Gesangverein in 1876 and the Singakademie in 1878, was a teacher at the conservatory from 1902 and directed the Wiener Männergesangverein, 1902–9. He was also a music critic, writing for the *Neue Wiener Tagblatt* from 1881, the Munich *Allgemeine Zeitung* from 1889, and succeeding Hanslick on the important and influential *Neue freie Presse* (1896–1901); he also edited the *Musikbuch aus Österreich* (1904–6). Besides collections of his criticisms, he published a biography of Schubert (1902). He composed two ballets, four operas and several operettas, and achieved considerable renown in his day with his choral and orchestral works; he is now remembered almost exclusively for his operetta *Der Opernball* (1898). This remains a mainstay of the German operetta repertory, esteemed especially for the insinuating duet 'Geh'n wir ins Chambre séparée' (for soprano and mezzo-soprano). Otherwise his stage works had little success, and when he was offered the libretto of *Die lustige Witwe* he was unable to supply music to suit the management of the Theater an der Wien, who thereupon handed it over to the young Lehár.

See also OPERNBALL, DER.

operettas unless otherwise stated

Die Abenteuer einer Neujahrsnacht op.29 (Komische Oper, 3, F. Schaumann, after H. Zschokke), Leipzig, Stadt, 12 Jan 1886
Manuel Venegas (op, 3, J. V. Widmann, after P. de Alarcon: *El niño de la bola*), Leipzig, Stadt, 27 March 1889
Mirjam [Das Maifest] (op, 3, L. Ganghofer), Vienna, Hofoper, 20 Jan 1894
Der Opernball op.40 (3, V. Léon and H. von Waldberg, after A. Delacour and A. Hennequin: *Les dominos roses*), Vienna, An der Wien, 5 Jan 1898 (Leipzig and Vienna, 1898)
Ihr Excellenz (3, Léon and Waldberg, after Hennequin and A. Millaud: *Niniche*), Vienna, An der Wien, 28 Jan 1899
Der Sechsuhrzug (3, Léon and L. Stein, after H. Meilhac: *Décoré*), Vienna, An der Wien, 20 or 21 Jan 1900
Das Baby (3, Waldberg and Willner, after A. W. Pinero), Vienna Carl, 3 Oct 1902
Barfüssele (op, prelude, 2, Léon, after B. Auerbach), Vienna, Volksoper, 22 Dec 1905
Der Fürst von Düsterstein (3, Gaudeamus), Vienna, Johann Strauss Theater, 3 March 1909
Don Quichotte (2, H. Reichert and F. Grünbaum, after M. de Cervantes), Vienna, Hölle, 1 Dec 1910

*

MGG (H. Wamlek)
O. Schneidereit: *Operette von Abraham bis Ziehrer* (Berlin, 1966)
ANDREW LAMB

Heure espagnole, L' ('The Spanish Hour'). *Comédie musicale* in one act by MAURICE RAVEL after the play by FRANC-NOHAIN; Paris, Opéra-Comique (Salle Favart), 19 May 1911.

Torquemada *a clockmaker*	tenor ('Trial')
Concepcion *Torquemada's wife*	soprano
Gonzalve *a bachelor*	tenor
Ramiro *a muleteer*	baritone ('Martin')
Don Inigo Gomez *a banker*	bass

Setting The interior of Torquemada's shop in Toledo in the 18th century

Franc-Nohain's comedy *L'heure espagnole* had been a great success at the Odéon in Paris in 1904, and Ravel made only some small cuts and revisions in refashioning it as a libretto. The director of the Opéra-Comique, Albert Carré, had doubts as to whether his clientèle would accept the risqué story line and on these grounds delayed acceptance for some time after Ravel finished the vocal score in October 1907. He agreed only at the insistence of Mme Jean Cruppi, the wife of a cabinet minister, and Ravel dedicated the work to her.

The cast of the première included Geneviève Vix as Concepcion and Jean Périer as Ramiro. Vix was a well-known Carmen, and Périer had been the original Pelléas nine years earlier: this casting emphasized the parodic element in Ravel's score, as did the pairing in a double bill after Massenet's *Thérèse*. Press reaction was mixed. Pierre Lalo found that Ravel's air of detached superiority spoilt his enjoyment, while Reynaldo Hahn, referring to Ravel's technique as 'a sort of transcendent jujitsu', preferred those diatonic moments in the score which the composer had failed to hide beneath the Hispanic chromaticism. The opera reached Covent Garden in 1919, Chicago and New York in 1920, the Opéra in 1921 (with Fanny Heldy) and La Scala in 1929 (with Conchita Supervia). Heldy's 78 r.p.m. recording of 'Oh! la pitoyable aventure' stands as an unrivalled example of clear diction and sexual verve.

During an orchestral introduction clock noises (taken, according to Roland-Manuel, from Ravel's projected opera *Olympia*, where they accompany the entry of Coppelius) prepare the audience for the sight of Torquemada at his work-bench, his back to the audience. The simultaneous ticking of three clocks at different speeds, but coinciding every 15 seconds, acts as a symbol of the struggle between order and chaos which informs the opera at many levels.

Ramiro enters with a watch to be mended which once belonged to his uncle the toreador and saved him from the bull's horns. The explosion of Spanish colour as Ramiro tells his tale not only serves an obvious referential purpose but marks Ramiro out also as a man of action. Concepcion enters and reminds Torquemada that it is Thursday, the day when he has to spend an hour ('l'heure espagnole', indeed) going round winding up the municipal clocks. He leaves, asking Ramiro to await his return and declaiming importantly 'l'heure officielle n'attend pas' – a phrase which has gestural and psychological similarities with Golaud's 'Je suis le prince Golaud, le petit fils d'Arkel le vieux roi d'Allemonde' in the first scene of *Pelléas et Mélisande*. Ramiro's continuing presence suits neither Concepcion, who likes to have this hour each week free in order to keep her male friendships in good repair, nor Ramiro, who knows he ought to indulge in light conversation but can't think of anything to say. However, Concepcion takes advantage of having a strong man around the place and asks him to carry a grandfather clock up to her bedroom. As he ascends the staircase with his load, the voice of the poet Gonzalve is heard offstage singing a roulade.

Gonzalve enters, and the roulade turns into a song of no literary merit whatever ('Enfin revient le jour si doux'), to which Ravel responds with equally tired Spanish clichés. This emphasizes the high level of Ravel's hispanicisms so far and, more importantly, informs the audience that Gonzalve is a dolt; though it goes against the composer's wishes to play the part for laughs. Concepcion urges Gonzalve to take advantage of the few moments the muleteer's absence allows them, but Gonzalve is intoxicated with his own poetic images,

and before she can bring him down to earth Ramiro returns, his mission accomplished. Astonished by Ramiro's despatch, Concepcion decides that, after all, she has asked him to move the wrong clock. Would he be kind enough to fetch it down again and take up another one instead? Ramiro is perfectly obliging. As he departs, Gonzalve 'with a disdainful look' says 'les muletiers n'ont pas de conversation', unwittingly copying the admission Ramiro has already made to Concepcion. Ravel sets Gonzalve's version to almost the same music, not surprisingly, but the effect is very different since Gonzalve's part must be sung (Ravel says in a preface to the score) 'lyrically, with affectation', whereas Ramiro's, like the rest, must be sung in the manner of recitative in Italian *opera buffa*. Gonzalve's bitchy comment comes over as dry and inexpressive within the context of his overall vocal style, Ramiro's admission as lyrical within the context of his. This is but one example out of many of Ravel's almost abstract game-playing in the opera.

Concepcion persuades Gonzalve to insert himself in the clock that Ramiro will shortly be carrying up to her bedroom. Gonzalve expatiates on the 'sensations neuves' the experience is likely to afford. Don Inigo enters, to a dotted rhythm similar to that of the pompous peacock in Ravel's song cycle *Histoires naturelles*. His oratory is well into its stride when Ramiro returns. Concepcion explains him away to Don Inigo as a removal man. Ramiro lifts the clock containing Gonzalve on to his shoulders and Concepcion goes up the stairs after him, ostensibly to oversee Gonzalve's welfare. Don Inigo decides that his only chance of being alone with Concepcion is to hide, in a clock; he squeezes himself in with difficulty, while the orchestra underlines the ridiculous nature of the exercise with a surrealistically nonchalant waltz (all the more effective because the bar lengths have been constantly changing until this point).

Ramiro descends alone and muses on the complex mechanisms of clocks and women. Concepcion rejoins him, distraught because, she says, the clock now in her room is not functioning properly. Ramiro goes to bring it down again. Don Inigo's cuckoo imitations do not amuse Concepcion, and she pleads with him to come out of his clock; but this is easier said than done. Ramiro returns, bearing both clock and Gonzalve, and soon it is Don Inigo who is on his way upstairs. Gonzalve has still not recovered from his attack of poetry and refuses to leave his clock. Concepcion walks off in a huff. Alone, Gonzalve sings of the delights of imprisonment.

Ramiro returns and sings of Concepcion's charms; if he were not a muleteer he would be a watchmaker. Concepcion enters, and she has only to say 'Monsieur!' for Ramiro to divine her command. With Gonzalve silently immured, Concepcion delivers a tirade against her two established lovers ('Oh! la pitoyable aventure!') as the awful prospect of fidelity stretches before her. Ramiro descends with Don Inigo's clock and offers still further service as a clock remover, but this time Concepcion asks for his services 'sans horloge' and follows him up the stairs.

Don Inigo and Gonzalve are left on stage, each in his clock. Don Inigo is unable to extricate himself and retires inside. Gonzalve emerges easily enough and sings a lyrical farewell to his prison, but he too retires inside on seeing Torquemada returning. Torquemada capitalizes on Don Inigo's close interest in his clock by selling it to him and assures Gonzalve that he has just the clock for him too. Torquemada and Gonzalve try unsuccessfully to set Don Inigo free.

Ramiro and Concepcion descend from her room. After one further attempt with Concepcion's assistance, Ramiro finally pulls Don Inigo free without apparent effort. Finally, the five characters step forward in a ceremonial gesture to address the audience. The moral is taken from Boccaccio: 'in the pursuit of love there comes a moment when the muleteer has his turn'.

*   *   *

In a letter of 17 May 1911, two days before the première, Ravel wrote: 'What I've tried to do is fairly ambitious: to breathe new life into the Italian *opera buffa*: following only the principle … the French language, like any other, has its own accents and inflections of pitch.' At the same time he referred to Musorgsky's *Zhenit'ba* ('The Marriage') as the work's only real ancestor. It also forms part of a larger group of Spanish works that spanned Ravel's whole career, and the necessary Spanish colouring provided him with a reason for a virtuoso use of the modern orchestra, which he felt was 'perfectly designed for underlining and exaggerating comic effects'. Brilliant though his orchestration is, there is some truth in the oft-repeated comment that the clocks are more human than the humans. In the theatre, it is often hard to disguise a calculating coldness at the heart of the opera or to resist the charge, so unjustly levelled at many of his other works, that here Ravel was indeed just a little too clever for his own good.

For a design for *L'heure espagnole*, see PONNELLE, JEAN-PIERRE.

ROGER NICHOLS

Hewitt, James (*b* ?Dartmoor, 4 June 1770; *d* Boston, 2 Aug 1827). American conductor, composer and publisher of English birth. He played in the orchestra at Astley's Amphitheatre in London, one of the forerunners of the modern circus. In 1792 he travelled to New York, where he lived until 1811. From 1792 until the end of March 1808, he was conductor of the orchestra at the Park Street Theatre; his duties included arranging and composing music for ballad operas and other musical productions. He also operated his own 'musical repository', where he gave lessons and sold music and musical instruments. His first opera, *Tammany, or The Indian Chief*, with a satirical, anti-Federalist libretto had its première at the John Street Theatre on 3 March 1794.

Although Hewitt's musical activities in Boston began as early as 1805, the family did not move there until 1811. He pursued the same musical interests there as in New York, conducting the orchestra at the Federal Street Theatre, giving lessons, composing and publishing music; he was also the organist at Trinity Church. In 1816 he returned to New York, taking his two eldest sons with him. During the last two years of his life he was afflicted with a facial cancer. In later 1826, an unsuccessful operation was performed in New York, and in early 1827 he was brought back to his family in Boston, where he died.

Hewitt published at least 639 compositions, the majority by such British composers as William Shield, Michael Kelly and James Hook, though he also issued works by Handel, Haydn and Mozart, and approximately 160 of his own compositions. These include instrumental pieces, songs, pantomimes and 19 ballad operas, of which only excerpts survive; a 20th ballad opera, *The Tars from Tripoli*, based on the ballad opera *The Naval Pillar* with new music by John Morehead, is the only work at least partly by Hewitt for which the complete music is published.

ballad operas; first performed, and printed works published, in New York unless otherwise stated

Tammany, or The Indian Chief (A. J. Hatton), John Street, 3 March 1794, 1 song (1794)
The Patriot, or Liberty Asserted, 1794
Flash in the Pan, 1798, 1 song (1798), 1 song (1800)
Columbus, or The Discovery of America, 1799
The Mysterious Marriage, or The Heirship of Roselva, 1799
The Spanish Castle, or The Knight of Guadalquivir (comic opera), Park, 5 Dec 1800
Pizarro in Peru, or The Death of Rolla, 1800
Robin Hood, or Sherwood Forest, 1800
The Wild Goose Chase, 1800, 1 song (1801)
The Cottagers, 1801
The Comet, or He would be a Philosopher, 1802
Don Raphael, 1804, 1 song (1804)
The Blind Bargain, 1805, 1 song (1805)
The Honeymoon, 1805, 1 song (1805), 1 song (Boston, 1814–15)
The Finger Post, or Five Miles Off, 1806, 1 song (1807)
The Hunter of the Alps, 1807, 2 songs (1807)
Wood Daemon, Boston, 1808
Who Wins, 1810, 1 song (1810)
The Snow Storm, Atlanta, 1823

Music in: The Tars from Tripoli (2, after J. Morehead: The Naval Pillar); (*c*1806)

*

EwenD
W. Dunlap: *History of American Theatre* (New York, 1832), 108–9
O. G. T. Sonneck: *Early Opera in America* (New York, 1915)
J. W. Wagner: *James Hewitt: his Life and Works* (diss., Indiana U., 1969)
——: 'James Hewitt, 1770–1827', *MQ*, lviii (1972), 259–76
JOHN W. WAGNER

Hidalgo, Elvira de (*b* Aragon, 27 Dec 1892; *d* Milan, 21 Jan 1980). Spanish soprano. She studied in Barcelona and Milan, making her début in 1908 at the S Carlo as Rosina, the role of her Metropolitan début in 1910, when she also sang Amina. She appeared at La Scala, Rome, Buenos Aires and Covent Garden, where she sang Gilda in 1924 with the British National Opera Company. Returning to the Metropolitan (1924–6), she sang Gilda and Lucia. At San Francisco (1925) she sang Rosina, Violetta and Martha, then toured the USA in *Il barbiere* with Shalyapin. Her repertory included Elvira (*I puritani*), Linda di Chamounix and Marguerite de Valois (*Les Huguenots*). She retired in 1932, then taught in Athens (where her pupils included Maria Callas), Ankara and Milan. Her recordings show her bright, agile soprano voice to advantage.

*

GV (R. Celletti; R. Vegeto)   ALAN BLYTH

Hidalgo, Juan (*b* Madrid, 28 Sept 1614; *d* Madrid, 31 March 1685). Spanish composer. In 1630 or 1631 he was received into the Spanish royal chapel as harpist responsible for the accompaniment of both sacred and secular music. Around 1645, he began to serve as chief composer of secular songs, theatrical songs and vernacular sacred pieces (*villancicos*), and as leader of the court's chamber musicians. Prolific, cooperative, dedicated and generally admired in his employment, he dominated secular and theatrical music at court until his death and was probably the most influential composer of his time in Spain.

Although a brief autobiographical memorandum indicates that Hidalgo's work as a theatrical composer began in the 1640s, this essential focus of his activity

Stage design by Baccio di Bianco for the celebration scene from the semi-opera 'Fortunas de Andrómeda y Perseo' (attributed to Hidalgo), first performed at the Madrid court in 1653

cannot be otherwise confirmed until the 1650s. He wrote music for at least nine *autos sacramentales* (allegorical religious plays performed in public for Corpus Christi); his work for the court stages included songs for spoken plays (*comedias*), partly-sung zarzuelas and semi-operas, and two exceptional fully sung operas. Among the surviving songs for *comedias*, the lament for the nymph Canente from the pastoral *Pico y Canente* (L. de Ulloa, 1656) is a striking example of his originality and distinctive approach to text expression. He probably collaborated with the dramatist Pedro Calderón de la Barca on productions of the first zarzuelas, beginning with *El laurel de Apolo* (1657). Songs for a later zarzuela, *Los celos hacen estrellas* (1672; for illustration *see* MADRID, fig.1) to a text by Juan Vélez de Guevara, survive; of the semi-operas, some of his music for Calderón's *La estatua de Prometeo* (c1670–75) is available, and the entire extant vocal score to the monumental *Fortunas de Andrómeda y Perseo* (Calderón, 1653), with its recitatives in triple metre, has been attributed to Hidalgo.

Hidalgo's most extensive and innovative works were the mythological semi-operas and the two operas he created with Calderón. *La púrpura de la rosa* and *Celos aun del aire matan* were composed to commemorate the Peace of the Pyrénées (1659) and the Spanish-French royal wedding of 1660. Several versions of Calderón's librettos for the operas survive, but Hidalgo's score to the one-act *La púrpura de la rosa* (?1660) is lost. A complete score for the three-act *Celos aun del aire matan* (?1660) survives. Although it is often stated that Hidalgo modelled his theatrical style on that of Italian opera, this contention is not supported by an informed analysis of his works. During his years as court composer the strongest Italian influence upon the Spanish court plays is found in the visual effects created by imported stage designers. In Hidalgo's music, the tradition of Iberian secular song dominates, although he followed the non-technical advice of the Italian stage designer Baccio di Bianco and adapted recitative monologue for the weighty dialogues and speeches of the gods in the court semi-operas (beginning around 1652) and for specially significant moments in *Celos aun del aire matan*. This work survives as the earliest extant complete Spanish opera, exceptional in the context of 17th-century Spanish theatrical music only because it is wholly sung. Hidalgo approached this extraordinary commission by exploiting familiar Spanish musical and theatrical conventions developed for the semi-operas. The basic texture is of strophic airs whose forward motion and continuity are only interrupted by dramatic recitative monologues for the most intensely charged moments or as the expression of supernatural power. Hidalgo's operatic conventions and his musical style clearly differ from any of the several contemporary kinds of opera cultivated in Italy. His sparing, specific use of recitative and approach to the shaping and rhythm of recitative melodies are distinctive in comparison to other 17th-century dramatic composers. In songs and airs which are almost exclusively syllabic, diatonic and laced with syncopation and hemiola, his adaptation of Spanish dances (such as the *jácara* and the *seguidilla*) for characterization and verisimilitude is especially important. Moreover, the absence of italianate affective devices or gestures and of formulaic or strophic bass patterns distances them stylistically from the practices of contemporary Italian composers. During Hidalgo's career, Italian opera was not performed in Madrid, Italian operatic composers did not seek employment in Madrid, nor did Spanish composers study abroad. It is doubtful that Hidalgo knew contemporary Italian opera, except for his work with Baccio di Bianco and possible contact with the Roman librettist Giulio Rospigliosi, who stayed several years in Madrid as papal legate.

Hidalgo's place in the history of Spanish theatrical music is comparable to that of Lully in France or Purcell in Britain. Like Purcell, he worked with the greatest dramatist of his age and composed mainly for partly-sung productions designed to appeal both to royal patrons and to a broad but sophisticated public. Like Lully, he not only composed for the most important political occasions but was charged with developing a national theatrical music suitable to the characteristic histrionic style of the Spanish actors, the stylized dignity of the highly symbolic dramatic texts and their exquisite visual effects. As composer he wielded less influence than the dramatist and the scenic designer, but he was fortunate to work with Calderón, arguably the strongest dramatist in Europe, and to benefit from the sponsorship of the ambitiously artistic Marquis de Eliche whose productions, for a brief period, were said to be some of the most daring, opulent and innovative in Europe.

See also CELOS AUN DEL AIRE MATAN; CELOS HACEN ESTRELLAS, LOS; and PÚRPURA DE LA ROSA, LA.

Pico y Canente (comedia, 3, L. de Ulloa), Madrid, Buen Retiro, 1656, 1 song *E-Mn*; ed. Stein 1986, 1987 and 1992
Triunfos de amor y fortuna (comedia, 3, A. de Solís), 1658, collab. Galán, songs *Bc* and *Mn*; excerpts ed. Stein 1987 and 1992
Celos aun del aire matan (3, P. Calderón de la Barca), Madrid, Buen Retiro, ? 5 Dec 1660, *P-EVp*; excerpts ed. Stein 1987, 1991 and 1992; ed. Subirá 1933 (Act 1 only)
Ni amor se libra de amor (comedia, 3, Calderón), 1662, songs *E-Mn* and *Mcns*; excerpts ed. Stein 1987 and 1992
La estatua de Prometeo (semi-op, 3, Calderón) ? 1670 or 1674, songs *Mn*; ed. Stein 1986, 1987 and 1992
Los celos hacen estrellas (zar, 2, J. Vélez de Guevara), 1672, songs *Mn*, *V* and *I-Vnm*; ed. Varey, Shergold and Sage 1970
Los juegos olímpicos (zar, 2, A. de Salazar y Torres), 1673, songs *D-Mbs*, *E-Mn* and *US-NYhsa*; excerpts ed. Stein 1987 and 1992
Endimión y Diana (zar, 2, M. Fernández de León), 1675, songs *E-Mn*
El templo de Palas (zar, 2, F. de Avellaneda), 1675, songs *Mn*
Alfeo y Aretusa (zar, 2, J. B. Diamante), ?1674; rev., 1678, collab. Galán; songs *US-NYhsa*; excerpts ed. Stein 1987 and 1992
Contra el amor desengaño (zar, 2), 1679, songs *E-Mn*
Hado y divisa de Leonido y Marfisa (comedia, 3, Calderón), 1680
Icaro y Dédalo (comedia, 3, Fernández de León), 1684, songs *Bc* and *Mn*; excerpts ed. Stein 1987 and 1992
Apolo y Leucotea (comedia, 3, P. Scotti de Agoiz), 1684
El primer templo de amor (comedia, 3, Fernández de León), before 1685

Attributed works [see Stein 1992]: Fortunas de Androméda y Perseo (semi-op, 3, Calderón), 1653, *US-CA*, excerpts ed. Stein 1987 and 1992; El laurel de Apolo (zar, Calderón), 1657; La púrpura de la rosa (1, Calderón), Madrid, Buen Retiro, ? 17 Jan 1660; Fieras afernina amor (semi-op, 3, Calderón), 1670, ? collab. J. del Vado

*

J. Subirá, ed.: *'Celos aun del aire matan': ópera del siglo xvii* [with edn of Act 1] (Barcelona, 1933)
——: 'El operista español Don Juan Hidalgo: nuevas noticias biográficas', *Las ciencias*, i (1934), 615
——: 'Una tonada del operista Don Juan Hidalgo', *Las ciencias*, ii (1935), 166
O. Ursprung: '"Celos aun del aire matan": Text von Calderón, Musik von Hidalgo, die älteste erhaltene spanische Oper', *Festschrift Arnold Schering* (Berlin, 1937), 223–40
J. Moll: 'Nuevos datos para la biografía de Juan Hidalgo, arpista y compositor', *Miscelánea en homenaje a Monseñor Higinio Anglés*, ii (Barcelona, 1961), 585–9
J. Subirá: 'Calderón de la Barca, libretista de ópera: consideraciones literario-musicales', *AnM*, xx (1965), 59–73
R. E. L. Pitts: *Don Juan Hidalgo, Seventeenth-Century Spanish Composer* (diss., George Peabody College, Nashville, TN, 1968)
J. E. Varey, N. D. Shergold and J. Sage: *Juan Vélez de Guevara: 'Los celos hacen estrellas'* (London, 1970)
J. Sage: 'Nouvelles lumières sur la genèse de l'opéra et la zarzuela en Espagne', *Baroque*, v (1972), 107–14
——: 'The Function of Music in the Theater', *Pedro Calderón de la Barca: Comedias*, xix: *Critical Studies of Calderón's Comedias*, ed. D. W. Cruickshank and J. E. Varey (London, 1973), 209–30
M. D. Stroud: *Pedro Calderón de la Barca: Celos aun del aire matan: an Edition with Introduction, Translation and Notes* (San Antonio, TX, 1981)
L. K. Stein: 'Música existente para comedias de Calderón de la Barca', *Congreso internacional sobre Calderón y el teatro español del siglo de oro: Madrid 1982*, 1161–72
E. López de Saa: 'Juan Hidalgo', *Ritmo*, xv (1985), 11
L. K. Stein: '*La plática de los dioses*: Music and the Calderonian Court Play, with a Transcription of the Songs from *La estatua de Prometeo*', introduction to P. Calderón de la Barca: *La estatua de Prometeo*, ed. M. R. Greer (Kassel, 1986), 13–92
——: *Music in the Seventeenth-Century Spanish Secular Theater, 1598–1690* (diss., U. of Chicago, 1987)
C. Caballero: 'Nuevas fuentes musicales de *Los celos hacen estrellas* de Juan Vélez de Guevara', *Cuadernos de teatro clásico*, iii (1989), 119
A. Cardona, D. Cruickshank and M. Cunningham, eds.: *Pédro Calderón de la Barca and Tomás de Torrejón y Velasco, 'La púrpura de la rosa'* (Kassel, 1990)
L. K. Stein: 'Opera and the Spanish Political Agenda', *AcM*, lxiii (1991), 125–66
——: *Songs of Mortals, Dialogues of the Gods: Music and Theatre in Seventeenth-Century Spain* (Oxford, 1992)

LOUISE K. STEIN

Hieronymus Knicker. *Komisches Singspiel* in two acts by CARL DITTERS VON DITTERSDORF to his own libretto; Vienna, Theater in der Leopoldstadt, 7 July 1789.

The old miser Knicker (bass) intends to dispose of his two wards by marrying his niece Louise (soprano) to another aged merchant, Tobias Filz (bass), and enlisting his nephew Ferdinand (tenor) in the army. He himself intends to marry young Röschen (soprano), Ferdinand's beloved. After a foiled double elopement, Louise's betrothed Carl (tenor) contrives a new stratagem involving a treasure buried in Knicker's cellar. It, too, fails, but Louise's chambermaid Henriette (soprano) forces the miser's hand by reminding him of an old promise of marriage he had once made to her.

Hieronymus Knicker, one of Dittersdorf's most popular works, reproduces nearly all the tried and true dramatic and musical elements of his earlier German operas. Cheerful ensembles and ample, lively finales mix with a great diversity of aria types – the folklike, comic, sentimental, mock-heroic, virtuoso and even a 'Turkish' song sung by Ferdinand disguised as an Armenian.

THOMAS BAUMAN

Hiestermann, Horst (*b* Ballenstedt, 14 Aug 1934). German tenor. In 1955 he joined the chorus at Brandenburg, becoming a soloist there in 1957. After engagements in Leipzig and Weimar, in 1964 he joined the Staatsopern of both Berlin and Dresden. In 1976 he moved to Düsseldorf, and in 1984 to Zürich; in the latter year he took part in the première of Reimann's *Gespenstersonate* in Berlin. He has also sung in Hamburg, Munich, Salzburg and Dallas and at the Opéra and La Scala. A powerful actor, he has a repertory including Monostatos, Loge, Mime (the role of his Metropolitan début in 1987), David, the Witch (*Hänsel* *und Gretel*), Aegisthus, Herod, Valzacchi, Shuysky, Robespierre (*Dantons Tod*) and Edmund (Reimann's *Lear*).   ELIZABETH FORBES

Higgins, Harry [Henry] **Vincent** (*b* London, 10 April 1855; *d* London, 21 Nov 1928). English administrator. By profession a solicitor and director of the Carlton and Ritz Hotel companies and of the Ritz Hotel, Paris, he was educated at the Oratory School, Edgbaston, and at Oxford. From 1888, in conjunction with Lady de Grey, he found financial backing for Augustus Harris at the Royal Opera House, Covent Garden, securing the patronage of the aristocracy and a system of regular subscriptions. On Harris's death in 1896, he became chairman of the Grand Opera Syndicate, which kept Covent Garden financially viable for 30 years and provided money for improvements to the theatre. The syndicate gave regular summer seasons, bringing to London all the greatest singers, and let the theatre or acted in association with other companies for autumn seasons. Higgins incurred some displeasure by his insistence on giving opera in its original language on the grounds that to give it in English was financially impractical. He was appointed CVO in 1905.

H. Klein: *The Golden Age of Opera* (London, 1920)
H. V. Higgins: Letters to *The Times* (19 Feb 1924, 23 Feb 1924)
J. D. Chamier: *Percy Pitt of Covent Garden and the BBC* (London, 1938)   FRANCES DONALDSON

Higglety Pigglety Pop! Fantasy opera in one act, op.21, by OLIVER KNUSSEN to a libretto by Maurice Sendak after his book; incomplete version (five scenes), Glyndebourne, 13 October 1984; preliminary version, Glyndebourne, 5 August 1985; definitive version, Los Angeles, Music Center, 5 June 1990.

Sendak's subtitle was 'There Must be More to Life', and his libretto concerns the search of Jennie (mezzo-soprano), a pampered but discontented sealyham terrier who already has 'everything', to discover what this might be. Voraciously in quest of her next meal she encounters a number of animal and human characters (five solo singers) on her travels, including a pig who tells her of the World Mother Goose Theatre, which is looking for a leading lady with experience. Desperate for the job, Jennie seeks experience as nurse to the recalcitrant Baby (soprano) which, in an unthinking act of courage, she protects from a hungry lion by putting her head in its jaws. But ultimately she finds herself alone in a wood with 'nothing' and, apparently, dies. In the highly ambiguous final scenes, she is awakened by the other characters and proclaimed leading lady; they all journey to Castle Yonder and embark upon an endlessly repeating performance of their new production, *Higglety Pigglety Pop!*

Composed in 1984–5 and revised in 1989–90, the opera was conceived as a companion piece, with similar forces, to *Where the Wild Things Are*, although the score is longer, at just over an hour, and more intricately structured; Knussen complements the luminous impressionism of the earlier work with a drier, more parodic manner full of sophisticated allusions from Mozart to Britten, though not lacking in poetic equivalents of the narrative's more troubling undertones. The opera's second interlude was performed as a concert item at the 1988 Aldeburgh Festival, and Knussen has since linked it to the first to make an eight-minute sequence entitled *The Ride to Castle Yonder* (op.21a).
                                         BAYAN NORTHCOTT

Hildesheim. City in northern Germany, in Lower Saxony. The theatre 'Im Sacke', built in 1770, was used for the earliest performances by touring companies. In the 19th century operatic performances were given only sporadically in Hildesheim; for example, in 1838 a performance of Weber's *Der Freischütz* was made possible by the efforts of the Verein der Musikfreunde. In 1870 a new theatre was opened in the former St Paulikirche, which had been renovated, but two years later performances were discontinued owing to the small stage and a lack of interest among the inhabitants of Hildesheim. The Stadttheater opened on 2 October 1909 and was run privately until 1922, when it was taken over by the city. In March 1945 bombing left only the exterior walls standing; in September 1945, however, the first postwar season began in a temporary theatre in the hall of the State Technical Building College. Hildesheim was one of the first German cities to rebuild its theatre after war damage: a new one opened on 10 September 1949 with G. E. Lessing's play, *Nathan der Weise*. The main auditorium seats 673 and the Studio Theatre 99. An orchestra of 31 players and a chorus of 18 perform under the Musical Director Werner Seitzer.   SABINE SONNTAG

Hilgermann, Laura (*b* Vienna, 13 Oct 1867; *d* Vienna, 1937). Austrian contralto and soprano. She studied in Vienna, and in 1885 made her début as Azucena in Prague, where she remained till 1889. For the next decade she sang in Budapest, then in 1900 joined the distinguished company assembled by Mahler at the Vienna Opera, leaving it in 1920. Her wide range and adaptability proved useful: in *Die Walküre* she could sing Sieglinde in one performance and Fricka in the next. Her mezzo roles included Adriano in *Rienzi*, Ortrud and Dorabella, and as a soprano she sang such roles as Countess Almaviva and Elisabeth in *Tannhäuser*. She later taught in Vienna and Budapest, her pupils there including the soprano Gitta Alpar. Her few and early recordings, representative of both her soprano and mezzo roles, suffer from uncertainties of intonation but show the warmth of her tone.
                                            J. B. STEANE

Hill, Aaron (*b* London, 10 Feb 1685; *d* London, ?8 Feb 1750). English playwright and manager. At the age of 24 he was named manager of Drury Lane by William Collier – an astonishing appointment for a theatrical novice. His relations with the actors were predictably stormy, and Hill was forcibly evicted from the theatre in the celebrated riot of June 1710. He bounced back the following season, becoming Collier's manager at the Haymarket. Hill was summarily fired on 3 March 1711, for reasons unknown, but not before he had staged the première of Handel's *Rinaldo* (24 February 1711) – the first Italian opera designed especially for London, and over which the composer himself presided. Hill collaborated on the libretto, although the precise nature of his contribution remains disputed. Whether he actually wrote the libretto in English or designed the plot for Giacomo Rossi and then translated Rossi's libretto is relatively immaterial. In a variety of ways *Rinaldo* shows the influence of English opera traditions, and in particular of George Granville's *The British Enchanters* (1706). The fact that Hill abandoned the world of opera management in 1711 does not lessen the significance of his attempt to meld English and Italian operatic conventions.

In the remaining 39 years of his chequered career Hill dabbled in schemes to sell beech-mast oil and to colonize Georgia; he wrote some innovatory and not very successful plays, including the tragedy *Zara* (1736) set by Arne; and he tried several times to regain a position in theatre management. He also tried journalism, most notably in *The Prompter*, a periodical he produced from 1734 to 1736 with William Popple. His contributions to the theory of acting are among the best in early 18th-century England. The several issues he devoted to Italian opera are exceedingly hostile: he resented the sums paid to castratos and deplored the lack of moral substance in opera. He positively gloated over rumours of the demise of opera in London during 1735–6. Nonetheless, he maintained friendly relations with Handel. In a letter of 5 December 1732 Hill urged Handel 'to deliver us from our *Italian bondage*; and demonstrate, that *English* is soft enough for Opera' – a statement reflecting his oft-expressed conviction that opera should have a moral point and that it should be presented in English.

D. Brewster: *Aaron Hill: Poet, Dramatist, Projector* (New York, 1913)
W. W. Appleton and K. A. Burnim, eds.: *The Prompter: a Theatrical Paper (1734–1736)* (New York, 1966) [selections]
J. Milhous and R. D. Hume, eds.: *Vice Chamberlain Coke's Theatrical Papers, 1706–1715* (Carbondale, IL, 1982)
W. Dean and J. M. Knapp: *Handel's Operas 1704–1726* (Oxford, 1987)
C. Price: 'English Traditions in Handel's *Rinaldo*', *Handel: a Tercentenary Collection*, ed. S. Sadie and A. Hicks (London, 1987), 120–37
J. Milhous and R. D. Hume: 'The Haymarket Opera in 1711', *EMc*, xvii (1989), 523–37
ROBERT D. HUME

Hill, Alfred (Francis) (*b* Melbourne, 16 Nov 1870; *d* Sydney, 30 Oct 1960). Australian composer and conductor. He spent his formative years (from 1872) in New Zealand and established a leading position both there and in Australia as a composer of attractively melodious romantic operas that were quite the equal of those of his European contemporaries. His success in this genre was based on professional training as a violinist and as a composer at the Leipzig Conservatory, 1887–91, during which period he absorbed the music he heard at the Leipzig Opera House, finding a special sympathy with Wagner, after whose characters he named his three children: Isolde, Elsa and Tristan. Hill played the violin in the Leipzig Gewandhaus orchestra under many notable conductors and composers (including Brahms and Tchaikovsky), but, encouraged by his teacher Gustav Schreck, he decided to become a composer.

In 1892 Hill returned to Wellington, where the acclaim which greeted his cantata *Hinemoa* (1896) led him to become absorbed in Maori music and dance. His opera *Tapu, or The Tale of a Maori Pah* describes the improbable escapades of an Australian politician who falls into the hands of the Maori. First performed in Wellington in 1903, it was taken on a successful tour throughout New Zealand by the indigenous Pollard Opera Company. This had been preceded by the apprentice works *The Whipping Boy* (unfinished) and *Lady Dolly*. Hill then turned to a fictional desert world for his comic opera *A Moorish Maid* (1905). Although never revived, the opera is remembered for its association with the New Zealand-born singer Rosina Buckman, whose performance as La Zara, Queen of the Riffs, launched her on an international career. After the

romantic tragic opera *Teora: the Enchanted Flute* (composed 1913), for which he wrote his own libretto, Hill became deeply involved in more eclectic subjects. The romantic comic opera *Giovanni, the Sculptor* was first performed in Sydney on 3 August 1914, shortly before the outbreak of World War I, with Fritz Hart's *Pierrette*. These were the first offerings of the newly formed Opera League, whose aims included the provision of opportunities for Australian composers to write and perform opera on a modest and practical scale. 'We are a musical people: it is in our blood', said Hill (Sydney *Daily Telegraph*, 12 February 1914). The wartime mood and atmosphere brought the enterprise to an end, despite initial success and support from the state, press, leading musicians and a fairly large section of the public. Hill returned to familiar themes in his comic opera *The Rajah of Shivapore* (composed 1913), which was first performed in December 1917 and warmly received.

After the war Hill's remaining two operatic works, *Auster* and *The Ship of Heaven*, seemed survivors from another age. Although the latter contained fresh and charming incidents (Hill told his librettist, the poet and artist Hugh McCrae, that he had composed it in three weeks), it proved impossible to find further backers for such a highly individualistic extravaganza.

Hill's long career embodied a prodigious output and included almost every genre. His talents best expressed themselves in spontaneous, shorter stretches; individual arias in his operas can be telling and expressive, and he could shape a melody with a distinct nostalgic touch of his own. Hill was a child of his age, an indomitable trouper, brought up in the era of travelling opera companies, whose musicians had taught him and with whose orchestras he regularly played. Although his operas now seem beyond revival, their plots and dialogues having become irretrievably dated, individual numbers deserve rediscovery.

The Whipping Boy, 1895 (comic op, A. Adams), inc., unperf.
Lady Dolly, 1898 (romantic comic op, M. Browne), Sydney, 31 March 1900
Tapu, or The Tale of a Maori Pah (romantic op, 2, Adams, rev. J. C. Williamson), Wellington, Opera House, 16 Feb 1903
A Moorish Maid, or The Queen of the Riffs (comic op, 2, J. Y. Burch), Auckland, 26 June 1905
Teora: the Enchanted Flute, 1913 (grand op, 1, Hill), Sydney, 23 March 1929
Giovanni, the Sculptor (romantic comic op, 3, H. Callan), Sydney, 3 Aug 1914
The Rajah of Shivapore, 1913 (comic op, 2, D. Souter), Sydney, 15 Dec 1917
Auster, 1919 (romantic op, 3, E. Congeau), concert perf., Sydney, 31 Aug 1922; stage, Melbourne, 1935
The Ship of Heaven (musical fantasy, 2, H. McCrae), frags., private perf., Sydney, 1923; complete, stage, Sydney, 7 Oct 1933

A. D. McCredie: 'Alfred Hill (1870–1960): Some Backgrounds and Perspectives for an Historical Edition', *MMA*, iii (1968), 181–258
J. M. Thomson: 'The Role of the Pioneer Composer: Some Reflections on Alfred Hill 1870–1960', *SMA*, iv (1970), 52–61
——: *A Distant Music: the Life and Times of Alfred Hill 1870–1960* (Auckland, 1980)
——: *Biographical Dictionary of New Zealand Composers* (Wellington, 1990)
J. Commons: 'The Operas of Alfred Hill', *Opera in New Zealand: Aspects of History and Performance* (Wellington, 1991)
J. M. Thomson: *The Oxford History of New Zealand Music 1840–1990* (Auckland, 1991)
J. M. THOMSON

Hill, Karl (*b* Idstein im Taunus, 9 May 1831; *d* Sachsenberg bei Schwerin, 12 Jan 1893). German baritone. He studied in Frankfurt, making his début in 1868 as Jacob

(Méhul's *Joseph*) at Schwerin, where he was engaged until 1890. He sang Alberich in the first *Ring* cycle, at Bayreuth in 1876, and Klingsor in the first performance of *Parsifal* (1882). His repertory included the Dutchman and Hans Sachs as well as Mozart's Count Almaviva, Don Giovanni and Leporello. Signs of insanity forced him to retire from the opera house.   ELIZABETH FORBES

Hillebrecht, Hildegard (*b* Hanover, 26 Nov 1927). German soprano. She studied in Düsseldorf and made her début in 1951 at Freiburg as Leonora (*Il trovatore*). After engagements at Zürich (where she sang the Daughter in the première of the revised version of *Cardillac*, 1952), Düsseldorf and Cologne, she joined the Bayerische Staatsoper in 1961. At Salzburg (1956–64) she sang Ilia, Ariadne and Chrysothemis, and at San Francisco (1965) Elsa and Ariadne. She also sang at the Deutsche Oper, Berlin, where she created Anticlea in Dallapiccola's *Ulisse* (1968). Her roles included Tosca, Amelia (*Ballo*), Hélène (*Les vêpres siciliennes*), Elisabeth de Valois and Desdemona, as well as Leonore, Senta, Elisabeth, Sieglinde, Jenůfa and Ursula (*Mathis der Maler*). A dignified actress, she had a vibrant, creamy-toned voice, especially well suited to Strauss. Her best roles were the Empress, which she sang at Covent Garden in 1967, the Marschallin, which she sang in Copenhagen (1970), and Ariadne, which she recorded for Böhm. She made her farewell in Munich in 1977 as the Second Norn.   ALAN BLYTH

Hillemacher, Paul (Joseph Guillaume) (*b* Paris, 29 Nov 1852; *d* Versailles, 13 Aug 1933). French composer. He and his brother Lucien (Joseph Edouard) (*b* Paris, 10 June 1860; *d* Paris, 2 June 1909), known as the 'frères Hillemacher', must be unique in the history of opera: two brothers who collaborated in the composition of several successful operas. Questioned about the nature of their collaboration, the brothers revealed that they would each work on the same portion of text, and decide afterwards whose setting was the more successful. It is thus hardly surprising that they were dubbed 'the Goncourts of music'. Paul studied with François Bazin at the Paris Conservatoire and won the Prix de Rome in 1876; Lucien, a pupil of Jules Massenet and a contemporary of Bruneau at the Conservatoire, won the Prix de Rome in 1880. The brothers published under the pen name Paul-Lucien Hillemacher from 1881 to 1909. Their music shows a considerable debt to Wagner, especially in the use of rhythmic and melodic leitmotifs.

Saint-Mégrin is a historical opera set in the 16th century during the reign of Henri III; *Une aventure d'Arlequin* is a light *commedia dell'arte* piece. *Le Drac*, set on the Provençal coast, is the tale of a man with magical powers related to the sea: 'his voice is the thunder, his look, the lightning'; played by a soprano, Le Drac is rival to Bernard (tenor) in his love for Francine (soprano). The work was revived at the Paris Opéra in 1942. *Orsola*, the story of a Grecian princess, is set in the Cyclades during the Venetian and infidel occupations; *Circé*, in which Maggie Teyte created the role of Glycère, is a classical tale set in three distinct tableaux.

printed works published in Paris

Saint-Mégrin (oc, 4, E. Dubreuil and E. Adenis, after A. Dumas *père*: *Henri III et sa cour*), Brussels, Monnaie, 2 March 1886, vs (1887)
Une aventure d'Arlequin (oc, 1, L. Judicis), Brussels, Monnaie, 22 March 1888 (1888)

Le régiment qui passe (oc, 1, M. Hennequin), Royan, 11 Sept 1894
Le Drac (drame lyrique, 3, L. Gallet, after G. Sand and P. Meurice); as Der Flutgeist (trans. E. Klingenfeld), Karlsruhe, 14 Nov 1896, vs (?1896)
Orsola (drame lyrique, 3, P. B. Gheusi), Paris, Opéra, 21 May 1902, vs (1902)
Circé (poème lyrique, 3, E. Haraucourt), Paris, OC (Favart), 17 April 1907, vs (1907)
Fra Angelico (tableau musicale, 1, M. Vaucaine), Paris, 9 June 1924

*

A. Jullien: 'Orsola à l'Opéra', *Le théâtre*, no.83 (1902), 7–8
C. Oulmont: 'G. Hüe, les frères Hillemacher, Roger Ducasse', *Le théâtre lyrique en France* (Paris, 1939), iii, 138–48
          RICHARD LANGHAM SMITH

Hillemacher, Paul-Lucien. Pen name used by PAUL HILLEMACHER and Lucien Hillemacher.

Hiller, Ferdinand (von) (*b* Frankfurt, 24 Oct 1811; *d* Cologne, 11 May 1885). German composer. The son of a wealthy Jewish merchant, he revealed a talent for music at an early age. His principal piano teacher was Alois Schmitt; in 1825–7 he was a pupil of Hummel in Weimar, where he played in concerts at court and at Goethe's home and composed incidental music for the theatres. In 1828 he went to Paris, staying almost seven years; he gave concerts and won praise both as pianist and composer. Berlioz, Chopin and Liszt became his close friends; the older generation, including Mendelssohn, Cherubini and Rossini, gave him encouragement. In 1836 he conducted in Frankfurt and in the following year he went to Italy, but his opera *Romilda*, performed in Milan, was not a success. In 1843–4 he replaced Mendelssohn as conductor of the Leipzig Gewandhaus Orchestra.

In 1844 Hiller was active in Dresden, where he composed two operas; like his next three, they were unsuccessful. His salon was the meeting place for Dresden's intellectual circle. He went to Düsseldorf in 1847 and from 1850 was city Kapellmeister in Cologne. He reorganized the music school, directed the Gürzenich concerts and played an important role in the Rhenish music festivals. He retired in 1884. His successor introduced works by Wagner, Liszt and Richard Strauss, all of whom Hiller had avoided. In his last year he was ennobled.

Hiller was a productive, versatile and cultured composer; however, as Schumann recognized, 'despite mastery of formal techniques' (and occasional originality) his music 'lacked that triumphant power which we are unable to resist'. Even his last two operas, *Die Katakomben* and *Der Deserteur*, are unadventurous in their harmonic vocabulary and structure, consisting of self-contained numbers linked by recitatives. There is also little evidence of Wagner's influence in matters of phrase structure and shaping of the vocal line.

The public rejection of nearly all Hiller's operas (only the serious *Die Katakomben*, in the style of Meyerbeer, was staged in several cities) was a disappointment to him. His lively exchange of letters with the librettist Robert Reinick concerning *Konradin* (on which Eduard Devrient, Schumann and Wagner gave critical advice), regarded as his most dramatically moving, widestranging opera (it is close to Wagner's *Tannhäuser*), shows Hiller's artistic scope and experience in the best light. To Moritz Hartmann, with whom he engaged in an even livelier exchange of ideas about operatic themes and their artistic forms, he wrote: 'My deepest musical desires occur in the striving towards a dramatic poem, where the most genuine people, without aristocratic, historical or even mythological make-up, without pomp of any kind, could sing out, straight from the heart, their suffering and their joy, so pure, true and heartfelt that one could not but be touched and moved'.

Romilda (os, G. Rossi), Milan, Scala, 8 Jan 1839, selections (Milan, c1839)
Der Traum in der Christnacht (3, C. Gollmick, after E. Raupach), Dresden, 9 April 1845 (Leipzig, c1845)
Konradin, der letzte Hohenstaufen (R. Reinick), Dresden, 13 Oct 1847
Der Advokat (komische Oper, 2, R. J. Benedix), Cologne, 21 Dec 1854
Die Katakomben (ernste Oper, 3, M. Hartmann), Wiesbaden, 15 Feb 1862 (Cologne, 1862)
Der Deserteur (komische Oper, 3, E. Pasqué), Cologne, 17 Feb 1865 (Mainz, 1865)

*

MGG (R. Sietz); StiegerO
W. Neumann: 'Ferdinand Hiller', Die Componisten der neueren Zeit, xliii (Kassel, 1857), 69–121
'Dr. Ferdinand von Hiller', Neue Musik-Zeitung, i (1880), no.16, pp.1–2; no.17, p.1
Obituary, Neue Musik-Zeitung, vi (1885), 121
T. Kwast-Hiller: 'Ungedruckte Briefe ein politisches Programm von Ferdinand Hiller', Frankfurter Zeitung, nos.192–5 (1896)
E. Wolff: 'Ferdinand Hiller', NZM, lxxviii (1911), 553–5
R. Sietz, ed.: Aus Ferdinand Hillers Briefwechsel (Cologne, 1958–70)
R. Sietz: Der Nachlass Ferdinand Hillers (Cologne, 1970)
REINHOLD SIETZ/R

Hiller, Friedrich Adam (*b* Leipzig, *c*1767; *d* Königsberg [now Kaliningrad], 23 Nov 1812). German composer, son of J. A. Hiller. He was trained in music by his father and by 1783 had given successful performances in Leipzig. In 1789 he made his stage début in Rostock as Romeo in *Romeo und Julie* (perhaps Georg Benda's setting). In 1790 he was appointed director of a music society in Schwerin, where his incidental music for the allegorical drama *La Biondetta* was enthusiastically received (1792). When the Nationaltheater in Altona was completed (1796) he was summoned as music director of its carefully selected orchestra, and in 1799 he took over the musical direction of the theatre in Königsberg. His vocal works closely resemble his father's. Only a few items survive from his stage works.

Adelstan und Röschen (operetta, 2, J. F. Schink), Güstrow, Rathaus, 6 Sept 1792
Das Nixenreich (3, H. Schmieder), int for Kauer: Das Donauweibchen, Altona, 1801, arias arr. pf (Hamburg, 1802)
Das Schmuckkästchen (Spl, 1, ?E. Jester), Königsberg, 1804
Die drei Sultane [Sultaninen] (Spl, 1, E. Bornschein), Königsberg, 1809
ELLWOOD DERR

Hiller, Johann Adam (*b* Wendisch-Ossig, 25 Dec 1728; *d* Leipzig, 16 June 1804). German composer and writer on music. His father, a schoolmaster, died when his son was only six. His successor taught the boy some rudiments of music, and Hiller may have acquired further training during his five years at the Gymnasium in nearby Görlitz. He attended the Kreuzschule in Dresden on a scholarship and in 1751 entered Leipzig University as a law student. In both cities Hiller participated actively in musical life. The *galant* manner embodied in the serious operas of J. A. Hasse and C. H. Graun, which he experienced first-hand at Dresden, informed his musical taste and remained his musical ideal for the rest of his life. He became a principal preserver and propagator of this ideal among his countrymen, not through direct creative emulation but rather through his enormous organizational talents, through writing, editing and translating, and through his avid interest in pedagogical matters, particularly as they bore on fine singing.

In 1754 Hiller began his first attempt at opera (a setting of Gellert's *Das Orackel*, never completed), published his first piece of musical journalism (an essay on imitation, in Marpurg's *Historisch-kritische Beyträge zur Aufnahme der Musik*), and secured a position in the service of Count Brühl of Dresden. He left this post in 1760 owing to recurrent fits of depression.

After the Seven Years War (1756–63) the theatrical company of Heinrich Gottfried Koch established itself at Leipzig, and Koch lost little time in soliciting the aid of the poet Christian Felix Weisse to update some of the German comic operas his troupe had performed in the 1750s. He also turned to Hiller for new music. In so doing he created German opera's most fruitful and long-lived partnership of the era. Hiller's first operas with Weisse, produced in 1766, were modifications of *Der Teufel ist los* and *Der lustige Schuster*, composed by Johann Standfuss, who based them on ballad operas by Charles Coffey. Weisse, who had spent the war in Paris, adapted the tone and techniques he had grown to admire in *opéra comique* to the German stage. Hiller retained some of Standfuss's numbers, but tempered their unpolished vigour with a simple, tuneful charm derived from Hasse's melodic grace and with a refinement of popular song styles.

At this time Hiller was also busy with the Grosses Concert series at Leipzig, which he had re-established in 1763, and with editing the *Wöchentliche Nachrichten und Anmerkungen die Musik betreffend* (Leipzig, 1766–70). Nonetheless, the instant popularity of his first operas for Koch encouraged him to attempt a more serious German opera based on a medieval tale, *Lisuart und Dariolette* (1766), and a classical afterpiece, *Die Muse* (1767), both with the young poet Daniel Schiebeler; both met with only moderate success. Hiller's next operas, written in collaboration with Weisse, turned directly to French models, especially those embodying Rousseau's vision of uncorrupted rural virtue: the contrast with courtly artificiality of manners is especially strong (and receives musical delineation) in *Lottchen am Hofe* (1767), while rustic innocence is piled high in *Die Liebe auf dem Lande* (1768). A happy synthesis of these tendencies and some of Hiller's finest music appear in the greatest and most enduring of his operas, *Die Jagd*, first performed in early 1770 before the music-loving Duchess Anna Amalia at the Weimar court. The role of music remains somewhat restricted in all these works, owing in part to the indifferent skills of the singers and to Koch's own wishes. Weisse, too, saw German opera as an essentially spoken genre that could also take as its goal 'to introduce the little social song among us'.

In 1773 the Koch company moved permanently from Leipzig to Berlin, and with *Die Jubelhochzeit* of that year Weisse and Hiller concluded their association with the troupe. Other composers in northern and central Germany were now closely following the model for German opera they had created. Hiller himself had guided the first operatic efforts of younger composers such as C. G. Neefe (who contributed music to Hiller's *Der Dorfbalbier* of 1771) and J. F. Reichardt. During the 1770s Anton Schweitzer and Georg Benda deepened and broadened the scope of German opera as superior singers emerged and court sponsorship increased. Hiller participated little in this development. He added a few numbers to the two-act version of Benda's *Der Jahrmarkt* in 1775, and later that year tentatively agreed to serve as music director of the estimable theatrical company of Abel Seyler, active in Leipzig and Dresden; but after an immediate falling out with Seyler he turned these duties over to his protégé Neefe.

Thereafter Hiller directed his energies chiefly towards concerts, teaching and church duties. The few operas he completed after 1775 were clearly secondary projects and are retrospective in style. *Poltis*, begun in 1773, was not performed until 1777; *Das Grab des Mufti*, begun for Seyler in 1776, received its première only three years later. Hiller collaborated with his old friend Weisse on a one-act children's operetta, *Die kleine Ährenleserinn*, in 1778, but a second such project, *Das Denkmal in Arkadien*, if it was ever completed, has not been traced.

In his analysis of *Die Jagd* in *Über die deutsche comische Oper* (1774), the young J. F. Reichardt summed up aptly Hiller's contribution to German opera: 'He knew French and Italian comic opera; he took from them what pleased him, rejected what was unfit, and created a form that was closer to Nature and to our language, but more especially one that was necessary owing to our wretched singers'. Reichardt further remarks on Hiller's unique handling of aria form and his superior powers of characterization. German audiences and critics agreed; during the decade after 1766 Hiller's operas competed with and often supplanted the best *opéras comiques* on most German stages, and several remained in repertories to the end of the century, by which time their modest musical dimensions stood in sharp contrast to prevailing styles everywhere in Germany. Their continued favour depended not just on a nationalistic sense of nostalgia and the direct appeal of his music, but also on the strength of Weisse's librettos as independent dramas (they were in fact occasionally performed without music).

Hiller worked all his operatic life within simple dimensions. In his arias and ensembles he observed a strict protocol of moderation. On the one hand, excess of vocal artifice was ruled out by the capabilities of his executants, and on the other, the moral temper of Weisse's texts did not allow the grotesque or exaggerated. Yet within these bounds the stock characters are artfully fleshed out by the expressive aptness of the music. Hiller was the first great practitioner of the operatic *Romanze* in Germany, and many of his numbers in this narrative genre became and remain virtual folksongs in German popular culture. While his other simple, multi-strophic lieder often deal in little more than homiletic asides, his more ambitious arias are always dramatically relevant. His ensembles, too, always reflect the dramatic situation, although they are modest in dimensions and very seldom advance the plot.

Hiller's writings reveal a sound, well-trained musical mind but also very traditional tastes (he, like many other North German musicians, had no enthusiasm for Gluck's reform operas). Although the limitations Weisse, Koch and German singers imposed on him seriously circumscribed his Hasse-like ideals for German opera, he did little to escape these constraints. In the end, it was the absence of a strong native operatic tradition in Germany that decisively conditioned his development.

See also JAGD, DIE; LISUART UND DARIOLETTE; LOTTCHEN AM HOFE; and VERWANDELTEN WEIBER, DIE; for illustration see LEIPZIG, fig.1.

first performed at Rannstädter Thore, Leipzig, unless otherwise stated

Die verwandelten Weiber, oder Der Teufel ist los, erster Theil (comische Oper, 3, C. F. Weisse, after C. Coffey: *The Devil to Pay, or The Wives Metamorphos'd* and M.-J. Sedaine: *Le diable à quatre*), Leipzig, Quandt's Court, 28 May 1766, *D-Mbs, RU-KAu*, vs (Leipzig, 1770) [12 of 36 nos. by J. Standfuss]

Der lustige Schuster, oder Der Teufel ist los, zweyter Theil (comische Oper, 3, Weisse, after Coffey: *The Merry Cobler*), 1766, vs (Leipzig, 1771) [32 of 39 numbers by J. Standfuss]

Lisuart und Dariolette, oder Die Frage und die Antwort (romantisch-comische Oper, 2, D. Schiebeler, after C.-S. Favart: *La fée Urgèle*), 25 Nov 1766; rev. in 3 acts, 7 Jan 1767, *B-Bc, D-B, W, RU-KAu, US-Wc*, vs (Leipzig, 1768)

Lottchen am Hofe (comische Oper, 3, Weisse, after Favart: *Le caprice amoureux, ou Ninette à la cour*), 24 April 1767, *CH-Zz* (pts), *D-B, Mbs, US-Wc*, vs (Leipzig, 1769)

Die Muse (Nachspiel, 1, Schiebeler), 3 Oct 1767, *Bp*, vs (Leipzig, 1771)

Die Liebe auf dem Lande (comische Oper, 3, Weisse, after Favart: *Annette et Lubin* [Acts 1, 3] and L. Anseaume: *La clochette* [Act 2]), 18 May 1768, *D-LEm, Rtt*, vs (Leipzig, 1769)

Die Jagd (comische Oper, 3, Weisse, after C. Collé: *La partie de chasse de Henri IV* and Sedaine: *Le roi et le fermier*), Weimar, Kleines Schloss, 29 Jan 1770, *CH- Zz* (pts), *D-B, Dlb, US-Wc*, vs (Leipzig, 1771)

Der Dorfbalbier (comische Operette, 1, Weisse, after Sedaine: *Blaise le savetier*), 18 April 1771; rev. in 2 acts, 1 Aug 1771, *B-Bc*, vs (Leipzig, 1771) [10 of 23 nos. by C. G. Neefe]

Der Aerndtekranz (comische Oper, 3, Weisse), April/May 1771, *A-Wn, D-B, US-Wc*, vs (Leipzig, 1772)

Der Krieg (comische Oper, 3, Weisse and C. W. Ramler, after C. Goldoni: *La guerra*), Berlin, Behrenstrasse, 17 Aug 1772, vs (Leipzig, 1773)

Die Jubelhochzeit (comische Oper, 3, Weisse), Berlin, Behrenstrasse, 5 April 1773, *D-Dl*, vs (Leipzig, 1773)

Poltis, oder Das gerettete Troja (Operette, 3, G. S. Brunner and Magister Steinel), 1777, vs (Leipzig, 1782)

Die kleine Ährenleserinn (Operette für Kinder, 1, Weisse), unperf., *A-Wn*, vs (Leipzig, 1778)

Das Grab des Mufti, oder Die zwey Geizigen (comische Oper, 2, A. G. Meissner, after F. de Falbaire: *Les deux avares*), 17 Jan 1779, vs (Leipzig, 1779)

Das Denkmal in Arkadien (ländliches Schauspiel für die Jugend mit untermischten Gesängen, 1, Weisse, after G. Keate: *The Monument in Arcadia*), lost

*

J. F. Reichardt: *Über die deutsche comische Oper* (Hamburg, 1774)

J. F. Schink: 'Die Jagd', *Dramaturgische Monate*, iii (Schwerin, 1789), 653–63

K. Peiser: *Johann Adam Hiller* (Leipzig, 1894)

G. Calmus: *Die ersten deutschen Singspiele von Standfuss und Hiller* (Leipzig, 1908)

L. Schiedermair: *Die deutsche Oper* (Leipzig, 1930; 2/1940)

G. Sander: *Das Deutschtum im Singspiel Johann Adam Hillers* (diss., U. of Berlin, 1943)

K. Kawada: *Studien zu den Singspielen von Johann Adam Hiller (1728–1804)* (Marburg, 1969)

T. Bauman: *North German Opera in the Age of Goethe* (Cambridge, 1985)

THOMAS BAUMAN

Hiller, Lejaren (Arthur, jr) (*b* New York, 23 Feb 1924). American composer. Renowned as an innovator in computer music, he has also composed a great many theatre works, few of which employ computers in any capacity. He learnt the piano, clarinet and saxophone during his adventurous and bohemian childhood (which included travel to the USSR and a run-in with Mexican bandits), and had ample opportunity to observe the elaborately staged *tableaux-vivants* favoured by his father, a photographer. From these he acquired a sense of theatre-as-tableau that may be detected in all his work for the stage. Though he had begun composing at school, he studied chemistry at Princeton (PhD 1947), where he also had composition lessons with Roger Sessions and Milton Babbitt; he continued to compose while working as a research chemist. In 1952 he became a chemistry research associate at the University of Illinois, Urbana-Champaign. His work with computers soon led to musical experiments, and in 1956 he produced the first computer composition. His sudden fame in this area coincided with a permanent shift to music as a career; he moved to the university's music department and set up an electronic music studio there. From 1968 until his retirement in 1989 he taught at the State University of New York at Buffalo.

As a composer Hiller has remained a determined eclectic, his work at all times characterized by an Ivesian humour and density of incident. His theatrical works range from incidental music and a film score to multimedia extravaganzas, including *HPSCHD* (1968), and the fully staged melodramas *Ponteach* (1977) and *John Italus* (1989), but have only accidentally entered the realm of opera. Both *The Birds* (Urbana, Illinois, University Theater, 12 March 1958) and *Chang Fu, the Witch of Moon Mountain* (W. Smalley; Austin, University of Texas, 29 November 1982) lie on the border between opera and incidental music, each containing about 30 minutes of music in a 90-minute work – music demanding enough to require performers who are primarily musicians rather than actors. *The Birds* is a 'musical' in two acts in modified Broadway idiom, while *Chang Fu*, a 'fantasy for young people in the tradition of ancient Chinese theater', is based on Beijing Opera models and reveals the influence of Lou Harrison.

See also BIRDS, THE.

*

EwenD; VintonD
'Lejaren Hiller', *Compositores de América/Composers of the Americas*, xviii (1972), 33–45
C. Gagne and T. Caras: *Soundpieces: Interviews with American Composers* (Metuchen, NJ, 1982)　　ANDREW STILLER

Hill Smith, Marilyn (*b* Carshalton, Surrey, 9 Feb 1952). English soprano. After studying at the Guildhall School, in 1978 she joined the ENO, for which her roles have included Adele, Despina, Blonde, Susanna, Olympia, Zerbinetta, Fiakermilli, Thérèse (*Les mamelles de Tirésias*), and Venus and Chief of Secret Police in the British première of *Le Grand Macabre* (1982). She made her Covent Garden début in 1981 as First Niece in *Peter Grimes*. She sang Musetta and Konstanze for the WNO, Angèle (*Der Graf von Luxemburg*) and Countess Maritza for New Sadler's Wells Opera and Cunegonde (*Candide*) for Scottish Opera. Her bright, flexible voice and charming appearance are perfect for operetta, and she has also sung Handel roles, particularly light and florid ones, with success.　　ELIZABETH FORBES

Hilverding [Hilferding] **van Wewen, Franz** (**Anton Christoph**) (bap. Vienna, 17 Nov 1710; *d* Vienna, 30 May 1768). Austrian dancer, choreographer and impresario. His principal training, at the emperor's expense, was with the dancer Blondy in Paris during the mid-1730s. While there he probably witnessed performances of Fuzelier and Rameau's *opéra-ballet Les Indes galantes*, an entrée of which, 'Le Turc généreux', he later imitated in a pantomime ballet. By 1737 he was engaged as a dancer at the Habsburg court, where he soon began composing ballets, and dances for operas, alongside Alexander and Franz Anton Phillebois. Following the Viennese theatres' reorganization under court control in 1752, Hilverding was named choreographer for both the German and French theatres, with responsibility also for Italian operas; Joseph Starzer composed the music. In the Italian manner, Hilverding's ballets for *opere serie* were often unrelated to the main

plot, but some were linked, as with the 'conflagration' in Adolfati's *La clemenza di Tito* (1753) and the dances in Gluck's *L'innocenza giustificata* (1755).

It was Hilverding's independent pantomime ballets that most impressed his contemporaries. Arteaga, writing much later, mentions danced versions of plays by Racine, Crébillon and Voltaire given about 1740, of which no trace remains today. More reliably, his pupil Angiolini describes a long process of reflection and experimentation (begun during the theatrical inactivity following the death of Charles VI), by which Hilverding purged ballet of trivial and licentious elements, and by 1752 arrived at 'complete pantomimic action[s] with a beginning, a middle and an end'. One ballet of that year was *Psiché et l'Amour*, the *merveilleux* of which was expressly linked to French operatic practice in the 1757 *Répertoire* of Viennese theatre offerings. Hilverding, whom the *Journal encyclopédique* described as equally gifted in comic and serious dancing, composed literally hundreds of ballets during this period, depicting mainly artisans and peasants in works for the German theatre, mainly mythological and newly invented subjects for the French. Two of his best-known works, *Pygmalion* and *Le Turc généreux* (for illustration *see* ORCHESTRA, fig.8), date from 1758, towards the end of which year he was called to the Russian court at St Petersburg, where Starzer soon followed. There they revived some of their Viennese works and created several new pantomime ballets and ballets for Italian operas. Hilverding was succeeded in the Burgtheater by Angiolini, who over the next several years, in collaboration with Ranieri de' Calzabigi, produced a series of major dance dramas (to music by Gluck) informed by their knowledge of ancient pantomime. Hilverding worked alongside his former pupil following his return to Vienna in 1764, but in a more pastoral, allegorical vein. After the *Hoftrauer* for Emperor Francis Stephen (*d* 18 August 1765), Hilverding served briefly as the lessee of the Kärntnertortheater, but retired in 1767 because of ill health. His successor as impresario, Giuseppe d'Afflisio, in that year inaugurated a new era of Viennese ballet by hiring the reformist choreographer (and rival of Angiolini) Jean-Georges Noverre.

Hilverding left no theoretical writings, nor, according to Angiolini, was he in the habit of writing programmes. But some of his precepts (e.g. thorough integration of pantomime and dance) are evident in descriptions of his ballets by journalists, and in in-house scenarios prepared by Durazzo's chronicler Philipp Gumpenhuber. Hilverding's mature works share with reform operas of Gluck a concern for dramatic continuity (at its most pronounced in finales), a subservience of technical display to expression, and a seriousness of approach – even to the point of ending tragically. His superiority over other ballet-masters of his time (many of whom imitated his work) is traceable in part to his high culture; he was well versed in literature, and a capable draughtsman and composer of music.

Ballets in (given in Vienna unless otherwise stated): La fedeltà sin alla morte, 1742; Hasse: Ipermestra, 1744; Gluck: La Semiramide riconosciuta, 1748; Hasse: Leucippo, 1748; Bernasconi and Jommelli: Ezio, 1749; Wagenseil and others: Euridice, 1750; Wagenseil and others: L'Armida placata, 1750; Perez: Vologeso, 1750; Wagenseil: Vincislao, 1750; Adolfati: La clemenza di Tito, 1753; Gluck: La danza, 1755; Favart: Les amours de Bastien et Bastienne, 1755; Wagenseil: Le cacciatrici amanti, 1755; Favart: La vengeance inutile, 1755; Gluck: L'innocenza giustificata, 1755; Favart: Tircis et Doristée, 1756; Reutter: L'amor prigionero, 1756; A. Bret: Le déguisement pastoral, 1756; Gluck: Il re pastore, 1756; Gluck: La fausse esclave, 1758; Gluck: Le monde renversé, 1758; Starzer and Raupach: Pribezhishche dobrodeteli [L'asile de la vertu], St Petersburg, 1759; Raupach: Siroe, St Petersburg, 1760; V. Manfredini: L'Olimpiade, Moscow, 1762; Manfredini: Carlo Magno, St Petersburg, 1763; Gassmann: Il trionfo d'Amore, 1765; Gassmann: L'Olimpiade, 1765; Hasse: Partenope, Innsbruck, 1765

*

Reports from Vienna in *Journal encyclopédique* (Jan 1756–Dec 1759)

Répertoire des théâtres de la ville de Vienne depuis l'année 1752 à l'année 1757 (Vienna, 1757)

J. von Stählin: 'Nachrichten von der Musik in Russland', *Beylagen zum neuveränderten Russland*, ed. J. J. Haigold [A. L. von Schlözer] (Riga and Leipzig, 1769–70)

G. Angiolini: *Lettere … a Monsieur Noverre sopra i balli pantomimi* (Milan, 1773)

——: *Riflessioni sopra l'uso dei programmi nei balli pantomimi* (Milan, 1775)

S. Arteaga: *Le rivoluzioni del teatro musicale italiano* (Bologna, 1783–8)

R. Haas: 'Die Wiener Ballet-Pantomime im 18. Jahrhundert und Glucks Don Juan', *SMw*, x (1923), 6–36

——: *Gluck und Durazzo im Burgtheater* (Vienna, 1925)

——: 'Der Wiener Bühnentanz von 1740 bis 1767', *JbMP 1937*, 77–93

A. Michel: 'Two Great XVIII Century Ballet Masters, Jean-Baptiste de Hesse and Franz Hilverding: *La guinguette* and *Le turc généreux* seen by G. de St. Aubin and Canaletto', *Gazette des beaux-arts* (1944–5), 271–86

R.-A. Mooser: *Opéras, intermezzos, ballets, cantates, oratorios joués en Russie durant le XVIIIe siècle* (Basle, 1945, 3/1964)

——: *Annales de la musique et des musiciens en Russie au XVIIIe siècle* (Geneva, 1948–51)

M. H. Winter: *The Pre-Romantic Ballet* (London, 1974)

B. A. Brown: *Gluck and the French Theatre in Vienna* (Oxford, 1991)

BRUCE ALAN BROWN

Himmel, Friedrich Heinrich (*b* Treuenbrietzen, 20 Nov 1765; *d* Berlin, 8 June 1814). German composer. Together with Seidel he received his first instruction from Klaus, the organist in Treuenbrietzen. In 1785 he began studying theology in Halle, but from 1786 he devoted himself entirely to music. Friedrich Wilhelm II gave him a year's salary and permission to study with J. G. Naumann in Dresden. After Himmel's return the king appointed him chamber composer and financed a journey to Italy, which Himmel probably began in spring 1793. In 1794 his pastorale *Il primo navigatore* was performed in Venice and on 12 January 1795 *La morte di Semiramide* (probably composed in Germany) was performed in Naples for the birthday of Ferdinand IV. Himmel travelled on to Sicily, but returned to Berlin when he was made royal Kapellmeister in place of Reichardt, who had fallen into disfavour. In spring 1795 music from *Semiramide* were performed in Berlin. A cantata for the wedding of Princess Auguste of Prussia and the Prince Elector of Hesse in February 1797 was followed closely by another performance of the opera.

Himmel's plan to revive German opera in Berlin in collaboration with the actor, theatre director and dramatist A. W. Iffland did not interest the court. Financial difficulties forced him to travel to the courts of Russia, Denmark and Sweden, beginning in July 1797. *Alessandro* had its first performance in St Petersburg at the beginning of 1799. The journey was a financial and artistic success and Himmel was back in Berlin in January 1800. *Semiramide* was performed again on 12 January, cut by one and a half hours but still widely thought too long. By February he was in Hamburg with Reichardt and Righini, and from March to May 1800 in Dresden with Naumann. *Vasco da Gama* was performed on 12 January 1801 in Berlin; the rivalry

with Reichardt's *Rosmonda*, which followed on 6 February 1801, led to a dispute similar to that between Piccinni's and Gluck's followers in Paris, with Himmel as a representative of the neo-Neapolitan school and Reichardt as a defender of Gluck's principles attacking each other, not without personal animosity. After further concert tours Himmel's Singspiel *Fanchon das Leyermädchen* (1804) achieved a triumphant, lasting success far exceeding that of the Liederspiel *Frohsinn und Schwärmerey* (1801) or the opera *Die Sylphen* (1806). He made further journeys to (among other places) Munich, Leipzig and Rome before returning to the Prussian court (then at Königsberg). His last opera, *Der Kobold*, was performed in Vienna in 1813 and in Berlin on 23 March 1814. Ten weeks later Himmel died, of dropsy.

Throughout his career Himmel enjoyed the favour of the Prussian royal family, although his improprieties and requests for financial support often taxed their goodwill. He was on friendly terms with Prince Louis Ferdinand, at whose residence he first met J. L. Dussek (later to be his close friend). The Privy Chamberlain Rietz, whose wife was the mistress of Friedrich Wilhelm II, was also an influential patron. According to Rellstab, in the 1790s Himmel was 'decidedly a representative of the modern age: elegantly dressed, lightly powdered, somewhat portly but very agile, red-cheeked, his delicate white hands covered with splendid rings'. Either his ability as a Kapellmeister was limited or it too often deteriorated under the influence of champagne; during rehearsals for *Semiramide* in 1800, the director of the court theatre requested the king to remove this 'partly drunken and partly demented man' from the theatre, especially as his opera could be produced perfectly well without his assistance. This was probably part of an intrigue which failed: after Friedrich Wilhelm II's death Himmel retained favour with the new king, and he could always rely on royal understanding.

Apart from *Fanchon*, which was performed repeatedly in Berlin up to 1853, Himmel's works were soon forgotten. His Italian operas are of the neo-Neapolitan school, but he surpassed their modifications of the Metastasian opera by incorporating melodrama, then very new. Some of his German stage works are offshoots of Reichardt's Liederspiel (*Frohsinn und Schwärmerey*) or the Singspiel in the style of Hiller with influence from Italian *opera buffa* (*Fanchon*). *Die Sylphen*, however, has been described as a forerunner of *Der Freischütz* and 'a fully developed monument of Berlin early Romanticism' (Moser, Bücken); it has also been speculated that it represents – or at least is a notable part of a general trend that does so – the beginnings of the rise of German Romanticism from 18th-century tradition and practice, with its anticipation of many of E. T. A. Hoffmann's ideas on the role of the marvellous world of the spirits, as stated in *Der Dichter und der Komponist* (1813; it is significant that Himmel's libretto draws on Gozzi, an author whom Hoffmann himself was to recommend as an ideal source for the Romantic spirit).

Il primo navigatore (pastorale, A. S. Sografi), Venice, Fenice, 1 March 1794, frags. *D-Mbs*

La morte di Semiramide [Sémiramis] (os, 2, ?P. Giovannini or A. di Benedetto, after Voltaire), Naples, S Carlo, 12 Jan 1795, *Bds*, *Dlb*

Alessandro (os, 2, F. Moretti), St Petersburg, Hermitage, Jan 1799, *Dlb*

Vasco da Gama (os, 3, A. de Filistri), Berlin, Kgl, 12 Jan 1801, *Bds*

Frohsinn und Schwärmerey (Liederspiel, 1, C. A. Herklots), Berlin, National, 9 March 1801, *Bds*, *Mbs*

Fanchon das Leyermädchen (Spl, 3, A. von Kotzebue, after Fr. vaudeville), Berlin, National, 16 May 1804, *A-Wn*, *D-Bds*; vs (Leipzig, ?1805), ov. (Offenbach, ?1811)

Die Sylphen (Zauberoper, 3, L. Robert [M. Levin], after C. Gozzi: *La donna serpente*), Berlin, National, 14 April 1806; (Mainz, n.d.), ov. as op.22 (Leipzig, 1807)

Der Kobold (komische Oper, 4, after F. W. Gotter), Vienna, An der Wien, 22 May 1813, *Bds*; vs (Vienna, n.d.)

*

J. E. F. Arnold: 'Friedrich Heinrich Himmel: seine kurze Biographie und ästhetische Darstellung seiner Werke', *Gallerie der berühmtesten Tonkünstler des 18. und 19. Jahrhunderts*, ii/5 (Erfurt, 1810)

E. T. A. Hoffmann: 'Der Opern Almanach des Hrn. A. v. Kotzebue', (Leipzig, 1814), *AMZ*, xvi (1814), cols.720–21, 735–41

L. Rellstab: *Aus meinem Leben* (Berlin, 1861)

M. Steuer: 'Die Erstaufführung von Himmels "Fanchon": ein Gedenkblatt zum 16. Mai', *Signale für die Musikalische Welt*, lxii (1904), 580–81

A. Weissmann: *Berlin als Musikstadt* (Berlin, 1911)

A. Kohut: 'Friedrich Heinrich Himmel (ein Gedenkblatt zu seinem 100. Todestage, 8. Juni)', *NZM*, Jg.81 (1914), 344–7

L. Odendahl: *Friedrich Heinrich Himmel: Bemerkungen zur Geschichte der Berliner Oper um die Wende des 18. und 19. Jahrhunderts* (diss., Bonn U., 1914; excerpts, Bonn, 1917)

H. J. Moser: *Geschichte der deutschen Musik* (Stuttgart and Berlin, 1920–24), ii/1, 393; ii/2, 78

E. Bücken: *Die Musik des 19. Jahrhunderts bis zur Moderne* (Potsdam, 1928), 59

V. Reising: *Phantastische Gestalten in der deutschen Oper von 1790 bis 1840* (diss., Berlin U., 1975)

A. S. Garlington jr: 'German Romantic Opera and the Problem of Origins', *MQ*, lxiii (1977), 242–60   GERHARD ALLROGGEN

Hinckley, Allen C(arter) (*b* Gloucester, MA, 11 Oct 1877; *d* Yonkers, NY, 28 Jan 1954). American bass. He studied in New York and then with Siegfried Wagner at Bayreuth, and made his début in 1903 at Hamburg as King Henry (*Lohengrin*). He first sang at Covent Garden in 1904, taking the roles of Pogner, King Mark and the Landgrave, and returned in 1907 and 1910. At Bayreuth he sang Hagen in 1906 and Hunding and King Henry in 1908; 1908 was also the year of his début at the Metropolitan Opera, where he sang until 1914. Although his dark-coloured voice was particularly suited to the operas of Wagner, he also sang other roles, including Rocco, Caspar and Tommaso (*Tiefland*).

ELIZABETH FORBES

Hindemith, Paul (*b* Hanau, nr Frankfurt, 16 Nov 1895; *d* Frankfurt, 28 Dec 1963). German composer. He was born into a poor family, and it was through his precocious talent as a violinist that Hindemith gained his musical education. He attended the Hoch Conservatory in Frankfurt as a scholarship pupil from 1909 to 1917, and in 1915 joined the orchestra of the Frankfurt Opera, with which he remained until 1923. After his father's death in 1915, he supplemented the family income with private teaching and by playing in taverns and cinemas. This practical approach to music-making remained with him throughout his life; besides his composing, he performed as a solo violist or in various chamber music ensembles, organized music festivals in Donaueschingen and Baden-Baden (1923–9), taught at the Hochschule für Musik, Berlin (1927–38), Yale University (1940–53) and Zürich University (1951–56), and in 1953 began a new career as orchestral conductor. He also spent three years (1935–7) organizing musical life in Turkey.

Though most of his music was written for concert performance, Hindemith was no less interested in dramatic genres. His years of service in the Frankfurt Opera orchestra aroused in him the ambition to develop an operatic form more in keeping with modern times than the post-Wagnerian Romanticism of his older contemporaries, and his first operatic works were one-act structures based on expressionist texts. Though later disowned by Hindemith, these operas made a strong impression when first produced (*Mörder, Hoffnung der Frauen* and *Das Nusch-Nuschi* in Stuttgart in 1921, *Sancta Susanna* in Frankfurt, 1922); indeed an irreverent quotation from Wagner's *Tristan und Isolde* in *Das Nusch-Nuschi* and the erotic subject of *Sancta Susanna* provoked some scandal.

Music for a children's play, *Tuttifäntchen*, and a short dance-pantomime, *Der Dämon* (both 1922), preceded his first full-length opera, *Cardillac* (1926), in which Ferdinand Lion's economical libretto enabled him to design his music in a series of tightly controlled, mainly polyphonic numbers in the Handelian tradition. This became the musical pattern for all his subsequent operas, though it was not always so rigorously applied.

Hindemith had provided evidence before *Cardillac* (notably in his 1923 song cycle *Das Marienleben*) of a deepening seriousness of purpose, but this had not lessened his interest in experiment. The theme of the 1926 Donaueschingen Festival was mechanical music, and for Oskar Schlemmer's *Das triadische Ballett* he devised a score which he punched directly on to paper rolls for player piano. Several film scores for mechanical instruments were composed in this and the following year. For the 1927 Baden-Baden Festival he devised a series of 'miniature operas', his own contribution being *Hin und zurück*.

The comic *Neues vom Tage* (1929) represented a return to his earlier iconoclastic period, with its broad satire on modern social behaviour and its soprano heroine singing in her bath. By this time he had reached a new stage in his development based on a desire to widen public interest, and above all active participation, in contemporary music. The music of this period (1927–32), labelled *Gebrauchsmusik*, is more aptly characterized by the title he gave to a series of pieces for amateurs, *Sing- und Spielmusik* ('Music to Sing and Play'). To this category belong *Lehrstück* (1929) and *Wir bauen eine Stadt* (1930), a small-scale children's opera written in close cooperation with schoolchildren in Berlin.

When the Nazis came to power in Germany in 1933 Hindemith found himself under suspicion for the 'decadence' of his early work (Hitler himself had once been shocked by the sight of a naked soprano in her bath in *Neues vom Tage*). His own feelings about the responsibilities of an artist in times of political upheaval were an important factor in drawing his attention to the German painter Matthias Grünewald, who lived in the 16th century at the time of the Peasants' War, and who became the subject of Hindemith's next opera, *Mathis der Maler*. He wrote the libretto himself, relishing the opportunity of fitting the words to the music and not the other way round. The *Mathis der Maler* Symphony (1934) was completed well in advance of the opera on which it is based. He completed that in 1935, having written some of the scenes out of order. It is Hindemith's operatic masterpiece and is notable not only for the humanity of its characters (as distinct from the 'types' of his previous operas) but also for its use of folk music and church chorales, the importance of which he had come to recognize in his *Sing- und Spielmusik* period. Early church music also had an influence on the full-length ballet he wrote for Léonide

Massine, *Nobilissima visione*, based on the life of St Francis of Assisi (1938).

Hindemith's emigration to the USA in 1940 virtually put a halt to his operatic output owing to the lack of production possibilities, though he had worked on the text of an opera about the astronomer Johannes Kepler before he left Europe. Instead he turned his attention to ballet. Initially he had scant success and the only work to reach the stage during the war years was *Hérodiade*, written in 1943 for Martha Graham. *Die vier Temperamente*, commissioned by George Balanchine and first performed in the concert hall in 1944, was not staged until 1946. Hindemith's operatic activity in these years was confined to 'an attempt at a reconstruction of the first performance of Monteverdi's *Orfeo*', given with and for members of the music school at Yale University in 1943. With some changes in the orchestration, it was first performed (in a concert version) in Vienna in 1954.

During one of his annual visits to Europe, Hindemith decided, after seeing a performance in Venice, to revise *Cardillac* drastically (1952), subsequently wishing this new version to be regarded as definitive (a request posterity has preferred to ignore). A less radical revision of *Neues vom Tage* followed in 1954. Meanwhile, his Kepler opera, *Die Harmonie der Welt*, still languished in neglect, though he had assembled sufficient musical ideas for it to make a symphony (as with *Mathis der Maler*), which was first performed in Basle in 1952. He did not apply himself fully to the opera until 1956, by which time he had returned from the USA to settle in Blonay, Switzerland. Illness and conducting engagements hampered his work, and the opera was completed only ten weeks before the Munich première (1957). It was an immensely ambitious project, in which Hindemith's recurring theme of the artist's responsibility to the world in which he lives (as in *Cardillac* and *Mathis der Maler*) is taken into mystical spheres, though it undoubtedly suffered from the haste with which it was written and staged.

Hindemith's last opera, *The Long Christmas Dinner* (1961), a gentle saga of an American family seen over a period of 90 years, was clearly conceived as a graceful tribute to the country in which he had spent his years of exile.

See also CARDILLAC; HARMONIE DER WELT, DIE; HIN UND ZURÜCK; LEHRSTÜCK; LONG CHRISTMAS DINNER, THE; MATHIS DER MALER; MÖRDER, HOFFNUNG DER FRAUEN; NEUES VOM TAGE; NUSCH-NUSCHI, DAS; and SANCTA SUSANNA.

Edition: *P. Hindemith: Sämtliche Werke*, ed. K. von Fischer and L. Finscher, i: Bühnenwerke (Mainz, 1979–) [H]

printed scores published in Mainz

Mörder, Hoffnung der Frauen op.12, 1919 (1, O. Kokoschka), Stuttgart, Landes, 4 June 1921 (1921), H i/1

Das Nusch-Nuschi op.20 (1, F. Blei), Stuttgart, Landes, 4 June 1921 (1921), H i/2

Sancta Susanna op.21 (1, A. Stramm), Frankfurt, Opernhaus, 26 March 1922 (1921), H i/3

Cardillac op.39 (3, F. Lion, after E. T. A. Hoffmann: *Das Fräulein von Scuderi*), Dresden, Staatsoper, 9 Nov 1926 (1926), H i/4; rev. version (4, Hindemith, after Lion), Zürich, Stadt, 20 June 1952 (1953)

Hin und zurück op.45a (Sketch mit Musik, 1, M. Schiffer), Baden-Baden, 15 July 1927 (1927), H i/6

Neues vom Tage (lustige Oper, 3 pts, Schiffer), Berlin, Kroll, 8 June 1929 (1929); rev. version (2, Hindemith, after Schiffer), Naples, S Carlo, 7 April 1954, vs (1954)

Lehrstück (music theatre work, B. Brecht), Baden-Baden, 28 July 1929 (1929), H i/6

Wir bauen eine Stadt (Spiel für Kinder, R. Seitz), Berlin, 21 June 1930 (1930)

Mathis der Maler, 1933–5 (7 scenes, Hindemith), Zürich, Stadt, 28 May 1938 (1937) [sym. Mathis der Maler, 1934, drawn from material in the opera]

Die Harmonie der Welt (5, Hindemith), Munich, Prinzregent, 11 Aug 1957 (1959) [sym. Die Harmonie der Welt, 1952, drawn from material in the opera]

The Long Christmas Dinner (1, T. Wilder), as Der lange Weihnachtsmahl (Ger. trans. Hindemith), Mannheim, National, 17 Dec 1961, vs (1961), H i/11

F. Willms: *Führer zur Opera Cardillac von Paul Hindemith* (Mainz, 1926)

F. Lion: 'Cardillac I and II', *Akzente*, iv (1957), 126–32

H. L. Schilling: *Paul Hindemiths Cardillac* (Würzburg, 1962)

F. Wöhlke: '*Mathis der Maler' von Paul Hindemith* (Berlin, 1965)

I. Kemp: *Hindemith* (London, 1970)

A. Briner: *Paul Hindemith* (Zürich and Mainz, 1971)

A. Zabrsa: 'Hindemiths Opernprojekte', *Hindemith-Jb*, i (1971), 42–62

E. Padmore: 'Hindemith and Grünewald', *MR*, xxxiii (1972), 190–93

A. Briner: 'Die erste Textfassung von Paul Hindemiths Oper "Die Harmonie der Welt"', *Festschrift für einen Verleger: Ludwig Strecker* (Mainz, 1973), 203–41

G. Skelton: *Paul Hindemith: the Man behind the Music* (London, 1975)

J. E. Paulding: 'Mathis der Maler – the Politics of Music', *Hindemith-Jb*, v (1976), 102–22

N. J. Schneider: 'Prinzipien der rhythmischen Gestaltung in Hindemiths Oper *Mathis der Maler*', *Hindemith-Jb*, viii (1979), 7–48

C. M. Zenck: 'Zwischen Boykott und Anpassung an den Charakter der Zeit', *Hindemith-Jb*, ix (1980), 65–129 [*Mathis der Maler*]

A. Lehmann: 'Hindemiths Lehrstück', *Hindemith-Jb*, xi (1982), 36–76

N. J. Schneider: 'Thornton Wilder und Paul Hindemith', ibid, 147–88 [*The Long Christmas Dinner*]

D. Rexroth: 'Paul Hindemith und Brechts *Lehrstück*', *Hindemith-Jb*, xii (1983), 41–52

A. Briner: 'Ergänzungen und Berichtigungen zu Thornton Wilder und Paul Hindemith', ibid, 96–103

J. D'Angelo: 'Tonality symbolism in Hindemith's opera *Die Harmonie der Welt*', *Hindemith-Jb*, xiv (1985), 99–128

A. Laubenthal: *Paul Hindemiths Einakter-Triptychon* (Tutzing, 1986)

D. Neumeyer: *The Music of Paul Hindemith* (New Haven, 1986)

A. Briner, D. Rexroth, G. Schubert: *Paul Hindemith: Leben und Werk* (Zürich and Mainz, 1988)

S. C. Cook: *Opera for a New Republic: the Zeitopern of Krenek, Weill and Hindemith* (Ann Arbor and London, 1988)

GEOFFREY SKELTON

Hines [Heinz], **Jerome (Albert Link)** (*b* Hollywood, CA, 8 Nov 1921). American bass and composer. He studied in Los Angeles and made his début in 1941 at San Francisco as Nerone, then sang Biterolf. In nearly 40 years with the Metropolitan from 1946 he sang a huge number of roles including Méphistophélès, Sparafucile, Boris, Sarastro, Hunding, Don Basilio, the Grand Inquisitor, Philip II and Swallow (*Peter Grimes*). He sang Nick Shadow at Edinburgh in the British stage première of *The Rake's Progress* (1953), Don Giovanni in Munich (1954), Handel's Hercules at La Scala (1958), Gurnemanz, King Mark and Wotan at Bayreuth (1958–63) and Boris at the Bol'shoy (1962). His later roles included Arkel in Rome (1984), the blind father in *Iris* at Newark (1988) and Ramfis at New Orleans (1989), 45 years after he first sang there. He was a fine actor with an imposing stage presence, a huge voice and solid technique. His careful preparation of the historical and psychological aspects of each role led to especially vivid projections of such parts as Boris and Philip II. Hines's own opera on the life of Christ, *I am the Way*, (1969, Philadelphia), in which he sang the protagonist, has been given in several cities. He has published an autobiography, *This is my Story, this is my Song* (1968),

and a book of interviews, *Great Singers on Great Singing* (1982).
RICHARD BERNAS, ELIZABETH FORBES

Hinrichs, Gustav (*b* Ludwigslust, 10 Dec 1850; *d* Mountain Lake, NJ, 26 March 1942). American conductor, impresario and composer of German birth. He studied first with his father and later in Hamburg with Marxsen. He began conducting at the age of 15 and five years later moved to San Francisco, where he taught and conducted the Fabbri Opera. In 1885 he became assistant to Theodore Thomas in New York as director of the American Opera Company. After its failure he established his own company in Philadelphia in 1888, and during the ten seasons of its existence conducted the American premières of Mascagni's *Cavalleria rusticana* (1891) and *L'amico Fritz* (1892), Bizet's *Les pêcheurs de perles* (1893) and Puccini's *Manon Lescaut* (1894). He also directed his own opera, *Onti-Ora*, at its première on 28 July 1890. Hinrichs was later active in New York, where he taught and conducted at the National Conservatory and at Columbia University (1895–1906); he conducted at the Metropolitan Opera during the 1899–1900 and 1903–4 seasons. He seems to have retired by 1910. His other compositions include a symphonic suite and some vocal works, none of which was published. He was married to the soprano Katherine Fleming.
BRUCE CARR

Hinsch [Hintz, Hintze], **Hinrich** [Heinrich, Henricus] (*b* Stade, ? *c*1650–60; *d* Hamburg, 5 May 1712). German librettist. After studying theology and law, he settled at Hamburg as an advocate and became one of the most prolific librettists of the Gänsemarkt opera. His vocabulary and verbal forms in no way depart from 17th-century traditions; a typical feature is the large number of *e*-insertions and elisions. Because of its regular and sometimes rather awkward use of Baroque imagery and standard poetic patterns, Hinsch's writing may seem somewhat uninspired, but he was able to work out effective plots. His opera *Philippus*, set to music by Georg Bronner for the emperor's name-day in 1701, raised a scandal at the Viennese court because in the play an emperor appeared as a ladies' man; nevertheless, the work was staged in 1702, as *Beatrix*. Another work of 1701, *Thassilo*, to be performed to celebrate the coronation of the Prussian king, Friedrich I, was withdrawn for unknown reasons.

Hannibal, J. W. Franck, 1681; *Semiramis*, Franck, 1683 (also attrib. Strungk); *Der irrende Ritter Don Quixotte*, Förtsch, 1690; *Venus, oder Die siegende Liebe*, Bronner, 1694; *Mahumeth II*, Keiser, 1696; *Als der aller-durchlauchtigste ... Philippus*, Bronner, 1701 (staged as Beatrix, 1702); *Thassilo*, 1701, lost; *Victor Hertzog der Normannen*, J. C. Schieferdecker, Mattheson and Bronner, 1702; *Der Tod der grossen Pans*, Bronner ? and Mattheson, 1702; *Berenice*, Bronner, 1702; *Claudius*, Keiser, 1703; *Minerva*, Keiser, 1703; *La fedeltà coronata, oder Die gekrönte Treue*, Keiser, 1706; *Dido, Königin von Carthago*, Graupner, 1707; *Der beglückte Florindo*, Handel, 1708; *Die verwandelte Daphne*, Handel, 1708

*

H. Schröder: *Lexikon der hamburgischen Schriftsteller*, iii (Hamburg, 1857), 271

H. C. Wolff: *Die Barockoper in Hamburg*, i (Wolfenbüttel, 1957)

H. Rupp and C. L. Lang, eds.: *Deutsches Literatur-Lexikon*, vii (Berne and Munich, 3/1979), 1223
DOROTHEA SCHRÖDER

Hinshaw, William Wade (*b* nr Union, IA, 3 Nov 1867; *d* Washington, DC, 27 Nov 1947). American baritone and impresario. He made his début as Gounod's Méphistophélès with Henry Savage's company in St Louis in 1899. He then moved to Chicago, where he founded a school of opera and drama which merged with the Chicago Conservatory in 1903. With the tenor James F. Sheehan, Hinshaw formed the Metropolitan Grand Opera Company to produce opera in English at the International Theatre in Chicago; it opened in January 1908 with *Lohengrin* in which Hinshaw sang Telramund. He became a leading baritone at the Metropolitan (1910–13), where he sang Wotan, at the Wagner festivals in Graz (1912) and Berlin (1914). He had a strong and sonorous voice; his repertory included more than 50 roles, and he sang in a number of premières, among them Horatio Parker's *Mona* (1912, as Gloom) and *Fairyland* (1915, as Corvain) and Walter Damrosch's *Cyrano de Bergerac* (1913, as Le Bret).

Hinshaw is chiefly remembered, however, as an enthusiastic promoter of opera in English. He presented hundreds of performances of *opéra comique* and grand opera, as president of the Society of American Singers in New York (1918–20) and with his own company in tours of the USA, Canada and Cuba (1920–26).

*

O. Thompson: *The American Singer* (New York, 1937), 245
ANNE MINKO

Hin und zurück ('There and Back'). Sketch with music, op.45a, by PAUL HINDEMITH to a libretto by Marcellus Schiffer; Baden-Baden, 15 July 1927.

Robert (tenor), returning home unexpectedly, catches his wife Helene (soprano) with a letter from her lover, and he shoots her in a jealous rage. As the body is carried off by the Professor (baritone) and the Ambulance Man (bass), Robert throws himself out of the window. A Wise Man (tenor) enters. Deploring the tragedy, he causes time to run backwards, and the whole scene is played in reverse (including the music) to its happy beginning.

Written for a series of 'miniature operas' featured at the 1927 Baden-Baden Festival, this work takes only 12 minutes to perform. It pokes fun in both story and music at conventional opera, with a coloratura ariette for Helene, a jealousy duet and a mournful, chromatic terzet for the men after the shooting. To that extent it can be described as a reversion to Hindemith's youthful iconoclastic period, but the music is now more rigidly controlled and the mirror construction represents a considerable tour de force. The reversal process is carried out phrase by phrase rather than note by note. It is scored for a small instrumental ensemble, including two pianos and a harmonium.
GEOFFREY SKELTON

Hippolyte et Aricie ('Hippolytus and Aricia'). *Tragédie en musique* in a prologue and five acts by JEAN-PHILIPPE RAMEAU to a libretto by SIMON-JOSEPH PELLEGRIN after JEAN RACINE's *Phèdre*, EURIPIDES' *Hippolytos* and Seneca's *Phaedra*; Paris, Opéra, 1 October 1733.

Rameau's controversial first opera had a troublesome early history. Although the cast included Chassé de Chinais (Theseus) and Antier (Phaedra), with Dupré and Camargo among the dancers, some of the performers were unable or unwilling to master the work's difficulties. This, along with criticism of the dramatic structure, led to a series of cuts, which severely blunted the work's dramatic impact. Though successfully revived in 1742 and 1757 and again posthumously, it never enjoyed the reputation of Rameau's other *tragédies*. Nowadays, though, it is rightly regarded as one of the peaks of his output.

Aricie [Aricia]	soprano
Hippolyte [Hippolytus] *Theseus's son by a previous marriage*	haute-contre
Phèdre [Phaedra] *Theseus's wife, Hippolytus's step-mother*	soprano
Thésée [Theseus] *King of Athens*	bass
Oenone *Phaedra's confidante*	soprano
Arcas *Theseus's confidant*	haute-contre
Diane [Diana]	soprano
L'Amour [Cupid]	soprano
Jupiter	baritone
Tisiphone *a Fury*	haute-contre
Pluton [Pluto] *King of the Underworld*	bass
Mercure [Mercury]	tenor
Neptune	bass
The High Priestess of Diana	soprano
Three Fates	haute-contre, tenor, bass
A Follower of Cupid	haute-contre
A Priestess	soprano
A Sailor Girl	soprano
A Huntress	soprano
A Shepherdess	soprano

Diana's nymphs, forest dwellers, Diana's priestesses, underworld gods, Troezenians, sailors, hunters and huntresses, shepherds and shepherdesses

Setting The Spartan city of Troezen; Hades; the Forest of Aricia

The first modern staging of *Hippolyte* took place at Geneva on 28 March 1903. The previous year Charles Bordes had organized a concert performance at the Schola Cantorum, Paris, and was eventually to mount the first revival at the Paris Opéra (13 May 1908). Among later productions, that at Birmingham University in 1965 led to the earliest near-complete recording of the work (L'Oiseau-Lyre), a powerful and committed performance conducted by Sir Anthony Lewis with John Shirley-Quirk (Theseus) and Janet Baker (Phaedra) in the cast.

PROLOGUE *The forest of Erymanthus* Jupiter persuades Diana to let her chaste forest dwellers serve Cupid on one day each year. Diana pledges to protect Hippolytus and Aricia.

ACT 1 *The temple of Diana* Theseus has secured the Athenian throne, compelling Aricia, the last of his enemy Pallas's line, to take vows of chastity. Before the ceremony, she and Hippolytus discover their mutual love, Aricia having first expressed her anguish in the monologue 'Temple sacré'. As the priestesses perform airs and dances in Diana's honour, Phaedra arrives to enforce Theseus's order. Outraged at Aricia's defiance and suspecting that Hippolytus (whom she secretly loves) loves the princess, Phaedra orders her guards to sack the temple. As the priestesses appeal to the gods, thunder is heard, graphically represented by Vivaldian tremolandos and sharp dynamic contrasts. Diana descends; to Phaedra's chagrin, she reaffirms her protection of the lovers. Phaedra learns that Theseus has descended to Hades. Oenone suggests that, now that she is effectively a widow, Phaedra may declare her love to Hippolytus.

ACT 2.i *The entrance to Hades* Theseus's comrade Peirithous has tried to abduct Pluto's wife. As Theseus

attempts to rescue him, Tisiphone bars his way, his spiteful threats contrasting with Theseus's eloquent pleas. Their altercation includes a terse duet, 'Contente-toi d'une victime'.

2.ii *Pluto's court* Pluto declares that, as Peirithous's accomplice, Theseus must share his suffering. He commands a trial, whereupon he and his court call on the rivers of hell to avenge the outrage ('Que l'Averne, que le Ténare, le Cocyte, le Phlégéton'), their imprecations barked out over a turbulently undulating accompaniment. As the Furies dance, the underworld gods prepare vengeance. When Theseus pleads to be reunited with Peirithous, the Fates reveal that he must await his hour. Their stark, homophonic trio (the first Trio des Parques), 'Du Destin le vouloir suprême', is modelled on the Furies' Trio in Lully's *Isis*. Theseus, his mission clearly hopeless, appeals to Neptune: his prayer 'Puisque Pluton est inflexible', an arioso of Bach-like intensity with a figured accompaniment of rising arpeggios, reveals that Neptune had sworn to assist his son three times. Mercury descends and persuades Pluto that Neptune's oath must be upheld. Before Theseus leaves, however, the Fates warn that he will find hell in his own home. Their second trio, with its sweeping upward scales, aggressive dotted rhythms and sudden silences, is justly renowned for its bizarre enharmonic progressions, introduced by Rameau 'to inspire dread and horror'.

ACT 3 *Theseus's palace near the sea* As she prepares to reveal her guilty love to her stepson, Phaedra prays to Venus that Hippolytus might yield to her passion ('Cruelle mère des amours', a monologue in which her conflicting emotions are conveyed by subtle changes of pace and harmonic intensity). When Hippolytus arrives, Phaedra pretends that her former anger was feigned. Taking his expressions of relief and his support for her son's claim to the throne as a sign of tenderness, Phaedra offers him 'throne, son and mother'. Unaware of what she is really offering, Hippolytus rejects the throne: he longs only for Aricia. In her fury, the queen tactlessly describes Aricia as her rival. Appalled, Hippolytus calls down divine retribution, at which point Phaedra realizes her love is hopeless and commands him to pierce her heart. When he refuses, she seizes his sword; he seizes it back. At that moment Theseus enters. Finding his son apparently threatening his wife's honour, the king recalls the Fates' prediction. He is made none the wiser by what follows: Hippolytus is too honourable to accuse his stepmother, Phaedra appears defiant, while Oenone insinuates that Hippolytus had indeed threatened the queen. Theseus is prevented from further questioning by the arrival of his subjects to thank Neptune for his safe return. During their celebration – a colossal chorus ('Que ce rivage retentisse'), several dances and an air – the king must conceal his anguish. Eventually dismissing his subjects, he prays again to Neptune: for his outrage Hippolytus must die ('Puissant maître des flots', a tortured monologue as powerful as his earlier prayer). The sea boils: Neptune has heard Theseus's prayer.

ACT 4 *Diana's grove by the sea* Bewailing his fate ('Ah! faut-il, en un jour'), Hippolytus realizes he cannot reveal the truth to his father. He asks Aricia to share his exile. Hunters and huntresses arrive to give thanks to Diana. Their celebration, characterized by hunting horns, is interrupted by a sea monster which carries off Hippolytus. Aricia is escorted away, fainting. As the onlookers react to his apparent death ('O disgrace cruelle'), Phaedra reveals her guilt. Her confession, in which the claps of thunder and the quaking earth that reflect her feelings are vividly painted by the orchestra, leads up to a powerful invocation underpinned by sustained double-stopped strings.

ACT 5.i *Diana's grove by the sea* Theseus, having learnt the truth from the dying Phaedra, is about to throw himself into the sea when Neptune reveals that, through Diana's intervention, Hippolytus is alive. For too readily accepting his son's guilt, Theseus is condemned never to see him again. Grief-stricken, the king nevertheless accepts his punishment ('Je ne te verrai plus! O juste châtiment!', another Bach-like arioso, with drooping flute arpeggios and poignant suspensions).

5.ii *The forest of Aricia* Awakening to harmonious sounds, Aricia is nevertheless inconsolable. Shepherds and shepherdesses assemble as Diana descends; she announces the arrival of a king who will be Aricia's husband. Initially refusing to look at him, Aricia turns – to discover Hippolytus. The woodspeople celebrate their reunion, while a shepherdess sings the coloratura *air du rossignol*.

*　　*　　*

In reworking the story of Phaedra's incestuous love, Pellegrin borrowed elements (including several lines) from Racine's *Phèdre* and Racine's classical models. His setting, however, alters the balance between the characters. It is not the eponymous lovers who dominate the drama but the tragic figures of Theseus and Phaedra. That of Theseus is the more powerful. It gains immensely from the decision to devote Act 2 to his selfless mission and subsequent trial. In Act 3 Pellegrin deliberately places the welcoming *divertissement* to prevent Theseus from learning the truth about what he has witnessed; the fact that the king must therefore suppress his anguish gives greater impact to his eventual outburst, the tragic consequences of which are felt in Act 4. (During the first run the *divertissement* was moved, against Rameau's wishes, to the more conventional but dramatically weaker position at the end of the act.) Theseus's attempted suicide and dignified acceptance of Neptune's punishment provide a fitting end to one of the most monumental characterizations in Baroque opera. The smaller role of Phaedra suffers from comparison with Racine's more subtle study in the psychology of jealousy. Nevertheless, the queen's revelation of her love is certainly worthy of Racine, while her expression of remorse at his apparent death is among the outstanding passages in 18th-century opera.   GRAHAM SADLER

Hiroshima no Orufe ('Orpheus in Hiroshima'). Opera in one act by YASUSHI AKUTAGAWA to a libretto by Kenzaburō Ōe; NHK Television, 27 August 1967 (revision of *Kurai kagami* ('Dark Mirror'; NHK Radio, March 1960, staged Tokyo, Yomiuri Hall, 27 March 1960).

The action, in seven scenes, takes place in postwar Japan. A Young Man (baritone) with keloid scars caused by the atomic bomb meets a middle-aged Prostitute (contralto), who is actually a medium. She hands him a dark mirror through which he sees a mirror land, where he meets a Girl (soprano) with whom he falls in love. In order to have a happy life with her, he decides to undergo surgery to treat his keloids. But she is actually a messenger from the land of death, and eventually a car with a Chauffeur (tenor) arrives to take him

there. The Girl, however, moved by the Young Man's earnest love, decides to give him another chance. Back in the real world the Young Man goes to the hospital, where he finds the Girl as a nurse and the Chauffeur as a surgeon. The curtain falls as the surgeon raises his scalpel, leaving the result of the operation in doubt.

This highly psychological drama, with many fantastical elements, is enhanced by effective use of the orchestra and the backstage chorus. The final stage version of the opera has enjoyed a number of revivals and, after a successful performance at the 1984 International Music Festival in Moscow, was included in the repertory of the Stanislavsky–Nemirovich-Danchenko Music Theatre, Moscow, 1985.   MASAKATA KANAZAWA

Hislop, Joseph (*b* Edinburgh, 5 April 1884; *d* Upper Largo, Fife, 6 May 1977). Scottish tenor. He studied with Gillis Bratt in Stockholm, making his début there as Faust at the Royal Opera (12 September 1914). After five years in Scandinavia he spent a season in Italy at the S Carlo, Naples, before making his Covent Garden début on 14 May 1920 in *La bohème*, eliciting the commendation 'my ideal Rodolfo' from Puccini. He appeared in Chicago (1920–21) and at the Manhattan in New York (1921) and then joined Antonio Scotti's US tour. In 1923 he sang at La Fenice in Venice and the Regio in Turin, and became the first British tenor to take a leading role at La Scala (Edgardo in *Lucia di Lammermoor*). At the Colón (1925) and the Opéra-Comique he impressed by his convincing acting and vocal style. He appeared in a film, *The Loves of Robert Burns* (directed by Herbert Wilcox), and made over 120 records for HMV and Pathé before retiring in 1937. In a new career in teaching at Stockholm, his pupils included Birgit Nilsson and Jussi Björling. From 1947 he was artistic adviser at Covent Garden and then Sadler's Wells, and he later taught at the Guildhall School.

*

M. F. Bott: 'Joseph Hislop', *Record Collector*, xxiii (1976–7) 198–237; xxv (1979–80), 36–42

M. T. R. B. Turnbull: *Joseph Hislop – Gran Tenore* (Aldershot, 1992) [incl. complete discography]
                            MICHAEL T. R. B. TURNBULL

Histories of opera. For a bibliography of histories of opera, see OPERA, bibliography.

Hlobil, Emil (*b* Veselí nad Lužnicí, 11 Oct 1901; *d* Prague, 25 Jan 1987). Czech composer and teacher. After studying philosophy at Prague University (1920–24) and composition with Křička at the Prague Conservatory (1920–23), he attended Suk's master classes (1924–5, 1927–30). He taught in Prague at the women teachers' institute (1930–41), then at the conservatory, and in 1958 was appointed professor of composition at the Prague Academy of Music. At first a follower of the Czech impressionism of Suk and Novák, he turned his attention to newer trends before World War II. During the German occupation he evolved a synthesis of techniques introduced during the 1920s and 1930s, while at the same time his music came to express more intense nationalist feelings; after the war he simplified both the form and the expression of his work. A prolific composer, his extensive output includes three operas for which he wrote the librettos: *Anna Karenina* (op. 60, 1963; 3, after L. N. Tolstoy; České Budějovice, 16 April 1972); *Mešt'ák šlechticem* ('Le bourgeois gentilhomme', op.68, 1965; 3, after Molière; Liberec,

20 September 1986); and *Král Václav IV.* ('King Wenceslas IV', 1981; 5, after Arnošt Dvořák; unperf.), which was composed to celebrate the 100th anniversary of the National Theatre. The melodic language of Hlobil's operas is built up from the briefest of motivic fragments, which are superimposed to dynamic effect. The rapid, rhythmic, conversational dialogue of these tautly constructed works is contained within a musical setting closely linked to the stage action.

MÍLAN KUNA, HELENA HAVLÍKOVÁ

HMS Pinafore [*HMS Pinafore; or, The Lass that Loved a Sailor*]. Operetta in two acts by ARTHUR SULLIVAN to a libretto by W. S. GILBERT; London, Opera Comique, 25 May 1878.

Gilbert's libretto originates in several of his *Bab Ballads*, particularly 'Captain Reece' and 'The Bumboat Woman's Story'. Ralph Rackstraw (tenor), a humble sailor, loves Josephine (soprano), daughter of Captain Corcoran (baritone), who has hopes that she will marry Sir Joseph Porter (baritone), First Lord of the Admiralty (reputedly modelled on W. H. Smith who, under Gladstone, had attained that position by way of a commercial career). Their elopement thwarted, the lovers are united when Ralph's true social position is revealed: Little Buttercup (contralto), when foster mother to the Captain and Ralph, had inadvertently 'mixed those children up'. Among the celebrated songs in one of Sullivan's most directly melodious scores are 'For I'm called Little Buttercup', 'I am the Captain of the Pinafore!' and 'When I was a lad' and the ballads 'Sorry her lot' and 'Fair moon'. The vivacious trio, 'Never mind the why and wherefore', features prominently in the overture arranged by Alfred Cellier.

The fourth collaboration between Sullivan and Gilbert, *HMS Pinafore* achieved unprecedented success and set the seal on their creative partnership. It also established their popularity in the USA, initially through unauthorized versions which were successfully challenged when the collaborators' production was mounted in New York. Significant features of Gilbert's meticulous direction were the realism of naval detail, providing an essential foil to verbal and narrative absurdities, and the prominent role of the chorus. Satirizing both the navy and the British class system, the work is also rich in theatrical burlesque, Gilbert's main target being the old nautical melodramas. In the music the burlesque element is also prominent, particularly in the Handelian recitatives and the elopement scene (evocative of so many nocturnal operatic conspiracies), but best of all is the travesty of the big patriotic tune in 'For he is an Englishman!'

For illustration *see* OPERETTA, fig.3.   DAVID RUSSELL HULME

Hmyrya, Borys (Romanovych) [Gmïrya, Boris Romanovich] (*b* Lebedin, Kharkiv region, 23 July/5 Aug 1903; *d* Kiev, 1 Aug 1969). Ukrainian bass. He studied under Golubev at the Kharkiv Conservatory, graduating in 1939 and becoming a soloist in the Kiev Opera, where he had already made his début in 1936. His roles included Boris Godunov, Méphistophélès, and Maxim Kryvonis in Dan'kevych's *Bohdan Khymel'nyts'ky*. He appeared at the Bol'shoy in Moscow and toured widely in eastern Europe and China. A very musical singer, he was admired for the psychological insights he brought to his best roles; his voice had a wide range and a mellow, rich timbre.

P. Golubev: *B. R. Gmïrya* (Moscow, 1959)
I. Stebun: *Boris Romanovich Gmïrya* (Kiev, 1960)
B. S. Buryak, ed.: *Borys Hmyrya: statty, lysty, spohady* [Borys Hmyrya: Essays, Letters, Reminiscences] (Kiev, 1975)
VIRKO BALEY

Hnatyuk, Dmytro (*b* Starosiliya, Chernivets'ka region, 28 March 1925). Ukrainian baritone. After graduating from the Kiev Conservatory he became a member of the company of the Kiev Theatre of Opera and Ballet. His roles include Rigoletto, Rossini's Figaro, Ostap in Lysenko's *Taras Bulba* and the title roles in *Yevgeny Onegin* and *Mazepa*, which give scope to his strong and penetrating voice. He has toured in the USA, Japan and Australia. He serves as principal stage director of the Kiev Shevchenko Opera and Ballet Theatre.

*
M. Stefanovych: *Dmytro Hnatyuk* (Kiev, 1961)
VIRKO BALEY

Hoare, Prince (*b* Bath, 1755; *d* Brighton, 22 Dec 1834). English playwright. A son of the artist William Hoare, he studied painting at the Royal Academy and in Italy, where he met Stephen Storace, who was also interested in art. Hoare tried unsuccessfully to establish himself as a painter, though he became honorary foreign secretary to the Royal Academy in 1799. No doubt encouraged by Storace, he took to theatrical writing, initially specializing in plots that mixed clever farce and romance. *No Song, No Supper* (1790), his first success and one of Drury Lane's as well, exemplifies that blend (lawyers thrust into sacks and spouses who will not bar the door, disguised lovers and lost-and-found fortunes). His later works emphasized either farce or romance. In *The Three and the Deuce!* (1795) one person acts three roles, to everyone else's confusion; *The Captive of Spilburg* (1798), on the other hand, capitalizes on the gothic.

aft – *afterpiece*

No Song, No Supper (comic op aft), S. Storace, 1790; The Cave of Trophonius (comic op aft), Storace, 1791; Dido, Queen of Carthage (dramatic op), Storace, 1792; The Three and the Deuce! (musical farce), Storace, 1795; The Prize, or 2, 5, 3, 8 (aft), Storace, 1793; My Grandmother (aft), Storace, 1793; Lock and Key (aft), Shield, ov. by W. Parke, 1796; Mahmoud, or The Prince of Persia (musical drama), Storace, compilation completed by M. Kelly and N. Storace, 1796; A Friend in Need (comic op aft), Kelly, 1797; The Italian Villagers (comic op), Shield, 1797; The Captive of Spilburg (musical drama aft), Dussek and Kelly, 1798; The Children, or Give Them their Way (aft), Kelly, 1800; Chains of the Heart, or The Slave By Choice (comic op), Mazzinghi and Reeve, 1801; The Paragraph (aft), Braham and Reeve, 1804

*
DNB (W. Wroth)
D. Baker and others: *Biographia Dramatica; or A Companion to the Playhouse* (London, 1764, 3/1812)
M. Kelly: *Reminiscences of Michael Kelly* (London, 2/1826); ed. R. Fiske (London, 1975)
L. Hughes and A. H. Scouten, eds.: *Ten English Farces* (Austin, 1948)
R. Fiske, ed.: Preface to S. Storace: *No Song, No Supper*, MB, xvi (London, 1959)
R. Fiske: 'The Operas of Stephen Storace', *PRMA*, lxxxvi (1959–60), 29–44
——: *English Theatre Music in the Eighteenth Century* (London, 1973, 2/1986)
LINDA V. TROOST

Hobart. Capital of the Australian island state of Tasmania. It was the second major white settlement (established 1803) after Sydney and the only other significant musical and theatrical centre in early colonial times. John Phillip Deane, a former London instrumentalist, and his family (from 1826) and Vincent Wallace (1835) were among the early organizers and directors of Hobart music. Jerome Carandini, an aristocratic opera singer and dancer from Modena who had become a political refugee, took part in the four-year Tasmanian sojourn (1842–5) of Mrs Michael Clarke's opera-drama company; he married Marie Burgess, who as Marie Carandini became a renowned contralto and entrepreneur. Much of the musical-theatrical life of Hobart centred on the well-equipped Theatre Royal, built in traditional English style in 1837 with 600 seats but passing through many modifications by which its capacity has varied from 1200 (1912) to its present 700. Many singers, including Catherine Hayes, Anna Bishop, Amy Sherwin (début as Norina, 1878) and Clara Butt, and opera companies such as the Lyster, Montague-Turner, Nobili, Simonsen and Musgrove (Royal Grand) appeared at the Theatre Royal between the 1840s and 1914. The subsidized National Theatre and Fine Arts Society (NATFAS) took over the theatre in 1950, acting as sponsor of general theatre activity and generating, with the help of the Elizabethan Theatre Trust and the ABC, a degree of operatic enterprise, beginning in 1960 when the Australian première of Orff's *Die Kluge* took place there.   ROGER COVELL

Hochberg, Hans Heinrich XIV, Bolko Graf von (*b* Schloss Fürstenstein, Silesia, 23 Jan 1843; *d* Salzbrunn, 1 Dec 1926). German administrator and composer. The younger son of Prince von Pless, he was intended for a career in the diplomatic service. He studied law and political science in Bonn and Berlin and spent two years at the Prussian Embassy in St Petersburg (1867–9) before returning home to pursue musical studies. His Singspiel *Claudine von Villa Bella* (3, M. Garve, after Goethe) was performed at Schwerin on 25 February 1864 (vocal score, Berlin and Posen, 1864), followed at Hanover on 24 November 1876 by a Romantic opera, *Die Falkensteiner* (3, P. Frohberg; vocal score, Offenbach, 1875), revised as *Der Wärwolf* for Dresden in 1881. Afterwards he turned to composing instrumental works and songs, some published under the pseudonym Johann Heinrich Franz. In 1878 he founded the Silesian music festivals held in Görlitz, which he continued to assist until 1925. He was appointed successor to Hulsen as director of the Berlin Royal Theatre in 1886. He retired suddenly from this post in December 1902, officially from overwork though in fact as a result of a legal disagreement over the libretto to Richard Strauss's *Feuersnot*, of which Wilhelm II disapproved on moral grounds.

Although Hochberg contributed nothing original as a composer, he exerted considerable influence as founder of the Silesian music festivals and especially as director of the Berlin theatre. He reorganized the opera, attracting important conductors such as Joseph Sucher, Felix Weingartner, Carl Muck and Strauss, thus raising the standards of musical performance. Not pandering to popular taste, he also broadened the repertory and established a continuing place for Wagner's works.

*

NDB (J. Wilcke)

C. Weigelt: *Die Grafen von Hochberg zum Furstenstein* (Breslau, 1896)

J. Landau: 'Bolko Graf von Hochberg: zum 80. Geburtstag', *Deutsche Bühne*, xv (1923)

J. Kapp: *Geschichte der Staatsoper Berlin* (Berlin, 1937)

R. Strauss: *Betrachtungen und Erinnerungen*, ed. W. Schuh (Zürich, 1949)

M. Koch: *Das Königliche Schauspielhaus in Berlin unter der Leitung*

von Bolko Graf von Hochberg (1886–1902) (diss., Free U. of Berlin, 1957)
                                GAYNOR G. JONES

Hochzeit des Camacho, Die ('Camacho's Wedding'). Opera in two acts, op.10, by FELIX MENDELSSOHN to a libretto probably by Friedrich Voigt after an episode in MIGUEL DE CERVANTES' *Don Quixote*; Berlin, Schauspielhaus, 29 April 1827.

Mendelssohn received the libretto early in 1824 and wrote the first act between 11 June and 11 December 1824; the overture was finished on 12 February 1825 and the second act, begun on 5 March, was composed by 10 August. The opera was produced 20 months later, during which period Mendelssohn carried out a thorough revision. The original version vividly illustrates the rapidity with which his gifts were developing; by the time he came to write Act 2 he seems to have recognized that he was already a far more mature composer and he made particularly extensive changes to Act 1, including the deletion of several numbers. The second finale, too, was largely rewritten.

Quiteria (soprano) is in love with Basilio (tenor), but her father Carrasco (bass) wants to marry her to Camacho (tenor), a rich neighbour. Lucinda (soprano) and Vivaldo (tenor) determine to help Basilio. Sancho Panza (bass) and his master Don Quixote (baritone) arrive, in search of the haunted cave of Montesinos, and are invited to Camacho's lavish wedding feast. Meanwhile, Basilio hides in the forest while Vivaldo attempts to convince Carrasco that Basilio has inherited a fortune. Quiteria, on her way to join Basilio, meets Don Quixote and is terrified. When the angry Carrasco and Camacho go in search of the lovers, Basilio confronts them disguised as the ghost of Montesinos and Act 1 ends in general confusion. As part of Camacho's wedding feast Vivaldo provides an entertainment, a barbed allegory designed to show the superiority of love to wealth; this is brought to an abrupt end by the crazy intervention of Don Quixote. Just as Quiteria, in despair, is about to sign the marriage contract, Basilio arrives; in accordance with Vivaldo's plan he pretends to stab himself and is allowed to marry Quiteria so that he can die happy. But as soon as the marriage is solemnized he leaps to his feet. Camacho reluctantly accepts the situation and the wedding feast is allowed to proceed.

Camacho shows Mendelssohn's familiarity with the classical German opera tradition and the latest developments in Romantic opera. The brilliance and dramatic flair of *Der Freischütz* made a powerful impact on him in 1821. While he was writing *Camacho* he also came under the spell of Spohr's *Jessonda*. In accordance with the aims of Spohr and Weber, Mendelssohn sought to produce a work that went beyond the bounds of conventional Singspiel. This is evident not only in his meticulous workmanship and seriousness of purpose, but especially in his use of musical motif and reminiscence. Don Quixote has a personal motif, usually played by brass. Reminiscence is effectively employed at various points, notably the opening section of no.15, where the music of the lovers' opening duet is recalled. Further, Mendelssohn adopted an individual approach to the musical structure which is different from that used by Spohr, Weber or anyone else at this period; the whole opera is enclosed within Don Quixote's motif, which begins the overture and appears in the closing bars of the finale. In addition, reference to the music of the overture concludes both finales and the

David Hockney's design for Stravinsky's 'The Rake's Progress': Act 3 scene i from the 1975 Glyndebourne production showing the auctioning of the Rake's possessions by Sellem (John Fryatt)

ballet in Act 2. Other musical cross-references abound. As the dates on the score indicate, the overture was not left until last but was integral to the musical thought of the opera. The musical characterization is as skilful and inventive as the structure, and the choruses, which play an important part in the opera, are handled with variety and imagination.

For the 1827 production Mendelssohn seems to have been persuaded to make cuts and alterations. These he evidently later regretted; in the 1829 vocal score he partly reverted to material that had been cut in 1827 and refined and recomposed portions of the opera. The full score edited by Julius Rietz for the Breitkopf & Härtel collected edition largely reproduces the conductor's score of 1827 and does not, therefore, agree with Mendelssohn's own vocal score. The first complete staging of Mendelssohn's final version of the opera was at the Playhouse in Oxford on 24 February 1987. No definitive copy of the spoken dialogue is known, but what appears to be a working draft, lacking the first eight pages, is in the Bodleian Library, Oxford.

CLIVE BROWN

Hockney, David (*b* Bradford, Yorks., 9 July 1937). English painter. He studied at Bradford Art School (1957–9) and the Royal College of Art, London (1959–62). In 1961 he gained recognition through the Young Contemporaries Exhibition, London; he received the Guinness Award for etching and first prize for painting at the John Moores Liverpool Exhibition, both in 1961. His first solo exhibition, 'A Rake's Progress and Other Etchings', was in London in 1963.

His first stage designs were for Alfred Jarry's *Ubu Roi* in 1966 in London. In opera he has designed *The Rake's Progress* (1975, Glyndebourne; see illustration), *Die Zauberflöte* (1978, Glyndebourne) and two triple bills at the Metropolitan Opera House, in 1981 (Satie's *Parade*, Poulenc's *Les mamelles de Tirésias* and Ravel's *L'enfant et les sortilèges*; and Stravinsky's *Rite of Spring*, *The Nightingale* and *Oedipus rex*). In 1987 he designed *Tristan und Isolde* for the Los Angeles Music Centre.

Hockney is noted for a witty use of the engraver's art of line and hatch (*Rake's Progress*), one-point perspec-

tive and throbbing colour (*Die Zauberflöte* and *L'enfant et les sortilèges*), and collage (*Les mamelles de Tirésias*). A child-like simplicity disguises a sophisticated awareness of text, but his designs often overwhelm other elements of a production.

*

N. Stangos, ed.: *David Hockney by David Hockney* (London, 1976)
Hockney Paints the Stage (Minneapolis, 1983) [pubn of Walker Arts Centre]
David Hockney: a Retrospective (Los Angeles, 1988) [pubn of Los Angeles County Museum of Art]   DAVID J. HOUGH

Hoddinott, Alun (*b* Bargoed, Glam., 11 Aug 1929). Welsh composer. He was educated at University College, Cardiff, and also studied privately with Arthur Benjamin in London. After teaching at the Cardiff (now the Welsh) College of Music and Drama (1951–9), he was appointed lecturer at University College, Cardiff, becoming professor there in 1967. In that year he founded the Cardiff Festival of Music (originally of 20th-century music), remaining its artistic director. He resigned from University College in 1987.

Until 1974 Hoddinott's reputation as a composer rested mainly on his orchestral and chamber music although his output also included a masque, *The Race of Adam* op.23, given in Llandaff Cathedral in 1961, and incidental music for films and radio. The opportunity to compose opera came with a commission from the WNO which resulted in *The Beach of Falesá*, followed during the next six years by four more operas, of which *What the Old Man Does is Always Right* has been the most successful. Like Britten's *The Little Sweep*, it mixes adult roles with smaller parts and choruses for children.

The librettist of *What the Old Man Does*, Myfanwy Piper, worked with Hoddinott on two further operas; here the collaboration proved less successful, perhaps because Hoddinott's music (unlike Britten's in *The Turn of the Screw* and *Death in Venice*) is not well suited to the rapid succession of short scenes into which Piper likes to organize her literary adaptations. Also, Hoddinott came to opera comparatively late, with his style already fully formed. He brought to the genre a mastery of abstract structures, a keen ear for orchestral

729

textures and a distinct personal idiom which uses 12-note serialism freely within a tonal framework. The most memorable moments in the operas occur when a dramatic, or better still melodramatic, incident provides the context for striking orchestral comment.

See also BEACH OF FALESÁ, THE.

The Beach of Falesá op.83 (3, G. Jones, after R. L. Stevenson), Cardiff, New, 26 March 1974, vs (London, 1974)
The Magician [Murder, the Magician] op.88 (television op, 1, J. Morgan), Harlech Television, 11 Feb 1976, vs (London, 1978)
What the Old Man Does is Always Right op.93 (1, M. Piper, after H. C. Andersen), Fishguard, 27 July 1977, vs (London, 1980)
The Rajah's Diamond op.99 (television op, 1, Piper, after Stevenson), BBC, 24 Nov 1979
The Trumpet Major op.103 (3, Piper, after T. Hardy), Manchester, RNCM, 1 April 1981

*

M. Boyd: 'The Beach of Falesá', *MT*, cxv (1974), 207–9
A. J. H. Rees and A. Hoddinott: 'The Beach of Falesá', *Welsh Music*, iv/6 (1972–5), 8–19
M. Burtch: '*What the Old Man Does is Always Right*: Hoddinott's New Opera for Children', *Welsh Music*, v/7 (1975–8), 77–81
B. Deane: *Alun Hoddinott* (Cardiff, 1977), 56–8
——: 'Alun Hoddinott: the Seventies and After', *Soundings*, ix (1979–80), 6–12
M. Boyd: 'The Trumpet Major', *MT*, cxxii (1981), 237–9
R. Fawkes: *Welsh National Opera* (London, 1986), 169–70

MALCOLM BOYD

Hodgson [Hudgson, Hudson; née Dyer], **Mary** (*b* ? London, bap. 26 Dec 1673; *d* after 1718). English soprano. She was a leading singer on the London stage and in concerts from 1693 to 1706. Probably the daughter of the dancing-master Benjamin Dyer, she married the actor John Hodgson on 16 May 1692, two weeks after singing in the première of Purcell's *The Fairy-Queen*. Purcell's song 'Though you make no return to my passion' in *The Maid's Last Prayer* (February 1693) is shown as sung by her under her maiden and married names in different sources. Mrs Hodgson sang in a revival of Purcell's *The Prophetess* and in the second part of *The Comical History of Don Quixote*. With her husband, she joined the breakaway Betterton company in 1695 and subsequently sang music by Eccles in *Macbeth*, *The Rape of Europa* and *The Loves of Mars and Venus*. Congreve praised her performance as Juno in the Eccles setting of his *Judgment of Paris* (1701). Her career appears to have ended in 1706 but there were benefit performances for her up to 1719.

*

BDA; *LS*
O. Baldwin and T. Wilson: 'Purcell's Sopranos', *MT*, cxxiii (1982), 602–9
C. A. Price: *Henry Purcell and the London Stage* (Cambridge, 1984)

OLIVE BALDWIN, THELMA WILSON

Hoë, Johann Joachim (*fl c*1680–1730). German librettist. Between 1711 and 1718, this otherwise unknown writer produced seven librettos for the Gänsemarkt opera at Hamburg, four of which were adaptations of Italian texts. In his own works (*Henrico IV*, *Trajanus*, *Jobates und Bellerophon*), Hoë developed a naturalistic style based on 'sound thoughts' (*gesunde Gedancken*) rather than 'sublime words and diffuse allusions' (*sublime Worte und weitläufftige Allusiones*, foreword to *Henrico IV*). Characteristic of his librettos are long, learned forewords, scenes expressing the local colour (such as the bullfight in *Henrico IV* with the spectators shouting Spanish exclamations), and elaborate stage settings that show by the detailed representation of con-temporary and ancient places the author's strong – possibly professional – interest in history and topography. *Trajanus*, written for the emperor's name-day in 1717, earned Hoë the title of *poeta laureatus caesareus*. The first performance of *Augustus* (1722) at Copenhagen, as well as the revival there of part of *Julia* (as *Antonius, Römischer Kaiser*), may indicate that he spent some time at the Danish court.

Die geheimen Begebenheiten Henrico IV, Mattheson, 1711; *Achilles*, Keiser, 1716; *Julia*, Keiser, 1717; *Tomyris*, Keiser, 1717; *Trajanus*, Keiser, 1717; *Jobates und Bellerophon*, Keiser, 1717; *Il trionfo dell'amore e della costanza* [Der Triumph der Liebe und Beständigkeit] (after Ballerini), Conti, 1718; *Augustus*, Keiser, 1722

*

H. Schröder: *Lexikon der hamburgischen Schriftsteller*, iii (Hamburg, 1857), 284–5
H. C. Wolff: *Die Barockoper in Hamburg*, i (Wolfenbüttel, 1957)
K. Zelm, ed.: Introduction to R. Keiser: *Die grossmütige Tomyris* (Munich, 1976)
H. Rupp and C. L. Lang, eds.: *Deutsches Literatur-Lexikon*, vii (Berne and Munich, 3/1979), 1291

DOROTHEA SCHRÖDER

Hoekman, Guus (*b* The Hague, 16 Oct 1913). Dutch bass. He studied in Hilversum and Antwerp, where he made his début in 1951 as Osmin. Engaged by Netherlands Opera, he sang a wide repertory including the King (*Die Kluge*), Don Basilio, Baculus (*Der Wildschütz*), Rocco, the Grand Inquisitor, Sarastro and the Doctor (*Wozzeck*). He sang in the stage première of Martin's *Le mystère de la Nativité* at Salzburg (1960), then joined Deutsche Oper am Rhein (1961–2). He sang Arkel, undoubtedly his finest role, at Glyndebourne (1962–3, 1969), La Roche (*Capriccio*) for New York City Opera (1965), Monteverdi's Seneca in Oslo (1967) and Duke Bluebeard in Boston (1969). After teaching in the USA for some years he returned to Netherlands Opera in 1980, his voice unimpaired, to create Lumey in Jan van Gilse's *Thijl*; he also sang Schigolch (*Lulu*), Titurel and Trulove (1985). A superb singing actor, he was as effective in comic as in tragic roles.

TRUUS DE LEUR, ELIZABETH FORBES

Hoengen, Elisabeth. *See* HÖNGEN, ELISABETH.

Hof. Town in central Germany. The first municipal theatre was opened in 1821 in the chancel of a former monastery church. In 1894 a private hall was erected on the site of the present theatre, in Schützenstrasse. The town acquired it in 1925, named it the Stadttheater and renovated it extensively (1929–30). It was reopened on 11 July 1930 with *Die Meistersinger* and in 1933 allotted a new function as a 'frontier theatre'. It remained undamaged throughout World War II and was used as a theatre for the American military until 1945. Renamed the Zweckverband Nordostoberfränkisches Städtebundtheater (501 seats), it reopened on 4 October 1948 with *La traviata*. Despite the small dimensions of the stage, it has mounted large operatic productions including *Les contes d'Hoffmann*, *Carmen*, *Tosca* and *Fidelio*, as well as operetta, drama and ballet. The season runs from mid-August to the end of May. The company performs in the theatre for about half the season and spends the other half touring the region, playing in towns such as Erlangen, Bamberg, Schweinfurt, Bayreuth, Selb and Marktredwitz.

KLAUS J. SEIDEL

Hofburg. The imperial palace in Vienna. Opera performances were given there for the court during the 17th and 18th centuries. The ballrooms of the palace, the Redoutensäle, have occasionally been used for opera since. *See* VIENNA, §§1, 2 and 4(i).

Hofer [née Weber; Mayer], (**Maria**) **Josepha** (*b* Zell, 1758; *d* Vienna, 29 Dec 1819). German soprano, sister of Aloysia Lange. She was the eldest daughter of the singer and violinist Fridolin Weber (1733–79). After her father's death she moved to Vienna, and was then engaged as a soprano at Graz, 1785–7. On 21 July 1788 she married the court musician Franz de Paula Hofer (1755–96), and began performing at the suburban Theater auf der Wieden the next January. According to contemporary reports, she commanded a very high tessitura but had a rough edge to her voice and lacked stage presence. In September 1789 Mozart wrote for her the bravura insertion aria 'Schon lacht der holde Frühling' (K580, for a German version of Paisiello's *Il barbiere di Siviglia*). Two years later he composed the role of the Queen of Night in *Die Zauberflöte* for her; she finally ceded the part to Antonia Campi in 1801. Josepha's second husband, from 1797, was (Friedrich) Sebastian Mayer (1773–1835), who created Pizarro in Beethoven's *Fidelio* (*Leonore*) in 1805. In that year Josepha retired from the stage, to be replaced by her daughter Josefa Hofer.

C. Groag-Belmonte: *Die Frauen im Leben Mozarts* (Augsburg, 1905, 2/1924)

E. K. Blümml: *Aus Mozarts Freundes- und Familienkreis* (Vienna, 1923), 119–39
THOMAS BAUMAN

Høffding, (Niels) Finn (*b* Copenhagen, 10 March 1899). Danish composer. He studied the violin, organ and composition in Copenhagen and in Vienna, where he came into contact with the Schoenberg circle. Initially, however, he drew his strongest inspiration from the tradition around Nielsen, whom he admired, and from modernist contemporaries such as Stravinsky and Bartók. The 1920s saw the composition of Høffding's first major works, including the Symphonies nos.1–3 and the operas *Kejserens nye klæder* and *Kilderejsen*. From around 1930 he became involved in educational work: in 1931 he was co-founder of the Københavns Folkemusikskole, and his music, including the choral school opera *Pasteur* (1935), was predominantly for teaching purposes. Throughout his career choral arrangements and songs occupied a central role. He taught at the Royal Danish Conservatory from 1931, becoming professor in 1949 and director in 1954, and held many administrative and honorary offices; he was awarded the Carl Nielsen Prize in both 1956 and 1958.

Kejserens nye klæder [The Emperor's New Clothes] op.8 (Høffding, after H. C. Andersen), Copenhagen, Kongelige, 29 Dec 1928
Kilderejsen [Spring Journey] op.16, 1930–31 (V. Andersen, after L. Holberg), Copenhagen, Kongelige, 13 Jan 1942
Pasteur op.27, 1935 (school op, Høffding and O. Gelsted), Copenhagen, Oddfellows, 9 March 1938

G. Heerup: 'Kejserens nye Klæder', *Dansk musiktidsskrift*, iv (1929), 12–15

R. Hove: 'Finn Høffding: "Kilderejsen"', *Dansk musiktidsskrift*, xiii (1938), 6–14

A. Agerby: 'Finn Høffdings ny opera "Pasteur"', ibid, 30–35
NIELS MARTIN JENSEN

Höffer, Paul (*b* Barmen, 21 Dec 1895; *d* Berlin, 31 Aug 1949). German composer. He studied at the Cologne Conservatory and then with Schreker at the Berlin Hochschule für Musik; subsequently he taught at the Hochschule, becoming director in 1948. With Josef Rufer he founded the Musikinstitut für Ausländer in Berlin in 1945.

Höffer belonged to the New Berlin School of the 1920s and 30s. His work falls into two general categories; besides serious art music, notably the operas *Borgia* op.28 (composed 1931) and *Der falsche Waldemar* op.39, ballets and incidental music, he wrote a great deal of *Gebrauchsmusik*, including music for six radio plays and three children's plays. *Der falsche Waldemar*, in four acts, first performed in Stuttgart on 10 December 1934, was subsequently banned by the Nazis, and political pressure drove him to a period of silence from 1942 to 1944.
CHARLOTTE ERWIN

Höffgen, Marga (*b* Mülheim an der Ruhr, 26 April 1921). German contralto. She studied at the Berlin Hochschule für Musik and with Weissenborn. She appeared mostly as a concert singer and for some years her only operatic roles were Erda and the First Norn in the *Ring*. She first sang Erda on stage at Covent Garden in 1959, subsequently singing the part at Bayreuth, Vienna and Buenos Aires. Her expressive and beautifully focussed voice is particularly well suited to Wagner and she has recorded roles in *Parsifal* and *Die Meistersinger*.
PETER BRANSCOMBE

Hoffman [Hoffmann, Hofman, Hofmann], **François-Benoît(-Henri)** (*b* Nancy, 11 July 1760; *d* Passy, nr Paris, 25 April 1828). French librettist, critic and playwright. Though his name appears in various forms in early newspapers and modern library catalogues, he always spelt it 'Hoffman'. After winning the Nancy Académie's poetry prize in 1784, he decided to follow a literary career in Paris. During the 1780s, *épigrammes* and poems published in the *Almanach des muses* and other journals brought him some attention in literary circles. The patronage of Megret de Serilly, *trésorier général de la guerre*, helped him to achieve his first major public success: *Phèdre*, set by Lemoyne in 1786, was rehearsed at Serilly's chateau and given its première at Fontainebleau. After a trip to Italy in 1787, Hoffman and Lemoyne collaborated again: *Nephté* was praised for its dramatic integrity, although it did not remain in repertory long. The two fell out. Hoffman offered his next libretto, *Adrien*, first to Cherubini (who declined it, but accepted the next, *Médée*) and then to Méhul, who became his favourite partner during the 1790s.

In 1789–90 Hoffman had the first of many disagreements with theatres. He opposed the Opéra's wish to add what he felt were unsuitable *divertissements* to *Nephté*, and threatened to press for legislation to force recognition of authors' rights to maintain control over their published works. Although he won on both points, it proved a Pyrrhic victory, for, partly in retaliation, the Opéra rejected the *Médée* libretto in 1790. The same strength of character is clear in his public declarations during the 1792 *Adrien* controversy. Exceptionally for the time of the Revolution, few of his works had a clear political message (even *Callias* is more patriotic than partisan). More typical are his librettos for Méhul, Solié and Dalayrac, which range from the *chevaleresque* to *comédie héroïque*, bourgeois comedy, satire and *drame*. In spite of the great variety of subjects, they all show Hoffman's attention to character development, well-constructed plot, finely paced dramatic action and finesse in language (with, however, a tendency to verbosity).

In 1797 Hoffman became the editor and principal writer of the periodical *Le menteur*, in which he ridiculed, often by outlandish praise, current literary fashions and those who misused political power (with the result that it was soon banned). During the Consulate, he continued to champion the author's cause: active in the Société des Auteurs Dramatiques, he became its Opéra-Comique representative. His librettos thereafter tended more to the genre's comic and sentimental sides, and he collaborated successfully with Isouard, whose light, italianate musical style well matched the slight dramatic requirements of the text. He also wrote plays performed at several Parisian theatres, some of which were moderately successful.

In the autumn of 1807 Hoffman virtually retired from the theatre (the two operas produced after this date were written earlier) and joined the *Journal de l'empire* as a literary critic. Although his insistence on upholding certain traditional principles of style made him unsympathetic to some of the early French Romantics, he was respected for his independence and thoroughness – a rarity when favourable reviews were frequently bought. After his death he was remembered as one who appreciated that a work for the Opéra-Comique was not merely a play with music added, as many of his contemporaries assumed. As the writer of his obituary noted, 'The majority of Hoffman's works are distinguished by a perfect understanding of the stage and by ingenious schemes to introduce situations suitable for musical effects. Few dramatists have known so well the method and structure of verses for vocal pieces.'

Phèdre (tragédie lyrique, after Euripides and J. Racine), Lemoyne, 1786; *Nephté* (tragédie lyrique, after T. Corneille: *Camma*), Lemoyne, 1789; *Euphrosine, ou Le tyran corrigé* (comédie mise en musique), Méhul, 1790; *Adrien, empereur de Rome* (opéra, after P. Metastasio), Méhul, 1790–91 and 1799; *Stratonice* (comédie héroïque, after *De Dei Syria* [attrib. Lucian] and T. Corneille: *Antiochus*), Méhul, 1792; *Le jeune sage et le vieux fou* (comédie mêlée de musique), Méhul, 1793

Callias, ou Nature et patrie (drame héroïque mêlé de musique), Grétry, 1794; *La soubrette, ou L'étui de harpe* (cmda), Solié, 1794; *Le brigand* (drame mêlé de musique), R. Kreutzer, 1795; *Le jockey* (cmda), Solié, 1796; *Le secret* (comédie mêlée de musique), Solié, 1796; *Azéline* (comédie mêlée de musique, after B. Imbert: *Les ruses innocentes*), Solié, 1796; *Médée* (tragédie lyrique), Cherubini, 1797; *Léon, ou Le château de Monténéro* (drame mêlé d'ariettes), Dalayrac, 1798

La femme de quarante-cinq ans (comédie mêlée de musique), Solié, 1798; *Ariodant* (drame mêlé de musique, after L. Ariosto: *Orlando furioso*), Méhul, 1799; *Bion* (comédie mêlée de musique, after E. F. de Lantier: *Voyages d'Anténor*), Méhul, 1800; *Le trésor supposé, ou Le danger d'écouter aux portes* (comédie mêlée de musique), Méhul, 1802; *La boucle de cheveux* (opéra), Dalayrac, 1802; *La statue, ou La femme avare* (opéra), Isouard, 1802

Louise, ou La malade par amour (comédie mise en musique, after Hoffman's own Stratonice), Solié, 1804; *La ruse inutile* (opéra), Isouard, 1805; *Idala, ou La sultane favorite* (opéra), Isouard, 1806; *Les rendez-vous bourgeois* (opéra bouffon), Isouard, 1807; *Abel* (tragédie lyrique), Kreutzer, 1810, also as La mort d'Abel; *Le dilettante d'Avignon* (oc, with L. Halévy), F. Halévy, 1829

*

Obituary, *Revue encyclopédique, ou analyse raisonnée des productions les plus remarquables dans les sciences, les arts industriels, la littérature et les beaux-arts*, xxxviii (Paris, 1828), 820–21

L. Castel, ed.: *Oeuvres de F.-B. Hoffman* (Paris, 1828–9, 2/1831) [incl. biographical notice by Castel]

P. Jacquinet: *François Benoît Hoffman: sa vie, ses oeuvres* (Nancy, 1878)

A. Pougin: *Méhul: sa vie, son génie, son caractère* (Paris, 1889, 2/1893)

M. E. C. Bartlet: *Etienne Nicolas Méhul and Opera during the French Revolution, Consulate, and Empire: a Source, Archival and Stylistic Study* (diss., U. of Chicago, 1982)

——: 'On the Freedom of the Theatre and Censorship: the *Adrien* Debate (1792)', *Musique, histoire, démocratie: Paris 1989*

M. ELIZABETH C. BARTLET

Hoffman, Grace [Goldie] (*b* Cleveland, 14 Jan 1921). American mezzo-soprano. She studied with Schorr at the Manhattan School of Music, Basiola in Milan and Maria Wetzelsberger in Stuttgart, making her début in 1951 as Mascagni's Lola with a small touring company in the USA. She sang at Florence (1951–2) and Zürich (1953–5). She joined the Württemberg Staatsoper in 1955, the year of her Scala début as Fricka (*Die Walküre*). In addition to making regular guest appearances in Vienna and other European cities, she sang for 13 years (1957–70) at Bayreuth as Brangäne, Fricka and Waltraute; she made her Covent Garden début as Eboli (1959) and her Opéra début as Fricka (1962). Although she appeared at the Metropolitan, making her début in 1958 as Brangäne, she sang principally in Europe. With her smooth, steady, ample voice and dignified stage presence, she was particularly distinguished in the Wagner mezzo roles. From 1978 she taught in Stuttgart, where she sang Mary (*Der fliegende Holländer*) in 1989.

HAROLD ROSENTHAL/R

Hoffmann, E(rnst) T(heodor) A(madeus) [Ernst Theodor Wilhelm] (*b* Königsberg [now Kaliningrad], 24 Jan 1776; *d* Berlin, 25 June 1822). German composer and writer, a central figure in the development of German Romanticism.

1. Life. 2. Writings. 3. Music.

1. LIFE. Hoffmann was brought up chiefly by aunts and an uncle, Otto Wilhelm Doerffer, who took responsibility for his musical education. The boy studied keyboard, violin, harmony and counterpoint under different masters, and later had lessons with J. F. Reichardt in Berlin (1798–1800). He studied law at Königsberg University, graduating in 1795, afterwards practising in Glogau (1796–8), Berlin (1798–1800), Posen (now Poznań), Płock and Warsaw (1804–6). He adopted the name 'Amadeus' in 1804, in homage to Mozart.

During these years Hoffmann was very active as a composer, and to some extent as a painter. As well as stage works, he wrote a number of masses and other vocal pieces, a symphony in E♭ (1805–6), which he conducted in Warsaw, and chamber music. Following the expulsion of civil servants after the French invasion of Warsaw in 1806, he secured the musical directorship of the Bamberg theatre, submitting the opera *Der Trank der Unsterblichkeit* as his credentials. His arrival in September 1808 was followed by disagreements with the musicians (who were chiefly mediocre), so he decided simply to compose for the theatre, to teach music and to write. His now-famous story *Ritter Gluck* appeared in the *Allgemeine musikalische Zeitung* in 1809, and his celebrated review of Beethoven's Fifth Symphony in 1810. Later writings include the dialogue *Der Dichter und der Komponist* (1813), central to his theory of opera, and the essay *Alte und neue Kirchenmusik* (1814).

In 1811–12 Hoffmann was active in theatre production and design, inventing realistic effects for plays by Kleist and Calderón. His 'grosse romantische Oper' *Aurora* stemmed from the same period. In spring 1813 he was appointed musical director to the opera company of Joseph Seconda operating in Leipzig and Dresden. The many works he conducted there have been documented by Schnapp (1981); they included operas by Mozart, Cherubini and Salieri. At the same period he began to write larger-scale fiction, and he worked on his opera *Undine*. Having been sacked, following an argument, in 1814, Hoffmann moved to Berlin and resumed his legal career, subsequently becoming Supreme Court judge; he was much in demand as a writer. *Undine* was successfully staged in 1816, but Hoffmann never realized his plans for a further opera.

2. WRITINGS. Although remembered as a distinctive contributor to Romantic literature with such works as *Fantasiestücke in Callots Manier* (1814–15), *Die Elixiere des Teufels* (1815–16), *Die Serapions-Brüder* (1819–21) and *Lebens-Ansichten des Katers Murr* (1820–21), Hoffmann also played a crucial role in the development of musical criticism, notably through his contributions to the theory and practice of opera. His theory of Romantic opera concerned subject matter, musical articulation of the drama, and 'total effect'. Proper subject matter was that which gave rise to music 'as a necessary product' of itself. It was not limited to any one genre and might indeed be tragic. The essential point was that it should convey an 'overall imaginative idea', making manifest the influence of 'higher natures' on human life. This could involve unforeseen events or the supernatural. The dramatic fairy-tales of Gozzi, especially *Il corvo*, were to be taken as a model.

Musical articulation of a drama was to convey its inner impulses at every point, not the superficial verbal structure. Here the model was to be Gluck, especially the *Iphigénie* tragedies. The example of Mozart's works was to be followed by the few (most composers, in Hoffmann's view, imitated Mozart's techniques, not his Romanticism). *Don Giovanni* remained for Hoffmann 'the opera of all operas'. 'Total effect' was Hoffmann's ideal for any theatre production; he demanded the coherent collaboration of all involved, to 'transport the spectator … to the fantastical land of poetry' (see 'Der vollkommene Maschinist' from *Fantasiestücke*).

In *Der Dichter und der Komponist* Hoffmann analysed the creative interaction of words and music in opera. The 1819 edition of this dialogue in *Die Serapions-Brüder* emphasized the view that a single person could create both words and music of an opera, and 'at the same instant'. Although *Undine* and *Aurora* each employed a separate librettist, Hoffmann had earlier written both words and music for several Singspiels.

At Spontini's instigation, Hoffmann translated *Olimpie* (1819) into German for the Berlin première (1821), also writing the words for the new final scenes required by Spontini. Antigonus's death scene particularly bears his imprint.

3. MUSIC. In his review of Hoffmann's most important composition, the opera *Undine*, Weber (*AMZ*, 19 March 1817) praised the swift pace and forward-pressing dramatic action and had kind words for Hoffmann's restraint in avoiding excessive and inapt melodic decoration (though he criticized the tendency towards abrupt endings, which he thought partly spoilt the effectiveness of individual numbers). Unfortunately, circumstances mitigated against a revival of the opera. Soon after Hoffmann's death a rumour appeared that not only the costumes and sets but also the score and parts had been destroyed in the fire that disrupted the

Berlin production. Throughout the 19th century all his music passed gradually into oblivion, but it again aroused interest at the turn of the century when his writings were attracting the attention of literary historians. Studying the Berlin autographs, Ellinger (1894) regarded Hoffmann as having based his music entirely on Mozart and Gluck (the two masters who, besides Beethoven, he acclaimed most often in his writings), and tirelessly hunted out Mozart reminiscences in every work. Not until 1906, when Pfitzner edited a vocal score of *Undine*, did a major work of Hoffmann's come to public notice; but admirers of the fantastic tales expecting his music to be in a Berliozian style were disappointed. Schiedermair (1907) considered the work as a Singspiel containing arias, romances and choruses in addition to songs, and thus as partaking of the formal variety that marked Italian and French opera of its time. The demonic world was represented by the dramatic means peculiar to the late Neapolitan operatic style: the nobility and seriousness of tone, the striking choral effects and the musical depiction of nature derived from Gluck; the characterization and the depth of feeling in the music owed something to Mozart; the orchestral prominence and harmonic peculiarities were related to Beethoven; and finally certain instrumental effects came, via Spontini, from the school of Mayr. However, Schiedermair emphasized individual features of style in which Hoffmann departed from his models and already evinced some of the characteristic traits of German Romantic opera, while the patriotic German literature on Weber and Wagner, trying to define a distinctive national style, advanced the idea of a consistent historical development from Hoffmann, Weber and Spohr, by way of Marschner, to Wagner.

Indeed, from a formal standpoint it is only a short step from the number operas *Undine* and *Aurora* to *Euryanthe* and *Lohengrin*. But Hoffmann's two serious operas deserve consideration as more than precursors. In them he went beyond merely transferring the forms of *opera buffa* to German Singspiel, partly by giving greater scope to the ensembles and a more prominent role to the chorus. Even the lighter operas, such as *Der lustigen Musikanten* and *Liebe und Eifersucht*, ought not simply to be viewed as the rearguard of Mozartian *opera buffa* but also as ranking among the few significant German contributions to the genre. Hoffmann's six surviving operas show his sure theatrical instinct, with dramatic climaxes always accompanied by musical ones and the musical progression carefully timed to the stage action.

See also UNDINE (i).

AV – no. from Allroggen Verzeichnis (1970)

Die Maske AV4 (Spl, 3, Hoffmann), 1799, *D-Bds*, excerpts ed. F. Schnapp, vs (Berlin, 1923)

Scherz, List und Rache AV8 (Spl, 1, Hoffmann, after J. W. von Goethe), Posen, 1801, lost

Die lustigen Musikanten AV19 (Spl, 2, C. Brentano), Warsaw, 6 April 1805, *F-Pn*, ed. in G. von Dadelsen and others: E. T. A. Hoffmann: Ausgewählte musikalische Werke, iv–v (Mainz, 1975–6)

Die ungebetenen Gäste, oder Der Kanonikus von Mailand AV21, 1805 (Spl, 1, Rohrmann, after A. Duval: *Le souper imprévu*), lost

Liebe und Eifersucht AV33, 1807 (Spl, 3, Hoffmann, after P. Calderón de la Barca: *La banda y la flor*), *D-Bds*

Der Trank der Unsterblichkeit AV34, 1808 (romantische Oper, 4, J. von Soden), *Bds*

Dirna AV51 (melodrama, 3, Soden), Bamberg, 11 Oct 1809, *BAs*

Wiedersehen! AV53, 1809 (prol., 1, Hoffmann)

Aurora AV55, 1811–12 (grosse romantische Oper, 3, F. von Holbein), rev. and reorchd L. Böttcher, Bamberg, 5 Nov 1933,

BAs, WÜsa, ed. in DTB, v (1984); orig. version, Bamberg, 9 Sept 1990

Saul, König in Israel AV59 (melodrama, 3, J. Seyfried, after L. C. Caigniez: Le triomphe de David), Bamberg, 29 June 1811, BAs, WÜsa

Roderich und Kunigunde, oder Der Eremit vom Berge Prazzo, oder Die Windmühle von der Westseite, oder Die triumphierende Unschuld AV63 (Parodie, prol., 2, I. F. Castelli), Bamberg, 23 Feb 1812, lost

Undine AV70, 1813–14 (Zauberoper, 3, F. H. C. de la Motte Fouqué), Berlin, 3 Aug 1816, B, Bds, ed. in Dadelsen, i–iii (1971–2)

Thassilo AV74 (chorus and melodrama, Fouqué), Berlin, 22 Oct 1815, lost; rev. as drama (1), Berlin, 18 Jan 1817, lost

Der Liebhaber nach dem Tode AV85, 1818–22 (3, C. W. Salice-Contessa, after Calderón: El galan fantasma), inc., lost

LITERARY WORKS ON WHICH OPERAS HAVE BEEN BASED

Fantasiestücke in Callots Manier (stories and essays, 1814–15)
  Der goldne Topf: Braunfels, comp. 1906; W. Petersen, 1941; Kósa, 1945, as Anselmus diák [The Scholar Anselmus]
  Die Abenteuer der Sylvester-Nacht: die Geschichte vom verlornen Spiegelbilde: Offenbach, 1881, as Act 2 of Les contes d'Hoffmann
  Die Gesellschaft im Keller (1815): Offenbach, 1881, a source for Les contes d'Hoffmann

Die Elixiere des Teufels (novel, 1815–16): G. Rodwell, 1829, as The Devil's Elixir, or The Shadowless Man

Nachtstücke (stories, 1816–17)
  Der Sandmann: Adam, 1852, as La poupée de Nuremberg; Offenbach, 1881, as Act 1 of Les contes d'Hoffmann; Audran, 1896, as La poupée; J. Weir, 1989, as Heaven Ablaze in his Breast
  Das Majorat: J. Weigl, 1823, as Die eiserne Pforte

Klein Zaches genannt Zinnober (story, 1819): Offenbach, 1881, a source for Les contes d'Hoffmann; S. von Hausegger, 1898, as Zinnober; Harsányi, 1949, as Illusions, ou L'histoire d'un miracle

Die Serapions-Brüder (stories linked by dialogue, 1819–21)
  Die Bergwerke zu Falun: Schumann, planned op, 1831; lib. by Wagner for planned op by J. Dessauer, 1842; Holstein, 1868, as Der Haideschacht; Stanford, comp. 1888, as The Miner of Falun; Wagner-Régeny, 1961
  Signor Formica: Rastrelli, 1832, as Salvator Rosa, oder Zwey Nächte in Rom; E. Schütt, 1892; Gruenberg, comp. 1910
  Nussknacker und Mausekönig: Szeligowski, 1956, as Krakatuk
  Rat Krespel: J. Cadaux, as Le violon de Crémone (unperf.); Offenbach, 1881, as Act 3 of Les contes d'Hoffmann
  Doge und Dogaresse: Schumann, planned op, 1840; Reznícek, 1931
  Meister Martin, der Küfner, und seine Gesellen: Bizet, planned op, 1859, as Le tonnelier de Nuremberg; Weissheimer, 1879; Blockx, 1892, as Maître Martin; Lacombe, 1897, as Meister Martin und seine Gesellen
  Das Fräulein von Scuderi: Offenbach, arr. J. Stern and A. Zamara, 1919, as Der Goldschmidt von Toledo; Hindemith, 1926, as Cardillac
  Die Brautwahl: Busoni, 1912
  Die Königsbraut: Offenbach, 1872, as Le roi Carotte

Prinzessin Brambilla (novella, 1821): Braunfels, 1909; Malipiero, 1942, as I capricci di Callot

*

MHG – Mitteilungen der E. T. A. Hoffmann-Gesellschaft

SOURCE MATERIAL

F. Schnapp, ed.: E. T. A. Hoffmann: Schriften zur Musik: Nachlese (Munich, 1963, 2/1978)

——: E. T. A. Hoffmanns Briefwechsel, i–iii (Munich, 1967–9) [see also errata and suppl. remarks, MHG, xvii (1971), 36]

G. Allroggen: E. T. A. Hoffmanns Kompositionen: ein chronologisch-thematisches Verzeichnis seiner musikalischen Werke mit einer Einführung (Regensburg, 1970)

F. Schnapp, ed.: E. T. A. Hoffmann: Tagebücher (Munich, 1971)

J. C. Sahlin, ed.: Selected Letters of E. T. A. Hoffmann (Chicago and London, 1977)

F. Schnapp, ed.: Der Musiker E. T. A. Hoffmann: ein Dokumentenband (Hildesheim, 1981)

G. R. Kaiser: E. T. A. Hoffmann (Stuttgart, 1988) [incl. full bibliography]

D. Charlton, ed.: E. T. A. Hoffmann's Musical Writings: 'Kreisleriana', 'The Poet and the Composer', Music Criticism (Cambridge, 1989)

BIOGRAPHICAL AND GENERAL STUDIES

G. Ellinger: E. T. A. Hoffmann: sein Leben und seine Werke (Hamburg and Leipzig, 1894)

H. W. Hewett-Thayer: Hoffmann: Author of the Tales (Princeton, 1948)

R. Taylor: Hoffmann: a Study in Romanticism (London, 1963)

K. Negus: E. T. A. Hoffmann's Other World (Philadelphia, 1965)

E. Sams: 'E. T. A. Hoffmann, 1776–1822', MT, cxvii (1976), 29–32 [incl. list of works based on Hoffmann's fiction]

J. M. McGlathery: Mysticism and Sexuality: E. T. A. Hoffmann, i: Hoffmann and his Sources (Las Vegas, 1981); ii: Interpretations of the Tales (New York, 1985)

HOFFMANN AS MUSICIAN

G. Abraham: 'Hoffmann as a Composer', MT, lxxxiii (1942), 233–5; repr. in Slavonic and Romantic Music (London, 1968), 233–8

A. R. Neumann: 'Musician or Author? – E. T. A. Hoffmann's Decision', Journal of English and Germanic Philology, lii (1953), 174–81

H. Ehinger: E. T. A. Hoffmann als Musiker und Musikschriftsteller (Olten and Cologne, 1954); see also Ehinger's postscript, SMz, xciv (1954), 369–70

L. Siegel: 'Wagner and the Romanticism of E. T. A. Hoffmann', MQ, li (1965), 597–613

R. M. Schafer: E. T. A. Hoffmann and Music (Toronto and Buffalo, 1975)

F. Schnapp: 'Der Musiker E. T. A. Hoffmann', MHG, xxv (1979), 1–23

N. Miller: 'E. T. A. Hoffmann und die Musik', Zu E. T. A. Hoffmann, ed. S. S. Scher (Stuttgart, 1981), 182–98

H. Schulze: E. T. A. Hoffmann als Musikschriftsteller und Komponist (Leipzig, 1983)

A. Montandon, ed.: E. T. A. Hoffmann et la musique (Berne, 1987)

HOFFMANN AND OPERA

Reviews of Undine in Vossische Zeitung, Dramaturgisches Wochenblatt, AMZ, xviii (1816): see Schnapp 1981, 442–57

C. M. von Weber: 'Ueber die Oper, Undine', AMZ, xix/12 (1817), cols. 201–8; see Schnapp 1981, 476–80; Eng. trans. in J. Warrack, ed.: Carl Maria von Weber: Writings on Music (Cambridge, 1981), 200–05

H. von Chézy: Unvergessenes, ii (Leipzig, 1858), 162–74 [on Der Liebhaber nach dem Tode]

H. Pfitzner: 'E. T. A. Hoffmanns Undine', Süddeutsche Monatshefte, iii (1906), 370–80; repr. in Gesammelte Schriften, i (Augsburg, 1926), 55–75

L. Schiedermair: Review of Pfitzner's vocal score of Undine, ZIMG, viii (1906–7), 253

K. Thiessen: 'E. T. A. Hoffmanns Zauberoper Undine und ihre Bedeutung für die Entwicklung der deutschen romantischen Oper', Neue Musikzeitung, xxviii (1907), 491–3

E. Kroll: 'E. T. A. Hoffmann als Bühnenkomponist', Die Musik, xv/1 (1922), 99–115 [on Aurora]

——: 'E. T. A. Hoffmanns Opern', Almanach der Deutschen Musikbücherei auf das Jahr 1924–25 (Regensburg, 1924), 178–95 [on Aurora]

F. Schnapp: 'E. T. A. Hoffmanns letzte Oper', SMz, lxxxviii (1948), 339–45 [on Der Liebhaber nach dem Tode]

——: 'E. T. A. Hoffmanns Textbearbeitung der Oper "Olimpia" von Spontini', Jb des Wiener Goethe-Vereins, lxvi (1962), 126–43

M. M. Raraty: E. T. A. Hoffmann and the Theatre: a Study of the Origins, Development, and Nature of his Relationship with the Theatre (diss., U. of Sheffield, 1963)

J. Giraud: '"Die Maske", ein bereits typisches Hoffmann-Werk', MHG, xiv (1968), 18–30

G. Allroggen: 'Die Opern-Ästhetik E. T. A. Hoffmanns', Beiträge zur Geschichte der Oper, ed. H. Becker (Regensburg, 1969), 25–33

——: 'E. T. A. Hoffmanns Musik zur "Dirna"', MHG, xv (1969), 4–30

A. S. Garlington jr: 'Notes on Dramatic Motives in Opera: Hoffmann's Undine', MR, xxxii (1971), 136–45

M. M. Raraty: 'Wer war Rohrmann? Der Dichter und der Komponist', MHG, xviii (1972), 9–16 [on Der Kanonikus von Mailand]

H. Dechant: E. T. A. Hoffmanns Oper 'Aurora' (Regensburg, 1975)

A. S. Garlington, jr: 'E. T. A. Hoffmann's "Der Dichter und der Komponist" and the Creation of the German Romantic Opera', MQ, lxv (1979), 22–47

J. Schläder: 'Undine' auf dem Musiktheater: zur Entstehungsgeschichte der deutschen Spieloper (Bonn and Bad Godesberg, 1979)

G. Rienäcker: *Finali in Opern von E. T. A. Hoffmann, Louis Spohr, Heinrich Marschner und Carl Maria von Weber* (diss., Humboldt U., Berlin, 1984)

H. Dechant: 'Entstehung und Bedeutung von E. T. A. Hoffmanns Oper *Aurora*', *MHG*, xxxi (1985), 6–14

J. Rohr: *E. T. A. Hoffmanns Theorie des musikalischen Dramas* (Baden-Baden, 1985)

F. Ferlan: *Le thème d'Ondine dans la littérature et l'opéra allemands au XIXe siècle* (Berne, 1987)

D. Krickeberg: 'Die Ästhetik von E. T. A. Hoffmann und die Instrumentation der *Undine*: einige Bemerkungen', *E. T. A. Hoffmann et la musique*, ed. A. Montandon (Berne, 1987), 159–67

M. Walter: 'Hoffmann und Spontini: zum Problem der romantischen Oper', ibid, 85–119

R. L. Wilson: *Text and Music in the Operas of E. T. A. Hoffmann* (diss., U. of Southern California, 1990)

DAVID CHARLTON (1,2), GERHARD ALLROGGEN (3)

Hoffmann(-Onegin), Lilly. *See* ONEGIN, SIGRID.

Hoffmeister, Franz Anton (*b* Rothenburg am Neckar, 12 May 1754; *d* Vienna, 9 Feb 1812). Austrian composer. By 1785 he had established a music publishing firm in Vienna, publishing his own works and music by Haydn and Mozart; it was apparently successful until 1791. In 1801 he joined Ambrosius Kühnel in founding the Bureau de Musique in Leipzig, eventually taken over by C. F. Peters.

As a composer of chamber and orchestral music, Hoffmeister was extraordinarily prolific. Many of his Viennese works were also popular in foreign cities: by 1803 his most successful opera, *Der Königssohn aus Ithaka* (1795, Vienna), had been performed in Pest, Hamburg, Prague, Temesvar (now Timişoara), Warsaw and Weimar. Although his symphonies were admired for their flowing melodies and his lighter works for being both pleasant and instructive, his style is generally lacking in originality and depth.

See also KÖNIGSSOHN AUS ITHAKA, DER.

all first performed in Vienna

Der Alchimist, *c*1790

Die bezauberte Jagd, *c*1790

Der Schiffbruch (G. Korndorfer, after W. Shakespeare: *The Tempest*), 1792

Der Haushahn, *c*1795

Der Königssohn aus Ithaka [Telemach, der Königssohn von Ithaka] (heroisch-komische Oper, 2, E. Schikaneder), Wieden, 27 June 1795, *A-Wgm, D-Bds, DS,* vs (Brunswick, n.d.)

Rosalinde, oder Die Macht der Feen (Zauberoper, 3, S. Mayer), 23 April 1796, vs (Brunswick, n.d.)

Der erste Kuss (M. Stegmayer), 7 Feb 1797, ov. arr. 2 vn, va, b (Vienna, n.d.)

Drei Vater und zwei Kinder (komische Oper, 1, Stegmayer), Freihaus, 21 Dec 1798

Music in Die Liebe macht kurzen Prozess, oder Die Heirat auf gewisse Art (1798)

Addns to Gluck: La Cythère assiégée, in Ger. as Die Belagerung von Cythere, Wieden, 19 Jan 1796

Hofmann, Heinrich (Karl Johann) (*b* Berlin, 13 Jan 1842; *d* Gross-Tabarz, Thuringia, 16 July 1902). German composer. He studied in Berlin, with Kullak, Dehn and others, and was later active as a pianist and teacher. His comic opera *Cartouche* (1869) enjoyed great success, suggesting that he stood on the brink of a distinguished career as a composer. His next two operas, *Armin* and *Ännchen von Tharau*, as well as his choral and orchestral music, assured his growing fame in the 1870s and 80s throughout Germany. However, the fashionable eclecticism of his work did not provide a basis for continuing success; he was able to absorb current trends but not to enrich them. Hanslick described him as 'a reliable, skilled practical musician, able to present commonplace ideas in a tastefully refined form'.

Cartouche (komische Oper, 1, W. Fellechner), Berlin, 2 July 1869, vs (Berlin, *c*1870)

Der Matador (Operette, 1, Simmel), Berlin, Friedrich-Wilhelmstrasse, 13 April 1872

Armin (grosse Oper, 5, F. Dahn), Dresden, Hof, 13 Oct 1877

Ännchen von Tharau (romantische Oper, 3, R. Fels), Hamburg, 6 Nov 1878

Wilhelm von Oranien (grosse Oper, 3, Fels), Hamburg, 5 Feb 1882

Donna Diana (komische Oper, 3, E. Wittkowski), Berlin, Kgl, 5 Nov 1886

THOMAS M. LANGNER

Hofmann, Ludwig (*b* Frankfurt, 14 Jan 1895; *d* Frankfurt, 28 Dec 1963). German bass. He studied in Frankfurt and Milan, and made his début in 1918 at Bamberg. After engagements in Dessau, Bremen, Wiesbaden and Berlin he sang with the Vienna Staatsoper (1935–55). He also worked at Bayreuth (1928–42), where he sang King Mark, Gurnemanz, King Henry, Hunding, Fafner, Hagen and Daland. In 1932 he made his débuts at both Covent Garden (as Wotan) and the Metropolitan (as Hagen). He later sang in the première of Einem's *Der Prozess* at Salzburg (1953). A versatile singer, he included in his repertory the roles of Osmin, the Commendatore, Hans Sachs, Procida, Fiesco and Padre Guardiano.

ELIZABETH FORBES

Hofmann, Peter (*b* Mariánské Lázně, 12 Aug 1944). German tenor. A rock singer as a student, he took singing lessons during military service and afterwards at the Karlsruhe Conservatory. He joined the Lübeck Opera, making his début as Tamino in 1972, but from the time of his first appearance as Siegmund, at Wuppertal in 1974, his career developed into that of a leading Wagner Heldentenor. Since singing Siegmund in the centenary *Ring* (1976), followed by Parsifal, he has had regular engagements at Bayreuth, and his débuts at Covent Garden and in the USA (at San Francisco) were both as Siegmund in 1977. He first sang at the Metropolitan Opera in 1980 as Lohengrin, recorded and filmed *Tristan* with Bernstein (1983) and appeared as Schnorr von Carolsfeld, the first Tristan, in a television biography of Wagner. From time to time he has sought to combine operatic work with rock singing, not always to the advantage of an operatic voice which, at its best, is of virile tonal splendour and heroic commitment.

S. von Buchau: 'Tales of Hofmann', *ON*, xlviii/2 (1983–4), 17–20

NOËL GOODWIN

Hofmannsthal, Hugo von (*b* Vienna, 1 Feb 1874; *d* Vienna, 15 July 1929). Austrian poet, dramatist and librettist. If he was not, as has sometimes been claimed, the greatest of librettists, few writers of comparable distinction, and with an already firmly established literary reputation, have applied themselves so conscientiously and over so long a period to the composition of operatic librettos. During the 23 years of his collaboration with Richard Strauss, Hofmannsthal not only restored the words in opera to their former position of creative equality with music but also wrote librettos which are among the few that can be enjoyed as literature.

Hofmannsthal was born into a cultured Viennese family of Austrian, Italian, Swabian and Jewish origins, from whom he inherited a naturally cosmopolitan spirit and an instinctive sympathy with all that was best in the arts. A boy of precocious literary gifts and an abnormally sensitive intelligence, by the age of 17 he had astonished artistic circles in Vienna and throughout the German-speaking world with a steady stream of lyric poems of a mature beauty and perfection of form that inevitably suggested comparisons with the young Rimbaud. By his mid-20s Hofmannsthal's seemingly spontaneous poetic flow had run dry, provoking a crisis of intellect and sensibility; rejecting the extreme aestheticism of his earlier poetry, and stimulated by his rediscovery of Baroque theatre, especially Calderón, he emerged with a new faith in the ability of drama to fulfil a social and humanizing role. By presenting an experience of life as it ought to be, he believed that poetry, drama and music together could both transform the way people lived their lives and provide a cure for the moral ills of industrial society; these ideals lay behind his foundation, with Max Reinhardt, of the Salzburg Festival in 1920, and equally pervaded his major plays, such as *Jedermann* (1912) or *Der Turm* (1925), and his librettos.

Although Hofmannsthal was not particularly sensitive to music, he later acknowledged that even the short lyrical dramas of his youth were secretly designed as 'fantastic little operas and Singspiels without music'. In 1900 he approached Strauss with the scenario for a ballet, *Der Triumph der Zeit*, but the composer felt unable to set it. Six years later, however, Strauss suggested that they should make an opera together out of the free adaptation of Sophocles' *Electra* that Hofmannsthal had produced in 1903, thus inaugurating the collaboration that was to continue until the poet's death. Since they rarely met, they left in their correspondence what is probably the most detailed documentation of the creative interaction of a composer and a librettist (in the case of *Der Rosenkavalier* their letters must be supplemented by the correspondence between Hofmannsthal and Harry, Count Kessler). Whereas Strauss had the sharper theatrical sense, Hofmannsthal possessed the greater taste and subtlety, insisting that as much care should be given to decor, costumes and production as to text and music. In each of his librettos, whether in the comedy of manners of *Der Rosenkavalier* and *Arabella*, the symbolic myth of *Die Frau ohne Schatten* and *Die ägyptische Helena* or the interaction of comedy and tragedy in *Ariadne auf Naxos*, Hofmannsthal set Strauss a different compositional problem. Yet his librettos also form a consistent whole in their continuously developing exploration of love, not in the sense of what he once described as the 'intolerable erotic screamings' of Tristan and Isolde, but in the humane fusion of mature friendship, comparison and mutual understanding. The supple beauty of the poetry, the fluid precision of the conversational interchanges and the symbolic allusiveness that gives to each work a dimension beyond its stage reality are absorbed into a vivid delineation of character and personality. It was to Hofmannsthal's memory that Auden and Kallman dedicated their libretto for Henze's *Elegy for Young Lovers*.

For illustration *see* DRESDEN, fig.7.

Librettos (all set by Richard Strauss): Der Rosenkavalier, 1911; Ariadne auf Naxos, 1st version 1912, 2nd version 1916; Die Frau ohne Schatten, 1919; Die ägyptische Helena, 1928; Arabella, 1933; Die Liebe der Danae (draft, written out by J. Gregor), dress rehearsal for cancelled première, 1944

Plays on which operas have been based: Der Tor und der Tod (1893), H. Brehme, 1928; Alkestis (1893), Wellesz, 1924; Das

Bergwerk zu Falun (1899), Wagner-Régeny, 1961; Die Hochzeit der Sobeide (1899), A. Tcherepnin, 1933; Elektra (1903), R. Strauss, 1909; Oedipus und die Sphinx (1905), Varèse, comp. 1909–13

*

K. J. Krüger: *Hugo von Hofmannsthal und Richard Strauss* (Berlin, 1935)
M. Hottinger, T. Stern and J. Stern, eds.: *H. von Hofmannsthal: Selected Writings*, i: *Selected Prose* (London and New York, 1952); iii: *Selected Plays and Libretti* (London and New York, 1963)
F. Strauss and A. Strauss, eds.: *R. Strauss und H. von Hofmannsthal: Briefwechsel* (Zürich, 1952; Eng. trans., 1961)
E. Wellesz: 'Hofmannsthal and Strauss', *ML*, xxxiii (1952), 239–42
H. Hammelmann: *Hofmannsthal* (Cambridge, 1957)
W. Pfeiffer-Belli, ed.: *Harry, Graf Kessler: Tagebücher 1918–1937* (Frankfurt, 1961)
G. Baum: *Richard Strauss und Hugo von Hofmannsthal* (Berlin, 1962)
W. Schuh: *Hugo von Hofmannsthal und Richard Strauss: Legende und Wirklichkeit* (Munich, 1964)
H. Burger, ed.: *H. von Hofmannsthal und Harry, Graf Kessler: Briefwechsel 1898–1929* (Frankfurt, 1969)
P. J. Smith: *The Tenth Muse* (London, 1971)
W. H. Auden: 'A Marriage of True Minds', *Forewords and Afterwords* (London, 1973), 345–50 [on the Strauss-Hofmannsthal correspondence]
ROBERT HENDERSON

Hofoper (Ger.: 'court opera'). The term used for any opera company in the German-speaking lands that was supported by a court establishment, for example an imperial or royal court (such as those in Vienna and Berlin), an electoral one (as in Dresden, Munich or Mannheim) or a smaller princely or ducal court. They were chiefly taken over as national or state opera companies (Staatsoper) or as municipal ones (Städtische Oper) as the courts were supplanted, some in the 19th century, the remainder about the time of World War I.

Hogarth, George (*b* Carfrae Mill, Berwicks., 1783; *d* London, 12 Feb 1870). Scottish writer on music. Initially a lawyer in Edinburgh, where he was joint secretary of the Edinburgh Musical Festivals from 1815, he moved to London in 1830; there he contributed to the *Harmonicon* and later became joint editor and music critic for the *Morning Chronicle*, then music critic of the *Daily News*, 1846–66. His writings were valuable in their day in introducing music to a wide public, and remain interesting for their vivid and open-minded account of Victorian musicians and musical life. His *Memoirs of the Musical Drama* (London, 1838, 2/1851 as *Memoirs of the Opera*) is an important source for the study of London operatic life of the period.

JOHN WARRACK

Hoher Bass (Ger.: 'high bass'). Term used by Wagner and others for a voice of the BASS-BARITONE type, for such roles as Wotan and Hans Sachs.

Hoiby, Lee (*b* Madison, WI, 17 Feb 1926). American composer. He studied the piano with Egon Petri and composition with Menotti at the Curtis Institute. A recipient of several major awards, he has achieved wide acclaim as both composer and pianist. In addition to operas, his works for the theatre include ballets and incidental music for more than 20 stage productions.

Hoiby's first opera, *The Scarf* (1958), was commissioned by the Curtis Institute's founder, Mary Louise Curtis Bok. In one act, it is based on Chekhov's *The Witch* and tells the story of a Circe-like enchantress who strangles her betrayed husband with a crimson scarf. It was given its American première by the New York City

Opera in 1959 and has been performed in Japan, Italy, Germany, the Netherlands and Australia. *Beatrice* (1959), commissioned by WAVE-TV in Louisville and recorded for the Louisville Orchestra First Edition Series, was broadcast on 23 October 1959; it was staged by Kentucky Opera Association a week later. The moving tale of a medieval nun's fall from grace and her mystical redemption derives from Maeterlinck's *Soeur Béatrice*.

Commissioned by the New York City Opera, *Natalia Petrovna* (1964) was inspired by Turgenev's *A Month in the Country*. It was directed by the opera's librettist, William Ball, and conducted by Julius Rudel, with Maria Dornya and John Reardon in the main roles. The opera was revised as *A Month in the Country* and presented in Boston in 1981. *Summer and Smoke*, from the play by Tennessee Williams, was first performed by the St Paul Opera, Minnesota, in 1971 and produced by the New York City Opera the following year.

Hoiby also wrote the children's opera *Something New for the Zoo* (1982) and two humorous monodramas, *The Italian Lesson* (1985) and *Bon Appetit!* (1986). The latter, based on a chocolate cake recipe by Julia Child, was composed as a curtain-raiser or a companion piece to *The Italian Lesson*. The premières of the monodramas were given by the actress Jean Stapleton. Hoiby's *The Tempest* (1986), the first commissioned opera of the Des Moines Metro Opera, contains traditional preludes, trios, large ensembles and arias that are haunting and dramatic; John Rockwell wrote of its 'lush, beautiful and stratospherically difficult music' for the leading soprano (*New York Times*, 12 July 1986).

Hoiby writes in a conservative, tonal and post-Romantic idiom that shows his heritage from Menotti, Barber, Mahler and Debussy. He has an innate sense of melody, and his long flowing lines are lyrical, expressive and at times deeply melancholic. Highlighted by a rich orchestral fabric, Hoiby's characters are often given individual identification through thematic association and other musical means.

See also SUMMER AND SMOKE.

The Scarf op.12, 1955 (1, H. Duncan, after A. P. Chekhov: *The Witch*), Spoleto, 20 June 1958
Letter to Morocco (1, Hoiby), 1955
Beatrice op.18 (3, M. Nardi, after M. Maeterlinck: *Soeur Béatrice*), WAVE-TV, 23 Oct 1959; stage, Louisville, Columbia Auditorium, 30 Oct 1959
Natalia Petrovna op.24 (2, W. Ball, after I. Turgenev: *A Month in the Country*), New York, City Center, 8 Oct 1964, vs (New York, 1965); as A Month in the Country, Boston, Jan 1981
Summer and Smoke op.27 (2, L. Wilson, after T. Williams), St Paul, O'Shaughnessy Auditorium, 19 June 1971, vs (New York, 1972)
Something New for the Zoo op.31, 1979 (ob, 1, D. Huppler), Cheverly, MD, 17 May 1982, vs (New York, 1989)
The Italian Lesson op.34 (monodrama, 1, after R. Draper), Baltimore, Peabody Conservatory, 23 Jan 1985
Bon Appetit! op.45, 1986 (monodrama, 1, after J. Child), Washington DC, Kennedy Center, 8 March 1989 [companion piece to The Italian Lesson]
The Tempest (3, M. Shulgasser, after W. Shakespeare), Indianola, IA, Blank Performing Arts Center, 21 June 1986, vs (New York, 1991)

*

I. Kolodin: 'Hoiby on Turgenev's Natalia Petrovna', *Stereo Review* (24 Oct 1964)
L. Hoiby: 'Making Tennessee Williams Sing', *New York Times* (13 June 1971)
B. Fischer-Williams: '"Summer and Smoke" – On the Wings of Music with Lee Hoiby', *City Center Arts*, ii/2 (1971–2), 3, 6

G. Schmidgall: 'A Long Voyage', ON, l/17 (1985–6), 10–13 [on *The Tempest*]
'Lee Hoiby', *Current Biography*, xlviii/3 (1987), 17–21
W. Krusemark: *Two Early Operas by Lee Hoiby, 'The Scarf' and 'A Month in the Country': a Stylistic Analysis and Commentary* (diss., U. of Missouri, Kansas City, 1989)
R. H. Kornick: *Recent American Opera: a Production Guide* (New York, 1991), 145–9
ELISE K. KIRK

Höiseth, Kolbjörn (*b* Börsa, 29 Dec 1932). Norwegian tenor. He studied in Stockholm and was engaged at the Royal Opera there in 1959, making his début as Siegmund. His repertory contained all Wagner's tenor roles, from Tannhäuser and Lohengrin, which he sang at Covent Garden (1963), to Siegfried and Parsifal, which he sang at the Deutsche Oper, Berlin (1966). His repertory included Florestan, Don Carlos, Albert Gregor (*The Makropulos Affair*) and Laca (*Jenůfa*), which he sang at the 1974 Edinburgh Festival. His voice, though it had the range and power of a heroic tenor, lacked ideal fullness of tone for the heavier Wagner roles, but he was especially convincing in semicharacter parts such as Herod (*Salome*), Aegisthus (*Elektra*) and Mephistopheles (Busoni's *Doktor Faust*).

ELIZABETH FORBES

Holbrooke, Joseph [Josef] (*b* Croydon, 5 July 1878; *d* London, 5 Aug 1958). English composer. He studied at the RAM, then worked as a conductor and pianist. An eccentric with a penchant for monumental conceptions, he was considered by some the great hope of English music. He thrived on controversy and repeatedly castigated the English public for their apathy towards young English composers, himself included. His career as a composer began with the first performance of his orchestral poem *The Raven* at the Crystal Palace in 1900; provincial festivals then commissioned large-scale choral works. Holbrooke's influential supporters included Henry Wood and Thomas Beecham; Beecham's advocacy did much to influence public and critical opinion.

Holbrooke's first opera, the allegorical *Pierrot and Pierrette*, shows an uncharacteristic paring of resources, with only four major characters and a small orchestra. It deals with the resilience of the love of Pierrot and Pierrette despite the Stranger's temptation of Pierrot with worldly pleasures. His later opera-ballet *The Enchanter* (commissioned for Chicago as *The Enchanted Garden*) is most noteworthy for combining opera, mime and ballet in a single dramatic work.

Holbrooke's association with Lord Howard de Walden (T. E. Ellis) exerted the greatest influence on his music and resulted in an operatic trilogy of mammoth proportions, *The Cauldron of Annwn* (based on Welsh myths from *The Mabinogion*). The first opera to be composed was *Dylan*. Later Ellis provided two further librettos, placing *Dylan* at the central chronological point of the trilogy, which concerns the playing out of the effects of a cauldron whose fumes magnify emotion to the point of obsession. Ellis links two quite distinct tales by invoking a metaphysical reincarnation: the third opera, *Bronwen*, is a replaying not of the actual events of the first two, but of the interactions of personalities. Holbrooke musically underwrites the convoluted literary connections with an extensive system of leitmotifs. Much of his thematic material is diatonic, and a few Welsh folktunes are employed, but the harmony is typical of his other works (essentially late Romantic, with wide-ranging chromaticism, irregular resolutions of dissonance and ambiguous tonal centres). Through-composed recitative-arioso occasionally leads to a definable aria. Holbrooke's wide experience of choral writing is evident in his consummate handling of the chorus, particularly in *Dylan* and in the highly effective boys' chorus that closes *Bronwen*. The latter (not performed until 1929, by the touring Carl Rosa company) is musically and dramatically the most satisfying of the trilogy. All three very long operas demand extensive resources; they all suffered inadequate performances, but the critics were encouraging, finding fault primarily with the complex and often obscure librettos. *Dylan* was championed by Beecham and performed in his Drury Lane season of 1914; *The Children of Don* was revived by Weingartner for Vienna in 1923. Excerpts of the trilogy were recorded in the 1930s, but its large scale discourages revivals, and the operas have never become widely popular. Holbrooke's two comic operas remain unperformed, though *The Snob* has a delightful libretto, in which tramps capitalize on the gullible snobbery of the new Squire by claiming to be society folk on a gypsy vacation. *The Sailor's Arms* is based on sea shanties.

Pierrot and Pierrette op.36 (lyrical drama, 2 scenes, W. E. Grogan), London, His Majesty's, 11 Nov 1909, vs (London, 1909); as The Stranger, Liverpool, 13 Nov 1924, vs (London, 1923)
Dylan: Son of the Wave op.53, 1909 (3, T. E. Ellis [Lord Howard de Walden], after *The Mabinogion*), London, Drury Lane, 4 July 1914 (London, 1911) [pt 2 of trilogy The Cauldron of Annwn]
The Children of Don op.56 (prol., 3, Ellis, after *The Mabinogion*), London Opera House, 15 June 1912 (London, 1913) [pt 1 of trilogy The Cauldron of Annwn]
The Enchanter op.70 (opera-ballet, 3, D. Malloch, after M. Rabinoff), Chicago, Auditorium, spr. 1915, vs (London, 1914, as The Wizard)
Bronwen op.75, 1920 (3, Ellis, after *The Mabinogion*), Huddersfield, 1 Feb 1929 (London, 1929) [pt 3 of trilogy The Cauldron of Annwn]
Unperf.: The Sailor's Arms (comic op, A. P. Herbert); The Snob op.49 (comic op, 1, C. McEvoy; G. K. Chesterton and H. H. Ryan); Tamlane

*

H. Klein: 'Mr Joseph Holbrooke's New Opera *The Children of Don*', MT, liii (1912), 309
W. Wearenear-Yeomans: 'An English Opera for America', *Musical Standard*, v (1915), 331 [on The Enchanted Garden]
F. G. Webb: 'Holbrooke's New Opera-ballet, *The Enchanted Garden*', MT, lvi (1915), 402–3
G. Lowe: *Josef Holbrooke and his Work* (London, 1920)
T. E. Ellis: *The Cauldron of Annwn* (London, 1922)
N. Demuth: 'Holbrooke and his New Opera', *Sackbut*, x (1928–9), 276–7 [on Bronwen]
N. V. Dagg: 'Josef Holbrooke and his Music', *The Search*, i (1931), 56–7
Josef Holbrooke: Various Appreciations by Many Authors (London, 1937)
G. Davidson: *Standard Stories from the Operas* (London, 1944), 250–84
C. Scott: 'A Tribute to Josef Holbrooke', MT, xcix (1958), 425–6
K. L. Thompson: 'Holbrooke – Some Catalogue Data', ML, xlvi (1965), 297–305
P. Washtell: 'The Operas of Josef Holbrooke', *British Opera in Retrospect* (n.p., 1986) [pubn of the British Music Society], 89–91
L. Foreman: *From Parry to Britten: British Music in Letters 1900–1945* (London, 1987), 125–7   ANNE-MARIE H. FORBES

Holcombe, Henry (*b* ?Salisbury, *c*1690; *d* London, *c*1750). English singer. He was a chorister at Salisbury and then sang at Drury Lane from February 1705, billed first as the 'new Boy'. He often sang Purcell's music, including Cupid in the masque in *Timon of Athens*. He had substantial roles in two English operas in the Italian style, Prenesto in Bononcini's *Camilla* (1706) and the Page in Clayton's *Rosamond* (1707). He later taught the

harpsichord and singing, making only a few concert appearances as a singer from 1709, and published a number of songs.

*

BDA; BurneyH; DNB (R. F. Sharp); HawkinsH; LS
J. Sainsbury, ed.: *Dictionary of Musicians* (London, 2/1825)
          OLIVE BALDWIN, THELMA WILSON

Holland, Charles (*b* Norfolk, VA, 27 Dec 1909; *d* Amsterdam, 7 Nov 1987). American tenor. He studied in Hollywood and in New York with Clyde Burrows, and performed in Virgil Thomson's *Four Saints in Three Acts*. Having moved to France in 1949, he made his European début as Monostatos in *Die Zauberflöte* at the Opéra in 1954; the following year he became the first black singer to appear at the Opéra-Comique. He enjoyed a successful career in French, German and Dutch theatres in such roles as Faust and Nadir. He also sang in Italy, Switzerland, Scandinavia, Australia and Canada.   CHARLES JAHANT

Holland, Jan Dawid [Johann David] (*b* St Andreasberg, nr Hanover, 17 March 1746; *d* Vilnius, 26 Dec 1827). Polish composer of German birth. After holding an ecclesiastical post in Hamburg he left for Poland, and by about 1780 was in Warsaw for the first performance of *Cudzy majątek nikomu nie służy* ('Another Person's Property is Good for No One', 2; *PL-Wn*). He became a Kapellmeister in Prince Karol Radziwiłł's residence in Nieśwież in 1782. On 17 September 1784, during King Stanisław August Poniatowski's visit to Nieśwież, Holland's opera *Agatka czyli przyjazd pana* ('Agatha, or The Arrival of the Master', 3, M. Radziwiłł; *PL-Kp*) was performed; the work was later reduced as *Pan dobrý jest ojcem poddanych* ('A Good Host is the Father of Service') and given at Lwów on 17 July 1796. After the properties in Nieśwież had been confiscated by Catherine the Great, Holland settled in Vilnius and lectured at the university, 1802–26. He made extensive use of Polish folk music, particularly in his operas. In *Cudzy majątek nikomu nie służy* there is an extended polonaise aria 'alla Polacca' with virtuoso accents. The music in *Agatka* displays the tangle of various stylistic mannerisms of the late 18th century: the overture is in sonata form, but instead of a development section a 'new idea' is introduced, and the arias are mostly in the *opera buffa* tradition but contain clear elements of Polish folk music, such as rhythms of the krakowiak, oberek and polonaise.

*

SMP
J. Bieliński: *Uniwersytet Wileński* [Vilnius University] (Kraków, 1899–1900)
W. Zahorski: *Pamiętniki Dr Józefa Franka ... przetl. z francuskiego* [Memoir of Dr Joseph Frank] (Vilnius, 1913)
A. Nowak-Romanowicz: 'Muzyka polskiego oświecenia i wczesnego romantyzmu' [Polish Music in the Age of the Enlightenment and Early Romanticism], *Z dziejów polskiej kultury muzycznej*, ii (Kraków, 1966)   ALINA NOWAK-ROMANOWICZ

Holland Festival. Festival of music, opera, dance and the visual arts. It was founded in 1947 by H. J. Reinink, with Peter Diamand as secretary and, from 1950 to 1965, artistic director. At first, events were held concurrently in Amsterdam, The Hague and other Netherlands cities, but since 1980 opera has been virtually restricted to Amsterdam. The first operas performed, in 1948, were *Pelléas et Mélisande* and *The Beggar's Opera* (in the English Opera Group production). Since the formation in 1949 of Netherlands Opera, that company has staged a large proportion of the operatic events, the rest being provided by visiting companies from abroad. During its early years the festival ran from mid-June to mid-July; from the mid-1970s the dates were altered to cover the month of June.

The festival has staged an impressive number of operatic premières, including those of Hendrik Andriessen's *Philomela* (1950), Françaix's *L'apostrophe* (1951), Dresden's *François Villon* (1958), Badings's *Martin Korda DP* (1960), Ton de Leeuw's *De droom* (1965), Schat's *Labyrinth* (1966), the collaborative work *Reconstructie* (1969), Kruyf's *Spinoza* (1971), Reinbert de Leeuw's *Axel* (1977), Gilse's *Thijl* and Schat's *Aap verslaat de knekelgeest* (1980), Daniel Kessner's *The Tell Tale Heart* and Ian McQueen's *Mirror of Truth* (1982), Loevendie's *Naima* (1985) and *Gassier* (1991) and Louis Andriessen's *De materie* (1989).

The festival has sought to re-establish Haydn's operas with productions of *Il mondo della luna* (1959), *L'infedeltà delusa* (1963), *Le pescatrici* (1965) and *La fedeltà premiata* (1970). It has been important for the dissemination of Britten's works on the Continent, having given the first foreign performances of several operas and the church parables. More recently, it has featured music-theatre pieces by Peter Maxwell Davies and has revived neglected 20th-century works such as Hindemith's *Mörder, Hoffnung der Frauen* and *Sancta Susanna*. The festival gave the first performance outside Germany of Zimmermann's *Die Soldaten* (1971), celebrated the American bicentenary with the presentation of Floyd's *Of Mice and Men* (1976) and staged the European première of John Adams's *Nixon in China* (1988).

Peter Diamand, who had done so much to build up the success of the festival, was succeeded as artistic director in 1966 by Jaap den Daas, who encouraged experimental forms of music theatre by younger composers seeking a break with traditional forms. Productions of this kind have included *To You* (Schat), *Apocalypse* (Studio Laren and Theater Unie), *Cain and Abel* (Breuker and Lodewijk de Boer) and *Cheap Imitation* (Cage) in 1972, *Het vijfde seizoen* (Schat) and *Night* (William York) in 1973, and *Zwei-Mann-Orchester* (Kagel) in 1974. The composer Jan van Vlijmen was appointed artistic director in 1991.

See also NETHERLANDS, THE.

NOËL GOODWIN, ELIZABETH FORBES

Hölle, Matthias (*b* Rottweil, 8 July 1951). German bass. He studied in Stuttgart and in Cologne, where he made his début in 1976 and took part in Matthus's *Omphale* in 1979. Between 1981 and 1989 he sang the Nightwatchman, Hunding, Fasolt and Titurel at Bayreuth; in 1984 he created roles in Stockhausen's *Samstag aus Licht* at La Scala and Ostendorf's *Murieta* in Cologne. He has also sung at Bologna, Turin, Florence, Geneva, Houston, the Metropolitan and Stuttgart. His darktoned voice is especially suited to Wagner's King Mark and Hunding, which he sang at Bayreuth (1990), but his repertory also includes Sarastro, the Commendatore, Dikoj (*Kát'a Kabanová*), Raimondo (*Lucia di Lammermoor*) and Henry VIII (*Anna Bolena*).

ELIZABETH FORBES

Höller, York (George) (*b* Leverkusen, 11 Jan 1944). German composer. He entered the Cologne Hochschule für Musik in 1963, and studied composition there under

B. A. Zimmermann (1968–70), having assisted at the première of Zimmermann's *Die Soldaten* in Cologne in 1965. Between 1969 and 1972 he worked in the electronic music studios of Herbert Eimert and Stockhausen. He first met Boulez at Darmstadt in 1965 and in the mid-1970s was one of the first composers invited to work at IRCAM in Paris; his *Arcus* for chamber orchestra and electronics (1978) became one of the most celebrated early products of the research centre.

Höller's compositional techniques draw on the serialism of Boulez as well as elements of Zimmermann's stylistic pluralism, but it is Stockhausen's use of melodic formula that appears to lie behind his concept of 'Klanggestalt', the development of a 'macro series' from which the parameters of a composition may be determined and which enables electro-acoustic transformations to be integrated with melodic and harmonic manipulations. The Klanggestalt employed in *Schwarze Halbinseln* for orchestra (1982) and in the Strindberg setting *Traumspiel* was also used to determine the organization of his two-act opera *Der Meister und Margarita*, based on Bulgakov's surreal allegorical novel. The opera, which Höller worked on from 1984 to 1988, includes sections for pre-recorded tape (realized at IRCAM and in Cologne) juxtaposed with richly varied orchestral and vocal writing. It received its première in Paris on 20 May 1989.

See also MEISTER UND MARGARITA, DER (ii).

Y. Höller: 'Resonance: Composition Today', *Contemporary Music Review*, i/1 (1984), 67–76
J. Stenzl: 'York Höller's *The Master and Margarita*: a German Opera', *Tempo*, no.179 (1991), 8–15   ANDREW CLEMENTS

Holliday, Melanie (*b* Houston, 12 Aug 1951). American soprano. After study at Indiana University she moved to Europe, where she sang in Hamburg from 1973. Her reputation has been established in the coloratura repertory and in operetta; among her best roles are Adina, Zerbinetta, Olympia, Nicolai's Mrs Ford and Konstanze. She sang with the Vienna Volksoper from 1976, appearing with the company in its tours of Japan in 1979, 1982 and 1985. Her operetta repertory includes roles in *Die lustige Witwe* and *Die Fledermaus* (Adele at Barcelona, 1984). In 1986 she sang Musetta at the Theater am Gärtnerplatz, Munich.

DAVID CUMMINGS

Hollingsworth, Stanley [Hollier] (*b* Berkeley, CA, 27 Aug 1924). American composer. He studied with Milhaud at Mills College and with Menotti at the Curtis Institute, where he taught composition and assisted Menotti. He was a musical director for the Spoleto Festival of Two Worlds in 1960. After teaching at San Jose College (1961–3), he joined the faculty of Oakland University, Rochester, Michigan, where he became professor of music and composer-in-residence. His first opera, *The Mother* (1954), commissioned by the Curtis Institute and first performed there, is based on the Hans Christian Andersen fairy-tale about a mother who makes an arduous journey to rescue her child from Death. Hollingsworth was the youngest composer of his time to write an opera for American national television, *La grande Bretèche* (NBC, 1957). A popular trilogy was formed when his children's operas *The Selfish Giant* and *Harrison Loved his Umbrella* were first staged, together with *The Mother*, at the Spoleto Festival in Charleston, South Carolina, in 1981.

Hollingsworth's operas are lyrical and poetic with well-paced narrative movement and direction. His style has been described as 'Italianate with an almost Parisian proclivity for coloristic nuances' (N. Malitz, *Detroit Free Press*, 15 June 1987). According to Menotti, with whom he has been compared, his talents include a 'natural sense of melody and an exquisite awareness of musical form'.

The Mother (1, Hollingsworth and J. Fandel, after H. C. Andersen), Philadelphia, Curtis Institute of Music, 29 March 1954

La grande Bretèche (television op, 1, Hollingsworth and H. Duncan, after H. de Balzac), NBC, 10 Feb 1957

The Selfish Giant (1, Hollingsworth and H. Moulton, after O. Wilde), Charleston, SC, Dock Street, 24 May 1981

Harrison Loved his Umbrella (musical cartoon, 1, R. Levine), Charleston, Dock Street, 24 May 1981

B. Land: 'A Composer Serious about Television Music', *New York Times* (12 Feb 1957)

P. Affelder: 'Italian High Spots', *ON*, xxviii/2 (1963–4), 29

C. Babcock: 'Opera Trilogy Rousing Success', *Evening Post* [Charleston, SC] (25 May 1981)

J. Guinn: 'Director Finds Secret to Staging an Opera', *Detroit Free Press* (12 June 1987)

R. H. Kornick: *Recent American Opera: a Production Guide* (New York, 1991), 149–52

ELISE K. KIRK

Holloway, Robin (Greville) (*b* Leamington Spa, 19 Oct 1943). English composer. He studied with Alexander Goehr and read English and music at Cambridge University (1961–4), where he became lecturer in music in 1975. His early music (1962–9) was predominantly constructivist and motoric, including his first stage piece, a short setting for speakers and jazz-like ensemble of Eliot's *Sweeney Agonistes* (1965). In the 1970s his admiration for Wagner and a series of works based on Schumann lieder inspired a recension of a more Romantic sensibility, culminating in his two-act opera, *Clarissa* op.30 (1976), after Richardson's novel. Since then he has tended to mix Romantic and modernistic procedures, laced with a generous range of musical quotations, in varying proportions according to genre.

Clarissa was uncommissioned, and its failure to reach the stage for 14 years diverted Holloway's theatrical aspirations into hybrid concert projects, notably the 'dramatic ballad' *Brand* (1981), after Ibsen's play, and a large 'concert opera' on *Peer Gynt* (begun 1984), after the precedent of Berlioz's *La damnation de Faust*. However, the 1990 staging of *Clarissa* at the London Coliseum and a further ENO commission have given new impetus to his intention of composing a full-length comic opera. Since the publication of his dissertation, *Wagner and Debussy* (London, 1979), he has also contributed many illuminating opera articles to books and periodicals, notably on Wagner, Strauss, Berg and Britten.

See also CLARISSA.

P. P. Nash: '"Cantata on the Death of God" and "Clarissa"', *Tempo*, no.129 (1979), 27–34, [Holloway issue]

A. Bye: 'Holloway's "Clarissa"', *MT*, cxxxi (1990), 243–6

BAYAN NORTHCOTT

Hollreiser, Heinrich (*b* Munich, 24 June 1913). German conductor. After studying at the Munich Academy, he worked in Wiesbaden, Darmstadt, Mannheim and Duisburg, and then joined the Munich Opera in 1942 at the recommendation of Krauss. During the era of the illustrious actor-director Gustaf Gründgens he was for seven years Generalmusikdirektor in Düsseldorf. In 1952 he became principal Kapellmeister at the Vienna Staatsoper and from 1961 to 1964 he held the same post at the Deutsche Oper in Berlin, where he led the premières of Klebe's *Alkmene* (1961) and Sessions's *Montezuma* (1964). In 1969 he conducted the première in Berlin of Blacher's *Zweihunderttausend Taler*. He won respect as an advocate of *Wozzeck*, *Mathis der Maler* and *Bluebeard's Castle*, and was admired in Wagner and Richard Strauss. He conducted *Tannhäuser* at the Bayreuth Festival (1973–4) and *Die Meistersinger* (1975), and continued to be active into the 1990s at Munich, Berlin and Vienna, conducting the Vienna Staatsoper in *Parsifal* at Tokyo in 1989. His recordings include *Der Zigeunerbaron* (1960), and his consideration for singers and reliable partnership with them put him in demand for operatic recital discs, of which those with Della Casa in Richard Strauss and Handel are much admired.   HANS CHRISTOPH WORBS, NOËL GOODWIN

Hollweg, Ilse (*b* Solingen, nr Düsseldorf, 23 Feb 1922; *d* Solingen, 9 Feb 1990). German soprano. She was a student with Gertrude Förstel at the Musikhochschule in Cologne and made her operatic début in 1942 at Saarbrücken as Blonde in *Die Entführung*. After World War II she joined the Düsseldorf Opera as principal coloratura soprano. In 1950 she sang Konstanze at Glyndebourne, followed by Zerbinetta at the Edinburgh Festival. In the next years she sang at Hamburg, Berlin and Vienna, making her Covent Garden début as Gilda in 1951, also singing the Queen of Night there. In 1954 she returned to Glyndebourne, repeating her acclaimed Zerbinetta. She sang Konstanze at Salzburg in 1955 and for several years was Bayreuth's Woodbird in *Siegfried*. Her recordings include a highly accomplished performance of Zerbinetta's solo, and in *Die Entführung* under Beecham (1956) she is a charming Blonde.   J. B. STEANE

Hollweg, Werner (*b* Solingen, 13 Sept 1936). German tenor. He prepared for a commercial career but took up singing in 1958 and studied in Detmold, Lugano and Munich, making his début with the Vienna Kammeroper in 1962. He joined the Bonn Opera for four seasons from 1963, and from 1968, when he sang Belmonte, appeared more widely in Germany, at the Vienna Staatsoper and regularly at the Salzburg Festival. He developed a close working relationship with Nikolaus Harnoncourt, with whom he recorded the title role in *Idomeneo* (1981) and Eisenstein in *Die Fledermaus* (1988). A stylish lyric tenor, particularly in Mozart, he made his Covent Garden début in 1976 as Titus; in 1989 he sang in the première of Höller's *Der Meister und Margarita* in Paris. He has long been a much-admired concert soloist.   NOËL GOODWIN

Holm, Grete (*b* Brno, *c*1882; *d* after 1920). Austrian soprano. She studied in Brno and in Vienna under Rosa Papier-Paumgartner. She was coached by Robert Stolz in Brno and in 1904 appeared in his *Manöverliebe* and became his first wife; she also appeared as Marie in *La fille du régiment* at the German theatre there. She and Stolz moved to Vienna, singing principally at the Theater an der Wien, where she created the leading soprano roles in Straus's *Der tapfere Soldat* (1908; singing 'Komm', komm', Held meiner Träume') and Kálmán's *Ein Herbstmanöver* (1909). After separating from Stolz she went on to create the leading soprano roles of Zorika in Lehár's *Zigeunerliebe* (1910,

Carltheater) and Sári in Kálmán's *Der Zigeunerprimás* (1912, Johann Strauss Theater). Her roles also included Adele and, outside operetta, Aennchen and Philine (*Mignon*).   ANDREW LAMB

Holm, Renate (*b* Berlin, 10 Aug 1931). German soprano. She studied with Maria Ivogün in Vienna, where she made her début in 1957 in operetta. Engaged at the Volksoper and later the Staatsoper, she appeared there for over 20 years. At Salzburg (1961–3) she sang Blonde and Papagena. Her repertory included Zerlina, Despina, Marzelline, Norina, Mařenka, Sophie, Isotta (*Die schweigsame Frau*), Ighino (*Palestrina*) and Musetta, as well as Adele and many operetta roles. She sang in Berlin, Zürich, Lisbon and Buenos Aires. Her delightful personality and pure, well-focussed tone were perfect for soubrette roles.   ELIZABETH FORBES

Holm, Richard (*b* Stuttgart, 3 Aug 1912; *d* Munich, 20 July 1988). German tenor. He studied in Stuttgart with Rudolf Ritter and made his début at Kiel in 1937. After engagements at Nuremberg and Hamburg, in 1948 he joined the Staatsoper in Munich. In 1950 he sang Belmonte at Glyndebourne. He made his Metropolitan début in 1952 as David. At Covent Garden in 1953 he sang David and Flamand in the British première of *Capriccio*, given by the Munich company. He returned to London as Loge, 1958–60 and 1964–6; he also appeared at Bayreuth, Salzburg and Vienna. His extensive repertory included Tamino, which he sang in Felsenstein's 1954 production of *Die Zauberflöte* at the Komische Oper, Berlin, and Robespierre in *Dantons Tod*. At Munich he created Wallenstein in *Die Harmonie der Welt* (1957) and Black in *Die Verlobung in San Domingo* (1963), and in 1975 he sang Aschenbach in *Death in Venice*. His voice, though not large, was well schooled and pleasing, and he was a sensitive performer.   HAROLD ROSENTHAL/R

Holmès [Holmes], Augusta (Mary Anne) (*b* Paris, 16 Dec 1847; *d* Paris, 28 Jan 1903). French composer of Irish parentage. She first studied with Henri Lambert and in 1875 became a pupil of César Franck. By then, having heard *Das Rheingold* in 1869, she was already a devotee of Wagner's music, which is the dominant influence, with that of Franck, over her own. Much of it is conceived on an ample scale for large forces, based on strong classical or mythological subjects, and even in her songs the conception is often orchestral. She wrote a one-act opera *Héro et Léandre* in 1875 (she wrote all her own librettos), followed by *Astarté* and *Lancelot du lac* (MSS in *F-V*). None of these was performed, and her last opera, the four-act *La montagne noire* (vs, Paris, 1895), had a poor reception on its première at the Opéra, 8 February 1895. A tale of love and duty set in the Balkans in the 17th century, this work was criticized for its Wagnerian conception; but despite Holmès's avowed admiration for Wagner, the music is only partially reminiscent of Bayreuth. Although her music has great breadth and virility, her harmony has none of Wagner's fluency and moves too much in static blocks. Ethel Smyth, who was by no means wholly sympathetic to her music, nevertheless declared that it contained 'jewels wrought by one who was evidently not among the giants, but for all that knew how to cut a gem'. Holmès's songs have indeed survived longer than anything else of her output.

The impact of Holmès's music was less striking than that of her personality, which dominated the musical and literary salons of her day. Saint-Saëns, whose offer of marriage she declined, said 'we were all in love with her', and she was admired by Franck, Wagner, d'Indy, De l'Isle-Adam, and Mallarmé; she was for many years the mistress of Catulle Mendès, by whom she had three daughters.

P. Barillon-Bauché: *Augusta Holmès et la femme compositeur* (Paris, 1912)
R. Myers: 'Augusta Holmès: a Meteoric Career', *MQ*, liii (1967), 365–76   HUGH MACDONALD

Holmes, Eugene (*b* Brownsville, TN, 7 March 1934). American baritone. He studied at Bloomington and made his début in 1963 with the Goldovsky Opera Theater in Ward's *The Crucible*. Later he sang Uncle Alfred in Schuller's *The Visitation* in San Francisco (1967), the title role of Delius's *Koanga* in its first performance in the USA (1970, Washington, DC) and in London (1972), and Tolme in the première of Menotti's *The Most Important Man* with the New York City Opera (1971). Engaged at Düsseldorf from 1971 to 1985, he had a wide repertory including Escamillo, John the Baptist (*Salome*), Scarpia, Lescaut and Porgy; his fine voice was especially well suited to Verdi's Macbeth, Luna, Rigoletto, Posa, Renato, Don Carlo (*La forza del destino*), Boccanegra, Amonasro and Iago.

ELIZABETH FORBES

Holoubek, Ladislav (*b* Prague, 13 Aug 1913). Slovak composer. He studied composition at the Bratislava Conservatory under Moyzes before working as conductor at the opera houses of Bratislava and Košice. The first three of his six operas contributed to the creation of Slovak opera in the 20th century. *Svitanie* ('Dawn') is the most original: its use of absolute forms, Slovak folk colouring and balladic elements make it a forerunner of Suchoň's *Krútňava*. *Túžba* ('Aspiration') is a Slovak variation on the Cinderella story.

Holoubek's postwar operas deal with events of the recent past. *Rodina* ('The Family') portrays the Slovak countryside after collectivization; its music derives from Wagnerian and Janáčekian principles. *Professor Mamlock* concerns the rise of Nazism in Germany; here Holoubek uses Schoenbergian techniques in an individual way. The short comic opera *Bačovské žarty* ('Shepherds' Games') is a genre painting of the life of Slovak shepherds in the 1930s.

first performed at the Slovak National Opera, Bratislava, unless otherwise stated

Stella (L. Holoubek, after R. Haggard: *Stella Frigelius*), 18 March 1939; rev. 1948–9, 1954–5
Svitanie [Dawn] (J. Elen-Kaiser), 12 March 1941
Túžba [Aspiration] (F. Gabaj), 12 Feb 1944; rev. 1963, 1969
Rodina [The Family] (Holoubek, after I. Prachař: *Domov je u nás*), 12 Nov 1960
Professor Mamlock (Holoubek, after F. Wolf), 21 May 1966
Bačovské žarty [Shepherds' Games], 1975, Košice, State Opera, 16 Jan 1981

I. Vajda: *Slovenská opera* (Bratislava, 1988), 32–4, 119–25, 208–9, 233–4   IGOR VAJDA

Holst, Gustav(us Theodore von) (*b* Cheltenham, 21 Sept 1874; *d* London, 25 May 1934). English composer. He was a pupil of Stanford and a friend and colleague of Vaughan Williams. His early career as a trombone player (with the Carl Rosa Opera Company) was superseded by teaching, mainly at St Paul's Girls' School, Hammersmith, where he was employed from 1905 until his death. The principal influences on his mature music were the unlikely pairing of Sanskrit literature and English folksong. His most characteristic works are the orchestral *The Planets* (1914–16) and *Egdon Heath* (1927), and the choral *Hymn of Jesus* (1917).

Holst's nine completed operas span his composing life, although few would regard him primarily as an opera composer. When he began his studies at the RCM, in 1893, he had already composed an operetta, *Lansdown Castle*, which had been performed in Cheltenham; it was soon followed by another, *The Revoke*, which he designated his op.1. Both of these, and the later children's operetta, *The Idea* (?1896), were strongly influenced by Sullivan, and not unsuccessful on their own unadventurous terms.

Holst's growing passion for Wagner first became evident in the fragment, which was all that he composed, of *The Magic Mirror* (1896); Wagner's influence dominates *The Youth's Choice* (1902), a ponderously serious 'musical idyll in one act' which Holst soon withdrew, and overwhelms *Sita* (?1899–1906). This three-act opera, based on the Hindu epic, the Ramayana, was his main preoccupation during the period when he was beginning to develop his own musical language. *The Mystic Trumpeter* (1904), a scena for soprano and orchestra to words by Walt Whitman, and the orchestral *A Somerset Rhapsody* (1906–7) both mark significant advances in self-discovery. But, apart from some striking music in Act 3, *Sita* is derivative and lacking in spontaneity; its chief fault lies in its libretto, which is all too redolent of contemporary translations of Wagner.

Entered for the Ricordi prize in 1908, *Sita* was placed third (the winning opera was Edward Naylor's *The Angelus*) and was never performed. Holst turned what could have been a major setback to advantage by rejecting the Wagnerian apparatus, and, in part influenced by the simplicity of the folk music he had recently discovered, began to compose with much greater economy and directness. A set of *Choral Hymns from the Rig Veda* (1908) already pointed in this direction, but with the opera *Sāvitri* (1908–9) Holst achieved a remarkable volte-face. Having little in the way of precedent to guide him, he contrived a one-act chamber opera using only three singers, minimal staging (he suggested performance in the open air) and an orchestra of no more than 12 players. Like *Sita*, *Sāvitri* is based on a Sanskrit text – an episode from the Mahābharata – but in writing his own libretto Holst achieved far greater subtlety, avoiding the bombast of the earlier work, even though occasional archaic usages (e.g. Sāvitri's 'Dost thou not feel? Ah! Canst thou not see?') fail to match the economy of the music. The opera begins and ends with the unaccompanied voices of Death and Sāvitri; the use of an offstage wordless female chorus is equally innovatory.

Holst reached maturity as a composer only with the completion of *The Planets* in 1916, the year in which *Sāvitri* was first staged. Although he had conceived his next opera, *The Perfect Fool*, as early as 1908, it was not until 1918–19, while acting as musical organizer for demobilized troops in the Middle East, that he was able to draft the libretto. The ballet music with which the opera begins was adapted from incidental music written in 1918 for *The Sneezing Charm*, a play by Clifford Bax; the opera was completed in 1922 and first performed in 1923 at Covent Garden. Although *The Perfect Fool* was widely toured until late in 1924 (in a double bill with *Sāvitri*), it never re-entered the repertory. For that, Holst's clumsy scenario and naive sense of humour are perhaps to blame. With the notable exception of the ballet music – well established as an independent concert work – the score does not deserve revival.

For his remaining two operas Holst chose not to be his own librettist. In a letter to a friend at the time of the composition of *At the Boar's Head* (1924) he remarked, characteristically, that 'as the critics have decided that I can't write a libretto, the words of my new opera have been written by Shakespeare'. The 'new opera' was no more of a critical success, however, than *The Perfect Fool*, although it deserved a better reception. In threading together the Falstaff scenes from *Henry IV*, Holst created a libretto whose richness of words was almost a bar to their comprehension, and whose uneventfulness in dramatic terms was disconcerting. But his use throughout the opera of traditional country-dance tunes and folksongs is masterly, and achieved without any suggestion of pastiche. Shakespeare's characters are not sentimentalized, but portrayed with an acid wit, while, with the exception of a soliloquy for the Prince which uses one of Shakespeare's sonnets, the pace of the music is unrelenting.

The uneven quality of these two operas from Holst's middle years reflects the unevenness of his output as a whole. But his major achievements of the period, *The Hymn of Jesus* (1917), *Ode to Death* (1919), *First Choral Symphony* (1923–4), *Egdon Heath* (1927) and *Hammersmith* (1930), are matched by the fine balance of wit and economy achieved in his final opera, *The Wandering Scholar*. This was composed in 1929–30 to a libretto by Clifford Bax after a story from Helen Waddell's *The Wandering Scholars*, and first performed just before his death. A return to the chamber orchestra of *Sāvitri* foreshadows Britten's operas composed for the English Opera Group, and indeed Britten adapted it in 1951 for performances under his direction.

Holst is an isolated figure in English music, and his operatic output is characteristic of that isolation, neither influenced by nor influencing contemporary fashions. The singlemindedness which caused him to make errors of judgment also gave him the strength of purpose to continue to write in a genre to which he was perhaps temperamentally unsuited, and the individuality that informs at least three of his four mature operas sets him strikingly apart from the rest of his contemporaries, even his close friend Vaughan Williams, whose description of Holst as 'uncompromisingly direct' is very apt.

See also AT THE BOAR'S HEAD; PERFECT FOOL, THE; SĀVITRI; and WANDERING SCHOLAR, THE.

H – *no. in Holst, 'Thematic Catalogue' 1974*

Lansdown Castle, or The Sorcerer of Tewkesbury, HAppxI/21 (operetta, 2, A. C. Cunningham), Cheltenham, Corn Exchange, 7 Feb 1893

The Revoke op.1, H7, 1895 (1, F. B. Hart), unperf.

The Magic Mirror, HAppxII/12, 1896 (Hart, after G. Macdonald: *Phantastes*), Gb-Lbl* (frag.)

The Idea H21, ?1896 (children's operetta, Hart), unperf. (London, 1903)

Sita op.23, H89, ?1899–1906 (3, Holst, after the Ramayana), unperf., Lbl*

The Youth's Choice op.11, H60, 1902 (musical idyll, 1, Holst), unperf.; Lbl*

Sāvitri op.25, H96, 1908–9 (chamber op, 1, Holst, after the Mahābharata), London School of Opera, 5 Dec 1916, Ob* (London, 1923)

The Perfect Fool op.39, H150 (1, Holst), London, CG, 14 May 1923, *Lbl** (London, 1923)

At the Boar's Head op.42, H156 (musical interlude, 1, after W. Shakespeare: *King Henry IV*), Manchester, Opera House, 3 April 1925, *Lbl** (London, 1925)

The Wandering Scholar [The Tale of the Wandering Scholar] op.50, H176 (chamber op, 1, C. Bax, after H. Waddell), Liverpool, 31 Jan 1934, Aldeburgh, Britten-Pears Library* (London, 1971)

*

A. Bennett: 'Gustav Holst's *The Perfect Fool*', *Adelphi*, i/1 (1923), 58–60

A. Einstein: 'The Perfect Fool', *MT*, lxiv (1923), 389–93

D. F. Tovey: 'The Perfect Fool or the Perfect Opera', *MT*, lxiv (1923), 464–5

E. Newman: 'At the Boar's Head', *MT*, lxvi (1925), 413–4

E. Rubbra: 'Holst's Last Opera', *The Listener* (30 Dec 1948)

I. Parrott: 'Holst's *Sāvitri* and Bitonality', *MR*, xxviii (1967), 323–8

I. Holst: Introduction to Holst: *Sāvitri* and *The Wandering Scholar*, Collected Fascimile Edition, i (London, 1974)

——: *A Thematic Catalogue of Gustav Holst's Music* (London, 1974)

M. Hurd: 'Holst's Operas', *Music in Education*, xxxviii (1974), 168–70

H. Ottaway: 'Holst as an Opera Composer', *MT*, cxv (1974), 473–4

I. Holst: 'Holst's *At the Boar's Head*', *MT*, cxxiii (1982), 321–2

——: *The Music of Gustav Holst (Revised 3rd Edition) and Holst's Music Reconsidered* (Oxford, 1986)

M. Short: *Gustav Holst: the Man and his Music* (Oxford, 1990)

COLIN MATTHEWS

Holstein, Franz von (*b* Brunswick, 16 Feb 1826; *d* Leipzig, 22 May 1878). German composer. The son of an officer, he studied music with Griepenkerl while serving as a cadet in the army, and composed a two-act opera in Singspiel manner, *Zwei Nächte in Venedig* (1844–5). During a term as adjutant in Seesen he continued composing, and in 1852 was able to show an opera, *Die Gastfreunde*, to Moritz Hauptmann, who encouraged him to leave the army and take up a musical career. Holstein then studied at the Leipzig Conservatory with Moscheles, Richter and Hauptmann (1853–6), and later visited Rome (1856–7), Berlin (1858) and Paris (1859). On Hauptmann's death in 1868 he became chairman of the Bachgesellschaft. Also in 1868 he produced his most successful opera, *Der Haideschacht* (based on Hoffmann), in Dresden; this was taken up by 46 other German theatres and proved to be one of the most popular operas of the late 19th century.

Holstein, who generally wrote the texts for his own operas, was a gifted and many-sided figure. His childhood attraction to Scott found practical expression in *Der Erbe von Morley*, and he made an attempt to incorporate folktunes in his operas not merely as local colour but as part of the more continuous structure for which he strove. However, he was essentially a traditionalist, a follower of Weber and Marschner and later of Mendelssohn, who failed to appreciate the value for his purposes of Wagner's development and handling of leitmotif. Most of his unpublished manuscripts are in the Musikwissenschaftliches Institut of Leipzig University.

Zwei Nächte in Venedig (2, E. Materne), Brunswick, 1845, vs (n.d.)

Der Erbe von Morley op.30, 1852 (3, Holstein, after W. Scott), Leipzig, Neues, 24 Jan 1872 (Leipzig, 1872)

Wawerley, 1852 (grosse Oper, 5, Holstein, after Scott), ?unperf.

Die Gastfreunde, *c*1852 (5), ?unperf.

Der Haideschacht (3, Holstein, after E. T. A. Hoffmann: *Die Bergwerke zu Falun*), Dresden, Hof, 28 Oct 1868 (Leipzig, 1869)

Die Hochländer op.36 (historisch-romantische Oper, 4, Holstein), Mannheim, 16 Jan 1876 (Offenbach, 1875)

Im Norden (romantische Oper, 1), ?unperf., vs (n.d.)

Inc.: Marino Faliero (grosse romantische Oper, 4, after Byron), 1877, 4 pieces pubd (Leipzig, 1881); Der Gesandte (komisch-romantische Oper), excerpts pubd (n.d.); St Roger (romantische Oper, 3), excerpts pubd (n.d.)

Projected operas: Ekkehart (after Scheffel); Ingo (after G. Freytag); Iwan; Nonnerich

*

MGG (W. Kahl); *StiegerO*

G. Glaser: *Franz von Holstein: ein Dichterkomponist des 19. Jahrhunderts* (diss., U. of Leipzig, 1930)

JOHN WARRACK

Holý, Ondřej František [Holly; Holli, Andreas Franz] (*b c*1747; *d* Breslau, 4 May 1783). Czech composer and theatre orchestra director. His name is not listed in baptismal registers of anywhere that could be the 'Böhmisch Luba' given as his birthplace in earliest sources. It has been suggested that he attended the Jesuit Gymnasium in Prague and was later a novice of the Franciscan order. In 1768 or 1769 Holý joined the theatrical troupe of Johann Joseph Brunian at the Kotce theatre in Prague as co-répétiteur; he became its Kapellmeister in April 1772. He set several Singspiel texts by an actor of the troupe, Karl Franz Henisch (1745–76). When Henisch left Prague Holý followed him to Berlin, where he became music director of the Koch troupe about 1773, and then to Breslau, where he was music director of the Wäser troupe from about 1774 until his death.

Because Prague audiences in the late 1760s were not enthusiastic about Italian *opera seria*, Holý modelled his stage works on the type of German comic operas initiated by J. A. Hiller and C. F. Weisse. At about the same time as his fellow Czech Georg Benda, he contributed to the development of Singspiel not only in northern Germany but also in Vienna, where his most successful comic opera *Der Kaufmann von Smyrna* was staged in 1776 and 1781. Most of the manuscripts are lost, although the Breitkopf catalogues (1779–84; see Brook) list extant scores and parts of a number of the Singspiels.

Singspiels unless otherwise stated

Die Verwechslung, oder Der Teufel in allen Ecken (3, ? K. F. Henisch), Prague, 1769

Der lustige Schuster (3, Henisch, after C. Coffey), Prague, 1770 [sequel to Die Verwechslung]

Das Gespenst (3, Henisch), Prague, Kotce, 3 Dec 1771, *CS-Pu*

Die Jagd (3, C. F. Weisse, after C. Collé), Prague, Kotce, 10 May 1772

Der Zauberer (1, Henisch), Prague, 1772

Der Kaufmann von Smyrna (1, C. F. Schwan, after S. Chamfort), Berlin, Koch's, 13 Nov 1773, vs (Berlin, 1775); as Wohltaten gewinnen die Herzen, Vienna, Kärntnertor, May/June 1776; as Der Sklavenhändler von Smyrna, Vienna, Burg, 13 Feb 1781

Der Bassa [Pascha, Baron] von Tunis (1, Henisch), Berlin, Koch's, 6 Jan 1774, *B-Bc*; according to Eitner, vs (Berlin, 1775)

Das Gärtnermädchen (3, ? K. A. Musäus), Breslau, 1775

Gelegenheit macht Diebe (3, Henisch), Breslau, 1775

Das Opfer der Treue (Vorspiel with songs, 1, K. E. Schubert), Breslau, Wäser's, 24 Jan 1776

Deukalion und Pyrrha (melodrama, 2, Schubert), Berlin, 1776

Der Patriot auf dem Lande (Schubert), Breslau, 1777

Der Irrwisch (3, C. F. Bretzner), Breslau, 1779

Der Tempel des Friedens, Breslau, 1780

Die Zigeuner (? H. F. Möller) [listed in Breitkopf catalogue, 1781]

*

EitnerQ; *LoewenbergA*; *StiegerO*; *WurzbachL*

C. F. Cramer, ed.: *Magazin der Musik*, ii (1784), 37

G. J. Dlabacž: *Allgemeines historisches Künstler-Lexikon*, i (Prague, 1815), 661

H. M. Schletterer: *Das deutsche Singspiel* (Augsburg, 1863), 226–7

O. Teuber: *Geschichte des Prager Theaters*, i (Prague, 1883), 297, 322–3, 374–5; ii (Prague, 1885), 19, 23–4

O. G. Sonneck: *Catalogue of Opera Librettos Printed before 1800* (Washington DC, 1914)

B. S. Brook, ed.: *The Breitkopf Thematic Catalogue, 1762–1787* (New York, 1966)

O. E. Deutsch: 'Das Repertoire der Höfischen Oper, der Hof- und der Staatsoper', *ÖMz*, xxiv (1969), 369–421

O. Michtner: *Das alte Burgtheater als Opernbühne* (Vienna, 1970), 95, 373, 465
MILAN POŠTOLKA

Holzbauer, Ignaz (Jakob) (*b* Vienna, 17 Sept 1711; *d* Mannheim, 7 April 1783). Austrian composer. An autobiographical sketch, written in 1782 and first published in 1783, provides basic information about his life. He studied singing, keyboard instruments, the violin and the cello with students in the choir at St Stephen's Cathedral, Vienna. Later, he taught himself counterpoint by studying Fux's *Gradus ad Parnassum*. After a short trip to Venice, undertaken probably in the mid-1730s, he accepted a post in Moravia as Kapellmeister to Count Rottal of Holešov. There he married the singer Rosalie Andreides on 30 April 1737. From then until 1751 his life is not well documented. Some time before 1742 he and his wife were engaged by the imperial court in Vienna; he directed the court theatre and composed several ballets, and she sang there. Possibly in 1744, they went to Italy for about three years, during which time Rosalie sang in Milan, Venice and other cities. The couple must have returned to Vienna by 1747, for in that year Holzbauer provided ballet music for Hasse's *Arminio*. From Vienna they moved to Stuttgart; according to a decree dated 29 November 1751, Holzbauer succeeded Brescianello as Oberkapellmeister, a position he held for almost two years.

Following the successful première of his opera *Il figlio delle selve* at the rococo theatre at Schwetzingen, on 26 July 1753 Holzbauer was appointed Kapellmeister at Mannheim by decree of the Elector Carl Theodor. His duties included the provision of music for operas and pastorals for the court theatre. These years of intensive work included three more trips to Italy: in 1756 he travelled to Rome, stopping in Bologna and Florence en route and returning through Venice and Vienna; in 1758 he wrote *Nitteti* for Turin and then visited the Opéra and the Concert Spirituel in Paris; and in 1759 he wrote *Alessandro nell'Indie* for Milan. On this last trip he probably heard Traetta's *Ippolito ed Aricia* (1759, Parma) and brought back to Mannheim a copy of Frugoni's libretto; Holzbauer's own setting – possibly based on Traetta's – was performed in November 1759. Near the end of his tenure at Mannheim, he collaborated with the librettist Anton Klein on what was to be the culmination of his career, *Günther von Schwarzburg* (1777). He remained in Mannheim when the court moved to Munich in 1778; he produced the one-act opera *La morte di Didone* in 1779 and his last opera, *Tancredi*, was completed only a few months before his death.

Contemporary writers, notably Schubart and Mozart, remarked on the dramatic and expressive range of Holzbauer's music. There is evidence of a genuine melodic gift in his operas, but his transitional material is not as accomplished as that in other works of the period. His accompaniments tend to be laden with detail, reflecting the abilities of the virtuoso Mannheim orchestra. He often rose above the ordinary in his concertante arias, duets and choruses, and his accompanied recitatives employ often striking orchestral effects. Many individual arias can be found in the Pretlack Collection (in *D-B*), but few of his operas have survived

complete; *Günther von Schwarzburg* is the only one available in a modern critical edition.

See also GÜNTHER VON SCHWARZBURG.

dm – *dramma per musica*

Lucio Papirio dittatore (dm, A. Zeno), Holešov, 12 Oct 1737, lib. Milan, Pinacteca di Brera

Il figlio delle selve (favola pastorale, 3, C. S. Capece), Schwetzingen, 15 June 1753, lib. *US-Wc*; rev. Mannheim, Hof, 1771, lib. *D-MHrm*; pts *B*

L'isola disabitata (azione comica per musica, 2, P. Metastasio), Schwetzingen, 16 June 1754, arias *B*

L'Issipile (dm, 3, Metastasio), Mannheim, Hof, 4 Nov 1754, arias *B*

Don Chisciotte (opera serio-ridicola, 2, after M. de Cervantes), Schwetzingen, 16 June 1755, DI

I cinesi (componimento drammatico, 1, Metastasio), Mannheim, Hof, spr. 1756, lib. *HEu*, *MHrm*

Le nozze d'Arianna (festa teatrale, 2, M. Verazi), Schwetzingen, 29 Aug 1756, lib. *HEu*, *MHrm*

La clemenza di Tito (dm, 3, Metastasio), Mannheim, Hof, 4 Nov 1757, arias *B*

Nitteti (dm, 3, Metastasio), Turin, Regio, carn. 1758; rev. Mannheim, Hof, 5 Nov 1758, *Rp*, *P-La*

Alessandro nell'Indie (dm, 3, Metastasio), Milan, Regio Ducal, carn. 1759, arias and sinfonia *I-Nc* (*R*1982: IOB, lxxix), *P-La*

Ippolito ed Aricia (dm, 5, C. I. Frugoni), Mannheim, Hof, 5 Nov 1759, lib. *D-HEu*, *MHrm*, *US-Wc* [?rev. of T. Traetta's Ippolito ed Aricia, 1759, Parma]

Adriano in Siria (dm, 3, Metastasio), Mannheim, Hof, 5 Nov 1768, libs. *D-MHrm*, *US-Wc*

Günther von Schwarzburg (Spl, 3, A. Klein), Mannheim, Hof, 5 Jan 1777, *D-B*, (Mannheim, 1777); edn in DDT, viii–ix (1902)

La morte di Didone (dm, 1, Metastasio), Mannheim, National, 6 July 1779, *B*; rev. as Tod der Dido (Klein), 1780, *US-Wc*

Tancredi (dm, 3, Balbis, after Voltaire), Munich, Residenz, Jan 1783, lib. *Wc*; aria *GB-Lbl*

Music in Euridice (favola pastorale), Vienna, 26 July 1750, *A-Wn* (*R*1982: IOB, lxxv)

*

BurneyGN

J. G. Meusel, ed.: *Miscellaneen artistischen Inhalts*, iii (Erfurt, 1780), 18–22

Pfälzisches Museum, ed. A. Klein, i (Mannheim, 1783), 460–77 [autobiographical sketch]

C. F. D. Schubart: *Ideen zu einer Ästhetik der Tonkunst* (Vienna, 1806)

F. J. Lipowsky: *Baierisches Musiklexikon* (Munich, 1811)

J. Sittard: *Zur Geschichte der Musik und des Theaters am Württemburgischen Hofe* (Stuttgart, 1890–91)

F. Walter: *Geschichte des Theaters und der Musik am kurpfälzischen Hofe* (Leipzig, 1898)

H. Kretzschmar: Preface, DDT, viii–ix (1902)

R. Würtz: *Verzeichnis und Ikonographie der kurpfälzischen Hofmusiker zu Mannheim nebst darstellenden Theaterpersonal, 1723–1803* (Wilhelmshaven, 1975)

A. D. McCredie: 'Operatic Reform before Gluck, and the German Heroic Music Theatre of the *Sturm und Drang*', *Musicology*, vi (1980), 51–61; It. trans., *Ricerche musicali*, v (1981), 86–108

R. Würtz: 'Ignaz Holzbauer and *Das Teutsche*', *Studies in Music from the University of Western Ontario*, vii (1982), 89–98

H. Lühning: 'Aufkündigung einer Gattungstradition: das Metastasianische Drama, Wielands Singspielkonzept, und die deutsche Oper *Günther von Schwarzburg*', *Mannheim und Italien: zur Vorgeschichte der Mannheimer*, ed. R. Würtz (Mainz, 1984), 162–99

K. Hortschansky: 'Ignaz Holzbauers *Ippolito ed Aricia* (1759): zur Einführung der Tragédie lyrique in Mannheim', *Aufklärungen: Studien zur deutsch-französischen Musikgeschichte im 18. Jahrhundert*, ed. W. Birtel and C.-H. Mahling (Heidelberg, 1986), 105–16

P. Corneilson: *Opera at Mannheim, 1770–1778* (diss., U. of North Carolina, 1992)
PAUL CORNEILSON

Holzdieb, Der ('The Poacher'). Singspiel in one act by HEINRICH AUGUST MARSCHNER to a libretto by JOHANN FRIEDRICH KIND; Dresden, Hoftheater, 22 February 1825.

Master Lorenz (bass), the village blacksmith, has promised the hand of his cousin and ward Suschen (soprano) to the rich peasant Barthel (baritone), his landlord and the owner of the finest workshop in the village. In return, Barthel has promised to allow Lorenz to buy the smithy from him. But Suschen loves the youthful hunter Felix (tenor), godchild of Lorenz's wife, Barbara (contralto). Suschen, Felix and Barbara hatch a plot to force Barthel to break his contract with Lorenz: Suschen will flirt with Barthel, then demand that he give her for Whitsunday a straw hat she has long admired. According to local custom, he must cut a May tree and deliver it to her door with the hat fastened to it. But a new law has made it illegal to remove anything from the forest. Unaware of this, Barthel disappears into the woods, armed with an axe provided by Suschen. He soon returns with a birch on his back, crying out that he has been ambushed by woodsmen who caught him chopping it down. Pouncing on the now motionless Barthel, the woodsmen, tipped off earlier by the three conspirators to track him into the forest, threaten punishment if he does not allow Lorenz to buy the smithy without penalty. Reluctantly Barthel consents, freeing Lorenz to offer Suschen's hand to Felix.

Der Holzdieb is tightly constructed and fast-paced dramatically. Though short, its characters are well defined, particularly Barbara, an archetypal comic contralto. Musically, it is in the same conventional diatonic style that pervades the nearly contemporaneous works of Lortzing and Kreutzer. The single act comprises eight arias, the most famous of which is Suschen's 'Mein Herz ist voll Wonne', and five ensembles. All 13 separately numbered pieces are in relatively simple, closed forms. Its bourgeois comedy on village life and peasant marriage customs makes *Der Holzdieb* reminiscent of the Singspiels of Hiller, Schenk and Weigl, but it is devoid of the supernatural elements found in the Viennese 'magic' Singspiel. In the wake of the commercial success achieved by stage works such as those in Winkler's *Dramatisches Vergißmeinnicht*, Hartmann of Dresden issued *Der Holzdieb* with eight other compositions in a pocketbook anthology entitled *Polyhymnia* (1825). An instant success at its première, *Der Holzdieb* was produced in other German centres and was later published separately by Bote & Bock in a revision entitled *Geborgt* for a performance in Berlin (1853). It was revived in English as *The Poacher* (1935, Rochester) and in the same year in Dutch as *De meiboom*, in Amsterdam. Richard Strauss listed it in 1945 among his proposed repertory for the smaller of the two opera houses he believed should be present in every major German city. 　　　　　A. DEAN PALMER

Hölzel, Gustav (*b* Budapest, 2 Sept 1813; *d* Vienna, 3 Dec 1883). Austrian bass-baritone. The son of an actor-singer, he made his stage début at the age of 16 in Sopron, then sang in Graz, Berlin and Zürich. Engaged at the Vienna Hofoper in 1840, he remained there for more than 20 years. In 1843 at the Kärntnertortheater he created Di Fiesco in Donizetti's *Maria di Rohan*. Dismissed from the Hofoper in 1863 for altering the words of Friar Tuck's song in *Der Templer und die Jüdin*, he appeared at Darmstadt, Nuremberg, the Theater an der Wien and the Munich Hofoper, where he created Beckmesser in *Die Meistersinger* in 1868. In New York he took part in the American première of *Der Schauspieldirektor* (1870). An excellent comic actor, he sang Baculus (*Der Wildschütz*) at his farewell

performance in 1877. Other roles included Leporello, Don Basilio and Van Bett (*Zar und Zimmermann*).
　　　　　ELIZABETH FORBES

Homer. Greek poet or poets of uncertain date, traditionally responsible for *The Iliad* and *The Odyssey*. The two epics deal with the end of the Trojan War and the return of Odysseus (Ulysses) to Ithaca. The Troy of King Priam was probably destroyed *c*1250 BC, by the confederation of peoples who later wrought havoc on the Hittite empire and continued their marauding as far as the Egypt of Ramesses III (1198–1166 BC), where they were known as the 'Sea People'. Smyrna (now Izmir) and Chios have traditionally claimed to be the birthplace of Homer, and the dialect of the poems, basically Ionic with an underlay of Aeolic, is supporting evidence. At what stage the manifold elements that make up the epics were worked into an artistic whole it is impossible to say, although it is plausible that it was in the late 8th century BC. Tradition has Peisistratus, tyrant of Athens (560–27 BC), responsible for a Homeric recension that was recited annually at the festival of the Panathenaea. Aristarchus of Samothrace, head of the library at Alexandria, is credited with a meticulous edition of the poems in *c*150 BC; this is substantially the text known to the modern world. If the medical expert Hippocrates and the philosopher Aristotle quote as 'Homeric' lines no longer to be found in the epics, that only illustrates the problem.

Opera has treated subjects not only integral to the Trojan War but also prior to its outbreak, such as the marriage of Peleus and Thetis (the Greek warrior Achilles was their child) and the elopement of Paris and Helen. August Bungert planned a series of nine operas to be called *Homerische Welt*, five to deal with the *Iliad* and four with the *Odyssey*. The latter set was completed (1896–1903), but an *Achilleus* and *Klytämnestra* were only sketched. The characters of the *Iliad* form the staple of Greek tragedy, and Aeschylus is said to have described his plays as 'slices from the great banquet of Homer'. The *Iliad* inspired Schoeck to *Penthesilea* (1927) and Tippett to *King Priam* (1962); but it is the *Odyssey*, with the faithful Penelope at its core, and the wondrous adventures befalling the hero and his son Telemachus, that has been more frequently used as the basis for opera, from Monteverdi to Fauré and Dallapiccola. Calypso, Nausicaa, the cyclops Polyphemus and especially Circe (Keiser, Gazzaniga, Paer, Egk) have provided much material. 　ROBERT ANDERSON

Homer [née Beatty], **Louise** (Dilworth) (*b* Shadyside, Pittsburgh, 30 April 1871; *d* Winter Park, FL, 6 May 1947). American contralto. She studied music at Philadelphia and Boston, then married the composer Sidney Homer in 1895 and went to Paris, where she studied singing and acting with Fidèle Koenig and Paul Lhérie, the first Don José. She made her operatic début at Vichy in 1898, as Léonor in *La favorite*. At Covent Garden in 1899 she sang Lola and Amneris, returning in 1900 for Ortrud and Maddalena after a busy winter season at the Monnaie in Brussels. Her American début (1900) was with the Metropolitan Opera on tour in San Francisco as Amneris, in which role she also made her first New York appearance. During a long and successful Metropolitan career, she sang at first chiefly in Italian and French opera but soon assumed leading Wagnerian roles; she was also a notable Orpheus in Toscanini's 1909 revival of Gluck's opera, created the

Witch in Humperdinck's *Königskinder* (1910) and was the first to sing the title role in Parker's *Mona* (1912). After resigning from the Metropolitan in 1919, she sang with other major American companies including the Chicago Grand Opera (1920–25) and the San Francisco and Los Angeles operas (1926). She returned to the Metropolitan in 1927 and made her last appearance there in 1929, as Azucena. A performer of the highest artistic integrity, she had a beautiful voice and a majestic stage presence. Among her many recordings the ensembles with Caruso, Martinelli, Gigli and others are particularly successful. Samuel Barber was her nephew.

GV (J. B. Richards, with discography)

S. Homer: *My Wife and I* (New York, 1939)

D. Reutlinger: 'Louise Homer: a Discography', *The Maestro*, iv–v (1972–3), 62–5

A. Homer: *Louise Homer and the Golden Age of Opera* (New York, 1974)   HERMAN KLEIN, DESMOND SHAWE-TAYLOR, KATHERINE K. PRESTON

Honegger, Arthur (*b* Le Havre, 10 March 1892; *d* Paris, 27 Nov 1955). Swiss composer. As a child, before receiving harmony lessons in Le Havre, he wrote two operas, *Philippa* and *Sigismond*, and started a third, *Esmeralda* (after Victor Hugo: *Notre-Dame de Paris*), but nothing of these survives. After studying at the Zürich Conservatory (1909–11) he enrolled at the Paris Conservatoire and continued there until 1918, apart from a brief interruption at the beginning of World War I (1914–15), when he was required to serve as a frontier guard in Switzerland because he held dual Swiss-French nationality. He made his home in Paris (Montmartre), but visited Switzerland for holidays and for performances of music he wrote for Swiss institutions.

He had composed ballets and incidental music for several plays before he came to international attention with the incidental music he wrote for René Morax's 'drame biblique', *Le roi David* (1921; the music was subsequently rescored as a 'psaume symphonique' for concert performance). In the early 1920s he accompanied the French mezzo-soprano Claire Croiza in recitals that often included his own songs, and in 1925 Croiza sang the title role in his music for Morax's biblical drama *Judith*. Later that year Honegger composed more music to create his opera of the same title. Croiza bore him a son, but despite their close liaison he married the French pianist Andrée Vaurabourg in 1926.

The music for *Le roi David* is characterized by an extensive series of thematic and tonal correspondences and by the vivid and resourceful use of restricted instrumental forces. A basic dichotomy between the simple and the complex is apparent in each of Honegger's mature works and manifests itself in all the components of his musical language. In *Le roi David* it is most evident in the melodic content – the simple diatonic lines, the 'chorale' themes and the vocalise passages contrast sharply with melodies that involve a rapid juxtaposition of tonal planes. The same is true of *Judith*, but here the musical items are larger in size and fewer in number; this, together with the presence of a central character, meant that the task of reworking the score as an *opéra sérieux* was not a difficult one. In *Judith* there are still passages whose tender and relaxed lyricism reflects the influence of Fauré and Debussy, which Honegger had found to be a good counterbalance to the diet of Wagner, Richard Strauss and Reger he had

experienced in Zürich. These passages contrast strikingly with the massive, complex and powerful textures which, while reflecting the influence of his teachers in Paris – particularly d'Indy's passion for severe classical form and symmetry, Gédalge's advocacy of vigorous counterpoint and Widor's expansion of Franck's harmonic idiom – are more characteristic of Honegger's mature style.

In 1924 Honegger had started work on an opera based on Cocteau's adaptation of Sophocles' *Antigone*, which he first encountered when he was commissioned to write incidental music for a production in 1922. A personal and original concept of prosody, evident in *Judith*, gives *Antigone* (completed in 1927) much of its distinctive musical character. In the preface to the vocal score (Paris, 1927) Honegger expressed three aims:

(1) to envelop the drama with a tight symphonic construction without the-movement seeming heavy; (2) to replace the recitatives by a melodic vocal line which does not consist of sustained high notes – which always renders the text incomprehensible – or by purely instrumental lines; but, on the contrary, with a melodic line created by the word itself, which, due to its clean plasticity, is designed to raise the contours and augment the relief; and (3) to look for the correct accentuation in the 'consonnes d'attaque' as opposed to the conventional prosody which treats them as an anacrusis.

Cocteau's version of the story of Antigone is unique not only because of the radical intensification of pace but also because of the language used, which is contemporary and engagingly colloquial. The dynamism, dramatic thrust and relentlessly intense lyricism of Cocteau's libretto are well matched by the music, which is characterized by a discipline and refinement of language and form that is severe even for Honegger. The unbroken flow of incisive rhythmic figures resulting from Honegger's unorthodox prosody and the almost impenetrable symphonic logic underpin a melodic and harmonic style favouring 2nds and 7ths. The result is a stylistic complexity more akin to the Second Viennese School than any of Honegger's other music. The music is of the highest quality and consistency; nevertheless *Antigone* proved to be one of his least popular works.

Although Honegger was discouraged by the poor reception accorded to *Antigone* at its première in 1927, the phenomenal success of his first operetta, *Les aventures du roi Pausole* – which ran for almost 500 performances after its première on 12 December 1930 – undoubtedly encouraged him to compose incidental music in a similar style for Morax's lighthearted *La belle du Moudon* (1931). Plans to create an operetta out of it never came to fruition, but Honegger later shared with Jacques Ibert the composition of two other operettas, *L'aiglon* (1936–7) and *Les petites Cardinal* (1937). He also composed a 'stage oratorio', *Jeanne d'Arc au bûcher*, first performed in Basle in 1938.

Louÿs' original story for *Les aventures du roi Pausole* is distinctly erotic and was intended for Debussy. While the music clearly reflects the various influences of the operetta styles of Chabrier, Gounod, Lecocq, Messager and Offenbach, Honegger himself pointed out that 'my score, which is solid but of a likable nature, evolves, if you like, into a Mozartian style – gay, bright, alert and melodic' (Bruyr 1947). An assured use of counterpoint, judicious touches of bitonality, careful and systematic structuring of the large-scale numbers, and a wide-ranging palette of orchestral colours are all features of Honegger's personal style which give this score a clear stamp of originality. Similar stylistic features characterize *L'aiglon* (for which Honegger wrote Acts

2–4, Ibert Acts 1 and 5) and *Les petites Cardinal*. The division of work is not specified for the latter, although manuscript evidence shows that, of the 27 items, Honegger composed at least nos. 2, 4, 12, 13, 14, 15 and 21.

After collapsing in New York while on a tour of the Americas in 1947, Honegger suffered from heart disease. He continued to compose and to write, although his last works and the books *Incantation aux fossiles* (Lausanne, 1948) and *Je suis compositeur* (Paris, 1951; Eng. trans., 1966) show marked evidence of a pessimistic and depressed mental state exacerbated by his physical condition. He said that 'my dream would have been to compose nothing but operas; but that would have been labour lost in an age when the lyric theatre is on the way to disappearing' (1966, p.81). He attached importance to *Antigone* because 'it embodies my ambitions and my lyric efforts. Without shallow pride or false modesty, I believe that *Antigone* brought a little pebble to the lyric theatre', but he also noted that 'this pebble has since fallen to the bottom of the pit and remained there' (1966, p.99).

Although Honegger was one of Les Six, he stressed that there was never any group aesthetic and his independent musical style demonstrates the arbitrary nature of the grouping. Nevertheless, the spirit of the music associated with the group permeates some of his instrumental and vocal chamber works, the Piano Concertino, the Cello Concerto and the three operettas.

See also AIGLON, L'.

Judith (opéra sérieux, 3, R. Morax), Monte-Carlo, Opéra, 13 Feb 1926
Antigone (tragédie musicale, 3, J. Cocteau, after Sophocles), Brussels, Monnaie, 28 Dec 1927
Les aventures du roi Pausole (operetta, 3, A. Willemetz, after P. Louÿs), Paris, Bouffes-Parisiens, 12 Dec 1930
L'aiglon [Acts 2–4] (drame musical, 5, H. Cain, after E. Rostand), Monte Carlo, Opéra, 10 March 1937 [Acts 1 and 5 by Ibert]
Les petites Cardinal (operetta, 2, Willemetz and P. Brach, after L. Halévy), Paris, Bouffes-Parisiens, 13 Feb 1938, collab. Ibert

Lost: Philippa; Sigismond; Esmeralda

*

P. Collaer: *Arthur Honegger: Antigone 1928 (Etude)* (Paris, 1928)
P. Claudel and others: *Arthur Honegger* (Paris, 1942)
C. Gérard: *Arthur Honegger: catalogue succinct des oeuvres* (Brussels, 1945)
J. Bruyr: *Arthur Honegger et son oeuvre* (Paris, 1947)
M. Delannoy: *Honegger* (Paris, 1953; enlarged G. K. Spratt, 1986) [incl. catalogue of works]
W. Tappolet: *Arthur Honegger* (Zürich, 2/1954)
A. Honegger: 'Note sur *Antigone*', *Melos*, xxiii (1956), 282–3
J. Matter: *Honegger ou la quête de joie* (Lausanne and Paris, 1956)
J. Rochat: 'La prosodie dans la musique d'Arthur Honegger', *Feuilles musicales: Revue musicale romande et Courrier suisse du disque*, x/Jan (1957)
A. Gauthier: *Arthur Honegger* (Lyons, 1957)
M. Landowski: *Honegger* (Paris, 1957)
W. Reich, ed.: *Arthur Honegger, Nachklang, Schriften, Photos, Dokumente* (Zürich, 1957)
Y. Guilbert: *Honegger* (Paris, 1959)
A. Szőllősy: *Honegger* (Budapest, 1961, 2/1980)
J. Feschotte: *Arthur Honegger* (Paris, 1966)
K. von Fischer: 'Arthur Honegger: Grundlagen seines Stils', *Schweizer Jb 'Die Ernte'* (Basle, 1966), 158–79
P. Meylan: *René Morax et Artur Honegger au Théâtre du Jorat* (Lausanne and Paris, 1966)
L. Rappoport: *Artur Onegger* (Leningrad, 1967)
L. Schrade: 'Vom Sinn der Musik in Honegger's Werk', *De scientia musicae studia atque orationes* (Berne, 1967), 556–69
P. Meylan: *Arthur Honegger: humanitäre Botschaft der Musik, Wirkung und Gestalt*, viii (Frauenfeld, 1970)
K. von Fischer: *Arthur Honegger* (Zürich, 1978)
G. Kalošina: 'Principles of Symphonism in the Large Vocal Works of Arthur Honegger', *Teoretičeskie voprosy vokal'noj muzyki*, compiled N. Tiftikidi (Moscow, 1979)
E. Myszowski: 'Problems of Rendering Symphonic Vocal-Instrumental Form in the Compositions of Honegger, using as an Example his *Antigone*', *Ogólnopolska Sesja Naukowa (VII) na temat: muzyka oratoryjna i kantatowa w aspekcie praktyki wykonawczej: Wrocław 1980*
G. K. Spratt: *The Music of Arthur Honegger* (Cork, 1987)

GEOFFREY K. SPRATT

Höngen, Elisabeth (*b* Gevelsberg, Westphalia, 7 Dec 1906). German mezzo-soprano. She studied in Berlin with Ludwig Horth and made her début at Wuppertal in 1933, singing Lady Macbeth during her first season; after engagements at Düsseldorf and Dresden, in 1943 she became a member of the Vienna Staatsoper. She appeared at Salzburg (1948–50) as Orpheus, Britten's Lucretia and Clairon (*Capriccio*) and in 1959 as Bebett in the première of Erbse's *Julietta*. She sang at Covent Garden in 1947 with the Vienna company as Dorabella, Herodias and Marcellina, returning in 1960 as Clytemnestra. In 1951 she sang Fricka and Waltraute at Bayreuth; in 1952 she appeared at the Metropolitan Opera, making her début as Herodias. Her repertory also included Eboli, Amneris, Carmen, Venus, Baba the Turk, the Nurse and the Dyer's Wife, and Adriano (*Rienzi*). She retired in 1971. Her voice, not large but well trained and beautiful, was always used most musically, and her dramatic gifts were remarkable.

*

GV (R. Celletti and L. Riemens; L. Riemens)

HAROLD ROSENTHAL/R

Hong Kong. British colony (since 1841) in south-east Asia. It is important as a port and as a banking and commercial centre. During the late 19th and early 20th centuries Hong Kong was visited by various touring opera companies, most of them Italian, and formed part of a circuit that also included Manila, Batavia (now Jakarta), Shanghai and sometimes Singapore. The first visit, in 1870, was by a company led by the impresario Giovanni Pompei. On 28 March they gave *Lucia di Lammermoor*, followed by *Il barbiere di Siviglia*, *Il trovatore*, *Don Pasquale*, *La traviata*, *La sonnambula*, *La favorite*, *Ernani* and *Rigoletto*. Augusto Cagli's company followed in 1879 and 1880, and that of the Gonsalez brothers in 1915. Performances usually took place in the City Hall (seating 800).

The Hong Kong Festival, founded in 1972, began early on to include opera in its programmes. In 1975 the Swedish Royal Opera gave three performances each of *Così fan tutte* (with Söderström and Kerstin Meyer) and *Die Entführung*, all in the City Hall. During the festival of February 1980, Opera Rara gave four performances of a 'composite' Offenbach opera, *Christopher Columbus*, at the Baptist College. One of the first locally produced opera productions was of *Cavalleria rusticana* and *Pagliacci* at the City Hall in 1980, with the local soprano Ella Kiang as Santuzza and Nedda, directed by Lo King-man, a local artist who had worked in Rome; the same company presented *Lucia di Lammermoor* in 1985. These works were sung in Italian with 'side titles' in Chinese characters projected on to the proscenium arch. The American group Ambassadors of Opera started using Hong Kong as one of their bases from 1983. Performing with American principals, in 1983 they presented *Madama Butterfly*, *Carmen* (with Joann Grillo and Richard Kness), *Il barbiere di Siviglia* and *Tosca*. They returned in 1984 with *La bohème* and in 1985 with *Aida* with Aprile Millo.

The Hong Kong Cultural Centre, built in 1989 (including the opera house, inaugurated on 6 November 1989)

In 1986 the Hong Kong Academy of the Performing Arts was opened; the larger of its two theatres, the Lyric Theatre, seating 1181, was inaugurated during the festival the same year by Glyndebourne Festival Opera with *Don Giovanni* and *A Midsummer Night's Dream*. During the festival of 1988 Beijing Central Opera presented *Madama Butterfly* and *Carmen* in Mandarin Chinese; this was the first time that the colony had heard Western opera sung in Chinese. A new Cultural Centre was built in 1989 (see illustration), with a Grand Theatre (seating 1750, sometimes known as the Hong Kong Opera House) which is used for both Western and Chinese opera. This was inaugurated on 6 November 1989 with *Fidelio*, performed by the Cologne Opera under Janowski, with Lisbeth Balslev as Leonore, followed by *Il barbiere di Siviglia* under Alberto Zedda, with Alberto Rinaldi as Figaro.   CHARLES PITT

Honolulu. City on the island of Oahu, Hawaii. The first known opera performances were amateur productions given in 1854 at the wooden Varieties Theatre in King Street and noted in the journal of a merchant sea captain. In 1862 a professional touring company from Sydney en route to San Francisco performed excerpts from *Lucrezia Borgia* and *Ernani*, with piano accompaniment, at the Royal Hawaiian Theatre. In 1871 Agatha States's Italian Opera gave complete performances of *Il trovatore*, *Don Pasquale* and other operas with piano accompaniment. A larger Music Hall was built in 1881 and opera and drama productions were regularly imported from San Francisco. The Music Hall burnt down in 1895; it was rebuilt in 1896 and reopened as the New Hawaiian Opera House with a performance of *Il trovatore*. The Lambardi touring company gave 14 operas in a three-week season in 1913 and other Italian companies followed. In 1917 the house was demolished, and visits by touring companies ceased.

A new era of operatic activity began in 1961 with the founding of the Opera Committee under the aegis of the Honolulu SO, but the city remained without a civic music auditorium until 1964, when Blaisdell Concert Hall was opened, inspiring a new period of growth for the fledgling opera enterprise. In 1964 the company was renamed the Hawaii Opera Theatre and engaged Robert LaMarchina as music director; in 1981 it became a corporate entity, separate from the orchestra, presenting three productions in an annual winter festival from January to March. In 1990 Terence Knapp directed a Hawaiian monarchy period *Così fan tutte*, renamed *Pela no ho'i na wahine*, in the island's Hawaiian-English dialect.   NANCY MALITZ

Honzovo království ('Johnny's Kingdom'). Musical play in a prologue and seven scenes, op.25, by OTAKAR OSTRČIL to a libretto by Jiří Mařánek after LEV NIKOLAYEVICH TOLSTOY's fairy-tale *Skazka ob Ivane-durake i evo dvukh bratiyakh* ('The Tale of Ivan the Simpleton and his Two Brothers'); Brno, National Theatre, 26 May 1934.

The Prologue shows the Devil (bass) looking for the best place in which to sow envy, hate and fratricide. His eye falls on a small Czech village where a Father (bass) lives with his three sons: Ivan (tenor), the eldest, a soldier, Ondřej (baritone), a merchant, and the youngest, Honza (tenor, the 'Johnny' of the title). In Scene 1 Ivan and Ondřej and their wives (soprano and contralto) visit Father in his cottage. Though condescending to Honza, they are in financial trouble and are mainly interested in the value of Father's farm. The Devil then tempts Honza while he is working in the field (Scene 2), and when Honza succumbs the Devil gives him a magic plant, soldiers and gold in exchange for liberty. Honza hands the soldiers and the gold over to his brothers and goes on working as before.

The Princess (soprano) is wasting away, and in Scene 3 the King (bass) offers his kingdom and his daughter to whoever cures her. Ivan and Ondřej try and fail. Honza decides to visit the Princess as well, using the magic plant to cure a Beggar (tenor) on the way. Only someone of pure heart can cure the Princess. Honza becomes her saviour (Scene 4), marries her and becomes king. As he does not want to rule, he takes the advice of one of his courtiers, the Devil, and hands his power and riches over to his brothers. When in Scene 5 the people complain about the unjust rule of Ivan and Ondřej, Honza stands up on their behalf and the Princess calls on everybody to love each other in peace. Eventually the Devil's schemes fail (Scene 6). All the devils discuss how to drive Honza to anger and injustice and his kingdom to hell; war is their last resort. In Scene 7, however, Ivan's army invades a village where a fair is being held, and the soldiers, refusing to fight against humble countrymen, put down their arms and join in the dancing and merrymaking. Everybody is happy and the Devil sinks back into hell in fury.

Johnny's Kingdom was composed between 1928 and 1933, much later than Ostrčil's other operas. The Russian theme, Tolstoy's ideal of non-violent resistance to evil, is transformed here into a Czech folktale. As with Ostrčil's other operas, the libretto is in prose. The work represents a synthesis of his development. The dramatic peaks are underlined by expressive music; individual voices are woven into complex polyphonic and often bitonal chains. In the lyrical passages the composer created new melodic forms, suggesting inner links with the tender lyricism of *Poupě* ('The Bud'). Besides effective musical structures there are moving passages in simple folk style and (mostly) in polka rhythm. Ostrčil, in accordance with the Czech character of his theme, seems to be a conscious follower of Smetana. *Johnny's Kingdom* may be considered a statement of his credo and his response to the campaigns waged against him by right-wingers in the last decade of his position as head of the National Theatre opera company. The première turned into a manifesto against the rising force of fascism, and the Prague performance in 1934, a year before Ostrčil's death, had a similar impact. Of his five operas, this is the one most frequently staged in Czech opera houses.

EVA HERRMANNOVÁ

Hood, Basil (*b* nr Croydon, Surrey, 5 April 1864; *d* London, 7 Aug 1917). English librettist. He studied at Wellington College and the Royal Military College at Sandhurst and was an army officer until his retirement in 1898. As a dramatist, he provided librettos for more than a dozen comic operas and musical comedies performed in London, particularly at the Prince of Wales's Theatre. With his first important musical partner, Walter Slaughter, he wrote musical comedies including *Gentleman Joe, the Hansom Cabby* (1895), *The French Maid* and *Dandy Dan the Lifeguardsman* (both 1897). Hood was introduced to Arthur Sullivan by the composer Wilfred Bendall, with whom he had collaborated on *The Gypsies* (1890). For the Savoy Theatre Hood and Sullivan produced *The Rose of Persia, or The Story-Teller and the Slave* (1899) and *The Emerald Isle, or The Caves of Carig-Cleena* (1901, music completed by Edward German). After Sullivan's death in 1900 Hood began a successful partnership with German, providing librettos for *Merrie England* (1902) and *A Princess of Kensington* (1903), both produced at the Savoy.

Hood was second only to Gilbert as a collaborator of Sullivan's. Like most comic-opera librettists, he was widely perceived as an imitator of Gilbert; yet he had a talent for picturesque verse and colourful dialogue, and many of his pieces met with popular success.

FREDRIC WOODBRIDGE WILSON

Hoof, Jef Van [Josef Bonefacius Emilius Michaël] (*b* Antwerp, 8 May 1886; *d* Antwerp, 24 April 1959). Belgian composer. He studied composition at the Royal Flemish Conservatory with Mortelmans and Gilson, and was influenced by Peter Benoit; he won a second Prix de Rome in 1911 with his one-act lyrical play *Tycho-Brahé*. He later achieved outstanding technical virtuosity. He was a vigorous champion of Flemish national music and his songs are known by every patriotic Fleming. As well as liturgical and symphonic works he wrote three operas, combining a late Romantic style with a talent for spontaneous melody.

Meivuur ('Fire of May'), 1916 (landelijk zangspel, 2, P. De Mont), Antwerp, Koninklijke Vlaamse Opera, 12 Jan 1924
Vertraagde film ('Slow-motion film'), 1922 (2, H. Teirlinck), NIR (Radio Antwerp), 26 Feb 1937 [concert perf.]
Jonker Lichthart ('Squire Lightheart'), 1928 (comical-dramatical op, 1, E. Denhaene), Antwerp, Koninklijke Vlaamse Opera, 11 Nov 1961
CORNEEL MERTENS/R

Hook, James (*b* Norwich, ? 3 June 1746; *d* Boulogne, 1827). English composer. He was born in the parish of St John, Maddermarket, and although it has been suggested that he was the son of John Hook, minister of the Norwich Tabernacle, evidence shows him to have been the son of James Hook, razor-grinder and cutler. He showed remarkable musical talent at an early age, and before he was eight he had composed his first opera, to a libretto by a Miss Williams of Norwich. Containing 36 airs, it was considered by connoisseurs as an 'extraordinary instance of infantine genius' (Mann), but the music is lost.

At some time between June 1763 and February 1764 Hook moved to London, and before October 1766 had married his first wife, Miss Madden. He began to make a name for himself as an organist, piano teacher and composer of light attractive music, particularly songs. These were performed at the New Theatre, Richmond, and at many of the pleasure gardens. By 1768 he had been appointed organist and composer to Marylebone Gardens, and from 1774 to 1820 he was engaged in a similar capacity at Vauxhall Gardens. Hook contributed music to the dramatic works of other composers in addition to composing his own works. His wife and his two sons, James (1772–1828) and Theodore Edward (1788–1841), provided many of the librettos. His first wife died on 18 October 1805; on 4 November 1806 he married Harriet Horncastle James (*d* 1873).

Hook's positions at the pleasure gardens were important since, besides songs, he was expected to write short dramatic pieces for the concerts. These provided scope for the principal soloists in addition to concerted items. The stage at Marylebone was large enough for some dramatic interpretation, but that at Vauxhall, being smaller, allowed only for gestures. Although his dramatic works have not stood the test of time, they nevertheless contain much appealing music. Hook was fully conversant with the musical styles of his day and successfully exploited the *style galant*. In some ways his theatre and Vauxhall music became intermixed. The opera overtures were standard items in the Vauxhall concerts, Vauxhall songs and musical entertainments were sometimes performed between the main works in the theatres, and some of his popular Vauxhall songs were introduced into the dramatic works of contemporary authors. He did not hesitate to re-use portions of music in different works, an interesting example being the glee 'Saw you the nymph whom I adore' (autograph, *GB-Cu*), which was first entered for the prize contest of the Noblemen and Gentlemen's Catch Club in London in 1782, then used as a finale at Vauxhall in 1785, used again, with altered words, as the conclusion to Act 2 of *The Fair Peruvian* in 1786, and further utilized with altered words in *Safe and Sound* of 1809.

all first performed in London; printed editions in vocal score, published in London

LCG – *Covent Garden*   LDL – *Drury Lane*
LLH – *Little Theatre, Haymarket*   LMG – *Marylebone Gardens*
LSW – *Sadler's Wells*   LVG – *Vauxhall Gardens*

me – *musical entertainment*

Love and Innocence (pastoral serenata, 2), LMG, 10 Aug 1769, ?unpubd

Dido (comic op, ? T. Bridges), LLH, 24 July 1771, ?unpubd

The Country Courtship op.2 (pastoral dialogue, 1), LSW, 1772 (1772)

Trick Upon Trick op.3 (pantomime), LSW, 17 July 1772 (1772), possibly based on entertainment of same name given at Yeates, Warner and Rosoman's Great Theatrical Booth, May Fair, 9–16 May 1743

Cupid's Revenge op.8 (pastoral farce, 2, F. Gentleman), LLH, 27 July 1772 (1772)

The Divorce (me, 2, D. Dubois), LMG, 28 July 1772 [first documented perf.] , ?unpubd

Il dilettante (burletta), LMG, 28 Aug 1772, ?unpubd

Apollo and Daphne (serenata, J. Hughes), LMG, 27 Aug 1773, ?unpubd

The Dutchman (me, 2, T. Brydges [Bridges]), LLH, 21 Aug 1775, ?unpubd

The Lady of the Manor op.20 (comic op, 3, W. Kenrick, after C. Johnson: *The Country Lasses*), LCG, 23 Nov 1778, *GB-Cu** [incl. revisions dated 1815–17], vs (1778); rev. LCG, 28 Jan 1788, addl songs (1788); rev. LDL, 23 April 1818

The Volunteers, or Taylors to Arms! (musical prelude, 1, G. Downing), LCG, 19 April 1780, ?unpubd

Too Civil by Half op.25 (farce, 2, J. Dent), LDL, 5 Nov 1782 (1783)

The Cryer [The Crier of Vauxhall] (interlude, 1, M. P. Andrews), LVG, 12 June 1783 (1783)

The Double Disguise op.32 (farce, 2, Mrs Hook), LDL, 8 March 1784, song *Cu**, song *Ob** (Harding Mus.c.16); (1784)

The Love Wrangle, 1783 (pastoral interlude, 1), LVG, 20 May 1784, *Lbl**; 4 songs in Hook: Favourite Songs (1784)

The Country Wake op.36 (interlude, 1, Andrews), LSW, 21 June 1784 (1784)

The Poll Booth op.34 (me, 1), LVG, 29 June 1784 (1784)

A Word to Wives, or The Cryer's Sequel op.41 (me, 1), LVG, 19 May 1785 (1785)

The Fair Peruvian [The Peruvian] op.45 (comic op, 3, after J. F. Marmontel: *L'amitié à l'épreuve*), LCG, 18 March 1786, glee *Cu**; (1786)

The Triumph of Beauty op.46 (me, 1, ?Mrs Hook), LVG, 1 June 1786 (1786)

The Queen of the May (me, 1), LVG, 22 May 1787 (1787)

The Feast of Anacreon op.53 (serenata, 1), LVG, 24 May 1788 (1788)

The Effusions of Loyalty (me, 1, Andrews), LVG, 19 May 1789, ?unpubd

The Shepherds Festival (me, 1), LVG, 18 May 1790, ?unpubd

The Man Millener (me, 1, Andrews), LVG, 14 Aug 1790, ?unpubd

The Village Festival (me), LVG, 1791, ?unpubd

Look ere you Leap op.69 (serenata, 1, Vint), LVG, 2 June 1792 (1792)

The Soldier's Adieu (finale, 1), LVG, 25 May 1793, glee (1793)

The Ladies in Haste (comic finale), LVG, 10 Aug 1793, ?unpubd

Great Britain Triumphant (finale, 1, R. Houlton), LVG, 1794, London, Shepherd's Bush Library, ?unpubd

Jack of Newbury op.80 (comic op, 3 with masque, J. Hook jr), LDL, 6 May 1795, Act 1 finale *Cu**; (1795)

Diamond Cut Diamond, or Venetian Revels op.89 (comic op, 2, J. Hook jr), LCG, 23 May 1797 (1797)

Maids and Bachelors (finale), LVG, 1797, *Lbl**, ?unpubd

The Wreath of Loyalty, or British Volunteer op.94 (serenata, 1, Houlton), LVG, 31 July 1799 (1799)

Wilmore Castle op.96 (comic op, Houlton), LDL, 21 Oct 1800 (1800)

The Fane of Pleasure (finale), LVG, 6 Aug 1801, ?unpubd

Summer (finale), LVG, 1801, ?unpubd

Britannia's Invocation (finale), LVG, 1803, ?unpubd

The Soldier's Return, or What can Beauty Do? op.108 (comic op, 2, T. E. Hook), LDL, 23 April 1805, ov. *Cu**, duet *Ob** (Harding Mus.c.16); (1805)

The Invisible Girl op.112 (operatic farce, 1, T. E. Hook), LDL, 28 April 1806 (1806)

Catch him who Can op.113 (farce, 2, T. E. Hook), LLH, 12 June 1806, chorus, song and finale *Cu**, song *Ob** (Harding Mus.c.15); (1806)

Tekeli, or the Siege of Montgatz op.114 (melodrama, 3, T. E. Hook, after R. C. G. de Pixérécourt: *Tékéli, ou Le siège de Montgatz*), LDL, 24 Nov 1806, *Cu**; (1806); rev. (2), Lyceum, 10 Aug 1809

The Fortress op.117 (melodrama, 3, T. E. Hook, after Pixérécourt: *La forteresse du Danube*), LLH, 16 July 1807 (1807)

Music Mad op.119 (comic sketch, T. E. Hook), LLH, 27 Aug 1807 (1808)

The Siege of St Quintin, or Spanish Heroism op.122 (drama, 3, T. E. Hook, after Pixérécourt: *Les mines de Pologne*), LDL, 10 Nov 1808, *Cu**, recit and air *Ob** (Harding Mus.c.15); (1808)

Killing no Murder op.129 (farce, 2, T. E. Hook), LLH, 21 Aug [?1 July] 1809, *Ob** (Harding Mus.c.13); (1809)

Safe and Sound op.130 (comic op, T. E Hook), Lyceum, 28 Aug 1809 (1809)

The Jovial Crew, Lyceum, 15 July 1813, ?unpubd

Sharp and Flat op.140 (operatic farce, D. Lawler), Lyceum, 4 Aug 1813 (1813)

2 Unnamed operas: inc. (Lawler), 1813, *Ob** (Harding Mus.c.14, 15); finale dated 5 Aug 1819, *Cu**

Music in: Marriage a-la-mode, or Conjugal Douceurs, 1767; The Double Falsehood, 1770; St Patrick's Day, or The Scheming Lieutenant, 1775; She Stoops to Conquer, 1775; The Snuff Box, or A Trip to Bath, 1775; The Sheep-Shearing, 1777; The Fairy Tale, 1777; A Fete, 1781; The Sultan, or A Peep into the Seraglio, 1782; An Harmonic Jubilee, 1786; Love and War, 1787; Le matin, midi, et le soir, 1788; Comus, 1791; Tippoo Saib, or British Valour in India, 1791; The Union, or St Andrew's Day, 1791; Harlequin and Faustus, or The Devil will Have his Own, 1793; The Irishman in London, 1794; Inkle and Yarico, 1797; The Anacreontic Society Revived, 1798; Belle's Stratagem, 1799; Daphne and Amintor, *c*1800; The Lyric Novelist, 1804

*

LS

J. Genest: *Some Account of the English Stage from the Restoration in 1660 to 1830*, vii–viii (Bath, 1832)

A. H. Mann: Notebooks on East Anglian Music and Musicians (MSS, *GB-NWr*)

R. Fiske: *English Theatre Music in the Eighteenth Century* (London, 1973, 2/1986)
PAMELA McGAIRL

Hopf, Hans (*b* Nuremberg, 2 Aug 1916). German tenor. He studied in Munich with Paul Bender and in Oslo with Ragnvald Bjärne. In 1936 he made his début as Pinkerton with the Bayerische Landesbühnen, a touring ensemble; engagements followed in Augsburg (1939–42), Dresden (1942–3) and Oslo (1943–4). He joined the Berlin Staatsoper in 1946 and in 1949 was engaged by the Staatsoper in Munich. At Bayreuth in 1951 he sang Walther; between 1961 and 1966 he returned as Siegfried, Tannhäuser and Parsifal. At the 1954 Salzburg Festival he sang Max (*Der Freischütz*). He appeared at Covent Garden (1951–3) as Radames and Walther and at the Metropolitan, where he made his début in 1952 as Walther and sang mostly in the Wagner repertory. He made his La Scala début in 1963 as Siegfried and first appeared at the Teatro Colón in 1958 as Walther. His repertory also included Otello and the Emperor (*Die Frau ohne Schatten*). His voice and performances were both solid and reliable.

HAROLD ROSENTHAL/R

Höpken, Arvid Niclas, Friherr von (*b* Stockholm, 7 July 1710; *d* Stralsund, 28 July 1778). Swedish composer. A member of Sweden's minor nobility, he was taught art and music in Stockholm during his youth; it is possible that he studied under the Kassel

Kapellmeister Fortunato Chelleri during military service in Hesse, 1730–35. As an officer in the Swedish army, he spent most of the rest of his career outside Sweden – in Finland and in Swedish Pomerania – though he maintained close connections with Stockholm through his brother, the State Councillor. While in Stralsund he composed two *opere serie* and an intermezzo, possibly intended for Mingiotti's troupe, which made periodic visits to Stockholm. His naturally lyrical style draws heavily on Neapolitan opera of the period, mixed with influences of German composers like C. H. Graun and Hasse. In the few larger ensemble numbers, as in his surviving oratorio of 1751, the influence of Handel is in evidence.

all MSS in S-Skma

Il re pastore, 1752 (os, 2, P. Metastasio)
Catone in Utica, 1753 (os, 2, Metastasio)
Il bevitore, 1755 (int, 2)

*

E. Sundström: 'Arvid Niklas von Höpken och hans komiska opera Il bevitore', *STMf*, xviii (1936), 24–42   BERTIL H. VAN BOER

Hopkins, Antony (*b* London, 21 March 1921). English composer, conductor and broadcaster. He studied the organ and piano at the RCM (1939–42), winning the Chappell Gold Medal as a pianist. In 1944 he wrote his first incidental music for the BBC drama department, achieving well-merited success with scores for Louis MacNeice's productions of *The Golden Ass* and *Cupid and Psyche*. Many commissions for radio, film and theatre followed. In 1948 his first opera, *Lady Rohesia*, was produced at Sadler's Wells. He directed the Intimate Opera Company, for which he wrote *Three's Company* and *Hands across the Sky*, from 1953 to 1960. In latter years, his radio series 'Talking about Music' introduced countless listeners to the major works of the classical and contemporary repertory. He was made a CBE in 1976.

Hopkins is an eclectic who composes fluently in many styles. In his operas, music serves the drama effectively but unobtrusively, while his own personality emerges in his often adventurous choice and treatment of subjects. *Lady Rohesia*, which delighted some critics and outraged others, is based on one of E. H. Barham's *Ingoldsby Legends*, and owes more to the American comedy film *Hellzapoppin* than to traditional operatic models. Lady Rohesia (mezzo-soprano) rises from her death-bed to chastise her husband (baritone) as he offers his heart to their serving-maid (soprano); Hopkins adds a sequel, in which the situation is reversed, the husband lying on his death-bed while the wife flirts with the priest (tenor). A distracted prompter makes frequent interventions during the course of the action. *Three's Company* is set in a London office with a typist for its heroine; the witty libretto is matched by music of Offenbachian verve and fluency, with patter songs, waltzes and ensembles in familiar styles. *Dr. Musikus* is designed to be performed in schools by professionals, with improvisatory audience participation; Bach and Mozart appear on stage to join the composer-hero in the final ensemble, which ends with a lesson in notation. *A Time for Growing*, a pageant opera involving several hundred children, is a brief history of man's evolution and of his attempts to reconcile the conflicting claims of religion and science in his search for a meaning in life.

Lady Rohesia (1, Hopkins, after E. H. Barham: *Ingoldsby Legends*), London, Sadler's Wells, 17 March 1948, vs (London, 1947)

The Man from Tuscany (op for choirboys, 1, C. Hassell), Canterbury, Chapter House, 20 July 1951
Scena (op for broadcasting, 1, P. Dickinson), BBC Radio, 1 May 1953
Three's Company (1, M. Flanders), Crewe, Cheshire County Training College, 10 November 1953, vs (London, 1955)
Ten O'Clock Call (1, W. Radford), Cheltenham, Opera House, 11 July 1956
Hands across the Sky (1, G. Snell), Cheltenham, Town Hall, 8 July 1959
A Time for Growing (3, N. Pain), Norwich, St Andrew's Hall, 5 June 1967
Rich Man, Poor Man, Beggar Man, Saint (op for young people, 2, D. Nixon), Stroud, Trinity Church, 1968
Dr. Musikus (1, Hopkins), London, Arts, 20 March 1969, vs (London, 1970)   HUGO COLE

Hopp, Julius (*b* Graz, 18 May 1819; *d* Vienna, 28 Aug 1885). Austrian composer and translator. He was the son of the actor and dramatist Friedrich Hopp (1789–1869). He first appeared as a composer in 1836 at the Theater an der Wien with music to his father's play *Die Bekanntschaft im Paradeisgartel*. He wrote three more scores for the Theater an der Wien in 1837–8, but there followed a long gap before other scores by him were heard in Vienna. In 1858 he established a regular connection with the Theater in der Josefstadt, furnishing some two dozen scores in six or seven years; he composed regularly for the Theater an der Wien from 1863 to 1868, and occasionally in the mid- and late 1870s. In the mid-1860s he wrote for the Carl, Strampfer and Fürst theatres, and in 1879–80 produced a final flurry of scores for the Josefstadt.

The most important of Hopp's achievements is the series of 16 Offenbach translations and adaptations he made, mostly for the Theater an der Wien but some for the Carltheater, between 1865 and his death (one, *Tulipatan* – after *L'île de Tulipatan* – was not staged until 1888). These Offenbach versions include, in descending order of their success, *La belle Hélène* (as *Die schöne Helena*, 1865), *Barbe-bleue* (as *Blaubart*, 1866), *La Grande-Duchesse de Gérolstein* (as *Die Grossherzogin von Gerolstein*, 1867), *Le voyage dans la lune* (as *Die Reise in den Mond*, 1876) and *Madame l'archiduc* (as *Madame Herzog*, 1875).

Among Hopp's successful original works (for a number of which he wrote both words and music) are the operettas *Ein Deutschmeister* (1, K. Elmar; Vienna, Fürst's Singspiel-Halle, 1864) and *Das Donauweibchen und der Ritter vom Kahlenberg* (3, Hopp and P. Krone; Vienna, An der Wien, 14 April 1866), and a series of burlesques and parodies including *Fäustling und Margarethl* (1864), *Der Freischütz* (1867) and *Hammlet* (1874), for all of which he wrote both words and music. He provided Suppé with the libretto for *Der Teufel auf Erden* (1878).

*

SchmidlDS; StiegerO; WurzbachL
F. Hadamowsky: *Das Theater in der Wiener Leopoldstadt* (Vienna, 1934)
F. Hadamowsky and H. Otte: *Die Wiener Operette* (Vienna, 1947)
A. Bauer: *150 Jahre Theater an der Wien* (Zürich, 1952)
——: *Opern und Operetten in Wien* (Graz and Cologne, 1955)
——: *Das Theater in der Josefstadt zu Wien* (Vienna, 1957)
PETER BRANSCOMBE

Horaces, Les ('The Horatii'). *Tragédie lyrique* in three acts by ANTONIO SALIERI to a libretto by NICOLAS-FRANÇOIS GUILLARD after PIERRE CORNEILLE's tragedy *Horace*; Versailles, 2 December 1786.

Rome is at war with the neighbouring town of Alba Longa. The leaders of the opposing forces have agreed to let the quarrel be settled by personal combat in which three soldiers chosen by each side will fight to the death. Rome chooses Horace [Horatius] (tenor) and his two brothers as its champions; Alba chooses Curiace [Curiatius] (tenor) and his brothers. They agree to fight even though Curiatius is betrothed to Camille (soprano), Horatius's sister. The champions of Alba kill both of Horatius's brothers, but Horatius is eventually victorious, killing all three of his enemies. The Romans congratulate him, but Camille tearfully berates him for having killed her beloved Curiatius. Enraged by Camille's weeping for an enemy of Rome, Horatius is about to kill his sister when she is saved by her rejected lover, Valère [Valerius] (tenor). The festivities resume, and the opera ends with a chorus of celebration.

After the success of his first *tragédie lyrique* for Paris, *Les Danaïdes* (1784), Salieri was commissioned to write two more operas, *Les Horaces* and *Tarare*. Despite many fine passages and dramatic moments, *Les Horaces* has serious weaknesses, which include the ending. Corneille, following Roman history, had Horatius kill his sister; by sparing Camille, Guillard introduced inconsistencies that neither he nor Salieri could resolve. *Les Horaces* failed to please and was withdrawn after a few performances.
                                                              JOHN A. RICE

Horbowski, Mieczysław Apolinary (*b* Doleck, 23 July 1849; *d* Vienna, 26 Jan 1937). Polish baritone. He studied in Warsaw, Florence, in Milan with Lamperti and others, and in Paris with Roger. In 1872 he appeared in Italy under the name Francesco Ranieri, and the next year made his Warsaw début in *Il barbiere di Siviglia*; he later sang throughout Poland and at La Scala. His repertory centred on lyrical roles in operas by Moniuszko, Gounod, Meyerbeer, Donizetti, Verdi and Flotow. From 1886 to 1912 he taught successively at Warsaw, Moscow, Kraków and Vienna; he also contributed articles to *Echo muzyczne i teatralne* (1884) and published the two-volume *Szkoła śpiewu teoretyczno-praktycznego* ('Theoretical and Practical Teaching Methods in Singing', Warsaw, n.d.).
                                                              IRENA PONIATOWSKA

Horenstein, Jascha (*b* Kiev, 6 May 1898; *d* London, 2 April 1973). Russian conductor, naturalized Austrian, then American. He studied music theory with Joseph Marx and composition with Schreker in Vienna, from 1917. In 1928 he became chief conductor and later director of music at the Düsseldorf Opera, where his repertory included *Wozzeck*, given in 1930 under Berg's supervision. The Nazis forced him to leave in 1933. Moving to the USA in 1940, he conducted in North and South America and subsequently took American citizenship. After the war, through some notable concert performances, he introduced *Wozzeck* (1950) and Janáček's *From the House of the Dead* (1951) to Paris, and Busoni's *Doktor Faust* to the USA (American Opera Society, 1964). He conducted at the Städtische Oper in West Berlin and at Covent Garden (*Fidelio* in 1961 and *Parsifal* shortly before his death in 1973).
                                                              RONALD CRICHTON

Horký, Karel (*b* Štěměchy u Třebíče, 4 Sept 1909; *d* Brno, 27 Nov 1988). Czech composer. At the age of 14 he played the bassoon in the army band in Znojmo and he played in various orchestras before joining the

theatre orchestra in Brno in 1937. He studied composition with Haas (1937–9) and took part in Křička's masterclasses at the Prague Conservatory (1941–4); he then taught composition at the Brno Conservatory (as professor from 1961 and director from 1964) and at the Janáček Academy of Music.

Horký's command of orchestral writing and of individual instruments equipped him to compose in large forms, especially opera, in which he showed his sense of theatre. The music in his operas is essentially written to lend support to the text. He was interested in stories with a strong social-ethical content and often sought parallels between past and present. The quasi-oratorio *Jan Hus* is a broad fresco expressing opposition to the subjugation of the Czech nation by the Nazis. The exigencies of cultural politics during the 1950s led Horký to compose the romantic folk opera *Hejtman Šarovec* and, later, *Svítání* ('Daybreak'), which is about the birth of the workers' movement in Czechoslovakia. He responded to conditions prevailing in the 1960s in his music drama *Jed z Elsinoru* ('Poison from Elsinore'). His last opera, *Atlantida* ('Atlantis'; composed for the 100th anniversary of the establishment of the original National Theatre in Brno), deals with existential questions about the future of mankind.

Jan Hus, 1944–9 (oratorio-opera, 6, V. Kantor), Brno, 27 May 1950, rev. 1959
Hejtman Šarovec, 1951–2 (folk opera, 5, F. Kožík), Brno, 5 Dec 1953
Jed z Elsinoru [Poison from Elsinore], 1967–8 (2, V. Renč, after M. Rejnuš and W. Shakespeare), Brno, 11 Nov 1969
Svítání [Daybreak], (4, J. Nezval, after A. Zápotocký), Brno, Janáček, 4 July 1975
Atlantida [Atlantis] (4, E. Bezděková, after V. Nezval), Brno, Janáček, 30 Sept 1983   JIŘÍ FUKAČ, HELENA HAVLÍKOVÁ

Horn, Charles Edward (*b* London, 21 June 1786; *d* Boston, MA, 21 Oct 1849). English composer and singer of German parentage. He was taught music by his father, the composer Karl Friedrich Horn (1762–1830), and Venanzio Rauzzini and played the double bass and cello in the London theatres: as a singer he first appeared on the stage in 1809, in M. P. King's opera *Up All Night*. The next year he withdrew from the stage to study singing with Thomas Welsh, reappearing in 1814 in Storace's *The Siege of Belgrade* with more success. Meanwhile he had begun in 1810 to compose music for the theatre; his first great success was *The Devil's Bridge* (1812), which enjoyed many revivals in England, Ireland and the USA.

Horn continued to succeed as both a composer and a singer, though judging from contemporary accounts his voice was a poor one, its chief merit being a wide compass covering the tenor and baritone ranges. He became known especially for his performances as Macheath, Artabanes (in Arne's *Artaxerxes*) and Caspar (rewritten as a high baritone) in an English version of *Der Freischütz*. As a composer he was exceeded in productivity only by his exact contemporary, Henry Bishop; like Bishop he had several successes with songs originally introduced in dramatic pieces, notably 'On the banks of Allen Water' (*Rich and Poor*, 1812), 'I know a bank' (*The Merry Wives of Windsor*, 1824), 'The deep, deep sea' (*Honest Frauds*, 1830) and, above all, 'Cherry Ripe', apparently first sung by Lucia Elizabeth Vestris in *Paul Pry* (1826), an opera attributed to a Mr Poole with which Horn was not otherwise connected. He was accused of plagiarizing this last from Attwood, but cleared himself in court – according to one story by singing Attwood's song and his own to the jury.

Horn paid several visits to Dublin and staged some of his operas there. In 1827 he sailed to New York, where he appeared in *The Siege of Belgrade*, directed *The Devil's Bridge* (already known in New York since 1820) and adapted *Le nozze di Figaro* and other works for the American stage. In 1828 he visited Boston and Philadelphia. He was back in London in 1830 for the première of *Honest Frauds*, and in 1831–2 was musical director at the Olympic Theatre. Returning to New York in 1832, he became musical director at the Park Theatre, where he conducted operas from the piano, adapted *La Cenerentola* and *Die Zauberflöte* and successfully introduced several English operas. He lost his voice through illness in 1835, but continued to compose, to play the piano and organ in public, and to give singing lessons. Several of his operas were first performed in New York; it was said that he was the first composer with a substantial reputation in the Old World to go to live in America. In 1843 Horn returned once more to England, where for a time he was musical director at the Princess's Theatre, but he returned to the USA in 1847.

Horn's dramatic pieces cannot be taken seriously as operas: typically, they consist of a perfunctory overture, a string of a dozen independent songs with perhaps a duet and a glee, and a finale in one rondo movement. Most of the music is poor, but occasionally one or two of the songs are found to possess great charm, such as 'Cherry Ripe' in his favourite rondo form with coda. *Rich and Poor* (1812) is an astounding example of tasteless eclecticism. The overture incorporates the entire fugue in Eb major from book 2 of the '48' (which Horn's father had recently edited with Samuel Wesley), interspersed with Horn's less than sublime improvisations on the same subject. One song is lifted from Mozart (K596), another is based on 'All through the night', a third is a medley of Italian operatic songs and English folktunes, and the finale is an instrumental version of 'Adeste fideles'; yet the same work contains one of his most charming songs, 'On the banks of Allen Water'. He had a gift for incorporating and imitating elements of folksong (or, as it was termed in his day, 'national song'), and it was this that gave many of his songs their appeal.

In his more ambitious efforts at composition Horn was unsuccessful. *Dirce* is now believed to have been the first all-sung English opera since *Artaxerxes* (1762); only one number from it has survived. His one attempt at 'grand opera', *Ahmed al Ramel* (1840), has not survived.

first performed in London unless otherwise stated; music lost unless otherwise stated; all printed works published in city and year of first performance

LCG – *Covent Garden*   LDL – *Drury Lane*
LLY – *Lyceum (English Opera House)*
LHY – *Little Theatre, Haymarket*   LVG – *Vauxhall Gardens*

† – *partly adapted*   †† – *wholly adapted*

Tricks upon Travellers (comic op, J. B. Burges), LLY, 9 July 1810; collab. Reeve

The Magic Bride (dramatic romance, L. St G. Skeffington), LLY, 26 Dec 1810

The Bee Hive (musical farce, 2, J. G. Millingen, after C. A. G. Pigault-Lebrun), LLY, 19 Jan 1811, vs pubd

The Boarding House, or Five Hours at Brighton (musical farce, S. Beazley the younger), LLY, 26 Aug 1811, vs pubd

M. P., or The Blue Stocking (comic op, 3, T. Moore), LLY, 9 Sept 1811, vs pubd; collab. M. P. King

The Devil's Bridge (operatic romance, 3, S. J. Arnold), LLY, 6 May 1812, *GB-Lcm*, vs pubd; collab. Braham, M. Corri

†Rich and Poor (comic op, M. G. Lewis), LLY, 22 July 1812, *D-Ha*, vs pubd

Narensky, or The Road to Yaroslaf (seriocomic op, 3, C. A. Brown), LDL, 11 Jan 1814; collab. Braham, Reeve

†The Woodman's Hut (melodramatic romance, 3, Arnold), LDL, 12 April 1814, vs pubd

The Ninth Statue, or The Irishman in Bagdad (musical romance, 2, after *The Thousand and One Nights*), LDL, 29 Nov 1814

The Election (Arnold, after J. Baillie), LLY, 7 June 1817

The Wizard, or The Brown Man of the Moor (melodramatic romance, Arnold, after W. Scott: *The Black Dwarf*), LLY, 26 July 1817

The Persian Hunters, or The Rose of Gurgistan (seriocomic op, T. Noble), LLY, 13 Aug 1817, vs pubd; collab. G. Perry

Lalla Rookh, or The Cashmerian Minstrel (M. J. Sullivan, after T. Moore), Dublin, Theatre Royal, ?1818, vs pubd

Justice, or The Caliph and the Cobbler (musical drama, 3, J. S. Faucit), LDL, 28 Nov 1820

Therese, the Orphan of Geneva (melodrama, J. H. Payne), LDL, 2 Feb 1821

Dirce, or The Fatal Urn (serious recitative drama, after P. Metastasio: *Demofoonte*), LDL, 2 June 1821, 1 duet pubd

†Annette, Dublin, Royal, 1822; ? after Rossini: La gazza ladra

The Two Galley-Slaves, or The Mill of St Aldervon (melodrama, Payne), LCG, 6 Nov 1822; collab. T. S. Cooke

Actors al fresco (burletta, W. T. Moncrieff), LVG, 1823, only lib. pubd; collab. Blewitt, Cooke; rev. as vaudeville, LVG, 9 June 1827

Philandering, or The Rose Queen (comic op, Beazley), LDL, 13 Jan 1824; collab. Braham

The Merry Wives of Windsor (comedy, after W. Shakespeare), LDL, 20 Feb 1824; collab. J. Parry, S. Webbe and others

The Shepherd of Derwent Vale, or The Innocent Culprit (musical drama, J. Lunn), LDL, 12 Feb 1825

Faustus (romantic drama, 3, D. Terry and G. Soane, after J. W. von Goethe), LDL, 16 May 1825, vs pubd; collab. H. R. Bishop, Cooke; ov. from Weber's Euryanthe

The Wedding Present (comic op, 2, ? J. Kenney), LDL, 28 Oct 1825

Benyowsky, or The Exiles of Kamschatka (operatic play, 3, Kenney, after A. von Kotzebue), LDL, 16 March 1826; collab. Cooke, M. Kelly, B. Livius, Stevenson

The Death Fetch, or The Student of Göttingen (operatic romance, J. B. Buckstone), LLY, 25 July 1826

Peveril of the Peak (musical drama, I. Pocock, after W. Scott), LCG, 21 Oct 1826, *US-Bp*, vs pubd

Pay to my Order, or A Chaste Salute (vaudeville, J. R. Planché, W. H. Armstrong), LVG, 9 July 1827

††The Marriage of Figaro, New York, Park, 21 Jan 1828; after Mozart: Le nozze di Figaro

††Dido, New York, Park, 9 April 1828; after various Rossini operas

†Isidore de Merida, New York, Park, 9 June 1828; after Storace: The Pirates

††Oberon, New York, Park, 9 Oct 1828; after Weber's opera

The Quartette, or Interrupted Harmony (1), New York, Bowery, 27 April 1829

†Il trionfo della musica, Philadelphia, Chestnut Street, 5 May 1829; after Mayr: Che originali; in Italian

Honest Frauds (musical farce, 2, Lunn), LHY, 29 July 1830

†The Love Spell, or The Flirts of the Village (comic op), Olympic, 27 Oct 1831; after Auber: Le philtre

††Cinderella, New York, Park, 20 Dec 1832; after Rossini: La Cenerentola

Nadir and Zuleika, New York, Park, 27 Dec 1832

††The Magic Flute, New York, Park, 17 April 1833; after Mozart: Die Zauberflöte

Ahmed al Ramel, or The Pilgrim of Love (grand op, H. J. Finn, after W. Irving: *Alhambra*), New York, National, 12 Oct 1840

The Maid of Saxony (3, G. P. Morris, after M. Edgeworth), New York, Park, 23 May 1842

*

The Examiner (10 May 1812), 301 [*The Devil's Bridge*]

J. Sainsbury, ed.: *A Dictionary of Musicians*, i (London, 2/1825), 375

New York Mirror (6 Oct 1827, 14 Aug 1830, 22 Dec 1832, 14 March 1835, 16 Oct 1841)

American Musical Journal, i (1834–5), 45, 238

Monthly Supplement to the Musical Library, iii (1835), 23

Obituary, Musical World, xxiv (1849), 741

H. C. Lahee: *Annals of Music in America* (Boston, 1922)

E. W. White: *The Rise of English Opera* (London, 1951)

G. Chase: *America's Music* (New York, 1955), 164, 172

R. A. Montague: *Charles Edward Horn: his Life and Works* (diss., Florida State U., 1959)

J. Mattfeld: *A Handbook of American Operatic Premières 1731–1962* (Detroit, 1963)

B. Carr: 'The First All-Sung English Opera', *MT*, cxv (1974), 125–6

NICHOLAS TEMPERLEY

Horne, Marilyn (Bernice) (*b* Bradford, PA, 16 Jan 1934). American mezzo-soprano. She studied at the University of Southern California, taking part in Lotte Lehmann's masterclasses. She sang the dubbed voice of Dorothy Dandridge in the film *Carmen Jones* in 1954, the year of her début at Los Angeles (as Háta in *The Bartered Bride*), then spent three seasons at Gelsenkirchen (1956–9), singing soprano and mezzo roles. In 1960 she first appeared at San Francisco, as Marie in *Wozzeck* (the role of her Covent Garden début in 1964). An association with Sutherland, which began in New York in 1961 with a concert performance of *Beatrice di Tenda* in which she sang Agnese, brought many notable performances – as Arsace to Sutherland's *Semiramide* (1965, Boston), and as Adalgisa to her *Norma* (1967, Covent Garden; her Metropolitan début, 1970). She sang Neocles in *Le siège de Corinthe* at La Scala (1969), Carmen at the Metropolitan (1972), and Handel's *Rinaldo* in Houston (1975). Among other Rossini roles she has sung are Malcolm in *La donna del lago* (1981, Houston; 1985, Covent Garden), Falliero in *Bianca e Falliero* (1986, Pesaro), Andromache in *Ermione* (1987, Pesaro), Calbo in *Maometto II* (1988, San Francisco) and Isabella in *L'italiana in Algeri* (1989, Covent Garden). In the latter part of her career she has sung Mistress Quickly (1988, San Francisco) and Delilah (1988, Théâtre des Champs-Elysées). Horne has a voice of extraordinary range, rich and tangy in timbre, with a stentorian chest register and an exciting top. Her recordings include several Rossini roles, Laura in *La Gioconda*, Gluck's Orpheus, Anita in Massenet's *La Navarraise* and Zerlina. She has written an autobiography, *My Life* (New York, 1984).

M. R. Scott: 'Marilyn Horne', *Opera*, xviii (1967), 963–7

J. B. Steane: *The Grand Tradition* (London, 1974), 387ff

ALAN BLYTH

Horneman, Christian Frederik Emil (*b* Copenhagen, 17 Dec 1840; *d* Copenhagen, 8 June 1906). Danish composer. He studied at the Leipzig Conservatory (1858–60) with Moscheles, Ernst Richter, Moritz Hauptmann and others, and there he met Grieg, who became a lifelong friend. After his return to Copenhagen he and his father, the composer J. O. E. Horneman, established a music publishing firm where he issued, partly under pseudonyms, his own arrangements and potpourris of popular music. For more than 20 years (1865–87) he worked on the four-act opera *Aladdin*, his most important work. To a libretto by B. Feddersen, after A. Oehlenschlaeger, it was first performed at the Kongelige Teater in Copenhagen on the occasion of King Christian IX's 25th anniversary (18 November 1888). The opera was not well received, but a revival in 1902 won acclaim. Its overture (1864) became a popular concert work. Horneman also wrote incidental music for the stage (notably for a Danish version of Beaumarchais' *Le barbier de Séville*, 1893) and a string quartet as well as helping found two music societies and a conservatory.

SIGURD BERG

Horovitz, Joseph (*b* Vienna, 26 May 1926). British composer of Austrian birth. After early studies in Vienna he moved to Britain in 1938. He studied at Oxford (MA, BMus), at the RCM with Gordon Jacob and in Paris with Boulanger. A one-act ballet won him the Farrar Prize at the RCM, and in 1959 he won the Commonwealth Medal for composition. He is a composer of remarkable versatility, graceful wit and an enviable ability to communicate, whether in his refreshingly light or more serious styles. In the 1950s he won praise for his ballets and operas, the latter performed by the Intimate Opera Company, with which he was associated as an adapter of other operas, conductor and pianist. He wrote two comic operas for the company: *The Dumb Wife* (1, P. Shaffer, after F. Rabelais), produced in Lowestoft in 1953, and *Gentleman's Island* (1, G. Snell), produced in London in 1958.

ERNEST BRADBURY

Horusitzky, Zoltán (*b* Pápa, 18 July 1903; *d* Budapest, 25 April 1985). Hungarian composer. He graduated in 1926 from the Budapest Academy of Music as a composition pupil of Kodály and in law from Budapest University in 1927. He then taught the piano at the Budapest Upper School of Music, of which he was the director, 1945–9, and at the Budapest Academy of Music, 1946–69.

Horusitzky was a prolific writer of chamber, piano and, above all, vocal music, including songs, cantatas and oratorios. His main stage work is the three-act 'Hungarian historical opera' *Báthory Zsigmond* ('Zsigmond Báthory'), drafted in 1944 to his own libretto. It took concrete form only after 1950, with the help of the librettist József Romhányi. It was broadcast on Hungarian Radio in 1955, staged in Greiz in 1957 and presented in its definitive form on 11 June 1960 at the Hungarian State Opera House in Budapest. In *Báthory*, Horusitzky attempted to fuse his folk-inspired Hungarian style with the formal vestiges of 19th-century operatic 'realism' (Verdi, Erkel and, above all, Musorgsky). He has also written a children's opera (*Csipkerózsika*, 'Sleeping Beauty', Romhányi, 1971) and three radio operas: *A fekete város* ('Black City', 3, J. Erdődy and Horusitzky), after the novel by Kálmán Mikszáth (1982), though originating in a 1953 radio ballad; *Egyetlenegy éjszakán* ('On a Single Night', Romhányi), 1974; and *Palotai álmok* ('Palota Dreams', T. Török, after G. Krúdy), 1979.

A. Boros: *Harminc év magyar operái 1948–1978* [30 Years of Hungarian Opera, 1948–78] (Budapest, 1979)

G. Staud, ed.: *A budapesti operaház száz éve* [100 Years of the Budapest Opera House] (Budapest, 1984)

TIBOR TALLIÁN

Hosenrolle (Ger.). BREECHES PART.

Hostile Power. Opera by A. N. Serov; *see* VRAZH'YA SILA.

Hostinský, Otakar (*b* Martiněves u Budyně, Bohemia, 2 Jan 1847; *d* Prague, 19 Jan 1910). Czech aesthetician, writer and librettist. He was lecturer in aesthetics at the Charles University in Prague from 1877 (professor from 1882) and one of the most remarkable and influential cultural figures in Bohemia of the time. A personal friend of Smetana and Fibich, he promoted their works assiduously and published biographies of both. His espousal of what he considered to be the progressive line of Czech opera was to the detriment of Dvořák (whom he hardly noticed) and set the critical agenda for Czech writing on opera for much of the next century. He covered many fields such as history, literary theory, theatre studies and art history, but music was a major interest from his youth (when he composed songs and even began an opera), and he wrote important articles on many topics tangential to opera. He wrote the librettos *Nevěsta messinská* ('The Bride of Messina', after F. von Schiller's play *Die Braut von Messina*, 1881), set by Fibich (1884), and *Popelka* ('Cinderella', after the fairy-tale), set by Rozkošny (1885).

Bedřich Smetana a jeho boj o moderní českou hudbu [Smetana and his Struggle for Modern Czech Music] (Prague, 1901, 2/1941, ed. B. Hostinský)
Antonín Dvořák ve vývoji naší hudby dramatické [Antonín Dvořák in the Development of our Music for the Stage] (Prague, 1908)
Česká hudba 1864–1904 [Czech Music 1864–1904] (Prague, 1909)
Hostinský o hudbě [Hostinský on Music] (Prague, 1961)
Studie a kritiky [Studies and Reviews] (Prague, 1974)
Otakar Hostinský o divadle [Otakar Hostinský on Theatre] (Prague, 1981)
Z hudebních bojů let sedmdesátých a osmdesátých: výbor z operních a koncertních kritik [From the Musical Battles of the 1870s and 80s: Selection of Opera and Concert Reviews] (Prague, 1986)

*

ČSHS
V. Helfert: 'Smetanismus a Wagnerianismus', *Smetana*, i (1911), 167–73, 188–97, 253–5 [correspondence, O. Zich], 305–6 [reply]
M. Jůzl: *Otakar Hostinský* (Prague, 1980)
Pocta Otakaru Hostinskému: Brno 1980 [In Honour of Otakar Hostinský]
E. Vítová: '70. léta – doba zrání Otakara Hostinského' [The 1870s – the Time of Otakar Hostinský's Maturing], in O. Hostinský: *Z hudebních bojů let sedmdesátých a osmedsátých* (Prague, 1986), 5–27
J. Tyrrell: *Czech Opera* (Cambridge, 1988)   JOHN TYRRELL

Hans Hotter as Hans Sachs in Wagner's 'Die Meistersinger von Nürnberg', Covent Garden, 1948

Hotter, Hans (*b* Offenbach am Main, 19 Jan 1909). Austrian bass-baritone of German birth. He studied with Matthäus Römer and made his début at Troppau in 1930. He sang his first Wotan in 1937 at Munich, where he became a member of the company, remaining one until 1972.

Hotter's international career was delayed by the war, but from his first appearances at Covent Garden (as Mozart's Count Almaviva and Don Giovanni with the Vienna Staatsoper, in September 1947) he became a favourite with British audiences. He made his Metropolitan début in 1950 as the Dutchman and in 1952 began a 12-year association with Bayreuth. During the 1950s and 60s he was generally recognized as the world's leading Wagnerian bass-baritone, renowned especially as Hans Sachs and as Wotan, embodying the grandeur of Wagner's conception in a style at once rhetorical and noble. He was also known for his interpretations of the Grand Inquisitor (*Don Carlos*) and Boris Godunov. Although he made many recordings, it is to be regretted that he did not in his prime record Wotan, or such other of his finest parts as Borromeo in *Palestrina*, Sachs and the Dutchman. Among the roles he created are the Commandant in Strauss's *Friedenstag* (1938, Munich), Olivier in *Capriccio* (1942, Munich) and Jupiter in *Die Liebe der Danae* at the unofficial première (1944, Salzburg).

Hotter directed the *Ring* at Covent Garden (1962–4) and has appeared elsewhere as a director. He sang his last major stage role in 1972, subsequently appearing in small character parts – though he sang Schigolch in *Lulu* at San Francisco in 1989 and in Paris in 1991. An artist of intelligence and dedication, he was able to reduce his warm, ample voice to meet the demands of lighter roles. Though his voice could be unsteady and lack focus, its unmistakable quality, matched with his intense declamation and his commanding physical presence, made him one of the greatest operatic artists of the mid-20th century.

*

GV (L. Riemens; R. Vegeto)
P. Francis: 'Hans Hotter', *Opera*, iv (1953), 589–95
B. W. Wessling: *Hans Hotter* (Bremen, 1966)
D. Cairns: 'Hotter's Farewell', *Responses* (London, 1973)
P. Turing: *Hans Hotter: Man and Artist* (London, 1983)
                                            PETER BRANSCOMBE

Houston. City in Texas, the fourth largest city in the USA. Only two years after the Mexican general Santa Ana lost the Battle of San Jacinto (1836), Houstonians celebrated their new town in the Republic of Texas by staging a play. The first documented dramatic performance with music took place on 11 June 1838; a theatre was completed in early 1839. During the first 80 years of its existence, the city relied heavily on visiting opera companies, which performed the standard repertory. Complete grand opera performances took place for the first time in April 1867, presented by the Roncari Opera Troupe at the Perkins Opera House. The Italian cast and repertory (including *La traviata* and *Il trovatore*) were received with little enthusiasm, and two years later the Marie Friederici Grand German Opera Troupe fared only slightly better with Flotow's *Martha*. Emma Juch introduced Wagner to Houston in 1892 with a production of *Tannhäuser* at the Sweeney and Coombs Opera House. The discovery of oil in 1901 at Spindletop in nearby Beaumont ushered in the rapid development of the city as a petroleum centre and eventually as a major port. The date also marks the first visit to Houston of the Metropolitan Opera, with Emma Eames and Ernestine Schumann-Heink in *Lohengrin*. The event was to be the city's cultural turning-point. After the Metropolitan production of *Parsifal* at the Winnie Davis Auditorium, in 1905, the company did not return to Houston until 1947; but meanwhile the city had become the cultural and financial centre of Texas.

Until the foundation of the Houston Grand Opera in 1955, the city continued to rely on performances by touring groups. The company has since then acquired an international reputation and is regarded as one of the leading opera companies in the USA. It was guided from its inception until 1972 by Walter Herbert, who in the first season presented *Salome* and *Madama Butterfly* on a budget of approximately $40000. The basic tenets of Herbert's tenure have been retained: high performance and production levels of works in the standard repertory and innovatory presentation of 20th-century works, including American or world premières. David Gockley was appointed general manager in 1972; under him the budget has risen from $420000 to $15 million and the number of performances has increased from 30 to more than 250. The company's diverse activities include a light opera series in English; free staged performances in its Spring Opera Festival (it was this series that presented the highly acclaimed productions of Joplin's *Treemonisha* in 1975 and Gershwin's *Porgy and Bess* the following year); and the management of Texas Opera Theater, a touring subsidiary, and the Houston Opera Studio for young American singers, sponsored by the University of Houston. National and international tours have received favourable notice, and since 1973 each season has included either a world première or the presentation of a 20th-century masterpiece such as *Lulu*, *Wozzeck* and *Peter Grimes*. The conductor John DeMain was initially appointed to the Houston Grand Opera in 1977, becoming Music Director in 1980; his long tenure has produced an enviable musical standard as far as the quality of the orchestra and ensemble are concerned.

In October 1987 the company moved to its new permanent residence, the Wortham Theater Center in central Houston, consisting of two auditoriums: the Cullen Theater with a seating capacity of 1100 and the larger Brown Theater accommodating 2300. The building, costing $72 million, was erected with private funds during one of the worst economic periods in Houston's history. The first three productions in the new residence were *Aida*, the world première of John Adams's *Nixon in China*, and *Die Entführung aus dem Serail*. *Nixon in China* was later taken to the Edinburgh Festival.

Since 1974 the company has presented nine world premières, seven of them by American composers. Gockley was instrumental in securing the first transatlantic triple co-commission with La Scala, Milan, and the John F. Kennedy Center for Leonard Bernstein's *A Quiet Place*; the opera received its première on a double bill with *Trouble in Tahiti* in June 1983. Other premières have included Pasatieri's *The Seagull* (1974), Floyd's *Bilby's Doll* (1976), *Willie Stark* (1981) and the revised *Passion of Jonathan Wade* (1991), Glass's *Akhnaten* (1984) and *The Making of the Representative for Planet 8* (1988), Stewart Wallace's *Where's Dick?* (1989), Tippett's *New Year* (1989) and Meredith Monk's *Atlas* (1991). Among the performers and directors who have worked with the company are Marton, Te Kanawa, Sutherland, Pavarotti, Sills, Domingo, Scotto, Milnes, Behrens, Carreras, Vickers, Price, Sir Peter Hall, Hal Prince, Jonathan Miller, Jean-Pierre Ponnelle, Ken Russell, Stephen Sondheim, Nicholas Hytner and Peter Sellars.

*

L. M. Spell: *Music in Texas: a Survey of One Aspect of Cultural Progress* (Austin, TX, 1936)

D. G. McComb: *Houston: the Bayou City* (Austin, TX, 1969)

D. W. Pugh: *Music in Frontier Houston, 1836–1876* (diss., U. of Texas, 1970)

D. W. Looser: *Significant Factors in the Musical Development of the Cultural Life in Houston, Texas 1930–1971* (diss., Florida State U., 1972)

R. I. Giesberg: *Houston Grand Opera: a History* (Houston, 1981)

PAUL COOPER

Hovhaness [Hovaness], **Alan** [Chakmakjian, Alan Hovhaness] (*b* Somerville, MA, 8 March 1911). American composer of Armenian and Scottish descent. He began composing in his youth and continued without interruption into his 80s. Throughout his career, a mystical and spiritual intent has prevailed, while his style has changed according to varying harmonic and textural interests with particular reference to international and ethnic attractions. In works of the 1940s his Armenian heritage predominates; in later pieces the language relates to one Asian culture or another.

Hovhaness has written prolifically for voices, and his concern for melody is intense, yet his operatic output – some dozen works out of more than 400 – is disproportionately small. Indeed his most convincing *arioso* writing is found in unstaged works, such as the *Magnificat* (1958) and several works in cantata design. Among these, *Lady of Light* (1969, mounted 1974) may be given operatic staging and *Wind Drum* (1962) lies somewhere between ballet and opera. Only two of his works qualify as full-scale operas. *Etchmiadzin* (1945) was performed at the Armenian cathedral in New York soon after its composition but has been largely withdrawn, although several sections of it survive in other works. *Pericles* (1975) remains unperformed in its entirety.

In the 1960s Hovhaness wrote a number of chamber operas in the style of Japanese and Korean theatre music. The harmonic language is spare and sometimes entirely static; vocal lines feature slides as often as discrete intervals. Instrumentation is sparse and clearly profiled. The texts – always by the composer himself and always in English – are terse, allegorical and often concerned with isolation and exile. When a definite modal vocabulary applies, it is usually pentatonic but with the inclusion of semitones, thus suggesting more the influence of Japan than of China. Hovhaness is married to the Japanese coloratura soprano Hinako Fujihara; his short operas of the 1970s and 80s retain oriental features and often call for a very high voice. Despite many general similarities to Japanese noh drama, or Korean *ah-ak* or *p'ansori*, Hovhaness has not adhered strictly to the arcane conventions of those genres, and the subject matter generally has no particular geographical or local mythological origin.

all to librettos by the composer

Etchmiadzin op.62, New York, St Vartan's Cathedral, 1945

Afton Water (operetta, after W. Saroyan), 1951

Blue Flame op.172 (musical fairy-tale), San Antonio, 15 Dec 1959

Wind Drum op.183 (dance-opera), Honolulu, U. of Hawaii, 1962; Gatlinburg, TN, Union College, 23 May 1964

Spirit of the Avalanche op.197 (chamber op, 1), Tokyo, 15 Feb 1963

The Burning House op.185 (1), Gatlinburg, TN, Union College, 23 Aug 1964

The Leper King op.219, 1965 (music drama), Chicago, 1969

Pilate op.196 (chamber op, 1), Los Angeles, Pepperdine College, 26 June 1966

The Travelers op.215 (chamber op), San Francisco, Foothill College, 22 April 1967

Lady of Light op.227, 1969 (opera-oratorio), concert perf., Montana, 1974

Pericles op.283, 1975 (after W. Shakespeare), excerpts perf. Shippensburg, PA, 1979

Tale of the Sun Goddess Going into the Stone House op.323 (chamber op), Salinas, CA, 1978; rev. 1990

The Frog Man, 1987 (chamber op), unperf.   ARNOLD ROSNER

Hovhanisian [Oganesyan], **Edgar (Sergey)** (*b* Erevan, 14 Jan 1930). Armenian composer. He graduated in 1953 from the conservatory in Erevan, where he studied composition with Grigor Egiazaryan; he completed postgraduate studies at the Moscow Conservatory under Aram Khachaturyan in 1957. From 1962 to 1968 he was director of the Alexander Spendiaryan Theatre of Opera and Ballet in Erevan, and in 1979 he received a State Prize of the USSR for his opera-ballet *David Sasunskiy* ('David of Sasun'). He has been Artistic Director for Armenian radio and television, and since 1986 principal of the Erevan Conservatory and professor of composition; in 1986 he was made a People's Artist of the USSR.

Stage works, chiefly ballets, occupy a fundamental place in Hovhanisian's output. His early music shows the influence of Bartók and Stravinsky. In the 1970s he began to mix vocal and choreographic action, strikingly so in the opera-ballet *David of Sasun* (3, V. Galstyan after an Armenian epic; Erevan, Spendiaryan Theatre, 5 September 1976). Here the composer turns to the 9th-century Armenian epic about the folk hero David of Sasun, blending dance, song, speech and mime suggested by the original text. With its alternation of solo, ensemble and choral music, the work tends more towards oratorio than opera; the choral frescoes in particular lend it a typically monumental character. Hovhanisian's only other opera, the three-act *Puteshestviye v Arzrum* ('Journey to Erzrum'; Erevan, Spendiaryan Theatre, 27 December 1987), is to a libretto by G. Ansimov and the composer after the story of the same title by Pushkin. Verse by Griboedov and incidents from the lives of these poets also govern the historical nature of the opera and its appeal. With economical action, thematic threads are interwoven with psychological ones (e.g. the depiction of the Armenian people striving to free themselves from Persian and Turkish bondage), using personification, symbolism and techniques resembling cinematic close-ups and flashbacks. Two languages are used: Russian, thus observing Russian operatic traditions, and Armenian in the choruses using material drawn from folklore.

*

S. Sarkisyan: 'Djutsaznavep operai ev baleti lezvov' [The Epic in the Language of Opera and Ballet], *Garun Yerevani*, iii (1977), 83–9

M. Rukhkyan: 'Geroiko-patrioticheskaya epopeya' [A Heroic and Patriotic Epic], *SovM* (1977), no.10, 26–31

G. Tigranov: *Armyanskiy muzikal'niy teatr*, iv (Erevan, 1988), 29–59

S. Sarkisyan: 'Zhanrovo-stilisticheskiye sintezï v teatral'nom tvorchestve armyanskikh kompozitorov' [Synthesis of Genre and Style in the Stage Works of Armenian Composers], *Muzikal'niy teatr: sobïtiya, problemï*, ed. M. Sabinina (Moscow, 1990), 103–20   SVETLANA SARKISYAN

Howard, Ann [Giles, Ann Pauline] (*b* Norwood, London, 22 July 1936). English mezzo-soprano. She began her career in musical theatre, then joined the Covent Garden chorus and received a grant to study in Paris. After making her début as Azucena with the WNO in 1964, she joined Sadler's Wells Opera; her first role there, also in 1964, was Czipra (*Der Zigeunerbaron*). Her many roles with British companies include Carmen for Sadler's Wells (1970), which led to her American début in the role at New Orleans (1971), and Amneris at Covent Garden (1973). In Europe, North America, Mexico and South Africa her roles have ranged from operetta to Delilah, Clytemnestra and Eboli, and, in the Wagner repertory, Ortrud, Fricka and Brangäne. She created Leda in Bennett's *The Mines of Sulphur* at Sadler's Wells (1965), Mrs Danvers in *Rebecca* (Josephs) for Opera North in 1983, and Mrs Elsie Worthing in *The Plumber's Gift* (Blake) for the ENO in 1989. She also sang for the ENO the role of Mescalina in the first UK production of Ligeti's *Le Grand Macabre* (1982). A long association with Santa Fe culminated in her creation of Caliban in Eaton's *The Tempest* (1985). In 1990 she played Cinderella's Stepmother in Sondheim's *Into the Woods*. Her vivid stage personality, strong in comedy or in sinister character, is combined with clear articulation and a full and flexible voice over a wide compass.

NOËL GOODWIN

Howard, Brian (*b* Sydney, 3 Jan 1951). Australian composer and conductor. He studied composition at the universities of Sydney and Adelaide, where his teachers included Peter Sculthorpe and Richard Meale, and afterwards in Darmstadt at the Internationale Ferienkurse für Neue Musik and with Peter Maxwell Davies at the Cantiere d'Arte in Montepulciano. He took the conductor's course at the Musik-Akademie in Basle, and was a répétiteur with the Australian Opera, later conducting at the Adelaide, Canberra and Perth festivals. He has been composer-in-residence at the Cité Internationale des Arts in Paris and with the Royal Danish Ballet. He received the highest award at the 1978 Trieste International Competition for Symphonic Composition.

Howard's literary interests are the basis for much of his music in all forms and his three operas demonstrate his strength in translating dramatic action into music. In the programme notes for *Inner Voices* he explains that the division of the three ensembles supports the superstructure of the scores in the same way that the structure of each scene is supported by a pitch system that is cyclic and hierarchical; the rhythmic structure of the vocal parts allows the singers to follow normal speech patterns, producing a declamatory style aligned to the pervasive pitch system. In *Metamorphosis* Gregor's transformation from human to insect movement is reflected in the changing mobility of string harmonic figurations; the tragic situation is symbolized by harmonic structures built on minor 3rds. In the mystical, romantic *Whitsunday* the music closely follows the libretto's characterization, mood changes and spiritual focus, producing a work of unusual dramatic strength. Meticulously self-critical, Howard has destroyed much of his earliest work. In 1989 he completed the first act of a musical, *The Enchanted Rainforest*.

Inner Voices (chamber op, 10 scenes, L. Nowra), Sydney, Nimrod, 25 Feb 1977

Metamorphosis (2, S. Berkoff and Howard, after F. Kafka), Melbourne, St Martin's, 1 Oct 1983

Whitsunday (3, Nowra), Sydney Opera House, Drama Theatre, 2 Sept 1988
THÉRÈSE RADIC

Howard, Kathleen (*b* Clifton, Ont., 17 July 1880; *d* Hollywood, CA, 15 Aug 1956). Canadian mezzo-soprano. Her vocal studies were in Buffalo, New York, Berlin and (with Jean de Reszke) in Paris. After making her début as Azucena in Metz in 1907, she sang in Darmstadt (1909–12), as well as appearing in London and St Petersburg (1911). She sang with the New York Century Opera Company, 1914–15. Her Metropolitan Opera début was in 1916 as the Third Lady in *Die Zauberflöte*, and she remained a company comprimario until 1928, singing 39 roles, including Zita in the première of *Gianni Schicchi* (1918). She recorded for Edison and Pathé. After retiring from singing, she appeared in several films opposite W. C. Fields and was fashion editor of *Harper's Bazaar*. She published an autobiography, *Confessions of an Opera Singer* (New York, 1918).
CORI ELLISON

Howard, Samuel (*b* 1710; *d* London, 13 July 1782). English composer. As a boy he had lessons from Pepusch. He sang tenor in the chorus for Handel from 1732 until 1735 (*Alcina*), but later became an organist. Most of his published music is secular, and his early theatre music is so good that his later mediocrity is puzzling. The music for the pantomime *Robin Goodfellow* (London, Drury Lane, 30 October 1738) is lost, except for one song and three 'comic tunes' (music for miming), published with music from Lampe's *Orpheus and Euridice*. However, much of Howard's music for another pantomime, *The Amorous Goddess* (London, Drury Lane, 1 February 1744), appeared in vocal score (London, 1744), including a charming song in gavotte rhythm and an outstanding overture. About 1785 Harrison & Co. published a new vocal score of *The Amorous Goddess*, though it had never been revived; presumably the music was still in demand. Apart from one new song for Arne's pastiche *Love in a Village* (1762) and two for Richard Cumberland's *The Summer's Tale* (1765), Howard never again wrote for the playhouses. He was clearly unable to switch from the Handelian style in which he excelled to the *galant* style of Galuppi and Piccinni so admired in London in the 1750s and 1760s.
ROGER FISKE/R

Howarth, Elgar (*b* Cannock, Staffs., 4 Nov 1935). English conductor. He studied at Manchester University and the RMCM and began his career as a trumpeter in the Royal Opera House and other London orchestras, while also composing works for brass. An unplanned conducting début with the London Sinfonietta in Italy and further concert work led to his engagement by Ligeti to conduct *Le Grand Macabre* at its première at the Stockholm Royal Opera (1978); he then conducted the same work in Hamburg and Paris and in the ENO production (1982). He made his Covent Garden début with *King Priam* (1985), and was principal guest conductor for Opera North, 1985–8, where he also conducted the first British professional production of Nielsen's *Maskarade* (1990). A close association with Harrison Birtwistle led to his conducting the premières of *The Mask of Orpheus* (1986) for the ENO, and *Gawain* (1991) for the Royal Opera. His performances are marked by powerful concentration and a clear communication of sometimes complex scores.
NOËL GOODWIN

Howell, Gwynne (Richard) (*b* Gorseinon, 13 June 1938). Welsh bass. He studied at the RMCM, where he sang on stage the roles of Hunding, Fasolt and Pogner. In August 1968 he joined Sadler's Wells, making his début as Monterone (*Rigoletto*), and playing, among other parts, the Commendatore, Colline, and the Cook (*The Love for Three Oranges*). His Covent Garden début was as First Nazarene in *Salome* (1970); his many parts there have included Richard Taverner in the première of Maxwell Davies's *Taverner*, Timur, the Landgrave, Sarastro, Pimen and Padre Guardiano. With the ENO he has sung leading roles including Hans Sachs (1984), Gurnemanz (1986) and Philip II (1992). A voice of mellow, well-rounded timbre (slightly less imposing at the bottom of its compass) and a tall, dignified figure aid his natural aptitude for *basso cantante* roles.

A. Blyth: 'Gwynne Howell', *Opera*, xlii (1991), 1018–25
MAX LOPPERT

Howells, Anne (*b* Southport, 12 Jan 1941). English mezzo-soprano. She studied at the RMCM, singing Helen in the British première of Gluck's *Paride ed Elena* (1963) while a student. She made her professional début in 1966 as Flora (*La traviata*) with the WNO. At Glyndebourne (1966–89), she created Cathleen in Maw's *Rising of the Moon* (1970) and has also sung Erisbe (*Ormindo*), Dorabella, the Composer, Diana (*Calisto*), Clairon and Baba the Turk. She made her Covent Garden début in 1967 as Flora, created Lena in Bennett's *Victory* (1970) and has sung Hermia, Rosina, Cherubino, Siébel, Mélisande, Helen (*King Priam*), Olga, Thea (*The Knot Garden*), Despina and Clairon (1991). She made her Chicago (1972), Metropolitan (1975) and San Francisco (1979) débuts as Dorabella. At Geneva she sang Octavian, Idamantes, Régine in the première of Liebermann's *Forêt* (1987) and Leokadja Begbick in *Mahagonny* (1992). For Scottish Opera her roles have included Poppaea. She has sung Nicklausse in Salzburg (1980) and Rameau's Phaedra and Ravel's Concepcion in Paris (1985). Her voice, once light in tone, has developed a full, warm timbre; she is an excellent actress.

H. Canning: 'Anne Howells', *Opera*, xl (1989), 271–7
ALAN BLYTH

Howlett, Neil (*b* Mitcham, 24 July 1934). English baritone. After studying at Cambridge University, he took lessons with Otakar Kraus in London, with Tino Pattiera in Vienna, and in Stuttgart and Milan. He sang with the English Opera Group and Glyndebourne Touring Opera, spent a season at Bremen, and joined Sadler's Wells Opera (later the ENO) in 1966, appearing first as Agamemnon (*La belle Hélène*). He has since sung almost every leading baritone role in the Italian repertory, with special success as Scarpia in Jonathan Miller's production of *Tosca* (1987), and as Golaud. In contemporary opera he has sung Hector in *King Priam* (with the Royal Opera on tour in Athens, 1985) and King Fisher in *The Midsummer Marriage* (with Scottish Opera, 1968); he created the Commander in *The Plumber's Gift* (ENO, 1989). He sang Amfortas at Buenos Aires in 1986, later returning for the Dutchman; his versatile character and dramatic commitment have also brought him appearances in France, Germany and the Netherlands, where he sang Ruprecht (*The Fiery Angel*) in 1990.

NOËL GOODWIN

Howson, Emma. *See* ALBERTAZZI, EMMA.

Hrabovsky [Grabovsky], **Leonid (Oleksandrovych)** (*b* Kiev, 28 Jan 1935). Ukrainian composer. He studied composition with Levko Revuts'ky and Borys Lyatoshyns'ky at the Kiev Conservatory and received early praise from Shostakovich for his choral writing. Of all the Soviet composers who emerged on the international scene in the mid-1960s, Hrabovsky has the reputation of being the most adventurous and outrageous and the most interested in formal experimentation: for him form is content. Influenced at first by Bartók and Stravinsky and later by Stockhausen, Xenakis, the Polish avant garde and Cage, Hrabovsky's music is weighty and spacious if somewhat devoid of sensuality. His first two operas, *Medved'* ('The Bear', 1963) and *Predlozheniye* ('The Proposal', 1964), both based on Chekhov, are written in the experimental language associated with the first post-Stalinist generation of composers. Neither opera has yet secured performance and the scores remain only in piano reduction form. In 1971 Hrabovsky started work on a projected series of music theatre pieces to be performed over six evenings. Tentatively titled *Vechera v gorodskom teatre daleko ot Dikan'ki* ('Evenings in a Town Theatre far away from Dikanka'), the work features characters from Gogol who confront their author, questioning him and condemning him for bringing them to life.

*

V. Baley: 'The Kiev Avant Garde: a Retrospective in Midstream', *Numus-West*, no.6 (1974)

S. Savenko: 'Ornamenty na byelom pole' [Ornaments against a White Background], *Muzyka v SSSR* (1989), Oct–Dec

VIRKO BALEY

Hra o láske a smrti [*Das Spiel von Liebe und Tod*] ('The Play of Love and Death'). Music drama in one act by JÁN CIKKER to a libretto by the composer after ROMAIN ROLLAND's play, *Le jeu de l'amour et de la mort* (1925); Munich, Nationaltheater, 1 August 1969.

Set in the Paris of 1792, at the height of Robespierre's reign of terror, the opera concerns the last day in the lives of Jérome de Courvoisier (baritone) and his estranged wife Sophie (soprano). Jérome has effectively condemned himself to death by refusing to support Robespierre's demand that Danton be executed. Claude Vallée (tenor), a former friend of the couple, seeks refuge in their house. Realizing that Claude and Sophie are lovers, Jérome gives them the passports that were to bring him and Sophie to safety abroad. However, Claude leaves alone when Sophie tears up her passport to await arrest (and execution) with her husband.

Cikker adds to the original play an offstage chorus that functions like the chorus in Greek tragedy, commenting on the action and breaking up the work into more or less independent scenes. Outwardly, therefore, the work resembles a rondo, and the structure is further tightened by the use of a cyclical technique: when Courvoisier's narration about the National Convention reaches its climax, the music is similar to that both at the beginning and end of the opera. The large orchestra is used illustratively, uncovering inner truths about the characters of which they themselves may not be aware. The vocal writing is often declamatory, in the style of Janáček. Václav Neumann conducted the

successful première (in German), and the cast included Keith Engen and Donald Grobe.

IGOR VAJDA

Hřímalý, Vojtěch (*b* Plzeň, 30 July 1842; *d* Vienna, 15 June 1908). Czech composer and conductor. He started his career in the theatre during his studies at the Prague Conservatory, as a violinist at the Estates Theatre, and (1861) as leader of the opera orchestra in Rotterdam, under František Škroup. In 1868 he returned to operatic activity as leader and director of the Czech theatre orchestra at the Provisional Theatre in Prague. In spite of his outstanding organizational abilities, after disagreements with the management of the Czech theatre he transferred to the German (Estates) theatre in Prague as second conductor in 1873, and in 1874 he left Bohemia. Until the end of his career he was active in Czernowitz, Austria-Hungary (now Chernovtsy, Ukraine), as administrator, teacher and violinist, and sometimes as an opera conductor.

Apart from incidental music he composed two stage works. His comic fairy-tale opera *Zakletý princ* ('The Enchanted Prince', 3, J. Böhm, after J. von Plötz; autograph *CS-Pnd*) won considerable popularity; after its première at the New Town Theatre in Prague on 13 May 1872 it received 49 performances in the city and was later revived at the National Theatre (1933) and in Plzeň (1939), Brno and Ostrava; abroad it was staged in Graz (in 1875, in German) and Zagreb (1885, in Croatian). On the other hand, Hřímalý's lyric-romantic opera *Švanda dudák* ('Švanda the Bagpiper', 1884, prol., 3, Böhm, rev. K. Želenský, after J. K. Tyl's play *Strakonický dudák*, 'The Bagpiper of Strakonice'; *Pnd*) was turned down by the Prague National Theatre and produced in his native Plzeň (Town Theatre, 20 January 1896) and later in Czernowitz (1897). Hřímalý tended to use simple musical structures, and the polka and other dance patterns in his operas met the contemporary demand for folklike music. *The Enchanted Prince* rivalled Smetana's *The Two Widows* as the leading Czech national opera in conversational style.

*

V. Hřímalý: *Národní Divadlo a čeští skladatelé* [The National Theatre and Czech Composers] (Prague, 1894)

V. Hornové and J. Hornové: *Česká zpěvohra* [Czech Opera] (Prague, 1903)

J. Bartoš: *Prozatímní divadlo a jeho opera* [The Provisional Theatre and its Opera] (Prague, 1938)

J. Němeček: *Opera Národního divadla v období Karla Kovařovice 1900–1920* [The Opera of the National Theatre during the Kovařovic Era 1900–20] (Prague, 1968–9)

O. Hostinský: *Z hudebních bojů let sedmdesátých a osmdesátých: výbor z operních a koncertních kritik* [From the Musical Battles of the 1870s and 80s: Selection of Opera and Concert Reviews], ed. E. Vítová (Prague, 1986)

J. Tyrrell: *Czech Opera* (Cambridge, 1988)

MARTA OTTLOVÁ, MILAN POSPÍŠIL

Hristić, Stevan (*b* Belgrade, 19 June 1885; *d* Belgrade, 21 Aug 1958). Serbian composer and conductor. He studied at the Leipzig Conservatory and in Moscow, Rome and Paris. In 1912 he returned to Belgrade, where he conducted at the National Theatre, 1913–14; he conducted the Belgrade Opera from its inception in 1920 and was its director, 1925–35. He was also an orchestral conductor. He composed in a late Romantic style that included impressionist elements, lyrical ideas, inventive melodic writing and refined orchestration. His musical drama *Suton* ('The Twilight'; after I. Vojnović: *Dubrovačka trilogija*, pt 2) deals with the decay of the noble Beneša family in Dubrovnik in the 19th century;

the personalities are characterized by the use of a kind of *recitativo accompagnato* which transforms into arioso at dramatic moments. It is a chamber opera without chorus whose symphonic orchestration carries leitmotifs representing, for example, twilight (a harmonic idea), conflict and love. The composer extended the original one-act version (Belgrade, 26 November 1925) to three acts with a ballet *divertissement* (Belgrade, 5 July 1954). Hristić also composed incidental music for several plays and a very popular ballet, *Ohridska legenda* ('The Legend of Ohrid'), which was successfully performed abroad.

*

S. Đurić-Klajn: 'Razvoj muzičke umjetnosti u Srbiji' [The Development of the Art of Music in Serbia], in J. Andreis, D. Cvetko and S. Đurić-Klajn: *Historijski razvoj muzičke kulture u Jugoslaviji* [The Historical Development of Musical Culture in Yugoslavia] (Zagreb, 1962), 529–709

V. Peričić: *Muzički stvaraoci u Srbiji* [Musical Creators in Serbia] (Belgrade, 1969)

Stevan Hristić i njegovo delo: Zbornik radova studenata muzikologije Fakulteta muzičke umetnosti [Stevan Hristić and his Work: Anthology of Articles by Students of Musicology at the Faculty of Musical Art] (Belgrade, 1985)

ROKSANDA PEJOVIĆ

Hry o Marii ('The Plays of Mary'). Operatic cycle by BOHUSLAV MARTINŮ comprising four mystery plays: Part 1: *Prolog: Panny moudré a panny pošetilé* ('Prologue: The Wise and Foolish Virgins'), to a libretto by Vítězslav Nezval after a 12th-century French liturgical drama; Part 2: *Mariken z Nimègue* ('Mary of Nijmegen'), to a libretto by Henri Ghéon after a Flemish text, translated into Czech by Vilém Závada; Part 3: *Narození Páně* ('The Nativity of Our Lord'), from Moravian folk poetry; Part 4: *Sestra Paskalina* ('Sister Pasqualina'), to a libretto by the composer after Julius Zeyer's play and folk texts; Brno, Provincial Theatre, 23 February 1935.

The Plays of Mary build on the stylized folk theatre encountered in Martinů's ballet *Špalíček* (1932), which incorporated the legend of St Dorothy. Martinů was attracted by Ghéon's modern versions of medieval religious plays and completed a first version of *Mary of Nijmegen* on 18 July 1933. This was revised the next year and followed rapidly by the completion of the other plays: *The Nativity* on 1 April, *The Wise and Foolish Virgins* on 22 April and *Sister Pasqualina* on 26 June 1934.

The prologue is a stylized presentation of the tale of the wise and foolish virgins, consisting largely of choral interchanges, with a small part for the Archangel Gabriel (contralto). The two choruses framing the play which tell of the coming of Christ have a hieratic quality with suggestions of archaic counterpoint.

The miracle of Mariken (soprano) tells of the seduction of a young woman by the Devil (baritone) and her eventual repentance and salvation. This long episode includes a spoken part, Principál, which introduces the story and a play in which the Mother of God (mezzo-soprano) intercedes with her Son (baritone) on behalf of the sinner and triumphs over the arguments of the Devil's advocate, Maškaron (tenor).

The third part is a tale of the Nativity, which starts with the Virgin (soprano) going from house to house asking for room. The story includes the miraculous restoration of hands to the daughter of the village smith; much of the telling of the Virgin's story involves a children's chorus.

After this pastoral interlude the legend of Sister Pasqualina is, by contrast, broadly developed and highly dramatic. In the power of a demon, Pasqualina (soprano/mezzo-soprano) leaves her convent to follow a life of sin. She is not missed, since the Virgin (mimed) takes her place in the convent. The climax comes when the fundamentally good Pasqualina is saved from the stake by the Virgin and returns to the nunnery. Having had her keys returned by the Virgin, who resumes her place in heaven, Pasqualina dies.

The Plays of Mary are rich in theatrical experiment incorporating elements of folk drama, ballet and pantomime and employing devices such as the replacement of a character at key points (e.g. Mariken) with chorus. Musically, apart from a slight debt to Stravinsky, the work is entirely characteristic of Martinů in boldly juxtaposing dramatic writing and hieratic-archaic elements. The opera shows also the composer extending the folk idiom, already apparent in *Špalíček*, which anticipates the late cantatas and *The Greek Passion*.

JAN SMACZNY

Hubarenko, Vitaly Serhiyovych [Gubarenko, Vitaly Sergeyevich] (*b* Kharkiv, 13 June 1924). Ukrainian composer. He studied with Dmytro Klebanov at the Kharkiv Conservatory, where he later taught theory and composition (1961–72). Since then he has worked as an independent composer. His output has been prolific and varied and he has been especially productive in the field of opera. He achieved recognition following the production of his first opera, *Zahybel' eskadry* ('The Destruction of the Squadron'), which exhibits a neo-romantic style not unlike that of Samuel Barber or Vaughan Williams. Indeed the lyrical-dramatic style is well suited to Hubarenko's carefully structured dramaturgy. One of his most successful and original ventures, *Pys'ma lyubvi* ('Letters to Love'), is a series of four monologues for soprano, strings, four flutes, harp and piano. In it he achieves a truly dramatic synthesis of words and music with a strong psychological portrait of the heroine.

Zahybel' eskadry [The Destruction of the Squadron] (music drama, 2, Hubarenko and V. Bychko, after O. Korniychuk), Kiev, 1 Oct 1967, vs (Kiev, 1970)

Mamay (music drama, 3, Bychko and Hubarenko, after Yu. Yanovs'ky: *Duma pro Brytanku*), Kiev, 24 April 1970

Pys'ma lyubvi [Letters to Love] (monodrama, Hubarenko, after H. Barbusse), Kiev, 29 Nov 1972, vs (Kiev, 1976)

Vozvrashchonyy May [Reborn May] (lyric drama, 2, R. Levin and Hubarenko, after Y. Yezhova), L'viv, 11 July 1974

Kriz' polumya [Through Flames] (3, Ye. Kushakova, B. Paliychuk and P. Synhaïvs'ky), Donets'k, 15 May 1976

Viy (opera-ballet, prol., 3, epilogue, M. Cherkashyna and L. Mykhaylova, after N. V. Gogol), Odessa, 19 Aug 1984

Svat mymovoli [The Reluctant Matchmaker] (lyric comedy, 2, Cherkashyna, after H. Kvitka-Osnovyanenko), Kharkiv, 24 March 1985

Al'piyskaya ballada (lyric scenes, 2, Cherkashyna, after N. Bïkov), Kharkiv, Kotlyarevs'ky Institute, 7 May 1985

V stepakh Ukraïny, or *Komu posmikhayut'sya zori* [In the Steppes of Ukraine, or On whom the Stars Smile], 1986–7 (lyric comedy, 2, Cherkashyna, after Korniychuk)

Zhadayte, bratiya moya [Remember, my Brotherhood], 1990–91 (opera-oratorio, Cherkashyna, after T. H. Shevchenko)

*

E. Yavors'ky: *Vitaly Hubarenko* (Kiev, 1972)   VIRKO BALEY

Hubay [Huber], **Jenő** [Eugen] (*b* Budapest, 15 Sept 1858; *d* Budapest, 12 March 1937). Hungarian composer. He studied the violin with his father and with Alajos Gobbi at the Budapest National Conservatory, and later with Joachim in Berlin. In 1882 he was appointed principal violin professor at the Brussels Conservatory and in 1886 he took over the chair of violin at the Budapest Academy of Music (director, 1919–34). His pupils included Szigeti and d'Arányi.

As a composer, his output was enormous. All of his operas were composed (or at least drafted) before the end of World War I, and the first two were influenced by French lyric opera. His greatest stage success, *A cremonai hegedűs* ('The Violinist of Cremona'), is a modestly written piece of *opéra comique*-like dimensions and of genuine melodic charm. It was the first opera from Budapest to be performed outside the country. Around 1900 Hubay responded to the challenge of nationalism in Hungary with two essays in 'Hungarian' romantic style, *A falu rossza* ('The Village Vagabond') and *Lavotta szerelme* ('Lavotta's Love'). His later operas are more ambitious, and show more international influence; he achieved considerable success with *Anna Karenina*, which was staged in several German theatres and also in Vienna.

all first performed at the Royal Hungarian Opera House, Budapest

Alienor op.28 (3, E. Harancourt, trans. A. L. Várady), 5 Dec 1891
A cremonai hegedűs [The Violinist of Cremona] op.40 (2 [1/2], F. Coppée and H. Beauclair, trans. E. Ábrányi), 10 Nov 1894
A falu rossza [The Village Vagabond] op.50 (3, after E. Tóth and Várady), 20 March 1896
Moharózsa [The Moss Rose] op.85 (3, after Ouida and M. Rothauser, trans. B. Cziglányi), 21 Feb 1903
Lavotta szerelme [Lavotta's Love] op.96 (3, Á. Berczik and I. Farkas), 17 Nov 1906
Anna Karenina op.112 (3/4, after L. Tolstoy and S. Góth), 10 Nov 1923
Az álarc [The Mask] op.106 (3, after F. Martos, R. Lothar and Góth), 26 Feb 1931
A milói Vénusz [Die Venus von Milo] op.107 (1/3, after P. Lindau, Góth and Farkas), 1 March 1935

*

E. Haraszti: *Hubay Jenő élete és munkái* [Jenő Hubay's Life and Work] (Budapest, 1913)
G. Staud, ed.: *A budapesti operház száz éve* [100 Years of the Budapest Opera House] (Budapest, 1984)   TIBOR TALLIÁN

Huber, Franz Xaver (*b* Beneschau, Bohemia, 10 Oct 1755; *d* Mainz, 25 July 1814). German playwright. After living in Prague, Huber moved to Vienna in 1781, where he worked in a newspaper office. He was so outspoken in his liberal opinions, especially his support of the French and Napoleon, that he was forced to flee to Bavaria in 1809. In addition to satirical novels he wrote opera texts for Vienna's suburban theatres and also the libretto for Beethoven's oratorio *Christus am Oelberge* (1803).

Another Franz Xaver Huber, born in 1760 at Munderfing, Upper Austria, may be the author of some of the librettos attributed to the Bohemian Huber. He died in Vienna about 1809.

Armida und Rinaldo (melodrama), 1793; *Die edle Rache* (komische Oper), Süssmayr, 1795; *Das unterbrochene Opferfest* (heroisch-komische Oper), Winter, 1796 (rev. as *Das Opferfest*, in 4 acts, by C. A. Vulpius, 1798); *Der Wildfang* (komische Oper), Süssmayr, 1797; *Soliman der Zweite, oder Die drei Sultaninnen* (Spl), Süssmayr, 1799; *Der Bettelstudent* (Spl), W. Müller, 1800; *Ende gut, Alles gut*, Lichtenstein, 1800; *Samori* (grosse heroische Oper), G. J. Vogler, 1804; *Der Zerstreute* (Spl), Franz Teyber, 1805   THOMAS BAUMAN

Huber, Hans (*b* Eppenburg, Solothurn, 28 June 1852; *d* Locarno, 25 Dec 1921). Swiss composer. Trained at the Leipzig conservatory, he worked as a music teacher and pianist in Alsace and in Basle, where he settled in 1877; in 1896 he was appointed director of the Basle

Allgemeine Musikschule. There were frequent performances of his works, which include operas, *Festspiele*, incidental music and pieces in every other musical genre; they display a thoroughly Romantic technique following Liszt, Brahms and Richard Strauss. Because of his unusually wide-ranging output he can perhaps be regarded as the most important Swiss composer of the 19th century.

first performed in Basle, Stadttheater, unless otherwise stated

Festspiel der Kleinbasler Gedenkfeier, 1892
Weltfrühling (Liederspiel, 3, R. Wackernagel), 28 March 1894
Kudrun (3, S. Born), 29 Jan 1896
Der Simplicius, 1899 (3, A. M. Mendelssohn-Bartholdy), 21 Feb 1912
Die schöne Belinda (romantische Oper, 3, G. Bundi), Berne, Stadt, 2 April 1916
Frutta di mare (F. Kamin), 24 Nov 1918

*

Stieger O   LUISE MARRETTA-SCHÄR

Huber, Klaus (*b* Berne, 30 Nov 1924). Swiss composer. Having first worked as a schoolteacher, he studied composition at the Zürich conservatory with Willy Burkhard, whose music and philosophy strongly influenced his own; he was also taught by Blacher in Berlin. From 1961 he taught at the Basle Musikakademie; in 1973 he became professor of composition at the Freiburg Hochschule für Musik. He received the medal of the Arnold Bax Society in 1962 and the Beethoven Prize of Bonn in 1970. His opera *Jot, oder Wann kommt der Herr zurück* (P. Oxman, trans.) was staged at the Deutsche Oper, Berlin, on 27 September 1973. Huber uses avant-garde techniques; his music attempts to bring together a modern conception of time with medieval mysticism and to achieve a conjunction of all arts in a primordial experience of creation.

*

F. Muggler: 'Das Porträt: Klaus Huber', *Melos*, xli (1974), 339–44
G. R. Koch: 'Klaus Huber (1924)', *Swiss Composers in the 20th Century* (Zürich, 1990), 46–51   ANDRES BRINER

Huberdeau, Gustave (*b* Paris, 1874; *d* Paris, 1945). French bass-baritone. He studied at the Paris Conservatoire and made his début at the Opéra-Comique, gaining experience in a wide variety of secondary roles and taking part in premières such as that of Massenet's *Grisélidis* (1901), in which he sang Gondebaud. His career prospered further when he joined the Manhattan Company in 1909; for the American première of *Grisélidis* he played the Devil, and he also sang Orestes in the American première of *Elektra* (1910). From 1913 to 1920 he appeared with the Chicago Opera Company and was a visitor to Covent Garden, where he sang Méphistophélès, Arkel, and the Father in the British première of Mascagni's *Iris* (1919). He also took part in the première of *La rondine* at Monte Carlo in 1917. He continued to sing throughout France in the 1920s, appearing at Monte Carlo in 1927, still in a wide repertory, including Hunding in *Die Walküre*. His recordings are rare and show a sturdy voice, somewhat dry in quality.   J. B. STEANE

Huberty, Albert (*b* Seraing-sur-Meuse, Feb 1881; *d* Ostend, 10 March 1955). Belgian bass. He studied in Brussels and Paris, making his début in 1903 at Antwerp. In 1909 he sang Sparafucile at Covent Garden. After appearances at New Orleans, Montreal, Liège and the Opéra-Comique, in 1916 he was engaged at the Paris Opéra, where he remained until 1940, singing over 60 roles, many of which were ostensibly for baritone. They included Méphistophélès, Marcel (*Les Huguenots*), Balthazar (*La favorite*), Friar Laurence, Don Inigo Gomez (*L'heure espagnole*) and Fabio Conti, which he created in Sauguet's *La chartreuse de Parme* (1939); Boris, Pimen and Varlaam; Pogner, Hans Sachs, Hagen, Hunding, Wotan, King Mark, Ochs, Sarastro and Falstaff.   ELIZABETH FORBES

Hubička. Opera by Bedřich Smetana; *see* KISS, THE.

Hübner, Fritz (*b* Sachsengrün, Czechoslovakia, 25 April 1933). German bass of Czech birth. He studied in Dessau, making his début in 1957 at Bernburg. After two seasons in the Leipzig Opera chorus, in 1962 he was engaged at the Komische Oper, Berlin. In 1974 he joined the Staatsoper, where his repertory has included Sarastro, Osmin, Rossini's Don Basilio, Khan Konchak, the King in Dessau's *Die Verurteilung des Lukullus* and Rocco, which he also sang at Covent Garden in 1983. His Wagner roles include Daland, the Landgrave (*Tannhäuser*), Fafner and Hagen, which he sang at Bayreuth in 1978–80 and again in 1985. He has a fine voice and good stage presence.   ELIZABETH FORBES

Huc-Santana, (André) [Santana, Huc] (*b* Argentina, 1911; *d* Paris, 21 Jan 1982). Argentine bass of French parentage. He made his début in 1939 at Marseilles in *Louise*. In 1943 he was engaged at the Paris Opéra, making his début as Sparafucile and later singing Ramfis, the Old Hebrew (*Samson et Dalila*), Friar Laurence (*Roméo et Juliette*), the Commendatore, Phanuel (*Hérodiade*), both Gounod's and Berlioz's Méphistophélès, Hunding and Boris. At the Opéra-Comique (1946) he sang Rossini's Don Basilio and in Monte Carlo (1947–51) the four villains in *Les contes d'Hoffmann*, Don Quichotte and Don Giovanni. At the Théâtre de la Monnaie (1954–8) his roles included Salieri (*Mozart and Salieri*), Peachum (Britten's version of *The Beggar's Opera*) and the Abbé (Tomasi's *Don Juan de Mañara*). A stylish singer, he was particularly noted as the Grand Inquisitor.   ELIZABETH FORBES

Hudson [Hudgson], Mrs. *See* HODGSON, MARY.

Hüe, Georges (Adolphe) (*b* Versailles, 6 May 1858; *d* Paris, 7 June 1948). French composer. Born into a celebrated family of architects, he was encouraged by Gounod and later studied counterpoint with Paladilhe and the organ with Franck. In 1879 he won the Prix de Rome with a cantata, *Médée*, and two years later won acclaim for his comic opera, *Les pantins* ('The Jumping-Jacks'). A plotless sequence of set pieces for four singers doubling various roles, this piece established Hüe on a path which totally ignored fashionable realist trends in favour of fantastic and historical themes.

In 1901 his first full-scale opera, *Le roi de Paris*, was performed. A historical work centring on the unsuccessful attempt by the Duke of Guise to usurp the throne of Henri III, the work has many heroic choruses with a story of unrequited love woven in, as well as a *divertissement* for which Hüe supplied quasi-Baroque dances – a Sarabande, Rigaudon and Menuet. A court scene is similarly underpinned by a pastiche Pavane. *Titania*, in direct contrast, returned to the world of fantasy and employed extended choral forest scenes where the impressionistic orchestral and musical style is reminiscent of the Forest Murmurs from Wagner's *Siegfried*.

Le miracle, returning to a historical setting, concerns a sculptor who has produced a naked image of St Agnes too reminiscent of a local courtesan; the miracle occurs when the statue transforms into a more appropriately pious image, now miraculously draped. Musically, the work employs a good deal of plainsong for the Bishop's music, as well as massive organ effects. His next opera, *Dans l'ombre de la cathédrale* (1921), set in Toledo and based on the celebrated novel by Blasco Ibañez, also makes considerable use of ecclesiastical effects but attempts to add a political element of conflict between socialism and catholicism. The liturgical atmosphere is augmented by local custom, where choirboys dance a 'Menuet de la vierge'. In *Siang-Sin*, a Chinese spring festival is portrayed with appropriate pastiche: a result of Hüe's own travels. His final opera *Riquet à la houppe* ('Prince Riquet with the Tuft') is based on a Perrault fable and concerns the exploits of an ugly prince in a fantasy world of fairies.

Hüe's work met with only limited success; its style, not adapted to changing tastes, quickly dated. *Dans l'ombre de la cathédrale*, his most successful work, was revived several times during the 1920s. Among Hüe's critics was Debussy, who admired the orchestration of *Titania* and found a considerable debt to Weber. Fauré also admired this work.

all first performed in Paris

Les pantins (oc, 2, E. Montagne), OC (Favart), 28 Dec 1881
Le roi de Paris (opéra, 3, H. Bouchut), Opéra, 26 April 1901
Titania (opéra, 3, L. Gallet and A. Corneau), OC (Favart), 20 Jan 1903
Le miracle (opéra, 5, P. B. Gheusi and A. Mérane), Opéra, 14 Dec 1910
Dans l'ombre de la cathédrale (opéra, 3, M. Léna and H. Ferrare, after Blasco Ibañez), Opéra, 7 Dec 1921
Siang-Sin (ballet-pantomime, 2, P. Jobbé-Duval), Opéra, 12 March 1924
Riquet à la houppe (comédie-musicale, 3, R. Gastambide, after Perrault), OC (Favart), 17 Dec 1928

*

J. Crisolles: 'Le roi de Paris', *Le théâtre*, no.59 (1901), 18–20
C. Debussy: 'Le roi de Paris', *La revue blanche* (15 April 1901); repr. in *M. Croche et autres écrits* (Paris, 1971, 2/1987), 40
——: 'A l'Opéra-Comique: Première représentation de Titania ...', *Gil Blas* (21 Jan 1903); repr. in ibid, 83
A. Jullien: 'Titania', *Le théâtre*, no.101 (1903), 5–10
L. Vuillemin: 'Alfred Bruneau, Gustave Charpentier, Georges Hüe', *Le ménestrel*, lxxxii (1920), 181
J. Bruyr: 'Un entretien avec ... Georges Hüe', *Guide du concert*, ix (1934)
C. Oulmont: 'Georges Hüe, les frères Hillemacher, Levadé', *Le théâtre lyrique en France* (Paris, 1937–9) [pubn of Poste National/Radio-Paris], iii, 138–48
P. Landormy: *La musique française après Debussy* (Paris, 1943)
P. Bertrand: *Le monde de la musique* (Geneva, 1947)
G. Samazeuilh: *Musiciens de mon temps* (Paris, 1947)
R. Dumesnil: *Histoire de la musique*, iv (Paris, 1958)
                                    RICHARD LANGHAM SMITH

Hueffer, Francis [Hüffer, Franz] (*b* Münster, 22 May 1843; *d* London, 19 Jan 1889). English author and music critic of German birth. He studied philology and music in London, Paris, Berlin and Leipzig, gaining the doctorate at Göttingen for a critical study of the troubadour Guillem de Cabestanh (Berlin, 1869). Moving to London, he began writing for periodicals, including the *Musical World*, which he also edited. He was music critic of *The Times* (1878–89) and in 1878 published *The Troubadours*, a history of medieval Provençal life and literature. He edited the Great

Musicians series of composers' lives, initiating it with his own *Richard Wagner* (London, 1881). He also wrote librettos for *Colomba* (after Mérimée) and *The Troubadour* (originally entitled *Guillem le troubadour* and based on Cabestanh) for Mackenzie, and made an adaptation of Verdi's *Otello* using as much as possible of Shakespeare's original.

Hueffer was, with Dannreuther, one of the first critics to draw English attention to Wagner, Liszt and Berlioz, and his first book on Wagner (*Richard Wagner and the Music of the Future*, London, 1874) was a pioneering attempt, before the first Bayreuth Festival, to declare the nature of Wagner's genius in England. He followed the study of Wagner's artistic principles with a life of Wagner designed to arouse popular interest and with a translation of the Wagner–Liszt correspondence (London, 1888) that very serviceably reproduces Wagner's prose. His *Half a Century of Music in England: 1837–1887* (London, 1889) significantly dates the revival of music as an English national art from Queen Victoria's accession.

JOHN WARRACK

Huehn, Julius (*b* Revere, MA, 12 Jan 1904; *d* Rochester, NY, 8 June 1971). American baritone. He studied at the Juilliard School in New York and in 1934 made his début as Kurwenal in *Tristan und Isolde* at the Philadelphia Opera. On New Year's Eve 1935 he appeared at the Metropolitan as the Herald in *Lohengrin*, thus opening a promising career there. Subsequent roles included Köthner in *Die Meistersinger*, the title role in *Gianni Schicchi* and Escamillo in *Carmen*, and he gained credit for his singing, though less for his acting, as Telramund in *Lohengrin* and Gunther in *Götterdämmerung*. In 1939 he added John the Baptist in *Salome* and Wotan in *Die Walküre* to his repertory, having been coached by Friedrich Schorr. He also appeared in San Francisco and Chicago. On his return in 1945 from war service his voice was out of condition, and the following year he retired to teach at the Eastman School of Music. Technically inferior recordings of broadcasts from the Metropolitan suggest a bright, well-projected voice probably being worked too hard.

J. B. STEANE

Hughes, Arwel (*b* Rhosllanerchrugog, 25 Aug 1909; *d* Cardiff, 23 Sept 1988). Welsh composer and conductor. He was educated at Ruabon Grammar School and at the RCM, where he studied with C. H. Kitson and Vaughan Williams. He then became organist at the church of St Philip and St James, Oxford, and in 1935 joined the BBC's music department in Wales, becoming head of music in 1965. He was appointed OBE in 1969.

For some years Hughes also conducted performances by the WNO, and his own two operas were produced by the company at the Sophia Gardens Pavilion, Cardiff: *Menna*, a tragedy based on a Welsh folk legend (3, W. Griffith, 1950–51) was given on 9 November 1953, and *Serch yw'r Doctor* ('Love's the Doctor'; 3, S. Lewis, 1959), based on Molière's *L'amour médecin*, on 1 August 1960. The vocal writing was praised, but *Love's the Doctor* at least was felt to be dramatically weak. Notwithstanding their importance for the development of opera in Wales and the opportunity they gave him for attractive lyricism, it is Hughes's music for chorus and orchestra, such as the oratorio *Pantycelyn*, that is most characteristic.

MALCOLM BOYD

Hughes [Hughs, Hues], **Francis** (*b* 1666 or 1667; *d* London, 16 March 1744). English countertenor. He sang at Drury Lane from February 1700, when he was in Daniel Purcell's dramatic opera *The Grove*. He played the hero in the first all-sung English opera in the Italian style, Clayton's *Arsinoe* (1705), and then in Bononcini's *Camilla* (1706) and Clayton's *Rosamond* (1707). For the pasticcio *Thomyris* arranged by Pepusch (1707) he apparently alternated with the castrato Valentini, who soon replaced him as the leading man in the operas. His voice, reaching up to *b'* and occasionally *c"*, was clearly no match for the Italian. He performed opera arias at Nottingham during the races in July 1707 and left the stage to join the Chapel Royal Choir in September 1708. Hawkins reported that Hughes's strong voice could break a drinking glass 'with ease'.

BDA; LS   OLIVE BALDWIN, THELMA WILSON

Hughes, Gervase (**Alfred Booth**) (*b* Birmingham, 1 Sept 1905). English composer, conductor and writer on music. He studied at Corpus Christi College, Oxford (BA and BMus, 1927). From 1926 to 1929 he was on the staff of the British National Opera Company and conducted *Carmen*, *Faust* and *Samson et Dalila*. In 1929–30 he arranged and conducted Handel's *Giulio Cesare* for the London Opera Festival. Giving up music as a profession in 1933, he continued however to compose. Hughes completed one opera, *Imogen's Choice* (*Twelfth Night*, after Shakespeare, was not finished) and three operettas, *Castle Creevey* (1, A. Booth and S. Evernden; vs, London, 1930), *Penelope* and *Venetian Fantasy*. He also wrote books on Sullivan (1960) and Dvořák (1967) and a volume on *Composers of Operetta* (1962).

Hughes, John (*b* Marlborough, Wilts., 29 Jan 1677; *d* London, 17 Feb 1720). English librettist. He was one of the first 18th-century Englishmen to write intelligently about setting English words to music, as well as composing texts himself – 18 cantatas, four odes, a serenata, two masques (*Cupid and Hymen's Holiday* and *Apollo and Daphne*) and an opera. He may have written much of the text of Handel's *Acis and Galatea* and possibly some of *Esther* (both 1718; see B. Trowell, in *Music and Theatre: Essays in Honour of Winton Dean*, 1987). He was also a violinist.

In the Preface to *Six Cantatas or Poems for Musick after the Manner of the Italians* (*c*1710) Hughes tried to show that English could be just as suitable for music as Italian and that the sister arts of poetry and music must be closely allied. For him, recitative was 'a kind of improv'd Elocution, or pronouncing of the Words in Musical Cadences ... like the reading of Verse, which is not everyone's Talent'. Passions came through the 'different Tones of the Voice ... without approaching to what we call a *Tune* or *Air*'. In the preface to *Calypso and Telemachus* (his only opera, set by J. E. Galliard, 1712), he emphasized how 'Dramatical Entertainments ... shou'd be perform'd in a Language understood by the Audience', and how an opera 'is to be consider'd as a Species of Poetry, compounded out of *Lyrick* and *Dramatick* Kinds, admitting of all the Beauty of the first, united with part of the latter'.

Hughes wrote essays for the *Tatler*, the *Spectator* and the *Guardian*, and was closely allied with Addison and Steele in various theatrical and literary ventures.

J. MERRILL KNAPP

Hughes, Spike (Patrick Cairns) (*b* London, 19 Oct 1908; *d* London, 2 Feb 1987). English composer and critic. From 1923 to 1925 he studied composition in Vienna with Egon Wellesz and reported on Viennese musical activities for London periodicals. After leaving Vienna he spent some time in Cambridge and wrote incidental music for productions of Congreve's *Love for Love* (1926) and W. B. Yeats's *The Player Queen* (1927). An interest in jazz led him to form a dance orchestra with which he made many recordings (1930–33); an offshoot of this was the jazz ballet *High Yellow* (1932).

From 1933 to 1936 he was music critic of the *Daily Herald*, and in the latter year his first radio plays were heard. He wrote the incidental music for a musical version of Ferenc Molnar's *The Swan*, and on 29 December 1938 his television opera, *Cinderella* (after Perrault), was first broadcast by the BBC. Although criticized for its lack of originality, this work was deemed 'a pleasant entertainment' by *The Times*. Excerpts from a later opera, *St Patrick's Day* (after R. B. Sheridan), were broadcast in 1947, and in 1950 his musical *Frankie and Johnny* was televised.

Hughes was best known as a broadcaster and writer on music: his handbooks on operas are successful in their popular approach and the two volumes of his autobiography contain much information on famous contemporaries.

Opening Bars (London, 1946) [autobiography]
with B. McFadyean: *Nights at the Opera* (London, 1948)
Second Movement (London, 1951) [autobiography]
Great Opera Houses (London, 1956)
Famous Mozart Operas (London, 1957)
Famous Puccini Operas (London, 1959)
The Toscanini Legacy (London, 1959, 2/1969)
Glyndebourne: a History of the Festival Opera (London, 1965, 2/1981)
Famous Verdi Operas (London, 1968)

Hugh the Drover [*Hugh the Drover, or Love in the Stocks*]. Romantic ballad opera in two acts by RALPH VAUGHAN WILLIAMS to a libretto by Harold Child; London, Royal College of Music, 4 July 1924.

The opera, composed between 1910 and 1914, is set in a small English Cotswold town in about 1812, when invasion by Napoleon is expected. Mary (soprano) is to marry John the butcher (bass-baritone) against her will; her Aunt Jane (contralto) persuades her to accept the situation. A stranger, Hugh the Drover (tenor), arrives; he and Mary fall in love at first sight. In his 'Song of the Road' he offers her a life of freedom and toil instead of the comfort she would have with John. Hugh challenges John to fight for her hand. The butcher loses but accuses Hugh of being a French spy. The Constable (bass), Mary's father, orders Hugh to be put in the stocks.

An optional scene, which the composer disowned but did not withdraw, may be inserted at the start of Act 2. In the customary version, John and his friends return from a night out and taunt Hugh as they pass. Mary, who has stolen the keys from her father, comes to release Hugh. They are on the point of escaping when they hear the voices of the returning men who have been Maying. Hugh returns to the stocks with Mary hiding under his cloak. John now arrives at Mary's home to wake her, bringing a spray of mayflowers. But she is missing. The Constable and Aunt Jane find her in the stocks with Hugh. Her father disowns her. Soldiers who

have been called to arrest Hugh now arrive, but the Sergeant (baritone) recognizes him as an old and loyal comrade; instead, he pressgangs John as a soldier. The Constable apologizes to Hugh, and the townsfolk beg Hugh and Mary to stay. But they prefer a roaming life and leave the town.

Although not strictly a ballad opera, *Hugh the Drover* quotes several English folksongs and the original melodies have the flavour of folksong. The love duet between Hugh and Mary has a Puccinian warmth.

MICHAEL KENNEDY

Hugo, John Adam (*b* Bridgeport, CT, 5 Jan 1873; *d* Bridgeport, 29 Dec 1945). American composer. He entered the Stuttgart Conservatory in 1888 and later appeared as a concert pianist in Europe. In 1899 he returned to the USA, where he taught in Baltimore and from 1906 devoted his time to composition and private teaching in his native city. Hugo's student work *The Hero of Byzanz* (composed in 1891–3 to his own libretto) was never produced, but his one-act opera *The Temple Dancer*, to a libretto by Jutta Bell-Ranske after her story of a Hindu woman who loves a man not of her faith, was first performed at the Metropolitan on 12 March 1919 and won the David Bispham Medal in 1925. A picturesque use of modal harmony and exotic percussion lightly flavour the otherwise conventional idiom of this and of Hugo's third and last (unperformed) opera, *The Sun God* (1925; B. James), a full-length work about the Incas of Peru. Hugo's MSS are in the Bridgeport Public Library, Connecticut.

MICHAEL MECKNA

Hugo, Victor(-Marie) (*b* Besançon, 26 Feb 1802; *d* Paris, 22 May 1885). French author. In a long, tumultuous life he wrote vast quantities of every sort of literature. Awarded the Légion d'honneur by Charles X on his coronation in 1825, elected to the Académie Française in 1841 and made a Peer of France by Louis-Philippe four years later, he nonetheless identified himself above all with the common man. After striving for political prominence, he was obliged to flee France with the collapse of the Second Empire but returned when Napoleon III fell in 1870.

Hugo's literary works inspired many operas, in particular his novel *Notre-Dame de Paris* (from which he also created the libretto *La Esmeralda*). The first setting, by Louise Bertin in 1836, was a failure, as were several later ones. Felice Romani provided Donizetti with the libretto of *Lucrezia Borgia* in 1833, the year Hugo's prose play on which it was based had its première. Verdi's *Ernani*, to a libretto by F. M. Piave based on the verse tragedy *Hernani* (highly controversial on its première at the Comédie-Française in 1830), dates from 1844; Piave also wrote the libretto for the highly successful *Rigoletto* (1851), inspired by Hugo's *Le roi s'amuse*, which had fallen foul of the censor in 1832 because its philandering hero (the Duke of Mantua in the opera) was François I of France.

Han d'Islande (novel, 1823): Musorgsky, 1856 (projected)
Amy Robsart (drama, 1828): Donizetti, 1829, as Elisabetta, o Il castello di Kenilworth
Marion de Lorme (verse drama, 1829): J. A. Heller, 1856; Bottesini, 1862; Pedrotti, 1865; F. E. Barbier, 1875; E. Perelli, ?1880s; Ponchielli, 1885; L. Tarantini, 1910
Hernani (verse drama, 1830): Bellini, 1830, inc.; V. Gabussi, 1834; Mazzucato, 1843; Verdi, 1844; Laudamo, 1851; Hirschmann, 1908

Notre-Dame de Paris (novel, 1831); as *La Esmeralda* (libretto, 1836): Bertin, 1836; Rodwell, 1836, as Quasimodo; Mazzucato, 1838; E.-P. Prévost, ? 1840; Valero, 1843; Poniatowski, 1847; Dargomïzhsky, 1847; V. Battista, 1851, as Ermelinda; Lebeau, 1857; Bizet, 1859 (projected); Fry, 1864; Massenet, 1865 (sketched); Wetterhahn, 1866; F. Müller, 1867; Campana, 1869; F. Pedrell, 1875, as Quasimodo; Camps y Soler, 1879; A. G. Thomas, 1883; C. de Mesquita, 1888; M. Giró, 1890, as Nuestra Señora de París; Granados, 1901, as Picarol; M. Zanon, 1912; F. Schmidt, 1914; Honegger (sketched)

Le roi s'amuse (verse drama, 1832): Verdi, 1851, as Rigoletto

Lucrèce Borgia (prose drama, 1833): Donizetti, 1833

Marie Tudor (prose drama, 1833): Schoberlechner, 1839, as Rossane; G. B. Ferrari, 1840, as Maria d'Inghilterra; G. Pacini, 1843, as Maria regina d'Inghilterra; Bognar, 1856; Kashperov, 1859; Balfe, 1863, as The Armourer of Nantes; Gomes, 1879; Blaramberg, 1888, as Marie de Bourgogne; Wagner-Régeny, 1935, as Der Günstling

Angelo, tyran de Padoue (prose drama, 1835): Mercadante, 1837, as Il giuramento; Villate, comp. 1867; Ponchielli, 1876, as La Gioconda; Cui, 1876, as Andzhelo; E. Albert, 1902, as Der Improvisator; R. Halm, 1905; Bruneau, 1928

Ruy Blas (verse drama, 1838): Poniatowski, 1843; Besanzoni, 1843; N. de Giosa, 1851, as Folco d'Arles; G. Rota, 1858; Glover, 1861; Chiaromonte, 1862, as Maria di Nuremburgo; Zenger, 1868; G. Braga, 1868; F. Franchetti, 1868; F. Marchetti, 1869; B. Godard, 1891; Pietri, 1916, as Il signor Ruy Blas

Les Burgraves (verse drama, 1843): M. Salvi, 1845; d'Indy, 1869–72, inc.; Orsini, 1881; Podesta, 1881; Lekeu, 1887, inc.; L. Nielson, 1917–20, as Lola; Sachs, 1924

La légende des siècles (epic episodes, 1859): Mancinelli, 1884, as Isora di Provenza [after part xviii: L'Italie-Ratbert]; Gilson, 1904, as Zeevolk [after part lii: Les pauvres gens]

Les misérables (novel, 1862): Duniecki, 1864, as Nedznicy; Bonsignore, 1925

La grand-mère (verse comedy, 1865): Silver, 1930

L'homme qui rit (novel, 1869): P. Ronzi, 1894, as Dea; Enna, 1920, as Komedianter; Pedrollo, 1920

Quatre-vingt-treize (novel, 1874): Silver, 1935; Belov, 1973; Duhamel, 1989

Torquemada (verse drama, 1882): N. Rota, 1976 (comp. 1943)

*

R. Brancour: 'Le sentiment de la musique chez Victor Hugo', *RMI*, xxii (1915), 447–82

J. Tiersot and J. Sergent: 'Victor Hugo et la musique', *ReM*, no. 159 (1935) [whole issue]

J.-B. Barrère: *Hugo, l'homme et l'oeuvre* (Paris, 1952)

L. Gschöpf: *Die Dramen Victor Hugos in der Operndichtung* (diss., U. of Vienna, 1952)

A. Maurois: *Olympio, ou La vie de Victor Hugo* (Paris, 1954)

G. Franceschetti: 'La fortuna di Hugo nel melodramma italiano dell' ottocento', *Contributi del seminario di filologia moderna, serie francese*, ii (Milan, 1961) [pubn of Università cattolica del Sacro Cuore]

A. Laster: 'Victor Hugo, la musique et les musiciens' and introduction to La Esmeralda, *V. Hugo: Oeuvres complètes*, v (Paris, 1967)

A. Gerhard: *Die Verstädterung der Oper* (Stuttgart, 1992)

CHRISTOPHER SMITH

Huguenots, Les ('The Huguenots'). Grand opera in five acts by GIACOMO MEYERBEER to a libretto by EUGÈNE SCRIBE and Emile Deschamps; Paris, Opéra, 29 February 1836.

On hearing the soprano Cornélie Falcon sing the part of Alice in *Robert le diable* during summer 1832, Meyerbeer resolved that she would take a leading role in his next opera, together with the tenor Adolphe Nourrit and the bass Nicholas Levasseur. The groundwork for *Léonore, ou La Saint Barthélemy*, as *Les Huguenots* was initially called, was set out in discussions with Scribe and the Opéra director Louis Véron in September 1832. The subject matter was very much in fashion: the period of confrontation between Huguenots (French Protestants) and Catholics in the late 16th century had been the setting for several plays in the late 1820s, as

Raoul de Nangis *a Huguenot gentleman*	tenor
Marcel *his servant*	bass
Marguerite de Valois *betrothed of Henry of Navarre*	soprano
Urbain *her page*	soprano
Valentine *daughter of the Count of Saint-Bris*	soprano
Count of Saint-Bris ⎱ *Catholic noblemen*	bass
Count of Nevers ⎰	baritone
De Retz ⎫	bass
Cossé ⎪	tenor
Méru ⎬ *Catholic gentlemen*	bass
Thoré ⎪	bass
Tavannes ⎭	tenor
Bois-Rosé *a Huguenot soldier*	tenor

Protestant and Catholic soldiers, courtiers, and burghers

Setting Touraine, then Paris, August 1572

well as for Mérimée's novel, *Chronique du règne de Charles IX* (1829), which in turn provided material for Hérold's *opéra comique*, *Le pré aux clercs* (1832).

Contrary to what has been sometimes suggested, there is little evidence that Scribe modelled *Les Huguenots* upon Mérimée's book. Both novel and libretto do, however, feature prominently a real historical event, the St Bartholomew massacre of over 3000 French Protestants in Paris on the night of 23 August 1572. Meyerbeer signed a contract with Véron on 23 October 1832 and began composing immediately. He had drafted much of the work before he decided upon major revisions during a trip to Italy in summer 1834: an expansion of the role of the servant Marcel (which Meyerbeer came to consider his most successful characterization up to that time) and the creation of more numbers with female voices. To address the latter problem – and possibly influenced by the leading role of the soprano in the 'Guerra! guerra!' chorus of Bellini's *Norma* – Meyerbeer added the figure of Catherine de Medicis to the 'Bénédiction des poignards'. He called upon Gaetano Rossi, a previous collaborator, to provide Italian verse so that he could begin to compose new music immediately. Because Scribe had little time in autumn 1834 and was reluctant to act as a mere adapter of another's work, Meyerbeer turned to the poet Emile Deschamps, who made substantial contributions to the libretto.

Rehearsals at the Opéra began in June 1835. Among the most noteworthy alterations made during the rehearsal period was a recasting of the slow section of the duet between Valentine and Raoul in Act 4 at the insistence of Adolphe Nourrit, who was offended by the directness of the language between the adulterous couple in a previous version. Also significant was an order from the government censor that forbade the appearance of Catherine de Medicis, doubtless to avoid any association of royal authority with intolerance in an era when a monarchy of the *juste-milieu* was consciously trying to project the opposite image; her music was taken by Saint-Bris. *Les Huguenots* proved as successful as *Robert le diable* and was the first work to be performed more than a thousand times at the Opéra. The unflattering portrait of Catholic fanaticism caused the libretto to be rewritten in certain towns during its rapid conquest of Germany: in Munich it was first performed as *Anglikaner und Puritaner* and in Kassel as *Die Ghibellinen vor Pisa*.

ACT 1 *A hall in the chateau of the Count of Nevers*
After a brief overture, based on the chorale 'Ein feste
Burg', Nevers launches a buoyant mood-setting chorus
about the pleasures of youth and tells his Catholic
comrades that, in the spirit of a recent peace treaty
between the Protestant faction and the royal house, he
has invited a Huguenot nobleman, Raoul de Nangis, to
join their revelry. Raoul's entry is highlighted by a
change of musical character and tonality in an extended
solo that lies high in the tenor voice, a heartfelt expression of gratitude in a predominantly comic context. The
multi-sectional introduction is brought to a close by a
drinking chorus ('Bonheur de la table') with a
frenzied coda containing a twofold increase in tempo and rapid
patter singing. When prodded to reveal past amorous
exploits, Raoul responds that he has fallen in love with
an unknown woman whom he recently rescued; he
describes her beauty in a strophic *romance*, 'Plus
blanche que la blanche hermine', the intimacy of which
is sustained by elegant *fioritura*, chromatic passing notes
in the melody and, above all, a solo viola accompaniment in the changing part of each strophe.

The Catholic gentlemen make light of Raoul's love
and of Marcel, his serious and abstemious manservant,
who appears soon after to a strain in the bassoons and
double basses. Marcel, horrified to see Raoul with
Catholics, appeals to his conscience with the chorale
'Ein feste Burg'. At the request of the bemused company,
Marcel sings an old Huguenot song, 'Piff, paff', with a
grotesque accompaniment that highlights piccolo,
bassoon, cymbal and drums. His macabre account of
Catholic misfortune during the battle of La Rochelle
evokes nothing more than laughter. A valet enters with
news that a beautiful woman has arrived to speak with
Nevers. The men fall over themselves with offers to go
in his place and then peer through a window to watch
the *tête-à-tête* ('L'aventure est singulière'). The comic
atmosphere is momentarily dissipated by an orchestral
explosion and sudden tonal shift when Raoul himself
follows suit: he identifies the woman as the one he
rescued but declares he is no longer enamoured of her.
In a monologue Nevers reveals that the mysterious
woman is his betrothed, a lady-in-waiting to the
Catholic Queen Marguerite. She has come to inform
him that, by order of the queen, their marriage cannot
take place. The queen's page, Urbain, enters with a note
requesting Raoul's presence at a secret rendezvous.
Nevers and his companions identify the seal as Queen
Marguerite's and, in a comical canon, affectedly congratulate him. In a concluding chorus Raoul expresses
his bewilderment with a halting melodic line, Marcel
delivers a prayer in long notes and the Catholic gentlemen remark, in quick anapaestic rhythms, upon Raoul's
good fortune.

ACT 2 *The gardens of the chateau of Chenonceaux* Queen Marguerite sings a multi-sectional
entrance aria about her desire to see the heart take
precedence over political disputes ('O beau pays de la
Touraine'). She then informs Valentine, her lady-in-
waiting, that she has asked her to break off her engagement with Nevers so that she may marry Raoul. Before
he arrives the ladies of the court take a swim in the river,
while the page Urbain secretly looks on with delight.
The *choeur dansé*, 'Jeunes beautés sous ce feuillage', has
obvious erotic appeal and, together with the women's
chorus sung as the blindfolded Raoul is led into the
garden, serves as a counterweight to the male choruses

in the first act. When the blindfold is lifted Raoul
expresses wonder at his surroundings and the beauty of
the queen in the duet 'Beauté divine, enchanteresse'. The
stiffness of their encounter, suggested by two parallel
strophes sung in succession, gives way to a scherzo-like
section where the two voices combine; this is followed
by an F major *cabalette* in which Raoul delivers an
impassioned strain, in the distant key of Gb major, and
Marguerite laughingly warns him not to fall in love with
her.

In a recitative, she informs him that his hand will be
given in marriage to the daughter of the Catholic Count
of Saint-Bris as a gesture of reconciliation between the
religious groups. Catholic and Protestant notables have
been invited to witness the ceremony and both groups
appear in her gardens. They swear eternal peace to a
dramatic alternation of *a cappella* singing and full
orchestral accompaniment, the slow section of a multi-
sectional *final*. But when Valentine appears with her
father, Raoul recognizes her as the woman who visited
Nevers and refuses to conclude the pact. The *strette* of
the *final* begins quietly in unison, as the entire assembly
gives voice to its astonishment, and concludes with
boisterous expressions of renewed hatred between the
two religious factions.

ACT 3 *The Pré-aux-clercs on the bank of the Seine*
After an introductory chorus of Parisian pleasure-
seekers, the Huguenot soldier Bois-Rosé leads his
comrades in a *rataplan*. The wedding procession of
Valentine and Nevers, accompanied by a choral litany,
is seen making its way to the chapel. *Rataplan* and litany
are combined and superimposed upon a chorus of the
Catholiic populace who demand that the Huguenots
show respect for their ritual. Huguenots and Catholics
adopt a menacing posture towards each other, but tension is unexpectedly relieved by the appearance of a
colourful band of singing and dancing gypsies.

Marcel intercepts Saint-Bris as he leaves the chapel
and presents him with a challenge for a duel from
Raoul. The signal for the nightly curfew is given, a
passage coloured evocatively by chimes, horn octaves
and woodwind chords. As night descends, Valentine
and Marcel appear, unaware of each other's presence
(duet, 'Dans la nuit où seul je veille'). The situation is at
first treated comically, with popping octave leaps in
bassoons and horns and Marcel's exaggerated (and
therefore suspect) claim that he does not fear women.
Valentine reveals the Catholics' plan to ambush Raoul
before the duel; during the slow section of the duet she
sings of her will to save Raoul's life and Marcel gives
voice to his agitation with rapid declamation beneath
her lyrical line. In the *cabalette* she expresses her distress
at having betrayed her father and, with a shift to the
major mode, Marcel attempts to comfort her.

Raoul and Saint-Bris appear with their witnesses and
prepare for the duel during a septet propelled by motor-
rhythmic dotted figures suggestive of the determination
of each party ('En mon bon droit j'ai confiance').
Raoul's life is saved because, just as Saint-Bris's henchmen arrive, a band of Huguenot soldiers is unexpectedly
heard in the distance singing the *rataplan*; knowing that
an ambush is imminent, Marcel calls out to them.
Bloodshed between the two groups is prevented by the
equally unexpected arrival of Queen Marguerite. Raoul
discovers the real purpose of Valentine's earlier visit to
Nevers. As a nuptial march sounds in the distance,
Saint-Bris tells Raoul with great satisfaction that a

'*Les Huguenots*'
(*Meyerbeer*), *Act 2 (the
gardens of the chateau of
Chenonceaux): design by
Edouard Despléchin for
the original production at
the Paris Opéra, 29
February 1836;
lithograph by C.
Deshayes*

wedding between Nevers and his daughter has already taken place. Nevers arrives in a sumptuously decorated and illuminated boat to escort Valentine; Catholic students and Protestant soldiers exchange insults.

ACT 4 *Outside Valentine's bedroom in Nevers' residence* Valentine sings a *romance*, 'Parmi les pleurs', about her continuing love for Raoul. Suddenly he appears, prepared to give up his life by trespassing in a rival Catholic household. When others are heard approaching she begs him to hide.

Saint-Bris, Nevers and a group of Catholic gentlemen enter and discuss plans to massacre the Protestant population of Paris. This scene of the Consecration of the Swords is in two large sections. The first, in E major, ends when Nevers is led off after refusing to participate in the massacre. At its core lie two renditions of the ensemble 'Pour cette cause sainte', separated by Nevers' act of breaking his sword. The principal dramatic action of the second section, centred on G♯ minor/A♭ major, is the appearance of three monks bearing white scarves, to serve as identification tags for Catholics, and the oath-taking itself, led by Saint-Bris and the monks. This last action stands out against the prevailing harmonic vocabulary through repeated alternation of chords whose roots lie a 3rd apart. The end of the second section is articulated by a homorhythmic ensemble in the fastest tempo of the number, as the entire assembly advances to the front of the stage brandishing swords ('Dieu le veut, Dieu l'ordonne'). This ensemble is not closed tonally, however, but rather opens into a reprise – in unison and even more fully scored than before – of 'Pour cette cause sainte', a spectacular conclusion to the number.

When the conspirators depart, Raoul emerges and runs to warn the Protestants. But Valentine stops him in his tracks and in the duet 'O ciel! où courez-vous?' she begs him not to leave; for the first time she declares her love directly to him. This gives rise to the slow section of the duet, Raoul's impassioned *cavatine*, 'Tu l'as dit'. He is awakened from his amorous reverie by the sound of

bells, the signal for the start of the massacre, and, mirroring the plunge to reality, the music abruptly turns from G♭ to C major. In the *cabalette* he declares his intention to join his co-religionists, and though he vacillates once again following that section, he finally dashes off.

ACT 5.i *A ballroom in the Hôtel de Nesle* Protestants have gathered to celebrate the marriage of Queen Marguerite to Henry of Navarre. Raoul bursts in bearing news of the massacre and urges the Protestants to take up arms in defence of their brethren.

5.ii *A Protestant cemetery, with a church in the background* The wounded are taken into the church. Raoul meets Marcel and both are soon joined by Valentine. She urges Raoul to save himself by donning a white scarf. When he refuses she declares, in a passage of true heroic stature ('Ainsi je te verrai périr?'), that she will adopt his faith – an example of the dramatic cogency Meyerbeer was capable of at his best moments: recitative merges seamlessly into declamatory measured writing as the melodic line rises gradually to ab'', first sounding as the root of the harmony, and then transformed, *pianissimo*, into the 3rd of E major. In a final burst of energy the line rises to c''' and descends two octaves within the space of a single bar. Marcel performs an impromptu marriage ceremony to the sparing and mournful accompaniment of a single bass clarinet. As Catholic murderers enter the church, Marcel is seized with a vision of heaven; Valentine and Raoul are themselves transported by Marcel's ecstatic music and the passage culminates in a unison rendition by all three of 'Ein feste Burg'.

5.iii *A street* Valentine and Marcel support Raoul, who is mortally wounded. Saint-Bris appears and orders his soldiers to execute the three immediately. Only after the shots have been fired does he realize that he has ordered the execution of his own daughter. Finally, Queen Marguerite arrives to put a stop to the massacre.

*   *   *

In *Les Huguenots* Meyerbeer successfully transposed the formula of a highly variegated succession of scenes connected by a well-integrated plot from the good-versus-evil morality play of *Robert le diable* to a historical setting that prominently features public political turmoil. In the first three acts some of the most effective scenes blend comedy into the mix, for example the Valentine–Marcel duet in Act 3: first the two grope in the dark and then Marcel moves from comic gynophobia to staunch loyalty and paternal solicitude. Neither Valentine nor Raoul is as richly drawn in the music. As often with Meyerbeer, the most remarkable sequence in the opera, the fourth-act Consecration of the Swords and the ensuing duet for the lovers, does not depend on effective characterization: in a bold stroke he reversed the usual progression towards the massed finale by placing the large choral set piece at the middle of the act. This produces a tinder-box setting for the duet, in which the love music is projected as an escapist reverie in a distant key; and Raoul's subsequent hesitations, though they have never earned him many admirers, create the sparks that kept generations of opera-goers enthralled. Even Meyerbeer's detractors (such as Wagner, later in his career) have grudgingly admired the act. In its juxtaposition of reverential Protestant victims and fanatical Catholics – both invoking the name of the Lord – the fifth act is a *locus classicus* for the vivid ironical contrasts characteristic of Meyerbeerian grand opera.

For further illustration *see* DORUS-GRAS, JULIE.   STEVEN HUEBNER

Huguet, Josefina [Giuseppina] (*b* Barcelona, 22 Sept 1871; *d* Barcelona, 1951). Spanish soprano. She studied in Barcelona where she made her début as Lakmé at the Teatro Liceo in 1888. She toured Spain, South America and Italy, appearing first at La Scala in 1896 as Ophelia in Thomas' *Hamlet*. She was also popular in Russia, where she sang several times opposite Mattia Battistini. She appeared at the New York Academy of Music in 1898. Her repertory centred on coloratura roles such as Rosina, Elvira and Amina, but she also sang such lyric parts as Mimì, and her recordings include excerpts from *Lohengrin*. Today she is remembered principally on account of her numerous recordings, which range from the Queen of Night's arias to Desdemona's 'Ave Maria' and include the role of Nedda in the first complete recording (under the composer's supervision) of *Pagliacci*, made in 1907. Sweet, firm and musical, her voice and style give more consistent pleasure than do those of several of her more celebrated contemporaries.

J. B. STEANE

Hulak-Artemovsky, Semyon Stepanovych. *See* GULAK-ARTEMOVSKY, SEMYON STEPANOVICH.

Hulda. Opera in four acts and an epilogue by CÉSAR FRANCK to a libretto by Charles Grandmougin after a play by Bjørnstjerne Bjørnson; Monte Carlo, 4 March 1894.

The action takes place in 11th-century Norway. Hulda (mezzo-soprano), whose father and brothers have been slaughtered by Aslak (bass) and some of his sons during a tribal feud, swears vengeance. Gudleik (baritone), her own captor and bridegroom, is killed by Eioff (tenor), the King of Norway's representative. Hulda incites three of Aslak's other sons to kill Eioff,

who after paying court to Hulda has returned to Swanhilda (soprano), his first love. Having accomplished her revenge, she kills herself by jumping into the fjord.

Little of the violence in the text is reflected either in the stage action or in the richly worked score which, though deeply influenced by Wagner, is in a style inherently lacking in drama. The fourth-act ballet, 'L'hiver et le printemps', is musically attractive but again undramatic in context.

ELIZABETH FORBES

Hullah, John Pyke (*b* Worcester, 27 June 1812; *d* London, 21 Feb 1884). English composer and teacher. He studied composition with William Horsley and singing, at the RAM, with Crivelli. In 1835 he became friends with Charles Dickens, who agreed to collaborate on what Hullah at first planned to be the completion of an already begun work, *The Gondolier*. Almost immediately Dickens informed Hullah that he was dissatisfied with the subject: 'remembering the popularity and beauty of many of the old English operas, I am strongly prejudiced in favour of a simple rural story'. It became *The Village Coquettes*, set in an English village in 1729. Billed as an 'operatic burletta', it opened in December 1836 at the St James Theatre with John Braham as Squire Norton and Elizabeth Rainforth, then at the beginning of her career, as Lucy Benson. Hullah remembered it as a 'very decided' success, but press reports were mixed. The *Athenaeum* (December 17) asserted that the music gave 'fair promise of future excellence', but warned that Dickens (whose *Pickwick Papers* had just begun to appear in serial form) was 'likely rather to diminish than increase his reputation by his dramatic efforts'. In 1843 Dickens wrote to R. H. Horne that he 'devoutly' wanted his share in the opera to be forgotten. Hullah composed two subsequent operas, *The Barbers of Bassora* (1837) and *The Outpost* (1838), both performed at Covent Garden.

From about 1838 Hullah began to devote his time increasingly to his life's work, music education, in which field he became very influential; he was professor of vocal music at King's College, London (1844–74) and government music inspector from 1872.

*

Grove6 (B. Rainbow)

F. Hullah: *Life of John Hullah* (London, 1886)

M. House and G. Storey, eds.: C. Dickens: *Letters* (Oxford, 1965), esp.i   ROBERT BLEDSOE

Hummel, Ferdinand. (*b* Berlin, 6 Sept 1855; *d* Berlin, 24 April 1928). German composer and harpist. A child prodigy, he appeared in public as a harpist at the age of seven and was given a subsidy by Wilhelm I of Prussia to study in Vienna (1862–3). In 1864–7 he toured Germany, Scandinavia and Russia with his father, a flautist in the Prussian royal chapel. From 1868 to 1875 he attended first Kullak's academy and then the Berlin Hochschule für Musik and the Akademie der Künste. After a period as an orchestral harpist he became music director of the Königliches Theater in 1892, and royal Kapellmeister in 1897.

Hummel's compositions reach about 120 opus numbers, including seven *verismo* operas; of these, *Mara* (1893, Berlin) was quite successful. His operatic achievements were, however, overshadowed by d'Albert's *Tiefland* (1903) and his works are all but forgotten.

Mara op.61 (1, A. Delmar), Berlin, Kgl, 11 Oct 1893 (Berlin, 1893)

Angla op.60 (1, Delmar), Berlin, Kgl, 9 June 1894 (Berlin, 1893)

Ein treuer Schelm op.64 (lyrisch-komische Oper, 2, Delmar), Prague, 25 Oct 1894

Assarpai op.65 (3, D. Duncker [Drucker]), Gotha, Hof, 6 April 1898 (Berlin, 1898)

Sophie von Brabant (3, E. von Frankenberg), Darmstadt, Hof, 14 Feb 1899

Die Beichte op.69 (Opernmysterium, 1, Delmar), Berlin, Kgl, 10 April 1900 (Leipzig, n.d.)

Das Gefilde der Seligen (1, G. Witte), Altenburg, Hof, 19 Jan 1917

MGG (T.-M. Langner); *StiegerO*　ALICE LAWSON ABER-COUNT

Hummel, Johann Nepomuk (*b* Pressburg [now Bratislava], 14 Nov 1778; *d* Weimar, 17 Oct 1837). Austrian composer. Although best known as a pianist and composer of piano music he wrote a substantial number of works for the stage. Hummel studied composition with Mozart, Albrechtsberger and Salieri in Vienna, where his father became music director of the Freihaus-Theater auf der Wieden in the late 1780s. His first attempts at theatrical composition date from the late 1790s, but it was after his appointment as Konzertmeister to Prince Nikolaus Esterházy in 1804 that he began to produce a steady stream of stage works. The first version of *Mathilde von Guise* survived only three performances when produced in Vienna in 1810. He was dismissed from the Esterházy court in 1811 but continued to write Singspiels and various occasional pieces for the Viennese theatres; *Die Eselshaut*, a *Feenspiel*, enjoyed considerable success despite its poor libretto. After leaving Vienna, Hummel virtually ceased operatic composition. As Kapellmeister in Weimar (1819–37) he worked seriously on only one new opera, *Attila*, which he probably never completed. A substantial revision of *Mathilde von Guise* in 1821, however, gained favourable recognition and was his only opera to be published in vocal score. During his later years he wrote a number of substitutions and insertions for other people's operas. Hummel's relative lack of operatic success resulted largely from the fact that, in spite of his lifelong theatrical experience, he did not develop a sufficiently bold musical style to be effective in the theatre. As a reviewer of the first version of *Mathilde von Guise* remarked: 'he has no real "theatre style"; in several of his choruses we thought we were listening to a Credo or Gloria from a modern mass' (*AMZ*, xii, 1810, col.491).

s – number from Sachs (1973–4)
z – number from Zimmerschied (1971)

Il viaggiator ridicolo s25/z30, 1797 (komische Oper), inc.

Dankgefühl einer Geretteten s29 (monodrama), 21 March 1799

Demagorgon s41, *c*1800 (komische Oper), frag.; used in s42

Don Anchise Campione s42, ?*c*1800 (ob, ? G. B. Lorenzi), inc.

Le vicende d'amore s56/z26, 1804 (ob, 2); rev. as s71/z27

Die beyden Genies s65, 1805 (Lustspiel), lost

Die vereitelten Ranke s71/z27, Eisenstadt, Sept 1806

Die Messenier s61/z29, ?*c*1805–10 (grosse heroische Oper, 3)

Pimmalione s62/z33, ?*c*1805–15 (azione teatrale, after J.-J. Rousseau)

Mathilde von Guise op.100 (3, after L. E. F .C. Mercier-Dupary), Vienna, Kärntnertor, 26 or 27 March 1810; rev. Weimar, 17 Feb 1821, vs (Leipzig, *c*1826)

Stadt und Land s85, *c*1810 (Spl), Vienna, An der Wien, *c*1810

Dies Haus ist zu verkaufen s90/z28 (Spl, 1, A. Klebe, after A. Duval: *Maison à vendre*), Vienna, Leopoldstadt, 5 May 1812; based on music from s71/z27

Der Junker in der Mühle s97 (Spl, 1, ? H. Schmidt), Nov 1813

Die Eselshaut, oder Die blaue Insel s101 (Feenspiel, 3, Geway), Vienna, An der Wien, 10 March 1814

Die Rückfahrt des Kaisers op.69 (Spl, 1, E. Veith), Vienna, An der Wien, 13 or 15 June 1814, vs (Vienna, *c*1814)

Attila s163, *c*1825–7 (V. J. Etienne de Jouy), ? never completed, lost

Music in: Fünf sind Zwey, 1813 [aria]; Die gute Nachricht, 1814 [ov., qt, duet, trio]; Jeannot et Colin, 1815 [duet, qt]; Hadrian, 1819 [march]; Armide, 1832 [epilogue]; Zampa, 1833 [Act 3 finale]; Gustav III, 1836 [finale]

*

J. Batka and E. Wodianer: *Johann Nepomuk Hummel: biographische Skizze* (Bratislava, 1887)

A. Bartels: *Chronik des Weimarischen Hoftheaters, 1817–1907* (Weimar, 1908)

K. Benyovszky: *J. N. Hummel: der Mensch und Künstler* (Bratislava, 1934)

J. Harich: *Esterházy-Musikgeschichte im Spiegel der zeitgenössischen Textbücher* (Eisenstadt, 1959)

D. Zimmerschied: *Thematisches Verzeichnis der Werke von Johann Nepomuk Hummel* (Hofheim, 1971)

J. Sachs: 'A Checklist of the Works of Johann Nepomuk Hummel', *Notes*, xxx (1973–4), 732–54　CLIVE BROWN

Humperdinck, Engelbert (*b* Siegburg, 1 Sept 1854; *d* Neustrelitz, 27 Sept 1921). German composer.

1. Up to *Hänsel und Gretel*. 2. Later operas.

1. UP TO 'HÄNSEL UND GRETEL'. Humperdinck is remembered largely for his first opera, the much-loved *Hänsel und Gretel*; his later, more ambitious operas have never quite succeeded in gaining a firm place in the repertory. He began his musical education with piano lessons at the age of seven. His first experience of opera was in 1868 when he heard Lortzing's *Undine*. The consequences were immediate: in the same year he began working on two Singspiels, *Perla* and *Claudine von Villa Bella*, and on the music drama *Harziperes*. In later life Humperdinck continued to refer to Lortzing as one of his models. His father was alarmed by these distractions from serious study, but, on the enthusiastic advice of the composer Ferdinand Hiller, he agreed to let his son enter the Cologne Conservatory in 1872. Humperdinck was most successful as a music student, winning the Mozart Prize of Frankfurt in 1876, the Mendelssohn Prize of Berlin in 1879 and the Meyerbeer Prize of Berlin in 1881. When he moved to the Munich Königliche Musikschule in 1877 new influences began to disturb his adherence to the Schumannesque traditions of his teachers. He heard Wagner's *Ring* in 1878 and joined the Munich Wagnerian society 'Orden vom Gral'. A visit to Wagner in 1880 during Humperdinck's scholarship tour of Italy proved even more decisive; Wagner invited him to come to Bayreuth in 1881 to help with the first production of *Parsifal*. Though friends feared such contact would inhibit Humperdinck's creativity, the composer said he would willingly give up 'originality' if it meant he could write choruses like those in *Parsifal*. He also pointed out that there were lighter sides to Wagner's writing not incompatible with his own more Mendelssohnian inclinations.

It was ten years before Humperdinck was able to show the fruit of these new influences. Although he successfully pursued his career as a teacher and critic, becoming a lecturer at the Cologne Conservatory in 1887 and later at the Hoch Conservatory in Frankfurt, all his operatic plans came to nothing. Significantly, the inhibition caused by Wagner was overcome by a request from Humperdinck's sister, Adelheid Wette, to set some folksongs for *Hänsel und Gretel*. The simplicity of the proposal suited the composer's unpretentious nature. (Many of his later works were also written in response to personal requests.) As *Hänsel und Gretel* developed from folksongs to Singspiel and finally to opera, the composer began to question the aesthetic wisdom of his choice. The public's response to the work, however, confirmed that its spontaneity and naivety were among its greatest assets. Even those who complained of the inappropriateness of the Wagnerian scoring could not deny the music's immediate melodic appeal or the skill with which the quoted or invented folksongs were integrated into the action. The significance of the fairy-tale content was heightened by the contrast it offered to the craze for Italian *verismo*. The opera was frequently compared to *Der Freischütz* as another German monument in the battle against the influx of Italian opera. The genre of fairy-tale opera had the advantage of being approved by Wagner, in advice he had given to Alexander Ritter, while it also administered a much-needed antidote to misguided imitations of Wagnerian music drama.

Title-page of the vocal score of Humperdinck's 'Die sieben Geislein' (Magdeburg: Heinrichshofen, 1895)

The immense success of *Hänsel und Gretel* (performances being given in at least 72 theatres within the first year) proved difficult for Humperdinck to follow. His first recourse was to another Grimm fairy-tale, *Die sieben Geislein*, once again adapted by Adelheid Wette. On this occasion, however, the work remained a simple series of songs, for soprano, bass, children's chorus and piano. After what he called this 'Satyrspiel' on *Hänsel und Gretel*, the composer became more thoroughly involved with a fairy-tale of a quite different nature. *Königskinder*, by Ernst Rosmer (the pseudonym of Else Bernstein-Porges), first shown to the composer in 1894, was permeated by contemporary allegorical messages, such as the alienation of the artist from society. Much of the action grew from didactic

arguments on the nature of true nobility and was hardly self-explanatory, being seen through the eyes of adults rather than children. Humperdinck claimed that everything in the text could be set to music – indeed, that it needed music to realize its symbolism – but he failed to convince his librettist of this. She wished him to keep to the original exercise of providing incidental music. He turned to melodrama as a compromise, believing that spoken recitation would make the dialogue more realistic. According to his new kind of melodrama, the actors were to recite in fixed rhythms and to follow a given melodic line, the degree of their deviation from it depending on how much they chose to sing or speak each verbal phrase. Humperdinck believed he was bringing music nearer to Wagner's ideal of Sprechgesang and responding to contemporary demand for realism in opera. The practical difficulties proved immense, however, and many critics, echoing Wagner's words on melodrama, called it an unaesthetic mishmash.

2. LATER OPERAS. After an unfruitful collaboration in 1902 on the Sleeping Beauty story (*Dornröschen*), undertaken out of friendship rather than for artistic reasons, Humperdinck left fairy-tale opera to return to an old ambition of writing a comic opera. He wished to revive the light touch of the early Romantics, Lortzing, Auber and Rossini. His wife's libretto for *Die Heirat wider Willen*, however, was not ideal for such treatment: the third act in particular was too long and weighty in tone. As this opera confirmed, Humperdinck's strengths lay in conveying mood and atmosphere, rather than in creating the pace of comic action and dialogue. The later comic opera *Die Marketenderin* (1914) was no more successful, though Humperdinck now left a great deal of the action to spoken dialogue and used music only to highlight the most important moments. But *Die Marketenderin* reveals the continuing influence of incidental music on Humperdinck's operatic writing. His most significant achievements in this genre were the collaborations with Max Reinhardt, for whose productions of four Shakespeare plays he composed incidental music in 1905. The pantomime *Das Mirakel* of 1911, also commissioned by Reinhardt, overlapped the two genres of opera and incidental music. Even when composing fully-fledged opera, Humperdinck tended to consider his texts as a series of disparate lyrical numbers, relying on his skills of polyphonic extension and transition to disguise the closed nature of his structures.

These compositional skills became particularly important with the transformation of *Königskinder* from melodrama to opera, a task of revision that began in 1907. Humperdinck extended the existing scenes of the melodrama and bound them together with newly composed dialogue so that the seams were barely noticeable. The revised work proved to be the most rigorously through-composed of Humperdinck's operas. Whereas in *Hänsel und Gretel* each scene or section tended to have a different motif, in *Königskinder* Humperdinck transformed and varied the same motifs throughout the opera in the manner of Wagner. The continuous juxtaposing and interweaving of diatonic and chromatic harmonies also played a large part in conveying the story's symbolism of innocence overshadowed by evil. At the opera's première in New York in 1910, it was considered by the critics to be a stylistic advance on *Hänsel und Gretel*; some said it was the most significant opera since *Parsifal*. Its subsequent neglect must be attributed to the problem that dogged much of Humperdinck's operatic work, the use of inappropriate or second-rate dramatic texts. The impact of the impassioned lyricism of *Königskinder* was undoubtedly diminished by some of the plot's obscurity.

The story of *Hänsel und Gretel* corresponded more precisely to the strengths of Humperdinck's style. All his melodic writing, not just that related to folksong, is striking for its directness and simplicity. Although the melodic lines are often expanded by richly varied orchestral sonorities, by sequences and by polyphonic combinations, the clarity of each melodic shape remains. The diatonic basis and strongly marked rhythmic character of his themes give stability to the fullest orchestral textures; they remain lyrically contained and lack the long-term dramatic tension associated with Wagner. With Humperdinck the music always seems ready to resolve into a folklike phrase. The composer might thus find a more appropriate place in operatic history by the side of Cornelius or Wolf than by that of Wagner. Like them he adopted some aspects of Wagner's style and ignored others, taking song not symphony as the basis of his dramatic structures; unlike them, however, Humperdinck succeeded in writing an opera of lasting popularity.

See also HÄNSEL UND GRETEL *and* KÖNIGSKINDER.

Hänsel und Gretel (Märchenspiel, 3, A. Wette, after J. L. and W. C. Grimm), Weimar, Hof, 23 Dec 1893 (Mainz, 1894)
Die sieben Geislein (Märchenspiel, Wette, after Grimm), Berlin, Schiller, 19 Dec 1895, vs (Magdeburg, 1895)
Dornröschen (Märchenoper, 3, E. Ebeling and B. Filhès, after C. Perrault), Frankfurt, Stadt, 12 Nov 1902 (Leipzig, 1902)
Die Heirat wider Willen (komische Oper, 3, H. Humperdinck, after A. Dumas (i): *Les demoiselles de Saint-Cyr*), Berlin, Kgl, 14 April 1905 (Leipzig, 1905)
Bübchens Weihnachtstraum (melodramatisches Krippenspiel, G. Falke), Berlin, Zirkus Busch, 30 Dec 1906 (Berlin, 1906)
Königskinder (Märchenoper, 3, E. Rosmer [E. Bernstein-Porges]), New York, Met, 28 Dec 1910 (Leipzig, 1910)
Das Mirakel [Das Wunder] (pantomime, 3, K. Vollmöller), London, Olympia, 23 Dec 1911 (Berlin, 1912)
Die Marketenderin (Spieloper, 2, R. Misch), Cologne, Stadt, 10 May 1914 (Berlin, 1914)
Gaudeamus: Szenen aus dem deutschen Studentenleben (Spieloper, Misch), Darmstadt, Landes, 18 March 1919 (Berlin, 1919)

*

W. Klatte: 'Hänsel und Gretel', *Freie Bühne*, xi (1894), 204–5
E. Hanslick: 'Hänsel und Gretel', *Die moderne Oper*, vii: *Fünf Jahre Musik (1891–1895)* (Berlin, 1896), 132–9
R. Batka: 'Der Kampf um's Melodram', *Neue musikalische Rundschau* (1897), March
——: 'Singen und Sagen', *Kunstwart* [Munich] (1897), June
——: 'Von Hänsel und Gretel', *Musikalische Streifzüge* (Leipzig, 1899), 139–56
A. Seidl: *Wagneriana, erlebte Aesthetik*, iii: *Die Wagner-Nachfolge im Musik-Drama* (Berlin and Leipzig, 1902), 114–29
W. Pastor: 'Engelbert Humperdincks "Heirat wider Willen"', *Kunstwart*, xviii (1905–6)
A. Friedenthal: 'Humperdinck als Komponist der Shakespeare-Dramen', *Deutsche Tonkünstlerzeitung*, ix (1911)
O. Besch: *Engelbert Humperdinck* (Leipzig, 1914)
H. Kuhlmann: *Stil und Form in der Musik von Humperdincks Oper 'Hänsel und Gretel'* (Borna and Leipzig, 1930)
L. Kirsten: *Motivik und Form in der Musik zu Engelbert Humperdincks Oper 'Königskinder'* (diss., U. of Jena, 1942)
L. Stucki: *Max Reinhardts Shakespeare-Inszenierungen* (diss., U. of Vienna, 1948)
W. Humperdinck: *Engelbert Humperdinck* (Frankfurt, 1965)
E. Thamm: *Stilkritische Bemerkungen zum Schaffen Engelbert Humperdincks* (Cologne, 1974)
H. J. Irmen: *Die Odyssee des Engelbert Humperdinck: eine biographische Dokumentation* (Siegburg, 1975)
E. F. Kravitt: 'The Joining of Words and Music in Late Romantic Melodrama', *MQ*, lxii (1976), 571–90
L'avant-scène opéra, no.104 (1987) [*Hänsel und Gretel* issue]

AMANDA GLAUERT

Hundertmark, Lothar. See LOTHAR, MARK.

Hungarian State Opera House. Theatre in BUDAPEST, built in 1884 as the Royal Hungarian Opera House.

Hungary (Hung. Magyarország). Before 1918, Hungary was approximately three times its present size. It was united under Habsburg rule during the 17th century. After the abortive War of Independence that began in 1848, the dual Austro-Hungarian monarchy was established in 1867 and survived until World War I; the country was then reduced to its present size with the cession of a large part of Transylvania to Romania and the establishment of Czechoslovakia (of which the Hungarian-ruled Slovakia became a part) and Yugoslavia (which incorporated regions linked with Hungary). Hungary was a 'people's republic' from 1948 until 1989.

1. Origins. 2. 19th century. 3. 20th century.

1. ORIGINS. The operatic history of Hungary has three distinct sources. The earliest of these is the ecclesiastical school drama, recorded first in an anonymous *Comico tragoedia* of 1646 from Nagyvárad (now Oradea, Romania); school dramas were at first written in Latin, sometimes in German and then in Hungarian. The oldest surviving example with music, from 1736, to a text by the Piarist K. Kátsor, includes melodies also surviving in the oral tradition. Another Piarist, B. Benyák (1745–1829), philosopher and linguist, composed his own music for his dramas. The earliest complete surviving example is János Paczelt's setting of the story of Castor and Pollux (1743, Sopron: *CS-Mnm*).

Visiting Italian companies provided a second starting-point. The earliest company came in 1648, on the coronation of the second wife of Ferdinand III, to perform Sances's *I trionfi d'Amore* (Pozsony, now Bratislava, Slovakia). The Mingotti company visited Pozsony at the time of Maria Theresa's coronation in 1740–41. German troupes also visited Hungary. Felix Berner's children's company paid repeated visits to Pozsony and Sopron between 1768 and 1786. Performances in Pozsony were at first at inns and from 1764 in a private house; from 1776 a theatre built by Count György Csáky was used (it survived until 1884). Theatres were built in Sopron in 1769 (from a mill), in Pest in 1773–4 (from a fort; cap. 500) and in Buda in 1787 (from a church), among other Hungarian cities; these were initially used for spoken theatre in German, but later for opera – also in German, by German, Italian and French composers.

They in turn were stimulated by a third source, opera performances at the Hungarian aristocratic courts. The initiator here was Prince Nikolaus Esterházy; his opera company, which initially performed at Kismarton (now Eisenstadt, Austria), was powerfully stimulated by the opening of the new theatre at Eszterháza in 1768 (cap. 400), open only to the princely family and their guests. Most of Haydn's operas were composed for this house. The singers were predominantly Italian, the orchestra predominantly German. There was also a puppet opera at Eszterháza. Dittersdorf's presence at the court of Bishop Patachich in Nagyvárad in the late 1760s led to the erection of a theatre where Latin opera was given.

Another patron of opera was Count Batthyány (1727–99), the Pozsony archbishop and primate of Hungary, who engaged opera troupes, in particular that of Hubert Kumpf, to perform with his Kapelle in Pozsony and elsewhere, stimulating Count János Erdődy to establish a theatre in Pozsony in the 1780s. After Erdődy's death Kumpf's company played in Buda and Pest during 1789, in German; opera has been given there continuously since then. László Kelemen (1760–1814) organized a company there in 1790 which lasted until 1796; in 1793 it gave the first Hungarian Singspiel, *Pikkó Hertzeg és Jutka Perzsi* ('Duke Pikko and Judy Perzsi'), by the company's conductor, József Chudy (1753–1813). At much the same time, a company was founded in Kolozsvár (now Cluj-Napoca, Romania) by the literary man János Kótsi Patkó (1763–1843), which performed in Marosvásárhely (now Tirgu Mureş, Romania) and Debrecen at different times of year, with a repertory of Hungarian and other works, all sung in Hungarian.

2. 19TH CENTURY. In 1807 part of the company in Kolozsvár moved to Pest, performing Hungarian opera there while the Town Theatre gave performances in German. They re-formed into travelling troupes, but those remaining in or near Kolozsvár performed from 1821 in the new Hungarian National Theatre (cap. 1200, with 50 boxes on three levels). In 1822 József Ruzitska, the conductor, composed the first true Hungarian opera, *Béla futása* ('Béla's Escape'), to words by Kótsi Patkó; it was followed the same year by his *Kemény Simon*. These took their place in a large international repertory (including works by Mozart, Weigl, Rossini, Méhul, Weber and others) and were given on tour in Transylvania and beyond. Another part of the company, travelling westward, played in Baja (giving a new Hungarian opera, György Arnold's *Kemény Simon*, in 1826–7), Kolozsvár, Szeged and Pest (the German Town Theatre). Yet another section of the company had moved eastward, to Miskolc and then Kassa (now Kosiče, Slovakia), for a time the country's leading operatic centre, with a modern repertory (Rossini, Mercadante, Auber); some of this group moved to the Castle Theatre in Buda in 1833, where with Erkel as conductor and some distinguished singers (notably the soprano Róza Déry) regular performances began. That provoked the building of a new Hungarian theatre in Pest in 1837, for which Erkel and the soprano Róza Schodel were engaged the next year. Support was provided by the National Assembly, and the building became the National Theatre, which soon established its superiority over the Town Theatre.

The ensuing years saw the building of many new theatres in Hungarian cities, providing more stages for the travelling troupes, though Kolozsvár and Kassa remained the principal centres (they preceded Pest in Bellini and Meyerbeer premières). German companies were based in Temesvár (now Timişoara, Romania) and Pozsony; the former in particular flourished, with an international repertory, in the 1850s and early 60s. Hungarian companies needed to excel or to present novelties, as for example did J. Szabó's troupe in 1852 when it introduced six Hungarian works (one each by Bartay and Thern, two each by Erkel and Császár); it specialized too in the *népszínmű* (a rural comedy akin to the ballad opera).

Erkel, chief conductor of the National Theatre and the most talented composer, was the central figure in Hungarian opera throughout the period from 1837 (when he was appointed) until 1884. His influence was powerful. Among the lesser composers of the time were András Bartay (1799–1854), Mihály Mosonyi (1815–70), György Császár (1813–50), Károly Thern (1817–86), Ferenc Doppler (1821–83), Gusztáv Fáy (1824–66), Károly Doppler (1825–1900), Károly Huber (1828–85), the Croatian August Adelburg (1830–73), Bódog Orczy (1831–92) and Ferenc Sárosi (1855–1913). Of these only Császár and Ferenc Doppler were successful, the former primarily with *A kunok* ('The Cumanians', 1848), the latter with *Ilka* (1849); these works both achieved repertory status for half a century. Karl Goldmark (1830–1915) enjoyed success outside Hungary. During this central part of the century no fewer than 17 theatres were erected in Hungarian cities; the Italian repertory predominated but German, French (including operetta) and native works were also heard. Increasing attention was given to operetta towards the end of the century.

Erkel ceased composing in the 1880s, but his influence persisted in the operas of Géza Zichy (1849–1924), Ödön Farkas (1851–1912), Jenő Hubay (1858–1937), Nándor Rékai (1879–1943) and (along with Verdi's influence) Sárosi. Wagner's influence is represented in Hungary by Ödön Mihalovich (1842–1929) and, coupled with Italian influences, Zichy and Farkas, and with French ones, Károly AgghÁzy (1855–1918); other francophile composers include Hubay, Béla Szabados (1867–1936) and (along with Hungarian and Italian influences) Ede Poldini (1869–1957), while Emil Ábrányi (1882–1970) represents Italian influences. Hubay's *A cremonai hegedűs* ('The Violinist of Cremona', 1894) and Poldini's *Csavargó és királylány* ('The Vagabond and the Princess', 1903) stand as the most distinguished products of this generation.

3. 20TH CENTURY. Touring troupes remained active in the 20th century and the building of new theatres continued. At the end of World War I, however, when Hungary lost much of her former territory, several centres remaining within the country – Budapest, Debrecen, Szeged, Pécs and to some extent Miskolc (from 1921) and Győr (from 1935) – continued to accommodate opera performances on a more or less regular basis. Conditions during the interwar years and since World War II have not been conducive to the building of new theatres; examples at Nagykanizsa (1928), Eger (1963) and Győr (1978) are among the few to have been erected.

The most prominent Hungarian opera composers of the era, Béla Bartók (1881–1945) and Zoltán Kodály (1882–1967), were influenced first of all by folk music, from which each was able to develop an individual style. Ernő Dohnányi (1877–1960) remained closer to Romantic tradition, while László Lajtha (1892–1963) was affected both by folk music and contemporary French influences. Ferenc Farkas (*b* 1905) contributed to the native repertory, while Sándor Veress (1907–92), with his two ballets, was affected both by Hungarian folk music and the modern tradition of Switzerland, where he lived. Among a younger generation, András Szőllősy (*b* 1921) has composed much music for the stage, showing a certain Italian influence. György Ligeti (*b* 1925) is a leading European experimental composer, in music theatre as in other realms. Jószef Soproni (*b* 1930) draws his subject matter from Greek mythology and makes no use of folk music. The most productive of opera composers in the country is Sándor Szokolay (*b* 1931), whose highly original and individual style is seen at its most telling in his large-scale ensembles. By contrast, Attila Bozay (*b* 1939) draws on native material for his subject matter and uses the rhythmic patterns of the Hungarian language as a basis for his music. Other Hungarians to have contributed to opera include Emil Petrovics (*b* 1930), Zsolt Durkó (*b* 1934), Sándor Balassa (*b* 1935) and János Vajda (*b* 1949). Among operetta composers Kálmán, Kacsóh and Lehár have been prominent.

For further information on operatic life in the country's principal centres *see* BUDAPEST; DEBRECEN; ESZTERHÁZA; PÉCS; and SZEGED. *See also* BANSKÁ BYSTRICA; BRATISLAVA; CLUJ-NAPOCA; KOŠICE; and TIMIŞOARA.

S. K. Nagy: *A váradi színészet története 1799–1884* [History of the Theatrical Art of Várad] (Nagyvárad, 1884)

B. Váli: *Az aradi színészet története, 1774–1889* [History of the Theatrical Art of Arad] (Budapest, 1889)

F. Ferenczi: *A kolozsvári színészet és színház története* [History of Theatrical Art and Theatre in Kolozsvár] (Kolozsvár, 1897)

M. Fekete: *A temesvári színészet története* [History of the Theatrical Art of Temesvár] (Temesvár, 1911)

I. Vatter: *A soproni német színészet története 1841–ig* [History of the German Theatrical Art of Sopron to 1841] (Budapest, 1929)

D. Bartha: *Erdély zenetörténete* [History of Transylvanian Music] (Budapest, 1936)

M. Horlay: *Olasz operák Magyarországon* [Italian Operas in Hungary] (Budapest, 1943)

R. A. Murányi: 'Két XVIII. századi iskoladráma dallamai' [Songs of two School Dramas from the 18th Century], *Zenetudományi Tanulmányok*, ii (1954), 501–7

P. Réz, ed.: *Déryné emlékezései* [Memoirs of Mrs Déry] (Budapest, 1955)

J. Vigué and J. Gergely: *La musique hongroise* (Paris, 1959, 2/1976)

D. Legány: *A magyar zene krónikája: zenei művelődésünk ezer éve dokumentumokban* [A Chronicle of Hungarian Music: 1000 Years of Music History in Documents] (Budapest, 1962)

M. Pándi: *Száz esztendő magyar zenekritikája* [A Century of Hungarian Music Criticism] (Budapest, 1967)

F. Katona: *A miskolci Nemzeti Színház 1823–1973* [The National Theatre of Miskolc] (Budapest, 1973)

J. Breuer: *Harminc év magyar zenekultúrája* [30 Years of Hungarian Musical Culture] (Budapest, 1975)

G. Kroó: *A magyar zeneszerzés 30 éve* [30 Years of Hungarian Composition] (Budapest, 1975)

G. Staud: *Adelstheater in Ungarn* (Vienna, 1977)

K. Bárdos: *Győr zenéje a 17–18. században* [Music in Győr in the 17th–18th Centuries] (Budapest, 1980)

——: *Sopron zenéje a 16–18. században* [Music in Sopron in the 16th–18th Centuries] (Budapest, 1984)

L. Ballova: 'Hudba v školských hrách na Slovensku' [Music of School Dramas in Slovakia], *Zbornik slovenského narodného muzea LXXXI: historia*, xxvii (Bratislava, 1987), 313–38 [with Ger. and Russ. summaries]

K. Bárdos: *Eger zenéje 1687–1887* [Music in Eger] (Budapest, 1987)

A. Németh: *A magyar opera története a kezdetektől az Operaház megnyitásáig* [History of the Hungarian Opera from its Beginnings to the Opening of the Opera House] (Budapest, 1987)

M. Pintér and I. Kilián, eds.: *Iskoladráma és folklor* [School Drama and Folklore] (Debrecen, 1989)   DEZSŐ LEGÁNY

Hüni-Mihaczek, Felice (*b* Pécs, 3 April 1891; *d* Munich, 26 March 1976). Hungarian soprano. She studied in Vienna with Rosa Papier, making her début there at the Staatsoper in 1919 as the First Lady (*Die Zauberflöte*). She remained a member of the Vienna company until 1926, when she joined the Staatsoper in Munich, singing there regularly until 1944 with occasional postwar appearances until 1953. Originally a coloratura soprano, taking such roles as the Queen of Night and Fiordiligi, she gradually assumed lyric-dramatic roles, including Donna Anna, the Marschallin, Eva and Elsa. She was generally considered one of the outstanding Mozart sopranos of the inter-war period.

HAROLD ROSENTHAL/R

Hunt, (James Henry) Leigh (*b* Southgate, nr London, 19 Oct 1784; *d* Putney, London, 28 Aug 1859). English critic. He was the son of a Unitarian and Universalist preacher. In 1808, together with his elder brother John, he founded the weekly *Examiner*, a liberal journal that contained political essays and literary and theatrical criticism. The brothers went to gaol (1812–14) for a libel against the future George IV, yet with the help of friends the journal not only survived but became famous. Hunt's articulate criticism of both English (1808–12, 1815–21) and Italian (1817–21) opera performances in London did much to arouse public interest in opera, while his writing, marked by wit, clarity and independent thinking, helped raise the literary standard in contemporary periodicals.

T. Fenner: *Leigh Hunt and Opera Criticism: the 'Examiner' Years, 1808–1821* (Lawrence, NE, 1972)

J. Thompson: *Leigh Hunt* (Boston, 1977)

T. Fenner: *Opera in London: Views from the Press, 1785–1830* (Carbondale, IL, forthcoming)   THEODORE FENNER

Hunter, Rita (Nellie) (*b* Wallasey, 15 Aug 1933). English soprano. She studied with Edwin Francis in Liverpool and Redvers Llewellyn in London, and after two years in the chorus at Sadler's Wells became a principal there in 1960, making her début as Marcellina; other roles included Senta, Santuzza and Odabella (*Attila*). However, it was not until the first vernacular performance of the *Ring* at the Coliseum (beginning with *Die Walküre*, 1970), in which she was Brünnhilde, that the potential of her well-defined, vibrant dramatic soprano began to be realized. Flexibility, of both style and timbre, also allows her to encompass Verdi roles – in particular Amelia (*Ballo*) and Leonora (*Il trovatore*). Her first original-language Brünnhilde was at the Metropolitan, in December 1972; she returned there as Santuzza and Norma, and has also sung in San Francisco, Munich and Nice. She later settled in Australia, curtailing her European and North American operatic activities. She has recorded Brünnhilde, in German and English, and Eglantine in the first complete *Euryanthe*. She was made a CBE in 1980.

E. Forbes: 'Rita Hunter', *Opera*, xxvii (1976), 14–20

MAX LOPPERT

Hunyadi László. Opera in four acts by FERENC ERKEL to a libretto by BÉNI EGRESSY after Lőrinc Tóth's play *Hunyadi László*; Pest, National Theatre, 27 January 1844.

Hunyadi László is a historical opera set in the mid-15th century. János Hunyadi, László's father, was a famous Hungarian general who gained a decisive victory over the Turks at Nándorfehérvár (now Belgrade) in July 1456 but died shortly afterwards. The story was also the subject of a drama by Vörösmarty, a poem by Petőfi and many other Hungarian works. Independently of the opera, Erkel first wrote the fine *Hattyúdal* ('Death Song') for piano, which he later orchestrated and used as the introduction to Act 4. He began to compose the opera as a whole at the beginning of 1841 or earlier. At its première many numbers in the eventual score had not yet been composed. The overture was written one and a half years later and first performed in context on 2 October 1845; Erkel revised and reorchestrated it in 1878, and this version, the one now widely known, was first heard on 7 November 1878. The wedding song (Act 3) was composed for the soprano Kornélia Hollósy and the flautist Franz Doppler and first performed on 13 November 1847. Erkel conceived the celebrated 'La Grange' aria for Mme La Grange, who first sang it on 18 July 1850; the ballet in Act 3 was introduced at the same performance. He enlarged the role of the King for Ferenc Stéger in 1859 and that of Mária Gara for Désirée Artôt in 1862. The full opera was first performed in the Royal Hungarian Opera House in Budapest on 19 February 1885 under Erkel himself, with a few minor omissions and in fast tempos. In 1935 the directors of the opera house rewrote the libretto to fit the music more closely, and also revised the dramaturgy, the scenery and to some extent the music itself. *Hunyadi László* has been performed in this version since then, though a 1985 recording uses Erkel's original music with improvements only in the libretto.

The opera has been performed by all the Hungarian opera companies. Abroad, it was staged in Vienna on 14 August 1856, incomplete and with poor singers; it was performed successfully in Bucharest on 4 June 1860 and in Zagreb on 21 July 1860. The overture was first conducted abroad by Liszt in Vienna on 17 May 1846. The 'La Grange' aria was widely sung in the 19th century, mainly by Marie Wilt and Etelka Gerster as well as by La Grange herself.

Act 1 takes place inside the citadel of Nándorfehérvár and before its walls. László (tenor) returns from the national assembly to learn that Count Ulrik Cilley (bass), the powerful regent, has promised his head and that of his younger brother Mátyás (soprano) to the Prince of Serbia. The Habsburg King of Hungary and Bohemia (tenor) enters with Cilley, who persuades him to arrest László, but his agent Rozgonyi (baritone) informs László of the plan to kill him, and it is Cilley himself who is eventually killed. The King, alarmed, promises forgiveness to all. The choral finale 'Meghalt a cselszövő' ('The intriguer is dead') became one of the most popular numbers in the opera; when in 1848 the revolution in Paris took hold in Vienna and brought to an end the despotism of Metternich, its melody was sung in the streets of Buda and Pest.

In Act 2, set in the fortress of the Hunyadi family in Temesvár (now Timişoara, Romania), János Hunyadi's widow Erzsébet Szilágyi (soprano) describes a vision she has had of László being executed. The king assures her of his goodwill towards her son, but catches sight of László's fiancée, Mária (soprano), daughter of the palatine (governor-general) Gara (baritone); he is jealous of their love. Gara expresses his thirst for power. The Hunyadi brothers enter; their mother sings the 'La Grange' aria and László and Mária sing of their love. The King swears that he will not avenge Cilley's death.

Act 3 scene i (later omitted by Erkel) includes a duet in which Gara guarantees László the King's benevolence. In scene ii (in the King's hall at Buda) Gara promises Mária to the King if he will have László executed as a traitor; the King agrees. Scene iii includes a wedding party for László and Mária, Mária's cabaletta and a ballet (a *csárdás*); but then Gara and his soldiers rush in and carry László off.

After the fine Death Song for orchestra, Act 4 scene i shows László in a dungeon. Trusting the King's promise, he refuses Mária's offer of rescue. Gara finds them, and Mária prays in vain for mercy. Scene ii is set in Buda castle. The execution procession enters with László to a fine funeral march (later often performed at state burials). László's mother tries unsuccessfully to save him. She sees the executioner strike three times with his sword, but László is unhurt; by law he must therefore be pardoned. The crowd cries for mercy, but Gara again shouts 'Strike!' and László is executed.

Erkel, who conducted many French and still more Italian operas (especially those of Bellini and Donizetti), was of course influenced by them; he also had the greatest respect for Mozart and Beethoven. *Hunyadi László* includes numbers that clearly show Italian influence. More important, while some of the roles are mere types, several are well-characterized figures who are often differentiated by the use of motifs (among other devices). Erkel had considerable skill as dramatist and was able to employ a symphonic technique to achieve an organic unity. There is also a strikingly large amount of recitative, all of it accompanied; the motifs, used in both the lyrical music and the recitative to characterize situations, individuals and states of mind, to a large extent assure the dramatic coherence of *Hunyadi László*. Erkel later wove these motifs into an overture in the classical style, which was the first important Hungarian symphonic work, and into the 'La Grange' aria; motifs from the earlier Death Song are scattered throughout the opera. Some of the motifs derive from the Rákóczi March and the *torborzó* (recruiting music); all are typically Hungarian in style.

DEZSŐ LEGÁNY

Hurd, Michael (*b* Gloucester, 19 Dec 1928). English composer. Despite an early interest in music, his formal musical education did not begin until 1950, when he studied at Pembroke College, Oxford. From 1953 to 1959 he studied composition with Lennox Berkeley, at the same time teaching theory at the Royal Marines School of Music. Since then he has worked as a freelance composer, writer and lecturer. He has written two children's operas, both to his own librettos: *Little Billy* (Newham-on-Severn, Brightlands School, 25 March 1964) and *Mr Punch* (Gothenburg, 3 April 1970), which was commissioned by the Institutet for Rikskonserter. The Stroud Festival commissioned his chamber opera *The Widow of Ephesus* (1, D. Hughes and Hurd; Stroud, 23 October 1971). Hurd takes a traditional approach to opera, in which melody predominates in a tonal context and the orchestra accompanies the singers. Word setting and characterization are handled simply but effectively. He has written many books on music, including a biography of Britten (London, 1966, 2/1984), *Young Person's Guide to Opera* (London, 1963), *Immortal Hour: the Life and Period of Rutland Boughton* (London, 1962, 2/1993) and *Tippett* (London, 1978).

GEOFFREY BUSH

Hurlebusch, Conrad Friedrich (*b* Brunswick, *c*1696; *d* Amsterdam, 17 Dec 1765). German composer. After matriculating in 1715 he spent two years in Hamburg and Vienna, and from 1718 he travelled in Italy as a harpsichord virtuoso. In August 1721 he returned to Brunswick, where he composed his first Italian opera, *L'innocenza difesa*. He was Kapellmeister to the King of Sweden (1722–5) and wrote several occasional works for the court; an Italian opera, *Arminio*, is either lost or (according to Mattheson) was never completed because of the poor libretto. After his resignation he travelled in Germany, visiting Hamburg, Hanover, Kassel, Eisenach and Gotha. In 1726 he was in Bayreuth, where the margrave invited him to write dramatic music for the carnival; music for *Gunderich*, *Dorinda* and *Etearchus*, now lost, may have been written there. Back in Brunswick, he finished his opera *Flavio Cuniberto* and a treatise, and in November 1727 he moved to Hamburg, hoping to establish himself there. But he was disappointed: his opera remained unperformed and there are records of only two concerts that he gave at the beginning of his stay. In 1736 he was attacked in a pamphlet (copy, *D-Bds*) and left Hamburg, and in 1743 he was appointed organist of the Oude Kerk in Amsterdam, where he remained until his death. Besides his operas, none of which has survived, Hurlebusch wrote much keyboard and choral music.

L'innocenza difesa (dramma per musica, 3, F. Silvani), Brunswick, ?1722
Arminio, ?Stockholm, 1722–5
Dorinda, ?Bayreuth, carn. 1726
Etearchus, ?Bayreuth, carn. 1726
Gunderich, ?Bayreuth, carn. 1726
Flavio Cuniberto (dramma per musica, 3, M. Noris), Brunswick, ?1727

J. Mattheson: *Grundlage einer Ehren-Pforte* (Hamburg, 1740); ed. M. Schneider (Berlin, 1910)
J. W. Lustig: 'Hurlebusch', *Kritische Briefe über die Tonkunst*, i, ed. F. W. Marpurg (Berlin, 1759–63)
M. Seiffert: 'Konrad Friedrich Hurlebusch (ca. 1695–1765): biographische Skizze', *TVNM*, vii/4 (1904), 264–77
G. F. Schmidt: *Neue Beiträge zur Geschichte der Musik und des Theaters am herzoglichen Hofe zu Braunschweig-Wolfenbüttel* (Munich, 1929)
AREND KOOLE

Hurník, Ilja (*b* Poruba, nr Ostrava, 25 Nov 1922). Czech composer. He studied composition with Novák (1941–4) and has worked as a pianist and writer. His sophisticated and thoughtful wit and his gift for parody can be heard in his neo-classical operas, for which he wrote his own librettos. He uses traditional operatic procedures but eliminates their pathos by relating them to everyday situations and twisting their meaning in an absurdist manner; humour and easy-going joviality are used to illuminate human feeling. His style springs from folk music and the influence of Janáček and Martinů, but he uses anachronisms, paraphrased quotations from well-known works and imitative effects as sources of polished humour. *Dáma a lupiči* ('The Lady and the Robbers'), a setting of the script of the English film *The Ladykillers*, is about a group of bank robbers (tenor, two baritones, bass) who, disguised as a string quartet, try to hide in the house of an old woman (soprano). They kill each other after she has found them out, while the police investigate in vain. *Mudrci a bloudi* ('Wise Men and Fools') is a set of three anecdotal one-act operas about the biblical character Solomon (bass-baritone), a medieval juggler (tenor), and a modern fireman (tenor) and water nymph (soprano); the works are connected by the idea of the similarity of wise men and fools. The chamber opera *Diogenes* paraphrases the ancient theme of an ascetic philosopher (baritone) who is struck by the power of music. The beauty of music is also a theme of *Rybáři v síti* ('Fishermen in the Fishing Net'), depicting the experience of people who encounter music and acquire a taste for it. *Oldřich a Boženka* ('Oldřich and Boženka') is a comic operatic fable based on an old Czech legend.

Dáma a lupiči [The Lady and the Robbers] (tragicomic op, 4, Hurník, after W. Rose: *The Ladykillers*), Plzeň, Great, 17 Dec 1966
Mudrci a bloudi [Wise Men and Fools], 1968 (3 1-act ops, Hurník, after Hasidic legend and A. France), unperf.
Diogenes, 1973 (1, Hurník), Brno, Reduta, 24 Feb 1976
Rybáři v síti [Fishermen in the Fishing Net], 1981 (comic op, 3, Hurník), Plzeň, Tyl, 4 June 1983
Oldřich a Boženka, 1985 (comic op, 3, Hurník), unperf.

M. Pospíšil: 'Hurníkova opera Dáma a lupiči v Plzni' [Hurník's Opera *The Lady and The Robbers* in Plzeň], *Divadlo*, xviii (1967), 73–5
V. Pospíšil: 'Dáma a lupiči', *HRo*, xx (1967), 46–7
V. Koula: 'Ironie a něha' [Irony and Tenderness], *HRo*, xxi (1968), 255–7
E. Herrmannová: 'Není malých oper' [There are no Insignificant Operas], *Tvorba* (1976), no.17, p.9
L. Šíp: *Česká opera a její tvůrci* [Czech Opera and its Composers] (Prague, 1983), 317–23
V. Pospíšil: 'Hurníkovi Rybáři v síti', *HRo*, xxxvii (1984), 14–15
HELENA HAVLÍKOVÁ

Hurry, Leslie (*b* London, 10 Feb 1909; *d* London, 20 Nov 1978). English painter and designer. He was trained at St John's Wood Art School and the Royal Academy Schools, London. He was introduced to theatre design by Robert Helpmann who, impressed by an exhibition of his paintings, persuaded Hurry to design his ballet *Hamlet* (1941, Sadler's Wells). The production established Hurry as the most controversial English designer of his generation and, despite uncertain health, he went on to design another 59 productions, chiefly at the Old Vic and, from 1964, at the Stratford Festival, Ontario. He designed a series of 'chamber operas' for the Sadler's Wells company, *La forza del destino* (directed by Ebert for the Glyndebourne company at the Edinburgh Festival, 1951), and four Covent Garden productions: *Turandot* (1947), the *Ring* (1954), *Tristan und Isolde* (1958) and Searle's *Hamlet* (1969).

Hurry did not always impose his disturbing view of the world in his work for the stage, but his most memorable designs were essentially the transference of his painter's vision from canvas to three-dimensional space, and when his surreal vision was engaged he designed masterpieces: the ballets *Hamlet* (1941) and *Swan Lake* (1943); Marlowe's *Tamburlaine the Great* (1951); and the bristling, barbaric *Turandot*, in which gilded mythic beasts presided over a luridly coloured setting of flowing, anthropomorphic architectural forms and hallucinatory perspectives, embracing the protagonists, clad in vast, painted costumes, in a coherent nightmare (see illustration overleaf). The Theatre Museum, London, the Victoria and Albert Museum, and the Metropolitan Ontario Library, Toronto, have good collections of his work.

Leslie Hurry: a Painter for the Stage (Stratford, Ont., 1982) [touring exhibition catalogue]
MARINA HENDERSON

Hüsch, Gerhard (*Heinrich Wilhelm Fritz*) (*b* Hanover, 2 Feb 1901; *d* Munich, 21 Nov 1984). German baritone. He studied with Hans Emge and made his début at Osnabrück in *Der Waffenschmied* in 1923. Engagements followed at Bremen, Cologne (1927–30) and Berlin (1930–42), first at the Städtische Oper and then at the Staatsoper. He sang at Covent Garden in 1930 as Falke (*Die Fledermaus*), returning in 1931 and 1938 as Papageno. At Bayreuth in 1930 and 1931 he sang an outstanding Wolfram. His repertory included Count

Leslie Hurry's design for the finale of Act 2 of Puccini's 'Turandot' (Covent Garden, London, 1947), with Eva Turner as Turandot and Walter Midgley as Calaf

Almaviva, Germont, Sharpless, the title role in *Jonny spielt auf* and Storch (*Intermezzo*). Hüsch possessed a lyric baritone which could be soft and sweet in Italian opera, sonorously warm and resonant in German.

D. Hammond-Stroud: 'Gerhard Hüsch – an Appreciation', *Opera*, xxxvi (1985), 164–6　　　　　HAROLD ROSENTHAL/R

Ḥusni, Daoud (*b* Cairo, Aug 1870; *d* Cairo, 10 Dec 1937). Egyptian composer. Attracted to classical Arabic music, he left his family at the age of 11 to join musical troupes. The 1890s saw his first attempts at composition; he wrote over 500 songs, all in the 'Āmmīyya dialect, and for these he is now chiefly remembered. In 1917, when Salāma al-Ḥigāzi (1852–1917), a pioneer of musical drama in Egypt, became ill, Ḥusni completed two of his operettas, *Romeo and Juliet* and *Aida*. Thereafter he largely abandoned song in favour of the new medium; he wrote over 25 operettas.

In 1922 he was commissioned to compose the first full-length opera written in Egypt, *Shamshoun wa Dalīlah* ('Samson and Delilah'). Its overwhelming success was more sociological and patriotic than artistic, reflecting Egypt's longing for liberation from Western influence, but it marked a turning-point in Arabic music. Its success led to the commission of his second opera, *Lāylat Kilubātra* ('The Night of Cleopatra'), influenced by the biblical dialogues of King Solomon and the Shulamite, written in verse and in the 'Āmmīyya dialect. In 1923 he revised *Huda*, an operetta by Sayyid Darwīsh, as an opera, as a tribute on Darwīsh's untimely death. His fourth opera, *Semiramis*, was a joint venture, initiated by the singer and actress Munīra al-Mahdīyya, who commissioned three composers to write a three-act opera (*c*1935); Ḥusni completed the second act.

Shamshoun wa Dalīlah [Samson and Delilah], Cairo, Azbekīya, 1922

Lāylat Kilubātra [The Night of Cleopatra] (H. Fawzi, after A. Shāwqi: *Antūniu waKilubātra*), mid-1920s
Huda, 1923 [completion of an operetta by S. Darwīsh]
Semiramis (3), mid-1930s [Act 2; Acts 1 and 3 by Kāmil al-Khōl'i and Riyāḍ al-Sunbāṭi]

Recueil des traveaux du Congrès de musique arabe (Cairo, 1932)
'M. Dawāra Daoud Ḥusni', *Al-Gumhouriyya* (14, 21, 28 June, 5 July 1973)　　　　　WILLIAM Y. ELIAS

Hussey, Dyneley (*b* Deolali, India, 27 Feb 1893; *d* Cheltenham, 6 Sept 1972). English critic. After serving in World War I and as a civil servant he worked at the National Gallery. Expert knowledge of the visual arts and of European culture in general lent a valuable perspective to his music criticism in the *Saturday Review*, the *Spectator* and *The Times* (1923–46). His criticism in the *Listener*, after he had left *The Times*, showed a special interest in Italian opera. Well-informed and balanced judgment and an urbane style mark his books on Mozart and Verdi.

Wolfgang Amade Mozart (London, 1928)
Eurydice; or the Nature of Opera (London, 1929)
Some Composers of Opera (London, 1940)
Verdi (London, 1940, 3/1963)　　　　　MARTIN COOPER

Huszka, Jenő (*b* Szeged, 24 April 1875; *d* Budapest, 2 Feb 1960). Hungarian composer. At the Budapest Academy of Music he studied with Hubay (violin) and Koessler (composition), and he also studied law. He was for a time a first violinist in the Lamoureux Orchestra, and then worked in the Ministry of Culture in Budapest, where he met Ferenc Martos, who became his librettist. Huszka's first operetta, *Tilos a bemenet* ('No Entry'), was produced in 1899. With *Bob herceg* ('Prince Bob', 1902), set in London and later produced in Vienna, Italy and the USA, he successfully challenged the dominance of Viennese and British works and helped pave the way for a Hungarian school of operetta. Huszka was held in high esteem in Hungarian artistic circles; he served as president of the Hungarian Society of Composers and Authors and was vice-president of the International Composers' Federation congress in Budapest in 1930.

all operettas, first performed in Budapest, unless otherwise stated

Tilos a bemenet [No Entry] (musikalisches Lustspiel, A. Mirai), Magyar, 2 Sept 1899; Bob herceg [Prince Bob] (3, F. Martos and K. Bakonyi), Nép, 20 Dec 1902; Aranyvirág [Golden Flower] (3, Martos and Bakonyi), Király, 6 Nov 1903; Gül-Baba (Spl, 3, Martos and Bakonyi), Király, 6 Dec 1905; Tündérszerelem [Fairy Love] (3, Martos and Bakonyi), Nép-Vigopera, 21 Dec 1907; Rébusz báró [Baron Rebus] (3, F. Herzeg), Király, 20 Nov 1909
Nemtudomka [Night-club Girl] (3, Bakonyi and Harsanyi), Király, 14 Jan 1914; Lili Bárónő [Baroness Lili] (3, Martos), Vársoi, 9 March 1919; Hajtóvadászat [Riding to Hounds] (Martos), Vársoi, 20 Oct 1926; Erzsébet [Elizabeth] (Spl, 3, L. Szilágyi), Magyar, 4 Jan 1939; Gyergyói bál [Ball at Gyergyoi] (Szilágyi), Magyar, 4 Jan 1941; Mária főhadnagy [Corporal Maria] (3, Szilágyi), Fővárosi Operett, 16 Sept 1942
Szabadsag, szerelem [Freedom, Love] (Spl, 3, S. Fischer, after M. Jókai), 1 April 1955; Szép Juhászné [Beautiful Mrs Juhasz] (K. Kristof), Szeged, Nemzeti, 8 May 1955

*

L. Tordai: *Dalmuvek könyve* (Budapest, 1936)
G. S. Gal and V. Somogyi: *Operettek könyve* (Budapest, 1959)
R. Traubner: *Operetta: a Theatrical History* (New York, 1983)
ANDREW LAMB

Hutt, Robert (*b* Karlsruhe, 8 Aug 1878; *d* Berlin, 5 Feb 1942). German tenor. He studied in Karlsruhe, where he made his début in 1903. Düsseldorf and Frankfurt claimed him from 1910 to 1917, and he then began a ten-year engagement with the Berlin Staatsoper. Though he sang a wide range of heroic parts, such as Manrico in *Il trovatore*, he became principally associated with Wagner and Strauss. At Covent Garden in 1913 and 1914 he sang Walther in *Die Meistersinger* and Parsifal (at the British stage première), and at Drury Lane appeared as Bacchus in the last four of the performances in which Beecham introduced *Ariadne auf Naxos* to English audiences. In 1920 he sang the Emperor in the Berlin première of *Die Frau ohne Schatten*. He was also a member of the German opera company led by Leo Blech which played at the Manhattan Opera House, New York, in 1923, and the following year he sang there in the New York première of d'Albert's *Die toten Augen*. His recordings include songs by Richard Strauss in which he is accompanied by the composer, and excerpts from a performance of *Die Meistersinger* showing his style assured and his voice still sturdy at the age of 50.
J. B. STEANE

Hüttenbrenner, Anselm (*b* Graz, 13 Oct 1794; *d* Ober-Andritz, nr Graz, 5 June 1868). Austrian composer. The son of a landowner, he studied at the University of Graz. He was an accomplished pianist and was already composing by the time he went, in April 1815, to study with Salieri in Vienna; there he and his brother Josef (1797–1882) became friendly with Beethoven and Schubert. He was director of the Steiermärkischer Musikverein, 1825–39. In March 1827 he visited the dying Beethoven, and later in the year helped to make Schubert's stay in Graz a happy one. After his wife's death, in 1848, he became a recluse. Besides his operas, now mostly lost, his compositions include sacred music, symphonies, chamber music and songs.

Die französische Einquartierung (komische Oper, K. Schütz), 1819, lost
Armella, oder Die beiden Viceköniginnen (I. Kollmann), Graz, Franzens, 6 Feb 1827, lost except for ov., 1 aria and lib.

Lenore (2, K. G. von Leitner and Kollmann, after Bürger), Graz, Franzens, 22 April 1835
Oedip zu Colonos (3, N. F. Guillard, trans. C. Herklots), 1836, ?unperf.
Der Rekrut (3, Schütz), lost, mentioned in *Grazer Tagespost* (7 Aug 1863)
Die Drachenhöhle zu Röthelstein (Operette, Kollmann), lost
Claudine von Villa Bella (J. W. von Goethe), inc., lost except for ov. arr. pf 4 hands

*

H. Kundigraber: 'Anselm Hüttenbrenner: ein steirischer Tondichter', *Grazer Tagespost* (30 July 1942, 13 Oct 1944)
MAURICE J. E. BROWN

Huttenlocher, Philippe (*b* Neuchâtel, 29 Nov 1942). Swiss baritone. He studied at Fribourg with Juliette Bise, and later became a professor of singing at Neuchâtel Conservatory. He made his operatic début in the title role of Monteverdi's *Orfeo* at the Zürich Opera in 1975. Other engagements have taken him to Vienna, Berlin, Hamburg and Milan. His recordings include *Orfeo*, Charpentier's *David et Jonathas*, Marais' *Alcyone* (Peleus), Rameau's *Castor et Pollux* and *Les Indes galantes*, *Così fan tutte*, *Pénélope* and *L'enfant et les sortilèges*. He sang Lucan in the video of Ponnelle's Zürich production of *L'incoronazione di Poppea*. He is noted for his light but warm baritone, his clear articulation and his keen sense of style.
NICHOLAS ANDERSON

Huxley, Aldous (*b* London, 26 July 1894; *d* Los Angeles, 22 Nov 1963). English writer. A member of a distinguished scientific family, he became a major literary figure after World War I, with such novels as *Crome Yellow* (1921), *Antic Hay* (1923) and *Brave New World* (1932). He moved to California in 1937 and continued to write fiction, as well as essays, travel works and a number of historical studies, the most celebrated of which is *The Devils of Loudun* (1952), a study in sexual hysteria which was adapted by John Whiting for his play *The Devils*, in turn the basis for Penderecki's opera (1969). In California Huxley became a friend of Stravinsky, to whom he proposed W. H. Auden as librettist for *The Rake's Progress*.

*

J. Aplin: 'Aldous Huxley and Music in the 1920s', *ML*, lxiv (1983), 25–36
ANTHONY PARR

Hvorostovsky, Dmitry (*b* Krasnoyarsk, Siberia, 16 Oct 1962). Russian baritone. He studied in Krasnoyarsk, making his début there in 1986. He appeared at the Kirov (1987) and in 1989 won the Singer of the World Competition at Cardiff and made his West European début at Nice as Yeletsky. Subsequently he sang in Venice (as Yevgeny Onegin), Barcelona (in *Pagliacci*) and at Covent Garden, where he made his début in 1992 as Riccardo (*I puritani*); his American début was in *War and Peace* in San Francisco. His repertory includes Don Giovanni, Rossini's Figaro and Germont. He has a beautiful, well-schooled voice of moderate size.
ELIZABETH FORBES

Hydaspes. Opera given in London in 1710, based on GL' AMANTI GENEROSI by Francesco Mancini.

Hyde, Walter (*b* Birmingham, 6 Feb 1875; *d* London, 11 Nov 1951). English tenor. He studied at the RCM under Gustave Garcia and as a student appeared in *Euryanthe* and Stanford's *Much Ado about Nothing*. He made his début at Terry's Theatre, London, in *My Lady Molly*, and in 1906 sang in the première of Liza

Lehmann's *Vicar of Wakefield*. In 1908 he sang Pinkerton, and Siegmund in the English *Ring* under Richter, at Covent Garden, where he appeared regularly until 1923–4; he also sang Siegmund in his Metropolitan début in 1910. A distinguished Mozartian, he was a member of the Beecham and the British National Opera companies. He sang Sali in the first London performance of *A Village Romeo and Juliet* (1910) and took part in the première of Holst's *The Perfect Fool* (1923). His repertory also included Walther and Parsifal.   HAROLD ROSENTHAL/R

Hynninen, Jorma (*b* Leppävirta, 3 April 1941). Finnish baritone. He studied in Helsinki, making his début there in 1969 with the Finnish National Opera as Tonio. He created Topi in Sallinen's *The Red Line* (1978, Helsinki), and sang that role with the Finnish National Opera in London (1979), Moscow (1982) and New York (1983) and at Savonlinna, where he created the King in Sallinen's *The King Goes Forth to France* (1984). In 1984 he became artistic director of the company. As well as appearing in Vienna, Stockholm and Barcelona and at the Metropolitan, he has sung Pelléas at La Scala and the Opéra and in Strasbourg and Madrid. His repertory includes Guglielmo, Count Almaviva, Papageno, the Speaker, Don Giovanni, Wolfram, Yeletsky, Yevgeny Onegin, Germont, Rigoletto, Ford, Hindemith's Mathis and the title role of Aarre Merikanto's *Juha* (1978, Edinburgh). He created the title roles of Rautavaara's *Thomas* at Joensuu in 1985, *Vincent* in 1990 and Sallinen's *Kullervo* at Los Angeles in 1992. He is a stylish singer and actor with outstanding diction.   ELIZABETH FORBES

Hyperion. *Lirica in forma di spettacolo* by BRUNO MADERNA, to a text arranged by Maderna and Virginio Puecher after Friedrich Hölderlin, with phonemes by H. G. Helms; Venice, Teatro La Fenice, 6 October 1964 (revised versions, Brussels, Monnaie, 17 May 1968; Bologna, Palazzo Bentivoglio, 18 July 1968).

Hyperion was Maderna's first work for the stage. In collaboration with the producer Virginio Puecher, Maderna arranged around a group of existing works or parts of works – *Le rire* and *Dimensioni II* on tape, *Dimensioni IV* for orchestra and *Aria* for soprano and orchestra – a 'dramatic action' in which a flautist attempts to perform an expressive solo. He is frustrated first by the appearance of a cage in which he is trapped, then by a monster Machine, and lastly by a Woman (soprano) who sings *Aria* on a Hyperion text by Friedrich Hölderlin.

This first version, performed by Severino Gazzelloni and Catherine Gayer, was poorly received by its audience, and four years later two largely different versions appeared, in Brussels and Bologna. In Brussels, as *Hyperion en het geweld* ('Hyperion and Violence'), the work was amalgamated with a dramatic idea called 'Morituri' by Hugo Claus. The setting was no longer a bare stage but a military bunker in a Vietnamesque war, in which soldiers confront the enemy's 'Rats'. After a battle, the rats are victorious, and the Woman appears once more to sing *Aria*. In Bologna, Maderna placed the five 'scenes' of the Venice *Hyperion* in alternation with the five sections of Domenico Belli's 1616 *intermedi Orfeo dolente*: the solitary flautist-artist here became identified with the artist Orpheus in a search for consolation and inspiration.

The musical fabric of each version of *Hyperion* was largely a matter of ad hoc assembly of material (the later versions incorporating some newly composed sections) which, in the case of the Brussels version, is not now easily identifiable. Maderna also made several concert versions. After his death the Italian conductor and composer Marcello Panni assembled a composite concert work incorporating the essentials of the 'Hyperion idea'.   RAYMOND FEARN

Hytner, Nicholas (*b* Manchester, 7 May 1956). English director. After studying at Cambridge University (1974–7), where he directed for the Footlights, he began a career divided between the spoken and lyric theatres. One of the most original and intellectually wide-ranging of younger theatre directors, his first opera production was *The Turn of the Screw* for Kent Opera (1979), for whom he also directed *Figaro* (1981) and *King Priam* (1983). For the ENO he has directed a *Rienzi* (1983) that explored the work's totalitarian resonances, a *Serse* in 1985 that re-created the ancient Persian setting in the antiquarian spirit of Handel's contemporaries, and a wittily inventive *Zauberflöte* (1988). His *Knot Garden* for the Royal Opera House (1988) exemplified his gift for lucid exposition effected by powerfully acted performances. Other notable productions include *Giulio Cesare* for the Paris Opéra (1987), *Figaro* at Geneva (1989) and *La clemenza di Tito* for Glyndebourne in 1991. He was appointed an associate director of the National Theatre in 1989.

'"The Purpose of Playing"', *Opera*, xxxix (1988), 419–23
'Opera Production', *Kent Opera: Twentieth Anniversary 1969–1989*, ed. M. Bewick and J. Platt (1989), 53–5
*
M. Loppert: 'Nicholas Hytner', *Opera*, xlii (1991), 754–61
               BARRY MILLINGTON

I

Iași (Fr. Jassy). Town in north-eastern Romania. Formerly the capital of Moldavia, it was founded in 1387. It has a strong academic and cultural tradition: the Conservatorul Filarmonic-Dramatic (Dramatic and Philharmonic Conservatory) was founded in 1836, and the first state artistic institution, the Conservatorul de Musică și Declamațiune (Conservatory of Music and Declamation) as well as the first Romanian university, were established in 1860. Foreign opera companies visited the town from the 18th century; these later stimulated students of the Dramatic and Philharmonic Conservatory to present *Norma* (February 1838). An Italian opera company was founded in 1851 and the first Romanian company, the Societatea Lirică (Lyrical Society), in 1878. From 1840 performances took place in the Teatrul Național (National Theatre), which was reconstructed as one of the most beautiful and sumptuous buildings in Romania, and reopened on 1 December 1896. Today the Opera de Stat (State Opera of Iași), founded on 1 November 1956, performs on the same stage. While the permanent repertory consists of works by Mozart, Beethoven, Verdi, Bellini, Rossini, Wagner, Puccini, Bizet, Musorgsky and Tchaikovsky, world premières have been given of works by Doru Popovici, Mansi Barberis, Teodor Bratu, Vasile Spătărelu, Viorel Doboș and others. Singers who have appeared include Giovanni Dimitrescu, Aldo Protti, Theo Adam, Nicola Rossi-Lemeni and Viorica Cortez, and conductors, Eduard Caudella, Ion Baciu, Radu Botez and Corneliu Calistru.   VIOREL COSMA

Ibert, Jacques (François Antoine) (*b* Paris, 15 Aug 1890; *d* Paris, 5 Feb 1962). French composer. He studied composition at the Paris Conservatoire with Paul Vidal and after war service won the Prix de Rome (1919). In Rome he wrote his first opera, *Persée et Andromède* (1921), to a libretto by Nino (pseudonym of Michel Veber), his brother-in-law, after one of Jules Laforgue's *Moralités légendaires*. It is based on a satirical reworking of the myth, with set pieces between the various characters. Perseus rescues Andromeda from the monster Cathos but is dismayed to find her pining for the beast. He leaves her, his pride clearly wounded, and the monster is miraculously transformed into a handsome suitor. Despite Ibert's youth, this concise work (lasting under an hour) already shows his understanding of the theatre, for he had studied drama before turning to music.

Ibert vehemently refused to ally himself to any particular school, proclaiming that 'all systems are valid', a claim which has caused his detractors to accuse him of eclecticism. His most successful opera, the farce *Angélique* (1927), displays this eclectic style and his accomplished writing of pastiche set pieces. *Le roi d'Yvetot* (1930) is also full of farcical situations, misunderstandings and overemphases. Set in an 'unspecified epoch, between the invention of gunpowder and our days', it concerns a king who has been deposed from his village. The opera has much choral writing for the villagers, composed in a simple folklike style. The *opéra bouffe Gonzague* (1931) recounts the adventures of a piano tuner who replaces a missing guest at a bourgeois dinner party.

L'aiglon (1937) was the first of two operas written in conjunction with Honegger. It treats the historical subject lightly, introducing *commedia dell'arte* characters with several musical pastiches. This accessible style of writing was continued in the farcical *Les petites Cardinal* (1938), a family tale of two daughters. Faust and Mephisto enter the proceedings, and the music is provided in set pieces in the manner of an operetta. A play within a play sees the daughters taking the roles of a gramophone and a light bulb; there is a 'migraine trio' and music is provided for the audience to exit. Mild moralizing leads to a finale which concludes that life has its own demands and should not be taken too seriously.

Le chevalier errant (1935), a choreographic epic with chorus and two reciters, was first performed at the Paris Opéra in 1950, choreographed by Serge Lifar.

See also AIGLON, L', and ANGÉLIQUE.

Persée et Andromède, ou Le plus heureux des trois, 1921 (2, Nino [Michel Veber], after J. Laforgue), Paris, Académie Nationale de Musique, 15 May 1929
Angélique (farce, 1, Nino), Paris, Bériza, 28 Jan 1927
Le roi d'Yvetot (oc, 4, J. Limozin and A. de la Tourrasse), Paris, OC (Favart), 15 Jan 1930
Gonzague (opéra bouffe, 1, R. Kerdyck, after P. Veber), Monte Carlo, Opéra, 17 Dec 1931
L'aiglon [Acts 1 and 5] (drame musical, 5, H. Cain, after E. Rostand), Monte Carlo, Opéra, 10 March 1937 [Acts 2–4 by A. Honegger]
Les petites Cardinal (operetta, 2, A. Willemetz and P. Brach, after L. Halévy), Paris, Bouffes-Parisiens, 12 Feb 1938, vs (Paris, 1946), collab. Honegger
Barbe-bleue (opéra bouffe for radio, W. Aguet), Radio Lausanne, 10 Oct 1943

J.-G. Prod'homme: 'Gustave Doret, Paul Ladmirault, Louis Aubert, Jacques Ibert', *La théâtre lyrique en France* (Paris, 1937–9) [pubn of Poste-National Radio-Paris], iii, 172–81

P. Landormy: *La musique française après Debussy* (Paris, 1943, 2/1948)

R. Dumesnil: *La musique en France entre les deux guerres* (Paris, 1946)

J. Feschotte: *Jacques Ibert* (Paris, 1958)

G. Michel: *Jacques Ibert* (Paris, 1967)

RICHARD LANGHAM SMITH

Ibsen, Henrik (*b* Skien, 20 March 1828; *d* Christiania [now Oslo], 23 May 1906). Norwegian dramatist. He is generally regarded as the father of modern prose drama, with such plays as *A Doll's House* (1879), *Ghosts* (1882) and *Hedda Gabler* (1891). His early verse plays, written in the 1850s, attracted opera composers at the turn of the century – for instance, Stenhammar (*Gildet på Solhaug*, 1899) and Karel Moor (*Hjördis*, 1905). The subjects of these plays are epic and patriotic, evoking Norway's greatness during the Viking and medieval periods; and Ibsen's use of the *Volsung-Saga* in *Haermaendena på Helgeland* ('The Vikings at Helgeland'; 1858) clearly aligns the play with a Wagnerian tradition. His later and more innovatory work had less appeal for composers, though the revolutionary *Brand* (1866) leaves its mark on d'Indy's *L'étranger*; and Mark Brunswick's opera *The Master Builder* (1959–67) is based on Ibsen's 1892 play of the same name. *Hedda Gabler* has inspired recent settings by Robert Ward (1978) and Edward Harper (1985).

Ibsen had little feeling for music, although he made some early attempts at opera criticism, in which he expressed strong views on librettos (and wrote a verse parody of Bellini's *Norma*). His attempt in 1861 to rewrite his *Olaf Liljenkraus* (1857) for the operatic stage was abandoned (the play was later turned into a very successful opera by Arne Eggen in 1940), and he turned down a request for a libretto from Grieg, who had written music for his play *Peer Gynt* in 1876.

Gildet på Solhaug [The Feast at Solhaug] (verse play, 1856): Stenhammar, 1899

Olaf Liljekrans (play, 1857): A. Eggen, 1940

Haermaendena på Helgeland [The Vikings at Helgeland] (play, 1858): Moor, 1905, as Hjördis

Brand (play, 1866): d'Indy, 1903, as L'étranger

Peer Gynt (play, 1867): L. Heward, 1922, inc.; V. Ullmann, 1928, inc.; Egk, 1938

Hedda Gabler (play, 1891): Ward, 1978, as Claudia Legare; Harper, 1985

Bygmester Solness [The Master Builder] (play, 1892): M. Brunswick, 1959–67, inc.

*

M. Meyer: *Henrick Ibsen* (London, 1967–71)
ANTHONY PARR

Ice and Steel. Opera by V. M. Deshevov; *see* LYOD I STAL'.

Ice Break, The. Opera in three acts by MICHAEL TIPPETT to his own libretto; London, Covent Garden, 7 July 1977.

Tippett's fourth opera, commissioned by Covent Garden and composed between 1973 and 1976, is a study of the imprisoning character of stereotypes. The wide-ranging scenario encompasses conflicts of race and generation in particular. Although the location is not specified, it is clear that much of the opera arose directly from Tippett's fascination with the USA in the late 1960s and early 1970s. At the same time he identifies with persecuted Russian writers, so that his Lev (bass) is an exiled poet who has spent 20 years in a concentration camp. He flies to the 'new world' to join his wife Nadia (lyric soprano) and their son Yuri (baritone).

Nadia has been sustained by hope, love for her lost husband and nostalgia for the past. Yuri, however, knows nothing of this and belongs entirely in the vibrant if dangerous world which we take to represent America. His friends Gayle (dramatic soprano), the nurse Hannah (rich mezzo) and the athletic champion Olympion (tenor) symbolize a generation at once free but in danger of generating explosive tensions. Yuri rejects his father and in following his friends is almost killed in a horrific race riot. Nadia dies peacefully, to some of Tippett's most ravishing visionary music, and after fighting for his life Yuri and his father are reconciled in a moving scene.

The disturbing cinematic realism of Tippett's score, with its violent, splintered music, is tempered by moments of surrealism culminating in a bizarre interlude in the Paradise Garden (Act 3 scene v). Woven alongside the contemporary issues, however, are rich references to Shakespeare's late plays of forgiveness and Goethe's *Wilhelm Meister*. The scenic intercutting of this shortest of Tippett's operas is his most daring, involving the complex redistribution of a large masked chorus. Tippett's darkest operatic vision is certainly his riskiest but issues in music of genuine, if fragile hope.

GERAINT LEWIS

Iceland. For discussion of opera in Iceland *see* REYKJAVÍK.

Idalma [*L'Idalma, overo Chi la dura la vince* ('Idalma, or Whoever Perseveres will Win')]. *Commedia per musica* in three acts by BERNARDO PASQUINI to a libretto by GIUSEPPE DOMENICO DE TOTIS; Rome, Palazzo Capranica, 6 February 1680.

The Roman libretto has no dedicatee, and it names no author, composer or singers. It was a private production, perhaps sponsored by the Accademici Sfaccendati, a small group which included Giuliano Capranica (whose theatre became public in 1692). Between 1684 and 1693 the work was revived (with alterations) in Bologna, Florence, Genoa and Ferrara.

Act 1 begins in a wood near Rome. Lindoro (tenor) sighs for his former beloved, Irene (soprano), rather than his new wife, Idalma (soprano), with whom he has eloped. He and his servant, Pantano (bass), abandon his sleeping wife, who awakens to find the stranger Almiro (tenor), brother of Irene, admiring her beauty. Lindoro and Pantano arrive at the courtyard of the villa of Celindo (contralto) and his wife Irene, who rejects Lindoro's advances. In a gallery at the villa, Almiro introduces the sorrowing Idalma to the shocked Irene, who employs Celindo's page, Dorillo (soprano), in her scheme to recall Lindoro to his senses. In Act 2 Irene's attempt fails, misunderstandings abound, and the enraged Celindo enters the closing scene with dagger drawn. In Act 3 Celindo and Almiro swear to kill Lindoro and Irene; but the long-suffering Idalma prevents this disaster, Lindoro reaffirms his love for her, and Dorillo proclaims that future ages will learn from Idalma that 'whoever perseveres will win'.

Each act has 20–22 brief set pieces, supplemented by the numerous ariosos and ensembles that terminate recitative passages. A quarter of the 53 solos and ten duets are accompanied by four-part strings, and many others are followed by four-part ritornellos. Ostinato basses and strophic forms are more prominent than da capo forms.

LOWELL LINDGREN

Idaspe fedele. Opera by Francesco Mancini; *see* AMANTI GENEROSI, GL'.

Idiota, L' ('The Idiot'). *Opera lirica* in three acts (seven scenes) by LUCIANO CHAILLY to a libretto by Gilberto Loverso after FYODOR MIKHAYLOVICH DOSTOYEVSKY's novel; Rome, Teatro dell'Opera, 18 February 1970.

Chailly's opera, composed in 1966–7, follows Dostoyevsky's novel more or less faithfully. Apparently cured of his epilepsy, Prince Lev Nikolayevich Myskin (tenor), known because of his naivety as 'the idiot', returns to St Petersburg from Switzerland. On seeing the portrait of Nastasia Filipovna Baraskova (mezzo-soprano), the fiancée of Gavrila Ardalionich Ivolgin (tenor), he asks Gavrila if he may meet her. Nastasia is left troubled by their meeting and, surprisingly, confides in Myskin as to the advisability of marrying Gavrila; Myskin counsels her against doing so. Nastasia breaks off her engagement, to general dismay. The wealthy Parfen Rogozin (baritone) then offers 100 000 rubles for Nastasia's hand, and Myskin too proposes marriage. Fearful of hurting Myskin, Nastasia follows Rogozin, whom she nevertheless soon leaves. Sensing that this anguished love will lead to Nastasia's death, Myskin falls prey to an epileptic attack.

During the second and third acts, his fears are realized. Aglaya Ivanovna (soprano) falls in love with him, coming into conflict with Nastasia and departing, bereft and weeping, after a convulsive confrontation with her in the presence of Myskin and Rogozin. Nastasia, having promised Myskin that she will marry him, elopes on the day of the wedding with Rogozin, at whose hands she meets her death. Rogozin awaits arrest with resignation. The opera ends with the wild ravings of Myskin, whose fragile mental balance has finally given way.

Beginning in the 1950s with a series of operas in neoclassical style and traditional dramatic outlook, Chailly moved closer with *Era proibito* (1963) to 12-note principles, which he explored in a fairly free and undogmatic way. *L'idiota*, composed in that vein, nonetheless reasserts his essential fidelity to formal operatic tradition while displaying dramatically motivated developments in language and usage as well as using electronic and aleatory techniques; these, however, are denied the negative ideological significance assigned to them by the avant garde.

RAFFAELE POZZI

Idomenée ('Idomeneus'). *Tragédie en musique* in a prologue and five acts by ANDRÉ CAMPRA to a libretto by ANTOINE DANCHET; Paris, Opéra, 12 January 1712.

Idomenée is best known today as the principal source of the libretto to Mozart's *Idomeneo*. G. B. Varesco, Mozart's librettist, simplified Danchet's plot and changed the tragic ending to a happy one. At the end of Campra's opera Idomeneus (bass) goes mad, slays Idamantes (*haute-contre*) and is prevented from suicide by his retinue.

The most impressive musical features in *Idomenée* are in Campra's use of the chorus and orchestra. There is, for example, an offstage chorus of shipwrecked people (Act 2 scene i), a device used 37 years later by Rameau in *Zoroastre*. In this scene the orchestra's storm music constantly penetrates the chorus and the recitative 'Vents orageux, cessez', sung by Neptune (bass). The same motif recurs in the prelude to Act 3 scene i to evoke the 'storm' in Idomeneus's heart. In *Idomenée* Campra increased his use of rapid modulations and expressive harmonies (especially in the accompanied

recitatives), and sometimes used rare tonalities: Act 5, for example, ends in Bb minor.

See also IDOMENEUS.

JAMES R. ANTHONY

Idomeneo, re di Creta ('Idomeneus, King of Crete'). *Dramma per musica* in three acts, K366, by WOLFGANG AMADEUS MOZART to a libretto by GIOVANNI BATTISTA VARESCO after ANTOINE DANCHET's *Idomenée*; Munich, Residenztheater, 29 January 1781.

Idomeneus *King of Crete*		tenor
Idamante [Idamantes] *his son*		soprano castrato
Ilia *Trojan princess, daughter of Priam*		soprano
Elettra [Electra] *princess, daughter of Agamemnon*		soprano
Arbace [Arbaces] *confidant of the king*		tenor
High Priest of Neptune		tenor
Oracle		bass

Trojan prisoners; sailors; people of Crete

Setting Mycenaean Crete: the Royal palace at Kydonia (Sidon), by the sea, and the temple of Neptune

Mozart received the commission from the Munich Intendant, Count Seeau, during the summer of 1780. Danchet's five-act libretto of 1712 was adapted by the Salzburg cleric Varesco in three acts, on the pattern of the 'reformed' operas of Jommelli and Gluck, balancing the introduction of Italian arias by retaining a strong choral element, ballet, a high proportion of orchestrated recitative, scenic effects, and some ensemble writing. The influence of Gluck's *Alceste* is felt in hieratic scenes, particularly the speech for the High Priest and the utterance of the oracle, but also in the prevailing seriousness. Mozart had witnessed the synthesis of French forms and Italian music in Piccinni's *Roland*, the effect of which, and perhaps of Jommelli, was to encourage what Gluck tended to repress: highly developed aria forms with the bloom of italianate lyricism.

The tenor Anton Raaff (Idomeneus) may have been instrumental in obtaining the commission for Mozart, and other singers, as well as the orchestra, were known to Mozart from Mannheim. He was therefore able to start work before leaving Salzburg on 5 November. His completion of the work in Munich is documented in letters home; his father, besides supplying trumpet mutes, had to act as intermediary between composer and librettist. Mozart is constantly concerned with theatrical effect and timing. The libretto required severe pruning: the oracle must have fewer words; the recitatives were too long; there were too many arias (at the last minute, two were dropped from the third act).

Mozart also reported the singers' reactions, and the elector's approval of the music in rehearsal. The first performance, attended by Leopold Mozart, was well received. The designs were by Lorenzo Quaglio and the ballet-master was Le Grand, who in the absence of the librettist may have acted as director. Raaff, already 66, was tactfully nursed by the composer; his music contrives to be brilliant and expressive without placing exceptional demands on breath-control. The Wendling sisters-in-law, Dorothea (Ilia) and Elisabeth, were capable and experienced; Elisabeth, the younger, must have been a formidable singer to have inspired Electra's music. Unfortunately Idamantes (Vincenzo dal Prato) was relatively inexperienced; Mozart had to teach him his part 'as if he were a child'; and Domenico de Panzacchi insisted on the unnecessary development (with two arias) of the confidant Arbaces.

There were three performances in 1781. In September of that year Mozart wrote to his father from Vienna that he would like to revise *Idomeneo* 'more in the French style', but with a German text (by J. B. von Alxinger, who had translated Gluck's *Iphigénie en Tauride*). Idomeneus must be a bass (Ludwig Fischer). Various numbers were included in concerts in his first year in Vienna, as if sowing seeds for a new production; but the only other performance in Mozart's lifetime, at Prince Auersperg's palace in Vienna, was probably a concert performance, given by amateurs. The chief alteration actually made was to recast Idamantes as a tenor. Mozart added two new numbers, rewrote the ensembles involving Idamantes, produced a simplified version of Idomeneus's showpiece ('Fuor del mar'), and made further cuts including Arbaces's arias and a good deal of recitative: so much, indeed, as at times to endanger intelligibility.

Idomeneo was not performed again until the 19th century, when various translations appeared in the repertory of German companies. The first of these was in Kassel (1802), followed by Vienna and Berlin (1806). The music was occasionally employed in 19th-century *pasticcios*, but there were few recognizable performances outside Austria and Germany until the 20th century, the first in Paris (in concert form) being in 1902, in Britain (Glasgow) 1934, in Italy and the USA 1947. The 150th anniversary (1931) was mostly recognized by productions in German, still more or less 'arranged', notably Richard Strauss's version for Vienna (published in vocal score). In the last 30 years most major companies have produced *Idomeneo*, but as an opera in need of perpetual revival rather than a repertory item.

The Trojan war is over; the legendary misfortunes of the returning Greek chieftain Idomeneus closely parallel the biblical story of Jephtha. Ilia and other Trojan captives have been sent to Crete ahead of him. Electra is there, following the murder of Agamemnon by her mother. Both have fallen in love with Idamantes.

The overture, in D major, is a boldly truncated sonata movement of majesty and suffering. It ends with a controlled dissonant diminuendo making repeated use of a significant motif first heard in the ninth bar, which occurs throughout the opera and has been identified as a 'Sacrifice' or 'Idamantes' motif. The minor-mode plagal cadence prefigures the tonality of the first aria and allows Ilia to sing without further introduction.

ACT 1 *Ilia's apartment in the palace* Ilia bewails her fate: orphaned, a prisoner, in love with her captor's son and certain that he must prefer his compatriot Electra to a foreign slave. She explores her dilemma in a subdued lament in G minor, its moderate tempo as characteristic of her as an *allegro* is of Electra (recitative and aria, 'Padre, germani, addio!'). This introduces the standard aria design of *Idomeneo*, corresponding in key-scheme and thematic design to binary sonata form (*see* MOZART, WOLFGANG AMADEUS). When Ilia considers her own disloyalty to her father, Priam, in loving a Greek, Mozart introduces the 'Idamantes motif' in the cellos.

Idamantes enters with words of comfort and even affection, but she proudly rejects him. In a short, majestic Adagio Idamantes protests that he has committed no

fault, and in a driving Allegro he blames the gods for his suffering ('Non ho colpa'). As evidence of his kindly intentions, he frees the Trojan prisoners (chorus, 'Godiam la pace'). Electra protests at this action and is suspicious of his motives. Arbaces brings news of Idomeneus's shipwreck and Idamantes rushes off. In obbligato recitative, Electra gives vent to her jealousy: with Idomeneus dead, who will prevent his son marrying Ilia? Her D minor aria ('Tutte nel cor vi sento') writhes between fury and self-pity. The daring reprise in C minor not only symbolizes her mental disturbance but anticipates the storm of the next scene: although decorum is restored in that the aria ends in D, the music continues without interruption or change of speed, modulating again to C minor for the next scene.

The sea-shore, strewn with wreckage A distant chorus of sailors echoes the chorus on shore ('Pietà! Numi, pietà'). In pantomime Neptune is seen calming the waters; the king lands and dismisses his followers. He can think only of the impending sacrifice, for the price of his escape is that Neptune must be offered the first person he meets; he imagines himself haunted by the innocent victim ('Vedrommi intorno'). The 'Idamantes motif' reappears in the Andantino, as do images of the storm in the Allegro. The victim appears: it is Idamantes searching for his father. At his ecstatic recognition simple recitative explodes into orchestral figures. But Idomeneus breaks away and leaves Idamantes a prey to fear and longing; the atmosphere of the storm again affects Idamantes' aria ('Il padre adorato'). The Cretan soldiers make land and the populace comes to greet them (ballet sequence with choral chaconne, 'Nettuno s'onori').

ACT 2 *A royal apartment* [1786 only: orchestrated dialogue and aria K490. Ilia yields Idamantes to Electra but asks to be remembered. His reply, 'Ch'io mi scordi di te?', and subsequent rondò, 'Non temer, amato bene', with obbligato violin, also provided the text for the later, independent aria K505.]

Idomeneus tells Arbaces everything; he resolves that Idamantes must escape sacrifice by taking Electra back to Argos. Arbaces responds sententiously, in an energetic Allegro ('Se il tuo duol', omitted in 1786). Ilia approaches the king. In Mozart's most tenderly poised melodic vein, and in a warm E♭ major with muted strings and four obbligato winds, she accepts Idomeneus as a second father ('Se il padre perdei'). He now sees that the sacrifice will ruin two lives beyond that of the victim; his recitative underlines his concern by its orchestral use of motifs from her aria. His own aria ('Fuor del mar'), majestic in D major (the opera's tonic), exists in a simplified (1786) version as well as the more flamboyant original destined for Raaff. Freed from the sea, he finds a worse storm in his own heart. In the middle section he asks why a heart so near to shipwreck cannot find it; Mozart risked a heartstopping enharmonic modulation before the full reprise. Electra is transformed by the thought of Idamantes escorting her home; her aria is a serene invocation of love ('Idol mio, se ritroso'), accompanied by strings only, and utterly unlike the remainder of her role. A distant march, beginning with muted brass, grows to *fortissimo* to mark the change of scene.

The port of Kydonia Electra and the chorus welcome the propitious calm ('Placido è il mar, andiamo'). Idomeneus bids farewell to his sorely perplexed son (trio, 'Pria di partir, o Dio!'). As they are about to

Opening from the first printing (early January 1781) of Mozart's 'Idomeneo' showing part of the Act 2 finale in Italian and German (a further libretto in Italian only was printed before the first performance, incorporating cuts)

=== 76 ===

Tuttti.

a 3. { Deh, cessi il scompiglio;
Del Ciel la Clemenza
Sua man porgerà. (vanno verso le navi.)

Mentre vanno ad imbarcarsi sorge improvisa tempesta. Il Popolo canta il seguente

C O R O.

Qual nuovo terrore!
Qual rauco mugito!
De' Numi il furore
Hà il Mare infierito.
Nettuno, mercè!

Incalza la tempesta, il Mare si gonfia, Il Cielo tuona, e lampeggia, e i frequenti fulmini incendiano le navi. Un Mostro formidabile s'appresenta fuori dell' onde. Il Popolo canta il seguente

C O R O.

Qual odio, qual ira
Nettuno ci mostra!
Se il Cielo s'adira,
Qual colpa è la nostra?
Il Reo qual è?

Idomeneo.

Eccoti in me, barbaro Nume! il reo,
Io solo errai, me sol punisci, e cada
Sopra di me il tuo sdegno. la mia morte
Ti sazi al fin; ma s'altra aver pretendi
Vittima al fallo mio, una innocente
Darti io non posso, e se pur tu la vuoi,
Ingiusto sei, pretenderla non puoi.

La

=== 77 ===

Alle.

O Himmel! reich uns deine Hand
Erhöre unsre Bitte,
Thu unserm Unglück Widerstand
Erzeig uns Gnad und Güte.

(Sie gehen den Schifen zu.)

Während daß sie sich den Schifen nähern, um einzusteigen, erhebet sich unvermuthet ein gewaltiger Sturm. Dann singet das Volk' diesen

Chor.

O welch ein neuer Schrecken!
Der Zorn der Götter will auß neu
Die Wuth des Meers erwecken:
Weh uns, Neptun! ach steh uns bey!
Der Sturm wird immer häftiger, das Meer schwillt auf, es donnert, es blizet, wiederholte Donnerkeile zünden die' Schife an. Ein fürchterliches Ungeheuer steigt aus dem Meere heraus. Das Volk singt folgenden

Chor.

Was will, Neptun! dein Zorn und Wüthen!
Wer raubet uns der Götter Huld?,
Was ist an uns für eine Schuld
Welch sträflicher soll sie vergüten?

Idomeneus.

Sieh da; unbarmherzige Gottheit! an mir den Schuldigen; ich allein habe gesündiget, ich allein muß bestrafet seyn; laß allen deinem Zorn über mich fallen, mein Tod mag dich endlich besänftigen. Aber wenn du ein anders, ein unschuldiges Opfer von mir begehrest; so werde ich dirs nicht geben, und wenn du es mit Gewalt verlangst; so ist deine Foderung höchst ungerecht.

Der

embark, a tempest breaks out (represented in music of barely repressed violence) and a terrible sea-monster appears (storm, with chorus, 'Qual nuovo terrore'): the people demand who has brought this upon them by angering the gods. Without naming Idamantes, Idomeneus publicly confesses (obbligato recitative) that he is the sinner; he has the temerity to accuse the gods of injustice. Terrified at the revelation, the crowd flies in confusion ('Corriamo, fuggiamo').

ACT 3 *The palace garden* In a tender E major aria, Ilia bids the winds bear her message of love to Idamantes ('Zeffiretti lusinghieri'). When he appears she is unable to suppress her feelings, and they declare themselves (duet, 'S'io non moro' – omitted at the première; replaced in 1786 by a shorter duet with some of the same material, including the 'Idamantes motif', 'Spiegarti non poss'io' K489). Idomeneus and Electra find the lovers. The varied emotions of all four are embodied in the harrowingly beautiful harmonic and contrapuntal web of one of Mozart's supreme achievements, the quartet ('Andrò, ramingo e solo'). Ilia's heart is still divided; Electra is full of suppressed jealousy; Idamantes, again banished without learning the reason, is deeply saddened, and Idomeneus wishes the gods would kill him instead. Each has reached the limit of suffering; their voices unite at 'soffrir più non si può'. Idamantes repeats his opening phrase, an emblem of loneliness and misery, and leaves the stage. Arbaces begs the king to help his suffering people and laments the condition of his country in a magnificent obbligato recitative ('Sventurata Sidon!'), usually retained when the role is reduced. His aria ('Se colà ne' fati è scritto', omitted in 1786) is more conventional, a broadly conceived piece accompanied by strings.

A large public place before the palace The high priest confronts the king (recitative, 'Volgi intorno la sguardo, o Sire'): the monster has devoured thousands and laid the country to waste. Only Idomeneus can save them by naming the sacrificial victim. To the longest development of the 'Idamantes motif' he confesses the truth; the Cretans are awed and deeply moved ('O voto tremendo'). The collision of triplet violin quavers with the duple rhythms of the voices, the ominous fanfares of muted brass, and a melancholy chromatic fragment, form a picture of desolation without equal in 18th-century music.

The temple of Neptune, both exterior and interior being visible The king and priests process to the temple (march) and prepare the sacrifice (chorus of priests with Idomeneus, 'Accogli, o rè del mar'). A jubilant cry is heard (fanfare); Idamantes has slain the monster. Idomeneus fears worse will befall them, but Idamantes enters robed for sacrifice. Interrupted only by the first of the arias Mozart planned to omit before the 1781 performances, but may ultimately have included (Idamantes's 'Nò, la morte io non pavento': he has no fear of death but dies willingly), these scenes unfold in orchestrated recitative of unprecedented length and expressiveness. At the moment of sacrifice Ilia enters and offers herself instead; the confusion is ended only when the oracle commands the abdication of Idomeneus in favour of his son, who is to marry Ilia. Electra invokes the Furies (her stupendous rage aria, 'D'Oreste, d'Ajace', was replaced in 1781 by a recitative powerful even by the standards of *Idomeneo*). Idomeneus welcomes his retirement (recitative, 'Popoli! a voi l'ultima legge'). His exquisitely beautiful aria ('Torna la pace al core') was also cut in 1781, but its serene glow perfectly concludes the action. The brisk final chorus ('Scenda

Amor, scenda Imeneo') is followed by an extended ballet (K367).

* * *

Idomeneo is divided from its French model by the spread of Enlightenment. Danchet's libretto includes another love tangle (Idomeneus loves Ilia), and involves Electra closely in the plot (jealous of Ilia, she reveals to the priests Idomeneus's scheme to save Idamantes). It also ends tragically, with Idamantes dead and Idomeneus driven mad by Nemesis. Varesco, undoubtedly influenced by Metastasio, made myth into *opera seria*, an allegory of enlightened monarchy; flawed by his vow, rather than his failure to fulfil it, Idomeneus is unfitted to reign, but the god permits the organic transfer of power to the new generation and the reconciliation of former enmities by dynastic marriage. This restoration of harmony is movingly captured in Idomeneus's final aria (on which see Heartz 1974, 'Raaff's Last Aria') so that Mozart's omission of 'Torna la pace' is particularly regrettable. This theme also reflects the father-son relationship which is considered to have been the source of much creative tension in Mozart.

The letters to his father, and the cuts on which he insisted, demonstrate Mozart's growing theatrical judgment as well as the powers of persuasion he exercised upon the singers. Most remarkable is his willingness at the last moment, following the dress rehearsal, to sacrifice superlative music for a theatrical end. In view of his intended and actual reworkings, it seems safe to say that *Idomeneo* never reached a form with which he would have been completely satisfied. Unfortunately some performances with tenor Idamantes ignore not only the 1786 aria and duet in Act 2 but also Mozart's careful revision of the great Act 3 quartet, whose texture is ruined by simply placing the original line an octave too low.

Even within the repertory of 'reform' opera (Italian, French and German), *Idomeneo* is remarkable for its orchestration. Mozart used clarinets here for the first time in an opera, and four horns, but the music for flutes, oboes, bassoons and trumpets is equally striking, as are the brass mutes in the Act 2 march and the scene where the Cretans learn that the sacrificial victim must be Idamantes. The varied but almost continual use of all the wind instruments creates an unprecedentedly rich palette, although trombones are confined to the oracle's speech (and these may have been omitted in the event: Mozart made four different settings of the oracle's words, one using only woodwind and horns). Most remarkable is the deployment of wind instruments during critical passages of recitative, notably those preceding the two final arias. The strings are treated with equal resourcefulness; for instance the tremolando in the High Priest's recitative, the hammering c''' in 'O voto tremendo', responding to the muted trumpet calls, and the harp-like pizzicato in the invocation of Neptune at the beginning of the last scene.

Instrumental inventiveness is matched by harmonic daring; even the simple recitatives make expressive use of enharmonic progressions and remote tonalities. *Idomeneo* is also notable for its continuity, again beyond what was normal in 'reform' operas. Several numbers have no final cadence but move into the next recitative as if to avoid leaving time for applause; Mozart added such an ending to the simpler version of 'Fuor del mar'. Continuity, expressed in long periods without simple recitative, is particularly apparent towards the ends of the second and third acts and in the middle of the first (from Electra's aria to Idomeneus's landing).

Idomeneo is also the first Mozart opera in which the arrangement of tonalities seems deliberately calculated. Recognition of certain recurring keys is not only assisted by instrumentation but by the use of distinct motifs; the descending arpeggio of the central showpiece for the title-role, 'Fuor del mar', inverts the opening of the overture and recurs in the final chorus, all three numbers being in D major. The same arpeggio is transformed in the final chorus of Act 2 ('Corriamo, fuggiamo') when the crowd reacts to Idomeneus's confession.

The use of significant motifs is more highly developed than in any previous opera. Although it is unlikely that every instance that has been detected (Floros 1964; Cairns 1973; Heartz 1974; Rushton 1991) was intentional, Mozart cannot have overlooked the 'Idamantes motif': from the overture to the sacrifice scene its most clearly identifiable recurrences all relate to the young hero. Nevertheless, most of the opera consists of discrete numbers which reflect Mozart's determination that music should govern the poetry. With this end in view, he did not reject virtuosity, but turned its musical qualities to dramatic ends. Despite detectable influences within it, and from it (for instance in *Don Giovanni* and *La clemenza di Tito*), *Idomeneo* is an opera *sui generis*, occupying a special place in the affections of its composer who went on to other achievements as vital and significant, but never returned to its dignified, heroic, yet thoroughly human world.

See also IDOMENEUS.

JULIAN RUSHTON

Idomeneus. Libretto subject, used several times in the 18th century. Idomeneus was King of Crete during the time of the Trojan War. Beset by a violent storm as he returned to Crete, he vowed to Neptune that if he escaped shipwreck he would sacrifice to the god the first living thing he saw on his safe arrival; that thing turned out to be his own son. Idomeneus carried out his vow; the inhumanity of his deed caused such horror that he was forced to abdicate and leave Crete. This story, whose parallels with the story of Agamemnon and Iphigenia and the biblical stories of Abraham and especially Jephtha are obvious, is unmentioned by Homer. It may not have been associated with Idomeneus until late antiquity, and probably under the influence of other legends. The 4th-century grammarian Servius, in his commentary on Virgil's *Aeneid*, is the author of what is apparently the earliest surviving account.

François de Salignac de la Mothe Fénelon (1651–1715) recounted the story of Idomeneus's tragic vow in his didactic novel *Télémaque* (1696); six years later it became the subject of a spoken tragedy, *Idoménée*, by Prosper Jolyot de Crébillon. In 1712 an opera by the same title was performed in Paris, with a libretto by Antoine Danchet and music by André Campra. Danchet's libretto served as G. B. Varesco's model for the libretto for Mozart's *Idomeneo* (1781); Varesco condensed the action from Danchet's five acts to three and contrived a happy ending. Among other Italian librettos on this subject is the anonymous one set by Galuppi as *Idomeneo* (1756, Rome); Giuseppe Sertor's libretto of the same name was set by Gazzaniga (1790, Padua) and Paer (1794, Florence); and Gaetano

Rossi's version was set by Giuseppe Farinelli (1811, Venice).

See also IDOMENÉE [Campra] and IDOMENEO, RE DI CRETA [Mozart]. For bibliography *see* MOZART, WOLFGANG AMADEUS.   JOHN A. RICE

Ifigenia in Tauride (i) ('Iphigenia in Tauris'). *Opera seria* in three acts by TOMMASO TRAETTA to a libretto by MARCO COLTELLINI; Vienna, Schönbrunn, 4 October 1763.

Predating Gluck's *Alceste* (1767), Traetta's *Ifigenia* was the first full-length *opera seria* performed in Vienna to incorporate French elements. Choruses figure prominently as independent pieces and in combinations with soloists and ensembles, contributing collective commentary. The scene complexes are various, drawing on the options of chorus, dance, obbligato recitative, ensemble, cavatina and aria. The opera has much French-inspired spectacle including a storm and a ghost scene for chorus with a Dance of the Furies. The dramaturgy is otherwise Italianate. Wind instruments are prominent in obbligato recitatives and arias, intensifying ghostly imaginings, frightful memories, terrifying spectres and dread of future events. The sinfonia in D major foreshadows a happy outcome, but the G minor aria for Pilade [Pylades] (soprano castrato) in the first scene casts a gloomy tone. The tritone relationship between the A major of Iphigenia's ministers and the E♭ major of the soldiers of Toante [Thoas] (tenor) announcing Pylades' death immediately identifies the opposing forces. Flat keys, particularly E♭, persist, and the first two acts conclude in C major. Iphigenia sings in A major as she kills the tyrant Thoas, preparing for a resolution at last in the key of D.

Traetta's most successful serious opera, *Ifigenia* was performed three times in Florence (1767 under Gluck, 1776 and 1782), twice in Mantua (1768 and 1777), once in Milan (1768) and finally at Eszterháza under Haydn's direction (1786).

See also IPHIGENIA IN TAURIS.   MARITA P. McCLYMONDS

Ifigenia in Tauride (ii) ('Iphigenia in Tauris'). *Opera seria* in three acts by GIAN FRANCESCO DE MAJO to a libretto by MATTIA VERAZI; Mannheim, Hoftheater, 5 November 1764.

Verazi's libretto, which differs markedly from Coltellini's for Traetta, overburdens the ancient story with massive scenes of lavish spectacle. A storm, shipwreck, landing and battle on the shores of Tauris, where Iphigenia (soprano) is high priestess, are mimed during the sinfonia (an opening that Guillard later adopted for Gluck's *Iphigénie en Tauride*, 1779, Paris). Merodate [Merodates] (tenor), the king of Sarati, arrives amid a magnificent procession of sumptuous gifts, slaves and wild animals to press his suit with the Princess Tomiri (soprano). Terrifying wild beasts threaten Oreste [Orestes] (soprano castrato) in a gladiatorial amphitheatre; later he endures elaborate preparations for sacrifice, Merodates storms the gates of the city, and the tyrant Toante [Thoas] (bass) dies amid flames and destruction (as did Metastasio's Dido). The opera is one of the earliest to cast the principal male role, Thoas, for a bass singer (G. B. Zonca).

Majo's opera, one of a number of extravagant, spectacular works performed at Mannheim in the early 1760s, challenged not only the theatrical architect and machinist but also the roots of Metastasian opera. The two duets for Pilade [Pylades] and Orestes, one with an interjection from Iphigenia, would remain anomalies for another 25 years. Also totally foreign to the conventions of *opera seria* are the expansive scene complexes of arias and choruses without the customary exits, and the many ensembles (two duets, two trios and a quartet). In both the trios one or two of the participants exit before the end of the number, and all the ensembles are infused with action, a feature more common in a comic opera finale. Majo rose to the dramatic challenge by writing through-composed arias and ensembles as well as elaborate antiphonal choruses to enhance the dynamic nature of the texts. The sinfonia, the battle music and the many obbligato recitatives have dramatic intensity and the requisite programmatic effects.

See also IPHIGENIA IN TAURIS.   MARITA P. McCLYMONDS

Ifigenia in Tauride (iii) ('Iphigenia in Tauris'). *Opera seria* in three acts by NICCOLÒ JOMMELLI to a libretto by MATTIA VERAZI; Naples, S Carlo, 30 May 1771.

Verazi's original libretto, set by Majo (1764, Mannheim), contained several innovations. Besides the programmatic sinfonia, Verazi had provided at least one choral scene in each act as well as a quartet, two duets (one with an interjection by a third character) and two trios. The opera closes, like Metastasio's *Didone abbandonata*, in flames and ruins. Jommelli admired this libretto and asked Verazi to revise it for production in Naples. The result was an 'aria' opera; all of the ensembles and choruses were eliminated. Iphigenia's 'ghost' scene and aria were moved to the end of Act 1, and a new duet for Oreste [Orestes] (soprano castrato) and Iphigenia (soprano) concluded Act 2. The programmatic sinfonia and the extraordinary ending were retained.

Verazi's final revisions of *Ifigenia* could not have reached Naples before late April. Jommelli had only one month to compose and rehearse the work. Considering the lavish chromatic harmonies, the rhythmic and textural complexity of the orchestration, and the elaborately embellished and technically difficult singing roles it was too little time. The opening night was a disaster. Arcangelo Cortoni (Toante [Thoas], tenor) and Anna Lucia De Amicis (Iphigenia) had sung in Jommelli's *Armida abbandonata* the previous year, but the primo uomo, Gaspare Pacchierotti, was still inexperienced and unable to carry the demanding role of Orestes. Nor was the orchestra able to contend with Jommelli's unfamiliar and unusually demanding musical style. As a result, further performances were cancelled, and *Armida* was revived instead. Despite its initial lack of success, *Ifigenia* enjoyed a vogue in fashionable salons, and a production was mounted at Salvaterra for the Portuguese court during Carnival 1776.

See also IPHIGENIA IN TAURIS.   MARITA P. McCLYMONDS

Igrok. Opera by Sergey Prokofiev; *see* GAMBLER, THE.

Igroki. Opera by Dmitry Shostakovich; *see* GAMBLERS, THE.

Ikonomov, Boyan Georgiev (*b* Nikopol, 14 Dec 1900; *d* Sofia, 27 March 1973). Bulgarian composer and conductor. He studied in Sofia (1920–26) and later in Paris with d'Indy and Guy de Lioncourt at the Schola Cantorum, and with Boulanger and Roussel; he also took a conducting course with Weingartner in Basle in

1934. In 1937 he returned to Bulgaria where he held various appointments, working with the Bulgarian Film Institute (1948–56) and Sofia Radio (head of the music department, 1957–60). During his stay in Paris, Ikonomov had fruitful contacts with Stravinsky, Honegger and Milhaud. Predominantly a composer of instrumental music, he nevertheless wrote several works for the stage, including a historical opera in 1960 in the mainstream Bulgarian tradition (*Indzhe voyvoda* [Indzhe the Resistance Fighter], prol., 5 scenes, 1969, Stara Zagora) and a children's operetta *Malkite hitreci* ('The Cunning Little Boys', 1960). He also wrote film music, a ballet and two dance dramas. MAGDALENA MANOLOVA

Ile de Merlin, L' [*L'île de Merlin, ou Le monde renversé* ('Merlin's Island, or The World Upside-down')]. *Opéra comique* in one act by CHRISTOPH WILLIBALD GLUCK to a libretto based on the *opéra comique Le monde renversé* (1718) by Alain René Le Sage and d'Orneval (on a plan by JOSEPH DE LA FONT), as revised by LOUIS ANSEAUME (1753); Vienna, Schönbrunn Schlosstheater, 3 October 1758.

The second of Gluck's French *opéras comiques* for Vienna, *L'île de Merlin* is an episodic piece, in which Pierrot (bass) and Scapin (baritone), visitors to their master Merlin's realm, comment satirically on the inhabitants, most of whom are inversions of types found in Paris. There is a musical philosopher (tenor); an honest lawyer, M. de La Candeur (tenor); a woman doctor, Hippocratine (soprano); a 'reasonable' *petit-maître*, the Chevalier de Catonville (tenor); and a notary, M. Prud'homme (bass). The plot proper concerns the visitors' courtship of Merlin's remarkably uncoquettish nieces Argentine and Diamantine (both sopranos); the matches are contested by Hanif (tenor) and Zerbin (who only sings vaudevilles), but Merlin intervenes on behalf of his valets.

Gluck later reused the descriptive overture, with changes, as the storm which opens *Iphigénie en Tauride*. His 24 *airs nouveaux* replaced some pieces in Anseaume's 1753 all-vaudeville version of what had originally been a work in vaudevilles and prose. Several former vaudevilles he combined into impressive ensembles governed by sonata procedure. As in his other *opéras comiques*, Gluck draws on both French and Italian musical styles as well as dance rhythms of his native Bohemia. BRUCE ALAN BROWN

Iliev, Konstantin (*b* Sofia, 9 March 1924; *d* Sofia, 6 March 1988). Bulgarian composer and conductor. In 1946 he graduated from the Sofia State Academy of Music, where he studied composition with Vladigerov and conducting with Goleminov. He later studied composition with Jaroslav Řídký and Alois Hába at the Prague Conservatory, as well as conducting with Dedecek and Talich. Until 1952 he was Chief Artistic Director of the Ruse SO and State Opera. From 1952 to 1956 he conducted the Varna State SO and from 1956 to 1972 the Sofia PO. In 1970 he was appointed professor of conducting at the Bulgarian State Conservatory. Together with Lazar Nikolov, Iliev added new dimensions to Bulgarian music in the 1950s and 60s, building on the foundation laid by Pipkov. Having renounced Romantic pathos, they embraced the rational-constructive aesthetics of free tonal thinking and 12-note and aleatory techniques. Iliev wrote two operas, *Boyanskyat maïstor* ('Boyana's Master' op.196,

4, M. Hadjimishev, after S. Zagorchinov; Sofia, National Opera, 3 Oct 1962), and *Elenovo zarstvo* ('The Kingdom of the Deer', Iliev; Ruse, 1976). MAGDALENA MANOLOVA

Illica, Luigi (*b* Castell'Arquato, nr Piacenza, 9 May 1857; *d* Colombarone, 16 Dec 1919). Italian librettist. At an early age he ran away to sea; in 1876 he fought against the Turks. Three years later he settled in Milan and became well known in literary circles. An ardent republican, he was associated with the poet Giosuè Carducci on a radical literary review. In 1882 he produced a collection of prose sketches, *Farfalle, effetti di luce*, and the following year wrote his first play, *I Narbonnier-Latour*, in collaboration with Ferdinando Fontana. His greatest success in this field was a comedy in Milanese dialect, *L'eriditàa di Felis* (1891).

Illica's activity as a librettist began in 1889 with the crudely melodramatic *Il vassallo di Szigeth* written for Smareglia. The association with Puccini began in 1892, when Leoncavallo suggested that Illica complete the much tormented libretto of *Manon Lescaut*. As much of Domenico Oliva's work remained in the final text, including the entire fourth act, Illica tactfully withheld his name from the title-page, and the libretto was published without an attribution. In Puccini's next three operas – *La bohème*, *Tosca* and *Madama Butterfly* – Illica worked in partnership with the playwright Giacosa, who versified the dialogue that his colleague had drafted out. When Giacosa died in 1906 Puccini turned to other librettists, though he continued to keep Illica employed on the book of a *Maria Antonietta* which he never set; his failure to do so led to a permanent breach between them.

Illica's 35 librettos run the gamut of contemporary fashions, from near-*verismo* to historical drama, from *art nouveau* symbolism to evocations of the *commedia dell'arte*, and range as far afield as an adaptation of Thomas Hardy's *Tess of the D'Urbevilles*. Though negligible as literature, they show considerable stage sense as well as invention (he was one of the earliest librettists to devise his own plots, as in *Andrea Chénier* and *Siberia*). He was especially skilful with what could be termed the 'dynamic' or 'kinetic' ensemble during which the action moves forward (e.g. the roll-call of the prostitutes in *Manon Lescaut*, the Café Momus scene in *La bohème*, the parade of the People's Representatives in *Andrea Chénier*). Above all he was instrumental in breaking down the rigid system of Italian operatic metres into lines of irregular length, which Giacosa jokingly referred to as 'illicasillabi' but which were eminently suited to the prevailing musical style.

Il vassallo di Szegith (with Francesco Pozza), Smareglia, 1889; *La Wally*, Catalani, 1892; *Cristoforo Colombo*, Alberto Franchetti, 1892; *Manon Lescaut* (with Domenico Oliva), Puccini, 1893; *Cornelius Schütt*, Smareglia, 1893; *La martire*, Samaras, 1894; *Nozze istriane*, Smareglia, 1895; *La bohème* (with G. Giacosa), Puccini, 1896; *Andrea Chénier*, Giordano, 1896; *Iris*, Mascagni, 1898; *Tosca* (with Giacosa), Puccini, 1900; *Anton*, Galleotti, 1900; *Medioevo Latino*, Panizza, 1900
Le maschere (commedia lirica e giocosa), Mascagni, 1901; *Il cuore della fanciulla*, Buongiorno, 1901; *Lorenza*, Mascheroni, 1901; *Germania*, Franchetti, 1902; *Nadeya*, Cesare Rossi, 1903; *Siberia*, Giordano, 1903; *Madama Butterfly* (tragedia giapponese, with Giacosa), Puccini, 1904; *Cassandra*, Gnecchi, 1905; *Tess*, Erlanger, 1906; *Aurora*, Panizza, 1908; *Il principe Zilah*, Alfano, 1909; *Héllera*, Montemezzi, 1909; *La Perugina*, Mascheroni, 1909; *Isabeau* (leggenda drammatica), Mascagni, 1911; *Giova a Pompei* (with E. Romagnoli), Franchetti and Giordano, 1921

G. Adami: *Giulio Ricordi e i suoi musicisti* (Milan and Rome, 1933)
E. Gara, ed.: 'Il carteggio Puccini – Illica – Ricordi', *Carteggi pucciniani* (Milan, 1958)
M. Morini: *Luigi Illica* (Piacenza, 1961)
——: 'Illica e Mascagni nell' esperienza dell' "Iris" ', *Musica d'oggi*, new ser., vi (1963), 58–66   JULIAN BUDDEN

Ilosfalvy, Róbert (*b* Hódmezővársárhely, 18 June 1927). Hungarian tenor. He studied under Andor Lendvai at the Budapest Academy of Music, and made his début at the Budapest Opera in 1954 in the title role of Erkel's *Hunyadi László*. An international career has taken him to San Francisco, New York, Vienna, and all over Germany; at Covent Garden in 1968 he was Des Grieux in Puccini's *Manon Lescaut*. He was a member of the Cologne Opera from 1966 to 1982. A voice of both lyric grace and dramatic power equips him for Tamino, Rodolfo, Dick Johnson (*La fanciulla del West*), Don Alvaro, Manrico, Don José and Walther, which he sang in Florence (1986). His many recordings include the title role in Donizetti's *Roberto Devereux*, the Duke (*Rigoletto*) and Alfredo.   PÉTER P. VÁRNAI

Ilosvay, Maria von (*b* Budapest, 8 May 1917; *d* Hamburg, 16 June 1987). Hungarian mezzo-soprano. She studied in Budapest and Vienna where in 1937 she won first prize in the International Song Competition. She then travelled with the North American Salzburg Company until the outbreak of war, and in 1940 joined the Hamburg Opera. Guest appearances in Vienna confirmed her position as one of the most promising mezzo-sopranos of the day, and her début at Covent Garden as Fricka in *Die Walküre* remained, with Waltraute in *Götterdämmerung*, among the most valued memories of the 1953 *Ring* cycle and its repetitions in following years. Less happily cast were her Venus in *Tannhäuser* and Ulrica in *Un ballo in maschera*. At Bayreuth she was an admired Erda, and at Salzburg she took part in the première of Orff's *Antigonae*. Her voice was of exceptionally beautiful quality, and her aristocratic stage presence distinguished her Fricka from the termagant of more commonplace representations. The record companies were unduly neglectful, but her performance of Gertrud in *Hänsel und Gretel* under Karajan provides enduring evidence of her merit.   J. B. STEANE

Imbrie, Andrew (Welsh) (*b* New York, 6 April 1921). American composer. He studied composition with Roger Sessions (1937–47), and received the BA at Princeton University (1942). After serving in the US Army (1942–6), he continued his studies with Sessions at the University of California at Berkeley (MA 1947). He joined the faculty of Berkeley two years later, and has taught there for over 40 years. He was also appointed chairman of the composition department at the San Francisco Conservatory and visiting professor of composition at Brandeis. As a composer, he has received numerous honours and awards, including two Guggenheim fellowships, the Brandeis University Creative Arts Medal, and election to the National Institute of Arts and Letters. He has written influential analytical and theoretical articles, especially on the music of Sessions and on meter and accent in Beethoven.

Imbrie's work embodies a sophisticated post-tonal idiom, a preoccupation with contrapuntal textures and an abiding fascination with subtle phrasing details and coherent large forms. He has written two operas: the

first, *Three against Christmas*, was renamed *Christmas in Peebles Town* (4 scenes, R. Wincor) and was first performed at Berkeley on 3 December 1964. It presents a comic story, about the banning and eventual rehabilitation of the Christmas holiday, in a serious compositional idiom. His second opera, the three-act *Angle of Repose* (O. Hall, after W. Stegner), is more ambitious. It presents the story of a California historian, Lyman Ward, who is himself writing a historical narrative of the settling of the West in the 1870s by his ancestors. This story, interwoven with that of Lyman's personal tribulations, centres around the historian's grandfather, an engineer who operates a mercury mine, and his grandmother, a literary figure of some renown in the East. Imbrie weaves banjo tunes, work songs, Viennese waltzes and English reels into the fabric of his own atonal idiom, demonstrating an impressive sensitivity to characterization and the opera's historical disjunctions. It was first performed in San Francisco on 6 November 1976.

A. Boucher: 'Christmas in Berkeley', *ON*, xxix/11 (1964–5), 32
R. Commanday: 'Angle of Repose', *ON*, xli/5 (1976–7), 54–6
R. H. Kornick: *Recent American Opera: a Production Guide* (New York, 1991), 152–4   MARTIN BRODY

Imeneo ('Hymen'; 'Hymenaeus'). Opera in three acts by GEORGE FRIDERIC HANDEL to a libretto anonymously adapted from SILVIO STAMPIGLIA's *Imeneo* (1723, Naples); London, Lincoln's Inn Fields, 22 November 1740.

Handel drafted the score of *Imeneo* between 9 and 20 November 1738, while he was working on his oratorio *Saul*. As there was no immediate prospect of an opera season it may have been his intention to have something ready to use for celebrating the wedding of the Princess Mary, whose betrothal was then rumoured. The opera was never used for this purpose, however, and was not finished for performance until 10 October 1740, when for the last time Handel attempted to arrange an opera season, at Lincoln's Inn Fields. He had already used some of the music from the draft score in the pasticcio *Giove in Argo* and his op.6 concertos. The libretto, written as a two-part *componimento dramatico* for a ducal marriage in 1723, was originally set by Porpora and performed by a cast including two singers who later worked for Handel (Antonia Merighi and Annibale Pio Fabbri) as well as the 18-year-old Farinelli. It elaborates the traditional myth relating how Hymen, a youth of Athens, became the god of marriage by rescuing his beloved from a ship captured by pirates and living with her in wedded bliss. In Handel's production Imeneo [Hymen or Hymenaeus] was sung by William Savage, his beloved Rosmene by Elisabeth Duparc ('La Francesina'), her betrothed lover Tirinto [Tirinthus] by the castrato Giovanni Andreoni, her friend Clomiri [Clomiris] by Miss Edwards and the Athenian senator Argenio [Argenius], father of Clomiris, by Henry Reinhold. After the first performance Francesina became ill, and *Imeneo* was given only once more, on 13 December. Handel did however prepare a concert version for his Dublin season and performed it there on 24 and 31 March 1742, probably with Susannah Cibber as Tirinthus and Christina Avoglio as Rosmene. There were no further revivals until the production of an arrangement by Waltraud Lewin and K. Hübenthal at Halle on 13 March 1960. The first British revival, in a version by Sir Anthony Lewis, was at the Barber Institute, University of Birmingham, on 23 March 1961. The Handel Opera Society gave the first revival of Handel's own version of 1740 on 31 October 1984 at Sadler's Wells Theatre, London.

Rosmene (soprano) and Clomiris (soprano), sent to take part in the Eleusian rites in honour of Ceres, have failed to return to Athens. Hymen (bass or baritone) arrives and relates that, disguised as a girl, he travelled with the Athenian maidens to witness the Eleusian mysteries; when the ship was captured he slew the pirates single-handed and brought the ship home, rescuing Rosmene and Clomiris; in reward, he claims Rosmene's hand. Argenius (bass) supports him, but Tirinthus (mezzo-soprano), Rosmene's betrothed, is distraught. Hymen reminds Rosmene what she owes to him, upsetting Clomiris, who has fallen in love with him. Rosmene's attempt to reassure the jealous Tirinthus is mixed with a non-commital response to Hymen. Clomiris drops hints to Hymen about one who loves him but gets nowhere and leaves Hymen confidently expecting his reward. In Act 2 Rosmene finds herself torn by the conflicting demands of her promise to Tirinthus and her gratitude to Hymen; Argenius makes it plain that Athens expects her to choose gratitude. The distress of both Tirinthus and Clomiris increases. At the start of Act 3 Hymen and Tirinthus insist that Rosmene make her choice; she does so as if in a delirium. She describes a journey to the underworld, where she is brought before the judge Rhadamanthus; his sword divides her heart and releases her soul; to whom does it fly? Emerging from the trance, Rosmene gives the answer: Hymen. The Athenians comment that the heart should always yield to the dictates of reason.

* * *

Though modest in scope, *Imeneo* is one of Handel's most delightful dramatic works. All the music is of high quality and the characters are brought sharply to life. The agonies of Tirinthus emerge in a series of passionate and often profound arias, nicely contrasting with the lively and matter-of-fact style of Hymen's music. Rosmene's progression from doubt to calm resolution is movingly depicted, her final accompanied recitative and the exquisite little arioso in which she confirms her decision ('Al voler di tua fortuna') being a perfect climax. There is also a touching portrait of the hapless Clomiris, whose 'V'è un infelice' in Act 1 is perhaps the most delectable of Handel's songs in minuet style. Argenius has two sturdy arias, the first ('Di cieca notte', erroneously allocated to Hymen in Chrysander's Händel-Gesellschaft edition) with a meandering chromatic line anticipating 'The people that walked in darkness' in *Messiah*. A fine trio brings Rosmene and her two suitors together near the end of Act 2, and each act is concluded by a chorus.

For the Dublin version of 1742 Handel changed Hymen to a tenor role (as in his first draft), added two arias adapted from *Deidamia* to Tirinthus's part and cut most of Clomiris's music. These changes were hardly improvements, but the Dublin version has the attraction of two additional duets for Rosmene and Tirinthus, one from *Faramondo* (Act 1) and one from *Sosarme* (Act 3) – except that the heartbreaking beauty of the latter, 'Per le porte', as a farewell for Tirinthus and Rosmene, upsets the deliberately cool conclusion of Stampiglia's and Handel's original conception. Handel's alterations to *Imeneo* over a period of four years left both the autograph and the conducting score in confusion, which Chrysander's edition reflects all too well by mixing fragments of Handel's first draft with sections of his London and Dublin versions. Lewis's edition (London, 1980) unfortunately follows a similar policy, though in a more orderly fashion; any new edition should probably reflect the 1740 text, with the option of adding the Dublin duets.   ANTHONY HICKS

Imer, Teresa. *See* CORNELYS, THERESA.

Immortal Hour, The. Music drama in two acts by RUTLAND BOUGHTON to a libretto after Fiona Macleod's play and poems; Glastonbury, Assembly Rooms, 26 August 1914.

Three characters are wandering in a forest: Dalua, Lord of Shadow (baritone), outcast of gods and men, whose touch brings madness and death; Etain, a fairy princess from the land of youth (soprano) who does not remember her origin; and Eochaidh, the king (baritone), who is searching for the Immortal Hour, beauty and love such as the world cannot provide. Dalua tells Etain that in her the king will have found his desire, and as she goes on her way Eochaidh approaches, to be led further into the forest by Dalua. In scene ii the king meets and falls in love with Etain, sheltering from a storm in a peasant hut, but distant voices singing the 'Faery Song' call to her as the curtain falls.

In Act 2 Eochaidh celebrates his year of joy with Etain in a Druid feast, but both are weary and troubled with forebodings and she retires. A stranger enters and asks if he may touch the queen's hand. It is Midir (tenor), her rightful lord, whom, on re-entering, she does not recognize but who sings the 'Faery Song' to her, reclaiming her for the land of heart's desire. She follows him in a trance. Eochaidh, left alone, is struck dead by Dalua, his wish that his joy might suffer no twilight having thus been granted.

Despite obvious similarities not just to Wagner but to *Pelléas et Mélisande*, *The Immortal Hour* is less an essay in the symbolist aesthetic than a folk parable of Celtic setting and universal appeal in its poignant depiction of love's inevitable ending in loss. Boughton's music stays close to the ground, its Wagnerian continuity and thematic premises largely modified by a simple modal style which makes few demands on either performers or listeners yet conveys the dramatic essence perfectly well. There is a substantial role for the chorus. One can hardly begrudge the work its formidable success in the 1920s.   STEPHEN BANFIELD

Importance of Being Earnest, The [*L'importanza di esser Franco*]. Comic opera in three acts by MARIO CASTELNUOVO-TEDESCO to his own libretto after OSCAR WILDE's play; New York, La Guardia Theatre, 22 February 1975 (in Italian, Florence, Chiostro delle Donne, 1984).

Set in Victorian London, this comedy of manners concerns two friends, Algernon Moncrieff (tenor) and John Worthing (tenor), who are in love with two young girls, Gwendolen Fairfax (soprano) and Cecily Cardew (soprano). Gwendolen's mother, Lady Bracknell (contralto), cannot agree to John (nicknamed Jack) marrying her daughter until he can satisfactorily substantiate his eligibility as to age, money, education and, most importantly, parentage; he was found as a baby in a handbag at Victoria Station and then adopted by Lord Worthing. To further complicate matters, John Worthing assumes the names of 'Ernest in town and Jack in the country [where he lives]', while Algernon, who lives in town, 'invents' a permanent invalid named Bunberry whom he uses as an excuse to absent himself from the city to visit Cecily, John Worthing's ward.

Eventually, during a visit from the Rev. Canon Chasuble (bass), Cecily's governess, Miss Prism (mezzo-soprano), attests to the fact that the baby discovered in the handbag (Jack) is the son of Lady Bracknell's sister. This establishes his parentage and eligibility for Gwendolen's hand while his persistence proves the importance of being earnest.

The opera is scored for eight singers, two pianos and percussion, the libretto based entirely on Wilde's text (a metrical version in Italian was later created by the composer). Wilde's sophisticated humour is matched by Castelnuovo-Tedesco's musical humour in quoting melodies from more than 50 compositions by almost as many composers: in addition to obvious opportunities indicated in the text, such as Algernon's piano-playing at the opening (Chopin's Nocturne in F♯ major) and Lady Bracknell's 'Wagnerian ring' on the doorbell ('The Ride of the Valkyries'), a Bach chorale, 'Wachet auf', is heard in the accompaniment each time Canon Chasuble enters. In spite of his heavy cutting of the original play the opera suffers from being rather too long for the type of musical humour and substance involved.   NICK ROSSI

Impresario (Ger. *Schauspieldirektor*). A manager, originally Italian, of an opera season; later applied to an agent, often based in the USA or Britain, who arranged tours and other engagements for musicians or theatre or opera companies.

'Impresario' in Italian derives from 'impresa', 'enterprise', and basically means 'entrepreneur', though the existence of a related word, 'imprenditore' (often applied to building contractors), has tended to restrict its meaning. In the early 17th century, when opera began, an impresario was a person who undertook to provide a service and kept part or all of the proceeds; he generally was granted the right to do this by way of a concession ('appalto') from a magnate or an institution. An impresario, for instance, could take on the collection of certain taxes (e.g. on salt, a state monopoly) for a term of years in exchange for paying the state a fixed sum. His function as concessionaire of an opera season originated in Venice, where the first public opera houses belonged to noble families who did not as a rule wish to run seasons themselves, partly for reasons of dignity but mostly because direct management by nobles was reckoned to bring high expenditure: nobles were expected to be lavish. The system rapidly spread to other Italian towns and to many parts of Europe (with France the notable exception); in 18th-century Germany in particular Italian impresarios were active.

The usual arrangement was for the impresario to contract for one or more seasons, undertaking to provide a specific number and kind of operas; there were often highly detailed conditions specifying the standard of singers, costumes, scenery etc. and the composers to be used. The impresario paid rent (up until the late 18th century, and in Rome later still); he could as a rule dispose of only part of the auditorium, as many of the boxes were private property and not in the control of the theatre owner. In exchange the impresario was given the use of stock scenery and, often, an endowment ('dote') provided by the theatre owner or the box holders or the government (or a combination of those), in the form of boxes for him to dispose of, or a gambling concession attached to the theatre, or – increasingly

from the late 18th century – in cash. The impresario was thus a semi-dependent intermediary rather than a purely risk-taking entrepreneur, though there was an element of risk and some impresarios failed.

Impresarios, many of them from the theatrical or allied professions, were as a rule men (very occasionally women) of few or no resources and little reputation, though a few in the first half of the 19th century, notably Domenico Barbaia, Alessandro Lanari and Bartolomeo Merelli, made a considerable mark. Some impresarios also acted as agents, nurturing and exploiting artists, singers and dancers in particular. This aspect of their work was central to the careers of some late 19th-century and 20th-century agents, known as impresarios, who operated especially in the USA and a few of whom, for instance Maurice Grau and Maurice Strakosch, also ran opera seasons.

See also SOCIOLOGY OF OPERA.

ES (R. Celletti)
G. Valle: *Cenni teorico-pratici sulle aziende teatrali* (Milan, 1823)
E. Rosmini: *La legislazione e la giurisprudenza dei teatri* (Milan, 1873)
G. Monaldi: *Impresari celebri del secolo XIX* (Rocca S Casciano, 1918)
B. Brunelli: 'L'impresario in angustie', *Rivista italiana del dramma*, v (1941), 311–41
B. Cagli: 'Verdi and the Business of Writing Operas', *The Verdi Companion*, ed. W. Weaver and M. Chusid (London, 1980), 106–20
J. Rosselli: *The Opera Industry in Italy from Cimarosa to Verdi: the Role of the Impresario* (Cambridge, 1984)   JOHN ROSSELLI

Impresario, The. Opera by W. A. Mozart; *see* SCHAUSPIELDIREKTOR, DER.

Impresario delle Canarie, L' ('The Impresario from the Canary Islands'). Libretto by PIETRO METASTASIO, first set by Domenico Sarro (1724, Naples). Versions of the libretto also appear under the titles *Dorina e Nibbio*, *L'impresario*, *L'impresario dell'isole Canarie* and *L'impresario e la cantante*.

PART 1 Dorina, a prima donna, is impatient with her attendants because she cannot find a 'modern' piece, with embellishments on every word, to sing at an embassy function. Nibbio, the impresario from the Canary Islands, calls on Dorina, reassures her that texts are unimportant in opera, and coaxes her to sing for him. Enraptured, he presents her with a cantata of his own, the airing of which occupies the remainder of the interview until Dorina contrives an escape.

PART 2 Dorina is upbraiding the wardrobe assistants when she is again visited by Nibbio to whom she explains the miseries of pleasing an audience; she is also concerned that, in having to show extreme emotion on stage, she may damage her voice. She obliges Nibbio with an excerpt from *Cleopatra*, and his surprise at finding a scene with no exit aria and no reference to 'butterflies' or 'ships', leads him to demonstrate an example from one of his own works. Dorina, unimpressed, lists her conditions for a contract: she must always have leading roles, librettos written by friends and, in addition to her fee, ice cream, coffee, chocolate etc. on demand, and at least two presents weekly. Nibbio's ready acceptance of these demands prompts Dorina to suspect infatuation; this she dismisses, suggesting that negotiations be resumed some other time.

*   *   *

This two-part intermezzo, Metastasio's only attempt at comedy, was written to be performed between the acts of *Didone abbandonata*. The satirical content echoes Benedetto Marcello's *Il teatro alla moda*, published no more than four years previously, and identifies practices with which Metastasio had to contend. Although clearly aware of the foibles of contemporary serious opera and its performance at this the outset of his career, Metastasio was to achieve certain reforms while working from within the genre itself, not as an overt antagonist. His letters reveal lifelong complaints about the mistreatment of his librettos by composers, singers and theatre directors. There appear to be six settings of *L'impresario delle Canarie*, all written between 1724 and 1744, the most popular being Leo's (1741). As this was one of four written for Venice, it seems that the text enjoyed a certain popularity there, possibly because it had particular relevance to that same Venetian opera at which Marcello's satire had been aimed. Padre Martini's setting (1744) was one of four comic intermezzos that he wrote for Bologna, presumably for private performance.

For a list of settings *see* METASTASIO, PIETRO.   DON NEVILLE

Impresario in angustie, L' ('The Impresario in Distress'). *Farsa per musica* in one act by DOMENICO CIMAROSA to a libretto by GIUSEPPE MARIA DIODATI; Naples, Teatro Nuovo, 1786.

In a theatre near Naples, three sopranos, a librettist (Don Perizonio Fattapane, bass), a composer (Gelindo Scagliozzi, tenor), and an impresario (Don Crisobolo, bass) await the production of a new opera. As the text and music are in the process of being written, the singers (the *prima buffa* Fiordispina, the 'prima donna giocosa' Merlina and the 'prima donna seria' Doralba) request roles and music especially suited to each of them, as well as placing demands on the frustrated impresario. Fiordispina, who is wooed by both the poet and the impresario, is not happy with the impresario's choice of composer, since his music previously resulted in a fiasco for her. Merlina, on the other hand, is capitalizing on the composer's amorous feelings towards her. To everyone's general dismay, the opera is not produced because of the impresario's bankruptcy.

While devoid of dramatic action, this short comic entertainment provides an insight into the behind-the-scenes preparation of an 18th-century opera. It pokes fun at the vanity of singers whose only goal is to be popular with the audience, the ignorance of librettists (Don Perizonio is depicted as an uncultured and somewhat crude Neapolitan speaking his native dialect) and the dishonesty of impresarios.

At its original Neapolitan performance this *farsa* featured seven characters and contained a total of eight musical numbers (the opening quartet, a duet, four arias, a quintet and a duet which ends the work). Goethe, who heard the work in Rome in 1787 as a five-voice intermezzo for male voices, was impressed with its naturalness and the overall spirit of the interpretation by castratos dressed in women's clothing. In his diary he commented on the hilarity of the quintet in which the poet, who is reading his libretto, is praised by the impresario and the prima donna, while simultaneously being criticized by the composer and Merlina, the whole resulting in a clamorous ensemble.

When Goethe took over the management of the court theatre in Weimar in 1791, he translated *L'impresario in angustie* into German and arranged text and music for local performances as *Die theatralischen Abenteuer*, adding two of his own lieder, 'Die Spröde' and 'Die Bekehrte'. In 1797 he incorporated selections from Mozart's *Der Schauspieldirektor*. Two years later, a third arrangement by Vulpius transformed *Die theatralischen Abenteuer* into a Singspiel which continued to be performed until 1810.

Between 1786 and the end of the century *L'impresario in angustie* was performed as far south as Lisbon and north to Copenhagen, with a cast varying from five to seven, as a one- as well as a two-act opera. The music, however, was reworked with practically each new presentation, the most noteworthy in addition to Goethe's being Haydn's alterations in 1790 in preparation for its Eszterháza performance, which included a substitute aria for Merlina's 'Il meglio mio carattere'.

Cimarosa's music is light and bubbly, with the orchestra (horns, oboes and strings) providing a transparent texture which for the most part functions as accompaniment to the voice. Humorous characterization is particularly evident in Crisobolo's *buffo* aria 'Vado, e giro nei palchetti', as well as Merlina's 'Il meglio mio carattere', the simplicity of which characterizes her demands to be cast as an uneducated peasant girl.   GORDANA LAZAREVICH

Im weissen Rössl ('At the White Horse Inn'). Singspiel in three acts by RALPH BENATZKY to a libretto by Hans Müller, with lyrics by Robert Gilbert, after the comedy by Oskar Blumenthal and Gustav Kadelburg; Berlin, Grosses Schauspielhaus, 8 November 1930.

Josepha (soprano), proprietress of the White Horse Inn on the Austrian Lake Wolfgang, is an attractive widow who dismisses the advances of her head waiter, Leopold (tenor), in favour of the wealthy Dr Siedler (tenor buffo). Josepha finally realizes that Siedler's amorous interests lie elsewhere and, helped by intervention from the visiting Emperor Franz Joseph II (spoken), settles for Leopold. The lively song-and-dance numbers in the score include Benatzky's 'Es muss was wunderbares sein', 'Im weissen Rössl am Wolfgangsee' and 'Im Salzkammergut' and two Robert Stolz interpolations, 'Die ganze Welt ist Himmelblau' and 'Mein Liebeslied muss ein Walzer sein'. Bruno Granichstaedten and Robert Gilbert also each composed a number, while further interpolations were added for subsequent productions. The original Berlin cast included Camilla Spira (Josepha), Max Hansen (Leopold) and Paul Hörbiger (Franz Joseph II); in London the cast was led by Lea Seidl, Clifford Mollison and Bernard Clifton.   ANDREW LAMB

Inbal, Eliahu (*b* Jerusalem, 16 Feb 1936). Israeli conductor, of Israeli and British citizenship. After studying the violin at the Jerusalem Conservatory, he took part in Sergiu Celibidache's conducting classes in Siena and studied conducting at the Paris Conservatoire, winning the 1963 Guido Cantelli conducting prize at Novara. In a busy orchestral career he made his opera début with *Elektra* at Bologna in 1969; this was followed by *Don Carlos* at Verona the same year. In Siena (1971) he conducted the first performance since 1803 of Cherubini's *Anacréon* with the original French text (concert performance). Besides his appointment as chief conductor of the Frankfurt RSO (1974), he became chief conductor at the Teatro La Fenice, Venice (1984), where in 1986 he conducted performances on the same day of

Verdi's *Stiffelio* and *Aroldo*, winning praise for the orchestral playing more than for the vocal share. His recordings include Donizetti's *Maria de Rudenz* with La Fenice.   ARTHUR JACOBS, NOËL GOODWIN

Incledon, Charles [Benjamin] (*b* St Keverne, Cornwall, bap. 5 Feb 1763; *d* Worcester, 11 Feb 1826). English tenor. The son of a medical practitioner, he disliked his baptismal name and took the name Charles instead. He was a chorister at Exeter Cathedral under William Jackson, and then joined the navy, where he attracted attention as a singer. In 1784 he made his stage début in Southampton as Alphonso in Arnold's *Castle of Andalusia* and the next year moved to Bath, where he studied with Rauzzini, who helped him get an engagement at Vauxhall Gardens. He sang at Covent Garden (1790–1815) and in spite of limited acting abilities established himself as the leading English tenor. He appeared in many operas and afterpieces by Shield and others. Incledon was popular in Dublin, particularly as Young Meadows in *Love in a Village* and Orpheus in an adaptation of Gluck's *Orfeo ed Euridice*, and sang extensively in the provinces, sometimes in his own one-man show. He toured with success in North America in 1817–18. An accomplished oratorio singer, he was a soloist in the first London performance of *The Creation* (1800). Haydn had heard him in Shield's *The Woodman* (1791) and noted: '[Incledon] has a good voice and quite a good style, but he uses the falsetto to excess. He sang a trill on high C and ran up to G'. Robson (1846) remembered that 'never was so sound, so rich, so powerful, so sweet an English voice as Incledon's'.

BDA; *DNB* (L. M. Middleton); *LS*
A. Pasquin [pseud. of J. Williams]: *The Children of Thespis*, ii (London, 13/1792)
[F. G. Waldron]: *Candid and Impartial Strictures on the Performers* (London, 1795)
J. Roach: *Authentic Memoirs of the Green Room* (London, 1796)
C. H. Wilson: *The Myrtle and Vine* (London, 1802)
'First Lines of Vocal Criticism', *Quarterly Musical Magazine*, i (1818), 78–80
J. Sainsbury, ed.: *Dictionary of Musicians* (London, 2/1825)
W. Robson: *The Old Play-Goer* (London, 1846)
T. J. Walsh: *Opera in Dublin 1705–1797* (Dublin, 1973)
                OLIVE BALDWIN, THELMA WILSON

Incontro improvviso, L' ('The Unexpected Meeting'). *Dramma giocoso* in three acts by JOSEPH HAYDN to a libretto by CARL FRIBERTH after L. H. Dancourt's *opéra comique La rencontre imprévue*; Eszterháza, 29 August 1775.

Ali *Prince of Balsóra, in love with Rezia*		tenor
Rezia *Princess of Persia, favourite of the Sultan*		soprano
Balkis	*Rezia's slaves and confidantes*	soprano
Dardane		soprano
Osmin *Ali's slave*		tenor
A Calender (Dervish) *supervisor of the caravan storehouse*		bass
Three Calenders		basses
Sultan of Egypt		bass
An Officer		tenor

Male and female slaves, janissaries

Setting Cairo

Among the many festive entertainments that took place at Eszterháza during the four-day royal visit of Archduke Ferdinand and Maria Beatrice d'Este, described in detail in the *Pressburger Zeitung*, this 'abduction' opera appealed to the current Austrian fascination with Turkish subjects. An 18th-century *gouache* (in *D-Mth*), frequently reproduced and described as depicting a performance of *L'incontro improvviso* at Eszterháza, must be discounted since it contradicts evidence derived from surviving costume receipts. The two principals, Carl Friberth (Ali) and his wife Maddalena (Rezia), wore costumes trimmed in silver and embroidered with numerous roses; Christian Specht (the Calender) wore grey fustian and a grey beard, accompanied by three calenders dressed in grey linen and black beards; Leopold Dichtler (Osmin) wore red and green fustian; and the six members of the janissary chorus wore costumes made of yellow, red, blue and flesh-coloured linen. Accessories only are listed in the costume receipts for Barbara Dichtler (Balkis), Elisabeth Prandtner (Dardane) and Melchior Griessler (Sultan). Five of these singers – the Friberths, the Dichtlers and Specht – had appeared in Haydn's *L'infedeltà delusa* (1773).

Friberth's libretto represents much more than a translation of Dancourt's French text (set by Gluck; 1764, Vienna). A few roles are cut, including that of Amine, Rezia's third slave, and M. Vertigo, a mad painter. Only a vestige of the 'original genius' of the latter character remains in Ali's Act 3 aria ('Ecco un splendido banchetto'), in which the prince, indulging in extensive text painting, sings in the guise of an artist. In keeping with the Italian tradition, Friberth also constructed longer *buffo* finale texts at the end of the first two acts. The opera was translated into German as *Die unverhoffte Zusammenkunft*, with spoken recitative by Franz Xaver Girzik for the Erdődy Theatre, Pressburg, but no record of any performance there survives. Following Jens Peter Larsen's discovery of the autograph in Leningrad in 1954, the opera was broadcast in Russian by Leningrad Radio (1956) and eventually performed in Moscow (1982). It was staged at the St Pancras Festival in London (1966) in an English translation by Andrew Porter.

ACT 1.i *A storehouse with various kinds of merchandise and food* In a convivial introduction, the Calender and the dervishes who work under him drink wine, smoke tobacco and sing merrily of their life as beggars and deceivers.

1.ii *A public square near the seraglio* Osmin, penniless, is distracted by the Calender begging in the streets. The bare octaves and awkward rhythms of his E minor nonsense chant ('Castagno, castagna') help establish the local colour. He has little trouble in persuading the famished Osmin to become a mendicant dervish.

1.iii *A room in the seraglio* Rezia, informed that her long-lost lover has been sighted in Cairo, shares the good news with Balkis and Dardane. They join together in the beautiful, lyrical trio in E♭ major (Andantino, 3/8), 'Mi sembra un sogno, che diletta'. Accompanied by muted strings and english horns, the spacious musical lines of this expressive trio lend it a timeless quality, anticipating and celebrating the long-awaited reunion.

1.iv *A square* In a solo scene, Ali explains how, betrayed by his brother, he fled to Persia where he fell in love with Princess Rezia. Though betrothed to another, Rezia eloped with Ali, only to be captured by pirates and then separated. Ali, who has been searching for Rezia for two years, laments his fate in the aria 'Deh! se in ciel pietade avete'. Ali watches as Osmin, in the company of the Calender, learns a variant of the familiar chant, 'Castagno, castagna'. The Calender recognizes Ali as the Prince of Balsóra and leaves to fetch him a calender's cloak as Osmin praises the dervish way of life. Balkis greets Ali with news that a certain woman, having observed him through a window in the seraglio, wishes to meet him. But Ali is resolute; amid Osmin's protestations, he simply states that he loves another. Balkis continues to press her case until Ali relents and follows her.

1.v *A room containing a banquet table* A gluttonous Osmin is already enjoying the feast when Ali reluctantly arrives with Balkis. Throughout the tripartite finale, the regularity of the poetic rhyme and incessant eight-syllable lines hamstring the composer, as does the limited stage action centring on an increasingly inebriated Osmin who provokes Ali's ire.

ACT 2.i *A room with a sofa* Ali and Osmin reflect on their good fortune at having been shown such courtesy. Dardane tries to charm Ali in order to test his faithfulness. The slave then praises Ali's resolve in her aria 'Ho promesso oprar destrezza', saying that the god of love has reserved Ali's affection for her mistress. Having been convinced of the prince's fidelity, Rezia herself enters, taking Ali and Osmin by surprise. Friberth and Haydn have been criticized for showing a lack of theatrical timing in failing to provide the lovers with a reunion duet, as Dancourt and Gluck do, at this point in the drama. Instead, Rezia, Balkis and Dardane tell of their unfortunate travels that brought them to Cairo, their long narrative, interrupted by Rezia's comic canzonetta, 'Non piangete, putte care', in which she imitates their pirate abductor, nullifying the tender moment of reunion. The scene ends with Rezia's grand C major aria, 'Or vicina a te, mio cuore' (published separately by Artaria in 1783 and reviewed by Johann Friedrich Reichardt in *Studien für Tonkünstler und Musikfreunde*, 1793). Its large scale and extended coloratura passages, calculated to show Rezia's resolve against the Sultan rather than her tenderness towards Ali, reveal her to be equally faithful and worthy of Ali's love.

2.ii *The Calender's room* Osmin informs the Calender that Ali's recently found lover is none other than Rezia herself. Over a bottle of wine, which the dervish praises in a short canzonetta, Osmin solicits the Calender's help in preparing for the couple's escape.

2.iii *A garden* While final preparations are made for the banquet preceding their departure, Rezia and Ali sing a love duet, 'Son quest'occhi un stral d'Amore'. This profession of love, a lyrical statement in E major, proceeds directly into the finale, thereby creating an even longer stretch of continuous music. The finale's tranquil opening mood is broken by the anxious arrival of Balkis and Dardane, who announce that the Sultan has returned unexpectedly from the hunt. Following Osmin's advice, everyone flees via a secret staircase.

ACT 3.i *The Calender's storehouse at night* News of the Sultan's reward for Rezia's recovery reaches the greedy Calender who, in order to win the bounty, betrays the trust placed in him and leads the Sultan's guards to the hiding place of Rezia and Ali in the storehouse. In a last-ditch effort to escape detection, Ali dis-

guises himself as an eccentric French painter, but he is detected. An officer reads the death warrant for the fugitives and their accomplices. But in a second note which the officer gives to Ali, the Sultan forgives the escapees, summons them to his apartments and promises death to the traitorous Calender.

3.ii *An illuminated hall* The Sultan pardons Rezia and Ali and gives them his blessing. In the closing chorus the Sultan, at the couple's request, pardons the Calender but banishes him from Cairo.

* * *

The opera's themes of chance meeting, thwarted rescue and royal clemency are shared by other 'abduction' operas, including *Die Entführung aus dem Serail*. Common to these operas are exotic elements of the 'Turkish' style: leaping melodies based on reiterated 3rds, grace notes, unusual chromatic touches, harmonically static bass lines and percussive notes. Such stylistic features are most prominent in the Act 3 Turkish march, scored for triangle and tambourine in addition to strings and pairs of oboes and horns. Tambourine, trumpets and drums are also used in the overture and closing chorus, but these were removed when the overture was published by Artaria in a set of six overtures (Vienna, 1782–3).   CARYL CLARK

Incoronazione di Poppea, L' [*Coronatione di Poppea, La*] ('The Coronation of Poppaea'). *Dramma musicale* in a prologue and three acts by CLAUDIO MONTEVERDI and others to a libretto by GIOVANNI FRANCESCO BUSENELLO primarily based on Tacitus's *Annals* (books 13–16) but also Suetonius, *The Twelve Caesars* (book 6); Dio Cassius, *Roman History*, (books 61–2); and pseudo-Seneca, *Octavia*; Venice, Teatro SS Giovanni e Paolo, 1643.

PROLOGUE

La Fortuna [Fortune]	soprano
La Virtù [Virtue]	soprano
Amore [Cupid]	soprano

OPERA

Ottone [Otho] *most noble lord*		mezzo-soprano
Poppea [Poppaea] *most noble lady, mistress of Nero, raised by him to the seat of empire*		soprano
Nerone [Nero] *Roman emperor*		soprano
Ottavia [Octavia] *reigning empress, repudiated by Nero*		soprano
Drusilla *lady of the court, in love with Otho*		soprano
Seneca *philosopher, preceptor to Nero*		bass
Arnalta *aged nurse and confidante of Poppaea*		alto
Nutrice *nurse of the empress Octavia*		alto
Lucano [Lucan] *poet, intimate of Nero, nephew of Seneca*		tenor
Valletto *page of the empress*		soprano
Damigella *lady-in-waiting to the empress*		soprano
Liberto *Captain of the praetorian guard*		tenor
Due soldati pretoriani [two praetorian soldiers]		tenors
Littore [Lictor] *officer of imperial justice*		bass
Pallade [Pallas Athene] *goddess of wisdom*		soprano
Mercurio [Mercury] *the gods' messenger*		bass
Venere [Venus]		soprano

Friends of Seneca, consuls, tribunes, Graces, Cupids

Setting Rome, AD 65

This was Monteverdi's last opera, probably his last work altogether. Although the identity of only one of the original singers, Anna Renzi, in the role of Ottavia, is known for certain, several others can be tentatively identified from the cast of the opera with which *L'incoronazione di Poppea* shared the stage of the Teatro SS Giovanni e Paolo during the 1642–3 season, *La finta savia*, with music by several different composers on a libretto by Giulio Strozzi. These include the soprano Anna di Valerio (possibly as Poppaea), and the castratos Stefano Costa (possibly Nero) and 'Rabocchio' or 'Corbacchio' (possibly the Page). The only documented revival took place in Naples in 1651, for which a libretto was published. Both of the surviving manuscript scores of the work (in *I-Vnm* and *Nc*) can be associated with that revival. Only one, possibly two, of the remaining sources reflect the original Venetian production: a scenario published in 1643 and a manuscript libretto recently discovered at Udine (*I-UDc*). The other libretto sources include five manuscripts (at *I-TVco, Fn, RVI, UDc* and *Vmc*) and one print, published in a collection of Busenello's works (*Le hore ociose*, 1656), which was evidently supervised by the librettist and represents his final – though not necessarily original – version of the text. The differences among the various sources are extensive enough to require historical explanation, and they must be resolved before a definitive performance text can be established. Inconsistencies in the scores, in particular, which clearly post-date Monteverdi's death, have raised questions about the authenticity of the music they contain. It is now generally agreed that some sections were written by other, younger composers such as Sacrati, Benedetto Ferrari and Cavalli. The score has been edited frequently since the beginning of this century, usually in connection with performances: by Hugo Goldschmidt (in *Studien zur Geschichte der italienischen Oper im 17. Jahrhundert*, ii, 1904/R1967), Vincent d'Indy (Paris, 1908), Charles van den Borren (Brussels, 1914), Gian Francesco Malipiero (*Claudio Monteverdi: Tutte le opere*, xiii, 1931), Giacomo Benvenuti (Milan, 1937), Krenek (Vienna, 1937), Ghedini (Milan, 1953), Hans F. Redlich (Kassel, 1958), Walter Goehr (Vienna and London, 1960), Raymond Leppard (London, 1966) and Alan Curtis (London, 1990). Curtis's edition is the first to attempt a scholarly collation and rationalization of the sources. The opera can be said to have entered the operatic mainstream in the early 1960s with performances at, among other places, Aix-en-Provence (1961), Glyndebourne (1962) and La Scala, Milan (1967).

PROLOGUE *In the heavens* Fortune, Virtue and Cupid contest their primacy; in a closing duet, Fortune and Virtue grant the victory to Cupid, who responds that they will have occasion to observe his powers this very day.

ACT 1.i *Outside Poppaea's palace* At daybreak, Otho, returning from abroad, stands outside Poppaea's palace and sings of his love, first in a brief aria ('E pur io torno') that in form (*ABA*) and musical material (circling around the tonic) portrays the idea of returning, then in a longer aria ('Apri un balcon') whose third strophe terminates abruptly and pathetically in recitative as he sees Nero's sleeping soldiers and understands that Nero is inside and that Poppaea has betrayed him.

1.ii Overhearing him, the soldiers awaken, curse the love of Poppaea and Nero, and gossip about the court. Monteverdi increases the naturalism of this scene by overlapping its opening with the end of Otho's monologue.

1.iii Poppaea and Nero come out into the early morning light, where they bid passionate farewell to one another. Monteverdi intensifies the sensuality of their relationship by interlacing their texts where Busenello had given them successively. Musical elaboration of particular keywords, languid chromaticism and aria-like lyricism portray the lovers' pleasure in one another. But by judicious repetition of words and interrupted lines, Monteverdi manages to portray the nature of Poppaea's power over Nero.

1.iv Poppaea talks with Arnalta about her ambitions for the crown, boasting that Cupid will assure her success ('Speranza, tu mi vai … per me guerreggia Amor'), but her old nurse warns against trusting great men, Love or Fortune.

1.v *Rome (?the imperial apartments)* In one of the musical peaks of the opera, the recitative lament 'Disprezzata regina', Octavia bewails her fate: rejected by Nero, she is furious at the danger she faces of losing both husband and kingdom. She firmly dismisses her nurse's advice that she distract herself by taking a lover, and vows to remain steadfast in her sorrow.

1.vi Seneca attempts to console Octavia, urging her to stand firm. The page, remarking on the impotence of Seneca's advice, ridicules him for his pedantry; Octavia leaves to pray in the temple.

1.vii Seneca muses on the pain caused by the trappings of royalty.

1.viii He is joined by Pallas Athene, who, from the heavens, foretells his impending death, promising to warn him again through Mercury. In an unusually florid passage, Seneca expresses his willingness to embrace death whenever it comes.

1.ix Seneca is then joined by Nero, who insists, against his old tutor's advice, that he will do exactly as he wishes: he will send Octavia into exile and crown Poppaea empress. This is one of the most dramatic moments in the opera as the two men, the one mature, thoughtful and moral, the other passionate, headstrong and immature, pit their wits against each other. Monteverdi escalates the conflict by once again interlacing the characters' lines rather than presenting their speeches successively throughout, and he portrays the intensity of the conflict with his characteristic *stile concitato* (or warlike style), consisting of rapid repeated notes and forceful arpeggios. Nero finally dismisses Seneca, but the philosopher has the last word: the worst is to be expected when power wages war against reason.

1.x In a succession of sensual evocations of their pleasure in one another, Poppaea and Nero, overheard by Otho, discuss their happiness; he promises to make her empress and she, manipulating his weakness, insinuates that he is ruled by Seneca, whereupon Nero orders one of his soldiers to carry a death sentence to the philosopher, closing the scene with an echo of Cupid's message in the prologue: today Poppaea will see what Cupid can do.

1.xi In a strophic aria ('Ad altri tocca in sorte') Otho, overheard by Arnalta, reveals to Poppaea his despair at having been replaced in her affections by Nero, and she answers each of his strophes with one of her own, on the same bass, justifying her change of heart as the effect of Fortune's favour. A more intense recitative exchange, which Monteverdi heightens through repetition and intercalation of Otho's and Poppaea's final lines, concludes abruptly with Poppaea's curt dismissal: 'No more, no more. I am Nero's.'

1.xii Left alone, Otho vents his despair and rage against Poppaea in recitative bursts. He even contemplates murdering her.

1.xiii He is overheard by Drusilla, who complains that he is still obsessed by Poppaea. He assures her that he will henceforth cast Poppaea from his mind and heart and think only of *her*, but he expresses himself in a lyrical aria style that seems forced and artificial when compared with the recitative of the previous scene. Although Drusilla is suspicious, she is finally reassured and departs. But Otho, knowing he cannot maintain his vow, confesses that his lips may say Drusilla but that Poppaea is in his heart.

Act 2.i *The garden of Seneca's villa outside Rome* Mercury, sent to earth by Pallas Athene, announces to Seneca that the day of his death has arrived. Seneca rejoices in the news, and Mercury departs on the wings of his highly elaborate, melismatic song.

2.ii Liberto haltingly attempts to inform Seneca of Nero's death sentence, but his information is unnecessary. Seneca assures him that he is ready to die and asks him to inform Nero that he is already dead and buried.

2.iii Seneca gathers the members of his household around him and in a poignant lyrical effusion ('Amici è giunta l'ora') informs them of his decision. They urge him to reconsider in a strikingly expressive madrigal chorus whose first section ('Non morir Seneca') is built on the imitative treatment of an ascending chromatic scale but whose much more cheerful, diatonic second section ('Questa vita è dolce troppo') suggests a certain lack of sympathy with his gesture. He is unaffected by their pleas and orders them to prepare his fatal bath.

[A scene for Seneca and a chorus of Virtues is given here in some of the libretto sources, including Busenello's print of 1656, but it is not set in either of the scores or mentioned in the published scenario of 1643 and thus was probably never set to music.]

2.iv *Rome* Relieving the dramatic intensity generated by Seneca's impending death, and providing the time necessary for the death to take place, the page and lady-in-waiting exchange a series of flirtatious arias. He begins with two strophes in lively duple metre ('Sento un certo non so che'); she responds with a single strophe in compound metre ('Astutello garzoncello'), and they join in a final lascivious duet ('O caro, o cara') featuring short imitative phrases and longer passages of parallel 3rds and 6ths in a style similar to that of the closing duet of the opera (see below).

2.v Nero, having heard of Seneca's death, joins with his friend Lucan in an extended, sensuous duet of continuously overlapping lines in praise of Poppaea's beauty. The second section of the duet, 'Bocca, bocca', is built on a major descending tetrachord ostinato, the same bass line as that of the closing duet of the opera (see below); in both cases it is surely the traditional association of that pattern with sexual love that is being invoked. This duet is one of the erotic peaks of the opera. Nero ends the scene alone, with an aria ('Son rubin preziosi') that is musically something of a letdown. (The sources disagree on the extent of this aria.)

2.vi Otho berates himself for thinking of harming Poppaea. In a rather subdued three-strophe aria ('Sprezzami quanto sai') he recognizes that his passion for her will remain hopeless.

2.vii He is joined by Octavia, who commands him to kill Poppaea and to disguise himself as a woman so as not to be apprehended. When he initially rejects her command, she threatens him with blackmail. Although they both speak entirely in recitative, Monteverdi distinguishes powerfully between Otho's unfocussed hesitancy and Octavia's forceful determination.

2.viii Reassured by Otho's declaration of love, Drusilla rejoices in an aria-like section enclosed by a refrain ('Felice cor mio'). The page teases Octavia's nurse about her age, taunting her with the vision of Drusilla in love. In a two-strophe aria ('Il giorno feminil') the nurse philosophically agrees that spring is the season for love.

2.ix Otho reveals that Octavia has ordered him to kill Poppaea and asks Drusilla for her clothes so that he can disguise himself in them. Although disturbed by Otho's willingness to commit so heinous an act, she readily agrees, responding with two reprises of her joyful refrain from the previous scene (a convincing dramatic touch added by Monteverdi that underscores Drusilla's love for Otho).

2.x *Poppaea's garden* Poppaea, rejoicing at the death of Seneca, whom she recognized as the last obstacle to her ambitions, prays that Cupid ensure her marriage to Nero ('Amor, ricorro a te'). She expresses undying affection to her nurse Arnalta, who, characteristically, cautions her mistress against too much ambition. Feeling drowsy, Poppaea repeats her prayer to Cupid and is lulled to sleep by Arnalta's lullaby, whose circular melody and frequent, extended cadences actually produce a soporific effect.

2.xi Cupid, descended from Heaven to prevent Poppaea's death, hides near her. He sings an extended aria ('O sciocchi, o frali'), the four strophes of which elicit three different musical settings. Except for its added string accompaniment, the fourth strophe is the same as the first, thus creating a large-scale refrain form and one of the most extended arias in the opera.

2.xii Disguised as Drusilla, Otho enters the garden and reluctantly attempts to kill the sleeping Poppaea, but Cupid stays his hand. Poppaea awakens in time to identify the fleeing Otho as Drusilla, Arnalta calls the guards to pursue 'her', and Cupid declares that he has saved Poppaea and wishes to make her empress.

Act 3.i *Rome* Drusilla rejoices in the hope that her rival will soon be dead and that Otho will be hers alone. The expansive enthusiasm of her refrain, 'O felice Drusilla', ironically underscores her ignorance of the outcome of the previous scene.

3.ii Arnalta, the lictor and a number of his colleagues come to seize Drusilla, who sadly recognizes that her enthusiasm was mistaken and that she must now pay for lending Otho her clothes.

3.iii Drusilla is brought before Nero and, when questioned about the murder attempt, decides to shield Otho and pleads guilty. Nero furiously sentences her to death.

3.iv Otho, refusing to allow Drusilla to accept the blame for his act, confesses to the crime and blames Octavia for instigating it. This gives Nero the excuse to repudiate Octavia, whom he orders to leave Rome in a ship. He spares Otho's life and commutes Drusilla's sentence, allowing them to go into exile together.

3.v After informing her of Octavia's guilt and exile, Nero joyfully tells Poppaea that they will be married this very day. This highly lyrical scene culminates in an expansive duet in which the two lovers sing together for the first time ('Ne più s'interporà').

3.vi Octavia sadly divests herself of the imperial garments and bids farewell to Rome in a highly expressive recitative monologue, 'Addio Roma'.

3.vii Arnalta exults in Poppaea's success and in her own improved station but remarks that she would have preferred to be born a lady and die a servant so that death would be more welcome.

3.viii *Nero's palace* After a lengthy expressive conversation between Nero and Poppaea filled with lyrical outpourings of love and contentment, Poppaea, hailed by the tribunes and consuls in chorus, is crowned empress. Then Cupid, descending from heaven with Venus, the Graces and the Cupids, crowns Poppaea as goddess of beauty on earth. The opera concludes with a duet for the lovers built on a descending tetrachord ostinato, 'Pur ti miro'. With melodic lines that are very close to one another and continually overlap, this duet has been considered the perfect embodiment of the eroticism of the opera. Although it is generally agreed that the text of this duet is not by Busenello and the music not by Monteverdi – the text is certainly by Benedetto Ferrari, and the music may be too – it was probably introduced soon after the première of the opera. To a 17th-century Venetian audience no less than a modern one, it evidently served a crucial dramatic function.

*   *   *

The historical context of the opera helps to explain its extraordinary glorification of lust and ambition at the expense of reason and morality. Its libretto was the product of a libertine intellectual movement in Venice that was specifically concerned with the relative value of religion and sensuality. But the intellectual issues in the libretto become charged with feeling in Monteverdi's music. He portrays the characters as human beings with strong emotions, fears and desires, who express themselves in distinctly different ways: Poppaea and Nero are prone to hedonistic lyricism in arioso, aria and duet; Octavia speaks only in strongly etched recitative; Otho's music lacks focus, is hesitant and is limited in range; Seneca's is bold and strongly directional. And their conflicts touch the very depth of their beings. For its broad moral compass and its psychological conviction, *L'incoronazione di Poppea* stands as the first in a long, if broken, tradition of operatic monuments that includes *Don Giovanni* and *Don Carlos*.   ELLEN ROSAND

Indes galantes, Les ('The Amorous Indies'). *Opéra-ballet* in a prologue and four entrées by JEAN-PHILIPPE RAMEAU to a libretto by LOUIS FUZELIER; Paris, Opéra, 23 August 1735.

At its première, Rameau's first *opéra-ballet* consisted only of a prologue and two entrées, 'Les Incas du Pérou' and 'Le turc généreux', the entrée 'Les fleurs' being added at the third performance. After criticism of what was seen as the absurdity of disguising the hero as a woman, this entrée was replaced with a version in which the plot and all the music except the *divertissement* was new. With the addition of a final entrée 'Les sauvages' (10 March 1736) the work took on something like a definitive form. In the course of many revivals, however,

the number and order of entrées was frequently altered. The last complete contemporary performance was in 1761; at subsequent revivals, individual entrées were replaced with those from other works, not all by Rameau. The prologue stayed in the repertory until 1771, 'Les Incas' and 'Les sauvages' respectively until 1772 and 1773.

The vogue at the Opéra during the 1730s was for *opéras-ballets* on mythological themes. *Les Indes galantes* reverts to a type involving believable modern characters, a type initiated by Campra's *L'Europe galante* (1697) and fashionable during the first 20 years of the century. The prologue retains its allegorical character in introducing the work's theme, aspects of love in far-flung lands: the young men of four allied European nations forsake the goddess Hébé [Hebe] (soprano) and, despite the advice of L'Amour [Cupid] (soprano), are led off to war. The Cupids, realizing that Europe is deserting them, decide to fly to the various 'Indies' (a generic term at that time for any exotic land).

These Indies become the settings for the ensuing entrées. 'Le turc généreux' is set on an island in the Indian Ocean. A French girl, Emilie (soprano), has been sold as a slave to the pasha Osman (bass), who has fallen in love with her. When Emilie's beloved Valère (*haute-contre*) is shipwrecked and captured, Osman recognizes him as the one who freed him from slavery. Though envious of the lovers' happiness, Osman shows his gratitude by releasing them.

'Les Incas' takes place during a Sun Festival in the shadow of a Peruvian volcano. Huascar (bass), the Incan master of ceremonies, loves the princess Phani (soprano), though she loves the Spaniard Don Carlos (*haute-contre*). To convince Phani that the Sun god disapproves of her love, Huascar causes the volcano to erupt. When Carlos foils Huascar's attempt to abduct her, the frenzied Incan causes a further eruption and is crushed by molten rocks.

In the original version of 'Les fleurs', the young Persian prince Tacmas (*haute-contre*) and his confidant Ali (bass) are each in love with the other's slave – Tacmas with Zaïre (soprano), Ali with Fatima (soprano). On the day of the flower festival, the four meet in a confusing encounter where Tacmas is disguised as a woman and Fatima as a Polish slave; but when Zaïre and Fatima reveal that each loves the other's master, the men exchange slaves and all take part in the festival. In the revised version, Fatima (here Sultana rather than slave) suspects her husband Tacmas of infidelity with Atalide (soprano). Disguised as a slave, she gains Atalide's confidence and discovers that her suspicions are unfounded. The happy couple take part in the festival.

In 'Les sauvages' a tribe of North American Indians prepares to make peace with its European vanquishers. The Spaniard Don Alvar (bass) and Frenchman Damon (*haute-contre*) vie for the hand of the chief's daughter Zima (soprano). But she, declaring that the jealous Spaniard loves too much and the fickle Frenchman too little, follows her innocent 'savage' instincts and chooses an honourable Indian brave, Adario (tenor). The shamefaced Europeans join the Indians in the Great Peace-Pipe ceremony.

Fuzelier's libretto, though much criticized in Rameau's day, has considerable merits. Each entrée has its distinctive character, while except in the prologue there are no supernatural interventions. Fuzelier generates the necessary visual and dramatic interest by means of his cleverly chosen locations and the indigenous ceremonial they provide. (Certain details of the latter were culled from published reports of recent events or from first-hand experience.) In the process he manages to contrast European and other cultures, not always to the former's advantage, as the episode of the generous Turk and the lighthearted but moving tribute to the 'noble savage' demonstrate.

Rameau's magnificent response to this material raised the traditionally lightweight genre of *opéra-ballet* to a new level. To 'Les Incas' he brings an intensity no less than that of the *tragédies*: from the start of the eruption to the end of the entrée is an almost unbroken sequence of 350 bars, during which voices and orchestra interact with extraordinary vehemence. The entrée is dominated by Huascar, whose fanatical but wholly credible character Rameau establishes with a sureness not found outside *Hippolyte*. Elsewhere it is the grace and variety of the *airs* and dances that impress most. 'Les sauvages', which proved particularly popular, includes a reworking of Rameau's harpsichord piece *Les sauvages*, inspired by the dancing of two American Indians in Paris in 1725. The first complete modern revival of *Les Indes galantes*, at the Paris Opéra on 18 June 1952, was notable for the lavishness of its staging.   GRAHAM SADLER

India. Although the British Raj was not particularly noted for operatic activity, its rich capital, Calcutta, 'City of Palaces', had by the beginning of the 19th century four or five theatres, the principal one being the Chowringhee Theatre. It was built by public subscription in 1813 and held about 800 in the boxes and 200 in the pit. In 1833 a group of six Italian singers offered their services, forming an Italian Music Society and opening a subscription for ten performances. The company began with *L'italiana in Algeri* (15 Jan 1834) and continued with *Il barbiere di Siviglia*, Paer's *Agnese*, Rossini's *L'inganno felice*, *Tancredi*, *Otello*, *La gazza ladra*, *Eduardo e Cristina*, Mercadante's *Elisa e Claudio* and Rossini's *La Cenerentola* – all no doubt first performances in India. Each was given two or three times, with an orchestra made up of musicians from local bands, led by M. Planel, a prominent figure in musical life in Calcutta. That the operas were somewhat arranged to suit resources can be deduced from the fact that Domingo Pizzoni, who sang Figaro, Dandini and Mustafà, also sang the title role in *Otello*. Many of the male leading roles – Almaviva, Lindoro, Ramiro and others – were sung by the contralto Margarita Caravaglia; the prima donna was Teresa Schieroni, and the only tenor was a local one, Mr Linton, who usually sang second tenor roles and occasionally conducted. Secondary and choral roles were taken by locals. The Italian Music Society continued for 15 months, after which the singers returned to Europe; the Chowringhee Theatre was destroyed by fire in 1839.

The Grand Opera House in Calcutta was inaugurated in 1867 with a gala performance of *Il trovatore*, with ballet (the first time ballet had been seen in India), by Augusto Cagli's Grand Italian Opera Company. The company consisted of ten principal singers and eight instrumentalists (section professors from La Scala) who led the local players. The resulting orchestra was thought a great improvement on anything previously heard in India. At the opening a typhoon hit Calcutta, robbing the event of much of its news value. Cagli's company also presented 20 other popular Italian works, returning each year until 1872. In 1875 Miss Alice

May's English Opera Company gave a season including Offenbach's *Barbe-bleue* and *La Grande-Duchesse de Gérolstein*, *Der Freischütz*, *La sonnambula*, *Fra Diavolo* and *The Lily of Killarney*. Amy Sherwin (the 'Tasmanian Nightingale') and her company appeared in 1888. The D'Oyly Carte Company performed six seasons at this theatre, and in 1896–7 Pollard's Lilliputian Opera Company (31 juvenile singers who performed light works) played there. In 1916 the Italian Grand Opera Company, under the musical direction of the Gonsalez brothers, gave over 20 operas (mostly popular Italian) with 40 singers and an orchestra of 25. After this the Grand Opera House, which still stands, became the Globe Cinema. Opera found a new home at the Empire Theatre where in 1925 the Italian Grand Opera Company returned, giving 20 operas. In the 1950s Alexander Shemansky, a Russian emigré who had sung with an Italian company in Calcutta before World War II, formed his own company, performing *La traviata*, *Carmen*, *Faust*, *Tosca* and *Pagliacci*. In 1965 the Empire Theatre became the Roxy Cinema, as it remains. From 1940 to 1965 the (now defunct) Calcutta Light Opera Group and Society gave annual productions of Gilbert and Sullivan and other light opera.

When Simla became the Raj's summer capital, opera was occasionally given there in the Gaiety Theatre, part of the Town Hall complex; Loewenberg lists a performance of *Cavalleria rusticana* in 1901. Most of the operatics were, however, amateur (as was one in which Robert Baden-Powell starred).

Opera came later to Bombay than to Calcutta. Probably the first company to perform there was Cagli's; it gave a season at the Grant Road Theatre, later called the Theatre Royal. The late 19th-century Excelsior and New Empire Theatres both had orchestral pits; European companies, often on their way to Australia, occasionally stopped to perform there. In 1954 the Bombay Madrigal Singers presented a fully staged *Mikado* and in 1961 a concert performance of *Il trovatore*; their success led to a staged *La traviata* in 1962. *Il trovatore* followed in 1963, inaugurating a series of performances with foreign guest singers (including Luigi Infantino, Boris Carmeli, Paolo Silveri, Rowland Jones and Otello Borgonova), conducted by Cesar Coelho with Celia Lobo, a local soprano, in the prima donna roles. Each work was performed three or four times, at the old Cowasjee Jenagir Hall and from 1966 at the Bhulabbai Desai Auditorium. Occasional performances of operetta followed, but both opera and operetta were discontinued after 1985 as no Government subsidy was available for Western music.

A neo-classical Royal Opera House was built in Charni Road, Bombay, in 1925 by a Parsee businessman and theatre lover, Jahangir Fardoonji Karaka. Principally a playhouse (although the Bandman Opera Company was billed there in the late 1920s), it became a cinema in 1935. Around 1900 there were some 30 Indian opera houses in Bombay giving performances of spectacular musical shows, sung in Marathi, using a mixture of Indian and Western music mostly by Parsee composers. Linley's *The Duenna* was performed in Bombay in Marathi in 1925 (according to Loewenberg). This genre was patronized by the Parsee community whose musical tradition continues in the Mehta family, notably in the conductor Zubin Mehta. Other attempts to combine Indian and Western music in dramatic form were made by the Bengali poet and composer Rabindranath Tagore (1861–1941), whose music dramas, the most successful of which was *Shyama* (1939), are analogous to ballad operas, combining traditional Indian music with European folksong. In Delhi, the Indian composer Param Vir (*b* 1952) founded the Music Theatre Workshop in 1979 and mounted a series of large-scale productions of music theatre allying Indian subjects to Western music: *Kidstuff* (1979), *The Demons of Bara Tooti* (1980), *Besura Desh* (1982), *Fall Out* (1984) and *Krishna* (1988). In the early 1990s there were plans to build a new opera house in Bombay.

CHARLES PITT

Indianapolis. American city, capital of Indiana. It is the home of the Indianapolis Opera. The idea for a professional opera company began with Miriam Ramaker, a singing teacher at Indiana Central University who wanted an opportunity for her students to perform. Between 1975 and 1977 four productions were presented on the university campus. Subsequently the company performed at the Murat Temple (1800 seats). Under the artistic director Robert B. Driver, who served simultaneously as artistic director of the Syracuse Opera Company, the company developed in the early 1980s a pattern of shared productions to save costs. In 1984 Driver became artistic director of Opera Memphis in Tennessee and Indianapolis-Memphis pairings were established. In 1988 the company moved to the Clowes Memorial Hall at Butler University, a proscenium theatre (2182 seats) built in 1963. By 1989 the season consisted of eight performances of four productions, usually one light opera or musical and three grand operas. In 1990 the company served 10 000 patrons. The Indianapolis SO regularly accompanies productions.

NANCY MALITZ

Indiana University Opera Theatre. American educational institution, based in BLOOMINGTON, Indiana.

Indianola. American city, in Iowa, 12 miles from the state capital, Des Moines. It is the home of the Des Moines Metro Opera, the largest performing arts organization in Iowa. This summer repertory company was founded in 1973 by Douglas J. Duncan, the managing director, and Robert L. Larsen, chairman of the music department at Simpson College in Indianola, an institution with an emphasis on performing arts. The first season consisted of *La rondine*, *The Medium*, Arthur Benjamin's *Prima Donna* and *Albert Herring*, with Larsen as conductor and stage director. The company has maintained a pattern of 18 performances in English of three operas: it stages both standard and contemporary repertory and gives prominence to American works and emerging American singers. The season runs for four weeks in June and July. Performances are given in the Blank Performing Arts Center (488 seats), built in 1969. An unusual feature of the auditorium is a second performance area in front of the orchestra pit, connected to the proscenium stage by two bridging ramps. Notable productions have included Robert Ward's *The Crucible* (1974), Carlisle Floyd's *Susannah* (1976), Menotti's *The Consul* (1978), Douglas Moore's *The Ballad of Baby Doe* (1981) and Floyd's *Of Mice and Men* (1985). The company gave the première of Lee Hoiby's *The Tempest* in 1986, and the production was repeated in 1987 at the Lyric Opera of Kansas City. The company has also used the Civic Center (2750 seats) in Des Moines for productions of *Aida* (1984) and *Hänsel und Gretel* (1991). In 1987 a

small, educational touring subsidiary, Opera Iowa, was developed to travel throughout Iowa and surrounding states from February to May; Opera Iowa presented the première of Stephen Paulus's *Harmoonia* on 23 February 1991.

NANCY MALITZ

Indian Queen, The. Semi-opera in a prologue and five acts by HENRY PURCELL, adapted from the heroic play of JOHN DRYDEN and Sir Robert Howard; London, Theatre Royal, Drury Lane, probably late autumn 1695.

Purcell's last major work, it included much less music, dancing and scenic spectacle than his previous semi-operas and was probably left unfinished at the time of his death. Owing to a managerial crisis, almost all the leading Theatre Royal players had left the company before the première; *The Indian Queen* was therefore performed by very young and inexperienced actors and singers. The score, however, is among Purcell's most refined and dramatic.

The play text, which was rather carelessly adapted from Dryden and Howard's original tragedy of 1664 (cut down from 1400 lines to 640), concerns the Mexican Queen Zempoalla in her struggle against the Peruvians. The invaders are led by Montezuma, a mercenary of unknown origin, who decamps to the Mexican side, where he discovers that Zempoalla has usurped the throne of the rightful queen – who turns out to be his long-lost mother. Purcell transformed this historically and geographically preposterous story, which is told entirely in heroic couplets, into a powerful tragedy by focussing most of the music on the Indian Queen herself. Though she never sings, Zempoalla is surrounded by music which conveys her unspoken turmoil and guilt.

Purcell's music is concentrated into four scenes: the prologue; a masque of Fame and Envy in Act 2; an incantation in Act 3; and a sacrifice scene in Act 5. The final hymeneal masque, which was set by 'Mr Daniel Purcell, Mr Henery Purcell being dead' (as an early manuscript notes), was not part of the original drama and represents a rather feeble attempt to provide a happy ending. Besides these large musical scenes, the score includes Henry's fine overture and act tunes, as well as the masterful soprano songs 'I attempt from Love's sickness to fly' and 'They tell us that you mighty powers', whose exact locations in the play are unknown.

Purcell broke up Dryden and Howard's spoken dialogue into a series of songs and duets for an Indian boy and girl, beginning with 'Wake, Quivera'; the pieces prophesy certain events in the drama and present in miniature the tonal scheme of the whole work. The first major musical interpolation into the play is the masque in Act 2. Fame, an alto ('I come to sing great Zempoalla's story'), is pitted against Envy, a bass, who in the memorable aria 'What flatt'ring noise is this' is joined by two countertenor attendants reinforcing the sibilant word in the line 'at which my snakes all *hiss*'. The vivid music is probably meant to represent Zempoalla's struggle of conscience.

The longest and most important musical scene is in Act 3. Zempoalla, worried by a portentous dream, consults Ismeron the magician, a role created by the bass Richard Leveridge at the beginning of a long and distinguished career. He sings the charm 'You twice ten hundred deities' (which Burney called 'the best piece of recitative in our language') and a bizarre accompanied aria, 'By the croaking of the toad'. The rest of the scene

797

comprises a series of no less impressive pieces for the God of Dreams (soprano) and aerial spirits, notably 'Ah how happy are we', whose ironic melancholy only deepens Zempoalla's depression. The music for the sacrifice scene in Act 5 concludes with the contrapuntal chorus 'All dismal sounds thus on these off'rings wait', a dissonant and sombre piece.

The incorporation of a trumpet symphony from *Come ye Sons of Art Away* (April 1694), a dance from *The Fairy-Queen* and another which is almost certainly not by Purcell, not to mention the final masque supplied by his younger brother, all point to the probability that Purcell died before the première. The finished pieces are, however, of the highest quality. The style is decidedly conservative: *The Indian Queen* is an extended exercise in traditional English chromatic counterpoint, which gives lie to the idea that Purcell's music was becoming ever more italianate during his last year.   CURTIS PRICE

Indonesia. French opera companies visited Batavia (now Jakarta), the capital of Indonesia, with some frequency during the middle of the 19th century. A typical company arrived in August 1865, having previously been to Saigon and Manila, and stayed for slightly over a year. They gave some 36 operas at the Theatre Batavie, mostly from the standard repertory but also including such rarities as *La reine de Chypre*, *Charles VI* and *Jérusalem*. Of the operas given 22 were by French composers, 11 by Italians and one (*Martha*) by a German. Some companies also went on to Soerebaya (now Surabaya) and other centres.

The first Italian opera company arrived by way of Singapore in June 1869. They stayed in Batavia for three months, then toured Java with stops in Semarang, Solo (now Surakarta) and Soerebaya, returning to Batavia twice during additional tours of the island. 18 operas were given, including such relative rarities as *Nabucco*, *I due Foscari*, *Attila* and *Maria di Rohan*. After a further tour of the island, some of the artists joined another impresario in Melbourne while others returned to Italy.

More French companies visited during the 1870s, to be followed by another Italian company in 1879. This troupe, which returned in 1880 and 1881, was headed by the impresario AUGUSTO CAGLI, who specialized in giving opera in far-flung places. Such companies returned fairly frequently until World War II. Some might stay in Batavia for a few months, then tour the island, possibly visiting Sumatra. Others split a season between Batavia and Manila. Still others, such as the Gonsalez company in 1915, went to Java as part of a wider tour (*see* GONSALEZ, GIUSEPPE). They had arrived in Batavia in June 1915, and then went on to Solo, Soerebaya and Semarang. The company, with changes of personnel, returned to Batavia, revisited Singapore, then Sumatra and Rangoon, India and the Antipodes. Gonsalez' company continued to tour the Far East occasionally; the companies of his successor, Carpi, were active in the 1920s and early 30s and visited Batavia frequently as part of tours of the entire region, including Japan.   TOM KAUFMAN

Indy, (Paul Marie Théodore) Vincent d' (*b* Paris, 27 March 1851; *d* Paris, 2 Dec 1931). French composer, teacher, theorist and writer on music. He is remembered as a founder of the Schola Cantorum, as the propagator of the symphonic ideals of Franck, and as the champion of classicism and Wagner in France. His aristocratic ancestors came from the Vivarais (Ardèche), but after

his mother's death he was raised by his paternal grandmother, the Countess Rézia d'Indy. Her insistence on strict moral and intellectual discipline marked d'Indy for life. The musical influence came from his uncle, Viscount Wilfrid d'Indy, an amateur composer and pupil of Franck. D'Indy studied the piano, proving something of a child prodigy, and began harmony lessons with Lavignac in 1865. In 1869 it was decided that he should become a professional musician. After the Franco-Prussian war of 1870–71, in which he served, d'Indy threw himself into Parisian musical life. In 1872, on Duparc's advice, he submitted some compositions to Franck; the reaction, 'You have ideas, but cannot do anything!', came as a blow, and d'Indy entered the Paris Conservatoire to study counterpoint and composition with him. He determined to learn his craft at first hand, playing in the band of the Théâtre Italien and becoming timpanist for Edouard Colonne in 1873. Through Franck and Duparc he was introduced to German music, including Wagner, and that summer he toured the Germanic countries, meeting Liszt at Weimar and seeing Wagner at Bayreuth.

In January 1874 he made his début as a composer. The next year he became organist at St Leu-la-Forêt and choirmaster for Colonne, and his symphony *Jean Hundaye* was performed at the Société Nationale; he also acted as prompter in Bizet's *Carmen*. 1876 proved no less eventful, for his pilgrimage to Bayreuth for the first *Ring* cycle made him a perfect Wagnerite. Many operas were projected in this decade, though on Wagner's advice his aim became a successful adaptation of the master's principles to a French legendary or nationalistic subject. In 1882 he heard what he regarded as the ideal dramatic work, *Parsifal*, about which he was writing on the day he died. Some years later his earlier operatic project *Axel* was converted into *Fervaal*, often known as 'the French Parsifal'. Like his *Symphonie sur un chant montagnard français*(1886), systematically based on a folksong collected in the Ardèche and one of his greatest works, *Fervaal* is set in the Cevennes district of southern France; d'Indy established a summer residence at Faugs (in the upper Ardèche) where he composed much of his later music.

After several years as effective head of the Société Nationale, d'Indy was invited in 1893 to assist with a commission to reorganize the Paris Conservatoire's teaching methods. His far-sighted proposals, rejected as too revolutionary, were later used in the Schola Cantorum, of which he was a founder in 1894. His activities included the revival of early opera, and the modern popularity of the operas of Monteverdi, Rameau and Gluck owes much to d'Indy's pioneering editions and revivals. D'Indy came increasingly to public attention after the production of *Fervaal* (1897) and *L'étranger*(1903) in Brussels and Paris, and he came to head the official opposition to the then flourishing Debussyism, openly declaring *Pelléas et Mélisande* 'formless'. In the next decade his reputation worsened, largely as a result of his eclectic *La légende de Saint Christophe* (1908–15), in which all his artistic and political prejudices were combined in a monumental, anti-semitic and propagandist libretto – part Wagnerian music drama, part medieval mystery play.

As Debussy noticed with *L'étranger* in 1903, there is far less of Wagner in d'Indy's operas than is often thought. *Fervaal*, the prime candidate, uses a vast orchestra and leitmotifs, and its original libretto is based on an ancient legend symbolizing the victory of love and

Christian purity over pagan beliefs. There is more of Wagner musically in *Le chant de la cloche*, the *Wallenstein* overtures, and the romantic legend *La forêt enchantée*, and it was d'Indy's clear, luminous scoring, owing much to Berlioz in its use of pure tone-colours, which saved him time and again. The plot of *L'étranger* shows similarities to that of *Der fliegende Holländer* in its allegorical ending and its all-important soprano role of Vita, but the buoyant, accessible score, which includes folksong themes and is scored for smaller orchestra, is quite another matter. Very far distant also are the two comedies which straddle d'Indy's operatic career: the insignificant *Attendez-moi sous l'orme*, and *Le rêve de Cinyras*, a rare but unsuccessful attempt at musical relaxation.

See also ETRANGER, L'; FERVAAL; and LÉGENDE DE SAINT CHRISTOPHE, LA.

Les burgraves du Rhin, 1869–72 (R. de Bonnières), inc.
Les abencérages, 1874 (after F. R. de Chateaubriand) [project]
Mahomet, 1874 (after J. W. von Goethe) [project]
Les maîtres-sonneurs, 1874 (after G. Sand) [project]
Attendez-moi sous l'orme op.14, 1876–82 (oc, 1, J. Prével and de Bonnières, after J. F. Régnard), Paris, OC (Favart), 11 Feb 1882
Axel, ?1878 (d'Indy, after E. Tegnér) [project, only lib. completed, later used as basis for Fervaal]
Peau d'âne, 1879 (opéra féerie, after C. Perrault) [project]
Le chant de la cloche op.18, 1879–83 (légende dramatique, prol., 7 tableaux, d'Indy, after F. von Schiller), Brussels, Monnaie, 21 Nov 1912 [stage version of choral work]
L'organiste de Harlem, ?c1880 (oc, 3, d'Indy), lib. F-Pn [project]
Fervaal op.40, 1889–93, orchd 1893–5 (action musicale, prol.,3, d'Indy), Brussels, Monnaie, 12 March 1897
L'étranger op.53, 1898–1901 (action musicale, 2, d'Indy), Brussels, Monnaie, 7 Jan 1903
La légende de Saint Christophe op.67, 1908–15 (drame sacré, 3, d'Indy, after J. de Voragine: *Legenda Aurea*), Paris, Opéra, 9 June 1920
Le rêve de Cinyras op.80, 1922, orchd 1922–3 (comédie musicale, 3, X. de Courville), Paris, Petite Scène, 10 June 1927

OPERA EDITIONS
A.-C. Destouches and M.-R. de Lalande: *Les élémens* (Paris, 1883)
C. W. Gluck: *Iphigénie en Aulide* (Paris, 1908); *L'ivrogne corrigé* (Paris, 1925)
C. Monteverdi: *L'incoronazione di Poppea* (Paris, 1908); *Orfeo* (Paris, c1905); *Il ritorno d'Ulisse in patria* (Paris, 1926)
J.-P. Rameau: *Hippolyte et Aricie* (Paris, 1900); *Dardanus* (Paris, 1905)

WRITINGS
Cours de composition musicale (Paris, 1903–50) [vol.iv ed. G. de Lioncourt]
César Franck (Paris, 1906; Eng. trans., 1909)
Beethoven (Paris, 1911)
Emmanuel Chabrier et Paul Dukas (Paris, 1920)
Richard Wagner et son influence sur l'art musical français (Paris, 1930)
Introduction à l'étude de 'Parsifal' de Wagner (Paris, 1937) [inc.]
Many articles in *Le figaro* (1892–1900), *Guide musical* (1897–1904), *Tribune de St Gervais* (1897–1909), *L'art moderne* (Brussels, 1900–03), *Courrier musical* (1902–31), *Musica* (1902–13), *Comoedia* (1907–28), *BSIM* (1909–14), *Tablettes de la Schola* (1909–24) etc.

*

MONOGRAPHS AND COLLECTIONS OF ARTICLES
E. Destranges: *Le chant de la cloche* (Paris, 1890)
——: *Fervaal* (Paris, 1896)
P. de Bréville and H. Gauthier-Villars: *Fervaal: étude analytique et thématique* (Paris, 1897)
E. Destranges: *L'étranger* (Paris, 1904)
A. Sérieyx: *Vincent d'Indy* (Paris, 1914)
C. Saint-Saëns: *Les idées de M. Vincent d'Indy* (Paris, 1918)
ReM (1932), no.122 [special issue]
L. Vallas: *Vincent d'Indy, i: La jeunesse (1851–86)* (Paris, 1946)
—— : *Vincent d'Indy, ii: La maturité, la vieillesse (1886–1931)* (Paris, 1950)
J. Canteloube: *Vincent d'Indy* (Paris, 1951)

N. Demuth: *Vincent d'Indy 1851–1931, Champion of Classicism* (London, 1951)

OTHER LITERATURE
M. Kufferath: 'Fervaal: Action musicale en trois actes et un prologue par Vincent d'Indy', *RMI*, iv (1897), 313–27
P. Lalo: 'Fervaal et la musique française', *Revue de Paris* (15 May 1898)
C. Debussy: 'L'étranger, à Bruxelles', *Gil Blas* (12 Jan 1903)
L. Laloy: 'Le drame musical moderne: Vincent d'Indy', *BSIM*, i (15 May 1905)
J. Marnold: 'La résurrection d'Iphigénie en Aulide', *Comoedia* (5 Jan 1908)
——: 'L'ouverture d'Iphigénie et M. d'Indy', *Mercure de France* (16 Feb 1908)
R. Rolland: 'Vincent d'Indy', *Musiciens d'aujourd'hui* (Paris, 1908), 97–118
M. Ravel: 'Fervaal', *Comoedia illustré* (20 Jan 1913)
P. Dukas: *Ecrits sur la musique* (Paris, 1948)
M. Cooper: *French Music from the Death of Berlioz to the Death of Fauré* (London, 1951)
L. Davies: 'The French Wagnerians', *Opera*, xix (1968), 351–7
——: *César Franck and his Circle* (London, 1970)
R. Myers: *Modern French Music* (Oxford, 1971)
G. B. Paul: 'Rameau, d'Indy and French Nationalism', *MQ*, lviii (1972), 46–56
ROBERT ORLEDGE

Ines de Castro (i). *Opera seria* in two acts by NICCOLÒ ANTONIO ZINGARELLI to a libretto by A. Gasperini; Milan, Teatro Carcano, 11 October 1798.

This is neither a cheerful opera nor a *semiseria*, as some lists suggest, but a gloomy drama with an unexpected happy ending. The story deals with the persecution of innocent lovers, Don Pedro, Infante of Portugal (soprano), and Ines de Castro (soprano), his secret wife and mother of his children, by unjust authority. Don Pedro's refusal to marry the Infanta of Spain, and the unrequited love of Don Rodrigo (tenor) for Ines provide a series of dramatic events culminating in a great prison scene (2.xii), with an attempt by the queen mother (soprano) and Don Rodrigo to poison Ines, who is threatened with the death of her children. One of Zingarelli's most famous operas, it has often been revived in Italy. The most successful numbers circulated in manuscript: the aria with cabaletta for King Alfonso (tenor), 'Avrai la sorte amica' (1.i); the trio 'Non ricercar perdono' (2.iii); and especially Ines's pathetic farewell to her children in the poisoning scene, 'Sento nel dirvi addio' (2.xii).
MARIA CARACI VELA

Ines de Castro (ii). *Tragedia lirica* in three acts by GIUSEPPE PERSIANI to a libretto by SALVADORE CAMMARANO; Naples, Teatro S Carlo, 28 January 1835.

The plot is based loosely on 14th-century history, and has been the basis of over 20 operas. The action takes place in Coimbra (Portugal) in 1349. King Alfonso (baritone) has intended that his son, Don Pedro (tenor), marry Bianca (soprano), the infanta of Castile; Don Pedro has refused, angering his father. Gonzales (tenor), an adviser (and villain), suggests the reason: Don Pedro has loved another, Ines de Castro (soprano), even during his marriage to the late Costanza. Alfonso threatens to disinherit Don Pedro. In Ines's garden, Don Pedro marries Ines and proclaims their two sons legitimate. Gonzales (scorned by Ines) appears, seeking revenge. The couple dismiss him contemptuously; Gonzales kidnaps the children. At court, before a silent Alfonso, Ines pleads for her children. The king is indifferent to her entreaties until she declares that the kidnapped are his heirs. Alfonso puts Don Pedro and Ines in chains.

In Act 2 Ines is greeted in prison by her rival, Bianca, who offers an alternative to death: exile. Ines agrees to leave, if she can once more embrace her sons. Her farewell scene with them convinces Bianca and eventually Alfonso that she is truly innocent.

In Act 3 some time has passed; courtiers narrate how the king had found pleasure temporarily with his newfound family. Then Gonzales murdered the grandchildren; the king, when told, had a near fatal stroke. Vowing revenge, Don Pedro comes to bid farewell to his father, but he is too late. Ines, quite mad, wanders in the graveyard near the tomb of her predecessor, Costanza. She is confronted by the courtiers, Don Pedro and the captured Gonzales. This miscreant admits he has given a slow deadly poison to Ines. In her torturous death scene she is comforted that soon she will see her children.

The music is structured in the Donizetti style, with four-part arias ending in virtuoso cabalettas. The vocal style is very difficult; the role of Ines has a range of over two octaves.   MARVIN TARTAK

Infedeltà delusa, L' ('Deceit Outwitted'). *Burletta per musica* in two acts by JOSEPH HAYDN to a libretto by MARCO COLTELLINI, possibly revised by CARL FRIBERTH; Eszterháza, 26 July 1773.

Vespina *a girl of spirit, sister of Nanni, and in love with Nencio*	soprano
Sandrina *a simple girl, in love with Nanni*	soprano
Filippo *an old peasant, father of Sandrina*	tenor
Nencio *a well-to-do peasant*	tenor
Nanni *a peasant, in love with Sandrina*	bass

Setting A small village in the Tuscan countryside in the 18th century

---

The first documented performance of this work was on the name-day (26 July) of the Dowager Princess Esterházy, as the first edition of the libretto – printed at Ödenburg (Sopron) by Joseph Siess – indicates. The cast featured Maddalena Friberth, Barbara Dichtler, Carl Friberth, Leopold Dichtler and Christian Specht. The libretto was reprinted with a new title-page, 'nell'occasione del gloriosissimo arrivo quìvi de Sua Maestia L'Imperatrice Maria Theresia … nel mese di Settembre dell'Anno 1773'. This famous performance ('If I wish to hear a good opera, I go to Eszterháza', as Maria Theresa is supposed to have said) took place on 1 September, and the work was revived once more, on 1 July 1774, during the visit of two distinguished Italians. No other revivals are known during Haydn's lifetime.

L'infedeltà delusa has enjoyed considerable esteem, even popular success, since World War II. Before the war it had been arranged as a Singspiel, *Die Liebe macht erfinderisch*, with a German text by Hermann Goja, and the music edited by Gottfried Kassowitz (Vienna, c1930). Performances in its original form began with a broadcast by Hungarian Radio in 1952 and a production at the State Opera, Budapest, in 1959. Since publication of the editions by H. C. Robbins Landon (1960) and by Dénes Bartha and Jenő Vécsey (1964) it has been staged at the Holland Festival, and several times in Germany, England, France, Sweden and the USA. It has also been easily the most favoured Haydn opera in both number and quality of recordings: conducted by Antonio de Almeida (1969) – still perhaps the finest of all Haydn operatic recordings – Frigyes Sándor (1976), Antal Dorati (1980) and Sigiswald Kuijken (1989).

ACT 1 *Outside Filippo's house* Filippo, Vespina, Nencio and Nanni are enjoying the beauty of a summer evening, but Vespina senses that Nencio is hatching a plot with Filippo, and Nanni is concerned about Sandrina's absence. Sandrina enters, perturbed by her father's plan to marry her to Nencio. The F major quintet, 'Bella sera ed aure grate', that opens the work is by far the largest number in the opera; it is also the most beautiful of all Haydn's opera ensembles. Structurally, it consists of two sections, a Moderato followed by an Allegro in 3/8 time, the change in tempo and time signature coinciding with Sandrina's entrance and plea to her father. In an imaginative touch Haydn has her solo accompanied solely by strings, her father's otherwise identical music accompanied solely by winds. Brother and sister, then all four characters, take up the same melody. Filippo drags out of Sandrina her reluctant agreement to marry Nencio and rebuff Nanni, to whom she admits her predicament in an uncharacteristically vehement *presto* aria in A major ('Che imbroglio è questo!'). Nanni's anger finds expression in a brilliant aria, 'Non v'è rimedio' (Allegro di molto, 3/4 time, F minor), virtually a challenge to the absent Filippo: one or the other of them must die. The number ends with frenetic rising violin figuration and vivid flourishes from oboes and horns.

The kitchen of Nanni's house Vespina, preparing supper, sings of the grief brought on by love. When her brother returns, equally dejected by the loss of Sandrina, they express their desire for vengeance in a dashing D major duet ('Son disperato').

Outside Filippo's house Nencio serenades Sandrina in a very long and slow-moving aria, with pizzicato strings suggesting his guitar; his theme is the flirtatious unsatisfactoriness of town girls compared with those of the countryside; a poignant dissonance at the word 'guai' ('woe'; bar 114) reveals something more than a stock response to a conventional topos. While Vespina and Nanni listen from the shadows, Nencio tries in vain to persuade Sandrina to love him. It is all too much for Vespina, who steps forward and slaps Nencio, thus setting the finale in motion, a busy G major ensemble of perplexity (Allegro di molto, followed by Presto).

ACT 2 *Outside Filippo's house, the following morning* Vespina has a plan and, disguised as a frail old woman, begins to put it into action. Her brother slips away as Filippo and Sandrina come out, the former intent on lodging a complaint against Nanni. With feigned reluctance Vespina tells them that Nencio married her daughter and then abandoned her; the long scene of *secco* recitative is exquisitely lightened by five passages of accompanied recitative as the distraught 'old woman' tries to find consolation in resorting to proverbs. Her mock-pathetic Adagio aria, 'Ho un tumore', lists her infirmities. (Haydn deleted 38 bars from it, presumably for the performance the empress attended; the musical loss is more than offset by the dramaturgical gain.) Seeing Nencio approach, father and daughter re-enter their house and lock the door. The bemused Nencio is told to look after his wife and children; Filippo berates him soundly in a *presto* outburst, 'Tu sposarti alla Sandrina?', offset by tender phrases that reveal his love for his daughter. The bewildered Nencio suspects a trick, but before he can knock on the door, a tipsy German servant (Vespina, in her second disguise) tells him in pidgin Italo-German that 'his' master is going to marry Sandrina that day. In a rollicking F major aria in 6/8 time, 'Trinche vaine allegramente', Vespina urges Nencio to enjoy the celebrations. This is the shortest, and also the wittiest, number in the opera. Nencio now thinks he understands Filippo's changed attitude, but he hardly gets his breath back before Vespina enters again, this time as the pretended bridegroom, the Marchese di Ripafratta, who tells Nencio that Sandrina is to be fobbed off with his servant. Nencio, wanting to see Filippo's discomfort, agrees to act as witness at the wedding, and in an aria gleefully anticipates his revenge. Vespina emerges from the house to tell Nanni that Filippo has taken the bait, and in an E major aria, 'Ho tesa la rete' (Allegretto, 2/4), which makes charming use of muted violins, she tells him that if she is careful she will lure more than one bird into the net. (As in the aria earlier in the act, Haydn again cut 38 bars.)

A room in Filippo's house All of Filippo's attempts to convince his daughter of the advantages of her fine match are vain; Sandrina wants only a simple life with Nanni (aria, 'È la pompa un grand'imbroglio'). Nanni enters, announcing himself as the Marquis's servant, accompanied by the notary (Vespina, in her last disguise) to prepare the contract; the Marquis will join them when he has completed arrangements for his bride's wardrobe and the honeymoon. The finale (C major, Poco adagio, Presto) opens with the notary drawing up the contract, which Nencio and Nanni sign as witnesses. Nanni reveals himself to the 'notary' as proxy for the bridegroom. Vespina, singing snatches from two of her disguised roles, explains her part in the proceedings, and there is nothing Filippo can do other than accept the double wedding of Sandrina and Nanni, Vespina and Nencio.

*　　*　　*

This work marks an important step forward in Haydn's development as an opera composer. Compared with its predecessor, *Le pescatrici* (1769), *L'infedeltà delusa* reveals a marked degree of concentration: the five characters are all from the peasant class, the chorus is excluded and the work is limited to two acts of equal length. The orchestra is of modest size, including oboes, horns and strings, augmented by bassoons (specified only in the opening quintet). Timpani are used only in the three C major pillars of the structure (where they are combined with horns): the overture, Filippo's aria early in Act 2 and the finale. A gift of 25 ducats from Prince Nikolaus to Haydn at the end of May was probably a thank-offering for the new opera, and it may have received a private performance in the early summer (Landon 1978).

PETER BRANSCOMBE

Inganni felici, Gli ('The Happy Deceptions'). *Dramma per musica* in three acts by CARLO FRANCESCO POLLAROLO to a libretto by APOSTOLO ZENO after Herodotus; Venice, Teatro di S Angelo, 25 November 1696.

Clistene [Cleisthenes], King of Siconia (alto), has promised his daughter Agarista (soprano) to the winner of the Olympic Games. Demetrio [Demetrius], King of Athens (soprano), wins and is crowned by Cleisthenes. Agarista does not realize that Demetrius is the same person as her painting teacher Armidoro with whom she is in love. The loser Orgonte, Prince of Thrace (soprano), in love with Agarista, has gained access to the court as her music teacher Sifalce, while his former love Oronta, Princess of Thessaly (soprano), masquerades as an astrologer named Alceste. 'Sifalce' courts Agarista

and decides to abduct her during the hunt, with the help of his aide Arbante (tenor). 'Armidoro' witnesses her abduction and saves her by defeating 'Sifalce', who is reconciled to Oronta. Though known as Zeno's first libretto, it is not yet a reform libretto but reflects the conventional taste for disguise and mistaken identity; it still has a servant role, though a minor one (Brenno, tenor). The predominant texture of the musically conservative score is four parts. For the arias, Pollarolo used continuo accompaniment twice as much as orchestral; most are exit arias. With four soprano roles, the higher tessituras dominate, but the ranges and technical requirements are modest.

OLGA TERMINI

Inganno felice, L' ('The Happy Deception'). *Farsa* in one act by GIOACHINO ROSSINI to a libretto by GIUSEPPE MARIA FOPPA; Venice, Teatro S Moisè, 8 January 1812.

The opera enjoyed huge popularity in Rossini's day; its designation *farsa* is misleading in the light of its *semiseria* status as a romantic melodrama with *buffo* elements. Set in a seaside mining community, the drama is concerned with the discovery and rehabilitation of Isabella (soprano), the wronged and, it is thought, long-dead wife of Duke Bertrando (tenor). The villains of the piece are Ormondo (bass), a confidant of the Duke, and his henchman Batone (bass). It was Ormondo who, years before, had attempted to dispose of Isabella after she had refused his sexual advances. She had floated out to sea but was rescued by Tarabotto (bass), the respected leader of the mining community. The arrival of the Duke, Ormondo and Batone in the village where Isabella now mysteriously resides triggers an action which culminates in a spaciously conceived denouement in which Tarabotto and the Duke (now no longer estranged from his wife) set a night-time trap for Ormondo and Batone amid the mines and mining-galleries. Much of Isabella's music, the fine nocturnal trio towards the end of the opera and the *buffo* lunacy of the duet for Tarabotto and Batone in which each tries unsuccessfully to find out what the other knows about the mysterious girl, all contribute to the quality and variety of one of Rossini's most original early scores.

RICHARD OSBORNE

Inghelbrecht, D(ésiré)-E(mile) (*b* Paris, 17 Sept 1880; *d* Paris, 14 Feb 1965). French conductor, composer and writer on opera. The son of a viola player at the Opéra, he studied at the Paris Conservatoire with Taudou before first appearing as a conductor at the Théâtre des Arts in 1908. He became friendly with Debussy and directed the chorus for the première of *Le martyre de St Sébastien* in 1911. As director of music at the Théâtre des Champs Elysées (1913) he directed the first production in French of *Boris Godunov*, and went on to conduct at the Ballets Suédois, the Opéra-Comique (1924–5 and 1932–3), the Pasdeloup concerts (1928–32), the Algiers Opera (1929–30) and the Paris Opéra (1945–50). Both in his conducting career and in his writings on music he was an ardent champion of the work of Debussy (particularly *Pelléas et Mélisande*), Ravel, Roussel and Florent Schmitt, whose *Tragédie de Salomé* he directed at the Théâtre des Arts. The style of his compositions is richly eclectic, at times suggestive of Fauré or Debussy, but frequently with echoes from further afield, and sometimes intentionally eccentric. Even if stylistically unoriginal, his polished, often masterly orchestration makes his work worthy of closer attention. *La nuit vénitienne* (after A. de Musset, 1908) is a predictable comic opera, and lacks the harmonic inventiveness of later works. The operetta *Leïla* (or *Virage sur l'aile*, 1947) is a hilarious and eminently singable entertainment, somewhat in the manner of an updated, Gallic Gilbert and Sullivan. The opera-ballet *Le chêne et le tilleul* (after La Fontaine, 1960), set in ancient Greece, is the climax of the composer's output. Its colourful plot raises philosophical issues, discussed by Mercury and Jupiter. Harmonies in the style of Debussy, charming and directionless, give no hint of the impending Bacchic frenzy of a wild dance with its pungently rhythmic, virile accompaniment.

Comment on ne doit pas interpréter Carmen, Faust et Pelléas (Paris, 1933)
Diabolus in musica (Paris, 1933)
Mouvement contraire, souvenirs d'un musicien (Paris, 1947)
Le chef d'orchestre et son équipe (Paris, 1950)
Le chef d'orchestre parle au public (Paris, 1957)

*

J. Bruyr: 'D.-E. Inghelbrecht', *Musica*, no.21 (1955), 24
G. Inghelbrecht: *D. E. Inghelbrecht et son temps* (Neuchâtel, 1978)
ARTHUR HOÉRÉE, NICHOLAS KAYE

Inghilleri, Giovanni (*b* Porto Empedocle, Sicily, 9 March 1894; *d* Milan, 10 Dec 1959). Italian baritone. He trained first as a pianist and discovered his voice while working as a répétiteur. In 1919 he made his début as Valentin in *Faust* at the Carcano, Milan, and then went on to sing with considerable success throughout Italy, at the Costanzi in Rome, the S Carlo in Naples (the first of many seasons in 1922, the last being 1948) and La Scala. He was enthusiastically received at his début in *Pagliacci* at Covent Garden in 1928, and returned there for the next two seasons and again in 1935. A highlight of his career in London was the 1930 *Traviata* with Ponselle and Gigli where his 'steadiness of tone, flawless phrasing and ease of manner' were commended as a model. He sang at Chicago in 1929, and later in France and Spain. In 1936 he appeared in the première of Malipiero's *Giulio Cesare* in Genoa. He continued to prove his worth as a musicianly singer (he was also a composer of opera, ballet and songs) until his retirement in 1953, after which he taught singing in Milan. Recordings show the fine voice and authoritative style that distinguished him in the 1920s; when he returned to the studios after the war his style had deteriorated, though his tone remained impressive.
J. B. STEANE

Ingram, Lance [Lancelot Albert]. *See* LANCE, ALBERT.

Inimico delle donne, L' ('The Misogynist'). *Dramma giocoso* in three acts by BALDASSARE GALUPPI to a libretto by GIOVANNI BERTATI; Venice, Teatro S Samuele, autumn 1771.

On the island of Kibin-kin-ka in the Chinese sea, the crown prince Zon-Zon hates all women, but if he does not marry on this last day of opportunity he loses the crown. He is criticizing various possible brides, including Xunchia and Kam-si (cousins, related to the prince's steward, Si-Sin) and Zyda (daughter of Ly-Lam, the high priest), when he meets Agnesina, an Italian girl, and her uncle Geminiano; Agnesina is fleeing from her many suitors at home and hates all men. Zon-Zon and Agnesina have much in common, therefore, and they fall in love. Geminiano dresses as a village god and blesses the pair, but the ceremony becomes dangerous and he flees. Zon-Zon's potential polygamy is resolved when Agnesina swears him to loyalty, and Zon-Zon decrees that Xunchia should marry Geminiano.

This exotic comedy, inspired by similar *opera seria* librettos, was a path-breaking, experimental work for Bertati, pointing towards him *Il matrimonio segreto* of 20 years later, and displays an enormous variety of poetic forms. Galuppi's music is similar to that of his comedies of 15 years earlier, tied to relatively short melodic cells, brief development and great concern for singers.
DALE E. MONSON

Inkle and Yarico. Comic dialogue opera, op.30, in three acts by SAMUEL ARNOLD to a libretto by George Colman the younger (*see* COLMAN family, (3)) after Richard Steele's essay; London, Little Theatre in the Haymarket, 4 August 1787.

The action is set in the West Indies and was so up to date as to touch on the slavery problem which had just become the subject of parliamentary agitation by William Wilberforce. Inkle (tenor), an English adventurer, does not know whether to marry his fiancée, Narcissa (soprano), a wealthy English heiress, whom he does not love, or the 'noble savage' Yarico (soprano), who has saved his life. His servant Trudge (baritone) feels no inhibitions about loving Yarico's maid Wowski (soprano). Of course love triumphs, though avarice gives it a sharp tussle; Narcissa marries the more deserving Captain Campley (baritone). The plight of Yarico, when Inkle prepares to sell her to slavers, stirred up great public feeling and Fanny Kemble's portrayal was praised by Robert Burns. This piece, which came to be taken as the first English anti-slavery play, was popular for at least 50 years (it seems to have been the genesis of George Eliot's short story *Brother Jacob*, 1878). Colman's libretto derives from Steele's essay (published in *The Spectator*, 13 March 1711) which is an embellishment of an account in Richard Ligon's *A True Exact History of the Island of Barbadoes* (London, 1657). Steele's Yarico is ruthlessly sold into slavery, whereas in Colman the Governor of Barbados refuses to permit the sale. In Steele, Inkle is not called to account, but in Colman he is made to reform in the last scene, suddenly acknowledging his commitment to Yarico. Arnold's music consists mainly of short ensembles and simple airs, some with descriptive musical accompaniments. Arnold wrote two additional songs, 'Simplicity, thou fav'rite Child' and 'What Citadel so proud can say' (full score, London, 1788), for John Johnstone (tenor) when he took over the role of Inkle from John Bannister for the opera's transfer to Covent Garden; it was most unusual for a winter playhouse to take over a piece from the Little Theatre.
ROBERT HOSKINS

Innocente, L' [O Inocente] ('The Innocent'). Opera in three acts by FRANCISCO MIGNONE to a libretto by ARTURO ROSSATO after Concha Espina Tagle's novel; Rio de Janeiro, Teatro Municipal, 5 September 1928.

The action takes place in Cantabria, Spain, at the beginning of the 20th century. Irene (mezzo-soprano) abandons her son at the door of a couple, Andrés (tenor) and Marcella (soprano), whose defective first son was recently born. Andrés, who had a love affair with Irene, is the father of the abandoned child. Marcella exchanges the boys, so that her rival will appear as the mother of the defective baby. Three years later, Irene's supposed son dies in a mountain snow storm and she grieves for him. Remorsefully, Marcella finally reveals that Irene's true son is alive and well and then renounces her household.

The opera dates from the composer's early period when his music showed a strong Romantic Italian influence. The overly dramatic and theatrical story results in a somewhat histrionic setting, not always well-balanced, but with effective expressive passages. Mário de Andrade, the spokesman of modernism in Brazilian music, took exception to this opera, stating that it belonged to Italy and therefore had no national value. Nevertheless Luiz Heitor Corrêa de Azevedo considered it a truly outstanding and singular work.

GERARD BÉHAGUE

Innocenza risorta, L' [*L'innocenza risorta, ovvero Etio* ('Innocence Resuscitated, or Aetius')]. *Dramma per musica* in three acts by PIETRO ANDREA ZIANI to a libretto by ADRIANO MORSELLI; Venice, Teatro S Cassiano, week before 6 February 1683.

The cast has nine characters, including one servant, and there is little spectacle. The historical characters include the Emperor Valentinian III, his wife Licinia Eudoxia, and Aetius, commander of the imperial army. The plot, largely fanciful, focusses almost exclusively on love entanglements: Valentiniano [Valentinian] (soprano castrato) loves Flavia (soprano), Massimo's wife; Massimo [Maximus] (tenor) loves Eudossa [Eudoxia] (soprano), Valentinian's wife; Ezio [Aetius] (soprano castrato) loves Sabina (soprano), who during his absence has fallen in love with Onorio (soprano or tenor). Aetius eventually foils Maximus's attempt to overthrow Valentinian, who, after banishing Maximus and Flavia, swears to remain faithful to Eudoxia.

This, Ziani's last opera, was produced twice in 1683. Three months after its première in Venice, it was re-staged under the title *Il talamo preservato dalla fedeltà di Eudossa* in Reggio Emilia, where it was performed seven times between 1 and 11 May. For the 1686 carnival in Naples, Alessandro Scarlatti also set Morselli's libretto, entitled simply *Etio*. Extensive documentation survives for the Reggio Emilia production (in the Archivo di Stato, Modena).

There are 63 arias, only 12 of which are accompanied by upper melodic instruments in addition to continuo. The score from the Reggio Emilia production calls for four-part strings and trumpets with continuo; the orchestra consisted of two harpsichords, theorbo, five violins, three violas, violoncello, contrabass and two trumpets. At Reggio, Margherita Salicola assumed the role of Eudossa, the female lead. During the 1683 carnival she had sung at the Teatro S Giovanni Grisostomo in Venice, in Pallavicino's *Il re infante* (as had one other cast member, Giovanni Buzzoleni). At least three arias from *Il re infante* were inserted, and several other substitute arias can be identified from other operas of the early 1680s. HARRIS S. SAUNDERS

Innsbruck. Austrian city, capital of the Tyrol. As the province's capital since the 15th century and, at times, the Habsburg residence, Innsbruck and the nearby Schloss Ambras were the sites of early performances of interludes, *trionfi*, ballets and operas; Antonio Cesti composed for the court between 1652 and 1665 (though he was in Rome 1658–61). The court's first opera theatre, the Ballhaus, could be flooded with water for plays with ships. In 1654 the Archduke Ferdinand Karl (1646–62) had a Komödienhaus built in the Venetian style with 'many machines, flies and settings'; it was the first self-contained opera house in a German-speaking country, and the first to have a permanent company.

The Tyrolean line of the House of Habsburg ended in 1665 with the death of Archduke Siegmund Franz and the court was transferred to Vienna, but some of the court performers remained at Innsbruck to serve visiting royalty. The last court opera performance, the première of Hasse's *Romulo ed Ersilia*, was in 1765. The Komödienhaus was subsequently leased by outside contractors; the first of these was known as the Kaiserliches und Königliches Hoftheater, and performed operas, Singspiels and plays. The theatre was replaced in 1846 by a new classical-style building on the same site. In 1886 the theatre came under the control of the town, becoming the Stadttheater; from 1918 it had once again a permanent opera company. Its name was changed to the Tiroler Landestheater in 1945. After extensive alteration and expansion (1961–7) the main house could seat 794. Since then more than 80 operas, operettas, musicals and ballets have had their local premières there, including a 12-part comprehensive Richard Strauss cycle, little-known works by Haydn and Mozart, *Wozzeck*, *Pelléas et Mélisande*, Franz Schmidt's *Notre Dame*, and works by Egk, Shostakovich and Bresgen. The company staged the world première of *Ninive* by the Tyrolean composer Erich Urbanner in 1988. A Festival of Ancient Music, including early operas, was established in the 1980s.

*

F. Waldner: 'Nachrichten über die Musikpflege am Hofe zu Innsbruck', *MMg*, xxix–xxx (1897–8), suppl., 1–64; xxxvi (1904), 143

A. Einstein: 'Italienische Musik und italienische Musiker am Kaiserhof und an den erzherzöglichen Höfen in Innsbruck und Graz', *SMw*, xxi (1934), 3–52

W. Senn: *Musik und Theater am Hof zu Innsbruck* (Innsbruck, 1954)

E. Berlanda: 'Die Opernpflege im Innsbrucker Theater', *110 Jahre Innsbrucker Theater*, ed. K. Paulin and H. C. Pfeiffer (Innsbruck, 1955–6)
HARALD GOERTZ, WALTER SENN

Insanguine [Monopoli], **Giacomo** (**Antonio Francesco Paolo Michele**) (*b* Monopoli, nr Bari, 22 March 1728; *d* Naples, 1 Feb 1795). Italian composer. He studied in Naples with Abos, Feo and Durante. In 1756 he had his first opera, *Lo funnaco revotato*, performed at the Teatro dei Fiorentini; it is said to have been highly successful and was revived there in 1760. His production of operas thereafter was somewhat intermittent, but he seems also to have done considerable hackwork, patching up operas by other composers. According to remarks supposed to have been made much later by Paisiello, 'Monopoli was the *maestro delle pezze*, that is, [he wrote] those numbers that were added in revising other composers' scores at the impresario's expense, as a result of which he lost standing among professional musicians'. The full extent of his work of this sort is not known. Most of his own operas written before 1770 were comic ones performed at Neapolitan theatres, and of these only *Lo funnaco revotato* is known to be extant. *L'osteria di Marechiaro* (1768) was particularly successful. In 1770 he had a work performed at the S Carlo for the first time, a setting of *Didone abbandonata*. According to Prota-Giurleo, this commission began as an assignment to revise and direct Galuppi's setting, and only when Galuppi's work proved impossible of adaptation to the needs of the S Carlo was Insanguine asked to set the text anew. Perhaps because of the success of this work he then composed mostly *opere serie*, including four for the S Carlo (as well as his completion with Errichelli of Gian

Francesco de Majo's last opera, *Eumene*, which was performed there in 1771). His last two operas for the S Carlo, *Medonte* (1779) and *Calipso* (1782), were not successful. Something of his standing at this time may perhaps be seen in the fact that he was paid only 230 ducats for *Calipso*, while among the composers of the other three operas performed that season, the popular Cimarosa, making his S Carlo début, received 340, the young Francesco Bianchi 250 and only the little-known Curci less (the minimum fee of 200 ducats). Insanguine also taught at the S Onofrio conservatory, becoming *primo maestro* in 1785; in 1793 he was given Salvatore Rispoli as special *secondo maestro*. Meanwhile he was organist and *maestro di cappella* at the Tesoro di S Gennaro.

The scanty references to Insanguine in contemporary lexicons suggest that he was little known outside Naples except as the composer of a few popular arias. The disrespect for him in Naples reflected in Paisiello's remark above (Paisiello is known to have been particularly lacking in charity towards most of his fellow composers) perhaps also appears in Villarosa's judgment, repeated by Florimo and later writers, that he had 'a style lacking in inspiration [estro] and taste'. Insanguine was an expert craftsman and always up to date (an aria in the library of the Royal College of Music, London, sung by Aprile in an unidentified *opera seria* at Palermo in 1766, is in a modern style more common in the 1770s and has no trace of *galant* intricacies); however, his music usually has a slightly perfunctory quality, reflected in the excessively regular working out of his aria forms.

NC – *Naples, Teatro di S Carlo* NF – *Naples, Teatro dei Fiorentini*
NN – *Naples, Teatro Nuovo*

Lo funnaco revotato (oc, B. Saddumene or P. Mililotti, after F. Oliva), NF, sum. 1756, *GB-Cfm*
La Matilde generosa (oc), NF, aut. 1757
Demetrio (os, P. Metastasio), Rome, Argentina, carn. 1759, *P-La*
Le sorelle tradite (oc), NN, sum. 1759
La giocatrice bizzarra (oc, A. Palomba), NN, spr. 1764, collab. G. Gabellone
Il nuovo Belisario (oc), NF, carn. 1765
La vedova capricciosa (oc, G. Palomba), NN, carn. 1765 [1 aria by C. de Franchi]
Le quattro malmaritate (oc, G. Palomba), NN, carn. 1766
L'osteria di Marechiaro (oc, F. Cerlone), NF, wint. 1768
La finta semplice, ossia Il tutore burlato (oc, Mililotti), NN, aut. 1769
Pulcinella vendicato nel ritorno di Marechiaro (farsetta), NF, wint. 1769 [perf. with L'osteria di Marechiaro]
Il natal di Telefo (prol., S. Mattei), NC, 12 Jan 1770, *I-Nc*
La Didone abbandonata (os, Metastasio), NC, 20 Jan 1770, *Nc, P-La*
La dama bizzarra (oc, G.C.), NF, wint. 1770
Eumene [Act 2] (os, A. Zeno), NC, 20 Jan 1771, *I-Nc* [Act 1 by G. F. de Majo, Act 3 by P. Errichelli]
Merope (os, Zeno), Venice, S Benedetto, 26 Dec 1772, *P-La*
Arianna e Teseo (os, P. Pariati), NC, 20 Jan 1773, *I-Nc, P-La*
Adriano in Siria (os, Metastasio), NC, 4 Nov 1773, *I-Nc, P-La*
Le astuzie per amore (ob, Mililotti), NF, carn. 1777, *I-Nc*
Eumene (os, Zeno), Turin, Regio, carn. 1778, *Tf, P-La* [apparently a new, complete setting]
Medonte (os, G. de Gamerra), NC, 30 May 1779, *I-Nc, P-La*
Motezuma (os, V. A. Cigna-Santi), Turin, Regio, carn. 1780, *I-Tf, P-La*
Calipso (os), NC, 30 May 1782, *I-Nc, P-La*

Music in: Monte Testaccio, 1760; L'astuto balordo, 1761; La furba burlata, 1762; L'innamorato balordo, 1763; Le viaggiatrici di bell'umore, 1763; Monsieur Petitone, 1763

ES (U. Prota-Giurleo); *FlorimoN*; *GiacomoC*; *RosaM*

S. di Giacomo: 'Paisiello e i suoi contemporanei', *Musica e musicisti*, lx (1905), 762–8; repr. in *Napoli: figure e paesi* (Naples, 1909) and *Opere*, ii (Milan, 1946)
E. Dent: 'Ensembles and Finales in 18th-century Italian Opera', *SIMG*, xi (1909–10), 534–69; xii (1910–11), 112–38
A. Mondolfi: 'Destino e stile di Giacomo Insanguine detto Monopoli', *Gazzetta musicale di Napoli*, iv (1958), 4
A. Giovine and U. Porta-Giurleo: *Giacomo Insanguine detto Monopoli, musicista monopolitano: cenno biografico, elenco di rappresentazioni, bibliografia, indice vari e iconografia* (Bari, 1969) DENNIS LIBBY (text), JAMES L. JACKMAN (work-list)

Intendant (Ger.). A term used in German-speaking countries since the 18th century to denote the officially appointed supervisor of a court or state or municipal theatre. Up until 1914 the Intendant was generally a nobleman; his work might be largely administrative or more actively artistic. In recent times the Intendant has been declaredly in charge of artistic as well as administrative direction, working, in an opera house, alongside a conductor termed *Generalmusikdirektor*. In English-speaking countries the equivalent figure is the general manager or managing director, in Italy the *sovrintendente*.

ES (P. Chiarini)
'Intendant', *Das grosse Brockhaus* (Leipzig, 1930)
JOHN ROSSELLI

Interlude (Fr. *entr'acte*; Ger. *Zwischenspiel*; It. *intermezzo*). A short instrumental number or passage, usually for orchestra, to be played between two scenes or acts of a theatrical work. There is no clear distinction in size or function between numbers called 'interlude' or one of its synonyms and those called SINFONIA, PRELUDE or the like. Weber, for instance, opens the third act of *Der Freischütz* with an independent orchestral number that he calls an 'entr'acte', though it might as easily have been called a 'prelude'. Most often 'interlude' and its synonyms are applied to orchestral movements used to maintain continuity through a change of scene, such as the 'intermezzi' in Mascagni's *Cavalleria rusticana* and Leoncavallo's *Pagliacci*, or the 'intermedium' in the first act of Berg's *Lulu*. (In *Pelléas et Mélisande*, Debussy was obliged to extend his interludes during rehearsals as the original ones allowed insufficient time for scene changes.) There are, however, many sections of similar function in other operas that are given no specific designation at all. STEPHEN C. FISHER

Intermède (Fr.). A French musical entertainment or theatrical work, usually including singing and dancing, often performed between the acts of a play or as an operatic programme filler, a counterpart to the Italian INTERMEZZO and INTERMEDIO. The 16th-century French *intermède* (or *divertissement*) was a courtly diversion with often elaborate costumes and machines. Important royal occasions, such as marriages and victories, were celebrated metaphorically in *intermèdes* in honour of love, virtue or other attributes. Plots or characters drawn from mythology and allegorical figures were common. Members of the royal family and the court participated. The French love of dancing assigned ballet a prominent role; indeed, the dividing line between *intermède* (in this sense) and the early *ballet de cour* is sometimes difficult to draw, although continuity in, or even presence of, a plot was more characteristic of the latter. In addition, court performances of plays sometimes included *intermèdes* between the acts.

The *théâtre à machines*, including works by Pierre Corneille, made extensive use of *intermèdes* virtuoso in their staging. At Jesuit colleges, in the 17th century and the early 18th, *intermèdes*, dominated by dance but also including singing, were given between the acts of Latin and, more rarely, French plays; their themes were related to those of the play so that they provided a vernacular gloss on the main work and an entertainment pleasing to the eye. Plays at court continued to make use of *intermèdes* between or at the end of acts. The experiments of Molière and Lully in the *comédie-ballet*, with the aim of improving the coordination between the musical and spoken parts, were an important model for their successors. In the *tragédie* Racine, in part inspired by the spirit of Greek classical theatre, included *intermèdes* featuring the chorus in several works, including *Esther* (1689) and *Athalie* (1691), written for the Maison Royale St-Louis de St-Cyr and later given at court (music by J.-B. Moreau; *Athalie* was later reset by Gossec). While the *comédie-ballet* and *intermèdes* in spoken *comédie* and *tragédie* were significant features of 'private' performance in the late 17th century and the 18th, public ones had a more restrictive, less elaborate use of music, often better described as incidental music. M.-A. Charpentier's difficulties in revising *Le malade imaginaire* so as to reduce the number of performers and thus avoid transgressing Lully's *lettres patentes* are one example. The Académie Royale de Musique's monopoly on works with choruses prevented the public staging of the original versions of Racine's masterpieces until the law on 'the freedom of the theatres' (1791) abolished it. Furthermore, during the course of the 18th century the trend was towards a thorough integration of all aspects of a theatrical work (for example, Lindor's serenade and the music lesson, both functioning dramatically as such, in Beaumarchais' *Le barbier de Séville*, 1775).

In 18th-century French opera *intermède* had two related meanings. It was the translation of the Italian *intermezzo*. When Pergolesi's *La serva padrona* was performed in Paris in French translation as *La servante maîtresse* (1754), it was termed a 'comédie mêlée d'ariettes, intermède italien'. When Rousseau defined 'intermède' as 'a work of music and dance inserted between the acts of an opera, or sometimes a comedy', he was describing the French practice for the latter but only the original Italian one for the former. In France these translations were always given as independent works – one of two or three on an evening's programme. By extension *intermède* was also applied to works in a similar lighthearted spirit and generally in one or two acts originally written in French. They were performed at either the Académie Royale de Musique (e.g. J.-J. Rousseau's own *Le devin du village*, 1752, and Joseph Pouteau's *Alain et Rosette*, 1777), sung throughout, or the Opéra-Comique (e.g. E. Duni's *Nina et Lindor*, 1758) or other theatres, with spoken dialogue. By the late 18th century the term had virtually disappeared.

*

D. Diderot: 'Intermède', *Encyclopédie, ou Dictionnaire raisonné des sciences, des arts et des métiers*, ed. D. Diderot and others (Paris, 1751–80)

J.-J. Rousseau: *Dictionnaire de musique* (Paris, 1768)

Castil-Blaze [F. H. J. Blaze]: *Dictionnaire de musique moderne* (Paris, 1821, 2/1825)

L. E. Reichenburg: *Contribution à l'histoire de la 'querelle des bouffons'* (Paris, 1937)

F. A. Yates: 'Poésie et musique dans les "Magnificences" au mariage du duc de Joyeuse, Paris, 1581', *Musique et poésie au XVIe siècle* (Paris, 1954), 241–64

R. Lebègue: 'Les représentations dramatiques à la cour des Valois', *Les fêtes de la Renaissance*, i, ed. J. Jacquot (Paris, 1956), 85–91

I. Mamczarz: *Les intermèdes comiques italiens au XVIIIe siècle en France et en Italie* (Paris, 1972)   M. ELIZABETH C. BARTLET

Intermedio [*intromessa, introdutto, tramessa, tramezzo, intermezzo*] (It.; Fr. *intermède*). Musico-dramatic entertainment inserted between the acts of plays in the Renaissance and Baroque periods. In scale, *intermedi* could range from simple musical interludes played out of sight of the audience ('intermedi non apparenti') to costumed extravaganzas ('intermedi apparenti') which were important predecessors of opera. They reached their peak in Florence in the late 16th century as the Medici exploited court entertainments to manifest the glory and permanence of the ducal state. The French counterpart is the INTERMÈDE; the preferred term in Italy by the 18th century is INTERMEZZO.

The *intermedi* had obvious precedents in the choruses of classical tragedy and comedy: the practice was discussed by such theorists as G. B. Giraldi, G. G. Trissino and A. Ingegneri. Philippe Verdelot set the choruses of Machiavelli's *Clizia* (1525) and *La mandragola* (1526, ed. in Slim 1972); experiments were made with recitative styles in G. Bombasi's *Alidoro* (1568, Reggio Emilia); and Andrea Gabrieli adopted classicizing homophony for Sophocles' *Oedipus tyrannus* (1585, Vicenza, ed. in Schrade 1960). Such *intermedio* choruses could comment on the action and delineate the temporal perspective of the play. Thus Antonio Landi's *Il commodo*, for the wedding of Duke Cosimo I de' Medici and Eleonora of Toledo (1539, Florence), had *intermedi* (music by Francesco Corteccia; ed. in Minor and Mitchell 1968) representing specific times of day, with the prologue recited by Dawn and the epilogue by Night. The *intermedi* also served a pragmatic function: according to Bernardino Daniello (1536), between the acts of a play 'so that the stage will not be empty, music, songs, dances and jesters are customarily introduced and mingled'. But under the Medici, the *intermedi* rapidly expanded. 'Once *intermedi* were made to serve the comedy, but now comedies are made to serve the *intermedi*', the playwright Antonfrancesco Grazzini complained, lamenting 'la meraviglia, ohimè, degli intermedi' ('the wonder, alas, of the *intermedi*').

As newly created dukes (later grand dukes) of Tuscany, the Medici consolidated their position by carefully calculated dynastic marriages. A Medici wedding was celebrated with elaborate entertainments, generally culminating in a performance of a comedy with *intermedi*. Usually there were six *intermedi* (prologue, four entr'actes and epilogue) exploiting scenic conventions – encompassing the heavens, earth, sea and inferno – that were clearly chosen with spectacle in mind. The thematic content combined complex classical allusions and allegory (no doubt often lost on the audience) with none too subtle Medici propaganda. The *intermedi* were invariably set to music to enhance their visual detachment from the play, to reinforce the mythological and pastoral aura, to emphasize the magical effect of the stage transformations and doubtless to cover the sound of the machinery.

The *intermedi* for Francesco d'Ambra's *La Cofanaria*, for the wedding of Prince Francesco and Johanna of Austria (1565–6), were devised 'with the intention of making it appear as if that which is enacted by the gods in the fable of the *intermedi* is likewise enacted – as it were, under constraint of a higher power – by the mortals in the comedy'. Here the thematic unity (the story of Cupid and Psyche, after Apuleius) leads the *intermedi* to adopt an almost operatic guise, as does the range both of musical genres and styles (including an archetypal lament, ed. in Brown 1972) and of instrumental effects (with instruments linked to specific scenes). However, such unity could go against the raison d'être of the *intermedi*, and in 1586 Giovanni de' Bardi was ordered to abandon his idea of a linking theme because 'before everything else, one has to seek variety'.

The *intermedi* reached their peak at the wedding of Grand Duke Ferdinando I and Christine of Lorraine in 1589. Ferdinando was anxious to emphasize the 'new start' of his reign, and his wedding was celebrated with the most magnificent entertainments ever seen in the city, in which Girolamo Bargagli's comedy *La pellegrina* with spectacular *intermedi* served as climax (texts largely by G. B. Strozzi and Ottavio Rinuccini; music by Cristofano Malvezzi, Luca Marenzio and others). The theme of the *intermedi* (devised by Giovanni de' Bardi, with stage effects by Bernardo Buontalenti) was the power of music: the third and fifth dealt specifically with the mythological musicians Apollo and Arion. Significantly, Apollo soon reappeared in the first opera, *Dafne*; while Jacopo Peri's music for Arion provided important precedents for the coming generation of operatic Orpheuses. The 1589 *intermedi* (ed. in Walker 1963) included a wide range of instrumental and vocal music – highly ornamented solo songs (one by Giulio Caccini), madrigals and sinfonias, large-scale polychoral

The first intermedio in 'La liberazione di Tirreno e d'Arnea' (designed by Giulio Parigi), performed at Bernardo Buontalenti's theatre in the Uffizi Palace for the wedding of Ferdinando Gonzaga, Duke of Mantua, and Catherine de' Medici, 6 February 1617: etching by Jacques Callot

settings – concluding with a grand ballet in the French manner with music (the 'Aria di Firenze') by Emilio de' Cavalieri.

Rinuccini, Peri, Caccini and Cavalieri were soon associated with the rise of opera in Florence. But the *intermedi* retained their potency for symbolic articulation well into the 17th century, due to the palpable failure of early opera to accommodate itself to princely modes of celebration: for the wedding of Prince Cosimo and Maria Magdalena of Austria in 1608, the Medici court deliberately abandoned opera in favour of a traditional set of *intermedi*. The genre also influenced other kinds of entertainments in the early Baroque period in terms of subject matter, scenic effects and musical techniques: Monteverdi's *Orfeo* has close links (in both content and structure) with the *intermedio* tradition, as do the tournaments, ballets and masques that dominate 17th-century court entertainments in Italy and northern Europe. Similarly, *intermedi* entered operas: Stefano Landi's *Il Sant'Alessio* (1632), *Chi soffre speri* by Virgilio Mazzocchi and Marco Marazzoli (1639) and Marco Scacchi's *La santa Cecilia* (1637) each have *intermedi* between two or more of the acts; and in Rome in the 1670s, Alessandro Stradella composed *intermedi* for revivals of operas by Cavalli, Cesti, Sartorio and others. The practice continued into the early 18th century, where such *intermezzi* (by then the preferred term) had a profound influence on the emergence of comic opera.

For further illustration *see* CIGOLI; COSTUME, fig.1; ORCHESTRA, fig.1; PRODUCTION, fig.2; and STAGE DESIGN, fig.1.

*

B. Daniello: *La poetica* (Venice, 1536)

G. B. Giraldi Cinthio: *Discorsi intorno al comporre de i romanzi, delle comedie, e delle tragedie, e di altre maniere di poesie* (Venice, 1554); ed. G. Antimaco, in *G. B. Giraldi Cinthio: scritti estetici*, Biblioteca rara, lii-liii (Milan, 1864)

G. G. Trissino: *La 5a et la 6a divisione della poetica* (Venice, 1562)

A. Ingegneri: *Della poesia rappresentativa et del modo di rappresentare le favole sceniche* (Ferrara, 1598)

A. Warburg: 'I costumi teatrali per gli intermezzi del 1589', *Commemorazione della riforma melodrammatica* (Florence, 1895), 103–46; rev. with notes by G. Bing, in A. Warburg: *Gesammelte Schriften*, i (Leipzig, 1932), 259–300, 394–438

A. Solerti: *Gli albori del melodramma* (Milan, 1904)

——: *Musica, ballo e drammatica alla corte medicea dal 1600 al 1637* (Florence, 1905)

O. Sonneck: 'A Description of Alessandro Striggio and Francesco Corteccia's Intermedi "Psyche and Amor", 1565', *MA*, iii (1911), 40-53; repr. in O. Sonneck: *Miscellaneous Studies in the History of Music* (New York, 1921), 269–86

L. Schrade: *La représentation d'Edippo tiranno au Teatro olimpico* (Paris, 1960)

D. P. Walker: *Les fêtes du mariage de Ferdinand de Médicis et de Christine de Lorraine, Florence 1589: musique des intermèdes de 'La Pellegrina'* (Paris, 1963)

A. M. Nagler: *Theatre Festivals of the Medici, 1539–1637* (New Haven, CT, and London, 1964)

A. C. Minor and B. Mitchell: *A Renaissance Entertainment: Festivities for the Marriage of Cosimo I, Duke of Florence* (Columbia, MI, 1968)

C. Molinari: *Le nozze degli dèi* (Rome, 1968)

G. Gaeta Bertelà and A. Petrioli Tofani, eds.: *Feste e apparati medicei da Cosimo I a Cosimo II: mostra di disegni e incisioni* (Florence, 1969)

O. Jander: 'The Prologues and Intermezzos of Alessandro Stradella', *AnMc*, no. 7 (1969), 87–111

W. Osthoff: *Theatergesang und darstellende Musik in der italienischen Renaissance* (Tutzing, 1969)

W. F. Kümmel: 'Ein deutscher Bericht über die florentinischen Intermedien des Jahres 1589', *AnMc*, no. 9 (1970), 1–19

H. M. Brown: 'Psyche's Lament: some Music for the Medici Wedding in 1565', *Words and Music, the Scholar's View: a*

Medley of Problems and Solutions Compiled in Honor of A. Tillman Merritt by Sundry Hands (Cambridge, MA, 1972), 1–27

W. Kirkendale: *L'aria di Fiorenza id est Il Ballo del Gran Duca* (Florence, 1972)

H. C. Slim: *A Gift of Madrigals and Motets* (Chicago, 1972)

F. W. Sternfeld: 'La technique du finale: des intermèdes à l'opéra', *Les fêtes de la Renaissance*, iii (Paris, 1972), 267–80

——: 'Les intermèdes de Florence et la genèse de l'opéra', *Baroque*, v (1972), 25–9

H. M. Brown: *Sixteenth-Century Instrumentation: the Music for the Florentine Intermedii*, MSD, xxx (1973)

F. W. Sternfeld: 'Aspects of Italian Intermedi and Early Opera', *Convivium musicorum: Festschrift Wolfgang Boetticher* (Berlin, 1974), 359–66

L. Zorzi and others, eds.: *Il luogo teatrale a Firenze* (Milan, 1975)

G. M. Bergman: *Lighting in the Theatre* (Stockholm, 1977)

H. W. Kaufmann: 'Music for a *Favola Pastorale* (1554)', *A Musical Offering: Essays in Honor of Martin Bernstein* (New York, 1977), 163–82

I. Fenlon: *Music and Patronage in Sixteenth-Century Mantua*, i (Cambridge, 1980)

L. Zorzi, ed.: *Il teatro dei Medici*, Quaderni di teatro, ii/7 (Florence, 1980)

R. Donington: *The Rise of Opera* (London, 1981)

N. Pirrotta: *Music and Theatre from Poliziano to Monteverdi* (Cambridge, 1982)

T. Carter: 'A Florentine Wedding of 1608', *AcM*, lv (1983), 89–107

N. Pirrotta: 'I cori per l' "Edipo tiranno"', *Andrea Gabrieli e il suo tempo: Venice 1985*, 273–92

K. Newman: 'The Politics of Spectacle: *La Pellegrina* and the Intermezzi of 1589', *MLN* [*Modern Language Notes*], ci (1986), 95–113

T. Carter: 'Giulio Caccini (1551–1618): New Facts, New Music', *Studi musicali*, xvi (1987), 13–31

——: '"Non occorre nominare tanti musici": the Politics of Spectacle in Late Sixteenth-Century Florence', *I Tatti Studies: Essays in the Renaissance*, iv (forthcoming) TIM CARTER

Intermezzo (It.). Literally, an entr'acte. The term was applied during the 18th century, in place of the earlier INTERMEDIO, to a miniature comic opera in Italian (the French counterpart is the INTERMÈDE) involving two characters (rarely three or more), performed in segments between the acts of a larger work, usually an *opera seria*. The genre flourished during the first half of the 18th century, then gradually disappeared, giving way to the fully-fledged comic opera (*see* OPERA BUFFA). Often, especially in earlier years, its name appeared in the plural as 'intermezzi', sometimes also 'intermedii', 'scherzi musicali' etc. This referred to its performance during the entr'actes (hence the plural) of the larger work; but from the very beginning the intermezzo was unified by a single plot and cast of characters. The segments (in effect, the 'acts' of the intermezzo) were known as 'parti', as in 'intermezzo di due (tre) parti'. Two such 'parts' (performed between Acts 1 and 2 and Acts 2 and 3) were commoner than three; a third 'part', if present, was performed before the final change of scene in the main presentation.

The intermezzo traces its ancestry to the comic scenes of *seicento* opera which, towards the end of the century, were beginning to fade away. Venice took the lead in 'expurgating' the librettos of the *dramma per musica* of its 'improprieties' in an attempt to lend it some of the dignity of classical tragedy. Comic scenes were glaring instances of such breaches of taste; hence their gradual removal. By the first years of the 18th century, comic scenes had become rare in Venice, though not entirely absent. One important consequence of their reduction was to deprive the specialized *buffo* singers of their niche.

It is therefore not surprising that the earliest known intermezzos were performed in Venice. The very first one appears to have been *Frappolone e Florinetta*, performed at the S Cassiano theatre in February 1706 between the acts of the opera *Statira* by Francesco Gasparini. The libretto was not printed; it survives as an anonymous manuscript (*I-Vnm*) but may be ascribed with certainty to Pariati (the music, now lost, was most probably by the composer of the main opera, Gasparini). There may well have been other intermezzos performed, but not published, at about that time: only in October 1707 did the Venetian censorship require publication of intermezzo librettos, thus placing them under its supervision.

The S Angelo theatre briefly entered the field, but during the next few years it was the S Cassiano, with Pariati as poet and Gasparini and (later) Albinoni as composers, that presented the most successful intermezzos. At least three of these were to gain widespread fame as their interpreters, the Mantuan *basso buffo* G. B. Cavana and the Bolognese contralto S. Marchesini, set out on their travels: Gasparini's *Erighetta e Don Chilone* and *Parpagnacco* (both 1707), and Albinoni's *Pimpinone* (1708), the score of which is the earliest specimen of its kind to survive. *Erighetta* is loosely modelled on *Le malade imaginaire* by Molière, who was to become a favourite source of subjects for intermezzos.

In contrast to the Venetian practice of only sporadically performing such independent intermezzos with *opere serie*, the Neapolitan custom during the first two decades of the 18th century was to incorporate comic scenes into nearly every new opera; local composers, including Giuseppe Vignola, Francesco Mancini, Francesco Feo and Leonardo Leo, added the traditional *scene buffe* to works first produced elsewhere without them. After 1720, when the comic elements finally gained complete independence from the *opera seria* libretto, the Neapolitan intermezzo entered a golden age, exemplified in the works of such composers as Domenico Sarro (intermezzos of *Brunetta e Burlotto* frequently revived under the title *La capricciosa e il credulo*, 1720), Hasse (*La contadina*, 1728), Pergolesi (*La serva padrona*, 1733) and Giuseppe Sellitto (*La vedova ingegnosa*, 1735). Neapolitan librettists of that time include Bernardo Saddumene, G. A. Federico and Tommaso Mariani, all of whom were at the same time providing texts for the new, full-length *opere buffe* playing in that city's smaller theatres.

Substantial contributions to the intermezzo repertory were made by the Bolognese composer G. M. Orlandini, whose works, including the enormously successful *Il marito giocatore* (1719), had their first performances in different Italian cities and seem to belong to no particular local tradition. Important figures active outside Italy include Francesco Conti (Vienna) and Telemann (Hamburg).

Apart from Molière's comedies, at least six of which were adapted as librettos for intermezzos (e.g. Antonio Salvi's version of *Le bourgeois gentilhomme*, published at Florence in 1722 as *L'artigiano gentiluomo*), librettists made use of a variety of other sources. Situations from the *commedia dell'arte* were ready to hand, and there is no doubt that intermezzo singers learnt much from their confrères in the matter of acting; unwritten *lazzi* (sight gags) were part of their stock-in-trade, as several contemporary writers testify. 'These buffoons cry, roar with laughter, throw themselves about, indulge in all manner of pantomime, and never deviate from the beat by so much as an eighth of a second', wrote Pré-

Performance of an intermezzo in a Venetian theatre: painting by an unknown artist (? mid-18th century)

sident de Brosses from Rome in 1740. And the English traveller Edward Wright, in an account of intermezzo singers he heard at Venice about 1720, wrote: 'They laugh, scold, imitate other Sounds, as the cracking of a Whip, the rumbling of Chariot Wheels, and all to Music'. Although some of these effects were doubtless improvised by the performers, musical scores furnish abundant examples of written-out portrayals of laughter, sneezing, weeping, the palpitations of a love-sick heart and the like. Other important characteristics of the *buffo* style exemplified in the intermezzo include a lively, frequently disjunct vocal line; constant repetition of short, balanced phrases; parody effects directed mainly at the musical conventions of *opera seria*; and – above all – absolute fidelity of music to text, frequently manifested by extreme changes of tempo and style within a single aria or duet. As a contrast to the prevailing *buffo* style, composers sometimes introduced mock-pathetic numbers and arias modelled on dance rhythms. From their texts and occasional stage directions, it appears that the latter were sometimes actually danced by the *parti buffe*, whose favourite step seems to have been the minuet.

Stock comedy figures, such as the old man and the braggart captain, people the world of the intermezzo. By far the most common of the intermezzo's stock types is the cunning servant girl, widow or shepherdess who, despite her humble station, through feminine wiles plays a *burla* (trick) on her male partner or ensnares him in matrimony. Often the soubrette's name indicates her sharp cunning, as, for example, Serpina ('little snake') in Federico's *La serva padrona* (1733) or Vespetta ('little wasp') in Pariati's *Pimpinone* (1708). Other common dramatic themes include the supernatural, probably deriving from the close connection between the comic characters and transformations of the *intermedi* in 17th-century opera, and satire directed at the *opera seria* (e.g. Sarro's *L'impresario delle isole Canarie*, 1724, attributed to Metastasio).

The intermezzo exhibits nearly as rigid a standard musical format as contemporary *opera seria*. Each 'part' customarily contains one or two arias for each of the two singing roles (one or more mute roles frequently appear) and a final duet, all in da capo form and separated by *secco* recitatives. Accompanied recitative appears infrequently and usually in a parody context, while overtures and other types of independent instrumental music are lacking altogether or confined to short, concluding dance pieces. But stylistically it is more progressive; its simple harmonies, homophonic accompaniments, general melodiousness and symmetrical phrase structure are clear harbingers of later 18th-century Classical style.

The vogue of intermezzos spread quickly to the playhouse, where *commedia dell'arte* companies were fighting a losing battle to retain some of the audience they had lost to opera. As early as 1711, comedians inserted musical intermezzos between the acts of their plays at the S Samuele theatre, Venice. And in the 1730s, Carlo Goldoni served his theatrical apprenticeship as purveyor of intermezzo librettos to another company acting at that theatre.

During the first half of the 18th century, travelling singers, among them the celebrated team of Antonio Ristorini and Rosa Ungarelli, spread the intermezzo repertory throughout Italy and to nearly every European city that supported Italian opera; intermezzos performed between the acts of *commedia dell'arte* plays at Moscow in 1731 preceded by five years the earliest *opere serie*, heard in Russia. Intermezzo performances by itinerant troupes are recorded as early as 1716 in Wolfenbüttel, 1717 in Brunswick and Dresden, 1724 in Prague, 1726 in Mannheim, 1727 in Breslau and 1737 in London. The process of diffusion continued with the tours of Angelo and Pietro Mingotti's opera companies in Austria, Germany and Denmark betwen 1737 and 1760 and in conjunction with the pantomimes presented by the impresario Nicolini's troupe of Piccoli Olandesi (Dutch children) in central Europe between about 1745 and 1750. Perhaps the most significant of the intermezzo's extraterritorial conquests was Paris. Performances of *opere buffe* and intermezzos there during the seasons of 1752–4 by a troupe of singers brought from Strasbourg by Eustachio Bambini precipitated the QUERELLE DES BOUFFONS, a literary polemic which inspired many musical parodies and imitations that opened a new chapter in the history of French opera.

By 1750, ballets had almost completely supplanted intermezzos as the principal entr'acte diversions in performances of *opere serie*, although works to music by such composers as Rinaldo da Capua, Gioacchino Cocchi, Niccolò Piccinni and Baldassare Galuppi continued to figure occasionally between the acts of Italian spoken plays throughout the remainder of the 18th century. Because of the size of their casts (up to seven), which permitted large-scale ensembles and concerted finales, these intermezzos, or 'farsette' as they were often called, differ little from contemporary *opere buffe* except in length and function. Many, in fact, were simply versions of full-length comic operas shortened to fit between the acts of a play and reduced to fit the number of available singers (e.g. *Il filosofo di campagna*, an *opera buffa* by Goldoni and Galuppi, Venice, 1754, and *La serva astuta*, a condensed version performed as an intermezzo at Venice in 1761).

A. Perrucci: *Dell'arte rappresentativa premeditata, ed all'improviso* (Naples, 1699)

Raccolta copiosa d'intermedj, parte da rappresentarsi col canto, alcuni senza musica, con altri in fine in lingua milanese (Milan, 1723)

F. Quadrio: *Della storia e della ragione d'ogni poesia* (Bologna and Milan, 1739–52)

R. Colomb, ed.: *Le Président de Brosses en Italie: lettres familières écrites d'Italie en 1739 et 1740 par Charles de Brosses* (Paris, 1858)

P. Toldo: *L'oeuvre de Molière et sa fortune en Italie* (Turin, 1910)

J. Pulver: 'The Intermezzi of the Opera', *PMA*, xliii (1916–17), 139

H. Nietan: *Die Buffoszenen der spätvenezianischen Oper* (diss., U. of Halle, 1924)

L. Reichenburg: *Contribution à l'histoire de la 'Querelle des Bouffons'* (Philadelphia, 1937)

G. Lazarevich: *The Role of the Neapolitan Intermezzo in the Evolution of Eighteenth-century Musical Style: Literary, Symphonic and Dramatic Aspects, 1685–1735* (diss., Columbia U., 1970)

O. Landmann: *Quellenstudien zum 'intermezzo comico per musica' und zu seiner Geschichte in Dresden* (diss., U. of Rostock, 1972)

I. Mamczarz: *Les intermèdes comiques italiens au XVIIIe siècle en France et en Italie* (Paris, 1972)

M. F. Robinson: *Naples and Neapolitan Opera* (Oxford, 1972)

R. Strohm: *Die italienische Oper im 18. Jahrhundert* (Wilhelmshaven, 1979)

C. E. Troy: *The Comic Intermezzo: a Study in the History of Eighteenth-Century Opera* (Ann Arbor, 1979)

M. Talbot: Introduction to T. Albinoni: *Pimpinone*, RRMBE, xliii (1983)

P. Weiss: 'Venetian Commedia dell'Arte "Operas" in the Age of Vivaldi', *MQ*, lxx (1984), 195–217

CHARLES E. TROY, PIERO WEISS

Intermezzo. *Bürgerliche Komödie mit sinfonischen Zwischenspielen* in two acts by RICHARD STRAUSS to his own libretto; Dresden, Staatsoper, 4 November 1924.

In the spring of 1916 Strauss was still composing *Die Frau ohne Schatten*, as well as finishing the new prologue for the full-opera version of *Ariadne auf Naxos*, but an idea struck him for a new opera of his own. Not another collaboration with Hofmannsthal, nor a substantial art-work at all: rather, it would be a light domestic comedy, almost operetta, with a story based on a marital *contretemps* of his own (in 1903), and leading roles modelled upon himself and his wife Pauline. For a libretto he approached the critic and play-

Christine	soprano
Robert Storch *her husband, a conductor*	baritone
Anna *their maid*	soprano
Franzl *their eight-year-old son*	spoken
Baron Lummer	tenor
The Notary	baritone
His Wife	soprano
Stroh *another conductor*	tenor
A Commercial Counsellor ⎱ *Robert's Skat*	baritone
A Legal Counsellor ⎰ *partners*	baritone
A Singer	bass
Fanny *the Storchs' cook*	spoken
Marie and Therese *maids*	spoken
Resi *a young girl*	soprano

Setting Partly in Grundlsee, partly in Vienna

wright Hermann Bahr, who made sketches but found Strauss so intent upon strict verisimilitude that he finally suggested that Strauss should be his own librettist – a role he had abandoned after his first opera, *Guntram*. He took it up again with delight, if not much urgency; the whole opera was completed, during a South American tour, only in the summer of 1923.

Intermezzo proved to be something more than a self-regarding jest – though the composer did have Lotte Lehmann, the first 'Christine', visit his family to observe Pauline's ways, the Dresden sets copied their Garmisch home, and the first 'Robert' (Joseph Correck) wore a Strauss-mask. Fritz Busch conducted. There was of course gossip about 'doubtful taste', especially because the volatile, petulant Pauline was faithfully drawn, and her husband depicted as buoyantly sensible and generous. Yet Strauss could hardly have seen that as a *risqué* new departure: for 30 years he had portrayed himself in his music, along with Pauline in *Ein Heldenleben* and the *Sinfonia domestica*, and already in the latter their son Franz as the noisy baby-in-the-bath (he appears in *Intermezzo*, like their maid Anna, under his own name). Much more interesting is the actual form of the opera, a string of short scenes in quick alternation with vivid orchestral interludes – often longer than some of the scenes, more lyrically elaborated, and variously ironic, cartoon-pictorial (the toboggan scene) or vehemently impassioned. The latter passages have been thought 'excessive', as if Strauss ought to have trimmed the emotional storms to a bourgeois scale of propriety; but his adored Pauline never did, and he would have scorned the notion that mythical opera-heroes were entitled to stronger feelings than middle-class musicians.

The opera has had a fitful career. Its three-hours-plus probably exceed Strauss's original intention. Though his modest strings, double winds and standard percussion are reinforced by harp, piano, harmonium and a third horn, they must work hard and sonorously. The opera demands much from its stage hands too, for part of the theatrical joke is the rapid succession of contrasted settings briefly glimpsed. Above all, it depends upon an appealing pair of character-comedians who can sing: like Hermann Prey and Hanny Steffek, for many years the ideal Storch couple.

ACT 1.i *The dressing-room at home in Grundlsee* Robert is packing for a two-month engagement in Vienna while Christine fusses, bridles, berates the servants and bemoans her lot. When Robert has

'Intermezzo' (Richard Strauss), Act 1 scene ii (the ski slopes) of the original production at the Staatsoper, Dresden, 4 November 1924

gone, the maid Anna tries in vain to placate her; but a telephone invitation to go skating improves her mood. A brisk orchestral interlude in D develops her voluble tunes and ends with glissando sweeps: toboggans whizzing downhill.

1.ii   *The ski slopes*   On the slope is young Baron Lummer on skis; Christine on her toboggan runs him over. She blames him vociferously, but then discovers that their parents know each other. The interlude mingles the Baron's slight tune with Robert's and Christine's before settling into a lengthy waltz (tongue-in-cheek plain).

1.iii   *The Grundlsee inn*   A ball is in progress. The Baron and Christine stop dancing – she is theatrically exhausted; they chat, agree to meet next day, and go back refreshed for the next waltz. The orchestra continues with suave passion in Db, fades away and drops suddenly into blunt C major …

1.iv   *A furnished room in the Notary's house* Christine is vetting the room for her new protégé and in minute, peremptory detail she enjoins the Notary's wife to take motherly care of him. Interlude: the Baron's and Christine's tunes, cautiously and decorously romantic.

1.v   *The Storchs' dining-room*   Christine is writing a letter to Robert, mentioning her penurious new protégé, the migraines which have delayed his university studies, and her promise to help him. He pays his daily visit, dropping unsubtle hints about how useful a loan (or gift) would be – but Christine's prudent instincts are subliminally aroused, and she confines her response to praising her husband's dependable kindness (brightly in A, then devoutly in Bb). After the Baron departs she falls to mellow musing in Ab, and the orchestra warms the idyll into an elaborate rhapsody.

1.vi   *The Baron's lodgings*   The Baron, alone, smokes a cigarette and considers whether he should press the Frau Hofkapellmeister harder. Indiscreetly, his girl-friend Resi arrives; he sends her out while he drafts a note to Christine. His tone of bland bluster is continued in the interlude.

1.vii   *The Storchs' house*   Christine expostulates about the Baron's stupid letter, with its shameless request for 1000 marks. He enters, and is duly and loftily rebuked. But then the maid Marie brings a note addressed to the Hofkapellmeister Robert Storch. It proves to be a plea from a certain Mitzi Meier for opera tickets, with a promise to meet her 'angel' afterwards in the bar as usual. Christine explodes with anger and the Baron retreats. She dispatches a telegram to her faithless husband announcing that she knows about Mitzi and is leaving forever – and orders poor Anna to pack everything at once. There are orchestral paroxysms (of saintly trust betrayed) in F minor, the basic key for the rest of the act.

1.viii   *Franzl Storch's bedroom*   Descending tearfully upon their son, Christine explains that his wicked father has betrayed her; he will never see him again, because they are going away. Little Franzl ('Bubi') obstinately defends Papa. His mother stays to pray for this fatherless child, and herself, until he is asleep again. (Opinions differ about which is the more embarrassing, this scene or the Act 2 finale; here, Strauss supplies a poignant lyrical plaint without any saving hint of irony.)

ACT 2.i   *The house of the Commercial Counsellor* The Commercial Counsellor is playing Skat (Strauss's adored betting game with cards, something between bridge and poker: the orchestra represents the shuffling and dealing) with the Legal Counsellor, an opera singer and the conductor Stroh, and they discuss Storch's daunting wife. Robert, arriving late from rehearsal, protests that her abrasive temperament is just what he needs, and sings a little eulogy to her in F# – whereupon her telegram reaches him. Dumbfounded, without any idea (unlike Stroh) who Mitzi Meier might be, he rushes off; his friends continue serenely with their *Skatpartie*. There is a frantic orchestral interlude.

2.ii   *The Notary's offices*   Christine descends upon the Notary to demand a divorce. First he suspects her relationship with his lodger the Baron to be germane; then he doubts her evidence against his friend Robert to be adequate. She flounces out. In the interlude, a violent thunderstorm blows up.

2.iii   *The Prater*   Wet and distraught, Robert wanders in the Prater. Stroh rushes up to confess: it is *he* who knows Mitzi Meier – but she was vague about his name, and hit upon the wrong Kapellmeister when she consulted the telephone directory. Robert insists absolutely that Stroh must tell this to Christine in person. Interlude: joyous, hyper-excited relief in honest C major, subsiding into gentle confidence.

2.iv *The Storchs' house* Amid volatile chromatics, the packing up proceeds in some disarray. Christine has sent the Baron off to Vienna to play detective. As she discusses that with the maids, a telegram comes from Robert: unfortunate confusion, Stroh on his way to explain it all! – and indeed the unlucky Stroh is at the door. She doubts whether she wants to be persuaded, but the last interlude – an exuberant 6/8 affair in E – recycles the main themes with an air of finality.

2.v *The same* Robert arrives, expecting complete forgiveness; but it is Christine who demands apologies. He goes off in a fury and she declares that she always knew it would end like this.

2.vi *The same* The Baron reports upon his mission, but his vague findings have been pre-empted. Christine dismisses him brusquely. Though Robert, back again, makes fun of her illusions about him, she accepts the teasing almost meekly: like Barak's Wife in Strauss's previous opera, *Die Frau ohne Schatten*, she has been deeply stirred by the sight of her husband in real anger. They bill and coo at length in A, with a rapturous F♯ coda.

* * *

If the cheerful triviality of the *Intermezzo* story is in radical contrast to the lofty concerns of *Die Frau ohne Schatten*, so is its musical form. Hofmannsthal's dramaturgy had dictated long Wagnerian paragraphs and continuous development; in *Intermezzo* Strauss gave himself room to play with the mercurial conversation style he had devised for the *Ariadne* prologue, and to veer away from through-composed music drama towards a new kind of number opera. There are at least as many distinguishable themes in *Intermezzo* as in any other of his operas, and assiduously developed as always – but in a string of bright, separate little inventions, each with a neat theatrical point. (The score is also spiced with jokey quotations, from his own and other composers' music.) With a feather-light plot, anecdotal detail had to provide the life of the piece. Given the strictly naturalistic text, no vocal 'numbers' were feasible beyond the odd lyrical effusion; otherwise, the distinct set pieces had to be orchestral, and mostly between the scenes. They supply more than just a frame: *Intermezzo* depends upon them for due variety of colour and rhythm (and some of its better jokes), as both its title and its subtitle imply. Among the singing roles, the Christine/Pauline character is brilliantly fixed by her music (full of irascible leaps like the part of Barak's Wife, which Pauline had also inspired unawares). Robert/Richard is pleasantly idealized; the Baron is no more than languid cartoon, and the lesser characters fare worse. For the next two decades Strauss would attempt nothing remotely like this piece – until his last opera, *Capriccio*, which capitalized upon lessons learnt from the *Intermezzo* experiment.   DAVID MURRAY

Interval (Amer. intermission; Fr. *entr'acte*; Ger. *Pause*; It. *intervallo*). A break between the acts, with the curtain down and the auditorium emptied, seems to be a modern device, though the subject is ill documented. Until the 19th century (in some places late in the century) continuous but varied entertainment was probably the norm in theatres with both spoken and musical repertories; the interval pianist, who lingered on

in some British theatres into the 1970s, was its last manifestation.

Opera houses until about 1850 were centres of social life for an audience of which many members expected in the course of a season to hear the same work several times over. They did not pay attention continuously to the stage action; the auditorium was lit throughout; visits, conversations and, in Italy, eating, drinking and gambling went on during the performance, in the boxes as well as in the foyers; often the stalls too allowed some promenading. Sets, until the late 18th century or after, consisted mainly of flats that could be moved in view of the audience. In such conditions, a total break was scarcely called for; the pause needed to rest the singers was given over to another genre, which at times could rouse more interest than the opera it was interleaved with: a comic INTERMEZZO, instrumental music, and especially ballet.

More solid three-dimensional sets required changing with the curtain down, a new departure said to have been made at the Paris Opéra from 1831. With the coming of repertory opera, audiences were less likely to hear the same work repeated in quick succession. A general trend towards greater attentiveness (at concerts too) culminated in Wagner's darkening the theatre and requiring total concentration during the acts, with intervals given over to refreshment and socializing. After some initial resistance from audiences, attentiveness became the new norm, with a corresponding need for a clear break. In recent years some houses have lengthened their intervals, probably so as to maximize bar takings; a common length is 12 to 20 minutes, but 45 minutes or more may be allowed, for example, during a long Wagner opera, so that a meal may be taken; and at Glyndebourne there is a 'dinner interval' of 75 to 90 minutes.

*

ES ('Intervallo'; 'Intermezzo', C. Casini)
A. Pougin: 'Entr'acte', *Grande Encyclopédie* (Paris, 1887–98)
                    JOHN ROSSELLI

In the Well. Opera by Vilém Blodek; *see* V STUDNI.

Intimate Opera Company. English company founded 'to revive unknown opera of the chamber music genre'. It was established in 1930 by Frederick Woodhouse, who launched the company with Arne's *Thomas and Sally*; collaborating with him were Margaret Ritchie and Geoffrey Dunn, who was later to edit and arrange many of the company's operas. The company established itself successfully and in 1937 visited Spain and the USA. During World War II it gave performances for both the forces and civilians. In 1953 Woodhouse was succeeded as musical and artistic director by Antony Hopkins, with Joseph Horovitz as his assistant. This change in directorship resulted in a break in tradition, and works were commissioned from young composers including Horovitz's *The Dumb Wife*, Geoffrey Bush's *If the Cap Fits*, and Hopkins's *Three's Company*. In 1960 Winifred Radford, a member of the company until 1950, returned as director, and in 1973 the baritone William Dickie became the general manager. Additions to the repertory after 1970 include Egidio Duni's *La clochette* (as *The Sheep Bell*), produced by Anthony Besch; and Purcell's *Don Quixote* and the pasticcio *Il maestro di musica* (formerly attributed to Pergolesi), both produced by Dennis Arundell.   HAROLD ROSENTHAL

*'Intolleranza 1960'
(Nono): stage picture
produced by the
projection of Emilio
Vedova's collages and
abstract images on to
screens designed and
arranged by Josef
Svoboda for the original
production at La Fenice,
Venice, 13 April 1961*

Intolleranza 1960 ('Intolerance 1960'). *Azione scenica* in two parts by LUIGI NONO after an idea by Angelo Maria Ripellino, to texts by Ripellino, Henri Alleg, Bertolt Brecht, Aimé Césaire, Paul Eluard, Vladimir Mayakovsky, Julius Fucik and Jean-Paul Sartre, assembled by the composer; Venice, Teatro La Fenice, 13 April 1961.

Intolleranza 1960 was conceived and written within the space of three months in response to an invitation from the director of the Venice Biennale, Mario Labroca. For nearly a decade Nono had been fascinated by the experimental theatre of pre-Stalinist Russia, above all that of Meyerhold, as described in the writings of Ripellino. He therefore requested a text from Ripellino reflecting that tradition, but found the result difficult to work with. In consequence he substituted a collage of fragments from a wide range of sources, some poetic (Eluard, Mayakovsky), others documentary (Alleg, Fucik). Each text defined an emblematic 'situation' conducive to reflection; they were linked by a skeletal narrative that carried contemporary political resonances.

The unnamed protagonist (tenor) is defined simply as a migrant worker (exemplified for an Italian audience by the many southern Italians who sought work in the industrial towns of the north). In Part 1, overcome by the oppressive environment of a mining town, he resolves to return home, leaving behind the woman who has cared for him. But he finds himself caught up in a demonstration, and is arrested, interrogated and tortured. He is placed in a concentration camp, but contrives to escape with an Algerian. (At the time of composition the Algerian crisis was at its height.) In Part 2, after a collage representing the absurdities of everyday life, the immigrant encounters on his travels a female companion (soprano): together they find the will to confront social fanaticism. Finally, they find themselves near a town whose river, dammed in order to provide hydro-electric power, has become perilously swollen. The river breaks through the dam, sweeping all before it including the two principal characters.

The visual aspect of *Intolleranza 1960* aimed at the dynamization of the whole stage space and owed much to Josef Svoboda's 'magic lantern' techniques – multiple simultaneous projections on to moving curtains of various shapes – which Nono had encountered when visiting Prague in 1958. Svoboda came to Venice, but his selection of photographic slides (details of architecture, gardens, etc.) did not coincide with Nono's conception. Nono's friend, the painter Emilio Vedova, provided a mixture of collage and abstraction to project on to Svoboda's screens instead. The music of *Intolleranza 1960* throws into opposition many of Nono's most characteristic procedures to date: documentary materials are presented in a direct, realistic fashion (often spoken), whereas poetic texts are sometimes 'dissolved', syllable by syllable, into complex choral textures that echo (if in somewhat simplified form) Nono's daring choral experiments of the previous few years. Solo lines echo the eloquent, impassioned lyricism of such earlier works as *Il canto sospeso* (1956). While the orchestra at times reactivates the fragmented textures of *Il canto sospeso* (and at one pertinent point between interrogation and torture in Part 1 scene iv, quotes directly from that setting of letters from condemned resistance fighters), it is also used by Nono to create stark, vigorous gestures and massive, teeming blocks of musical material, both kinds of texture strongly recalling techniques in the paintings of Vedova. In 1960 Vedova's work had also been the inspiration for Nono's first experiments with electronic resources, now put to dramatic use by placing loudspeakers so as to surround the audience.

A work so overtly confrontational both courted and received a stormy reception, even though some part of the furore surrounding its first performance was orchestrated by opposing political groups. Since part of its impact depended upon contemporary resonances, when revising the work as a one-act opera for performance in 1974 Nono allowed modifications to the scenario and changed the work's name to *Intolleranza 1970*.   DAVID OSMOND-SMITH

Into the Storm. Opera by T. N. Khrennikov; *see V BURYU*.

Intrepidi. Theatre in Florence, properly the Regio Teatro degl'Intrepidi detto Palla a Corda, built in the late 18th century by a group of nobility and common citizens; *see* FLORENCE, §§6–7.

Introduzione (It.: 'introduction'). A title often given to the opening number of an opera when it involves more than two characters. An early example is 'Che lieto giorno' (*La finta giardiniera*, Mozart, 1775), which parades the whole cast. Sometimes it may consist merely of a chorus with or without the intervention of a minor character, as in *Tancredi* (Rossini, 1813), *I Capuleti e i Montecchi* (Bellini, 1830) and *Maria Padilla* (Donizetti, 1841); but already in *Il barbiere di Siviglia* (1816) Rossini had evolved a more complex structure incorporating a tenor cavatina and ending with a stretta. A still more elaborate scheme is found in *Semiramide* (1823), proceeding from an initial recitative through a trio and quartet interspersed with brief choral movements to a headlong 'stretta dell'introduzione'. The commonest formula during the first half of the 19th century, however, is that of the 'Introduzione e cavatina', consisting of an opening chorus, a recitative and 'cantabile' for the soloist, a *tempo di mezzo* with dialogue and finally a cabaletta with choral support (after which the stage empties). Examples include *Maria Stuarda* (Donizetti, 1834), *Lucia di Lammermoor* (1835), *Ernani* (Verdi, 1844) and *Il corsaro* (Verdi, 1848). In *Il bravo* (Mercadante, 1839) it is extended to include a *romanza* sung by another character; in *Stiffelio* (Verdi, 1850) it follows a pattern akin to that of *Semiramide*, comprising a 'settimino'; while in *Rigoletto* (1851) it covers the entire action of the first scene up to and including Monterone's curse. The 'introduzione' of *Un ballo in maschera* (1859) contains two cavatinas and a canzone together with an opening chorus and closing stretta. With the coming of Italian grand opera during the 1870s the 'introduzione' ceased to exist as a formal unit. A rich parody, however, is to be found in *The Gondoliers* (Sullivan, 1889). JULIAN BUDDEN

Invisible City of Kitezh, The Legend of the. Opera by N. A. Rimsky-Korsakov; *see* LEGEND OF THE INVISIBLE CITY OF KITEZH AND THE MAIDEN FEVRONIYA, THE.

Inzenga (y Castellanos), José (*b* Madrid, 3 June 1828; *d* Madrid, 28 June 1891). Spanish composer. After studying with his father and at the Madrid Conservatory with Pedro Albéniz, he spent 1842–8 in Paris, where he was a composition pupil of Carafa at the Conservatoire. Through Auber's influence, he was in 1847 appointed a chorus master at the Opéra-Comique, but the next year was driven back to Madrid by the Revolution of 1848.

Although betraying French influences, his first zarzuela, the one-act *El campamento* (1851), dedicated to the Duke of Osuna, who had subsidized his Parisian studies, won immediate and lasting acclaim. As a result, he was invited to join forces with Barbieri, Gaztambide, Hernando, Oudrid, the poet Luis Olona the younger, and the actor-singer Francisco Salas in forming a zarzuela company. Their intention was to contract performers and promote zarzuelas at the Teatro del Circo; Inzenga was appointed the company's archivist. In collaboration with Hernando, Inzenga next composed *El confitero de Madrid* (1851) and with

Barbieri, Gaztambide, Hernando and Oudrid the highly successful *Por seguir a una mujer* (1851) and the less popular *Don Simplicio Bobadilla* (1853) that ran for only 14 consecutive days. He also collaborated on *Un día de reinado* (1854) but independently composed no successes from 1851 until his last zarzuela, *¡Si yo fuera rey!* (6 Sept 1862), which was decently applauded. From 1860 to his death he taught singing at the Madrid Conservatory. His importance in music history is as a collector of folk music.

all first performed in Madrid

El campamento (1, L. Olona), Circo, 8 May 1851 (Madrid, 1851)
El confitero de Madrid (2 or 3, Olona), Circo, 7 Nov 1851, collab. Hernando
Por seguir a una mujer (4, Olona), Circo, 24 Dec 1851, collab. F. A. Barbieri, Gaztambide, Hernando and Oudrid
Don Simplicio Bobadilla (3, M. and V. Tamayo y Baus), Circo, 7 May 1853, collab. Barbieri, Gaztambide and Hernando
Un día de reinado (3, J. García Gutiérrez and Olona), Circo, 15 Feb 1854, collab. Barbieri, Gaztambide and Oudrid
¡Si yo fuera rey! (3, M. Pina and M. Pastorfido), Circo, 6 Sept 1862

*

A. Peña y Goñi: *La ópera española y la música dramática en España en el siglo XIX* (Madrid, 1934), 480ff
J. M. Esperanza y Sola: *Treinta años de crítica musical: colección póstuma de los trabajos* (Madrid, 1906), ii, 394–402, 616–21
E. Cotarelo y Mori: *Historia de la zarzuela, o sea el drama lírico* (Madrid, 1934), 315, 467, 509
F. Asenjo Barbieri: *Documentos sobre música española y epistolario (Legado Barbieri)*, ed. E. Casares (Madrid, 1986), 393, 661–7, 1174 [incl. letters to Barbieri]
J. Henken: *Francisco Asenjo Barbieri and the Nineteenth-Century Revival in Spanish National Music* (diss., UCLA, 1987), 57, 70, 84, 92, 98, 551 ROBERT STEVENSON

Iolanta ('Iolanthe'). Lyric opera in one act by PYOTR IL'YICH TCHAIKOVSKY to a libretto by MODEST IL'YICH TCHAIKOVSKY after Henrik Hertz's play *Kong Renés Datter* ('King René's Daughter'), translated from the Danish by Fyodor Miller, adapted for the Maliy Theatre (Moscow) by Vladimir Rafailovich Zotov; St Petersburg, Mariinsky Theatre, 6/18 December 1892.

Iolanta *blind daughter of King René*		soprano
René *King of Provence*		bass
Vaudémont *Count, Burgundian knight*		tenor
Ibn-Hakia *Moorish physician*		baritone
Robert *Duke of Burgundy*		baritone
Alméric *armour-bearer to King René*		tenor
Bertrand *doorkeeper to the castle*		bass
Martha *Bertrand's wife, Iolanta's nursemaid*		contralto
Brigitta	*Iolanta's girl friends*	soprano
Laura		mezzo-soprano

Iolanta's servant-girls and girl friends, the king's retinue, the duke's regiment, men-at-arms

Setting The mountains of southern France, 15th century

Tchaikovsky began work on *Iolanta* on 28 June/10 July 1891 with the decisive confrontation between Iolanta and Vaudémont, culminating in their big duet in praise of light. Although he complained to his librettist brother of a loss of facility after the huge access of inspiration that carried him through *The Queen of Spades*, the opera was finished in short score by 25 August/5 September and the orchestration was completed on 8/20 November. The composer was not entirely happy with the result. He accused himself of self-repetition (notably of *The Enchantress*), and a passage in a letter he wrote to a would-be librettist in February 1892 ('medieval dukes and knights and ladies capture my imagination but not my heart') is often taken as evidence of his attitude to his last opera. Rimsky-Korsakov, who attended the dress rehearsals, recalled it scathingly in his memoirs. Yet at the première, so the composer reported, *Iolanta* – conducted by Eduard Nápravník, with Nikolay Figner as Vaudémont and Medea Figner in the title role – fared much better with the audience than *The Nutcracker* (as a companion-piece to which it had been commissioned by the Imperial Theatres).

A lush garden with hedge roses and fruit trees, its gate at the rear overgrown with green The introduction, scored for woodwind and horns, is intensely chromatic, evocative of Iolanta's world of darkness. The opening of the scene, like that of *Yevgeny Onegin*, pits vocal *parlante* against background music, in this case a solo string quartet (muted) and harp, which serenade the blind princess and her companions as they pick fruit in the garden. Iolanta confides in Martha that she senses she is lacking something, but does not know what. The musicians are silenced and she expresses her doubts more fully in an arioso ('Otchego eto prezhde ne znala': 'Why did I not know this before'). Her girl friends and ladies in waiting try to comfort Iolanta with flowers. Finally Brigitta, Laura and Martha, followed by the chorus, sing Iolanta to sleep. All exit except Iolanta, who sleeps at the rear of the stage, behind the overgrowth, through the next pair of scenes.

Alméric enters, having presented credentials to Bertrand. He announces the impending arrival of King René, accompanied by the Moorish physician Ibn-Hakia, who will see whether Iolanta's blindness may be cured. They enter, and after Ibn-Hakia has been led off to examine the sleeping Iolanta, the king prays for his daughter's recovery ('Gospod' moy, yesli greshen ya': 'O Lord, if I have Sinned'). Ibn-Hakia returns and informs the king that it may be possible to restore Iolanta's sight, but only if she is made aware of her misfortune and desires a cure. The king is unwilling to risk his daughter's unhappiness. To 'modal' oriental strains (compare the 'Arabian Dance' in *The Nutcracker*), the physician gives the king some ancient metaphysical advice: he is unwise to consider the world of the flesh apart from the world of the spirit; Iolanta can only be made whole if her spirit grasps the idea of light and prepares her eyes to receive it. They make for the castle.

Robert and Vaudémont wander into the garden, lost. They have no idea that they are in the grounds of King René or that Iolanta sleeps nearby. In fact Robert is preparing to ask to be released from his childhood betrothal to Iolanta because he has fallen in love with Countess Mathilde of Lorraine, to whom he sings an impassioned encomium ('Kto mozhet sravnit'sya s Matil'doy moyey': 'Who may compare with my Mathilde'). Vaudémont declares that he is uninterested in physical charms but rather looks for a woman of perfect purity; this romance, composed during rehearsals at Nikolay Figner's request, is optional.

The two intruders begin looking around and Vaudémont stumbles on the nook where Iolanta is sleeping. He is immediately thunderstruck, recognizing the answer to his just-uttered prayer. Robert takes fright at what he perceives to be an enchantment. He insists that they leave. The ensuing quarrel awakens Iolanta. She comes out, meets the two knights, and rushes off to fetch some wine to entertain them. While she is offstage

Robert leaves, so that when she returns Vaudémont is alone. He sings to her of his infatuation and asks for a rose the colour of her cheeks. She picks him a white one. He points out her error and asks specifically for a red one; she does not know what that means. He asks her how many roses he is holding; when she answers that she cannot tell without touching them, he knows that she is blind. He extends sympathy; she is uncomprehending. He describes to her what she is missing; she understands at last but insists that she does not need light in order to praise the Creator (duet, 'Chudnïy pervenets tvoren'ya': 'Wondrous firstling of creation').

The stage fills with the remaining characters, except Robert. When King René finds out that Iolanta has learnt of her blindness in the course of finding love he is at first in despair, but Ibn-Hakia points out that his condition has now been met, and nothing stands in the way of a cure. The assembled characters join voices in a brief octet expressing hope, at the end of which the king, believing in the cure at last, threatens Vaudémont with execution if the operation is unsuccessful. Ibn-Hakia understands that the king is providing Iolanta with the incentive she needs to gain her sight.

Vaudémont asks for Iolanta's hand in marriage, but King René informs him that she is pledged to another. Robert, returning with his retinue (who at last provide a male chorus), requests release from his promise of marriage in favour of Vaudémont, a request the king is now only too happy to grant. Iolanta returns, cured. All raise their voices in praise of light and its creator, partly to a reprise of the main tune from the duet, whose resemblance to Anton Rubinstein's song *Zhelaniye* ('Longing'), after Lermontov (op.8 no.5), so annoyed Rimsky-Korsakov. The resemblance was probably a deliberate double homage: the first line of Lermontov's poem – 'Open up my gaol cell, let me see the light of day!' – is singularly apt to the dramatic situation (ex.1).

Ex.1
(a) Rubinstein

Allegro moderato *Appassionato*

Ot - vo - ri - te mne tem - ni - tsu, [etc.]

(b) Tchaikovsky

Moderato mosso

VAUDÉMONT

Chud - nïy per - ve - nets tvo-ren'- ya, per - vïy mi - ru dar tvor-tsa,

sla - vï bozh'- yey pro-yav-len'- ye, luch-shiy perl e - go ven-tsa!

['Wondrous firstling of creation, the creator's first gift to the world, manifestation of God's glory, finest pearl in His crown!']

* * *

The dramatic confrontations and arias in *Iolanta*, despite the fact that several of the latter (Iolanta's opening arioso, King René's prayer, Robert's aria) achieved an independent recital-stage popularity, are fairly routine and in at least one case, the king's, downright trite. Ibn-Hakia's monologue-aria, too, is pretty much thrown-off; the mysterious East did not beckon Tchaikovsky as it did his teacher Rubinstein or his 'kuchkist' contemporaries, nor did the composer respond in any special way to the libretto's metaphysical trappings. The magic in this opera is to be found in its decorator colours.　　　　　RICHARD TARUSKIN

Iolanthe [*Iolanthe; or, The Peer and the Peri*]. Operetta in two acts by ARTHUR SULLIVAN to a libretto by W. S. GILBERT; London, Savoy Theatre, 25 November 1882.

Phyllis (soprano) loves Strephon (baritone), an Arcadian shepherd. A ward of court, she requires the consent of the Lord Chancellor (baritone) to her marriage. This he refuses, being enamoured of her himself. Strephon's mother is a fairy, Iolanthe (mezzo-soprano), who has just been released from the banishment to which the Fairy Queen (contralto) committed her for breaching fairy law by marrying a mortal. Strephon's fairy parentage causes problems with Phyllis but gains him the fairies' support for a controversial parliamentary career. Meanwhile Phyllis deliberates: should she now marry Lord Tolloller (tenor) or Lord Mountararat (baritone)? To salvage Strephon's happiness, Iolanthe reveals herself to her mortal husband, the Lord Chancellor, thereby reinvoking the death penalty which, but for the Fairy Queen's mercy, would have been her original punishment. Fortunately an amendment to the fairy law saves the situation: 'every fairy shall die who *doesn't* marry a mortal'. Strephon and Phyllis are reunited and the love-struck fairies and peers all fly off to Fairyland.

A remarkable blend of whimsical fantasy and satire, *Iolanthe* exhibits an emotional range rare in the Savoy operas. This, together with its originality, variety, subtlety and unity of creative purpose, makes it one of the finest in the series. Sullivan's entrancing score is rich in contrast, setting the delicacy of the Mendelssohnian fairy music against the grandiloquent March of the Peers and the patriotic 'When Britain really ruled the waves', and the gaiety of the trio 'If you go in' against the pathos of the scene in which Iolanthe confronts the Lord Chancellor – at the heart of which is the hauntingly beautiful 'He loves!' The political musings of guardsman Private Willis (bass) remain apposite, though some topical references need clarification, as in the Fairy Queen's lyrical 'Oh, foolish fay'. Among Savoy patter songs, 'When you're lying awake' is particularly original, its inventive instrumental colouring illustrating Sullivan's orchestral mastery, which is especially evident in this work.　　　　　DAVID RUSSELL HULME

Ionian Islands. *See* CORFU.

Ipermestra ('Hypermnestra'). Libretto by PIETRO METASTASIO, first set by Johann Adolf Hasse (1744, Vienna).

ACT 1　Danao [Danaus], King of Argos, is informed by an oracle that he will lose his life at the hands of a son of Aegyptus. He therefore commands his daughter, Hypermnestra, betrothed to Linceo [Lynceus], a son of Aegyptus, to murder him on their wedding night; but, unable to commit such a crime, Hypermnestra decides to reject Lynceus. Told of this action by Adrasto [Adrastus], his confidant, Danaus condemns his daughter, who still refuses Lynceus when next she meets him.

ACT 2　Danaus instructs Adrastus to tell Elpinice, his niece, that she will inherit the throne if she convinces Hypermnestra to change her mind. Unsure of what to do, Elpinice seeks counsel. Meanwhile, Hypermnestra

pleads in vain with her father to spare Lynceus. She learns from Lynceus himself that he plans suicide; she begs him to refrain, but refuses to admit that she still loves him.

ACT 3　Elpinice tells Hypermnestra of the king's offer. At their next meeting, Hypermnestra and Lynceus reaffirm their love. Lynceus agrees to leave Argos, but when Elpinice tells Plistene [Pleisthenes], her betrothed, about the king's schemes, Pleisthenes encourages Lynceus to revolt instead. Realizing Hypermnestra's safety might be at stake, Lynceus consents. Danaus hears of the uprising and again accuses Hypermnestra of betrayal, but when Lynceus and Pleisthenes break into the king's chambers, it is Hypermnestra who rescues him and who subsequently pleads for the lives of the traitors when the rebellion is suppressed. Danaus pardons them, and graciously gives permission for the wedding of Hypermnestra and Lynceus.

*　　　*　　　*

Accounts of the events that provide the basic action for this drama may be found in the Apollodorus, *Bibliotheca* (book 2) and the Hyginus, *Fabulae* (no.168). Aeschylus covered the myth surrounding the 50 sons of Aegyptus and the 50 daughters of Danaus in his Danaid trilogy, but of this work, only the first play, *The Suppliant Women*, remains. Prior to Metastasio's drama, Théodore de Gombauld's *Les Danaïdes* (1644), Gaspard Abeille's *Lyncée* (1678) and Théodore de Riupeirous' *Hypermnestre* (1704) were all based upon this story, as were Giovanni Moniglia's libretto for Cavalli's opera *Hipermestra* (1658, Florence) and Antonio Salvi's text for Giacomelli's *Ipermestra* (1724, Venice). Of the contemporary sources, however, Metastasio's plot has its closest parallels with Joseph de Lafont's *livret* for Charles-Hubert Gervais' *Hypermnèstre* (1716, Paris). Metastasio claims to have written his *Ipermestra* in 18 days for Hasse to set as part of the celebrations that honoured the wedding of the Archduchess Maria Anna of Austria to Charles Alexander, Duke of Lorraine. The opera was first performed at a private court gathering before its première at the Hoftheater on 25 January 1744. Gluck's setting opened in Venice in November of the same year, and although *Ipermestra* never achieved more than moderate popularity, with just on 30 settings, it was set in the 19th century by three different composers; Mercadante's version for Naples (1825) was revised for a subsequent performance. With the violent elements of the classical story suppressed, Metastasio's libretto inspired settings markedly different from such operas as Salieri's *Les Danaïdes* (1784, Paris), a setting of a French translation of an Italian libretto originally written by Calzabigi for Gluck.

For a list of settings *see* METASTASIO, PIETRO.　　　DON NEVILLE

Iphigenia in Aulis. Libretto subject used in the 18th century. Its source is the *Iphigeneia in Aulis* of EURIPIDES, but Racine's *Iphigénie* (1674) is of equal importance. Librettos on the subject were written in French (*Iphigénie en Aulide*), German (*Iphigenie in Aulis*) and Italian (*Ifigenia in Aulide*).

In Euripides' account, the Greek fleet is becalmed at Aulis where it has assembled to sail for Troy. An oracle demands that Agamemnon sacrifice his daughter Iphigenia, in order that the winds may blow. Agamemnon vacillates; Clytemnestra protests; Achilles defends Iphigenia; Iphigenia goes willingly to the altar.

At the last minute Diana carries her off, leaving a deer in her place. This version permits a sequel, IPHIGENIA IN TAURIS. According to Racine there is a second Iphigenia, known as Erifile [Eriphyle]. At the last moment the high priest realizes that Eriphyle is the one who must die; she kills herself, and Iphigenia and Achilles marry. The third common variant is a compromise, in which, without Eriphyle, Iphigenia is saved by divine intervention and marries Achilles.

The earliest surviving libretto is by Postel, for Keiser (1699): *Die wunderbahr-errettete Iphigenia*. Some further unimportant librettos followed in the early 18th century before Zeno's *Ifigenia in Aulide* (1718), which became the most popular Iphigenia libretto of the century. It is based on Racine, but Eriphyle is now called Elisena. It was set first by Caldara (1718) and then by Orlandini (1732), Giovanni Porta (1738), Porpora (1735), Abos (1745), Sarti (1777), Tarchi (1785) and Giuseppe Giordani (1786). Verazi's *Ifigenia* for Jommelli (1751) is a new adaptation of Racine, while V. A. Cigna-Santi's libretto, set by Bertoni (1762) and Franchi (1766), follows Euripides.

There was some interest in the story of Iphigenia in Aulis as a subject for reform opera in the middle of the century. Villati's *Ifigenia in Aulide* for Graun (1748) uses the third plot variant. In 1755 Algarotti included a detailed scenario (in French prose) for a libretto based on Euripides as an appendix to his *Saggio sopra l'opera in musica*. This text was never set, but it became part of the thinking on reform opera. Gluck's *Iphigénie en Aulide*, with libretto by Bailli du Roullet (1774), uses the third variant, although the goddess appears on stage only in the 1775 revision.

After Gluck, two late *opera seria* librettos entitled *Ifigenia in Aulide* had some popularity: Luigi Serio's was set by Martín y Soler (1779) and Prati (1784); Moretti's was set by Zingarelli (1787) and Cherubini (1788, his last opera for Italy).

See also IPHIGÉNIE EN AULIDE [Gluck].   JULIE E. CUMMING

Iphigenia in Tauris. Libretto subject popular in the 18th century. Its source is the *Iphigenia in Tauris* of EURIPIDES, although Guimond de la Touche's spoken drama *Iphigénie en Tauride* (1757) was also influential. Librettos on the subject were written in Italian (*Ifigenia in Tauride*), French (*Iphigénie en Tauride*) and German (*Iphigenie in Tauris*); they were sometimes named after the two principal male characters (*Oreste*; *Oreste e Pilade*; *Pilade e Oreste*) or their friendship (*La forza dell'amicizia*).

Iphigenia is a priestess at the temple of Diana in the barbarian kingdom of Tauris, having been transported there after her supposed sacrifice in Aulis. Her brother Orestes arrives in Tauris with his faithful friend Pylades. He is being pursued by the Furies for having killed his mother, Clytemnestra, and must do penance by finding the statue of Diana in Tauris and returning it to Greece. They are captured and the tyrant, Thoas, demands that they be sacrificed. Iphigenia does not recognize them, but feels a strange affinity with Orestes; there is a recognition scene, an attempt to escape, and a final *dea ex machina* to save the day. In some versions the goddess is replaced by human intervention; some librettos, for example Verazi's for G. F. de Majo (1764), contain several additional characters and episodes.

The first opera on the subject was a *tragédie lyrique* begun by the librettist Duché de Vancy and the composer Desmarets, and completed by the librettist Danchet and the composer Campra (1704). Iphigenia in Tauris also enjoyed modest popularity as an *opera seria* libretto: Pasqualigo's libretto for Orlandini (1719) was set again by Vinci (1725), Mazzoni (1756) and Carlo Monza (1784). But after De la Touche's spoken drama of 1757 Tauris became a popular subject for reform opera. The Desmarets-Campra opera was revived in 1762 (revised by Pierre-Montan Berton), and hard on its heels came Italian reform settings: Marco Coltellini's libretto for Traetta (1763, set again by Galuppi in 1768), and Verazi's for Majo (1764, set again by Monza, as *Oreste*, in 1766 and in a revised version by Jommelli in 1771). Guillard's libretto for Gluck's *Iphigénie en Tauride* (1779), based on the De la Touche tragedy, was followed by Dubreuil's libretto for Piccinni (1781). These two operas provoked the Querelle des Gluckistes et Piccinistes.

See also IFIGENIA IN TAURIDE (i) [Traetta]; IFIGENIA IN TAURIDE (ii) [Majo]; IFIGENIA IN TAURIDE (iii) [Jommelli]; IPHIGÉNIE EN TAURIDE (i) [Gluck]; IPHIGÉNIE EN TAURIDE (ii) [Piccinni]; and ORESTE [Handel].

JULIE E. CUMMING

Iphigénie en Aulide ('Iphigenia in Aulis'). *Tragédie* in three acts by CHRISTOPH WILLIBALD GLUCK to a libretto by MARIE FRANÇOIS LOUIS GAND LEBLANC ROULLET after JEAN RACINE's *Iphigénie en Aulide*, itself after EURIPIDES; Paris, Opéra, 19 April 1774.

Agamemnon *King of Mycenae and Argos*		baritone
Clitemnestre [Clytemnestra] *his wife*		soprano
Iphigénie [Iphigenia] *their daughter*		soprano
Achille [Achilles] *a Greek hero in love with* *Iphigenia*		tenor
Patrocle [Patroclus] *a Greek chieftain and friend* *of Achilles*		bass
Calchas *High Priest*		bass
Arcas *Captain of Agamemnon's guards*		bass
Three Greek women		sopranos
Slave from Lesbos		soprano

Greek officers, warriors and people, guards, Thessalian warriors, women from Argos and Aulis, slaves from Lesbos and priestesses of Diana

Setting Aulis, a town on the island of Euboea off the coast of Greece at the time of the Trojan War

Iphigénie en Aulide was the first of the seven operas that Gluck composed for Paris, although it was not actually commissioned by the Académie Royale de Musique. After *Paride ed Elena* failed to meet with success in Vienna in 1770, Gluck's thoughts turned elsewhere. He had already written and adapted several French *opéras comiques* for Vienna and he had admired and studied the *tragédies lyriques* of Lully and Rameau; their influence can certainly be seen in Gluck's three Viennese 'reform' operas, *Orfeo ed Euridice*, *Alceste* and *Paride ed Elena*. So it was inevitable that, having incorporated many features of French opera into his latest works, Gluck should be drawn to the French stage itself.

So, in the early 1770s, with no certainty of a production, Gluck set the libretto of *Iphigénie en Aulide* written by Roullet, an attaché to the French Embassy in Vienna. The two men then began to plan their conquest of Paris, a matter involving artistic politics and diplomatic letters to the Académie Royale and the French press. The directors of the Académie Royale, fearing that *Iphigénie en Aulide* would drive existing French operas off the stage, were reluctant to accept the work unless Gluck agreed to write five more operas for them. However, with the support of the Dauphine, Gluck's former singing pupil Marie Antoinette, the composer arrived in Paris in 1773 and, after six months of strenuous rehearsals, *Iphigénie en Aulide* finally reached the stage. The original principals were Henri Larrivée (Agamemnon), Mlle du Plant (Clytemnestra), Sophie Arnould (Iphigenia), Joseph Legros (Achilles), Durand (Patroclus), Nicolas Gélin (Calchas) and Beauvalet (Arcas).

Sophie Arnould as Iphigenia in Gluck's 'Iphigénie en Aulide': bust by Jean-Antoine Houdon (1741–1828)

Gluck revised *Iphigénie en Aulide* after the first run of performances, introducing the goddess Diana (soprano) at the end of the opera as a *dea ex machina*, and altering and expanding the *divertissements* for a 1775 revival. So, broadly speaking, there are two versions of the opera; but the differences are by no means so great or important as those between *Orfeo ed Euridice* and *Orphée et Euridice* or between the Italian and the French *Alceste*. The Gluck collected edition (1987) opts for the later version, with the omitted 1774 music printed in the second volume. The differences are indicated in the synopsis below.

Iphigénie en Aulide was much performed in France in the 18th century and in the first part of the 19th, since when it has not been revived as regularly as, for example, *Orphée et Euridice* or *Iphigénie en Tauride*. Wagner realized the importance of the work and made his own version in German for performances in Dresden in 1847, with Wilhelmine Schröder-Devrient in the title role. He rescored the opera, made numerous cuts and added recitatives and other music of his own; he also changed Act 3 and gave it a new ending, with Diana (called Artemis, her Greek name, by Wagner) ordering Iphigenia to go to Tauris as her High Priestess there, thus effecting a link between *Iphigénie en Aulide* and

Iphigénie en Tauride which was certainly not Gluck's intention. This version of the opera was often performed in Germany; Mahler conducted a famous revival of it in Vienna in 1907, the year Lucienne Bréval scored great success in the title role in Paris. *Iphigénie en Aulide* was not performed in England until 1933, in Oxford. In a revival at the Maggio Musicale Fiorentino in 1950 Boris Christoff sang Agamemnon, repeating his performance in 1959 at La Scala with Giulietta Simionato as Iphigenia. Christa Ludwig sang the title role at the Salzburg Festival in 1962; Elisabeth Söderström sang it at Drottningholm in 1965. It was conducted by Sir Charles Mackerras at the Vienna Staatsoper in 1987. A performance at the Spitalfields Festival, conducted by Richard Hickox, took place in London in 1987 with Isabelle Poulenard as Iphigenia and John Aler as Achilles, a role he recorded that year with Lynne Dawson (Iphigenia), Anne Sofie von Otter (Clytemnestra) and José van Dam (Agamemnon); conducted by John Eliot Gardiner, this is the first recording of the 1775 version of the opera. There has also been a recording of Wagner's version conducted by Kurt Eichhorn with Anna Moffo and Dietrich Fischer-Dieskau.

ACT 1 *The Greek camp on one side in the background, a wood on the other* The Greek fleet, led by Agamemnon, is becalmed on its way to Troy. The High Priest Calchas has consulted the oracle and says that to obtain favourable winds Agamemnon must sacrifice his daughter Iphigenia to appease the goddess Diana, whose favourite stag he killed. Agamemnon has sent to Greece for Iphigenia on the pretext of marrying her to Achilles but, after a change of heart, he has also sent Arcas to turn her back with the news that Achilles has been unfaithful to her.

The overture suggests the violently contrasting emotions to be encountered in the opera itself; and at the point where its opening bars return Agamemnon sings – a surprising, highly dramatic gesture which hastens on the action and anticipates the very fluid style of the opera's music, which moves from air to recitative to dance or chorus with few breaks in the action or the music. In this opening arioso Agamemnon calls defiantly to Diana that he will not sacrifice his daughter: it leads into his air 'Brillant auteur de la lumière'. The music remains fluid, with tempo changes and passages of recitative within the air. Agamemnon has done all he can, and admits that if Iphigenia comes to Aulis nothing can save her.

The Greeks ask Calchas how the gods may be placated. Calchas and Agamemnon sing of the severity of the necessary sacrifice; a prayer to Diana ensues. The Greeks demand to know the victim; without disclosing Iphigenia's name, Calchas promises that the sacrifice will be made that very day.

Alone with Calchas, Agamemnon asks if the gods can really command a father to kill his daughter (air, 'Peuvent-ils ordonner qu'un père'). Calchas's reference in the ensuing recitative to Iphigenia's already being on her way is immediately answered by a brief chorus of Greeks announcing the arrival of Clytemnestra and Iphigenia. In a march-like air, 'Au faîte des grandeurs', Calchas reflects on the feebleness of mortals, even at the height of splendour; and in a minuet-like chorus the Greeks welcome Iphigenia and her mother ('Que d'attraits, que de majesté'). An expression of grief is heard from Agamemnon under the beginning of the chorus: Arcas has failed to prevent Iphigenia from coming. Agamemnon leaves just before Clytemnestra and Iphigenia enter. After Clytemnestra's short air of gratitude ('Que j'aime à voir ces hommages flatteurs'), there is a *divertissement*, a series of dances and choruses (shorter and more succinct in the 1775 version than in the original), during which Iphigenia herself has a short air, 'Les voeux dont ce peuple m'honore'.

Clytemnestra interrupts: she has been told by Agamemnon, in a last desperate measure to save his daughter, that Achilles has been unfaithful to Iphigenia, and Clytemnestra, in a fierily indignant da capo aria, 'Armez-vous d'un noble courage', urges her to prepare to leave. Left alone, Iphigenia is at first incredulous, then laments that she ever loved Achilles (air, 'Hélas! mon coeur sensible et tendre'). Achilles now enters, amazed to see Iphigenia in Aulis, and even more so to hear of his supposed infidelity. He refutes her accusations and assures her of his love in a dialogue in recitative and arioso, incorporating an air for each of them before a final duet in which they call on the god of marriage to unite them that very day ('Ne doutez jamais de ma flamme').

ACT 2 (as Act 1) Iphigenia's attendants reassure her that Achilles will marry her, although he has been told that Agamemnon suspected he had scorned her love (chorus, 'Rassurez-vous, belle Princesse'; in the 1774 version a short simile air follows for one of the Greek women, 'L'indomptable lion ardent', and the chorus is repeated). Iphigenia responds reflectively but becomes more animated when she sings of her changing emotions, Agamemnon's pride and Achilles' anger ('Par la crainte et par l'espérance').

Clytemnestra tells Iphigenia that preparations are being made for her marriage, to which Agamemnon has now consented. Achilles enters with his friend Patroclus, and after a march for the Thessalians Achilles presents Patroclus to Iphigenia and leads the Thessalians in a rousing military chorus in her praise: 'Chantez, célébrez votre reine!'. A *divertissement* follows (much longer in the 1775 revision, where the dances and choruses are a celebration of Achilles' valour, during which Iphigenia frees the slaves whom he has brought from Lesbos). After a ceremonial quartet and chorus to Diana ('Jamais à tes autels'), Arcas enters and, unable to control himself any longer, tells them that Agamemnon is waiting at the altar not to marry Iphigenia to Achilles but to sacrifice her. Arcas's words at the crucial disclosure (unaccompanied, so that they are clearly heard) are greeted with outbursts of horror from the other principals and the chorus. Clytemnestra poignantly begs Achilles to save Iphigenia (air, 'Par un père cruel à la mort condamnée'); then Iphigenia herself leads a trio in which she expresses her love for her father while Clytemnestra and Achilles rant against him, the three of them finally uniting in an appeal to the heavens ('C'est mon père, Seigneur').

Clytemnestra and Iphigenia leave, and in a short air which veers between anger and tenderness (Allegro and Lento) Achilles sends Patroclus to tell Iphigenia that he will contain his fury and respect her father ('Cours, et dis-lui'). But in the next scene Achilles' confrontation with Agamemnon becomes more and more heated until it erupts into a fiery duet ('De votre audace téméraire'). Achilles tells Agamemnon that he will have first to kill him before he sacrifices his daughter.

Alone, Agamemnon wavers between his duty to Greece and his love for his daughter. He sends Arcas to take Iphigenia and Clytemnestra to Mycenae; then follows an arioso with abrupt changes of mood and tempo, leading to an air whose sighing phrases and desolate minor key express Agamemnon's love for his daughter ('O toi, l'objet le plus aimable'); this extended scene ends with Agamemnon resolute and defiant as he tells the goddess to take his life rather than Iphigenia's.

ACT 3.i (as Act 1) The assembled Greeks brutally demand the sacrifice in a diatonic, homophonic chorus (which returns several times in this act). Iphigenia has refused to leave with Arcas and tells him to take care of Clytemnestra during the sacrifice. Achilles hurries in and calls on Iphigenia to leave with him. She replies that she must submit to her destiny ('Il faut de mon destin') and, after further pleas from Achilles, she declares her love for him and bids him farewell ('Adieu, conservez dans votre âme'). But Achilles is still determined to save her, as he makes clear in a heroic bravura air, with prominent horns and trumpets: 'Calchas, d'un trait mortel percé'.

Alone, Iphigenia reflects, but is interrupted first by the impatient Greeks and then by Clytemnestra, who also expresses her willingness to die for her daughter. Iphigenia's farewell to her mother ('Adieu, vivez pour Oreste') is also twice interrupted, by Clytemnestra herself and by the Greeks. She goes, and Clytemnestra gives vent to her rage in a recitative; an extraordinary arioso follows in which she has a vision of the sacrifice. She begins hesitantly, 'Ma fille! Je la vois', becoming more impassioned, her voice rising with the oboe phrases, until she sees Agamemnon about to kill Iphigenia; then she bursts into a passionate plea to Jupiter, her father, to send his thunderbolts into the Greek camp ('Jupiter, lance la foudre!'). When she has finished, she hears offstage the Greeks singing a processional hymn on their way to the sacrifice; her anguished comments are heard over the chorus, much as Agamemnon's were in Act 1.

3.ii *A seashore with an altar* Iphigenia is kneeling on the altar steps; behind her is the High Priest holding the sacred knife, his hands stretched out towards the heavens. The Greeks' hymn is broken off at the arrival of Achilles and his Thessalians, determined to save Iphigenia, who nevertheless begs the gods to take their victim ('Grands Dieux! Prenez votre victime!'). Most of the music of this scene is based on the Greeks' chorus, heard earlier. Calchas interrupts the skirmish between Greeks and Thessalians: he tells them that Diana has changed her mind and a sacrifice is no longer required. (Gluck replaced this denouement in the 1775 revision by having the goddess herself appear, thus removing the ambiguity of Calchas' change of heart in the face of a challenge to his divine powers by Achilles; the only gain in the 1775 version is that Diana gives her blessing both to the wedding of Achilles and Iphigenia and to the Greeks' voyage to Troy.) There is a quartet of rejoicing for Iphigenia, Clytemnestra, Achilles and Agamemnon ('Mon coeur ne saurait contenir'), which leads to a chorus ('Jusques aux voûtes étherées').

The original version ended with a lengthy *divertissement* including an air for a Greek woman ('Heureux guerriers') and a chaconne, interrupted just before the end by Calchas, exhorting the Greeks to great conquests. In 1774 the opera ended with a sinister war chorus, 'Partons, volons à la victoire', with stark, bare octaves and crude thumps on the bass drum, perhaps with a hint of irony; this was omitted from the 1775 version, which had an expanded final *divertissement* including the magnificent passacaglia from the Act 1 *divertissement* of 1774.

* * *

While *Iphigénie en Aulide* may lack the unity of conception, construction and style of *Iphigénie en Tauride*, in its original version it is one of Gluck's most powerful dramas; to an extent the revision, with its alterations to suit French taste, can be regarded as something of a compromise. The continuity of the opera's action is ensured by the long stretches of continuous music as Gluck elides in a masterly fashion the free forms of recitative and arioso with arias and ensembles. The three extended *divertissements* are not integrated into the drama as thoroughly as in some of Gluck's other Paris operas, but the dramatic irony of that in Act 1 is highly effective.

Of the opera's characters, Agamemnon and Clytemnestra are no less important than Iphigenia, and all of them are among Gluck's most memorable creations: Agamemnon with his two great monologues in the first two acts which are without precedent in the history of opera, Clytemnestra with her passionate arias and her visionary scene in Act 3, and Iphigenia herself, whose growth from the young lover of Act 1 to her heroic exaltation at the thought of dying for her father and her country in the third is so effectively conveyed in her music. The music broke new ground too with its combination of Italian lyricism and melody and French declamation, a formula Gluck was to use in various ways in all his Paris operas and of which he was justifiably proud. 'I have found a musical language fit for all nations', he wrote to the *Mercure de France* in February 1773, 'and hope to abolish the ridiculous distinctions between national styles of music'.

See also IPHIGENIA IN AULIS.   JEREMY HAYES

Iphigénie en Tauride (i) ('Iphigenia in Tauris'). *Tragédie* in four acts by CHRISTOPH WILLIBALD GLUCK to a libretto by NICOLAS-FRANÇOIS GUILLARD after Guymond de la Touche's *Iphigénie en Tauride*, itself based on EURIPIDES; Paris, Opéra, 18 May 1779.

Iphigénie [Iphigenia] *High Priestess of Diana*		soprano
Oreste [Orestes] *King of Argos and Mycenae,*		
Iphigenia's brother		baritone
Pylade [Pylades] *King of Phocis, Orestes' friend*		tenor
Thoas *King of Tauris*		bass
Diane [Diana] *goddess of hunting*		soprano
First Priestess		soprano
Second Priestess		soprano
A Scythian		bass
A Minister		bass
A Greek woman		soprano

Priestesses, Scythians, Eumenides, guards and Greeks

Setting Tauris (modern Crimea), after the Trojan War

Iphigénie en Tauride was the sixth of Gluck's seven operas for Paris. The subject (*see* IPHIGENIA IN TAURIS), a popular one, had already been used for several French and Italian operas (Desmarets, 1704; Traetta, 1763; Majo, 1764; and Jommelli, 1771) and by a strange coincidence Goethe's *Iphigenie auf Tauride* was first performed in Weimar the year Gluck's opera had its première in Paris. Gluck had conducted Traetta's 'reform

opera' *Ifigenia in Tauride* in Vienna in 1763. The first known reference to Gluck's setting is in a *pro memoria* he drafted before signing his contract with the Académie Royale de Musique in 1775; two of his letters from that year make it clear that Roullet, his collaborator for *Iphigénie en Aulide* and the French *Alceste*, was at work on the libretto. It is not clear why or at what stage Roullet passed it on to the young Parisian poet Guillard. The evidence suggests that it was in 1776, but it is impossible to be certain, partly because Gluck's behaviour concerning the libretto and the music for the opera appears to have been secretive to the point of deviousness. This was probably to keep the subject of his next opera a secret from Niccolò Piccinni, who had been brought to Paris by the directors of the Académie Royale de Musique as a rival to Gluck. In the event the Académie gave Piccinni a different libretto on the Iphigenia in Tauris story, by A. de Congé Dubreuil, but this opera was a comparative failure when it was first performed in 1781 while Gluck's had been an unqualified success two years before. The principals in the first performance were Rosalie Levasseur (Iphigenia), Henri Larrivée (Orestes), Joseph Legros (Pylades) and Moreau (Thoas).

Gluck made a German version of the opera for performance in Vienna on 23 October 1781. The translation was made by the young Viennese writer Johann Baptist Edler von Alxinger; Gluck altered the music to fit the new German libretto and amended the orchestration where the text required it. The major revisions were the transposition of the part of Orestes from baritone to tenor and the replacement of Iphigenia's last recitative and the chorus of priestesses at the end of Act 2 by an instrumental sinfonia.

Iphigénie en Tauride has always been one of Gluck's most frequently performed operas. It was first seen in London in 1796 in Da Ponte's Italian translation. One of the most important interpreters of the title role in the 19th century was Wilhelmine Schröder-Devrient. Richard Strauss made his own version for the Weimar Hoftheater in 1889, rewriting many of the recitatives, altering certain of the numbers in Act 1, joining the third and fourth acts together and revising the end of the opera; he linked many of his elaborate revisions by a new musical motif of his own. Like Wagner's revision of *Iphigénie en Aulide*, Strauss's of *Iphigénie en Tauride* is of interest as one great composer's view of another; but although it was quite often performed at the beginning of the century (it was the version used for the work's première at the Metropolitan Opera in 1916), it is now rarely heard. It was recorded in 1961 with Montserrat Caballé in the title role.

Revivals of *Iphigénie en Tauride* this century have included performances conducted by Carlo Maria Giulini in Aix-en-Provence in 1952 with Patricia Neway as Iphigenia and Léopold Simoneau as Pylades, later recorded. Another famous production which also found its way on to record, albeit 'privately', was that directed by Luchino Visconti at La Scala in 1957 with Maria Callas (sung in Italian). In 1961 Rita Gorr sang Iphigenia at Covent Garden with Sir Georg Solti conducting; that year she recorded excerpts from it conducted by Georges Prêtre. Régine Crespin sang it at the Paris Opéra in 1965; a new production there in 1984 featured Shirley Verrett as Iphigenia and Thomas Allen as Orestes. Productions in Britain have been conducted by Roger Norrington at the Edinburgh Festival in 1979 and John Eliot Gardiner, at Covent Garden in 1973 with Sena Jurinac; Gardiner also conducted it in Lyons in 1983 with Diana Montague and this production was subsequently recorded.

ACT 1 *The sacred wood of Diana with the entrance to her temple in the background* The opera begins with a gentle minuet (called 'Le calme'), suddenly interrupted by a tempestuous Allegro which depicts the approaching storm. The orchestral tumult is crowned by the entry of the piccolo, and then – when the storm is at its height – by the voice of Iphigenia, soon joined by her priestesses, begging the gods to help them. This is one of the most remarkable openings in the history of opera. In the preface to *Alceste*, Gluck and Ranieri de' Calzabigi had said that the overture should forewarn the audience of the nature of the drama to follow; although he had done this in *Alceste* and *Iphigénie en Aulide*, Gluck went much further in *Iphigénie en Tauride* by introducing the voice in the middle of what seems to be an instrumental overture with a slow introduction. The orchestral tempest symbolizes Iphigenia's inner torment, as she explains in the recitative that follows when the storm has died away. She describes her dream the previous night in which she saw first her father, Agamemnon, fleeing from his murderer, her mother Clytemnestra; then she saw her brother Orestes, but a fatal power forced her to kill him. So, in a succinct recitative, Gluck explains the events so far, as well as preparing for what is to follow. After a short lament for the priestesses, Iphigenia bewails the hopelessness of her situation, and then in an intense, almost serenely despairing air, begs the goddess Diana to take her life so that she can be with Orestes once again ('O toi qui prolongeas mes jours').

After another sorrowful chorus for the priestesses, Thoas rushes in. He too has been frightened by the storm and, having consulted the oracles, demands that Iphigenia does her duty and sacrifices a stranger to appease the gods. Thoas's air 'De noirs pressentiments', with its restless dotted rhythms and almost incessant semiquavers in the bass, depicts his obsession. The Scythians crowd in and press Thoas's demands for a sacrifice. One of them reveals that two Greeks have been cast up on to their shore during the storm, and despite Iphigenia's protests Thoas sends her to prepare for their sacrifice. The Scythians' choruses and the short dances that follow are in the exotic, so-called Turkish style so popular in the 18th century, with piccolos, tambourine, triangle and cymbals to the fore.

Orestes and Pylades are brought in. Thoas tells them of their fate; as they are led away, Orestes, in an expressively harmonized phrase, blames himself for bringing Pylades to his death.

ACT 2 *A chamber in the temple set aside for victims; on one side is an altar* Orestes and Pylades are in chains. Orestes is prey to guilt and remorse: the music of his exclamation, 'Dieux! à quelles horreurs m'aviez-vous réservé', echoes Iphigenia's entry in the first act. Orestes' recitative culminates in an agitated air, 'Dieux qui me poursuivez', with horns, trumpets, timpani and tremolando strings, in which he begs the gods to cast him into hell for his crimes. Pylades responds with a serene, lyrical air in which he assures Orestes of his undying friendship ('Unis dès la plus tendre enfance').

A minister of the sanctuary enters and takes Pylades away. Believing that Pylades has gone to his death, Orestes calls furiously on the gods to strike him down in an anguished recitative, restless in rhythm and unstable in harmony. This yields to more tranquil music before

Orestes' arioso 'Le calme rentre dans mon coeur!'; that the calm is illusory is made clear by the violas' uneasy ostinato rhythm, on the same note for 28 bars.

Orestes sinks into sleep, only to dream that he is possessed by the Eumenides, come to torment him for killing his mother (Gluck specifies that the Furies should be seen on the stage; they appear to the same music as began Orestes' previous recitative, but enriched by the addition of three trombones, and sing a chorus which seems like a parody of Baroque polyphony: 'Vengeons et la nature'). Orestes begs them to have pity; then, at the climax of the scene, he awakens, thinking that he sees his mother. But it is actually Iphigenia (a dramatic masterstroke, Gluck's idea rather than Guillard's). So many years have passed that neither recognizes the other. Iphigenia asks Orestes for news of Mycenae: he tells her of the murder of Agamemnon by Clytemnestra and how Orestes in turn killed his mother – adding that at last Orestes had found the death he had looked for. Iphigenia, overcome, tells him to leave her; after a short chorus for the priestesses she sings a grief-laden air, 'O malheureuse Iphigénie'. Like several other laments by Gluck, including 'Che farò senza Euridice', it is in a major key. Again there are persistent accompaniment figures in the orchestra, and the syncopated first violins are as obsessive here as the violas were, in a different context, earlier in the act. Iphigenia and her priestesses now perform funeral rites for Orestes in a ceremonial chorus.

'Iphigénie en Tauride' (Gluck): drawing by Gabriel de Saint-Aubin showing the appearance of the goddess Diana at the denouement of Act 4 in the original production at the Paris Opéra (Académie Royale de Musique, Palais-Royal), 18 May 1779

ACT 3 *Iphigenia's apartment* Iphigenia tells her priestesses that she will yield to their wishes and send one of the captives to Greece to tell her sister Electra what they are suffering in Tauris. She is struck by one of the prisoners' resemblance to her brother Orestes, and laments that she will be reunited with her brother only when she dies (air, 'D'une image, hélas!'). Orestes and Pylades are brought in; Iphigenia is moved by their mutual devotion. In a trio 'Je pourrais du tyran', the three characters express different emotions: Iphigenia her indecision, and the two friends their eagerness to die for each other. Finally Iphigenia announces that Orestes will take the message to Greece, and leaves the men arguing for the right to die ('Et tu prends encore').

The music of the Furies returns as Orestes begs Pylades to let him be the one to die, so that he can escape the Furies. In a more lyrical air ('Ah, mon ami'), Pylades begs Orestes to abide by Iphigenia's decree; but when she returns Orestes threatens to kill himself unless she changes her mind and sends Pylades instead of him. She has to agree; as Orestes is led away, Iphigenia gives Pylades the letter for Electra. He ends the act with a rather conventional, heroic, bravura air ('Divinité des grandes âmes').

ACT 4 *The interior of the temple of Diana; the statue of the goddess is mounted on a dais, and to one side is the sacrifical altar* Iphigenia, in anguish, prays to Diana to give her strength to perform the sacrifice ('Je t'implore et je tremble': a virtuoso, italianate aria based on the Gigue from J. S. Bach's Partita no.1 in B♭). The priestesses, singing to Diana, lead Orestes in. The proximity of the relief of death has given him a new serenity which finds expression in a short, very French air ('Que ces regrets touchants'). The priestesses sing a processional hymn to Diana ('Chaste fille de Latone') as they prepare him for the sacrifice.

Orestes is led to the altar. Iphigenia once more calls on the gods to give her strength, and takes the sacrificial knife. 'Iphigénie, aimable soeur! C'est ainsi qu'autrefois tu péris en Aulide' ('My beloved sister Iphigenia, thus did you too perish in Aulis'), mutters Orestes as she is about to strike the fatal blow. 'Mon frère ... je me meurs' ('My brother ... I feel I am dying'), she replies, followed by an outburst of astonished joy from the priestesses. This recognition takes merely a few bars of recitative, lightly accompanied; and Iphigenia's air of jubilation is then cut short when a Greek woman comes to warn them of the approach of Thoas who has heard that one of the captives has left Tauris.

In the confusion that follows, Thoas determines to sacrifice Orestes himself, even when he knows his true identity; but then Pylades returns with an army of Greeks and kills Thoas. To the music of the tempest from Act 1, there is a brief skirmish between the Greeks and Thoas's army of Scythians; then Diana herself appears, halts the fighting, and tells the Scythians to return her statues to the Greeks. She tells Orestes that his remorse has effaced his guilt, and sends him to rule as King of Mycenae, taking Iphigenia to Greece with him. Orestes offers his thanks in a brief, minor-key arioso 'Dans cet objet charmant'. The opera ends with a chorus of departure and a return (or allusion) to the calm sea of the opening, 'Les Dieux, longtemps en courroux'. Gluck wrote no music for the customary concluding ballet, which was supplied by Gossec.

*   *   *

Iphigénie en Tauride was the crowning achievement of Gluck's career, a result of the combination of his life-long experience as an opera composer and a libretto which is arguably the best he ever set. The opera is one of Gluck's most tightly constructed, and although the action moves quickly and the tension is seldom relaxed for long, there was still room for dramatic and lyrical expansion. Each of Gluck's late operas is unique; even in his 60s he was a tireless experimenter. *Iphigénie en Tauride* has an unusual number of ensembles, and although there are more arias than, for example, in *Armide*, he strikes a balance between these more italianate set pieces and the French declamation and short airs, leading to a comparable fluidity of musical structure which always serves the development of the drama. Of all Gluck's operas, *Iphigénie en Tauride* is the one in which he was most successful in bringing his theories of operatic reform to life in a memorable combination of music and drama in which every detail is subordinate to the whole.

For further illustration *see* STAGE DESIGN, fig.9.   JEREMY HAYES

Iphigénie en Tauride (ii) ('Iphigenia in Tauris'). *Tragédie lyrique* in four acts by Niccolò Piccinni (see PICCINNI family, (1)) to a libretto by A. du Congé Dubreuil; Paris, Opéra, 23 January 1781.

This opera, produced in Paris two years after the pre-mière of Gluck's opera on the same story, was intended by the Piccinnistes to compete directly with it. Although it did not achieve the success of Gluck's, Piccinni's *Iphigénie* was performed more than 30 times during its first run in Paris and was revived there in 1785 and 1790. It had reached Copenhagen by 1787 and, according to Loewenberg, was given in a concert performance in St Petersburg in 1791.

The story derives originally from Euripides (*see* IPHIGENIA IN TAURIS). In Dubreuil's libretto the Scythian ruler Thoas (bass) is an unwelcome suitor to Iphigenia (soprano), and the work opens with Iphigenia lamenting her fate as a chorus of priestesses tries to comfort her. She then describes to her confidante Elise (soprano) a dream in which she sees the bloody, disfigured bodies of her parents. A storm arises, bringing a distant ship into danger. As the principals and chorus retire, the second act begins without a break; the scene changes to a furious ocean, from which Pilade [Pylades] (tenor) emerges. He laments the loss of his friend Oreste [Orestes] (bass), but eventually sees him and jumps into the ocean to save him. Orestes wishes that he had not been saved: he has a vision of his mother Clytemnestra pointing a dagger at him. Thoas demands that the two strangers be sacrificed. In Act 3, set in the Temple of Diana, Orestes tells Iphigenia the gruesome news from Greece and says that Orestes is also dead; Iphigenia reacts with horror. She tells the men that she can save one of them and, although Pylades wants to save his friend, Orestes prefers to die for his crimes. They agree that Orestes will be sacrificed and express their grief in a trio. Act 4 opens with a ceremonial scene preparing the sacrificial altar in the Temple. Iphigenia senses a bond between her and Orestes, and eventually brother and sister discover their true identities. Thoas interrupts and is about to kill Orestes himself when Pylades appears with the Greek army and kills Thoas. The goddess Diana (soprano) abolishes the Scythian ritual of slaying strangers and sends Orestes back to Greece to govern his people.

Though more loosely constructed than Gluck's work, Piccinni's nevertheless has its strengths. The parallel between Iphigenia's dream and Orestes' vision is striking, and the chorus, used both as participant and commentator, is specially important. Piccinni's choral writing is also particularly effective: the priestesses' 'O jour fatal' (3.iii), for example, with its opening section of two-bar units for the chorus followed by one-bar unison responses by the strings, is quite moving.

Piccinni used a wide variety of aria forms. In both tone and length, his arias are better integrated into the flow of the drama than they were in his first *tragédie lyrique, Roland*. A number are in *ABA* form with a central contrasting section, which belies the precepts of the Piccinnistes in expressing a single mood in an aria; nevertheless they do accurately express the text. Also quite common is a flexible two-part form, in which the second half refers to or recalls (but does not repeat) music from the first half, giving an impression of eloquence and naturalness. Most texts are not repeated in their entirety, but individual lines often return at crucial moments. The recitatives are full of orchestral devices that illustrate the passionate content of the text. But the predictability of some of these and the rather routine way in which they alternate with the voice somewhat reduce their effect.   MARY HUNTER

Ipocrita felice, L'. Opera by G. F. Ghedini; *see* LORD INFERNO.

Ippolito ed Aricia ('Hippolytus and Aricia'). *Tragedia* in five acts by TOMMASO TRAETTA to a libretto by CARLO INNOCENZO FRUGONI after SIMON-JOSEPH PELLEGRIN's *Hippolyte et Aricie*; Parma, Teatro Ducale, 9 May 1759.

Hippolytus (soprano castrato), son of the King of Athens Teseo [Theseus] (tenor), loves Aricia (soprano), whose deceased father was Theseus's rival. Theseus's wife Fedra [Phaedra] (soprano) loves Hippolytus, her stepson, but confesses to Enone [Oenone] (soprano) the fear that he will take power from her own son. Theseus asks his father Neptune to destroy Hippolytus, whom he believes has betrayed him. He learns the truth only after a sea monster causes Hippolytus's death. Phaedra poisons herself, and Theseus reconciles himself to the grieving Aricia. Diana (soprano) restores Hippolytus to life and reunites the couple.

Traetta was among the first to attempt to create a new kind of Italian opera by infusing it with French elements as advocated by Algarotti. He advised Frugoni on the final form of the libretto, which relies heavily on Pellegrin's text for Rameau's opera but also borrows additional scenes from Racine's drama *Phèdre*. From its French source the opera takes its five-act format, the superfluous underworld scene and the appearances of deities in machines accompanied by choruses, dances and sinfonias. It follows the conventions of Italian *opera seria* in maintaining a fixed number of characters in each scene and in punctuating the action with exit arias. Most of the choruses and dances appear in scenes that serve as entr'actes and are not incorporated into the action in the French manner. Following Rameau's example, Traetta composed the dance music and programmatic sinfonias himself, a task normally left to a secondary composer in Italian opera companies. Also following Rameau, Traetta's violas occasionally step out of their supporting role to provide solo accompaniment and obbligato commentary in two parts.

Obbligato recitative heightens the terrifying effect of the sea monster's appearance. The choruses are sizable and of some textural complexity, particularly when soloists are involved. Traetta abridged the usual form of da capo arias by placing a sign either at the initial entry of the singer or within the second setting of the first strophe. A variety of orchestral accompaniment amplifies a few of the most dramatic moments. The solo scenes in obbligato recitative at the beginning of Acts 1 and 3 are unusual. Apart from their use in the dance music, wind instruments are not as prominent as they were to be in Traetta's later operas.   MARITA P. McCLYMONDS

Ippolitov-Ivanov, Mikhail Mikhaylovich (*b* Gatchina, nr St Petersburg, 7/19 Nov 1859; *d* Moscow, 28 Jan 1935). Russian composer, conductor and educator. His real surname was Ivanov (pronounced Ivánov), to which he added his sister's married name to avoid confusion with Mikhail Mikhaylovich Ivanov (pronounced Ivanóv; 1849–1927), a composer and detested critic. After studying the double bass at the St Petersburg Conservatory he switched to composition and was the pupil of Rimsky-Korsakov, graduating in 1882. While still a student he had begun attending, at first with his teacher, the latterday meetings of the Balakirev circle, of which he remained a lifelong epigone. From the year of his graduation until 1893 he lived in Tbilisi in the Caucasus, heading the local branch of the Imperial Russian Musical Society, which meant both conducting orchestral concerts for the cultivated European-Russian colony there (from 1884 performances of opera as well) and teaching in the local music school, where his pupils included Dimitri Arakishvili and Zakhary Paliashvili, early representatives of the Georgian 'national school' on the Russian model.

In 1893 Ippolitov-Ivanov settled in Moscow as opera director and composition teacher at the conservatory, with which institution he remained associated to the end of his life, directing it from 1905 to 1922. His pupils included Vasilenko, Glier, and Yuly (Joel) Engel', a leader of the short-lived Jewish national school. As operatic conductor Ippolitov-Ivanov maintained a busy schedule not only at the conservatory but also with the two major private troupes in Moscow, those of Zimin and Mamontov, conducting the first performances of three of Rimsky-Korsakov's operas (*The Tsar's Bride, The Tale of Tsar Saltan* and *Kashchey the Deathless*).

In his own operas Ippolitov-Ivanov at first naturally adopted the traditional Russian 'oriental' idiom, which he had imbibed both at the source (Balakirev) and *in situ* (Tbilisi), and which formed the basis of his most famous work, the *Caucasian Sketches* of 1894. Three of his operas – *Ruf* ('Ruth'), *Azra* and *Izmena* ('The Betrayal') – have Near-Eastern or Islamic settings. (In the last-named Islam and Christianity are shown in conflict during the 16th-century occupation of Georgia by the Persians.) Genre painting in strong national colours marks Ippolitov-Ivanov's remaining operas as well. In *Asya*, after Turgenev's updating of Pushkin's *Yevgeny Onegin* set among Russians abroad, the German ambience is garishly depicted with beer-garden songs, sentimental ballads and even *Gaudeamus igitur*. In *Ole iz Nordlanda* ('Ole from the Northland'), the Norwegian idiom of Grieg is made to bear a crushing dramatic weight. Ippolitov-Ivanov's final opera, the unperformed and unpublished *Poslednyaya barrikada* ('The Last Barricade'), is set in the Paris commune of 1871. Adapting his old methods to Soviet conditions, the composer made use of *La Carmagnole* and other revolutionary songs, some of which he claimed to have heard sung by a French worker installing the Moscow Conservatory organ in 1897.

In 1931, the 50th anniversary of Musorgsky's death, Ippolitov-Ivanov, as the last living link with Musorgsky, was commissioned by Sergey Lopashyov of the Soviet Radio to complete Musorgsky's declamatory setting of Gogol's prose comedy *Zhenit'ba* ('Marriage') and orchestrate the whole. (Six years earlier, the Bol'shoy Theatre had entrusted him with orchestrating the newly rediscovered scene at St Basil's for insertion into Part 4 of *Boris Godunov*.) Despite the pronounced (and deliberate) disjuncture in style between Musorgsky's 'realistically harsh, dry recitative' (as Ippolitov-Ivanov described it) and his own tamely lyric ariosos, the new version of *Marriage* was considered successful enough to be recorded.

Ruf' [Ruth] op.6, 1883–6 (lyric op or biblical scenes, prol., 3, A. Tolstoy & A. Ostrovsky), Tbilisi, 23 Jan/4 Feb 1887, vs (Moscow, 1888)

Azra (dramatic op, 3, Ippolitov-Ivanov, after Moorish legend and A. Mickiewicz), Tbilisi, 22 Nov/4 Dec 1890, lib. (Tbilisi, 1890), score destroyed by composer

Asya op.30 (lyric scenes, 3, N. Maníkin-Nevstruyev, after I. Turgenev), Moscow, Solodovnikov (Mamontov opera company), 28 Sept/11 Oct 1900, vs (Moscow, 1905)

Izmena [The Betrayal] op.43, 1908–9 (dramatic op, 4, A. Sumbatov [Yuzhin], after his own tragedy), Moscow, Solodovnikov (Zimin opera company), 4/17 Dec 1910, vs (Moscow, 1910)

Ole iz Nordlanda [Ole from the Northland] op.43 (4, Ippolitov-Ivanov, after M. Jersen, trans. M. Ippolitova), Moscow, Bol'shoy, 8/21 Nov 1916, vs (Moscow, 1915)

Zhenit'ba [Marriage] op.70 (musical comedy, 4, after N. V. Gogol), Moscow, Radio Theatre, 18 Oct 1931, vs (Moscow, 1934) [Act 1 by Musorgsky]

Poslednyaya barrikada [The Last Barricade] op.74, 1933 (3, N. Krasheninnikov), photocopy of holograph, *RU-Mcm*

*

N. Kashkin: 'Teatr i muzïka: "Asya": novaya opera M. M. Ippolitova-Ivanova', *Moskovskiye vedomosti*, no.268 (25 Sept 1900)

I. Lipayev: 'Iz Moskvï: M. Ippolitov-Ivanov kak opernïy dirizhyor' [From Moscow: Ippolitov-Ivanov as an Opera Conductor], *RMG* (1900), no.5, p.151

——: '"Asya" – opera M. Ippolitova-Ivanova', *RMG* (1900), no.41

Yu. Engel': '"Ole iz Nordlanda" Ippolitova-Ivanova', *MS* (1916), nos.9–10, pp.17–23

M. Ippolitov-Ivanov: *50 let russkoy muzïki v moikh vospominaniyakh* [50 Years of Russian Music in my Reminiscences] (Moscow, 1934)

S. D. Krebs: *Soviet Composers and the Development of Soviet Music* (New York, 1970)

N. Sokolov, ed.: *M. M. Ippolitov-Ivanov: Pis'ma, stat'i, vospominaniya* [Letters, Articles, Reminiscences] (Moscow, 1986)

S. Neef: *Handbuch der russischen und sowjetischen Oper* (Kassel, 1989)

RICHARD TARUSKIN

Iradier [Yradier], **Sebastián** (*b* Sauciego, Álava, 20 Jan 1809; *d* Vitoria, 6 Dec 1865). Spanish composer. He is said to have been professor of solfège at the Madrid Conservatory, lived for a time in Paris, where he taught singing to Empress Eugénie, and travelled to Cuba, where he became much interested in Creole music. In Madrid he collaborated on various theatrical works, among them the zarzuela *La pradera del canal* (1847; with Oudrid and Cepeda), but he is noted particularly for his popular Spanish songs, which were immensely successful in both Europe and the Americas and were performed by Viardot, Patti and other famous singers. The best known is *La paloma*, but in addition his *Aÿ*

chiquita was sung in Meilhac's *L'attaché d'ambassade* (1861), the source of Lehár's *Die lustige Witwe*, and his *El arreglito* was adapted by Bizet for the habanera in the first act of *Carmen* (1875). Bizet apparently thought it was a folksong, and, when he learnt his mistake, added a note in the vocal score acknowledging the source.

*

W. Dean: *Georges Bizet* (London, 1965), 215, 228–9 [quotes music of *El arreglito*]

ANDREW LAMB

Iran. For discussion of opera in Iran *see* TEHERAN.

Ireland. In 18th-century Ireland, European music was cultivated by an élite group in selected cities, while the ancient Gaelic culture prevailed elsewhere. The prosperity and elegance of Georgian Dublin rivalled that of many continental cities. A vibrant concert life flourished from 1740, attracting many eminent composers and singers. Handel was fêted in the city in 1741–2. In the decade that followed, his oratorios were prominent; his operas were ignored, although he had directed a concert performance of *Imeneo* during his visit.

The Beggar's Opera, heard in Dublin within weeks of its London première in 1728, set a fashion and created intense theatrical rivalry. The term 'opera' denoted a one-act play with songs (ballads) performed after the main drama; its repertory reflected London tastes. Among the works of local composers Thomas Roseingrave's *Phaedra* (1753) and Kane O'Hara's *Midas* (1762) were satirical pieces. Thomas Arne was twice a resident of Dublin; his *Comus* (heard in Dublin in 1741) maintained its popularity for 40 years.

A travelling group of Italians including the De Amicis family introduced a burletta, *Cascina*, in December 1761 and similar pieces by Galuppi, Pergolesi and Jommelli up to 1764 with scant success. Tenducci's singing of the title role in Arne's *Artaxerxes* in 1765 was adjudged superior. Tommaso Giordani, with *L'eroe cinese* (1766), gave Dublin its only *opera seria* of the century. John Stevenson and Philip Cogan (born in Cork) were musical contributors in the next decades. Richard Brinsley Sheridan's *The Duenna* with music by Thomas Linley (given in Dublin in 1777) excelled. Two further Italian ventures ensued between 1777 and 1782, Gazzaniga's *L'isola d'Alcina* being the first complete Italian opera heard in Ireland. The companies included in their repertory works by Anfossi, Cimarosa, Paisiello and Piccinni. In January 1784 Tenducci organized a production in English of Gluck's *Orfeo ed Euridice* in the version with additions by J. C. Bach. The vivacious tenor Michael Kelly was prominent in the last decade of the century.

The Act of Union of 1800, by abolishing the Irish Parliament, transferred power and patronage to London and made Dublin an impoverished provincial town. Thomas Cooke (1782–1848) and William Rooke (1794–1847) led the exodus of Irish composers who were to struggle in London. But Michael Balfe (1808–70), a Dubliner, and Vincent Wallace (1812–65), from Waterford, enjoyed a vogue that extended into Europe. From the 1820s Dublin audiences enthusiastically acclaimed the operas of Rossini, Bellini, Donizetti and later Verdi, many of them based on English historical figures or on Scott's Waverley novels. Julius Benedict's *The Lily of Killarney* (1862) was the first to capitalize on an Irish background. It may well have stimulated Stanford, also born in Dublin, to write his *Shamus O'Brien* (1896). From the 1880s touring companies led by Carl Rosa, Joseph O'Mara and Moody Manners regularly visited Irish cities.

The intense patriotic fervour that emerged with the new century prompted O'Brien Butler (1862–1916) to write *Muirghéis*, the first opera to a Gaelic text. Staged in 1903, its music is continuous, the airs reflecting the modal character of Irish folk melody. Robert O'Dwyer's *Eithne* (1909) is more assured, with some fine ensembles. World war and civil strife suspended musical endeavours, but when a new Irish state emerged, introspective isolationism prevailed for a generation. Éamonn Ó'Gallchobhair (1906–78) alone provided operas in the Irish language from *Nocturne sa Chearnóig* ('Nocturne in the Square', 1942) to *Traghadh na Taoide* ('The Ebb Tide', 1950).

Although seasons of opera have been given in Dublin each year since 1941 and there has been a festival in Wexford since 1951, Ireland yet awaits a resident opera company. The national broadcasting service has been the true Maecenas of music in the country. Three senior composers have cultivated opera with English texts. Their musical idioms rarely converge. Gerard Victory (*b* 1921), the most prolific, has himself provided librettos for six of his eight operas. *Chatterton* (1971) and *Eloise and Abelard* (1972) are on a large scale and reveal his interest in avant-garde techniques. Archie Potter (1918–80) in his television opera *Patrick* (1963) deals with racial tension; James Wilson (*b* 1922) has based two recent works on Van Gogh and Karen Blixen. The post-1950 generation is exemplified by Gerald Barry (*b* 1952), a pupil of Stockhausen and Kagel, in his adoption of the concept of music theatre. His use of flexible combinations of instrumental groupings, often with tapes, has helped secure performances and recognition. Barry's puzzling and fascinating *The Intelligence Park*, ten years in gestation, was heard at the Almeida Festival in London in 1990; it is set in the 18th century with Tenducci a central figure.

For further information on operatic life in the country's principal centres *see* CORK; DUBLIN; and WEXFORD; *see also* BELFAST.

*

M. Kelly: *Reminiscences of Michael Kelly* (London, 1826); ed. R. Fiske (London, 1975)

C. K. Kenny: *A Life of Michael William Balfe* (London, 1875)

S. M. Ellis: *The Life of Michael Kelly, Musician, Actor and Bon Viveur* (London, 1930)

A. G. Fleischmann, ed.: *Music in Ireland: a Symposium* (Cork, 1952)

T. J. Walsh: *Opera in Old Dublin, 1819–1838* (Wexford, 1952)

I. M. Hogan: *Anglo-Irish Music, 1780–1830* (Cork, 1966)

T. J. Walsh: *Opera in Dublin, 1705–1797* (Dublin, 1973)

B. Harris: *Catalogue of Irish Contemporary Music* (Dublin, 1982)
ANTHONY G. HUGHES

Irino, Yoshirō (*b* Vladivostok, 13 Nov 1921; *d* Tokyo, 23 June 1980). Japanese composer. He studied economics at Tokyo University (1941–3) while taking composition lessons privately with Saburō Moroi. He won a Mainichi Music Competition prize with his Piano Trio in 1948, and received many composition prizes throughout the 1950s. Irino taught at the Tōhō Gakuen School of Music as a lecturer (1952), assistant professor (1955), professor (1959) and director (1960). In 1973 he became professor of composition at the Tokyo College of Music. He promoted various musical

activities by organizing the Institute of Twentieth-Century Music (1957), becoming chief administrator of the Amis de la Musique du 20ème Siècle (1967) and founding the Japan Music Life (1972). Primarily a composer of orchestral and chamber music, Irino was a representative of the serial movement in Japan. However, he also distinguished himself as a composer of dramatic music. His first success in the genre was a radio operetta *Kamisama ni shikarareta otoko* ('The Man in Fear of God'), broadcast by the NHK in 1954. Later the NHK commissioned a number of dramatic works, including a television opera *Aya no tsuzumi* ('The Damask Drum'), based on a noh play depicting the desperate love of an old medieval court servant; it won a Salzburg Television Opera Prize in 1962 and was revised for the stage in 1975. His most important opera, however, is *Sonezaki shinjū* ('The Lovers' Suicide at Sonezaki'), a chamber opera based on a famous puppet play, in which he successfully used Japanese instruments together with flutes and piano. He wrote much incidental music for plays, including several by Brecht, Synge's *Riders to the Sea* (1956), *Anna Karenina* (1966) and *King Lear* (1972).

broadcast by NHK unless otherwise stated

Kamisama ni shikarareta otoko [The Man in Fear of God] (radio operetta, N. Uno, after S. Komada), 25 May 1954

Fuefuki to Ryūō no musumetachi [The Piper and the Dragon King's Daughters] (radio op, M. Takeuchi), 1959

Sarudon no mukoiri [The Marriage of Mr Monkey] (radio op, M. Yokomichi, after I. Wakabayashi), 26 Nov 1961; stage, Tokyo, Metropolitan Festival Hall, 15 March 1962 [pt 2 of Mittsuno mukashiko (Three Old Tales); pt 1 by Moroi; pt 3 by Shimizu]

Aya no tsuzumi [The Damask Drum] (television op, H. Mizuo, after a noh play), 9 Aug 1962; stage, Tokyo, Yūbin Chokin Hall, 26 March 1975

Sonezaki shinjū [The Lovers' Suicide at Sonezaki] (chamber op, after M. Chikamatsu), Osaka, Morinomiya Pirot Hall, 10 April 1980

MASAKATA KANAZAWA

Iris. *Melodramma* in three acts by PIETRO MASCAGNI to a libretto by LUIGI ILLICA; Rome, Teatro Costanzi, 22 November 1898.

In 1896 Mascagni met Luigi Illica, from whom he had commissioned a new libretto and who suggested a tragedy set in Japan, a country which until then had inspired only Gilbert and Sullivan's operetta *The Mikado* in spite of the current vogue for exotic subjects. Mascagni asked him for a tragedy that could be treated realistically but in which the setting could colour the music. The libretto was ready as requested in the following April; fired by the subject, Mascagni completed the opera a year later.

Iris (soprano) is the only support of her blind father (bass). The young Osaka (tenor) is attracted by her and with the help of his friend Kyoto (baritone) abducts her. Iris repulses him, and he allows Kyoto to imprison her in his brothel. Iris's voice is recognized in the crowd by her father, who curses her, and she kills herself by throwing herself into a ravine.

Mascagni said of *Iris* that he did not want the music to be only 'arid comment' on the drama but that it should 'develop it with its own inexorable force'. This ingenuous declaration fails to conceal the true problem with the subject, the thinness of the action. In the third act, a protracted depiction of Iris's anguish in its symbolic relationship with the egoism of the three male characters, there is virtually none. The almost inevitable consequence is the introduction of an excessive number of character-pieces, among which is the grandiloquent Hymn to the Sun, a sort of orchestral-choral prologue with dances, arias and serenades. The static nature of the plot in relation to the exoticism of the setting was to pose a number of problems for Puccini in *Madama Butterfly* (1904), and it is obvious that some solutions common to both were first found by Mascagni. In the search for realistic orchestral sounds he made use of the shamisen, a long-necked Japanese lute with a piercing tone, and enriched the percussion with several Japanese instruments (bells, tam-tam, gong). All of these are used in the travelling-theatre scene in the first act. This is the most colourful part of the whole score, together with the beginning of Act 2, when a Japanese play is performed on the stage, a theatrical device often used after *Pagliacci*. It is neatly interwoven with the abduction of Iris, using the dancers as an allegory of what is happening and at the same time serving as cover for the deed. The dominant features of the writing are the dynamic nuances, lyrical vocal texture and harmonic blends of unusual delicacy and originality, although Mascagni could not match what Puccini's greater skill and shrewdness were later to accomplish. His unremitting search for inspired melodies does not, however, fall into empty mannerism but serves the subject, on the lines of *Cavalleria rusticana*, and contributes to the success of the work as a whole.   MICHELE GIRARDI

Irmelin. Opera in three acts by FREDERICK DELIUS to his own libretto; Oxford, New Theatre, 4 May 1953.

The subject of Delius's first completed opera was chosen during a walking tour in Norway with Grieg and Sinding. Composed in 1890–92, *Irmelin* uses some material planned for the unfinished incidental music (1888) to Bulwer Lytton's *Zanoni*. A vocal score was made by Florent Schmitt (1893–4), but the first full publication was Dennis Arundell's vocal score of 1953. An orchestral *Irmelin* Prelude (1931), based on four themes from the opera, was published in 1938.

The six scenes of Act 1 take place in Irmelin's room at the royal castle. Irmelin (soprano), advised by a Voice in the Air, is waiting for the man of her dreams; but the King, her father (bass), insists she must be wed at the end of six months. He announces three knightly suitors, each of whom she swiftly rejects; as twilight descends, she returns to her reveries.

Act 2 begins by a forest swamp where Nils (tenor), swineherd to the robber chieftain Rolf, is despondent: he has lost the Silver Stream that was guiding him to the princess of his dreams. Rolf (bass-baritone) summons him to the castle; darkness sets in, a storm threatens, and Nils approaches the brilliant light of the banqueting hall. In scene ii, Rolf's men are drinking with their chief. Rolf sings of the days he went to sea with a Viking band; now, feared by the King, he is ready to woo the princess. Nils is asked for a song but refuses, saying he must search for the Silver Stream. The women of the castle dance in an attempt to prevent Nils's departure, but he perseveres. Scene iii moves to the mountains, where the Silver Stream glitters in the morning sun. As Nils approaches the stream, wood-nymphs try to beguile him to their haunts of pleasure, but he continues climbing the rocks.

Act 3 opens six months later than Act 1; it is now Irmelin's betrothal day in the royal palace, and the King has chosen for her the Third Knight (bass). Irmelin is abstracted yet still hopes her waiting may not be in vain.

Nils appears at the entrance to the hall, and Irmelin is instantly transfixed. The King asks him to sing and cheer the company; Nils tells of his upbringing by Rolf among the swine. He is dismissed among the servants, and the royal party prepares for the chase. Irmelin is alone on the balcony as night falls and bids a maid summon the swineherd. Nils returns, and he and Irmelin declare their love. As the huntsmen return, they plan to meet by moonlight in the garden. A lengthy prelude leads to the garden of scene ii, where Nils and Irmelin are reunited. He has found his princess, and she knows him to be a prince. As dawn breaks, they wander hand in hand into the woods, and the castle disappears.

According to Beecham, the libretto unites two stories: that of the princess who rejects 100 noble suitors and the fairy-tale of the princess and the swineherd. The libretto's undoubted charm is somewhat obscured by its naivety and the banality of Delius's attempts at rhyme. The music, on the other hand, has telling use of motifs that are memorable and apt, economy in the setting of atmosphere, and ability to fill convincingly the large span of the three acts with an admirable sense of flow. The vocal lines cultivate safety rather than adventure, and the chorus tends to sing four-square. But already the Wagnerian influence has been assimilated into a personal idiom of deeply felt nostalgia.

ROBERT ANDERSON

Iron Chest, The. Mainpiece play in three acts with music by STEPHEN STORACE to a text by George Colman the younger (*see* COLMAN family, (3)), after William Godwin's novel *Caleb Williams*; London, Drury Lane, 12 March 1796.

The Iron Chest is unique among Storace's compositions because it is a complete set of music for a staged drama that is not an opera. The work was most commonly described in contemporary publications as a play with music. Storace composed music exclusively for the subplot and almost entirely for minor characters. Most of the main roles are non-singing, and the major singers play subsidiary acting roles. Drury Lane's two highest-paid singers, Nancy Storace (as Barbara) and Michael Kelly (the robber captain) had only one solo each.

The Drury Lane management commissioned Colman, owner and manager of the Little Theatre in the Haymarket, to write *The Iron Chest*. He based his text on Godwin's *Caleb Williams* (London, 1794), a contemporary political novel, to which he made major modifications including the addition of a comic subplot. Colman's adaptation received overwhelmingly adverse criticism from the daily press.

Colman was so dissatisfied with the progress of the production at Drury Lane that he vented his feelings in a vituperative preface to the first edition of his text. Above all he blamed John Philip Kemble, who played the non-singing anti-hero, and saved faint praise for Storace, who had died before the text was published. After an unsuccessful first season, Colman took *The Iron Chest* to his own theatre, where it was much better received. In the 19th century the work was revived at Drury Lane, often as a vehicle for Edmund Kean in the leading role. Probably little if any of Storace's music survived the revivals.

The plot revolves around Sir Edward Mortimer's secret that, although he has been found innocent of the murder of his lover's brutish uncle, he was in fact guilty.

His secretary Wilford (baritone) discovers the fact in papers hidden in an iron chest, and decides he cannot live in the house with the burden of his new knowledge; however, Sir Edward refuses to release him from service. Wilford escapes, only to be found by a band of robbers, one of whom betrays his whereabouts. He is dragged back to the house and wrongly accused of theft, but Sir Edward's brother discovers the entire truth. Sir Edward is taken mortally ill and Wilford is reunited with his lover, Barbara (soprano).

Storace's music was published a year after his death in a joint volume with his last opera *Mahmoud* as a memorial to him and to benefit his widow and son. The music consists of an overture and 12 vocal numbers (4 airs and 8 ensembles). The overture is Storace's only one composed in two independent movements, with the first movement including a slow minor introduction of the type Storace had recently adopted. The ensembles include finales to all three acts and an opening glee, 'Five times by the taper light', which became popular in print. Although a few small action ensembles are included, they are short, of a domestic nature and peripheral to the plot.

JANE GIRDHAM

Irrelohe. Opera in three acts by FRANZ SCHREKER to his own libretto; Cologne, 27 March 1924.

The last opera in Schreker's highly charged middle-period style contained some of his finest music but fuelled critical disaffection. The characteristic scenario, set in the 18th century, focusses upon Irrelohe Castle, where Count Heinrich (tenor) lives a reclusive life, fearing hereditary madness should he give way to sexual desire. His love for the forester's daughter, Eva (soprano), painfully confronted in their remarkable Act 2 duet, inspires the violent jealousy of her ineffectual suitor, Peter (baritone), and the vengeance of old Christobald (tenor), the wedding-fiddler. Long ago, Christobald's own fiancée, Peter's mother Lola (contralto), had been raped by Heinrich's father on their wedding day. During the festivities following Heinrich's and Eva's marriage, Peter, beside himself, attempts to snatch Eva back, but Heinrich fights and kills him, unaware that they are brothers. Christobald has meanwhile set fire to Irrelohe Castle. Heinrich is broken, but Eva assures him of the redemptive power of love. They embrace as the sun rises above the smoking ruin.

PETER FRANKLIN

Irrlicht, Das [*Das Irrlicht, oder Endlich fand er sie* ('The Will-o'-the-Wisp, or He Found her at Last')]. Singspiel in three acts by IGNAZ UMLAUF to a text by GOTTLIEB STEPHANIE after CHRISTOPH FRIEDRICH BRETZNER's libretto *Der Irrwisch, oder Endlich fand er sie* (1779); Vienna, Burgtheater, 17 January 1782.

Alwin (tenor), Prince of the Green Island, has been placed under a fairy's curse for the liberties he has taken with the ladies at his court. The curse requires him to wander through the swamps each night as a will-o'-the-wisp, presenting himself as a humble shepherd to the maidens he meets until he finds a pure innocent who will love him for himself alone. He finds her in Blanka (soprano), adopted daughter of the foolish fisherman Berthold (bass) and his scheming wife Rosa (soprano). Rosa attempts to gain the prince's hand by substituting herself for Blanka, but fails a ceremonial test of virtue. Blanka passes the test by firmly rejecting the prince until he dons his shepherd's disguise.

Stephanie, who was making more thorough-going changes to another of Bretzner's librettos for Mozart at the same time (*Belmont und Constanze*), limited his alterations for Umlauf to the musical texts of *Der Irrwisch*. Umlauf's setting, although soon eclipsed by *Die Entführung*, enjoyed considerable success during the 1780s. His strophic variations for the opera's *Romanze*, 'Zu Stephen sprach im Traume', became his most popular musical creation.

THOMAS BAUMAN

Isaac [Lelong], **Adèle** (*b* Calais, 8 Jan 1854; *d* Paris, 22 Oct 1915). French soprano. She studied with Gilbert Duprez in Paris, making her début in 1870 at the Théâtre Montmartre in Massé's *Les noces de Jeannette*. In 1873 she first sang at the Opéra-Comique, as Marie (*La fille du régiment*). She also sang Gounod's Juliet and Mozart's Susanna, and in 1881 created Olympia and Antonia in *Les contes d'Hoffmann*. From 1883 to 1885 she was engaged at the Opéra, where her roles included Ophelia (*Hamlet*), Marguerite (*Faust*), Adèle (*Le comte Ory*), Zerlina, Marguerite de Valois (*Les Huguenots*), Isabelle (*Robert le diable*), Thomas' Francesca da Rimini and Mathilde (*Guillaume Tell*). In 1887 she created Minka in Chabrier's *Le roi malgré lui* at the Opéra-Comique. She retired in 1894. Her brilliant, flexible voice was especially suited to Mozart.

ELIZABETH FORBES

Isabeau. *Leggenda drammatica* in three parts by PIETRO MASCAGNI to a libretto by LUIGI ILLICA; Buenos Aires, Teatro Coliseo, 2 June 1911.

In an interview given in 1910 Mascagni emphasized his 'return to the romanticism which inspired so much of Italian opera', but in the crucial moments of his sweetened version of the medieval English legend of Lady Godiva he was not deterred from using a strenuous vocal line and heightened dynamics.

On the advice of his minister Cornelius (baritone), the old king Raimondo (bass) holds a tourney to find a husband for his beautiful and chaste daughter Isabeau (soprano), but she refuses all her noble suitors. The king compels her to ride naked through the city, but the people respect her and demand from him an edict condemning to blindness anyone who dares to look at her. Unaware of this, the falconer Folco (tenor) is the only person to see her. Isabeau visits him in prison and falls in love with him, and she goes to beg her father to pardon him. But Cornelius stirs up the people against him, and they execute summary justice; Isabeau returns in time to share his fate.

Mascagni tried to concentrate interest on the orchestra; *Isabeau*'s survival for 15 years was thanks to tenors such as Hipolito Lazaro and Bernardo De Muro. Despite the effectiveness of such passages as the flowing Intermezzo which accompanies Isabeau's ride, characterized by an incessant use of bells, the opera depends too much on 19th-century devices whose forced rhetoric is often evident; similarly, the attempts at musical sophistication in the work fail to conceal its essential conservatism.

MICHELE GIRARDI

Ishii, Kan (*b* Tokyo, 30 March 1921). Japanese composer. A son of Bac Ishii, a leading Japanese ballet dancer, he was educated to become a composer of ballet music, opera and orchestral works. He learnt counterpoint while studying the piano at the Musashino School of Music (1939–43). His first ballet, *Kami to Bayadēre*

('The God and the Bayadère'), choreographed by his father, was performed in Tokyo in 1950. After further studies with Orff in Munich (1952–4) he taught at the Tōhō Gakuen School of Music (1954–66), at the Aichi Prefectural Arts University, Nagoya (1966–86), and then at Showa Music College, Tokyo (from 1986). He has won several composition prizes and has also served as head of the Japan Composers' Federation (1964–70) and president of the All-Japan Chorus League. While he is better known for his choral works and ballets, of which *Marimo* (1962) is the most successful, the highly emotional quality of his music, its vital energy and strong sense of rhythm, as well as Ishii's colourful orchestration, are perhaps best realized in his operatic works. After composing two lighter operas based on folktales, he proceeded to write a full-scale opera, *En no Gyōja*, based on the story of a legendary 7th-century Japanese magician. The work did not achieve as much success as was hoped, but it paved the way for his masterpiece, *Kesa to Moritō* ('Kesa and Moritō'), of which performances have been given continuously since its première in 1968, in Japan and abroad. In his later operas he has returned to his lighter vein.

See also KESA TO MORITŌ.

Nyngyo to akai rōsoku [The Mermaid and the Red Candle] (1, after M. Ogawa), Tokyo, Asahi Shinbun Kōdō, Nov 1961
Kaguya-hime [Princess Kaguya] (1, Ayako Sōno), NHK TV, Nov 1963
En no Gyōja (3, Shikō Tsubouchi, after Shōyō Tsubouchi), Tokyo, Metropolitan Festival Hall, 20 March 1965
Kesa to Moritō [Kesa and Moritō] (3, Y. Yamanouchi, after *Heike monogatari* and *Genpei seisuiki*), Tokyo, Metropolitan Festival Hall, 20 Nov 1968
Onna wa suteki [Women are Wonderful] (comic op, 1, Yamanouchi), Tokyo, Iino Hall, 27 Oct 1978
Kantomi (3, K. Nakata), Kagoshima, Bunka Centre, 10 Oct 1981
Aojishi [Blue Lion] (operetta, 2, K. Hoshino, after a folktale), Komagane, City Hall, 3 Nov 1989   MASAKATA KANAZAWA

Ishiketa, Mareo (*b* Wakayama, 26 Nov 1916). Japanese composer. He studied composition with Kan'ichi Shimofusa and in 1939 graduated from the Tokyo Music School (now the Tokyo National University of Fine Arts and Music), where he was appointed lecturer in 1946 and professor of composition in 1952. His music, particularly for voices and chamber groups, reveals a personal style of lyricism, influenced by both Impressionism and Japanese traditional music. This tendency is also apparent in his four operas, all based on traditional Japanese subjects: *Sotoba Komachi*, a collaboration with the novelist Mishima based on a noh play; *Gyofukuki*, a folktale about a village girl who is turned into a small fish; *Koshamain ki* ('Tale of Koshamain'), a story of an Ainu hero; and *Kakekomi*, an opera accompanied by both Japanese and European instruments. In addition, Ishiketa has written two operettas, *Kappa-banashi* ('Tale of the Water Imps', 1954) and *Yappari ningen* ('Human after All', 1955).

Kappa-banashi [Tale of the Water Imps] (operetta), Tokyo, Haiyū-za, 24 Dec 1954
Yappari ningen [Human after All] (operetta), NHK Radio, 1955
Sotoba Komachi (1, Y. Mishima, after a noh play), Tokyo, Daiichi Seimei Hall, 12 Nov 1960
Gyofukuki (1, K. Hashimoto, after O. Dazai), Tokyo, NHK Hall, 1 Oct 1963
Koshamain ki [Tale of Koshamain] (T. Tsuruta and H. Takahashi), Tokyo, NHK Hall, Nov 1967
Kakekomi (T. Endō), Tokyo, Toshi Centre Hall, 28 Nov 1968
                                    MASAKATA KANAZAWA

Isis. *Tragédie en musique* in a prologue and five acts by Jean-Baptiste Lully (*see* LULLY family, (1)) to a libretto by PHILIPPE QUINAULT after OVID's *Metamorphoses*; St Germain-en-Laye, court, 5 January 1677.

The story of *Isis* is set entirely in pastoral and divine realms; there are no mortal heroes or worldly kingdoms here. Jupiter (baritone) courts the nymph Io (soprano). The jealous Junon [Juno] (soprano) imprisons Io under the hundred watchful eyes of Argus (baritone). Mercure [Mercury] (*haute-contre*) helps Io to escape and turns Hiérax [Hierax] (baritone), Io's former lover, into a bird when he tries to interfere. Juno then orders a Fury (*haute-contre*) to torment Io. After a series of tortures Io desperately invokes Jupiter in the monologue *air* 'Terminez mes tourments, puissant maître du monde'; Jupiter promises Juno that he will be faithful to her if she will spare Io. Juno transforms Io into an immortal, the Egyptian goddess Isis.

According to Le Cerf de la Viéville, *Isis* was known as 'the musicians' opera': he called the music 'learned'. The work contains a multiplicity of inventive *divertissements*. The prologue, set in the palace of Fame, is an immense static tableau of particularly intricate musical design. The Act 3 *divertissement* – a theatrical representation of the Pan and Syrinx story, staged to put Argus to sleep – occupies most of the act; it involves a double chorus and double dance troupe, and culminates in a much praised lament for Pan (bass), 'Hélas, hélas! quel bruit'. In Act 4 the Fury drags Io from the frozen north to the flaming forges of the Chalybes and on to the den of the Fates; the chorus and dance troupe appear at each location. The chorus of 'Trembleurs' – People from the Frozen Climates, whose teeth chatter in slurred tremolos (*see* Carter, *EMc*, xix, 1991, p.54) unaccountably marked 'lentement' in Lajarte's vocal score – was celebrated for its pantomime ballet as well as for its music.

Isis caused a scandal at its première, resulting in Quinault's temporary banishment from court: Io and Juno were understood to represent Mme de Ludres, the king's new favourite, and Mme de Montespan, his jealous mistress. Though it was the first work by Lully to be published (in partbooks, 1677), *Isis* had relatively few Paris Opéra productions (1677, 1704, 1717 and 1732).
                                              LOIS ROSOW

Island Princess, The. Semi-opera in five acts by Jeremiah Clarke, RICHARD LEVERIDGE and DANIEL PURCELL to a libretto by PETER ANTHONY MOTTEUX after plays of the same title by John Fletcher and Nahum Tate; London, Theatre Royal, Drury Lane, early February 1699.

One of the most popular English music dramas before *The Beggar's Opera* (only the 1674 version of *The Tempest* was performed more often), *The Island Princess* remained in repertory until 1739. It was rushed into production following the unexpected success of John Dennis and John Eccles's semi-opera *Rinaldo and Armida* (1698), which was given by the rival theatre in Lincoln's Inn Fields. The libretto of *The Island Princess* is based on Fletcher's original play of 1621, which had already been anonymously adapted in 1668 and again in 1687 by Tate. The heroic story of love and honour is set in the East Indies and centres on the struggle between Armusia and Ruy Dias (Portuguese colonists) for the hand of Princess Quisara. The play is action-filled, with characters in disguise, rescue scenes, bombardment, the triumph of Christianity and True Love. The original play had very little music, yet most of Motteux's added masques and entertainments grow naturally from the drama: shepherds celebrate the king's release from prison (Act 2); Quisara is comforted with a song (Act 3 scene iii); chanting Brahmins predict the future (Act 4 scene ii). By Motteux's own admission, the rustic dialogue in Act 4 is a poor fit, having been designed for the pastoral masque in Act 2 and moved against his wishes. The fifth-act finale, 'The Four Seasons or Love in every Age', was composed by Clarke in 1696 (probably as an homage to Henry Purcell) and does not relate to the drama in any sense.

The remarkable success of *The Island Princess* was due largely to its highly varied music. Clarke's overture and act tunes are especially fine; the second entr'acte is the famous Trumpet Tune in D (originally scored for strings alone) which was long misattributed to Henry Purcell. While he was clearly indebted to the great composer, Clarke was no mere imitator; rather, he developed an original, cleaner though no less vigorous style. Daniel Purcell's contribution is probably his finest theatre score, even though the words of the second-act pastoral were added after the music had been composed. In the preface to the word-book, Motteux wrote: 'What Mr. Daniel Purcell has set is so fine, that as he seems inspir'd with his Brother's wonderful Genius, it cannot but be equally admir'd'. The hyperbole should not detract from the excellence of 'All the pleasures Hymen brings', a simple, graceful song of near-faultless construction.

By far the most popular piece in the opera was the so-called Enthusiastic Song, 'Oh cease, urge no more', composed and performed by the bass Richard Leveridge. It is a long cantata in several contrasting sections which prophesies the horrors to befall the island kingdom should Armusia's blasphemy of the pagan gods go unpunished. Leveridge's singing and acting were much praised, but the song itself, which is in the Italian style with athletic violin parts, generates tremendous momentum, dissipated dramatically in the last section. Though perhaps inspired by 'You twice ten hundred deities' in *The Indian Queen*, the Enthusiastic Song helps explain the continuing popularity of semi-opera even after the death of Henry Purcell.

CURTIS PRICE

Ismagilov, Zagir Garipovich (*b* Verkhne-Sermenevo, now Beloretsky region of Bashkortostan, 26 Dec 1916/8 Jan 1917). Bashkir composer. He was a folk performer before being sent to the Moscow Conservatory in 1937 for formal studies, initially in the Bashkir national division with V. Beliy and V. Fere; after an interruption during the war years, he graduated in 1954. An important figure in Bashkir cultural life and the recipient of numerous awards and honours, he has contributed substantially to the national music theatre. His best-known opera, *Salavat Yulayev*, to a libretto by the Bashkir dramatist Bayazit Bikbay, takes its title from a local hero of the 1773–4 Pugachyov rebellion against tsarist authority. In this and subsequent operas, the dramatic and musical framework is based on Russian classical models enhanced with pentatonic modes, and on original and stylized folk material.

first performed at the Bashkir Theatre, Ufa

Salavat Yulayev (4, B. G. Bikbay), 15 April 1955
Shaura, 1963

Gyul'zifa, 1967
Vol'nïy Agideli [Free Agideli] (rev. version of Gyul'zifa), 1972
Poslï Urala [Ambassadors of the Urals], 1982
Akmulla, 1988

LAUREL E. FAY

Isola, Anna (*b* Naples or Genoa, *fl* 1728–45). Italian soprano. She sang in *commedie per musica* in Neapolitan dialect and in comic intermezzos and operas in Italian, and contributed to the stylistic interaction between the various genres. In Naples in 1728–9 she performed in Neapolitan comedies and in 1730 moved north to perform intermezzos with Domenico Cricchi and others. She joined Pietro Gaggiotti's company to sing in Graz (1737), and in 1744–5 she played her part in the unexpected success of Neapolitan, Roman and Florentine comic opera in Venice together with the best *buffo* singers of the day: Grazia Mellini, Francesco Baglioni, Anna Querzoli, Filippo Laschi and Pietro Pertici.

E. H. Müller: *Angelo und Pietro Mingotti* (Dresden, 1917)
P. Weiss: 'La diffusione del repertorio operistico nell'Italia del settecento: il caso dell'opera buffa', *Civiltà teatrale e settecento emiliano*, ed. S. Davoli (Bologna, 1986), 241–56

FRANCO PIPERNO

Isola, Gaetano (*b* Genoa, 1754; *d* Genoa, 17 July 1813). Italian composer. It is known from a letter he wrote to Padre Martini (in *I-Bc*) that he spent about ten years at the Palermo Conservatory studying for a diploma as *maestro di cappella*. Returning to Genoa in 1775 he began a career as a composer and music director. From 1777 to 1796 he was *maestro di cappella* at various churches and from 1789 *maestro al cembalo* at the Teatro di S Agostino, of which he also seems to have been director at least for the last years of his life.

Between 1785 and 1797 six operas and an oratorio by him were performed in Genoa, Turin, Florence and Lisbon to public acclaim. Two in particular were big spectacle pieces. For *La conquista del vello d'oro* Boggio chose a mythological subject on which to construct an opera in the French style. It incorporates a dance of the infernal spirits and some machine spectacle in the form of a fire-breathing dragon and a temple of the sun appearing in mid-air. The trio that closes Act 2 contains programmatic storm music, generously scored for percussion and wind including solo bassoon, clarinet and trumpet in addition to the usual oboe and horn. In *Le danaidi*, the innovatory librettist Sertor provided a formally more fluid work including many ensembles, choruses and pantomime. Two of the ensembles involve some action, and several include chorus.

Besides operas Isola wrote songs and sacred and instrumental music. Of his stage works, in most cases only the librettos and a few arias survive. His pupils included the English tenor and composer John Braham.

Medonte, Genoa, S Agostino, carn. 1785, scena and rondo *I-Gl*, and *MOe*
L'isola dei portenti (dg per musica, 2, P. Calvi), Voltri, nr Genoa, Palazzo Brignole Sale, aut. 1788
Lisandro (dramma serio per musica, 3, F. Ballani), Genoa, S Agostino, carn. 1790, duet *I-MOe*, scena and rondo *Gl*
La conquista del vello d'oro (dramma per musica, 3, G. Boggio), Turin, Regio, 26 Dec 1790, aria *Gl* and *Tn*, aria *Tf*, *P-La*
Le danaidi (dramma per musica, 3, G. Sertor), Florence, Pergola, aut. 1792
'Melodramma patriottico' (G. Sauli), Genoa, S Agostino, 9 July 1797

Arias for insertion in: Artaserse, 1794 [comp. unknown], *I-Gl, Rsc*; Nasolini: La morte di Cleopatra, 1795, *Gl*; Virginia, 1798 [various comps.], *Gl*; Mayr: Lodoiska, 1799, *Gl*; Mayr: Ginevra di Scozia, 1802, *Gl*; Cimarosa: Penelope, 1803, *Gl*; Paisiello: I zingari in fiera, 1806, *Gl*; others for unspecified operas, *CMbc, Gl, PAc*

*

C. Gervasoni: *Nuova teoria di musica* (Parma, 1812), 164
L. Grillo: 'Gaetano Isola', *Giornale degli studiosi di lettere, scienze, arti e mestieri*, i (1869), 209
A. Basso: *Storia del Teatro regio di Torino*, v: *Cronologie* (Turin, 1988), 151
C. Bongiovanni: *Il fondo musicale dell'Archivio capitolare del duomo di Genova* (Genoa, 1990), 44–54

CARMELA BONGIOVANNI, MARITA P. McCLYMONDS

Isola di Alcina, L' ('The Island of Alcina'). *Dramma giocoso* in three acts by GIUSEPPE GAZZANIGA to a libretto by GIOVANNI BERTATI after LUDOVICO ARIOSTO's poem *Gerusalemme liberata*; Venice, Teatro S Moisè, Carnival 1772.

The opera is a satire on Ariosto's story of the seductive sorceress Alcina (soprano). A Frenchman (La Rose, tenor), a Spaniard (Don Lopez, bass), a German (Barone di Brik Brak, bass), an Englishman (James, baritone) and an Italian (Brunoro, tenor) are shipwrecked on Alcina's magical island. On discovering where they are, they ask about the other characters in the famous legend and swear not to be taken in by Alcina's enchantments. All but the German gradually succumb and compete for the hand of the lovely witch. She enslaves two of them but they are rescued (with the assistance of her two nymphs) by the German, who plucks a hair from the sleeping Alcina's head. The men escape with the nymphs, and Alcina departs in her customary manner – in her chariot, raging. For each of the five gentlemen, Gazzaniga's music parodies the national and affective stereotypes in a clever and attractive way. This opera achieved immediate and widespread popularity, receiving at least seven productions in the year of its appearance, and remaining in the repertory until 1785. At Eszterháza, Haydn inserted 'Sono Alcina' for the heroine, one of his most famous insertion arias.

MARY HUNTER

Isola disabitata, L' (i) ('The Deserted Island'). *Dramma giocoso per musica* in three acts by Giuseppe Scarlatti (*see* SCARLATTI family, (3)) to a libretto by CARLO GOLDONI; Venice, Teatro Grimani di S Samuele, autumn 1757.

A young Chinese woman, Gianghira (soprano), is abandoned by her father on an uninhabited island because she refuses to marry the man chosen by him. A Dutch vessel carrying its captain, Valdimonte (tenor), his friend Garamone (tenor), their two brides-to-be, Carolina (soprano) and Giacinta (soprano), the cowardly elderly servant Panico (bass), the Dutchman Roberto (alto) and Marinella (soprano) arrives at the island. All are under the impression that they are the only inhabitants, until Garamone meets Gianghira. He immediately develops designs on her, and in order to keep her for himself tells Roberto and Gianghira seperately, in asides, that the other is mentally unbalanced. His ruse is soon uncovered, and Gianghira and Roberto fall in love.

Panico incites Carolina's and Giacinta's anger at their bridegrooms by telling them that both Valdimonte and Garamone have been entertaining another woman. After a series of intricate and bizarre developments, Valdimonte and Garamone, each of whom is courting

Gianghira, appear in Chinese disguise pretending to be emissaries from Gianghira's father. To complete the slapstick situation, Panico, Carolina and Giacinta also enter in Chinese costume, as presumed emissaries of Gianghira's jilted bridegroom. The five pretenders engage in an extended pantomine scene in which they dance and use mock Chinese words. Once the ruse is disclosed, Roberto and Gianghira declare their love for each other, while Valdimonte and Garamone pair off with their original brides. Before the standard happy ending, however, Gianghira's Chinese bridegroom is seen approaching the island with his navy. After an ocean battle in which the Dutch are victorious, all the characters unite onstage to sing the final chorus, 'Viva la pace'.

The opera is permeated with elements of slapstick, buffoonery and disguise. Using orientalisms as a veneer, Goldoni and Scarlatti created several likeable and believable characters, for example the well-meaning, cowardly Panico and the sentimental heroine, Gianghira, who resembles Cecchina in Goldoni's *La buona figliuola*. The opera won considerable success at its première through its interpretation by members of the popular Baglioni family, Francesco Carattoli and Catterina Ristorini in particular. It was also performed in Genoa (1760), as *La cinese smarrita* ('The Bewildered Chinese Woman'), and was well received in Vienna in 1773.

GORDANA LAZAREVICH

Isola disabitata, L' (ii) ('The Deserted Island'). *Azione teatrale* in two parts by JOSEPH HAYDN to a libretto by PIETRO METASTASIO; Eszterháza, 6 December 1779.

This opera, written for the name-day of Prince Nikolaus Esterházy, was performed only three weeks after the fire that destroyed the Eszterháza opera house. Haydn's autograph has not survived, although its precise fate is unclear; parts of it were available to Artaria in the early 1780s, and four pages of the overture still exist. Our knowledge of the majority of the opera comes from several authentic copies. It was performed twice at Eszterháza, and enjoyed a few performances, mostly in German translation, outside Eszterháza. In 1909 it was revived by Felix Weingartner at the Vienna Hofoper as part of the centenary commemoration of Haydn's death, under the title *Die wüste Insel*.

The only complete text by Metastasio that Haydn set, the story involves two sisters, Costanza (soprano) and Silvia (soprano), who have lived alone on an island for 13 years. They were left there by Costanza's husband, Gernando (tenor), after they had landed on the island to escape a storm at sea. Unknown to Costanza and Silvia, Gernando was actually abducted by pirates and enslaved for 13 years. Gernando has now freed himself, and he and a companion, Enrico (bass), have come in search of the sisters.

The opera opens with a strong overture in G minor; published separately in Haydn's lifetime, it still enjoys an independent existence. Its manner resembles that of Haydn's *Sturm und Drang* symphonies, and it sets up the anguished opening of the drama, in which Costanza finishes an inscription that describes her suicide. Silvia, who has little sympathy with her sister's misery, interrupts Costanza's accompanied recitative with innocent stories about her pet fawn. Costanza leaves just as Enrico and Gernando arrive, discussing their search for the two abandoned women. Silvia observes them from a hiding-place, and decides that these beings are too attractive to be men; she has had no direct contact with males since she was brought to the island as an infant. Gernando sees Costanza's inscription, and believes her dead; he decides that he too will die on the island. Enrico decides that he must take Gernando back to their boat in order to save his life. But before they return to the boat, Silvia and Enrico meet and fall in love. Gernando finds Costanza, who faints in horror at seeing the man who betrayed her. He rushes off in despair, but the confusion is quickly resolved, and both couples celebrate their good fortune.

The libretto invokes many Enlightenment figures and themes. Costanza, the abandoned woman, harks back to classical mythology, but 'donne abbandonate' appear in operas of all kinds throughout the 18th century. Silvia, the innocent young maiden attuned to nature, is altogether in the style of Rousseau; Enrico, the trustworthy companion, recalls Rinaldo's colleagues in Tasso's *Gerusalemme liberata*, similar to Ubaldo in Haydn's *Armida* (1784); and Gernando is the typical noble lover who seeks his lost love in faraway places, such as Prince Ali in Haydn's *L'incontro improvviso* (1775). The deserted island recalls Defoe's *Robinson Crusoe* as well as the late 18th-century German tradition of female 'Crusoes'. *L'isola disabitata* also displays the typically Metastasian characteristics of symmetry and smoothness of plot. Within the Eszterháza repertory it joins a group of 'island' operas, some comic and some serious. Its brevity and its reliance on accompanied recitative is shared by Luigi Bologna's *L'isola di Calipso abbandonata* (1784).

Haydn's opera follows Metastasio's original libretto exactly, except for two arias and the final quartet, which replaces Metastasio's brief chorus. The additional arias occur in scene v, where Enrico reflects on his duty to aid Gernando in his search, and scene x, where Silvia (originally sung by Luigia Polzelli) is left alone to consider her new feelings for Enrico. Enrico's aria, 'Chi nel cammin d'onore', comes from Metastasio's *festa teatrale Il tempio dell'Eternità* (or *Enea negli Elisi*), and may have been an early substitution in the libretto's peregrinations. Silvia's aria, 'Come il vapor s'ascende', may have been a 'stock' text of the time; it is also used in longer form in Anfossi's *Il curioso indiscreto* (performed in Vienna in 1782 and at Eszterháza in 1783). The final quartet brings Metastasio's original chorus up to date, insofar as it includes individual utterances reminiscent of the third-act finale of an *opera buffa*.

Haydn's accompanied recitative avoids his characteristic musical picture-painting; indeed the text affords rather few opportunities for this sort of display. Rather, Haydn subtly suggests the characteristics of the different roles – Costanza's introspectiveness and despair, Silvia's cheerful innocence and Gernando's trembling desire to see his wife. The arias range from deeply felt lyrical numbers (Costanza's 'Se non piange un infelice') to a more heroic idiom (Enrico's 'Chi nel cammin d'onore'). All are notable for their absence of vocal display and their formal restraint; there are no two-tempo arias, and emotional progression is suggested by means of the varied reprise rather than by striking contrasts. Wind instruments are used with particular beauty throughout the work. The final quartet is a celebration of the princely orchestra as well as of the happy end; in concertante style, it includes solos for violin, cello, flute and bassoon. Haydn's revision of this piece in 1802 (with a view to publication by Breitkopf) drastically shortened the orchestral episodes.

MARY HUNTER

Isouard, Nicolas [Nicolò; Isoiar, Nicolò; Nicolò de Malte] (*b* Valletta, 18 May 1773; *d* Paris, 23 March 1818). Maltese composer of French origin. As a composer he often used the names Nicolò or Nicolò de Malte. A patron financed Isouard's early journey to Paris and education at the Pensionnat Berthaüd, a preparatory school for the Engineers and Artillery, where he had piano lessons. In 1789 the Revolution forced him to leave; back in Malta his father placed him in a merchant's office. He played the piano in society and studied composition with Michel-Ange Vella and counterpoint with Azzopardi. Sent to Palermo as a merchant's assistant, he took harmony lessons with Giuseppe Amendola; later, in Naples, he completed composition studies with Sala and received practical advice from Guglielmi.

In June 1794 Isouard's début as a composer took place in Florence with the opera *L'avviso ai maritati*, which was enthusiastically received and later given in Lisbon, Dresden and Madrid. From this time he abandoned commerce and called himself Nicolò de Malte in order not to compromise his family. On the death of Vincenzo Anfossi (brother of the composer) Isouard was appointed organist of the church of St John of Jerusalem, Malta, where he stayed until the French invasion in June 1798, composing serious and comic Italian operas for the Maltese theatre. He became secretary to the governor of the French garrison, Vaubois, and accompanied his family on their return to Paris before the hostilities were ended.

Le petit page, Isouard's first Parisian *opéra comique*, was given in the Théâtre Feydeau in February 1800, composed in collaboration with Rodolphe Kreutzer, who acted as Isouard's manager and patron. Their second work, the serious opera *Flaminius à Corinthe* (1801), was a failure; this induced Isouard to rework his earlier *opéras comiques*, *L'improvvisata in campagna* (as *L'impromptu de campagne*) and *Le tonnelier*, and these were successful. He also became friendly with the librettist F.-B. Hoffman, who influenced the direction his work was taking; Isouard acknowledged the thorough grounding in dramatic art that Hoffman gave him. Isouard's first major success, however, was *Michel-Ange* (1802), to a libretto by Delrieu.

With *Un jour à Paris* (1808) Isouard began his long collaboration with the librettist C.-G. Etienne, editor of the *Journal des deux mondes*. Together they had an unprecedented success at the Opéra-Comique in 1810 with the fairy-tale opera *Cendrillon*. This accomplishment reconciled Isouard with his father, who came from Malta for his son's wedding in 1812 to Claudine Berthault. Although *Cendrillon* was set later in the same year by Steibelt, Isouard's work was revived periodically and reorchestrated by Adam in 1845. Isouard's activity in opera continued almost to the end of his life. *Jeannot et Colin* (1814) was a triumph both for its expressive melodies and for its fine interpretation, but *Joconde* (1814), also to a libretto by Etienne, finally confirmed Isouard's international reputation and remained in the repertory until the close of the century. Isouard's creativity had been stimulated by the return in 1811 of his chief competitor, Boieldieu, from eight years in Russia. In the later works Isouard showed extraordinary power of expression, which the levity and rapid composition of earlier operas had not admitted. His rivalry with Boieldieu came to a head when both applied for membership of the Institut de France (1817). Boieldieu received the nomination, and Isouard broke off relations with his old friend. Isouard died at the age of 44. His opera *Aladin* was completed by Benincori, who himself died shortly before the première on 6 February 1822. The work was successful (seen up to 1830) and was the first opera in Paris to be produced with gas lighting, and to include an ophicleide in its pit orchestra.

Isouard played an important part in the Italian influence on French music between the Empire and the beginning of the Restoration. Up to 1811 he had limited competition (Dalayrac was at the end of his career; Méhul, Berton and Kreutzer had sporadic successes) but did not win the public's consistent support, in spite of the effectiveness of his work. Secure craftsmanship, gained through the study of Neapolitan practice, went hand in hand with his melodic gift, the mainstay of his reputation; and he had an unfailing instinct for matching in music the tone of the words. *Cendrillon* brought about a vogue for fairy-tale operas; though carefully composed it lacks the qualities that made *Jeannot et Colin* his most perfectly shaped and moving piece, and *Joconde* his masterpiece, wherein poet and composer sound as one. Martine (1813) denied Isouard's music any 'appropriate colour' or 'expression', but this was a manifestation of the long rivalry between French and Italian music. Others levelled criticism at the effective monopoly created by his partnership with Etienne. But Isouard helped to give French *opéra comique* its essentially final form. Most of his mature works were performed throughout Europe; some reached the USA. *Michel-Ange* was translated into five languages and *L'intrigue aux fenêtres* into seven. *Les rendez-vous bourgeois* was still revived in the 1860s, *Cendrillon* and *Joconde* in the 1870s. In Paris many of Isouard's works survived until the late 1820s, and the Opéra-Comique revived *Les rendez-vous bourgeois* and *Joconde* after World War I.

See also CENDRILLON (i); JOCONDE; and RENDEZ-VOUS BOURGEOIS, LES.

first performed in Paris by the Opéra-Comique at the Théâtre Feydeau unless otherwise stated; printed works published in Paris

L'avviso ai maritati (2, F. Gonella), Florence, Pergola, 4 June 1794, *F-Pc*

Artaserse re di Persia (3, P. Metastasio), Livorno, Avvalorati, Sept 1794

Il barbiere di Siviglia (ob, after P.-A. Beaumarchais), Malta, *c*1796

Rinaldo d'Asti (G. Carpani, after J.-B. Radet and P.-Y. Barré: *Renaud d'Ast*), Malta, *c*1796

L'improvvisata in campagna (ob, after E. J. B. Delrieu), Malta, 1797; rev. as L'impromptu de campagne (1, Delrieu), Paris, OC (Favart), 30 June 1801 (1801)

Il tonneliere, Malta, 1797; rev. as Le tonnelier (1, Delrieu and F. A. Quêtant), Paris, OC (Favart), 19 May 1801

I due avari (ob), Malta, *c*1797

Il barone d'Alba chiara (ob), Malta, *c*1798

Ginevra di Scozia (after L. Ariosto), Malta, *c*1798

Le petit page, ou La prison d'état (cmda, 1, R. C. G. de Pixérécourt and L. T. Lambert), Paris, Feydeau, 14 Feb 1800, (n.d.), collab. R. Kreutzer

Flaminius à Corinthe (opéra, 1, Pixérécourt and Lambert), Paris, Opéra, 27 Feb 1801, *Po* (inc.), collab. Kreutzer

La statue, ou La femme avare (1, F.-B. Hoffman), 26 April 1802

Michel-Ange (opéra, 1, Delrieu), 11 Dec 1802 (1802)

Les confidences (comédie mêlée de chants, 2, A. J. Jars), 31 March 1803 (1803)

Le baiser et la quittance, ou Une aventure de garnison (3, L. B. Picard, M. Dieulafoy and C. de Longchamps), 18 June 1803, *B-Bc, F-Pn*, collab. E.-N. Méhul, A. Boieldieu and Kreutzer

Le médecin turc (opéra-bouffon, 1, P. Villiers and A. Gouffé), 19 Nov 1803 (1804)

L'intrigue aux fenêtres (opéra bouffon, 1, J.-N. Bouilly and L. E. F. C. Mercier-Dupaty), Paris, OC (Favart), 25 Feb 1805 (1805)

La ruse inutile, ou Les rivaux par convention (opéra, 2, Hoffman), Paris, OC (Favart), 30 May 1805 (1805)

Léonce, ou Le fils adoptif (comédie mêlée de musique, 2, B.-J. Marsollier), 18 Nov 1805 (1805)

La prise de Passau (2 or 3, Mercier-Dupaty), 8 Feb 1806

Le déjeuner de garçons (cmda, A.-F. Creuzé de Lesser), 24 April 1806 (*c*1806)

Idala, ou La sultane (3, Hoffman), 1 Aug 1806

Les rendez-vous bourgeois (opéra-bouffon mêlé d'ariettes, 1, Hoffman), 9 May 1807 (1807)

Les créanciers, ou Le remède à la goutte (3, J.-B.-C. Vial), 10 Dec 1807

Un jour à Paris, ou La leçon singulière (oc mêlé de musique, 3, C.-G. Etienne), 24 May 1808 (1808)

Cimarosa (oc, 2, Bouilly), 28 June 1808 (1808)

Zélomir, ou L'intrigue au sérail (3, Etienne), 25 April 1809

Cendrillon (opéra-féerie, 3, Etienne, after C. Perrault: *Contes de ma mère l'oye*), 22 Feb 1810 (*c*1810)

La victime des arts, ou La fête de famille (2, L.-M. d'Estourmel), 27 Feb 1811, collab. H.-M. Berton and J.-P. Solié

La fête de village, ou L'heureux militaire (1, Etienne), 31 March 1811

Le billet de loterie (cmda, 1, Creuzé de Lesser, J.-F. Roger), 14 Sept 1811 (*c*1811)

Le magicien sans magie (oc, 2, Creuzé de Lesser and Roger), 4 Nov 1811 (*c*1811)

Lully et Quinault, ou Le déjeuner impossible (oc, 1, P. C. Gaugiran-Nanteuil), 27 Feb 1812 (?1812)

Le prince de Catane (opéra, 3, R. R. L. Castel, after Voltaire: *L'éducation d'un prince*), 4 March 1813 (*c*1813)

Le français à Venise (oc, 1, J. Gensoul), 14 June 1813 (1813)

Bayard à Mézières, ou Le siège de Mézières (oc, 1, Mercier-Dupaty and A. R. P. Allisan de Chazet), 12 Feb 1814, vs (1814), collab. Boieldieu, C.-S. Catel and L. Cherubini

Joconde, ou Les coureurs d'aventures (comédie mêlée de chants, 3, Etienne), 28 Feb 1814 (*c*1814)

Jeannot et Colin (oc, 3, Etienne), 17 Oct 1814 (*c*1814)

Les deux maris (oc, 1, Etienne), 18 March 1816 (1816)

L'une pour l'autre ou L'enlèvement (oc, 3, Etienne), 11 May 1816 (*c*1816)

Aladin, ou La lampe merveilleuse (opéra-féerie, 5, Etienne), Paris, Opéra, 6 Feb 1822 (*c*1822), completed by A. M. Benincori

Une nuit de Gustave Wasa (opéra, 2), inc. [sketches and chorus for Act 1], completed by F. Gasse, 1825

*

'Nicolo (Nic. Isouard, dit)', *Dictionnaire historique des musiciens*, ed. A. E. Choron and F. Fayolle (Paris, 1811)

J. D. Martine: *De la musique dramatique en France* (Paris, 1813), chap. 21

Castil-Blaze: 'Nicolo', *Le ménestrel*, xxviii (1860), 17

E. Wahl: *Nicolo Isouard: sein Leben und sein Schaffen auf dem Gebiet der Opéra Comique* (Munich, 1906)

J. Tiersot: *Lettres de musiciens écrites en français du XVe au XXe siècles*, i (Turin, 1924), 423ff

M. Pincherle: *Musiciens peints par eux-mêmes: lettres de compositeurs écrites en français* (Paris, 1939), 73–4

A. S. Garlington jr: *The Concept of the Marvelous in French and German Opera 1770–1840* (diss., U. of Illinois, 1965)

C. Nazloglou: *Le goût musical en France à travers l'art lyrique, 1815–1840* (diss., U. of Nice, 1975)

K. A. Hagberg: *'Cendrillon' by Daniel Steibelt: an Edition with Notes on Steibelt's Life and Operas* (diss., Eastman School of Music, 1976)

B. V. Daniels: 'Cicéri and Daguerre: Set Designers for the Paris Opéra, 1820–1822', *Theater Survey*, xxii (1981), 69–90

J. Warrack, ed.: *Carl Maria von Weber: Writings on Music* (Cambridge, 1981) [incl. reviews of Isouard's operas]

C. J. Robison: *One-act Opéra-Comique from 1800 to 1810: Contributions of Henri-Montan Berton and Nicolo Isouard* (diss., U. of Cincinnati, 1986)
DAVID CHARLTON, MARIE BRIQUET

Ispirazione, L' ('Inspiration'). *Melodramma* in three acts by SYLVANO BUSSOTTI to his own libretto after Ernst Bloch's short story *Die gutmachende Muse* from his *Spuren* (1930); Florence, Teatro Comunale, 26 May 1988.

In the year 2031, a new opera is being rehearsed by the director Harno Lupo (bass) at his theatre. A chorus of computers and robots under the baton of a

'Kapellmeister' (bass) is rehearsing an absurd score when Mastro Wolfango (baritone), an old violinist, is heard snoring; the enraged conductor interrupts the rehearsal and leaves. Mastro Wolfango is fired from his position; his wife Argía (soprano) criticizes him, while his daughter Serena (soprano) is clandestinely copying the parts for an opera that Mastro Wolfango has written in secret during years of poverty and lack of recognition. Mastro Wolfango surprises Serena, and after a scene she leaves the house of her parents. Later, found in extreme poverty, Mastro Wolfango is brought by a messenger (baritone) to the opera house where Serena – who has become a famous singer – is performing for the first time the leading role in his opera. Mastro Wolfango witnesses the triumphant success of his work.

Bussotti's opera, a musical legend about poverty and musical success projected into the future, is based on a short philosophical text by Ernst Bloch. As well as incorporating material from his composition *Nympheo* of 1984, Bussotti included two of his other works, *In memoriam (Cathy Berberian)* (1984) and *Studia sempre* (from *Due ballabili*, 1983), thereby adding an autobiographical dimension to the opera which may be read as a hidden glorification of his own music.

JÜRGEN MAEHDER

Israel. Operatic traditions in the area of the Jewish state date back to well before the achievement of statehood in 1948: performances were given between 1923 and 1927 in Tel-Aviv by a Palestine Opera Company, beginning with *La traviata* and including works of special local significance such as *Samson et Dalila*, *La Juive* and Rubinstein's *Die Maccabäer* (all translated into Hebrew). The company's founder and conductor, Mordechai Golinkin, also founded a Palestine Folk Opera in 1941, and a Chamber Opera was formed under Benno Frankel in 1933; but it was not until 1948 that a national company, the Hebrew (later Israel) National Opera, came into being, founded by the singer Edis de Philippe (who sang Massenet's Thaïs in the company's inaugural production). The company functioned up to 1953 and then from 1957 until 1982; the New Israel Opera was established in 1985 and three years later moved to the Noga Theatre in Jaffa. Italian, French and Russian opera have predominated in the repertory, Wagner and to some extent Strauss being excluded.

In the light of the country's limited scope for operatic life, it is understandable that few Israeli composers have been active in opera. Most of the leading figures have been first-generation immigrants from central Europe. Among the earliest was Karel Salmon, composer in 1930 of a marionette opera on the story of David and Goliath, who made use of regional folk music in his operas. Like Salmon, Abel Ehrlich, an intensely prolific writer of small-scale operas, came from Germany. Another composer influenced by local folk idioms, both east European and eastern Mediterranean, was Marc Lavry, in his two operas *Dan Hashomer* (1945) and *Tamar* (1958). Among the more widely successful composers are Menahem Avidom, whose operas range from parody to early Jewish history and psychological drama; his success however has been largely local, whereas Josef Tal (like Avidom of Polish birth) has had his operas seen on a wider stage, with performances in Hamburg, Berlin and elsewhere in Germany, writing in a basically European musical language although most of his operas draw on Jewish legend and history. The next

generation of Israeli opera composers is represented by Mark Kopytman, whose opera *Chamber Scenes from the Life of Susskind von Trimberg* was first given in Jerusalem in 1983, and the native Ami Maayani.

Issé. *Pastorale héroïque* in a prologue and three acts by ANDRÉ CARDINAL DESTOUCHES to a libretto by ANTOINE HOUDAR DE LAMOTTE; concert performances at Fontainebleau, 7 October, and Versailles, Trianon, 17 December 1697 (stage performance, Paris, Opéra, 30 December 1697).

Apollo (*haute-contre*), wishing to win the nymph Issé (soprano), disguises himself as Philemon, a shepherd, with whom Issé duly falls in love. When an oracle discloses that Apollo wants Issé, she declares her loyalty to her simple shepherd; Apollo, delighted, reveals his true identity. Parallel with this plot is a more lighthearted secondary intrigue between Doris (soprano) and Pan (bass). The changes made by Destouches for a revival in 1708 (involving an expansion to five acts) reflect developing tastes in the first decade of the 18th century: the role of dance in the *divertissements* is increased, the choruses extended and enriched, and some vocal *airs* are rewritten in a more ornate style related to the cantata. *Issé* launched Destouches' composing career and was considered his *chef d'oeuvre*. Revivals continued at the Opéra until 1757 and at court until 1773, Madame de Pompadour playing Issé in the 1749 performance at the Théâtre des Petits Cabinets.

CAROLINE WOOD

Issipile ('Hypsipyle'). Libretto by PIETRO METASTASIO, first set by Francesco Conti (1732, Vienna).

ACT 1 Delayed in Thrace, the men of Lemnos have made concubines of the young Thracian women. In revenge, the women of Lemnos vow to murder their menfolk upon their return. Toante [Thoas], King of Lemnos, has a particular enemy in the widowed princess, Eurinome [Eurynome], whose son, Learco [Learchus], he banished for the harassment of his daughter, Hypsipyle. When Hypsipyle vows to murder her father to satisfy Eurynome, she secretly plans to warn him not to land, but is too late. Thoas is surprised at his daughter's cool public greeting, but she explains all privately when she bids him hide in the sacred grove of the goddess Diana.

ACT 2 Unknown to all, Learchus has returned with a band of pirates and, unrecognized, tells Thoas to flee the grove for his daughter's sake. Masquerading as Thoas, Learchus plans to seize Hypsipyle and leave Lemnos. Meanwhile, Hypsipyle sacrifices another Lemnian in place of her father, passing the body off as that of Thoas. So convincing is her deception that Giasone [Jason], betrothed to Hypsipyle and just returned to Lemnos, renounces her when he learns of her patricidal act from Eurynome.

ACT 3 Hypsipyle, mistaking Eurynome for Rhodope, her confidante, reveals her deception regarding Thoas. Eurynome demands that the king be hunted down and is awestruck when Learchus is found instead. Rhodope, in love with Learchus, releases him, and his immediate attempt to murder the sleeping Jason is prevented only by the timely arrival of Hypsipyle; Jason awakes to find her with dagger in hand. He rebuffs her further as his attempted murderess, but later realizes his errors when he encounters Thoas. Left alone while Jason searches for Hypsipyle, Thoas is taken as captive to the pirate ship. Here, Learchus threatens to kill the king if Hypsipyle does not join him.

Jason counters, however, by taking Eurynome hostage. Defeated, Learchus stabs himself and plunges into the sea.

*   *   *

From among the classical sources, the most complete accounts of the Hypsipyle legend are contained in the Apollonius *Argonautica* (book 1) and the Valerius Flaccus *Argonautica* (book 2). Other sources include Apollodorus, *Bibliotheca* (book 1); Herodotus, *Historiae* (book 6); Hyginus, *Fabulae* (no.15); Ovid, *Heroïdes* (no.6); and Statius, *Thebaid* (book 5). Metastasio combined the Thoas and Jason incidents as related in these sources and possibly drew upon Thomas Corneille's *Camma* (1661) for the circumstances of a would-be assassin's identity being mistaken. Dramas by Aeschylus (*Hypsipyle*) and Sophocles (*Lemnians*) are lost, and the *Hypsipyle* of Euripides, existing only in scant fragments until 1908, focusses upon situations surrounding Hypsipyle after her banishment from Lemnos. Metastasio may, however, have had recourse to Aurelio Aureli's *L'Issifile amazone di Lenno* which, in a setting by Pietro Porfiri, was performed in Pesaro in 1697. Certainly, Metastasio's libretto served Pierre Belloy's drama *Zelmire* (1762). *Issipile* was Metastasio's second drama for Vienna; given in the Kleines Hoftheater in February, it was probably part of the carnival festivities. It was given a grand presentation with settings by Giuseppe Galli-Bibiena and gained for its author the approval of his patron, Charles VI. This setting by Conti was his last opera, and although the text was to be set four times in its first year, it was to gain only moderate popularity, with fewer than 30 subsequent realizations.

For a list of settings *see* METASTASIO, PIETRO.   DON NEVILLE

Istanbul [Constantinople]. Former capital of Turkey. As Constantinople the city was the seat of the sultans of the Ottoman Empire from 1453. Selim III was the first sultan to attend an opera performance in Turkey: this was given in 1797 in the courtyard of the ancient Topkapi Sarayi Palace, probably by musicians invited by the French embassy.

The city's first purpose-built opera house (cap. 400) was opened in 1840 by an Italian named Bosco and used by visiting Italian companies, but in 1844 the management was assumed by Mihail Naum, a local businessman. The Naum Theatre, as it came to be called, burnt down in 1846 but Naum had it restored with the assistance of Sultan Abd al-Mejid. It burnt down again in 1870 and was not rebuilt.

Meanwhile the Sultan had built a private opera house (cap. 300) near the Dolmabahçe Palace. It staged operas from the standard Italian repertory. The building burnt down in 1864. Sultan Abd al-Hamid II opened a theatre in Yildiz Palace in 1889, and operatic performances continued there until 1908. Armenian and Italian operas and French operettas were also given at the Opera Tiyatrosu (Opera Theatre, opened 1874) and the Gullu Agop Tiyatrosu (opened 1883). The Republic of Turkey was established in 1923 with Ankara as the new capital. Constantinople's name was changed to Istanbul in 1930; performances by visiting troupes continued, but locally based operatic activity was not undertaken until 1957, when an opera studio was founded in cooperation with the German contralto Ruth Michaelis. In 1960 the city sponsored a series of performances on the stage of the old Dramatic Theatre with both Turkish and foreign singers.

The new municipal opera house, whose foundations had been laid in 1946, was finally opened in 1968 as part of the Istanbul Kültür Sarayi (Istanbul Palace of Culture). Two years later the building was gutted by fire. Performances were held in a converted night-club until the theatre was reopened in 1977, as the Atatürk Kültür Merkezi (Atatürk Cultural Centre); this has two auditoriums, seating 1250 and 600. In 1970 the sponsorship of operatic activity was transferred from the city to the state.

Performances by the Istanbul State Opera Company are given from October to June in a stagione pattern. Three new opera productions are presented each year along with two or more operettas or musicals. At least one Turkish opera is included in the annual repertory, among the most popular being Saygun's *Köroğlu*, which had its première in Istanbul in 1973, and Okan Demiriş's *Murat IV*, first performed there in 1980.

*

A. C. Konuralp: *Devlet Opera v Balesi: Ankara, Istanbul, Izmir* [The State Opera and Ballet: Ankara, Istanbul, Izmir] (Ankara, 1991)   FARUK YENER

Istel, Edgar (*b* Mainz, 23 Feb 1880; *d* Miami, FL, 17 Dec 1948). German musicologist and composer. After studying composition with Fritz Volbach and with Thuille and Sandberger in Munich, he took the doctorate in 1900 with a dissertation on Rousseau's music to *Pygmalion* and worked as a lecturer, music critic and essayist. In 1920 he moved to Madrid, where he represented the Verband deutscher Bühnenschriftsteller und Bühnenkomponisten; he emigrated in 1936 to England and in 1938 to the USA. He established his reputation with his work on the history of opera, especially librettos; his book on the libretto (1914) is one of the best accounts of the outlines and characteristics of opera texts. His major compositions include several operas and incidental music.

Der fahrende Schüler (komisch-romantisches Spiel, 1, after M. de Cervantes and others), Karlsruhe, 24 March 1906; rev. as Maienzauber, Gera, Reussisches, 18 Oct 1919

Des Tribunals Gebot (komisch-romantisches Bühnenspiel, 3, F. Halm), Mainz, Stadt, 16 Nov 1916; rev. as Verbotene Liebe, (1), Gera, 1919

Endlich allein (burlesk-romantische Oper, 1), Schwerin, Landes, 11 Jan 1920

Wenn Frauen träumen (musikalisches Lustspiel, 3), Berlin, Komische Oper, 4 April 1920

Wie lernt man lieben? (musikalisches Lustspiel, 3), Duisburg, Jan 1931

Spanisches Abenteuer (Spl), unpubd

WRITINGS

Jean-Jacques Rousseau als Komponist seiner lyrischen Scene 'Pygmalion' (Leipzig, 1901)

Das deutsche Weihnachtsspiel und seine Wiedergeburt aus dem Geiste der Musik (Langensalza, 1901)

Die komische Oper (Stuttgart, 1906)

Die Entstehung des deutschen Melodramas (Berlin and Leipzig, 1906)

Das Kunstwerk Richard Wagners (Leipzig, 1910)

Das Libretto (Berlin, 1914, 2/1915; Eng. trans., rev., as *The Art of Writing Opera Librettos*, 1922)

Die moderne Oper seit dem Tode Richard Wagners bis zum Weltkrieg (Leipzig, 1915, 2/1923)

Das Buch der Oper (Berlin, 1919, 2/1920)

Revolution und Oper (Regensburg, 1919)

Bizet und 'Carmen' (Stuttgart, 1927)   ALFRED GOODMAN

Italiana in Algeri, L' ('The Italian Girl in Algiers'). *Dramma giocoso* in two acts by GIOACHINO ROSSINI to a libretto substantially derived from ANGELO ANELLI's libretto for Luigi Mosca's *L'italiana in Algeri* (1808, Milan); Venice, Teatro S Benedetto, 22 May 1813.

Mustafà	*Bey of Algiers*	bass
Elvira	*wife of Mustafà*	soprano
Zulma	*slave, confidante of Elvira*	mezzo-soprano
Haly	*Captain of the Algerian Corsairs*	bass
Lindoro	*young Italian, favourite slave of Mustafà*	tenor
Isabella	*Italian lady*	contralto
Taddeo	*companion of Isabella*	bass

Eunuchs of the harem, Algerian corsairs, Italian slaves, pappataci (tenors 1 and 2, basses); women of the harem, European slaves, sailors (supernumeraries)

Setting Algiers, about 1805

The opera is Rossini's first *buffo* masterpiece in the fully fledged two-act form. It quickly won widespread popular acclaim in Italy and it was the first Rossini opera to be produced in Germany (1816, Munich) and France (1817, Paris). Paradoxically, it was the failure with Venetian audiences of Rossini's own *La pietra del paragone* that prompted a crisis in the schedule of the Teatro S Benedetto in late April 1813, a crisis exacerbated by the non-appearance of a promised opera by Carlo Coccia. To fill the gap, Rossini was commissioned to re-work Anelli's libretto for *L'italiana in Algeri*, first set to music by Mosca for La Scala, Milan, in August 1808. Rossini completed the work in 27 days, in time for the *prima* on 22 May 1813. Predictably, there were those in the audience during the opera's initial run ready to proclaim that the opera was a rehash of Mosca and secondhand Rossini. In fact, nothing could be further from the truth, as informed Venetian critical opinion rapidly acknowledged. This is not only one of Rossini's most brilliant scores but also one of his most original, with most of the music, including the famous overture, freshly written by him. The only music in the score farmed out to his anonymous collaborator are the secco recitatives, Ali's Act 2 aria 'Le femmine d'Italia' and, possibly, the original Act 2 cavatina for Lindoro, 'Oh come il cor di giubilo'. It is not known for certain who helped Rossini adapt Anelli's libretto. What is clear is that the changes reflect Rossini's desire to strengthen and modify the character of the heroine Isabella and to bring to the big ensembles – the Act 1 finale, the stretta to the Act 2 quintet – the kind of manic verbal onomatopoeia that he delighted in setting to music.

The singers at the first performance included two leading artists for whom Rossini had already written important roles: Marietta Marcolini (Isabella) and Filippo Galli (Mustafà). The rest of the cast was: Luttgard Annibaldi (Elvira), Annunziata Berni Chelli (Zulma), Giuseppe Spirito (Haly), Serafino Gentili (Lindoro) and Paolo Rosich (Taddeo). The strength of the cast was said to have been an important factor in the opera's initial success; indeed, it was Marcolini's decision on 19 June to use the occasion of a charity night gala to sing Mosca's setting of 'Pensa alla patria' as well as Rossini's that finally scotched all talk of plagiarism by Rossini. When the production transferred to Vicenza in the summer of 1813, Marcolini commissioned from Rossini a new Act 1 cavatina, 'Cimentando i venti e l'onde', more closely aligned to the demands of her voice

and technique than 'Cruda sorte!'; it has not, however, supplanted the original cavatina. For the Milanese *prima* in 1814 Rossini made changes to the orchestration of 'Cruda sorte!' and substituted an obbligato flute for an obbligato cello in Isabella's Act 2 cavatina 'Per lui che adoro'. The Act 2 cavatina for Lindoro, 'Concedi, amor pietoso', partly based on music from *Tancredi* and also new to the score, is a more substantial piece than 'Oh come il cor di giubilo' and is more certainly a genuine Rossini composition than its predecessor. Rossini's final modification to the score came in Naples in 1815 when the politically inflammatory Rondo for Isabella in Act 2, 'Pensa alla patria' ('Think of your country'), was replaced by 'Sullo stil de' viaggiatori'; this, incorporating the overture's second theme, is certainly by Rossini himself – though nowadays there is little likelihood of 'Pensa alla patria' being banned by the censor. All Rossini's variants can be found in the appendices to Azio Corghi's definitive critical edition published in 1981 by the Fondazione Rossini, Pesaro.

The opera was frequently performed in Europe, and in the USA, in the period up to 1830 and rarely left the repertory even in the later years of the 19th century when Rossini's reputation was in widespread decline. Its revival in modern times dates from 1925 and a Turin production, conducted by Vittorio Gui, with Conchita Supervia as Isabella. Richard Strauss was among those reported to have been 'mad with enthusiasm' about the opera and Supervia's performance of the title role, something she repeated with equal success during famous revivals in Paris in 1929 and at the Royal Opera House, Covent Garden, in 1935. She recorded Isabella's three arias and part of the Act 1 finale ('O che muso') in Barcelona in 1927. Gui was also the conductor when the opera was produced at Glyndebourne in 1957 with Oralia Dominguez in the title role. Distinguished Isabellas of more recent times have included Teresa Berganza, Marilyn Horne, Lucia Valentini-Terrani and Agnes Baltsa. During the 1970s and 80s the opera was directed a number of times by Jean-Pierre Ponnelle, whose ability to reproduce on stage the patterns and rhythms of Rossini's score was as gratifying as it was amusing.

ACT 1.i *Mustafà's palace – a small hall in the Bey's apartments* Elvira laments the decision of her husband, the Bey Mustafà, to reject her. Zulma and the court eunuchs try to comfort her but the arrival of Mustafà confirms their worst fears. His Andantino 'Delle donne l'arroganza', full of grotesque intervals and elaborate coloratura, shows him to be arrogant and domineering. Mustafà orders Haly to arrange for Elvira to be married to Lindoro, his Italian slave; he also orders Haly, on threat of instant impalement, to find him an Italian girl to replace Elvira. Lindoro, meanwhile, laments his separation from the beautiful Isabella (cavatina, 'Languir per una bella'). In their duet 'Se inclinassi a prender moglie', Mustafà and Lindoro swap opinions on the desirability of the proposed match.

1.ii *The seashore* Haly and his men have sunk a ship and captured the survivors, among them an Italian girl, Isabella. In her cavatina 'Cruda sorte!' she grandly mourns her ill-fortune. But at Rossini's insistence a further element is added to the text of the cavatina; in the fleeting 'Già so per pratica' we encounter the wily, feline side of Isabella's nature. Isabella is determined to find her beloved Lindoro and is irked by the constant amorous attentions of her travelling companion

Title-page of the first edition of the vocal score of Rossini's 'L'italiana in Algeri', with a scene from the opera engraved by Cöntgen (Mainz: Schott, c1819; this copy bears the stamp of the selling agent Ricordi)

Taddeo. In the duet 'Ai capricci della sorte' they begin by wrangling but come to the reluctant conclusion that their present parlous state is not best served by arguing. The duet is an early locus classicus of Rossini's genius for using musical forms and conventions as the springboard of his comedy; the contrast between this and the almost unrelieved patter of the earlier Mosca setting is especially instructive.

1.iii *A small hall in Mustafà's palace* Haly reports the capture of a beautiful Italian girl and Lindoro is told he can return to Italy provided he takes Elvira with him. Mustafà's aria 'Già d'insolito ardore' reveals him aroused to fever-pitch as he comtemplates the arrival of the Italian girl.

1.iv *A magnificent hall in Mustafà's palace* The philandering Mustafà is brought face to face with Isabella. As Isabella enters the hall the music makes a furtive step-by-step ascent from C to E♭ as if following Isabella's gaze as it travels upwards to Mustafà's face. A slow round begins with the words 'O che muso' ('My god, what a mug!'), a line that Conchita Supervia made as memorable as Edith Evans's exclamation about the handbag in Wilde's *The Importance of Being Earnest*. In the music that follows wonder, solemnity and barely suppressed laughter wittily coexist. Taddeo, intervening, narrowly escapes death by impalement. When Lindoro, Elvira and Zulma come to make their farewells, Isabella and Lindoro enter to a minuet-like Andantino in G major, leading to a transition of Mozartian poignancy as the lovers, astonished, recognize each other. It is a transition that stands at the very heart of the opera, the lovers' suppressed ardour touchingly juxtaposed with Mustafà's bumbling expression of earthbound bemusement. Isabella guilefully announces that she could never love a man who treated his wife as Mustafà is treating Elvira. She also insists that Lindoro, being Italian, should be detailed to remain with her. The announcement sends the entire company into a state of delirium, their heads full of the sounds of

bells ('din din', the women), a hammer ('tac tac', Lindoro), crowing ('cra cra', Taddeo) and a cannon ('bum bum', Mustafà).

ACT 2.i *A small hall* (as Act 1.i) Everyone is amused at the antics of Mustafà, who has become a besotted lover. But Zulma is confident that things could work to Elvira's advantage, and it is Elvira who informs Isabella that Mustafà has invited Isabella to take coffee with him. Having convinced Isabella of his absolute fidelity to her, Lindoro is overjoyed when she agrees to attempt to escape (the alternative versions of his cavatina are discussed above). Further to ingratiate himself with Isabella, Mustafà proposes to appoint Taddeo to the position of Kaimakan, protector of the Muslims. Taddeo finds both the idea and the lavish costume quite unbearable ('Ho un gran peso sulla testa') but prudence in the face of Mustafà's anger persuades him to accept the position.

2.ii *A magnificent ground floor apartment; behind it a loggia opens to the sea* Isabella tells Elvira to follow her advice. While she dresses in anticipation of her reunion with Lindoro she is secretly watched by Mustafà, Taddeo and Lindoro; but in fact she is aware of their presence, and her aria 'Per lui che adoro' is both a love song to Lindoro and a deception at Mustafà's expense. In the quintet 'Ti presento di mia man' Mustafà vainly tries to be alone with Isabella, but Lindoro and Taddeo refuse to leave. When Isabella invites Elvira to coffee in an attempt to reconcile her with her husband, Mustafà is beside himself with anger and frustration. In an interlude, Haly sings of the wiles of Italian women. Isabella now plays her master card. As a token of her love, she offers to bestow upon Mustafà the Order of Pappataci, an order whose members lead a life exclusively given over to eating, drinking and sleeping. They also take a vow to keep silent, whatever dramas are playing around them. The 'Pappataci' trio for Mustafà, Taddeo and Lindoro is an excellent piece of foolery and one of the score's most diverting episodes. Isabella now rallies Mustafà's Italian servants, appealing to their sense of patriotism so that they become accomplices in her escape. Her rallying call, the recitative and Rondo 'Pensa alla patria', has great power and a glorious, long-breathed solemnity of utterance, though she is also able to cope on the side with the cackling Taddeo. The asides to Taddeo apart, this is the kind of highly effective *opera seria* piece that no Italian composer before Rossini would have had the wit to include in a *buffo* entertainment. Lindoro announces that the Pappataci ceremony is about to begin. Mustafà's capacity for silence is tested as Isabella openly flirts with Taddeo; he fails and is quickly reprimanded. The scene is now set for Isabella and Lindoro to make their escape. A ship is to hand and under cover of the Pappataci ceremony Mustafà and Taddeo are easily duped. Realizing too late what is happening, Taddeo tries to alert Mustafà, who recognizes that Italian girls are too clever for him. He begs forgiveness of his wife, gives the lovers his blessing and leads the company in wishing them a safe journey home.

* * *

L'italiana in Algeri is a work of great richness and sophistication. Formally it is an innovative piece, drawing Rossini's experience from his single-act *farse* into a larger context. It is also, despite being written at speed, notably free from any kind of self-borrowing. The numbers that were farmed out to another composer, gracious and decorous in an 18th-century style, are by contrast a reminder of how fiercely the flame of Rossini's own comic invention burns in this remarkable opera, which transcends Mosca's earlier effort as surely as Rossini's *Il barbiere di Siviglia* was shortly to transcend Paisiello's.   RICHARD OSBORNE

Italiana in Londra, L' ('The Italian Girl in London'). *Intermezzo comico per musica* in two parts by DOMENICO CIMAROSA to a libretto by GIUSEPPE PETROSELLINI; Rome, Teatro Valle, 28 December 1779.

The Neapolitan Don Polidoro (bass), the Dutch merchant Sumers (tenor) and Milord Arespingh (baritone) have assembled at the London inn of Madama Brillante (soprano). All three have become infatuated with the beauty of Madama Brillante's house-guest from Genoa, Livia (soprano), who is in London under a false name in order to seek her lover Arespingh, who has abandoned her. Arespingh is torn between his filial duty to marry his father's choice and his love for Livia. Livia, on the other hand, believes that Arespingh is unfaithful to her. Polidoro's wish to marry Livia frustrates Madama Brillante, who wants him for herself. The gullible and simple-minded Polidoro is used as a scapegoat by Madama Brillante who makes him believe that Livia, with the help of a magic stone, has become invisible and is continually by his side. After a number of comic situations, quarrels and misunderstandings the lovers reaffirm their commitment to each other, while Madama Brillante's marriage proposal to Polidoro ends in a promise for both of them to live in Naples.

The frothy plot reflects late 18th-century values in its use of characters representing the middle classes and coming from various parts of the world and in its conflict between filial obligation and freedom of choice. Polidoro, who pines for Naples in folklike music in the first finale, is the least stereotyped character. At its Rome première this intermezzo was given by an all-male cast, including the 17-year-old castrato Girolamo Crescentini. A popular work, it enjoyed revivals for more than three decades. In many German-speaking cities it was sung in German translation as *Die Italienerin zu London* and *Näntchen, oder Das deutsche Mädchen in London* with revisions by H. C. Pleissner and J. C. Bock. A French version, published as a three-act *opéra comique*, includes arias by Cherubini and Mingozzi. The intermezzo was also performed at the Burgtheater, Vienna (1783 and 1786–7), and in one of these revivals – though it is not clear which from the undated score in *A-Wn* – Cimarosa's part 2 duet between Livia and Arespingh 'Caro amico, deh permetti' was replaced by a duet by Fernando Paer. It was also revived at Eszterháza in 1783 and in 1787–8, with revisions by Haydn which included replacing the same Cimarosa duet with the composer's trio 'Son qual cervo'. Cimarosa revised the work himself for Naples (1794).

The melodies, predominantly in the violins, exude lightness, verve and humour. Particularly noteworthy are the arias of Sumers ('Vi parlo all'olandese') and Polidoro ('Oh che gusto, che piacere') in part 2. The long chain finales, with their excellent dramatic and musical pacing, are the work's strongest assets.
                    GORDANA LAZAREVICH

Italian overture. A type of OVERTURE common from the late 17th century to the late 18th, usually in three movements, fast–slow–fast. The texture is generally homophonic and the outer movements are normally in major keys, most often D major. Initially, the first movements tended to be in duple metre; the slow movements were often quite short; and the finales were dance-like, often resembling fast minuets or gigues. As the form developed, the first movements tended to incorporate fanfare elements and came increasingly to follow the pattern of sonata form without a development section; the slow movements became longer and more lyrical.

The Italian overture became established in the works of Alessandro Scarlatti in the 1690s (his earliest use of the form is in *Tutto il mal non vien per nuocere*, 1681) and spread throughout Europe until it became the standard operatic overture in the middle decades of the 18th century. Alternatives to the three-movement pattern among multi-sectional italianate overtures include the REPRISE OVERTURE and a two-movement design, fast–slow, in which the first number after the curtain serves as the finale of the overture (Mozart, *La finta giardiniera*, 1775). After 1760 these types gradually gave way to other patterns, particularly the familiar one-movement design, which represents the first movement of the earlier Italian overture.

*

H. Livingston: *The Italian Overture from A. Scarlatti to Mozart* (diss., U. of North Carolina, 1952)
H. Hell: *Die neapolitanische Opernsinfonie in der ersten Hälfte des 18. Jahrhunderts* (Tutzing, 1971)
S. C. Fisher: *Haydn's Overtures and their Adaptations as Concert Orchestral Works* (diss., U. of Pennsylvania, 1985)
                    STEPHEN C. FISHER

Italien [Théâtre Italien]. Companies active in Paris; the term stood equally for the theatres in which they performed. Théâtre Italien was the name often used for the Comédie-Italienne (or Opéra-Comique), based at the Hôtel de Bourgogne during the 18th century; *see* Paris, §§2(iii) and 3(i). In the period 1801–78 it was a company specializing in Italian opera and performing at various theatres including the first Salle Favart, the

Théâtre de l'Odéon and the Théâtre Louvois; *see* PARIS, §4(v).

Italy.

1. History and geography. 2. Structure of operatic life: (i) The decentralized structure (ii) The mobility of singers (iii) Output (iv) Repertory (v) Typology of sources (vi) Circulation in Italy (vii) The spread abroad. 3. Drama and form: a historical outline: (i) The 17th century (ii) The 18th century (iii) The early 19th century (iv) After unification (v) Since World War I.

1. HISTORY AND GEOGRAPHY. Like Germany, but unlike France and Great Britain, Italy achieved political unity late. The kingdom was formed only in 1861, through the so-called Risorgimento; by 1870 it included most of the territory now belonging to the Italian Republic established in 1946. The sense of a national cultural identity, however, was ancient and strong, rooted since the 13th century in a mature, modern literary language, although this was spoken only by a small élite in a country in which even today most of the population is effectively bilingual in the national language and a local dialect. There have always been contradictions between the unity suggested by geographical and literary maps and the separateness resulting from physical topography and political frontiers.

Over the four centuries of opera in Italy, this fragmentation – still visible in the country's economic and social structure, in the imbalance between the industrial wealth of the north and the subsidized economy of the south – has been a constant influence, both in the centrifugal impetus it imparted to the national operatic structure and in the benefits accrued through the participation of so many peripheral centres.

About 1650, when Venetian opera was spreading and taking root with sensational rapidity from Milan to Palermo, opera invaded a dozen or more states, and before the end of the 17th century over 40 towns and cities had more or less permanent opera houses (see

TABLE 1: Opera houses in Italy

region (ruling house)	late 17th century	1785–6 (according to Indice de' teatrali spettacoli)
Duchy of Savoy (Kingdom of Sardinia)	Turin	Acqui, Alessandria, Intra, Nice, Novara, Turin*
Duchy of Milan (Spanish; Austrian)	Milan, Cremona, Lodi, Pavia	Abbiategrasso, Casalmaggiore, Chiavenna, Como, Cremona, Gallarate, Lodi, Mantua, Milan*, Monza, Pavia, Varese
Duchy of Mantua (Gonzaga; Austrian)	Mantua	
Venetian Republic	Bergamo, Brescia, Crema, Padua, Rovigo, Treviso, Udine, Venice*, Verona, Vicenza	Bassano, Bergamo*, Brescia, Capodistria, Legnago, Mestre, Padua*, Romano, Rovigo, Salò, Treviglio, Treviso, Udine, Venice*, Verona, Vicenza, Zara
Archbishopric of Trent		Bolzano, Borgo Valsugana, Mori, Rovereto, Trent
Duchy of Parma and Piacenza (Farnese; Bourbon-Parma)	Parma, Piacenza	Parma, Piacenza
Duchy of Modena and Reggio (Este)	Modena, Reggio	Castelnuovo di Garfagnana, Correggio, Modena, Reggio
Republic of Genoa	Genoa	Finale, Genoa*, Novi
Principality of Massa (Cybo)	Carrara	Carrara
Republic of Lucca	Lucca	Lucca*
Grand Duchy of Tuscany (Medici; Lorraine)	Florence, Livorno, Pisa, Siena	Florence*, Livorno, Pisa, Siena
Papal State	Ancona, Bologna*, Fano, Ferrara, Macerata, Perugia, Pesaro, Ravenna, Rimini, Rome*	Ancona, L'Aquila, Bologna*, Castelgandolfo, Cento, Fano, Fermo, Ferrara, Forlì, Jesi, Imola, Lanciano, Lugo, Osimo, Perugia, Pesaro, Ravenna, Rimini, Rome*, Senigallia, Urbino
Kingdom of Naples (Spanish; Austrian; Bourbon)	Naples	Barletta, Naples*
Kingdom of Sicily (Spanish; Austrian; Neapolitan)	Palermo, Messina	Palermo
free cities		Savona
Austrian possessions		Gorizia, Trieste

* – more than one opera house

TABLE 2: Italian opera seasons, 1830–40

	regular	intermittent	sporadic
Kingdom of Sardinia (Piedmont, incl. Genoa)	24	11	11
Kingdom of Lombardo-Veneto (administered by Austria)	33	18	31
Duchy of Parma	3	—	2
Duchy of Modena	2	4	1
Duchy of Lucca	2	1	1
Grand Duchy of Tuscany	11	4	6
Papal State	32	14	15
Kingdom of the Two Sicilies (Naples, Sicily)	7	4	4
Fiume, Trent, Trieste	3	1	3
total	117	57	74

Table 1); most had the system of tiered boxes still typical of the modern 'teatro all'italiana'. In the 18th century, Austrian hegemony replaced Spanish, to the benefit of the development of cities such as Naples, Florence and Milan; but at the end of the century, before the upheavals caused by Napoleon's Italian campaigns (1796), the states forming the political and civic map remained substantially the same. Yet the number of towns and cities with opera houses doubled. The annual *Indice de' teatrali spettacoli* records almost 100 theatres active in 1785–6; many of these played host to sporadic productions of *opera buffa*, for a single season or for several. Taking into account the entire series of the *Indice*, from 1764 to 1823, the total number of Italian towns concerned is well above 200.

With the political and territorial reorganization after the Congress of Vienna (1815), just at the time of Rossini's breathtaking national success, Italy was re-divided into ten or so states with about 15 'capitals'. But under the reactionary governments of the 1815 Restoration there was a boom in theatre building; about 100 houses were built between 1821 and 1847. In the decade 1830–40, theatres and their seasons were approximately as shown in Table 2. Cities with at least two opera houses regularly in use were still as shown in Table 1, with the addition of Treviso, Livorno and Perugia. There was a tendency towards expansion: in 1830 there were around 175 opera seasons across Italy, and ten years later the number had increased by about 50. The cities in which a successful opera such as Verdi's *Ernani* (1844) was seen in 1846 are shown in Table 3; operas of ten or fifteen years earlier, such as Bellini's *Norma* or Donizetti's *Belisario*, reached small towns such as Casale Monferrato, Chivasso, Faenza, Moncalvo, Oleggio, Pontevico, Pontremoli, Reggio Calabria and San Giovanni in Persiceto.

After unification, with the recurrent economic and political crises of a modern state in a poor and backward country and with the tendency of the Left to resent an expensive and élitist entertainment, the market for opera contracted. Nonetheless, in the 1890s the official count for 755 municipalities was 1055 theatres (for both spoken drama and opera: the repertories cannot be separated in the 19th century). However, only 11 were rated first-class theatres, reserved for opera: the Comunale in Bologna, the Bellini in Catania, the Pergola in Florence, the Carlo Felice in Genoa, La Scala in Milan, the S Carlo in Naples, the Bellini in Palermo, the Argentina and Costanzi in Rome, the Regio in Turin and La Fenice in Venice.

In spite of political unity the market continued to be decentralized, and the new capital, Rome, did not play a leading role. If anything, theatres such as La Scala, La Fenice, the S Carlo and, in certain respects, the Comunale in Bologna and the Regio in Turin led in the number, quality and novelty of their productions (though not without eclipses, short or long). It is symptomatic and ironic that even in 1967 Law no.800 (still in force), dealing with the organization of the 13 public 'Enti Lirici' (opera authorities), acknowledged to the Teatro dell'Opera in Rome a special role 'for the representative function carried out by the theatre in the capital of the state', but went on to declare La Scala, an autonomous 'Ente Lirico' since 1920, to be 'a body of particular national interest in the field of music', indicating an official diarchy (as the size of state subsidies confirms). But this is contradicted by the varying importance of Milan, and still more of Rome, compared with the opera houses of Bologna, Florence, Genoa, Naples, Palermo, Trieste, Turin and Venice, not to mention the Arena in Verona (of the other two 'Enti Lirici', one in Rome is concerned only with concerts, one in Cagliari primarily so). The activity of the leading 'Enti Lirici' is often rivalled by the artistic vitality and imaginative programming of some of the 'teatri di tradizione', which receive considerably less state subsidy (see Table 4). Finally, an important role in operatic enterprise is played by festivals, particularly at Alessandria (Laboratorio Lirico), Martina Franca (Festival della Valle d'Itria), Montepulciano (Cantiere Internazionale d'Arte), Pesaro (Rossini Opera Festival), Siena (Settimana Musicale Senese), Spoleto (Festival dei Due Mondi) and Torre del Lago (Festival Pucciniano), and the small theatres which specialize in revivals of 18th- and 19th-century operas (Savona, Lugo, Vicenza).

2. STRUCTURE OF OPERATIC LIFE. The decentralized geography of Italy has had its effect on the history and

TABLE 3: Places in Italy where Verdi's *Ernani* (1844) was seen in 1846

Carnival	Ancona, Cagliari, Crema, Florence, Foligno, Fossombrone, Lodi, Milan, Novara, Pallanza, Pesaro, Pisa, Pistoia, Prato, Rieti, Rome, Saluzzo, Spoleto, Terni, Trieste, Venice
Spring	Asti, Civitavecchia, Ferrara, Fiume, Florence, Foggia, Genoa, Mantua, Padua, Piacenza, Reggio Emilia, Rovereto, Tortona, Turin, Voghera
Summer	Brescia, Milan, Monza, Naples, Recanati, Senigallia, La Spezia, Trieste, Vicenza
Autumn	Ascoli Piceno, Castiglione delle Stiviere, Cento, Chiari, Codogno, Cremona, Florence, Guastalla, Milan, Mortara, Nice, Soresina, Stradella, Treviso, Trieste, Venice, Verona

development of the country's operatic structure. The exchange of artists, texts and scores between various theatres and centres, with different artistic, political and administrative traditions, has been vital to the system, which could better survive and prosper if it satisfied a range of expectations and could balance the resources of patronage – princely or civic – which in any case tended to be narrow and fragmented. (As late as 1860 no city in Italy had a population of half a million – a total reached by Paris and London in the 17th century; at the end of the 18th century only Milan, Venice and Rome had more than 100 000 inhabitants and only Naples and Palermo, with their endemic poverty, over 200 000.)

(i) The decentralized structure. Any attempt to co-ordinate production on a national scale, or to impose exclusive rights, has been rare in Italian opera. Opera as a public spectacle was 'born' in Venice (1637) – a city without a court – from a compromise between the opulent splendour of a 'princely' spectacle and the commercial profit of a private business enterprise; the first theatres were halls already equipped for inexpensive *commedia dell'arte* productions and corresponded to the established model of professional theatre as opposed to the splendour of aristocratic salons. Although the management of opera houses in most of Italy had been financially supported by local government and under police supervision since the end of the 17th century, and although in the 18th groups of noblemen were formed to hold shares and act as guarantors (and sometimes managers) of the theatre, and although governments of the post-1815 era concerned themselves with the good management of the local theatre (as an appropriate venue for high society, easily subject to political control), historically speaking the main stimulus was always private initiative.

In fact, there were significant attempts in the 19th century to coordinate different operatic centres (which gave a powerful impulse to unifying and consolidating the repertory); but these came from only the most forward-looking impresarios, such as Domenico Barbaia and Alessandro Lanari, who respectively managed simultaneous seasons in Milan, Naples,

Palermo and Vienna, and in Florence, Venice, Naples, Parma, Rome, Lucca and other towns, maximizing the yield for the singers and from scores (to which they often had exclusive rights). The important Milanese publishers, especially Ricordi (who shrewdly organized premières of Verdi, Ponchielli and Puccini in Italy and abroad) and Sonzogno, were strengthened by the introduction of copyright into Italy, permitting a better coordinated distribution of productions. But even today plurality of programming – which can lead to the staging in the same season of two different productions, less than 100 km apart, of an opera of such specialized taste as Strauss's *Capriccio* – is an unwritten law which remains unquestioned in the world of Italian opera.

(ii) The mobility of singers. In Italy the casting of an opera, whether new or well established, was and still is the result of negotiations begun afresh for every new production. The large number of theatres provided each opera singer (and in the 18th and 19th centuries each *maestro di cappella*) with the possibility of stipulating as many contracts as there were seasons. In the mid-19th century there were normally four; at the end of the 17th century, when nearly every city planned only one, they had been distributed through the calendar so that, for example, the same outstanding singers who were to sing in Venice, Rome or Bologna for the carnival season (from 26 December to Shrove Tuesday; in Naples the season traditionally began on the feast of S Carlo, 4 November, continuing until carnival) were available to Reggio Emilia in May, to Milan in June–July, to Pratolino (Florence) in the summer, Modena in October and Genoa in November. Indeed, early 19th-century impresarios tried to fix contracts for a number of years, which made it possible to arrange the circulation of package deal entertainments in their theatres. In the 17th and 18th centuries singers depended on a variety of forms of noble patronage (many sought-after singers were in the service of the dukes of Modena, Mantua and Parma and of the heir apparent of Tuscany), whereas in the 19th the often ambiguous figure of the theatrical agent appeared, promoting and exploiting the careers of young singers. Some particular restrictions – such as the

TABLE 4: State-funded opera houses in Italy today

Enti Lirici	Milan, Rome; Bologna, Cagliari, Florence, Genoa, Naples, Palermo, Trieste, Turin, Venice, Verona (Arena)
Teatri di tradizione (a) independent	Bari, Bergamo, Brescia, Catania, Como, Cosenza, Cremona, Jesi, Lecce, Lucca, Macerata, Mantua, Novara, Pisa, Rovigo, Treviso
(b) Associazione teatri Emilia Romagna	Ferrara, Modena, Parma, Piacenza, Ravenna, Reggio Emilia

prohibition of the appearance of female singers in public in Rome, annulled only in 1797 – and the increase in the number of theatres which was accompanied by a gradual differentiation of 'first rank' circuits and 'second rank' ones, with artists frequently passing from one level to the other, on the way up or down, introduced limits and further opportunities in a market of singers as specialized professionals.

It was singers' mobility that ensured artistic variety in Italian operatic life. Up to the late 19th century – before the dominance of the repertory began to determine the choice of singers – the singers' engagement by the impresario was the first decisive step in the process leading to a new opera: the configuration of the cast – the number of main roles, their relative importance (shown by the 'convenienze teatrali', or the quota of solo or ensemble numbers assigned to each) and their vocal and dramatic characteristics – formed the basic material with which librettist and composer had to work, and might even dictate the choice of dramatic subject. A last-minute change in the list of singers or their preferences (an example from 1816: 'the leading male singer does not want a cavatina but an entrance duet; … avoid the duet between the two basses … as one is a great actor, the other a lesser actor but a better singer') could force the librettist and composer to start again from scratch with a different subject (as late as 1842 Donizetti suggested preparing various dramatic subjects in outline, proceeding only at the last moment to versification of the libretto, which could be adjusted to suit the company).

Major singers pressed for the parts they preferred: in Venice in 1666 the soprano Giulia Masotti, dissatisfied with the role offered her in P. A. Ziani's *Alciade*, proposed instead *Argia* or *Alessandro* by Cesti, and finally sang her speciality, the title role in a production of his *Dori*, revived for her; in the 18th century some singers specialized in one or another character from Metastasio, irrespective of the score that might be used (memorizing the recitative text was probably harder than memorizing the music of the new arias); and in the 19th certain operas and roles became the stock-in-trade of stars who had enough contractual power to put them into many theatres (the success of Federico Ricci's *Luigi Rolla*, 1841, was linked to the career of Napoleone Moriani, 'the tenor with the fine death', who also triumphed in scenes of sung agony in *Lucia di Lammermoor* and *Pia de' Tolomei*).

At certain periods and in some genres, the existence of travelling companies, taking advantage of the theatre circuit, was conducive to a standardization of the repertory. Between 1644 and 1652 the Febiarmonici and the Accademici Discordati toured from Turin to Naples with early Venetian operas, such as Sacrati's *La finta pazza* and Cavalli's *Egisto* and *Giasone*. In the early 18th century, travelling pairs of *buffi* gave intermezzos between the acts of any serious drama; at this period too, and up to the age of revolution, troupes, mainly comic, penetrated beyond the Alps (for example the Bambini family, the unwitting cause of the Querelle des Bouffons in Paris in 1752, and the Mingotti brothers, who established the cult of Italian opera from Graz to Copenhagen). In the 19th century, without actually forming into a company, the 'quartetto dei Puritani' – Giulia Grisi, Rubini (later replaced by Mario), Tamburini and Lablache – dominated for some 20 years the billboards of the Théâtre Italien, Her Majesty's and later Covent Garden, moulding the operatic taste of Paris and London with a repertory largely of Bellini and Donizetti. Between 1930 and 1942 the Carro di Tespi Lirico (an allusion to the travelling players of the *commedia dell'arte*) operated in fascist-promoted cultural programmes. Finally, after World War II, the success enjoyed by such specialists as Sciutti, Bruscantini and Corena gave a powerful stimulus to the regeneration of 18th- and 19th-century *opera buffa*.

(iii) Output. The number of operatic scores launched year by year in Italian theatres is hard to determine. In the second half of the 17th century and throughout the 18th the record for output belonged to Venice, which kept an average of four or five theatres active with two or more operas each, most of them new and specially composed. In the 18th century Rome, Naples, Turin, Milan and Bologna normally staged a couple of new works each year, with revivals of operas already given elsewhere, retouched and restored as necessary; other, mostly northern, cities of medium size would pride themselves on opening the main season with a new opera (or at least a new pasticcio). The proportion of new operas falls in the early 19th century, but considering the boom in the number of theatres and seasons the absolute quantity remains high until the middle of the century when, in the turmoil of war and politics after 1848 and the economic difficulties during the struggle for unification, there was a sharp contraction of the operatic market, coinciding with a move towards homogeneity and stability in the repertory. (On 26 December 1880, for example, of the 32 theatres that opened this carnival season only two gave new works; four gave a success from the previous year, such as Usiglio's *Le donne curiose*, four gave *Aida*, four each gave works by Gomes, Petrella and Meyerbeer, and Rossini's *Semiramide* was still among those given.) For a century and a half, Italy had produced about 50 new opera scores a year: most never survived beyond their first staging, while the others were brought into the theatrical circuit by singers (keen to shine in their favourite roles) or by *maestri di cappella* (eager to get the most from them with the minimum effort), or through business connections between impresarios.

The concern of singers, as of *maestri*, was to obtain the maximum number of contracts. So the rate of production sustained by Italian opera composers comes as no surprise: for 15 or 20 years without a break, such composers as Alessandro Scarlatti, Vivaldi, Hasse, Piccinni, Paisiello, Cimarosa, Mayr, Rossini, Pacini, Donizetti and Mercadante produced an average of three or four new scores annually, often while maintaining a steady employment at court or in church music; while famous theatrical poets such as Salvadore Cammarano or Gaetano Rossi – often based at a leading theatre, where they also oversaw the staging – turned out four or five librettos a year. Bellini was the first who could boast of negotiating contracts so lucrative as to allow him to compose no more than one opera a year; after *La traviata*, Verdi composed no more than one every two years, and even 'rapid' musicians such as Leoncavallo (a writer of operettas as well as operas) or G. F. Malipiero (his own librettist) did not surpass these rates.

Behind the remarkable productivity of Italian opera stood a robust but tacit set of formal and operational conventions, which allowed the librettist and composer to come quickly to terms, saving time and effort in planning the opera and drafting the verbal and musical text. The theatre-going public, aware of such implicit conventions, would gauge each opera's novelty on the basis of past years' performances. The result is a tendency towards stylistic uniformity: the vastness and continuity of the new output almost precluded any daring or abrupt formal and stylistic innovations or publicly proclaimed theoretical programmes (the figure of the composer-as-publicist, such as Berlioz or Wagner, is virtually unknown in Italy before Boito).

In cities with several theatres the distribution of new works (as well as of revivals) among the different theatres was hierarchical, also taking account of the special requirements of different genres and seasons. In Turin in the late 18th century, for example, the Teatro Regio (the court theatre) gave two *opere serie* – usually new works – in December and January, but the *società di cavalieri* that managed it also organized an autumn season of four comic operas in the less grand Teatro Carignano, using specialists in comedy and scores imported from Milan, Venice and Florence (profits from the *buffa* season partly compensated for the deficit on the *seria* one). Theatrical competition could also give rise to great homogeneity of style, as in Naples in the 1830s and 40s, when six city theatres gave 700 performances in a year, staging 150 works – but on no fewer than 194 evenings in 1842 the citizen or tourist could have attended one or more Donizetti performances, *serie*, *buffe* or *semiserie*, new or old, in surroundings ranging from the splendid S Carlo down to the modest Partenope. One can imagine the powerful standardization of collective musical taste brought about by so unvaried a diet, the more so in the light of the fact that it was normal throughout Italy to go regularly to the theatre – indeed for certain classes and certain theatres a duty of etiquette. (An English traveller describes having attended, with his hosts, 16 consecutive performances of the same Cavalli opera in Venice during the 1656 carnival; in the town theatre at Sassuolo, the autumn residence of the Este court, the holidaying Modena nobility attended a full 42 performances of two works to librettos by Metastasio from 22 August to 4 November 1750: one by Galuppi, very new to Italy, the other by Vinci and 20 years old.)

(iv) Repertory. A stable, enduring repertory was late to emerge in Italy. The entertainments given for great dynastic or civil occasions – such as Melani's *Ercole in Tebe* for the Medici-Orléans wedding in 1661 or *Europa riconosciuta* by Salieri which inaugurated La Scala in 1778 – were by their nature majestic but not repeatable. However, the mobility of singers and the existence of numerous operatic centres allowed operas of mere entertainment a meagre survival: as a rule, in the 17th century, *drammi per musica* were not repeated in the city in which they had already been given, and they lasted only ten or 15 years in the national circuit. Works such as Cavalli's *Giasone* (1649), which with much retouching remained in circulation until 1690, or Cesti's *La Dori* (1657), which lasted until 1689 (both given more than once in Venice), are exceptions.

It is easier to compose new scores than to invent new differing plots. Very soon composers resorted to the expedient of setting new music to librettos of established effectiveness on the stage, often dissimulating the fact in the title: in 1678, for example, Stradella set a successful libretto sent to him in Genoa by his Venetian sponsors (Minato's *Seleuco* of 1666), which with his music became *La forza dell'amor paterno*. In the 18th century a stock of long-lived *drammi per musica* was built up,

ready to wear ever differing musical clothing and flexible enough to undergo partial or total rewriting of the text in order to suit changing musical forms (particularly the introduction of ensemble numbers). *Drammi per musica* such as *Astianatte* by Antonio Salvi (1701), an imitation of Racine's *Andromaque*, or *Teseo in Creta* by Pariati (1715) reappeared, variously modernized, more than 40 times on Italian and foreign stages up to 1800.

This initially sporadic phenomenon became the norm with Metastasio's *drammi per musica*, which, from *Didone abbandonata* (1724) to *Il trionfo di Clelia* (1762), passed through the hands of tens (and in some cases hundreds) of composers well into the 19th century, Meyerbeer in 1819 and Mercadante in 1827 being among the last. In ever more up-to-date musical garb, certain of Metastasio's dramas imprinted themselves permanently on the consciousness and the cultural horizon of every moderately educated Italian. There must have been Neapolitan opera-goers who at S Carlo listened to *Artaserse* with music by Vinci (1738), Manna (1743), Perez (1749), Hasse (1760 and 1762), Piccinni (1768), Mysliveček (1774) and Alessandri (1783). But Metastasio's success was also literary, and that consolidated his cultural impact: whereas in 1697 the preface to a Roman libretto declared that 'the poetry of the stage is very different from that for simple reading, and the dramas of today are heard, not read', a century later the theatre of Metastasio, with its tumult of tender and tormented but noble and limpid affections, was required reading for the literate three per cent of the Italian population.

The remake was an enduring phenomenon: just as in the 1840s Cammarano and Mercadante re-used such subjects as *La vestale* and *Gli Orazi e i Curiazi*, which had enjoyed great success in the masterpieces of Spontini (1807; first Italian performance, 1811) or of Cimarosa (1796), so the Boito-Verdi *Otello* was a 'remake', taking the place vacated by Rossini's work of the same title. Its prevalence confirms that the repertory was first constituted as an ideal collection more of well-known dramatic subjects than of specific scores. Whereas in Rossini's day an anomalous cast (such as the six tenor roles in *Armida*, 1817) prejudiced the chances of a score's circulation and survival from the outset, with Donizetti a successful opera could impose new vocal types on the theatrical world (the early success of *Lucia di Lammermoor* owed much to the specialized star Fanny Tacchinardi-Persiani, who hence became pioneer of a new vocal type).

The first Italian operas to claim a permanent place in the repertory were Rossini's *Il barbiere di Siviglia* (1816), Bellini's *La sonnambula* and *Norma* (1831), and Donizetti's *L'elisir d'amore* (1832) and *Lucia di Lammermoor* (1835). On a provincial stage, such as that of Piacenza (where no Mozart opera has ever been given), it was unthinkable that as much as 15 years could elapse without those works' being heard. Rossini, in 1816, certainly did not foresee that *Il barbiere* would live on in this way, for at the culminating point of *Otello* he re-used an orchestral motif from the calumny aria and later had to remove it to avoid comic effect. From Verdi onwards, with the benefit of a strong publishing trade and of modern copyright, the Italian opera composer aimed for immediate popularity, as the first step towards an established place in the repertory; he was seldom successful. A Florentine born about 1830 could have seen Verdi's successful (but not outstandingly so) *Macbeth* in ten or so productions, 1847, 1851, 1854, 1857, 1862, 1864, 1870, 1872, 1875, 1878 and 1904.

In the 20th century, besides new indigenous works (ever fewer and more ephemeral) and the fairly rapid reception granted to international successes (*Salome* arrived in 1906, *Pelléas* in 1908, *Boris* and *Elektra* in 1909, *Rosenkavalier* in 1911, *Wozzeck* in 1942), resuscitations of older operas and restorations of interrupted traditions have found their way in: the gradual rediscovery of the comic Rossini (since 1925), of Monteverdi, of the 18th-century *opera buffa*, of 'minor' Donizetti, of Vivaldi as an opera composer, of 17th-century Venetian works, and finally of the serious Rossini, marks the course of theatrical life since the 1920s (some areas remain hidden: 18th-century *opera seria* and the theatrical work of Malipiero, for example, still await proper rediscovery). Restoration of the old has also benefited those foreign traditions that the Italian system's very exuberance denied a welcome in their time. Handel's London operas remained a dead letter in Italy (only *Rinaldo* was given in Naples in 1718, in a pasticcio assembled by Leo); Gluck's Viennese 'reform' operas – an attempt to regenerate Italian opera, not of course to reject it – had a selective and lukewarm reception in their day, and mainly in noble institutions and Austrophile theatres; *opéra comique* could never find a lasting place in a wholly sung theatrical tradition like the Italian (Giuseppe Carpani made an attempt at the theatre of the Villa Reale at Monza beginning in 1787, with translations of works by Grétry and Dalayrac); and as for Gluck's French works and for Cherubini, they remained in oblivion until almost 1900.

(v) Typology of sources. In a theatrical system with so great a turnover, in a realm where voices are so pre-eminent, and in a society where musicians form a profession both large and discrete, it is not surprising that the written tradition of operatic music was, for the first two centuries, essentially one of manuscripts and, for the next two, essentially one of vocal scores. The public text of the *opera in musica* was above all that of the libretto, which until about 1860 was freshly printed for each new version; later, standard librettos sold by the publisher took their place; nowadays, the programme published by the theatre, often luxurious and sometimes even scholarly, has taken over its functions. In the libretto, the dramatist – from Ottaviano Castelli to Arrigo Boito – used the preface to declare the aims of his conception; the impresario listed the performers in the opera and any intermezzos or dances given as entr'actes or as an afterpiece; the sovereign offered it to his guests and to friendly courts abroad as a testimony of the remarkable theatrical events he had promoted (in such cases reproductions of scenes and accounts of the staging and the ceremonial of the entourage might be included); the ordinary spectator acquired it at the door and skimmed through it in his box or in the stalls during the performance (auditoriums were not completely darkened until about 1900); the music lover looked through it again at home, memorizing those arias whose words have entered into the daily speech of every Italian (from 'È la fede degli amanti' to 'La donna è mobile'); the well-read man collected it and perhaps even made it an object of bibliographic compilation or regarded it as an item of historical reportage.

The full score, however, while indispensable for producing or reproducing the operatic performance, went only to whoever was in charge, and had no wider circulation. A dozen or so scores issued in printed form bear witness to the dawn of Italian opera, from the two of *Euridice* by Peri and Caccini (Florence, 1600–01) to the Mantuan *Dafne* by Marco da Gagliano (Florence, 1608), and from F. Vitali's *Aretusa* (Rome, 1620) to Michelangelo Rossi's *Erminia sul Giordano* (Rome, 1637); but these editions were designed to commemorate particular theatrical ventures, not to facilitate revivals. Yet at least one of them enjoyed some publishing success, since it was reprinted (*Orfeo* by Monteverdi, Venice, 1609 and 1615), and the availability of Roman scores by Domenico Mazzocchi (*La catena d'Adone*, 1626), by Landi (*Sant'Alessio*, 1634) and by the castrato L. Vittori (*Galatea*, 1639) gave rise to public or private performances in other localities (*Sant'Alessio* was also imitated in Warsaw in 1636). In the 18th century, the only opera given and printed in full score in Italy was *Orfeo* by Ferdinando Bertoni (Venice, 1776, reprinted 1783); it is a direct imitation of Gluck's opera, adopting its text.

In fact, within the system of entrepreneurs' regular seasons, established throughout Italy after 1637, for nearly two centuries manuscript scores became the property of the impresario or whoever else commissioned them, and the owner could claim an exclusive right, negotiating transfer or copying of them for the benefit of other theatres: it was therefore crucial not to divulge the scores through publication. (Most important surviving collections of scores, such as that at the Naples Conservatory, probably have local theatrical origins.) But some more perceptive composers, seemingly conscious of their works' artistic worth, assembled private collections of original autographs or authentic copies (for example Cavalli and Hasse; their collections are housed in the Biblioteca Nazionale Marciana, Venice, and the Milan Conservatory respectively). Equally, in the 17th and 18th centuries there were aristocratic collectors who out of pride or enthusiasm collected operas they had commissioned or whose manuscripts had been presented to them, or which were acquired in existing book collections: this was how the Chigi collection (in the Vatican Library, Rome) was constituted, as were the Borromeo (Stresa), Estense (Modena, where works by Stradella were bought after his death) and Durazzo (now Foà-Giordano, Turin, with operas by Vivaldi) collections.

The English custom of publishing the favourite songs of a successful opera was almost unknown in Italy (the collections of arias by Laurenzi and Lucio, Venice, 1643, 1655, were not imitated). But from about 1670 up to the mid-18th century a trade flourished in manuscripts giving selected arias from one or more operas, intended for domestic use: to be sung in a convent, say, by nuns of noble family, or sold to foreign tourists. The publishers Marescalchi and Canobbio, in Venice from 1773 to about 1775, published in score single numbers from successful *seria* and *buffa* operas; other publishers, notably in Venice but also in Florence and Naples, continued the practice intermittently up to 1794 – a simple extension of the small trade in manuscript pieces transacted on the side by theatre copying workshops.

The decisive step towards a true Italian operatic publishing trade was made in the next century by another copyist, who held the sole right to copy material for the Teatro Carcano in Milan (and who also obtained it in 1814 for La Scala and in 1816 for the Teatro Re). In

1808 Giovanni Ricordi published the complete (or almost so) vocal score of Mayr's *Adelasia ed Aleramo* without the composer's knowledge; following the example of German publishers, he adopted an oblong format and a system of bound fascicles, one for each number in the opera, which could also be offered for individual sale. It was a system that satisfied both a professional market (singers and répétiteurs) and an amateur one (dilettantes, for whom reductions for piano and various chamber groups were also provided), without prejudicing the exclusive rights to the full score and orchestral material, which was hired out in manuscript and never put on sale (during the 19th century, such rights passed from the theatre impresario to the publisher-distributor, who organized their hire, national and later international, paying the composer a percentage of the fees).

Several years passed before the new publishing system took root in Italy. The earliest publications of Rossini's operas, at the height of their overwhelming European success, were the vocal scores issued north of the Alps: Schott in Mainz began in 1816–18 with *Tancredi* and *L'italiana in Algeri* and was soon followed by Simrock in Bonn and Cologne, Breitkopf & Härtel in Leipzig, Carli and Boieldieu in Paris and Artaria in Vienna. But with the advent of Mercadante (about 1820) and above all of Bellini with *Il pirata*, Donizetti with *Anna Bolena* and Verdi with *Nabucco*, the vocal scores of Ricordi – the firm opened a branch in Florence in 1824, acquired the archive of La Scala in 1825, and in the 1830s and 40s made exclusive contracts with the theatres of Venice and Naples – promptly embraced the new works of the greatest composers and imposed themselves as the dominant form of publication of Italian opera (fewer than two dozen standard Ricordi study scores have ever been offered for public sale).

It is not surprising that the first 'collected works' devoted to an Italian opera composer, the monumental *Nuova compiuta edizione di tutte le opere teatrali* by Rossini, prepared by Tito Ricordi (1854–66), should have taken the form of sumptuous oblong format vocal scores (the modern upright format came a little later). A handful of orchestral scores were published by copyists or musicians turned publishers – the eight Rossini operas issued by Ratti & Cencetti (Rome, 1825–36), Bellini's *Beatrice di Tenda* from P. Pittarelli (Rome, *c*1837), the pioneering but barely successful pocket scores from G. G. Guidi (Florence, from 1858; this firm pursued a historical publishing programme, exhuming Paisiello's *Il barbiere di Siviglia* to put it next to Rossini's *Barbiere* and Meyerbeer's *Les Huguenots*), and also *La traviata* from Del Monaco (Naples, 1882). But such isolated attempts had no impact on a field dominated by the Milan publishers' vocal scores: by the end of the century, Ricordi had absorbed Artaria & Longo in Milan, Girard and Clausetti in Naples, Guidi in Florence, and Lucca, the Italian agent of Wagner and Meyerbeer, also in Milan, while Edoardo Sonzogno, publisher of the Giovane Scuola and Italian agent for *Carmen* and Massenet, had become established in 1874.

Ricordi's domination of the Italian theatrical world – with its weighty catalogue including Verdi, Ponchielli, Catalani and Puccini – also imposed itself on journalism (it owned the leading Italian music periodical, the *Gazzetta musicale di Milano*, 1842–1912) and scenic taste: having from 1820 to 1830 published in lithograph the large *Raccolta di varie decorazioni sceniche* by Alessandro Sanquirico, stage designer at La Scala,

Ricordi introduced to Italy in 1855, with the Italian edition of Verdi's *Les vêpres siciliennes*, Parisian-style 'disposizioni sceniche' describing the staging of the première as a model for later productions. In the 20th century, besides Sonzogno and Ricordi (who published Zandonai, Pizzetti and Malipiero, and later Nono, Bussotti and Sciarrino), Suvini Zerboni (with Malipiero, Dallapiccola and Petrassi) have risen to eminence together with foreign houses issuing Italian music, such as Chester and Universal Edition.

Dictated by the practice of reading at the piano and the enduring vitality of the 19th-century repertory, the predominance of the vocal score long delayed the application of scholarly method to the masterpieces of the past (even certain scholarly editions of Pergolesi and Piccinni have appeared as vocal scores); following the deserving but controversial Monteverdi edition prepared by G. F. Malipiero after World War I, it was necessary to wait for the critical edition of Rossini's *Il barbiere* prepared by Zedda in 1969 before Ricordi conscientiously returned to authentic texts (alongside critical editions of Vivaldi, Pergolesi, Rossini, Donizetti, Verdi and Puccini, Ricordi have issued a collection of 17th- and 18th-century facsimiles, *Drammaturgia musicale veneta*). Not by chance, this scholarly awareness was gaining hold just when the last living repositories of that technical *savoir faire* and those tricks of the trade learnt through an oral tradition were fast disappearing, embodied in the great conductors of the generation after Toscanini (Serafin, Gui, De Sabata, Votto, Previtali, Gavazzeni, Patanè).

(vi) Circulation in Italy. The system of Italian opera, based on a free market of performers and new works, has tended towards expansion and homogeneity. At its apogee, it allowed an opera as successful as *Il trovatore* (19 January 1853, Rome) to reach 27 Italian cities in its first 12 months; by the end of 1855 the number had doubled, the opera having been given also in Corfu, Malta, Constantinople, Athens, Madrid, Oporto, Lisbon, Vienna, Barcelona, Valencia, Odessa, Warsaw, Cádiz, Málaga, Rio de Janeiro, Budapest, Paris, Iaşi, Puerto Rico, Buenos Aires, Timişoara, Bucharest, Alexandria (Egypt), Montevideo, Brunswick, New York, London, Boston, Seville, Saragossa, Havana, Liverpool, Manchester, Brno, Dublin, Graz, Nice, Palma (Majorca), Bratislava, Zara, St Petersburg and Darmstadt in the same time-span; by 1860 it had arrived in Mexico, Belgium, Chile, Peru, the Netherlands, Venezuela, Switzerland, Canada, Australia, Colombia, Guatemala and Sweden; by 1870 Norway, Finland, India, Indonesia, China, the Philippines and South Africa. (Verdi wrote to a friend in 1862: 'When you go to India and to the heart of Africa, you will hear *Il trovatore*'.)

It was not always so. Between 1650 and 1750, the circulation of *opera seria* was widespread and rapid, but beside it flourished forms of comic operatic theatre rooted in local customs and much less inclined to enter the national circuit. The 'opere musicali alla spagnola' which Monsignor Rospigliosi extracted from *comedias de capa y espada* for performance at the Palazzo Barberini in Rome in the 1650s, the 'drammi civili e rusticali' (with characters speaking Tuscan dialect) devised by G. A. Moniglia for Cardinal Giovanni Carlo de' Medici in Florence about 1660, the 'opere musicali' of Spanish extraction that Maggi wrote for the Borromeo counts in Milan around 1670, the 'favole drammatiche musicali' written by Pasquini and Agostini for the holidays of the Chigi princes at Ariccia near Rome and in Siena in the 70s, and the 'melodrami' on adventurous subjects which Provenzale, *maestro di cappella* of the city of Naples, also wrote in that decade, not for the court-sponsored public theatre but to a commission from the nobility: all these were responses to the initiative and taste of a civic aristocracy which sought no resonance beyond the original context. And in the 18th century the opening up of a national market for comic opera – to be a pan-European business by the end of the century – was anything but rapid.

The intermezzos were first to create a professional circuit for themselves – parallel to, but independent of, that of the *dramma per musica*: starting from Venice (where their use from 1706 may be credited in particular to Pariati, Gasparini and Albinoni), intermezzos invaded northern and central Italy from 1709, reaching Vienna and Dresden (1714, 1717), and in Rome and Naples, from 1715, supplanting the 'scene buffe' or 'contrascene' integrated into the ends of the acts of *opere serie*. From there, the intermezzos of Hasse and Pergolesi began to spread into Europe.

In Naples, meanwhile, quite independently, the *commedia per musica* in local argot had emerged in 1709 from the houses of the nobility and installed itself in the Teatro dei Fiorentini (and later the Teatro Nuovo); it took 20 years to reach (in Italianized form) the theatres of Rome, mostly the Valle and the Pace, and only in 1743 did it catch on in Venice (at the S Moisè, S Angelo and S Cassiano theatres; from 1726 to 1743 the S Samuele had cultivated indigenous 'drammi eroicomici' and 'opere bernesche', which lacked any real market outside the Laguna). A true Italian *opera buffa*, not restricted to particular regions, began only with the gradual propagation northwards of the Neapolitan *commedia per musica*, as well as with the spread, quick by contrast, of the highly successful series of 'drammi giocosi per musica', staged by Goldoni and Galuppi in Venice between 1749 and 1755 – a phenomenon that from the S Angelo and S Samuele ran over into Milan, Turin, Bologna and later Florence, reached Dresden, Leipzig, Prague, Mannheim and Bonn before Rome, was to reach Munich, St Petersburg, Moscow and London by 1760 and by 1770 Lisbon, Vienna and Warsaw, without ever reaching Naples or Palermo. Instead, Palermo and Naples (which was itself fertile in the production of indigenous comic opera) were to have *La buona figliuola* by Goldoni and Piccinni (1760, Rome), but only in 1773 and 1778 respectively, by which time this most celebrated of *opere buffe* had made several circuits of Enlightenment Europe.

This comparative impermeability between north and south relates not only to comic opera: the opera scores of Alessandro Scarlatti, considered even at Naples 'most difficult' and more apt for chamber than theatrical performance, found favour with a princely patron, Ferdinando de' Medici (who gave five of them in his Pratolino villa, 1702–6), but had meagre success north of Florence and were hissed in Venice. Towards the middle of the century the spheres of influence were tending to separate: while Vinci's setting of Metastasio's *Artaserse* (1730, Rome) circulated mostly south of the Apennines, Hasse's setting (1730, Venice) predominated in the north (Galuppi's *Artaserse* succeeded them both in the 1750s).

Similarly constrained and uneven, whether through local resistance or the practical difficulties of performance, was the spread and assimilation in 19th-century Italy of works by European composers. Mozart's last four Italian operas (variously rearranged) had some success, mostly after 1810, in Austrian-ruled cities such as Milan, Florence and Trieste, as well as in Naples, Rome and Turin (although Italians found their orchestration difficult); but no less a theatre than the Comunale in Bologna never gave *Don Giovanni*, an opera that however affected the young Verdi and also the greatest Italian novel of the time, Manzoni's *I promessi sposi* (1827). In Florence there was an early following for Meyerbeer (*Robert le diable* and *Les Huguenots* were given in 1840 and 1841); but, sporadic revivals of *Robert* in the 40s apart (Parma, Venice, Bologna, Milan), only in the 50s did the theatre bills of Turin, Genoa, Milan and Naples, and only in the 60s those of Bologna, Parma, Palermo and Venice, herald the intense and lasting Meyerbeer fever that made possible the developments of the period 1870–90: the flowering of *opera-ballo* (the Italian variant of *grand opéra*), the immense success of Gounod's *Faust*, the variable passion for Wagner (*Lohengrin* had 68 stagings over 25 years in 34 cities, but otherwise the response was more lukewarm) and the rise of the modern conductor as the authoritative artistic coordinator of a complex performance (a prominent pioneer here was Angelo Mariani).

In the 20th century, the repertory of Italian theatres has itself become international while Puccini's dominance in Italian programming (which in the first 30 years of the century marginalized even Verdi) has overflowed into Europe and beyond (even today, *Bohème*, *Tosca* and *Madama Butterfly* head the lists of the world's – and of course Italy's – most frequently performed operas). The space for avant-garde musical theatre at home has grown narrower, although Italians have occupied a distinct place in the International Society for Contemporary Music. It is not surprising that for many years the premières of works by G. F. Malipiero (not to mention Busoni or Wolf-Ferrari) should far more often have taken place in German rather than Italian theatres.

(vii) The spread abroad. Opera is an Italian invention which an admiring modern Europe has made its own. At first a princely spectacle, it was soon imitated by sovereigns north of the Alps, as a display of pomp and splendour and a demonstration and symbol of power and munificence. In this, it depended in foreign courts more than in Italy on the direct will of the sovereign and on dynastic events. The Viennese court between 1650 and about 1740 provides a large-scale example of continuity and stability: it made constant use of an Italian team of librettists (Sbarra, Minato, Stampiglia, Zeno, Pariati and Metastasio), composers (Cesti, Draghi, Bononcini, Conti and Caldara), singers, dancers and stage designers (the Burnacinis and the Galli-Bibienas), producing operas at a frenetic rate, which codified within the calendar and the ceremonial – done autonomously, and much as it came to be done in Italian theatres. In Paris, on the other hand, Cardinal Mazarin's programme of italianization, which included the importation of Venetian operas such as *La finta pazza* (1645) and *Xerse* (1660) and the commissioning of new Italian operas such as Luigi Rossi's *Orfeo* (1647) and Cavalli's *Ercole amante* (1662), was broken off by the young Louis XIV's express political wish to instigate a grandly self-sufficient national taste in every field of the

arts, learning and politics; the result was that Italian opera was lastingly ostracized in France. Elsewhere, as in Warsaw in 1635–48 (with Puccitelli and Scacchi), Innsbruck in 1654–65 (with Apolloni and Cesti) or Hanover in 1678–97 (with Mauro and Steffani), Italian opera flourished and died out as if by magic, simply on the accession of sovereigns inclined or disinclined towards this kind of entertainment.

Throughout the 17th century and up to the middle of the 18th, the establishment of Italian opera outside Italy represented the adoption of an alien form of art, using imported specialist personnel and imitating styles and genres tried out elsewhere. But it mostly involved acceptance from above: in the years around 1740, in ambitious residences such as Mannheim, Stuttgart, Bayreuth and Berlin, enlightened music-loving autocrats built splendid court theatres, using Italian architects, and employed eminent composers (such as Jommelli), with the conscious aim of leaving a mark on the history of opera (whether their subjects wanted it or not), by participating in its development.

By the mid-17th century, frequenting the opera house in Italian cities had become a social custom of the élite (and also of the court, when there was one). North of the Alps this did not take root until after 1740, because of the crises over succession faced by the absolutist regimes – earlier in those cities where the taste for opera depended on patricians and aristocrats who had encountered it in Italy than where the operatic initiative had come exclusively from the court (Munich, Dresden and Vienna moved to a system of entrepreneurial theatres licensed by the sovereign, ensuring the court certain privileges but divesting it of its monopoly). This happened in Hamburg, for example, from 1678 (with the Theater am Gänsemarkt, which staged a varied bill of fare in German, including translations of Italian operas); in London from 1705 (with the opening of the new theatre in the Haymarket, where Bononcini, Handel, Galuppi, J. C. Bach, P. A. Guglielmi and Sacchini triumphed); and in Prague in 1724 (with Count F. A. Sporck's theatre, whence numerous musicians, many of them from minor Venetian theatres and under Vivaldi's influence, spread across the imperial domains).

In all these cities there was a flourishing theatrical life before opera arrived: opera had therefore to occupy a limited space (as opposed to its all-encompassing one in Italy) and found itself running alongside spoken theatre, and forced to compete with it. Composers could not ignore the audience's ability to compare the conventions of *dramma per musica* with the sublime world of literary tragedy or the histrionic vivacity of Hanswurst, and singers had to compensate with theatrical bravura for the loss of intelligibility that the use of a foreign language entailed. It is no coincidence that certain outstanding achievements in Italian opera in the 18th century – the musical eloquence of Handel, the evocation of a mythic classicism in Gluck, the flagrant vitality of Mozart's characters – took place outside Italy. To be sure, from the 17th century, Italian became the international *lingua franca* of opera; that, together with the availability of an Italian workforce, assured a continual interchange of personnel and repertory between the system in Italy and the subsystems of other countries, where it was guaranteed a long, tenacious flowering. Indeed, in the 19th century, distinct enclaves developed in metropolitan performing life, as with the Théâtre Italien in Paris, in competition with the Opéra and the Opéra-Comique, the King's Theatre and Covent Garden in London, where operas by German and French composers were also given in Italian, the Kärntnertortheater in Vienna, run by impresarios who secured exchanges with Naples and Milan, and the Bol'shoy in St Petersburg, where in 1843 Nikolay I engaged the tenor Rubini as artistic director, direct from his Paris and London successes. Such international prosperity for Italian opera in the mid-19th century could not have occurred without the intense Rossini fever which spread unremittingly from 1815 (by 1824 the 'epidemic' had reached Mexico City and Rio de Janeiro) and paved the way for the success of Bellini, Donizetti and, more controversially, Verdi.

Meanwhile the artistic autonomy enjoyed by Italian opera in European capitals condemned it to a long isolation by comparison with opera in the vernacular, which grew more vigorous, feeding on the aversion of local composers and many intellectuals towards the preponderant Italian influence; this was marked in the German-speaking countries and later in Russia. In France, the exclusion of *opera seria* from 18th-century Paris and the sporadic performances of intermezzos and comic operas at the Académie Royale de Musique (in 1729, 1752–4 and 1778–9) had made Italian opera a polemical and ideological issue among intellectuals and had also stimulated assimilation and mimicry, whether of genre (*opéra comique* arose in 1757, with E. R. Duni, as a synthesis of indigenous theatrical forms and alien musical styles) or of artistic personality (Piccinni, Sacchini and Salieri became French composers for a few years, Cherubini and Spontini for a lifetime). The French operatic tradition was solid enough to withstand the establishment under the Revolution of comic opera and under Napoleon of serious Italian opera (at the Théâtre Italien, from 1801). At the height of his career, Rossini virtually transformed himself into a French opera composer (1826–9), while Donizetti and Verdi were to take on the role for some of their masterpieces (*La fille du régiment*, *La favorite*; *Les vêpres siciliennes*, *Don Carlos*); in the German operatic world, which began its emancipation from Italian dominance only with Weber and Marschner, such an assimilation would have been inconceivable.

In the post-revolutionary European settlement the position of opera reflected the political idea of the 'concert of nations' of the Congress of Vienna, with Italian opera acquiring a pre-eminent role alongside increasingly sharply delineated national operatic forms, within a context of wider internationalization. (It later became possible for such 'Italian' singers as Adelina Patti or Rosa Ponselle to be born, make their débuts and triumph abroad without having set foot in Italy before reaching the zeniths of their careers in London, Paris or New York.) The wider international scene was monopolized by Italian opera up to World War I (markedly in Central and South America, somewhat less in North America): while this gave renewed impetus to the economy of Italian opera on its home ground, through the seasonal to-and-fro of singers and the export of scores, it gave rise to no significant artistic development.

At the dawn of the 20th century, Italian opera – which even today has more titles in the international repertory than any other country – gave European opera a last, brief but intense artistic stimulus through the vitality of the Giovane Scuola; but later it increasingly assumed the role of a mental 'locus' willingly used to house the theatrical inspiration and poetic conception of those who, like Busoni or Stravinsky, wished to contest, in their outlook and their music, the prevailing culture of Wagnerian music drama.

3. DRAMA AND FORM: A HISTORICAL OUTLINE. There is no hidden essence that unites Peri's *Euridice* (1600) and Bussotti's *Lorenzaccio* (1972). But one may say that, over the four centuries of Italian opera, certain features have remained prominent: (1) the metric poetic structure of the text (mixed forms of spoken prose and sung verse are virtually unknown); (2) the prevailing realism of the subject matter (the fantastic, the fairy-tale, the grotesque and the satirical are rare); (3) the tendency to reduce the drama to its pathetic and affective dimension (the clash of passions prevails over any conflict of ideas); (4) the individuation of the characters through their voices (solo singing prevails over all other elements in the aesthetic hierarchy); and (5) the remarkable autonomy granted to musical forms (satisfying the listener's formal and stylistic expectations is no less important than interesting the follower of the drama). In this light, we may review the principal historical phases of Italian opera.

(i) The 17th century. The poet Ottavio Rinuccini, who wrote the verse for the first true operas in Florence around 1600, adopted without question the metrical system used in the Italian literary theatre, in particular in pastoral fables such as Tasso's *Aminta* and Guarini's *Il pastor fido*; adapted as necessary, this became the basic system for Italian opera librettos until the 20th century. As a rule the dramatic dialogue is conducted in *versi sciolti*, a rough equivalent of blank verse, in a free sequence of whole hendecasyllables and broken ones (septenaries) of quite flexible rhythm (only the accent on the penultimate metric syllable is fixed) and without a fixed rhyme scheme (a rhyming couplet is however often used to mark speakers' cues in dialogues or salient clauses in a protracted speech). Historically, recitative corresponds to this system in music. (The double septenaries used for example in certain colloquial scenes in *La bohème* – both Puccini's and Leoncavallo's – and the hendecasyllables with a dactylic ending which for the Prologue of *Pagliacci* Leoncavallo modelled on the comedies of Ariosto, are extensions of the same principle.) For the interventions of the chorus, for individual characters' sad or comic effusions of song, for ritual moments and assertions of universal moral significance, closed metric forms are used instead. Here the stanzas are either of hendecasyllables and septenaries (such as the octave, the quatrain, the canzone, the madrigal and sometimes the sonnet, the standard Italian poetic forms since the 14th century, which however almost disappear from opera after the mid-17th century), or of the measured metres with a regular and fixed stress scheme, which in Italian art poetry reached their own zenith around 1600, above all in the hands of Chiabrera (the *quaternario* or line of four syllables, *quinario*, *ottonario*, from about 1630 the *senario*, from about 1670 the *decasillabo*, and sporadically in the 17th century and from the late 19th onwards the *novenario*). Historically these strophic structures, in the most varied combinations, give rise to the aria and the other closed forms of Italian opera, and find their antecedents in the theatre music of the 16th century (particularly in the spectacular *intermedi* sung between the acts of festal comedies and tragedies, mostly at the Florentine court). From Rinuccini to Dallapiccola the proportion of recitative verse ('sciolti') to metrical verse ('lirici') varies, but this double diet, with its different dramatic functions, remains. When Peri, in the preface to his *Euridice*, declares that he wants to 'imitate with singing whoever speaks (and without doubt one never spoke singing)', he is pointing to the melodic potential of a poetic language that is already in itself rhythmically organized and stylized.

That this invention ('as if talking in harmony', over the chordal support of a simple and partly improvised *basso continuo*) was a specifically Florentine one, that it suited the spectacular celebrations of festive occasions, and that the supposed chant of ancient tragedy might be revived within it, are convictions that crystallized early in the historical consciousness of Italian opera: for example, the printed account of *Ercole in Tebe* by Moniglia and Melani (1661, Florence), a nuptial *festa teatrale* whose subject goes back to Euripides and Seneca, describes the 'natural recitation of the naked words' (the recitative) as the effect of a *genius loci*. 60 years after Peri, the system had spread from Florence to Mantua, Rome, Venice, Naples and Palermo and had tended to become specialized, leaving the development of the action to light and free recitative punctuated with frequent *canzonette* or *ariette* which relieved its musical 'tedium' (a risk that had been warned against as early as 1626, in the score of Domenico Mazzocchi's *Catena d'Adone*). Poets contributed to the formal variety of the arias by providing often capricious and extravagant strophic schemes (from 1660 increasingly often polymetric), furnished with ritornellos ('intercalari'), while composers supplied a host of brief rhythmic-melodic patterns that lent themselves to reiteration and combination at various pitches. The uses of some of these – for example the dactylic *quinario* for scenes of incantation, magic or the world beyond – soon became conventions and recurred as recognizable musical commonplaces (Medea's spell in Cavalli's *Giasone*, 1649, is the first of many demonic and infernal scenes, right down to Gluck's *Orfeo ed Euridice*, to be frequently parodied in *buffo* scenes and in intermezzos and comic operas).

From 1600 to 1640, operas often drew their subjects from classical mythology, in particular Ovid's *Metamorphoses*. The contemporary theoretical debate (set out by G. B. Doni) turns in particular on plausibility, on the credibility of an action that is entirely sung: in the fabulous golden world of Arcadia it is so much more plausible that the passions of men and their miraculous transformations should be represented in musical sound rather than naked words (the choice of mythical subjects thus masks an implicitly realistic standpoint). But by 1630 the anonymous manuscript treatise *Il corago* (its author may have been Rinuccini's son, Pier Francesco), summing up the early Florentine operatic experiments, implies that, if 'le rappresentazioni armoniche' continued to be cultivated, audiences 'would become accustomed to enjoy anything performed in music' – even the glory or ruin of sovereigns in tragedies, or the attraction of young lovers and the opposition of their fathers in comedies. This is confirmed by the operas given in Rome between 1631 and 1643 by the Barberini, nephews of Urban VIII: Rospigliosi's dramas draw variously on hagiography (as in Landi's *Sant'Alessio*), on Tasso's and Ariosto's chivalric epics (as in Luigi Rossi's *Palazzo d'Atlante*) and on Boccaccio's realistic narrative (as in *Chi soffre speri* by Virgilio Mazzocchi and Marco Marazzoli).

From 1640 in Venice, after a wave of mythological and chivalric subjects (fostered by Ferrari, both poet and musician) which perpetuated the taste of princely entertainments, heroic themes from Homer and Virgil began to appear, centring on the Trojan war (Troy was the mythical precursor of Venice); these included *Il ritorno d'Ulisse in patria* by Badoaro and Monteverdi and *La finta pazza* by Strozzi and Sacrati. From a musico-dramatic viewpoint, there are many scenes of sadness and great laments sung by heroes and abandoned heroines (modelled on Ovid's *Heroides* and Monteverdi's 'Lamento d'Arianna'); dramaturgically, the conscious breaches of the rule of the three Aristotelian unities are intensified (*Didone* by Busenello and Cavalli, which shows the fall of Troy in Act 1 and Aeneas's African love affairs in the remaining two acts, spans a variety of times, places and actions – to justify himself the librettist invokes the 'Spanish custom', promoted by Lope de Vega, of depicting in a single drama 'years, not hours'). Operatic dramaturgy of the mid-17th century is intentionally 'disorderly'; in this it is no different from such other forms of 17th-century professional theatre as the *commedia dell'arte*, Elizabethan drama or Spanish *comedia*, all far removed from the 'classical' literary tragedy, then at its peak particularly in France.

The standard three-act *dramma per musica* of Cicognini, Faustini, Aureli, Minato and Noris aimed for entertainment by means of the capricious: strangeness, the astonishing, a multiplication of plots and subplots and the juxtaposition of the serious and the facetious. The result is an ambivalent position for music – a language incapable of false utterances – in adventurous subjects (such as Cicognini's *Orontea*, set to music by Lucio, Cirillo, Cesti and Vismarri) or political ones (such as Noris's *Flavio Cuniberto*, set by Partenio, Gabrielli, Mancia, Alessandro Scarlatti and later Handel) where disguises or deceptions and tangled misunderstandings abound, and where, in keeping with the political ideology of Tacitism, the characters systematically dissimulate to attain their own ends and thus ensnare themselves in a web of conflicts. In a deceitful, illusory world, singing may thus be the only credible language in which the emotions secretly tormenting the characters may be expressed, or it may be the instrument of fiendishly sinful enticement, mostly wielded by female singers (one thinks of the protagonist in Busenello's *L'incoronazione di Poppea*, 1643, with music attributed to Monteverdi), but also used in those operas which, in Venice around 1680, boldly indulged in cheeky representations of the 'vice of Venus' (to which the censor turned a blind eye as long as there was no offence to the State). But in accordance with early-established convention, drama intended for music should have a happy ending (concluding with bloodshed did not suit so pleasing and harmonious a language as music). Accordingly, Italian opera was much more lax than the *tragédie lyrique* or the Spanish *comedia* in observing poetic justice; in the general joy, reprobates and the wicked mend their ways *in extremis* (and sometimes they triumph absolutely, as in *L'incoronazione di Poppea*); Jason, moved by Hypsipyle's desperate lament, and Medea marry their respective suitors; the dissolute Heliogabalus (in the opera by Aureli and Boretti) is unexpectedly converted to justice and virtue. Finally, the music of *ariette* – from 1670 onwards increasingly often in two strophes, the first repeated da capo and lending itself to extemporized melodic variation by the singer – provided the caricatural and clownish standard for

comic roles, always present up to about 1700.

The scores however include no instrumental accompaniment to the wonders of stage technology that also enriched certain *drammi per musica* in the middle of the century, such as those put on by Jacopo Torelli in 1641–3 at the Teatro Novissimo in Venice (where he introduced scene changes with sliding panels in the sight of the audience, later adopted throughout Europe) or those given in the grandest, most sumptuous of the Venetian theatres, the S Giovanni Grisostomo, which opened in 1678. Nor do the scores contain music for the entr'acte dances, which also – whether linked to the action or free standing – were a standard ingredient of an evening's opera in Italy until the end of the 19th century (the main curtain was not closed during the performance). This is explained by division of labour, since the music for the dances was provided by the choreographers themselves or by specifically engaged composers, not by the composer of the opera.

In the last 30 years of the 17th century the influence of the Spanish *comedia* of Calderón and fellow writers became more direct (mostly in such 'Spanish' centres as Milan and Naples, or noblemen's theatres in Rome with Spanish links), as in the last ten years did that of the French *tragédie* of Corneille and Racine (mostly in Venice and particularly in the hands of the nobleman G. Frigimelica Roberti, who attempted various kinds of *tragedia per musica* in five acts). But the librettists, who soon outgrew the concept of discrete scenes, had by the mid-17th century adopted the constructional rationalistic principle of *liaison des scènes*: increasingly, the juncture between one scene and the next was marked by an aria on which the character embarks before re-entering between the wings. Occasionally, a sequence of scenes might begin with a short aria, usually a brief but often moving monologue. This allowed a profusion of brief, very varied *ariette* (as many as 50) which, with the singing of the *prime donne* and castratos, were the primary attraction of the opera.

(ii) The 18th century. The founding of the Arcadian Academy in Rome in 1690, influencing the whole of Italy through its poetic 'colonies', gave the Italian intellectual world its first common collective programme of stylistic and ideological renewal, embracing all branches of the arts.

Opera in musica felt its influence in several ways. The 18th century saw endless discussion of opera among literary men, often of a highly polemical kind attacking its supposed abnormality. Any historian of Italian poetry, when dealing with dramatic literature, has had to come to terms with the theatrical form long predominant in Italian civic life which has drained dry the soil of literary theatre and subjugated poetry to singing. Measured against contemporary French classical theatre of the time (favoured among the literati and on academic stages) or against the Italian tragic theatre of the 16th century, the *drammi per musica* seemed poor in their versification, strained in their dramatic texture, monotonous in the pre-eminence of amorous feeling and unseemly in their mixture of serious and facetious characters. The 18th century struggles in words against the abuses, the cosy conventions and habitual prerogatives (those 'convenienze teatrali' satirized by Benedetto Marcello and in numerous *opere comiche*) to establish within opera a rational taste and a unified artistic plan, all solidly entrusted to the dramatist, a poet who might govern all aspects of the performance, from the scenic setting (minutely prescribed by Zeno and above all Metastasio in their stage directions) to the staging (until after 1850 it was the theatre poet's job to manage stage movement and control the singers' whims), from distributing the affections in the sequence of arias to planning the effects produced by alternating the main and supporting roles. The most astute handbook of operatic dramaturgy is the dialogue *Della tragedia antica e moderna* (Rome, 1715) by Martello, who as a librettist shared the Arcadians' ideals of a purified francophile classicism. Algarotti's *Saggio sopra l'opera in musica* (Venice, 1755), viewing the scene from a European standpoint at a time when Metastasio's international success was at its height, supports the transalpine model of court theatre as the only one that, exempt from the economic pressures of entrepreneurial theatre, may escape the double tyranny of the singers' caprices and the need to indulge public taste. Finally, in his judicious *Dell'opera in musica* (Naples, 1772), Planelli sets out a synthesis of enlightened thinking on musical theatre.

As regards dramaturgy, the Arcadians' influence was felt in the respect paid to the three unities and in the preference for subjects dealing with ancient Roman, Greek and even Persian history, to the exclusion of the medieval or 'barbaric' that the late 17th century, with its love of the picturesque, had not disdained; that influence is even more apparent in the exaltation of ancient heroes as embodiments of ideal virtue and morals, exposed to the harsh tests of fortune and politics but finally triumphant. With the *buffo* characters appropriately relegated to 'contrascene' and later to intermezzos, the texture of the drama became centred on a single strand, albeit tangled as it inextricably entwines four leading characters in one knot. There are usually two or three sopranos and a contralto, either women or castratos, and sometimes a tenor antagonist, as in Gasparini's *Bajazet* of 1719 (a source for Handel's *Tamerlano*), and two or three supporting parts; in a number of arias, between 25 and 35, they give vent to their changing feelings. The comic element becomes a kind of stylistic spice, which occasionally finds its way into the plot or into the personality of one of the roles. Whereas in his early drama *I rivali generosi* (1697, Venice) Zeno gave a wartime setting (the Byzantine conquest of Ravenna) to the playful, even humorous whirl of military reversals and amorous mishaps that afflict the two leading characters, in the late drama *Caio Fabbricio* (1729, Vienna) he sketches in the ancient Roman protagonist a grim picture of inflexible ethical and political integrity, a marmoreal character whose patriotic ideals freeze any tenderness in his environment.

In his poetry, Metastasio – an attentive reader of Racine and of Spanish playwrights – excelled in his amiable, subtle and indulgent representation of the difficulties which give rise to 'inconstancy and rages' and 'amorous cravings' in his younger and more impetuous characters: the system of solo arias (there are no more than one or two duets and choruses in each drama) is the artistic apparatus with which an analysis is developed, precise rather than severe, of the 'mille affetti insieme / tutti raccolti al cor' (*Demetrio*, 1731) tormenting the interlocutors. The system ranges from the more abstract comparison arias, which in two stanzas develop a parallel between the love portrayed and various physical phenomena, suitably echoed in the music (the impetus of the steed, the little boat at the mercy of the waves and so forth), to the *parlante* arias, which give voice to a flood of throbbing emotion: sometimes these

latter take an irregular form (like the three-stanza 'Se cerca, se dice', which in 12 lines depicts a playing-out of the torment and alienation of the three main characters in *Olimpiade*, 1733, and which moved Metastasio himself to tears) – and often the composer stresses their urgency by beginning them directly, without the customary orchestral ritornello. In particular the brilliant early dramas of Metastasio, of 1724–30 – those that earned him the summons to Vienna as imperial court poet – depict the fatal havoc that politics can wreak on the emotions, and particularly on love (reasons of state in *Didone abbandonata*, infiltration and tyrannicide in *Siroe*, civil war in *Catone in Utica*, palace intrigues in *Ezio*, the *coup d'état* in *Semiramide*, the war of conquest and occupation in *Alessandro nell' Indie* and the struggles for succession in *Artaserse*); in the Viennese dramas, on the other hand, such values as patriotism (*Temistocle*, *Attilio Regolo*), equality in adversity (*Demofoonte*, *Il re pastore*) and the duty of sovereigns to their subjects (*Adriano in Siria*, *La clemenza di Tito*) prevail, destined as much to satisfy enlightened monarchs' consciences as the intellectual schemes of Enlightenment thinkers or the need for tenderness nurtured by European sensibility in the latter half of the 18th century.

As regards style, the Arcadian movement made itself felt in the formal regularizing of poetry and in the elegant litheness that propelled the musical language. The da capo aria – which, while expanding in size and then contracting in the crucial juncture of the repeat, persisted at least until the 1790s – ensured a formally ordered and balanced frame for the most tumultuous emotions or (in *commedia*) for less reverent feelings: the character sets his or her feelings within it, organizing them logically and thus revealing the capacity for reason that remains man's central quality. While Zeno and Stampiglia still made desultory use of the polymetric stanzas that increased the impetus of pathos (swift in C. F. Pollarolo, coaxing in Giovanni Bononcini, laborious in Alessandro Scarlatti), Metastasio opted for constant metre, favouring septenary verse, the most flexible of the lyric forms and, with its variable stress, the most congenial to the new musical style cultivated from the 1720s by Vivaldi, Orlandini and Porta in the north and (with considerable artistic success) by Vinci, Pergolesi and Hasse in the south. It is a style based less on the contrapuntal procession of the voice and continuo on equal terms, with or without solo or *ripieno* instruments, than on the clear division of responsibility between the vocal melody – slender, open and able to shift between laughter and tears at the turn of a bar – and the orchestral accompaniment, laid out in broad harmonic brushstrokes, often with quivering repeated notes. This same stylistic evolution appears in intermezzos and the Neapolitan *commedia per musica*, which (in classical plots that owe much to Terence) treat their family rows according to the very same system as was used in *dramma per musica*: da capo arias in a highly diverse series of affections with jokes from the lower characters (often in dialect) and very few ensembles.

About 1750, the *dramma giocoso per musica* of Goldoni and Galuppi took two decisive steps towards the musical representation of the dramatic material that forms the core of any *opera buffa* – the obstacles which conspiring family and pecuniary interests place in the way of the love, finally granted, of two young people (who invariably have a love duet at a crucial moment in the third act, shortly before the denouement). First, while the arias and any duets for the serious characters (mostly nobility) generally remain in da capo form, those of the comic or lowly characters take binary or ternary forms, with sections in different metre and tempo to mark the successive stages of an often ridiculous or caricatured piece of reasoning (perhaps addressed to another speaker who, speechless or out of patience, does not reply). Secondly, the scuffles, altercations and machinations of the comic characters give way, in the finales of the first two acts, to protracted ensembles with sections that differ in metre, tempo and key and in character (some in dialogue and propulsive, others sung as 'asides'; the last is always a noisy commotion).

The initially rigid hierarchic and formal separation between the two or three serious roles and the four or five comic ones gradually became less marked with the use of tear-jerking subjects such as that of Goldoni's *La buona figliuola* (drawn from Richardson's *Pamela*), with its touching appeal to that classless value, natural goodness of feeling, and also in plots about purity threatened by the devious lust of the powerful, by turns cynically malicious and tenderly sorrowful. In *Le nozze di Dorina* by Goldoni and Galuppi (1755, Bologna) the musical numbers are divided among the seven characters (the Count and Countess, the housekeeper and the steward, two servants and the gardener) as follows: the two serious parts sing two duets and six da capo arias, the two middle-ranking parts have two duets and, with the three *buffo* parts, a total of 15 arias (mostly binary or ternary) and take part in the Act 1 and 2 finales (of 48 and 37 lines respectively) from which the serious characters are excluded. In other words, the Count's plotting to win the housekeeper for himself and the manoeuvres of the Countess to thwart him are expressed only in recitative and do not take on an articulated musical form. Adapted, to suit a Roman custom, into two intermezzos for five singers in the intervals of a comic play, *Le nozze di Dorina*, given at the Valle in 1760, does away with the two serious characters: the *dramma giocoso* is reduced to a farce involving scurrilous characters squabbling about maidservants. But in the reworked version for La Scala in 1782, *Fra i due litiganti il terzo gode* (set by Sarti), the ensemble numbers are increased to six, the serious characters join the *buffo* ones in the introduction and the lengthy first and second finales (141 and 184 lines), the only duet involves *buffo* characters (who divide up ten arias, in one of which the Count is reduced to a bit-part, commenting on an outburst made by his servant), and of the four long *seria* arias the biggest and most exacting goes not to the nobility but to the main *buffa*, the housekeeper. And while in *Le nozze* the locations limit the sphere of action of the characters (the hall for the nobility, the threshing-floor for the servants, with middle-rank characters here and there), in *Fra i due litiganti* the Act 1 finale involves all seven characters in a communal run in the garden and an 'indecorous' intrusion into Dorina's private room, and the Act 2 finale sees them all chasing one another in the dark in a 'thick wood' amid 'horrible caves', threatened by a thunderstorm in the orchestra at the height of the confusion (so that Nature participates in the amorous turmoil).

The formal pliability of *opera buffa* in keeping up with the fluctuations of fortune had reached such a degree as to allow the more or less literal translation of comic stage plays rich in peripetias into opera librettos, such as those made by an unknown St Petersburg writer

for Paisiello in 1782 and Da Ponte for Mozart in 1786 from Beaumarchais' *Le barbier de Séville* and *Le mariage de Figaro*, granting unforeseen musical prominence to that third-estate agitator whose creation was to play such a part in the political turmoil of the late 18th century. (It was a coincidence that the thunderstorm in the Act 2 finale of Sarti's opera should precede by a single day a similar meteorological outbreak in Paisiello's *Barbiere*, of which Rossini's comic operas embody so many illustrious descendants; but it was not fortuitous that in Milan in 1782 the *prima buffa* and *primo buffo caricato* should have been Nancy Storace and Francesco Benucci, the future Viennese Susanna and Figaro.)

In the 1780s, such critical observers as Borsa and Mattei (and in France A.-C. Quatremère de Quincy) boasted of the tight relationship in *opera buffa* between the intricate stage action, the lively musical form of the ensemble numbers and the singers' gestural vitality: these very qualities were thought to be lacking in *opera seria*, which was busy re-elaborating Metastasio's dramaturgy in various ways without disputing or subverting it. In 1769 Jommelli, about to set Metastasio's *Ezio* for the third time, complained that 'to have to draw out so many diverse thoughts ... ever from the same words' posed a real problem to the composer. Composers faced up to it in the culminating moments of the drama by devising texts for vocal numbers in three or more parts which combine in one rousing musical tableau the emotional conflicts that Metastasio unravels analytically in three or more separate successive arias.

The best-known example of this method of emotional synthesis and amplification at key dramatic points – with a corresponding expansion of forms that at the end of the century often led to the fusion of three acts into two – is Mozart's *La clemenza di Tito*; but already in Paisiello's *opere serie* from 1773 onwards, whether to new librettos or to revisions of Metastasio's, there is at least one trio or quartet in addition to the usual duets, and in *Elfrida* (1792, libretto by Calzabigi) there are two trios, two quartets and a septet. These ensembles, Calzabigi wrote, are 'essentially a kind of chorus, and much more interesting since these are chiefly characters singing from passion', often recoiling from an event that has left them angry or dismayed. Here he is articulating in operatic terms a theatrical idea from his years of working with Gluck and Angiolini, and which he had declared in 1783 in a public letter to Vittorio Alfieri, a writer of tragedies (who was to influence the language of 19th-century librettists): 'Tragedy', wrote Calzabigi, 'must be none other than a series of pictures', of 'situations capable of revealing the personalities of the characters ... and the passions that bestir them' so as to 'strike at the hearts of the audience and effectively rouse them'. The principle is equally valid for the musical theatre, where indeed it was to find an unexpected resonance. Calzabigi exemplifies this theory in the story of Iphigenia in Aulis: this amounts to a renewed link with the taste for the statuesque nature and dramatic concision of ancient tragedy and the mythological plots which, as an alternative to Metastasio's intrigues of love and politics, Algarotti and Diderot had advocated from the 1750s. To this vein, open to the thematic and formal influence of *tragédie lyrique* (particularly in the use of choruses and dancing), belong such exacting operas as Traetta's *Ifigenia in Tauride* (1763, Vienna; revived in 1767 under Gluck's direction, in Florence) and Jommelli's *Armida abbandonata* (1770, Naples), as well as the early imitations of Rameau's *tragédies lyriques* by C. I. Frugoni and Traetta in the francophile court of Parma in 1759–60.

But Jommelli recognized in 1769 that 'in a tragedy, historical fact is always better than anything fictitious', since 'the former must touch while the latter can at best surprise: in the former the listeners' hearts are all passion, in the latter all amazement'. This view, almost axiomatic for Italian opera of all times, was well served by the vogue for tragedies with fatal endings (such as *La vendetta di Nino o sia La morte di Semiramide*, which Giovannini took from Voltaire; set by Prati, 1786, Florence) and for ancient Roman subjects, which explore lacerating emotions in the most human of characters who yet are located in a remote, quasi-mythical historical world. The masterpiece of this genre was the highly successful *Gli Orazi e i Curiazi* by Sografi and Cimarosa (1796, Venice; much revived, at times with some delicate arias by Portugal for the *prima donna* role, Grassini's *pièce de résistance*). The tragic story, drawn from Corneille and the ballet by Noverre, moves inexorably forward, terrible and heartbreaking, from the irreparable rupture of amorous and family affections during the military action that founds the state. The score contrasts, with irreconcilable styles of singing and orchestral writing, the fierce patriotism of Horatio (played by Babbini, the first heroic tenor in Italian opera) with the plaintive romantic pathos of his unsuccessful opponent Curiatius (played by such castratos as Crescentini and Velluti and such prima donnas as Pasta and Giuditta Grisi) and of the unfortunate Horatia. The arias, duets and trios, often with choruses and martial music from offstage, together with scenes in obbligato recitative, create vivid and formally quite free musical pictures; the drama ends unresolved, in conflict, with a mute tableau uniting survivors' 'confusion, mirth and consternation'.

(iii) The early 19th century. The years of revolution and Napoleonic domination (1796–1814) did not on the whole upset the working of Italian operatic life. The new regimes brought about changes in the ruling class and therefore to some extent in the composition of the theatrical public, but wealthy Italians' fondness for luxury entertainment remained. Nor was there an immediate change in the neo-classical and pathetic orientation of the prevailing taste for *opera seria*. After a long period of peace, the war and political turbulence would have made the fragility of human affections and intentions seem the more acute to those endangered by misfortune and the malice of usurpers. The dramatic form that best expresses this sense is the comic opera on a *semiserio* subject, which – as in Paer's *Camilla* (1799, drawn from an *opéra comique* of 1791), or Rossini's *La gazza ladra* (1817, from a Parisian *mélodrame* of 1815) – depicts tragedy, in a setting civil and modern rather than heroic and remote, narrowly averted with the liberation of the innocent and the condemnation (or pardoning) of the wicked. (The *semiserio* drama, which in Rossini's *Barbiere* Dr Bartolo deplores as a tiresome fashion, does not form a separate class within the dramatic system: a La Scala competition in 1816 for the best libretto provided for only two genres, *serio* and *giocoso* or *buffo*, saying of the latter that it was sufficient for there to be 'at least one *giocoso* character'.) But in the same period, the 'dictatorship' exercised by French dramaturgy over librettists' decisions was strengthened. It was a domination which, helped by the

Italian literati's good knowledge of French, lasted the rest of the century (both Rossini's *Otello* and that of Boito and Verdi came from French translations, the Classical one by Ducis and the Romantic one by F.-V. Hugo), and it met the need for dramatic subjects created by increased operatic output and the changing roles of librettist and composer. For by now the true dramatist was the person who chose the subject and drew from an already dramatized source the theatrical situations that could be adapted to Italian opera, and this, increasingly, was the composer; the librettist fell in rank to become a clever arranger of someone else's work (Gaetano Rossi described himself as 'a hack rather than a poet').

Also from France, in the first years after the revolutionary era, came the impetus for the first literary polemic on Romanticism, Madame de Staël's essay 'De l'esprit des traductions' in the Milanese *Biblioteca italiana* (1816): it spoke of the benefit that Italian culture would gain by translating German and English poetry, particularly the plays of Schiller and Shakespeare, instead of 'rummaging around in the ancient ashes'. In Italy the discussion of Romanticism (1816–19) barely touched the musical world, but the crucial question of the aesthetic legitimacy of historical drama touched a vital chord concerning the choice of operatic themes. Conflict between the Classicists and Romanticists flared up in the 1830s, a reflection of the controversy provoked in Paris by Hugo's *Cromwell* and *Hernani*. This time opera was involved – directly in the clamorous arguments for and against Bellini's *Norma* (1831), indirectly in Mazzini's *Filosofia della musica* (1836), which declared Italian opera's 'need to spiritualize itself' as well as its need for 'the historic element', 'the colour of the age' and 'the character of the settings'.

In fact, while the composer exercised absolute control over that major source of pleasure, the vocal melody ('Cantilena, always cantilena: beautiful, new, magical and rare' was for Carpani the prime ingredient of Italian opera), it was the staging alone that took care of the local colour: there is nothing Polish, Babylonian, Swiss, Scottish or Aragonese in the music of Mayr's *Amor coniugale* (1805, from Bouilly's *opéra comique Léonore*), Rossini's *Semiramide* (1823, after Voltaire), Bellini's *La sonnambula* (1831, from a *ballet-pantomime* by Scribe), Donizetti's *Lucia di Lammermoor* (1835, from a French dramatization of Scott's novel) or Verdi's *Ernani* (1844, after Hugo). Paradoxically, it was to be a contemporary subject, Verdi's *La traviata* (1853, from the play by Alexandre Dumas *fils*), that provided Italian opera with the first realistic portrayal to have its ambience contained within the music (though the achievement was frustrated by the practice – still current until around 1880 – of moving the action back to 1700, since the chorus, people of humble extraction, would never in modern dress pass for ladies and gentlemen of high society).

Above all, early 19th-century librettists and composers drew from contemporary French drama their abundant use of *coups de théâtre* – sensational and alarming events, which unleash conflicting reactions and quicken, retard or redirect the action. This technique was moreover profoundly in agreement with the Romanticist view of theatrical effect, which 'works over a host of assembled men, rousing their attention, exciting their interest', a view that Italians would be familiar with above all from Schlegel's *Vorlesungen über dramatische Kunst und Literatur* (which was translated in 1817 by the librettist of *La gazza ladra*). Not surprisingly, 'effect' is the dramaturgic concept that recurs perhaps most often in Verdi's letters, with an almost obsessive frequency – as when he telegraphs from home about the first performance of *Aida*, demanding news of the theatrical effectiveness of this or that scene. Henceforth Italian opera drew indiscriminately on any source of drama, even Schiller and, from Verdi's *Macbeth* (1847), Shakespeare.

The *coup de théâtre* – and this is the essential innovation – is integrated into the musical form and triggers off moments of abundant vocal melody. The forms of the musical numbers are enlarged and if necessary more complex. Different tempos alternate. In the active ('kinetic') sections, the action moves forward, time passes as represented, the musical substance serves the rapid succession of dialogue and events and the orchestra is kept busy (sometimes, in the 'parlante', the melody leads, with the voices reciting their cues syllabically) and at crucial points the key changes, the metre comes to a halt, and the singing flares up or breaks off. In the 'static' sections the action pauses, 'real' time is suspended, the dialogue proceeds in 'asides' or adopts statuesque gestures and poses, while the singing takes wing, the orchestra supports it, the metre becomes regular and the harmony stable within a closed tonal area. Dramaturgically these static sections, often the most memorable melodically, represent the sung reaction in the heat of the moment of characters struck by a reversal of fortune in the last bars of the preceding 'kinetic' section: a piece of news, a revelation, an insult, an internal shock expressed in a few lapidary words 'which clearly and evidently express the situation' (the formula of the famous 'parola scenica' which Verdi required of his librettist for the Aida–Amneris duet), but it could well be a musical signal from offstage, a roll of drums, a festive or military fanfare, a chorus of jubilation or mourning, or a ballad that we know heralds the unexpected approach of a loved or hated character.

Offstage music is a characteristic feature of 19th-century *melodramma*, drawn from late 18th-century *opéra comique*: there was a great fondness for enlarging the stage rectangle acoustically, with the visible setting overpowered by a disquieting space beyond: from it erupts the clamour of gendarmes bent on arresting Almaviva in Rossini's *Il barbiere di Siviglia* (there is no such scene in Beaumarchais or Paisiello); from it too comes the call by which the two infatuated women recognize the crusader, their hearts missing a beat, in the delightful treble *terzettino* in Meyerbeer's *Il crociato in Egitto*; from it come the holy bells inexorably punctuating Pollione and Norma's fate, Alfredo's love song

from beneath Violetta's balcony (or from within her heart?) and indeed, in the 'Miserere' from *Il trovatore*, the highly skilful interlacing of the funeral chorus, Manrico's song of farewell to life and the tolling of the passing bell which floods with anguish the heart (and the singing) of Leonora, alone on the stage.

The basic scheme of musico-dramatic relationships is summarized in Table 5 (contemporary terminology for the constituent movements shows the variation typical of practical jargon: that of Basevi's *Studio sulle opere di G. Verdi*, 1859, is used here). This 'customary form' is the fundamental structure of Italian *melodramma* in the first 60 or 70 years of the 19th century. Act 1 of *Ernani*, for example, after a brief *adagio* orchestral prelude and the usual introductory chorus in a single tempo, is developed entirely by an almost slavish fivefold reiteration of the pattern: a tenor cavatina (an entrance aria); a soprano cavatina; a soprano-baritone duet which becomes a trio with the addition of the tenor; a bass cavatina at the opening of the finale (the *tempo di mezzo* and the cabaletta were later joined); and then the finale in the true sense (with a *scena* leading directly into the Largo). The three or four sections in each number are always settings of lyric verse, organized in more or less symmetrical stanzas and laisses. The connective tissue is provided by the scenas, in free verse, realized as recitatives with orchestral participation and interjection. ('Recitativo secco', accompanied by cellos and basses with or without harpsichord, had disappeared at the S Carlo in Naples by about 1812, and elsewhere in Italy around 1820.)

This system of conventional forms, equally valid for *opera seria* and *buffa*, governed the audience's expectations and their sense of surprise. It was not however rigid. In the first place, after the disappearance of the da capo aria, there were nevertheless forms in a single movement (simple ariettas, songs as such, ballades, choruses), or in two, slow–fast (arias, 'duettini', 'terzettini'): in *Semiramide* – which stayed in the repertory until the 1880s and was a significant influence on Donizetti and Verdi – half the numbers are in two movements (in the same key), the other half in three or four, the first and the last in the same key (following a rule no longer absolute for Bellini, Donizetti and Verdi) with the slow section of four-part numbers in a key a third away. (A shift of a third, major or minor, upwards or downwards, is by far the favourite in 19th-century Italian opera, either between one movement and another or within a movement; another strict rule, up to the Introduction to *Il trovatore*, decrees that movements and numbers in the minor should end in the tonic major, except for the final number of an opera that ends tragic-

TABLE 5: Sectional structure in Italian opera of the early 19th century (Basevi 1859)

		gran duetto	*aria or cavatina*	*finale primo*
		Scena [versi sciolti; recitative]	Scena [versi sciolti; recitative]	[Chorus, ballet, scena, aria or arietta, duet or duettino, march etc.]
kinetic section:	1	Tempo d'attacco	—	Tempo d'attacco
static section:	2	Adagio (Cantabile)	Adagio (Cantabile)	Pezzo concertato (Largo)
kinetic section:	3	Tempo di mezzo	Tempo di mezzo	Tempo di mezzo
static section:	4	Cabaletta	Cabaletta	Stretta

ally, such as *Norma*. The Largo concertato in Rossini's finales is almost always in A flat major; he was not the only composer fond of very flat keys.)

Secondly, virtually any section could be omitted from the quadripartite 'customary form' without disturbing the music-dramatic relationships. An aria consisting of only a cantabile was often called a 'romanza', providing an oasis of radiant melody. In *Il trovatore*, an opera considered formally very conventional, half the numbers do not conform to the canonical pattern. The Act 1 finale of Donizetti's *Maria Stuarda* begins directly with the Largo concertato. Largo concertato is lacking in the Introduction to Verdi's *Rigoletto*, which has all the other characteristics of a finale. There is no true *tempo di mezzo* in the Act 1 finale of Rossini's *Otello*. Verdi, from Act 3 of *Ernani* (1844) onwards, liked occasionally to finish an intermediate finale with a powerful Largo concertato, and from *Luisa Miller* (1849) onwards sometimes cut short the dramatic thread with a *tempo di mezzo* leading directly into the final cadence, eliminating the *stretta* that in Rossini's hands formed the tumultuous 'general tableau', the chaotically frenzied outburst of musical energy which a moment earlier had been stored up in the 'picture of amazement' of the Largo concertato. Stendhal described (*Vie de Rossini*) the 'folie organisée' of the great finales of which, beginning with *Tancredi* and *L'italiana in Algeri* in 1813, Rossini was the supreme craftsman, even if not the inventor; for instance, in the Largo concertato of Mayr's *La rosa bianca e la rosa rossa*, given the same season, a supporting character proclaims 'Ah, fra poco tanta calma / in furor si cangerà' and in 1812 the librettist of Manfroce's *Ecuba*, translated from a *tragédie lyrique*, confessed to being put off it in the Act 1 finale (a perfect Rossini finale before its time) by 'the need to make the end of this ensemble number noisy, and to throw in the chorus, to serve current Italian theatre fashion'.

Finally, the standardization of forms allows the composer to use them in ways against their grain, to manipulate them so as to mislead the audience's expectations. At one extreme there is the alienating effect of a cabaletta that is slow and dream-like instead of vehement and impetuous (used by Donizetti for his most romantically melancholy creations, such as 'Verranno a te sull'aure', in the Lucia-Edgardo duet). At the other there is the comic disappointment evoked by a Largo concertato which in the finale to Act 1 of Rossini's *Il turco in Italia* (1814) fails to happen at the 'right' moment: 'V'è il sedile, e non si sviene: / colle regole non va' ('There's a seat and no-one's fainting: this is quite against the rules') proclaims the crestfallen Poet, expecting dismayed stupor from the first calamity when it in fact comes about only with the subsequent one. The joke is already there in the opera of the same title by Seydelmann (1788), the model for Rossini's *Turco*, confirming that Rossini was indeed the codifier rather than the inventor of the dramatic and formal mechanisms of 19th-century *melodramma*, which in fact drew heavily on the techniques of late 18th-century *opera buffa*. More intricate examples include the formidable 'terzettone' attempted by Rossini in Act 1 of *Maometto II* (1820), with no fewer than nine different movements from the Adagio to the cabaletta in the same key and spanning a change of scene (the composer himself thinned it out for the Venice revival of 1823), and the *scena*, *romanza* and *terzetto* in *Il trovatore* (no. 3) where the forms are telescopically compressed: the Count sings a *scena* which would flow naturally into its cavatina if

Manrico's offstage *romanza* did not cool the melody on his lips; the beginning of the *terzetto* has the formal characteristics of a *tempo d'attacco*, including modulation to the submediant, but the grafting on of the final wrathful *stretta* reveals that it has assumed the function of a *tempo di mezzo*.

In the 19th century the variety of available forms and the abundance of ensembles in place of arias (expressly preferred, for example, in the announcement of the La Scala libretto competition in 1816) called for careful agreement between librettist and composer over the distribution of the dramatic material: the letters and notebooks of Bellini, Donizetti and Verdi, of Romani, Rossi and Cammarano provide ample testimony to this (there is no reason to suppose it was any different for Rossini). This crucial phase in the creative process took the form of an agreed plan or 'programma' (Ferretti, Cammarano and Verdi), 'schizzo' (Mercadante and Verdi), 'traccia' (Mercadante), 'orditura' (Romani and Cammarano), 'tessitura' (Sterbini), 'ossatura' (Rossi), 'piano de' pezzi' (Bellini), 'scheletro delle situazioni drammatiche' (Noseda) or 'selva' (Donizetti, Verdi and Piave). There were several stages before the librettist could proceed with the versification: the enumeration of pieces, taking account of the 'convenienze' (the wishes, specialities and prerogatives of the singers) and the dramatic situations (called 'posizioni' or 'punti di scena'); next a scenario that defined the salient points of the dialogue; and then a rough prose draft. This gradual evolution, from the narrative pattern to the story and thence to the plot, assumes that the librettist, the composer or both had applied the reverse procedure to their external source, in a process of progressive abstraction – from source text to the plot, thence to a story and to the pattern of basic relationships that support the conceptual structure of the drama. 'Musical colour' ('tinta musicale'), to which Verdi alludes in a famous letter (24 August 1850), is a part of this process, this 'general concept of the drama' (Basevi); here, more than in the application of clever technical devices to hold the work together (large-scale tonal relationships, motivic echoes), resides the unifying principle for a construction including so many closed numbers possessing such remarkable morphological autonomy. With the 'ossatura' established and the 'selva' drafted, the librettist organized the text for the numbers into rigorously isometric strophes and laisses, favouring strong, vigorous accentuation of the metrically constant lines (with a renewed fondness for verses of six, eight or ten syllables), which the composer transformed into symmetrical melodic elements (normally two bars to a line), often enriched with appoggiaturas, in long and balanced though cadentially predictable phrases (12, 16, 24, 32 or even 40 bars), clear in outline and capable of being taken in on first hearing.

Isorhythm – the reiteration of a fixed melodic and rhythmic motif in the vocal line over a standard accompaniment – provides a 'musico-economic system' (Basevi) which gives great clarity to the phrase. Rossini tempers it with an unfailing regard for good prosody and impeccably elegant phrasing, adopted in turn by Donizetti, while Verdi's 'almost savage nature' (Rossini's term of approval) sharpens it, sometimes with violent distortions of the accentuation ('Lá donna è móbile') or brutally wrenching syllabification ('Arpa d'ór – déi – fatí — díci vá——tí'). Only rarely, but with elevating effect, ethereal phrases – 'melodie lunghe lunghe lunghe' – escape into flight, gliding for a minute

or more before alighting on a firm cadence (Anna/
Pamira's prayer in *Maometto II*, Norma's first invoca-
tion, Elizabeth's delirious final cabaletta in *Roberto
Devereux*, Leonora's first cantabile in *Il trovatore*).

At the same time, Rossini devised and applied on a
large scale a structural principle, distinct from that of
vocal phrases with symmetrical elements: the obsessive,
mechanical reiteration of a motif, in regular two- or
four-bar groups, alternately in the tonic and the
dominant (or in a sequence such as I–V–VI–III–IV–I). It
is the systematic extension of a procedure already used
by Haydn and Mozart for closing sections or for
transitions, the 'reproduction continuelle d'une formule
de cadence' or 'cadence à retour périodique', which so
angered Berlioz. It gives rise to a propulsiveness that is
hypnotic in slow tempos (as in the Largo in the Act 1
finale of *L'italiana in Algeri*) and nerve-wracking in fast
ones (as in the tumultuous *stretta* of the Act 1 finale of
Tancredi), a frenzied whirling at breakneck speed
which, combined with an orchestral crescendo, also
crowns the final sections of sinfonias and brilliant vocal
numbers. It produced an almost physical sensation in
audiences; Rossini was likened to a new Napoleon, an
invincible musical conqueror of Europe (Carpani,
Stendhal). The same principle is used, more sparingly,
by Bellini, Mercadante, Donizetti and Verdi; they,
beginning with the Act 2 finale of *Norma*, practised
another celebrated type of crescendo – a powerful rising
phrase which expands and hugely prolongs the cadence,
creating a double melodic and harmonic climax (what
Budden and Kerman have called a 'groundswell') – at
the emotional and musical apex of the great ensemble
numbers: their contemporaries found it 'electrifying'.

The early 19th century saw a revolution in the
development of voices with decisive implications for
drama. When Rossini began his career, the demise of the
castrato was complete. (Velluti, who played the leads in
Rossini's *Aureliano in Palmira*, Morlacchi's *Tebaldo e
Isolina* and Meyerbeer's *Il crociato in Egitto*, was a
curious relic when he left the stage at the age of 48 in
1829.) It was the female contralto, equally skilled in
serio and *buffo* roles, whether feminine or manly (but
decidedly not asexual), who was to inherit in Rossini's
operas the hermaphrodite quality of the castrato's voice,
with its dramatic pre-eminence, nobility, agility,
elegance and (as exploited in Cimarosa's day) its leaning
towards the pathetic. As with the Rossini contralto, who
with an upward extension of her range gave rise to the
Romantic soprano (Malibran and Pasta were initially
contraltos), the tenor – whether in a character role (Iago
and Rodrigo) or an amorous one (Otello) – arose from a
robust, deep baritonal register and by agility and the
resort to falsetto climbed to dizzying heights. (The voice
of Nozzari, who in *La donna del lago* took a *c″* at a leap
several times, seemed to Rossini 'suitable and
opportune' for Fernando in *La gazza ladra*, originally
conceived for a bass, Filippo Galli, the first Mustafà in
L'italiana and Assur in *Semiramide*.) A similar upward
evolution applies to the bass voice: it was, except in
name, already the modern baritone – a man's voice
plain and simple, representing the true, realistic driving
force in *Il barbiere di Siviglia* and later *Guillaume Tell*.

With Bellini and Donizetti the tenor was confirmed as
the foundation of the vocal and dramatic system: relatively unnatural in leaping towards the high range, it is
the idealizing and Romantic voice *par excellence*,
whether for elegiac emotion (as of Arturo in *I puritani*
who reaches a falsetto *f″*) or for fomenting rebellion (of

which Duprez' chest-voice *c″* in the Italian première of
Guglielmo Tell, 1831, was the emblem): 'It is precisely
the replacement of the 18th-century equation *love =
pleasure* by its Romantic counterpart *love = pain* that
leads the tenor to declare the ideal motives of his passion, and to eliminate among other things the sensuality
of his embellishments' (F. d'Amico). The counterpart to
the Romantic tenor as man of destiny and mournful
hero is the soprano: her ethereal voice gives full vent to
the fragile vulnerability of the woman in love who, deciding alone on sacrifice, finds the courage to sustain an
actual defeat that represents a moral victory. The baritone voice (initially known as 'basso cantante'), now
distinct from the deep bass, forms a counterbalance: a
noble man, mature, energetic, possibly wicked or
treacherous, the opposite of the tenor. He is the cornerstone of Verdi's operas: the clash between this virile,
paternal and realistically deeper voice and that of the
idealistic, impetuous tenor proves the sharper when bel
canto singing is disturbed by drama and emotional
impulse (with irregular breaths, sudden changes of
register and harsh unisons against a noisy orchestra).

The basic pattern of Romantic opera is the vocal
triangle which, while subject to variation and expansion
(by the addition of another soprano or another bass),
was time and again repeated: long before Bernard Shaw,
a Florentine reviewer deplored in 1852 the 'threadbare
plots' of Italian operas 'where the tenor loves a soprano
of whom the bass is jealous', contrasting them with the
great historical frescoes of Meyerbeer's *grands opéras*.
Verdi, however, enriched and complicated the pattern
by choosing subjects which add an ethical edge to the
conflict between social and emotional values (overturn-
ing, in *Rigoletto*, the relationship between moral worth
and the social hierarchy as far as baritone and tenor are
concerned) or which appealed to the audience's patriotism, in the sense of a group (the audience) conceptually
extended to an entire nation: the Verdi heroine,
romantically bent on sacrifice in her amorous destiny, is
willingly caught up in the struggle for liberty against
foreign foes (*Nabucco, Attila*) or against factional
tyranny or caste oppression (*Simon Boccanegra, Aida*).

(iv) After unification. With the formation of the kingdom of Italy in 1861 and the achievement of national
unity (with Rome as capital from 1870), the social and
cultural position of opera changed profoundly. For the
theatre-going élite, opera had been a substitute throughout the long political Risorgimento 'for a life dreamt of
but not lived' (Mila), a shared imaginary world of feelings and modes of conduct, and of exemplary ideals (not
however to be acted upon): this functioned as a potent
catalyst, even if only subconsciously. In the modern
state, *opera lirica* had now become the theatrical *locus*
of a desire for cultural modernity, along with the great
European powers: the more strongly the desire was
professed, the sharper the perception that the golden age
of Italian opera, economically and artistically, was near-
ing its end. The relationship with tradition was changed,
for the public and for the operatic world: the well-
established canon of the operatic repertory assured the
coexistence of the new with the old, of progress with a
sense of proprietorship. The search for novelty and the
systematic rejection of traditional formulae became, for
the first time, a rallying-point for librettists, composers
and journalists. Boito's *Mefistofele* (a fiasco in Milan in
1868, only moderately successful in the reworked version of 1875 for Bologna) was the first youthfully noisy

manifesto of a phenomenon unprecedented in Italian opera – an avant garde, determined to subvert convention and to seek the taste of the future rather than satisfy that of the present (Boito was involved in the so-called *scapigliatura* in Milan, an anticonformist literary movement akin to the Parisian *bohème*).

With Donizetti dead, Mercadante silent and Pacini worn out by endless work, Verdi's colossal preeminence in the 1850s and 60s – strengthened by foreign successes, by the Milan publishing industry's control over Italian theatres, and by the new copyright legislation (1865), to which Verdi, as a parliamentary deputy, had himself contributed – amounted to an absolute domination, unknown before, even in Rossini's day. The success of a handful of operas – Apolloni's *L'ebreo* (1855), De Ferrari's *Pipelè* (1855), Ponchielli's *I promessi sposi* (1856), Pedrotti's *Tutti in maschera* (1856), Petrella's *Jone* (1858) and *La contessa d'Amalfi* (1864), Cagnoni's *Michele Perrin* (1864), Usiglio's *Le educande di Sorrento* (1868) and Marchetti's *Ruy Blas* (1869) – could not jeopardize, and indeed confirmed, the overwhelming ascendancy of Verdi, which gave rise to a sort of 'father complex' in the Italian musical world, beginning with *Aida* (which had its Italian première in Milan in 1872), the opera which for many years everyone, including Verdi, thought would be his last. It was Verdi himself who twice broke through the pall which his own operas had cast over the last 30 years of the century, with that champion of renewal Boito, now turned librettist, at his side: *Otello* (1887) and *Falstaff* (1893) are among the ten or so truly successful Italian operas to illuminate the long twilight that followed *Aida*. They are a good deal more complex than Verdi's earlier operas, in a literary sense (their metrical and lexical sophistication), compositionally (their pliant, fragmented forms, the demands they make on vocal skill, their rich orchestral textures) and dramatically (in their idiosyncratic characterization and the strong musical and theatrical momentum, which can become tumultuous when contrasting events are juxtaposed, as in the Act 3 finale of *Otello* and the Act 1 finale of *Falstaff*). These works, products of an intense and protracted collaboration between composer and librettist, demand exceptional artistic and technical resources for their realization; they presuppose a degree of overall control that only the evolution of the modern conductor (established in Italy in the 1860s) could provide, while productions further depended on the 'disposizioni sceniche' which show a binding record of every detail of the staging.

The yearning for modernity that afflicted Italian culture after unification is best seen in the increasing weight that non-Italian opera assumed in the repertory, and in its supply of models and ideals worthy of emulation: this massive embracing of foreign opera was new and impinged deeply on the self-awareness of musicians and the public. The dominant models, in chronological order, were (beginning mainly in the 1860s) the *grand opéra* of Meyerbeer and Halévy, with Gounod's *Faust* in *dramma lirico* form (1862, Milan); Wagner's romantic operas, particularly *Lohengrin* (1871, Bologna); Bizet's *Carmen* as a *dramma lirico* (1879, Naples); and Massenet's operas – his two *opere-ballo Il re di Lahore* (1878, Turin) and *Erodiade* (1882, Milan), and the *dramma lirico Werther* (1895, Milan), were particularly popular. The *opera-ballo* was the Italian variant of *grand opéra*, with its shock-propelled action, its great choral scenes and *tableau* ensembles, picturesque

flavour drawing on the exotic and the historical, all sumptuously filled with choreographic and choral *divertissements* (a novelty in Italian opera, which had traditionally resisted the incorporation of dance, keeping ballet in isolated entr'actes): distinguished examples, besides *Aida*, are Gomes's *Il Guarany* (1870), Ponchielli's *La Gioconda* (1876), Puccini's *Le villi* (1884) and Catalani's *Loreley* (1890). From Wagner and his ideas, championed by such critics as the perspicacious Filippi and many other literary enthusiasts, Italians drew the idea of inspired melodic declamation and pervasive poeticizing of the drama, whether in a grand style (Wagner reconceived à la Meyerbeer, as in Franchetti's *Cristoforo Colombo*, 1892), or morbidly romantic (Catalani's *La Wally*, 1892) or indeed symbolic (Smareglia's *Oceàna*, 1903), while the use of leitmotif (especially by Puccini) mostly followed the example of Massenet's flexible and allusive variation. *Carmen*, in turn, became the direct progenitor of *verismo* in opera, which strives to portray in strong colours a slice of life, using 'low' subjects and the ruinous tumult of the instincts in erotic seduction.

The concept of *verismo* was ready to hand in the Franco-Italian literary debate of the 1880s (as early as 1884 Amintore Galli, editor of *Il teatro illustrato*, the organ of Sonzogno – the Italian publisher of Bizet and Massenet, and later of Mascagni and Leoncavallo – wrote a disquisition 'Dell'opera verista del Bizet'). The affiliation of *verismo* opera with literary *verismo* was bound to seem the more obvious as the phenomenon erupted in Mascagni's one-act *Cavalleria rusticana* (1890), drawn from the 1884 play by Verga (known as the Italian Zola), itself taken from a short story of 1880. But the operas of the Giovane Scuola – the name given, around 1892, to the *verismo* movement in music, to which Giordano (*Mala vita*, 1892; *Andrea Chénier*, 1896; *Fedora*, 1898) and Cilea (*Tilda*, 1892; *L'arlesiana*, 1897; *Adriana Lecouvreur*, 1902) also belonged – adhered only superficially to the social-psychological critical theories of literary *verismo*, which aimed to represent 'the facts pure and simple' (Verga) from within the action, without the author's intervention.

Musical *verismo* (an art 'wrought of slashes of the knife and fawnings, of criminal gangs and shrill chatterings, of blasphemies and entreaties' in the indignant words of the Wagner enthusiast E. Thovez, 1896) was concerned less with the 'logically necessary development of passions and actions towards catastrophe' than with the actual 'effect of the catastrophe', and thus with the ineluctable power of fate and the unbridled vehemence of passion in elementally erotic plots: hence the clear polarization of the key roles – the soprano as *femme fatale*, the tenor as victim who unsuccessfully rebels – and a preference for the short opera involving swift, fiery conflict. The *veristi* sought to enlist the audience's sympathies for the unfortunate lovers in a sometimes hysterical drama, often using wide-spanning melodies, an impetuous, discontinuous rhythmic flow that may often disrupt the harmonic pace, obsessively reiterated themes and successive peaks of melodic and sonic tension, with the orchestra reflecting the expression of the voices (it was often used to perorate a salient theme, a device introduced by Ponchielli in Act 3 of *La Gioconda* and picked up by Verdi at the end of *Otello* and by Puccini at the end of *La bohème*, 1896, and *Tosca*, 1900); they draw on hammered syllabification, forceful attack, and the sob and cry achieved by straining the top of the central register, on moments of vocal expansiveness and on the use of music within the action (in *Cavalleria rusticana*, stornellos, canzonas, prayers, toasts, canticles and hymns amount to almost half the score).

In doing this, however, Mascagni and the others made no attempt to develop an intrinsically realistic musical language. The popular nature of their dramatic subjects (limited to very few titles, and maintaining the taste for the exotic and the historical) never led them to draw on folk melody, still less on the phonetic structure of spoken language (nowhere among the *veristi*, nor elsewhere in Italian opera, with its literary background, is there a Janáček, a Falla or a Bartók). Equally, the insertion of music with an 18th-century flavour, in *Andrea Chénier* and *Adriana Lecouvreur*, is limited to stylistic pastiche, which homogenizes the materials. What is *veristico* in the dramatic strategy is the agonizing moment towards which the action is impelled: the dying hero is denied the catharsis of a swansong, and instead of the consolatory utterance with which Verdi's men and women bid farewell to the world, they are starkly snatched by death to blunt and unadorned *parlato*. The notion that life and art both give rise to death, dear to European decadentism, is sealed by the sudden breaking off of singing, that essential medium of all musical drama: while in *Pagliacci* life, or rather death, bursts howling into the fiction that is sung from theatre to theatre, and while in Act 3 of *Andrea Chénier* the shouting all but drowns the music, in *Adriana Lecouvreur* the famous actress's unsung declamation of a soliloquy from Racine's *Phèdre* abruptly turns into song for an outraged invective addressed to her rival, the princess, as though (in a remarkable reversal of function) the unforeseen return of the melody represents the destruction of life through art.

The person to venture furthest in the world where naturalism and decadence met was Puccini. The radical portrayal of love as intrinsically destructive and of death as the accomplishment of a senseless destiny is already to be found in *Manon Lescaut* (1893): the myth of the inconstant woman, elusive and devouring, as in Prévost's story or in Massenet's opera (*Manon*, 1884, which reached Italy only after Puccini's work appeared), gives way to a blind, fateful eroticism, an ever downward slide. The lovers are more (or perhaps less) than just morally individuated characters: they are the contrasting poles of an elemental discourse. It is symptomatic that Puccini should have wanted to delete the scenes of Des Grieux and Manon living together in poverty (and her subsequent betrayal), and Manon's returning to seduce Des Grieux in the seminary of St Sulpice (Acts 2 and 3.ii in Massenet): Puccini's is not a story of dissolute lovers but an elliptic account of four phases of a progressive mortal disintegration. The couple's love is persecuted (as is the sensibility of the audience) by recurrent themes in the orchestra and the voices, obsessively repeated and juxtaposed, but neither varied nor developed. Puccini breaks the narrative continuity, but he also transforms the Verdian metrical stereotypes into surging, wide-ranging and mostly diatonic melodic contours, dissolving the standard vocal forms into a propulsive musical prose except when they can be justified as music within the action or to establish an ambience; he aims to capture reality naturalistically, as an active process. To prevent the prostitutes' Act 3 embarkation at Le Havre (a scene created at Puccini's request) from descending into the 'ensemble across the forestage' beloved of 19th-century opera, with its obligatory assembly of opposed choruses and asides from the main roles, the librettist Illica (one of seven involved) had the idea of interweaving the principal characters' dialogue with the rough comments of the townsfolk with the roll-call of the prostitutes as they go on board, producing an unprecedented natural vitality and motion; to the pulse of the ostinato – rhythmic and melodic, but above all dramatic – the tension increases as the final parting approaches.

In subsequent operas, too, Puccini exploits suspense at culminating moments and the audience's identification with the characters in their agonized expectation of the inevitable. Thus it is for Mimì's death in *La bohème*, the mock execution of Cavaradossi in *Tosca*, the card game in *La fanciulla del West* and the solving of the riddles in *Turandot*. Such suspense was later to be codified by the cinema, the art form which was to inherit the wealth of ideas and techniques of opera most directly, and which in Italy from the 1920s was to take opera's place within popular culture. But the working out of Puccini's naturalistic musical dramaturgy in the pre-cinema era was no simple matter, and the bewilderment and annoyance felt by his librettists is symptomatic. Even his publisher, Giulio Ricordi, took exception to Act 3 of *Tosca*, and particularly the duet: 'A fragmented duet, in short lines which diminish the characters ... three passages in succession, but broken off and hence ineffective'. But that was precisely what Puccini wanted (and got) – simplicity, 'little episodes', illusions of tenderness and elation on the edge of moral transgression, the dream of youth that becomes exhausted and fades without seeking or achieving adulthood: such fragments of naturalistic observation are welded into an agonizing unitary picture by means of a montage of images and a musical syntax designed to be tenuous and yielding. Of the national characteristics of the Italian *fin de siècle*, the clear but 'weary' melodies of Puccini's poor heroes embody one above all, 'victimism' – the predisposition to a kind of failure that is both actual and (unlike in Verdi) moral.

Aestheticism and decadentism, implicit from the outset, are accentuated in *La fanciulla del West*, which, as Aldrich observed after the New York première in 1910:

involves a more or less detached and formless paragraphic, sometimes a rapid and staccato vocal utterance, projected against an equally expeditious and hastily sketched orchestral background, to which is given the task of accentuating, emphasizing and intensifying – if it can – the significance of the dialogue with points or broad stretches of color, thematic fragments, quickly shifting, kaleidoscopic harmonies.

These themes culminate in *Turandot* (1926), where the drama is consumed in deadly dissension between unshakeable and incompatible human and musical worlds: at one extreme, a chillingly sadistic modal and timbral *chinoiserie* for Turandot, with her terrible, cruel ceremonial display (involving, too, the revival of clearly perceptible 19th-century closed forms) and, at the other, a sorrowful transcaucasian exoticism for Prince Calaf and the slave-girl Liù, from which Puccini's characteristic melos arises like death's release.

(v) Since World War I. With *verismo* burnt out and Puccini's naturalism transformed into decadentism, Italian opera at the beginning of the 20th century presented an eclectic and rambling picture. The search continued for popularity along the lines of Mascagni and Puccini, but this was ever harder to come by (even

Mascagni, after his *verismo* phase, vainly tried every approach and style). But among younger composers cultivating spiritual and cultural refinement there spread an experimentalism in avowed opposition to the sloppy immediacy of 'commercial' opera and the historical 'falsity' of Puccini's work, which in a famous 1912 pamphlet Torrefranca condemned as 'international' opera, a degenerate departure from the 'authentic' Italian tradition – that of Renaissance polyphony and the instrumental sonata of the 17th and 18th centuries – which had been trampled underfoot in the 19th century by the triumphant operatic monoculture. This rediscovery of the remoter past of Italian music, stimulated by aestheticism as well as by scholarship, drew heavily on the prevailing enthusiasm for the writings of D'Annunzio in literary, artistic and political circles before World War I. D'Annunzio was in contact with all the major Italian opera composers: he supplied Mascagni with the Renaissance-flavoured libretto for his most pretentious opera, *Parisina* (1913); he planned more than one opera plot with Puccini (these were never realized); he allowed Franchetti, Zandonai and the young Pizzetti (who in 1908 had composed incidental music for his tragedy *La nave*) respectively to set, virtually unaltered, the plays *La figlia di Iorio* (1906), *Francesca da Rimini* (1914) and *Fedra* (1915), rare examples of a species (identical with the German *Literaturoper*) otherwise alien to Italian opera and attempted previously only by the eclectic Mascagni in *Guglielmo Ratcliff* (1895) to a translation of Heine's tragedy; and finally, with the young G. F. Malipiero, he oversaw an important series of editions of early music. These composers reacted in different ways to D'Annunzio. Mascagni and Zandonai were driven to musical sumptuousness, melodic excess and antiquarian colour (in Act 1 of *Francesca da Rimini* the long scene of love at first sight, all glances and nothing uttered, takes place against an orchestral background enriched with 'ancient' instruments); Pizzetti responded by retreating to a simple vocality, with austere, ascetic syllabic writing and a contemplative melodic abstinence, the sound reduced to a rarefied halo of timbre and harmony covering the words, whose every nuance is observed and whose hellenic nudity is revealed by a monotonous recitation (reminiscent of Debussy's *Pelléas*).

While Malipiero's musical and dramatic imagination avoids such shriven severity, it is nevertheless given to a radical pessimism and is often deliberately bizarre and troubling in its renunciation of narrative and plot. Its contemplative gaze fixes on musical objects in themselves: the *Sette canzoni* (1920, Paris), seven miniatures taking three-quarters of an hour, are both musical and pantomimic in their effect, which results from a clash of different songs, on and off stage, mostly settings of Renaissance poetry; his ghostly *Torneo notturno* (1931, Munich) is permeated by the ostinato singing of a moralistic memento of human vanity, to poems by Serafino Aquilano, whose simple scansion is disrupted by a confusion of its relation to the strong beat of the bar. In Malipiero's best theatrical works, the aesthetic and the expressionistic impulses approach one another, collide and trigger off a tragic effect: the evocation of unblemished ancient beauty set against the fatal threat of decay. The search for abstract categories, for allegorical personifications and figures stripped of psychological individuation, led Malipiero to draw on the theatrical work of two Venetian spirits, Monteverdi and Goldoni, but reducing it to the fable in the first case

and the mask in the second, so making the realistic component unnatural. This merely evocative and metaphysical debt to Goldoni is quite remote from the taste for vernacular comedy and costume which, at the height of a flourishing *fin de siècle* Venetian neo-rococo, had given rise to Wolf-Ferrari's *Le donne curiose* and *I quattro rusteghi* (1903 and 1906, Munich), forebears in turn of a long revival of comic operas which reached a height of Rossinian lightness and freshness in Rota's *Il cappello di paglia di Firenze* (composed in 1946 and given in Palermo in 1955). Malipiero's theatrical work – like that of Casella (*La donna serpente*, after Gozzi, 1932) and the expatriate Busoni (*Arlecchino* and *Turandot*, 1917, Zürich, reaching Italy only in 1940) – had a limited impact on Italian operatic life under fascism, which continued wearily on a post-*verismo* and post-Puccini track.

From the 1930s, there was no longer in any real sense a specifically Italian operatic tradition. While operas certainly continued to be composed in Italy, there was no entity that could be called 'Italian opera'. The crisis was twofold, affecting demand as well as supply. Throughout the world opera entered a critical phase as the post-tonal vocabulary of contemporary music undermined the very basis of cantabile, on which opera had always depended, and nowhere more clearly than in Italy; there was also a crisis of an art that was wedded, politically as well as aesthetically, to such institutions as the publicly subsidized opera houses, which were increasingly concerned with the preservation of the traditional repertory and impervious to modern works, and which thus, in the view of the avant garde, deserved more than ever to be challenged. Official incentives for the production of new operas and special seasons (like the Festival di Musica Contemporanea affiliated to the Venice Biennale from 1930 and the Teatro delle Novità at Bergamo from 1937) by no means remedied such contradictions, but they did at least ensure a certain regular output, most of it ephemeral and inflexibly eclectic.

After World War II high points in contemporary Italian opera were few. Particularly striking, though, is the figure of Dallapiccola, whose *Il prigioniero* (1950, Florence; composed from 1944 onwards), a horrifyingly sinister expressionistic fable of fascist tyranny, gains its agonizing musical potency from the use of 12-note technique, its first use by an Italian opera composer but kept, so to speak, skin deep (the series are sometimes audible, and indeed integrated into a melodic context that owes much to Verdi). Attendance each summer at the Darmstadt Ferienkurse – an obligatory pilgrimage for the young Italian avant garde of the 1950s – set an ideological and technical seal on the final draining dry of Italian opera: with its propensity for immediate expressiveness and its large-scale forms, opera was constitutionally resistant to Webernian serialism, pointillism and the aleatory. In this context, forms of musical theatre prevailed in which the narrative, when it existed, was devoted to civil and political commitment (as in Nono's *Intolleranza 1960* and *Al gran sole carico d'amore*, 1961 and 1975), or was reduced to a pretext for intellectualism (as in Berio's *Opera*, an 'opera aperta' from an idea by Umberto Eco served up as a pastiche, in which images of death and exhaustion are intertwined, from the sinking of the *Titanic* to Monteverdi's *Orpheus*), or functioned as a weak support for a luxuriant, voluptuous and mournful ceremonial (as in Bussotti's 'mistero da camera' *Passion selon Sade*, 1965, and *Lorenzaccio*, 1972, after Musset

– which successfully cloaks the radical language of serialism with histrionically exhibitionistic exuberance and effete visual elegance, but at the same time points towards the *Gesamtkunstwerk*, open to dance, pantomime and cinema).

In 1984 two works appeared which epitomize, in their titles, the position in which Italian musical theatre finds itself as the millennium ends. In *Un re in ascolto*, Italo Calvino and Berio use the Shakespearian figure of Prospero in the guise of a dying impresario to display a hallucinatory meditation on the impotence of the theatre, musical and otherwise; in *Prometeo*, intended for an extra-theatrical setting, Nono and the philosopher M. Cacciari (using texts from Hölderlin, Benjamin, Nietzsche and Rilke) weave what the subtitle calls a 'tragedy of listening', the tragedy of an intellectual faculty destroyed by the alienation of contemporary society. An ephemeral 'neo-romantic' trend (Ferrero, Tutino) enjoyed something of a success, but not an enduring one, in the 1980s.

In the last half-century, with the internationalization of the repertory and of the movement of singers, and with the performance of opera – in Italy as elsewhere – largely reduced to a living museum, an Italian strand may be discerned more clearly than anywhere in the tradition of production and scene design, which in Italy had long remained (until the 1960s) entrusted to the highly expert but unadventurous directors and scene designers permanently affiliated to individual theatres (for example the director of scene design Mario Frigerio at La Scala, 1930–62, and the scene designer Nicola Benois, there 1936–70). Controversial but culturally important were the experiments at the Maggio Musicale in Florence – the home since 1933 of many revivals of ancient operas – where the *mise en scène* was entrusted to painters such as Casorati, De Chirico and Savinio. The modern 'director's opera', using the production as the vehicle for a conscious critical re-reading of the musical and dramatic text, arose in Italy in the mid-1950s, and – with the militant higher criticism wielded by musicologists such as D'Amico and Mila, and distinguished dilettantes such as the poets Montale and Vigolo – contributed significantly to the returning to opera of something that the unvarying round of productions had largely taken from it: a seal of intellectual dignity among a cultivated and lettered public. Leading pioneers in director's opera were two film directors of a neo-realist bent, Luchino Visconti (his 1954–5 productions at La Scala with Callas were memorable and seminal) and later his former assistant Franco Zeffirelli (admired for the vividness of his great crowd scenes), as well as two directors from the prose theatre, Giorgio Strehler (of a 'critical', Brechtian bent) and later Luca Ronconi (who aims to make the dead conventions of opera collide with the spatial and gestural provocations of contemporary theatre). Italy – where the audience's relationship with opera is mostly of an ingenuous, direct kind – has offered relatively little success to the vogue for the irreverent, topicalized production, such as that mounted by the novelist Alberto Arbasino in the extra-terrestrial *Carmen* which caused a sensation in Bologna in 1967. More successful is a certain elegant mannerism based on a pastiche of historical figured styles, freely evoked and combined (as in the work of Pier Luigi Pizzi), and a search for relationships, not always pertinent from a historical point of view, between opera and the tradition of Italian popular theatre (Roberto De Simone).

For further information on operatic life in the country's principal centres *see* ALESSANDRIA; ANCONA; ASSISI; BARGA; BARI; BATIGNANO; BERGAMO; BOLOGNA; BOLZANO; BRESCIA; BUSSETO; CAGLIARI; CASALMAGGIORE; CATANIA; CITTÀ DI CASTELLO; CREMONA; FAENZA; FANO; FERRARA; FLORENCE; FOLIGNO; GENOA; GUBBIO; LIVORNO; LUCCA; LUGO; MACERATA; MANTUA; MARTINA FRANCA; MESSINA; MILAN; MODENA; MONTEPULCIANO; NAPLES; ORVIETO; PADUA; PALERMO; PARMA; PERUGIA; PESARO; PIACENZA; PIAZZOLA SUL BRENTA; PISA; RAVENNA; REGGIO EMILIA; ROME; SIENA; SPOLETO; TORRE DEL LAGO; TREVISO; TRIESTE; TURIN; UDINE; VENICE; VERONA; VICENZA; and TRAVELLING TROUPES, §1.

*

*In view of the extent of the literature
on Italian opera, the present
bibliography covers only writings since 1950.*

GENERAL

StiegerO

U. Rolandi: *Il libretto per musica attraverso i tempi* (Rome, 1951)

F. d'Amico: *I casi della musica* (Milan, 1962)

F. Mancini: *Scenografia italiana dal rinascimento all'età romantica* (Milan, 1966)

F. Mancini, M. T. Muraro and E. Povoledo, eds.: *Illusione e pratica teatrale: proposte per una lettura dello spazio scenico dagli intermedi fiorentini all'opera comica veneziana* (Vicenza, 1975)

S. Leopold: 'Bibliographie der italienischen Literatur zur Szenographie des Musiktheaters', *AnMc*, no. 17 (1976), 296–309

A. L. Bellina: 'Rassegna di studi sul libretto d'opera (1965–1975)', *Lettere italiane*, xxix (1977), 81–105

F. Degrada: *Il palazzo incantato: studi sulla tradizione del melodramma dal barocco al romanticismo* (Fiesole, 1979)

A. Giovine: *Bibliografia di teatri musicali italiani* (Bari, 1982)

F. Lippmann, ed.: 'Die stilistische Entwicklung der italienischen Musik zwischen 1770 und 1830 und ihre Beziehungen zum Norden', *AnMc*, no. 21 (1982) [whole issue]

R. Celletti: *Storia del belcanto* (Fiesole, 1983; Eng. trans., as *A History of Bel Canto*, 1991)

A. L. Bellina: *L'ingegnosa congiunzione: 'melos' e immagine nella 'favola' per musica* (Florence, 1984)

M. Mila: *I costumi della 'Traviata'* (Pordenone, 1984)

A. Asor Rosa, ed.: *Letteratura italiana*, vi: *Teatro, musica, tradizione dei classici* (Turin, 1986), 356–437 [incl. L. Bianconi: 'Il cinquecento e il seicento', 318–63; R. di Benedetto: 'Il settecento e l'ottocento', 365–410; S. Sablich: 'Il novecento: dalla "generazione dell'80" a oggi', 411–37]

W. Osthoff: 'Musica e versificazione: funzioni del verso poetico nell'opera italiana', *La drammaturgia musicale*, ed. L. Bianconi (Bologna, 1986), 125–41

L'opera tra Venezia e Parigi: Venice 1986

L. Bianconi and G. Pestelli, eds.: *Storia dell'opera italiana*, iv: *Il sistema produttivo e le sue competenze* (Turin, 1987)

N. Pirrotta: *Scelte poetiche di musicisti: teatro, poesia e musica da Willaert a Malipiero* (Venice, 1987)

J. Rosselli and others: 'Condizioni materiali e forme di trasmissione del sapere musicale: il caso delle scuole di canto', *IMSCR, xiv Bologna 1987*, ii, 171–225

'Literature and Opera', *Italica*, lxiv/4 (1987) [whole issue]

L. Bianconi and G. Pestelli, eds.: *Storia dell'opera italiana*, v: *La spettacolarità* (Turin, 1988)

L. Bianconi and G. Pestelli, eds.: *Storia dell'opera italiana*, vi: *Teorie e tecniche, immagini e fantasmi* (Turin, 1988)

W. Dean: *Essays on Opera* (Oxford, 1990)

Opera & Libretto, i (Florence, 1990)

C. Sartori: *I libretti italiani a stampa dalle origini al 1800* (Cuneo, 1990–)

F. d'Amico: *Un ragazzino all'Augusteo: scritti musicali* (Turin, 1991)

D. Kimbell: *Italian Opera* (Cambridge, 1991)

J. Rosselli: *Singers of Italian Opera: the History of a Profession* (Cambridge, 1992)

L. Bianconi and G. Pestelli, eds.: *Storia dell'opera italiana*, ii: *Lo spazio europeo* (Turin, 1993)

17TH CENTURY

N. Pirrotta: 'Temperaments and Tendencies in the Florentine Camerata', *MQ*, xl (1954), 169–89

——: ' "Commedia dell'arte" and Opera', *MQ*, xli (1955), 305–24

H. S. Powers: '"Il Serse trasformato"', *MQ*, xlvii (1961), 481–92; xlviii (1962), 73–92

W. Osthoff: 'Maske und Musik: die Gestaltwerdung der Oper in Venedig', *Castrum peregrini*, lxv (1964), 10–49; It. trans. in *NRMI*, i (1967), 16–44

C. Molinari: *Le nozze degli dèi: un saggio sul grande spettacolo italiano nel seicento* (Rome, 1968)

C. V. Palisca: 'The Alterati of Florence, Pioneers in the Theory of Dramatic Music', *New Looks at Italian Opera: Essays in Honor of Donald J. Grout* (Ithaca, 1968), 9–38

N. Pirrotta: *Li due Orfei: da Poliziano a Monteverdi* (Turin, 1969, 2/1975; Eng. trans., 1981)

H. M. Brown: 'How Opera Began: an Introduction to Jacopo Peri's "Euridice" (1600)', *The Late Italian Renaissance, 1525–1630*, ed. E. Cochrane (New York, 1970), 401–43

C. V. Palisca: 'The "Camerata Fiorentina": a Reappraisal', *Studi musicali*, i (1972), 203–36

Venezia e il melodramma nel seicento: Venice 1972

L. Bianconi: 'Dalla "Finta pazza" alla "Veremonda": storie di Febiarmonici', *RIM*, x (1975), 379–454; Eng. trans. in *DMV*, i [forthcoming]

S. Leopold: '"Quelle bazzicature poetiche, appellate ariette": Dichtungsformen in der frühen italienischen Oper (1600–1640)', *HJbMw*, iii (1978), 101–41

B. Russano Hanning: 'Glorious Apollo: Poetic and Political Themes in the First Opera', *Renaissance Quarterly*, xxxii (1979), 485–513

F. W. Sternfeld: 'The Birth of Opera: Ovid, Poliziano and the "lieto fine"', *AnMc*, no. 19 (1979), 30–51

B. Russano Hanning: *Of Poetry and Music's Power* (Ann Arbor, 1980)

S. Leopold: 'Die Hierarchie Arkadiens: soziale Strukturen in den frühen Pastoralopern und ihre Ausdrucksformen', *Schweizer Jb für Musikwissenschaft*, new ser., i (1981), 71–92

L. Bianconi: *Il seicento* (Turin, 1982, 2/1991; Eng. trans. as *Music in the Seventeenth Century*, 1987), chap. 4

A. L. Bellina and T. Walker: 'Il melodramma: poesia e musica nell'esperienza teatrale', *Storia della cultura veneta, iv/1: Il seicento*, ed. G. Arnaldi and M. Pastore Stocchi (Vicenza, 1983), 409–32

P. Fabbri and A. Pompilio, eds.: *Il corago, o vero Alcune osservazioni per metter bene in scena le composizioni drammatiche* (Florence, 1983)

L. Bianconi and T. Walker: 'Production, Consumption and Political Function of Seventeenth-Century Opera', *Early Music History*, iv (1984), 209–96

N. Pirrotta: *Music and Culture in Italy from the Middle Ages to the Baroque* (Cambridge, MA, 1984) [essays]

C. V. Palisca: *Humanism in Italian Renaissance Musical Thought* (New Haven and London, 1985), 408–33

R. Strohm: 'Italienische Barockoper in Deutschland: eine Forschungsaufgabe', *Festschrift Martin Ruhnke zum 65. Geburtstag* (Stuttgart and Neuhausen, 1985), 348–63

R. Katz: *Divining the Powers of Music: Aesthetic Theory and the Origins of Opera* (New York, 1986)

S. Harris: 'The Significance of Ovid's "Metamorphoses" in Early Seventeenth-Century Opera', *MR*, xlviii (1988), 12–20

P. Weiss: 'Opera and Neoclassical Dramatic Criticism in the Seventeenth Century', *Studies in the History of Music*, ii (New York, 1988), 1–30

M. G. Accorsi: 'Problemi testuali dei libretti d'opera fra sei e settecento', *Giornale storico della letteratura italiana*, clxvi (1989), 212–25

P. Fabbri: *Il secolo cantante: per una storia del libretto d'opera nel seicento* (Bologna, 1990)

——: 'Drammaturgia spagnuola e drammaturgia francese nell'opera italiana del sei-settecento', *AcM*, lxiii (1991), 11–14

E. Rosand: *Opera in Seventeenth-Century Venice: the Creation of a Genre* (Berkeley, 1991)

18TH CENTURY

R. Giazotto: *Poesia melodrammatica e pensiero critico nel settecento* (Milan, 1952)

A. Yorke-Long: *Music at Court: Four Eighteenth-Century Studies* (London, 1954)

N. Burt: 'Opera in Arcadia', *MQ*, xli (1955), 145–70

E. Battisti: 'Per una indagine sociologica sui librettisti napoletani buffi del settecento', *Letteratura*, viii (Rome, 1960), 114–64

H. Hucke: 'Die neapolitanische Tradition in der Oper', *IMSCR*, viii New York 1961, i, 253–77

F. A. Gallo: 'L'estetica dell'opera buffa nel saggio sulla "Musica imitativa teatrale" di Matteo Borsa', *RaM*, xxxii (1962), 56–65

D. Heartz: 'From Garrick to Gluck: the Reform of Theatre and Opera in the Mid-Eighteenth Century', *PRMA*, xciv (1967–8), 111–27

R. S. Freeman: 'Apostolo Zeno's Reform of the Libretto', *JAMS*, xxi (1968), 321–41

E. Surian: *A Checklist of Writings on 18th-century French and Italian Opera* (Hackensack, NJ, 1970)

S. Kunze: *Don Giovanni vor Mozart: die Tradition der Don-Giovanni-Opern im italienischen Buffa-Theater des 18. Jahrhunderts* (Munich, 1972)

M. F. Robinson: *Naples and Neapolitan Opera* (Oxford, 1972)

W. Osthoff: 'Die Opera buffa', *Gattungen der Musik in Einzeldarstellungen: Gedenkschrift Leo Schrade* (Berne and Munich, 1973), 678–743

Venezia e il melodramma nel settecento: Venice 1973–5

A. L. [Saletta] Bellina: 'Personaggio e linguaggio nel libretto comico del '700', *Atti dell'Istituto veneto di scienze, lettere ed arti*, cxxxiii (1974–5), 331–45; cxxxiv (1975–6), 1–24

R. Strohm: 'Italienische Opernarien des frühen settecento (1720–1730)', *AnMc*, no. 16 (1976) [whole issue]

D. Heartz: 'The Creation of the Buffo Finale in Italian Opera', *PRMA*, civ (1977–8), 67–78

——: 'Mozart and his Italian Contemporaries: 'La clemenza di Tito', *MJb* 1978–9, 275–93; repr. in *Mozart's Operas* (Berkeley, 1990), 299–317

R. Strohm: *Die italienische Oper im 18. Jahrhundert* (Wilhelmshaven, 1979; It. trans., enlarged, as *L'opera italiana nel settecento*, 1991)

C. E. Troy: *The Comic Intermezzo* (Ann Arbor, 1979)

P. Weiss: 'Pier Jacopo Martello on Opera (1715): an Annotated Translation', *MQ*, lxvi (1980), 378–403

R. S. Freeman: *Opera Without Drama: Currents of Change in Italian Opera, 1675–1725* (Ann Arbor, 1981)

H. Hucke: 'Die Entstehung der Opera buffa', *GfMKB: Bayreuth 1981*, 78–85

L. Bianconi and G. Morelli, eds.: *Antonio Vivaldi: teatro musicale, cultura e società* (Florence, 1982)

'Crosscurrents and the Mainstream of Italian Serious Opera, 1730–1790' *Studies in Music* [U. of W. Ontario], vii/1–2 (1982)

G. Muresu: *La parola cantata: studi sul melodramma italiano del settecento* (Rome, 1982)

F. Piperno: 'Buffe e buffi (considerazioni sulla professionalità degli interpreti di scene buffe ed intermezzi)', *RIM*, xvii (1982), 240–84

P. Simonelli: 'Lingua e dialetto nel teatro musicale napoletano del '700', *Musica e cultura a Napoli dal XV al XIX secolo: Naples 1982*, 225–37

G. Folena: *L'italiano in Europa: esperienze linguistiche del settecento* (Turin, 1983)

F. Lippmann: 'Haydn e l'opera buffa: tre confronti con opere italiane coeve sullo stesso testo', *NRMI*, xvii (1983), 223–46

H. Lühning: '"Titus"-Vertonungen im 18. Jahrhundert: Untersuchungen zur Tradition der Opera seria von Hasse bis Mozart', *AnMc*, no. 20 (1983) [whole issue]

P. Gallarati: *Musica e maschera: il libretto italiano del settecento* (Turin, 1984)

P. Weiss: 'Venetian Commedia dell'Arte "Operas" in the Age of Vivaldi', *MQ*, lxx (1984), 195–217

L'opera italiana a Vienna prima di Metastasio: Venice 1984

A. L. Bellina and B. Brizi: 'Il melodramma', *Storia della cultura veneta, v/1: Il settecento*, ed. G. Arnaldi and M. Pastore Stocchi (Vicenza, 1985), 337–400

D. Goldin: *La vera fenice: librettisti e libretti tra sette e ottocento* (Turin, 1985)

R. Strohm: *Essays on Handel and Italian Opera* (Cambridge, 1985)

R. Verti: 'The "Indice de' teatrali spettacoli", Milan, Venice, Rome 1764–1823', *Periodica musica*, iii (1985), 1–7; Fr. trans., abridged, in *FAM*, xxxii (1985), 209–11

P. Weiss: 'La diffusione del repertorio operistico nell'Italia del settecento: il caso dell'opera buffa', *Civiltà teatrale e settecento emiliano: Reggio Emilia 1985*, 241–56

S. Henze-Döhring: 'Opera seria, Opera buffa und Mozarts "Don Giovanni": zur Gattungskonvergenz in der italienischen Oper des 18. Jahrhunderts', *AnMc*, no.24 (1986) [whole issue]

M. Hunter: 'The Fusion and Juxtaposition of Genres in Opera Buffa 1770–1800: Anelli and Piccinni's "Griselda"', *ML*, lxvii (1986), 363–80

M. T. Muraro, ed.: *Metastasio e il mondo musicale* (Florence, 1986)

F. Degrada: 'La commedia per musica a Napoli nella prima metà del settecento', *IMSCR, xiv Bologna 1987*, iii, 263–74

M. P. McClymonds: '"La morte di Semiramide, ossia La vendetta di Nino" and the Restoration of Death and Tragedy to the Italian Operatic Stage in the 1780s and 90s', *IMSCR, xiv Bologna 1987*, iii, 285–92

G. Mangini: 'Le passioni, la virtù, la morale nella concezione tardosettecentesca dell'opera metastasiana', *RIM, xxii* (1987), 114–44

R. Strohm: '"Tragédie" into "Dramma per musica"', *Informazioni e studi vivaldiani*, ix (1988), 14–24; x (1989), 57–101; xi (1990), 11–25; xii (1991), 47–74

B. M. Antolini: 'Editori, copisti, commercio della musica in Italia: 1770–1800', *Studi musicali*, xviii (1989), 273–375

M. T. Muraro and D. Bryant, eds.: *I vicini di Mozart*, i: *Il teatro musicale tra sette e ottocento*; ii: *La farsa musicale veneziana (1750–1810)* (Florence, 1989)

J. Platoff: 'Musical and Dramatic Structure in the Opera Buffa Finale', *JM*, vii (1989), 191–229

J. Joly: *Dagli Elisi all'inferno: il melodramma tra Italia e Francia dal 1730 al 1850* (Florence, 1990)

J. Platoff: 'The Buffa Aria in Mozart's Vienna', *COJ*, ii (1990), 99–120

M. F. Robinson: 'The Da Capo Aria Seria as Symbol of Rationality', *La musica come linguaggio universale*, ed. R. Pozzi (Florence, 1990), 51–63

M. Hunter: 'Some Representations of *opera seria* in *opera buffa*', *COJ*, iii (1991), 89–108

F. Lippmann: 'Die Entwicklung der "Aria marziale" in der italienischen und französischen Oper im zeitlichen Umkreis der französischen Revolution', *Musica senza aggettivi: studi per Fedele d'Amico* (Florence, 1991), 253–96

EARLY 19TH CENTURY (TO VERDI)

F. Schlitzer: *Mondo teatrale dell'ottocento* (Naples, 1954)

M. Mila: 'La vita della musica nell'ottocento italiano', *Belfagor*, xii (1957), 485–505

T. Serafin and A. Toni: *Stile, tradizioni e convenzioni del melodramma italiano del settecento e dell'ottocento* (Milan, 1958)

G. Gavazzeni: *Problemi di tradizione dinamico-fraseologica e critica testuale, in Verdi e in Puccini* (Milan, 1961)

L. Dallapiccola: 'Parole e musica nel melodramma', *QRaM*, no.2 (1965), 117–39; rev. in *Appunti, incontri, meditazioni* (Milan, 1970), 5–28; Eng. trans. in *The Verdi Companion*, ed. W. Weaver and M. Chusid (New York, 1979), 193–215

W. F. Kümmel: 'Aus der Frühzeit der Mozart-Pflege in Italien', *AnMc*, no. 7 (1969), 145–63

F. Lippmann: 'Vincenzo Bellini und die italienische Opera seria seiner Zeit: Studien über Libretto, Arienform und Melodik', *AnMc*, no. 6 (1969) [whole issue]; It. trans., rev., in M. R. Adamo and F. Lippmann: *Vincenzo Bellini* (Turin, 1981), 313–555; see also *JAMS*, xxiv (1971), 301–6; xxv (1972), 280–83; xxvi (1973), 175–7

——: 'Zum Verhältnis von Libretto und Musik in der italienischen Opera seria der ersten Hälfte des 19. Jahrhunderts', *GfMKB: Bonn 1970*, 162–8

J. Budden: *The Operas of Verdi* (London, 1973–81, 2/1992)

L. Baldacci: *Libretti d'opera* (Florence, 1974)

B. Bentivoglio: 'Preliminari sul linguaggio dei libretti nel primo ottocento', *Italianistica*, iv (1975), 330–41

R. A. Moreen: *Integration of Text Forms and Musical Forms in Verdi's Early Operas* (Ann Arbor, 1975)

A. Fabrizi: 'Riflessi del linguaggio tragico alfieriano nei libretti d'opera ottocenteschi', *Studi e problemi di critica testuale*, no.12 (Bologna, 1976), 135–55

J. Mitchell: *The Walter Scott Operas: an Analysis of Operas Based on the Works of Sir Walter Scott* (Birmingham, AL, 1977)

G. Pestelli, ed.: *Il melodramma italiano dell'ottocento: studi e ricerche per Massimo Mila* (Turin, 1977)

F. Lippmann, ed.: 'Mozart und Italien: Rom 1974', *AnMc*, no.18 (1978) [whole issue]

J. Budden: 'Verdi and the Contemporary Italian Operatic Scene', *The Verdi Companion*, ed. W. Weaver and M. Chusid (New York, 1979), 67–105

B. Cagli: 'Verdi and the Business of Writing Operas', *The Verdi Companion*, ed. W. Weaver and M. Chusid (New York, 1979), 106–20

A. Ziino: 'Luigi Romanelli ed il mito del classicismo nell'opera italiana del primo ottocento', *Chigiana*, xxxvi (1979), 173–215

M. G. Accorsi: 'Il melodramma melodrammatico', *Sigma*, xiii (1980), 109–27

W. Weaver: *The Golden Century of Italian Opera from Rossini to Puccini: a Documentary Study* (London, 1980)

M. Ambrose: 'Walter Scott, Italian Opera and Romantic Stage-Setting', *Italian Studies*, xxxvi (1981), 58–78

D. R. B. Kimbell: *Verdi in the Age of Italian Romanticism* (Cambridge, 1981)

F. Portinari: *Pari siamo! Io la lingua, egli ha il pugnale: storia del melodramma ottocentesco attraverso i suoi libretti* (Turin, 1981)

M. Conati and M. Pavarani, eds.: *Orchestre in Emilia Romagna nell'ottocento e novecento* (Parma, 1982) [mainly on opera orchestras]

E. Surian: 'Organizzazione, gestione, politica teatrale e repertori operistici a Napoli e in Italia, 1800–1820', *Musica e cultura a Napoli dal XV al XIX secolo: Naples 1982*, 317–67

S. Henze-Döhring: '"Combinammo l'ossatura ...": Voltaire und die Librettistik des frühen Ottocento', *Mf*, xxxvi (1983), 113–27

J. Rosselli: 'Verdi e la storia della retribuzione del compositore italiano', *Studi verdiani*, ii (1983), 11–28

J. Black: *The Italian Romantic Libretto: a Study of Salvadore Cammarano* (Edinburgh, 1984)

J. Rosselli: *The Opera Industry in Italy from Cimarosa to Verdi: the Role of the Impresario* (Cambridge, 1984; It. trans., with biographical appx, as *L'impresario d'opera: arte e affari nel teatro musicale italiano dell'ottocento*, 1985)

S. L. Balthazar: *Evolving Conventions in Italian Serious Opera: Scene Structure in the Works of Rossini, Bellini, Donizetti and Verdi, 1810–1850* (Ann Arbor, 1985)

J. Maehder: '"Banda sul palco": variable Besetzungen in der Bühnenmusik der italienischen Oper des 19. Jahrhunderts als Relikte alter Besetzungstraditionen?', *Alte Musik als ästhetische Gegenwart: Stuttgart 1985*, ii, 293–310

R. Verti: 'Dieci anni di studi sulle fonti per la storia materiale dell'opera italiana nell'ottocento', *RIM*, xx (1985), 124–63

P. Weiss: '"Sacred Bronzes": Paralipomena to an Essay by Dallapiccola', *19th Century Music*, ix (1985–6), 42–9

A. L. Bellina and B. Brizi: 'Il melodramma e la musica strumentale', *Storia della cultura veneta*, vi: *Dall'età napoleonica alla prima guerra mondiale*, ed. G. Arnaldi and M. Pastore Stocchi (Vicenza, 1986), 429–60

F. Lippmann: *Versificazione italiana e ritmo musicale: i rapporti tra verso e musica nell'opera italiana dell'ottocento* (Naples, 1986); Ger. orig. in *AnMc*, no. 12 (1973), 253–69; no.14 (1973), 324–410; no.15 (1975), 298–333

G. W. Harwood: 'Verdi's Reform of the Italian Opera Orchestra', *19th Century Music*, x (1986–7), 108–34

G. Tomlinson: 'Italian Romanticism and Italian Opera: an Essay in their Affinities', *19th Century Music*, x (1986–7) 43–60

H. R. Cohen, M. Conati and others: 'L'opéra italien du dix-neuvième siècle à travers la presse contemporaine', *IMSCR, xiv Bologna 1987*, ii, 7–18 (expanded, with statistics, in *Periodica musica*, vi, 1988; vii, 1989)

F. Della Seta: 'Affetto e azione: sulla teoria del melodramma italiano dell'ottocento': *IMSCR, xiv Bologna 1987*, iii, 395–400

H. S. Powers: '"La solita forma" and "The Uses of Convention"', *AcM*, lix (1987), 65–90

B. M. Antolini: 'L'editoria musicale in Italia dal settecento al novecento: fonti e bibliografia', *Le fonti musicali in Italia*, iii (1989), 33–55

S. L. Balthazar: 'Music, Poetry and Action in *ottocento* Opera: the Principle of Concurrent Articulation', *Opera Journal*, xxii (1989), 13–34

——: 'The *primo ottocento* Duet and the Transformation of the Rossinian Code', *JM*, vii (1989), 471–97

——: 'Ritorni's "Ammaestramenti" and the Conventions of Rossinian Opera', *Journal of Musicological Research*, viii (1988–9), 281–311

J. Kerman and T. S. Grey: 'Verdi's Groundswells: Surveying an Operatic Convention', *Analyzing Opera: Verdi and Wagner*, ed. C. Abbate and R. Parker (Berkeley, 1989), 153–79

V. Bernardoni: 'La teoria della melodia vocale nella trattatistica italiana (1790–1870)', *AcM*, lxii (1990), 29–61

A. Roccatagliati: 'Libretti d'opera: testi autonomi o testi d'uso?', *Quaderni del Dipartimento di linguistica e letterature comparate*, vi (Bergamo, 1990), 7–20

S. L. Balthazar: 'Analytic Contexts and Mediated Influences: the Rossinian *Convenienze* and Verdi's Middle and Late Duets', *Journal of Musicological Research*, x (1990–91), 19–45

——: 'Mayr, Rossini, and the Development of the Early *concertato*

Finale', *JRMA*, cxvi (1991), 236–66

M. Conati: '"L'oltracotata turba che s'indraca": inforestieramenti dell'opera italiana nel secondo ottocento', *Musica senza aggettivi: studi per Fedele d'Amico* (Florence, 1991), 345–53

J. Rosselli: *Music and Musicians in 19th-Century Italy* (London, 1991; It. trans., enlarged, as *Sull'ali dorate: il mondo musicale italiano dell'ottocento*, 1992)

S. Huebner: 'Lyric Form in Ottocento Opera', *JRMA*, cxvii (1992), 123–47

G. Pestelli: 'Riflessi della rivoluzione francese nel teatro musicale italiano', *L'eredità dell'ottantanove in Italia*, ed. R. Zorzi (Florence, 1992), 261–78

LATE 19TH CENTURY AND 20TH CENTURY

P. Salviucci: *La musica e lo stato* (Milan and Rome, 1953)

R. Allorto: 'Il consumo musicale in Italia, ii: L'opera e il concerto', *NRMI*, i (1967), 534–58

C. Annibaldi: 'Musica gestuale e nuovo teatro: ritorno alla teatralità', *Musica moderna*, iii/106 (Milan, 1969), 145–54

P. Santi: 'Passato prossimo e remoto nel rinnovamento musicale italiano del novecento', *Studi musicali*, i (1972), 161–86

U. Jung: *Die Rezeption der Kunst Richard Wagners in Italien* (Regensburg, 1974)

F. d'Amico: 'Il regista d'opera', *Visconti: il teatro*, ed. C. d'Amico de Carvalho (Reggio Emilia, 1977), 9–32

R. Tedeschi: *Addio, fiorito asil: il melodramma italiano da Boito al verismo* (Milan, 1978)

E. Voss: 'Verismo in der Oper', *Mf*, xxxi (1978), 303–13

J. Nicolaisen: *Italian Opera in Transition, 1871–1893* (Ann Arbor, 1980)

Musica italiana del primo novecento: la generazione dell'80: Florence 1980, ed. F. Nicolodi

G. Azzaroni: *Tra riforme e compromessi: il teatro musicale in Italia tra il 1920 e il 1980* (Bologna, 1981)

F. Nicolodi: 'Parigi e l'opera verista: dibattiti, riflessioni, polemiche', *NRMI*, xv (1981), 577–623; repr. in *Gusti e tendenze del novecento musicale in Italia* (Florence, 1982), 1–66

L. Pestalozza: 'Lo stato dell'organizzazione musicale: la svolta del fascismo e la sua lunga durata', *Musica/realtà*, ii, no.5 (Aug 1981), 143–60

F. Quadri: *Il teatro degli anni settanta: tradizione e ricerca* (Turin, 1982), 159–85

G. Rostirolla, ed.: *Wagner in Italia* (Turin, 1982)

R. Curci and G. Gori: *La dolcissima effigie: manifesti italiani dell'opera lirica* (Trieste, 1983)

L. Trezzini and A. Curtolo: *Oltre le quinte: idee, cultura e organizzazione del teatro musicale in Italia* (Venice, 1983)

M. S. Miller: 'Wagner, Wagnerism, and Italian Identity', *Wagnerism in European Culture and Politics*, ed. D. C. Large and W. Weber (Ithaca and London, 1984), 167–97

F. Nicolodi: *Musica e musicisti nel ventennio fascista* (Fiesole, 1984)

E. Sanguineti: 'Teatro con musica, senza musica', *Intersezioni*, iv (1984), 68–80

V. Bernardoni: *La maschera e la favola nell'opera italiana del primo novecento* (Venice, 1986)

B. Bianchini: *La disciplina degli Enti Lirici e Istituzioni Concertistiche assimilate* (Milan, 1986)

J. Budden: 'Wagnerian Tendencies in Italian Opera', *Music and Theatre: Essays in Honour of Winton Dean* (Cambridge, 1987), 299–332

J. Maehder: 'Il libretto patriottico nell'Italia della fine del secolo e la raffigurazione dell'antichità e del rinascimento nel libretto prefascista italiano', *IMSCR, xiv: Bologna 1987*, iii, 451–66

Opera '87 [etc.]: annuario EDT dell'opera lirica in Italia (Turin, 1988–) [yearbook]

D. Bryant, ed.: *Il novecento musicale italiano tra neoclassicismo e neogoticismo* (Florence, 1988)

A. Guarnieri Corazzol: *Tristano, mio Tristano: gli scrittori italiani e il caso Wagner* (Bologna, 1988)

J. Maehder: 'The Origins of Italian *Literaturoper*', *Reading Opera*, ed. A. Groos and R. Parker (Princeton, 1988), 92–128

'Il teatro musicale contemporaneo', *Il Verri*, nos.5–6 (March–June 1988) [whole issue]

F. Nicolodi: *Orizzonti musicali italo-europei 1860–1980* (Rome, 1990)

J. Stenzl: *Von Giacomo Puccini zu Luigi Nono: italienische Musik 1922–1952: Faschismus – Resistenza – Republik* (Buren, 1990)

A. Lanza: *Il secondo novecento* (Turin, 1991), 68–83, 150–60, 168–89

LORENZO BIANCONI

Ivan IV. *Opéra* in five acts by GEORGES BIZET to a libretto by François-Hippolyte Leroy and Henri Trianon; Mühringen Castle, Württemberg, 1946.

Bizet appears to have worked intensively on *Ivan IV*, a libretto originally intended for Gounod, in the winter of 1862–3 in expectation of a performance at Baden-Baden. He may have begun it earlier, after Gounod had renounced interest. The Baden performances never took place, but negotiations with Carvalho for a production at the Théâtre Lyrique, Paris, were carried on in 1864–6. These, too, came to nothing. The autograph reached the Paris Conservatoire in 1929, and the first performances took place after World War II. The vocal score was first published, in Büsser's adaptation, in 1951.

This is Bizet's largest and longest work, conceived in the manner of Meyerbeer's operas for a large cast and orchestra, with a setting in the Caucasus and the Kremlin in the 16th century. Hostilities between Caucasians and Russians and between various Kremlin factions are fuelled by the marriage of Tsar Ivan (baritone) to Marie (soprano), daughter of the Caucasian king. The libretto is confused and confusing, full of villainy, usurpation, revenge, vows of fidelity to race and family, poison, dissembling, and scenes of entertainment and fantasy. There is no attempt to disguise the grand opera clichés. Bizet responded with his customary prodigality of invention, although some scenes are perfunctory or sentimental. He used many passages in later works. The orchestration of Act 5 remained unfinished.

HUGH MACDONALD

Ivanoff [Ivanov], **Nicola** [Nikolay] (**Kuz'mich**) (*b* Poltava, 10/22 Oct 1810; *d* Bologna, 7 July 1880). Russian tenor. He studied with Eliodoro Bianchi, Andrea Nozzari and Heinrich Panofka in Naples, making his début at the S Carlo in 1832 as Percy (*Anna Bolena*). First heard in Paris at the Théâtre Italien in 1833 as Gianetto (*La gazza ladra*), he made his London début in 1834 as Percy at the King's Theatre. In 1840 he sang Arnold in *Guillaume Tell* (given as *Rodolfo di Sterlinga*) at Bologna. Engaged at Palermo, he sang Riccardo in the première of Pacini's *Maria, regina d'Inghilterra*, then made his début at La Scala in the same opera (1843). In 1844 he sang at the Kärntnertortheater, Vienna, in Donizetti's *Maria di Rohan* and *Roberto Devereux* and at Parma in the title role of *Ernani*, which he repeated at the Teatro Apollo, Rome, in 1845. In 1846 at Trieste he sang Foresto in *Attila*. He retired in 1852. At the beginning of his career Ivanoff had a very sweet-toned voice which, when later he attempted heavier roles, lost its bloom.

*

H. Panofka: *Voix et chanteurs* (Paris, *c*1870)

O. Tiby: *Il Real Teatro Carolino e l'ottocento musicale palermitano* (Florence, 1957)

F. de Filippis and R. Arnese: *Cronache del Teatro di S Carlo* (Naples, 1961)

J. Budden: *The Operas of Verdi*, i: *From 'Oberto' to 'Rigoletto'* (London, 1973)

D. Brown: *Mikhail Glinka* (London, 1974)   ELIZABETH FORBES

Ivanov, Lev Ivanovich (*b* St Petersburg, 18 Feb/2 March 1834; *d* St Petersburg, 11/24 Dec 1901). Russian choreographer. After graduating from the Imperial Theatre School in St Petersburg in 1852 he performed extensively in ballet and opera at the Imperial Theatres, though his work in opera, which theatre officials took for granted, is scantily documented. Krasovskaya attributes to him the bolero in Auber's *La muette de Portici* (1858) and the dances in Halévy's *La Juive* (1859). In 1861 Ivanov himself claimed that he had 'always tried to be useful to the direction by staging dances for various operas'. In 1899 he noted in his memoirs many trips to Moscow and one to Warsaw for this purpose.

Ivanov's promotions to ballet régisseur (1882) and second ballet-master (1885) increased his duties in opera; he shared responsibility with the first ballet-master, Marius Petipa, for restaging dances of operas in repertory and for creating those of new productions. He staged Russian dances for 12 operas by Russian composers, notably Tchaikovsky's *Mazepa* (1884), *Yevgeny Onegin* (1884) and *The Enchantress* (1887), Rubinstein's *Kupets Kalashnikov* (1889) and Nápravník's *Dubrovsky* (1895). His most important opera dances, pendants to his work on *Swan Lake* and *The Nutcracker*, were those for Borodin's *Prince Igor* (1890) and Rimsky-Korsakov's *Mlada* (1892). Historians continue to debate whether Ivanov's creative gifts were stifled by the prejudicial treatment of Russians in a troupe dominated by foreigners, particularly the wilful Petipa. This claim must be weighed against his problems with short-sightedness, his reputed alcoholism, a disabling shyness and the contemporary opinion that his gifts, while laudable, were second to Petipa's.

*

Yu. Slonimsky and others: 'Writings on Lev Ivanov', *Dance Perspectives*, ii/2 (1959) [whole issue]

V. Krasovskaya: *Russkiy baletnïy teatr vtoroy polovinï XIX veka* [Russian Ballet Theatre of the Second Half of the 19th Century] (Moscow and Leningrad, 1963), 26–62

ROLAND JOHN WILEY

Ivanov, Mikhail Mikhaylovich (*b* Moscow, 11/23 Sept 1849; *d* Rome, 20 Oct 1927). Russian critic and composer. He graduated from the Institute of Technology in St Petersburg in 1869 and then studied at the Moscow Conservatory, where he attended Tchaikovsky's composition classes. From 1870 to 1875 he studied with Giovanni Sgambati in Rome and associated with Liszt and his circle. On his return to St Petersburg, he began to write articles on musical topics and in 1879 edited a musical journal; the following year he was engaged as music critic on the *Novoye vremya*, where he remained until 1918. Conservative in his outlook on music, he earned the dislike of many composers for his often ironic and scathing reviews of new works. After the Revolution he emigrated to Italy.

Ivanov wrote four operas, three of which were performed with some success. His compositional style has been described as a pale imitation of that of Tchaikovsky. His writings include a history of music in Russia and *Pushkin v muzïke* ('Pushkin in Music'; St Petersburg, 1889).

Zabava Putyatishna, Moscow, Novïy, 15 Jan 1899
Potyomkin Holiday, St Petersburg, 16 Dec 1902
Kashirskaya starina [Kashirskaya Antiquity], St Petersburg, 1905
Gore ot uma [Woe from Wit] (after A. S. Griboyedov), St Petersburg, Mariinsky, May 1910   JENNIFER SPENCER

Ivanov-Boretsky, Mikhail Vladimirovich (*b* Moscow, 4/16 June 1874; *d* Moscow, 1 April 1936). Russian music historian and composer. He studied law at St Petersburg University, graduating in 1896, and music at the St Petersburg Conservatory, where his teachers included Rimsky-Korsakov. In 1901 he went to Italy to study with A. Falconi at the Florence Conservatory. Returning to Russia in 1905, he undertook teaching commitments in Moscow and was a council member of the music department at the Institute for the History of the Arts in St Petersburg. At about the same time he produced a number of compositions, including the comic opera *Adol'fina* (*c*1906; 3, W. A. Powolski; pubd 1909), first performed in Moscow on 27 November/10 December 1908, and the opera *Koldun'ya* ('The Sorceress', 1913; 3, Ivanov-Boretsky); initially prohibited by tsarist censorship, this work was first performed after the October Revolution, on 14 August 1918 at the Public Opera House in Petrograd.

In 1922 he was appointed dean of the faculty of theory and composition at the Moscow Conservatory, and under his supervision the research department was founded (1923). He was the first Russian musicologist to write extensively on Western music. His publications include pamphlets on Handel, Beethoven, Rossini, Schumann and Mendelssohn, *Karmen: opera Bize* ('Bizet's *Carmen*'; Moscow, 1924) and the article 'Ot operï, k oratorii' ('From Opera to Oratorio'), to commemorate the 250th anniversary of Handel's birth (*SovM*, 1935, no.3, pp.30–37).   IGOR BELZA

Ivanovich, Cristoforo (*b* Budva, Dalmatia, 1628; *d* Venice, before 6 Jan 1689). Italian librettist and theatre chronicler of Dalmatian birth. He went to Italy in the mid-1650s to escape the war over Crete. He settled first at Verona, where he was a member of the Accademia Filarmonica, and from 1657 lived in Venice. Soon after moving there he became secretary to Leonardo Pesaro, one of the procurators of St Mark's, where in 1676 he obtained the position of *sotto-canone* and in 1681 that of *canone*. He wrote librettos for Venice, Vienna and Piacenza; he also adapted Moniglia's Florentine extravaganza *Ipermestra* to Venetian taste as *La costanza trionfante*. His exchange of letters with Pagliardi (*Poesie*, Venice, 1675) contains an interesting and rare description of that taste: 'The character of this city likes the heroic to be serious but lively, the pathetic not excessively languid, and the comic full of vigour but easy-going'. His principal contribution to musical theatre is a catalogue of Venetian opera performances from 1637 to 1681 (continued, in a second edition, to 1687), 'Le memorie teatrali di Venezia', published as an appendix to his *Minerva al tavolino* (Venice, 1681, 2/1688). Although it contains many inaccuracies (see Walker), it is a valuable source of information about 17th-century operatic repertory and is the basis for all subsequent catalogues; it also contains an extensive discussion of contemporary theatre practice. Ivanovich's will was proved on 6 January 1689.

L'amor guerriero (dramma per musica), P. A. Ziani, 1663; *La Circe* (dramma per musica), Ziani, 1665 (D. Freschi, 1679); *Coriolano* (dramma), F. Cavalli, 1669; *La costanza trionfante* (dramma per musica), G. D. Partenio, 1673 (B. Pasquini, 1679, as *Dov'è amore è pietà*); *Lisimaco* (dramma per musica), G. M. Pagliardi, 1673

*

M. Velimirovic': 'Cristoforo Ivanovich from Budva: the First Historian of the Venetian Opera', *Zvuk: Jugoslovenska muzička revija* [Sound: Yugoslavian Music Review] (1967), 135–45

T. Walker: 'Gli errori di "Minerva al tavolino": osservazioni sulla cronologia delle prime opere veneziane', *Venezia e il melodramma nel seicento: Venice 1972*, 7–20

M. Milosevic': 'Il contributo dei libretti e della corrispondenza di Cristoforo Ivanovich nell'evoluzione del melodramma seicentesco', *Il libro nel bacino adriatico (secc. XV–XVIII): Venice 1989*

I. Cavallini: 'Questioni di poetica del melodramma del seicento nelle lettere di Cristoforo Ivanovich', *Giovanni Legrenzi: Clusone 1990*
THOMAS WALKER, NORBERT DUBOWY (bibliography)

Ivan Susanin. Opera by M. I. Glinka; *see* LIFE FOR THE TSAR, A.

Ivan the Terrible. Opera by N. A. Rimsky-Korsakov; *see* MAID OF PSKOV, THE.

Ivey, Jean Eichelberger (*b* Washington DC, 3 July 1923). American composer. She studied the piano at the Peabody Conservatory and composition at the Eastman School and the University of Toronto. She is director of the electronic music studio founded by her (1969) at the Peabody Conservatory and is coordinator of the composition department there. As a pianist she has toured Europe, Mexico and the USA.

Ivey has composed works in most genres, but is particularly fond of writing for the voice, often to her own texts, and her non-vocal music often has literary or dramatic connotations. Her early style was tonal and neo-classical, influenced by Bartók and Ravel. In the 1960s she began to incorporate atonal and electronic elements, which gave her style fluidity. She has pointed out that the modern composer, with access to music not only of the past but of many cultures, can be and possibly should be eclectic, 'but always in the service of the effective communication of humanistic ideas and intuitive emotion'. Her monodrama *Testament of Eve* (Ivey; Baltimore, 21 April 1976) presents a highly dramatic dialogue, accompanied by orchestra, between Eve (mezzo-soprano) and Lucifer, whose voice is on tape, as Eve tries to decide for the whole human race whether or not to eat of the fruit of the Tree of Knowledge. This is presented as a heroic decision, choosing knowledge and courage in preference to remaining a pampered pet in the Garden of Eden. *The Birthmark* (composed 1980–82; 1, Ivey, after Nathaniel Hawthorne) deals with a dedicated scientist of some centuries ago who becomes obsessed with the idea of removing a birthmark from the face of his beautiful wife. Having tried many methods without success, he offers her a potion which causes the birthmark to fade away – but she dies as it fades.

*

C. Ammer: *Unsung – A History of Women in American Music* (Westport, CT, 1980), 187–9, 283
J. W. Le Page: 'Jean Eichelberger Ivey', *Women Composers, Conductors and Musicians of the 20th Century*, i (Metuchen, NJ, 1980), 85–102
M. Stewart-Green: *Women Composers – A Checklist of Works for the Solo Voice* (Boston, 1980), 38
R. M. Muennich: *The Vocal Works of Jean Eichelberger Ivey* (diss., Michigan State U., 1983) [incl. catalogue of works]
SAM DI BONAVENTURA

Ivogün, Maria [Kempner, Ilse] (*b* Budapest, 18 Nov 1891; *d* Beatenberg, Switzerland, 2 Oct 1987). Hungarian soprano. She was the daughter of the singer Ida von Günther, from whom she derived her own stage name. Heard by Bruno Walter at an unsuccessful audition for the Vienna Opera, she was instantly engaged for Munich, where she appeared in 1913, first as Mimì and then as the Queen of Night. She remained at Munich until 1925, singing lyrical roles as well as the high coloratura parts for which she became famous, such as Mozart's Konstanze and Strauss's Zerbinetta. Strauss described her in this role as 'simply unique and

without rival', and made a point of having her engaged for *Ariadne* productions whenever possible; it was as Zerbinetta that she made her Covent Garden début in 1924. In 1925 she followed Bruno Walter to Berlin, and remained a member of the Städtische Oper until 1932; until 1934 she appeared at the Staatsoper as Zerbinetta. In 1921 she married the Munich tenor Karl Erb, with whom she often appeared; the couple were divorced in 1932, and the following year Ivogün married the pianist Michael Raucheisen, who became her recital accompanist. Her records, though mostly pre-electric, are good; a smaller group made for HMV by the electrical process includes a version of the Zerbinetta scene that justifies the composer's praise.

*

A. Frankenstein: 'Maria Ivogün', *Record Collector*, xx (1971–2), 98–119 [with discography by J. Dennis], 283–4
A. Blyth: 'Maria Ivogün – an Appreciation', *Opera*, xxxviii (1987), 1372–3
DESMOND SHAWE-TAYLOR

Ivrogne corrigé, L' ('The Drunkard Reformed'). *Opéra comique* in two acts by CHRISTOPH WILLIBALD GLUCK to a libretto after LOUIS ANSEAUME and Jean-Baptiste Lourdet de Santerre's *L'ivrogne corrigé, ou Le mariage du diable* (1759); Vienna, Burgtheater, April 1760.

Gluck's music for this work (in prose, vaudevilles and *ariettes*) replaced that by Jean-Louis Laruette for the original Parisian production. In Anseaume's libretto (based on La Fontaine), the drunkard Mathurin (tenor) wishes to marry his niece Colette (soprano) to his companion in debauchery, Lucas (baritone). In order to frustrate this plan, Mathurin's wife Mathurine (soprano), Colette and her lover Cléon (tenor), and a chorus of peasants masquerade as furies, so that on awakening the drunkards think they are in hell, rather than Mathurin's wine cellar. Cléon, as 'Pluto', offers to suspend punishment if Mathurin will renounce drink and accord his niece to Cléon. Mathurin signs the marriage contract, whereupon the players unmask. Lucas, who has promised nothing, reverts to his former ways.

Internal evidence suggests Gluck's involvement in shaping the Viennese libretto. Formally, *L'ivrogne corrigé* is the most advanced of his *opéras comiques*, with a nearly continuous underworld tableau which anticipates that of *Orfeo ed Euridice*. The musical style ranges from sentimental (Cléon), to grotesque (the furies), to rustic (Lucas). The opera's two drinking songs (placed prominently just within the overall frame of overture and final chorus) reveal Gluck's sympathy for the unreformed drunkard.
BRUCE ALAN BROWN

Ivry, Paul Xavier Désiré, Marquis d' [Yrvid, Richard] (*b* Beaune, 4 Feb 1829; *d* Hyères, 18 Dec 1903). French composer. Self-taught as a musician, he wrote five operas. Of the first four, composed between 1850 and 1860, only one, *La maison du docteur*, to a libretto also used by Bizet, was performed, at the Grand Théâtre, Dijon (1855). His last and most ambitious opera, *Les amants de Vérone*, for which he wrote the text himself, was based on Shakespeare's *Romeo and Juliet*. Privately performed in Paris on 12 May 1867, Ivry's version of the tragedy suffered by comparison with that of Gounod, produced at the Théâtre Lyrique the previous month. Later, an interest taken in *Les amants* by the tenor Victor Capoul resulted in a professional production at the Théâtre Ventadour in 1878, with Capoul as Romeo and Marie Heilbronn as Juliet. The same singers took part in the production at Covent Garden on 24 May 1879, which received three performances. The text, apparently closer to Shakespeare than the version set by Gounod, earned Ivry the accusation of coarseness. His music, especially a duet in Act 2 for the lovers, won mild praise.

Fatma, *c*1850, unperf.
Quentin Metsys, 1854 (oc, 1, Ivry), unperf.
La maison du docteur (oc, 1, H. Boisseaux), Dijon, Grand, 1855
Omphale et Pénélope, ?1860 (1), unperf.
Les amants de Vérone (5, Ivry, after W. Shakespeare: *Romeo and Juliet*), private perf., Paris, Salle Duprez, 12 May 1867; Ventadour, 12 Oct 1878   ELIZABETH FORBES

Izaht. Opera in four acts by HEITOR VILLA-LOBOS to a libretto by Azevedo Júnior and the composer (using the pseudonym Epaminodas Villalba Filho); Rio de Janeiro, Teatro Municipal, 13 December 1958 (first performed in concert, Rio de Janeiro, Teatro Municipal, 6 April 1940).

A history of partial, concert, and abortive performances of *Izaht*, which culminated in the stage première less than one year before his death, typifies the ill-fortune which dogged Villa-Lobos as an opera composer. *Izaht* was composed between 1912 and 1914 by amalgamating fragments of two earlier, unperformed operas, *Aglaia* (1909) and *Elisa* (1910), both written while he was a cellist in the orchestra of a small opera company. The composer constructed *Izaht*'s libretto around a fantastic story of underworld life, telling of gypsies, espionage, intrigue and banditry, and opening unpromisingly 'in the Tavern of Death, badly built in the vaults of an abandoned castle, in an outer suburb of Paris'.

The long, tortuous and extremely complicated plot and the need for 11 soloists, a chorus, a ballet and large orchestra all militated against early performances. The orchestral Prelude and Act 4 were heard in Brazil in 1918, and Acts 3 and 4 in 1921; Villa-Lobos then disregarded the work until the 1940 concert performance. Critical reaction was mixed: the bizarre and rough-hewn orchestration was generally considered the result of youthful inexperience, while the vocal lines were perceived as extremely difficult. The incipient traits of Brazilian nationalism in the music were thought out of place in the context, but the grandness and unashamed daring of Villa-Lobos's conception underwrote his stated aim in composing the work: to alleviate the tedium and monotony which he saw as opera's chief pitfall.   SIMON WRIGHT

Izmir. City in western Turkey on the Aegean Sea, formerly called Smyrna. Italian companies visited the city in the 19th century, and in 1861 an opera house was opened by an Italian named Barbieri. Visiting Italian and Armenian companies presented operas, as also did the Spor Kulubu (Sporting Club), which was active from 1850 until 1922. Beginning in 1946 the Ankara Devlet Opera ve Balesi (Ankara State Opera and Ballet Company) gave performances in Izmir. From 1979 opera and ballet were given in the Elhamra Theatre, seating 650 (formerly a cinema, built in 1887). The Izmir Devlet Opera ve Balesi (Izmir State Opera and Ballet) was established in 1982. A wide variety of operas has been produced, ranging from the standard Italian repertory to Pergolesi's *La serva padrona*, Menotti's *The Consul* and Lehár's *Die lustige Witwe*, as well as Turkish operas such as *Van Gogh* by Nevit Kodallı and *Midas in Kulaklari* ('Midas's Ears') by Ferit Tüzün.

A. C. Konuralp: *Devlet Opera v Balesi: Ankara, Istanbul, Izmir* [The State Opera and Ballet: Ankara, Istanbul, Izmir] (Ankara, 1991)   FARUK YENER

Izzo d'Amico, Fiamma (*b* Rome, 1964). Italian soprano. After winning the Toti Dal Monte Competition, she made her début in 1984 at Treviso as Mimì, repeating the role at Philadelphia, Houston, Modena, Genoa, Geneva and Oslo (1988). She also sang Violetta at Bologna. At Salzburg in 1986 she sang Elisabeth de Valois (Easter) and Micaëla (summer), returning for Tosca in 1988. She sang Massenet's Manon at Turin (1989) and Nedda in 1990 at the Baths of Caracalla. She has a delightful personality and a beautiful voice.

ELIZABETH FORBES

J

Jachino, Carlo (*b* San Remo, 3 Feb 1887; *d* Naples, 23 Dec 1971). Italian composer. After studies in Lucca and with Riemann in Leipzig (1909–10), he held teaching posts in Parma (1928–33), Naples (1933–8) and Rome (1938–51), then became director of the conservatories of Naples (1951–3) and Bogotá, Colombia (1953–6). From 1961 he was artistic director of the S Carlo, Naples. As a composer he was an unpredictable eclectic and wrote much instrumental music as well as operas. He made his name with *Giocondo e il suo re* (1915–21; 3, G. Forzano, after Ariosto: *Orlando furioso*; Milan, Dal Verme, 24 June 1924), the only one of Jachino's operas that seems ever to have been performed. *Giocondo* was frequently revived in Italy, though criticized in some quarters for failing to respond adequately to the subtle irony of the story, and for its overt indebtedness to such established composers as Puccini and Zandonai. Jachino's unperformed operas include four early works (1903–14), one of them unfinished, three projects dating from the period 1925–40, all of which were abandoned before completion; and the late comic opera *I due nasi* (1970).

A. Lualdi: ' "Giocondo e il suo re" di C. Jachino al Dal Verme', *Serate musicali* (Milan, 1928), 130–35

F. Lunghi: *Quando la vita diventa romanzo* (Rome, 1970) [incl. full work-list, 46–50]   JOHN C. G. WATERHOUSE

Jackson. American city, capital of Mississippi. One of the earliest opera productions took place in 1916, an abridged performance of *Madama Butterfly* featuring the local singer Catherine Stewart Power. In 1927 the Chicago Civic Grand Opera made the first of several visits. Local opera received its first major impetus when the Jackson Opera Guild was organized in 1945 (incorporated 1947). At the time it was among only 12 such institutions in the USA. Mascagni's *Cavalleria rusticana* was the first opera it produced (27 November 1945), in the Bailey Junior High School Auditorium, and since 1948 at least one opera has been presented each year. Reorganization in 1970 resulted in the formation of the Mississippi Opera Association (renamed the Mississippi Opera Guild in 1977).

In 1958 the company presented the first staged production of *The Soldier* by Lehman Engel, a locally born composer. The company's production of Carlisle Floyd's *Flower and Hawk* was televised by Mississippi Educational Television in 1979. As in most regional companies, major roles are generally sung by national artists. Mississippi singers who have taken leading roles include John Alexander, Julian Patrick and Gail Robinson. The Mississippi Opera also has a studio theatre (established 1977), designed to give experience to local and regional artists, and a schools programme ('Opera in Blue Jeans'). An educational ensemble for touring throughout the state was established in 1989.

The Bailey Auditorium remained the principal venue until 1957; productions were then mainly in Millsaps Auditorium and Murrah Auditorium until 1968, when the company opened a new Municipal Auditorium (seating 2418) with *Aida* (starring Richard Tucker as Radames). Two productions are presented there each year.

Opera South, a national black company, was founded in Jackson in 1970 largely through the efforts of a white nun of the Catholic order the Sisters of the Blessed Sacrament, Sister Mary Elise. She organized the company in conjunction with three constituents of the Mississippi Intercollegiate Opera Guild: Jackson State University, Utica Junior College and Tougaloo College. The company generally uses students and nonprofessionals in the choruses and ballet ensembles and nationally prominent professionals in the principal roles. Appearing with the company has helped several singers (including William Brown, Esther Hinds and Florence Quivar) to find engagements with major American and European companies. The company has also given opportunities to black conductors, stage directors and technicians.

Opera South has not limited itself to traditional repertory. It has mounted operas by black composers, among them Ulysses Kay's *The Juggler of Our Lady* (1972) and *Jubilee* (première, 20 November 1976) and William Grant Still's *Highway No.1, USA* and *A Bayou Legend*. The première of *A Bayou Legend* (composed 1941) was given by Opera South on 15 November 1974. In 1981 this production became the first opera by a black composer to be televised on a national network, the Public Broadcasting Service.   DERRICK HENRY

Jackson, William [Jackson of Exeter] (*b* Exeter, 29 May 1730; *d* Exeter, 5 July 1803). English composer. The son of a respected grocer, he studied music at Exeter Cathedral and in London. He first ventured into opera with *Lycidas* (Jackson, after J. Milton; London, 4 Nov 1767), a one-act cantata afterpiece for Covent Garden that lamented the death of Edward, Duke of York; it received one performance in London and one in Bath. He also wrote both sacred and secular music, two of his tunes appearing in the Linleys' comic opera *The Duenna* (1775). In 1777 he became organist and master of the choristers at Exeter Cathedral.

Jackson's next opera, *The Lord of the Manor* (comic op, 3, J. Burgoyne, after J. F. Marmontel; London, Drury Lane, 27 Dec 1780), saw well over 30 performances and appeared in both vocal and full score (as op.12, London, 1781). The songs echo the rural English setting by avoiding italianate bravura and favouring simple melody in the English style. For example, Rashly's lament for his dead wife ('Encompass'd in an angel's frame') charmed audiences precisely because of its simplicity. Jackson received about £200 from the three benefit performances; this was unusual because the author, not the composer, generally claimed such profits. Songs from the opera were later revised by Thomas Dibdin and Henry Bishop (London, c1812). In 1783 Jackson wrote both music and lyrics for *The Metamorphosis* (comic op, 3, R. Tickell; London, Drury Lane, 5 Dec 1783; vs, as op.14, London, 1783), which failed. He achieved some notoriety, however, with *Observations on the Present State of Music in London* (London, 1791), which attacked italianate music and Handel-worship, both of which he saw as destroying the English melodic tradition. His own operatic music sought to redress the imbalance by emphasizing lyrical melody over ornamentation, discord and modulation.

DNB (R. Sharp); *LS*

J. Burgoyne: Preface, *The Lord of the Manor* (London, 1781)

J. Cranch: *Memoirs of the Life with Observations on the Genius and Works of William Jackson, of Exeter* (Frome, 1813)

R. Lonsdale: *Dr. Charles Burney: a Literary Biography* (Oxford, 1965)

J. Hayes: 'William Jackson of Exeter: Organist, Composer and Amateur Artist', *The Connoisseur*, clxxiii (1970), 17–24

R. Fiske: *English Theatre Music in the Eighteenth Century* (London, 1973, 2/1986)

G. Jackson, ed.: *William Jackson, of Exeter: a Short Sketch of my Life (1802)* (Vienna, 1974)

L. Troost: 'The Characterizing Power of Song in Sheridan's *The Duenna*', *Eighteenth-Century Studies*, xx (1986–7), 153–72

LINDA V. TROOST

Jacobacci, Vincenzo. See JACOVACCI, VINCENZO.

Jacobi, Frederick (*b* San Francisco, 4 May 1891; *d* New York, 24 Oct 1952). American composer. He studied composition with Goldmark and Bloch in New York and Paul Juon in Berlin. From 1913 to 1917 he was assistant conductor of the Metropolitan Opera. His three-act opera *The Prodigal Son* (1943–5), which won him the David Bispham Medal, is based on four early American prints found in a New England tavern, in which the biblical characters wear American 19th-century garb. Jacobi added the character of Johnny Appleseed to reinforce his American vision of the ancient story. The opera was a vehicle for Jacobi and his librettist, the Canadian playwright Herman Voaden, to express their wartime idealism, revealed most sharply in the prodigal son's final aria, 'Now the darkness lifts from my eyes'. The opera received a concert performance in Chicago in 1947 and the second act was fully staged at Stanford University on 19 August 1949. The stage première of the whole work was at the Arts and Letters Club in Toronto on 22 April 1952; the

opera was revived in 1959 at the Forest Hill Auditorium. This drama and Jacobi's other works, both instrumental and vocal, reveal a modernism informed by intense American, Judaic and Romantic traditions.

M. Bauer: *Twentieth Century Music* (New York, 1933, 2/1947)

D. Diamond: 'Frederick Jacobi', *MM*, xiv (1936–7), 124–31

C. Reis: *Composers in America: Biographical Sketches of Living Composers* (New York, 1938, enlarged 2/1947), 192–4

O. Downs: 'American Composer: Contribution of F. Jacobi to his Time and Art', *New York Times* (2 Nov 1952)

MARJORIE MACKAY-SHAPIRO

Jacobi, Georg [Jacoby, Georges] (*b* Berlin, 13 Feb 1840; *d* London, 13 Sept 1906). German conductor and composer. He first studied the violin at the age of six in Berlin, moving to Brussels in 1849 to study with Bériot. He later joined Massart's class at the Paris Conservatoire (1852) and studied composition with Réber, Gevaert and Chéri. After winning a *premier prix* for violin in 1861 he played for two years at the Opéra-Comique and then won the competitive post of first violin at the Opéra, where he played in many notable productions, including *Tannhäuser*.

In 1869 Jacobi became conductor at the Bouffes-Parisiens, where he directed many Offenbach performances as well as composing operettas (according to Fétis, two or three 'without value or consequence'). On the outbreak of the Franco-Prussian War he moved to London to conduct at the Alhambra Theatre for the 1871–2 season; he remained for 26 years, composing 103 ballets and *divertissements*, which were also widely performed abroad. His comic operas include *The Black Crook* (which ran for 310 performances) and *Mariée depuis midi*; he also wrote incidental music for Henry Irving's productions at the Lyceum. In 1898 he transferred to the Crystal Palace, for which he wrote two ballets, and was briefly conductor at the London Hippodrome. He taught at the RCM from 1896.

Le feu aux poudres (opérette, 1), Paris, 21 March 1869

La nuit du 15 octobre (opérette, 1, A. Vanloo and E. Letterier), Paris, Bouffes-Parisiens, 25 Oct 1869

Violà le plaisir mesdames (opérette, Florent), Paris, 1869

The Black Crook (grand opéra bouffe féerie, 4, H. Paulton and J. Paulton, after *La biche au bois*), London, Alhambra, 23 Dec 1872, collab. F. Clay; rev. version, London, Alhambra, 3 Dec 1881

Mariée depuis midi (opérette, 1, W. Busnach and A. Liorat), Marseilles, 20 Aug 1873 (Paris, 1874)

La forêt enchantée, London, 1873

Don Juan (Christmas extravaganza, 7 scenes, H. J. Byron), London, Alhambra, ? 19 Jan 1874, collab. Clay, incl. music by Lecocq and Offenbach

The Demon's Bride (grand opéra bouffe, 3, H. J. Byron, after Vanloo and Letterier), London, Alhambra, 7 Sept 1874

Rothomago [Act 4] (grand opéra bouffe féerie, 4, H. B. Farnie), London, 22 Dec 1879 [Act 1 by E. Solomon, Act 2 by P. Bucalossi, Act 3 by G. Serpette]

Boccaccio, ?unperf., song (London, 1882)

Le clairon (opérette, 3, E. Philippe, G. Marot and F. Friebault), Paris, Renaissance, 7 Nov 1883

Cinderella (school operetta, S. Wensley), London, 1898 (London, 1898)

The Babes in the Wood (comic operetta, 2, Wensley), London, 1905 (London, 1905)

Am Hochzeitstag (solo operetta), ?unperf.

Claudine et Trusquin (opérette), ?unperf.

FétisB; *GänzlBMT*; *MGG* (H. F. Redlich); *StiegerO*

Jacobi, Johann Georg (*b* Düsseldorf, 2 Sept 1740; *d* Freiburg im Breisgau, 4 Jan 1814). German librettist.

The elder brother of the philosopher Friedrich Wilhelm Jacobi, he studied theology and later philology and literature at Göttingen. In 1766 he was appointed professor of philosophy at Halle. His early works, including his popular one-act opera *Elysium*, explore an extreme of sentimental preciosity, with reconciliation as a persistent theme. In 1784 Jacobi accepted a professorship at Freiburg (the first Protestant ever to hold such a post). At the age of 52 he married a woman less than half his age; he used this relationship as the model for his libretto *Phaedon und Naide*.

Elysium (Vorspiel mit Arien), Schweitzer, 1770; *Apollo unter den Hirten* (Vorspiel mit Arien), Schweitzer, 1770; *Phaedon und Naide* (Spl), Bierey, 1793 (G. Bachmann, 1795); *Der Tod des Orpheus* (Spl), Bachmann, 1798   THOMAS BAUMAN

Jacobin, The [*Jakobín*]. Opera in three acts by ANTONÍN DVOŘÁK to a libretto by MARIE ČERVINKOVÁ-RIEGROVÁ; Prague, National Theatre, 12 February 1889 (revised version, Prague, National Theatre, 19 June 1898).

Count Vilém of Harasov *retired general*	bass
Bohuš of Harasov *his son*	baritone
Adolf of Harasov *his nephew*	baritone
Julie *the wife of Bohuš*	soprano
Filip *the count's steward*	bass
Jiří *a young hunter*	tenor
Benda *teacher, choirmaster and composer*	tenor
Terinka *his daughter*	soprano
Lotinka *old housekeeper of the castle*	contralto

Townspeople, school children, musicians, musketeers, country folk

Setting A country town in Bohemia during the French Revolution, in 1793

The libretto was the second by Červinková-Riegrová set by Dvořák and the first she had written expressly for him; it went through several stages before reaching its final form. Dvořák approved a very early version in October 1882. In 1883 he wrote to her, while revising the fourth act of *Dimitrij*, that he liked *The Jacobin* but wanted to show it to Hanslick. Dvořák continued to assure Červinková-Riegrová that he was looking forward to setting the text, but with the prospect of international success beckoning, he looked for subjects of more cosmopolitan interest. On 1 August 1887 Červinková-Riegrová asked him to return the text if he was dissatisfied. Three months later (10 November 1887) Dvořák began work on *The Jacobin* and he completed the full score on 18 November 1888.

The opera had some success at its première but criticism of the music, text and organization led Dvořák to request revisions from Červinková-Riegrová in 1894 during his return to Europe from the USA. These were supplied by the author, but Dvořák did not work on them until February 1897, after she had died. František Rieger, who had helped his daughter with the early drafts of the work, assisted Dvořák by adding verse for Terinka's song in the second act ('Na podzim v ořeší'). Structural changes involved moving a conversation between Benda and Count Vilém to the last act and revising parts of the choral ballet at the end of the opera, rather in the manner of changes made to the second version of *King and Charcoal Burner* in 1887. This new version (performed in June 1898) was a success, and remains the definitive form of the opera. A performance

in Czech was given by a company from Bratislava in Vienna on 5 May 1929, and in a German translation in Teplitz-Schönau on 12 December 1931. The first professional staging in Great Britain was a joint production by the WNO and the Royal Northern College of Music in an English translation by Rodney Blumer at the Cardiff New Theatre on 14 May 1980.

ACT 1 *A town square, with a church visible* As is the case with Dvořák's earlier comic operas, *The Jacobin* is a through-composed, number opera reflecting a pattern established in the final version of Smetana's *The Bartered Bride*. Dvořák makes use of several recurrent motifs employed both as reminiscences and as part of the textural fabric. The first of these, associated with Bohuš, the estranged son of Count Vilém, is heard in the first scene. The theme is a song which Bohuš's mother sang to him – an early version of the libretto was called *The Mother's Song* – and which his wife Julie now sings to their child. Bohuš is returning to his native town with Julie, a foreigner. Moved by the sound of singing from a church, he tells Julie that he longs for the love of his father who, through the wiles of his cousin Adolf, has turned against him, thinking Bohuš a revolutionary – a Jacobin. Bohuš only wanted justice for the people of the estate and now hopes for reconciliation. The townspeople come out of church and greet each other. Filip, the pompous steward, after effusively flattering the choirmaster, Benda, attempts to turn the head of his daughter, Terinka. His clumsy efforts at love-making enrage Jiří, who is also in love with Terinka. Egged on by the town lads, Jiří makes fun of the steward. Terinka attempts to calm Jiří, to no avail, and Filip reacts by threatening the young men with conscription. Jiří and Terinka declare their love for each other in an extended duet, but they are frequently and sarcastically interrupted by Filip. Bohuš and Julie arrive and, introducing themselves as travelling players, ask to see Count Vilém. Filip is suspicious, but the scene is interrupted by the entrance of Count Vilém, who announces that Bohuš is disowned and Adolf now his heir.

The arias and choruses – the latter have a perceptibly national accent – hide sophistication in their melodic symmetry and formal construction. The combination of the steward's aria with the taunts of the town lads is especially effective. Dvořák's musical characterization is also more acute than before. Particularly successful is the minuet parody mocking the steward's oily courtesy and the rapid and repetitive delivery of the choirmaster.

ACT 2 *A school room* The act opens with a rehearsal of a serenade for performance in the manor. This scene owes its inspiration to *Zar und Zimmermann*, but Dvořák makes it his own with archaic classical references in his music, simple rustic melody, tuning violins and naive ornamental coloratura. Terinka worries that her father would prefer her to marry Filip rather than Jiří. The lovers sing a long and ravishing duet. Benda discovers them and demands that Terinka marry Filip. Jiří and Terinka threaten to wreck Benda's serenade, but the row is interrupted by the town girls who bring news that soldiers are searching for revolutionaries. Bohuš and Julie enter and ask for lodging. They sing a richly emotive number ('My cizinou jsme bloudili': 'We wandered in foreign lands'), which describes how music sustained them in their struggles. Benda is won over and allows them to stay. Filip arrives to woo Terinka, finds Jiří and prepares to conscript him, ignoring Benda's plea to spare him so that he can take the tenor lead. Adolf enters and supports Filip. Bohuš intervenes and denounces Adolf, who arrests him as a dangerous revolutionary.

ACT 3 *A hall in the castle of Count Vilém* Jiří attempts to tell the count of his son's return, but Adolf has him thrown out. Lotinka, the old housekeeper, admits Julie and Benda who hope to plead with the count on behalf of Bohuš. Benda presents his serenade to the count but fails to reconcile him to his son, and Julie makes a final attempt. As the count reflects on how he could not be persuaded of his son's innocence, he hears from another room the sound of his dead wife's harp and Julie singing a favourite lullaby ('Synáčku můj květe': 'Little son, my flower'), an exquisite piece in which a chromatically inflected melody is set over a gentle drone bass. Julie persuades the count of Bohuš's innocence by showing him a document promulgated by the Jacobins sentencing Bohuš to death. The count hears that his son is imprisoned in the castle, and as the serenade begins he resolves to see Bohuš. Father and son are reconciled, and in an eloquent arioso, added in the later revision, Bohuš sings that he wishes to remain at home forever. The plot of Adolf and Filip is frustrated, and all ends in general rejoicing in an extended choral ballet.

* * *

The sentimental action and outcome of *The Jacobin* suited Dvořák well, with numerous opportunities for the kind of open-hearted lyricism at which he was most adept. The dramatic exchanges, supported by arioso and conventional accompanied recitative, are brisk and credible. All of the set pieces are fully rounded, confirming that number opera was Dvořák's natural mode of expression. The richer, slightly Wagnerian, colouring of the later revision adds to what is one of Dvořák's most effective operas.

JAN SMACZNY

Jacobs, Arthur (David) (*b* Manchester, 14 June 1922). English writer on music and translator. He studied at Merton College, Oxford. He worked as a music critic, from 1952 mainly freelance, for many newspapers and journals, including the *Sunday Times* and especially *Opera*, of which he was deputy editor, 1961–71. In 1964 he was appointed professor at the RAM, and from 1979 to 1984 he was head of the music department at Huddersfield Polytechnic; he has also taught in Canada, the USA and Australia.

Jacobs's wide interests are reflected in his publications. Opera is prominent among them: he has been much concerned with new forms of music theatre, and a vigorous advocate of the performance of opera in English. He has translated more than 20 operas, including works by Handel, Rossini, Berlioz, Tchaikovsky, Strauss and Berg (the complete *Lulu*), generally in a brisk and fluent style; he also wrote the libretto for Nicholas Maw's *One Man Show* (1964). Victorian musical life and Sullivan's life and music in particular have been the central topics of his research.

Gilbert and Sullivan (London, 1951)
with S. Sadie: *The Pan Book of Opera* (London, 1964, 2/1969)
Arthur Sullivan: a Victorian Musician (London, 1984, 3/1992)
The Penguin Dictionary of Musical Performers (London, 1990)
STANLEY SADIE

Jacobs, René (*b* Ghent, 30 Oct 1946). Belgian countertenor and conductor. He studied classical philology at the University of Ghent, later taking singing lessons from Louis Devos in Brussels and Lucie Frateur in The Hague and attending Alfred Deller's masterclasses. He has performed with many of the leading early and Baroque ensembles including those directed by Alan Curtis (with which he made his début in 1974 as Clerio in Cavalli's *Erismena*, in Amsterdam), Nikolaus Harnoncourt, Gustav Leonhardt and Sigiswald Kuijken. During the 1970s he founded his own group, Concerto Vocale, which he has successfully directed in operas by Cavalli and Handel. He conducted *L'incoronazione di Poppea* in his own performing edition at Montpellier in 1989, and at the Innsbruck Festival of Ancient Music the following year. Jacobs also teaches performing practice in Baroque singing at the Schola Cantorum, Basle. His recordings as a singer include Cesti's *Orontea*, Lully's *Le bourgeois gentilhomme*, Charpentier's *David et Jonathas*, and Handel's *Admeto*, *Alessandro* and *Tamerlano*. Recordings under his direction include *L'incoronazione di Poppea*, Cavalli's *Giasone* and Handel's *Flavio* and *Giulio Cesare*. He both directed and sang the title role in Cavalli's *Serse*.

NICHOLAS ANDERSON

Jacovacci [Jacobacci], Vincenzo (*b* Rome, 14 Nov 1811; *d* Rome, 30 March 1881). Italian impresario. As a youth he was interested in the theatre, though he made his living as a fishmonger. His first contract to manage a theatrical season was in 1835 at the Teatrino Fiano, Rome. Gradually he moved to larger Roman theatres: in 1838 the Valle, in 1840 the Apollo, and in 1846 the Argentina, the Alibert and the Corea Amphitheatre (which he had restored). Not all of his enterprises were successful: he was arrested when too many tickets were sold for the première of Donizetti's *Adelia* (February 1841; sung by Giuseppina Strepponi), and in 1848 he was bankrupt though he survived through handling his creditors cleverly.

With Barbaia, Lanari and Merelli, Jacovacci was one of the most celebrated impresarios of the 19th century. His fame was tied to the Apollo theatre, then the largest in Rome, and his reputation rested on spectacular and dignified performances, ballets with classical subjects and an uncanny ability to sidestep the obstacles of the papal censors. Most of the operas he mounted were traditional; only under pressure did he present *Lohengrin* and Massenet's *Le roi de Lahore*. He had absolute confidence in Verdi from *Nabucco* onwards and in 1848 dedicated the season to his works. He gave the premières of *Il trovatore* (1853) and *Un ballo in maschera* (1859), and the first Italian performance of *La forza del destino* (1863). Verdi complained that stinginess had made Jacovacci engage for *Ballo* inadequate singers unsuited to their roles, and he haggled for cheaper rates from the publisher, Ricordi. He wrote the impresario a letter (5 June 1859) ironically suggesting he avoid further talk of new operas and put on instead the works of Paisiello, Gluck and Lully – all in the public domain.

*

C. Montani: 'Tre impresari: Jacovacci, Baracchini, Canori', *Il messaggero* (Rome, 1927)
MARVIN TARTAK

Jacquet de la Guerre, Elisabeth-Claude (*b* 1666–7; *d* Paris, 27 June 1729). French composer. She was the daughter of the Parisian organ builder Claude Jacquet, and wife (from 1684) of the organist Marin de la Guerre. So exceptional was her talent as a harpsichordist that Louis XIV relaxed the convention restricting women instrumentalists from performing at court or in public. According to the Marquis of Dangeau, in the summer of 1685 the dauphin hosted a performance of a miniature opera by Mlle Jacquet. Two years later she became the first French woman to publish a collection of harpsichord pieces. She was one of several progressive composers (and the only woman) who experimented with Italian genres, notably the sonata and cantata, in the early 1690s. Simultaneously, she sought a place among the post-Lullian composers of large-scale music by writing first a ballet for the dauphin, *Les jeux à l'honneur de la Victoire* (1691, lost), then a five-act *tragédie lyrique*, *Cephale et Procris*, to a libretto by Duché de Vancy, first performed by the Académie Royale de Musique on 15 March 1694. The opera was dedicated to Louis XIV and engraved in a reduced score by the royal printer Christophe Ballard. Although it was not well received in Paris, its prologue was arranged by Sébastien de Brossard for a performance in 1696 by the music academy at Strasbourg. A chorus of demons appears in Act 4, preceded by the kind of subterranean rumbling that Marais later made famous in *Alcyone* (1706). While deeply indebted to Lully, La Guerre infused her music with a new degree of virtuosity, and added violin accompaniment to many of the *airs*. Her achievements were acknowledged by Titon du Tillet, who accorded her a place on his 'Mount Parnassus', next to Lalande and Marais and just below Lully.

Her collection of *Cantates françoises* (1710) includes a duet known as *Le raccommodement comique de Pierrot et de Nicole* (for soprano, baritone and continuo), performed as part of the *comédie La ceinture de Vénus* at the Théâtre de la Foire in 1715. During the Regency she composed further music for the Théâtre de la Foire (excerpts were published in 1721).

*

E. Titon du Tillet: *Le Parnasse françois* (Paris, 1732), 635–6
M. Brenet: 'Quatre femmes musiciennes, I: Mademoiselle Jacquet de la Guerre', *L'art*, lix/Oct (1894), 108–12
E. Borroff: *An Introduction to Elisabeth-Claude Jacquet de La Guerre* (Brooklyn, NY, 1966)
J. A. Sadie: '*Musiciennes* of the Ancien Régime', *Women Making Music*, ed. J. Bowers and J. Tick (Urbana and Chicago, 1986), 191–223
JULIE ANNE SADIE

Jadin, Louis-Emmanuel (*b* Versailles, 21 Sept 1768; *d* Montfort-l'Amaury, Yvelines, 11 April 1853). French composer. He was trained in music at Versailles, where his first opera, *Guerre ouverte*, was staged in 1788. In 1789 he became second keyboard player at the newly founded Théâtre de Monsieur (later Théâtre Feydeau), and in 1792 joined the musical corps of the National Guard. Famous as a pianist, he taught at the Paris Conservatoire and in 1824 was made a Chevalier of the Légion d'honneur. Jadin wrote some 40 operas and, judging from their printed scores, he was proficient in several styles.

In *Guerre ouverte* a young Marquis, who is in love with Lucile, makes a pact with her uncle, the Baron, saying that he will prevent her marriage to a rival and win her heart by midnight, while the Baron will try to make the rival succeed. The music, in an Italian style reminiscent of Cimarosa, is intended less to comment on the characters than to enhance the witty and fast-paced action. The variety of aria forms, the rhythmical complexities and the carefully structured ensemble finales can easily sustain comparison with other examples of contemporary comic opera, such as M.-A. Désaugier's *Le rendez-vous* (1792). A farcical element is also prominent in *Le défi hasardeux* (1796), in which a husband absorbed by his scholarly work begins to take his wife seriously after she has feigned an affair to arouse his jealousy (the theme of a character adapting to his social surroundings is a recurrent one in Jadin's operas). In its song-like melodies and *couplets*, *Le défi* is closer to the French style than *Guerre ouverte*; the husband's dramatic and richly scored fury aria ('Où suis-je quelle phrénesie') is in the manner of serious opera. This aria also shows features of sonata form.

A stylistic ambiguity can again be detected in *Le coin du feu* (1793). Here a woman successfully sets a trap for her husband to prevent his disloyalty. While the plot suggests the genre of *opera semiseria*, the finale is a crude example of Italian *buffo* style. Furthermore, the characters remain ill-defined in the music and the denouement takes place in spoken dialogue. It is normal in the operas mentioned for the orchestra simply to support the vocal line in parallel motion. The aria 'Ne crois pas que je pardonne' from *Le coin du feu* is a noteworthy exception, since its musical form employs two independent orchestral motifs; the second, which is dominant in the middle section, even undergoes some thematic development. In the year of *Le coin du feu* Jadin also composed the patriotic *Le siège de Thionville* for the Opéra. After the undistinguished *Le grand-père* (1805), Jadin set out to use a modern style in *La partie de campagne* (1810), based on a farcical plot by Lamartelière. Here string and wind instruments are almost equally important to the musical texture, and all compositional devices, such as the gradual introduction of a theme and the use of unison, appear to have a specific dramatic function. Jadin's setting provides a commentary on every step of the dramatic development. Later in this work, however, he falls back into a more conventional idiom, and his last performed opera, *Fanfan et Colas* (1822), does not reach the musical quality of the better part of *La partie de campagne*. Here, as elsewhere, Jadin's harmonic invention is limited. The operas under consideration rarely use keys with more than three sharps or flats.

first performed in Paris unless otherwise stated; all printed works published in Paris

Guerre ouverte, ou Ruse contre ruse (cmda, 3, Dumaniant [A.-J. Bourlin]), Versailles, 1788, excerpts *F-Pn*; (1789)

Constance et Gernand (1, P. Desriaux), Français Comique et Lyrique, 15 July 1790

Joconde (3, Desforges [P.-J.-B. Choudard], after La Fontaine), Monsieur, 14 Sept 1790, excerpts (1790)

La religieuse danoise, ou La communauté de Copenhague (3, A.-L. Bertin d'Antilly), Montansier, 13 Dec 1790; also as Le duc de Waldeza

La vengeance du bailli, ou La suite d'Annette et Lubin (cmda, 2, C.-S. Favart and C.-N.-J. Favart), Monsieur, 30 April 1791

L'heureux stratagème (comédie lyrique, 2, G. Saulnier), Opéra, 13 Sept 1791, *Po*, ov. *Pc**

Amélie de Monfort (3, Cottereau, after N. B. de La Dixmerie), Feydeau, 13 Feb 1792

Il signor di Pursognac (after Molière), Feydeau, 23 April 1792, *Pc**, excerpt *Pc**

L'avare puni (1, Verneuil), Feydeau, 4 Aug 1792

Les talismans (opéra à grand spectacle, 3, P.-U. Dubuisson), Louvois, 12 Jan 1793

Le coin du feu (comédie, 1, E.-G.-F. de Favières), OC (Favart), 10 June 1793 (n.d.)

Le siège de Thionville (drame lyrique, 2, Saulnier and Dutilh), Opéra, 14 June 1793, *Po*, 1 air (n.d.)

Le congrès des rois (cmda, Desmaillot [A. F. Eve]), OC (Favart), 26 Feb 1794, collab. Dalayrac, Grétry, Méhul and 8 others

Alisbelle, ou Les crimes de la féodalité (3, Desforges), National, 27 Feb 1794, *A*, excerpt (n.d.)

L'apothéose du jeune Barra (tableau patriotique, 1, F.-P.-A. Léger), Feydeau, 5 June 1794

Agricol Viala, ou Le jeune héros de la Durance (fait historique et patriotique, 1, L. Philipon de la Madeleine), Amis de la Patrie, 1 July 1794, ov. and airs (n.d.)

L'écolier en vacances (comédie, 1, L. B. Picard), OC (Favart), 13 Oct 1794

Le cabaleur (cmda, 1, J.-A. Lebrun-Tossa), OC (Favart), 11 Jan 1795

Le lendemain de noces (1, Léger), Feydeau, 18 April 1795

La supercherie par amour, ou Le fils supposé (comédie mêlée de musique, 3, C.-J. Loeuillard d'Avrigny), OC (Favart), 12 May 1795

Loizerolles, ou L'héroïsme paternel (1, Ducaire), Amis de la Patrie, 25 Dec 1795

Le mariage de la veille (1, Loeuillard d'Avrigny, after Voltaire: *La femme qui avoit raison*), OC (Favart), 2 Jan 1796, excerpts (n.d.)

Le négociant de Boston (comédie mêlée de musique, 1, Loeuillard d'Avrigny and Dejaure, after Mercier: *Le libérateur*), OC (Favart), 4 March 1796

Les deux lettres (1, E.-J.-B. Delrieu), OC (Favart), 4 Aug 1796

Le défi hasardeux (2, Delrieu), Louvois, 8 Aug 1796 (1797), *Mc*

Les bons voisins (fait historique, 1, B. Planterre), Feydeau, 1 Nov 1797

Candos, ou Les sauvages du Canada (3, Delrieu), Feydeau, 2 Jan 1798, ov. *Pc*

Mahomet II (tragédie lyrique, 3, Saulnier), Opéra, 9 Aug 1803, *Po*, Acts 1 and 2 *Pc**, excerpts *Pc**

Jean Bart et Patoulet (1, Léger), OC (Feydeau), 21 Jan 1804

Mon cousin de Paris (oc, 1, Léger), Molière, 23 June 1804, *Pc**

La grand-mère (2, E.-G.-F. de Favières), Molière, 17 Oct 1804, *Pc**

Les trois prétendus (1, T. Pein), Montansier, 29 April 1805

Le grand-père, ou Les deux âges (oc, 1, A. de Favières), OC (Feydeau), 14 Oct 1805, *Pc**; (n.d.)

Charles Coypel, ou La vengeance d'un peintre (1, Léger), Montansier, 26 Oct 1805

Les arts et l'amitié (oc, A. de Bouchard), OC (Feydeau), 9 June 1807

La partie de campagne (comédie mêlée de chants, 1, J. H. F. Lamartelière), OC (Feydeau), 26 June 1810, *Pc**; (n.d.)

L'auteur malgré lui, ou La pièce tombée (1, Claparède, after J.-F. Marmontel: *Le connoisseur*), OC (Feydeau), 16 May 1812, ov. *Pc**

L'inconnu, ou Le coup d'épée viager (oc, 3, Vial and E.-G.-F. de Favières), OC (Feydeau), 30 March 1816, ov. *Pc**

Fanfan et Colas, ou Les frères de lait (1, A. Jadin, after Beaunoir [A.-L.-B. Robineau]), OC (Feydeau), 29 Oct 1822 (n.d.)

Unperf: Jean et Geneviève, 1 air pubd

Doubtful: La rosière de Cholet (1), Montansier, 16 Aug 1796

*

E. de Briqueville: 'L. Jadin, compositeur versaillais', *Echo de Versailles* (6 Nov 1908)

D. P. Charlton: *Orchestration and Orchestral Practice in Paris, 1789–1810* (diss., U. of Cambridge, 1973)

MICHAEL FEND (text, bibliography), MICHEL NOIRAY (work-list)

Jadlowker, Hermann (*b* Riga, 17 July 1877; *d* Tel-Aviv, 13 May 1953). Latvian tenor. He studied at the Vienna conservatory with Joseph Gänsbacher and made his début at Cologne in 1899 as Gomez in Kreuzer's *Nachtlager in Granada*. In 1900 he went to Stettin, then to Riga, and in 1906 to the court theatre in Karlsruhe, where he began to attract international attention. The German emperor heard him during a Wiesbaden festival and arranged for his engagement at the Berlin Hofoper in 1909. From 1910 to 1912 he sang at the Metropolitan, where he made his début as Faust, created the King's Son in Humperdinck's *Königskinder* opposite Farrar and sang Rodolfo, Turiddu, Canio, Lohengrin, Max and Pinkerton. In 1912 Strauss chose him for Bacchus in the première of *Ariadne auf Naxos*.

Although intrinsically a lyric tenor with amazing coloratura agility, Jadlowker sang such roles as Florestan, Tannhäuser, Parsifal and Otello, which gradually took their toll. He left the Berlin company in 1921 and thereafter seldom appeared in opera, though he sang

Armand Mirabeau in the first performance of Lehár's *Frasquita*.

*

A. Frankenstein: 'Hermann Jadlowker', *Record Collector*, xix (1970–71), 5–31 [with discography by T. Kaufmann, D. Brew and J. Dennis]
LEO RIEMENS, ELIZABETH FORBES

Jagd, Die ('The Hunt'). *Comische Oper* in three acts by JOHANN ADAM HILLER to a libretto by CHRISTIAN FELIX WEISSE, after Charles Collé's play *La partie de chasse de Henri IV* and MICHEL-JEAN SEDAINE's *opéra comique Le roi et le fermier*; Weimar, Kleines Schlosstheater, 29 January 1770.

The village judge Michel (tenor) and his wife Marthe (soprano) prepare for the arrival in the country of the King (bass) and his hunting party. Their daughter Röschen (soprano) is in love with the village lad Töffel (bass), but they cannot marry until her older brother Christel (tenor) has wed. He loves the farmer's daughter Hannchen (soprano), recently abducted by the sinister Count von Schmetterling (spoken). She escapes and convinces a hesitant Christel of her fidelity. A storm separates the King from his party and he comes to Michel's humble home, posing as one of his own retinue. He learns of the universal love for him and also of Schmetterling's attempt on Hannchen. When the count appears, the King reveals himself, banishes Schmetterling, and settles a handsome dowry on the two young couples.

Weisse's story is more fully steeped than its sources in a healthy, idealized rustic milieu; the moralizing, the tearful scenes of reunion and reconciliation, and the easy intercourse between monarch and subjects are additional emblems of German sentimental comedy. The opera was first performed by H. G. Koch's theatrical troupe, with singers of limited ability. Hiller's music for them became the very epitome of simple directness of expression in German comic opera. Variously cheerful, tender or noble in tone, his short arias deftly colour Weisse's standard character types. Röschen's *Romanze* 'Als ich auf meiner Bleiche' became a popular song in its own right.
THOMAS BAUMAN

Jagel, Frederick [Jeghelli, Federico] (*b* Brooklyn, NY, 10 Jan 1897; *d* San Francisco, 5 July 1982). American tenor. After war service in France, he studied singing in New York and Milan; he made his début in 1924 at Livorno in *La bohème*. As Federico Jeghelli he sang for three years in Italy and with an Italian company in the Netherlands. Resuming his own name, he made his American début at the Metropolitan in 1927 as Radames, the part he sang most frequently there; in the same season, he made a strong impression in the local première of Alfano's *Risurrezione*. He remained with the Metropolitan until 1950, also singing in Chicago, San Francisco and South America, and with the New York City Opera (1947–9). His most important new role at the Metropolitan (and his last) was probably Peter Grimes, which he sang in the first production there of Britten's opera in 1948; other American premières in which he took part include Musorgsky's *Fair at Sorochintsï* (1930). His repertory also included the Drum Major in *Wozzeck* and Luka in *From the House of the Dead* (which he sang in a televised performance in 1969). His singing of Alfredo with Ponselle as Violetta can be heard in a primitive recording of a Metropolitan performance in 1935, the voice clearly projected, the bright tone sensitively shaded.
J. B. STEANE

Jäger, Ferdinand (*b* Hanau, 25 Dec 1839; *d* Vienna, 13 June 1902). German tenor. He studied in Dresden, where he made his début in 1865. Engagements in Cologne, Hamburg, Stuttgart and Kassel followed. Recommended to Wagner as a possible Siegfried, Jäger did not sing in the first *Ring* cycle at Bayreuth (1876) although coached in the role by the composer. But he sang Siegfried in both *Siegfried* and *Götterdämmerung* in the Vienna premières (1878–9), at the Munich Hofoper in private performances before King Ludwig II and at the Viktoria Theater, Berlin (1881). He sang Parsifal at Bayreuth (1882), after Winkelmann and Gudehus. Despite his fine voice and a physique perfect for the role, he never quite obtained real success as Siegfried.
ELIZABETH FORBES

Jahn, Gertrude (*b* Zagreb, 13 Aug 1940). German mezzo-soprano. She studied in Vienna, then made her début in 1963 at Basle as Gluck's Orpheus. Engaged at the Vienna Staatsoper for over 20 years, she also appeared at Munich, Barcelona, Innsbruck and Glyndebourne, where she sang Olga (1968). At Salzburg she sang Margret (*Wozzeck*) in 1971 and created the Countess in Penderecki's *Die schwarze Maske* (1986). Her repertory included Cherubino, Meg Page (*Falstaff*), Maddalena (*Rigoletto*), Eboli, Carmen, Magdalene, Larina, Santuzza, Varvara (*Kát'a Kabanová*), Octavian, Clairon, Adelaide (*Arabella*) and Geschwitz, which she sang at Madrid in 1988. An excellent actress, she had a warm, full-toned voice.
ELIZABETH FORBES

Jahrmarkt, Der ('The Annual Fair'). *Komische Oper* in one act by Georg Benda (*see* BENDA family, (1)) to a libretto by FRIEDRICH WILHELM GOTTER, with Johann Jakob Engel; Gotha, Schloss Friedenstein, 10 February 1775.

Begun as an adaptation of Engel's sentimental afterpiece *Der dankbare Sohn*, the text was drastically altered when the famous actor Konrad Ekhof objected to the debasing of one of his favourite roles. There resulted a one-act farce centred on a minor episode in the original: the recruiting sergeant Fickfack (bass) gets the despondent lover Lukas (tenor) drunk and enlists him before his betrothed, Bärbchen (soprano), can prevent it; a benevolent colonel resolves the matter in the end.

Benda's first German opera follows many of the conventions already established by J. A. Hiller and C. F. Weisse – a text substantially independent of the musical numbers, important non-singing roles (the Colonel, the Jew Nathan), and music aimed at deepening character rather than situation. The music ranges from short lieder in popular style to large-scale arias for Bärbchen, written for the splendid voice of Josepha Hellmuth. For the two-act version (named *Der Dorfjahrmarkt*; Leipzig, Theater am Rannstädter Tor, 26 April 1775) Benda added new numbers to texts by Gotter, and Hiller composed several more to texts by Engel.
THOMAS BAUMAN

Jaime [Gem], **Louis-Adolphe** (*b* Paris, 1824; *d* Paris, 4 March 1901). French librettist. The son of Ernest Jaime (1802–84), who worked with Ludovic Halévy, Philippe Dumanoir and others on several *comédies-vaudevilles* and *comédies*, he adopted the same lighthearted forms with some success, collaborating with a number of different writers, including H.-J. Crémieux, Philippe Gille and Jules Noriac, over a career of nearly 40 years.

In the late 1850s he wrote librettos for Offenbach, including *Croquefer* (1857) with Etienne Tréfeu, *Dragonette* (1857) with E. Mestépès, *Une demoiselle en loterie* (1857) with Crémieux and, most notably, *Geneviève de Brabant* (1859) with Tréfeu, which was revised by Crémieux in 1867. Jaime was also associated with Delibes, Hervé and Lecocq, as well as many lesser composers.

DBF (H. Blémont)
CHRISTOPHER SMITH

Jakobín. Opera by Antonín Dvořák; *see* JACOBIN, THE.

Jakova, Prenkë (*b* Shkodër, Albania, 27 June 1917; *d* 16 Sept 1969). Albanian composer. His family were photographers and he also worked in the studio. He started his musical activities in the 1940s in Shkodër, playing the clarinet, composing and, most importantly, encouraging music-making among children. From 1942 to 1944 he studied the clarinet in Rome, but as a composer was self-taught. Much of his early music was written for the town choirs and this led him to compose vocal dramas such as *Shkodran Wedding* and *Light over Albania*. In July 1956 he began work on the first Albanian opera ever written, *Mrika*, which received its première in Shkodër on 16 December 1958.

Later Jakova wrote *Gjergj Kastrioti-Skënderbeu*, on a libretto by Llazar Siliqi, to celebrate the 500th anniversary of the death of the national hero who won many battles against the Turks in the 14th century. First performed at the Theatre of Opera and Ballet, Tirana, on 17 January 1968, it is an epic-heroic work on an unprecedentedly large scale. Much use is made of recitative in a style closely linked to the characteristics of popular speech. The theme of national warfare, with a large cast of Albanians and Turks interweaving their individual conflicts, makes this a powerfully dramatic work. The children are not forgotten, however, and their songs and dances bring a happy freshness to the opening of Act 2. Jakova's musical style is 'of the people', taking themes from popular folk music, and is lyrical and communicative.

S. Kalemi: *Arritjet e artit tonë muzikor* [The Arrival of our Musical Art] (Tirana, 1982)
J. Emerson: *Albania: the Search for the Eagle's Song* (Studley, Warwicks., 1990)
JUNE EMERSON

Jakowicka-Friderici, Teodozja. *See* FRIDERICI-JAKOWICKA, TEODOZJA.

James, Eirian (*b* Cardigan, 7 Sept 1952). Welsh mezzo-soprano. She studied at the RCM and made her début in 1977 as Olga with Kent Opera, for which she also sang Cherubino, Meg Page, Friday (*Robinson Crusoe*), Nero (*Agrippina*), Poppaea, Rosina and Purcell's Dido. Her roles for the ENO include Kitchen Boy (*Rusalka*) and Flora. She sang Medea (Cavalli's *Giasone*) and Ariodante at Buxton; Fatima (*Oberon*) and Isolier at Lyons; and Olga, Hänsel and Cherubino at Geneva. After her Covent Garden début as Annina (*Der Rosenkavalier*) in 1987, she returned for Javotte (*Manon*), Smeton and Nancy (*Albert Herring*, 1989), as well as Tisbe (*La Cenerentola*) in 1990. At Edinburgh (1987) she sang Babette (*The English Cat*). Her attractive appearance, keen sense of humour and warm-toned voice are delightfully displayed as Dorabella, which she sang at Aix-en-Provence (1988).
ELIZABETH FORBES

James, Henry (*b* New York, 15 April 1843; *d* London, 26 Feb 1916). American novelist. He received an eclectic and cosmopolitan private education, thus gaining the intimate knowledge of Europeans and Americans that he displays so prominently in his writings. He ranks as one of the most acclaimed writers and critics of the USA, but after 1876 he made his home in England and in 1915 became a British citizen. The best-known operatic adaptations of James's fiction are Britten's *The Turn of the Screw* (1954) and *Owen Wingrave* (1971), both based on novels of the same titles. Other well-known operas include Thea Musgrave's *The Voice of Ariadne* (1974; based on the short story *The Last of the Valerii*) and Douglas S. Moore's *The Wings of the Dove* (1961). The novel *Washington Square* was the basis of operas by Catherine Sloper (1978) and Thomas Pasatieri (1976).

P. H. Lang: 'Current Chronicle: *The Wings of the Dove*', *MQ*, xlviii (1962), 101–2

M. Schneider: 'Henry James et Benjamin Britten', *Nouvelle revue française*, xiii/4 (1965), 713–16

R. G. Deavel: *A Study of Two Operas by Benjamin Britten: Peter Grimes and The Turn of the Screw* (diss., U. of Rochester, 1970)

R. E. Long: 'Adaptations of Henry James's Fiction for Drama, Opera, and Films: with a Checklist of New York Theatre Critics' Reviews', *American Literary Realism*, iv (1971), 268–78

S. Corse: 'From Narrative to Music: Benjamin Britten's *The Turn of the Screw*', *University of Toronto Quarterly*, li (1981–2), 161–74

MICHAEL HOVLAND

Janáček, Leoš [Leo Eugen] (*b* Hukvaldy, Moravia, 3 July 1854; *d* Moravská Ostrava [now Ostrava], 12 Aug 1928). Czech composer. He was a late developer, with his first distinctive opera (*Jenůfa*) given in his 50th year, and his greatest operas written after the age of 65. His reputation was equally slow in coming. He was almost 62 when Prague first performed *Jenůfa*, and although it became a repertory piece in Czechoslovakia and the German-speaking world during the 1920s and 30s, it was not until the 1950s that it, or any other Janáček opera, was given in Britain. Since then his reputation has continued to grow steadily throughout the world. As the 20th century draws to a close he has become accepted as one of its most substantial, original and immediately appealing opera composers.

1. Early life and studies. 2. Early operas. 3. Later operas. 4. Style and conventions.

1. EARLY LIFE AND STUDIES. Janáček's family background hardly destined him for opera. Both his grandfather and his father were village schoolmaster-musicians – part of the 'kantor' tradition that Charles Burney much admired and that kept Czech culture alive through the lowest ebb of the nation's fortunes. It was, however, essentially a village or small-town tradition and one that produced church and instrumental musicians rather than opera composers. In 1848 Janáček's father took up a teacher's post in the village of Hukvaldy, northeastern Moravia, remote from any large cultural centre, where Leoš was born six years later. By contrast, earlier Czech opera composers – Smetana, Fibich, Bendl, Šebor, Rozkošný and Blodek – all came from town or city backgrounds, usually from Prague. Only Dvořák hailed from a village background, and for him opera was an uncertain medium well into his maturity.

Janáček's move to the town and his first exposure to opera came sooner than expected. At the age of 11, to relieve the crowded household (he was the seventh child of the surviving nine), he was sent to be a chorister at the Augustinian 'Queen's' monastery in Brno. One of his first musical experiences there was to take part in a performance of Meyerbeer's *Le prophète* at the German theatre. This, however, was an isolated experience. The monastery choir school was in decline and was further disrupted by the Austro-Prussian War of 1866. When it reassembled the effects of the Cecilian movement began to be felt: instrumental teaching ceased and the choristers became a purely vocal ensemble. The monastery, however, played a vital role in Janáček's development; in particular its choirmaster Pavel Křížkovský, a leading Moravian composer, took a keen interest in his musical education. Later, Janáček underwent two periods of study with Skuherský at the Prague Organ School (1874–5; June–July 1877). He also studied at the conservatories in Leipzig (October 1879–February 1880) and Vienna (April–June 1880). During the time of his studies poverty prevented him from taking full advantage of his surroundings. In Prague and Leipzig he seems never to have gone to the opera. In Vienna he went twice, seeing *Der Freischütz* and Cherubini's *Les deux journées*; he enjoyed neither.

Janáček was to follow his family's teaching tradition and he studied in Brno at the Czech Teachers' Institute (1869–72). After several years as an apprentice teacher there, he taught at the institute as a 'full teacher of music' from 1880 until his early retirement at the age of 50 in 1904. He also taught singing at the Old Brno Gymnasium (1886–1902). His most influential post, however, was as director of the Organ School in Brno (1881–1919), which he had founded after the model of the Prague Organ School.

Janáček's musical activities went far beyond the classroom. During the 1870s and 80s he contributed to the musical life of Brno as conductor of choral societies, first (1872–6) of the male-voice Svatopluk, then (1876–88) at the Beseda ('Club'), the cultural centre of middle-class Czech society in Brno. With help from the monastery choir and pupils from the Teachers' Institute, he was able to muster a force of 250 singers for performances of large-scale choral works such as Mozart's Requiem (1877) and Beethoven's *Missa solemnis* (1879). It was for Svatopluk that he wrote his first secular compositions, simple four-part settings of folk texts.

2. EARLY OPERAS. Another cultural venture was Janáček's founding of a musical journal, *Hudební listy* (1884–8), published by the Beseda. Janáček was editor and a chief contributor, reviewing most of the operatic events in Brno in the newly opened Provisional Czech Theatre. Soon, Janáček began to think of composing operas himself. The first indication was a sketch-scenario (1884) on the unlikely subject of Chateaubriand's *Les aventures du dernier Abencérage*. In 1887 Janáček began to compose his first opera, *Šárka*, to a verse libretto by Julius Zeyer based on Czech mythology. Zeyer had intended the work for Dvořák and consequently refused the unknown and inexperienced Janáček permission to use his text. By then Janáček had already written the work in piano score, shown it to Dvořák, and revised it; undaunted by Zeyer's refusal he went on to score two of the three acts. *Šárka* remained unperformed until 1925, when it was staged in a revised version with the orchestration completed by his former student, Osvald Chlubna.

While working on *Šárka*, Janáček was invited by František Bartoš, a fellow teacher at the Old Brno Gymnasium, to help him collect folksongs (1888). This visit to Janáček's native region was decisive. He turned his back abruptly on the gauche Romanticism of *Šárka* and for a few years immersed himself completely in Moravian folk music. The many works that he wrote in the early 1890s popularizing Moravian folk music included a folk ballet *Rákos Rákoczy*, hurriedly put together for the 1891 Jubilee Exhibition in Prague, and a one-act opera, *Počátek románu* ('The Beginning of a Romance', 1891), which consists predominantly of folksongs and folkdances with added voice parts. The libretto was adapted from a short story by Gabriela Preissová, who also wrote the play *Její pastorkyňa* ('Her Stepdaughter'), which provided the subject of Janáček's third opera. Both works were set in the same ethnographically-rich region of southern Moravia but were worlds apart in their dramatic potential. It was probably when Janáček realized the greater possibilities of the play that he became dissatisfied with his unassuming but favourably received earlier opera. Withdrawing it after four performances (1894), he set to work on *Jenůfa* (as the work has become known outside Czechoslovakia).

The long period of composition of *Jenůfa* (1894–1903) cannot be explained merely by Janáček's other activities. There was an interval of perhaps four years between the composition of the first act and the rest of the opera, during which time much of Janáček's approach to composing opera seems to have been rethought; even after the première (1904) Janáček made extensive changes before the vocal score was published (1908). He had previously submitted the score to the Prague National Theatre; its chief conductor, Karel Kovařovic, eventually went to see *Jenůfa* in Brno but still declined to take it up. Possibly he remembered Janáček's sarcastic criticism of his own opera *Ženichové* ('The Bridegrooms', 1884) many years earlier, in 1887. Kovařovic's refusal held up Janáček's operatic career outside Brno for a decade.

Janáček's next opera, *Osud* ('Fate', 1903–7), a semi-autobiographical work depicting the social, domestic and professional life of a composer, was accepted by the Brno Theatre in 1906. But when the Vinohrady Theatre opened in Prague in 1907 (as a rival to the National Theatre, where Kovařovic presided), Janáček withdrew *Fate* from Brno and submitted it instead to the Vinohrady Theatre, where despite promises and a contract it was declared unperformable and was eventually withdrawn by Janáček himself. He never lived to see it staged. His fifth opera, *Výlety páně Broučkovy* ('The Excursions of Mr Brouček'), did little better, at least at first. Problems with the libretto (based on a novel satirizing both anti-cultural and over-cultured attitudes in late 19th-century Prague) and with a series of reluctant 'librettists' prolonged work from 1908 to 1913, when Janáček finally gave up with only two acts complete of what was then planned as a single excursion in three acts.

In 1915 a campaign by Janáček's friends and admirers to get *Jenůfa* performed in Prague finally bore fruit. Kovařovic grudgingly reversed his decision and accepted *Jenůfa*, subject to revisions (which he had routinely made, for instance, to Dvořák's operas). Janáček gave his joyous acquiescence and at once returned to *Brouček*, a process encouraged by the huge success *Jenůfa* gained with the Prague public in May 1916. A few months later the Viennese publisher Universal Edition successfully bid for the foreign-language rights. From then on Janáček's operas were published by Uni-

versal Edition, usually in Czech-German editions, and his operas began to be staged abroad. By Janáček's death in 1928 *Jenůfa* had been performed in more than 60 theatres outside Czechoslovakia.

It was some while, however, before Janáček's next opera reached the stage. With the impending break-up of the Austro-Hungarian Empire and consequent establishment of an independent Czechoslovak Republic, Janáček added a whole new, much more patriotic 'Excursion' to *Brouček*. The newly extended work was virtually complete by the end of 1917, but Prague was in no hurry to stage this strange opera; it was finally given in Prague under Kovařovic's successor, Otakar Ostrčil, in 1920. It was Janáček's only operatic première in Prague, where it was popular with neither the singers nor the public and was taken off after ten performances.

1. *Page of autograph score from the final scene of Janáček's 'The Cunning Little Vixen' showing the moment when the Forester sees the Vixen Cub in his dream; typical are the many erasures and the double page number indicating the replacement of two pages in the previous version*

3. LATER OPERAS. *Brouček* and its unhappy première was a watershed in Janáček's career. Thereafter he no longer sought librettists, but did his adaptations himself. This is true both of works such as *Kát'a Kabanová* (1920–21) and *Věc Makropulos* ('The Makropulos Affair', 1923–5), which are based on plays, and of *Příhody Lišky Bystroušky* ('The Cunning Little Vixen', 1922–3) and *Z mrtvého domu* ('From the House of the Dead', 1927–8), which are based on novels. Similarly Janáček no longer looked to Prague for premières for his operas, but with Czechs now installed in the fine German opera house in Brno, headed by Janáček's choice of conductor (František Neumann), Janáček settled for a pattern of Brno premières followed a year or so later by Prague, and then by foreign productions. This allowed him to tinker with the orchestration at Brno rehearsals, adjusting the balance or even filling out scene-change music where necessary. These last years, from 1920 to 1928,

were tremendously fertile, astonishingly so for a man past 65, when in addition to four major operas he completed many other of his best-known works including the Sinfonietta, the Glagolitic Mass and two string quartets. He died at full vigour at the age of 74, his last opera recently completed in fair copy.

A distinctive feature of Janáček's post-*Jenůfa* operas is his willingness and ability to explore territory not normally cultivated by opera composers. *Kát'a Kabanová*, on Ostrovsky's tale of adultery, played safe, possibly after the difficulties of *Fate* and *Brouček*, but all the others are extraordinary subjects for opera. 'Soon he'll even be setting the local column in the newspaper', Karel Čapek is said to have declared when he heard that Janáček wished to set his play *The Makropulos Affair*, much of which is taken up with the exposition of a complicated legal case. But that was one of the more conventional. The local newspaper, Brno's *Lidové noviny*, did in fact provide the basis for Janáček's previous opera, about the adventures of a clever vixen. Dostoyevsky's prison memoirs, lightly disguised as reportage, was the subject of Janáček's final opera, *From the House of the Dead*, which he set straight from the Russian novel, with only the sketchiest of scenarios before him.

4. STYLE AND CONVENTIONS. Janáček began writing operas in the familiar moulds of Czech nationalist opera. *Šárka*, a serious opera based on Czech mythic history, was inspired by Smetana's *Libuše* (1881; in terms of story *Šárka* is actually its continuation). *The Beginning of a Romance*, a comic one-act village opera, is usually said to resemble Dvořák's *Tvrdé palice* ('The Stubborn Lovers', 1881), though Janáček himself likened it to Blodek's *V studni* ('In the Well', 1867). The serious village opera that Janáček attempted in *Jenůfa* is sometimes regarded as a new departure but even here there were Czech models at hand, most obviously by J. B. Foerster (e.g. his *Debora*, 1893). Foerster's *Eva* (composed 1895–7, performed 1899) furthermore was based on a play by Gabriela Preissová. What set apart Janáček's *Jenůfa* and Foerster's *Eva*, written almost simultaneously, were three factors. Though both composers attempted to evoke a Moravian atmosphere, Janáček, with his Moravian roots, his extensive fieldwork, and his absorption of the patterns of Moravian folksong at a deep level, was able to present folk music not as a colourful exoticism but as part of his distinctive style. Second, while Foerster turned Preissová's prose play into verse before he began work, Janáček left *Her Stepdaughter* in prose, so writing the first Czech prose opera. The third factor is that Janáček began to cast adrift from obvious set numbers. The remains are there, ranging from simultaneous duets and a trio, to song-based folk scenes and a full-scale slow concertato ensemble for four soloists and chorus.

Ensembles persist into *Fate* and *Brouček*, but by *Kát'a* and *Makropulos* there are few passages where solo voices combine for more than a bar or two; when they overlap there is usually a naturalistic explanation. Janáček thus became more dependent on the monologue, and most of his librettos from *Jenůfa* onwards provide many such confessional or narrative opportunities. Their frequency in *From the House of the Dead* is one reason why he was so attracted to this seemingly unoperatic material.

During the writing of *Jenůfa* Janáček began to formulate his ideas about 'speech-melody' which were to influence his approach to the voice line and indeed his whole musical idiom for the rest of his life. From about 1897 he took down examples of everyday speech in conventional musical notation and studied them, trying to establish the influence of moods and emotions as well as external factors on their rhythm and pitch. He wrote up his 'research' both in theoretical articles and in whimsical evocations of tiny scenes brought to life by the inclusion of snatches of notated speech. He frequently stressed how important such work was to an opera composer. Speech melodies were in no sense potential thematic material for Janáček but, rather, study material to help him produce sung stylizations of the irregular patterns of everyday speech. The result was a gradual move away from the regular metrical structure in the voice parts of his operas (regular phraseology generally remains in the orchestra) to a more varied and irregular approach using a greater variety of rhythms. The process is graphically demonstrated by the revisions that Janáček made in 1918 to the 1888 voice parts of his first opera, *Šárka* (see Tyrrell 1988, pp.292–7).

In the play-based operas such as *Jenůfa*, *Kát'a Kabanová* and *The Makropulos Affair*, Janáček could rely on a ready-made dramatic structure, though he occasionally overrode the act climaxes (*Kát'a Kabanová*). But in *Brouček* and in particular in *The Vixen* and *From the House of the Dead*, he was able to make tiny scenes cohere by bedding them into the orchestral continuum, a process facilitated by the increasing structural importance of the orchestra in his post-speech-melody works. He made little use of leitmotif and only sporadic use of a few reminiscence themes. Instead his approach was to build up sections – often a whole scene – on a single motif subjected to ostinato and variation techniques, sometimes contrasted with another theme in a type of loose rondo. The second half of Act 2 of *The Vixen* is bonded by the structural arch of the offstage chorus; the first half consists of a set of variations of the theme of the opening prelude.

In *Jenůfa* Janáček came to terms with Moravian folksong and his notion of speech-melody. The next two operas, *Fate* and *The Excursions of Mr Brouček*, show a further development in their reactions to fashionable European composers such as Charpentier and Puccini. Janáček much admired *Louise*, and learnt from its urban setting and characters (and the urban waltzes that go with them). In Act 1 of *Fate* he imitated Charpentier's large individualized chorus. Much longer-lasting, however, was Janáček's use of offstage symbolic chorus: the 'voice of the Volga' in *Kát'a Kabanová*, the 'voice of the forest' in *The Cunning Little Vixen* and the mysterious male-voice chorus that repeats Marty's words at the end of *The Makropulos Affair*. All this can be traced back to the 'call of Paris' (an offstage chorus) that finally lures Louise away from her home. Puccini's influence can be detected in *Brouček* and *Kát'a Kabanová*. Later, Janáček seems to have picked up something of Debussy (in *The Vixen*) and even of Berg (in *From the House of the Dead*).

The uncertainty suggested by the extensive revisions that Janáček made to *Jenůfa*, *Fate* and *The Excursions of Mr Brouček* contrasts strikingly with the confidence he showed in the last four operas. By now he was belatedly acknowledged as one of the most important composers in Czechoslovakia, in whose independence in 1918 he took an almost personal pride. His marriage in 1880 to Zdeňka Schulzová (1865–1938) was unhappy from the start and further embittered by the death of

2. *Page of autograph score from Act 3 scene ii of Janáček's 'From the House of the Dead' showing the moment when Alexandr Petrovič sings of his resurrection 'from the dead' and the prisoners celebrate his freedom in chorus; the page illustrates Janáček's conversion to self-ruled paper for his final opera and the inclusion by one of his copyists of bar numbers and crosses indicating the page turns*

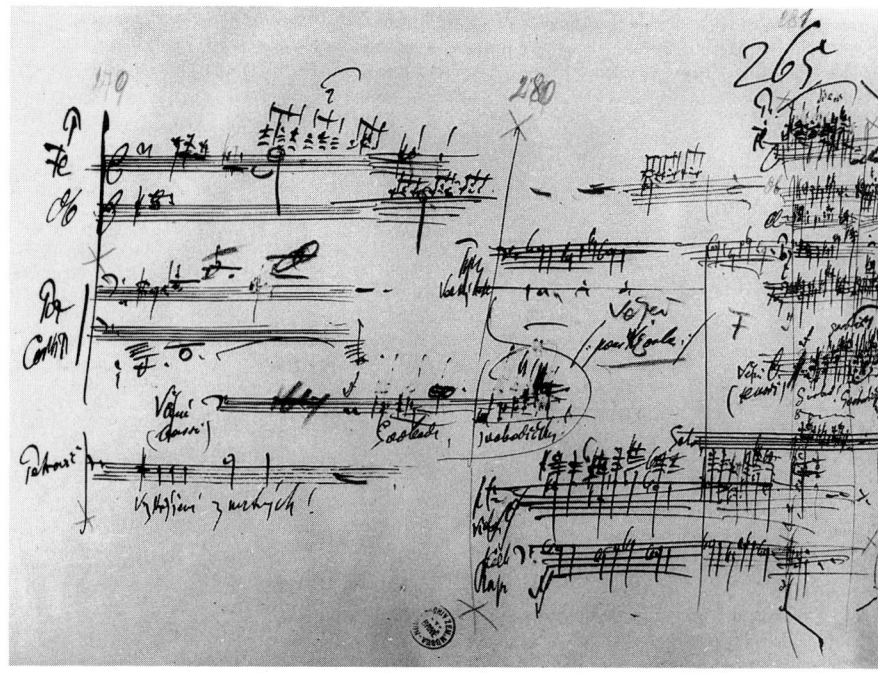

both his children. But from 1917 an ever-deepening friendship with Mrs Kamila Stösslová (1892–1935) provided the incentive and inspiration for many of his later works.

By the time of his final four operas Janáček had consolidated an individual style and a set of operatic conventions. The musical language is essentially tonal, though coloured by modal inflections and in places surprisingly dissonant. But even in his harshest works, such as the final two operas, there are sudden and intense lyrical flowerings: this tension between extremes is one of the sources of Janáček's creative energy. Janáček's melodic style was sometimes dismissed by early commentators as 'short-breathed'. Concision in all aspects is now seen to be one of his chief virtues: most of the operas are over in two hours. The dramaturgy of the later ones is engagingly direct, achieving striking effects by means of stark juxtapositions. In *From the House of the Dead*, Luka's tale of his horrific beating is followed by the return of Petrovič after similar treatment by the prison guards. The torment and release of the eagle is juxtaposed with the torturing and release of Petrovič. With a few deft additions, including the death of its main protagonist, Janáček turned Těsnohlídek's light-hearted tale of a vixen and a forester into a profound tragicomic fable that can comprehend and come to terms with death. In *The Makropulos Affair* the death (another addition) of Emilia Marty became one of Janáček's most magnificent finales, his music investing Čapek's conversation piece with a moving grandeur and monumentality. *From the House of the Dead*, his slackest libretto in terms of events, is fuelled by music of an intense driving force, startling even for Janáček. The means of his art often seem trivial when analysed, the dramaturgy occasionally clumsy or even amateurish, but such factors pale into insignificance in the light of the immense dramatic instincts that Janáček brought to life in his operas.

See also CUNNING LITTLE VIXEN, THE; EXCURSIONS OF MR BROUČEK, THE; FROM THE HOUSE OF THE DEAD; JENŮFA; KÁŤA KABANOVÁ; MAKROPULOS AFFAIR, THE; and OSUD.

---

first performed at Brno, National Theatre, unless otherwise stated
full scores (Universal Edition) unless otherwise stated are updated reproduced scores for hire only; detailed source information for works in CS-Bm is listed by A. Němcová, S. Přibáňova and T. Straková (1980)

title	genre, acts	libretto	date	first performance	remarks, publication, sources
Šárka	heroic opera, 3	J. Zeyer	1887, rev. 1888, 1918–19, 1924–5	11 Nov 1925	Act 3 orchd O. Chlubna, 1918; full score (Vienna, 1977) [reproduced MS]; A-Wn
Počátek románu [The Beginning of a Romance]	romantic opera, 1	J. Tichý, after G. Preissová's story	1891	10 Feb 1894	sections later destroyed by Janáček; reconstructed B. Bakala; full score ed. E. Holis (Prague and Vienna, 1978) [reproduced MS]; CS-Bm

title	genre, acts	libretto	date	first performance	remarks, publication, sources
Její pastorkyňa [Her Stepdaughter; Her Foster Daughter; Jenůfa]	opera, 3	Janáček, after Preissová's play	1894–1903, rev. before 1908	21 Jan 1904	vs (Brno, 1908), full score ed. C. Mackerras and J. Tyrrell (London, 1991) [reproduced MS]; rev. version, reorchd K. Kovařovic (Vienna, 1917), ed. J. M. Dürr (Vienna, 1969); *A-Wn*
Osud [Fate; Destiny]	novelesque scenes, 3	F. Bartošová and Janáček	1903–6; rev. 1907	Brno Radio, 13 March 1934 (abridged), 18 Sept 1934 (complete); Brno, National, 25 Oct 1958	1958 production = re-arranged version by V. Nosek; full score, orig. version, ed. V. Nosek (Prague and Vienna, 1978) [reproduced MS]; *CS-Bm*
Výlety páně Broučkovy [The Excursions of Mr Brouček]	opera, 2 pts		1908–17	Prague, National, 23 April 1920	vs (Vienna, 1919); *Bm**
Part 1: Výlet pana Broučka do měsíce [Mr Brouček's Excursion to the Moon]	2	Janáček, with addns by F. Gellner, V. Dyk, F. S. Procházka and others, after S. Čech's novel	1908–17		orig. in 3 acts: 'epilogue' act discarded when 2nd excursion added
Part 2: Výlet pana Broučka do XV. stoleti [Mr Brouček's Excursion to the 15th Century]	2	Procházka, after Čech's novel	1917		
Kát'a Kabanová	opera, 3	Janáček, after A. N. Ostrovsky: *Groza* [The Storm], trans. V. Červinka	1920–21	23 Nov 1921	full score (Vienna, 1922), ed. C. Mackerras (Vienna, 1971); *Bm**
Příhody Lišky Bystroušky [The Adventures of the Vixen Bystrouška; The Cunning Little Vixen]	opera, 3	Janáček, after R. Těsnohlídek's novel	1922–3	6 Nov 1924	vs (Vienna, 1924); *Bm**
Věc Makropulos [The Makropulos Affair; The Makropulos Case]	opera, 3	Janáček, after K. Čapek's play	1923–5	18 Dec 1926	vs (Vienna, 1926); full score, ed. C. Mackerras (Vienna, 1970); *Bm**
Z mrtvého domu [From the House of the Dead]	opera, 3	Janáček, after F. M. Dostoyevsky's novel	1927–8	12 April 1930 [version by O. Chlubna and B. Bakala]	rev. and reorchd O. Chlubna and B. Bakala, vs and full score (Vienna, 1930); vs with orig. ending as appx (Vienna, 1964), full score (Vienna, 1991); *Bm**

Projected operas with musical sketches: Gazdina roba [The Farm Mistress] (Preissová), 1904, 1907; Paní mincmistrová [The Mintmaster's Wife] (L. Stroupežnický), 1906–7; Anna Karenina (L. N. Tolstoy), 1907 [in Russ.]; Živá mrtvola [The Living Corpse] (Tolstoy), 1916

Other projected operas, with only scenario, annotated play or novel etc.: Poslední Abencerage (F. R. de Chateaubriand: *Les aventures du dernier Abencérage*), 1885; Andělská sonata [The Angel Sonata] (J. Merhaut), 1903; Divoška [The Tomboy] (V. Krylov), 1920–21 [class exercise: corrections to composition pupils' versions]; Dítě [The Child] (F. X. Šalda), 1923

CATALOGUES, BIBLIOGRAPHIES, DISCOGRAPHIES, LISTS OF PERFORMANCES

J. Racek, ed.: *Leoš Janáček: obraz života a díla* [A Picture of Janáček's Life and Works] (Brno, 1948) [incl. list of works (T. Straková and V. Veselý), 31–54; list of writings (T. Straková), 55–61; systematic bibliography (O. Fric), 62–88; iconography (J. Raab), 89–104]

Leoš Janáček na světových jevištích [Janáček on the World Stages] (Brno, 1958) [exhibition catalogue; incl. list, by town, of performances of operas outside Czechoslovakia, 15–30]

V. Telec: *Leoš Janáček 1854–1928: výběrová bibliografie* [Select Bibliography] (Brno, 1958)

B. Štědroň: *Dílo Leoše Janáčka: abecední seznam Janáčkových skladeb a úprav* [Janáček's Works: an Alphabetical Catalogue of Janáček's Compositions and Arrangements] (Prague, 1959; Eng. trans., 1959, as *The Work of Leoš Janáček*; Ger. trans., *BMw*, ii, 1960, pp.120–53, iii, 1961, pp.34–77)

ČSHS [list of works and bibliography to 1962]

W. D. Curtis: *Leoš Janáček* (Utica, NY, 1978) [discography]

J. Kratochvílová: *Dílo Leoše Janáčka: výběrová bibliografie* (Brno, 1978)

Z. Tomanová: 'Leoš Janáček a Národní divadlo v předhledech' [Janáček and the National Theatre Surveyed], *HRo*, xxxi (1978), 234–8 [detailed list of productions at Prague National Theatre]

J. Procházka: *Hudební dílo Leoše Janáčka* [Janáček's Musical Works] (Frýdek-Místek, 1979) [chronological list of works, newly numbered; chronological list of editions 1877–1930]

A. Němcová: 'Na okraj Janáčkovy Její pastorkyně: úvaha před zahajením příprav ke kritickému vydání opery' [On the Margin of *Jenůfa*: a Reflection before the Commencement of Preparations towards a Critical Edition of the Opera], *ČMm*, lxv (1980), 159–64 [incl. list of sources]

S. Přibáňová: 'Operní dílo Janáčkovo vrcholného údobí' [The Operas of Janáček's Culminative Period], *ČMm*, lxv (1980), 165–71 [incl. list of musical sources for *The Excursions of Mr Brouček*, *Kát'a Kabanová*, *The Cunning Little Vixen*, *The Makropulos Affair* and *From the House of the Dead*]

T. Straková: 'Janáčkovy opery Šárka, Počátek románu, Osud a

hudebnědramatická torza: ke genezi děl, stavu pramenů and jejich kritické intepretaci' [Janáček's Operas Šárka, The Beginning of a Romance, Fate and the Musico-Dramatic Fragments: on the Genesis of the Works, State of the Sources and their Critical Interpretation], ČMm, lxv (1980), 149–57

S. Přibáňová: 'Productions of "Kát'a Kabanová"', Leoš Janáček: Kát'a Kabanová, ed. J. Tyrrell (Cambridge, 1982), 209–24

——: 'Opery Leoše Janáčka doma a v zahraničí' [The Operas of Leoš Janáček at Home and Abroad], Program [Státního divadla v Brně] (1984) [special no.] [list of productions of each opera; list of translations]

N. Simeone: The First Editions of Leoš Janáček: a Bibliographical Catalogue (Tutzing, 1991)

ICONOGRAPHY

J. Raab: 'Janáčkova ikonografie', Leoš Janáček: obraz života a díla, ed. J. Racek (Brno, 1948), 89–104 [documented list]

B. Štědroň: Leoš Janáček v obrazech [Janáček in Pictures] (Prague, 1958, enlarged 2/1980)

T. Straková, ed.: Iconographia janáčkiána (Brno, 1975)

P. Eckstein, ed.: Leoš Janáček a Národní divadlo [Janáček and the National Theatre] (Prague, 1978)

S. Jareš: 'Obrazová dokumentace Janáčkovy Její pastorkyně v Národním divadle roku 1916' [Pictorial Documentation of Jenůfa, National Theatre, 1916], HV, xv (1978), 358–64

LIFE AND WORKS

M. Brod: Leoš Janáček: život a dílo [Life and Works] (Prague, 1924; Ger. orig., 1925, 2/1956)

D. Muller: Leoš Janáček (Paris, 1930)

A. E. Vašek: Po stopách dra Leoše Janáčka [On the Track of Dr Leoš Janáček] (Brno, 1930)

V. Helfert: Leoš Janáček, i (Brno, 1939)

J. Vogel: Leoš Janáček: Leben und Werk (Prague, 1958; Eng. trans., 1962, 2/1981; Cz. orig., 1963) [expanded version of Leoš Janáček: dramatik (Prague, 1948)]

J. Šeda: Leoš Janáček (Prague, 1961)

J. Racek: Leoš Janáček: Mensch und Künstler (Leipzig, 1962, 2/1971; Cz. orig., 1963, as Leoš Janáček: člověk a umělec)

H. Hollander: Leoš Janáček: his Life and Work (London, 1963; Ger. orig., 1964)

M. Černohorská: Leoš Janáček (Prague, 1966) [in Eng.; also in Fr., Ger., Russ., 1966]

B. Štědroň: Leoš Janáček: k jeho lidskému a uměleckému profilu [Janáček's Image as Man and Artist] (Prague, 1976) [incl. chronology of life and works in Cz. and Ger. and bibliography, chiefly post-1965 literature]

G. Erismann: Janáček ou La passion de la vérité (Paris, 1980, 2/1990)

I. Horsbrugh: Leoš Janáček: the Field that Prospered (Newton Abbot, 1981)

J. Vysloužil: Leoš Janáček: für Sie porträtiert (Leipzig, 1981)

K. Honolka: Leoš Janáček: sein Leben, sein Werk, seine Zeit (Stuttgart and Zürich, 1982)

A. Gozenpud: Leosh Yanachek (Moscow, 1984)

S. Přibáňová: Leoš Janáček (Prague, 1984)

LETTERS, MEMOIRS, DOCUMENTARY

J. Kunc: 'Leoš Janáček', HR, iv (1911), 121–34, 185–9

L. Janáček: 'Výlety páně Broučkovy: jeden do měsíce, druhý do XV. století' [The Excursions of Mr Brouček: One to the Moon, the Other to the 15th Century], Lidové noviny (23 Dec 1917); repr. in Janáček 1958, 52–5; Eng. trans. in Zemanová, ed. 1989, 92–6

——: 'Výlety páně Broučkovy' [The Excursions of Mr Brouček], HR, xiii (1919–20), 177–9

L. Janáček and others: 'Liška Bystrouška na divadle' [Liška Bystrouška in the Theatre], Lidové noviny (1 Nov 1924); repr. in Janáček 1958, 316–25; Eng. trans. in Tausky 1982, 145–54

R. Těsnohlídek: 'Mladistvý kmet' [The Youthful Old Man], Lidové noviny (3 July 1924); abridged repr. in Štědroň 1946, 218–19

A. Veselý, ed.: Leoš Janáček: pohled do života a díla [Leoš Janáček: a View of the Life and Works] (Prague, 1924) [= Janáček's autobiography], repr., ed. T. Straková, in OM, xx (1988), 225–40

M. Calma[-Veselá]: 'Z boje pro Janáčkovou Pastorkyni' [From the Battle for Janáček's Jenůfa], Listy Hudební matice, iv (1924–5), 137–47

F. Mareš: 'K sedmdesátinám Leoše Janáčka' [For Leoš Janáček's 70th Birthday], HRo, i (1924–5), 33–5

O. Chlubna: 'Vzpomínky na Leoše Janáčka' [Reminiscences of Leoš Janáček], Divadelní list, vii (1931–2), 101–4, 125–7, 169, 172, 289–90

V. Jiřikovský: 'Vzpomínky na Leoše Janáčka' [Reminiscences of Leoš Janáček], Divadelní list, vii (1931–2), 248–50

V. Kaprál: 'Vzpomínky na první provedení "Její pastorkyně"' [Reminiscences of the First Performance of Jenůfa], Divadelní list, vii (1931–2), 197–9; abridged repr. in Štědroň 1946, 155–6

V. Helfert: 'Něco o vzniku "Její pastorkyně"' [Something on the Origin of Jenůfa], Divadelní list, ix (1933–4), 65–72; repr. in V. Helfert: O Janáčkovi [About Janáček], ed. B. Štědroň (Prague, 1949), 45–50

J. Kunc: 'Vzpomínky na premiéru Její pastorkyně' [Reminiscences of the Première of Jenůfa], Divadelní list, ix (1933–4), 78–90; repr. in Štědroň 1946, 153–5

Janáčkův archiv, 1st ser., ed. V. Helfert (i) and J. Racek (ii–ix) (Prague, 1934–53): i Korespondence Leoše Janáčka s Artušem Rektorysem (1934, enlarged 2/1949 = iv); ii Korespondence Leoše Janáčka s Otakarem Ostrčilem (1948); iii Korespondence Leoše Janáčka s F. S. Procházkou (1949); v Korespondence Leoše Janáčka s libretisty Výletů Broučkových [Janáček's Correspondence with the Brouček Librettists] (1950); vi Korespondence Leoše Janáčka s Gabrielou Horvátovou (1950); vii Korespondence Leoše Janáčka s Karlem Kovařovicem a ředitelstvím Národního divadla [Janáček's Correspondence with Kovařovic and the Directorate of the National Theatre] (1950); viii Korespondence Leoše Janáčka s Marií Calmou a MUDr Františkem Veselým (1951); ix Korespondence Leoše Janáčka s Maxem Brodem (1953) [i–vi, ed. A. Rektorys; vii–ix, ed. J. Racek and A. Rektorys]

L. Firkušný: Leoš Janáček kritikem brněnské opery [Leoš Janáček as Critic of the Brno Opera] (Brno, 1935) [repr. of Janáček's reviews in Hudební listy, 1884–8]

——: 'Poslední Janáčkova opera Z mrtvého domu' [Janáček's Last Opera From the House of the Dead], Divadelní list, xii (1936–7), 358–68, 386–400; printed separately (Brno, 1937); repr. in Firkušný 1939, 54–70

M. Calma[-Veselá]: 'Ze vzpomínek na Leoše Janáčka' [From my Recollections of Leoš Janáček], Hudební výchova, xix (1938), 99–100

V. Červinka: 'Jak vznikla Kát'a Kabanová' [How Kát'a Kabanová came into Being], Národní politika (18 Oct 1938)

L. Firkušný, ed.: 'Dopisy Leoše Janáčka z archivu Družstva Národního divadla v Brně' [Janáček's Letters from the Archive of the Družstvo of the National Theatre in Brno], Musikologie, i (1938), 130–39

L. Firkušný: Odkaz Leoše Janáčka české opeře [Janáček's Legacy to Czech Opera] (Brno, 1939)

P. Dědeček: 'Karel Kovařovic a "Její pastorkyňa"' [Karel Kovařovic and Janáček], Vzpomínáme Karla Kovařovice, ed. J. Petr (Prague, 1940), 91–4

F. Mareš: 'Vzpomínky na Leoše Janáčka' [Reminiscences of Leoš Janáček], Lidové noviny (17 Feb 1940); abridged repr. in Štědroň 1946, 182–3

G. Preissová: 'Má setkání s Thalií' [My Encounters with Thalia], Divadlo a hudba, i/8 (1942), 49–51

B. Štědroň: 'Leoš Janáček a František Neumann', Smetana, xxxiv (1942), 58–60, 72–4, 89 [correspondence]

——, ed.: Janáček ve vzpomínkách a dopisech [Janáček in Reminiscences and Letters] (Prague, 1946); rev. and Eng. trans. as Leoš Janáček: Letters and Reminiscences (Prague, 1955)

F. Bartoš, ed.: 'Janáčkovy dopisy dr. Fr. Skácelíkovi' [Janáček's Letters to Dr František Skácelík], Tempo, xx (1947–8), 244–8

L. Kundera: Janáček a Klub přátel umění [Janáček and the Friends of Art Club] (Olomouc, 1948)

R. Smetana: Vyprávění o Leoši Janáčkovi [Stories about Leoš Janáček] (Olomouc, 1948)

F. Pala: 'Janáček a Národní divadlo' [Janáček and the National Theatre], HRo, vi (1953), 882–91

J. Racek: 'Leoš Janáček a Praha' [Janáček and Prague], Musikologie, iii (1955), 11–50 [incl. Janáček's comments on operas he saw in Prague]

T. Straková: 'Janáčkova opera Osud' [Janáček's Opera Fate], ČMm, xli (1956), 209–60; xlii (1957), 133–64 [incl. correspondence]

O. Chlubna: 'K úpravě opery "Z mrtvého domu"' [On the Revision of the Opera From the House of the Dead], Opery Leoše Janáčka na brněnské scéně, ed. V. Nosek (Brno, 1958) [unpaginated]

——: 'Několik slov k Janáčkově "Šárce"' [A Few Words on Janáček's Šárka], ibid

L. Kundera: 'Janáčkova "Věc Makropulos"' [Janáček's The Makropulos Affair], ibid

L. Janáček: Fejetony z Lidových novin [Feuilletons from the Lidové noviny], ed. J. Racek (Brno, 1958; partial Eng. trans. by V.

Tausky and M. Tausky as *Leoš Janáček: Leaves from his Life*, London, 1982)

I. Stolařík, ed.: 'Jan Löwenbach a Leoš Janáček: vzájemná korespondence' [Mutual Correspondence], *Slezský sborník*, lvi (1958), 360–411

T. Straková: 'Setkání Leoše Janáčka s Gabrielou Preissovou' [Janáček's Encounter with Gabriela Preissová], *ČMm*, xliii (1958), 145–63 [incl. correspondence]

B. Štědroň: 'K Janáčkově opeře Osud' [Janáček's Opera *Fate*], *Živá hudba*, i (1959), 159–83 [incl. correspondence]

M. Trkanová: *U Janáčků: podle vyprávění Marie Stejskalové* [At the Janáčeks': After the Account of Marie Stejskalová] (Prague, 1959, 2/1964)

B. Štědroň: 'Ke korespondenci a vztahu Leoše Janáčka a Karla Kovařovice', *Sborník prací filosofické fakulty brněnské university*, F6 (1960), 31–69

A. Němcová and S. Přibáňová: 'Příspěvek k dějinám opery Národního divadla v Brně 1884–1919', *ČMm*, xlviii (1963), 261–82

B. Štědroň: 'Leoš Janáček kritikem brněnské opery v letech 1890–1892' [Leoš Janáček as Critic of the Brno Opera 1890–92], *Otázky divadla a filmu*, i (1970), 207–48 [repr. reviews of 1890–92]

——, ed.: 'Janáčkova korespondence s Universal-Edition v letech 1916–1918 týkající se Její pastorkyně' [Janáček's Correspondence with Universal Edition 1916–18 over *Jenůfa*], *Otázky divadla a filmu*, ii (1971), 249–309

A. Němcová: 'Brněnská premiéra Janáčkovy Její pastorkyně' [The Brno Première of *Jenůfa*], *ČMm*, lix (1974), 133–46; Ger. trans. in Knaus 1982, 7–22 [incl. letters and reviews]

K. Blaukopf: 'Gustav Mahler und die tschechische Oper', *ÖMz*, xxxiv (1979), 285–8 [incl. letters]

D. Plamenac: 'Nepoznati komentari Leoša Janáčeka operi "Katja Kabanova"' [Unknown Commentaries on Leoš Janáček's Opera *Kát'a Kabanova*], *MZ*, xvii/1 (1981), 122–31; Eng. trans. of documents in John 1985, 83–6

J. Knaus, ed.: *Leoš Janáček-Materialien* (Zürich, 1982)

V. Tausky and M. Tausky, eds.: *Leoš Janáček: Leaves from his Life* (London, 1982)

J. Tyrrell: *Leoš Janáček: Kát'a Kabanová* (Cambridge, 1982) [incl. letters and other documents]

C. Susskind: *Janáček and Brod* (New Haven, CT, and London, 1985) [incl. correspondence]

Z. E. Fischmann, ed.: *Janáček-Newmarch Correspondence* (Rockville, MD, 1986)

B. Štědroň, ed.: *Leoš Janáček: vzpomínky, dokumenty, korespondence a studie* [Reminiscences, Documents, Correspondence] (Prague, 1986)

E. Hilmar, ed.: *Leoš Janáček: Briefe an die Universal Edition* (Tutzing, 1988)

M. Kuna and others, eds.: *Antonín Dvořák: korespondence a dokumenty*, ii (Prague, 1988) [incl. letters to Janáček]

M. Zemanová, ed.: *Janáček's Uncollected Essays on Music* (London, 1989)

S. Přibáňová, ed.: *Hádanka života (dopisy Leoše Janáčka Kamile Stösslové)* [The Riddle of Life (Leoš Janáček's Letters to Kamila Stösslová)] (Brno, 1990; Eng. trans., forthcoming)

J. Tyrrell: *Janáček's Operas: a Documentary Account* (London, 1992)

HISTORICAL, ANALYTICAL AND AESTHETICS

M. Brod: *Sternenhimmel: Musik- und Theatererlebnisse* (Prague and Munich, 1923, 2/1966 as *Prager Sternenhimmel …*) [incl. chaps. on *Jenůfa* and *Kát'a Kabanová*]

V. Helfert: 'Janáčkovy neznámé opery: 1. Šárka' [Janáček's Unknown Operas: 1. *Šárka*], *HRo*, i (1924–5), 48–55; repr. in V. Helfert: *O Janáčkovi*, ed. B. Štědroň (Prague, 1949), 23–38

O. Chlubna: 'Dr Leoš Janáček: Z mrtvého domu' [Dr Leoš Janáček: *From the House of the Dead*], *Divadelní list Národního divadla v Brně*, v (1929–30), 177, 189–94

H. Kašlík: 'Retuše Karla Kovařovice v Janáčkově opeře Její pastorkyně' [Karel Kovařovic's 'Retouchings' in Janáček's Opera *Jenůfa*], *Hudební věstník*, xxxi (1938), 112–13, 130–31, 142–3, 159–60; repr. separately (Prague, 1938)

L. Firkušný: *Odkaz Leoše Janáčka české opeře* [Janáček's Legacy to Czech Opera] (Brno, 1939) [chaps. on all Janáček's operas]

J. Vysloužil: 'Janáčkova opera "Počátek románu"' [Janáček's Opera *The Beginning of a Romance*], *HRo*, v (1954), 743–4

Musikologie, iii (1955) [incl. F. Pala: 'Jevištní dílo Leoše Janáčka' [Janáček's Stage Works], 61–210; J. Burjanek: 'Janáčkova Kát'a Kabanová a Ostrovského Bouře' [Janáček's *Kát'a* and

Ostrovsky's *The Storm*], 345–416; T. Straková: 'Janáčkovy operní náměty a torsa' [Janáček's Operatic Projects and Fragments], 417–49]

Leoš Janáček a soudobá hudba: mezinárodní hudebně vědecký kongres: Brno 1958 [Leoš Janáček and Contemporary Music: International Musicological Conference, Brno 1958]

V. Nosek, ed.: *Opery Leoše Janáčka na brněnské scéně* [Janáček's Operas on the Brno Stage] (Brno, 1958) [articles on each opera]

J. Racek: 'Janáček – dramatik', *SH*, ii (1958), 6–12, 49–55, 91–9, 142–8; abridged Ger. trans. in *DJbM*, v (1960), 37–57

F. Pala: 'Postavy a prostředí v Její pastorkyni' [Characters and Environment in *Jenůfa*], *Leoš Janáček: sborník statí a studií* (Prague, 1959), 29–70

K. Wörner: 'Katjas Tod: die Schlussszene der Oper "Katja Kabanowa" von Janáček', *SMz*, xcix (1959), 91–6; also in *Leoš Janáček a soudobá hudba: Brno 1958*, 392–8 [see also K. H. Wörner: 'Natur, Liebe und Tod bei Janáček', *Die Musik in der Geistesgeschichte* (Bonn, 1970), 131–43; 'Leoš Janáček', *Das Zeitalter der thematischen Prozesse in der Geschichte der Musik* (Regensburg, 1969), 146–53; Eng. trans. in J. Tyrrell: *Leoš Janáček: Kát'a Kabanová* (Cambridge, 1982), 174–84]

M. Očadlík: 'Dvě kapitoly k Janáčkovým Výletům pana Broučka na měsíc' [Two Chapters on Janáček's *Mr Brouček's Excursion to the Moon*], *MMC*, no.12 (1960), 133–47

Z. Sádecký: 'Celotónový charakter hudební řeči v Janáčkově "Lišce Bystroušce"' [The Whole-tone Character of the Musical Language of Janáček's *Cunning Little Vixen*], *Živá hudba*, ii (1962), 95–163 [with Ger. summary]

A. Závodský: *Gabriela Preissová* (Prague, 1962) [incl. chap. on the play on which Janáček based *Jenůfa*]

O. Fiala: 'Libreto k Janáčkově opeře Počátek románu' [The Libretto of Janáček's *The Beginning of a Romance*], *ČMm*, xlix (1964), 192–222 [with Ger. summary]

T. Straková: 'Mezihry v Káti Kabanové' [The Interludes in *Kát'a Kabanová*], *ČMm*, xlix (1964), 229–36; Ger. trans. in *Operní dílo Leoše Janáčka: Brno 1965*, 125–30, repr. in *Leoš Janáček – Materialien*, ed. J. Knaus (Zürich, 1982), 39–49; abridged Eng. trans. in J. Tyrrell: *Leoš Janáček: Kát'a Kabanová* (Cambridge, 1982), 134–43

T. Straková and others, eds.: *Operní dílo Leoše Janáčka: Brno 1965* [Janáček's Operatic Works]

J. Procházka: 'Z mrtvého doma: Janáčkův tvůrčí i lidský epilog a manifest' [*From the House of the Dead*: Janáček's Creative and Human Epilogue and Manifesto], *HV*, iii (1966), 218–43, 426–37

J. Tyrrell: 'The Musical Prehistory of Janáček's *Počátek románu* and its Importance in Shaping the Composer's Dramatic Style', *ČMm*, lii (1967), 245–70

G. Abraham: 'Realism in Janáček's Operas', *Slavonic and Romantic Music* (London, 1968), 83–98

R. Pečman, ed.: *Colloquium Leoš Janáček et musica europaea: Brno III 1968* [incl. section on operas]

L. Polyakova: *Opernoye tvorchestvo Leosha Yanacheka* [Janáček's Operas] (Moscow, 1968)

Z. Sádecký: 'Výstava dialogu a monologu v Janáčkově Její pastorkyni' [Dialogue and Monologue Structure in Janáček's *Jenůfa*], *Živá hudba*, iv (1968), 73–146 [with Ger. summary]

B. Štědroň: *Zur Genesis von Leoš Janáčeks Oper Jenůfa* (Brno, 1968, 2/1972); extracts in Eng. in *Sborník prací filosofické fakulty brněnské university*, H3 (1968), 43–74; H5 (1970), 91–104 [incl. extensive bibliography]

A. Mazlová: 'Zeyerova a Janáčkova Šárka' [Zeyer's and Janáček's *Šárka*], *ČMm*, liii–liv (1968–9), 71–88 [with Eng. summary]

J. Tyrrell: 'Mr Brouček's Excursion to the Moon', *ČMm*, liii–liv (1968–9), 89–124

K. von Fischer: 'Zu Leoš Janáčeks "Das Schlaue Füchslein"', *Jb 70/71 Opernhaus Zürich*, xlix (1970), 10–18; repr. in *Leoš Janáček-Gesellschaft: Mitteilungsblatt 1972*, no.3

L. Polyakova: 'Russkiye operï Yanacheka' [Janáček's Russian Operas], *Puti razvitiya i vzaimosvyazi russkogo i chekhoslovatskogo*, ed. Institut istorii iskusstv (Moscow, 1970), 190–206; Cz. trans. in *Cesty rozvoje a vzájemné vztahy ruského a československého umění* (Prague, 1974), 247–69

J. Tyrrell: 'Janáček and the Speech-melody Myth', *MT*, cxi (1970), 793–6

E. Chisholm: *The Operas of Leoš Janáček* (Oxford, 1971)

J. Knaus: 'Leoš Janáček und Richard Strauss', *NZM*, Jg.133 (1972), 128; rev. in *Richard-Strauss-Blätter*, new ser., no.3 (1980), 74–9

M. Štědroň: 'Janáček a opera Groza Vladimíra Nikitiče Kašperova na libreto N. A. Ostrovského (1867)' [Janáček and Kashperov's

Opera *The Thunderstorm* to Ostrovsky's Libretto (1867)], *Svazky – vztahy – paralely* (Brno, 1973), 128–33

J. Tyrrell: 'How Domšík Became a Bass', *MT*, cxiv (1973), 29–30

T. Kneif: *Die Bühnenwerke von Leoš Janáček* (Vienna, 1974)

T. Straková: 'Janáčkova opera Její pastorkyňa: pokus o analýzu díla' [Janáček's *Jenůfa*: an Attempt at an Analysis], *ČMm*, lix (1974), 119–26 [with Ger. trans., 126–32]

R. Cígler: *Příhody Lišky Bystroušky: příspěvek k poznání díla a původnosti nové Janáčkovy operní koncepce* [The Cunning Little Vixen: a Contribution to Knowledge of the Work and the Originality of Janáček's New Operatic Conception] (diss., U. of Brno, 1975)

F. Pulcini: 'Le opere teatrali inedite di Leoš Janáček', *NRMI*, ix (1975), 552–67

M. Štědroň: 'K analýze vokální melodiky Janáčkovy opery Věc Makropulos s využitím samočinného počítače' [The Analysis of the Voice Part of Janáček's Opera *The Makropulos Affair* with the Aid of a Computer], *HV*, xii (1975), 46–61 [with Ger. summary]; see also *Musicologica slovaca*, vi (1978), 187–98

M. Ewans: *Janáček's Tragic Operas* (London, 1977; Ger. trans., 1981)

F. Pala: 'Osud', *HRo*, xxxi (1978), 41–5; see also 231–3

R. Pečman: 'Námětová geneze Věci Makropulos (Cesta od Shawa k Čapkovi a Janáčkovi)' [The Genesis of the Subject of *The Makropulos Affair*: the Journey from Shaw to Čapek and Janáček], *Leoš Janáček ac tempora nostra: Brno XIII 1978*, 245–65; abridged Ger. trans. in *Sborník prací filozofické fakulty brněnské univerzity*, H17 (1982), 21–40

——, ed.: *Colloquium Leoš Janáček ac tempora nostra: Brno XIII 1978* [incl. papers on the operas]

L. Peduzzi: 'Janáček, Haas a Divoška' [Janáček, Haas and The Tomboy], *OM*, x/8 (1978), pp.i–iv; xii/7 (1980), pp.i–iv, viii

L. Polyakova: *Cheshskaya i slovatskaya opera XX. veka* [Czech and Slovak Opera of the 20th Century], i (Moscow, 1978)

A. Gozenpud: 'Janáček a Musorgskij', *OM*, xii (1980), no.4, 101–9; no.5, suppl. pp.i–v, vii–viii; Ger. trans. in *Leoš Janáček-Gesellschaft: Mitteilungsblatt 1984*

J. Tyrrell: 'Mr Brouček at Home: an Epilogue to Janáček's Opera', *MT*, cxx (1980), 30–33 [on the discarded act of the *Excursion to the Moon*]

A. Gozenpud: *Dostoyevskiy i muzikal'no-teatral'noye iskusstvo* [Dostoyevsky and the Art of Music Theatre] (Leningrad, 1981), 202–12

C. Dahlhaus: *Musikalischer Realismus: zur Musikgeschichte der 19. Jahrhunderts* (Munich, 1982; Eng. trans., 1985) [contains discussion of *Jenůfa*]

F. Pulcini: *Per una ricognizione italiana del teatro musicale di Leoš Janáček: aspetti della drammaturgia di 'Da una casa di morti'* (diss., U. of Turin, 1982)

J. Tyrrell: *Leoš Janáček: Kát'a Kabanová* (Cambridge, 1982)

——: *Příhody Lišky Bystroušky* (Decca D257D 2, 1982) [record notes]

——: 'The Tower of Babylon Collapses', Welsh National Opera programme book (Cardiff, 1982) [on *From the House of the Dead*]

——: *Jenůfa* (Decca D276D 3, 1983) [record notes]

A. Němcová: 'Otázníky nad Její pastorkyní' [A *Jenůfa* Questionnaire], *OM*, xvi (1984), 24–7

R. Pečman, ed.: *Colloquium Dvořák Janáček and their time: Brno XIX 1984* [incl. papers on the operas]

N. John, ed.: *Leoš Janáček: Jenůfa/Katya Kabanova* (London and New York, 1985) [librettos and essays]

L'avant-scène opéra, no.84 (1986) [*The Cunning Little Vixen* issue; Fr. libretto and essays]

M. Melnikova: 'Interpretace Dostojevského textu v libretu poslední Janáčkovy opery' [The Interpretation of Dostoyevsky's Text in the Libretto of Janáček's Last Opera], *HV*, xxiii (1986), 43–55

——: 'Opera Leosha Janacheka Katya Kabanova', *Sborník prací filozofické fakulty brněnské univerzity*, H21 (1986), 85–91

M. Štědroň: 'Janáček a Zeyerův verš v opeře Šárka' [Janáček and Zeyer's Verse in the Opera *Šárka*], ibid, 41–48

J. Tyrrell: 'From Meiningen to Moravia: *Jenůfa* in Context', Covent Garden programme book (London, 1986)

J. Vysloužil: 'Zur Bedeutung der Prosa bei Leoš Janáček', *Sborník prací filozofické fakulty brněnské univerzity*, H21 (1986), 73–84

L'avant-scène opéra, no.102 (1987) [*Jenůfa* issue; Fr. libretto and essays]

J. Bužga: 'Demytologizace přírody a mýtus přírody v Janáčkově opeře "Příhody lišky Bystroušky"' [The Demythologizing of Nature and the Myth of Nature in Janáček's Opera *The Cunning Little Vixen*], *OM*, xix (1987), 193–5

J. Tyrrell: 'The Cathartic Slow Waltz, and Other Finale Conventions in Janáček's Operas', *Essays on Drama and Music in Honour of Winton Dean* (Cambridge, 1987), 333–52

R. Vonásek: 'Osud' [*Fate*], *OM*, xix (1987), 206–9

L'avant-scène opéra, no.107 (1988) [*From the House of the Dead* issue; Fr. libretto and essays]

L'avant-scène opéra, no.114 (1988) [*Kát'a Kabanová* issue; Fr. libretto and essays]

M. Beckerman: '"Pleasure and Woes": the Vixen's Wedding Celebration', *Leoš Janáček and Czech Music: St Louis, Missouri 1988* (forthcoming); Cz. trans., *OM*, xx (1988), 306–11

L. Faltus and M. Štědroň: 'Janáčkův Houslový koncert – torzo nebo vrcholné dílo posledního údobí skladatele?' [Janáček's Violin Concerto – Torso or Culminative Work of the Composer's Final Period?], *OM*, xx (1988), 89–96 [on the orig. version of the ov. to *From the House of the Dead*]

J. Tyrrell: *Czech Opera* (Cambridge, 1988)

——: 'Fate, Louise and the Hidden Agenda', *Leoš Janáček and Today: Brno XXIII 1988* (forthcoming)

——: 'Janáček's Concept of Recitative', *Leoš Janáček and Czech Music: St Louis, Missouri 1988* (forthcoming)

R. Klos: 'Rozsudek nad Kostelničkou' [Verdict on the Kostelnička], *OM*, xxi (1989, no.iii, suppl.; Eng. trans. in *Glyndebourne Festival Opera Book 1989*, ed. H. O'Neill (Glyndebourne, 1989), 126–7

J. Procházková: 'Duše v očarovaném kruhu' [Soul in the Charmed Circle], *OM*, xxi (1989), 200–207 [on Janáček's Violin Concerto, the original version of the ov. to *From the House of the Dead*]

J. Tyrrell: 'The Kostelnička: a Life Before and After', *Glyndebourne Festival Opera Book 1989*, 121–5 [on Preissová's later novel on the *Jenůfa* topic]

——: 'The Making of the Libretto', Welsh National Opera programme book (Cardiff, 1989) [on *Fate*]; repr. with EMI recording (CDC 7 49993 2, 1990)

A. Němcová, ed.: *Leoš Janáček: chaque son, c'est un déferlement de passion* (Prague, 1990) [essays]

J. Tyrrell: '"A Merry Thing with a Sad End": *The Vixen* as Tragicomedy', Covent Garden programme book (London, 1990)

——: *Věc Makropulos* (Decca 430 372–2, 1991); *Z mrtvého domu* (Decca 430 375–2, 1991) [record notes]

PERFORMANCE, INTERPRETATION AND RECEPTION

E. Nováková: *Opera v Prozatímním divadle v Brně v letech 1884–1894* [Opera in the Provisional Theatre in Brno 1884–94] (diploma diss., U. of Brno, 1956)

F. Pala: *Opera Národního divadla v období Otakara Ostrčila* [The Opera of the (Prague) National Theatre during the Time of Otakar Ostrčil], i–iv (Prague, 1962–70); V. Pospíšil: ibid, v–vi (Prague, 1983–9)

A. Němcová-Grulichová: *Opera českého Národního divadla v Brně v letech první světové války* [The Opera of the Czech National Theatre in Brno in the Years of World War I] (MS, Brno, 1963; copy deposited with Český hudební fond, Prague)

J. Telcová: articles on the scenography of Janáček's operas in *ČMm*, xlix (1964), 259–83 [on *Jenůfa*]; ibid, l (1965), 261–78 [on the Vixen]; ibid, li (1966), 345–59 [*Kát'a Kabanová*]; lii (1967), 315–30 [*Brouček*]; liii–iv (1968–9), 155–67 [*Věc Makropulos*]; lvi (1971), 153–62 [*Šárka* etc.] [all with Ger. summaries and illustrations]; general survey in *Otázky divadla a filmu*, iii (Brno, 1973), 39–53 [with Eng. summary]

Operní dílo Leoše Janáčka: Brno 1965 [incl. sections on interpretation and staging, notably articles by J. Vogel, 145–7, and C. Mackerras, 102–4; further article by Mackerras in J. Tyrrell: *Leoš Janáček: Kát'a Kabanová* (Cambridge, 1982), 143–54]

S. Přibáňová: 'Janáčkovy opery ve světle zahraničních kritik' [Janáček's Operas in the Light of Foreign Criticism], *ČMm*, l (1965), 231–42 [with Ger. summary]; see also *Janáčkiana '78 a '79*, ed. K. Steinmetz (Ostrava, 1980), 25–30

Sborník Janáčkovy akademie múzických umění, v (1965) [on questions of performance and interpretation of Janáček's works]

J. Němeček: *Opera Národního divadla v období Karla Kovařovice 1900–1920* [The Opera of the (Prague) National Theatre in the Time of Karel Kovařovic 1900–20] (Prague, 1968–9)

A. Němcová: *Profil brněnské opery v kontextu s dějinami českého divadla v Brně v letech 1894–1904* [A Profile of the Brno Opera in the Context of the History of the Czech Theatre in Brno 1894–1904] (diss., U. of Brno, 1971)

S. Přibáňová: *Opera českého Národního divadla v Brně v letech před první světovou válkou* [The Opera of the Czech National Theatre in Brno in the Years before World War I] (diss., U. of Brno, 1971)

R. Pečman, ed.: *Leoš Janáček ac tempora nostra: Brno XIII 1978* [incl. section on reception history]

O. Pulkert: 'Dramatické dílo Leoše Janáčka na scénách Národního divadlo v Praze' [Janáček's Stage Works at the Prague National Theatre], *HRo*, xxxi (1978), 218–24

S. Přibáňová, A. Simpson and B. Hampton Renton: 'Stage History and Reception', *Leoš Janáček: Kát'a Kabanová*, ed. J. Tyrrell (Cambridge, 1982), 111–33   JOHN TYRRELL

Janáček Theatre. Theatre in BRNO, opened as the Stadttheater in 1882, known as the National Theatre, or sometimes the Theatre on the Ramparts from 1918 to 1945, then named after Janáček; a new Janáček Theatre was opened in 1965.

Janků, Hana (*b* Brno, 25 Oct 1940). Czech soprano. After study with Jaroslav Kvapil in Brno she made her début at the Brno Opera in *Lucerna* by Vítězlav Novák. A powerful singer in the lyric-dramatic repertory, she was soon heard in such roles as Turandot, Libuše, Milada (*Dalibor*) and Leonora (*Il trovatore*). She made her La Scala début in 1967 and sang at the Deutsche Oper in Berlin from 1970. Her Covent Garden début was in 1973 as Tosca. Other roles include Leonora (*La forza del destino*), Ariadne, Kundry, Rusalka and La Gioconda.   DAVID CUMMINGS

Janowitz, Gundula (*b* Berlin, 2 Aug 1937). German soprano. She studied in Graz and made her début in 1960 as Barbarina at the Vienna Staatsoper, where she was engaged for 30 years. Early roles there included Pamina, Purcell's Dido, Mimì, Marzelline and, in 1964, the Empress (*Die Frau ohne Schatten*). At Bayreuth (1960–62) she sang a flowermaiden and Woglinde; at Aix-en-Provence (1963), Pamina; and at Glyndebourne (1964), Ilia. She made her Metropolitan début in 1967 as Sieglinde, which she also sang at the Salzburg Easter Festival (1967–8) and recorded for Karajan. At Salzburg she sang Donna Anna, Countess Almaviva, Fiordiligi (1968–72), the Marschallin and Ariadne (1978–81). She appeared at Frankfurt, Hamburg, Munich, Berlin, Paris, La Scala and Covent Garden, making her début in 1976 as Donna Anna, then singing Ariadne (1987). Her roles included Leonore (which she recorded under Bernstein), Agathe, Elisabeth, Eva, Freia, Arabella, the Countess (*Capriccio*), Aida, Odabella and Amelia (*Boccanegra*). Her full-toned, lyric soprano, with its very beautiful timbre, had become more dramatic by 1988, when she sang Clytemnestra (*Iphigénie en Aulide*) at Vienna. In 1990 she was appointed opera director at Graz, but resigned the following year.   ALAN BLYTH

Janowski, Marek (*b* Warsaw, 18 Feb 1939). Polish conductor. He left Poland as a child with his German-born mother and was brought up in Germany, studying in Cologne with Sawallisch and later in Siena. He worked in the opera houses of Aachen, Düsseldorf and Cologne, and made his London début with the Cologne company at Sadler's Wells in 1969 in the first British performances of Henze's *Der junge Lord*. He was first conductor at Hamburg, then music director at Freiburg (1973–4) and Dortmund. Apart from isolated works he has conducted all the standard repertory. At Hamburg he took over Penderecki's *The Devils of Loudun* and conducted its recording (1970, as *Die Teufel von Loudun*); his other recordings include the first *Euryanthe* (1975) and the first *Ring* on CD, with the Dresden Staatskapelle (1984), which was much praised

for sustained momentum and sense of line. Following his American début in San Francisco in 1983, and his Metropolitan début the next year in *Arabella*, he conducted more Wagner in Paris and Chicago. He has also worked at the Colón in Buenos Aires, and has appeared often at the Vienna Staatsoper.   NOËL GOODWIN

Jansen [Toupin], **Jacques** (*b* Paris, 22 Nov 1913). French baritone. He studied in Paris and made his début at the Opéra-Comique in 1941 as Pelléas, which became his most famous role. He sang it in many places, including the Theater an der Wien, Vienna (1946), the Holland Festival, Amsterdam (1948), Covent Garden and the Metropolitan (1949). At the Opéra-Comique he also sang Valérien in Hahn's *Malvina* (1945) and the title role in Pierné's *Fragonard* (1946). At the Opéra he appeared as Ali in Rameau's *Les Indes galantes* (1952), and at Aix-en-Provence he sang Cithaeron in Rameau's *Platée*. He was also a notable Danilo in *Die lustige Witwe*. A sensitive artist, he had a small but well-projected voice.   ELIZABETH FORBES

Janssen, Herbert (*b* Cologne, 22 Sept 1892; *d* New York, 3 June 1965). German baritone. After serving as an officer in World War I, he studied with Oskar Daniel in Berlin and made his début at the Staatsoper in 1922, as Herod in Schreker's *Der Schatzgräber*; he remained with the company until 1938. At Covent Garden (1926–39) and at Bayreuth (1930–37) he was regarded as the outstanding exponent of the lighter Wagnerian baritone parts – notably Wolfram, Kurwenal and Amfortas – with a warmly sympathetic timbre, fine legato, clear enunciation and clever acting; he also sang Prince Igor and Strauss's Orestes. Distaste for the Nazi regime caused him to leave Germany in 1938. He made his début with the Metropolitan Opera in Philadelphia on 24 January 1939 as Wotan in *Siegfried*, and sang regularly with the company until 1952. After Schorr's retirement in 1943 he reluctantly took over the heavier roles of Wotan and Hans Sachs, to which his voice was not so happily suited. Except for his Bayreuth Wolfram of 1930, the Wagner roles in which he excelled are rather poorly represented in his recordings.

T. Hart: 'Herbert Janssen', *Record Collector*, xvi (1964–6), 243–63 [with discography]; xxi (1973–4), 84

DESMOND SHAWE-TAYLOR

Janus [*Der bey dem allgemeinen Welt-Friede von dem grossen Augustus geschlossene Tempel des Janus* ('The Temple of Janus Closed at the Universal Peace by the Great Augustus')]. *Singe-Spiel* in three acts and an epilogue by REINHARD KEISER to a libretto by CHRISTIAN HEINRICH POSTEL; Hamburg, Theater am Gänsemarkt, 1698.

The title, which refers to the Roman custom of keeping the Temple of Janus open in times of war and closing it in times of peace, has little to do with the main plot but reflects the opera's occasional purpose of celebrating the Treaty of Ryswick, concluded in 1697. Livia (soprano), wife of the Emperor Augustus (bass), has decided that Tiberius (contralto), her son by a previous marriage, should marry Augustus's daughter Julia (soprano) in order to improve his prospects of becoming emperor. The only problem with the plan is that Tiberius is betrothed to Agrippina (soprano), whom he adores. Livia arranges to have Agrippina abducted and imprisoned and tells Tiberius that she has thrown herself into the Tiber. There is a long and moving prison scene for Agrippina, who believes Tiberius has betrayed her but continues to love him (Act 1 scene xi), and a scarcely less striking sequence in which she is allowed to pay Tiberius a final visit in the guise of a silent apparition (Act 3 scenes iv–vi). At last Livia reveals that Agrippina is alive but cannot marry Tiberius, since she is his twin sister. This leaves Tiberius free to marry Julia, while Agrippina returns to her faithful former love Valerius (contralto). The action concludes with the closing of the Temple of Janus by Augustus. In the earliest librettos there follows an epilogue for Fama, the music of which has not survived.

Janus, which was revived as late as 1722, is one of the most impressive of Keiser's early operas. C. F. Hunold observed in his *Theatralische, galante und geistliche Gedichte* (Hamburg, 1706) that the aria 'Holde Schatten' (which Handel reworked for his oratorio *La resurrezione*) was alone worth a visit to the theatre.

JOHN H. ROBERTS

Japan (Jap. Nihon). Documentary evidence suggests a comic opera was performed among Dutch residents of Nagasaki in 1820, but the first reliable record of an opera performance is that by amateurs of Sullivan's *Cox and Box* at the Chinese Theatre in Yokohama in 1870. In the early years operatic activities were supported by American and European residents in Yokohama, but the movement was gradually transplanted to Tokyo and drew the interest of Japanese audiences. The Tokyo Music School, established in 1887, sponsored early ventures, including a partial performance of Gounod's *Faust* (1894) and the first performance by a Japanese cast of Gluck's *Orfeo* (1903). Activities during the 1910s were dominated by the vain attempt of the impresario G. V. Rosi to establish regular opera seasons in Tokyo and by the rise of comic operas at Asakusa theatres. After World War I, the composer-conductor Kósçak Yamada began to promote opera, founding the Nihon Gakugeki Kyōkai (Japan Music Drama Society) in 1920. From about this time a number of visiting opera companies and singers gave performances in Tokyo; they included the Russian Grand Opera (1919), the Carpi Italian Opera (1923), Schumann-Heink (1921), Fleta (1925), McCormack (1926), Galli-Curci (1929), and Shalyapin (1936). The NHK (National Broadcasting Company), founded in 1925, started its opera programme in 1927 and did much to popularize opera throughout Japan. The Fujiwara Opera Company, the only pre-war group still active, gave its first performance, of *La bohème*, in 1934. At this time almost all new opera societies were initiated in Tokyo, and it was only after World War II that any real provincial activity was found. The only exception may be the popular, successful Takarazuka Girls' Opera, founded in 1914 at Takarazuka Spa, near Osaka, which specializes in light musicals.

After World War II, the Fujiwara quickly resumed activity; between 1946 and 1950 it gave 428 performances of 15 operas, *La traviata* and *Carmen* being the most popular. There were now other groups: the Nagato Miho Opera Company gave its first performance in 1946 (*Madama Butterfly*), and the Tokyo Opera Kyōkai in 1950 (*Turandot*). The Kansai Opera Company, founded in Osaka in 1949, became the first major group outside Tokyo. But most important was the Niki Kai, which was inaugurated with a performance of *La bohème* in 1952 and whose

influence spread throughout Japan; eventually it founded local branches, including the Kansai (Osaka), the Nagoya and the Chūgoku-Shikoku groups. Japanese composers were now interested in writing operas, of which Dan's *Yūzuru* ('The Twilight Heron', 1952) and Shimizu's *Shuzenji monogatari* ('Tale of Shuzenji', 1954) scored outstanding successes and remained in the standard repertory. The NHK, which started television programmes in 1953, encouraged and supported opera productions, invited artists from abroad, and commissioned new works, including radio operas (such as the works of Shimizu) and television operas (such as *Kaguya-hime* by Ishii, 1963).

Since the late 1950s several important European and American companies, among them the Vienna Staatsoper, the Paris Opéra, the Deutsche Oper and the Staatsoper, Berlin, the Bol'shoy, Covent Garden, La Scala and the Metropolitan, have performed in Tokyo and Osaka. The Lirica Italiana visited Japan for the first time in 1956 and returned seven times up to 1976.

In 1969 the Tokyo Shitsunai Kagekijō (Tokyo Chamber Opera) gave its first performances with works by Galuppi and Orff; since then it has specialized in small-scale works of all periods. The Nihon Opera Kyōkai (Japan Opera Society), which began as the Nihon Opera Kenkyūkai (Japan Opera Research Group) in 1958 and was renamed in 1970, has made efforts to produce new operas by Japanese composers. After 1970 a number of local opera groups which like to have native works in the repertory were founded; notable are the Kagoshima Kenmin Opera and the Ōita Kenmin Opera, both active in Kyūshū district. New works have been written for them by composers such as Bekku, Dan, Hara, Hayashi, Ishii, Ishiketa, Makino, Miki and Shimizu. Some of these have been staged in Europe or the USA, including Dan's *Yūzuru*, Ishii's *Kesa to Moritō* and Miki's *Ada* and *Jōruri*.

For further information on operatic activity in the country's principal centre *see* TOKYO.

*

K. Masui: *Nihon no Opera – Meiji kara Taisho e* [Opera in Japan – from the Meiji to the Taisho Period] (Tokyo, 1984)
Nihon no opera shi [Opera History in Japan] (Tokyo, 1986) [pubn of the Nihon Opera Shinkōkai] MASAKATA KANAZAWA

Jaques-Dalcroze, Emile (*b* Vienna, 6 July 1865; *d* Geneva, 1 July 1950). Swiss composer and music educationist. He studied in Paris with Fauré and Delibes, in Vienna with Bruckner and Fuchs and in Geneva at the conservatory, to which he returned in 1892 as professor of harmony. Through his efforts to broaden the basis of musical education, he evolved his system of eurythmics. He founded the Institut Jaques-Dalcroze at Geneva, and specialist schools were started in other major cities. The principles underlying the method have been applied in varying degrees to his theatrical and operatic productions. These include elaborate outdoor pageants commemorating special events (*Festival vaudois*, *La fête de juin*), in addition to *opéras* and more intimate, often humorous operettas and *saynètes enfantines*. Many works mix a popular folk style with classical elements; in tone they are often light and vivacious, characterized by conventional harmony but clear orchestration, abundant melody and rhythmic vitality.

La soubrette (oc, 2, P. Monnier), Geneva, 1880 or 1881
Riquet à la houppe (opérette, R. Yve-Plessis), vs (Lausanne, 1883)

L'écolier françois villon, 1887 (comédie lyrique, 1, Monnier), vs pubd, unperf.

Par les bois (pièce, 3, Monnier), vs (Vienna, 1888)

Le violon maudit (opéra, 3, A. Ponthieu and Jaques-Dalcroze), Geneva, 25 Jan 1893 [concert perf. of one act]

Janie, oder Der Leiermann (idylle musicale, 3, P. Godet, after G. de Peyrebrune), Geneva, Grand, Feb 1894 (Leipzig, 1894)

Printemps (kermesse, Jaques-Dalcroze), vs (Geneva, 1895)

Le poème alpestre (Festspiel, D. Baud-Bovy), Geneva, Exposition, 27 May 1896 (Lausanne, 1896)

Sancho Pança (comédie lyrique, 4, Yve-Plessis, after M. de Cervantes: Don Quixote), Geneva, Grand, Dec 1897, vs (Geneva, 1896)

Respect pour nous (opérette, Jaques-Dalcroze), Geneva, April 1898

Le jeu du feuillu, 1900 (poème printanier, Jaques-Dalcroze), Radio-Genève, 21 June 1943, vs (Paris, 1900)

Festival vaudois (Festspiel, 5, Jaques-Dalcroze), Lausanne, 4 July 1903, vs (Neuchâtel, 1903)

Le bonhomme Jadis, ou Onkel Dazumal (oc, 1, Franc-Nohain, after H. Mürger), Cologne, 25 May 1905 (Paris, 1905)

L'eau courante (opéra, prol., 5, Jaques-Dalcroze, after E. Rod), Geneva, 4 Feb 1907, vs (1907)

Les jumeaux de Bergame (oc, 2, M. Léna, after J. P. C. de Florian), Brussels, Monnaie, 30 March 1908 (Paris, 1910)

La fête de juin (spectacle patriotique, 4, Baud-Bovy and A. Malsch), Geneva, 2 July 1914, vs (Lausanne, 1914)

Les premiers souvenirs (poème en images, J. Chenevière), Geneva, Institut Jaques-Dalcroze, vs (Paris, 1924)

La fête de la jeunesse et de la joie (Festspiel, Chenevière, Jaques-Dalcroze and P. Girard), Geneva, Palais Électoral, 7 June 1923, vs (Lausanne, 1923)

Le petit roi qui pleure (féerie enfantine musicale, 3, Jaques-Dalcroze, after H. C. Andersen), Geneva, Grand, 21 Feb 1932, vs (Geneva, 1932)

Le savetier et le financier (saynète, M. Grange) (Lausanne, 1933)

Le joli jeu des saisons (revue, Jaques-Dalcroze), Geneva, Grand, 30 May 1934, vs (Geneva, 1934)

Ces bonnes dames (saynète enfantine, Grange), vs (Lausanne, 1935)

Riquet à la houppe (saynète enfantine, Grange), vs (Lausanne, 1935)

Blanche-Neige (opérette, prol., 2, Jaques-Dalcroze)

La cigale et la fourmi (saynète, Grange), vs (Lausanne, n.d.)

Le laboureur et ses enfants (saynète, prol., 1, Grange), vs (Lausanne, n.d.)

Perette et le pot au lait (saynète, 2, Grange), vs (Lausanne, n.d.)

*

K. Storek: Emile Jaques-Dalcroze: seine Stellung und Aufgabe in unserer Zeit (Stuttgart, 1912)

H. Brunet-Lecomte: Jaques-Dalcroze: sa vie, son oeuvre (Geneva, 1950) [incl. list of compositions]

A. C. van Deventer: Dalcroze (Amsterdam, 1965)

H. Gagnebin: 'Jaques-Dalcroze compositeur', Emile Jaques-Dalcroze: l'homme, le compositeur, le créateur de la rythmique, ed. F. Martin (Neuchâtel, 1965), 159–288

W. R. Volbach: 'The Collaboration of Adolphe Appia and Emile Jaques-Dalcroze', Paul A. Pisk: Essays in his Honor (Austin, TX, 1966), 192–202

G. Giertz: Kultus ohne Götter: Emile Jaques-Dalcroze und Adolphe Appia: Versuch einer Theaterreform auf der Grundlage der rhythmischen Gymnastik (Munich, 1975)

Jarboro, Caterina [Yarborough, Katherine] (b Wilmington, NC, 24 July 1903; d New York, 13 Aug 1986). American soprano. After leaving school she went to New York in 1916. She began her stage career singing and playing the trombone in all-black musical comedies, Sissle and Blake's Shuffle Along (1921) and James P. Johnson's Runnin' Wild (1923). In the late 1920s she went to Europe to study and made her début in Milan at the Teatro Puccini as Aida (1930–31). She sang in France, Poland and Switzerland, adding the title roles of Gounod's La reine de Saba and Meyerbeer's L'Africaine to her repertory before returning to the USA, where she sang Aida in Chicago and New York (at the Hippodrome, with Jules Bledsoe as Amonasro). After several further years in Europe, based in Belgium, she eventually settled in New York, where she gave her first recital at Town Hall, 16 January 1942, including arias by Piccinni, Gluck, Weber and Wagner. She continued to sing in recital until the early 1950s. Jarboro seems to have been the first Afro-American singer to have achieved a significant career on the opera stage. 'A beautiful woman,' wrote Virgil Thomson (New York Herald-Tribune, 17 January 1942), 'superb of presence, gifted with a lyrico-dramatic voice handsome in range and quality, she is also the possessor of a truly great dramatic temperament.'

*

SouthernB

W. Bolcom and R. Kimball: Reminiscing with Sissle and Blake (New York, 1973)

A. F. Block and C. N. Bates: Women in American Music (Westport, CT, 1979)

J. Gray: Blacks in Classical Music (Westport, CT, 1988)

PATRICK O'CONNOR

Jarda, Tudor (b Cluj [now Cluj-Napoca], 11 Feb 1922). Romanian composer. He studied music in Cluj and Timişoara (1941–5, 1945–8) and from 1945 to 1948 also played the trumpet at the Romanian Opera in Cluj. He then taught harmony at the Cluj Conservatory (1949–88) and for a time was secretary of the Composers' Union in Cluj (1954–7). His music for the stage consists of three operas, a lyrical allegory and a ballet. Rooted in the sounds of Transylvanian folk music, his works are characterized by modal harmony, polyphonic features and lyrical passages; traditional patriotic songs are used in Pădurea vulturilor ('The Forest with Vultures') and Dreptul la viaţă ('The Power of Life'). His operas bear the genuine stamp of the Romanian ethos.

Neamul Şoimăreştilor [The Şoimaru Kin] (3, I. Balea, after M. Sadoveanu), Cluj, 1 Nov 1956

Pădurea vulturilor [The Forest with Vultures] (1, C. Rusu and P. Gâlmeanu), Cluj-Napoca, 9 May 1961; rev. 1964

Dreptul la viaţă [The Power of Life], 1965 (lyrical allegory, prol., 2, D. Drăgan), Cluj-Napoca, 20 Aug 1984

Inger şi demon [Angel and Demon] (4, N. Pîrvu and Jarda, after M. Eminescu), Cluj-Napoca, 23 June 1989   VIOREL COSMA

Jardín de Oriente ('Garden of the Orient'). Opera in one act, op.25, by JOAQUÍN TURINA to a libretto by Gregorio Martínez Sierra; Madrid, Teatro Real, 6 March 1923.

Following the success of his first opera Margot in 1914, Turina travelled to North Africa and there experienced the exotic geographical and historical atmosphere. He made notes and sketches and secretly transcribed a prayer he found in a mosque in Tangier. It was from music inspired by this experience that he produced the first version of a new work he called Laberinto, and after redrafting, amplifying and improving this it became the Jardín de Oriente. The première was part of a season of important new works, and although the orchestra was good, the chorus and ballet were not, old scenery was used, Conchita Supervia did not take part as she had promised, and only three performances were given. Turina's enchanting music received the appreciation it deserved, but the libretto, a short tale of love and conflict which takes place in the palace of a conventional sultan surrounded by uninteresting characters, was considered ingenuous and undramatic. Turina himself published several numbers from the opera, arranged for voice and piano. The work was restaged at the Teatro de la Zarzuela in Madrid on 23 February 1982 to celebrate the centenary of the composer's birth.   CARLOS GÓMEZ AMAT

Jarecki, Henryk (*b* Warsaw, 6 Dec 1846; *d* Lwów, 18 Dec 1918). Polish composer and conductor. He took lessons in composition with Moniuszko at the Warsaw Music Institute from 1864, also studying conducting and the organ; while in Warsaw he played the double bass at the Wielki Theatre. From 1872 he was deputy conductor and from 1877 to 1900 principal conductor and director of the Opera Theatre in Lwów; it was through his artistic judgment and organizational ability that the Lwów Opera became the leading opera company in Poland. He directed Polish operas (including his own) as well as the first series in Poland of operas in the standard repertory (Bellini, Donizetti, Mascagni, Leoncavallo, and especially Verdi and Wagner). Between 1878 and 1900 he and his company made short tours each year to other cities in Poland, particularly to Kraków.

Jarecki is known to have completed six operas, on subjects from Polish history and literature. These have certain dramatic qualities, though fundamentally his idiom is unoriginal and strongly influenced by Moniuszko. The operas are characterized by short orchestral introductions, leitmotifs, short monologues and lyrical duets; there are few ensembles but often extended dances (mainly Polish ones: polonaises, mazurkas, cracoviennes and the *oberek* and *kujawiak* folk dances). *Mindowe* (1879) is the only contemporary Polish opera to approach Wagner in style.

first performed in Lwów, Count Skarbek Theatre, unless otherwise stated

Mindowe, król litewski [Mindowe, King of Lithuania] (4, Jarecki, after J. Słowacki), 1 April 1880, *PL-Wn**, *Wtm*

Wanda, 1881 (4, W. Bełza), unperf., withdrawn, autograph frags. *Wn*

Jadwiga, królowa polska [Jadwiga, Queen of Poland] (4, Jarecki, after J. Szujski), 16 Jan 1886, *Wn**

Barbara Radziwiłłówna, 1888–9 (prol., 4, ?A. Kitschman, after D. Magnuszewski), 18 March 1893, *Wn**

Powrót taty [The Father's Return], 1896 (opera-ballade, 3, J. Gołębiowski, after A. Mickiewicz), 19 Jan 1897, *Wn**, *Wtm**

List żelany [The Iron Letter], 1900–01 (5, Kitschman, after A. Małecki), unperf., *Wn**, *Wtm**

Nowy Don Kiszot, czyli Sto Szalenstw [The New Don Quixote, or 100 Extravagances], *c*1901 (farce, 3, ? after A. Fredro), ?unperf., autograph frag. *Wn*

*

K. Michałowski: *Opery polskie* (Kraków, 1954)

W. Poźniak: 'Opera po Moniuszce' [Opera after Moniuszko], *Z dziejów polskiej kultury muzycznej*, ed. A. Nowak-Romanowicz and others, ii (Kraków, 1966), 272–3, 298ff

E. Wasowska: 'Twórczość operowa Henryka Jareckiego' [Henryk Jarecki's Operas], *Muzyka*, xxxiv/4 (1989), 3–29

BARBARA CHMARA-ŻACZKIEWICZ

Järnefelt, (Edvard) Armas (*b* Viipuri, 14 Aug 1869; *d* Stockholm, 23 June 1958). Swedish conductor of Finnish birth. He studied under Wegelius and Busoni in Helsinki, Becker in Berlin and Massenet in Paris. Following guest engagements at the Helsinki and Stockholm opera houses, he settled in Stockholm in 1907 as conductor of the Royal Opera. In 1910, on his additional appointment as court conductor, he took Swedish nationality, and in 1923 he became the Royal Opera's principal conductor. He returned to Finland as director of the Finnish National Opera (1932–6), where he played an important part in broadening the repertory, especially with operas by Mozart and Wagner.

ERIK WAHLSTRÖM

Jaroměřice nad Rokytnou. Town in Moravia. Among the theatres at all the castles belonging to Count Johann Adam Questenberg (1678–1752), the one at Jaroměřice was the most important. It was first opened to the local public in 1722, and completely rebuilt in 1731; the stage was altered in 1739. There was also a garden theatre, built in 1735. Some of the scenery, notably in the 1730s, was designed by Giuseppe Galli-Bibiena. The first opera performance took place in 1723. The repertory consisted not only of Italian opera and German Singspiel, mostly imported from Vienna, but also of works in the Czech language; composers included Brivio, Bioni, Pergolesi, Caldara, Giacomelli, F. B. Conti, I. M. Conti, D. N. Sarro, Vinci, Leo, Hasse and the count's Kapellmeister, the singer and composer František Antonín Míča. Míča's *L'origine di Jaromeriz in Moravia* was given in Czech in 1730. Most of the singers, dancers and musicians in the count's company were members of his household or local people, especially from the Míča and Frey-Svoboda families. Others visited Jaroměřice from Vienna and Brno. The count's band of music existed from around 1706; in 1725 it had 25 and in the 1740s up to 50 members. Opera performances at Jaroměřice stopped immediately after the count's death. The music archive, particularly rich in Italian MSS, is now lost.

*

V. Helfert: *Hudba na jaroměřickém zámku* [Music in the Castle of Jaroměřice] (Prague, 1924)

T. Straková: 'Jaroměřice nad Rokytnou', *OM*, v (1973), 57–60

——: 'Jaroměřice nad Rokytnou a jejich význam v hudebním vývoji Moravy' [Jaroměřice nad Rokytnou and its Importance in the Musical Development of Moravia], *O životě a umění: listy z jaroměřické kroniky 1700–1752* (Jaroměřice nad Rokytnou, 1974), 393–404

J. Trojan: 'Jak to dopadlo v Jaroměřicích: německý tisk libreta opery L'origine di Jaromeriz in Moravia' [A German Print of the Libretto of the Opera *L'origine di Jaromeriz in Moravia*], *OM*, vi (1974), 82–5

——: 'Čeština na zámecké scéně v Jaroměřicích' [Czech Language on the Stage of the Castle of Jaroměřice], *OM*, xvi (1984), 101–5

MICHAELA FREEMANOVA

Jarred, Mary (*b* Brotton, Yorks., 9 Oct 1899). English contralto. She was educated at the RAM and RCM in London. Her rich, resonant voice and sound artistry led to her engagement as a regular member of the Hamburg Städtische Oper, then an unusual honour for an English singer. She remained there from 1929 to 1932, singing with success all the standard contralto parts. She appeared at the Covent Garden international season in Wagnerian roles, notably Erda, and at Sadler's Wells as Gluck's Orpheus. She belonged to a long tradition of English contralto singing, solid, even somewhat massive in style, but of impressive quality in music of large utterance.

DESMOND SHAWE-TAYLOR

Järvefelt, Göran (*b* Bollnäs, 3 Aug 1947; *d* Stockholm, 30 Nov 1989). Swedish director. He was trained as an actor and worked with the Swedish National Theatre from 1970 to 1975, during which time he was strongly influenced by Ingmar Bergman. Having directed Stradella's *San Giovanni Battista* at the Vadstena Academy in 1974, he made his début at the Swedish Royal Opera with *Il barbiere di Siviglia* (1977). His stagings as chief opera director at Gelsenkirchen (1977–9) included *Don Carlos*, *Il trovatore*, *La forza del destino* and *Die Zauberflöte*, the last of which was acquired by the WNO (1979); its success led to a fruitful association with the company, which included productions of *Un ballo in maschera* (1982), the *Ring* (1983–5), *La* *bohème* (1984) and *La traviata* (1988). At his untimely death Järvefelt was engaged on a Strauss cycle at Santa Fe, which had included such rarities as *Die ägyptische Helena, Feuersnot* and *Friedenstag*. He had also done notable work at Drottningholm (five Mozart operas), Houston, Stockholm and Sydney; his double bill of *Erwartung* and *Bluebeard's Castle* was staged at the Metropolitan in 1989. His productions were characterized by their simplicity of outline, cogent unfolding of narrative and striking theatricality.

R. Milnes: 'People, 146: Göran Järvefelt', *Opera*, xxxvii (1986), 1243–7

G. Järvefelt: *Opera regi: ett sökande efter människan* [Opera Direction: a Search for Man] (Stockholm, 1990)

R. Milnes: Obituary, *Opera*, xli (1990), 34   BARRY MILLINGTON

Järvi, Neeme (*b* Tallinn, 7 June 1937). Estonian conductor. He studied in Tallinn (percussion and choral conducting) and with Mravinsky at the Leningrad State Conservatory, making his opera début with *Carmen* at the Kirov Theatre. From 1963 he was music director of the Estonian Opera Theatre where, during 13 seasons, he conducted a wide repertory including the first Soviet performances of *Il turco in Italia* and *Der Rosenkavalier*. He conducted opera and ballet in Moscow and Leningrad, and made his Metropolitan début in *Yevgeny Onegin* in 1979. In 1980 he emigrated to the USA. He first appeared at the Stockholm Royal Opera in 1982 (*Salome*) and held orchestral posts in Göteborg and Glasgow. A prolific recording conductor in the concert repertory, he is admired in opera mainly for a symphonic approach, favouring warm, lyrical feeling more than dramatic urgency.   NOËL GOODWIN

Jasager, Der ('The Affirmer'). *Schuloper* in two acts by KURT WEILL to a libretto by BERTOLT BRECHT after the Japanese noh play *Taniko*; Berlin, Zentralinstitut für Erziehung und Unterricht, 23 June 1930.

The Boy	treble
The Mother	mezzo-soprano
The Teacher	baritone
First Student	treble/tenor
Second Student	treble/tenor
Third Student	treble/baritone
Large chorus	

Setting No specific time or place

After the success of *Der Lindberghflug* (text by Brecht, music by Hindemith and Weill) at the Baden-Baden Festival in July 1929, Weill and Brecht planned another project for the festival of new music in Berlin the following year. The Baden-Baden piece had been an experiment using radio. But despite (and partly because of) having worked as a correspondent for the magazine *Der deutsche Rundfunk*, Weill had become disillusioned with that medium. 'On the radio,' he said, 'an anonymous community of adults is available from the most diverse circles, with whom little can be done. One cannot offer these adults anything, because their opinions diverge too much' ('Aktuelles Zwiegespräch über die Schuloper', *Die Musikpflege*, i, 1930, pp.48–53). For Berlin he developed the 'school opera', with which he associated three aims: 'a schooling for composers or a generation of composers, in order to

place the genre of "opera" on new foundations'; 'a schooling in operatic presentation' requiring 'simplicity and naturalness'; and the placing of music 'at the service of institutions' such as schools, 'rather than its being created as an end in itself' ('Über meine Schuloper *Der Jasager*', *Die Scene*, xx, 1930, pp.232–3). *Der Jasager* is a Lehrstück whose didactic content is both political (albeit not in any party political sense) and artistic. Furthermore, as a reflection of the then prevailing philosophy of *Gebrauchsmusik* (utility music), it is, as Weill stated, 'a full-blooded work of art'. It is based on Elisabeth Hauptmann's translation of the 15th-century noh play *Taniko*. Hauptmann's source was itself a translation, Arthur Waley's English version, which is a free rendering of the Japanese original. Brecht uses about 90% of Hauptmann's text; the principal change is the introduction of the concept of *Einverständnis* ('active consent'), extolled in the chorus's exordium at the beginning of each act. The boy demonstrates *Einverständnis* in his willingness to act in the interests of the community, to the point of sacrificing his own life. In the original play, his suicide is justified by his unquestioning obedience to convention; the new version attempts a demythologization. Tradition and custom are subjected to rational scrutiny.

The piece, as planned, encountered two obstacles. First, the première did not take place at the festival of new music. Another of Brecht's Lehrstücke, *Die Massnahme* (with music by Hanns Eisler), had been rejected by the festival's committee on account of its text. By way of protest, Brecht and Weill withdrew *Der Jasager*. Instead it was performed by pupils of the Akademie für Kirchen- und Schulmusik under the auspices of the Berlin Zentralinstitut für Erziehung und Unterricht, and broadcast simultaneously on radio. The second obstacle was the critical reception. A number of critics with differing political views appeared to misconstrue the intended message: some greeted favourably what they saw as confirmation of their conservative Christian principles, while others interpreted the piece as lending support to authoritarian and reactionary tendencies. It also provoked discussion among the performers themselves. As a result, Brecht made two separate revisions. In the first, the changes mainly serve to stress the autonomy of the boy's decision. In the second, *Der Jasager* ('the affirmer') is complemented by *Der Neinsager* ('the refuser'). In this alternative version the boy contravenes convention by refusing to commit suicide. The additional music supplied by Weill for the first revision has never been published, no doubt because it disrupts his original design, and there is no musical setting of *Der Neinsager*. In its original form *Der Jasager* was one of Weill's most successful compositions in Germany, receiving more than 300 performances before 1933.

ACT 1.i The chorus, standing on either side of the stage (as it does throughout), sings the exordium (a musical and moral canon): 'Above all, it is important to learn consent'.

1.ii The teacher visits one of his pupils to bid farewell before a school trip across the mountains. He learns that the boy's mother is ill.

1.iii The mother reassures the teacher about her condition. The teacher says the journey will take him to a town in which the great doctors live, but the route is too dangerous for the boy to accompany him.

1.iv The boy urges the teacher to allow him to

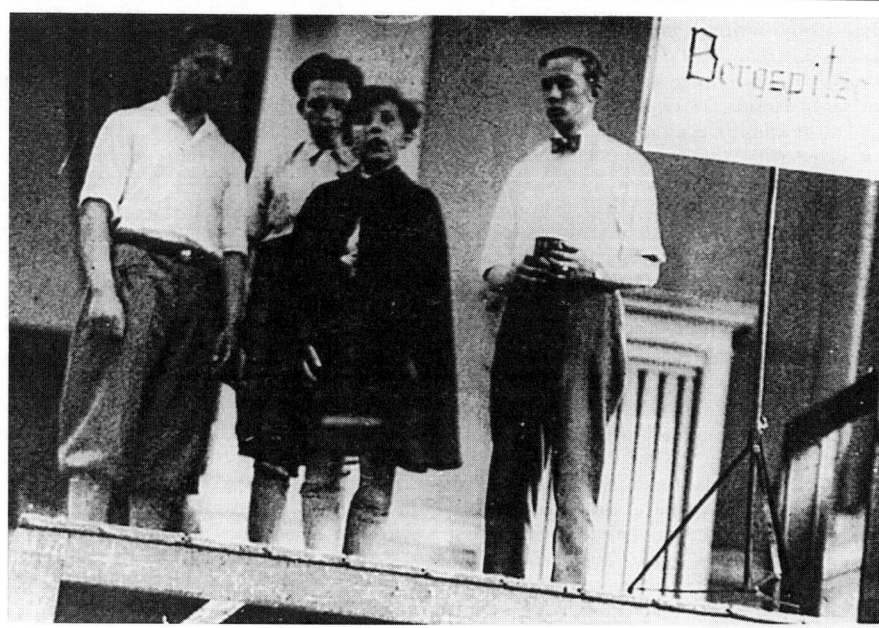

'Der Jasager' (Weill), Act 2 (the mountain peak): scene from the original production at the Zentralinstitut für Erziehung und Unterricht, Berlin, 23 June 1930, showing the Three Students and the Boy (centre) before he is hurled into the valley

join the group so that he can obtain medicine for his mother.

1.v The mother is reluctant to let her son go. The boy, however, is adamant. All finally agree that he shall go.

1.vi The chorus confirms the boy's resolve. The mother and teacher sing, 'Such profound consent! Many accept what is wrong; yet he does not accept the illness but rather that it should be cured'.

ACT 2.i The chorus repeats its exordium.

2.ii The chorus comments on the journey; the boy is not equal to it.

2.iii The boy tells the teacher and three other pupils that he is feeling unwell. The teacher suggests a short rest and the pupils ask whether they should follow the old custom and hurl the sick boy into the valley.

2.iv The boys repeat their question. The teacher reminds them that the custom also requires that he who has fallen ill must be asked whether the others should turn back on his account. If the boy agrees to that, the students will still want to hurl him into the valley.

2.v The teacher explains the custom, adding that it also requires that the answer to the question should be not to turn back. The boy complies, explaining that he had been aware of the possible consequences, and asks that the others should fill his jug with medicine for his mother. The chorus concludes: 'Thereupon the friends took the jug and bemoaned the sad ways of the world and its harsh law and hurled him down. Foot to foot they stood at the edge of the abyss and hurled him down with closed eyes, none more guilty than his neighbour, and flung down clods of earth and flat stones as well!'

*   *   *

Der Jasager consolidates stylistic changes in Weill's musical language already evident in *Aufstieg und Fall der Stadt Mahagonny*. As Weill said, 'the rhythms are no longer expressly dance rhythms, but have been transformed, "digested"' ('Aktuelles Zwiegespräch'). The simplicity and restraint, a function of the Lehrstück, go hand in hand with the urge towards a new 'classicality' (to use Busoni's term). The literary scholar Peter Szondi has rightly drawn attention to Brecht's

probable motives for adding *Der Neinsager* to the original libretto ('Nachwort', in B. Brecht: *Der Jasager und Der Neinsager: Vorlagen, Fassungen, Materialien*, ed. P. Szondi (Frankfurt, 1978)). In a political climate in which *Der Jasager* could be misconstrued as underwriting sacrifice to the wrong cause, it was just a matter of months before nay-sayers would not be tolerated. But neither Brecht nor Szondi considers the music, which has its own integrity. To follow them is to ignore the ambiguous light which Weill's music characteristically casts on any of the work's potentially misconstrued messages. The boy's sacrifice has nothing to do with the legacy of Bismarckian 'blood and iron'. It occasions immense human grief expressed by the sparse orchestral commentary – notably the major 7th clash on an accented upper auxiliary note – in the poignant D minor conclusion.

STEPHEN HINTON

Jassy (Fr.). IAŞI.

Jazz opera. Jazz and opera are generally viewed as separate traditions, too diverse in cultural origin to come together successfully. Yet throughout the 20th century both traditions have borrowed from each other, and have spawned a number of cross-breeds, which often find no home in either camp and end up on Broadway. In most cases musicians have tended to incorporate gestures rather than develop common ground.

1. Afro-American origins. 2. European opera. 3. The merging of cultures, and later developments.

1. AFRO-AMERICAN ORIGINS. Jazz, an amalgamation of tribal African musics with Euro-American styles, emerged at the beginning of the 20th century; created mainly by black musicians, it was essentially an urban American folk art. Aspirations to western art-music respectability came less from mainstream New Orleans jazz or blues musicians than from ragtime composers. This is not surprising, as ragtime itself is a hybrid of African rhythm and European harmony, and its best-known publicist, Scott Joplin, was trained by a German music teacher. Having started as an improvising bordello pianist, Joplin earned modest fame for his rag-

time compositions which he disseminated as sheet music. Gaining confidence from his success, he soon formed his own opera company, for whom he wrote *A Guest of Honor* (1903, St Louis), now lost. His second and more ambitious attempt at elevating ragtime to high art came with *Treemonisha* (composed 1908–11), the plot appropriately concerning emancipation from error and superstition by way of education. The music is, however, hardly operatic (there is virtually no recitative or arioso) and draws on rags for dance music while the vocal numbers rely on recollections of spirituals and plantation songs with just a touch of blues. Joplin published and mounted a concert performance of *Treemonisha* at his own expense but its disastrous failure broke him, and he died lunatic as well as young.

James P. Johnson (1891–1955), also a composer-pianist, with a reputation for 'ragging' the music of classical composers in his improvisations, composed a string of musicals for the New York stage before embarking on his one-act 'blues opera', *The Organizer*. The harlem intellectual Langston Hughes produced a blank-verse libretto based on Theodore Brown's play *Natural Man* and the opera was performed at Carnegie Hall in 1940. In subject matter *The Organizer* went beyond problems of racial equality, tackling ideas of unionization and social reform but without resorting to stereotypes. Sadly, the music of only one number, 'Hungry blues', survives. Duke Ellington, having composed a number of successful stage musicals (e.g. *Jump for Joy*, 1941), also attempted an opera, *Boola*. It remains unfinished, but became the source for a number of important concert works, including the *Black, Brown and Beige* suite.

The only full-scale opera to fuse black blues successfully with sophisticated stagecraft and an orchestral expertise more akin to that of Puccini or Ravel was *Porgy and Bess* (1935) – written by a white American Jew, George Gershwin. Revealing parallels between his own alienation and that of the black American, *Porgy* came out of the composer's longstanding interest in black life and musical culture, previously expressed in his musicals and his one-act opera *Blue Monday* (performed once in 1922, then withdrawn). *Porgy* emerged as a great, even grand, opera, though in Broadway terms it was a box-office failure, having little in common with the musical comedy tradition of Irving Berlin and Jerome Kern. Whereas *Porgy* is written throughout in the spirit of blues-jazz, Kern's *Show Boat* (1927), also set in the South, uses music demotically. The distinction is best shown, perhaps, by Kern and Oscar Hammerstein's consideration of turning Edwin DuBose Hayward's novel *Porgy*, Gershwin's source, into a musical for Al Jolson in the early 1930s.

2. EUROPEAN OPERA. Jazz first emerged as a significant influence on European opera in the 1920s, having infiltrated ballet (Satie's *Parade*, 1916) and music theatre (Stravinsky's *Soldier's Tale*, 1918). Composers' understanding of its essence varied widely, owing in no small part to the diversity of sources available: visiting and recorded bands presented an authentic early jazz style but Paul Whiteman's pretentious and watered-down 'symphonic jazz', with its elaborate arrangements and rescoring using violins, initially had the greater impact. Laying aside Parisian experiments such as Ravel's *L'enfant et les sortilèges* (1925), jazz took root more seriously in the opera of the Weimar Republic. Krenek's *Der Sprüng über den Schatten* (1924) was the first German opera to insert 'hot' rhythms and jazz dances into an atonal structure. Three years later his *Jonny spielt auf* enjoyed a *succès de scandale*, veering theatrically between grand opera, musical comedy and cinematic slapstick in its portrayal of Jonny, a black jazz-band leader. The score requires a banjo and saxophones and introduces rhythms characteristic of early jazz, yet Krenek objected to the label 'jazz opera', stressing that the jazz elements were superimposed and not integrated into the music. What *Jonny* lacked most was sheer quality of musical invention, in the absence of which it proved to be ephemeral.

As Hindemith showed in his comic *Neues vom Tage* and Max Brand in *Maschinist Hopkins* (both 1929), jazz soon became a potent means of addressing the audience directly. Composers could use it to shock, or to reconcile listeners who felt alienated by contemporary music, or even as a vehicle for political messages. Weill's early collaborations with Brecht exploited decadent Berlin cabaret music more than jazz, though *Die Dreigroschenoper* (1928) exudes more than a hint of blues amid the tango rhythms. Unsurprisingly, jazz influences surfaced again in his American works, most notably in *Street Scene* (1946) and his last completed stage work, set in South Africa, *Lost in the Stars* (1949).

3. THE MERGING OF CULTURES, AND LATER DEVELOPMENTS. With the advent of World War II, European composers emigrating to the USA found themselves on jazz's 'home territory', creating a further melding of musical styles. Marc Blitzstein, who later adapted and translated *Die Dreigroschenoper* into the language of 1950s America, found in Brecht and Weill's work a model for his deeply American 'plays in music' *The Cradle will Rock* (1937) and *No for an Answer* (1941). In 1949 his *Regina*, an adaptation of a Lillian Hellman play about corruption in the Deep South, was staged successfully in New York. Featuring leading black characters, it mixes spirituals, blues and Dixieland jazz with arias and choruses. Originally performed on Broadway, *Regina* is the only 'jazz opera', save *Porgy*, to work efficaciously in a legitimate opera house.

Nodding references to jazz may be found in Antheil's *Transatlantic* (composed 1927–8), Copland's *The Second Hurricane* (1937), Virgil Thomson's *Four Saints in Three Acts* (1934) and *The Mother of Us All* (1947) and various operas by Menotti, but perhaps Blitzstein's most direct musical heir was Leonard Bernstein, a classically trained musician steeped in popular music. His amusing one-act opera *Trouble in Tahiti* (1952) features a trio of scat singers who function as a 'Greek chorus', interspersing instrumental writing suggestive of big-band music. Bernstein incorporated the piece into *A Quiet Place* in 1983, a full-scale opera to a libretto by Stephen Wadsworth, which the composer believed to be his own best work. Bernstein's attempt to write a musical on a weightier dramatic subject resulted in his 1957 masterpiece *West Side Story*, described by Wadsworth as a 'jazz Singspiel'; in it, choreographed rituals of dancing and fighting mixed with American speech-rhythms are delivered through Stephen Sondheim's tightly constructed lyrics, in an exploration of the sociological and psychological tensions of urban life. With intelligent craftsmanship, Bernstein combines angular jazz riffs with a Puccinian lyricism, achieving a surprisingly consistent overall style.

More firmly in the realm of serious opera, B. A. Zimmermann's multi-media *Die Soldaten* (1965) juxtaposes plainchant, chorales and modern jazz – a walking bass with sizzling percussion – against jagged vocal lines. In England Michael Tippett has evolved a highly personal idiom from a jazz-influenced balance of melodic flow, harmonic rhythm and metrical beat. After the latent jazz implications in his first opera *The Midsummer Marriage* (1955) came more recognizable styles (e.g. blues and boogie) in *The Knot Garden* (1970), *The Ice Break* (1977) and *New Year* (1989). Springing more directly from the world of jazz, recent notable achievements include *X* (1985, Philadelphia), an opera based on the life of Malcolm X, by the jazz pianist and composer Anthony Davis, and *The Mother of Three Sons* by Leroy Jenkins, first performed at the Munich Biennale in 1990.

E. Berlin: *Ragtime* (London, 1980)
S. E. Brown: *James P. Johnson: a Case of Mistaken Identity* (Metuchen, NJ, 1986)
S. Wadsworth: 'Librettist's Notes', *A Quiet Place* (Deutsche Grammophon 419 761–2, 1986) [record notes]
R. Kimball: 'The Roots of "Porgy and Bess"', *Porgy and Bess* (EMI EX165 7 49568 1, 1989) [record notes]
WILFRID MELLERS, WALTER WELLS, MADELEINE LADELL

Jean de Paris ('John of Paris'). *Opéra comique* in two acts by ADRIEN BOIELDIEU to a libretto by Claude de Saint-Just; Paris, Opéra-Comique (Théâtre Feydeau), 4 April 1812.

The Dauphin (tenor), wishing to meet and get to know the bride chosen for him by the king, introduces himself to the Princess of Navarre (soprano) as Jean, a bourgeois from Paris who would be happy to escort her to the French capital. During the journey he falls in love with the princess and she, though still unaware of his identity, with him.

Boieldieu's score was much admired by Weber, who conducted *Jean de Paris* in Prague on 1 January 1814. 'What places this composer above his rivals,' he wrote, 'are his flowing and well-proportioned melodies; the design of the separate numbers, as well as the overall design of his operas; the excellence and finish of his instrumentation: qualities that distinguish the master and give him the right to an everlasting success in the realm of art.' Even in France Boieldieu's success has not been everlasting, but many musicians agree with Weber that the score of *Jean de Paris* is a minor masterpiece.

ELIZABETH FORBES

Jeanie Deans. Grand opera in four acts by HAMISH MACCUNN to a libretto by Joseph Bennett after WALTER SCOTT's novel *The Heart of Midlothian*; Edinburgh, Lyceum Theatre, 15 November 1894.

Effie Deans (soprano) has borne a son by her lover, George Staunton (tenor), alias the bandit nobleman Geordie Robertson. The child has been spirited away by the mother of the crazed gypsy Madge Wildfire (soprano), whom Staunton has also ruined. Falsely accused of infanticide, Effie is imprisoned in the Tolbooth Prison under sentence of death. Her sister, Jeanie (soprano), resolves to save her by seeking a royal pardon. To this end she walks to London where, aided by the Duke of Argyle (tenor), she successfully intercedes with Queen Caroline (mezzo-soprano) on Effie's behalf. She then walks back to Edinburgh, arriving only just in time to stay the execution. The opera and the novel are based on a true story; central to both are the Porteous riots in Edinburgh, in 1736, caused

by the execution of a smuggler who had won popular sympathy.

Jeanie Deans was commissioned by Carl Rosa and remained in that company's repertory until 1914. Its London première took place at Daly's Theatre on 22 January 1896. It has been revived several times in the 20th century, and received strongly favourable reviews in performances by Opera West at the Gaiety Theatre, Ayr, in 1986 (5–8 February). It is arguably the finest serious opera of the late Victorian period, possessing great dramatic and musical integrity. MacCunn's idiom is uniquely personal and prophetic of the realism which has informed 20th-century British opera. The work is permeated by an unobtrusive Scottish nationalism which imparts genuine life to its characters; the conception of a simple farm girl emerging as a courageous and redeeming heroine dominates the opera and reflects MacCunn's admiration for Wagner.

NIGEL BURTON

Jeghelli, Federico. *See* JAGEL, FREDERICK.

Její pastorkyňa. Opera by Leoš Janáček; *see* JENŮFA.

Jelmoli, Hans (*b* Zürich, 17 Jan 1877; *d* Zürich, 6 May 1936). Swiss composer. He studied at the Hoch Conservatory, Frankfurt, with Ivan Knorr, Bernhard Scholz and Humperdinck. After working as a conductor of theatre orchestras in Mainz and Würzburg he settled in Zürich, where he was a music critic, accompanist and teacher. Principally a vocal composer, he regarded musical drama as the most important genre and wrote six stage works; his idiom is close to folk music.

Sein Vermächtnis (lyrische Komödie, 1, E. Scribe, trans. Jelmoli), Zürich, Stadt, 6 Oct 1904
Prinz Goldhaar und die Gänsehirtin (Weihnachtsmärchen, 3, A. Rohner), Zürich, Stadt, 23 Dec 1909

?Unperf.: Die Schweizer, 1913 (K. Falke); Die Badener Fahrt, 1921 (Spl, E. Eschmann); Das Gespenst auf dem Petersturm, 1921 (Spl, Eschmann); Die Wunderkur, 1931 (Spl, Eschmann)
PETER ROSS

Jélyotte, Pierre de (*b* Lasseube, 13 April 1713; *d* 12 Oct 1797). French singer and composer. He received his early training at Toulouse, studying singing, the harpsichord, guitar, cello and composition. He made his début at the Paris Opéra in Collin de Blamont's *Les festes grecques et romaines* in 1733. He continued to sing minor roles there and his popularity quickly grew. In 1738 he took the main part in Lully's *Atys*, and subsequently created many of Rameau's leading roles, usually with the soprano Marie Fel, with whom he also sang in Mondonville's *Daphnis et Alcimadure* (1754).

One of the extraordinary features of Jélyotte's voice was the ease with which he traversed the upper register of the *haute-contre* range ($f\sharp$ to d''). Some of Rameau's roles (such as Castor, revised for him in 1754) demand a high tessitura and agility in rapid runs. One of the most difficult ariettes in all of Rameau's works, 'Règne, Amour' from *Zaïs* (1748), was written specially for him. Rameau's librettist, Cahusac ('Chanteur', *Encyclopédie*, iii, 1751), pointed to the talents of Fel and Jélyotte as an important factor in the success of the composer's works.

For illustration *see* PLATÉE.

J.-G. Prod'homme: 'Pierre de Jélyotte (1713–1797)', *SIMG*, iii (1901–2), 686–717
A. Pougin: *Un ténor de l'opéra au XVIIIe siècle: Pierre Jélyotte et les chanteurs de son temps* (Paris, 1905)

G. Sadler: 'Rameau's Singers and Players at the Paris Opéra: a Little-known Inventory of 1738', *EMc*, xi (1983), 453–67

MARY CYR

Jenbach, Béla (*b* Miskolc, 1 April 1871; *d* Vienna, 21 Jan 1943). Austrian librettist. Originally an actor at the Burgtheater in Vienna, he turned to writing; among several of his librettos for operettas produced in Leipzig was that of Charles Cuvillier's *Der lila Domino* (1912), which enjoyed considerable success in English translation. In Vienna he collaborated on some of the major operetta librettos of the World War I years and after; with Leo Stein he achieved a major international success with Kálmán's *Die Csárdásfürstin* (1915). He also wrote the librettos for two of Lehár's late successes, *Paganini* (1925) and *Der Zarewitsch* (1927, with Reichert), the latter of which was also offered to both Mascagni and Künneke.

operettas unless otherwise stated

Madame Troubadour (Vaudeville-Operette, with R. Pohl), F. Albani, 1907; *Die Barfusstänzerin*, Albani, 1909; *Biribi* (with Pohl), F. Korolanyi, 1909; *Die Liebesschule* (with Pohl), Korolanyi, 1909; *Die romantische Frau* (with C. Lindau), C. Weinberger, 1911; *Der Natursänger* (with L. Stein), E. Eysler, 1911; *Der lila Domino* (with E. von Gatti), C. Cuvillier, 1912; *Der tolle Kosak* (with H. Hall), S. Ehrlich, 1912; *Die Premiere* (musikalische Schwank, with Stein), J. G. Hart, 1912; *Der fliegende Rittmeister* (with Stein), H. Dostal, 1912; *Ein Tag im Paradies* (musikalische Posse, with Stein), Eysler, 1913

Liebesgeister (musikalische Schwank, with Oesterreicher), E. Steffan, 1915; *Die Csárdásfürstin* (with Stein), Kálmán, 1915; *Die – oder keine* (with Stein), Eysler, 1915; *Urschula* (Spl, with J. Wilhelm), H. Dostal, 1916; *Das Hollandweibchen* (with Stein), Kálmán, 1920; *Die blaue Mazur* (with Stein), Lehár, 1920; *Rinaldo* (with Oesterreicher), A. Szirmai, 1921; *Die Siegerin* (musikalische Komödie, with O. Friedmann and F. Lunzer), R. Klein, after Tchaikovsky, 1922; *Die Ballkönigin* (E. von Gatti), K. Stigler, 1923; *Clo-Clo* [Cloclo], Lehár, 1924; *Paganini* (with P. Knepler), Lehár, 1925; *Der Zarewitsch* (with H. Reichert), Lehár, 1927; *Die kluge Mama* (musikalische Komödie), L. Lajtai, 1931

ANDREW LAMB

Jenkins, Graeme (James Ewers) (*b* London, 31 Dec 1958). English conductor. He was a chorister at Dulwich College, and studied at Cambridge University, where he conducted the first British production of *Stiffelio*, and the RCM, conducting College productions of *Albert Herring* and *The Turn of the Screw*. He joined the music staff at Kent Opera, making his professional début with *The Beggar's Opera* (1982). From 1986 to 1991 he was music director of Glyndebourne Touring Opera, making his Glyndebourne Festival début with *Carmen* in 1987. He has conducted the Scottish, Geneva, Netherlands, Canadian and Australian Opera companies, and at the Hong Kong festival. His début with the ENO was in *Così fan tutte* (1988); he also conducted the première of Stephen Oliver's *Timon of Athens* (1991), following the London production of Oliver's *Beauty and the Beast* for Musica nel Chiostro (1985). His performances are marked by a concern for detail and balance, giving sympathetic support to the voices.

NOËL GOODWIN

Jenkins, Neil (*b* St Leonards, Sussex, 9 April 1945). English tenor. He studied at Cambridge and in London. With Kent Opera (1972–88) he sang Monteverdi's Ulysses, Don Ottavio, Ferrando, Count Ory, Robinson Crusoe and Achilles (*King Priam*). He has sung Almaviva for the WNO (1974), Nadir, Goro, Tamino and Monostatos and the Shepherd (*Oedipus rex*) for Scottish Opera and Monsieur Triquet for Opera North.

At Glyndebourne (1985) he took part in Knussen's *Higglety Pigglety Pop!* and *Where the Wild Things Are*. He has appeared at Berlin, Frankfurt, Edinburgh, Geneva, Lyons and Wexford, where in 1989 he sang Don Jerome (Prokofiev's *Betrothal in a Monastery*). His repertory includes Peter Quint, Lord Puff (Henze's *The English Cat*), Weber's Oberon and Ravel's Torquemada. A versatile singing actor, he has a lyrical voice with excellent diction.

ELIZABETH FORBES

Jenkins, Newell (Owen) (*b* New Haven, CT, 8 Feb 1915). American conductor. He studied in Dresden, Freiburg and Munich, at Yale University, and in New York with Leon Barzin. His début was in 1935 with *Dido and Aeneas* at the Städtisches Theater, Freiburg, and in 1940 he founded the Yale Opera Group, New Haven. From 1948 to 1956 he worked in Bologna and Florence, where he formed and directed the Piccola Accademia Musicale (1952), and in the 1970s he was guest conductor at the Stockholm Royal Opera. Meanwhile, in 1958, he started the Clarion Concerts series in New York which broadened into concert and semi-staged performances of rare Baroque operas, among them *Aeneas i Cartago*, *Croesus*, *Giasone*, Vivaldi's *Farnace*, Hasse's *L'olimpiade*, Piccinni's *Didon* and five works by Steffani up to *Le rivali concordi* in 1987. His recordings include operas by Simon Mayr and Rossini.

DENNIS K. McINTIRE, NOËL GOODWIN

Jenkins, Speight (*b* Dallas, 31 Jan 1937). American administrator. He was educated at the University of Texas (BA, 1957) and Columbia University (LLB, 1961). After working as an editor for *Opera News* (1967–73) and as music critic for the *New York Post* (1973–81), from 1981 to 1983 he was host for the 'Live From the Met' broadcasts on public television. He was appointed general director of the Seattle Opera in 1983 and, with productions of the *Ring* cycle in 1986, 1987 and 1991 and such new ventures as Prokofiev's *War and Peace* and Poulenc's *Dialogues des Carmélites* in 1990, revived the company's artistic standing and financial fortunes.

NANCY MALITZ

Jenko, Davorin (*b* Dvorje, nr Kranj, 9 Nov 1835; *d* Ljubljana, 25 Nov 1914). Slovene composer. He was educated in Ljubljana and Trieste, and studied law in Vienna. In 1865 he accepted the post of conductor of the Belgrade Choral Society. He studied composition in Prague (1869–70) before returning to Belgrade, where he conducted at the National Theatre (1871–1902), adapting and arranging incidental music by various composers and also composing his own. He was involved in more than a hundred stage works, including collaborations with other composers and rearrangements of operas into spoken plays with music. Jenko made a significant contribution to Serbian music and was largely responsible for the creation of a uniquely Serbian Singspiel, the *Komad s pevanjem* ('play with singing'). His *Vračara* ('The Sorceress') was the first Serbian operetta; *Pribislav i Božana*, his most ambitious work, comes close to Weberian Romantic opera. Jenko's melodic idiom was much influenced by folk music, and some of his works achieved great popularity; a chorus from *Markova sablja* ('Marko's Sword') later became the Serbian national anthem. Manuscripts of many of Jenko's works can be found in Ljubljana (Narodna in Univerzitetna Knjižnica) and Belgrade (Arhiv Narodnog Pozorišta).

*

D. Cvetko: *Davorin Jenko i njegovo doba* [Jenko and his Time] (Belgrade, 1952)   BOJAN BUJIĆ, ROKSANDA PEJOVIĆ

Jensen, Adolf (*b* Königsberg [now Kaliningrad], 12 Jan 1837; *d* Baden-Baden, 23 Jan 1879). German composer. In 1857–8 he worked as a Kapellmeister at theatres in Posen (now Poznań), Bromberg and in Copenhagen. By 1861 he was second director of the music academy in Königsberg; after his resignation in 1862 he continued to make frequent appearances as a pianist. Eventually in 1868 he settled in Dresden to devote himself to composing. An enthusiastic admirer of Wagner, he campaigned for *Die Meistersinger* on the occasion of the rehearsals under Julius Rietz. Because of his poor health he went to Meran in 1869, to Graz in 1870 and to Baden-Baden in 1875.

Jensen's delicate sensibilities were employed to greatest advantage in his piano music and many songs. He was less successful in larger forms, and his only opera, the two-act *Die Erbin von Montfort* (composed 1858–65 to his own libretto; excerpts of the full score in *D-Mbs*), remained unperformed. After his death it was revised by Wilhelm Kienzl and Elsbeth Jensen as a three-act opera with ballet, *Turandot*, which also was not performed (complete full score in *Mbs*). The vocal score of the revised work was published in Leipzig in 1888.

*

A. Niggli: *Adolf Jensen* (Berlin, 1879)   ROBERT MÜNSTER

Jenůfa [*Její pastorkyňa* ('Her Stepdaughter'; 'Her Foster Daughter')]. Opera in three acts by LEOŠ JANÁČEK to his own libretto after GABRIELA PREISSOVÁ's play *Její pastorkyňa*; Brno, National Theatre, 21 January 1904. (*Pastorkyně* – in dialect, *pastorkyňa* – means simply 'not own daughter'; in the play and the opera, Jenůfa is both stepdaughter and foster daughter to the Kostelnička. Janáček, when approving the German translation, was anxious to promote *Stieftochter*, 'stepdaughter', rather than *Ziehtochter* or *Pflegetochter*, 'foster daughter'. 'Stepdaughter' and 'stepmother' have consequently been used in this article.)

Gabriela Preissová's play *Her Stepdaughter* was first given in Prague in 1890. The next year, Janáček set a libretto made from one of her short stories as his second opera, *The Beginning of a Romance*, and by 1893 seems to have been considering *Her Stepdaughter* as a possible libretto. He began preliminary work on 18 March 1894; by the end of the year he had written the overture 'Žárlivost' ('Jealousy'), originally conceived to open the opera though never used that way during Janáček's lifetime. Act 1 was probably written in full score between 1895 and 1897 but Janáček then dropped the opera for

Grandmother Buryjovka *retired mill owner and now housekeeper at the mill*	contralto
Kostelnička Buryjovka *her daughter-in-law*	soprano
Jenůfa *stepdaughter of the Kostelnička*	soprano
Laca Klemeň *grandson of Grandmother Buryjovka*	tenor
Števa Buryja *half-brother to Laca*	tenor
Foreman (*at the mill*)	baritone
Jano *a herdboy*	soprano
Barena *servant girl at the mill*	soprano
Herdswoman	mezzo-soprano
Mayor	bass
Mayor's Wife	mezzo-soprano
Karolka *their daughter*	mezzo-soprano

Recruits, musicians, people from the mill, mill workers, country-folk, children

Setting A remote village in Slovácko (Moravian Slovakia), with a stream and a mill; some time between 1868 and 1890

---

several years. When he took up the work late in 1901 it went faster; he completed Act 2 by summer 1902 and the whole opera by March 1903. He was able to play it to his daughter Olga on her deathbed; it is dedicated to her memory.

Janáček first offered it to the Prague National Theatre in March 1903. It was immediately rejected, possibly because of an antagonism towards him by the head of opera, Karel Kovařovic. The opera, however, was performed in Brno early the next year, conducted by Janáček's pupil Cyril Metoděj Hrazdira. Despite a tiny orchestra of 34, it achieved some popular success, and continued to be played in Brno and on provincial tours up to 1913. Prague, however, refused to take it up until 1915, when under great pressure from several friends of Janáček, Kovařovic's resistance weakened, and he consented to stage the work subject to his revisions (chiefly cuts and some reorchestration). Janáček agreed (he was 61, and had waited long enough), and the work was given a fine performance under Kovařovic on 26 May 1916. Soon afterwards, *Jenůfa* was translated into German by Max Brod (who thereafter translated most of Janáček's operas) and was given in Vienna in 1918. It was, however, the Berlin Staatsoper production of 1924 under Kleiber which really established the work's reputation in Germany and which led to over 50 more performances before Janáček's death in 1928.

The vocal score, published by the Club of the Friends of Art in Brno (1908), incorporated revisions made by Janáček in 1906–7 (including several cuts suggested by Hrazdira). After the Prague production, the rights were acquired by the Czech publishing firm Hudební Matice, which issued a vocal score (May 1917) based on the original plates but also indicating Kovařovic's cuts. The German score issued by Universal Edition (December 1917) reproduced only the Kovařovic version. It is in this form that the opera was known until Charles Mackerras's reconstruction of the Brno score, which was recorded by Decca in 1982 and made available as a hire score by Universal Edition in a revised form by Charles Mackerras and John Tyrrell (1991).

ACT 1 *The Buryjovka mill, towards evening* The turning of the mill-wheel is represented at the beginning of the short prelude by a repeated xylophone note, a sound Janáček returned to several times during the act. The mill and what it represents is an important element in the motivation of the characters. After the death of his parents, the mill now belongs to Števa, while his elder half-brother Laca, having only a small inheritance, is forced to work there as a common labourer. Both are in love with their cousin Jenůfa, an orphan brought up by her stepmother. Jenůfa loves Števa, by whom she is pregnant, and as the curtain goes up she is seen waiting anxiously for his return from the annual conscription ceremony, 'Už se večer chýlí' ('Night is already falling'). If Števa is drafted into the army Jenůfa will not be able to marry him and her pregnancy will be discovered. Laca watches her suspiciously and in a bitter aria, 'Vy stařenko' ('You, Grandmother'), expresses his frustration and jealousy at the better lot, in love and in fortune, of his half-brother.

This opening scene also introduces three minor figures connected with the mill. There is Grandmother Buryjovka, its former owner now living at the mill as a pensioner. She is harsh towards Laca but indulgent towards her two direct grandchildren, Števa and Jenůfa, and is easily pacified by Jenůfa when the latter apologizes for being unable to concentrate on her work, 'Stařenko, nehněvejte se!' ('Don't be cross, Grandmother!'). Next the herdboy Jano, whom Jenůfa has taught to read, runs on to announce his achievement. Finally there is the mill Foreman, a sympathetic older man, who gives Laca the opportunity to talk about Jenůfa (Laca denies, naturally, that he likes her at all). The Foreman also sharpens Laca's blunt knife for him, an incident whose significance is made clear only at the end of the act. At the end of this dialogue the Foreman announces the dramatic news that Števa has not, after all, been conscripted.

This produces a hubbub of reaction: Jenůfa is overjoyed, Laca furious. And soon the recruits can be heard approaching, singing a familiar anti-conscription song, 'Všeci za ženija' ('All are getting married'), to a stage-band accompaniment, Janáček's skilful and authentic evocation of Moravian folk instrumental ensembles.

At the climax of this ensemble, Števa enters. However glad she is to see Števa back, and not recruited, Jenůfa cannot help reproaching him for being drunk. This makes him show off, boasting of his conquests, and throwing money around for more music. He demands to hear Jenůfa's favourite song, 'Daleko široko' ('Far and wide'), here set as three stanzas sung by the chorus with instrumental music for dancing in between. The pace quickens and turns into a wild dance. At the climax a stern figure comes forward and with a single gesture silences the musicians. This is Jenůfa's stepmother, known as the Kostelnička. This word describes her honorary office at the local chapel, where she serves as sacristan. She is a woman of little means, but immense moral authority. She orders Jenůfa to wait a year before marrying Števa, during which time he must not get drunk. In an aria 'Aji on byl žlutohřívý' ('He too was also golden-haired') that Janáček cut before it could be published in 1908, but which has been printed in the Universal score of 1969 and reinstated in several productions since, the Kostelnička explains her reasons. She had married Jenůfa's widowed father, the ne'er-do-well but attractive brother of the miller. Her husband soon squandered their wealth and died, leaving her to bring up his young daughter. The Kostelnička saw parallels between Jenůfa and herself and was anxious to spare her stepdaughter this fate. She leaves as abruptly

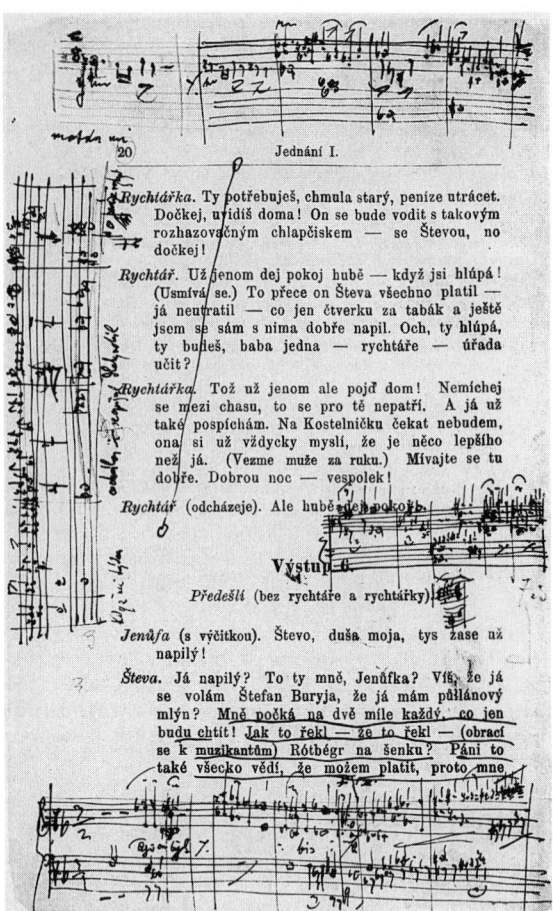

Page from the printed libretto of Janáček's 'Jenůfa' showing part of Act 1, with annotations and marginal notes in the author's hand; the exchange between Jenůfa and Števa about his drunkenness can be seen at the bottom of the page

as she entered. Grandmother Buryjovka sends away the musicians, tells Števa to get some sleep, and attempts to comfort Jenůfa with the thought that every young couple has to endure hard times. This gives rise to one of the more old-fashioned elements of the score, a full-scale slow concertato ensemble for four soloists and chorus composed on the Grandmother's words 'Každý párek si musí svoje trápení přestat' ('Every couple must get over its problems'). At its end the sound of the xylophone is heard once again, now rather more urgently and ominously.

The rest of the act is a series of confrontations between Jenůfa and her two admirers. The first is with the drunken Števa, who, scarcely penitent or aware of the full implications of the Kostelnička's ban, reacts angrily to Jenůfa's reproaches, even when they settle into a pleading Andante, 'Beztoho bude od mamičky těch výčitek dost, dost' ('Even so, there will be many, many reproaches from my mother'). His anger, however, soon dissolves into praise of Jenůfa's rosy cheeks ('Už pro tvoje jablúčkovy líce'), a lyrical moment in which Grandmother Buryjovka's voice joins those of Števa and Jenůfa for a brief trio before she hauls her grandson off to bed.

All this has been observed by Laca who, after another xylophone intervention, spitefully reminds Jenůfa of how Števa boasted of his conquests. She refuses to be upset and Laca, goaded to distraction, takes out the knife the Foreman had been sharpening earlier. If all Števa cared for was Jenůfa's rosy cheeks how might he react if her beauty were disfigured? In a flash his knife does its work. Laca is immediately horrified by his action, and in a brief ensemble his slow lyrical pain is poured out above the faster reactions of Barena the servant girl, and the Grandmother. The final voice is that of the mill Foreman, who declares that Laca did this on purpose.

ACT 2 *A room in the Kostelnička's cottage, half a year later* The gloomy prelude (two bassoons meandering in 3rds provide its chief melodic content) is punctuated by sharp chords and leads to a *fortissimo* tutti outbreak before sinking back again – an evocation of despair and fear in the depths of winter. The Kostelnička has hidden Jenůfa away at her cottage where, eight days earlier, she gave birth to a son. She is still weak and, after a short appearance notable for its tender 'baby music' (as Jenůfa contemplates her child) and a rare moment of duetting between the two women, Jenůfa is sent to bed with a sleeping draught. Alone, the Kostelnička sets to work. Her first plan is to beg Števa to marry Jenůfa. He reluctantly appears at her command and is subjected to urgent and even tender pleading, 'Pojd' se Števo, přece naň podívat' ('Come, Števa, do look at him'). She even kneels to him. But Laca's knife has done its work too well: Števa no longer thinks Jenůfa beautiful. He is going to marry the Mayor's daughter instead. He offers money, but not marriage, and hurries out.

The next visitor is Laca. He has come to see the Kostelnička frequently during the past months, to inquire about Jenůfa, whom he believes, like the rest of the village, to be in Vienna. Only now does he learn that Jenůfa has been at home all this while and has given birth to a child – Števa's child. Laca still wants to marry Jenůfa, but is so dismayed to hear about the child that the Kostelnička, in a fateful moment of decision, tells him that the child died. She then sends him away on an errand. She must now prove her lie correct. After a highly dramatic monologue, one of the key moments of the opera in which she wrestles with her conscience and screws up her courage, 'Co chvíla' ('In a moment'), she runs from the cottage, taking the child with her. Almost immediately Jenůfa wakes up from her drugged sleep and notes the absence of both her stepmother and the child. She concludes that the Kostelnička must have taken him to show to the people at the mill. Calm at last, she offers up a prayer to the Virgin, a touching setting of the *Salve regina* in Czech ('Zdrávas královno').

When the Kostelnička returns alone from her expedition to the icy millstream, she tells Jenůfa that she has been delirious for two days during which the child died, a fact that Jenůfa accepts with tender resignation, 'Tož umřel' ('So he died'). And when Laca arrives soon after, she similarly accepts unresistingly his earnest proposal of marriage, urged on by the Kostelnička. As the Kostelnička blesses the union and then curses Števa, the window is forced open by the wind and, filled with foreboding, she cries out in terror. The five-note rhythm of her final word 'načuhovalo' ('[as if death] were peering in') forms the basis for an ominous postlude to the act.

ACT 3 *A room in the Kostelnička's cottage, two months later* It is early spring and the cottage is filled with preparations for Jenůfa's wedding to Laca. Jenůfa has recovered her strength, whereas the Kostelnička is only a shadow of her former self and is helped out by a

Herdswoman. The Mayor and his wife arrive and while the Kostelnička shows them the trousseau, Laca and Jenůfa are left alone: a deep relationship is beginning to form between the two. Števa arrives with his betrothed – the Mayor's daughter Karolka – and Jenůfa adroitly manages a reconciliation between the half-brothers. Finally a group of girls from the village bring flowers and sing a wedding song 'Ej, mamko, mamko' ('Hey, mother') for Jenůfa. Grandmother Buryjovka gives her blessing to the pair and as the Kostelnička is about to add hers, a tumult is heard outside. Jano runs on with the news that workmen from the brewery sent to cut ice from the stream have discovered the frozen corpse of a little child. Jenůfa thinks it is her child, and the gathering crowd suspect her of murder. Laca holds off the mob but it is the Kostelnička who silences the people with her own confession of guilt, 'To můj skutek' ('It's my deed'). At first appalled, Jenůfa begins to understand the motives behind the Kostelnička's terrible action. In one of the great moments of opera she forgives her stepmother, who is then led off to stand trial (and under Austrian law of the time, to her death). The crowd follows, leaving Laca and Jenůfa alone on the stage. Jenůfa thinks that Laca can no longer want her in these circumstances, but she is wrong, and as he pleads with her, the stubborn dissonant note that has clouded the tonality throughout this scene suddenly disappears – a token of Jenůfa's hard-won acceptance of his love.

* * *

This final scene is known in two forms, the canonic apotheosis that Kovařovic elaborated from it, and Janáček's more sober orchestration, much more in keeping with the spiritual growth that is depicted in the opera. It is wrong to emphasize the violent actions of the opera – Laca's slashing of Jenůfa's cheek, the Kostelnička's murder of Jenůfa's baby – in an attempt to link the opera to the wave of *verismo* works written at the same time by Czech composers. Nor should too much be made of the ethnographic scenes in the outer acts; Janáček was keen to stress that though the words were authentic, the music was in fact his own. This is not a folklore opera, as was its predecessor, and modern productions have sometimes dispensed with the traditional Moravian folk costumes to underline this. The opera instead belongs to a line in which the spiritual development of the characters is paramount, a line that can be seen in Smetana's late operas and before that in *Die Zauberflöte*. Laca and Jenůfa have quite visibly grown through the opera from obsessed and self-centred individuals in the first act to generous and understanding human beings in the last. The shocking course of events is not there for gratuitous violence, but as a depiction of the hard lessons they have had to learn. The Kostelnička has the hardest lessons of all and it is fitting that Janáček's title for the work should reflect that she is the main character.

JOHN TYRRELL

Jephté ('Jephtha'). *Tragédie en musique* in a prologue and five acts by MICHEL PIGNOLET DE MONTÉCLAIR to a libretto by SIMON-JOSEPH PELLEGRIN; Paris, Opéra, 28 February 1732.

This was the first 'biblical opera' performed at the Opéra, although the genre had existed in France since the end of the 17th century, cultivated especially by the Jesuits (e.g. Charpentier's *David et Jonathas*). Clément and Delaporte (*Les anecdotes dramatiques*, 1775) state that the opera was banned by the Cardinal of Noailles, but there is no mention of this interdict in the *Mercure*.

Produced during Lent (and thus allowing the Opéra to open its doors during that period), *Jephté* was immediately given a warm reception by the public. The main parts were taken by Antier (Almasie), Le Maure (Iphise), Chassé (Jephté) and Dun (Phinée).

Sources for the study of *Jephté* are extremely complex. The opera was frequently revived during Lent, probably because it was the only one that could be staged at the Opéra during this period. A *fête en action de grâce* (of which the libretto is extant but the music lost), added to Act 5 on 18 March and adversely criticized in the *Mercure* (March 1732), was suppressed and replaced by a chorus for the 1733 revival. Subsequent revivals were staged at the Opéra in 1734, 1735, 1737, 1738, 1740, 1741, 1744 and 1761 (without the prologue). *Jephté* was also performed at the Concert de la Reine in 1732, 1737 and 1741, and at court in 1751. Many extracts were given at the Concert Spirituel until 1760. The opera's success was so great that it was mentioned by Voltaire (letter to Thieriot, 14 April 1732), Saint-Simon and Rousseau (*Confessions*, book 5). Voltaire, however, wrote to Cideville on 8 March 1732, saying that it bored him to hear the Bible at the Opéra. Considered extremely modern when first produced, the work is thought to have had a great influence on Rameau. According to the *Mercure* (March 1761): 'The noble and distinguished character of this work struck him in points clearly analogous to the virile fecundity of his genius'. In the prologue the pagan deities sing of their power over humanity but are ousted by Truth and the Virtues (of Catholicism).

The subject of the main plot is taken from the Book of Judges. Jephtha (bass), rejected by his family, is recalled to his country to fight the Ammonites and dictates his conditions. If he wins the day, he will become leader of the Israelites. Before taking the field he makes a vow to the Lord: he will sacrifice the first creature he meets on returning victorious. Unfortunately the first person who runs to meet him is his daughter. Pellegrin adapted the biblical text to the taste of the period, allowing the daughter, Iphise (soprano), to live, employing the element of the marvellous in the descent of the Ark (1.iv), and adding a sentimental interest to the sombre story in the character of Ammon (tenor), as well as a tender part in that of Almasie (soprano), Iphise's mother.

Though the work is chiefly notable for choral singing, *Jephté* is also full of action and colourful incident – the parting of the River Jordan and the crossing of the Israelite army (Act 1), the news of Jephtha's victory, celebrated by all the people of Maspha (Act 2), Jephtha's coronation, rudely interrupted (Act 3), the singing and dancing of the happy shepherds (Act 4), and the storm and thunderbolts sent by God to halt the sacrifice of Iphise (Act 5). Montéclair's score is one of the most important of the century and contains much powerful writing. The string texture is usually four-part, although Montéclair includes sections in as few as one part and as many as eight. Flutes, oboes and trumpets are often used in an innovatory manner, both as solo instruments and in combination with others. Especially fine moments include a duet for a solo flute accompanied by unison violins (5.i), and the quintet for recorders (4.i), which appeared only in the original version. Among the most famous passages are Jephtha's aria with accompaniment 'Rivages du Jourdain' (1.i) and the chorus of exhortation, 'Tout tremble devant le Seigneur' (1.iv).

JEAN DURON, FANNIE VERNAZ

Jepson, Helen (*b* Titusville, PA, 28 Nov 1904). American soprano. She studied at the Curtis Institute with Queena Mario. After singing in Philadelphia (1928–30) and in Montreal, she made her début at the Metropolitan as Helene in John Laurence Seymour's *In the Pasha's Garden* in 1935 and the same year first sang with the Chicago Grand Opera as Thaïs and at San Francisco as Martha. She continued to appear regularly with both the Metropolitan and Chicago companies until 1942, her roles including Marguerite, Nedda and Eva. After retiring she taught for many years. Her few recordings, the most famous of which is of excerpts from *Otello* (with Martinelli and Tibbett), display a lyric instrument of beauty but limited dramatic intensity.

RICHARD LeSUEUR

Jeremiáš, Otakar (*b* Písek, 17 Oct 1892; *d* Prague, 5 March 1962). Czech composer and conductor. He received his earliest musical education from his father and his mother, the singer and pianist Vilma Jeremiášová, née Bakešová (1865–1953). He studied at the Prague Conservatory in 1907 and then had private composition lessons with Novák (1909–10). As a cellist he made several concert tours abroad, returning home in 1918 and settling in České Budějovice, where he directed the music school from 1919 and conducted concerts and opera.

In May 1945 Jeremiáš was appointed opera director of the National Theatre in Prague, where on 27 May 1945 he conducted Smetana's nationalist opera *Libuše*, the first performance after the Nazi occupation, when it had been prohibited. His withdrawal from this post in 1947 and a serious illness two years later prevented him from realizing all his artistic plans for the National Theatre, but he took an active part in cultural activities until the end of his life. In 1949 he was elected the first chairman of the Union of Czechoslovak Composers; having been a member of the Czech Academy of Sciences and Arts since 1928, he was awarded the title of National Artist in 1950 and the Order of the Republic in 1960.

Jeremiáš was a prolific composer, chiefly of choral and other vocal works in the late Romantic style. His three-act opera *Bratři Karamazovi* ('The Brothers Karamazov'), for which he wrote the libretto with Jaroslav Maria, is based on the novel by F. M. Dostoyevsky and was first given at the National Theatre, Prague, on 8 October 1928. Full of dramatic tension, warmly emotional music and keen psychological portrayals, it is his masterpiece and ranks among the best Czech operatic works. His other opera, *Enšpígl* ('Eulenspiegel'), in a prologue and seven scenes to a libretto by Jiří Mařánek after Charles de Coster, was composed between 1940 and 1944 and first performed at the National Theatre on 13 May 1949. In maintaining a balance between spontaneous and rational elements in his music, Jeremiáš was heir to Smetana, in whom he saw the embodiment of the genius of the Czech nation, a vision expressed in his booklet of essays on Smetana (Prague, 1924). With his generation, he witnessed social struggles to which he sensitively responded both as a performing artist and in his compositions. Like Janáček, he used texts by Czech poets of strong social conscience.

See also BRATŘI KARAMAZOVI.

J. Bartoš: 'Otakar Jeremiáš', *Listy hudebni matice*, viii (1928), 4–16
H. H. Stuckenschmidt: 'Brüder Karamasov als Oper', *Melos*, vii (1928), 561

J. Hutter and Z. Chalbala, eds.: *Českě uměni dramatické*, ii: *Zpěvohra* [Czech Dramatic Art: Opera] (Prague, 1941), esp. 346–9

J. Plavec: *Otakar Jeremiáš* (Prague, 1943)

——: 'Enšpigl', *Národni divadlo* (12 May 1949)

H. Havlová: *Otakara Jeremiáše 'Bratři Karamazovi'* (Prague, 1958)

J. Plavec: *Národní umělec: Otakar Jeremiáš* [National Artist: Otakar Jeremiáš] (Prague, 1964) [with list of works]

J. Smolka: 'Nově nalezené dílo náraodního umělce Otakar Jeremiáše' [Newly Discovered Work of the National Artist Otakar Jeremiáš], *HV*, iii (1966), 623–31 [with Eng. summary]

M. Jeremiášová-Budíková: 'Ze vzpomínek na Otakara Jeremiáše' [From my Memories of Otakar Jeremiáš], *Živá hudba*, iv (1968), 147–50 [with Ger. summary]   JIŘÍ VYSLOUŽIL

Jerger, Alfred (*b* Brno, 9 June 1889; *d* Vienna, 18 Nov 1976). Austrian bass-baritone. After studying musicology and conducting at the Vienna Music Academy, he joined the staff of the Zürich Opera in 1913; he conducted operetta performances, worked as an actor, and in 1917 sang Lothario in *Mignon*. That year he so impressed Strauss with his Ochs that he was invited to join the Munich Opera (1919), and after two seasons moved to the Vienna Staatsoper where he sang some 150 roles, including Don Giovanni, Leporello, Hans Sachs, Beckmesser, Méphistophélès, Scarpia, the Grand Inquisitor, Philip II and the title role of Krenek's *Jonny spielt auf*; his Pizarro and his Mozart roles were a familiar part of the Salzburg Festival. In 1924 he created the Man in Schoenberg's *Die glückliche Hand*. He was a renowned Strauss singer and created Mandryka in *Arabella* at Dresden in 1933. Jerger was also active as a director and editor, and at the end of World War II was appointed temporary director of the Vienna Staatsoper. He was largely responsible for its being able to perform *Figaro* as early as 1 May 1945. In 1947 he became a professor at the Vienna Music Academy and in his 80th year he was invited to sing the Notary in Solti's *Der Rosenkavalier* recording. Between the wars Jerger made a fine series of recordings.   PETER BRANSCOMBE

Jeritza, Maria [Mizzi; Jedlizka, Marie] (*b* Brno, 6 Oct 1887; *d* Orange, NJ, 10 July 1982). Czech soprano, later naturalized American. After studies in Brno and Prague, she made her début at Olmütz in 1910 as Elsa; she then joined the Vienna Volksoper, and in 1912 appeared at the Hofoper. She quickly became an immense favourite in Vienna, where she sang regularly for over two decades; she was an especially admired Tosca, Minnie and Turandot. Among her many Strauss roles she was the first Ariadne in both versions of *Ariadne auf Naxos* (1912, Stuttgart; 1916, Vienna; for illustration *see* ARIADNE AUF NAXOS (ii)), and the first Empress in *Die Frau ohne Schatten* (1919, Vienna). Having sung Marietta in the first Vienna performance of Korngold's *Die tote Stadt*, she repeated this role for her Metropolitan début later in the same year (19 November 1921). Of greater musical significance was her Jenůfa in both the first Viennese (1918) and first New York (1924) performances of Janáček's masterpiece. During the next 12 years she became recognized as the Metropolitan's most glamorous and beautiful star since the days of Geraldine Farrar, and appropriately introduced to New York both Puccini's *Turandot* and Strauss's *Die ägyptische Helena*. Her Covent Garden performances were confined to seven roles during 1925 and 1926, whereas at the Metropolitan she sang 290 performances in 20 roles. After World War II she made isolated appearances in Vienna and New York. Though endowed with an ample and lustrous voice, Jeritza belonged to the category of artist known as a 'singing actress', freely yielding both dramatically and vocally to impulses that were sometimes more flamboyant than refined. In her numerous records, faults of taste and technique co-exist with genuine vocal achievements.

*

GV (L. Riemens and R. Celletti; S. Smolian)

M. Jeritza: *Sunlight and Song: a Singer's Life* (New York, 1924)

R. Werba: *Maria Jeritza: Primadonna des Verismo* (Vienna, 1981)
     DESMOND SHAWE-TAYLOR

Jérusalem ('Jerusalem'). *Opéra* in four acts by GIUSEPPE VERDI to a libretto by ALPHONSE ROYER and GUSTAVE VAËZ after TEMISTOCLE SOLERA's and Verdi's earlier opera *I Lombardi alla prima crociata*; Paris, Opéra, 26 November 1847.

Gaston, Viscount of Béarn	tenor
The Count of Toulouse	baritone
Roger *the Count's brother*	bass
Hélène *the Count's daughter*	soprano
Isaure *her companion*	soprano
Adhemar de Monteil *Papal Legate*	bass
Raymond *Gaston's squire*	tenor
A Soldier	bass
A Herald	bass
The Emir of Ramla	bass
An Officer of the Emir	tenor

Knights, ladies, pages, soldiers, pilgrims, penitents, an executioner, Arab sheiks, women of the harem, people of Ramla

Setting Toulouse and Palestine, in 1095 and 1099

The great Paris opera house, the Académie Royale de Musique (or the Opéra), had been making overtures to Verdi for some two years when, in the summer of 1847, he signed a contract to supply the theatre with a 'new' work by November of that year. As had Rossini and Donizetti, Verdi offered for his début at the Opéra a revision of one of his earlier Italian operas; with the help of Royer and Vaëz, both of whom had considerable experience in such matters, he fashioned a French version from *I Lombardi*, first performed in 1843 and not previously seen in Paris. The librettists retained little of the original plot apart from its basis in a crusade: in vocal terms, the lovers Giselda and Oronte become Hélène and Gaston, the warring brothers Arvino and Pagano become the Count of Toulouse – now a baritone rather than tenor – and Roger. As well as adding the obligatory ballet, Verdi decided on some wide-ranging structural changes, adding much new music, cutting what he considered weak or inappropriate and leaving only a few of the original numbers in their former positions. *Jérusalem* was well received in Paris, its first cast including Gilbert Duprez (Gaston), Charles Portheaut (the Count), Adolphe-Joseph-Louis Alizard (Roger) and Mme Julian-Van-Gelder (Hélène). However, in spite of being in many ways superior to *I Lombardi*, the opera failed to establish itself in either the French or the Italian repertory and is today only occasionally revived. The following summary will mention musical detail only in passages new to the revised opera.

The prelude is new; in contrast with the disparate juxtaposition of musical elements in *I Lombardi*, it sets out to develop in a systematic manner aspects of its opening theme.

ACT 1 *A gallery connecting the Count of Toulouse's palace and his chapel* As the curtain rises, Hélène and Gaston are bidding each other farewell, Gaston assuring his beloved that he will be reconciled to the Count (who killed his father) if permission is granted for their marriage. Their brief duet, 'Adieu, mon bien-aimé', is unaccompanied except for solo horn. As Gaston leaves, Isaure appears and the two ladies kneel in prayer, Hélène offering a French version of 'Salve Maria' from *I Lombardi*, now entitled 'Vierge Marie'.

Hélène and Isaure depart and, as the orchestra depicts a sunrise, the stage fills with lords and ladies who join in a chorus celebrating the end of civil war, 'Enfin voici le jour propice'. The Count and all the other principals appear. They are about to go on a Crusade, and the Count offers peace to Gaston and his family, sealing the pact with his daughter's hand. All rejoice except Roger, who incestuously desires Hélène for himself. The principals explore their individual feelings in the quintet 'Je tremble encor, j'y crois à peine', a number that required some vocal redistribution from its model in *I Lombardi*. In a newly composed linking passage, Gaston swears allegiance to the Count, who is pronounced leader of the crusading army. The scene closes with a grand chorus, 'Cité du Seigneur!'

An organ sounds from inside the chapel; Roger appears and, in the cantabile 'Oh! dans l'ombre, dans le mystère', explores the nature of his incestuous love. The aria over, Roger instructs a soldier to seek out two knights in golden armour and to murder the one not wearing a white cloak. After a warlike chorus looking forward to the Crusade, Roger anticipates the murder of Gaston in a cabaletta new for the French version, 'Ah! viens! démon! esprit du mal!'. The action scene that follows is also new. Cries of 'Murder!' in the chapel precede the appearance of Gaston: it is the Count who has been attacked. Roger's hired assassin accuses Gaston of instigating the violence and all join in an accusatory concertato, 'Monstre, parjure, homicide!'. The Papal Legate sentences Gaston to exile and in a final stretta, 'Sur ton front est lancé l'anathême', all pronounce anathema on him.

ACT 2.i *The mountains of Ramla in Palestine* Four years have passed. At the opening, corresponding with Act 2 scene ii of *I Lombardi*, the disguised Roger is outside his cave, singing the Adagio 'O jour fatal! ô crime!'. Raymond enters, dying of thirst. At the news that others are in a similar plight, Roger hurries to the rescue. Hélène now appears, recognizes Raymond as Gaston's squire and learns that her beloved is alive and imprisoned in Ramla. She breaks into a joyous cabaletta, originally in Act 4 of *I Lombardi* and here retitled 'Quelle ivresse! bonheur suprême!', and leaves to seek out Gaston. A band of pilgrims, weak from lack of water, struggle on to deliver 'O mon Dieu! Ta parole est donc vaine!' (the French version of 'O Signore, dal tetto natio'). As in *I Lombardi*, a lively march introduces the Count (marvellously recovered, he tells us, from the assassination attempt), who asks the hermit's blessing. But Roger (still unrecognized) elects to accompany them into battle. All depart after a lively final chorus, 'Le Seigneur nous promet la victoire', new for the French version.

2.ii *A room in the Emir's palace at Ramla* Gaston, a prisoner, muses on Hélène in a revised version of his Act 2 Andante from *I Lombardi*, now entitled 'Je veux encor entendre'. The Emir appears,

quickly followed by Hélène, who has been captured nearby. The Act 3 lovers' duet from *I Lombardi* then ensues; Hélène and Gaston are about to escape to join the Crusaders but are at the last moment surrounded by guards.

ACT 3.i *The gardens of the harem at Ramla* This scene corresponds to Act 2 scene iii of *I Lombardi*, except that the opening chorus is followed by a full-length ballet. By the time the dancing is over, Crusaders are at the gates. Hélène prays for deliverance; Gaston appears at her side. The Crusaders rush in and the Count denounces Hélène for consorting with Gaston, the presumed assassin. Hélène, like her Italian counterpart, responds with a rondò finale, 'Non ... votre rage', at the close of which the Count drags her away.

3.ii *The public square at Ramla* In an impressive ensemble scene, new for the French version, Gaston is led on to the strains of a funeral dirge. The Legate informs the crowd that he is to be dishonoured and executed; Gaston pleads for mercy in the Andante mosso, 'O mes amis, mes frères d'armes'. But the accusers are unmoved: he will be executed the following day. In a closing stretta, 'Frapper bourreaux!', Gaston asks for immediate death, proud before God of his innocence.

ACT 4.i *On the edge of the Crusaders' camp in the valley of Jehoshaphat* The scene is based on the 'Coro della Processione' that opens Act 3 of *I Lombardi*, although the chorus is preceded by a recitative from Roger, looking over the valley at Jerusalem. As the procession moves away, Roger and Hélène remain behind to offer Gaston a final blessing. The tenor appears, and so the new plot links to the famous trio that ends Act 3 of *I Lombardi*: it is now entitled 'Dieu nous sépare, Hélène!', is shorn of its violin solo and boasts an exciting coda in which offstage sounds of battle cause Gaston and Roger to rush off into the fray.

4.ii *The Count's tent* The Count, accompanied by an unknown knight who has distinguished himself in battle, announces victory. The knight reveals himself as Gaston. Roger is now brought on, mortally wounded. The music links into the final scene of *I Lombardi*, with Roger's revelation of his true identity and his pleas that mercy be shown to Gaston, answered by the closing Hymne Général, 'A toi gloire ô Dieu de victoire'.

* * *

Although *Jérusalem* was soon converted into the Italian *Gerusalemme*, and published in Italy, Verdi's revision failed to oust *I Lombardi* from the Italian stage and gradually disappeared from the repertory. This is in some ways regrettable, as the opera simplifies somewhat the complex action of the Italian original, adds convincing new music (in particular the fine crowd scene of Act 3 scene ii), cuts some of the weaker portions and, by converting Arvino from a tenor to a baritone, solves one of the problems of vocal distribution that occurred in *I Lombardi*. Whatever its ultimate merits, *Jérusalem* serves as a fascinating first document in charting Verdi's relationship with the French stage, a relationship that was to become increasingly important during the next decade.

ROGER PARKER

Jerusalem, Siegfried (*b* Oberhausen, 17 April 1940). German tenor. After some years as a bassoonist he studied singing in Stuttgart and made his début there in 1975 as the First Prisoner in *Fidelio*. At Bayreuth he sang Froh, the Young Seaman (1977), Parsifal, Walther,

Lohengrin (1979–81), Siegmund (1983–6) and Siegfried (1988–90). He became a member of the Deutsche Oper, Berlin, in 1978 and has also appeared in Hamburg, Vienna, Munich, Zürich, Geneva, Barcelona and Madrid. He made his Metropolitan début in 1980 as Lohengrin and returned in 1987 as Loge; in 1986 he sang Parsifal (at very short notice) with the ENO and Erik at Covent Garden. As well as the Wagner roles to which his strong, expressive voice is so well suited, his repertory includes Tamino, Idomeneus, Gluck's Orestes (a high baritone role), Max (*Freischütz*) and Boris (*Kát'a Kabanová*). ELIZABETH FORBES

Jessner, Irene (*b* Vienna, 28 Aug 1901). Canadian soprano. She studied at the Neues Konservatorium in Vienna with Victor Fuchs. Her début was in Teplice in 1930 as Elsa in *Lohengrin*, after which she appeared in Brno, Buenos Aires, Chicago, Munich, Philadelphia, Prague and San Francisco. In 1936 she made her Metropolitan début as Ortlinde in *Die Walküre* and remained with the company until 1952, singing a broad repertory including Hänsel, Tosca and many Mozart, Strauss and the lighter Wagner roles. She recorded for Columbia and Victor. In 1952 Jessner joined the voice faculty at the University of Toronto, where her pupils included Teresa Stratas. CORI ELLISON

Jessonda. *Grosse Oper* in three acts by LOUIS SPOHR to a libretto by Eduard Gehe after Antoine-Marin Lemièrre's play *La veuve de Malabar*; Kassel, Hoftheater, 28 July 1823.

Jessonda *a rajah's widow*	soprano
Amazili *her sister*	soprano
Dandau *chief Brahmin*	bass
Nadori *a young Brahmin*	tenor
Tristan d'Acunha *a Portuguese general*	baritone
Pedro Lopes *a Portuguese colonel*	tenor
Indian Officer	tenor
Two Bayadères	sopranos

Brahmins, bayadères, Portuguese and Indian soldiers, townspeople

Setting In and around Goa on the coast of Malabar in the early 16th century

Spohr read Lemièrre's *La veuve de Malabar* during a visit to Paris in winter 1820–21 and drew up a rough scenario the following summer. It was made into a libretto by Eduard Gehe, a lawyer and literary amateur in Dresden. Spohr began serious work on the music in April 1822, shortly after taking up the post of Hofkapellmeister in Kassel, and completed the opera by the end of the year. At its première *Jessonda* was enthusiastically received, and its first performance in Leipzig, on 9 February 1824, was such a triumph that Peters doubled the agreed sum of 100 thalers for the publication rights. The vocal score was published by them in 1824 and there were several later editions. An extra aria for Amazili (no.19*a*, 'O Welt, so schön und blühend') was written during the mid-1820s and published by Schuberth in 1841, and a full score was issued by Peters, at Brahms's instigation, in 1881. By 1830 *Jessonda* was regarded as a repertory piece in Germany and the Austrian Empire, and during the succeeding decades it was staged in many other European countries. It remained in the German repertory until the early 20th

century. After its London première in 1840 the *Morning Chronicle* asserted: '*Jessonda* is not surpassed by any opera that we know, and it is equalled by very few'. In Paris in 1842, however, it was coolly received. There have been a number of modern revivals, including those at Kassel in 1959 and at Oxford in 1980. The opera was recorded by Austrian Radio (ORF) in 1986.

ACT 1.i *A temple in Goa* A ceremony of mourning for the recently deceased rajah is in progress. In a succession of choruses, accompanied by processions and dancing, the association of the Indians with the key of E♭ is established. In a recitative and duet, 'Aus dieses Tempels heil'gen Mauern', the characters of Dandau, the ruthless high priest, and Nadori, a young Brahmin who abhors the priesthood, are developed; the reluctant Nadori is required to go outside the temple for the first time in his life to deliver the message of death to the rajah's young widow, Jessonda, who must burn on the funeral pyre. A messenger arrives to say that a Portuguese army is advancing on the city. Dandau and the priests express their defiance.

1.ii *Jessonda's apartments* In conversation with her sister Amazili, Jessonda reveals that she was torn from her real love, a Portuguese general, to marry the old rajah. In the recitative and aria 'Als in mitternacht'ge Stunde' Jessonda moves from agitation to resignation. In the bipartite aria Spohr adopts the unusual procedure of following an Allegro in E minor with an Adagio in A♭. The finale begins when Nadori enters, accompanied by dancing bayadères, to deliver the message of death, but, overcome by Amazili's beauty, he falls immediately in love and vows to help save Jessonda.

ACT 2 *Outside the city* In a succession of male-voice choruses the Portuguese practise their warlike skills and greet their general, Tristan d'Acunha. D major is established as the principal key associated with the Portuguese. In the aria 'Der Kriegeslust ergeben' Tristan sorrows for his true love who had mysteriously disappeared from her home on the Ganges some years earlier. This aria, which has the rhythm of a polonaise, became enormously popular as a concert piece. In conversation with his friend Lopes, Tristan reveals that he has given his oath that the Indians can carry out what he believes to be harmless religious ceremonies without interference. Bayadères bring Jessonda to the sacred stream for purification. Jessonda and Amazili sing a duet as they weave flower garlands. Nadori, alone, renews his vow to save Jessonda in a recitative and rondo, 'Still lag auf meiner Seele'; like Tristan's aria it is in polonaise rhythm. During the recitative, as Nadori states his intention to rescue Jessonda, the oboe intones the phrase to which, in the Act 1 finale, Amazili had sung her plea for help, and his thoughts turn to his love for her. Amazili enters and together they sing a duet, 'Schönes Mädchen', which became one of the most popular items in the opera. Informed by Nadori of the gruesome purpose of the ceremonies, Tristan comes to investigate and discovers that Jessonda is his lost love; but before he can take action to save her, Dandau arrives and reminds him of his oath. After a tense confrontation Jessonda is taken back to the city.

ACT 3.i *The Portuguese camp outside the city* The orchestral introduction is based on the motif representing Tristan's oath heard in the finale of Act 2. Tristan

Design by Carl Wilhelm Gropius (inscribed on the back '2t Decor 1str Act Nr.2 Oper Jessonda'), possibly for the first Berlin performance (14 February 1825) of Spohr's 'Jessonda'

emerges from his tent and gives vent to his despair at the consequence of the oath in a freely constructed section which strikingly anticipates Tannhäuser's vision. Nadori arrives unexpectedly and informs him that the Indians have broken the truce by attacking the Portuguese ships. Released from his oath, Tristan prepares to enter the city by a secret passage known to Nadori.

3.ii *A square in the city* Outside the temple, choruses of bayadères and priests invoke the gods. A storm is raging, at the height of which a colossal image of Brahma is struck by lightning. This is taken as a sign that the god is angry, and Dandau decides to expedite the sacrifice. The stage clears and Jessonda, arrayed for the sacrifice, comes out, followed by two bayadères. In the aria 'Hohe Götter!' Jessonda begs the gods to intercede and save her from her fate. Amazili rushes in to tell her that rescue is at hand. Dandau returns with the Indians, and when an officer arrives to tell him that the Portuguese have entered the city he tries to kill Jessonda but is prevented by the timely arrival of Tristan and the Portuguese. The opera ends with the joyful union of Tristan and Jessonda and of Nadori and Amazili.

*   *   *

Jessonda differs considerably in several respects from Spohr's earlier operas, most significantly in its extensive use of chorus and ballet and in its replacement of spoken dialogue with recitative. The musical and dramatic action flow almost continuously with very few breaks between numbers. Musical motifs and reminiscence play an important part in strengthening the dramatic coherence, although they do not have as central a role as in Spohr's earlier opera, *Faust*. In an article 'Aufruf an deutsche Componisten', published in the *Allgemeine musikalische Zeitung* shortly before the première of *Jessonda*, Spohr set out in detail his views on the future course which he believed German opera should take. He clearly intended *Jessonda* to be an exemplar of what he thought German composers should be trying to achieve, and, more particularly, he intended to present an alternative to the approach Weber had taken in *Der Freischütz* (about which Spohr had mixed feelings). Weber's *Euryanthe*, first staged in October 1823, aimed to do many of the same things as *Jessonda*, but although

it contains some of Weber's finest music it was marred by an unwieldy libretto. Thus *Jessonda* enjoyed far greater success than *Euryanthe* and remained the standard-bearer of German grand opera until the advent of Wagner.   CLIVE BROWN

Jessye, Eva (*b* Coffeyville, KS, 20 Jan 1895; *d* Ann Arbor, 21 Feb 1992). American choral conductor. She studied at Western University, Kansas, and Langston University, Oklahoma, and then taught for a while before settling in New York in 1926. There she studied with Will Marion Cook and Percy Goetschius, and formed her own group, the Original Dixie Jubilee Singers (later the Eva Jessye Choir). She was choral director for King Vidor's film *Hallelujah* (1929), Virgil Thomson's *Four Saints in Three Acts* (1934) and Gershwin's *Porgy and Bess* (1935). She trained many professional black choruses and promoted interest in Afro-American musical forms, as well as composing oratorios.

*

SouthernB
D. Cooper: *Eva Jessye, Afro-American Woman: her Contribution to American Music and Theater* (thesis, Hunter College, City U., New York, 1979)   MARK TUCKER

Jesuit drama. Both universalist and emphatically humanist in outlook since its founding in 1540, the Society of Jesus has always functioned as one of the principal educational arms of the Catholic Church and the papacy. This role developed most fully in the colleges and seminaries established by the Jesuits in Catholic lands. Here instruction stressed not only theology and philosophy but also literature. As early as the 16th century, dramatic representations were staged at these institutions, drawing together elements from the humanist theatre, medieval mystery plays and Shrovetide entertainments. The Bible served as the basic source material, but secular and often local subjects were used too, invariably with a strong emphasis on the allegorical and symbolic, and music often had an important role.

Early examples of Jesuit drama with music are recorded from the Low Countries (*Josephus* by Georg Maropedius, given in 1544 in Antwerp and published in Utrecht, 1552–3), Spain (1558, Orcaña), Portugal (a drama by João Arias, given at the college of S Antão, Lisbon, in 1562; further examples at Coimbra and Evora), and Switzerland. In Italy, the tradition at the German College in Rome dates back at least to 1573. A surviving early work performed by the pupils of the Roman Seminary in 1606 is Agostino Agazzari's *Eumelio*, a three-act *dramma pastorale*. This is a moralizing tale, set mainly in recitatives and arias (with choruses at the ends of the acts), about a boy who is enticed away from the simple pastoral life but is ultimately restored. Also at the seminary, a version by Leone Santi of the story of David and Goliath was given in 1622 'con bellissimi intermedi'; in 1654 the seminarians gave a tragedy, *Ciro*, and Cardinal Pallavicino's *Ermengildo* was also given at the seminary. The seminarians of S Pietro gave *S Eustachio* in 1643. A five-act musical drama on the story of the Cyclops was acted at the German and Hungarian College in 1628 for the young Grand Duke of Tuscany and in 1653 the German College was the site of a *tragedia sacra musicale*. These Jesuit musical dramas in Italy represent a somewhat different tradition from the more moralistic and educational type of the German-speaking countries.

The most important institution for Jesuit theatre in France was the Collège de Clermont (from 1682 called Collège Louis-le-Grand in gratitude for the king's declaring it a royal foundation and endowing it handsomely). Other important colleges were the Collège d'Harcourt and those at Lyons, Avignon and Lille. Members of the order wrote the texts, students acted them, professional musicians and choreographers were hired, and no expense was spared on the scenery and costumes. *Intermèdes* in French were often used between acts of Latin tragedies with biblical, other sacred, mythological or historical plots, and they shared characters or themes with the play, though each act was independent from the rest. French tragedies with choruses and other incidental music were rarer.

Dance was part of the instruction, and a *ballet de cour* was traditionally given at the distribution of prizes in August, when the king was sometimes present. The ties with the monarchy were also sometimes reflected in the choice of subject; for example, in 1660 the *Ballet du lys et de l'impériale* accompanied Dozenne's *Clementia christiana* and celebrated Louis XIV's marriage. Collasse and M.-A. Charpentier were among the composers of Jesuit stage works. Occasionally from 1684 onwards, true operas (with coherent plots) were performed, still following the *intermède* pattern of intercalation. Thus, Charpentier's *David et Jonathas* (1688) was given with Chamillart's Latin tragedy *Saül*. Later, Campra contributed to numerous Jesuit works, but all the music appears to be lost. Indeed the French tradition was lost with the suppression of Jesuit colleges and their expulsion from the kingdom (1761–2).

In German-speaking lands, Jesuit dramas were most assiduously cultivated in Bavaria and Austria, where the order controlled most Gymnasia. Professional actors were very seldom involved, since a major purpose of the dramas was to train students in Latin in particular and in rhetoric and deportment in general. Normally responsibility for producing the text fell to a senior professor of rhetoric, who, like librettists of the day, also supervised its staging. Performances, given at the end of the school year (usually September), could be held out of doors for a large audience or 'in aula' for a smaller group. Some lasted up to eight hours. Synopses,

called *Periochen*, were distributed for those who did not understand Latin.

No means of enhancing the visual and emotional impact on the faithful was overlooked. After 1600, dramas began borrowing techniques from opera, including stunning stage effects where practicable, for example in the 27 dramas written by Nikolaus Avancini (1612–86) for Vienna. Authors did not shrink from presenting grisly scenes; in a play performed at Graz in 1640, for instance, an image of Jezebel composed of blood, bones and pieces of meat was torn to pieces on stage by dogs. Crowd scenes, processions, ballet, pantomime, *intermedi* and choruses also made their way into the Jesuit drama in the early 17th century. Solo numbers ranged from simple folksongs and aria-like laments to hymns, frequently sung during representations of acts of martyrdom.

In 1655, a large theatre built by Ferdinand III for the Jesuits, with elaborate stage machinery, was opened at the University of Vienna, with a lavish hall accommodating 3000 and a musicians' gallery. Initially the dramas were in Latin; from 1665 German was used in comic interludes. Musical and spoken portions were, by the end of the century, of approximately equal length and importance. The dramas used the same types of form and idiom as contemporary opera, including recitatives, arias and ensembles. Notable composers of Jesuit dramas were J. C. Kerll, whose five-act *Pia et fortis mulier* was given for Leopold I in 1677, and F. T. Richter.

Jesuit involvement with school drama ceased with the suppression of the order by Pope Clement XIV in 1773. When the Society was restored in 1814 it continued its central commitment to education, but without its former degree of emphasis on dramatic presentations.

*

E. Boysse: *Le théâtre des Jésuites* (Paris, 1880)

H. L. Bouquet: *L'ancien Collège d'Harcourt* (Paris, 1891)

J. Zeidler: *Studien und Beiträge zur Geschichte der Jesuitenkomödie und des Klosterdramas* (Hamburg and Leipzig, 1891)

P. Bahlmann: 'Das Drama der Jesuiten', *Euphorion*, ii (1895), 271–94

W. Flemming: *Geschichte des Jesuitentheaters in den Landen deutscher Zunge* (Berlin, 1923)

K. Adel: *Das Wiener Jesuitertheater und die europäische Barockdramatik* (Vienna, 1960)

M. M. McGowan: *L'art du ballet de cour en France, 1581–1643* (Paris, 1963)

C. H. Freches: *Le théâtre néo-latin au Portugal (1550–1745)* (Paris and Lisbon, 1964)

W. Kramer: *Die Musik im Wiener Jesuitdrama von 1677–1711* (diss., U. of Vienna, 1965)

R. W. Lowe: *Marc-Antoine Charpentier et l'opéra de collège* (Paris, 1966) [incl. list of perfs. at the Collège Louis-le-Grand, 1579–1761]

F. de Dainville, A. Stegmann and others: 'Le théâtre des Jésuites', *Dramaturgie et société*, ed. J. Jacquot, ii (Paris, 1968), 433–523

T. D. Culley: *Jesuits and Music: a Study of the Musicians connected with the German College in Rome during the 17th Century and of their Activities in Northern Europe* (Rome and St Louis, 1970)

H. E. Smither: *A History of the Oratorio*, i (Chapel Hill, NC, 1977)

T. F. Kennedy: *Jesuits and Music: the European Tradition, 1547–1622* (diss., U. of California at Santa Barbara, 1982)

P. Guillot: *Les Jésuites et la musique: le Collège de la Trinité à Lyon (1565–1762)* (Liège, 1991)

M. ELIZABETH C. BARTLET, THOMAS BAUMAN

Jeune Henri, Le ('The Young Henry'). *Drame lyrique* in two acts by ETIENNE-NICOLAS MÉHUL to a libretto by JEAN-NICOLAS BOUILLY; Paris, Opéra-Comique (Salle Favart), 1 May 1797.

Bouilly intended that the libretto (originally entitled *La jeunesse de Henri IV*) glorify the youth of one of the most popular French kings, and more particularly the role of the queen in his upbringing; by extension, he meant to allegorize Marie Antoinette and the dauphin. In 1791, the year of the opera's composition, events moved too quickly to allow its staging, and although royal references were later removed, the result pleased neither royalists nor republicans in 1797. The opera was a resounding failure at its only public performance, but Méhul's overture, nicknamed 'La chasse du jeune Henri', was a notable success. One of the best examples of 18th-century music representing a hunt, with its horn calls, repeated string figures imitative of horses' hooves and pastoral motifs, it became a staple as interval music at the Opéra-Comique and on concert programmes in France and elsewhere well into the 20th century.

In Act 1, several remark on the desire of Isaure (soprano) that her son be independent. When Henri (soprano) kills a wolf which had terrorized the village and saves a child, she lauds his courage, then gives him a lesson in patriotic duties. In Act 2, at a village *fête*, after homage is paid to an elder, Daniel (baritone), a race is held: Henri wins, but yields the prize to the runner-up, Fideli (tenor), so that Fideli can marry the woman of his choice. Méhul's music, except for the overture and the race ensemble (never performed), is old-fashioned, following the model of the *comédie mêlée d'ariettes*. But the chorus takes a more important role than was typical in *ancien régime* precedents, especially in Act 2. Though not among Méhul's best works of the 1790s, *Le jeune Henri* failed not because of its musical attainments but rather for political reasons – a case that was among many.   M. ELIZABETH C. BARTLET

Jílek, František (*b* Brno, 22 May 1913). Czech conductor. He studied with Jaroslav Kvapil and Zdeněk Chalabala at Brno, and with Vítězslav Novák at Prague. He was a répétiteur with the Brno Opera (1937–9) and then conductor of the Ostrava Opera (1939–48), where the director, Jaroslav Vogel, was an authority on Janáček. Jílek returned to the Brno Opera in 1948, working as artistic director, 1952–78. There he continued the Janáček tradition and was instrumental in presenting the complete operas at the 1958 festival, including *The Beginning of a Romance*. The stage première of *Osud* won special acclaim, along with *From the House of the Dead*, pioneer performances of Prokofiev's *Fiery Angel* and *War and Peace*, and Martinů's *Greek Passion*. Under him Brno Opera reached its postwar peak in the interpretation of Czech and 20th-century works. Jílek has appeared in many European centres, often giving the first local performances of works by Janáček. His interpretations are characterized by detailed attention to the score, fusing timbre and expressiveness into a musical and dramatic whole. In 1978 he became chief conductor of the Brno State Philharmonic Orchestra. He wrote an essay on the instrumentation of Janáček's operas for the collection *Janáčkovy akademie múzických umění* (Brno, 1965), and his recordings include *The Beginning of a Romance* (recorded 1976), *Osud* (1976), *Jenůfa* (1978) and *The Excursions of Mr Brouček* (1980) and Martinů's *Comedy on the Bridge* (1985) and *Alexandre bis* (1986).

V. Pospíšil: 'Jubileum dirigenta' [Conductor's Jubilee], *HRo*, xvi (1963), 394

J. Fukač: 'František Jílek', *OM*, iii (1971), 3

E. Dufková and B. Srba, eds.: *Postavy brněnského jeviště* [The Characters of the Brno Stage] (Brno, 1979–84), i, 317

E. Drlíková, ed.: *František Jílek* (Brno, 1987)   ALENA NĚMCOVÁ

Jiménez, Jerónimo. *See* GIMÉNEZ, JERÓNIMO.

Jiménez Mabarak, Carlos (*b* Tacuba, 31 Jan 1916). Mexican composer. He graduated in composition from the conservatory in Brussels, also earning a *premier prix* in piano, and studied in Rome and later in Paris (with René Leibowitz). His compositions include two symphonies (1945, 1962), a concerto for piano and percussion ensemble (1961), other piano pieces and, in particular, ballet music: his *Balada del venado y de la luna* and *El paraíso de los ahogados* are considered cornerstones of the Mexican dance repertory. He has written two operas: *Misa de seis* ('Mass at Six o'Clock') and *La güera* ('The Blonde'). These works, together with Bernal Jiménez's *Tata Vasco* and Moncayo's *La mulata de Córdoba*, are the most characteristic of 20th-century Mexican operas.

Misa de seis (1, E. Carballido) was first performed in the Palacio de Bellas Artes, Mexico City, on 21 June 1962. Lolita, standing outside a church with her friend Carmelita, hears gunshots in a nearby nightclub. While Carmelita runs, Lolita seeks refuge in the church, and a man who is escaping hides there too. When a policeman discovers him, Lolita pretends to be a relative and protects him. A maid arrives announcing the murder of a woman by her lover and the latter's escape with a gun; Lolita demands an explanation but gets only evasive answers, and decides to leave, giving the man what little money she has. As he turns to go she notices a small object under his clothes; she runs to him and touches it, but he stops her abruptly and escapes. Lolita slowly realizes what has taken place, opens her purse and finds she has not even bought bread. The church bell gives six strokes and Lolita re-enters the church, crying and shouting desperately.

La güera (3, J. Alejandro) was first performed on 26 September 1982, also in the Palacio de Bellas Artes. It presents moments in the life of Doña Ignacia Rodriguez, a historic character better known as 'La Güera', as an allegory of Mexico's struggle for independence from Spain (1810–21); the opera includes scenes such as her protest against the punishment of a slave – the abolition of slavery being one of the first aims of the political movement. She also gives a final farewell to a young Simón Bolívar, who leaves Mexico to become South America's liberator. La Güera symbolizes the Spain that wishes to mix its culture with that of Mexico, and the birth of La Güera's son in the last act represents the birth of Mexico as a new, independent country.

Jiménez Mabarak's music has undergone an interesting evolution, from an early style full of Spanish reminiscences to a modern language, producing in *El paraíso de los ahogados* and above all in *Misa de seis* some of the most advanced Mexican scores of the time. However, Jiménez Mabarak considers that he must not separate himself from his environment, and his later works are in a more classical style. In his own words, 'the discipline of a more conventional language allows me the greater possibility of freedom'. *La güera*, along with all his later works, uses a tonal language enriched not only by elements of Mexican folklore but also by a complex chromatic texture.   RICARDO MIRANDA-PÉREZ

Jin Xiang (*b* Manjing, Jiangsu, 20 April 1935). Chinese composer. He graduated from the Central Institute of Music in Beijing, then for political reasons was sent to Xingjiang, where he worked for 20 years as a farm labourer. In 1979 he became conductor of the Beijing

SO; in 1984 he joined the faculty of the Chinese Music Conservatory, where he is professor of composition and director of the Composition Research Centre. A widely recognized Chinese composer, Jin has written in all genres. His operas comprise *A Warm Breeze Outside* (1980), *Savage Land* (1987, First International Art and Music Festival, Beijing) and *Sunrise* (1990). In 1989 *Savage Land* won a prize at the Third International Music Theater Workshop in Munich. It was given its North American stage première in January 1992 by the Washington Opera (Eisenhower Theater, Kennedy Center, Washington, DC) to great acclaim, the first opera with a Chinese libretto (by Wan Fang, after her father's play *Wilderness*) to be presented by a major American company. A powerful romantic tragedy, it effectively integrates Western lyricism with traditional Chinese tonality and instrumentation (the orchestra includes Beijing opera drum, temple blocks and other Chinese percussion).   ELISE K. KIRK

Jirásek, Ivo (*b* Prague, 16 July 1920). Czech composer. He studied composition, conducting and opera production (with Pujman) at the Prague Conservatory, 1938–45, then worked as head of opera at the Z. Nejedlý Theatre in Opava, 1946–56. Since 1956 he has been engaged in organizational and pedagogic activity. His output consists mainly of operas and other vocal works. His first two operas conformed to the socialist ethos prevailing in Czechoslovakia in the 1950s. *Pan Johanes* ('Mr Johanes') is an allegorical fairy-tale in the Smetana tradition, with folklike songs and dances and patriotic symbols. It concerns the rescue of the Czech princess Kačenka from a German tyrant by a wandering student who enlists the help of the Czech people. *Svítání nad vodami* ('Dawn over the Waters') is based on a real event: during completion of a dam, a conflict comes to a head between superstitious villagers who are against the inundation of their old homes and unwittingly ally themselves with reactionary forces, progressive Communists and the police. Two chamber operas written in the 1960s are simple, lighter, scherzo-like miniatures. *Medvěd* ('The Bear') is about a farmer wooing a sorrowful widow; *Klíč* ('The Key') deals with a love triangle. The mystery opera *Danse macabre* (after Bergman's film *The Seventh Seal*, about a man seeking the meaning of life) uses 12-note and aleatory techniques. Jirásek's other operas show his development both as composer and man of the theatre. *Mistr Jeroným* ('Master Jeroným'; the opera was dedicated to the 100th anniversary of the National Theatre, Prague) concerns man's struggle with his conscience when choosing between moral purity and earthly existence. Jeroným, a 15th-century theology professor, criticizes church abuses and fights for the rights of the poor. He is imprisoned and recants his position but soon becomes aware of his weakness. Proclaiming his faith again, he is burnt to death. Throughout the opera a joker makes grotesque comments on the plot. Scenes are arranged so that declamation contrasts with restrained lyricism; the whole is organized into a two-part cyclic form with orchestral interludes, a procedure Jirásek also used in *Zázrak* ('The Miracle'), a witty Renaissance story about the punishment of a flirtatious clergyman.

Pan Johanes [Mr Johanes], 1951–2 (3, V. Šrámek, after A. Jirásek), Opava, Z. Nejedlý, 24 March 1956

Svítání nad vodami [Dawn over the Waters], 1960–61 (5, J. Procházka), Pilsen, Tyl, 16 Nov 1963

Medvěd [The Bear], 1962–3 (chamber op, 1, K. Berman, after A. P. Chekhov), Prague, Nusle Music Theatre, 25 Jan 1965

Klíč [The Key], 1968 (chamber op, 1, Berman, after A. T. Averchenko), Prague, Discus, 18 March 1971

Danse macabre: I byl večer a bylo jitro [Danse macabre: And an Evening Was and a Morning Was] (3, I. Jirásek and P. Eckstein, after I. Bergman: *The Seventh Seal*), Czech Radio, 1972

Mistr Jeroným [Master Jeroným], 1979–80 (prol., 10 scenes and epilogue, Jirásek), Prague, National, 27 Sept 1984

Zázrak [The Miracle], 1984 (1, J. Havel, after S. Straparolla), unperf., vs

*

ČSHS

V. Pospíšil: 'Soudobá opera na soudobé téma' [Contemporary Opera on a Contemporary Theme], *HRo*, xvi (1963), 989–90

V. Holzknecht: 'Hezké maličkosti' [Nice Trifles], *HRo*, xviii (1965), 149

L. Šíp: *Česká opera a její tvůrci* [Czech Opera and its Composers] (Prague, 1983), 329–35

V. Pospíšil: 'Jiváskův Mistr Jeroným' [Jirásek's 'Master Jeroným], *HRo*, xxxviii (1985), 55–6   HELENA HAVLÍKOVÁ

Jirko, Ivan (*b* Prague, 7 Oct 1926; *d* Dobříš, 20 Aug 1978). Czech composer. He read medicine at Prague University, at the same time studying composition with Karel Janeček (1944–9) and Pavel Bořkovec (1949–52). He worked as a psychiatrist from 1951 to 1977, and was also a music critic for Prague newspapers. From 1974 to 1978 he was a lecturer at the Prague Academy of Performing Arts; from 1976 to 1978 he was opera dramaturg at the National Theatre.

Jirko's music is characterized by its neo-classical stylistic orientation. Mozart was his ideal, and works such as the Piano Concerto no. 3 and the Trumpet Concerto have a Mozartian spontaneity of expression. Though he also wrote much programme music, he held opera to be the supreme art form and felt ready to attempt the genre only after he had been composing for more than 15 years. All four of his operas are to his own librettos. *Večer tříkrálový* ('Twelfth Night') is a neo-classical Singspiel, with arioso passages, recitatives and spoken dialogue, and shows Jirko to have had a definite theatrical flair. It is a musical symbiosis of lyric poetry and plebeian humour, focussing attention firmly on the voice through clarity of declamation and sparse orchestral textures. *Podivuhodné dobrodružství Arthura Rowa* ('The Wonderful Adventure of Arthur Rowe') is more dramatic, with its rapidly changing mini-scenes (similar to film 'takes'), economy of expression and theatrical verve. The two one-act chamber operas *Milionářka* ('The Millionairess') and *Děvka* ('The Strumpet') bear all the hallmarks of their source of inspiration, the cinematic style of Cesare Zavattini; these are pieces of musical 'reportage', with a rapid dramatic pace and a parlando delivery, on the empty life of the rich and on social inequality.

Večer tříkrálový [Twelfth Night], 1964 (3, Jirko, after W. Shakespeare), Liberec, F. X. Šalda, 25 Feb 1967

Podivuhodné dobrodružství Arthura Rowa [The Wonderful Adventure of Arthur Rowe] (3, Jirko, after G. Greene: *The Ministry of Fear*), Liberec, F. X. Šalda, 25 Oct 1969; rev. as Návrat [The Return], Prague, Tyl, 11 Oct 1979

Děvka [The Strumpet], 1970 (op divertimento, 1, Jirko, after Zavattini), Olomouc, O. Stibor, 23 June 1974

Milionářka [The Millionairess], 1970 (op divertimento, 1, Jirko, after C. Zavattini), Brno, Miloš Wasserbauer Opera Studio, 28 April 1977

*

ČSHS

B. Karásek: 'Pokus o operní komedii' [An Attempt at an Operatic Comedy], *HRo*, xx (1967), 206–7

V. Pospíšil: 'Greenovo "divertimento" jako opera' [Greene's 'Divertimento' as Opera], *HRo*, xxii (1969), 656

P. Zapletal: 'O životě a hudbě s Ivanem Jirko' [Life and Music with Ivan Jirko], *HRo*, xxvii (1974), 229–33

H. Vojtěchová: 'Na okraj operní tvorby I. Jirko' [On the Edge of Jirko's Operatic Output], *HRo*, xxxii (1979), 271–8

HELENA HAVLÍKOVÁ

Jiró, Manuel. *See* GIRÓ, MANUEL.

Jo, Sumi (*b* Seoul, South Korea, 22 Nov 1962). Korean soprano. She studied in Italy, making her début in 1986 at Trieste as Gilda. In 1988 she sang Thetis/Fortune in Jommelli's *Fetonte* at La Scala and Barbarina in Salzburg, where she returned in 1989 as Oscar. She has sung Zerbinetta in Lyons (1989), Oscar at Salzburg and the Queen of Night in Chicago (1990), her American début, and Olympia at Covent Garden (1991) where she also sang Adina and Elvira in *I puritani* (1992). She uses her pure, high-lying voice and its extreme facility in coloratura with great musicality.

ELIZABETH FORBES

Job. *Sacra rappresentazione* by LUIGI DALLAPICCOLA to his own libretto after the Book of Job; Rome, Teatro Eliseo, 30 October 1950.

In many ways *Job* is akin to the English mystery play, with its series of tableaux linked and introduced by a narrator. The work begins with the Narrator (spoken role) reciting the opening words of the Book of Job: 'There was a man in the land of Uz ... and that man was perfect'. Then comes the first encounter between God and Satan (two spoken choruses), ending with God's words: 'behold, all that he hath is in thy power – only upon himself put not forth thy hand'. Four Messengers (soprano, contralto, tenor and bass) tell Job (bass-baritone) that his worldly goods have been destroyed. Job answers 'The Lord gave, and the Lord hath taken away; blessed be the name of the Lord'. In the second encounter between God and Satan, God surrenders Job's body to Satan but orders that his life be saved. Satan covers Job in boils. Job curses the day in which he was born, after which his friends Elifàz (soprano), Baldad (contralto) and Zofàr (tenor) bring false comfort, advising him to repent and humbly ask God for forgiveness. Job, at the peak of his suffering, remembers his former prosperity, protests his innocence and cries 'Why do the wicked prosper?'. Out of the whirlwind God answers: 'Where wast thou when I laid the foundations of the earth?'. Job submits to God's power: 'I abhor myself, and repent in dust and ashes'. The narrator ends the story: 'the Lord blessed the latter end of Job more than his beginning'.

The title 'sacra rappresentazione' reflects Dallapiccola's interest in the music of Italy's past (he made a performing version of Monteverdi's *Il ritorno d'Ulisse in patria* in 1941), and also the nature of the commission: *Job* was written for the Associazione Anfiparnaso in Rome, which aimed to encourage the composition of short operas. Dallapiccola considered the Book of Job 'an epic of revolt', and like many of his works after *Il prigioniero* it deals with the metaphysical torment born of doubt, of sudden loss of faith. It also marks the beginning of the resolution of these doubts that was to reach its fullest form at the end of Dallapiccola's last opera, *Ulisse*. *Job* is Dallapiccola's first large-scale work to use a single 12-note row; it also uses the *Te Deum* as a cantus firmus. A particular feature is the use of speech, rather than singing, in the first, third and last sections. Indeed, the third section is merely a spoken discussion between God and Satan, accompanied by simple rhythmic ostinatos.

ANTHONY SELLORS

Jobin, André (*b* Quebec, 20 Jan 1933). Canadian tenor, the son of Raoul Jobin. He trained as an actor in Paris, then sang as a light baritone. In 1962 he took on the role of Pelléas, which he sang in Nice, Paris, Marseilles, San Francisco, Los Angeles and Madrid, with the New York City Opera and at Glyndebourne (1976). Meanwhile he became a tenor and sang Romeo, Don José, Werther, Des Grieux (*Manon*), Araquil (*La Navarraise*), Rodrigo (*Le Cid*), John the Baptist (*Hérodiade*), Hoffmann and Julien (*Louise*) in Quebec and in Lyons and other French provincial cities. His roles also included the Chevalier (*Dialogues des Carmélites*), Boris (*Kát'a Kabanová*) and Eisenstein (*Die Fledermaus*), which he sang in Chicago and Detroit. A fine actor, he had a lyric voice well suited to French music.

ELIZABETH FORBES

Jobin, Raoul (*b* Quebec, 8 April 1906; *d* Quebec, 13 Jan 1974). Canadian tenor. He studied first in Quebec, then in Paris. There Busser engaged him for the Opéra, where he made his début as Gounod's Tybalt in 1930 and sang minor roles for two years. After two seasons in Bordeaux, he returned to the Opéra in 1935; there he sang Romeo, Faust, Raoul and Lohengrin, and created Fabrice in Sauguet's *Chartreuse de Parme* (1939). At the Opéra-Comique he sang Don José, Julien, Werther, Hoffmann, Massenet's Des Grieux and Cavaradossi. He left France in 1939 and made his Metropolitan début in 1940 as Des Grieux, later singing Tonio (*La fille du régiment*), Faust and Canio. He also sang Gérald in San Francisco (1940) and Don José in Chicago (1941). He returned to the Opéra, where his roles (1949–52) included Mârouf, Walther, Radames and Boito's Faust. On retirement he opened a singing school in Montreal. His firm, bright-toned voice can be heard in a recording of Gluck's *Alceste*, in which he sings Admetus opposite Flagstad.

ANDRÉ TUBEUF, ELIZABETH FORBES

Jochum, Eugen (*b* Babenhausen, 1 Nov 1902; *d* Munich, 26 March 1987). German conductor. Like his brother, the choirmaster and composer Otto Jochum, he played the organ as a child and attended the Augsburg Conservatory. In 1922 he went to the Munich Academy of Music, chiefly as a composition student of Waltershausen, but later he studied conducting with Siegmund von Hausegger and worked as répétiteur at the Munich National Theatre and at Mönchengladbach. He spent three years at the Kiel Opera (1926–9), where he became principal conductor and acquired a repertory of more than 50 operas. He moved to Mannheim for a season (1929–30) and to Duisburg as Generalmusikdirektor (1930–32), then was appointed musical director for Berlin radio in 1932. In 1934 he succeeded Muck as Generalmusikdirektor at the Hamburg Staatsoper, avoiding much of the political pressure of the Nazi regime and continuing to perform works banned elsewhere in Germany. He returned to Munich in 1949 as music director for Bavarian radio. During the 1950s he increased his reputation as a guest conductor, and first appeared at Bayreuth in 1953 conducting *Tristan und Isolde*. His recordings include *Die Meistersinger von Nürnberg* with Fischer-Dieskau and Domingo (1976), which reflects his outstanding qualities as a Wagner conductor. Jochum drew from his players a warm, luminous sound though his relaxed, romantic approach was tempered by a keen feeling for underlying pulse.

NOËL GOODWIN

Joconde [*Joconde, ou Les coureurs d'aventures* ('Joconde, or The Adventurers')]. *Comédie mêlée de chants* in three acts by NICOLAS ISOUARD to a libretto by Charles-Guillaume Etienne; Paris, Opéra-Comique (Salle Feydeau), 28 February 1814.

Disappointed by the inconstancy of their lovers – Robert, Count of Martigue (tenor), and Joconde (baritone) – Mathilde (soprano) and her friend Edile (soprano) join in a scheme to arouse the men's jealousy. Bored with life at court, the men decide to test the fidelity of the two women by wooing each other's partner. Unaware of the women's conspiracy, the men are disillusioned by their easy success. They disguise themselves as troubadours and leave for the provinces, where they are attracted by Jeannette (soprano), a candidate for the 'rosière' prize to be awarded to a virtuous girl on the following day. Mathilde and Edile, who have secretly followed their lovers, warn Jeannette of the wicked intentions of Robert and Joconde. When the Village Mayor (tenor) overhears the men planning to abduct Jeannette, he assembles the militia. Jeannette comes as planned for the rendezvous, but her lover, Lucas (tenor), is the first to meet her. The militia deliver Robert and Joconde to prison, where they reveal their identity and claim that their journey was undertaken in pursuit of true morals. At the *rosière* ceremony the next morning Robert crowns Jeannette.

The story of the *rosière* competition had been used earlier (e.g. by Grétry in *La rosière de Salency*, 1773), but Etienne combined it with the story of Joconde, adapted from versions in the *Thousand and One Nights* and La Fontaine among other sources. The densely packed but somewhat incoherent drama is treated by Isouard in a rather simple style in which a fast pace and ensemble numbers prevail. The disappointment of the protagonists is expressed in speech rather than in music. The overall impression of musical homogeneity is, however, lifted by some attempts at historical *couleur locale*, as in a villanella melody (no.11, 'Je voudrais bien vous dire quelque chose') and a musette theme (no.12, 'Quand on attend sa belle'), and the transformation of simple numbers into dramatic scenes (nos.4, 'Pour votre fête le plaisir nous a réunis', and 10, 'C'est la fête qui s'apprête').

MICHAEL FEND

Jodelet [*Der lächerliche Printz Jodelet* ('The Ridiculous Prince Jodelet')]. *Schertzhaftes Sing-Spiel* in five acts by REINHARD KEISER to a libretto by Johann Philipp Praetorius after Matsen's *Jodelet, oder Sein selbst Gefangener*; Hamburg, Theater am Gänsemarkt, 1726.

Federic, Crown Prince of Sicily (bass), is fleeing from the soldiers of Fernando, King of Naples (bass), after killing the brother of Isabella, Princess of Salerno (soprano), during a tournament. To elude their pursuers, he and his companion, Octavius (bass), leave their clothes behind in a wood, where they are found by Jodelet (bass), a simpleton, and his bibulous friend Nicolo (tenor). Jodelet and Nicolo decide to masquerade as a prince and his steward and are immediately arrested. At the Neapolitan court Jodelet poses as Prince Federic, putting on absurd airs, while Federic disguises himself under the name Leonhard. Other notable characters include Fernando's daughter Laura (soprano), Federic's beloved, and Ermine (soprano), a coquettish lady of the court, who delights

in teasing Jodelet and Nicolo. The arrival of Federic's brother Eduard (bass) at last leads to the unmasking of both Jodelet/Federic and Federic/Leonhard. Fernando agrees to the union of Laura and Federic, and Isabella (who had been in love with Federic) marries Eduard.

Jodelet is one of Keiser's strangest and least satisfactory operas, a coarse and witless comedy in which half the arias are taken from serious operas by Italian composers. Of the 17 solo arias in Italian, only 'Ch'io ritorni, o luci care!' appears likely to be by Keiser. Although the role of Jodelet contains some extraordinary musical caricature – in which the influence of Telemann and particularly his *Der neumodische Liebhaber Damon* (1724) is strongly felt – the score does not on the whole show the composer at his best. Isabella's splendid aria 'Ein zärtlich liebendes Hertze', with its rich accompaniment including four muted violins, was originally composed for *Bretislaus* the previous year.

JOHN H. ROBERTS

Johannesburg. City in the Republic of South Africa. Some years after the discovery of gold (1884), opera was performed in Johannesburg by amateurs and visiting companies. According to Grobbelaar the city had 16 theatres by 1920. Until the formation of the Performing Arts Council of the Transvaal (PACT) in 1963, opera was given by visiting companies and various societies and amateur groups. Regular seasons were directed by John Connell from 1925 to 1950. PACT performed at the 1120-seat Johannesburg Civic Theatre, which had opened in 1962, until 1981 when its main venue became the State Theatre in Pretoria. The Civic Theatre began to undergo rebuilding in the early 1990s.

*

M. Grobbelaar: 'The Johannesburg Civic Theatre', *Scenaria* (Oct–Nov 1977), 12–13

L. Wolpavitz and J. P. Malan: 'Johannesburg, Music in', *South African Music Encyclopedia* (Cape Town, 1979–86)

JAMES MAY

Johnny's Kingdom. Opera by Otakar Ostrčil; *see HONZOVO KRÁLOVSTVÍ.*

Johns, William (*b* Tulsa, 2 Oct 1936). American tenor. He studied in New York and made his début in 1967 at Lake George as Rodolfo (*Bohème*). While engaged at Bremen he sang the Duke, the Prince (*The Love for Three Oranges*) and Chapelou (*Le postillon de Lonjumeau*); with the WNO he sang Radames (1970) and Calaf (1972). He has appeared in Dallas, Los Angeles, Trieste, San Diego, Vancouver, Cologne, Düsseldorf, Hamburg, Bregenz, Naples, Rome, Chicago, San Francisco, Houston, Vienna and Aix-en-Provence and at La Scala, the Opéra and the Metropolitan. In 1987 he made his Covent Garden début, singing Bacchus. His powerful voice is equally well suited to French, Italian and German parts; among those in his repertory are the title role of Mercadante's *Il bravo*, Mayr's Jason, Berlioz's Faust, Hoffmann, Don José, Huon, Walther, Lohengrin, Tannhäuser, Siegmund, Siegfried, Tristan, the Emperor (*Die Frau ohne Schatten*), Don Alvaro and Othello.

ELIZABETH FORBES

Johnsen, Hinrich [Henrik] **Philip** (*b* Gottorf, nr Schleswig, 1716; *d* Stockholm, 12 Feb 1779). German composer active in Sweden. He was appointed keyboard player to Duke Adolph Frederik of Holstein-Gottorf in

901

Eutin in 1735. In 1742 he composed a German comic opera, *Die verkaufte Braut*, and the following year he moved with the court to Sweden when his patron became king. In 1745 he became organist at the church of St Klara in Stockholm, and in 1753 *kammarmusikus*; he was employed as court organist from 1763 and also directed musical productions of the resident French theatre group, 1763–71. In 1771 he was elected archivist and teacher of harmony at the newly founded Swedish Royal Academy of Music, where he participated in the formation of the Royal Opera. During the last years of his life Johnsen was active in arranging music for various stage productions; he composed portions of the operas *Acis och Galathea*, *Procris och Cephal, Birger Jarl och Mechtilde* and *Aeglé*. His own one-act opera-ballet *Neptun och Amphitrite* was first performed in 1775. His vocal works abound in unusual part-writing and awkward harmonic structures, yet his last compositions display adept word-setting and extremely colourful orchestration.

See also Birger Jarl och Mechtilde.

all in MS in S-Skma and St

Die verkaufte Braut (comic opera, 5), Eutin, court, Dec 1742
Aeglé (op-ballet, 1, G. G. Adlerbeth, after P. Laujon), Stockholm, Bollhuset, 8 July 1774, collab. F. Uttini
Birger Jarl och Mechtilde (drama with music, 3, divertissement, G. F. Gyllenborg, after Gustavus III), Stockholm, Rikssalen, 8 July 1774, collab. Uttini
Neptun och Amphitrite (op-ballet, 1, Adlerbeth), Stockholm, Bollhuset, 24 April 1775

Music in: Acis och Galathea, 1773 [rev. of Handel: Acis and Galatea]; Procris och Cephal, 1778 [rev. of Grétry: Céphale et Procris]

Doubtful: Don Tabarano (int, 2), c1754

*

F. Dahlgren: *Anteckningar om Stockholms teatrar* (Stockholm, 1866)
E. Nordenfelt-Åberg: *Hinrich Philip Johnsen* (Stockholm, 1982)

BERTIL H. VAN BOER

John Socman. Opera in three acts by GEORGE LLOYD to a libretto by William Lloyd; Bristol, Hippodrome, 15 May 1951.

Richard, a young archer (tenor), returns home after taking part in the Battle of Agincourt in 1415 to find that his beloved Sybil (soprano) is being blackmailed by the magistrate, John Socman (baritone), into marriage; her father Warner (bass), a follower of Wyclif, is otherwise likely to be branded a heretic. But the marriage proves unlawful when it is discovered that Socman had previously married and abandoned a girl in France long ago.

The opera was commissioned for the Carl Rosa company by the Festival of Britain, along with Vaughan Williams's *The Pilgrim's Progress* (for Covent Garden) and Britten's *Billy Budd* (for Sadler's Wells). The strain of meeting the deadline told on Lloyd's health and it is generally thought that the music lacks the freshness of his earlier operas. Nevertheless, Lloyd's straightforward, buoyant style ensures that dramatic interest sustains itself on an engaging though not profound level.

STEPHEN BANFIELD

Johnson, Anthony Rolfe. *See* ROLFE JOHNSON, ANTHONY.

Johnson, David (Charles) (*b* Edinburgh, 27 Oct 1942). Scottish composer. He was educated at Aberdeen University, where he read English literature, and at Cam-

bridge, where he completed the doctoral dissertation later published as *Music and Society in Lowland Scotland in the Eighteenth Century*; as an editor, he has rediscovered and published the music of 18th-century Scottish composers such as the Earl of Kelly and William McGibbon. As a composer, Johnson has evolved a pungent, tonal idiom influenced by Robert Burns, Vaughan Williams, Hindemith, Weill, Britten and the Beatles. He has succeeded in writing genuinely humorous music, and deploys a variation technique which is both simple and sophisticated.

In the 1960s Johnson was much influenced by the social-realist dramatist Jack Ronder, who wrote the libretto for his first opera, *All There Was Between Them* (1969). His most significant operatic work, *Thomas the Rhymer* (1976), was successfully staged in Edinburgh by a company he formed and led. Here both plot and music are derived from the Scottish border ballad collected by Sir Walter Scott. The medieval story tells of a young poet's possession and eventual release by the Queen of Elfland. In this opera Johnson, whose aims are to put observed social reality into music and to explain past periods in present-day terms, achieves an eerily ironic double-focus by the subtle use of anachronism.

All There Was Between Them (1, J. Ronder), Cambridge, ABC, 22 Oct 1969
Building the City (1, Johnson), Edinburgh, Rudolf Steiner Hall, 11 July 1973
Thomas the Rhymer (4, Johnson), Edinburgh, George Square, 20 April 1976 (Edinburgh, 1979)
The Cow, the Witch and the Schoolmaster (1, Johnson), Edinburgh, Church Hill, 16 Aug 1978

*

C. MacDonald: 'Thomas the Rhymer', *MT*, cxvii (1976), 305–7

NEIL MACKAY

Johnson, Edward [Di Giovanni, Edoardo] (*b* Guelph, Ont., 22 Aug 1878; *d* Guelph, 20 April 1959). Canadian tenor and impresario. His father hoped he would become a lawyer, but in 1899 he went to New York to study music. In 1902 he was the hero in De Koven's *Maid Marian* in Boston, and he starred on Broadway (1908) in Straus's *A Waltz Dream*. On Caruso's advice he went to Florence (1909) to work with Vincenzo Lombardi. As Edoardo di Giovanni he made his operatic début in Padua (1912) in *Andrea Chénier*. He sang in premières of works by Pizzetti and Alfano, in *Parsifal* in Italian (his La Scala début, 1914) and in the Italian premières of Puccini's *Il tabarro* and *Gianni Schicchi* (1919, Rome).

Johnson left Italy to become the leading tenor of the Chicago Opera (1919–22, début as Loris in *Fedora*) and of the Metropolitan (1922–35, début as Avito in *L'amore dei tre re*), where he was a favourite as Pelléas, Romeo and Peter Ibbetson, a role he created in the Deems Taylor opera. Also in his repertory were Siegfried and Faust (Covent Garden, 1923). His musicianship, romantic appearance and ability to project a character were coupled with a lyric voice of good quality and range, a sound technique and a seldom-used but easy high E. He followed Herbert Witherspoon, Gatti-Casazza's successor, as general manager of the Metropolitan (1935–50), successfully guiding the company through the war period.

*

R. A. Simon: 'Profile: General Director', *New Yorker* (14 Dec 1935), 30–33
J. Bauer: 'Edward Johnson', *Canadian Review of Music and Art*, iii (1944), nos.7 and 8, pp.14–16

H. P. Court: 'Edward Johnson', *Record News* [Toronto], ii (1957–8), 193–202 [with discography]

N. A. Benson: 'Edward Johnson', *Canadian Music Journal*, ii (1958), 28–34

R. Mercer: *The Tenor of his Time: Edward Johnson of the Met* (Toronto, 1976)   RUBY MERCER

Johnson, Gertrude (*b* Hawksburn, Victoria, 1894; *d* Melbourne, 28 March 1973). Australian soprano and administrator. She was a pupil of Melba at the Albert Street Conservatorium in Melbourne and sang with the Consalez touring company in Australia (Gilda and Lucia, 1919) and the British National Opera Company in Britain (Micaela, Gounod's Marguerite, the Princess in Holst's *The Perfect Fool*). Her most enduring legacy to opera was her founding of the National Theatre Movement in Melbourne in 1936. This was envisaged as a national theatre that would not only accommodate a resident professional opera company, but also provide ballet and spoken drama. The first opera performances were given in 1939. Its peak of achievement came after World War II when it provided professional opportunities to many singers who subsequently had distinguished careers in Australia and abroad. It helped establish a new approach to operatic production in Australia. Johnson and her postwar counterpart, Clarice Lorenz of the Sydney-based National Theatre of Australia, both sat on the first board of the company established in 1956 (now the Australian Opera) that proved to be the lasting offspring of their rival enterprises.   ROGER COVELL

Johnson, Lockrem (*b* Davenport, IA, 15 March 1924; *d* Seattle, 5 March 1977). American composer. He studied composition with George Frederick McKay at the University of Washington (1938–42), where he later became a faculty member, and was music director of the Eleanor King Dance Company (1947–50) and pianist of the Seattle SO (1948–51). In 1951 he moved to New York, where he worked in the music publishing business, returning to Seattle in 1962 as head of the music department at the Cornish School of Music. An active composer throughout his career, Johnson wrote chiefly chamber and piano compositions in a lyrical and dramatic style. His one-act chamber opera *A Letter to Emily* (Johnson, after R. Hupton: *Consider the Lilies*), based on an incident in the life of Emily Dickinson, was one of his most successful works. Composed in 1951 and first performed at Cornish College on 24 April 1951, the work is predominantly diatonic with touches of mild dissonance; it was staged frequently during the 1950s.

A. Freed: 'Lockrem Johnson: Conservative Rebel', *American Composers Alliance Bulletin*, viii/4 (1959), 12–15

KATHERINE K. PRESTON

Johnson, Patricia (*b* London, 1934). English mezzo-soprano. She studied in London, then sang in the Covent Garden chorus before joining Sadler's Wells Opera in 1954; Carmen, Delilah and Azucena were among her early roles. After a season in Basle, in 1961 she joined the Deutsche Oper, Berlin. At Covent Garden she has sung Andromache (*King Priam*), the Queen (Searle's *Hamlet*), the Kostelnička, Marcellina, Baba the Turk and Mrs Sedley (*Peter Grimes*); her Glyndebourne roles include Jane Seymour (*Anna Bolena*) and Lady Billows (*Albert Herring*). She has also sung at Santa Fe, Aix-en-Provence and Salzburg. In Berlin she created Baroness

Grünwiesel in Henze's *Der junge Lord* (1965) and her roles have ranged from Cenerentola, Eboli and Lady Macbeth to Fricka, Herodias, and Claire (*Der Besuch der alten Dame*); more recently she has sung Adelaide (*Arabella*) and the Old Lady (*Candide*) in 1989 and Kabanicha, one of her finest interpretations, in 1991. She has a rich, flexible voice and sings with powerful dramatic conviction.   ELIZABETH FORBES

Johnson, Tom (*b* Greeley, CO, 18 Nov 1939). American composer. He studied composition with Morton Feldman during the late 1960s. In 1971 he was hired by the *Village Voice* to report on experimental music and during his tenure became one of the most influential critics in the USA, introducing Reich, Glass, Ashley and other important experimental composers to artists and musicians as well as to a mainstream audience. Active himself as a composer of experimental works in a variety of media, he has received several commissions. In *The Four-Note Opera*, one of his most successful works, only four notes (A, B, D and E) are employed; the text consists of the singers' description of the music they sing and of the delights and frustrations of their roles. His second opera, *The Masque of Clouds*, is scored for 12 performers, chamber ensemble and sextet of dancing clouds. Of his later works, *Riemannoper* has had particular success in Germany and the Netherlands.

The Four-Note Opera (1, Johnson and R. Kushner), New York, The Cubiculo, 16 May 1972

The Masque of Clouds (3, Johnson and Kushner), New York, The Kitchen, 10 Oct 1976

Five Shaggy-Dog Operas (Johnson), New York, 15 Oct 1978

Réservé aux sopranes (1, Johnson), Paris, American Center, March 1984

Riemannoper (2, Johnson, after H. Riemann: *Musiklexikon*), Berlin, Inventionen Festival, Feb 1986; rev. Bremen, 3 Nov 1988

200 Ans (1, Johnson), Avignon, 25 July 1989

GREGORY SANDOW

Johnston, Ben(jamin Burwell, jr) (*b* Macon, GA, 15 March 1926). American composer. He studied the piano and trombone when young, and attended the College of William and Mary, Williamsburg, Virginia, acquiring the equivalent of an undergraduate music training as a US Navy bandsman (1944–6); after completing the BA (1949) he attended the Cincinnati Conservatory (MMus 1950). Unhappy with the composition teaching there, he apprenticed himself for two years to Harry Partch, with whom he shared an interest in just intonation and microtones. He enrolled at Mills College, Oakland, for further study with Milhaud (MFA 1952), and as late as 1959 studied briefly with Cage. In 1951 Johnston was appointed to the faculty of the University of Illinois at Urbana-Champaign, where he remained until his retirement in 1983.

Johnston's musical development displays remarkable parallels with that of Lejaren Hiller, his longtime colleague at Illinois. Both began by writing incidental music and both created musical-opera hybrids, anticipating by a decade or more the current 'music theatre' movement. Johnston's compositions characteristically derive great intensity from the high level of ensemble co-operation and concentration they require; this has been expressed increasingly in the combining of microtonal just intonation with highly complex polyrhythms.

Johnston's operas are intimately connected to the career of the noted playwright and stage director

Wilford Leach, who commissioned all three. The two had met as undergraduates, collaborating immediately on *Carry Me Back*, which won an award for student musicals and was published (though Johnston has since withdrawn it). *Gertrude, or Would She be Pleased to Receive It?* was written when Johnston and Leach were both at Illinois, and is one of the peaks of the composer's neo-classical period. Since the opera is a surreal spoof of Gertrude Stein and Isadora Duncan, comparison with the Thomson-Stein operas is inevitable, though Johnston's leanly Stravinskian idiom owes nothing to Thomson. When Leach became director of the LaMama E. T. C. (Experimental Theatre Club) company in New York, he commissioned *Carmilla: a Vampire Tale* as a 'rock opera'; in fact, Johnston's score employs the rock idiom only sparingly, as part of a kaleidoscope of styles reminiscent of latter-day postmodernism. In typical Broadway (or here, off-Broadway) fashion, Johnston supplied lead sheets which were fleshed out and orchestrated by other hands. LaMama has retained *Carmilla* in its repertory, and revived it in 1976 and 1986. A recording of the first production was issued by Vanguard Records.

Carry Me Back (musical, W. Leach), Williamsburg, College of William and Mary, 1947, songs pubd; withdrawn

Gertrude, or Would She be Pleased to Receive It?, 1954 (chamber op, 1, Leach), Urbana, U. of Illinois, 1956

Carmilla: a Vampire Tale (rock op, 1, Leach, after J. S. Le Fanu), New York, Café LaMama, late Nov 1970

*

M. Gussow: 'Theater: "Gertrude" at LaMama Happily Fantastic', *New York Times* (13 Nov 1970)
——:'The Theater: Carmilla', *New York Times* (1 Dec 1970)
C. Gagne and T. Caras: *Soundpieces: Interviews with American Composers* (Metuchen, NJ, 1982)
G. Rogoff: 'Unsound', *Village Voice* (14 Oct 1986), 100–01
H. Von Gunden: *The Music of Ben Johnston* (Metuchen, NJ, 1986)
M. N. Grant: 'New York', *Opera*, xxxviii (1987), 158, 179
ANDREW STILLER

Johnston, James (*b* Belfast, 13 Aug 1903; *d* Belfast, 17 Oct 1991). Irish tenor. He studied privately and made his début in 1940 in Dublin as the Duke in *Rigoletto*. In 1945 he was engaged by Sadler's Wells, and while their leading tenor (1946–50) he sang Gabriele Adorno in the English première of *Simon Boccanegra* (1948). In 1949 he created Hector in *The Olympians* at Covent Garden; he went on to become a principal tenor there (1951–8), singing Radames, Don José and Manrico. He sang Macduff at Glyndebourne in 1952. His ringing tone and intensity of performance were rare among contemporary singers.
HAROLD ROSENTHAL/R

Johnstone, John (*b* Kilkenny, ?1 Aug 1749; *d* London, 26 Dec 1828). Irish tenor and actor. After several years in a cavalry regiment he became a singer on the Dublin stage in 1775, playing Lionel in *Lionel and Clarissa* and other musical heroes. From October 1783 he sang in London, making his début again as Lionel, followed by Macheath, Lord Ainsworth (*The Maid of the Mill*) and Dermot in the première of Shield's Irish opera, *The Poor Soldier*. He was tall, handsome, charming and a good actor. His upper voice, a very sweet falsetto, was much admired, but the transition to his lower voice was abrupt, and Haydn, hearing him in *The Woodman* (1791), found him most unmusical. With the coming of Incledon in 1790 he gradually lost his opera roles and became a specialist in the comic Irish parts in which, long before his retirement in 1820, he was considered unrivalled.

A. Pasquin [pseud. of J. Williams]: *The Children of Thespis*, ii (London, 1787, 13/1792)
M. Kelly: *Reminiscences* (London, 1826); ed. R. Fiske (London, 1975)
J. O'Keeffe: *Recollections* (London, 1826)
W. Oxberry: 'Memoir of John Johnstone', *Dramatic Biography*, iv (1826), 73–83
J. Adolphus: *Memoirs of John Bannister, Comedian* (London, 1839)
W. Robson: *The Old Play-Goer* (London, 1846)
T. J. Walsh: *Opera in Dublin 1705–1797* (Dublin, 1973)
OLIVE BALDWIN, THELMA WILSON

Jokl, Fritzi (*b* Vienna, 23 March 1895; *d* New York, 15 Dec 1974). Austrian soprano. She studied in Vienna and made her début at Frankfurt in 1917, appearing in small roles and achieving a first notable success in *Il barbiere*. After a season at Darmstadt she sang at the Volksoper in Berlin where her parts included Konstanze in *Die Entführung* and Violetta in *La traviata*. In 1926 she became principal soprano in Munich at the Bavarian Staatsoper. She enjoyed a spectacular success at Monaco as Zerbinetta in *Ariadne auf Naxos* and also became a favourite at Salzburg. Guest appearances at the Vienna Staatsoper in the 1930s seemed about to lead to a substantial career but as a Jew she found her way blocked, and after a heroic period with the Jewish Theatre in Berlin left Europe for America, where she married the writer Jack Siegel and gave up her public career. A delicately clear and beautiful voice combined with remarkable agility and an imaginative style help to place her few recordings among the most delightful of the period.
J. B. STEANE

Jolas [Illouz], **Betsy** (*b* Paris, 5 Aug 1926). French-American composer. After a childhood spent mostly in France, she moved to the USA in 1940. She studied composition with Paul Boepple and, after her return to Paris (1946), Milhaud and Messiaen. Since 1975 Jolas has been professor of composition and analysis at the Paris Conservatoire. Commissions and guest teaching appointments have been divided between France and the USA. Jolas's compositions include many instrumental and vocal works in a wide range of combinations. She uses strict compositional methods, including serialism, that result in lyrical and essentially melodic music. She reflects her background as the daughter of well-known literary parents by showing particular interest in the relationships between words and music.

Her first opera, *Le pavillon au bord de la rivière*, a 90-minute chamber work in four acts, received its première in Avignon (1975), directed by Bernard Sobel. It was seen in Paris, London, Brussels and several cities in the USA in 1976. The 13th-century Chinese text by Kuan Han Chin, adapted by Michele Raoul-Davis, concerns a beautiful young widow who has remarried. The new husband, a magistrate, threatened by one of her admirers who has secured a royal edict for his death, is saved by the heroine's cleverness. A soprano and six choristers are accompanied by seven instrumentalists (three trombones, two flutes, english horn and percussion), who appear on stage in costume and take part in the action. The vocal style emphasizes the spoken word and the opera combines elements of ancient Chinese popular theatre with contemporary Western composition.

Le Cyclope is a 90-minute opera using Euripides' *Cyclops* as a libretto. The première at Avignon (1986) was followed by 15 performances at the Théâtre de Chaillot in Paris, directed by Bernard Sobel and conducted by Annick Mink. The players consist of nine singers and eight instrumentalists. The choice of instruments reflects the use of jazz idioms in the score: two saxophones, three trombones, electric guitar, bass guitar and percussion. The historical text deals with the relationship between Cyclops, Ulysses and Silene. Satyrs comment on the action, which deals with the confrontation between civilization and non-civilization. In order to achieve flexibility in the setting of the text, actors rather than singers are called for and the conductor is required to follow their flexible tempos.

Schliemann (composed 1988–9) is in three acts and of three hours' duration. The libretto, adapted by the composer and Bruno Bayen from a play by Bayen, tells the story of a childhood dream come true. It explores the unusual personality of the extraordinary 19th-century archaeologist, who at the age of 47 leaves New York City to discover Greece and marry Helen of Troy. A concert performance with four singers and piano was heard at the opening of the Bastille Opera in 1990.

Le pavillon au bord de la rivière (chamber op, 4, M. Raoul-Davis, after Kuan Han Chin), Avignon, 4 Aug 1975
Le Cyclope (1, after Euripides: *Cyclops*), Avignon, 27 July 1986
Schliemann (3, B. Bayen and Jolas, after Bayen), concert perf. Paris, Bastille, 4 April 1990

*

M.-J. Chauvin: 'Entretien avec Betsy Jolas', *Courrier musical de France*, xxvii (1969), 163–73
V. Perlis: Interview with Betsy Jolas, American Oral History Project, Yale U. Library, 1983
T. Beauvert: 'Le Cyclope', *Revue de musique* (1986), 105
R. Sabon: '"Le Cyclope" d'Euripide', *La gazette provençale* (25 July 1986)
'"Schliemann" de Betsy Jolas', *Salabert-Actuel*, ix (1988), 19

VIVIAN PERLIS

Jolie fille de Perth, La ('The Fair Maid of Perth'). *Opéra* in four acts by GEORGES BIZET to a libretto by JULES-HENRI VERNOY DE SAINT-GEORGES and JULES ADENIS after WALTER SCOTT's novel *The Fair Maid of Perth*; Paris, Théâtre Lyrique, 26 December 1867.

La jolie fille de Perth was commissioned by Carvalho, director of the Théâtre Lyrique, in July 1866, the choice of libretto being fixed by the terms of the contract. The commission confirmed Carvalho's faith in Bizet following *Les pêcheurs de perles* in 1863 and the unfinished *Ivan IV* in the intervening years. The librettists were experienced men of the theatre, especially Saint-Georges, yet the libretto is notoriously free in its treatment of Scott's novel and loose in its dramatic structure. Bizet was well aware of its faults and was unenthusiastic about the verse, yet he set to work with great energy and completed the score before the end of 1866. The soprano role, Catherine [Catharine] Glover, was composed for the coloratura of Christine Nilsson, although in the event it was Jeanne Devriès, not Nilsson, who sang it. The opera reached a public dress rehearsal on 10 September 1867, but for a variety of reasons the performances were postponed until December. Although it was well received, it did not draw good audiences and had only 18 performances, the same number as *Les pêcheurs de perles* had received in the same theatre four years before. A persistent criticism, with which Bizet privately agreed, was that the music had been 'sacrificed to the false gods of the quadrille, the *roucoulade*' and the 'concessions' of coloratura. The opera was played in Brussels in April 1868 but not revived until 1883, when it was subjected, like Bizet's other operas, to substantial posthumous disfigurement.

Act 1 takes place in the forge of Henri [Henry] Smith (tenor). He is in love with Catharine (soprano), daughter of Simon Glover (bass), whose name also indicates his profession. But Catharine is coquettish and likes to tease her admirers. Mab (soprano), the queen of the gypsies, suddenly rushes in. She sings some *couplets* ('Catherine est coquette'). Smith shelters her from her pursuers and hides her when Catharine, her father, and another admirer, Ralph (bass or baritone), all enter. Smith and Catharine are alone together when the Duc de Rothsay [Duke of Rothsay] (baritone) arrives to have his dagger-blade repaired. Catharine, to make Smith jealous, pretends to flirt with the Duke. Smith is about to strike him when Mab emerges from hiding and thus arouses Catharine's jealousy.

At the start of Act 2 Glover and his friends are on patrol in Perth's city square. The Duke and some revellers are celebrating the carnival. There is a gypsy dance. The Duke enlists Mab's aid in getting Catharine to come masked to the ball that night. Mab sings more *couplets* ('Les seigneurs de la cour') and swears to be avenged on him. Smith does not share everyone's joy, but sings a doleful Serenade ('A la voix d'un amant fidèle'). He is drawn into a tavern as midnight strikes. Ralph, also drinking, falls asleep in the street but wakes to see a woman, actually Mab dressed as Catharine, being led to the Duke's palace. He finds Smith and tells him what he has seen, causing Smith to run off in pursuit. Ralph then hears Catharine singing Smith's Serenade from her house and realizes his mistake.

In Act 3 the Duke entertains his guests with a cavatina ('Elle sortait de sa demeure'). When Mab is brought in she refuses to unmask until the lights are out. Smith arrives, convinced of Catharine's faithlessness even when she appears with her father and denies it furiously. When he sees the Duke wearing a silver rose which he, Smith, had given her (it had passed through Mab's hands), his convictions are redoubled.

In the first tableau of Act 4 Ralph and Smith dispute Catharine's honour and agree to fight. In the second tableau, Mab reports that the Duke stopped the fight. But Catharine has gone mad, singing a ballad ('Echo, viens sur l'air embaumé'). She thinks Smith is dead, but is brought to her senses when he sings his Serenade. Mab appears at the window in Catharine's clothes, and the whole imposture is revealed. Catharine thinks it was all a dream.

This libretto must be severely criticized not only for its remoteness from Scott and its garbling of his original characters but also for its dependence on such worn-out devices as mistaken identity, coincidence and wholly irrational events. It is hard to read the changing motivations and actions of Mab and Ralph, for example, although Smith, Glover and the Duke are all more consistent in character. Making Catharine coquettish justified her treatment as a coloratura, which in turn required a mad scene in the last act. It is hardly surprising that Bizet's dramatic gifts are given little scope, although he applies some deft motivic treatment at salient points. Nor did he attempt any Scottish colour at all, offering Bohemian and polonaise idioms instead. The strength of the opera lies in the vitality of its set pieces and individual numbers. Scenes of drinking and festivity, ensembles of bewilderment or challenge, duets and solos of different types: all this draws out the best from Bizet's muse, full of wonderful melodic, harmonic and instrumental invention. It is hard to accept that such a fresh score belongs to an unstageable opera, but its fate is always more likely to be in the form of extracts than as a dramatic continuum. Smith's Serenade, the best-known piece from the opera and well worthy of its celebrity, was borrowed from *Don Procopio*.

HUGH MACDONALD

Jolivet, André (*b* Paris, 8 Aug 1905; *d* Paris, 20 Dec 1974). French composer. Drawn as much to the visual arts, literature and drama as to music, he took some time to find his direction. At 15 he conceived a ballet, designing the scenery and costumes as well as composing the music. He was trained as a teacher and from 1927 taught in Paris schools, but at the same time he studied music with Le Flem and with Varèse. In 1936 he, Messiaen and others founded the contemporary music group Jeune France.

Jolivet's style in the 1930s, strongly influenced by Varèse, was esoteric, but during World War II it turned in more conventional directions. The change was marked in *Dolorès, ou Le miracle de la femme laide*, an *opéra bouffe* composed in 1942 (1, H. Ghéon; French radio, 1947). Set in Valence, *Dolorès* tells the story of the wife of a master-tailor, Alonzo (baritone or *buffo* bass), who beats Dolorès (soprano) simply because she is ugly. Amusing quartets result in the addition of a foreign tourist ('baryton Martin') and a sports enthusiast (tenor) passing by on the road. Vincent, a hermit, cures Dolorès of her ugliness, and she then is admired by other men. All this is treated by Jolivet with a highly refined sense of parody and characterization. This work was followed by the ballet *Guignol et Pandore* (1943).

Jolivet became director of music at the Comédie Française from 1943 to 1959, and while there wrote and conducted a quantity of incidental music. He founded the Centre Français d'Humanisme Musical at Aix-en-Provence (1959) and taught at the Paris Conservatoire, 1966–70. In 1951 he received the Grand Prix awarded by the city of Paris.

ARTHUR HOÉRÉE, RICHARD LANGHAM SMITH

Joll, Phillip (*b* Merthyr Tydfil, 14 March 1954). Welsh baritone. He studied at the RNCM, Manchester, and at the National Opera Studio in London. His début was as the Bonze (*Madama Butterfly*) with the ENO in 1978; in the same year he joined the WNO, with which he has sung major roles including Wotan in the company's *Ring* cycle, also Kurwenal and Amfortas (both of which he has recorded) and Coroebus. He made his Covent Garden début in 1982 in *Salome* and has sung Donner and other roles there. His first German appearance was in 1983 as Amfortas in Frankfurt; he sang Donner at the Metropolitan Opera in 1987, the Dutchman at Bregenz (1988–9), and John the Baptist (*Salome*) and Marcello at Brisbane (1989–90), earning praise for his amplitude of tone and commanding presence. NOËL GOODWIN

Jolli [Joli], **Antonio** (*b* Modena, *c*1700; *d* Naples, 29 April 1777). Italian stage designer. He studied first in Modena and then in Rome, where he was a pupil of G. P. Pannini. He won fame as a painter of landscapes and views as well as being active as a scene painter, and he travelled widely. He worked at Modena, Reggio Emilia and Padua while residing in Venice (1732–42), where he was the designer at the Teatro S Giovanni Grisostomo (Pergolesi's *Olimpiade*, 1738) and other houses (S Cassiano, 1737: Geminiano Giacomelli's *Arsace*; S Samuele, 1737: the première of Galuppi's

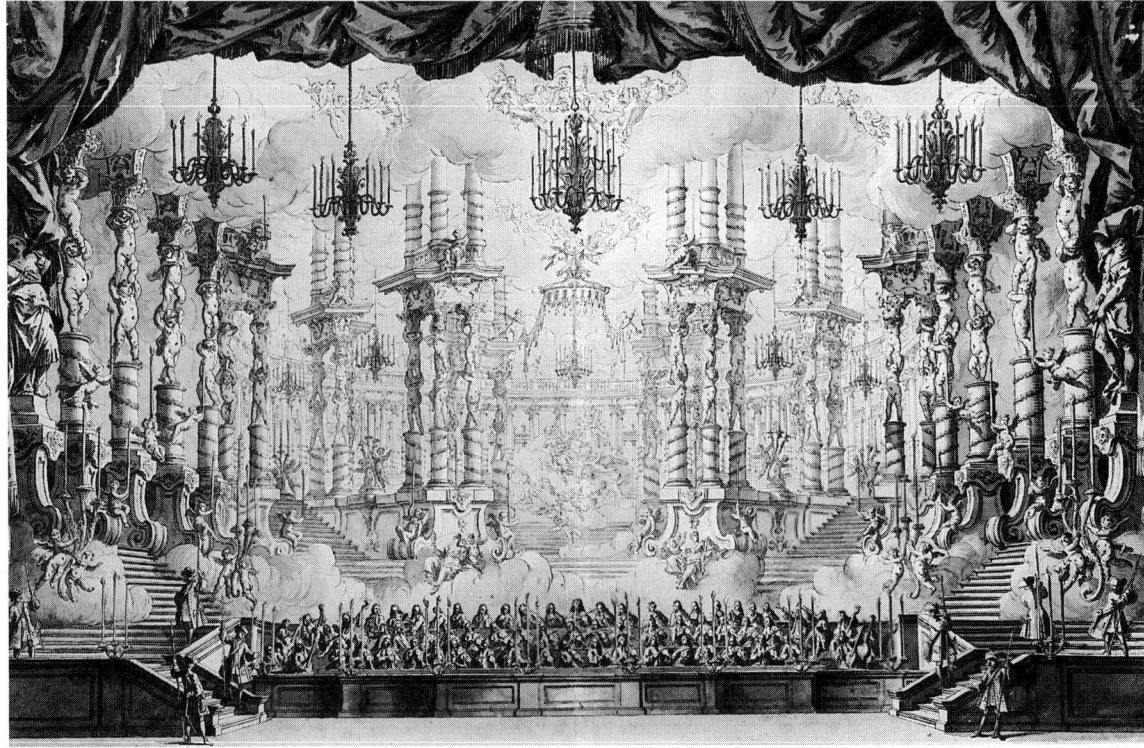

Stage design by Antonio Jolli for 'La reggia della Dea Flora', a festival at the Teatro S Giovanni Grisostomo, Venice, 1 March 1740, in honour of Friedrich Christian of Saxony

Alvilda). In 1740 he was responsible for the celebrations in Venice in honour of Friedrich Christian of Saxony. After that he spent time in Lombardy and in Germany, where he does not appear to have been active in the theatre; but in England he worked on the production of the pasticcio *Annibale in Capua* in 1746, and on D. M. B. Terradellas's *Bellerofonte* at the King's Theatre, London, the following year. He then went to France and to Madrid, where the musical life of the court was directed by the singer Farinelli. Jolli worked at the Teatro Buen Retiro, and for the marriage of the Infanta Maria Antonia Fernanda to Vittorio Amedeo III of Savoy in 1750 he collaborated with Jacopo Amiconi on the scenery for G. B. Mele's *Armida placata*, for which he contrived various festive devices. In about 1757 he moved to Naples for health reasons. On the death of Vincenzo Re (1762) he was appointed scenographer at the Teatro S Carlo, where his many productions included revivals of Traetta's *Armida* (1763), Hasse's *Ruggiero* (1772) and Gluck's *Orfeo e Euridice* (1774). Towards the end of his life he was assisted by Giuseppe Baldi. Few of his scene drawings survive, but his paintings show his skill and his ability to adapt to changes of fashion: *Samson Destroying the Temple of the Philistines* (Modena, Galleria Campori) is effectively an adaptation of a *diroccata* (collapse of a building), a stage device of Baroque origin, while the *Ruins of an Ancient Temple* (Naples, Capodimonte) is a faithful archaeological reconstruction in the new spirit of Classicism.

L'Adria festosa: Notizie storiche … del soggiorno di S. A. R. ed Elettorale Federico Cristiano … (Venice, 1740)

Il trionfo di Nettuno dio del mar su l'acque dell'Adria … a divertimento di S. A. R. … Federico Cristiano (Venice, 1740)

Relazione degli Sponsali celebrati in Madrid … tra Vittorio Amedeo di Savoia e Maria Antonia di Spagna (Bologna and Venice, 1750)

G. Tiraboschi: *Notizie de' pittori, scultori, … natii degli stati del duca di Modena* (Modena, 1786)

H. Tintelnot: *Barocktheater und Barocke Kunst* (Berlin, 1939)

F. Mancini: *Scenografia napoletana dell'età barocca* (Naples, 1964)

M. T. Muraro: *I teatri pubblici di Venezia (secoli XVII–XVIII)* (Venice, 1971) [exhibition catalogue]

C. Sorgato: 'Antonio Jolli', *L'arte del settecento emiliano: Architettura, scenografia, pittura di paesaggio* (Bologna, 1980), 227–30 [exhibition catalogue]

F. Mancini: *Il Teatro di S Carlo, 1737–1987*, iii: *Le scene, i costumi* (Naples, 1987)
MERCEDES VIALE FERRERO

Jommelli [Jomelli], Niccolò [Nicolò] (*b* Aversa, 10 Sept 1714; *d* Naples, 25 Aug 1774). Italian composer. He was important among those who initiated the mid-18th-century modifications to singer-dominated Italian opera. His greatest achievements represent a combination of German complexity, French decorative elements and Italian brio, welded together by an extraordinary gift for dramatic effectiveness.

1. Early career. 2. The Stuttgart years. 3. The final years.

1. EARLY CAREER. Jommelli's musical training began under Canon Muzzillo, director of the cathedral choir at Aversa. In 1725 he went to the Conservatorio S Onofrio, Naples, where he studied with Prota and Feo; he transferred to the Conservatorio Pietà dei Turchini in 1728, where his teachers included Nicola Fago. He was also influenced by the composers active in Naples during his student years, notably Hasse and Leo. Later, to Schubart, he admitted his debt to both Hasse and Graun. His public career began with two comic operas for Naples, *L'errore amorosa* in spring 1737 and *Odoardo* in winter 1738. The success of his first serious

opera, *Ricimero rè de' Goti*, at Rome in 1740 brought him to the attention of a wealthy and influential patron, Cardinal Henry Benedict, Duke of York.

An early exposure to Hasse's obbligato recitative must have impressed the young Jommelli with the capacity of motivic orchestral writing to create an intensified emotional effect at particularly dramatic moments. Speaking of Jommelli's obbligato recitative for *Ricimero*, Charles de Brosses declared that the force of the declamation, the variety of the harmony and the sublimity of the accompaniment created a sense of drama greater than the best French recitative and the most beautiful Italian melody.

For the production of his setting of Metastasio's *Ezio* in 1741, Jommelli moved to Bologna, where he met and studied with Giovanni Battista ('Padre') Martini, establishing a lifelong friendship (nine letters from Jommelli to Martini are in *I-Bc*). He was elected a member of the Accademia Filarmonica. Later that year he composed his first opera for Venice, *Merope*. Its first and second acts are linked with an unusual scene including chorus, obbligato recitative, ballet and pantomime, depicting war games, foreshadowing in startling fashion the French-inspired operas to come in the latter half of the century. In the next few years he wrote operas for Bologna, Venice, Turin, Ferrara and Padua, as well as two oratorios which were widely performed, *Isacco figura del Redentore* and *La Betulia liberata*. In 1743 he was appointed, on Hasse's recommendation, musical director of the Ospedale degli Incurabili, Venice. Much sacred music was written for the girls there, but opera continued to consume most of his creative energy.

The basic characteristics of his mature style were already emerging: the incursion of declamatory elements in the aria, audacious harmonic effects, abundant modulations, chromaticism, and the exploration of orchestral resources such as the use of the second violin as an independent textural element, the occasional independent viola parts, the abundant dynamic indications and the development of the crescendo effect, which reached Mannheim from Italy through Jommelli's Italian sinfonias, in which Johann Stamitz first heard the innovations since credited to him. Symphonic construction, without repeat signs and with a contrasting second theme in the dominant key, contrasting sections for pairs of instruments, sharp dynamic contrasts and the 'Mannheim' crescendo can all be found in Jommelli's opera sinfonias of the 1740s. The basic units of composition, at the level of motif and phrase in Jommelli's sinfonias, doubled (as Wolf has observed) in the 1740s: 2+2 becomes 4+4. The same process in vocal music led to a doubling in the length of the ordinary aria during the decade. Equally significant, Jommelli increasingly wrote arias in which the internal structure and function are clearly differentiated, using techniques associated with instrumental sonata procedures. Many of his arias of the 1740s have first themes, transitions, second and closing themes, clearly delineated by changes in texture, dynamics and orchestration. His interest in formal clarity was most pronounced during this decade, during which he was writing the most 'modern-sounding' music of anyone (Terradellas being a close second and Galuppi joining them around 1745); he also stands out for his interest and skill in the details of expression.

In 1747 Jommelli left Venice for Rome, where in 1749 he became *maestro coadiutore* to the papal chapel, a post secured for him by the cardinals Benedict and

Albani with a nomination to membership of the Accademia di S Cecilia. For the Vatican he produced a repertory of choral liturgical music. Besides operas for Rome, Jommelli fulfilled opera commissions for Naples, Spoleto, Turin, Bologna and Piacenza; but most important to his career was a commission Albani secured for him from Vienna in 1749. Here he composed *Achille in Sciro* and a second version of *Didone abbandonata* besides writing music for pasticcios. Metastasio, then court poet at Vienna, reported that Jommelli's *Achille* far exceeded expectations. He believed Jommelli to be unrivalled in his ability to seize the heart of the listener with his delicate and sensitive melody. The early Viennese symphonists, Dittersdorf and Wagenseil, later acknowledged Jommelli's influence on the formation of their symphonic style (see Hell 1971).

In Vienna Jommelli found a demand for chorus and ensemble scenes long out of vogue in Italy. *Achille in Sciro* is one of Metastasio's few librettos requiring a chorus. Although there are no ensembles in Jommelli's operas for Vienna, there are some in the pasticcios, for example a quartet in *Merope*. On his return to Italy in the early 1750s, Jommelli began incorporating ensembles and substantial final choruses into his operas. Mainly homophonic with solo and antiphonal sections, these have points of imitation and independent part-writing even in the traditionally homophonic final chorus.

In pursuit of the dramatic, Jommelli cut both recitative and aria from Metastasian librettos, increasing the number of obbligato recitatives. The most powerful obbligato solo scenes were written for Dido's death at the end of *Didone abbandonata* and for Regolus's farewell to Rome at the close of *Attilio Regolo*. Burney described the latter as producing such an uncommon effect during a production in London (1754) that it was encored, the only instance within his memory when a scene of recitative had inspired such a response.

Sofonisba (1745) and *Ifigenia in Aulide* (1751) anticipated by more than a decade efforts to restore staged death and tragedy to *opera seria*. In *Sofonisba* the plot is allowed to proceed to its tragic conclusion; the heroine dies of a poisoned drink on stage, as she would later in Traetta's 1762 setting of Mattia Verazi's text for Mannheim. Jommelli's libretto cites no author, but Verazi may well have penned this early staged suicide, for there is a parallel in his libretto for Jommelli's *Ifigenia* in which 'another Iphigenia' leaps into the sea, her shocking sacrifice paving the way for a happy ending.

Jommelli's concern for the musical realization of textual imagery found expression not only in a subtly responsive vocal line but also in orchestral word-painting, in sensitive textural variation suited to the changing moods of the poetry, and in programmatic effects such as those for Arbaces' shipwreck aria in *Artaserse*. He was among the first to use wind instruments in other than a supporting or obbligato role: they appear in solo sections, contribute motivic interest, create effective contrasts and combine for imaginative effects of colour.

In 1748 Jommelli wrote *L'amore in maschera*, his first comic opera for ten years. His few intermezzos followed within a few years. *L'uccellatrice* was written for Venice and performed there in May 1751. A reworked version, *Il parataio*, was presented by the Italian *buffo* troupe during its controversial appearance in Paris in 1753.

Thus Jommelli, along with Pergolesi and others, contributed fodder to the Querelle des Bouffons and to the clamour for more italianate elements in French opera voiced by the Encyclopédistes Rousseau, Grimm and Diderot.

2. THE STUTTGART YEARS. In 1753 Jommelli was at the height of his fame; he had received offers of positions at Mannheim and Lisbon at the time the Duke of Württemberg approached him about coming to Stuttgart. An interest in Italian opera had been established in Stuttgart before Carl Eugen came to power in 1744. The young duke had also developed a taste for French opera during his visit to Paris and Versailles in 1748: he was particularly attracted to the ensembles, choruses and ballet, the independent programmatic orchestral pieces and the elaborate staging and machinery. A new Stuttgart theatre had been completed in 1750 and a number of Jommelli's works were produced there. *Fetonte*, a French-inspired pasticcio containing Jommelli's music, was given there for the duke's birthday, 11 February 1753. During a trip to Italy early in the year, a firm friendship was established between Jommelli and the duke and it was arranged that Jommelli would move to Stuttgart in time for the production of *La clemenza di Tito* on 30 August, the birthday of the duchess, Friederike. Before leaving, Jommelli joined the Arcadian Academy in Rome under the pastoral name of Anfione Eteoclide; membership presupposed an ability to extemporize poetry and Jommelli is one of very few composers, if not the only one, to have held it.

On 1 January 1754, Jommelli officially assumed the duties of Ober-Kapellmeister at the Stuttgart court. Although Carl Eugen reserved the right to choose the subject of an opera and to decide the form it would take, Jommelli had control over all other aspects of its production. Under his strong leadership, no aspect of music or spectacle was ignored. He knew how to take advantage of the capacities of his singers and his orchestra, welding music, drama, decor and ballet into a powerfully unified whole calculated to make the maximum effect. No expense was spared in attracting the best instrumentalists, singers, dancers and designers. A succession of three French choreographers came to Stuttgart, among them Noverre, the pioneer of *ballet d'action*.

Jommelli's interest in the dramatic possibilities of the orchestra was allowed free rein. He built one of the finest orchestras in Europe. Numbering only 24 players in 1755, by 1767 it had grown to 47 including a lutenist, a double bass, paired wind (except clarinet), brass and percussion. Jommelli's obbligato recitative gained new strength of expression as he grew more skilled in developing the motivic material to paint the emotional state of his characters. The orchestra stepped out of its role as accompanist and became an equal partner with the singer. Schubart reported that Jommelli's programmatic orchestral effects overwhelmed his audiences.

In 1755 Jommelli collaborated with Verazi in two operas, *Pelope* and *Enea nel Lazio*. Following Carl Eugen's taste, these were a radical departure from the traditional succession of recitatives and exit arias. Built on mythological rather than historical subjects, the librettos freely combine obbligato recitative, aria, ensemble, chorus and programmatic orchestral music in dramatic scene complexes and spectacular, French-inspired finales. Among the unusually large number of

Design by Carlo Galli-Bibiena for the serenata 'Cerere placata' by Niccolò Jommelli, performed at the Perrelli Palace, Naples, 14 September 1772

ensembles in the two operas, the great quintet in *Enea* is outstanding. Jommelli used imitative counterpoint in his ensembles and choruses, but they are predominantly made up of solo, antiphonal and homophonic textures; they never reach the state of contrapuntal complexity that some of his biographers have indicated. The same may be said of his orchestral music which, while containing canonic imitation, is more accurately described as texturally than contrapuntally complex.

According to his contract, Jommelli had the right to return periodically to Italy, and he wrote and directed *Temistocle* for Naples and *Creso* for Rome in 1757. After the Stuttgart theatre was renovated in 1758–9, he devoted all his time to his duties there. Verazi had now moved to Mannheim, and Jommelli's operas were written on extensively modified Metastasian texts. French-style prologues were appended, scenes were tightened, eliminating much recitative and some arias, while new arias, ensembles, choruses and orchestral pieces were added. In a Metastasian libretto, a succession of exit arias left a single actor on stage for the final scene of each act (except the last); by combining the last few scenes, the act could be closed with an ensemble finale in which the participants expressed their separate emotions as in an aria.

Very little simple recitative remains in *Vologeso* or *Fetonte*, to texts by Verazi, Jommelli's last two serious operas for the Stuttgart court (given at the Ludwigsburg residence). Scenes of obbligato recitative are linked with a common key scheme. Declamatory elements invade the aria, although Jommelli's gift for melodic writing is still apparent. The da capo aria has all but disappeared, replaced by the dal segno (or partial da capo). There are many through-composed arias, some of them in two-part form rather than three-part. Shorter aria forms are scattered throughout the opera, serving to break up the long stretches of recitative with expressions of emotion intensifying the drama without stopping the action for the span of time required by full-length arias. Jommelli's ensembles show the same formal plasticity as his arias in response to dramatic demands. The last half of Act 2 is made up of two ensembles of diminishing personnel, each introduced with an aria, expanded to a quartet or trio, and then reduced to a duet when characters exit. The final trio of *Fetonte* is the most extensive spectacle scene in Jommelli's work: an action ensemble of a type usually found only in comic opera, it combines obbligato recitative, arioso, ensemble and chorus with a programmatic orchestral representation of a catastrophe. The flexibility of structure represents a radical departure from Metastasian conventions.

To meet the demand for lighter works, Jommelli wrote a series of serenatas and pastorales. Then, in 1766, he wrote two comic operas, *La critica* and *Il matrimonio per concorso*, both to texts by Gaetano Martinelli, the new court poet; their collaboration produced a warm friendship which lasted until Jommelli's death. Their next three operas, *Il cacciatore deluso* and *La schiava liberata* for Ludwigsburg and *Le avventure di Cleomede* for Lisbon, were termed *dramma serio-comico*. Jommelli's skill at musical caricature is shown to good advantage in these parody operas, where comedy is combined with pathos.

3. THE FINAL YEARS. By 1768, the situation in Ludwigsburg was such that Jommelli found it expedient to begin negotiations with the court of José I in Lisbon. According to an agreement of 1769, he was to send copies of earlier operas, to compose one serious and one comic opera each year, and to write unaccompanied sacred music for the royal chapel, for a yearly pension of 400 zecchini. In lieu of his own presence in Lisbon he sent his close friend, Martinelli, with whom he remained in constant correspondence about the detailed requirements (some of this correspondence, and Jommelli's letters to and from the director of the royal theatres of Portugal, survives: in *C-Lu*, *D-Sl*, *US-BE*, and the Portuguese Ministry of Finance Archives). The Naples-trained *mestre de capela*, João Cordeiro da Silva, was assigned the task of revising Jommelli's work according to production circumstances in Lisbon. At the same time, arrangements were made, in accordance with his

Stuttgart contract, for him to return to Aversa with his ailing wife in the hope that the southern climate would improve her health. His absence from Ludwigsburg gave his enemies an opportunity to intrigue against him, and Jommelli was cut off without his promised pension: moreover, he was refused not only the originals of his earlier works, but copies as well. In addition to his problems with Carl Eugen, Jommelli's wife died at the end of July 1769, a few months after they reached Italy.

On his return to Naples, Jommelli was immediately pressed into writing several new operas. In *Armida abbandonata*, his last spectacle opera, Jommelli incorporated ballet into the drama, wrote a great obbligato recitative scene for Armida, and concluded with a scene complex of cavatina, aria, ensemble and chorus. In a letter to his sister, Mozart judged *Armida* 'beautiful but too serious and old-fashioned for the theatre'. Mozart's reaction reflects the controversy that Jommelli's last opera for Naples inspired: a controversy represented on the one hand by Saverio Mattei, who felt that the depravity and decadence of popular taste rendered the modern audience incapable of comprehending the sublimity of Jommelli's music, 'full of harmony and contrivance', and on the other by those who stood for the unremitting trend towards a broader and less complex style. Jommelli, having already admitted to Vogler that he wished for himself Hasse's economy of means, and always concerned with the effect of his music on his audience, tried unsuccessfully to adapt his style to the Neapolitan taste.

Plagued with ill-health and gout, Jommelli completed a fourth version of *Demofoonte* (1770) for Naples; he then moved to Rome to write a second setting of *Achille in Sciro* and the comic opera *L'amante cacciatore* for Carnival 1771. At the same time, he was pressed to fulfil his obligations to the Portuguese court. A number of substitute arias and parts of a fourth version of *Ezio* had been sent before he went to Rome. *Le avventure di Cleomede* was completed shortly after he returned to Naples early in April. *Ifigenia in Tauride*, the sixth opera written in little more than a year, was finished on the day of the first performance (30 May 1771) in Naples: hastily and inadequately prepared, it was a complete disaster and had to be replaced within a few weeks by a new production of *Armida abbandonata*. Mattei observed that *Ifigenia* later came to be 'admired and thought far superior to the two former'.

The final arias for *Ezio* had been sent to Lisbon when, in August, Jommelli suffered a paralytic stroke. A year later he had recovered sufficient use of his hands to write, for private performance in Naples, the serenata *Cerere placata*, in the best tradition of his spectacular late style, and to begin work on a third opera for Lisbon. The final instalment of *Il trionfo di Clelia* arrived in Lisbon a month before the scheduled performance for the king's birthday on 6 June. From Carnival 1769 until the death of José I in 1777, the royal Portuguese theatres presented to appreciative audiences as many as four of Jommelli's operas each year. The enthusiastic report of the success of *Clelia* in Lisbon probably reached Jommelli little more than a month before his death in August. At the instigation of the *maestro*, Gennaro Manna, the musicians and poets of Naples collaborated in a grand public funeral to honour the passing of a great master.

At the time of his death, Jommelli was regarded as one of the greatest composers of his time. He was always among those cited when memorable composers of the century were named. In Stuttgart, Schubart declared:

> The great musical Pan is dead ... If richness of thought, glittering fantasy, inexhaustible melody, heavenly harmony, deep understanding of all instruments, and particularly the full magical strength of the human voice – if great art affects entirely each chord of the human heart, if all these – yet combined with the sharpest understanding of musical poetry – constitute a musical genius, then in him Europe has lost its greatest composer.

In *De la musique en Italie*, Alexandr Beloselsky wrote that Jommelli could 'be regarded universally as the most profound and the greatest artist who has ever distinguished himself in the harmonious profession'. Arteaga described him as 'truly original in having such excellent qualities as the felicity of his musical imagination, which earned him the appellation of the Chiabrera, and the Horace of composers, the coupling of expression and difficulty, the richness, and the energy and vivacity of his scoring'.

See also ARMIDA ABBANDONATA; DEMOFOONTE; FETONTE; IFIGENIA IN TAURIDE (iii); OLIMPIADE, L' (v); SCHIAVA LIBERATA, LA; UCCELLATRICE, L'; and VOLOGESO.

L'errore amoroso (ob, 3, A. Palomba), Naples, Nuovo, spr. 1737, lib. *I-Nc*, 3 arias *Nc* and *PLcon*
Odoardo (ob, 3), Naples, Fiorentini, wint. 1738, lib. *B-Bc* and *I-Nc*, 2 arias *B-Bc*, *F-Pn* and *GB-Lbl*
Ricimero re di Goti (os, 3, A. Zeno and P. Pariati), Rome, Argentina, 16 Jan 1740, *I-Nc* (inc.), 2 arias *D-MÜs*, *Rtt* and *GB-Cfm*
Astianatte [Andromaca] (os, 3, A. Salvi), Rome, Argentina, 4 Feb 1741, *B-Bc* (Act 3), *D-Sl**, *GB-Lbl*, *I-Nc* (without recits), *US-Cn*, *R*
Ezio [1st version] (os, 3, P. Metastasio), Bologna, Malvezzi, 29 April 1741, *D-Sl**, *GB-Lbl*, *I-Nc*
Merope (os, 3, Zeno), Venice, S Giovanni Grisostomo, 26 Dec 1741, *D-Dlb*, *Mbs*, *GB-Lbl*; with addns, ?Bologna, 1745, *D-Sl**, *F-Pn* (addns probably not by Jommelli)
Tito Manlio [1st version] (os, 3, G. Roccaforte), Turin, Regio, carn. 1742, *D-Sl**, *GB-Lbl*
Semiramide riconosciuta [1st version] (os, 3, Metastasio), Turin, Regio, 20 Jan 1742, *D-Sl**, *GB-Lbl*, *I-Nc*
Eumene [1st version] (os, 3, Zeno), Bologna, Malvezzi, 5 May 1742, *D-Sl** (Acts 1 and 2), *GB-Lbl*
Semiramide (os, 3, F. Silvani), Venice, S Giovanni Grisostomo, 26 Dec 1742, *D-Sl**
Don Chichibio (int, 2), Rome, Valle, 1742, *A-KR**, *GB-Lbl*
Ciro riconosciuto [1st version] (os, 3, Metastasio), Ferrara, Bonacossi, 20 Jan 1743, *I-Bc*; rev. Bologna, Formagliari, 4 May 1744, *D-Sl** (Acts 2 and 3), *GB-Lbl*, *I-Fc* (Act 3)
Demofoonte [1st version] (os, 3, Metastasio), Padua, Obizzi, 13 June 1743, *D-Sl** (Acts 1 and 2), *F-Pn* 778
Alessandro nell'Indie [1st version] (os, 3, Metastasio), Ferrara, Bonacossi, 26 Dec 1743, lib. *I-Bc*, 2 arias *D-Dlb*, *MÜs*, *F-Pn*, *GB-Lbl* (attrib. Galuppi), *I-Fc* and *PLcon*
Antigono (os, 3, Metastasio), Crema, Grande, Sept 1744, *D-Sl** (inc.), 2 arias *F-Pn*; rev. Lucca, 1746, aria *I-Nc* and *TLp*
Sofonisba (os, 3, A. Zanetti and G. Zanetti), Venice, S Giovanni Grisostomo, 26 Dec 1745, *Rp*
Caio Mario (os, 3, Roccaforte), Rome, Argentina, 12 Feb 1746, *A-Wgm*, *D-MÜs* (Acts 1 and 2), *F-Pn*, *GB-Lbl*, *I-Mc*, *Nc*, *Rsc*; rev. Bologna, 1751, *P-La*
Tito Manlio [2nd version] (os, 3, J. Sanvitale, after M. Noris), Venice, S Giovanni Grisostomo, aut. 1746, lib. *I-Bc* and *US-Wc*, 6 arias *A-Wn*, *D-B*, *BAR*, *Dlb*, *Mbs*, *Rtt*, *F-Pn*, *GB-Lbl*, *I-Mc*, *MC*, *MOe*, *Nc*, *PAc*, *PLc* and *Vc*
Didone abbandonata [1st version] (os, 3, Metastasio), Rome, Argentina, 28 Jan 1747, *Mc*, *Nc*
Eumene [2nd version] (os, 3, Zeno), Naples, S Carlo, 30 May 1747; as Artemisia, *F-Pn**; with revisions, *I-Nc*, *Rsc*
L'amore in maschera (ob, 3, Palomba), Naples, Fiorentini, carn. 1748, lib. *Nc* and *US-Wc*
Ezio [2nd version] (os, 3, Metastasio), Naples, S Carlo, 4 Nov 1748, *I-Mc**, *Nc* (without recits)
La cantata e disfida di Don Trastullo (int, 2), Rome, Pace, carn. 1749, *D-Mbs*, *F-Pn*, *GB-Lbl*, *Lcm*, *Lgc*, *I-BRc*, *Gl*, *MOe*, *Nc*, *Nlp*, *Rsc*; rev. Lucca, Pubblico, carn. 1762, *PAc*
Artaserse [1st version] (os, 3, Metastasio), Rome, Argentina, 6 Feb

1749, *D-Sl**, *Hs*, *F-Pn*, *GB-Lbl*, *I-Nc* (without recits); rev. Mannheim, 1751, *D-B*, *Bsp*

Demetrio (os, 3, Metastasio), Parma, Ducale, May 1749, *I-Nc** (inc.), 2 arias *B-Bc*, *D-Mbs*, *I-Nc* and *Vc*; rev. Madrid, Buen Retiro, 1751, 8 arias *D-B*, *MÜs*, *E-Zac*, *F-Pn*, *I-Gl* and *Nc*

Achille in Sciro [1st version] (os, 3, Metastasio), Vienna, Burg, 30 Aug 1749, *A-Wn*

Ciro riconosciuto [2nd version] (os, 3, Metastasio), Venice, S Giovanni Grisostomo, Nov 1749

Didone abbandonata [2nd version] (os, 3, Metastasio), Vienna, Burg, 8 Dec 1749, *Wn* 18282, *F-Pn*, *GB-Cfm*

L'uccellatrice (int, 2), Venice, S Samuele, 6 May 1750, *I-Gl*; rev. as Il parataio [La pipée] (int, 2, C. F. Clément), Paris, Opéra, 25 Sept 1753, *B-Bc*, *F-Po*, *H-Bn*, *I-Mc* (all without recits)

La villana nobile (ob, 3), Palermo, de' Valguarneri di S Lucia, carn. 1751, lib. *US-BE*

Ifigenia in Aulide (os, 3, M. Verazi), Rome, Argentina, 9 Feb 1751, *B-Bc** (Act 3), *F-Pn*, *GB-Lbl*, *I-Mc*, *Nc*, *P-La*; pasticcio, Naples, S Carlo, 18 Dec 1753, with arias by Traetta, *GB-Lbl* (Act 2), *I-MC*

Ipermestra (os, 3, Metastasio), Spoleto, Nobile, 9 Oct 1751, *GB-Lcm**, *I-Nc*, *US-Bp* (Act 1)

Talestri (os, 3, Roccaforte), Rome, Dame, 28 Dec 1751, *I-Mc**, *Nc*, *P-La*

I rivali delusi (int, 2), Rome, Valle, carn. 1752, *D-B*

Attilio Regolo (os, 3, Metastasio), Rome, Dame, 8 Jan 1753, *B-Bc*, *GB-Cfm*, *Lbl*, *I-BGc*, *Nc*, *P-La*, *US-Bp* (Act 1); pasticcio, London, 1753, *GB-Lbl*; pasticcio, Naples, S Carlo, 23 March 1761, *P-La*

Demofoonte [2nd version] (os, 3, Metastasio), Milan, Regio Ducal, 27 Jan 1753, *I-Nc**, *Nc*

Semiramide riconosciuta [2nd version] (os, 3, Metastasio), Piacenza, Ducale, April 1753, *Nc** (inc.), *P-La*

La clemenza di Tito [1st version] (os, 3, Metastasio), Stuttgart, Herzogliches, 30 Aug 1753, lib. *US-Wc*, 3 arias *D-Dlb*, *F-Pn*, *I-Bc*, *BGc* and *Nc*

Bajazette (os, 3, A. Piovene), Turin, Regio, 26 Dec 1753, *Nc*

Don Falcone (int, 2), Bologna, Rossi, 22 Jan 1754, *Gl*

Lucio Vero (os, 3, after Zeno), Milan, Regio Ducal, Jan 1754, *Nc**

Catone in Utica (os, 3, Metastasio), Stuttgart, Herzogliches, 30 Aug 1754, lib. *US-Wc*, 4 arias *B-Bc*, *F-Pn*, *I-Bc*, *Mc*, *MC*, *Nc* and *Rc*

Pelope (os, 3, Verazi), Stuttgart, Herzogliches, 11 Feb 1755, *Nc*; rev. J. C. da Silva, Salvaterra, Real, carn. 1767, *P-La*

Enea nel Lazio [1st version] (os, 3, Verazi), Stuttgart, Herzogliches, 30 Aug 1755, *F-Pn*; rev. Silva, Salvaterra, Real, carn. 1767, *P-La*

Artaserse [2nd version] (os, 3, Metastasio), Stuttgart, Herzogliches, 30 Aug 1756, *D-Sl*, *P-La*

Creso (os, 3, G. Pizzi), Rome, Argentina, 5 Feb 1757, *B-Bc* (Act 2), *GB-Cfm*, *Lbl*, *I-BGc*, *MAc*, *Mc*, *Nc**, *Nn*, *P-La*, *S-Skma*, *US-Wc*

Temistocle [1st version] (os, 3, Metastasio), Naples, S Carlo, 18 Dec 1757, *B-Bc* (Act 1), *Br*, *D-Hs*, *SWl*, *F-Pn**, *GB-Lbl*, *Lcm*, *I-MC* (without recits), *Nc*, *Nn*, *Tf*, *S-Skma*

Tito Manlio [3rd version] (os, 3), Stuttgart, Herzogliches, 6 Jan 1758 (Sittard 1890–91)

Ezio [3rd version] (os, 3, Metastasio), Stuttgart, Herzogliches, 11 Feb 1758, lib. *US-Wc*, arias *I-Nc* and *D-Dlb*

Nitteti (os, 3, Metastasio), Stuttgart, Herzogliches, 11 Feb 1759, 3 arias *I-MC* and *Nc*; rev. Silva, Lisbon, Ajuda, 2 June 1770, *P-La*

Endimione, ovvero Il trionfo d'Amore (pastorale, 2, after Metastasio), Stuttgart, Herzogliches, spr. 1759; rev. Queluz, Real, 29 June 1780, *La*

Alessandro nell'Indie [2nd version] (os, 3, Metastasio), Stuttgart, Herzogliches, 11 Feb 1760, 5 arias *I-MC* and *Nc*; rev. Silva, Lisbon, Ajuda, 6 June 1776, *P-La*

Caio Fabrizio (os, 3, Verazi), Mannheim, Hof, 4 Nov 1760, with arias by G. Colla, *I-Mc* (without recits), *US-R*, *Wc*

L'olimpiade (os, 3, Metastasio), Stuttgart, Herzogliches, 11 Feb 1761, *D-WRtl*, *I-Mc*, *Nc* (without recits), *A-Wn* (reduced, without recits), *Recueuil des opéra composés par Nicolas Iomelli* (Stuttgart, 1783) (without recits); rev. Silva, Lisbon, Ajuda, 31 March 1774, *P-La*

L'isola disabitata (pastorale, 2, Metastasio), Ludwigsburg, Schloss, 4 Nov 1761; rev. Queluz, Real, 31 March 1780, *La*

Semiramide riconosciuta [3rd version] (os, 3, Metastasio), Stuttgart, Herzogliches, 11 Feb 1762, *F-Pn*

Didone abbandonata [3rd version] (os, 3, Metastasio), Stuttgart, Herzogliches, 11 Feb 1763, *A-Wn** 16488, *D-B*; rev. Stuttgart, 1777–83, *Sl*

Il trionfo d'Amore (pastorale, G. Tagliazucchi), Ludwigsburg, Schloss, 16 Feb 1763 (Sittard 1890–91), lib. *US-Wc*, aria *D-B*

La pastorella illustre (pastorale, 2, Tagliazucchi), Stuttgart, Herzogliches, 4 Nov 1763; rev. Silva, Salvaterra, Real, carn. 1773, *P-La*

Demofoonte [3rd version] (os, 3, Metastasio), Stuttgart, Herzogliches, 11 Feb 1764, *B-Bc*, *D-Sl**; rev. Ludwigsburg, Schloss, 11 Feb 1765; rev. Silva, Lisbon, Ajuda, 6 June 1775, *P-La*

Il re pastore (os, 3, Metastasio), Ludwigsburg, Schloss, 4 Nov 1764; rev. Silva, Salvaterra, Real, carn. 1770, *La*

La clemenza di Tito [2nd version] (os, 3, Metastasio), Ludwigsburg, Schloss, 6 Jan 1765; rev. Silva, Lisbon, Ajuda, 6 June 1771, *La*

Imeneo in Atene (pastorale, 2, after S. Stampiglia), Ludwigsburg, Schloss, 4 Nov 1765; rev. Silva, Lisbon, Ajuda, 19 March 1773, *La* (attrib. Porpora)

Temistocle [2nd version] (os, 3, Metastasio), Ludwigsburg, Schloss, 4 Nov 1765

Enea nel Lazio [2nd version] (os, 3, Verazi), Ludwigsburg, Schloss, 6 Jan 1766, *F-Pn*, *I-Nc*

Vologeso (os, 3, Verazi, after Zeno: *Lucio Vero*), Ludwigsburg, Schloss, 11 Feb 1766, *A-Wgm*, *B-Bc*, *D-B*, *Sl*, *F-Pn*; rev. Silva, Salvaterra, Real, carn. 1769, *P-La*

Il matrimonio per concorso (ob, 3, G. Martinelli), Ludwigsburg, Schloss, 4 Nov 1766; rev. Silva, Salvaterra, Real, carn. 1770, *La*

La critica (ob, 1, Martinelli), Ludwigsburg, Schloss, 1766, *I-Nc*; rev. as Il giuoco di Picchetto (int), Koblenz, Hof, spr. 1772, *F-Pn*; rev. as La conversazione and L'accademia di musica (int, 2), Salvaterra, Real, carn. 1775, *P-La* (La conversazione)

Il cacciatore deluso [ovvero] La Semiramide in bernesco (dramma serio-comico, 3, Martinelli), Tübingen, 4 Nov 1767, *I-Nc** (inc.); rev. Silva, Salvaterra, Real, carn. 1771, *P-La*

Fetonte (os, 3, Verazi), Ludwigsburg, Schloss, 11 Feb 1768, *A-Wgm*, *B-Bc*, *D-B*, *Sl*, *F-Pn*; ed. in DDT, xxxii–xxxiii (1907)

La schiava liberata (dramma serio-comico, 3, Martinelli), Ludwigsburg, Schloss, 18 Dec 1768, *DK-Kk* (Acts 2 and 3), *F-Pn*, *I-Mc* (Act 1), *Nc*; rev. Silva, Lisbon, Ajuda, 31 March 1770, *P-La*

Armida abbandonata (os, F. S. de Rogatis, after T. Tasso: *Gerusalemme liberata*), Naples, S Carlo, 30 May 1770, *B-Bc*, *D-B*, *Dlb*, *Hs*, *Mbs*, *MÜs*, *F-Pn*, *GB-Ob*, *I-Fc*, *Mc*, *Nc*, *Rsc*, *P-La*; rev. Silva, Lisbon, Ajuda, 31 March 1773, *La*

Demofoonte [4th version] (os, 3, Metastasio), Naples, S Carlo, 4 Nov 1770, *D-B*, *F-Pn* D6231–3, *I-Mc*, *Nc*, *Nn*, *P-La*

L'amante cacciatore (int, 2, A. Gatta), Rome, Pallacorda, carn. 1771, lib. *I-Bc* and *Vgc*

Achille in Sciro [2nd version] (os, 3, Metastasio), Rome, Dame, 26 Jan 1771, *D-B*, *F-Pn*, *I-Mc* (Acts 1 and 2), *Nc*

Le avventure di Cleomede, April 1771 (dramma serio-comico, 3, Martinelli); rev. Silva, Lisbon, Ajuda, 6 June 1772, *P-La*

Ifigenia in Tauride (os, 3, Verazi), Naples, S Carlo, 30 May 1771, *D-B*, *Mbs*, *DK-Kk*, *I-Fc*, *Mc*, *Nc*; rev. Silva, Salvaterra, Real, carn. 1776, *P-La*

Ezio [4th version], July 1771 (os, 3, Metastasio), *A-Wn* SM9952, *F-Pn*, *I-Nc*; rev. Silva, Lisbon, Ajuda, 20 April 1772, *P-La*

Cerere placata (serenata, 2, Sarcone), Naples, Perrelli, 14 Sept 1772, *B-Bc*, *D-Sl*, *F-Pn*, *I-Mc*, *Nc*, *P-La*

Il trionfo di Clelia, early 1774 (os, 3, Metastasio), *F-Pn*, *I-Nc*; rev. Silva, Lisbon, Ajuda, 6 June 1774, *P-La*

La pellegrina (ob), sent to Lisbon, according to letter from Silva (see McClymonds 1980)

Music in pasticcios: La contessina, 1743, *B-Bc*; Catone in Utica, 1747; Merope, 1749, *A-Wn*; Andromeda, 1750, *Wn*; Euridice, 1750, *Wn*; Armida placata, 1750, *Wn*; César in Egipte (os, 3, after G. Bussani), Strasbourg, carn. 1751, lib. *US-Wc*; Fetonte (os, 3, L. Villati), Stuttgart, Herzogliches, 1753, lib. *D-Sl*; Il tre vecchi innamorati, 1768; ? Arcadia in Brenta, *A-Wgm*

*

BurneyFI; *BurneyH*; *EitnerQ*; *FlorimoN*; *RosaM*

S. Mattei: *Saggio di poesie latine, ed italiane*, ii (Naples, 1774), 268–79; Eng. trans. in *BurneyH*

G. J. Vogler: *Betrachtungen der Mannheimer Tonschule*, i (1778), 159–64

S. Mattei: *Elogio del Jommelli* (Colle, 1785), 59–140

G. Sigismondo: *Descrizione della città di Napoli*, ii (Naples, 1788), 119–25

C. Schubart: *Ideen zu einer Ästhetik der Tonkunst* (Vienna, 1806)

——: *Gesammelte Schriften und Schicksale* (Stuttgart, 1839)

P. Alfieri: *Notizie biografiche di Nicolò Jommelli* (Rome, 1845)

J. Sittard: *Zur Geschichte der Musik und des Theaters am Württembergischen Hofe* (Stuttgart, 1890–91)

H. Abert: Preface to *Fetonte*, DDT, xxxii–xxxiii (Leipzig, 1907)

——: *Niccolò Jommelli als Opernkomponist* (Halle, 1908)

R. Krauss: *Das Stuttgarter Hoftheater* (Stuttgart, 1908)

H. Goldschmidt: 'Die Reform der italienischen Oper des 18 Jahrhunderts', *IMusSCR, iii Vienna 1909*, 196–206

E. Celani: 'Musica e musicisti in Roma', *RMI*, xviii (1911), 1–63

M. Fehr: 'Zeno, Pergolesi und Jommelli', *ZMw*, i (1918–19), 281–7

S. Di Giacomo: *I quattro antichi conservatori di musica a Napoli* (Palermo, 1924–8), 243–9

H. Abert: 'Die Stuttgarter Oper unter Jommelli', *Neue Musikzeitung*, xlvi/24 (1925), 551–4

A. Yorke Long: *Music at Court: Four Eighteenth Century Studies* (London, 1954)

H. Hell: *Die Neapolitanische Opernsinfonie in der ersten Hälfte des 18. Jahrhunderts* (Tutzing, 1971)

M. Robinson: *Naples and Neapolitan Opera* (Oxford, 1972)

H. Brofsky: 'Jommelli e Padre Martini: anedoti e realtà di un rapporto', *RIM*, viii (1973), 132–46

L. Tolkoff: *The Stuttgart Operas of Niccolò Jommelli* (diss., Yale U., 1974)

R. Bossa: 'Luigi Vanvitelli spettatore teatrale', *RIM*, xi (1976), 48–70

C. Sprague: *A Comparison of Five Settings of Metastasio's Artaserse* (diss., U. of California, Los Angeles, 1978)

A. Schnoebelen: *Padre Martini's Collection of Letters* (New York, 1979)

R. Strohm: *Die italienische Oper im 18. Jahrhundert* (Wilhelmshaven, 1979), 292–304

M. McClymonds: *Niccolò Jommelli: the Last Years, 1769–1774* (Ann Arbor, 1980)

——: 'The Evolution of Jommelli's Operatic Style', *JAMS*, xxxiii (1980), 326–55

——: 'Haydn and his Italian Contemporaries: *Armida abbandonata*', *Haydn: Vienna 1982*, 325–32

——: 'Mattia Verazi and the Opera at Mannheim, Stuttgart and Ludwigsburg', *Studies in Music from the University of Western Ontario*, vii/2 (1982), 99–136

——: 'Jommellis Opernsinfonien der 1750er Jahre und ihre Beziehung zum Mannheimer Stil', *Mannheim und Italien*, ed. R. Würtz (Mainz, 1984), 97–120

E. K. Wolf: 'Zur Entstehungsgeschichte des Mannheimer sinfonischen Stiles', *Mannheim und Italien*, ed. R. Würtz (Mainz, 1984), 41–65

E. Weimer: *Opera Seria and the Evolution of the Classical Style, 1755–72* (Ann Arbor, 1984)

F. Dorsi: 'Un intermezzo di Niccolò Jommelli: *Don Falcone*', *NRMI*, xix (1985), 432–57

M. P. McClymonds: 'Jommelli's Last Opera for Germany: the Opera Seria-Comica *La schiava liberata* (Ludwigsburg, 1768)', *CMc*, no.39 (1985), 7–20

MARITA P. McCLYMONDS (with PAUL CAUTHEN)

Jonas, Peter (*b* London, 14 Oct 1946). English administrator. He studied at Sussex University (1965–8), and while a student was an extra and stagehand at Glyndebourne Festival Opera. From 1968 to 1971 he studied at the RNCM and the RCM, and in 1973 continued his education at the Eastman School of Music in Rochester, New York. He held administrative posts with the Chicago SO from 1974, becoming their director of artistic administration in 1976, then took up the post of general director of the ENO in 1985, succeeding the Earl of Harewood. During his tenure he expanded the company's repertory and brought about a series of commissions from British composers and librettists. He has been appointed Intendant of the Bavarian State Opera, Munich, to take effect from 1993.

Joncières, Victorin (de) [Rossignol, Félix-Ludger] (*b* Paris, 12 April 1839; *d* Paris, 26 Oct 1903). French composer and critic. At 16 he decided to study painting, but for his own amusement shortly afterwards wrote the *opéra comique Le sicilien*, which was well received when presented by Conservatoire students in 1859. On the recommendation of a music critic who attended the performance, he began to study music formally. He entered the Conservatoire to learn counterpoint and fugue with Leborne but left after a disagreement over Wagner early in 1860. An ardent Wagnerian, Joncières later made enemies through his partisan, sometimes acerbic music and theatre criticism in *La liberté* (1871–1900).

Both his *Sardanapale* (1867) and *Le dernier jour de Pompéï* (1869) failed at the Théâtre Lyrique, though the first featured Christine Nilsson. After years of silence, Joncières returned to the stage with his best opera, *Dimitri* (1876; revived at the Opéra-Comique in 1890). It was praised for its breadth, power, dramatic sense and brilliant orchestration, though some Wagnerian passages were duly noted in a score more indebted to French and Italian traditions. Pougin acknowledged that the work was accomplished, but did not feel the ideas were truly original; the general public did not respond to the work with great enthusiasm. Of Joncières' later operas, only *Le chevalier Jean* (1885) held the stage, largely in Germany (as *Johann von Lothringen*). Its revival at the Opéra-Comique was prevented by the disastrous 1887 fire which also burnt the sets brought to the theatre for that day's dress rehearsal with orchestra. The composer presented himself as a candidate for the Institut but was not elected, and at his funeral Paul Milliet lamented that his reputation had never equalled his true merit as an artist.

first performed in Paris unless otherwise stated; all printed works published in Paris

Le sicilien, ou L'amour peintre (oc, 1, ?Joncières, after Molière), Ecole lyrique, early Dec 1859, *F-Pc**

Sardanapale, 1864 (opéra, 3, H. Becque, after Byron), Lyrique, 8 Feb 1867, *Pc**, vs (1867)

Le dernier jour de Pompéï (opéra, 4, C. Nuitter and A. Beaumont, after E. Bulwer-Lytton), Lyrique, 21 Sept 1869, *Pc**, vs (1869)

Dimitri (opéra, 5, H. de Bornier, A. Silvestre and L. Carvalho, after F. von Schiller: *Demetrius*), Gaîté, 5 May 1876, *Pc**; (1877)

La reine Berthe (opéra, 2, J. Barbier), Opéra, 27 Dec 1878, *Po**, vs (1879)

Le chevalier Jean (drame lyrique, 4, L. Gallet and E. Blau), OC (Favart), 11 March 1885, *Pn**, *Pc**, vs (1885)

Lancelot (drame lyrique, 4, Gallet and Blau), Opéra, 7 Feb 1900, *Pn**, *Po**, vs (1899)

Music in: Le baron Frick (opérette, 1, E. Depré and Clairville), Cercle Artistique et Littéraire, 1885, collab. E. Guiraud and others

Unperf.: Suzette (opérette, 5 tableaux), *Pc**; Un mari pour 100 francs (oc, 1), *Pc**; unidentified opéra comique, inc., *Pc**

*

FétisBS

F. Clément and P. Larousse: *Dictionnaire lyrique* (Paris, 1867–81; 2/1897, 3/1905 ed. A. Pougin as *Dictionnaire des opéras*)

H. L.: 'Joncières', *La grande encyclopédie* (Paris, 1887–1901)

A. Soubies and C. Malherbe: *Histoire de l'Opéra Comique*, ii (Paris, 1892)

G. Vapereau: *Dictionnaire universel des contemporains* (Paris, 6/1893)

A. Jullien: *Musiciens d'aujourd'hui*, 2nd ser. (Paris, 1894), 328–49

A. Pougin: 'Victorin Joncières', *Le ménestrel*, lxix (1903), 348

C. Le Senne: 'Période contemporaine: Joncières', *EMDC*, I/iii (Paris, 1931), 1797–8

T. J. Walsh: *Second Empire Opera: the Théâtre Lyrique, Paris, 1851–1870* (London, 1981)

LESLEY A. WRIGHT

Jone [*Jone, o L'ultimo giorno di Pompei* ('Jone, or The Last Day of Pompeii')]. *Dramma lirico* in four acts by ERRICO PETRELLA to a libretto by GIOVANNI PERUZZINI, after EDWARD BULWER-LYTTON's novel *The Last Days of Pompeii*; Milan, Teatro alla Scala, 26 January 1858.

Jone is reasonably faithful to the bones of Bulwer-Lytton's novel. Jone (soprano) and Glauco (tenor) are Greeks living in Pompeii, in love with one another. She is the ward of Arbace (baritone), a villainous priest of Isis, who desires her for himself. He plots to win her, first by impugning Glauco's character, describing him as a debauchee; later, he seeks to beguile Jone by unveiling before her her statue in his temple. When Jone resists his temptations, Arbace sentences Glauco to a fate amid the beasts of the Circus. At the amphitheatre during the eruption of Vesuvius, the Thessalian slave Nidia (mezzo-soprano) stabs Arbace, thereby permitting Jone and Glauco to escape to the sea at the last minute. In Peruzzini's crudely melodramatic libretto scarcely anything remains of Bulwer-Lytton's erudition and atmosphere; the characters are one-dimensional and the setting, except for the odd detonation and the occasional archaicism, could be anywhere.

Petrella's score is largely cast in the conventions of the 1830s, including a brash sinfonia in sonatina form and arias and duets rounded off by jagged cabalettas. His melodies frequently possess a naive impetus, but the text-setting is often awkward. The accompaniments are simplistic, and Petrella's penchant for unison passages in ensembles irrepressibly manifest. His orchestration resembles that of a provincial bandmaster of the period. In view of its shortcomings, the viability of *Jone* for nearly half a century is not easy to explain. The opportunities for spectacle and for emphatic singing account for it in some measure, but so does the relentless demand for repertory-fodder in the numerous Italian opera houses of the years after unification. Two of Glauco's arias achieved popularity, enough at least to be recorded several times during the acoustic period. These are his bumptious *brindisi* in Act 1, 'Canti chi vuole', and his Act 4 *romanza*, 'O Jone, di quest'anima', arguably the most expressive passage in the entire work. While Verdi's stricture that Petrella was ignorant of music ('Petrella non sa la musica') may be an example of hyperbole, there is just enough truth in it to describe his insensitivity to all that makes for genuinely moving musical theatre.

WILLIAM ASHBROOK

Jones, Mrs. English contralto; *see* YOUNG family, (3).

Jones, Daniel (Jenkyn) (*b* Pembroke, 7 Dec 1912). Welsh composer. He began to compose when still a child, but his university studies at Swansea were in English literature (BA 1934, MA 1939). Between 1935 and 1938 he studied at the RAM and won the Mendelssohn scholarship (1935). During the pre-war years in Swansea Jones belonged to a circle which included the young Dylan Thomas. The two had first met as schoolboys, as recounted in Thomas's story *The Fight*. Jones made many settings of Thomas's early poems and wrote the music for the 1954 radio version of *Under Milk Wood*, which won the Italia Prize.

Jones has been a notably consistent composer, committed to traditional forms and to the principle of tonality. During and after World War II he turned increasingly to orchestral composition, the field in which he has made his major contribution. He has written two operas, both to his own librettos. *The Knife* (1961), a two-act piece in the Romantic mould, with lyrical solo lines, powerful choruses and effective orchestration, was performed by the New Opera Company at Sadler's Wells, London, on 2 December 1963; *Orestes* (1967) is based on Aeschylus and was commissioned by the BBC.

A. Stewart: 'Daniel Jones's Opera', *MT*, civ (1963), 790 [on *The Knife*]

ARNOLD WHITTALL

Jones, Della (*b* Neath, 13 April 1946). Welsh mezzo-soprano. She studied in London and in Geneva, where she made her début in 1970 as Fyodor (*Boris Godunov*), later singing Olga (*Yevgeny Onegin*) and the Schoolboy (*Lulu*). She sang Clytemnestra (*Iphigénie en Aulide*) at Oxford in 1972 and in 1977 joined the ENO. Her roles with the company have included Cherubino, Dorabella, Handel's Sextus, Rosina, Cenerentola, Isolier, Ninetta (*La gazza ladra*) and Suzuki; she created Dolly in Hamilton's *Anna Karenina* in 1981. With Scottish Opera she sang Hänsel, Clori (*Egisto*) and Preziosilla and with the WNO, Dido (*Les Troyens*) and Herodias (*Salome*); in her Covent Garden début (1983) she appeared as the Female Cat (*L'enfant et les sortilèges*). She has also sung in Venice, Bordeaux, Los Angeles, Antwerp and San Diego; her repertory includes Baba the Turk, Ruggiero (*Alcina*), Donna Elvira, Marcellina, Adalgisa, Magdalene and Monteverdi's Nero. She has a superb coloratura technique and is an excellent actress.

H. Canning: 'Della Jones', *Opera*, xli (1990), 1159–64

ELIZABETH FORBES

Jones, Dame Gwyneth (*b* Pontnewynydd, Mon., 7 Nov 1936). Welsh soprano. She studied at the RCM and in Siena and Geneva. Engaged as a mezzo at Zürich in 1962, she made her début as Annina (*Der Rosenkavalier*). After singing Lady Macbeth for the WNO, she joined the Royal Opera in 1963, singing Lady Macbeth and Octavian on tour. Established as a soprano, she made her Covent Garden début in 1964 as Leonore, then sang Leonora (*Il trovatore*), Elisabeth de Valois, Santuzza, Desdemona, Donna Anna, Aida, Tosca, Salome, Chrysothemis, the Marschallin and Sieglinde, her début role at Bayreuth (1966), where she has also sung Eva, Kundry, Elisabeth/Venus, Senta, and Brünnhilde in the 1976 Centenary *Ring*. She sang regularly at the Vienna Staatsoper, in Munich, Paris, Milan, San Francisco, Chicago and the Metropolitan, making her début in 1972 as Sieglinde. Her later repertory included Isolde, Ortrud, the Empress and the Dyer's Wife, Helen (*Die ägyptische Helena*), Electra and Turandot, which she sang with the Royal Opera at Los Angeles (1984). She sang Brünnhilde in the *Ring* at Covent Garden in 1991. Her strong, vibrant voice (which can develop an uncomfortable beat under pressure) and handsome stage presence, together with total emotional and dramatic involvement in her roles, give tremendous excitement to her performances. She was created DBE in 1986.

K. Loveland: 'Gwyneth Jones', *Opera*, xxi (1970), 100–06
A. Blyth: 'Gwyneth Jones', *Gramophone*, l (1972–3), 26
J. Rockwell: 'Gwyneth Jones', *ON*, xxxvii/7 (1972–3), 18–19

ALAN BLYTH

Jones, Inigo (*b* London, bap. 19 July 1573; *d* London, 21 June 1652). English architect and stage designer. He was the son of a London cloth worker; he was probably educated as a painter, and was given considerable stimulus by journeys abroad, to France, Germany and Italy (?1598–1601) and to Copenhagen in 1603. He entered royal service in 1604 when Queen Anne commissioned him to design the scenery for masques. He was festive decorator to the Earl of Salisbury (1606–9) and 'surveyor' to the Prince of Wales, designing his tournaments (1610–12). In 1613 he staged three royal wedding masques in London. After nearly two years in Italy, he became Surveyor of the King's Works in September 1615 to James I, an appointment confirmed

by Charles I in 1626: Jones thus became responsible for the royal building (including the Banqueting House, 1619–22, where masques were performed, and the Cockpit-in-Court Theatre, 1629–31, in Whitehall) and for the staging of court festivities and theatrical performances.

Jones was the most important architect of the English Renaissance and at the same time had a crucial influence on the theatre of the Stuart court. Between 1605 and 1640 he was involved with over 40 productions as stage and costume designer, machinery operator, director and co-author; his (often polemically opposed, but nonetheless fruitful) collaboration with the dramatist Ben Jonson, with the composers Alfonso Ferrabosco the younger, Giovanni Coprario, Robert Johnson the younger, Thomas Campion, Lanier, and William and Henry Lawes, and with choreographers, influenced the masque's development as a theatrical form. The masque, as the Stuarts' means of self-portrayal, depicted their claim to absolute power with primarily visual imagery, marked by Platonic hypostasization. Jones's most important tool was the perspective stage, which ensured an integrated visual effect; after experimenting with the *periaktos* system (1605, Oxford) he designed his own apparatus which illustrated the central theme of the masque, the transformation of chaos into the divinely sanctioned, absolute order, first using a *machina versatilis* (a wall, painted on both sides, rotating on a central pivot), then (possibly by 1611) with a *scena ductilis* (horizontally mobile pieces of scenery, flats and shutters, which ran along grooves in the floor). This transformation scene, perfectly displayed in a design for the anonymous pastorale *Florimene* (1635), was complemented with a scene of relief in the background, and an upper stage suspended above it with a flying gallery for cloud effects and apotheoses (first used in Jonson's *Chloridia*, 1631). He was iconographically close to Giulio Parigi's stage designs for Florentine *inter-*

medi and opera productions. His costume sketches, drawn in a free, spontaneous style, were largely based on models by Jacques Callot, as well as on contemporary iconologies (Ripa) and costume books (Vecellio). His stage art carried English music theatre to its first peak, and helped prepare the ground for its achievements during the time of Purcell and Handel.

See also STAGE DESIGN, §3 (ii); for further illustration see MASQUE.

W. R. Lethaby: 'Inigo Jones and the Theatre', *Architectural Review*, xxxi (1912), 189–90

P. Simpson and C. F. Bell, eds.: *Designs by Inigo Jones for Masques and Plays at Court* (Oxford, 1924)

J. A. Gotch: *Inigo Jones* (London, 1928)

O. Fischel: 'Inigo Jones und der Theaterstil der Renaissance', *Vorträge der Bibliothek Warburg*, ix (1932), 103–35

D. J. Gordon: 'Poet and Architect: the Intellectual Setting of the Quarrel between Ben Jonson and Inigo Jones', *Journal of the Warburg and Courtauld Institutes*, xii (1949), 152–78

J. Lees-Milne: *The Age of Inigo Jones* (London, 1953)

J. Summerson: *Inigo Jones* (Harmondsworth, 1966)

S. McMillin: 'Jonson's Early Entertainments: New Information from Hatfield House', *Renaissance Drama*, new ser., i (1968), 153–60

The King's Arcadia: Inigo Jones and the Stuart Court: a Quatercentenary Exhibition held at the Banqueting House, Whitehall, from July 12th to September 2nd 1973 (London, 1973) [catalogue by J. Harris, S. Orgel and R. Strong]

S. Orgel and R. Strong: *Inigo Jones: the Theatre at the Stuart Court* (London, 1973)

J. Peacock: 'Inigo Jones's Stage Architecture and its Sources', *Art Bulletin*, lxiv/2 (1982), 195–216

J. Orrell: *The Theatres of Inigo Jones and John Webb* (Cambridge, 1985)   MANFRED BOETZKES

Jones, Parry (*b* Blaina, Mon., 14 Feb 1891; *d* London, 26 Dec 1963). Welsh tenor. He studied at the RCM, and with Colli, Scheidemantel and John Coates. He joined the D'Oyly Carte Opera in 1915 and sang with the Carl Rosa Opera Company, 1919–22. He made his Covent Garden début with that company in 1921 as Turiddu, and later sang with the British National Opera and the Covent Garden English companies. He took part in the first English performances of *Wozzeck* (1934), Busoni's *Doktor Faust* (1937) and Hindemith's *Mathis der Maler* (1939), all concert performances for the BBC. From 1949 to 1953 he was a member of the Covent Garden Opera, where he sang such character roles as Shuysky, the Captain (*Wozzeck*) and Bob Boles (*Peter Grimes*).

HAROLD ROSENTHAL/R

Jones, Richard (*b* London, 7 June 1953). English director. After studying at the universities of Hull and London, he directed for the fringe theatre. The award of an Arts Council bursary in 1982 led to work with Scottish Opera. He began to make his reputation with *Mignon* at Wexford (1986), *Carmen* for Opera North (1987) and *Così* for Scottish Opera (1988). With his inaugural staging of Judith Weir's *A Night at the Chinese Opera* (Kent Opera, 1987), and his riotously amusing *Love for Three Oranges* (Opera North, 1988) featuring Dadaesque eccentrics and pantomime grotesques, he established himself as one of the most resourceful directors of his generation. A promising *Ring* cycle he initiated for Scottish Opera, with an irreverent, anarchic *Rheingold* of remarkable perception (the gods' ascent to power represented by a building-block staircase leading nowhere) and a vibrant, colourful *Walküre*, was subsequently abandoned.

BARRY MILLINGTON

Jones, Robert Edmond (*b* Milton, NH, 12 Dec 1887; *d* Milton, 26 Nov 1954). American designer. He graduated from Harvard University (1910), where he remained for two years as an instructor. On a trip to Europe (1913–14), he was much influenced by Max Reinhardt in Berlin, Jacques Coupeau in Paris, and by the work of Adolph Appia and Jaques-Dalcroze at Hellarau. He returned to Europe in 1922 with Kenneth Macgowan; they recorded their impressions in *Continental Stagecraft* (New York, 1923). With Lee Simonson (1888–1967) and Norman Bel Geddes, Jones was responsible for introducing a 'new stagecraft' to America: the fusion of acting, lighting and setting into a dramatic whole. His output over 25 years was prodigious and wide-ranging. His designs for *The Man who Married a Dumb Wife* (1915) for Harley Granville-Barker are said to be the first important, in-digenous expression of the new stagecraft and his *Macbeth* (1921) for Arthur Hopkins created a sensation for its use of expressionism.

Jones designed the first American productions of Schoenberg's *Die glückliche Hand* (1930), Berg's *Wozzeck* (1931) and Stravinsky's *Oedipus rex* (1931), all in Philadelphia, and the première of Douglas Moore's *The Devil and Daniel Webster* (1938, New York). Designs for his last production, *Der fliegende Holländer* (1950), were realized by Charles Elson at the Metropolitan on the occasion of Hans Hotter's début as the Dutchman. Jones's unity of craft elements with a unique style was never a formula but a constant endeavour to realize the rhythm of each production. A simplified realism and poetic use of light were his trademarks. 'When I go to the theatre, I want to get an eyeful,' he wrote.

*

R. E. Jones: *The Dramatic Imagination* (New York, 1941)
R. Pendleton: *The Theatre of Robert Edmond Jones* (Middleton, CT, 1958)

DAVID J. HOUGH

Jones, (James) Sidney (*b* London, 17 June 1861; *d* London, 29 Jan 1946). English composer. His father J. Sidney Jones (1838–1914) studied at Kneller Hall and was a military bandmaster before settling in Leeds and becoming musical director at the Grand Theatre and, from 1887 to 1902, conductor of the Harrogate Municipal Orchestra. The younger Sidney assisted his father in Leeds, played the clarinet in his orchestras and later took to conducting. He was spotted by the theatre producer George Edwardes and first made his name as a composer with the song 'Linger longer, Loo' for the burlesque *Don Juan* (1893). As conductor at the Prince of Wales Theatre he wrote the music for *A Gaiety Girl* (1893), an early musical comedy; it was followed by other stage works, of which *The Geisha* (1896) achieved enormous success not only in Britain but throughout Europe, where its popularity exceeded that of any other British operetta, including *The Mikado*.

Later works could not rival this success, although *San Toy* (1899) almost did so in London. Belonging to the older comic-opera school, Jones resented the extraneous interpolations that were increasingly a feature of London musical productions of the time and struck out on his own. The musical comedy *The Medal and the Maid* and the comic opera *My Lady Molly* were

Sketch by Robert Edmond Jones for 'Der fliegende Holländer', produced by the Metropolitan Opera, New York, 9 November 1950, using Charles Elson's sets realized from Jones's designs; watercolour and ink

agreeably free from such interpolations but achieved less success. The latter especially showed Jones's substantial abilities in the light-opera tradition of Sullivan, German and Liza Lehmann, and Jones was sufficiently fond of the work to revise it later. In 1905 he became conductor at the Empire Theatre, London, and composed some ballets. He also composed music for further musical plays but after *The Happy Day* (1916) went into retirement, feeling out of tune with changing tastes in the popular theatre. His unassuming nature was reflected in his works, particularly *The Geisha*, which is full of charming numbers, its opening chorus in particular being worthy of Sullivan.

See also GEISHA, THE.

all published in vocal score in London around time of original production
A Gaiety Girl (musical comedy, 2, O. Hall and H. Greenbank), London, Prince of Wales, 14 Oct 1893
An Artist's Model (comedy with music, 2, Hall and Greenbank), London, Daly's, 2 Feb 1895
The Geisha (musical play, 2, Hall and Greenbank), London, Daly's, 25 April 1896
A Greek Slave (musical comedy, 2, Hall, Greenbank and A. Ross), London, Daly's, 8 June 1898
San Toy (musical comedy, 2, E. Morton, Greenbank and Ross), London, Daly's, 21 Oct 1899
My Lady Molly (comedy op, 2, G. H. Jessop, P. Greenbank and C. H. Taylor), Brighton, Royal, 11 Aug 1902; London, Terry's, 14 March 1903
The Medal and the Maid (musical comedy, 2, Hall, Taylor, G. Rollitt and P. Rubens), London, Lyric, 25 April 1903
See, See (comic op, 2, C. H. Brookfield and Ross, after F. de Grésac and P. Ferrier: *La troisième lune*), London, Prince of Wales, 20 June 1906, collab. F. E. Tours
King of Cadonia (musical play, 2, F. Lonsdale and Ross), London, Prince of Wales, 3 Sept 1908, collab. F. Rosse
A Persian Princess (musical play, 2, L. Bantock, P. J. Barrow and P. Greenbank), London, Queen's, 27 April 1909, collab. M. Horne
The Girl from Utah (musical play, 2, J. T. Tanner, Ross, P. Greenbank and Rubens), London, Adelphi, 18 Oct 1913, collab. Rubens
The Happy Day (musical play, 2, S. Hicks, Ross and Rubens), London, Daly's, 13 May 1916, collab. Rubens

GänzlBMT
C. A. Davies: 'Sidney Jones', *MO*, lxix (1945–6), 166–7
G. Hughes: *Composers of Operetta* (London, 1962)
R. Traubner: *Operetta: a Theatrical History* (New York, 1983)
ANDREW LAMB

Jones [née Joyner], (**Matilda**) **Sissieretta** ['Black Patti'] (*b* Portsmouth, VA, 5 Jan 1869; *d* Providence, RI, 24 June 1933). American soprano. She studied singing at the Providence Academy of Music and the New England Conservatory in Boston, and privately in London. On 5 April 1888 she made her début at Steinway Hall, New York, and from 1890 to 1895 toured as soloist in the West Indies, Canada, the USA and Europe. She was engaged in 1892 by the Metropolitan Opera to sing Aida, and Sélika in *L'Africaine*, the first black singer to be engaged by the company, but the performances did not take place because the season was cancelled after the house burnt down. In 1896 she became the leading soprano of Black Patti's Troubadours, a newly organized vaudeville company, and she toured internationally with them until 1915. A feature of their shows was the operatic kaleidoscope, comprising arias and scenes from operas, staged and performed by Jones. Her voice was admired for its richness and power. Collections of memorabilia concerning her are in the library of Howard University, Washington, DC, and the Schomburg Center for Research in Black Culture, New York Public Library.

SouthernB
M. A. Majors: *Noted Negro Women* (Chicago, 1893), 228
L. A. Scruggs: *Women of Distinction* (Raleigh, NC, 1893), 325
G. Shirley: 'The Black Performer', ON, xxxv/14 (1970–71), 6–13
E. Southern and J. Wright: 'Sissieretta Jones', *Black Perspective in Music*, iv (1976), 191

Jones, Trevor Morgan (*b* Springhill, Nova Scotia, 13 June 1899). Canadian composer. In Toronto he studied at the conservatory and was a violinist in a visiting American orchestra. In 1923 the orchestra returned to the USA with Jones as pianist. He worked there playing the piano in dance bands, for radio and for vaudeville, and also played in Havana and Finland. In New York he studied composition with Clement Gale and on returning to Canada (1938) gave up his career as a pianist but continued to compose.

Jones's one-act folk opera, *The Broken Ring* (1953), is based on six Nova Scotia ballads from the collection of Helen Creighton. The libretto, by the Halifax writer Donald Wetmore, combines the story of the 1844 Saladin Mutiny off the coast of Nova Scotia with a tale of separated lovers each carrying half a broken ring. The opera was commissioned by the Nova Scotia Opera Association and first performed by them in Halifax on 15 August 1953. In 1974 Jones transcribed the overture for symphonic band. His one-act musical drama *Pictou Landing* (originally called *Scottish Landing*) was first performed by the Nova Scotia Centennial Committee on the Arts in Halifax on 27 November 1967.

EMC ('Broken Ring, The'; S. Willis)
'The Broken Ring', *CBC Times* (26 Feb–3 March 1956)
RUTH PINCOE

Jongen, Léon (Marie Victor Justin) (*b* Liège, 2 March 1884; *d* Brussels, 18 Nov 1969). Belgian composer. He studied at the Liège Conservatory, and in 1913 won the Belgian Prix de Rome. Thereafter he toured the world as a concert pianist. After a period as conductor of the Tonkin Opera, Hanoi (1927–9), he taught at the Brussels Conservatory and was later its director (1939–49). In 1945 he was elected to the Belgian Royal Academy; for a time he was joint rector of the Chapelle Musicale Reine Elisabeth. Jongen's operas demonstrate his fiery temperament. The highly coloured music of *Thomas l'Agnelet*, a story of 17th-century privateers, requires considerable vocal and instrumental forces.

L'Ardennaise, 1909 (action lyrique, 2, Théroigne de Méricourt), unperf.
Le rêve d'une nuit de Noël (féerie populaire, 3, J. F. Fonson), Paris, Champs-Elysées, 18 March 1918
Thomas l'Agnelet, gentilhomme de fortune (roman musical, 4, C. Farrère), Brussels, Monnaie, 14 Feb 1924
Les cinq filles de Benjamin (opérette, 3, L. Payen), unperf.

P. Tinel: 'Notice sur Léon Jongen', *Annuaire de l'Académie royale de Belgique*, cxxxix (1973), 301
D. von Volborth-Danys: *CeBeDeM and its Affiliated Composers* (Brussels, 1977–80)
HENRI VANHULST

Jongleur de Notre-Dame, Le ('The Juggler of Notre Dame'). *Miracle* in three acts by JULES MASSENET to a libretto by Maurice Léna based on the medieval legend as recounted by Anatole France in his collection of stories *L'étui de nacre* (1892); Monte Carlo, Opéra, 18 February 1902.

Le jongleur was the first of the series of Massenet operas that were first performed in Monte Carlo (the remaining six included *Chérubin*, *Thérèse* and *Don Quichotte*). The circumstances leading up to the première are unclear; the composer wrote in his memoirs that it resulted from a chance meeting with the impresario Raoul Gunsbourg, but it seems more likely that Gunsbourg made the first – financially very tempting – approach and that the composer then had to extricate himself from an existing agreement with Albert Carré at the Opéra-Comique, where the work received its first Paris performance two years later. In both cities the title role was taken by Adolphe Maréchal, creator of Julien in Charpentier's *Louise*; in Paris Lucien Fugère enjoyed a great success as Brother Boniface, the abbey cook. *Le jongleur* is unique in Massenet's output in having an exclusively male cast of principals, but in New York (1908) Mary Garden insisted on taking the title role *en travestie*, to Massenet's intense but only silkily expressed disapproval. This practice did not persist. The opera has lapsed from the postwar repertory, even in France, but occasionally surfaces – with considerable success – at festivals.

The setting is the Abbey of Cluny in the 14th century. Outside the Abbey, Jean, an aging and undernourished juggler (tenor), struggles to entertain a crowd more interested in buying vegetables and indulgences. They mock his conjuring and reject his suggestions for improving musical entertainment, insisting on a drinking song. After three verses of the vaguely sacrilegious 'Le vin, c'est Dieu', the Prior (bass) emerges angrily and threatens him with everlasting hellfire. The terrified juggler is told he must give up his trade to be forgiven, and is offered a place in the Abbey. He hesitates, singing rapturously of the freedom he enjoys as a strolling player ('Liberté! c'est elle que mon coeur pour maîtresse a choisi'), but the entry of Boniface (baritone) with supplies of food tips the balance. He enters the Abbey.

The second act is set in the cloister. Monks prepare for the Feast of the Assumption. The musician monk rehearses an anthem, the painter monk decorates a statue of the Virgin, a sculptor monk sculpts, a poet monk composes verses and Boniface peels vegetables. Jean gives thanks for his full stomach ('La cuisine est bon au couvent') but feels out of step with his brothers: he has no trade. The sculptor offers to teach him his skills, provoking a debate between the four artists as to which of their offerings will find most favour with the Virgin. After they have been silenced by the Prior, and have left for the chapel with the new statue, Boniface sings Jean the Legend of the Sage, telling how this most humble of plants concealed the infant Jesus from Herod's armies during the flight into Egypt and thereafter received the Virgin's special blessing.

In the final act Jean steals into the chapel to pay homage to the Virgin the only way he knows how – in song and dance. After a 'Chanson de Guerre' and the 'Pastourelle de Robin et Marion', he dances an energetic bourrée and falls down exhausted. The monks are prevented from interrupting and denouncing him by Boniface. The statue of the Virgin smiles and extends a hand in benediction. Jean dies to the sound of a heavenly choir singing his praises. 'Blessed are the simple,' intones the Prior, 'for they shall see God.'

The overwhelming – in every sense – religious sentiment of *Le jongleur* is saved from mere glueyness by a strain of gentle comedy running through the score. The quartet of quarrelling monks (gently mocked by their music), the more robust humour of Brother Boniface, even Jean's shy self-deprecation, all bring a whiff of astringency to the proceedings. The Prior's closing words could stand as the motto of the 90-minute score, in which Massenet pares down his musical language to its plainest, despite having obviously heard and profited from *Die Meistersinger* and *Parsifal* (the composer monk's music modulates with Wagnerian chromaticism). A 19th-century composer's idea of medieval music, which Massenet studied for the juggler's songs and dances, is not without a certain period charm: viol, chalumeau and portative organ have their place in the orchestra. Motifs are fielded and reminisced without the blatancy sometimes found in early Massenet, and an easily flowing passage in 5/4 neatly suggests how Jean feels out of step with abbey life. But the highlight of the opera, much recorded (notably by Vanni Marcoux), is Boniface's 'La légende de la sauge', one of those moments when Massenet's facility and craftsmanship aspire to – and reach – realms of genius.

RODNEY MILNES

Jonny spielt auf ('Jonny Strikes Up'). *Oper* in two parts by ERNST KRENEK to his own libretto; Leipzig, Neues Theater, 10 February 1927.

Max *a composer*	tenor
Anita *an opera singer*	soprano
Jonny *a negro jazz-band fiddler*	baritone
Daniello *a virtuoso violinist*	baritone
Yvonne *a hotel chambermaid*	soprano
Artists' manager	tenor
Hotel director	tenor
Railway employee	tenor
Policeman 1	tenor
Policeman 2	baritone
Policeman 3	bass

Hotel guests, travellers and audience

Setting A central European city, Paris and the Alps during the mid-1920s

Jonny is one of the most characteristic products of the Weimar Republic, embodying the mythology and fashions of its time and reflecting a growing conviction that music should be entertaining and relevant. Its overwhelming popular success established it as a model for a spate of 'Zeitopern', although it is fantastic and escapist compared with the more realistically ordinary settings of Hindemith. The plot, involving an opera, is laden with symbolism presenting contradictions in psychology, lifestyle and temperament between the old world and the new along an East–West axis. Although the opera is largely set in Paris (the work is Krenek's response to his experiences there in the early 1920s), it is the image of America that focusses European longing for a new land of freedom and promise. *Jonny* appeared to indicate a change of direction for Krenek, but in fact its kaleidoscopic nature draws on earlier compositions such as the jazz elements of *Der Sprung* and the *Weltschmerz* of the 1925 Rilke settings. Krenek, however, objected to the label 'jazz opera' for *Jonny* as jazz was idiomatically superimposed rather than absorbed in any integral way. His usage is closer to that of Milhaud and Stravinsky than to Weill's. Krenek's eclecticism, particularly the return to tonality and Puccinian lyri-

'*Jonny spielt auf*
(Krenek), Part 1, scene iii
(a hotel corridor in Paris):
scene from the original
production at the Neues
Theater, Leipzig, 10
February 1927

cism, reveals his sceptical attitude towards the role assigned to contemporary music by the Second Viennese School.

The original cast, conducted by Gustav Brecher, included Paul Beinert as Max, Fanny Eleve as Anita, Max Spilcker as Jonny, Theodor Horand as Daniello and Clare Schulthess as Yvonne. In its first season it was produced at 42 opera houses, including the Metropolitan, and performed 421 times in Germany alone, a record unmatched in a single season. By 1929 the libretto had been translated into 14 languages. Productions were lavish, with many special effects such as real cars and trains and film projection. The opera was eventually revived in Florence in 1963, and eight other productions have followed, notably the first British production, an English version by Opera North in 1984.

PART 1.i *On top of a glacier in the Alps* Max, a melancholic intellectual composer (either a self-portrait of the younger Krenek or a caricature of Webern), meets Anita, a glamorous singer who has performed a leading role in one of his operas. The bland Romantic clichés of Max's hymn to the glacier ally him with Oswald Spengler's apocalyptic 'abendländische Kultur'. Anita finds the atmosphere of these rarefied heights sterile and morbid and Max is obliged to rescue her, significantly neglecting to press on to the summit.

1.ii *Anita's house in the city* Anita has melted the heart of her 'Gletschermensch' and they have been having an affair. He presents her with the manuscript of his latest opera, which she is about to sing in Paris. They rehearse a sentimental aria 'Ich suchte mein Heim in der Träume Land' ('I sought my home in dreamland'). A car arrives and she almost forgets her banjo, a vital prop for the opera.

1.iii *A hotel corridor in Paris* Yvonne is tidying Daniello's room, to a shimmy in a quick 'gramophone tempo', when Jonny, the symbolic manifestation of the new man free from sexual and musical inhibitions with whom she is in love, arrives with his golden saxophone; he seems, however, more interested in Daniello's Amati violin. Daniello, a virtuoso womanizer, returns thronged by admirers and Yvonne joins them. Daniello persuades Anita to invite him to her room. Meanwhile Jonny steals the precious violin and hides it in Anita's banjo case.

1.iv *The following morning* Anita prepares to depart for home, leaving Daniello her ring as a keepsake, but taking Yvonne, dismissed after the theft, as her maid. Daniello, his ego bruised at losing both Anita and the violin, persuades Yvonne to deliver the ring to Max, ostensibly as payment following a bet. Jonny resigns from his employment in Paris to pursue the banjo case. The artists' manager arrives and offers Anita a contract to tour America.

PART 2.i *Anita's house that evening* Max has received a telegram from Anita and longs for her return. Her failure to arrive as promised prompts a tortured psychological monologue, which parodies the expressionism of Schoenberg's *Erwartung*.

2.ii *The next morning* Anita finally arrives, altered by the Parisian experience, and greets Max nervously. The 'gift' of Anita's ring from Daniello confirming that she has been unfaithful badly upsets Max, who rushes off. Jonny reclaims the violin with Yvonne's help and celebrates triumphantly with a cross between a negro spiritual and a Lutheran chorale.

2.iii *The glacier* The mysterious solace of the mountains induces in Max thoughts of suicide as he realizes that nature can no longer provide him with sufficient inspiration. Spurred on by the singing glacier, reiterating its message in canon, he realizes he must respond to life itself if his music is to be vital. Just then a broadcast of Anita singing the aria from his opera is relayed by loudspeaker from the hotel terrace below. Admitting the extent of his need for Anita's life-force, Max resolves to seek his salvation in her. Significantly, the ensuing item, to the great relief of the audience, is Jonny's jazz band, starring the stolen violin, which Daniello, a guest at the hotel, recognizes. The contrast of styles represents the past and future of music in which the new appropriates the best of the European tradition in the form of Daniello's violin.

2.iv *A city street* Jonny is on the run and heading for America; in his haste he drops his train ticket.

2.v *The railway station* The discovery of Jonny's lost ticket leads the police to the station where Max and Anita are also about to leave for America. Jonny places the violin among Max's luggage and Max is arrested instead. Assuming Anita and Yvonne to be accessories to the crime, Daniello tries to prevent them from leaving but falls on to the track and is crushed by the oncoming train.

2.vi *Outside the police station* With Jonny's help Max escapes by car.

2.vii *At the railway station* Max and Anita are reunited and with Yvonne and the manager they board the train, singing optimistically in a simple tonal and homophonic idiom, punctuated by the strains of the violin from Jonny, straddling the revolving globe on the station clock. In striking up the new note it is he who leads the people in the dance towards a new life where nothing is to be taken too seriously.

* * *

The tremendous success of *Jonny* put Krenek firmly at the forefront of European culture between the wars. This was not least because as sheer entertainment it created an unprecedented impact on the contemporary operatic scene, but also because it exposed key issues about musical modernism and brought them to public attention. The extent to which the work may be able to transcend its original historical context and continue to succeed in revival could depend on whether the questions it raises about the relative validity of different sorts of music remain as pertinent to future audiences as they did to Krenek himself at the time. There is, however, little doubt that the expertly crafted eclecticism and period flavour of the opera will continue to attract admirers.   CHARLOTTE PURKIS

Jonson, Ben (*b* London, 1572 or 1573; *d* London, 6 Aug 1637). English dramatist and masque librettist. Among his contemporaries he was second in repute only to Shakespeare. Best known as a dramatist, Jonson wrote plays from about 1598 to the early 1630s for a variety of London theatrical troupes. As a librettist his chief claim to fame rests on his development of the masque: he wrote more than 25 court masques between 1605 and 1631. He greatly lengthened the fable, or plot, beyond the brief prologue speeches of early Tudor times, expanded the cast of mythological and allegorical personages, varied the metrical shapes and contours of the lyrics and significantly amplified the overall design by the introduction of an antimasque or two to complement the main masque. Thus he elaborated the form from a simple plotless pageant to a complex symbolic drama in which the ideal and its opposite could be seen and measured against each other.

For none of his masques has a complete vocal score been preserved. Nicholas Lanier was reported in the libretto of *Lovers made Men* (1617) to have set and sung the entire masque in 'Stylo recitativo', and he probably also composed the recitative items so described in *The Vision of Delight* (1617). Arne's all-sung 'masque' of 1771, *The Fairy Prince*, was based on Jonson's masque *Oberon* (1611).

The most celebrated operatic adaptation from Jonson's plays is the libretto which Stefan Zweig wrote for Richard Strauss: *Die schweigsame Frau* (1935, Dresden), after *Epicoene, or The Silent Woman* (1609); the libretto alters the original considerably, moving the period to the 18th century. *Epicoene* also inspired Salieri's *Angiolina* (1800). Another play, *Volpone, or The Fox* (1605–6), was the source of operas of the same title by Norman Demuth (1949), George Antheil (1953) and Francis Burt (1960). Elgar, at the time of his death, was planning an opera to be called *The Spanish Lady*, derived from Jonson's *The Devil is an Ass* (1616), with lyrics from other Jonson plays and poems added to the libretto. Jonson's verse also appears in the arias and choruses of Vaughan Williams's *Sir John in Love* (1929).

See also MASQUE.

*

A. Mathis: 'Stefan Zweig and Richard Strauss', *ML*, xxv (1944), 163–76, 226–45

A. J. Sabol: *Songs and Dances for the Stuart Masque* (Providence, RI, 1959, enlarged 2/1978)

——: *A Score for 'Lovers made Men': a Masque by Ben Jonson* (Providence, RI, 1963)

D. Fuller: 'The Jonsonian Masque and its Music', *ML*, liv (1973), 440–52

M. Chan: *Music in the Theatre of Ben Jonson* (London, 1980)

P. M. Young: 'Elgar and The Spanish Lady', *MT*, cxxvii (1986), 272–6   ARTHUR JACOBS, ANDREW J. SABOL

Joplin, Scott (*b* nr Marshall, TX, or Shreveport, LA, 24 Nov 1868; *d* New York, 1 April 1917). American composer. The circumstances of his training and early career remain obscure, but by 1896 he had settled in Sedalia, Missouri. There, after studying at the George R. Smith College for Negroes to improve his musical technique, he began to issue, with the publisher John Stark, the numerous piano rags on which his reputation as the 'king of ragtime' largely rests. Ragtime had been a predominantly improvised folk genre, but Joplin wished to elevate it to 'classical' status – a goal he pursued energetically throughout his life – and the idea of a ragtime opera was an early obsession. Almost operatic is *The Ragtime Dance* of 1899, a six-minute display of ragtime dance steps with sung narration by a 'caller' (after the fashion of square dances) and an orchestral accompaniment.

In the wake of the success of *Maple Leaf Rag* (1899), Joplin married and moved (1901) to St Louis. There he composed *A Guest of Honor* (1903), a 'ragtime opera' in one act comprising 12 numbers, all rags. He formed the Scott Joplin Drama Company in April of that year, presenting a single performance of the opera in St Louis before taking it on tour. The renamed Scott Joplin Ragtime Opera Company, however, quickly collapsed, and the touring production was probably heard only in four small Midwestern towns. Stark proved reluctant to publish so ambitious a project, and the work is now lost. As late as 1950 there were still 'many people' who remembered the St Louis performance, but no reliable account of the opera's plot or subject has survived, though the titles of two numbers are known.

Joplin led an itinerant life until 1907, when he moved to New York with the express purpose of publishing and producing his next opera, the three-act *Treemonisha* (1908–11, orchestrated 1915). Unable to find either publisher or backers, he brought out the piano score (New York, 1911) at his own expense (attracting a single, laudatory review), and likewise mounted a poorly received concert performance with piano accompaniment. Three numbers were revised and issued separately in 1913 and 1915. *Treemonisha* was not staged, however, until 28 January 1972, in Atlanta; it is published in *The Complete Works of Scott Joplin* (vol.ii, New York, 2/1981), but the original orchestration is lost.

Joplin refrained from labelling *Treemonisha* a 'ragtime opera'. The style of both text (by the composer) and music is an uneasy but effective combination of ragtime and operetta. The identification of ragtime as a pop genre and Joplin as a 'minority' composer has tended to obscure the fact that *Treemonisha* is the earliest musically significant opera by an American (apart from Gottschalk's one-act *Escenas campestres*, 1860), and the earliest in an identifiably modern idiom.

In autumn 1916 Joplin, already seriously debilitated by his final illness, notified the New York *Age* that he had just completed a 'music comedy drama' entitled *If*; but this, if it existed, has vanished without trace.

See also TREEMONISHA.

*

SouthernB
'A Musical Novelty', *American Musician* [New York], xxvii/12 (1911), 7–8
R. Blesh and H. Janis: *They all Played Ragtime* (New York, 1950, 4/1971)
A. W. Reed: *The Life and Works of Scott Joplin* (diss., U. of North Carolina, 1973)
T. Waldo: *This is Ragtime* (New York, 1976)
J. Haskins and K. Benson: *Scott Joplin* (Garden City, NY, 1978)
A. W. Reed: 'Scott Joplin: Pioneer', *Ragtime: its History, Composers, and Music*, ed. J. E. Hasse (New York, 1985), 117–36
E. A. Berlin: 'On the Trail of *A Guest of Honor*: in Search of Scott Joplin's Lost Opera', *A Celebration of American Music: Words and Music in Honor of H. Wiley Hitchcock* (Ann Arbor, 1990), 51–65
ANDREW STILLER

Jordan, Irene (*b* Birmingham, AL, 25 April 1919). American soprano. She studied at Judson College and later in New York with Clytie Mundy. After making her Metropolitan début as a mezzo-soprano in the role of Mallika in *Lakmé* (1946), she studied as a soprano (1949–52). She sang at the Chicago Lyric Theatre (1954) as Donna Elvira and Micaëla and with the New York City Opera (1957); she returned to the Metropolitan in 1957, singing the Queen of Night. Her roles included Aida, Santuzza, Butterfly, Leonore (*Fidelio*), and Lady Macbeth. She had a large and flexible voice of great expressiveness.
RICHARD LeSUEUR

Jörn, Karl (*b* Riga, 5 Jan 1873; *d* Denver, 19 Dec 1947). Latvian tenor. He studied with Jacobs Ress in Berlin and in 1896 made his début in *Martha* at Freiburg. Appearances at Zürich and Hamburg led to his engagement at the Berlin royal opera in 1902, where he remained until 1908. Covent Garden first heard him in a British double première, in 1906, of Poldini's one-act *Vagabund und Prinzessin* and Cornelius's *Der Barbier von Bagdad*. In the two following seasons he sang Walther in *Die Meistersinger*; his Loge in *Das Rheingold* was considered one of the best ever heard. He joined the Metropolitan in 1908, proving his adaptability in Mozart and Wagner, Massenet (*Manon*) and Mascagni (*Cavalleria rusticana*) and in a special performance of Beethoven's Ninth Symphony under Toscanini. He also sang Jeník in the American première of *The Bartered Bride* (1909). Taking American citizenship in 1916, he retired from singing to develop an invention for mineral-divining; then, losing his fortune, he returned in 1928, joining Johanna Gadski's touring company and singing (with great success) his first Tristan and Siegfried. He taught in New York and Denver, and gave a final performance as Lohengrin shortly before his death. His sturdy voice and lyric style can be heard in many recordings; they cover a wide repertory and include two of the earliest made of complete operas, *Faust* and *Carmen*, both recorded in 1908 with Emmy Destinn.
J. B. STEANE

***Jōruri*.** Opera in three acts by MINORU MIKI to a libretto by COLIN GRAHAM after the puppet plays of Monzaemon Chikamatsu; St Louis, Loretto Hilton, 30 May 1985.

Jōruri is a narrative style of singing used in puppet or kabuki plays. Awa-no-Shōjō (bass), a blind master of *jōruri* singing and leader of a puppet company, has a devoted young wife, Otane (soprano), whom he once saved from the hands of a sadistic magistrate at the price of his eyesight. She, however, is in love with a young puppeteer, Yosuke (baritone), though they have not acknowledged it to each other. Yosuke carves a female head for a new *jōruri* play, which turns out to be an exact likeness of Otane. At the rehearsal of the play the young pair start a quarrel and by so doing reveal their true feelings to each other, while Shōjō becomes aware of their devotion by feeling the head which Yosuke has carved. The master writes a new *jōruri* play in which the best solution is suggested. Thereupon the young lovers start on their pilgrimage to a sacred waterfall, into which they disappear, while the old master is left to narrate their story and to mourn.

The music is a remarkable mixture of European and Japanese styles, with lyrically flowing melodic lines supported by a Western orchestra with three Japanese instruments added: shamisen, koto and shakuhachi.
MASAKATA KANAZAWA

Josefstadt [Theater in der Josefstadt]. Theatre in Vienna, opened in 1788 and used for opera during the first half of the 19th century. *See* VIENNA, §4 (ii).

***Joseph*.** *Drame mêlé de chants* in three acts by ETIENNE-NICOLAS MÉHUL to a libretto by Alexandre Duval after *Genesis* xxxvii–xlvi; Paris, Opéra-Comique (Théâtre Feydeau), 17 February 1807.

Although favoured by the pharaoh, Joseph (*haute-contre*), known in Egypt as Cléophas, misses his family and homeland. When famine brings his brothers there, he grants them his protection and hospitality. They fail to recognize him and this allows Joseph to test whether their remorse over selling him into slavery is genuine. When Ruben (tenor) mentions that their father is nearby, Joseph decides to go to the Israelites' camp outside Memphis. First he meets Siméon (tenor), now almost mad with feelings of guilt, and becomes convinced of his brother's repentance. The Israelites' morning prayers are heard in the distance. Joseph is so overcome by seeing his youngest brother Benjamin (soprano) and then his father Jacob (baritone) again that he almost reveals his identity; but, warned by Utobal (baritone), he has to leave to intercede with the pharaoh: Joseph's enemies have criticized his generosity towards foreigners. During Joseph's absence Siméon confesses his crime to Jacob. At first Jacob denounces him and his guilty brothers, but Benjamin and later Joseph (still incognito) plead for them. Jacob begins to relent; Joseph reveals his identity and forgives them. The pharaoh has granted them sanctuary on Joseph's request, and all thank God for his goodness and mercy.

In writing *Joseph*, Duval and Méhul sought to capitalize on two current French interests: an Egyptian craze, partly the result of Napoleon's campaign there (1798–9), and a marked religious revival, partly in reaction to the anti-clericalism of the Revolution. The result was Méhul's longest-lasting and most widely performed opera. Duval's libretto is intentionally austere. Unlike other contemporary theatrical treatments of the subject, it includes no love intrigue. The moral rectitude of Joseph and the God-fearing attitudes of all the Israelites

Costumes of Jacob (sung by Solié, right) and Benjamin (sung by Anne-Marie Jeanne Gavaudan) in Act 3 scene vi of the original production of Méhul's 'Joseph' at the Opéra-Comique (Théâtre Feydeau), 17 February 1807; engraving from A. Martinet, 'La petite galerie dramatique', plate 92

are constantly emphasized. Even Siméon's remorse and Joseph's forgiveness of his brothers are marked strongly by religious principles.

As the topic is unique among Méhul operas, so too is the score: *Joseph* is an atypical work. The religious atmosphere is strongest in the prayer chorus 'Dieu d'Israël! père de la nature'; here the virtually unaccompanied voices (the held notes in the trumpets and horns provide minimal support), the *alla breve* time signature, the homophonic, hymn-like texture and, in the last section, the restrained use of imitative phrase openings all contribute to a style suitable for a *cantique*. The prominence of choruses and ensembles generally lends emphasis to collective response rather than to individual concerns. Significantly, Méhul avoided the normal number of major solo *airs*. Only Joseph has one ('Champs paternel'), and its style is noble and sustained, not flamboyantly virtuoso. The other solo pieces are two *romances*, one for Joseph ('A peine au sortir de l'enfance') and one for Benjamin ('Ah! lorsque la mort trop cruelle'), in which the characters' innocence and essential goodness are reflected in the choice of the simplest type of *air*. As a further representation of the *stile antico*, Méhul wrote more strongly contrapuntal music than was his norm; the themes and motifs at times take on a quasi-fugal character, as in the overture and

the final section of the Act 2 finale. One detail of local colour is the presence of the tuba curva for the triumphal march in the latter. The instrument, invented during the early 1790s ostensibly following antique models, had been used in Revolutionary outdoor *fêtes*; its appearance in *Joseph* was one of its last.

Admired for the restrained treatment of the biblical subject, *Joseph* did not initially enjoy great popular success in Paris. Nevertheless, it was awarded in 1810 the prize, given every ten years, for the best work written for the Opéra-Comique (the prize-money was never delivered), and was frequently revived there and performed widely elsewhere as an opera or as an oratorio in the 19th and early 20th centuries.

M. ELIZABETH C. BARTLET

Joseph II (*b* Vienna, 13 March 1741; *d* Vienna, 20 Feb 1790). Holy Roman Emperor, Archduke of Austria, first son of Maria Theresa and Francis of Lorraine. As a patron of music and supervisor of the court theatres in Vienna, he helped to shape the city's operatic life. During the first part of his long reign he shared power with Maria Theresa, but even before her death in 1780 he exercised considerable influence over operatic policy. Especially fond of the young Antonio Salieri, Joseph supported him with commissions and recommendations from 1770 onwards.

In the mid-1770s Joseph dismissed the impresario who was struggling to present Italian opera in the court theatres, and transformed the Burgtheater into a national theatre for the performance of spoken plays in German. In 1778 he organized a troupe of German singers to perform Singspiels there and it was for this troupe that Mozart wrote *Die Entführung aus dem Serail* in 1782. Claiming that he found *opera seria* boring (and reluctant to pay for the more costly singers), Joseph assembled in 1783 one of the best *opera buffa* troupes in Europe, together with a skilful librettist, Lorenzo da Ponte. Composers commissioned to write for the company included Salieri, Mozart, Paisiello and Martín y Soler. Through his chamberlain Count Rosenberg he supervised the troupe closely, making important decisions about theatre finances, personnel and repertory. He thus helped to create the environment in which it was possible for Mozart and Salieri to produce some of their greatest operas. Both Da Ponte and the tenor Michael Kelly relate stories in their memoirs about Joseph and opera. Joseph is alleged to have thought that *Die Entführung* contained 'too many notes' and that *Don Giovanni* was 'too tough for the teeth' of his Viennese.

R. Payer von Thurn: *Joseph II. als Theaterdirektor* (Vienna, 1920)
O. Michtner: *Das alte Burgtheater als Opernbühne von der Einführung des deutschen Singspiels (1778) bis zum Tod Kaiser Leopolds II. (1792)* (Vienna, 1970)
F. Hadamowsky: *Die Josefinische Theaterreform und das Spielzeit 1776/77 des Burgtheaters* (Vienna, 1978)   JOHN A. RICE

Josephs, Wilfred (*b* Newcastle upon Tyne, 24 July 1927). English composer. After early musical studies with Arthur Milner he took a degree in dental surgery and worked as a dental officer during his two years' military service. He then studied at the GSM with Alfred Nieman (1954–6) and later with Max Deutsch in Paris. After his Requiem won first place in the First International Composing Competition of the city of Milan and La Scala in 1963, he abandoned dentistry for full-time composition.

Josephs's instrumental works include ten symphonies and 15 concertos, and he has composed much music for television. Early stage works include *The Nottingham Captain* (1962), a morality for narrator, voices and seven instruments, to a text by Arnold Wesker; *Pathelio* (1963), an opera-entertainment with libretto by Edward Marsh; *The King of the Coast* (1962–7), a children's musical with libretto by Gwen Marsh which won a prize in 1967; and *The Appointment* (1968), a television opera commissioned by the BBC with libretto by Bernard Kops. He has composed two children's operas for the Harrogate Festival based on Lewis Carroll's *Alice* books, for which he has written his own librettos: *Through the Looking Glass*, 1977–8, and *Alice in Wonderland*, 1985–8.

The full-length opera *Rebecca* (1981–3) was commissioned by Opera North, Edward Marsh's libretto being closely based on Daphne du Maurier's novel. The opera was enthusiastically received at its première in 1983 at Leeds, and was sold out for all performances that season. It was revived in 1988. Josephs's eclectic score plays for the most part a supportive, illustrative role; but taut construction, sympathetic vocal writing and the aptness of musical imagery contributed much to *Rebecca*'s popular success.

See also REBECCA.

HUGO COLE

Josif, Enriko (*b* Belgrade, 1 April 1924). Yugoslav composer of Jewish origin. He graduated from the Academy of Music in Belgrade in 1954 and was professor of composition there, 1957–89. His compositions are robust in character and tend to use the forms and sounds of past ages, expressed in modern musical language. *Smrt Stevana Dečanskog* ('The Death of Stevan Dečanski', 1956), a collection of motets for reciter, soloist, choir and chamber orchestra, was originally composed for Jovan Sterija Popović's drama of the same title, which deals with the sad fate of the 14th-century Serbian king. Later Josif extended and reworked it for stage performance as the dramatic chronicle *Stevan Dečanski*, bringing it close to the forms of total theatre and scenic oratorio (Belgrade, 7 October 1970). It uses Serbian medieval songs, and texts by Stevan Dečanski and Grigorije Camblak; it is scored as a melodrama including melodic recitative and arioso, with a reciter, sung and spoken chorus and orchestra. Characteristic of the composer's output, it combines religious theatre with modern theatre and comprises 22 parts ('Lamentatione', 'Fanfare', 'Danza', 'Ballatta', 'Organum', 'Salmodia', 'Motetto finale' etc.). Josif has also composed a ballet, other theatre music and film music.

*

V. Peričić: *Muzički stvaraoci u Srbiji* [Musical Creators in Serbia] (Belgrade, 1969)

ROKSANDA PEJOVIĆ

Joteyko, Tadeusz (*b* Poczujki, nr Kiev, 1 April 1872; *d* Cieszyn, 20 Aug 1932). Polish composer. He studied composition with Noskowski at the Warsaw Conservatory (1891–5). From 1900 to 1902 he was a cellist in the Wielki Theatre orchestra in Warsaw, his only direct link with opera performance. He worked as a choral conductor all his life, as well as conducting the Warsaw Philharmonic from 1914 to 1918, and from 1914 also taught at the conservatory. Joteyko's works are deeply rooted in the Polish 19th-century tradition of Moniuszko and Żeleński. The music has a more modern stamp, however, with broader tonal relations, chromati-

cism and partial through-composition, yet also including Polish dance rhythms. Except in the two earliest works, the subjects derive from Polish history; this and its simple dramatic music made *Zygmunt August* Joteyko's only really successful opera, which was widely performed in Poland before World War II.

librettos by the composer, and first performed at Warsaw, Wielki Theatre, unless otherwise stated

Rybacy [Fishermen] op.35, before 1919, unperf.

Grajek [The Folk Musician] op.31 (2, after H. Sienkiewicz: *Organista z Ponikły*), 23 Nov 1919

Zygmunt August op.33 (5, after L. Rydel), 29 Aug 1925, vs (Warsaw, 1929)

Królowa Jadwiga [Queen Jadwiga] op.53 (prol., 4), 7 Sept 1928, rev. 1929; excerpts, vs (Warsaw, 1929)

Jan Kiliński op.57, 1931 (4, Joteyko and A. Oppman), unperf.

*

M. Gliński: 'Zygmunt August, opera narodowa T. Joteyki', *Muzyka* (1925), no.10, pp.21–5

A. Wieniawski: 'Zygmunt August, opera w 5 aktach T. Joteyki', *Wiadomości muzyczne* (1925), nos.5–6, pp.148–51

ZOFIA CHECHLIŃSKA

Joubert, John (**Pierre Herman**) (*b* Cape Town, 20 March 1927). British composer of South African origin. He studied in London at the RAM (1946–50), then lectured and taught at the universities of Hull (1950–62) and Birmingham (1962–86), where he eventually became reader in music. Joubert's music is predominantly tonal and makes resourceful use of traditional processes. His operas reveal him as a master of large-scale musical architecture and a fine contrapuntist with a considerable lyrical gift, able to communicate clearly and directly with non-specialist audiences. Wilfrid Mellers's description of Joubert's music as being 'rooted in the conventions of the classical baroque' applies equally to abstract and dramatic works. His operas are typically divided into arias, duets and ensembles, with a connective tissue of arioso recitative. He frequently makes use of themes or intervals to stand for certain attributes of personality or character, while in *Silas Marner* (1961) and *Under Western Eyes* (1969) there are extended interludes in which the orchestra explores and develops the music of preceding scenes.

Joubert's choice of operatic subjects reflects his concern for humanity and his belief in the need for tolerance, understanding and forgiveness. Thus *In the Drought* (1956) tells the story of an erring wife harshly condemned by the Dutch Reformed Church; *Silas Marner* deals with the 'redemption by love' of a social outcast who only loves gold; and *Under Western Eyes* is about a revolutionary student who betrays a colleague and is driven by conscience to confess his crime and be punished for it. The children's opera *The Quarry* (1965) is concerned with man's need for desolate places and warns against the destruction of natural resources.

Antigone op.11 (radio op, 4 scenes, R. Trickett, after Sophocles), BBC, 21 July 1954

In the Drought op.17 (1, A. Wood), Johannesburg, 20 Oct 1956; London, 13 Dec 1959

Silas Marner op.31 (3, Trickett, after G. Eliot), Cape Town, 20 May 1961; London, 10 Dec 1961

The Quarry op.50 (op for young players, 1, D. Holbrook), London, 25 March 1965, excerpts, vs (London, 1967)

Under Western Eyes op.51 (3, C. Cliffe, after J. Conrad), London, St Pancras Town Hall, 29 May 1969, vs (London, 1969)

The Prisoner op.76 (children's op, 2, S. Tunnicliffe, after L. Tolstoy: *Dorogo stoit*), Barnet, 16 May 1973

The Wayfarers op.98 (op for young people, 2, Tunnicliffe, after G. Chaucer), Huntingdon, 4 April 1984

E. Chisholm: 'John Joubert's "Silas Marner"', *MT*, cii (1961), 550–56

W. Mellers: 'John Joubert and the Blessed City', *MT*, cv (1964), 814–17

M. Rose and others: 'Birth of an Opera', *Music in Education*, xxviii (1964), 269–70; xxix (1965), 23–5, 79–80, 132, 178 [on *The Quarry*]

E. Bradbury: 'Joubert's "Under Western Eyes"', *Opera*, xx (1969), 391–3

J. Joubert: 'Under Western Eyes', *MT*, cx (1969), 470–73

HUGO COLE

Joueur, Le. Opera by Sergey Prokofiev, originally given in French; *see* GAMBLER, THE.

Journet, Françoise (*b* Lyons; *d* Paris, 1720). French soprano. She sang at the Lyons opera for three or four years, moving to Paris shortly before 1700. The Parfaicts (MS, *F-Pn*) record her as singing Mélisse in the première of Destouches' *Amadis de Grèce* (1699), a role she repeated in 1711. At first she was not well received by the public, but was encouraged to persevere by Mlle Desmatins, with whom she seems to have alternated in the title role of Desmarets and Campra's *Iphigénie en Tauride*. She subsequently alternated with Mlle Armand as Clorinde in the first revival of Campra's *Tancrède* (1707), having previously appeared as Iole to Desmatins' Dejanira in Marais' *Alcide* (1705).

Journet created the title role in Marais' *Sémélé* (1709) and Ilione in Campra's *Idoménée* (1712) and sang in Lully revivals: as Hermione (*Cadmus*, 1711), Angélique (*Roland*, 1716), Io (*Isis*, 1717) and Stheneboea (*Bellérophon*, 1718). She took Polyxena in the only revival of Lully and Collasse's *Achille et Polyxène* (1712) and twice sang the title role in Destouches' *Issé* (1708 and 1719) and in Collasse's *Thétis et Pélée* (1708 and 1712). She repeated the title role of *Iphigénie en Tauride* in the 1711 revival and surpassed herself in the famous 1719 revival. The same year, she was the heroine in the revival of Marais' *Alcyone*. When she died, her roles were taken over by Antier.

She was said to have beauty of voice, nobility of presence and a particular personal fascination. Her tender, moving eloquence of gesture, combined with a majestic deportment, were recorded in a famous full-length portrait by Raoux. Her duets with Thévenard were apparently much admired.

A. Pougin: *Un ténor à l'Opéra: Pierre Jélyotte et les chanteurs de son temps* (Paris, 1905), 46–7

PHILIP WELLER

Journet, Marcel (*b* Grasse, 25 July 1867; *d* Vittel, 25 Sept 1933). French bass. He reportedly studied singing in Paris and made his operatic début at Béziers in 1891 in *La favorite*. He sang at La Monnaie, 1894–1900, and then was based in Paris, appearing both at the Opéra and at the Opéra-Comique, where he sang in the French première of Puccini's *La bohème* (1898). He made his Covent Garden début on 10 July 1897 as the Duke of Mendoza in d'Erlanger's *Inès Mendo*. That season he sang the Landgrave in a French version of *Tannhäuser*; he returned regularly until 1907 and again in 1927 and 1928. He was engaged at the Metropolitan Opera, 1900–08 (début as Ramfis on 22 December), and then sang at the Opéra until 1931. He appeared frequently in other centres, including Monte Carlo, Buenos Aires, Chicago, Madrid and Barcelona, and was heard regularly at La Scala, 1917–27, where on 1 May 1924 he created Simon Magus in Boito's posthumous *Nerone*. Endowed with a powerful, resonant

Marcel Journet as Klingsor in Wagner's 'Parsifal'

voice with a range which allowed him to sing such baritone parts as Tonio and Scarpia, he had a large repertory of French and Italian roles and many Wagnerian ones including Klingsor, Hans Sachs, Wotan, Titurel and Gurnemanz.

GV (R. Celletti; J. P. Kenyon and R. Vegeto)

HAROLD BARNES

Jouy, (Victor-Joseph-)Etienne de (*b* Jouy-en-Josas, nr Versailles, 12 Sept 1764; *d* St-Germain-en-Laye, 4 Sept 1846). French librettist. When only 17 he travelled to French Guiana as a sub-lieutenant, and later he served in India for three years as an artillery officer. Returning to France in 1790, he was at once caught up in the turmoil of the Revolution. He took part in the early campaigns, but eventually decided that there was no future for him in the army and retired, devoting himself to literature. As a dramatist he was successful both in light comedy interspersed with songs and in tragedy. In the latter he cleverly combined a traditional technique with a readiness to follow the French fashion for widening the scope of the genre by treating such themes as *Tippo-Saeb*. *Julien dans les Gaules*, like Alexandre Soumet's *Norma* (the basis of Bellini's opera), contrived to satisfy both convention and the demand for novelty by showing ancient Romans in Gaul.

The transitional nature of Jouy's drama, which may be seen as belonging to the long evolution from Voltaire's reforms to the advent of full-blown Romanticism with Dumas *père* and Victor Hugo, is also reflected in the librettos he devised. Spontini's *Milton* (1804), though called an opera, is little more than a *comédie-vaudeville*. Jouy's next collaboration with Spontini, *La vestale* (1807), was a sensation with its beguiling blend of restraint and high emotion, and *Fernand Cortez* (1809), said to have been written to glorify Napoleon, is set in Mexico, with impressive scenes in a temple and a mausoleum. Cherubini's *Les abencérages*, after Chateaubriand, is set in 15th-century Grenada. In Catel's *Les bayadères* (1810) the characters are once again temple maidens, this time in India, and for Méhul he wrote *Les amazones*. Towards the end of his career Jouy was called upon for the French revision of Rossini's *Mosè* and for the libretto of *Guillaume Tell*. The reprints of each of the librettos in his *Oeuvres complètes* (xviii-xxi; Paris, 1823–8) are preceded and followed by informative commentaries by the author. Jouy was elected to the Académie Française in 1815.

Milton (with A. M. Dieulafoy), Spontini, 1804; *La vestale* (tragédie lyrique), Spontini, 1807; *Le mariage par imprudence* (oc), M. P. Dalvimare, 1809; *Fernand Cortez, ou La conquête du Mexique* (tragédie lyrique, with J. A. d'Esmenard), Spontini, 1809; *Les bayadères*, Catel, 1810; *Les amazones, ou La fondation de Thèbes*, Méhul, 1811; *Les aubergistes de qualité* (oc), Catel, 1812; *Les abencérages, ou L'étendard de Grenade* (after F. R. de Chateaubriand), Cherubini, 1813; *Pélage, ou Le roi et la paix*, Spontini, 1814; *Zirphile et fleur de myrthe, ou Cent ans en un jour* (opéra-féerie, with N. Lefebvre), Catel, 1818; *Les courses de Newmarket* (oc, with M. Merle), J. Strunz, 1818; *Moïse et Pharaon* [Fr. version of *Mosè in Egitto*] (with L. Balocchi), Rossini, 1827; *Guillaume Tell* (with H.-L.-F. Bis and Marrast), Rossini, 1829

*

A. Gerhard: *Die Verstädterung der Oper* (Stuttgart, 1992)

CHRISTOPHER SMITH

Juch, Emma (**Antonia Joanna**) (*b* Vienna, 4 July 1863; *d* New York, 6 March 1939). American soprano. She studied in Detroit with Adeline Murio Celli. Engaged by Mapleson for Her Majesty's Theatre, London, she made her début in 1881 as Philine (*Mignon*), the role of her first American appearance at the New York Academy of Music later that year with Mapleson's company. In 1884 she joined the American, subsequently the National, Opera Company, which toured throughout the USA. In 1889 she established the Emma Juch Opera Company, which for two years travelled widely in the USA, Canada and Mexico. Her voice was one of exceptional purity and wide compass, able to undertake the Queen of Night and Senta with equal success.

*

O. Thompson: *The American Singer* (New York, 1937), 119–22

HAROLD ROSENTHAL/R

Judgment of Paris, The. Pastoral masque in one act, set by JOHN ECCLES, GOTTFRIED FINGER, DANIEL PURCELL and JOHN WELDON, to a libretto by WILLIAM CONGREVE; London, Dorset Garden Theatre, 21 March 1701 (Eccles), 28 March 1701 (Finger), 11 April 1701 (Purcell), 6 May 1701 (Weldon), 3 June 1701 (all four settings).

In 1701 a group of noblemen including the Earl of Halifax, the Duke of Somerset and other members of the Kit-Cat Club (a Whiggish group of writers and politicians) decided to hold a competition for 'the Encouragement of Musick'. They asked William Congreve to write a libretto on the Judgment of Paris, an ideal subject for a competition: Juno, Pallas Athene and Venus (all sopranos) compete in a beauty contest for the golden apple awarded by the shepherd Paris (alto in Eccles; bass in Purcell; alto in Weldon). Four settings were chosen for public performance, and prizes of 100, 50, 30 and 20 guineas were awarded by vote of the subscribers. The finalists were presumably screened from a pool of entrants (a fifth version by Johann Franck, now lost, was performed in concert in 1702).

The cards seemed stacked in favour of Eccles, house composer at Lincoln's Inn Fields Theatre. He was a good friend of Congreve and of the popular actress-singer Anne Bracegirdle, for whom he wrote the part of Venus. Daniel Purcell, music director at Drury Lane since the death of his brother Henry in late 1695, had suffered a gradual decline in popularity. The Moravian Finger had been supplying competent instrumental music for both London theatres for many years, but was not a particularly gifted composer of vocal music. Weldon, former pupil of Henry Purcell and organist of Magdalen College, Oxford, was a rank outsider. Perhaps because Purcell and Eccles were associated with rival theatres, a neutral venue was found – the old Dorset Garden Theatre at Blackfriars, which was hastily refurbished and decked out as for a ridotto, with a stand set up for refreshments. The stage was rebuilt to accommodate the exceptionally large forces – 85 chorus singers and instrumentalists who, along with specially prepared acoustical reflectors, would have left little room for the soloists and scenery. Though Congreve's libretto includes stage directions (e.g. 'Juno, Pallas, *and* Venus *are seen at a Distance descending in several Machines*'), it is uncertain whether any of the performances were actually staged, thereby leaving the exact genre of the work – opera or masque – in doubt.

The contest itself ended in fiasco. Weldon unexpectedly won first prize, with Eccles, Purcell and Finger following in that order. Finger immediately left the country in disgust, muttering that Purcell's score was the best (after his own, of course). John Walsh published sumptuous editions of the Eccles and Purcell scores but not, conspicuously, Weldon's; Finger's music is lost. A manuscript copy of Weldon's version was rediscovered by Stoddard Lincoln at the Folger Shakespeare Library in Washington, DC. Comparison shows that Eccles's version is indeed superior to Weldon's. As Lincoln observes, it shows an unjustly neglected composer 'at the height of his creative powers'. Roger Fiske also admired Eccles's version, but might have awarded the prize to Weldon for his simple, catchy songs and 'moments of deeper beauty, and even passion'. (In a re-staging of the contest by Anthony Rooley and the Consort of Musicke on 13 August 1989 at the Proms in London, the BBC declared Eccles the winner, by popular vote.)

The three surviving scores use basically the same forces and instrumentation (for example, trumpets to accompany the warlike Pallas and recorders for Venus). Each is written in a conservative idiom, with heavy reliance on ground basses and strophic or simple binary forms and general avoidance of italianate features such as the da capo aria and *secco* recitative. Yet the three composers take quite different approaches to the libretto.

Daniel Purcell conceives the drama as a series of grand tableaux, more like a pageant than an opera. Where the others prefer short triple-metre tunes, he writes expressive, florid recitatives modelled on the virtuoso declamatory songs of his brother. Trumpet sonatas and sinfonias are inserted at every opportunity. His style is less chromatic and dissonant than his brother's, but in *The Judgment of Paris* he paints with unusually vivid colours.

Weldon also attempts grand effects, yet his score shows a clarity of harmony and melodic line which the others lack, despite also being firmly rooted in the Purcellian tradition. What distinguishes this version is the more dramatic role assigned to the chorus. Moreover, Weldon transforms the beauty contest into a battle among the three sopranos. Each goddess is provided with bravura passage-work, though Venus's somewhat softer strains eventually prevail. Pallas's music is so brilliant that when this version was revived a few years later, Catherine Tofts, the leading British operatic soprano of the day, took this role rather than that of the victorious Venus.

Though stylistically the most conservative, Eccles produced a superior drama, concise and swiftly moving with carefully calculated moments of reflection. The three goddesses are sharply contrasted along classical lines and Venus's victory is foreshadowed in various subtle ways. For example, in the trio 'Hither turn thee gentle swain', hers is the dominant voice, though technically the least demanding – probably a concession to Mrs Bracegirdle, whose untrained voice was plaintive rather than powerful. Eccles's music is rarely complicated, but there are memorable pieces, Juno's starkly simple 'Let ambition fire thy mind', for instance. His best moments, however, owe much to Henry Purcell: Paris's aria 'O ravishing delight', in which the shepherd nearly dies of joy at first sight of the goddesses, is modelled on Dido's Lament, with four-part string accompaniment and chromatic ground bass.

The Music Prize, which was intended to wean English audiences and composers away from provincial semi-opera and to instil a taste for all-sung music drama, did little to encourage the development of native opera. Instead, it opened the door for *opera seria*, which first appeared in London in 1705 in the form of Thomas Clayton's *Arsinoe*, modern in its da capo arias and *secco* recitative but musically inferior to any of the surviving settings of *The Judgment of Paris*.   CURTIS PRICE

Judic [née Damiens], **Anna Maria Louise** (*b* Semur-en-Auxois, 11 July 1849; *d* Golfe-Juan, 14 April 1911). French soprano. She studied at the Paris Conservatoire. Apart from early appearances in Brussels (1870–71) and London (1873), she worked chiefly in Paris, where she created Princess Cunégonde in Offenbach's *Le roi Carotte* and the title roles in his *Madame l'archiduc* and *La Créole*. At the Variétés in 1877 she played the title role in a revival of *La belle Hélène*, following it with a fourth Offenbach creation, *Le docteur Ox*. Judic is remembered above all for her performances in the premières of Hervé's *Lili* and *Mam'zelle Nitouche*, both at the Variétés, where she was the resident prima donna for a decade, also creating roles in Lecocq's *La rousotte* and *Le grand Casimir* and Boullard's *Niniche*. She divided the later part of her career between operetta, *café-concert* and drama; her final appearance in 1909 as the Grandmother in Lecocq's *La belle au bois dormant*. Judic's high voice and her speciality in laughing songs inspired such numbers as 'Pi-ouit!' from *La rousotte* and 'Ne m'chatouillez pas' which she recorded for Pathé in the early 1900s. Reynaldo Hahn (*Notes: Souvenirs d'un musicien*, Paris, 1933) mentioned the 'grace and tact' of her performances in the 1900s.

A. Laroque: *Acteurs et actrices de Paris* (Paris, 1898)
J. Martin: *Nos artistes* (Paris, 1901)
F. Duquesnel: 'Anna Judic', *Le théâtre*, no.297 (1 May 1911), 4–5
R. Traubner: *Operetta: a Theatrical History* (New York, 1983)
                                        PATRICK O'CONNOR

Judith. Opera by A. N. E. Serov; *see* YUDIF'.

Jugar con fuego ('Playing with Fire'). Zarzuela in three acts by FRANCISCO ASENJO BARBIERI to a libretto by Ventura de la Vega, after the French comedy *La comtesse d'Egmont*; Madrid, Teatro del Circo, 6 October 1851.

This work, unprecedented in being in three acts, initiated the genre of the *zarzuela grande*. Like others of his early works, *Jugar con fuego* shows Italian influence in its melodies and structure; this is exemplified by the extended finale to Act 2. Felix (tenor), an ingenuous country lad, has caught the fancy of the young Duchess of Medina (soprano), who has passed herself off as a servant in order that he should not be inhibited from courting her. She is making her way through a holiday crowd to meet him, but is being followed by the lecherous Marquis of Caravaca (baritone), from whose importunities and those of his fellow-carousers she is saved by the appearance of her father (bass), who does not recognize her but helps her to escape, leaving Felix bewildered. As the son of one of the old Duke's soldiers, Felix has been invited to see him at court, but is at first denied admission there because of his rustic appearance. The Marquis, who has suspected the disguised Duchess's identity, tries to embarrass her (for his own advantage) by introducing Felix to her, and she has to resort to pretending not to know him. But the Marquis manages to get hold of an indiscreet letter of hers, and as the price of his silence demands an embrace. Felix surprises them, loudly denounces her and draws his sword, creating a scandal. He is seized and taken away as a madman. The Duchess, repentant and now truly in love, goes to help him escape from the asylum (romance, 'Un tiempo fué'): the Marquis suddenly appears, but he is set upon by the inmates, deprived of his clothes and held instead of Felix. All ends happily.   LIONEL SALTER

***Juha*.** Opera in three acts by AARRE MERIKANTO to a libretto by AÏNO ACKTÉ, after Juhani Aho's novel; Lahti Music College, Finland, 28 October 1963 (previously broadcast on Finnish Radio, 3 December 1958).

The history of Merikanto's *Juha*, now regarded as one of the masterpieces of Finnish opera, is somewhat melancholy. The original novel inspired the soprano Aïno Ackté – a natural dramatist, as it turned out – to convert it into a libretto. She boldly offered it to Sibelius but, after pondering it for two years, he rejected it. Having found nobody else, in 1919 Ackté turned to the young Merikanto. He completed the final version in 1922, only to have it rejected by the Finnish Opera as 'too modern' and 'radical'. Later they commissioned LEEVI MADETOJA to produce a 'safer' version; that work, given by Finnish Opera in Helsinki on 17 February 1935, is skilfully crafted, reflecting in its rich and bold orchestration and its graceful vocal lines the influence of Debussy, Ravel and Fauré.

Modern critical opinion, however, tends to put Madetoja's *Juha* in the shadow of Merikanto's, although the value of Merikanto's opera was not recognized until long after the composer's death. The work has since been performed at Savonlinna and in Germany and the USA in a production by the Finnish National Opera, who have also recorded it.

Marja (soprano), the pretty young wife of Juha (baritone), an elderly farmer in the east Finnish backwoods, is bored with her life. When a handsome and wealthy Karelian pedlar, Shemeikka (tenor), appears, she first rejects his advances but, stung by her mother-in-law's abuse, finally runs away with him. After a period of bliss with Shemeikka, Marja discovers to her horror that she is just a mere member of his harem; but it is too late to go back, for she is expecting Shemeikka's child. Her humiliation is complete when Shemeikka brings a new bride to his household.

The good-natured Juha cannot bring himself to believe that Marja had eloped. When she suddenly returns, he is overjoyed and blithely accepts Marja's lie that she was forcibly abducted by Shemeikka; he even offers to adopt Marja's illegitimate baby. He agrees to go along with Marja to Shemeikka's village to fetch the child. On the way they encounter Shemeikka and one of his girls. Enraged by Shemeikka's mockery, Juha maims and nearly kills him, but in the fracas the truth is revealed. With nothing more to live for, Juha throws himself into the nearby rapids.

The plot of *Juha* follows a classic pattern but is no less powerful for that. Merikanto's music is vividly expressionistic; if his orchestration is occasionally a little raw, it has great and utterly convincing dramatic impact. His vocal lines, especially for Marja and Shemeikka, are almost Puccinian in their intensity; at the same time they are as finely attuned to the Finnish language as are Janáček's to the Czech.   ERKKI ARNI

Juif polonais, Le ('The Polish Jew'). *Conte populaire d'Alsace* in three acts by CAMILLE ERLANGER to a libretto by HENRI CAIN and Pierre-Barthélemy Gheusi after ERCKMANN-CHATRIAN's novel of the same title; Paris, Opéra-Comique (Salle Favart), 11 April 1900.

Erlanger's second opera and first great success, *Le Juif polonais*, based on the same legend as *The Bells*, Sir Henry Irving's favourite drama, was given more than 50 times by the Opéra-Comique in 33 years. Mathis (baritone), the burgomaster haunted by the memory of a murder that he once committed, was created by Victor Maurel, whose highly dramatic performance no doubt accounted for much of the work's initial success. In the same way that *The Bells* lost its popularity after Irving's death, Erlanger's work, although well crafted and appropriate to the subject, was insufficiently strong to keep the opera in the repertory once the melodramatic text became outmoded. The same subject was used for an opera by Karel Weis.   ELIZABETH FORBES

Juive, La ('The Jewess'). *Opéra* in five acts by FROMENTAL HALÉVY to a libretto by EUGÈNE SCRIBE; Paris, Opéra, 23 February 1835.

Eléazar *a Jewish goldsmith*		tenor
Rachel *his daughter*		soprano
Cardinal Brogni *president of the Council*		bass
Léopold *prince of the Empire*		tenor
Princess Eudoxie *the Emperor's niece*		soprano
Ruggiero *the city provost*		baritone
Albert *sergeant in the Emperor's army*		baritone

Courtiers, clergymen, officers, soldiers, guards, heralds, town crier, hangman and citizens

Setting Konstanz, Switzerland, in 1414

The first production of *La Juive*, in 1835, with Cornélie Falcon as Rachel, Julie Dorus-Gras as Princess Eudoxie, Adolphe Nourrit as Eléazar and Nicolas Levasseur as Brogni, was one of the most spectacular ever seen at the Opéra. The Act 1 procession and the Act 3 festival became famous for their splendour. One newspaper thought the procession, with all the leading figures on horseback, was the eighth wonder of the world.

Nothing is missing in this prodigious resurrection of a distant century. The costumes of the warriors, civilians and ecclesiastics are not imitated but reproduced in the smallest detail. The armour is not paste-board, it is real metal. One sees men of iron, men of silver, men of gold! The Emperor is a glittering ingot from head to foot! The Opéra may become a power capable of throwing its armies into the balance of power in Europe.

The role of Eléazar was written in response to Nourrit's request for a tenor role that was for once not a faultless hero. It has been a vehicle for many famous tenors and was a favourite part of Caruso's. The opera won admiration from both Berlioz and Wagner; one of its greatest admirers was Mahler, who declared: 'I am absolutely overwhelmed by this wonderful, majestic work. I regard it as one of the greatest operas ever created'.

ACT 1 A Te Deum is heard from the church at one side of the city square while the jeweller Eléazar and his workmen are hammering in their workshop at the other. The citizens object to Jews working on a Christian festival. Rachel, Eléazar's daughter, is in love with a man she knows as Samuel, who is in fact Prince Léopold pretending to be a Jew. She is puzzled by his evident authority over the Emperor's soldiers in protecting the Jews from molestation by Ruggiero, the city provost, and by angry citizens.

ACT 2 Léopold has joined Eléazar and Rachel in celebrating the Passover, although Rachel becomes anxious when he discards the unleavened bread. Princess Eudoxie comes to buy a gold chain as a gift for her husband (Léopold) to mark his victory over the Hussites. Léopold confesses to Rachel that he is in fact a Christian. She agrees to give up everything for him even so, and Eléazar, though horrified at first, agrees to give him his blessing. Léopold hints at other difficulties.

ACT 3 At a fête in the Emperor's palace Léopold is honoured for his victory. Eléazar delivers the gold chain for Eudoxie to present. Rachel realizes that 'Samuel' is none other than Prince Léopold and publicly denounces him. For loving a Jewess both he and she may be sentenced to death. Cardinal Brogni goes further by including Eléazar in his anathema and having all three led away for trial.

ACT 4 Eudoxie pleads with Rachel to save Léopold; Brogni pleads with her to save them both by renouncing her faith, but she refuses. Eléazar also refuses, hinting that their deaths will avenge him on at least one Christian. Brogni's daughter, he explains darkly, was saved many years before by some Jews.

ACT 5 Eléazar and Rachel are led to the scaffold. She has saved Léopold by swearing his innocence, to Eléazar's horror. Despite her father's pleas Rachel refuses to renounce her Jewish faith. Brogni begs Eléazar to reveal where his (Brogni's) daughter is. As Rachel is hurled into the boiling cauldron, he cries 'La voilà' and goes himself to his death. Rachel was thus not a Jewess at all. (For illustration *see* GRAND OPÉRA, fig.3.)

*   *   *

The sensational dramaturgy of the libretto perfectly exemplifies Scribe's theatrical style. The plot is spring-loaded with inherently improbable facts (Rachel being in fact not Eléazar's daughter but Brogni's; her lover

'La Juive' (Halévy), Act 1 (procession through the city of Konstanz): design by Charles Séchan, Léon Feuchère, Jules Dieterle and Edouard Despléchin for the original production at the Paris Opéra (Salle Le Peletier), 23 February 1835; lithograph

being in fact not a Jewish artisan but a Christian emperor), the revelation of each of which creates a general *frisson* expressed normally by a large static ensemble. The background conflict between Christians and Jews provides a sense of menace sharpened by the emphasis on ceremony and spectacle; and, in Brogni and Eléazar, Scribe created two fanatics whose wills are doomed to end in collision. The success of *La Juive* must be attributed to these uninhibitedly stagy elements as well as to Halévy's music. He treated the Jewish scenes as local colour, not in any way identifying with them as a Jew. His orchestration is bold throughout, calling for left-hand pizzicatos in the violins and chromatic brass. The new valve trumpet has some prominent solos, including the melody in Rachel's 'O mon Dieu, que j'implore' in the finale of Act 1. Brogni's anathema in Act 3 is pronounced with valve trumpets and valve horns outlining his sombre descending scales. Anvils are heard from Eléazar's workshop. Halévy was to some extent hampered by Scribe's metric regularities and facile rhymes, but his melodic invention is strong and he proved himself well able to conjure up an atmosphere of desperate agitation (as in Eléazar's scene with Brogni in Act 4) or genial romantic passion (as in Léopold's Serenade in Act 1). Eléazar's great air, 'Rachel, quand du Seigneur' at the close of Act 4, is one of the opera's unforgettable scenes, a fine portrayal of Eléazar's tormented, fanatical soul.

For an illustration of Falcon as Rachel, *see* FALCON, CORNÉLIE.

HUGH MACDONALD

Julie. *Comédie mêlée d'ariettes* in three acts by NICOLAS DEZÈDE to a libretto by Jacques Marie Boutet de Monvel; Paris, Comédie-Italienne (Hôtel de Bourgogne), 28 September 1772.

Julie (soprano) is the daughter of Monsieur Marsanges (bass), a *seigneur*, who plans to marry her off to Le Comte (tenor), 60 years her senior. But Julie is in love with the poor, young Saint-Alme (tenor). When she sees her new relatives approaching the château, Julie escapes; she is found by the woodcutter, Michaut (baritone), in a forest at night, and he takes her to his cottage where he lives with his daughter Catau (soprano) and

son-in-law Lucas (tenor). There Julie is reunited with Saint-Alme, who had been searching for her, and a plan of action is drawn up. They all return to the château where Catau and Lucas pretend to be lovers pleading for Marsanges' protection against Michaut's unsuitable match-making. After taking the lovers' side against their parents, Marsanges comes to realize the foolishness of his own plan and consents to Julie's marriage to Saint-Alme.

The musical high point of the first act is the realistic portrayal of Le Comte's deafness and stammering; the grief of Julie and Saint-Alme, expressed in their speeches, has little echo in their music. The musical climax of the opera is Julie's remarkable scene of loneliness and desperation ('Amant malheureux et fidelle', 2.iii). The act begins with Michaut's song 'Lison dormant dans un bocage'; this was published separately and later used by Mozart as a theme for variations (K264). The third act is musically anticlimactic, although Catau's *ariette*, 'Je suis simple née au village', was also published separately. *Julie* marked Dezède's successful début and was performed in eight European countries during the 18th century.

MICHAEL FEND

Julien [*Julien, ou La vie du poète* ('Julien, or The Poet's Life')]. *Poème lyrique* in a prologue and four acts by GUSTAVE CHARPENTIER to his own libretto; Paris, Opéra-Comique (Salle Favart), 4 June 1913.

The opera is a sequel to *LOUISE* and deals with the artistic aspirations of Louise's suitor Julien (tenor). Like *Louise*, it is loosely autobiographical and incorporates elements of an earlier piece, in this case *La vie du poète*, a symphony-drama of 1888–9. In the prologue, subtitled 'Enthousiasme', Julien, as a recipient of the Prix de Rome, is at the Villa Medici in Rome, as Charpentier himself had been. Here, however, until the last tableau, set in Montmartre, the realistic element ends, for the main scenes are imaginary. Act 1, subtitled 'Au pays du rêve', is set first on the Holy Mountain, then in the Accursed Valley and finally in the Temple of Beauty; Act 2, in which Julien has creative doubts, is set in the Slovakian countryside; Act 3, headed 'Impuissance', is set in the wild countryside of Brittany; and the last act,

'Ivresse', ends in Montmartre, with the Temple of Beauty suddenly appearing in the Place Blanche.

Like *Louise*, *Julien* demands many characters and chorus roles: in the first performance Marguerite Carré played Louise (soprano) as well as Beauty, two different girls and a female ancestor. There is a chorus of 'filles du rêve', fairies and chimeras as well as various men's roles, mainly different kinds of worker. Charpentier described how, except for the prologue, 'Louise and the various characters who surround Julien are not so much real people as an exteriorized realization of their inner souls'. Fauré was one of the few to find admirable qualities in the work, which was otherwise considered largely unsuccessful. Apart from two productions in 1914, it has not been revived.

RICHARD LANGHAM SMITH

Julietta [*Snář* ('The Dream-Book')]. Opera in three acts by BOHUSLAV MARTINŮ to his own libretto after Georges Neveux's play *Juliette, ou La clé des songes*; Prague, National Theatre, 16 March 1938.

Julietta	soprano
Michel *a young travelling bookseller*	tenor
Small Arab	mezzo-soprano
Old Arab	bass
Woman Selling Poultry	mezzo-soprano
Woman Selling Fish	mezzo-soprano
Man in Fur Cap	bass
Man in Helmet	baritone
Police Officer	tenor
Three Gentlemen	sopranos
Old Man	bass
Grandfather	bass
Grandmother	contralto
Fortune Teller	contralto
Seller of Memories	bass-baritone
Forest Watchman/Police Officer	tenor
Young Sailor	mezzo-soprano
Old Sailor	bass
Old Woman	mezzo-soprano
Voice on Ship	baritone
Official	tenor
Messenger	mezzo-soprano
Blind Beggar	baritone
Voice (male) offstage	spoken
Convict	bass
Engine Driver	tenor
Nightwatchman	spoken

Townspeople, female chorus, offstage chorus, silent figures in grey

Setting A small seaside town and its surroundings

According to Šafránek, Martinů first encountered Neveux's play in 1932. After a controversial première on 7 March 1930 at the Théâtre de l'Avenue in Paris, it acquired a considerable following. Martinů was deeply impressed both by its subject matter and by the beauty of Neveux's language and made his own adaptation of the play with the author's enthusiastic approval. An initial setting in French was abandoned in favour of a Czech adaptation, composed between 17 May 1936 and 24 January 1937. This involved a change to the end of the play, which originally concluded with Michel remaining uncertain of re-entering his dream world; in the opera, he returns to the setting of the opening scene on hearing the theme associated with Julietta.

The opera had its première under Václav Talich in a production by Jindřich Honzl with set designs by František Muzika (see illustration). Neveux attended the first performance and accounted the musical setting superior to his prose original. Despite the considerable success of its première *Julietta* was not produced again in Prague until 5 April 1963, when it was conducted by Jaroslav Krombholc in a production by Václav Kašlík with set designs by Josef Svoboda. This production became the basis of the recording under Krombholc, with Ivo Žídek as Michel and Maria Tauberová in the title role. Productions outside Czechoslovakia have been infrequent. Martinů was present at the first German production, at the Hessisches Staatstheater in Wiesbaden on 25 January 1956, conducted by Ludwig Kaufmann and directed by Wilhelm Pohl. The first British production was given by the New Opera Company in association with the ENO at the London Coliseum on 5 April 1978 in a new translation by Brian Large. It was conducted by Charles Mackerras and directed by Anthony Besch with set designs by John Stoddart.

Martinů's response to the libretto is predominantly lyrical, although, paradoxically, there are no extended vocal solos and no big arias, even for the main characters. The action is advanced largely in telegraphic exchanges between a constantly shifting sequence of individuals. The musical language is the extended diatonicism typical of Martinů's maturity. The motoric rhythms associated with such works as the Double Concerto for two string orchestras, piano and timpani of 1938 are apparent in passages where the action requires brisk treatment, notably in the first act.

ACT 1 A bookseller, Michel, arrives in the square on the quayside in search of the girl whose voice he heard three years before and which has haunted him ever since. After a brief, confusing exchange with two Arabs, Michel enters the Sailors' Hotel. The townspeople begin to emerge, and in a brisk sequence of gossip it becomes clear that no one in the town has a memory lasting more than a few minutes. Michel's call for help brings a police officer to investigate. The police officer confirms that no one has a memory lasting any length of time. He asks Michel what his earliest memory of childhood is. Michel recounts, to music with a parodistic, almost neoclassical quality, that he remembers a toy duck. According to the town statutes, anyone with such a memory must become the town captain. The police officer leaves for the town hall to prepare for Michel to recite his tale of a toy duck to the assembled citizens. Martinů maintains the impetus in these wordy, comic exchanges with a free-flowing texture, occasionally involving speech, energized by dynamic rhythms and catchy ostinatos.

The musical characterization veers away from comedy as Michel, to the reduced accompaniment of the piano, recounts how he fell in love with the voice of a mysterious girl. He cannot make himself understood to an audience of townspeople who imagine memories rather than retaining real ones. After these confusing scenes a piano solo introduces the voice of Julietta singing a song of folklike simplicity ('Moje láska v dálce se ztratila': 'My love has vanished in the distance'), succeeded by an instrumental passage of extraordinary sweetness in which Martinů introduces one of his most characteristic fingerprints, a modified plagal cadence (identical with that at the end of Janáček's *Taras*

'Julietta' (Martinů): set design by František Muzika for the original production at the National Theatre, Prague, 16 March 1938

Bulba). After two passages of dialogue, Julietta asks Michel to meet her in the woods. The strangeness of their encounter is intensified by a meeting with the police officer, who is now a postman and has no recollection of his earlier exchange with Michel.

ACT 2   Michel's rendezvous with Julietta in scene v is preceded by the arrival at a woodland crossroads of various characters, all of whom suffer from the local lack of memory: three gentlemen in search of a party and, it emerges, Julietta; an old man who sells wine and delights his audience by prompting them with false memories; a Fortune Teller who makes little sense to Michel, but warns him to be careful. Julietta appears and builds a world of fantasy romance in contrast to Michel's reality. She fancies that the wood is empty, while Michel is certain that he hears voices. Julietta's music is rhapsodic and highly charged (the passage of repeated rising scales which concludes her first statement was quoted by Martinů in the finale of his Sixth Symphony, 1953). Julietta wishes to be told of a past, which does not exist, in which they were lovers.

Julietta's fantasies are fed further with the appearance of a pedlar in whose wares – photographs and postcards – Julietta sees a non-existent past with Michel. By contrast, she believes his story about hearing her voice three years ago to be fantasy rather than reality. At the climax of the scene Julietta runs into the woods and Michel fires a pistol after her. In response to Michel's shot the townspeople appear and threaten to execute him. To divert them Michel tells them more stories and, forgetting their fury, they wander into the woods. Michel arrives back in the town square. He finds Julietta's house inhabited by a fractious old woman who denies her existence. He once again hears Julietta's song from Act 1 and, reflecting on its strangeness, boards a ship about to leave the harbour.

ACT 3   An official at the Central Bureau of Dreams explains to Michel that he has been dreaming. A succession of dreamers – a messenger, a blind beggar, a convict and an engine driver – enter in pursuit of their fantasies. Each selects a different dream, but in each there is a girl who appears to be Julietta. Michel asks to return to his dream but is warned of the danger by the official. The hazard of returning is illustrated for Michel by a group of timorous grey figures: the personification of those trapped in their dreams. Michel prepares to leave his dream. He hears Julietta calling his name as the Nightwatchman announces that the office is closing. Michel asks to see behind the door; the Nightwatchman reveals that there is nothing there. As he prepares to leave once again, Michel hears Julietta calling him. In a passionate outburst, his longest in the opera, he tells of his desire to return to her. The setting of the opening and some of the townspeople from the beginning of the opera return as Michel re-enters his dream.

*   *   *

The music of Michel's climactic statement in Act 3 epitomizes the diatonic lyricism of the opera. To balance the frequently telegraphic and naturalistic word-setting, Martinů provides the accompaniment with the necessary melodic expansiveness. His strong sense of comic characterization brings a plethora of disparate small roles to life, and renders engaging and credible passages of dialogue which on the page seem to amount to little more than insubstantial nonsense. Impressionist colouring in the orchestration enhances the dreamlike qualities of this uniquely successful attempt to capture and amplify the fragile beauty of Neveux's play.

JAN SMACZNY

Julius Caesar. Libretto subject much used in the 17th and 18th centuries. Its principal sources are the historical accounts of the Roman leader Julius Caesar as recorded in Plutarch's *Lives*. Opera librettos have tended to focus either on Caesar's visit to Egypt, where he falls in love with Cleopatra (the subject of Bernard Shaw's play *Caesar and Cleopatra*), or on his assassination at the hands of his fellow Romans (as in WILLIAM SHAKESPEARE's tragedy *Julius Caesar*). They may be found under titles including *Giulio Cesare in Egitto*, *Cesare in Alessandra*, *Cesare e Cleopatra*, *Cesare in Egitto*, *La morte di Cesare* and *Il trionfo di Cesare*.

Possibly the first libretto featuring an episode from the life of Caesar was G. F. Busenello's *La prosperità infelice di Giulio Cesare dittatore* (libretto published in 1656; possibly intended for the Teatro SS Giovanni e Paolo, Venice, with music attributed to Cavalli, but possibly not composed). Probably the earliest setting on the Caesar and Cleopatra theme is Cesti's *Il Cesare amante*, given at Venice in Carnival 1651 (and later revised as *La Cleopatra*). But the libretto by G. F. Bussani, *Giulio Cesare in Egitto*, first set by Antonio Sartorio (1676), was by far the most popular version of the story. L. A. Predieri (1728), Giacomelli (1735), Antonio Colombo (1744), Jommelli (1751), Sarti (1763) and Piccinni (1770) also composed operas based on this libretto. The best-known setting is Handel's (1724), to an adaptation by Haym of the Bussani text. Other early variants on Julius Caesar in Egypt include J. S. Kusser's *Cleopatra* (1690, Brunswick), a German version of Bussani's text, G. A. V. Aldrovandini's *Cesare in Alessandria* (1699), F. A. Novi's *Cesare e Tolomeo* (1716) and C. H. Graun's *Cesare e Cleopatra* (1742).

The death of Caesar has been almost as popular a subject. One of the earliest works based on this topic was Keiser's *Der durch den Fall des grossen Pompejus erhöhete Julius Caesar* (1710). Herder's libretto *Brutus*, closely related to Plutarch and Shakespeare, was set by J. C. F. Bach (1774, music lost). Gaetano Sertor's libretto *La morte di Cesare* enjoyed a great vogue in the last decade of the 18th century with settings by Bianchi (1788), Andreozzi and Zingarelli (both 1790). Several operas on this subject, dating from the 19th and 20th centuries, rely heavily on Shakespeare's play, including those of José García Robles (1880), Alfredo Consorti (1923) and G. F. Malipiero (1936). A more recent setting is Klebe's *Die Ermordung Cäsars* (1959). One further work on Julius Caesar is Giuseppe Nicolini's *Guilio Cesare nelle Gallie* (1819; rev. as *Il trionfo di Cesare*, 1819), on his campaign against the Gauls.

See also GIULIO CESARE IN EGITTO (i) [Sartorio]; GIULIO CESARE IN EGITTO (ii) [Handel]; and MORTE DI CESARE, LA [Bianchi]. For a list of operas based on Shakespeare's *Julius Caesar see* SHAKESPEARE, WILLIAM.

PAUL CORNEILSON

Jullien, (Jean Lucien) Adolphe (*b* Paris, 1 June 1845; *d* St Pierre-les-Nemours, 30 Aug 1932). French writer on music. He studied music and took a degree in law, becoming a contributor to several Paris journals and newspapers; he was critic on *Français* from 1872 to 1887, remaining when it was amalgamated with the *Moniteur universel*, and from 1893 was critic of the *Journal des débats*. Jullien fought valiantly for musical 'progress' and took an advanced position in the controversies surrounding Wagner, his substantial biography of whom was for its time a monument of accurate, erudite information. He also made a close study of 18th-century musical theatre.

L'Opéra en 1788 (Paris, 1873)
Histoire du théâtre de Madame de Pompadour, dit Théâtre des petits cabinets (Paris, 1874)

Grandes nuits de Sceaux: le théâtre de la Duchesse du Maine (Paris, 1876)
Un potentat musical: Papillon de la Ferté, son règne à l'Opéra de 1780 à 1790 (Paris, 1876)
Airs variés: histoire, critique, biographies musicales et dramatiques (Paris, 1877)
Weber à Paris en 1826 (Paris, 1877)
La cour et l'Opéra sous Louis XVI: Marie-Antoinette et Sacchini, Salieri, Favart et Gluck (Paris, 1878)
L'Opéra secret au XVIIIe siècle (Paris, 1880)
Richard Wagner: sa vie et ses oeuvres (Paris, 1886; Eng. trans., 1892)
Musique: mélanges d'histoire et de critique musicale et dramatique (Paris, 1896)
Ernest Reyer: sa vie et ses oeuvres (Paris, 1909, 2/1914)

Jullien, Louis (George Maurice Adolphe Roch Albert Abel Antonio Alexandre Noé Jean Lucien Daniel Eugène Joseph-le-brun Joseph-Barême Thomas Thomas Thomas-Thomas Pierre Arbon Pierre-Maurel Barthélemi Artus Alphonse Bertrand Dieudonné Emanuel Josué Vincent Luc Michel Jules-de-la-plane Jules-Bazin Julio César) (*b* Sisteron, 23 April 1812; *d* Paris, 14 March 1860). French conductor and composer. He published under both his surname and his various Christian names – e.g. Roch-Albert – bestowed by his 36 godfathers, members of the Sisteron Philharmonic. He entered the Paris Conservatoire in 1831 or 1833 and left in 1836. Settling in England in 1838, he organized and flamboyantly conducted popular promenade concerts at London theatres and music for society balls. In December 1847 he embarked on an ill-planned season of grand opera at the Drury Lane Theatre, engaging Berlioz to conduct *Le nozze di Figaro*, *Lucia di Lammermoor*, *Linda di Chamounix* and the première of Balfe's *The Maid of Honour*. The season resulted in Jullien's first bankruptcy in England. Berlioz's grimly amusing account describes him as fundamentally honest but with 'the incontestable character of a madman'.

After a crash course in opera composition with Fétis in Brussels, Jullien composed an extravagant grand opera *Pietro il grande* to a libretto by Desmond Ryan, music critic of the *Morning Herald* and *Standard*. After five performances at Covent Garden in August 1852 the opera was withdrawn. The inclusion of three military bands and a small regiment of cavalry did nothing to please its critics. The music is 'one long plagiarism from beginning to end', said the *Illustrated London News*. The full score is lost, but a vocal score was published. Jullien became a household name in his heyday though latterly he became mentally unstable, ending his life in a lunatic asylum.

*

'A Sketch of the Life of Louis Jullien', *Musical World*, xxxi (1853), 307–469 passim
A. Carse: *The Life of Jullien* (Cambridge, 1951)

KEITH HORNER

Jumping Frog of Calaveras County, The. Comic opera in one act by LUKAS FOSS to a libretto by Jean Karsavina after Mark Twain's story *The Celebrated Jumping Frog of Calaveras County*; Bloomington, Indiana University, 18 May 1950.

The first scene takes place in a saloon during the California gold rush; the saloon-keeper, Uncle Henry (baritone), his niece Lulu (mezzo-soprano) and the regular patron Smiley (tenor) sing the praises of Smiley's frog Daniel Webster, the champion jumper in the county. A Stranger (bass) enters and wagers that a frog chosen at random can beat Daniel in a jumping contest. The local men leave to find another frog, and the Stranger flirts with Lulu. Finally, left alone in the saloon, he pours buckshot down Daniel's throat; the scene closes with his monologue ('Each time I hit a town') about his con games and amorous conquests.

The second scene takes place in the town square; two Crapshooters (tenor, bass), a Guitar Player (baritone) and an optional chorus of townspeople sing the folksong 'Sweet Betsy from Pike'. At Uncle Henry's urging, all rush to place what looks like a sure bet on Daniel Webster. The Stranger and Lulu enter arm in arm, to catcalls and mockery from the crowd, and the jumping contest begins. The Stranger's frog can manage only a small jump, but Daniel cannot move at all, despite the people's pleading. After the Stranger collects his winnings and slips away, Smiley discovers the trick. The crowd pursue the Stranger, recover the money and throw him out of town. All rejoice again in their champion jumping frog.

This 45-minute opera, one of several early works on frontier subjects by Foss, tells its fast-moving story mostly in dialogue and ensembles rather than solo arias. Influences on its style include folksongs of the Old West, Copland's populist works of the 1940s and the irony of Stravinsky's *Histoire du soldat*.   DAVID WRIGHT

Junca, Marcel (*b* Bayonne, 1818; *d* Lormes, nr Corbigny, 4 Oct 1878). French bass. He studied in Toulon and Paris, making his début in 1839 at Metz. After singing in Lyons, he went to Paris, where in 1852 he took part in the first performance of Adam's *Si j'étais roi*, at the Théâtre Lyrique. In 1859 he sang Procida in the American première of *Les vêpres siciliennes* at the Academy of Music, New York. At La Scala he created the title role of Boito's *Mefistofele* (1868) and sang Padre Guardiano in the revised version of *La forza del destino* (1869). He took part in the first performance of *Salvator Rosa* (Gomes) at Genoa in 1874. His repertory included Silva (*Ernani*), King Philip (*Don Carlos*), Alfonso (*Lucrezia Borgia*) and Cardinal Brogni (*La Juive*). He retired in 1877. A powerful singing actor, he had a fine, dark voice.   ELIZABETH FORBES

June, Ava (*b* London, 23 July 1931). English soprano. She joined the Sadler's Wells chorus in 1953, becoming a principal in 1957, and was thereafter permanently associated with the company (later the ENO); she was heard at Covent Garden in 1958 as the Heavenly Voice in *Don Carlos*. She sang with the WNO and at San Francisco, where she made her American début in 1974 as Ellen Orford. Her repertory included Purcell's Dido, Mozart's Countess Almaviva, Donna Elvira and Donna Anna, Beethoven's Marzelline and Leonore, Tatyana and Lisa, Micaëla, Violetta, Butterfly, Judith (*Bluebeard's Castle*) and Kát'a. She created Mrs Schomberg in Bennett's *Victory* (1970, Covent Garden) and sang Sieglinde in the English-language *Ring* cycle at the Coliseum (1973). An outstandingly musical singer, with impeccable diction, she had a lyric soprano voice that could sustain dramatic roles such as Elizabeth I, in both Britten's *Gloriana* and Donizetti's *Maria Stuarda*, and the Marschallin, which she first sang in 1976. She created Countess Vronskaya in Hamilton's *Anna Karenina* (1981, ENO).   ELIZABETH FORBES

Jung, Doris (*b* Centralia, IL, 5 Jan 1924). American soprano. She studied at Urbana and in New York and

Vienna, making her début in 1955 at Zürich as Vitellia (Mozart's *La clemenza di Tito*). Engaged at Freiburg, she sang Handel's Cleopatra, Fiordiligi, Ariadne, Arabella, Countess Madeleine (*Capriccio*) and the Lady (*Cardillac*). She also appeared in Hamburg, Munich, Frankfurt, Vienna, Copenhagen, Vancouver and Strasbourg. Among her other roles were Countess Almaviva, Leonore (*Fidelio*), Senta, Elisabeth, Elsa and Sieglinde; she sang the Marschallin for the New York City Opera in 1972. A very dramatic singer, she had a vibrant, warm-toned voice and excelled in Wagner and Strauss.   ELIZABETH FORBES

Jung, Manfred (*b* Oberhausen, 9 July 1940). German tenor. He studied at Essen and in 1967 sang Arindal (*Die Feen*) at the Bayreuth Youth Festival. A member of the Bayreuth chorus, 1970–73, he was engaged at Dortmund (1971), Kaiserslautern and, in 1977, Düsseldorf. Between 1977 and 1986 he sang Siegfried, Tristan, Parsifal and Loge at Bayreuth. He made his American début in 1980 at Tulsa as Siegmund and first sang at the Metropolitan Opera in 1981 as Siegfried. He has sung throughout Germany and in Vienna, Brussels, Zürich, Turin, Warsaw and Chicago; his roles include Florestan, Laca (*Jenůfa*) and Hermann (*The Queen of Spades*), but he has been most successful as an interpreter of Wagner.   ELIZABETH FORBES

Junge Lord, Der ('The Young Lord'). *Komische Oper* in two acts by HANS WERNER HENZE to a libretto by INGEBORG BACHMANN after Wilhelm Hauff's story 'Der Affe als Mensch' from *Der Scheik von Alexandria und seine Sklaven* (1826); Berlin, Deutsche Oper, 7 April 1965.

Sir Edgar	silent
His Secretary	baritone
Lord Barrat *Sir Edgar's nephew*	tenor
Begonia *his Jamaican cook*	mezzo-soprano
The Mayor	bass-baritone
Councillor Hasentreffer	baritone
Councillor Scharf	baritone
Professor von Mucker	buffo tenor
Baroness Grünwiesel	mezzo-soprano
Frau von Hufnagel	mezzo-soprano
Frau Hasentreffer	soprano
Luise *the Baroness's ward*	soprano
Ida *her friend*	soprano
A Maid	soprano
Wilhelm *a student*	tenor
Amintore La Rocca *a circus director*	dramatic tenor
A Lamplighter	baritone
Monsieur La Truiare *a dancing-master*	silent
Meadows *the butler*	silent
Jeremy *a Moor*	silent

Circus performers, a teacher, a military band, a dance band, ladies and gentlemen of society, men and women of the people, children

Setting Hülsdorf-Gotha in 1830

Henze's final collaboration with Bachmann was the product of a commission from the Deutsche Oper; the composition of the music occupied Henze for much of 1963 and 1964. At the première, which was conducted

by Christoph von Dohnányi and produced by Gustav Sellner, Loren Driscoll sang Barrat, Barry McDaniel the Secretary, Edith Mathis Luise and Donald Grobe Wilhelm. A recording with the same cast was subsequently released. The Italian première followed in Rome later the same year, conducted by Henze, and the American première was at San Diego in 1967. There were productions in a number of German-speaking houses in the late 1960s and early 70s: the Cologne production, conducted by Marek Janowski, provided the work with its British première when the company visited London in 1969.

The scenes are numbered independently of the acts.

ACT 1.i *The town square* The prominent citizens of Hülsdorf-Gotha await the arrival of a rich English gentleman, Sir Edgar, who has rented a house in the town. They rehearse their speeches of welcome while Luise, the town beauty, and Wilhelm embark on a rapturous love duet and school children practise their welcome song. As a carriage comes into sight the Mayor assembles his welcoming committee, but what emerges is Sir Edgar's household, starting with his menagerie, and moving on to his pages and servants and finally to Begonia, the rum-swilling cook.

They all assemble to await a grander, even more flamboyant carriage from which Sir Edgar finally appears, to orchestral greetings that include a quotation from the 'Turkish music' from Mozart's *Die Entführung*. Speaking through his secretary he refuses the town's hospitality and the scene descends into embarassed confusion, which Luise and Wilhelm exploit so they may continue their duet.

1.ii *Baroness Grünwiesel's salon* Although Sir Edgar has turned down all invitations, the Baroness hopes that because of her position at the head of society in Hulsdorf-Gotha she will be treated as an exception. But she is to be disappointed: Jeremy, the page, arrives with a message declining her hospitality. The Baroness is furious: she vows to have her revenge, and the following orchestral interlude points up the parallels with

Bartolo's thirst for vengeance in Mozart's *Le nozze di Figaro*.

1.iii *The town square* A circus has come to town. The director, La Rocca, is thanking the audience at the end of the show when Sir Edgar and his servants come out of their house to watch the performance. To the consternation and disapproval of the townspeople the Englishman acknowledges only the children: when the councillors attempt to ingratiate themselves, his secretary discourages them. As Wilhelm and Luise pursue their courtship La Rocca continues to woo his audience until the Council revokes the circus's licence to perform. Sir Edgar offers to pay for their licence, and invites some of the artistes into his house, pointedly ignoring the local dignitaries. The poor approve, the rich feel insulted, and as the orchestral textures thin down to percussion the word 'shame' is daubed across Sir Edgar's house.

ACT 2.iv *A winter evening outside Sir Edgar's house* The town has turned against Sir Edgar. Jeremy is pelted with snowballs as he returns from shopping; a Lamplighter hears screams and shouts coming from inside the house. Wilhelm and Luise at last have the opportunity to embark upon a large-scale love duet but they are interrupted by more shrieks and the arrival of the Mayor and his Council, summoned by the Lamplighter. The Mayor demands entry to investigate: the secretary explains that the door is open but that the noise was caused by the efforts of Sir Edgar's nephew, just arrived from England, to learn German. When he has mastered the language the townspeople will be invited to meet him. Everyone goes off, satisfied by the explanation.

2.v *The library of Sir Edgar's house* Sir Edgar's staff are preparing for a party; they are dominated by Begonia, who careers around with piles of food delivering a bilingual lecture on Napoleon's gastronomic tastes. Eventually everything is ready and the guests, led by the Baroness, are welcomed. The secretary confesses that Sir Edgar is still doubtful of his nephew's ability to speak German, but the problems are dismissed and Sir

Edgar and Lord Barrat appear on the stairs. Even though the young lord grabs Luise's handbag and throws it away, everyone seems impressed by his courtesy, and the Baroness asks Luise to offer him a cup of tea. That too is thrown away.

While the Mayor begins to pursue Begonia, Lord Barrat climbs on the tables; only Wilhelm is outraged. He goes off with Sir Edgar and the secretary to view the collection of exhibits – animal remains, statuary, maps – with which the library is crammed. All the ladies cluster around the young lord, who pulls a ribbon from Luise's dress and begins to dance, toying with Luise's shawl. Wilhelm is incensed: he confronts Lord Barrat, whom Sir Edgar and the secretary usher away; Luise faints and Wilhelm finds himself without friends.

2.vi *The ballroom at the casino* The final scene is unfolded over a vast passacaglia encompassing vocal set pieces which gradually expand from aria through duet, trio and quartet to full ensemble. Luise takes a moment off from dancing to sing of her new love for Lord Barrat: he arrives and gives her a rose whose thorns draw blood. Watched by Wilhelm, they celebrate their happiness in a duet. The news of their match spreads, and everyone is drawn into a dance: the Debutantes' Waltz. Eventually Luise and Lord Barrat take the floor. As his dancing becomes more frantic and his behaviour more extravagant (he swings from the chandeliers), good humour turns to panic: even Sir Edgar's arrival fails to calm things down. Eventually Luise collapses exhausted and the young lord begins to tear off his clothes, revealing a monkey beneath. Sir Edgar leads the animal from the room. Luise and Wilhelm embrace while confusion reigns again.

*   *   *

Der junge Lord is perhaps the most italianate of all Henze's stage works, the final product of his self-imposed exile in Italy and a loving tribute to the *opera buffa* tradition from Mozart through Rossini to Verdi. Its use of bel canto vocal lines and fast moving ensembles, as well as the knowing pastiches of salon dances and lean, classically trimmed orchestral writing, evoke a blackly comic 19th-century world with a sharp satirical edge.

ANDREW CLEMENTS

Jungwirth, Manfred (*b* St Pölten, 4 June 1919). Austrian bass. He studied in St Pölten and Vienna, making his début in 1942 at Bucharest as Méphistophélès and King Henry (*Lohengrin*). Engaged at Innsbruck (1945), Zürich (1948) and Frankfurt (1960), he also sang at the Komische Oper, Berlin, and Deutsche Oper am Rhein. He made his British début in 1965 at Glyndebourne as Ochs, which was also his début role at the Vienna Staatsoper (1967), San Francisco (1971), the Metropolitan (1974) and Dallas (1982); he also sang it at Munich, Nice, Rome and Trieste. He created the Vicar in Einem's *Besuch der alten Dame* (1971, Vienna). His repertory included Osmin, Rocco, which he sang at La Scala (1978), the King (*Aida*), Pietro (*Boccanegra*), Cuno (*Der Freischütz*), Sacristan (*Tosca*), Severolus (*Palestrina*), Truffaldino (*Ariadne auf Naxos*), Count Waldner (*Arabella*), the role of his Covent Garden début (1981), and La Roche (*Capriccio*), which he sang at Salzburg (1985) and Florence (1987). His ripe, dark-coloured voice and comic talents were displayed to best advantage as Ochs, which he recorded with Solti.

ALAN BLYTH

Juniper Tree, The. Chamber opera in two continuous acts with prologue, by PHILIP GLASS and ROBERT MORAN to a libretto by Arthur Yorinks after Jacob Ludwig and Wilhelm Carl GRIMM; Cambridge, Massachusetts, American Repertory Theater, 6 December 1985.

Glass's most popular operatic work, it had received more than a hundred performances by mid-1989. This success is partly due to its straightforward concision, but more to its highly effective alternation of styles. The contrast between Glass's lush minimalism and Moran's more naturalistic neo-romanticism is much like the alternating aria and recitative style of older operas. Moran set the more dramatic parts of the libretto, while Glass concentrated on points of stasis or slow unfolding.

The Prologue (composed by Glass, and largely mimed) introduces an unnamed husband and wife (called The Father and The Mother in the cast list) who have everything they want from life except children. When the Mother (lyric soprano) wishes intensely for a baby, she becomes pregnant but dies in childbirth. Some years later (Act 1 scene i; music by Moran), the Father (lyric baritone) has remarried, and provided his child, the Son (soprano) with a half-sister, the Daughter (soprano). The Stepmother (mezzo-soprano), pathologically jealous of the Son, sees his dead mother every time she looks at him. When the Daughter (Act 1 scene ii; Moran) expresses solicitude for her brother, the Stepmother resolves to kill him, decapitating him with the lid of a chest into which he has reached for an apple. She props the body in a chair, placing the severed head on its shoulders and the apple in its hands. When the Daughter asks for a piece of the apple there is of course no reply; vexed, she boxes the Son's ears and the head flies off. The Stepmother comforts her, saying no one need ever know of the 'accident', and proceeds to chop up the body. When the Father returns home (Act 1 scene iii; Glass) he is ravenously hungry, and insists on eating all of the stew his wife has prepared from the Son's body. The Daughter buries the bones under a nearby juniper tree, from which a bird emerges singing beautifully of the murder, in the Son's voice, its words understood only by the audience. Seeing and hearing it, the Daughter regains some of her spirits (Moran) and ventures to hope for a fortunate outcome.

The bird flies through the countryside (Act 2 scene i; Glass), where it encounters Three Craftsmen (tenor, baritone, bass) who reward its beautiful singing with emblems of their trades: a gold chain, a pair of red shoes and a millstone. Returning (Act 2 scene ii; Moran), the bird presents the chain to the Father, gives the shoes to the Daughter and drops the millstone on the Stepmother. The Son, magically returned to life, appears in her place, and all, presumably, live happily ever after.

ANDREW STILLER

Jurinac, Sena [Srebrenka] (*b* Travnik, 24 Oct 1921). Austrian soprano of Yugoslav birth. A pupil of Milka Kostrenčić, she made her début in 1942 at the Zagreb Opera as Mimì, and in 1945 joined the Vienna Staatsoper, in the role of Cherubino. In 1948 she made a deep impression as Dorabella with the Glyndebourne company at the Edinburgh Festival. Although best known early in her career for Mozart, she built up an extensive repertory covering a wide range of parts. She appeared at most of the world's leading opera houses, maturing from roles such as Octavian, Marzelline and Ilia (*Idomeneo*) to the Countess Almaviva, the Marschallin, Leonore and Electra. Among her other notable roles were the Composer, the two ladies in *Don Giovanni*, Elisabeth (*Tannhäuser* and *Don Carlos*), Jenůfa, Butterfly and Tosca, Desdemona, and later Marie (*Wozzeck*), Poppaea and the Taurian Iphigenia.

Jurinac's voice was beautifully pure, rich and even throughout its range, and although she did not always sound to best advantage in her numerous recordings, the finest of them faithfully convey her integrity, eloquence and commitment. Without doubt, she will be remembered as one of the outstanding operatic sopranos of her time, generous of voice and radiant of personality.

*

GV [with discography by R. Vegeto]

Earl of Harewood: 'Sena Jurinac', *Opera*, i/5/(1950), 26–9

U. Tamussino: 'Sena Jurinac', *Opera*, xvii (1966), 265–71

——: *Sena Jurinac* (Augsburg, 1971) [with discography]

PETER BRANSCOMBE

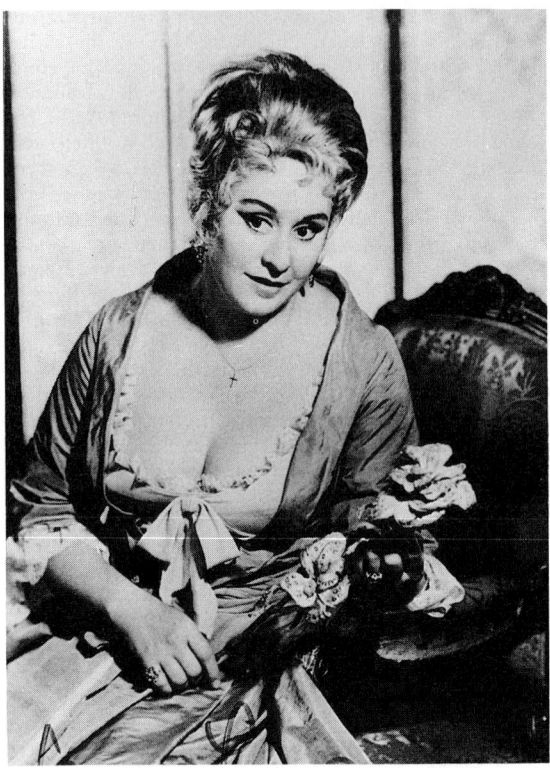

Sena Jurinac as Fiordiligi in Mozart's 'Così fan tutte'

Jurjevskaya, Zinaida (*b* Russia, ?1896; *d* Andermatt, Switzerland, ?3 Aug 1925). Russian soprano. She moved to Germany with her family in 1917 and studied in Berlin, making her début in 1922 at the Staatsoper in *The Golden Cockerel*. She quickly established herself as a leading lyric soprano and in 1924 sang the title role in the Berlin première of *Jenůfa*. At concerts in Paris, including one in which she was accompanied by Prokofiev, she was hailed as one of the supreme singers of the time. The following year her body was discovered in the river Reuss near Andermatt, in conditions that pointed to suicide. The promise of a distinguished career is well borne out by recordings, which include an exceptionally moving and beautifully sung account of Jenůfa's prayer.   J. B. STEANE

Just, Johann August (*b* Gröningen, *c*1750; *d* ?The Hague, Dec 1791). German composer. According to Burney, he studied with Kirnberger in Berlin. By 1767 he was at the court of William V, Prince of Orange and Nassau, where he served as music master to Princess Wilhelmine; he remained connected with the court throughout his career. A keyboard player and violinist, he composed largely for keyboard, but also wrote at least three Singspiels, of which *De Koopman van Smyrna* was performed in German translation in Bonn and Frankfurt in 1783 (the overture and selected songs were published separately: Amsterdam, n.d.). *Der gute Fürst und der Edelknabe* survives (3; *A-Wgm*), but the music of *De Sympathie* is lost. The authorship of the Singspiel *Günther von Schwarzburg* (cited by Eitner) is doubtful. Just's music reflects the simple, direct but expressive style which became prevalent from the 1760s. Despite Just's peripheral position geographically, it was evidently the popular and widely circulated stage works and song style of J. A. Hiller that provided the primary model for his Singspiels.

*

BurneyGN

M. de Smet: *La musique à la cour de Guillaume V Prince d'Orange (1748–1806)* (Utrecht, 1973)   RONALD R. KIDD

Jutland Opera. Danish company founded in 1947 in ÅRHUS.

Juvarra [Juvara], **Filippo** (*b* Messina, 16 June 1676; *d* Madrid, 31 Jan 1736). Italian architect, stage designer and engraver. He was trained for the Catholic priesthood while also studying architecture; he published his first artistic work in 1701 (see Sciavo). From about 1704 he studied architecture in Rome and in 1705 won the architecture prize of the Concorso Clementino and became a member of the Accademia di S Luca. In 1706 Juvarra was working in the S Bartolomeo opera house in Naples as assistant to the stage designer Giuseppe Capelli, a pupil of Francesco Galli-Bibiena. After returning to Rome he designed a new theatre for Cardinal Ottoboni in the Palazzo della Cancelleria in 1709 and renovated Prince Capranica's theatre in 1713. In the years following 1709 he built elaborate sets for operas and oratorios in these two theatres and the Queen of Poland's private theatre in the Palazzo Zuccari. He became chief architect to Vittorio Amedeo II of Savoy in 1714 and as such was in charge of the construction of several important buildings in Turin, Piedmont, Portugal and Spain. From the date of his appointment his theatrical activities were confined to directing festivities at the Turin court and to a few isolated building projects (plans for an opera house in Genoa, *c*1713; construction of a stage in the Palazzo Reale and renovation of the Teatro Regio in Turin, 1722).

Juvarra's application of contemporary techniques for illusion in art, especially his perfecting of the 'maniera di veder le scene per angolo' by means of asymmetrical placing of wings, resulted in architectural structures of extraordinary complexity. For all their fantasy, his sets are based on precise architectonic concepts, anticipating the demands of stage theory in the age of Enlightenment. Within the artificial confines of the stage he sought to create an autonomous aesthetic realm which drew its justification primarily from the musico-dramatic work itself, and therefore, like the designs of J. O. Harms, displayed a strong element of lyricism. A

Design by Filippo Juvarra for Filippo Amadei's 'Teodosio il Giovane' performed at the Teatro Ottoboni, Rome, in 1711

compositional technique that emphasized the picturesque, a virtuoso play of light and shadow and the deployment of characteristic architectural and landscape motifs, created an atmosphere appropriate to the opera in question and furnished enough local colour to set its scene. Juvarra's settings for Alessandro Scarlatti's pastoral *Il Ciro* (1712) are typical, creating an exotic Arcadia dotted with romantic ruins, foreshadowing the cult of nature and the sensibility of the second half of the century.

See also STAGE DESIGN, §4. For further illustration *see* LUCCA; ROME, fig.2; SCARLATTI, (1); and SOCIOLOGY OF OPERA, fig.1.

ES (M. Viale-Ferrero)

N. M. Sciavo: *Amore ed ossequio di Messina* (Messina, 1701) [with 8 engravings]
F. Juvarra: *Galleria architettonica … ossia Memorie e cenni diversi di architettura militare e civile* (MS, *I-Tr*, 1708)
[P. Ottoboni]: *Il Costantino Pio* (Rome, 1710) [with 13 engravings]
F. Amadei: *Teodosio il giovane* (Rome, 1711) [with 12 engravings]
Giunio Bruto overo La caduta de'Tarquinii (MS, *A-Wn*, 1711) [with 20 drawings]
[P. Ottoboni]: *Il Ciro* (Rome, 1712) [with 13 engravings]
P. A. Bernardoni: *L'Eraclio* (Rome, 1712) [with engraving of the Teatro Ottoboni proscenium]
S. Maffei: 'Elogio del signor abate D. Filippo Juvara', *Osservazioni letterarie*, iii (Verona, 1738), 193–204
F. Milizia: *Le vite dei più celebri architetti d'ogni nazioni e d'ogni tempo* (Rome, 1768), 409
L. Masini: *La vita e l'arte di Filippo Juvarra* (Turin, 1920)
L. Rovere, M. Viale and E. A. Brinckmann: *Filippo Juvarra* (Milan, 1937)
R. E. Stout: 'Filippo Juvarra: an Introduction', *Ohio State University Theatre Collection Bulletin*, xi (1964), 3–5
W. R. West: 'Some Notes concerning Staging at the Ottoboni Theatre through an Analysis of "Il Teodosio"', *Ohio State University Theatre Collection Bulletin*, xi (1964), 21–34
M. Viale: *Mostra di Filippo Juvarra architetto e scenografo, Università degli studi di Messina, 1966* (Turin, 1966) [exhibition catalogue]
M. Viale-Ferrero: *Filippo Juvarra scenografo e architetto teatrale* (Turin, 1970) [with catalogue of stage designs]
——: *Storia del Teatro Regio di Torino: la scenografia dalle origini al 1936* (Turin, 1980)
H. A. Millon: *Filippo Juvarra* (Rome, 1984)

MANFRED BOETZKES

Juvo, Nicola. *See* GIUVO, NICOLA.

Juzeliūnas, Julius (*b* Čepolė Žeimelìs region, 20 Feb 1916). Lithuanian composer. He graduated at the Kaunas Conservatory (1948) and completed postgraduate studies at the Leningrad Conservatory in 1952. From that year he taught composition at the Vilnius Conservatory, where he was made professor and doctor of art criticism. His early works are neo-romantic, but the mature music shows a combination of national elements with new techniques. He has written two operas: *Sukilėliai* ('The Rebels'; 4, V. Mykolaitis-Putinas), composed in 1957 and given in Vilnius in 1977, and *Žaidimas* ('The Game'; 1, Juzeliūnas, after Dürrenmatt: *Die Panne*), also given in Vilnius, in October 1991.

*

'Juzeliūnas, Julius', *Encyclopedia lituanica*, ii (Boston, 1972), 575

MARINA NEST'YEVA

K

Kaart, Hans (Johannes Jansen) (*b* The Hague, 10 May 1920; *d* Lugano, 18 June 1963). Dutch tenor. He came from a family of actors, and from 1944 to 1955 appeared in Shakespeare and Chekhov as well as in modern comedies. He then studied singing in Holland and Italy, and made his début as Canio at Karlsruhe in 1956. This was also the role of his début with the Netherlands Opera in 1957. At Covent Garden in 1958 he was heard as Calaf in *Turandot*, and later sang Don José and Canio. In 1962 and 1963 he sang Samson at Chicago. Much of his best work was done with the Oper am Rhein at Düsseldorf, where his acting ability served well such parts as Mephistopheles (*Doktor Faust*) and the Witch (*Hänsel und Gretel*). His Otello, which has been ranked as 'among the best of all times' (Leo Riemens, *Opera*), can be sampled in extracts on some impressive recordings. He died while undergoing an operation on his ear.   J. B. STEANE

Kabaivanska, Raina (*b* Burgas, 15 Dec 1934). Bulgarian soprano. She studied at the Bulgarian State Conservatory and made her début in Sofia in 1957 as Tatyana. In 1961, after further study in Italy, she appeared at La Scala in Bellini's *Beatrice di Tenda*; her American début was at San Francisco in 1962 as Desdemona. She returned regularly to La Scala, and also appeared at the Metropolitan (début in 1962 as Nedda), Covent Garden, Moscow, Salzburg and Vienna; in 1973 she sang Hélène in Callas's production of *Les vêpres siciliennes* at the rebuilt Teatro Regio, Turin. She made her Paris début in 1975 at the Opéra as Leonora (*La forza del destino*). Butterfly and Tosca are considered her greatest roles, and her repertory also includes the Countess (*Capriccio*), Elizabeth (*Roberto Devereux*), Adriana Lecouvreur and Francesca da Rimini. Her voice is a strong and agreeable lyric soprano, secure in the top register and capable of warm, expressive shading; she is a natural and highly individual actress with a fine stage presence, particularly suited to the *verismo* repertory.

MAGDALENA MANOLOVA, RODOLFO CELLETTI

Kabalevsky, Dmitry Borisovich (*b* St Petersburg, 17/30 Dec 1904; *d* Moscow, 14 Feb 1987). Russian composer. He studied composition and the piano at the Moscow Conservatory, where he returned in 1932 to teach theory and composition. From 1940 to 1946 he was chief editor of the journal *Sovetskaya muzika*, and from 1952 until his death he was on the governing board of the Union of Composers of the USSR, where he was especially concerned with pedagogical matters. During a long and distinguished career, he held many other responsible positions in national and international societies and received numerous prizes and honours. He was also active as a pianist and conductor.

In addition to his five operas, Kabalevsky composed a ballet, an operetta, four symphonies, and many choral and vocal works. A deep sense of patriotism often provided the inspiration for his compositions, as in his well-known Requiem op.72 (1962). Three of his operas – *V ogne* ('Into the Fire', 1943), *Sem'ya Tarasa* ('The Taras Family', 1947) and *Nikita Vershinin* (1955) – were written on patriotic subjects with contemporary resonances. *Into the Fire* and *The Taras Family* dealt with events and emotions still vivid from World War II: the defence of Moscow in the former, and the heroic exploits of a family living under occupation in the latter. In *Nikita Vershinin* he attempted to create a 'folk' music drama, using the establishment of Soviet power in the Far East during the Civil War as its basis. The inspirational spirit of revolutionary hymns and mass songs can often be found in his writing.

Another important facet of Kabalevsky's creative activity was his music for children, including songs and pedagogical piano music and, perhaps most notably, works designed to bridge the technical and aesthetic gaps between childhood and professional maturity. His demonstrated sensitivity to the needs of young listeners prompted Natal'ya Sats to request an opera from him to enrich the repertory of her newly established Children's Music Theatre in Moscow. His final opera, *Syostrï* ('The Sisters', 1969), about two sisters amid the hardships of Siberia and their search for the meaning of life, was written to meet her demand for a work dealing with a theme of contemporary relevance to adolescents.

Kabalevsky was not a stylistic innovator. His music is fundamentally tonal and his melodies diatonic; he modelled his operas on the work of Tchaikovsky and, to a lesser extent, Musorgsky. What contributes to the durability of his works, especially his first opera, *Kola Bryun'on* ('Colas Breugnon', 1938), is a gift for simple, irresistibly lyrical melodies and catchy rhythms, all fleshed out with brilliant but transparent orchestral colour. Although the 16th-century Burgundian setting seemed remote from Soviet realities in the 1930s, particularly in light of the notorious attack on

937

Shostakovich's opera *Lady Macbeth of the Mtsensk District* in 1936 and the inescapable political pressures subsequently brought to bear on Soviet composers, Kabalevsky was successful in combining the larger theme of social conflict between Colas and the supercilious Duke d'Asnois with the human dimension of wide-ranging contrasts between life's tragedies and joys.

See also COLAS BREUGNON *and* SEM'YA TARASA.

Kola Bryun'on: master iz Klamsi [Colas Breugnon: the Master of Clamecy] op.24 (prol., 3, V. G. Bragin, after R. Rolland), as Master iz Klamsi, Leningrad, Malïy, 22 Feb 1938; rev. as op.90, Leningrad, Malïy, 16 April 1970

V ogne: pod Moskvoi [Into the Fire: near Moscow] op.37 (4, Ts. S. Solodar'), Moscow, Bol'shoy Branch, 19 Sept 1943

Sem'ya Tarasa [The Taras Family] op.47 (4, S. A. Tsenin, after B. Gorbatov: *Nepokorennïye* [The Unvanquished]), Moscow, Stanislavsky–Nemirovich-Danchenko Music Theatre, 2 Nov 1947; rev., Leningrad, Kirov, 7 Nov 1950; rev., Moscow, Stanislavsky–Nemirovich-Danchenko Music Theatre, 17 Nov 1967

Nikita Vershinin op.53 (4, Tsenin, after V. V. Ivanov: *Bronepoyezd 14–69* [Armoured Train 14–69]), Moscow, Bol'shoy, 26 Nov 1955

Vesna poyot [Spring Sings] op.58 (operetta, 3, Solodar'), Moscow, Operetta Theatre, 4 Nov 1957

Syostrï [The Sisters] op.83 (prol., 3, epilogue, S. Bogomazov, after I. Lavrov: *Vstrecha s chudom* [Encounter with a Miracle]), Perm', State Academic, 31 May 1969

*

L. Danilevich: '"Master iz Klamsi": opera D. Kabalevskogo', *SovM* (1937), no.12, pp.35–47

M. Druskin: ' "Kola Bryun'on" v Leningradskom Malom opernom teatre' ['Colas Breugnon' in the Malïy Opera Theatre in Leningrad], *Teatr* (1938), no.6, p.104

A. Ostretsov: 'Master iz Klamsi', *SovM* (1938), no.3, pp.86–91

I. Sollertinsky: 'Kola Bryun'on', *Iskusstvo i zhizn'* [Art and Life] (1938), no.3, p.29

G. Abraham: *Eight Soviet Composers* (London, 1943), 70ff

Yu. Keldïsh: 'Na puti opernogo realizma D. Kabalevskogo' [In Search of Operatic Realism in Kabalevsky], *SovM* (1951), no.3, pp.13–24

T. Livanova: 'Kharakter geroya i opernaya ariya' [The Character of the Hero and the Operatic Aria], *SovM* (1951), no.8, pp.10–18

L. Polyakova: *Putevoditel' po opere 'Sem'ya Tarasa' D. Kabalevskogo* [Guide to Kabalevsky's 'The Taras Family'] (Moscow, 1953)

——: 'Dve operï D. Kabalevskogo' [Two Operas by Kabalevsky], *Sovetskaya muzika: stat'i i materiali* [Soviet Music: Articles and Documents], i (Moscow, 1956), 72–94 [on *The Taras Family* and *Nikita Vershinin*]

——: 'Novaya sovetskaya opera' [A New Soviet Opera], *SovM* (1956), no.1, pp.13–22 [on *Nikita Vershinin*]

G. Abramovsky: 'Osnovnïye muzikal'no-dramaturgicheskiye obrazï oper D. Kabalevskogo "Sem'ya Tarasa" i "Nikita Vershinin" ' [The Main Musico-Dramaturgical Images in Kabalevsky's Operas 'The Taras Family' and 'Nikita Vershinin'], *Ocherki po istorii i teorii muziki* [Studies in Music History and Theory], ed. M. Druskin and Y. Tyulin (Leningrad, 1958), 155–77

L. Khinchin: 'Opera Kabalevskogo "Sem'ya Tarasa" kak obrazets muzikal'noy dramï' [Kabalevsky's Opera 'The Taras Family' as an Example of Music Drama], *Nauchno-metodicheskiye zapiski Novosibirskoy konservatorii imeni M. I. Glinki* [Scientific-Methodical Notes of the Novosibirsk Glinka Conservatory], i (Novosibirsk, 1958)

P. Nazarevsky, ed.: *D. B. Kabalevsky: notograficheskiy i bibliograficheskiy spravochnik* [Kabalevsky: Work-list and Bibliography] (Moscow, 1969)

Z. Sokol'skaya: 'Dobrogo vam puti, "Syostrï" ' [Fare thee well, 'Sisters'], *SovM* (1969), no.11, pp.33–9

E. Dobrïnina: ' "Zhiv kurilka!": o novoy redaktsii "Kola Bryun'ona" D. Kabalevskogo' [There's Life in the Old Dog Yet!: on a New Edition of Kabalevsky's 'Colas Breugnon'], *SovM* (1972), no.2, pp.2–16

I. Prokhorova: 'Opera "Sem'ya Tarasa" ', *Sovetskaya muzikal'naya literatura* [Soviet Musical Literature], ed. M. Rittikh (Moscow, 1977), 454

LAUREL E. FAY

Kacsóh, Pongrác (*b* Budapest, 15 Dec 1873; *d* Budapest, 16 Dec 1923). Hungarian composer, teacher and writer on music. He studied the piano and flute at the University of Kolozsvár (now Cluj-Napoca), theory with Ödön von Farkas and organized a student orchestra. From 1892 to 1896 he studied physics, and he taught mathematics and physics in Budapest before turning to composition and criticism. As a contributor to the journal *Zenevilág* he was among the first to recognize Bartók's talent. The popularity of some songs and the musical play *Csipkerózsa* led to a commission for the operetta *János vitéz* (1904), which provided a welcome antidote to the Viennese works then in vogue and has remained the most popular Hungarian national operetta. It was followed by *Rákóczi* (1906), *Mary-Ann* (1908) and incidental music for Molnár's *Liliom* (1909). After a period in Kecskemét, Kacsóh returned in 1912, to Budapest, where he held various positions as a teacher and chorus master. He composed many songs and some choral and piano music and also published textbooks on music.

Csipkerózsa [Wild Rose] (Spl, 3, Kacsóh), Budapest, Málnai Academy, 1904

János vitéz [Hero John] op.5 (Spl, 3, K. Bakonyi and J. Heltai, after S. Petőfi), Budapest, Király, 18 Nov 1904

Rákóczi op.7 (Spl, 3, Bakonyi, S. Endrödy, Á. Pásztor and C. Sassy), Budapest, Király, 20 Nov 1906

A harang [The Bell] (legend, 3, Pásztor), Budapest, Király, 1 Feb 1907, collab. A. Buttykay

Mary-Ann op.14 (operetta, 3, S. Hajó and A. Gábor, after I. Zangwill), Budapest, Király, 5 Dec 1908

Pompei (3, Pásztor), 1913, inc.

Dorottya [Dorothea] (3, Kacsóh, after M. Csokonai Vitéz), Szeged, National, 1929

*

L. Koch: *Kacsóh Pongrác János vitéze* (Budapest, 1942)

ANDREW LAMB

Kadosa, Pál (*b* Léva [now Levice, Czechoslovakia], 6 Sept 1903; *d* Budapest, 30 March 1983). Hungarian composer. He studied composition with Kodály at the Budapest Academy of Music (1921–7). From 1927 until 1943 he taught the piano at the Fodor Conservatory, and in 1943–4 at the Goldmark School of Music in Budapest. In 1928 he was a joint founder of the Society of Modern Hungarian Musicians (later united with the Hungarian Association for New Music, the Hungarian section of the ISCM). In the 1930s his works began to appear in such international centres of new music as Amsterdam, Venice (the 1934 Biennale) and Strasbourg. After World War II, Kadosa's career continued to develop. He was awarded many composition prizes and as a pianist became one of the foremost Bartók interpreters. Kadosa wrote two comic operas: the one-act *Irren ist staatlich* (1931), to his own libretto, and the two-act *A Huszti kaland* ('The Adventure at Huszt', 1949–50) to a libretto by B. Szaboksi, which was first performed in Budapest on 22 December 1951.

FERENC BÓNIS

Kaffka [Engelmann], **Johann Christoph** (*b* Regensburg, 1759; *d* Riga, after 1803). German composer and librettist. He studied the violin with his father and later music theory with Joseph Riepel. After studying to become a Jesuit, then a Cistercian, he changed his name and began a long and chequered theatrical career in 1775 as music director of the Brunian company in Prague. He acted with various troupes in Nuremberg, Frankfurt (Marchand), Leipzig (Bondini), Regensburg,

Stuttgart (Schikaneder), Berlin (Döbbelin, 1779–81), Brno and finally Breslau (Maria Wäser, to 1789).

In addition to his seven operas, Kaffka composed incidental music, ballets, celebratory prologues and especially melodramas. As a composer he was keenly aware of current fashion. His allegorical prologue *Bitten und Erhörung* (for the birthday of Frederick the Great, 24 January 1783) drew a charge of plagiarism from one reviewer, as did his melodrama *Rosemund* (1782, Breslau) from another. He was also given to passing off librettos adapted from others as his own work. His greatest success as a composer and actor-singer came during his years at Breslau, where his 'extremely advantageous figure' won him an ardent female following.

first performed in Breslau by the Wäser company unless otherwise stated

Die Zigeuner (Lustspiel mit Gesang und untermischten Tänzen, 5, H. F. Möller, after M. de Cervantes: *La gitanilla*), Munich, Kurfürstliches, 1778
Antonius and Cleopatra (Duodrama mit Gesang, 2, B. C. d'Arien), Berlin, Döbbelins, 15 Nov 1779
Der Äpfeldieb, oder Der Schatzgräber (Operette, 1, C. F. Bretzner), Berlin, Döbbelins, 26 June 1780
Rosemund (Melodram, 1, Bretzner), Jan 1782
Das wütende Heer, oder Das Mädchen im Thurme (Operette, 3, Bretzner), Jan 1782, *D-Bhm*
Der Guck Kasten, oder Das Beste komt zulezt (komische Operette, 2, Kaffka), 1782
So prellt man alte Füchse (Operette, 1, Kaffka, after F. L. W. Meyer), 1782
Der blinde Ehemann (Operette, 2, J. F. Jünger), 1788
Der Talisman, oder Der seltene Spiegel (romantisch-komische Oper, 3, Bretzner), 1789, *Bhm*

*

C. F. Cramer, ed.: *Magazin der Musik*, ii (1784), 872–8
Allgemeine deutsche Bibliothek, lxxii/1 (1787), 163–4
R. M. Werner, ed.: *Gallerie von teutschen Schauspielern und Schauspielerinnen* (Berlin, 1910)
A. Mai: *Das Wäser'sche Schauspielergesellschaft in Schlesien (1772–97)* (diss., Friedrich-Wilhelm U., Breslau, 1928)
S. Färber: *Das Regensburger Fürstlich Thurn und Taxische Hoftheater und seine Oper 1760–1786* (Regensburg, 1936)
T. Bauman: *North German Opera in the Age of Goethe* (Cambridge, 1985)
                                    THOMAS BAUMAN

Kagel, Mauricio [Maurizio] (**Raúl**) (*b* Buenos Aires, 24 Dec 1931). Argentine composer. A film-maker and dramatist as well as a highly inventive and versatile composer, he has constantly explored new types of music theatre; his numerous compositions include stage works, chamber, vocal and orchestral music and pieces for specially constructed instruments, as well as film, television, radio, video and tape.

Kagel studied the piano, the cello, the organ, singing, conducting and theory with private teachers and on his own (in retrospect he remarked 'my encounters with substandard teachers trained me to become self-taught'), as well as literature and philosophy at Buenos Aires University. In 1949 he worked with an avant-garde group, the Agrupación Nueva Música; a year later he co-founded the Cinémathèque Argentine and wrote his earliest compositions. From 1952 to 1959 he was film and photography critic for two Buenos Aires journals. Having been head of studies at the Chamber Opera and director of the Teatro Colón, he moved to Cologne in 1957, succeeding Stockhausen as director of the Cologne Courses for New Music. Remaining until 1975, he taught music and radio, music therapy, music and image, children's instruments and other unconventional subjects. In 1974 he became Professor of New Music Theatre at the Cologne Musikhochschule. Kagel

has toured and lectured widely and directs premières of all his own stage works, films and radio plays.

In his very first compositions Kagel began to exploit the latent theatricality of musical performance and, working closely with the Cologne Ensemble for New Music, which he founded in 1961, began to integrate visual elements into his works, calling them 'instrumental theatre'; the scores contained not only the musical material but also specified the gestures of the performers, their movements, the stage blocking, lighting and sets. Kagel wrote in 1966:

As a composer I feel I have an increasing duty to non-aural materials. In this I see no substitute for actual composition, but on the contrary assert that the dictionary definition of the word 'composition' as 'setting together' or 'mixing' may be as much accepted as the more usual definition of 'tone setting'. Musical thought can be applied to theatrical thought – words, lights and movements articulated in the same way as pitch, timbre and tempo.

Among the most important examples of this 'instrumental theatre' are *Sur scène* (composed 1958–60), a 'chamber music play', *Match* (1964), *Tremens* (1963–5), a 'scenic montage of a test experiment', and the cycle of three pieces, *Camera obscura*, *Die Himmelsmechanik* and *Pas de cinq* (all composed 1965). Kagel's vocal style of writing in his early concert pieces (such as in the strictly serial *Anagrama* of 1957–8, written at the time he entered the West German avant garde) is deployed in subsequent stage works to define a dramatic character: the solo performer in *Phonophonie* (1963–4) alternates between singing voice, mimic, ventriloquist and deaf-mute to create the character of an opera singer in vocal decline; *Hallelujah* (1967–8) for 16–32 singers exists as both a concert piece in which a Latin text is sung in a wide range of vocal articulation, and as a stage work, the actions for which are to be derived exclusively from the vocabulary of religious gesture.

Staatstheater (1967–70), subtitled 'scenic composition' and commissioned by the Hamburg Staatsoper, is a culmination of these earlier preoccupations. Kagel's previous multi-media concerns are now contained within the opera-house framework: 'I don't want a one-dimensional stage, but a multi-dimensional one. Strange to say, I can achieve this best with a peep-show stage', he remarked. The work is an examination of opera as both genre and institution: Kagel divides up the apparatus and personnel of the opera house (musicians, chorus, props, costumes, scenery) into hundreds of individual activities and recombines them in virtuoso fashion. The composition comprises nine vocal, instrumental and scenic sections; apart from *Repertoire*, which should begin any performance of *Staatstheater*, their order and combination is left open. There is no one plot or libretto; instead most sections consist of single stage-actions (each lasting up to a minute, and described within one page of score) which explore the relationship between the performer and a prop or specially constructed 'sound-source'. There is also no text: the vocal sections *Ensemble*, for 16 voices, and *Debüt*, for 60 voices, are scored for soloists, dressed in costumes typical of operatic repertory, singing parts made up of elaborate vocal exercises. Despite the visual and aural density of *Staatstheater*, any production, in the words of the composer, should be presented with 'the utmost transparency and lucidity'.

These terms could equally well apply to Kagel's subsequent musical style, which tended to use regular rhythmic pulse (or what he called 'tonal rhythm' since it

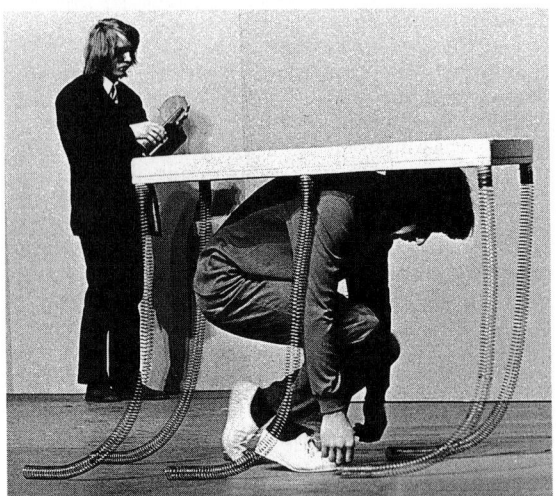

'Repertoire', numbers 78 (Hallraum, foreground) and 82 (Obertöne), from the original production of Kagel's 'Staatstheater' by the Hamburg Staatsoper, 25 April 1971

is based on rational proportions) and consonance (both melodic and harmonic) with instrumental ensembles chosen for their distinctive and associative timbral character. His compositional methods become much clearer and the treatment of particular musical 'objects' more obvious; they also tend to make overt his tackling of more complex subject matter: *Mare nostrum* (1973–5), subtitled 'discovery, pacification and conversion of the Mediterranean by an Amazonian tribe', is a fictional account of colonization in reverse, and *Kantrimiusik* (1973–5), a pastoral for voices and instruments, concerns the artificial world of commercial folk music. Both pieces include a substantial theatrical component and are focussed around a distinct stage design: the eight players in *Mare nostrum* sit in a set representing the Mediterranean; in *Kantrimiusik* the 'leading role' is played by a piece of stage machinery fitted with movable parts and representing characteristic folklore elements. In both music and text (the latter in a specially invented language of misunderstanding) the pieces are to be seen as Kagel's personal commentary on cultural misrepresentation and mishearing – the one as experienced by an imaginary South American colonizer as he makes his way from Portugal to the Middle East, the other as presented by a folkband in a programme of mock light entertainment.

Between 1976 and 1980 Kagel worked on two further operatic projects, much larger in scope and theme than anything before. *Die Erschöpfung der Welt*, a 'scenic illusion in one act', inverts the creation story as told in Genesis by substituting passages from the Apocalypse. In an attempt at 'Acoustic Theology', Kagel presents the world as a theatre in which Man has invented God (an invisible, negative figure throughout) as stage director. The German text deconstructs and filters original Bible verses, lines of prayer, chant and hymn in the manner of concrete poetry, to create a sadistic pseudo-liturgy. A small stage, hanging over the performing area, represents in a naive, picture-book fashion an 'Allegorical Space of Heaven' and acts as a counterpoint to the events onstage, which, illustrating the creation of music alongside Man, are depicted with typical Kagelian fantasy – God's 'Zoological Garden' is filled with animals wearing acoustic attributes as parts of their body. The orchestral music also illustrates the narrative, supplemented with taped sound effects of thunder, fire and water.

The libretto to *Aus Deutschland*, subtitled a 'Lieder-opera', is a collage of German lieder texts scored for soloists and chorus, accompanied principally by pianos. The *dramatis personae* are figures and allegories taken from the songs (an organ-grinder, Death, Night, the Mother, Hyperion, Mignon, Music) as well as the authors themselves (Goethe, Schubert); the narratives are staged as a sequence of 27 fast-moving tableaux vivants. The music is all original Kagel, deriving its forms and figures from characteristic piano accompaniment patterns. *Aus Deutschland* is Kagel's most thorough contribution to his ongoing engagement with the legacies of 19th-century music, begun with his homage to Beethoven in the film *Ludwig van* (1969); his motive is to demystify the world of the Romantic, by exposing its principal concerns – freedom and repression, experience and desire, alienation and tradition.

selective list

Sur scène, 1958–60 (Kammermusikalisches Theaterstück), Bremen, 6 May 1962
Antithèse, version for actor with elec and public sounds, Cologne, Schauspielhaus, 23 June 1963
Phonophonie, 1963–4 (4 melodramas), Munich, 1 Dec 1965 (London, 1976)
Tremens, 1963–5 (szenische Montage eines Tests), Bremen, 6 May 1966; Variaktionen über Tremens, 1963–5
Camera obscura, 1965 (chromatisches Spiel), Frankfurt, Hindemith Saal, 25 Aug 1989
Die Himmelsmechanik, 1965 (Komposition mit Bühnenbildern), Venice, 14 Sept 1969 (London, 1967)
Match, Berlin, 22 Oct 1965 (London, 1967)
Pas de cinq (Wandelszene), Munich, 14 June 1966 (London, 1967)
Variaktionen, Frankfurt, 5 June 1967; Musik aus Variaktionen, 1966–7
Kommentar + Extempore (Selbstgespräche mit Gesten), Frankfurt, 5 June 1967
Hallelujah, 1967–8, Stuttgart, 29 Jan 1969
Staatstheater, 1967–70 (szenische Komposition), Hamburg, Staatsoper, 25 April 1971; 9 sections: Repertoire (szenisches Konzertstück); Einspielungen; Ensemble; Debüt; Saison (Sing-Spiel in 65 Bildern); Spielplan (Instrumentalmusik in Aktion); Kontra-Danse (Ballett für Nicht-Tänzer); Freifahrt (gleitende Kammermusik); Parkett (konzertante Massenszenen)
Con voce, Berlin, Akademie der Künste, 23 Jan 1973
Mare nostrum, 1973–5 (Entdeckung, Befriedung und Konversion des Mittelmeerraumes durch einen Stamm aus Amazonien), Berlin, Hochschule der Künste, 15 Sept 1975 (London, 1975)
Kantrimiusik, 1973–5 (Pastorale für Stimmen und Instrumente), Donaueschingen, 18 Oct 1975 (London, 1975)
Quatre degrés, Metz, Municipal, 18 Nov 1977; 4 sections: Dressur (Schlagzeugtrio für Holzinstrumente); Présentation für zwei; Déménagement [Umzug] (stummes Schauspiel für Bühnenarbeiter); Variété (Concert-Spectacle für Artisten und Musiker)
Ex-position, Oslo, Høvikodden, 14 Sept 1978; 2 sections: Die Rhythmusmaschinen (Aktion für Gymnasten, Rhythmusgeneratoren und Schlagzeuger); Chorbuch (für Vokalensemble und Tasteninstrumente)
Die Erschöpfung der Welt (szenische Illusion, 1), Stuttgart, Württembergische Staatstheater, 9 Feb 1980
Aus Deutschland (Lieder-Oper), Berlin, Deutsche Oper, 9 May 1981
Der Tribun (Hörspiel für einen politischer Redner, Marschklänge und Lautsprecher), Aix-en-Provence, Cloître St-Louis, 1 Aug 1981
La Trahison Orale, (Musikepos über den Teufel), Paris, Chaillot, 27 Oct 1983

*

M. Kesting: 'Musikalisierung des Theaters – Theatralisierung der Musik', *Melos*, xxxvi (1969), 101–9
D. Schnebel: *Mauricio Kagel: Musik, Theater, Film* (Cologne, 1970)
J.-Y. Bosseur: 'Dossier Kagel', *Musique en jeu*, no.7 (1972), 88–126
M. Kagel: *Tamtam: Dialoge und Monologe zur Musik* (Munich, 1975)

N. Matossian: 'The New Music Theatre', *Music and Musicians*, xxv/1 (1976), 22–4

K.-H. Zarius: *Beiträge zur Theorie des Instrumentalen Theaters* (Bonn, 1976)

W. Gruhn: 'Die instrumentale Inszenierung des Klanges bei Mauricio Kagel', *Musik und Bildung*, ix (1977), 606–14

K.-H. Zarius: '*Staatstheater*' *von Mauricio Kagel: Grenze und Übergang* (Vienna, 1977)

'Kagelopéradiothéâtre', *Musique en jeu*, no.27 (1977) [whole issue]

H. Brodegg: *Marginalien zur 'Erschöpfung der Welt' Kagels* (Stuttgart, 1980)

W. Klüppelholz: *Schubert im Schosse Goethes in den Armen Freuds* (Berlin, 1980) [Deutsche Oper programme book]

——: *Mauricio Kagel 1970–1980* (Cologne, 1981)

M. Kagel: *Das Buch der Hörspiele* (Frankfurt, 1982)

——: *Das filmische Werk 1: 1965–85* (Amsterdam and Cologne, 1985)

M. Kagel: *Worte über Musik* (Munich, 1991)

W. Klüppelholz, ed: *M. Kagel…/1991* (Cologne, 1991)

DAVID SAWER

Kagen, Sergius (*b* St Petersburg, 9/22 Aug 1909; *d* New York, 1 March 1964). American composer of Russian birth. In 1921 he went to Berlin, where he studied composition with Paul Juon at the Hochschule für Musik. After emigrating in 1925 to the USA, he attended the Juilliard School. He taught singing and vocal literature at Juilliard from 1940 until his death, and composed over 70 songs. His three-act opera *Hamlet*, written in a lyrical twelve-note style using only a quarter of Shakespeare's text, was first performed in Baltimore on 9 November 1962. A second opera, *The Suitor* (based on Molière's *Monsieur de Pourceaugnac*), was never completed.

B. J. Woods: *Sergius Kagen: his Life and Works* (diss., George Peabody College for Teachers, 1969)   R. ALLEN LOTT

Kahn, Otto (Hermann) (*b* Mannheim, 21 Feb 1867; *d* New York, 29 March 1934). American arts patron. A banker from a banking family, he was an amateur violinist and cellist. His career took him first to London, where he became a naturalized British subject, then to New York (1893).

In 1903, when a new producing group was organized at the Metropolitan Opera, Kahn purchased stock and in 1907, with William K. Vanderbilt sr, he bought the company and reorganized it under Gatti-Casazza and Toscanini (both previously of La Scala); he personally made up its sizable losses for the next three years. He became chairman of the board in 1911 and president in 1918; he resigned both positions in 1931 but stayed on as a director. He became an American citizen in 1917. The period of his chairmanship was marked by financial solvency, growing artistic prestige and the performance of 14 operas by American composers. In 1926 he purchased land on West 57th Street for a new opera house for the Metropolitan, but box-holder opposition and rising costs thwarted this plan. In support of performances in English translation by American-born artists, he gave liberally to the short-lived American Opera and Century Opera companies. He was a founder of the first Chicago opera company and a director of the Boston Opera Company. He supported, often anonymously, many other arts organizations.

'Our Opera Best, Says Otto Kahn', *New York Times* (8 Aug 1911)

'In Tune with the Finite', *New Yorker*, ii (20 Feb 1926)

M. J. Matz: *The Many Lives of Otto Kahn* (New York, 1963)

M. Goldin: *The Music Merchants* (New York, 1969)

DAVID WRIGHT

Kaiserslautern. City in south-west Germany. Its first permanent theatre opened in 1862; before then touring companies gave occasional performances. The building was destroyed by fire in 1867, but was immediately rebuilt. Although its existence was seriously endangered by the Franco-Prussian War in 1870, it was saved when purchased by a joint-stock company in 1873. In 1897 the theatre passed into civic control; in 1944 the building was destroyed in an air raid. After the war, theatrical performances began again in a cinema, the company being known successively as the Städtische Bühnen (1945), Pfälzisches Landestheater (1946) and Pfalztheater (1948). The former cinema and café on the Fackelrondell was soon converted into a theatre, and opened in 1950 with *Fidelio*. This building is still in use, but construction has begun on a new, larger and technically more efficient theatre, which is planned for completion in the late 1990s. The Pfalztheater is financed by the Bezirksverband, an association of towns in the Palatinate, and by a grant from the *Land* of the Rhineland-Palatinate. The company also gives regular performances outside the city (in Ludwigshafen, Landau, Pirmasens, Zweibrücken, Frankenthal, Neustadt and elsewhere).

There are about 50 operatic performances in and outside Kaiserslautern every season. The repertory consists of six operas in the Grosses Haus (including one or two modern pieces and one or two *Spielopern*) and three modern chamber operas in the Studio. The old theatre on the Fackelrondell holds 514; the new theatre will have 450 seats in the stalls and 250 in the circles.

GÁBOR HALÁSZ

Kaiser von Atlantis, Der [*Der Kaiser von Atlantis, oder Der Tod dankt ab* ('The Emperor of Atlantis, or Death Abdicates')]. 'Legend' in four scenes by VIKTOR ULLMANN to a libretto by Petr Kien; Amsterdam, Bellevue Theatre, 16 December 1975.

The work was composed in 1943 in the Nazi concentration camp Theresienstadt (Terezín). Two versions of the libretto, one handwritten, the other typed, were made on the reverse side of prisoner information forms. The work is scored for seven singers and a medium-sized ensemble of available instruments. The cast includes Emperor Überall (baritone), Death (bass-baritone), Pierrot (tenor), a Loudspeaker (bass-baritone), a Drummer (mezzo-soprano), a Soldier (tenor), a Girl (soprano) and two female dancers. In the Prologue (melodrama) the Loudspeaker, after introducing the characters, describes the situation in which the living no longer laugh, the dying no longer die, and life and death have lost their customary meanings. Death finds this repulsive and goes on strike: henceforth no one is allowed to die. The opera comprises recitatives, arias and ensembles (duets and trios), and there are three dance numbers – a prelude and two intermezzos ('Dance of Death' and 'The Living Death'). Ullmann's music and Kien's text inevitably mirror much of the tension and anxiety which the Terezín inhabitants felt in the face of an unknown but threatening fate. As with Ullmann's music generally, the style of the work is eclectic, ranging from that of Weill to the Second Viennese School. With its rich harmonic and contrapuntal textures, and its varied instrumentation and idiomatic vocal writing, a convincing sense of theatre emerges. The quotation of music known to the Terezín audience would no doubt have had a powerful impact had the work been presented there. Ullmann quotes the 'Angel of Death' motif from Josef Suk's *Asräel* symphony and uses a distortion of *Deutschland über Alles*. The final chorale, sung to the melody of *Ein' feste Burg ist unser Gott*, urges that life's end should be through the dignity of natural death and not through meaningless killing. Although rehearsals began in Terezín in September 1944, both the censorship and the increasing transports to Auschwitz prevented a production. Since its 1975 première, however, performances have been given in Europe, Israel and North and South America.

DAVID BLOCH

Kaktiņš, Ādolfs (*b* Mazsalaca, Valmiera district, 26 July 1885; *d* San Francisco, 25 July 1965). Latvian bass-baritone. At first an actor, he made his operatic début in 1910 at Riga in Kreutzer's *Das Nachtlager von Granada*. Engaged at Nuremberg (1913–15), he sang Méphistophélès, Caspar and the bass roles in the *Ring*. He sang in Petrograd (now St Petersburg, 1915–17), then returned to Riga where he was a member of the Latvian National Opera (1919–44). He also appeared in Finland, Estonia, Lithuania, Sweden and at Prague and Dresden. In 1925 he sang Tonio and Rubinstein's Demon at Monte Carlo and Amonasro at the Paris Opéra. He sang Iago and the Dutchman at Munich and Rigoletto and Escamillo in Moscow. With a powerful voice of very wide compass, he had an immense repertory that included Luna, Renato, Scarpia, Prince Igor and Boris, his favourite and most impressive role.

ELIZABETH FORBES, ARNOLDS KLOTIŅŠ

Kalbeck, Max (*b* Breslau, 4 Jan 1850; *d* Vienna, 4 May 1921). German writer and librettist. He studied law and philosophy at Breslau university. Between 1875 and 1880 he worked in Breslau as a music critic and as assistant director of the Schlesisches Museum, then moved to Vienna and worked for the *Wiener allgemeine Zeitung* and other periodicals.

Kalbeck was an influential critic in Vienna and a partisan of Brahms. While his earliest published studies were devoted to Wagner's music dramas, his main work of musical scholarship was his biography of Brahms. He also wrote new librettos for Mozart's *Bastien und Bastienne* and *La finta giardiniera*, made translations of librettos, including *Don Giovanni* and Gluck's *Orfeo ed Euridice*, and wrote librettos for contemporary composers. Ede Poldini wrote three children's operas in 1899 based on Kalbeck's *Märchenspielen für die Jugend*.

LIBRETTOS

Jakuba, J. Strauss (operetta), 1894; Nubia, G. Henschel, 1899; Das stille Dorf, A. von Fielitz, 1900; Die Hochzeit zu Ulfosa, P. Caro, unperf.

CRITICISM

selective list

Richard Wagners Nibelungen (Breslau, ?1876, 2/1883)
Das Bühnenfestspiel zu Bayreuth (Breslau, 1877)
Richard Wagners Parsifal (Breslau, 1883)
Wiener Opernabende, Bibliothek für Ost und West, xiv (Vienna, 1885)
Opernabende, i–ii (Berlin, 1898)

*

A. Wurz: 'Max Kalbeck', ZfM, cxi (1950)
W. Kosch: 'Kalbeck, Max', *Deutsches Literatur-Lexicon* (Berne, 2/1953)
A. Bettelheim: 'Kalbeck, Max', *Österreichisches biographisches Lexicon* (Vienna, 1954)

R. J. PASCALL

Kale, Stuart (*b* Neath, 27 Oct 1944). Welsh tenor. He studied at the GSM and the London Opera Centre, then joined the WNO, with which he made his début in 1971 as the Prince in Berg's *Lulu*. He was then a resident principal with the ENO for 12 years, taking a variety of lyric and character roles from Don Ottavio to Nanki-Poo (in Jonathan Miller's production of *The Mikado*). He sang Siegfried at Bucharest in 1983, the Captain (*Wozzeck*) at Strasbourg in 1987, Glock/Agrippa/Doctor and Mephistopheles in Prokofiev's *The Fiery Angel* for State Opera of South Australia in 1988, and made his Covent Garden début that year as Guillot de Morfontaine (*Manon*). He also sings the Drum Major (*Wozzeck*), Boles (*Peter Grimes*), Lucan (*L'incoronazione di Poppea*), Shuysky (*Boris*) and Zinovy Izmaylov (*Lady Macbeth of the Mtsensk District*). In 1991 he sang Idomeneo at Drottningholm. He brings wit and intelligence to character roles, as well as a sturdy and expressive vocal technique.

NOËL GOODWIN

Kalenberg, Josef (*b* Cologne, 7 Jan 1886; *d* Vienna, 8 Nov 1962). German tenor. He studied at Cologne, where in 1911 he made his début as Turiddu in *Cavalleria rusticana*. There followed seasons at Krefeld, Barmen and Düsseldorf, with a return to Cologne in 1925. While there he sang Calaf in the local première of *Turandot*. From 1927 to 1942 he became the valued tenor-of-all-work at the Vienna Staatsoper, singing the Verdi repertory from *Traviata* to *Otello*, taking the title role in Strauss's revival of *Idomeneo*, and appearing in Wagner, Strauss and Korngold. He was also in demand at Salzburg where his roles included Tamino, Florestan and Tristan, a part he sang finally in Vienna at the age of 62. His recordings range almost as widely, though what they show principally is a tireless, weighty voice of no great beauty and used all too often at an unvarying forte.

J. B. STEANE

Kálik, Václav (*b* Opava, 18 Oct 1891; *d* Prague, 18 Nov 1951). Czech composer. He studied history and art history at Prague University (1909–14), and composition with Novák (1911–13), continuing his studies in Suk's master classes at the Prague Conservatory (1924–6). He also studied the piano, violin, singing and conducting. His studies took him abroad, principally to Italy, and some of his music was based on his Italian experiences. Between 1911 and 1923 he devoted much energy to work with choirs in Czechoslovakia. He became a member of the Czech Academy of Sciences and Art in 1946. His richly lyrical and intensely expressive music found wide popularity and many of his choral and chamber works show the depth of his humanitarian concerns. The operas *Jarní jitro* ('Spring Morning', 1933) and *Lásky div* ('The Miracle of Love', 1943) had successful premières, but have not remained in the repertory.

Jarní jitro [Spring Morning], 1933 (1, Kálik), Olomouc, 1 Oct 1943
Lásky div [The Miracle of Love], 1943 (1, J. Zeyer), Liberec, 20 Nov 1950
Posvěcení mládi [The Consecration of Youth], 1946 (3, J. Mahen), unperf.

JAN VRATISLAVSKÝ

Kaliningrad (Russ.). KÖNIGSBERG.

Kalisch, Alfred (*b* London, 13 March 1863; *d* London, 17 May 1933). English translator. He was one of the first British champions of Richard Strauss, with whom he became personally acquainted at the first performance in Berlin of *Feuersnot* (1912). His translation of *Der Rosenkavalier*, published in the vocal score and first performed in Birmingham in 1913, showed fluency and comic resource. He also made the authorized translations of Strauss's *Salome*, *Elektra* (1912, Hull) and *Ariadne auf Naxos* (1934, New York). He translated Johann Strauss's *Die Fledermaus* for a London production of 1910, and De Lara's *Les trois mousquetaires* for its first and only performances in England (1924, Newcastle upon Tyne and London).

ARTHUR JACOBS

Kalisch, Paul (*b* Berlin, 6 Nov 1855; *d* St Lorenz am Modensee, 27 Jan 1946). German tenor. He studied in Italy with Leoni and the younger Lamperti, and in 1879 made his début in Rome (under the name of Paolo Alberti) as Edgardo. After singing at Milan and Florence he appeared at Munich in 1883 as Raoul (*Les Huguenots*) and the Duke (*Rigoletto*). He was engaged at the Berlin Hofoper from 1884 to 1887, and made his Metropolitan début in the first New York performance of the Paris version of *Tannhäuser* (1889). At the Metropolitan he appeared frequently with his wife, the soprano Lilli Lehmann. With her he sang in *Die Walküre*, *Fidelio*, *La juive*, *Norma* and *Il trovatore*, but his lyric voice and refined style were perhaps better suited to Don Ottavio or to Nureddin, which he sang at the American première of Cornelius's *Der Barbier von Bagdad* (1890).

H. H. Krehbiel: *Chapters of Opera* (New York, 1908)
I. Kolodin: *The Story of the Metropolitan Opera 1883–1950* (New York, 1951) ELIZABETH FORBES

Kallenberg, Siegfried Garibaldi (*b* Bad Schachen, 3 Nov 1867; *d* Munich, 9 Feb 1944). German composer. He studied at the Stuttgart Conservatory and the Munich Königliche Musikschule. In 1892, he became director of a private music conservatory at Stettin (now Szeczin) and subsequently taught in Königsberg (Kaliningrad), Hanover and Munich, where he settled in 1910. Although a Kallenberg Society was founded in 1921 to promote the composer's music, he attained greater recognition as a writer on music and as a critic. His work was influenced by neo-Romanticism, and to a certain extent, his absorption of symbolic subjects can be related to the German expressionists. As a conservative nationalist, he displayed great sympathy for the Nazi regime, but this did not result in extensive performances of his work after 1933. Consequently his five operas, which include *Sun Liao* (1918), *Das goldene Tor* (1920), *Der Diener zweier Herren*, *Die lustigen Musikanten* and *Der Spielmann* were unpublished and, except for *Die lustigen Musikanten*, broadcast by Bavarian Radio in 1932 to mark the composer's 65th birthday, remained unperformed during his lifetime.

W. Zentner: 'Siegfried Kallenberg', *ZfM*, civ (1937), 1375–6
ERIK LEVI

Kalliwoda, Johann Wenzel [Kalivoda, Jan Křtitel Václav] (*b* Prague, 21 Feb 1801; *d* Karlsruhe, 3 Dec 1866). Bohemian composer. He studied composition and the violin at the Prague Conservatory, graduating with distinction in 1816. While on a tour of Germany, Switzerland and Holland, he met Prince Karl Egon II of Fürstenberg, who offered him the post of conductor for his orchestra in Donaueschingen, and at the end of 1822 he moved there with his family. At Donaueschingen he

staged Cherubini's *Les deux journées*, in which his wife Teresa (née Brunetti, 1803–92) appeared as Constance, as well as operas by Mozart and Rossini. In 1828 he staged his own three-act opera *Prinzessin Christine von Wolfenburg* (Keller, after H. Zschokke; vs, Leipzig, 1840). His only other opera, *Blanda, die silberne Birke* (3, J. F. Kind; ov. pubd, Leipzig, 1849), was first performed in Prague on 29 November 1847. The following year revolution caused the prince's orchestra to be dispersed, and in 1856 the theatre burnt down.

Kalliwoda was highly esteemed during his lifetime and was offered posts in the most famous musical institutions of Leipzig, Cologne, Mannheim, Dessau and Prague; he was also made an honorary member of many music societies in Europe. His large output includes many orchestral, chamber and piano works, but he succumbed to the fashionable demand for mere prettiness and many pieces fall into the category of popular music.

K. Strunz: *Johann Wenzel Kalliwoda* (Vienna, 1910)
ALENA NĚMCOVÁ

Kallman, Chester (*b* Brooklyn, New York, 7 Jan 1921; *d* Athens, 18 Jan 1975). American poet, librettist and translator. Auden said he 'was the person responsible for arousing my interest in opera, about which previously … I knew little or nothing'. Their collaborative works are discussed under W. H. AUDEN. Independently, Kallman – a witty, resourceful, and most 'musical' poet and an operatic erudite – wrote *The Tuscan Players* for Carlos Chávez (the opera was performed in 1957 under the title *Panfilo and Lauretta*) and made singing translations of, among other operas, *L'incoronazione di Poppea*, *Falstaff* and *Bluebeard's Castle* (Bartók).

ANDREW PORTER

Kálmán, Emmerich [Imre] (*b* Siófok, 24 Oct 1882; *d* Paris, 30 Oct 1953). Hungarian composer. At an early age he showed musical talent and an interest in the theatre, being a frequent visitor to the summer theatre in Siófok. He had high hopes of becoming a concert pianist, but he had to abandon these studies due to the onset of chronic neuritis. In 1900 he joined Koessler's composition class at the Budapest Academy of Music, where for a time he was a fellow student of Bartók, Kodály and Leo Weiner, as well as the future operetta composers Albert Szirmai and Viktor Jacobi. He also pursued law studies for a time. From 1904 to 1908 he was music critic for the daily *Pesti napló*, meanwhile presenting himself as composer of 'serious' works such as the symphonic poems *Saturnalia* (1904) and *Endre és Johanna* (1905). In 1907 he received the Franz Josef Prize of Budapest for his compositions, and was thereby enabled to visit Bayreuth. That same year the popularity of some humorous cabaret songs led him towards the composition of his first operetta, *Tatárjárás* ('The Gay Hussars', 1908). This achieved enormous success throughout Europe and the USA, and its reception in Vienna led to his settling there.

In Vienna, Kálmán began a sequence of successful works that in due course ranked him with Lehár as the leading exponent of the Viennese operetta genre in the period after World War I. *Die Csárdásfürstin* (1915) and *Gräfin Mariza* (1924) were the most successful, being produced around the world and remaining today among the best-loved examples of that time. Kálmán also created new works for Budapest, London, New

York and Zürich, but he remained based in Vienna until the Anschluss. He then moved to Paris in 1939 and, on the German occupation of that city, to the USA, where he worked unsuccessfully with Lorenz Hart on a musical. He retained his Hungarian nationality until 1942, becoming an American citizen only when the Hungarian government aligned itself definitely with Hitler. He returned to Europe in 1949, finally settling in Paris. His posthumously performed operetta, *Arizona Lady* (1954), was given its final form by his son Charles Emmerich Kálmán (*b* Vienna, 17 Nov 1929), himself the composer of various light pieces and musicals.

Kálmán's librettos were always carefully chosen – sometimes after years of searching – and were equally carefully set. Yet he managed to produce a rich vein of seemingly natural melody. In *Die Herzogin von Chicago* (1928) he experimented with jazz-flavoured American popular music, and in *Kaiserin Josephine* (1936) he attempted a more ambitious work, of which a projected production at the Vienna Staatsoper with Richard Tauber and Jarmila Novotná had to be abandoned for political reasons. However, Kálmán's most successful and typical works are those in which the Viennese waltz is mixed with the Hungarian popular style. His major international operetta successes all had Hungarian settings, while other works had sub-plots with opportunities for music in the Hungarian manner. Even in his last work, set on a ranch in Arizona, the heroine is a Hungarian. Thus he was able to add to his fund of melody an almost obsessive taste for Hungarian popular rhythms, set off by a penchant for opulent orchestral colouring and instrumental counterpoint. His orchestrators used a full orchestra, incorporating such distinctive instruments as glockenspiel, harp, celesta, tam-tam, cimbalom, banjo, guitar and (in *Die Bajadere* and *Der Teufelsreiter*) the native Hungarian tárogató. He provided some particularly rewarding solos for tenor and soprano, especially in *Gräfin Mariza* and *Die Zirkusprinzessin* (1926). His works also give important opportunities for the chorus, while his finales, often recapitulating themes heard earlier, are particularly well constructed and crafted to achieve maximum dramatic effect in the theatre.

See also Csárdásfürstin, die; Gräfin mariza; and Zirkus-prinzessin, die.

all operettas

WW – Vienna, Theater an der Wien

Tatárjárás [The Gay Hussars] (3, K. von Bakonyi and A. Gábor), Budapest, Vig, 22 Feb 1908; rev. as Ein Herbstmanöver (3, Bakonyi and R. Bodanzky), WW, 22 Jan 1909
Az obsitos [The Soldier on Leave] (3, Bakonyi), Budapest, Vig, 1910; rev. as Der gute Kamerad (2, V. Léon, after Bakonyi), Vienna, Bürger, 27 Oct 1911; rev. as Gold gab ich für Eisen [Her Soldier Boy] (Léon, after Bakonyi), WW, 16 Oct 1914
Der Zigeunerprimas [Sari] (3, F. Grünbaum and J. Wilhelm), Vienna, Johann Strauss, 11 Oct 1912
The Blue House (1, A. Hurgon), London, Hippodrome, 28 Oct 1912
Der kleine König (3, Bodanzky, after Bakonyi and F. Martos), WW, 27 Nov 1912
Kivándorlók [The Emigrants] (1, Gábor), Budapest, Modern, 1913
Zsuzsi kisasszony [Miss Springtime] (3, Martos and M. Bródy), Budapest, Vig, 23 Feb 1915
Die Csárdásfürstin [The Riviera Girl; The Gipsy Princess] (3, L. Stein and B. Jenbach), Vienna, Johann Strauss, 17 Nov 1915
Die Faschingsfee (3, A. M. Willner and R. Oesterreicher), Vienna, Johann Strauss, 21 Sept 1917 [partial musical reworking of Zsuzsi kisasszony]
Das Hollandweibchen [A Little Dutch Girl] (3, Stein and Jenbach), Vienna, Johann Strauss, 30 Jan 1920

Die Bajadere [The Yankee Princess] (3, J. Brammer and A. Grünwald), Vienna, Carl, 23 Dec 1921
Gräfin Mariza (3, Brammer and Grünwald), WW, 28 Feb 1924
Die Zirkusprinzessin (3, Brammer and Grünwald), WW, 26 March 1926
Golden Dawn (2, O. Harbach and O. Hammerstein II), Wilmington, Oct 1927, New York, Hammerstein's, 30 Nov 1927; collab. H. Stothart
Die Herzogin von Chicago (2, Brammer and Grünwald), WW, 5 April 1928
Das Veilchen vom Montmartre [Paris in Spring] (3, Brammer and Grünwald), Vienna, Johann Strauss, 21 March 1930; rev., WW, 25 July 1930
Ronny (film operetta, R. Schünzel, E. Pressburger, R. Schanzer and E. Welisch), Berlin, Gloria-Palast, 22 Dec 1931
Der Teufelsreiter (3, Schanzer and Welisch), WW, 10 March 1932
Kaiserin Josephine (8 scenes, P. Knepler and G. Herczeg), Zürich, Stadt, 18 Jan 1936
Miss Underground, 1943 (P. Gallico and L. Hart), inc.
Marinka (K. Farkas and G. Marion), New Haven, 1945, New York, Winter Garden, 18 July 1945
Arizona Lady (2, Grünwald and G. Beer), broadcast, Munich, Bayerische Rundfunk, 1 Jan 1954; stage, Berne, Stadt, 14 Feb 1954; completed C. Kálmán

*

R. Oesterreicher: *Emmerich Kálmán: der Weg eines Komponisten* (Vienna, 1954)
V. Kálmán: *Grüss' mir die süssen, die reizenden Frauen: mein Leben mit Emmerich Kálmán* (Bayreuth, 1966)
A. Lamb: 'Emmerich Kálmán – a Centenary Tribute', *Opera*, xxxiii (1982), 1009–15
R. Traubner: *Operetta: a Theatrical History* (New York, 1983)
ANDREW LAMB

Kálmán, Oszkár (*b* Kis-Szent-Péter, 19 June 1887; *d* Budapest, 17 Sept 1971). Hungarian bass. He studied at the Budapest Academy of Music with József Sík, making his début as Sarastro (1913) at the Budapest Opera House, where he later sang Bluebeard in the première of Bartók's opera (1918). In 1927 he joined the Kroll Opera, Berlin, at Klemperer's invitation, playing Leporello, Rocco, and Tiresias in Stravinsky's *Oedipus Rex* (1928); he also sang Hunding and Hermann at the Staatsoper. He sang at Hamburg, Vienna, Barcelona, Helsinki and Prague, returning to Budapest in 1929. A voice of wide range, particularly sonorous in its middle and high registers, and a strong acting ability fitted him for Wagner and character roles alike; he was a fine Guglielmo, Osmin and Colline. He often participated in Budapest oratorio performances, and introduced many of Kodály's songs to the public. PÉTER P. VÁRNAI

Kalmanoff, Martin (*b* Brooklyn, New York, 24 May 1920). American composer. He studied at Harvard with Walter Piston (1937–43). His one-act *Fit for a King* won first prize in the Robert Merrill Contest (1950), and *The Great Stone Face* won second prize in the Harvey Gaul Contest (1968). He received the Rodgers and Hammerstein Foundation grant in 1968 and the New York State Council on the Arts/American Music Center grant in 1978. Of his extensive operatic output, 15 works were written for children and seven received their premières on the WNYC radio network. His operas are usually in one act with a small cast and no chorus. Many of the plots use well-known stories: *Fit for a King* is based on *The Emperor's New Clothes*, *Godiva* parodies the Lady Godiva story and *Noah and the Stowaway* gives the biblical story a space-age twist.

first performed in New York unless otherwise stated

Fit for a King (1, A. Baer, after H. C. Andersen: *The Emperor's New Clothes*), WNYC, 13 Feb 1949; stage, Master, 21 June 1950
Noah and the Stowaway (1, Baer), WNYC, 18 Feb 1951; stage, Provincetown Theater, 12 Oct 1952

The Empty Bottle (mystery, 3, Baer), WNYC, 17 Feb 1952; stage, Judson Hall, Ruffino Opera Theatre, 4 Feb 1966

Godiva (3, Baer), WNYC, 15 Feb 1953

Brandy is my True Love's Name (children's op, 1, Baer), Blackfriars Theater, 17 June 1953

A Quiet Game of Cribble (1, Kalmanoff), WNYC, 8 June 1954

The Delinquents (tragedy, 1, Kalmanoff), WNYC, 26 April 1955

Opera, Opera (children's op, 1, W. Saroyan), WNYC, 22 Feb 1956

Videomania (musical farce, 1, Kalmanoff), Lincoln, NE, Lincoln College, 8 May 1958; rev. version, Denison, OH, Denison U., 18 Feb 1965

Lizzie Strotter (1, Kalmanoff, after Aristophanes: *Lysistrata*), Des Moines, IA, Drake U., 6 March 1959

The Bald Prima Donna (1, E. Ionesco, after his *La cantatrice chauve*), Community Opera, Brooklyn Museum, 15 Dec 1962

Young Tom Edison (children's op, 1, R. K. Adams), Greenwich Mews, April 1963

Half Magic in King Arthur's Court (children's op, 1, E. Eager), Wading River, NY, High School, 17 May 1963

Huck Finn and Tom Sawyer (children's op, 1, Thomas and G. Lebowitz, after M. Twain), Judson Hall, 15 Oct 1966

Mr Scrooge (children's op, 1, Lebowitz, after C. Dickens: *A Christmas Carol*), Judson Hall, 3 Dec 1966

Canterville Ghost (children's op, 1, after O. Wilde), Judson Hall, 11 March 1967

The Audition (aleatory op, 1, Kalmanoff, S. Spaeth and J. S. Harrison), Pittsburgh, PA, Chatham College Opera Workshop, 21 Aug 1968

The Victory at Masada (1, Kalmanoff), concert perf., Detroit, 10 Nov 1968

The Great Stone Face (1, Kalmanoff), Muncie, IN, Ball State U., 14 Nov 1968

Aesop, the Fabulous Fabulist (children's op, 1, Kalmanoff), Camp Pemiqewasset, NH, Aug 1969

King David and David King (children's op, 1, Kalmanoff), Temple Ansche Chesed, 12 Oct 1969

Legends Three (1, Kalmanoff, after M. Brenner), Jewish Heritage Theater, 11 Nov 1969

Photograph – 1920 (comedy, 5, after G. Stein), Lake Placid, NY, 27 July 1971

Hipopera: Mod Traviata, Mod Faust, Mod Carmen, Mod Aida (4, Kalmanoff); Mod Traviata, Mike Douglas Show, 4 May 1972; Mod Carmen and Mod Traviata, Boise, ID, Boise State U., 9 April 1977

The Magic Land of Opera (children's op, 1, Kalmanoff), 1972

Sganarelle (1, after Molière: *Le médecin malgré lui*), Manhattan School of Music, 18 May 1974

Give me Liberty or Give me Death (children's op, 1, Adams), Producer's Association, 2 Jan 1975

The Magic Beanstalk (children's op, 1, J. Cahalan), Monticello, NY, Delano Playhouse, 1976

Christopher Columbus (children's op, 1, Kalmanoff, after J. Forscher), Producer's Association [tour], March 1976–7

Smart Aleck and the Talking Wire (children's op, 1), Producers' Association [tour], 1976–7

Alexander Graham Bell (children's op, 1, Kalmanoff, after A. Drake), Producers' Association, March 1977

Beautiful Beast (children's op, 1, Cahalan, after the Beauty and the Beast story), Monticello, Delano Playhouse, 13 July 1977

Insect Comedy, 1977 (3, L. Allen, after K. Čapek and J. Čapek: *Ze života hmyzu* [From the Life of the Insects]), unperf.

Ralph and the Wonderful Goodtime Circus (children's op, 1, Kalmanoff and Cahalan), Monticello, Delano Playhouse, 1978

The Harmfulness of Tobacco (mono-opera, 1, E. Bentley, after A. P. Chekhov), Tully Hall, 22 March 1979

Ralph and the Stalking Bear (children's op, 1), Monticello, Delano Playhouse, 8 July 1979

You'll Never Get it Off the Ground (children's op, 1, Kalmanoff and Drake), 1980

*

E. Renard: 'The Operas of Martin Kalmanoff', *Opera Journal*, vii/3 (1974), 14–22
BRADLEY H. SHORT

Kalniņš, Alfrēds (*b* Cēsis, 23 Aug 1879; *d* Riga, 23 Dec 1951). Latvian composer. He studied the organ with L. Homilius and composition with Anatol Lyadov at the St Petersburg Conservatory (1897–1901) and then worked mainly as an organist in Estonia and Latvia. In 1919 he settled in Riga, where he was a member of the directorate of the Latvian National Opera. From 1927 to 1933 he held an appointment in New York and later he became a professor at the Latvian State Conservatory. His opera *Baņuta* was the first Latvian opera. Based on a historical-mythological plot, it concerns a woman's struggle against superstitions in defence of her love and is set against a background of Latvian folklore and tradition. Commentators have found a strong national flavour in *Baņuta*, despite the absence of recognizably folk-derived material: the music is lyrical, picturesque and psychologically dramatic, much in the spirit of Wagner. Kalniņš's music drama *Salinieki* ('The Islanders') uses allegory to show the struggle of a people against its oppressors and the self-sacrifice of heroes on behalf of freedom. The music is infused with leitmotifs and part-writing, and the chorus is closely integrated with the action.

first performed in Riga by the Latvian National Opera

Baņuta (4, A. Krūiņš), 29 May 1920, vs (Riga, 1968)

Salinieki [The Islanders] (music drama, 4, Krūmiņš), 10 Feb 1926; rev. as Dzimtenes atmoda [The Nation's Awakening'], 9 Sept 1933

*

L. Apkalns: *Lettische Musik* (Wiesbaden, 1977), 290–96
ARNOLDS KLOTIŅŠ, STEPHEN JOHNSON

Kalniņš, Imants (*b* Riga, 26 May 1941). Latvian composer. He graduated from Skulte's class at the Latvian State Conservatory in 1964 and was a prizewinner in the Third All-Union Competition for Young Composers in 1969. His early dramatic music includes the musical *Princis un ubaga zēns* ('The Prince and the Pauper'; after M. Twain), first performed in Liepāja in 1968, and the one-act opera *Vai tur ir kāds* ('Is Anybody There?', 1971). His one-act rock opera *Ei, jūs tur* ('Hey, You There', 1971; after W. Saroyan) was one of the first works in this genre in the East European countries; it was first performed in Liepāja in 1977. The basis of the opera *Spēlēju, dancoju* ('I play, I dance'; 3, after J. Rainis) is a symbolic drama of the role of a creative principle in a man, a separate nation and mankind in general. First performed in Rija in 1977, the work unites the folk drama genre with that of lyric-psychological opera in rock music form. Neoclassicism prevails in *Ifiģenija Aulīdā* ('Iphigenia in Aulis'; 2, after Euripides; Riga, 1982) and the character of the opera is oratorical. He has cultivated an individual style which combines innovation with classical tradition, and sometimes also with elements of rock.

*

V. Briede-Bulavinova: *Opernoye tvorchestvo latyshkih kompozitorov* [Operas of Latvian Composers] (Leningrad, 1979)
JĒKABS VĪTOLIŅŠ, ARNOLDS KLOTIŅŠ

Kalniņš, Jānis (*b* Pärnu, Estonia, 3 Nov 1904). Canadian composer of Latvian parentage. He was taught to play the piano and the organ by his father, Alfrēds Kalniņš, and studied composition with Jāzeps Vītols at the Latvian Conservatory (1920–24). In 1923 he began working at the National Theatre in Riga as music adviser and conductor, and in 1933 was appointed conductor at the National Opera. His works from the 1930s include the operas *Lolitas brīnumputns* ('Lolita's Wonderbird', 1934), *Hamlets* ('Hamlet', 1936) and *Ugunī* ('In the Fire', 1937), as well as ballets and incidental music. He fled from the advancing Soviets in 1944 and later settled in Canada, where he taught at the Fredericton College of Music, New Brunswick (1949–68), founded and conducted the

Fredericton SO (1953), and continued to compose, mainly instrumental music. His early style retained Latvian national characteristics while following contemporary trends as represented by Hindemith, Stravinsky and Prokofiev. Kalniņš was among the first to start an anti-romantic trend in Latvian music, but later incorporated traditions of romanticism into his operatic music.

Lolitas brīnumputns [Lolita's Wonderbird] (1, after A. Brigadere), Riga, 6 Dec 1934

Hamlets [Hamlet] (3, Kalniņš, after W. Shakespeare, trans. A. P. Chekhov), Riga, 17 Feb 1936

Uguni [In the Fire] (3, after R. Blaumanis), Riga, 20 March 1937

JOACHIM BRAUN, ARNOLDS KLOTIŅŠ

Kalomiris, Manolis (*b* Smyrna [now Izmir], 14 Dec 1883; *d* Athens, 3 April 1962). Greek composer. As the dominant figure of the national school of composition, he was largely responsible for the renewal of Greek art music, taking it away from the Italian models it had emulated in the 19th century and finding new inspiration in indigenous folk music. He studied in Athens (1894–9) and Constantinople (1899–1900), and then at the conservatory of the Gesellschaft der Musikfreunde in Vienna (1901–6), where he became a fervent Wagnerite; he then taught piano in Kharkiv (1906–10), gaining a knowledge of the Russian national school and opera. In Athens, he taught at the Athens Conservatory (1911–19) and founded the Hellenic Conservatory in 1919 and the National Conservatory in 1926, where he encouraged the study of opera. He also founded the short-lived Ethnikos Melodramatikos Omilos (National Opera Group) in 1933, and was the first director general of the state opera in Athens, the National Lyric Scene, when it became independent of the National Theatre in 1944. Kalomiris's programme notes for the first concert of his works (Athens Conservatory, 11 June 1908) were a manifesto of the Greek national school as he conceived it; he called for the deliberate blending of folk and traditional elements 'with all the technical means put at our disposal by . . . the musically advanced peoples, mainly German, French, Russian and Norwegian'. His instantly recognizable style consists of vocal lines or dense polyphonic textures based on Greek folksong modes and rhythms, chromatically expanded, impulsively harmonized and dazzlingly orchestrated, often driven forward exuberantly to dramatic climaxes. He followed textual shifts of tension, mood and atmosphere, turning the text into a kind of montage reminiscent of film music. His operas betray an acute sense of pace and timing and use Wagnerian models of *unendliche Melodie* and leitmotifs, the latter of which became increasingly chromatic over the years. In many cases chromatic climaxes are constructed from authentic folksong or Byzantine chant melodies familiar to Greek audiences that act as strong psychological stimuli.

autograph MSS and parts held in Manolis Kalomiris Society Archives, Athens

O Mavrianos ki o vassilias [Mavrianos and the King] 1907–8 (comic op, 2, Kalomiris, after a Gk. folksong), inc.

O protomastoras [The Master Builder] (music drama, 2 and int, Myrtiotissa [T. Drakopoulou], N. Poriotis and Y. Stefopoulos, after N. Kazantzakis), Athens, Municipal, 11 March 1916, vs (Athens, 1917); rev. 1929, 1940, 1944

To dakhtylidi tis manas [The Mother's Ring] (music drama, 3, A. Orfikos [Y. Stefopoulos], after Y. Kambyssis), Athens, Municipal, 8 Dec 1917, vs (Athens, 1937); rev., Berlin, Volksoper, 10 Feb 1940

Anatoli [Sunrise] (musical fairy-tale, 2, Kalomiris, after Kambyssis), Athens, Olympia, 18 Dec 1945; rev. 1948, vs (Athens, 1953)

Ta xotika nera [The Shadowy Waters] (musical dramatic poem, prol., 1, Kalomiris, after W. B. Yeats: *The Shadowy Waters*, trans. V. Pezopoulou), Athens, Olympia, 4 Jan 1951, vs (Athens, 1951)

Konstantinos o Palaeologos, i Piran tin Poli [Constantine Palaeologue, or They took the City] (musical tragedy-legend, 3, after Kazantzakis), Athens, Herod of Atticus Theatre, 12 Aug 1962, vs (Athens, 1961)

*

M. Kalomiris: 'I zoi mou ke i téchni mou' [My Life and My Art], *Nea hestia* [New Hearth], xxxv–xxxvii (1944–5), passim; incl. posth. frags (Athens, 1988)

F. Anoyanakis: *Katalogos ergon Manoli Kalomiri (1883–1962)* [Catalogue of the Works of Kalomiris] (Athens, 1964; Eng. trans. 1986)

G. J. Zack: *The Music of Manolis Kalomiris* (diss., Florida State U., 1972)

G. Leotsakos: 'O Protomastoras, megas stathmos tis ellinikis moussikis' [The Master Builder, a Milestone in Greek Music], *Moussikologhia*, ii (1986), 27–33; enlarged in notes, *O Protomastoras* (GCO CD 0304/90, 1990), 16–21

O. Frangou-Psychopedis: *I ethniki scholi moussikis – provlimata ideologhias* [The National School of Music: Problems of Ideology] (Athens, 1990)

P. Tsalahouris: *Manoli Kalomiri: ergo* [Manolis Kalomiris: Works] (forthcoming)

GEORGE LEOTSAKOS

Kalter [Aufrichtig], **Sabine** (*b* Jaroslaw, 28 March 1890; *d* London, 1 Sept 1957). Polish mezzo-soprano. She studied in Vienna and made her début at the Volksoper in 1911. From 1915 to 1935 she was engaged at Hamburg, where she was especially successful in Verdi and Wagner and as Delilah, Gluck's Orpheus, Fidès and Marina (*Boris Godunov*). She had to leave Germany in 1935 and settled in London, where she sang with much success at Covent Garden (1935–9) as Ortrud (her début role), Fricka, Waltraute, Brangäne, Herodias (*Salome*) and Háta (*The Bartered Bride*). She had a warm, beautiful voice and strong dramatic ability.

HAROLD ROSENTHAL/R

Kamenniy gost'. Opera by A. S. Dargomïzhsky; *see* STONE GUEST, THE.

Kamieński, Maciej (*b* ? between Hungary and Slovakia (Moson district), 13 Oct 1734; *d* Warsaw, 25 Jan 1821). Polish composer of Slovak origin. In his youth he lived at Sopron. In 1760 he moved to Vienna, and about 1770 he settled in Warsaw, giving music lessons and organizing public concerts. From 1778 he devoted himself mainly to opera: he composed the first Polish opera performed in a public theatre, *Nędza uszczęśliwiona* ('Sorrow Turned to Joy'). Kamieński also wrote keyboard and vocal music. Although he was influenced by the Viennese Classical school and the Italian *opera buffa*, his music gives early evidence of the emergence of the Polish national style. His 'Krótki rys egzystencji najpierwszej oryginalnej opery polskiej' ('A Short Outline of the Original Polish Opera') was edited in *Biblioteka Warszawska*, iv (Warsaw, 1878).

all Singspiels; first performed in Warsaw unless otherwise indicated; MSS in PL-Wn and Warsaw Music Society Library unless otherwise stated

Nędza uszczęśliwiona [Sorrow Turned to Joy] (2, W. Bogusławski, after F. Bohomolec), 11 July 1778

Prostota cnotliwa [Virtuous Simplicity] (Bohomolec), 1779, lost

Zośka czyli Wiejskie zaloty [Sophie or Country Courtship] (1, S. Szymański), 1779, lost

Balik gospodarski [The Burgher's Ball] (3, F. Zabłocki, after C.-S. Favart), 14 Sept 1783, lost

Anton und Antoinette, 1785 (1, after J. Desboulmiers), unperf., lost

Tradycja dowcipem załatwiona [Court Warrant Settled by Jest] (1, Zabłocki), 27 May 1789 [ov. by Antoni Wejnert, Kamieński's son-in-law]

Słowik czyli Kasia z Hanką na wydaniu [The Nightingale, or Kasia and Hanka, Two Marriageable Girls] (2, G. Witkowski), 19 Jan 1790 [ov. by Wejnert]

Sultan Wampum, oder Die Wünsche, 1794 (3, A. Kotzebue), unperf., lost

*

K. Michałowski: *Opery polskie*, Materiały do bibliografi muzyki polskiej, i (Kraków, 1954)   ALINA NOWAK-ROMANOWICZ

Kaminski, Heinrich (*b* Tiengen, nr Waldshut, 4 July 1886; *d* Ried, nr Benediktbeuren, 21 June 1946). German composer. His father, originally a priest, was of Polish descent, and his mother was an opera singer. His musical talent did not manifest itself until relatively late; in 1909 he went to Berlin, where he took composition lessons with Kaun and others, but he was largely self-taught. He lived quietly, taking pupils, among whom was Carl Orff in 1920. Kaminski composed incidental music for a play (performed in 1920) and the opera *Jürg Jenatsch*; this three-act music drama to his own libretto (after C. F. Mayer) was performed in Dresden on 27 April 1929. From 1930 to 1933 he taught composition at the Preussische Akademie der Künste in Berlin, in succession to Pfitzner; he also worked as a conductor. In later years performances of his music in Germany were made difficult, or even forbidden, because his origins were not 'pure Aryan'. His last major work was his second opera, *Das Spiel vom König Aphelius* (in a prologue, 5 scenes and an epilogue, completed 1946), also to his own libretto; it centred on the idea of the brotherhood of man after Europe emerged from World War II, but it only received its first performance, in Göttingen's Theater der Stadt, on 29 January 1950.

For Kaminski, music was not a 'craft', but a revelation of mysteries, of the fundamental laws of the universe and of life, and all his work must be considered in this sense 'religious'. He was essentially an untheatrical composer: *Jürg Jenatsch* is characterized by a mixture of spoken and sung words, and *Das Spiel vom König Aphelius* is a drama of ideas, without much action.

H. J. Moser: 'Heinrich Kaminski', *ZfM*, xcvi (1929), 601–7

E. Krieger: 'Heinrich Kaminski's Drama "Jürg Jenatsch"', *ZfM*, c (1933), 992–5

H. F. Redlich: 'In memoriam Heinrich Kaminski', *MMR*, lxxvii (1947), 185–8

K. Schleifer: 'Heinrich Kaminski, Leben und Werk', *Musica*, i (1947), 71–81

R. Schwarz-Schilling: '*Das Spiel von König Aphelius*: zur bevorstehenden Uraufführung in Göttingen', *Musica*, iii (1949), 429–32   KLAUS KIRCHBERG

Kamionsky, Oscar (*b* Kiev, 1869; *d* Yalta, 15 Aug 1917). Russian baritone. He studied in St Petersburg and Naples, where he made his début in 1892, returning to Russia the following year. After seasons in Kharkiv, Kiev and Tbilisi, he appeared in 1904 with a private opera company in St Petersburg, where he sang Iago to Nikolay Figner's Otello. From 1905 to 1908 and again in the 1913 season he was with Sergey Zimín's company in Moscow, singing in the Italian and French repertories as well as the Russian: his roles included Don Giovanni, Rossini's and Mozart's Figaro, Rigoletto, and Rubinstein's Demon. He was considered the finest Russian baritone of his period, often compared with Battistini; his recordings show a similar freedom and brilliance in the upper register with loss of resonance in the lower. Despite some over-emphasis, his style impresses as fervent and imaginative, his voice clear and firm.

J. B. STEANE

Kamy, Hassan (*b* Cairo, 1941). Egyptian tenor and administrator. He studied in Cairo with Geilane Rathle and then in Rome with Achille Braschi. In 1963 he made his début at the Cairo Opera House, as Edgardo, and the next year he joined the newly formed Cairo Opera Company, singing Alfredo (in Arabic) in the opening production. His international début was in Russia in 1970, as Rodolfo; he went on to sing Turiddu at the Bol'shoy in Moscow and in Leningrad, in 1972, and Cavaradossi in Warsaw, followed by performances in Sofia and other east European houses. He was the first Egyptian tenor to sing Radames, at Vilnius in 1974, going on to sing the role in Rome in 1976, before the Pyramids in Cairo in 1987 and at the Metropolitan, New York, in 1991. He has also performed in Barcelona, at the Paris Opéra and at the Chicago Lyric, and has sung in many Egyptian operettas and in films. He was appointed artistic director of the new Cairo Opera House in 1991.   CHARLES PITT

Kanawa, Kiri te. *See* TE KANAWA, KIRI.

Kancheli, Giya Alexandrovich (*b* Tbilisi, 10 Aug 1935). Georgian composer. In 1963 he graduated from the composition course at the Tbilisi Conservatory, where he taught orchestration from 1972. From 1971 he directed musical activities at the Rustaveli Dramatic Theatre, providing music to many productions by the director Robert Sturua. He has received numerous awards, including the USSR State Prize (1976) and the Georgian State Prize (1981); in 1980 he was named People's Artist of the Georgian SSR. Kancheli is best known as a composer of symphonic music. A common theme in his works is the transcendent contemplation of elemental conflicts between tenderness and brutality, beauty and ugliness, good and evil. This forms the focus of his unusual opera *Muzika dlya zhivïkh* ('Music for the Living'), a plotless, mixed-media work conceived in collaboration with the Georgian director, Robert Sturua, who wrote the libretto. The work received its première at the Paliashvili Theatre of Opera and Ballet in Tbilisi on 28 April 1984.

See also MUZÏKA DLYA ZHIVÏKH.

*

G. Kozhukhova: 'Music for the Living', *Music in the USSR* (1985), Jan–March, 79

K. Rudnitsky: 'A Brief Improvisation on Kancheli Themes', *Music in the USSR* (1985), Oct–Dec, 88–9   LAUREL E. FAY

Kandinsky, Alexey Ivanovich (*b* Moscow, 24 Feb 1918). Russian musicologist. From 1950 he has been on the staff of the Moscow Conservatory and from 1960 was head of the department of Russian music history there. A solid and conservative style critic, he has specialized in 19th-century Russian opera, with an emphasis on Rimsky-Korsakov. As an influential reviewer (for *Sovetskaya muzika* and *Pravda*) he has vigilantly policed productions of the classical repertory, defending authorial intentions against the vagaries of directors and designers.

'O muzikal'nïkh kharakteristikakh v tvorchestve Rimskogo-Korsakova 90-kh godov' [On Musical Characterization in Rimsky-Korsakov's Work of the 1890s], *Muzikal'noye nasledstvo: Rimsky-Korsakov: issledovaniya, materialï, pis'ma* [Musical Heritage: Rimsky-Korsakov: Research, Documents, Letters], ed. D. Kabalevsky and others, i (Moscow, 1954), 79–144

Problema narodnosti v opernom tvorchestve N. A. Rimskogo-Korsakova [Problems of National Identity in the Operatic Works of Rimsky-Korsakov] (diss., Moscow Conservatory, 1956)

Operï Rakhmaninova (Moscow, 1956, 2/1960)
Istoriya russkoy muziki, ii/2: *N. A. Rimsky-Korsakov* (Moscow, 1984)
RICHARD TARUSKIN

Kanne, Friedrich August (*b* Delitzsch, Saxony, 8 March 1778; *d* Vienna, 16 Dec 1833). Austrian composer of German birth. After studying medicine at Leipzig and theology at Wittenberg he devoted himself to music. In 1808 he settled in Vienna, where he worked as a music teacher, poet and journalist; he nevertheless failed to establish himself to the extent that his considerable talents promised. He turned down various permanent posts apart from a briefly held Kapellmeister appointment at Pressburg (Bratislava) in 1809, preferring to maintain a tenuous independence. Some of his contributions to the *Wiener allgemeine musikalische Zeitung* reveal the breadth of his sympathies, even if they have little to add to the by then well established Romantic aesthetic. He briefly edited that periodical, and reviewed musical events for several newspapers, showing a balanced judgment, and most notably a then uncommon awareness of the achievements of Beethoven's late works.

Kanne's works include a dozen operas and a similar number of other theatre scores, some of which were major successes. His opera *Orpheus* (to his own libretto) was performed 15 times in the Kärntnertortheater and Burgtheater in 1807–8; *Miranda* was staged at the Theater an der Wien in 1811; in 1814 he was represented (along with Mozart, Beethoven, Hummel, Gyrowetz and Weigl) in Treitschke's pasticcio *Die gute Nachricht* at the court theatres. His greatest popular success was achieved with his music for Bäuerle's *Lindane, oder Die Fee und der Haarbeutelschneider*, given 68 times at the Theater in der Leopoldstadt between 27 March 1824 and 1841. This parody of the Vestris ballet *Die Fee und der Ritter* (music by Rossini) was revived in the Theater in der Josefstadt as late as 1852. Although Kanne wrote other fairly successful scores for the Leopoldstadt, and a melodrama and incidental music for several plays in the Theater an der Wien, he lacked the application to develop his potential fully; his last years were clouded by penury and alcohol.

first performed in Vienna unless otherwise stated

Anakreon und Sappho (monodrama, D. Nöller), 1805
Orpheus (grosse Oper, 2, Kanne), Kärntnertor, 10 Nov 1807
Miranda, oder Das Schwert der Rache (heroisch-komische Oper, 3, Kanne), An der Wien, 14 Sept 1811
Die gute Nachricht (Spl, 1, F. Treitschke), Kärntnertor, 11 April 1814, incl. music by Mozart, Beethoven, Hummel, Gyrowetz and Weigl
Schloss Theben, oder Der Kampf der Flussgötter (Zauberoper, 2, Kanne), Josefstadt, 20 May 1817
Die eiserne Jungfrau (melodrama, 4, F. von Biedenfeld), An der Wien, 20 June 1822
Malvina, oder Putzerls Abenteuer (Zauberspiel, 2, A. Pfahler), An der Wien, 19 March 1823
Lindane, oder Die Fee und der Haarbeutelschneider (Zauberspiel, 3, A. Bäuerle), Leopoldstadt, 27 March 1824
Die Zauberschminke, oder Das Land der Erfindungen (Feenoper, 3, Bäuerle), Leopoldstadt, 28 Oct 1825
Philipp und Suschen, oder Der falsche Jupiter (mythologisches Zauberspiel, 2, J. Schickh), Leopoldstadt, 20 Oct 1832
Die Mainacht, oder Der Blocksberg, Berlin, Königstädter, 1832

StiegerO; WurzbachL
J. N. Vogl: 'Von einem Verschollenen: ein Stück aus Altwien', *Österreichischer Volkskalender*, xviii (Vienna, 1862), 163
R. Wallace: *Beethoven's Critics: Aesthetic Dilemmas and Resolutions during the Composer's Lifetime* (Cambridge, 1986)
PETER BRANSCOMBE

Kannen, Günter von (*b* Rheydt, 22 March 1940). German bass-baritone. He studied in Frankfurt, making his début in 1965 at Kaiserslautern. After engagements at Bonn, Gelsenkirchen and Karlsruhe, in 1979 he joined the Zürich Opera. He made his American début at Santa Fe in 1983 as Don Pasquale; he sang Osmin at Drottningholm (1985) and Aix-en-Provence (1987), and Mozart's Bartolo at Salzburg (1986). He has also appeared in Brussels, Paris, Vienna, Berlin and Munich. His repertory includes Rossini's Dr Bartolo, the Tutor (*Le comte Ory*), Don Magnifico, Dulcamara, Rocco, Nicolai's Falstaff, Varlaam, Ochs and Balstrode. Despite his vocal agility and talent for comedy, he is also formidable as Alberich (which he sang in 1988 at Bayreuth) and Klingsor (1990, Chicago).

ELIZABETH FORBES

Kansas City. American city in the state of Missouri. It was incorporated in 1850. Touring companies visited the city from the opening of the Coates Opera House in October 1870. Operas, plays and concerts were presented there until its destruction by fire on 3 January 1901; the Gillis Opera House (1902–17), the Shubert Theatre (1906–35), the Music Hall in the Municipal Auditorium (built 1935) and the Folly Theater (1900; renovated 1981) have been its principal successors. Since 1951 the Starlight Theatre Association has presented Broadway musicals in Swope Park. The Kansas City PO offered opera productions, both staged and unstaged, in the 1950s and 60s. In 1965–6 the Performing Arts Foundation gave performances of operas by Handel (*Giulio Cesare*) and Purcell.

The Lyric Opera of Kansas City was founded in 1958 by D. Russell Patterson, Henry Haskell and Morton Walker. Directed by Patterson, it gives annual opera seasons in English at the Lyric Theatre (cap. *c*2000) and tours under the auspices of the Missouri Arts Council and the Mid-America Arts Alliance. The company has recorded Vittorio Giannini's *The Taming of the Shrew* and Jack Beeson's *Captain Jinks of the Horse Marines* (of which it gave the première in 1975). It has also staged important subsequent productions of American operas, notably Barber's *Vanessa* (1963, 1965, 1979), Floyd's *Of Mice and Men* (1970), Ward's *The Crucible* (1974, 1986) and Hoiby's *The Tempest* (1988).

M. Crabb: *A History of Music in Kansas City, 1900–1965* (diss., U. of Missouri, Kansas City, 1967)
E. C. Krohn: *Missouri Music* (New York, 1971)   JACK RALSTON

Kapp, Eugen (*b* Astrakhan, 13 May 1908). Estonian composer. A son of Artur Kapp, he graduated from his father's composition class at the Tallinn Conservatory in 1931; in 1935 he joined the staff there. He lived in Yaroslavl (1941–4), where he founded the Estonian State Ensemble. He later became the leading figure in Estonian musical life, holding appointments at the Estonian Conservatory (from 1947; rector 1952–64) and with the composers' union (1948–65). He received many honours and was made People's Artist of the USSR (1956). Three works each earned Kapp a Stalin Prize, the operas *Tasuleegid* ('Flames of Vengeance', 1946) and *Vabaduse laulik* ('Bard of Freedom', 1950), and the ballet *Kalevipoeg* (1952). Simple harmonies, march rhythms and melodiousness characterize his music, which was particularly appreciated in the 1940s and 50s, conforming as it did to current political requirements of art.

Tasuleegid [Flames of Vengeance] (3, P. Rummo), Tallinn, 21 July 1945, vs (Moscow, 1958)
Vabaduse laulik [Bard of Freedom] (4, Rummo), Tallinn, 22 July 1950; rev. (prol., 3, epilogue) 1952, vs (Moscow, 1953)
Talvemuinasjutt [Winter Fairy-tale] (3, I. Nasalevitsi), Tartu, 28 Oct 1958, vs (Leningrad, 1963)
Tabamatu [Elusive Marta] (3, J. Galitsky), Tartu, 19 March 1961
Assol (operetta, I. Vsevolozhsky), 1965
Rembrandt (2, K. Süvalepp and J. Pessina), Tartu, 30 March 1975
Rukkilille suvi [The Summer of the Cornflower] (children's musical, Veske), Haapsalu, 1976
Kristallkingake [The Crystal Shoe] (children's musical, Gabbe and Laar), Haapsalu, 1980
Enneolematu ime [Unheard-of Wonder] (children's op, 2, J. Galitski), Tallinn, 8 May 1983   JOACHIM BRAUN

Kapp, Julius (*b* Steinbach, Baden, 1 Oct 1883; *d* Sonthofen, Allgäu, 18 March 1962). German writer on music. He studied chemistry and music, and worked as a freelance writer. He was adviser on productions to the Berlin Staatsoper and edited the *Blätter der Staatsoper*, 1921–45; he then held the same position with the Berlin Städtische Oper, 1948–54.

Kapp was a prolific writer, centring his work largely on the study of opera composers, Wagner in particular. His monumental biography was followed by editions of his writings and the first two volumes of his collected letters. His studies of Meyerbeer and Weber were also influential. While directing productions at the Berlin Staatsoper he edited several operatic texts for use there.

Richard Wagner und Franz Liszt: eine Freundschaft (Berlin and Leipzig, 1908)
ed.: *Der junge Wagner: Dichtungen, Aufsätze, Entwürfe, 1832–1849* (Berlin, 1910)
Richard Wagner: eine Biographie (Berlin, 1910, 32/1929; Eng., Fr., Russ. and Swed. trans.)
Richard Wagner und die Frauen: eine erotische Biographie (Berlin, 1912, 16/1929, rev. 1951; Eng. trans., 1951)
ed.: *Richard Wagner: Gesammelte Schriften und Dichtungen* (Leipzig, 1914)
ed.: *Richard Wagners gesammelte Briefe*, i–ii (Leipzig, 1914–33)
ed.: *Richard Wagner an Mathilde und Otto Wesendonk* (Leipzig, 1915, 2/1936)
Berlioz: eine Biographie (Berlin and Leipzig, 1917, 2/1922)
Das Dreigestirn: Berlioz, Liszt, Wagner (Berlin, 1920)
Giacomo Meyerbeer: eine Biographie (Berlin, 1920, 8/1932)
Franz Schreker: der Mann und sein Werk (Munich, 1921)
Carl Maria von Weber (Stuttgart and Berlin, 1922, 15/1944)
Die Oper der Gegenwart (Berlin, 1922)
Das Opernbuch (Leipzig, 1922, 18/1928, rev. 1939)
ed.: *Richard Strauss und die Berliner Oper* (Berlin, 1934)
Geschichte der Staatsoper Berlin (Berlin, 1937)   HUGH COBBE

Kapp, Villem (*b* Suure-Jaani, 25 Aug 1913; *d* Tallinn, 24 March 1964). Estonian composer. He was a nephew of Artur Kapp, his first teacher. In 1938 he completed organ studies at Tallinn Conservatory; he graduated from Eller's composition class there in 1944 and taught there from then until his death. In 1963 he was given the title People's Artist of the Estonian SSR. His only opera, *Lembitu* (A. Pirn) in four acts, is an epic set in the period of the crusades; it was first performed in Tallinn at the Estonian Theatre on 23 August 1961.

H. Tönson: *Villem Kapp* (Tallinn, 1967)   JOACHIM BRAUN

Kappel, Gertrude (*b* Halle, 1 Sept 1884; *d* Pullach, 3 April 1971). German soprano. She studied in Leipzig, making her début in 1903 as Leonore at Hanover, where she was engaged until 1924. At Covent Garden she sang Brünnhilde (1912–14) and also Isolde, Sieglinde, Senta, the Marschallin and Electra (1924–6).

She appeared at the Vienna Staatsoper (1921–7), at Salzburg, where she sang Donna Anna (1922), and the Staatsoper in Munich (1927–31). She made her Metropolitan début in 1928 as Isolde, later singing Ortrud, Fricka, Brünnhilde, the Marschallin and Electra (the first Metropolitan performance, 1932). She sang Isolde at San Francisco in 1933 and retired in 1937. Her 1924 recordings of 'Pace, pace, mio Dio' (*La forza*) and the closing scene of *Götterdämmerung* reveal the wide range of her voice and the richness and security of her singing.   ALAN BLYTH

Kapsperger, Giovanni Girolamo [Giovanni Geronimo; Kapsberger, Johann Hieronymus] (*b* ?Venice, *c*1580; *d* Rome, January 1651). Italian composer of German origin. Some time after 1604 he arrived in Rome where he worked for the Orders of St Stephen and St John, the Jesuits and the Bentivoglio family. His works of this period were probably intended for some of the more prestigious Roman academies, but his reputation extended to Florence, where his *Maggio* cantata was performed during Carnival 1612. From 1624 Kapsperger was in the service of Cardinal Francesco Barberini through the death of Urban VIII (Maffeo Barberini) in 1644 and until the subsequent flight of the Barberini nephews to France in 1645–6.

Although Kapsperger's first venture into opera was his Jesuit drama *Apotheosis sive Consecratio SS Ignatii et Francisci Xaverii* of 1622, it was during his years with the Barberini that he largely turned to dramatic works. Unfortunately, the bulk of these are lost, and since most were never printed they were probably only occasional pieces. In 1625 he wrote *La vittoria del principe Vladislao in Valacchia*, an opera on the subject of the Polish-Turkish war of 1621 for the visit of the Prince of Poland Vladislao Waza to the Barberini court (only the librtto survives). Allacci lists the opera *Fetonte* (1630), to a libretto by the court poet Ottavio Tronsarelli, and more settings of Tronsarelli's 33 librettos may have been included in Kapsperger's lost collection of *Drammi diversi*, also mentioned by Allacci. There is no evidence that any of these were part of the lavish operatic productions put on by the Barberini at the palace in via Quattro Fontane. Hammond has speculated, however, that Kapsperger may have composed the music for *Il contrasto di Apollo con Marsia*, based on Tronsarelli's libretto *Marsia*, given at the unfinished Quattro Fontane in 1628.

Specific knowledge of Kapsperger as an opera composer is limited to his *Apotheosis*; essentially a Jesuit drama, the text is in Latin and there is no dialogue between characters. Personifications of Rome and countries important in the lives of the two saints, Ignatius Loyola and Francis Xavier, come to the Temple of the Consecration to participate in the apotheosis. In the final act an earthquake gives way to an opening of the heavens in which the two saints appear and prayers of thanks and adoration are given to the Church and Pope Gregory XIV. Kapsperger's music for *Apotheosis* (probably representative of his other dramatic works) is in a rhythmically regular and undecorated recitative style with occasional arioso passages. In his secular dramatic works Kapsperger also may have relied on elaborately ornamented recitative, as he did in his books of *Arie passeggiate*. The occasional tediousness of the declamatory sections is broken up by choruses in dance rhythm and instrumental *sinfonie*, which were cited in Kircher's *Musurgia Universalis* (1650) as exemplary of the *stylus hyporchematicus* (for feasts and festivities) or *choraicus* (for dances and ballets). Highly praised then largely forgotten, Kapsperger's works reveal a high artistic and technical merit.

Apotheosis sive consecratio SS Ignatii et Francisci Xaverii (prol., 5, O. Grassi), Rome, Collegio Romano, 1622, *A-Wn, F-Pn**

La vittoria del principe Vladislao in Valacchia (3, G. Ciampoli), Rome, 1625, lib. in *Rime scelte di Monsignor Ciampoli* (Rome, 1666)

Fetonte (dramma recitato a più voci, 5, O. Tronsarelli), Rome, 1630, lib. in *Drammi musicali di Ottavio Tronsarelli* (Rome, 1632)

Doubtful: Il contrasto di Apollo con Marsia (Tronsarelli), Rome, palace in via Quattro Fontane, August 1628, lib. in *Drammi musicali di Ottavio Tronsarelli* (Rome, 1632)

L. Allacci: *Apes urbanae* (Rome, 1633), 159–60 [incl. bibliography of Kapsperger's works]

G. V. Verzellino: 'P. O. Grassi', *Memorie degli uomini illustri di Savona*, ii (Savona, 1891), 347–51

W. Ambros: *Geschichte der Musik*, iv (Leipzig, 3/1909), 469–89

P. Kast: 'Biographische Notizen über Johann Hieronymus Kapsberger aus den Vorreden zu seiner Werken', *Quellen und Forschungen aus italienischen Archiven und Bibliotheken*, xl (1960), 200–11

J. Forbes: *The Non-Liturgical Vocal Music of Johann Hieronymus Kapsberger* (diss., U. of North Carolina, Chapel Hill, 1978)

V. Coelho: 'G. G. Kapsberger in Rome, 1604–1645: New Biographical Data', *Journal of the Lute Society of America*, xvi (1983), 103–33

F. Hammond: 'More on Music in Casa Barberini', *Studi musicali*, xiv (1985), 241–2

A. Szweykowski and Z. Szweykowski: 'Un'opera ignota di G. G. Kapsperger in onore del Principe Vladislao Waza', *Studi in onore di Giuseppe Vecchi* (Modena, 1989), 221–32

VICTOR COELHO

Karajan, Herbert von (*b* Salzburg, 5 April 1908; *d* Anif, 16 July 1989). Austrian conductor and opera director. Though his reputation as the leading conductor of his time, universally if sometimes grudgingly acknowledged, lay mainly in his work in the orchestral repertory, both in the concert hall and on record, his career from first to last drew inspiration from opera.

Born into a musical family, the son of a doctor, Karajan showed precocious talent as a pianist, appearing in public from the age of five. In Vienna his uncle was technical director of the state theatres, and so was able to give the boy regular access to performances at the State Opera. As a student at the Vienna Academy he was much influenced by Arturo Toscanini's conducting of the visiting La Scala company, notably in *Lucia di Lammermoor*, a work Karajan had previously regarded as trivial. His first orchestral concert as a conductor, which he himself organized in his native Salzburg on graduating from Vienna, led directly to his appointment to the post of music director of the Stadttheater in Ulm, where he made his operatic début conducting *Le nozze di Figaro* on 2 March 1929. During his five years in Ulm (which had a very small theatre and an orchestra of 32 players) he learnt some 40 scores and even presented such ambitious operas as *Die Meistersinger*. He also gained valuable experience as répétiteur.

Karajan's appointment in 1934 to his next post, as music director at the much more important opera house in Aachen, followed an awkward gap in his career. In later years he openly acknowledged that in order to get the Aachen post he joined the Nazi party. He was very soon spotted as a rising star, and was asked in 1937 to conduct at the Vienna Staatsoper, but made conditions over the work to be chosen, which delayed his début. In the end he was denied the rehearsals promised to him for *Tristan*, but his success with it directly led to his historic début at the Berlin Staatsoper. He stipulated that he would conduct only three operas, *Fidelio*, *Tristan* and *Meistersinger*. Bold as that demand was from a young conductor, he had his way, winning the respect of the orchestra in *Tristan*, and being dubbed 'Das Wunder Karajan' by a critic. The expression followed him throughout the Nazi period, when he was regularly acclaimed as the young rival of Wilhelm Furtwängler, often for political reasons. For a time after the end of World War II he was prevented from conducting until he had faced a denazification tribunal. After 1946 his orchestral career quickly revived, at first mainly in the recording studio; from 1948 he conducted regularly at La Scala, where he also acted as director in important productions, starting with *Tannhäuser* in 1950. He conducted Gluck's *Orfeo* at the Salzburg Festival in 1948, and in 1951 conducted for the first time at the Bayreuth Festival, giving a memorable reading of *Die Meistersinger*, which has been preserved on record. The following year he conducted *Tristan*, but after disagreements with Wieland Wagner never worked there again.

After the death of Furtwängler Karajan took over as chief conductor of the Berlin PO; from 1956 he was artistic director of the Salzburg Festival, and in 1957 he succeeded Karl Böhm as director of the Vienna Staatsoper. One of his early successes there was his own production of *Lucia di Lammermoor*, which he had already conducted at La Scala, with Maria Callas memorable in the title role. Yet the Vienna association was not happy, and after much wrangling he finally resigned in 1964, after which he concentrated his opera conducting in Salzburg. He invariably acted as director as well, first at the Summer Festival, but later also at the Easter Festival (which he himself founded in 1967). Helped by the opening of the Grosses Festspielhaus, where the wide, spacious stage encouraged the most spectacular presentation, he was able to insist on almost ideal conditions. From his earliest days he would always rehearse the singers himself at the piano, and when he acted as stage director, he liked to make a recording first, to use during the long and intensive process of staging. Some found the results heavy, but within a solid conservative frame his Salzburg productions of such operas as *Don Carlos* and *Aida* were as memorable visually as they were musically. He conducted and directed the entire *Ring* cycle between 1967 and 1970 at the Easter Festival, though only *Das Rheingold* and *Die Walküre* were transferred to the Metropolitan in New York. In 1988 he officially gave up the artistic directorship of the festival but, still effectually in command, he continued with the production of *Un ballo in maschera* on which he was at work when he died.

Though Karajan was often regarded as a musical dictator, singers were glowing in their tributes to him as the most sympathetic of conductors, who always understood their problems. In casting, however, his preference for stretching voices to the limit was often criticized, though it regularly produced memorable results on recordings. Those made in preparation for stage productions in his later years did not always match the subsequent live performances. Most of his finest opera recordings were made earlier in his career, notably in London with the Philharmonia Orchestra and with Walter Legge, its founder, as recording producer. Outstanding among these are his classic recordings of *Der Rosenkavalier* and *Ariadne auf Naxos*, both with

Elisabeth Schwarzkopf. Though Karajan as an interpreter was often accused of being cold, that charge is regularly rebutted by his opera recordings, combining as they do characteristic polish with high-voltage electricity.

*

B. Gavoty: *Herbert von Karajan* (Geneva, 1956)

F. Herzfeld: *Herbert von Karajan* (Berlin, 1959)

K. Lobl: *Das Wunder Karajan* (Bayreuth, 1965)

E. Haeusserman: *Herbert von Karajan: Biographie* (Gütersloh, 1968, 2/1978)

P. Robinson: *Karajan* (London, 1976)

R. C. Bachmann: *Karajan: Anmerkungen zu einer Karriere* (Düsseldorf, 1983; Eng. trans., 1990)

R. Vaughan: *Herbert von Karajan: a Biographical Portrait* (London, 1986)

F. Endler: *Herbert von Karajan: my Biography as told to Franz Endler* (London, 1989)

R. Osborne: *Conversations with Karajan* (Oxford, 1989)

EDWARD GREENFIELD

Karamzin, Nikolay Mikhaylovich (*b* Mikhaylovka, Samara province, 1/12 Dec 1766; *d* St Petersburg, 22 May/3 June 1826). Russian prose writer and historian. As the official court historiographer from 1804, he produced an 11-volume history of Russia to the early 17th-century 'Time of Troubles'; its authority was not challenged until the 1860s. Many details from it found their way into the libretto of Musorgsky's *Boris Godunov*, especially the expanded version of 1872, which cites Karamzin, along with Pushkin, as a direct source.

Karamzin's other claim to literary fame was the introduction of the sentimental novel into Russia. This aspect of his work found contemporary operatic echo in *Natal'ya, boyarskaya doch'* ('Natalia, the Nobleman's Daughter', 1798) by Daniil Nikitich Kashin (1770–1841), a serf musician who was one of the early collector-arrangers of Russian folksong. In his opera after Karamzin, performed in Moscow in 1803, Kashin accommodated the folk idiom to the style of the contemporary sentimental romance, paving the way towards Tchaikovsky's *Yevgeny Onegin*, the *chef d'oeuvre* of that hybrid manner. Tchaikovsky probably knew Kashin's songs and romances, including the popular *Devitsï-krasavitsï* ('Maidens, pretty maidens'), a setting of a folk or folkish text Pushkin included in the third chapter of the novel *Yevgeny Onegin*, which Tchaikovsky retained in the third scene of his opera.

Karamzin unexpectedly resurfaced in the Russian musical theatre in 1981, when the young Leningrad composer Leonid Desyatnikov based a one-act opera on *Bednaya Liza* ('Poor Liza', 1792), Karamzin's most famous novel, portraying love thwarted by social difference; it was produced by the Moscow Chamber Opera Theatre.

*

M. Nest'yeva: 'Dva vechera v moskovskom kamernom' [Two Evenings at the Moscow Chamber Opera], *SovM* (1981), no. 6, pp. 57–67

A. Orlova and M. Schneerson: 'After Pushkin and Karamzin: Researching the Sources for the Libretto of *Boris Godunov*', *Musorgsky: In Memoriam 1881–1981*, ed. M. H. Brown (Ann Arbor, 1982), 249–70

R. Taruskin: 'The Present in the Past: Russian Opera and Russian Historiography, ca. 1870', *Russian and Soviet Music: Essays for Boris Schwarz*, ed. M. H. Brown (Ann Arbor, 1984), 77–146

C. Emerson: *Boris Godunov: Transpositions of a Russian Theme* (Bloomington and Indianapolis, 1986)

RICHARD TARUSKIN

Karayanis, Plato (*b* Pittsburgh, 26 Dec 1928). American administrator. He studied singing at Carnegie-Mellon University and opera at the Curtis Institute of Music in Philadelphia. He sang lyric baritone roles in European houses, where he also gained some experience as a director, before returning to America in 1964 to run the rehearsal department of the San Francisco Opera. A Martha Baird Rockefeller research grant enabled him to study opera administration and production technology at the Hamburg State Opera, after which he joined the touring Metropolitan Opera National Company as assistant stage director and company administrator in 1965. On the termination of the programme in 1967, he was hired by Affiliate Artists, Inc. (a career development programme for young artists), later becoming its executive vice-president and treasurer. In 1977 he was named general director of the Dallas Opera, which he nurtured artistically and financially. In 1980 the company mounted the first professional staged performance of a Vivaldi opera in America, *Orlando furioso*. In 1988 it gave the première of Dominick Argento's *The Aspern Papers*. By 1991 the company was presenting five productions annually.

NANCY MALITZ

Karayev, Kara (**Abul'faz-oglï**) (*b* Baku, 23 Jan/5 Feb 1918; *d* Baku, 13 May 1982). Azerbaijani composer. The leading figure in Azerbaijani music after World War II, he studied the piano at the Baku Music Technical School (1930–35), and then entered the Azerbaijan State Conservatory, where he studied composition with Rudol'f and Azerbaijani folk music with Hajibeyov. In 1938 he began studies with Alexandrov and Vasilenko at the Moscow Conservatory, after which he became a composition pupil of Shostakovich (1942–6). Karayev took an active part in the musical life of Azerbaijan, serving on committees, and from 1946 he taught at the State Conservatory (professor from 1959); he received the title National Artist of the USSR in 1959.

Some sources cite an early opera *Ayna* (I. Idayat-zade and E. Mamerchanly; 1941; unpubd). During the war he wrote the heroic-patriotic opera *Veten*, also called *Rodina* ('Fatherland'; Idayat-zade and M. Ragim; Baku, 4 May 1945) with Jevdet Hajiyev, which won a State Prize in 1946. He wrote a mono-opera, *Nezhnost'* ('Tenderness', 1972; Karayev, after A. Barbyus), for female voice and chamber orchestra, and a musical comedy, *Sirano de Berzherak* (1973; after E. Rostand). His large output includes ballets, incidental music and music for 20 films.

Besides expressive, at times romantically emotional, local colour, powerful tendencies towards neo-classicism are detectable in Karayev's music, notably in his form and contrapuntal development. His creative synthesis of Prokofievian chromaticism with Azerbaijani folk modality led to the establishment of a new modal harmonic system on which he was able to base his works of the 1940s and 50s. His later works show a more rational technique and a wide stock of expressive methods.

*

I. Abezgauz: 'Kara Karayev', *SovM* (1956), no.9, pp.19–27

YURY GABAY

Karczykowski, Ryszard (*b* Tczew, 6 April 1942). Polish tenor. He studied in Gdańsk and Berlin and made his début at Dessau in 1969 as Beppo. He then sang at Leipzig and Frankfurt, and wider engagements took him to the Vienna Staatsoper, Berlin, and other principal European centres, Moscow and Leningrad, and to the

USA, where he made his début at Boston in 1981 as the Duke (*Rigoletto*). His Covent Garden début was in 1977 as Alfred (*Die Fledermaus*). He sang Alwa in 1978 at Zürich and later in the three-act version of *Lulu* at Covent Garden (1981), Berlin (1982) and Vienna (1983). In 1981 he took part in the first staged performance of *Maddalena* (Prokofiev) at Graz. He has also appeared in Mozart roles. A lyric tenor of musical sensibility if sometimes variable technique, he has made recordings including Alfred and Camille (*Die lustige Witwe*) with the Vienna Volksoper ensemble.

NOËL GOODWIN

Karel, Rudolf (*b* Plzeň, 9 Nov 1880; *d* Terezín, 6 March 1945). Czech composer. In Prague he studied law at the university and composition at the conservatory, where he was Dvořák's last pupil. During World War I he was interned in Russia; he taught in music schools, becoming director of the Irkutsk school. In 1918 he joined the Czech legion, within which he established a symphony orchestra, which he conducted. From 1923 to 1941 he was professor of composition and orchestration at the Prague Conservatory. Arrested by the Gestapo in 1943, he died in the Terezín concentration camp. Karel's early compositions were greatly influenced by Dvořák and Tchaikovsky, but his mature style is complexly polyphonic, showing predilections for involved variation form, modally-tinged harmony and irregular rhythm: comparisons can be made with Reger. The difficulty of his music kept it from immediate acceptance, and in later years he tended towards simplification.

Karel's first opera, *Ilseino srdce* ('Ilsa's Heart', composed 1909), uses a psychological theme from aristocratic and artistic life, adding a hint of social comment. It is constructed on a system of leitmotifs, with variation techniques playing an important part. *Smrt kmotřička* ('Godmother Death', 1933), after a national fairy-tale, was one of his most successful works. Karel worked on his last opera, *Tři zlaté vlasy děda vševěda* ('The Three Golden Hairs of the Knowledgeable Old Man'), while he was in Pankrác prison; it was unfinished at his death. His pupil Zbyněk Vostřáák completed it and it was performed in Prague in 1948.

Ilseino srdce [Ilsa's Heart], 1909 (lyrical comedy, 3, A. Kropáček and K. H. Hilar), Prague, National, 11 Nov 1924, vs (Prague, 1921)

Smrt kmotřička [Godmother Death] (3, S. Lom), Brno, Provincial, 3 Feb 1933, vs (Prague, 1935)

Tři zlaté vlasy děda vševěda [The Three Golden Hairs of the Knowledgeable Old Man], 1944–5 (3, Karel, after folktales), inc.; completed and orchd Z. Vostřáák, Prague, National, 28 Oct 1948

JAN TROJAN

Karetnikov, Nikolay (*b* Moscow, 28 June 1930). Russian composer. He studied with Shebalin at the Moscow Conservatory (1948–53), then embraced the modernist influences which unofficially entered Russian musical life in the late 1950s and early 60s. After his Fourth Symphony of 1963 he embarked on two long-term operatic projects, with no foreseeable prospects of performance because of the element of thinly disguised political allegory.

Til' Ulenshpigel' ('Till Eulenspiegel'), completed in 1985, based on the novel by the Belgian Charles de Coster, tells of Till's adventures in 16th-century Flanders, where he is a thorn in the flesh of both the Dutch authorities and the occupying Spaniards. He is exiled, his father is burned at the stake and his mother is tortured to death. In Part 2 the Spaniards are defeated, Till has his revenge on the Fishmonger (an informer) and in a surreal conclusion he dies but returns to life. The music appeared in stages, in part as a film score, in part as 15 independent songs. In its final Singspiel-like form *Til' Ulenshpigel'* is a kaleidoscope of styles, all of them laconic and memorable. It was recorded in extraordinary circumstances – Karetnikov persuaded film orchestra musicians, singers and engineers to work after hours over a period of five years to create it – which led to its being dubbed (by Gerard McBurney on BBC Radio 3) 'the first *samizdat* opera'.

Karetnikov's *Misteriya apostola Pavla* ('The Mystery of St Paul'), an opera-oratorio, was composed between 1972 and 1987. Its subject is a mythical one, of St Paul brought before the Emperor Nero to justify his beliefs. Here the style is more uniformly austere and modernist. Neither opera has been staged.

DAVID FANNING

Karl Eugen. *See* CARL EUGEN.

Karlsruhe. City in south-west Germany, capital of Baden. Before Karlsruhe was founded, music was cultivated by the margraves of Baden-Durlach at the court of Durlach. From 1662 onwards there are records of Singspiels, ballets and plays being given. In 1715 Margrave Karl Wilhelm founded the city named 'Carolsruhe' after him, and in 1719 he took his Hofkapelle, his dancers and actors to the new capital, where a court theatre had been built. Early German opera was at the centre of theatrical activity here; of those composed and performed, only Casimir Schweizelsperg's *Die romanische Lucretia* is extant. After the Margrave's death in 1738 the court theatre was dissolved, and touring companies dominated the scene until the beginning of the 19th century. A turning point came in 1806, when Napoleon and Tsar Alexander I created the Grand Duchy of Baden. Two years later Grand Duke Carl Friedrich commissioned the architect Friedrich Weinbrenner to build 'a proper theatre' in the Schlossplatz. In 1810 he engaged Wilhelm Vogel's company for the court, thus effectively founding the Grand Ducal Baden Hoftheater.

In 1847 Weinbrenner's theatre, the pride of Karlsruhe, was destroyed in a fire killing 64 people. A temporary theatre was opened the same year, and by 1853 the handsome theatre designed by Heinrich Hübsch stood on the site of the old Weinbrenner building. Eduard Devrient's period as Intendant here, 1852–70, was a brilliant one. As early as 1853 Liszt conducted Beethoven's Ninth Symphony in the city, and Wagner appeared as a conductor in 1863. Of major importance for the operatic tradition of Karlsruhe was the work of two musical directors: Hermann Levi, the first conductor of *Parsifal* (1864–72), and Felix Mottl (1881–1903), during whose tenure Karlsruhe was regarded as a 'little Bayreuth'. Mottl was also a Berlioz enthusiast; the première of the whole of *Les Troyens* in Karlsruhe in 1890 was a cultural event of international significance. In the Mottl era also came the first performance of Schubert's *Fierrabras* (1897). In the early 20th century the theatre had close contacts with Strauss and with Siegfried Wagner, whose own *Banadietrich*, *Schwarzschwanenreich* and *Der Friedensengel* were first given there.

After World War I and the abdication of the Grand Duke the theatre became the Badische Landesbühne (1918), and in 1933 it was renamed the Badisches

Staatstheater, with the orchestra becoming the Badische Staatskapelle. Both names are still in use. Between the wars the musical directors Josef Krips (1926–33) and Joseph Keilberth (1935–40) maintained the Opera's high standards. There was a new start under Keilberth's successor, Otto Matzerath, after World War II – in the Konzerthaus, since the theatre in the Schlossplatz had been destroyed in 1944. Performances continued to take place in the Konzerthaus, converted into a theatre in 1953, until the new theatre on the Baumeisterstrasse opened on 29 August 1975 with *Die Zauberflöte*. A modern concrete structure with highly efficient stage machinery, it was designed by Helmut Bätzner. Opera is mainly performed in the Grosses Haus, but the Kleines Haus is also available. Both theatres consist of stalls and one circle. The asymmetrically arranged Grosses Haus has 1002 seats; the Kleines Haus can accommodate up to 550 people.

During its season, which lasts for about ten and a half months, the Badisches Staatstheater gives some 135 opera performances of about 20 works, including two or three modern operas, two to five *Spielopern* and about three Baroque operas, mainly by Handel. It is funded by the *Land* of Baden-Württemberg and by the city. Since 1975 Karlsruhe has worked closely with Opéra du Rhin of Strasbourg, the two companies sharing their repertories. The annual Handel Days began in Karlsruhe in 1978 (renamed the Handel Festival in 1985), and the European Days of Culture began in 1983. First performances after World War II have included Rainer Kunad's *Der Meister und Margarita* (1986), the German premières of Tippett's *King Priam* (1963) and *The Midsummer Marriage* (1973) and Cavalli's *Giasone* (1974), and the first production in West Germany of Siegfried Matthus's *Graf Mirabeau* (1989). Among the singers who had long-term engagements at Karlsruhe were the creators of the title roles in *Tristan und Isolde*, Ludwig Schnorr von Carolsfeld and his wife Malvina Garrigues; other famous performers have included Hermann Jadlowker, Erika Köth, Jess Thomas, Francisco Araiza and Wolfgang Brendel.

W. Harder: *Das Karlsruher Hoftheater* (Karlsruhe, 1889)

E. Kilian: *Beiträge zur Geschichte des Karlsruher Hoftheater* (Karlsruhe, 1893)

L. Schiedermair: 'Die Oper an den badischen Höfen des 17. und 18. Jahrhunderts', *SIMG*, xiv (1912–13), 191–207, 369–449, 510–50

W. Bauer: *Das Hoftheater zu Karlsruhe 1715–1810* (diss., U. of Heidelberg, 1923)

G. Haass: *Geschichte des ehemaligen Grossherzoglich-Badischen Hoftheaters Karlsruhe, 1806–52*, i (Karlsruhe, 1932)

GÁBOR HALÁSZ

Karl Theodor. *See* CARL THEODOR.

Karl V. Bühnenwerk mit Musik in two parts, op.73, by ERNST KRENEK to his own libretto; Prague, Neues Deutsches Theater, 22 June 1938.

Ostensibly a historical work, *Karl V* was also Krenek's contribution to the controversy within Austrian political ideology of the early 1930s. The work's emphasis on universal Catholicism as a political alternative to nationalism was thought to pose a fundamental ethical challenge to the reactionary tendencies dominating Austrian cultural politics even before the German fascist *Anschluss*. Although commissioned by the Vienna State Opera in 1930, preparations for a 1934 première were forcibly halted. Fragments were

performed outside Austro-Germany as op.73a in 1936 and 1937; eventually the German opera house in Prague produced it a year later.

Krenek experimented with a synthesis between music and drama which extended the operatic genre by incorporating recent theatrical innovations from epic theatre and cinema. The work is designed for montage presentation on a divided stage, so that the enactment and commentary can take place simultaneously. In the background, the events of Karl's life up to his abdication in 1556 are presented, not as a chronological narrative – but rather, like flashbacks in a film, as fragmented experiences which he, facing the last judgment shortly before his death in 1558, chooses to remember. The foreground is the arena for theological and ethical debate.

Karl V (baritone) is called by God (offstage voice) to account for himself. Through a confessor, the young monk, Juan de Regla (spoken), he examines the most important stages of his life, in which his task has been to unite the world in the Christian faith. Karl is simultaneously the subject of the narrative and the object of a divine plan. In addition, Krenek's presentation of Karl as a psychological subject – interacting with the conflicting motivations of the other main characters: Juana, his mother (alto), Isabella, his wife (soprano), Luther (baritone), Sultan Soliman (baritone), Franz I (tenor) and Pope Clement VII (spoken) – encourages the objective participation of the audience. There are parallels with Schoenberg's *Moses und Aron*, in content and musicodramatic style, but these are coincidental. However, Krenek did study the methods of earlier Second Viennese School composers during the composition of this his first 12-note opera. He exploited the alienating effects of the musical language to enhance reality and dispel illusion, articulating dimensions of Karl's dilemma which were beyond expressing in words.

CHARLOTTE PURKIS

Karmins'ky, Mark (*b* Kharkiv, 30 Jan 1930). Ukrainian composer. He studied initially philology at the University of Kharkiv, then went to the conservatory where he studied under Dmytro Klebanov and graduated in 1953. He has composed in a wide range of genres but has had a particular interest in opera, in which he has tried a number of experiments. The most notable is in *Desyat' dniv, shcho potryasly svit* ('Ten Days that Shook the World'), where he rejected the notion of creating a socialist-realist opera; rather, he mixed various genres and methods, creating a collage of styles that reflect the tumultuous events described in the opera. Epic choral sections contrast with a re-creation of agitprop theatre to give rise to an 'opera-spectacle'.

Bukovyntsi [People of Bukovyna] (4, epilogue, I. Muratov), Kharkiv, Lysenko Academic, 1957; rev. as Karpats'ka bil' [Carpathian Pain], Moscow, 1960 (concert perf.)

Desyat' dniv, shcho potryasly svit [Ten Days that Shook the World] (prol., 10 scenes, V. Dubrovsky, after J. Reed), Donets'k, 1970

Irkutskaya istoriya, 1977 (3, Dubrovsky, after A. Arbuzov), unperf.

Vsego odin den' [One Day Left] (prol., 2, Dubrovsky), L'viv, Ivan Franko, and Odessa, Academic, 1987   VIRKO BALEY

Kärntnertortheater [Kaiserlich-königliches Hoftheater nächst dem Kärntnerthor]. Theatre built in 1709 in Vienna, used for opera for much of the 18th and 19th centuries. It was used by the Hofoper until the company moved to its new opera house in 1869 and was demolished in 1870. *See* VIENNA, §§1–3 and 4(i).

Karsten, Christofer Christian (*b* Ystad, 9 Sept 1756; *d* Drottningholm, 7 Aug 1827). Swedish tenor. Following rudimentary training in Ystad, he was taken in 1771 by Queen Lovisa Ulrika to Stockholm, where he was employed in the chorus at the Royal Opera in 1776. After further singing lessons in Copenhagen, he made his début as Bores in the prologue to J. G. Naumann's *Amphion* in Stockholm in 1778. He performed major roles, such as Christiern in Naumann's *Gustaf Wasa*, until being pensioned in 1806. His dark tenor voice (closer to a baritone) was noted for its power, making him the ideal contrast to Carl Stenborg's lighter, more flexible voice; from 1786 the two often performed opposite each other.

F. Dahlgren: *Anteckningar om Stockholms teatrar* (Stockholm, 1866)

J. Flodmark: *Stenborgska skådebanorne* (Stockholm, 1893)

N. Personne: *Svenska teatern under Gustavianska tidehvarfvet* (Stockholm, 1913)   BERTIL H. VAN BOER

Kartousch, Louise (*b* Linz, 17 Aug 1886; *d* Vienna, 13 Feb 1964). Austrian soprano. After studying at the music school in Linz, she appeared at the provincial theatre there in juvenile roles. From 1902 she was second soubrette in Graz, appearing as a Valkyrie and as Mercédès in *Carmen*. She then became principal soubrette at the Theater an der Wien, from 1911 forming a famous partnership there and at other Viennese theatres with the *buffo* bass Ernst Tautenhayn (*b* Vienna, 3 April 1873; *d* Zlabing, 30 Aug 1944). She created principal roles in such works as Fall's *Die Dollarprinzessin* (1907) and *Die Rose von Stambul* (1916), Lehár's *Der Mann mit den drei Frauen* (1908), *Der Graf von Luxemburg* (1909), *Eva* (1911), *Die ideale Gattin* (1913), *Endlich allein* (1914), *Der Sterngucker* (1916), *Die blaue Mazur* (1920), *Die gelbe Jacke* (1923) and *Clo-Clo* (1924), and Kálmán's *Die Bajadere* (1921). She was noted for her excellent light-comedy performances, allied to intelligent musicality.   ANDREW LAMB

Kaschmann [Kašman], **Giuseppe** (*b* Lussimpiccolo [now Mali Lošinj], Istria, 14 July 1847; *d* Rome, 7 Feb 1925). Italian baritone. After studying in Rome, he made his début in Udine in 1868 (as a bass, Banquo), then appeared in 1869 at Zagreb, where in 1870 he sang the title role of Zacj's *Mislav*. He sang in 1876 at Turin as Alphonse (*La favorite*), then at Venice, Rome, Trieste and La Scala (1878, as Posa). In the inaugural season of the Metropolitan (1883–4), he sang Enrico Ashton, Don Giovanni and Thomas's Hamlet, a role he also sang at Lisbon and Madrid, and at the S Carlo, the Colón and La Fenice. He sang Wolfram and Amfortas at Bayreuth (1892, 1894) and returned to the Metropolitan (1895–6) as Kurwenal, Wotan and Telramund. His repertory included Valentine, Escamillo, Athanaël, Nélusko, William Tell, Riccardo (*I puritani*), Severo (*Poliuto*), Rigoletto, Macbeth, Amonasro, Don Carlo (*Ernani* and *La forza*), Iago, Barnaba, Tonio and Scarpia. In his 60s he turned to *buffo* roles such as Rossini's Dr Bartolo and Don Pasquale; his last performance was in Rome in Cimarosa's *Le astuzie femminili* (1921). His few records reveal a velvety voice of great beauty, employed with style.

GV (R. Celletti; R. Vegeto)   ALAN BLYTH

Kaschovska, Felicie (*b* Warsaw, 12 May 1867; *d* Bielsko-Biała, 18 July 1951). Polish soprano. She studied with Enrico Tamberlik, then at the Vienna Conservatory with Josef Gänsbacher and in Paris with Jean de Reszke. She made her début at the Warsaw Opera as Alice in *Robert le diable* (1888) and in the same season sang Wagnerian roles at the Metropolitan (her début there was as Urbain in *Les Huguenots*). After singing in Boston and St Louis she returned to Europe, appearing in France, Germany and Russia as Carmen, Aida, Norma and Brünnhilde. After her retirement she taught in Vienna and Poland; Maria Németh was among her pupils.   DAVID CUMMINGS

Kashchey the Deathless [*Kashchey bessmertnïy*]. Autumnal parable in one act (three scenes without pause) by NIKOLAY ANDREYEVICH RIMSKY-KORSAKOV to a libretto by the composer and his daughter Sofiya after a scenario by Yevgeny Maximovich Petrovsky; Moscow, Solodovnikov Theatre (Savva Mamontov's Private Russian Opera), 12/25 December 1902.

A seasonal allegory like his *Snow Maiden* or *Christmas Eve*, Rimsky-Korsakov's 12th opera is loosely based on a group of Russian folktales concerning Kashchey (tenor), an evil sorcerer who keeps captive the Princess Unearthly-Beauty (Nenaglyadnaya krasa; soprano) until she is rescued by Prince Ivan (Ivan-Korolevich or Ivan-Tsarevich, the Russian 'Prince Charming'; baritone), who has found the hiding place where Kashchey has secreted his death – here, in the tears of the sorcerer's hard-hearted daughter Kashcheyevna (mezzo-soprano), tears that she finally sheds for love of the prince.

Petrovsky, a music journalist, submitted a libretto called *Ivan-Korolevich* to Rimsky-Korsakov in November 1900, but the composer ('the compleat musical materialist', as Petrovsky called him) found its symbolism obscure. In the summer of 1901, after perusing Wagner's *Siegfried*, Rimsky's head began filling up with novel harmonic ideas that seemed to demand outlet in an opera about evil magic, so with his daughter's help he revised Petrovsky's libretto to meet his own standards of clarity and plunged in. The resulting text was sufficiently far from the original *Ivan-Korolevich* that Petrovsky saw fit to publish his libretto independently (St Petersburg, 1903), with a preface inviting any composer 'open to the possibility of creating a Russian symbolist opera' to help himself to it (there seem to have been no takers). The first performance was conducted by Mikhail Ippolitov-Ivanov, with Nadeshda Zabela as the Princess and Mikhail Bocharov as Prince Ivan. Rimsky-Korsakov revised the opera in 1906.

In March 1905, amid the widespread civil disturbances following the 'Bloody Sunday' massacre of political protesters, a performance of *Kashchey the Deathless* was organized by a group of St Petersburg Conservatory pupils under Glazunov's direction as a tribute to Rimsky-Korsakov, who had recently been dismissed from his professorship for supporting a student strike. (Rimsky was the single political liberal among the great Russian composers – something, it would seem, rather closely bound up in what Petrovsky called his 'materialism'.) It proved very easy to invest the opera's rather hoary conceptual dualism (icy-evil-supernatural chromaticism *versus* sunny-human-benign diatonics) with a new and topical metaphorical import, and the performances turned into a major political demonstration that had to be quelled by the tsarist police. The opera thus gained a 'revolutionary' aura that sustained it, despite its 'decadent' harmonic idiom (and also, perhaps, beyond its intrinsic deserts), in the Soviet repertory throughout the Stalinist period.

RICHARD TARUSKIN

Kashin, Daniil Nikitich (*b* nr Moscow, *c*1770; *d* Moscow, Dec 1841). Russian composer. A serf musician and an early folksong collector, in 1798 he composed the opera *Natal'ya, boyarskaya doch'* ('Natalia, the Nobleman's Daughter'; 1803, Moscow) after the novel by NIKOLAY MIKHAYLOVICH KARAMZIN.

Kashperov, Vladimir Nikitich (*b* Chufarovo, Simbirsk province, 25 Aug/6 Sept 1826; *d* Romantsevo, Podol'sk region, nr Moscow, 26 June/8 July 1894). Russian composer. Trained as a youth for a military career, he left the service on receiving his commission and devoted himself to music. After piano studies with Henselt in St Petersburg, he went to Berlin on Glinka's advice to study counterpoint and composition with Siegfried Dehn. Back in Russia, 1848–56, he briefly resumed his military career, commanding a company at Sevastopol during the Crimean War. He made his first stab at operatic composition with *Tsïgani*, a setting, begun in 1850 but never finished, of a libretto by Nikolay Ogaryov after Pushkin's *The Gypsies* (later the source for Rakhmaninov's *Aleko*).

In 1856 Kashperov returned to Berlin, resumed his studies with Dehn and became close to Glinka, who was there for a second educational visit. After Glinka's death the next year, Kashperov went on to Italy, where he lived until 1865 and produced three operas, the first by a Russian to be produced in Italy since the 18th century. He returned to Russia at Nikolay Rubinstein's invitation to join the faculty of the newly formed Moscow Conservatory, where he was professor of singing, 1866–72.

In Moscow he joined forces with Alexander Ostrovsky, whom he had met in Italy. The playwright, a great lover and connoisseur of Italian opera, eagerly arranged his own most famous play, *The Storm*, as a numbers libretto for Kashperov to set in his wonted Donizettian manner (*Groza*, 1867). The story was stripped down to the love intrigue, which, denuded of its social and cultural milieu (the most essential of its components for most readers), is reduced to a typical tale of a fickle woman, a spineless paramour and a ridiculous cuckold. Several roles are virtually eliminated, including that of Kabanova, the heroine's mother-in-law, often viewed as the play's central character. The individual, scattered speeches and admissions of the lovers Boris and Katerina are gathered into big expository arias, set, Italian-style, in sequences of mounting tempos. Each of the four acts is furnished with an impressive ensemble finale.

Most critics wrote off the result as a joke, and Kashperov lacked the wherewithal to captivate public taste. He was the main Russian epigone of Italian opera in the second half of the 19th century, but taste in Russia was veering sharply away from Italian opera in the period between the *Forza* débâcle (1862) and the advent of Adelina Patti (1869). Discouraged, 'Il signor maestro Kasperoff' (as Cui dubbed him) lapsed into indolence. It took him two decades to produce another luckless opera (*Taras Bulba*, after Gogol), and at his death he was deemed a walking anachronism.

Tsïgani, 1950 (N. Ogaryov, after A. S. Pushkin: *The Gypsies*), inc.

Maria Tudor (4, A. Ghislanzoni, after V. Hugo), Milan, Carcano, 7 Dec 1859
Cola di Rienzi (melodramma, 4, Ghislanzoni, after E. Bulwer-Lytton), Florence, Pergola, March 1863
Consuelo (after G. Sand), Venice, 1865
Groza [The Storm] (4, A. Ostrovsky, after his play), St Petersburg, Mariinsky, and Moscow, Bol'shoy, 30 Oct/11 Nov 1867
Taras Bulba (5, I. Shpazhinsky, after N. Gogol), Moscow, Bol'shoy, 20 April/2 May 1887

A. Serov: '"Groza", opera v 4-kh deystviyakh. Libretto A. N. Ostrovskogo. Muzïka V. N. Kashperova', *Izbrannïye stat'i*, ed. G. Khubov, ii (Moscow, 1957), 72–8 [orig. pubd 1867]
I. Turgenev: 'Ob opere "Mariya Tyudor" Kashperova', *Sankt-peterburgskiye vedomosti* (8 Feb 1868)
'V. N. Kashperova', *RMG*, i/8 (1894), 169–71
V. Kiselyov: 'A. N. Ostrovsky i V. N. Kashperov', *A. N. Ostrovsky i russkiye kompozitori*, ed. E. Kolosova and V. Filippov (Moscow and Leningrad, 1937), 67–92
R. Taruskin: *Opera and Drama in Russia* (Ann Arbor, 1981), 154–7
RICHARD TARUSKIN

Kašlík, Václav (*b* Poličná, 28 Sept 1917; *d* Prague, 4 June 1989). Czech composer, director and conductor. He studied composition with Karel and Hába, conducting with Talich and others and opera direction with Pujman at the Prague Conservatory (1936–40). He worked with E. F. Burian at the theatres D 40 and D 41, the Prague National Theatre (1941–3) and the People's Theatre in Brno (1943–5). In 1945 he and Alois Hába founded the Grand Opera of 5 May in Prague, then one of the most modern opera houses, at which he worked as principal, director and conductor (notably of Smetana's *The Brandenburgers in Bohemia*, 1945, and Prokofiev's *Betrothal in a Monastery*, 1947). In 1948 the company was incorporated into the National Theatre, where Kašlík worked until the end of his life, directing *The Cunning Little Vixen* (1954) and *The Makropulos Affair* (1956 and 1965), *Der fliegende Holländer* (1959), Martinů's *Julietta* (1963) and *The Greek Passion* (1967 and 1984) and *Don Giovanni* (1969). Abroad he made notable débuts with Nono's *Intolleranza 1960* (1961) and Hindemith's *Cardillac* (1964) in Venice, *Les contes d'Hoffmann* in Wiesbaden (1966), Berlin (1969) and Frankfurt (1970), *Pelléas et Mélisande* in London (1969) and *Boris Godunov* in Verona (1976). He also directed operas for film and television (*Rusalka*, 1963; *Julietta*, 1969; *Les contes d'Hoffmann*, 1970) and participated in productions by Laterna Magica (*Les contes d'Hoffmann*, 1963). Wherever he worked he showed a feeling for melody, art, characterization and experimental procedures, a rich imagination and great technical skill (with film and television projections, stage setting and dynamic action); he tried to fuse these elements in interesting ways to attract contemporary audiences. His style of direction, which matured in the 1960s, is known as kinetism.

Kašlík's experience and profound dramatic understanding are also apparent in all his operas, in which he sought to modernize the traditional form into complete music theatre; he also composed ballets and film music. *Zbojnická balada* ('The Brigand's Ballad'), drawing inspiration from the folklore of his native Valašsko and from Burian's Folk Suite, is a traditional narrative based on authentic and stylized folksongs and nursery rhymes, combining epic narration and dramatic scenes about love and betrayal, robbers fighting against oppression by the nobility and the humiliation of people. The unfinished *Křížová cesta* ('The Way of the Cross'), in the style of a folk Passion, is a metaphor of the suffering of a nation under Nazi occupation. The operas *Krakatit* and

La strada, on librettos after film scripts, alternate between simple diatonic writing, jazz, cabaret songs and circus songs and serial procedures, *musique concrète* and electronic music. These changes are reflected in the dramatic situations; the unifying elements are dynamism and theatricality. *Krakatit* was composed for television but is also suitable for the stage. It concerns the feverish visions of an injured inventor of explosives (tenor) who is involved in the fight against their possible misuse by militants, and the universal struggle for profit. *La strada* is based on Fellini's work about two wandering comedians, the tough Zampano (bass-baritone) and the simple-minded Gelsomina (soprano); it is a modern Singspiel with spoken dialogue and songs. Similar procedures are used in the concise opera *Krysař* ('Pied Piper'), a poetic adaptation of a medieval legend which represents a parable of the clash between dreams of pure love and freedom, and primitive self-interest.

Zbojnická balada [The Brigand's Ballad], 1939–42 (1, Kašlík, after V. Školaudy and folk poetry), Prague, Grand Opera of 5 May, 17 June 1948; rev. 1978 (3), Prague, National, 2 Oct 1986
Křížová cesta [The Way of the Cross], 1941–5 (13 stations, J. Bogner), inc., unperf.
Krakatit (2, O. Vávra, after K. Čapek), Czechoslovak TV, 5 March 1961
La strada, 1980 (Spl, Kašlík, after F. Fellini; lyrics P. Kopta, J. Kainar, V. Nezval and J. Wolker), Prague, Smetana, 13 Jan 1982
Krysař [Pied Piper] (Spl, Kašlík, after V. Dyk, lyrics J. Brukner), Plzeň, Chamber, 27 Oct 1984

*

V. Lébl: 'Operní quo vadis' [Operatic quo vadis], *Literární noviny*, x/11 (1961), 8
J. Bajer: 'Kašlíkův Krakatit', *HRo*, xix (1966), 404
I. Jirko: 'Olomoucký Krakatit', *HRo*, xxvi (1973), 244–5
J. Brožovská: 'Teď rozbiju měsíc' [Now I will Break the Moon], *Scéna*, vii/5 (1982), 4
E. Herrmannová: 'Nová česká opera ve Smetanově divadle' [A New Czech Opera in the Smetana Theatre], *Tvorba* (1982), no.7, p.9
J. Pávek: 'Silnice v operní podobě' [*La strada* in Operatic Form], *Gramorevue*, xviii/4 (1982), 2
H. Havlíková: 'Opera především jako divadlo' [Opera Mainly as Theatre], *Scéna*, xi/5 (1986), 4
E. Herrmannová: 'Zbojnická balada v Národním divadle' [*Zbojnická balada* at the National Theatre], *Tvorba* (1986), no.51, p.19
V. Bor: 'Zbojnická balada V. Kašlíka', *HRo*, xl (1987), 76–7
V. Kašlík: *Jak jsem dělal operu* [How I Made an Opera] (Prague, 1987)   HELENA HAVLÍKOVÁ

Kaspar der Fagottist ('Kaspar the Bassoonist') [*Der Fagottist, oder Die Zauberzither* ('The Bassoonist, or The Magic Zither')]. Singspiel in three acts by WENZEL MÜLLER to a libretto by JOACHIM PERINET after J. A. Liebeskind's tale *Lulu oder die Zauberflöte* (published in *Dschinnistan*, iii, 1789); Vienna, Theater in der Leopoldstadt, 8 June 1791.

Prince Armidoro comes to the castle of the fairy Perifirime; she commissions him to recover her magic tinder-box from the evil (but comically incompetent) magician Bosphoro. Equipped with magic ring and zither, accompanied by his comic child servant Kaspar, and to be assisted in crises by the genial child spirit Pizichi, he is sent on his way by balloon. After a protracted series of difficulties he wins the tinder-box – and also the love of Sidi, held captive by Bosphoro. Perifirime appears, and is revealed to be Sidi's mother. Bosphoro is punished, and the lovers (including the bassoon-playing Kaspar and Sidi's companion, Palmire) are united.

Originally entitled *Der Fagottist*, the piece was swiftly renamed after the popular actor Johann La Roche, who regularly played the stock character Kaspar or Kasperl. It was immensely popular for three decades, being given

nearly 130 times in Vienna, and very frequently throughout German-speaking lands. Though the action is feebly motivated, the light, satirical tone, broad comedy (especially of Kaspar and his opposite number, Zumio) and Müller's extensive (25 vocal numbers) and tuneful music account for the work's success. Armidoro's 'Der Lenz belebet die Natur' and Sidi's 'Alles liebet, was da lebet' were widely known, and Kaspar's songs and the bassoon-teaching duet also reveal Müller's sure hand. Following his visit to the fourth performance, Mozart commented: 'to cheer myself up, I went to the new opera *Der Fagottist* in the Kasperl Theatre, which everyone is talking about – but there's absolutely nothing to it' (letter of 12 June 1791). Despite frequent claims to the contrary, *Kaspar der Fagottist* did not influence *Die Zauberflöte*. That it is a pleasing Singspiel was amply borne out by the Vienna Kammeroper revival in 1970.   PETER BRANSCOMBE

Kassel [Cassel]. City in central Germany. It became the residence of the landgraves of Hesse in 1277 and the capital of Hesse-Kassel in 1567. Landgrave Moritz of Hesse-Darmstadt (1592–1627) began importing troupes of English actors in 1594, and constructed for them in 1604–6 the first permanent theatre in Germany, which he named the Ottoneum after his favourite son. Its heyday came to an abrupt end with the outbreak of the Thirty Years War (1618). Musical life revived on the accession of Landgrave Carl (1677–1730): the Hofkapelle was reorganized and the Kassel court began an Italian period with the appointment of Ruggiero Fedeli, a Venetian, as Kapellmeister in 1701. Fortunato Chelleri became conductor of the court orchestra in 1725, but musical life declined again after the landgrave's death. Another revival took place under Landgrave Friedrich II (1760–85): the Italian opera was expanded, the 30-strong Hofkapelle reorganized, and Kassel engaged outstanding artists, notably the court Kapellmeister Ignazio Fiorillo. Prince Maximilian's palace was converted into an opera house with extensive technical equipment; it opened in 1764 with Fiorillo's *Diana ed Endimione*. Soon after Gluck's visit in 1774 French opera (Grétry, Monsigny and Gluck) became dominant.

Under Elector Wilhelm I (1785–1806, 1814–21) all theatrical activity ceased; the opera, ballet and orchestra were disbanded, and the complete stock of costumes sold. However, modest theatrical performances were staged by touring companies such as G. F. W. Grossmann's Bohemian Troupe. A gradual revival of musical life began again in 1793 under the singer and theatrical director Carl Hassloch. *Die Zauberflöte* was staged on 29 December 1793, and thereafter followed *La clemenza di Tito* (1794), *Le nozze di Figaro* (1797) and *Idomeneo* (1802). In 1797 the opera house was renamed the Fürstliche Hoftheater. On 16 May 1803, when Wilhelm became elector, Hassloch's *Hesus, oder Lohn für Vaterlandsliebe* was performed there.

Kassel was occupied by French troops from 1806 to 1813, becoming capital of the Kingdom of Westphalia in 1807, with Jérôme Bonaparte, Napoleon's youngest brother, as king. A Théâtre Royal was built, and a dazzling new period of theatrical history in Kassel began. With Johann Friedrich Reichardt as court Kapellmeister, Mozart opera was much performed. Efforts to engage Beethoven as Kapellmeister failed when his Viennese patrons promised him material security, and so Felice Blangini became court

Kapellmeister in 1809. A small Hoftheater designed by Leo Klenze was built in 1808–9, and a ballet company was set up in 1810. The repertory of the Théâtre Royal was extensive: in 1811 it comprised 66 operas, 99 plays and 20 ballets, as well as *divertissements* and intermezzos. The excellent orchestra had 48 permanent members. In 1814, when the French had left, Elector Wilhelm I returned, and with him economy; the Hoftheater became a private enterprise with a grant from court funds.

Opera in Kassel flourished once more under Elector Wilhelm II (1821–32), when Louis Spohr was Kapellmeister. This period saw productions of Mozart, Weber and Spohr, French opera (Spontini, Boieldieu, Auber) and Italian (especially Rossini). Following the elector's death the theatre closed, 1832–3. There were occasional performances by the Bethmann company, but operatic activity was much reduced. Kassel was the second theatre to stage *Der fliegende Holländer*, on 5 June 1843, but the regent rejected the idea of staging *Tannhäuser* and Lortzing's *Der Waffenschmied*. Hesse ceased to be an electorate in 1866, when it became part of Prussia. The theatre was renamed the Königliche Schauspiele of Kassel and placed under the general administration of Berlin. Soon it saw another artistic revival. Gustav Mahler was musical director in 1883–5; Wilhelm Treiber became court Kapellmeister, and ambitious productions were staged. The old Hoftheater was demolished on the orders of Kaiser Wilhelm II, and a magnificent new building opened on 26 August 1909 with Lortzing's *Undine*. Despite World War I, the repertory remained stable. In 1918 ownership of the theatre was transferred from the royal court to the Prussian state, which became responsible for funding it. It became the Staatstheater Kassel in 1921. Under Paul Bekker (administrator, 1925–7), a progressive, modern repertory was introduced. Franz Ulbrich was administrator, 1935–44, with Robert Heger as Kapellmeister. The opera house was badly damaged in World War II and had to be demolished in 1950. To replace it, Paul Bode and Ernst Brunding designed a modern theatre with 953 seats. Work started in 1955 and on 12 September 1959 the theatre opened with *Prometheus*, specially commissioned from Rudolf Wagner-Régeny. Notable performances since then have included a spectacular production of the *Ring* (1970–73). The season runs from the end of September to the end of July. Adam Fischer became music director in 1987.

*

C. Engelbrecht and others: *Theater in Kassel* (Kassel, 1959)
R. Lebe: *Ein deutsches Hoftheater in Romantik und Biedermeier: die Kasseler Bühne zur Zeit Feiges und Spohrs* (Kassel, 1964)
KLAUS J. SEIDEL

Kastle, Leonard (*b* New York, 11 Feb 1929). American composer and director. He attended the Curtis Institute (1945–50) and later Columbia University, and studied composition with Szell, Scalero, Menotti and Barber. In 1950–51 he was music director for a Broadway revival of Menotti's *The Medium* and *The Telephone* and for Weill's *Lady in the Dark*. Shortly thereafter he was assistant music director for NBC television's Opera Theatre (1955–9); he has also directed his own operas. He taught at SUNY, Albany, from 1978 to 1988. Principally a vocal composer, Kastle has received several awards including an NEA grant; his opera *The Pariahs*, about whaling, was commissioned by the Deerfield Foundation. The *Mother Ann* operas are about the

Shakers, while *Desert* is based on the life of the Mormon prophet Brigham Young. His music, although harmonically modern, is romantic, tonal and melodic.

The Swing (television op, 1, Kastle), televised, NBC, 11 June 1956
Desert (3, A. H. Bailey), televised, NBC, 11 January 1961; rev. 1978
The Pariahs, 1966 (3, Kastle), excerpts perf., Albany, 1985
The Calling of Mother Ann (1, Kastle), Albany, 1985 [pt 1 of 5]; with pt 2, Potsdam, NY, 1987
The Journey of Mother Ann (1, Kastle), Potsdam, NY, 1987 [pt 2 of 5]
Professor Lookalike and the Children (children's op, 1, Kastle), Albany, 1988
KATHERINE K. PRESTON

Kastner, Jean-Georges [Johann Georg] (*b* Strasbourg, 9 March 1810; *d* Paris, 19 Dec 1867). French composer and theorist. He studied for a career in theology but abandoned this in the 1830s. He was composing by 1826 and in 1830 was put in charge of the Strasbourg National Guard band; between 1828 and 1835 he wrote four operas and numerous instrumental works. His first three operas were not performed, but after *Die Königin der Sarmaten* was played in Strasbourg (1835), the town council awarded him a stipend for study at the Paris Conservatoire. There he studied with Reicha (counterpoint and fugue) and H.-M. Berton (composition) and began work on the numerous treatises for which he was to become widely known. These include a *Méthode élémentaire* for voice and methods for nearly every wind instrument.

Kastner's marriage to a wealthy pupil, Léonie Boursault, enabled him to compose and write without financial worries. He wrote five operas in Paris, of which only *La maschera* (1841) was staged; details of other performances (listed in U. Manferrari: *Dizionario universale delle opere*, Florence, 1954–5) have not been verified. His primary importance for French opera of the period was perhaps his influence on Berlioz; the latter read and reviewed Kastner's works and writings, particularly his thoughts on orchestration and orchestral timbres, with much enthusiasm.

Die Königin der Sarmaten (5), Strasbourg, 13 June 1835
La maschera (oc, 2, A. J. F. Arnould and J. de Wailly), Paris, OC (Favart), 17 June 1841, vs (Paris, 1841)
Le dernier roi de Juda (biblische Oper, 2, M. Bourges), concert perf., Paris, 1 Dec 1844

Unperf.: Gustav Wasa, 1832 (5); Oskars Tod, *c*1833 (4); Der Sarazene, 1835 (komische Oper, 2); Beatrice, die Braut von Messina, 1839 (2, G. Schilling, after F. von Schiller); Juana, 1840 (oc, 2), inc.; Les nonnes de Robert-le-diable, 1845 (oc, 3, E. Scribe); Pépito, 1846 (oc, 3)

*

H. Ludwig: *Jean Georges Kastner* (Leipzig, 1886)
P. Spitta: 'Johann Georg Kastner', *Musikgeschichtliche Aufsätze* (Berlin, 1894)
THOMASIN LA MAY

Kastorsky, Vladimir (*b* Bol'shiye Saly, 2/14 March 1871; *d* Leningrad [now St Petersburg], 2 July 1948). Russian bass. He studied in St Petersburg and made his début in the provinces, going to the Mariinsky, St Petersburg, in 1895. There he remained until 1930, singing in a wide repertory which included Wagnerian roles such as Wotan and King Mark. In 1908 he sang Pimen at Paris in the first performances of *Boris Godunov* outside Russia. For many years he taught singing in Leningrad, and at an advanced age appeared at the Bol'shoy in a supporting role in *The Queen of Spades*. A voice of fine quality, almost baritonal in timbre, is heard in recordings, impressive also in the low register, evenly produced, tastefully directed and well preserved in later years.
J. B. STEANE

Kastu, Matti (*b* Turku, 3 Feb 1943). Finnish tenor. He joined the Stockholm Royal Opera in 1973, making his début as Laca Kleme (*Jenůfa*), which he also sang in Edinburgh (1974). In Stockholm his other roles included Rodolfo, Bacchus and the Emperor (*Die Frau ohne Schatten*), a part he subsequently sang in San Francisco (1976), Vienna and Düsseldorf (1977) and Munich (1978), and for the WNO (1981). He created the Guide in Sallinen's *The King Goes Forth to France* (1984, Savonlinna). His repertory encompasses Erik, Siegmund, Siegfried, Tannhäuser, Walther and Tristan, which he sang at Edinburgh (1990), but his brilliant, steel-toned voice is better suited to such roles as Menelaus (*Die ägyptische Helena*), which he has sung in New York and Munich and has also recorded.

ELIZABETH FORBES

Kas'yanov, Alexander Alexandrovich (*b* Bolobonovo, Simbirsk province [now Gor'kovskaya region], 18/30 Aug 1891; *d* Gor'kiy [now Nizhniy Novgorod], 13 Feb 1982). Russian composer. He studied composition with Nikolay Sokolov and the piano with Sergey Lyapunov at the St Petersburg (later Petrograd) Conservatory from 1912 to 1917, then moved to Nizhniy Novgorod, where he became active in many facets of the city's musical life, including the foundation of the People's Conservatory in 1918. Kas'yanov's operas form an important portion of a creative legacy deeply influenced by the classics of 19th-century Russian nationalist music. His vivid treatment of massed choral scenes and local folk colour is particularly noteworthy in his most important opera, *Stepan Razin*, which, along with *Foma Gordeyev* and *Yermak*, manifests the composer's affinity with epic and heroic subjects.

performed in Gor'kiy, Pushkin Theatre, unless otherwise stated

Iyola (Kas'yanov, after S. Zhulavsky), 1923, unperf. [never orchestrated]
Stepan Razin (folk music drama, prol., 4, N. G. Biryukov), 29 Dec 1939; rev., 28 Nov 1953; rev., 25 Nov 1977 (Moscow, 1978)
Molodyozh' [Youth], 1940–41 (I. Vsevolozhsky and M. Triger), inc.
Partizanka [The Partisan Girl], 1942 (P. Poluyanov), unperf.
Foma Gordeyev (4, G. A. Sannikov, after M. Gorky), concert perf., Moscow, 27 Jan 1946; stage, 12 June 1946; rev., 12 March 1966, vs (Moscow, 1970)
Na dal'nem severe [In the Far North], 1948 (N. Shapovalenko), unperf. [never orchestrated]
Yermak (4, V. M. Pukhnachev), Novosibirsk, 23 Feb 1957; rev., 17 Oct 1961 (Moscow, 1974)

I. Yeliseyev: *A. A. Kas'yanov* (Moscow, 1973)   LAUREL E. FAY

Kát'a Kabanová. Opera in three acts by LEOŠ JANÁČEK to his own libretto after ALEXANDER NIKOLAYEVICH OSTROVSKY's play *Groza* ('The Storm') in the Czech translation by Vincenc Červinka; Brno, National Theatre, 23 November 1921.

Vincenc Červinka's translation of Ostrovsky's play appeared in the spring of 1918; it may have been this, or the production of the play in Brno in March 1919, that drew Janáček's attention to it as a possible opera, but it was not until the autumn of 1919 that he began to inquire about permission to set it; he acquired the rights from Červinka early in January 1920 and began composition on 9 January. Janáček's autograph score was complete by 17 April 1921, though he continued to make small revisions up to the Brno première, on 23 November 1921. The work was subsequently dedicated to the woman who inspired it, Janáček's friend Kamila Stösslová.

Marfa Ignatěvna Kabanová (Kabanicha) *a rich merchant's widow*	contralto
Tichon Ivanyč Kabanov *her son*	tenor
Kateřina (Kát'a) *Tichon's wife*	soprano
Varvara *a foundling in the Kabanov household*	mezzo-soprano
Savël Prokofjevič Dikoj *a merchant*	bass
Boris Grigorjevič *Dikoj's nephew*	tenor
Váňa Kudrjáš *teacher, chemist and engineer employed by Dikoj*	tenor
Glaša *a servant in the Kabanov household*	mezzo-soprano
Fekluša *a servant*	mezzo-soprano
Kuligin *friend of Kudrjáš*	baritone
Woman from the Crowd	contralto
Passer-by	tenor
Drunk Passer-by	silent

Townspeople, offstage chorus

Setting The town of Kalinov on the bank of the Volga in the 1860s

The vocal score (made by Janáček's pupil Břetislav Bakala) was published in February 1922 and incorporated a few minor changes suggested by Max Brod, who provided the German translation. More substantial additions derived from Janáček's insistence on

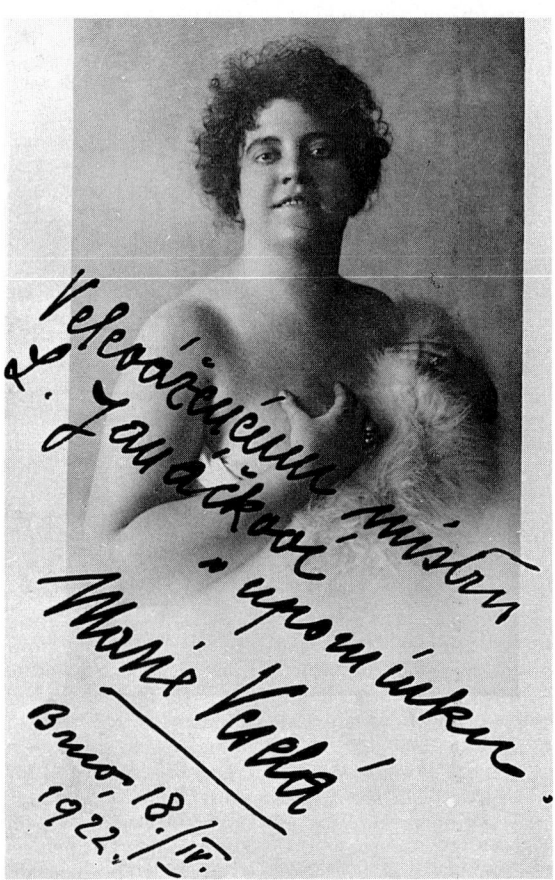

Marie Veselá, who sang the title role in the original production of Janáček's 'Kát'a Kabanová' at the National Theatre, Brno, 23 November 1921: photograph, with a dedication to the composer

attacca joins between the two scenes in Act 1 and Act 2, and the briefness of the music he provided for the scene changes. In November 1927 Janáček solved the problem by extending the interludes in these acts. In Act 1 he reworked existing material, but in Act 2 he wrote fresh music. The new interludes were first heard on 21 January 1928 at the Prague German Opera under William Steinberg, who also played the first two acts through without a break (a procedure enthusiastically endorsed by Janáček). Janáček did not attend the German première of the opera (under Klemperer in Cologne) in 1922 but was present at the much more successful Berlin première in 1926 under Fritz Zweig. *Kát'a Kabanová* was Janáček's first opera to be performed in Britain (under a very young Charles Mackerras) in 1951 and in 1976 it initiated Mackerras's cycle of recordings for Decca, with Elisabeth Söderström in the title role.

The overture to *Kát'a Kabanová* has one of the most evocative openings in opera. A long-held chord on the lower strings swells into a short melodic phrase and comes to rest on the eight-note timpani motif (ex.1). In

Ex.1 Moderato

the following Allegro ex.1 is speeded up and given to the oboe against the jingle of sleigh-bells and a whirling flute figure. This music will be associated with Tichon's departure: Kát'a's fate is sealed during his absence. The contrasting *espressivo* theme has associations with Kát'a. Each time it is heard it is quelled by the timpani theme – the course of the opera in miniature.

ACT 1.i *A park on the bank of the Volga in front of the Kabanovs' house: afternoon* Kudrjáš invites Glaša to admire the view of the afternoon sunlight on the Volga. They are soon distracted by the approach of Dikoj, rebuking his nephew Boris for his apparent idleness. Dikoj is looking for Kabanicha (the widowed matriarch of the Kabanov household) and, told that she is in the park, goes off to find her.

Left alone with Boris, Kudrjáš asks him why he is so submissive to Dikoj. Boris explains that after the death of his parents, his grandmother's will provides for him and his sister on condition that he lives with his uncle Dikoj and shows him respect. Boris accepts these humiliating conditions for his sister's sake. After a brief interruption as Fekluša praises Kabanicha's charity to Glaša, Boris reveals to Kudrjáš that he has fallen in love with a married woman. During an orchestral interlude they briefly observe from a distance the object of his passion, Kát'a Kabanová, as she returns from church with her husband Tichon, her mother-in-law Kabanicha and the Kabanovs' foster child Varvara.

This short interlude (Janáček's response to Puccini's entrance music for *Butterfly*) is the first lyrical moment in what has been an expository and rather wordy introduction and suggests Kát'a's gentle nature. The mood abruptly changes. Kabanicha orders Tichon to make the traditional trip to the market at Kazan', complaining

that Tichon now neglects her for his wife. Tichon denies this, as does Kát'a, whose first words (in regular, warmly-harmonized phrases) contrast strongly with Kabanicha's (in jagged recitative-like passages, accompanied by whole-tone chords). Kát'a goes indoors leaving Kabanicha to complain further. When Kabanicha herself leaves, Varvara defends Kát'a to a petulant Tichon and expresses sympathy for her. A brief interlude leads into scene ii.

1.ii *In the Kabanovs' house* Janáček moved this scene indoors to provide a more intimate setting for Kát'a's confession, in which she tells Varvara of her happier, carefree life before she married; she now longs to be free again, like a bird in the air. She remembers her daily routine, and especially her visionary trances in church. At this moment a regular lyrical melody forms, but as the pace quickens and the pitch rises, Kát'a's reminiscences become feverish as she describes how she feels herself to be on the brink of some disaster. Varvara wonders if Kát'a is ill. Kát'a replies that she would be less troubled if she were only ill, as the pace now relaxes. A more ominous depiction of her conflict begins: a sinuous theme initially on the english horn punctuated by *sforzando* stabs as Kát'a describes how the Devil seems to be whispering to her. When Varvara asks about her dreams Kát'a, in one of the great lyrical phrases of the opera, declares she cannot sleep ('Varjo! Nemohu spát'). Someone keeps on whispering in her ear, as if he were embracing her, and she goes off with him. Varvara urges her to tell her more, but Kát'a is ashamed.

With a repeat of sleigh-bell music from the overture Tichon comes in, preparing to leave. Kát'a flings herself into his arms and begs him either not to go or to take her with him. He refuses, unable to understand her distress. At this point ex.1 is heard continually in the orchestra, soon to be joined by another, even more ominous theme ending in a semitone clash – E♮ against an E♭ ostinato. After another lyrical appeal Kát'a, believing some misfortune will happen (the semitone ostinato), begs Tichon to make her swear an oath never to speak to, look at, or think of any stranger while he is gone. Low trombone chords heighten the sense of catastrophe.

As Tichon remonstrates, Kabanicha comes in announcing that everything is ready for his departure (the sleigh-bell music again). Through the mildly protesting Tichon Kabanicha dictates humiliating instructions as to how his wife should behave while he is away: she must be polite, obey Kabanicha, find work to do, and not look at other men. As in Act 1 scene i, the two women are sharply contrasted; Kabanicha gives her instructions against a whole-tone motif, Kát'a receives them from Tichon against a lyrical theme (on the viola d'amore), which at the end expands into a brief but radiant interlude. Left alone by Kabanicha, husband and wife have nothing to say. The ostinato begins again, and a complex of the sleigh-bell theme, semitone clash and ex.1 make up the increasingly tense orchestral background as Kabanicha returns. She forces Tichon to his knees to say goodbye to her and rebukes Kát'a for publicly embracing her husband. With a final word to Varvara, Tichon leaves against a triple *forte* version of ex.1.

ACT 2.i *A room in the Kabanovs' house, late afternoon* As they sit together, embroidering, Kabanicha reproaches Kát'a for not observing the tradition of displaying her sorrow publicly while her husband is away. She retires, leaving orders not to be disturbed. The mood changes with the first significant appearance of a theme associated with Varvara (ex.2, on the viola,

Ex.2

against sensuous flute and celesta off-beat chords). Before Varvara goes for a walk she gives Kát'a the garden gate key (which she has stolen from Kabanicha's hiding place). If she sees Boris, she tells Kát'a, she will ask him to come to the gate.

Kát'a's crisis of conscience is powerfully depicted in an alternation of moods. It is interrupted by a conversation offstage between Kabanicha and Dikoj, who has just arrived. Kát'a unthinkingly hides the key. When she is sure that she is alone again she realizes that 'fate' has made up her mind for her. She goes out, longing for nightfall.

Kabanicha enters with Dikoj, who is slightly drunk. While he proclaims his own soft-heartedness, telling of a worker whom he insulted and then begged for forgiveness, Dikoj suggestively sidles up to Kabanicha but is repulsed by her. The vigorous and cheerful interlude which Janáček added here in 1927 throws a comic slant on this encounter. It leads into scene ii.

2.ii *Outside the Kabanovs' garden gate, a summer night* A short prelude consists of the alternation of a hesitant theme and a lyrical one. Kudrjáš arrives with a guitar and as he waits for his sweetheart Varvara he sings a two-stanza song, 'Po zahrádce děvucha' ('Early one morning a girl went walking in the garden'), against a light, guitar-like accompaniment. The words (about a young woman courted by a handsome suitor but who has eyes for another) were a late substitution for Ostrovsky's original lyric, a grisly song about a Cossack who is contemplating killing his wife. Boris arrives and tells Kudrjáš that he met a girl who asked him to come to this spot: he has come in the hope of meeting Kát'a. Kudrjáš warns him of the risks for a married woman. Varvara comes out of the gate singing the words 'Za vodou, za vodičkou' ('Over the river my Váňa is standing') to the viola theme heard in the previous scene (ex.2). Kudrjáš responds with a second verse and the two go off to the river.

Left alone, Boris compares himself to the departing lovers, uncertain of his own situation. Soon Kát'a appears – to the hesitant first theme from the prelude – and guiltily repulses Boris's attempt to take her hand. But Boris declares his love for Kát'a; as the lyrical theme from the prelude is heard, Kát'a relents. To a soaring orchestral theme (and a vocal top C) Boris declares his passion. She is deeply troubled by her sense of sin but guardedly admits her love for him. Kudrjáš and Varvara return and discuss their hoodwinking of Kabanicha while in the distance Boris and Kát'a, who have gone for a walk, are heard declaring their love for one another. It is late and Kudrjáš soon calls the others back. He and Varvara then sing alternate verses of another song, 'Chod' si dívka, do času' ('So go here soon, my girl'). Boris and Kát'a return. To a *fortissimo* version of the soaring theme Kát'a goes in through the garden gate leaving Boris behind. On a radiant chord – E major

gently alternating with E minor – the curtain comes down.

ACT 3.i *Two days later, a ruined building overlooking the Volga; towards evening* An ostinato background with pattering chords suggests the beginnings of a storm. Kuligin and Kudrjáš shelter from the rain and are soon joined by others. Kuligin notices that the walls of the ruin are covered with barely discernible paintings depicting the punishment of the damned in Hell. Dikoj also takes shelter and is accosted by Kudrjáš. The two men clash about the nature of storms; Kudrjáš considers them 'electricity' (he has just urged the need for lightning conductors) while for Dikoj they are punishments sent from God. The rain stops and Dikoj walks out into the open air.

Varvara appears, and when Boris arrives she urgently attracts his attention. She tells him that Tichon has returned and that Kát'a has gone to pieces and is threatening to confess everything to her husband. When Kát'a enters, Boris and Kudrjáš hide from her while Varvara attempts to calm her. Her behaviour attracts the attention of passers-by (the only onstage chorus in the piece) and as Dikoj, Kabanicha and Tichon arrive the storm builds up (ex.1 is heard prominently). Kát'a falls on her knees and confesses her infidelity publicly. Kabanicha forces Kát'a to name her lover and finally she does so against a *fortissimo* version of ex.1. Kát'a collapses into Tichon's arms but immediately tears herself away and rushes out into the breaking storm. The storm music leads straight into scene ii.

3.ii *A bank of the Volga, dusk turning to night* Tichon and Glaša hurry in, searching for Kát'a, who is missing. No sooner have they left than Kudrjáš and Varvara arrive. She complains of being locked in her room by Kabanicha. Kudrjáš advises her to run away with him to Moscow. They leave together.

In the distance Tichon and Glaša can be heard calling for Kát'a. She enters alone. Against a lyrical theme on the oboe and viola d'amore Kát'a regrets her confession, seeing it as futile as well as humiliating for Boris. She dreads the emptiness of nights alone and longs for death (she interprets the brief wordless offstage chorus as a funeral lament) but her life continues, bereft of meaning except for her longing to see Boris. Suddenly he enters and embraces her silently against a gentle orchestral interlude. He is being sent to a trading post in Siberia; Kát'a, on the other hand, remains at the mercy of her vindictive mother-in-law and drunken husband. She has a special message for Boris: he must give alms to the beggars he meets on his journey. The wordless chorus returns, sounding here, in Janáček's instructions, like 'the sigh of the Volga' (its music was in fact heard during Kát'a's public confession). This theme and a recurring, searing *fortissimo* trill dominate the farewell as Boris's voice trails off in the distance. Then against a repeated timpani beat and a chirruping motif, Kát'a imagines her grave visited by birds and covered with flowers. She crosses her arms and throws herself into the river. Hearing the noise, a search party enters, followed by Kabanicha. Dikoj retrieves Kát'a's corpse against an excited orchestral background deriving from the sleigh-bell theme. Tichon blames his mother for Kát'a's death and flings himself on to her lifeless body. Kabanicha impassively thanks those assembled for their efforts. The wordless chorus is heard once more, *fortissimo*, combined with ex.1.

*　　*　　*

Kát'a Kabanová initiated the great final period of Janáček's career. With the confidence gained by the success of *Jenůfa* in Prague in 1916, Janáček first dealt with unfinished business: the completion of his previous opera, *The Excursions of Mr Brouček* and the radical revision of his first opera *Šárka*. He then proceeded, at the age of 65, to crown his career with the composition of four final operas, on which his reputation now rests. Of these, *Kát'a Kabanová* is the most conventional as far as its libretto is concerned, but it is also his most tender, as he was to tell its dedicatee, Kamila Stösslová, a few months before he died. Janáček's passion for her inspired the central portrait of Kát'a and is evident throughout the opera, welling up almost from nothing at the beginning of the overture and quelled only in the final notes of the opera by the brutal timpani theme and its connotations of fate and authoritarian repression.

JOHN TYRRELL

Kate and the Devil. Opera by Antonín Dvořák; *see* DEVIL AND KATE, THE.

Katerina Izmaylova. Opera in four acts, op.114, a revision of LADY MACBETH OF THE MTSENSK DISTRICT op.29 (1932), by DMITRY SHOSTAKOVICH to a libretto by the composer and Alexander Preys; Moscow, Stanislavsky–Nemirovich-Danchenko Music Theatre, 8 January 1963.

Katerina Izmaylova (soprano) is the heroine of Shostakovich's second opera which, after playing to phenomenal critical and popular acclaim for two years after its première in 1934, was repressed by Stalin's cultural watchdogs in 1936. The title *Katerina Izmaylova* was used for the opera's original Moscow production in 1934, directed by B. Mordvinov and Vladimir Nemirovich-Danchenko, and conducted by Georgy Stolyarov with designs by Vladimir Dmitriyev, although it is more often used to distinguish the revision of the opera, undertaken by Shostakovich in the mid-1950s and allocated a new opus number.

Although the plot, dramatic development and music remain substantially the same in both versions, in *Katerina Izmaylova* the vulgarity and rough naturalism of the libretto is virtually eliminated, replaced by more conventional dramatic euphemisms. This process of sanitization, however, was begun by Shostakovich in the published vocal score of 1935, even before the opera was attacked. The lengthy and controversial instrumental interlude of Act 1 scene iii, in which the love-making of Sergey (tenor) with Katerina was graphically portrayed, was replaced by a brief interlude conjuring up the threat of discovery by Boris Timofeyevich (high bass). Two of the orchestral entr'actes, between scenes i and ii, and between scenes vii and viii, were replaced with interludes with more obviously transitional motivation, the extremes of tessitura were smoothed, and many other small alterations were effected.

After its production, Shostakovich designated *Katerina Izmaylova* the definitive version of his opera, a claim accepted by Soviet critics at face value. In the West, however, since the rediscovery of the original 1932 version in the late 1970s, the later version has been routinely dismissed as an unfortunate product of political compromise.

LAUREL E. FAY

Katrena. Opera by Eugen Suchoň; *see* WHIRLPOOL, THE.

Katul'skaya, Yelena Kliment'yevna (*b* Odessa, 21 May/2 June 1888; *d* Moscow, 19 or 20 Nov 1966). Russian soprano. She studied privately in Odessa (1904) and St Petersburg (1905–7), then at the St Petersburg Conservatory. She made her début as Lakmé at the Mariinsky Theatre, where she sang until 1911, then went to the Bol'shoy (1913–45). Her roles included Rimsky-Korsakov's Swan-Princess (*Tale of Tsar Saltan*) and Snow Maiden, Marguerite and Juliet, Butterfly and Massenet's Manon. A sensitive, cultured musician, she had a lyrical voice of beautiful timbre and wide range. She was also well known as a recitalist.

*

E. Groshyova: *Y. K. Katul'skaya* (Moscow and Leningrad, 1957)
E. Groshyova, ed.: *Yelena Kliment'yevna Katul'skaya: sbornik statey* [Collection of Articles] (Moscow, 1973)

I. M. YAMPOL'SKY

Kauer, Ferdinand (*b* Klein-Thaya [Tayax; now Dyákovice], nr Znaim [now Znojmo], 18 Jan 1751; *d* Vienna, 13 April 1831). Austrian composer and conductor. The son of a schoolmaster, he was educated at Znaim; he then moved to the Jesuit seminary at Tyrnau (now Trnava), Hungary, as organist, studying philosophy and medicine. When the university was transferred to Ofen, Kauer went to Vienna (*c*1777) and established himself as a musician: first as a keyboard teacher, then as organist of the Servite church and reader to the music publishers Artaria. He studied composition with Heidenreich and Zimmermann and became a violinist and later leader of the orchestra of the Theater in der Leopoldstadt (probably soon after Marinelli opened it in 1781); he was appointed director of the theatre's newly founded music school. Although his name is connected with a few Singspiels given there in the 1780s, he did not become established as a composer until the early 1790s. For the next two decades he was second Kapellmeister to Wenzel Müller and, during Müller's Prague engagement, to Tuček. During these years he composed a succession of Singspiels and other theatre scores including *Das Faustrecht in Thüringen* (1796; together with its two sequels it received 157 performances in 20 years), *Die Löwenritter* (1799, with three sequels) and *Das Donauweibchen* (1798). This last is the work on which Kauer's fame was based; it held its place in the Leopoldstadt repertory for 40 years, being given over 100 times; the first sequel was even more successful. Goethe staged *Das Donauweibchen* at Weimar as *Die Saalnixe* and mentioned it in his novel *Die Wahlverwandtschaften*. It was frequently performed in various countries (including Scandinavia) for many years, giving rise to numerous imitations and sequels.

In 1810 Kauer went to Graz as Kapellmeister, staying there only one season (and writing some six new theatre scores) before returning to the Leopoldstadt theatre. In 1814 he moved to the Theater in der Josefstadt as Kapellmeister, but the resources of this theatre were not comparable with those of the Leopoldstadt (its orchestra, 25 strong, was not notably smaller than that in the Leopoldstadt, with 32, but the standards were much lower). Most of Kauer's successful scores from this period included leading roles for the principal actor and singer there, Ferdinand Raimund, especially the plays centring on the character of Adam Kratzerl, a violinist, first introduced in 1815 in *Die Musikanten am hohen Markt*. These and others of Kauer's scores for this theatre were written to texts by Joseph Alois Gleich,

Raimund's father-in-law and for a time the director of the theatre. In four seasons Kauer wrote more than 20 new scores for the Josefstadt theatre and revived about 30 of his older works.

In 1818 Kauer lost his post through a change in the management and financial difficulties at the theatre, and was deemed too old (and probably too feeble and old-fashioned as a composer) to be taken back into the Leopoldstadt company. He scratched out a miserable existence, occasionally having a new score accepted by the Josefstadt theatre, until he was admitted to the Leopoldstadt orchestra in 1821 as a lowly second violinist. His name appears among the orchestra members in the theatre's almanac until 1830. In the night of 28 February to 1 March 1830 he was among the victims of severe floods in the Leopoldstadt when a thaw caused the Danube to overflow its banks. He lost almost all he possessed, including his musical scores, and died in poverty little more than a year later.

The events of the Danube flood, but also certain personal characteristics, encourage the opinion that Grillparzer may have had Kauer in mind in his depiction of the old musician hero in his story *Der arme Spielmann*. Kauer typifies the once-popular composer pathetically outliving his fame, which, though modest enough viewed with the benefit of hindsight, brought him much artistic success if little financial gain. Goethe wrote a new text for Hulda's famous and touching air 'In meinem Schlösschen ist's gar fein' from *Das Donauweibchen*, and Gerber in 1813 revised his earlier dismissive comments on Kauer on the basis of better acquaintance with his works. Kauer is at his best and most characteristic in simple strophic songs and airs, whose melodies and instrumentation often have considerable charm. However, harmonic and contrapuntal predictability all too often diminishes the impact of a promising number, and the ensembles seldom carry much weight or distinction. There are frequent echoes of Mozart and Wenzel Müller in his scores; Weber (who conducted *Das Sternenmädchen* in Prague) and Lortzing in their turn probably owed a debt to Kauer.

Although important primarily for his music for some 200 stage works (including Singspiels, parodies, local plays, pantomimes etc.), Kauer also wrote examples of almost every musical genre then current and a number of instructional works.

all first performed in Vienna
pantomimes not included

WJ – *Theater in der Josefstadt* WL – *Theater in der Leopoldstadt*

Der Streit zwischen dem Zauberer Scionco und der Fee Galantine, oder Kasperl beleibt Kasperli (comedy with machines and music, 3), WL, 3 Feb 1784
Der unschuldige Betrug, oder Auf dem Lande kennt man die Rache nicht (Kinder-Operette, 1, L. Huber), WL, 22 June 1790
Bastien und Bastienne (Operette, after Fr. orig.), WL, 18 Aug 1790
Kaspars Zögling, oder Der Sieg der Bescheidenheit auf der Insel des Vergnügens (Spl, 2, J. Perinet), WL, 1 Feb 1791
Kasperl, der lustige Schafhirt, oder Das Maifest auf den Alpen (Spl, Huber), WL, 11 May 1791
Die Serenade, oder Der gefoppte Alte (Spl, 2), WL, 4 June 1792
Ritter Willibald, oder Das goldene Gefäss (romantisches Spl, 2, K. F. Hensler), WL, 13 June 1793
Das Faustrecht in Thüringen, pt 1 (Schauspiel, 4, Hensler), WL, 7 April 1796, ?D-Mbs; pt 2 (4), 28 June 1796; pt 3 (4), 17 Jan 1797
Der Waffenschmied (komische Oper, 2, Hensler, after Ziegler), WL, 25 July 1797
Das Donauweibchen, pt 1 (romantisch-komisches Volksmärchen, 3,

Hensler), WL, 11 Jan 1798, many MSS, vs (Brunswick, n.d.); pt 2, 13 Feb 1798
Die Löwenritter (Schauspiel, 4, Hensler), WL, 5 Sept 1799; pt 2, 17 Sept 1801; pt 3 (Schauspiel, 4, J. A. Gleich), 4 Oct 1804
Telemach Prinz von Ithaka (travestirtes Spl, 3, Hensler), WL, 29 April 1801
Ferrandino (Schauspiel, 3, Hensler), WL, 14 Aug 1800; pt 2, 17 July 1801; pt 3, 7 Jan 1802
Das Sternenmädchen im Meidlinger Walde (romantisch-komisches Volksmärchen, 3, Huber), WL, 20 Oct 1801, ov., songs (Offenbach, n.d.)
Die Nymphe der Donau (romantisch-komisches Volksmärchen, Hensler, sequel to *Das Donauweibchen*), WL, 4 Feb 1803
Die Waffenruhe in Thüringen (Schauspiel, 4, Hensler), WL, 22 July 1802; pt 2, 30 Nov 1803
Die Lazaroni (romantisches Schauspiel, 3, Hensler), WL, 15 Oct 1803
Philibert und Kasperl, oder Weiber sind getreuer als Männer (Zauberoper, 3, Hensler), WL, 7 Feb 1804
Das Loch in der Mauer (komische Oper, 1, Perinet), WL, 1 March 1804
Faschingswehen (Lustspiel, 3, J. F. Kringsteiner), WL, 4 March 1805
Die Kreuzerkomödie (Posse, 3, Kringsteiner), WL, 21 June 1805, ?Mbs
Der travestirte Telemach (Karikatur, 3, Perinet), WL, 29 Aug 1805; revision of his own Telemach Prinz von Ithaka (Hensler), 1801
Antiope und Telemach (Travestie, 2, Perinet), WL, 23 Oct 1805, second part of Der travestirte Telemach
Albert der Bär, oder Die Weiber von Weinsberg (Schauspiel, 3, Gleich), WL, 27 March 1806
Die eiserne Jungfrau (Schauspiel, 3, Gleich), WL, 30 April 1806
Der brave Mann, oder Die Gefahr am Donaustrome (komische Oper, 1, Gleich), WL, 26 June 1806
Konrad von Riesenburg (Schauspiel, 4, J. A. Schuster), WL, 16 Aug 1806
Heinrich der Stolze, Herzog von Sachsen (Schauspiel, 3, Gleich), WL, 5 Oct 1806
Die Dorfrichterin und ihre Liebhaber (komische Oper, 2, Huber), WL, 27 Nov 1806
Der Tanzmeister (Posse, 3, Kringsteiner), WL, 6 Feb 1807, collab. W. Müller and I. Schuster
Die Totenfackel, oder Die Höhle der Siebenschläfer (Schauspiel, 4, Huber), WL, 12 June 1807
Inkle und Yariko (Spl, 1, Gleich), WL, 9 April 1807
Der bezauberte Gasthof, oder Die Vermählung im Elysium (Posse, 3, J. A. Schuster), WL, 15 July 1807
Kunz von Kauffungen (Schauspiel, 3, Gleich), WL, 19 Nov 1807
Die Bewohner des glücklichen Tales, oder Das Fest der Freude (Zauberoper, 3, J. L. Werneck), WL, 13 Feb 1808
Götz von Berlichingen mit der eisernen Hand (Schauspiel, 4, T. von Ehrimfeld, after J. W. von Goethe), WL, 23 April 1808
Der Feldtrompeter, oder Wurst wider Wurst (Spl, 1, Perinet, after Hensler), WL, 16 May 1808
Das Turnier zu Ponthieu (Schauspiel, 3, Gleich), WL, 4 June 1808
Die Fürsten der Longobarden (Schauspiel, 3, Gleich), WL, 1 Sept 1808
Der gezwungene Bräutigam (Posse, 1, Gleich), WL, 9 Sept 1808
Grauhütchen (Schauspiel, 3, Gleich), WL, 4 Dec 1809
Hainz von Geyersburg (Schauspiel, 3), WL, 5 Oct 1811
Die Zauberin aus Liebe (comische Zauberoper, 3, Perinet), WL, 5 Dec 1812
Orpheus und Euridice, oder So geht es im Olympus zu (mythologische Karikatur, 2, K. Meisl), WL, 20 Feb 1813
Das Mädchen an der Silberquelle (heroisch-komische Zauberoper, 3, Kringsteiner), WL, 9 Oct 1813
Antonius und Cleopatra (Posse, 1, M. F. Perth, after A. Kotzebue), WJ, 25 Feb 1814
Die Schmiedstochter von Nürnberg, oder Die verfehlte Entführung (komische Oper, 2, Gleich), WJ, 2 July 1814
Der Narrenthurm (komisches Spl, 1, Perinet), WL, 13 Aug 1814
Prinzessin Eigensinn und König Bröselbart (heroisch-komische Oper, 2, Gleich), WJ, 21 Nov 1814

Bertha von Lilienstein, oder Die deutschen Ritter in Palästina (Schauspiel, Gleich), WJ, 19 Dec 1814

Die Musikanten am hohen Markt (Posse, 3, Gleich), WJ, 28 March 1815

Herr Adam Kratzerl von Kratzerlsfeld (Posse, 3, Gleich), WJ, 29 Aug 1815

Die Amazonen in Böhmen (grosse-heroisch-komische Oper, 3, Gleich), WJ, 30 Nov 1815

Herr Adam Kratzerl und sein Pudel (Posse, 3, Gleich), WJ, 18 Dec 1815

Herr von Hannsdampf, oder Die Zusammenkunft in der anderen Welt (Posse, 3, Gleich), WJ, 28 March 1816

Herr Adam und Frau Eva (Quodlibet, 2, J. Landner), WJ, 18 June 1816

Doktor Kramperl (Posse, 3, Gleich), WJ, 18 May 1816

Velasco de Gaston, oder Der Seeräuber-Admiral (Schauspiel, 3, Gleich), WJ, 22 Nov 1816; part 2, 24 Nov 1816

Herr Kratzerl und seine Familie, oder Der Pudel als Kindsweib (Posse, 3, Gleich), WJ, 20 Jan 1817

Herr Adam Kratzerl als Dorfrichter, oder Die Landkomödianten (Posse, 3, Gleich), WJ, 15 July 1817

Amor und Psyche (Karikatur, 2, Meisl), WL, 2 Oct 1817

Die Frau Mahm aus dem Pustertale (Posse, 2, Gleich), WJ, 10 Sept 1826

*

StiegerO

Autobiographical sketch (MS, *A-Wgm*) [incl. list of works, inc.]

L. Schmidt: *Zur Geschichte der Märchenoper* (Halle, 1895)

B. Glossy and R. Haas: *Wiener Comödienlieder aus drei Jahrhunderten* (Vienna, 1924) [incl. 3 arias by Kauer]

T. Haas: 'Ferdinand Kauer (1751–1831): ein Künstlerschicksal', *Neue Musik-Zeitung*, xlvi (1925), 273, 300

R. Haas: 'Singspiel und Volksmusik', *Almanach der deutschen Musikbücherei auf das Jahr 1926*, ed. G. Bosse (Regensburg, 1926), 152

K. Manschinger: *Ferdinand Kauer: ein Beitrag zur Geschichte des Wiener Singspiels um die Wende des 18. Jahrhunderts* (diss., U. of Vienna, 1929)

F. Hadamowsky: *Das Theater in der Wiener Leopoldstadt* (Vienna, 1934)

A. Bauer: *Opern und Operetten in Wien* (Graz and Cologne, 1955)

——: *Das Theater in der Josefstadt zu Wien* (Vienna, 1957)

PETER BRANSCOMBE

Kauffmann, Leo Justinius (*b* Dammerkirch [now Dannemarie, Alsace], 20 Sept 1901; *d* Strasbourg, 25 Sept 1944). German composer. After preliminary music studies in Strasbourg, he became a pupil of Jarnach in Cologne and also had lessons with Florent Schmitt during his military service. In 1929 he secured a teaching position at the Rheinische Musikschule in Cologne and from 1932 was director of music for broadcast drama and composer for Cologne Radio. During the Nazi era his music was condemned as 'modernistic' and he could only maintain his employment at the radio by writing under a pseudonym. Nevertheless, after winning prizes in two competitions for composition, he was allowed to resume his professional work and in 1940 moved to Strasbourg, where he became a teacher of composition at the Conservatory. It was there that he was killed during an air-raid.

Kauffmann's operas *Die Geschichte vom schönen Annerl* and *Das Perlenhemd* were written for the conductor Hans Rosbaud who remained an enthusiastic exponent of the composer's work. *Die Geschichte vom schönen Annerl* originated as a ballad for radio, written in 1936, which was expanded into a full-length opera four years later. Based on an episode of love and honour during the Thirty Years War, its expanded diatonic style with clearly delineated numbers, including some memorable popular songs, belongs to the category of the epic music theatre. The opera's direct appeal, enhanced at its Strasbourg première by Jürgen Fehling's distinguished production, encouraged several other German opera houses to perform the work during the war. *Das Perlenhemd*, which takes its material from a Chinese love story, presents an intriguing mixture of opera, melodrama, pantomime and stage play. Scored for modest forces, it employs a similarly direct musical idiom with tenderness and restraint. Three operas, including *Agnes Bernauer*, which was commissioned by the Dresden Staatsoper, were left incomplete at the composer's death.

Abenteuer in Kaschgar (Märchenoper), 1924

Liebe um Gloria (Operette), Vienna, 1924

Die Ardwibele (Spl), 1928

Das Zauberflötchen (Märchenspiel, Mathiesen), 1934

Gesang ins Glück (Operette), 1935

Die Serenade (Funkoper, H. Kranz), Cologne Radio, 2 July 1936

Das niegesehene Braut (Spl, Kranz), 1937

Liebe im Park (Operette, E. Wippermann), 1937

Frühere Verhältnisse (Rundfunkburleske, after J. N. Nestroy), 1939

Die Geschichte vom schönen Annerl (9 scenes, E. Reinacher and E. Bormann, after Brentano), Strasbourg, 20 June 1942 (Cologne and Vienna, 1941)

Das Perlenhemd (Kammeroper, 6 scenes, Bormann and Kauffmann), Strasbourg, 22 July 1944 (Vienna, 1947)

Agnes Bernauer, 1944 (Reinacher, after Hebbel), inc.

Hyppolitos, inc.

Der Verwandelte (Wippermann), inc.

*

H.-J. Seydel: 'Leo Justinius Kauffmann', *Musica*, v (1951), 186–9

H. von Radzibor: 'Kauffmann, Leo Justinius', *Rheinische Musiker*, iv (Cologne, 1966), 42

ERIK LEVI

Kaufmann, Julie (*b* Iowa, 20 May 1950). American soprano. She studied at Iowa University and at the Opera Studio, Zürich. After making her début in *Hagen* she appeared at the Frankfurt Opera in such soubrette roles as Oscar, Blonde, Norina and Despina; guest engagements followed in Hamburg, Berlin and Stuttgart. She sang Zerlina at Covent Garden in 1984 and was engaged with the Staatsoper in Munich the same year; she added Zdenka and Zerbinetta to her repertory and in 1988 appeared with the company in Tokyo as Despina. At the 1989 Ludwigsburg Festival she was heard as Susanna. The roles she has recorded include Cupid in *Orfeo ed Euridice* and Woglinde in the Haitink version of *Das Rheingold*.

DAVID CUMMINGS

Kaufmann von Smyrna, Der ('The Merchant of Smyrna'). Singspiel in one act by GEORG JOSEPH VOGLER to a libretto by CHRISTIAN FRIEDRICH SCHWAN after Nicolas Chamfort's one-act comedy *Le marchand de Smyrne*; Mannheim, Schauspielhaus auf dem Fruchtmarkt, summer 1771.

Der Kaufmann von Smyrna has some points of similarity with Mozart's *Die Entführung aus dem Serail*. The naive and sentimental story has an exotic, Turkish setting. A rich Turk, Hassan (tenor), has vowed to free a Christian slave. Among the slaves brought in on the ship of the villainous trader Kaled (bass) Hassan recognizes the Frenchman Dornal (tenor), who earlier had freed him from captivity in France. He buys his freedom; coincidentally Hassan's wife, Zayde (soprano), has arranged to buy Dornal's wife, Amalie (soprano). In the end Dornal and Amalie are reunited despite the protests of Kaled.

The work was originally performed by Theobald Marchand's company, and Vogler added two arias for the revival on 20 February 1778. The latter production probably featured Barbara Strasser as Zayde, Aloysia Weber as Amalie, and Ludwig Fischer as Kaled. Vogler's score juxtaposes the simple melodic idiom of comic opera with virtuoso orchestral and vocal writing characteristic of the Mannheim operatic tradition. Kaled's two arias include janissary music complete with cymbals, drums and triangles.

Schwan's sentimental text also found popularity in settings by C. D. Stegmann (1773, Königsberg), F. A. Holly (1773, Berlin) and Franz Seydelmann (1778, Dresden). Schwan's revision of the libretto in two acts, as *Der Sclavenhändler*, was set by Peter Ritter (1790, Mannheim). THOMAS BAUMAN, PAUL CORNEILSON

Kaun, Hugo (*b* Berlin, 21 March 1863; *d* Berlin, 2 April 1932). German composer. Born into a merchant family, he studied the piano and attended composition classes at the Preussische Akademie der Künste in Berlin. Following his father's death in 1886, he went to the USA and settled in Milwaukee, Wisconsin, where he worked as a teacher, composer and choral conductor. He returned to Berlin in 1902, and by the 1920s his fame as a composer had spread throughout German-speaking Europe. In 1912 he was elected a member of the Academy of Arts and from 1922 taught at the Berlin Conservatory. His operas are Wagnerian in style, and the Wagnerian harmonic language pervades all of his larger compositions. The many choral works enjoyed great popularity.

Der Pietist (1, W. Drobegg) Leipzig, 1895
Sappho (3, after F. Grillparzer), Leipzig, Neues, 27 Oct 1917
Der Fremde (4, F. Rauch), Dresden, Staatsoper, 24 Feb 1920
Menandra (3, Kaun, after F. Jansen), Kiel, 1926

*

MGG (R. Schaal); *StiegerO*
H. Kaun: *Aus meinem Leben* (Berlin, 1932)
R. Schaal: *Hugo Kaun, 1863–1932, Leben und Werk: ein Beitrag zur Musik der Jahrhundertwende* (Regensburg, 1946)
WILLIAM D. GUDGER

Kaunas (Pol. Kowno; Russ. Kovno). Second city of Lithuania and capital from 1920 to 1939. Following Lithuania's absorption by Russia in 1795, its cultural and musical life was irregular; it had no permanent opera theatre but was visited by companies from Poland, Germany, Italy and Vilnius. In 1920 – in the now independent Lithuania – the establishment in Kaunas of the Lietuvių Meno Kūrėjų Draugija (Creative Artists' Society) led to the foundation of the Operos Vaidykla (Opera Theatre). This opened on 31 December with *La traviata*, the staging of which on New Year's Eve became a tradition. The theatre came under state control in 1922; in 1925 it was merged with the drama company and renamed Valstybės Teatras (State Theatre). As well as the standard Italian, French, German and Russian repertory, lesser-known operas were given: d'Albert's *Tiefland* (1928) and *Die toten Augen* (1940), Wolf-Ferrari's *I gioielli della Madonna* (1928) and *I quatro rusteghi* (1935), and Rimsky-Korsakov's *Tsar Saltan* (1932) and *Legend of the Invisible City of Kitezh* (1936).

Only two works by Lithuanian composers had entered the repertory: Jurgis Karnavičius's historical-heroic opera *Gražina* (K. Inciūra, after A. Mickiewicz; 16 Feb 1933) and Antanas Račiūnas's fantasy opera *Trys talismanai* ('The Three Talismans'; 1936). Other landmarks were Karnavičius's second opera *Radvila*

Perkūnas (1937) and Stasys Šimkus's *Pagirėnai* (1941). The growing reputation of the State Theatre led to its leading singers being invited abroad and to visits from artists including Shalyapin, Albert Coates, Emil Cooper and Issay Dobroven. Outstanding singers of the company included the tenor Kipras Petrauskas. In 1941 the theatre was renamed Kauno Didysis Teatras (Great Theatre of Kaunas), in 1944 Lietuvos TSR Operos ir Baleto Teatras (Opera and Ballet Theatre of the Lithuanian SSR); it moved to Vilnius in 1948. From 1920 to 1944 about 70 operas and some operettas were performed (about 2700 performances in all). The season lasted from mid-September to mid-June.

The Kaunas Operetta Theatre opened in 1940. In 1959 it became Kauno Muzikinis Teatras (Kaunas Musical Theatre). Besides operettas and musicals it put on about 40 operas between 1951 and 1991. Among the operas by Lithuanian composers were Vitolis Baumilas's *Paskenduolė* ('The Drowned Maiden', 1957), Antanas Belazaras's *Kupriukas muzikantas* ('The Hump-Backed Musician', 1973), and Bronius Kutavičius's *Kaulo senis ant Geležinio kalno* ('Doddering Old Man on the Iron Mountain', 1983). Of great importance was the role of the composer, tenor and conductor Juozas Indra (1918–68), who worked at the theatre from 1954 to 1965. The Musical Theatre now occupies the former home of the Kaunas Opera Theatre. In 1925 and 1931 it was rebuilt and enlarged (*c*700 seats). Further reconstruction took place in 1976–84: more rooms were added, but the number of seats was reduced to 450.

*

S. Santvaras: 'Operos teatras', *Lietuvių enciklopedija*, xv (Boston, 1968) [incl. shortened version in Eng.]
——: 'Opera', *Encyclopedia lituanica*, iv (Boston, 1975)
D. Klimauskaitė, ed.: *Kauno valstybinis muzikinis teatras* [Kaunas State Musical Theatre] (Kaunas, 1980)
V. Mažeika: 'Opera', *Lietuvių teatras, 1918–1929* (Vilnius, 1981), 175–277 ADEODATAS TAURAGIS

Kavalier, Franziska Helena Appolonia. *See* CAVALIERI, CATERINA.

Kavatine (Ger.). CAVATINA.

Kavkazskiy plennik ('The Captive in the Caucasus'; 'The Prisoner in the Caucasus'). Opera in three acts by CÉSAR ANTONOVICH CUI to a libretto by VIKTOR ALEXANDROVICH KRÏLOV based on ALEXANDER SERGEYEVICH PUSHKIN's poem; St Petersburg, Mariinsky Theatre, 4/16 February 1883.

Acts 1 and 3 were composed in 1857–8, and in this form the opera was at first accepted by the Mariinsky Theatre for the 1859 season; but it was cancelled after the first orchestral rehearsal, so inadequate and amateurish was the orchestration. In 1881–2 Cui interpolated the second act, reorchestrated the whole, and resubmitted it. Shortly after the première in 1883 the opera became the first of Cui's works to be performed abroad (1883, Liège), under the auspices of the Countess Mercy Argenteau. The opera played in all the main Russian centres in various productions up to the Revolution.

The music is predictably given to hackneyed orientalism, beginning with an 'Eastern Prayer' replete with mullahs and augmented 2nds, culminating in a 'Circassian song' (Act 3) to original Pushkin verses that became a popular concert number in the wake of the première. (On the way there are the usual choruses and dances.) The suicide by drowning of Fatima (soprano), the Circassian girl in love with the Russian prisoner (tenor), so subtly and ambiguously handled by Pushkin ('And in the moonlight a circle of ripples/Disappears in the water'), is turned into a blatant denouement, with the Caucasian armies returning prematurely from their raid just in time to shout 'O horror!' as Fatima hurls herself into the river she has helped the prisoner ford to freedom.   RICHARD TARUSKIN

Kavrakos, Dimitri (*b* Athens, 26 Feb 1946). Greek bass. After studying in Athens, he made his début in 1970 as Zaccaria and sang with the Greek National Opera in Athens until 1980. He first sang at the Metropolitan in 1979 as the Grand Inquisitor. He has also appeared in Chicago, Dallas, Houston, San Francisco, Geneva, Aix-en-Provence, Lyons and Paris and at La Scala; he made his début at Glyndebourne as the Commendatore (1982) and at Covent Garden as Pimen (1984). Among the roles in his repertory are Mozart's Bartolo, Rocco, Don Fernando, Giorgio (*I puritani*), Oroveso, Henry VIII (*Anna Bolena*), Nilakantha, Prince Gremin, Wurm, Silva, Fiesco and Padre Guardiano, the last of which best displays the beauty and nobility of his bronze-toned voice.   ELIZABETH FORBES

Kay, Ulysses (Simpson) (*b* Tucson, AZ, 7 Jan 1917). American composer. He was born into a musical family; his maternal uncle was the celebrated jazz trumpeter and band director Joseph 'King' Oliver. He learnt the piano, violin and saxophone as a youth, and later studied composition with Bernard Rogers and Howard Hanson at the Eastman School of Music (MMus 1940), with Hindemith at Tanglewood (summer 1941) and at Yale University (1941–2) and with Otto Luening at Columbia University (1946–7). His teaching career included appointments at the University of California at Los Angeles (1966–7) and Lehman College of the City University of New York (1968–88). In 1954 he first attracted national attention as a composer with his Serenade for Orchestra. He visited the USSR four years later as a member of the first delegation of American composers on a cultural exchange. A prolific composer, he has been considered a notable voice in contemporary 20th-century American music.

Kay has written in a wide variety of forms, including opera. His stage works consist of three one-act operas, *The Juggler of Our Lady* (1962), *The Boor* (1968; commissioned by the Serge Koussevitsky Foundation and dedicated to Natalie Koussevitsky) and *The Capitoline Venus* (1971), and two full-length operas, *Jubilee* (1976) and *Frederick Douglass* (1991). While the subjects of his earlier operas are eclectic and based upon such diverse sources as a Chekhov novel, a Christmas morality play and a Mark Twain short story, his later works have dealt with themes rooted in black American experiences during the pre-Civil-War period. *Jubilee* was commissioned for the bicentenary of the USA by Opera South. His musical style emphasizes lyricism, supported by dissonant counterpoint that converges on a tonal centre, distinctive rhythmic vitality, and sonorous orchestration.

The Boor, 1955 (1, Kay, after A. P. Chekhov: *The Bear*), Lexington, KY, 12 April 1968 (New York, *c*1978)
The Juggler of Our Lady, 1956 (1, A. King), New Orleans, 23 Feb 1962 (New York, *c*1978)
The Capitoline Venus (1, J. Dvorkin, after M. Twain), Urbana, IL, 12 March 1971

Jubilee (3, D. Dorr, after M. Walker), Jackson State U., 20 Nov 1976
Frederick Douglass, 1985 (3, Dorr), Newark, NJ, Symphony Hall, 14 April 1991

N. Slonimsky: 'Ulysses Kay', *American Composers Alliance Bulletin*, vii/1 (1957), 3–11
L. Hayes: *The Music of Ulysses Kay (1939–1963)* (diss., U. of Wisconsin, 1971)
C. Laverne: *Black Idioms in Opera as Reflected in the Works of Six Afro-American Composers* (diss., U. of Southern California, 1974)
C. Davidson: *Operas by Afro-American Composers: a Critical Survey and Analysis of Selected Works* (diss., Catholic U. of America, 1980)   JOSEPHINE WRIGHT

Kayser [Keiser], Margaretha Susanna (*b* Hamburg, *c*1690; *d* Hamburg, *c*1748). German soprano. The daughter of the opera singer J. H. Vogel, in 1706 she married the Hamburg town musician Johann Kayser (not to be confused with Reinhard Keiser); she was known as 'Die Kayserin'. After her début in Graupner's *Antiochus*, she and her husband spent some time at the court of the Landgrave Ernst Ludwig of Hessen in Darmstadt. In 1717 she made her début at the Gänsemarkt Opera, singing the lead in Reinhard Keiser's *Tomyris*. She visited Brunswick and from 1721 to 1723 she and her husband, with his operatic company, were at the Copenhagen court. Possessing a talent for organization, she was a director of the Gänsemarkt Opera, 1729–37, having sung leading roles there, 1724–30, under Telemann's direction. Her repertory included Cleopatra in Handel's *Giulio Cesare*, ten Keiser operas and 17 operas and prologues by Telemann including *Margaretha, Königin von Castilien* (in which she appeared with her daughter Sophie Amalia). In 1736 she was 'still the most distinguished of [women singers], despite her age ... her person is theatrical, her voice still good, only she is a little too much inclined to the Italian style'.

W. Maertens: 'G. Ph. Telemann und seine Interpreten: Margaretha Susanna und Johann Kayser', *Magdeburger Telemann-Studien*, iv (1973), 68–85
H. J. Marx: *Johann Mattheson (1681–1764): Lebensbeschreibung des Hamburger Musikers, Schriftstellers und Diplomaten* (Hamburg, 1982), 64, 140, 152
K. Zelm: 'Die Sänger der Hamburger Gänsemarkt-Oper', *HJbMw*, iii (1978), 35–73, esp. 53–6   HANS JOACHIM MARX

Kayser, Sophie Amalia (*b* Darmstadt, 25 Sept 1711; *d* ?Brunswick, 12 May 1747). German soprano, daughter of the soprano Margaretha Susanna Kayser and the composer and violinist Johann Kayser (not to be confused with Reinhard Keiser's daughter, Sophia Dorothea Louisa). She is thought to have made her début in Hamburg, with her mother, in Telemann's *Margaretha, Königin von Castilien* (1730). In 1731 or 1732 she married the Italian violinist Giovanni Verocai, in Moscow, and seems to have followed him to St Petersburg in 1732. In 1735 she returned to Hamburg and in 1737 she became prima donna at the opera house of Brunswick-Wolfenbüttel. She played an important part, as an Italian-style soprano, in the rise of the opera under G. C. Schürmann.

MGG ('Verocai, Giovanni'; C. Sartori)
W. Maertens: 'G. Ph. Telemann und seine Interpreten: Margaretha Susanna und Johann Kayser', *Magdeburger Telemann-Studien*, iv (1973), 74–6   HANS JOACHIM MARX

Kazakhstan. For discussion of opera in Kazakhstan *see* ALMA-ATA.

Kazan'. Capital of Tatarstan, on the Volga river. Local opera history begins with the Kazanskiy Vol'nïy Teatr (Kazan' Free Theatre; 1791–1800) and the serf troupe of the nobleman P. P. Yesipov (1803–14), whose performances included the 1811 première of *Fingal* by the local composer A. V. Novikov. Touring companies from Russia and Italy appeared from 1833, undeterred even by the 1842 fire which destroyed the old Yesipov theatre; fire did cut short the August–December 1874 season of P. M. Medvedev's Astrakhan'-based troupe, although the theatre was rebuilt and the companies of Medvedev and A. A. Orlov-Sokolovsky appeared there until 1889. At the end of the century the Kazansko-Saratovskoye Operno-Dramaticheskoye Tovarishchestvo (Kazan'-Saratov Opera-Dramatic Company) under M. M. Boroday (1894–1901) and N. I. Sobol'shchikov-Samarin (1901–8), became one of the best in the Russian provinces; Shalyapin began his career as a chorister there. Although performing forces dispersed after the theatre was destroyed by fire in 1919, the first Tatar operas were produced between 1925 and 1930. The Tatarskiy Teatr Operï i Baleta, formed by members of the Moscow Conservatory and the local opera studio, opened on 17 June 1939 with a performance of N. G. Zhiganov's *Kachkïn* ('The Fugitive'). A new 1029-seat hall, the Tatarskiy Gosudarstvennïy Teatr Operï i Baleta imeni M. Dzhalilya (Dzhalil' Tatar State Theatre of Opera and Ballet), named after the Tatar poet M. Dzhalil', opened in 1956.

ME (G. M. Kantor)

Tatarskiy gosudarstvennïy teatr operï i baleta im. M. Dzhalilya [The Dzhalil' Tatar State Opera and Ballet Theatre] (Kazan', 1957)

I. Kruti: *Russkiy teatr v Kazani* [The Russian Theatre in Kazan'] (Moscow, 1958)

Ia. Girshman: 'Opera, balet i muzïkal'naya komediya', *Muzïkal'naya kul'tura Sovetskoy Tatarii* (Moscow, 1959)

N. Shumskaya: 'Tatarskomu opernomu teatru 20 let' [Tatar Opera Theatre is 20 Years Old], *SovM* (1959), no.10, pp.103–11

N. F. Taube: 'Chetvert' veka kazanskoy operï (1874–1901)' [25 Years of Kazan' Opera], *Iz muzïkal'nogo proshlogo* [From the Musical Past], i (Moscow, 1960), 234–87

G. Bernandt: *Slovar' oper vpervïye postavlennïkh ili izdannïkh v dorevolyutsionnoy Rossii i v SSSR 1736–1959* [Dictionary of Operas First Performed or Published in Pre-revolutionary Russia or in the USSR 1736–1959] (Moscow, 1962), 537

Yu. V. Keldïsh, ed.: *Istoriya muzïki narodov SSSR* [History of the Music of the Soviet Peoples], i–v (Moscow, 1970–74)

G. Kantor: 'Predïstoriya kazanskoy operï' [The Pre-history of Kazan' Opera], *Voprosï istorii, teorii muzïkii muzïkal'nogo vospitaniya* [Problems of History, Music History and Musical Cultivation] (Kazan', 1970)

——: 'Rol' russkogo teatra v formirovanii tatarskoy operï' [The Role of the Russian Theatre in the Development of Tatar Opera], *Muzïka i muzïkantï bratskikh narodov Sovetskogo Soyuza* [Music and Musicians of the Fraternal Nations of the USSR] (Leningrad, 1972)

N. N. Nigedzyanov, ed.: *Muzïka i sovremennost': aktual'nïye voprosi tatarskoy muzïki* [Music and Contemporary Life: Issues of Tatar Music] (Kazan', 1980)

S. I. Raimova: *Istoriya tatarskoy muzïki* (Kazan', 1986)

GREGORY SALMON

Kazaryan, Yuri. *See* GHAZARYAN, YURI.

Keane, David Roger (*b* Akron, OH, 15 Nov 1943). Canadian composer. He attended Ohio State University and was the first composer to use the university's electronic music studio. In 1967 he moved to British Columbia, where he taught music in schools (1967–9) and at Simon Fraser University, Vancouver (1969–70). From 1970 he taught at the Queen's University, Kingston, Ontario, where he became a professor of theory and composition and where he established and directed the university's electro-acoustic music studios. He became a Canadian citizen in 1984.

Much of Keane's work involves electronic music. His operas feature small forces, electronic sound and mixed media. The chamber opera *The Devil's Constructs* (1978), commissioned to provide an introduction to opera for schoolchildren, is scored for seven solo voices and two prepared tapes. *Carmina tenebrarum* (1983), which was commissioned by the soprano Karen Skidmore, uses projections and special lighting effects.

The Devil's Constructs (chamber op, 1, D. Fanstone), Napanee, Ont., Napanee District Secondary School, 16 Oct 1978; broadcast, CKWF-TV, 22 Jan 1981

Carmina tenebrarum (1, Keane and M. Cuddy), Montreal, 14 May 1983

Harlequins (chamber op, 2, Cuddy), Toronto, Comus Music Theatre, 15 May 1986

Lumina (short op, 1, Cuddy), Toronto, Du Maurier, 11 May 1988

RUTH PINCOE

Keene, Christopher (*b* Berkeley, CA, 21 Dec 1946). American conductor. He studied at the University of California, Berkeley, and made his conducting début there in 1965 with Britten's *The Rape of Lucretia*, given by a company organized by himself. After working as assistant conductor for the San Francisco and San Diego opera companies, he was invited by Menotti to conduct *The Saint of Bleecker Street* at the Spoleto Festival in 1968, his European début. He returned there during the period 1971–6, variously as music director or general manager. Keene first conducted for the New York City Opera in 1970 with Ginastera's *Don Rodrigo*, then made his Metropolitan début in 1971 with *Cavalleria rusticana* and *Pagliacci*, and his Covent Garden début in 1973 with *Madama Butterfly*.

From 1977 to 1980 Keene was associated with the American Spoleto Festival at Charleston, South Carolina, and from 1974 to 1989 was music director (president from 1985) at the ArtPark, Lewiston, New York, where his performances included an innovative *Ring* production, spread over the years 1985 to 1988. In these and other centres in the USA and Europe he had built up a repertory of more than 90 operas before he became music director at the New York City Opera (1983–6), succeeding Beverly Sills as general director in 1989. There he conducted Philip Glass's *Akhnaten* in 1984 (the year of its première), and became known as a persuasive advocate of Glass's music, including *Satyagraha*, which he recorded with the New York City Opera (1985). With this company he conducted the première of Jay Reise's *Rasputin* (1988) and in 1990 the first stage production in New York of *Moses und Aron*.

Keene is a resourceful, intelligent conductor and administrator, who brings strong commitment to new works and a fresh approach to repertory. In 1989 he was elected to the board of the nationwide management association Opera America.

RICHARD DYER, NOËL GOODWIN

Keil, Alfredo (*b* Lisbon, 3 July 1850; *d* Hamburg, 4 Oct 1907). Portuguese composer of German descent. His father was a German tailor who settled in Lisbon, his mother was of Alsatian descent. He studied in Lisbon, then in 1868 went to Nuremberg, where he studied painting with Kremling and music with Kaulbach. As a result of the Franco-Prussian War he returned to Portugal in 1870 and started to exhibit his paintings and to publish short compositions. His first important work, the comic opera *Susana*, was performed in Lisbon in 1883. His next dramatic work, *Donna Bianca*, given in 1888 by a remarkable cast, which included the brothers António and Francisco D'Andrade (tenor and baritone respectively), had about 30 performances; with a libretto based on a poem by the leading Portuguese Romantic poet Almeida Garrett, *Donna Bianca* represents the first step towards Keil's most important opera, *Serrana*, given in 1899 at the S Carlos theatre in Lisbon. Also at this time he wrote his most significant cantatas and a symphonic poem. (He also continued to paint, and collected about 400 musical instruments.) A cultivated man (he spoke six languages), he was in touch with some of the most important contemporary Italian and French composers, including Verdi, Puccini, Mascagni, Leoncavallo, Gounod, Massenet (the dedicatee of *Serrana*) and Ambroise Thomas.

As a representative of Portuguese nationalism in opera, in *Donna Bianca* and *Irene* Keil followed the trend of most of his predecessors, such as Francisco de Sá Noronha and Miguel Ângelo Pereira, in using subjects drawn from Portuguese Romantic literature or national history. *Serrana*, on the other hand, with its folk setting and characters, is aesthetically closer to *verismo*. All of Keil's operas were translated into Italian, as was usual at the S Carlos theatre. Side by side with Italian patterns (such as the use of choruses at the beginning of some acts and terminology such as 'scena ed aria') are French influences, for example the introduction of ballets, particularly in *Donna Bianca*.

See also SERRANA.

Susana (ópera cómica, 1, H. Lopes de Mendonça), Lisbon, Trindade, 1883
Donna Bianca (drama lírico, prol., 4, C. Fereal, after A. Garrett: *Dona Branca*), Lisbon, S Carlos, 10 March 1888, vs (Paris, 1889)
Irene (leggenda mistica/dramma lirico, 4, Fereal, after the popular legend *Santa Iria*), Turin, Regio, 22 March 1893, vs (Leipzig, 1895)
Serrana (ópera, 3, Lopes de Mendonça, after C. Castelo Branco: *Como ela amava*), Lisbon, S Carlos, 13 March 1899, *P-Lt*, vs (Leipzig, 1906)

Unfinished operas: A India; Simão o Ruivo

DBP
'Keil, Alfredo', *Grande enciclopédia portuguesa e brasileira* (Lisbon and Rio de Janeiro, n.d.)
F. Lopes Graça: *A música portuguesa e os seus problemas*, ii (Lisbon, 1959)
LUISA CYMBRON

Keilberth, Joseph (*b* Karlsruhe, 19 April 1908; *d* Munich, 20 July 1968). German conductor. He studied at Karlsruhe and joined the Staatstheater there in 1925 as a répétiteur, becoming general music director ten years later. He was appointed music director of the Dresden Staatsoper in 1945 and, in 1951, conductor at the Bayerische Staatsoper, Munich. His career reached its first peak in 1952 when he made his début at Bayreuth and appeared at the Edinburgh Festival with the Hamburg Staatsoper (in *Der Freischütz* and *Der Rosenkavalier*). At Bayreuth he conducted the *Ring* and other operas in successive years up to 1956, and he appeared regularly at the Salzburg and Lucerne festivals. In 1959 he succeeded Fricsay as general musical director

of the Bayerische Staatsoper, Munich, where he played a major part in the artistic direction of the rebuilt National-theater. He died after collapsing during a performance of *Tristan und Isolde* (as had his Munich predecessor, Felix Mottl, in 1911).

Keilberth was representative of German musical traditions in his direct, dynamic and solidly robust approach. His great understanding of style and purpose was heard to notable effect in Pfitzner's *Palestrina*, Strauss's *Arabella* and *Intermezzo*, and Hindemith's *Mathis der Maler*. Skilled in the direction of singers, he gave some fine performances of Mozart and Wagner operas, and among his numerous gramophone records were the first complete recordings of *Der Freischütz* and Hindemith's *Cardillac*.

R. Freyse: 'Joseph Keilberth: ein Schallplatten-Porträt', *NZM*, Jg.124 (1963), 435–9
J. Keilberth: 'Begegnungen mit Hans Pfitzner und seinem Werk', *Mitteilungen der Pfitzner-Gesellschaft*, no.18, (1967), pp.1–9
R. Hartmann: 'Joseph Keilberth, 1908–68', *Opera*, xix (1968), 799–802
W.-E. von Lewinski: *Joseph Keilberth* (Berlin, 1968)
GERHARD BRUNNER

Keiser, Reinhard [Cesare, Rinardo] (*b* Teuchern, nr Weissenfels, 10 or 11 Jan 1674 [bap. 12 Jan]; *d* Hamburg, 12 Sept 1739). German composer. He was the foremost composer of German Baroque opera.

1. LIFE. Keiser was the son of Gottfried Keiser (*d* before 1732), an organist and composer, and Agnesa Dorothea von Etzdorff (1657–1732), who had married only four months before his birth. The elder Keiser seems to have lost or given up his position as organist at Teuchern in 1674 or 1675 and departed, leaving his wife and two sons behind. On 13 July 1685 Keiser enrolled at the Thomasschule, Leipzig, for seven years, and it was there presumably that he received his principal musical education, studying under Johann Schelle and perhaps Johann Kuhnau. Mattheson observed, however, that he owed his composing skill almost entirely to natural ability and the study of the best Italian music.

After leaving the Thomasschule, Keiser probably soon made his way to Brunswick, where the court opera was flourishing under the leadership of Johann Kusser; by 1694 he had obtained an appointment as 'Cammer-Componist'. His opera *Procris und Cephalus*, on a text by the court poet F. C. Bressand, was performed in Brunswick that year, while another opera, *Basilius*, was done in Hamburg, perhaps at the invitation of Kusser, by then musical director of the Theater am Gänsemarkt. Between 1695 and 1698 Keiser produced five more operas for the Brunswick-Wolfenbüttel court, all with Bressand, but in 1696 or 1697 he moved to Hamburg as Kusser's successor at the Opera. There he found one of his most sympathetic literary collaborators in C. H. Postel, with whom he wrote eight operas, including *Adonis* (1697), *Janus* (1698) and the lost *Iphigenia* (1699).

Beginning in 1703 Keiser also tried his hand at managing the opera house, in partnership with one Drüsicke. According to Mattheson their administration got off to a good start but was soon beset by financial difficulties, at least partly precipitated by riotous living by Keiser and his friends. In spring 1704 the theatre was temporarily closed, and Keiser left briefly for Weissenfels, where he gave the first performance of his *Almira*, originally intended for Hamburg. Drüsicke apparently passed on the *Almira* libretto to the youthful Handel, a member of the opera orchestra, who scored a great success with his own setting in January 1705, leading to strained relations between the two composers that no doubt contributed to Handel's decision shortly afterwards to leave for Italy. *Octavia* (1705), Keiser's first opera after returning from Weissenfels, inaugurated an important series of eight historical dramas with librettos by Barthold Feind. Following the final collapse of his administration in 1707, Keiser appears to have absented himself from the opera house for more than a year, passing much of his time visiting the estates of noble friends. He may not have participated in the highly successful première of *Der Carneval von Venedig* in summer 1707, and he composed no new work for 1708. Whatever rift may have existed between him and the new director, J. H. Sauerbrey, seems to have been healed by 1709, and his dominance over the Hamburg repertory became more complete than ever. By the time Sauerbrey's long regime ended in bankruptcy in 1718, Keiser had composed more than 40 operas for the Gänsemarkt theatre.

Sauerbrey was succeeded as director by J. G. Gumprecht, a member of the family that owned the building, who undertook to reverse the company's declining fortunes. For reasons that can only be surmised, Keiser was not retained as musical director. Instead he sought unsuccessfully to obtain a position elsewhere as court Kapellmeister, visiting Gotha and Eisenach in June 1718 and lingering long (at least from April 1719 to November 1720) in Stuttgart in an effort to unseat the incumbent, Giuseppe Brescianello. In 1721 he may have conducted a performance of *Tomyris* in Durlach before returning to Hamburg, where his arrival was celebrated on 9 August with a performance of his oratorio *Der siegende David*. With the formation of a troupe of Hamburg musicians to provide operas for the Danish court Keiser saw another opportunity for a permanent position. Beginning in December 1721 he composed or revised seven operas for Copenhagen, but he was rewarded only with the empty title of Royal Danish Kapellmeister and lost six months' salary when the impresario, Johann Kayser, absconded in March 1723.

Meanwhile, perhaps as a result of the replacement of Gumprecht as director in May 1722, Keiser again began composing for the Hamburg Opera, presenting *Ariadne* in November 1722 and a much revised *Carneval von Venedig* in February 1723. Though Telemann was now musical director, Keiser soon regained much of his former prominence. In 1725 and 1726, while Telemann composed relatively little for that theatre, Keiser turned out five major new works, two revised versions, and parts of two intermezzos. The situation changed dramatically in 1727, however, as the opera house passed through one of its periodic crises. Thenceforth it was Telemann who composed most of the new operas, and Keiser seems to have withdrawn entirely until the première of his *Lucius Verus* in October 1728; he may well have left the city at that time, for when his *Masagniello* and *Nebucadnezar* were revised for revivals in 1727 and July 1728 respectively the new music was supplied by Telemann. Keiser's daughter Sophia (1712–68) sang at the Hamburg Opera during this period.

On 2 December 1728 Keiser succeeded Mattheson as Kantor of Hamburg Cathedral, an important post which nonetheless brought him meagre remuneration.

He never again composed a wholly new opera, though he did revise *Croesus* in 1730, provide German recitatives for Handel's *Partenope* in 1733, and put together the pasticcio *Circe* in 1734. His diminished productivity probably had less to do with the demands of his ecclesiastical duties than with the sorry state of the Hamburg Opera, which finally closed its doors in 1738. After the death of his wife in 1735, he 'found reason' (in Mattheson's words) 'to remain completely in retirement' until his own death four years later.

2. WORKS. Although Keiser produced music in various vocal and instrumental genres, he was always primarily an opera composer. Claims that he wrote well over a hundred operas (which he himself fostered) are certainly exaggerated, but he can be shown to have composed at least 66, several of which he drastically revised during his final Hamburg period, as well as many ballets, serenatas and other occasional works in dramatic form. Less than a third of this music has survived, but it includes largely complete scores of 19 operas and substantial portions of four others.

The subject matter of Keiser's librettos is extremely diverse. In addition to works with the usual mythological, historical and pastoral plots there are two biblical operas (*Salomon* and *Nebucadnezar*), a double opera dealing with two famous Hamburg pirates (*Störtebecker und Jödge Michaels*), and a drama built around a revolution that had taken place less than 60 years earlier (*Masagniello*). Many of the operas have comic characters, and in 1707 a new form of comic opera was inaugurated with *Der Carneval von Venedig*, an adaptation of a *comédie lyrique* (originally set by Campra) with some scenes in Plattdeutsch; it led eventually to three sequels built around popular German festivals, *Der Leipziger Messe*, *Der Hamburger Jahr-Marckt* and *Die Hamburger Schlacht-Zeit*. The last two works belong to a group of five comic operas or intermezzos dating from 1725–6, part of a larger wave of comedy at the Hamburg Opera, for which Telemann seems to have been largely responsible. In 1703, apparently at Keiser's instigation, 11 Italian aria texts were introduced into the libretto of *Claudius*, probably to counter competition from foreign theatrical players. The novelty proved immensely popular, and thereafter most Hamburg operas contained some numbers in Italian.

Guided by the example of his Hamburg predecessors and his own study of Italian music, Keiser developed from an early date a highly distinctive musical style. Over the course of his long career that style underwent a remarkable evolution. In part he was responding to changes in contemporary Italian opera, particularly in the 1720s, when he adopted many of the *galant* gestures then coming into vogue. But it is also clear that he steadily refined and enriched his compositional technique in a way that belies the picture of a brilliant but frivolous natural genius presented by Chrysander and others. The elaborate revisions made in *Croesus* when it was revived in 1730 seem to have stemmed as much from an urge to improve as from a need to adapt to altered tastes or conditions. In addition, Keiser's style varied greatly from one work to another, since he gave each opera a special individual colouring reflecting its dramatic character. Thus even scores composed more or less at the same time – *Claudius* and *Nebucadnezar* for example – can be quite dissimilar in musical language.

Title-page of the libretto of Keiser's 'Fredegunda', first performed at the Theater am Gänsemarkt, Hamburg, in 1715

Though Keiser's arias are mostly italianate in design, their idiom is hardly ever purely Italian, and he also wrote numerous French dance *airs* and, for the comic or lower-class characters, jolly songs reminiscent of German folksong. The early operas display the formal variety characteristic of the Hamburg tradition, as da capo arias alternate freely with those in strophic, sectional binary and through-composed forms, but increasing Italian influence in the 1710s led to an overwhelming preponderance of da capo structure. Ostinato arias, usually with some interruption or transposition of the bass, are common in *Adonis*, *Janus* and *La forza della virtù*; thereafter they become rare, though there are some fine later examples (e.g. 'Stille Düffte' in *Octavia*) as well as many arias with patterned basses. In keeping with the general trend in Italian opera the length of Keiser's arias grew somewhat over the years, but even in the 1720s his da capo arias are still of modest proportions and do not necessarily cadence out of the tonic during the first section. After initially employing the Lullian type of overture with a slow introduction leading to a faster, quasi-fugal section he gradually abandoned it in favour of various italianate forms, whose diversity is suggested by the multiplicity of their titles – 'Aria' (*Masagniello*), 'Sonata' (*Fredegunda*), 'Concerto' (*Tomyris* and *Circe*), 'Intrada' (*Ulysses*), 'Sinfonia' (*Cupido* and *Croesus*) and 'Burla' (*Jodelet*). The ballet music, when preserved, is invariably French.

Central to Keiser's approach to opera was an intense concern for the relationship between music and text. He gave the fullest statement of his views (which appear to have coincided closely with those of his friends Mattheson and Feind) in the prefaces to two vocal collections, *Componimenti musicali* (1706) and *Divertimenti serenissimi* (1713). The chief aim of music, he held, was the expression of the emotions (*Affecten*) contained in a poetic text, which in the case of opera meant not merely abstract states of feeling but the actual passions of the characters, 'after true Nature, with its constantly changing conditions' (*Divertimenti serenissimi*). As a musical dramatist he displayed great versatility, dealing equally well with comedy and pathos and with amorous and martial sentiments. He had a special affinity for suffering heroines, such as Agrippina (*Janus*), Octavia, Marianne (*Masagniello*) and Penelope (*Ulysses*), and the moments in which they give voice to inner anguish can be intensely vivid and genuinely moving. He took unusual care over characterization, an interest he shared with Feind. His depiction of the overbearing and unstable revolutionary Masagniello shows what original figures he was capable of creating when provided with an adequate literary foundation.

No small part of the dramatic impact of Keiser's operas derives from the recitatives, particularly those with orchestral accompaniment. An expressive recitative, he observed in *Divertimenti serenissimi*, often cost a good composer as much trouble as an aria. He attached great importance to the musical observance of the rhetorical 'distinctions' implied by marks of punctuation and was, according to Mattheson, the first composer (along with himself) to have adopted this 'oratorical and rational manner' of setting a text. In set numbers, Keiser made extensive use of word-painting, often introducing sharp contrasts to highlight particular words, without ever losing sight of the basic affection being expressed. He was especially responsive to images of nature, which inspired some of his most splendid arias, including 'Kühle Winde' in *Tomyris*, 'Ihr sanften Winde' in *Ulysses* and 'Klarer Spiegel' in *Cupido*.

Never a learned composer, Keiser had little interest in counterpoint or motivic development. He was above all a melodist, and his seemingly inexhaustible fund of lyrical ideas won high praise from his German contemporaries. C. P. E. Bach considered that 'in the beauty, novelty, expression, and pleasing qualities of his melody' he had nothing to fear from comparison with Handel. Along with an astonishing variety of contour and character and a comparative freedom from formula, Keiser's melodies tend to have strong elements of periodic structure. From the very beginning he favoured relatively short phrases and marked segmentation within longer ones, and as early as *Pomona* (1702) and *Claudius* (1703) symmetrical formations became prominent, especially in the numerous arias in 6/8 or 12/8 time. This tendency towards periodicity helps explain Hasse's remark to Burney in the 1770s that Keiser's melodies, 'though more than fifty years old, are such as would now be thought modern and graceful'.

He was also a master of orchestral colour, and particularly in the operas between *Octavia* (1705) and *Trajanus* (1717) he experimented with many rich and unusual sonorities, frequently writing three or more separate parts for oboes, recorders or bassoons. *Octavia* is the earliest Hamburg opera score to contain horns, the 1711 *Croesus* the first to include chalumeaux. In the later operas there are many arias in which the scoring or texture changes almost incessantly, a style seen at its most kaleidoscopic in 'Kühle Winde' in *Tomyris*. Some arias or sections have minimal accompaniment; 'Dieser Haare güldnes Schertzen' in *La forza della virtù*, the most extreme case, lacks any instrumental support and replaces the expected ritornellos with wordless passages intoned by the singer.

A number of Keiser's operas incorporate arias by other composers, a fact that is usually acknowledged explicitly (if often imprecisely) in the printed libretto. In his early years the borrowings are comparatively rare and generally involve only a few numbers, but in the 1720s and 1730s pre-existing Italian arias were inserted into at least six Keiser operas; in *Jodelet* and *Circe* the insertions make up half the score and so must have formed part of the original plan. Evidently Keiser found it impossible to resist the demands of the singers (who became much more important in Hamburg at this time) and the enthusiasm of the public for Italian music. Failure to recognize which portions of the late operas are Keiser's own has led to considerable misunderstanding regarding his stylistic development and the quality of his inspiration during his final period.

Keiser enjoyed a much greater reputation in the 18th century than he does today. Mattheson called him 'the greatest opera composer in the world', and Scheibe considered him 'perhaps the most original musical genius that Germany has ever produced'. He had a profound and lasting impact on the style of Handel, who, moreover, borrowed countless melodic ideas from *Claudius*, *Octavia* and other operas. Yet even at the height of his fame Keiser's operas were scarcely performed outside Hamburg and Brunswick, and after the collapse of the Hamburg Opera in 1738 they virtually disappeared from the stage and seem to have been largely forgotten except by connoisseurs. Since the late 19th century Keiser has found some eminent musicological champions, including Kretzschmar, Leichtentritt and Grout, but to date the modern revival of Baroque opera has largely passed him by, probably because he belongs to neither of the principal national traditions of the period and because he has often been approached with expectations based on the very different styles of Bach and Handel.

Keiser was the first great figure in German operatic history. If he failed to establish a truly national genre and even contributed to the increasing italianization of the existing form, he nonetheless raised German dramatic music to a new level, matching if not surpassing the achievements of his principal French and Italian contemporaries. Unfortunately, most of his operas are lost and some of those that survive suffer from the weakness of their librettos or the intrusion of arias by other composers. Yet there remains a handful of masterpieces, chief among them *Masagniello*, *Ulysses* and *Croesus*, that must be counted among the glories of Baroque opera.

See also CLAUDIUS; CROESUS; CUPIDO; JANUS; JODELET; MASAGNIELLO; OCTAVIA; TOMYRIS; and ULYSSES (i). For further illustration *see* HAMBURG, fig.1.

HG – *Hamburg, Theater am Gänsemarkt*

Basilius [Der königliche Schäfer, oder Basilius in Arcadien] (3, F. C. Bressand, after F. Parisetti: *Il re pastore*), HG, 1694; rev. as Arcadia, oder Die königliche Schäferey, Brunswick, Rathaus, 1699

Procris und Cephalus (Spl, 3, Bressand), Brunswick, Rathaus, 1694, 10 arias, duet *D-B*, *Bds*, *SWl*

Die wiedergefundenen Verliebten [Die beständige und getreue Ismene] (Schäferspiel, 3, Bressand), Salzthal, nr Wolfenbüttel, 24 May 1695

Clelia (Spl, 5, Bressand), Brunswick, Rathaus, 1695

Circe, oder Des Ulysses erster Theil (Spl, 3, Bressand), Brunswick, Rathaus, Feb 1696

Penelope, oder Des Ulysses anderer Theil [Penelope und Ulysses ander Theil] (Spl, 3, Bressand), Brunswick, Rathaus, Feb 1696

Mahumeth II (3, H. Hinsch), HG, 29 Feb 1696

Adonis [Der geliebte Adonis] (Spl, 3, C. H. Postel), HG, 1697, *B*/*R*1986: HS, i

Irene [Die durch Wilhelm den Grossen in Britannien wider eingeführte Irene] (Sing- und Tantz-Spiel, 1, Postel), HG, 10 Jan 1698

Orpheus (Spl, 5, Bressand), Brunswick, Rathaus, 1698; rev. as Die sterbende Euridice and Die verwandelte Leyer des Orpheus [Die sterbende Eurydice, oder Orpheus erster Theil and Orpheus ander Theil] (3, 3), Brunswick, Rathaus, 1699; rev. as Die biss in und nach dem Todt unerhörte Treue des Orpheus (5), HG, 1709, *B* [without recits.], duet in Divertimenti serenissimi (Hamburg, 1713)

Der güldene Apfel [Der aus Hyperboreen nach Cymbrien übergebrachte güldene Apfel] (3, Postel), HG, 1698

Janus [Der bey dem allgemeinen Welt-Friede von dem grossen Augustus geschlossene Tempel des Janus] (Spl, 3, epilogue, Postel), HG, 1698; rev. as Der von Othino dem Uhrheber des Dänischen Reichs geschlossene Tempel des Janus, Copenhagen, 30 Nov 1722; rev. version, HG, 1729; *B*/*R*1986: HS, i

Iphigenia [Die wunderbahr-errettete Iphigenia] (Spl, 5, Postel, after Euripides), HG, 1699

Hercules und Hebe [Die an dem glücklichen Vermählungs-Tage ... vorgebildete Verbindung des grossen Hercules mit der schönen Hebe] (Spl, 3, Postel), HG, 24 Feb 1699

Die Wiederkehr der güldnen Zeit (Spl, 3, Bressand), HG, 1699

La forza della virtù, oder Die Macht der Tugend (Spl, 3, Bressand, after D. David), HG, 1700, *B*, excerpts in Die auserlesensten Arien der Opera genannt La forza della virtù (Hamburg, 1701/*R*1986: HS, ii)

Endymion [Der gedemüthigte Endymion] (Spl, 3, Nothnagel), HG, 1700; rev. as Der siegende Phaeton, HG, 1702

Störtebecker und Jödge Michaels erster Theil (Spl, 3, Hotter), HG, 1701

Störtebecker und Jödge Michaels zweyter Theil (Spl, 3, Hotter), HG, 1701

Psyche [Die wunder-schöne Psyche] (Spl, 3, Postel), HG, 20 Oct 1701, 5 arias *SWl*, *W*

Pomona [Sieg der fruchtbaren Pomona (Streit der vier Jahres Zeiten)] (18 scenes, Postel), HG, 18 Oct 1702, *B*

Claudius [Die verdammte Staat-Sucht, oder Der verführte Claudius] (Spl, 3, Hinsch), HG, 1703, *B*/*R*1986: HS, iii; rev. as Claudius, römischer Kayser, HG, 17 July 1726

Minerva [Die Geburth der Minerva] (Spl, 3, Hinsch), HG, 28 Aug 1703, aria in Arsinoe, 1710

Salomon [Die über die Liebe triumphirende Weisheit, oder Salomon] (Spl, 3, Duke Anton Ulrich of Brunswick or J. C. Knorr von Rosenroth, rev. C. F. Hunold), HG, 1703, 3 arias *B*, *Hs*; incl. 8 arias by G. C. Schürmann, 1 aria by an unknown composer

Nebucadnezar [Der gestürtzte und wieder erhöhte Nebucadnezar, König zu Babylon] (Spl, 3, Hunold), HG, 1704, *B-Br*, *D-Gs*; rev. version, HG, 1709; rev. Telemann, HG, 1728, *B*/*R*1986: HS, iii

Almira [Der in Krohnen erlangte Glücks-Wechsel, oder Almira, Königin von Castilien] 1704 (Spl, 3, F. C. Feustking, after G. Pancieri: *Almira*), comp. for HG, unperf.; 2 arias *A-Wn*, *D-B*, excerpts in Componimenti musicali (Hamburg, 1706); rev. as Almira, Königin von Castilien, Weissenfels, Neu-Augustusburg, 30 July 1704; rev. as Der durchlauchtige Secretarius, oder Almira, Königin in Castilien (lib. rev. B. Feind), HG, 1706; with new epilogue Der Genius von Europa, HG, 26 July 1708; incl. 3 arias by R. Fedeli

Octavia [Die römische Unruhe, oder Die edelmühtige Octavia] (Spl, 3, Feind), HG, 5 Aug 1705, *PL-Kj**, excerpts in Componimenti musicali (Hamburg, 1706); ed. F. Chrysander and M. Seiffert, G. F. Händels Werke, suppl.vi (Leipzig, 1902); incl. 2 arias by P. Hebenstreit

Lucretia [Die kleinmühtige Selbst-Mörderin Lucretia, oder Die Staats-Thorheit des Brutus] (musicalisches Trauer-Spiel, 5, Feind), HG, 29 Nov 1705, 1 aria *A-Wn*

La fedeltà coronata [oder Die gekrönte Treue] (Spl, 3, Hinsch), HG, 1706, 2 arias *Wn*, *D-B*

Masagniello [Masagniello (Masaniello) furioso [oder] Die neapolitanische Fischer-Empörung] (drama musicale, 3, Feind), HG, June 1706; rev. Telemann, HG, 1727; *B**, ed. in EDM, 1st ser., lxxxix (1986)

Sueno [La costanza sforzata/Die bezwungene Beständigkeit, oder Die listige Rache des Sueno] (Spl, 3, Feind), HG, 11 Oct 1706

Der Carneval von Venedig [Der angenehme Betrug, oder Der Carneval von Venedig] (Spl, 3, [? J. A.] Meister and M. Cuno, after J. F. Regnard: *Le carneval de Venise*), HG, sum. 1707, 36 arias *A-Wn*, *D-HS*, *SWl* [? earlier version, Weissenfels, 1705]; rev. HG, 8 Feb 1723; rev. HG, 1733; ? some numbers by Graupner

Helena [La forza dell'amore/Die Macht der Liebe, oder Die von

Paris entführte Helena] (Spl, 3, Keiser, after A. Aureli: *Helena rapita da Paride*), HG, 1709; incl. 1 aria not by Keiser

Heliates und Olympia [Die blut-durstige Rache, oder Heliates und Olympia] (Spl, 3, Keiser), HG, 1709, 3 arias *A-Wn*; partly by Graupner

Desiderius, König der Longobarden (musicalisches Schauspiel, prol., 3, epilogue, Feind), HG, 26 July 1709, *PL-Kj**

Arsinoe [La grandezza d'animo, oder Arsinoe] (Spl, 5, Breymann), HG, 1710, *D-B**, aria in Divertimenti serenissimi (Hamburg, 1713)

Die Leipziger Messe [Le bon vivant, oder Die Leipziger Messe] (Singe- und Lust-Spiel, 3, C. F. Weidemann), HG, 1710

Aurora [Der Morgen des europäischen Glückes, oder Aurora] (Schäffer-Spiel, 5, Breymann), HG, 26 July 1710, 10 arias *A-Wn*, *D-B*, *SWl*, chorus in Trajanus, 1717

Julius Caesar [Der durch den Fall des grossen Pompejus erhöhete Julius Caesar; Der Fall des grossen Pompejus] (Spl, 3, Feind), HG, Nov 1710, 1 aria *SWl*

Croesus [Der hochmüthige, gestürzte und wieder erhabene Croesus] (Spl, 3, L. von Bostel, after N. Minato: *Creso*), HG, 1711, 4 arias *B*, *SWl*; rev. HG, 6 Dec 1730; *PL-Kj**, ed. in DDT, xxxvii–xxxviii (1912)

Cato [L'amore verso la patria/Die Liebe gegen das Vaterland, oder Der sterbende Cato] (musicalisches Schauspiel, 3, Feind, after M. Noris: *Catone uticense*), HG, 1711, 1 aria *D-B*

Carolus V [Die oesterreichische Grossmuth, oder Carolus V] (musicalisches Schauspiel, 3, epilogue, J. U. von König), HG, 1712, 10 arias *A-Wn*, *D-B*, *SWl*

Diana [Die entdeckte Verstellung, oder Die geheime Liebe der Diana] (pastoral, 3, König, partly after F. de Lemene: *Endimione*), HG, April 1712, 7 arias *B*, *Bds*, *SWl*; rev. as Cupido [Der sich rächende Cupido], HG, 9 July 1724, *B*, incl. 7 It. numbers by other composers

Heraclius [Die wiederhergestelle Ruh, oder Die gecrönte Tapferkeit des Heraclius] (Spl, prol., 5, epilogue, König, after N. Beregan: *Heraclio*), HG, June 1712, *PL-Kj*

L'inganno fedele, oder Der getreue Betrug (heroisches Schäfer-Spiel, 3, König), HG, Oct 1714; as Die gecrönte Tugend, 15 Nov 1714; 2 arias *D-B*, excerpts in Erlesene Sätze aus der Opera L'inganno fedele (Hamburg, 1714), ed. in DDT, xxxvii–xxxviii (1912); rev. 1726

Fredegunda (musicalisches Schau-Spiel, 5, König, after F. Silvani: *Fredegonda*), HG, 1715, *Bds*

Artemisia (musicalisches Schau-Spiel, 3, ? G. H. Stölzel and others), HG, 1715

Das römische April-Fest (musicalisches Lust- und Tantz-Spiel, 5, Feind), HG, June 1716

Achilles [Das zerstörte Troja, oder Der durch den Tod Helenen versöhnte Achilles] (musicalisches Spl, 5, J. J. Hoë, after U. Rizzi: *Achille placato*), HG, Nov 1716, 2 arias *A-Wn*, *D-B*

Julia [Die durch Verstellung und Grossmuth über die Grausamkeit siegende Liebe, oder Julia] (Spl, 5, Hoë, after G. F. Bussani: *Antonio e Pompeiano*), HG, Feb 1717; Acts 1–2 rev. as Antonius römischer Kayser, Copenhagen, 30 Jan 1722, 1 aria

Tomyris [Die grossmüthige Tomyris] (Spl, 3, Hoë, after D. Lalli: *L'amor di figlio non conosciuto*), HG, July 1717, *B* [2 copies]; ed. in Die Oper, i (Munich 1975); rev. HG, 1723, with 2 arias by G. Bononcini

Trajanus [Der die Vestung Siebenbürgisch-Weissenburg eroberde und über die Dacier triumphirende Kayser Trajanus] (Spl, 3, epilogue, Hoë), HG, Nov 1717, *B*

Jobates und Bellerophon [Das bey seiner Ruh und Gebuhrt eines Printzen frolockende Lycien unter der Regierung des Königs Jobates und Bellerophon] (Spl, prol., 3, epilogue, Hoë), HG, 28 Dec 1717, 3 arias *A-Wn*, *D-B*, duet in Jodelet, 1726

Cloris und Tirsis (3, epilogue, various), Copenhagen, 18 Dec 1721

Psyche [Die unvergleichliche Psyche] (musicalisches Schauspiel, prol., 3, Postel, rev. F. M. Lersner), Copenhagen, 16 April 1722

Augustus [Der durch Grossmuth und Gnade siegende Augustus] (Spl, prol., 3, epilogue, Hoë), Copenhagen, ?Oct 1722

Ulysses (musicalisches Schau-Spiel, prol., 3, Lersner, after H. Guichard: *Ulysse*), Copenhagen, Court, ?Nov 1722, *B*; incl. 2 It. arias by Orlandini

Ariadne [Die betrogene und nachmals vergötterte Ariadne] (Spl, prol., 3, Postel), HG, 26 Nov 1722, aria in Ulysses, 1722

Der Armenier, 1722 (Lersner), comp. for Copenhagen, ?unperf.

Sancio, begun 1723 (König, after F. Silvani: *Il miglior d'ogni amore per il peggiore d'ogni odio*), intended for HG, ? not completed

Cupido: see Diana, 1712

Bretislaus, oder Die siegende Beständigkeit (Spl, prol., 3, epilogue,

J. P. Praetorius), HG, 7 Feb 1725; incl. several It. arias by other composers, aria in Jodelet, 1726

Der Hamburger Jahr-Marckt, oder Der glückliche Betrug (schertzhafftes Spl, 5, Praetorius), HG, 20 June 1725

Die Hamburger Schlacht-Zeit, oder Der missgelungene Betrug (Spl, prol., 5, Praetorius), HG, 22 Oct 1725; banned after 1 perf.

Mistevojus (Spl, 5, J. S. Müller, after A. Zeno and P. Pariati: *Antioco*), HG, 1726; incl. a few arias by other composers

Jodelet [Der lächerliche Printz Jodelet] (schertzhaftes Spl, 5, Praetorius, after Matsen), HG, 1726, *B*, ed. in PÄMw, xviii, Jg. xxi–xxii (1892); incl. 16 It. arias by other composers

Buchhöfer, der stumme Printz Atis (int, 2, Praetorius), HG, 1726, parody of Croesus, 1711, ? arr. by another composer

Barbacola (Zwischen-Spiel, 1, Praetorius), HG, 1726, ? partly by Lully

Lucius Verus, oder Die siegende Treue (Spl, 3, Hinsch, after Zeno: *Lucio Vero*), HG, 18 Oct 1728; ? a few It. arias by other composers

Circe (Spl, 5, Praetorius and J. J. van Mauritius), HG, 1 and 3 March 1734 in 2 pts, *B**; incl. 22 It. numbers by other composers

Aria, Durch Tugend, Rach' und Güte, for Graupner: L'amore ammalato/Die krankende Liebe, oder Antiochus und Stratonica, HG, 1711, *Bds**

11 numbers and addl recits. for Handel: Oriana [Amadigi di Gaula], HG, Sept 1717, 2 arias *A-Wn*, *D-B*; aria Ein Glässgen Wein in Ulysses, 1722

Prol. to F. Amadei, G. Bononcini and Handel: Muzio Scevola, HG, 7 Jan 1723

Recits. for Handel: Partenope, HG, 28 Oct 1733

For other possible addl arias, see Schulze 1938

MGG (H. Becker); PEM (K. Zelm)

J. Mattheson: *Grundlage einer Ehren-Pforte* (Hamburg, 1740); ed. M. Schneider (Berlin, 1910)

E. O. Lindner: *Die erste stehende deutsche Oper* (Berlin, 1855)

F. Chrysander: 'Geschichte der Braunschweig-Wolfenbüttelschen Capelle und Oper vom sechzehnten bis zum achtzehnten Jahrhundert', *Jahrbücher für musikalische Wissenschaft*, i (1863), 147–286

——: 'Mattheson's Verzeichniss Hamburgischer Opern von 1678 bis 1728, gedruckt im ''Musikalischen Patrioten'', mit seinen handschriftlichen Fortsetzungen bis 1751, nebst Zusätzen und Berichtigungen', *AMZ*, new ser., xii (1877), 198–282

——: 'Adonis: Oper von Reinhard Keiser (1697)', *AMZ*, new ser., xiii (1878), 65–101

——: 'Geschichte der Hamburger Oper vom Abgange Kusser's bis zum Tode Schott's (1695–1702)', *AMZ*, new ser., xiv (1879), 433–533

——: 'Geschichte der Hamburger Oper unter der Direction von Reinhard Keiser (1703–1706)', *AMZ*, new ser., xv (1880), 17–88

H. Leichtentritt: *Reinhard Keiser in seinen Opern* (diss., U. of Berlin, 1901)

P. A. Merbach: 'Das Repertoire der Hamburger Oper von 1718 bis 1750', *AMw*, vi (1924), 354–72

T. Krogh: 'Reinhard Keiser in Kopenhagen', *Musikwissenschaftliche Beiträge: Festschrift für Johannes Wolf* (Berlin, 1929), 79–87

W. Schulze: *Die Quellen der Hamburger Oper (1678–1738)* (Hamburg, 1938)

H. C. Wolff: *Die Barockoper in Hamburg (1678–1738)* (Wolfenbüttel, 1957)

R. Brockpähler: *Handbuch zur Geschichte der Barockoper in Deutschland* (Emsdetten, 1964)

A. D. McCredie: *Instrumentarium and Instrumentation in the North German Baroque Opera* (diss., U. of Hamburg, 1964)

R. D. Brenner: *The Operas of Reinhard Keiser in their Relationship to the Affektenlehre* (diss., Brandeis U., 1968)

W. Dean: 'Handel and Keiser: Further Borrowings', *CMc*, no.9 (1969), 73–80

R. D. Brenner: 'Emotional Expression in Keiser's Operas', *MR*, xxxiii (1972), 222–32

B. Deane: 'Reinhard Keiser: an Interim Assessment', *Soundings*, iv (1974), 30–41

K. Zelm: *Die Opern Reinhard Keisers: Studien zur Chronologie, Überlieferung und Stilentwicklung* (Munich, 1975)

H.-J. Theill: 'Reinhard Keisers Masaniello furioso: Notizen zur Herausgabe einer Hamburger Barockoper', *Schweizer Beiträge zur Musikwissenschaft*, iii (1978), 107–42

K. Zelm: 'Die Sänger der Hamburger Gänsemarkt-Oper', *HJbMw*, iii (1978), 35–73

B. Baselt: 'Händel auf dem Wege nach Italien', *G. F. Händel und seine italienischen Zeitgenossen* (Halle, 1979), 10–21

R. D. Lynch: *Opera in Hamburg, 1718–1738: a Study of the Libretto and Musical Style* (diss., New York U., 1979)

C. Dahlhaus: 'Zum Affektbegriff der frühdeutschen Oper', *HJbMw*, v (1981), 107–11

S. Leopold: 'Feinds und Keisers Masagniello furioso: eine politische Oper?', *HJbMw*, v (1981), 55–68

K. Zelm: 'Reinhard Keiser und Georg Philipp Telemann: zum Stilwandel an der frühdeutschen Oper in Hamburg', *Die Bedeutung Georg Philipp Telemanns für die Entwicklung der europäischen Musikkultur im 18. Jahrhundert: Magdeburg 1981*, 104–13

——: 'Zur Verarbeitung italienischer Stoffe auf der Hamburger Gänsemarkt-Oper', *HJbMw*, v (1981), 89–106

——: 'Stilkritische Untersuchungen an einem Opernpasticcio: Reinhard Keiser's *Jodelet*', *Festschrift Heinz Becker* (Laaber, 1982), 10–25

R. Meyer: *Die Hamburger Oper, 1678–1730: Einführung und Kommentar zur dreibändigen Textsammlung* (Millwood, NY, 1984)

K. Zelm: 'Georg Philipp Telemann und Reinhard Keiser: zur Konzeption der Opernarie um 1730', *Telemann und seine Freunde: Kontakte, Einflüsse, Auswirkungen: Magdeburg 1984*, ii, 3–14

J. H. Roberts: 'Handel's Borrowings from Keiser', *Göttinger Händel-Beiträge*, ii (1986), 51–76

J. D. Arnn: *Text, Music, and Drama in Three Operas by Reinhard Keiser* (diss., Rutgers U., 1987)

B. Baselt: 'Georg Friedrich Händels "römische" Kadenzen: zu Entstehung und Weiterwirkung zweier characteristischer Schlusswendungen aus Händels Kompositionen der italienischen Reisezeit', *Festschrift Wolfgang Rehm* (Kassel, 1989), 51–61

K.-P. Koch: *Reinhard Keiser (1674–1739): Leben und Werk* (Teuchern, 1989)

——: 'Zu Reinhard Keisers Spätschaffen', *HJb 1990*, 91–105

J. H. Roberts: 'Keiser and Handel at the Hamburg Opera', *HJb 1990*, 63–87

D. Schröder: 'Zu Entstehung und Aufführungsgeschichte von Händels Oper "Almira": Anmerkungen zur Edition des Werkes in der Hallischen Händel-Ausgabe', *HJb 1990*, 147–53

JOHN H. ROBERTS

Keiser, Sophia (**Dorothea Louisa**) (*b* Hamburg, bap. 21 Oct 1712; *d* Copenhagen, 1768). German soprano. The daughter of the composer Reinhard Keiser and his wife Barbara, a singer, she made her début at the age of 12 in the part of Amour in Telemann's version of Destouches' *Omphale*. She was employed at the Hamburg Opera, 1724–30, and shared the leading soprano roles with Margaretha Susanna Kayser (the latter was described as 'Mme Kayser', Sophia as 'Mlle Keiser'). From the end of 1738 to the beginning of 1741 she was engaged at the Copenhagen court with a salary of 400 reichsthalers.

Keiser sang principally in her father's operas (including *Cupido*, 1724; *Die Hamburger Schlacht-Zeit*, 1725; and *Jodelet*, 1726) and in the operas of Telemann, then also musical director of the Hamburg Opera (including *Die Amours der Vespetta*, *Sancio* and *Das jauchzende Grossbritannien*, all 1727; *Die verkehrte Welt*, 1728; *Flavius Bertaridus*, 1729; *Das neubeglückte Sachsen*, 1730; and *Der wohlgetroffene Wettstreit*, 1743).

*

W. Maertens: 'Georg Philipp Telemann und seine Interpreten: Margaretha Susanna und Johann Kayser', *Magdeburger Telemann-Studien*, iv (1973), 68–85

K. Zelm: 'Die Sänger der Hamburger Gänsemarkt-Oper', *HJbMw*, iii (1978), 35–73, esp. 57–8

HANS JOACHIM MARX

Kékszakállú herceg vára, A. Opera by Béla Bartók; *see* BLUEBEARD'S CASTLE.

Keldïsh, Yury [Georgy] **Vsevolodovich** (*b* St Petersburg, 16/29 Aug 1907). Russian musicologist, administrator and educator. He began his career as a member of the Russian Association of Proletarian Musicians (RAPM), the 'left' organization of the early Soviet period, hostile to the institutions and artworks of bourgeois culture. Since the dissolution of the RAPM Keldïsh has risen to the summit of the Soviet musicological establishment, serving as director of the Leningrad Institute of Theatre and Music (1955–7), head of the department of the Institute of Arts History of the Soviet Ministry of Culture devoted to the music of the peoples of the USSR (1961–74), editor of *Sovetskaya muzïka* (1957–60), general editor of the Soviet musical encyclopedia (from 1967), of the ten-volume official history of Russian music (*Istoriya russkoy muzïki v desyati tomakh*, 1983–), and of the series Monuments of Russian Music (*Pamyatniki russkogo muzïkal'nogo iskusstva*, 1972–), which has included several early Russian operas. In addition, he has been the executive secretary of the Union of Soviet Composers since 1974 and has taught continuously at the Moscow Conservatory since 1930, except for a period in the 1950s when he was living in Leningrad. His pupils have included a number of important specialists in the history of Russian music (and Russian opera in particular), including A. I. Kandinsky and Yevgeny Levashov.

Keldïsh has written prolifically and generally on Russian music history, including a long-standard textbook (*Istoriya russkoy muzïki*, 3 vols., 1947–54). His major areas of specialization relevant to operatic history have been the 18th century, which he approaches from a nationalistic standpoint typical of his generation of Soviet scholars, and the early 19th century.

Russkaya muzïka XVIII veka (Moscow, 1965), chap. 6

'Vozniknoveniye i razvitiye russkoy operï v XVIII v.' [The Rise and Development of Russian Opera in the 18th Century], *Musica antiqua Europae orientalis I: Bydgoszcz 1966*, 489–506

'Neizvestnaya opera russkogo kompozitora' [An Unknown Opera by a Russian Composer], *SovM* (1966), no.12, pp.39–50; repr. in *Ocherki i issledovaniya po istorii russkoy muzïki* (Moscow, 1978), 113–29, 486–94

'Opera', *Istoriya muzïki narodov SSSR*, iv (Moscow, 1973)

'K istorii operï "Yamshchiki na podstave"' [On the History of the Opera *Postal Coachmen*], *Ocherki i issledovaniya po istorii russkoy muzïki* (Moscow, 1978), 130–40

'Ital'yanskaya opera', *Istoriya russkoy muzïki v desyati tomakh*, ii (Moscow, 1984), 91–128

'Ye. I. Fomin', 'D. S. Bortnyansky', *Istoriya russkoy muzïki v desyati tomakh*, iii (Moscow, 1985), 84–110, 161–93

'Opernïy teatr', 'K. A. Kavos i russkaya opera', 'S. I. Davïdov', *Istoriya russkoy muzïki v desyati tomakh*, iv (Moscow, 1986), 25–61, 123–44, 145–67

'A. N. Verstovsky', 'Muzïkal'nïy teatr', 'Muzïkal'no-kriticheskaya mïsl'', *Istoriya russkoy muzïki v desyati tomakh*, v (Moscow, 1988), 97–131, 283–321, 370–410

'A. S. Dargomïzhsky', 'Opernoye tvorchestvo A. N. Serova', *Istoriya russkoy muzïki v desyati tomakh*, vi (Moscow, 1989), 83–133, 134–66

RICHARD TARUSKIN

Kelemen, Milko (*b* Podravska Slatina, Croatia, 30 March 1924). Croatian composer. He studied at the Zagreb Academy of Music from 1945 to 1952 (composition with Šulek); he continued his compositional studies at the Paris Conservatoire with Messiaen and Aubin (1954–5), with Frazzi in Siena and with Fortner at the Freiburg Musikhochschule. After teaching in Zagreb, he studied at the Siemens electronic studio in Munich, 1966–8, and spent the years 1968–9 in Berlin. He was then professor of composition at the Düsseldorf Conservatory (1970–73) and at the Stuttgart Musikhochschule (from 1973). Kelemen founded the Zagreb Biennale (1961) and was largely responsible for paving the way for avant-garde music in Yugoslavia. In

1968 he was awarded a major prize by Yugoslav television for his opera *Der neue Mieter*.

At first Kelemen was influenced by folk music and by neo-classicism. Under the influences of his studies with Fortner and his participation in Darmstadt summer courses, he developed an original style, closely combining the newest compositional procedures with archetypal elements. A large part of his work – particularly since around 1960 – has been music for the stage, in which he creates rich sonorities based on small intervals. His opera *Der neue Mieter* is a work typical of the 'theatre of the absurd', while in *Der Belagerungszustand* he used a range of styles, including avant-garde expressive means and effects, to stress the central idea: the necessity of fighting every form of tyranny. In the multi-media ballet-opera *Apocalyptica* Kelemen and his collaborators used dispersed dramaturgy and allegory to portray some of the enduring and essential problems of the human condition within modern civilization. For the music he employed vocal soloists, instrumental chamber groups, narrators and tape, amalgamating traditional and new styles of expression. Several ballets and film scores are among his other works.

Der neue Mieter (musical scene, after E. Ionesco), Münster, 15 Sept 1964; as Novi stanar, Zagreb, 18 May 1965
Der Belagerungszustand (2, after A. Camus), Hamburg, 13 Jan 1970; as Opsadno stanje, Zagreb, 9 May 1971
Apocalyptica (multi-media ballet-opera, F. Arrabal and E. Kieselbach) [based on *Opera Bestial*, 1973–4, unperf.]; concert perf., Graz, 10 Oct 1979; stage perf. of ballet version, Dresden, 10 May 1982; pantomime version by M. Sládek, Cologne, 2 Nov 1989

*

M. Cadieu: 'Sartre chantant, Ionesco dansant par Milko Kelemen', *Nouvelles littéraires* (Paris, 1965)
M. Kelemen: 'Muzička scena, opera i multi-media opera', *Zvuk*, nos.119–20 (1971), 437–8
J. Andreis: *Music in Croatia* (Zagreb, 1974)
S. Erding: *Apocalyptica: eine multimediale Balletoper von Fernando Arrabal (Text), Milko Kelemen (Musik) und Edmund Kieselbach (Objekte)* (Nagold, 1979)
N. Turkalj: 'Apocalyptica: multimedijalna opera ballet Milka Kelemena', *Zvuk* (1980), no.3, pp.51–6
RUDOLF LÜCK, KORALJKA KOS

Kelemen, Zoltán (*b* Budapest, 12 March 1926; *d* Zürich, 9 May 1979). Hungarian bass-baritone. He studied at Budapest and Rome, making his début in 1959 at Augsburg as Kecal. After an engagement at Wuppertal, in 1961 he joined the Cologne Opera, remaining there until his death; he took part in the première of Zimmermann's *Die Soldaten* (1965) and made his London début with the company at Sadler's Wells (1969) as the Mayor in *Der junge Lord*. He first appeared at Bayreuth in 1962 as Ortel and a Nobleman (*Lohengrin*); in 1964 he sang Alberich, the role of his Salzburg (1965), Metropolitan (1968) and Covent Garden (1970) débuts, and which he recorded for Karajan. He sang in Paris, Vienna, Hamburg, Munich and Düsseldorf; his repertory included Mozart's Bartolo, Osmin, Leporello, Don Alfonso, Pizarro, Don Magnifico, Falstaff (Nicolai and Verdi), Dulcamara, the Grand Inquisitor, Ochs, Gianni Schicchi, Rangoni and Klingsor, which he also recorded. A powerful actor, he coloured his rich, agile voice to suggest humour or malevolence as a character required.
ALAN BLYTH

Keller, Gottfried (*b* Zürich, 19 July 1819; *d* Hottingen, 15 July 1890). Swiss poet and novelist. He studied art in Munich and philosophy in Heidelberg. After a first

volume of poems (1846), he made his reputation with the novel *Der grüne Heinrich* (1851–3). He returned to Switzerland in 1855 after a five-year period in Berlin and became friendly with Wagner. He published studies of Swiss provincial life in two volumes entitled *Die Leute von Seldwyla* (1856, 1874), some of which provided librettos for Georg Haeser (*Hadlaub*), Delius (*A Village Romeo and Juliet*), Zemlinsky (*Kleider machen Leute*) and Kelterborn (*Julia*).

ROBERT ANDERSON

Kellgren, Johan Henrik (*b* Floby, Västergötland, 1 Dec 1751; *d* Stockholm, 20 April 1795). Swedish librettist. He attended Åbo University in Finland, where he began to write poetry and theatre criticism, earning a position as docent in Åbo in 1774. In 1777 he followed his comrade A. N. Edelcrantz to Stockholm, where his poetry attracted the attention of Gustavus III, who engaged him as his personal secretary and entrusted him with versifying his opera sketches. In 1778 Kellgren participated in a polemical debate in the Stockholm newspapers on the aesthetics of opera, during the course of which his views changed from those of a Voltairian to those of an ardent supporter of Gluck. His first opera text, *Adonis och Proserpina* (1778), was revised in 1781 for J. M. Kraus; the subsequent decade was devoted to a grand opera *Aeneas i Cartago* (1782–90) and to the Swedish nationalist work *Gustaf Wasa* (1786). His last important work was a tragedy, *Olympie* (1792), based on Voltaire, to which Kraus wrote incidental music. His correspondence contains a colourful description of operatic life in Stockholm during the Gustavian period.

Adonis och Proserpina, 1778 (J. M. Kraus, 1781, as Proserpina); Aeneas i Cartago [Dido och Aeneas], 1782–90 (tragédie lyrique), Kraus, 1799; Gustaf Wasa (tragédie lyrique), J. G. Naumann, 1786 (F. Berwald, 1828); Gustav Adolph och Ebba Brahe (drama with song and dance), G. J. Vogler, 1788
BERTIL H. VAN BOER

Kellogg, Clara (Louise) (*b* Sumterville [now Sumter], SC, 9 or 12 July 1842; *d* New Hartford, CT, 13 May 1916). American soprano. She studied in New York with Muzio and others, making her début as Gilda in *Rigoletto* at the Academy of Music (27 February 1861). She sang Marguerite in the New York première of Gounod's *Faust* (25 November 1863) and made her London début (2 November 1867) in the same role at Her Majesty's Theatre; later she appeared at Drury Lane and then spent four years touring the USA. In 1872 she organized a short-lived company with Pauline Lucca, and in 1873 another of her own, the English Opera Company, for which she supervised the translations, sets and rehearsals. Kellogg had immense stamina: during the 1874–5 season alone, she sang in 125 performances. After further appearances in England and the USA she retired in 1887. Her repertory encompassed over 40 roles, her favourites being Aida and Carmen. She published her memoirs in 1913 (*Memoirs of an American Prima Donna*).

*

H. P. Spofford: 'Clara Louise Kellogg', *Our Famous Women* (Hartford, CT, 1884), 359
E. E. Hipser: *American Opera and its Composers* (Philadelphia, 1934), 37–8, 46
O. Thompson: *The American Singer* (New York, 1937), 71–8
H. WILEY HITCHCOCK

Kelly, Michael (*b* Dublin, 25 Dec 1762; *d* Margate, 9 Oct 1826). Irish tenor, composer, theatre manager and music publisher. The eldest of the 14 children of Thomas Kelly (Master of the Ceremonies at Dublin Castle, and a wine merchant), Michael Kelly grew up amid the rich musical life of Dublin, and received singing lessons from various immigrant Italians, notably Passerini and Rauzzini. His piano teachers included Michael Arne. Having made his earliest operatic appearances in Piccinni's *La buona figliuola*, Dibdin's *Lionel and Clarissa* and Michael Arne's *Cymon*, Kelly left Dublin in 1779, on Rauzzini's advice, to study in Naples.

His most influential teachers were Finaroli and Aprile. Equally important, perhaps, was the patronage of Sir William Hamilton. Kelly made his way northwards, obtaining engagements in many opera houses. In Venice his fortunes took a decisive turn. Early in 1783 the Austrian Emperor Joseph II intended to build up an Italian opera company at his court and instructed Count Durazzo, his ambassador in Venice, to recruit singers, and he offered engagements to Kelly, Nancy Storace, Benucci and Mandini. The four years that Kelly spent in Vienna were to prove the climax of his musical career. Not only did he create the parts of Don Curzio and Don Basilio in *Le nozze di Figaro*, but he also met most of the great composers and singers of the day. Kelly and Storace were the only singers from the British Isles to sing in any first performance of a Mozart opera.

In his *Reminiscences* he left a vivid picture of his acquaintance with Mozart, both socially and in the opera house. Although Kelly's comments on musical life in Vienna are often superficial, he saw humanity in the round with keen observation and humorous detachment. It is these qualities which make the book so attractive: its first volume, particularly, is a valuable source of information about the music and manners of the time. Even if written with the aid of a rough diary or notes, the *Reminiscences*, which run to some 170 000 words, are a remarkable testimony to Kelly's memory. They were ghosted, not long before Kelly's death, by Theodore Hook, who was described by his great-great-nephew, the English music critic Martin Cooper (1910–86), as 'a man of the theatre, professional writer, almost a professional wag and something of a crook'. Perhaps some of Hook's character colours Kelly's narrative.

In February 1787, with the Storaces and Attwood, Kelly left Vienna for London, visiting Mozart's father in Salzburg en route. Kelly quickly established himself, and his services as a singer were in continual demand throughout the British Isles during the next 30 years. He won greater approval for his technique than for the quality of his voice. In his *Memoirs of the Life of John Philip Kemble* (1825), James Boaden wrote:

His voice had amazing power and steadiness, his compass was extraordinary. In vigorous passages he never cheated the ear with the feeble wailings of falsetto, but sprung upon the ascending fifth with a sustaining energy that often electrified an audience.

Lord Mount Edgcumbe, however, no mean judge, expressed a less favourable view in his *Musical Reminiscences* (1825):

Though he was a good musician and not a bad singer, having been long in Italy, yet he had retained, or regained, so much of the English vulgarity of manner that he was never greatly liked at this theatre [Drury Lane].

As a composer, Kelly claimed to have written over 60 theatre pieces between 1797 and 1821. But for many of these he contributed just a few songs; at other times he wrote in collaboration. He commanded a limited but prolific vein of melodic invention and seems to have relied on others for harmony and orchestration. In 1801, Thomas Moore wrote: 'Poor Mick is rather an imposer than a composer. He cannot mark the time in writing three bars of music: his understrappers, however, do all that for him'. Kelly himself says (i, 133–4) that the German bandmaster R. T. Eley provided the wind accompaniment for the march in *Blue Beard*. He caught the current taste so well that his music became widely popular: it was extensively pirated in America, resulting in some 200 separate issues. *Blue Beard* remained in the repertory for 26 years. In 1801 Kelly set up as a publisher, in premises so close to the King's Theatre that he could offer patrons a private entrance through the shop, directly on to the stage. His publications included operas in vocal score and a considerable number of single songs. But the business seems to have needed more time than he could spare and was declared bankrupt in 1811. Kelly also engaged in the wine trade which, added to the suspicion that some of his compositions came from abroad, induced Sheridan to suggest that his shop-sign should read 'Michael Kelly, composer of wines and importer of music'.

Much of Kelly's time and energy was devoted to the King's Theatre in the Haymarket; he became its stage manager in 1793 and served it with little intermission for nearly 31 years. Thus as singer, publisher and manager, he lived in the heart of London's musical life. He never married, though he lived with ANNA MARIA CROUCH for some years in what seems to have been a platonic relationship. Kelly was buried in the churchyard of St Paul's, Covent Garden. His niece, Frances Maria Kelly (1790–1882), was an actress and singer of considerable distinction.

The Garrick Club possesses two portraits of Kelly, one by De Wild, showing him in costume as Cymon, the other a half-length by James Lonsdale. The frontispiece to the *Reminiscences* was engraved by H. Meyer from a drawing by A. Wivell, which cannot now be traced. The Garrick Club also has two letters in Kelly's autograph.

Blue Beard (grand dramatic romance, 2, G. Colman (ii)), London, Drury Lane, 16 Jan 1798, vs (London, 1798), collab. R. T. Eley and others

The Captive of Spielberg [Spilberg] (musical drama, 2, P. Hoare), London, Drury Lane, 14 Nov 1798, selections (London, 1798), collab. J. L. Dussek

The Wood Demon [One o'clock, or The Knight and the Wood Daemon] (grand dramatic romance, 3, M. G. Lewis), London, Drury Lane, 1 April 1807, song (1807), rev. M. P. King, 1811

Contribs to: False Appearances, 1789; Fashionable Friends, 1789; A Friend in Need, 1797; The Last of the Family, 1797; The Chimney Corner, 1797; The Castle Spectre, 1797; The Outlaws, 1798; Aurelio and Miranda, 1798; Feudal Times, 1799; Pizarro, 1799; Of Age To-morrow, 1800; De Montfort, 1800; The Indians, 1800; Deaf and Dumb, 1801; Adelmorn the Outlaw, 1801; The Gipsey Prince, 1801; Urania, 1802; Algonah, 1802; A House to be Sold, 1802; The Hero of the North, 1803; The Marriage Promise, 1803; Love Laughs at Locksmiths, 1803; Cinderella, or The Little Glass Slipper, 1804; The Counterfeit, 1804; The Hunter of the Alps, 1804; The Gay Deceivers, 1804; The Blind Bargain, 1804; The Land We Live In, 1804; The Honey Moon, 1805; A Prior Claim, 1805; Youth, Love and Folly, 1805; We Fly by Night, 1806; The Forty Thieves, 1806; Adrian and Orilla, 1806; The Young Hussar, 1807; Town and Country, 1807; Adelgitha, 1807; Time's a Tell-tale, 1807; The House of Morville, 1807; The Jew of Mogadore, 1808; The Africans, 1808; Vernoni, 1808; The Foundling of the Forest, 1809; The Jubilee, 1809; Gustavus Vasa, 1810; The Peasant Boy, 1811; The Royal Oak, 1811; The Absent Apothecary, 1813; The Russians, 1813; Polly, or The Sequel to Beggar's Opera, 1813; The Illusion, 1813; Harlequin Harper, 1813; Remorse, 1814; The Unknown Guest,

1815; The Conquest of Taranto, 1817; The Bride of Abydos, 1818; Abudah, 1819; The Lady and the Devil, 1820

DNB (L. M. Middleton)
Reminiscences of Michael Kelly, of the King's Theatre, and Theatre Royal, Drury Lane (London, 1826, 2/1826/R1968 with introduction by A. H. King); ed. R. Fiske (London, 1975)
S. M. Ellis: *The Life of Michael Kelly, Musician, Actor and Bon Viveur* (London, 1930)   ALEC HYATT KING

Kelterborn, Rudolf (*b* Basle, 3 Sept 1931). Swiss composer. He was a pupil of Walther Müller von Kulm at the Basle Musikakademie, and later took private lessons with Burkhard and worked as a conductor. In 1953 he attended Blacher's composition course in Salzburg, and in 1955 studied with Fortner and Bialas in Detmold. He also studied with the conductor Igor Markevich. He has taught at the Basle Musikakademie (1955–60), the Nordwestdeutsche Musikakademie in Detmold (1960–68) and the Zürich Musikhochschule (1968–75, 1980–83). He was also professor of composition at the Karlsruhe Musikhochschule (1980–83) and head of the music division of the Swiss-German Broadcasting Corporation (1974–80). He edited the *Schweizerische Musikzeitung* (1969–75). In 1983 he became director of the Basle Musikakademie. His writings include an article 'Funktion und Wirkung des zeitgenössischen Musiktheaters' (*Melos*, xli, 1974, pp.21–3) and two books, *Zum Beispiel Mozart: ein Beitrag zur musikalischen Analyse* (Kassel, 1980) and *Musik im Brennpunkt* (Kassel, 1988).

Kelterborn was strongly influenced by the avant garde of the 1950s and 60s, and established himself initially as a composer of orchestral music. It was not until the 1970s and 80s that he became widely known as an opera composer. Serialism plays a central role in his first two operas, *Die Errettung Thebens* (1963) and *Kaiser Jovian* (1967), and also features prominently in his later works, but in a more personal style. *Ein Engel kommt nach Babylon* (1977) shows his command of structure and an individual use of 12-note rows. His Chekhov opera *Der Kirschgarten* (1984) places greater emphasis on tone colour and vocal melody. *Julia* (1991), a chamber opera written for the 700th anniversary of Switzerland, is a fast-moving collage based on the Romeo and Juliet story, drawing on Shakespeare's drama, Gottfried Keller's novella and the fate of a contemporary Julia in the Israeli-occupied territories, with Romeo a Palestinian and Julia an Israeli. All his stage works are well-crafted, but dry in their musical effect.

Die Errettung Thebens (3, Kelterborn), Zürich, Theaterhaus, 23 June 1963
Kaiser Jovian (4, H. Meier), Karlsruhe, 4 March 1967
Ein Engel kommt nach Babylon (3, F. Dürrenmatt), Zürich, Opernhaus, 5 June 1977
Die schwarze Spinne (television op, H. Schneider), Zürich, 1984
Ophelia (5 scenes, Meier, after W. Shakespeare), Schwetzingen, Schlosstheater, 2 May 1984
Der Kirschgarten (4, Kelterborn, after A. Chekhov), Zürich, Opernhaus, 4 Dec 1984
Julia (chamber op, Kelterborn and D. Freeman, after Shakespeare and G. Keller), Zürich, Opernhaus, 18 April 1991

D. Larese: *Rudolf Kelterborn* (Amriswil, 1970)
W.-E. von Lewinski: 'Rudolf Kelterborn: ein Porträt', *Musica*, xxiv (1970), 121
K. von Fischer: 'Rudolf Kelterborn', *Swiss Composers in the 20th Century*, ed. A. Briner (Zürich, 1990), 52–6   ANDREW CLARK

Kemble, Adelaide (*b* London, 1814; *d* Warsash, Hants., 4 Aug 1879). English soprano. After appearances in concerts she studied in Paris, Germany and with Pasta in Italy, making a successful début in 1838 as Norma at La Fenice. In 1840 she sang at Trieste, Milan, Padua, Bologna and Mantua with increasing reputation. She returned to England in 1841 and on 2 November appeared at Covent Garden in an English version of *Norma* in which both her singing and her acting were acclaimed. The following year she sang there in *Le nozze di Figaro*, *La sonnambula*, *Semiramide* and *Il matrimonio segreto*. She retired on marrying in 1843.

H. F. Chorley: *Thirty Years' Musical Recollections* (London, 1862), i, 112, 213

Kemp [Mikley-Kemp], **Barbara** (*b* Cochem, 12 Dec 1881; *d* Berlin, 17 April 1959). German soprano and director. She studied at the Strasbourg Conservatory (1902–5), becoming an 'apprentice' at the Strasbourg Opera and making her début in 1903 as an offstage priestess in *Aida*. She was engaged at Rostock (1906–8), Breslau (1908–13), and, from 1913, at the Berlin Hofoper (later Staatsoper), remaining a member of the ensemble until 1932. In 1922 she made her Metropolitan début in the title role of Max von Schillings's *Mona Lisa*. The next year she married the composer and sang again at the Metropolitan, as Elsa, Isolde – a role in which she was admired for her stage presence but considered deficient in range and power – and Kundry. She sang Senta at Bayreuth in 1914 (as Barbara Mikley-Kemp) and Kundry from 1924 to 1927. In 1938–9 she directed Von Schillings's *Ingwelde* and *Mona Lisa* in Berlin.

O. Bie: *Barbara Kemp* (Berlin, 1921)   HAROLD ROSENTHAL/R

Kempe, Rudolf (*b* Niederpoyritz, Saxony, 14 June 1910; *d* Zürich, 12 May 1976). German conductor. He studied at the Dresden Musikhochschule and made his conducting début at the Leipzig Opera in 1935 with Lortzing's *Der Wildschütz*, as a result of which he joined the opera staff as a répétiteur. From 1942 he was employed at the Chemnitz Opera, first as répétiteur then as conductor, and finally as music director, 1946–8. After a year at the Weimar Opera he went as general music director to Dresden (1949–52), and to the Staatsoper in Munich (1952–4) in succession to Georg Solti. Kempe's international recognition began when he opened the 1951–2 season at the Vienna Staatsoper. He made his British début conducting *Arabella* during a guest season by the Bavarian company at Covent Garden in September 1953, and first conducted the Covent Garden company in *Salome* the next month. He never accepted their pressing invitation to a resident appointment but remained a frequent guest conductor until 1974. Kempe made his Metropolitan Opera début in 1954 and his Bayreuth début in 1960. His performances were marked by clarity of rhythm and phrasing allied to restraint and subtlety of expression, and these qualities, along with his broad command of pacing and texture, led to his being regarded as an outstanding interpreter of Wagner, the *Ring* and *Parsifal* in particular. He recorded, most notably, *Lohengrin*, *Die Meistersinger von Nürnberg* and *Ariadne auf Naxos*. He was married to the soprano Elisabeth Lindermeier.

H. D. Rosenthal: 'Rudolf Kempe', *Opera*, x (1959), 713–18
C. Kempe-Öttinger: *Rudolf Kempe: Bildnis eines Lebens* (Munich, 1977)   NOËL GOODWIN

Kennedy, Mrs. *See* FARRELL, MARGARET.

Kennedy, (George) Michael (Sinclair) (*b* Chorlton-cum-Hardy, Manchester, 19 Feb 1926). English writer on music. He joined the Manchester staff of the *Daily Telegraph* in 1941 and from 1950 to 1989 served on the music staff (as well as a period as northern editor), then becoming chief critic of the *Sunday Telegraph*. A percipient and prolific writer, he has specialized in English music, with sensitive, carefully researched biographies of Vaughan Williams (1964), Elgar (1968) and Britten (1980); his sympathy for the music of the early 20th century has also drawn from him valuable and balanced studies of Mahler (1974) and Richard Strauss (1976). Kennedy has also published extensively on the musical history of Manchester and musicians active there and is editor of the *Concise Oxford Dictionary of Music* (1980, rev. 1985). He has done much to foster musical and operatic activity in the north of England.

Kennedy, Roderick (*b* Birmingham, 7 May 1951). English bass. He studied in London with Otakar Kraus and was engaged in 1978 at Covent Garden, where his roles have included Zuniga, Angelotti, Ashby (*La fanciulla del West*), Cuno, Lieutenant Ratcliffe, Dr Grenvil and Fasolt. He has also sung at Glyndebourne, Wexford and Aldeburgh; with the WNO, the ENO and Scottish Opera; and in San Francisco, Paris, Florence, Chicago, Berlin, Barcelona and Vienna. The possessor of a resonant voice and a fine stage presence, he includes in his repertory Pogner, the Doctor (*Wozzeck*), the Animal Tamer and the Athlete (*Lulu*), Swallow (*Peter Grimes*), Bottom, Gualtiero (Puccini's *Edgar*), Don Fernando, Rocco, Sparafucile, Seneca, Phanuel (*Hérodiade*), Arkel and Konchak. ELIZABETH FORBES

Kennedy Center. Complex of performing halls, including an Opera House, opened in WASHINGTON, DC, in 1971; properly called the John F. Kennedy Center for the Performing Arts, it is the home of Washington Opera.

Kenny, Sean (*b* Tipperary, 23 Dec 1932; *d* London, 11 June 1973). Irish designer. He trained as an architect in Dublin and for two years with Frank Lloyd Wright in the USA before settling in London, where he worked as an architect, interior decorator and, from 1960, as a maverick, inspirational designer for the stage. In the next ten years he designed 32 major London productions (and, among other enterprises, an all-glass underwater restaurant in Nassau, a 13-platform set, controlled by only two technicians, for a revue at Las Vegas in 1962, and the 'Gyroton' thrill-ride through the 1967 Montreal Expo). Kenny sought to revolutionize stage design, arguing that theatres should be built 'from the inside out', that settings were essentially pieces of moving architecture (the single-unit timber set for the musical *Oliver!*, 1960), that three-dimensional kinetic forms should be used to fill theatrical space (*Der fliegende Holländer*, 1966, Covent Garden), that colour should be achieved by light (and gelatins) reflected on natural, unpainted materials (*King Priam*, 1962, Coventry). His theories, especially on changing stage-levels and spaces controlled by simplified machinery, are still being absorbed in the development of contemporary stage design.

For illustration *see* KING PRIAM.

ES (J. Kaufman)
Obituary, *The Times* (12 June 1973) MARINA HENDERSON

Kenny, Yvonne (*b* Sydney, 25 Nov 1950). Australian soprano. She studied in Sydney and Milan and made her début in 1975 at the Queen Elizabeth Hall, London, in the title role of Donizetti's *Rosmonda d'Inghilterra*. After her Covent Garden début in the première of Henze's *We Come to the River* (1976), she sang many roles there, including Ilia, Pamina, Oscar, Susanna, Aennchen, Sophie (*Der Rosenkavalier* and *Werther*), Helena (*A Midsummer Night's Dream*), Semele, Micaëla, Adina and in 1991 Aspasia (*Mitridate, rè di Ponto*). She has also worked with Australian Opera and Scottish Opera and has sung at Vienna, Zürich, Glyndebourne, Schwetzingen, Aix-en-Provence, Paris and La Scala and at Lyons, where she created the title role of Gavin Bryars's *Medea* (1984). Her repertory includes Gilda, Mélisande, Massenet's Manon, Donna Elvira, Fiordiligi and Handel's Alcina. A stylish singer, she has a full, rich and flexible voice with an excellent coloratura technique. ELIZABETH FORBES

Kent Opera. English company active in the period 1969–89. It was founded by Norman Platt (artistic director) and Roger Norrington (musical director until 1984), to bring professional opera to centres outside London, and it initiated the idea of regionally based opera companies in England under the auspices of the Arts Council of Great Britain. It performed regularly in Kent (where its principal venues were Tunbridge Wells and Canterbury), as well as on tour throughout southern England and at festivals and engagements abroad. Productions included well-known operas by Verdi, Mozart, Sullivan and Britten; less familiar works by Handel (*Atalanta*, 1970; *Agrippina*, 1982), Telemann (*Der geduldige Socrates*, as *The Patience of Socrates*, 1974) and Monteverdi (*L'incoronazione di Poppea*, 1969, 1974, 1975; *Orfeo*, 1976); Tippett's *King Priam* (1984); commissioned works (Alan Ridout's *The Pardoner's Tale* and *Angelo*, 1971; Judith Weir's *A Night at the Chinese Opera*, 1987); and a number of new translations into English.

The company received critical acclaim for the clarity and imagination of its productions by Platt, Jonathan Miller, Adrian Slack and Nicholas Hytner, for the specialist interpretation which Roger Norrington brought to its performances, for its authentic orchestral forces and for its singers, carefully chosen from among both established and little-known names. In December 1989 the Arts Council, in a controversial decision, withdrew its funding and the company was forced to close. CAROLINE BENT

Kentucky Opera. American company based in LOUISVILLE.

Ķepītis, Jānis (*b* Trikata, Valka district, 2 Jan 1908; *d* Riga, 10 Aug 1989). Latvian composer. He graduated from the Latvian State Conservatory in Riga, where his teachers included Jānis Mediņš, and then continued piano studies in Paris and Wiesbaden. He was a member of the Jāzeps Vītols trio, 1934–44, and from 1945 taught at the Latvian State Conservatory. His compositions include two operas. The first is a three-act lyric comedy, *Minhauzena precības* ('Münchhausen's Wedding', 1945, after M. Zīverts), first performed at

Liepāja in 1960. *Indulis un Ārija* (1969, after Rainis) is a psychological drama which reflects the conflict between love and patriotic duty during the medieval wars. The music of both operas reflects naive, epigonic romanticism.   JĒKABS VĪTOLIŅŠ, ARNOLDS KĻOTIŅŠ

Kercel. See KERZELLI.

Kerem. Opera in three acts by AHMED ADNAN SAYGUN to a libretto by Selahattin Batu after an old Turkish legend; Ankara, State Opera, 22 March 1953.

Set in Anatolia, the story concerns Kerem (tenor), the son of the Khan (bass), who falls in love with Asli (soprano), the daughter of the Vizier (bass). Their love is thwarted by the Khan because the Vizier has betrayed his country; on being forbidden to marry Asli, Kerem picks up his instrument and leaves home. One day he dreams that he meets an old man (bass) who offers him a drink. Pouring it on the ground, Kerem has a vision of Asli. A caravan train then appears, and he is told that his suffering will soon end. He returns home to take part in a minstrel contest that includes a riddle set by the Khan. He relates how his mother and the Vizier's wife met an old man who cut an apple in half, offering it to each of the women and prophesying that their children would marry. The Khan declares the riddle solved and the Vizier, now forgiven, leaps up to embrace Kerem, who slowly walks away towards the sound of Asli's call.

FARUK YENER

Kerkado, Mlle Le Sénéchal de (*b* c1786; *d* 1805 or later). French composer. She was one of a small group of women composers who wrote opera in France. The archives of the Opéra-Comique in 1805 record that she was then 19 years of age. Her one-act *comédie mêlée d'ariettes, La méprise volontaire, ou La double leçon*, was first given on 24 June 1805 at the Opéra-Comique (not on 5 June as stated on the libretto issued in 1807, when the work was revived on 2 January); the libretto was by Alexandre Duval.   DAVID CHARLTON

Kerker, Gustave A(dolphe) (*b* Herford, Germany, 28 Feb 1857; *d* New York, 29 June 1923). American composer. He began studying the cello at the age of seven. In 1867 his family emigrated to the USA and settled in Louisville, where he played the cello and directed several theatre orchestras. In 1879 he wrote his first stage work, *The Cadets*, which was performed on a four-month tour of the South by the Herman Grau English Opera Company. He went to New York in 1880 as conductor of the H. V. B. Mann Opera Company, then transferred to the Thalia Theatre (1883) and the Bijou Opera House (1884); finally, the producer E. E. Rice arranged for him to become music director of the Casino Theatre.

Kerker's first Broadway operetta was *The Pearl of Pekin* (1888), after Lecocq, and by 1912 he had written at least 23 comic operas, musical comedies or revues, as well as dances, marches and songs for other shows. In 1890 he adapted a French operetta for *Castles in the Air*. *The Belle of New York* (1897) had only a modest run in New York but became Kerker's most popular work and the one by which he is best remembered, with almost 700 performances in London and many more on tours; several of its melodies are inspired by marches or lively dances, and the vocal lines have an unusually restless character with dotted rhythms and repeated notes.

In his later works Kerker incorporated more of the Tin Pan Alley style of lyrical, graceful waltz songs and sentimental ballads. On the whole, his scores convey the gaiety and giddiness of New York's young, fashionable and European-orientated society at the turn of the century.

all operettas; dates are of first New York performance, Casino Theatre unless otherwise stated

The Cadets, 1879; The Pearl of Pekin (C. A. Byrne, after A. C. Lecocq: La fleur de thé), Bijou, 1888; Castles in the Air (Byrne, after J. Offenbach: Les bavards), Broadway, 5 May 1890; Prince Kam, or A Trip to Venus (Byrne and L. Harrison), 29 Jan 1894; Kismet (R. F. Carroll), Herald Square, 8 Dec 1895; The Lady Slavey (H. Morton), 3 Feb 1896; An American Beauty (Morton), 28 Dec 1896; The Whirl of the Town (Morton), 25 May 1897; The Belle of New York (Morton), 28 Sept 1897; The Telephone Girl (Morton), 27 Dec 1897

The Girl from up There (Morton), Herald Square, 7 Jan 1901; A Chinese Honeymoon (G. Dance), 2 June 1902; The Billionaire (H. B. Smith), Daly's, 29 Dec 1902; The Blonde in Black (Smith), Knickerbocker, 8 June 1903; Winsome Winnie (F. Ranken), 1 Dec 1903; The Social Whirl (J. W. Herbert), 7 April 1906; The Tourists (R. H. Burnside), Daly's, 25 Aug 1906; The White Hen, or The Girl from Vienna (P. West), 16 Feb 1907; Fascinating Flora (Burnside, Herbert), 20 May 1907; The Lady from Lane's (G. Broadhurst), Lyric, 19 Aug 1907; Two Little Brides (A. Anderson and H. Atteridge), 23 April 1912

*

J. W. McSpadden: *Light Opera and Musical Comedy* (New York, 1936)
G. Hughes: *Composers of Operetta* (New York, 1962)
D. Ewen: *New Complete Book of the American Musical Theater* (New York, 1970)
G. Bordman: *The American Musical Theatre* (New York, 1978)

DEANE L. ROOT/R

Kerkyra (Gk.). CORFU.

Kerll, Johann Caspar (*b* Adorf, Saxony, 9 April 1627; *d* Munich, 13 Feb 1693). German composer. He was in the service of Archduke Leopold Wilhelm in Vienna and studied with the Hofkapellmeister Giovanni Valentini before 1647, the year in which the archduke left for his new residence in Brussels. Kerll apparently followed him in 1648 but was sent to Rome to study composition with Carissimi in the same year. In 1651 and 1652 he was in Vienna to assist at the preparations and performance of the opera *La gara* (8 January 1652; composer unknown); he then returned to Brussels. In 1656 he was appointed Kapellmeister to the Elector Ferdinand Maria of Bavaria in Munich; in 1657 his first opera, *Oronte*, was produced there. Up to 1673 he provided the music for several *drammi musicali*; only three librettos list him as the composer, but some others of this period were probably also set by him. In 1673 Kerll left Munich because of quarrels with the Italian musicians there. He returned to Vienna where from 1674 to 1677 he was organist at St Stephen's Cathedral and, without appointment, at the imperial court. From 1677 he took on the duties of court organist, but from 1683 until his death he was mostly in Munich, where he settled in 1688.

Kerll's operas are lost; his operatic style can be traced only in the incidental music for the school play *Pia et fortis mulier in S. Natalia S. Adriani martyris coniuge expressa* (Vienna, 24 February 1677; *A-Wn, D-Mbs*), the first Viennese Jesuit drama with extant music. There are instrumental ritornellos and accompaniments, including a sleep aria accompanied by three violas, the only one with da capo design. A quartet for four basses displays interesting timbre and tone painting.

first performed at the Munich Hofoper

Oronte (drama musicale, 3, G. J. Alcaini), 13 Feb 1657, lib. *GB-Lbl*

Erinto (drama regio musicale, 3, P. P. Bissari), 1661, lib. *Lbl*

Le pretensioni del sole (introduttione musicale, 1, D. Gisberti), 6 Nov 1667

Doubtful: Applausi festivi (barriera, 1, G. B. Maccioni), 28 Aug 1658; Ardelia (drama musicale, 3, Maccioni), 1660, lib. *I-Vgc*; Fedra incoronata (drama regio musicale, 3, Bissari), 24 Sept 1662, lib. *D-W*; Antiopa giustificata (drama guerriero, 1, Bissari), 26 Sept 1662, lib. *W*; L'amor della patria superiore ad ogni altro (drama musicale, 3, F. Sbarra), 1665, lib. *GB-Lbl*; Atalanta (attione dramatica, R. Pallavicino), 30 Jan 1667, lib. *B-Bc*; I colori geniali (torniamento di luce, 1, Gisberti), 6 Nov 1669, lib. *GB-Lbl*; Amor tiranno, overo Regnero innamorato (poesia dramatica-comica-nuova rappresentata in musica, Gisberti), 31 Oct 1672, lib. *Lbl*

*

Court documents: Hofquartierresolutionen 1679, Hofquartierbuch 1688 (Vienna, Hofkammerarchiv)

F. M. Rudhart: *Geschichte der Oper am Hofe zu München* (Freising, 1865)

W. Kramer: *Die Musik im Wiener Jesuitendrama von 1677–1771* (diss., U. of Vienna, 1961)

R. Schaal: *Quellen zu Johann Kaspar Kerll* (Vienna, 1962)

H. Bolongaro-Crevenna: *L'Arpa festante: die Münchner Oper 1651–1825* (Munich, 1963)

H. Knaus: *Beiträge zur Geschichte der Hofmusikkapelle des Erzherzogs Leopold Wilhelm* (Vienna, 1966), 158, 159

——: *Die Musiker im Archivbestand des kaiserlichen Obersthofmeisteramtes (1637–1705)*, ii (Vienna, 1968)

HERBERT SEIFERT

Kerman, Joseph (Wilfred) (*b* London, 3 April 1924). American scholar and critic. He studied at New York University and at Princeton (PhD 1950). He has been on the faculty of the University of California at Berkeley since 1951, except for a brief period (1971–4) when he was Heather Professor of Music at Oxford University. He was a founder-editor of the journal *19th Century Music* (1977–89). Kerman's forceful critical voice and pliant prose style have given new life to a discipline that has traditionally emphasized 'scientific' methods. His polemic views on that discipline were expressed in *Contemplating Music* (Cambridge, MA, 1985; as *Musicology*, London, 1985). His remarkable and provocative first book, *Opera as Drama* (New York, 1956, 2/1989), secured his position as one of the most trenchant voices in operatic criticism.   PHILIP BRETT

Kern, Adele (*b* Munich, 25 Nov 1901; *d* Munich, 6 May 1980). German soprano. She studied in Munich, making her début there in 1924 as Olympia in *Les contes d'Hoffmann*. She was a member of the famous Clemens Krauss ensembles, first in Frankfurt, later in Vienna and finally in Munich from 1937 to 1943, and again briefly after World War II. She appeared frequently at Salzburg between 1927 and 1935, as Susanna, Despina, Marzelline and Sophie; she also sang at the Teatro Colón (1928) and Covent Garden (1931, 1934). She possessed a light, high, silvery voice of great charm: her Zerbinetta was a highlight of the Munich summer festivals in the late 1930s. She retired in 1947.   HAROLD ROSENTHAL/R

Kern, Jerome (David) (*b* New York, 27 Jan 1885; *d* New York, 11 Nov 1945). American composer. He learnt the piano from his mother, and then went to the New York College of Music in 1902 to study harmony, theory and the piano. He continued his studies of music theory and composition in Heidelberg in 1903, returning via London to New York, where in 1904 he began working as a song-plugger (notably for T. B. Harms) and as a rehearsal pianist in Broadway theatres. He also began providing additional songs for American adaptations of European musical shows, his first major success being with 'How'd you like to spoon with me?' for Ivan Caryll's *The Earl and the Girl* (1905). His success in this line was furthered by visits to London, where in 1906 several songs were performed, notably two with words by P. G. Wodehouse for Herbert E. Haines's musical play *The Beauty of Bath*. His London visits enabled him to see European works before their American productions, for which he was commissioned by the American impresario Charles Frohman to compose suitable songs. By World War I over 100 of Kern's songs had been interpolated into about 30 shows, among which the most noteworthy was 'They didn't believe me', for the 1914 New York version of the British musical *The Girl from Utah* by Paul Rubens and Sidney Jones. This song in particular set the pattern for the American 20th-century popular song that set everyday speech in a natural way, and it greatly inspired Gershwin and others.

Meanwhile the first shows entirely of Kern's composition achieved little success. However, between 1915 and 1918, four musicals were performed at the Princess Theatre in New York that provided sharp contrasts with the large-scale, Ruritanian imports then in vogue. The theatre seated only about 300 and accommodated an orchestra of about 12, necessitating a small cast, limited sets and an intimate style of production. With the librettist Guy Bolton, Kern took Rubens's 1905 London musical *Mr Popple (of Ippleton)*, already a show in which songs and story were more closely integrated than in the currently popular operettas, and adapted it with new music as *Nobody Home* (1915). It was followed by *Very Good Eddie* (1915), Kern's first internationally produced show, and *Oh Boy!* (1917). Though *Oh Lady! Lady!!* (1918) was not so popular, it remains significant as the show for which the song 'Bill' was originally written.

Thereafter Kern returned to more traditional song-and-dance musical comedies, which introduced various songs that have become classics, such as 'Look for the silver lining' from *Sally* (1920) and 'Who?' from *Sunny* (1925). However, in 1927 came his most important work, *Show Boat*, a musical play with words by Oscar Hammerstein II, perhaps the most lastingly successful and influential Broadway musical play ever written. At least six songs have become standard favourites, including 'Ol' man river', 'Can't help lovin' dat man' and 'Why do I love you?'. More important was the degree to which it adapted existing conventions of music theatre to a new style of show that used an American subject and integrated music, speech, drama and characterization to a hitherto unprecedented degree. Kern composed further works with parts for operatic voices, notably *The Cat and the Fiddle* (1931) and *Music in the Air* (1932), while others were more notable for developing the art of popular song, as in *Roberta* (1933), with 'Smoke gets in your eyes', and his final stage work, *Very Warm for May* (1939), with 'All the things you are'. In addition Kern turned to composition for Hollywood film musicals such as *Swing Time* and *Cover Girl*, producing for them several lastingly popular songs.

It is for such songs that Kern's name remains celebrated above all, though the importance of *Show Boat* for the American music theatre has never been questioned. It was the first musical to enter an opera company's repertory (New York City Opera, 1954), and the rediscovery of the original performing material, with orchestrations by Robert Russell Bennett (Kern's regular orchestrator from 1923), led to a large-scale recording in 1987 and widespread opera-house productions. This rediscovery served to highlight all the more forcibly the importance of Kern's work in providing a bridge between the old European tradition of opera and operetta and that of the modern American music theatre.

musicals unless otherwise stated; librettists indicated as (book author; lyricist)

Mr Wix of Wickham (2, H. Darnley; J. H. Wagner), New Haven, Hyperion, 12 Sept 1904; New York, Bijou, 19 Sept 1904; collab. others

La Belle Paree (2, E. Smith; E. Maddern), New York, Winter Garden, 20 March 1911, collab. others

The Red Petticoat [Look Who's Here] (3, R. J. Young; P. West), Philadelphia, Adelphi, 24 Oct 1912; New York, Daly's, 13 Nov 1912

Oh, I Say! (3, S. Blow and D. Hoare, after Keroul and Barré; H. B. Smith), Albany, 27 Sept 1913; New York, Casino, 30 Oct 1913

Ninety in the Shade (2, G. Bolton), Syracuse, Empire, 31 Dec 1914; New York, Knickerbocker, 25 Jan 1915

Nobody Home (2, Bolton, after P. Rubens), New York, Princess, 20 April 1915, collab. others

Very Good Eddie (2, P. Bartholomae and Bolton; S. Green), Schenectady, 9 Nov 1915; New York, Princess, 23 Dec 1915

Love o' Mike [Girls Will Be Girls] (2, T. Sidney; H. B. Smith), Philadelphia, Lyric, 20 Nov 1916; New York, Shubert, 15 Jan 1917

Have a Heart (2, Bolton and P. G. Wodehouse), Atlantic City, Apollo, 28 Dec 1916; New York, Liberty, 11 Jan 1917

Oh Boy! (2, Bolton; Wodehouse), Schenectady, Van Curler Opera House, 13 Jan 1917; New York, Princess, 19 Feb 1917

Head over Heels [Houp-La] (E. A. Woolf, after N. Bartley), Hartford, Parsons', 25 June 1917; New York, George M. Cohan, 29 Aug 1918

Leave It To Jane (2, Bolton, after G. Ade: *The College Widow*; Wodehouse), Atlantic City, Apollo, 30 July 1917; New York, Longacre, 28 Aug 1917

Miss 1917 (revue, 2, Bolton; Wodehouse), New York, Century, 5 Nov 1917, collab. V. Herbert

Toot, Toot! (2, Woolf, after R. Hughes: *Excuse Me*; B. Braley), Wilmington, Playhouse, 25 Dec 1917; New York, George M. Cohan, 11 March 1918

Oh Lady! Lady!! (2, Bolton; Wodehouse), Albany, Harmanus Bleecker Hall, 7 Jan 1918; New York, Princess, 1 Feb 1918

Rock-a-bye Baby (3, Woolf, after M. Mayo: *Baby Mine*; H. Reynolds), New Haven, Shubert, 8 April 1918; New York, Astor, 22 May 1918

She's a Good Fellow [A New Girl] (3, A. Caldwell), Washington, National, 6 April 1919; New York, Globe, 5 May 1919

Zip Goes a Million (Bolton, after G. B. McCutcheon: *Brewster's Millions*; B. De Sylva), Worcester, MA, 8 Dec 1919

The Night Boat (2, Caldwell, after A. Bisson), Baltimore, Academy of Music, 29 Dec 1919; New York, Liberty, 2 Feb 1920

Hitchy Koo, 1920 (revue, 2, G. MacDonough and Caldwell), Boston, Colonial, 6 Sept 1920; New York, New Amsterdam, 19 Oct 1920

Sally (3, Bolton; C. Grey), Baltimore, Academy of Music, 29 Nov 1920; New York, New Amsterdam, 21 Dec 1920, ballet music by Herbert

Good Morning, Dearie (2, Caldwell), Atlantic City, Apollo, 12 Oct 1921; New York, Globe, 1 Nov 1921

The Cabaret Girl (3, G. Grossmith and Wodehouse), London, Winter Garden, 19 Sept 1922

The Bunch and Judy (2, Caldwell and H. Ford; Caldwell), Philadelphia, Garrick, 6 Nov 1922; New York, Globe, 28 Nov 1922

The Beauty Prize (3, Grossmith and Wodehouse), London, Winter Garden, 5 Sept 1923

Stepping Stones (2, Caldwell and R. H. Burnside), New Haven, Shubert, 16 Oct 1923; New York, Globe, 6 Nov 1923

Sitting Pretty (2, Bolton; Wodehouse), Detroit, Shubert, 23 March 1924; New York, Fulton, 8 April 1924

Dear Sir (2, E. Selwyn; H. Dietz), Philadelphia, Forrest, 3 Sept 1924; New York, Times Square, 23 Sept 1924

Sunny (2, O. Harbach and O. Hammerstein II), Philadelphia, Forrest, 9 Sept 1925; New York, New Amsterdam, 22 Sept 1925

The City Chap (2, J. Montgomery, after W. Smith: *The Fortune Hunter*; Caldwell), Philadelphia, Garrick, 28 Sept 1925; New York, Liberty, 26 Oct 1925

Criss Cross (2, Caldwell and Harbach), New Haven, Shubert, 21 Sept 1926; New York, Globe, 12 Oct 1926

Lucky (2, Harbach; B. Kalmar), Philadelphia, Garrick, 8 March 1927; New York, New Amsterdam, 22 March 1927, collab. H. Ruby

Show Boat (2, Hammerstein, after E. Ferber), Washington, National, 15 Nov 1927; New York, Ziegfeld, 27 Dec 1927

Blue Eyes (2, Bolton and G. John), Southsea, King's, 9 April 1928; London, Piccadilly, 27 April 1928

Sweet Adeline (2, Hammerstein), Atlantic City, Apollo, 19 Aug 1929; New York, Hammerstein's, 3 Sept 1929

The Cat and the Fiddle (2, Harbach), Philadelphia, Garrick, 23 Sept 1931; New York, Globe, 15 Oct 1931

Music in the Air (2, Hammerstein), Philadelphia, Garrick, 17 Oct 1932; New York, Alvin, 8 Nov 1932

Roberta [Gowns by Roberta] (Harbach, after A. D. Miller), Philadelphia, Forrest, 21 Oct 1933; New York, New Amsterdam, 18 Nov 1933

Three Sisters (3, Hammerstein), London, Drury Lane, 19 April 1934

Gentlemen Unafraid [Hayfoot, Strawfoot] (3, Hammerstein and Harbach, after E. Boykin), St Louis, Municipal Opera, 3 June 1938

Very Warm for May (2, Hammerstein), Wilmington, Playhouse, 20 Oct 1939; New York, Alvin, 17 Nov 1939

Many songs for other shows

*

GänzlBMT

P. G. Wodehouse and G. Bolton: *Bring on the Girls* (New York, 1953)

D. Ewen: *The World of Jerome Kern* (New York, 1960)

S. Green: *The World of Musical Comedy* (New York, 1960, 4/1980)

A. Wilder: *American Popular Song* (New York, 1972)

H. Wilk: *They're Playing Our Song* (New York, 1973)

M. B. Kreuger: *Show Boat: the Story of a Classic American Musical* (New York, 1977)

M. Freedland: *Jerome Kern: a Biography* (London, 1978)

G. Bordman: *Jerome Kern: his Life and Music* (New York, 1980)

A. Lamb: *Jerome Kern in Edwardian London* (Littlehampton, 1981, 2/1985)

J. P. Swain: *The Broadway Musical: a Critical and Musical Survey* (New York, 1990), 15–49

R. H. Kornick: *Recent American Opera: a Production Guide* (New York, 1991), 158–60
ANDREW LAMB

Kern, Patricia (*b* Swansea, 4 July 1927). Welsh mezzo-soprano. From 1949 to 1952 she studied with Parry Jones at the Guildhall School, London. She began her career with Opera for All (1952–5). In 1959 she joined Sadler's Wells, making her début in *Rusalka*; for ten seasons she was a valued and busy member of the company, her most notable achievement being her interpretations, at once mischievous and sensitive, of Cenerentola, Rosina, Isolier (*Le comte Ory*) and Isabella (*L'italiana in Algeri*). Her Iolanthe, Hänsel, Cherubino, Pippo (in Rossini's *La gazza ladra*), Messenger (in Monteverdi's *Orfeo*) and Josephine (in the première of Malcolm Williamson's *The Violins of St Jacques*, 1966) were also much admired. She made her Covent Garden début in 1967 as Zerlina. Her American début was at Washington, DC, in 1969 and in 1987 she sang Marcellina in Chicago. Kern possessed a smooth, creamy voice, imaginative of phrase and easily capable of negotiating Rossinian fioritura – her account of Cenerentola's final rondo was a tour de force. Her stage personality was engaging and sympathetic.

ALAN BLYTH

Kerns, Robert (*b* Detroit, 8 June 1933; *d* Vienna, 15 Feb 1989). American baritone. He studied at the University of Michigan and made his début in 1955 at Toledo, Ohio, as Sharpless. After a year with the New York City Opera, in 1960 he was engaged at Zürich. From 1963 he sang in Vienna and in 1964 made his Covent Garden début as Billy Budd. He sang at the Spoleto, Aix-en-Provence and Salzburg festivals, at the Paris Opéra, San Francisco and the Deutsche Oper, Berlin, where from 1973 he was a permanent guest. His earlier repertory included Mozart's Count Almaviva, Don Giovanni, Papageno and Guglielmo, as well as Rossini's Figaro and Donizetti's Belcore. Later he took on heavier roles, Verdi's Germont, Posa, Guy de Montfort, Ford and Falstaff, and also Yevgeny Onegin, Scarpia and Marcello. His Wagner roles included Donner, Amfortas and Wolfram. A stylish singer with a firmly placed though not very large voice, he excelled in parts such as the Barber in Strauss's *Die schweigsame Frau* where acting ability is paramount.

ELIZABETH FORBES

Kersters, Willem (*b* Antwerp, 9 Feb 1929). Belgian composer. He studied at the royal conservatories of Antwerp and Brussels, then taught until 1961, when he became programming director of Belgian Radio and Television in Hasselt. In addition he was appointed a harmony teacher at the conservatory in Antwerp in 1962. He left Belgian Radio in 1968 to become a lecturer at the conservatory in Maastricht, and in 1971 he began to teach composition at the conservatory in Antwerp. He has received several national and international awards.

Kersters has written numerous vocal and orchestral works, including an opera-oratorio, *Marianna Alcoforado* (1961), and a three-act tragicomic opera, *Gansendonk* (Kersters and B. De Nijs, after H. Conscience: *Baes Ganzendonck*; Antwerp, Opera voor Vlaanderen, 19 September 1984). *Gansendonk* tells the story of an innkeeper whose aspirations to higher social standing lead him to send his daughter to a finishing-school; she is driven to despair and eventual madness by her rejection at the hands of her own villagers and failure to be accepted by the nobility. Musically *Gansendonk* combines impressionist colour and expressionist power, with occasional recourse to 12-note techniques.

DIANA VON VOLBORTH-DANYS

Kertész, István (*b* Budapest, 28 Aug 1929; *d* nr Tel-Aviv, 16 April 1973). German conductor of Hungarian birth. He studied with Kodály and Weiner at the Franz Liszt Academy, Budapest, and took further conducting instruction from Somogyi. Having absorbed the influence of Klemperer (then at the Budapest Opera) and Walter, he became resident conductor at Györ in 1953, and two years later joined the Budapest Opera as conductor and répétiteur. He left Hungary with his family after the 1956 uprising and settled in Germany. Kertész was general music director at Augsburg (1958–63), and at Cologne from 1964 where his wide repertory included *Tristan und Isolde*, Verdi's *Stiffelio* (the German première) and *La clemenza di Tito*. He first appeared at Covent Garden (conducting Verdi's *Un ballo in maschera*) in 1966. His performances were characterized by direct, unexaggerated interpretations that may at times have lacked some extra quality of imagination or individuality. He showed a special concern for the music of Bartók, Henze, Stravinsky and Britten, introducing *Billy Budd* to Germany. His gramophone records include the first western European recordings of the full *Háry János* and *Duke Bluebeard's Castle*, as well as the first complete recording of *La clemenza di Tito* (with the Vienna Staatsoper).

NOËL GOODWIN

Kerzelli [Kercel, Kerzel, Kerzell]. Family of musicians, possibly Czech, active in Moscow in the late 18th century. Information about them is meagre and their works are a notorious bibliographical fog. At least four of them made noteworthy contributions to the Russian musical stage.

(1) **Ivan** [Johann, Iosif] **Kerzelli** (*fl* 1773–80). His middle initial is given variously as B. or I. Composer. As the musical director at the theatre on the Znamenka (1773–80), it fell to him to arrange the music for *Derevenskoy vorozheya* ('The Village Soothsayer', December 1777, Moscow), Vasily Maikov's influential 'intermediya' after *Le devin du village* by Rousseau, which spawned a host of imitations including the most popular of all Russian Singspiels, *Mel'nik – koldun, obmanshchik i svat* ('The Miller who was a Magician, a Cheat and a Matchmaker'). Its vocal score – 'Overture and Songs from the Intermezzo The Village Soothsayer' (Moscow, 1778) – was the first publication of its kind in Russia. Almost as popular was *Rozana i Lyubim* ('Rozana and Lyubim', 1778, theatre on the Znamenka; one song in Ginzburg), in which Kerzelli supplied music for a conflated adaptation by Nikolay Nikolev of two of Charles Favart's most successful *comédies mêlées d'ariettes* (*Annette et Lubin* and *Ninette à la cour*). Both plays to which Kerzelli contributed, now considered classics of early Russian drama, were of the type in which the score consists of folk and popular tunes (*golosi*) sung to new words. The extent to which Kerzelli's music was original, and the precise nature of his source tunes, are still matters of debate. What is not debated is the bad impression Kerzelli's treatment of *Rozana and Lyubim* made on connoisseurs both then and since. Nikolev himself declared, in the preface to the printed libretto, that the primitive music 'tormented' his play: 'where three or four should be singing together, two sing and one or two yawn; what should be sung is spoken and what should be spoken is left out'. Other comic operas in the pastoral tradition of Rousseau to which Kerzelli (or possibly some other member of his family) contributed music *na golosï* include *Lyubovnik – koldun* ('The Lover who was a Wizard', 1, Nikolev, 1777) and *Derevenskiy prazdnik, ili Uvenchannaya dobrodetel'* ('The Village Festival, or Virtue Crowned', 2, Maikov, 1777). In various sources the music for all four works is attributed to M. F. Kerzelli, perhaps Ivan Kerzelli's nephew (see below). While this is thought to be a fallacy originating with Gerber, similarly conflicting attributions remain unresolved for *Finiks* ('The Phoenix', 3, Nikolev; ?1779, Moscow) and *Arkas i Irisa* ('Arcas and Iris', 1, Maikov; 1780, Moscow).

(2) **Frants Kerzelli** (*fl* 1794). Composer and cellist, ?brother of (1) Ivan Kerzelli. His best-known work is the comic opera *Tri svad'bï vdrug, ili Kak auknetsya, tak i otkliknetsya* ('Three Weddings at Once, or The Echo Responds to the Call', 2, A. Zheltov), first performed in Moscow in 1794.

Two other members of the family, Mikhail Frantsevich Kerzelli (*b* c1740; *d* 1804) and Ivan Frantsevich Kerzelli (*b* c1760; *d* 14/26 May 1820), perhaps sons of (2) Frants Kerzelli, composed for the theatre. From 1801 to 1820 Ivan directed the orchestra at the Petrovsky Theatre; Mikhail was occupied with directing and instructing horn bands. Both were prolific composers of comic operas. No two authorities agree as to which wrote which. On the basis of the title-page of Vasily Levshin's collected librettos (Kaluga, n.d.),

Mooser confidently asserted Ivan to be the author of the operas on Levshin's texts; yet Findeyzen, citing the same document, attributed them to Mikhail. *Svad'ba gospodina Voldïryova* ('Mr Voldïryov's Wedding'), a sequel to the perennial crowd-pleaser *Sbiten'shchik* ('The Hot-Mead Vendor') by Knyazhnin and Bullant, was the most popular of these Singspiels.

attributed to M. F. or I. F. Kerzelli; first performed in Moscow unless otherwise stated

Gulyan'ye, ili Sadovnik Kuskovskoy [Merrymaking, or The Gardener of Kuskovo] (1, V. Kolïchev), estate of Count Sheremet'yev, Kuskovo, 1780 or 1781

Plenira i Zelim [Plenira and Selim] (3, trans. B. Blank), 1789

Korol' na okhote [The King Goes Hunting] (3, V. Levshin, after Sedaine), 1793 or 1794

Svad'ba gospodina Voldïryova [Mr Voldïryov's Wedding] (1, Levshin), 1793 or 1794; extract from ov. in Findeyzen

Mnimïye vdovtsï [The Make-Believe Widowers] (3, Levshin, after the Ger.), 1794

Svoya nosha ne tyanet [One does not Mind a Burden of one's Choice] (2, Levshin), c1794

Molodïye poskoreye starïkh mogut obmanut' [Youth will Sooner Cheat than Age] (1, Levshin), estate of Prince Shcherbatov, Litvinovo, 1795

*

GerberNL

N. F. Findeyzen: *Ocherki po istorii muziki v Rossii s drevneyshikh vremyon do kontsa XVIII veka* [Studies in the History of Music in Russia from Ancient Times to the End of the 18th Century], ii (Moscow and Leningrad, 1929)

R.-A. Mooser: *Annales de la musique et des musiciens en Russie au XVIIIme siècle*, ii (Geneva, 1951)

T. N. Livanova: *Russkaya muzïkal'naya kul'tura XVIII veka v eyo svyazyakh s literaturoy, teatrom i bïtom* [Russian Musical Culture of the 18th Century and its Connections with Literature, the Theatre and Everyday Life], ii (Moscow, 1953)

A. A. Gozenpud: *Muzikal'niy teatr v Rossii ot istokov do Glinki: ocherk* [The Musical Theatre in Russia from its Origins up to Glinka: a Study] (Leningrad, 1959)

G. Bernandt, ed.: *Slovar' oper* [Dictionary of Opera] (Moscow, 1962)

S. Ginzburg: IRMO, i, 452–5

S. Karlinsky: *Russian Drama from its Beginnings to the Age of Pushkin* (Berkeley and Los Angeles, 1985)

Yu. V. Keldïsh and others: *Istoriya russkoy muzïki v desyati tomakh* [The History of Russian Music in Ten Volumes], iii–iv (Moscow, 1985–6) RICHARD TARUSKIN

Kesa to Moritō ('Kesa and Moritō'). Opera in three acts by KAN ISHII to a libretto by Yasuo Yamanouchi after the Japanese epics *Heike monogatari* and *Genpei seisuiki*; Tokyo, Metropolitan Festival Hall, 20 November 1968.

The story is based on a historical incident in Kyoto around 1137. Endō Moritō (baritone), a young warrior, brings a Magician (bass) to a flower-viewing party held by his close friend Watanabe-no-Wataru (tenor). The Magician sees a bad omen on Wataru's face and then disappears mysteriously. At the height of the party Wataru's wife, Kesa Gozen (soprano), appears and greets the guests; Moritō is struck by her beauty. Desperately in love, Moritō tries to see Kesa, but their meeting is interrupted by his angry fiancée, Shiragiku (soprano). Kesa, seeing the impossibility of the situation, tells Moritō to kill Wataru in his bedroom; Moritō follows her instructions. But it is Kesa herself who is in Wataru's bed and whom Moritō kills. After a long period of torments, reflections and meditation, Moritō decides to become a priest, assuming the name of Mongaku. *Kesa to Moritō* is a psychological melodrama with violently emotional music using the full orchestra.

MASAKATA KANAZAWA

Ketting, Otto (*b* Amsterdam, 3 Sept 1935). Dutch composer and conductor. He studied composition with his father, Piet Ketting, and later with K. A. Hartmann in Munich. He taught composition at the conservatories of Rotterdam (1967–71) and The Hague (1971–4).

As a composer Otto Ketting has been active in concert, stage (opera, theatre and ballet) and film music. He has written two operas. *Dummies* (B. Schierbeek; Scheveningen, Kurzaal, 14 November 1974), a chamber opera for three singers and nine instrumentalists, is experimental, with moments of quasi-improvisation, block chords and layers of sound; its music is severe and yet playful. *Ithaka*, based on the poem of the same name by Cavafy, is extremely lyrical and expressive, though never exuberant. Stylistically it looks backwards, with reminiscences of Alban Berg. *Ithaka* was composed for the inauguration of the Muziektheater in Amsterdam (23 September 1986).

*

L. Samama: *Zeventig jaar Nederlandse muziek (1915–1985)* (Amsterdam, 1986), 282–3 LEO SAMAMA

Keurvels, Edward (Hubertus Joannes) (*b* Antwerp, 8 March 1853; *d* Ekeren, nr Antwerp, 29 Jan 1916). Belgian conductor and composer. He studied at the Flemish Music School in Antwerp, and completed his training with its director Peter Benoit. In 1871 he was appointed répétiteur and accompanist there; in 1882 he became conductor of the Dutch Theatre, Antwerp, and composed music for its productions. A staunch supporter of Benoit, he worked hard to promote spoken lyric drama and in 1890 was closely involved in setting up the Netherlands Lyric Theatre, where many of Benoit's works were introduced and for which Keurvels composed the lyric drama *Parisina* (with a text by F. Gittens, after Byron). From this theatre developed the Vlaamse Opera (1893), which he conducted for many years. His work for the theatre was prolific and included excellent translations of Wagner. Besides working closely with Benoit, he was also active in founding the Royal Flemish Conservatory (1898) and in 1902 set up the Peter Benoit-Fonds for promoting Benoit's works.

MARIE-THÉRÈSE BUYSSENS

Khaikin [Khaykin], Boris (Emmanuilovich) (*b* Minsk, 13/26 Oct 1904; *d* Moscow, 10 May 1978). Russian conductor. After studying at the Moscow Conservatory he became influenced by Stanislavsky, at whose opera theatre he conducted (1928–35), preparing productions of *Il barbiere di Siviglia* and *Carmen*. In 1936 he was appointed principal conductor and artistic director of the Malïy Opera Theatre, Leningrad; there he conducted the première of Kabalevsky's *Colas Breugnon* and the Leningrad première of Dzerzhinsky's *Podnyataya tselina* ('Virgin Soil Upturned'), as well as notable productions of operas by Rimsky-Korsakov, Musorgsky and Tchaikovsky. From 1943, as principal conductor and artistic director of the Kirov Theatre, he conducted the local première of Prokofiev's *Betrothal in a Monastery* and the private first performance in 1948 of *The Story of a Real Man*. He also staged Kabalevsky's *Sem'ya Tarasa* ('The Taras Family') and Dzerzhinsky's *Knyaz'-ozero* ('The Prince-lake'). In 1954 he became conductor at the Bol'shoy Theatre. His occasional foreign appearances included *Khovanshchina* in Florence (1963) and *The Queen of Spades* in Leipzig (1964). Khaikin possessed a sure understanding of style and, in opera, used the drama inherent in the music to heighten the characterization on stage.

I. M. YAMPOL'SKY

Kharkiv (Russ. Khar'kov). City in Ukraine. The Kharkivs'kyy Derzhavnyy Akademichnyy Teatr Opery ta Baletu imeni M. V. Lysenka (Lysenko Kharkiv State Academic Theatre of Opera and Ballet) is one of the oldest in Ukraine, being the successor of the first permanent opera theatre in the city, established in 1880. Two of Mykola Lysenko's operas received their premières here, *Chornomortsy* ('Black Sea Sailors') and *Rizdv'yana nich* ('Christmas Eve'), both in 1883. In 1918 the theatre was known as the Narodnaya Opera (National Opera), in 1920 the Russkaya Gosudarstvennaya Opera (Russian State Opera); and in 1925 it became the Ukraïns'ka Derzhavna Stolychna Opera (Ukrainian State Capital Opera – Kharkiv was the capital of the Ukrainian SSR from 1919 to 1934). In 1931 the theatre became the Kharkivs'kyy Teatr Opery ta Baletu; in 1934 'Academic' was added to the title and finally in 1944 the Lysenko Kharkiv State Academic Theatre of Opera and Ballet was born. In 1924 the first Ukrainian-language opera, Lysenko's *Taras Bulba*, was given its première, and in the early years after the Revolution a number of important productions were given. Some were in a cubist style: *Guillaume Tell* as staged by Volodymyr Manzy and Borys Lyatoshyns'ky's *Zolotyy obruch* ('The Golden Ring') as staged by Olexander Khvostenko-Khvostov; others were nearer to drama (Joseph Lapitsky's setting of *Carmen*) or were done in the style of Ukrainian folk art (Serhy Karhalsky's productions of *Prince Igor* and *Rusalka*, brought from Kiev). All stage productions at this time were influenced to a certain extent by the brilliant Berezil' theatre of Les' Kurbas, which made its home in Kharkiv from 1926 to 1933. The relatively short period of experimentation came to a halt when Moscow declared the new order of 'socialist realism'. Singers who have appeared in the city include Aleksander Myszuga, Ivan Kozlovsky, Mariya Lytvynenko-Vol'hemut and Borys Hmyrya. The conductors Antin Rudnytsky and Lev Steinberg, the directors Panas Saksahansky and Nicolay Smolych and the designer Anatoly Petrytsky have also worked here.

ME ('Khar'kov', Yu. L. Shcherbinin; also 'Khar'kovskiy teatr operï i baleta', Yu. A. Stanishevsky)

K. Myloslavs'ky, P. Ivanovs'ky and H. Shtol': *Kharkivs'kyy derzhavnyy akademichnyy teatr opery ta baletu im. M. V. Lysenka* (Kiev, 1965)

Yu. Stanyshevs'ky: 'Traditsii i novatorstvo: Kharkivs'kyy operi – 40 rokiv' [Tradition and Experimentation: 40 Years of Kharkiv Opera], *Prapor* (1965), no.11

——: *Ukraïns'kyy radyans'kyy muzychnyy teatr 1917–1967* [Soviet Ukrainian Music Theatre 1917–1967] (Kiev, 1970)

——: *Opernyy teatr Radyans'koï Ukraïny* [Opera Theatre of Soviet Ukraine] (Kiev, 1988)

VIRKO BALEY

Khessin, Alexander Borisovich (*b* St Petersburg, 7/19 Oct 1869; *d* Moscow, 3 April 1955). Russian conductor and teacher. He studied composition at the St Petersburg Conservatory, and conducting under Nikisch in Leipzig and Mottl in Karlsruhe. He conducted opera at the People's House in Petrograd (1915–17), and at the Mariinsky Theatre (1918–19). From 1935 to 1941 he was director of the opera studio at the Moscow Conservatory. As director of the Soviet Opera Company of the All-Russian Dramatic Society (1943–53) Khessin introduced to Moscow Prokofiev's *War and Peace*, Koval's *Sevastopol'tsï* and Kas'yanov's *Foma Gordeyev*

(all in concert performances), and staged other operas not performed in the Moscow repertory, such as *Porgy and Bess*, Moniuszko's *The Haunted Manor*, Smetana's *Dalibor* and Taneyev's *Oresteya*. He wrote *Iz moikh vospominaniy* ('From my Reminiscences', Moscow, 1959).

I. M. YAMPOL'SKY

Khokhlov, Pavel (Akinfiyevich) (*b* Spassky, Tambov, 21 July/2 Aug 1854; *d* Moscow, 20 Sept 1919). Russian baritone. He made his début at the Moscow Bol'shoy as Valentin (3 March 1879), remaining with the company until his retirement in 1900; he also appeared at the Mariinsky in St Petersburg (1881, 1887–8). His rich, warm voice and generous artistry quickly made an impression, and he was particularly successful as Yevgeny Onegin (singing the role at the first public performance, 23 January 1881, and thereafter 138 times in Moscow alone) and as Rubinstein's Demon; he also appeared in Prague (1889) in those two roles. His repertory also included Don Giovanni, Verdi's Anckarstroem (Renato), Luna and Germont, Wagner's Wolfram and Telramund, Meyerbeer's Nélusko and Nevers, Weber's Ottokar, and many Russian roles including Boris and Prince Igor. A scrupulous stylist, conscientious in his constantly refreshed study of a role, he was a master both of bel canto and of a more flexible declamatory style, and had a fine stage presence. Various factors, including overwork and alcohol, led to an early vocal decline.

S. Durilin: *P. A. Khokhlov 1854–1919* (Moscow and Leningrad, 1947)

Y. Yakovlev: *P. A. Khokhlov* (Moscow and Leningrad, 1950)

JOHN WARRACK

Kholminov, Alexander Nikolayevich (*b* Moscow, 8 Sept 1925). Russian composer. He graduated from Golubev's class at the Moscow Conservatory in 1950. In addition to the composition of cantatas and mass songs on patriotic themes, he has devoted most of his career to opera. His first and best-known opera, *Optimisticheskaya tragediya* ('An Optimistic Tragedy', 1965), a tuneful treatment of a heroic-romantic subject from the Civil War period, achieved wide acclaim in the USSR after its première in 1965. In more recent operas he has turned to Russian literary classics. His chamber operas, based on works by writers such as Gogol, Chekhov and Dostoyevsky, were all first performed by the Chamber Opera Theatre in Moscow, and are notable for their spectacular theatricality. In 1978 he was awarded the USSR State Prize for his chamber-opera diptych after Gogol's *Shinel'* ('The Overcoat') and *Kolyaska* ('The Carriage'), and in 1984 he was named People's Artist of the USSR.

See also OPTIMISTICHESKAYA TRAGEDIYA.

performed in Moscow, Chamber Opera Theatre, unless otherwise stated

Optimisticheskaya tragediya [An Optimistic Tragedy] (3, Kholminov and A. Mashistov, after V. Vishnevsky), Frunze, Kirghiz Theatre of Opera and Ballet, 20 Nov 1965

Anna Snegina (2, Mashistov, after S. Yesenin), Gor'kiy, Musical Theatre, 1967

Shinel' [The Overcoat], 1971 (chamber op, 1, Kholminov, after N. V. Gogol), 1975

Kolyaska [The Carriage], 1971 (chamber op, 1, Kholminov, after Gogol), 25 Dec 1975

Chapayev, 1974 (5 scenes, Kholminov, after D. Furmanov), Moscow Radio, 20 Oct 1977

Dvenadtsataya seriya [The Twelfth Series] (chamber op, 3 scenes, Kholminov, after V. M. Shukshin), 28 Dec 1977

Svad'ba [The Wedding] (chamber op, after A. P. Chekhov), 25 Feb 1984

Van'ka (monodrama, after Chekhov), 25 Feb 1984

Brat'ya Karamazovï [The Brothers Karamazov] (chamber op, 2, Kholminov, after F. M. Dostoyevsky), 31 March 1985

Goryachiy sneg [Hot Snow] (4 frescoes, after Y. Bondarev), Sïktïvkar, Komi Republic, April 1985

*

V. Vinogradov: 'Revolyutsionno-romanticheskaya opera' [A revolutionary-romantic opera], *SovM* (1966), no.5, pp.44–8 [on *Optimisticheskaya tragediya*]

I. Nest'ev: 'V traditsiyakh Gogolya i Musorgskogo' [In the Traditions of Gogol and Musorgsky], *SovM* (1975), no.1, pp.12–18 [on *Shinel'* and *Kolyaska*]

A. Bretanitskaya: 'Vnimaniye – na stsene Gogol: "Shinel'" i "Kolyaska" A. Kholminova' [Attention – Gogol on Stage: 'The Overcoat' and 'The Carriage' by Kholminov], *Muzïka Rossii* [The Music of Russia], ii (Moscow, 1978), 198–212

V. Zarudko: 'Komicheskoye i ser'yoznoye v "Dvenadtsatoy serii"' [The Comic and the Serious in 'The Twelfth Series'], *SovM* (1979), no.2, pp.50–54

M. Manuilov: 'New Operas by Alexander Kholminov', *Music in the USSR* (1986), July–Sept, 91–3   LAUREL E. FAY

Khovanshchina ('The Khovansky Affair'). 'National music drama' (*narodnaya muzïkal'naya drama*) in six scenes, traditionally given in five acts, by MODEST PETROVICH MUSORGSKY to his own libretto, compiled with VLADIMIR VASIL'YEVICH STASOV from historical sources; St Petersburg, Amateur Musical-Dramatic Club in Kononov Auditorium, 9/21 February 1886, in Rimsky-Korsakov's version (given by Imperial Theatres, St Petersburg, Mariinsky Theatre, 7/20 November 1911; Ravel-Stravinsky version, Paris, Théâtre Champs-Elysées, 5 June 1913 [with Stravinsky's final chorus, 16 June 1913]; Shostakovich version, Leningrad, Kirov Theatre, 25 November 1960).

Prince Ivan Khovansky *head of the strel'tsï* (*musketeers*)	bass
Prince Andrey Khovansky *his son*	tenor
Prince Vasily Golitsïn	tenor
The Boyar Shaklovity	baritone
Dosifey *leader of the schismatics ('Old Believers')*	bass
Marfa *a schismatic, a young widow*	mezzo-soprano
Susanna *an old schismatic*	soprano
A Scrivener	tenor
Emma *a girl from the German quarter*	soprano
Pastor	bass
Varsonof'yev *Golitsïn's attendant*	bass
Kuz'ka *a musketeer*	baritone
Streshnev *a young boyar*	tenor
Three *Strel'tsï*	basses
Golitsïn's Minion	tenor

Refugees, musketeers, their wives, Old Believers, immured maidens and Persian slave girls of Ivan Khovansky, Tsar Peter's guard, crowd

Setting Various locations in and near Moscow at a time roughly corresponding to that of the second 'revolt of the Strel'tsï' (1689)

Musorgsky conceived the work in 1872 and began its composition the next year; it was left unfinished, and (except for two fragments) unorchestrated at his death in 1881. A vocal score transmitting Musorgsky's manuscripts as he left them was published in 1931, edited by Pavel Lamm. The first performing edition was made by Rimsky-Korsakov (published 1883) and this was the version given at the 1886 première, under

Eduard Goldshteyn, and at the Mariinsky Theatre in 1911 under Albert Coates, with Shalyapin as Dosifey, Ivan Yershov as Golitsïn and Yevgeniya Zbruyeva as Marfa. A variant of this version by Ravel and Stravinsky was used for the Paris performance in 1913, directed by Dyagilev, under Emil Cooper, with Shalyapin and with Yelizaveta Petrenko as Marfa. In 1952 Shostakovich orchestrated the scenes omitted by Rimsky for the Kirov Theatre, and in 1958 he re-orchestrated the rest of the opera for a film version (1959, with Mark Reyzen as Dosifey and Yevgeny Kibkalo as Shaklovity, conducted by Yevgeny Svetlanov). Shostakovich's score was published in 1963; at the stage première Boris Khaikin conducted, with Boris Shtokolov as Dosifey.

It is significant that Musorgsky's second historical opera was conceived in Tsar Peter I's bicentenary year, for it reflects the moral controversy that has always swirled around 'Peter the Great', the first Russian Emperor, through whose reforms the modern Russian state was created after Western European bureaucratic models; who built his capital, in which Musorgsky lived, on marshes at the cost of untold thousands of indentured lives; and who has been regarded by a divided posterity as either the best thing that ever happened to Russia or the worst. The letter to Vladimir Stasov in which Musorgsky first mentioned being 'pregnant' with the new opera (16–22 June/28 June–4 July 1872) also contains enigmatic musings about 'the power of the black earth' and its resistance to ploughing 'with tools wrought of alien materials'. These dark ruminations are virtually all we have to go on if we want to understand, as a work of history, the sprawling, unprecedented opera-chronicle that gestated over the nine years that remained to the composer, since his early death from alcoholism left crucial holes in the scenario. There is reason to believe that the melioristic viewpoint subsequently built into the opera by its revisers was not the one intended by its creator.

It was inevitable that Musorgsky, in writing an opera that would contain a judgment of Peter, should have concentrated on the period of the so-called 'Strel'tsï Revolts', the convulsions out of which the modern Russian state emerged. It was impossible to base a libretto on the life and actions of the tsar himself; the Russian censorship prohibited the representation of any member of the Romanov dynasty on the dramatic stage. His opponents (with one royal exception) could be shown in action, however, and it was on them that Musorgsky fastened.

In order to assert full power, Peter had to overcome opposition from three quarters. First there were the *strel'tsï* (musketeers), the crack Moscow militia, represented in the opera by their leader Ivan Khovansky and his son Andrey. A crisis of succession was created in 1682 by the death of Tsar Fyodor Alexeyevich (Romanov) at the age of 20, leaving a sickly and half-witted 16-year-old brother Ivan, and also his half-brother Peter, then not quite ten. The families of the two royal mothers competed viciously for the throne. The *strel'tsï* backed Ivan's family and secured the installation of the two young heirs as joint sovereigns, with Ivan's sister Sophia as regent. Khovansky now tried to use his troops to force the new régime to abrogate the recent church reforms; some thought he coveted the throne either for himself or for Andrey. This threatened revolt was the 'Khovansky affair' (*Khovanshchina*). Sophia, formerly the *strel'tsï*'s protégée, now turned around and had both Khovansky and his son beheaded. Her agent in

'Khovanshchina' (Musorgsky): design by Apollinary Vasnestsov for scene vi (secluded hermitage in a pine forest; the Old Believers' immolation) in the first Moscow production by Mamontov's Private Opera Company at the Solodovnikov Theatre, 12/24 November 1897

this perfidy was a boyar, Fyodor Shaklovity, whom Sophia installed as Khovansky's successor at the head of the *strel'tsï*. (In the opera, as in history, Shaklovity eliminates Khovansky, but seemingly as Peter's agent rather than Sophia's.)

Peter's second opponent, Sophia herself, is represented in the opera by Prince Vasily Golitsïn, Sophia's chief minister (and former lover), himself an eager reformer who envisaged the abolition of serfdom and the institution of mass education. These plans were doomed when a second *strel'tsï* revolt, organized by Shaklovity at Sophia's behest to murder Peter and his family and install the regent as actual hereditary ruler, failed. As a result of this offensive against the 17-year-old tsar, Sophia was sent off to a convent, Shaklovity was executed and Golitsïn was exiled. By 1696 Peter's mother and half-brother had died and the 24-year-old tsar assumed his full responsibilities as head of the Russian church and state. (A third *strel'tsï* revolt in 1698 was punished with unprecedented severity: after prolonged torture, more than 1000 mutineers were executed, their bodies gruesomely displayed in Red Square as an admonition.)

The last of Peter's opponents were the so-called Old Believers, religious recusants who had been persecuted from the time of Peter's father Alexey. Their representative in the opera, Dosifey, had to be invented, for they had no organized clergy. The libretto identifies Dosifey with Prince Mïshetsky, an Old Believer of noble birth whose narrative *Glïb'* ('The Depths') explicitly identified Peter as Antichrist. The Old Believers, never a serious threat to the royal power, responded to the events herein recounted with an epidemic of mass suicides, chiefly by burning.

One major character remains to be accounted for. In order to make their assemblage of historical portraits jell into some semblance of a plot, Musorgsky (and Stasov, his collaborator) resorted to the most conventional, and in this case blatantly anachronistic, sort of operatic glue: romantic love. Andrey Khovansky's love interest (though he is chiefly seen betraying her) is his fiancée Marfa, a figment of the libretto but its most important prop. She is an Old Believer, a specially favoured member of Dosifey's spiritual community; she

is linked by amorous bonds to the *strel'tsï*; and she is a soothsayer with a fatal influence on Prince Golitsïn, to whom she foretells Sophia's downfall and his own. She alone, in other words, inhabits all the worlds of the opera and links them. Her constant tone of keening lamentation symbolizes the doom that overhangs everything and everyone, the doom that is the core and essential message of this most pessimistic of historical operas.

Khovanshchina accumulated gradually in vocal score, scene by scene, but not in order. Until 1879, when Musorgsky finally wrote out a fair copy of the existing texts (it is called the 'blue notebook') and linked them as a guide to completing the opera (and, possibly, for submission to the censor), there was no libretto, properly speaking. Only two tiny excerpts from the third scene were ever orchestrated by the composer. When the manuscripts were finally put in blue-notebook order after the composer's death, it was found that two scenes remained unfinished: Act 2 lacked a conclusion and Act 5 was little more than a sheaf of sketches. No wonder the action has seemed to exude an air of pointless confusion and ambiguity, and has been so susceptible to contradictory readings – though one interpretation, arguably at variance with the composer's, has been gradually built into the opera by its revisers. A brief account of this process must be included here, since unlike *Boris Godunov* (which has two), *Khovanshchina* has no complete 'original' version to which one can revert.

The standard interpretation of the Petrine reforms is one that casts all of the variously contending political and social factions portrayed in the opera – Sophia's regency, the *strel'tsï*, the Old Believers – into the dustbin of history. All of them, but particularly the Old Believers, were viewed as the symbol of everything that was outmoded and antiquated, 'petty, wretched, dull-brained, envious, evil and malicious' (as Stasov put it of the character Susanna in a letter to Musorgsky). This melioristic view was fixed once and for all by Rimsky-Korsakov, who had to fill the gaps in *Khovanshchina* as well as orchestrate (and cut and 'correct') it. His method was that of symbolic reprise. At the end of Act 2, he followed the break-up of the colloquy at Golitsïn's, involving representatives of all three anti-Peter factions, with an impressively developed reprise of the melody of the opera's prelude ('Dawn over the Moskva River'). At a stroke all ambiguities were resolved: Peter is 'day'; the Muscovite opposition, in all its manifestations, is 'night', a view driven home again at the very end of the opera, where Rimsky trumped his own final chorus (composed on an Old Believers' melody Musorgsky had transcribed and designated for the opera's conclusion) with a brassy reprise of the March that had represented the unseen Peter in the Act 4 finale. Shostakovich, when it came his turn to revise *Khovanshchina*, ratified Rimsky's view and even managed to strengthen it. Retaining Rimsky's final chorus, he replaced Rimsky's ending for Act 2 with a foreshadowing of the Act 4 march, and transferred Rimsky's reprise of the 'Dawn' theme to the very end of the opera, where it casts an even more conclusively optimistic judgment on the whole of the opera's action.

Without all these reprises, first of Peter's march and then of the 'Dawn', the Old Believers would have the fifth act of *Khovanshchina* all to themselves; and, as they trudge off to their mass suicide, accompanied by the sober strains of their psalm, the opera would end on a note of quiet pessimism, a sense of loss. Act 5, as Musorgsky evidently intended it (and as realized

uniquely in the version of the opera Sergey Dyagilev presented to Paris in 1913 with the help of Ravel and Stravinsky), acts as a gloss on the rest of the drama – a conservative and nationalistic judgment that calls the necessity of the political events portrayed in the other four acts severely into question, implying that what for some may have been a dawn was for others the veritable end of the world.

The cluttered action of *Khovanshchina* can best be grasped by conceptualizing the six scenes in the blue notebook in two groups. (Musorgsky himself never specified a grouping; the conventional five-act format was Rimsky-Korsakov's idea.) The first three scenes are chiefly centred on each of Peter's opponents in turn: *strel'tsï* (Khovansky), Golitsïn (representing the unseen Sophia) and Old Believers. The last three then show them eliminated in the same order. Soviet researchers have proposed regrouping the scenes to make this scheme clearer: Scene i = Act 1; Scenes ii and iii = Act 2; Scenes iv–vi = Act 3. The division is attractive for the further reason that both intervals, as well as the final curtain, follow choruses. In the synoptic table that follows, the constituent units are the individual manuscripts. Their dates are given ('Old Style') so that the opera's creative history may be reconstructed.

Prelude 'Dawn over the Moskva River'	MS dated 4 Sept 1874; first mentioned in letter to Dmitry Stasov, 2 Aug 1873
SCENE i *Red Square, Moscow*	
a *Strel'tsï* keep watch; after singing an old marching tune the sentry Kuz'ka dozes off, is awakened and reprimanded.	mentioned in letter to D. Stasov, 2 Aug 1873
b A scrivener arrives and sets up shop; Shaklovïty dictates denunciation of the Khovanskys (its text is from an actual historical document).	mentioned in letter to Vladimir Stasov, 23 July 1873
c Settlers violently compel the scrivener to read them a posted notice detailing penalties imposed by the *strel'tsï* on perfidious nobles; they lament that punishing the rich does not help the poor (the offstage opening chorus is based on a folksong from the Villebois collection, 1860).	MS 2 Jan 1875; omitted in Rimsky version, orch. Ravel for 1913 version, orch. Shostakovich, 1952
d Ivan Khovansky enters to thunderous acclaim and vows to crush Sophia's enemies and punish treason.	
e Emma, a young Lutheran from the German quarter, rushes in pursued by Andrey Khovansky; Marfa intercedes and is threatened with a dagger.	
f Ivan Khovansky returns and demands Emma; Dosifey enters, puts an end to the quarrel and entrusts Emma to Marfa for protection.	much cut by Rimsky, restored by Ravel and Shostakovich
g Dosifey prays, with chorus, for preservation of the faith.	MS 30 July 1875; whole scene described as finished in letter to V. Stasov, 18 May 1876
SCENE ii *Golitsïn's study*	
a Golitsïn reads Sophia's love letter (its text is derived from a historical document) and wonders if he can still trust her.	*a*, *b*, *c* dated by letters, Aug–Dec 1875; *b* omitted by Rimsky and in 1913 (where
b He reads a letter from his mother.	Act 2 was cut), restored by
c A Lutheran pastor arrives and pleads for Emma and a Lutheran church.	Shostakovich; Musorgsky had planned to cut *c* (it is not in the blue notebook), but it is in Lamm and thence Shostakovich
d Marfa enters and reads Golitsïn's fortune in a bowl of water, predicting imminent disgrace and exile (Divination, 'Silï potainïye': 'O mysterious forces').	MS 20 Aug 1870, originally for a planned opera *Bobïl*; final version, 24 July 1878
e Golitsïn dismisses Marfa, whispering instructions to his attendant Varsonof'yev that she be drowned. Ivan Khovansky arrives and they quarrel over the boyars' hereditary rights.	*e*, *f*, *g* dated by letters, Aug 1876; much abbreviated by Rimsky, restored by
f Dosifey enters; he reveals his past identity as Prince Mïshetsky (offstage, the Old Believers sing a folksong, from the 1866 Balakirev collection). He exhorts Golitsïn and Khovansky to join forces with him to restore old ways.	Shostakovich via Lamm; to supply the unwritten conclusion to the scene, Rimsky repeats 'Dawn' and Shostakovich foreshadows Peter's march

g   Marfa returns, in fright, telling of the attempts on her life and its thwarting by passing bodyguards of Peter.

h   Shaklovity enters and announces that a denunciation (his own) has been received and acted upon by Peter, who has vowed to clean up the 'Khovansky mess' (*khovanshchina*).

SCENE iii   *Strel'tsï quarter, across the Moskva River*

a   The Old Believers sing (the Balakirev-derived melody cited above).   MS 31 Dec 1875

b   Marfa laments her lost love ('Iskhodila mladyoshen'ka vse luga i bolota': 'A girl went out walking in the fields and marshes' – based on a folksong in the Villebois collection).   MS vocal score 18 Aug 1873, orchestral score 24–5 Nov 1879

c   Susanna reproaches Marfa for her unclean passion.   MS 5 Sept 1873

d   Dosifey intervenes, sending Susanna away; Marfa confesses her love for Andrey and her wish to immolate herself with him; Dosifey counsels patience.   MS 1 Feb 1876

e   Shaklovity, alone, muses on Russia's troubled history (aria, 'Spit streletskoye gnezdo': 'The nest of *strel'tsï* sleeps').   MS 6 Jan 1876

f   The *strel'tsï* awaken, with hangovers, and immediately start thinking about wine.   *f, g, h, i, j*, MS vocal score 29 May 1880; *f* exists in undated autograph full score

g   Their wives nag them about their drinking.   abbreviated by Rimsky, restored Ravel and Shostakovich

h   Kuz'ka sings to his balalaika, with chorus (the Rumour Song).   omitted by Rimsky, orch. Ravel, 1913, and Shostakovich, 1952

i   The scrivener rushes in with news of mercenary attacks on the *strel'tsï*.

j   The *strel'tsï* appeal to Khovansky, who declines to fight Peter, and they pray for deliverance.

SCENE iv   *Refectory on Ivan Khovansky's estate*

a   Khovansky is at home, awaiting news; his servant girls entertain him (the choruses of immured maidens are based on folksongs from the Melgunov collection, 1879). A warning arrives from Golitsïn; Khovansky ignores it, calling for more entertainment.   MS of choruses 5 Aug 1880

b   Khovansky's Persian slave girls dance for him.   MS 3 April 1876

c   Shaklovity arrives with a summons to a meeting with Sophia; as Khovansky dons his robes the girls sing a chorus in praise of their master (based on a chorus Musorgsky learnt from Shishko, lighting director of the Mariinsky Theatre, included in Rimsky's 1876 collection). At the doorway, Shaklovity stabs Khovansky, then gloats over the corpse by continuing the interrupted song.   MS 5 Aug 1880

SCENE v   *Red Square, before St Basil's shrine*   MSS undated (except *b*)

a   Golitsïn's exile is mourned by Moscow settlers.

b   Dosifey laments (in an aria) the fate of Khovansky and Golitsïn; he and Marfa decide the time has come for immolation.   25–6 June 1879; first mentioned in letter to V. Stasov, 25 Dec 1876

c   Andrey confronts Marfa over Emma; she tells him the girl has been sent beyond the frontier. Andrey calls for the *strel'tsï*.   mentioned in V. Stasov letter to Musorgsky, 15 Aug 1873

d   The *strel'tsï* enter with axes and blocks, ready for execution; Marfa offers Andrey asylum and they depart.

e   In a double chorus, the *strel'tsï* pray for divine mercy and their wives plead against their husbands' pardon.

f   Peter's guard enters, to a march with onstage band; his pardon of the *strel'tsï* is announced.

SCENE vi   *Secluded hermitage in a pine forest; moonlight*

a   Dosifey mourns the outcome of his struggle with Peter and appeals to his followers to prepare for death.   MS 2 April 1880; expanded in Rimsky version

b   Andrey enters, disconsolate; Marfa lovingly leads him to the pyre ('Lyubovnoye otpevaniye': 'Love Requiem').   mentioned in letters as early as 23 July 1873; MS lost, partly reconstructed by Rimsky to his own text; recently found copy of Andrey's part published 1976 in a new vocal score of Lamm edition revised by A. Dmitriyev and A. Vul'fson

c   Dosifey leads the faithful into the hermitage.   MS Aug 1880
     A final chorus, unwritten, was to have been based on an Old Believer melody Musorgsky had taken down from the singing of his friend Lyubov' Karmalina.   Rimsky added orch. figure representing flames and reprised march; Shostakovich retained Rimsky version, adding reprise of 'Dawn'; Stravinsky based his chorus on the designated tune and two other themes associated with Old Believers

* * *

Khovanshchina is an aristocratic tragedy, and this is reflected in its musical style. But for the scenes involving the lowborn scrivener, it is full of 'noble' melody in place of the radically realistic speech-song one finds in Musorgsky's songs or in the earlier version of *Boris*. In part this is a continuation of a tendency, already noticeable in the revised *Boris*, towards a more heroic scale and a more authentically tragic tone – in short, towards a more traditionally operatic style. But Musorgsky refused to call it a retrenchment; on the contrary, in one of his late letters to Stasov he pointed with pride to his *advancement* towards what he called 'thought-through and justified melody', meaning a kind of melody that would embody all the expressive potential of speech. Yet these sinuous melodies, unlike the idiosyncratic recitatives of his earlier manner, are curiously impersonal. The characters who sing them (Marfa throughout, Shaklovity in Scene iii, Dosifey in Scenes iii and vi) do not speak, it seems; rather, something akin to a Tolstoyan notion of impassive historical forces (what Musorgsky, in his sphinx-like way, had called 'the power of the black earth') speaks through them. And this is perhaps the central message of an opera in which personal volition is everywhere set at nought; in which everyone plots and strives and everyone loses; in which the final stage picture shows the last survivors of the old order, the opera's only morally undefiled characters, resolutely stepping out of history and into eternity, where Peter cannot touch them.

RICHARD TARUSKIN

Khrennikov, Tikhon Nikolayevich (*b* Yelets, 28 May/10 June 1913). Russian composer. He studied composition with Mikhail Gnesin at his music school from 1929 to 1932, when he enrolled at the Moscow Conservatory, studying composition with Shebalin and the piano. Even before his graduation in 1936, he had attracted attention with his compositions. From 1936 he was active as a composer of incidental music, chiefly for the Vakhtangov Theatre in Moscow. In 1939 he won critical praise with his first opera, *V buryu* ('Into the Storm'), which satisfied the pressing need for Socialist Realist works transcending mediocre levels of dramatic and musical integrity. Khrennikov infused the traditional forms of operatic arias, duets and ensembles with the familiar rhythms and melodic style of folk and urban songs. *Into the Storm* remained the most exemplary and appealing model for the Stalinist 'song opera'. It also introduced the character of Lenin – in a brief speaking role – to the operatic stage.

During World War II, Khrennikov composed his Second Symphony and many patriotic songs. In 1948 he was prominent as Andrey Zhdanov's right-hand man in the purge of Soviet musicians, condemning Shostakovich, Prokofiev and Khachaturian, among others. Shortly thereafter he became General Secretary of the Union of Composers of the USSR, a position of unprecedented influence and power which he retained for more than 40 years (from 1957 as First Secretary). He has also served in many other official capacities, notably as a deputy to the Supreme Soviet from 1974, and he has taught composition at the Moscow Conservatory from 1961. He is also active as a pianist. His numerous honours are more indicative of political stature than a purely artistic evaluation.

Khrennikov's style has remained consistent throughout his career. His forms are conventional, and his language, with its emphasis on accessible melodies, is tonal and derivative. A number of songs taken from his music for films and television have met with independent success. He turned again to a revolutionary subject in his opera *Mat'* ('Mother'), which was staged as part of the celebration of the 40th anniversary of the October Revolution in 1957. In setting Gorky's story dealing with events during the abortive revolution of 1905, the composer drew extensively on old revolutionary songs and anthems. He has also written two ballets and two operettas, *100 chertey i odna devushka* ('100 Devils and One Girl') and *Belaya noch'* ('White Night'). His so-called comic operas undoubtedly have more in common with turn-of-the-century operetta than with any other model. There has been little development in their anachronistic formula of sentimental waltzes and other standard dance and song forms, their varied repetition of a limited amount of original material and their repertory of stock comic clichés.

See also V BURYU.

V buryu [Into the Storm] op.8 (4, A. Fayko and N. Virta, after Virta: *Odinochestvo* [Loneliness]), Moscow, Nemirovich-Danchenko Music Theatre, 10 Oct 1939; rev. version, Moscow, Stanislavsky–Nemirovich-Danchenko Music Theatre, 12 Oct 1952

Frol Skobeyev op.12 (comic op, 4, S. A. Tsenin, after D. Averkiyev), Moscow, Stanislavsky–Nemirovich-Danchenko Music Theatre, 24 Feb 1950; rev. as Bezrodnïy zyat' [The Low-born Son-in-law] (2), Novosibirsk, 29 Dec 1966

Mat' [Mother] op.13 (4, Fayko, after M. Gorky), Moscow, Bol'shoy, 26 Oct 1957

100 Chertey i odna devushka [100 Devils and One Girl] op.15 (operetta, 3, after E. Shatunovsky), Moscow, Operetta Theatre, 16 May 1963

Belaya noch' [White Night] op.17 (musical chronicle, 3, after Shatunovsky), Moscow, Operetta Theatre, 23 May 1967

Mal'chik-velikan [The Boy Giant] op.18 (fairy-tale op, 3, N. Shestakov), Moscow, Children's Music Theatre, 19 Dec 1969

Mnogo shuma … iz-za serdets [Much Ado about Hearts] (comic op, 2, B. Pokrovsky, after W. Shakespeare: *Much Ado about Nothing*), Moscow, Chamber Music Theatre, 11 March 1972

Doroteya op.27 (comic op, 2, Y. Khaletsky, after R. B. Sheridan: *The Duenna*), Moscow, Stanislavsky–Nemirovich-Danchenko Music Theatre, 26 May 1983

Zolotoy telyonok [The Golden Calf] op.29 (comic op, 2, Khaletsky and I. Sharoyev, after I. Il'f and E. Petrov), Moscow, Stanislavsky–Nemirovich-Danchenko Music Theatre, 9 March 1985

Golïy korol' [The Naked King] (comic op, 2, R. Rozhdestvensky and I. Sharoyev, after E. Shvarts), Leningrad, Malïy, May 1988

*

A. Fayko: 'Rabotaya nad libretto' [Working on the Libretto], *Muzikal'naya zhizn'* [Musical Life] (1957), nos.19–20

E. Ivanov: *Opera T. Khrennikova 'V buryu'* [Khrennikov's opera 'Into the Storm'] (Moscow, 1961)

Y. Kremlyov: *Tikhon Khrennikov* (Moscow, 1963)

B. Schwarz: *Music and Musical Life in Soviet Russia, 1917–1970* (London, 1972)

D. M. Person: *T. N. Khrennikov: notograficheskiy spravochnik* [Khrennikov Work-list] (Moscow, 1973, 2/1978)

I. I. Martïnov: *Tikhon Khrennikov: stat'i o tvorchestve kompozitora* [Tikhon Khrennikov: Articles about the Composer's Works] (Moscow, 1974)

I. Shekhonina: *Tvorchestvo T. N. Khrennikova* [Khrennikov's Works] (Moscow, 1985)

I. I. Martïnov: *Tikhon Nikolayevich Khrennikov* (Moscow, 1987)

LAUREL E. FAY

Kibkalo, Yevgeny (Gavrilovich) (*b* Kiev, 12 Feb 1932). Russian baritone. He graduated from Vladimir Politkovsky's class at the Moscow Conservatory in 1956, was engaged that year as a soloist by the Bol'shoy, then studied at the La Scala opera school in 1963. His distinctive qualities are his beautiful, even voice and warm tone, his musicality and his excellent sense of ensemble. He sang in the first Bol'shoy performances of Prokofiev's *War and Peace* (Andrey) and *The Story of a Real Man* (Alexey); his other roles include Tchaikovsky's Yeletsky, Mazepa and Yevgeny Onegin; Rossini's and Mozart's Figaro; and Demetrius in Britten's *A Midsummer Night's Dream*. He has performed in many countries, and was made People's Artist of the RSFSR in 1959.   I. M. YAMPOL'SKY

Kiel. City in northern Germany, on the Baltic Sea. The first theatre for opera productions, the Opern- und Komödienhaus, was opened in 1764. It was demolished in 1840 and replaced by the Altes Stadttheater. The Neues Stadttheater opened on 1 October 1907; entirely destroyed in 1944, it was rebuilt, and reopened in 1953 with *Fidelio*. Conductors of note who have worked in Kiel include Eugen Jochum, Hans Zender and Klaus Tennstedt. Under its Intendant Joachim Klaiber (1963–76), Kiel became one of the most important centres of modern music drama in the Federal Republic of Germany, staging, for instance, the first performances of Aribert Reimann's *Ein Traumspiel* (1965) and Renato de Grandis's *Gloria al re* (1967, as *Es lebe der König*). Menotti's *The Medium* and Milhaud's *La mère coupable* had their first German performances in the city. More recently, the Kiel Opernhaus has given support to contemporary music drama, giving 13 first performances between 1971 and 1981. The house (866 seats) employs an orchestra of 75 and a chorus of 36. Klaus-Peter Seibel was appointed musical director in 1988.

*

G. Junge: *Die Geschichte des Theaters in Kiel unter der dänischen Herrschaft bis zur Errichtung einer stehenden Bühne, 1774–1841* (Kiel, 1928)

R. Meyer and H. Niederauer: *Festschrift zum 50jährigen Bestehen des Hauses am Kleinen Kiel* (Kiel, 1957)

W. Danielsen: *Hundert Jahre Kieler Theater, 1841–1944* (Kiel, 1961)

W. Pfannkuch: 'Opernaufführungen in Kiel, 1780–1798', *Opernstudien: Anna Amalie Abert zum 65. Geburtstag* (Tutzing, 1975), 91–102

P. Dannenberg: *Immer wenn es Abend wird: dreihundert Jahre Theater in Kiel* (Hamburg, 1983)   SABINE SONNTAG

Kienlen, Johann Christoph (*b* Ulm, bap. 14 Dec 1783; *d* Dessau, 7 Dec 1829). German composer. The son of a Stadtmusicus at Ulm, he appeared as a prodigy pianist and singer at the age of seven. With the help of rich patrons he studied at Munich (1802) and Paris (*c*1803–6, under Cherubini) and was then briefly Stadtmusikdirektor in his native town. He returned to Paris in 1809, travelled to Munich in 1810 (producing his *Claudine von Villa Bella*) and then to Stuttgart and Vienna. He was appointed music director to Baron Zinnicq, who ran a private theatre at Baden and also at Pressburg (now Bratislava), returning to Vienna in 1815. From 1817 he lived for several years in Berlin, at first without an official appointment; in 1823 he became singing instructor at the royal theatre. He is said to have died insane and in poverty.

Claudine von Villa Bella (Spl, 3, J. W. von Goethe), Munich, Hof- und National, 9 Sept 1810, *D-B*

Die Kaiserrose (Zauberoper, 3, J. S. von Menner), Vienna, Leopoldstadt, 13 Jan 1816

Petrarca und Laura (3, A. Eckschlager), Pressburg, March 1816, *B*

*

LoewenbergA; StiegerO

X. Schnyder von Wartensee: *Lebenserinnerungen* (Zürich, 1888)

E. Holzer: 'Ein vergessener schwäbischer Musiker', *Die Musik*, viii/3 (1908–9), 145–51

          ALFRED LOEWENBERG, DAVID CHARLTON

Kienzl, Wilhelm (*b* Waizenkirchen, 17 Jan 1857; *d* Vienna, 3 Oct 1941). Austrian composer. His experience of the theatre began in early childhood, when he was taken from his home in Graz to Vienna to see a comedy at the Theater an der Wien. As a music student at Graz University his tastes were widened by von Hausegger, the respected Wagnerian aesthetician. Together they travelled to Bayreuth for the first performance of the *Ring* in 1876. Although Wagnerian music drama remained the most important influence upon Kienzl's work, he did not identify himself exclusively with Wagnerian circles. His studies took him to the universities of Prague and Leipzig, to Liszt's circle at Weimar and finally to Vienna University, where he completed a doctoral dissertation on musical declamation. Kienzl's independence of mind, when he refused to give up his advocacy of Schumann, led to a disagreement with Wagner in 1879. His early Romantic leanings were reflected in his first opera, *Urvasi*, composed in 1884, which combined Wagnerian leitmotifs with a more lyrical style. The symbolism of the story, earthly love being compared with the heavenly love between the king and heaven's daughter, Urvasi, certainly owes much to Wagner. But even in this early music drama, Kienzl's idealism was offset by a realistic grasp of the demands of the theatre, his practical sense enhanced by his wide-ranging activities as a conductor and critic. His second opera, *Heilmar der Narr*, anticipated his success with more down-to-earth settings, though in stressing the self-sacrifice of the main character it still bore a close relationship to Wagner's *Parsifal*.

The full release from Wagner's shadow came with the composition of *Der Evangelimann* in 1894. Kienzl was planning to make a satirical, philosophical music drama out of Immermann's novel *Münchhausen*, but became gripped by the graphic tale of an evangelist's forgiveness of his treacherous dying brother, and he wrote both text and music of *Der Evangelimann* as though under compulsion. He called his creation a 'musical play' as an indication of its new simplicity of style and construction. Its success far outstripped that of his previous two operas, audiences responding enthusiastically to its moral message and to the interweaving of lighter folklike scenes into the emotional drama. The opera swept the stages of Germany and Austria and was performed as far away as Turkey and Russia. Resisting publishers' demands that he write another such opera, in 1897 Kienzl composed *Don Quixote*, once more on the grander scale of music drama, though without resorting to Wagnerian techniques. He identified closely with the opera's subject matter, seeing himself in Cervantes's idealistic hero. But his experiments with the mixing of comic and tragic scenes confused his audiences and led to the work's failure. In reaction, Kienzl withdrew from operatic composition for a period of 13 years, except for the creation of the children's Christmas fairy-tale *In Knecht Ruprechts Werkstatt* in 1907.

When Kienzl embarked on a new series of operas, in 1911, he showed a greater awareness of his operatic strengths and concentrated more on folk material. *Der Kuhreigen* centred on the nostalgic folksong that Swiss soldiers were not allowed to sing lest homesickness would make them desert. In *Das Testament* of 1916 Kienzl introduced Styrian dialect, giving the opera a realistically Austrian character. Comic scenes were now more prominent, though Kienzl also retained his ethical concerns; the main character begins by being obsessed with his will and with money, but learns that love and well-being are of greater importance. Such allegorical content represented a modernist aspect in Kienzl's folk operas; in *Sanctissimum* of 1922 a poor fiddler becomes the symbol of the 20th-century composer, forced to prostitute his art. But in matters of musical style Kienzl was not in tune with contemporary trends. His operas have indeed tended to be valued more for their theatrical effectiveness than for their musical invention, much of his musical language relying upon the past models of Wagner, Schumann and Lortzing.

Urvasi op.20, 1884 (3, A. Gödel, after Kalidasa), Dresden, 20 Feb 1886; rev. 1909
Heilmar der Narr op.40 (prelude, 3, W. Kienzl sr, after M. Hartmann), Munich, 8 March 1892, vs (Berlin, 1892)
Der Evangelimann op.45 (musikalisches Schauspiel, 2, Kienzl, after L. F. Meissner), Berlin, 4 May 1895, vs (Berlin, 1894)
Don Quixote op.50 (musikalische Tragikomödie, 3, Kienzl, after M. de Cervantes), Berlin, 18 Nov 1898 (Berlin, 1898)
In Knecht Ruprechts Werkstatt op.75 (Weihnachtsmärchenspiel, 1, H. Voigt), Graz, 25 Dec 1907
Der Kuhreigen op.85 (musikalisches Schauspiel, 3, R. Batka, after R. H. Bartsch), Vienna, 23 Nov 1911 (Vienna, 1911)
Das Testament op.90 (musikalische Komödie, 2, Kienzl, after P. Rosegger), Vienna, 6 Dec 1916, vs (Leipzig, 1916)
Hassan der Schwärmer op.100, 1921 (3, H. Bauer, after A Thousand and One Nights), Chemnitz, 27 Feb 1925, vs (Leipzig and Vienna, 1922)
Sanctissimum op.102, 1922 (melodramatische Allegorie, 1, Bauer), Vienna, 14 Feb 1925 (Vienna, 1922)
Hans Kipfel op.110 (Spl, 1, Bauer, after old Viennese story), Vienna, 1926

*

PEM (H.-J. Bauer)
E. Hanslick: 'Der Evangelimann', *Am Ende des Jahrhunderts (1895–1899): die moderne Oper*, viii (Berlin, 1899), 1–9
R. Batka: 'Don Quixote', *Kranz* (Leipzig, 1903), 232–6
J. Korngold: 'Der Kuhreigen', 'Das Testament', *Deutsches Opernschaffen der Gegenwart: kritische Aufsätze* (Leipzig and Vienna, 1921), 256–69
W. Kienzl: *Meine Lebenswanderung: Erlebtes, Erschautes* (Stuttgart, 1926)
K. Trambacher: *Wilhelm Kienzls Opernstoffe* (diss., U. of Vienna, 1950)
H. Sittner: *Kienzl – Rosegger: eine Künstlerfreundschaft* (Zürich, 1953) [incl. diaries, work-list and correspondence]
I. Samlick-Hagen: *Lehr- und Wanderjahre Wilhelm Kienzls (1874–1897)* (diss., U. of Vienna, 1979)   AMANDA GLAUERT

Kiepura, Jan (*b* Sosnowiec, 16 May 1902; *d* Harrison, NY, 15 Aug 1966). Polish tenor. He studied in Warsaw with Tadeusz Leliva, making his début in Lwów as Faust in 1924. He sang at the Vienna Staatsoper (1926–37) as Cavaradossi, Calaf, Rodolfo, Manrico, Don José and created the Stranger in Korngold's *Das Wunder der Heliane* (1927, Hamburg). In 1928 he sang Cavaradossi at the Paris Opéra and Calaf at La Scala, where he created Marchese Mascarille in Lattuada's *Le preziose ridicole* (1929). He made his American début at Chicago in 1931 as Cavaradossi and his Metropolitan début in 1938 as Rodolfo, singing there until 1942 as Don José, the Duke, Massenet's Des Grieux and Cavaradossi. He also sang in Chicago (1939–42). With his wife, the soprano Marta Eggerth, he appeared on Broadway, on tour and in London at the Palace Theatre (1955) in *The Merry Widow*. A natural actor and a very handsome man, he had a velvet-toned, lyric voice with superb top notes. He made many films and records.

*

GV (R. Celletti; R. Vegeto)   LEO RIEMENS, ELIZABETH FORBES

Kiev. Capital of Ukraine. In the 17th and 18th centuries school theatres played an important part in training performers. Ukrainian performers participated in serf theatres, which on occasion produced entire grand operas. Unfavourable circumstances and economic hardships however prevented the development of an independent Ukrainian operatic culture, in a national and territorial sense, until after the 1917 revolutions. The national aspirations that swept Europe and Russia in the 19th century were dealt with in the Ukraine with increasing harshness by the tsarist regimes, culminating in the Ems Ukase of 1876, which forbade the printing in Ukrainian of anything except historical documents. The restrictions applied to musical and theatrical productions as well. Towards the close of the 19th century Ukrainian musical life was confined to travelling troupes with a repertory reflecting peasant life. The era did produce the composer Mykola Lysenko, who laid the foundation for the future development of a Ukrainian musical style.

Professional operatic activities can be traced to 1803, although touring companies from Poland visited Kiev even earlier, performing in private buildings on makeshift stages. The first opera house built with city funds was completed in 1805–6 and had a seating capacity of 470. From 1816 to 1830 a Polish company headed by Lenkawski was in residence, performing both the theatrical and the operatic repertory. It was replaced during 1829–30 by the Russian company of Ivan Stein, which became the first truly resident company and continued the mixed diet of theatrical and operatic productions, including the popular *Der Freischütz*. In 1851 the theatre was closed, and in 1856 a new city theatre was built on the site of the present Kyïvs'kyy Derzhavnyy Akademichnyy Teatr Opery ta Baletu imeni T. H. Shevchenka (Shevchenko State Academic Theatre of Opera and Ballet). The new theatre had 849 seats and was run by a special committee. Although the official opening was on 20 September/2 October 1856, the first operatic production took place on 16/28 October with the opera *Ukraïntsi* ('The Ukrainians') by M. Karol. Opera became the rage during the three seasons of 1863–6, when the Italian company of Ferdinand Berger was invited to Kiev. In that first season they mounted 14 productions. Their success was so great that in 1865 the performances continued throughout the summer months. In 1867, under the auspices of the Kiev branch of the Russian Music Society, a permanent opera company, the Teatr Russkoy Operï (Russian Opera Company), was formed. This was the first official theatre to be organized in a province, only two opera theatres for the whole Russian empire existing at that time, in St Petersburg and in Moscow. The opening took place on 15/27 December 1867 with Verstovsky's *Askold's Grave*.

The history of the Russian Opera Company in Kiev is by many accounts a splendid one. Tchaikovsky wrote that the company had 'a beautifully organized chorus, a good ballet troupe and a number of designers. ... As to the wealth, refinement and historical accuracy of its costumes the Kiev company is in no way inferior to the St Petersburg [company] and infinitely superior to the Moscow' (*P. Chaykovsky: muzikal'no-kriticheskiye stat'i*, ed. T. Sokolova, Moscow, 1953, pp.219–22). The company gave many important early performances in Russia: *Oprichnik* (27 November/9 December 1874) and *The Queen of Spades* (7/19 December 1890), *The Snow Maiden* by Rimsky-Korsakov (December 1895), and *Aleko* by Rakhmaninov, conducted by the composer (6/18 October 1893). During its existence, until 1917, a number of important singers appeared on its stage, among them Fyodor Stravinsky (the father of Igor) and Shalyapin.

After the Russian Opera Company was disbanded in 1917, on 15 March 1919 the Opera Ukraïns'koï Radyanskoï Respubliky imeni K. Liebknekhta (Liebknecht Opera of the Ukrainian SSR) was established. It was at this time (until 1925) that operas were first sung in Ukrainian. In 1925, in an attempt to overcome the enormous difficulties of creating a national opera theatre, the three principal opera companies in Ukraine, at Kiev, Kharkiv and Odessa, formed a three-part company that shared singers and productions, but this lasted for one season only. By 1926 each company felt strong enough to go its independent way, and the Kyïvs'ka Derzhavna Akademichna Ukraïns'ka Opera (Kiev State Academic Opera) was inaugurated. In 1934 it became the Kyïvs'kyy Derzhavnyy Akademichnyy Teatr Opery ta Baletu (Kiev State Academic Theatre of Opera and Ballet) and finally, in 1939, adopted the title Shevchenko State Academic Theatre of Opera and Ballet. Before World War II it cultivated a number of Ukrainian singers, such as Mariya Lytvynenko-Vol'hemut, Mariya Sokil, Ivan Kozlovsky, Mykhaylo Hryshko, Borys Hmyrya and others. The repertory became varied – in addition to the standard Italian and Russian fare, a limited number of French and German operas were presented, and even Berg's *Wozzeck* was seriously considered – but few Ukrainian operas were produced. In the late 1920s a wave of experimentation swept Ukrainian opera theatre, with productions including *Jonny spielt auf*, *Turandot*, *Tiefland* (d'Albert) and *Guillaume Tell*. Of special interest were Serhy Karhalsky's productions of *Prince Igor* and *Rusalka*, in the spirit of Ukrainian folk art. One of the main achievements of this period was the production of Borys Lyatoshyns'ky's *Zolotyy obruch* ('The Golden Ring'). As the war reached Ukraine the Kiev Opera was evacuated to Irkutsk in 1942, where it combined with the Kharkiv Theatre of Opera and Ballet. It remained there until the end of 1943, resuming productions in Kiev in 1944. In the 1950s and 60s the Kiev Opera expanded its activities and again achieved an international reputation. It began to tour in countries such as Yugoslavia, Bulgaria, East Germany, Romania, Spain and, more recently, in France, Italy, Egypt and Japan. The Kiev Opera was chosen by Shostakovich when the revival of his epoch-making *Lady Macbeth of the Mtsensk District* was filmed.

*

ME (L. B. Arkhimovich; also 'Ukrainskiy teatr operï i baleta', Yu. A. Stanishevsky)

'Istoricheskaya spravka "Kiyevskiy teatr"', *Kiyevlyanin* (15 Aug 1901)

'Do istorii ukraïns'koï opery v Kyyevi' [Towards a History of Ukrainian Opera in Kiev], *Muzyka* (1923), no.2

M. Stefanovych: *Kyïvs'kyy derzhavnyy ordena Lenina akademichnyy teatr opery ta baletu URSR imeni T. H. Shevchenka* (Kiev, 1960)

L. Arkhimovych: *Shlakhy rozvytku ukraïns'koï radyans'koï opery* [Paths of Development of Ukrainian Soviet Opera] (Kiev, 1970)

Yu. Stanyshevs'ky: *Ukraïns'kyy radyans'kyy muzychnyy teatr 1917–1967* [Soviet Ukrainian Music Theatre 1917–1967] (Kiev, 1970)

M. Hordiychuk: 'Na shlyakhu do stvorennya ukraïns'koï opery v Kyyevi' [On the Way to the Creation of the Ukrainian Opera in Kiev], *Ukraïnske muzykoznavstvo*, x (1975), 93–113

Yu. Stanyshevs'ky: *Opernyy teatr Radyans'koï Ukraïny* [Opera Theatre of Soviet Ukraine] (Kiev, 1988)

VIRKO BALEY

Killebrew, Gwendolyn (*b* Philadelphia, 26 Aug 1939). American mezzo-soprano. She studied at the Juilliard School and the Metropolitan Opera Studio, making her début in 1967 as Waltraute (*Die Walküre*). During 1973 she sang Baba the Turk (*The Rake's Progress*) at Washington, DC, and Léonor (*La favorite*) and Marina (*Boris Godunov*) at San Francisco. She made her Santa Fe début in 1975 as Carmen, a role she later repeated at the Metropolitan. In 1976 she became a member of the Deutsche Oper am Rhein, Düsseldorf, where her roles included Gluck's Orpheus, Isabella (*L'italiana in Algeri*), Azucena, Preziosilla and Frau Leimberger in Klebe's *Der jüngste Tag* (1988). Her powerful rich-toned voice made her an ideal interpreter of Amneris and Mistress Quickly, which she sang in Amsterdam (1980) and Zürich (1981). She also had several Wagner roles in her repertory, including Fricka and Waltraute (*Götterdämmerung*), in which she made her Bayreuth début in 1978.

ELIZABETH FORBES

Killmayer, Wilhelm (*b* Munich, 21 Aug 1927). German composer. After tuition from Waltershausen (1945–50) and Orff (1953), he taught in Munich, and was ballet conductor at the Staatsoper (1961–5). Around this time he composed several works for the stage, including *Yolimba*. In 1974 he was appointed professor of composition at the Staatliche Musikhochschule, Munich. He won an Italia Prize (for *Une leçon de français* in 1965) and other prizes. His creative work, influenced by Orff, has developed independently, drawing on other types of new music but retaining a direct expressive power. A Hölderlin opera was planned in the late 1980s.

La buffonata, 1959–60 (Ballettoper, T. Dorst), Heidelberg, 30 April 1961, vs (Mainz, 1961)

La tragedia di Orfeo (after A. Poliziano), Munich, 9 June 1961

Yolimba, oder Die Grenzen der Magie, 1962–3 (musikalische Posse, 1, Dorst and Killmayer), Wiesbaden, 25 March 1964; rev., Munich, 9 May 1970, vs (Mainz, 1965)

Une leçon de français, 1964, Stuttgart, 19 Oct 1966

PAUL GRIFFITHS

Kimm, Fiona (*b* Ipswich, 24 May 1952). English mezzo-soprano. A member of the Covent Garden chorus from 1975 to 1977, she made her début in 1978 at Glyndebourne as the Third Lady (*Die Zauberflöte*) with the Glyndebourne Touring Opera. In 1979 she joined the ENO, where her roles included Hänsel, Mercédès, Rosalind (*The Mines of Sulphur*), Fyodor, Siébel, the Kitchen Boy (*Rusalka*), Nicklausse, Smeraldina and Lola. She made her Covent Garden début in 1983 as the Shepherd (*L'enfant et les sortilèges*) and has also sung with Opera North and Scottish Opera and at Lyons and Geneva; she took part in the premières of Cowie's *Kate Kelly's Road* (1983, Chester) and Turnage's *Greek* (1988, Munich). Her other roles include Olga, Hermia, the High-School Boy and the Groom (*Lulu*), and in 1992 she sang the Old Woman, the Spanish Girl and the Waitress in *Der ferne Klang* for

Opera North at Leeds. A versatile artist with a voice of unusual resonance, she is particularly effective in trouser roles.   ELIZABETH FORBES

Kincses, Veronika (*b* Budapest, 8 Sept 1948). Hungarian soprano. She studied with Jenő Sipos at the Liszt Academy of Music, Budapest, 1968–73, and with Gianna Pederzini at the Accademia di S Cecilia in Rome, 1974. Her début was in 1974 at the Budapest Opera as Zerlina. She has made guest appearances in Vienna (Staatsoper) in 1983, San Francisco and Boston in 1984, West Berlin and Montreal in 1985, Barcelona (Liceo) and Venice (Fenice) in 1986, Buenos Aires (Colón) in 1987, Pittsburgh in 1989 and Rome in 1990. An excellent lyric soprano with some dramatic roles in her repertory, she is at her best in Puccini, especially as Butterfly; she is also a fine Mozart singer. Her greatest strength lies in the softness and beauty of her sound.
                                                    PÉTER P. VÁRNAI

Kind, Johann Friedrich (*b* Leipzig, 4 March 1768; *d* Dresden, 25 June 1843). German writer. He studied at the Thomasschule (1782), where he came to know Johann August Apel and began writing poetry; then, settling in Dresden (1792), he published novels and poetry, also doing some occasional writing and journalism. He was a member of the 'Dichter-Thee', later 'Liederkreis', that included Helmina von Chezy and subsequently Weber, for whose *Freischütz* he wrote the libretto. His play *Van Dycks Landleben* was produced in Dresden in 1816, and in the same year he took on the editing, with Carl Winkler, of the *Dresdner Abendzeitung*. Weber's triumph at the première of *Der Freischütz* (1821, Berlin) embittered Kind, as he felt that insufficient credit was given to his libretto; a result was to stimulate him to a series of more ambitious literary projects that earned him some renown in his day. He withdrew from the *Abendzeitung* in 1826, and retired from literary life in 1832.

Kind wrote the libretto for Marschner's Singspiel *Der Holzdieb* (1825, Dresden) and for Kalliwoda's opera *Blanda, die silberne Birke* (1847, Prague). His play *Das Nachtlager von Granada* was the basis for Conradin Kreutzer's opera of the same title (1834, Vienna). He is remembered, however, only as the author of the text for *Der Freischütz*. Though he insisted that he found the story in a 'browning, dusty quarto' in the Leipzig Ratsbibliothek with Apel (*Unterredungen von der Reiche der Geister*, by Otto von Graben zum Stein – not a quarto), he almost certainly took it not from there but from Apel and Laun's treatment in their popular *Gespensterbuch* (1810) and other sources. He gave his version of the events, together with the original text and much other relevant *Freischütz* material, in his *Freischützbuch* (Leipzig, 1843).

J. G. T. Grässe: *Die Quelle des Freischütz* (Dresden, 1870)
H. W. von Waltershausen: *Der Freischütz: ein Versuch über die musikalische Romantik* (Munich, 1920)
F. Hasselberg: *Der Freischütz: Friedrich Kinds Operndichtung und ihre Quellen* (Berlin, 1921)
T. Cornelissen: *Weber's 'Freischütz' als Beispiel einer Operhandlung* (Berlin, 1940)
H. Schnoor: *Weber auf dem Welttheater: ein Freischützbuch* (Dresden, 1942, 4/1963)   JOHN WARRACK

Kindermann, August (*b* Potsdam, 6 Feb 1817; *d* Munich, 6 March 1891). German bass-baritone. In 1836 he joined the chorus of the Berlin Hofoper, and in 1839 he was engaged at Leipzig, where he took part in the first performance of Lortzing's *Caramo*. He also created the title role of Lortzing's *Hans Sachs* (1840) and Eberbach in *Der Wildschütz* (1842). In 1846 he went to Munich, where he was engaged at the Hofoper until his retirement in 1889. His very large repertory included Mozart's Figaro and Sarastro, Hidraot in Gluck's *Armide*, Indra (*Le roi de Lahore*) and many of Wagner's baritone and bass roles. He sang Wotan in the first performances of *Das Rheingold* (1869) and *Die Walküre* (1870); his repertory also included King Henry (*Lohengrin*), Fafner, Hunding, Hagen, King Mark and Titurel, which he sang at the first performance of *Parsifal* at Bayreuth (1882). For the 40th anniversary of his engagement at Munich he sang Stadinger in Lortzing's *Der Waffenschmied* (1886). His son and three daughters all became singers, the best known of them being Hedwig Reicher-Kindermann.   ELIZABETH FORBES

Kindermann, Hedwig Reicher-. *See* REICHER-KINDERMANN, HEDWIG.

King, James (*b* Dodge City, KS, 22 May 1925). American tenor. After study with Martial Singher and Max Lorenz he began his career as a baritone. As a winner of the American Opera Auditions in Cincinnati, he was sent to Europe in 1961 where he made his professional début in Florence, singing Cavaradossi. His first resident appointment took him to the Deutsche Oper, Berlin (1962), and engagements followed at Salzburg (1962), Vienna (1963), Bayreuth (1965) and La Scala (1968). In the USA he has sung at San Francisco, making his début in 1961 as Don José, and at the Metropolitan, where he first appeared in 1966 as Florestan. He sang the Emperor in both the Metropolitan and Covent Garden premières of *Die Frau ohne Schatten*. His bright, slender tone, easy top voice and remarkable stamina have made him particularly successful in the lighter Wagner roles such as Walther von Stolzing, Parsifal and Lohengrin; his repertory also includes Otello, Siegmund (which can be heard in Böhm's Bayreuth recording of the *Ring*) and the title role in Pfitzner's *Palestrina*. In 1983 at La Scala he sang the title role in the revival of Cherubini's *Anacreon*; he sang Aegisthus at Salzburg in 1989 and the Drum-Major at the Metropolitan in 1990.

                                                    MARTIN BERNHEIMER

King, Matthew Peter (*b* London, *c*1773; *d* London, Jan 1823). English composer. Little is known of him beyond a catalogue of his works, though he was probably a child prodigy, as his earliest compositions appeared under the name of 'Master King'. Before 1800 he published a series of keyboard works, and around the turn of the century several theoretical treatises. When he was about 30 he began composing songs for plays and 'operas', mostly written by James Kenney and S. J. Arnold, and staged at the two patent houses (Drury Lane and Covent Garden) and at Arnold's Lyceum theatre (the English Opera House). Kelly, Braham and Davy also wrote songs for some of the plays – Braham exclusively for himself to sing – though they were not collaborations in any real sense. King was undoubtedly a talented musician, but most of his theatrical songs were incidental to their dramatic context. Musically they exhibit a short-breathed, harmonically simplistic charm similar to the stage music of Henry Bishop. After the enormous success of Bishop's *The Miller and his*

Men in 1813, King wrote no further works for the stage and returned to more serious music (his music in J. Tobin's 1819 melodrama *The Fisherman's Hut* was probably not originally composed for it). The aria 'Eve's Lamentation' from King's oratorio *The Intercession* was especially successful and was widely circulated. His son C. M. King was also a composer.

all performed in London and published in year of performance

LCG – *Covent Garden*   LDL – *Drury Lane*

Matrimony (comic op, 2, J. Kenney), LDL, 20 Nov 1804
Too Many Cooks (musical farce, 2, Kenney), LCG, 12 Feb 1805
The Weathercock (comic op, 2, J. T. Allingham), LDL, 18 Nov 1805
False Alarms, or My Cousin (comic op, 3, Kenney), LDL, 12 Jan 1807, collab. J. Braham
Ella Rosenberg (melodrama, 2, Kenney), LDL, 19 Nov 1807, *GB-Lbl*
Up All Night, or The Smuggler's Cave (comic op, 3, S. J. Arnold), Lyceum, 26 June 1809, Act 2 *Lbl*
Oh, This Love, or The Masqueraders (comic op, Kenney), Lyceum, 12 June 1810
Plots!, or The North Tower (melodramatic op, Arnold), Lyceum, 3 Sept 1810
The Americans (comic op, 3, Arnold), Lyceum, 27 April 1811, collab. Braham
Timour the Tartar (melodrama, M. G. Lewis), LCG, 29 April 1811
One o'clock, or The Knight and the Wood Daemon (grand romantic op, 3, Lewis), Lyceum, 1 Aug 1811, rev. of M. Kelly
Turn Him Out, or Tyrant and Parasite (musical farce, 2, Kenney), Lyceum, 7 March 1812
The Fisherman's Hut (melodrama, J. Tobin), LDL, 20 Oct 1819, collab. J. Davy

*

EitnerQ; *FétisB*
J. Sainsbury, ed.: *A Dictionary of Musicians* (London, 2/1825)
J. D. Brown and S. S. Stratton: *British Musical Biography* (Birmingham, 1897)
The Stage Cyclopaedia (London, *c*1910)
CHARLES CUDWORTH/BRUCE CARR

King and Charcoal Burner [*Král a uhlíř*]. Comic opera in three acts by ANTONÍN DVOŘÁK to a libretto by B. J. Lobeský [Bernard Guldener]; Prague, Provisional Theatre, 24 November 1874 (original version (1871), Prague, National Theatre, 28 May 1929).

Lobeský's story, based on older sources including the puppet plays of Prokop Konopásek, tells of the friendship that grows between King Matyáš (baritone) and the charcoal burner, Matěj (baritone). In the first act Matěj entertains a stranger lost in the forest. The love interest is provided by Matěj's daughter, Liduška (soprano), and a young charcoal burner, Jeník (tenor). Jeník mistakenly thinks Liduška is consorting with the stranger when she is only telling him of Matěj's unwillingness to permit her love for Jeník. Jeník's jealousy drives him to become a soldier, and eventually captain, of the king's guard. All is resolved in Act 3 when Matěj and his family are invited to Prague, where the king returns his hospitality, but only after the charcoal burner's family is accused of mistreating the stranger. King Matyáš finally admits that he was the stranger, Liduška and Jeník are reunited and all ends happily.

Two distinct versions of the opera exist. Dvořák's first attempt, composed in 1871 (but not performed until 1929), was far too difficult for the performers of the Provisional Theatre when it went into rehearsal. Musically, the work is one of Dvořák's most adventurous operas, incorporating Wagnerian elements and bold harmonic experiment. The opera also shows clear signs of an idiomatic approach to the setting of Czech. The second version, composed (and performed) in 1874, is substantially different and in a simpler style, more reminiscent of Lortzing. In 1886 Dvořák asked V. J. Novotný to make revisions to the libretto. Apart from removing a subplot in Act 3 involving a lady of the court and a dignitary, Novotný improved Lobeský's versification; the revision was performed in Prague at the National Theatre on 15 June 1887.   JAN SMACZNY

King Arthur [*King Arthur, or The British Worthy*]. Semi-opera in five acts by HENRY PURCELL and JOHN DRYDEN; London, Queen's Theatre, Dorset Garden, late May–early June 1691.

Dryden wrote *King Arthur* in 1684 in anticipation of the celebration of the 25th anniversary of the restoration of Charles II. It was a play in blank verse intended to be 'adorn'd with Scenes, Machines, Songs and Dances' – what Dryden called a 'dramatick opera'. But the king specifically requested a French-style opera, so the original sung prologue to the play, entitled *Albion and Albanius*, was expanded and set to music by Luis Grabu; *King Arthur* was then abandoned. Greatly impressed by Purcell's music for *Dioclesian* in 1690, Dryden revised the script for him a year later. By far the most popular and enduring of Purcell's stage works, with revivals throughout the 18th century and even into the 19th, *King Arthur* is his only semi-opera specifically designed as such rather than adapted from a spoken play. David Garrick produced a heavily altered version in 1770 with new music by Thomas Arne.

The plot, while drawing on Geoffrey of Monmouth's *Historia regum Britanniae* and other sources of Arthurian legend, is essentially Dryden's. Arthur and the Britons fight Oswald and the Saxons to establish a united kingdom. Most of the story concerns Arthur's attempts (assisted by Merlin) to free his beloved Emmeline from the clutches of Oswald and his evil magician Osmond. Purcell's music consists of six separate scenes, distributed throughout the play. Unlike the self-contained masques of the other semi-operas, most of the musical episodes are integral and advance the plot, even though the main characters (Arthur, Osmond, Emmeline and others) do not sing. The vocal forces are led by the spirits Philidel (soprano) and Grimbald (baritone) who, unusually for semi-opera, also speak.

The first musical scene (Act 1 scene ii) is the sacrifice offered by the Saxons on the eve of battle. Purcell constructed this exactly like a verse anthem, with solemn choral responses interspersed between solo incantations which lead to longer, developed choruses. The battle follows immediately, with the Britons' taunting air and chorus 'Come if you dare, our trumpets sound'; Purcell's vivid setting of Dryden's line 'the double, double, double beat of the thundring drum' was imitated by Handel in his treatment of the similar line in his setting of Dryden in his Ode for St Cecilia's Day.

The second act opens with the Britons in hot pursuit of the routed Saxons, whose evil spirit Grimbald misdirects the attackers into perilous rivers and 'dreadful downfalls'. In the most overtly operatic scene of the work, 'Hither this way', Philidel and his followers try to redirect Arthur's men to safety while Grimbald's forces pull in the opposite direction; the lithe music graphically points the way. The second musical episode of this act is a pastoral entertainment for Emmeline – two air-and-chorus pairs which remind the shepherds of the consequences of sexual pleasure.

In Act 3 the blind Emmeline, held by Oswald, has her sight restored by Philidel in a mysterious and apparently symbolic episode for which no music survives. The heroine steadfastly refuses the advances of Osmond who, frustrated, gives a demonstration of his magical powers by showing her 'a Prospect of Winter in Frozen Countries'. Then follows the famous Frost Scene, which includes one of Purcell's greatest pieces, 'What power art thou', a remarkable chromatic aria for the Cold Genius (baritone). The composer underscored the string and voice parts with wavy lines whose exact meaning is unknown, though the desired effect is obvious. The passage is supposedly inspired by the shivering chorus in Lully's opera *Isis* (1677), but Purcell's daring harmonic technique and intensity of expression are of a completely different magnitude.

The fourth act finds Emmeline still in captivity, with Arthur's rescue attempts thwarted by Saxon magic. The centrepiece of the act (indeed, of the entire work) is the massive passacaglia 'How happy the lover', one of Purcell's longest compositions. It is built on a four-bar ground bass (repeated 59 times in various forms) with a succession of solos, duets, trios, choruses and instrumental interludes. The passacaglia far exceeds Dryden's stage direction for a 'minuet' and was clearly influenced by the chaconnes in Lully's *tragédies en musique*.

The fifth-act entertainment, played out after Arthur has comprehensively defeated the Saxons and forgiven Oswald, is a miscellaneous pageant in celebration of Britannia, who rises on an island 'with Fisherman at her Feet' during the performance of the virtuoso bass aria 'Ye blust'ring brethren of the skies'. Britannia is then entertained by a hotch-potch of music which includes the rollicking and blasphemous folksong 'Your hay it is mow'd' followed by the nostalgic air 'Fairest isle', sung by Venus (soprano), whose noble melody is supported by richly dissonant harmony.

Dryden hinted that *King Arthur* was a political allegory whose exact meaning is probably irrecoverable, a design which may account for the ambiguous tone of the drama. The music, by contrast, is consistently fine and, apart from the thumping patriotism of the finale, on a more intimate scale than either *Dioclesian* or *The Fairy-Queen*. (Purcell used only two or three solo singers who doubled up on roles, and the orchestra did not include kettledrums.) Yet in spite of the skilful integration of music and drama, *King Arthur* remains a play with music; it is not an opera.   CURTIS PRICE

Kingdom for a Cow, A. Musical play by KURT WEILL to a book by Reginald Arkell with lyrics by Desmond Carter (after Weill's unfinished operetta *Der Kuhhandel* to a libretto by Robert Vambery); London, Savoy Theatre, 28 June 1935.

In the republic of Santa Maria, half of an imaginary Caribbean island (the other half is the republic of Ucqua), Leslie Jones (baritone), an arms dealer, has instructions to start an arms race between the two halves. But President Mendez of Santa Maria (tenor *buffo*) is a pacifist. He allows himself to be bribed, however, and orders an assignment of arms that he has no intention of using. Jones sounds the alarm in Ucqua, which responds by planning to invade its neighbour. The President in turn responds by calling a peace conference. Jones then organizes a *coup d'état* by General Conchas (high baritone), Santa Maria's War Minister. War seems inevitable. The emergency impinges on everyone, even the villagers Juan (lyric tenor) and Juanita (lyric soprano), who are romantically engaged (hence the work's Kleistian subtitle: *Die Verlobung von Santa Maria*). The metaphorical *Kuhhandel* ('shady dealing', or 'horse

trading') of the original title turns into a literal one ('cow trading'): Juan and Juanita's livelihood, a cow, is confiscated twice in lieu of extra taxes for the war effort (the money for the second cow is earned by unloading armaments); Juan is conscripted, and Juanita forced to work in a brothel. After refusing to swear allegiance to the General and instead heroically clipping him round the ear, Juan is sent before a firing squad. But none of the weapons works, whereupon the General extols the virtues of peaceful coexistence, pardons Juan and, amid rejoicing, blesses the couple.

The process whereby the two-act operetta *Der Kuhhandel* became *A Kingdom for a Cow* reflects the turbulent circumstances of the years between Weill's abrupt departure from Germany in March 1933 and his emigration to the USA in September 1935. Like the biblical pageant *Der Weg der Verheissung* (which became *The Eternal Road*), *Der Kuhhandel* began life in German but was completed and first performed in English. The topicality of its libretto hardly needs stressing. Its satirical format draws on the conventions of operetta, lending substance to the otherwise tenuous comparison between Weill and Offenbach. Weill worked on *Der Kuhhandel* in France between February and December 1934, initially with hope of a première in Zürich, but other projects intervened. When he resumed work, including the orchestration, in January 1935, he had moved to London. *A Kingdom for a Cow* resulted from an unsuccessful attempt to turn the satirical operetta into a modern West End musical comedy. The London production closed after three weeks but Weill did not wholly discard the music. Borrowings crop up in several of his American stage works, the best-known being 'September Song', the opening melody of which first appeared in *Der Kuhhandel* ('Seit ich in diese Stadt gekommen bin'). Attempts to reconstruct the original German version, which has never been staged, initially met with opposition from the librettist. Vambery's revised libretto of 1977 forms the basis of the performing edition completed by Lys Symonette from the disparate sources. A concert performance using fragments from the original German version was given at the Düsseldorf Tonhalle on 23 March 1990 as part of the Weill festival.   STEPHEN HINTON

King Goes Forth to France, The [*Kuningas lähtee Ranskaan*]. Opera in three acts by AULIS SALLINEN to a libretto by Paavo Haavikko; Savonlinna, 7 July 1984.

Sallinen's third opera was a joint commission from the Savonlinna Festival, the Royal Opera, Covent Garden (where it was given on 1 April 1987), and the BBC. It is a somewhat enigmatic work best described as a parable that deals with power and war and their effect on people. A new ice age overwhelms a future England. The young Prince (baritone) wrests power from his complacent Prime Minister (bass) and crowns himself King. He decides to lead his court, his four prospective brides and his people across the frozen English Channel to France. Once they are across, events go back to the Hundred Years' War. The Battle of Crécy is refought; the King besieges Calais with frightful cruelty and finally leads his hordes on a march towards Paris and the south (which seem to symbolize the future and its uncertainties).

The King Goes Forth to France has aroused somewhat conflicting responses. Haavikko's libretto, laden with symbolism, has been condemned as obscure and praised as a relevant warning of the consequences of the nuclear age. Sallinen's music has met equally divided opinions: it has been criticized as cliché-ridden and complimented for its colourful inventiveness. It contains unashamedly lyrical passages, but the underlying dark message of warning is often clad in sharp irony – for instance in the way Sallinen burlesques one of Schubert's *Marches militaires* as a troop of doomed Genoese cross-bowmen march towards Crécy. Sallinen reserves his most poignant scoring for two of the victims, an English Archer (baritone), who is brutally tortured on the King's orders, and one of the ladies, The Caroline with the Thick Mane (mezzo-soprano), who loses her reason as the world around her slides towards degradation and squalor.

ERKKI ARNI

King Priam. Opera in three acts by MICHAEL TIPPETT to his own libretto after HOMER's *Iliad*; Coventry, Belgrade Theatre (Royal Opera, Covent Garden), 29 May 1962.

Priam *King of Troy*	bass-baritone
Hecuba *his wife*	dramatic soprano
Hector *their eldest son*	baritone
Andromache *Hector's wife*	lyric dramatic soprano
Paris *Priam's second son*	boy soprano/tenor
Helen *wife to Menelaus of Sparta, then*	
wife in adultery to Paris	mezzo-soprano
Achilles *a Greek hero*	heroic tenor
Patroclus *his friend*	light baritone
Nurse	mezzo-soprano
Old Man *also Greek chorus*	bass
Young Guard	lyric tenor
Hermes *messenger of the gods*	high light tenor

Hunters, wedding guests, serving women

Setting The royal palace, walls, plain and environs of Troy, and the royal palace at Sparta

King Priam (1958–61), Tippett's second opera, was in many respects a carefully considered reaction to *The Midsummer Marriage*, composed, without any real prospect of production, between 1946 and 1952. This experience of a prolonged gestation and period of composition, and an unfavourable response when it was eventually produced at Covent Garden in 1955, did not deter Tippett. His mind had already turned to considering Greek theatre in some radio talks in 1953 about the effect of music in the theatre. Three years later he read a book by Lucien Goldmann, *Le dieu caché*, which, he wrote, 'determined the tragic nature of my new opera *King Priam*' through its analysis of tragedy in the dramas of Racine. He was also influenced by Brecht's concept of epic theatre, the visit to London in 1956 of the Berliner Ensemble and the Barrault production of Claudel's *Christophe Colomb*.

In 1957 a commission from the Koussevitzky Foundation for a large-scale choral and orchestral work brought from Tippett an initial idea of a work in 'eight, somewhat unrelated scenes' concerned with man's progress from birth to death. He was persuaded that this was in reality an operatic scenario and advised to discuss the project with the director Peter Brook. In the aftermath of *The Midsummer Marriage*, in which Tippett had created his own heavily symbolic scenario, it was suggested that he should now take a familiar story and present it simply. He found his ideal material in Homer's *Iliad*, though it is characteristic that, given his instinctive pull towards the Greek world, he should view the scenario from the Trojan perspective. He was able to change the scope of the commission to one for an opera, and it was later agreed that it would be produced by the Royal Opera, Covent Garden, who gave the première at the Coventry Festival of 1962 which marked the consecration of the new cathedral. *King Priam*, one of the most war-torn of all operas, was thus heard for the first time a day before the première of Britten's *War Requiem*.

PRELUDE   As in *The Midsummer Marriage*, *King Priam* opens with a vivid musical 'frame' for the orchestra and chorus. In this instance the piercing trumpets of war speak for themselves, as do the fusillades of timpani-fire. According to authoritative commentators, the offstage cries of the chorus represent the anguished sounds of labour, taken over by the lower brass as a jolting pattern of contractions.

ACT 1.i   *The royal palace at Troy*   A final heave and a gentle oboe introduces a baby in his cot – we have been present at the birth pangs of Paris. The musical drama is stark and uncompromising and, though harsh, has a sense of visceral excitement. Tippett's command of grand dramatic gesture is here at its most impressive, and just as brilliantly calculated is the intimacy of the darkened nursery and the gentle sounds of a nurse calming the crying baby.

It is in this domestic context that Tippett introduces King Priam and his queen, Hecuba. She is troubled by a dream and cannot attend to the child. Her musical line is jerky and haughty, in distinct contrast to the soothing tone of the nurse and the regal entry of Priam. This initial scene comes to a point of focus when the king summons an Old Man to interpret the dream. He reads it as a premonition that the child Paris will in time cause his father's death. Hecuba's reaction, violent and hysterical, is to call for the child's immediate death. Her frenzied singing is accompanied by a wild, insistent ostinato from the violins, which is to be her characterizing musical gesture. When Priam is asked to react he sings against a warm and deeply moving chordal pattern from the lower strings, and his attitude is initially one of torn humanity – 'a father and a King'. It is clear from the music that his conscience tells him one thing, but that his duty as a king compels him to follow a ruthless course, and the child is ordered to be killed. In his response Priam touches on what is for Tippett the central theme of the opera – the conflict between human choice and the actions of Fate: 'O child who cannot choose to live or die, I choose for you'. Ian Kemp has pointed to the origin of this topic for Tippett in a passage from *The Midsummer Marriage*: 'Fate and freedom propound a paradox/Choose your fate but still the god/Speaks through whatever acts ensue'.

Interlude 1 begins as the king and queen leave to the sound of a royal fanfare. Tippett now introduces one of the most significant dramatic devices of the opera. The Nurse, Old Man and Young Guard (who goes briefly offstage with the child as if to dispose of him, though in fact he ensures his survival) come to the front of the stage and address the audience directly. They comment on the action in the manner of a Greek chorus but also adopt a Brechtian trait in examining the moral and philosophical (but in no direct sense political) issues raised so far. By implication, we are invited to ponder these issues ourselves, at a subtle remove from the enmeshed world of the opera's protagonist. This is Tippett's adaptation of the technique of alienation, and the interjection also serves to move the action forward.

1.ii *The countryside outside Troy* The pastoral timbre of woodwind punctuated by bucolic horn calls conjures up a world of 'hunting and the arts of peace'. Priam and his eldest son, Hector, are seen at their recreation. Attention focusses on an alluring young boy discovered by Hector, who performs dazzling feats. His ambition is to leave his shepherd father and graduate to Troy as a 'young hero' like Hector. Priam accepts him and on asking his name is answered 'Paris'. As at the foretelling of the Old Man in scene i, time momentarily stands still, for which Tippett finds a clipped, dislocated sound from woodwind and gentle chiming percussion. This momentous discovery enables Priam to release the feelings he had clearly felt when making his initial choice: 'So I'd hoped it might be; that accident or god reversed the choice'. Priam now has an extended monologue of reflection and consideration of his position. Haunted by echoes of his earlier contemplation, he decisively accepts Paris as his son, whatever the consequences.

Interlude 2 (like the first interlude) serves a dual purpose. As Chorus, the characters reflect on life as 'a bitter charade', and their tone, as was true of Priam's monologue, is here intensified. They then go on to fill in a stretch of the story with the help of a chorus of wedding guests who report on Hector's wedding to Andromache. Paris's growth from boy, to youth, to beautiful young man is sketched, and we learn of his rift with his father and brother and that he has sailed to Greece, 'where Menelaus keeps open house in Sparta with his wife, Daughter of Zeus, Queen Helen'.

1.iii *Menelaus's palace at Sparta* In one of Tippett's most vivid dramatic coups the onward flow of this narrative is cut short by the unmistakable sounds of ecstatic love-making. The male voice has a line derived from the birth pangs of the opening, and the same frisson of physical excitement is uncannily created. This adulterous passion of Paris and Helen is soon put in context by her invocation of her husband Menelaus. Paris is outraged that she could possibly return to him and so asks her to choose between them. She indicates that she chooses Paris, if he so wishes. His reflection is suffused with the acceptance that if he sails with her back to Troy there will be a grim avenging war. As he prays to Zeus for guidance, the god Hermes suddenly appears in his role as a messenger of the gods. Another striking theatrical moment is now prepared – the Judgment of Paris – in which he is asked to choose between three goddesses, Athene, Hera and Aphrodite. He relates the first two to Hecuba and Andromache (though she has not yet appeared to us in the opera) and Aphrodite, as if by reflex action, to Helen. He chooses her, is cursed by the others and takes her away to Troy. This decisive end to Act 1 is dramatically very effective: a crucial personal choice has been made which will trigger an irrevocable war and a further chain of seemingly inevitable events.

ACT 2.i *Troy* We are plunged directly into this climate of conflict and violence. Act 2 has been described as a 'war' act, scored only for men's voices and an ensemble of wind, brass and percussion, with a prominent role for the piano. This is a theatrically telling deployment of resources, and it creates a fine dramatic balance. Tension mounts as Hector and Paris quarrel. Hector is

'King Priam' (Tippett), Act 3 scene iii (Achilles' tent): King Priam (Forbes Robinson, left) pleads with Achilles (Richard Lewis) to allow him to take back the body of his son Hector (Covent Garden, London, 1962; design by Sean Kenny)

the embodiment of the Trojan 'young hero' annoyed by 'Prince handsome Paris', whose adulterous affair is the cause of the war. Troy's very masculinity and sovereignty are at stake, and the accompanying music has a hectoring muscular quality – its memorability enhanced by extensive quotation in the Second Piano Sonata (1962) and the Concerto for Orchestra (1962–3). Priam emerges to command the situation, and his sons run off to fight.

2.ii *Achilles' tent* The first interlude of this act sees Hermes taking the Old Man from the walls of Troy through to the Greek battle lines. The clear threat to Troy is the Greek war-hero Achilles, who however has retreated to his tent because of a trivial snub administered by Agamemnon. He is now seen ensconced with his friend Patroclus, and it is implied that their emotional relationship is of the closest, Patroclus being the key to Achilles' heart. In musical terms Tippett manages the most effective contrast. As if intensified by the surrounding barrage of warlike noises, the episode in the tent has a moving intimacy – Achilles sings to the accompaniment of his guitar, and Patroclus is moved to tears by his song. They decide to dress Patroclus in Achilles' celebrated armour and to send him to battle in order to confound the Trojans, who imagine Achilles, for a time, to be passive.

2.iii *Troy* A second 'war' interlude reversing the journey of the first leads to a final scene of reportage. Paris tells Priam of Hector's fight with a figure in Achilles' armour, Patroclus is killed, and Priam, Paris and Hector enact a gruesome ceremony of blood-lust over the dead body, only to be overshadowed by the far more blood-curdling sound of Achilles' war-cry of revenge, which closes this central act.

The shaping of this act as an independent entity was an addition and revision to the original two-act scenario, as is revealed by Eric Walter White, who corresponded with the composer at the time of composition. Others prefer the two-act structure and see the final result as afflicted by 'structural imbalance' and 'faults in construction' (Ian Kemp). The composer's judgment however seems theatrically and dramatically acute. Act 3 may be lengthy, but its purpose is not so much one of action, of which there has been plenty, as of restitution and contemplation.

ACT 3.i *The royal palace at Troy* In a suitable counterbalance to the counterpointing of women and goddesses at the end of Act 1, the final act opens with a tableau for the women – as wives and mistress. Andromache is visited by a premonition of Hector's death at the hand of Achilles, and with her mother-in-law Hecuba she berates the adulterous Helen, who is indirectly the instrument of his death. In an imposing aria, 'Let her rave', Helen asserts her authority and near-divinity, and the three women join in a trio addressed to their associated goddesses.

3.ii *The royal palace at Troy* After Interlude 1, in which a chorus of serving women briefly confirm the death of Hector, scene ii is a graphic and revealing treatment of King Priam's reaction to this blow. Paris breaks the news and is severely rebuked for his trouble – he goes to kill Achilles in further revenge. An extended monologue allows Priam to reflect on the tricks of Fate.

3.iii *Achilles' tent* The profound and purely instrumental Interlude 2 which precedes this scene shifts the action back to Achilles' tent. Achilles is disturbed by Priam, who brings the body of Achilles' beloved

Patroclus to trade for that of his own beloved son Hector. This is the overwhelming moment of human emotion in the opera: the two enemies, united in grief, find a bond of common humanity. The almost schematic pattern of deaths is outlined as if in premonition: Paris will kill Achilles, Agamemnon will kill Paris, and Neoptolomus (Achilles' son) will kill Priam. In making these seem like gratuitous events, Tippett concentrates the final stages of his opera on two extended moments. In Interlude 3 Hermes, as Messenger of Death, sings a lyrical hymn to the divine power of music as an instrument of healing and love. It has been objected that this holds up the action, but the objection misses the point that the 'action' is now secondary.

3.iv *Troy* The final scene focusses on the withdrawal of Priam into a private world of grief and preparation for death. He refuses to speak to the avenging Paris, his wife Hecuba and daughter-in-law Andromache. Only Helen melts his heart, as if in acknowledgment of her mysterious near-divinity. He is killed as if inevitably, but in acknowledgment of his humanity the opera's last gesture reflects our tears of compassion for the nobility of his suffering. The musical and dramatic gesture, as throughout this opera, is uncannily meshed.

* * *

King Priam is in some respects an exception among Tippett's five operas in that it is set in the past and based on a familiar story. But it is entirely characteristic in the way in which he presents his carefully honed scenario as a paradigm of chequered humanity. The eternal conflict of love in the shadow of death and violence is present in one form or another in every Tippett opera, and the probing of the individual psyche and of human interaction in *King Priam* is as profoundly explored as in any of the others. The opera's musical language, while sharply differentiated from the lyrical luxuriance of *The Midsummer Marriage*, is directly related to the heroic and tragic subject it serves and has a compelling unity of purpose which Tippett was later to eschew. *King Priam* is one of the most powerful operatic experiences of the modern theatre and a landmark in the history of British opera.

GERAINT LEWIS

King Roger [*Król Roger*; *Pasterz* ('The Shepherd')]. Opera in three acts by KAROL SZYMANOWSKI to a libretto by Jarosław Iwaszkiewicz and the composer very loosely based on EURIPIDES' *Bacchae*; Warsaw, Wielki Theatre, 19 June 1926.

Król Roger II [King Roger] *King of Sicily*		baritone
Shepherd		tenor
Roxana *Queen of Sicily*		soprano
Edrisi *Arabian sage*		tenor
Archbishop		bass
Deaconess		contralto

Priests, monks, nuns, acolytes, courtiers, guards, eunuchs, Shepherd's disciples

Setting Sicily in the 12th century

The earliest discussions about *King Roger* took place in the summer of 1918 when Jarosław Iwaszkiewicz visited Szymanowski at Yelisavetgrad (now Kirovograd). The first version of the libretto was completed by Iwaszkiewicz (partly following sketches prepared by Szymanowski) in June 1920, but in the course of

*'King Roger'
(Szymanowski), Act 1 (the
interior of a church) of
the original production at
the Wielki Theatre,
Warsaw, 19 June 1926,
with sets designed by
Wincenty Drabik*

composition Szymanowski made substantial alterations to the libretto, in particular rewriting the whole of the last act. He had originally intended to call the opera *Pasterz* ('The Shepherd'), and the changes he made reflected the shift of focus from the Shepherd to the King. Work on the music began in 1920, but the opera was completed only in August 1924. The first performance was conducted by Emil Młynarski, produced by Adolf Popławski and designed by Wincenty Drabik. The composer's sister, Stanisława Szymanowska, sang Roxana. Later performances include Duisburg (1928), Prague (1932), Palermo (1949), Warsaw (1965), Gdańsk (1974) and London (1975). A vocal score was published in 1926, with a German libretto appearing two years later, and the full score was published in 1973. The opera has been recorded under Mieczysław Mierzejewski and under Robert Satanowski.

ACT 1 *The interior of a church* In some ways *King Roger* is as close to oratorio as to opera and the first act has the character of a static tableau stylizing the Byzantine religious-cultural world. The music is continuous, but there are definable formal units, somewhat in the nature of very extended set numbers. The atmosphere is tellingly conveyed by Szymanowski's notes on the stage setting: 'Golden mosaics, shadows. Marble ... an early Roman ceiling – as in the Palatina ... choirs – the clergy in gilded robes, stiffly hieratic – incensories. A severe, formal splendour with oriental overtones'. A solemn mass is taking place as the curtain rises, and against the background of choral incantations (the importance of the chorus strengthens the work's oratorio connections) the Archbishop and Deaconess describe how the people are being led away from the church towards a new faith. The Arabian sage Edrisi describes to King Roger the Shepherd who advocates this new faith. As the Archbishop demands retribution the voice of Roxana the queen is heard interceding on the Shepherd's behalf and suggesting that he be summoned to the church to explain himself.

The arrival of the Shepherd immediately transforms the scene and the music, and the choral archaisms are replaced with a song of serene and limpid beauty in which he proclaims his creed of love and beauty. This represents the second of the three major formal units of the act, and its opening phrase becomes one of the Shep-

herd's two leitmotifs. The motivic links between this phrase and earlier Byzantine themes help to clarify the symbolic meaning of the opera and of its characters. It is apparent already that the conflict between the Church and the Shepherd – between medieval scholastic conventions and the Dionysian cult of self-abandoning joy – is really an externalization of opposing forces within Roger himself. Much of the opera works on this symbolic level. Edrisi, for instance, might be viewed as a symbol of wisdom or rationality and Roxana as an embodiment of the allurements of love.

As Roxana is increasingly captivated by the Shepherd's song the third and final formal unit in the act begins. The voices of Roxana and the Shepherd soar above the choral music in a mounting ecstasy of expression which is dramatically interrupted by Roger's call for silence. For the first time the King is characterized musically by an independent theme, later to be associated with him, and the contrast between the restless urgency of this theme and the suavity and sensuous appeal of the Shepherd's music epitomize the dramatic and symbolic conflict at the heart of the work. The act ends as Roger asks the Shepherd to return that night to stand trial.

ACT 2 *The inner courtyard of the palace* The second act is an oriental (Arab-Indian) tableau centred on two extended set numbers: Roxana's aria, in which she pleads for clemency for the Shepherd, and the ritual dance of the Shepherd's followers. In general the richly dissonant harmonic language, the oriental stylizations and the sumptuous orchestral impressionism (recalling the Ravel of *Daphnis et Chloé*) give to this act a quality of sustained ecstasy which is in sharp contrast to the Byzantine archaisms of Act 1. Szymanowski's tone painting in the opening section is masterly, conveying the heavy heat of the Sicilian night by dense, slowly moving harmonies supporting melodic strands of faintly oriental hue. The curtain rises on Roger and Edrisi, with Roger's music already betraying the unsettling influence of the Shepherd. The latter's imminent arrival, heralded by the distant sound of tambourine and zither, immediately evokes a response from Roxana, whose hauntingly beautiful aria, strophic in design, has become the best-known music from the opera (familiar above all in the violin transcription by Paweł Kochański).

The appearance of the Shepherd is a moment of considerable dramatic intensity, as the orchestra works the Shepherd's two leitmotifs into an impassioned climax. As he describes his faith and origins his themes mingle with Roxana's in yet another ecstatic climax, culminating in his call for music and dancing. The dance of the Shepherd's followers is the clearest example of oriental stylization in the opera, its wordless chorus, percussion ostinatos and metrical irregularities directly reminiscent of the central sections of the Third Symphony (1916). As the dance becomes ever more abandoned, the voices of Roxana and the Shepherd rise above the chorus and orchestra, their ecstasy once more interrupted by Roger. An attempt to seize the Shepherd and chain his hands proves unsuccessful, and he leaves, followed by Roxana and eventually by Roger himself.

ACT 3 *In the ruins of an ancient theatre* All three acts of the opera are built around a confrontation between Roger and the Shepherd. In Act 3 this takes place in the ruins of a Greek amphitheatre: 'Rows of semicircular benches towering above each other … then the sky with brilliant stars … in the centre the altar of Dionysus'. Here the symbolism of the opera is made even more explicit as the Shepherd appears to Roger as Dionysus and the King makes a sacrifice to him, no longer suppressing the Dionysian within himself. In the passage that follows the voices of Roxana and the Shepherd once more soar above the chorus in the most powerful and sustained climax of the opera, before they depart and leave the King alone.

For the most part the third act is centred on Roger's character, and it is significant that his is the only part in the opera which truly grows musically, in contrast to the archetypes of Roxana and the Shepherd. He emerges only inconclusively in the first act, travels through his 'dark night of the soul' in the second to his final hymn to the sun at the end of Act 3, when the 'dream is over … the beautiful illusion passed'. In the final pages, as Roger salutes the rising sun, his vocal line achieves a dignity and strength that had formerly eluded it. In a departure from Euripides' play obviously influenced by Nietzsche, he emerges 'strong enough for freedom', enriched and transformed by the truths of Dionysus but no slave to them. At the end he stands alone as a powerful symbol of modern Nietzschean man.   JIM SAMSON

King's Theatre. A leading London opera house, in the Haymarket, from 1705 to 1910; it was known as the Queen's Theatre during Anne's reign, and Her Majesty's during Victoria's. *See* LONDON, §II, 2.

Kingston, Morgan (*b* Wednesbury, Staffs., 16 March 1881; *d* London, 4 Aug 1936). English tenor. His voice was discovered while he was a miner, and his singing career began in concert and oratorio. In opera his reputation was made first in the USA, where he sang Manrico and the Duke at the Metropolitan in 1917. He was a member of the Scotti Grand Opera which toured America in the early 1920s. In 1924 he made his Covent Garden début as Canio, strengthening favourable opinion with his Siegmund the following season. Herman Klein praised his 'clear, ringing tones and experienced art'. Records, mostly made in the USA, have variable stylistic merit but show a strong, serviceable voice.   J. B. STEANE

Kingston, William Beatty. *See* BEATTY-KINGSTON, WILLIAM.

Kinkakuji [*The Golden Pavilion*; *Der Tempelbrand*]. Opera in three acts by TOSHIRŌ MAYUZUMI to a libretto in German by Claus H. Henneberg after a novel by Yukio Mishima; Berlin, Deutsche Oper, 23 June 1976.

The action takes place in Kyoto, Japan, in the 1940s. Mizoguchi (baritone) is a young priest at the Kinkakuji, a temple in Kyoto. His deformed hand has marked him for life and, disturbed in mind, he reflects on his past. In Act 1 he recalls his devout father (tenor) and adulterous mother, and also the time when his father took him to the temple to make him a disciple of Abbot Dōsen (bass). Still he cannot find peace of mind, and he remains apathetic even at his father's death and when spoken to by his friend Tsurukawa (baritone). In Act 2 he is forced by an American GI to kick a pregnant prostitute (contralto), causing her to miscarry, then denies the deed to Tsurukawa. Kashiwagi (tenor), another friend, tells him that all values are changeable and that it is possible to find pleasure in destruction and ridicule of beauty. He turns his own girlfriend over to Mizoguchi. In Act 3 Mizoguchi hopes to be destroyed with the temple by a typhoon, but it leaves both of them unharmed. He is elected to succeed Abbot Dōsen, but the ceremony holds no meaning for him, and Abbot Dōsen is found to be dishonourable. After reading letters by Tsurukawa, who has killed himself, and recalling in visions all the people and events of his past, Mizoguchi realizes that only his own actions can change the pattern of his life. He decides to set fire to the Golden Pavilion. *Kinkakuji* is a highly psychological drama, with expressionistic writing containing elements of Buddhist music. A Japanese-language version of the opera was first performed in the Metropolitan Festival Hall, Tokyo, on 18 October 1983.

MASAKATA KANAZAWA

Kipnis, Alexander (*b* Zhitomir, Ukraine, 1/13 Feb 1891; *d* Westport, CT, 14 May 1978). American bass of Ukrainian birth. After studying conducting at the Warsaw Conservatory and singing with Ernst Grenzebach in Berlin, he appeared at Hamburg (1915) and at Wiesbaden (1917–22). He became leading bass with the Berlin Städtische Oper (1919–29); thereafter he joined the Berlin Staatsoper (1930–35) and the Vienna Staatsoper (1935–8). He became known as an outstanding Wagner and Mozart bass and a fine interpreter of Italian and Russian roles, appearing at Bayreuth (1927–33) and at the 1937 Salzburg Festival. By then he was familiar in most of the world's leading opera houses, especially in North and South America; he became an American citizen in 1931. From 1923 to 1932 he was a regular member of the Chicago company. He sang often at Covent Garden (first as Marcel in *Les Huguenots*, 1927) and for one season at Glyndebourne as Sarastro (1936); he repeated the latter role under Toscanini in Salzburg (1937). He made a surprisingly late début at the Metropolitan, in 1940, as Gurnemanz, remaining on its roster until 1946. Kipnis had a voice of unusual refinement and flexibility for a bass. The best of his many operatic records are those made in Berlin in the early 1930s, especially Osmin's first song from *Die Entführung* and 'Il lacerato spirito' from *Simon Boccanegra*.

GV (L. Riemens; J. Stratton)

A. Frankenstein, E. Arnosi and J. Dennis: 'Alexander Kipnis', *Record Collector*, xxii (1974–5), 53–79 [with discography]; xxiii (1976–7), 166–71   DESMOND SHAWE-TAYLOR

Kirchhoff, Walter (*b* Berlin, 17 March 1879; *d* Wiesbaden, 26 March 1951). German tenor. He studied with Lilli Lehmann in Berlin, making his début there at the Hofoper in 1906 as Faust. He was engaged in Berlin, apart from two short absences, until 1931. At Bayreuth he sang Walther (1911–12) and Parsifal (1914). He made his Covent Garden début in 1913 as Walther, returning in 1924 as Loge, the role of his début in 1927 at the Metropolitan, where he sang until 1931. His repertory included Tannhäuser, Lohengrin, Tristan, Siegmund, Siegfried, the King's Son (*Königskinder*), Alfonso (Korngold's *Violanta*), Menelaus (*Die ägyptische Helena*) and Max, which he sang at the New York première of *Jonny spielt auf* (1929). He had a powerful, grainy voice, well suited to Wagner.

ELIZABETH FORBES

Kirchner, Alfred (*b* Göppingen, nr Stuttgart, 22 May 1937). German director. After a period as co-director of the Stuttgart Staatstheater (1972–9) he was appointed co-director of the Bochum Schauspielhaus (1979–86) and then of the Burgtheater in Vienna (1986–9). In 1989 he became Generaldirektor of the Staatliche Schauspielbühnen in Berlin.

During the years of the Gielen–Zehelein regime at the Frankfurt Opera (1977–87) he was a key member of the team of guest directors – also including Ruth Berghaus, Hans Neuenfels and Christof Nel – who established the company at the forefront of European opera production with their provocatively radical stagings. Kirchner, who has maintained a dual career in the spoken and lyric theatres, is notable for his psychologically acute, dramatically tense productions, in which a strongly visual element often makes use of surreal images and dislocated planes of reality. His productions for Frankfurt have included *Jenůfa* (1979), *Die Soldaten* (1981), *Ballo* (1982), *Yevgeny Onegin* (1984) and Zender's *Stephen Climax* (1986). He has also worked in Santa Fe (*We Come to the River*, 1984), Amsterdam (*Don Giovanni*, 1987) and Vienna (*Khovanshchina*, 1988); a new production of the *Ring* is scheduled for Bayreuth in 1994.   BARRY MILLINGTON

Kirchner, Leon (*b* Brooklyn, 24 Jan 1919). American composer and conductor. A pupil of Schoenberg and Sessions, Kirchner has composed in all genres except ballet. His highly expressive, advanced tonal language draws on a full range of 20th-century compositional techniques and is characterized by linear chromaticism, asymmetric rhythms and phrases, contrasting textures, evocative timbres and virtuosity.

Lily, Kirchner's only opera, is set to a libretto by the composer based on Saul Bellow's novel *Henderson, the Rain King*. An allegorical tale of one civilization's well-intentioned decimation of another, *Lily* depicts the millionaire Gene Henderson's accidental destruction of an African tribe's water supply, an allusion to President Lyndon Johnson and American involvement in the Vietnam War. Conceived as a *Gesamtkunstwerk*, the one-act, mixed-media *Lily* employs film, electronics, speech collages, improvisation, aleatory techniques and a variety of virtuoso vocal styles, including quasi-pop and gradations between speech and song. Material from three of Kirchner's concert works – *Music for Orchestra*

(1969), *Flutings* for solo flute (1973) and *Lily* for soprano, chamber ensemble and tape (1937) – is incorporated into the opera's score. Commissioned by the New York City Opera, *Lily* received its first performance there on 14 April 1977, conducted by the composer and staged by the Broadway director Tom O'Horgan.

*

GroveAM (A. L. Ringer and J. Wierzbicki)
H. Heinsheimer: 'Zeroing In', *ON*, xli/23 (1976–77), 13–15
L. Kerner: 'Kirchner Writes his Opera at Last', *Village Voice* (11 April 1977)   MARY LOU HUMPHREY

Kïrgïstan. For discussion of opera in Kïrgïstan *see* BISHKEK.

Kirkby, (Carolyn) Emma (*b* Camberley, Surrey, 26 Feb 1949). English soprano. She studied classics at Oxford and singing with Jessica Cash. Her pure, light-textured voice and natural declamation have been widely admired by interpreters of early and Baroque music and have served as a model for many specialists in this repertory. She made her début as Mother Nature in Locke and Christopher Gibbons's *Cupid and Death* at Bruges in 1983 and her first American appearances as Dorinda in Handel's *Orlando* in a 1989 tour. She has sung frequently under the direction of Andrew Parrott, Anthony Rooley and Christopher Hogwood in a repertory ranging from 14th-century Italian songs to arias by Haydn and Mozart. In 1989 she sang Venus in Daniel Purcell's, Weldon's and Eccles's settings of *The Judgment of Paris* at the BBC Promenade Concerts. Her recordings include *Dido and Aeneas*, *Venus and Adonis*, *Orlando*, Monteverdi's *Orfeo* and Hasse's *Cleofide*.

NICHOLAS ANDERSON

Kirov. Theatre in St Petersburg, built in 1860 as the Mariinsky; it was known as the State Academic Theatre of Opera and Ballet from 1917 and became the Kirov in 1935. In 1991 it reverted to the name Mariinsky. *See* ST PETERSBURG, §§3, 4.

Kirsten, Dorothy (*b* Montclair, NJ, 6 July 1907). American soprano. She first studied at the Juilliard School and then with Astolfo Pescia in Rome. She made her operatic début as Poussette in *Manon* with the Chicago Grand Opera in 1940; she then appeared in major parts with the New York City Opera and at San Francisco. Her début at the Metropolitan was in 1945 as Mimì, and she sang there frequently until 1975 when she gave her farewell performance as Tosca. Her other roles with the company included Butterfly, Minnie (*La fanciulla del West*), Manon Lescaut, Nedda and Louise (which she had studied with the composer). She made guest appearances in France, England, the Soviet Union and South America. Kirsten had a clear but not voluminous lyric soprano that could also undertake *lirico spinto* roles, a coolly assured voice that was employed with much security if not with overwhelming effect. She published an autobiography, *A Time to Sing* (1982).

*

L. Rasponi: 'The Great Lyrics', *The Last Prima Donnas* (New York, 1982), 284

Kishineu (Russ. Kishinyov; Romanian Chişinău). Capital of Moldova. Musical life in the first half of the 19th century was centred on private homes and salons;

the Moldavian composer Alexander Flechtenmacher made his operatic career abroad, and the city became a stop for touring Italian and Russian opera troupes only in the latter part of the century. An attempt in 1919–21 to form an opera theatre was unsuccessful, but the Moldavskiy Muzikal'nïy-Dramaticheskiy Teatr performed occasional lyric works and finally in 1955 formed the basis for the Moldavskiy Teatr Operï, Baleta i Dramï imeni A. S. Pushkina (Pushkin Moldavian Theatre of Opera, Ballet and Drama). Operatic activities began on 8 June 1956 with the first national opera, D. G. Gershfel'd's *Grozovan*; in July 1957 the opera and ballet troupes separated from the dramatic and formed the Moldavskiy Teatr Operï i Baleta. Premières have included operas by Gershfel'd, A. G. Strycha and E. L. Lazarev. The troupe received a new 1200-seat theatre (designed by A. Gorshkov) in 1980.

*

ME (L. A. Aksyonova and N. I. Shekhman; also 'Moldavskiy teatr operï i baleta', N. I. Shekhman)

A. Kirtoka and M. Manuilov: *Moldavskiy gosudarstvennïy teatr operï i baleta: kratkiy ocherk* [The Moldavian State Opera and Ballet Theatre: a Short Study] (Kishineu, 1960)

G. Bernandt: *Slovar' oper vpervïye postavlennïkh ili izdannïkh v dorevolyutsionnoy Rossii i v SSSR 1736–1959* [Dictionary of Operas First Performed or Published in Pre-revolutionary Russia and in the USSR 1736–1959] (Moscow, 1962), 538

A. Beylina: 'Opernoe tvorchestvo moldavskikh kompozitorov' [The Operatic Works of Moldavian Composers], *Muzikal'naya kul'tura sovetskoy Moldavii* (Moscow, 1965), 289

B. Kotlyarov: *Muzïkal'naya zhizn' dorevolyutsionnogo Kishinyova* [Musical Life in Pre-revolutionary Kishineu] (Kishineu, 1967)

D. I. Prilepov: *Moldavskiy teatr* (Kishineu, 1967)

N. Rozhkovskaya: *Teatral'naya zhizn' Kishinyova XIX–nachala XX vv* [Theatrical Life in Kishineu in the 19th and Early 20th Centuries] (Kishineu, 1979)

N. D. Sebov: *Stanovleniye moldavskogo muzïkal'nogo teatra* [The Founding of the Moldavian Music Theatre] (Kishineu, 1983)

L. M. Chermotan: *Stanovleniye moldavskogo sovetskogo teatra: stranitsï istorii* [The Founding of the Moldavian Soviet Theatre: Pages from History] (Kishineu, 1986)   GREGORY SALMON

Kiss, The [*Hubička*]. Folk opera in two acts by BEDŘICH SMETANA to a libretto by ELIŠKA KRÁSNOHORSKÁ after the short story by Karolina Světlá; Prague, Provisional Theatre, 7 November 1876.

Father Paloucký	bass
Vendulka *his daughter*	soprano
Lukáš *a young widower*	tenor
Tomeš *his brother-in-law*	baritone
Martinka *an old aunt of Vendulka's*	contralto
Matouš *an old smuggler*	bass
Barče *servant girl at Paloucký's house*	soprano
Guard	tenor

Neighbours, girls, musicians, smugglers

Setting A village in the Krkonoš mountains

Eliška Krásnohorská drew Smetana's attention to Karolina Světlá's short story (1871) in the winter of 1872 (soon after he completed *Libuše*), but he saw no operatic potential in it then. Instead he first took up and completed his fifth opera, *The Two Widows*, and then began work on *Viola* (Krásnohorská's *Twelfth Night* libretto) before deafness struck and he restricted himself to non-vocal works. When he received Krásnohorská's libretto on 11 November 1875, he liked it and began work on it before the end of the month. Despite his deaf-

ness, Smetana finished the piano sketch in a few months, by the end of February 1876. The orchestration of Act 1 was complete by 27 April 1876, Act 2 by 23 July and the overture by 31 August. After its première in November 1876 Smetana revised the vocal score and full score in February and March 1877; the vocal score appeared in October 1880.

The Kiss was the first of his works that Smetana did not conduct himself. Instead it was entrusted to his former deputy at the Provisional Theatre, Adolf Čech, who thereafter conducted all Smetana operatic and symphonic premières. The cast were all stalwarts from Smetana's time at the Provisional Theatre and the director was another of Smetana's protégés, Edmund Chvalovský. The première was the happiest and most successful of all of Smetana's operas and the work soon established itself as his most popular opera after *The Bartered Bride*. It led to two more operas with the same librettist.

The overture, while based mostly on motifs from the opera (in varying metres and tempos), gives the impression of a symphonic structure going beyond a mere potpourri. An introduction (including exx.1 and 2)

leads into a symphonic Allegro which develops ex.1 and a further theme. This culminates in an 'à la polka' section (ex.3), a climactic crescendo (based on ex.2) and a return to the opening.

ACT 1 *The sitting-room of Paloucký's house* The opening bustling *moto perpetuo* accompanies the breathless arrival of Martinka with the news that Lukáš is coming to ask for Vendulka's hand in marriage. Vendulka is thrilled and touched. She and Lukáš had long been in love but, respecting his parents' wishes, he married another woman who soon died, leaving him with a baby. Vendulka's father, Paloucký, expresses his doubts. The bustling music resumes with the arrival of Lukáš and his companions, and Vendulka slips discreetly out of the room. Lukáš's brother-in-law Tomeš announces their business in a forthright *ABA* aria and to

'The Kiss' (Smetana): Edmund Chvalovský's design for Act 1 (the sitting-room of Paloucký's house) of the original production at the Provisional Theatre, Prague, 7 November 1876

Lukáš's joy (ex.1), Paloucký gives his consent, but then expresses reservations in an imposingly solemn solo characterized by trills, flourishes and double dots: Lukáš and Vendulka are both too obstinate. Lukáš brushes aside these objections and Paloucký invites the company to toast the pair in a lighthearted 2/4 version of ex.1, taken up by the chorus. Vendulka is brought in and Lukáš greets her in heroically ringing tones. This gives way immediately to a radiantly tender duet, 'Jsme svoji' ('We belong to one another'). The chorus comments softly 'They are made for one another' and Lukáš tries to kiss Vendulka. She abruptly pushes him aside. This incident – which gives the opera its title – signals a full-scale concertato of male soloists' comments above a choral background. Tomeš attempts to rescue the situation with another toast (the chorus respond in turn) and suggests they should leave the couple together. All withdraw.

The scene that follows is one of Smetana's finest dialogues, its many sections beautifully crafted to the emotional temperature of the words. It begins with a tender orchestral interlude as the sunset glows through the window. The voices enter to an Andante amoroso, and Vendulka explains that as a mark of respect for the child's mother she should not kiss Lukáš until they are married (Barče and Martinka now bring in the crib with the baby). In the *dolcissimo* section that follows, Lukáš once again tries to kiss Vendulka and once again she repulses him. This sets off the second, agitated part of the dialogue as the shortening note values and increasing pace convey the rising anger of the pair. Eventually, Lukáš resorts to violence, creating a disturbance which brings on Paloucký with one of the opera's best-known numbers, 'Jak jsem to řek' ('Just as I said'), the Baroque implication of his previous solo now reinforced by the circle of 5ths harmony and vocal melismata. Lukáš stumps off. Martinka solicits Vendulka's help with her operations as a smuggler, but she refuses and Martinka gruffly departs.

Left alone Vendulka sings two lullabies to the child.

The first is a well-known pastorella song 'Hajej, můj andílku' ('Go to sleep my little angel'), with its original tune. The second, as the moon shines in, is a folk imitation by Smetana, 'Letěla bělounka holubička' ('A little white dove flew'), in two verses. Vendulka falls asleep over the crib only to be woken up by sounds from outside. Lukáš has returned, rather the worse for wear, from the pub, and, accompanied by musicians, sings an ironic polka (ex.3) through the window. Tomeš (also at the window) reproaches Lukáš, to a choral commentary. Vendulka can take no more and, leaving the baby with Barče, runs off – presumably to Martinka.

ACT 2.i *Deep forest near the border; darkest night* A prelude, developed chiefly from ex.3, leads into the chorus of smugglers headed by Matouš – an atmospheric piece with a Baroque crotchet tread and hushed voices above. After their whistled signal the smugglers leave the scene to Lukáš, who rushes on in a state of profound remorse. His scena gives way to an Andante amoroso (he remembers Vendulka's love) and then a tempestuous close (the remorse returns). But Tomeš has followed him and in the ensuing duet 'Jen odpros ji' ('Just ask for her forgiveness'), based on ex.2, he convinces Lukáš that his proposed marriage can be saved, the two voices coming more and more together as Lukáš's hopes grow. They go off, but they have been overheard by Matouš (the smugglers' chorus is repeated) waiting for Martinka. She turns up with her new recruit, Vendulka. After a trio dwelling on Vendulka's blighted love, Matouš hands over his parcel to Martinka and, as he confides to the audience, he goes off to tell Lukáš.

The dawn breaks (a radiantly orchestrated and prolonged chord of C major) and no sooner has Martinka hidden away the package in her pear-basket than the two are accosted by the Guard, looking out for smugglers. Martinka adroitly fools him – that their encounter will turn out happily is predicted by the cheerful polka music to which it is set. Then Martinka reproaches Vendulka for her foolishness and, in a 6/8 duet, tells her how best to manage men. But when at the end Martinka tries again, Vendulka replies with a passionate flourish that she hates Lukáš.

2.ii *Martinka's forest cottage and garden, early morning* Barče runs in having heard Matouš's news of Lukáš, which she wants to pass on to Martinka. But it is only the lark's voice that answers her and, while waiting, she sings a two-verse 'lark song', 'Hlásej, ptáčku' ('Announce, little bird'), full of trills and melismatic flourishes. Then, led by Matouš, the entire village descends upon Martinka's cottage. Paloucký sings a spirited aria in which he declares he will forgive Lukáš for the sake of peace and quiet. Eventually Vendulka and Martinka appear. Despite her last statement Vendulka is overjoyed to see Lukáš: they express their love in ecstatic high notes. She embraces him and wants to kiss him. But now it is Lukáš who pulls away. A puzzled ensemble builds up, after which he explains himself: he must be forgiven before receiving the kiss (ex.2 returns). This is joyfully conceded (ex.1) and the whole ensemble comment happily on the reconciliation (ex.2).

* * *

Non-Czech commentators have often dismissed the plot of *The Kiss* as trivial and improbable, hinging as it does on Vendulka's refusal to grant her future husband a kiss. Nevertheless this opera is one of Smetana's most successful. Its fervent lyricism is unforced (remarkably so, considering that this was Smetana's first stage work after he became deaf), the psychological penetration of the characters profound. Its appeal to Czech audiences ever since its first performance owes something to its genre description as a 'folk opera' (underpinned by Lukáš's polka, Vendulka's two lullabies and other genre pieces), but equally to its gentle message of reconciliation, a feature of all of Smetana's late operas and those of many later Czech composers.   JOHN TYRRELL

Kistler, Cyrill (*b* Grossaitingen, nr Augsburg, 12 March 1848; *d* Bad Kissingen, 1 Jan 1907). German composer and writer on music. After attending a teachers' seminary in Lauingen he spent eight years as an assistant master in Augsburg and neighbouring villages. A patroness finally enabled him to study for three years at the Königliche Musikschule in Munich, where he was taught the organ and composition by Rheinberger, Wüllner and Franz Lachner. He taught theory at the Fürstliche Konservatorium in Sondershausen from 1883 to 1885 when he retired to Bad Kissingen, directing a private music school and living as a freelance composer and writer.

Kistler initially agreed with Lachner's conservative attitude, but his friendship with Wagner in Bayreuth crucially affected his views. He adopted Wagner's musical language but could not go beyond mere imitation, and though respected by Wagner's followers he failed to achieve lasting recognition. His arrangements of excerpts from Wagner operas are noteworthy and his own most successful work was the *Volksoper Röslein im Hag*, which demonstrated his preference for popular subjects. This nationalist inclination was also present in his writings (he was editor of the neo-German *Musikalische Tagesfragen*), in which he expressed views hostile to everything un-German.

Alfred der Grosse, 1876 (Körner), unperf. (repudiated by composer)
Lichtenstein, 1878, unperf. (repudiated by composer)
Kunihild, oder Der Brautritt auf Kynast (romantische Oper, 3, F. Sporck), Sondershausen, 20 March 1884
Eulenspiegel (komische Oper, 2, after A. Kotzebue); rev. H. Levi and L. Sauer (1), Würzburg, 5 April 1889
Baldurs Tod, 1891 (Musikdrama, 3, von Sohlern), Düsseldorf, 25 Oct 1905
Im Honigmond op.112 (Idyll, 1, B. Wieland), Bad Kissingen, 1900
Arm Elslein op.117 (Märchenoper, 1), Schwerin, 2 March 1902
Röslein im Hag (Volksoper, 3, T. A. Kolve), Elberfeld, 13 Oct 1903
Der Vogt auf Mühlstein (tragische Oper, 3, B. Straub, after H. Hansjakob), Düsseldorf, 19 April 1904
Faust I. Teil (Musiktragödie, 4, J. W. von Goethe: *Faust*), 1905
Die Kleinstädter (komische Oper, 3, B. Luovsky)
Die Grossstädter (komische Oper, 3), inc.

*

M. Chop: 'C. Kistler', *Zeitgenössische Tondichter*, ii (Leipzig, 1890), 274–98
C. Kistler: 'Selbstbiographie', *Musikalische Tagesfragen*, xv (1906), 37
Obituary, *Die Musik*, vi (1906–7)
H. Ritter: 'C. Kistler', *Lebensläufe aus Franken*, ii, ed. A. Chroust (Würzburg, 1922), 228–34   HORST LEUCHTMANN

Kittel, Hermine (*b* Vienna, 2 Dec 1879; *d* Vienna, 7 April 1948). Austrian contralto. She began her career as an actress, then studied singing with Amalie Materna in Vienna. At the Vienna Hofoper she sang at first under Mahler's direction, and later in the première of the revised version of *Ariadne auf Naxos*. At Bayreuth (1902, 1908) she sang Erda and various minor roles, and at the early Salzburg Festivals she was often heard as Marcellina in *Figaro*.   DAVID CUMMINGS

Kittl, Jan Bedřich [Johann Friedrich] (*b* Orlík nad Vltavou, 8 May 1806; *d* Lissa, Prussia [now Leszno, Poland], 20 July 1868). Bohemian composer. A lawyer by profession, he studied composition under Tomášek and from 1843 to 1865 was director of the Prague Conservatory; in that capacity he cooperated with the Estates Theatre in Prague, giving consent for students to play in the orchestra and thus making possible, for example, the Prague première of Wagner's *Tannhäuser* (25 November 1854). One of the first Romantic composers in Prague, he combined German fervour and tenderness with typically French acuity of characterization and vivacity of tone (see Gut 1848). All Kittl's operas have interesting orchestration, with rich wind writing; he was criticized for overburdening singers' voices. His first opera, *Daphnis' Grab*, written in his student years, has not survived. Kittl's greatest success was *Bianca und Giuseppe*. He received the libretto from Wagner in 1846, and the opera was performed in Prague in 1848, 1852 and 1854; a Czech translation (by Bedřich Pešek) was performed at the Provincial Theatre in Prague on 20 September 1875. It is set in 1793 in Nice in Savoy, then besieged by the French Republican army. Another opera, *Die Waldblume*, is set in France at the time of Louis XIV and has a comic plot based on mistaken identities; the overture was frequently played as a concert piece. The tragic opera *Die Bilderstürmer* is set in Valenciennes on the French-Netherlands border in 1567, during a battle between Orange and Calvinist factions.

See also BIANCA UND GIUSEPPE.

Daphnis' Grab, c1825 (idyllische Oper, 1, H. Poeschl), destroyed
Bianca und Giuseppe, oder Die Franzosen vor Nizza (4, R. Wagner, after H. König: *Die hohe Braut*), Prague, Estates, 19 Feb 1848, Cs-Pk*, vs (Leipzig, n.d.)
Die Waldblume (lyrische komische Oper, 3, J. Hickel), Prague, Estates, 20 Feb 1852, Pk*

Die Bilderstürmer (grosse tragische Oper, 3, J. E. Hartmann), Prague, Estates, 20 April 1854, *Pk**

*

LoewenbergA

B. G. [B. Gut]: 'Theater', *Bohemia* (22 and 24 Feb 1848) [on *Bianca und Giuseppe*]

V. [F. Ulm]: 'Theater', *Bohemia* (22 and 29 Feb 1852) [on *Die Waldblume*]

——: 'Theater', *Bohemia* (21 and 23 April 1854) [on *Die Bilderstürmer*]

R. Procházka: 'Die böhmischen Musikschulen', *Musikalische Streiflichter aus alten und neuen Tagen* (Dresden, 1897), 74–5 [letter from Wagner]

E. Rychnovsky: *Johann Friedrich Kittl* (Prague, 1904)

E. Newman: *The Life of Richard Wagner* (New York, 1933), 221–3

J. Plavec: *František Škroup* (Prague, 1940) [on the Prague Conservatory and the Estates Theatre]

M. Tarantová: *Jan F. Kittl* (Prague, 1948)

J. Arbes: *Z divadelního světa* [From the World of Theatre] (Prague, 1958), 87–8

Dějiny českého divadla [History of the Czech Theatre], ii (Prague, 1969), 327–9

J. Tyrrell: *Czech Opera* (Cambridge, 1988), 67   JITKA LUDVOVÁ

Kiurina, Berta (*b* Linz, 18 Feb 1882; *d* Vienna, 3 May 1933). Austrian soprano. At the Vienna Academy she turned to singing after studying the piano; in 1904 she made her operatic début at Linz. Shortly afterwards she moved to Vienna on Mahler's invitation and appeared regularly at the Staatsoper until 1927. Her roles included both the Empress and the Dyer's Wife in *Die Frau ohne Schatten* and Octavian in *Der Rosenkavalier* but were mostly of the coloratura and lyric type such as Gilda, Marguerite, Konstanze and the three soprano parts in *Les contes d'Hoffmann*. In 1919 she sang Ighino in Pfitzner's *Palestrina* and in 1926 was Liù in *Turandot*, both Viennese premières. She also appeared at the Colón, at the Salzburg Festival, and in many European cities in both operatic and concert work. An artist of great charm and accomplishment, she made some attractive recordings, displaying a light but resourceful voice, with occasional uncertainty of intonation but considerable sensitivity and expressiveness.

J. B. STEANE

Klafsky, Katharina [Katalin] (*b* Mosonszentjános, 19 Sept 1855; *d* Hamburg, 22 Sept 1896). Hungarian soprano. She studied briefly with Mathilde Marchesi, and in 1875 sang small parts at Salzburg. In 1876 she was engaged at Leipzig, where she studied further with Josef Sucher. She sang Waltraute (*Die Walküre*) and the Third Norn in the Leipzig première of the *Ring* (1878), as well as Venus (1879) and Brangäne (1882). She sang Wellgunde and Waltraute (*Die Walküre*) at Her Majesty's Theatre in the first complete London *Ring* (1882), and Sieglinde and Brünnhilde with Angelo Neumann's touring company (1882–3). After appearances in Bremen and Vienna she was engaged at Hamburg (1886), where in addition to her Wagner roles, she sang Santuzza, Valentine (*Les Huguenots*), Norma, Agathe, Eglantine (*Euryanthe*), Donna Anna and Countess Almaviva. Her dramatic temperament, allied to a magnificent, full-toned voice and a secure technique, enabled her to sing German, French and Italian roles with equal success. She died suddenly while still in her vocal prime.

*

H. Klein: *Thirty Years of Musical Life in London* (London, 1903)

L. Ordemann: *Aus dem Leben und Wirken von Katharina Klafsky* (Hameln, 1903)

A. Neumann: *Erinnerungen an Richard Wagner* (Leipzig, 1907; Eng. trans., 1909)

H. Chevalley: *100 Jahre Hamburger Stadttheater* (Hamburg, 1927)

ELIZABETH FORBES

Klagenfurt. Austrian town, capital of the southern province of Carinthia. From 1709 a Ballhaus was used for performances by Italian theatre troupes on their way from Venice to Vienna. Since 1811 the Stadttheater has offered a wide opera repertory including works by Verdi and Wagner. Works performed since 1945 include Wagner's *Ring* cycle, Menotti's *The Consul* and Weill's *Aufstieg und Fall der Stadt Mahagonny*. The present theatre building, with a seating capacity of 770, was opened in 1910. The Stadttheater is owned by the township of Klagenfurt and is subsidized by both the town and the province. In recent decades the company has attracted many young singers and its repertory has gained momentum. Klagenfurt's music-theatre activities extend over the borders into northern Italy and Slovenia, where guest performances are reciprocated by visits of local ensembles.

HARALD GOERTZ

Klarwein, Franz (*b* Garmisch, Ober-Bayern, 8 March 1914). German tenor. He studied in Frankfurt and in Berlin, where in 1937 he joined the Grosse Volksoper (Theater des Westens) as a lyric tenor. After moving to the Staatsoper in Munich, he created the Italian Tenor in *Capriccio* (1942), sang the title role in Sutermeister's *Raskolnikoff* (1949), took part in the première of Hindemith's *Die Harmonie der Welt* (1957) and created Timoleon in Cikker's *Hro o láske a smrti* ('The Play of Love and Death', 1969). He also sang a variety of character roles during his 35 years with the Munich company, including Count Elemer (*Arabella*) sung on tour at Covent Garden in 1953. His final appearance, in 1977, was as an Officer in *Ariadne auf Naxos*.

ELIZABETH FORBES

Klausenburg (Ger.). CLUJ-NAPOCA.

Klebe, Giselher (**Wolfgang**) (*b* Mannheim, 28 June 1925). German composer. He studied composition with Kurt von Wolfurt (1941–3), Josef Rufer (from 1946) and Boris Blacher (1946–51) in Berlin. In 1957 he was appointed to take a composition class at the Nordwestdeutsche Musik-Akademie in Berlin, and seven years later was nominated a member of the West Berlin Akademie für Künste.

Initially influenced by the post-serial styles as cultivated in the early 1950s in Darmstadt and Donaueschingen, Klebe, like his exact contemporary Henze, has achieved a rapprochement with wider audiences through his successful assimilation of a more eclectic idiom as manifested in his numerous operas. The first of these works, *Die Räuber*, occupied the composer for five years and set a precedent for future compositions in that its libretto is based around an established work of literature. Schiller's text is drastically reduced to present a tense internal drama between the four major characters. The composer employs two central note-rows, one with closed intervals, the other widely spaced, to represent the constructive and destructive elements of the plot. A large orchestra, which includes parts for two harpsichords and a vast array of percussion instruments, underpins the musical argument often in strict contrapuntal forms such as canon, ricercare and fugue. Yet despite the complexity of the musical language, which remains heavily dependent upon the Second Viennese School, *Die Räuber*, like many of Klebe's later operas, is in essence a traditional 'number' opera. Both *Die tödlichen Wünsche* and *Die Ermordung Cäsars* represent a stylistic advance in that a more personal idiom is cultivated, with ironic references to the music of the 19th century in the former work and a greater economy of means, a harsher instrumentation (including the use of electronic tape) and a dramatically effective treatment of variation technique in the latter. In his fourth opera, *Alkmene*, commissioned for the opening of the new Deutsche Oper in Berlin, the composer precedes Kleist's drama *Amphitryon* with a prologue on Mount Olympus which provides the opportunity to present a grand spectacle, incorporating extensive choral writing and an erotic ballet. Aleatory devices are often used to highlight more complex dramatic situations although the score suffers to a certain extent from understated emotion. A lighter touch is revealed in *Figaro lässt sich scheiden*, written for Rolf Liebermann and the Hamburg Opera. Horváth's comedy represents a continuation of Beaumarchais' world, as depicted in *Le barbier de Séville* and *Le mariage de Figaro*, which is brought to an abrupt end by revolution and transports the main characters into the 20th century to confront the problems and disillusionments experienced by present-day refugees. While the opera, constructed in a series of short numbers of arias and ensembles, includes some highly effective moments such as Cherubino's sentimental 12-note pop song set in the hotel bar of a sports resort, a certain lack of characterization detracts from its impact. This flaw was somewhat overcome in *Jacobowsky und der Oberst*, also performed at Hamburg, since the composer had begun to attempt an integration of serial and tonal elements. Werfel's autobiographical tragi-comedy, brought to a wider audience through Peter Glenville's film *Me and the Colonel* (1958), inspired Klebe to write in a more demonstrative manner. In particular, there is a G minor theme, representing Jacobowsky and appearing at crucial moments in the drama, which is peculiarly affecting. The composer seemed unable to recapture such simplicity in his later operas, where a desire to present too much detail on the stage detracts from the dramatic vitality. Thus *Das Mädchen aus Domrémy*, a portrait of Joan of Arc which invites obvious comparisons with Verdi, Tchaikovsky and Honegger, is disfigured by an over-reliance upon rather discursive sections of recitative and *Sprechgesang*. Similarly, *Der jüngste Tag* lacks contrast in that the supernatural elements in Horváth's drama are surprisingly understated. On the other hand, in *Die Fastnachtsbeichte*, based on Zuckmayer's tale of a murder at carnival time in Mainz, Klebe has written a genuinely popular opera in which the flexibility of styles and the variety of modes of singing are used to great effect.

Die Räuber op.25 (4, Klebe, after F. von Schiller), Düsseldorf, 3 June 1957, vs (Berlin, 1957, 2/1962)

Die tödlichen Wünsche op.27 (3, Klebe, after H. de Balzac: *La peau de chagrin*), Düsseldorf, 14 June 1959, vs (Berlin, 1959)

Die Ermordung Cäsars (1, Klebe, after W. Shakespeare), Essen, 20 Sept 1959, vs (Berlin, 1960)

Alkmene op.36 (3, Klebe, after H. von Kleist), Berlin, Deutsche Oper, 25 Sept 1961, vs (Berlin, 1961)

Figaro lässt sich scheiden op.40 (2, Klebe, after Ö. von Horváth), Hamburg, Staatsoper, 28 June 1963, vs (Berlin, 1963)

Jacobowsky und der Oberst op.49 (4, Klebe, after F. Werfel), Hamburg, Staatsoper, 2 Nov 1965, vs (Berlin, 1965)

Das Märchen von der schönen Lilie op.55 (2, Klebe, after J. W. von Goethe), Schwetzingen, Schloss, 15 May 1969, vs (Kassel, 1968)

Ein wahrer Held (3, Klebe, after J. M. Synge: *The Playboy of the Western World*), Zürich, 18 Jan 1975, vs (Kassel, 1975)

Das Mädchen aus Domrémy (2, Klebe, after Schiller), Stuttgart, 19 June 1976, vs (Kassel, 1976)

Das Rendez-vous (Klebe, after M. Soschtschenko), Hanover, 7 Oct 1977

Der jüngste Tag (3, Klebe, after Horváth), Mannheim, 12 July 1980

Die Fastnachtsbeichte (2, L. Klebe, after C. Zuckmayer), Darmstadt, 20 Dec 1983

*

G. Klebe: 'Über meine Oper "Die Räuber"', *Melos*, xxiv (1957), 73–6

——: 'Meine Oper "Alkmene"', *Melos*, xxviii (1961), 272–5

W. E. von Lewinski: 'Der Dramatiker Giselher Klebe', *Melos*, xxviii (1961), 4–7

C. H. Bachmann: 'Der Barbier von Grosshadersdorf: Uraufführung von Giselher Klebes "Figaro-Oper" in Hamburg', *OW*, iv/9 (1963), 21–3

H. Ehinger: '"Figaro lässt sich scheiden": Klebe-Uraufführung in Hamburg', *Das Orchester*, xi (1963), 284–6

A. D. McCredie: 'Giselher Klebe', *MR*, xxvi (1965), 220–35

A. Goléa: '"Jacobowsky und der Oberst" von Giselher Klebe uraufgeführt', *Das Orchester*, xiv (1966), 10–13

W. E. von Lewinski: 'Der Opernkomponist Giselher Klebe', *SMz*, cix (1969), 337–40

——: 'Konzentration auf einen ewigen Konflikt: Anmerkungen zu Giselher Klebes Oper "Das Mädchen aus Domrémy"', *Musica*, xxx (1976), 305–8
ERIK LEVI

Klee, Bernhard (*b* Schleiz, 19 April 1936). German conductor. A chorister at St Thomas's, Leipzig, he later studied piano, composition and conducting at Cologne, where he joined the opera music staff and made his conducting début with *Die Zauberflöte* (1960). He held conducting appointments at Berne, Salzburg, Oberhausen and Hanover before becoming music director at Lübeck, 1966–73, by which time he had a repertory of over 80 operas. His British début was with the Hamburg Staatsoper at the Edinburgh Festival in 1969 conducting *Der fliegende Holländer*, and his Covent Garden début was with *Così fan tutte* in 1972. He was appointed Generalmusikdirektor in Düsseldorf (1977), chief guest conductor with the BBC PO (1985–9) and a conductor with the Bavarian State Opera in Munich (from 1990). His performances have secure control and assiduous attention to musical character without interposing any distraction of personality.
NOËL GOODWIN

Kleiber, Carlos (*b* Berlin, 3 July 1930). Argentine conductor of German birth, son of the conductor Erich Kleiber. His parents settled in Buenos Aires in 1935, and he began music lessons in 1950, making his début at La Plata in 1952. On the family's return to Europe, Kleiber was advised by his father against a musical career and studied chemistry in Zürich, but he began his opera career at the Theater am Gärtnerplatz, Munich, in 1953. He was appointed conductor at Potsdam (1954), and at the Deutsche Oper am Rhein, Düsseldorf and Duisburg (1956–64), Zürich Opera (1964–6) and the Stuttgart Staatsoper (from 1966). In Stuttgart he was particularly successful in Berg's *Wozzeck* (of which his father had conducted the 1925 première), and in operas by Strauss, Wagner, Verdi, Bizet and Weber, whose *Der Freischütz* he recorded in 1973. From 1968 he made regular appearances at the Staatsoper in Munich, and conducted *Tristan und Isolde* at his débuts at the Vienna Staatsoper in 1973, and the Bayreuth Festival in 1974, the year he first appeared at Covent Garden, in *Der Rosenkavalier*. He recorded all these works and *Die Fledermaus*, either on record or video, with outstanding success during the 1980s. Other works that form part of his limited repertory, which he has seemed chary of expanding, are *La bohème* and *Otello*, both of which he has conducted with exceptional success at Covent Garden. Kleiber prefers not to hold a resident appointment, as his rigorous artistic demands restrict his appearances. A passionately eloquent conductor, he sustains strong musical and dramatic tension in an expressive range from refined lyrical poetry to frenzied ecstasy, but his instinctive approach to a work is controlled by his intellectual grasp of its character.

WOLFRAM SCHWINGER/ALAN BLYTH

Kleiber, Erich (*b* Vienna, 5 Aug 1890; *d* Zürich, 27 Jan 1956). Austrian conductor. He was educated in Vienna, where he was deeply impressed by performances at the court opera during the last years of Mahler's directorship. After studying at the conservatory in Prague, he was appointed chorus master at the German Theatre there in 1911, but in 1912 he moved to Darmstadt, where he conducted at the court theatre for seven years. Further appointments followed at Barmen-Elberfeld (now Wuppertal) in 1919, Düsseldorf in 1921 and Mannheim in 1922. An outstanding success on his Berlin début in 1923, with Frida Leider and Friedrich Schorr in *Fidelio*, led to his appointment as Generalmusikdirektor of the Berlin Staatsoper; here his 1924 production of Janáček's *Jenůfa* was regarded as decisive for the composer's wider success. It was followed by Krenek's *Zwingburg* in 1924 and in 1925 by the première, after 137 painstaking rehearsals, of Berg's *Wozzeck*. Other new works included Schreker's *Der singende Teufel* (1928) and Milhaud's *Christophe Colombe* (1930), and he also conducted Wagner's *Das Liebesverbot* and various operettas. Following the Nazi regime's embargo on such operas as Berg's *Lulu*, he resigned his post in 1934, conducting the première of the *Lulu* Suite at his last concert before leaving.

Kleiber became a frequent visitor to European cities, and in 1938 made his Covent Garden début conducting *Der Rosenkavalier* with Lotte Lehmann. Meanwhile he had begun to make a new home in Buenos Aires, where he had first appeared in 1926. He took charge of the German opera seasons at the Teatro Colón between 1937 and 1949, and virtually made a second career as a pioneering conductor in countries such as Chile, Uruguay, Mexico and Cuba. From 1950 to 1953 he was on a regular contract at Covent Garden, where he conducted the British stage première of *Wozzeck* in 1952, and his presence became of crucial importance to the development of the postwar company. At the 1951 Maggio Musicale, Florence (his first opera performance in Italy), he conducted Haydn's *Orfeo ed Euridice* (its first known performance) and a memorable *Les vêpres siciliennes*, both with Callas. Plans for his appointment to the Vienna Staatsoper did not materialize, and his only operatic engagement there was *Der Rosenkavalier* in 1951, when the company was at the Theater an der Wien. In 1955 his reappointment at the Berlin Staatsoper was announced, but he resigned before taking up the post in protest against political intrusion.

Kleiber rehearsed with an almost fanatical ardour and aimed at the utmost possible precision. He was outstanding as a conductor of Mozart, Beethoven and Richard Strauss, refusing to indulge in romantic interpretation as a means of self-projection, ignoring false performing traditions and studying the scores assiduously. He never lost his whole view of a work, and his approach was strictly non-sentimental. He won the lasting devotion of orchestral players as well as singers, and as Russell well said 'there was no such thing, to him,

as an unimportant musician'. His intellect enabled him to balance structural and emotional elements in model performances, including highly regarded recordings of *Der Rosenkavalier* and *Le nozze di Figaro*.

*

K. Blaukopf: 'Erich Kleiber', *Grosse Dirigenten* (Teufen, 1954)
D. Webster: 'Kleiber: an Appreciation', *Tempo*, new ser., no.39 (1956), pp.5–6
J. Russell: *Erich Kleiber – a Memoir* (London, 1957)
W. Reich: 'Erich Kleiber und Alban Berg', *SMz*, xcviii (1958), 374–77
F. F. Clough and G. J. Cuming: 'Erich Kleiber: a Discography', *Gramophone Record Review*, no.74 (1959), 117

GERHARD BRUNNER

Kleider machen Leute ('Clothes Make the Man'). *Musikalische Komödie* in a Vorspiel and three acts by ALEXANDER ZEMLINSKY to a libretto by Leo Feld after GOTTFRIED KELLER's novella; Vienna, Volksoper, 2 December 1910 (revised version, Prague, Neues Deutsches Theater, 22 April 1922).

In the Vorspiel Strapinski (tenor), a downcast tailor, is seen leaving Seldwyla to seek his luck elsewhere. A passing coachman gives him a lift to the neighbouring town of Goldach.

Act 1 introduces Böhni (baritone) and Nettchen (soprano), the daughter of the local magistrate. Nettchen has romantic notions about marrying a foreign nobleman and rejects Böhni's advances. When the coach arrives in Goldach, Strapinski, whose principal assets are his stylish clothes, is mistaken for an aristocrat. After consuming a large meal, he is treated to cigars by the local worthies in a scene underpinned by a delightful waltz. Strapinski at first plays the role assigned to him rather unwillingly, even after he has been introduced to Nettchen. His attempt to escape is thwarted by the innkeeper and the worthies, who arrive with replacements for his supposedly lost luggage.

Act 2 takes place at the magistrate's house. Nettchen hints at her feelings for Strapinski by singing a Heine song. After dinner Strapinski once more tries to escape. This time it is Nettchen who thwarts his plans. After an extended and lyrical scene of parting, they are discovered by Böhni, and Nettchen at once persuades Strapinski to marry her. The news is greeted with some incredulity, but is then celebrated with a rousing waltz. After an interlude, 'Der arglistige Böhni' ('Crafty Böhni'), the scene changes to the Waldhaus, where the festivities are due to continue. Böhni is seen finalizing arrangements with Strapinski's former employer for a play entitled *Kleider machen Leute*, which retraces a tailor's transformation into a Polish count. His identity revealed, Strapinski rushes out into the snow. Nettchen follows him, and he confesses to deceiving her. Once more there is a lyrical scene of parting. However, there is a happy ending. When her father and Böhni arrive Nettchen declares that she intends to marry Strapinski, despite his lowly origins.

Kleider machen Leute juxtaposes some soaring lyricism with various kinds of grotesque humour that are effectively rendered in musical terms, and a number of very Viennese waltzes. Much of the musical material makes play with 4ths (they are introduced at the very beginning of the Vorspiel), a feature that derives from Schoenberg's first Chamber Symphony.

ALFRED CLAYTON

Klein, Peter (*b* Zündorf, nr Cologne, 25 Jan 1907). Austrian tenor of German birth. After study at the

Cologne Conservatory and a season in the Cologne Opera chorus he sang at Düsseldorf, Kaiserslautern and Zürich. In 1937 he was engaged at the Hamburg Opera and in 1942 moved to Vienna where he became a professor of opera and operetta at the Conservatory in 1956. He first sang at Covent Garden with the visiting Vienna Staatsoper in September 1947, as Jaquino; the next year he returned to sing Mime in the *Ring*, and for more than a decade was the outstanding exponent of the part. He took part in the première of Einem's *Der Prozess* (1953, Salzburg). He was excellent in a host of character parts – Pedrillo and Monostatos, Dr Blind (*Die Fledermaus*), Valzacchi in *Der Rosenkavalier* (his début role at the Metropolitan in 1949), Monsieur Taupe (*Capriccio*) – and was impressive in vital but small roles in such modern operas as *Wozzeck* and *Dantons Tod*; in 1965 he sang Beckmesser at the Vienna Staatsoper.   PETER BRANSCOMBE

Kleinmichel, Richard (*b* Posen [now Poznán], 31 Dec 1846; *d* Charlottenburg, 18 Aug 1901). German pianist, composer and arranger. He received his first instruction from his father, F. H. H. Kleinmichel (1827–94), a military and operatic conductor. He studied at the Leipzig Conservatory, 1863–6, before settling in Hamburg, where he published many works, mostly for his own instrument. For a time he was Kapellmeister at the Leipzig Stadttheater, and he subsequently held similar appointments at Danzig (now Gdańsk) and Magdeburg. His first opera, *Schloss de l'Orme* (romantische Oper, 4, E. Henle, based on Prévost's *Manon Lescaut*), was successfully produced at Hamburg on 8 October 1883, and his *Pfeifer von Dusenbach* (W. Wulff and W. Warneke) at Hamburg on 21 March 1891. He is best known for his simplified piano arrangements for vocal scores of Wagner's operas, published mostly during the 1880s; in his last decade he also made vocal scores of works by Paisiello, Mozart, Grétry, Isouard, Méhul, Cherubini, Berlioz, Lortzing and Humperdinck.

Kleist, (Bernd) Heinrich (Wilhelm) von (*b* Frankfurt an der Oder, 18 Oct 1777; *d* Wannsee, nr Potsdam, 21 Nov 1811). German writer. He was the great-nephew of the poet Ewald Christian von Kleist. Orphaned at an early age, he joined the army in 1792 but resigned in 1799. He travelled extensively, visiting Dresden and Paris (1801), Berne, Königsberg (1805–6), Dresden (1807–9) and Berlin, near where he and his incurably ill mistress committed suicide. Many of his plays and stories have been used as the basis for operas and other musical compositions, with no sign of diminishing interest in the 20th century.

Amphitryon (play, 1807): G. Klebe, 1961, as Alkmene
Das Erdbeben in Chili (story, 1807): J. Cikker, 1979, as Rozsudok: zemetrasenie v Chile
Die Marquis von O … (story, 1808): H. Erbse, 1959, as Julietta
Michael Kohlhaas (story, 1808): P. von Klenau, 1933
Penthesilea (play, pubd 1808): O. Schoeck, 1927
Das Käthchen von Heilbronn (play, 1810): F. Lux, 1846; K. Reinthaler, 1881
Die Verlobung in San Domingo (story, 1811): W. Zillig, 1957; W. Egk, 1963
Der Prinz Friedrich von Homburg (play, 1821): P. Graener, 1935; H. W. Henze, 1960

A. Schaefer: *Historisches und systematisches Verzeichnis sämtlicher Tonwerke zu den Dramen … Kleists* (Leipzig, 1886)
E. L. Stahl: *Heinrich von Kleist's Dramas* (Oxford, 1948)
D. De La Motte: *Hans Werner Henze: Der Prinz von Homburg* (Mainz, 1963)

K. Kanzog and H. J. Kreutzer, eds.: *Werke Kleists auf dem modernen Musiktheater* (Berlin, 1977) [incl. complete list of settings]
M. R. Griffel: *Operas in German: a Dictionary* (New York, 1990)
                                        PETER BRANSCOMBE

Klemperer, Otto (*b* Breslau, 14 May 1885; *d* Zürich, 6 July 1973). German conductor. He studied the piano with James Kwast and composition and conducting with Pfitzner in Berlin where he conducted Max Reinhardt's production of *Orphée aux enfers* at the Neues Theater in 1906. In 1907, on Mahler's recommendation, he was appointed chorus master and subsequently conductor at the Neues Deutsches Theater in Prague, making his début in *Der Freischütz*. Further appointments followed at Hamburg (1910–12), Barmen (1913–14), Strasbourg (1914–17), where he was Pfitzner's deputy, and as first conductor at Cologne (1917–24) and Wiesbaden (1924–7).

Klemperer declined the music directorship of the Berlin Staatsoper but in 1927 became director of its second house, the Staatsoper am Platz der Republik, usually known as the Kroll Theatre. Though more modest than its parent house on Unter den Linden, the Kroll reached high standards under its conductors Fritz Zweig, Zemlinsky and Klemperer. New operas performed there included Stravinsky's *Oedipus rex* and *Mavra* (both directed by Klemperer), Schoenberg's *Erwartung* and *Die glückliche Hand*, Hindemith's *Cardillac* and *Neues vom Tage*, Janáček's *The House of the Dead* and Weill's *Der Jasager*. After the Prussian government shut the Kroll in July 1931, Klemperer remained with the Staatsoper until 1933, when he conducted *Tannhäuser* on the 50th anniversary of Wagner's death. His next regular operatic engagement was at the Budapest Opera (1947–50). In 1961 he made his Covent Garden début, conducting and directing *Fidelio*; *Die Zauberflöte* followed in 1962, and *Lohengrin* in 1963.

Klemperer's later performances were notable for their heroic dimensions and architectural grasp (the slow tempos for which he became known were a feature only of his last years). His interpretation of Mozart remained controversial in Britain – detractors found it too plain and lacking in nimbleness while admirers praised its simplicity and directness. Klemperer took a few lessons in composition with Schoenberg in the mid 1930s and his output includes an opera, *Das Ziel* (composed 1915, revised 1970), which received a concert performance in Berlin in 1931.

P. Heyworth: *Conversations with Klemperer* (London, 1973)
H. Curjel, ed. E. Kruttge: *Experiment Krolloper* (Munich, 1975)
P. Heyworth: *Otto Klemperer, his Life and Times* (Cambridge, 1983)
                                        PETER HEYWORTH

Klenau, Paul (August) von (*b* Copenhagen, 11 Feb 1883; *d* Copenhagen, 31 Aug 1946). Danish composer and conductor. After initial studies in composition with Otto Malling in Copenhagen, he became a pupil of Max Bruch at the Berlin Hochschule für Musik (1901–3) and moved to Munich in 1903 to work under Ludwig Thuille. After Thuille's death in 1907, he was appointed Kapellmeister at the Freiburg Opera; however in 1908 he went to study with Max von Schillings in Stuttgart, where he obtained his first conducting post, at the Hofoper, in 1909. He became conductor of the Frankfurt Bach Society in 1912 before taking up a position at the Freiburg Opera, where he remained until

1917. On returning to Copenhagen during World War I he participated in the formation of the Danish Philharmonic Society, which he conducted from 1920 to 1926. Following a final period of study with Schoenberg, he conducted the Vienna Konzerthausgesellschaft from 1922 to 1930.

Klenau's early operas *Sulamith*, based on the Song of Solomon, and *Kjarten und Gudrun*, derived from Icelandic themes, are conceived in a conventional late-Romantic idiom owing much to the examples of Schillings and Richard Strauss. Neither work created much impression despite the fact that Furtwängler gave the first performance of *Kjarten und Gudrun* during his tenure at Mannheim. *Die Lästerschule* represented an advance through its more sophisticated handling of form, although its straightforward musical idiom hardly suggests that the composer had become a proponent of Schoenberg's music. Yet after this work, Klenau embarked upon a thorough re-examination of his musical style and subsequently incorporated elements of 12-note technique into his compositions. This change of direction coincided with the advent of the Nazis and provoked a certain degree of controversy when his next opera, *Michael Kohlhaas*, was first performed at the Stuttgart Opera in November 1933. Since Schoenberg and his technique had been vilified by the new regime, the composer had to employ all means, including political obeisance, to circumvent charges of decadence against his work. A series of articles appeared in Nazi periodicals in which the composer defended his use of 12-note rows, claiming historical precedence in Wagner and avoiding all mention of Schoenberg. *Michael Kohlhaas* was deemed to be acceptable to the authorities because Klenau had treated Kleist's classic drama with respect and juxtaposed atonal passages with episodes based on German folk melodies and Lutheran chorales. Nevertheless in *Rembrandt van Rijn*, performed in Berlin in 1937, his 12-note technique was somewhat modified in order to avoid further discussion. Both this work and Klenau's last opera, *Elisabeth von England* (1939), failed to secure more than a handful of performances despite receiving positive reviews from the critics. The latter work had to be presented under the title *Die Königin* when it was heard in Berlin in 1940, as the original title was considered to be subversive in view of hostilities against England.

Sulamith (1, after the Bible), Munich, 16 Nov 1913 (Vienna and Leipzig, 1914)

Kjarten und Gudrun (3, Klenau), Mannheim, 4 April 1918, vs (Vienna and Leipzig, 1918); rev. as Gudrun auf Island, Hagen in Westfalen, 27 Nov 1924

Die Lästerschule (komische Oper, 3, R. S. Hoffmann, after R. B. Sheridan: The School for Scandal), Frankfurt, 25 Dec 1926, vs (Vienna and New York, 1926)

Michael Kohlhaas (4, Klenau, after H. von Kleist), Stuttgart, 4 Nov 1933, vs (Vienna, 1933); rev. version, Berlin, Staatsoper, 7 March 1934

Rembrandt van Rijn (4, Klenau), Berlin, Staatsoper, 23 Jan 1937, vs (Berlin, 1936)

Elisabeth von England (4, Klenau), Kassel, 29 March 1939, vs (Vienna and Leipzig, 1938); rev. as Die Königin, Berlin, Staatsoper, April 1940; as Drønningen, Copenhagen, 1941

König Tannmor, unpubd

*

P. von Klenau: 'Handwerk und Inspiration', Die Musik, xxviii (1935–6), 645–62

F. Stege: 'Musik in Berlin: Rembrandt van Rijn', ZfM, civ (1937), 284–9

P. von Klenau: 'Das Wesen des Tragischen', ZfM, cvi (1939), 243–6

W. Matthes: 'Paul von Klenau', ZfM, cvi (1939), 237–43

——: 'Elisabeth von England', ZfM, cvi (1939), 492–6

P. Hamburger: 'Paul von Klenau', Aschehougs musiklexikon, ii (Copenhagen, 1958), 36

H.-G. Klein: 'Ideologisierung von Werken Kleists im Opern aus dem 20. Jahrhunderts', Norddeutsche Beiträge, i (1978), 44–65

H.-G. Klein: 'Atonalität in den Opern von Paul von Klenau und Winfried Zillig: zur Duldung einer im Nationalsozialismus verfemten Kompositionstechnik', Bericht über den Internationalen Musikwissenschaftlichen Kongress Bayreuth 1981 (Kassel, 1984), 490–94   ERIK LEVI, WILLIAM H. REYNOLDS

Kletzel, Martin (*d* Dresden, 1699). German stage designer. His first documented activity is his participation with J. O. Harms in designing a ballet with music by Christoph Bernhard for the Dresden court in 1678. Ten years later he was formally engaged as theatrical engineer and principal scenic artist at the Dresden court theatre, replacing Harms who went to Brunswick in 1686. For Carnival 1693 Kletzel designed 16 sets for C. L. P. Grua's *Camillo generoso* (they were engraved by Moritz Bodenehr and accompanied the first edition of the libretto). Kletzel appears to have been influenced by Harms: although he exploited the full width of the stage, he continued to use the 'box' shape typical of his predecessor, breaking up the stage space with a divided and asymmetrical background.

M. Fürstenau: Zur Geschichte der Musik und des Theaters am Hofe der Kurfürsten von Sachsen, i (Dresden, 1861)

U. Thieme and F. Becker, eds.: Lexikon der bildenden Künstler, xxi (Leipzig, 1947)

G. Rudloff-Hille: Katalog der Staatliche Kunstsammlung Dresden: Abteilung Barocktheater (Dresden, 1954), 15

H. Richter: Johann Oswald Harms: ein deutscher Theaterdekorateur des Barock (Emsdetten, 1963)

H. C. Wolff: Oper: Szene und Darstellung von 1600 bis 1900 (Leipzig, 1968, 2/1979), 80–81   EVAN BAKER

Klimentova, Maria Nikolayevna (*b* Moscow, 1857; *d* Moscow, 1946). Russian soprano. She studied at the Moscow Conservatory and while still a student there, in 1879, she created Tatyana in *Yevgeny Onegin* at the Maliy Theatre. She joined the Bol'shoy in 1880 and sang there for a decade. She took part in another Tchaikovsky première, as Oxana in *Cherevichki* (1887), and continued to sing Tatyana throughout her career, as well as Tamara (*The Demon*) and other Russian and French roles. Later she taught in Paris, and remained there until near her death.

For illustration *see* YEVGENY ONEGIN.   ELIZABETH FORBES

Klobucar, Berislav (*b* Zagreb, 28 Aug 1924). Croatian conductor. He studied in Salzburg with Lovro von Matačić and Clemens Krauss, and was on the conducting staff at the Zagreb Opera, 1943–51. His Vienna Staatsoper début was in 1953, and during the late 1950s he was invited by Carl Ebert to work at the Städtische Oper, Berlin. He was general director at Graz, 1960–71. During this time he began to tour more widely and made his début at the Metropolitan in 1968, where he was admired in the Wagner repertory. He was music director at the Stockholm Royal Opera, 1972–81, and at Nice, 1983–8, taking the Nice Opéra production of the *Ring* to Paris (Théâtre des Champs-Elysées) in 1988. In 1989 he conducted Montemezzi's now rarely-heard *L'amore dei tre re* at Palermo. He favours broad, steady tempos and close integration of voices and orchestra, in performances regarded as competent and secure more than inspirational.   NOËL GOODWIN

Klose, Friedrich (*b* Karlsruhe, 29 Nov 1862; *d* Ruvigliana, Lugano, 24 Dec 1942). German-Swiss composer. As a schoolboy he received instruction from Vinzenz Lachner and was definitively influenced by Mottl. His studies continued in Geneva (he became a Swiss citizen in 1886) and, most importantly, with Bruckner in Vienna (1886–9). Thereafter he taught in Geneva, Basle and Munich, where he succeeded Thuille at the Akademie der Tonkunst and from 1910 to 1919 served as professor. Increasing attention to his work was reflected in the Friedrich Klose Week celebrated in Munich in 1918, but in that year he stopped composing. His music was always written in response to pictorial or poetic ideas, and the symphonic poems contain much of his best work. He remained rooted in the Romantic tradition, particularly in the opera *Ilsebill: das Märlein von dem Fischer und seiner Frau* (H. Hoffmann, after J. L. and W. C. Grimm; Karlsruhe, 7 June 1903), which he called a *dramatische Symphonie*. Klose had himself written the texts for five of his nine earlier, uncompleted operatic projects. Among his writings, *Meine Lehrjahre bei Bruckner* (Regensburg, 1927) contains aesthetic reflections on, for example, the conception of the 'Gesamtkunstwerk', which Klose thought might be renewed along the lines of *Carmen*.   PETER ROSS

Klose, Margarete (*b* Berlin, 6 Aug 1902; *d* Berlin, 14 Dec 1968). German mezzo-soprano. After study in Berlin with Marschalk and Bültemann she made her début at Ulm in 1927. She was a member of the Mannheim Opera (1928–31), then of the Berlin Staatsoper. In 1935 she sang Ortrud under Beecham at Covent Garden and in 1936 she began to appear at Bayreuth. She was heard in London again in 1937, as Fricka, Waltraute and Brangäne, and in 1939 in Rome. After the war she sang in North and South America, at the Salzburg Festival and in Italy, Spain, London and Vienna. In 1949 she moved from the Berlin Staatsoper to the Städtische Oper, returning to her old company in 1958 and retiring in 1961. Klose's clear, rich voice and dignified stage bearing fitted her admirably for the Wagnerian mezzo roles in which she was best known; she was a distinguished Clytemnestra in *Elektra* and *Iphigénie en Aulide*, and she also appeared with success as Carmen, the Kostelnička (*Jenůfa*), Delilah and Mrs Herring (*Albert Herring*), as well as in many Verdi roles.

GV (L. Riemens; R. Vegeto)   PETER BRANSCOMBE

Kluge, Die [*Die Geschichte von dem König und der klugen Frau* ('The Story of the King and the Clever Young Woman')]. Opera in 12 scenes by CARL ORFF after the fairy-tale *Die kluge Bauerntochter* by the brothers Jacob Ludwig and Wilhelm Carl GRIMM; Frankfurt, Städtische Bühnen, 18 February 1943.

The Clever Girl (soprano) is the daughter of a Peasant (bass). He finds a golden mortar while ploughing a field and, against his daughter's wishes, has taken it to the King (baritone). The King immediately locks up the Peasant in a tower because he does not produce the golden pestle which is supposed to go with the mortar. Together with the Prison Governor (bass), he presses the Peasant to tell him where the pestle is hidden. However, the Peasant simply reiterates the warnings delivered by his daughter. In exasperation, the King demands to see the daughter. She appears and is asked three riddles which she solves with no difficulty. Without hesitation, he asks for her hand in marriage.

Meanwhile, a Man with a Donkey (tenor) and a Man with a Mule (baritone) have been quarrelling over the ownership of a colt which had been born to the donkey during the night but which had been found lying near the mule. The dispute is brought before the King who decides in favour of the man who owns the mule. The Clever Girl consoles the man with the donkey and offers advice as to how to recover his colt. Furious that his orders have been contradicted, the King tells the Clever Girl that he has had enough of her and that she must leave. As a concession, she can keep a trunk and put her most precious possession into it. She prepares the King one last meal and, having drugged his wine, puts him into the trunk as the object she holds most dear. At the end, she claims that her cleverness was just a pose since 'no one can both love and be clever'. As the plot unfolds, three Vagabonds (tenor, baritone and bass) regularly appear to exchange remarks and comment upon the situation, much in the manner of figures from the *commedia dell'arte*.

Die Kluge was Orff's second opera and shares with its predecessor, *Der Mond*, a naive yet refreshing simplicity. Of all Orff's stage compositions, it has enjoyed the widest currency, partly through its skilfully delineated characterization and partly through its entertaining mixture of comedy, satire, irony and profound home truths.   ERIK LEVI

Klughardt, August (Friedrich Martin) (*b* Cöthen, 30 Nov 1847; *d* Rosslau, nr Dresden, 3 Aug 1902). German conductor and composer. He studied in Cöthen, Dessau and Dresden. After working as a theatre conductor in Posen (now Poznań, 1867–8), Neustrelitz (1868–9) and Lübeck (summer 1869), he became court music director at Weimar (1869), where he formed a friendship with Liszt. His compositions of these years include incidental music for theatre productions. At the première of Liszt's *Christus* in 1873 he met Wagner, to whom he dedicated his symphonic poem *Lenore*; his Symphony in F minor was composed under the impact of hearing the *Ring* at the first Bayreuth Festival in 1876. Having returned to Neustrelitz in 1873 as music director, he moved on to succeed his teacher Thiele at Dessau in 1882; he brought the ensemble to a high standard, giving the *Ring* in 1892 and 1893. In his own operas Klughardt attempted to absorb a Wagnerian influence into number opera; his concert works also show his enthusiasm for the New German School at the same time as his loyalty to classical practice.

Mirjam op.15 (grosse Oper, 3, A. Formey), Weimar, Hof, 1 April 1871
Iwein op.35 (grosse Oper, 3, K. Niemann), Neustrelitz, 28 March 1879 (Leipzig, n.d.)
Gudrun op.38 (grosse Oper, 3, Niemann), Neustrelitz, 29 Jan 1882, vs (Berlin and Posen, 1883)
Die Hochzeit des Mönchs (4, E. Pasqué), Dessau, 10 Nov 1886, vs (Berlin and Posen, 1886); as Astorre, Prague, 19 April 1888; rev. version, Dessau, 15 Nov 1889

*

MGG (W. Pfannkuch); *Stieger*O
L. Gerlach: *August Klughardt* (Leipzig, 1902)   JOHN WARRACK

Kmentt, Waldemar (*b* Vienna, 2 Feb 1929). Austrian tenor. He studied at the Vienna Academy. While a student he toured the Netherlands and Belgium with an ensemble from the Academy in *Die Fledermaus* and *Le nozze di Figaro*. In 1951 he sang the Prince in *The Love for Three Oranges* at the Vienna Volksoper. He was soon singing Mozart roles at the Theater an der Wien and in 1955 sang Jaquino at the opening performance of the rebuilt Staatsoper. From 1955 he sang regularly at the Salzburg Festival, where his roles included Idamantes, Ferrando, Gabriel (Martin's *Le mystère de la Nativité*) and Tamino. In 1968 he sang Idomeneus at La Scala. He sang Walther at Bayreuth (1968–70) and his repertory included Erik, Bacchus and the Emperor (*Die Frau ohne Schatten*).   HAROLD ROSENTHAL/R

Knapp, Peter (*b* Aylesbury, 4 Aug 1947). English baritone. He was a choral scholar at Cambridge, then studied in London and with Tito Gobbi in Italy. After his début in 1973 as Almaviva with the Glyndebourne Touring Opera, he worked with Kent Opera, sang the title role in Szymanowski's *King Roger* for the New Opera Company in 1975 and first appeared with the ENO the next year as Don Giovanni. In 1977 he won the first Benson and Hedges Gold Award at Aldeburgh, and in 1978 he formed and directed the Singers' Company (later the Travelling Opera), which toured with small-scale performances of opera in English. He created Maxim in *Rebecca* (Josephs) for Opera North (1983), and has sung in Bulgaria, Germany, Switzerland, Hong Kong and Australia. He sang Wolfram for New Sussex Opera in 1990. His secure, warm-toned singing and excellent diction have also contributed to a successful concert career.   NOËL GOODWIN

Knappertsbusch, Hans (*b* Elberfeld, 12 March 1888; *d* Munich, 25 Oct 1965). German conductor. After studying conducting with Steinbach at the Cologne Conservatory he conducted at the Mülheim/Ruhr theatre from 1910–12, spending the summers as assistant to Siegfried Wagner and Richter at Bayreuth. From 1913 to 1918 he was opera director at Elberfeld (taking part in the Wagner Festivals of 1913–14 in the Netherlands). In 1918 he went to Leipzig and in the following year to Dessau, where in 1920 he was made music director; in this capacity he served at Munich from 1922 before conducting at the Vienna Staatsoper, 1937–44. After the war he returned to Munich, where he regained his former eminence, and was a leading conductor at the Bayreuth Festivals between 1951 and 1957.

Knappertsbusch made guest appearances in various European countries (he conducted *Salome* in the 1936–7 Covent Garden season) but was generally content to stay at home, a fact which increased his popularity in Munich even if it partly robbed him of more international fame. In music he was a conservative in a broad sense and the unhurried stride of his conducting of Wagner made him appear to be one of the last representatives of the old school. He was not particularly interested in contemporary music, though he conducted many premières in Munich including *Samuel Pepys* by Albert Coates (1929) and Pfitzner's *Das Herz* (1931). His conducting of *Parsifal* (recorded in 1951 and 1962) was among the highest musical achievements of the postwar regime at Bayreuth.

F. F. Clough and G. J. Cuming: 'Hans Knappertsbusch Discography', *Gramophone Record Review* (1960), no.85, p.18
H. Hotter: 'Hans Knappertsbusch 1888–1965: in Memoriam', *Opera*, xvii (1966), 21–3
H. C. Schonberg: *The Great Conductors* (London, 1968)
                     RONALD CRICHTON

Knayfel', Alexander Aronovich (*b* Tashkent, 28 Nov 1943). Russian composer. He studied the cello at the Secondary Music School of the Leningrad Conservatory

from 1950 to 1961, before enrolling in Mstislav Rostropovich's class at the Moscow Conservatory. A hand injury forced him to give up the instrument in 1963 and the following year he entered the Leningrad Conservatory, studying composition with Boris Arapov and graduating in 1967.

Nearly all of his works derive from some literary or dramatic impulse. Even his instrumental works often involve visual or theatrical elements that he sometimes requires the performer to internalize. Considered one of the leading representatives of the Soviet avant-garde, his style has evolved from his explorations of serialism in the 1960s to a rarified and highly symbolic language. His only opera, *Kentervil'skoye privedeniye* ('The Canterville Ghost'), was composed in 1965–6 to a libretto by T. Kramarova after Oscar Wilde's comic horror story. Written in a prologue and three acts, it received its première at the Leningrad House of Composers on 26 February 1974. Knayfel' simultaneously fashioned a suite for soloists and chamber orchestra from the opera subtitled 'Romantic Scenes', which was published with an English translation in 1977. *The Canterville Ghost* is a vivid and colouristic work with rhythmic qualities and grotesque effects reminiscent of Shostakovich's *The Nose*. The organ passacaglia, which marks the dramatic climax, can be performed independently of the opera.

T. Voronina and B. Kats: 'Eskizï k portretu' [Sketches for a Portrait], *SovM* (1975), no.4, pp.49–54   LAUREL E. FAY

Knecht, Justin Heinrich (*b* Biberach, 30 Sept 1752; *d* Biberach, 1 Dec 1817). German composer. He was mainly self-taught. The writer C. M. Wieland, who lived near Biberach until 1769, was a friend and his tutor. By the age of 12 or 13 Knecht had had two operas produced in Biberach and in 1771 he was appointed music director and organist there; he remained in Biberach all his life apart from a short interlude as court conductor at Stuttgart (1806–8). He enjoyed a great reputation as composer, organist and theorist of the Vogler school. His works for the stage are mostly Singspiels in the style of Hiller. *Die Entführung aus dem Serail* (1787) is of interest as a setting of the libretto which Mozart had used five years earlier. As well as 11 operas of various kinds, he wrote a duodrama after J.-J. Rousseau's *Pygmalion* (1807, Stuttgart) and a melodrama on Schiller's *Das Lied von der Glocke* (1807).

first performed in Biberach unless otherwise stated

Joshua (geistliche Oper), Liebhaber, 1764
Kain und Abel (geistliche Oper), Liebhaber, 1765
Der Kohlenbrenner (Lustspiel mit Gesang, 1, L. Ysenburg von Buri), Neuwied, Hof, 1779
Die treuen Köhler (operetta, 2, G. E. Heermann), Evangelischen Meister Sänger Gesellschaft, 2 Feb 1786
Die Entführung aus dem Serail (Spl, 3, C. F. Bretzner, rev. G. Stephanie), 2 Feb 1787
Der Erntekranz (Spl, 3, C. F. Weisse), 1788
Der lahme Husar (comische Oper, 2, F.H. Koch), 1789
Scipio vor Karthago (grosse heroische Oper, 3), 1789
Die Aeolsharfe, oder Der Triumph der Musik und Liebe (romantische Oper, 4, Remele), 1795
Der Schulze im Dorfe, oder Der verliebte Herr Doktor (comische Oper, 3), Liebhaber, 1810
Feodora (Spl, A. Kotzebue), 1812

StiegerO
A. Bopp: *J. H. Knecht* (Biberach, 1917)
——: *Das Musikleben der freien Reichsstadt Biberach* (Kassel, 1930)

Knife, The. Opera by Paavo Heininen; *see* VEITSI.

Knight, Gillian (*b* Redditch, Worcs., 1 Nov 1939). English mezzo-soprano. She studied in London, then in 1959 joined the D'Oyly Carte Opera. In 1968 she joined Sadler's Wells Opera, making her début as Ragonde (*Le comte Ory*). She made her Covent Garden début in 1970 as the Page (*Salome*); during the next 20 years her roles included Maddalena (*Rigoletto*), Fenena (*Nabucco*), Lola, Flosshilde, Waltraute, Siegrune, Spirit of Antonia's Mother (*Les contes d'Hoffmann*), Madame Larina, Fortune Teller (*Arabella*), Juno/Ino (*Semele*), Emilia (*Otello*) and Zulma (*L'italiana in Algeri*). She created Rose Parrowe in *Taverner* (1972) and took part in the première of *We Come to the River* (1976). For the WNO she sang Carmen (1970) and the Nurse in *Die Frau ohne Schatten* (1989). She sang Ulrica at Frankfurt and Marguerite (*La dame blanche*) at Wexford in 1990. A reliable artist, she has a vibrant voice, strongest in the lower register.

ELIZABETH FORBES

Kniplová [née Pokorná], **Naděžda** (*b* Ostrava, 18 April 1932). Czech soprano. She studied singing at the Prague Conservatory with Jarmila Vavrdová and at the Academy of Musical Arts with Ungrová and Otava. After engagements at Ústí nad Labem (1957–9) and the Janáček Opera, Brno (1959–64), she became a principal of the Prague National Theatre. From her Brno days she was noted for the dramatic force of her performances; the sonorous, metallic, dark timbre of her voice was particularly well suited to roles such as Smetana's Libuše, Milada (*Dalibor*) and Anežka (*Two Widows*), and Janáček's Kostelnička and Emilia Marty. She has also sung Tosca, Aida, Ortrud and Brünnhilde. In Brno she created splendid characterizations of Prokofiev's Renata (*The Fiery Angel*), Katerina in Martinů's *The Greek Passion*, and Shostakovich's Katerina Izmaylova. Her many international appearances, notably those at Vienna, Munich, Hamburg, San Francisco and New York, have been praised for their dramatic intensity.

ALENA NĚMCOVÁ

Knipper, Lev Konstantinovich (*b* Tbilisi, 21 Nov/3 Dec 1898; *d* Moscow, 30 July 1974). Russian composer. In 1922, after five years' military service, he adopted music as a career and entered the Gnesin School of Music in Moscow, where his teachers included Glier. During the 1921–2 season he also worked as a stage manager with the Moscow Art Theatre. He continued his compositional studies with Philipp Jarnach in Berlin and Julius Weismann in Freiburg, returning in the mid-1920s to Moscow where he held, among other posts, that of musical adviser to the Nemirovich-Danchenko Music Theatre (1929–30). Throughout his life Knipper held occasional posts in the music section of the Red Army.

As a young composer in the mid-1920s Knipper aligned himself with the German-influenced avant garde. He was a member of the Association of Contemporary Music in Moscow, and under its auspices had some of his early works performed in the West. His most sophisticated composition – and his most important work historically – is the opera *Severnïy veter* ('The North Wind', 1929–30). Based on Kirshon's tragic tale of the mass execution of commissars in Baku during the Civil War, the opera is in a declamatory, satirical style, musically advanced for its time. It was staged in Moscow in March 1930, but thereafter, along with Shostakovich's *The Nose*, with which it has certain affinities, it was strongly criticized for its irrelevant modernism. Knipper's musical idiom underwent a radical change at the beginning of the 1930s when, in keeping with party policy, he turned to the ideals of realist music. From that time he became increasingly interested in the national musics of the outer republics of the USSR; his opera *Na Baykale* ('On Lake Baykal', 1946–8) is based on Mongolian themes. His main achievements as a composer were his 14 symphonies (1929–54).

Kandida, 1926–7 (op-ballet, after Voltaire)
Severnïy veter [The North Wind] (Knipper, after W. Kirshon), Moscow, Nemirovich-Danchenko Music Theatre, 30 March 1930
Mariya, 1936–8 (P. Pavlenko and A. Kovalenkov)
Aktrisa [The Actress], 1942 (Knipper)
Na Baykale [On Lake Baykal] (G. Tsïdïnzhapov and L. Feynberg), Ulan-Ude, 25 June 1948; rev. 1958
Serdtse taygi [The Heart of Taiga], (A. Alexandrov and A. I. Mashistov); rev. as Koren' zhizni [The Source of Life], 1948–9 (4, A. I. Vitenson and Mashistov), concert perf., Moscow, 27 March 1958
Murat (3, S. Arungasiyeva and N. I. Imshenetsky), Frunze, 1 March 1959
Krasavitsa Angara [The Beautiful Angarà] (op-ballet), Ulan-Ude, 1962, collab. B. Yampilov
Malen'kiy prints [The Little Prince], 1964 (after A. de Saint-Exupéry), unperf.

G. Abraham: *Eight Soviet Composers* (London, 1943), 52ff
B. Schwarz: *Music and Musical Life in Soviet Russia 1917–1970* (London, 1972)

RITA McALLISTER

Knorr, Iwan (**Otto Armand**) (*b* Mewe, West Prussia, 3 Jan 1853; *d* Frankfurt, 22 Jan 1916). German composer. At the age of four he was taken to southern Russia, where he grew up surrounded by Russian folk music. The Knorr family settled in Leipzig in 1868, and Iwan studied composition with Reinecke at the conservatory. He then taught in Kharkiv and, after a recommendation from Brahms, at the Hoch Conservatory in Frankfurt (from 1883); in 1908 he succeeded Bernhard Scholz as director. He had a number of distinguished pupils, including Cyril Scott, Hans Pfitzner and Ernst Toch.

Knorr's three operas fall within what Bauer defined as his middle period of composition, devoted mainly to large orchestral works. For the two-act *Dunja* op.18 (Koblenz, 23 March 1904) he wrote his own libretto based on Gogol's *The Fair at Sorochintsï*. His second opera, *Die Hochzeit*, was produced at Prague in 1907, and his last, the one-act *Durchs Fenster* (again to his own libretto), at Karlsruhe in 1908.

MGG (H. Hartmann)
M. Bauer: *Iwan Knorr: ein Gedenkblatt* (Frankfurt, 1916)

R. J. PASCALL/R

Knote, Heinrich (*b* Munich, 26 Nov 1870; *d* Garmisch, 12 Jan 1953). German tenor. His long career was almost entirely centred on Munich, where he remained for nearly 40 years, until his farewell in *Siegfried* on 15 December 1931. Between 1901 and 1913 he made many successful appearances at Covent Garden, and was even more appreciated at the Metropolitan (1904–8), where his performance fees were, at one time, twice those earned by Van Rooy. Knote was a superior, if typical, Wagnerian Heldentenor, who made many pre-1914 recordings and a further Wagner series as late as 1930, demonstrating the amazing endurance of his vocal powers.

DESMOND SHAWE-TAYLOR

Knot Garden, The. Opera in three acts by MICHAEL TIPPETT to his own libretto; London, Covent Garden, 2 December 1970.

Faber *a civil engineer, aged about 35*	robust baritone
Thea *his wife, a gardener*	dramatic mezzo
Flora *their ward, an adolescent girl*	light high soprano
Denise *Thea's sister, a dedicated freedom-fighter*	dramatic soprano
Mel *a black writer in his late 20s*	lyric bass-baritone
Dov *his white friend, a musician*	lyric tenor
Mangus *an analyst*	high tenor baritone

Setting An enclosed garden with steps leading away over a high wall

Tippett composed this, his third opera, between 1966 and 1969. Following his treatment of a story from *The Iliad* in *King Priam* he reverts in *The Knot Garden* to creating his own modern scenario. Although the garden of the title can change before our eyes from a labyrinth to a rose garden, it would if visible probably be 'a high-walled house-garden shutting out an industrial city'. Tippett's word-play in this title has particular significance. The 'knot garden' can clearly stand as a metaphor for a tangle of psychological interrelationships. Although the time is the present, the metaphor stems directly from the Elizabethan knot garden, a special kind of intricate garden which could easily become a maze. As a counterpoint to his contemporary action (which can be related to Albee's *Who's Afraid of Virginia Woolf* and Shaw's *Heartbreak House*) Tippett refers directly to Shakespeare's *The Tempest*, which casts a shadow behind most of his own characters, and in the last act even surfaces as 'a play within the play'.

ACT 1 ('Confrontation') The opening of the opera immediately brings *The Tempest* to mind: as the curtain rises we appear to be caught in a storm, and when the solitary character on stage sings to the audience he says 'So if I dream, it's clear I'm Prospero, man of power. He put them all to rights'. Mangus is the psychoanalyst in Tippett's design who is present to witness and possibly advise the varied characters who are to populate the garden – he is a figure familiar from the novels of Iris Murdoch and even the films of Woody Allen and is a supposed voice of sanity, balance and potential therapy.

Two couples and two single women are involved and all meet in Act 1. Faber and Thea have been married for some time but have withdrawn into locked private worlds and do not communicate. It is characteristic of Tippett's tightly drawn scenario that Thea is obsessed with her garden, where she hides, and Faber is drawn to his work in the city to which he escapes. They have a neurotic adolescent ward, Flora, whom Thea imagines she has to protect from Faber's advances – another symptom of their failed marriage. This domestic mismatch is the opera's foundation. The other characters enter the garden from the outside world and bring their own problems, which either cause further chaos or act as catalysts towards a resolution and even catharsis.

Dov and Mel are a homosexual couple whose relationship is becoming fragile. Mel is the dominant partner, a black writer, while Dov is a gentle white musician and the character who develops most during the course of the opera. Their first appearance is comic, and they already play-act as Caliban and Ariel, reducing

Flora to Alice-like proportions. But tensions appear as Mel is sexually drawn towards Thea, leaving Dov to howl in despair and approach Faber. The entry of Denise, Thea's sister, stops all in its tracks and is one of Tippett's most dramatic theatrical gestures. As a committed freedom-fighter she is disfigured from the effects of torture, and her first aria is an outpouring of graphic anguish unequalled in Tippett's output. After this the characters all pour out their feelings in a remarkable blues ensemble, which while being a logical step forward from the spirituals of *A Child of our Time* belongs to a different world in terms of its sheer visceral power and raw expression.

ACT 2 ('Labyrinth') The garden acts as a labyrinthine maze and the characters are thrown together as if accidentally, thus activating many of the tensions implicit in Act 1. The very clearly delineated musical themes and motifs associated with each character and situation in Act 1 are whirled around with often violently disruptive effect. Faber does now virtually rape Flora, so that Thea takes a whip to her husband. He in turn is drawn experimentally to the distraught Dov, only to find Mel on the scene to taunt his lover for loving manhood and not the man himself. But this is Mel's excuse to end the affair, and his bisexuality comes to the fore as he becomes attracted to the other sister, Denise. In accepting him she softens her stance of stoic self-sufficiency, and their music blossoms with an undertone of 'We shall overcome', which blends perfectly and movingly with the opera's eclectic fabric.

A nightmarish climax leaves a sobbing and bewildered Flora onstage to be comforted by a heartbroken Dov in one of Tippett's most touching personal encounters, which is achieved in a magically stylized manner. Flora sings an innocent song of love from Schubert's *Die schöne Müllerin*, 'Die liebe Farbe', because she has no expression of her own. Dov can console her but cannot respond romantically to her. He performs a song of his own in a heightened pop idiom which comes from his personal experience of love, with references to California and a jazzy accompaniment featuring vibraphone and electric guitar.

ACT 3 ('Charade') The resolution of the drama is achieved through the enacting of certain scenes from *The Tempest*, watched by Denise and Thea with Mangus as Master of Ceremonies. The situations however often step outside the expected script or scenario, and the mirror set up to the problems of the real characters in the form of the Shakespearean characters is suddenly shattered. Thus Flora gains her freedom and bravery and Thea sees that Faber has achieved maturity; Denise berates the lusty Mel (as Caliban jumping on Miranda/Flora) only to learn that Dov was previously his lover – the tables are now turned, and all three characters have to accommodate and come to terms with their anguish. As a scene from the play is about to end in a riot, Mangus reveals that to him 'Prospero's a fake', and as he 'breaks his staff and drowns his book' he points to the profundity of love as the only answer to individual and collective problems. It is clear now that where Mozart's *Die Zauberflöte* was the operatic exemplar behind *The Midsummer Marriage*, the parallel with *The Knot Garden* is *Così fan tutte*. The deceptions and disguises are however for real and their overcoming accordingly more painful.

As the opera ends, in music of radiant splendour punctuated with quotations from Tippett's *Songs for*

Ariel (written for a production of *The Tempest* at the Old Vic in 1962), we see Mel going away with Denise, Flora confidently leaving alone, and Thea and Faber rediscovering the bond of marriage. Only Dov is seemingly left alone; but he has acquired enormous strength and self-knowledge, as we learn subsequently in the off-shoot from the opera, *Songs for Dov*, which traces his destiny as a creative artist, thus reinforcing the feeling that in some degree Dov is for Tippett an autobiographical figure.

* * *

The Knot Garden has claims to be considered Tippett's most perfect opera. It has a careful, felicitous balance of literary, textual, musical and dramatic elements, and the capacity to refer to both personal and collective issues on an intimate scale but with great power of vocal and orchestral gesture. Yet it is important to remember that when it was first staged its controversial cast of characters and eclectic blend of musical materials made it seem one of Tippett's most daring ventures.

A version of the opera with reduced instrumentation by Meirion Bowen was given in 1983 and successfully made the opera more accessible to smaller companies. The production by Opera Factory/London Sinfonietta at the Royal Court Theatre, London, found in it the character of a chamber opera without sacrificing its elemental power. In either context the score seems likely to emerge as a convincing example of mid-20th-century music theatre.

GERAINT LEWIS

Knoxville. American city in Tennessee. Staub's Opera House, the first permanent theatre in Knoxville, opened in 1872, although few important artists visited before the 1880s. During the 1890s the amateur Knoxville Home Opera Company (with its own orchestra) flourished. In the 20th century the city became the home of the Knoxville Opera. Founded in 1976, the company gave its first four seasons at the Bijou Theatre (800 seats) in downtown Knoxville. In 1979 it moved into the larger Tennessee Theater (1550 seats), a 1929 movie palace that had been restored in 1969, its shallow vaudeville stage deepened and orchestra pit enlarged. In 1982 Robert Lyall was appointed general director, artistic director and conductor. In 1986 the production of Carlisle Floyd's *Susannah* was televised for the Tennessee celebration of Appalachian culture. In 1989 the company presented a world première: *Rachel* by Kenton Coe, the state composer laureate. In 1991 the company moved into the Civic Theatre (2500 seats). All productions are accompanied by the Knoxville SO.

NANCY MALITZ

Knüpfer, Paul (*b* Halle, 21 June 1866; *d* Berlin, 4 Nov 1920). German bass. He studied at Sondershausen, where he made his début in 1885. He sang in Leipzig (1887–98), then from 1898 he was engaged at the Berlin Hofoper (later Staatsoper) until his retirement in 1920. He took part in the disastrous première of Leoncavallo's *Roland von Berlin* (1904) and sang Ochs in the Berlin première of *Der Rosenkavalier* (1911). He made his Bayreuth début in 1901, alternating as Gurnemanz and Titurel, then sang there regularly till 1906 as the Landgrave, Hunding and King Mark, and returned in 1912 as Pogner. At Covent Garden (1904–8 and 1913–14) he made his début as King Mark, then sang his Wagner roles, including King Henry and Hagen, as well as Nicolai's Falstaff, Abul Hassan in the first Covent Garden *Barbier von Bagdad* (1906), Ochs in the British

première of *Der Rosenkavalier* (1913) and Gurnemanz in the British stage première of *Parsifal* (1914). He was equally gifted in serious or comic roles. His voice was mellow and flexible; his many recordings give some idea of his expressive range. He was married to the soprano Marie Egli.

ALAN BLYTH

Knussen, (Stuart) Oliver (*b* Glasgow, 12 June 1952). English composer and conductor. Son of the double bass player Stuart Knussen, he studied in London with John Lambert and at Tanglewood with Schuller, initially attracting attention when he conducted the LSO in his own First Symphony at the age of 15. Over the next decade, which culminated in his vivid Third Symphony (1973–9), he was preoccupied with concert works, evolving a personal style of iridescent intricacy from such varied influences as Skryabin, Ives, Carter and Ligeti. But several pieces already emulated Carter's concept of the 'auditory scenario for players to act out with their instruments' or adapted techniques of cutting and timing from the cinema; after 1979 he turned to drama proper with a pair of one-act operas in collaboration with the American illustrator and author Maurice Sendak: *Where the Wild Things Are* (1979–83) and *Higglety Pigglety Pop!* (1984–90). From the late 1970s Knussen also emerged as one of the most sought-after English conductors of modern music, and as an animator of musical events. He was appointed Executive Artistic Director of the Aldeburgh Festival in 1983 and Co-ordinator of Contemporary Music Events at Tanglewood in 1986. He has also taught and advised many younger composers.

See also HIGGLETY PIGGLETY POP! *and* WHERE THE WILD THINGS ARE.

*

P. Griffiths: Interview, *New Sounds, New Personalities: British Composers of the 1980s* (London, 1985), 54–64

BAYAN NORTHCOTT

Knyazhnin, Yakov Borisovich (*b* Pskov, 3/14 Oct 1742 or 1740; *d* St Petersburg, 14/25 Jan 1791). Russian librettist. A neo-classical playwright, poet and translator, his contemporary reputation rested on his tragedies – imitations of Corneille and Metastasio. His main historical contribution however lay in his establishing the verse comedy genre in Russian and in his librettos for early Russian comic operas such as *Neschastiye ot kareti* ('Misfortune from a Coach', 1779, music by Pashkevich), *The Miser* (1781, music by Pashkevich) and *Sbiten'shchik* ('The Hot-Mead Vendor', 1784, music by Bullant). Adroitly manipulating themes derived from French comedies, both with and without music (Favart, Molière, Sedaine, Beaumarchais), Knyazhnin managed to invest his librettos with enough topicality and local colour to put historians (especially wishful Russian ones) off the scent of his sources for many decades.

A. Rabinovich: *Russkaya opera do Glinki* [Russian Opera Before Glinka] (Moscow, 1948)

R.-A. Mooser: *Annales de la musique et des musiciens en Russie au XVIIIme siècle*, ii (Geneva, 1951)

D. Lehmann: *Russlands Oper und Singspiel in der zweiten Hälfte des 18. Jahrhunderts* (Leipzig, 1958)

S. Karlinsky: *Russian Drama from its Beginnings to the Age of Pushkin* (Berkeley and Los Angeles, 1985), 116–49

RICHARD TARUSKIN

Knyaz' Igor'. Opera by A. P. Borodin; *see* PRINCE IGOR.

Koanga. Lyric drama in a prologue, three acts and an epilogue by FREDERICK DELIUS to a libretto by Delius and Charles F. Keary after George W. Cable's novel *The Grandissimes*; Elberfeld, Stadttheater, 30 March 1904 (previous incomplete concert performance, London, St James's Hall, 30 May 1899).

The action is set on a Louisiana plantation by the Mississippi in the second half of the 18th century. In the prologue, planters' daughters ask the old servant Uncle Joe (bass) for a tale of long ago. He agrees to tell the story of Koanga and Palmyra. In Act 1 the slave-girl Palmyra (soprano), maid to Clotilda (contralto), wife of the planter Don José Martinez (bass), prepares for the day's work. She is constantly pursued by Martinez's overseer, Simon Perez (tenor), who is determined to marry her. Slave songs from the chorus accompany the action as Perez announces to his master the arrival of a fine new captive, Koanga (baritone). Palmyra is greatly struck by Koanga's refusal to cooperate with his new masters and recognizes the attitudes of a Dahomey prince and Voodoo priest. Martinez urges her to make Koanga tractable, realizing the importance of such a priest to his workers. Palmyra succeeds, stirring Koanga to a powerful declaration of love. To the dismay of Perez and Clotilda (who knows the secret of Palmyra's birth), Martinez declares Palmyra shall marry Koanga.

Act 2 begins with wedding preparations. Clotilda reveals to Perez that Palmyra is her own father's daughter and must not marry a slave. Perez tries persuasion to prevent the wedding, telling Palmyra she is Clotilda's sister. She will not listen, and Perez decides on force. During the celebrations, 'La calinda' (known independently as an orchestral piece) is danced and sung. Perez abducts Palmyra. The enraged Koanga fells Martinez and calls on his gods to curse the plantation.

Act 3 opens at nightfall by a swamp. Voodoo rites are prepared and Koanga is expected. Sacrificial blood is poured and a vision is seen of the now desolate plantation, with the slaves in sorry plight. Koanga hears the voice of the grieving Palmyra and the scene changes to morning on the plantation. The slaves assure Martinez it is Koanga's curse that has brought them such affliction. Palmyra emerges from her cabin; as Perez attempts to embrace her, Koanga appears and slays him. Koanga is captured and tortured; he is carried in to die. Palmyra renounces the Christianity in which she has been brought up and stabs herself. The epilogue returns to the opening scene, with the girls saddened by Uncle Joe's tale; they await the sunlight of a morning when they hope true lovers will find happiness.

The opera suffers from inadequacies in the libretto and clumsy changes made by Delius and Keary to the Cable story. The directness and passion of the music deserve better. Delius made use of traditional black tunes in the work, harmonized in the poignant manner he had come to know on his Florida plantation, where he returned for a visit during the writing of the opera. As in *The Magic Fountain*, he used music from the *Florida* suite; it found place, for instance, in part of 'La calinda', a very Delian distillation from an originally obscene and violent dance. The characters of *Koanga*, and notably the hero himself, drew from Delius a heartfelt lyricism and range of colour that well match the exotic ingredients of the tale.

The Elberfeld performances were in German, to a translation by Jelka Delius. She redid the text into rather stilted English for Covent Garden performances under Beecham in 1935. The published vocal score (1935) had the libretto revised by Beecham and Edward Agate. A 1972 Sadler's Wells production had further text revision by Douglas Craig and Andrew Page; this version was used for the 1974 recording under Charles Groves and for the full score in the complete edition of Delius's works.

ROBERT ANDERSON

Kobbé, Gustav (*b* New York, 4 March 1857; *d* Babylon, Long Island, NY, 27 July 1918). American writer. He studied in Wiesbaden and New York, graduating from Columbia University in 1879. He was briefly editor of the *Musical Review*, then became music critic for several New York newspapers, including *The Sun*, the *Mail and Express* and *The Herald*. In 1882 he was sent to Bayreuth by *The World* to review the première of *Parsifal*. An interest in Wagner resulted in a two-volume biography (1890, 2/1896), and he edited *Wagner and his Isolde* (1905). Kobbé's best-known work, *The Complete Opera Book*, was published posthumously in 1919. This popular and widely loved collection of opera plots and descriptions was revised and updated by the Earl of Harewood in 1954; further enlarged editions (9/1976, 10/1987) have taken account of many contemporary operas and works by Monteverdi, Handel and others which were little known in Kobbé's day.

DAVID CUMMINGS

Kobekin, Vladimir Alexandrovich (*b* Sverdlovsk [now Yekaterinburg], 22 July 1947). Russian composer. He studied composition with S. M. Slonimsky at the Leningrad Conservatory, graduating in 1971. From 1971 to 1980 he taught at the Urals Conservatory and he was assistant chairman of the Urals branch of the Composers' Union, 1984–8. He has composed instrumental, choral and chamber music but has concentrated on opera, achieving noteworthy success with the graphically expressive mono-opera *Dnevnik sumasshedshego* ('Diary of a Madman') and the epic *Pugachyov*.

The dramatic and symbolic synthesis of themes in *Prorok: Pushkinskiy triptikh* ('The Prophet: a Pushkin Triptych', 1984) has helped to single out this work as one of the most unusual and interesting among recent Soviet operas. In the libretto Kobekin skilfully linked settings of Pushkin's *The Stone Guest* and *Feast in Time of Plague* with a scenic cantata, *The Death of Pushkin*, using excerpts from García Lorca's poetry, as well as reminiscences of Pushkin's contemporaries. The tragic symbiosis between the life and creative legacy of Russia's greatest poet is depicted in an expressive musical style that has been said to recall Musorgsky and Prokofiev. In 1987 Kobekin was awarded the USSR State Prize for *The Prophet* and was named Honoured Artist of the RSFSR.

librettos by the composer unless otherwise stated

Lebedinaya pesnya [Swan Song] (chamber op, 1, after A. P. Chekhov), Moscow, Chamber Music Theatre, 12 April 1980

Dnevnik sumasshedshego [Diary of a Madman] (mono-opera, 1, after Lu Hsün), Moscow, Chamber Music Theatre, 3 May 1980

Sapozhki [The Boots] (chamber op, 1, after V. Shukshin), 1981

Pugachyov (musical tragedy, 2, after S. Yesenin), Leningrad, Malïy, Dec 1983

Igra pro Maxa-Yemel'yana, Alyonu i Ivana [Play about Maximilian, Eleanor and Ivan], 1984 (roundelay op, 2, after S. Kirsanov), Moscow, Chamber Music Theatre, 19 Dec 1989

Prorok: Pushkinskiy triptikh [The Prophet: a Pushkin Triptych] (3, after A. S. Pushkin and others), Sverdlovsk, A. V. Lunacharsky Theatre, 1984

Shut i korol' [The Jester and the King] (chamber op, 1, after M. de Gelderode), *c*1991

Schastlivïy prints [The Happy Prince] (chamber op, 1, A. Parin, after O. Wilde), *c*1991

*

M. Nest'yeva: 'Dva vechera v Moskovskom kamernom' [Two Evenings at the Moscow Chamber Theatre], *SovM* (1981), no.6, pp.57–67

R. Fairman: 'A Visit to Leningrad and Moscow', *Opera*, xxxv (1984), 1184–6 [on *Pugachyov*]

M. Galushko: 'Ot partiturï k postanovke' [From Score to Production], *SovM* (1984), no.12, pp.62–8

N. Vil'ner: 'Soprikosnoveniye s Pushkïnïm' [Contact with Pushkin], *SovM* (1985), no.10, pp.25–30

A. Bayeva: 'Opernïy triptikh "Prorok" V. Kobekina' [The Operatic Trilogy 'The Prophet' by V. Kobekin], *Muzika Rossii: al'manakh*, viii (Moscow, 1989), 111–35

I. Kertész: Review of 'Prorok', *Opera*, xl (1989), 992

V. Kobekin: 'Koye-chto ob opere' [Something about Opera], *SovM* (1990), no.7, pp.28–31

A. Vlasov: 'Skazaniye pro …' [Tale about …], *SovM* (1990), no.5, pp.70–73 [on *Play about Maximilian, Eleanor and Ivan*]

S. Korobkov: 'Pereputannïe stranitsï' [Lost Pages], *SovM* (1991), no.9, pp.48–53   LAUREL E. FAY

Kobelius, Johann Augustin (*b* Waehlitz, nr Merseburg, 21 Feb 1674; *d* Weissenfels, 17 Aug 1731). German composer. His career was centred on his native Saxony, where he was born the son of a pastor. His mother was the daughter of Nicolaus Brause, a Weissenfels organist who became his first music teacher. Later Kobelius studied the organ with Christian Schieferdecker, Kantor and organist in Weissenfels, and, according to Gerber, composition with J. P. Krieger, court Kapellmeister. Gerber also stated that Kobelius travelled extensively as a student and visited Venice. In 1702 he was appointed organist at the Holy Trinity Church in Sangerhausen and in 1703 became director of the chorus there. In 1724 he also took on the direction of choruses in the neighbouring town of Querfurt. In 1725 he was named *Landrentmeister* (land steward) for the court of Saxe-Weissenfels.

Kobelius was the last important composer to write operas during the brief but brilliant period of music at the Weissenfels court. Among his distinguished predecessors had been Keiser, Heinichen and especially Krieger. Kobelius was active as a composer in Weissenfels as early as 1712, but from 1715 to 1729 he served as the only regular composer of operas for performances in the royal palace, writing at least one work each year. All this music seems to be lost and few of the librettists have been identified.

first performed in Weissenfels unless otherwise stated

Der unschuldig verdammte Heinrich, Fürst von Wallis, 1715

Der Irrgarten der Liebe, oder Livia und Cleander, 23 Feb 1716

Die auch im Unglück glückliche Liebe der Isabelle und Rodrigo, 1717

Die gerettete Unschuld, oder Ali und Sefira, 1717

Die bewährte und wohlbelohnte Treue, oder Cloelia und Pythias, 1718

Don Carlos und Sidonie, 1719

Das doppelte Glück getreuer Liebe zwischen Fernando und Bellamira, 1719

Die zwar gedrückte, doch wieder erquickte Liebe, oder Amine und Sefi, 1719

Die vom Himmel geschützte Unschuld und Tugend, oder Bellerophon, Neumeister, 1720

Das durch beständige Liebe mit Persien glücklich verknüpfte Numidien, oder Achmed und Almeide, 1721

Die triumphierende Liebe, 1723

Der Triumph der Treue, oder Bellinde, 24 June 1724

Die erhabene Tugend, oder Bozena, 1725

Das triumphierende Glück, oder Augustas und Livia, 27 Feb 1727

Selimone und Cloriden, 1727

Ismene und Menoikeus [Menalces; Menarcas], 23 Jan 1728

Marcus Antonius und Cleopatra, 26 Feb 1728

Die getreue Schäferin Doris, 1728

Meleager und Atalanta, 1729

Paris und Oenone, 1729

Theseus und Helene, 1729

Doubtful: Der glückliche Betrug, oder Clythia und Orestes, 1717; Damoetus und Euphrasia, Sangerhausen, 1720

*

GerberL; *WaltherML*

A. Werner: *Städtische und fürstliche Musikpflege in Weissenfels bis zum Ende des 18. Jahrhunderts* (Leipzig, 1911)

R. Brockpähler: *Handbuch zur Geschichte der Barockoper in Deutschland* (Emsdetten, 1964)   GEORGE J. BUELOW

København (Dan.). COPENHAGEN.

Koblenz [Coblenz]. City in western Germany, at the confluence of the Rhine and Mosel rivers. The theatre was built in 1787 by the architect P. J. Krahe at the instigation of Prince Clemens Wenzeslaus of Trier. Known as the Comödien- und Ballhaus, it opened with *Die Entführung aus dem Serail* on 23 November 1787. Some years earlier, touring companies had given plays and operas in the inn Zu den drei Reichskronen. As the Stadttheater, the building came under civic administration in 1867, but private entrepreneurs continued to control its repertory. Not until 1920 did the city take over entire responsibility for the theatre, now called Theater der Stadt Koblenz, including its repertory. The old building in Clemensstrasse is still in use; it was damaged in 1944, and restored after the war. Its auditorium, with stalls and two circles, has 460 seats. In a season lasting about nine and a half months, there are 70–75 opera performances of a repertory including one modern opera, one Baroque or early Classical work, and usually two *Spielopern*. The theatre is subsidized by the city and the Land of Rhineland-Palatinate.

*

W. J. Becker: *Gesammelte Beiträge zur Literatur und Theatergeschichte von Coblenz* (Koblenz, 1919)

GÁBOR HALÁSZ

Kochno [Kokhno], **Boris Yevgen'yevich** (*b* Moscow, 3/16 Jan 1904; *d* Paris, 9 Dec 1990). Russian-Ukrainian librettist and dance functionary. After emigrating from Russia to France at the end of the post-revolutionary civil war, he became personal secretary to Sergey Dyagilev (1921–9), during which time he also wrote scenarios for some of the most important works of the late Ballets Russes repertory: *Les fâcheux* and *Les matelots* (Auric), *Ode* (N. Nabokov), *La chatte* (Sauguet), *Le bal* (Rieti) and above all *L'enfant prodigue* (Prokofiev). After Dyagilev's death he served as executive or director of many Paris-based ballet enterprises, and also of the Ballets Russes de Monte Carlo. He retired in 1951 and devoted the remainder of his life to writing books about Dyagilev and on the history of dance.

Kochno was the librettist of Stravinsky's *Mavra* (1921–2). Intended originally for Nikita Baliyev's émigré cabaret Théâtre de la Chauve-souris and taken over by Dyagilev as a curtain-raiser to a Stravinsky retrospective, the work was a nostalgic evocation in poetry and music of its early 19th-century setting, contemporary with Pushkin, on whose comic novella in verse, *Domik v Kolomne* ('The Little House in Kolomna'), the scenario was based. Despite his extreme youth (he celebrated his 18th birthday during the project's gestation), Kochno adapted and imitated Pushkin's literary language with extraordinary elegance and resourcefulness.

B. Kochno: *Diaghilev and the Ballets Russes* (New York, 1970)

A. Kisselgoff: Obituary, *New York Times* (11 Dec 1990)

RICHARD TARUSKIN

Kodallı, Nevit (*b* Mersin, 12 Jan 1924). Turkish composer. He studied at the Ankara State Conservatory with Necil Akses, and from 1948 in Paris with Honegger and Nadia Boulanger. He returned to Turkey in 1953, and after teaching at the Ankara Conservatory for two years was appointed conductor at the Ankara State Opera, where his two operas, *Van Gogh* (1955) and *Gilgameş* (1963), have been produced regularly. He became a composer at the State Theatre in 1962 and continues to teach. Kodallı's works, including two symphonies and an oratorio (*Atatürk*, 1950), are characterized by a fidelity to tonality and Classical forms but make use of Turkish folk music material.

FARUK YENER

Kodály, Zoltán (*b* Kecskemét, 16 Dec 1882; *d* Budapest, 6 March 1967). Hungarian composer. While attending the grammar school in Nagyszombat he learnt to play the piano, violin and cello and taught himself the elements of composition. He studied German and Hungarian at the University of Budapest (1900–06) and composition at the Budapest Academy of Music with Hans Koessler (1900–05). In 1905 he began collecting and studying the folksongs of Hungary in collaboration with his friend Bartók. In 1907 he joined the Budapest Music Academy as a teacher of composition. During the revolutionary period in 1918–19 he was deputy director of the academy, for which he was suspended from teaching for two years by the counter-revolutionary government. A conciliatory gesture came in the form of an invitation to compose a piece for the concert given in 1923 to celebrate the 50th anniversary of the unification of Buda and Pest (*Psalmus hungaricus*). From 1925 Kodály was increasingly engaged in the musical education of the young and in the choral movement. In 1940 he took over from Bartók the direction of preparations for publication of the Corpus Musicae Popularis Hungaricae by the Hungarian Academy of Sciences, of which he was elected a member in 1943. After the end of World War II Kodály was the most highly respected figure in Hungarian cultural life, as president of the Budapest Academy of Music, of the Hungarian Council of Arts and of the Hungarian Academy of Sciences; he received several awards and honorary doctorates.

Kodály's musical style was formed under the influence of Hungarian folk music and the harmonic idiom of Debussy. Later it was enriched by other sources of inspiration including unaccompanied Renaissance polyphony, Bach and 19th-century Hungarian 'verbunkos'. He was primarily a composer of vocal music. In his songs and choruses he laid the foundations of Hungarian musical declamation, based on the melodic structures of folksong, but in spite of that his work in opera was limited, possibly because he sensed an incongruity between the lyricism of folksong (and of his own temperament) and modern musical drama. His stage works are based almost exclusively on genuine folksongs and other folklike material, warmly and colourfully orchestrated and organized into longer and dramatically complex musical forms (e.g. rondeau). In *Háry János* (1926) Kodály sets the musical numbers in a Singspiel-like context with spoken dialogue, but in the one-act 'lyrical play' *Székely fonó* ('The Transylvanian Spinning-Room', first produced in 1924 as a cabaret scene accompanied by a small instrumental ensemble, then enlarged and orchestrated for the Royal Hungarian Opera House in Budapest, where it was first performed on 24 April 1932) he dispensed wholly with dialogue, entrusting the representation of the rudimentary plot to mime artists. The much later *Czinka Panna* (Singspiel, 4, B. Balázs; Budapest, Hungarian State Opera, 15 March 1948) has a wildly romantic plot from the era of the anti-Habsburg revolts around 1700, a period of musical flowering in Hungarian folksong. The heroine of the work is the legendary gypsy musician, who allegedly wrote the famous 'Rákóczi' March; Kodály made a new arrangement of this piece but otherwise offered music rather sparingly.

See also HÁRYJÁNOS.

L. Eősze: *Zoltán Kodály: his Life and Work* (London, 1962)

F. Bónis, ed.: *Z. Kodály: Visszatekintés*, Magyar zenetudomány, v–vi (Budapest, 1964, 3/1984); vii (Budapest, 1989) [writings on musical topics]

J. Breuer: *Kodály-kalauz* [A Guide to Kodály] (Budapest, 1982)

G. Staud, ed.: *A budapesti operaház száz éve* [100 years of the Budapest Opera House] (Budapest, 1984)

I. Vargyas, ed.: *Z. Kodály: közélet, vallomások, zeneélet* [Public Life, Confessions, Musical Life] (Budapest, 1989)

TIBOR TALLIÁN

Koessler [Kössler], Hans (*b* Waldeck, 1 Jan 1853; *d* Ansbach, 23 May 1926). German composer. He was a cousin of Max Reger. He trained as a teacher but worked as an organist from 1871 to 1874, then studied in Munich with Rheinberger and Wüllner; he went with Wüllner to Dresden, where he taught at the conservatory until 1881. He was briefly conductor of the Stadttheater in Cologne, but the theatre did not suit him and in 1882 he moved to the Budapest Academy of Music, where he taught intermittently until 1925. His opera *Der Münzenfranz* (3, A. Schaefer) was staged in Strasbourg in 1903. He was a composer of highly accomplished technique, with a rare feeling for the virtuoso treatment of the voice; his choral works are specially worthy of attention. His contribution to Hungarian music as a teacher is indicated by his many pupils, who included Bartók, Dohnányi and Kodály.

VERA LAMPERT

Kogoj, Marij (*b* Trieste, 29 May 1895; *d* Ljubljana, 25 Feb 1956). Slovene composer. He studied with Schreker and Schoenberg in Vienna (1914–18) and was then coach and conductor at the Ljubljana Opera. Until 1932 he was also active as a music critic, but growing mental illness forced him to live in isolation. Kogoj was a pioneer of expressionism in Slovene music; his opera *Črne maske* ('Black Masks', 2, after L. Andrejev; Ljubljana, 7 May 1929) sets out to explore the inner psychic world, truly revealed only in acts of madness. The polyphonically conceived and richly orchestrated music takes Bergian liberties with strict 12-note technique, and there are parallels between this opera and *Wozzeck*, with which Kogoj was not acquainted. The libretto of his other opera, the five-act *Kar hočete* ('Twelfth Night', 1929), was adapted by the composer from O. Zupančič's translation of Shakespeare's play and located on the Adriatic. The music makes use of Slovene and Istrian folksong; while basically expressionist, it shows some neo-classical traits.

B. Loparnik: 'Dramaturška in kompozicijska zasnova Kogojeve opere "Kar hočete"', [The Dramatic and Musical Scheme of Kogoj's Opera 'Twelfth Night'], *MZ*, ii (1966), 77–94

I. Klemenčič: 'Zasnova in pomen Kogojeve opere "Črne maske"' [The Conception and Significance of Kogoj's Opera 'Črne maske'], *Slovenska opera v evropskem okviru: ob njeni 200-letnici: Ljubljana 1982*, 111–31
ANDREJ RIJAVEC

Kohaut [Kohault, Kohout], **(Wenzel) Josef (Thomas)** (*b* Saaz [now Žatec], Bohemia, 4 May 1738; *d* Paris, ?1793). Bohemian composer active in France. He was a trumpeter in the Austrian army but deserted and fled to France, where he joined the orchestra of the Prince of Conti, eventually becoming an *ordinaire de la musique* in the prince's employ. He composed a number of *opéras comiques*, of which *Le serrurier* (1764) was the most successful, containing several tuneful *ariettes*. It was revived regularly during the five years after its première, unlike Kohaut's two following works, *La bergère des alpes* (1766) and *Sophie* (1768), which remained in the repertory for less than a month each. The latter, based on Garrick's and George Colman the elder's *The Clandestine Marriage*, was a *drame bourgeois*, a new style of *opéra comique* emerging in the 1760s and influenced by English literature; earlier examples included Monsigny's *Le roy et le fermier* (1762) and Duni's *L'école de la jeunesse* (1765). Although Kohaut could compose agreeable melodies with ease, a frequent criticism was that his operas lacked real imagination and sustained originality; Grimm, at his most acerbic, wrote of *Sophie* that there was 'point de coloris, point de magie ni dans le chant ni dans les accompagnements'.

PCI – Paris, Comédie-Italienne (Hôtel de Bourgogne)

Le serrurier (oc, 1, A.-F. Quétant), PCI, 20 Dec 1764 (Paris, *c*1765)

Le tonnelier (oc, 1, N.-M. Audinot and Quétant, after La Fontaine: *Le cuvier*), PCI, 16 March 1765 (Paris, ?1767), collab. Alexandre, Ciapalanti, Gossec, Philidor, J. Schobert and J.-C. Trial

La bergère des alpes (pastorale mêlée de chant, 3, J. F. Marmontel), PCI, 19 Feb 1766, excerpts (Paris, n.d.)

Sophie, ou Le mariage caché (comédie, 3, after D. Garrick and G. Colman: *The Clandestine Marriage*), PCI, 4 June 1768 (Paris, *c*1768)

La closière, ou Le vin nouveau (opéra comique mêlé d'ariettes, 1, A. F. J. Masson de Pezay), Fontainebleau, 10 Nov 1770

*

M. Tourneux, ed.: *Correspondance littéraire, philosophique et critique par Grimm, Diderot, Raynal, Meister, etc.* (Paris, 1877–82)

G. Cucuel: *Les créateurs de l'opéra-comique français* (Paris, 1914)

J. Branberger: 'Aufgefundene Opern von Josef Kohout', *Der Auftakt*, ix (1929), 45–6

L. Vachulka: 'Josef Kohout', *České umění dramatické* [Czech Dramatic Art], ed. J. Hutter and Z. Chalabala, ii: *Zpěvohra* [Opera] (Prague, 1941), 37 [on *Le serrurier*]
ELISABETH COOK (text), MICHEL NOIRAY (work-list)

Kokhno, Boris Yevgen'yevich. See KOCHNO, BORIS YEVGEN'YEVICH.

Kokkonen, Joonas (*b* Iisalmi, 13 Nov 1921). Finnish composer. He studied at Helsinki University, the Sibelius Academy and abroad, and was later appointed professor at the academy. An accomplished pianist, he has long played a central role in the development of Finnish musical life. His achievements were recognized by his appointment in 1963 as a member of the Academy of Finland; he is highly respected as a musical elder statesman.

Kokkonen is known mainly as a symphonist, although his output also includes a cello concerto, chamber music and choral works. His music has been described as neo-classical, but he has consistently main-tained his individuality, eschewing experiments for their own sake. His only opera is the two-act *Viimeiset kiusaukset* ('The Last Temptations'), to a libretto by his cousin Lauri Kokkonen. It was first performed by the Finnish National Opera, Helsinki, on 2 September 1975. It has both modal and tonal elements, and in its symbolism shows the influence of Bartók, especially *Bluebeard's Castle*.

See also VIIMEISET KIUSAUKSET.

*

E. Tawaststjerna: '*Viimeiset kiusaukset* suurtapaus' [The Première of *The Last Temptations*], *Esseitä ja arvosteluja* [Essays and Criticism] (Helsinki, 1976), 196–203
ERKKI ARNI

Kola Bryun'on. Opera by D. B. Kabalevsky; *see* COLAS BREUGNON.

Kollo, René (*b* Berlin, 20 Nov 1937). German tenor. He studied in Berlin with Elsa Varena, making his début in 1965 at Brunswick as Oedipus Rex; he was engaged at Düsseldorf from 1967 to 1971. At first he sang lyric roles such as Froh, Eisenstein, Mozart's Titus and Tamino, which he sang at Salzburg in 1974, Pinkerton and the Steersman, with which he made his Bayreuth début in 1969. Appearing in Munich, Vienna, Berlin and Hamburg, as well as in Venice and Milan, he gradually took on heavier roles, especially Wagner's Parsifal, Erik, Lohengrin, and Walther, which he sang at Bayreuth in 1973 and at the Salzburg Easter Festival in 1974. In 1976 he made his Metropolitan début as Lohengrin, his Covent Garden début as Siegmund, and sang the young Siegfried in the Bayreuth centenary *Ring*. His repertory includes Vladimir Igorevich (*Prince Igor*), Hermann (*Queen of Spades*), Lensky (*Yevgeny Onegin*), Laca (*Jenůfa*), Matteo (*Arabella*), Tristan, which he sang at Bayreuth in 1981, Tannhäuser, Siegfried (*Götterdämmerung*) and Otello, which he sang at Frankfurt in 1988.

*

B. Kayser: 'René Kollo', *Opera*, xl (1989), 1415–21
ELIZABETH FORBES

Kollo [Kollodzieyski], **(Elimar) Walter** (*b* Neidenburg, East Prussia, 28 Jan 1878; *d* Berlin, 30 Sept 1940). German composer. He studied music at Sondershausen and took up a position as a theatre conductor in Königsberg. Already known as a composer of popular songs, he moved to Stettin and then to Berlin, where he wrote for cabarets and, from 1908 onwards, composed operettas and other light works, primarily for the Berliner Theater. He later founded his own publishing company and several theatres. His most successful theatrical work was *Wie einst in Mai*, written with Willy Bredschneider, which reached the USA in 1917 as *Maytime*. He also composed music for revues and films. His son Willi Kollo, who several times served him as lyricist, was also a composer of light theatre music and film scores; the tenor René Kollo is his grandson.

Operetten and Possen, selective list; first performed in Berlin unless otherwise stated

Ali ben Mokka (2, Hardt, H. Frey and L. Hartmann), Apollo, 2 March 1907; Ein aufgelegtes Geschäft (3, Frey and Hardt), Komische Oper, 7 April 1912; Der Liebesonkel (3, Frey and Pordes-Milo), Hamburg, Neues, 3 Aug 1912, collab. W. Schütt; Filmzauber (4, R. Bernauer and R. Schanzer), Berliner, 19 Oct 1912; So wird's gemacht (Frey and Hardt), Hamburg, Neues, Dec 1912; Wie einst in Mai (4, Bernauer and Schanzer), Berliner, 4 Oct 1913, collab. W. Bredschneider

Der Juxbaron (Pordes-Milo, H. Haller and W. Wolff), Hamburg, Carl Schultz, 14 Nov 1913; Die tolle Komtesse (3, Bernauer and

Schanzer), Berliner, 21 Feb 1917; Drei alte Schachteln (4, Haller and Rideamus), Nollendorfplatz, 6 Oct 1917; Blitzblaues Blut (3, Bernauer and Schanzer), Berliner, 9 Feb 1918; Sterne, die wieder leuchten (Bernauer and Schanzer), Berliner, 6 Nov 1918; Fräulein Puck (3, F. Arnold and E. Bach), Munich, Volks, 25 June 1919; Marietta (3, R. Bodanzky and B. Hardt-Warden), Metropol, 22 Dec 1923

Die Frau ohne Kuss (3, R. Kessler and Willi Kollo), Metropol, 6 July 1924; Olly-Polly (3, Back and Arnold), 1925; Nur Du! (Hardt-Warden and Willi Kollo), 1925; Der vertauschte Frau, 1925; Drei arme kleine Mädels (H. Finer, Hardt-Warden and Willi Kollo), 1927; Kitty macht Karriere, 1928; Jettchen Gebert (R. Bruck and W. Wolff, after G. Hermann), 1929; Majestät lässt bitten (3, Rideamus [F. Oliven]), Hamburg, 1930; Derfflinger (Bredschneider, Frey and Willi Kollo), Metropol, 1933

Ein Kaiser ist verliebt (T. Halton), Hamburg, 1935; Heirat nicht ausgeschlossen, place unknown, 1935; Mädel ahoi!, place unknown, 1936; Das Schiff der schönen Frauen, Cologne, 1940

ANDREW LAMB

Köln (Ger.). COLOGNE.

Kolozsvár (Hung.). CLUJ-NAPOCA.

Koltai, Ralph (*b* Berlin, 31 July 1924). British stage designer of Hungarian descent. He was educated in Berlin and, after working with British Intelligence in World War II, studied at the London School of Arts and Crafts (where he was later head of the theatre department, 1965–73). Koltai has been a prolific designer, active in the spoken theatre as well as opera. As an associate artist of the Royal Shakespeare Company, he designed many classical and contemporary productions. The first opera he designed was Ibert's *Angélique* (1950, London, Fortune Theatre), but his long, fruitful association with Sadler's Wells began in 1957 with *Samson et Dalila*. His most important productions include *Aufstieg und Fall der Stadt Mahagonny* (1963), *Volpone* (1964), *From the House of the Dead* (1965), *Bluebeard's Castle* (1972) and *Anna Karenina* (1981). His *Ring* (1970–73) was admired for its 'moonscape', with attractive textures and a strictly controlled palette of colours. For Covent Garden he has had two notable successes: the designs for the premières of Peter Maxwell Davies's *Taverner* (1972; for illustration *see* TAVERNER) and Michael Tippett's *The Ice Break* (1977). In 1976 he designed memorable sets for the WNO production of Tippett's *The Midsummer Marriage*. Koltai has designed many productions for Scottish Opera, beginning with the first British staging of Dallapiccola's *Volo di notte* (1963) and including *Boris Godunov* (1965), *The Rake's Progress* (1967), Henze's *Elegy for Young Lovers* (1970), *Tristan und Isolde* (1973) and a controversial *Macbeth* (1976).

Internationally, Koltai has designed for opera houses in Buenos Aires (*A Midsummer Night's Dream*, 1962), Amsterdam (*Wozzeck*, 1973), Munich (*Fidelio*, 1974), Sydney (*Tannhäuser*, 1974) and Geneva (*Tannhäuser*, 1986). In 1987 he made his début as a director in Hong Kong with *Der fliegende Holländer*.

Koltai is a most individual designer, combining powerful theatrical images with the practicalities of the stage. Always looking for a new direction, he frequently uses contemporary materials and technology in his spacious and often futuristic decor. He was made a CBE in 1983.

DAVID J. HOUGH

Komische Oper (Ger.: 'comic opera'). A term for either a comic work (opera or Singspiel) or one of two opera companies in Berlin: the first existed from 1905 to 1911, the second (unconnected with it) was founded in 1947 under Walter Felsenstein and is noted for its advanced, politically committed style of production. *See* BERLIN, §§2(ii) and 3(iii).

Komissarzhevsky, Fyodor Petrovich (*b* Kiev province, 1838; *d* Sanremo, 1/14 March 1905). Russian tenor. After studying in St Petersburg and with Repetto in Milan, he made his début in 1863 at the Mariinsky Theatre, where he quickly attained the rank of leading tenor, a position he held until 1880. Among the many roles he created were Don Juan (*The Stone Guest*, 1872), Grigory (*Boris Godunov*, 1874), Sinodal (*The Demon*, 1875) and the title role in *Vakula the Smith* (1876). He had a small voice of velvety timbre, heard to advantage in parts such as Gennaro (*Lucrezia Borgia*), Faust, Fra Diavolo and Jontek (*Halka*). He was noted for his impeccable diction and his refined phrasing and characterization. From 1883 to 1888 he was a professor at the Moscow Conservatory, teaching drama as well as singing; Stanislavsky was one of his pupils.

BORIS SEMEONOFF

Komlóssy, Erzsébet (*b* Budapest, 9 July 1933). Hungarian mezzo-soprano. After studying at the Budapest Conservatory, she joined the Szeged National Theatre in 1955, remaining there for three years. She then became a member of the Budapest State Opera (until 1974), playing leading mezzo-soprano roles as well as the Mother in Szokolay's *Vérnász*; she has also appeared in Berlin, Cologne, Moscow and Vienna, and sang Azucena at Covent Garden in 1970. Her many recordings include operas by Erkel and Kodály. A truly dramatic artist, she can create an emotionally tense atmosphere, but has also had significant success in lyrical roles.

PÉTER P. VÁRNAI

Komorous, Rudolf (*b* Prague, 8 Dec 1931). Canadian composer of Czechoslovak birth. He studied the bassoon at the Prague Conservatory (1946–52) and at the Prague Academy of Musical Arts, where he also studied composition with Bořkovec (1952–9). During the latter period he was also first bassoonist at the Prague Opera. In 1957 he won the Concours International for performers at Geneva, which led to an appointment at the Beijing Conservatory (1959–61). After returning to Prague he co-founded the ensemble Musica Viva Pragensis. He emigrated in 1969 and taught in the USA for two years before being appointed professor of composition at the University of Victoria, British Columbia. In 1989 he became director of the School for the Contemporary Arts at Simon Fraser University in Burnaby, British Columbia.

Komorous's first opera, *Lady Blancarosa*, composed in 1967 (Buffalo, 28 January 1970), explores many of the concerns of the Czech avant garde of the 1960s. The libretto consists of a collage of phrases from various works by the Czech writer Jan z Wojkowicz. Except for a solemn fanfare for five trumpets played on a gramophone, the one-act opera is scored for voices alone. The notation is approximate, showing the direction of the melodic lines but not the precise pitch; in the revised version (1987) the composer notated the specific pitches and altered certain passages of text.

In Komorous's second opera, *No No Miya* (Vancouver, East Cultural Centre, 30 September 1988), elements of traditional Japanese noh theatre are combined with Western operatic traditions. The poetic libretto, rich in imagery, was written by the composer

1017

after extensive research in Kyoto and is based on an adaptation of a play attributed to Motokiyo Zeami (1363–1443). The opera incorporates many of the formalized stage practices and gestures of noh theatre, subtly altered. The music, uniting vocal lines of exquisite elegance with an enigmatic, shifting chordal palette, evokes the aesthetic purity and economy of Eastern art while remaining essentially Western in its language and instrumentation. The scores of Komorous's operas are at the Canadian Music Centre in Toronto.

D. Zapf: 'Thoughts on No No Miya and Composition', *No No Miya* (Vancouver, 1988), 12 [programme notes]

R. Chatelin: 'Rudolf Komorous' Melodic Journeys', *Canadian Composer*, no. 240 (1989), 28   JOAN BACKUS

Komorzynski, Egon Ritter von (*b* Vienna, 7 May 1878; *d* Vienna, 16 March 1963). Austrian musicologist. He studied musicology and German philology, graduating at Vienna in 1900, and was professor of German language and literature at the Vienna Handelsakademie, 1904–34, and for 40 years music critic of the *Österreichische Volkszeitung*. The majority of his published writings are concerned with Mozart, and especially with *Die Zauberflöte*. His first book, *Emanuel Schikaneder: ein Beitrag zur Geschichte des deutschen Theaters* (Berlin, 1901, 2/1951), contains the essence of his long life's work: in it he demonstrated – against current opinion – Schikaneder's authorship, and became the nature and worth, of the *Zauberflöte* libretto. He published a book and many articles on Mozart (several treating the sources, the background and the original production of *Die Zauberflöte*), and articles on other German operatic topics, returning to Schikaneder in *Der Vater der Zauberflöte: Emanuel Schikaneders Leben* (Vienna, 1948). Komorzynski's work is not free of errors, but his great virtue lay in his tireless search for new facts. His place in Mozart studies is secure.

PETER BRANSCOMBE

Kondorossy, Leslie (*b* Pozsony [now Bratislava], 25 June 1915; *d* Cleveland, 22 April 1989). American composer and conductor of Hungarian birth. He studied at the Franz Liszt Music Academy in Budapest and conducted concerts of his own music at Bayreuth and Salzburg. In 1951 he emigrated to the USA, became an American citizen and settled in Cleveland. He established the American New Opera Theatre Society in 1954 to encourage the production of one-act operas by contemporary composers, and in 1955 he founded the series 'Opera of the Air' for the Cleveland radio station WSRS. Kondorossy's own operas have been heard on Radio Free Europe, Voice of America and WSRS.

Kondorossy specialized in one-act operas which were lyrical and dramatic, yet simple to stage. His musical style shows influences of Bartók and Stravinsky. The story of *The Voice*, which takes place in New York City, resembles aspects of both *The Telephone* and *The Medium* by Menotti. In *The Pumpkin*, Kondorossy paints a musical picture of American farm life, while *A Night in the Puszta* draws images of the Magyar lowlands. Elements of jazz are employed in *The Two Imposters*. Kondorossy wrote several children's operas, such as *Shizuka's Dance* and *Kalamona and the Four Winds*, which were commissioned by schools for exceptional or handicapped children. His wife, Elizabeth Davis, under the pseudonym Shawn Hall, wrote the

librettos for many of his operas. Copies of Kondorossy's MSS are held at Cleveland Public Library.

first performed in Cleveland unless otherwise stated

A Night in the Puszta (1, Kondorossy), Auditorium, 28 June 1953

The Pumpkin (1, C. Kulin, after B. Pasztor), concert perf., Severance Chamber Music Hall, 15 May 1954; stage, American New Opera, June 1954

The Voice (1, S. Lenek and S. Hall [E. Davis]), concert perf., Severance Chamber Music Hall, 15 May 1954; stage, Duxbury, MA, 11 Aug 1954

The Midnight Duel (1, Kondorossy and Hall), Mayfield, OH, Gates of Hope Temple, 8 March 1955

The Two Imposters (1, Kondorossy), WSRS, 10 April 1955; stage, Little, 21 Oct 1956

The String Quartet (1, Kondorossy), WSRS, 8 May 1955

The Mystic Fortress (1, Kondorossy), WSRS, 12 June 1955

The Unexpected Visitor (1, J. Kemeny, Hall and Kondorossy, after Kemeny), Little, 21 Oct 1956

The Fox (1, Hall, after K. Mikszath), 28 Jan 1961

Nathan the Wise (poetic drama, 3, Hall), Sunbeam School for Crippled Children, 1964

The Poorest Suitor (children's op, 1, Hall, after a Blackfoot Indian tale), Sunbeam School for Crippled Children, 24 May 1967

Shizuka's Dance (children's op, 1, Hall, after a tale of Prince Bantam), Sunbeam School for Crippled Children, 22 April 1969

Kalamona and the Four Winds (children's op, 1, Hall, after a Hungarian fairy-tale), WSRS, 12 Sept 1971, vs (Cleveland, 1972)

Ruth and Naomi (1, Hall and R. Glass, after the Bible), Cleveland Heights, Church of the Master, 28 April 1974

'Kondorossy of Cleveland, Composer, Conductor, Teacher, Champions One-Act Opera Premières', *Musical Leader* (May 1956), 7

R. Widder: 'The Listener always knows it is Kondorossy', *Musical Courier*, clvii/4 (1958), 7

'Their Music Strikes "One World" Note', *Sun Press* [Cleveland] (22 Oct 1970)

'Leslie Kondorossy, was Music Composer', *Plain Dealer* [Cleveland] (24 April 1989)   ELISE K. KIRK

Kondrashin, Kirill (Petrovich) (*b* Moscow, 21 Feb/6 March 1914; *d* Amsterdam, 7 March 1981). Russian conductor. He was taught music theory by Nikolay Zhilyayev, who greatly influenced his artistic development, then began his conducting career in 1931 at the Children's Music Theatre, Moscow. From 1934 he was assistant conductor at the Nemirovich-Danchenko Music Theatre, making his début with Planquette's *Les cloches de Corneville* (1934). He studied conducting at the Moscow Conservatory with Boris Khaikin (1932–6), and was then conductor at the Malïy Theatre, Leningrad (1936–43), where he gave promising performances of *La fanciulla del West*, Pashchenko's *Pompadour* and Mikhail Cheryomukhin's *Kalinki*. In 1943 he moved to the Bol'shoy Theatre, where contacts with Samosud, Pazovsky and Nikolay Golovanov helped to improve his opera performances and widen his practical experience; he also staged a number of new productions. After leaving the Bol'shoy in 1956 Kondrashin won recognition as an outstanding concert conductor, most notably with the Moscow Philharmonic. He emigrated to the West in 1978.

I. M. YAMPOL'SKY

Konetzni(-Wiedmann) [Konerczny], **Anny** (*b* Ungarisch-Weisskirchen, 12 Feb 1902; *d* Vienna, 6 Sept 1968). Austrian soprano, sister of Hilde Konetzni. After a short period in the Volksoper chorus, she studied at the Vienna Conservatory with Schmedes and made her stage début at Chemnitz in 1927 as a contralto. After guest appearances in the *Ring* at Paris in 1929 she joined the Berlin Staatsoper in 1931, singing Helena (*Les vêpres siciliennes*), Ariadne and the Feldmarschallin in her first season. In 1933 she appeared at Buenos Aires, then became a member of the Vienna Staatsoper. In 1935 she sang Brünnhilde under Beecham at Covent Garden, returning in three of the next four seasons, and was invited back for *Die Walküre* in 1951. This was her début role at the Metropolitan, where she appeared in the 1934–5 season as Brünnhilde, Venus, Ortrud and Isolde. She also sang several roles at Salzburg, including Reiza (*Oberon*) under Bruno Walter in 1934 and Isolde for Toscanini in 1936, and appeared in Rome, Paris and other leading centres. Her voice, in its prime a strong, pure dramatic soprano, was not supported by a particularly impressive stage presence.

PETER BRANSCOMBE

Konetzni [Konerczny], Hilde (*b* Vienna, 21 March 1905; *d* Vienna, 20 April 1980). Austrian soprano, sister of Anny Konetzni. She studied at the Neues Konservatorium in Vienna and made her début at Chemnitz in 1929 as Sieglinde to her sister's Brünnhilde. In 1932 she joined the German Theatre in Prague, and after a successful guest appearance as Elisabeth in *Tannhäuser* in Vienna joined the Staatsoper in 1936, where she sang regularly for many years, becoming an outstanding exponent of Wagner and Strauss. Also in 1936 she first sang at Salzburg, as Donna Elvira. She made her Covent Garden début in May 1938, when she appeared as the First Lady in *Die Zauberflöte* and as Chrysothemis, and is remembered for taking over from Lotte Lehmann as the Feldmarschallin during a performance when Lehmann was taken ill; she returned as Leonore (*Fidelio*) in 1947 and as Sieglinde and Gutrune in the 1955 *Ring*. She also created the title role in Sutermeister's monodrama *Niobe* in Zurich in 1946. Towards the end of her career she added to an extensive repertory, principally of lyrical roles, a number of small character parts, including one in the Salzburg première in 1961 of Wagner-Régeny's *Das Bergwerk zu Falun*.

PETER BRANSCOMBE

Kongelige Teater. Royal theatre in COPENHAGEN, founded in 1770; the term is also used for the company based there.

König, Johann Ulrich von (*b* Esslingen, Swabia, 8 Oct 1688; *d* Dresden, 14 March 1744). German poet, dramatist and librettist. He studied theology at Tübingen and law at Heidelberg. He settled in Hamburg (1710–16), where he rapidly achieved a leading position in the direction of the opera and began a fruitful career as librettist to many prominent German composers, including Keiser, Melchior Hoffmann, Telemann and, at Brunswick, G. C. Schürmann and C. H. Graun. He became closely associated with Brockes and Richey, with whom he founded the Teutschübende Gesellschaft. In 1720 he became court poet and private secretary at the Dresden court. He was elected a member of the Berlin Academy of Sciences in 1729, and in 1730 returned to Hamburg. In 1735 he was made director of court ceremonies and court librarian in Dresden. He was ennobled by the King of Saxony in 1740.

König occupies an important position in the history of German opera for, as the list of settings of his librettos proves, he was highly respected by composers as a poet and dramatist. Mattheson (*Critica musica*, 1722–3), extolled him as an 'incomparable poet'. Although several 19th-century writers on German opera condemned him as the untalented creator of tasteless and bombastic Baroque texts, he was, in fact, a gifted experimenter who sought to revitalize the German language and its poetry. Many of his librettos are translated and adapted from French and Italian texts, a not unusual practice for early 18th-century German opera. He subscribed to the taste of the time by retaining large numbers of arias in Italian, which created the curious mixture of languages to be found in the works of Keiser, Telemann and Schürmann. While his librettos rely on many characteristic dramatic stereotypes of the early 18th century and depend heavily on the conventions of stage decoration, machines and ballets, they are often models of straightforward, uncomplicated plot development, excelling in comedy, and with a realistic, natural and frequently folklike language. König also wrote many sacred texts, including one of the most important oratorio texts of the 18th century, the Passion oratorio *Der zum Tode verurteilte und gecreuzigte Jesus.*

Die entdeckte Verstellung, oder Die geheime Liebe der Diana (Schäferspiel), Keiser, 1712, as Diana (Keiser, 1724, as Cupido); *Die oesterreichische Grossmuth, oder Carolus V*, Keiser, 1712, as Carolus V; *Die wiederhergestellte Ruh, oder Die gecrönte Tapferkeit des Heraclius*, Keiser, 1712, as Heraclius; *L'inganno fedele, oder Der getreue Betrug*, Keiser, 1714; *Rhea Sylvia*, M. Hoffmann, 1714; *Fredegunda*, Keiser, 1715; *Heinrich der Vogler*, pt 1, G. C. Schürmann, 1718; *Die getreue Alceste*, Schürmann, 1719; *Der geduldige Socrates*, G. P. Telemann, 1721; *Heinrich der Vogler*, pt 2, Schürmann, 1721; *Cadmus*, J. P. Kunzen, 1725; *Sancio und Sinilde*, C. H. Graun, 1727 (Telemann, 1727, as Sancio, oder Die siegende Grossmuth)

*

H. C. Wolff: *Die Barockoper in Hamburg* (Wolfenbüttel, 1957)

D. I. Lindberg: *Literary Aspects of German Baroque Opera: History, Theory and Practice* (diss., UCLA, 1964)

G. Flaherty: *Opera in the Development of German Critical Thought* (Princeton, 1978)

GEORGE J. BUELOW

König, Klaus (*b* Beuthen [now Bytom, Poland], 26 May 1934). German tenor. He studied in Dresden and made his début in 1970 at Cottbus. After a period in Leipzig he moved to Dresden (1982), where in 1985 he sang Max in the performance of *Der Freischütz* that reopened the Semper Oper, also appearing as the Italian singer in *Der Rosenkavalier*. His repertory included Florestan, Radames, Don Carlos, Don Alvaro, Don José, Bacchus, Erik, Lohengrin, Walther, Tristan and Parsifal. In his débuts at Covent Garden and La Scala (1984) and the USA (1988, Houston) he sang Tannhäuser, the role that best suits his powerful, steel-toned voice and unusual stamina. He has also appeared in Brussels, Paris, Buenos Aires and in Munich, where he sang Strauss's Guntram and Menelaus (*Die ägyptische Helena*) in the festival of 1988.

ELIZABETH FORBES

König Hirsch ('The Stag King'). Opera in three acts by HANS WERNER HENZE to a libretto by Heinz von Cramer after the fable by CARLO GOZZI; Berlin, Städtische Oper, 23 September 1956 (severely cut); revised as *Il re cervo, oder Die Irrfahrten der Wahrheit*, Kassel, Staatstheater, 10 March 1963; first performance of complete score, Stuttgart, Staatsoper, 5 May 1985.

Henze began discussions on a successor to his first stage opera, *Boulevard Solitude*, in 1952; Cramer's libretto was prepared by the following year and the composition of *König Hirsch* occupied Henze between 1953 and 1955. It was the first of his works to be composed during his self-imposed exile in Ischia, and its teeming, many-hued textures reflect the optimism of this

Leandro *the king* — tenor
Costanza *his lover* — soprano
Tartaglia *the chancellor* — bass-baritone
Scolatella I — coloratura soprano
Scolatella II — soubrette
Scolatella III — mezzo-soprano
Scolatella IV — contralto
Checco *a melancholy musician* — tenor buffo
Coltellino *an unsuccessful murderer* — tenor buffo
Six Alchemists — silent
Two Statues — contraltos
Cigolotti *a magician* — spoken
The Stag — spoken

Voices of the wood, voices of the people, voices of the wind, courtiers, pages, wild animals, people from the city, soldiers, huntsmen

(characters named as in *Il re cervo*; see below)

Setting Near Venice, between sea and forest, in antiquity

period in Henze's life. The original score contained more than five hours of music, and its arias in particular were severely cut by the conductor Hermann Scherchen for the Berlin première in 1956, which was directed by Leonard Steckel; the cast included Sándor Kónya as the king, Helga Pilarczyk as Costanza, Tomislav Neralic as Tartaglia and Nora Jungwirth as Scolatella I. The same version was also presented at Darmstadt in 1959 (conducted by Hans Zanotelli and directed by Harro Dicks) and at Bielefeld the following year. In 1962 Henze prepared a revised version, reducing the score to approximately half the original length and restoring the italianate names of Gozzi's fable. The revision involved substantial recomposition: new blocks of material replaced larger structures (the original finale of Act 2 became Henze's Fourth Symphony) and Cramer and the composer created a speaking role, the magician Cigolotti, to 'ensure that the plot remains comprehensible even though it is compressed'. In general it was the supernatural, 'magical' aspects of the score that were excised. The Kassel première of *Il re cervo* was conducted by Henze himself and the same production by Hans Hartleb was also seen in Munich two years later, conducted by Christoph von Dohnányi; Claude Heater was Leandro, Felicia Weathers Costanza, Hans Günter Nöcker Tartaglia and Ingeborg Hallstein Scolatella I. In 1985 the uncut, original version of *König Hirsch* was at last performed; the Stuttgart staging was conducted by Dennis Russell Davies and produced by Hans Hollmann with a cast led by Toni Krämer, Julia Conwell, John Bröcheler and Karin Ott. The following synopsis is of the version published in 1963 as *Il re cervo*.

ACT 1: 'The Castle'

1.i Everything is being prepared for the coronation of the new king, Leandro, who has been raised in the forest among the animals. As a storm rages (depicted in the orchestral introduction), Scolatella complains that the weather has ruined her clothes; she nurtures ambitions to become queen. Though the thunder terrifies her, she does not lose her self-confidence or her ambition, and from the looking-glass she summons her double, Scolatella II, who emerges equally full of complaints and

closely followed by Scolatella III and Scolatella IV; all are intent on winning the hand of the new king.

1.ii ('The Coronation Procession') Scolatella I dispatches her doubles and hides herself as the sounds of a carillon and a chorus of celebration herald the beginning of the ceremony. Tartaglia appears, also looking for a hiding place, from where he delivers a long sardonic commentary on the absurd sycophancy of the ceremony ('a lamb led to the slaughter') and rails against his own unjust treatment. From his imperious manner Scolatella assumes Tartaglia to be the king.

1.iii She takes the opportunity to introduce herself just before Costanza is brought in by her guards. Tartaglia offers her freedom, but she refuses to leave; she is keen to discover what the new king is like, but assumes that he has had her arrested and therefore must be far less compassionate than Tartaglia. The chancellor eagerly agrees with this assessment, and gives her a dagger and tells her to kill Leandro with it. When Costanza hesitates, he forces her to hide the weapon and orders her to remain outside.

1.iv As the sound of the bells that dominated the previous scene dies away, the animals of the forest gather around Leandro to say goodbye; he delivers his farewell in a slowly moving, expressive aria. When he is left alone, two statues, singing in rhythmic unison and accompanied by harp and celesta, warn him of the dangers of the human world he is joining; they promise to warn him (by laughing) whenever anyone lies to him.

1.v ('Finale') Fanfares announce Tartaglia's entrance; he tells the new king that he must choose a bride. He is followed by a vivid carnival procession that also includes the four Scolatellas, each of whom is already confident she will be crowned queen. Leandro questions them, assisted by the statues; none of them meets his exacting standards.

1.vi Tartaglia introduces Costanza, and Leandro is immediately intrigued; the silence of the statues convinces him that she is suitable, and the couple begin a long, slow love duet. As it ends, Leandro breaks the statues so they cannot reveal his lover's untruths, but Tartaglia 'discovers' Costanza's hidden dagger, and insists that she must be executed. Leandro decides he must abdicate, and is led back to the forest by Cigolotti, disguised as a parrot.

1.vii Tartaglia's plan has succeeded: he is triumphant. The spirits of the wind whirl around the stage, and Tartaglia orders Coltellino to follow Leandro and kill him; he will not accept the excuse that the spirits have blown away the assassin's dagger and pistol, and provides him with replacements. The act ends with the sounds of a percussion band and the entry of six alchemists, who have arrived, belatedly, to welcome the new king.

ACT 2: 'The wood'

2.i An orchestral prelude of 'magical' textures — woodwind, horns, celesta — evokes the living, breathing sounds of the forest, and the voices of the woods warn of the presence of a stranger among them; suddenly the forest is full of men. Leandro is dogged by Scolatella, who clings to the idea that she is queen, though he tries to shake her off. Everyone — human, animal and the alchemists disguised as animals — appears to be both predator and prey; in the general confusion that culminates in a violent stretta, Tartaglia attempts to stab Leandro, but fails.

'König Hirsch' (Henze), Act 2 (the wood): scene from the original production at the Städtische Oper, Berlin, 23 September 1956, with Checco and the alchemists disguised as animals

2.ii Cigolotti wishes to give Checco the secret of magical transformation; he can then pass it on to the king and save his life. As the sounds of the voices of the wood die away, Checco begins a beautifully expressive aria accompanied by solo guitar.

2.iii Tartaglia wounds a stag, but the animal escapes, and the chancellor demands that Checco tell him where Leandro is hiding.

2.iv They have a magical vision of the stag's death, but Tartaglia also learns of the transformational spell, which he uses to change into the king's shape while Leandro himself is turned into a stag. Checco and Cigolotti are horrified by the events they have inadvertently set in train.

2.v Tartaglia now assumes the powers of the king; in a fierce declamation he imposes his dictatorial rule on the country, and organizes a stag hunt that will finally destroy Leandro, as a storm breaks over the forest.

Act 3: 'The City'

3.i Under Tartaglia's despotic rule the city has become a ghost town. While an offstage chorus cries for deliverance, Leandro, still transformed as the Stag King, wanders the streets. He receives no response to his calls, which are set against Coltellino's lament for his failure as an assassin.

3.ii Percussion again heralds the alchemists, who find themselves as hounded as the rest of the population.

3.iii Costanza enters the city searching for Leandro and, in an aria of high-lying legato lines over the sounds of the chorus, recalls her short-lived love for him.

3.iv Costanza finds the Stag King, and they manage to sing a second love duet, before the stag flees as Tartaglia arrives.

3.v Tartaglia pretends to be Leandro, but Costanza is not deceived and rejects his advances; the false king, now thoroughly paranoid, summons his soldiers to repel the enemies he sees on every side.

3.vi The people have become aware of the presence of the stag; an ancient legend holds that the arrival of a stag will restore peace to the city. Tartaglia still demands the animal be shot on sight, but just as he is about to do the deed himself he is shot by Coltellino, who mistakes him for the king. Leandro is transformed back to his real self, and the work ends with a general choral celebration, framing a short duet in which Leandro and Costanza are finally united.

*   *   *

In both its versions, but especially the original, *König Hirsch* is the most luxuriant of all Henze's operatic scores. Henze has acknowledged the italianate flavour of much of his writing, citing Bellini's example for some of the scoring. At the beginning of the opera, he wrote: 'rudiments of serial technique can still be found. They seem to mobilize the harmony, and rhythm, in order to release the material with greater freedom'. The opera is made up of self-contained numbers, highly varied – arias and cabalettas, duets and ensembles, music for the hunts and for the mimes – but it is connected by vivid bridge passages into a continuous whole, so that each act gives the impression of being through composed.

ANDREW CLEMENTS

Königin von Saba, Die ('The Queen of Sheba'). Opera in four acts by KARL GOLDMARK to a libretto by SALOMON HERMANN MOSENTHAL, after I Kings 10; Vienna, Hofoperntheater, 10 March 1875.

Goldmark's most famous work was inspired by the striking mezzo-soprano voice of his pupil, Caroline Bettelheim; a chance remark comparing her beauty to that of the Queen of Sheba led Goldmark to embark on the opera, whose principal character is sung by a mezzo. (However, Bettelheim never sang the role she inspired.) A libretto written in 1863 proved unsuitable, and Goldmark did not proceed with the project until 1865, when Mosenthal provided him with a new libretto. He wisely jettisoned the latter's plans for a happy end. The main roles were created by Amalie Materna (Queen of Sheba), Marie Wilt (Sulamith) and Gustav Walter (Assad). The première was a great success, partly because Goldmark had been persuaded to make sizable cuts after the dress rehearsal. Performances in many European operatic centres followed, notably in Italy.

'Die Königin von Saba'
(Goldmark), Act 2 scene
ii: design by Carlo
Brioschi for the original
production at the
Hofoperntheater, Vienna,
10 March 1875

The plot centres on a love-triangle. In Act 1, set in a hall in Solomon's palace, Sulamith (soprano) and her father, the High Priest (bass), await the return of her betrothed, Assad (tenor), who has been on a diplomatic mission to prepare for the visit of the Queen of Sheba (mezzo-soprano) to the court of Solomon (baritone). When Assad enters, he reveals that his feelings for Sulamith have changed, and tells Solomon of how he met a beautiful unknown woman among the cedars of Lebanon. The Queen of Sheba enters with her retinue. When, in a dialogue with Solomon, she lifts her veil, Assad recognizes in her the unknown beauty he had encountered earlier. He is aghast when the Queen pretends not to recognize him. Solomon wisely counsels him to proceed with his marriage to Sulamith.

Act 2 is set in the garden of the palace at night. The Queen has escaped from the festivities in her honour to ponder Assad's imminent marriage. Her slave Astaroth (soprano) brings news that Assad is in the vicinity, and lures him towards the Queen with an entrancing oriental vocalise. After a passionate dialogue that culminates in a duet, the Queen and Assad embrace. They are interrupted by the Guardian of the Temple (bass), who calls the Sons of Israel to prayer at daybreak. The Queen leaves. Assad, distraught again, is discovered and taken to the temple, where the priests and Levites are seen at prayer. He is about to be married to Sulamith when the Queen appears, ostensibly to give the latter a wedding present. Assad is more distraught than ever, and again the Queen denies any knowledge of him. In front of the Ark of the Covenant Assad commits blasphemy by stating that the Queen is his god. There is general consternation, and Assad is led off to await punishment.

In Act 3 the festivities in honour of the Queen continue with a ballet, 'Bienentanz der Almeen', and a bacchanale. The Queen pleads unsuccessfully with Solomon for Assad's life and leaves, threatening revenge. News arrives that Assad has been condemned to death. Sulamith and her companions appear, singing a song of mourning. Before retiring to the desert to bewail her fate, she pleads for Assad's life in a moving passage that develops into a large ensemble. Solomon utters a dark prophecy about her future.

Act 4 is set in the vicinity of Sulamith's retreat. Assad, who has been banished to the desert, is pursued by the Queen, who attempts to persuade him to follow her. Once more she exercises all her charms, but this time Assad rejects her advances. In the penultimate scene he longs for death, hoping in this way to expiate his blasphemy. He prays for Sulamith, and as he does so is overwhelmed by a violent sandstorm. In the final scene he is discovered by Sulamith and her companions. After a brief and tender duet of reconciliation he dies in Sulamith's arms.

Although Goldmark was never a slavish disciple of Meyerbeer or Wagner, the debt he owed to them is clear. Die Königin von Saba is a skilful combination of the stock-in-trade features of grand opera – the historical subject matter, the crowd and ensemble scenes, the judicious application of local colour, the ballet – with the formal fluidity and orchestral effects Goldmark admired in Wagner. The vocal writing ranges from solo recitative and arioso passages to duets and large-scale choruses (as Hanslick noted, the stretta at the end of Act 2 is particularly effective). Carlo Pedrotti described Assad's short arietta 'Magische Töne' in Act 2 as 'una vera Belliniana'. It is something of an exception, though there are other moments of great lyricism, such as in the final duet. Although Goldmark never adopted a fully-fledged system of leitmotifs, certain passages are reminiscent of Tristan. The most striking feature of the opera is the use of various kinds of oriental local colour. On the one hand there is the sultry eroticism of the Queen of Sheba, and on the other the sturdy nobility of the Jewish religious music, particularly that of the High Priest, who at times recalls Sarastro, and that of the Ark of the Covenant. The religious character of this part of the opera may well have been influenced by the ideas of the great Viennese cantor Salomon Sulzer, who was concerned to restore Jewish music to its oriental origins.

ALFRED CLAYTON

Königsberg (Russ. Kaliningrad). Capital of East Prussia until 1946, when it became part of the USSR and was renamed Kaliningrad. Musical dramatic allegories were performed there in the 17th century, with Heinrich Albert's *Cleomedes* (1635) and *Sorbuisa, oder Prussiarchus* (1645), both to texts by Simon Dach; but it was not until 1753 that a theatre was built there, by C. E. Ackermann, and Singspiels were performed. It is supposed that the patronage of Austrian officers held captive in the city in the 1760s during a period of Russian occupation helped establish Viennese music there. Mozart operas were performed in 1793 (*Don Giovanni*) and 1794 (*Die Zauberflöte*); among local composers were Friedrich Ludwig Benda, three of whose Singspiels to texts by the local poet E. F. Jester were given in 1790–92. A troupe run by the Schuch family played a prominent part in the city's operatic life, but in 1799 Friedrich Adam Hiller (son of J. A. Hiller) took over the musical direction of the theatre. A new Schauspielhaus was opened in 1806 but burnt down two years later; it was many times rebuilt and modernized in the 19th century and again in 1910; this, the Ostpreussischer Landestheater, has a capacity of 1225 seats with additional standing places. Wagner was in the city during the period 1836–7, when his wife was an actress at the theatre and he was briefly Kapellmeister. That post had earlier been held by H. L. E. Dorn, a native of the city, and later by Weber's pupil F. E. Sobolewski; operas by these two men were in the theatre's repertory, but Wagner was particularly favoured. *Tannhäuser* was given in 1853 with Johanna Wagner as Elisabeth; Angelo Neumann's travelling troupe visited the city in 1882; and between 1889 and 1900 there were 206 performances of ten Wagner operas.

Native Königsberg composers of this period include Otto Nicolai and Hermann Goetz. Among the musicians active in the city were the university music director and cathedral organist Otto Fiebach (1851–1937), whose seven operas enjoyed only moderate success, and the conductors Karl Rankl (1927–8) and Hermann Scherchen (1928–33). Günther Rennert was chief director there, 1939–42. Among the operas to have had premières in Königsberg is Ernst Toch's *Der Fächer* (1930).

Königskinder ('The King's Children'). *Märchenoper* in three acts by ENGELBERT HUMPERDINCK to a libretto by ERNST ROSMER (pseudonym of Else Bernstein-Porges) after her play of the same name; New York, Metropolitan Opera, 28 December 1910.

In 1894 Heinrich Porges asked Humperdinck to provide incidental music for the play written by his daughter, Else Bernstein-Porges, under the pseudonym Ernst Rosmer. When the author refused to allow the material to be expanded into an opera, Humperdinck decided to adopt the medium of melodrama, mixing spoken dialogue and song with a new kind of rhythmically notated Sprechgesang. The work was produced at the Munich Hoftheater on 23 January 1897, with Hedwig Schako as the Goose Girl. Despite the practical difficulties created by the new idiom, the melodrama appeared on over 130 stages before lapsing into obscurity.

In 1907, finally gaining the author's consent to transform it into an opera, Humperdinck set about revising the work. He reworked each melodramatic scene into a continuous musical fabric, replacing the Sprechgesang with sung dialogue. The American public

Goose Girl	soprano
Witch	contralto
King's Son	tenor
Fiddler	baritone
Woodcutter	bass
Broom-maker	tenor
Stable Girl	contralto
Innkeeper's Daughter	mezzo-soprano
Two Gatekeepers	baritone
Innkeeper	bass
Broom-maker's Daughter	soprano
Senior Councillor	baritone
Tailor	tenor

Townspeople, councillors and their wives, artisans, musicians, girls, youths, children

Setting The town of Hellabrunn and surrounding forest of Hellawald in the Middle Ages

responded with great enthusiasm to the opera's New York première, which Alfred Herz conducted with Geraldine Farrar as the Goose Girl, Hermann Jadlowker as the King's Son, Louise Homer as the Witch and Otto Goritz as the Fiddler. The Berlin première on 14 January 1911, with Leo Blech conducting, Lola Artôt de Padilla as the Goose Girl and Walter Kirchhoff as the King's Son, seemed equally successful. The critics were guarded in their praise, however, comparing the work unfavourably with *Hänsel und Gretel*. More recent performances have been rare. A recording by Heinz Wallberg helped to revive interest in the opera, and Albert Rosen conducted it at the Wexford Festival in 1986.

ACT 1 *Outside the Witch's hut in Hellawald* A prelude depicts the heroic wanderings of the King's Son, focussing on a single figure, the first in an elaborate scheme of leitmotifs. The energetic sequences built from this motif contrast with the peaceful mood as the curtain rises, revealing the Goose Girl under a lime tree, surrounded by her geese. Dark chromatic chords usher in the first suggestions of evil forces as the Witch, her 'grandmother', calls the Goose Girl to bake poisoned bread. The Goose Girl's melodic lines also become chromatically tinged as she notices one of her lilies has not opened, a symbol of her own unfulfilment. Her baking-song, 'Meine weissen Blumen tragen Tau', develops into a plea for freedom, until the Witch reminds her of the spell holding her. The Goose Girl's lament 'O liebe Linde' begins as a sorrowful echo of her first motif, but as she is left alone to her reverie the melodic web expands, climaxing with the appearance of the King's Son. Music from the prelude reappears as he introduces himself ('Bin ein lustiger Jägersmann'), complemented by a new hymnlike motif suggesting his nobility. As he confesses his growing love for the Goose Girl ('Willst du mein' Maienbuhle sein'), his first leitmotif is lyrically transformed. Their passion is interrupted by the power of the Witch's spell, yet the King's Son protests that their courage should conquer it. He believes that the Goose Girl's fear is a sign that she does not yet deserve to share his nobility ('Königsblut und Bettelblut'); she will not see him again until a falling star opens her lily.

The threatening rhythms of the spell, as the Witch triumphs over the deserted Goose Girl, are interrupted by the arrival of the Fiddler. The folklike idiom of his

Geraldine Farrar as the Goose Girl in the original production of Humperdinck's 'Königskinder' at the Metropolitan Opera House, New York, 28 December 1910

song, 'Drei Narren zogen aus', relates sympathetically to the simplicity associated with the Goose Girl. His stupid companions, the Woodcutter and the Broom-maker, caricature the folk style with a heavy march. The Fiddler has a clearer vision than they of the king or queen they are seeking for Hellabrunn. He provokes the Witch into prophesying how a sovereign will enter Hellabrunn ('Wenn morgen die Mittagsglokken schlagen'); the music is significantly akin to the Goose Girl's motif. The Witch also reveals the Goose Girl's parentage, in a sinister narrative reminiscent of the Witch's Ride in *Hänsel und Gretel*, 'Dein Vater der hat vor sechzehn Jahren'. It releases the Goose Girl from her fear, as she realizes that her father too was 'royal', since he had died to save his people from a tyrant. As a star falls into the lily, she leaves with the Fiddler to seek the King's Son.

ACT 2 *Within the gates of Hellabrunn* The festive folkdances of the prelude continue throughout the act as the townspeople prepare for the arrival of their sovereign. Only the King's Son seems musically at odds, haunted by lyrical reminiscences of the Goose Girl. He has three encounters in Hellabrunn. The first, with the flirtatious Innkeeper's Daughter, makes him determined to leave ('Ei ist das schwer ein Bettler sein'); only the magical stirrings of flowers from the Goose Girl in his breast hold him back. After his second dialogue, with the Innkeeper, the King's Son withdraws to dream under a lime tree ('Lass die Nachttropfen deiner Zweige'). Only the innocent Broom-maker's Daughter succeeds in drawing him into a dance, 'Roter Ringelrosenbusch'.

The conflict breaks as the townspeople gather, and the King's Son contrasts his own view of nobility with the pompous march of the Woodcutter and Broom-maker. At the climax the gates open to reveal the Goose Girl as the expected sovereign; the King's Son's lyrical dream of her is fulfilled, even though they are now chased in scorn from the town.

ACT 3 *Outside the Witch's hut in winter* A prelude represents the Fiddler's last song, as he keeps vigil for the King's children in Hellawald. A transformation in

his music prepares for the changed wintry scene. The arrival of the children of Hellabrunn, expressing faith in the Fiddler in their simple song 'Lieber Spielmann', renews his desire to search for the King's children ('O du liebheilige Einfalt du!'). The accompanying Woodcutter and Broom-maker can only think of sheltering in the now deserted hut.

The Fiddler's folksong as he takes the children into the forest, 'Wohin bist du gegangen', contrasts with the return to the mood of the prelude as the King's Son and Goose Girl enter. Their recapitulated love music is tinged with deathly chromaticism ('Weisst noch das grosse Nest'), and the Goose Girl's unnaturally bright folksong, 'Kommt mein Geselle', ends in her collapse. The unclouded lyricism of the first act returns only when they eat the Witch's poisoned bread, offered to them by the Woodcutter from the hut in exchange for the King's Son's crown. The Fiddler and children reappear, but only in time to make up a funeral procession, accompanied by the Fiddler's last song, 'Verdorben! Gestorben!'.

*   *   *

The opera's bleak and uncompromising ending does not fulfil the usual expectations of *Märchenoper*; for Else Bernstein-Porges, *Königskinder*'s Romantic imagery of woodland idyll and heroic young lovers was only a thin covering for a symbolic message of alienation, in particular the artist's separation from the rest of society. Allegorical meaning and simple folklike narrative exist side by side in the text, creating a difficult mixture for the composer to resolve. The beauty of Humperdinck's melodic writing greatly strengthens the opera's folklike qualities, though one notices he takes unusual care to bind contrasting musical material together. The lovers' lyrical melodies are nearly always coloured with chromaticism, the musical symbol for the opera's forces of evil. Such efforts at creating a seamless transition between opposites was a new musical achievement for the composer, outstripping the more simple variation techniques he used in *Hänsel und Gretel*. It reveals how seriously Humperdinck approached this libretto, although the text is largely responsible for the opera's relative lack of popularity.   AMANDA GLAUERT

Königssohn aus Ithaka, Der [*Telemach, der Königssohn aus Ithaka* ('Telemachus, the Prince from Ithaca')]. *Heroisch-komische Oper* in two acts by FRANZ ANTON HOFFMEISTER to a libretto by EMANUEL SCHIKANEDER; Vienna, Theater auf der Wieden, 27 June 1795.

Kalypso [Calypso] has fallen in love with Telemachus, the son of her former lover Odysseus. Telemachus, despite the admonitions of his tutor Mentor, is attracted to one of Calypso's nymphs, Tillina, while his squire Colifonio cavorts with another nymph, Pratschina. Calypso's efforts to win Telemachus's heart all fail; with the escape of Mentor, Telemachus and Tillina, she is left a tragic, abandoned woman.

Hoffmeister's only collaboration with Schikaneder was by far the most successful of his eight operas. Like the poet's other librettos of the period, this one makes ample allowance for spectacular effects and includes a dozen different stage sets. Schikaneder himself created the part of the vainglorious but cowardly Colifonio.

THOMAS BAUMAN

Konink [Koninck, Kooninck, Coning, Cooninck, Koning etc], **Servaas de** (*b* Dendermonde, bap. 9 Oct 1654; *d* Amsterdam, bur. 15 July 1701). Netherlands composer. He studied in Leuven (1675) and lived in Brussels in the early 1680s before settling permanently in Amsterdam. During the 1690s he worked as a theatre musician. His instrumental and vocal compositions were published in Amsterdam by Estienne Roger between 1696 and 1699, among them two volumes with trio pieces that may have served as introductory and entr'acte music for plays given at the Amsterdam Stadsschouwburg. Konink's op.2 consists of three-part settings of the choruses of Racine's *Athalie* (1697). In addition, he composed the music (now lost) to two *zangspelen* (light theatre plays with a mixture of spoken texts and songs): *De vryadje van Cloris en Roosje* (1688, libretto by Dirk Buysero, performed annually at Christmas at the Stadsschouwburg from 1707 onwards) and *Hardersspel ter bruiloft van Frederik Wilhelm Mandt en Maria van Blyswyk* (1699, libretto by Abraham Alewijn).

His son Servaas de Konink the younger (*b* Brussels, bap. 8 Sept 1682; *d* Amsterdam, bur. 13 Feb 1718) was an Amsterdam theatre musician as well (hitherto, father and son have always been taken for the same person). Servaas the younger provided the music (lost) for the *zangspel Piramus en Thisbe* (1714, libretto by Hendrik van Halmael) and edited the first three volumes of a series of collections of tunes related to the theatre, entitled *Hollantsche Schouburg en Plugge Dansen* (Amsterdam, 1715–16).

R. A. Rasch: 'De Dendermondse componist Servaas de Konink (1654–1701)', *Gedenkschriften van de oudheidkundige kring van het Land van Dendermonde*, 4th ser., x (1992), 5–35

RUDOLF A. RASCH

Koninklijke Muntschouwburg (Flem.). Theatre in BRUSSELS, the home of the national opera of Belgium, also known as the Théâtre Royal de la Monnaie.

Koninklijke Vlaamse Opera. Theatre in ANTWERP. Built in 1907 to house the Vlaamse Opera company, it was called the Vlaamsch Lyrisch Toneel until 1920, when it took its present name.

Konjović, Petar (*b* Čurug, Bačka, 5 May 1883; *d* Belgrade, 1 Oct 1970). Serbian composer. After studying composition in Prague he was director of the National Theatre in Zagreb (1921–6, 1933–5) and of theatres in Osijek, Split and Novi Sad (1927–33). A follower of Steven Mokranjac, he was inspired by the Serbian national idiom and used folk melodies and dances in his own music. His operas, based on historical subjects and individuals, are composed in a late Romantic style, with vocal lines derived from the intonations of the spoken word (in the style of Musorgsky and Janáček), as well as with folk rhythms and colourful orchestration. His first opera, *Ženidba Miloša Obilića, ili Vilin veo* ('The Marriage of Miloš Obilić, or The Fairy's Veil', 1917) is an immature Romantic work, but *Knez od Zete* ('The Prince of Zeta') is a true musical drama about the unhappy love between the Montenegrin prince Maksim and Andjelija, the daughter of the doge of Venice; the lives of Montenegrins and Venetians are portrayed by the contrast of Romantic musical language and barcarolle rhythms with Montenegrin songs and the chant of the *guslari* (singers of Serbian epic folksongs, who accompanied themselves with bowed instruments called *gusle*).

In the opera *Koštana*, the Balkan-oriental atmosphere of the small Serbian town of Vranje is evoked by three tragic characters: Mitke, mourning for youth, the violent Toma, who sings impressively about a young Turkish woman, and Koštana, the beautiful and unhappy young gypsy girl. National songs and dances with frenetic rhythms are features of this famous work. The related *Symphonic Triptych* (1935) is 'full of lavish, picturesque dance rhythms, contrasted with the intense melancholy of the intermediate movement' (Peričić); it is performed as a concert piece or on stage as a ballet. The unpretentious opera *Seljaci* ('The Peasants') combines folk music and original musical ideas to portray life in a Serbian village. The plot of Konjović's last opera, *Otadžbina* ('The Fatherland'), deals with a mother who has lost nine sons and a husband in the battle of Kosovo in 1389. It has an oratorio-like form, with static choruses and ensembles (in a polyphonic style inspired by Serbian church music), but is intended for stage performance. Konjović's music is enriched with oriental elements.

Ženidba Miloša Obilića, ili Vilin veo [The Marriage of Miloš Obilić, or The Fairy's Veil] (romantic op, 3, D. Ilić), Zagreb, 25 April 1917, vs (Vienna, 1917); rev., Belgrade, 4 Oct 1922, vs (Belgrade, 1926)

Knez od Zete [The Prince of Zeta] (musical drama, 4, after L. Kostić: *Maksim Crnojević*), Belgrade, 1 June 1929; rev., 29 Dec 1946, vs (Zagreb, 1965)

Koštana (3, after B. Stanković), Zagreb, 16 April 1931; rev., Belgrade, 29 May 1940, vs (Belgrade, 1946); rev., Belgrade, 4 April 1948 (Belgrade, 1948)

Seljaci [The Peasants] (national op, 3, J. Konjović, after J. Veselinović and D. Brzak: *Djido*), Belgrade, 3 March 1951, vs (Novi Sad, 1964)

Otadžbina [The Fatherland], 1960 (solemn sacred spectacle, 3 chantings, after I. Vojnović: *Smrt majke Jugovića* [The Death of Mother Jugović]), Belgrade, 19 Oct 1983

*

S. Đurić-Klajn: 'Razvoj muzičke umjetnosti u Srbiji' [The Development of the Art of Music in Serbia], in J. Andreis, D. Svetko and S. Đurić-Klajn: *Historijski razvoj muzičke kulture u Jugoslaviji* [The Historical Development of Musical Culture in Yugoslavia] (Zagreb, 1962), 529–709

V. Peričić: *Muzički stvaraoci u Srbiji* [Musical Creators in Serbia] (Belgrade, 1969)

N. Mosusova: 'O "Koštani" Petra Konjovića', *Arti musices*, ii (1971), 153–67

Život i delo Petra Konjovića: Belgrade 1983 [The Life and Work of Petar Konjović] ROKSANDA PEJOVIĆ

Kono, Kristo (*b* Korçë, 17 July 1907; *d* Tirana, 22 Jan 1991). Albanian composer. He was one of the small group of musicians who began to be active during the first few years after the proclamation of Albanian independence in 1913. From the simple harmonization of local songs he proceeded to write choral and orchestral works, and became gradually involved with the promotion of socialist ideals through his music. He wrote the first Albanian operetta, *Agimi* ('The Dawn'; K. Jakova; Korçë, 22 November 1954), but his first true opera was *Lulja e kujtimit* ('The Flowers of Remembrance'; A. Mara and A. Skali, after F. Postoli; Tirana, 5 November 1961). The work describes the breaking-down of the social prejudices which separate Dhmiter, a poor apprentice, from Olimba, a merchant's daughter, whom he loves. The opera interweaves the love story with a theme of patriotic struggle, using leitmotifs to point the drama. Much of the thematic material is based on the lyrical music of the town of Korçë.

S. Kalemi: *Arritjet e artit tonë muzikor* [The Arrival of our Musical Art] (Tirana, 1982)

J. Emerson: *Albania – The Search for the Eagle's Song* (Studley, Warwicks., 1990) JUNE EMERSON

Kont, Paul (*b* Vienna, 19 Aug 1920). Austrian composer. He studied in Vienna, with Krips and Swarowsky (1945–8), in Paris with Milhaud, Honegger and Messiaen (1952) and was trained in Webernian methods of analysis. He taught at the Vienna Musikhochschule from 1969 to 1986, specialising in composition for audio-visual media, and appeared frequently as a pianist and conductor in performances of his own music. His large output of works for radio, television and the stage began in the early 1950s, when he first used 12-note methods; these include *Kammertanzspiele* and the operas *Peter und Susanne*, composed for the 1959 Salzburger Opernkongress, *Lysistrate* (1961, Dresden) and *Libussa* (1969, Vienna). He received the Austrian State Prize in 1964 for the musical fairy-tale *Traumleben*.

Indische Legende (Kurzoper, J. Mauthe), broadcast, 1951; stage, Vienna, Kammeroper, 1954

Peter und Susanne, oder Die österreichische Schwermut (komische Oper, G. Fritsch), televised ORF, 1959; stage, Innsbruck, Landes, 1968

Lysistrate (3, Kont, after Aristophanes), Dresden, Radebeul, 19 March 1961

Traumleben (musikalische Märchen, Mauthe, after F. Grillparzer: *Der Traum ein Leben*), Salzburg, Landes, Dec 1963

Inzwischen, 1965 (Mysterienspiel für unsere Zeit, after W. H. Auden: *For the Time Being*), televised ORF, 24 May 1967

Libussa, Vienna, 1969

Plutos (after Aristophanes), Klagenfurt, Stadt, 10 Feb 1977

Die Paare [Grosse Amouren], 1985–8

*

MGG (R. Klein)

W. Szmolyan: 'Paul Kont', *ÖMz*, xix (1964), 591-3

R. Klein: 'Paul Konts Vision einer neuen Tonalität', *ÖMz*, xxvi (1971), 253–6

P. Kont: 'Die kleine Götterdämmerung: Bemerkungen zu *Plutos*', *ÖMz*, xxxii (1977), 87–8 JOSEPH CLARK

Konwitschny, Franz (*b* Fulnek, Northern Moravia, 14 Aug 1901; *d* Belgrade, 28 July 1962). German conductor. After studying at the Leipzig Conservatory he began his career as a string player, and played the viola in the Gewandhaus Orchestra under Furtwängler. Turning to conducting in 1927, he worked his way up from répétiteur to chief conductor at Stuttgart by 1930. He was appointed music director at Freiburg (1933), Frankfurt (1938), and Hanover (1946); from 1950 to 1955 he worked simultaneously as conductor of the Dresden Staatsoper and the Leipzig Gewandhaus. His appointment in 1955 as music director of the rebuilt Staatsoper in Berlin placed him at the head of East Germany's conductors.

Konwitschny, a conductor of Furtwängler's type, gained an international reputation through his guest appearances which included a Covent Garden *Ring* cycle in 1959. Indeed, he was outstanding in passionately fiery interpretations of Wagner (*Meistersinger*, *Tristan* and the *Ring* cycle) and of Strauss (*Die Frau ohne Schatten*), which he projected with broad dimensions and infused with great intensity.

WOLFRAM SCHWINGER

Kónya, Sándor (*b* Sarkad, 23 Sept 1923). Hungarian tenor. He studied in Budapest, Detmold and Milan, making his début in 1951 at Detmold as Turiddu, before singing at Darmstadt. In 1955 he joined the Städtische (later Deutsche) Oper, Berlin. In 1956 he created Leandro in Henze's *König Hirsch*, and sang Nureddin (*Der Barbier von Bagdad*) at Edinburgh. He made his Bayreuth (1958), Paris (1959), Florence, Metropolitan (1961) and Covent Garden (1963) débuts as Lohengrin, his best-known role. At La Scala (1960) he sang Parsifal; at San Francisco (1960–65) he appeared as Dick Johnson, Lohengrin, Pinkerton, Radames, Don Alvaro and Riccardo (*Ballo*). At the Metropolitan, where he sang until 1975, his roles included Walther, Parsifal, Erik, Max, Edgardo (*Lucia*), Don Carlos, Cavaradossi and Calaf. His strong, clear voice, equally suitable for German or Italian roles, lay between the lyrical and the heroic.

ALAN BLYTH

Koppel, Herman D(avid) (*b* Copenhagen, 1 Oct 1908). Danish composer of Polish parentage. A member of one of the foremost musical families of Denmark, he is the father of the singer Lone Koppel; another daughter and a son are also professional musicians. He began piano studies at the age of six and started to compose while still a child. In 1926 he entered the Copenhagen Conservatory, where he attracted the attention of Nielsen; he later became an authoritative interpreter of Nielsen's piano music. He served as répétiteur for the Kongelige Teater and for Danish radio in the late 1930s. He continued to work as an accompanist and soloist, and held a teaching appointment at the Royal Institute for the Blind (1940–49), taking refuge from the German invaders in Sweden (1943–5). He then taught the piano at the Copenhagen Conservatory, becoming professor there in 1955. The circumstances surrounding his flight into Sweden made a deep impression on his compositional attitudes, evident in the music he wrote for the play *Niels Ebbesen*, by Kaj Munk (1943, Göteborg), and in the music for a documentary film (1944).

Koppel has written one opera, *Macbeth* op.79, composed in 1967–8. The libretto of this five-act work is by the composer and his son, Anders Koppel, based on the Danish translation of Shakespeare's play by V. Østerberg. At the first performance, which took place at the Kongelige Teater on 1 February 1970, Lady

Macbeth was sung by Lone Koppel. The composer was praised for the varied musical setting, which ranges from motoric rhythms and block chords, underscoring the more dramatic passages, to a harsh lyricism, adapted to the mood of the text in the more sombre scenes.

G. Colding-Jørgensen: 'Koppels "Macbeth"', *Dansk musiktidsskrift*, xliv (1969), 111–12

F. Behrendt: *Fra et hjem med klaver: Herman D. Koppels liv og erindringer* [From a Home with a Piano: Koppel's Life and Reminiscences] (Copenhagen, 1988)　WILLIAM H. REYNOLDS

Koppel [Koppel Winther], **Lone** (*b* Copenhagen, 20 May 1938). Danish soprano. She studied in Copenhagen, making her début there in 1961 as Musetta. In 1973 she accompanied her husband, John Winther, to Australia, where he became manager of the new Sydney Opera House. She was a leading singer in Sydney and her repertory included Donna Anna and Donna Elvira, Leonore, Elisabeth, Venus, Ortrud, Amelia (*Ballo*), Abigaille, Elisabeth de Valois and Tosca. Later she returned to Copenhagen, where in 1991 she sang Katerina Izmaylova and Amneris. With a powerful voice and a dramatic temperament, she excelled in roles such as Jenůfa and Marie (*Wozzeck*).　ELIZABETH FORBES

Kopytman, Mark (*b* Kamyanets' Podil's'kyy, 6 Dec 1929). Israeli composer of Ukrainian origin. He studied in Chernovtsy, Ukraine, then at the L'viv Academy of Music (1952–5) and the Tchaikovsky Academy. His prize-winning first opera, *Kasa Mare* (2, V. Teleuke and V. Tatarinova, after I. Drutze), received its première on 20 December 1968. It concerns a love affair between Vassilutza (mezzo-soprano), a middle-aged widow, and Pavalake (baritone), a fickle peasant boy. When the young, glamorous Sofika (soprano) steals the attentions of Pavalake, Vassilutza decides it is time to leave him and find her own 'kasa mare' (a Moldavian term for a 'joyful corner' in a household).

Kopytman emigrated to Israel in 1972 and the following year started teaching at the Rubin Academy of Music, Jerusalem, where he became professor in 1975. Since 1972 he has gradually abandoned his adherence to the Russian school of composition and has explored aleatory techniques, often notated graphically. *Chamber Scenes from the Life of Susskind von Trimberg* (1, R. Freier) is a medieval tale about a Jewish poet, Susskind (baritone), who is forced to adopt Christianity in order to escape persecution. He is coerced by the Christian knight, Konradin (tenor), and yet is drawn to Judaism through his love for his wife Rose-Marie (contralto) and the Jewish people. The action is observed under the watchful eye of the Devil (bass), who knows that he will have ultimate control over Susskind's soul. The opera, which includes ancient instruments in its scoring, was first performed in Jerusalem on 1 February 1983.

　WILLIAM Y. ELIAS

Korchmaryov, Klimenty Arkad'yevich (*b* Verkhne-Dneprovsk, 21 June/3 July 1899; *d* Moscow, 7 April 1958). Ukrainian composer. He graduated from the Odessa Conservatory (gold medal, 1919), where his teachers included Maliszewski. From 1923 he lived in Moscow and from 1939 to 1947 in Turkmenia, where he established the first Turkmenian National Ballet and collected folksongs of the region. He was one of the first Soviet composers to write on revolutionary subjects.

Ivan-Soldat [Ivan the Soldier], 1925–7 (D. Smolin), Moscow, Bol'shoy Branch, 3 April 1927

Desyat' dney, kotorïye potryasli mir [Ten Days that Shook the World], 1929–31 (S. Gorodetsky)

Opasnïy kvartal [Dangerous Quarter], 1934 (operetta)

Rannyaya krasavitsa [The Early Beauty]/Ganna (operetta, S. Vetlugin and L. Oshanin), Khabarovsk, 1939

Bagttlï yashlïik/Schastlivaya molodost' [Happy Youth], 1942 (comic op, A. Afinogenov and R. Seidov)

Pan-zabiyaka [Mr Bully], 1945 (operetta, Ya. Galitsky and L. Cherkashinaya)

Ditya radosti [Child of Joy], 1953 (Cherkashinaya and A. Zhadov, after Chinese music drama: *The Whitehaired Girl*), Ulan-Ude, 21 April 1955

E. Braudo: *Ivan Soldat* (Moscow, 1927)

D. Gojowy: *Neue sowjetische Musik der 20er Jahre* (Laaber, 1980)

　DETLEF GOJOWY

Kord, Kazimierz (*b* Pogórze, 18 Nov 1930). Polish conductor. He took first prize for piano at the Leningrad Conservatory and studied composition and conducting at Kraków. He joined the Warsaw Opera and made his début there in 1960. He was artistic director at the Kraków Opera, 1962–8, where he produced and conducted works. He directed and toured abroad with the Polish Radio-Television Orchestra, 1968–73, during which time he made his début at the Metropolitan on 27 December 1972 in *The Queen of Spades* (the first Russian opera to be sung in its original language at that theatre) and conducted *Boris Godunov* at San Francisco the next year. His Covent Garden début was in *Yevgeny Onegin* in 1976; since then he has held mainly orchestra appointments, with the Warsaw PO (from 1977), the South-West German Radio Orchestra, Baden-Baden (from 1980), and the Cincinnati SO (1980–82). His operatic conducting drew praise for its commitment and precision, sometimes with more attention to detail than to overall character.　NOËL GOODWIN

Korea. Country in east Asia, divided after World War II into the Republic of Korea (South Korea) and North Korea. While retaining their traditional arts of music, dance and theatre, Koreans have become fascinated with Western techniques and instruments. The Korean National Opera, based in the South Korean capital, Seoul, was founded in 1962 by Ahn Hyong-il under the auspices of the Ministry of Information and Culture. Since that time it has performed over 50 operas, mostly Italian but including Korean works such as Yon-taek Hong's *Nongae* (1975) and Il-nam Chang's *Choyong* (1987). Currently two and sometimes three operas are given each season by Korean singers, some of whom have gained experience in Europe and America, with foreign guest directors and conductors. The works are usually sung in Korean and are accompanied by the National SO. The National Opera is one of eight companies that perform at the National Theatre (architect Lee Hi-tae), in a park on the outskirts of Seoul. It was completed in 1973, the main theatre having 1518 seats, the small experimental theatre, 344 seats.

A second company, the Seoul Metropolitan Opera Theatre, was founded in 1985 and gives one or two productions a year at the Sejong Cultural Centre Main Theatre (nearly 4000 seats) in central Seoul. *Andrea Chénier* was sung in 1985 with Italian guest singers alternating with Koreans in the principal roles, but with a mainly Korean cast. It was followed by *Chunhyang Chon* ('The Tale of the Maiden Chunhyang'), an opera with libretto and music by the Korean composer Junsang Pahk, then *Nabucco* (1986), *La Gioconda* (1987), *Aida* (1988) and *Adriana Lecouvreur* (1989). These productions are accompanied by the Seoul PO. The Royal Opera, Covent Garden, visited Seoul in 1979, giving *Peter Grimes*, *Die Zauberflöte* and *Tosca*, and returned in 1986 with *Turandot*, *Carmen* and *Samson et Dalila*, all at the Sejong Cultural Centre. A new theatre, seating 2500, in which opera is performed opened in 1992 as part of the Seoul Arts Centre.

At Taegu in South Korea, the Taegu Opera was founded in 1972 by Kim Keum Hwan. The company gives two or three performances of a different popular, usually Italian, opera each year, in Korean with Korean artists. Some Korean singers have become internationally famous, notably Sumi Jo, Helen Kwon and Jungwhon Park.

The North Koreans founded their own Russian-orientated opera company in Pyongyang in 1959, and by the 1970s this company was appearing in East European opera houses. CHARLES PITT

Koréh, Endre (*b* Sepsiszentgyörgy, 13 April 1906; *d* Vienna, 20 Sept 1960). Hungarian bass. He studied in Budapest under Árpád Palotay, making his début at the Budapest Opera House as Sparafucile in 1930. His rich, dark bass voice soon attracted attention in Wagner roles (notably Hunding, Hagen and Fafner), but he also sang Mozart and Verdi. In 1948, after guest performances in Vienna, he became a member of the Staatsoper. He made appearances at Glyndebourne (Osmin, 1950), the Metropolitan (Ochs, 1953) and the Salzburg and Florence festivals, and was the first Caliban in Martin's *Der Sturm* (1956). PÉTER P. VÁRNAI

Kořínek, Miloslav (*b* Brno, 21 Jan 1925). Slovak composer. He studied at the Bratislava Academy with Alexander Moyzes and later was appointed professor of music at the Academy (by then called the State Conservatory). His two-act opera, *Ako išlo vajce na vandrovku* ('As the Egg went A-wandering'), was originally written for radio and uses a libretto by Jela Krčméry-Vrteľová after Slovak folktales. This humorous opera is like a Singspiel in that spoken dialogue alternates with musical numbers in a simple yet inventive style; the work is organized in the form of a rondo, with a repeated march song sung by the animals on their journey through the world. It exists in versions for adult and child singers; only the first has been performed to date, by the Slovak National Opera in Bratislava on 31 December 1960.

I. Vajda: *Slovenská opera* (Bratislava, 1988), 213–6, 239
IGOR VAJDA

Korn, Artur (*b* Wuppertal, 4 Dec 1937). German bass. He studied in Cologne, Munich and Vienna, making his début in Cologne in 1963 as Samuel. After singing in Graz, he joined the Vienna Volksoper (1968), where his roles included van Bett (*Zar und Zimmermann*), Sleep and Hymen (*The Fairy-Queen*), Lothario (*Mignon*) and Nicolai's Falstaff. He first sang at Glyndebourne as Ochs (1980), at Covent Garden as Mozart's Bartolo (1981), at the Metropolitan as Osmin and in Chicago as Waldner (1984). He has also sung in San Francisco, Detroit, Munich, Buenos Aires, Bregenz and Salzburg (*Moses und Aron*, 1987). An excellent actor, he sings

Sarastro, Rocco, Pimen, Sherasmin, Fasolt and Fafner, but his finest role is certainly Ochs. ELIZABETH FORBES

Körner, (Karl) Theodor (*b* Dresden, 23 Nov 1791; *d* Gadebusch, Mecklenburg, 26 Aug 1813). German poet and librettist. After studying geology, philosophy and law at Freiberg, Leipzig and Berlin, he went to Vienna in 1811 to work as a Dramaturg. He met Eichendorff, Beethoven, Weber, Moscheles and Meyerbeer and wrote a quantity of dramas and poems. He also discussed opera projects with Beethoven and Spohr but in 1813, before bringing these ideas to fruition, he enlisted in Lützow's volunteer corps and fell in battle. His most popular and perhaps also his best works are the soldiers' songs he wrote in the months before his death. Schubert set the libretto *Der vierjährige Posten* in 1815, as did Reinecke in 1855; J. P. S. Schmidt set *Das Fischermädchen* (1818) and *Alfred der Grosse* (1830). Flotow's settings of *Die Bergknappen* and *Alfred der Grosse*, however, were unperformed, and Dvořák's setting of the latter was not staged during his lifetime. A number of other composers (including A. R. von Adelburg, F. X. Grutsch, F. X. Kleinheinz, Karl Steinacher and C. T. Weinlig), now largely forgotten, based operas on Körner's dramas and librettos.

*
A. Schaefer: *Historisches und systematisches Verzeichnis sämtlicher Tonwerke zu den Dramen ... Körners* (Leipzig, 1886)
R. Musiol: *T. Körner und seine Beziehungen zur Musik* (Ratibor, 1893)
K. Berger: *T. Körner* (Bielefeld, 1912) PETER BRANSCOMBE

Körner, Thomas (*b* Breslau, 3 Nov 1942). German writer and librettist. He studied medicine and jurisprudence at the Humboldt University of East Berlin, qualifying with a diploma in law. He moved to West Germany in 1979, and was drama adviser to the Deutsche Theater in Hamburg, 1985–8.

After trying his hand at journalism and short scripts for a cartoon film and a documentary, Körner turned to librettos, libretto translations, scenarios and related scripts for music drama in the widest sense of the term. In 1973 the Deutsche Staatsoper, Berlin, commissioned him to write the libretto for *R. Hot bzw. Die Hitze*, after Jakob Lenz's *Der Engländer*, for the five-act opera of the same name composed by Friedrich Goldmann (1974). In 1976 Körner was again commissioned by the Deutsche Staatsoper, to adapt Büchner's play *Leonce und Lena* for Paul Dessau. After moving to West Germany, Körner wrote librettos for the Württembergische Staatstheater, Stuttgart: in 1979 *Das Märchen von Fanferlieschen Schönefüsschen* (in collaboration with his wife Karin Körner) for the Viennese composer Kurt Schwertsik; in 1983 *M. Pineda*, a new version of the Orpheus and Eurydice story, for Cristobál Halffter; in 1987 an adaptation of the text of *Bremer Freiheit*, after Rainer Werner Fassbinder, for the Stuttgart-based Romanian composer Adriana Hölszky, and the libretto for Schwertsik's *Das Friedensbankett – eine Operette*; in 1990 *Die spurlose Beseitigung des Zuschauers*, for the Viennese composer Otto M. Zykan; and in 1991 *Les paravents*, after Jean Genet, for Hölszky.

*
S. Neef: 'R. Hot von Thomas Körner und Friedrich Goldmann', *Theater der Zeit*, viii (1978), 64
G. Rienäcker: 'Letzte Seite im Opernvermächtnis: *Leonce und Lena*', *Musik und Gesellschaft*, xii (1979), 709–15
REINHARD OEHLSCHLÄGEL

Korngold, Erich Wolfgang (*b* Brno, 29 May 1897; *d* Hollywood, 29 Nov 1957). American composer of Austro-Hungarian birth. Although born in Moravia, he was brought up in Vienna, where his father Julius was assistant to the music critic Eduard Hanslick. When at the age of nine Erich demonstrated his precocious talent with a cantata, *Gold*, he was sent to study with Robert Fuchs at the Vienna Conservatory; eventually he came to the notice of Mahler, who declared him a genius and recommended that he should study with Zemlinsky. Under Zemlinsky's tutelage Korngold produced a pantomime, *Der Schneemann*, the première of which (at the Vienna Hofoper on 4 October 1910) led to its composer being hailed as the *Wunderkind* of the age. Korngold continued to compose prolifically, and with great success, throughout his teens: his *Schauspiel Ouvertüre* was performed by Nikisch in 1911, and Nikisch, Weingartner and Richard Strauss all conducted his Sinfonietta the following year. In 1916, Bruno Walter presented Korngold's one-act operas, *Der Ring des Polykrates* and *Violanta*, as a double bill at the Munich Staatsoper. In addition, there were chamber works and songs, as well as incidental music to a production of *Much Ado About Nothing* which ran for some 80 performances at the Vienna Burgtheater. Korngold's most celebrated opera, *Die tote Stadt*, was completed in 1920, and received premières simultaneously in Hamburg and Cologne in December of that year. His last two operas, *Das Wunder der Heliane* (1927, Hamburg) and *Die Kathrin* (scheduled for performance in Vienna in 1937, but due to political circumstances eventually given its première in Stockholm in 1939), received less critical acclaim and failed to gain a foothold in the repertory. In the meantime, Korngold's other activities included re-orchestrating, re-arranging and in some cases re-composing classical operettas by Johann Strauss, Offenbach and Leo Fall; he travelled around the theatres and opera houses of Europe conducting these as well as his own operatic works.

In 1934 Korngold went to Hollywood to work on a film version of *A Midsummer Night's Dream*, for which he was to adapt Mendelssohn's music. This was the start of his distinguished association with the American film industry: in 1935 he returned to compose (in collaboration with Oscar Hammerstein II) an original film-operetta, *Give us this Night*, and while he was there was asked by Warner Brothers to provide the score for the adventure film, *Captain Blood*. 18 original film scores followed over the next 12 years, most notably for the handsome series of Errol Flynn costume dramas, culminating in *The Sea Hawk*. World War II prevented Korngold's return to Europe and he remained in America after his retirement from film-composing in 1947. The last ten years of his life were largely devoted to composing concert pieces (including a Violin Concerto, a Symphonic Serenade for strings, a Cello Concerto and a Symphony), although at the time of his death he was making plans for a sixth opera.

Korngold's eclectic late-Romantic style crystallized early. Already established in *Violanta*, thereafter it preserved an undeviating identity, neither stagnating nor following any characteristic pattern of development, but rather exploring similar areas of feeling in changing perspectives. Richard Strauss and Puccini were its chief influences; Korngold showed no interest in the Second Viennese School, and traces of contemporary *Angst* are almost totally absent from his music. In this respect he is remote from contemporaries such as Zemlinsky or Schreker. His strong points are lyrical melody, rich textures and virtuoso orchestration; the music has a strong sense of the theatre and of theatrical effectiveness, but is deficient in contrapuntal vitality. His emotional directness and lack of inhibition, his unashamedly grand manner and the sheer exuberance of his invention breathed new life into a moribund tradition and have ensured the renewed and growing interest in his work which the last few years have witnessed.

See also TOTE STADT, DIE and VIOLANTA.

Der Ring des Polykrates op.7 (1, after H. Teweles), Munich, Staatsoper, 28 March 1916 (Mainz, 1916)
Violanta op.8 (1, H. Müller), Munich, Staatsoper, 28 March 1916 (Mainz, 1916)
Die tote Stadt op.12 (3, Paul Schott [E. W. Korngold and J. Korngold], after G. Rodenbach: *Bruges la morte*), Hamburg and Cologne, 4 Dec 1920 (Mainz, 1920)
Das Wunder der Heliane op.20 (3, Müller, after H. Kaltneker), Hamburg, 7 Oct 1927, vs (Mainz and Leipzig, 1927)
Die Kathrin op.28 (E. Decsey), Stockholm, 7 Oct 1939, vs (Vienna and Leipzig, 1937)

*

L. Korngold: *Erich Wolfgang Korngold* (Vienna, 1967)
B. G. Carroll: *The Operas of Erich Wolfgang Korngold* (diss., U. of Liverpool, 1975)
——: *Erich Wolfgang Korngold: His Life and Works* (Paisley, nr Glasgow, 1984)   CHRISTOPHER PALMER

Környei, Béla (*b* Krumau [now Český Krumlov], 18 May 1875; *d* Budapest, 22 April 1925). Hungarian tenor. He sang bass in the Folk Theatre chorus, later taking solo parts at Temesvár (now Timişoara, Romania) as a baritone and returning to the Folk Theatre in 1907 as Don José. The heroic power and beauty of his voice, which compensated for dramatic deficiencies, assured his success, principally in Verdi and Puccini. From 1915 to 1918 he was a member of the Vienna Staatsoper, where he created Bacchus in the second version of *Ariadne auf Naxos*. In 1918 he returned to Budapest, where he died while still at the height of his career. Numerous recordings preserve his art.   PÉTER P. VÁRNAI

Kórodi, András (*b* Budapest, 24 May 1922; *d* Venice, 17 Sept 1986). Hungarian conductor. He studied conducting with János Ferencsik at the Budapest Conservatory, and joined the Budapest Opera as répétiteur in 1946. The same year he made his conducting début there with Kodály's *Háry János*, was appointed conductor, and became principal conductor in 1963. He conducted several premières, including those of Hungarian operas such as Szokolay's *Blood Wedding* (1964), which led to his British début with the Hungarian company at the 1973 Edinburgh Festival. He also appeared at Cologne, Paris, Stockholm and Vienna. He was the first Hungarian to conduct the Bol'shoy Opera in Moscow, with *Carmen* in 1957; that year he was appointed a professor of conducting at the Budapest Academy. He was named Artist of Merit in 1960, appointed president conductor of the Budapest PO in 1967 and received the Kossuth Prize in 1970.

PÉTER P. VÁRNAI

Köroğlu. Opera in three acts by AHMED ADNAN SAYGUN to a libretto by Selahattin Batu; Istanbul, 1973.

Köroğlu is based on an old Turkish legend in which Beyoglu (tenor), the cruel son of the Bey (baritone), attacks a village to carry off the beautiful Günayim (soprano) but is thwarted in his attempt by the Groom's son (bass), the girl's fiancé. On hearing of the incident, the Bey summons the Groom (bass) and asks about his magic horse Kırat; unable to believe the account of the horse's extraordinary qualities and convinced that he is lying, he has the Groom's eyes put out. Meanwhile, the Bey's men kidnap Günayim, whereupon the Groom's wife (mezzo-soprano) summons her son and, giving him the horse Kırat, asks him to avenge his father. Addressing her son for the first time as Köroğlu ('blind man's son') she sends him to Çamlıbel. Under Köroğlu's leadership the local peasants surround the Bey's dwelling and demand an end to oppression and Günayim's release, but instead of freeing the girl the Bey gives orders for her execution. The peasants are routed and return to their village. But Köroğlu never abandons his desire for revenge. After some time the peasants lose all hope. Köroğlu appears and announces that the Bey and his men have all been killed. When asked about Günayim he tells them that she is living in a world of dreams, and leaves in obedience to a call from Kırat.

Saygun displays great skill in his handling of the main lines of the legend. A generally impressionistic approach is sometimes combined with speech-song. Köroğlu's famous aria in the last act contains certain modal elements.   FARUK YENER

Korsoff, Lucette (*b* Genoa, 1 Feb 1876; *d* Brussels, 14 Feb 1955). Russian soprano. Her father, a baritone, was impresario of a Russian opera company with which she made her début in *La serva padrona*, at the age of 16. She then trained in Paris and joined a French company touring Egypt in 1900. There she sang Ophelia in Thomas' *Hamlet* with Maurice Renaud, who recommended her to the Opéra-Comique in Paris. Her début role with the company was Lakmé and she sang Mařenka in the French première of *The Bartered Bride*, but she was most famed for her Queen of Night. She was also popular at La Monnaie, Brussels, where appeared from 1906 to 1908. In 1912 she sang in Chicago, Boston and New Orleans, and gave concerts in New York. She spent the war years in Italy, sang at Monte Carlo in 1918 and retired in 1921. Later she taught in Paris and Brussels, her pupils including Gina Cigna and Joseph Rogachevsky. Her many recordings of the lyric-coloratura repertory are highly accomplished in technique, fresh of tone and animated in presentation.
                                                    J. B. STEANE

Korsov, Bogomir Bogomirovich [Gering, Gottfried] (*b* St Petersburg, 19 Feb/3 March 1843; *d* Tbilisi, 1920). Russian baritone. After studies in St Petersburg with Piccioli and in Milan with Corsi, he made his début in Turin in 1868. He returned to Russia the following year, singing at the Mariinsky until 1882, and thereafter at the Bol'shoy until 1904. In Moscow he created the roles of Mazeppa (1884), the Fiend (Tchaikovsky's *The Slippers*, 1887) and Aleko (1893). Other important roles included the title roles in *Boris Godunov*, Rubinstein's *The Demon* and Saint-Saëns' *Henry VIII* (Russian première, 1897, Moscow). His German antecedents were said to be reflected in the care he applied to all aspects of his characterizations.   BORIS SEMEONOFF

Kortes, Sergey. *See* CORTES, SERGEY.

Koryakin, Mikhail Mikhaylovich (*b* Kochetka, Kharkiv province, 19/31 March 1850; *d* St Petersburg, 18/30 Jan 1897). Russian bass. After completing his studies with Alexandrova-Kochetova at the Moscow Conservatory in 1878, he made successful débuts that year in both Moscow and St Petersburg, remaining at the Mariinsky Theatre until his untimely death at the height of his career. He took part in the premières of important Russian operas, notably as Konchak in *Prince Igor* (1890) and as Bermyata in *The Snow Maiden* (1882). A true *basso profondo*, he excelled in comic and fantastic parts, but his extensive repertory also embraced more conventional roles, such as Ivan Susanin and the Village Head (*May Night*).   BORIS SEMEONOFF

Kósa, György (*b* Budapest, 24 April 1897; *d* Budapest, 16 Aug 1984). Hungarian composer. At the age of ten he became a pupil of Bartók, and he studied composition with Kodály at the Budapest Academy of Music (1908–12); he also studied the piano at the academy (1908–15) and with Dohnányi (1915–16). In 1916–17 he was co-répétiteur at the Royal Opera House in Budapest, where he took part in the first performance of Bartók's *The Wooden Prince*. He undertook concert tours in Europe and north Africa, and in 1920–21 was a theatre conductor in Tripoli. He then settled in Budapest and from 1927 was professor of piano at the academy. He was awarded the Erkel Prize (1955) and other national awards.

In outlook, Kósa showed marked affinities with Mahler, combining complexity with an almost childlike naivety. Man's greatest problems stand at the centre of his work, and this preoccupation is reflected in the subtitles of his symphonies (e.g. 'Man and the Universe'). Existence, fate and men's beliefs, and beauty and inspiration drawn from the widest possible cultural background, embracing Greek and Chinese, Old French and Scandinavian civilizations, coloured his thought. His music was influenced neither by folk music nor by serialism. The striving gestures of a believing soul in conflict with the world characterize his type of expressionism, in which the eruptive statement of his experience appears more important than the form that the statement takes.

A király palástja [The King's Cloak], 1926 (3, M. Kósa, after H. C. Andersen: *The Emperor's New Clothes*)
Az két lovagok [The Two Knights], 1934 (comic op, 3, A. Keleti), Budapest, 1937
Cenodoxus, 1942 (mystery op, 3, M. Kósa, after J. J. Biedermann and J. Gregor)
Anselmus diák [The Scholar Anselmus], 1945 (3, G. Devecseri, after E. T. A. Hoffmann: *Der goldne Topf*)
A méhek [The Bees], 1946 (1, R. Meller)
Tartuffe, 1951 (comic op, 3, F. Jankovich and G. Kósa, after Molière), Budapest Radio, 1952
Pázmán lovag [Knight Pázmán], 1962–3 (comic op, L. Hollós-Korvin)
Kocsonya Mihály házassága [The Marriage of Mihály Kocsonya], 1971 (comic op, after Hung. 18th century)
Kiálts, város [City, Shout!], 1980–81 (G. Kósa, after M. Szabó)
                                                    FERENC BÓNIS

Koshetz [Koshits], **Nina** (**Pavlovna**) (*b* Kiev, 18/30 Dec 1894; *d* Santa Ana, CA, 14 or 15 May 1965). Ukrainian soprano. The daughter of Pavel Koshitz, a leading tenor at the Bol'shoy, she was trained in Moscow, first as a pianist, and then as a singer under Sergey Taneyev. She made her début as Tatyana in *Yevgeny Onegin* with the Zimin Private Opera company in 1913, and remained with the company until 1919. During this period she also toured Russia and in 1917 appeared as Tatyana at the Mariinsky, Petrograd. Other roles included Lisa in *The Queen of Spades*, Marina in *Boris Godunov*, Tosca, and Electra in Taneyev's *Oresteya*. In 1920 she left Russia and joined the Chicago Opera Association, singing Fata Morgana in the première of *The Love for Three Oranges* in 1921. She sang as a guest artist with the Russian Opera Company in New York and on tour in 1922, and in 1924 was at the Colón, Buenos Aires. The later 1920s were spent largely in France, where she sang at the Paris Opéra in 1925, and at the Trocadéro in 1927 in the first Paris production of Rimsky-Korsakov's *Sadko*. There were further concert seasons and occasional operatic appearances in Europe and the USA; in 1940 she retired to Hollywood, where she managed a restaurant and appeared in several films. Her few recordings, prized by collectors, show a clear, steady voice excitingly combined with an imaginative, emotionally charged style.

J. Dennis: 'Nina Pavlovna Koshetz', *Record Collector*, xvii (1967–8), 53–61 [with discography by V. Liff]
M. Scott: *The Record of Singing*, ii (London, 1979), 23–5
J. B. STEANE

Košice (Hung. Kassa). Town in eastern Slovakia, formerly under Austro-Hungarian government. As Kassa, it was an important centre for Hungarian opera troupes in the early 19th century, with a resident company, 1828–33; it remained a leading centre up to World War I. A new theatre was built in 1899.

The Košice State Opera was founded in 1945. It performs the standard repertory as well as native compositions. Conductors include Tibor Frešo, Ladislav Holoubek, Ján Kende, Zdeněk Bílek and Richard Zimmer; directors include Drahomíra Bargárová and Blažena Hončarivová. Košice Opera's major artistic achievements include productions of Cikker's *Beg Bajazid* (1957), Suchoň's *Svätopluk* (1960), Fibich's *Bouře* ('The Tempest', 1961), Iša Krejčí's *Pozdvižení v Efesu* ('Revolt in Ephesus', 1963), Cikker's *Vzkriesenie* ('Resurrection', 1963), Ferenczy's *Nevšedná humoreska* ('Uncommon Humoresque', 1969), Suchoň's *The Whirlpool* (1975), Cikker's *Mr Scrooge* (1984) and Milan Novák's *Prestávka* ('The Interval', 1986).

Hudobné divadlo v Košiciach (1789–1989) [Music Theatre in Košice (1789–1989)] (Košice, 1991)   IGOR VAJDA

Košler, Zdeněk (*b* Prague, 25 March 1928). Czech conductor. He studied at the Prague Academy. In 1948 he joined the Prague National Theatre, where he made his conducting début with *Il barbiere di Siviglia* (1951), and he toured with the National Theatre company to Moscow (1955) and Brussels (1958). He won the 1956 International Conducting Competition at Besançon and the 1963 Mitropoulos Competition in New York, where he worked as assistant to Leonard Bernstein in 1963–4. He was artistic director of the Olomouc Opera (1958–62) and the Ostrava Opera (1962–6), and Generalmusikdirektor of the Berlin Komische Oper in association with Walter Felsenstein (1966–8). He conducted *Salome* at the Vienna Staatsoper in 1965, has toured in other European countries and since 1968 has been a frequent guest conductor in Japan. He was chief conductor of the Slovak National Opera, Bratislava, 1971–6, and artistic director and chief conductor at the Prague National Theatre from 1980–85, and again from 1989–91. He took part in the 1990 Martinů centenary season there, conducting *The Greek Passion*. His recordings include *The Bartered Bride* (1982) and *Libuše* (1983). His performances are deeply emotional yet balanced in character and his wide repertory includes much 20th-century music. He was named Artist of Merit in 1974 and National Artist in 1984.

I. Jirko: 'Třikrát Zdeněk Košler' [Three Times Zdeněk Košler], *HRO*, xxiii (1970), 195
'Košlerův nástup v Bratislavě' [Košler's Appearance in Bratislava], *HRO*, xxv (1972), 109
V. Pospíšil, ed.: *Národní divadlo a jeho předchůdci* [The National Theatre and its Predecessors] (Prague, 1988)
ALENA NĚMCOVÁ, NOËL GOODWIN

Kospoth, Otto Carl Erdmann, Freiherr von (*b* Mühltroff, Vogtland, 25 Nov 1753; *d* Mühltroff, 23 June 1817). German composer. He attended the Ritterakademie at Leignitz (now Legnica). In 1776 he became chamberlain and *maître des plaisirs* at the Prussian court, where he often played the violin or cello in performances with Frederick the Great. He was also an excellent keyboard player. In 1783 he visited Italy, spending at least six months in Venice. Kospoth remained a chamberlain at the court of Friedrich Wilhelm II, but in 1789 returned to his estates at Mühltroff. In 1790 he was made a Reichsgraf. Whereas earlier he had appeared a typically versatile Enlightenment figure, engaging in chemical, physical and mechanical experiments and literary activities as well as music, in the 1790s he turned increasingly to necromancy, alchemy, spiritualism and other eccentric pursuits with a strong megalomaniac colouring. He lavished a great deal of money on his estates, which he eventually lost apart from the right to an apartment in the castle. When the castle caught fire in 1817 he refused to leave it, claiming to be impervious to fire.

Kospoth's music is agreeable and fluent. Several of his Singspiels had long runs and several productions. According to Gerber, who judged him 'among the most industrious and inventive dilettantes', he was working on a Singspiel on Lessing's *Emilia Galotti* in 1790, but it was never produced.

Der Freund deutscher Sitten (Operette, 3, G. W. Burmann), Berlin, Döbbelin's, 25 Sept 1778
Adrast und Isidore, oder Die Serenate (komische Oper, 2, C. F. Bretzner, after Molière: *Le sicilien*), Berlin, Döbbelin's, 16 Oct 1779, *D-Bds*, songs (Berlin, n.d.)
Der Irrwisch, oder Endlich fand er sie (komische Oper, 3, Bretzner), Berlin, Döbbelin's, 2 Oct 1780, songs (Berlin, n.d.)
Timante ed Emirene, oder Die Macht der Liebe, 1783, unperf.
Das Fest der Schäfer (divertimento), Berlin, 18 Oct 1787
Der kluge Jakob (komische Oper, 3, J. Wetzel), Berlin, National, 26 Feb 1788, *Bds*
Bella und Fernando, oder Die Satyr (Operette, 1, C. A. Vulpius), Berlin, 1790
Der Mädchenmarkt zu Ninive (komische Oper, 2, K. A. Herklots), Hamburg, Gänsemarkt, 3 Sept 1793, excerpts (Leipzig, 1795)

Undated: Il trionfo d'Arianna, *Dlb*; Karoline, oder Die Parforcejagd (Operette, 4, C. A. G. Seidel), unperf.

GerberL; *MGG* (T. M. Langner)
C. H. Richter: *Die Herrschaft Mühltroff und ihre Besitzer* (Leipzig, 1857)
T. Bauman: *North German Opera in the Age of Goethe* (Cambridge, 1985)

Kostić, Dušan (*b* Zagreb, 23 Jan 1925). Serbian composer. He studied at the Academy of Music in Belgrade, where he later taught. Although mainly interested in composing orchestral works and cantatas, he wrote a musical burlesque, *Majstori su prvi ljudi* ('Craftsmen are Top People'; Belgrade, 23 April 1962), to a libretto by Jovan Putnik based on Kosta Trifković's comedies *Čestitam* ('I Congratulate') and *Ljubavno pismo* ('The Love's Letter'). In this stage work, which has elements of operetta, farce and incidental music, the composer displays his leanings towards caricature, the grotesque, irony and parody, which are also found in his other compositions; he emphasizes the social intrigues of 19th-century Novi Sad by the use of urban songs and *parlando*.

V. Peričić: *Muzički stvaraoci u Srbiji* [Musical Creators in Serbia] (Belgrade, 1969)
ROKSANDA PEJOVIĆ

Koszut, Urszula (*b* Pszczyna, 13 Dec 1940). Polish soprano. She studied in Katowice and Warsaw and made her début in 1967 at Stuttgart in the title role of *Lucia di Lammermoor*, then sang in Frankfurt, Warsaw, Vienna and Munich. After her American début at New Orleans as Norina in 1969, she sang the Queen of Night at Glyndebourne (1970), Zerbinetta in Amsterdam, Oscar in Chicago (1972), Mimì in Toronto (1972) and Violetta for Scottish Opera (1973). Her repertory includes the four soprano roles in *Les contes d'Hoffmann*, Gilda, Aminta (*Die schweigsame Frau*), Electra (*Idomeneo*), Konstanze and Countess Almaviva, which she sang at Covent Garden (1982). Her light, agile voice encompasses both lyrical and coloratura roles.
ELIZABETH FORBES

Köth, Erika (*b* Darmstadt, 15 Sept 1927; *d* Speyer, 21 Feb 1989). German soprano. She began her musical studies in Darmstadt in 1942 with Elsa Blank and after an interruption resumed them in 1945. She made her début in 1948 at Kaiserslautern as Philine in *Mignon*; engagements followed at Karlsruhe (1950–53), Munich (from 1953) and Berlin (from 1961). She sang at Covent Garden in 1953 with the Munich company as the Fiakermilli (*Arabella*) and the Italian Soprano in the English première of *Capriccio*. She appeared regularly at Salzburg (1955–64) as the Queen of Night and Konstanze, and at Bayreuth (1965–8) as the Woodbird. It was as a coloratura singer that she established herself in Germany. Her repertory included Lucia, Donna Elvira, Susanna, Violetta, Gilda, Sophie and Zerbinetta. She also sang Stravinsky's Nightingale and Anne Trulove.
HAROLD ROSENTHAL/R

Kott, František Bedřich (*b* Zběšičky, 15 April 1808; *d* Brno, 29 April 1884). Czech composer. He was a member of the Brno theatre company. Most of his works are small in scale, but they include two operas. The two-act *Žižkův dub* ('Žižka's Oak'), on a libretto by M. Mikšíček, after a play by V. K. Klicpera, was given its première in Brno on 28 November 1841. In 1863 Kott submitted a three-act adaptation of it, with the title *Poklad* or *Nejdražší poklad* ('The Treasure' or 'The Dearest Treasure', libretto by A. A. Pozděna), for Count Jan Harrach's competiton for the best original Czech opera and libretto. His second opera, *Dalibor* (*Dalibor in Gefängnissthurm auf den Hradschin in Prag*; *Dalibor, Die Gefängnisse auf den Hradschin in Prag*), in three acts to a libretto by Perger, is believed lost; only one scene was performed, in Brno in 1844. Kott's operas failed to receive critical acclaim: they were considered lacking in weight, too eclectic and too obviously based on folk melodies.

A. Bezdíčková-Ingerlová: *František Bedřich Kott a jeho zpěvohra Žižkův dub* [Kott and his Opera Žižka's Oak] (thesis, U. of Brno, 1975)

P. Daněk and J. Vyšohlídová: 'Dokumenty k operní soutěži o cenu hraběte Harracha' [Documents concerning Count Harrach's Opera Prize Competition], *MMC*, no.30 (1983), 147–50

J. Tyrrell: *Czech Opera* (Cambridge, 1988)
MICHAELA FREEMANOVÁ

Kotzebue, August von (*b* Weimar, 3 May 1761; *d* Mannheim, 23 March 1819). German dramatist, diplomat and man of letters. His adventurous career included appointments as lawyer and theatre secretary, Russian court councillor and editor, poet and Russian consul. His satires, quarrels, and above all his duty to report to the Tsar of Russia on all affairs of interest in Germany and France, made him many enemies, and he was assassinated in 1819 by a student who suspected him of being a traitor and spy.

Kotzebue's immense output of plays includes a majority of ephemera, yet he dominated the repertory of German and Austrian (and many foreign) theatres for a considerable part of the 19th century, and the best of his comedies (including *Die deutschen Kleinstädter*, the first of a prodigious number of plays set in the self-important country town of Krähwinkel, the German equivalent of Gotham) are still effective. Beethoven wrote music for his *Die Ruinen von Athen* and *König Stephan*; Boieldieu, Kreutzer, Lortzing, Reichardt and Spohr are among composers who set his works; and Schubert wrote two operas to Kotzebue texts: *Der Spiegelritter* (?1812, incomplete), and *Des Teufels Lustschloss* (1813–14).

plays; parenthesized dates are publication dates

Der Eremit auf Formentara (1784): composer unknown, 1784; E. W. Wolf, 1786; P. Ritter, 1788; C. L. Dieter, 1791; M. Stegmayer, 1793

Menschenhass und Reue (1789): P. Generali, 1805, as Misantropia e pentimento; C. Conti, 1823

Der Papagey [*Der Papagei*] (1792): Wolf, c1790

Sultan Wampum, oder Die Wünsche (1794): J. Elsner, 1787, as Sultan Wampum, czyli Nieroztropne życzenie; C. D. Stegmann, 1791; C. D. von Dittersdorf, 1795, as Der Schach von Schiras

Graf Benjowsky, oder Die Verschwörung auf Kamtschatka (1795): A. Boieldieu, 1800, as Béniowski, ou Les exilés du Kamchatka; T. Welsh, 1811, as Kamchatka, or The Slave's Tribute; T. S. Cooke and others, 1826, as Benyowsky, or The Exiles of Kamschatka; F. Doppler, 1847, as Benyovsky, vagy Akamcsatkai száműzött

Das Dorf im Gebirge (1798): J. Weigl, 1798; K. T. Eisrich, 1812

Der Wildfang (1798): F. X. Süssmayr, 1797; A. L. H. Ohmann, c1810, as Der fürstliche Wildfang

Der Schreiner: P. Wranitzky, 1799

Johanna von Montfaucon (1800): Wranitzky, 1799

Die kluge Frau im Walde, oder Der stumme Ritter (1801): I. Seyfried, 1813

Des Teufels Lustschloss (1801): I. Walter, 1797; composer unknown, 1799, as Das bezauberte Schloss; Dieter, 1802; J. F. Reichardt, 1802, as Das Zauberschloss; Schubert, comp. 1813–14; Seyfried, 1816, as Der Rosenhügel am Blocksberg

Die Kreuzfahrer (1802): Reichardt, 1802; Seyfried, 1809; Spohr, 1845

Der Spiegelritter (1802): V. Mašek, 1784; Walter, 1791; C. C. Agthe, 1795; J. K. Mainberger, 1796; A. H. Hinze, 1797; F. Schubert, comp. c1812

Fanchon, das Leiermädchen (1805): F. H. Himmel, 1804

Eulenspiegel (1806): T. Ferguson, 1801; J. P. S. Schmidt, 1806

Die gefährliche Nachbarschaft (1806): ?F. Stein, 1815

Das Lustspiel am Fenster (1807): L. Gastinel, 1857

Das Gespenst (1808): K. Guhr, 1808 (rev. 1815 as Deodata)

Das Grenzstädtchen: P. J. Riotte, 1808

Der blinde Gärtner, oder Die blühende Aloe (1809): P. J. von Lindpaintner, 1813 or 1815

Das Sammtrock (1811): A. Gyrowetz, 1809

Das zugemauerte Fenster (1811): Gyrowetz, 1810

Feodora [*Feodore*] (1812): Seyfried, 1811; Guhr, 1811; Eisrich, 1811; L. K. Reinecke, 1812; Schmidt, 1812; C. Kreutzer, 1812

Das unsichtbare Mädchen (1812): G. B. Bierey, 1811
Belas Flucht (1813): J. Ruzitska, 1822
Die Alpenhütte (1815): Kreutzer, 1815; J. Miller, 1815; Schmidt, 1816
Hans Max Giesbrecht von der Humpenburg (1815): W. Müller, 1814; J. A. Gürrlich, 1815; Lindpaintner, 1816
Der Käficht [Käfig] (1815): F. X. Kleinheinz, 1816; J. Fusz, 1816
Pervonte, oder Die Wünsche (1815): Reinecke, 1814; Lindpaintner, 1816
Die Prinzessin von Cacambo (1815): Ohmann, 1812; Lindpaintner, 1814; Müller, 1814
Der Rehbock, oder Die schuldlosen Schuldbewussten (1816): A. Lortzing, 1842, as Der Wildschütz, oder Die Stimme der Natur
Alfred der Grosse (1817): Reinecke, 1818
Der gerade Weg [ist] der Beste (1817): Walter, 1790
Die hölzernen Säbel (1817): Riotte and P. Röth, 1822, as Staberl als Freischütz
Der Kyffhäuser Berg (1817): Schmidt, 1817; H. A. Marschner, 1822
Hermann und Thusnelda (1819): Miller, 1815; B. A. Weber, 1819
Das Rosenmädchen (1819): Lindpaintner, 1818

*

A. von Kotzebue: *Sämtliche dramatische Werke* (Leipzig, 1827–9)
W. von Kotzebue: *A. von Kotzebue: Urtheile der Zeitgenossen und der Gegenwart* (Dresden, 1881)
C. Rabany: *Kotzebue, sa vie et son temps, ses oeuvres dramatiques* (Paris and Nancy, 1893)
K. Goedeke: *Grundriss zur Geschichte der deutschen Dichtung*, v (Dresden, 2/1893), 270–88; xv (Berlin, 2/1966), 151–278, 1138–40
L. F. Thompson: *Kotzebue: a Survey of his Progress in France, and England* (Paris, 1928)
F. Stock: *Kotzebue im literarischen Leben der Goethezeit* (Düsseldorf, 1971)   PETER BRANSCOMBE

Koukos, Periklis (*b* Athens, 3 Jan 1960). Greek composer. He studied composition with Yannis Andreou Papaioannou and Dimitris Dragatakis in Athens and with Hans Werner Henze and Paul Patterson in London. Since 1990 he has taught composition at the Athens Conservatory. His first opera, *Merlinos o magos* ('Merlin the Magician'), is a one-act children's *opera buffa*. *O Conroy ke i kopies tou* ('Conroy's Other Selves', 1990), which deals with the relationship between an artist and his creations, is conceived as a set of numbers following each other in flowing succession. Behind the subtle and captivating melodies and themes, sometimes with remote echoes of Weill and Stravinsky, lies a strictly organized tonal and harmonic plan. Koukos completed the vocal score of a three-act opera based on Tassos Roussos' novel, *Ta hirografa tou Manuel Salinas* ('The Manuscript of Manuel Salinas'), in September 1991 and that to *Oniro kalokerinis nychtas* ('A Midsummer Night's Dream') in February 1992.

Merlinos o magos [Merlin the Magician], 1987–9 (children's ob, 1, Y. Seferis)
O Conroy ke i kopies tou [Conroy's Other Selves] (1, A. Mouriki), Athens, Olympia, 4 March 1990 (Athens, 1990)
Ta hirografa tou Manuel Salinas [The Manuscript of Manuel Salinas], 1991 (3, after T. Roussos)
Oniro kalokerinis nychtas [A Midsummer Night's Dream] (opéra-ballet, 2, Y. Karahissaridis, after W. Shakespeare), Piraiévs, Municipal, May 1992

*

A. Kostios: 'Me aformi to ergo ke ya to ergo' [On the Occasion of the Work and About the Work] (Athens, 1990) [programme notes for Conroy's Other Selves]
G. Leotsakos: 'Periklis Koukos: O Conroy ke i kopies tou', *Prin* (Athens, 18 March 1990)
A. Kostios: Introduction to P. Koukos: *O Conroy ke i kopies tou* (Athens, 1991)   GEORGE LEOTSAKOS

Koulhaas, Christina Louisa (*b c*1700; *d* after 1735). German soprano. She and her husband, the bass Johann Ferdinand Koulhaas, were in the Kapelle of Duke August Wilhelm in Brunswick. In 1722 she went to the Hamburg Gänsemarkt Opera as a substitute for one of the Hamburg singers engaged by the Copenhagen court. She sang the roles of Statira in Orlandini's *Arsace*, Placidia in Telemann's *Sieg der Schönheit* and Lucinda in F. B. Conti's *Don Chisciotte*, all in 1722. She was re-engaged by the Gänsemarkt Opera for six months in 1726, at a salary of 400 Reichsthalers, and probably sang in Handel's *Ottone* (in the German translation by J. G. Glauche).

*

G. F. Schmidt: *Die frühdeutsche Oper und die musikdramatische Kunst Georg Caspar Schürmanns*, i (Regensburg, 1934), 124, 127ff, 131
K. Zelm: 'Die Sänger der Hamburger Gänsemarkt-Oper', *HJbMw*, iii (1978), 35–73, esp.58–9   HANS JOACHIM MARX

Kounadis, Arghyris (*b* Constantinople, 14 Feb 1924). Greek composer. He studied the piano at the Athens Conservatory (graduating in 1952) and composition with Yannis Andreou Papaioannou at the Hellenic Conservatory (graduating in 1956). He pursued his studies at the Freiburg Hochschule für Musik, where his composition teacher was Wolfgang Fortner. In 1963 he was appointed director of the 'Musica Viva' concerts and assistant professor to Fortner, becoming professor in 1972. His operas represent by far the most important phase of his career. They are mostly extended one-act works for chamber ensemble and, recently, tape (first used in *Die Bassgeige*, which involves a 'salon orchestra' plus tapes with music for nine double basses). The make-up of the ensemble is dictated by the specific needs of the text, whose language (German or Greek) also conditions the vocal writing. The music, although essentially atonal, tends to incorporate a great variety of codes, and even quotations – in *Teiresias*, for instance, from Bellini's *Norma*, Maillart's *Les dragons de Villars*, Saint-Saëns' *Samson et Dalila* and Donizetti's *Lucia di Lammermoor*. Similarly, in *Die Bassgeige* Kounadis had recourse to Verdi as well as to dance forms including gavottes, tangos and waltzes, while in *Lysistrate* he used elements of Greek folk music and Byzantine melos. In *The Return*, a modern approach to the myth of Orestes and Electra, he used speech and singing to contrast two different psychological climates. Kounadis has also composed seven ballets and many songs.

The Return (1, K. Cicellis and C. Clerides, after Cicellis: *The Way to Colonos*), 1961; rev. 1974 and 1987–8 as O Gyrismos, Athens, National, 23 March 1991
Der Gummisarg, 1962 (1, V. Ziogas, Ger. trans. O. Steininger), Bonn, Stadt, 8 April 1968
Die verhexten Notenständer (music theatre, 1, after K. Valentin), Freiburg, Städtische Bühnen, 26 June 1971
Teiresias (revue, 10 scenes, Kounadis and S. Schoenbohm), Heidelberg, Städtische Bühnen, 18 April 1975
Der Ausbruch (1, W. Jens), Bayreuth, Städtische Bühnen, 25 Aug 1975
Die Bassgeige (opera semiseria, 5 scenes, Schoenbohm, W. Reuter, L. Lütkehaus and Kounadis, after A. P. Chekhov), Freiburg, Städtische Bühnen, 13 Jan 1979
Lysistrate (1, Lütkehaus and Kounadis, after Aristophanes), Lübeck, Bühnen der Hansastadt, 31 March 1983
Der Sandmann, 1983–4 (1, P. Sievert, after E. T. A. Hoffmann), Hamburg, Staatsoper, 7 Feb 1987

*

M. Dounias: *Moussikokritika* (Athens, 1963)
N. Slonimsky: 'New Music in Greece', *MQ*, li (1965), 225–35, esp. 231

G. Leotsakos: 'Kounadi "Gyrismos" ke ... gyrismos' [Kounadis's O *Gyrismos* and Homecoming], *Epikerotita* (27 March 1991)

GEORGE LEOTSAKOS

Koussevitzky [Kusevitsky], **Sergey (Alexandrovich)** (*b* Vïshniy-Volochyok, Tver', 14/26 July 1874; *d* Boston, MA, 4 June 1951). American conductor of Russian birth. He joined the Bol'shoy Theatre Orchestra in 1894 as a double bass player but gradually turned to conducting, having acquired some knowledge of method from watching Nikisch. His successful public début in 1908 launched an international career and after the 1917 Revolution he left the USSR for Europe. In Paris he conducted *Boris Godunov*, *Khovanshchina*, *Prince Igor* and *The Queen of Spades*, but otherwise was seldom concerned with opera. He later set up the Koussevitzky Music Foundation in the USA (his home from 1924), its funds to be used to commission new works from composers of all nationalities. *Peter Grimes* (1945) was the foundation's first commissioned opera.

NOËL GOODWIN

Kouznetsov, Maria. *See* KUZNETSOVA, MARIYA NIKOLAYEVNA.

Koval' [Kovalyov], **Marian Viktorovich** (*b* Pristan' Vozneseniya, Olonets province, 4/17 Aug 1907; *d* Moscow, 15 Feb 1971). Russian composer. He studied in Nizhniy Novgorod (1918–21), in Petrograd and at the Moscow Conservatory (1925–30) with M. F. Gnesin; he also studied composition privately with N. Ya. Myaskovsky. In the 1920s he was a member of Prokoll, a 'production collective' of composers whose aim was to write music in the spirit of the new revolutionary era, and of the Russian Association of Proletarian Musicians (RAPM), 1925–32. He began his creative career as a composer of choral pieces, and such works were to form the greater part of his output. From 1957 to 1961 he was artistic director of the Pyatnitsky Choir. His style has its roots in folk music, with distinctively Russian, lyrical melodies.

Koval' began *Zemlya vstayot* ('The Earth Arises') in 1932. Conceived in four acts, the work, which reflects the ideology of RAPM, was never completed. The first act of a later version of the opera was performed at the small hall of the Moscow Conservatory by an amateur group. *Volk i semero kozlyat* ('The Wolf and Seven Kids') was first conceived for a radio performance, although it has often been staged. It was revived in Leningrad in 1966, the same year that it was produced in a new version at the Children's Music Theatre in Moscow. The most celebrated composition by Koval' is the monumental oratorio, *Yemel'yan Pugachyov* (1938), which the composer subsequently converted into a five-act opera of the same name. The libretto, by the Ural poet V. Kamensky and based on one of his poems, is rich in metaphor and shows a folk mentality which had attracted the composer as early as 1934. When Koval' revised this folk-historical drama in the mid-1950s, the poet N. Aseyev contributed to the libretto. *Sevastopol'tsï* ('Inhabitants of Sevastopol') is based on M. Tevelev's story *Posledniy kater* ('The Last Cutter'). Koval' began to work with this story in 1943, initially completing a one-act opera, *Posledniy kater*, which received a concert and radio performance that year. The composer continued with the idea, and in 1945 completed the four-act *Sevastopol'tsï*, which incorporates *Posledniy kater* as the third act.

Usad'ba [The Farmstead], 1929 (comic op, 3, J. Anisimov, after A. S. Pushkin: *Graf Nulin*); rev. as Graf Nulin, 1949 (S. Gorodetsky); unpubd
Zemlya vstayot [The Earth Arises], 1932 (4, after A. Hidas: *Megmozdul a Föld*, Russ. trans. by L. Kochetkov), inc., unperf.; rev. (musical-dramatic scene), Act 1 only, Moscow, Conservatory Small Hall, *c*1932, vs (Moscow, 1932)
Volk i semero kozlyat [The Wolf and Seven Kids], 1939–40 (children's op, prol., 3, Koval' and E. Manucharova), Tashkent, 1 July 1941; rev. 1951; rev., Moscow, Children's Music Theatre, 1966, vs (Moscow, 1969)
Yemel'yan Pugachyov, 1940 (folk-historical drama, prol., 4, V. Kamensky), Perm', 7 Nov 1942 [orchd D. Rogal'-Levitsky], vs (Moscow, 1946); rev. (added text by N. Aseyev), Moscow, Stanislavsky–Nemirovich-Danchenko Music Theatre, 1 Feb 1959, vs (Moscow, 1955) [based on the composer's oratorio of the same name]
Posledniy kater [The Last Cutter] (1, after M. Tevelev), concert perf., 1943 [became Act 3 of Sevastopol'tsï]
Sevastopol'tsï [Inhabitants of Sevastopol], 1943–5 (4, epilogue, N. L. Braun and S. D. Spassky, after Tevelev: *Posledniy kater*), concert perf., Moscow, 9 May 1945, vs (Moscow, 1945); stage, Perm', 28 Nov 1946; rev. 1949 [Posledniy kater incorporated as Act 3]

*

D. Kabalevsky: 'Volk i semero kozlyat', *SovM* (1940), no.11, pp.43–9
B. Yarustovsky: 'O "Yemel'yane Pugachyove" M. Kovalya' [On 'Yemel'yan Pugachyov'], *SovM* (1940), no.2, pp.22–44
——: 'Novoye i staroye v "Yemel'yane Pugachyove"' [Old and New in 'Yemel'yan Pugachyov'], *SovM* (1959), no.4, pp.30–40
J. G. Polyanovksy: *Marian Koval'* (Moscow, 1968)

GALINA GRIGOR'YEVA

Kovařovic, Karel (*b* Prague, 9 Dec 1862; *d* Prague, 6 Dec 1920). Czech conductor and composer. He studied the clarinet, piano and harp at the Prague Conservatory (1873–9) and composition with Fibich (1878–82). From 1879 to 1885 he played the harp in the orchestra of the Provisional (later National) Theatre in Prague. In 1885 he was appointed conductor at the Czech Theatre in Brno and in 1886 headed the newly founded Jan Pištěk Opera Company at Plzeň. Later he was a singing coach at, then director of, František Pivoda's Prague school for singers (1896–8); he was also one of the first conductors of the Czech Philharmonic Orchestra. In view of his conducting and theatre experience Kovařovic was appointed head of opera at the National Theatre in Prague, a post he held until his death. His theatre duties after 1900 all but halted his activities as a composer.

Kovařovic was the first great conductor at the National Theatre and he significantly raised the level of performance. He devoted a great deal of time to Czech opera (he conducted the première of Dvořák's *Rusalka* in 1901) and was interested in French and German composers, particularly Wagner and Strauss. After 1910 attacks were made on his choice of repertory. He rejected the first version of Janáček's *Jenůfa*, which in 1903 he returned as unperformable, but in 1916 conducted it in a version which he himself had revised, a performance which marked the beginning of Janáček's renown. Kovařovic also revised Dvořák's operas for dramatic reasons, and for publication.

As an opera composer, Kovařovic was not particularly original, but he had an intimate knowledge of how a theatre should be run and understood how to write for orchestra and voices. He was influenced by Dvořák (to a lesser extent by Smetana and Fibich) and also by French opera composers, such as Delibes and

Massenet. For a Czech, this French orientation was quite exceptional and did not meet with understanding among Czech critics, who were more used to music based on German and Austrian models. The blend is apparent in *Psohlavci* ('The Dogs'-heads'), which deals with a rebellion against a landowner in south-west Bohemia that took place in 1695; here Kovařovic used French-style music to characterize aristocratic society and elements of folk music for the Czech rustic environment. It is also a feature of *Na Starém bělidle* ('At the Old Bleachery'), a series of four scenes stressing the idyllic quality of Czech country life. Kovařovic's honours included membership of the Czech Academy of Sciences, and in 1910 he was made an Officer of the Académie Française.

first performed at Prague, National Theatre, unless otherwise stated

Ženichové [The Bridegrooms] (comic op, 3, A. Koukl, after K. Š. Macháček), 15 May 1884, *Cs-Pnm*, selections arr. pf (Prague, *c*1884)

Cesta oknem [The Way through the Window] (comic op, 1, E. Züngel, after E. Scribe and G. Lemoine), 11 Feb 1886, *Pnm**, vs (Prague, 1885); rev. 1914, 1920

Noc Šimona a Judy [The Night of SS Simon and Jude] (comic op, 3, K. Šípek, after P. d'Alarcón: *El sombrero de tres picos*), 5 Nov 1892, *Pnm**, selections arr. pf (Prague, *c*1893)

Edip král [King Oedipus] (opera-parody, 3, A. Nevšímal), Prague, Žofín Hall, 19 March 1894, vs (Prague, 1895)

Psohlavci [The Dogs'-heads] (3, Šípek, after A. Jirásek), 24 April 1898, *Pnm*, vs (Prague, 1898)

Na Starém bělidle [At the Old Bleachery] (4 scenes, Šípek, after B. Němcová: *Babička*), 22 Nov 1901, vs (Prague, 1910); reorchd version, 17 Dec 1916, *Pnm** (Prague, 1951)

Slib [The Promise], *c*1905 (Šípek, after O. Feuillet), inc.; prol. only, orchd R. Zamrzla, 9 Dec 1921; MS Prague, National Theatre Archive

Incomplete and unperformed: Armida, 1888–95 (J. Vrchlický, after T. Tasso) [4 acts planned, only 1 completed; further frag. in sketch]; Crespo (after P. Calderón de la Barca) [frag.]; Flétna [The Flute], *c*1905 (J. Kvapil) [sketch]

*

Z. Nejedlý: *Česká moderní zpěvohra po Smetanovi* [Modern Czech Opera after Smetana] (Prague, 1910), 221–85

H. Doležil: 'Karel Kovařovic', *České umění dramatické*, ii: *Zpěvohra* [Czech Dramatic Art: Opera], ed. J. Hutter and Z. Chalabala (Prague, 1941), 182–95

O. Šourek: 'Karel Kovařovic a Vrchlického Armida', *Smetana*, xxxvi (1943), 53–5

F. Pala: *Opera Národního divadla v období Otakara Ostrčila* [The Opera of the National Theatre at the Time of Ostrčil], ii (Prague, 1964), 41, 43, 80–86

J. Němeček: *Opera Národního divadla v období Karla Kovařovice* [The Opera of the National Theatre at the Time of Kovařovic] (Prague, 1968–9)

J. Tyrrell: *Czech Opera* (Cambridge, 1988)   JITKA LUDVOVÁ

Koven, (Henry Louis) Reginald de. See DE KOVEN, REGINALD.

Kovno (Russ.). KAUNAS.

Kowalski, Henri (*b* Paris, 1841; *d* Bordeaux, 8 July 1916). French pianist and composer of Polish and Irish descent. At the Paris Conservatoire he studied the piano under Marmontel, Prudent and Anatole Petit and composition under Carafa and Samuel David. He worked as a pianist at the Opéra before embarking on a concert career in 1858. His first opera, *Gilles de Bretagne*, was produced unsuccessfully by Vizentini in Paris in 1877 and revived at Brest in 1880. That year he travelled to Melbourne to give a series of concerts and subsequently toured widely in Australia. His *Vercingétorix* was performed in Sydney and Melbourne

in 1881 and was also given in June 1899 at the Casino di Dinan, Brittany. While working as the overseas correspondent to *Le Figaro*, he began to work on his 'Australian' opera, *Moustique*, to a libretto by the Melbourne writer Marcus Clarke. *Moustique* had its première in Brussels in 1883 and was performed in Sydney in 1889. Kowalski's music was once widely performed and fashionable but now even his fame as 'the Prince of the Pianoforte' has been forgotten. The manuscripts of most of his operas are held in the Kowalski archives in the Bibliothèque de Dinan, Brittany.

Gilles de Bretagne (4, A. Péronnet and A. Silvestre), Paris, Lyrique, 24 Dec 1877, vs (Paris, 1878)

Vercingétorix, or Love and Patriotism (lyric drama, 3, M. Mainiel), Sydney, Garden Palace, 1 April 1881

Moustique (comic op, 3, M. Clarke), Brussels, Alcazar Royal, 1883

Les Laveuses de Minuit (comic op, 3), Dinan, Salle Philharmonique

Les Crétois, Montreal, Dec 1908

Le chevalier cupide (comic op), unperf.

DENNIS DAVISON, ELIZABETH WOOD

Kowalski, Jochen (*b* Wachow, Brandenburg, 30 Jan 1954). German countertenor. He studied in Berlin, making his début while still a student as David in *Die Meistersinger* with the Komische Oper, and then joined the company. He has appeared in Hamburg, Vienna, Munich, Houston, Amsterdam, Paris and Düsseldorf. His repertory includes the title roles of Handel's *Giustino* and *Giulio Cesare*, Ptolemy, Annius (*La clemenza di Tito*), Fyodor (*Boris*), Orlofsky and Britten's Oberon. He sang Gluck's Orpheus at Covent Garden during the Komische Oper's visit in 1989 and with the Royal Opera in 1991, when he also sang Orlofsky and Pharnaces (*Mitridate, re di Ponto*). Kowalski's voice, strong, sweet and flexible, is equally well suited to Baroque, Classical and 20th-century music, and he is a powerful and expressive actor.

ELIZABETH FORBES

Kowno (Pol.). KAUNAS.

Kox, Hans (*b* Arnhem, 19 May 1930). Dutch composer. After studies at the Utrecht Conservatory and with Henk Badings (1951–5), he became director of the Doetinchem Music School (1957–71) and thereafter returned to the Utrecht Conservatory to teach. He wrote his first large orchestral work in 1956 to a commission from the Concertgebouw Orchestra, and in 1970 *In Those Days*, a piece for two choral and three instrumental groups, won the Prix Italia. Kox's first opera, *Dorian Gray*, in two acts to his own libretto after Oscar Wilde's novel, was first performed at the Circustheater at Scheveningen (The Hague) on 30 March 1974. He revised the opera in 1976; the music is lyrical, colourful and theatrically effective. In 1991 he completed a second opera begun in 1980, *Das grüne Gesicht* (6 scenes, Kox, after G. Meyrink and L. Jacobowski).

*

W. F. Bon: 'Hans Kox's Opera Dorian Gray', *Sonorum Speculum*, no.54 (1973), 4–14

F. van Rossum: 'Dorian Gray, an Opera to strike Joy into a Director's Heart', *Key Notes* [Amsterdam], no.6 (1977), 12–18

A. van der Ven: 'Dutch Opera in Progress', *Key Notes*, no.19 (1984), 30–33

L. Samama: *Zeventig jaar Nederlandse muziek (1915–1985)* (Amsterdam, 1986), 211–15   JOS WOUTERS/LEO SAMAMA

Kozeluch [Koscheluch, Koželuh], **Johann Antonín** [Jan Evangelista Antonín Tomáš] (*b* Velvary, 14 Dec 1738; *d* Prague, 3 Feb 1814). Bohemian composer, a cousin of

Leopold Kozeluch. He studied music at school in Velvary, as a chorister at the Jesuit college in Březnice and in Prague with J. F. N. Seger. He then worked for a short time as Kapellmeister in Rakovník and cantor in Velvary. Between about 1763 and 1766 he lived in Vienna, where he studied composition with Gluck and Gassmann and recitative with Hasse. After his return to Prague he soon became renowned as a music teacher and was subsequently Kapellmeister at St Francis's Church at the Crusaders' monastery. He was appointed *cappellae magister* at St Vitus's Metropolitan Cathedral in 1784, and held this position until his death. Among his pupils were Václav Praupner and Leopold Kozeluch; he also taught composition to his two sons, Wenzel Franz (*b* 1784, a teacher of Joseph Proksch) and Vinzenz Emanuel (1780–1839), and to his daughter Barbara, a singer and pianist.

Kozeluch was one of the most important Bohemian composers in the second half of the 18th century and his music was performed well into the 19th century. His two operas, both in three acts to librettos by Metastasio, were performed in Prague, where previously Mysliveček had been the only native Czech composer to have had works staged. *Alessandro nell'Indie* (MS in *A-Wn*, fragments in *CS-Pnm*) was given in the spring of 1769 and *Il Demofoonte* (holograph in *Pnm*, 2 arias edited in Němeček) in the spring of 1771. They are in the *opera seria* style of Jommelli, with alternating recitatives and arias in abridged da capo form. Kozeluch made considerable use of accompanied recitative, especially in *Il Demofoonte*, and he used the orchestra to depict the dramatic situation and add harmonic depth to the accompaniments. Despite Italian inspiration and some traces of French *opéra comique* in the melodies, the fundamental Czech colouring of his idiom is unmistakable. His church music of this period is in the same operatic style and he adapted some opera arias for use in church.

AMZ, ii (1799–1800), 499; ix (1806–7), 67, 628

O. Kamper: *Hudební Praha v xviii. věku* [18th-Century Musical Prague] (Prague, 1936), 39–40, 195ff

R. Fikrle: *Jan Ev. Ant. Koželuh: život, dílo a osobnost svatovítského kapelníka* [J. E. A. Kozeluch: Life, Work and Personality of the St Vitus Kapellmeister] (Prague, 1946) [incl. list of works]

J. Němeček: *Zpěvy xvii. a xviii. století* [17th- and 18th-Century Songs] (Prague, 1956), 208ff

M. Poštolka: *Leopold Koželuh: život a dílo* [L. Kozeluch: Life and Works] (Prague, 1964) [incl. list of works]

W. Vetter: 'Tschechische Opernkomponisten', *Sborník prací filosofické fakulty brněnské university*, F9 (1965), 353

K. Hálová: *Opera Demofoonte J. A. Koželuha* (diss., U. of Prague, 1989)
MILAN POŠTOLKA

Kozeluch [Kotzeluch, Koželuh], **Leopold** [Jan Antonín, Ioannes Antonius] (*b* Velvary, 26 June 1747; *d* Vienna, 7 May 1818). Bohemian composer. He received his basic music education in Velvary and then studied music and law in Prague, where his first ballets and pantomimes were successfully performed, between 1771 and 1778. In 1778 he went to Vienna, quickly making a reputation as an excellent pianist, teacher and composer, and in 1785 he founded a music publishing house. After the accession of Emperor Franz II he was appointed Kammer Kapellmeister and Hofmusik Compositor (1792), posts he held until his death.

Kozeluch was one of the foremost representatives of Czech music in 18th-century Vienna. As a composer he devoted himself almost exclusively to instrumental works (especially for piano) and secular vocal music, though he also composed for the stage. His achievement in opera is difficult to assess, however, because only one work survives, *Gustav Wasa*, a typical one of its period.

Mazet [Le Muzet] (französische komische Oper, 2, L. Anseaume, after J. de La Fontaine), Vienna, Kärntnertor, 1780 ? or 1786

Didone abbandonata, before 1790 (os, 3, P. Metastasio), Vienna, Hof, 1795

Gustav Wasa, after ?1792 (grosse heroische Oper, 3), *CS-Pk*

G. J. Dlabacž: 'Versuch eines Verzeichnisses der vorzüglichern Tonkünstler in oder aus Böhmen', *Materialien zur alten und neuen Statistik von Böhmen*, ed. J. A. Riegger, xii (Leipzig and Prague, 1794), 249–50

Jb der Tonkunst von Wien und Prag (Prague, 1796), 33

G. J. Dlabacž: *Allgemeines historisches Künstler-Lexikon* (Prague, 1815)

O. E. Deutsch: 'Kozeluch ritrovato', *ML*, xxvi (1945), 47–50

M. Poštolka: *Leopold Koželuh: život a dílo* [Life and Works] (Prague, 1964) [with thematic catalogue, bibliography; Eng. and Ger. summary]
MILAN POŠTOLKA

Kozlovsky, Alexey Fedorovich (*b* Kiev, 2/15 Oct 1905; *d* Tashkent, 9 Jan 1977). Ukrainian composer. He began to compose at the age of six, and studied at the Kiev Conservatory (1917–19), the First Moscow Music Technical College and the Moscow Conservatory; he took conducting lessons from Khessin. On graduating in 1931 he made his début as a conductor at the Stanislavsky Opera Theatre, where he worked for several years, meanwhile making a reputation in the USSR and the USA as a composer. In 1936 he moved to Tashkent where he collected examples of Uzbek and Karakalpak folk music; he also composed in all genres and wrote articles on Uzbek folk music. He taught at the Tashkent Conservatory from 1944 and was principal conductor of the Uzbek Philharmonic SO (1949–57, 1960–66).

Kozlovsky was one of a number of leading Soviet composers working in Uzbekistan in the 1930s who tried to achieve a creative synthesis of European and Uzbek traditions. Though he was brought up on the music of the Russian Romantics and the French impressionists, he displayed a rare insight into the essence of Asian folklore. An inventive harmonist and orchestrator, he was drawn to programmatic orchestral genres, which provided opportunities for imaginative sonorities, and to the musical theatre. His works include Uzbek music dramas, written in collaboration with Uzbek composers. His chief opera is the heroic-historical *Ulugbek* (1942), whose subject is the fate of the grandson of Timur, the famous medieval thinker.

Khamza Khakim-Zade Niyazi, 1936, inc.

Davron ata (music drama, S. Abdul and K. Yashen), Tashkent, 8 Nov 1941, collab. T. Sadikov

Sherali (music drama, Kh. Gulyam), Tashkent, 15 Jan 1942, collab. S. N. Vasilenko and M. Ashrafi

Ulugbek (Kozlovsky and G. Gerus), Tashkent, 19 Nov 1942; rev. version, 1958

Afdal', 1942 (Gerus), unperf.

Mat' [The Mother], 1942, inc.

Podvig Bektasha [The Heroic Deed of Bektash], 1942 (M. Tursunov), unperf.

Tanavar [The Oriole] (Gerus), 1971
L.M. BUTIR

Kozlovsky, Ivan Semyonovich (*b* Mar'yanovka, Kiev province, 11/24 March 1900). Ukrainian tenor. He graduated from the Kiev Institute of Music and Drama in 1920, having made his début in 1918 at Poltava. He joined the Bol'shoy Theatre in 1926 and was made People's Artist of the USSR in 1940. Kozlovsky was the most popular Soviet singer of his time. The distinctive features of his singing were his clear, silvery tone and flexible upper register extending to *e″*, his remarkable technique, expressive use of words and finished phrasing. A versatile artist and a fine actor, he sang such contrasting roles as Lensky, Berendey (*The Snow Maiden*), Lohengrin and the Holy Fool (*Boris Godunov*). From 1938 to 1941 Kozlovsky directed his own opera company and took part in Gluck's *Orfeo ed Euridice* and Massenet's *Werther*.

G. Polyanovsky: *Ivan Semyonovich Kozlovsky* (Moscow and Leningrad, 1945)

V. S. Slyotov: *I. Kozlovsky* (Moscow and Leningrad, 1951)
I. M. YAMPOL'SKY

Krainik, Ardis Joan (*b* Manitowoc, WI, 8 March 1929). American director and administrator. She received the BA in speech from Northwestern University in 1951 and went on to study music there. She sang with the Lyric Opera of Chicago in supporting roles (1954–9) and became its assistant manager in 1960. In 1975 she was named artistic administrator, becoming general director in 1981, and has restored the company to financial health. Her 'Towards the 21st Century' initiative aims to encourage the performance of 20th-century opera; new works have included Argento's *The Voyage of Edgar Allan Poe* (1990) and Barber's *Antony and Cleopatra* (1991).
NANCY MALITZ

Kraków (Cracow; Ger. Krakau). City in southern Poland. It was the country's capital from the late 11th century to 1596 and was under Austrian domination, 1795–1918. The first private opera performances were presented by Stanisław Lubomirski and Kajetan Sołtyk, 1725–50, and the first public ones by visiting Italian and German companies under Domenico Toniolli and Karl Ludwig Wothe from about 1780. The Italian troupe staged mainly comic operas by Anfossi, Cimarosa, Duni, Gossec, Paisiello, Piccinni, Sacchini and Salieri, while the German troupe presented Haydn, Mozart, Süssmayr, Dittersdorf, W. Müller, J. Weigl and others until 1798. In 1787 the proprietor of the Kraków Theatre, Jacek Kluszewski (1761–1841), formed the city's first permanent public opera company from the singers of Toniolli's troupe and an orchestra of 20 local musicians. Performing at the Spiski Palace, it first continued with the Italian repertory, but later (1789–94) staged Polish operas by Kamieński and Gaetano, using singers from the Warsaw National Theatre.

In 1795, at the third partition of Poland, Kraków was seized by the Austrians, who enforced German language and repertory in the opera house. But in 1800 Kluszewski succeeded in founding a new theatre (now the Stary Teatr), organizing occasional performances of Polish operas and vaudevilles by Stefani, Elsner and Gaetano. Wojciech Bogusławski's theatrical troupe visited Kraków in 1809, during the short-lived liberation of the city, and gave a number of operas. In the 1820s Kluszewski engaged the Kamiński company from Lwów and Skibinski's from Wilno, who, besides the most popular contemporary works of Rossini, Cherubini, Auber, Weber and others, presented operas by Elsner, Kurpiński, Baszny and Damse, and by the Kraków composers Franciszek Salezy Dutkiewicz, Józef Wygrzywalski and Baltazar Boguński. Performances were less frequent in the 1830s and 40s.

After the suppression of the 1846 revolution Kraków was annexed, and the theatre was taken over by the Austrians in 1853. A revival of Polish opera took place in the 1860s under Adam Skorupka and Stanisław Duniecki (music director, 1864–7), who staged operas by Moniuszko as well as operettas by Offenbach and Lecocq; Duniecki was succeeded by Kazimierz Hofmann, who favoured the lighter repertory. From 1875 to 1913 the Opera at Lwów (now L'vov) staged regular summer seasons in Kraków, performing the standard repertory in addition to modern and Polish operas. Finally, after several unsuccessful attempts to set up a permanent company, Opera Krakowska (Kraków Opera Society) was founded in January 1915. Under the direction of the composer and conductor Bolesław Wallek-Walewski, and with Polish singers and conductors, the Opera performed in the municipal J. Słowacki Theatre (cap. 900); an operetta company, under Tadeusz Pilarski, also flourished. From 1924 to 1931 there was a break in activity, but the Opera reopened in September 1931 under the direction of Eugeniusz Bujański and Wallek-Walewski. In the eight seasons to 1939, 184 operas were staged, including 30 premières during the first four years. The Nazi occupants mounted German opera during World War II, permitting only a few Polish productions in 1944.

Native operas (mostly by Moniuszko) were presented again in Kraków from June 1945. The newly founded Society of Opera Friends, under the excellent direction of Walerian Bierdiajew, gave three seasons of twice-weekly performances from August 1946 in the Słowacki Theatre, including ten premières. Between 1948 and 1954 operas were given only by visiting companies. In October 1954 the Kraków Opera Society formed a repertory company under J. Katlewicz and Z. Chwedczuk, giving 272 performances and eight premières before the end of 1957. The Miejski Teatr Muzyczny: Opera i Operetka (Municipal Music Theatre) was set up in 1958 by M. Drobner; his successor, Kazimierz Kord (1962–8), made a notable contribution to opera in Kraków. The city is planning to build a new opera house with two auditoria (cap. 2000).

J. W. Reiss: *Muzyka w Krakowie w XIX wieku* (Kraków, 1931)

——: *Jak Kraków walczyt o operę* [How Kraków Fought for Opera] (Kraków, 1934)

S. Lachowicz: *Dwadzieścia lat opery i operetki w Krakowie 1954–1974* [20 Years of Opera and Operetta in Kraków, 1954–1974] (Kraków, 1974)

M. Drobner and T. Przybylski, eds.: *Kraków muzyczny 1918–1939* (Kraków, 1980)

Z. Jabłoński: *Dzieje teatru w Krakowie w latach 1781–1830* [History of the Theatre in Kraków, 1781–1830] (Kraków, 1980)

J. Got: *Das österreichische Theater in Krakau im 18. und 19. Jahrhunderts* (Vienna, 1984)

J. Michalik: *Dzieje teatru w Krakowie w latach 1893–1915* [History of the Theatre in Kraków, 1893–1915] (Kraków, 1985)
KORNEL MICHAŁOWSKI

Král a uhlíř. Opera by Antonín Dvořák; *see* KING AND CHARCOAL BURNER.

Krämer, Günter (*b* Neustadt an der Weinstrasse, 2 Dec 1940). German director. After studying at the universities of Heidelberg and Freiburg and working as a teacher in Mannheim, he became increasingly involved in drama production. He made his début as a stage director in 1972, and turned to opera in 1979 with Krenek's *Karl V* in Darmstadt. He was head of drama in Bremen before being appointed Intendant of the

Cologne Schauspielhaus from 1990. Krämer achieved an international reputation with his stagings in Düsseldorf of Korngold's *Die tote Stadt* (1986) and Schreker's *Die Gezeichneten* (1987). He has also staged productions for the Deutsche Oper, Berlin, and in 1989 he became the first West German stage director to be invited to work at the Komische Oper in East Berlin. His opera stagings tend to be highly stylized, with a delicate balance between intellectual and emotional content.

ANDREW CLARK

Krämer, Toni (*b* Malsch, 14 Sept 1935). German tenor. He studied in Karlsruhe and made his début in 1965 as Nathanaël (*Les contes d'Hoffmann*) at Stuttgart, where he was engaged to sing minor roles. As his voice developed he took on Pinkerton, Max, Don Alvaro, Florestan, Grigory and the title role of *König Hirsch*. He also began to sing Wagner: Erik, Lohengrin, Walther and Parsifal. Having sung Eisslinger, a Noble (*Lohengrin*) and a Knight (*Parsifal*) at Bayreuth (1980), he appeared as Siegfried there (1985) and at Wiesbaden (1986) and Seattle (1987), and at the Metropolitan (1988). His repertory also includes the Emperor (*Die Frau ohne Schatten*) and Tannhäuser. Though not a very convincing actor, he has a strong, ringing voice and much stamina.

ELIZABETH FORBES

Krása, Hans (*b* Prague, 30 Nov 1899; *d* ?Auschwitz, 1944). German composer. After taking composition lessons with Zemlinsky, he worked as an accompanist at the Neues Deutsches Theater in Prague and made several foreign tours. He continued his compositional studies in Berlin and with Roussel in Paris, and in the 1920s became attracted to the music of Stravinsky and contemporary French composers, influences demonstrated in his mature works. He finally settled in Prague but was interned under the Nazis at Terezin concentration camp. On 16 October 1944 he was taken to Auschwitz and no more is known of him.

His first opera, the two-act *Verlobung im Traum*, uses a libretto by Rudolf Fuchs and Rudolf Thomas based on Dostoyevsky's *Dvadushkin son* ('Uncle's Dream'). A mixture of psychological opera and *opéra-bouffe*, it combines neo-classicism with Schoenbergian atonality, mollifying the stylistic disparity through a reduced musical language with an expressive reserve. George Szell conducted the première at the Neues Deutsches Theater on 18 May 1933 as part of the Prague May festival. Krása's children's opera, *Brundibár* ('The Bumble Bee'), after a story by Karel Hoffmeister, was composed in 1938–9. It was studied by Jewish children in a Prague orphanage and, following their deportation to the concentration camp at Terezin, staged by them on 23 September 1943 under the direction of Rudolf Freudenfeld with an instrumental ensemble drawn from the camp. In *Brundibár* Krása took into consideration the limited possibilities of the singers, using a simple and modest technique.

E. Steinhard: 'Hans Krása: "Verlobung im Traum"', *Der Auftakt*, xiii (1933), 73–4
V. Helfert and E. Steinhard: *Die Musik in der Tschechoslowakischen Republik* (Prague, 1936), 175–6
M. Kuna: *Hudba na hranici života* [Music on the Border of Life] (Prague, 1990)
JOSEF BEK

Krásnohorská, Eliška [Pechová, Alžběta] (*b* Prague, 18 Nov 1847; *d* Prague, 26 Nov 1926). Czech librettist and writer. She was a friend of the writer Karolina Světlá, who introduced her into feminist literary circles. She worked as an editor of the magazine *Ženské listy* ('Women's Letters') and took part in the founding of the first Czech girls' gymnasium, Minerva, in 1890. Her writings include books for children and two plays, but she is best known today for her poetry and her librettos, written chiefly for Smetana and Bendl.

She was a woman of forthright views and was not afraid to voice them. Her article on Czech prosody 'O české deklamaci hudební' ('On Czech Musical Declamation', *Hudební listy*, ii, 1871, pp.1–4, 9–13, 17–19) contained criticisms of Smetana's word-setting which had an immediate impact on his work; in the light of it he revised his current opera (*Libuše*) and thereafter took great trouble with the setting of Czech. Krásnohorská wrote the librettos of Smetana's three last operas (suggesting the subjects herself) and that of his unfinished *Viola*. She was responsible for many of their conventions (for instance the use of duets, trios and ensembles) and in some cases for the voice types that Smetana used. She took great care with her work, ensuring that different metres were used for characterization and other effects, for instance Kalina's multi-metre scene in Act 2 of *The Secret*. Her librettos were criticized by Smetana's friends for their lyrical nature; nevertheless Smetana responded warmly to them: 'I have grown together with your lines and with that music which I always feel in them and which I no longer hear in any other lines'.

Her other writings on music include 'Český básník a hudební drama' ('The Czech Poet and Music Drama', *Hudební listy*, i, 1870, pp.293–301, 306–10) and a biography of Smetana (Prague, 1885), both reprinted in Z. Pešat and J. Křesálková 1956, vol.ii; and memoirs of Bendl's early years ('Z mladých let Karla Bendla: osobní vzpomínky', *Osvěta*, xxvii, 1897, pp.959–76).

Lejla, Bendl, 1868; *Jaroslav ze Šternberku*, Skuherský, comp. 1868, inc.; *Žena Vršovcova*, Bendl, comp. 1868–74, inc.; *Kassandra* [before 1870; for H. Palla but not set]; *Břetislav a Jitka*, Bendl, 1870; *Lumír* [?1870; for Smetana but not set]; *Vlasta*, Palla, comp. ?1870–81, inc.; *Viola*, Smetana, comp. 1874 and 1883–4, inc.; *Hubička*, Smetana, 1876; *Tajemství*, Smetana, 1878; *Blaník*, Fibich, 1881; *Čertova stěna*, Smetana, 1882; *Karel Škreta*, Bendl, 1883; *Dítě Tábora*, Bendl, 1892

*
ČSHS [incl. further bibliography]
E. Krásnohorská: *Memoirs: i, Z mého mládí* [From my Youth] (Prague, 1920); ii–iii, *Co přinesla léta* [What the Years Brought], ed. F. Strejček (Prague, 1928)
M. Očadlík, ed.: *Eliška Krásnohorská – Bedřich Smetana: vzájemná korespondence* [Mutual Correspondence] (Prague, 1940)
——, ed.: *Eliška Krásnohorská: Hubička* [The Kiss] (Prague, 1942) [critical edn]
——, ed.: *Eliška Krásnohorská: Čertova stěna* [The Devil's Wall] (Prague, 1946) [critical edn]
M. Očadlík: 'Mezi Shakespearem a Smetanou' [Between Shakespeare and Smetana], *Eliška Krásnohorská*, ed. P. Antošová (Brno, 1947), 93–114
——: *Smetanovi libretisté* [Smetana's Librettists] (Prague, 1948), 30–36
Z. Pešat and J. Křesálková, eds.: *Eliška Krásnohorská: výbor z díla* [Selected Works], i–ii (Prague, 1956)
Z. Vokurka: 'Ještě k vavřínům Smetanovy Hubičky' [Once more about the Laurels of Smetana's *The Kiss*], *OM*, ii (1970), 198–203
R. Šťastný: *Čeští spisovatelé deseti století* [Czech Writers of Ten Centuries] (Prague, 1974) [incl. bibliography]
M. Suchá and M. Ulčová: 'Plzeňské počátky libretistické spolupráce Elišky Krásnohorské s Bedřichem Smetanou' [The Plzeň Beginnings of Krásnohorská's Collaboration with Smetana as Librettist], *Bedřich Smetana: Plzeň 1840–1843* (Plzeň, 1974), 97–117
J. Tyrrell: *Czech Opera* (Cambridge, 1988), 105–12, 273–6

J. Jiránek: *Smetanova operní tvorba* [Smetana's Operatic Works], ii
(Prague, 1989)
JOHN TYRRELL

Krásová, Marta (*b* Protivín, 16 March 1901; *d* Vráž u
Berouna, 20 Feb 1970). Czech mezzo-soprano. She
studied with Borová-Valoušková, Maturová and, in
Vienna, Ullanovský. In 1922 she joined the Slovak
National Theatre in Bratislava, where she changed from
soprano to mezzo roles. She made her Prague National
Theatre début as Amneris (1927) and was a member of
the company from 1928 to 1966. To her musicality,
excellent technique and wide range was allied a great
acting talent and a rich imagination. She was an outstanding Isabella in Fibich's *Bride of Messina*, Róza in
The Secret, Witch in *Rusalka* and Death in Karel's
Death the Neighbour; her non-Czech roles included
Azucena, Eboli, Carmen, Gluck's Orpheus and the
Countess in *The Queen of Spades*. Her finest
performance was the Kostelnička in Janáček's *Jenůfa*.
She sang in Hamburg, Dresden, Madrid, Paris, Moscow
and Warsaw, and toured the USA. She made many
recordings.

L. Šíp: *Pěvci před mikrofonem* [Singers before the Microphone]
(Prague, 1960), 55ff
V. Šolín: *Marta Krásová* (Prague, 1960)
E. Kopecký and V. Pospíšil: *Slavní pěvci Národního divadla*
[Famous Singers of the National Theatre] (Prague, 1968), 164ff
Národní divadlo a jeho předchůdci [National Theatre and its Pre-
decessors] (Prague, 1988), 244ff [incl. list of operatic repertory
and discography]
ALENA NĚMCOVÁ

Kraus, Alfredo (*b* Las Palmas, Canary Islands, 24 Sept
1927). Spanish tenor. A pupil of Mercedes Llopart, he
made his début in 1956 at Cairo in *Rigoletto* and was
soon appearing in various Italian theatres. He then sang
in Spain, at Covent Garden (1959, Edgardo opposite
Sutherland's Lucia) and at La Scala (1960, Elvino),
where he has frequently returned. He has also appeared
in the USA, particularly at the Metropolitan where he
made his début in 1966 in *Rigoletto*. Kraus's voice is
smooth, bright and well schooled, with an extensive top
register up to *d"*. He is considered the best light, lyric
tenor of his generation, and the elegance and stylishness
of his singing, combined with warmth of expression and
a handsome stage presence, make him the ideal interpreter of such aristocratic roles as Don Ottavio,
Almaviva, Alfredo, Faust and Massenet's Des Grieux,
Werther and Hoffmann, which he sang at Covent
Garden in 1991.

R. Celletti: 'Alfredo Kraus', *Opera*, xxvi (1975), 17–21
RODOLFO CELLETTI

Kraus, Auguste. *See* SEIDL-KRAUS, AUGUSTE.

Kraus, Ernst (*b* Erlangen, 8 June 1863; *d* Wörthsee, 6
Sept 1941). German tenor. He studied in Munich with
Schimon-Regan, and later in Milan with Cesare
Galliera. He made his début at Mannheim in 1893 as
Tamino; after two seasons with the Damrosch Opera
Company in the USA he was engaged as leading
Heldentenor at the Berlin Hofoper (later Staatsoper)
from 1898 to 1924. He sang regularly at Bayreuth from
1899 to 1909 as Walther, Erik, Siegmund and Siegfried,
and created Heinrich in Ethel Smyth's *Der Wald* (1902).
He sang the title role in the German première of *Dalibor*
(1904) and Herod in the first London *Salome* at Covent
Garden in 1910, having already appeared there between
1900 and 1907 in the Wagnerian repertory. He sang at

the Metropolitan during the 1903–4 season, making his
début as Siegmund. Kraus was generally considered the
finest Wagner tenor of the century until the advent of
Lauritz Melchior.
HAROLD ROSENTHAL/R

Kraus, Felix von (*b* Vienna, 3 Oct 1870; *d* Munich, 30
Oct 1937). Austrian bass. He studied in Vienna and,
after three years as a concert singer, made his stage
début at Bayreuth in 1899, singing Hagen and
Gurnemanz. He sang there regularly until 1909, adding
the Landgrave (*Tannhäuser*), Titurel and King Mark to
his repertory. In 1907 he sang in the German opera
season at Covent Garden as King Henry (*Lohengrin*),
the Landgrave and King Mark. He was married to the
contralto Adrienne von Kraus-Osborne.
ELIZABETH FORBES

Kraus, Joseph Martin (*b* Miltenberg am Main, 20 June
1756; *d* Stockholm, 15 Dec 1792). German-Swedish
composer. He received his earliest musical education in
the central German town of Buchen im Odenwald and
during the years 1768–73 was educated in Mannheim,
where his teachers included members of the Mannheim
Kapelle. He attended the universities of Mainz
(1773–4), Erfurt (1774–5) and, after an interruption
due to family troubles, Göttingen (from 1776); he
became acquainted with members of the Göttinger
Hainbund, a *Sturm und Drang* literary circle under
whose influence he wrote the treatise *Etwas von
und über Musik fürs Jahr 1777* (Frankfurt, 1778; facs.
with commentary by F. W. Riedel, Munich, 1977),
which devotes a large section to a thorough critique of
Anton Schweitzer's opera *Alceste*. In 1778 a Swedish
student, Carl Stridsberg, persuaded Kraus to accompany
him to Stockholm and try his fortune at the court of
Gustavus III.

After three years of poverty, Kraus was elected to the
Swedish Royal Academy of Music in 1781; his opera
Proserpin then won him the post of assistant
kapellmästare at the Swedish court. A commission to
provide the inaugural work for the Royal Opera's new
theatre in 1782 (*Aeneas i Cartago*) was undermined at
the last minute, and he was sent by Gustavus III on a
study journey throughout Europe to observe the latest
trends in the theatre. His four-year grand tour took him
to Germany, Austria, Italy, France and England. In
Vienna he met Haydn, who considered him an original
genius, Salieri and Gluck, who stated: 'That man has a
great style, the like of which I have found in no one else'
(according to Kraus's biographer F. S. Silverstolpe).
In Italy he wrote elaborate descriptions of the theatres
in Naples and Rome, and his lengthy review of
Piccinni's *Didon*, which he saw in Paris in 1785, was
published (Mannheim, 1786). In London he attended
the second Handel Commemoration before returning
late in 1786 to Stockholm, where he succeeded Uttini as
hovkapellmästare in 1788. A popular composer for the
Stockholm theatres, he produced works like the ballet
Fiskarena (1789), the drama with music *Soliman den
andra* (1789) and a large portion of the pasticcio
Äfventyraren (1791), in addition to numerous shorter
stage works. He also became a close friend of the poet
and singer Carl Michael Bellman, with whom, along
with with other intellectuals, he formed the
Diktarkretsen (Poetry Society), a literary and musical
circle. He died of tuberculosis shortly after the
assassination of his patron GUSTAVUS III.

Kraus can be considered the most original and notable composer in Sweden during the Gustavian period. His German education, coupled with his experiences during his grand tour, gave him a cosmopolitan outlook that was absorbed into his music. As early as 1778 he declared himself to be an ardent admirer of Gluck and Grétry, who served as his models. His participation in the debate on opera in the Stockholm newspapers *Stockholms posten* and *Dagligt allehanda*, 1778–82, shows much concern with the fusion of drama and music. He was, however, not always successful in his early years in getting his theatrical works performed; his first opera *Azire* was ignored, and *Proserpin* was given only a single private performance. His greatest work, *Aeneas i Cartago*, was subjected to intrigues that prevented its première until 1799, seven years after his death. During the period 1787–92, on the other hand, he was a popular composer whose music for the stage was highly prized.

Kraus's musical style is highly original, though his through-composed recitatives and extensive use of choruses and ballet show his relationship with Gluck. His works display a highly developed sense of lyrical melody and employ bold harmonies which often anticipate Beethoven or Schubert; he was a sensitive and precise orchestrator, using a rich palette to create varying textures. He developed dramatic unity through the use of motivic devices, and he had a keen sense of the inner feelings of his characters, whose moods are often underscored at the expense of virtuoso display. In his serious operas, his writing can be terse and emotional, while the comic ones show a lightness of touch.

See also AENEAS I CARTAGO; PROSERPIN; and SOLIMAN DEN ANDRA.

unless otherwise stated, first performed in Stockholm, MSS in S-Uu

Azire, 1778 (Spl, 3, C. Stridsberg), unperf., only autograph frags. extant
Proserpin (1, J. H. Kellgren, after Gustavus III and P. Quinault), Ulriksdal Castle, 1 June 1781, *S-St*
Aeneas i Cartago, eller Dido och Aeneas, 1782 (lyric tragedy, prol., 5, Kellgren after Gustavus III and J.-J. le Franc de Pompignan: *Didon*), Royal Opera, 18 Nov 1799, *A-Wn, S-Skma, St*
Le bon seigneur, 1784–6 (oc, 1)
Oedip, 1785 (3), 1 act completed, lost
Zélia, ou L'origine de la félicité (melodrama, 1, J. d'Invilliers), Paris, 1786, lost
Fintbergs bröllop [Fintberg's Marriage] (comedy with song, 2, C. G. von Holthusen), Munkbro, 7 Jan 1788
Fricorpsen, eller Dalkarlarne [The Free Corps, or Men from Dalacarlia] (comedy with song, 1, D. Björn), Bollhuset, 1 Nov 1788, lost
Soliman den andra, eller De tre sultaninnorna [Soliman II, or The Three Sultanas] (drama with music, 3, divertissement, J. G. Oxenstierna, after C.-S. Favart), Royal Dramatic, 22 Sept 1789, *St*
Födelsedagen [The Birthday] (comedy with song, 1, Gustavus III and Björn), Royal Opera, 20 Nov 1790, lost
Marknaden [The Market Place] (Spl, 1, Björn), Munkbro, 8 Oct 1792, lost

Music in: Äfventyraren, eller Resan till månens ö [The Adventurers, or The Journey to the Isle of the Moon], 1791

F. S. Silverstolpe: *Biographie af Kraus* (Stockholm, 1833)
E. Sundström: 'Ett melodram av Joseph Martin Kraus?', *STMf*, xv (1933), 169–72
R. Engländer: 'Kraus' Proserpin, ett bidrag till Kraus' musikdramatiska stil', *STMf*, xxi (1939), 48–67
A. Mayer-Reinach: 'Lannerstiernas "Äfventyraren", musik av Kraus med flera', *STMf*, xxi (1939), 101–118
R. Engländer: *Joseph Martin Kraus und die Gustavianische Oper* (Uppsala, 1943)
——: 'Die Gustavianische Oper', *AMw*, xvi (1959), 314–27
I. Leux-Henschen: *Joseph Martin Kraus in seinen Briefen* (Stockholm, 1978)
F. Riedel, ed.: *Joseph Martin Kraus in seiner Zeit* (Munich, 1982)
H. Åstrand, ed.: *Kraus und das Gustavianische Stockholm* (Stockholm, 1984)
B. van Boer: *Die Werke von Joseph Martin Kraus: systematisch-thematisches Werkverzeichnis* (Stockholm, 1988)
——: 'Joseph Martin Kraus's *Soliman den andra*: a Gustavian Turkish Opera', *STMf*, lxx (1988), 18–29

BERTIL H. VAN BOER

Kraus, Otakar (*b* Prague, 10 Dec 1909; *d* London, 28 July 1980). British baritone of Czech birth. He studied in Prague and with Fernando Carpi in Milan, made his début at Brno in 1935 as Amonasro, then sang with the Bratislava Opera (1936–9). He settled in England in 1940 and appeared at the Savoy Theatre in that year in Musorgsky's *The Fair at Sorochintsï*; from 1943 to 1946 he sang with the Carl Rosa Opera Company, and joined the English Opera Group in 1946, creating Tarquinius in *The Rape of Lucretia* (for illustration *see* RAPE OF LUCRETIA, THE). After a season with the Netherlands Opera (1950–51), he joined the Covent Garden company and sang there until 1973, creating Diomede in *Troilus and Cressida* (1954) and King Fisher in *The Midsummer Marriage* (1955). He was also an outstanding Alberich, his Italian training having made him more lyrical than many German singers; he sang the role at Bayreuth (1960–62). In 1951 he created Nick Shadow in *The Rake's Progress* at Venice and repeated the part at La Scala and Glyndebourne. Kraus established himself as a first-rate singing actor, always a vital and striking stage figure and a master of make-up.

H. Rosenthal: 'Otakar Kraus', *Opera*, xxiv (1973), 1067–72

HAROLD ROSENTHAL/R

Kraus, (Wolfgang Ernst) Richard (*b* Berlin, 16 Nov 1902; *d* Walchstadt, 11 April 1978). German conductor, son of Ernst Kraus. After studying in Berlin with Erich Kleiber his first engagements were in Kassel, Hanover, Stuttgart and (from 1937) as music director in Halle, where he contributed to the German revival of Handel stage works with performances of *Agrippina*. He conducted *Der fliegende Holländer* at Bayreuth in 1942, and at the Berlin Staatsoper in 1944. After a period in Düsseldorf, in 1947 he was appointed general music director in Cologne, where his performances of Pfitzner's *Palestrina* were particularly admired. From 1952 he had no permanent post, but conducted frequently at the Städtische Oper (now the Deutsche Oper), Berlin. There his performances of Busoni's *Doktor Faust* (1955), with Fischer-Dieskau in the title role, saw the reinstatement of an almost completely forgotten work. Kraus's sense of theatre, broad musical sympathies and reliability made him an especially successful interpreter of Wagner and Strauss.

HANS CHRISTOPH WORBS

Krause, Tom (*b* Helsinki, 5 July 1934). Finnish baritone. He studied at the Vienna Akademie für Musik and made his operatic début in Berlin (1959) as Escamillo, the part with which he became most closely associated throughout Germany and Scandinavia. His career was then based in Hamburg where, in addition to the standard repertory of Mozart, Verdi and Wagner, he appeared in such rarities as Rossini's *La pietra del paragone* (1963), Handel's *Jephtha* (1964) and Searle's *Hamlet*, the title role of which he created in 1968. The Herald in *Lohengrin* was his first role at Bayreuth (1962) and the Count in *Capriccio* his first in England

(1963, Glyndebourne). In 1967 he made his Metropolitan début as Mozart's Count Almaviva, and reappeared there in every season up to 1973. He has also sung at La Scala, Covent Garden and the Paris Opéra, and since his début as Don Giovanni in 1968 has appeared regularly at Salzburg. Throughout his long career disappointments have been rare (his Nick Shadow at Geneva was one), and in 1990 *Opera* magazine described his Don Alfonso (*Così fan tutte*) as 'unforgettable' and sung 'in wonderful voice'. His recordings show a firm, resonant voice, a sound technique and a power of vivid characterization.

J. B. STEANE

Kraus-Osborne [née Eisbein], **Adrienne von** (*b* Buffalo, 2 Dec 1873; *d* Zell am Ziller, 15 June 1951). American, later Austrian contralto. She studied in Leipzig, where she made her début in 1893 as Mignon. She was engaged in Leipzig until 1908 and also sang in Munich. She first sang at Bayreuth in 1899 as Grimgerde and an Esquire in *Parsifal*, under the name of Osborne. Later that year she married the bass Felix von Kraus. Returning to Bayreuth (1904–9), she added Flosshilde, First and Second Norn and Waltraute (*Götterdämmerung*) to her repertory. In 1907 she sang at Covent Garden in the German opera season as Mary (*Der fliegende Holländer*), Magdalene (*Die Meistersinger*) and Mrs Page (*Die lustigen Weiber von Windsor*).   ELIZABETH FORBES

Krauss, Clemens (*b* Vienna, 31 March 1893; *d* Mexico City, 16 May 1954). Austrian conductor. He was the son of the Viennese actress and singer Clementine Krauss, and great-nephew of the soprano Gabrielle Krauss. In 1912 he went to Brno as chorus director, conducting his first opera there the following year. He was at Riga (1913–14), Nuremberg (1915–16) and Sczeczin (1916–21), which gave him frequent opportunities of hearing Nikisch in Berlin, before returning to Austria in 1921 as conductor of the Graz Opera. The following year he became conductor of the Vienna Staatsoper and from 1924 to 1929 was Intendant at Frankfurt. In 1929 he returned to his post in Vienna, where he conducted the Viennese première of *Wozzeck* in 1930. He became director of the Berlin Staatsoper in 1935. The climax of his official career came in 1937 with his appointment as Intendant of the Munich Opera. During the war he was active at Salzburg with the festivals and the direction and reorganization of the Mozarteum. He left Munich in 1943 after the destruction in an air raid of the National Theatre.

Krauss was a born opera conductor with a sharp eye for visual as well as musical detail and a gift for administration. The flair he showed in his operatic career deserted him where decisions of a political nature were concerned: he was ready to take over the première of Strauss's *Arabella* (1933) when Fritz Busch, for whom the opera was intended, had been hounded out of Dresden, and his immediate predecessors in Berlin (Kleiber) and Munich (Knappertsbusch) had both resigned for political reasons. Against these acts of public indiscretion must be weighed private deeds of kindness to Jewish artists in trouble. After the war he was forbidden to conduct until 1947, when he resumed opera directing at the Theater an der Wien, Vienna (the Staatsoper was not yet rebuilt). He made many visits abroad (his Covent Garden début had taken place in 1934) with the Vienna Opera or as guest conductor. His sudden death occurred on one of these tours.

Krauss was closely associated with Richard Strauss both as friend and interpreter. Apart from *Arabella*, he gave the premières of *Friedenstag* (1938, Munich), *Capriccio* (1942, Munich), of which he helped write the libretto, and *Die Liebe der Danäe* (1952, Salzburg). He married Viorica Ursuleac, a noted exponent of Strauss soprano roles. Krauss had a wide repertory, embracing the German-Austrian Classics and much beyond. For the music of the other Strauss, Johann, he had an exceptionally light and happy touch. The Clemens Krauss Archive in Vienna contains his non-commercial as well as commercial recordings.

*

J. Gregor: *Clemens Krauss: eine musikalische Sendung* (Vienna and Zürich, 1953)
O. von Pandor: *Clemens Krauss in München* (Munich, 1955)
D. Wooldridge: *Conductor's World* (London, 1970)
E. Maschat: 'Clemens Krauss', *Recorded Sound* (1971), no.42–3, p.740 [with list of non-commercial recordings]
C. Höslinger: ' "… nicht als ein Wiener Musikant": eine Erinnerung an Clemens Krauss aus Anlass seines 80. Geburtstages am 31. März von Clemens Höslinger', *Fonoforum*, xviii (1973), 322–7 [with discography of commercial recordings]

RONALD CRICHTON

Krauss, (Marie) Gabrielle (*b* Vienna, 24 March 1842; *d* Paris, 6 Jan 1906). Austrian soprano. She studied at the Vienna Academy with Mathilde Marchesi and made her début in 1859 as Mathilde (*Guillaume Tell*) at the Vienna Hofoper. She was engaged by the Théâtre Italien, Paris (1859–70); in 1875 she sang Rachel in *La Juive* at the inauguration of the Palais Garnier and remained a member of the Opéra company until the end of 1888. She became famous for her portrayals of Meyerbeer heroines, and as Leonore, Aida and Donna Anna; she created a number of roles, including Pauline in Gounod's *Polyeucte* (1878), Hermosa in Gounod's *Le tribut de Zamora* (1881) and Catherine of Aragon in Saint-Saëns' *Henry VIII* (1883). At La Scala she created the title role in Gomes's *Fosca* (1873). She was acclaimed for the dramatic intensity of her performances, to which she brought a tragedienne's passion and nobility. She retired in 1888.

*

ES (L. Riemens and R. Celletti)
G. de Charnacé: *Les étoiles du chant* (Paris, 1868–9)
M. Strakosch: *Souvenirs d'un imprésario* (Paris, 2/1887)
H. de Curzon: 'Mme Gabrielle Krauss', *Le théâtre: revue illustrée des théâtres et concerts*, ix (1906)   HAROLD ROSENTHAL/R

Krauze, Zygmunt (*b* Warsaw, 19 Sept 1938). Polish composer. He studied composition with Kazimierz Sikorski at the Warsaw Conservatory and with Nadia Boulanger in Paris (1966–7). He is known in Poland and abroad for his commissioning zeal and performance with the ensemble Warsztat Muzyczny (Music Workshop), which flourished in the 1960s and 70s, and for his use of folk melodies and instruments in orchestral and chamber music. His chamber opera *Die Kleider* (known in Poland as *Gwiazda*, 'The Star'), to a libretto by H. Kajzar, was first performed in Mannheim in 1982. The work maintains the highly concentrated use of minimal material prevalent elsewhere in his output. Its female protagonist is given several alter egos as she and they explore, sometimes in surreal fashion, many facets of a woman's life today.

*

O. Pisarenko: '*Gwiazda*', *Ruch muzyczny*, xxix (1985), no.18, pp.9–10
ADRIAN THOMAS

Krebs, Helmut (*b* Dortmund, 8 Oct 1913). German tenor. He studied at the Dortmund Conservatory and the Berlin Hochschule für Musik, and started a concert career before his stage début at the Berlin Volksoper in 1938. He was engaged at Düsseldorf from 1945 and returned to Berlin as a member of the Städtische (later Deutsche) Oper from 1947, where he remained for over 40 years. His British début was at Glyndebourne in 1953 as Belmonte and Idamantes; the next year he sang Aaron in the first complete concert performance of *Moses und Aron* in Hamburg under Rosbaud. He also sang at La Scala, the Vienna Staatsoper and Covent Garden. Krebs was a lyric tenor of vocal elegance and style, as is evident from his recording of Monteverdi's *Orpheus* under Wenzinger (1955). He was made *Kammersänger* in 1963.   NOËL GOODWIN

Krebs [Miedke], Karl August (*b* Nuremberg, 16 Jan 1804; *d* Dresden, 16 May 1880). German conductor and composer. The son of A. and Charlotte Miedke of the Nuremberg Theatre company, he took, on his mother's death in 1805, the name of his adoptive father, the tenor and composer Johann Baptist Krebs (1774–1851). He first appeared as a pianist at the age of six, and his first opera, *Feodora*, was composed the following year. He studied with Johann Schelble, then in Vienna with Seyfried (1825). After acting as third Kapellmeister at the Kärntnertortheater, he went to Hamburg as Kapellmeister in 1827, remaining until 1850. He then moved to Dresden as Kapellmeister at the Hofoper in succession to Wagner; here he staged *Lohengrin* in 1852. He retired from the theatre in 1872 and took over the directorship of Dresden's Catholic church. He was an enthusiastic supporter of Spontini and Meyerbeer, with a taste for large choirs and orchestras. Wagner, whose early music he also championed, wrote from Hamburg about the *Rienzi* production there, describing him as 'a really excellent conductor … I could have no better conductor for my opera' (letter to Minna Wagner, 17 March 1844); later Wagner lost confidence in him (describing his *Lohengrin* production as 'mindless') and was affronted by his demand for an extra number in *Rienzi* for his wife. His works include four operas, but he is best known for his many songs, which were once very popular.

In 1850 Krebs married Aloyse Michalesi (*b* Prague, 29 Aug 1826; *d* Dresden, 5 Aug 1904), daughter of the singer Wenzel Michalesi (*d* 1836). She was a mezzo-soprano who made her début in Brno in 1843 and moved to Hamburg in 1846; at Meyerbeer's request, she went to Dresden in 1849 to sing Fidès in *Le prophète*. She retired from the stage in 1870 but continued to sing in concerts and to teach.

Feodora, 1811 (1, A. von Kotzebue)
Der Kosakenoffizier, 1815 (1, Krebs)
Sylvia, oder Die Macht des Gesanges (2), Hamburg, 4 Feb 1830
Agnes Bernauer [Herzog Albrecht] (4, A. Lewald), Hamburg, 8 Oct 1833; rev. as Agnes Bernauerin, der Engel von Augsburg, Dresden, Hof, 17 Jan 1858

*

A. Lewald: 'Geschichte einer deutschen Oper', *Europa*, iv (1836), 139–41
A. Ehrlich: *Berühmte Sängerinnen der Vergangenheit und Gegenwart* (Leipzig, 1895)
H. von Brescius: *Die königliche sächsische musikalische Kapelle von Reissiger bis Schuch (1826–1898)* (Dresden, 1898)
H. Chevalley: *Hundert Jahre Hamburger Stadt-Theater* (Hamburg, 1927)
P. Adolph: *Vom Hof- zum Staatstheater Dresden* (Dresden, 1932)
                JOHN WARRACK

Krefeld. Town in western Germany, in Nordrhein-Westfalen. The first theatre was built in 1779, a wooden structure which burnt down after three months and was replaced by a stone building in 1780. In 1825 a new theatre was built in the Rheinstrasse and opened with Boieldieu's *La dame blanche*. It was rebuilt in 1828, closed after the fire at the Vienna Ringtheater in 1881 and rebuilt again in 1886. The theatre was destroyed on 23 June 1943. In 1946 performances of opera were resumed in temporary accommodation, and in 1951 work began on a new building. The new theatre opened on 7 October 1952 with *Lohengrin*, and the present house opened on 12 January 1963 with *Don Giovanni*.

The association with the neighbouring town of Mönchengladbach goes back to 1862 when the Krefeld company began giving guest performances. Until 1923 the association between them was based on private agreements. A more formal arrangement, an early example of German theatrical cooperation, was made in 1950; the two companies merged, and their first production was *Carmen* on 27 September 1950. The amalgamated companies play in the Krefeld Stadttheater (cap. /32) and the Stadthalle Reydt (cap. 811) in Mönchengladbach. The latter was built between 1928 and 1930 and opened in October 1930 with *Der Freischütz*. After the war it was not used for opera until 1984 when it was rebuilt, opening with Berg's *Lulu* on 29 November 1984. It became the official centre for the Vereinigte Städtische Bühnen Krefeld und Mönchengladbach.

Among the outstanding artists who have performed and worked in Krefeld and Mönchengladbach are the singers Astrid Varnay, Kurt Böhme, Franz Crass, Hermin Esser and Donald Grobe. Of the opera productions, high points have been the German premières of Richard Rodney Bennett's *The Ledge* (as *Am Abgrund*, 1963) and Moniuszko's *Straszny dwór* ('The Haunted Manor'; as *Das Gespensterschloss*, 1971). More recently the company has begun to expand its repertory, performing new as well as historically important operas, including the first performance in West Germany of Siegfried Matthus's *Judith* (1986), Zandonai's *I cavalieri di Ekebù* (1987) and Rameau's *Platée* (as *Platäa*) and Massenet's *Thérèse* (both 1989). Eike Gramss was appointed Generalintendant in 1986. In Krefeld there are some 130 operatic performances annually and in Mönchengladbach around 90.
                SABINE SONNTAG

Krehbiel, Henry (Edward) (*b* Ann Arbor, 10 March 1854; *d* New York, 20 March 1923). American critic and writer on music. He studied law but soon turned to journalism and became music critic of the *Cincinnati Gazette*, 1874–80, and then for the *New York Tribune*, a post he held until his death. He occupied a position of authority and influence among American critics and did much to advance the understanding and love of Wagner's later music dramas in the USA. Among his writings the revised and completed edition of Thayer's *Life of Beethoven* (1921), published for the first time in English, is pre-eminent.

Studies in the Wagnerian Drama (New York, 1891)
Chapters of Opera (New York, 1908, 3/1911)
A Book of Operas (New York, 1909)
A Second Book of Operas (New York, 1917)
More Chapters of Opera (New York, 1919)

*

R. Aldrich: 'Henry Edward Krehbiel', *ML*, iv (1923), 266–8

Kreidekreis, Der ('The Chalk Circle'). Opera in three acts by ALEXANDER ZEMLINSKY to a libretto after Klabund's *Der Kreidekreis*; Zürich, Stadttheater, 14 October 1933.

Der Kreidekreis is an adaptation by the German playwright Klabund (1889–1928) of Li Hsing-tao's *Hui-lan-chi*, a play written during the time of the unpopular Yüan dynasty (1278–1368). Klabund altered and simplified Li Hsing-tao's depiction of injustice and corruption in order to heighten the element of social criticism; his version was later used by his friend Bertolt Brecht as the basis of *Der kaukasische Kreidekreis*. Zemlinsky's opera compresses the five acts of the play into seven scenes divided into three acts. It is a work of great immediacy and represents a successful fusion of jazz (there is a striking similarity between the opening saxophone melody and a similar one in *Jonny spielt auf*) and Chinese music (pentatonic harmony and sonorities, as in the courtesans' music in scene i). Spoken dialogue and melodrama clearly set off the lyrical moments of introspection against the rest of the plot. The first performance in 1933 was conducted by Robert Kolisko, the main roles being created by Maria Madien Madsen (Haitang), Arthur Cavara (Pao) and Fred Destal (Ma).

Act 1 scene i is set in a teahouse owned by Tong (tenor), a nauseous pimp. Frau Tschang (contralto) and her daughter Haitang (soprano) enter. The latter is about to be sold to Tong because the family has been ruined by a ruthless mandarin, Ma (Heldenbariton). Tschang-Ling (baritone), Haitang's brother, tries in vain to prevent the deal, and strikes Haitang when she offers to help him financially. In scene ii, set in another room of the teahouse, Pao (tenor) displays an interest in Haitang, and they discuss the various meanings of the chalk circle, which is rendered musically by a four-bar theme immediately followed by its inversion. Haitang maintains that whatever lies outside the ring is nothing, and inside is the universe. Appropriately, the 'chalk circle' motif can be regarded as the source of much of the opera's musical material. Pao and Haitang are rudely interrupted by Ma, who thrusts his head through the circle Haitang has drawn on the paper partition. When he hears that Haitang is still a virgin he buys her on the spot. Haitang resigns herself to her fate.

Act 2 scene iii takes place about a year after the events in Act 1. Haitang's meekness has triumphed over Ma's brutality, and she has borne him a son, Li, thereby infuriating his first wife, Yü-Pei (soprano), who has remained barren. Yü-Pei and her lover Tschao (baritone) plot to murder Ma. Tschang-Ling, a member of a secret society that has condemned Ma to death, appears disguised as a beggar. After consulting the oracle of the chalk circle, Haitang begs him to reconsider their verdict. In scene iv, Yü-Pei unsuccessfully accuses Haitang of having been unfaithful to Ma. Having heard from Tschao that Ma is planning to divorce her, Yü-Pei slips poison into Ma's tea. The police arrive, and Yü-Pei convinces them that Haitang's son is in fact hers.

Act 3 scene v takes place in the local court. The corrupt judge Tschu-Tschu (spoken role) is seen accepting money from Yü-Pei, who also bribes the witnesses. The court duly condemns Haitang to death. She is saved by a *deus ex machina* in the shape of a messenger from Peking, who arrives with the news that the new emperor has ordered a judicial review of all recent sentences. Haitang and her brother, who declares that the new sovereign will be no better than the old, are taken to the capital in chains. In scene vi, which begins and ends with a marching song, Haitang expresses her despair. In the final scene, set in the Imperial throne room, the wheel of fate turns full circle. After releasing Tschang-Ling, the emperor turns to Haitang, who at once recognizes that he is Pao. By means of the oracle of the chalk circle the emperor establishes that Yü-Pei is not the mother of Haitang's son. Yü-Pei and Tschao are led off to await punishment. He then reveals that he secretly made love to her at Ma's house, something Haitang had taken to be a dream, and makes her his empress. Lifting up Li, she says: 'May justice be your highest aim, For that's the moral of the chalk circle's play'.

ALFRED CLAYTON

Krejčí, Iša [František] (*b* Prague, 10 July 1904; *d* Prague, 6 March 1968). Czech composer and conductor. Son of the philosopher František Krejčí, he studied history and musicology at Charles University and composition with Jirák and Novák at the Prague Conservatory (1927–9). He learnt conducting under Václav Talich. He became répétiteur at the National Theatre in Prague (1933–4), conductor and sound director at Prague Radio (1934–45) and conductor of the Orchestral Association. His period as conductor-in-chief of the Olomouc Opera (1945–58) was characterized by polished performances and innovatory programming. As Dramaturg of the Prague National Theatre from 1958, he sought to increase opportunities for the performance of contemporary works for the stage.

Krejčí attracted attention as a composer in 1925 with a work for wind quintet, and went on to become an outstanding figure in contemporary Czech music. Much of his output consists of chamber and symphonic music. His style is classically transparent, his music highly melodious, full of humour and, particularly on spiritual themes, deeply contemplative. He twice used the theme of Sophocles' *Antigone* – first in a 'musical tragedy', then over 20 years later in a 'dramatic cantata'. His most successful and most frequently staged opera is *Pozdvižení v Efesu* ('Scandal in Ephesus'), based on Shakespeare's *The Comedy of Errors*. It is a typical *buffo* piece with lively, witty action, refined music and delightful lyrical passages; musical scenes are combined with spoken prose. It is composed in neo-classical style, of which Krejčí was the leading Czech representative.

Antigona (musical tragedy, 1, Krejčí, after Sophocles), Prague, Estates, 9 May 1934; rev. 1958–62, Czechoslovak TV, 24 May 1964; Olomouc, Stibor, 20 March 1965
Pozdvižení v Efesu [Scandal in Ephesus], 1939–43 (ob, 2, J. Bachtík, after W. Shakespeare: *The Comedy of Errors*), Prague, National, 8 Sept 1945
Temno [The Darkness], 1944 (dramatic scenes, Krejčí and Bachtík, after A. Jirásek); rev. 1951, concert perf., Olomouc, 8 Jan 1955

*

L. Vachulka: 'Iša Krejčí', *České umění dramaticke*, ii: *Zpěvohra* [Czech Dramatic Art: Opera], ed. J. Hutter and Z. Chalabala (Prague, 1941), 378
I. Krejčí: 'Skladatel o sobě' [The Composer on Himself], *Rytmus*, ix (1943–4), 29–30
J. Kasan: *Novoklasicismus v díle I. Krejčího* [Neo-Classicism in the Work of Iša Krejčí] (diss., Charles U., Prague, 1956)
I. Vojtěch: 'Pozdvižení v Efesu', *Divadlo* (1963), no.2, p.79
EVA HERRMANNOVÁ

Krejčí, Miroslav (*b* Rychnov nad Kněžnou, 4 Nov 1891; *d* Prague, 29 Dec 1964). Czech composer. He learnt the piano, the organ and theory at home, before studying natural history, geography and music at Prague University (1910–14), where he also took composition lessons with Novák (1911–13). He taught in secondary schools (1915–53) and also taught composition at the

Prague Conservatory (1943–53). In 1946 he became a member of the Czech Academy of Sciences and Art.

Krejčí's output of several hundred pieces, in most genres, includes two operas: *Léto* op.41 ('Summer', composed 1937; 3, F. Šrámek), first performed at the Prague National Theatre on 4 December 1940, and *Poslední hejtman* op.62 ('The Last Hetman', composed 1944; 5, E. Klenová, after A Jirásek: *Brotherhood*), first performed at the same theatre on 18 March 1948. His style is derived from Novák's and, in his mature compositions, is notable for a fully developed polyphonic technique within a tonal harmonic framework. Eschewing the developments of the interwar avant garde, Krejčí maintained a measured, basically lyrical expressive quality, which eventually took the form of a kind of Novák-Foerster synthesis. The effect is tasteful, if unenterprising.

F. Bartoš: 'Miroslav Krejčí', *České umění dramatické*, ii: *Zpěvohra* [Czech Dramatic Art: Opera], ed. J. Hutter and Z. Chalabala (Prague, 1941), 355–8   OLDŘICH PUKL

Kremsmünster. Benedictine abbey in Upper Austria, founded in 777. Theatrical music can be traced from 1647, when a Stiftstheater was built. Incidental music for allegorical scenes, ballets and final choruses connected with Latin school dramas and dialogues became increasingly elaborate until these forms of entertainment were banned in 1765. Such performances were given for visiting nobility, for the prelate and at the cloister school or, after 1744, the Ritterakademie. Although personnel, including poets and composers, were drawn usually from the abbey's community, the influence of the theatre of Salzburg University was strong from the beginning.

Musical drama flourished between 1747 and 1783 under the direction of Franz Sparry (1715–67), a pupil of Leo, and Georg Pasterwiz (1730–1803), a pupil of Eberlin. After 1771 the repertory was expanded to include Italian *opere buffe* and *opere serie* (Pergolesi, Piccinni, Gluck, Salieri) along with German operettas and Singspiels, some of the latter composed by Pasterwiz. This brilliant period faded with the reforms of Emperor Joseph II, and finally the theatre itself was demolished in 1804 to make room for a boarding school.

A. Kellner: *Musikgeschichte des Stiftes Kremsmünster* (Kassel, 1956)
A. Sturm: *Theatergeschichte Oberösterreichs im 16. und 17. Jahrhundert*, Theatergeschichte Österreichs, i/1 (Vienna, 1964)
F. Fuhrich: *Theatergeschichte Oberösterreichs im 18. Jahrhundert*, Theatergeschichte Österreichs, i/2 (Vienna, 1968) [incl. repertory]
H. Boberski: *Das Theater der Benediktiner an der alten Universität Salzburg (1617–1778)*, Theatergeschichte Österreichs, vi/1 (Vienna, 1978)   ROBERT N. FREEMAN

Krenek [Křenek], Ernst (*b* Vienna, 23 Aug 1900; *d* Palm Springs, CA, 23 Dec 1991). American composer of Austrian birth. He became a pupil of Schreker in Vienna at the age of 16, and continued to study with him in Berlin until 1923, entering a circle which included Busoni. His first dramatic work, *Die Zwingburg* (composed 1922), originated during the time which Krenek later described as the heydey of musical expressionism when everything was intended to be 'radical', meaning autonomous and abstract. Yet the representation of social upheaval in this scenic cantata revealed a sympathy for radical change which was far from irrelevant to central Europeans in the aftermath of the Russian Revolution. Krenek's setting of a plot in the

expressionist mode, concerning oppressed workers ruled by a tyrant whose decision to liberate them for a day drives them into a delirium, marked the beginning of a life-long involvement with the nature and implications of different kinds of freedom without promoting any particular ideology. Many of his 20 other operatic compositions explore philosophical ideas and human problems, several in a satirical or allegorical manner. In 1922–3 he composed a comic opera, *Der Sprung über den Schatten*, about a psychologist who liberates an individual from his shadow, or inhibitions, and brings about the overthrow of a regime. This was followed by a setting of a Kokoschka play, *Orpheus und Eurydike*.

Krenek's first experience of professional operatic work was at Kassel and Wiesbaden (1925–7) as assistant to Paul Bekker, who introduced him to new socio-aesthetic ideas. Contact with the less self-consciously esoteric approaches of composers such as Milhaud during a visit to Paris and the more relaxed artistic environment he experienced in Italy and Switzerland (1923–5), combined with practical experience of the theatre, caused Krenek to reconsider the relevance of entertainment. The result was *Jonny spielt auf*, his best-known work and the greatest box-office success of the entire Weimar period (see illustration). Its overwhelming impact in 1927 made the composer and his hero household names and enabled him virtually to retire from earning a living. Three satirical one-act operas – *Der Diktator*, a parody of the rise of fascism in Italy, *Das geheime Königreich*, about a king who chooses to abdicate from worldly power in the face of threatened rebellion, and *Schwergewicht*, inspired by the mass popularity of boxing – were swiftly composed in the afterglow of *Jonny*, sharing some 'Zeitoper' traits. In spite of their unconnected subject matter and different classifications as tragic, fairy-tale and burlesque works, the three operas were designed to be presented together (they were revived at the Vienna Festival in 1990).

On his return to Vienna in 1928 Krenek revived grand opera in his *Leben des Orest*, in which he speculated on the value of an unbridled existence. Influenced, perhaps, by finally meeting his hero Karl Kraus in 1930, some of whose poems he set to music, Krenek went rather too far in his comic satire, *Kehraus um St Stephan*. The work was rejected because of fears that it would provoke offence, since not only did it poke fun at every political principle of the time, but its subject, the collapse of the Austrian regime of 1918, was badly timed. Just as Krenek was considering giving up composition for writing, Clemens Krauss, the director of the Vienna Opera, encouraged him to continue exploring his vision of the regeneration of a disintegrating society by commissioning *Karl V*. The result was a historical work, which used techniques of epic theatre to propose Catholicism as the basis of a cultural alliance capable of challenging the barbarism of Nazism. Not surprisingly, the proposed 1934 Vienna première was banned, though the work was eventually staged in 1938 in Prague as the Nazis marched into Austria.

Krenek was forced to emigrate, and he returned to the USA (which he had visited in 1937 with his adaptation of Monteverdi's *L'incoronazione di Poppea*), beginning a distinguished teaching career. At first he turned to church and chamber composition, writing several small-scale operas: *Tarquin*, *What Price Confidence?* (his first English libretto) and *Dark Waters*. It was 20 years before he resumed large-scale operatic composition. Two works for the Hamburg Staatsoper, marking

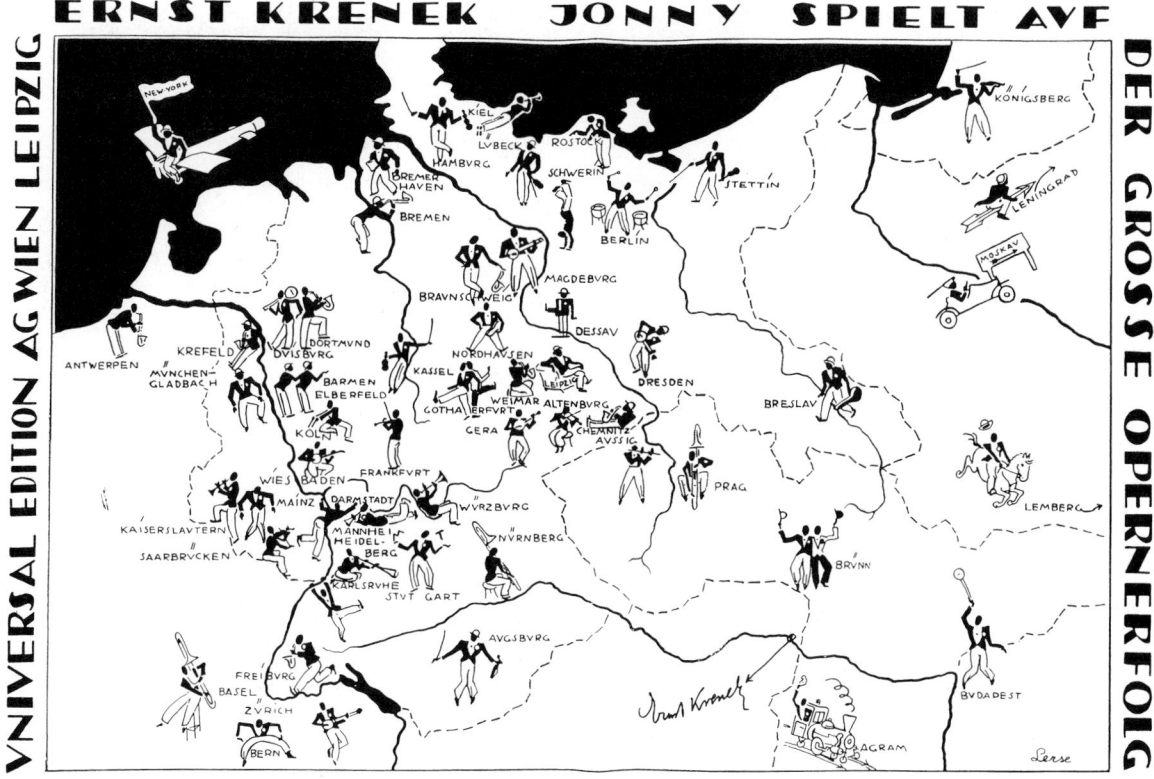

Map showing all the places where Krenek's 'Jonny spielt auf' was performed: drawing by Rudolf Smirzitz issued by Universal Edition on the occasion of the opera's first Vienna performance (1927)

a return to classical mythology applied to contemporary sociological issues, appeared in the 1950s and 60s: *Pallas Athene weint*, a treatment of the downfall of democracy in Athens reflecting the concerns of postwar Europe, and *Der goldene Bock*, a surrealistic setting of the legend of the Argonauts. Krenek became a pioneer of television opera in the 1960s, writing *Ausgerechnet und verspielt* and *Der Zauberspiegel* for European companies. Both these and the chamber work *Sardakai* are heavily ironic and reflect his increasing scepticism about the genre, bringing it closer to the theatre of the absurd. His individual treatment and expansion of the capacities of opera has led to an increase in the popularity of the genre. Composing mostly to his own librettos he demonstrated both his desire for total control over the dramatic material and his need for verbal expression, the latter also manifested in his extensive literary output. His designation of works under various types was indicative of his continual revaluation of the genre.

Krenek's response to, and initiation of, musical and intellectual innovations resulted in a stylistic vocabulary characteristic of the age. Initially he renounced the sensual lyricism of Schreker for the ascetic radicalism of the Second Viennese School, scoring successes at contemporary festivals with, for example, the Second Symphony (1922). *Die Zwingburg* and *Der Sprung* are also atonal, sharply rhythmic works unified by means of motivic relationships. *Der Sprung*, however, is self-critical in the satirical way it contrasts avant-garde modernism with the fashionable modernity of entertainment music, anticipating features of *Jonny* and the three one-act operas. These attempts to bridge the divide between élite and popular music divested opera of its

subjectivity more in the manner of the French neo-classicists than of Eisler. In *Orpheus* Krenek devised musical tone-symbols to represent the ideas, events and emotions in Kokoschka's play. *Leben des Orest* continues the reconciliation of italianate Romanticism with the jazz characteristic of *Jonny*, but in grander form. *Karl V* is elaborate yet simple, due to the juxtaposition of traditional dance types with cantabile melodies and smooth rhythms. Using distancing effects it reflects on the then current psychological preoccupation with historical objectivity and subjective truth. Following the successful completion of this early operatic work in the 12-note method (where ironically Schoenberg, writing *Moses und Aron* at the same time, had failed) Krenek went on to explore serial devices anticipating techniques of Boulez and Stockhausen. By the time of the television operas Krenek's serialism was fully developed. Lyricism is the prominent stylistic feature of *Der goldene Bock*, and entertainment and topicality are the essence of *Sardakai*, which seems to bring Krenek's operatic work full circle. Its characters could be the counterparts of *Der Sprung*, his first real opera, and it contains the ultimate neo-classical joke: a transistor playing Mozart at a beach party.

See also JONNY SPIELT AUF; KARL V; and ORPHEUS UND EURYDIKE.

librettos by the composer unless otherwise stated

Die Zwingburg op.14, 1922 (szenische Kantate, 1, F. Werfel, after F. Demuth), Berlin, Staatsoper, 20 Oct 1924, vs (Vienna and New York, 1923)

Der Sprung über den Schatten op.17, 1923 (komische Oper, 3), Frankfurt, Opernhaus, 9 June 1924, vs (Vienna and New York, 1923)

Orpheus und Eurydike op.21, 1923 (Schauspiel, 3, O. Kokoschka), Kassel, Staats, 27 Nov 1926, vs (Vienna and New York, 1925)

Bluff op.36 (musikalische Komödie, C. von Levetzov, after G. Gribble), 1924–5, *A-Wst**

Jonny spielt auf op.45, 1925 (2 pts), Leipzig, Stadt, 10 Feb 1927 (Vienna and Leipzig, 1927)

Der Diktator op.49, 1926 (tragische Oper, 1), Wiesbaden, Staats, 6 May 1928, vs (Vienna and Leipzig, 1928)

Das geheime Königreich op.50, 1926–7 (Märchenoper, 1), Wiesbaden, Staats, 6 May 1928 (Vienna and Leipzig, 1928)

Schwergewicht, oder die Ehre der Nation op.55 (burleske Operette, 1), Wiesbaden, Staats, 6 May 1928 (Vienna and Leipzig, 1928)

Leben des Orest op.60, 1928–9 (grosse Oper, 5), Leipzig, Neues, 19 Jan 1930 (Vienna and Leipzig, 1930)

Kehraus um St Stephan op.66, 1930 (Satire mit Musik, 2), Vienna, Ronacher, 6 Dec 1990, *Wst**

Karl V op.73, 1931–3 (Bühnenwerk mit Musik, 2 pts), Prague, Neues Deutsches, 22 June 1938, vs (Vienna, 1933), full score [fragments] (Vienna, 1936); rev. 1954, Düsseldorf, Deutsche Oper, 11 May 1958

Cefalo e Procri op.77 (Fabel, prol., 3 scenes, R. Küfferle, Ger. trans. by Krenek), Venice, Goldoni, 15 Sept 1934

Tarquin op.90, 1940–1 (drama with music, 2 pts, Eng. text by E. Lavery, Ger. text by M.-C. Schulte-Strathaus and P. Funk), reading, Poughkeepsie, NY, Vassar College, 13 May 1941; stage, Cologne, Kammerspiele, 16 July 1950, vs and lib. *Wst**

What Price Confidence? [Vertrauenssache] op.111, 1945–6 (komische Kammeroper, 9 scenes), Saarbrücken, Stadt, 23 May 1962; Eng. trans. perf. 1968

Dark Waters [Dunkle Wasser] op.125, 1950 (1, after H. Melville: *The Confidence Man*), Los Angeles, UCLA, 2 May 1951

Pallas Athene weint op.144, 1952–5 (prol., 3), Hamburg, Staatsoper, 17 Oct 1955, vs (Vienna and Mainz, 1955)

The Bell Tower [Der Glockenturm] op.153, 1955–6 (1, after Melville), Urbana, IL, U. of Illinois, 17 March 1957

Ausgerechnet und verspielt op.179 ('spiel' Oper [television], 1), Österreichisches Fernsehen, 25 July 1962

Der goldene Bock [Chrysomallos] op.186, 1962–3 (4), Hamburg, Staatsoper, 16 June 1964, lib. pubd

Der Zauberspiegel op.192, 1963–6 (Fernsehoper, 14 scenes), Bayerischer Fernsehen, 23 Dec 1968

Sardakai, oder Das kommt davon [Wenn Sardakai auf Reisen geht] op.206, 1967–9 (11 scenes), Hamburg, Staatsoper, 27 June 1970, lib. pubd; rev. 1971

SELECTED WRITINGS

'Zum Problem der Oper', *Von Neuer Musik* (Cologne, 1925), 39–43

'"Materialbestimmtheit" der Oper', *Musikblätter des Anbruch*, ix (1927), 48–52

'Über Sinn und Zweck des Theaters', ibid, ix (1927), 281–2

'"Jonny spielt auf" und die Ausführenden', *Staatstheater Wiesbaden* (Oct 1927)

'Wege des Theaters', *Neue Schweizer Rundschau*, xxi (1928), 235–40

'Meine drei Einakter', *Musikblätter des Anbruch*, x (1928), 158–61

'Opernerfahrung', *Anbruch*, xi (1929), 233–7

Leben des Orest, ibid, xii (1930), 1–4

'Zur Situation der Oper', *Frankfurter Zeitung* (20 May 1932); repr. in *Auftakt*, xii (1932), 131–7

'Zur musikalischen Bearbeitung von Monteverdis *Poppea*', *SMz*, lxxvi (1936), 545–55

'The New Music and Today's Theatre', *MM*, xiv (1937), 200–03; repr. in *The Essence of Opera*, ed. U. Weisstein (New York, 1964), 348–54

Über neue Musik: sechs Vorlesungen zur Einführung in die theoretischen Grundlagen (Vienna, 1937) [rev. as *Music Here and Now* (New York, 1939)]

'New Opera Style', *National Federation of Music Clubs: Official Bulletin*, xx/4 (1941), 7–8

'Where to begin? Operatic production or produce', *Opera News*, vi/14 (1942–3), 8–10, 30

'Opera between the Wars', *MM*, xx (1943), 102–11

Selbstdarstellung (Zürich, 1948); rev. and enlarged as 'Self Analysis', *University of New Mexico Quarterly*, xxiii (1953), 5–57

'*The Neighbours* or *The Test*', *Freundesgabe für Friedrich T. Gubler zum sechzigsten Geburtstag am 1. Juli 1950* (Winterthur, 1950), 103–26 [text for a chamber op (not composed)]

'Freiheit und Rechtfertigung', *Oper* (Frankfurt am Main, 1951), 2–4 [programme book]

'Pallas Athene weint', *ÖMz*, x (1955), 8–9

Zur Sprache gebracht (Munich, 1958) [essays]

'Musik im Schauspiel', *ÖMz*, xx (1965), 415–18

Horizons Circled: Reflections on my Music (Berkeley, 1974)

Das Musikdramatische Werk (Vienna, 1974–82)

'Zur Vollendung von Alban Berg's *Lulu*-Fragment', *Musica*, xxxi (1977), 401–3

'Jonny erinnert sich', *ÖMz*, xxxv (1980), 187–9

'Marginal remarks to *Lulu*', *Alban Berg Symposium: Wien 1980*, 8–11

'Persönliches zur Oper', *Jahrbuch des Wiener Goethe-Vereins* (1980–1), 275–81

'Aus der Mappe eines Opernkomponisten', *ÖMz*, xxxix (1984), 506–9

'Studien zu meinem Bühnenwerk *Karl V*', *Ernst Krenek*, ed. H. K. Metzger and R. Riehn (Munich, 1984), 20–34

'Meine Zusammenarbeit mit Oskar Kokoschka', *ÖMz*, xlv (1990), 337–9

Autobiographical MSS in *US-Wc* [withheld until 15 years after Krenek's death]

*

H. H. Stuckenschmidt: 'Ernst Kreneks Opern', *Melos*, v (1925–6), 365–8

A. Aber: 'Ernst Krenek: Jonny spielt auf', *Musikblätter des Anbruch*, ix (1927), 127–32

A. Baresel: 'Jonny spielt auf: Leipziger Uraufführung der neuen Krenek-Oper', *Neue Musik-Zeitung*, xlviii (1927), 293–4

R. Hartmann: 'Operndramaturgische Glossen über Kreneks "Jonny spielt auf"', ibid, 382–4

W. Jacob: 'Über den Realismus in Kreneks "Jonny spielt auf"', *Die Musik*, xx (1927–8), 182–5

W. Harry: 'Zeitliches und Überzeitliches in "Jonny spielt auf"', *Musikblätter des Anbruch*, x (1928), 14–17

R. Majut: 'Kreneks Jonny-Dichtung im geistesgeschichtlichen Zusammenhang des Weltschmerzes und des Rousseauismus', *Germanisch-Romanische Monatsschrift*, xvi/11–12 (1928), 437–59

A. Heuss: 'Wo stehen wir heute? Zur Uraufführung von Ernst Kreneks grosser Oper in 5 Akten: "Das Leben des Orest"', *NZM*, xcvii (1930), 163–8

H. F. Redlich: 'Heimat und Freiheit: zur Ideologie der jüngsten Werke Ernst Kreneks', *Musikblätter des Anbruch*, xii (1930), 54–8

P. Bekker: *Wandlungen der Oper* (Zürich and Leipzig, 1934)

H. H. Stuckenschmidt: 'Kreneks *Karl V*', *Prager Tageblatt* (22 June 1938)

R. Erickson: 'Křenek's Later Music', *MR*, ix (1948), 29–44

C. Dahlhaus: 'Aschylos und Jazz: Kreneks "Leben des Orest" in Darmstadt aufgeführt', *Theater heute*, ii/4 (1961), 10–11

L. Knessl: 'Das dunkle Wasser: Krenek zwischen "Jonny" und Zeitfragen', *NZM*, cxxv (1964), 553–4

W. Rogge: *Ernst Kreneks Opern: Spiegel der zwanziger Jahre* (Wolfenbüttel, 1970)

W. W. Bruchhäuser: 'Ein unabhängiger Musiker – Krenek 70 Jahre', *Das Opernjournal* (1970–72), 12

H. W. Schwab: '"Jonny spielt auf": Berichte und Bilder vom Auftreten des schwarzen Musikers in Europa', *Opernstudien* (Tutzing, 1975), 175–87

H. Knoch: *Orpheus und Eurydike: der antike Sagenstoff in den Opern von Darius Milhaud und Ernst Krenek* (Regensburg, 1977)

C. Maurer-Zenck: 'Unbewältigte Vergangenheit: Kreneks "Karl V" in Wien: zur nicht bevorstehenden Wiener Erstaufführung', *Mf*, xxxii (1979), 273–88

N. Tschulik: 'Die verhinderte Uraufführung von Kreneks *Karl V*', *ÖMz*, xxxiv (1979), 122–9

O. J. Bailey: *The Influence of Ernst Krenek on the Musical Culture of the Twin Cities* (diss., U. of Minnesota, 1980)

C. Maurer-Zenck: *Ernst Krenek: ein Komponist im Exil* (Vienna, 1980)

——: 'Musikalisches Welttheater: Kreneks *Karl V*: zur konzertanten Wiedergabe der Oper den Salzburger Festspielen', *ÖMz*, xxxv (1980), 370–2

W. Molkow: 'Der Sprung über den Schatten: zum Opernschaffen Ernst Kreneks in den 20er und 30er Jahren', *Musica*, xxxiv (1980), 132–5

W. Rogge: 'Oper als Quadrator des Kreises: zum Opernschaffen Ernst Kreneks', *ÖMz*, xxxv (1980), 453–7

P. Stadlen: 'Krenek: a Lifetime of Opera', *Opera*, xxxi (1980), 876–82

J. L. Stewart: 'Frauen in den Opern Ernst Kreneks', *Musica*, xxxiv (1980), 136–8

E. Hilmar, ed.: *Dank an Ernst Krenek: Katalog zur Ausstellung* (Vienna, 1982)

O. Kolleritsch, ed.: *Ernst Krenek* (Vienna and Graz, 1982)

G. Schubert: 'Hindemith und Krenek', *Mf*, xxxv (1982), 277–82

W. J. Schweiger: 'Vom anderen Orpheus ...', *Parnass*, ii/4 (1982), 69

H.-K. Metzger and R. Riehn, eds.: *Ernst Krenek* (Munich, 1984)

J. Sams: '"Jonny" – the First Jazz Opera', *Opera*, xxxv (1984), 1085–90

C. Maurer-Zenck: 'The Ship Loaded with Faith and Hope: Krenek's *Karl V* and the Viennese Politics of the Thirties', *MQ*, lxxi (1985), 116–34

S. C. Cook: *Opera for a New Republic: the 'Zeitopern' of Krenek, Weill and Hindemith* (Ann Arbor and London, 1988)

J. Warren: 'Ernst Krenek and Max Brand: Two Austrians at the "Court" of Weimar', *German Life and Letters*, xli (1987–8), 467–78

G. H. Bowles: *Ernst Krenek: a Bio-bibliography* (New York and London, 1989)

R. Bletschacher: 'Zur Uraufführung von Kreneks "Kehraus um St Stephan"', *ÖMZ*, xlv (1990), 702–3

P. Dickinson: 'Ernst Krenek', *The Independent* (28 December 1991) [obituary]

W. Mellers: 'In tune with the century', *The Guardian* (31 December 1991) [obituary]

J. L. Stewart: *Ernst Krenek, the Man and His Music* (Berkeley, 1991)   CHARLOTTE PURKIS

Krenn, Fritz (*b* Vienna, 11 Dec 1887; *d* Vienna, 17 July 1964). Austrian bass-baritone. He studied in Vienna, making his début at the Volksoper in 1917 as Alfio. After singing at Bratislava and Liberec, he was engaged at the Vienna Staatsoper (1920–25) and the Berlin Staatsoper (1927–43). He appeared in the première of Hindemith's *Neues vom Tage* (1929, Kroll-Oper). In 1936 he sang Ochs at Salzburg and also made his début at Covent Garden as the Devil (*Švanda Dudak*); he returned there to sing Ochs, Pizarro and Kecal. In 1938 he returned to Vienna. His repertory included Escamillo, Falstaff, Gianni Schicchi, the Dutchman and Count Almaviva, but his finest role was Ochs, which he sang at the Metropolitan Opera in 1952, at the age of 65.   ELIZABETH FORBES

Krenn, Werner (*b* Vienna, 21 Sept 1943). Austrian tenor. He was a member of the Vienna Boys' Choir and studied with László Somogy, making his début in Purcell's *The Fairy-Queen* at the 1966 Berlin Festival. He first sang at Salzburg in 1967 as Aceste in Mozart's *Ascanio in Alba*. He sang Don Ottavio at Aix-en-Provence in 1969 and made his British début with Scottish Opera in 1970, singing Jaquino and Don Ottavio. He sang Idamantes at the Vienna Staatsoper (1971) and at Scheveningen (1973). His light, smooth and flexible voice was ideal for Mozart. He recorded roles in several early Mozart operas, as well as Titus for Kertesz. He sang Belmonte in a film of *Die Entführung*.
                                                                        ALAN BLYTH

Kreutzer [Kreuzer], Conradin [Conrad, Konradin] (*b* Messkirch, Baden, 22 Nov 1780; *d* Riga, 14 Dec 1849). German composer and conductor. The son of a Swabian burgher, he received his earliest musical training from the local choirmaster, J. B. Rieger. From 1789 he studied theory and the organ with Ernst Weinrauch and learnt to play a number of instruments at the Benedictine monastery of Zwiefalten. In 1798 or 1799 he became a student of law at the University of Freiburg, but after his father's death in 1800 he turned entirely to music. While still students he and friends performed his one-act Singspiel *Die lächerliche Werbung*. For the next three or four years he was probably in Switzerland; in 1804 he went to Vienna, where he met Haydn and was probably a pupil of Albrechtsberger. He gave music

lessons and concerts in order to maintain himself, and continued to compose. From 1810 he toured Germany and elsewhere demonstrating Franz Leppich's semi-mechanical 'panmelodicon'. He spent the winter of 1811–12 in Stuttgart, where the operas *Konradin von Schwaben* and *Feodora* were successfully staged. Following Danzi's resignation Kreutzer was appointed Hofkapellmeister with effect from 10 July 1812. That autumn he married for the first time; his daughters Cäcilie and Marie (the latter from his second marriage) became singers. Although he gave up his Stuttgart post in 1816 owing to intrigues, his friendship there with the Swabian poet Johann Ludwig Uhland, one of Germany's foremost lyricists and ballad writers, was of far-reaching importance for his later development.

After he left Stuttgart Kreutzer spent some time at Schaffhausen before becoming Kapellmeister (1818–22) to Prince Carl Egon of Fürstenberg at Donaueschingen. He made several tours while still nominally engaged there, and following the successful production of his opera *Libussa* in Vienna in 1822 was appointed Kapellmeister at the Kärntnertortheater; he held the post until 1827 and from 1829 to 1832. Between these spells at the Vienna court opera he was in Paris. In 1833 he moved to the suburban Theater in der Josefstadt, in response to an invitation from the ambitious director, Stöger. He was Kapellmeister there from 1833 to 1835, the period that saw the first performances of his two greatest successes, *Das Nachtlager in Granada* and *Der Verschwender*. Although he was back at the Kärntnertortheater from 1835, it was at the Josefstadt that the opera *Die Höhle bei Waverley* was given in 1837. In the 1840s he accompanied his daughters on concert tours and was city music director at Cologne, 1840–42, as well as working in Mainz, 1844–5. He was mentioned in 1846 as Nicolai's likely successor at the Vienna Opera, but the negotiations came to nothing and in 1848 he moved to Riga.

During the 1840s a number of German theatres staged Kreutzer's operas, though these were more *succès d'estime* than triumphs: Brunswick, Wiesbaden, Darmstadt, Hamburg and (posthumously) Kassel each staged one of his new operas in the years following his final departure from Vienna, but none of these houses seems to have invited him back to mount another. Tastes were changing; the esteemed master of *Das Nachtlager* and *Der Verschwender* had nothing original to offer a public that was experiencing the early operas of Wagner.

Kreutzer's music has never been entirely forgotten. His Uhland settings for male-voice chorus long remained popular. *Das Nachtlager* used to be revived occasionally in Germany and a few of the solo songs are still sometimes heard; above all, his score for Raimund's 'romantic magic tale' *Der Verschwender* continues to be performed regularly in Austria. Despite the power of some of the big numbers in *Das Nachtlager* and the sure sense of dramatic timing and instrumental colour in *Der Verschwender* (the beggar's song 'O hört des armen Mannes Bitte' is, with its haunting, melancholy beauty, not unworthy of Schubert; its insertion within a roistering chorus is a touch that Weber would have admired), Kreutzer is at his most characteristic in simple, expressive songs, such as the beggar's 'Habt Dank, ihr guten Leute' and Valentin's 'Da streiten sich die Leut herum' from *Der Verschwender*, and the once-famous romance 'Ein Schütz bin ich' from *Das Nachtlager*. Many works have effective instrumentation and a lively feeling for rhythm and local colour.

See also NACHTLAGER IN GRANADA, DAS and VERSCHWENDER, DER.

*performed in Vienna and printed works published as vocal scores,
unless otherwise stated; principal sources for MSS and published
works are A-Wdtö, Wgm, Wn, Wst; D-DO, Mbs, Rp*

WJ – *Theater in der Josefstadt*   WK – *Kärntnertortheater*
WW – *Theater an der Wien*

Die lächerliche Werbung (Spl, 1), Freiburg, *c*1800
Aesop in Phrygien [Aesop in Lydien], 1808; rev., Stuttgart, *c*1816
Die zwei Worte, oder Die Nacht im Walde (1, after B.-J. Marsollier
    des Vivetières), Stuttgart, 1808 [or ? Vienna, 1803]
Jery und Bätely (Spl, 1, J. W. von Goethe), WK, 19 May 1810
Konradin von Schwaben, 1810 or before (3, B. von Guseck); with
    new text by K. R. Weitzmann, Stuttgart, 30 March 1812; rev. as
    Konradin, der letzte Hohenstaufe, 1847
Panthea, 1810 (3), unperf.
Feodora (1, A. von Kotzebue), Stuttgart, 1812 (Leipzig, n.d.)
Die Insulanerin (2, J. F. Schlotterbeck, after P. Metastasio),
    Stuttgart, 25 March 1813; rev. as Die Insulanerinnen, WK, 11 Feb
    1829
Der Taucher (romantische Oper, 2, S. G. Bürde, after F. Schiller),
    Stuttgart, 19 April 1813; rev. 1823 (Vienna, n.d.)
Alimon und Zaide, oder Der Prinz von Katanea (3), Stuttgart, 24
    Feb 1814 (Mainz, n.d.)
Die Nachtmütze (komische Oper, after Kotzebue: *Die Schlafmütze
    des Propheten Elias*), Stuttgart, 1814
Die Alpenhütte (1, Kotzebue), Stuttgart, 1 March 1815 (Augsburg,
    n.d.)
Der Herr und sein Diener (1, after Fr. orig.), Stuttgart, 30 Nov 1815
Orestes (lyric tragedy, 3), ? Prague, 1818
Adele von Budoy (Spl, 1), Königsberg, 1821; rev. as Cordelia
    (lyrisch-tragische Oper, 1, P. A. Wolff), WK, 15 Feb 1823, arias
    (Berlin, 1823)
Libussa [Primislav] (romantische Oper, 3, J. K. Bernard), WK, 4 Dec
    1822 (Vienna, n.d.)
Sigune (Nordic legend, 3, A. Schumacher), WW, 20 Nov 1823
    (Vienna, n.d.)
Die erfüllte Hoffnung (ländliche Szene, 1), WW, 2 Dec 1824
Die lustige Werbung (komische Oper, 2, C. B. [? R. B.], after Fr.
    orig.), WW, 27 June 1826
La folle de Glaris (2, T.-M.-F. Sauvage), Paris, Odéon, 21 April
    1827 [? same as Cordelia; additional music by J.-M. Payer]
L'eau de jouvenance (comic op, 2, F.-A. Duvert and Xavier [X. B.
    Saintine]), Paris, Odéon, 13 Oct 1827; as Die Verjüngungs-Essenz
    (Operette, 1, trans. K. von Braun), WK, 24 Sept 1838
Das Mädchen von Montfermeuil, oder Denise, das Milchmädchen
    (komische Oper, 5, Schumacher), WK, 3 Oct 1829
Baron Luft (Spl, 1, after Fr. orig.), WK, 20 Jan 1830
Die Jungfrau (romantische Oper, 3, Schumacher, after Mélesville
    [A.-H.-J. Duveyrier]), Prague, Nov 1831
Die Hochländerin, 1831 (1), unperf.
Der Lastträger an der Themse (3, H. Herzenskron), Prague, 16 Feb
    1832
Melusine (romantische Oper, 3, F. Grillparzer), Berlin, König-
    städtisches, 27 Feb 1833
Der Ring des Glückes, oder Die Quellenfürstin im Alpentale
    (Zauberspiel, 3, F. K. Weidmann), WJ, 19 Dec 1833
Das Nachtlager in [von] Granada (romantische Oper, 2, von Braun,
    after J. F. Kind), WJ, 13 Jan 1834 (Vienna, n.d.)
Der Verschwender (Zaubermärchen, 3, F. Raimund), WJ, 20 Feb
    1834 (Vienna, n.d.)
Tom Rick, oder Der Pavian (komische Oper, 3, J. Kupelwieser, after
    Fr. orig.), WJ, 1 July 1834
Der Bräutigam in der Klemme (Spl, 1, Herzenskron), WJ, 24 June
    1835
Traumleben, oder Zufriedenheit, die Quelle des Glückes
    (Zauberspiel, 3, F. X. Told), WJ, 10 Oct 1835
Die Höhle bei Waverley (3, G. Ott, after A. Oehlenschläger), WJ, 6
    April 1837
Der Gang nach dem Eisenhammer [Fridolin] (romantische Oper, 3,
    J. A. F. Reil, after Schiller), WK, 16 Dec 1837
Die beiden Figaro (komische Oper, 2, G. F. Treitschke, after J. F.
    Jünger), Brunswick, 13 Aug 1840 (Brunswick, n.d.)
Der Edelknecht (4, C. von Birch-Pfeiffer), Wiesbaden, 21 June 1842
    (Brunswick, n.d.)
Des Sängers Fluch (1, E. Pasqué, after J. L. Uhland), Darmstadt, 17
    May 1846
Die Hochländerin am Kaukasus (romantische Oper, 3, Guseck),
    Hamburg, 6 or 16 Nov 1846 [? connected with Die Hochländerin,
    1831]

Aurelia, oder Die Prinzessin von Bulgarien (romantische Oper, 3, C.
    Gollmick, after J. F. von Weissenthurn), ? Kassel, 20 Aug 1851

Undated works: Der Apollosaal (Spl, 1); Zenobia, unperf.
    [Kreutzer's final opera]; Das Bild der Landesmutter (occasional
    piece)

[H. Weber]: *58. Neujahrsstück der Allgemeinen Musikgesellschaft
    in Zürich* (Zürich, 1870)
W. H. Riehl: *Musikalische Charakterköpfe*, i (Stuttgart, 5/1876),
    263–74
R. Krauss: *Das Stuttgarter Hoftheater von den ältesten Zeiten bis
    zur Gegenwart* (Stuttgart, 1908)
A. Prümers: 'Aus Kreutzers Briefwechsel', *Neue Musikzeitung*,
    xxxiii (1912), 290
R. Rossmayer: *Konradin Kreutzer als dramatischer Komponist*
    (diss., U. of Vienna, 1928)
A. Bauer: *150 Jahre Theater an der Wien* (Zürich, 1952)
K. Goedeke: *Grundriss zur Geschichte der deutschen Dichtung*, xi/2
    (Düsseldorf, 2/1953)
A. Bauer: *Opern und Operetten in Wien* (Graz and Cologne, 1955)
——: *Das Theater in der Josefstadt zu Wien* (Vienna, 1957)
R. Heinemann: 'Kreutzer, Konrad', *Rheinische Musiker*, iv, ed.
    K. G. Fellerer (Cologne, 1966), 59–64   PETER BRANSCOMBE

Kreutzer, Léon Charles François (*b* Paris, 23 Sept 1817;
d Vichy, 6 Oct 1868). French writer on music and
composer, nephew of Rodolphe Kreutzer. He studied
the piano and composition privately. His cultural interests and independence of thought led him to music criticism; according to Fétis (*Biographie universelle*) he
began writing for *L'union* in 1840, concentrating on
aspects of opera and operatic history. The series of
articles 'De l'opéra en Europe' was published in the
Revue et gazette musicale de Paris between 4 February
and 23 September 1849. His work also appeared in the
Revue contemporaine (from 1854), *L'opinion publique*
and *Le théâtre*. In collaboration with Edouard Fournier
he wrote the articles 'Opéra' and 'Opéra-Comique' in
the *Encyclopédie du XIXe siècle*, later published as
Essai sur l'art lyrique au théâtre (Paris, 1849). In addition to two symphonies, songs and chamber music,
Kreutzer composed two operas, *Serafine* and *Les filles
d'azur*; neither was performed or published.

K. J. Ellis: *La revue et gazette musicale de Paris (1834–1880): the
    State of Music Criticism in Nineteenth-Century France* (diss., U.
    of Oxford, 1991)   DAVID CHARLTON

Kreutzer, Rodolphe (*b* Versailles, 16 Nov 1766; *d*
Geneva, 6 Jan 1831). French composer and violinist. He
studied with his father, a musician in the Swiss Guards
of the Duke of Choiseul, and from 1778 with Anton
Stamitz. On 25 May 1780 he performed a concerto by
Stamitz at the Concert Spirituel, Paris, and was received
as a prodigy. Influenced by Viotti's style of composition
and playing, Kreutzer performed his own First Violin
Concerto at the Concert Spirituel in May 1784. He
came under the influence of Marie Antoinette and the
Count of Artois, who probably arranged his acceptance
into the king's music in 1785. He wrote chamber music
and played more of his own violin concertos, and by
1789 was a leading virtuoso.

No primary evidence has been discovered for Fétis's
assertion that two operas by Kreutzer were privately
produced under the queen's patronage in the closing
years of the *ancien régime*. But a series of operatic works
was brought out by Kreutzer from 1790, chiefly at the
Comédie-Italienne, later Opéra-Comique. The two
pieces which established his stage reputation were *Paul
et Virginie* and *Lodoïska*; the latter was preferred in

France to Cherubini's work of the same name, also first given in 1791.

Kreutzer was professor at both the Conservatoire (until 1826) and its forerunner the Institut National de Musique and sat on the Conservatoire council from 1825 to 1830. He made a successful concert tour of Italy in 1796 and during a second tour he was attached to Bernadotte's party on the latter's appointment as French ambassador to Vienna in February 1798; his activities included the removal of Italian manuscripts to France on Napoleon's orders. A Beethoven letter of 4 October 1804 reveals that Beethoven heard Kreutzer play; the 'Kreutzer' Sonata of 1802–3, published in 1805, was dedicated to him. Kreutzer's career in Paris from 1798 was marked by particularly successful concert appearances at the Théâtre Feydeau and the Opéra, where he became solo violin in 1801; he joined Napoleon's chapel orchestra in 1802 and his private orchestra four years later.

The opera *Astyanax* (1801) was fairly successful; but Kreutzer's first ballet score, *Paul et Virginie* (1806), using music from the earlier opera, held the stage for 15 years. *Aristippe* (1808), a comedy on the popular Anacreon theme, and the ballet *Les amours d'Antoine et Cléopatre* (1808), also proved successful and the former was given until 1830. The biblical opera *Abel* (1810), though at first indifferently received, was revived (minus its second act) in 1823; Berlioz wrote the composer an ecstatic letter of appreciation.

His career as a soloist ended when he broke his left arm in 1810, although he continued to play in ensembles and retained his official positions. After the Restoration in 1815 Kreutzer was named *maître de la chapelle du roi*; the next year he was created second conductor of the Opéra and chief conductor in 1820. From 1824 to 1827 he took overall direction of music at the Opéra. In the spring of 1826 Berlioz approached him unsuccessfully with a view to having *La révolution grecque* performed at the Opéra's series of *concerts spirituels*. But by this time Kreutzer's own style could find little public favour and his last opera, *Matilde*, was refused by the Opéra. His health declined from 1826, when he retired from most of his public positions.

In his stage works, Kreutzer achieved a measure of originality without ever producing a work of lasting value. His harmonic language is not without variety, and his melodies themselves betray Romantic turns of phrase even in the 1790s, though they are not often memorable. *Lodoiska* and *Abel* are his worthiest achievements; the former is vivid in drama and colour, and has warmth of melody. *Astyanax* contains some striking final pages depicting the Greeks leaving Troy, and in *Abel* the purely musical quality runs at a consistently higher level. Biblical subject matter was topical (cf Méhul's *Joseph*, 1807, and Le Sueur's *La mort d'Adam*, 1809); in Kreutzer's opera the devils who forge the club of human destruction are the tempters of Cain, and as an apotheosis Abel is carried heavenwards. There are pages of large-scale conception, but the opening of the original Act 3, in which an exhausted Cain prays for sleep ('Doux sommeil'), contains some of Kreutzer's best music. At the Opéra-Comique, *Jadis et aujourd'hui* was given until 1826, *L'homme sans façon* until 1833 and the 1791 version of *Paul et Virginie* was revived in 1830 and 1846.

Kreutzer is best remembered, however, for his *42 études ou caprices* (1796) for unaccompanied violin,

unique in their anticipation of the demands of 19th-century violin technique and their continuing utility as training material.

first performed and published in full score in Paris unless otherwise stated

Jeanne d'Arc à Orléans (drame historique mêlé d'ariettes, 3, Desforges [P. J. B. Choudard]), Comédie-Italienne (Salle Favart), 10 May 1790, unpubd

Paul et Virginie (cmda, 3, E. G. F. de Favières), Comédie-Italienne (Salle Favart), 15 Jan 1791 (1791)

Lodoiska, ou Les tartares (cmda, 3, J. E. B. Dejaure), Comédie-Italienne (Salle Favart), 1 Aug 1791 (1792)

Charlotte et Werther (comédie, 1, Dejaure), Comédie-Italienne (Salle Favart), 1 Feb 1792, unpubd

Le franc breton (comédie, 1, Dejaure), Comédie-Italienne (Salle Favart), 3 Nov 1792 (1803–10); collab. J.-P. Solié

Le siège de Lille [Cécile et Julien] (trait historique, 1, L. A. B. d'Antilly), Feydeau, 14 Nov 1792, extracts (1792)

Le déserteur de la montagne de Ham (fait historique, 1, Dejaure), Comédie-Italienne (Salle Favart), 6 Feb 1793, unpubd

Le congrès des rois (cmda, 3, Desmaillot [A. F. Eve]), OC (Favart), 26 Feb 1794; collab. N.-M. Dalayrac, A.-E.-M. Grétry, E.-N. Méhul and 8 others, unpubd

Le lendemain de la bataille de Fleurus (impromptu, 1, d'Antilly), Egalité, 15 Oct 1794, unpubd

Encore une victoire, ou Les déserteurs liégeois (1, d'Antilly), OC (Favart), 30 Oct 1794, unpubd

On respire (cmda, 1, C. L. Tissot), OC (Favart), 9 March 1795, lib. (c1795)

Le brigand (drame mêlé d'ariettes, 3, F.-B. Hoffman), OC (Favart), 25 July 1795, *F-Pc*

La journée du 10 août 1792, ou La chute du dernier tyran (opéra, 4, G. Saulnier and Darrieux), Opéra, 10 Aug 1795, lib. (1795)

Imogène, ou La gageure indiscrète (cmda, 3, Dejaure), OC (Favart), 27 April 1796, unpubd

Le petit page, ou La prison d'état (cmda, 1, R. C. G. de Pixérécourt and L. T. Lambert), Feydeau, 14 Feb 1800 (c1800); collab. N. Isouard

Flaminius à Corinthe (opéra, 1, Pixérécourt and Lambert), Opéra, 27 Feb 1801, *Po* (inc.); collab. Isouard

Astyanax (opéra, 3, Dejaure), Opéra, 12 April 1801, *Po*

Le baiser et la quittance, ou Une aventure de garnison (oc, 3, L. B. Picard, M. Dieulafoy and C. de Longchamps), OC (Feydeau), 18 June 1803, *B-Bc*; collab. A. Boieldieu, Isouard and Méhul

Harmodius and Aristogiton, 1804 (tragédie lyrique, E.-J.-B. Delrieu), unperf., lost

Les surprises, ou L'étourdi en voyage (2, C. A. B. Sewrin), OC (Feydeau), 2 Jan 1806, unpubd

Paul et Virginie (ballet-pantomime, 3), St Cloud, 12 June 1806, *F-Po*

François I, ou La fête mystérieuse (cmda, 2, Sewrin and A. de Chazet), OC (Feydeau), 14 March 1807 (c1807)

Aristippe (comédie lyrique, 2, P. F. Giraud and M. T. Leclercq), Opéra, 24 May 1808 (c1808), ov. ed. D. Charlton, *The Symphony 1720–1840*, ser. D, vii (New York and London, 1983)

Jadis et aujourd'hui (opéra bouffon, 1, Sewrin), OC (Feydeau), 29 Oct 1808 (c1808)

La fête de Mars (divertissement-pantomime, 1), Opéra, 26 Dec 1809, *Po*

Abel (tragédie lyrique, 3, Hoffman), Opéra, 23 March 1810, *Po*; rev. as La mort d'Abel (2), Opéra, 17 March 1823, vs (c1824)

Le triomphe du mois de mars (opéra-ballet, 1, E. M. Dupaty), Opéra, 27 March 1811, *Po*

L'homme sans façon, ou Les contrariétés (cmda, 3, Sewrin), OC (Feydeau), 7 Jan 1812 (c1812)

Le camp de Sobieski, ou Le triomphe des femmes (comédie mêlée de chant, 2, Dupaty), OC (Feydeau), 19 April 1813

Constance et Théodore, ou La prisonnière (oc, 2, B.-J. Marsollier des Vivetières), OC (Feydeau), 22 Nov 1813

L'oriflamme (opéra, 1, C.-G. Etienne and L. P.-M.-F. Baour-Lormian), Opéra, 1 Feb 1814, *Pn*, *Po*, *I-PAc*; (1814); collab. H.-M. Berton, Méhul and F. Paer

Les Béarnais, ou Henri IV en voyage (comédie mêlée de chants, 1, Sewrin), OC (Feydeau), 21 May 1814; collab. Boieldieu

La perruque et la redingote (oc, 3, A. E. Scribe), OC (Feydeau), 25 Jan 1815; collab. C. F. Kreubé

La princesse de Babylone (opéra, 3, L. J. B. E. Vigée), Opéra, 30 May 1815, *F-Po*

Les dieux rivaux (opéra-ballet, 1, C. Briffaut and Dieulafoy), Opéra, 21 June 1816, *Po*; collab. G. Spontini, L.-L. L. Persuis and Berton

Le maître et le valet (oc, 3, M. A. J. Gensoul), OC (Feydeau), 8 Aug 1816

Clari, ou La promesse de mariage (ballet-pantomime, 3), Opéra, 19 June 1820, Po

Blanche de Provence, ou La cour des fées (opéra, 1, M. E. G. M. Théaulon and de Rancé), Tuileries, 1 May 1821, Po; collab. Berton, Boieldieu, L. Cherubini and Paer

Le négociant de Hambourg (oc, 3, J. B. C. Vial and J. A. de R. St-Cyr), OC (Feydeau), 15 Oct 1821

Le paradis de Mahomet (oc, 3, Scribe and Mélesville [A.-H.-J. Duveyrier]), OC (Feydeau), 23 March 1822; collab. Kreubé

Ipsiboé (opéra, 4, M. de St-Lyon), Opéra, 31 March 1824, Po

Pharamond (opéra, 3, J. A. P. F. Ancelot, P. M. T. A. Guiraud and L. A. Soumet), Opéra, 10 June 1825, Pn, Po, R(m), vs (Paris, n.d.); collab. Berton and Boieldieu

Matilde, c1826–7 (3), unperf.

*

FétisB

Review of 'Ipsiboé', AMZ, xxvi (1824), 305–7

Review of 'Pharamond', AMZ, xxvii (1825), 597–8

F. J. Fétis: Obituary, Revue musicale (15 Jan 1831), 298–303

A. Jullien: Paris dilettante au commencement du siècle (Paris, 1884)

M. Dietz: Geschichte des musikalischen Dramas in Frankreich während der Revolution bis zum Directorium (Vienna, 2/1886)

H. Kling: Rodolphe Kreutzer (Brussels, 1898)

J. Hardy: Rodolphe Kreutzer (Paris, 1910)

J. Tiersot: Lettres de musiciens écrites en français du XVe au XXe siècle, i (Turin, 1924), 292–4

F. Friebe: 'Rodolphe Kreutzer als Opernkomponist', Chigiana, xxiii (1966), 149–62

M. E. C. Bartlet: 'Opera as Patriotic Ceremony: the Case of L'Oriflamme', IMSCR, xiii Strasbourg 1982, i, 327–39

W. Dean: 'French Opera', The Age of Beethoven 1790–1830, NOHM, viii (London, 1982), 26–119

D. Charlton: 'The Tragic Seascape: Sapho and its 12–note chord', JbO (1985), 46–72

——: 'On Redefinitions of Rescue Opera', Music and the French Revolution, ed. M. Boyd (Cambridge, 1992), 169–88

DAVID CHARLTON

Křička, Jaroslav (b Kelč, Moravia, 27 Aug 1882; d Prague, 23 Jan 1969). Czech composer. He grew up in an atmosphere imbued with folk traditions. After studying at the Prague Conservatory (1902–5) and in Berlin he taught at the Imperial School of Music in Yekaterinoslav (now Dnipropetrovs'k; 1906–9). He then returned to Prague, where he worked as a choirmaster and later as a professor of composition at the conservatory. Křička's talent manifested itself best in small forms (songs and choral works), and closer inspection of his larger pieces reveals that he conceived them in terms of smaller parts. His large output of compositions for the stage is varied and sometimes difficult to categorize. Beside musical interludes, operettas and musical comedies he wrote a lyrical opera, Hypolita, of which the instrumentation and vocal writing were influenced by Gustave Charpentier's Louise. He experimented with novel forms, including a Christmas play Ceské jesličky ('Bohemian Nativity'), a Singspiel with dancing, Král Lávra ('King Lávra'), a television opera, Kalhoty ('The Trousers'), and others. He achieved his greatest success with his children's operas, which have been frequently performed by professional and amateur ensembles, both in his own country and abroad; Clemens Krauss staged Max Brod's version of Bílý pán ('The Gentleman in White'), Spuk im Schloss, at the Staatsoper in Vienna in 1932. In his music Křička declined to sacrifice everything to originality and innovation, and his writing, though fresh and lively, reveals his strong folk background. His works have clearcut melodic structures close to the simplicity of folksongs, which he adapted in large numbers. There is also much humour in his music, often brimming over into parody or grotesque. His early compositions show Russian influence; later ones reflect elements from Smetana and Dvořák as well as from Janáček and Novák and many contemporary trends abroad, including jazz.

Hipolyta (comic op, 3, J. Munk [pseud. of J. Křička and P. Křička], after M. Hawlett: Ippolita in the Hills), Prague, National, 10 Oct 1917

Ogaři [Country Boys and their Games] (children's op, 2, O. Kalda), Nové Město na Moravě, 7 Sept 1919

Bílý pán, aneb Těžko se dnes duchům straší [The Gentleman in White, or No Haunts Left for Ghosts] (comic op, prol., 3, epilogue, J. L. Budín, after O. Wilde: The Canterville Ghost), Brno, National, 27 Nov 1929; rev. as Spuk im Schloss, oder Böse Zeiten für Gespenster, 1930 (M. Brod), Breslau, Stadt, 14 Nov 1931

Dobře to dopadlo, aneb Tlustý pradědeček, lupiči a detektivové [It Turned Out Well, or The Fat Great-Grandfather, Robbers and Detectives] (comic Spl for children, 2, J. Čapek), Prague, National, 29 Dec 1932

Král Lávra [King Lávra] (Spl with dancing, prol., 3, epilogue, Křička and J. Jenčík, after K. H. Borovský), Prague, National, 7 June 1940

Oživlé loutky [Revived Puppets] (Spl for children, J. Křička, after M. Lopecký: Krásná Dišperanda and Doktor Faust), Prague, Vinohrady, 26 April 1943

Psaníčko na cestách [Travelling Letter] (Spl for children, 5 scenes, J. Křička and P. Křička, after K. Čapek: Postman's Tale), Prague, Vinohrady, 15 Jan 1944

Jáchym a Juliana, 1947–8 (folk romance, 5 scenes, J. Křička, after B. Beneš-Buchlovan), Opava, Civic Theatre of Zdeněk Nejedlý, 22 Dec 1951

České jesličky [Bohemian Nativity] (Christmas op, prol., 3, epilogue, J. Port and B. Stejskal), Prague, Grand Opera of the Fifth of May, 15 Jan 1949

Kolébka [Cradle] (musical comedy, 3, J. Křička, after A. Jirásek), Opava, Civic Theatre of Zdeněk Nejedlý, 25 Nov 1951

Kalhoty [The Trousers] (television op, J. Křička, after P. Lambrosi), Czechoslovak TV, 25 Aug 1962

*

O. Šourek: 'Jaroslav Křička dramatik' [The Dramatist Jaroslav Křička], Národní a Stavovské divadlo (1933–4), no.3, pp.4–5

J. Hutter and Z. Chalabala, eds.: České umění dramatické, ii: Zpěvohra [Czech Dramatic Art: Opera] (Prague, 1941), 330–36

J. Dostál: Jaroslav Křička (Prague, 1944)

J. Fialka: Soupis skladeb J. Křičky [List of J. Křička's Works] (Bystřice pod Hostýnem, 1957)

J. Plavec: 'Přínos Jaroslava Křičky' [Jaroslav Křička's Contribution], HRo, x (1957), 657–9

EVA HERRMANNOVÁ

Krieger [Kruger], **Johann** [Kriegher, Giovanni] (b Nuremberg, bap. 1 Jan 1652; d Zittau, 18 July 1735). German composer, younger brother of Johann Philipp Krieger. Mattheson stated that he began his musical training with Heinrich Schwemmer, Kapellmeister at the church of St Sebald, Nuremberg. He participated in a children's ballet in 1664, and from 1661 to 1668 had keyboard lessons from G. C. Wecker. The early years of Krieger's career are closely connected with the fortunes of his brother, through whom he obtained most of his positions and with whom he may have studied; he took over as court organist at Bayreuth in the mid-1670s and later was Kapellmeister to Count Heinrich I at Greiz (1678–80). After a period as Kapellmeister of the neighbouring court of Duke Christian at Eisenberg he became organist of St Johannis and director chori musici at Zittau; he held this post for 53 years.

In addition to keyboard music and a large number of sacred vocal pieces, Krieger composed ten dramatic works, now mostly lost. Part iii of his collection of songs to texts by Christian Weise, Neue musicalische Ergetzligkeit (Frankfurt and Leipzig, 1684), contains arias – in fact strophic songs – from five Singspiels performed during the traditional Zittau Shrovetide festival in 1683 and 1684. There also survive some texts and arias from three other dramatic works by Krieger, performed at Zittau in 1688, 1717 and 1721 respectively, and he probably wrote at least one opera for the Eisenberg court. Zittau did not have its own opera; the Singspiels were performed by the pupils of the Gymnasium.

Edition: *Neue musicalische Ergetzligkeit, das ist: Unterschiedene Erfindungen welche Herr Christian Weise, in Zittau von geistlichen Andachten, Politischen Tugend-Liedern und Theatralischen Sachen bishero gesetzet hat* (Frankfurt and Leipzig, 1684) [NME]

Jakobs doppelte Heirat (Spl), Zittau, 1682
Der verfolgte David (Spl), Zittau, 2 March 1683, 3 arias in NME
Die sicilianische Argenis (Spl), Zittau, 3 March 1683, 3 arias in NME
Von der verkehrten Welt (Lustspiel), Zittau, 4 March 1683, lib. *D-ZI*
Nebucadnezar (Spl), Zittau, 15 Feb 1684, 7 vocal and inst movts in NME
Der schwedische Regner (Spl), Zittau, 16 Feb 1684, 3 arias in NME
Der politische Quacksalber (Spl), Zittau, 17 Feb 1684, 2 arias in NME
Die vierte Monarchie (Spl), ?Eisenberg, 1684 [see Böhme]
Der Amandus-Tag (Spl), Zittau, 26 Oct 1688, lib. *ZI*
Friedrich der Weise, Zittau, 23 Nov 1717, arias and lib. *ZI*
Die vormahlige Zittauische Kirchen Reformation (Dramate), Zittau, 4 Nov 1721, lib. *ZI*

*

J. Mattheson: *Grundlage einer Ehren-Pforte* (Hamburg, 1740); ed. M. Schneider (Berlin, 1910)
M. Seiffert: Introduction to DTB, xxx, Jg. xviii (1917)
E. W. Böhme: *Musik und Oper am Hofe Herzog Christians von Sachsen-Eisenberg (1677–1707)* (Stadtroda, 1930), 115–22
H. E. Samuel: *The Cantata in Nuremberg during the Seventeenth Century* (Ann Arbor, 1982)   HAROLD E. SAMUEL

Krieger [Kriger, Krüger, Krugl], **Johann Philipp** [Kriegher, Giovanni Filippo] (*b* Nuremberg, bap. 27 Feb 1649; *d* Weissenfels, 6 Feb 1725). German composer, elder brother of Johann Krieger. The chief sources for his biography, Doppelmayr (*Historische Nachricht*, Nuremberg, 1730) and Mattheson (*Grundlage einer Ehren-Pforte*, Hamburg, 1740), both state that as a child he made outstanding progress in keyboard playing. At the age of 14 or 16 he went to Copenhagen to study the organ and composition; after four or five years he returned to Nuremberg. He then served at the Bayreuth court, but was given permission to travel to Italy, where he probably stayed for about two years. Mattheson stated that he studied composition with Rosenmüller, A. M. Abbatini and Bernardo Pasquini. Krieger left Bayreuth for Frankfurt am Main and Kassel, and then in 1677 became court organist at Halle. When Duke August died in 1680 his successor, Johann Adolph I, moved the court to Weissenfels. Krieger went with him as Kapellmeister; he held this position until his death, bringing the cultivation of court music to a very high level.

Before leaving for Weissenfels, Krieger sold some music to the Marienkirche, Halle; an inventory is extant (printed in DDT, liii–liv). He compiled a more important document during his years at Weissenfels (also in DDT, liii–liv): beginning in 1684 he maintained a catalogue of every vocal work he performed. After his death his son Johann Gotthilf continued it until 1732. The catalogue includes about 2000 of his own works, 225 by his brother Johann and 475 by other German and Italian composers. Some of his teachers and the musicians he met in Italy – Förster, Rosenmüller, Carissimi, Francesco Foggia, Legrenzi and P. A. Ziani – are represented with several works each. Other Italian composers in the catalogue are Bertali, Cazzati,

Ruggiero Fedeli, Filippini, Giannettini, Gratiani, Alessandro Melani and Peranda; among the German composers are Beer, Bernhard, Capricornus, Erlebach, Kerll, Knüpfer, Printz and Theile.

Krieger was one of the outstanding German composers of his time. While the largest part of his output consisted of church cantatas, he also composed secular vocal and instrumental works. He is known to have written 24 stage works of various kinds (some are described as 'Tafelmusik') to German texts, of which only some librettos and two published collections of arias are extant. Although some of his operas were performed at Brunswick, Halle, Eisenberg and Hamburg, most of them were written for the court at Weissenfels, where Italian opera was not allowed. His arias, like those of Boxberg, Erlebach, Löhner and Strungk, are strophic songs with a syllabic setting of the text and simple harmony and rhythms; unlike those of J. W. Franck, Keiser and Kusser, they show no influence of the more developed Italian arias, in spite of Krieger's sojourn in Italy.

Editions: *Auserlesene in denen dreyen Sing-Spielen Flora, Cecrops und Procris enthaltene Arien* (Nuremberg, 1690) [A]
Auserlesener Arien Anderer Theil; Welcher gezogen aus folgenden vier Sing-Spielen als Dem wiederkehrenden Phöbus, Der gedruckt- und wieder erquickten Ehe-Liebe, Dem wahrsagenden Wunderbrunnen, und Dem grossmüthigen Scipio (Nuremberg, 1692) [AA]

WFH – *Weissenfels, Hoftheater*

Die drey Charites (serenata), Halle, Hof, 4 June 1681
Orpheus und Euridice, oder Der Höllen stürmende Liebeseifer, Eisenberg, 7 May 1683
Die bewährte Liebeskur, Eisenberg, 1684 [see Böhme]
Der Ursprung der römischen Monarchie, Eisenberg, 1684
Phöbus und Iris, WFH, 1685
Die glückliche Verbindung des Zephyr mit der Flora, WFH, 16 May 1687, arias in A, lib. pubd
Cecrops mit seinen drei Töchtern (3), WFH, 2 Nov 1688, arias in A, lib. pubd
Daniel in der Löwengrube, WFH, 1688
Flora, Ceres und Pomona (Masquerade), WFH, 1688, lib. pubd [see Wagner]
Die gedrückte und wieder erquickte Eheliebe (Trauer-Freudenspiel), WFH, 1688, arias in AA, lib. pubd
Die ausgesöhnte Eifersucht, oder Cephalus und Procris (3), Weissenfels, 1689, arias in A, lib. pubd
Der grossmüthige Scipio (3, after N. Minato: *Scipio affricano*), Weissenfels, 2 Nov 1690, arias in A, lib. pubd
Der wahrsagende Wunderbrunnen (3), WFH, 1690, arias in AA, lib. pubd
Mars und Irene (Tafelmusik, P. C. Heustreu), 1692, lib. pubd
Der wiederkehrenden Phöbus (Spl), 1692, arias in AA [may be identical with Phöbus und Iris]
Ganymedes und Juvental (Tafelmusik: serenata, Heustreu), WFH, 1693, lib. pubd
Herkules unter den Amazonen (5, F. C. Bressand), Brunswick, Hof, 1693, lib. pubd
Der Wettstreit der Treue (3, Bressand), Brunswick, Hof, 1693, lib. pubd
Chronus, Apollo, Fortuna, Constantia (Tafelmusik: serenata, Heustreu), WFH, 1695, lib. pubd
Die lybische Thalestris, Weissenfels, 1696, lib. pubd
Unterthänigstes Freuden-Opffer (Tafelmusik, A. Bohse), 1696, lib. pubd
Tafelmusik bei der Rückkehr Johann Georgens und Friderica Elisabeth aus dem Emser Bade (Tafelmusik, J. A. Meister), 1707, lib. pubd
Adelheid (3), WFH, 1710
Schleiffers Comoedia, lost [see Mersmann, pp.11, 18 and Schwarzbeck, p.108]

*

StiegerO
R. Eitner: 'Johann Philipp Krieger', *MMg*, xxix (1897), 114–17; suppl., 1–128
A. Werner: *Städtische und fürstliche Musikpflege in Weissenfels* (Leipzig, 1911)

H. Mersmann: *Beiträge zu Ansbacher Musikgeschichte* (Leipzig, 1916)

R. Wagner: 'Beiträge zur Lebensgeschichte Johann Philipp Kriegers und seines Schülers Nikolaus Deinl', *ZMw*, viii (1925–6), 146–60

E. W. Böhme: *Musik und Oper am Hofe Herzog Christians von Sachsen-Eisenberg (1677-1707)* (Stadtroda, 1930)

F. W. Schwarzbeck: *Ansbacher Theatergeschichte* (Emsdetten, 1939)

H. E. Samuel: *The Cantata in Nuremberg during the Seventeenth Century* (Ann Arbor, 1982)

C. H. Parsons: *The Mellen Opera Reference Index* (Lewiston, NY, 1986–9)   HAROLD E. SAMUEL

Krïlov, Viktor Alexandrovich (*b* Moscow, 29 Jan/10 Feb 1838; *d* Moscow, 28 Feb/13 March 1906). Russian librettist. A classmate of César Cui at engineering school, he began his career as a dramatist and poet by furnishing his friend with librettos for his early operas *Kavkazskiy plennik* ('The Captive in the Caucasus', after Pushkin, 1857–8) and *Sïn mandarina* ('The Mandarin's Son', 1859); the latter is an operetta, a genre in which Krïlov specialized. For the Imperial Theatres he translated Offenbach's texts – *Prekrasnaya Yelena* (*La belle Hélène*) was especially successful – and also furnished the words for *Bogatïri* ('The Heroic Warriors'), the farce-pastiche with music by Borodin that was given at the Bol'shoy Theatre, Moscow, once only (6/18 November 1867).

As an employee of the Theatres with well-established 'kuchkist' connections Krïlov was the natural choice to write the libretto for the collective opera-ballet *Mlada* on which four of the Russian Five collaborated in 1872 (only Cui's act – the first – was eventually completed and published with the original text, 1911). Krïlov was also the intended librettist for Cui's most important opera *William Ratcliff*, after Heine – but acquaintance with Dargomïzhsky's *The Stone Guest* impelled the composer to aspire higher than a light opera à la Auber. He scrapped Krïlov's text for the later acts and based them directly on the text of the original play as translated by Alexey Pleshcheyev. Krïlov published a short piece on Cui in the periodical *Istoricheskiy vestnik* in 1894 (no.2; reprinted in the collected edition of his writings, ii, 1908, pp.291–300).   RICHARD TARUSKIN

Krilovici, Marina (*b* Bucharest, 11 June 1942). Romanian soprano. She studied in Bucharest and with Maria Caniglia and Luigi Ricci in Rome, making her début with the Romanian National Opera in Bucharest in 1967 as Donna Anna. In the same year she won competitions in 's-Hertogenbosch and Montreal, and took leading Italian lyric-dramatic roles with the Romanian National Opera. She made her Covent Garden début as Aida in 1971, and sang Mimì with the Chicago Lyric Opera the next year. These and appearances at the Vienna Staatsoper, the Deutsche Oper in Berlin and elsewhere in Europe established her as a singer of fine vocal character and expressive ardour.   NOËL GOODWIN

Krips, Henry (*b* Vienna, 10 Feb 1912; *d* Adelaide, 25 Jan 1987). Australian conductor of Austrian birth, brother of Josef Krips. He studied at the Vienna Conservatory and University, and made his début in 1932 at the Burgtheater there. In 1933 he moved to Innsbruck, then to Salzburg, 1934–5. He returned to Vienna and remained there until 1938, when he emigrated to Australia. He took Australian citizenship in 1944, having formed the Krips-de Vries Opera Company there.

From 1947 he worked for the ABC, and for more than 20 years played a leading part in Australian and New Zealand musical life. In 1972 he gave up his Australian appointments to live in London, where he had appeared as a guest conductor with the Sadler's Wells Opera from 1967, notably in Johann Strauss and Lehár. His compositions include the opera *Fiordaliso*, ballets, songs and instrumental pieces.   NOËL GOODWIN

Krips, Josef (*b* Vienna, 8 April 1902; *d* Geneva, 13 Oct 1974). Austrian conductor, brother of Henry Krips. After studying at the Vienna Academy with Weingartner he made his opera début in 1921. He joined the Vienna Volksoper under Weingartner as chorus master and répétiteur (1921–4), and then went to the city theatres at Aussig an der Elbe (1924–5) as head of the opera department; he was at Dortmund (1925–6) and at Karlsruhe as music director (1926–33). In 1933 he became a resident conductor at the Vienna Staatsoper but lost this position on the Nazi annexation of Austria in 1938. After a season with the Belgrade Opera his musical activities were suspended by the war. From 1945 Krips played a leading part in reorganizing postwar musical life in Vienna, conducting the resumed performances by the Vienna Staatsoper at the Volksoper and the Theater an der Wien. His conducting of *Don Giovanni*, which reopened the Salzburg Festival in 1946, marked the first of many visits there. He also conducted it for his début at Covent Garden in 1963 (having first visited Britain with the Vienna Staatsoper in 1947). Krips toured many European countries and was a guest conductor at the Chicago Lyric Opera from 1959, the Metropolitan from 1967 and the Deutsche Oper, Berlin, from 1970. He had a reputation as a benevolent despot, whose unaffected interpretations and warmth of expressive feeling served as ideal introductions to the Viennese classics (especially Mozart) for a postwar generation of concert-goers.   NOËL GOODWIN

Kristiania. OSLO.

Kroll Oper. Company established in Berlin in 1927 to perform new and standard works in a non-traditional manner at the theatre opened by Josef Kroll in 1844 (enlarged 1924); *see* BERLIN, §§2(ii) and 3(i).

Król Roger. Opera by Karol Szymanowski; *see* KING ROGER.

Krombholc, Jaroslav (*b* Prague, 30 Jan 1918; *d* Prague, 16 July 1983). Czech conductor. He studied privately with Ostrčil and at the Prague Conservatory and the Master School (1937–42) with Novák and Talich, and attended Alois Hába's quarter-tone classes and, at Prague University, Zdeněk Nejedlý's lectures. He joined the National Theatre staff in 1940, and in 1942 Talich entrusted him with the première of Bořkovec's *Satyr*. He also worked at the E. F. Burian Theatre. In 1944 he became head of the Ostrava Opera, but in 1945 he returned to Prague, where he was appointed conductor and a member of the management of the National Theatre, eventually becoming one of its leading musical personalities. His conducting repertory was based on 19th-century Czech opera; he preferred Smetana and the lyricism of such works as *Kát'a Kabanová* to more conspicuously dramatic pieces. In 1949 and 1955 he won state prizes for his outstanding performances of *Dalibor* and *Libuše*, and his interpretation of Fibich was regarded as a model. He achieved significant success with Ostrčil's *Honzovo království* ('Johnny's Kingdom'), Foerster's *Eva*, Martinů's *Julietta*, Jeremiáš's *Bratři Karamazovi*, Burian's *Maryša*, Rafael Kubelík's *Veronika* and the operas of Novák, Cikker and Suchoň. He also conducted Mozart, Musorgsky, Shostakovich, Prokofiev and a very individual *Wozzeck*. On tour he visited Budapest, Stuttgart, Holland and Edinburgh. He first appeared at the Vienna Staatsoper in 1959, the same year he conducted *Boris Godunov* at Covent Garden, and in 1978 conducted a revival of *Don Giovanni* at the ENO. Krombholc was also well known as the conductor of the Czech National Theatre company on its foreign tours and for his many excellent recordings. He was married to the singer Maria Tauberová.

J. Burghauser: *Slavní čeští dirigenti* [Famous Czech Conductors] (Prague, 1963)

B. Karásek: 'Český dirigent' [The Czech Conductor], *HRo*, xxi (1968), 22–3

V. Pospíšil, ed.: *Národní divadlo a jeho předchůdci* [The National Theatre and its Predecessors] (Prague, 1988), 251

ALENA NĚMCOVÁ

Kronstadt (Ger.). BRAŞOV.

Krstić, Petar (*b* Belgrade, 18 Feb 1877; *d* Belgrade, 21 Jan 1957). Serbian composer. He studied in Vienna with Robert Fuchs and later worked as a conductor of opera and other theatrical music. He taught at the Serbian music school in Belgrade, 1911–14, before becoming its director, 1914–21. He was the director of the Stanković music school, 1921–4, and in 1922 became editor of *Muzički glasnik* ('Music Herald').

Like most of his compositions, his theatre music shows the influence of urban folk music that includes oriental elements. The musical drama *Zulumćar* ('The Hooligan'; 3, after S. Ćorović; Belgrade, 23 Nov 1927), is Romantic in style. It is a lyrical work with distinct solo and ensemble numbers, subordinate orchestral accompaniment and simple harmony, and includes two songs on poems by Aleksa Šantić ('Emina' and 'Nimfa'). His other opera, the three-act *Ženidba Janković Stojana* ('The Marriage of Janković Stojan', composed 1948), has similar characteristics. Both operas were published in vocal score. Krstić also composed music for a number of plays performed in Belgrade, in some cases using arrangements of folktunes.

V. Peričić: *Muzički stvaraoci u Srbiji* [Musical Creators in Serbia] (Belgrade, 1969)

Petar Krstić: zbornik radova [Petar Krstić: Anthology of Works] (Belgrade, 1986) [pubn of the Belgrade Faculty of Musical Art]

ROKSANDA PEJOVIĆ

Kruger, Johann. *See* KRIEGER, JOHANN.

Krüger [Krugl], Johann Philipp. *See* KRIEGER, JOHANN PHILIPP.

Krull, Annie [Maria Anna] (*b* nr Rostock, 12 Jan 1876; *d* Schwerin, 14 June 1947). German soprano. She studied in Berlin and made her début at Plauen in 1898. In 1901 she sang in the premières of Strauss's *Feuersnot* and Paderewski's *Manru*, both in Dresden, where she established herself as principal dramatic soprano until 1912. She created the title role in Strauss's *Elektra* in 1909, repeating the role in 1910 under Beecham at Covent Garden, where she was compared to her dis-

advantage with London's first Electra, Edyth Walker. Salome was another role in which she was much admired. She spent her last seasons at Mannheim, Weimar and Schwerin, where in 1916 she retired to teach. Her recordings include Act 2 of *Tannhäuser* (1909) in which her Elisabeth is strongly characterized and finely sung.

For illustration *see* ELEKTRA.   J. B. STEANE

Salomea Krusceniski in the title role of Richard Strauss's 'Salome'

Krusceniski [Kruszelnicka], Salomea [Krushel'nytska, Solomiya] (*b* Bilyavyntsi, Halychyna [now Tarnopol'] province, 11/23 Sept 1872; *d* L'viv, 16 Nov 1952). Ukrainian soprano, later naturalized Italian. She studied in Leopoli, making her début at L'viv in 1892, and continued her studies at Milan in 1895 with Fausta Crespi. During the 1895–6 season at Cremona she appeared in Puccini's *Manon Lescaut* and in *Les Huguenots*. Until 1902 she sang mostly in Russia, but a brilliant début at the S Carlo, Naples, in 1903 inaugurated her career in the leading Italian theatres (La Scala in 1907, 1909 and 1915), Spain and Buenos Aires (1906–13). She became Italian by marriage in 1910 and retired in 1925.

A woman of singular beauty and complex personality, she had a flexible, warm and well-focussed voice. At first a fine interpreter of Meyerbeer and Verdi, she later appeared in Catalani's *Loreley*, as Butterfly (in the revised version at Brescia in 1904), Adriana Lecouvreur, Strauss's Salome and Electra, and in Wagner roles, particularly Brünnhilde. Though passionate and vigorous in temperament, she avoided the vulgar over-exuberance of many singers. She was guided by original and subtle ideas which in roles such as Aida and Salome led her to a highly stylized characterization, marked by hieratic attitudes or an enigmatic oriental languor.

For further illustration *see* FEDRA (ii).

GV (R. Celletti; R. Vegeto)

E. Arnosi and J. Dennis: 'Salomea Kruszelnicka', *Record Collector*, xviii (1968–9), 77–88 [with discography by R. L. Autrey]

M. Holovashchenko, ed.: *Solomiya Krushel'nytska: spohady, materiyaly, lystuvannya* [Recollections, Documents, Correspondence] (Kiev, 1978–9)   RODOLFO CELLETTI

Krútňava. Opera by Eugen Suchoň; *see* WHIRLPOOL, THE.

Kruyf, Ton de (*b* Leerdam, 3 Oct 1937). Dutch composer. He was self-taught until 1966, when he studied composition with Fortner, having won a major success with *Einst dem Grau* for mezzo-soprano and ensemble (1964). Around 1970, 12-note serialism gave place to a freer technique in which timbre has served an increasingly important function. The music of his first opera *Spinoza* (2, D. F. Frank; Amsterdam, 15 June 1971), decorative and atmospheric, characterizes each of the principal characters with an individual instrumentation and in some cases an individual compositional technique. The radio opera *Quauhquauhtinchan* (1, H. Mulisch; Dutch Radio, 3 June 1972), based on an old Mexican tale, uses a large orchestra and some unconventional instruments to evoke naturalistic sounds. Kruyf's other work for the stage is a monodrama, *Inaugurazione* (1974), for mezzo-soprano and orchestra.

E. Vermeulen: 'Ton de Kruyf: Spinoza', *Sonorum speculum*, no. 47 (1971), 1–14   JOS WOUTERS/LEO SAMAMA

Kryukov, Vladimir Nikolayevich (*b* Moscow, 9/22 July 1902; *d* Staraya Rusa, nr Moscow, 14 June 1960). Russian composer. He studied at the Moscow Conservatory and later worked for short periods as a broadcasting editor, music director of the Theatre of the Revolution, director of the Moscow PO and (1957–9) composition teacher at the Gnessin Institute. His compositions are moderately progressive in technique.

Korol' na ploshchadi [The King on the Square], 1925 (after A. Blok)

Stantsionnïy smotritel' [The Postmaster] op. 30, 1936–9 (4, M. Aliger, after A. S. Pushkin), Moscow, Stanislavsky Opera Theatre Studio, 30 Oct 1940

Metel' [Blizzard], 1941 (after Pushkin), inc.

Lev Gurïch Sinichkin, 1945 (musical comedy, E. Gal'perin and M. Gal'perin, after V. Lensky)

Dmitry Donskoy op. 40, 1945–7 (4, G. V. Kristi), Moscow, Stanislavsky-Nemirovich-Danchenko Music Theatre, 5 Sept 1947

Razlom [Breakage], 1948 (B. Lavrenyov)

*

V. Belaiev: 'Moskauer Komponisten' (untitled suppl.), *Musikblätter des Anbruch*, vii (1925), 173   DETLEF GOJOWY

Kubelík, Rafael (Jeronym) (*b* Býchory, nr Kolín, 29 June 1914). Swiss conductor and composer of Czech birth. He studied at the Prague Conservatory, made his conducting début in 1934 with the Czech PO and was music director at the Brno Opera from 1939 to 1941. He appeared with the Glyndebourne Festival Opera in *Don Giovanni* at the 1948 Edinburgh Festival, an engagement that enabled him to leave Czechoslovakia after the Communist Party took control there. He settled first in London and later in Switzerland, taking Swiss nationality in 1973. After concert work with the

Chicago SO and elsewhere he conducted a memorable production of Janáček's *Kát'a Kabanová* for the Sadler's Wells Opera in 1954 and was appointed music director at Covent Garden (1955–8). There his repertory included the first London productions of *Jenůfa* (1956) and *Les Troyens* (1957), both sung in English as the basis for a potential national ensemble capable of giving good performances in the vernacular. The policy was discontinued after Kubelík resigned following a scathing attack by Thomas Beecham on the Covent Garden company and management.

Apart from a brief (six months) appointment as the first music director of the Metropolitan Opera in 1973, when he conducted the first production there of *Les Troyens*, he preferred to concentrate on concert work in Munich and elsewhere, but his operatic performances are remembered for dynamism, commitment and lyrical appeal on a basis of intensive rehearsal. His own compositions include five complete operas, of which *Veronika* (1943–4; D. C. Faltis) was staged at Brno in 1947, and *Cornelia Faroli* (1966; Faltis, after the life of Titian) at Augsburg in 1972; Kubelík conducted both of these performances. He wrote two operas in 1946 – *Císařovy nové šaty* ('The Emperor's New Clothes'; K. Koval, after H. C. Andersen) and *Květinky malé Idy* ('The Flowers of Little Ida') – and one in 1967 (*Tiziano*). His recordings include *Rigoletto*, Weber's *Oberon* and Orff's *Antigonae* and *Oedipus der Tyrann*. He has received numerous awards in different countries, including honorary membership of the RAM.

ARTHUR JACOBS, NOËL GOODWIN

Kubiak, Teresa (*b* Łódź, 26 Dec 1937). Polish soprano. She studied in Łódź, making her début there in 1965 as Halka in Moniuszko's opera. In 1970 she sang Sulamith in a concert performance of Goldmark's *Die Königin von Saba* at Carnegie Hall, New York, and the following year appeared at San Francisco, Chicago, and Glyndebourne, where she sang Lisa (*The Queen of Spades*) and Juno (Cavalli's *Calisto*). In 1972 she made her début at Covent Garden as Butterfly, and the next year sang Lisa at the Metropolitan and Elsa in Vienna. Her repertory includes Aida, Senta, Tatyana, Tosca, Giorgetta, Ellen Orford and Jenůfa. Her strong, lyrical voice is particularly well suited to Puccini, while her dramatic involvement has increased since her early appearances.

ELIZABETH FORBES

Kubín, Rudolf (*b* Ostrava, 10 Jan 1909; *d* Ostrava, 11 Jan 1973). Czech composer. He studied composition with Hába at the Prague Conservatory (1924–9). In 1929 he joined the Prague RO as a cellist and from 1935 was music director of Czech Radio. After World War II he helped establish several institutions in Ostrava, including the music teaching college which later became the conservatory (Kubín was director, 1958–60). In recognition he received the Order of Work in 1959.

His early works, influenced by Hába, employed quarter-tones and also took ideas from contemporary dance music: his interest in light music is reflected in his musical comedy *Letní noc* ('Summer Night'), the first Czech radio opera. The 1930s brought a change to a style marked by expressionism. His postwar works are simpler and tend to synthesize his earlier techniques; they are also touched by the socialist realist aesthetic. *Naši furianti* ('Our Defiant Fellows') is a direct prototype of the socialist/folk comic opera. Its eclectic Smetana-like style, realism and folklike musical language were intended to make it as appealing as possible to a working-class audience.

Among his operettas and folk operas, *Děvčátko z kolonie* ('The Girl from the Mining Settlement', 1942) was especially successful; its subject is the life of the mining colony in Ostrava. After the première of the revised version (10 September 1955) some of its songs became popular and were published and recorded separately. Kubín was awarded a prize for this work (Ostrava, 1954).

Žena, která zdělila muže [The Woman who did down Men]/Ženich z prérie [The Bridegroom from the Prairie] (operetta, 3, F. Lašek and F. Balej), Prague, Vinohrady Comic Opera, 29 March 1930
Tři mušketýři [The Three Musketeers]/Královnin náhrdelník [The Queen's Necklace] (musical comedy, 3, K. Musil and V. Nečas, after A. Dumas), Prague, Uranie, 19 April 1931
Letní noc [Summer Night] (radio op, 1, M. Kareš), Czech Radio, 26 Sept 1931
Kavalír [The Cavalier], 1932 (operetta, 3, L. Pohl), unperf.
Cirkus života [Circus of Life] (operetta, 3, Kareš), Prague, Big Operetta, 15 May 1933
Ta česká muzika, ta srdce proniká [That Czech Music, it Speaks Straight to the Heart], 1933 (folk play with songs, 3, Lašek and Balej), unperf.
Zasnoubení na paloučku [A Greenwood Betrothal], 1933 (folk play with song and dance, 3, Lašek and Balej), unperf.
Ondráš, 1936–7, inc.
Zpěv uhlí [Song of Coal] (1, Kubín), inc., ov. perf., Brno, 1941
Děvčátko z kolonie [The Girl from the Mining Settlement] (operetta, 3, V. Poláček and V. Ruml), Ostrava, Moravian-Silesian, 22 March 1942; rev. (lib. by K. Melichar-Skoumal), Ostrava, 10 Sept 1955
Naši furianti [Our Defiant Fellows], 1942–3 (comic op, 3, Pohl, after L. Stroupežnický); rev. version, Ostrava, 18 Sept 1949
Selský kníže [The Village Prince] (operetta-burlesque, 3, Pohl), Prague, Comic Opera, 10 April 1947
Koleje mládí [The Ways of Youth] (play with song and dance, 2, J. Plachetka), Brno, Reduta, 15 Sept 1949
Pasekáři [People of the Glades], 1950–51 (operetta, 3, Kubín, M. Vyoral and A. Koreček, after F. Sokol-Tůma); rev. version, Ostrava, State, 30 April 1954
Jiříkovo vidění [Jiřik's Vision], 1952 (folk op, 5, Kubín, after J. K. Tyl), inc.
Heva, 1955–64 (folk operetta, 5, Pohl, after Sokol-Tůma), unperf.

*

J. Válek: 'Naši furianti', *HRo*, ii (1949–50), 114
R. Kubín: 'Má nová opera Pasekáři', *HRo*, iii (1950–51), 9
V. Pospíšil: 'Nové znění Kubínovy havířké operety', *HRo*, viii (1955), 826–7
V. Gregor: *Rudolf Kubín: obraz života a díla* (Ostrava, 1975)
OLDŘICH PUKL, HELENA HAVLÍKOVÁ

Kuchta, Gladys (*b* Chicopee, MA, 16 June 1923). American soprano. She studied in New York and in Italy, making her début in 1951 at Florence as Donna Elvira. In 1958 she joined the Städtische (later Deutsche) Oper, Berlin, where her repertory included Amelia (*Simon Boccanegra*, *Ballo*), Lady Macbeth, Donna Anna, Leonore (*Fidelio*), Ariadne and the Marschallin. She made her Covent Garden début as Chrysothemis (1960) and her Metropolitan début as Sieglinde (1961), later singing Gutrune and Senta; she also sang Abigaille (*Nabucco*) and the Dyer's Wife (*Die Frau ohne Schatten*) at San Francisco (1964), and Brünnhilde at Bayreuth and Isolde in Munich (1968). She retired from the stage in 1975. Her powerful voice and dramatic talent were best displayed as Strauss's Electra and Turandot.
ELIZABETH FORBES

Kuen, Paul (*b* Sulzberg bei Kempten, 8 April 1910). German tenor. He studied in Munich and made his début in 1933 at Konstanz. After singing in Bamberg, Freiburg, Nuremberg and Dresden, in 1947 he was engaged at the

Munich Staatsoper. A fine singer and a superb actor, he had a wide repertory that included Monostatos (*Die Zauberflöte*), Don Basilio (*Le nozze di Figaro*), David (*Die Meistersinger*), Kilian (*Der Freischütz*), Valzacchi (*Der Rosenkavalier*), Baba Mustapha (*Der Barbier von Bagdad*) and the Captain (*Wozzeck*). His most successful part was Mime (*Das Rheingold* and *Siegfried*), which he sang at Bayreuth (1951–7), Covent Garden (1953–4), the Metropolitan (1961–2) and at many other opera houses. He also sang the Witch in *Hänsel und Gretel*.
ELIZABETH FORBES

Kuhhandel, Der. Operetta by Kurt Weill; *see* KINGDOM FOR A COW, A.

Kuhlau, Friedrich (Daniel Rudolph) (*b* Uelzen, nr Hanover, 11 Sept 1786; *d* Copenhagen, 12 March 1832). Danish composer of German birth. He was the son of a poor military bandsman whose family settled in Hamburg about 1803. When the French occupied Hamburg in 1810 he fled to Copenhagen, and here became court chamber musician (1813), with the duty of composing dramatic works for Det kongelige Teater (the Royal Theatre), at which he was chorus master in 1816–17. In 1828 he was appointed an honorary professor. His last years were embittered by his continual economic problems, by a fire which destroyed his house and by a chest ailment which caused his death. He made several journeys abroad, including concert tours in Sweden, but went mostly to Germany and Austria for pleasure, meeting Beethoven in 1825.

Kuhlau is known mainly for his many flute and piano compositions, but in Denmark he was most important for his stage works: five Singspiels and incidental music to three plays. His earliest extant opera, *Røverborgen* ('The Robbers' Castle', 1814), a kind of 'rescue' opera, draws on the principal operatic genres and forms of the time: Italian *opera seria* and *opera buffa* and French *opéra comique* as well as German, Austrian and Danish Singspiel. *Trylleharpen* ('The Magic Harp') caused a scandal in 1817 because part of the libretto had been used by another composer and was thought, wrongly, to have been stolen. It is rather in the manner of French opera, with many through-composed scenes. *Elisa* (1820), set in the time of the crusades, suffers from a very undramatic text. Kuhlau's chief operatic work is the fairy or magic opera *Lulu* (1824), which has the same literary source as Mozart's *Die Zauberflöte*; the music is richly coloured both melodically and harmonically. His last opera, *Hugo og Adelheid* (1827), is based on a static love story but is enlivened by the inclusion of many subordinate characters and situations (thieves, competing knights and merchants, a nightwatch and prisoners) and contains some of Kuhlau's most personal operatic music.

Kuhlau's incidental music includes his evocative music to C. J. Boye's romantic play *William Shakespeare* (1826), which is very similar to (and dates from the same year as) Weber's *Oberon*. Still more Romantic in character is his music to J. L. Heiberg's famous play *Elverhøj* ('The Elf Hill', 1828), the most often performed play in the Danish repertory. This was Kuhlau's most successful work. It is largely based on old Danish and Swedish folktunes skilfully arranged to fit the dramatic situations, above all the tune *Kong Christian stod ved højen mast* ('King Christian [IV] stood by the lofty mast'), which became the Danish national anthem. He also composed music with 'Turkish' effects to Oehlenschlaeger's comedy *Trillingbrødrene fra Damask* ('The Triplet Brothers from Damascus', 1830), the lyric-dramatic scene *Euridice in Tartarus* (1816) and several other works.

Unlike C. E. F. Weyse, the other principal Danish composer of the period, Kuhlau was extrovert and modern. His style, although cosmopolitan, contains many elements of the Danish musical tradition. A conspicuous feature is his parody technique, in which themes, passages and whole movements by other composers function as a catalyst for his own compositions. Though he was strongly influenced by his principal model, Mozart, by Cherubini, Paer and Beethoven and later also by Rossini and Weber, he had his own artistic character, and must be considered the greatest Danish opera composer of the first half of the 19th century.

See also LULU (i).

first performed in Copenhagen, Det kongelige Teater, unless otherwise stated; MSS of full scores in DK-Kk unless otherwise stated

Amors Triumph, 1803–4, ov., Hamburg, 3 March 1804, lost

Røverborgen [The Robbers' Castle] (Spl, 3, A. Oehlenschlaeger, after C. L. Heyne), 26 May 1814, vs (Copenhagen, 1815), ov., Samfundet til udgivelse af dansk musik, 3rd ser., ci (Copenhagen, 1948)

Euridice in Tartarus op.47 (lyric-dramatic scene, J. Baggesen), 17 June 1816 [partly re-used in Lulu]

Trylleharpen [The Magic Harp] op.27 (Spl, 2, Baggesen), 30 Jan 1817, autograph; ov. (Leipzig, 1820)

Alfred, 1817 (3, A. von Kotzebue, trans. L. C. Sander), unperf., inc., lost

Aandsprøven, eller Krigseventyret [The Mental Trial, or The War Adventure], 1819 (Spl, 2, L. Kruse), unperf., inc., lost

Elisa, eller Venskab og Kjærlighed [Elisa, or Friendship and Love] op.29 (lyrisk Drama, 3, C. J. Boye), 17 April 1820, vs (Copenhagen, 1820–21)

Lulu op.65 (romantische Oper, 3, C. C. F. Güntelberg, after A. J. Liebeskind: *Lulu, oder Die Zauberflöte*), 29 Oct 1824, vs (Hamburg, 1825; Copenhagen, 1825)

Hugo og Adelheid op.107 (Spl, 3, Boye), 29 Oct 1827, vs (Copenhagen, 1838)

2 songs in W. Thrane: Fjeldeventyret [The Mountain Adventure], 1825

*

DBL (G. Busk); *LoewenbergA*; MGG (R. Sietz)

'Die Räuberburg', *AMZ*, xlvii (1822), 757–61

L. Rellstab: 'Hugo og Adelheid', *Iris im Gebiete der Tonkunst*, vii–ix (Berlin, 1840), 25–7, 29–31, 33–4

T. Overskou: *Den danske Skueplads*, iv–v (Copenhagen, 1862–4)

C. Thrane: *Danske Komponister* (Copenhagen, 1875), 71–192, 271–82; Ger. trans. as *Friedrich Kuhlau* (Leipzig, 1886)

K. Graupner: *Friedrich Kuhlau* (Remscheid, 1930)

T. Krogh: 'Kong Christian', 'Omkring Elverhøj-Musikens Tilblivelse', *Dansk musiktidsskrift*, xvii (1942), 26–32, 70–76; 162–76

K. Å. Bruun: *Dansk musiks historie*, i (Copenhagen, 1969), 186–250

D. Fog, ed.: *Kompositionen von Fridr. Kuhlau: thematisch-bibliographischer Katalog* (Copenhagen, 1977)

G. Busk: *Friedrich Kuhlau: en biografi og en kritisk analyse af hans musikdramatiske produktion* (diss., U. of Copenhagen, 1986)

——: *Friedrich Kuhlau: hans liv og værk* (Copenhagen, 1986)

——, ed.: *Kuhlau: breve* [Letters] (Copenhagen, 1990)

GORM BUSK

Kuhlmann, Kathleen (*b* San Francisco, 7 Dec 1950). American mezzo-soprano. After attending the Chicago Lyric Opera School, she made her début in 1979 as Maddalena (*Rigoletto*) with the Lyric Opera, with which she also sang Bersi (*Andrea Chénier*) and Princess Clarice (*The Love for Three Oranges*). She made her European début in 1980 at Cologne as Preziosilla (*Forza*), then sang at La Scala (1981), Covent Garden and San Francisco (1982). She sang the title role in *La*

Cenerentola at Glyndebourne in 1983. Other roles in her repertory include Rosina, Pauline (*The Queen of Spades*), Gluck's Orpheus, Meg Page, Nicklausse (*Les contes d'Hoffmann*), Nancy (*Martha*), Dorabella, Charlotte (*Werther*), Arsace, Isabella (*L'italiana in Algeri*), Carmen, Bradamante (*Alcina*) and Juno/Ino in Handel's *Semele*. Her vibrant, supple voice is as effective in florid music as it is in the more dramatic repertory.

ELIZABETH FORBES

Kuhn, Gustav (*b* Turrach, nr Spittal, 28 Aug 1947). Austrian conductor. He studied at the Salzburg Mozarteum and with Swarowsky, Maderna and Karajan in Vienna. He was first conductor at the Turkish State Opera, Istanbul, 1970–73, making his début with *Fidelio*; artistic director, Netherlands Opera Forum, 1974–5; and first conductor, Dortmund Opera, 1975–7. He conducted *Elektra* for his Vienna Staatsoper début in 1977 and remained as resident conductor until 1980. While music director at Berne, 1979–83, he made his début at Glyndebourne (*Die Entführung*, 1980), Covent Garden (*Don Giovanni*, 1981), the Opéra and Chicago Lyric Opera. Subsequent engagements were at Bonn (from 1983), La Scala (*Tannhäuser*, 1984), Rome (1985) and the S Carlo (1986). A versatile conductor, praised for his command and conviction in Strauss and Wagner, his Italian experience included the Pesaro revival of Rossini's *Ermione* (1987), and he has also staged some productions himself (*Der fliegende Holländer* in Trieste, *Parsifal* in Naples).

NOËL GOODWIN

Kuhnau [Kuhn, Cuno], **Johann** (*b* Geising, Erzgebirge, 6 April 1660; *d* Leipzig, 5 June 1722). German composer. After early study in Dresden, he continued his education at the Gymnasium in Zittau, where he came into close association with the Rektor, Christian Weise, and wrote music (now lost) for some of Weise's school dramas. In 1682 he became a law student at the University of Leipzig and meanwhile increased his activity as a composer and performer. In 1684 he was appointed organist at the Thomaskirche; from 1701 until his death he was Kantor of the Thomasschule. As well as music for Weise's plays, Kuhnau's secular works included a *dramma per musica* for the welcome of Elector-Prince Johann Georg (Michaelmas 1683); the opera *Orpheus*, mentioned in Kuhnau's satirical novel *Der musicalische Quack-Salber* (Dresden, 1700) and written probably for Weissenfels; and a Singspiel (according to Scheibe). All are lost.

*

R. Münnich: 'Kuhnau's Leben', *SIMG*, iii (1901–2), 473–527

B. F. Richter: 'Eine Abhandlung Joh. Kuhnau's', *MMg*, xxxiv (1902), 147–54

GEORGE J. BUELOW

Kuhse, Hanne-Lore (*b* Schwann, Mecklenburg, 28 March 1925). German soprano. She studied at Rostock and Berlin, making her début in 1951 at Gera as Leonore (*Fidelio*). After engagements at Schwerin and Leipzig, in 1963 she joined the Berlin Staatsoper. She made her American début at Philadelphia in 1967, as Isolde, and sang the title role of Busoni's *Turandot* at Philharmonic Hall, New York. Her extensive repertory included Donna Anna, Abigaille (*Nabucco*), Lady Macbeth, Aida, all the Wagner soprano roles from Irene (*Rienzi*) to Kundry, Tosca, Turandot, Ariadne, the Marschallin and Marie (*Wozzeck*). She sang Mita in the first British performance of Siegfried Wagner's *Der Friedensengel* (1975, Queen Elizabeth Hall). Her powerful voice, a real dramatic soprano, was admirably suited to such roles as Isolde, Leonore and Turandot.

ELIZABETH FORBES

Kuibyshev. SAMARA.

Kuks. Palace and spa town in north-east Bohemia, Czech Republic. It was built as a summer residence by Count Franz Anton Sporck (1662–1738), beginning in 1692. Theatre performances date from 1697, but the first attempt to introduce opera was not made until 1724, when the count acquired for his Prague and Kuks theatres the company of Antonio Denzio from Venice, through the Peruzzi family of impresarios. Opera performances took place in the summer seasons of 1724 (15 August to September) and 1725 (July to mid-September). During this period, as in Prague, the repertory consisted mostly of pasticcios using the music of, among others, Albinoni, Antonio Bioni and Vivaldi, who was in contact with Denzio's company. After the death of Count Sporck's wife in 1726, performances at Kuks ceased, but they continued until 1734 at his theatre in Prague.

J. Krupka: 'František Antonín hrabě Špork a jeho opera v Praze a Kuksu' [Count Franz Anton Sporck and his Opera in Prague and Kuks], *Dalibor*, xxxix (1922–3), 77–9, 89–91, 105–7, 145–7; xl (1923–4), 15–17, 113–15, 125–8
H. Benedikt: *Franz Anton Graf von Sporck (1662–1738): zur Kultur der Barock Zeit in Böhmen* (Vienna, 1923)
P. Nettl: 'F. A. Sporcks Beziehungen zur Musik', *Mf*, vi (1953), 324–34
J. Hůlek: 'Opera F. A. Sporcka v Kuksu a v Praze', *Ročenka Státní knihovny ČSR 1979–80* (Prague, 1982), 218–31
D. E. Freeman: *The Opera Theater of Count Franz Anton von Sporck in Prague (1724–35)* (diss., U. of Illinois, 1987)

MICHAELA FREEMANOVÁ

Kuljerić, Igor (*b* Šibenik, 1 Feb 1938). Croatian composer. He graduated from the Zagreb Academy of Music in 1965 after studying composition with Šulek, and continued his studies in the electronics studio of RAI in Milan. He has subsequently held conducting posts in Zagreb.

Kuljerić is one of the most successful avant-garde Croatian composers. In his works for the stage he uses a variety of new compositional and technical procedures to promote dramatic development. In his first opera, *Moć vrline* ('The Power of Virtue'; 1, D. Miladinović, after M. Božić; Zagreb, 8 May 1977), the plot concentrates on the tragic isolation of a 'small man'. The music consists of two contrasting layers, employed at times simultaneously and at times in alternation. One uses new sound procedures to portray the psychological world and real-life crowd scenes; the other, based on deliberately trivial ideas, symbolizes alienation, manipulation and cynicism. In his second opera, *Rikard III* (2, N. Turkalj, after W. Shakespeare; Zagreb, 16 April 1987), the scenes focus on the ritual-archetypal layers of human consciousness; the music is based on emotional, melodious vocal lines, while the short transitions between the scenes, which serve to comment on and connect them, are realized on tape. Among Kuljerić's other works are ballets, incidental music and *Balade Petrice Kerempuha* ('The Ballads of Petrica Kerempuh', 1973).

J. Andreis: *Music in Croatia* (Zagreb, 1974)   KORALJKA KOS

Kullervo. Opera in two acts by AULIS SALLINEN to his own libretto after the play of the same title by Aleksis Kivi; Los Angeles, Music Center, 25 February 1992.

Sallinen finished *Kullervo* in 1988. It had been commissioned by the Finnish National Opera to celebrate the opening of their new house in Helsinki, but because the planned completion of the building was delayed, the soloists and chorus of the company were invited to present the première jointly with the Los Angeles Music Center Opera.

In a feud, Untamo (baritone), also called Unto and Untamoinen, has destroyed the family of his brother Kalervo (bass) except for Kullervo (baritone), whom he has kept as a slave. He sells Kullervo to a smith, whose young wife (mezzo-soprano) tries to seduce him. Humiliated and provoked by the woman, Kullervo murders her. His friend Kimmo (tenor) has found Kullervo's parents alive, but when Kullervo arrives their relations are strained, although his mother (mezzo-soprano) has retained her love for him. In a dream sequence, a Blind Singer (variety artist) describes how Kullervo unwittingly seduced his own long-lost sister. Now he has no option but to leave his stricken family. With the help of a group of men he encounters, Kullervo destroys Unto's family in a raid. He goes to search for Kimmo, but finds that his friend has lost his reason. With nothing more to live for, he throws himself into the fire.

The basis of the libretto, Kivi's play of 1864, derives in turn from the Finnish national epic, the Kalevala. Although his libretto principally follows the play, Sallinen makes effective use of the poem: the chorus sings passages from it as either a form of recitative or a comment on the action. As usual in Sallinen's operas, the music has a strongly tonal basis; Max Loppert described it as 'a conception of the medium perhaps old-fashioned (at least to some) but made potently modern, and tinglingly dramatic, by the accuracy and security of Sallinen's theatrical instinct' (*Financial Times*, 3 March 1992). Its boldly colourful effects are enhanced by some imaginative instrumentation (including a synthesizer), and Sallinen does not hesitate to use a jazz-flavoured idiom in the Blind Singer's ballad, the 'Song of a Sister's Ravishing'.

ERKKI ARNI

Kullman, Charles (*b* New Haven, CT, 13 Jan 1903; *d* New Haven, 8 Feb 1983). American tenor. He studied at Yale University and the Juilliard School. After making his début with the American Opera Company as Pinkerton in 1929 he went to Europe and sang the same role with the Kroll Opera in Berlin in 1931. He later appeared at the Berlin Staatsoper and Covent Garden, and in Vienna and Salzburg. He made his Metropolitan début in 1935 in Gounod's *Faust*. For 25 seasons he sang with the company while still making guest appearances elsewhere. Kullman was one of the most versatile tenors ever to sing with the Metropolitan. He was able to adapt his lyric voice to heavy roles, and his repertory ranged from Tamino and Rinuccio to Tannhäuser and Parsifal. He had an appealing vocal quality and a pleasing stage personality.

Kunad, Rainer (*b* Chemnitz, 24 Oct 1936). German composer. He began studying composition as a 16-year-old schoolboy. After a year at the Dresden Conservatory he studied with Finke and Gerster in Leipzig, 1956–9, then lectured on music theory at the Zwickau Conservatory before becoming director of incidental music for the Dresden theatres. From 1971 he was a permanent member of the Berlin and Dresden Staatsopern. He was appointed professor of composition at the Dresden Musikhochschule in 1978 and was visiting professor at the Salzburg Mozarteum, 1982–4. With Matthus and Udo Zimmermann he became one of the best-known composers of his generation in the German Democratic Republic; he received many prizes (including the National Prize in 1975) and was made a member of the Berlin Academy of Arts. Alone among prominent East German composers, Kunad left the Democratic Republic in 1984, settling in Tübingen.

After producing youthful works influenced by Orff, and while he was still studying, Kunad set himself against the classicism of such composers as Prokofiev, Stravinsky and Egk. His creative work was influenced chiefly by Lutosławski, and to some extent also by Penderecki and Henze. Initially he concentrated on symphonic forms before proving himself a man of the theatre *par excellence* with the comedy *Maître Pathelin* (1969), which paved the way to his success as a much-performed operatic composer. His large-scale first opera on the Faust theme, *Sabellicus*, followed in 1974. The striking 'opera for actors', *Litauische Claviere* (1976), shows Kunad as a master of cogent brevity and the sparing use of numerous compositional methods. Until the mid-1970s his music drama, shunning the clichés of traditional opera, aimed for 'functionality', with libretto, direction and music being closely interconnected. Kunad's musical language, however, remains accessible to a broad opera-going public; his compositions are marked by musicianship, a melodic vocal line is maintained, and the dodecaphonic organization and use of clusters and aleatory elements are sometimes so well hidden behind familiar sound patterns as to be almost imperceptible. Latterly he has attempted to escape the danger of functionalist rigidity by relaxing his style. The impressive drama *Vincent* (1979), on the life of Van Gogh, is constructed on strictly dodecaphonic lines. As early as *Litauische Claviere* Kunad employed parodic reminiscences of light music, a technique he developed further in the ballet *Münchhausen* (1981). After the neo-tonal comedy *Amphitryon* (1984) he made positive use of traditional forms, often for paradoxical dramatic ends, especially in his second Faust opera, *Der Meister und Margarita* (1986).

Because of Kunad's application to emigrate, *Amphitryon* was performed only once, and all his works were removed from the repertories of East German theatres. Since living in the West he has composed sacred and eschatological music (unthinkable in East Germany at the time of his emigration) of the utmost simplicity, including dramatic oratorios and cosmic pieces which, like *Parsifal*, are not intended for the standard operatic repertory. Banned in East Germany until the reunification of the country in 1990, and largely unappreciated in West Germany because of the composer's turning away from the operatic mainstream, Kunad's operas are performed hardly at all, having fallen victim to German disintegration in a manner almost unparalleled in art.

In numbering his compositions, Kunad has used the term 'conatum' ('attempt', 'undertaking') rather than the usual 'opus'.

See also MAÎTRE PATHELIN; MEISTER UND MARGARITA, DER (i); and VINCENT (i).

numbers in square brackets are conatum numbers

Bill Brook [23] (music-theatre piece, 1, Kunad, after W. Borchert), Dresden-Radebeul, Landesbühne, 14 March 1965

Old Fritz [28] (music-theatre piece, 1, Kunad), Dresden-Radebeul, Landesbühne, 14 March 1965

Maître Pathelin, oder Die Hammelkomödie [41] (8 scenes, Kunad, after H. U. Wendler: *Wer zuletzt lacht*), Dresden, Staatsoper, 30 April 1969

Sabellicus [53] (9 scenes, Kunad, after Faust legends), Berlin, Staatsoper, 20 Dec 1974

Der Eiertanz [62] (mini-op, 1, S. Böhmel and Kunad, after F. Pocci), DDR TV, 1975 [with puppets]; stage, Tübingen, Landes, 7 June 1986

Litauische Claviere [59] (op for actors, 8 scenes, G. Wolf, after J. Bobrowski), Dresden, Staats, 4 Nov 1976

Vincent [63] (10 scenes, Kunad, after A. Matusche: *Van Gogh*), Dresden, Staatsoper, 22 Feb 1979

Amphitryon [74] (musical comedy, 9 scenes, I. Zimmermann, after Hesiod), Berlin, Staatsoper, 26 May 1984

Der Meister und Margarita (romantic op, 10 scenes, H. Czechowski, after M. Bulgakov), Karlsruhe, Staats, 9 March 1986

WRITINGS

'Der Komponist im zeitgenössischen Musiktheater', *Gestaltung und Gestalten*, iv (1968–9)

'Über die Oper: Realismusprobleme in der zeitgenössischen Oper', *Theater der Zeit*, xxv/5 (1970), 37–40

'Realismusprobleme in der zeitgenössischen Oper (zu *Maître Pathelin*)', *Sammelbände zur Musikgeschichte der DDR*, ed. H. A. Brockhaus and K. Niemann, ii (Berlin, 1971), 77–100

*

W. Rösler: 'Zur musikalischen Dramaturgie der Oper *Sabellicus* von Rainer Kunad', *Musikbühne 75: Probleme und Information*, ed. H. Seeger (1975), 67–81

'*Maître Pathelin*', *Sammelbände zur Musikgeschichte der DDR*, ed. H. A. Brockhaus and K. Niemann, v (Berlin, 1979), 254–6

H. J. Schneider: 'Rainer Kunad', *Musiker in unserer Zeit*, ed. D. Brennecke and others (Leipzig, 1979), 262–72

P. Wittig: 'Mit dem Leben Ernst machen: Rainer Kunad's *Vincent*', *Oper heute*, iii (Berlin, 1980), 21–54

H. J. Schaefer: 'Rainer Kunad', *OW*, xxiii/8–9 (1982), 23–6

JOCHEN SCHÖNLEBER

Kunc, Zinka. *See* MILANOV, ZINKA.

Kuningas lähtee Ranskaan. Opera by Aulis Sallinen; *see* KING GOES FORTH TO FRANCE, THE.

Künneke, Eduard (*b* Emmerich, 27 Jan 1885; *d* Berlin, 27 Oct 1953). German composer. In Berlin he attended university lectures on theory and was a composition pupil of Bruch at the Hochschule für Musik. In 1907 he was appointed chorus master at a Berlin operetta theatre, after which he was conductor for Max Reinhardt at the Deutsches Theater. During the war he played the horn in an infantry regiment, and afterwards went to the Friedrich-Wilhelmstädtisches Theater. The success of Heinrich Berté's Schubert pastiche *Das Dreimäderlhaus*, which Künneke conducted, led him to operetta. In this field he enjoyed conspicuous international acclaim with *Der Vetter aus Dingsda* (1921), especially for the tenor solo 'Ich bin nur ein armer Wandergesell'. In the wake of this huge success, Künneke was engaged in 1924 and 1925 to compose works for the Shuberts in New York and one for the Gaiety Theatre in London. These achieved little notice, however, and his further recognition was confined largely to Germany, where he remained the leading exponent of operetta, writing some works in traditional style and others in a more modern dance idiom. His sympathetic and rewarding writing for the operatic voice has kept his music popular with German singers, not least *Die grosse Sünderin* (1935), a more ambitious operetta composed for the Berlin Staatsoper and first performed with Tiana Lemnitz and Helge Roswaenge.

Besides his theatre pieces, Künneke composed a string quartet, orchestral suites, two piano concertos and choral and vocal music.

Operetten unless otherwise stated

Robins Ende op.1 (komische Oper, 1, M. Moris), Mannheim, National, 5 May 1909; Coeur-As op.2 (Oper, 3, E. Tschirch and C. Berg, after E. Scribe), Dresden, Hof, 31 Oct 1913; Tobias Kopp op.5 (komische Oper, E. F. Maikowsky, after W. Busch), unperf.; Das Dorf ohne Glocke op.10 (3, A. Neidhart, after Á. Pásztor: *A harang* [The Bell]), Berlin, Friedrich-Wilhelmstädtisches, 5 April 1919; Der Vielgeliebte op.11 (3, H. Haller and Rideamus [F. Oliven]), Berlin, Nollendorfplatz, 17 Oct 1919

Wenn Liebe erwacht op.12 (3, Haller and Rideamus, after F. Schönthan and F. Koppel-Ellfeldt), Berlin, Nollendorfplatz, 3 Sept 1920; Der Vetter aus Dingsda op.13 (3, Haller and Rideamus, after M. Kempner-Hochstädt), Berlin, Nollendorfplatz, 15 April 1921 (rev. as Caroline, New York, 1923); Die Ehe im Kreise op.14 (3, Haller and Rideamus, after Molière), Berlin, Nollendorfplatz, aut. 1921; Verliebte Leute op.16 (3, Haller and Rideamus), Berlin, Nollendorfplatz, 15 April 1922

Casino-Girls op.17 (Extravaganza-Operette, 3, G. Okonkowski), Berlin, Metropol, 15 July 1923; The Love Song (H. B. Smith), New York, Century, 13 Jan 1925 [after Offenbach]; Lover's Lane op.18, New York, 1925; Die hellblauen Schwestern op.19 (romantische Operette, 3, A. Salfeld and F. Richthoff), Berlin, Nollendorfplatz, 22 Aug 1925; Mayflowers [Not So Long Ago] op.21 (A. Richman and C. Grey), New York, Forrest, 24 Nov 1925

Riki-Tiki op.22 (musical play, 3, L. Stiles), London, Gaiety, 1 May 1926; Lady Hamilton op.23 (3, R. Bars and L. Jacobson), Breslau, Schauspielhaus, 25 Sept 1926; Die blonde Liselott op.24 (Spl, R. Kessler, after H. Stobitzer), Altenburg, Landes, 25 Dec 1927 (rev. as Liselott, Berlin, Admiralspalast, 17 Feb 1932); Die singende Venus op.25, Breslau, Schauspielhaus, 9 June 1928; Der Tenor der Herzogin op.27 (3, Kessler, after H. Ilgenstein), Prague, German, 8 Feb 1930

Nadja op.28 (Oper, 4, R. Lauckner), Kassel, Staats, 28 Feb 1931; Glückliche Reise op.29 (3, M. Bertuch and K. Schwabach), Berlin, Kurfürstendamm, 23 Nov 1932; Klein-Dorrit op.30 (Spl, Kessler, after C. Dickens), Stettin, Stadt, 28 Oct 1933; Fahrt in die Jugend op.31 (B. Jenbach and L. Hirschfeld), Zürich, Stadt, 26 March 1933; Die lockende Flamme op.32 (romantisches Spl, P. Knepler and M. Welleminsky), Berlin, Westens, 25 Dec 1933

Herz über Bord op.33 (E. van der Becke), Zürich and Düsseldorf, 30 March 1935; Die grosse Sünderin op.37 (K. Stoll and H. Roemmer), Berlin, Staatsoper, 31 Dec 1935; Walther von der Vogelweide op. 39 (Oper, U. R. Hirt), unperf.; Zauberin Lola op.40 (musikalische Komödie, 3, A. Brieger and S. Graff), Dortmund, Stadt, 24 April 1937; Hochzeit in Samarkand op.42, Berlin, Volkes, 14 Feb 1938; Der grosse Name, Düsseldorf, Operettenhaus, 14 May 1938

Traumland op.49 (E. Rhein), Dresden, Albrechtsplatz, 15 Nov 1941; Die Wunderbare op.50 (K. Adalbert and J. Scheu), Fürth, Stadt, Jan 1941; Hochzeit mit Erika op.59 (W. Webels), Düsseldorf, Opera, 31 Aug 1949

*

O. Schneidereit: *Eduard Künneke: der Komponist aus Dingsda* (Berlin, 1978)   ANDREW LAMB

Kunz, Erich (*b* Vienna, 20 May 1909). Austrian bassbaritone. A pupil of Theo Lierhammer and Hans Duhan at the Vienna Akademie für Musik, he made his début at Troppau in 1933 as Osmin. After various provincial engagements he became a member of the Vienna Staatsoper in 1940. In 1943 he first sang Beckmesser at Bayreuth, and he soon became a regular singer at Salzburg and other festivals. Covent Garden heard him as Leporello and Figaro during the 1947 Vienna Staatsoper season, and in 1948 and 1950 he sang Guglielmo at Glyndebourne. In 1952 he sang at the Metropolitan for the first time, as Leporello.

An accomplished singing actor with a fine sense of humour and a gift for timing, he excelled in such roles as Papageno, Beckmesser and Figaro. He was a firm favourite with Viennese audiences from the beginning, often playing small parts in operetta or Volksoper

performances with consummate gusto and vocal skill. He was also an accomplished singer of popular Viennese songs.

GV (G. Baldini; R. Vegeto)   PETER BRANSCOMBE

Kunze, Stefan (*b* Athens, 10 Feb 1933). German musicologist. He studied musicology at the universities of Heidelberg and Munich under Rudolph von Ficker and Thrasybulos Georgiades. At the same time he attended the Trapp Conservatory in Munich where he took a performer's diploma in flute in 1955. In 1961 he took the doctorate from Munich University with a dissertation on the instrumental music of Giovanni Gabrieli, and in 1970 he completed his *Habilitation* there with a study of 18th-century Italian *opera buffa*. In 1973 he accepted the chair of musicology at Berne University. His other areas of research include instrumental music and opera from the 16th century to the 19th and questions of music historiography and analysis. He has edited Mozart's *Arien, Szenen, Ensembles und Chöre mit Orchester* in the Neue Ausgabe sämtlicher Werke (Kassel, 1967–72), and Gazzaniga's *Don Giovanni o sia Il convitato di pietra (1787)* (Kassel, 1973).

Don Giovanni vor Mozart: die Tradition der Don-Giovanni-Opern im italienischen Buffa-Theater des 18. Jahrhunderts (Munich, 1972)
Der Kunstbegriff Richard Wagners: Voraussetzungen und Folgerungen (Regensburg, 1983)
Mozarts Opern (Stuttgart, 1984)
ed., with H. J. Lüthi: *Auseinandersetzung mit Othmar Schoek: ein Symposium* (Zürich, 1986)   HANS HEINRICH EGGEBRECHT

Kunzen [Kuntzen], **Friedrich Ludwig Aemilius** (*b* Lübeck, 4 Sept 1761; *d* Copenhagen, 28 Jan 1817). German composer, grandson of Johann Paul Kunzen. In 1781 he began studies in law at the University of Kiel, but he moved to Copenhagen, where he was a successful keyboard performer, composer and organizer of concerts from 1784 to 1789. After the failure of his opera *Holger Danske* (1789) he moved to Berlin, where he founded a music shop with Reichardt and in 1791 edited the journal *Musikalisches Wochenblatt*. In 1792 he became Kapellmeister at the theatre in Frankfurt am Main, where he performed his Singspiel *Das Fest der Winzer, oder Die Weinlese* in 1793. In 1794 he took up a similar post in Prague. He succeeded J. A. P. Schulz as royal Kapellmeister in Copenhagen in 1795, performing many of his own operas and Singspiels there and also directing the oratorio society Det Harmoniske Selskab.

Kunzen presents a many-sided musical personality who was well versed in the music of his time, especially Mozart's operas, which he often presented. The unsuccessful *Holger Danske*, composed to Wieland's proto-Romantic *Oberon* with Schulz as adviser, mixes the styles of grand opera and Singspiel: simple strophic songs, situation comedy, tone-painting of nature, janissary music, energetic dance rhythms and dramatic scenas are all combined in the work, which recalls Gluck and Mozart.

unless otherwise stated, first performed at the Kongelige Teater, Copenhagen, MSS in DK-Kk, printed works published in Copenhagen

Holger Danske [Ogier the Dane] (3, J. Baggesen, after C. M. Wieland: *Oberon*), 31 March 1789, vs (1790)
Das Fest der Winzer, oder Die Weinlese (ländlich-komische Oper, 3, J. Ihlee), Frankfurt, 3 May 1793, *D-Bds, Dlb*; perf. as Viinhøsten, Copenhagen, Dec 1796; vs (1798)

Hemmeligheden [The Secret] (comisk syngestykke, 1, A. G. Thoroup, after Quétant), 22 Nov 1796, vs (?1797)
Dragedukken [The Dragon Doll] (syngestykke, 4, E. Falsen), 14 March 1797, vs (?1797)
Jokeyen (Spl, 1), 14 Dec 1797
Erik Eiegod (3, Baggesen), 30 Jan 1798, ov. (Leipzig, n.d.), vs (?1798)
Naturens røst [The Cry of Nature] (Spl, 3, Falsen, after Armand), 3 Dec 1799, ov. (Leipzig, 1812)
Min bedste moder [My Grandmother] (2, Falsen), 15 May 1800, aria (n.d.)
Ossians Harfe, c1800, aria (Leipzig, 1800)
Hiemkomsten [The Homecoming] (syngespil, 1, T. Thaarup), 1802, vs (?1802)
Eropolis (grosse Oper, 3, L. C. Sander), Jan 1803
Den Logerende [The Lodgers] (Spl, 1, L. Kruse), 1804
Gyrithe (L. Kruse), 1807, vs (n.d.)
Kaerlighed paa landet [Love in the Country] (3, N. T. Bruun, after Weisse), 23 March 1810; excerpts in Polyhymnia, ed. Kunzen (?1780–90) [c8 vols.]

Other stage works: Festen i Valhal [Festival in Valhalla] (prol.), 1796; Hussitterne [The Hussites] (incidental music), 1806; Kapertoget [The Pirates] (occasional piece), 1808; Husarerne paa frieri [The Hussars out Courting] (Posse), 1813

*

StiegerO
C. A. Martienssen: '"Holger Danske", Oper von Fr. L. Ae. Kunsen', ZIMG, xiii (1911–12), 225–32
B. Friis: Friedrich Aemilius Kunzen: sein Leben und Werk I. Bis zur Oper 'Holger Danske' (1761–1789) (diss., U. of Berlin, 1943)
S. Lunn: 'Oberon's Tryllehorn', Dansk Musiktidskrift, xix (1944), 75–80
GEORG KARSTÄDT

Kunzen, Johann Paul (b Leisnig, Saxony, 31 Aug 1696; d Lübeck, 20 March 1757). German composer. He distinguished himself on the violin and on keyboard instruments while at school in Torgau and Freiberg, and from 1716 to 1718 was a student in Leipzig, where he was decisively influenced by Kuhnau and Telemann. A gifted singer and instrumentalist, he performed in both capacities at the Leipzig opera, and stood in for the organist of the Nikolaikirche. In 1718 Kunzen became a Kapellmeister in Zerbst and in 1719 he went to Wittenberg, where his opera Die über Eyffersucht und List triumphirende beständige Liebe was given in concert form about 1720. After several concert tours he took over in 1723 the direction of the opera in Hamburg, where he performed several of his own compositions, including Critique des Hamburgischen Schauplatzes (1725, to a libretto by Schwemschuh); he also added music to a translation of Giovanni Porta's Numitore, which was given there in 1724 as Die heldenmüthigen Schäfer Romulus und Remus. A fourth opera, Cadmus (3, J. U. König), may have been staged there in 1725 (or perhaps in February 1720 at Brunswick, according to Sonneck). When Kunzen's two-year contract expired he remained in Hamburg as a private music teacher. He journeyed to England in 1728–9 and met Pepusch and Handel. From 1732 he was organist of the Marienkirche, Lübeck, and wrote numerous occasional pieces as well as works for the Advent Abendmusiken. The music of his operas has not survived.

*

MGG (G. Karstädt)
J. Mattheson: Grundlage einer Ehren-Pforte (Hamburg, 1740); ed. M. Schneider (Berlin, 1910)
O. G. T. Sonneck: Library of Congress: Catalogue of Opera Librettos Printed before 1800 (Washington DC, 1914)
H. C. Wolff: Die Barockoper in Hamburg (1678–1738) (Wolfenbüttel, 1957)
GEORG KARSTÄDT

Kupets Kalashnikov ('The Merchant Kalashnikov'). Opera in three acts by ANTON GRIGOR'YEVICH RUBIN-STEIN to a libretto by Nikolay Ivanovich Kulikov after MIKHAIL YUR'YEVICH LERMONTOV'S poem Pesnya pro tsarya Ivana Vasil'yevicha, molodogo oprichnika i udalogo kuptsa Kalashnikova ('Song of Tsar Ivan Vasil'yevich, the Young Oprichnik and the Brave Merchant Kalashnikov', 1838); St Petersburg, Mariinsky Theatre, 22 February/5 March 1880.

Lermontov's poem tells how Kalashnikov (baritone in the opera), a Moscow merchant, with his bare fists kills Sergey Kiribeyevich (tenor, originally sung by Josef Paleček), a young member of the personal guard of Ivan the Terrible (bass, originally sung by Fyodor Stravinsky), for abducting his wife Alyona Dmitriyevna (soprano, first sung by Wilhelmina Raab) and is then unjustly condemned to death. It is famous for its adoption of the diction and metre of the old Russian epic songs contemporary with its subject. Following suit, Rubinstein's opera, which conserves many of the poet's original verses, is composed in what is for him an unusually national idiom, for which reason alone it has gone down in biased history as one of his best works. The ban on the opera – it was suppressed after two performances – was the result of unfortunate timing: a would-be assassin of Alexander II had just been sentenced to death and it was feared that the tragic sentencing of Kalashnikov in the opera's finale might arouse sympathy for him. In 1889, revived at the Mariinsky under Nápravník, the opera was again banned by a squeamish tsar after two performances, to the composer's intense chagrin. Thereafter it played in Russia only on provincial and private stages.
RICHARD TARUSKIN

Kupfer, Harry (b Berlin, 12 Aug 1935). German director. After studying theatre science at the Hans Otto Theaterhochschule in Leipzig, he became an assistant at the Landestheater in Halle, where he made his début with Rusalka in 1958. He was then successively Oberspielleiter at the Theater der Werftstadt in Stralsund (1958–62), senior resident producer at the Städtische Theater in Karl-Marx-Stadt (now Chemnitz; 1962–6) and opera director of the Nationaltheater in Weimar (1966–72); from 1967 to 1972 he also taught at the Franz Liszt Musikhochschule in Weimar.

In 1971 Kupfer made his début at the Deutsche Staatsoper, Berlin, with Die Frau ohne Schatten, and the following year was appointed opera director and chief producer at the Staatsoper, Dresden. He remained at that post until 1981, winning wide renown for himself and the opera house. His adventurous programming there resulted in the premières of Udo Zimmermann's Levins Mühle (1973) and Der Schuhu und die fliegende Prinzessin (1976) and of Rainer Kunad's Vincent (1979), as well as challenging productions of such works as Moses und Aron (1975), Tristan (1975) and Simon Boccanegra (1980).

Kupfer came to international attention in 1978 with a Fliegender Holländer at Bayreuth that provided both an incisive psychological reassessment of Senta's predicament, in terms of socially induced alienation and neurosis, and an electrifying theatrical experience. In the same year he made his British début with a savage, sanguineous Elektra (WNO, 1978), returning with a highly praised Pelléas et Mélisande (ENO, 1981) and a characteristically polemical Fidelio (WNO, 1981) which alluded in its final tableau to freedom fighters past and present. In 1981 he became chief producer at the Komische Oper, Berlin. Two of his many productions there were taken on the company's visit to Covent

Garden in 1989: a *Bartered Bride* that penetrated behind the folksy façade to the underlying social realities, and an *Orfeo ed Euridice* that addressed the dilemma of the artist in society, relocating the myth against a bleak background of contemporary urban decline.

The two greatest avowed influences on Kupfer's dramaturgy were Felsenstein (though Kupfer was not his associate) and Brecht. The fusion of the former's principles of realistic music theatre, emphasizing the importance of motivation and immediacy in stage movement, with the latter's contrasting theory of 'alienation', resulted in a style both powerfully engaging and intellectually rigorous. Those qualities were strikingly evident in his most notable staging to date, that of the *Ring* at Bayreuth (1988): a densely allusive, socially critical exploration of the work that integrated mythological and contemporary planes so as to address the issues of accumulated wealth and power, ruination of the natural environment and global destruction while remaining faithful to the work's timeless universality.

Kupfer collaborated with Penderecki on the libretto of Penderecki's *Die schwarze Maske*, first performed at the Salzburg Festival on 15 August 1986.

*

N. Ely and S. Jaeger, eds.: *Regie heute: Musiktheater in unserer Zeit* (Berlin, 1984), 161–82
D. Kranz: '*Ich muss Oper machen': der Regisseur Harry Kupfer* (Berlin, 1988)
M. Lewin: *Harry Kupfer* (Vienna and Zürich, 1988)
H. Canning: 'Kupfer and the Komische', *Opera*, xl (1989), 913–18 [interview]
——: 'The Path of History', *Opera* (1989), festival issue, 71–5 [review of Bayreuth *Ring*]
R. Hutton: 'The 1988 Bayreuth "Ring" as Theory and as Theatre', *Wagner*, x (1989), 66–80
R. Lummer: *Regie im Theater: Harry Kupfer* (Frankfurt, 1989)
BARRY MILLINGTON

Kupferman, Meyer (*b* New York, 3 July 1926). American composer. Self-taught in music, he was appointed to teach composition and chamber music at Sarah Lawrence College in 1951. He is a prolific composer whose operas reflect his versatility and his range. The earliest, *In a Garden*, is a 20-minute chamber piece for three singers, based on a book of plays for children by Gertrude Stein. The second, *Doctor Faustus Lights the Lights* (1953), again drawn from Stein, is by contrast a three-act work in the style of grand opera, with big arias, big sets and a large cast and chorus. In 1957 two one-act operas, *Voices for a Mirror* and *The Curious Fern*, were first performed, as a double bill, in New York City by the Living Theatre at the Master Theatre Institute.

In his operas as in his other compositions Kupferman has shown a marked interest in formal experimentation. *The Judgment*, a choric opera based on the biblical story of Lot, calls for a large cast and chorus but dispenses with orchestra or other instrumental participation. This opera is no.18 in Kupferman's *Infinities* series, so-called because of the infinite compositional possibilities found in the single 12-note row on which the entire series of works, using varied instrumental and vocal combinations, is based. *Prometheus* (1977), with a libretto partly in German, drawn from Goethe, and partly in English, written by Kupferman, is cast in five scenes divided into two acts, yet it might also be heard as five separate but related one-act operas. Each scene tells the Prometheus story in its own way, with its own highly contrasting music and staging, thereby creating a set of operatic

Prometheus variations. Act 1 scene i, 'Prometheus Primus' (in German), is set for bass voice and small orchestra; Act 1 scene ii, 'Prometheus', is for onstage percussion ensemble and dancers; Act 1 scene iii, 'Prometheus Condemned' (in German and English), is for tenor, bass, chorus, percussion ensemble and small orchestra; Act 2 scene i, 'Prometheus and Pandora' (in German), is for soprano, tenor, baritone, bass and small orchestra; the final scene, 'Prometheus Profundus' (in German and English), calls for large chorus, brass and percussion ensemble.

In a Garden (children's op, 1, after G. Stein: *First Reader*), New York, Finch Junior College, 29 Dec 1949, vs (New York, 1952)
Doctor Faustus Lights the Lights (3, after Stein: *Three Plays*), Bronxville, NY, Sarah Lawrence College, 5 April 1953
Voices for a Mirror, 1955 (1, A. Reid), New York, The Master Theatre Institute, 5 June 1957, vs (New York, 1957) [double bill with The Curious Fern]
The Curious Fern (comic op, 1, Reid), New York, The Master Theatre Institute, 5 June 1957, vs (New York, 1957) [double bill with Voices for a Mirror]
Draagenfut Girl (2, Kupferman, after Cinderella fairy-tale), Bronxville, NY, Sarah Lawrence College, 8 May 1958, vs (New York, 1964)
The Judgment, 1966 (3, P. Freeman), vs (New York, 1967), unperf. [no.18 of Infinities series]
Antigonae (opera-monodrama, 1, F. Hölderlin, after Sophocles), Stockbridge, MA, Lenox Art Center, 1973
Prometheus (2, J. W. von Goethe and Kupferman, in Ger. and Eng.), Act 1 scene ii, New York, Manhattan School of Music, 1978
The Proscenium: ... on the Demise of Gertrude (chamber op, 1, Kupferman), New York, Columbia U., Miller Theatre, 3 Nov 1991
JEROME ROSEN

Kupka, Karel (*b* Rychvald, nr Karviná, 19 June 1927; *d* Ostrava, 26 Oct 1985). Czech composer. After early studies at the Ostrava Institute of Music and Singing and at the Prague Conservatory (1940–46), he studied composition with Kvapil and Petrželka in Brno (1946–52). In 1948 he was appointed headmaster of the Karviná music school, and he held a similar position in Petřvald, Moravia, until 1954, when he became répétiteur and conductor of the opera company at the Zdeněk Nejedlý Theatre in Ostrava. His musical style was initially influenced by Janáček and Bartók. During the late 1950s and early 1960s, Kupka's operas gained attention through their use of atypical classical themes; their style of expression came close to that of the contemporary Polish school (*Taškář*, *Lysistrata* and *Sokratova smrt*). In the later 1960s he began to make use of the sonorities of more recent music, but without losing his tendency to write in extended forms. A terse vehemence and dramatic power are combined in his music with a lyrical melodiousness which has its roots in Moravian folksong.

unperformed unless otherwise stated

Taškář [Jester] (1, Kupka, after Plautus), excerpts, Ostrava, Zdeněk Nejedlý, 21 Oct 1956
Má lásko [My Love], 1956 (television op)
Lysistrata (4, Kupka, after Aristophanes), excerpts, Ostrava, Zdeněk Nejedlý, 28 Sept 1958
Když tančí růže [When the Roses Dance] (3, Kupka, after D. Petrov), Ostrava, Zdeněk Nejedlý, 3 Feb 1962
Idiot, 1962 (after F. M. Dostoyevsky)
Jeptiška [The Nun], 1964
Sokratova smrt [The Death of Socrates], 1965
A z celé duše miluji [I Love You With All My Heart], 1967
Tirésiovy prsy [Les mamelles de Tirésias], 1970 (anti-op, after G. Apollinaire)
Mít vlastní pokoj v rezidenci [To Have One's Own Room in the Residence] (L. Slíva), 1982
Noční hlídka [Night Guard], 1983
Opus Odysseus, 1984 (opera-suita, M. Nekušil)

Č. Gregor: 'Rozhovor o nové opeře' [Interview on the New Opera], *Červený květ*, iii (1958), 68 [on *Lysistrata*]

E. Sýkorová: 'Nová opera Karla Kupky', *Červený květ*, vii/2 (1962), 61 [on *Když tančí růže*]

OLDŘICH PUKL, HELENA HAVLÍKOVÁ

Kupper, Annelies (Gabriele) (*b* Glatz, 21 July 1906; *d* Munich, 8 Dec 1987). German soprano. She studied in Breslau and made her début there in 1935 as Second Boy in *Die Zauberflöte*. After engagements at Schwerin and Weimar, in 1940 she joined the Hamburg Staatsoper, singing there until 1945; for the next 15 years she was a member of the Staatsoper in Munich, where she continued to sing occasionally until 1966. In 1944 she sang Eva at Bayreuth, returning as Elsa in 1960. At Salzburg she was the Female Chorus in *The Rape of Lucretia* in 1950 and two years later created the title role in the first public performance of *Die Liebe der Danae*. At Covent Garden in 1953 she sang Chrysothemis and, in the Munich company's London season, Danae. She made guest appearances throughout Europe. In addition to the Mozart and Strauss repertory, Kupper sang Aida, Desdemona and Tatyana. Her musicianship, sensitivity and feeling for words were admirably suited to contemporary works.

HAROLD ROSENTHAL/R

Kurai Kagami. Opera by Yasushi Akutagawa; *see* HIROSHIMA NO ORUFE.

Kurka, Robert (Frank) (*b* Cicero, IL, 22 Dec 1921; *d* New York, 12 Dec 1957). American composer. He studied briefly with Otto Luening and Milhaud but was principally self-taught. His honours include a Guggenheim Fellowship (1951–2) and an award from the National Institute of Arts and Letters (1952). Although he wrote a quantity of orchestral and chamber music in neo-classical style, Kurka is best known for his orchestral suite *The Good Soldier Schweik* (1956), a set of six character pieces inspired by Jaroslav Hašek's satirical anti-war novel about a conscript who pretends feeblemindedness in order to outwit his superiors. The suite is often compared with Weill's *Kleine Dreigroschenmusik* suite (1929); not only are the instrumentation and tonal language similar, but both works combine references to popular musical idioms (dances, marches, the ballad style) with pungent dissonances and brittle rhythms for ironic effect. In 1957, with the librettist Lewis Allan, Kurka expanded the suite into a two-act opera, the orchestration of which was completed after the composer's death by Hershy Kay. It was first performed, to great acclaim, by the New York City Opera on 23 April 1958, and has since been given frequently in both the USA and Europe.

JAMES WIERZBICKI

Kurofune ('The Black Ships') [*Yoake* ('The Dawn')]. Opera in three acts by KŌSÇAK YAMADA to a libretto by the composer and Atsuo Ōki after Percy Noël; as *Yoake*, Tokyo, Takarazuka Theatre, 28 November 1940.

On a summer day in 1856 at a restaurant near the wharf of Shimoda, people are enjoying a feast, in spite of the news that the Black Ships are coming to negotiate a peace treaty, while Omatsu (soprano) sings. Okichi (soprano) joins the party, but the merrymaking is interrupted by Yoshida (baritone), a samurai who is faithful to the emperor and against the treaty. Okichi is attracted to Yoshida. The Black Ships arrive and the American Consul (tenor) appears, singing an aria in

praise of Japan. Yoshida approaches Okichi and persuades her to kill the Consul with a dagger hidden in a fan. In Act 2, six months later Yoshida and his comrades are in the restaurant discussing their plan to assassinate the Consul. Okichi arrives, and Yoshida confirms their plan. Later Okichi entertains the Consul, who is depressed. The Secretary (tenor), himself in love with Omatsu, suggests that the Consul is interested in Okichi. The Magistrate (bass) tells Okichi to become the Consul's mistress and arrests her at her refusal. Act 3 begins in the Consul's office in a Buddhist temple; the Consul is irritated because the negotiations have been delayed. Okichi, released and now sympathetic to the Consul, consoles him, but a message from Yoshida reminds her of the assassination plan. Okichi takes the Consul to an island, following Yoshida's instruction. While she tries to kill the Consul, a storm breaks out and he rescues her. Back in the temple the people applaud the Consul's bravery, and Okichi is confessing her sin when the Magistrate brings the news that the shogun invites the Consul to Edo to negotiate the treaty. Yoshida tries to kill the Consul himself, but, after learning that the emperor is also in favour of peaceful negotiation, commits suicide. The people pray for the dead and for the dawn of a new peaceful age. Written in a post-Romantic Straussian style with some Japanese elements, including pentatonic scales, *Kurofune* is virtually the first full-scale opera written by a Japanese composer.

MASAKATA KANAZAWA

Kurpiński, Karol Kazimierz (*b* Włoszakowice, Wielkopolska, 6 March 1785; *d* Warsaw, 18 Sept 1857). Polish composer and conductor. He studied with his father Marcin Kurpiński, an organist at Włoszakowice, and became organist himself at nearby Sarnów in 1797. Three years later he was employed as a second violinist at the estate of Feliks Polanowski, where his uncle was a member of the small private orchestra. In 1808 he took a post as tutor to the Rastawiecki family in Lwów, where he heard a number of Italian and German operas, and in 1810 he settled in Warsaw. There he met the dramatist Wojciech Bogusławski, the so-called father of Polish theatre, who was at that time looking for a deputy conductor to work alongside Józef Elsner at the National Theatre. Kurpiński was appointed initially as chorus master, and then deputy conductor. With Elsner's help he became an increasingly influential figure in Warsaw's musical life. In 1824 he was appointed principal conductor at the National Theatre (on Elsner's dismissal) and in that capacity, to 1840, he presented a repertory of the highest quality, notably Mozart and Rossini, to Polish audiences. In addition he regularly conducted orchestral concerts, including the first performances of Chopin's two piano concertos.

Kurpiński was also active as a teacher, establishing the School of Singing and Declamation at the National Theatre in 1835 as a replacement for the conservatory, closed down after the 1830 insurrection. In a modest way he was a man of letters, with a work of philosophy as well as books of music pedagogy to his name. He founded and contributed regularly to the journal *Tygodnik muzyczny* ('Music Weekly') – later *Tygodnik muzyczny i dramatyczny* ('Music and Drama Weekly') – the main forum for musical debate in Warsaw in the first half of the century. In 1823, just before his appointment as principal conductor at the National Theatre, he embarked on a European tour that took in all the major musical centres. Kurpiński's creative work slackened noticeably following the tour, and it seems possible that he felt his own music to be somewhat anachronistic in relation to the new musical styles of the 1820s. His later life was given mainly to teaching. Kurpiński died in Warsaw, largely forgotten, on 18 September 1857, three months before Moniuszko's *Halka* had its Warsaw première.

Kurpiński was the major Polish opera composer before Moniuszko, and his output (most of it for the National Theatre in Warsaw) was considerable. Many of his operas received only a few performances before disappearing from the repertory, but some had more lasting success, notably *Szarlatan, czyli Wskrzeszenie umarłych* ('The Charlatan, or The Raising of the Dead'), *Jadwiga królowa Polska* ('Jadwiga, Queen of Poland') and *Zamek na Czorsztynie, cyli Bojomir i Wanda* ('The Castle of Czorsztyn, or Bojomir and Wanda'). For the most part his stage works were vaudevilles or Singspiels, interleaving songs and choruses with spoken dialogue. These were popular genres in Poland in the early 19th century, with vaudevilles by Polish composers as prominent in the repertory as foreign works.

Nine of Kurpiński's 26 known stage works survive complete, and there are extracts from a further eight. It is clear from the surviving works that their stylistic profile was distinctly Italian, influenced both by late 18th-century composers such as Cimarosa and Paisiello and by later masters such as Rossini. At the same time, Kurpiński helped lay the foundations of a national operatic style by drawing on themes from Polish history and folklore, notably in *Jadwiga, Jan Kochanowski w Czarnym Lesie* ('Jan Kochanowski at Czarny Las') and *Oblężenie Gdańska* ('The Siege of Gdańsk'). In some works he also made use of Polish national dances and folksongs. The overture (the only surviving music) to *Marcinowa w Seraju* ('Marcin's Wife in the Harem') is based on an *oberek* (fast mazurka) rhythm. Similarly, *Szarlatan* contains an extended polonaise aria, and *Zabobon, czyli Krakowiacy i górale, albo Nowe Krakowiaki* ('Superstition, or Krakowians and Mountaineers, or The New Krakovians') make use of several folk melodies.

His most ambitious stage work was probably *Jadwiga*, a full-scale opera similar in its broad design to the historical operas of Spontini. More than his other surviving operas *Jadwiga* registers the influence of Rossini (whose operas Kurpiński frequently conducted at the National Theatre), not least in its florid coloratura arias. Its overture is also more integral to the opera than is usual in Kurpiński. In recent years there have been attempts to revive some of his operas in Poland, with notable success in the cases of *Pałac Lucypera* ('Lucifer's Palace'), *Szarlatan* and *Zabobon*. *Henryk VI na łowach* ('Henry VI Goes Hunting'), a pasticcio from several Kurpiński works, was made by Jerzy Dobrzański and first given in Łódź in 1972.

Pigmalion, *c*1800–08 (1, J. J. Rousseau, trans. K. Węgierski), lost

Dwie chatki [Two Cabins] (1, L. Dmuszewski), Warsaw, 26 May 1811, lost except ov. (Kraków, 1950)

Pałac Lucypera [Lucifer's Palace] (operetta, 4, A. von Kotzebue and J. M. Loaisel, trans. A. Żółkowski), Warsaw, 9 Nov 1811, *PL-Wn*

Oblężenie Gdańska [The Siege of Gdańsk] (melodrama, 3, J. E. Boirie and J. C. A. Cuvelier, trans. Dmuszewski), Warsaw, 13 Dec 1811, lost

Ruiny Babilonu [The Ruins of Babylon] (melodrama, 3, R. C. G. de Pixérécourt), Warsaw, 6 March 1812, lost except ov. (Leipzig, 1820)

Marcinowa w Seraju [Marcin's Wife in the Harem] (3, W. Pękalski), Warsaw, 20 March 1812, lost except ov. (Leipzig, 1820)

Szarlatan, czyli Wskrzeszenie umarłych [The Charlatan, or The Raising of the Dead] (2, Żółkowski), Warsaw, 23 Jan 1814, ov. and 9 excerpts (Warsaw, 1828)

Łaska Imperatora [The Emperor's Staff] (1, Kotzebue, trans. Dmuszewski), Warsaw, 11 March 1814, *Wn*

Agar na puszczy [Agar in the Forest] (melodrama, 1, S. F. Genlis), Warsaw, 19 May 1814, lost

Jadwiga królowa Polska [Jadwiga, Queen of Poland] (3, J. U. Niemcewicz), Warsaw, 23 Dec 1814, *Wtm*, ov. (Leipzig, 1820)

Aleksander i Apelles [Alexander and the Apelles] (melodrama, 1, A. de la Ville de Mirmont, trans. Dmuszewski), Warsaw, 17 March 1815, *Wn*

Nagroda [The Reward] (operetta, 2, Dmuszewski), Warsaw, 1815, lost except ov. (Warsaw, 1820)

Mała szkoła ojców [The School Founder] (1, Dmuszewski), Warsaw, 15 March 1816, lost

Zabobon, czyli Krakowiacy i górale, albo Nowe Krakowiaki [Superstition, or Krakowians and Mountaineers, or The New Krakovians] (3, J. Kamiński), Warsaw, 16 June 1816, *Wtm*, ov. and excerpts (Warsaw, 1826)

Dziadek i Wnuk [Grandfather and Grandchild] (?melodrama, 2, A. de Favieres, trans. L. Osiński), Warsaw, 13 Oct 1816, lost

Hero i Leander [Hero and Leander] (melodrama, 1, J. P. C. de Floris, trans. S. Starzyński), Warsaw, 6 Dec 1816, lost

Jan Kochanowski w Czarnym Lesie [Jan Kochanowski at Czarny Las] (2, Niemcewicz), Warsaw, 1 Jan 1817, excerpts (Warsaw, 1817)

Bateria o jednym żołnierzu [A Troop of One Soldier] (melodrama, 1, Żółkowski), Warsaw, 9 Nov 1817, frags. *Kj*

Czaromysł książę słowiański [Czaromys the Slav Prince] (1, Żółkowski), Warsaw, 27 March 1818, *Kj*, *Wtm*

Zamek na Czorsztynie, czyli Bojomir i Wanda [The Castle of Czorsztyn, or Bojomir and Wanda] (2, J. W. Krasiński), Warsaw, 5 March 1819 (Kraków, 1968)

Zbigniew (3, Niemcewicz), Warsaw, 5 Nov 1819, lost

Kalmora, czyli Prawo ojcowskie Amerykanów [Kalmora, or The Paternal Right of the Americans] (melodrama, 2, K. Brodziński), Warsaw, 10 Feb 1820, *Wtm*, ov. (Leipzig, 1826)

Sąd ostateczny [The Last Court] (genre unknown, E. Young, trans. F. Dmochowski), Warsaw, 9 March 1821, lost

Cień Księcia Józefa Poniatowskiego [The Ghost of Józef Poniatowski] (?melodrama, 1), Warsaw, 13 Sept 1821, lost

Leśniczy z Kozienickiej Puszczy [The Foresters of Kozienice] (1, Krasiński), Warsaw, 28 Oct 1821, *Wn*

Cecylia Piaseczyńska (2, Dmuszewski), Warsaw, 31 May 1829, ov. and excerpts (Warsaw, 1830)

*

K. Kurpiński: *Karol Kurpiński: dziennik podrozy, 1823* [Karol Kurpiński: Diary of a Journey], ed. J. Jachimecki (Kraków, 1954)

A. Lisowska: 'Karol Kurpiński jako pisarz, dzialacz i organizator muzyczny w Warszawie' [Karol Kurpiński as Writer, Promoter and Organizer of Musical Life in Warsaw], *Szkice o kulturze muzycznej xix wieku*, ed. Zofia Chechlińska, ii (Warsaw, 1973), 181–231

T. Przybylski: *Karol Kurpiński, 1785–1857* (Warsaw, 1975)

——: 'Karol Kurpiński: kronika życia i twórzosci' [Karol Kurpiński: Chronicle of his Life and Works], *Szkice o kulturze muzycznej xix wieku*, ed. Zofia Chechlińska, iv (Warsaw, 1980), 276–489

JIM SAMSON

Kurt(-Deri), Melanie (*b* Vienna, 8 Jan 1880; *d* New York, 11 March 1941). Austrian soprano. She studied in Vienna with Fannie Müller and in 1902 made her début at Lübeck as Elisabeth. After a season in Leipzig she withdrew for further study with Lilli and Marie Lehmann in Berlin. She joined the Brunswick Staatsoper in 1905 and was engaged at Berlin (1908–15). She sang at Covent Garden in 1910 as Sieglinde and Brünnhilde (*Die Walküre*) and in 1914 as Kundry. From 1915 to 1917 she sang at the Metropolitan Opera, making her début as Isolde and singing, as well as the Wagner repertory, the title role in *Iphigénie en Tauride*, Leonore (*Fidelio*), Pamina, Santuzza and the Marschallin. In 1920 she joined the Berlin Volksoper, where she sang until 1925. She possessed a rich, powerful dramatic soprano voice and had outstanding dramatic presence.

GV (L. Riemens)   HAROLD ROSENTHAL/R

Kurz [Kurtz, Kurz-Bernardon, Bernardon], **(Johann) Joseph Felix von** (*b* Vienna, 22 Feb 1717; *d* Vienna, 3 Feb 1784). Austrian comic actor, singer, dramatist and theatre manager. The son of the actor-manager Felix Kurz, he grew up in the theatre, and by the age of 20 he was performing leading roles with the German troupe at the Kärntnertortheater in Vienna. From 1740 to 1744 he performed in Germany. Back in Vienna (1744–53) he developed and perfected the kind of magic burlesque, generously larded with songs, choruses, ensembles and incidental music, that dominated the popular repertory in most of the southern German lands. He became known as Bernardon, the name of the comic character through which he made his acting reputation. After the imperial ban on extemporization, Kurz moved in 1753 to Prague, where he was Locatelli's sub-lessee and director at the Kotzentheater. He returned to Vienna in 1754, earning notoriety for his lavish spectacles and lasting renown for the high standard of the music offered in his company's performances (Haydn was Kurz's collaborator in *Der (neue) krumme Teufel*; earlier Ignaz Holzbauer had written a score for a comedy by Weiskern, 1746). Kurz was in Prague again in 1760, and subsequently he appeared at Venice and Pressburg (now Bratislava) and in a number of German cities. During 1769–71 Kurz was in Vienna again, as co-lessee with Gluck; his productions included *La serva padrona* and a revival of *Der krumme Teufel*. In 1771 he toured via Breslau and Danzig to Warsaw, where he directed the theatre and, after his retirement, ran a paper factory.

In 1743 Kurz married Franziska Toscani, and in 1758, three years after her death, he married Teres(in)a Morelli. Both his wives and his numerous children were members of his troupe; Teresa especially was an important artist in her own right, being chosen in 1770 to create the role of Cupid in Gluck's *Paride ed Elena*. Kurz himself was a versatile singer; in one of his own comic operas he sang the three principal parts (falsetto, tenor and bass). He was also brilliantly successful as a comic actor. As a theatre impresario Kurz did not ignore the growing demand for regular plays and serious operas, but he is best remembered as an inventive comic dramatist and actor, with a full and remarkably early appreciation of the role of music in the theatre; he may indeed be said to have introduced the first works that can be recognized as modern Singspiels.

C. H. Schmid: *Chronologie des deutschen Theaters* (Leipzig, 1775); ed. P. Legband (Berlin, 1902)

O. Teuber: *Geschichte des Prager Theaters*, i (Prague, 1883)

——: *Das k.k. Hofburgtheater seit seiner Begründung* (Vienna, 1896)

F. Raab: *Johann Joseph Felix von Kurz, gennant Bernardon* (Frankfurt, 1899)

A. von Weilen: *Geschichte des Wiener Theaterwesens* (Vienna, 1899)

——: 'Johann Joseph Felix von Kurz, genannt Bernardon', *Euphorion*, vi (1899), 350–61

M. Pirker, ed.: *Teutsche Arien* (Vienna, 1927)

O. Rommel, ed.: *Die Maschinenkomödie* (Leipzig, 1935)

——: *Die Alt-Wiener Volkskomödie* (Vienna, 1952)

U. Birbaumer: *Das Werk des Joseph Felix von Kurz-Bernardon und seine szenische Realisierung* (Vienna, 1971)

G. Zechmeister: *Die Wiener Theater nächst der Burg und nächst dem Kärntnerthor von 1747 bis 1776* (Vienna, 1971)

P. Branscombe: 'Music in the Viennese Popular Theatre of the Eighteenth and Nineteenth Centuries', *PRMA*, xcviii (1971–2), 101–12
                    PETER BRANSCOMBE

Selma Kurz in the title role of Delibes' 'Lakmé'

Kurz, Selma (*b* Biala, Silesia, 15 Oct 1874; *d* Vienna, 10 May 1933). Austrian soprano. Although she made her début in Hamburg as Mignon in 1895, her first appearance at Vienna during the Mahler epoch in the same role in 1899 established that city as the centre of her artistic and private life. She was highly successful in many and varied roles, including Tosca and even Sieglinde, but became particularly famous in the coloratura repertory, notably as Verdi's Gilda and Oscar. Gifted with a voice of remarkable purity, sweetness and ease, she also possessed a shake of amazing perfection and duration, which she was accustomed to display – not inappropriately – in an inserted cadenza to Oscar's teasing 'Saper vorreste'. Between 1904 and 1907, and again in 1924, she dazzled Covent Garden audiences in these and other parts. In 1916 she became the first Zerbinetta in the revised version of Strauss's *Ariadne auf Naxos* in Vienna, where she continued to sing until 1926. Among her many successful recordings are the unaccompanied 'Lockruf' from Goldmark's *Königin von Saba* and numerous versions of her *cheval de bataille*, 'Saper vorreste'.

GV (R. Celletti; R. Vegeto)

D. Halban (as told to A. E. Knight): 'Selma Kurz', *Record Collector*, xiii (1960–61), 53–6 [with discography by A. E. Knight]; xvii (1966–8), 46

D. Halban: 'My Mother Selma Kurz', *Recorded Sound*, no. 49 (1973), 128–40 [with discography by A. Kelly, J. F. Perkins and J. Ward]
                    DESMOND SHAWE-TAYLOR

Kurzbach, Paul (*b* Hohndorf, Erzgebirge, 13 Dec 1902). German composer. He attended the Leipzig Conservatory (1925–8) and while teaching in a primary school (1921–33) he conducted workers' choirs in Chemnitz (later Karl-Marx-Stadt). Through his advocacy of Hanns Eisler's works he got to know the composer personally, but it was the influence of Orff, with whom he was associated between 1939 and 1943, that was of decisive significance for his own music. After 1945 he held various posts in cultural administration, becoming a vice-president of the Composers' Union in 1968; subsequently he supported himself as a freelance composer. In the 1950s his involvement with the general effort to establish a national opera in his country resulted in the completion of two operas, *Thomas Müntzer* and *Thyl Claes*, both musically revealing the influence of Orff. In later works he gradually toned down the Orffian percussive style of his work in favour of a consistently tonal 'friendly tendency', to use his own words.

Junge Liebe, 1932 (H. Kurzbach and P. Kurzbach, after G. Keller: *Romeo und Julia auf dem Lande*), unperf.
Historia de Susanna, 1946–7 (P. Kurzbach, after the Book of Daniel), Göttingen, 1948
Thomas Müntzer (P. Kurzbach), 1948–50, Magdeburg, 24 June 1955; rev. version, Dresden, Radebeul, 26 Oct 1974
Thyl Claes, 1955, Görlitz, 7 Dec 1958
Jean, der Soldat (P. Kurzbach)

*

E. Rebling: 'Die Oper "Thomas Müntzer" von Paul Kurzbach', *Musik und Gesellschaft*, v/9 (1955), 3–4
J. Wiecke: 'Paul Kurzbachs Oper "Thyl Claes"', *Musik und Gesellschaft*, viii/11 (1958), 18
P. Kurzbach: 'Bemerkungen zur Situation der Gegenwartsoper', *In eigener Sache: zehn Jahre Verband deutscher Komponisten und Musikwissenschaftler* (Berlin, 1961)   HELLMUT KÜHN

Kürzinger, Paul Ignaz (*b* Mergentheim, Württemberg, 28 April 1750; *d* Vienna, after 1820). Bavarian composer. As a violinist he joined the orchestra of the electoral court at Munich in 1775, where in the same year his opera *La contessina* was produced. Two years later he went to Regensburg to play in the orchestra of the Prince of Thurn and Taxis, and he directed the court opera theatre there from 1780 to 1783. While in Regensburg he wrote a number of operas and ballets. Later he moved to Vienna, where he continued to write theatrical works, including the opera *Die Illumination* for the Burgtheater in 1787. He became music director at a private school in Vienna, and remained there for the rest of his life.

MSS in D-Rtt unless otherwise stated
La contessina (dg per musica, C. Goldoni), Munich, 1775
Robert und Kalliste (komische Oper, J. J. Eschenburg), Regensburg, 15 Oct 1780
Julie [Die dankbare Tochter] (Spl, 1, F. G. von Nesselrode), Regensburg, 1780
Minerven's Ankunft bei den Musen (Spl, 1, Nesselrode), Regensburg, 1780
Cora und Alonzo (melodrama, d'Albonico-Roland), Regensburg, 1781
Die Bergknappen (P. Weidmann), Regensburg, 1782
Die Illumination (Spl, 2), Vienna, Kärntnertor, 25 Nov 1787, lost

*

MGG (O. Kaul)
O. Kaul: *Geschichte der Würzburger Hofmusik im 18. Jahrhundert* (Würzberg, 1924)
K. G. Fellerer: *Beiträge zur Musikgeschichte Freisings* (Freising, 1926)   GEORGE J. BUELOW

Kusche, Benno (*b* Freiburg, 30 Jan 1916). German bass-baritone. He studied at Karlsruhe and made his début at Koblenz in 1938 as Melitone (*La forza del destino*). The next year he was engaged at Augsburg. In 1946 he was engaged by the Staatsoper in Munich,

where he sang for over 30 years. At Salzburg in 1949 he took part in the first performance of Orff's *Antigonae*. He made his Covent Garden début in 1952 as Beckmesser; the following year he appeared there with the Munich company, as La Roche in the British première of *Capriccio*. At Glyndebourne he sang Leporello (1954), Don Fernando in *Fidelio* (1963) and La Roche (1963 and 1964). In 1971 he made his Metropolitan début as Beckmesser. Kusche's repertory included Papageno (which he sang in Felsenstein's 1954 production of *Die Zauberflöte* at the Komische Oper, Berlin), Alberich, Faninal, Figaro, Don Alfonso and Gianni Schicchi. He was one of the best character singers in postwar German opera, being specially effective in comic roles.   HAROLD ROSENTHAL/R

Kuss, Der ('The Kiss'). *Tragisch-komische Oper* in three acts by Franz Danzi (*see* DANZI family, (2)) to a libretto by Matthias Georg Lambrecht; Munich, Hoftheater, 27 June 1799.

Der Kuss is a *Zauberoper*, a type especially popular in southern Germany and Austria in the 1790s. Like Mozart's *Die Zauberflöte*, it has an exotic setting, blends serious and comic elements and requires special scenic effects. Danzi's choice of harmonic relationships is striking, especially the modulations to 3rd-related keys and shifts between major and minor modes. Inventive orchestration, especially wind accompaniment, enhances his musical characterization. The first performances received mixed reviews; one writer found the eclectic music 'very masterful, but more artistic than pleasing'. The original cast included the composer's wife, Margarethe Marchand-Danzi, who made her final stage appearance in the prima donna role.

PAUL CORNEILSON

Kusser, Johann Sigismund [Cousser, Jean Sigismond] (*b* Pressburg [now Bratislava], bap. 13 Feb 1660; *d* Dublin, Nov 1727). Composer of Hungarian parentage active in Germany, England and Ireland. Walther established the highly significant fact that he spent six years in Paris studying with Lully, which must have been between 1674, when he moved to Stuttgart, and 1682, when he was appointed to the court at Ansbach. He left Ansbach in 1683, and may then have travelled throughout Germany before becoming opera Kapellmeister at the court of Brunswick-Wolfenbüttel in 1690. A man of volatile temperament, he quarrelled there with F. C. Bressand, court poet and manager of the opera, who wrote the librettos for several of his works: he openly criticized both the quality of Bressand's poetry and the efficiency of his management of the opera, and this probably led to Kusser's departure from the court in 1694, when he moved to Hamburg.

In Hamburg Kusser seems almost immediately to have quarrelled with Jakob Kremberg, the manager of the opera, who denied him the opera theatre for a performance of his *Porus*. Kusser, with the aid of Gerhard Schott, performed his opera in the refectory of Hamburg cathedral in competition with Kremberg's theatre, and his considerable success deepened Kremberg's animosity. When Kremberg gave up the opera management some time in 1695 Kusser became Hamburg opera Kapellmeister, but only until 1696. Kusser quickly formed his own travelling opera company, visiting Kiel for performances. He soon began to travel more widely with his company: he is known to have performed in Nuremberg and Augsburg during the

1697–8 season, in 1698 he appeared in Stuttgart and he apparently made several more journeys from there as a guest conductor and opera impresario, including one to Munich. On 17 April 1700 he was appointed Oberkapellmeister at the court at Stuttgart; he visited Italy in 1701 to find musicians for the court. New disagreements led him to abandon his post at Stuttgart in 1704, and towards the end of that year or early in 1705 he arrived in London. He spent the remaining 22 years of his career in England and Ireland. After a few years as a private tutor he went in 1709 to Dublin, where he later became 'Master of the Musick attending his Majesty's State in Ireland' (1717). On 30 October 1727 his birthday ode for George II, a *serenata theatrale*, was fully staged as an opera, apparently the only such dramatic representation of Kusser's music in Ireland (see Walsh for a detailed description of the libretto).

The lack of information about the major part of Kusser's career in London and Dublin, and the apparent loss of virtually all the music he wrote from 1705 onwards, make any judgment of him as a composer tentative. Two collections of arias, from his operas *Erindo* and *Ariadne*, and some orchestral suites, make up virtually all of his surviving oeuvre. It is apparent that his close relationship with Lully and his considerable experience with Italian operas at Wolfenbüttel made him an exponent of the most recent developments in French and Italian music. Furthermore he learnt from Lully the superiority of the French orchestral discipline, especially the brilliant violin playing for which the French court orchestra under Lully's direction was famous: not only did he teach the French style of violin playing at Ansbach, but much of his career grew out of his talent and experience as an outstanding director of opera.

Wolff is one recent writer who has claimed that Kusser brought the French operatic style to Hamburg, but this distinction must be given to Kusser's predecessor at Hamburg, J. G. Conradi. It can certainly be said, however, that Kusser consolidated and reinforced the introduction of the French style, which was already known to and probably much admired by Hamburg audiences. He was a lesser composer than his successors at the Hamburg opera, Keiser and Telemann. However, his surviving music shows sensitivity, and his simple strophic songs are often of great charm, very much in the tradition of the late 17th-century lied. He also excelled in longer arias of more dramatic appeal, with expressive vocal line and striking harmonic strength. He was far less influenced by Italian operatic practice than one might expect: although many of his arias are in da capo form, there are, for example, few lengthy melismatic passages. Much of his music is based on French dance forms, and like Conradi he frequently employed chaconne basses, both in individual arias and in longer, climactic scenes at the end of acts. The arias from *Erindo* show his predilection for solo instrumental passages in his arias, and both collections contain a number of homophonic duets in the French style.

An important contribution that Kusser made to Hamburg musical life was his introduction of operas by non-German composers, including Gianettini, Carlo Pallavicino and especially Steffani. It was this, coupled with his exceptional ability as an orchestra director, more than his own operas, that changed the course of the Hamburg opera by raising the standards of musical performance and by developing a more cosmopolitan repertory.

music lost unless otherwise stated

Cleopatra (prol., 3, ? F. C. Bressand, after G. Bussani: *Giulio Cesare in Egitto*), Brunswick, April 1690

Julia (?Bressand), Brunswick, 1690, songs D-SWl [according to MGG]

La Grotta di Salzdahl (divertimento, 1, F. Parisetti), Brunswick, spr. 1691

Narcissus (prol., 3, G. Fiedler), Brunswick, 4 Oct 1692, pubd lib. HAu

Andromeda (Spl, 3), Brunswick, ?1692

Ariadne (5, Bressand), Brunswick, 1692, arias pubd as Heliconische Musen-Lust (Stuttgart, 1700)

Jason (Spl, 5, Bressand), Brunswick, 1692

Porus (Spl, 5, Bressand, after Racine), Brunswick, 1693; as Der durch Gross-Muth und Tapfferkeit besiegte Porus (lib. rev. C. H. Postel), Hamburg, 1694

Erindo, oder Die unsträfliche Liebe (Schäferspiel, 3, Bressand), Hamburg, 1694; [44] Arien aus der Opera Erindo (Hamburg, 1695); ed. H. Osthoff, EDM, 2nd ser., iii (1938)

Der grossmütige Scipio Africanus (3, Fiedler, after N. Minato), Hamburg, 1694

Pyramus und Thisbe getreue und festverbundene Liebe (C. Schröder), Hamburg, 1694 [possibly not perf.]

Der verliebte Wald (Spl, 1), Stuttgart

The Man of Mode (G. Etherege), London, Little Lincoln's Inn Fields, 9 Feb 1705

Doubtful: Gensericus, als Rom und Karthagens Überwinder (Postel), Hamburg, ?1694 [according to Mattheson; also attrib. J. G. Conradi]

WaltherML

J. Mattheson: *Der musicalische Patriot* (Hamburg, 1728)

F. Chrysander: 'Geschichte der Braunschweig-Wolfenbüttelschen Capelle und Oper vom 16. bis zum 18. Jahrhundert', *Jb für Musikalische Wissenschaft*, i (1863), 147–286

H. Scholz: *Johann Sigismund Kusser: sein Leben und seine Werke* (Leipzig, 1911)

H. C. Wolff: *Die Barockoper in Hamburg* (Wolfenbüttel, 1957)

T. J. Walsh: *Opera in Dublin, 1705–1797: the Social Scene* (Dublin, 1973)

W. Braun: *Vom Remter zum Gänsemarkt* (Saarbrücken, 1987)

GEORGE J. BUELOW

Kutavičius, Bronislovas [Bronius] (*b* Molainiai, Panevėžys region, 13 Sept 1932). Lithuanian composer. He studied at the Vilnius College of Music and the Lithuanian State Conservatory (until 1964) and teaches composition in the M. K. Čiurlionis School of Arts. In his compositions he experiments a great deal with rhythm, sound space and unconventional structures. *Malen'kiy spektakl'* ('A Little Performance', 1971), for example, is scored for a near and a remote violin, a near and a remote piano and a crooning actress.

Kutavičius's first opera, *Strazdas: žalias paukštis* ('The Thrush is a Green Bird'), is a setting of his own libretto, based on a poem by the contemporary Lithuanian poet Sigitas Giada. The plot centres on the priest and rebel Antanas Strazdas, an exceptional national poet of the early 19th century and a man of powerful emotions. The opera is in three parts: the first, 'Intimacy', describes the closeness of man and nature, of the man to the bird; Part 2, 'The Revelation of Space', is about the tragic lot of Lithuania under serfdom and the persecution of independent thinkers; and Part 3, 'Inchoate Songs', concerns the poet's death and immortality. The scoring is for soprano and bass (as Woman and Man), mixed chorus, chamber orchestra, Lithuanian folk instruments and organ; certain elements are supplied using audio equipment and *musique concrète* techniques. Composed in 1981, the work was first performed at the Dramatic Theatre, Kaunas, in December 1984. His second opera, *Kauto senis ant Geležinio kalno* ('Doddering Old Man on the Iron

Mountain'), was produced at the Kaunas Operetta Theatre in 1983.

*

V. Landsbergis: 'Opera-poema na dramaticheskoy stsene', *SovM* (1987), no.2, pp. 29–31   MARINA NEST'YEVA

Kuusik [Kuuzik], **Tiyt** (**Ditrikh Yanovich**) (*b* Pärnu, Estonia, 11 Sept 1911). Estonian baritone. He graduated from the Tallinn Conservatory in 1938, and that year won the Vienna International Singing Competition. In the 1940–41 season and then from 1944 he was a soloist at the Opera in Tallinn. He also sang at the Staatstheater in Kassel, 1942–4. Kuusik is outstanding among Estonian singers. Along with fine musical and dramatic talents, he had a flexible, velvety voice, and considered that learning the cello as a boy contributed to his attainment of a true cantabile. Among his best roles were Boris and Tonio, and he gave captivating, sharp performances of Petruccio in Shebalin's *Ukroshcheniye stroptivoy* ('The Taming of the Shrew') and Vambo in Eugen Kapp's *Tasuleegid* ('Flames of Vengeance'). From 1940 he taught at the Tallinn Conservatory; among his pupils was Georg Ots.

*

E. Kurbatova: 'Tiyt Kuuzik: teatral'nïy portret' [Kuusik: Theatrical Portrait], *Teatr* (1962), no.8
H. Körvits: *Tiyt Kuusik* (Tallinn, 1963)   I. M. YAMPOL'SKY

Kuybïshev [Kuibyshev]. SAMARA.

Kuznetsova, Mariya Nikolayevna (*b* Odessa, 1880; *d* Paris, 26 April 1966). Russian soprano. She first went into ballet at St Petersburg, then trained as a singer with Joakim Tartakov. Her operatic début at the Mariinsky Theatre as Marguerite in *Faust* was a triumph, and she remained with the company until 1913. Among the premières in which she took part was Rimsky-Korsakov's *The Legend of the Invisible City of Kitezh* (1907). From 1908 she developed a reputation abroad, and Paris became her second artistic home. At the Opéra she appeared in Chabrier's *Gwendoline* (1910), Massenet's *Roma* (1912; she had sung in the first performance earlier that year at Monte Carlo), as Aida and Norma, and created roles in Gunsbourg's *Venise* (1913) and Massenet's *Cléopâtre* (1914). She made her Covent Garden début in 1909 and took part in the famous Beecham Russian season at Drury Lane in 1914; there she sang Yaroslavna in the first performances of *Prince Igor* in England. As a dancer she also had a great success with her appearances in 1914, first in Paris then at Drury Lane, as Potiphar's wife, in Richard Strauss's ballet *Josephs-Legende*, a role which she created. In the USA she sang with the Manhattan Company and at Chicago, where in 1916 she created a sensation in the first production in America of *Cléopâtre*. She returned to Russia but fled from the Revolution to Sweden, disguised as a cabin-boy and hidden in a trunk. Her operatic career continued and she also sang operetta for a while (at Paris in 1934 she replaced Supervia in Lehár's *Frasquita*). She was still singing in 1936, when a company of Russian émigrés she had formed in 1929 visited Japan. Her repertory ranged from Salome, Aida and Norma to the lighter lyric roles such as Mimì and Gounod's Juliet. With an expressive voice and excellent technique she was the first Russian singer after Shalyapin to attach as much importance to acting as to singing. She made 36 recordings (1905–28).

E. Stark: *Peterburgskaya opera i evo mastera* [The St Petersburg Opera and its Stars] (Leningrad, 1940)
D. I. Pokhitonov: *Iz proshlovo russkoy operï* [From the Past of the Russian Opera] (Leningrad, 1949)
S. Yu. Levik: *Zapiski opernogo pevtsa* [Notes of an Opera Singer] (Moscow, 1955; enlarged 2/1962)
D. C. Kinrade: 'Marija Nikolaevna Kuznecova', *Record Collector*, xii (1958–60), 156–9 [with partial discography by H. Barnes]
J. B. STEANE, HAROLD BARNES

Kuznets Vakula. Opera by P. I. Tchaikovsky; *see* CHEREVICHKI.

Kvapil, Jaroslav (i) (*b* Chudenice u Klatov, Bohemia, 25 Sept 1868; *d* Prague, 10 Jan 1950). Czech poet, dramatist and librettist. From 1900 he was a director and Dramaturg at the Prague National Theatre, where he introduced plays by Chekhov, Ibsen and Gorky into the repertory. Later he was a director at the Vinohrady Theatre (1921–8). He wrote six plays, but is today chiefly remembered as the librettist of Dvořák's opera Rusalka (*see* RUSALKA (iii)). Before then he adapted Mosenthal's *Deborah* for his friend Foerster, and was to have undertaken a similar adaptation for him of Preissová's *Gazdina roba* ('The Farm Mistress'), work which in the end Foerster did himself (in *Eva*).

Perdita, Nešvera, 1893 [orig. for Kovařovic but not set by him]; *Debora*, Foerster, 1893; *Selská bouře* [The Peasants' Revolt], Lošťák, 1898; *Rusalka*, Dvořák, 1900

*

ČSHS
J. Kvapil: Introduction to the libretto of *Rusalka* (Prague, 1901), 5–8
——: 'O vzniku "Rusalky" ' [On the Genesis of *Rusalka*], *HR*, iv (1911), 428–30
J. Borecký: *Jaroslav Kvapil* (Prague, 1918)
J. Kvapil: *O čem vím* [What I Know About] (Prague, 1932, 2/1946–7) [memoirs]
R. Šťastný: *Čeští spisovatelé deseti století* [Czech Writers of Ten Centuries] (Prague, 1974)
V. Procházka, ed.: *Národní divadlo a jeho předchůdci: slovník umělců divadel Vlastenského, Stavovského, Prozatímního a Národního* [The National Theatre and its Predecessors: a Dictionary of Artists of the Patriotic, Estates, Provisional and National Theatres] (Prague, 1988) [incl. list of productions and bibliography]
J. Tyrrell: *Czech Opera* (Cambridge, 1988), 150–51
JOHN TYRRELL

Kvapil, Jaroslav (ii) (*b* Fryšták, Zlin district, 21 April 1892; *d* Brno, 18 Feb 1959). Czech composer and conductor. He studied with Janáček at the Brno Organ School, graduating in 1909, and later studied with Reger at the Leipzig Conservatory (1911–13). He taught in Brno at the organ school and the conservatory, and was professor of composition at the academy. Kvapil was an excellent accompanist, and as choirmaster and conductor of the Brno Beseda (1919–47) he gave the Czech première of Honegger's biblical opera *Judith* (1933). He received the Award of Merit in 1955. In his music Kvapil worked best in traditional forms, particularly variation form, and showed a partiality for contrapuntal textures. His romantic style included few immediate references to folk music, but he achieved a simple and direct expression. His opera *Pohádka máje* ('A May Fairy-tale'; 3, F. Kožík and B. Polách, after V. Mrštík) was composed in 1943 and first performed at the National Theatre in Prague on 12 June 1950. It is a lyrical opera in the tradition of Dvořák, eminently singable, with outdoor settings and effective choral scenes.
JAN TROJAN

Kyreyko, Vitaly (*b* Shyroke, Dnipropetrovs'k district, 23 Dec 1926). Ukrainian composer. He studied under Revuts'ky at the Kiev Conservatory, graduating in 1949. He has written in a variety of genres, among which opera and ballet have been particularly important to him. His operas are closely tied to Ukrainian folklore and the classics of literature and drama. His lyrical bent is specially apparent in "*U nedilyu rano zillya kopala ...*" ('On Sunday Morning she gathered Herbs', 1966), where the national spirit, melodic content and reliance on clear and simple characterization established his style. His is a conservative talent, very traditional and well attuned to the basic tenets of socialist realism.

Lisova pisnya [Forest Song] (fairy op, 3, Kyreyko, after L. Ukraïnka), L'viv, Franko Academic Theatre of Opera and Ballet, 27 May 1958
"U nedilyu rano zillya kopala ..." ['On Sunday Morning she gathered Herbs'] (4, M. Zotsenko, after O. Kobylyans'ka), L'viv, Franko Academic Theatre of Opera and Ballet, 1966
Marko v pekli [Marko in Hell], 1966 (3, Kyreyko, after I. Kocherha), unperf.

*

K. Mayburova: *Vitaly Kyreyko* (Kiev, 1979)   VIRKO BALEY

Kyurkchiiski, Krasimir (*b* Troyan, 22 July 1936). Bulgarian composer. He studied composition with Vladigerov at the Bulgarian State Conservatory, graduating in 1962, and with Shostakovich at the Moscow State Conservatory. Later he worked as conductor of the Filip Kutev State Folksong and Dance Ensemble and the Folksong Ensemble of the Bulgarian Committee for Radio and Television, then taught at the conservatory before becoming a freelance composer. Kyurkchiiski's works cover a broad range of genres, including two ballets. His spontaneous and emotional nature, as well as the expressive and romantic tension in his works, show a close identification with Vladigerov's style and his musical language owes much to the folk music of the Shopski area around Sofia. He has written two operas, which are both in a traditional and accessible style. *Yula*, a two-act psychological opera to a libretto by Petar Filchev, was first performed at Stara Zagora in 1969. *Nasledstvo* ('Heritage'; also known as *A votre santé*), to a libretto by Molen Paunov, received its première in Sofia on 30 November 1986. The plot centres on the family of Stefan Boasier, a writer, and the confusion which arises from his feigned death.

*

M. Manolova: 'Nasledstvo', *Plamuk*, viii (1986), 80
                    MAGDALENA MANOLOVA

L

La Barre, Michel de (*b* Paris, *c*1675; *d* Paris, 15 March 1745). French composer. An excellent performer on the 'German' or transverse flute, he had a brilliant career as an instrumentalist in Paris and at court, where from 1703 to 1730 he played in the Musique de l'Ecurie et de la Chambre. It is not known when he joined the orchestra of the Paris Opéra, but he was there in 1700 and by 1704 his annual salary was 600 livres; in 1713 he had the honour of featuring among the best soloists of the *petit choeur*. From 1694 onwards he composed instrumental and vocal pieces, trios and *airs sérieux et à boire*. In collaboration with the librettist Antoine Houdar de Lamotte, he wrote two scores for performance at the Opéra. The first was *Le triomphe des arts* (*F-Po*), an *opéra-ballet* for which he was paid 3000 livres; according to remarks in the *Lettre d'un lanterniste de Thoulouze à l'autheur du ballet des arts*, it was a failure at its first performance (16 May 1700), being 'attacked from beginning to end'. The second work, the *ballet La Vénitienne* (26 May 1705; *F-Pn*), seems to have been received more warmly, since one of its acts was subsequently revived in 1711 at the Opéra, on which occasion Marie Antier made her début. La Barre's dramatic music shows the influence of Campra.

See also VÉNITIENNE, LA.

H. Guiscardi [H. Guichard]: *Lettre d'un lanterniste de Thoulouze à l'autheur du ballet des arts, représenté sur le theatre de l'Opéra* (n.p., n.d.)
F. Parfaict and C. Parfaict: *Histoire de l'Académie royale de musique depuis son établissement jusqu'à présent* (MS, 1741, *F-Pn*)
J.-G. Prod'homme, ed.: 'Michel de La Barre', *Ecrits de musiciens (XVe–XVIIIe siècles)* (Paris, 1912), 241–5
M. Benoit: *Musiques de cour: chapelle, chambre, écurie, 1661–1733* (Paris, 1971)
J. de La Gorce: 'L'Académie royale de musique en 1704, d'après des documents inédits conservés dans les archives notariales', *RdM*, lxv (1979), 160–91
JÉRÔME DE LA GORCE

Labarre [Berry], Théodore(-François-Joseph) (*b* Paris, 24 March 1805; *d* Paris, 9 March 1870). French composer, foster-brother of Napoleon III. He studied with Dourlens, Fétis and Boieldieu. In 1823 he won second prize in the Prix de Rome and subsequently embarked on concert tours of England, Italy and Switzerland. On his return to France in 1831 he began writing operas, ballets and incidental music. There are two *opéra comiques*, *L'aspirant de marine* (1, Rochefort and Decomberousse), first performed at the Théâtre des Nouveautés (OC) on 2 June 1834, and *Le ménétrier, ou Les deux duchesses* (3, A. E. Scribe), given at the Théâtre Favart (OC) on 9 August 1845; and an *opéra bouffe*, *Pantagruel* (2, H. Trianon), performed at the Opéra on 24 December 1855. Their musical style derives from the works of Boieldieu and Adam, and anticipates those of Offenbach. Labarre also wrote harp music (and included harp parts in some of his scores), as well as romances, some of which became extremely popular. After marrying the singer Mlle Lambert in 1837, he divided his time between France and England. A conductor at the Opéra-Comique, 1847–9, he later held posts in the imperial chapel and at the Conservatoire, and finally was music critic for *Paris illustré*.

Obituary, *Revue et gazette musicale* (13 March 1870)
FRÉDÉRIC ROBERT

Labbette, Dora [Perli, Lisa] (*b* Purley, 4 March 1898; *d* Selsey, 3 Sept 1984). English soprano. She studied at the GSM and with Liza Lehmann on a Melba Scholarship. Established as a concert singer she began her operatic career, under the name of Lisa Perli, as Mimì at Covent Garden (1935). Her voice was true, pure and youthful, and she was an outstanding actress, ideal for Gounod's heroines, Mélisande, Delius's Vreli (*A Village Romeo and Juliet*) and Verdi's Desdemona. The war cut short her London career. She recorded Act 4 of *La bohème* (with Heddle Nash as Rodolfo) under Beecham.

ALAN JEFFERSON

Labia, Maria (*b* Verona, 14 Feb 1880; *d* Malcesine, Lake Garda, 10 Feb 1953). Italian soprano. She studied with her mother, Cecilia Labia, making her début in 1905 as Mimì in Stockholm. In 1907 she appeared at the Komische Oper, Berlin, as Tosca, returning subsequently as Carmen, Marta (*Tiefland*) and Salome, among other roles. She sang at the Manhattan Opera House, New York (1908–9), La Scala (1912) and the Paris Opéra (1913). In 1916 she was imprisoned for a year in Ancona as a suspected German agent. Resuming her career after the war, she sang Giorgetta in the first European performance of *Il tabarro* (1919, Rome), repeating the role in that year in Buenos Aires. In the first Scala production of *I quattro rusteghi* (1922) she played Felice, a role that became her favourite and in which she continued to appear until 1936. Her performances in *verismo* operas were said to be impulsive and, for their day, 'shamelessly sensual'. She used her warm, not especially large voice with particular reliance on the chest register.

Her elder sister Fausta (*b* Verona, 3 April 1870; *d* Rome, 6 Oct 1935) had a relatively short career (1892–1912), which included performances as Sieglinde under Toscanini at La Scala. She retired shortly after her marriage to the tenor Emilio Perea.

R. Celletti: 'Maria Labia', *Record News*, iii (Toronto, 1958–9), 32–4 [with discography]   HAROLD ROSENTHAL/R

Labinsky, Andrey (*b* Kharkiv, 14/26 July 1871; *d* Moscow, 8 Aug 1941). Russian tenor. He studied with Stanislaus Gabel at the St Petersburg Academy and sang in the chorus of the Mariinsky Opera. There he made his début as a soloist in 1897, remaining till 1911 and singing in a wide repertory which included Lohengrin and Don José as well as the Russian operatic roles. In 1907 he sang in the première at St Petersburg of Rimsky-Korsakov's *The Invisible City of Kitezh*. From 1912 to 1924 he was a leading tenor at the Bol'shoy in Moscow where he appeared in such diverse roles as Radames and Almaviva. In 1920 he was appointed professor at the Moscow Conservatory and at the time of his death was principal vocal coach at the Bol'shoy. His records include some brilliant performances and also show him to have been a creative, sensitive interpreter.   J. B. STEANE

Lablache, Luigi (*b* Naples, 6 Dec 1794; *d* Naples, 23 Jan 1858). Italian bass. The son of an expatriate French merchant and an Irishwoman, he became the most famous bass of his generation. He entered the conservatory when he was 12 and began his operatic career as a *buffo* at the Teatro S Carlino in 1812, making his début in Fioravanti's *La molinara*. After further study and an engagement as *buffo* at Messina, in 1813 he became first *basso cantante* at Palermo. His reputation grew, and in 1817 he made a triumphant début at La Scala as Dandini (*La Cenerentola*). He remained there for six seasons, also appearing at Rome, Turin, Venice and, in 1824, Vienna, where he was a leading member of Barbaia's company. Ferdinand I of Naples appointed Lablache to his royal chapel and had him engaged for the S Carlo, where for several years he appeared in new operas by Bellini and Donizetti, as well as distinguishing himself in such roles as Assur in Rossini's *Semiramide*.

On 30 March 1830, Lablache made a brilliant London début as Geronimo (*Il matrimonio segreto*) at the King's Theatre, where he appeared nearly every season until 1852 (except for 1833–4). Mount Edgcumbe described him as 'a bass of uncommon force and power. His voice was not only of deeper compass than almost any ever heard, but when he chose, absolutely *stentorian*, and he was also gigantic in his person; yet when he moderated its extraordinary strength, he sang pleasingly and well'. While his reputation rested chiefly on his comic roles, in which he excelled, he was equally impressive as Henry VIII (*Anna Bolena*) and Oroveso (*Norma*). In 1839 Wagner wrote an additional aria for this latter role for him, but Lablache declined to sing it. His Paris début was in 1830 at the Théâtre Italien, where he appeared regularly until 1851 and created his most important roles, including Giorgio in *I puritani*, and the title role in *Marino Faliero* (1835). *I puritani* enjoyed such success that for the next seven years this opera opened and closed each season

with its original cast of Giulia Grisi, Rubini, Tamburini and Lablache. He was the first Don Pasquale in Donizetti's opera (Théâtre Italien, 1843), and his interpretation, in which he displayed 'real comic genius' (Chorley), became definitive.

After the opening in 1847 of the Royal Italian Opera, Covent Garden, Lablache was one of the few artists to remain faithful to Her Majesty's (where he created Massimiliano in *I masnadieri* in 1847). With his readiness to take small roles without condescension he acquired an unusually large and varied repertory for a singer of his standing. Lumley described him as 'the greatest dramatic singer of his time'. On the closure of Her Majesty's in 1852 Lablache visited St Petersburg, and in 1854, after his return, he became a leading member of Gye's company at Covent Garden. In 1855, over 60, he was still singing some of his most famous roles, including Leporello, Don Pasquale, Dr Bartolo (*Il barbiere*) and Balthazar (*La favorite*). He retired from the stage in 1856.

Lablache wrote a *Méthode de chant*, published in Paris. His eldest son, Federico Lablache, was an operatic bass, and his daughter-in-law, Demeric Lablache, was a mezzo-soprano with Mapleson's company. One of his daughters, Cecchina, married the pianist Thalberg.

For illustration *see* DON PASQUALE; ELISIR D'AMORE, L'; MASNADIERI, I; and NORMA.

Castil-Blaze: *Biographie de Lablache* (Paris, n.d.)
J. d'Ortigue: Obituary, *Le journal des débats* (24 Feb 1858)
G. Widen: *Luigi Lablache* (Göteborg, 1897)   PHILIP ROBINSON

Labò, Flaviano (Mario) (*b* Borgonovo, nr Piacenza, 1 Feb 1927; *d* Milan, 13 Feb 1991). Italian tenor. While in the army, he came to the notice of the conductor Antonino Votto, and subsequently studied with Ettore Campogalliani in Parma, Renato Pastorino in Milan and Valentino Metti in Piacenza. In 1954 he made his début at the Teatro Municipale, Piacenza, as Cavaradossi. He went on to sing in many of the principal Italian opera houses, as well as in several German and other European cities and in Buenos Aires. He made his first appearance at the Metropolitan Opera in 1957 as Don Alvaro in *La forza del destino* and sang there for eight seasons in 13 roles. He continued to make guest appearances at many houses into the 1980s. His final appearance was as Macduff in Verona in 1982. Labò's robust, typically italianate tenor voice and outgoing manner were well suited to Verdi and *verismo* roles, and his repertory included Calaf, Don Carlos, Enzo Grimaldi (*La Gioconda*), Manrico, Radames and Turiddu.   CORI ELLISON

La Borde [Laborde], Jean-Benjamin(-François) de (*b* Paris, 5 Sept 1734; *d* Paris, 22 July 1794). French composer and writer on music. Born into an aristocratic family, he studied the violin with Dauvergne and composition with Rameau and made a successful début as a stage composer at the age of 14. He entered Louis XV's service in 1762 and during the next 12 years acquired the title of *premier valet du chambre* and worked primarily as a composer. The majority of his stage works are *opéras comiques*, but he also wrote pastoral operas, such as *Annette et Lubin*, *La meunière de Gentilly* and *La cinquantaine*. Their short *airs*, hardly allowing the singers time to express any sentiment, are mostly composed in regular periods, with a string and basso continuo accompaniment, resembling the *ari-*

ettes or chansons that La Borde published separately in collections with great success. The *pastorales* convey less a sense of drama than an agreeable lyrical atmosphere.

La Borde's best work is possibly the concisely written, lively *Gilles, garçon peintre, z'amoureux-t-et-rival*, a parody of Duni's *Le peintre amoureux de son modèle*; it is characterized by irregular rhythms, continuous dynamic changes, ensembles and unaccompanied *airs*. He also composed *tragédies lyriques* that bear witness to his close relationship with Rameau, and he revised operas by Lully and Collasse, documenting his interest in updating the 'classics' of French opera. According to Lajarte, *Ismène* and *Amadis* enjoyed 23 performances and *La cinquantaine* 26 (although the *Mercure de France* reports that the audience whistled at its première). Some of his operas were performed only privately. Grimm was openly hostile towards him: after the première of *Les amours de Gonesse* he called him a 'barbouilleur de notes infatigable' (see Tourneux, vi, 302); he frequently found La Borde's music lacking in 'goût' and 'génie' (viii, 200; ix, 237; xi, 162), and labelled him an 'amateur' (vii, 457).

When La Borde's relationship with the famous dancer Marie-Madeleine Guimard came to an end in 1773, he travelled through France, Italy and Switzerland; on his return Louis XV promoted him to Governor of the Louvre. In 1780 La Borde published his four-volume *Essai sur la musique ancienne et moderne*, an extremely valuable source of information on 18th-century music and that of earlier periods. During the Revolution he escaped from Paris; meanwhile his palace, with its library of 25 000 volumes and extensive collection of scores, was burnt down. He was eventually arrested in Rouen, brought back to Paris and guillotined five days before Robespierre's downfall.

unless otherwise stated, opéras comiques performed and printed in Paris; works without performance details were performed privately; MSS in F-Pc and Po

PCI – *Comédie-Italienne (Hôtel de Bourgogne)*
PO – *Opéra*

La chercheuse d'oiseaux (parodie, Derozée), Mons, 1748 (Mons, 1748)
Le rossignol, ou Le mariage secret (1, C. Collé), Château de Berny, 18 Nov 1751, Théâtre de Société, 1751 (The Hague, 1777)
Gilles, garçon peintre, z'amoureux-t-et-rival (parade, 1, A. H. H. Poinsinet, after E. Duni: Le peintre amoureux de son modèle), 2 March 1758 (1758)
Les épreuves de l'amour (1, L. Anseaume), Foire St Germain, 1759
Les trois déesses rivales, 1760, unperf.
Les bons amis [Les bons compères] (1, M.-J. Sedaine), Opéra-Comique (Foire), 5 March 1761 (1761); rev. as L'anneau perdu et retrouvé, PCI, 8 Aug 1764 (?1764)
Annette et Lubin (pastorale, 1, J. F. Marmontel), Théâtre du Maréchal de Richelieu, 30 March 1762 (1762)
Ismène et Isménias, ou La fête de Jupiter (tragédie lyrique, 3, P. Laujon), Choisy, 13 June 1763 (?1770)
Le dormeur éveillé (2, Ménilglaise and La Borde), Fontainebleau, 27 Oct 1764 (1764)
Les amours de Gonesse, ou Le boulanger [Le mitron et la mitronne] (opéra bouffon, 1, C.-S. Favart and S.-R.-N. Chamfort), PCI, 18 May 1765 (?1765)
Fanny, 1765 (Chamfort), unperf.
Thétis et Pélée (tragédie lyrique, 3, B. B. de Fontenelle), Fontainebleau, 10 Oct 1765 (1765) [rev. of Collasse]
Zénis et Almasie (ballet-héroïque, 1, Chamfort and Duc de La Vallière), Fontainebleau, 2 Nov 1765 (1765), collab. B. de Bury
Le coup de fusil, 1766
La mandragore, 1766
Le revenant (Desfontaines [F. G. Fouques]), 1766
Pandore (tragédie lyrique, 5, Voltaire and M.-P.-G. de Chabanon), Menus-Plaisirs, 14 Feb 1767 (1767)

Amphion (ballet-pastorale-héroïque, 1, Thomas), PO, 13 Oct 1767 (1767)
Colette et Mathurin (Desfontaines), 1767
La meunière de Gentilly (pastorale, L.-A. Lemonnier), PCI, 13 Oct 1768 (1768)
Candide [Le prieur], 1768
Le chat perdu et retrouvé (1, Carmontelle), PCI, 1769 (1769)
Alix et Alexis (2, Poinsinet), Choisy, 6 July 1769 (1769)
Jeannot et Colin (Desfontaines), 1770
La cinquantaine (pastorale, 3, Desfontaines), PO, 13 Aug 1771 (?1771)
Amadis de Gaule (tragédie lyrique, 5, P. Quinault), PO, 26 Nov 1771, collab. P.-M. Berton [rev. of Lully]
Le billet de mariage (Desfontaines), PCI, 31 Oct 1772
Adèle de Ponthieu (tragédie lyrique, 3, Raziens de Saint-Marc), PO, 1 Dec 1772 (1772), collab. Berton
Le projet (N. E. Framéry), 1772
L'amour quêteur (Beaunoir [Robineau]), Trianon, 1779
La chercheuse d'esprit (Favart)

*

ES (F. Lesure)
M. Tourneux, ed.: *Correspondance littéraire, philosophique et critique par Grimm, Diderot, Raynal, Meister, etc.* (Paris, 1877–82)
T. de Lajarte: *Bibliothèque musicale du Théâtre de l'Opéra* (Paris, 1878)
J. de Visme: *Un favori des dieux* (Paris, 1935)
E. Closson: 'Les notes marginales de Grétry dans l' "essay sur la musique" de Laborde', *RBM*, ii (1948), 106–24
J. Warmoes: *L'exemplaire de l''Essai sur la musique ancienne et moderne' de J.-B. de Laborde annoté par Grétry* (diss., U. of Louvain, 1956)
MICHAEL FEND

Labradoras de Murcia, Las ('The Farm-Girls of Murcia'). Zarzuela in two acts by ANTONIO RODRÍGUEZ DE HITA to a libretto by Ramón de la Cruz; Madrid, Teatro del Príncipe, 16 September 1769.

It is a seminal work in the history of the Spanish zarzuela for the successful way composer and librettist linked regionalistic folkloric and linguistic traditions with italianate operatic conventions. The plot centres on a silkworm farm in Murcia run by the matronly Doña Nicolasa (contralto), where Don Vicente (baritone) works as foreman. He is a distinguished Valencian who has been forced to take refuge from the law because he has been falsely accused of a murder he knows the hero, Narciso (tenor), in fact carried out. Operatic demands for conventional emotional conflicts are met by the love Don Vicente's daughter Teresa (soprano) feels for Narciso, as well as by the suit of the foppish rival lover, Leandro (tenor), Nicolasa's son. The resolution is achieved by one of Ramón de la Cruz's favourite substitutes for the traditional *deus ex machina*: an official letter exonerating Narciso. The most celebrated scene is that which ends Act 1: all the cast sing and dance a *jota* in order to drown out a thunderstorm, the noise of which, according to local folklore, would make the silkworms die of fright.
JACK SAGE

La Bruère, Charles-Antoine Le Clerc de (*b* Crespy-en-Valois, 1714; *d* Rome, 18 Sept 1754). French librettist. An amateur of noble birth, he began his literary career at the age of 20 with the comedy *Les mécontents* (1734) and is said later to have written an *Histoire de Charlemagne*. From 1744 to 1750 he held the privilege (jointly with Louis Fuzelier) of the *Mercure de France*, to which he contributed. He was eventually appointed first secretary to the Duke of Nivernois; when the duke became French Ambassador to the Papal Court in 1749 La Bruère followed him to Rome, where he remained until his death.

It was generally agreed that La Bruère had a flair for elegant and memorable verse. Voltaire praised the libretto of *Les voyages de l'Amour* as 'plein de grâces & d'esprit' (letter to Berger, 5 April 1736) and other contemporaries, including D'Alembert, quoted passages from *Dardanus* with genuine admiration. La Bruère was less secure in his treatment of the plot. The original libretto of *Dardanus* has been described, justly, as 'without contradiction the most inept' in the history of the genre (Girdlestone 1972). Even by contemporary French standards it is overcharged with supernatural elements, which include a sorcerer who can stop the sun in its tracks, a magic wand that allows the hero to assume another form, a dream sequence, and two combats with monsters (one in a dream, the other in reality). For the first revival, in 1744, La Bruère made extensive changes (with help, it is said, from the Abbé Pellegrin), so that Acts 3, 4 and 5 had an entirely new plot. In La Bruère's lifetime this version excited remarkably little comment; but when the work was revived in 1760 with only minor revisions, it had come to be regarded as one of French opera's chief glories.

Of La Bruère's other librettos, only the one-act *Bacchus et Erigone* had any lasting success. It was originally written for Mme de Pompadour's amateur theatricals in her Théâtre des Petits Appartements (the marquise herself played Erigone), and later incorporated into the *opéra-ballet Les fêtes de Paphos* (1758).

Les voyages de l'Amour (opéra-ballet), Boismortier, 1736; *Dardanus* (tragédie), Rameau, 1739 (Sacchini, 1784); *Bacchus et Erigone* (acte de ballet), Mondonville, 1747; *Le Prince de Noisy* (ballet-héroïque), Francoeur and Rebel, 1749; *Linus* (tragédie), Rameau, before 1752 (Dauvergne, Berton and Trial, comp. 1775)

A. de Léris: *Dictionnaire portatif des théâtres* (Paris, 1754, 2/1763)
L.-F. Beffara: *Dictionnaire de l'Académie royale de musique* (MS, 1783–4, *F-Po* Rés 602)
C. Malherbe: 'Commentaire bibliographique', *Jean-Philippe Rameau: Oeuvres complètes*, x (Paris, 1905), xvii–cxxxiv
P.-M. Masson: *L'opéra de Rameau* (Paris, 1930)
C. Girdlestone: *Jean-Philippe Rameau: his Life and Work* (London, 1957, 2/1969)
W. H. Kaehler: *The Operatic Repertoire of Madame de Pompadour's Théâtre des petits cabinets (1747–1753)* (diss., U. of Michigan, 1971)
C. Girdlestone: *La tragédie en musique (1673–1750) considérée comme genre littéraire* (Geneva, 1972)   GRAHAM SADLER

Labyrinth, Das [*Das Labyrinth, oder Der Kampf mit den Elementen* ('The Labyrinth, or The Battle with the Elements')]. *Heroisch-komische Oper* in two acts by PETER WINTER to a libretto by EMANUEL SCHIKANEDER; Vienna, Freihaus-Theater auf der Wieden, 12 June 1798.

Among the numerous sequels to *Die Zauberflöte* that appeared in the 1790s, this work served as the official 'second part' to Mozart's opera, Schikaneder himself providing the libretto and producing the opera. It earned only a fraction of the widespread acclaim of Mozart's work. As the story opens on the marriage ceremony of Tamino (tenor) and Pamina (soprano), the Queen of Night (soprano) announces her plans to send an army to lay waste the temple of Sarastro (bass). Before the battle ensues, Sarastro directs Tamino and Pamina into opposite ends of a labyrinth to fulfil their final trial of initiation. The Queen and her followers abduct Pamina in the maze. Tamino and Pamina are reunited only after several battles between the forces of good and evil. In the prominent subplot, Monostatos (tenor) dresses like a bird to woo Papagena (soprano). Papageno (bass), with the help of his large family and his glockenspiel, succeeds in capturing 'the black bird'

and winning back his new wife. Winter draws heavily on the characteristic styles of *Die Zauberflöte*, though he depends less on polyphonic passages and is often less succinct.

LINDA TYLER

Lac des fées, Le ('The Fairy Lake'). *Opéra* in five acts by DANIEL-FRANÇOIS-ESPRIT AUBER to a libretto by EUGÈNE SCRIBE and MÉLESVILLE [A.-H.-J. Duveyrier]; Paris, Opéra, 1 April 1839.

The subject is drawn from a German ballad in which a group of students come upon an enchanted lake in the Harz Mountains, where they see swans transformed into fairies. Albert (tenor) immediately falls in love with the fairy Zéïla (soprano). While she and her sisters bathe, he takes her veil as a souvenir, unwittingly depriving her of her immortality. Unable to rejoin her companions, she finds work in an inn run by Marguerite (mezzo-soprano), who dismisses Zéïla when she notices Albert's attraction to her. A wealthy libertine, Rodolphe (bass-baritone), courts Marguerite, then Zéïla, and he has Albert imprisoned, thus removing his rival. Touched by Albert's misfortune and Zéïla's plight, Marguerite retrieves the veil for Albert, who gives it back to Zéïla rather than see her marry Rodolphe. Her restored immortality saves her from an unhappy marriage.

The opera is more important for its *mise en scène* than for its music. The descent of the fairy-sisters to the lake is a vehicle for elaborate stage effects and ballet sequences. That scene and a madness–dream sequence in Act 4 reflect the strong influence that the convent scene from Meyerbeer's *Robert le diable* continued to wield at the Opéra. Though the opera had only 30 performances, its overture, one of Auber's best, remained popular in France throughout the 19th century.

LAURIE C. SHULMAN

Lachmann, Hedwig (*b* Stolp, Pomerania [now Słupsk, Poland], 21 Aug 1865; *d* Krumbach, Swabia, 21 Feb 1918). German translator and poet. She worked initially as a governess, living in England, Dresden, and then in Berlin (1889), where her writings first attracted attention through the circle of the poet Richard Dehmel. In 1891 she began to contribute to periodicals, and her translations of Rossetti, Swinburne, Verlaine and Wilde put her among the first to bring English and French symbolist poetry to Germany. Her 1903 translation of Wilde's *Salomé* became the libretto for Richard Strauss's opera of 1905. After her marriage to Gustav Landauer in 1903 she and her husband collaborated on several translations, including works of Wilde, Balzac, Poe and Conrad. She was considered 'a poet of tender and constant individuality, a translator of the first order' (J. Bab: *Richard Dehmel*, 1926).

Lachner, Franz Paul (*b* Rain am Lech, Upper Bavaria, 2 April 1803; *d* Munich, 20 Jan 1890). German composer. After three years as organist of the Evangelical Church in Vienna he became deputy Kapellmeister at the Kärntnertortheater in 1826 and principal Kapellmeister (with Konradin Kreutzer) in 1829. He was made director of the Mannheim Court Opera in 1834 and from 1836 was conductor of the Munich Opera. There he advocated performances of classic Viennese and contemporary opera and conducted (albeit reluctantly) the Munich premières of Wagner's *Tannhäuser* (1855) and *Lohengrin* (1858). Following disagreements with Wagner he retired in 1868.

Lachner's two most popular operas, *Catarina Cornaro* and *Benvenuto Cellini*, were composed in the style of grand opera, rather in the manner of Spohr and Meyerbeer; this contributed to the continuing success of *Catarina Cornaro* in Germany for a span of 40 years. The vocal writing, particularly for the lead soprano, was skilful, but dramatic tension and characterization were lacking.

Contemporary opinion undoubtedly over-estimated Lachner as a composer, misled by his abilities as a conductor and, above all, as the trainer and developer of an orchestra, without whose preparation Wagner's works could not have been fully realized in Munich. Although he took Beethoven and Schubert as models, he lacked dramatic ability, conciseness and genuine sensitivity as opposed to Biedermeier sentimentalism.

See also CATARINA CORNARO, KÖNIGIN VON CYPERN.

Die Bürgschaft (3, K. von Biedenfeld, after F. von Schiller), Budapest, Várósi Színház, 30 Oct 1828
Alidia (3, O. Prechtler, after E. Bulwer-Lytton: *The Last Days of Pompeii*), Munich, Hofoper, 12 April 1839
Catarina Cornaro, Königin von Cypern (tragische Oper, 4, J.-H. Vernoy de Saint-Georges), Munich, Hofoper, 3 Dec 1841, vs (Mainz, 1842)
Benvenuto Cellini (4, A. Barbier and A. F. L. de Wailly), Munich, Hofoper, 7 Oct 1849

*

W. Neumann: *Franz, Vinzenz, Ignaz Lachner* (Cassel, 1856)
F. Stetter: 'Verzeichnis der Werke von Franz Lachner', *Zeitgenössische Tondichter*, ed. M. Chop (Leipzig, 1890), 78–88
M. Zenger: 'Franz Lachner', *Die Musik*, ii/13 (1902–3), 3–12
A. Würz: *Franz Lachner als dramatischer Komponist* (Munich, 1927)
HORST LEUCHTMANN

Lachner, Ignaz (*b* Rain am Lech, Upper Bavaria, 11 Sept 1807; *d* Hanover, 24 Feb 1895). German composer. He had his earliest musical training in Augsburg and Munich, and then went to Vienna to study with his brother Franz, whom he succeeded as organist of the Lutheran church there. In 1828 he became assistant Kapellmeister of the Vienna Hofoper, moving to Stuttgart three years later as deputy Hofkapellmeister. He went to Munich in 1836, becoming assistant Kapellmeister of the Hofoper in 1842. He then became principal Kapellmeister of the Hamburg theatre in 1853, but accepted a post as court Kapellmeister in Stockholm five years later. From 1861 until his retirement in 1875 he was chief conductor in Frankfurt. His most significant compositions are his chamber music and dramatic works, of which the *Alpenszenen*, close in form to Singspiels, enjoyed considerable success in their day.

Die verkaufte Bärenhaut (Spl, 1), Vienna, Kärntnertor, 10 Sept 1827
Zenobia vor der Römerschlacht (Spl, 1), Vienna, Kärntnertor, 3 March 1830
Der Geisterturm (3, K. Hanisch), Stuttgart, Hof, 14 April 1837
Die Regenbrüder (E. Mörike and H. Kurz), Stuttgart, Hof, 20 May 1839
Loreley (E. W. Molitor and Wendling), Munich, Hof, 6 Sept 1846, vs (Heidelberg, c1846)
Alpenszenen, all first perf. Munich, Hof, c1850: 'S letzti Fensterln (J. G. Seidel and W. von Kobell), Drei Jahrln nach'm letzten Fensterln (Seidel), Die beiden Freier, Der Freiherr als Wildschütz, Der Ju-Schroa

*

StiegerO
H. Müller: *Ignaz Lachner: Versuch einer Würdigung, mit Werkverzeichnis* (Celle, 1974)
HORST LEUCHTMANN

Lachnith [Lachnitt, Lachnicht], **Ludwig Wenzel** [Louis-Wenceslas] (*b* Prague, 7 July 1746; *d* Paris, 3 Oct 1820). Bohemian composer. He visited Paris in 1773 to per-form at the Concert Spirituel and settled there about 1780 after leaving the service of the Duke of Zweibrücken. After studying composition with F.-A. D. Philidor he wrote a number of orchestral and chamber works and several operas. Lachnith was exiled during the Revolution; on his return in 1801 he was appointed *instructeur* at the Opéra, holding this post for ten months and again from 1806 to 1816.

Lachnith wrote few original stage works, most of which were unsuccessful, although some received encouraging reviews in the contemporary press. His first, *L'heureuse réconciliation*, apparently offered evidence of a sound technique but was marred by a weak libretto and was therefore performed only twice. Several elaborate pasticcio arrangements proved more popular: *Les mystères d'Isis*, his first experiment with the style, was based on *Die Zauberflöte*. It acquired the nickname 'Les misères d'ici' and was criticized by Berlioz as a 'wretched French hotchpotch', but it was an enormous success, receiving regular performance in Paris for more than 25 years. Other pasticcios were based on religious subjects and presented at the Opéra during Holy Week as oratorios *en action* in place of orchestral concerts.

all first performed in Paris
L'heureuse réconciliation (oc, 1, A. M. D. Devismes, after J. F. Marmontel), Comédie-Italienne (Favart), 25 June 1785
Eugénie et Linval, ou Le mauvais fils (oc, 2, Devismes), Montansier, 1798
Les fêtes lacédémoniennes, 1808 (opéra, 3, J.-B. Lourdet de Santerre), unperf.
Pasticcios: Les mystères d'Isis (opéra, 4, E. Morel de Chédeville, after E. Schikaneder: *Die Zauberflöte*), Opéra, 20 Aug 1801, F-Po; (1801); Saul (oratorio mis en action, 3 pts, Morel de Chédeville, E. Deschamps and J. B. D. Desprès), Opéra, 6 April 1803, collab. C. Kalkbrenner, Pc*, Po; La prise de Jéricho (oratorio, 3 pts, Morel de Chédeville, Deschamps and Desprès), Opéra, 11 April 1805, collab. Kalkbrenner, Pc*; Le laboureur chinois (opéra, 1, Morel de Chédeville, Deschamps and Desprès), Opéra, 5 Feb 1813, collab. M. Berton, Po

Additions to works by others: 7 airs in Sacchini: Oedipe à Colonne, 1786, acc. hpd (n.d.); ov., airs in Salieri: Tarare, 1787, arr. hpd, vn (n.d.); ov., airs, duos in Sacchini and Rey: Arvire et Evelina, 1788, acc. hpd (c1788); ov., airs, duos in Deux prétendus, acc. hpd (n.d.)

Doubtful: L'antiquaire, 1789 [? by Anfossi]

*

EitnerQ; FétisB
L. Petit de Bachaumont: *Mémoires secrets* (London, 1780–89)
A. J. B. d'Origny: *Annales du théâtre italien depuis son origine jusqu'à ce jour* (Paris, 1788)
A. Choron and F. Fayolle: *Dictionnaire historique des musiciens* (Paris, 1810–11)
H. Berlioz: *Mémoires de Hector Berlioz* (Paris, 1870; Eng. trans. 1969, 2/1970)
M. Tourneux, ed.: *Correspondance littéraire, philosophique et critique par Grimm, Diderot, Raynal, Meister, etc.* (Paris, 1877–82)
J. Mongrédien: 'Les *Mystères d'Isis* (1801) and Reflections on Mozart from the Parisian Press at the Beginning of the Nineteenth Century', *Music in the Classic Period: Essays in Honor of Barry S. Brook* (New York, 1985), 195–211
ETHYL L. WILL/ELISABETH COOK

Lacombe [Trouillon-Lacombe], **Louis** (*b* Bourges, 18 Nov 1818; *d* St Vaast-la-Hougue, 30 Sept 1884). French composer. Far better known in his lifetime as a virtuoso pianist than as a composer, he nonetheless left a significant amount of music, including several works for the stage. Only two were performed in his lifetime. The first, *La madone*, received a lukewarm response at its première. In many respects it was a thoroughly modern *opéra comique*, with only a small amount of spoken dialogue, consequent musical continuity across the act, as well as elaborate writing for the orchestra. Other operatic works were given posthumous premières, including *Winkelried* (1892) and *Le tonnelier de Nuremberg* (1897). Lacombe considered the former 'his most individual work'. Motivation to write a four-act opera with the Swiss hero Winkelried as protagonist came from the many professional contacts and friendships that Lacombe had in that country; the autograph shows that the opera was begun in 1876 and completed five years later. Musically the score is worth more recognition than it has received. It betrays none of the influence of Gounod seen in so many French operas of the period. Though it is conservative in form, the orchestration and harmonic style are rich, the latter arguably more so than in the works that the young Massenet was writing at the same time. Stirring homorhythmic choruses make *Winkelried* a fine vehicle for Swiss patriotic sentiment.

La madone (oc, 1, P. F. de Carmouche), Paris, Lyrique, 16 Jan 1861
Winkelried, 1876–81 (opéra, 4, L. Bonnemère and Moreau-Sainti), Geneva, Grand, 17 Feb 1892, vs (Paris, 1892)
Madame Boniface (2, E. Dupré and Clairville), Paris, Bouffes-Parisiens, aut. 1883
Le tonnelier de Nuremberg (oc, 2, C. Nuitter, after E. T. A. Hoffmann), in Ger., as Meister Martin und seine Gesellen, Koblenz, 7 March 1897
La Corrigane, ou La reine des eaux (opéra, 3, Nuitter), in Ger., as Die Korrigane, Sondershausen, 14 March 1901
Le festin de pierre (comic op, 1, Clairville), in Ger., as Der Kreuzritter, Sondershausen, 21 March 1902

STEVEN HUEBNER

Lacome [Lacôme d'Estalenx], **Paul(-Jean-Jacques)** (*b* Le Houga, Gers, 4 March 1838; *d* Le Houga, 12 Dec 1920). French composer. He studied with José Puig y Absubide, organist in Aire-sur-Adour, 1857–60. He won a prize in a magazine competition, with an operetta, *Le dernier des paladins*, and settled in Paris, where he wrote music criticism and had over 20 operettas performed between 1870 and the end of the century, when he returned to his native Gascony. The most successful of them in France was *Jeanne, Jeannette et Jeanneton* (1876), the libretto of which had been turned down by Offenbach, but *Ma mie Rosette* (1890) achieved greater popularity in Britain. Lacome was a close friend of Chabrier, whose high opinion of him is evident from his letters. He has been criticized for a certain affected and showy quality to his invention, and it may be this that prevented his music from achieving still greater success.

opérettes, performed in Paris

L'épicier par amour (1), Marigny, July 1870; Il veux mon peignoir (1, G. Mancel), Tertulia, 11 May 1872; En Espagne (1, Mancel), Tertulia, 28 May 1872; La dot mal placée (3, Mancel), Athénée-Lyrique, 28 Feb 1873; Le mouton enragé (1, Jaime and Noriac), Bouffes-Parisiens, 27 May 1873; Amphytrion (oc, 1, C. Nuitter and Beaumont), Tailbout, 5 April 1875; Jeanne, Jeannette et Jeanneton (3, C. Clairville and M. Delacour), Folies-Dramatiques, 27 Oct 1876
Paques fleuries (3, Clairville and Delacour), Folies-Dramatiques, 21 Oct 1879; Le beau Nicolas (3, A. Vanloo and E. Letterier), Folies-Dramatiques, 8 Oct 1880; La nuit de Saint-Jean (oc, 1, M. de Lua-Lusignan and Delacour, after Erckmann-Chatrian), OC (Favart), 13 Nov 1882; Madame Boniface (3, Clairville and E. Depré), Bouffes-Parisiens, 20 Oct 1883; Myrtille (oc, 4, Erckmann-Chatrian and M. Drack), Gaîté, 27 March 1885
Les saturnales (3, A. Valabrègue), Nouveautés, 26 Sept 1887; La gardeuse d'oies (3, Letterier and Vanloo), Renaissance, 26 Oct 1888; Ma mie Rosette (3, J. Préval and A. Liorat), Folies-Dramatiques, 4 Feb 1890; La fille de l'air (féerie, 3, Coignard brothers, after Liorat), Folies-Dramatiques, 30 June 1890;

Mademoiselle Asmodée (3, P. Ferrier and Clairville), Renaissance, 24 Nov 1891, collab. V. Roger; Le cadeau de noces (4, Liorat, Stop and A. Hue), Bouffes-Parisiens, 20 Jan 1893
Le baiser de Monsieur (1, J. Pradels and Mancel), Eldorado, 15 Sept 1895; La fiancée en loterie (3, A. Douane and C. de Roddaz), Folies-Dramatiques, 18 Feb 1896, collab. Messager; Le maréchal Chadrou (oc, 3, H. Chivot, J. Gascogne and de Roddaz), Gaîté, 27 April 1898; Les quatre filles Aymon (3, Liorat and M. A. Fontenay), Folies-Dramatiques, 20 Sept 1898, collab. Roger; Un histoire de brigands (saynète, Stop)

ANDREW LAMB

La Coruña [Corunna]. City and provincial capital in Spain. The arrival of Italian opera in La Coruña, historically the seat of political, judicial and military power in Galicia, coincided with a time of economic expansion. In December 1768 a Teatro Público (designed by Nicolà Setaro) was inaugurated, but it was destroyed the following year. In 1770 Setaro built a new theatre, which the city acquired in 1772 when performances of opera were suspended; but in 1776 regular opera performances by Setaro's company (also active in Oporto until the end of the 18th century) were resumed under the direction of his son-in-law Alfonso Nicolini and the choreographer Nicolà Ambrosini. In 1842 a new theatre (now the Teatro Rosalia Castro) was built, and from 1847 until the end of the 19th century operas were given under the direction of the Berea family. Italian opera predominated, yielding in the last third of the century to French and, to a lesser degree, German opera. From 1916 the Teatro Rosalia Castro was used as a cinema, but after the Spanish Civil War the old routine was re-established, and regular modest festivals began in 1953 with the support of the Sociedad Amigos de la Opera. Local composers including Marcial del Adalid y Gurrea, Andrés Gaos Berea and Eduardo Rodríguez-Losada, and the singers Benita Moreno and María-Luisa Nache, have helped perpetuate a fine operatic tradition.

X. M. Carreira: 'Apuntes para la historia de la ópera en Galicia', *La ópera en España* (Oviedo, 1984)
L. I. de Souza: 'Algunas referencias a la ópera en La Coruña en el siglo XIX', *Abrente*, xiii-xv (1986)
X. M. Carreira: 'Centralismo y periferia en el teatro musical español del siglo XIX', *España en la música de Occidente*, ii (Madrid, 1987)
——: 'La tasa y regulación del coliseo de óperas y comedias fabricado por Setaro (La Coruña, 1772)', *RdMc*, x (1987), 601–21
——: 'El teatro de ópera en la Península Ibérica ca. 1750–1775: Nicolà Setaro', *De musica hispanica et aliis: miscelánea en honor al Prof. Dr. José Lopez-Calo* (Santiago, 1990), ii, pp.27–117

XOÁN M. CARREIRA

Lacoste, Louis de (*b* c1675; *d* before 1753). French composer. At the Paris Opéra in 1704 he was among the chorus members paid an annual salary of 400 livres, which rose to 1000 livres when he was appointed *batteur de mesure* (orchestral conductor) in 1713. The following year he gave up this position to Jean-Féry Rebel before becoming *maître de musique*, a post he held until 1717. His duties consisted of rehearsing the singers and supervising them during performances. He composed seven works for the Parisian stage – an *opéra-ballet* and six *tragédies en musique*. Inspired by the examples left by Colasse, Marais and Campra, his instrumentation reflected the different situations proposed in the librettos. But it is chiefly by the quality of his recitatives that he is distinguished, and he is today considered one of the most faithful disciples of Lully.

See also PHILOMÈLE.

tragédies en musique, first performed in Paris, at the Opéra, and published there the same year, unless otherwise stated

Aricie (opéra-ballet, prol., 5, Abbé Pic), 9 June 1697
Philomèle (prol., 5, P.-C. Roy), 20 Oct 1705, F-Po
Bradamante (prol., 5, Roy, after L. Ariosto), 2 May 1707
Créuse l'athénienne (prol., 5, Roy), 5 April 1712
Télégone (prol., 5, S.-J. Pellegrin), 6 Nov 1725, Po
Orion (prol., 5, Pellegrin and J. de La Font), 17 Feb 1728
Biblis (prol., 5, Fleury), 6 Nov 1732
Pomone (opéra), lost [cited by Fétis]

*

FétisB

T. Raimond: *Lettre critique sur Philomèle, tragédie nouvelle mise en musique* (Paris, 1705)
E. Campardon: *L'Académie royale de musique au XVIIIe siècle* (Paris, 1884)
M. Benoit and N. Dufourcq: 'Documents du minutier central: musiciens français du XVIIIe siècle', *RMFC*, ix (1969), 216–38
J. de La Gorce: 'L'Académie royale de musique en 1704, d'après des documents inédits conservés dans les archives notariales', *RdM*, lxv (1979), 160–91
                                              JÉRÔME DE LA GORCE

Lacy, Michael Rophino (*b* Bilbao, 19 July 1795; *d* London, 20 Sept 1867). English theatre musician. His mother was Spanish, his father an Irish merchant. A child prodigy on the violin, he took lessons from Kreutzer in Paris. In about 1804 he performed before Napoleon, and in 1805 he gave concerts in London. A few years later, at his father's insistence, he left the musical profession for that of the theatre and performed genteel comedy parts at the theatres of Dublin, Edinburgh, Glasgow and other cities. In 1818 he became leader of the Liverpool concerts, and at the end of 1820 returned to London and was leader of the ballet orchestra at the King's Theatre. From 1827 to 1833 Lacy adapted over a dozen plays (mostly French) and operas for the English stage, translating the words and arranging the music, and frequently taking great liberties with them, as was the contemporary practice. During the last decade of his life he wrote several original plays in London.

all first performed in London

LCG – *Covent Garden*   LDL – *Drury Lane*

Adaptations: The Turkish Lovers (comic op, after F. Romani: *Il turco in Italia*), LDL, 1 May 1827 [Rossini]; Love in Wrinkles, or The Russian Stratagem (comic op, after E. Scribe and G. Delavigne: *La vieille*), LDL, 4 Dec 1828 [Fétis]; The Maid of Judah, or The Knights Templars (after E. Deschamps and G. G. de Wailly: *Ivanhoé*), LCG, 7 March 1829 [Rossini]; The Casket (comic op, after *Les premières amours*), LDL, 10 March 1829 [Mozart: Idomeneo]; Cinderella, or The Fairy Queen and the Glass Slipper (comic op, after J. Ferretti), LCG, 13 April 1830, vs (London, 1830) [Rossini: La Cenerentola, incl. music from Maometto II, Armida and Guillaume Tell]; Fra Diavolo, or The Inn of Terracina (3, after Scribe), LCG, 3 Nov 1831 [Auber]; The Fiend Father, or Robert of Normandy (after Scribe and Delavigne: *Robert le diable*), LCG, 21 Feb 1832 [Meyerbeer]; The Coiners, or The Soldier's Oath (after Scribe and E. J. E. Mazères: *Le serment*), LCG, 23 March 1833 [Auber]

*

DNB (E. Heron-Allen); *FétisB*; *NicollH*   BRUCE CARR

Laderman, Ezra (*b* Brooklyn, New York, 29 June 1924). American composer. He studied composition with Stefan Wolpe, 1946–9, Miriam Gideon and with Otto Luening and Douglas Moore at Columbia University. Between 1971 and 1982 he taught at SUNY, Binghamton. He has written nine operas, on a variety of biblical, historical and fantastic subjects. *Goodbye to the Clowns* (composed 1956) portrays the imaginative world of a child faced with the challenge of death. *The Hunting of the Snark* (1958) is based on the nonsense poem by Lewis Carroll and makes frequent use of jazz and blues idioms. His biblical opera *Sarah* (1959) depicts the story of Abraham's barren wife. These early works are characterized by vibrant and colourful orchestrations and eminently singable vocal lines. His later operas focus on more realistic subjects. *Shadows Among Us* (1967) is set in a European refugee camp. *And David Wept* (1970) is the story of David and Bathsheba seen through the eyes of Bathsheba's husband, Uriah the Hittite; this tormented husband must decide to die with honour or live in shame. The work uses a mixture of song and spoken recitation. Expertly orchestrated, with an inventive use of percussion passages to heighten the drama, the piece has a lyrical attractiveness.

Laderman's best-known opera is *Galileo Galilei* (1978), a revision of his oratorio *The Trials of Galileo* (1967). The restructuring added about 45 minutes of music. Joseph Darion's libretto is tightly constructed, presenting a biography of Galileo told mostly in flashback. The music is strongly rhythmic, dissonant and highly contrapuntal; lyricism does not prevail. The drama is static, but purposeful in a Brechtian manner.

Jacob and the Indians, 1954 (3, E. Kinoy, after S. V. Benét), Woodstock, NY, 24 July 1957
Goodbye to the Clowns, 1956 (1, Kinoy), New York, Kaufmann Auditorium, 22 May 1960
The Hunting of the Snark, 1958–61 (opera-cantata, 1, L. Carroll), concert perf., New York, Hunter College, 25 March 1961; stage, New York, Queens College, 13 April 1978
Sarah (1, C. Roskam), CBS TV, 29 Nov 1959
Air Raid, 1965 (1, A. MacLeish)
Shadows Among Us, 1967 (2, N. Rosten), Philadelphia, Academy of Vocal Arts, 14 Dec 1979
And David Wept (opera-cantata, 1, J. Darion), CBS TV, 11 April 1971; stage, New York, Kaufmann Auditorium, 31 May 1980
The Questions of Abraham (opera-cantata, 1, Darion), CBS TV, 30 Sept 1973
Galileo Galilei (3, Darion), Binghamton, NY, Forum, 3 Feb 1979

*

Anderson2; *Baker7*
R. H. Kornick: *Recent American Opera: a Production Guide* (New York, 1991), 163–7
                                              JAMES P. CASSARO

Ladmirault, Paul (Emile) (*b* Nantes, 8 Dec 1877; *d* Kerbili en Kamoel, St Nazaire, 30 Oct 1944). French composer. His first opera, *Gilles de Retz*, in three acts to a libretto by his mother, was first performed in Nantes on 18 May 1893. In 1895 he went to Paris, where he studied composition at the Conservatoire with Fauré. Between 1899 and 1902 he worked on the opera *Myrdhin* (4, L. Ladmirault and A. Fleury); it remained incomplete, although he later extracted two orchestral suites from it, the *Suite bretonne* and *Brocéliande au matin*. He also wrote an opérette, *Glycère*, which was given in Paris in 1928. Ladmirault became professor and later director of the conservatory in Nantes and he wrote for several musical journals. He is best remembered as a regionalist, whose compositions display the atmosphere of his native Brittany, much as Séverac's music reflects the Languedoc region.

*

C. Debussy: 'De l'opéra et de ses rapports avec la musique', *Gil Blas* (9 March 1903)
M. Courtonne: *Un siècle de musique à Nantes et dans la région nantaise, 1850–1950* (Nantes, 1953)
                                              ELAINE BRODY

Ladurner, Ignace Antoine (François Xavier) [Ignaz Anton Franz Xaver/Joseph] (*b* Aldein, nr Bolzano, 1 Aug 1766; *d* Villain, nr Massy, 4 March 1839). French composer of Tyrolean descent. He studied music with his uncle at the nearby monastery of Benediktbeuren and in 1782 succeeded his father as organist at Algund. Two years later he went to Munich to study at the Lyceum Gregorianum, and from there moved to Longeville with Countess Heimhausen, a distinguished pianist. He arrived in Paris in 1788 and soon developed a reputation as an outstanding teacher; his most famous pupils include Auber and Boëly. From 1797 until 1802 he taught the piano at the Conservatoire.

Ladurner wrote two operas: the *drame lyrique Wenzel, ou Le magistrat du peuple* (3, F. Pillet; Paris, National, 10 April 1794; ov., airs, acc. pf, Paris, 1795–1800), and the *opéra comique Les vieux fous, ou Plus de peur que de mal* (1, J. A. de Ségur; Paris, OC (Feydeau), 15 or 16 Jan 1796; *F-Pc*). Most of his compositions were for the piano.   FRÉDÉRIC ROBERT

Lady in the Dark. Musical play in two acts by KURT WEILL to a book by Moss Hart and lyrics by IRA GERSHWIN; Boston, Colonial Theatre, 30 December 1940, New York, Alvin Theatre, 21 January 1941.

Despite achieving success as editor of a popular fashion magazine, Liza Elliott (high mezzo-soprano) feels at odds with male-dominated and success-orientated society. Moreover, she is unable to decide between the rival attractions of the three men in her life, her business colleague Charlie Johnson (baritone), her publisher and current lover Kendall Nesbitt, and glamorous film star Randy Curtis (baritone). She consults her psychiatrist, and at each of four sessions relives a dream. In the first ('Glamour Dream') she becomes the glamorous, sought-after woman that in real life she never feels. In the second ('Wedding Dream') her plan to marry Kendall Nesbitt is interrupted when Randy Curtis appears. In the third ('Circus Dream') she undergoes a trial in a circus ring, accused of being unable to make up her mind between her three admirers. Russell Paxton (high baritone), a photographer on the magazine, is the ringmaster. In the fourth dream ('Childhood Dream') she finally recalls the traumatic childhood incidents that are at the root of her problems and bursts forth with the haunting childhood song ('My Ship') that has appeared fragmentarily throughout the score.

The show's music is confined almost entirely to the dream sequences, where it is virtually continuous. It includes such numbers for Liza as the lilting 'One Life to Live' and the bluesy 'The Saga of Jenny', as well as the lyrical 'My Ship'. Paxton (as the ringmaster) has an irrelevant but highly effective tongue-twister patter song, 'Tschaikowsky', with a refrain in which the names of 49 Russian composers are rattled off within some 40 seconds. The first production included Gertrude Lawrence (Liza), Danny Kaye (Russell Paxton) and Victor Mature (Randy Curtis), with Maurice Abravanel conducting. A 1944 Paramount film version virtually eliminated Weill's music. In 1986 David Loud and John Mauceri compiled a new, extended score based upon the autograph full score and rehearsal material and significantly differing from the original published vocal score edited by Albert Sirmay. This new, fuller score was conducted by Mauceri at the Edinburgh Festival in August 1988.   ANDREW LAMB

Lady Macbeth of the Mtsensk District [*Ledi Makbet Mtsenskogo uyezda*]. Opera in four acts, op.29, by DMITRY SHOSTAKOVICH to a libretto by the composer and Alexander Preys, after the short story by Nikolay Leskov; Leningrad, Malïy Opernïy Teatr, 22 January

1934 (revised as *KATERINA IZMAYLOVA*; Moscow, Stanislavsky–Nemirovich-Danchenko Music Theatre, 8 January 1963).

Katerina L'vovna Izmaylova *wife of Zinovy Borisovich*	soprano
Boris Timofeyevich Izmaylov *a merchant*	high bass
Zinovy Borisovich Izmaylov *his son, a merchant*	tenor
Millhand	baritone
Sergey *the Izmaylovs' worker*	tenor
Coachman	tenor
Aksin'ya *the Izmaylovs' worker*	soprano
Shabby Peasant	tenor
Steward	bass
Porter	bass
Three Workers	tenors
Priest	bass
Apparition of Boris Timofeyevich	bass
Chief of Police	baritone
Policeman	bass
Teacher	tenor
Drunken Guest	tenor
Old Convict	bass
Sentry	bass
Sonetka *a convict*	contralto
Woman Convict	soprano
Officer	bass

Workers, policemen, guests, convicts

Setting The Russian provinces in the mid-19th century

Shostakovich began the composition of his second opera in autumn 1930, as his first opera, *The Nose*, was completing its short run at the Malïy Theatre, Leningrad. Turning once again to 19th-century Russian literature for a subject, he chose Leskov's tale of the passion, greed and brutality of a provincial merchant's wife. The composer and his co-librettist Alexander Preys made small but significant alterations to Leskov's story, all designed to humanize the central character of Katerina, to find justification for her crimes and make her a positive, sympathetic figure. Shostakovich referred to his opera as a 'tragedy-satire'; his chief technique in winning the spectator's sympathy for his heroine was by caricaturing those around her with excessively grotesque and parodistic music. With the conspicuous exception of the convicts in the final act, Katerina is the only character in the opera treated to music of genuine lyrical feeling.

Shostakovich completed *Lady Macbeth* in December 1932, dedicating it to his new bride Nina Varzar. The work was projected as the first of a trilogy or tetralogy of operas, a cycle dealing with the fates of women from different periods of Russian history. Interest in staging *Lady Macbeth* came from both the Malïy Theatre in Leningrad and from the Nemirovich-Danchenko Music Theatre in Moscow. In the event, the Leningrad production, staged by Nikolay Smolich, designed by Vladimir Dmitriyev and conducted by Samuil Samosud – the same team responsible for producing *The Nose* – beat their Moscow rival to the première by two days: Vladimir Nemirovich-Danchenko's production, which took a less satirical reading of Shostakovich's work and made some cuts and alterations, opened under the title *Katerina Izmaylova* on 24 January 1934.

The opera, in both its productions, was an immediate critical and, especially, popular success; its earthy approach to sex, its graphic language and extreme violence gave it powerful veristic appeal. The composer's confident mastery of the musical and dramatic idiom was indisputable. Despite minor criticisms, *Lady Macbeth* was widely hailed as the first major opera of the Soviet period. Over the next two years it received nearly 200 performances in Moscow and Leningrad. During the same period, it was exported and performed, either in concert or staged versions, in many cities including Buenos Aires, Cleveland, London, New York, Philadelphia, Stockholm and Zürich. In December 1935, a new production, similar to that of Leningrad's Maliy theatre, was staged in the Bol'shoy Theatre filial in Moscow. For a brief period in early January 1936, when the Maliy theatre company was on tour in Moscow, the city played host to three different productions simultaneously.

On 26 January 1936, Stalin, accompanied by a delegation of high-ranking government officials, attended a performance of the Bol'shoy production of Shostakovich's opera. The dignitaries did not stay for the fourth act. Two days later, an unsigned editorial, 'Sumbur vmesto muziki' ('Muddle instead of Music'), an uncompromising attack on Shostakovich's opera, appeared unexpectedly in the government newspaper *Pravda*: 'From the very first moment, listeners are stunned by the deliberately dissonant and confused stream of sounds ... singing is replaced by screaming ... the music quacks, hoots, pants and gasps in order to express the love scenes as naturally as possible ...'. The editorial censured the opera's pretensions as social satire, its rejection of the principles of classical opera and of 'a simple, accessible musical language'. It equated the opera's flaws with petty-bourgeois, leftist distortions in the other arts, contrasting this with the realistic, wholesome character of the 'true' art demanded by the people.

The timing and context of the editorial – its proximity, for instance, to Stalin's highly-publicized approbation of Dzerzhinsky's opera *Quiet Flows the Don* earlier in the month – left no doubt in the artistic community that this was a strategically planned official assault whose sights extended well beyond this particular opera or the field of music. It was the opening salvo in a campaign that resulted in the explicit subjugation of the individual creative freedom of Soviet artists to the repressive control of the Communist Party and State, through their obligatory adherence to the aesthetic doctrine of Socialist Realism.

Shostakovich's opera quickly disappeared from the repertory, not to return for nearly 30 years and then only in a significantly revised version. In the mid-1950s, after Stalin's death, Shostakovich made revisions to his opera but it was not approved for production until 1963, when it was rehabilitated, as *Katerina Izmaylova* op.114, at the Stanislavsky–Nemirovich-Danchenko Music Theatre in Moscow on 8 January 1963. Ironically, perhaps, some of the most controversial aspects of the first version – the crude, naturalistic language and musical effects, especially the musically explicit seduction scene – had already been sanitized in the vocal score published in 1935, before the opera was repressed. In the revised version Shostakovich took the sanitizing process still further, modifying the extremes of tessitura and replacing two of the orchestral entr'actes.

In the late 1970s, the original 1932 version of *Lady Macbeth* was rehabilitated; it was staged, published and recorded in the West to great acclaim. Since then, the original version has replaced the revised *Katerina Izmaylova* in the repertory of Western opera houses. In the Soviet Union, however, where the composer's substitution of the revised version was accepted at face value, the revised version was recognized as definitive.

The following synopsis corresponds to the original 1932 version of the opera.

ACT 1.i *Katerina's bedroom* Katerina, the young wife of provincial merchant Zinovy Izmaylov, tries to fall asleep, but gives up. She reflects instead on the source of her perpetual boredom and depression. In a brief arioso, she reveals her feeling of uselessness. The arrival of her father-in-law, Boris Timofeyevich, is announced by a steady, ominous pulse that punctuates an awkward bassoon melody. He asks if they will have his favourite dish of mushrooms for supper and Katerina nods curtly. Bridling at Katerina's apathy, Boris berates her for laziness and for failing to produce a child after nearly five years of marriage. Katerina defensively blames her husband but Boris accuses her of frigidity and warns her not to try to cuckold his son. As he departs, he tells her to prepare some rat poison. To his back, she retorts that he is the rat.

Informed that the dam at the mill has broken, a reluctant Zinovy decides he must oversee repairs himself. Boris scolds the tittering workers and bullies them into a choral apotheosis of their master, 'Zachem, zhe, ti uyezzhayesh', khozyain?' ('Why are you leaving us, master?'), its patent hypocrisy underscored by coarse waltz rhythms. As Zinovy prepares, at a gallop, for his departure, he points out to his father the new worker Sergey. Boris cruelly officiates the otherwise tender farewell between husband and wife, convincing the guileless Zinovy that Katerina must swear her fidelity in public. Her humiliation reaches its pinnacle as Boris forces her to her knees. The brief, somewhat ominous, entr'acte between scenes grovels in the low range of cellos and basses.

1.ii *In the Izmaylovs' yard* The scene begins abruptly with the high-pitched screams of Aksin'ya as a group of male workers roughly manhandle and molest her. In the seething turmoil, Sergey takes command of the assault and is cheered on by his companions. The arrival of their mistress, Katerina, puts an immediate end to the abuse; she delivers a proud defence of women's value in her arioso 'Mnogo vi, muzhiki' ('You men are all so conceited'), and threatens to beat them. Sergey convinces her instead to wrestle. Almost overwhelmed by desire, Sergey pins Katerina; on his arrival, Boris Timofeyevich discovers them in this compromising position and demands an explanation. Katerina invents a story to protect Sergey and Boris barks at everyone to get back to work. In stark contrast to the tone of the music that immediately precedes and follows it, the entr'acte is a rollicking, circus-like romp.

1.iii *Katerina's bedroom* Katerina prepares for bed, lonely and bored. Making his rounds, Boris keeps tabs on her. In her aria, 'Zherebyonok k kobïlke toropitsya' ('The foal runs after the filly'), a lyrical and emotional effusion central to the perception of the heroine as a sympathetic figure, Katerina gives vent to the full measure of her frustrated passion and despair. Over an ominous drum roll, Sergey knocks at the door, throwing Katerina into fear and confusion. He persuades her to admit him and asks to borrow a book. Sergey searches awkwardly for topics to prolong the conversation, admitting to his own boredom and sympathy for her position. Sergey's refusal to depart marks the beginning of a gradual, but inexorable, build-up of dramatic tension. He suggests that they wrestle again and, disregarding her protestations, embraces the struggling Katerina. She eventually succumbs to his seduction, and the union is consummated boisterously in a brassy instrumental interlude. The graphic musical representation of the sexual act in this lengthy passage, in particular the explicit trombone slides, proved the opera's most notorious feature, one that was tempered by the composer in his vocal score as early as 1935. In the languorous aftermath of lovemaking, Katerina half-heartedly tells Sergey to leave, but she acknowledges him now as her only husband. The curtain falls with a brief reprise of the rollicking music of the previous entr'acte.

ACT 2.iv *A courtyard in the Izmaylovs' house* The sleepless Boris patrols for burglars, and reminisces about his youth. As the music breaks into a brisk galop, he remembers fondly his prowess at the seduction of married women. When Boris notices a light on in Katerina's bedroom, the music shifts to a crude parody of a Viennese waltz; Boris persuades himself that, with Zinovy absent, he himself should go to her. At that moment he overhears Sergey and Katerina as they exchange tender farewells. Furious at the betrayal, Boris seizes Sergey as he departs and raises a rumpus. The workmen gather and Boris sends for a whip, calling Katerina to observe the relentless, rhythmic thrashing. Locked in her room Katerina is unable to defend her lover. Finally she climbs down the drainpipe to intercede, but it is only his exhaustion which causes Boris to stop. He has Sergey locked in the storeroom and orders Katerina to bring him some of the leftover mushrooms, meanwhile sending someone to fetch Zinovy. Against a romantic obbligato for solo violin, Boris greedily consumes the mushrooms, unaware that Katerina has laced them with rat poison. Soon his stomach begins to burn but Katerina defiantly rejects his order to bring water. As Boris writhes on the ground and calls for a priest, Katerina removes his keys and runs to free Sergey. A chorus of passing labourers sings as they go to the fields, 'Vidno, skoro uzh zarya' ('See, the dawn is almost breaking'), and Boris sends one of them to fetch the priest. In his confession, Boris tells the priest about the rat poison and points to Katerina as he dies, but all think he is merely raving. The hypocrisy of Katerina's grief shows through her grotesque parody of the supplication music from the prologue to Musorgsky's *Boris Godunov*. As the priest tries to comprehend the cause of death, he launches into jaunty, and utterly inapt, dance music. By contrast, the massive chordal tutti which opens the entr'acte and the extended passacaglia which gradually builds and peaks in intensity, are more tragic in tone.

2.v *Katerina's bedroom* Katerina wakes Sergey and begs him to kiss her passionately. Sergey warns her that soon her husband will return; he whines that he is not content to be her secret lover, that he wants her as his wife. She vows to make him both a merchant and her husband. Her resolve and new sense of courage, underscored by a resolute pulse, evaporate when she spies the threatening ghost of Boris Timofeyevich in the corner. He curses her. Katerina wakes Sergey in fear, but he cannot see the ghost and calms her. They go back to sleep. Later, sensing the approach of her husband, Katerina wakes Sergey and, in a whisper, tells him to

hide. Trumpets herald Zinovy as he knocks insistently at the door and demands entry. Katerina delays him as long as she can. When she finally admits him, she responds to his suspicious questions with sarcasm in a heated, fast-paced exchange. When Zinovy begins to beat her, Katerina calls upon Sergey to protect her. Zinovy tries to escape, but Katerina strangles him while Sergey holds him down. Zinovy dies after Sergey strikes him over the head with a candlestick. To a vamp-like accompaniment, Sergey carries the body to the cellar as Katerina lights the way. She then embraces Sergey as her husband.

ACT 3.vi *The Izmaylovs' house* On their wedding day, while standing outside the cellar, Katerina confesses to Sergey that she is afraid. He tells her not to fear the dead, only the living. Looking to the future, they depart for the church. The shabby peasant enters and, in a grotesquely comic song punctuated with drunken hiccups, 'U menya bïla kuma' ('Once I had a ladyfriend'), he expounds on characteristically Russian fashion the joys of drinking. His desire for a drink prompts him to break the lock on the cellar; the stink at first repels him, but then, to the bouncy, dance-like accompaniment of trumpets and drums, he discovers the corpse of Zinovy and runs off to the police. The entr'acte extends the sprightly, colourful atmosphere.

3.vii *At the police station* In a song in conspicuous strophic form, 'Sozdan politseyskiy bïl vo vremya ono' ('The police were created in the days of old'), the Chief of Police impresses on his men the significance of their profession. In the lilting, waltz refrain, the chorus of policemen lament the low pay and the scarcity of bribes. The Chief is annoyed that Katerina has not invited him to her wedding and promises to get even. Saying he has caught a socialist, a policeman drags in a teacher who has been experimenting to see if frogs have souls. He is thrown in jail. The bored Chief resumes his song. The shabby peasant arrives and informs them that there is a corpse in the Izmaylovs' cellar, news which is greeted with enthusiasm. The policemen make haste to depart. The entr'acte alternates the police's bustling music with unrelated dance-like episodes.

3.viii *In the Izmaylovs' garden* In fugal entries, the wedding guests wish the married couple long life, health and happiness. According to Russian custom, the priest periodically calls for the couple to kiss. In a rather tipsy manner, he extols Katerina's beauty. Gradually, the drunken guests fall asleep. Suddenly, Katerina notices that the lock on the cellar has been broken. Terrified, she tells the reluctant Sergey that they have not a minute to waste. Sergey fetches the money, but their escape is cut off by the march of the approaching police. Impatient with the Chief's self-important dawdling, Katerina begs Sergey's forgiveness and extends her hands for the handcuffs. Sergey, however, tries to escape and is beaten. Both are led away.

ACT 4.ix *On the banks of a river* A column of convicts settles down for the night, separated by the sexes and guarded by sentries. In an affecting, folk-inspired lament in Musorgskian vein, 'Verstï odna za drugoy' ('Verst by verst, one after another'), an Old Convict reflects philosophically on the endless road; his resignation to a cheerless fate is reinforced by the chorus of convicts. Slipping the sentry a bribe, Katerina makes her way to Sergey and snuggles up to him tenderly. Initially ignoring her, Sergey snaps at her for ruining his life. Tormented by his rejection, Katerina begs his forgive-

'Lady Macbeth of the Mtsensk District' (Shostakovich): Act 3 scene viii (the arrest) from the original production at the Maliy Opera Theatre, Leningrad, 22 January 1934; set by Vladimir Dmitriyev

ness and returns to her place. In counterpoint with solo english horn, she intones a plaintive lament 'Nelegko posle pochyota da poklonov' ('It's hard after being honoured and respected'). Sergey steals up to the pretty young convict, Sonetka, and flirts with her. They make fun of Katerina. To win her favour, Sonetka demands that Sergey get her a new pair of stockings. Sergey fawns on Katerina, pretending that without the stockings he will not be able to travel further. Selflessly, she takes off and gives him her own pair, which he promptly delivers to Sonetka. Katerina watches helplessly as Sergey carries Sonetka off in triumph; she is forced to endure the shrill mockery of the other women. Over an ominous, low sustained tremolo, the heroine, numb with grief, examines her black conscience in the arioso 'V lesu, v samoy chashche yest' ozero' ('In the forest, right in a thicket, there is a lake'). Sergey and Sonetka return from their tryst and jauntily tease Katerina. A steady drumbeat is heard and the sentries muster the column of convicts for departure. Slowly, Katerina approaches Sonetka on the bridge and pushes her, screaming, into the river, throwing herself in after. Both women are swept away by the strong current. The convicts are quickly formed back into ranks and are marched away to a reprise of the Old Convict's lament.

*   *   *

Musically and dramatically, Lady Macbeth is more immediately accessible than The Nose. It shares with the earlier opera a dynamic, fast-paced momentum – unified by instrumental interludes that connect the scenes within each act – as well as frequent, often comic, allusions to the aesthetic of music hall, theatre and circus. Here, however, Shostakovich places these features within a realistic plot and grounds them in a more conventional tonal idiom. He makes it difficult not to empathize with the suffering and downfall of Katerina, a misguided but, in the context of her social milieu, singularly strong and noble spirit.

Although Lady Macbeth has finally and firmly established itself among the few operatic masterpieces of the 20th century, its fate as tragic victim of Soviet political repression also caused an irreparable loss for the history of opera. Still under the age of 30 and one of the most naturally gifted theatrical composers of his generation, Shostakovich abandoned his ambition to create a tetralogy of operas about women after the work's condemnation. Despite a lifelong attraction to the genre and frequent fitful starts, he never completed another opera.

LAUREL E. FAY

Ładysz, Bernard (b Vilnius, 24 July 1922). Polish bass. He studied at the Fryderyk Chopin Music School in Warsaw. In 1950 he was engaged as a soloist by the Warsaw Opera where he remained for more than 20 years. After he won the Viotti Competition in Vercelli (1956) he began to appear at Italian opera houses, including Palermo, Parma and the S Carlo in Naples, and at the Bol'shoy Theatre in Moscow. His main roles included the Grand Inquisitor and Philip II in Don Carlos, Méphistophélès in Faust and the title role in Boris Godunov; and he sang in Szymanowski's King Roger and Penderecki's The Devils of Loudun. He recorded arias by Verdi and by Russian and other composers. He had a voice of wide range and possessed considerable talent as an actor.   MIECZYSŁAWA HANUSZEWSKA

La Ferté, Denis Pierre Jean Papillon de. *See* PAPILLON DE LA FERTÉ, DENIS PIERRE JEAN.

Lafitte, Léon (*b* St Genies, 28 Jan 1875; *d* Paris, Sept 1938). French tenor. He studied at the Paris Conservatoire and made his début in 1898 at the Opéra, as David in *Die Meistersinger*; later roles there included Beppe in *Pagliacci* and Mime in the local première of *Siegfried* (1908). At Covent Garden in 1906 he was heard as Renaud in Gluck's *Armide* and Jean in Massenet's *Le jongleur de Notre-Dame*, both British premières. He sang in the dramatic repertory for 15 seasons at the Brussels Opéra and appeared in North and South America from 1913. His last major roles at the Paris Opéra were Samson and the Berlioz Faust (1923).
DAVID CUMMINGS

Lafont, Jean-Philippe (*b* Toulouse, 11 Feb 1951). French bass-baritone. He studied in Paris, in 1977 singing Nick Shadow at the Opéra-Studio and Guglielmo at Albi. He has appeared in Paris, Geneva, Nîmes, Brussels, Perugia, Rome, Naples, Bonn and Aix-en-Provence, where in 1982 he sang Boreas (Rameau's *Les boréades*). As well as parts in Philidor's *Les femmes vengées* and *Tom Jones* his repertory includes the High Priest (*Alceste*), Thoas (*Iphigénie en Tauride*), Leporello, Count Almaviva, Creon (*Médée*), Astor (Cherubini's *Démophon*), Assur (*Semiramide*), the four villains (*Les contes d'Hoffmann*), Ourrias, Golaud, Ramiro (*L'heure espagnole*), Michele (*Il tabarro*), Escamillo, which he sang at the Metropolitan in 1988, and the title roles of *Guillaume Tell* and Busoni's *Doktor Faust*. Lafont created roles in Antoine Duhamel's *Gambara* (1978, Lyons) and Landowski's *Montségur* (1985, Paris). A fine actor, he has a well-focussed voice as effective in contemporary music as in the standard repertory.
ELIZABETH FORBES

La Font, Joseph de (*b* Paris, 1686; *d* Passy, 30 March 1725). French librettist and playwright. His masterpiece is the *opéra-ballet Le triomphe ou les fêtes de Thalie* (1714). Although not, as Loewenberg and others have claimed, the work in which the 'comic element was first introduced into the sphere of French opera' (compare for example *Les Muses* of 1703 and *Les fêtes vénitiennes* of 1710), *Les fêtes de Thalie* deals with flesh-and-blood characters, soubrettes, *petits maîtres* and coquettish widows. La Font stated that this was the 'first Opéra where one sees the women dressed *à la Françoise*'. The frequently mentioned *scandale* arose from La Font's bold stroke, in the prologue, of having Thalia (muse of Comedy) triumph over Melpomene (muse of Tragedy) in a setting representing the stage of the Paris Opéra. La Font and Mouret lost no time in composing another entrée, *La critique des fêtes de Thalie*, and in changing the name of the *opéra-ballet* to *Les fêtes de Thalie* – all of which appeared to placate the aestheticians. In 1722 a new entrée, 'La provençale', was added, proving the most popular of all, and holding the stage until 1778. La Font's other works for the lyric stage include two *tragédies en musique*, *Hypermnestre* (1716) and *Orion* (1728, completed by S.-J. Pellegrin), and the ballet *Les amours de Protée* (1720). In addition, he collaborated with Lesage and d'Orneval for the Opéra-Comique.

Although known for the 'kindness of his heart', as the *Mercure* reported, La Font led a dissipated life, in cafés and around gambling tables, which contributed to his early death.

Danae, ou Jupiter Crispin (comédie), 1707; *Le naufrage ou La pompe funèbre de Crispin* (comédie), Gillier, 1710; *Les fêtes de Thalie* (opéra-ballet), Mouret, 1714; *Hypermnèstre* (tragédie), Gervais, 1716; *Le monde renversé* (oc, with Lesage and d'Orneval), Gillier, 1718; *La querelle des théâtres* (prol., with Lesage), Gillier, 1718; *Les amours de Protée* (opéra-ballet), Gervais, 1720; *La décadence de l'Opéra-Comique* (prol.), 1721; *Le jugement d'Apollon et de Pan par Midas* (oc), 1721; *La réforme du régiment de la calotte* (oc), J. Aubert, 1721; *Les fourberies d'Arlequin* (oc), 1722; *Ourson et Valentin* (oc), 1722; *La provençale* (entrée for Les fêtes de Thalie), Mouret, 1722; *Le ballet des vingt-quatre heures* (prol.), Legrand, 1722; *Pierrot fée* (oc), 1726; *Le retour de la chasse du cerf* (oc), 1726; *Orion* (tragédie, Acts 4 and 5 by S.-J. Pellegrin), Lacoste, 1728

Jullien-Desboulmiers: *Histoire de la théâtre de l'Opéra-comique* (Paris, 1769)
J. Carmody: *Le répertoire de l'Opéra-Comique en vaudevilles de 1708 à 1764* (Berkeley, 1933)
JAMES R. ANTHONY

La Fontaine [Lafontaine], **Mlle de** (*b* 1655; *d* 1738). French dancer. She was called 'la première des premières danseuses' because she was the highest-ranked of the first ballerinas permitted to appear in public at the Paris Opéra. She danced the leading role in Lully's *Le triomphe de l'Amour* at the Opéra (1681) and, each year until Lully's death, created leading roles in others of his operas and ballets, including *Persée* (1682), *Phaëton* (1683), *Amadis* (1684), *Roland* (1685), *Le temple de la paix* (1685), *Armide* (1686), *Acis et Galatée* (1686) as well as revivals. She retired to a convent in about 1696. According to Titon du Tillet (*Le Parnasse françois*), she was considered remarkable for her beauty and the nobility of her dancing.
MAUREEN NEEDHAM COSTONIS

La Garde [Lagarde, Garde], **Pierre de** (*b* nr Crécy-en-Brie, Seine-et-Marne, 10 Feb 1717; *d c*1792). French composer. His fine bass voice was praised by La Borde, and it was as a singer that he first gained entry to court and opera house, subsequently securing positions in both spheres, including that of music teacher to Louis XV's children from 1755. His composing career was compressed into a short space of time; he wrote just four operatic works, all having their premières between 1748 and 1751. He was assistant conductor at the Paris Opéra between 1750 and 1755. His *pastorales-héroïques* were written for Madame de Pompadour's Théâtre des Petits Cabinets at Versailles; his *divertissement comique* was performed at her country house. Only *Aeglé* was given at the Opéra (in 1751, and with various companion pieces in subsequent revivals). La Garde's lyrical talents were shown to best effect in his many smaller-scale vocal works – cantatas, *airs* and duets.

all printed works published in Paris

Aeglé (pastorale-héroïque, 1, P. Laujon), Versailles, 13 Jan 1748, vs (1751)
Silvie (pastorale-héroïque, 3, Laujon), Versailles, 26 Feb 1749, *F-Pn, Po*
La journée galante (opéra-ballet, 3, Laujon), Versailles, 25 Feb 1750, lib. pubd in *Divertissemens du Théâtre des petits appartemens pendant l'hiver de 1749 à 1750* [incl. Aeglé as Act 2]
L'impromptu de la cour de marbre (divertissement comique, 1, C.-S. Favart), Bellevue, 28 Nov 1751

J.-B. de La Borde: *Essai sur la musique ancienne et moderne* (Paris, 1780)
T. Lhuillier: 'Note sur quelques artistes musiciens dans La Brie', *Bulletin de la Société d'archéologie, sciences, lettres et arts de Seine et Marne*, v (1868), 317–40

N. Dufourcq: *La musique ... de Louis XIV et de Louis XV d'après les mémoires de Sourches et Luynes 1681–1758* (Paris, 1970)

W. H. Kaehler: *The Operatic Repertoire of Madame de Pompadour's Théâtre des petits cabinets (1747–1753)* (diss., U. of Michigan, 1971)

R. Machard: 'Les musiciens en France au temps de Jean-Philippe Rameau, d'après les actes du Secrétariat de la Maison du roi', *RMFC*, xi (1971), 5–177   CAROLINE WOOD

Lagrange-Chancel, François-Joseph de [Chancel, François-Joseph de, Sieur de La Grange] (*b* Antoniac, Dordogne, 1 Jan 1677; *d* Antoniac, 26 Dec 1758). French librettist. He was a protégé of Racine and supplied texts in verse (mainly tragedies on Greek themes) for the Théâtre Français and the Académie Royale de Musique. He wrote the librettos of *Médus, roi des Mèdes* (set by Bouvard, 1702), *Cassandre* (Bertin de la Doué and Bouvard, 1706) and, with Roy, *Ariane* (Mouret, 1717) for the Académie Royale. The final edition of his works (1758) included the tragedies *Pirame et Thisbé*, *La mort d'Ulysse* and *Le crime puni*, intended for the Opéra. Though strongly influenced by Corneille and Racine, Lagrange-Chancel, initially considered an infant prodigy, came to be regarded as a mediocre writer with a style sometimes verging on the clumsy and trivial.

H.-C. Lancaster: *French Tragedy in the Time of Louis XV and Voltaire* (Baltimore, 1950)

J.-P. de Beaumarchais, D. Conty and A. Rey: *Dictionnaire des littératures de langue française* (Paris, 1984)   JÉRÔME DE LA GORCE

Laguerre [Lagarde, Legar, Legard, Legare, Leguar, Leguerre etc.], **John** (*d* London, 28 March 1748). English baritone. Son of the mural painter Louis Laguerre and himself an artist, he first appeared as a minor singer in the Italian Opera and had roles in Handel's *Radamisto* (1720) and the première of *Giulio Cesare* (1724). Most of his career was spent in John Rich's company at Lincoln's Inn Fields and Covent Garden, where from 1721 he sang in pantomimes, afterpieces, ballad operas and burlesques. His most popular roles were Hob in *Flora* and Gaffer Gubbins in *The Dragon of Wantley*. He sang Coridon in the first public performance of *Acis and Galatea* (1731). 'Honest Jack Laguerre' had a reputation as a wit, a mimic and an amusing companion.

BDA; *LS*

Vertue Note Books, v, ed. Walpole Society (Oxford, 1938)   OLIVE BALDWIN, THELMA WILSON

Laguerre, Marie-Joséphine (*b* Paris, 1755; *d* Paris, 14 Feb 1783). French soprano. She joined the Opéra as a chorister in 1771–2 and in 1776 took the title roles in La Borde's *Adèle de Ponthieu* and Gluck's *Alceste*. A pure-voiced and expressive singer, she shared leading roles with Rosalie Levasseur from 1778, and created the title role in Floquet's *Hellé* (1779), Sangaride in Piccinni's *Atys* (1780), Iphigenia in Piccinni's *Iphigénie en Tauride* (1781) and the Countess in Grétry's *La double épreuve* (1782). Her early death was apparently the result of loose living. In a famous incident at the second performance of Piccinni's *Iphigénie*, she was incoherent through drink, giving rise to the witticism (sometimes attributed to Sophie Arnould) that it was 'Iphigénie en Champagne', and was imprisoned until the following performance.

H. Audiffret: 'Laguerre (Marie-Joséphine)', *Biographie universelle*, ed. L. G. Michaud (Paris, 1843–65)

D. Denne-Baron: 'Laguerre (Marie-Sophie)', *Nouvelle biographie générale*, ed. J. C. F. Hoefer (Paris, 1852–66)

C. Davillier: *Une vente d'actrice sous Louis XVI: Mlle Laguerre* (Paris, 1870)   JULIAN RUSHTON

Laibach (Ger.). LJUBLJANA.

Lainati, Carlo Ambrogio. *See* LONATI, CARLO AMBROGIO.

Lais, François. *See* LAYS, FRANÇOIS.

Lajarte, Théodore (Edouard Dufaure de) (*b* Bordeaux, 10 July 1826; *d* Paris, 20 June 1890). French musicologist and composer. He is best remembered for his work as an archivist at the Paris Opéra. Following his appointment as librarian in 1873, he brought order to the theatre's historical scores and parts and in 1876 published an inventory of the collection, the *Bibliothèque musicale du théâtre de l'Opéra* (Paris, 1876). He also made frequent contributions to newspapers as a music historian. Late in life he launched an initiative to publish a series of French operatic classics in piano reduction with an edition of Lully's *Thésée*. While alive he had a modest reputation as a composer, primarily of military band music but also of *opéras comiques*. His stage career embraced more than a dozen works; most were one-act curtain-raisers that did not survive beyond a handful of performances. The greatest success was *Le secret de l'oncle Vincent* (1855) which achieved 45 performances; with only two players it was conceived as a vehicle for the baritone Edmond Meillet and a recent Conservatoire graduate, the soprano Esther Caye. Lajarte's works all fall on the lighter side of the spectrum of the musically variegated genre that was *opéra comique* after 1850. They are generally characterized by a simple harmonic vocabulary and stereotypical orchestral textures; his style underwent little change from the beginning of his career to the end.

first performed in Paris unless otherwise stated

On guérit de la peur (oc, 1, H. Boisseaux), private perf., 1853

Le secret de l'oncle Vincent (oc, 1, Boisseaux), Lyrique, 24 Nov 1855 (Paris, *c*1855)

Le duel du commandeur (oc, 1, Boisseaux), Lyrique, 10 June 1857

Mam'zelle Pénélope (oc, 1, Boisseaux), Lyrique, 3 Nov 1859

Le neveu de Gulliver (oc, 3, Boisseaux), Lyrique, 22 Oct 1861

La farce de maître Villon (oc, 1, M. Delaporte and F. Langlé), Athénée, 30 Dec 1872

Pierrot ténor (operette, 1, Langlé and J. Ruelle), Enghien, Casino, 1 July 1876

Les oiseaux en cage (oc, 1, C. Nuitter), 1878

Monsieur de Floridor (oc, 1, Nuitter and E. Tréfeu, after L. Anseaume: *L'ivrogne corrigé*), OC (Favart), 11 Oct 1880, vs (Paris, *c*1881)

Le portrait (oc, 2, M. Laurencin and J. Adenis), OC (Favart), 18 June 1883, vs (Paris, *c*1883)

Le roi de carreau (oc, 3, E. Leterrier and A. Vanloo), Nouveautés, 26 Oct 1883, vs (Paris, *c*1883)

La boîte à musique (oc, 1, Nuitter and A. de Beaumont), 1884 (Paris, *c*1884)

Les deux Toinon (oc, 1, Adenis), OC (Favart), spr. 1885/6 (Paris, *c*1886)

Madam Scapin, unperf., unpubd

Doubtful: Maître Patholin, 1855; Mlle Marguerite s.v.p., 1868; La rose pompom, 1888; La devineresse   STEVEN HUEBNER

Lake George Opera Festival. Summer festival held in QUEENSBURY, New York.

Lakes, Gary (*b* Dallas, TX, 26 Sept 1950). American tenor. He studied at Seattle, where he made his début in 1981 as Froh. After winning the Melchior Auditions at

'Lakmé' (Delibes): scenes from the original production at the Opéra-Comique (Salle Favart), Paris, 14 April 1883; engraving from 'L'illustration' (28 April 1883)

the Juilliard School, New York, he sang Florestan in Mexico City (1983), Achilles (*Iphigénie en Aulide*) at Waterloo, New Jersey (1984), and Samson in Charlotte, North Carolina (1985). He made his Metropolitan début in 1986 as the High Priest (*Idomeneo*), returning as Walther von der Vogelweide, Bacchus, Grigory, Siegmund, Florestan and Parsifal. He sang Aeneas at Lyons (1987) and Samson at the Châtelet, Paris (1991). Magnard's *Guercoeur* is among his recordings. With an imposing stage presence and a powerful, brilliant tone, he excels in French as well as German heroic tenor roles.

ELIZABETH FORBES

Laki, Krisztina (*b* Budapest, 16 Sept 1944). Hungarian soprano. She studied in Budapest and made her début in 1976 at Berne as Gilda. Engaged next at Düsseldorf and Cologne, she made her British début in 1979 at Glyndebourne as Aminta (*Die schweigsame Frau*), and later sang Lucile (*Dantons Tod*) at Salzburg (1980) and Sophie (*Der Rosenkavalier*) at the Opéra (1984). She has also sung in Milan, Oslo, Stuttgart and Prague. Her repertory includes Clymene (Jommelli's *Fetonte*), the Queen of Night, Zerlina, Susanna, Carolina (*Il matrimonio segreto*), Marzelline, Nannetta and Zdenka. She has a voice of exceptional range and flexibility.

ELIZABETH FORBES

Lakmé. Opéra in three acts by LÉO DELIBES to a libretto by EDMOND GONDINET and PHILIPPE GILLE after PIERRE LOTI's novel *Rarahu*; Paris, Opéra-Comique (Salle Favart), 14 April 1883.

The idea for *Lakmé* came from Edmond Gondinet. He wanted to write an opera libretto for the young American soprano Marie van Zandt, whose success in Thomas' *Mignon* in 1880 had created a great stir. He

suggested to Delibes an adaptation of Pierre Loti's recent novel, *Rarahu*, also known as *Le mariage de Loti*. Delibes read the novel on a train journey to Vienna and immediately agreed. He composed the score between July 1881 and June 1882, and the première the following April was a resounding success. Jean-Alexandre Talazac sang the role of Gérald. *Lakmé* remained in the repertory of the Opéra-Comique for some 80 years and was quickly produced on other stages.

The setting is British India. Lakmé (soprano) is the daughter of Nilakantha (bass-baritone), a Brahmin priest who thirsts for revenge against the occupying British. A group of English people wander near Nilakantha's home: two officers, Frédéric (baritone) and Gérald (tenor), Miss Ellen, Gérald's fiancée (soprano), her cousin Rose (soprano) and their governess Mistress Bentson (mezzo-soprano). When the others move on, Gérald remains behind and is discovered by Lakmé as she returns to her house. He is instantly entranced by her mysterious beauty. Lakmé too is moved. But he has to flee at the approach of Nilakantha, who swears vengeance when he finds his ground has been profaned by unknown intruders.

Act 2 is set in a market place. The two officers are shortly to be posted to a distant province. Mingling with the crowd is Nilakantha who has asked his daughter Lakmé to sing to attract the intruder. She breaks off, fainting, when she sees Gérald in the crowd. Gérald rushes forward to support her: Nilakantha stabs him and flees.

In Act 3 Lakmé's loyal servant Hadji (tenor) has sheltered the wounded Gérald in the forest, where Lakmé comes to tend him. While she is fetching water from the sacred spring that will seal their love, Frédéric comes to recall Gérald to his duty. Gérald agrees.

Lakmé, returning, knows that he will desert her, so she snatches a poisonous datura leaf and swallows it. When Gérald realises that she is dying for her love, he drinks from the sacred cup as a vow of fidelity as she dies, and Nilakantha is thwarted.

The opera brings together many favourite features of the age: an exotic location (already popular from Bizet's *Les pêcheurs de perles* and Massenet's *Le roi de Lahore*), a fanatical priest figure, the mysterious pagan rituals of the Hindus and their bewitching flora, and the novelty of exotically colonial English people. There are many similarities with Meyerbeer's *L'Africaine*. The plot rests on the conflicts felt by both lovers: her loyalty to her religion, his obligations to his regiment. Both yield to the fatality of love. Delibes treats the passionate elements in his story with warm and expressive music and reserves oriental colour for scenes of incantation and ceremony, for prayers and dances and for the tumultuous market scene, often with modal scales. The music is always reserved and tasteful, deftly orchestrated and imbued with many subtle harmonic colours. The most celebrated numbers are the duet 'Dôme épais' for Lakmé and her servant Mallika (mezzo-soprano) in Act 1 and Lakmé's 'Légende' in Act 2, 'Où va la jeune Hindoue', known as the Bell Song, with its tinkling coloratura. The characters of Nilakantha and Gérald are firmly, if conventionally, drawn. The influence of Meyerbeer and Bizet is clear, yet Delibes shows a distinctive original gift in *Lakmé* at a higher level than in the more familiar ballets *Coppélia* and *Sylvia*.

HUGH MACDONALD

Lalande [La Lande, de La Lande, Delalande], **Michel-Richard de** (*b* Paris, 15 Dec 1657; *d* Versailles, 18 June 1726). French composer. From Alexander Tannevot's *Preface, ou Discours sur la vie et les ouvrages de M. De la Lande* in the 1729 edition of Lalande's *grands motets* we learn that the composer came from a family of tailors and that his brother François also became a musician. From the mid-1660s Michel-Richard studied with François Chaperon at the choir school of St German-l'Auxerrois. After leaving the school in 1672 Lalande pursued a career as a violinist until Lully rejected his application to play in the Opéra orchestra, when he turned instead to the organ and sacred music. While exact dates are uncertain, in the late 1670s and early 1680s Lalande served as organist in four churches in Paris: St Gervais, Petit St Antoine, St Paul and St Jean-en-Grève. In the early 1680s he also composed *intermèdes* for spoken tragedies for the Jesuit school in Paris, a collaboration which undoubtedly led to his only commission in Paris for a secular work, the divertissement *L'amour berger* for the Duc de Duras in 1683.

Lalande's first employment at court was as harpsichord teacher to the two daughters of Louis XIV and Mme de Montespan, Mlle de Nantes and Mlle de Blois. Montespan and her sister Mme de Thianges supported the composer's first secular works for court, *La sérénade* (1682), *Les fontaines de Versailles* (1683) and *Le concert d'Esculape* (1683). In 1683 he also received his first continuing appointment, as *maître* in the royal chapel, where he eventually occupied seven posts. He married the court singer Anne Rebel in July 1684; their two daughters, Marie Anne (*b* 1686) and Jeanne (*b* 1687), also became singers. In 1685 Lalande attained the first of his seven positions in the court's *musique de la chambre*, as *compositeur*, and consequently wrote *Epithalame* for the wedding of the Duc

de Bourbon and Mlle de Nantes. His court production *Le ballet de la jeunesse* replaced Lully's *Armide* as the official carnival entertainment in 1686, perpetuating the rivalry between the two composers. Lalande's ballet *Le palais de Flore* (1689) confirmed his position at court as the leading composer for the stage and coincided with his nomination as *surintendant de la musique de la chambre*.

Throughout the remainder of Louis XIV's reign Lalande steadily acquired additional positions in the *musique de la chambre*, as *compositeur* in 1690, 1700 and 1709 and as *maître* in 1695 and 1709. In the 1709 appointments he succeeded Collasse, Lully's student. Only two short secular compositions are known to have been composed by Lalande in the early 1690s, the *Ballet de M. De la Lande* and the *Ballet de St Louis*. With the close of the War of the League of Augsburg the scope of his stage works expanded somewhat in the pastorals *Adonis* (1696) and *L'amour, fléchy par la constance* (1697), both of which remained under Louis' direct sponsorship but were performed at Fontainebleau rather than Versailles. His next stage works, the ballets *Mirtil et Mélicerte* (1698) and *La comédie des fées* (1699), also at Fontainebleau, were officially endorsed by Louis' son, the Dauphin, while Mme de Maintenon sponsored his final three secular works honouring Louis XIV, the *mascarade Hymen Champestre* (1700) at Marly, the *Ode* (1704) at Sceaux, and *Divertissement sur la Paix* (1713) at Marly. According to the Marquis de Sourches, in 1710 Lalande suffered a stroke. The following year the composer's daughters died during the same smallpox epidemic that claimed several members of Louis' family.

Revitalized artistic life in Paris after Louis XIV's death in 1715 granted Lalande more public recognition for his stage works than he had ever known previously. His three Regency-period court ballets, *L'inconnu* (1720), *Les folies de Cardenio* (1720) and *Les élémens* (1721, with Destouches), were grand productions designed to present the young Louis XV to the court and the city. The composer eventually resigned several court positions and named his students André Destouches and François Collin de Blamont to succeed him in others on his death. Anne Rebel died in 1722 and the following year Lalande married Marie-Louise Cury, by whom he had a daughter, Marie Michelle, in 1724. He died of pneumonia in 1726 after 43 years in service to the court.

Lalande's 19 known secular works are a good index of musical stage productions at court during the generation after Lully, since they reflect vacillations in the artistic and financial priorities of the court. Some of his early works are among his grander ones, produced in a court still for the most part at peace, while the smaller middle-period productions reflect the country's straitened wartime finances. The Regency court ballets, Lalande's most lavish productions, appropriately marked the end of the career of one of the court's most valued musicians.

Lalande wrote no *tragédies lyriques*, undoubtedly because of Lully's domination of the genre. Instead, his secular theatrical works, all non-tragic, can be classified generally as either ballets (works with dance) or *concerts*. Most were based on subjects related to current court events and so were not revived after their initial cycle of performances. On the other hand, his *grands motets* were among the most frequently performed compositions at the Concert Spirituel throughout the 18th century.

Unlike the motets, Lalande's stage works are stylistically conservative: they did not significantly advance beyond the Lullian approach to non-tragic stage entertainment. Furthermore, there is little musical distinction between his ballets and his *concerts*, the major difference being that the *concerts* were not staged, and generally included no dance, pantomime, costumes or scenery. His vocal writing emphasizes solo recitative and air, particularly in the *concerts*. Choruses, which appear in most works, are in a typically Lullian homophonic, four- and five-voice texture, usually with orchestral accompaniment. Ensembles are the least common of the vocal passages. Instrumental writing is usually in five-part string texture, with pairs of woodwinds, continuo and sometimes percussion. The ballets contain a higher proportion of instrumental music than the *concerts*. Most works are sectional, the *concerts* usually in several scenes performed without interruption, the ballets containing on average four to six independent entrées, allowing *Jeunesse*, *Mirtil*, *Fées*, *Inconnu* and *Cardenio* to be performed between the acts of spoken stage plays.

Lalande collaborated with other artists on all productions. Nine different authors have been identified, among them Florent Dancourt, the Abbé Genest and Antoine Morel. Pierre Beauchamps choreographed at least four of the earlier ballets, including *Jeunesse* and *Palais*, and Jean Balon the three Regency productions, while the Bérain workshop probably created any stage sets and costumes.

The number of identified performers in Lalande's productions ranged widely: 10 to 20 in some of the *concerts*, such as *Esculape* and *Ode*, but 100 to 175 in ballets such as *Jeunesse* and *Cardenio*. Singers and instrumentalists were from the court's chamber music establishment, while some of the ballets, produced during the final decades of the 150-year tradition of court ballet in France, included both courtiers and professional dancers. Performance sites varied from small chambers such as Mme de Maintenon's Versailles apartment to theatres, including the tiny Salle de Comédie at Versailles for *Jeunesse* and the immense Salle des Machines in the Tuileries Palace for *Cardenio*.

See also AMOUR, FLÉCHY PAR LA CONSTANCE, L' and ELÉMENS, LES.

La sérénade (?concert, L'abbé Genest), Fontainebleau, aut. 1682
L'amour berger (?ballet, prol., 3, Marquis de Lomagne), Paris, Hôtel de Duras, carn. 1683, 2 airs in *Mercure galant* (1683)
Les fontaines de Versailles (concert, 5 scenes, A. Morel), Versailles, 5 April 1683, *F-Pn*
Le concert d'Esculape (concert, 1, Morel), Versailles, May 1683, *Pn*
Epithalame (?concert, 1, L'abbé Genest), Versailles, 25 July 1685
Le ballet de la jeunesse (ballet, prol., 3 intermèdes, F. Dancourt), Versailles, 28 Jan 1686, *Pa*, *V* (R forthcoming: FO, ix)
Le palais de Flore (ballet, 5 entrées), Trianon, 5 Jan 1689, *Pn*
Ballet de M. De la Lande (?concert), ?Versailles, 1690–91, *Pn*
Ballet de St Louis (?concert), ?Versailles, 1690–91, *Pn*
Adonis (concert, 10 scenes), Fontainebleau, aut. 1696, *Pn*
L'amour, fléchy par la constance (pastorale, 9 scenes), Fontainebleau, aut. 1697, *LYm*
Mirtil et Mélicerte (ballet, prol., 3 intermèdes, N. A. M. Guérin), Fontainebleau, Oct 1698, *Pn*
La comédie des fées (ballet, prol., 3 intermèdes, Dancourt), Fontainebleau, 24 Sept 1699, *Pn*
Hymen Champestre (ballet, 4 entrées, [?J.-B.] Rousseau), Marly, 13 Feb 1700, *Pn*
Ode (concert, ?1 scene, Genest), Sceaux, Oct 1704, *Pn*
Divertissement [Ballet] sur la Paix (concert, 4 entrées, H.-B. de Roqueleyne), Marly, July 1713, *Pn*
L'inconnu (ballet, 6 entrées, Dancourt), Paris, Tuileries, Feb 1720, *Pn*, vocal and inst airs (Paris, 1720); incl. music by Campra, Bertin de la Doué, Destouches, Rebel

Les folies de Cardenio (ballet, prol., 3 entrées, C. A. Coypel), Paris, Tuileries, Dec 1720, *Pn*
Les élémens (opéra-ballet, prol., 4 entrées, P.-C. Roy), Paris, Tuileries, 31 Dec 1721; rev. version, Paris, Opéra, 29 May 1725, *Pn* (R forthcoming: FO, xvi), reduced score (Paris, 1725, 2/1742); collab. Destouches; ed. in *Chefs-d'oeuvre classiques de l'opéra français*, xiv (Leipzig, 1880)

E. Barbier: *Journal historique et anecdotique du règne de Louis XV* (Paris, 1847–56)
P. Dangeau: *Mémoires de la cour de France* (Paris, 1854)
M. Marais: *Journal et mémoires sur le régence et le règne de Louis XV (1715–37)* (Paris, 1863–8)
N. Dufourcq, ed.: *Notes et références pour servir à une histoire de Michel-Richard Delalande* (Paris, 1957)
——: 'Quelques réflexions sur les ballets et divertissements de Michel Delalande,' *Divertissements de cour au XVIIe siècle* (Paris, 1957), 44–52
H. Bert: 'Un Ballet de Michel-Richard Delalande,' *XVIIe*, xxxiv (1957), 58–72
B. Coeyman: *The Stage Works of Michel-Richard Delalande in the Musical-Cultural Context of the French Court, 1680–1726* (New York, 1987)
——: Preface to M.-R. Delalande: *Ballet de la jeunesse*, FO, ix (in preparation)
BARBARA COEYMAN

Lalli, (Benedetto) Domenico [Biancardi, (Nicolò) Sebastiano] (*b* Naples, 27 March 1679; *d* Venice, 9 Oct 1741). Italian librettist. He fled from Naples in 1706, when he was accused of having taken money from the treasury of the brotherhood of the Annunziata, where he had been employed. Seeking refuge in Rome, he met the composer Emanuele d'Astorga, and together they wandered throughout Italy. He adopted the pseudonym Domenico Lalli in 1709. In Venice Lalli wrote several poems and librettos and was impresario at the S Samuele and S Giovanni Grisostomo theatres. In the early 1720s he worked at the archiepiscopal court at Salzburg, and from 1727 to 1740 served as court poet to the Elector of Bavaria. During these years he made the acquaintance of Metastasio and Goldoni, and the latter often praised him for his 'poetic genius'.

One of Lalli's greatest achievements was in 1711, when his *Elisa* (with music by G. M. Ruggieri) became the first comic opera to be performed in Venice. In fact *opera buffa* had existed as early as 1706 in Naples (Faggioli's *La Cilla*), and at least one scholar considers that the text of *Elisa* may have been taken from an even earlier Neapolitan comedy by N. Amenta. Yet regardless of where Lalli acquired his understanding of the genre, and despite the fact that comic opera did not flourish in Venice until later, his importance lay in the initial step he took in presenting comic opera to the Venetians. With the exception of *Elisa* most of his texts adhered faithfully to the 18th-century convention of developing character relationships. In addition to the works listed below, he adapted texts by Minato, Zeno and Metastasio which were set by Hasse and Galuppi, and also wrote texts and some music for serenatas, cantatas, festive occasions, dedications and sacred and other works.

L'amor tirannico, F. Gasparini, 1710 (Feo, 1713; Orlandini, 1713; Handel, 1720, as *Radamisto*; Chelleri and G. Porta, 1722); *Elisa*, G. M. Ruggieri, 1711; *I veri amici* (with F. Silvani), A. Paulati, 1713 (A. M. Bononcini, 1715; Vivaldi, 1720, as *Candace*; Albinoni, 1722; Fiorè and Giai, 1728; Leo, 1731, as *Evergete*; Lampugnani, 1732, as *Candace*; Galuppi, 1747, as *Evergete*); *Il gran mogol*, F. Mancini, 1713 (Porta, 1717, as *Argippo*; Fiorè, 1722, as *Argippo*); *Ottone in Villa*, Vivaldi, 1713; *Il Pisistrato*, L. Leo, 1714
Il Tigrane (dramma), A. Scarlatti, 1715 (Albinoni, 1716, as *L'amor di figlio non conosciuto*; Keiser, 1717, as *Tomyris*); *Arsilda regina di Ponto*, Vivaldi, 1716; *Farnace*, C. F. Pollarolo, 1718 (Leo,

1736); *Il Cambise* (dramma), Scarlatti, 1719; *Il pentimento generoso*, Fiorè, 1719; *Gli eccessi dell'infedeltà*, A. Caldara, 1720; *La verità in cimento* (with G. Palazzi), Vivaldi, 1720; *Filippo re di Macedonia*, Vivaldi and G. Boniventi, 1721; *Camaide, imperatore della China*, with int *La marchesina di Nanchin*, Caldara, 1722

Gli eccessi della gelosia, Albinoni, 1722; *Timocrate*, Leo, 1723; *Damiro e Pitia*, N. Porpora, 1724; *Ulisse*, Porta, 1725 (Treu, 1726, as Ulisse e Telemacco); *Turia Lucrezia*, A. Pollardo, 1726; *L'Epaminonda* (dramma per musica), P. Torri, 1727; *Argene*, Leo, 1728; *Nicomede* (dramma per musica), Torri, 1728; *Edippo* (tragedia per musica), Torri, 1729; *Onorio* (with G. Boldini), F. Ciampi, 1729; *Sulpizia fedele* (with Boldini), A. Pollarolo, 1729; *L'Ippolito* (tragedia per musica), Torri, 1731

*

ES (M. Bogianckino)

O. G. Sonneck: *The Library of Congress: Catalogue of Opera Librettos Printed before 1800*, ii (Washington DC, 1914), 1300–01

F. Walker: 'Astorga and a Neapolitan Librettist', *MMR*, lxxxi (1951), 90–96

B. Brizi: 'Domenico Lalli librettista di Vivaldi?', *Vivaldi veneziano europeo*, ed. F. Degrada (Florence, 1980), 183–204

J. W. Hill: Introduction to Vivaldi: *Ottone in villa*, DMV, xii (Milan, 1983)

L. Bianconi and G. La Face Bianconi, eds.: *I libretti italiani di Georg Friedrich Händel e le loro fonti* (Florence, 1992–)

WENDY N. GIBNEY

Lallouette [Lalouette], **Jean François** (*b* Paris, 1651; *d* Paris, 31 Aug 1728). French composer. He studied composition with Lully, who appointed him as his secretary and as time-beater at the Opéra and asked him to fill in the inner parts of certain of his works, a task at which he became so adept that he began to attract attention. When he reportedly boasted of having written some of the best parts of Lully's *Isis* (1677) he was dismissed. *Isis*, however, displeased Louis XIV because of its thinly disguised and unflattering portrayal of Mme de Montespan in the character of Juno. The work was withdrawn, not to be performed again until 1704, and Philippe Quinault, the librettist, also was dismissed. Lully came through the affair unscathed, and one must wonder if Lallouette was a scapegoat. He was appointed composer of French music to the Savoy court at Turin in 1678, but was dismissed in 1679, possibly because in over a year he had produced only one composition, a three-part serenata, performed on 14 May 1678. He probably returned to Paris, where he composed an opera (*c*1678–80, Paris; lost); on 27 January 1681 the king's secretary wrote to a M. de la Régnie informing him that the king forbade further performances of it on the grounds that it violated Lully's privilege. Lallouette competed unsuccessfully in 1683 for one of the four positions of *sous-maître* at the royal chapel. The post was awarded to Pascal Collasse, who had succeeded him as Lully's secretary; it is likely that Lully intervened on Collasse's behalf and against Lallouette.

Lallouette later visited Rome and served in ecclesiastical posts in Paris and Rouen; between 1695 and 1700, according to one source, he was busy with a four-act opera, *Europe*. In 1700 he became choirmaster of Notre Dame, Paris, succeeding Capra. In his day Lallouette was a respected and popular musician and teacher. Among his stage works, all now lost, were also ballet airs and incidental music; most of his surviving music is sacred. His works were thought to be well composed and to display a certain originality.

*

Mercure galant (1677–1728)

J. L. Le Cerf de la Viéville: *Comparaison de la musique italienne et de la musique françoise* (Brussels, 1704–6; repr. in P. Bourdelot

and P. Bonnet-Bourdelot: *Histoire de la musique et de ses effets*, ii–iv (Amsterdam, 1721)

P. Bourdelot and P. Bonnet-Bourdelot: *Histoire de la musique et de ses effets*, ed. J. Bonnet (Paris, 1715, 7/1743)

E. Titon du Tillet: *Le Parnasse françoise* (Paris, 1732)

J.-B. de La Borde: *Essai sur la musique ancienne et moderne* (Paris, 1780)

L. E. S. J. de Laborde: *Musiciens de Paris, 1535–1792*, ed. Y. de Brossard (Paris, 1965)

M.-T. Bouquet: 'Quelques relations musicales franco-piémontaises au XXVIIe et au XVIIIe siècles', *RMFC*, x (1970), 5–18

M. Benoit: *Musiques de cour: chapelle, chambre, écurie, 1661–1733* (Paris, 1971)

R. M. Isherwood: *Music in the Service of the King* (Ithaca, NY, and London, 1973)

WILLIAM HAYS, ERIC MULARD

Lalo, Edouard(**-Victoire-Antoine**) (*b* Lille, 27 Jan 1823; *d* Paris, 22 April 1892). French composer. He studied at the Lille Conservatoire and then went at the age of 16 to Paris. He attended Habeneck's violin class at the Conservatoire and made a living for many years as a violinist and teacher. He was a founder member of the Armingaud quartet in which he played the viola and later second violin. His early compositions were songs and chamber music; two early symphonies were apparently destroyed. His interest in opera was aroused by his marriage in 1865 to a singer, Julie Besnier de Maligny. He at once embarked on his first stage work, the *grand opéra Fiesque*, which was completed in 1868 and submitted to a competition for performance at the Théâtre Lyrique. Its failure to win the prize or to be staged in any theatre had a deeply discouraging effect on Lalo. Success might have led to a productive career as an opera composer, but he made his name instead in the field of instrumental music, which was fortunately then, in the 1870s, experiencing a bright renaissance in France under Saint-Saëns' leadership. His friendship with Pablo Sarasate led him to write a number of violin concertos, including the popular *Symphonie espagnole*.

In 1875 he composed a second opera, *Le roi d'Ys*, on a Breton legend (his wife was from Brittany), but this too, like *Fiesque*, was refused a performance. The commission of a ballet, *Namouna*, by the Opéra in 1881 was intended as compensation for this refusal. *Le roi d'Ys* was not staged until 1888, when Lalo finally, at the age of 65, experienced success in the theatre. Ironically, now that theatres were opening their doors to his music, his creativity had all but withered, so that his last two stage works were neither original nor successful. *Néron* (1891) was a *pantomime* drawn almost entirely from recycled parts of *Fiesque*; and *La jacquerie*, an opera set during the French peasants' revolt of 1358, also drew on *Fiesque*. Lalo lived to complete only Act 1; it was staged in Monte Carlo in 1895 with the remainder composed by Arthur Coquard.

Lalo's style is robust and forceful, and his fresh rhythmic and harmonic invention make his two early operas impressive, stageworthy works. He was accused, like all progressive composers of his time, of imitating Wagner, but although he admired Wagner, their styles have little in common. As Lalo himself said: 'It's hard enough doing my own kind of music and making sure that it's good enough. If I started to do someone else's I'm sure it would be appalling'. It is certainly a pity that circumstances did not encourage him to compose more for the stage, and a pity too that *Fiesque* still awaits its first performance.

See also FIESQUE and ROI D'YS, LE.

printed works published in Paris

Fiesque, 1866–8 (grand opéra, 3, C. Beauquier, after F. von Schiller: *Die Verschwörung des Fiesco zu Genua*), unperf., vs (1872)
Le roi d'Ys, 1875–88 (opéra, 3, E. Blau), Paris, OC (Favart), 7 May 1888, vs (1888), full score (n.d.)
Néron (pantomime, 3, P. Milliet), Paris, Hippodrome, 28 March 1891, *F-Pn* [drawn from Fiesque and other works]
La jacquerie, 1891–2 [Act 1] (opéra, 4, Blau and S. Arnaud); completed by Coquard, Monte Carlo, 9 March 1895, vs (1894)

*

A. Pougin: 'Edouard Lalo', *Le ménestrel*, lviii (1892), 139
M. Dufour: *Edouard Lalo* (Lille, 1908)
O. Seré [J. Poueigh]: *Musiciens français d'aujourd'hui* (Paris, 1911, 8/1921) [incl. bibliography to 1921]
P. Dukas: 'Edouard Lalo', *ReM*, iv/5 (1923), 97–107
A. Jullien: 'Quelques lettres inédites de Lalo', *ReM*, iv/5 (1923), 108–17
P. Lalo: 'La vie d'Édouard Lalo', *ReM*, iv/5 (1923), 118–24
G. Servières: *Edouard Lalo* (Paris, 1925)
G. Schulz: 'A Northern Legend', *ON*, xxiv/14 (1959–60), 12
L'avant-scène opéra, no.65 (1984) [*Le roi d'Ys*]
H. Macdonald: 'A Fiasco Remembered: *Fiesque* Dismembered', *Slavonic and Western Music: Essays for Gerald Abraham* (Ann Arbor, 1985), 163–85
E. Lalo: *Correspondance*, ed. J.-M. Fauquet (Paris, 1989)
HUGH MACDONALD

Laloy, Louis (*b* Gray, Haute-Saône, 18 Feb 1874; *d* Dôle, 4 March 1944). French musicologist and administrator. He studied at the Schola Cantorum, Paris. From 1914 he was secretary general of the Paris Opéra (coinciding with Jacques Rouché's long reign as director). Between 1936 and 1941 he was professor of music history at the Conservatoire. He was also an influential music critic for several French journals. A friend of many leading French composers, Laloy provided the scenario for Ravel's ballet *Ma mère l'oye*, the text for Debussy's *Ode à la France* and the libretto for Roussel's opera-ballet *Padmâvatî*. Among his writings are books on Debussy, Rameau, Chinese music and dance at the Opéra.   RONALD CRICHTON

Lamb, Andrew (Martin) (*b* Oldham, 23 Sept 1942). English writer. He studied mathematics at Oxford; by profession an investment manager, he is a noted authority on the lighter forms of music theatre. He has written lucidly and extensively on the musical comedy and the zarzuela as well as the operetta and has published many articles in reference works (including the *Grove* dictionaries) and periodicals on the American musical theatre, Sullivan and particularly Offenbach; he was one of the collaborators on *Gänzl's Book of the Musical Theatre* (London, 1988) and has written a short study *Jerome Kern in Edwardian London* (Brooklyn, 1985).

Lambardi, Mario (*fl* 1895–1915). Italian impresario. His touring group, the Lambardi Opera Company, were active in the Caribbean and the USA from late 1896 until 1913 or 1914. Their first tour started in the small seaport of Puerto Cabello, Venezuela, in December 1896, and eventually included stops in San José, Curaçao, Maracaibo, Barranquilla, Cartagena, Panama City, Guayaquil, Quito and Lima. They were on the road for at least a year, and probably much longer. In 1899–1901 they toured Mexico, the USA, Cuba, Jamaica and Peru. During the next few years they appeared mostly in Latin America, going as far south as Lima and Valparaíso in 1904. They returned to the USA in 1906–7, performing primarily on the west coast. Several more tours followed, during which they frequently combined destinations in the USA with others in Central America or the Caribbean. In March 1913 they went to Hawaii, giving 14 works in a three-week season.   TOM KAUFMAN

Lambelet, Edouardos [Edoardo] (*b* ?1820; *d* Piraeus, 6 May 1903). Greek composer, father of Napoleon Lambelet. He studied reportedly in Bologna (possibly at the Liceo Filarmonico), and in Corfu with Mantzaros, becoming one of that composer's most renowned disciples. From an undated letter (reproduced by Grekas) written by Isabella Galleti-Gianoli, who sang the leading soprano role in *Olema la schiava*, it is clear that after 1857 Lambelet had settled in Naples, where his operas are said to have been performed; he later returned to Greece, however, where most of his manuscripts were lost during a flood. His three operas, all on Italian texts, were important items of the early Greek opera repertory. Both *Olema la schiava* and *Il castello maledetto* were composed for the S Giacomo Theatre, Corfu. Galleti-Gianoli praised *Olema la schiava* for its 'nobility of inspiration, the perfection of the form and the sensitive and flowing melody'.

L'orfana, ? before 1857, lost
Olema la schiava (3, L. Chierici), Corfu, S Giacomo, 1857, lost, lib. (Corfu, n.d.)
Il castello maledetto (3, G. Markoras), Corfu, S Giacomo, 25 Dec 1862, lost, lib. (Corfu, 1862)

*

A. S. Theodoropoulou: 'Lambelet, Edouardos', *Megali elliniki engyklopaedia* [Great Greek Encyclopaedia] (Athens, 1931)
G. Leotsakos: 'Lambelet, Napoleon', *Ekpedeftiki elliniki engyklopaedia* [Educational Greek Encyclopedia], v: *Pangosmio viografiko lexiko* (Athens, 1986)

For further bibliography *see* LAMBELET, NAPOLEON.
GEORGE LEOTSAKOS

Lambelet, Napoleon (*b* Corfu, 27 Feb 1864; *d* London, 25 Sept 1932). Greek composer and conductor. After studying at the S Pietro a Majella Conservatory in Naples he taught singing at the Athens Conservatory (1886–7). In 1887 he established a private music school and a chorus, which led to the formation of the so-called First Elliniko Melodrama, the earliest all-Greek opera company. He conducted the company in the Athenian première of Xyndas's *O ypopsifios vouleftis* ('The Candidate Deputy') in Boukourous on 14 March 1888, generally considered to be the 'birthday' of Greek lyrical theatre. His manifold activities (choral concerts, composition, and performance of stage music and opera) created a climate which prompted the Greek public to embrace the cause of a national lyric theatre. His music for the stage included *komidhyllia*, musical comedies based on foreign archetypes but using characters and manners from Greek life. In 1894 he was in Alexandria, teaching and conducting.

In June 1895, at the instigation of a music-loving English nobleman, he left Egypt to direct the choir of the Greek orthodox church of St Sophia in London. At least five of his works were presented at London theatres. As well as a keen theatrical sense, these display the ease with which he entered the world of Sullivan, Edward German and Sidney Jones (into whose score for *The Geisha* one of Lambelet's songs was interpolated). Yet, whenever the subject allowed, Lambelet did not forget his Greek identity; passages or whole numbers in modes with augmented 2nds give to the gypsies in *Fenella*, for example, a quintessentially Greek character.

I mylonades [The Millers] (komidhyllion, after an It. comedy), Athens, Euterpe, 22 July 1888, lost

I ikoyenia Paradarmenou [The Paradarmenos Family] (komidhyllion, H. Anninos), Athens, Omonoia, 9 Sept 1892, lost

The Yashmak, a Story of the East (2, C. Raleigh and S. Hicks; R. Carse, Hicks, A. J. Morris and others), London, Shaftesbury, 31 March 1897, vs (London, 1897), collab. 11 others

The Transit of Venus (musical comedy, 2, J. T. Tanner; A. Ross), Dublin, 9 April 1898, vs (London, 1898)

Pot-pourri, an 1899 Review (Tanner; W. H. Risque), London, Avenue, 1899, vs (London, 1899)

The Shadow Dance (operetta, B. Landek), London, Princess's, Oct 1901

Fenella (operetta, 1, A. N. Cleveland), London, Coliseum, 18 Dec 1905, vs (London, 1906)

Yellow Fog Island (musical and satirical play, 2, A. Sturgess), London, Terry's, 29 Sept 1906

To oniro tou Pierrotou [Pierrot's Dream], Athens, 9 Feb 1916

Valentine (romantic comedy op, 2, A. Davenport and C. Wibrow; Davenport), London, St James's, 24 Jan 1918, vs (London, 1918)

*

GänzlBMT

N. I. Laskaris: Istoria tou neoellinikou theatrou [History of Modern Greek Theatre] (Athens, 1938–9)

A. Hadjiapostolou: Istoria tou ellinikou melodramatos [History of Greek Melodrama] (Athens, 1949)

I. Grekas: 'Mia megali ikoyenia moussikon stin Ellada' [An Important Family of Musicians in Greece], Piraeus 1960: zoi ke techni (Piraeus, 1960), 161–80

T. Hadjipandazis: To komidhyllio [The Komidhyllion] (Athens, 1981)

G. Leotsakos: 'Lambelet, Napoleon', Ekpedeftiki elliniki engyklopaedia [Educational Greek Encyclopedia], v: Pangosmio viografiko lexiko (Athens, 1986)   GEORGE LEOTSAKOS

Lamberti, Giorgio (Casellato-) (b Adria, 9 July 1938). Italian tenor. He studied in Mantua, and made his début in 1964 at the Rome Opera as Henri (Les vêpres siciliennes). In 1965 he sang in the première of Zafred's Wallenstein in Rome and made his American début as Radames in Chicago. He has sung at La Scala and all the other principal Italian theatres, and in Vienna, Berlin, Hamburg, Paris, Brussels, Zürich, Geneva, Bonn and Buenos Aires. After his Metropolitan début in 1974 as Cavaradossi, he returned as Enzo (La Gioconda) and Turiddu; he first sang at Covent Garden in 1979, as Don Carlos. His repertory ranges from Donizetti's Edgardo and Poliuto to Lohengrin and Tannhäuser, and from Pollione to Calaf and Des Grieux; it includes Verdi's Jacopo Foscari, Arvino (I Lombardi), Ernani, Manrico, Riccardo, Gabriele Adorno and Don Alvaro. He has a strong, supple voice, but lacks dramatic involvement.

ELIZABETH FORBES

Lament (It. lamento). Usually, a vocal piece based on a mournful text, often built over a descending tetrachord ostinato and common in operas of the Baroque period.

Originating in ancient Greek drama and further developed in Latin poetry, the lament topos enjoyed a privileged status in European literature. Set apart as an exceptional moment of emotional climax of particularly intense expression, it provided an occasion for special formal development and for the display of expressive rhetoric and of affective imagery.

Librettists and composers of early opera acknowledged the special dramatic position and affective responsibility of the lament, distinguishing it from the narrative flow of its context: librettists imposed greater formality through using more strongly metred and rhymed texts in which particularly emotive lines often recurred as refrains; and composers interpreted these texts with greater freedom, repeating or otherwise enhancing specially expressive words or phrases with melodic sequence, dissonance or textural conflicts, often imposing an overall tonal coherence to create structural self-sufficiency. One of the most effective and clearly the most influential of early 17th-century laments was Monteverdi's Lamento d'Arianna from his opera to a libretto by Ottavio Rinuccini, performed in Mantua in 1608. Its musical isolation from its context was recognized immediately in contemporary descriptions of the opera's performance and confirmed by the publication of monodic Ariadne laments by other composers, as well as Monteverdi's own arrangement of it as a madrigal.

In the Venetian opera repertory of the 1640s an association between lament and tetrachord became explicit. Cavalli's 27 operas, the most comprehensive surviving musical documentation of Venetian opera from 1640 to 1660, confirm this association. Cavalli's earliest laments, like those of Monteverdi's operas, are in continuous recitative style, heightened by dissonance and affective text repetition and structured primarily by refrains. But after Apollo's lament from Gli amori di Apollo e di Dafne (1640), partly in free recitative, partly based on the descending tetrachord, Cavalli began to employ the bass pattern consistently in laments, which initially occupied a specific position at the dramatic climax immediately preceding the resolution of the plot. Characterized by a slow tempo, highly accented triple metre and usually accompanied by strings, they use the tetrachord in a variety of ways, ranging from strict ostinato treatment of the simple pattern to freer treatment of one of its variants, such as a chromatic or inverted version. They all exploit the tetrachord as a source of harmonic, melodic and rhythmic dissonance created by suspensions, syncopation and overlapping phrases between the voice and the bass. The popular success of such arias is indicated by their proliferation – accompanied by a loss of specific dramatic function – during the 1650s and 1660s, to the point where some operas contain as many as four laments spread over their three acts (e.g. Cavalli's Statira, 1655, and Eliogabalo, composed 1668).

Pathetic lament arias, many of them associated with some form of the tetrachord bass, continued to occur in operas of the late 17th and early 18th centuries; indeed, with the development of other aria types, they tended to reassume their former specific dramatic position. Purcell's Dido and Aeneas and The Fairy-Queen both contain a lament based on a chromatically descending tetrachord just before the resolution of the plot, and several Handel operas, such as Orlando (1733), have similarly placed laments in which the tetrachord bass plays a significant role.

*

E. Wellesz: 'Cavalli und der Stil der venezianischen Oper 1640–1660', SMw, i (1913), 1–103

C. Gallico: 'I due pianti di Arianna di Claudio Monteverdi', Chigiana, xxiv (1967), 29–42

N. Pirrotta: 'Early Opera and Aria', New Looks at Italian Opera: Essays in Honor of Donald J. Grout (Ithaca, 1968), 39–107

M. Murata: 'The Recitative Soliloquy', JAMS, xxxii (1979), 45–73

G. Tomlinson: 'Madrigal, Monody, and Monteverdi's via naturale alla immitatione', JAMS, xxxiv (1981), 60–108

P. Fabbri: Il secolo cantante: per una storia del libretto d'opera nel seicento (Bologna, 1990)

E. Rosand: Opera in Seventeenth-Century Venice: the Creation of a Genre (Berkeley and Los Angeles, 1991)   ELLEN ROSAND

Lammers, Gerda (*b* Berlin, 25 Sept 1915). German soprano. She studied in Berlin. After 15 years as a concert singer, she sang Ortlinde at the 1955 Bayreuth Festival; that autumn she joined the Kassel Opera, making her début as Marie in *Wozzeck*, and singing there until 1968 in such roles as Alcestis, Medea, Isolde, Brünnhilde and Electra. In this last role she made a triumphant, unheralded London début at Covent Garden in 1957, never forcing her voice or making an unpleasant sound. In 1958 she sang Purcell's Dido at Ingestre Hall, Staffordshire, and in 1959 returned to Covent Garden as Kundry. Her only American appearance was as Electra at the Metropolitan Opera in 1962.
                                                    HAROLD ROSENTHAL/R

La Montaine, John (*b* Chicago, 17 March 1920). American composer. He studied composition with Bernard Rogers and Howard Hanson at the Eastman School, with Bernard Wagenaar at the Juilliard School and with Nadia Boulanger in Fontainebleau. He was composer-in-residence at the American Academy in Rome in 1962 and visiting professor at the Eastman School in 1964–5. In 1977 he was named Nixon Distinguished Scholar and holder of the Nixon chair at Whittier College.

He has composed five operas, the central core being the trilogy of pageant-operas for Christmas: *Novellis, Novellis* (1962), *The Shephardes Playe* (1967) and *Erode the Great* (1969). These works are symptomatic of the American discovery of the appropriateness of biblical stories as subjects for opera, a province hitherto dominated by 20th-century British composers. Telling the story of the birth of Christ from the Annunciation to the slaughter of the Innocents, the librettos (by the composer) are based on Middle English texts and the King James Bible. La Montaine's study of Machaut's music before composing this trilogy has left its mark on the musical style. He also uses terraced dynamics, canonic imitation and some leitmotif-like themes to represent characters and recurring ideas. Vocal lines are clearly melodic with a supportive orchestral accompaniment. Reminiscent of the medieval miracle play, each work was first performed in a church.

Be Glad then America (1976), written for the American Bicentennial, has been heralded as a 'grand pageant of the Revolution'. In it, La Montaine shows a skilful understanding of vocal writing, both solo and choral. The orchestral writing borrows from music of the period, particularly from William Billings, whose *Chester* and *Anthem for Fast Day* are featured. There is an emphasis on panoramic pageantry rather than dramatic continuity.

all librettos by La Montaine; first performed at National Cathedral, Washington, DC, unless otherwise stated

Spreading the News op.27, 1957 (1), unperf.
Novellis, Novellis op.31 (Christmas pageant-opera, 1, after Middle Eng. text), 24 Dec 1962
The Shephardes Playe op.38 (Christmas pageant-opera, 1, after Middle Eng. text), 24 Dec 1967
Erode the Great op.40 (Christmas pageant-opera, 2, after Middle Eng. text), 31 Dec 1969
Be Glad then America op.43, Pennsylvania State U., 6 Feb 1976

*

H. A. Daugherty: *A Study of John La Montaine's 'Trilogy of Pageant-Operas for Christmas'* (diss., U. of Southern California, 1976)
B. R. Smedley: *Contemporary Sacred Chamber Opera: a Medieval Form in the Twentieth Century* (diss., George Peabody College for Teachers, 1977)

J. La Montaine: 'Life on the Edge', *Music Educators Journal*, lxix/7 (1983), 41–3
R. H. Kornick: *Recent American Opera: a Production Guide* (New York, 1991), 162–3
                                                    JAMES P. CASSARO

Lamotte [La Motte], **Antoine Houdar** [Houdart, Houdard] **de** (*b* Paris, 17 Jan 1672; *d* Paris, 26 Dec 1731). French librettist and aesthetician. He received an education in Latin and French literature at a Jesuit school, then attended law school but never practised law. At the age of 21 he saw his first play (a comedy) fail miserably and reacted by attempting to join a monastery. Two months later he emerged, but he spent some time reading and writing religious texts before returning definitively to the theatre. He wrote nearly all his opera librettos between 1697 and 1708, as well as three brief spoken comedies. Wishing to enter the Académie Française, he wrote a book of odes (1707); he was received by the Académie in 1710. His subsequent output includes cantata texts, spoken plays (four tragedies, five comedies), fables, a free translation of the *Iliad* with accompanying 'Discours' (which led to a long pamphlet war), other essays in literary criticism and miscellaneous non-fiction. He remained productive until his death, even though he had been blind and infirm for many years.

As a philosopher Lamotte's name is often coupled with that of his mentor, Fontenelle. Lamotte was a 'moderne' in the 'querelle des Anciens et des Modernes'. He favoured writing spoken tragedy in prose rather than alexandrines, aiming to please rather than 'instruct', and replacing the traditional unities with unity of 'interest'. Although his aesthetic writings concentrate on spoken tragedy, many of his recommendations (for instance, that spectacle be exploited) reflect his experiences as a librettist.

His first achievement as a librettist was to invent a new genre, the *opéra-ballet*. (The term appeared later; Lamotte used the simple designation 'ballet'.) The characters in *L'Europe galante* are contemporary Europeans, not heroes of mythology or chivalric legend; only the prologue features allegorical figures. Each act ('entrée') has a separate plot and its own *divertissement*; the entrées are loosely connected by a common theme (stereotype images of love-making in different countries). Cahusac later characterized the separate entrées as 'piquant miniatures'. Lamotte's only other *opéra-ballet*, *Le triomphe des arts*, returns to mythological characters; the five entrées represent architecture, poetry, music, painting and sculpture. The fifth entrée, which presents the legend of Pygmalion, is better known in Rameau's later setting than in La Barre's original.

Issé, in keeping with the conventions of the *pastorale-héroïque*, includes a pastoral love triangle involving a combination of a god and two mortals. There are three acts in the original version, but for the revised version of 1708 Lamotte lengthened the *divertissements* and superficially reorganized the structure by splitting Acts 1 and 3 into two acts each. D'Alembert later explained that Lamotte had been advised to put his three-act pastorale into five acts to give it 'the dignity of grand opera'; general critical opinion was that Lamotte might better have achieved 'dignity' by suppressing the comic subplot, which is a burlesque love intrigue for the confidants. The two pieces labelled *comédie-ballet* (a term used differently by Molière) have continuous plots, with the customary *divertissement* in each act. *Le*

Carnaval et la Folie has mythological characters (and therefore the expected supernatural events), whereas those of *La vénitienne* are contemporary Europeans. Both pieces are light comedies.

Lamotte's first *tragédie en musique*, *Amadis de Grèce*, is based on the same chivalric romance as Quinault's *Amadis de Gaule*. His next five works in that genre borrow from ancient mythology. Finally, *Scanderberg* (begun in 1711 and completed by La Serre after Lamotte's death) is based on an episode in Turkish history. In his youth Lamotte had written a manuscript study of Quinault's librettos, and the general style of these 'tragedies' is based closely on Quinault. The most important difference, one that had far-reaching influence on the next generation of French librettists, was the increased importance of the *divertissements*. The plots are simple, allowing lengthy *divertissements* (frequently ceremonial celebrations) to become the centre of gravity for each act. Lamotte often borrowed Quinault's occasional device of introducing the *divertissement* by interrupting the drama at a moment of great tension; the return to the story often involves a similarly violent contrast between static celebration and high drama.

L'Europe galante (opéra-ballet), Campra, 1697; *Issé* (pastorale-héroïque), A. C. Destouches, 1697; *Amadis de Grèce* (tragédie en musique), Destouches, 1699 (Handel, 1715, as Amadigi di Gaula); *Marthésie, reine des Amazones* (tragédie en musique), Destouches, 1699; *Le triomphe des arts* (opéra-ballet), La Barre, 1700 (Act 5, Rameau, 1748, as Pygmalion); *Canente* (tragédie en musique), Collasse, 1700 (Dauvergne, 1760); *Omphale* (tragédie en musique), Destouches, 1701 (Cardonne, 1769); *Le Carnaval et la Folie* (comédie-ballet), Destouches, 1703; *La vénitienne* (ballet), La Barre, 1705 (Dauvergne, 1768); *Alcyone* (tragédie en musique), Marais, 1706; *Sémélé* (tragédie en musique), Marais, 1709; *Scanderberg* (tragédie en musique, completed by J.-L.-I. de La Serre), Francoeur and Rebel, 1735; *Les âges* (comédie-ballet, prol., 4 entrées), prol. only, Mondonville, 1753, in Titon et l'Aurore; *Les fées* (comédie-ballet, 3 entrées), not set; *Climène* (pastorale-héroïque), not set

A. de Lamotte: *Oeuvres de théâtre* (Paris, 1730, 2/1765 as *Pièces de théâtre*)
E. Titon du Tillet: 'Antoine Houdart de la Motte', *Le Parnasse françois* (Paris, 1732), 655–7
Abbé Trublet: 'Mort de M. H. de La Motthe', *Mercure de France* (Jan 1732), 62–74
L. de Cahusac: *La danse ancienne et moderne*, iii (The Hague, 1754)
A. de Lamotte: *Oeuvres complètes* (Paris, 1754)
Abbé Trublet: *Mémoires pour servir à l'histoire de la vie et des oeuvres de M. de Fontenelle et de M. de La Motte* (Amsterdam, 1759)
J. le Rond d'Alembert: 'Eloge de La Motte', *Histoire des membres de l'Académie françoise, morts depuis 1700 jusqu'en 1771, pour servir de suite aux éloges imprimés et lus dans les séances publiques de cette compagnie*, i (Paris, 1787), 235–83
A. de Lamotte: *Oeuvres choisies* (Paris, 1811)
P. Dupont: *Un poète philosophe au commencement du dix-huitième siècle, Houdar de La Motte* (Paris, 1898)
M. Beaufils: *Par la musique vers l'obscur* (Marseilles, 1942)
M. Barthélemy: 'L'opéra français et la querelle des anciens et des modernes', *Les lettres romanes*, x (1956), 379–91
R. Finch: *The Sixth Sense* (Toronto, 1966)
C. Girdlestone: *La tragédie en musique (1673–1750) considérée comme genre littéraire* (Geneva, 1972)
J. R. Anthony: *French Baroque Music from Beaujoyeulx to Rameau* (London, 1973, 2/1978)
R. Fajon: Introduction to A. C. Destouches: *Issé: pastorale héroïque*, FO, xiv (1984); review by L. Rosow, *JAMS*, xl (1987), 548–57
P. Russo: '"L'isola di Alcina": funzioni drammaturgiche del "divertissement" nella "tragédie lyrique" (1699–1735)', *NRMI*, xxi (1987), 1–15

LOIS ROSOW

Lamoureux, Charles (*b* Bordeaux, 28 Sept 1834; *d* Paris, 21 Dec 1899). French conductor. He studied at the Paris Conservatoire and held short appointments at the Opéra-Comique (1876) and the Opéra (1877–9), resigning both posts following disagreements. In 1881 he instigated a series of concerts at the Théâtre du Château d'Eau in which he promoted Wagner's music by introducing single acts of *Lohengrin* and *Tristan*. He visited Bayreuth, where it seems that Wagner finally authorized him to produce *Lohengrin*. This he did in 1887 at the Eden-Théâtre, Paris, where he had established himself two years before. However anti-Wagner extremists staged a street demonstration and Lamoureux gave up the venture before the second performance. In 1891 he was made music director for the Opéra's production of *Lohengrin*. Lamoureux curtailed his orchestral conducting career in order to give more time to the theatre but his projects were not successful and he never built the French Bayreuth of his dreams. He did, however, succeed in producing *Tristan und Isolde* at the Nouveau-Théâtre in 1899, and by the time of his death he had seen the anti-Wagner sentiment of the 1870s and 1880s begin to evaporate.

ELISABETH BERNARD

Lampe, Mrs. English soprano; *see* YOUNG family, (2).

Lampe, Johann Friedrich (*b* Wolfenbüttel, 1744; *d* after 1788). German composer and singer. He was musical director of the Hamburg theatre from 1773 to 1777 and apparently stayed on as a singer. In 1788 he was a member of the court theatre at Schwedt (Pomerania). His works include incidental music for the stage and *Das Mädchen in Eichthale*, a three-act Singspiel adapted from Bickerstaff's *Love in a Village* and Burgoyne's *The Maid of the Oaks*, first performed at the Hamburg Gänsemarkt (19 August 1776) and later at Berlin and elsewhere (score in *D-Bdhm*).

Lampe, John Frederick [Johann Friedrich] (*b* Saxony, late 1702 or early 1703; *d* Edinburgh, 25 July 1751). German composer who spent most of his life in Britain. Nothing is known for sure of his life before he was admitted to the University of Helmstedt on 2 May 1718, when he was described as 'Brunsvicensis' ('from Brunswick'). He graduated in law in March 1720 and arrived in London in or shortly before 1726, when Henry Carey, later his regular librettist, described him in a poem as 'my Lamp obscure, because unknown' who 'shines in secret (now) to friends alone'. Fame was predicted for him ('Light him but up! let him in publick blaze,/ He will delight not only but amaze'), but he did not attract much public attention until 1732–3, when he joined Carey, Arne and J. C. Smith in a project to produce English operas at the Little Theatre in the Haymarket.

Lampe wrote three full-length serious operas 'after the Italian manner' for this company within a year: Carey's *Amelia*, *Britannia* by Thomas Lediard (a diplomat who had perhaps met Lampe in Germany) and *Dione*, a text adapted by the composer from a 'pastoral tragedy' by John Gay; only two airs from *Amelia* survive, though ten numbers from *Britannia* and eight from *Dione* exist in manuscript full score. Lampe's fourth work for the company, *The Opera of Operas, or Tom Thumb the Great*, adapted from Fielding's burlesque *The Tragedy of Tragedies* and produced at the Little Theatre in May 1733, has often been confused

'The Dragon of Wantley' (J. F. Lampe): engraving, possibly based on an early production, accompanying the air 'On Losing their Toast and Butter', from George Bickham's 'The Musical Entertainer', i (London, 1737)

with Arne's rival setting of the same text, put on at Lincoln's Inn Fields in October that year, though there is little doubt that the 16 surviving songs are by Lampe; further confusion has been caused by Lampe's revision of his work as an afterpiece for Drury Lane, first performed on 7 November 1733. The English opera company was not a failure, as is often said. Its productions mostly achieved respectable runs, and it launched a number of new singers and composers on successful theatrical careers. In spring 1734 Lampe wrote incidental music for two plays, a 'dramatic performance' (masque) to celebrate Princess Anne's wedding to the Prince of Orange entitled *Aurora's Nuptials* and his first major success, the pantomime *Cupid and Psyche, or Columbine Courtezan*.

For some reason Lampe disappeared from the London theatre at this moment of success, and did not reappear until his burlesque opera *The Dragon of Wantley* was produced at the Little Theatre in 1737. He may merely have been busy teaching and writing his thoroughbass treatise, published in September that year, though so complete an absence suggests that he spent part of the time out of London. But he returned in triumph, for *The Dragon* was the sensation of the season: Carey's libretto was reprinted 14 times in little more than a year, the work was taken up by other companies, and it held the stage until 1782; it is his only opera to survive complete. Carey ridiculed Italian opera by transferring its artificial conventions and high-flown sentiments to a down-to-earth English folktale set in his native Yorkshire; the legend of Moore of Moore Hall and the dragon of Wantley would have been familiar to his audience through the ballad printed in D'Urfey's *Pills to Purge Melancholy*. Lampe's music added an extra dimension to the comedy by setting Carey's inane lines to elaborate and seemingly serious music.

With such a hit on their hands it was inevitable that Carey and Lampe would produce a sequel; and like most sequels, *Margery, or A Worse Plague than the Dragon*, produced at Covent Garden in 1738, was less effective and less successful. But Lampe was now one of London's most prominent theatre musicians, a position he consolidated by marrying his leading lady, Isabella Young, in December 1738, thus becoming Thomas Arne's brother-in-law (Arne had married Isabella's sister Cecilia in 1737). His subsequent works were all

comedies – he evidently discovered his true *métier* just as Arne turned from comedy to the serious subject of Milton's *Comus* – and several were successful. The pantomime *Orpheus and Euridice*, first produced at Covent Garden in February 1740, received 46 performances in that season alone, though the crowds were probably drawn more by a 17-foot clockwork snake that devoured Euridice (it moved with 'a velocity scarcely credible') than by Lampe's music; only one song and some 'comic tunes' survive. In 1741, however, audiences dwindled for music as the public's attention was caught by the revolution in Shakespearean acting initiated by Charles Macklin and David Garrick. Lampe's *The Sham Conjuror*, a 'Comic Masque of Speaking, Singing and Dancing' to a lost anonymous text, failed after three performances at Covent Garden in April, though its music was published in full score. As a result his company tried its luck in the provinces, and Charles Burney recalled with pleasure its visit to Chester that summer. The years 1741 to 1744 were largely empty for Lampe in the theatre, apart from two operas given at the Little Theatre in spring 1744, *The Queen of Spain* and *The Kiss Accepted and Returned*, both lost.

Lampe's last opera, *Pyramus and Thisbe*, was first performed at Covent Garden in 1745. The text, derived in part from one set by Richard Leveridge in 1716, is an ingenious adaptation of the play-within-a-play in *A Midsummer Night's Dream*, with Italian opera and opera singers made the object of ridicule instead of plays and players. The airs are once again largely deadpan (the recitatives are lost), though the clichés of the Handelian style are parodied in typical rage and revenge numbers. *Pyramus* was a steady if unspectacular success, and was taken up by provincial companies. It did not, however, lead to further opportunities in the London theatre, a few contributions to plays excepted, and in September 1748, Lampe and his family went to Dublin for two years, where he wrote the serenata *Damon and Anathe* (now lost), and then Edinburgh for the 1750–51 season. He died there of a fever and was buried in Canongate churchyard; he had been converted to Methodism a few years earlier, and his death was commemorated by Charles Wesley in the hymn *Tis done! The Sov'reign will's obey'd*.

As a composer Lampe displays a consistent technical facility that was beyond the grasp of many of his colleagues in the English theatre; he inevitably invites comparison with his fellow-Saxon Handel, who employed him as a bassoonist in his opera orchestra and is said to have admired *The Dragon of Wantley*. Yet Lampe's surviving operas, perhaps because most of them are comedies, are closer to Arne than to Handel in style, except when the intention was clearly to parody Italian opera; he followed his brother-in-law in introducing elements of British popular song into his airs, including the Scotch snaps that proliferate in *Pyramus and Thisbe*. The few surviving fragments of his serious operas, notably the arias for *Britannia* and *Dione*, suggest that he was also capable of deeper things.

See also DRAGON OF WANTLEY, THE and PYRAMUS AND THISBE.

printed works published in London

LCG – *Covent Garden*   LLT – *Little Theatre in the Haymarket*

Amelia (Eng. op, H. Carey), LLT, 13 March 1732, 2 airs (*c*1732)
Britannia (Eng. op, T. Lediard), LLT, 16 Nov 1732, 10 airs *GB-Lbl*
Dione (Eng. op, Lampe, after J. Gay), LLT, 23 Feb 1733, 8 airs *Lbl*
The Opera of Operas, or Tom Thumb the Great (burlesque, E. Haywood, after H. Fielding), LLT, 31 May 1733; rev. (afterpiece), London, Drury Lane, 7 Nov 1733; airs (1733)
Aurora's Nuptials (masque), London, Drury Lane, ?15 March 1734
The Dragon of Wantley (burlesque op, 3, Carey), LLT, 16 May 1737, *Lcm*, full score without recits. (1738)
Margery, or A Worse Plague than the Dragon (burlesque, Carey), LCG, 9 Dec 1738, full score without recits. (1739)
Roger and Joan, or The Country Wedding (comic masque), LCG, 20 March 1739
The Sham Conjuror (comic masque), LCG, 18 April 1741, full score (1741)
The Queen of Spain, or Farinelli at Madrid (burlesque scene, J. Ayres), LLT, 19 Jan 1744
The Kiss Accepted and Returned (operetta, Ayres), LLT, 16 April 1744
Pyramus and Thisbe (mock op, 1, ? Lampe, after W. Shakespeare and R. Leveridge), LCG, 25 Jan 1745, full score without recits., dance and chorus (1745/*R*1988)
Damon and Anathe (serenata, T. Cibber), Dublin, Smock Alley, 12 March 1750

*

BurneyH; NicollH

P. Lord: 'The English-Italian Opera Companies 1732–3', *ML*, xlv (1964), 239–51
R. Fiske: *English Theatre Music in the Eighteenth Century* (London, 1973, 2/1986)
R. B. Price: *A Textual, Dramatic and Musical Analysis of Two Burlesque Operas, 'The Dragon of Wantley' and 'Margery, or A Worse Plague than the Dragon'* (diss., U. of Texas, Austin, 1975)
D. R. Martin: *The Operas and Operatic Style of John Frederick Lampe* (Detroit, 1985)
W. J. Burling and R. D. Hume: 'Theatrical Companies at the Little Haymarket, 1720–1737', *Essays in Theatre*, iv (1986), 98–118
B. Boydell: *A Dublin Musical Calendar 1700–1760* (Dublin, 1988)

PETER HOLMAN

Lampedo. Melodrama in one act by GEORG JOSEPH VOGLER to a libretto by Christian Friedrich Lichtenberg; Darmstadt, Hoftheater, 11 July 1779.

The text of *Lampedo* is drawn from the story of the Amazon queen's victory over her rival, King Argabyses, and the Scythians. Lampedo (spoken role) raises the sacrificial dagger to kill Argabyses (spoken role) but she finds herself unable to strike him. Angry and frustrated, she attempts to take her own life, but thunder prevents her from succeeding. Her wrath subsides, she forgives Argabyses and makes a pact with the Scythians.

Following in the wake of Georg Benda's popular German melodramas *Ariadne auf Naxos* and *Medea*, Vogler's *Lampedo* emphasizes aspects of *Sturm und Drang* theatre. The libretto has stage directions indicating gestures for virtually every phrase of the text. Crown Princess Louise Karoline Henriette, who played

the title role at Darmstadt, must have been an accomplished pantomimist. Vogler's orchestral accompaniment is modelled on that found in obbligato recitative: jagged arpeggios, dotted rhythms, sustained chords and motivic melodic figures dominate the texture. His score also includes several programmatic pieces, among them an 'Ouverture Gueriere' (pitting an onstage band against the orchestra) followed by a triumphal march, and in scene iii, storm music. The work concludes with a lengthy chaconne, inspired by French opera, celebrating Lampedo's noble clemency.

PAUL CORNEILSON

Lampugnani, Giovanni Battista (*b* ?Milan, 1708; *d* Milan, 12 June 1788). Italian composer. He was of middle-class origin; his father Virgilio may have been a composer. In 1732 his first opera, *Candace*, was given at the Teatro Regio Ducale, Milan, and during the ensuing years several of his operas were frequently performed, particularly in northern Italy. He was appointed resident composer in 1743 at the King's Theatre, London; his first opera production there was *Rossane* (15 November 1743), a pasticcio including music by Handel. Lampugnani wrote two further operas for London in the early months of 1744, *Alfonso* and *Alceste*. He was back in Italy in 1745–6; his *Semiramide* was performed in June 1745 in Padua, and *Il gran Tamerlano* on 20 January 1746 in Milan. In the years after his return from London he travelled throughout Italy, organizing performances of his works in Milan, Venice, Florence, Reggio Emilia, Turin, Piacenza and Genoa. In 1753 he composed *Vologeso* for Barcelona and probably visited that city. His *Siroe, re di Persia* was performed in London in 1755, but it is not certain that he was present.

In 1758 Lampugnani was appointed harpsichordist at the Teatro Regio Ducale, Milan, where he wrote his first comic operas; in 1760 his *Amor contadino* was performed in Venice. About this time he must have made the acquaintance of J. C. Bach and Padre Martini; Bach mentions him in a letter to Martini written in 1759. He became increasingly active as a teacher of singing and less as a composer: his last known opera was performed in Turin in 1769. He also wrote instrumental music, including concertos and symphonies. When Mozart was in Milan to finish his *Mitridate, rè di Ponto* in 1770, Lampugnani helped rehearse the singers, including the prima donna Antonia Bernasconi. During the first three performances he played second harpsichord and in subsequent performances directed the orchestra himself. Lampugnani continued his activity as harpsichordist, performing at the inauguration of the Regio Ducal Teatro alla Scala in August 1778 and a year later at that of the Canobbiana; he was still harpsichordist at La Scala for the performance of Cimarosa's *Il marito disperato* in the autumn of 1786.

In spite of popular approval Lampugnani's music gained only lukewarm acclaim from 18th-century critics. He acquired a reputation for providing his arias with over-energetic orchestral accompaniments; Arteaga, in particular, accused him of giving all his attention to them. The best-considered judgment of his music was passed by Burney. Writing about his *Alfonso* (1744), Burney commented on the large amount of bravura in the arias for the leading singer Monticelli, thought the work lacked dignity, but conceded nonetheless that 'there is a graceful gaiety in the melody of his quick songs, and an elegant tenderness in the slow, that

1091

resemble no other composer's works of that time'. In fact the arias of Lampugnani's early heroic operas contain many of the usual melodic formulae of the period. Not so usual, however, is the curious combination within several arias of elaborate melodic ornamentation – usual in heroic opera – on the one hand and a catchy tunefulness and a light, buoyant style – suitable for comic opera – on the other. The gay and elegant qualities that Burney noticed in *Alfonso* are present in Lampugnani's last extant opera, and incidentally his only surviving comic opera, *Amor contadino* (1760). In this work Lampugnani minimized the comical, grotesque nature of the characters and relied on tunefulness to gain his effects. Unlike his earlier heroic operas, in which the da capo form is preferred for the arias, he here adopted a variety of different forms for his vocal items, and never used an exact da capo. The ensembles, consisting of several sections in differing time signatures and speeds, may owe something to the example of Galuppi, who during the 1750s constructed ensembles in a similar way.

drammi per musica in 3 acts, unless otherwise stated

Candace (D. Lalli and F. Silvani: *I veri amici*, after P. Corneille: *Héraclius, empereur d'Orient*), Milan, Regio Ducale, 26 Dec 1732
Antigono (G. Marizoli), Milan, Regio Ducale, 16 Dec 1736
Arianna e Teseo (P. Pariati), Alessandria, Solerio, aut. 1737
Ezio (P. Metastasio), Venice, S Angelo, 1737, *I-Bas*; rev. version, Venice, S Samuele, Ascension 1743
Demofoonte (B. Vitturi), Piacenza, Ducale, carn. 1738
Angelica (C. Vedova, after L. Ariosto), Venice, S Samuele, 11 May 1738
Didone abbandonata (Metastasio), Padua, Obizzi, June 1739; rev. version, Naples, S Carlo, 20 Jan 1753, *E-Mn* (ov., Acts 1, 2)
Adriano in Siria (Metastasio), Vicenza, Grazie, May 1740
Semiramide riconosciuta (Metastasio), Rome, Dame, 1741, *I-Nc* (without recits), *P-La*
Arsace (A. Salvi), Crema, Sept 1741, *I-Fc* (Act 1)
Farasmene, re di Tracia, Genoa, Falcone, carn. 1743
Alfonso (P. A. Rolli, after S. B. Pallavicino), London, King's, 3 Jan 1744, Favourite Songs (London, c1744)
Alceste (Rolli, after Metastasio: *Demetrio*), London, King's, 28 April 1744, Favourite Songs (London, c1744)
Semiramide, Padua, Obizzi, June 1745
Il gran Tamerlano (A. Piovene), Milan, Regio Ducale, 20 Jan 1746
Tigrane (C. Goldoni, after Silvani: *Virtù trionfante dell'Amore e dell'Odio*), Venice, S Angelo, 10 May 1747, Favourite Songs (London, c1747)
L'Olimpiade (Metastasio), Florence, Pergola, carn. 1748
Andromaca (Salvi), Turin, Regio, 26 Dec 1748
Artaserse (Metastasio), Milan, Regio Ducale, 26 Dec 1749
Alessandro sotto le tende di Dario (G. Riviera), Piacenza, Ducale, spr. 1751
Vologeso, re de' Patri, Genoa, Falcone, carn. 1752
Vologeso (after A. Zeno), Barcelona, 1753 [possibly rev. of Vologeso, re de' Patri, 1752]
Siroe, re di Persia (Metastasio), London, King's, 14 Jan 1755, Favourite Songs (London, c1755)
Il re pastore (Metastasio), Milan, Regio Ducale, April 1758, *P-La*
Le cantatrici (dg), Milan, Regio Ducale, aut. 1758; as La scuola delle cantatrici, Modena, 1761; also as La scuola di musica
Il conte Chicchera (dg, Goldoni), Milan, Regio Ducale, aut. 1759
La contessina (dg, Goldoni), Milan, Regio Ducale, aut. 1759
Amor contadino (dg, Goldoni), Venice, S Angelo, 12 Nov 1760, *GB-Cfm* (*R*1982: IOB, lxxxii)
Enea in Italia (?G. Bussani), Palermo, 1763
L'illustre villanella (dg), Turin, Regio, spr. 1769

Music in: Alessandro in Persia, 1741; Meraspe, o L'Olimpiade, 1742; Gianguir, 1742; Rossane, o Alessandro nell'Indie, 1743; La finta schiava, 1744; Annibale in Capua, 1746; Catone, 1747–8; Didone, 1748; L'ingratitudine punita, 1748; Semiramide, 1748; Catone in Utica, 1749; Ipermestra, 1754; Andromaca, 1755; Orazio, c1755; Tito Manlio, 1756; La Giulia, 1760; Le pescatrici, 1761; L'Issipile, 1763; The Summer's Tale, 1765

BurneyFI; BurneyH
J.-B. de La Borde: *Essai sur la musique ancienne et moderne*, iii (Paris, 3/1780), 195–6
S. Arteaga: *Le rivoluzioni del teatro musicale italiano*, ii (Venice, 2/1785), 256–7
F. Piovano: 'Un opéra inconnu de Gluck', *SIMG*, ix (1907–8), 231–81
K. Hortschansky: 'Gluck und Lampugnani in Italien: zum Pasticcio "Arsace"', *AnMc*, no.3 (1966), 49–64
M. Donà: 'Dagli archivi milanesi: lettera di Ranieri de' Calzabigi e di Antonia Bernasconi', *AnMc*, no.14 (1974), 268–300, esp. 297
E. Weimer: Preface to G. B. Lampugnani: *L'amor contadino*, IOB, lxxxii (1982)
C. Vitali: 'Giovanni Battista Lampugnani', *The Symphony 1720–1840*, ser. A, iv (1983)
F. Maffei: *Giovanni Battista Lampugnani (c1708–1788): notizie biografiche e un catalogo ragionato della musica* (diss., U. of Pisa, 1988)
MICHAEL F. ROBINSON, FABIOLA MAFFEI

Lanari, Alessandro (*b* S Marcello di Iesi, 1790; *d* Florence, 3 Oct 1862). Italian impresario. His first appointment as impresario was at Lucca in 1819. For the next 40 years he was active in central and northern Italy, sometimes controlling several theatres simultaneously. He was associated mainly with the Teatro della Pergola in Florence, which he managed during the periods 1823–8, 1830–35, 1839–48 and 1860–62. With Barbaia, Merelli and Jacovacci, he was among the leading impresarios of 19th-century Italy and in general was the best liked of the four. His breadth of vision and skilful use of resources earned him the nickname (shared according to some sources with Merelli) 'the Napoleon of the impresarios', and he was warmly praised by Donizetti and Mercadante. His career was not free from reverses: the theatre at Senigallia burnt down under his management; he lost a lawsuit against the mezzo-soprano Giuditta Grisi; and in Rome he was ousted successively from the Apollo and Argentina theatres by Jacovacci. Because of financial difficulties he resigned from the direction of the Pergola shortly before his death. His letters (in *I-Fn*) shed an interesting light on the theatrical conditions of the time and also on the career of Giuseppina Strepponi, whom he managed for several years. Important premières given under his direction were Bellini's *I Capuleti e i Montecchi* (1830, Venice), *Norma* (1831, Milan) and *Beatrice de Tenda* (1833, Venice), Donizetti's *L'elisir d'amore* (1832, Milan), *Pia de' Tolomei* (1837, Venice) and *Maria di Rudenz* (1838, Venice), and Verdi's *Macbeth* (1847, Florence). Lanari also mounted the first Italian performances of *Robert le diable* (1840) and *Der Freischütz* (1843) at the Pergola.

Jarro [pseud. of G. Piccini]: *Memorie di un impresario fiorentino* (Florence, 1892)
M. De Angelis: *Le carte dell'impresario: melodramma e costume teatrale nell'ottocento* (Florence, 1982)
——, ed.: *Le cifre del melodramma: l'archivio inedito dell'impresario teatrale A. Lanari nella Biblioteca Nazionale Centrale di Firenze (1815–1870)* (Florence, 1982)
J. Rosselli: *The Opera Industry in Italy from Cimarosa to Verdi* (Cambridge, 1984)
JULIAN BUDDEN

Lance, Albert [Ingram, Lance(lot Albert)] (*b* Menindie, South Australia, 12 July 1925). Australian tenor. He was a pupil of Greta Callow. His audition with Gertrude Johnson of the National Theatre Movement brought him leading engagements with her company, including his 1954 appearances as Hoffmann. The prospect of studies with Dominique Modesti took him to Paris where, as Albert Lance, he made his début as Cavaradossi at the Opéra-Comique in 1956. Leading roles at the Opéra, beginning with Faust, followed quickly. He sang with Sutherland in *Rigoletto* at Covent Garden (1958) and became the resident Don José in *Carmen* at the Opéra from 1959. He appeared with Tebaldi in *Tosca* (1960) and with Rita Gorr in *Médée* (1962) and performed throughout Europe (Bol'shoy, 1965–6) and in North and South America. He sang with the Opéra du Rhin, Strasbourg, from 1972 to 1976. His recordings include complete sets of *Tosca*, *Madama Butterfly*, *Werther* and Roussel's *Padmâvatî*.

ROGER COVELL

Lancetti [Lanzetti], **Lucia** (*b* Venice; *fl* 1722–37). Italian contralto. In 1722–5 she sang in five operas in Venice, including the title role of Orlandini's *Antigona* (1724), one of the few female parts she ever played. She appeared in two operas during Carnival 1725–6 at Turin and two more in 1726–7 at Florence, where she was in the service of Princess Violante Beatrice. She sang the title roles of Vivaldi's *Orlando furioso* and *Farnace* in Venice in autumn 1727, returned to Turin for Carnival 1729–30 and appeared in four more operas in Venice in 1736–7.

R. Strohm: 'Vivaldi's Career as an Opera Producer', *Antonio Vivaldi: teatro musicale, cultura e società: Venice 1981*, i, 11–63
S. Mamy: 'La diaspora dei cantanti veneziani nella prima metà del Settecento', *Nuovi studi vivaldiani: edizione e cronologia critica delle opere*, ed. A. Fanna and G. Morelli (Florence, 1988), ii, 591–631
COLIN TIMMS

Lanciani, Flavio Carlo (*b* Rome, 1661; *d* Rome, 14 July 1706). Italian composer. His dramatic works include at least 15 two-part oratorios (ten of which were in Latin, written for S Marcello between 1683 and 1706), five three-act dramas (three more are attributed to him), one secular serenata and two serenatas for Christmas Eve performances at the Vatican. Between 1685 and 1688 he set two three-act texts and two oratorios written by his future father-in-law, the playwright G. A. Lorenzani. He was employed as a 'virtuoso' from 1688 by the most munificent of Roman patrons, Cardinal Ottoboni, and by 1704 he was *maestro di cappella* at both S Maria in Trastevere and S Agostino. Ottoboni supplied texts for five of the three-act dramas attributed to Lanciani; two (*Il martirio di S Eustachio* and *La costanza nell'amor divino*) are on religious subjects, but were staged like operas. The MS libretto of *L'amante del suo nemico*, intended for Rome in 1688, has alterations probably in Ottoboni's hand, and names Lanciani as the composer, but it is possible that the production was cancelled before any of the text was set. Lanciani also wrote additional arias for Scarlatti's *La Statira* (1690; MSS in *F-Pn* and *I-Rvat*). His tuneful arias flow gracefully, and their accompaniments resemble Corelli's solo and trio sonata textures.

Il Visir, amante geloso, overo Le disgrazie di Giurgia (introduzione drammatica per un lotto, 3, G. A. Lorenzani), Rome, Palazzo del Ugo e Fabio Accoramboni, Jan 1685
La forza del sangue, o vero Gl'equivoci gelosi (op musicale, 3, Lorenzani), Rome, Casa del Lorenzani, Jan 1686, arias *F-Pn* and *I-Rvat*
Il martirio di S Eustachio (oratorio per musica, 3, P. Ottoboni), Rome, Divoto Teatro del Prince Antonio Ottoboni, Feb 1690; Palazzo della Cancelleria, 26 Feb 1690, *F-Pc*, *GB-Lcm*
Amore e Gratitudine (dramma pastorale, 3, Ottoboni), Rome, Palazzo della Cancelleria, 3 Sept 1690, *D-Hs*, arias *I-Rli*
La costanza nell'amor divino, overo La Santa Rosalia [Act 2] (dramma sacro per musica, 3, Ottoboni), Rome, ? Palazzo della Cancelleria, ?carn. 1696, arias *F-Pn*, *GB-Ob* and *I-PAVu*; rev.

Ottoboni as L'amante del cielo, Rome, Collegio Nazareno, carn. 1699, *Rsp* [Act 1 by S. De Luca, Act 3 by F. Gasparini]

Doubtful: L'amante del suo nemico (dramma per musica, 3, Ottoboni), intended for Rome, 1688, ?not set, lib. *I-Rvat*; L'amante combattuto (dramma per musica, 3, ?G. Vaini), Rome, Casa Vaini, Jan 1695, arias *D-Dlb* and *I-Bc* [only one in *I-Bc* attrib. Lanciani]; Il console tutore (dramma per musica, 3, Ottoboni), Rome, ? Collegio Romano, carn. 1698, arias *F-Pn* [only one attrib. Lanciani], rev. Ottoboni as Il console in Egitto, 1701

Arias in: A. Scarlatti: La Statira, 1690

H. J. Marx: 'Ein neuer Fund zur römischen Operngeschichte des ausgehenden Seicento [*Amore e Gratitudine*]', *AnMc*, no.3 (1966), 43–8
G. Morelli: 'Giovanni Andrea Lorenzani: artista e letterato romano del seicento', *Studi secenteschi*, xiii (1972), 193–251
L. E. Lindgren and C. B. Schmidt: 'A Collection of 137 Broadsides Concerning Theatre in Late Seventeenth-Century Italy: an Annotated Catalogue', *Harvard Library Bulletin*, xxviii (1980), 202, 216
W. C. Holmes: '*La Statira*' by Pietro Ottoboni and Alessandro Scarlatti: the Textual Sources, with a Documentary Postscript (New York, 1983), 65–9
A. Lanfranchi and E. Careri: 'Le cantate per la natività della B.V.: un secolo di musiche al Collegio Nazareno (1681–1784)', *Handel e gli Scarlatti a Roma*, ed. N. Pirrotta and A. Ziino (Florence, 1987) 309, 328
S. Franchi: *Drammaturgia romana: repertorio bibliografico cronologico dei testi drammatici pubblicati a Roma e nel Lazio, secolo xvii* (Rome, 1988)
F. Carboni, T. M. Gialdroni and A. Ziino: 'Cantate ed arie romane del tardo seicento nel Fondo Caetani della Biblioteca Corsiniana: repertorio, forme e strutture', *Studi musicali*, xviii (1989), 49–192
K. Watanabe and H. J. Marx: 'Händels italienische Kopisten', *GHB*, iii (1989), 195–234
LOWELL LINDGREN

Lanctin, Charles-François-Honoré. *See* DUQUESNOY, CHARLES-FRANÇOIS-HONORÉ.

Land des Lächelns, Das ('The Land of Smiles'). *Romantische Operette* in three acts by FRANZ LEHÁR to a libretto by Ludwig Herzer and FRITZ LÖHNER; Berlin, Metropoltheater, 10 October 1929.

This operetta, a revised version of *Die gelbe Jacke* (Vienna, Theater an der Wien, 9 February 1923), was the greatest international success among Lehár's later pieces, and the most successful of the works he created for Richard Tauber, whose leading lady was Vera Schwarz. The setting of Vienna and China had popular appeal, and Lehár was able to combine his popular Viennese waltz style with ambitious vocal writing and a more serious plot. Tauber sang the role of Sou-Chong in London and New York, as well as under Lehár's baton at the Theater an der Wien in 1930 (again with Schwarz) and the Vienna Staatsoper in 1938 (with Maria Reining as Lisa, Adele Kern as Mi and Alfred Jerger as Tschang). The song 'Dein ist mein ganzes Herz' became virtually Tauber's signature tune and has remained a popular favourite of tenors ever since, attracting many eminent singers to the role on stage, among them Giuseppe di Stefano, Nicolai Gedda and Siegfried Jerusalem.

The librettist of the original *Die gelbe Jacke*, Victor Léon, dedicated it to the memory of his daughter, whom he credited with the idea for the work. *Das Land des Lächelns* was an extensive reworking, but with several numbers taken over from *Die gelbe Jacke* virtually unchanged ('Immer nur lächeln', 'Von Apfelblüten einen Kranz' – which includes lines adapted from a Chinese poet – 'Ich möcht' wieder einmal die Heimat seh'n', 'Zig, zig, zig!', 'Liebes Schwesterlein') or with a new text

('Meine Liebe, deine Liebe'). Other songs were completely new: Lisa's waltz 'Gern, gern wär' ich verliebt', 'Bei einem Tee à deux', 'Wer hat die Liebe uns ins Herz gesenkt?', 'Im Salon zur blau'n Pagode' and, above all, 'Dein ist mein ganzes Herz', worked up from a few bars in the original. The discarded numbers included a shimmy with the topical lines 'Wir woll'n in's Kino geh'n und den Charlie Chaplin seh'n'. In *Die gelbe Jacke*, Hubert Marischka was Sou-Chong, Betty Fischer was Lea (whose name was changed to Lisa in the revised version) and Louise Kartousch was Mi.

The action opens in Vienna in 1912, where a ball is taking place at the home of Count Lichtenfels (spoken) in honour of his daughter Lisa (soprano). She is, however, disenchanted with the empty flirting of such occasions ('Gern, gern wär' ich verliebt'). Her greatest admirer is Count Gustl von Pottenstein of the dragoons (tenor *buffo*), but his attentions are somewhat overshadowed by the gift of a magnificent Chinese statuette from a Chinese admirer, Prince Sou-Chong (tenor), who keeps his true feelings hidden behind a mask of Chinese inscrutability ('Immer nur lächeln'). The difference in their backgrounds makes for difficulties in communication. He doesn't touch alcohol, but common ground is found in a cup of tea ('Bei einem Tee à deux'), and he captivates the young ladies with his account of how courting takes place in China ('Von Apfelblüten einen Kranz'). He is then suddenly summoned back to China to take up the position of Prime Minister, but by that time he and Lisa have expressed their feelings in ways that both understand.

Act 2 takes place in Sou-Chong's palace in Peking, where he is installed in office with the ceremonial yellow jacket. Lisa is living with him, and their love for each other is profound ('Wer hat die Liebe uns ins Herz gesenkt?'). But the differences between the restrictions women suffer in the East and the freedom to which Lisa is accustomed in the West are pointed up by Sou-Chong's sister Mi (soprano) ('Im Salon zur blau'n Pagode'). She nevertheless seems to have managed to strike up an instant friendship with Gustl, who has arrived from Vienna in pursuit of Lisa ('Meine Liebe, deine Liebe'). Sou-Chong is reminded by his uncle Tschang (baritone) that, according to Chinese custom, he must take four wives, but the Prince declares that his whole heart belongs to Lisa ('Dein ist mein ganzes Herz'). For Lisa's part, the sight of Gustl excites a longing for home ('Ich möcht' wieder einmal die Heimat seh'n'). She decides to leave, but Sou-Chong forbids it, instantly turning from western lover to eastern master.

Act 3 begins a week later, when Gustl comes up with a plan to help Lisa escape. This arouses an ambivalent response in Mi – joy for Lisa but regret at the imminent departure of Gustl ('Zig, zig, zig!'). But Lisa's and Gustl's attempt to escape through the sacred temple of Buddha is foiled when they find their way barred afresh by Sou-Chong. Lisa pleads with him, and finally he relents, committing Lisa to Gustl's care and hiding his own sorrow at Lisa's departure behind the enigmatic Chinese smile.
ANDREW LAMB

Landi, Lamberto (*b* Lucca, 2 Sept 1882; *d* Lucca, 6 July 1950). Italian composer. After early studies at the Pacini Institute in Lucca, he graduated from the Milan Conservatory in 1908. His first opera, *Bianca*, was staged in Lucca two years later. Landi was active principally as a teacher, for example at the Pescia Conservatory (1923–43); his operas, which sometimes used 19th-century literary sources as their basis, were written at irregular intervals throughout his life and at least two remain unperformed.

Bianca, Lucca, Giglio, 20 Jan 1910
Nelly, 1916 (R. Simoni and E. Cavacchioli, after C. Dickens), Lucca, 1947
Il Pergolese (C. Marsili), Milan, Carcano, 7 June 1919
Lauretta (G. Adami, after A. de Vigny), Pisa, 1927
Gorgona, *c*1933 (S. Benelli), unperf.
Nausica, *c*1942 (M. Lombardi Lotti), unperf.

Landi, Marco. *See* ANELLI, ANGELO.

Landi, Stefano (*b* Rome, bap. 26 Feb 1587; *d* Rome, 28 Oct 1639). Italian composer and singer. The second son of Matteo Mattei and Cecilia Landi, he became a boy soprano at the Collegio Germanico, Rome, in 1595. After studying at the Seminario Romano, 1602–7, he built a career in Rome as an organist and singer, obtaining the post of *maestro di cappella* at S Maria della Consolazione (1614–17); he also took steps towards the priesthood. He began to move among princes and powerful cardinals with Cardinal Marco Cornaro in Padua (*c*1618–1619), and returned to Rome (by summer 1620) as *maestro di cappella* to Paolo Savelli, Prince of Albano (1619–*c*1622). In 1622 Landi was noted as 'servitore' of Pope Gregory XV's nephew Cardinal Lodovico Ludovisi, with regard to carnival entertainments for 1623. This may have involved him in *Il ritorno d'Angelica nell'India* (libretto by O. Tronsarelli), performed that season for Nicolò Ludovisi's marriage to Isabella Gesualdo.

By the end of 1624 Landi was *maestro di cappella* at S Maria ai Monti in Rome, musician to Cardinal Maurizio of Savoy and a composer with four published volumes of music to his credit. Among them, as op.2, was his first opera, the 'tragicomedia pastorale' *La morte d'Orfeo* (Venice, 1619; libretto edited in Solerti, music extracts edited in Goldschmidt, 188ff), which was possibly staged in the Veneto region in 1619. In 1629 his former singing pupil Angelo Ferrotti was admitted to the papal choir, and Landi began to teach the boy castrato Girolamo Zampetti for Cardinal Francesco Barberini, the pope's nephew. Both Zampetti and Ferrotti performed in the operas that the Barberini staged in Rome.

Landi's reputation is most strongly linked to the Barberini on account of their first major opera production, *Sant'Alessio*, to a libretto by Giulio Rospigliosi (libretto edited in Della Corte, 195–265). This is Landi's only major surviving work for his demanding patrons. Cardinal Francesco was hoping as early as June 1630 to employ Ferrotti in 'una comedia in musica'. There is a single notice of a musical representation on the life of St Alexis given at the Palazzo Barberini ai Giubbonari on 2 March 1631, but no details are known. An eye-witness cited Landi as the composer of the *Sant'Alessio* that was staged in the new Palazzo Barberini alle Quattro Fontane on 18 February 1632, a production considered to have begun a tradition of seasonal operatic performances in Rome. Its producer was a cardinal; its librettist, a prelate; its composer, a cleric. The scenographer, Pietro da Cortona, was a leading artist of the Roman high Baroque (the oft-repeated attribution of the scenography to G. L. Bernini was discounted by Lavin, 1964); and the visitor honoured on the occasion, Hans Ulrich von Eggenberg, was a prince of the Holy Roman Empire. A sign of the continuing influence of the

Counter-Reformation, the subject was the last trial of a 4th-century saint, a noble Roman ascetic who lived incognito in his family's palace, and refused riches and love in order to follow the way of the blessed to a humble death. Cardinal Francesco Barberini restaged the opera with additional characters, scenes and stage machines in 1634, also subsidizing the publication of the score, which had engravings representing eight of the scenes (Rome, 1634/*R*1970: BMB, xi).

Landi's two operas, separated by at least 12 years, resemble one another in the style of the recitative, which dominates both works, although the scenes in *Orfeo* are substantially shorter and fewer. His fondness for suspended 7ths, dissonant chords over prolonged bass notes and chromatic shifts of cadential centre all give the affective moments a characteristic poignancy. Some melodic figures recur in both operas. Both also show Landi's ability to differentiate between characters through the rhythms and intonation of their recitative, and both make extensive use of festive choral ensembles – interlacings of solos and duets with homophonic double chorus and lively madrigalian polyphony. Each of the five acts in *Orfeo* and the three in *Sant'Alessio* moves towards a typically classical release of emotion in such closing ensembles. Both operas include few arias: there are but six each in *Orfeo* and in the 1634 version of *Sant'Alessio*, not counting its prologue. In the earlier opera, four are sets of solo strophic variations; in the later, straight repeated strophes are the norm. The six in *Sant'Alessio* include a humorous duet for two lazy page-boys and two trios, the first of which leads to the closing chorus of Act 2; the second trio is a madrigalian lament for Alexis's parents and wife, its three separate sections forming an emotional part of both the dramatic and the harmonic architecture of the purgative denouement. The score of *Sant'Alessio*, unlike *Orfeo*, includes the instrumental music for multi-sectional sinfonias before each act, *balletos*, and concertato parts in choral ensembles. The required instruments are bowed and plucked strings, including harps, which were in frequent use in the Barberini establishment.

Sant'Alessio may not have been Landi's last encounter with musical drama. He must certainly be considered a possible composer of the Barberini opera of 1635 *I Santi Didimo e Teodora*, in which Ferrotti and Zampetti both sang. In that same year he served as musical director (and possibly composer) for a drama staged by Pietro Della Valle, and he also collaborated with Ottaviano Castelli on *I pregi di primavera*, music for a May Day representation (1635; MS libretto in *I-Rvat*). Circumstantial evidence that Landi may have set the opera-cantata *La vittoria del Principe Vladislao in Valacchia*, performed in Rome in 1625 for the Crown Prince of Poland, needs reconsideration in favour of J. H. Kapsberger.

See also MORTE D'ORFEO, LA and SANT'ALESSIO.

*

G. B. Doni: 'Trattato della musica scenica', *Lyra Barberina amphichordos*, ii: *De' trattati di musica di G. B. Doni*, ed. A. F. Gori and G. B. Passeri (Florence, 1763), 14–15; excerpts in A. Soletri: *Le origini del melodramma* (Turin, 1903), 202–3

R. Eitner: 'Die weiteren Entwicklung der Oper', *MMg*, xiv (1882), 98–100

A. Ademollo: *I teatri di Roma nel secolo decimosettimo* (Rome, 1888), 7–20

J. Grand-Carteret: 'Les titres illustrés et l'image au service de la musique', *RMI*, v (1898), 24–8

G. Canevazzi: *Papa Clemente IX, poeta* (Modena, 1900), 65–76

H. Goldschmidt: *Studien zur Geschichte der italienischen Oper im 17. Jahrhundert*, i (Leipzig, 1901)

R. Rolland: 'La première représentation du "San Alessio" de Stefano Landi, en 1632, à Rome, d'après le journal manuscrit de Jean-Jacques Bouchard', *RHCM*, ii (1902), esp.29–36

G. Canevazzi: *Di tre melodrammi del secolo XVII* (Modena, 1904)

A. Soletri: *Gli albori del melodramma*, iii (Milan, 1904), 293–339

A. Salza: 'Drammi inediti di G. Rospigliosi', *RMI*, xiv (1907), 480–89

G. Pavan: 'Un dramma musicale a Roma nel 1634: il *S. Alessio* del Landi', *Musica d'oggi*, iii (1921), 274–77

U. Rolandi: 'Un tricentenario . . . contestato: l'apertura del teatro Barberini (18 febb. 1632)', *Rassegna dorica*, iii (1931–2), 70–72

F. Vatielli: 'Operisti-librettisti dei secoli XVII–XVIII', *RMI*, xliii (1939), 1–16

A. A. Abert: *Claudio Monteverdi und das musikalische Drama* (Lippstadt, 1954)

A. Della Corte: *Drammi per musica dal Rinuccini allo Zeno*, i (Turin, 1958), 195–265

S. A. Carfagno: *The Life and Dramatic Music of Stefano Landi with a Transliteration and Orchestration of the Opera Sant'Alessio* (diss., U. of California, Los Angeles, 1960)

I. Lavin: Review of C. d'Onofrio, ed.: G. L. Bernini: *Fontana di Trevi*, *Art Bulletin*, xlvi (1964), 568–72

I. Küffel: *Die Libretti Giulio Rospigliosis: ein Kapitel frühbarocker Operngeschichte in Rom* (diss., U. of Vienna, 1968)

N. Pirrotta: 'Early Opera and Aria', *New Looks at Italian Opera: Essays in Honor of Donald J. Grout* (Ithaca, 1968), 87, 99–102

A. Ziino: '"Contese litterarie" tra Pietro della Valle e Nicolò Farfaro sulla musica antica e moderna', *NRMI*, iii (1969), 101–20

R. Lebègue: 'Peiresc témoin de la vie dramatique de son temps', *Mélanges historiques et littéraires sur le XVIIe siècle offerts à Georges Mongrédien* (Paris, 1974), 284–6

M. A. Lavin: *Seventeenth-century Barberini Documents and Inventories of Art* (New York, 1975)

S. Leopold: *Stefano Landi: Beiträge zur Biographie, Untersuchungen zur weltlichen und geistlichen Vokalmusik* (Hamburg, 1976); review by H. Meister, *Mf*, xxxiii (1980), 105–6

T. Tallián: 'Archivdokumente über die Tätigkeit S. Landis in Rom in den Jahren von 1624 bis 1629', *SM*, xix (1977), 267–95

S. Leopold: 'Das geistliche Libretto im 17. Jahrhundert: zur Gattungsgeschichte der frühen Oper', *Mf*, xxxi (1978), 245–57

——: 'Quelle bazzicature poetiche appellate ariette: Dichtungsformen in der frühen italienischen Oper (1600–1640)', *HJbMw*, iii (1978), 101–41

M. K. Murata: *Operas for the Papal Court, 1631–1668* (Ann Arbor, 1981)

G. Panofsky-Sorgel: 'Nachträge zu Stefano Landis Biographie', *AnMc*, xxii (1984), 69–129

V. Kapp: 'Das Barberini-Theater und die Bedeutung der römischer Kultur unter Urban VIII', *Literaturwissenschaftliches Jahrbuch*, new ser., xxvi (1985), 75–100 MARGARET MURATA

Landon, H(oward) C(handler) Robbins (*b* Boston, 6 March 1926). American musicologist. After studying with Karl Geiringer and Hugo Norton at Boston University (1945–7), he worked as a music critic for American newspapers in England, France, the Netherlands and Austria (1947–9). In 1949 he founded the Haydn Society, of which he became secretary general (1949–51). He has also lectured at Queens College, New York, the University of California at Davis and University College, Cardiff, and edited the *Haydn Yearbook*, 1962–70.

After his book on Haydn's symphonies (1955), a landmark in Haydn scholarship, Landon drew fresh public and scholarly attention to other Haydn works, notably his operas, several of which he published in new critical editions, stimulating performances and provoking a reappraisal of Haydn as a dramatic composer. He has published many articles on the operas and the background to their composition and performance, and has also written illuminatingly on Mozart and his mature operas.

'Haydn's Marionette Operas and the Repertoire of the Marionette Theatre at Esterház Castle', *Haydn Yearbook*, i (1962), 111–97

[with thematic catalogue, list of marionette operas and marionette productions at Eszterháza 1773–83]
ed.: *Haydn Yearbook* (1962–70)
'Opera in Italy and the Holy Roman Empire: the Operas of Haydn', *NOHM*, vii (1973), 172–99
Haydn: Chronicle and Works (London, 1976–80)
1791: Mozart's Last Year (London, 1988)
Mozart: The Golden Years (London, 1989)

Landowski, Marcel (*b* Pont L'Abbé, Finistère, 18 Feb 1915). French composer. He studied at the Paris Conservatoire with Noël Gallon, Büsser and Gaubert, and also had tuition from Monteux; later, after military service in World War II (1939–40), he benefited from the advice of Honegger. He lived in Boulogne-sur-Seine after the war, serving as director of the conservatory from 1959 to 1962. He then became music director for the Comédie-Française (1962–5), inspector-general for music education (1965) and music director for the Ministry of Cultural Affairs (1966).

As a composer Landowski has sought a middle path between conservatism and the avant garde. His stage works, which include incidental music and ballets as well as operas, reveal the influence of Honegger married with the dramatic realism of Menotti. The subjects of his operas are varied. *Le rire de Nils Halérius*, based on Indian philosophy, shows an involvement with metaphysical thought and its hero sees only one possible attitude to the absurdity of life: laughter. *Le fou*, which includes electro-acoustic passages, concerns the social responsibilities of scientists, while *L'opéra de poussière* deals with a misunderstood composer; the protagonist of *Adieux* is a girl who renounces love for the sake of her idealism and thirst for the absolute; and *Montségur* is a tale of incompatible love between two characters of differing religions – a Cathar and a Christian knight. Landowski's intentions are evident from his statement that 'the future will, like the past, belong to works which are clear and direct, and which issue from the heart of the artist to be understood by the hearts of all'.

Le rire de Nils Halérius, 1944–8 (légende lyrique et chorégraphique, 3, G. Caillet and Landowski), Mülhausen, Opéra, 19 Jan 1951
Le fou, 1949–54 (3, Landowski), Nancy, 1 Feb 1956
Le ventriloque (comédie lyrique et chorégraphique, 1, P. Arnold and Landowski), Paris, Sarah Bernhardt, 6 Feb 1956
L'opéra de poussière, 1958–62 (drame lyrique, prol., 2, Caillet and Landowski), Avignon, 25 Oct 1962, vs (Paris, 1964)
Les adieux, 1959 (drame lyrique, 1, Landowski), Paris, OC (Favart), 8 Oct 1960, vs (Paris, 1960)
Montségur, 1980–85 (2, Landowski, Caillet and G. P. Saindérichin, after Duc de Lévis-Mirepoix), Toulouse, Halle aux Grains, 1 Feb 1985
La sorcière du placard aux balais, 1983 (mini-opera for children, 1, P. Gripari), concert perf., Sévres, 2 May 1983; staged, Boulogne-Billancourt, 8 March 1984

*

A. Goléa: *Marcel Landowski* (Paris, 1969)
P. Ancelin: 'Marcel Landowski – le musicien de l'espérance', *ReM*, nos. 372–4 (1984), 5–8
F. Andrieux: 'Marcel Landowski et le théâtre lyrique', *Le théâtre lyrique français 1945–1985*, ed. D. Pistone (Paris, 1987), 243–53
L'avant-scène opéra (1991) [*Montségur*, *Le fou* issue]
RICHARD LANGHAM SMITH

Landré, Guillaume (*b* The Hague, 24 Feb 1905; *d* Amsterdam, 6 Nov 1968). Dutch composer. He was one of the most prominent pupils of Pijper, with whom he studied composition concurrently with his law studies at Utrecht University. He worked for many years in Amsterdam as a teacher of commercial law and as a music critic, and later held important administrative posts in

Dutch musical life. He was awarded the Sweelinck Prize in 1965.

Landré's first compositions clearly show Pijper's influence, notably the comic opera *De snoek* (1934). It is a surrealist piece, containing a number of humorous, shrewdly typified scenes in a colourful, polytonal idiom. A change of style is apparent in subsequent works, where broad, expressive melodies began to replace the short motifs characteristic of the Pijper style. Landré's last years saw the composition of two more operas, *Jean Lévecq* (1963) and *La symphonie pastorale* (1964); the latter was first performed during the Gide celebrations at Rouen in 1968.

Guillaume's father, Willem Landré (*b* Amsterdam, 12 June 1874; *d* Eindhoven, 1 Jan 1948), also a composer (and his son's first teacher), wrote two operas, *De roos van Dekama* (1897), and *Beatrijs* (libretto by F. Rutten), which, after its première in The Hague in 1925, was performed a year later at the Paris Opéra.

De snoek [The Pike], 1934 (3, E. van Lockhorst), Amsterdam, 1938
Jean Lévecq, 1963 (1, G. Smit, after G. de Maupassant: *Le retour*), Amsterdam, 6 June 1965
La symphonie pastorale, 1964 (prol., 3, epilogue, C. Rostand, after A. Gide), Rouen, Arts, 31 March 1968

*

C. Rostand: 'La symphonie pastorale: Opera by Guillaume Landré', *Sonorum speculum*, no.34 (1968), 1–10
JOS WOUTERS/LEO SAMAMA

Lane, Gloria (*b* Trenton, NJ, 6 June 1930). American mezzo-soprano, later soprano. She studied in Philadelphia and made her début there as the Secretary in the première of Menotti's *The Consul* (1950), the opera of her London début (Cambridge Theatre) the next year. She sang Desideria in another Menotti première, *The Saint of Bleecker Street*, on Broadway (1954), was Baba the Turk in the Glyndebourne revival of *The Rake's Progress* (1958), and Carmen at Covent Garden (1960). Other engagements took her to La Scala, the Vienna Staatsoper, the Deutsche Oper, Berlin, and to France, Denmark and Italy as well as Boston, Chicago and San Francisco. Changing to dramatic soprano, she first sang Santuzza with the New York City Opera in 1971, and Ariadne and Lady Macbeth at Glyndebourne the next year. She combines a forceful stage personality with a strong voice in both registers, and a keen sense of rhythm if not very subtle shading.
NOËL GOODWIN

Lanetin, Charles-François-Honoré. *See* DUQUESNOY, CHARLES-FRANÇOIS-HONORÉ.

Lanfranchi Rossi, Carlo Giuseppe (*fl c*1750–*c*1800). Italian librettist. Attributions to him in contemporary printed librettos attest to his noble Pisan origins. He was educated in Pisa and made his literary career in Florence, then Venice. Composers who set his librettos include Galuppi, Gazzaniga and Martín y Soler. His Arcadian name was Ergesippo Argolida.

Il Muzio Scevola (dm), Masi, 1760 (Galuppi, 1762); Telemaco nell' isola di Calipso (dramma), G. V. Meucci, 1773; Le cognate in contesa (dg), Zannetti, 1780 (Trento, 1791); L'amante per bisogno (dg), ?Gazzaniga, 1781; La sposa bizzarra (ob), A. Santi, 1781; Il trionfo d'Arianna (dm), Anfossi, 1781; Gli amanti canuti (dg), Anfossi, 1781; Telemaco nell'isola di Calipso (dm), ?V. Meucci; In amor ci vuol destrezza (ob), Martín y Soler, 1782; La vergine del sole (dramma), Tritto, 1786

*

G. G. Bernardi: 'L'opera comica veneziana del secolo XVIII', *Atti dell' Accademia virgiliana di Mantova: Mantua* 1908

M. Maylender: *Storia della accademia Italia* (Bologna, 1926)

E. Cristiani: *Nobiltà e popolo nel commune di Pisa dalle origini del podestariato alla signoria dei Donoratico* (Naples, 1962)

PATRICIA LEWY GIDWITZ

Lang, Paul Henry [Láng, Pál] (*b* Budapest, 28 Aug 1901; *d* Lakeville, CT, 21 Sept 1991). American musicologist of Hungarian birth. He studied in Budapest (where he was briefly assistant conductor at the Budapest Opera), Heidelberg, Paris and the USA, where he took the PhD at Cornell with a dissertation, *A Literary History of French Opera* (1934). He taught at Columbia University from 1933. His *Music in Western Civilization* (New York, 1941) is one of the outstanding 20th-century contributions to cultural history and probably his finest achievement. He was editor of the *Musical Quarterly*, 1945–73, and served from 1954 to 1963 as chief music critic of the *New York Herald-Tribune*; a volume of his writings was issued as *Critic at the Opera* (New York, 1971). He was early among those who drew attention to the operas of Haydn (*MQ*, xviii (1932), 274), and his substantial study *George Frideric Handel* (New York, 1966) includes much critical discussion of the operas.

Langdon, Michael [Birtles, Frank] (*b* Wolverhampton, 12 Nov 1920; *d* Hove, E. Sussex, 12 March 1991). English bass. He joined the Covent Garden chorus in 1948, making his solo début in 1950 as the Nightwatchman (*The Olympians*) in Manchester. Graduating to principal roles he created Lieutenant Ratcliffe in *Billy Budd* (1951), the Recorder of Norwich in *Gloriana* (1953), the He-Ancient in *The Midsummer Marriage* (1955) and the Doctor in *We Come to the River* (1976). His roles included Fafner, Hunding, Hagen, Daland, Don Basilio, Rocco, Kecal, Varlaam, the Grand Inquisitor (*Don Carlos*), Bottom, Waldner (*Arabella*) and Ochs, his best-known part, which he studied in Vienna with Jerger and sang over 100 times, at Hamburg, Berlin, Budapest, Paris, San Francisco, the Metropolitan, Brussels, Vienna and Geneva. His repertory also included Méphistophélès, Osmin, Sarastro, the Commendatore, Rossini's Moses, Nicolai's Falstaff, Nielsen's Saul and Don Pasquale; for Scottish Opera he created the title role of Orr's *Hermiston* at Edinburgh (1975). His final appearances were as Frank in *Die Fledermaus* at Covent Garden in 1985. He was a notable Claggart (*Billy Budd*) on television. He had a large, rather dry-toned voice, equally suitable to comic or tragic parts. On retiring from the stage he became director of the National Opera Studio (1978–86). His autobiography, *Notes from a Low Singer*, was published in 1982.

For illustration *see* MIDSUMMER MARRIAGE, THE.

*

H. Rosenthal: 'Michael Langdon', *Opera*, xxvi (1975), 1111–16

E. Downes and E. Forbes: 'Michael Langdon (1920–1991)', *Opera*, xlii (1991), 511–5

ALAN BLYTH

Lange [née Weber], **(Maria) Aloysia** [Aloisia, **Lange, Aloysia** Louise] (**Antonia**) (*b* Zell or Mannheim, *c*1761; *d* Salzburg, 8 June 1839). German soprano. She was the sister of Josepha Hofer, and sister-in-law of Mozart, who married her sister Constanze in 1782. She studied in Mannheim with Vogler and with Mozart, her association with whom produced seven concert arias and a role in *Der Schauspieldirektor* (as well as a series of letters by Mozart notable for their elucidation of his views on vocal performance and training). Their first encounter, during Mozart's stay in Mannheim in 1777–8 (when he fell in love with her) resulted in the concert arias K294, 316/300*b* and probably 538. She moved from Mannheim to Munich in 1778, where she made her début as Parthenia in Schweitzer's *Alceste* (Carnival 1779); she was then engaged for the new National Singspiel in Vienna, where she made her début on 9 September 1779 as Hännchen in a German adaptation of Philidor's *Le rosière de Salency*. She married the court actor and painter Joseph Lange on 31 October 1780.

When in 1782 Joseph II removed German opera to the neighbouring Kärntnertortheater and reinstated Italian comic opera at the Burgtheater, she was retained as a leading singer of the Italian troupe. For her début, as Clorinda in Anfossi's *Il curioso indiscreto* (1783), Mozart composed two substitute arias, K418 and 419. Lange participated regularly in Italian opera for only eight months; probably she fell out of favour because of disagreements over salary and roles as well as missed performances. In 1785 she was among the German singers transferred to the less prestigious Kärntnertortheater, where she revived many roles of her early career with the important addition of Konstanze in Mozart's *Die Entführung* (1785–8). Lange continued to appear occasionally at the Burgtheater, notably for a German revival in 1785 of Gluck's *La rencontre imprévue*, for the Vienna première of Mozart's *Don Giovanni* (as Donna Anna) and for Cimarosa's *Il fanatico burlato*, both in 1788. She was retained by Leopold II for his *opera seria* venture in Vienna in 1790, as a seconda donna. In 1795 Aloysia undertook a concert tour with her sister Constanze, continuing her successes as Mozart's Sextus, a role she had performed in Vienna.

A report in the *Deutsches Museum* (1781) states that she 'has a very pleasing voice, though it is too weak for the theatre', and Gerber pronounced her voice 'more suited for an ordinary room than the theatre'. Leopold Mozart corroborates this view in a letter to his daughter of 25 March 1785:

> It can scarcely be denied that she sings with the greatest expression: only now I understand why some persons I frequently asked would say that she has a very weak voice, while others said she has a very loud voice. Both are true. The held notes and all expressive notes are astonishingly loud; the tender moments, the passage work and embellishments, and high notes are very delicate, so that for my taste the one contrasts too strongly with the other. In an ordinary room the loud notes assault the ear, while in the theatre the delicate passages demand a great attentiveness and stillness on the part of the audience.

Mozart's compositions give the clearest picture of her voice. His sensitivity to Lange's small instrument may be seen in the light orchestration and relatively high tessitura. Her music exploits expressive, cantabile delivery and gives ample opportunity for portamento and the addition of ornaments. Her *fioriture* consist primarily of scale work and *abbellimenti* spun out in varied, flexible rhythmic configurations, and there is an almost casual assaying of her remarkable upper range, extending to *g'''* (as Blanka in Umlauf's *Das Irrlicht*, 1782, she sang to *a'''*). Gebler regarded her as 'a splendid singer, [with] a tone and an expression that goes to the heart [and] an extraordinary upper range; she correctly performs the most difficult passages and blends them with the song as it should be done'.

*

R. M. Werner: *Aus dem Josephinischen Wien: Geblers und Nicolais Briefwechsel während der Jahre 1771–1786* (Berlin, 1888)

R. P. von Thurn: *Joseph II. als Theaterdirektor* (Vienna and Leipzig, 1920)

J. H. Eibl: 'Wer hat das engagement Aloisia Webers an die Wiener Oper vermittelt?', *MJb 1962–3*, 111–14

O. Michtner: *Das alte Burgtheater als Opernbühne* (Vienna, 1970)

P. Lewy Gidwitz: *Vocal Profiles of Four Mozart Sopranos* (diss., U. of California, Berkeley, 1991) PATRICIA LEWY GIDWITZ

Lange-Müller, Peter Erasmus (*b* Frederiksberg, 1 Dec 1850; *d* Copenhagen, 26 Feb 1926). Danish composer. After leaving school in 1870 he enrolled at Copenhagen University (to read political science) and at the conservatory, but ill-health soon forced him to give up his studies. Throughout his life he suffered from constant headaches, which affected both his personal relations and his musical development. He was largely self-taught, and his isolation meant that he could more readily develop the original and untraditional characteristics of his music.

A romantic by temperament and artistic inclination, he was strongly influenced by the music of his countrymen Hartmann and Heise and by that of Schumann. He evolved an individual late Romantic style built around emotionally concentrated tonal effects on a dark harmonic background, reminiscent of Brahms and contemporary French developments – an expression of nostalgia that was not directly followed in Danish music. His incidental music for Holger Drachmann's romantic comedy *Der var engang* ('Once upon a time', 1887) was his most successful work for the stage and helped to ensure the play's enduring popularity in Denmark. His substantial output is dominated by vocal music. He hoped for success as a composer of opera, but his most ambitious work, *Vikingeblod*, in which Wagnerian influences are evident, was also his greatest disappointment; the critics found the style and subject outdated, and this judgment may partly account for the decline in his output after 1900 and its virtual cessation by 1910.

first performed at the Kongelige Teater, Copenhagen; all printed works published in Copenhagen; MSS in DK-Kk

Tove op.7 (Spl, 3, Lange-Müller), 1878, abridged vs (1879)

Spanske studenter op.22 (oc, 2, V. Faber), 1883, vs (1883)

Fru Jeanna op.30, 1886 (tragic op, 4, E. von der Recke), 1891, vs (1892)

Middelalderlig [Medieval] op.55 (melodrama, H. Drachmann), 1896, abridged vs (1903)

Vikingeblod op.50, before 1897 (4, E. Christiansen), 1900, vs (1897)

Renaissance op.59 (melodrama, Drachmann), 1901, vs (1903)

*

DBL (E. Abrahamsen)

P. E. Lange-Müller: Autobiography, *Illustreret tidende* (27 Nov 1910)

G. Lynge: 'P. E. Lange-Müller', *Danske komponister i det 20. aarhundredes begyndelse* (Århus, 1916, 2/1917), 170ff

H. Bonnén: *P. E. Lange-Müller* (Copenhagen, 1946)

K. A. Bruun: 'P. E. Lange-Müller', *Dansk musiks historie fra Holberg-tiden til Carl Nielsen* (Copenhagen, 1969), ii, 243–79

N. Schiørring: 'Lange-Müller', *Musikkens Historie, Danmark*, iii (Copenhagen, 1978), 89–94 NIELS MARTIN JENSEN

Lange Weihnachtsmahl, Das. Opera by Paul Hindemith; *see* LONG CHRISTMAS DINNER, THE.

Langlade, Sieur de. *See* LA SERRE, JEAN-LOUIS-IGNACE DE.

Langlé, Honoré (François Marie) (*b* Monaco, 1741; *d* Villiers-le-Bel, nr Paris, 20 Sept 1807). French composer. He studied at the Conservatorio della Pietà dei Turchini in Naples from 1756 to 1764. After managing the theatre and the noblemen's concerts in Genoa (1764–8), he made a career as a teacher and composer in Paris where his first works were performed at the Concert Spirituel. He wrote several stage works, but only two of them were performed. *Antiochus et Stratonice*, a skilfully orchestrated work, shows early hints of romanticism. The score of *Corisandre* demonstrates the composer's solid technique and characteristic style: highly coloured orchestration and an alternation of action scenes with poetic reflections. Langlé was appointed professor of singing at the Ecole Royale de Chant et de Déclamation (later the Conservatoire) in 1784; he retired in 1802. His compositions, which include *symphonies militaires*, motets, and many miscellaneous instrumental and vocal pieces, were far less successful than his theoretical and didactic works.

Antiochus et Stratonice (opéra, 3, Durosoi), Versailles, 30 Dec 1786, *F-Pn*; (Paris, 1786)

Corisandre, ou Les fous par enchantement (comédie-opéra, De Linières and A. F. Lebailly, after Voltaire: *La pucelle*), Paris, Opéra, 8 March 1791, *Po*; (Paris, 1791)

Unperf., scores in *Pn*: Oreste et Tyndare, 1783; Soliman et Eromine [Mahomet II], 1792; L'auberge des volontaires, 1793; La choix d'Alcide, 1800; Médée; Tancrède; Les vengeances

*

F. Fayolle: *Eloge de Langlé* (Paris, 1808)

A. Adam: *Souvenirs d'un musicien* (Paris, 1857)

L. Canis: 'Honoré-François-Marie Langlé, compositeur monégasque', *Le petit monégasque* (5 Aug 1923), 1

R. Valette: 'A propos d'Honoré Langlé', *Le petit monégasque* (12 Aug 1923), 1

J. Tiersot: *Lettres de musiciens*, i (Turin, 1924) PAULE DRUILHE

Langridge, Philip (Gordon) (*b* Hawkhurst, Kent, 16 Dec 1939). English tenor. He studied at the RAM with Bruce Boyce and later with Celia Bizony, making his début in 1964 as a Footman (*Capriccio*) at Glyndebourne, where he returned as Don Ottavio, Florestan (for the Glyndebourne Touring Opera), Idomeneus, Laca (*Jenůfa*), Titus and Pelegrin in the British première of *New Year* (1990). Roles for the ENO have included Peter Quint; Zivny (*Osud*), for which he won an Olivier Award in 1984; the title role of Birtwistle's *The Mask of Orpheus*, which he co-created in 1986; and Gregor (*The Makropulos Affair*), as well as Captain Vere, Stravinsky's Oedipus and Berlioz's Benedick. He made his Covent Garden début in 1983 as the Fisherman (*The Nightingale*) and the Teapot (*L'enfant et les sortilèges*), later singing Shuysky, Laca, Peter Grimes and Aschenbach (1992). He has sung Tom Rakewell, Shuysky, Oberon, Idomeneus and Andres (*Wozzeck*) at La Scala. He made his Metropolitan début in 1985 as Ferrando and first sang at Salzburg in 1987 as Aaron (*Moses und Aron*), which he recorded, winning a Grammy Award (1985). He has appeared in Vienna, Zürich, Aix-en-Provence, Paris, Wexford, Buxton, with Scottish Opera and the WNO. His firm voice, clear diction, incisive articulation and lively dramatic sense are of particular value in the Britten, Janáček and Stravinsky repertory in which he excels. He was made a CBE in 1992. ELIZABETH FORBES

Lanier, Nicholas (*b* London, bap. 10 Sept 1588; *d* London, bur. 24 Feb 1666). English composer and singer. He came from a family of musicians associated with the court and joined the King's Musick as a lutenist in 1616; he was later appointed Master of the King's Musick to Charles I. The court sent him to Italy several times to buy pictures, and he published sets of his own etchings. He was an innovatory composer of songs and is claimed by some scholars to have been the first composer of opera in England. That claim is made with reference to his music, none of which is extant, for Ben Jonson's *Lovers Made Men* (1617, London), based on the description of the masque in the Second Folio (1640) of Jonson's *Works*, which includes the comment that 'the whole Maske was sung (after the Italian manner) *Stylo recitativo*, by Master *Nicholas Lanier*'. This passage does not, however, occur in the 1617 quarto of the masque, and it is usually thought that only in retrospect did Jonson think of the masque as sung in recitative. The songs are more likely to have been declamatory ayres. Another masque by Jonson and Lanier, *The Vision of Delight* (1617, London), performed at court a month before *Lovers Made Men*, and whose description survives only in the 1640 folio, begins with the character Delight, who is described as having 'spake in song (*stylo recitativo*)'. One song survives from this masque (*GB-Lbl*), in the style of declamatory ayre rather than recitative. His later vocal piece *Hero and Leander*, however, written about 1630 after his visits to Italy, has been described as the first use of true recitative in English music.

Lovers Made Men was the first masque to be described as having been sung throughout. Indeed, far more than any other Jonson masque, it is a little drama enclosed by the self-contained fiction of its perspective set and with no antimasque. Both these characteristics, whether or not the music was recitative, may give the piece some claim to being an early English opera. Besides writing music on his own for *Lovers Made Men* and *The Vision of Delight*, Lanier is known to have provided music, with John Coprario, for Thomas Campion's *Maske ... at the Marriage of ... the Earle of Somerset* (26 Dec 1613, London) and, with Alfonso Ferrabosco the younger, for Jonson's *The Masque of Augurs* (1622, London; dance *Lbl*). Callon suggests that Lanier also composed music for some or all of the three performances of Jonson's *The Gypsies Metamorphos'd* (1621, Burley-on-the-Hill), but Randall gives evidence which disputes this. Callon also discusses the evidence for proposing Lanier's participation in Townshend's two masques of 1632, *Albion's Triumph* and *Tempe Restored*.

J. P. Cutts: 'Ben Jonson's Masque "The Vision of Delight"', *Notes and Queries*, new ser., iii (1956), 64–7

R. W. Ingram: 'Operatic Tendencies in Stuart Drama', *MQ*, xliv (1958), 489–502

A. J. Sabol, ed.: *Songs and Dances for the Stuart Masque* (Providence, RI, 1959, enlarged 2/1978)

M. Emslie: 'Nicholas Lanier's Innovations in English Song', *ML*, xli (1960), 13–27

A. J. Sabol: Introduction to *A Score for 'Lovers Made Men': a Masque by Ben Jonson* (Providence, RI, 1963)

V. Duckles: 'English Song and the Challenge of Italian Monody', in V. Duckles and F. B. Zimmerman: *Words to Music* (Los Angeles, 1967), 3–42

S. Orgel, ed.: *Ben Jonson: the Complete Masques* (New Haven and London, 1969)

D. B. J. Randall: *Jonson's Gypsies Unmasked: Background and Theme of 'The Gypsies Metamorphos'd'* (Durham, NC, 1975)

M. Chan: *Music in the Theatre of Ben Jonson* (Oxford, 1980)

G. J. Callon: *Nicholas Lanier, his Life and Music: a Study and Edition* (diss., U. of Washington, 1983)   MARY CHAN

Lanigan, John (*b* Seddon, Victoria, 7 Jan 1921). Australian tenor. He studied in Melbourne and London, making his début at the Stoll Theatre in 1949 as Fenton and Rodolfo. In 1951 he sang Thaddeus (*The Bohemian Girl*) at Covent Garden and began a 25-year engage-

ment with the Royal Opera, first appearing as the Duke (*Rigoletto*). For a decade he sang lyric roles, Tamino, Alfredo, Pinkerton, Des Grieux (*Manon*), Jeník, Essex (*Gloriana*), Almaviva and Laca (*Jenůfa*). He created Jack in *The Midsummer Marriage* (1955) and Hermes in *King Priam* (1962, Coventry). Later he displayed rare vocal and dramatic versatility in character parts: as Mime, Spalanzani (*Les contes d'Hoffmann*), Pandarus (*Troilus and Cressida*), Il 'Tinca' (*Il tabarro*), Dr Caius, the Drunken Guest (*Katerina Ismaylova*), the Rector (*Peter Grimes*), Flute, Sir Philip (*Owen Wingrave*) and Shuysky, his most effective role. He created Jones in Bennett's *Victory* (1970), the Cardinal/Archbishop in Maxwell Davies's *Taverner* (1972) and the Soldier/Madman in Henze's *We Come to the River* (1976).

ELIZABETH FORBES

Lankow [Rosenberg], Edward (*b* Tarrytown-on-the-Hudson, NY, 1883; *d* New York, 29 Jan 1940). American bass. He took his professional name in honour of his teacher Anna Lankow and appeared first in concerts, including an American tour with Adelina Patti. In 1906 he made his operatic début in Dresden as Sarastro in *Die Zauberflöte*. From 1908 to 1911 he sang at the Frankfurt Opera, also appearing in Vienna and Paris. On his return to America he appeared first with the Boston Opera Company, his roles including King Mark in *Tristan* and a much-praised Arkel in *Pelléas et Mélisande*. He made his Metropolitan début as Sarastro in 1913, greeted with superlatives by critics. His later career was confined to recital work and teaching. Lankow's voice possessed rare quality and depth, and his range was said to cover three octaves. Though he made a few recordings, they do scant justice to the distinction to which all who heard him paid tribute.

M. F. Bott: 'Edward Lankow', *Record Collector*, xxv (1979–80), 88–95   J. B. STEANE

Lantino, Liviano. *See* VILLANI, ANTONIO.

Lanzelot. Opera in 15 scenes by PAUL DESSAU to a libretto by Heiner Müller and Ginka Cholakowa after themes of HANS CHRISTIAN ANDERSEN and Yevgeni Schwartz's fairy-tale comedy *Der Drache*; Berlin, Deutsche Staatsoper, 19 December 1969.

Intended as a parable of society, attacking the exploitation of man by man throughout human history, *Lanzelot* also criticizes anarchist strategies of liberation and calls for collective revolutionary action. The opera opens following a cholera epidemic. A dragon (bass) has helped to eliminate the disease by breathing fire to 'boil away' the infected water; in return, however, he demands annual payment of a young maiden. Lanzelot (baritone) proposes to fight the dragon, to rid the town of his controlling influence and to save Elsa (soprano), the dragon's latest intended victim. Without the support of the frightened townsfolk, Lanzelot slays the dragon, but while he is recovering from his wounds the Bürgermeister (tenor) proclaims himself president and demands Elsa's hand in marriage. It seems that nothing has changed. Inspired by Lanzelot, the people rise up, depose the president, and celebrate their new-found freedom.

Dessau uses large musical forces, adding stereophonic taped sound to the large orchestra, but he employs them flexibly and for purposes of characterization: exaggeration of sound denotes criticism, while reduced sound expresses the positive factor. The music is largely composed on the collage principle, with clever use of quotation; indeed, a quotation from Dessau's own Spanish song 'Die Thälmannkolonne' plays an important symbolic part.   FRITZ HENNENBERG

Lanzetti, Lucia. *See* LANCETTI, LUCIA.

Laparra, Raoul (*b* Bordeaux, 13 May 1876; *d* Suresnes, 4 April 1943). French composer. Born into an artistic family, he studied with Gédalge, Fauré, Lavignac and Diemer although his music, with its constant reference to Spanish dance, must surely owe a lot to Albéniz. Two operas, *La habañera* (1908) and *La jota* (1911), have dance scenes built into the librettos. Both are tales which deal with Latin concepts of honour. In *La habañera* two brothers are in love with the same woman, who is to wed one of them; the other kills him during a village dance on the eve of the marriage. The murderous brother, who eventually takes his brother's place in marriage, is haunted by his spectre and is swallowed up by his tomb while a *Dies irae* mysteriously emanates from the grave. Two versions of the vocal score exist, with different music for the prologue and interludes.

In *La jota* the dance theme is even more ingeniously woven in. A priest is in love with a girl, Soledad, a folk-heroine with magic powers. He realizes his passion while a *jota* is being danced on the eve of her fiancé's departure for war. The fiancé returns as a carlist to attack the church. As the priest tries to embrace Soledad, the church crumbles, letting the invading carlists enter. The priest appears hanging from the crucifix and the falling building has thrown the lovers together, dead but standing as if dancing the *jota*.

Laparra writes vivid Spanish pastiche, with many different kinds of dance and *cante jondo*. He uses these to unify scenes and successfully superimposes the action on them. For the religious episodes, by contrast, he writes evocative but essentially simple ecclesiastical music.

Le joueur de viole (1925) abandons the Spanish settings in favour of an allegory. A luthier has been trying to make an instrument where each of the four strings represents one of the seasons. His son, previously considered a good-for-nothing, overtakes him in the project, producing an instrument on which the strings represent the joys and trials of life: love, fame, pain and death. In this, as in the other operas, Laparra gives detailed indications of various possibilities regarding scenery, as well as notes on the interpretation of the music. In style, his music looks back to Massenet, absorbing few of the innovations of the earlier part of the century. *Le joueur de viole* contains many pastiche movements in the style of Baroque dances, while *L'illustre Frégona* (1931) returns to purely Spanish pastiche in the form of a zarzuela combining Spanish songs and dances in many styles with spoken dialogue. Laparra met an untimely death during an air-raid.

Peau d'âne, Bordeaux, Grand, 3 Feb 1899
La habañera (drame lyrique, prol., 3), Paris, OC (Favart), 26 Feb 1908
La jota (conte lyrique, 2), Paris, OC (Favart), 26 April 1911
Le joueur de viole (4, Laparra), Paris, OC (Favart), 24 Dec 1925
Las torreras (zar, 1, after T. de Molina), Lille, Grand, 17 Jan 1929
Amphitryon, 1929
L'illustre Frégona (zar, 3, Laparra, after M. de Cervantes), Paris, Opéra, 16 Feb 1931

*

H. Rebois: *Les grands prix de Rome de musique* (Paris, 1932)

P. le Flem: 'G. Dupont, R. Laparra, F. Casadesus, Marcel Samuel-Rousseau', *Le théâtre lyrique en France* (Paris, 1937–9) [pubn of Poste Nationale/Radio-Paris], iii, 163–71
P. Landormy: *La musique française après Debussy* (Paris, 1943)
P. Bertrand: *Le monde de la musique* (Geneva, 1947)
G. Samazeuilh: *Musiciens de mon temps* (Paris, 1947)
                                        RICHARD LANGHAM SMITH

Lapierre, (Joseph) Eugène (*b* Montreal, 8 June 1899; *d* Montreal, 21 Oct 1970). Canadian composer. He studied the organ with Benoit Poirier and was then appointed organist at various churches, later achieving success both as a performer and as a journalist. He studied in Europe from 1924 to 1928; his teachers there included Vincent d'Indy (composition) and Marcel Dupré (organ). On his return to Montreal Lapierre was appointed director of the Conservatoire National de Montréal in 1928, where he remained until his death. He became well known for his books (all published in Montreal) on music and musicians – including *Le rôle social de la musique* (1930), *Les vedettes de la musique canadiennes* (1931) and *Un style canadien de musique* (1942) – and for his journalism and teaching.

He wrote one comic opera, *Le père des amours*, which was first performed at the Monument National in December 1942. This opera concerns Joseph Quesnel, a Frenchman of varied skills, composer of two operas (*Colas et Colinette* and *Lucas et Cécile*), whose life ended in Montreal. *Le père des amours* was performed as part of the tricentenary celebrations of the foundation of Montreal. Lapierre is also known for his lyrics, cantatas and songs, published in France and Canada.

*

EMC (C. Huot)
Soeurs de Sainte-Anne: *Dictionnaire biographique des musiciens canadiens* (Lachine, 1935)
H. Kallmann: *A History of Music in Canada, 1534–1914* (Toronto, 1960)   CÉCILE HUOT

Lapis [Lapi, Lappi], Santo [Sante] (*b* Bologna; *fl* 1725–64). Italian composer. According to archival documents (*I-Baf, Bas*), he studied in Bologna at the S Onofrio conservatory and in 1720 was admitted to the Accademia Filarmonica as an organist. He probably left Bologna after 1724. He wrote the first two acts of the three-act *dramma La generosità di Tiberio* (the third act was by Cordans) to a libretto by Minato, performed at the S Cassiano, Venice, in autumn 1729; and he partly reset Francesco Gasparini's *L'amor generoso* as *La fede in cimento*, performed during Carnival 1730, again at the S Cassiano. In 1732 he composed a cantata, *Le nozze di Psiche e Cupido*, for a celebration at St Mark's. In 1739 he may have been in Prague, where part of the music for a production of *Ginevra* (libretto by Antonio Salvi) was ascribed to him. He lived in the Netherlands from about 1752 to 1756, in 1754 presenting his opera *L'infelice avventurato*, probably in Amsterdam (the score was once in Breitkopf's possession). Lapis seems to have been in London in 1758–60, when some instrumental music and songs by him were published there. The last record places him in Edinburgh, as harpsichordist of a visiting Italian intermezzo company which performed Pergolesi's *La serva padrona* in June 1763, and he may have gone with the same company to York in October 1763 and to Dublin in the spring of 1764.

Laporte, André (*b* Oplinter, 12 July 1931). Belgian composer. He studied at the Lemmens Institute in Mechelen and then at the Catholic University in

Louvain. In 1963 he was appointed producer at Flemish Radio and Television, where he has been in charge of contemporary music and the radio orchestra. He is also professor of composition at the Brussels Conservatory.

Laporte's works include chamber and solo works as well as large orchestral pieces and cantatas. In 1976 he was awarded the Prix Italia for his oratorio *La vita non è sogno*. He has composed one opera, *Das Schloss*, for which he wrote the libretto, based on an adaptation by Max Brod of Kafka's novel. It is in three acts and was first performed at La Monnaie on 16 December 1986. The 12 singing characters (who always sing individually) are given different vocal timbres; there is an eclectic use of vocal style, including melodrama, speech-song and coloratura. The acts are through-composed with orchestral transitions linking the scenes. Very much in the tradition of Wagner and Berg (both of whom are quoted), the music interprets the events through the use of leitmotif and intricate, clustered textures representing moods of uncertainty and fatality. The leitmotif of the principal character, K., is a 12-note set which is transformed as K. pursues his quest in vain. The music throughout is imaginative and varied, employing chromatic and whole-tone scales, expressive sighing inflections, chordal and rhythmic leitmotifs and imitations of Viennese waltzes. To some extent the opera integrates many of the techniques used by Laporte in earlier works while combining lyrical expression with narrative drama.

DIANA VON VOLBORTH-DANYS

Laporte [Delaporte], **Pierre François** [Francis] (*b* ?Paris, 1799; *d* Soisy-sous-Etiolles, Corbeil, nr Paris, 25 Sept 1841). French actor and impresario. He came from a theatrical family; his father, Jacques François Laporte (1775–1841), was the celebrated Harlequin of the Théâtre du Vaudeville in Paris for over 30 years. The younger Laporte also appeared in comic French roles at the Vaudeville, 1822–6, and in Brussels (1823) and London (1824), making his début on the English stage at Drury Lane in November 1826. The following year he joined the Haymarket company and by the beginning of 1828 was involved with one Laurent, the manager of the Italian opera in Paris, in a scheme to run the King's Theatre, London. Laurent soon withdrew and Laporte actively managed the theatre for the next 13 years (apart from the 1832 season, when Monck Mason was in charge and Laporte himself was lessee of Covent Garden).

Laporte's tactics for reducing salaries (particularly of the orchestra), raising box and pit prices, and negotiating with star singers were tough and made him unpopular with some. But to his credit, he also hired Michael Costa as conductor (in N. C. Bochsa's place), introduced Sontag, Lablache, Rubini, Grisi, Persiani, Viardot and Mario to London audiences, and mounted the London premières of *Le comte Ory*, *Il pirata*, *I puritani*, *La sonnambula*, *Anna Bolena* and *Norma* (the last three with Pasta). Latterly he had great difficulty opposing his artists' power: after the 'Tamburini row' of 1841 (*The Times*, 4 May) he was forced by public demand to rehire a singer he had resolved to do without. Four months later he died of heart disease at his father's country house; Benjamin Lumley, his legal and financial adviser since 1835, succeeded him.

*

An Explanation of the Differences existing between the Manager of the Italian Opera and the non-conforming Members of the late Orchestra, written among Themselves (London, 1829)

Obituary, *The Times* (29 Sept 1841)
B. Lumley: *Reminiscences of the Opera* (London, 1864)
[J. E. Cox]: *Musical Recollections of the Last Half-Century* (London, 1872)
J. R. Planché: *Recollections and Reflections: a Professional Autobiography* (London, 1872, 2/1901)
H. Lyonnet: *Dictionnaire des comédiens français: biographie, bibliographie, iconographie* (Paris, then Geneva, 1904–8)

LEANNE LANGLEY

Lappas, Ulysses (*b* Athens, 1881; *d* Athens, 26 July 1971). Greek tenor. He studied in Athens and made his début there in 1913. Further study in Italy led to successful appearances in major houses including La Scala, where he sang in the première of De Sabata's *Il macigno* (1917). His Covent Garden début as Cavaradossi in 1919 won him great praise for his acting and stage presence as well as for his robust voice. He returned in 1920, 1925 (singing Loris to Jeritza's Fedora in Giordano's opera) and in 1933 in some generally poor performances of *Don Carlos*. He also sang with the Chicago Opera and at La Scala took the title role in Felice Lattuada's *Don Giovanni* in 1934. From 1935 to 1952 he sang mainly in Athens, where he also taught. His recordings date from the promising 1920s and show an impressive voice with a style both impassioned and thoughtful.

J. B. STEANE

Lappi, Santo [Sante]. *See* LAPIS, SANTO.

Lara, Isidore de. *See* DE LARA, ISIDORE.

Large, Brian (*b* London, 16 Feb 1939). English director. He studied at the RAM and at London University, then in Munich and Vienna. In the 1960s he worked at the National Theatre, Prague, during which period he also translated Smetana's diaries and letters. He returned to England, where he joined the BBC as a television producer; he was promoted to chief opera producer in 1974. Although initially concerned with the studio production of operas for broadcast (such as *Owen Wingrave*, 1971, and *Der fliegende Holländer*, 1976), he always preferred to film singers live rather than allow them to mime to pre-recorded tapes. Later he chose to work in the opera house, recording stage performances both for broadcast by television companies and for commercial release on video and laser disc. He has videotaped *Ring* cycles at Bayreuth (1980 and 1991), and at the Metropolitan (1990), where his many recordings include Nilsson's last appearances as Electra (1980) and *Les Troyens* (1988). At Covent Garden he worked on the broadcast of *Les contes d'Hoffmann* (1981). He is a pioneer in the use of High Definition Television (HDTV) for opera and has become well known for his work in this medium including Meyerbeer's *Les Huguenots* (Deutsche Oper, Berlin production, 1990). Always sympathetic to singers, Large pays as much attention to the musical as to the dramatic aspects of opera direction. He is also the author of books on Smetana and Martinů.

Largo concertato. *See* PEZZO CONCERTATO.

Laroon, Marcellus (*b* London, 2 April 1679; *d* Oxford, 1 June 1772). English baritone. Laroon made soldiering his career and achieved fame as an artist, but for a few years in his youth he appeared on the London stage. He sang in Daniel Purcell's *The Grove* (1700), *The Rival Queens* (D. Purcell and Finger), *Macbeth* (Leveridge) and Fedeli's opera *The Temple of Love* (1706) in which he played the hero Sylvander.

BDA; LS
R. Raines: *Marcellus Laroon* (London, 1966)
OLIVE BALDWIN, THELMA WILSON

La Roque, Sieur de. Pseudonym of SIMON-JOSEPH PELLEGRIN.

Larrivée, Henri (*b* Lyons, 9 Jan 1737; *d* Paris, 7 Aug 1802). French baritone. At first a singer in the Opéra chorus, he began his career as a soloist in 1755 when he played a High Priest in Rameau's *Castor et Pollux*; later he sang Jupiter and finally Pollux. Apart from other roles in operas of Rameau and Lully, he created Ricimer in Philidor's *Ernelinde* (1767) and the title role in Gossec's *Sabinus* (1773). For Gluck he sang Agamemnon (in *Iphigénie en Aulide*), Hercules (in *Alceste*), Ubalde (in *Armide*) and Orestes (in *Iphigénie en Tauride*); he also played Orestes in Piccinni's *Iphigénie*, Grétry's *Andromaque* and Lemoyne's *Electre*. He venerated Gluck and overcame a lack of sympathy with Piccinni to sing Roland with such success as to give rise to Framery's 'Épître à M. Larrivée' (*Journal de Paris*, 4 February 1778). Subsequently he created Danaus in Salieri's *Les Danaïdes* (1784). He last appeared as Agamemnon in 1797. He had a wide range and a flexible voice which, according to Fétis and others, became nasal on high notes.

Larrivée's wife, Marie Jeanne Larrivée (née Le Mière) (*b* Sedan, 29 Nov 1733; *d* Paris, Oct 1786), was a soprano who appeared at the Opéra from 1750, mostly in minor roles, but she created the title role of Philidor's *Ernelinde* (1767) and Eponine in Gossec's *Sabinus* (1773).

JULIAN RUSHTON

Larsen [Reece], **Libby** [Elizabeth] (**Brown**) (*b* Wilmington, DE, 24 Dec 1950). American composer. She grew up in Minneapolis, a city of lakes; their presence, combined with her feeling for nature and the open air, have found expression in her music. She studied at the University of Minnesota, where her children's opera *Some Pig* (1973) was submitted for a master's degree and received workshop and Minneapolis Park Board performances. Among her teachers was Dominick Argento, by whom she was influenced, notably in her one-act opera *The Words upon the Windowpane* (1977, submitted as a doctoral thesis), in its lyric-declamatory style and handling of flashback realized through the device of a séance, with seamless integration of the ensemble episodes.

Before *Frankenstein*, however, Larsen followed a searching path in the evolution of her operatic style. Early in her career, on the production of *Tumbledown Dick, or The Taste of the Times* (1980), she declared an intention of transforming opera into music theatre, resolving 'to make it more of a play and less of a convention'. She deviated from that position in the mid-1980s, creating what was intended as her last conventional work for the stage, *Clair de lune* (1985), a two-act opera based on a libretto by the poet Patricia Hampl. The romantic story, about an ageing female aviator, makes use of the feminist subject matter increasingly recurrent in her works, especially the music-theatre piece *Ghosts of an Old Ceremony*, composed in 1991 for dancers and orchestra, written in collaboration with the choreographer Brenda Way. *Clair de lune*, commissioned by Arkansas Opera Theatre, marked a parting with traditional romantic subject matter; Larsen has declared that 'the love and death profile, and the man/woman stereotype, are no longer valid'.

While contemplating the experimental *Frankenstein* Larsen wrote *Christina Romana*, a multi-media chamber opera that positions the chorus in the balcony and combines acoustic instruments with electronic sound. *Frankenstein, or The Modern Prometheus* (after Mary Wollstonecraft Shelley's novel) followed two years later. Dealing with contemporary themes, such as the moral dilemmas of technological society, and drawing a parallel between early alchemy and nuclear research, it proceeds from the premise that film and video editing have drastically altered audience perceptions. The multi-layered presentation, relying heavily on a video and slide system to project details of character and mood, compresses the unbroken action into a prologue and 14 terse scenes. The score blends a chamber orchestra of 15 instruments with electronically mixed sounds, and a sound system projects a backstage chorus and amplifies the singers' body microphones. However, the overriding lyricism and tonally orientated harmonies of the music do not significantly depart from the manner of Larsen's earlier dramatic works.

Some Pig (children's op, 1, Larsen, after E. B. White: *Charlotte's Web*), Minneapolis, U. of Minnesota, 6 June 1973
The Words upon the Windowpane (1, Larsen, after W. B. Yeats), Minneapolis, 1 June 1977
The Silver Fox (children's op, 1, J. Olive), St Paul, 20 April 1979
Tumbledown Dick, or The Taste of the Times (2, V. Sutton, after H. Fielding), Minneapolis, 16 May 1980
Clair de lune (romantic fantasy, 2, P. Hampl), Little Rock, AR, 22 Feb 1985
Christina Romana (chamber op, 2, V. Sutton), Minneapolis, U. of Minnesota, 13 May 1988
Frankenstein, or The Modern Prometheus (musical drama, 1, Larsen, after M. W. Shelley), St Paul, MN, 25 May 1990

MARY ANN FELDMAN

Larsén-Todsen, Nanny (*b* Hagby, 2 Aug 1884; *d* Stockholm, 26 May 1982). Swedish soprano. She studied in Stockholm, Berlin and Milan and made her début in 1906 with the Royal Opera, Stockholm, where she continued to sing until 1923, first in lyric roles, including Donna Anna, Reiza, Aida, Tosca and the Feldmarschallin, before taking on the heavier Wagner repertory. At La Scala (1923–4) she sang Isolde under Toscanini; at the Metropolitan (1925–7) she made her début as Brünnhilde (*Götterdämmerung*) and, as well as Wagner, also sang Fidelio, Rachel (*La Juive*) and Gioconda. At Covent Garden (1927 and 1930) she sang Brünnhilde, while at Bayreuth (1927–31) her roles were Isolde, Kundry and Brünnhilde. She also appeared at the Paris Opéra and with the state operas of Berlin and Vienna. On record her very powerful voice had a slow beat, but this was hardly noticeable in her stage performances.

LEO RIEMENS/ELIZABETH FORBES

Laruette (Fr.). Term for an old man's role sung by a high tenor. In the later part of his career as an *haute-contre*, JEAN-LOUIS LARUETTE of the Opéra-Comique specialized in comic roles for elderly gentlemen, which came to be known as 'laruettes'. As early as Mozart and Rossini old men's roles were generally for a bass rather than a high tenor, but the tradition survived in *opéra comique* until the late 19th century (*see also* TENOR). Relics of it may be found in *Turandot*, where the aged Emperor's part is written for tenor, and in the part of Dr Manette in Arthur Benjamin's *A Tale of Two Cities*.

J. B. STEANE

Laruette [La Ruette], **Jean-Louis** (*b* Paris, 7 March 1731; *d* Paris, 10 Jan 1792). French *haute-contre* and composer. He first became known as a singer in the Théâtres de la Foire, where he made his début in September 1752, shortly after Monnet opened the Théâtre de la Foire St-Laurent. He was thus one of the first to perform in *opéras comiques mêlées d'ariettes* at a time when librettists were mingling vaudevilles and parodies of Italian arias; his most important such role was probably the part of the Magician in Sedaine's *Le diable à quatre* (1756). His first ventures into composition are harder to date because the arrangers of pasticcios and vaudevilles generally remained anonymous; however, pieces attributed to him are the final vaudeville of Parmentier's *Le plaisir et l'innocence* (14 August 1753), a new air in Louis Anseaume and Farin de Hautemer's *Le boulevard* (24 August 1753) and the final quartet of Anseaume and P. A. L. de Marcouville's *La fausse aventurière* (22 March 1757). The nature of his contributions to Anseaume and Marcouville's *Les amans trompés* (1756) and Sedaine's *Le diable à quatre* is uncertain. Laruette fully assumed the role of composer with *Le docteur Sangrado*, an *opéra comique* with *ariettes* and vaudevilles written jointly with Duni. His first important operas, *Le médecin de l'amour*, *Cendrillon* and *L'yvrogne corrigé*, owe much to their librettos, in which Anseaume contrived a skilful mixture of vaudevilles, *ariettes* and vocal ensembles. Laruette's last three operas, while musically more ambitious (they contain no vaudevilles at all) were less successful than his mixed-genre works – indeed, *Le dépit généreux* and *Les deux compères* were total failures.

Laruette also pursued a brilliant career as a singer; after playing such juvenile leads as Alberti in Duni's *Le peintre amoureux de son modèle* (1757) and Azor in his own *Cendrillon* (1759), he specialized in the often unsympathetic parts of fathers and financiers, for instance Monsieur Pince in Philidor's *Blaise le savetier* (1759). He and his wife, Marie-Thérèse (née Villette) (1744–1837), were among the five members of the Opéra-Comique company authorized to join the Comédie-Italienne in 1762, and he contributed to the success of operas by Philidor (he sang Blifil in *Tom Jones*) and Grétry (as Cassandre in *Le tableau parlant*). Laruette retired from the Comédie-Italienne in March 1778, and thereafter sang only in concerts and at the Théâtre des Beaujolais, as a printed score of Anfossi and Cambini's *Le tuteur avare*, 1787, shows. His high voice was not particularly attractive, but his acting ability and the care composers took in writing music for him made him one of the most popular singers of his time. His name remained linked to a type of *opéra-comique* role which persisted until the end of the 19th century (*see* LARUETTE).

Laruette belonged to the first generation of French composers of *opéra comique* in the sense that term assumed during the 1750s under the influence of the *intermèdes* performed in Paris by the Bouffons. However, he never embraced the Italian *opera buffa* style, although his work does contain a few examples, such as Jacqueline's *ariette* 'De la médecine' in *Le docteur Sangrado* and the trio 'Sotte carogne' in *L'yvrogne corrigé*. These apart, he borrowed techniques directly from *tragédie lyrique* and *opéra-ballet*. His melodic writing is inseparable from its frequently lavish ornamentation, while the accompaniment displays a linear conception reminiscent of Rameau, although Laruette's harmony is less dissonant and his orchestral texture much less dense. Also French in style are his frequent recourse to dance metres, changes of time in recitatives and illustrative vocal writing of the kind found in the *divertissements* of *grand opéra*. The second act of *L'yvrogne corrigé* is very humorous, ushering in a series of pieces in which composers of *opéra comique* parody the serious style. *Le guy de chesne* is more in the pastoral tradition and, unusually, is set in pre-Roman Gaul.

printed works published in Paris
PCI – *Paris, Comédie-Italienne (Hôtel de Bourgogne)*
PSG – *Paris, Foire St-Germain*   MPSL – *Paris, Foire St-Laurent*

Le docteur Sangrado (oc, 1, L. Anseaume and J.-B. Lourdet de Santerre, after A.-R. Lesage: *Gil Blas*), PSG, 13 Feb 1758; rev. version, PCI, 5 May 1762 (1763), airs (1764); collab. Duni

L'heureux déguisement, ou La gouvernante supposée (oc mêlé d'ariettes, 2, P. A. L. de Marcouville), PSL, 7 Aug 1758, airs (1758, 1763)

Le médecin de l'amour (oc, 1, Anseaume and Marcouville), PSL, 22 Sept 1758; PCI, 25 April 1762 (n.d. [after 1762; with revisions]), excerpts (1766)

Cendrillon (oc, 1, Anseaume, after C. Perrault), PSG, 20 or 21 Feb 1759; rev. version, PCI, 14 July 1762 (1762), airs (1764); collab. Duni

L'yvrogne corrigé, ou Le mariage du diable (oc, 2, Anseaume and Lourdet de Santerre, after J. de La Fontaine: *L'ivrogne et sa femme*), PSL, 23 or 24 July 1759 (n.d.), airs (1771)

Le dépit généreux (cmda, 2, Anseaume and A.-F. Quétant), PCI, 16 July 1761

Le guy de chesne, ou La feste des druides (comédie mise en musique, 1, J.-B. de Junquières), PCI, 26 Jan 1763 (n.d.), excerpts (1763, 1766)

Les deux compères (cmda, 2, Lourdet de Santerre or Anseaume, after La Fontaine: *L'ivrogne et sa femme*), PCI, 3 Sept 1772, excerpts (1772)

*

G. Cucuel: *Les créateurs de l'opéra-comique français* (Paris, 1914), 104–8

F. Rühlman: Preface to C. W. Gluck: *L'ivrogne corrigé*, Sämtliche Werke, iv/5 (1951), 5–9

P. Letailleur: 'Jean-Louis Laruette: chanteur et compositeur', *RMFC*, viii (1968), 161–89; ix (1969), 145–61; x (1970), 57–86

K. M. Smith: *Egidio Duni and the Development of the Opéra-comique from 1753 to 1770* (diss., Cornell U., 1980), 113–21

B. A. Brown: *Gluck and the French Theatre in Vienna* (Oxford, 1991), 254–61
MICHEL NOIRAY

Laschi, Anna Maria Querzoli. *See* QUERZOLI LASCHI, ANNA MARIA.

Laschi, Filippo (*b* Florence, *fl* 1739–89). Italian tenor. He was a singer and actor of unusual ability and a champion of Italian comic opera in the mid-18th century, mentioned in admiring terms by Mozart and Burney. Initially he sang serious roles but from 1741 (Chinzer's *La serva favorita*) preferred comedy parts. He was a leading figure in the success of Neapolitan, Roman and Florentine comic opera in Venice between 1743 and 1745, singing with Pietro Pertici, Francesco Baglioni, Grazia Mellini, Pellegrino Gaggiotti and other specialists in the genre. With a company directed by G. F. Crosa, and initially including Pertici and the soprano Anna Maria Querzoli (whom he married; Luisa Laschi was their daughter), he introduced this repertory to London (1748–50), Brussels (1749) and Amsterdam (1750), and from 1753 he was involved in first performances of many of Goldoni's *commedie per musica*. The Goldoni repertory remained a constant element in his activity until the mid-1760s, after which he worked in Vienna (1765–8) where, among other works, he sang in Gluck's *Alceste*. Laschi sang in various Italian centres in the 1770s and was a teacher of the Mozart bass Luigi Bassi and the tenor Michael Kelly; he was also the composer of arias sung in pasticcios (such as *The Maid of the Mill*, 1765) and in 1780 played the cembalo at the Pergola Theatre in Florence. He held posts as a *virtuoso di camera* of the Grand Duke of Tuscany and Charles of Lorraine.

P. Weiss: 'La diffusione del repertorio operistico nell'Italia del settecento: il caso dell'opera buffa', *Civiltà teatrale e settecento emiliano*, ed. S. Davoli (Bologna, 1986), 241–56

RICHARD G. KING, FRANCO PIPERNO, SASKIA WILLAERT

Laschi [Mombelli], **Luisa** (*b* Florence, 1760s; *d* 1789). Italian soprano. When she made her Viennese début, in 1784 in Cimarosa's *Giannina e Bernardone*, the *Wiener Kronik* said: 'she has a beautiful clear voice, which in time will become rounder and fuller; she is very musical, sings with more expression than the usual opera singers and has a beautiful figure'. In 1785 she sang Rosina in Paisiello's *Il barbiere di Siviglia* 'very well, and was much applauded' (Zinzendorf). Joseph II grudgingly released her for the 1785 season in Naples, but she returned in 1786 and sang at the Viennese court opera during its finest period. On 1 May 1786 she created Countess Almaviva in *Le nozze di Figaro*. She had a further success on 15 May as Barbarina in Anfossi's *Il trionfo delle donne*, and in August appeared, probably for the first time in Vienna, with her future husband, the tenor Domenico Mombelli, in Sarti's *I finti eredi*. In November she created the role of Queen Isabella in Martín y Soler's *Una cosa rara*, and in 1787 created Cupid in his *L'arbore di Diana*, a role that required her to appear alternately as a shepherdess and as Cupid. A contemporary reviewer described her portrayal: 'Grace personified ...; ah, who is not enchanted by it, what painter could better depict the arch smile, what sculptor the grace in all her gestures, what singer could match the singing, so melting and sighing, with the same naturalness and true, warm expression?'

In January 1788 she appeared in the première of Salieri's *Axur, rè d'Ormus* and in May sang Zerlina in the first Vienna performance of Mozart's *Don Giovanni*; Mozart composed a new duet to be sung by her and Benucci. She was already seven months pregnant but continued singing until the day before her confinement and reappeared four weeks later. But there were difficulties between the Italian company and the management and the emperor gave the Mombellis notice. In September Luisa created the role of Carolina in Salieri's *Il talismano* and in February 1789 she made her farewell appearance as Donna Farinella in *L'ape musicale*; nothing further seems to be known about her, but in 1791 Domenico, apparently a widower, married the ballerina Vincenza Vigano, by whom he had 12 children.

CHRISTOPHER RAEBURN

Laserna, Blas de (*b* Corella, Navarre, bap. 4 Feb 1751; *d* Madrid, 8 Aug 1816). Spanish composer. At 23 he began his career as a theatrical composer in Madrid and by 1776 his fame was such that the impresario Eusebio Ribera contracted him to write 63 *tonadillas* every year. In 1790 he succeeded Esteve as conductor at the Teatro de la Cruz, remaining there until 1808. Despite being one of the most prolific composers of his time, he was constantly underpaid and after 1800 had to resort to menial copying and teaching to secure a livelihood.

Laserna's speciality was the *tonadilla* or skit for one to four actors, of which he wrote at least 700, some to his own texts. 684 of these along with 78 *sainetes* are in Madrid (*E-Mm*), and several were circulated as far as Lima, Mexico City and Caracas; manuscript copies of six *tonadillas* are held in the Biblioteca Nacional de Venezuela. Usually showing piquant scenes from contemporary middle and low life, these genre pieces lasted no more than 20 minutes and were inserted between acts of a play or opera. Although *El majo y la italiana fingida* (1778; ed. in Subirá 1930) involves a girl who, to pose as an Italian, sings in Italian operatic style, Laserna's early *tonadillas* on the whole were exempt from the influence of bel canto (in 1790 he even proposed founding a school to preserve authentic Spanish traditions). In his last period, however, he had to adopt the Italian vogue in order to have his pieces produced. Laserna also wrote the music for eight *melólogos* (melodramas; 1791–7) and for several zarzuelas, as well as instrumental pieces and prologues. Two excerpts from his *melólogos* are edited in Subirá (1950) and five vocal selections appear in Joaquín Nin's *Classiques espagnols du chant* (Paris, 1926).

ES (J. Subirá)

J. Gómez García: *Don Blas de Laserna: un capítulo de la historia del teatro lírico español visto en la vida del último tonadillero* (diss., U. of Madrid, 1916; extracts in *Revista de la Biblioteca, Archivo y Museo del Ayuntamiento de Madrid*, ii–iii, 1925–6)

J. Subirá: *La tonadilla escénica*, iii (Madrid, 1930), 69ff, esp.117–45

——: *El compositor Iriarte (1750–1791) y el cultivo español del melólogo*, ii (Barcelona, 1950), 265–6, 272ff, 422ff

J. Gómez, J. L. de Arrese and E. Aunós: *El músico Blas de Laserna* (Corella, 1952)

J. Subirá: *Catálogo de la Sección de música de la Biblioteca municipal de Madrid* (Madrid, 1965), i, 105ff, 337ff

R. Stevenson: *Renaissance and Baroque Musical Sources in the Americas* (Washington DC, 1970), 113

——: 'National Library Publications in Brazil, Peru and Venezuela', *Inter-American Music Review*, iii/1 (1980), 39–48, esp.44

ROBERT STEVENSON

La Serre. Pseudonym of PELLEGRIN, SIMON-JOSEPH.

La Serre [Laserre], **Jean-Louis-Ignace de** (*b* Cahors, 1662; *d* Paris, 1756). French librettist. He is described in most biographical sources simply as 'Sieur de Langlade, Gentilhomme de la Province de Quercy'. He apparently turned to writing only after he had gambled away his personal fortune. He lived with the novelist Mlle de Lussan and for some time was assumed to be the author of one of her novels. Similar doubts surround the attribution of some of his librettos: La Serre's name appears on the title-page of *Polidore* (1720) but, like the tragedy *Ataxare* (1718), the libretto is probably by Pellegrin (Girdlestone believes this is confirmed on the grounds of its superior quality). The name 'Seguineau' has likewise been associated with the libretto of *Pirithous*.

Judgments on La Serre's librettos have been harsh: 'models of triviality and mediocrity', according to one writer. Most of the operas based on his texts failed – not an uncommon fate for the *tragédie en musique* of this period. *Pirame et Thisbé*, however, launched the important partnership of 'Rebel, fils, et Francoeur le cadet' (François Rebel and François Francoeur).

tragédies en musique

Polyxène et Pyrrhus, P. Collasse, 1706; *Diomède*, T. Bertin de la Doué, 1710; *Pirithous*, J.-J. Mouret, 1723; *Pirame et Thisbé*, F. Rebel and F. Francoeur, 1726; *Tarsis et Zélie*, Rebel and Francoeur, 1728; *Scanderberg*, Rebel and Francoeur, 1735 [prol., Act 5]; *Nitétis*, C.-L. Mion, 1741

C. M. Girdlestone: *La tragédie en musique (1673–1750) considérée comme genre littéraire* (Geneva, 1972)

CAROLINE WOOD

Las Palmas. Capital of Gran Canaria in the Canary Islands. Opera has been given there since the middle of the 19th century. The present theatre, seating 1500, now called the Pérez Galdos in honour of a local writer, was built in 1918 to replace an earlier 19th-century structure. Since 1967 opera has been presented during an annual festival (January–February), when five or six works, largely drawn from the popular Italian repertory, are each given two performances. A frequent visitor has been the tenor Alfredo Kraus, who was born in the city. Other singers have included Pavarotti, Chiara, Caballé, Cossotto, Carreras, Martinucci, Managuerra, Aragall, Tomowa-Sintov, Bruson and Dimitrova. Samuel Ramey made his European début there in *Don Carlos*. Performances are accompanied by the Las Palmas SO, which for the rest of the year gives weekly concerts in the theatre. CHARLES PITT

Lassalle, Jean (*b* Lyons, 14 Dec 1847; *d* Paris, 7 Sept 1909). French baritone. He studied at the Paris Conservatoire and made his début as St Bris in *Les Huguenots* at Liège in 1868. There followed four years in the Netherlands and the French provinces; then, in 1872, he was engaged for the reopening of the Paris Opéra, where for a while he was the highest-paid male singer and where he remained as the leading baritone until his retirement in 1901. Premières in the house included Massenet's *Le roi de Lahore* and Saint-Saëns' *Henry VIII*, and in Brussels he sang in the première of Reyer's *Sigurd*. In 1879 he appeared at La Scala and in Madrid. At Covent Garden, where he was closely associated with the De Reszke brothers, he was heard from 1879 to 1881 and again from 1888 to 1893. Lassalle had a great success, as both singer and actor, as Nélusko in *L'Africaine* and another in the London première of Rubinstein's *Demon*. Other roles in London included Don Giovanni, William Tell, Hamlet and Rigoletto, with the later addition of Hans Sachs, the Dutchman, and Telramund in *Lohengrin*. Of these Wagnerian roles, the last two, along with Wolfram in *Tannhäuser*, were in his repertory at the Metropolitan, where he made his début in 1892 and sang for the last time in 1897. His few and rare recordings were made after his retirement, but they still show a well-preserved voice and, in the aria from *Le roi de Lahore*, a fine example of the elegant style for which his period is known. J. B. STEANE

Lassen, Eduard (*b* Copenhagen, 13 April 1830; *d* Weimar, 15 Jan 1904). Belgian composer and conductor of Danish descent, active in Germany. He entered the Brussels Conservatory in 1842 where he studied composition with F.-J. Fétis. His cantata *Belthasar* won the Belgian government's Grand Prix in 1851, enabling him to travel to Düsseldorf, Leipzig and Kassel (where he met Spohr), then to Weimar (where he enjoyed Liszt's hospitality), Dresden and Berlin, and finally to Italy.

The five-act opera *Le roi Edgard*, written upon his return to Brussels in 1855, was rejected by the Théâtre Royal as unstageable. It was revised and presented as *Landgraf Ludwigs Brautfahrt* under Liszt's supervision at Weimar in 1857. Its success led to Lassen's appointment at Weimar in 1858 as music director and in 1859 as court music director, a position he occupied until his retirement in 1895. He soon composed a second opera, *Frauenlob*, which was well received at its 1860 première in Weimar but then disappeared from the repertory. His final opera, *Le captif* (about Cervantes and his capture

by the Moors), did not find favour at its Brussels première in 1865 or at Weimar in 1869 where it was staged as *Der Gefangene* in a German translation by Peter Cornelius. Perhaps as a result of these failures, Lassen turned to writing incidental music and ballet. In particular his music to Goethe's *Faust* (1876) enjoyed great popularity.

While Lassen's stage works exhibit moments of great beauty, he did not possess an innate sense of dramatic effectiveness and was hindered by weak librettos based on historical texts; the librettists (Pasqué and Cormon) could not introduce the necessary continuity and tension in the narrative that would result in dramatically interesting or even believable texts. Texts for Lassen's other stage works were successful, however, since they involved unaltered dramas by distinguished playwrights (Goethe, Sophocles, Hebbel and Calderón).

Musically Lassen is most successful when writing illustrative and lyrical scenes, always inventing music appropriate to the text. Noteworthy scenes in the operas include the love duet in *Landgraf Ludwigs Brautfahrt*, the spirit scene in *Frauenlob* and Maryam's air with chorus in *Le captif*. In general the music is characterized by sensitive declamation, diatonic harmonies, closed forms and transparent orchestration. Its style is more closely related to French opera of the period than to operas by Wagner or by pupils of Liszt. After 1870, despite an increasing Wagnerian influence, the later stage works retain a certain French grace, especially in the ballet scenes. Lassen remained a composer working within a basically conservative style.

Le roi Edgard, 1855 (romantic op, 5, Lassen and E. Pasqué), unperf.; rev. as Landgraf Ludwigs Brautfahrt, Weimar, Hof, 10 May 1857, *D-WRdn**
Frauenlob (romantic op, 3, Pasqué), Weimar, Hof, 22 May 1860, *WRdn**
Le captif (oc, 1, E. Cormon, after M. de Cervantes: *El captivo*), Brussels, Monnaie, 24 April 1865, *vs* (Paris, 1866), *B-Ba**, *D-WRdn**; rev. as Der Gefangene, Weimar, Hof, 8 April 1869, *Mbn**

                                        *

P. Cornelius: 'Landgraf Ludwigs Brautfahrt', *NZM*, xlvii (1857), 15–18
B. Michel: 'Chronique Théâtrale', *Le Bulletin* (Brussels), 30 April 1865 [on *Le captif*]
H. Mendel: 'Lassen', *Musikalisches Conversations-Lexicon*, vi (Berlin, 1876), 253–4
A. O. E.: 'Biographisches: Eduard Lassen,' *Mw*, xxi (1890), 315–16
La Mara [pseud. of M. Lipsius], ed.: *Franz Liszt's Briefe* (Leipzig, 1893–1905)
——: *Briefe hervorragender Zeitgenossen an Franz Liszt*, ii (Leipzig, 1895)
P. Bachmann: 'Eduard Lassen', *Die Musik*, iii (1903–04), 270–1
A. Bartels: *Chronik des Weimarer Hoftheaters 1817–1907* (Weimar, 1908)
A. von Schorn: *Das nachklassische Weimar*, ii: *Unter der Regierungszeit von Karl Alexander und Sophie* (Weimar, 1912)
L. Schrickel: *Geschichte des Weimarer Theaters von seinen Anfängen bis heute* (Weimar, 1928)
W. Schuh: *Richard Strauss: Jugend und frühe Meisterjahre: Lebenschronik 1864–1898* (Zürich, 1976; Eng. trans., 1982)
W. Huschke: *Musik im klassischen und nachklassischen Weimar* (Weimar, 1982)
H. R. Jung, ed.: *Franz Liszt in seinen Briefen* (Berlin, 1987)
A. Walker: *Franz Liszt*, ii: *The Weimar Years 1848–1861* (New York, 1989)   JAMES A. DEAVILLE

Lasser, Johann Baptist (*b* Steinkirchen, 12 Aug 1751; *d* Munich, 21 Oct 1805). Austrian composer. He studied at Linz before moving to Vienna, where he probably continued his studies but also taught. In 1781 or 1782 he married the singer Johanna Roithner (who continued to sing at the Munich Opera until at least 1811). The couple were at Brünn (now Brno) in 1783 as members of Waizhofer's company, and in 1785 they moved on to Linz, where Lasser directed the company in the 1786–7 season. In 1788, after a brief season as director at Eszterháza, he rejoined Waizhofer, then at Graz. In 1791 the Lassers went to Munich, where he distinguished himself at court by singing arias in all four registers, and by playing a violin concerto. Apart from an appearance in Berlin in 1797 he remained in Munich for the rest of his life, well loved and respected as both man and musician.

Despite the vocal feat of his Munich court concert it is difficult to reconcile the opinions of Lipowsky and Wurzbach that he was a tenor with statements in later books that he was a bass. Apart from a *Vollständige Anleitung zur Singkunst* (Munich, 1798), he achieved some renown with a handful of Singspiels (mostly lost) dating mainly from his Graz years, and several masses.

Die kluge Witwe (Spl), Brünn, 1782
Die glückliche Maskerade (Spl), Graz, 1788
Der Kapellmeister (Spl, 2, J. C. Bock), ?Graz, 1789, and Vienna, Freihaus, 2 July 1790
Das wüthende Heer (Spl, C. F. Bretzner), Graz, 1789
Die Modehändlerin (Spl, F. Ebert), Graz, 1790
Die unruhige Nacht (Spl, after C. Goldoni: *La notte critica*), Vienna, Kärntnertor, 28 May 1790, D-Bds
Die Huldigung der Töne [?Treue] (Spl, W. von Bube), ? Graz, c1790
Der Jude (Spl), Graz, 1791
Cora und Alonzo, ? Munich, after 1791

ADB (J. Kürschner); *WurzbachL*
F. J. Lipowsky: *Baierisches Musik-Lexikon* (Munich, 1811)
C. d'Elvert: *Geschichte des Theaters in Mähren und Oesterreichisch Schlesien* (Brno, 1851)
——: *Geschichte der Musik in Mähren und Oesterr.-Schlesien* (Brno, 1873)
F. Grandaur: *Chronologie des königlichen Hof- und Nationaltheaters in München* (Munich, 1878)
H. Mendel and A. Reissmann: *Musikalisches Conversations-Lexikon*, vi (Berlin, 1881), 254
A. Rille: *Die Geschichte des Brünner Stadttheaters* (Brno, 1885)
F. Fuhrich: *Theatergeschichte Oberösterreichs im 18. Jahrhundert*, Theatergeschichte Österreichs, i/2 (Vienna, 1968)
PETER BRANSCOMBE

Last Temptations, The. Opera by Joonas Kokkonen; *see* VIIMEISET KIUSAUKSET.

László, Magda (*b* Marosvásárhely, 1919). Hungarian soprano. She studied at the Liszt Academy of Music, Budapest, then joined the Budapest Opera (1943–6), where her roles included Elisabeth, Lauretta and Amelia (*Simon Boccanegra*). In 1946 she settled in Italy, where she sang Isolde, Strauss's Daphne, and the Mother in the première of Dallapiccola's *Il prigioniero* for Italian radio. She also sang in the opera's first stage performance at the 1950 Florence Maggio Musicale. Her intelligent musicianship gained her many parts in contemporary Italian works by Malipiero, Ghedini, Casella and Lualdi. At Glyndebourne she appeared as Gluck's Alcestis (1953–4), Dorabella (1954) and Monteverdi's Poppaea (1962–3). In 1954 she created Cressida in *Troilus and Cressida* at Covent Garden. Other roles in her repertory included Marie (*Wozzeck*), Busoni's Turandot, Senta and Norma.

For illustration *see* PRIGIONIERO, IL and TROILUS AND CRESSIDA.
HAROLD ROSENTHAL/R

Latanzio, P. *See* ANELLI, ANGELO.

Latilla, Gaetano (*b* Bari, 12 Jan 1711; *d* Naples, 15 Jan 1788). Italian composer. As a boy he sang in the choir of Bari Cathedral. He then moved to Naples where in March 1726 he enrolled as a student in the conservatory of S Maria di Loreto; he must have been a pupil of Francesco Mancini or Giovanni Veneziano. He began his professional career in 1732 by composing a comic opera, *Li marite a forza*, for the Teatro Fiorentini in Naples, and wrote other comic operas for that theatre during the next five years. His *Gismondo* (more widely known as *La finta cameriera*) and *Madama Ciana* were two of the relatively few full-length comic operas successfully exported from Naples in the 1730s. Along with others such as Rinaldo di Capua's *La commedia in commedia* and Auletta's *Orazio*, they were highly influential in shaping the Italian comic opera tradition that was to culminate in the Venetian *drammi giocosi* of the late 1740s and 50s. Latilla's early fame was largely built on the rapid dissemination and pasticcio arrangements of these two operas.

Latilla also held church appointments at various stages of his career: S Maria Maggiore, Rome (1738–41); *maestro di coro* at the Pietà in Venice (1753–66); and assistant *maestro* at St Mark's, Venice, under Galuppi (from 1762). He probably composed a quantity of church music for these institutions, although few such works survive. His success as an opera composer continued until the mid-1750s, but thereafter his popularity with theatre audiences declined. By 1774 he had left Venice and was in Naples again, where he spent the last years of his life. One of his composition pupils during this period was Thomas Attwood, who later took lessons from Mozart in Vienna.

Few of Latilla's operas remain intact. The earliest, the comic opera *Angelica ed Orlando* of 1735, dates from the same period as the operas of his almost exact contemporary Pergolesi, although its music bears less resemblance to Pergolesi's than to that of another Neapolitan, Leonardo Leo. Over the following decades Latilla changed his style considerably, to conform with new tastes. The lyrical items of his heroic opera *Antigono* of 1775, the last of his compositions to have survived, are characterized by longer melodic lines and heavier accompaniments than those of his earlier works, and the more urgent, less lilting style he adopted seems to have been an attempt to come to terms with the latest music of Niccolò Piccinni, Antonio Sacchini and others among the new generation of Neapolitan composers.

dg – *dramma giocoso*   dm – *dramma per musica*
int – *intermezzo*   os – *opera seria*

Li marite a forza (commeddeja, 3, B. Saddumene), Naples, Fiorentini, spr. 1732
L'Ottavio (commedia per musica, 3, G. A. Federico), Naples, Fiorentini, wint. 1733
Gl'ingannati (commedia per musica, 3, Federico), Naples, Fiorentini, wint. 1734
Angelica ed Orlando (commedia per musica, 3, T. Fonsaconico [F. A. Tullio], after L. Ariosto), Naples, Fiorentini, aut. 1735, *GB-Lbl*
Lo sposo senza moglie [I due supposti conti] (dg, 3, C. Palma), Naples, Nuovo, aut. 1736
Temistocle (dg, 3, P. Metastasio), Rome, Tor di Nona, carn. 1737, *A-Wgm*
Gismondo (commedia per musica, 3, Federico), Naples, Fiorentini, sum. 1737; rev. as La finta cameriera (3, G. Barlocci), Rome, Valle, spr. 1738, *B-Bc*, *I-Fc*; rev. as Don Calascione (3), London, King's, 21 Jan 1749, Favourite Songs (London, 1749); rev. as La finta cameriera (int, 2), Naples, Nuovo, aut. 1745, *B-Bc*; Paris, Opéra, 1752, *F-Po*; rev. as La giardiniera contessa (1), *B-Bc*

Demofoonte (dm, 3, Metastasio), Venice, S Giovanni Grisostomo, carn. 1738

Polipodio e Rocchetta (int, 2), Rome, Argentina, carn. 1738

Madama Ciana (commedia per musica, 3, Barlocci), Rome, Pallacorda, Feb 1738; rev. as Gli artigiani arricchiti (int, 2), Paris, Opéra, 25 Sept 1753, F-Po, Pn

Romolo (dm, 3), Rome, Dame, carn. 1739, extracts D-Dlb, I-BGi; attrib. Latilla and Terradellas

Siroe (dm, 3, Metastasio), Rome, Dame, carn. 1740, A-Wgm

Olimpia nell'isola di Ebuda (dm, 3, A. Trabucco), Naples, S Carlo, 20 Jan 1741

La vendetta generosa (dm, 3), Naples, Fiorentini, aut. 1742

Zenobia (dm, 3, Metastasio), Turin, Regio, aut. 1742, arias in D-Dlb and I-Nc

La gara per la gloria (divertimento teatrale, 3, B. Vitturi), Venice, S Moisè, carn. 1744

Amare e fingere (dm, 3), Naples, Nuovo, carn. 1745

Il concerto (melodramma per musica, 3, Partenio Chriter [P. Trinchera]), Naples, Nuovo, spr. 1746

Catone in Utica (dm, 3, Metastasio), Rome, Capranica, carn. 1747, aria P-Lc

Il vecchio amante (dg, 3, Barlocci), Turin, Carignano, carn. 1747; also as La commedia in commedia

Adriano in Siria (dm, 3, Metastasio), Naples, S Carlo, 19 Dec 1747, aria I-G(l)

Il barone di Vignalunga (commedia per musica, 3, A. Palomba), Naples, Nuovo, 1747

Ciascheduno ha il suo negozio (dg), Madrid, Buen Retiro, 1747

La Celia (commedia per musica, 3, Palomba), Naples, Fiorentini, aut. 1749

La vecchia mmaretata (commeddeja, Trinchera), Naples, Pace, carn. 1750

Amore in Tarantola (dg, 3, Abate Vaccina), Venice, S Moisè, aut. 1750

Il giuoco de' matti (dg, 3, Palomba), Naples, Nuovo, aut. 1750

La maestra (commedia per musica, 3, Palomba), Naples, Fiorentini, carn. 1751 [rev., with G. Cocchi and G. Cordella, of Cocchi's La maestra, 1747]

L'opera in prova alla moda [Urganostocar] (dg ['tragedia tragichissima di lieto fine'], 3, G. Fiorini), Venice, S Moisè, carn. 1751

La pastorella al soglio (dm, 3, G. C. Pagani), Venice, S Moisè, Ascension 1751, D-Wa

Griselda (dm, 3, A. Zeno), Venice, S Cassiano, aut. 1751, arias Dlb

Gl'impostori (dg), Venice, S Moisè, aut. 1751

L'isola d'amore (commedia in musica, 3, A. Rigo), Venice, S Moisè, carn. 1752

Olimpiade (dm, 3, Metastasio), Venice, S Cassiano, aut. 1752, arias Dlb

Alessandro nell'Indie (dm, 3, Metastasio), Venice, S Cassiano, carn. 1753, collabs. unknown

Antigona (dm, 3, G. Roccaforte), Modena, Corte, 1753

Il protettor del poeta (int, 2, G. Piccinelli), Rome, Valle, carn. 1754

Venceslao (dm, ?3, Zeno), Barcelona, 1754

Tito Manlio (dm, 3, Roccaforte), Rome, Capranica, carn. 1755, P-La

La finta sposa (dg, 3), Bologna, Formagliari, 1755

Ezio (dm, 3, Metastasio), Naples, S Carlo, 10 July 1758, La, US-CA

L'amore artigiano (dg, 3, C. Goldoni), Venice, S Angelo, carn. 1761, I-Tco

Merope (dm, 3, Zeno), Venice, S Benedetto, carn. 1763, BGi

La buona figliuola supposta vedova (dramma comica per musica, 3, A. Bianchi), Venice, S Cassiano, carn. 1766

Gl'inganni amorosi (commedia per musica, 3, P. Mililotti), Naples, Fiorentini, carn. 1774

Il maritato fra le disgrazie (dg, 3, G. Palomba), Naples, Fiorentini, aut. 1774

Antigono (dm, 3, Metastasio), Naples, S Carlo, 13 Aug 1775, Nc, P-La

I sposi incogniti (commedia per musica, 3, Mililotti), Naples, Nuovo, 1779

Doubtful: L'astuzia felice (dg, 3, Goldoni), Turin, Carignano, spr. 1750; or c1777

*

BurneyFI; BurneyH; FlorimoN

G. G. Ferrari: Aneddoti piacevoli e interessanti occorsi nella vita di G. G. F. da Roveredo (London, 1830); ed. S. Di Giacomo (Milan, 1929)

T. Wiel: I teatri musicali veneziani del settecento (Venice, 1897)

M. Bellucci La Salandra: 'Saggio cronologico delle opere teatrali di Gaetano Latilla', Japigia, v (1935), 310

D. Arnold: 'Orphans and Ladies: the Venetian Conservatories (1680–1790)', PRMA, lxxxix (1962–3), 31–47, esp. 46

G. Ellero: 'Origini e sviluppo storico della musica nei quattro grandi ospedali veneziani', Nuova rivista musicale italiana, xiii (1979), 160–67

S. Mamy: L'influence des chanteurs napolitains sur l'évolution de l'opéra baroque tardif vénitien au théâtre San Giovanni Grisostomo de Venise (1701–1755) (diss., U. of Paris, 1983)

MICHAEL F. ROBINSON, DALE E. MONSON

Lattuada, Felice (b Caselle di Morimondo, nr Milan, 5 Feb 1882; d Milan, 2 Nov 1962). Italian composer. He embarked on a teaching career in primary schools in Milan and was at first self-taught musically, but in 1907 he entered the Milan Conservatory where he studied with V. Ferroni. In 1928 his opera Don Giovanni won the Concorso Nazionale della Pubblica Istruzione, judged by Alfano, Casella, Gasco and Mascagni. He was director of the Scuola Civica di Musica in Milan from 1935 to 1962. From his earliest works Lattuada showed a preference for a musical idiom deriving from late-Romantic tradition. In his theatre music his style remains close to verismo and is often emphatic, as Riccardo Allorto observed (Ricordiana, 1957) about his opera Caino. Lattuada's son Alberto (b 1914) is a well-known film director, for whose films Felice wrote much music.

See also PREZIOSE RIDICOLE, LE and TEMPESTA, LA.

La tempesta (prol., 3, A. Rossato, after W. Shakespeare), Milan, Dal Verme, 23 Nov 1922

Sandha (tragedia indiana, 1, F. Fontana), Genoa, Carlo Felice, 21 Feb 1924

Le preziose ridicole (commedia, 1, Rossato, after Molière), Milan, Scala, 9 Feb 1929

Don Giovanni (4, Rossato, after J. Zorrilla y Moral: Don Giovanni Tenorio), Naples, S Carlo, 18 May 1929

La caverna di Salamanca (1, V. Piccoli, after M. de Cervantes), Genoa, Carlo Felice, 1 March 1938

Caino (1, Lattuada and G. Zambianchi, after Byron), Milan, Scala, 10 Jan 1957

*

A. Procida: '"Don Giovanni" di Rossato e Lattuada', Musica d'oggi, vi (1929), 270–71

A. Fino: La Civica scuola di musica di Milano (Milan, 1978)

RAFFAELE POZZI

Latvia. The first operatic performances in Latvia took place in Jelgava (Ger. Mitau), the capital of the duchy of Courland, at the end of the 17th century. Travelling troupes performed in Riga after 1760. The first opera performed in the Latvian language was J. B. Schenk's Der Dorfbarbier; the first Latvian opera, composed by Jēkabs Ozols (1863–1902), the one-act Spoku stunda ('In the Hour of Ghosts'), was staged in the drama theatre in 1893.

The Latviešu Opera (Latvian Opera), for which Latvian composers wrote the first national Romantic operas, was founded in 1913. After World War I these included Alfrēds Kalniņš's Baņuta, which has become the most popular Latvian opera, with seven productions in Riga between 1920 and 1979 as well as concert performances in Germany and the USA, and Jānis Mediņš's symbolic music drama Uguns un nakts ('Fire and Night', 1921). Kalniņš's second opera, Salinieki ('The Islanders', 1926), was an expressionist historical and allegorical drama. Mediņš's Dievi un cilvēki ('Gods and Men', 1922) and Jāzeps Mediņš's Vaidelote ('The Priestess', 1927) can be characterized as psychological dramas set against a historical background, in a late Romantic musical style. Jānis Mediņš's next two operas,

Sprīdītis ('Tom Thumb', 1927) and *Luteklīte* ('The Little Darling', 1939) are psychologically nuanced children's operas of an impressionistic character. Jānis Kalniņš's operas *Lolitas brīnumputns* ('Lolita's Wonderbird', 1934), *Hamlets* (1936) and *Uguni* ('In the Fire', 1937) represent a stylistic turning-point in Latvian opera with their new level of theatricality and psychological characterization; they are set in an austere, anti-Romantic style, in the spirit of the *Neue Sachlichkeit*, infused with sentimental musical idioms.

After the annexation of Latvia in 1940 the ideological pressures on opera composers over the next 40 years caused an impoverishment of new works. Marģers Zariņš's opera *Uz jauno krastu* ('Towards the New Shore', 1954) follows a *verismo* style, which is also evident in Zariņš's subsequent operas, *Zaļās dzirnavas* ('The Green Mill', 1958), *Nabagu opera* ('Beggar's Opera', 1965) and *Svētā Mauricija brīnumdarbi* ('The Miracle of St Mauritius', 1974), which are dominated by vivid theatricality, paradoxical games with historical musical styles and frequent provocative aestheticism. Also popular have been Arvīds Žilinskis's children's operas *Zelta zirgs* ('The Golden Horse', 1965) and *Pūt, vējiņi* ('Blow, Wind'), which deliberately simplify the principal national classic works and rely on epigonic musical clichés of the Romantic style. An innovatory and original style has been developed by Imants Kalniņš in *Ej, jūs, tur* ('Hey, you, there', 1971), *Spēlēju, dancoju* ('I played, I danced', 1977) and *Ifiģenija Aulīdā* (1982), in which he creates a synthesis of 18th-century classical elements, folklore material and rock music.

For further information on operatic life in the country's principal centres see LIEPĀJA and RIGA.

L. Viduleja: *Latviešu padomju opera* [Latvian Soviet Operas] (Riga, 1973)
V. Briede-Bulavinova: *Opernoye tvorchestvo latishskiy kompozitorov* [Operas of Latvian Composers] (Leningrad, 1979) [in Russ.]
V. Briede: *Latviešu operateātris* (Riga, 1987)

ARNOLDS KLOTIŅŠ

Latymer, Lord. *See* MONEY-COUTTS, FRANCIS BURDETT.

Laubenthal [Neumann], Horst (Rüdiger) (*b* Eisfeld, Thuringia, 8 March 1939). German tenor. He studied in Munich and with Rudolf Laubenthal, whose name he adopted for professional purposes. He made his début at the Würzburg Mozart Festival in 1967 as Don Ottavio. Engagements followed in Stuttgart (1967–73), the Deutsche Oper, Berlin (from 1973), and at the festivals of Salzburg, Aix-en-Provence, Munich and Glyndebourne, mainly in the Mozart roles (Belmonte, Tamino, Ferrando) in which he specialized. His repertory included Jaquino, Lensky, Narraboth, the Prince (*Rusalka*), the title role of Pfitzner's *Palestrina*, which he sang at the Vienna Staatsoper (1978), the Painter (*Lulu*) and Wilhelm (*Der junge Lord*). He sang the Steersman at Bayreuth (1970), Walther von der Vogelweide (*Tannhäuser*) at Covent Garden (1984), Erik at Lisbon and Telemachus (Henze's version of *Il ritorno d'Ulisse in patria*) at Salzburg (1987). His performances, although stiff dramatically, were notable for intrinsic musicianship and for well-schooled, supple singing.

HAROLD ROSENTHAL/R

Laubenthal, Rudolf (*b* Düsseldorf, 18 March 1886; *d* Pöcking, Starnberger See, 2 Oct 1971). German tenor. He studied with Lilli Lehmann in Berlin and made his

début in 1913 at the Deutsche Oper, where he remained until 1923, the year of his Metropolitan début as Walther. He sang in the first American performances of *Jenůfa*, *Die ägyptische Helena* and *Švanda the Bagpiper*. At Covent Garden (1926–30) he sang Erik, Siegfried, Tristan and Walther. He continued to appear in Munich, Vienna and other European theatres until 1937. His repertory included Arnold (*Guillaume Tell*), Hoffmann and John of Leyden (*Le prophète*). A handsome man and an intelligent actor, he had a voice of heroic proportions, somewhat lacking in lyric beauty.

HAROLD ROSENTHAL/R

Laufer, Beatrice (*b* New York, 27 April 1923). American composer. At the Juilliard School (1942–50) she studied composition with Marion Bauer and Roger Sessions and orchestration with Vittoria Giannini. She has composed in a variety of instrumental and vocal genres. In 1952 she received permission to convert Eugene O'Neill's play *Ile* into a one-act opera. The story tells of a sea captain's obsession with whaling and its destructive effect on his wife, leading to a threat of mutiny. Sung in Swedish, *Ile* was first performed at the Royal Opera House, Stockholm, on 28 October 1958 and received ten further performances there. The first American production, directed by Phyllis Curtin, was at the Yale School of Music (1977). It was videotaped for the National Public Radio festival of one-act operas and broadcast in 1980. In June 1988, *Ile* had ten performances in Chinese at the Shanghai Opera House. The music, in keeping with O'Neill's stormy style, is dramatic and colourful.

MARJORIE MACKAY-SHAPIRO

Launis [Lindberg], Armas (Emanuel) (*b* Hämeenlinna, 22 April 1884; *d* Nice, 7 Aug 1959). Finnish composer. He studied in Berlin and with von Baussnern in Weimar, and taught theory (1906–14) and singing (1916–29) in Helsinki. In 1922 he founded the Helsinki Folk Conservatory, which he directed until 1930. Thereafter he lived in France. He was principally a composer of operas, in a rather unimaginative and derivative style drawing on Finnish and other folk music.

librettos by the composer

Seitsemän veljestä [The Seven Brothers] (4, after A. Kivi), Helsinki, National, 11 April 1913, vs (Helsinki, 1920)
Kullervo (3, after Kivi and the Kalevala), Helsinki, National, 28 Feb 1917, vs (Helsinki, 1919)
Aslak Hetta, 1922 (3, Launis), unperf., vs (Paris, 1930)
Noidan laulu [The Sorcerer's Song], 1932 (4), inc. [sketches only]
Kesä jota ei koskaan tullut [The Summer which Never Came], *c*1936 (3), inc. [sketches only]
Karjalainen taikahuivi [The Karelian Magic Kerchief], 1937 (2), unperf.
Oli kerran [Once upon a Time], *c*1939 (3), unperf.
Theodoora, 1939 (3)
Jeduhith, 1940 (3)
Jäiset liekit [The Icy Flames], *c*1957 (ballet-op), unperf.

H. Tomasi: *Armas Launis: notes biographiques* (London, 1940)
Armas Launis: henkilötietoja 60-vuotispäivän johdosta (Helsinki, 1944)

HANNU ILARI LAMPILA

Laurence, Elizabeth [Scott, Elizabeth Jane] (*b* Harrogate, 22 Nov 1949). English mezzo-soprano. She studied at Trinity College, London. In 1986 she sang Mallika (*Lakmé*) at Monte Carlo, Jocasta (*Oedipus rex*) in Madrid and Nancy (*Albert Herring*) with Glyndebourne Touring Opera, for whom she created Anna Arild (Osborne's *Electrification of the Soviet Union*) in 1987. She also created Behemoth in Höller's

Der Meister und Margarita at the Paris Opéra (1989). Her Covent Garden début was as Second Audition in the British première of *Un re in ascolto* (1989), which she also sang at Opéra Bastille (1991). Her roles include Cherubino, Erda, Bartók's Judith and Ravel's Concepcion. With her warm-toned, flexible voice and handsome appearance, she excels in parts such as Lady de Hautdesert in Birtwistle's *Gawain*, which she created at Covent Garden (1991).
ELIZABETH FORBES

Laurenti [Novelli], **Antonia Maria** ['La Coralli', 'Corallina'] (*fl* 1714–41). Italian contralto. She belonged to the famous musical Laurenti family of Bologna and may have been the daughter of Bartolomeo Girolamo Laurenti (1644–1726). Her first recorded appearance in opera was in 1714, in Padua. Until 1719 she was active on the stage in several Italian cities, taking leading roles. Veracini recruited her (at the high salary of 2375 thalers) for the company that performed at Dresden in 1719. In 1720 she resumed her career in Italy. Under her nickname 'La Coralli' she is referred to obliquely in Benedetto Marcello's satire *Il teatro alla moda* (1720). Antonio Denzio invited her to Prague in 1726. There she married the tenor Felice Novelli on 8 March 1727. The pair returned to Italy and thereafter often performed in the same productions. Of especial note is the appearance of Novelli and Laurenti as a comic pair in Francesco Mancini's intermezzo *La serva favorita* (1730, Turin). Laurenti's last known appearance was in the pasticcio *Sirbace* (1741, Ferrara).

*

D. Freeman: *The Opera Theater of Count Franz Anton von Sporck in Prague* (New York, 1990)
MICHAEL TALBOT

Laurenti, Pietro Paolo (*b* Bologna, 26 July 1675; *d* Bologna, 25 March 1719). Italian composer and singer. The information given by Fétis that he was a Franciscan is not confirmed by documentary sources. The son of the composer and violinist Bartolomeo Girolamo Laurenti, he was a violinist at S Petronio, Bologna, from 1692 to 1695, but he eventually played the viola (1701–11). He studied counterpoint with Perti and in 1698 was admitted to the Accademia Filarmonica as a cellist and a little later as a composer. His first opera, *Attilio Regolo in Africa*, was written in 1701. He was elected *principe* of the academy in 1701 and again in 1716, and held many minor posts. From 1703 he was *maestro di cappella* at the Collegio dei Nobili, Bologna. Active as a singer from at least 1705 (when he appeared in Giannettini's *Artaserse* in Bologna) until the year of his death, Laurenti performed in the theatres of Venice (1718–9), Florence (1716), Brescia (1718) and Piacenza. He is described in librettos as 'virtuoso of Prince Antonio of Parma' from 1718. His activity as opera composer was limited to Bologna, but it embraced various genres, including contributions to the Bolognese tradition of *opera buffa* in dialect. His sacred music, as well as 11 oratorios, was composed exclusively for the Accademia Filarmonica.

Attilio Regolo in Africa, Casa Bevilacqua, Bologna 1701
Esone ringiovenito, Bologna 1706
L'Iride dopo la tempestà, 1709
Li diporti d'amore in villa, 1710
Sabella mrosa d'Travlin, 1710
Il teatro in festa, 1714

*

FétisB
O. Penna: *Catalogo degli aggregati della Accademia Filarmonica* (MS, *I-Baf*, 1736/R1971) [sometimes attrib G. B. Martini]

G. B. Martini: 'Serie cronologica de' principi dell'Accademia de' filarmonici di Bologna', *Diario bolognese* (1776)
F. Vatielli: *Arte e vita musicale a Bologna*, 1927)
O. Gambassi: *La cappella musicale di S Petronio* (Florence, 1987)
SERGIO DURANTE

Laurenzi [Laurenti, Lorenzi], **Filiberto** [Filibertus de Laurentiis] (*b* Bertinoro, nr Forlì, ? 1619–20; *d* after 1659). Italian composer. From late spring 1631 to 30 September 1633 he was a soprano at S Luigi dei Francesi, Rome. He may have begun his career as an opera composer at Rome, for in a manuscript source (*F-Pn*) of Ottaviano Castelli's libretto he is credited with the musical setting (now lost) of *Il favorito del principe*, which was first performed at Rome at the residence of the French ambassador in 1640 (see Murata). Late in 1640 he moved to Venice together with the singer Anna Renzi, who was his pupil and with whom he remained associated until at least 1644. At Venice he collaborated with Arcangelo Crivelli, Benedetto Ferrari, Alessandro Leardini and Tarquinio Merula in writing the music for the opera *La finta savia* (libretto by Giulio Strozzi), which was performed at the Teatro SS Giovanni e Paolo during Carnival 1643. The arias that Laurenzi wrote for this opera were published at Venice in 1644 as *Arie ... raccolte da G. B. Verdizotti nel dramma della Finta savia*. In 1647 Laurenzi wrote for Rome a *carro musicale*, *Il trionfo della fatica*, the libretto of which ends with the same duet as that found at the conclusion of the surviving manuscripts of Monteverdi's *L'incoronazione di Poppea*. His last known opera, *L'esiglio d'Amore* (libretto by Francesco Berni) was again a collaboration, this time with Andrea Mattioli, for performance in 1651 at the Teatro di Cortile, Ferrara. The course of Laurenzi's career after 1651 is uncertaiin, though he may have been the Filiberto Laurenti mentioned in connection with a performance at S Petronio, Bologna, in 1659.

See also FINTA SAVIA, LA.

*

G. Strozzi: *Le glorie della signora Anna Renzi romana* (Venice, 1644)
W. Osthoff: 'Neue Beobachtungen zu Quellen und Geschichte von Monteverdis "Incoronazione di Poppea"', *Mf*, xi (1958), 129–38, esp.135
C. Sartori: 'La prima diva della lirica italiana: Anna Renzi', *NRMI*, ii (1968), 430–52
N. Pirrotta: 'Early Venetian Libretti at Los Angeles', *Essays in Musicology in Honor of Dragan Plamenac* (Pittsburgh, 1969), 233–43; repr. in *Music and Culture in Italy from the Middle Ages to the Baroque* (Cambridge, MA, 1984), 317–24
A. Schnoebelen: 'Performance Practices at San Petronio in the Baroque', *AcM*, xli (1969), 37–55, esp.49
W. Osthoff: 'Filiberto Laurenzis Musik zu "La finta savia" im Zusammenhang der frühvenezianischen Oper', *Venezia e il melodramma nel seicento*, ed. M. T. Muraro (Florence, 1976), 173–97
M. Murata: *Operas for the Papal Court, 1631–1668* (Ann Arbor, 1981), 6, 41
J. Lionnet: 'La Musique à Saint-Louis des français de Rome au XVIIe siècle', *NA*, new ser., iii (1985), suppl., 62, 76, 77
P. Fabbri: *Il secolo cantante: per una storia del libretto d'opera nel seicento* (Bologna, 1990)
JOHN WHENHAM

Lauri-Volpi [Volpi], **Giacomo** (*b* Rome, 11 Dec 1892; *d* Valencia, 17 March 1979). Italian tenor. He studied in Rome at the Accademia di S Cecilia with Cotogni and later with Rosati. He made his début (under the name Giacomo Rubini) at Viterbo in 1919 as Arturo (*I puritani*) and in 1920 sang Des Grieux (*Manon*) under his own name in Rome. Engaged at La Scala as the Duke in 1922, he sang there regularly in the 1930s and 40s.

He was a member of the Metropolitan Opera from 1923 to 1933, singing in 232 performances of 26 operas; his roles included Calaf in the American première of *Turandot* (1926) and Rodolfo in the first Metropolitan *Luisa Miller* (1929). His only Covent Garden appearances were in 1925 as Chénier and 1936 as the Duke, Radames and Cavaradossi. He sang Boito's Nero to open the Teatro dell'Opera, Rome, in 1928 and Arnold in the centenary production of *Guillaume Tell* at La Scala in 1929. His repertory also included Raoul (*Les Huguenots*), Otello and Manrico. He continued to sing in public until 1959. His bright, ringing tone and beautiful legato made him one of the finest lyric-dramatic tenors of his day. He wrote a number of books, including *Voci parallele* (Milan, 1955) and *Misteri della voce umana* (Milan, 1957).

C. Williams and T. Hutchinson: 'Giacomo Lauri-Volpi', *Record Collector*, xi (1957), 245–72; xii (1958–60), 34–5, 66–7, 108; xx (1971–2), 239 [with discography]
R. Celletti: '"Il tenore eroico" del melodramma celeste', *Musica e dischi*, no.143 (1958), 47; no.145 (1958), 47; no.146 (1958), 39
P. Caputo, ed.: 'Tre generazioni di artisti festeggiano Lauri-Volpi', *Musica e dischi*, no.200 (1963), 44   HAROLD ROSENTHAL/R

Lausanne. City in western Switzerland, on Lake Geneva. The Salle Dupleix, in the suburb of Marterey, had occasional performances of opera until it closed in 1859. The Casino-Théâtre de Lausanne (now the Théâtre Municipal, cap. 920), which opened on 10 May 1871 with *Il barbiere di Siviglia*, initially gave an opera season each spring; Stravinsky's *Histoire du soldat* received its première there in 1918. Jacques Beranger, director from 1928 to 1959, oversaw a complete renovation of the theatre in 1932, during which some of its elegance was sacrificed to increased seating capacity. The opening in 1954 of the suburban Théâtre de Beaulieu (cap. 1800) led to the inauguration of an annual festival of Italian opera (1955–72), featuring companies from Bologna, Rome and Venice. This theatre also became the centre for the annual Festival de Lausanne (1956–84), which included guest appearances by major European companies. Renée Auphan, who became director of the Théâtre Municipal in 1983, replaced the early summer festival with a winter season, launching the Opéra de Lausanne in 1988. The company has no permanent ensemble, but mounts a stagione of up to five productions, each given three or four performances, between September and June. In addition to the two Lausanne theatres, the company also uses the Théâtre du Jorat at Mézières, a village in the countryside above Vevey. Built by René Morax and his brothers in 1908, this all-wood theatre (cap. 1060) is unheated and used only in summer. The first opera staged there was Gluck's *Orfeo ed Euridice* in 1911, with Ernest Ansermet playing the timpani.

Le Théâtre du Jorat et René Morax (Lausanne, 1963)
J.-P. Pastori: *Le Théâtre de Lausanne 1869–1989* (Lausanne, 1989)
          ANDREW CLARK

Lauters, Pauline. *See* GUÉYMARD-LAUTERS, PAULINE.

Laval, Michel-Jean (*b* Paris, 1725; *d* 1777). French choreographer and dancer. He was the son of Antoine Bandieri de Laval (*b* Paris, 1688; *d* Paris, 20 Oct 1767), who had been a noted exponent of the *danse sérieuse* and had choreographed many revivals of operas by Campra and others. Michel-Jean joined the *corps de ballet* at the Opéra in 1746, and from 1765 shared with his father the choreographic duties there. Together they choreographed more than 20 ballets, including those in the premières of several operas by Rameau, notably *Zaïs* (1748), *Naïs* (1749), *Zoroastre* (1749) and *Acante et Céphise* (1751). Father and son danced or choreographed more than a hundred ballets and operas during a period of 71 years.   MAUREEN NEEDHAM COSTONIS

Lavallée, Calixa (*b* Ste Théodosie de Verchères [now Calixa-Lavallée], Quebec, 28 Dec 1842; *d* Boston, 21 Jan 1891). Canadian composer. He received his early musical training in St Hyacinthe and Montreal. From about 1857 he worked in the USA as a travelling theatre musician and in 1861–2 was enrolled as a bandsman in a northern regiment during the American Civil War. Later (*c*1870–72) he was conductor and artistic director of the New York Grand Opera House (more minstrel-show theatre than opera house); his comic opera *Lou-Lou* was to have been staged there in 1872, but the production was cancelled when the theatre owner was murdered. After a period at the Paris Conservatoire (1873–5), where his teachers included Bazin and Boieldieu *fils*, he returned to Canada with the intention of founding a state-supported conservatory and opera company. He set up a studio (an embryonic conservatory) with Franzt and Rosita Jehin-Prume in Montreal. Performances of Barbier's *Jeanne d'Arc* (1877, with music by Gounod) and Boieldieu's *La dame blanche* (1879) under Lavallée's direction enchanted the public but failed to convince the Quebec authorities that music education should be subsidized. In about 1880 Lavallée moved once again to the USA, where he received the recognition he had missed at home. His *opéra comique The Widow* (3, F. H. Nelson), published in Boston in 1881, was performed in several American cities in 1882. Many of his other works were published as well, including in 1883 *Tiq* ('The Indian Question'), a melodramatic satire on the Indian issue and its solution by the American government.

Lavallée was a serious musician, at home in the classics as much as in the operetta music of his day. His greatest talent lay in melodic invention; his song *O Canada* (1880) became the Canadian national anthem. According to Logan, he was the 'first native-born Canadian creative composer – first in time, in genius … and in meritorious musicianship'.

Tiq, or Settled at Last, 1865–6 (melodramatic musical satire, 2, W. F. Sage and P. Hawley), ?unperf., vs (Boston, 1883)
Lou-Lou, 1872 (comic op, 3), unperf., lost
The Widow (oc, F. H. Nelson), Springfield, IL, Chatterton's, 25 March 1882, vs (Boston, 1881)
Salomon, *c*1886, 2 frags., lost

EMC ('Lavallée, Calixa', 'The Widow'; G. Potvin)
D. J. Logan: 'Canadian Creative Composers', *Canadian Magazine*, xli (1913)   HELMUT KALLMANN

Lavelli, Jorge (*b* Buenos Aires, 1931). French director. In Paris he studied economic science, then theatre at the Université du Théâtre des Nations. In the 1960s and early 70s he was closely associated with the playwrights Witold Gombrowicz and Fernando Arrabal. His first opera productions were *Idomeneo* (Angers), *Faust* (Paris) and Campra's *Le carnaval de Venise* (Aix), all in 1975. With the designer Max Bignens, he produced for the Paris Opéra *Pelléas et Mélisande* (1977), *Madama Butterfly* (1978), *L'enfant et les sortilèges* and *Oedipus rex* (both 1979); *L'enfant* and *Butterfly* were also given at La Scala. Lavelli's feel for movement and the effective distribution of chorus and extras across the stage floor in crowd scenes (notably the *kermesse* in *Faust*) make his productions memorable. His 1981 production of Rameau's *Dardanus* at the Opéra was marred by the use of masks and references to an alien, modern punk-disco culture, but in *Le carnaval de Venise* (designed by Claudio Segovia), the mixture of vaudeville and *commedia dell'arte* costumes was striking. Later productions include Nono's *Al gran sole, carico d'amore* (1982, Lyons), *Salome* (1985, Zürich), *Norma* (1983, Bonn) and Maurice Ohana's *La Célestine* (1988, Paris). Like Chéreau, Lavelli has been one of the most influential and admired, although consistently controversial, directors working in Paris during the operatic renaissance there in the 1970s and 80s.

P. Norès and C. Godard: *Lavelli* (Paris, 1970)
A. Satgé and J. Lavelli: *Lavelli, opéra et mise à mort* (Paris, 1979)
PATRICK O'CONNOR

Lavigna, Vincenzo (*b* Altamura, nr Bari, 21 Feb 1776; *d* Milan, 14 Sept 1836). Italian composer and teacher. He studied in Naples at the Conservatorio di S Maria di Loreto under Fenaroli and Saverio Valente. In 1801 he moved to Milan, where, thanks to the protection of Paisiello, his first opera, *La muta per amore, ossia Il medico per forza*, was performed at La Scala in 1802. In the same year he became *maestro al cembalo* at La Scala, and from 1823 taught at the Milan Conservatory. Between 1802 and 1810 he wrote several operas and two ballets, with some success, for La Scala and other north Italian opera houses.

Verdi studied counterpoint privately under Lavigna. In a letter to Florimo (1871) Verdi wrote of him: 'He was very good at counterpoint, a little pedantic, and didn't care for any music but Paisiello's … In my three years with him I did nothing but canons and fugues, fugues and canons in all kinds of sauces … He was a learned man, and I wish all teachers were equally so'.

La muta per amore, ossia Il medico per forza (farsa giocosa, 1, G. M. Foppa), Milan, Scala, 14 June 1802
L'idolo di se stesso, Ferrara, Communale, carn. 1803
L'impostore avvilito (melodramma giocoso, L. Romanelli), Milan, Scala, 11 Sept 1804
Coriolano, Turin, Regio, 15 Jan 1806
Le metamorfosi (dramma eroicomico, 1, Foppa), Venice, Fenice, spr. 1807
Hoango (G. Boggio), Turin, Regio, 1807; rev., as Orcamo (melodramma serio, Romanelli), Milan, Scala, 28 Feb 1809
Di posta in posta (melodramma giocoso, Romanelli), Milan, Scala, 2 July 1808
Palmerio e Claudia (? after Romanelli), Turin, Regio, 20 Jan 1809
Chi s'è visto s'è visto (dramma, A. Anelli), Milan, Scala, 23 April 1810

Doubtful: Zaira, Florence, Risoluti, 1809

DEUMM (P. Mioli)
G. De Napoli: *La triade melodrammatica altamurana: Giacomo Tritto, Vincenzo Lavigna, Saverio Mercadante* (Milan, 1931)
GIOVANNI CARLI BALLOLA

Lavirgen, Pedro (*b* Bujalance, 31 July 1930). Spanish tenor. He studied singing with Miguel Barrosa in Madrid. He made his operatic début as Radames in Mexico City in 1964, before making his first appearance in Spain, as Don José, at the Teatro del Liceo, Barcelona. His American début was with the Metropolitan Opera as Cavaradossi (1969). In 1975 he first appeared at La Scala as Radames and at Covent Garden as Don José. He returned to Covent Garden in 1978 to sing Pollione opposite Caballé's Norma, and in the same year sang Don José at the Edinburgh Festival opposite Teresa Berganza's Carmen. Lavirgen has specialized in Italian lyric tenor roles, notably Verdi and Puccini, to which he brings a warm vibrancy and dramatic strength.

Lavrangas, Dionyssios (*b* Argostólion, 17 Oct 1860 or 1864; *d* Razata, Cephalonia, 18 July 1941). Greek composer, conductor and teacher. Following early studies in Greece he went to Naples in 1882 where he became a private pupil of Mario Scarano and Augusto Ross, later attending the composition courses of Lauro Rossi and Paolo Serao at the S Pietro a Majella Conservatory. According to his own *Memoirs* (Athens, 1940) and other Greek sources he moved to Paris in autumn 1885; there he studied with Delibes and Massenet at the Conservatoire and privately with Dubois, E.-J.-B. Anthiome and Franck. However, his name does not appear in the extant lists of students in the Conservatoire archives. Lavrangas earned his living as a touring opera conductor until 1898, when he was offered co-directorship with Ludovicos Spinellis (?1871–1904) of the Elliniko Melodhrama (Greek Opera) in Athens. The company made its début in 1900 with *La bohème* under Spinellis, and Lavrangas conducted numerous productions before retiring in 1935. He was also active as a teacher and was artistic director of the opera school at the Hellenic Conservatory from 1919 to 1924.

Lavrangas's own operatic compositions remain regrettably unknown: *Dido* (1909, Athens) enjoyed popularity until 1930 but was last staged in 1952. It seems that his earlier works, *Ta dyo adelfia* ('The Two Brothers'), *Mayissa* ('The Sorceress') and *O lytrotis* ('The Redeemer') have proved more influential in the evolution of the Greek opera of the Ionian School than that of the National School. Stylistically he is substantially indebted to Massenet and other French composers, but he learnt from Italian opera his flowing melody, effective at moments of drama (e.g. the Puccinian touches in the conflagration scene in *Dido*) or comedy (e.g. the Rossinian *Fakanapas*). Manuscripts of several of Lavrangas's works are scattered in private collections, others were probably destroyed during the 1953 earthquakes in the Ionian islands.

MSS in Athens at the Dionyssios Lavrangas Archive or at the National State Opera Library, unless otherwise stated

Elda di Vorn, ?1886 (3, ?F. Guidi), Naples, Mercadante, *c*1890, lost
La vita è un sogno, 1887 (4, E. Golisciani, ?after P. Calderón de la Barca), unperf., lost; Act 4 rev. as Mayissa [Sorceress] (1, Lavrangas), Athens, Varieté, 8 Oct 1901
Galatea, ?1887 (5, Guidi, after S. Vassiliadis), lost
Ta dyo adelfia [The Two Brothers] (3 tableaux, I. Tsakassianos and Lavrangas), Athens, Municipal, 24 April 1900
O lytrotis [The Redeemer], ?1900–03 (3, Z. Papandoniou), Corfu, 24 Feb 1934
Dido, 1906–09 (4, P. Dimitrakopoulos), Athens, Municipal, 10 April 1909
Mavri petaloudha [Black Butterfly], 1923 (1, S. Sperantzas), Athens, Olympia, 25 or 26 Jan 1929
Aida, ?1928 (parody, N. Laskaris), lost
Ikaros, ?1930, lost
Ena paramythi [A Fairy Tale], 1930 (comic op, 3, D. Bogris)
Fakanapas, 1935 (comic op, 2, Lavrangas, after E. Scribe), Athens, National State Opera, 2 Dec 1950
Frosso, 1938 (3, Lavrangas), unperf.

Operettas: I aspri tricha [The White Hair] (3, N. Laskaris and H. Anninos), Athens, Municipal, 22 March 1917; Sporting Club (3,

Lavrangas and V. Vekiarellis), Athens, 4 August 1917; Dhipli Fotià [Double Flame] (3, Dimitrakopoulos), Athens, Municipal, 10 Jan 1918; Satore (3, A. Doxas [N. Drakoulidis]), lost; O Tragoudistis tou Kazinou [The Casino Singer] (3, Doxas and Sylvio [A. Papadopoulos]), Athens, Rialto, 7 July 1934, collab. 9 others

I. A. Tsitselis: 'Lavrangas, Dionyssios', *Kefalliniaka symmikta* [Cephallonian Miscellanea], ed. P. Leonis (Athens, 1904), i, 285–7

G. Sklavos: 'Dionyssios Lavrangas', *Pangefalliniakon imerologion* [All-Cephallonian Calendar], i (1937), 114–20

A. Hadjiapostolou: *Historia tou Ellinikou melodhramatos* [A History of the Hellenic Opera Company] (Athens, 1949)

S. Motsenigos: *Noelliniki moussiki, symvoli is tin istorian tis* [Modern Greek Music: a Contribution to its History] (Athens, 1958), 255–60

S. Evanghelatos: *Historia tou Theatrou en Kefallinia, 1600–1900* [A History of the Theatre in Cephallonia] (diss., Athens U., 1970)

GEORGE LEOTSAKOS

Lavrovskaya [Lawrowska], **Yelizaveta Andreyevna** (*b* Kashin, Tver province, 1/13 Oct 1845; *d* Petrograd [now St Petersburg], 4 Feb 1919). Russian mezzo-soprano. She studied in St Petersburg, singing Gluck's Orpheus at a student performance in 1867, greatly impressing the Grand Duchess Elena. Her professional début was in 1868 as Vanya (*Ivan Susanin*) at the St Petersburg Court Opera, where she also sang Ratmir (*Ruslan and Lyudmila*), Siébel in Gounod's *Faust*, Azucena, Carmen, Mignon and Serov's Rogneda. In 1872 she went to Paris to study further with Viardot and develop her concert career. She appeared again in St Petersburg (1879–80) and at the Bol'shoy during the 1890 season. It was Lavrovskaya who in 1877 suggested to Tchaikovsky the subject of *Yevgeny Onegin*.

B. Yagolim: 'E. A. Lavrovskaya: k 30-letiyu so dnya smerti' [On the 30th Anniversary of her Death], *SovM* (1949), no.3, pp.76–9

JENNIFER SPENCER/ELIZABETH FORBES

Lavry, Marc (*b* Riga, 22 Dec 1903; *d* Haifa, 24 March 1967). Israeli composer and conductor of Latvian birth. He studied at the Riga and Leipzig conservatories and privately with Glazunov. After various appointments as an opera and ballet conductor in Germany and Latvia, he emigrated to Israel (then Palestine) in 1935. He conducted the Palestine Folk Opera between 1941 and 1947. His works were greatly influenced by both East European Jewish folktunes and Eastern (or Arabic) regional folklore, and occasionally by the Arabic *māqām*. The arias of his operas and oratorios are highly melismatic. The influence of Jewish history and the new State of Israel is also to be found in his compositions, especially the symphonic poems, many of which are operatic in conception.

Lavry wrote two operas: *Dan Hashomer* ('Dan the Guard'; M. Brod, after S. Shalom), first performed in Tel-Aviv on 17 February 1945; and *Tamar* (3, L. Newman), based on the biblical story of Judah and Tamar, composed in 1958 (concert performance in New York, 22 March 1970). The most distinctive feature of Lavry's music is its diatonic-modal oriental melody, although the invention is generally limited. Aiming at popularity, the composer often failed to distinguish between simplicity and banality, and some of his work is marred by a quasi-orientalism. Though genuinely expressive of a certain period in Israeli history, his music has not retained its popularity.

WILLIAM Y. ELIAS

Lawrence [first name unknown] (*fl* 1706–18). English tenor. He played Thyrsis in Fedeli's *The Temple of Love* (1706) and sang in other operas in the Italian style until, in January 1710, he became the first English male singer to perform in Italian on the English operatic stage when he played Rustano in *Almahidi*. He sang the Herald in Handel's first London opera, *Rinaldo* (1711). That April, Addison in the *Spectator* satirically suggested that opera need not be confined to Italian: '*Lawrence* can learn to speak *Greek*, as well as he does *Italian*, in a Fortnight's time'. Lawrence continued to appear in Italian operas until 1716; he also taught singing and sang in a few English stage works.

J. Milhous and R. D. Hume: *Vice Chamberlain Coke's Theatrical Papers 1706–1715* (Carbondale, IL, 1982)

OLIVE BALDWIN, THELMA WILSON

Lawrence, Marjorie (**Florence**) (*b* Dean's Marsh, nr Melbourne, 17 Feb 1909; *d* Little Rock, AR, 13 Jan 1979). Australian soprano, later naturalized American. She studied in Paris and made her opera début at Monte Carlo in 1932 as Elisabeth in *Tannhäuser*. In 1933 she first appeared, as Ortrud, at the Paris Opéra, where, during the next three years, she sang Brünnhilde, Salome (*Hérodiade*), Rachel (*La Juive*), Aida, Donna Anna, Brunehild (*Sigurd*), Brangäne and Valentine. She made her Metropolitan début as the *Walküre* Brünnhilde on 18 December 1935, continuing to appear there for six seasons, mostly in the Wagnerian repertory but also as the heroines of *Alceste*, *Salome* and *Thaïs*. Although she had polio in 1941, she resumed her career in 1943 in specially staged performances during which she was always seated. In 1946 she returned to Paris as Amneris. Lawrence possessed a large, vibrant and expressive voice of mezzo-soprano quality. Her singing, though not always secure, gave pleasure because of its physical impact and distinctive sound.

M. Lawrence: *Interrupted Melody: the Story of My Life* (New York, 1949)

J. Rockwell: Obituary, *New York Times* (15 Jan 1979)

MAX DE SCHAUENSEE/R

Lawrenceville. American town in central New Jersey. It is the home of the June Opera Festival of New Jersey, a summer company whose productions are given at the Allan P. Kirby Arts Center (cap. 890) at the Lawrenceville School. The company was founded in 1984 by Michael Pratt (who became artistic director), John Ellis and Peter Westergaard. The company gives three or four productions, sung in English, each season, in June and early July. In 1989 the festival gave the first American performance of *Le nozze di Figaro* to use period instruments.

STEVEN P. METCALF

Laxenburg. Palace outside Vienna used as an imperial summer residence. Opera performances for the court were occasionally given there during the 18th century. *See* VIENNA, §1.

Lays [Lay, Lais], **François** (*b* Barthe-de-Nestes, 14 Feb 1758; *d* Ingrande, Angers, 30 March 1831). French baritone. He studied at the monastery of Guaraison, then in 1779 was engaged at the Paris Opéra, where he remained until his retirement in 1823. He sang Husca in Grétry's *La caravane du Caire* (1784) and created the title roles in that composer's *Panurge dans l'île des lanternes* (1785) and *Anacréon chez Polycrate* (1797).

He also took part in premières of two works by Spontini, as Cinna in *La vestale* (1807) and Télasco in *Fernand Cortez* (1809). Though a poor actor and not, apparently, a very good singer, he was greatly admired for the warmth and beauty of his voice, baritonal in quality, but which extended into the tenor range.

ELIZABETH FORBES

Lazaridis, Stefanos (*b* Dire-Dawa, Ethiopia, 28 July 1944). British stage designer of Greek descent. He studied in Geneva (1960–62) and then at the Central School of Speech and Drama, London. Though known mostly as an opera designer, he has also created designs for the Royal Ballet and the Royal Shakespeare Company. With the director John Copley, he designed *Le nozze di Figaro* for Covent Garden in 1971; this was followed by an anti-romantic, visually unconventional *Don Giovanni* two years later. In 1978 he designed the sets for the Royal Opera's first *Idomeneo*, in a weighty, grandiose manner (directed by Götz Friedrich), and 1979 for *Werther*, a production shared with the ENO, for which, as an Associate Artist, he has designed more than 25 productions.

Other Copley-Lazaridis associations for the ENO include *Die Entführung* (1971) and a Velasquez-inspired *Il trovatore* (1972). Then began a series of collaborations with John Blatchley – an atmospheric *Kát'a Kabanová* (1973), *Dalibor* (1976) and *Euryanthe* (1977) – before a very Egyptian *Aida* (1979) with Copley. Lazaridis has worked with the director David Pountney on *Der fliegende Holländer* (1982), a poetically imaginative *Rusalka* (1983; see illustration), a striking *Madama Butterfly* with Graham Vick (1984) and a series of highly admired productions including Janáček's *Osud* (1984), an elaborate, claustrophobic *Doktor Faust* (Busoni; 1986) and a bold, ingenious *Hänsel und Gretel* (1987). Under Jonathan Miller's idiosyncratic direction, he designed *The Mikado* (1986) and *Tosca* (1986, Florence, revived in London and Houston), on a skew setting in 1940s style. He has also had successful productions for Opera North, including *Nabucco*

(1980) and *Oedipus Rex* (1981). It was in the latter work in tandem with *Bluebeard's Castle* that he made his directorial début, in 1990, for Scottish Opera.

He has designed a number of controversial productions for Yuri Lyubimov: *Tristan und Isolde* (1983, Bologna), *Rigoletto* (1984, Florence) and *Fidelio* (1985, Stuttgart). Other productions include *Ariane et Barbe-bleue* (with Steven Pimlott) for Krefeld (1986) and *Der fliegende Holländer* (with David Pountney) for the Bregenz Festival (1989). His *Carmen* (1989) was seen by capacity audiences in London (Earl's Court), Tokyo, Melbourne and Sydney. His first production for La Scala was *La fanciulla del West* (with Miller) in 1991.

Lazaridis has always been noted for his sumptuous costumes. His early designs reflected a tradition of decorative escapism. Beginning with the designs for Lyubimov, he has emphasized broad theatrical effect in his structural, atmospheric and visually arresting sets.

For further illustration *see* POUNTNEY, DAVID.   DAVID J. HOUGH

Lázaro, Hipólito (*b* Barcelona, 13 Dec 1887; *d* Barcelona, 14 May 1974). Spanish tenor. Success in amateur zarzuela performances led to his operatic début at Barcelona in *La favorita*. He then studied with Enrico Colli in Milan. In 1913 he sang in Mascagni's *Isabeau* at Genoa under the composer, who subsequently engaged him for the première of his *Parisina* at La Scala. In 1914 he made his first tour of South America where he enjoyed some of his greatest successes. He appeared at the Metropolitan in 1918, making a strong impression there with the high tessitura of *I puritani*. Back in Italy he received acclaim for his part in the première of Mascagni's *Il piccolo Marat* at the Costanzi, Rome, in 1921, and he repeated his success, also under Mascagni, in Paris in 1928. He was in the première of *La cena delle beffe* in 1924, but withdrew from further performances after disagreements with the composer, Giordano. His contentious disposition probably hindered the development of his career in the 1930s, though he continued to sing to the end of his life, giving a farewell concert in

New York in 1944 and making his final operatic appearances in Havana in 1950. A bright, penetrating voice with magnificent high notes is heard on recordings that also show him to have been capable of some delightful as well as some deplorable stylistic effects. He also wrote an egotistical autobiography *El libro de mi vida* (Havana, 1949, 2/1968).

J. B. Richards: 'Hipolito Lazaro', *Record Collector*, xvi (1964–6), 53–94

J. B. STEANE

Lazarus, Daniel (*b* Paris, 13 Dec 1898; *d* Paris, 27 June 1964). French composer and conductor. He studied at the Paris Conservatoire, where his teachers included Leroux; after this he was musical director at the Théâtre du Vieux Colombier (1921–5), artistic director of the Opéra-Comique (1936–9), choirmaster of the Paris Opéra (1946–56) and lastly professor at the Schola Cantorum. His long association with the theatre as a conductor was complemented by his compositional activity: his output includes four operas, three ballets and incidental music.

L'illustre magicien, 1924 (drame musical, J. R. Bloch, after Gobineau), Paris, 1937
La véritable histoire de Wilhelm Meister [from themes by Schumann], Paris, 1927
Trumpeldor, 1935 (épopée lyrique, 3), concert perf., Paris, 30 April 1946
La chambre bleue (comédie musicale, H. Prunières, after P. Mérimée), Paris, OC (Favart), 20 May 1938   ANNE GIRARDOT

Lazzari, (Joseph) Sylvio [Silvio; Lazzari, Josef Fortunat Sylvester] (*b* Bozen [Bolzano], 30 Dec 1857; *d* Suresnes, nr Paris, 10 June 1944). French composer of Austro-Italian parentage. The only son of a wealthy family, he travelled widely during his youth and entered the Paris Conservatoire in 1883, studying with Gounod, Guiraud and later Franck. He became a French national in 1896. Respected as a conductor, he held several posts in French theatres including the Gaîté-Lyrique in Paris. His most important works were incidental music and operas on Christian themes.

Armor was the first of several operas set in Brittany. Clearly echoing *Tristan*, it concerns Armor (tenor), a Breton knight who is nominated by the ghost of King Arthur (baritone) to inherit his crown. But Ked (dramatic soprano), fairy Queen of the Korriganes, guards the crown and will yield it only to a man with whom she falls in love at first sight. Lifting Armor's visor, she is struck by his handsomeness and offers him her love. But he has vowed to serve God alone. He breaks his vow and Ked her allegiance to the fairies. A hurricane engulfs the island leaving only the two sinners. The *prélude* was widely performed as a concert piece.

La lépreuse, which several critics considered Lazzari's finest work, is based on a Breton legend concerning Aliette (soprano) who is tainted with leprosy. Discovering that her suitor Ervoanik (tenor) is already married she drinks with him, and by turning her side of the cup to him, she ensures that he also is tainted. Breton folk melodies are employed and unaccompanied plainsong from the requiem mass is introduced as well as a carillon scene as the lovers die.

La tour de feu, the first opera to use cinema as an integral part, also has a Breton theme. It concerns the newly wed Naïc (dramatic soprano) who has married Yves (tenor), a lighthouse keeper. Don Jacintho (baritone), a rich Portuguese sailor, courts her, offering escape from her island prison. At first resistant, she eventually

succumbs, planning to be picked up at a pre-arranged signal. But Jacintho's boat is wrecked in the dangerous straits as Naïc sings desperately to him. *La tour de feu* was revived in Innsbruck in 1984.

Lulu (pantomime, 1, F. Champsaur), Paris, May 1889
Armor (3, E. Jaubert), Prague, Landes, 7 Nov 1898, *F-Po*, vs (Paris, 1897)
La lépreuse, 1900–1 (tragédie légendaire, 3, H. Bataille), OC (Favart), 7 Feb 1912, *Pn*; (Paris, 1912) [also known as L'ensorcelé]
Melaenis (5, G. Spitzmüller, after L. Bouilhet), Mulhouse, Municipal, 25 March 1927, vs (Paris and Leipzig, 1913)
Le sauteriot, 1913–15 (drame lyrique, 3, H. P. Roché and M. Périer, after E. de Keyserling), Chicago, Opera, 19 Jan 1918, *Po*, vs (Paris, 1920)
La tour de feu, 1925 (drame lyrique, 3, Lazzari), Paris, Opéra, 28 Jan 1928, *Po*, vs (Paris, 1928)

L. Schneider: 'Armor', *Le théâtre*, no.169 (1906), 22–4
G. Baudin: 'L'affaire de La lépreuse', *BSIM*, vi (1910), suppl., 395-6
G. Pioch: 'Alfred Bruneau, Sylvio Lazzari, Ernest Moret', *Le théâtre lyrique en France* (Paris, 1937–9) [pubn of Poste National/Radio-Paris], iii, 37–49
P. Landormy: *La musique française après Debussy* (Paris, 1943)
——: *La musique française de Franck à Debussy* (Paris, 1943)
P. Bertrand: *Le monde de la musique* (Geneva, 1947)
G. Samazeuilh: *Musiciens de mon temps* (Paris, 1947)
W. Asholt: 'La lépreuse von H. Bataille/S. Lazzari (1896/1912)', *Oper als Text: romanistische Beiträge zur Libretto-Forschung*, ed. A. Gier (Heidelberg, 1986), 299–318

RICHARD LANGHAM SMITH

Lazzari, Virgilio (*b* Assisi, 20 April 1887; *d* Castel Gandolfo, 4 Oct 1953). Italian bass, later naturalized American. He sang with the Vitale Operetta Company, 1908–11, then studied in Rome with Cotogni. He made his operatic début at the Teatro Costanzi, Rome, in 1914. After singing in South America, in 1917 he made his North American début at Boston. He sang with the Chicago Opera (1918–33), then made his Metropolitan début as Don Pédro (*L'Africaine*), remaining with the company until 1951 and singing 20 roles. From 1934 to 1939 he appeared at the Salzburg Festival, where he sang Pistol (*Falstaff*), Bartolo and Leporello, the role of his only Covent Garden appearance (1939). His most famous role was that of Archibaldo (Montemezzi's *L'amore dei tre re*), which he sang first in 1916 in Mexico City and as late as 1953 in Genoa. Although not blessed with a great voice, Lazzari was considered one of the best singing actors in his particular repertory.

HAROLD ROSENTHAL/R

Leak [Leake], Elizabeth (*b* East Beckham, Norfolk, bap. 18 Sept 1776; *d* after 1808). English soprano. She was articled to Dr Arnold, sang in London concerts in 1793 and made her stage début as Rosetta in *Love in a Village* in January 1794 when, according to the *Monthly Mirror*, she was 'not yet 15'. She sang at Drury Lane, with summer seasons at the Haymarket or in the provinces, until June 1800, creating the roles of Fanny in Storace's *The Cherokee*, Phebe in his *The Three and the Deuce* and the heroine in Arnold's *The Shipwreck*. In 1795 Waldron described her as 'a bewitching little syren, and a very pretty actress', but her voice was worn out by 1800 and she later taught music.

[F. G. Waldron]: *Candid and Impartial Strictures on the Performers* (London, 1795)
'Biographical Sketch of Miss Leak', *Monthly Mirror*, vii (1799), 5–7
The Thespian Dictionary (London, 1802, 2/1805)
M. J. Young: *Memoirs of Mrs Crouch* (London, 1806)
T. Gilliland: *The Dramatic Mirror*, ii (London, 1808)

OLIVE BALDWIN, THELMA WILSON

Leal Moreira, António. *See* MOREIRA, ANTÓNIO LEAL.

Lear. Opera in two parts by ARIBERT REIMANN to a libretto by Claus H. Henneberg after WILLIAM SHAKESPEARE's tragedy *King Lear*; Munich, Nationaltheater, 9 July 1978.

King Lear	baritone
King of France	bass-baritone
Duke of Albany	baritone
Duke of Cornwall	tenor
Earl of Kent	tenor
Earl of Gloucester	bass-baritone
Edgar *Gloucester's son*	tenor/countertenor
Edmund *Gloucester's bastard son*	tenor
Goneril ⎫	soprano
Regan ⎬ *Lear's daughters*	soprano
Cordelia ⎭	soprano
Fool	spoken
A servant	tenor
Gentleman	spoken

Servants, guards, soldiers

Setting England

Reimann's third opera was commissioned in 1975 by the Bayerische Staatsoper, after the success of its predecessor *Melusine* in West German opera houses in the early 1970s; the title role was conceived very much with the voice of Dietrich Fischer-Dieskau in mind. Fischer-Dieskau created the role at the première, when the cast also included Julia Varady, Colette Lorand and Helga Dernesch as Lear's daughters, David Knutson (Edgar), Werner Götz (Edmund), Rolf Boysen (Fool) and Hans Gunter Nöcker (Gloucester); the conductor was Gerd Albrecht, the director Jean-Pierre Ponnelle. The same cast subsequently made a recording of the work for Deutsche Grammophon. A production with Günter Reich as Lear was staged in Düsseldorf later the same year; Albrecht conducted the American première (in English translation) in San Francisco in 1981 with Thomas Stewart in the title role, and the French première took place in Paris in 1982. In 1989 it was staged by English National Opera at the London Coliseum; the cast was headed by Monte Jaffe, and the performances were conducted by Paul Daniel.

The two parts into which Reimann and Henneberg cast Shakespeare's tragedy divide into four and seven scenes respectively, though the placing of the orchestral interludes (between each of the scenes in Part 1, after i, iv and v in Part 2) imposes a musical symmetry on the score.

PART 1.i *A square in front of the castle* In a measured, weary monologue, Lear summons his court to witness the division of his kingdom between his three daughters, according to how much they love him. In arias which define their vocal characters, Goneril (fierce, declamatory) and Regan (extravagant coloratura) are effusive in their declarations of affection and are suitably rewarded, but Cordelia (lyrical and poised) cannot articulate her love. Despite Gloucester's intervention she is disinherited and banished by her father. The King of France claims Cordelia as his wife, and as the couple leave, they join Goneril, Regan, Lear, Gloucester, Edmund and Edgar in an ensemble,

punctuated by wry comments from the Fool. Goneril and Regan divide Cordelia's inheritance between them. The Fool observes Gloucester as Lear's mirror image – 'He's easy to betray. Old age has made him foolish and soft'. Edmund, his lines characterized initially by repeated notes, persuades Edgar to desert his father and then uses a forged letter to turn Gloucester against him.

1.ii *A palace courtyard* After the short, wild orchestral Interlude 1, Lear and his followers celebrate their new, carefree existence. Kent, in disguise, is recruited to Lear's service. Goneril and Regan round on their father; Kent is led away to be punished in the stocks and Lear forced to abandon his retinue. Humiliated and furious, he is led away by Kent and the Fool.

1.iii *A heath, in a storm* During the preceding Interlude 2 the storm breaks, and Lear's rage explodes in a declamatory monologue, high in tessitura (centred on *d'*) and characterized by leaping 7ths. As the storm subsides, the Fool and Kent plan a journey to Cordelia.

1.iv *A hovel* Interlude 3, led off by a flute melody spiralling upwards chromatically through two octaves, changes the mood and underpins the scene. Edgar, now disguised as the mad Poor Tom, is first heard as a disembodied offstage countertenor; he gives refuge to Lear who is close to madness himself. Edgar's line extends to *e''* and Lear's ravings become ever more hysterical before Gloucester and his followers arrive to escort him to meet Cordelia at Dover.

PART 2.i *Gloucester's castle* Gloucester is accused of treachery by Cornwall and Regan, whose vocal lines become ever more florid and hysterical. They tear out Gloucester's eyes; a servant who tries to intervene stabs Cornwall and is killed himself. When Gloucester calls out for Edmund's help he realizes that his son has joined the conspiracy; Cornwall dies from his wound, and Gloucester is thrown out.

2.ii/iii/iv *Albany's palace/The French camp near Dover/The country* After the briefest fugal interlude for a quartet of muted strings, three scenes are interwoven. Goneril seduces Edmund and plans to marry him when Albany is dead, while Cordelia is seen searching for her father. Albany unsuccessfully reproaches Goneril as she celebrates the news of Cornwall's death and Gloucester's fate. Edgar, still disguised as Poor Tom, encounters Gloucester, who fails to recognize his son and asks to be led to Dover, while Edgar's wailing lament gradually permeates the orchestral textures.

2.v *Open country, the coast* After a more extended Interlude 4, Edgar and Gloucester arrive at what the latter thinks are the cliffs at Dover. Gloucester attempts to throw himself off, and Edgar convinces him that he has been miraculously saved. Lear approaches; his voice is recognized by Gloucester, but the king only gradually regains his senses; when the French soldiers arrive to escort him to Cordelia, madness overtakes him again.

2.vi *In the French camp* Interlude 5 leads to the reconciliation of Cordelia and Lear, in an aria for Cordelia whose freely notated simplicity recalls Lear's opening monologue.

2.vii *A camp near Dover* Edmund celebrates the capture of Lear and Cordelia and orders them to prison. As Albany demands clemency for the pair Regan dies, poisoned by Goneril who is jealous of her liaison with Edmund. Edgar appears as an unknown knight to challenge Edmund to single combat; as Edmund is killed, Goneril stabs herself. Lear brings forward the body of Cordelia, who has been hanged on the orders of Goneril and Edmund. In an extended lament which brings back the flute threnody from Interlude 3, Lear mourns his daughter; as he dies the melody is submerged by an orchestral chord that slowly ebbs away.

* * *

Reimann's score is based on serial principles and founded on a pair of related hexachords (*c-b-c♯-d-e♭-f*, *e-f♯-g-a♭-b♭-a*). They furnish the note row of Cordelia's theme and are reversed to form Edgar's, as well as appearing melodically to articulate crucial monologues throughout the opera. Other elements, especially the Fool's 'folksongs' which punctuate his spoken utterances in the first act, are tonally based, though these are accompanied by serially derived textures that obscure their tonality. Vocal patterns are derived from speech rhythms; those for Lear are the most varied, ranging from freely notated parlando to precisely specified declamation, while the music for his daughters and Edgar (changing gradually from tenor to countertenor and back again) is the most conventionally operatic.

The instrumental writing, for a vast orchestra that includes a string section sometimes divided into 48 parts and a formidable array of percussion, is bold and highly dissonant, favouring massive chord clusters (including quarter-tones) and textures generated by micro-polyphony. Though many of his effects are massively rhetorical, Reimann ensures balance and coherence through the vocal characterization of each character outlined above, and by the deployment of recurrent motifs, particularly in the use of the chromatic flute melody as an anchor for the final scenes of each part, to provide the score's most abiding musical image.

ANDREW CLEMENTS

Lear [née Shulman], **Evelyn** (*b* Brooklyn, NY, 8 Jan 1926). American soprano. She studied at the Juilliard School and later in Berlin. Engaged by the Berlin Städtische (later Deutsche) Oper, she made her début in 1959 as the Composer. In 1961 she created the title role in Klebe's *Alkmene* in Berlin and in 1963 Jeanne in *Die Verlobung in San Domingo* at the opening celebrations of the rebuilt Nationaltheater, Munich. She made her Metropolitan début as Lavinia in the first performance of *Mourning Becomes Electra* (1967). With her first performance in Vienna of Berg's Lulu in 1962 she became closely associated with the role, singing it in London with the Hamburg company that year. She made her Covent Garden début in 1965 as Donna Elvira. Her repertory included both Cherubino and Countess Almaviva, Fiordiligi, Pamina, Handel's Cleopatra, Mimì, Desdemona, Tatyana, Marie (*Wozzeck*), Emilia Marty and Octavian. From 1972 she began to undertake heavier roles, including Tosca and the Marschallin. She created Arkadina in Pasatieri's *The Seagull* (1974), Magda in Robert Ward's *Minutes to Midnight* (1982) and Ranyevskaya in Kelterborn's *Kirschgarten* (1984, Zürich). Her voice, though not large, was of distinctively warm and affecting quality, well produced and projected. In 1985 she made her farewell at the Metropolitan as the Marschallin and sang Countess Geschwitz at Florence, repeating the role in Chicago (1987) and San Francisco (1989). She married the baritone Thomas Stewart.   HAROLD ROSENTHAL/R

Leblanc [first name unknown] (*b* ?*c*1750; *d* Paris, March 1827). French composer. He wrote light works for the Paris stage, beginning with *La noce béarnaise* in 1787. He was director of the orchestra of the Théâtre-Français Comique et Lyrique until at least 1791, and was a composer of operas and pantomimes for the Théâtre d'Emulation until 1801. At least the overture and accompaniments for Beffroy de Reigny's extremely popular *Nicodème dans la lune* (1790) are by him, but it was his misfortune to compose for the short-lived, smaller theatres, and his successes were quickly forgotten. He composed much music, often anonymously, for the pantomimes, ballets and melodramas of the boulevard theatres. A fall in his fortunes obliged him to accept the position of second violin at the Théâtre sans Prétention, and he was later reduced to copying music to support himself.

first performed in Paris

La noce béarnaise (oc, 3, Lutaine), Beaujolais, 14 Nov 1787, ov., entr'acte arr. hpd/pf, vn (Paris, n.d.), 2 ariettes (Paris, n.d.)

Gabrielle et Paulin, ou Les amours du printemps (vaudeville, 1), Beaujolais, 10 May 1788, 2 airs (Paris, n.d.)

Le lord et son jockey (opéra bouffon, 3, Lutaine), Beaujolais, 8 Oct 1788

La soubrette rusée (opéra bouffon, 1), Beaujolais, 3 Oct 1789

La folle gageure (cmda, 1, F.-P.-A. Léger), Français Comique et Lyrique, 30 June 1790

Rosine et Zély (oc), Français Comique et Lyrique, 4 Sept 1790

Le berceau d'Henri IV (oc, 2), Français Comique et Lyrique, 1 Dec 1790

Le mariage de Nanon, ou La suite de Madame Angot (oc, 1, A. F. Eve), Emulation, 1796

La fausse mère, ou Une faute d'amour (opérette), Emulation, 1798

La bergère de Saluces, ou La vertu à l'épreuve (drame-pantomime, 4, Noël), Jeunes Artistes, 29 Jan 1799

Le sérail, ou La fée du Mogol (féerie, 3, Hapdé and Dabaytua), De la cité, 23 Dec 1799

La forêt enchantée, ou Isaure et Florestan (féerie), Gaîté, 1800

Les deux nuits (oc, 2, Coffin-Rosny and Béraud), Gaîté, 31 May 1802

Ecbert, premier roi d'Angleterre, ou La fin de l'heptarchie (mélodrame, 3, P.-A.-L.-P. Plancher [V. Valcour]), *c*1802

Esther (mélodrame, 3, Plancher), 1802 or 1803

La belle Milanaise, ou La fille-femme, page et soldat, Gaîté, 28 June 1804

Le sabot miraculeux, ou L'isle des Nains, Salle de Jeux Forains, 8 Jan 1811

Saphirine, ou Le réveil magique (mélo-féerie, 2, J.-T. Merle and E. T. M. Ourry), Gaîté, 25 July 1811

Riquet à la houpe (mélo-féerie, 2, Simonnin), Gaîté, 28 Sept 1811

L'armure, ou Le soldat moldave (mélodrame, 3, J.-G.-A. Cuvelier de Trie and Léopold [L. Chandezon]), Gaîté, 20 Oct 1821

Azémire, ou Les réfugiés péruviens (mélodrame), ?unperf.

Elisa, ou Le triomphe des femmes (mélodrame), ?unperf.

Contribs to: L.-A. Beffroy de Reigny: Nicodème dans la lune, 1790

*

FétisB; GerberNL

P. L. Jacob, ed.: *Bibliothèque dramatique de Monsieur de Soleinne* (Paris, 1843–5)

F. Clément and P. Larousse: *Dictionnaire lyrique* (Paris, 1867–9, 2/1897, 3/1905 ed. A. Pougin as *Dictionnaire des opéras*)

C. S. Brenner: *A Bibliographical List of Plays in the French Language 1700–1789* (Berkeley, 1947)   LELAND FOX

Leblanc, Georgette (*b* Tancarville, 8 Feb 1875; *d* Le Cannet, nr Cannes, 27 Oct 1941). French soprano. She studied in Paris, making her début in 1893 at the Opéra-Comique as Françoise in the first performance of Bruneau's *L'attaque au Moulin*. She also sang Fanny in Massenet's *Sapho*. Engaged at the Théâtre de la Monnaie (1894–6), she sang Anita (*La Navarraise*), Thaïs and Carmen. In Brussels, she began a 20-year association with Maurice Maeterlinck, who wanted her to create the heroine of *Pelléas et Mélisande*; Debussy, however, insisted that Mary Garden should sing the role. Instead, Leblanc sang Ariane at the first performance of Dukas' *Ariane et Barbe-bleue* at the Opéra-Comique (1907). She first sang Mélisande in 1912 at Boston, where she also acted in the play.

ELIZABETH FORBES

Leborne, Aimé (Ambroise Simon) (*b* Brussels, 29 Dec 1797; *d* Paris, 1 or 2 April 1866). French composer of South Netherlands birth. He entered the Paris Conservatoire in 1811, where his teachers included H.-M. Berton and Cherubini. In 1820 he won the Prix de Rome, enabling him to travel in Italy and Germany for three years. On his return to Paris he taught at the Conservatoire and attempted several *opéras comiques*, on his own or with others. He was named librarian of the Opéra in 1829 and of the royal chapel five years later. After Reicha's death in 1836 Leborne became professor of counterpoint and fugue at the Conservatoire, and from 1840 he taught composition, retaining this post until his death.

Leborne was a renowned teacher; several of his pupils won the Prix de Rome. He brought out a new edition of Catel's *Traité d'harmonie* (1848), and wrote his own (unpublished) treatise on harmony. His operas, which displayed much coloratura writing, were produced between 1827 and 1838 with little success.

all *opéras comiques, first performed in Paris*

Les deux Figaro (3, V. Tirpenne), Odéon, 22 Aug 1827, collab. Carafa
Le camp du drap d'or (3, P. de Kock), OC (Feydeau), 23 Feb 1828, collab. Baton and Rifaut
La violette [finales to Acts 1 and 2 only] (3, F. A. E. de Planard, after Comte de Tressan: *Gérard de Nevers*), OC (Feydeau), 7 Oct 1828 (Paris, ?1829), collab. Carafa
Cinq ans d'entracte (2, A. Féréol), OC (Nouveautés), 15 June 1833
Lequel? (1, P. Duport and J.-A. F.-P. Ancelot), OC (Nouveautés), 21 March 1838   MARIE LOUISE PEREYRA, JEFFREY COOPER

Le Bovier de Fontenelle, Bernard. *See* FONTENELLE, BERNARD LE BOVIER DE.

Lebrun, Franziska (Dorothea). *See* DANZI family, (1).

Lebrun, Louis-Sébastien (*b* Paris, 10 Dec 1764; *d* Paris, 27 June 1829). French composer. He studied composition and singing at Notre Dame until 1783, when he became musical director of St Germain-l'Auxerrois. Encouraged to take up theatrical singing, he made his début at the Opéra in 1787 as Polynices in Sacchini's *Oedipe à Colone*. In the same period he appeared at the Concert Spirituel in the dual role of singer and composer. He transferred to the Théâtre Feydeau in 1791 and then rejoined the Opéra as an understudy, becoming a singing tutor in 1803. In 1807 he was admitted into the imperial chapel, where he was promoted to director of singing after three years.

Among his stage works, most of which are *opéras comiques, Marcelin* (1800) and *Le rossignol* (1816) were quite successful. The former was presented in Madrid, Vienna, St Petersburg, Budapest, Prague and Stockholm. *Le rossignol* was famed for its virtuoso exchanges between the soprano and the solo flute, and was performed 227 times in Paris up to 1852, though Clément and Larousse ascribed its longevity merely to the general shortage of operas brief enough to precede an evening of ballet. During its performance at the Théâtre Louvois on 13 February 1820, Charles Ferdinand de Bourbon, the Duke of Berry and heir to the throne, was assassinated. *Le rossignol* was played in New York (1833) and London (Drury Lane, 1846). As well as operas, Lebrun composed sacred works, songs and an oratorio.

opéras comiques unless otherwise stated; all first performed in Paris

L'art d'aimer au village, ou L'enchère amoureuse (cmda, 1, [?L.-H.] Dancourt), Montansier, 16 June 1790
Ils ne savent pas lire (1, Lasalle), Montansier, ? 20 June 1791
Emilie et Melcour, ou La leçon villageoise (1, L. Hennequin), Louvois, 3 July 1795, autograph frags. *F-Pc* (some dated 1791), aria (*c*1796)
Le bon fils (opéra mêlé de vaudevilles, 1, Hennequin), Feydeau, 17 Sept 1795, autograph frags. *Pc*
L'astronome (opéra, 1, Desfaucherets), Feydeau, 1798, *F-Po**, extracts arr. pf (*c*1799)
Le menteur maladroit (1), Molière, 1798
Un moment d'erreur (1), Louvois, 1798
Le maçon (oc, 1, C. A. B. Sewrin), Feydeau, 4 Dec 1799, *Pc*
La veuve américaine (opéra, 2), Louvois, 1799, *Pc*
Marcelin (opéra, 1, F. Bernard-Valville), Feydeau, 22 March 1800, *Pc*; (*c*1800)
Eléonore et Dorval, ou La suite de la cinquantaine (1), Montansier, 1800
Les petits aveugles de Franconville (1, A. Croizette and A. F. Chateauvieux), Montansier, 1802
Le rossignol (opéra or oc, 1, C. G. Etienne), Opéra, 23 April 1816 (n.d.)
Zéloïde, ou Les fleurs enchantées (opéra-ballet, 2, Etienne), Opéra, 19 Jan 1818, *Po*
Unperf., frags. *Pc*: L'an II (5); Charlemagne (opéra); Rosalie (opéra); Rosenberg (opéra, 4); Le Syst (opéra)

*

LoewenbergA
A. Choron and F. Fayolle: *Dictionnaire historique des musiciens* (Paris, 1810–11)
F. Clement and P. Larousse: *Dictionnaire lyrique* (Paris, 1867–81; 2/1897, 3/1905 ed. A. Pougin as *Dictionnaire des opéras*)
F. Lesure, ed.: *Catalogue de la musique imprimée avant 1800 conservée dans les bibliothèques publiques de Paris* (Paris, 1981)
M. Noiray: 'Les créations d'opéra à Paris de 1790 à 1794: chronologie et sources parisiennes', *Orphée phrygien: Les musiques de la Révolution*, ed. J.-R. Julien and J.-C. Klein (Paris, 1989), 193–203   DAVID CHARLTON

Le Cerf de la Viéville, Jean Laurent, Seigneur de Freneuse (*b* Rouen, 1674; *d* Rouen, 10 Nov 1707). French writer on music. He was educated by the Jesuits and studied philosophy and law before assuming his father's post as Keeper of the Seals of the Parliament of Normandy in 1696. This sinecure left him free to write and he became a frequent, if pedantic, contributor to the Jesuit journal, *Mémoires de Trévoux*. Music was for him a passion and, accordingly, he habitually spent his parliamentary recesses in Paris, even travelling out to Versailles.

Spurred on by the appearance of the *Paralèle des italiens et des françois* (1702) of his Normandy neighbour, FRANÇOIS RAGUENET, but nevertheless cautious enough to publish his own views in Brussels rather than Paris, Le Cerf brought out in 1704 the Première Partie of his *Comparaison de la musique italienne et de la musique françoise* modelled on the writings of Claude and Charles Perrault. In a series of three dialogues conducted by a count, a countess and a chevalier (representing Le Cerf's own voice), he began to limn out the musical aesthetic prevailing in France during the late 17th century. Taking Raguenet's *Paralèle* (which is, in fact, a rejection of French music and its practice in favour of Italian counterparts) as a point of departure, Le Cerf espoused a simple, rational, 'natural' art over one based primarily on sensual beauty, an art that finds its expression in the ideals inherent in the music of Lully. A review appeared in the 1 August 1704 issue of the

Journal des Sçavans, the periodical in which the physician and medical journalist, Nicolas de Boisregard Andry, later wrote critically of Le Cerf (7 December 1705 and 12 August 1706).

Raguenet swiftly and systematically replied in scornful and ironic tones to Le Cerf in his *Défense du parallèle* (Paris, 1705). At least in musical-aesthetic terms, he proved no match for the fluent though often digressive Le Cerf, who was proceeding with the publication, again in Brussels, of the compendious Seconde Partie of the *Comparaison*. In addition to three further dialogues, it includes a potpourri of song texts, historical surveys of music, opera and Lully, and a 'traité du bon goût en musique'. More particularly, he produced in 1705 a *Réponse à la Défense du Parallèle*, which – perhaps in view of its topicality – he published in Paris. Such was the speed with which he dispatched the *Réponse* that, within weeks of Andry's first piece, Le Cerf was able to quote disputed passages from it as well as from Raguenet's six-month-old *Défense*. Le Cerf, it must be said, admired the Italian music he heard in Rouen and Paris, especially the latest sonatas of Corelli and cantatas of Bononcini, as well as the older music of Rossi, Carissimi and Lorenzani. The Troisième Partie of the *Comparaison* (Brussels, 1706) begins with a fragmentary text for a sacred opera followed by two series of essays, one on church music, the other on the differences between French and Italian music; the final essay, 'Jugement sur les Italiens & sur les François', is written in a spirit closer to that of Raguenet's *Paralèle* than any other part.

Piqued by the impertinence of Andry, who Le Cerf referred to alternately as 'Mr. le Journalist' and 'Mr. le Médecin', he produced a scathing essay, *L'art de décrier ce qu'on n'entend point, ou Le médecin musicien* (1706), in which he devoted 25 pages to a rigorous 'Exposition de la mauvaise foi d'un extrait du Journal de Paris'. According to Philippe Le Cerf, a Benedictine monk who provided unique details of his brother's life in the April 1726 *Mercure galant*, Le Cerf intended to produce a fourth part to the *Comparaison*, which was to have included a critical catalogue of French operas, but died of a cerebral haemorrhage before completing it.

The appearance of a 'Dissertation sur la musique italienne et sur la musique françoise', signed by 'M. de L. T.' in the November 1713 *Mercure*, served to cloud the dissemination and perception of Le Cerf's views. Jacques Bonnet included it in the first volume of his *Histoire de la musique et de ses effets* (Paris, 1715) and devoted the subsequent three volumes to Le Cerf's three *parties* (Amsterdam, 1721). Many people have assumed the first was also by Le Cerf and annotated German translations of it were misleadingly juxtaposed with those of Raguenet's *Paralèle* in the inaugural issues of Mattheson's *Critica musica* (1722) and the first volume of Marpurg's *Kritische Briefe über die Tonkunst* (1759).

Comparaison de la musique italienne et de la musique françoise (Brussels, 1704–6); repr. in P. Bourdelot and P. Bonnet-Bourdelot: *Histoire de la musique et de ses effets*, ed. J. Bonnet, ii–iv (Amsterdam, 1722); Eng. trans. of extract from 6th dialogue in O. Strunk: *Source Readings in Music History* (New York, 1950), 489–507

Réponse à la Défense du Parallèle (Paris, 1705)

L'art de décrier ce qu'on n'entend point, ou Le médecin musicien (Brussels, 1706)

*
J. Ecorcheville: *De Lulli à Rameau 1690–1730: l'esthétique musicale* (Paris, 1906)

H. Prunières: 'Lecerf de la Viéville et l'esthétique musicale classique au XVIIe siècle', *BSIM*, iv (1908), 619–54

P.-M. Masson: 'Musique italienne et musique française: la première querelle', *RMI*, xix (1912), 519–45

R. Wangermée: 'Lecerf de la Viéville, Bonnet-Bourdelot et l'Essai sur le bon goust en musique de Nicolas Grandval', *RBM*, v (1951), 132–46

M. B. Ellison: *The 'Comparaison de la musique italienne et de la musique françoise' of Le Cerf de la Viéville: an Annotated Translation of the First Four Dialogues* (diss., U. of Miami, 1973)

G. Cowart: *The Origins of Modern Musical Criticism: French and Italian Music 1600–1750* (Ann Arbor, 1981)

ALBERT COHEN, JULIE ANNE SADIE

Leclair, Jean-Marie [l'aîné] (*b* Lyons, 10 May 1697; *d* Paris, 22 or 23 Oct 1764). French composer. He is considered the founder of the French violin school. In his youth Leclair studied not only as a violinist but as a dancer. Indeed, ballet provided him with his first known professional appointment: in 1716 he was listed among the dancers at the Lyons opera. He was in Turin as a freelance musician during the royal wedding festivities of 1722, providing ballet music for Orlandini's *Semiramide*. In 1727 he was again in Turin, where he supplied ballets (almost certainly the same as in 1722) for two further operas at the Teatro Regio Ducale. All the Turin music is now lost.

For most of the next two decades, Leclair devoted himself to his career as virtuoso violinist and composer of instrumental music. But at the age of 50, having largely retired from playing, he produced his only full-length opera, the *tragédie en musique Scylla et Glaucus* (in a prologue and five acts, to a libretto by D'Albaret after Ovid's *Metamorphoses*). First given at the Paris Opéra on 4 October 1746, it had a total of 18 performances; it was published in Paris in the same year (the manuscript score in *F-Po* contains corrections possibly in the hand of the composer).

Around 1748 the Duke of Gramont, a former pupil, persuaded the composer to end his semi-retirement. The duke gave Leclair a pension and appointed him *premier violon* of the ducal orchestra, an appointment the composer held until his murder in 1764. Leclair soon became involved in the theatrical entertainments that were a feature of the duke's house at Puteaux, near Paris. One contemporary noted the parallel between these extravagant entertainments, involving the duke's mistress, and those of Mme de Pompadour's Théâtre des Petits Cabinets.

The duke's theatre was evidently equipped with enough stage machinery to cope with transformation scenes and descents of supernatural characters. Both are used extensively in the first two works to which Leclair is known to have contributed: a lengthy *divertissement* for a play attributed to La Porte, *Le danger des épreuves* (1749), and one complete entrée, 'Apollon et Climène', for the *opéra-ballet Amusements lyriques* (1750). Leclair's other known activities at Puteaux mainly involved the resetting of existing librettos, or perhaps the refurbishing of their original settings. Apart from one fragment (see Sadler and Zaslaw 1980), none of the music for Puteaux can be positively identified; some, however, may have survived in Leclair's trios op.13 and op.14, which contain other known arrangements including the overture to *Scylla et Glaucus*.

Although Leclair's reputation as a composer rests securely on his violin sonatas and other instrumental music, he was at various times extensively occupied in writing music for the theatre. Much of this music is now lost, but it originally made up a substantial proportion of his output. His operatic idiom, as revealed in *Scylla*, is strongly rooted in French tradition and is somewhat less italianate than that of his instrumental music. In its boldness and variety, its harmonic intensity and in many of its melodic turns of phrase, it most closely resembles Rameau's style, though it is by no means a pale imitation. Leclair's opera maintains a consistently high level of invention: not surprisingly, the ballet music shows a dancer's sensitivity to pace and gesture, while the violin writing is often extremely elaborate. Many of the choruses, for example, are accompanied by strings in five parts with the first violins maintaining continuous independent figuration.

See also SCYLLA ET GLAUCUS.

Mercure de France (Oct 1746), 152–60
B. F. de Rosoi: 'Lettre à M. de La Place', *Mercure de France* (Nov 1764), 190–96
L.-F. Beffara: *Dictionnaire de l'Académie Royale de Musique* (MS, 1783–4, F-Po)
L. Vallas: *Un siècle de musique et de théâtre à Lyon 1688–1789* (Lyons, 1932)
M. Pincherle: *Jean-Marie Leclair l'aîné* (Paris, 1952)
H. Lagrave: 'René Louis de Voyer de Paulmy, Marquis d'Argenson: Notices sur les oeuvres de théâtre', *Studies on Voltaire and the Eighteenth Century*, nos. 42–3 (1966)
N. Zaslaw: *Materials for the Life and Works of Jean-Marie Leclair l'aîné* (diss., Columbia U., 1970)
——: 'Leclair's "Scylla and Glaucus"', *MT*, cxx (1979), 900–04
G. Sadler and N. Zaslaw: 'Notes on Leclair's Theatre Music', *ML*, lxi (1980), 147–57　　　　GRAHAM SADLER

Le Clerc de La Bruère, Charles-Antoine. *See* LA BRUÈRE, CHARLES-ANTOINE LE CLERC DE.

Lecocq, (Alexandre) Charles (*b* Paris, 3 June 1832; *d* Paris, 24 Oct 1918). French composer. He first came to notice at the age of 24 when his setting of the text to *Le Docteur Miracle* tied for first place with that of his Conservatoire contemporary, Georges Bizet, in a contest organized by Offenbach for the Théâtre des Bouffes-Parisiens. He continued to write for the theatre and during the next 15 years turned out as many pieces, principally one-act *opérettes*, but also several longer works, with some success but without forcing his way through to the first rank of operetta composers.

The most popular of these early pieces was the three-act oriental *opéra comique Fleur-de-thé* (1868), which was given a good Parisian run and was played thereafter in all the main theatrical centres of the world. *Le carnaval d'un merle blanc* succeeded in a botched version in London as *Loo, or The Party who Took Miss*; the short pieces *Liline et Valentin* (1870, Gaiety), *Les ondines au champagne* (1877) and *Le rajah de Mysore* (1878, Gaiety) also played in England while *Gandolfo, Le rajah de Mysore, Le beau Dunois* and *Le testament de M. de Crac* all won German-language productions.

Lecocq's breakthrough came when he composed the music for a low comic text by Chivot, Duru and Clairville for the Fantaisies-Parisiennes in Brussels, where he was then living. *Les cent vierges* (1872) was a splendid success in Belgium and within two months it appeared on the Paris stage before being exported world-wide, often bowdlerized, as *To the Green Isles Direct, The Island of Bachelors* and *Hundert Jungfrauen*. A second piece for the Belgian theatre, *La fille de Madame Angot*

(1872), was even more successful, and firmly established Lecocq and his light, comic-opera style of writing at the forefront of the French and international musical theatre scene, previously dominated by the outrageous frivolities of the *opéra bouffe* of Offenbach and Hervé.

La fille de Madame Angot, a combination of a dramatic libretto and music which offered one melodious song and ensemble after another, went round the world and proved itself the most durable work of the period. Britain was so avid for more such pieces that unscrupulous directors fabricated their own Lecocq operettas – *The Black Prince* (1874), *Una* (1875), *Angela* (1878) – with music from his lesser-known works, and the composer's next genuine piece, *Giroflé-Girofla*, also produced in Belgium, was brought to London by the company of the Fantaisies-Parisiennes in November 1874 (with Jeanne Granier scoring her first resounding success) even before the show had been seen in Paris. This delicious comic opera, much more in the old-fashioned low comic vein of *Les cent vierges* than in the historical/political mode of *La fille de Madame Angot* with its true-to-life characters, proved a third consecutive international hit for Lecocq.

With the Paris theatres now crying out for his services, Lecocq returned to France, and following the moderately successful *Les prés Saint-Gervais* (1874) at the Variétés and the less memorable *Le pompon* (1875, Folies-Dramatiques) he teamed up with one of the librettists of *La fille de Madame Angot*, Victor Koning, now the director of the Théâtre de la Renaissance. Over the next six years Lecocq composed, Koning presented and Granier – now the reigning queen of Parisian operetta – mostly starred in eight new *opéras comiques*, beginning with *La petite mariée* (1875), reaching a peak in *Le petit duc* (1878) and including other successes such as *La petite mademoiselle, La marjolaine* and *La Camargo*. The dismal failure of *Janot* (1881), written after a period of illness and unhappiness, led to a split between the two men, and it seemed that Lecocq, accused now of turning out works too much like one another, might be on the downward slope. A change of venue, producer and cast, however, proved to be a salutary one, and Lecocq's next two pieces, *Le jour et la nuit* (1881) and *Le coeur et la main* (1882), produced at the Théâtre des Nouveautés, were both splendid successes which, like his earlier triumphs, were played throughout the world. *La princesse des Canaries* (1883) had a limited home success but exported well. Thereafter, however, without his favourite teams of librettists, Leterrier and Vanloo and Meilhac and Halévy, the works he produced were less successful. Over the last 20 years of his career he failed to produce anything that approached his great works of the 1870s and early 1880s, and only one work, *Ninette* (1896), had any kind of a run.

A master of the charming and even the beautiful in light theatre music, as is best witnessed by the numbers written for the hero and heroine of *Le petit duc*, Lecocq could also turn his hand to lustier strains, such as those of the celebrated Quarrelling Duet and 'Marchande de marée' in *La fille de Madame Angot*, and to swirling dance music as in the waltzing finale to the second act of the same piece. His work did not in any way lack humour, but his turn of musical phrase in comic situations was always more genteel than the cheerfully vulgar and burlesque effects of such as Hervé. It is perhaps this lack of very obvious colouring that has led to his works being disproportionately neglected in modern times; only *La fille de Madame Angot* and, to a lesser extent, *Le petit duc* remain in the repertory, to the exclusion of his other half-dozen major successes.

See also FILLE DE MADAME ANGOT, LA.

operettas, first performed in Paris, and published there in vocal score, unless otherwise stated

ob – *opéra bouffe*   oc – *opéra comique*
optte – *opérette*

Le Docteur Miracle (oc, 1, L. Battu and L. Halévy), Bouffes-Parisiens, 8 April 1857 (1877)
Huis-clos (1, A. Guénée and A. Marquet), Folies-Nouvelles, 28 or 29 Jan 1859
Le baiser à la porte (optte de salon, 1, J. de la Guette), Folies-Nouvelles, 26 March 1864 (c1890)
Liline et Valentin (optte de salon, 1, de la Guette), Champs-Elysées, 25 May 1864 (?c1864)
[Les] ondines au champagne (optte, 1, H. Lefèbvre, Pélissié and Merle), Folies Marigny, 3 Sept 1865 or 1866 (1876)
Le myosotis (optte bouffe, 1, Cham and W. Busnach), Palais-Royal, 2 or 3 May 1866 (1866)
Le cabaret de Ramponneau (1, Lesire), Folies Marigny, 11 Oct 1867 (?c1867)
L'amour et son carquois (ob, 2, Marquet and Delbès), Athénée, 30 Jan 1868 (1868)
Fleur-de-thé (ob, 3, Chivot and Duru), Athénée, 11 April 1868 (1868)
Les jumeaux de Bergame (oc, 1, Busnach), Athénée, 20 Nov 1868 (1876), orch score (1884)
Le carnaval d'un merle blanc (folie parée et masquée, 3, H. Chivot and A. Duru), Palais-Royal, 10 Dec 1868
Gandolfo (optte, 1, Chivot and Duru), Bouffes-Parisiens, 16 Jan 1869 (1869)
Deux portières pour un cordon (1, Lucian [L. Dubuis and Lefèbvre]), Palais-Royal, 19 March 1869 (?c1869)
Le rajah de Mysore (optte bouffe, 1, Chivot and Duru), Bouffes-Parisiens, 21 Sept 1869 (1869)
Le beau Dunois (ob, 1, Chivot and Duru), Variétés, 13 April 1870 (1870)
Sauvons la caisse (1, de la Guette), Tertulia, 22 Sept or Dec 1871 (?c1871)
Le testament de M. de Crac (ob, 1, J. Moinaux), Bouffes-Parisiens, 23 Oct 1871 (1872)
Le barbier de Trouville (bluette bouffe, 1, A. Jaime and Noriac), Bouffes-Parisiens, 19 Nov 1871 (1872)
Les cent vierges (ob, 3, Clairville, Chivot and Duru), Brussels, Fantaisies-Parisiennes, 16 or 17 March 1872 (1872)
La fille de Madame Angot (oc, 3, Clairville, V. Koning and P. Siraudin), Brussels, Fantaisies-Parisiennes, 4 Dec 1872 (1873)
Giroflé-Girofla (opéra bouffe, 3, E. Leterrier and A. Vanloo), Brussels, Fantaisies-Parisiennes, 21 March 1874 (1874)
Les prés Saint-Gervais (oc, 3, V. Sardou and P. Gille), Variétés, 14 Nov 1874 (1874)
Le pompon (oc, 3, Chivot and Duru), Folies-Dramatiques, 10 Nov 1875 (1875)
La petite mariée (ob, 3, Leterrier and Vanloo), Renaissance, 21 Dec 1875 (1876)
Kosiki (oc, 3, Busnach and A. Liorat), Renaissance, 18 Oct 1876 (1877)
La marjolaine (ob, 3, Leterrier and Vanloo), Renaissance, 3 Feb 1877 (1877)
Le petit duc (oc, 3, H. Meilhac and Halévy), Renaissance, 25 Jan 1878 (1878)
La Camargo (oc, 3, Leterrier and Vanloo), Renaissance, 20 Nov 1878 (1879)
Le grand Casimir (optte, 3, J. Prével and A. de Saint-Albin), Variétés, 11 Jan 1879 (1879)
La petite mademoiselle (oc, 3, Meilhac and Halévy), Renaissance, 12 April 1879 (1879)
La jolie Persane (oc, 3, Leterrier and Vanloo), Renaissance, 28 Oct 1879 (1879)
Janot (oc, 3, Meilhac and Halévy), Renaissance, 21 Jan 1881 (1881)
La roussotte (vaudeville-opérette, 3, Meilhac, Halévy and A. Millaud), Variétés, 26 or 28 Jan 1881 (1881), collab. Hervé and M. Boulard
Le jour et la nuit (ob, 3, Leterrier and Vanloo), Nouveautés, 5 Nov 1881 (1882)

Le coeur et la main (oc, 3, C. Nuitter and A. Beaumont), Nouveautés, 19 Oct 1882 (1883)
La princesse des Canaries (ob, 3, Chivot and Duru), Folies-Dramatiques, 9 Feb 1883 (1883)
L'oiseau bleu (oc, 3, Chivot and Duru), Nouveautés, 16 Jan 1884 (1884)
La vie mondaine (ob, 3, E. de Najac and P. Ferrier), Nouveautés, 13 Feb 1885 (1885)
Plutus (oc, 3, Millaud and Jollivet), OC (Favart), 31 March or May 1886 (1886)
Les grenadiers de Mont-Cornette (3, Daunis, Delormel and E. Philippe), Bouffes-Parisiens, 4 Jan 1887 (?c1887)
Ali-Baba (oc, 4, Vanloo and Busnach), Brussels, Alhambra, 11 Nov 1887 (1887)
La volière (oc, 3, Nuitter and Beaumont), Nouveautés, 11 or 12 Feb 1888 (?1888)
L'égyptienne (oc, 3, Chivot, Nuitter and Beaumont), Folies-Dramatiques, 8 Nov 1890
Nos bons chasseurs (vaudeville, 3, P. Bilhaud and M. Carré), Casino de Paris, 10 April 1894
Ninette (oc, 3, Clairville, Hubert, Lebeau and C. de Trogoff), Bouffes-Parisiens, 28 Feb 1896 (1896)
Ruse d'amour (saynète, 1, S. Bordèse), Boulogne, Casino, 26 June 1898 (1897)
La belle au bois dormant (oc, 3, G. Duval and Vanloo), Bouffes-Parisiens, 19 Feb 1900 (1900, 2/c1905)
Yetta (oc, 3, F. Beissier), Brussels, Galeries St-Hubert, 7 or 8 March 1903 (1903)
Rose Mousse (comédie-musicale, 1, A. Alexandre and P. Carin), Capucines, 28 Jan 1904 (1904)
La salutiste (opéra monologue, 1, Beissier), Capucines, 14 Jan 1905
Le trahison de Pan (oc, 1, Bordèse), Aix-les-Bains, Casino, 13 Sept 1911 (1912)

Undated: Le chevrier (oc, 2, C. Narrey and M. Carré *fils*) (c1888)

Unperf.: Renza; Ma cousine

*

L. Schneider: *Les maîtres de l'opérette française: Hervé, Charles Lecocq* (Paris, 1924), 125–283
G. Lebas, ed.: 'Lettres inédites de Lecocq à Saint-Saëns', *ReM*, v/4 (1924), 119–31; v/10 (1924), 121–44; vi/8 (1925), 216–24
L. Schneider: *Une heure de musique avec Charles Lecocq* (Paris, 1930)
P. Landormy: *La musique française de Franck à Debussy* (Paris, 1943, 2/1948)
R. Traubner: *Operetta: a Theatrical History* (New York, 1983)
KURT GÄNZL (text), ANDREW LAMB (work-list)

Ledi Makbet Mtsenskogo uyezda. Opera by Dmitry Shostakovich; *see* LADY MACBETH OF THE MTSENSK DISTRICT.

Lee, Dai-Keong (*b* Honolulu, 2 Sept 1915). American composer. He was a pupil of Frederick Jacobi at the Juilliard Graduate School (1938–41), and also studied with Sessions, Copland and Otto Luening. Among his awards are two Guggenheim fellowships (1945, 1951) and many commissions. Lee writes in a variety of styles, but is best known for his instrumental music with Polynesian colouring and incidental music for *Teahouse of the August Moon* (New York, 15 October 1953). In 1951 he wrote *Open the Gates*, an opera based on the life of Mary Magdalene, commissioned and produced by the Blackfriars Theater Guild of New York; he has since written a number of short operas in the tradition of Weill, such as *Ballad of Kitty the Barkeep*, often as revisions of previously withdrawn works.

The Poet's Dilemma (1), New York, Juilliard School, 12 April 1940, withdrawn
Open the Gates (3, R. Payne), New York, 22 Feb 1951
Phineas and the Nightingale, 1952 (R. Healey), withdrawn
Newport by the Sea, c1952 (musical play, 2, Healey)
Speakeasy (Healey), New York, 8 Feb 1957, withdrawn
2 Knickerbocker Tales, 1957, (operas, 1, Healey and Lee)
Noa Noa, 1972 (musical play)

Ballad of Kitty the Barkeep, 1979 (1, Healey and Lee) [based on Speakeasy]

Jenny Lind, 1981 (musical play, after P. T. Barnum: *Recollections*) [based on Phineas and the Nightingale]   ALLAN B. HO

Lee, George Alexander (*b* London, 1802; *d* London, 8 Oct 1851). English composer. He began his career as a tenor and conductor at Dublin in 1822 and in 1826 returned to London, where his first engagement was at the Haymarket Theatre. The following year he began to write incidental music for plays at Covent Garden; his opera *The Sublime and the Beautiful* was produced there in 1828, and another, *The Nymph of the Grotto, or A Daughter's Vow*, written in collaboration with Giovanni Liverati, in 1829. Lee also became involved in managerial ventures, at the Tottenham Theatre (1829–30), Drury Lane (1831–2) and the Strand Theatre (1834); later he was conductor at the Olympic Theatre (1845) and Vauxhall (1849). He adapted two of Auber's operas for the English stage: *Fra Diavolo* as *The Devil's Brother* (Drury Lane, 1831) and *Le lac des fées* as *The Fairy Lake* (Strand, 1839). His output included music for about 20 plays, burlettas and melodramas.

DNB (R. F. Sharpe)

Lee, Ming Cho. *See* MING CHO LEE.

Leeds. English city. The opening of the Grand Theatre and Opera House on 18 November 1878 created an immediate demand for opera: the Carl Rosa and D'Oyly Carte companies soon became regular visitors. Designed by George Corson and built by a consortium under Sir Andrew Fairbairn, the Grand was reckoned one of the best-equipped theatres in Europe, with seats for 2600 and standing room for 200 on five levels with 28 boxes. Capacity has since been reduced to 1554, with 80 standing; extensive refurbishment in the 1980s under Clare Ferraby, with ornate maroon and gold decoration, confirmed its reputation as the most elegant Victorian theatre in the north of England.

The first *Ring* cycle in the English provinces was staged at Leeds by the Denhof Opera Company in March and April 1911, with John Coates as Siegfried and Michael Balling conducting. The British National Opera Company began to include the city on its tours from 1923, and Covent Garden Opera from 1955. The centrepiece of the Leeds Centenary Music Festival in 1958 was a Graf production of *Samson* conducted by Leppard, with Sutherland and Vickers.

A city council trust took over the theatre in 1971. Plans for a new opera company there, originally mooted in 1963, were announced by Lord Harewood in 1975 but local authorities withheld essential financial support. Only in late 1977 could a company be founded, under the aegis of the Arts Council of Great Britain. Conceived as an offshoot of the ENO, with Harewood as managing director of both companies, it was initially known as English National Opera North. It opened on 15 November 1978 with *Samson et Dalila*, conducted by its music director David Lloyd-Jones, with a resident orchestra (the English Northern Philharmonia) of 62 players and a chorus of 40. Its founding administrator was Graham Marchant, with Patrick Libby as director of productions. Ten operas were mounted during the first season, four of them in new productions; all but two were sung in English. A similar balance continues today, with regular tours to Hull, Manchester, Nottingham and York.

The company became independent of the ENO in 1981, as Opera North, and quickly achieved a reputation for its vigorous chorus and versatile orchestra. Nicholas Payne took over as general administrator in late 1982. In its first decade, Opera North gave 70 operas by 40 different composers, including the première of Wilfred Josephs's *Rebecca* (1983), and the first British stagings of Krenek's *Jonny spielt auf* (1984) and Strauss's *Daphne* (1987). Verdi's *Jérusalem* received its British première in 1990 under the company's new music director, Paul Daniel.   MARTIN DREYER

Lees, Benjamin (*b* Harbin, China, 8 Jan 1924). American composer of Russian parentage. He studied at the University of Southern California (1945–8) with Halsey Stevens, Ernst Kanitz and Ingolf Dahl. He also studied privately with George Antheil. His honours include a Guggenheim fellowship (1954), a Fulbright grant (1956), awards from the Fromm Foundation (1953) and the NEA (1981), and many commissions. From 1954 Lees travelled and studied in Europe, his aim being to create an individual style that did not rely on trends then fashionable in America. He returned to the USA in 1961 with many mature and impressive works, thereafter dividing his time between composition and teaching.

Lees writes in a vigorous rhythmic style which uses an extended tonality. While he is recognized particularly for his craftsmanship in orchestral and chamber works, his contribution to opera, although modest, is noteworthy. His first opera, *The Oracle* (composed 1955–6; 1, Lees), based on a computer fantasy story, was to have been performed on British Independent Television under Barbirolli, but financial difficulties prevented this. A longer opera, *The Gilded Cage* (composed 1970–72; 3, A. Reid), has now been withdrawn. Lees's chamber opera *Medea in Corinth* (composed 1970; 1, R. Jeffers) is based on the Greek myth of the abandoned Medea taking revenge on her husband Jason by murdering their two children and exhibiting them to him. Written for four voices and the economical but effective ensemble of wind quartet and optional timpani, the music is mostly in a flexible, expressive arioso or recitative style, with a highly developed motivic structure in the instrumental parts. The work was presented in a concert performance in London in 1971 by the Grosvenor Ensemble under Harry Legge, and subsequently staged in Antwerp in 1973 and, in a broadcast performance, by CBS Television in New York on 26 May 1974, with Rosalind Elias in the title role.

D. Cooke: 'The Music of Benjamin Lees', *Tempo*, new ser., no.51 (1959), 16–29

N. Slonimsky: 'Benjamin Lees in Excelsis', *Tempo*, new ser., no.113 (1975), 14–21   NIALL O'LOUGHLIN

Leeuw, Ton de (*b* Rotterdam, 16 Nov 1926). Dutch composer. He studied composition with Badings, Messiaen and others, then studied ethnomusicology for four years. He was a music producer for Dutch radio (1954–60), and taught composition at the Amsterdam Conservatory (director 1971–3). He also teaches modern music and ethnomusicology at Amsterdam University.

Leeuw's earliest compositions appeared in the immediate postwar period. His first opera, *Alceste* (1961–2), is based on Euripides but concentrates entirely on the character of Admetos [Admetus] (bass), husband of Alcestis (silent role). A tightly integrated combination of music, text and dance, it is scored for chamber orchestra, and includes writing for speaking voices and male chorus. A journey to India in 1961 brought Leeuw into closer contact with eastern thought, which from that time has exerted an important influence on his work. A noteworthy piece from the early 1960s is the one-act opera *De droom* (1963), for which Leeuw wrote his own text, based on several East-Asian legends. The most important episode is a dream scene, a dance accompanied by choral singing of haiku in English translation; the final scene is a retrograde of the first.

Alceste (TV op, 3, de Leeuw, after Euripides), TV, 13 March 1963
De droom, 1962–3 (3 scenes, de Leeuw), Amsterdam, Stadsschouwburg, 16 June 1965
Antigone, 1989–91 (2 pts, de Leeuw, after Sophocles)

*

J. Wouters: 'Ton de Leeuw', *Dutch Composers' Gallery* (Amsterdam, 1971), 17–49
L. Samama: *Zeventig jaar Nederlandse muziek* (Amsterdam, 1986), 230–41   JOS WOUTERS/LEO SAMAMA

LeFanu, Nicola (Frances) (*b* Wickham Bishops, Essex, 28 April 1947). English composer, daughter of Elizabeth Maconchy. She studied at Oxford and the RCM and attended composition masterclasses with Petrassi in Siena and Maxwell Davies at Dartington. In 1972 she was appointed director of the music-theatre group at Morley College, London, and moved to a lectureship at King's College, London, in 1977.

As well as composing much instrumental and vocal music, LeFanu showed an early affinity with the stage. Her first theatre piece, *Anti-World* (1972), established many characteristics of her work: a distinctive selection of texts (Gorbanevskaya and Voznesensky), chamber scoring with instruments dispersed round the stage, and a strong choreographic element, exploring ideas of freedom and control in society. The chamber opera *Dawnpath* (1977) is based on two American Indian myths, where the creation of the world is shown as a choice between light and dark, night and day. An even closer fusion of the performing elements is aimed at, with only two singers, five instrumentalists and a dancer.

LeFanu's growing interest in the position of women in society is reflected in the concerns of her subsequent works: female sexuality and old age are explored in *The Old Woman of Beare* (1981), a monodrama adapted from an ancient Irish poem; larger orchestral forces and atmospheric scoring illustrate the wild Irish coast of the setting. *The Story of Mary O'Neill* (1986) charts, through the medium of a radio opera for 17 voices, a woman's reaction to the appeal of two different types of civilization, the colonised and the Indian in South America. This medium particularly suits the intimate aspects of LeFanu's style: her ideas are always expressed with precision and sensitivity; economy of forces allows her to bring out the characteristics of performer or instrument. The involvement of school projects suggested in Kevin Crossley-Holland's libretto for *The Green Children* (1990) answered LeFanu's longstanding interest in working with younger musicians, backed by her teaching experience. She later turned to Lorca's *Blood Wedding* to fulfil an opera commission from the Women's Playhouse Trust.

first performed in London unless otherwise stated
Anti-World (music-theatre piece, 1, N. Gorbanevskaya and A. Voznesensky), Cockpit, June 1972
Dawnpath (chamber op, 1, LeFanu), Collegiate, 29 Sept 1977
The Old Woman of Beare (monodrama, 1, LeFanu), St John's, Smith Square, 3 Nov 1981
The Story of Mary O'Neill, 1986 (radio op, 3, S. McInerney), BBC, 4 Jan 1989
The Green Children (children's op, 2, K. Crossley-Holland), King's Lynn, 18 July 1990
Blood Wedding (2, D. Levy, after F. García Lorca), Jacob Street Studios, 26 Oct 1992

*

R. Cooke: 'Nicola LeFanu', *MT*, cxvi (1975), 961–3
V. O'Brien: 'Living British Women Composers', *The Musical Woman: an International Perspective*, ed. J. L. Zaimont (Westport, CT, 1983), 209–34, esp. 216–18
J. W. LePage: 'Nicola LeFanu, Composer', *Women Composers, Conductors and Musicians of the Twentieth Century*, iii (Metuchen, NJ, 1988), 115–28
K. Crossley-Holland: 'Singing Green Songs', *Times Educational Supplement* (6 July 1990)
A. Clements: 'Greening of the Opera', *Financial Times* (21 July 1990) [review of *The Green Children*]   CHRISTOPHER WINTLE

Lefebvre, Charles Edouard (*b* Paris, 19 June 1843; *d* Aix-les-Bains, 8 Sept 1917). French composer. The son of artist Jules Lefebvre, he was largely self-taught in music. The establishment of Jules Pasdeloup's Concerts Populaires in 1861 was a great inspiration to him, and in the same year he began lessons with Gounod, on whose recommendation he joined Ambroise Thomas' composition class at the Conservatoire in 1863. He failed to win the Prix de Rome the following year but, following a change in the age limits for entry, obtained it in 1870.

Lefebvre gained much inspiration from numerous visits to Italy (between 1866 and 1890) and also Greece and Asia Minor. When in Paris he was a regular visitor to the Viardots' Thursday salon and to Saint-Saëns' Monday gatherings. Musical influences included Gounod, Mendelssohn and Wagner, but he felt that Wagner's works and theories were too German to be absorbed wholesale into the French aesthetic. He nonetheless visited Bayreuth several times from 1882. His own stage career was brief. Of his six works, *Djelma* received performances at the Opéra (the title role being created by Rose Caron). Appointed a professor at the Conservatoire in 1895, he was created Chevalier of the Légion d'honneur in 1896.

Le florentin, 1868 (oc, 3), unperf., unpubd
Le voile de Sainte Walburge, 1877–8 (1, E. Blau), unperf., unpubd
Lucrèce, 1877–8 (3, Blau), unperf., unpubd
Le trésor (oc, 1, F. Coppée), Angers, Grand, 28 March 1883, vs (Paris, 1884)
Zaïre (4, P. Collin, after Voltaire), Lille, de Lille, 3 Dec 1887, vs (Paris, 1887)
Djelma (3, C. Lomon), Opéra, 25 May 1894, vs (Paris, 1894)

*

H. Imbert: 'Charles Lefebvre', *L'art musical*, xxxiii (1894), 161–2
——: *Profils d'artistes contemporains* (Paris, 1897)
A. Lavignac: *Le voyage artistique à Bayreuth* (Paris, 1897)
Orbus: 'La vie intime d'un grand musicien: Charles Lefebvre', *Revue des deux mondes*, lviii (1930), 346–76   JOHN WAGSTAFF

Lefèbvre, Joseph (*b* Berlin, 20 July 1761; *d* ?Paris, after 1822). French composer. A brother of Louise-Rosalie Dugazon, he wrote the music to two comic operas given in Paris at the Comédie-Italienne. The first, *Le prix, ou L'embarras du choix* (10 December 1788), was saved only by the presence of Mlle Renaud and Mme Dugazon in the cast, while *Caroline de Lichtfield* (2 December 1789) so displeased the audience that the performance had to be abandoned. Several songs from these operas were published separately. In 1790 Lefèbvre was a violinist at the Comédie-Italienne. He became first violinist at the Théâtre Feydeau and joint *chef d'orchestre* in 1791, and in 1801, when the Feydeau and Favart troupes united to form the Opéra-Comique, he was made *chef d'orchestre*. He retired in 1822.

J. J. Olivier: *Madame Dugazon de la Comédie-Italienne, 1755–1821* (Paris, 1917), 15
PHILIP ROBINSON

Lefèbvre, Louise-Rosalie. *See* DUGAZON, LOUISE-ROSALIE.

Leffler-Burckhardt, Martha (*b* Berlin, 16 June 1865; *d* Wiesbaden, 14 May 1954). German soprano. After studying in Dresden and Paris, she made her début in 1888 at Strasbourg. Successively engaged in Breslau, Cologne, Bremen, Weimar and Wiesbaden, from 1913 she sang in Berlin. She made her Covent Garden début in 1903 as Brünnhilde, then returned in 1907 for Isolde and Leonore (*Fidelio*). At Bayreuth (1906–9) she sang Kundry, Ortrud and Sieglinde. She sang one season at the Metropolitan (1908–9) and retired in 1919. Renowned as an interpreter of Wagner, she had a beautiful and powerful voice.
ELIZABETH FORBES

Le Flem, Paul (*b* Lézardrieux, 18 March 1881; *d* Trégastel, 31 July 1984). French composer. He studied at the Paris Conservatoire and, after spending time in Russia, at the Schola Cantorum with d'Indy and Roussel; he succeeded the latter as professor of counterpoint there, and also worked as a choral conductor. Later he was chorus-master of the Opéra-Comique.

His early works have a gracious melancholy that reflects the landscape of his native Brittany; this quality continued to form an important constituent of his music, as in the choral fable and shadow play *Aucassin et Nicolette* (1908), which unfolds in a series of tableaux and has songs for several characters, and the *fantaisie lyrique Le rossignol de Saint-Malo* (1938). This opera is set in the 13th century, and is based on a medieval tale of a capricious wife Azénor (soprano) who leaves her older husband Jacquemin (baritone) alone in bed every night, going to the ramparts to listen to a nightingale whose song brings a 'young and handsome servant of love' ('jeune et beau servant d'amour') (tenor). Her jealous husband shoots the nightingale only to find that it is always replaced by another. *Magicienne de la mer* is set on a quayside in Brittany and is based on the Breton legend of Dahut (dramatic soprano), a dissolute woman long since drowned who lures handsome sailors to participate in her orgies. An orchestral episode portrays her feverish passions and only when the bells of the submerged cathedral of Ys are heard is she stripped of her evil powers. Le Flem was also strongly influenced by the sobriety and technical mastery of d'Indy's music, and all his work is marked by solid craftsmanship. Nonetheless he admitted something of the poetic spirit of Debussy. Although his music remained tonal and cast in established forms and genres, he always took a keen interest in later developments, from dodecaphony to the innovations of young French composers.

Endymion et Sémélé (légende lyrique, Le Flem), Paris, 1903
Aucassin et Nicolette, 1908 (chante-fable, 1, Le Flem), private perf., Paris, 19 May 1909; stage, Beriza, 1924
Le rossignol de Saint-Malo, 1938 (fantaisie lyrique, 1, J. Gandrey-Réty), Paris, OC (Favart), 5 May 1942
La clairière des fées, 1944 (fantaisie lyrique, 1, F. Divoire), broadcast, 1964

Magicienne de la mer, 1946 (légende lyrique, 3 tableaux, J. Bruyr), Paris, OC (Favart), 29 Oct 1954
ANNE GIRARDOT, RICHARD LANGHAM SMITH

Le Froid de Méreaux, Nicolas-Jean. *See* MÉREAUX, NICOLAS-JEAN LE FROID DE.

Legard [Legar, Legare, Leguar, Leguerre etc.], **John.** *See* LAGUERRE, JOHN.

Légende de Saint Christophe, La ('The Legend of Saint Christopher'). *Drame sacré* in three acts, op.67, by VINCENT D'INDY to his own libretto after Jacobus de Voragine's *Legenda Aurea*; Paris, Opéra, 9 June 1920.

In Act 1 the giant Auférus (tenor) seeks the most powerful master he can find: the King of Kings. First he serves the King of Gold (bass), before Sathanaël (Prince of Evil, tenor) appears and liquefies his assets. Sathanaël's miserable kingdom is peopled with d'Indy's foes who are vanquished by the King of Heaven, whose sign of the cross Auférus diligently seeks in Act 2.

During his long quest, Auférus is exposed to faith, hope and charity. Scene iii tells the familiar story of the giant transporting, across a raging torrent, a child who turns out to be the infant Jesus (soprano). Jesus rebaptizes Auférus as Christopher (the carrier of Christ).

In Act 3 Saint Christopher is condemned to death because of his miracles and dangerous popularity. His previous masters appear at his trial and he is tempted by 'la reine de volupté' (Nicéa, soprano), whom he finally converts to Christianity through his unrepentant and exultant martyrdom.

D'Indy had been attracted to the *Legenda Aurea* of Jacobus de Voragine since his youth, but it was not until 1908–13 that he made his own eclectic adaptation of it, completing the orchestration in December 1915. Its reception ranged from deferential respect to outright hostility, and not surprisingly it has never entered the repertory, for beneath the cloak of a monumental religious drama, the increasingly chauvinistic and reactionary d'Indy attacked all his enemies: Jews, freemasons, atheists, socialists, even modern composers (such as Ravel). In a combination of Wagnerian music drama, oratorio and medieval mystery play, the elements of propaganda and prejudice made it a turning-point from which his reputation never really recovered.

There is, however, much to admire in this visionary, Trinitarian 'cathédrale sonore', which can only loosely be described as an opera, and really amounts to an almost superhuman act of faith. Its 24 themes are treated symphonically in a massive integrated tapestry, some deriving from plainchant, some from medieval or folksong sources. As always with d'Indy, the orchestration and tonal planning are masterly, and the textures and counterpoint are generally lighter than one might expect.
ROBERT ORLEDGE

Legend of Shota Rustaveli, The. Opera by Dmitri Arakishvili; *see* TKMULEBA SHOTA RUSTAVELZE.

Legend of the Invisible City of Kitezh and the Maiden Fevroniya, The [*Skazaniye o nevidimom grade Kitezhe i deve Fevronii*]. Opera in four acts by NIKOLAY ANDREYEVICH RIMSKY-KORSAKOV to a libretto by VLADIMIR NIKOLAYEVICH BEL'SKY conflated from the so-called Kitezh Chronicle of I. S. Meledin, the novel *V*

1123

lesakh ('In the Woods') by Pavel Ivanovich Mel'nikov (Pechersky), songs and epics collected by Kirsha Danilov and several traditional tales, including *The Life of Peter, Prince of Murom, and his Wife Fevroniya* (as set down in 1547, the year of their canonization); St Petersburg, Mariinsky Theatre, 7/20 February 1907.

Prince Yury Vsevolodovich *ruler of Kitezh*	bass
Princeling Vsevolod Yur'yevich *his son*	tenor
Fevroniya	soprano
Grishka Kuter'ma	tenor
Fyodor Poyarok	baritone
A Boy *Prince Yury's page*	mezzo-soprano
Two Upper-Crusters	tenor, bass
Bard *(psaltery player)*	bass
Bear Trainer	tenor
Singing Beggar	baritone
Bedyay	*Mongol warriors*	bass
Burunday		bass
Sirin	*vatic birds*	soprano
Alkonost		contralto

The Prince's musketeers, wedding party, domra players, upper-crusters, mendicant brothers, miscellaneous crowd, Tatars

Setting The Volga woods near Lesser Kitezh, in Lesser and Greater Kitezh, on Lake Svetlïy Yar, in the woods of Kerzhenets and in the Invisible City, in the year 6751 from the creation of the world

The 16th-century *zhitiye* (hagiography) of St Fevroniya of Murom has always been a prime document of Russian religious syncretism, in which Christian elements coexist with remnants of pre-Christian Slavonic mythology. The libretto of Rimsky-Korsakov's penultimate opera, combining history (the Mongol invasion of 1223), pantheistic folklore and Christian mystery, is another such document. Bel'sky, the librettist, had originally planned a dramatization of the *zhitiye* itself, but this Rimsky-Korsakov disallowed. His own reverent sentiments, already memorably embodied in *The Snow Maiden*, were pantheistic (and not so much metaphysical as aesthetic). These, bolstered with a strong dose of patriotism, dominated the opera to the extent that it held the stage in Soviet times with only minimal alterations to its text (although Sergey Gorodetsky, who sanitized the libretto of Glinka's *Life for the Tsar* for Soviet consumption, did propose a similar overhaul of the *Kitezh* libretto). Although the miracle by which the city of Kitezh was saved from the 'Tatars' is clearly wrought by the Christian God (and is announced by the spontaneous ringing of church bells), the only supernatural agencies to appear in the opera are Sirin and Alkonost, the traditional prophet-birds of Slavonic mythology. Fevroniya herself is turned into an apostle of pantheism: when asked in Act 1 whether she attends church she answers, 'Is not God everywhere? You may think [my forest] is an empty place, but no – it is a great church, where day and night we celebrate the Eucharist'. And the music to which she sings these lines comes back in Act 4 to accompany her transfigured soul – after an apotheosis that harks deliberately back to the Snow Maiden's nature ecstasies – into the Invisible City. There, the mystical rites are inextricably bound up with a folk wedding ceremony – the very one that had been interrupted by the Tatars in Act 2, of which the melody is recapitulated. Thus Christian religion is treated in

Kitezh as an aspect of folklore, which is probably how Rimsky-Korsakov, an enthusiastic positivist, viewed it.

Rimsky-Korsakov composed the opera in 1903–4, but it was not performed until 1907. The première was conducted by Felix Blumenfeld; the sets and costumes were by Apollinary Vasnetsov and Konstantin Korovin, and the cast included Andrey Labinsky as Vsevolod, Mariya Kuznetsova as Fevroniya, Ivan Yershov as Grishka Kuter'ma, Vladimir Kastorsky as the Bard, Nadeshda Zabela as Sirin and Yevgeniya Zbruyeva as Alkonost.

ACT 1 *A forest* After a prelude entitled 'In Praise of the Wilderness', the curtain rises on a dense forest, where Fevroniya lives with her brother, a woodsman. She sings of its mysteries and communes with the birds and beasts, her song culminating in a jubilus: 'A- oo!', the traditional folk-poetic ejaculation of wordless nature ecstasy. Suddenly she spies a stranger who has lost his way on a hunt. They immediately fall in love, he with her spiritual wisdom and beauty, she with his heroic mien. He claims her for his bride but, hearing hunting horns approach, leaves her to join his party, promising to send matchmakers to her brother. His men enter in pursuit of him, and Fevroniya learns from the huntsman Fyodor Poyarok that she has been betrothed to his master, Vsevolod, son of Prince Yury of Kitezh.

ACT 2 *The town of Lesser Kitezh* A holiday crowd turns out to greet Princess Fevroniya as her wedding cortège passes through Lesser Kitezh on the way to Greater Kitezh. A trained bear entertains them. An old bard sings a prophetic song to his psaltery, foretelling woe. A group of rich citizens express their discontent with Vsevolod's choice of a low-born bride and persuade the drunken Grishka Kuter'ma to mock her on her arrival. A group of mendicant brothers sing a song of praise to the rich citizens, a song of mockery at Grishka. The bridal party enters, announced by Poyarok; the ritual of the 'bride's ransom' is performed, followed by a song of praise to the bride. Suddenly the Tatars attack. They take two prisoners: Fevroniya, as a prize, and Grishka, who in fear for his life agrees to guide them to Greater Kitezh. The populace disperses in horror. Fevroniya prays for a miracle: that Greater Kitezh be made invisible to the enemy.

ACT 3.i *The Cathedral Square of Greater Kitezh* The people are assembled at dead of night. Poyarok, whom the Tatars have blinded, comes with news of their pillage. Prince Yury leads his people in prayer. A page is sent up to a tower to watch for the advancing host; when he spies them Prince Yury appoints a militia, headed by his son, to defend the city. As the soldiers march off, singing, a golden mist descends on Kitezh, accompanied by the ringing of the church bells.

The bloody battle of Kerzhenets is depicted in the entr'acte, which pits the soldiers' song against the Tatars' leitmotifs, all accompanied by a musical motif suggesting wild hoofbeats.

3.ii *Lake Svetlïy Yar* Grishka leads the Tatars, with Fevroniya, to the banks, where Greater Kitezh should be visible on the opposite shore. Since there is nothing to be seen but golden haze, the Tatars accuse him of deception, tie him up, and threaten death by torture the next day. They muse on the day's events, regretting that the noble Vsevolod, though he sustained 40 wounds, would not allow himself to be taken as an

'Legend of the Invisible City of Kitezh and the Maiden Fevroniya' (Rimsky-Korsakov), final scene (the invisible city, with the prophet-birds Sirin and Alkonost, centre right): design by Apollinary Vasnetsov for the original production at the Mariinsky Theatre, St Petersburg, 7/20 February 1907

honoured prisoner but preferred to perish on the battlefield. They make fires and fall to dividing their booty. In a dispute over Fevroniya the Tatar warrior Burunday slays his companion Bedyay. The group finish their division of spoils while singing a gruesome song about the ravens flocking over the field of carnage. The Tatars fall asleep. Grishka, raving with guilt and remorse, implores Fevroniya to untie him. Although he has not only betrayed Kitezh but has blamed her for his own misdeed, Fevroniya shows him kindness. Grishka's head is ringing with the Kitezh church bells. To put an end to their ear-splitting sound he runs to the lake to drown himself but stops short as the first rays of dawn come up and show the reflection of the invisible city in its waters; he runs off in terror, taking Fevroniya with him. The Tatars, awakened by his cries, see the reflected city and disperse in fright.

ACT 4.i *A forest; the next night* Fevroniya and Grishka are struggling through the wilderness (the opening forest music returns, dissonantly harmonized). Grishka is still raving; Fevroniya tries to comfort him with scriptural verses, but he finally goes mad, does a violent dance and runs off howling. Fevroniya, left alone, falls asleep, and as she does so the forest is transformed into a magical place: lighted candles appear in the trees and illuminate the night; fantastic flowers blossom forth and unearthly birds begin to sing, among them Alkonost, who tells Fevroniya that she is to die. The ghost of Vsevolod appears to lead her to the Invisible City. The prophet-bird Sirin foretells her eternal life.

The transfiguration of Fevroniya's soul on the way to the Invisible City is portrayed in the entr'acte, a magnificent orchestral carillon.

4.ii *The Invisible City* Fevroniya is greeted by Prince Yury and her wedding party, who resume the ceremony broken off in Act 2. Vsevolod leads her to the altar. She remembers Grishka, asks that he too be saved, but is told that he is not ready. She sends a message of consolation to him to inspire him to achieve eternal life with her in the Invisible City.

* * *

Kitezh is often called the 'Russian Parsifal', and this is justified insofar as Wagner's last opera was clearly among its models. The miracle music in Acts 3 and 4

resonates with the basso ostinato from the Good Friday Spell, and there is even a sort of Dresden Amen in the last scene, which takes place in the transfigured realm (ex.1), having been foreshadowed when Fevroniya had

Ex.1 Act 4 scene ii

spoken to Grishka of God's mysterious greatness, and again when she partakes of the Eucharistic bread offered her by the ghost of Vsevolod and is spiritually transformed. The opera's opening scene, of which the music is often reheard later, is rightly compared with the Forest Murmurs in *Siegfried* (although it is organized around a Balakirevesque key scheme, B minor alternating with Db major, and although it contains the same typically Russian cadences that inform much of the vocal writing); the appearance of Alkonost and Sirin to Fevroniya as disembodied voices in Act 4 was probably inspired by the Forest Bird episode in the same scene from Wagner's opera. Another ostensible echo from the *Ring* is the episode where the oafish Burunday kills Bedyay, as Fafner kills Fasolt, in a dispute over spoils.

Of course, there are also many resonances in *Kitezh* from earlier Russian opera, of which there was by the early 20th century a distinguished body of 'classics'. Chief among them was Glinka's *A Life for the Tsar*; the collision of national forces in Rimsky's opera was modelled on Act 3 of Glinka's, in which the Poles break in on a betrothal ceremony just as the Tatars do in *Kitezh*, their approach being telegraphed to the audience by a preliminary snatch of their leitmotif between the strains of a wedding song. The other important Russian model was Musorgsky, from whom Rimsky derived, or attempted to derive, the declamatory style in which he cast the role of Grishka Kuter'ma, whose music is full of resonances from the role of the Pretender (another Grishka!) in the Cell and Inn Scenes from *Boris Godunov*. Since Rimsky's musical imagination was heavily dependent on parallel rhythmic periods and melodic sequences, the imitation is flawed, and

Grishka's music came out sounding (surely inadvertently) as if modelled on that of Pyotr Il'ich, the tormented anti-hero of Serov's *The Power of the Fiend*, an opera Rimsky did not hold in very high esteem. A third musical precedent from earlier Russian opera is that of the Republican Council scene in Rimsky-Korsakov's first opera, *The Maid of Pskov*, on which the final chorus in Act 2 is modelled, showing the inhabitants of Lesser Kitezh in a state of panic. Here Rimsky's choral writing is of a 'realistic' declamatory complexity he had not attempted since his early 'kuchkist' days. Depending on the stress patterns of the various lines of text, the 9/8 metre is continually reinterpreted in beat patterns involving freely intermixed crochets and dotted crotchets. Of actual quoted folksongs there are only two: the song of the mendicant brothers in Act 2 and the famous historical song 'Pro tatarskiy polon' ('On the Mongol Captivity', published by Balakirev and also used by Tchaikovsky and Taneyev), which, suitably dressed up with augmented 2nds, provided one of the leitmotifs of the invaders (ex.2), the other being a descending tone-semitone

Ex.2

(a) Rimsky-Korsakov, *One Hundred Russian Folksongs* (1877), no. 8

Kak za rech - ko - yu, da za Dar' - ye - yu, zlī ta -

-ta - ro - ve du-van du - va - ni - li.

['Beyond the river, beyond the Dar'ya, the evil Tartars divided their spoils.']

(b) *Kitezh*, Act 2

BURUNDAI

Ta - koy kra - sī v ste - pi ne bu - det,

sve - zyom v Or - du tsve - tok bo - lot - nīy

['Such a beauty you won't find in the steppe; we'll take this field blossom back to the Horde']

(octatonic) scale, long associated in Rimsky's work with exotic, usually supernatural, evil (ex.3).

Ex.3 *Kitezh*, Act 2

etc.

The music of the opera is wholly continuous. While it is essentially composed in lyric set pieces, they are never allowed to come to full closes and are never extracted (hence they are not listed individually in the synopsis above). Even the pairs of scenes that make up the third and fourth acts are connected by the entr'actes in such a way that there is no musical close before the end of the act – and not even then in the case of Act 2, which fades out on an unresolved tritone.

RICHARD TARUSKIN

Leggate, Robin (*b* West Kirby, Cheshire, 18 April 1946). English tenor. He studied at Oxford and Manchester and made his début in 1975 as Richard II (*Wat Tyler*) at Sadler's Wells Theatre. He first sang at Covent Garden in 1977 as Cassio; his subsequent roles

there have included Joe (*La fanciulla del West*), Gaston, Elemer, Tamino, Narraboth, the Novice (*Billy Budd*), Malcolm, Jaquino, the Painter and the Negro (*Lulu*), Andrey Khovansky (*Khovanshchina*), Paris (*King Priam*), Edmondo (*Manon Lescaut*), Lysander, Ovlur (*Prince Igor*), and the Holy Fool (*Boris Godunov*). He has sung with Opera North, the WNO and Scottish Opera, in Hamburg, Paris and at Glyndebourne. A versatile character actor with a smooth, well-focussed voice, he also sings lyric roles such as Don Ottavio, Ferrando, Lensky, Oberon, Gonzalve (*L'heure espagnole*) and Bob Cratchit (Musgrave's *A Christmas Carol*).

ELIZABETH FORBES

Legge, Walter (*b* London, 1 June 1906; *d* St Jean, Cap Ferrat, 22 March 1979). English music administrator and writer. He had no formal musical training but in 1927 began to write literary material for the HMV record company. Later he worked as a music critic, and in 1938–9 he was Thomas Beecham's assistant at the Royal Opera House, Covent Garden. After World War II he created the Philharmonia Orchestra and Chorus in London, and worked extensively for record companies, in particular the Gramophone Company (Columbia). He supervised a number of important operatic recordings, including the Columbia Bayreuth recordings of 1951, *Tosca* conducted by De Sabata, *Der Rosenkavalier* and Verdi's *Falstaff* conducted by Karajan, Mozart's *Così fan tutte* conducted by Karl Böhm, Maria Callas's many records and the operetta series involving Elisabeth Schwarzkopf (Legge's second wife). He was a director of the Royal Opera House, 1968–73. Legge worked to raise standards of musical execution and interpretative artistry, and the opera recordings he made set new standards of interpretation, style and polish.

Leggenda di Sakùntala, La. Opera by Franco Alfano; *see* SAKÙNTALA.

Leghorn (Eng.). LIVORNO.

Leginska [Liggins], Ethel (*b* Hull, 13 April 1886; *d* Los Angeles, 26 Feb 1970). American composer and conductor of English birth. A pianist of prodigious ability, she adopted the name Leginska early in her professional career and became widely known as the 'Paderewski of woman pianists'. In the USA, where she achieved her greatest success in 1916–17, she began to compose, studying formally with Bloch in 1918. From the 1920s to the mid-30s Leginska established herself as one of the first woman conductors, directing major orchestras in Europe and America, and women's orchestras in Boston, Chicago and New York. In 1930–31 she conducted at leading European opera houses. She composed songs, piano and chamber music, some orchestral music and two operas. *The Rose and the Ring* (1932) was performed in Los Angeles on 23 February 1957, while the one-act *Gale*, which Leginska herself conducted, was first given by the Chicago City Opera on 23 November 1935.

CAROL NEULS-BATES

Legley, Vic(tor) (*b* Hazebrouck, 18 June 1915). Belgian composer. In 1934 he went to the Brussels Conservatory, where he won prizes in counterpoint, fugue, chamber music and viola. After his demobilization he studied composition and took the Belgian second Prix de Rome in 1943. He worked as a viola player, then as a music producer for Belgian radio; he was appointed head of serious music for the third programme in 1962. He has also been active as a teacher, notably as professor of harmony (from 1949) and composition (from 1959) at the Brussels Conservatory. He was made president of the Belgian Royal Academy in 1972 and was president of the Société Belge des Auteurs, Compositeurs et Editeurs from 1980 to 1992.

Legley has steadily developed an individual style in which highly charged emotion is kept in check by firm technique and refined taste. His opera *La farce des deux nues* (composed 1939–63; 4 scenes, H. Closson), based on the legend of Lady Godiva, was performed in Flemish by the Royal Opera, Antwerp, in 1966, as *De Cluyte der Twee Naakten*. Most of his other pieces are instrumental.
CORNEEL MERTENS/R

Legouix, (Isidore) Edouard (*b* Paris, 1 April 1834; *d* Boulogne, 15 Sept 1916). French composer. His father was the founder of a Parisian publishing house whose management later passed to Edouard's brother Gustave (1843–1916) and Gustave's son Robert. Edouard studied at the Paris Conservatoire with Henri Reber (harmony) and Ambroise Thomas (composition), winning the *premier prix* for harmony in 1855 and an honourable mention in the Prix de Rome in 1860. He soon devoted himself to a career in light opera and operetta; his one-act *Un Othello* (1863) was the first of several successes. The craftsmanship of his works is notable and, according to Feschotte, they survive in part in the French broadcast repertory. The operas tended to be fashionable and escapist; Clément and Larousse particularly noted the extravagance of the plot and incoherence of ideas in *Les dernières grisettes*.

first performed in Paris and printed works published in Paris, unless otherwise stated

Un Othello (?opérette, 1, C. Nuitter and A. Beaumont [A. Beaume]), Champs-Elysées, 1863, vs (?1863); Le lion de St-Marc (opéra-bouffe, 1, Nuitter and Beaumont), Cluny, St-Germain, 24 Nov 1864 (1866); Ma fille (opérette, 1, A. Bouvier), Délassements-Comiques, 20 March 1866; Marlbrough s'en va-t-en guerre [Act 2] (opéra-bouffon, 4, W. Busnach and P. Siraudin), Athénée, 13 Dec 1867, collab. Bizet, E. Jonas and Delibes

Le vengeur (opéra-bouffe, 1, Nuitter and Beaumont), Athénée, 20 Nov 1868, vs (1869); Deux portières pour un cordon (pochade, 1, Lucian [L. Dubuis and Lefèbvre]), Palais-Royal, 19 March 1869, vs (?c1869), collab. Hervé, Lecocq and G. Maurice; L'ours et l'amateur des jardins (bouffonnerie musicale, 1, Busnach and Marquet), Bouffes-Parisiens, 1 Sept 1869, vs (1869); La tartane (opérette, 1), ? London, c1872, vs pubd as The Crimson Scarf (London, 1872)

Les dernières grisettes (opéra-bouffe, 3, Nuitter and Beaumont), Brussels, Fantaisies-Parisiennes, 12 Dec 1874; Le mariage d'une étoile (opérette, 1, V. Bernard and E. Grangé), Bouffes-Parisiens, 1 April 1876, vs (1876); Madame Clara, somnambule (folie, 1), Palais-Royal, March 1877; Une nouvelle Cendrillon (opérette bouffe, 1, E. Adenis), 1885, vs (1885)

Unperf. [pubd in vs in *Magasin des demoiselles*]: Quinolette, c1870 (opérette, 1, P. Nac); La clef d'argent, c1870 (opérette, 1, Beaumont); La fée aux genêts (opérette)

Doubtful: Après la noce (1, P. Boisselot) [listed in *StiegerO*]

*

FétisBS; *MGG* (J. Feschotte); *StiegerO*
F. Clément and P. Larousse: *Dictionnaire lyrique* (Paris, 1867–81, 2/1897, 3/1905 ed. A. Pougin as *Dictionnaire des opéras*)
W. Dean: *Bizet* (London, 1975)
DAVID CHARLTON

Legrenzi, Giovanni (*b* Clusone, nr Bergamo, bap. 12 Aug 1626; *d* Venice, 27 May 1690). Italian composer. He was one of the most important opera composers in Venice in the late 1670s and early 1680s.

1. LIFE. From 30 July 1645 he served as organist at S Maria Maggiore in Bergamo. He entered the priesthood in 1651. Five years later, he left Bergamo for Ferrara, where he served as *maestro di cappella* of the Accademia dello Santo Spirito (1657–64). His three operas for Ferrara reflect aristocratic connections cultivated in that city. Marchese Ippolito Bentivoglio, an active member of the academy, was the librettist of at least two of these works. Legrenzi's whereabouts between June 1665, when he left Ferrara, and 1670 are undocumented, but the applications he submitted for various posts make clear that he enjoyed high esteem in Italy and abroad. By 1670, at the latest, he had settled in Venice. Appointed *maestro di coro* at the Ospedale dei Derelitti (1670–76) and at the Ospedale dei Mendicanti (1676–83), he also served as *maestro di cappella* at the oratory of the Congregazione dei Filippini at S Maria della Fava (1671–80), where he was responsible for composing and directing oratorios. He succeeded Sartorio as vice-*maestro di cappella* at St Mark's in 1681, and became *maestro di cappella* there on 23 April 1685.

Two of Legrenzi's Ferrarese operas were restaged in Venice: *Achille in Sciro* at the Teatro S Salvatore in 1664, and *Zenobia e Radamisto* (with a revised libretto, as *Tiridate*) on the same stage in 1668. Legrenzi's commissions for the S Salvatore in 1675 and 1676 may be connected with the absence of Sartorio, the house composer for this theatre, who was in Hanover for much of this time and presumably unavailable for carnival productions. *Totila* (1677) was Legrenzi's only opera for the Teatro SS Giovanni e Paolo, which was owned by the Grimani family. In 1681, after an interval of three seasons during which he wrote no operas, Legrenzi began his most productive period of operatic composition, monopolizing the season at the Grimani's luxurious new theatre, the S Giovanni Grisostomo, with two works, *Antioco il grande* and *Creso*. For three years after 1681, he wrote two operas each season for the S Salvatore (controlled, at least for Carnival 1683, by the Grimani family). Legrenzi thus replaced Sartorio not only at St Mark's, but also at the S Salvatore. His most productive period of operatic activity coincided with his tenure as vice-*maestro di cappella* at St Mark's; after his appointment as *maestro di cappella*, he focussed on liturgical music, writing only one more opera, *Ifianassa e Melampo*, which was commissioned by Grand Prince Ferdinando de' Medici and performed at the private theatre in his villa at Pratolino.

2. WORKS. Legrenzi's operatic activity was intermittent, and his output small compared to that of Antonio Sartorio and Carlo Pallavicino, his contemporaries. Before his first original operas for Venice in 1675, he was known principally as a composer of liturgical music and violin sonatas, and the ease with which he accommodated himself to the accessible operatic style of the day occasioned some surprise. Fattorini, his first Venetian librettist, praised him for the way he 'exceeded the expectation of many in cultivating charm and delight, violating his own genius, which was accustomed to hard and studious matters'. The principal characteristic of the style forged by Legrenzi and his contemporaries was the predominance of many short arias, in stark contrast to Cavalli's work, which was dominated by recitative interspersed with arioso passages and infrequent arias. Some of Legrenzi's operas of the 1670s include more than 90 arias, and those of the 1680s usually more than 60. Opportunities for lyric

effusion occur at many points in the course of a scene; recitative is minimal. Like his Venetian contemporaries, he focusses on the vocal part, but, in contrast to them, often favours active continuo parts: he uses ground basses (some of them modulatory) more frequently than, for example, Pallavicino. Arias are usually in da capo form; the high number with two strophes in the 1670s declines by the 1680s. Motto arias are frequent. The vocal parts respond flexibly to the wide variety of moods and emotions that the operas encompass: tragic lamentation and martial exhortation alternate with gallant love complaints; servants alternately imitate and deride their masters. Legrenzi uses the supple triple metre so important to Cavalli's generation alongside the sharply defined common time melodies of his own. Modal variety is important; arias in major and minor mode are almost equally balanced. Legrenzi negotiates rapid contrasts smoothly because recitatives and the vast majority of arias are supported by continuo alone. He uses upper melodic instruments in connection with arias in a strictly compartmentalized fashion, mostly in homorhythmic ritornellos after the singer has concluded his or her continuo aria. Occasionally ritornellos precede rather than follow the aria. Upper melodic instruments used in the course of an aria nearly always alternate with the voice. The texture in which instruments sound simultaneously with the voice is limited to certain well defined situations that invoke an appropriately shadowy atmosphere, such as night, foreboding, incantation, oncoming sleep and lamentation. The largest standard ensemble calls for five-part strings (two violins, two *violette* and violoncello) with basso continuo (at least two harpsichords, as well as lutes and theorbos), as well as two trumpets. The parts for *violette* fill the polarized outer parts and are sometimes omitted in scores. Librettos occasionally indicate trumpet fanfares that are not notated in scores. Opening sinfonias, several of which stem from Legrenzi's sonatas and dances, are multi-sectional and do not conform to any standard sequence of tempos.

Several of Legrenzi's operas incorporate a great deal of spectacle: *La divisione del mondo*, *Germanico sul Reno* (*see* MACHINERY, fig.7), *Totila*, *Ottaviano Cesare Augusto* and *Giustino*. Even less spectacular operas have one or two special effects, such as fires or storms. Most require many supernumeraries. They were well received in his own day, and at least one work, *Giustino*, continued to be performed in the decade after his death. However, musical and dramatic changes during the 1690s caused works by Legrenzi and his contemporaries to be superseded by those of younger composers such as Carlo Francesco Pollarolo and Giacomo Antonio Perti.

See also DUE CESARI, I; ETEOCLE E POLINICE; GIUSTINO (i); and TOTILA.

unless otherwise indicated, drammi per musica in 3 acts, first performed in Venice

Nino il giusto (prol., 3, ? I. Bentivoglio), Ferrara, S Stefano, 1662
Achille in Sciro (prol., 3, Bentivoglio), Ferrara, S Stefano, carn. 1663, arias in *GB-Och* and *I-Nc*
Zenobia e Radamisto (Bentivoglio), Ferrara, S Stefano, 1665; as Tiridate (rev. N. Minato), Venice, S Salvatore, carn. 1668; *Nc*
La divisione del mondo (G. C. Corradi), S Salvatore, carn. 1675, *F-Pn*
Eteocle e Polinice (T. Fattorini), S Salvatore, carn. 1675, *Pn* (R: DMV, vi, forthcoming), *I-MOe*, *Nc*
Adone in Cipro (after G. M. Giannini: *Adone*), S Salvatore, carn. 1676, arias in *MOe*, *Nc*, *Rc*, *Rvat* and *Vqs*

Germanico sul Reno (introduzione, 3, Corradi), S Salvatore, carn. 1676, *MOe*
Totila (M. Noris), SS Giovanni e Paolo, carn. 1677, *Vnm* (R1978:IOB, ix)
Antioco il grande (G. Frisari), S Giovanni Grisostomo, carn. 1681, arias in *GB-Lbl*, *I-Bca*, *MOe*, *Nc*, *Rvat*, *Vlevi* and *Vqs*
Creso (Corradi), S Giovanni Grisostomo, carn. 1681, arias in *GB-Lbl*, *Ob*, *I-Bca*, *Rvat* and *Vqs*
Pausania (Frisari), S Salvatore, aut. 1681, arias in *B-Bc*, *D-Bds*, *I-MOe*, *Rvat*, *Tn* and *Vqs*
Lisimaco riamato da Alessandro (G. Sinibaldi, rev. A. Aureli), S Salvatore, carn. 1682, arias in *I-Tn* and *Vqs*
Ottaviano Cesare Augusto (N. Beregan), Mantua, Ducale, May 1682
I due cesari (Corradi), S Salvatore, carn. 1683, arias in *B-Bc* and *I-Vqs*
Giustino (Beregan), S Salvatore, 12 Feb 1683, *Nc*, *Rc* (ed. in Collezione settecentesca Bettarini, xii, Milan, 1980), *Vnm*
L'anarchia dell'imperio (T. Stanzani), S Salvatore, aut. 1683, arias in *GB-Lbl* and *I-MOe*
Publio Elio Pertinace (P. d'Averara), S Salvatore, 22 Jan 1684, arias in *GB-Lbl* and *I-MOe*
Ifianassa e Melampo (G. A. Moniglia), Pratolino, aut. 1685

*
Mercure galant (August 1677), 75–86 [on *Totila*]; (March 1683), 232–50; (April 1683), 20–89
H. C. Wolff: *Die venezianische Oper in der zweiten Hälfte des 17. Jahrhunderts* (Berlin, 1937)
C. Sartori: 'Due Legrenzi ricuperati', *AcM*, xlvi (1974), 217–21
H. C. Wolff: 'Italian Opera from the later Monteverdi to Scarlatti', NOHM, v: *Opera and Church Music 1630–1750* (London, 1975), 1–72, esp. 34–9
E. H. Tarr and T. Walker: '"Bellici carmi, festivo fragor": die Verwendung der Trompete in der italienischen Oper des 17. Jahrhunderts', *HJbMw*, iii (1978), 143–203
Arte e musica all'Ospedaletto (Venice, 1978) [exhibition catalogue]
C. Vitali: 'Una lettera vivaldiana perduta e ritrovata, un inedito monteverdiano del 1630 e altri carteggi di musicisti celebri, ovvero splendori e nefandezze del collezionismo di autografi', *NRMI*, xiv (1980), 404–12
R. Emans: *Die einstimmigen Kantaten, Canzonetten und Serenaden Giovanni Legrenzis* (diss., U. of Bonn, 1984)
B. Glixon: *Recitative in Seventeenth-Century Venetian Opera: its Dramatic Function and Musical Language* (diss., Rutgers U., 1985)
R. Bossard: *Giovanni Legrenzi: 'Il Giustino': eine monographische Studie* (Baden-Baden, 1988)
D. Swale: 'Legrenzi's Operas: Dramatic Structures for an Autocratic Age', *MMA*, xv (1988), 89–99 [Galliver Festschrift]
E. Rosand: *Opera in Seventeenth-Century Venice: the Creation of a Genre* (Berkeley, 1991)
HARRIS S. SAUNDERS

Legros [Le Gros], Joseph (*b* Monampteuil, Laon, 7 or 8 Sept 1739; *d* La Rochelle, 20 Dec 1793). French tenor and composer. Having been a choirboy at Laon Cathedral, Legros developed a powerful, sweet-toned *haute-contre* suited to the high tessitura of French opera. Recruited by Rebel and Francoeur, he made his début at the Paris Opéra in 1764, shortly before the retirement of Jélyotte, in Mondonville's *Titon et l'Aurore*. Although a stiff actor he became the Opéra's leading *haute-contre* until his retirement (accelerated by obesity) in 1783.

Legros played the title roles in Rameau's principal *tragédies lyriques*, and created over 30 other roles. He adapted without apparent difficulty to the new italianate style, singing Sandomir in Philidor's *Ernelinde* in 1767 and at subsequent revivals. He was the first Achilles in Gluck's *Iphigénie en Aulide* (1774) and on its revival the following year led a patriotic demonstration with the aria 'Chantez, célébrez votre reine'. His popularity influenced the adaptation of the castrato role of Orpheus in the French version of Gluck's opera to suit his range (exceptionally, the compass is extended to *eb''*). Legros subsequently created the principal tenor roles in Gluck's *Alceste*, *Armide*, *Iphigénie en Tauride* and Cynire (rather than Narcissus) in *Echo et Narcisse*. For Piccinni he created Médor (*Roland*), the title role in *Atys* and Pylades (*Iphigénie en Tauride*); his last role was the eponymous hero in Sacchini's *Renaud*.

Legros was director of the Concert Spirituel from 1777, and promoted music by Haydn and Mozart; but too often he allowed commercial considerations to outweigh his artistic judgment. With L.-B. Desormery he rewrote the second entrée of F. L. Grenet's *opéra-ballet*, *Le triomphe de l'harmonie* (performed at the Opéra as *Hylas et Eglé* in 1775). He composed another opera, *Anacréon*, which was not performed.

ES (F. Serpa)   JULIAN RUSHTON

Lehane, Maureen (*b* London, 18 Sept 1932). English mezzo-soprano. She studied at the GSM and in Berlin. She made a speciality of Handel, and sang leading roles – often castrato roles, which she sang with much spirit – in some 20 of his stage works for the Handel Opera Society in London and elsewhere, mostly during the 1960s and 70s. Her Glyndebourne début was in 1967 as Melide in Cavalli's *L'Ormindo*, and her repertory includes operas by Vivaldi, J. C. Bach, Purcell (*Dido and Aeneas*) and Rossini (*La Cenerentola*) as well as works by Hugo Cole, Alan Ridout and her husband, Peter Wishart. With a voice admired for range, flexibility and fullness of tone, she toured Europe, the Middle and Far East and the USA; she has also given masterclasses in Handel interpretation and, with her husband, edited three volumes of Purcell songs.   NOËL GOODWIN

Lehár, Franz (Christian) (*b* Komáron, Hungary, 30 April 1870; *d* Bad Ischl, 24 Oct 1948). Austro-Hungarian composer and conductor. He was the leading operetta composer of the 20th century, being primarily responsible for giving the genre renewed vitality. His most successful operetta, *Die lustige Witwe*, has established a lasting place in the opera, as well as the operetta, repertory.

The family came originally from the eastern Sudetenland. His father, also Franz (1838–98), received his music education in Sternberg (now Šternberk) in Moravia, played in the orchestra of the Theater an der Wien, and was for nearly 40 years a military bandmaster and composer of dances and marches. In 1869 he married a Hungarian, Christine Neubrandt, and in the following years they moved between various Hungarian garrison towns. To improve his German their son was sent to Sternberg, where his uncle was the town's musical director. During the summer he played the violin in his uncle's orchestra at Bad Ullersdorf, and at the age of 12 he entered the Prague Conservatory, studying the violin with Bennewitz and theory with Foerster. He also took some private lessons in composition from Fibich and received some advice from Dvořák.

In autumn 1888 the young Lehár took up a position as theatre violinist at Barmen-Elberfeld in the Rhineland. Then, called up for military service, he joined the band of the 50th Austrian infantry regiment, playing under his father and alongside his future operetta colleague Leo Fall. In 1890 he was made bandmaster of the 25th infantry regiment in Losoncz and in 1894 of the naval corps in Pola. He gave up the position when his opera *Kukuška* was about to be performed, but its failure in Leipzig in 1896 forced him to return to military service. Having reached Vienna, he finally left military service in 1902. That year his waltz *Gold und*

Silber was first performed at a society ball, and he became conductor at the summer theatre in the Prater and at the Theater an der Wien. There, and at the rival Carltheater, his operettas *Wiener Frauen* (originally entitled *Der Klavierstimmer*) and *Der Rastelbinder* were performed within the year with real success. Their successors, *Der Göttergatte* and *Die Juxheirat* (both 1904), were both failures, but in 1905 Lehár was called in to set *Die lustige Witwe*. Its success in Vienna and abroad was the greatest in operetta history, and it heralded a new era for Viennese operetta through the works of Lehár, Fall, Oscar Straus and Kálmán.

In 1909–10 three of Lehár's works were produced within the space of three months, of which *Der Graf von Luxemburg* (1909) and *Zigeunerliebe* (1910) again achieved international acclaim. Far from allowing his success to let him settle into the production of routine works, Lehár was intent on developing his style and producing original and more ambitious works. *Zigeunerliebe* contained elements of melancholy and fantasy, *Eva* featured a factory girl and dealt with social relationships, while the whole of Act 2 of *Endlich allein* (1914) has the leading couple alone on a mountain top. However, with World War I a hindrance to international currency, these failed to attract the same wide public, and after the war the arrival of new styles of popular music from the USA increasingly suggested that Lehár's period of great popularity was over. His attempts to raise the quality of operetta inevitably brought accusations of pretentiousness, and his attempts to incorporate the popular musical styles of the time (blues, foxtrot, onestep, tango and shimmy) merely exacerbated the problem.

A new era of success then arrived with an association with Richard Tauber, which began when the latter sang in *Zigeunerliebe* at Salzburg in 1921. Tauber took over the leading role in *Frasquita* (1922), and Lehár subsequently wrote several works with leading roles for him. At a time when the musical content of operetta was being widely trivialized, these caught the public fancy, especially through the virile 'Tauber-Lied' that became a standard feature. These works sometimes also featured an unhappy ending, something almost without precedent in Viennese operetta. Tauber provided a focal point for a series that began in 1925 with *Paganini* (though, in the event, the tenor lead at the Viennese première was Carl Clewing) and continued with *Der Zarewitsch* (1927) and *Friederike* (1928; more a play with music than an operetta, in which Tauber played Goethe) before the most widely popular, *Das Land des Lächelns* (1929). This was a revision of *Die gelbe Jacke* (1923), reinforced by several new numbers, including the most famous of all Lehár's Tauber songs, 'Dein ist mein ganzes Herz'. If Lehár's melodic flow was now less profuse, the increased strength of his vocal writing was readily apparent. The Tauber songs, with their initial upward thrust ('O Mädchen, mein Mädchen' in *Friederike*, 'Dein ist mein ganzes Herz' in *Das Land des Lächelns*) may themselves have inclined to a stereotype, but they have provided rewarding material for tenors ever since.

At this time Lehár was much involved with revisions and film versions of his operettas, and he also composed some original film numbers. His only entirely new stage work after 1928 was *Giuditta*, an ambitious work written for the Vienna Staatsoper, where it was produced in 1934 with Tauber and Jarmila Novotna in the leading roles and 120 radio stations relaying the performance. It was with *Giuditta* that Lehár found the final resolution between his ambitions and the essentially popular requirements of operetta. He never again found the subject or the frame of mind for a new work. In 1935 he founded his own publishing house, Glocken Verlag, to take over the rights to many of his stage works from the bankrupt Karczag publishing house. From other publishers he also acquired the rights to most of his other works, with the notable exception of *Die lustige Witwe*, the lucrative rights to which were retained by Doblinger. Apart from a revision of *Zigeunerliebe* for Budapest as *Garabonciás diák*, he thereafter concentrated on preserving his works for posterity.

During World War II Lehár remained in Vienna and Bad Ischl, in the equivocal situation where, although his wife was Jewish and several of his friends and collaborators died in concentration camps, *Die lustige Witwe* was one of Hitler's favourite works. Always wrapped up in his music and unwilling to become involved in politics, his failure to protest against Nazi atrocities made him an object of suspicion outside Germany. Suffering ill-health, he moved in 1946 to Zürich, where his wife died in September 1947, and in summer 1948 returned to Bad Ischl where he died soon afterwards. His villa in Bad Ischl is now a Lehár museum, and memorials were erected in front of the Kursaal, Bad Ischl in 1958 and in the Stadtpark, Vienna in 1978.

Lehár was not only a superb melodist, but also, by the standards of operetta composers, unusually well equipped technically. The extent of the development of his musical style was probably unique for an operetta composer. Where his earlier works are distinguished by a sparkling fund of melody, his later ones are notable more for their ambitious vocal writing, with the Tauber songs at their centre. Like the younger Johann Strauss he had the ability to make melodies take an unexpected but natural-sounding turn. Though the waltz was the centrepiece of his operettas, it was a more tender, swaying, sensuous waltz than had typified the previous generation of waltz composers. Lehár was unusual for his time in orchestrating his own scores, which he did with notable skill and imagination, having learned from the innovations of Dvořák, Debussy, Puccini and Richard Strauss. He took a particular delight in portraying local colour (Slav in *Der Rastelbinder*, Balkan in *Die lustige Witwe*, Polish in *Die blaue Mazur*, Spanish in *Frasquita*, Russian in *Der Zarewitsch* and Chinese in *Das Land des Lächelns*). He was also himself an excellent violinist and eagerly seized the opportunity for violin solos (in *Zigeunerliebe*, *Die blaue Mazur* and *Paganini*, for instance), and the solo violin was always a particular feature in heightening the sensuousness of his love-scene waltzes.

See also GIUDITTA; GRAF VON LUXEMBURG, DER; LAND DES LÄCHELNS, DAS; LUSTIGE WITWE, DIE; PAGANINI; and ZAREWITSCH, DER.

Operetten unless otherwise stated

WW – *Vienna, Theater an der Wien*

Der Kürassier, 1891–2 (Oper, G. Ruther), inc.

Rodrigo, 1893 (Oper, 1, R. Mlčoch), unperf.

Kukuška (Oper, 3, F. Falzari), Leipzig, Stadt, 27 Nov 1896; rev. as Tatjana (Falzari and M. Kalbeck), Brünn, Stadt, 21 Feb 1905

Arabella, die Kubanerin, 1901 (G. Schmidt), inc.

Das Club-Baby, 1901 (V. Léon), inc.

Der Klavierstimmer [Wiener Frauen] (3, O. Tann-Bergler and E. Norini), WW, 21 Nov 1902, vs (Vienna, 1902); rev. as Der Schlüssel zum Paradies (3, Norini and J. Horst), Leipzig, Stadt, Oct 1906

Der Rastelbinder (prelude, 2, Léon), Vienna, Carl, 20 Dec 1902, vs (Vienna, 1902)

Der Göttergatte (prelude, 2, Léon and L. Stein), Vienna, Carl, 20 Jan 1904, vs (Vienna, 1904); rev. as Die ideale Gattin (3, J. Brammer and A. Grünwald, after L. Fulda: *Die Zwillingsschwester*), WW, 11 Oct 1913, vs (Vienna, 1913); rev. as Die Tangokönigin (Brammer and Grünwald), Vienna, Apollo, 9 Sept 1921, vs (Vienna, 1921)

Die Juxheirat (3, J. Bauer), WW, 22 Dec 1904, vs (Vienna, 1904)

Die lustige Witwe (3, Léon and Stein, after H. Meilhac: *L'attaché d'ambassade*), WW, 30 Dec 1905, vs (Vienna, 1906)

Peter und Paul reisen ins Schlaraffenland (Zaubermärchen, 1, F. Grünbaum and R. Bodanzky), WW, 1 Dec 1906, 7 nos. (Vienna, 1906)

Mitislaw der Moderne (1, Grünbaum and Bodanzky), Vienna, Die Hölle, 5 Jan 1907, 3 nos. (Vienna, ?1907)

Der Mann mit den drei Frauen (3, Bauer), WW, 21 Jan 1908, vs (Vienna, 1908)

Das Fürstenkind (prelude, 3, Léon, after E. About), Vienna, Johann Strauss, 7 Oct 1909, vs (Vienna, 1909); rev. as Der Fürst der Berge, Berlin, Nollendorfplatz, 23 Sept 1932

Der Graf von Luxemburg (3, A. M. Willner and Bodanzky), WW, 12 Nov 1909, vs (Vienna, 1909); rev. version, Berlin, Volkes, 4 March 1937, vs (Vienna, 1937)

Zigeunerliebe (romantische Operette, 3, Willner and Bodanzky), Vienna, Carl, 8 Jan 1910 (Vienna, 1910); rev. as Garabonciás diák [The Wandering Scholar] (E. Innocent Vincze), Budapest, Király, 20 Feb 1943

Eva [Das Fabriksmädel] (3, Willner and Bodanzky), WW, 24 Nov 1911, vs (Vienna, 1911)

Rosenstock und Edelweiss (Spl, 1, Bauer), Vienna, Die Hölle, 1 Dec 1912

Endlich allein (3, Willner and Bodanzky), WW, 30 Jan 1914, vs (Vienna, 1914); rev. as Schön ist die Welt! (3, L. Herzer and F. Löhner), Berlin, Metropol, 3 Dec 1930, vs (Vienna, 1930)

Der Sterngucker (3, Löhner), Vienna, Josefstadt, 14 Jan 1916; rev. version (3, Löhner and Willner), WW, 27 Sept 1916, vs (Vienna, 1916); rev. as La danza delle libellule (3, C. Lombardo), Milan, Lirico, 3 May 1922; as Libellentanz (Lombardo and Willner), Vienna, 31 March 1923, vs (Vienna, 1923); rev. as Gigolette (Lombardo and G. Forzano), Milan, Lirico, 30 Oct 1926

A pacsirta [The Lark] (3, F. Martos), Budapest, Király, 1 Jan 1918; as Wo die Lerche singt (Willner and H. Reichert, after Martos), WW, 27 March 1918, vs (Vienna, 1918)

Die blaue Mazur (2, Stein and B. Jenbach), WW, 28 May 1920, vs (Vienna, 1920)

Frühling (Spl, 1, R. Eger), Vienna, Die Hölle, 20 Jan 1922, vs (Berlin, 1922); rev. as Frühlingsmädel (3, Eger), Berlin, Zoo, 29 May 1928

Frasquita (3, Willner and Reichert), WW, 12 May 1922, vs (Vienna, 1922); rev. version, Paris, OC (Favart), 5 May 1933

Die gelbe Jacke (3, Léon), WW, 9 Feb 1923, vs (Vienna, 1923); rev. as Das Land des Lächelns (romantische Operette, 3, Herzer and Löhner, after Léon), Berlin, Metropol, 10 Oct 1929, vs (Berlin, 1929)

Cloclo (3, Jenbach), Vienna, Bürger, 8 March 1924; rev. version, Vienna, Johann Strauss, 4 Sept 1924, vs (Berlin, 1924)

Paganini (3, P. Knepler and Jenbach), Vienna, Johann Strauss, 30 Oct 1925, vs (Berlin, 1925)

Der Zarewitsch (3, Jenbach and Reichert, after G. Zapolska), Berlin, Deutsches Künstler, 16 Feb 1927, vs (Berlin, 1927)

Friederike (Spl, 3, Herzer and Löhner), Berlin, Metropol, 10 Oct 1928, vs (Berlin, 1928)

Giuditta (musikalische Komödie, 5 scenes, Knepler and Löhner), Vienna, Staatsoper, 20 Jan 1934 (Vienna, 1933)

*

E. Decsey: *Franz Lehár* (Munich, 1924, 2/1930)

G. Knosp: *Franz Lehár: une vie d'artiste* (Brussels, 1936)

S. Czech: *Franz Lehár: sein Weg und sein Werk* (Berlin, 1940, 2/1948)

M. von Peteani: *Franz Lehár: seine Musik, sein Leben* (Vienna, 1950, 2/1985)

I. Kwasnik-Teuber: *Franz Lehár: sein Leben und Werk* (Kevelaer, 1953)

W. Macqueen-Pope and D. L. Murray: *Fortune's Favourite* (London, 1953)

S. Czech: *Schön ist die Welt: Franz Lehárs Leben und Werk* (Berlin, 1957)

B. Grun: *Gold and Silver: the Life and Times of Franz Lehár* (London, 1970)

M. Schönherr: *Franz Lehár: Bibliographie zu Leben und Werk* (Vienna, 1970) [summary in 'Beiträge zu einer Franz-Lehár-Bibliographie', *ÖMz*, xxv (1970), 330–3]

——: 'Die Instrumentation bei Lehár', *Franz Lehár Congress: Bad Ischl 1978*; abridged and with Eng. summary in A. Lamb, ed.: *Light Music from Austria* (New York, 1992), 93–101, 195–7

A. Lamb: 'Opera on the Gramophone: *Die lustige Witwe*', *Opera*, xxxii (1981), 128–37, 243–7

L'avant-scène opéra, no.45 (1982) [*Die lustige Witwe* issue]

A. Lamb: 'Lehár's "Count of Luxembourg" ', *MT*, cxxiv (1983), 23–5

G. V. R. van Ham: *Franz Lehár* (Madrid, 1984)

O. Schneidereit: *Franz Lehár: eine Biographie in Zitaten* (Berlin and Innsbruck, 1984)

Franz Lehár: Thematic Index (London, 1985)   ANDREW LAMB

Lilli Lehmann as Brünnhilde

Lehmann, Lilli (*b* Würzburg, 24 Nov 1848; *d* Berlin, 17 May 1929). German soprano. She studied with her mother, Marie Loewe, in Prague, and made her début there in 1865 as the First Boy (*Die Zauberflöte*), later singing Pamina. In 1868 she was engaged at Danzig, and in 1869 sang for the first time at the Berlin Hofoper, as Marguerite de Valois (*Les Huguenots*). She was then engaged permanently in Berlin. She took part in the first complete *Ring* cycle at Bayreuth (1876), singing Woglinde, Helmwige and the Woodbird. She made her London début at Her Majesty's Theatre in 1880 as Violetta and also sang Philine (*Mignon*). In 1884 she appeared at Covent Garden as Isolde and Elisabeth.

In 1885 Lehmann broke her contract with the Berlin Hofoper and went to New York, making her début at the Metropolitan as Carmen. During her first season she also sang Brünnhilde (*Die Walküre*), Sulamith (Goldmark's *Die Königin von Saba*), Berthe (*Le prophète*), Marguerite (*Faust*), Irene (*Rienzi*) and Venus. During subsequent Metropolitan seasons, she took part in the American premières of *Tristan und Isolde* (1886), Sieg-

fried (1887) and *Götterdämmerung* (1888), as well as the first complete *Ring* cycle given in the USA (1889). In 1891 she returned to Berlin and in 1896 sang Brünnhilde at Bayreuth. During her final season at the Metropolitan (1898–9) she sang Fricka (*Das Rheingold*), and in 1899 made her last appearances at Covent Garden as Isolde, Sieglinde, Ortrud, Leonore, Donna Anna and Norma. Between 1901 and 1910 she sang at the Salzburg Festival (Donna Anna and the First Lady) and also became the festival's artistic director.

Lehmann's enormous repertory ranged from light, coloratura parts to the dramatic roles which she sang with superb authority and technical skill. As it grew more powerful, her voice retained its flexibility, and she could turn from Wagner or Verdi to Mozart or Bellini with astonishing ease.

Lilli's younger sister, the soprano Marie Lehmann (*b* Hamburg, 15 May 1851; *d* Berlin, 9 Dec 1931), made her début in 1871 at Leipzig as Aennchen (*Der Freischütz*) and then sang at Breslau, Cologne, Hamburg and Prague. In 1876 she took part in the first complete *Ring* cycle at Bayreuth, singing Wellgunde and Ortlinde. From 1882 to 1896 she was engaged at the Vienna Hofoper. Her repertory included Marguerite de Valois, Donna Elvira, Adalgisa, and Antonina in Donizetti's *Belisario*. She returned to Bayreuth in 1896 to sing the Second Norn (*Götterdämmerung*).

*

A. Ehrlich: *Berühmte Sängerinnen der Vergangenheit und Gegenwart* (Leipzig, 1895)

L. Lehmann: *Meine Gesangskunst* (Berlin, 1902, 3/1922; Eng. trans., 1902, as *How to Sing*, enlarged 3/1924)

——: *Mein Weg* (Leipzig, 1913, 2/1920; Eng. trans., 1914)

E. Newman: *The Life of Richard Wagner* (London, 1933–47)

I. Kolodin: *The Story of the Metropolitan Opera* (New York, 1951)

H. Fetting: *Die Geschichte der Deutschen Staatsoper* (Berlin, 1955)

H. Rosenthal: *Two Centuries of Opera at Covent Garden* (London, 1958)

G. Skelton: *Wagner at Bayreuth* (London, 1965, enlarged 2/1976)

L. M. Lai: 'Lilli Lehmann', *Record Collector*, xxvi (1980–81), 149–89, 199–214 [discography by J. Dennis]

ELIZABETH FORBES

Lehmann, Lotte (*b* Perleberg, 27 Feb 1888; *d* Santa Barbara, CA, 26 Aug 1976). German soprano, later naturalized American. She studied in Berlin, and began her career in 1910 with the Hamburg Opera. In 1916 she moved to Vienna, scoring an instant success as the Composer in the newly revised version of Strauss's *Ariadne auf Naxos*; she was later to be his first Dyer's Wife in *Die Frau ohne Schatten* (1919, Vienna) and Christine in *Intermezzo* (1924, Dresden). She remained in Vienna until 1938, when political events drove her from Austria. During her long Viennese career she sang a wide range of French and Italian as well as German roles. From 1924 she was a great favourite at Covent Garden, returning almost every year until 1938, by which time she had also established herself in the USA. Internationally, her most famous roles were Beethoven's Leonore, and Wagner's Elisabeth, Elsa, Eva and above all Sieglinde. But the part with which she became increasingly identified was that of Strauss's Marschallin – a portrayal of which Richard Capell wrote: 'The lyric stage of the time knew no performance more admirably accomplished; it seemed to embody a civilization, the pride and elegance of old Vienna, its voluptuousness, chastened by good manners, its doomed beauty'. Especially after her American début she developed and refined her lieder style, and her recitals, which continued until 1951, won her a following no less devoted than her

Lotte Lehmann as the Marschallin in Richard Strauss's 'Der Rosenkavalier'

operatic public. The best of her many recordings convey a vivid impression of her voice and urgently dramatic style. She wrote a volume of autobiography, *Anfang und Aufstieg*, published in Vienna in 1937 (as *Wings of Song*, London, 1938), as well as several studies in interpretation.

*

B. Glass: *Lotte Lehmann: a Life in Opera and Song* (Santa Barbara, CA, 1988) [with discography by G. Hickling]
A. Jefferson: *Lotte Lehmann 1888–1976* (London, 1988) [with discography by F. Juynboll]   DESMOND SHAWE-TAYLOR

Lehnhoff, Nikolaus (*b* Hanover, 20 May 1939). German director. He studied at Munich and Vienna universities and worked as assistant to Wieland Wagner and Karl Böhm at Bayreuth in the mid-1960s. He made his début as an opera director in 1972 with *Die Frau ohne Schatten* at the Paris Opéra with Böhm conducting. The following year, again with Böhm, he directed Birgit Nilsson and Jon Vickers in *Tristan und Isolde* at Orange. He has made a speciality of working with leading German painters and sculptors as his designers – Günther Vecker for *Fidelio*, Heinz Mack for *Tristan* and Erich Wonder for *Der Ring des Nibelungen*. His most important productions to date are two distinct versions of the *Ring*, with John Conklin in San Francisco (1983–5) and Wonder at the Bayerische Staatsoper, Munich (1987), *Elektra* in Chicago (1975), *Salome* at the Metropolitan Opera (1989), and two Janáček productions at Glyndebourne, *Kát'a Kabanová* (1988) and *Jenůfa* (1989). He made his Salzburg Festival début in 1990 with *Idomeneo*. Lehnhoff favours an eclectic visual style in his productions through his use of in-

dividual designers. Although he has experimented with the fashionable abstract modernism of the German opera stage in the 1980s and 90s, his finest work, such as his Glyndebourne Janáček productions, is marked by an intense 'Personenregie' (direction of character) and striking naturalism.

*

N. Ely and S. Jaeger, eds.: *Regie Heute: Musiktheater in unserer Zeit* (Berlin, 1984), 183–202
N. Lehnhoff: *Es war einmal* (Munich, 1987)
C. H. Bachmann: 'Von Mythos der Gegenwart – Ein Ringelspiel Unausweichlichkeit der "Postmoderne" – drei "Ring"-Inszenierungen der "80er"', *Neue Musikzeitung*, xxxviii/3 (1989)
   HUGH CANNING

Lehrstück (Ger.: 'teaching piece'). A 20th-century term closely associated with the work of BERTOLT BRECHT, who probably invented it to describe a theatrical genre for amateur performance whose principal function was to teach the participants (through performance and discussion) rather than to engage the attention of an audience. Written when the Nazis were gaining power in Germany, Brecht's Lehrstücke attempt in particular to teach political attitudes, often explicitly Marxist.

Brecht wrote his texts when he was experimenting with novel yet highly simplified forms of presentation derived from agit-prop drama, *Gebrauchsmusik* and his theories of 'epic theatre'. Music plays an important part, and a dominant one in the Lehrstücke by Weill, Hindemith and Eisler. Their settings enlarged the boundaries of music-theatre by integrating a variety of techniques from conventional opera and theatre with elements from oratorio, revue, dance and film. The composers also underlined the didactic purpose of a Lehrstück, treating it as a means by which amateurs could be taught specific musical accomplishments and a new interpretative dimension added to the dialectic.

Brecht's attitude to his seven Lehrstücke was pragmatic, and he frequently revised them, the first three so extensively that their definitive texts do not correspond with those set to music. *Der Lindberghflug*, for example, was first published in 1929 as a radio play. It was set jointly by Hindemith and Weill and presented at the Baden-Baden Festival the same year, in a manner indicating that some parts of it were ideally to be supplied by the radio loudspeaker and some by the listener at home. Later in 1929 Weill alone composed a second setting, the published *Der Lindberghflug*, as a cantata that revealed little of its radio origins. In 1930 Brecht published an expanded text as *Flug der Lindberghs*, a 'Radio Lehrstück for boys and girls' (in 1950 he altered the title to *Der Ozeanflug*, added a prologue and suppressed the name of Lindbergh, a Nazi sympathizer; the title of Weill's cantata was also changed). This had no explicitly didactic content until Brecht made his 1930 version, and although suitable for amateurs Weill's cantata is thus not a true Lehrstück.

A work actually entitled *Lehrstück*, by Hindemith, was written for the same Baden-Baden Festival of 1929 and the vocal score was published that year. Brecht later published a revised and expanded version of the text as *Das Badener Lehrstück vom Einverständnis*. *Der Jasager*, with music by Weill, was written and first performed in 1930. After criticism from the children who performed it, Brecht wrote a second version and a complementary Lehrstück, *Der Neinsager*. Weill set neither of these texts. Brecht's most important Lehrstück, *Die Massnahme*, was first performed with music by Eisler in 1930. Paul Dessau composed the music for

Die Ausnahme und die Regel (1930) and Kurt Schwaen for *Die Horatier und die Kuriatier* (1934).

S. Günther: 'Lehrstück und Schuloper', *Melos*, x (1931), 410–13
M. Esslin: *Brecht: a Choice of Evils* (London, 1959)
J. Willett: *The Theatre of Bertolt Brecht* (London, 1959)
H. Braun: *Untersuchungen zur Typologie die Schul- und Jugendoper* (Regensburg, 1963)
B. Brecht: 'Zu den Lehrstücken', *Gesammelte Werke*, xvii (Frankfurt, 1967), 1022–35
R. Steinweg: *Das Lehrstück* (Stuttgart, 1972)   IAN KEMP

Lehrstück ('Lesson on Consent'). Music theatre work by PAUL HINDEMITH to a libretto by BERTOLT BRECHT; Baden-Baden, Stadthalle, 28 July 1929.

This work for two male singers, speaker, chorus, dancer, three clowns and orchestra can be fitted into no previously existing category. An air pilot, injured in a crash, appeals for help. He is brought to see that he does not deserve it, and instead is instructed on the need to reconcile himself with death by acknowledging his own insignificance. Hindemith was less interested in Brecht's didactic message than in ways of involving the audience as well as the (preferably amateur) actors and musicians on stage in the discussion, and the audience is invited to join in the singing of various responses. He wrote the orchestral score in high, middle and low 'voices' only, leaving the composition of the orchestra to the conductor's discretion, and in the preface to the score he gave permission for omissions, additions and changes in the running order, as well as for dispensing with whole scenes, if necessary. No costumes or stage settings (beyond an optional wrecked plane) were to be used.

The spoken clowns' knockabout scene, involving the dismemberment of a giant, caused a scandal at the first performance; Hindemith was in favour of removing it entirely, but Brecht refused. Consequently, the work was unavailable for performance until after the deaths of both composer and librettist. It has since established itself as one of the strongest works of Hindemith's period of *Gebrauchsmusik* (more aptly described as 'Music to Sing and Play').   GEOFFREY SKELTON

Leibowitz, René (*b* Warsaw, 17 Feb 1913; *d* Paris, 29 Aug 1972). French composer and musicologist of Polish origin. He studied with Schoenberg and Webern in Berlin and Vienna (1930–33), then with Ravel in Paris (1933), where he lived from 1945. He appeared as a conductor throughout Europe and the USA and was active as a teacher (notably of Boulez) and a writer. His major contribution was his work on behalf of the Second Viennese School, although he also wrote *Histoire de l'opéra* (Paris, 1957) and *Les fantômes de l'opéra* (Paris, 1973).

Leibowitz composed operas, vocal music and many orchestral and instrumental works. His compositions are close to Schoenberg and Berg in their classical serial procedures, displaying a certain intellectualism that also marked his work as a conductor. However, a new lyricism emerges in his opera *Les espagnols à Venise*, through a fusion of expressionism and rigorous method.

La nuit close op.17, 1947–50 (drame musical, 3 scenes, G. Limbour)
La rumeur de l'espace, 1950
Circulaire de minuit op.30, 1952–3 (3, Limbour)
Ricardo Gonfalano, 1953
Les espagnols à Venise op.60, 1963 (ob, 1, Limbour), Grenoble, 27 Jan 1970
Labyrinthe op.85, 1969 (1, after Baudelaire)
Todos caerán op.91, 1972 (3, Leibowitz, after a Goya painting)
        DOMINIQUE JAMEUX

Leider, Frida (*b* Berlin, 18 April 1888; *d* Berlin, 4 June 1975). German soprano. She made her début at Halle in 1915, and filled other engagements at Rostock, Königsberg and Hamburg until her move in 1923 to the Berlin Staatsoper, where she was principal dramatic soprano for some 15 years. She appeared there in numerous Mozart, Verdi and Strauss operas as well as in *Fidelio* and in the big Wagner roles that brought her international fame. In 1924 she made her Covent Garden début as Isolde and Brünnhilde, at once becoming the favourite Wagnerian soprano of the house, to which she returned every year until 1938; her other roles there included Donna Anna, Leonora (*Il trovatore*) and Gluck's Armide. Between 1928 and 1938 she was a regular Brünnhilde, Isolde and Kundry at Bayreuth. Her American career was centred on Chicago rather than on New York. Leider was a splendid artist with a dark-coloured, ample and well-trained voice of lovely quality and a fine-spun legato and purity of phrase that enabled her to excel in Mozart and Italian opera as well as in Wagner. During her best years she made many valuable recordings, often in company with Melchior, Schorr and her other regular Wagnerian associates.

F. Leider: *Das war mein Teil* (Berlin, 1959; Eng. trans., as *Playing my Part*, 1966) [with discography by H. Burros]
D. Shawe-Taylor: 'Frida Leider (1888–1975)', *Opera*, xxxix (1988), 905–8   DESMOND SHAWE-TAYLOR

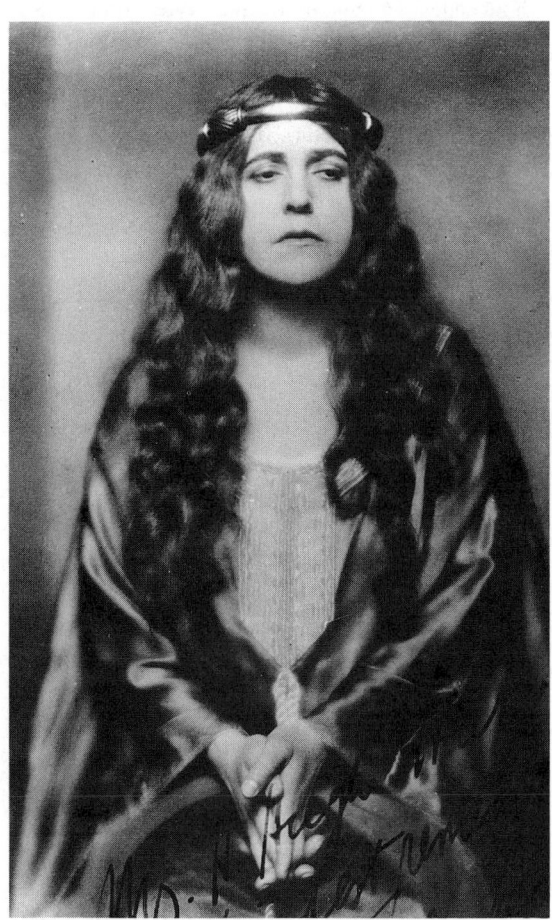

Frida Leider as Isolde in Wagner's 'Tristan und Isolde'

Leiferkus, Sergey (Petrovich) (*b* Leningrad [now St Petersburg], 4 April 1946). Russian baritone. He studied in Leningrad, where he was engaged at the Malïy Opernïy Teatr from 1972 to 1978; he first sang at the Kirov Theatre in 1977 as Prince Andrey (*War and Peace*). Among his earlier roles were Rossini's Figaro, Robert (*Iolanta*) and Don Giovanni. In 1982 he sang the Marquis in Massenet's *Grisélidis* at Wexford, where he returned as Hans Heiling, Boniface (*Le jongleur de Notre-Dame*) and the Fiddler (*Königskinder*). For Scottish Opera he has sung Don Giovanni and Yevgeny Onegin; for the ENO, Zurga (*Les pêcheurs de perles*) and Escamillo; for Opera North, Scarpia and Zurga. In 1987 he toured Britain with the Kirov Opera as Yevgeny Onegin and Tomsky (*The Queen of Spades*), opening at Covent Garden. He made his Royal Opera début as Luna (1989), returning as Prince Igor (1990) and Ruprecht in *The Fiery Angel* (1992). He sang Telramund at San Francisco (1989), Mazeppa at Bregenz (1991) and Tomsky at Glyndebourne (1992). His repertory includes Amonasro, Germont and Iago, but such roles as Yevgeny Onegin and Rangoni (*Boris Godunov*) best display his rich voice, fine diction and dramatic ability.

E. Forbes: 'Sergey Leiferkus', *Opera*, xli (1990), 175–80
ELIZABETH FORBES

Leigh, Adele (*b* London, 15 June 1928). English soprano. After studying drama she went to the Juilliard School and was a pupil of Maggie Teyte. From 1948 to 1956 she was a resident soprano at Covent Garden, making her début as Xenia (*Boris Godunov*) and having particular success as Cherubino, Pamina and Manon as well as creating Bella in Tippett's *The Midsummer Marriage* (1955). She returned in 1961 as Octavian, and in 1963 joined the Vienna Volksoper as principal operetta soprano, until 1972. Her American début was as Musetta at Boston in 1966. She later came out of retirement to sing Gabrielle (*La vie parisienne*) at the Brighton Festival in 1984 with Phoenix Opera, and Heidi Schiller in Sondheim's *Follies* in London in 1987. Her bright-toned lyric soprano and musical sensibility were widely admired, as were her personal charm and glamorous appearance.

H. Rosenthal: *Sopranos of Today* (London, 1956)
NOËL GOODWIN

Leigh, Mitch [Mitchnik, Irwin] (*b* Brooklyn, 30 Jan 1928). American composer. After studying with Hindemith at Yale, he began his career as a jazz musician. In 1954 he started composing for television and radio commercials and in 1957 founded Music Makers to produce them. After writing incidental music for a revival of Shaw's *Too True to be Good* (1963) and the Broadway play *Never Live Over a Pretzel Factory* (1964), he composed the musical play *Man of La Mancha* (D. Wasserman and J. Darion, after Cervantes; New York, Washington Square Theatre, 22 November 1965). This achieved wide international acclaim, but its successors, *Cry for us All* (1970), *Home Sweet Homer* (1976) and *Saravá* (1979), were less successful. At home in a wide range of styles, Leigh has put his versatility to effective use in his treatment of varied subjects.

S. Green: *The World of Musical Comedy* (New York, 1960, 4/1980)
G. Bordman: *American Musical Theatre* (New York, 1978, 2/1986)
ANDREW LAMB

Leinsdorf [Landauer], Erich (*b* Vienna, 4 Feb 1912). American conductor of Austrian birth. He studied in Vienna and in the USA at Rutgers and Columbia universities. He assisted Bruno Walter and Toscanini at the Salzburg Festival (1934–7), and worked in Italy. On Lotte Lehmann's recommendation he was engaged by the Metropolitan in 1937 as assistant to Artur Bodanzky, and made his conducting début there on 21 January 1938 in *Die Walküre* (with Kirsten Flagstad and Elisabeth Rethberg). After Bodanzky's death the next year, Leinsdorf took charge of the German repertory until 1943, and a performance of *Tristan und Isolde* with Flagstad and Lauritz Melchior in 1941 was recorded and commercially issued. His début at the San Francisco Opera was in *Pelléas et Mélisande*; he was music director for New York City Opera, 1956–7, then music consultant to Rudolf Bing at the Metropolitan, 1957–62. He conducted *Die Meistersinger* at Bayreuth in 1959.

While holding orchestral appointments (notably with the Boston SO, 1962–9), Leinsdorf appeared at the Teatro Colón, Buenos Aires and at the Vienna Staatsoper (where he conducted Krenek's *Karl V* in 1984), and continued guest appearances at the Metropolitan, where he conducted nearly 30 different operas, mainly Mozart, Wagner and Strauss but also *Orfeo ed Euridice*, *Pelléas* and *Macbeth*. He has given concert performances of Beethoven's *Leonore* and the original version of Strauss's *Ariadne auf Naxos*. His versatility and technical finesse have helped him achieve memorable performances of expressive eloquence when not constrained by undue rigidity. His numerous recordings include the second version of *Ariadne auf Naxos* (1959) with Sena Jurinac, Leonie Rysanek and Jan Peerce; *Turandot* (1960) with Birgit Nilsson; *Die Walküre* (1961) with Nilsson and Jon Vickers; *Lohengrin* (1966) with the Boston SO; and *Aida* (1970) with Leontyne Price. He has served on the National Endowment for the Arts, and is a member of the American Academy of Arts and Sciences. He has published an autobiography, *Cadenza: a Musical Career* (Boston, 1976).
MICHAEL STEINBERG, NOËL GOODWIN

Leipzig. City in Germany. A prosperous commercial centre, it gained considerable control over its own affairs from the Saxon court in the 15th century and, with its university (founded 1409) and pre-eminence in the publishing trade, became a leading intellectual centre by the 18th century.

1. To 1800. 2. After 1800.

1. TO 1800. Without a resident court, Leipzig attracted travelling theatre companies chiefly through its annual commercial fairs, but by the end of the 17th century there was some musical theatre at the university on special occasions. In 1693 the new elector at Dresden, Johann Georg IV, allowed his Kapellmeister, N. A. Strungk, to organize an Italian opera company to perform at Leipzig during the fairs. Strungk built a new theatre, the Opernhaus auf dem Brühl, inaugurated on 8 May 1693 with his own *Alceste*. Direction passed to Telemann in 1702; he left for Sorau in 1705 but continued to supply operas as late as 1719 (*Die Satyren in Arcadien*).

The Italian company was dissolved in 1720. Between then and the Seven Years War travelling companies, both German and Italian, visited Leipzig. In 1744 Pietro

Mingotti set up a wooden theatre in the Reithaus at the Rannstadt Gate, where his small company performed serious and comic Italian opera during the Easter fair. He returned, sometimes with his brother Angelo, four times in the next seven years; at the Easter fair in 1746 the elector himself attended Mingotti's performances.

In 1750 Heinrich Gottlieb Koch organized a German company at Leipzig and gave the English ballad opera *The Devil to Pay* in Borck's German translation. Koch then had the local poet C. F. Weisse retranslate the work, and his music director, J. G. Standfuss, composed new music. The success of the work at its first performance on 6 October 1752 began a new era of vernacular comic opera in Germany and prompted a vitriolic pamphlet war, initiated by J. G. Gottsched, university professor and self-appointed guardian of public morals. The lively exchange, which came to involve the Dresden court itself, ended with the Seven Years War and Koch's departure from Leipzig in 1756.

1. *'Die verwandelten Weiber' (Johann Adam Hiller), Act 1 scene vii: engraving by J. G. Geyser from Christian Felix Weisse, 'Komische Opern', ii (Leipzig, 1777)*

On his return after the war, Koch brought together Weisse and the composer J. A. Hiller, who conducted the Grosses Konzert at Leipzig, to create a new version of *Der Teufel ist los* (renamed *Die verwandelten Weiber*) in 1766. A fruitful period of collaboration followed. The works they produced, together with those

of Hiller's pupil C. G. Neefe and the Weimar composer E. W. Wolf, established the *komische Oper* as a distinctive sub-genre of cheerful, rustic plays interspersed with songs in a popular style, often resembling folksongs.

Since 1750 Koch had performed at Leipzig in the Theater an Quandts Hof in the Nicolaistrasse, built in the late 1740s to a plan, suggested by Gottsched, that involved a semicircular amphitheatre. A new theatre, the Theater am Rannstädter Tor, seating 1200, was constructed in 1766. This came to be known as Koch's Theatre, but the seasonal nature of the Leipzig theatrical year, along with competition from other German companies, led Koch to transfer his activities to Berlin by 1773. The Döbbelin company took over Koch's Theatre but eventually yielded to the stiff competition of the Seyler company, which first came to Leipzig in October 1774. Seyler had to perform at the Theater vor dem Grimma'schen Tor, a poor edifice built in 1770, but soon wrested Koch's Theatre from Döbbelin. When Seyler left for the Rhineland in 1776, a German company formed by Pasquale Bondini began coming from Dresden to perform at the fairs. In 1782 and ensuing years Bondini sent an Italian company from Prague to Leipzig for the summer; under Domenico Guardasoni's direction they brought *Don Giovanni* and *Figaro* in 1788. All these visiting troupes relied on a rather undistinguished local orchestra that numbered 21 in 1786; the chorus, made up of students, sang from behind the wings.

In 1786 Franz Seconda took over Bondini's German troupe. He gave spoken plays during the Easter and Michaelmas fairs, in winter rented the playhouse to his brother Joseph who gave German operas, and in summer turned the house over to Guardasoni's *buffa* troupe. This pattern continued until 1796, when other German companies replaced Joseph Seconda's troupe. In that year, too, the city government acquired and enlarged Koch's Theatre.

2. AFTER 1800. With the renovation and extension of Koch's Theatre completed, a permanent Stadttheater with an established company was founded in Leipzig in 1817, and the era of touring opera companies came to an end. The first leaseholder of the new theatre, until 1828, was Karl Theodor von Küstner, and under the first directors, Friedrich Schneider (1817–21), Heinrich Aloys Präger (1821–8) and Marschner (1827–31), the theatre became a centre for the performance of the Romantic operas of Weber, Spohr and Marschner himself. Among singers in Leipzig at this time were the young Wilhelmine Schröder-Devrient and Henriette Sontag. Economic difficulties between 1828 and 1832 forced the theatre to resume guest performances, including some by the Magdeburg company, and after 1829 Leipzig was in fact a branch of the Dresden Hoftheater, with Heinrich Dorn and Francesco Morlacchi as musical directors.

In 1833 Albert Lortzing was engaged as actor and singer at the Stadttheater, and was briefly Kapellmeister (1844–5). Eight of his operas had their premières there, including *Zar und Zimmermann* (1837), *Hans Sachs* (1840) and *Der Wildschütz* (1842). With Julius Rietz as Kapellmeister (1847–54) the long-delayed first performance of Schumann's only opera, *Genoveva*, took place in 1850, a theatrical event of the highest importance. In 1853–4 the first of Wagner's operas to be performed in his native city, *Tannhäuser* and *Lohen-*

2. Interior of the Neues Stadttheater, Leipzig, designed by C. F. Langhans and inaugurated in 1867: engraving from the Leipzig 'Illustrirte Zeitung' (1869)

grin, were produced, and Verdi entered the repertory of the Leipzig opera with *Ernani* in 1858.

By this time the building had become inadequate for the requirements of a large and expanding city, and 1865–7 the Neues Theater, designed by C. F. Langhans, was erected in the Augustusplatz (fig.2). Because of its large size it was used mainly by the opera company, while the older building (Altes Theater) was now seldom used for opera, although works by Mozart and *Spielopern* were sometimes produced there. Angelo Neumann, who was opera director from 1876 to 1882, introduced a great Wagnerian epoch at Leipzig with the third complete production (following those at Bayreuth and Munich) of the *Ring*, conducted by Joseph Sucher. Important conductors at this time included Anton Seidl (1879–82), Arthur Nikisch (chorus master 1878–82, principal Kapellmeister 1882–9) and Gustav Mahler (1886–8; the first performance of his version of Weber's *Die drei Pintos* was given at Leipzig in 1888).

In 1910 the leasing system in Leipzig was abandoned, and the city took responsibility for the administration of both its theatres. The first director under the new regime was Max Martersteig, who appointed Otto Lohse as director of opera and Kapellmeister (1912–23). Lohse's special enthusiasm was for naturalistic music drama, and in the first two decades of the 20th century (particularly with Ernst Lert as principal director of productions, 1912–19) Leipzig took the lead in reforming traditions of performing Mozart's operas. Under Guido Barthol (Intendant 1919–32) and Gustav Brecher (director of opera and Generalmusikdirektor 1923–33) there were premières of operas by Krenek (*Jonny spielt auf*, 1927; *Leben des Orest*, 1930) and Weill (*Der Zar*

lässt sich photographieren, 1928; *Aufstieg und Fall der Stadt Mahagonny*, 1930). With *Tamerlano* in 1926 the company resumed its Handel productions, which had begun at the end of the 19th century. As Generalmusikdirektor during a difficult period (1933–51), Paul Schmitz was able to organize a Mozart festival (1941) and to put on new works. There was a large-scale Wagner festival in 1938, with two complete cycles of the composer's stage works in chronological order.

In December 1943 all the buildings of the Städtisches Theater Leipzig were destroyed, and the rebuilding of an opera repertory after the war began in the Drei Linden variety theatre with *Fidelio* on 29 July 1945. The opera house in the Karl-Marx-Platz (now known again by its former name, the Augustusplatz), on the site of the former Neues Theater, was the first new theatre built in East Germany; it opened on 8 October 1960 with Wagner's *Die Meistersinger*. The temporary Drei Linden theatre was then renamed first the Kleines Haus and in 1964 the Musikalische Komödie. It has 1105 seats and is used mainly for operettas and musicals; *Spielopern* and contemporary opera were also presented there until 1980. From 1958 to 1989 all the Leipzig theatres, including those for spoken drama, came under a single organization, with Karl Kayser as Generalintendant. Heinz Rückert, director from 1947 to 1951, was succeeded by Heinrich Voigt (1950–59), Joachim Herz (1959–76) and Günther Lohse, who was made chief director of productions in 1976. Herz, a pupil of Felsenstein, applied the latter's principles of realistic music drama to the conditions of repertory theatre. With major productions of Mozart, Wagner (*Meistersinger* and the *Ring*) and Strauss, as well as revivals of forgotten works (including Weill's *Mahagonny*, which had caused an uproar at its Leipzig première in 1930), he helped the Leipzig opera to attain international standing, working with such conductors as Rolf Reuter, Václav Neumann, Paul Schmitz and Gert Bahner. The Leipzig Gewandhaus Orchestra plays in what is Germany's largest opera house.

In 1990 the composer Udo Zimmermann was made Intendant of the Leipzig opera, Fritz Hennenberg its chief dramatic adviser, Uwe Wand (first engaged in 1976) director of opera and Lothar Zagrosek Generalmusikdirektor; Zagrosek had been preceded in that post by Helmut Seydelmann (1951–62) and Johannes Winkler (1986–9), among others. Links with theatres in Moscow, Brno and Łódź, and guest performances in many European countries, have confirmed the international reputation of the company. Besides its own traditions of Mozart, Lortzing and Wagner, its repertory has placed emphasis on Slavonic (particularly Soviet Russian) and contemporary opera. Important premières, in addition to those mentioned above, have included works by Lehár, Weingartner, Eugen d'Albert, Reznicek, Dressel, Humperdinck, Orff and Alan Bush.

*

TO 1800

H. Blümer: *Geschichte des Theaters in Leipzig* (Leipzig, 1818)

G. Wustmann: *Quellen zur Geschichte Leipzigs: Veröffentlichungen aus dem Archiv und der Bibliothek der Stadt Leipzig* (Leipzig, 1889–95)

F. Berend: *Nicolaus Adam Strungk, 1640–1700: sein Leben und seine Werke, mit Beiträgen zur Geschichte der Musik und des Theaters in Celle, Hannover und Leipzig* (Freiburg, 1915)

E. H. Mueller von Asow: *Angelo und Pietro Mingotti: ein Beitrag zur Geschichte der Oper im XVIII. Jahrhundert* (Dresden, 1917)

G. F. Schmidt: 'Die älteste deutsche Oper in Leipzig am Ende des 17. und Anfang des 18. Jahrhunderts', *Festschrift zum 50. Geburtstag Adolf Sandberger* (Munich, 1918)

F. Reuter: *Die Geschichte der deutschen Oper in Leipzig (1693–1720)* (diss., U. of Leipzig, 1922)

A. Schering: *Musikgeschichte Leipzigs, iii: Das Zeitalter Johann Sebastian Bachs und Johann Adam Hillers (von 1723 bis 1800)* (Leipzig, 1941)

G. Rudloff-Hille: 'Das Leipziger Theater von 1766', *Maske und Kothurn*, xiv (1968), 217–38

——: *Das Theater auf der Ranstädter Bastei* (Leipzig, 1969)

B. van Boer: 'Coffey's *The Devil to Pay*, the Comic War, and the Emergence of the German *Singspiel*', *Journal of Musicological Research*, viii (1988), 119–39

AFTER 1800

K. T. Küstner: *Rückblick auf das Leipziger Stadttheater* (Leipzig, 1830)

E. Kneschke: *Zur Geschichte des Theaters und der Musik in Leipzig* (Leipzig, 1864)

G. H. Müller: *Das Stadttheater zu Leipzig* (Leipzig, 1887 and 91)

Jahresbericht der Städtischen Theater, i–xxiii (Leipzig, 1912–34)

F. Schulze: *Hundert Jahre Leipziger Stadttheater* (Leipzig, 1917)

Festschrift zur Eröffnung des neuen Leipziger Opernhauses (Leipzig, 1960)

'Leipzig', *Friedrichs Opernlexikon* (Velber, 1969) [with list of first performances]

I. Hempel and G. Hempel: *Musikstadt Leipzig* (Leipzig, 2/1984)

H. Seeger: *Opernlexikon* (Berlin, 1989)

THOMAS BAUMAN (1), DIETER HÄRTWIG (2)

Leisner, Emmi (*b* Flensburg, 8 Aug 1885; *d* Flensburg, 11 Jan 1958). German contralto. She came from a musical family and was trained first as a pianist. In Berlin she studied singing with Helene Breest and made her concert début in 1911. The following year she sang Gluck's Orpheus at Hellerau in the production by Alphonse Appia, and after appearances in Leipzig and Frankfurt was engaged by the Berlin Hofoper where she remained from 1913 to 1921. Her roles there included Amneris, Carmen, Brangäne and Fricka, and in 1925 she enjoyed a special success as Erda at Bayreuth. During the 1930s she confined herself increasingly to concert and oratorio work. At her London appearance in 1931 Ernest Newman found 'some noble notes' but little else to admire. Her records tend to support this judgment: the tone is deep and sumptuous, and so it remained until an advanced age, but her style is undependable and her interpretations lack interest.

J. B. STEANE

Leitmotif (from Ger. *Leitmotiv*: 'leading motif'). A term adopted by early commentators on Wagner's music dramas to highlight what they believed to be the most important feature contributing to comprehensibility and expressive intensity in those works. A leitmotif is a theme, or other coherent musical idea, clearly defined so as to retain its identity if modified on subsequent appearances, whose purpose is to represent or symbolize a person, object, place, idea, state of mind, supernatural force or any other ingredient in a dramatic work. The leitmotif may be musically unaltered on its return, or altered in rhythm, intervallic structure, harmony, orchestration or accompaniment, and may also be combined with other leitmotifs in order to suggest a new dramatic situation. A leitmotif is to be distinguished from a reminiscence motif (*Erinnerungsmotiv*), which, in earlier operas and in Wagner's works up to and including *Lohengrin*, tends to punctuate the musical design rather than provide the principal, 'leading' thematic premises for that design.

The earliest known use of the term 'leitmotif' (see Grey 1988) is by the music historian A. W. Ambros, who wrote, in or before 1865, that both Wagner in his operas and Liszt in his symphonic poems 'seek to establish a higher unity across the whole by means of consistent leitmotifs' (*durchgehende Leitmotive*). From Ambros the term gravitated, via F. W. Jähns's study of Weber (1871) to Hans von Wolzogen's thematic guide to the *Ring*, published in 1876 – the year of the cycle's first complete performance. Wagner used it in print in his essay *Über die Anwendung der Musik auf das Drama* (1879), in the course of a complaint that 'one of my younger friends [presumably Wolzogen] ... has devoted some attention to the characteristics of "leitmotifs", as he calls them, but has treated them more from the point of view of their dramatic import and effect than as elements of the musical structure'.

The use of the term 'motif' in writing about music goes back at least as far as the *Encyclopédie* (1765), and before 1879 Wagner had employed a variety of expressions when discussing thematic elements in his works: 'melodisches Moment', 'thematisches Motiv', 'Ahnungsmotiv', 'Grundthema', 'Hauptmotiv'. As Wagner's comments in 1879 indicate, he sensed that Wolzogen, whose 'guide' was little more than a pamphlet, was in danger of over-simplifying and trivializing his achievements in the interests of a desire to make the music dramas more accessible; his remarks reinforce the fact that 'leitmotif', and its subsequent usage, tells us as much (if not more) about the reception of his works as about his working methods or creative intentions.

Wagner, with his wide experience as a conductor, was undoubtedly aware of the extensive use of reminiscence motifs in earlier opera from Méhul and Cherubini to Marschner and Spohr, and his close friend, Theodor Uhlig, in writings on *Tannhäuser* and *Lohengrin*, had drawn attention to the role of recurrent thematic elements in Wagner's own work as early as 1850. Indeed, although Wagner was particularly concerned in *Oper und Drama* (written in 1851, before he had begun any extensive compositional work on the *Ring* cycle) to underline the importance of formal units (periods) constructed to ensure that all aspects of the music responded as vividly as possible to the promptings of the text, in practice he still recognized the necessity for a small number of easily identifiable and malleable motifs, along the lines of Beethoven's most pithy and memorable thematic cells. These would, however, originate in a melody quite different from the four-square and often florid vocal phrases of traditional opera, and embody such a power and directness of expression that the emotion concerned would be recalled when the motif itself returned, even if action or text no longer alluded directly to its original associations.

A major problem for motif-labellers has been that this original association is almost always multivalent – the music depicting the grandeur of Valhalla also portrays the nobility of Wotan, for example – and might well be ambiguous. It is now generally accepted that Wolzogen mislabelled the *Ring*'s principal love motif as 'Flight', taking over this designation from an earlier commentary by Gottlieb Federlein (1871). And the motif which, after Wolzogen, is invariably designated 'Redemption through Love' was seen by Wagner himself – at least in a letter of 1875 – as representing the 'glorification of Brünnhilde'. Such factors indicate why most commentators on Wagner express reservations about motif-labelling while finding it difficult to discard the activity altogether. After all, despite his own reservations about Wolzogen's efforts, Wagner's presentation and manipulation of his thematic material lay at the heart of his musico-dramatic technique, as he made clear in *Über die Anwendung der Musik auf das Drama*.

Discussing the 'simple nature-motif' (ex.1) and the

Ex.1

'equally simple motif' heard 'at the first appearance of the gods' castle Valhalla in the morning sunlight' in *Das Rheingold* (ex.2: Wagner transposed the motif from D♭

Ex.2

to C for ease of comparison), Wagner observes that 'having developed both these motifs in close correspondence with the mounting passions of the action, I was now able [in *Die Walküre*, Act 2] to link them – with the aid of a strangely distant harmonization – to paint a far clearer picture of Wotan's sombre and desperate suffering than his own words ever could' (ex.3). Later in the essay, seeking to emphasize the structural rather than the semantic role of his motivic techniques, Wagner describes how the 'remarkably simple' motif of the Rhinemaidens' innocent jubilation (ex.4) recurs in varied guises throughout the drama until, in Hagen's 'Watch' (*Götterdämmerung*, Act 1), 'it is

Ex.3

Ex.4

Rhein - gold!   Rhein - gold!

Ex.5

heard in a form which, to my mind at least, would be unthinkable in a symphonic movement' (ex.5). Wagner's point is that the malevolent, distorted versions of the gold motif that pervade the music at this point would sound like 'empty sensationalism' in a symphony, but the dramatic context justifies the nature of the musical transformation and the structural emphasis which requires its protracted employment in this 'distorted' form.

Wagner himself understandably sought to underline such larger-scale structural concerns. But the concentration of Wolzogen and others on the identification of local motivic associations is no less understandable, since their principal purpose was not to provide the most far-reaching analysis but to defend the composer against charges of illogicality and incomprehensibility. Just as commentaries on symphonies and sonatas can be valuable on all levels, from simple, non-technical programme notes to elaborate analyses (provided the simple and the elaborate are not confused), so there is room, and need, for such variety in commentaries on opera. There is no evidence that the activities of Wolzogen and his followers seriously inhibited attempts at more sophisticated analytical studies of Wagner's harmonic and formal procedures, though these were slower to emerge. And while the more sophisticated anti-Wagnerians were able to use such naive motif-spotting as Wolzogen's to support arguments about the essential crudity of Wagner's compositional principles (Hanslick, for example, wrote in praise of Verdi's *Falstaff* that 'nowhere is the memory spoonfed by leitmotifs'), many Wagner scholars have built on the foundations laid by Wolzogen, and Wagner himself, to refine and elaborate the study of musical meaning in the music dramas, and the role that leitmotifs play in establishing that meaning. It is motivic evolution and development, in the context of large-scale tonal structuring and formal organization, that has become the focus of attention in the attempt to understand the ways in which Wagner's musical language, and his attitude to drama, changed over the years between *Das Rheingold* and *Parsifal*.

From the very beginning of scene i of *Das Rheingold*, motifs 'lead' in the sense that they do not merely pervade the musical fabric but establish its expressive atmosphere and formal processes. They do not invariably originate in the vocal line as *Oper und Drama* had prescribed, and Wagner soon begins to move beyond their exact or varied repetition at textually appropriate moments into the kind of transformation that creates deeper dramatic resonances and larger-scale musical continuities, suggesting that musical thinking itself is beginning to promote dramatic associations. At the end of scene i of *Das Rheingold*, the motif associated with the ring, and with the world's wealth (Wagner's own interpretation of the idea, according to his sketches), is transformed orchestrally into the Valhalla motif at the start of scene ii, a process leading the listener to connect Alberich's precious acquisition with Wotan's no less highly valued possession, and the power they both embody. As the cycle proceeds, a clear contrast emerges between, on the one hand, the immediate connection of word – or visual image – and tone that first fixes important motivic elements and, on the other hand, the consequent power of music to reinforce a connection that text and action may leave implicit: for example, the use of Alberich's curse when Fafner kills Fasolt (*Das Rheingold*, scene iv), and the references to the Siegfried motif when Brünnhilde and Wotan proclaim the need for a fearless hero (*Die Walküre*, Act 3).

The interruption of work on the *Ring* in 1857 brought a significant change of direction. Up to that point, Wagner's aesthetic had centred on the belief that the most profound art work was a theatrical event to which words and music made significant contributions. But it now began to evolve, under the impact of Schopenhauer, and the sheer force of his own musical inspiration, to the point where music became the central feature – however important the initial conception of theatrical event and text remained in relation to the music he eventually composed. The result, in simple terms, is that leitmotifs become even less specific in meaning and even more subject to musical elaboration; in all the later dramas there is a sense in which the motifs 'lead' the music beyond literal and immediate signification while still, inevitably, remaining linked to, and helping to determine, the progress of the drama. Scholars have wrestled with the inherent complexity of this interaction between the 'symphonic' and the 'dramatic'. In particular, Ernst Kurth (1920) proposed a distinction between leitmotifs, which reflect the dramatic situation directly, and 'developmental motifs' (*Entwicklungsmotive*), which achieve independence not only of such representational functions but also of the kind of clearcut shaping that makes a leitmotif easily identifiable. 'Developmental motifs' are figures that promote the ongoing evolution of the music – a process quite distinct from the actual development (by sequential transposition or any other variation procedure) of the leitmotifs themselves.

Kurth recognized that leitmotivic analysis on its own cannot possibly do justice to the significatory power of Wagner's music. More recently, Carolyn Abbate (1989) has declared that his music 'actually projects poetry and stage action in ways far beyond motivic signs'; she has also asserted that 'Wagner's motifs have no referential meaning; they may, and of course do, absorb meaning at exceptional and solemn moments, by being used with elaborate calculation as signs, but unless purposely maintained in this artificial state, they shed their specific poetic meaning and revert to their natural state as

musical thoughts'. No doubt an analysis of *Tristan* that doggedly attempted to confine the meaning of every occurrence of the opening cello phrase to 'Tristan's suffering', or any other of the various tags that have been attached to it, would be absurdly naive and literal. But variation and diversity of meaning is not to be confused with meaninglessness; it seems undeniable that the listener 'comprehends' the intense, elaborate developments and derivations in *Tristan* subliminally, sensing meaning through the sheer force and insistence of its evolving musical logic.

One result of the increasing flexibility of motivic signification in the later Wagner is that the motifs themselves seem to invite reduction to a few unifying archetypes. Robert Donington, Deryck Cooke, Carl Dahlhaus and many others have shown how a few 'primal motifs' in the *Ring* – Donington (1974) has four, featuring Broken Chords, Conjunct Motion, Chromatic Intervals, and Changing Notes – may be regarded as generating a great number of offshoots. Robin Holloway (1986) has argued that in *Parsifal*, even more pervasively than in the *Ring* or *Tristan*, the leitmotifs grow from 'a sonorous image-cluster ... the nucleus that gives life to the work's expressive substance'. Holloway's interpretation illustrates the tendency of leitmotif analysis to seek out ever more intricate and all-embracing unifying factors. The role of leitmotif in Wagner's compositional design also remains a central topic in discussion of the extent to which his structures are 'tightly' or 'loosely' knit (see Abbate 1989, 1991). No less valuable has been the concern of scholars working in the field of German studies to re-examine the significance of Wagner's motivic theory and practice in the light of evolving concepts of drama (see Brown 1991).

One example of Wagner's importance in the history of music is the difficulty of avoiding the concept of leitmotif in studies of so many of his contemporaries and successors. Roger Parker has found it useful to discuss Verdi's *Aida* in the light of the observation that 'particularly in its treatment of "motive" and "recurring theme", it is the most nearly Wagnerian of Verdi's operas' (1989). Direct influence or attempted imitation are not implied in this case, but with slightly later composers the probability of literal influence is much stronger, whether the composer is relatively close in style to Wagner, as Richard Strauss was in *Salome* and *Elektra*, or strikingly distant, as with Debussy in *Pelléas et Mélisande*. There are in fact very few composers of significance on whom Wagner's stylistic influence was direct and extensive: Humperdinck is one such.

These composers' operas show that, whatever the musical style, through-composition renders some degree of leitmotivic working a useful means of achieving continuity and directedness. Yet discussion of the topic is bedevilled by the problems facing motivic analysis in general: that is, of recognizing the point at which 'connection' and 'derivation' cease to be more convincing than 'contrast' and 'difference'. John Tyrrell (1982) comments on K. H. Wörner's attempt to demonstrate all-embracing thematic connections in Janáček's *Kát'a Kabanová* that 'too wide an interpretation of permissible manipulations allows almost anything to creep in'. By contrast, Peter Evans (1979) has shown how the presence of pervasive motivic working can be plausibly demonstrated in Britten's operas, despite a style that owes more to Verdi than to Wagner.

George Perle (1980) has attempted to argue that

Alban Berg, in *Wozzeck*, used the leitmotif principle more effectively – that is, less predictably and mechanically – than Wagner himself had done. In his discussions of *Wozzeck* and *Lulu* Perle also distinguishes between leitmotif and 'Leitsektion': 'a total musical complex' that serves a referential function. The notion of referential musical function may be further elaborated if not only exact or near-exact recurrences but also the equivalences that are revealed by reduction to the unordered collections known as pitch-class sets are admitted: Allen Forte's work on *Wozzeck* (1985) and *Tristan* (1988) represents the most extensive demonstration of that procedure. Such manipulations might appear to have little to do with the leitmotif principle as it relates to Wagner, moving away as they do from the particular profile of the theme on the musical surface. So, too, Schoenberg's *Erwartung*, in its atonal athematicism, might be felt to be more a reaction against Wagner's influence than a celebration of it. Yet Carl Dahlhaus contends that the brief structural segments of *Erwartung*, 'not unlike Wagnerian periods, are not infrequently defined by means of a characteristic musical idea, which constitutes the predominant motif, albeit not the only one' (1987). If motivic elaboration of any kind is seen in terms of the leitmotif principle, then it becomes possible to extend the range of Wagner's 'influence' still further. The most ambitious operatic enterprise of the late 20th century, Stockhausen's *Licht*, could scarcely be less Wagnerian in style, yet the material of the entire seven-opera cycle derives from a 'super-formula', in which melodies representing the three central characters, Michael, Eva and Luzifer, are superimposed. The virtually constant presence, in the background, of these melodies may represent an approach to motivic composition very different from that of Wagner (see Kohl 1990). We might nevertheless sense a genuine bond with those 'plastic nature motifs, which, by becoming increasingly individualized, were to serve as the bearers of the emotional subcurrents within the broad-based plot and the moods expressed therein', to which Wagner referred in 1871, in the *Epilogischer Bericht* on the *Ring*, when he attempted to describe what he believed his first task had been when embarking on the work almost 20 years before.

*

A. W. Ambros: *Culturhistorische Bilder aus dem Musikleben der Gegenwart* (Leipzig, 1860, 2/1865)

F. Stade: 'Zur Wagner-Frage', *Musikalisches Wochenblatt*, i (1870), 529–95 passim

G. Federlein: '"Das Rheingold" von Richard Wagner: Versuch einer musikalischen Interpretation', *Musikalisches Wochenblatt*, ii (1871), 210–389 passim

F. W. Jähns: *Carl Maria von Weber in seinen Werken* (Berlin, 1871)

R. Wagner: *Gesammelte Schriften und Dichtungen* (Leipzig, 1871–83, 4/1907), iv, vi, x [incl. *Oper und Drama* (1851), *Epilogischer Bericht* (1871), *Über die Anwendung der Musik auf das Drama* (1879)]

G. Federlein: '"Die Walküre" von Richard Wagner: Versuch einer musikalischen Interpretation', *Musikalisches Wochenblatt*, iii (1872), 211–503 passim

H. von Wolzogen: *Thematischer Leitfaden durch die Musik von R. Wagners Festspiel 'Der Ring des Nibelungen'* (Leipzig, 1876; Eng. trans., 1882)

——: 'Die Motive in Wagners "Götterdämmerung"', *Musikalisches Wochenblatt*, viii (1877), 109–446 passim; ix (1878), 430–542 passim; x (1879), 249–531 passim

J. von Santen-Kolff: 'Erinnerungsmotiv-Leitmotiv', *Musikalisches Wochenblatt*, xiv (1883), 341–463 passim; xv (1884), 201–319

——: 'Geschichtliches und Aesthetisches über das Erinnerungsmotiv', *Bayreuther Blätter*, viii (1885)

T. Uhlig: *Musikalische Schriften* (Regensburg, 1913)

M. Seiling: 'Das indirekte Leitmotiv', *Bayreuther Blätter*, xl (1917)

R. Meister: 'Die Bedeutung der Leitmotive im Drama', *Bayreuther Blätter*, xli (1918)

E. Kurth: *Romantische Harmonik und ihre Krise in Wagners 'Tristan'* (Berne, 1920)

G. Abraham: 'The Leit-motif since Wagner', *ML*, vi (1925), 175–90

R. Engländer: 'Zur Geschichte des Leitmotivs', *ZMw*, xiv (1931–2), 356–7

K. H. Wörner: 'Beiträge zur Geschichte des Leitmotivs in der Oper', *ZMw*, xiv (1931–2), 151–72

L. Sabaneyev: 'Remarks on the Leit-motif', *ML*, xiii (1932), 200–06

H. Pleasants, ed.: *Eduard Hanslick: Vienna's Golden Years of Music 1850–1900* (New York, 1950, 2/1963 as *Music Criticisms 1846–99*) [selected writings]

J. M. Stein: *Richard Wagner and the Synthesis of the Arts* (Detroit, 1960)

J. Matter: 'La fonction psychologique du leitmotiv wagnérien', *SMz*, ci (1961), 317–20

R. Donington: *Wagner's 'Ring' and its Symbols* (London, 1963, 3/1974)

G. Knepler: 'Richard Wagners musikalische Gestaltungsprinzipien', *BMw*, v (1963), 33–43

C. Dahlhaus: *Die Musikdramen Richard Wagners* (Velber, 1971; Eng. trans., 1979)

——: *Zwischen Romantik und Moderne: Vier Studien zur Musikgeschichte des späteren 19. Jahrhunderts* (Munich, 1974; Eng. trans. 1980)

F. Noske: *The Signifier and the Signified: Studies in the Operas of Mozart and Verdi* (The Hague, 1977)

C. Dahlhaus: 'Ausdrucksprinzip und Orchesterpolyphonie in Schönbergs "Erwartung"', *Schönberg und andere: gesammelte Aufsätze zur neuen Musik* (Mainz, 1978), 189–94; Eng. trans., in *Schoenberg and the New Music* (Cambridge, 1987), 149–55

D. Cooke: *I Saw the World End: a Study of Wagner's 'Ring'* (London, 1979)

——: 'Wagner's Musical Language', *The Wagner Companion*, ed. P. Burbridge and R. Sutton (London, 1979), 225–68

P. Evans: *The Music of Benjamin Britten* (London, 1979, 2/1989)

C. Dahlhaus: *Die Musik des 19. Jahrhunderts* (Wiesbaden, 1980; Eng. trans., 1989)

G. Perle: *The Operas of Alban Berg*, i: '*Wozzeck*' (Berkeley, 1980)

J. Deathridge: Review of Wagner publications, *19th Century Music*, v (1981–2), 81–9

D. Borchmeyer: *Das Theater Richard Wagners: Idee – Dichtung – Wirkung* (Stuttgart, 1982)

J. Tyrrell: *Leoš Janáček: Kát'a Kabanová* (Cambridge, 1982)

R. Parker and M. Brown: 'Motivic and Tonal Interaction in Verdi's "Un ballo in maschera"', *JAMS*, xxxvi (1983), 243–65

J. Deathridge and C. Dahlhaus: *The New Grove Wagner* (London, 1984)

B. Millington: *Wagner* (London, 1984)

P. Britton: 'Stockhausen's Path to Opera', *MT*, cxxvi (1985), 515–21

A. Forte: 'Tonality, Symbol and Structural Levels in Berg's "Wozzeck"', *MQ*, lxxi (1985)

A. D. McCredie: 'Leitmotive: Wagner's Points of Departure and their Antecedents', *MMA*, xiv (1985), 1–28

R. Holloway: 'Experiencing Music and Imagery in "Parsifal"', *Parsifal*, ed. N. John (London, 1986), 23–41

A. Forte: 'New Approaches to the Linear Analysis of Music', *JAMS*, xli (1988), 315–48 [pp.324–38 concern the *Tristan* prelude]

T. S. Grey: *Richard Wagner and the Aesthetics of Form in the mid-19th Century (1840–60)* (diss., U. of California, Berkeley, 1988)

A. Groos and R. Parker, eds.: *Reading Opera* (Princeton, 1988)

C. Abbate: 'Wagner, "On Modulation" and "Tristan"', *COJ*, i (1989), 33–58

R. Langham Smith: 'Motives and Symbols', *Claude Debussy: Pelléas et Mélisande*, ed. R. Nichols and R. Langham Smith (Cambridge, 1989), 78–106

R. Parker: 'Motives and Recurring Themes in *Aida*', *Analyzing Opera*, ed. C. Abbate and R. Parker (Berkeley, 1989), 222–38

D. Puffett: '"Salome" as Music Drama', *Richard Strauss: Salome* (Cambridge, 1989), 58–87

S. Corse: *Wagner and the New Consciousness: Language and Love in the 'Ring'* (London and Toronto, 1990)

A. Forte: 'Musorgsky as Modernist: the Phantasmic Episode in "Boris Godunov"', *Music Analysis*, ix (1990), 3–45

J. Kohl: 'Into the Middleground: Formula Syntax in Stockhausen's *Licht*', *PNM*, xxviii (1990), 262–91

P. McCreless: 'Motive and Magic: a Referential Dyad in Parsifal', *Music Analysis*, ix (1990), 227–65

J. Riedlbauer: 'Erinnerungsmotive in Wagners "Der Ring des Nibelungen" ', *MQ*, lxxiv (1990), 18–30
C. Abbate: *Unsung Voices: Opera and Musical Narrative in the 19th Century* (Princeton, 1991)
H. M. Brown: *Leitmotiv and Drama: Wagner, Brecht and the Limits of 'Epic' Theatre* (Oxford, 1991)
M. C. Tusa: *Euryanthe and Carl Maria von Weber's Dramaturgy of German Opera* (Oxford, 1991)   ARNOLD WHITTALL

Leitner, Ferdinand (*b* Berlin, 4 March 1912). German conductor. He studied at the Berlin Hochschule für Musik and after working as an accompanist made his conducting début in 1943 at the Nollendorf Theater, Berlin. He was conductor at the Hamburg Staatsoper, 1945–6, and at the Munich Staatsoper, 1946–7. For more than 20 years he held an influential appointment at the Stuttgart Staatsoper, first as director of opera (from 1947), then as general music director (1950–69). He helped to make Stuttgart a leading European centre for opera, conducting 13 productions by Wieland Wagner (the last was Berg's *Lulu* in 1966) and many others by Günther Rennert, also the premières of Orff's *Oedipus der Tyrann* (1959) and *Prometheus* (1968). Leitner took the Stuttgart company to other European centres, and more than once to Vienna, Paris and Edinburgh (1958 and 1966).

He made annual visits to conduct German seasons at the Teatro Colón, Buenos Aires, for more than a decade, and continued appearances there into the 1980s, as he did at the Chicago Lyric Opera from 1969 (*Don Giovanni*) – including the Peter Sellars production of *Tannhäuser* (1988). He was principal conductor at the Zürich Opera, 1969–84, and made frequent appearances in Italy and elsewhere, especially in the operas of Mozart, Wagner, Strauss and Berg that were central to his repertory. His recordings include a Cologne broadcast performance of *Alcina* with Joan Sutherland, Orff's *Antigonae* and *Prometheus*, and the first recording of Busoni's *Doktor Faust* (1969). Leitner prefers to avoid emotional excess in his performances, and has a particular mastery in accompanying singers without restricting the music's symphonic character.

WOLFRAM SCHWINGER, NOËL GOODWIN

Lelio, Umberto di. *See* DI LELIO, UMBERTO.

Lemaire, Ferdinand (*fl* 1860–70). French librettist. When Saint-Saëns was planning to write an oratorio in the 1860s, an 'old music-lover' suggested the story of Samson, drawing attention to Voltaire's unperformed opera libretto of 1733. This libretto did not appeal to Saint-Saëns and subsequently he invited Lemaire to help him draft a suitable text. Lemaire, a young Creole from Martinique who had married a cousin of Saint-Saëns' wife, dabbled in poetry; the composer liked him, and showed an appreciation of his talent by setting two of his poems. Lemaire willingly agreed to collaborate, but insisted that the work should be an opera rather than an oratorio. Saint-Saëns accepted the proposal, and when they set to work on *Samson et Dalila* the composer drafted the plan while Lemaire was responsible for the versification. However, at the long-delayed first performance in Weimar (1877), a German translation was used and the French text was not heard in France until 1890.

H. Collet: '*Samson et Dalila*' *de C. Saint-Saëns* (Paris, 1922)
J. Harding: *Saint-Saëns and his Circle* (London, 1965)
CHRISTOPHER SMITH

Lemaure, Catherine-Nicole (*b* Paris, 3 Aug 1704; *d* Paris, 1786). French soprano. Entering the Paris Opéra chorus in about 1719, she sang Astraea in the 1721–2 revival of Lully's *Phaëton* in December, and was promoted to sing Libya in January. She quickly came to sing such principal parts as Hippodamie in the première of Mouret's *Pirithoüs* and the title role in Lacoste's *Philomèle* (both 1723). Her temperament was capricious and volatile, however, and she left the Opéra without warning in 1725 after a performance of Destouches and Lalande's *Les élémens*. She returned in 1726, only to cause an uproar when her rivalry with Mlle Pélissier caused acrimonious disputes among 'les politiques de l'Opéra' during the opening run of Francoeur and Rebel's *Pirame et Thisbé*. Lemaure disappeared again in 1727–30, returning to sing in Campra's *Hésione*. She sang Oriane (Lully's *Amadis*, 1731) with triumphant success, created Iphise (Montéclair's *Jephté*, 1732) and sang the title role in Destouches' *Issé* (1733 revival), in which she was considered 'miraculeuse' by Formont (see Besterman). She sang Iphigenia in the 1734 revival of Desmarets' *Iphigénie en Tauride*. Threatened with imprisonment if she did not appear in the 1735 revival of *Jephté*, Lemaure deliberately sang poorly and was hissed by the parterre. When she refused to continue, she was escorted (still in costume) to Fort l'Evêque, where she was detained overnight before returning the following day to take up her role with better grace. Her 1740 performances of Iphise and Oriane were greeted with enthusiastic ovations, and in 1744 she supplanted Pélissier as Iphise in Rameau's *Dardanus*, a role Pélissier had created.

Her personal fascination in performance, the 'transcendent beauty' of her voice, and the prodigious transformation which came over her as soon as she began to sing on stage, were vividly described by La Borde. Voltaire contrasted the rapturous physiological emotion of her voice with the supreme technical art of Pélissier. Lemaure retired in 1744, more by caprice than because of any vocal incapacity, but was still cited with admiration (by Voltaire and the *Mercure*) well into the 1760s and 70s.

ES (E. Borrel)
Mercure de France (Oct 1726), 2329ff; (Dec 1734), 2916ff
J.-B. de La Borde: *Essai sur la musique ancienne et moderne* (Paris, 1780), iii, 521–2
T. Besterman, ed.: *The Complete Works of Voltaire*, lxxxv-cxxxv: *Correspondence and Related Documents* (Geneva, 1968–77)
M. Benoit: *Versailles et les musiciens du roi* (Paris, 1971), 260
PHILIP WELLER

Lemberg (Ger.). L'VIV.

Lemene, Francesco de (*b* Lodi, 19 Feb 1634; *d* Lodi, 24 July 1704). Italian librettist. He came from a noble family (although the title of count was given him by the Duke of Mantua), and received a law degree at Pavia in 1655, having also studied at some time in Bologna. A career in the Spanish administration led him first to Milan as Public Orator and then to Lodi with the post of Decurion. His first stay in Rome was in 1661; he later established close relations there with the circle of Queen Christina of Sweden, for which he wrote *Il giudizio di Paride* (1666, lost), followed by *Il Narciso* (1676; presented in Rome in 1679) and *La ninfa Apollo* (1692). These works have a tender, comic-erotic character in the best style of Marino. Following a period of illness, and influenced by his friendship with the poet and playwright Carlo Maria Maggi, Lemene adopted in 1680 a typically Arcadian style and also wrote sacred poetry (*Il Dio*, 1684; *Il rosario*, 1691). He was a member of various academies and joined Arcadia in 1691 as Arezio Gateatico. Beyond their melodramatic structure, the *favole per musica* display the stylistic features of Marino, whose influence is still evident; there are shepherds and gods, a mood of refined sentiment but also a vitality reminiscent of Anacreon's verse, as well as Lemene's own somewhat learned experiments with metre. His last work was *Endimione*, an Arcadian pastoral full of symbolism and virtuous love. Lemene's lyric output was large, and his oratorios were easy-mannered and gallant. The dialectical comedy *La sposa Francesca* with its tender, everyday realism became justly famous.

Il Narciso (favola boschereccia), C. Borzio, 1676 (C. A. Badia, 1699); La ninfa Apollo (scherzo scenico per musica), Badia, 1692 (Gasparini and Lotti, 1709; F. Rossi, 1726; Galuppi, 1734; G. A. Paganelli, 1737, as Tirsi; A. Bernasconi, 1743); Endimione (favola per musica), P. Magni and G. Griffini, 1692 (G. C. Schürmann, 1700; G. Bononcini, 1706); Eliata (opera musicale); Dialogo pastorale, Borzio, 1689; Baccanale per cantarsi in Roma ne l'Accademia de la Maestà de la regina di Svezia

*

F. de Lemene: *Poesie diverse* (Milan and Parma, 1698–9)
T. Ceva: *Memorie d'alcune virtù del signor conte Francesco de Lemene con alcune riflessioni sulle sue poesie* (Milan, 1706)
L. A. Muratori: *Vita di Francesco de Lemene* (Rome, 1708)
C. Vignati: 'Francesco de Lemene e il suo epistolario inedito', *Archivio storico lombardo*, xix (1892), 345–76, 629–70
B. Maier: 'Lemene, Francesco de', *Dizionario critico della letteratura italiana*, ed. V. Branca (Turin, 1974)
M. G. Accorsi: *Pastori e teatro: dal melodramma al dramma ebraico in La Colonia Renia*, ii (Modena, 1988), 291–7
——, ed.: *F. de Lemene: Scherzi e favole per musica* (Modena, 1992)   MARIA GRAZIA ACCORSI

Lemeshev, Sergey (**Yakovlevich**) (*b* Knyazevo, Tver province, 27 June/10 July 1902; *d* Moscow, 26 June 1977). Russian tenor. He studied at the Moscow Conservatory and with Stanislavsky at the Bol'shoy Opera Studio. He made his début in 1926 in Sverdlovsk (now Yekaterinburg). In 1931 he joined the Bol'shoy Theatre. Lemeshev's lyrical voice, with its individual tone, and the integrity of his characterizations imbued his performances with special charm, and they were noted for their intelligence, fastidious detail and fine acting. His repertory included Lensky, Bayan (*Ruslan and Lyudmila*), Vladimir (*Prince Igor*), Berendey and Levko (*The Snow Maiden* and *May Night*), Vladimir Dubrovsky in Nápravník's *Dubrovsky*, Gounod's Faust and Romeo, the Duke and Almaviva. As a director he produced *La traviata* in 1951 at the Malïy Theatre, Leningrad (now St Petersburg), and *Werther* in 1951 at the Bol'shoy. He published *Put' k iskusstvu* ('The Path to Art', Moscow, 1968). He was made People's Artist of the USSR in 1950.

*

M. L'vov: *S. Ya. Lemeshev* (Moscow and Leningrad, 1947)
E. Groshyova: *S. Ya. Lemeshev* (Moscow, 1960)
                                        I. M. YAMPOL'SKY

Lemière [Larrivée, L'Arrivée], **Marie-Jeanne** (*b* Sedan, 29 Nov 1733; *d* Paris, Oct 1786). French soprano. She joined the Paris Opéra in the 1749–50 season and sang minor roles before withdrawing for four years (1753–7) in order to perfect her technique, which she did to prodigious effect. Hers was an agile, light voice of precision and beauty suited more to florid *ariettes* than to declamatory or passionate roles. La Borde (1780) con-

sidered her superior even to Petitpas in this genre, especially when she intertwined with the obbligato flute playing of Félix Rault. She regularly sang in the *divertissements* of *tragédies lyriques*, where most of the *ariettes* were located, but her voice also had a lyric quality and she sang tender or pastoral roles in many revivals. She was Lully's Oriane (*Amadis*) and Proserpina (*Proserpine*), both in 1759; Rameau's Zélide (*Zaïs*, 1761), Naïs (1764) and Chloë (*Anacréon*, 1766); Desmarets and Campra's Electra (*Iphigénie en Tauride*, 1762); Destouches' Omphale (1769); and Mondonville's L'Aurore (*Titon et l'Aurore*, 1763 and 1768). Her most significant title role was perhaps that she created in Philidor's epoch-making *Ernelinde* (1767), a part originally intended for Sophie Arnould. She was married to, though later estranged from, the eminent *basse-taille* Henri Larrivée. She retired in 1778.   PHILIP WELLER

Lemière [Le Mière, Lemierre] **de Corvey, Jean Frédéric Auguste** (*b* Rennes, 1770; *d* Paris, 19 April 1832). French composer. A military career led him to participate in many European campaigns (including the battle of Waterloo), and caused long breaks in his theatrical activities. One of his earliest operas, *Constance*, was written in 1790, probably while he was still in Rennes. He moved to Paris in 1792 and wrote a series of *opéras comiques* during the last decade of the 18th century. These were mainly one-act compositions of a light and humorous character which, compared with similar works by Boieldieu, Dalayrac and H.-M. Berton (under whom he studied composition), appear to have met with little success. Although his theatrical career continued well into the following century, culminating with arrangements of Rossini's operas in French, it lost much of its impetus. A review of *Les rencontres* (1828) in the *Mercure de France* suggests that his musical style had become outdated.

Very little of Lemière's music is extant. Contemporaries record that he occasionally lacked inspiration, but praised a number of his works for their spirited, melodious qualities, their elegant orchestration and the adept handling of comic situations. *Andros et Almona* (1794) appears to have been Lemière's most successful work and was particularly noted for large-scale choruses imitating the religious worship of Moslems and Brahmins.

opéras comiques, first performed in Paris, unless otherwise stated

Constance (?oc, 1), ? Rennes, 1790
Les chevaliers errants (1), Montansier, 20 March 1792
Crispin rival (1), Montansier, 1793
Le poëme volé (1), Montansier, 1793
La reprise de Toulon par les Français (fait historique, 1, A.-V. P. Duval), OC (Favart), 21 Jan 1794, ov. and 1 air (Paris, c1794)
Andros et Almona, ou Le Français à Bassora (3, L. B. Picard and Duval), OC (Favart), 5 Feb 1794
Le congrès des rois (comédie mêlée d'ariettes, 3, Desmaillot [A. F. Eve]), OC (Favart), 26 Feb 1794, collab. Dalayrac, Grétry, Méhul and 8 others
Scène patriotique, OC (Favart), 1794
Les suspects (1, Picard and Duval), Louvois, 19 May 1795
Babouc (4), Feydeau, 1795
La blonde et la brune (1), Feydeau or Louvois, 1795
La moitié du chemin (3), Louvois, 1796
La paix et l'amour (1), Lille, 5 Dec 1797
Les deux orphelines (1), Molière, 26 May 1798
Les deux crispins (1, Lemière de Corvey), Molière, 16 June 1798
La maison changée (1), Molière, 1798
Le porteur d'eau (1), 'en provence', 1801
Henri et Félicie (3), 'en provence', 1808
Les rivaux de village, ou La cruche cassée (1, J. B. R. Viollet

d'Epagny), OC (Feydeau), 24 Dec 1819 (Paris, ?*c*1819), arrs. pubd separately

La fausse croisade (2, Le Poitevin de Saint-Alme and Viollet d'Epagny), OC (Feydeau), 12 July 1825

Les rencontres (3, J. B. C. Vial and Mélesville [A.-H.-J. Duveyrier]), OC (Feydeau), 11 June 1828, *F-Pc*, collab. G. Catrufo

Spurious: L'écolier en vacances (1, Picard, M. F. Loraux), OC (Favart), 13 Oct 1794 [by L. E. Jadin]   ELISABETH COOK

Lemnitz, Tiana (Luise) (*b* Metz, 26 Oct 1897). German soprano. She studied with Anton Kohmann in Frankfurt and made her début at Heilbronn in 1920 in Lortzing's *Undine*; from 1922 to 1928 she sang at Aachen. She became leading lyric soprano at Hanover (1928–33) and then, after a year in Dresden, joined the Berlin Staatsoper in 1934, remaining there until she retired in 1957. In Berlin her roles ranged from Mimì and Micaëla to Aida and Desdemona, from Pamina and Mařenka to Sieglinde. Later she sang the Marschallin, Milada (*Dalibor*), Jenůfa and Nastas'ya (Tchaikovsky's *The Enchantress*).

Lemnitz made her Covent Garden début in 1936 as Eva and also sang Octavian, Elsa, Pamina and Sieglinde there; her career was otherwise mostly confined to central Europe. Her sensitive artistry, exquisite *pianissimo* and touching interpretations were greatly admired.

R. Seeliger: 'Tiana Lemnitz', *Record Collector*, xv (1963–4), 29–43 [with discography by R. Seeliger and B. Park]
   HAROLD ROSENTHAL/R

Lemonnier, Louis-Augustin (*b* 1793; *d* St-Sever, nr Mont-de-Marsan, 4 March 1875). French baritone. After singing in Brussels, in 1817 he joined the Opéra-Comique, Paris, where he was engaged for nearly 20 years. An excellent actor with a fine voice, he created roles in Henri-Montan Berton's *Les deux mousquetaires* (1824); Halévy's *L'artisan* and *Le roi et le batelier* and Carafa's *Masaniello* (all 1827); Boieldieu's *Les deux nuits* (1829); Adam's *Danilowa, Joséphine* (both 1830) and *Le grand prix* (1831); and Hérold's *Le pré aux clercs* (1832) and *Ludovic* (1833). He was married to the soprano Louise-Thérèse-Antoinette Lemonnier (*b* Brest, 24 Aug 1789; *d* St-Sever, 5 April 1866). She made her début in 1805 at Rouen and in 1809 joined the Opéra-Comique, where she sang until 1830. She took part in many premières: Isouard's *Cendrillon* (1810); Gaveaux's *L'enfant prodigue* (1811); Boieldieu's *Jean de Paris* (1812), in which she sang the Princess of Navarre; Carafa's *Jeanne d'Arc à Orléans* (1821); Auber's *Leicester* (1823); and, together with her husband, *Danilowa* and *Joséphine*.   ELIZABETH FORBES

Lemoyne [Moyne], Jean-Baptiste (*b* Eymet, 3 April 1751; *d* Paris, 30 Dec 1796). French composer. He was brought up by his uncle, who was the *maître de chapelle* at Périgueux. In 1770 he went to Berlin, and held a minor appointment with the Crown Prince of Prussia while he studied under J. G. Graun, Kirnberger and J. A. P. Schulz. He then obtained a post in Warsaw, where his opera *Le bouquet de Colette* was produced with his pupil Antoinette Clavel (Mme de Saint-Huberty) in the cast; she was later to contribute much to his first Parisian success, *Phèdre*, by her performance in the title role. Lemoyne was in Paris by about 1780. His first serious opera, *Electre*, was dedicated to Marie Antoinette with flattering references to Gluck, whose methods he claimed to follow. The work was poorly

received; Gluck dissociated himself from Lemoyne, and the latter accordingly took Piccinni as a model for *Phèdre*. In 1787 he visited Italy, presumably to study the musical style then rapidly coming into vogue in Paris.

In spite of its universal critical rejection, *Electre* is Lemoyne's most interesting work. It makes striking use of free, short and abbreviated musical forms, and in the heroine's role uses a highly expressive recitative, seasoned with musical repetitions akin to the technique of leitmotif. The orchestration is frequently crude, but the quiet ending, as Orestes is pursued off the stage by the Furies, is noteworthy; Lemoyne repeated the effect, with more subtlety, in *Phèdre* and *Nephté*. The weakest parts of *Electre* are those in which purely musical invention is required, rather than declamation and orchestral effects; the dances are poor, and the longer arias weak in melody and design. *Phèdre* contains only a residue of the leitmotif technique, and although Lemoyne improved in aria writing and his operas became less uneven in quality, his originality became diluted. *Nephté* contains some fine scenes, and was his greatest success in tragedy – he was called on to the stage after the first performance, a favour then quite unusual at the Opéra – and it gave rise to the Abbé Toscan's pamphlet in which Lemoyne is considered to have surpassed Gluck by adding melodic sweetness to dramatic power. Lemoyne had less talent for comedy, but the slight charms of *Les prétendus*, enhanced by the unusual orchestral use of the piano, kept it in the repertory for 294 performances until 1827. Lemoyne's later works, including some with Revolutionary themes, are of decreasing interest and aroused little enthusiasm.

Lemoyne's son, Gabriel Lemoyne (*b* Berlin, 14 Oct 1772; *d* Paris, 2 July 1815), wrote three *opéras comiques*, one (*L'entresol*, 1802) in collaboration with L. A. Piccinni.

PFE – *Paris, Théâtre Feydeau*   PO – *Paris, Opéra*

Le bouquet de Colette (opéra, 1), Warsaw, 1775
Electre (tragédie, 3, N. F. Guillard, after Voltaire: *Oreste*), PO, 2 July 1782 (Paris, n.d.)
Phèdre (tragédie lyrique, 3, F.-B. Hoffman), Fontainebleau, 26 Oct 1786 (Paris, n.d.)
Nadir, ou Le dormeur éveillé, 1787, unperf., *F-Po*
Les prétendus (comédie lyrique, 2, M. A. J. Rochon de Chabannes), PO, 2 June 1789 (Paris, n.d.)
Nephté (tragédie lyrique, 3, Hoffman, after T. Corneille: *Camma*), PO, 15 Dec 1789, *Po* (Paris, n.d.)
Les pommiers et le moulin (comédie lyrique, 1, N. J. Forgeot), PO, 20 Jan 1790 (Paris, n.d.)
Louis IX en Egypte (opéra, 3, Guillard and F.-G. J.-S. Andrieux), PO, 15 June 1790, *Po*, *Po*
L'ivrogne vertueux, *c*1791 (oc, 2, L.-A. Beffroy de Reigny), unperf.
Elfride [Elfrida] (drame héroïque, 3, Guillard), Paris, OC (Favart), 17 Dec 1792
Silvius Nerva, ou La malédiction paternelle, 1792 (Beffroy de Reigny), unperf., *Po*
Miltiade à Marathon (opéra, 2, Guillard), PO, 5 Nov 1793, *Po*
Toute la Grèce, ou Ce que peut la liberté (tableau patriotique, 1, Beffroy de Reigny), PO, 5 Jan 1794, *Po*
Le compère Luc (oc, 2, Beffroy de Reigny), PFE, 19 Feb 1794
Le batelier, ou Les vrais sans-culottes (tableau patriotique, 1, Rézicourt), PFE, 12 May 1794
Le mensonge officieux (1, Forgeot), PFE, ?13 March 1795
L'île des femmes, 1796 (opéra, 2), unperf.

Other stage works: Storm scene for Gossec: Toinon et Toinette, Berlin, 1772; many airs de ballet for productions at PO, *Po*; many excerpts from above operas pubd separately

G. L. G. Toscan: *De la musique et de Nephté: aux mânes de l'abbé Arnaud* (Paris, 1790)
M. Tourneux, ed.: *Correspondance littéraire, philosophique et*

critique par Grimm, Diderot, Raynal, Meister etc. (Paris, 1877–82)

J. Rushton: 'An Early Essay in "Leitmotiv": J. B. Lemoyne's "Electre"', *ML*, lii (1971), 387–401 JULIAN RUSHTON

Lenardo und Blandine. Melodrama in two acts by PETER WINTER to a libretto by Johann Friedrich von Göz after Gottfried August Bürger's ballad *Lenardo und Blandine*; Munich, Nationaltheater, 25 June 1779.

One of Winter's first compositions for the stage, this work reflects the strong influence of Georg Benda and his melodramas in Munich. The grisly plot centres on Blandine, whose father and fiancé murder her lover, Lenardo. She is driven to insanity and death after Lenardo's ring and heart are delivered to her room at the hour she was to escape with him. Winter portrays the story with generally compact, intense musical interpolations rather than the more discursive type preferred by other, mostly north German, composers. He follows Benda's model in many particulars (including his depiction of a storm), but depends much less on the recall of melodies and motifs. LINDA TYLER

Lenepveu, Charles Ferdinand (*b* Rouen, 4 Oct 1840; *d* Paris, 16 Aug 1910). French composer. He abandoned a projected legal career in 1862 and entered Ambroise Thomas' composition class at the Conservatoire, where he won the Prix de Rome in 1865. His stage career began in 1867–8, when he won a competition organized by the Académie des Beaux-Arts for a comic opera. Lenepveu had to fight hard to hold the Opéra-Comique to a performance of the piece, *Le florentin*, which finally received its première in 1874. Its comparative lack of success may have been due to lack of encouragement by the Opéra-Comique management: it enjoyed more success in French provincial theatres. Saint-Arroman detected the influence of Gounod, Verdi and Meyerbeer in both *Le florentin* and the larger-scale *Velléda* (1882), after which Lenepveu turned to a more meditative, religious mode of self-expression. He seems to have been diffident about promoting his stage works – *Velléda* was performed at Covent Garden mainly through the efforts of Adelina Patti, its dedicatee, while *L'anniversaire* and *Le retour de Jeanne* appeared in *Le magasin des demoiselles*, a publication specializing in operettas for salon performance. Possibly Lenepveu was put off by his struggles with the Opéra-Comique over *Le florentin*, but the fact that none of his contemporaries appears to have regarded either this work or *Velléda* as a masterpiece may also have played a part.

Le florentin (oc, 3, J.-H. Vernoy de Saint-Georges), OC (Favart), 25 Feb 1874, vs (Paris, ?1874)

L'anniversaire (oc, 1, A. Bisson), unperf., vs (Paris, 1876)

Le retour de Jeanne (oc, 1, Bisson), unperf., vs (Paris, 1881)

Velléda (4, A. Challemel and J. Chantepie, after F. R. de Chateaubriand: *Les martyrs*), London, CG, 4 July 1882, vs (London, 1883); separate numbers (London, 1882)

*

R. de Saint-Arroman: *Charles Lenepveu: étude biographique* (Paris, 1898) [orig. pubd as a series of articles in *Le journal musical*, iii (1898)]

H. R. Cohen, ed.: *Les gravures musicales dans L'illustration* (Quebec, 1982) [incl. picture of the *mise en scène* for *Le florentin* at the Opéra-Comique, 1874] JOHN WAGSTAFF

Leningrad. ST PETERSBURG.

Lenya [Lenia], **Lotte** [Blamauer, Karoline Wilhelmine] (*b* Vienna, 18 Oct 1898; *d* New York, 27 Nov 1981). American singing actress of Austrian birth. She studied

Lotte Lenya as Jenny in the 1954 New York production of Weill's 'Die Dreigroschenoper': painting (1954) by Saul Bolasni

dance in Zürich, before going in 1920 to Berlin, where she turned to spoken theatre. In 1926 she married Kurt Weill.

Her international reputation dates from her creation of Jenny in Weill's and Brecht's *Die Dreigroschenoper* (1928, Berlin), and from the subsequent recordings and film (directed by G. W. Pabst). She created three further roles in works by Weill, singing Anna I in the choral ballet *Die sieben Todsünden* (1933, Paris), Miriam in *The Eternal Road* (1937, New York), and the Duchess in *The Firebrand of Florence* (1945, New York).

After Weill's death in 1950 Lenya devoted much of her time to the revival of some of his most important works from the German years. Her live and recorded performances won for her and for Weill a new or renewed reputation in many lands, and established as 'classical' a performing style whose characteristics of timbre and tessitura were markedly different from those of her Berlin years. But that combination of dramatic insight and musical instinct, of intelligence, wit, coolness and passion had survived from those years, and most remarkably developed and matured.

Although her tastes in both popular and classical music were broad, as a performer she confined herself almost entirely to the songs of her husband, and to the one extended work he composed especially for her, *Die sieben Todsünden*; that was enough to establish her as one of the outstanding *diseuses* of her time.

C. Osborne: 'Berlin in the Twenties: Conversations with Otto Klemperer and Lotte Lenya', *London Magazine*, i/2 (1961), 44–51

H. Marx, ed.: *Weill – Lenya* (New York, 1976) DAVID DREW

Lenz. Opera in one act by LARRY SITSKY to a libretto by Gwen Harwood after the novella by GEORG BÜCHNER; Sydney, Opera House, 14 March 1974.

The opera is divided into a prologue, seven sections and an epilogue, which chart the psychological breakdown of the demented 18th-century poet Jakob Lenz (tenor). There are no set-changes or breaks in the action, which takes place in the village of Waldbach. In 1771 Lenz meets Goethe and falls in love with the poet's mistress, Friederike von Brion (mezzo-soprano); his eccentric behaviour eventually results in his being asked to leave. During the winter of 1777–8, while staying with Christoph Kaufmann (baritone), he experiences his first bout of insanity. He goes to live with the pastor Oberlin (bass) and his periods of madness become increasingly frequent. Lenz eventually attempts suicide, after which he is led away in protective custody. The story charts the poet's loss of spiritual and physical love: he comes to reject people, God and finally himself.

Sitsky acknowledges Berg's influence on this score, which is constructed from thematic rows and their inversions, used to underpin characters and express emotional states. Originally the opera included a prelude, which the composer now considers optional. The material for this prelude is from his *Homage to Stravinsky* (1968), but much of the orchestral writing from *Lenz*, as it now stands, derives from it. *Lenz* was first performed on a double bill with Felix Werder's *The Affair* by Australian Opera, the company's first presentation of opera by Australian composers.

THÉRÈSE RADIC

Lenz, Jakob Michael Reinhold (*b* Sesswegen, Livonia [now Latvia], 12 Jan 1751; *d* Moscow, 13/24 May 1792). German dramatist, writer and poet. His best-known dramas, *Der Hofmeister* (1774) and *Die Soldaten* (1774–5), show features of the *Sturm und Drang* and look forward towards the realism of the late 19th century, even to epic theatre (Brecht adapted *Der Hofmeister* for the Berliner Ensemble in 1950). Though he continued to write, Lenz's life from the late 1770s became increasingly dominated by mental instability (sympathetically portrayed in Büchner's prose study *Lenz*, 1835–6, published 1839). The most important operatic setting based on Lenz's plays is B. A. Zimmermann's *Die Soldaten* (1958–60, revised 1963–4), for which the composer wrote his own libretto, dividing the stage into five planes of action in the interest of condensing the fragmented structure of the original (in five acts and 34 scenes); it had been preceded in 1930 by Manfred Gurlitt's *Soldaten*. In 1978 Friedrich Goldmann's opera *R. Hot, bzw. Die Hitze* was performed at Stuttgart; its text was based by Thomas Körner on Lenz's little-known play *Der Engländer* (1776), which depicts the conflict between the English Lord Hot and his son Robert, and the latter's vain love for a Spanish princess. Lenz's life has also inspired operas. Larry Sitsky's *Lenz* (1974, Sydney), is based on Büchner's study; Wolfgang Rihm's *Jakob Lenz* (1979, Hamburg) also uses Büchner's account, focussing on the deranged poet's stay in the Vosges in February 1778.

PETER BRANSCOMBE

Leo, Leonardo (Ortensio Salvatore de [di]) (*b* San Vito degli Schiavi [now San Vito dei Normanni], nr Brindisi, 5 Aug 1694; *d* Naples, 31 Oct 1744). Italian composer. He went to Naples in 1709 and became a pupil of Nicola Fago at the Conservatorio S Maria della Pietà dei Turchini. At the beginning of 1712 his *S Chiara, o L'infedeltà abbattuta*, a *dramma sacro*, was performed there; from the fact that it was performed again in the viceroy's palace on 14 February it would seem that it attracted unusual attention. On finishing his studies he was appointed supernumerary organist in the viceroy's chapel, 1713, and at the same time was *maestro di cappella* in the service of the Marchese Stella and possibly of the church of S Maria della Solitaria. He was not yet 20 when his first opera, *Il Pisistrato*, was staged. There followed commissions for opera arrangements, intermezzos and serenatas, and in 1718 a second opera, *Sofonisba*. From *Caio Gracco* (1720) the list of his opera commissions continues without a break up to his death. In 1723 he wrote his first opera for Venice, and in the same year, with *La 'mpeca scoperta*, he turned for the first time to the developing genre of Neapolitan *commedia musicale*; from then on he was regarded as one of the leading composers of comedy.

On Alessandro Scarlatti's death in 1725 Leo was promoted to first organist of the viceregal chapel. In the following years he lost his supremacy as a composer of serious opera in Naples to his rivals Vinci and Hasse, and between 1726 and 1730 he apparently received no commissions for opera at the Teatro S Bartolomeo in Naples. He did, however, write serious operas for Rome and Venice, and in Naples he pursued his career as a composer of comic operas. After Hasse's departure and Vinci's death in 1730, Leo became the dominant figure in Neapolitan musical life. He succeeded Vinci as *provicemaestro* and on Mancini's death in 1737 became *vicemaestro* of the royal chapel. He was repeatedly given leave to fulfil commissions for operas elsewhere (1737 Bologna, 1739 Turin, 1740 Turin and Milan), and through the connections of the Neapolitan royal family he received commissions from the Spanish court. Even greater than his reputation as an opera composer was the esteem he acquired as a composer of oratorios. He also became prominent as a teacher, becoming *primo maestro* at the Conservatorio S Onofrio in 1739 and in 1741 taking over the duties of *primo maestro* at the S Maria della Pietà dei Turchini in succession to Fago. He was much concerned with the reform of church music, which was connected with his activities as a teacher; in both respects he was in competition with Francesco Durante, who taught at the two other conservatories in Naples. On Domenico Sarro's death (25 January 1744) Leo became *maestro di cappella* of the royal chapel. He immediately composed a series of *a cappella* compositions (with continuo) for the use of the royal chapel during Lent and reformed the orchestra of the royal opera, but he died after only nine months in office.

Leo's works, even those for the stage, reflected more than those of others of his generation the academic side of his training to the extent that his ecclesiastical style is echoed even in his *opere buffe* (albeit with parodistic intent). There was considerable rivalry in the Neapolitan school between the 'Leisti', the supporters of Leo, and the 'Durantisti', those of Francesco Durante, the first characterized by their 'scientific', almost cerebral, approach, with counterpoint to the fore, and the second by a more instinctive approach allied to a tendency to harmonic and melodic simplicity, free of the contrapuntal artifice of Leo's adherents. In opera, Leo was a great deal more conservative and bound by tradition than his contemporaries Hasse, Vinci and Porpora; the choral episodes of *L'olimpiade* and *Ciro riconosciuto*,

1145

for example, are closer to the motet style than to the celebratory choruses of contemporary *opera seria*. His comic operas likewise show a solid compositional technique, above all in the ensembles at the ends of acts; Leo is credited with having conferred on comic opera a musical dignity equal to that of *opera seria*, whose salient characteristics it borrowed. A typical example is the celebrated aria of the leading character, Fazio Tonti, in *Amor vuol sofferenza*, 'Io non so dove mi sto', accompanied by two orchestras in dialogue; its academic and pompous structure, as well as mocking the whole Metastasian style, ironically echoes Leo's ecclesiastical manner.

Tradition, inadequately supported by evidence (as so often with the biographies and teaching careers of musicians of the Neapolitan school), has it that Leo, besides being a pupil of Scarlatti in Naples, studied with Ottavio Pitoni in Rome (particularly 1726–31, when *Il trionfo di Camilla* and *Il Cid* were performed at the Teatro Capranica, and *Evergete* at the Teatro delle Dame); certainly his earliest operas (at least up to 1730) are characterized by elements clearly derived from the older style, including figured bass and ostinato typical of late Baroque opera and the use of strict contrapuntal techniques, including canon. This assiduous use of counterpoint provided a firm basis for his melodic phrase structure; and certainly Leo showed an innate gift for melody, with numerous borrowings from popular song, especially in comic operas. His *buffo* works show a care over form and technique, in melodic structure and in the management of ensembles, that hitherto had been the preserve of serious opera.

Of particular interest for the history of the diffusion of Leo's operas is that a manuscript of *Catone in Utica* (in *GB-Lam*) bears notes in Handel's handwriting and was used for a performance of the pasticcio *Catone* (London, King's Theatre, 1741) directed by Handel himself and including music by Hasse, Porpora, Vivaldi and Vinci as well as Leo.

See also AMOR VUOL SOFFERENZA; ANDROMACA (ii); CATONE IN UTICA (i); and OLIMPIADE, L' (iii).

NB – *Naples, Teatro di S Bartolomeo*
NF – *Naples, Teatro dei Fiorentini*
NC – *Naples, Teatro di S Carlo* NN – *Naples, Teatro Nuovo*

dm – *dramma/drama per musica*

Il Pisistrato (dm, 3, D. Lalli), NB, 13 May 1714, *I-MC*
Eumene (dm, 3, A. Zeno), Reggio Emilia, Pubblico, [May] Fair 1714, collab. F. Gasparini and others [prol., arias and comic scenes by Leo]
Sofonisba (dm, 3, F. Silvani), Naples, Real Palazzo, 22 Jan 1718; NB, carn. 1718
Caio Gracco (dm, 3, S. Stampiglia), Naples, Real Palazzo, 19 April 1720; rev., NB, 18 Nov 1720, 1 aria *F-Pc*
Arianna e Teseo (dm, 3, P. Pariati), NB, 26 Nov 1721 [perf. inc.]; Naples, Pace, carn. 1729, arias in *I-MC*, *PLcon* and *Rc*, 1 duet *Nc*
Bajazete, imperador de' Turchi (dramma tragico, 3, B. Saddumene, after A. Piovene), Naples, Real Palazzo, 28 Aug 1722, 2 arias *D-MÜs*, collab. others
Timocrate (dm, 3, Lalli), Venice, S Angelo, carn. 1723, 1 aria and 1 duet *MÜs*
La 'mpeca scoperta (commedia per musica, 3, F. Oliva), NF, 11 Nov 1723
L'ammore fedele (favola sarvateca, 3, Oliva), NF, 18 April 1724
Lo pazzo apposta (commedia per musica, 3, Oliva), NF, aut. 1724
Turno Aricino (dm, 3, Stampiglia), NB, 3 Dec 1724, 4 arias *MÜs*, collab. Vinci [recits. in Acts 2 and 3 by Leo]
Le fente zingare (commedia, 3, F. A. Tullio), NF, wint. 1724 [rev., with new arias, of 1717 opera by A. Orefice]
Zenobia in Palmira (dm, 3, Zeno and Pariati), NB, 13 May 1725, *I-Nc*

Il trionfo di Camilla, regina de' Volsci (dm, 3, Stampiglia), Rome, Capranica, 8 Jan 1726, *A-Wn*, *D-Dlb*, arias in *MÜs*, *I-Bc* and *PEsp* [music for ints also by Leo]
Orismene, ovvero Dalli sdegni l'amore (dm, 3, C. de Palma), NN, carn. 1726, *MC*
La donna violante (commedia, 3, Tullio), NF, aut. 1726, lib. *TAc*
La semmeglianza de chi l'ha fatta (commedia per musica, 3), NF, aut. 1726, *MC*, Act 2 *Nc**
Il Cid (dm, 3, G. G. Alborghetti), Rome, Capranica, 10 Feb 1727, arias in *D-MÜs* and *I-Rc* and *Rvat*
Lo matrimonio annascuso (commedia per musica, 3, S. de Maltrano), NF, spr. 1727
Argene (dm, 3, Lalli), Venice, S Giovanni Grisostomo, 17 Jan 1728, *GB-Lam*; NB, 28 Aug 1731, Acts 2 and 3 *I-MC**, arias in *D-MÜs*, *GB-Cfm* and *I-Vc*
La pastorella commattuta (chelleta ridicola, 3, T. Mariani), NN, aut. 1728
Catone in Utica (tragedia per musica, 3, P. Metastasio), Venice, S Giovanni Grisostomo, carn. 1729, *B-Bc*, *GB-Lam* (*R*1983: IOB, lxx), *US-Wc*, arias in *GB-Lcm*, *I-Mc* and *MAC*; as Catone, arr. Handel with addl arias by Hasse, Porpora, Vinci and Vivaldi, London, King's, 4 Nov 1732, *D-Hs* (*R*1983: IOB, lxxi), *GB-Lam*
La schiava per amore (commedia per musica, 3, Mariani), NN, aut. 1729, arias *Rc*
Semiramide (dm, 3, Metastasio), ?2 Feb 1730, 1 aria *Bc*
La Rosmene (commedia per musica, 3, Saddumene), NN, sum. 1730, arias *Rsc*
Evergete (dm, 3, Lalli and Silvani, after P. Corneille: *Héraclius empereur d'Orient*), Rome, Dame, 20 Jan 1731, *MC*, arias in *Rc* and *Rsc*
Il Demetrio [1st version] (dm, 3, Metastasio), NB, 1 Oct 1732, *F-Pc** (Act 1), *I-MC*, arias in *Mc*, *Nc* and *Vc*
La vecchia trammera (commedia per musica, 3, Tullio), NN, 1732, collab. A. Orefice
Amore mette sinno [Amor dà senno] (commedia pe museca, 3, Saddumene), NN, spr. 1733, collab. 1 other
Nitocri, regina d'Egitto (dm, 3, Zeno), NB, 4 Nov 1733, *I-MC*
La Rosilla (tragicommedia, 3, Tullio), NN, aut. 1733, collab. Orefice [rev. of Orefice: La Locinna, 1723]
Il castello d'Atlante (dm, 3, Mariani), NB, 4 July 1734 [ints by Feo], arias *Rc*
Il Medo (dm, 3, O. Frugoni), Palermo, 1734, *B-Bc*, collab. Vinci
Demofoonte (dm, 3, Metastasio), NB, 20 Jan 1735, *GB-Lbm* (attrib. entirely to Leo in catalogue), *I-MC*, Acts 1 and 2 *Nc*, arias in *Bc*, *Mc* and *Nc*, 1 duet *CATc*, collab. F. Mancini, Sarro and Sellitto
La clemenza di Tito (dm, 3, Metastasio), Venice, S Giovanni Grisostomo, 29 Jan 1735, *I-Nc*
Emira (dm, 3), NB, 12 July 1735 [ints by I. Prota], *GB-Bu* (Acts 1 and 3), *I-MC*, *Nc*, arias *Mc*
Il Demetrio [2nd version] (dm, 3, Metastasio), Castello di Torremaggiore, 10 Dec 1735
Lucio Papirio (dm, 3, S. Salvi), NB, 19 Dec 1735, 1 Act *B-Bc*
Onore vince amore (melodrama, 3), NF, aut. 1736
Farnace (dm, 3, Lalli), NB, 19 Dec 1736, *A-Wn*, *F-Pc*
L'amico traditore (dm, 3), NF, carn. 1737
Siface (dm, 3, Metastasio), Bologna, Malvezzi, 11 May 1737, *I-MC*, arias in *Bas*, *Bc*, *CAS*, *Mc*, *Nc*, *PAc* and *PLcon*; rev. as Viriate, Pistoia, sum. 1740, incl. music by others
La simpatia del sangue (dm, 3, P. Trinchera), NN, aut. 1737, *F-Pc*
L'olimpiade (dm, 3, Metastasio), NC, 19 Dec 1737, *B-Bc*, *F-Pc*, *D-Bds*, *Dlb*, *I-Mc* (*R*1978: IOB, xxxvi), *Nc*, *Vc*, *Vnm*, arias in *Bas*, *CAS*, *Gl*, *Ls*, *Mc*, *Nc*, *PAc* and *PLcon*
Il conte (dg per musica, 3, G. Federico), NF, spr. 1738
Sesostri re d'Egitto (Pariati), Lisbon, Trindade, 1738, lib. *P-C*
Il Ciro riconosciuto (dm, 3, Metastasio), Turin, Regio, carn. 1739, *D-Bds*, *F-Pc*, *I-Mc*, *MC*, *Nc*, arias in *Bc*, *Ls*, *Mc*, *Nc* and *PAc*
Amor vuol sofferenza [La frascatana; Il cioè] (commedia per musica, 3, Federico), NN, aut. 1739, *A-Wgm*, *F-Pc*, *GB-Lbl*, *I-Nc* (Act 1), *Mc*, arias in *Bc* and *Mc*, ed. G. A. Pastore (Bari, 1962); rev. with addns by M. Capranica as La finta frascatana (ob), NN, Nov 1744
Achille in Sciro (dm, 3, Metastasio), Turin, Regio, carn. 1740, *D-Bds*, *Tu*, *I-Mc*, *MC*, *Nc*, arias in *Bc*, *Mc* and *Nc*
Scipione nelle Spagne (dm, 3, Zeno), Milan, Ducale, carn. 1740, arias in *CATc*, *MC* and *Nc*
L'Alidoro (commedia per musica, 3, Federico), NF, sum. 1740, *MC*
L'Alessandro (commedia per musica, 3, Federico), NF, aut. 1741
Il Demetrio [3rd version] (dm, 3, Metastasio), NC, 19 Dec 1741, *F-Pc*, *I-Mc*

L'impresario delle Isole Canarie (intermezzi comici musicali, Metastasio), Venice, S Angelo, 1741

L'ambizione delusa (commedia pastorale, 3, D. Canica), NN, spr. 1742, *F-Pc*

L'Andromaca (dm, 3, Salvi, after J. Racine), NC, 4 Nov 1742, *D-LEm* (R1979: IOB, xxxix, *I-Nc**), arias in *Bc* and *PAc*

Issipile (dm, 3, Metastasio), NC, 19 Dec 1742, arias in *I-Bc, Mc* and *Nc*, collab. Hasse

Il giramondo (commedia per musica, 3, G. Palomba), Florence, Cocomero, aut. 1743, lib. *Bc*; rev. as I viaggiatori (int per musica, 3), Paris, Opéra, 1754, *F-Po*

Il fantastico, od Il nuovo Chisciotte (commedia per musica, 3, Federico, after M. de Cervantes), NN, 1743

Vologeso re de' Parti (dm, 3), Turin, Regio, carn. 1744, *I-Tci, Tf*, arias in *Mc* and *Nc*

La fedeltà odiata (commedia per musica, 3, Palomba), NF, spr. 1744

La caduta di Germanico (dm, 3), ?unperf., *BRc*

Arias for Naples perfs. of Gasparini: Sesostri, re d'Egitto, 1717; Handel: Rinaldo, 1718; Ristori: Temistocle, 1738; Perez: Siroe, re di Persia, 1740, *B-Bc*

Music in: Il Demetrio, 1738; Andromeda, 1750, *A-Wn*

Arias in *B-Bc, D-MÜs, F-Pn, GB-Cfm, Lam, I-Mc, Nc, Nf* and *PLcon*

Doubtful: Venturina e Sciarappa (int, Saddumene), 1722; Lo Simmele (commedia, 3, Saddumene), NN, 15 Oct 1724, collab. Orefice [possibly all by Orefice]; Carlo in Alemagna, Milan, Ducale, Jan 1740 (see *StiegerO*); Tiridate, NC, 19 Dec 1740 (see Marinelli Roscioni 1987, p.8)

*

ES (H. Hucke); *FlorimoN; GiacomoC; RosaM*

Avvisi di Napoli (1714–17, 1719–25, 1734–40), passim

J. F. Reichardt: 'Leonardo Leo', *Musikalisches Kunstmagazin*, i (1782), 39–41

[G. B. G. Grossi]: 'Leonardo Leo', *Biografia degli uomini illustri del regno di Napoli ornata de' loro rispettivi ritratti, compilata da diversi letterati nazionali*, vi (Naples, 1819)

M. Scherillo: *L'opera buffa napoletana durante il settecento: storia letteraria* (Naples, 1883, rev. 2/1916)

B. Croce: *I teatri di Napoli del secolo XV–XVIII* (Naples, 1891)

V. Leo: *Leonardo Leo e la sua epoca musicale* (Brindisi, 1894)

G. Leo: *Leonardo Leo celebre musico del sec. XVIII ed il suo omonimo Leonardo Leo di Corrado* (Naples, 1901)

——: *I signori Leo e Di Leo ricchi e poveri nel secolo XVII e XVIII in S. Vito de' Normanni ed il celebre musicista Leonardo Leo* (Naples, 1901)

——: *Leonardo Leo musicista del secolo XVIII e le sue opere musicali* (Naples, 1905)

E. Dent: 'Leonardo Leo', *SIMG*, viii (1906–7), 550–66

F. Piovano: 'A propos d'une récente biographie de Léonard Leo', *SIMG*, viii (1906–7), 70–95, 336

A. Della Corte: *L'opera comica italiana nel '700* (Bari, 1923)

U. Prota-Giurleo: *La grande orchestra del Teatro di S. Carlo nel settecento (da documenti inediti)* (Naples, 1927)

C. de Brosses: *Lettres familières sur l'Italie*, ed. Y. Bézard (Paris, 1931)

E. Faustini-Fasini: 'Leonardo Leo e la sua famiglia', *NA*, xiv (1937), 11–18

W. C. Smith: *A Bibliography of the Musical Works published by John Walsh during the Years 1695–1720* (London, 1948)

F. Walker: 'Cav. Giacomo Leo and his Famous "Ancestor"', *MR*, ix (1948), 241

U. Prota-Giurleo: 'Breve storia del teatro di corte e della musica a Napoli nei secoli XVII–XVIII', *Il teatro di corte del palazzo reale di Napoli* (Naples, 1952), 19–146

F. Schlitzer, ed.: *Tommaso Traetta, Leonardo Leo, Vincenzo Bellini: note e documenti*, Chigiana, ix (1952)

G. A. Pastore: *Leonardo Leo* (Galatina, 1957)

——: 'Manoscritti di musicisti salentini nelle biblioteche estere', *Informazioni archivistiche e bibliografiche sul Salento*, ii (1958)

G. Tintori: *L'opera napoletana* (Milan, 1958)

G. Roma: *Il brindisino Leonardo Leo* (Fasano, 1966)

W. C. Smith and C. Humphries: *A Bibliography of the Musical Works published by the Firm of John Walsh during the Years 1721–1766* (London, 1968)

S. H. Hansell: 'The Cadence in 18th-Century Recitative', *MQ*, liv (1968), 238–46

A. Trizza: *Leonardo Leo, i suoi genitori e la sua famiglia* (San Vito dei Normanni, 1969)

H. Hell: *Die neapolitanische Opernsinfonie in der ersten Hälfte des 18. Jahrhunderts* (Tutzing, 1971)

H. D. Clausen: *Händels Direktionspartituren ('Handexemplare')* (Hamburg, 1972), 126–8

M. F. Robinson: *Naples and Neapolitan Opera* (London and New York, 1972)

H. C. Wolff: 'Leonardo Leo's Oper "L'Andromaca" (1742)', *Studi musicali*, i (1972), 285–315

——: 'Un oratorio sconosciuto di Leonardo Leo', *RIM*, vii (1972), 196–213

G. Hardie: *Leonardo Leo (1694–1744) and his Comic Operas 'Amor vuol sofferenza' and 'Alidoro'* (diss., Cornell U., 1973)

R. S. Freeman: 'Farinello and his Repertory', *Studies in Renaissance and Baroque Music in Honor of Arthur Mendel* (Kassel and Hackensack, NJ, 1974), 301–30

R. Strohm: 'Händel's Pasticci', *AnMc*, no.14 (1974), 208–67

G. Hardie: 'Comic Operas performed in Naples, 1707–1750', *MMA*, viii (1975), 56–81

H. C. Wolff: 'Italian Opera 1700–1750', *Opera and Church Music, 1630–1750*, NOHM, v (1975), 73–168, esp. 108–16

G. Hardie: 'Gennaro Antonio Federico's *Amor vuol sofferenza* (1739) and the Neapolitan Comic Opera', *SMA*, x (1976), 62–6

R. Strohm: 'Italienische Opernarien des frühen Settecento', *AnMc*, no.16 (1976)

F. Degrada: 'L'opera napoletana', *Storia dell'opera*, ed. G. Barblan and A. Basso, i (Turin, 1977), 237–332

R. Zanetti: *La musica italiana del settecento* (Milan, 1978)

F. Degrada: 'Origini e destino dell'opera buffa napoletana', *Il palazzo incantato*, i (Fiesole, 1979), 41–65, esp. 50

R. Strohm: *Die italienische Oper im 18. Jahrhundert* (Wilhelmshaven, 1979)

Leonardo Leo, Il Punto (San Vito dei Normanni, 1979)

H. C. Wolff: *Geschichte der komischen Oper: Einführung* (Wilhelmshaven, 1981)

H. M. Brown: Preface to L. Leo: *Catone in Utica*, IOB, lxx (1983)

G. Hardie: 'Neapolitan Comic Opera, 1707–1750: some Addenda and Corrigenda for *The New Grove*', *JAMS*, xxxvi (1983), 124–7

R. Strohm: *Essays on Handel and Italian Opera* (Cambridge, 1985)

B. Cagli and A. Ziino, eds.: *Il Teatro di San Carlo 1737–1987*, ii: *La cronologia*, ed. C. Marinelli Roscioni (Naples, 1987) [incl. F. Degrada: '"Scuola napoletana" e "Opera napoletana": nascita, sviluppo e prospettive di un concetto storiografico', 9–20; H. Hucke: 'L' "Achille in Sciro" di Domenico Sarri e l'inaugurazione del teatro di San Carlo', 21–32; G. Morelli: 'Castrati, primedonne, e Metastasio nel felicissimo giorno del nome di Carlo', 33–60]

C. Sartori: *I libretti italiani a stampa dalle origini al 1800* (Cuneo, 1990–)

HELMUT HUCKE, ROSA CAFIERO

Léon [Hirschfeld], **Victor** (*b* Vienna, 4 Jan 1858; *d* Vienna, 3 Feb 1940). Austrian librettist. As stage manager of both the Theater in der Josefstadt and the Carltheater in Vienna, he was closely involved in various aspects of Viennese musical-theatre life and became a prolific writer of operetta librettos. These were of variable worth, his success being greatest when subjected to the more disciplined approach of Leo Stein, with whom he collaborated most notably on *Wiener Blut* (1899) and *Die lustige Witwe* (1905). Of his individual librettos, that for Lehár's *Die gelbe Jacke* (1923), which incorporates translations of Chinese poetry and was later adapted into *Das Land des Lächelns*, was based on an idea of his daughter Lizzi (the first wife of the tenor and director Hubert Marischka). Léon also prepared German versions of *The Yeomen of the Guard* (1889, with C. Lindau) and Edward Jakobowski's *Erminie* (1890, with F. Zell).

Operetten unless otherwise stated

Beim Schützenfest in Wien (Posse), M. von Weinzierl, 1880; *D'Artagnan* [*Die Drei Musketiere*], R. Raimann, 1881; *Tizianello*, E. Rosé, 1883; *O diese Götter!*, C. F. Stix, 1883; *Die Königin von Arragon* (komische Operette), Zamara, 1883; *Der Doppelgänger* (romantische komische Oper), Zamara, 1886; *Simplicius*, Johann Strauss, 1887; *Der Savoyarde* (Spl, with F. J. Brakl), O. Feyth, 1888; *Der Herr Abbé* (Spl, with Brakl), Zamara, 1889; *Der bleiche Gast* (with H. von Waldberg), J. Hellmesberger and Zamara, 1890; *Friedel mit der leeren Tasche*, M. J. Beer, 1892; *Gringoire* (Oper), I. Brüll, 1892; *Der Bajazzo* (with Waldberg), A. Czibulka, 1892

Schach dem Könige (Oper), Brüll, 1893; *Die Chansonette* (with Waldberg), Dellinger, 1894; *Das Modell* (with L. Held), Suppé, completed by J. Stern and Zamara, 1895; *Die Doppelhochzeit* (Vaudeville, with Waldberg), Hellmesberger, 1895; *Der Streik der Schmiede*, Beer, 1897; *Der Cognac-König* (with Held), F. Wagner, 1897; *Der Husar* (komische Operette), Brüll, 1898; *Der Opernball* (with Waldberg), R. Heuberger, 1898; *Katze und Maus* (with F. Gross), J. M. E. Strauss, 1898; *Die Pariserin [Das heimliche Bild]* (with Held), Suppé, 1898; *Ihre Excellenz* (with Waldberg), Heuberger, 1899; *Wiener Blut* (with L. Stein), A. Müller (jr), after Johann Strauss, 1899

Die Strohwitwe (with Waldberg), A. Kauders, 1899; *Der Sechsuhrzug* (with Stein), Heuberger, 1900; *Die verwunschene Prinzessin*, E. Gärtner, 1901; *Das Medaillon*, W. Mortier, 1901; *Tarok* (Posse), Raimann, 1901; *Der polnische Jude* (with R. Batka), K. Weis, 1901; *Der Rastelbinder*, Lehár, 1902; *Gräfin Pepi*, Josef Strauss and E. Reiterer, 1902; *Das gewisse Etwas* (Vaudeville-Operette, with Stein), C. Weinberger, 1902; *Der Herr Professor*, B. von Ujj, 1903; *Der Göttergatte* (with Stein), Lehár, 1904; *Vergeltsgott [Der Bettelgraf]*, L. Ascher, 1905; *Barfüssele* (Volksoper), Heuberger, 1905; *Die lustige Witwe* (with Stein), Lehár, 1905; *Kaisermanöver*, Ujj, 1905

Der fidele Bauer, Fall, 1907; *Die schönen von Fogaras* (Oper), A. Grünfeld, 1907; *Der Frauenmörder* (melodramatische Szene), Straus, 1907; *Die geschiedene Frau*, Fall, 1908; *Das Fürstenkind*, Lehár, 1909; *Der grosse Name* (Schauspiel mit Musik, with L. Feld), Stolz, 1909; *Didi*, Straus, 1909; *Das erste Weib*, B. Hartl, 1910; *Der gute Kamerad*, E. Kálmán, 1911, rev. as Gold gab ich für Eisen, 1914; *Die eiserne Jungfrau*, Stolz, 1911; *Der andere Herr war nicht so* (melodramatische Szene), Straus, 1911, as *Die anderen Herren sind nicht so*; *Die Studentengräfin*, Fall, 1913; *Der Nachtschnellzug* (Operette-Schwank, with Stein), Fall, 1913

Das Lumperl, Stolz, 1915; *Man steigt nach* (Posse, with H. Reichert), Straus, 1915; *Otto oder Otto* (Spl), H. Tegern, 1915; *Die Wachsfigur* (Spl), O. Stalla, 1916; *Liebeszauber*, Straus, 1916; *Liebchen am Dach*, Stojanović, 1917; *Der weisse Adler* (with H. Regel), R. Mader, 1917; *Wiener Kinder* (Spl, with Reichert), Stalla, after J. Schrammel, 1917; *Der Millionendieb*, F. Mayer, 1918; *Wiener Volkssänger* (Volksstück), R. Mahler, 1920; *Hol' mich der Teufel* (with Reichert), L. Reichwein, 1920; *Der Herzog von Reichstadt* (with Reichert), Stojanović, 1921; *Die gelbe Jacke*, Lehár, 1923; *Glück bei Frauen* (with Reichert), B. Granichstaedten, 1923; *Donna Gloria* (with Reichert), Nedbal, 1925

ANDREW LAMB

Leonati, Carlo Ambrogio. *See* LONATI, CARLO AMBROGIO.

Leoncavallo, Ruggero [Ruggiero] (*b* Naples, 23 April 1857; *d* Montecatini, 9 Aug 1919). Italian composer and librettist. The son of a well-to-do family in Naples – his father, Vincenzo, was a magistrate – he began his musical studies at the Conservatory in 1866. There he studied the piano with Beniamino Cesi and composition with Lauro Rossi, one of the best known opera composers of the day in the French tradition. He also studied composition under Serao until 1876. Formative in his development were the courses of the poet Giosuè Carducci, an enthusiastic Wagnerian, at Bologna University, which Leoncavallo followed from the autumn of 1876, breaking off, however, the following year without obtaining a degree. At the same time he was fired by the controversy over the art and aesthetic of *Wort–Ton–Drama* which led to the revival of the new version of Boito's *Mefistofele* and the Italian premières of *Rienzi* (1876) and *Der fliegende Holländer* (as *Vascello fantasma*, 1877), conducted by Mancinelli. Influenced by Wagner and grand opera, Leoncavallo wrote both the libretto and the music of his first opera, *Chatterton*, at about that time, although it was not performed until much later.

Encouraged by an uncle who was employed in the Italian Foreign Ministry, he then tried his fortune in Egypt, but on the outbreak of the Anglo-Egyptian War in 1882 he made his way to Marseilles and thence to Paris, where he lived a bohemian life, earning his living by giving music lessons and playing the piano at café-concerts. Thanks to the support of the baritone Victor Maurel, he received a commission for an opera from the publisher Giulio Ricordi. Leoncavallo had already decided to write a trilogy, to be entitled *Crepusculum*, which would be the Italian answer to Wagner's *Ring* cycle, as he claimed to have expounded to Wagner himself in 1876 when *Rienzi* received its first Italian performance in Bologna. His work on the project was erratic and he either could not or did not want to complete the task; the first opera, *I Medici*, took him a long time to write and caused serious difficulties with the publisher which continued until 1899. Meanwhile he made himself known in Paris with the performance of extracts from his symphonic poem *La nuit de mai*, after a poem by Alfred de Musset. After marrying the singer Berthe Rambaud he returned to Milan and became involved in the artistic life of the city, making a living by writing and occasional musical activity; he collaborated on the libretto for Puccini's *Manon Lescaut* (1893).

A decisive event for Leoncavallo's musical future was the success of Mascagni's *Cavalleria rusticana* in 1890. An acute analyst of market requirements, he recognized its significance and especially the potential of realism in opera as the quickest way to win popularity, but as with Mascagni, his fame was to rest on one opera into which he poured all his talent. *Pagliacci* was immediately successful with the Milanese audience at the Teatro Dal Verme in 1892 and paved the way for performances of his two earlier operas: *I Medici* was performed at the same theatre in the following year, and *Chatterton*, based on Alfred de Vigny's poem, was performed at the Teatro Argentina in Rome in 1896.

He completed his version of Murger's *Scènes de la vie de Bohème*, on which he had been working since 1892, and its first performance was carefully supervised by his new publisher Sonzogno in Venice in 1897. The long period of composition during which he sought to convey the realities of life in the Latin Quarter of Paris was preceded by fierce controversy with Puccini and the Ricordi publishing house. It was Leoncavallo who first had the idea of making it into an opera, but his *Bohème*, although it has pages full of vitality, is much more a social document of the period, and after the first years in which the two operas were performed almost side by side, it was Puccini's version that survived in the repertory. *Zazà*, on the other hand, the favourite role of Emma Carelli, first performed at the Teatro Lirico in Milan in 1900, was another opera with a theatrical setting and was an international success. But Leoncavallo's fortunes in Italy gradually declined, not least because being litigious by nature he frequently quarrelled with his publishers.

Although it became difficult for Leoncavallo to have his works performed in Italy they were very successful in Germany, where audiences were favourably inclined to works of the GIOVANE SCUOLA. After the success of *Pagliacci* (given in German as *Der Bajazzo*) and *I Medici*, Wilhelm II commissioned an opera from him to celebrate the Hohenzollern dynasty. The story chosen as subject, *Der Roland von Berlin*, had to be translated into Italian for Leoncavallo to dramatize it, and the result was then translated back into German, in which language it received great acclaim in 1904, with almost 40 performances.

This favourable episode gave him fresh confidence. His awareness of public media led him to the recording companies as early as 1904, and to compose his celebrated *Mattinata*, which Caruso recorded for the G & T Company. This was soon followed by *La jeunesse de Figaro*, his first operetta, for the American market. He returned to opera in 1910 with *Maià* at the Teatro Costanzi in Rome, based on a story by Paul de Choudens, who had written *Amica* for Mascagni (1905). This was followed by a return to the *verismo* of *Pagliacci* (as Mascagni was to do with *Il piccolo Marat* a few years later) with *Zingari* (1912, London).

The final phase of his career was concerned mainly with operettas, whose titles indicate their superficiality, from *Prestami tua moglie* to *A chi la giarrettiera?*. His last finished opera, *Goffredo Mameli* (1916), was a grand patriotic work, based on outmoded forms of expression and of little musical interest. More seriously, Leoncavallo had accepted a commission from the artistic director of the Chicago Lyric Opera, Cleofonte Campanini. The task of adapting as operas the plays of *Edipo re* (to a libretto by the experienced dramatist Giovacchino Forzano) and *Prometeo* were the most ambitious projects of his career, but his death in 1919 prevented him from completing them. He also left unfinished an opera on a Sardinian subject, *La tormenta*, which he had begun in 1914. *Edipo re* was performed in Chicago the year after his death, with Titta Ruffo in the title role. D'Annunzio described Leoncavallo's death as 'an excellent finale for that prolific composer of melodramas and operettas whose name combined two noble beasts and who died suffocated by melodic adiposity'.

See also Bohème, La (ii); Medici, I; Pagliacci; and Zazà.

all printed works published in Milan

Chatterton, *c*1876 (melodramma, 4, Leoncavallo, after A. de Vigny), unperf.; rev. (dramma lirico, 3), Rome, Argentina, 10 March 1896, vs (1896)
Pagliacci (dramma, prol., 2, Leoncavallo), Milan, Dal Verme, 21 May 1892 (1893)
Crepusculum (poema epico in forma di trilogia storica, Leoncavallo): I Medici (azione storica, 4), Milan, Dal Verme, 9 Nov 1893 (1893); pts 2, 3 not comp.
La bohème (commedia lirica, 4, Leoncavallo, after H. Murger), Venice, Fenice, 6 May 1897 (1897); rev. as Mimì Pinson (3), Palermo, Massimo, 14 April 1913, vs (1913)
Zazà (commedia lirica, 4, Leoncavallo, after P. Berton and C. Simon), Milan, Lirico, 10 Nov 1900 (1900); rev. R. Bianchi (1947)
Der Roland von Berlin (historisches Drama, 4, Leoncavallo, after W. Alexis; Ger. trans. G. Droescher), Berlin, Städtische Oper, 13 Dec 1904, vs (1904)
La jeunesse de Figaro (ob, 3, after V. Sardou and M. Vaucaire: Les premières armes de Figaro), ? New York, Nov 1906
Maià (dramma lirico, 3, A. Nessi, after P. de Choudens), Rome, Costanzi, 15 Jan 1910 (1908)
Malbruk (fantasia comica medioevale, 3, A. Nessi, after Boccaccio), Rome, Nazionale, 19 Jan 1910, vs (1910)
La reginetta delle rose (operetta, 3, Forzano), Rome, Costanzi, and Naples, Politeama Giacosa, 24 June 1912, vs (1912)
Zingari (dramma lirico, 2, E. Cavicchioli and G. Emanuel, after A. S. Pushkin), London, Hippodrome, 16 Sept 1912, vs (1912)
Are you There? (farce, 3, A. de Courville and E. Wallace), London, Prince of Wales, Nov 1913
La candidata (operetta, 3, Forzano), Rome, Nazionale, and Turin, Politeama Chiarella, 6 Feb 1915
Goffredo Mameli (azione storica, 2, Leoncavallo and G. Belvederi), Genoa, Carlo Felice, 27 April 1916
Prestami tua moglie (operetta, 3, E. Corradi), Montecatini, Casino, 2 Sept 1916
A chi la giarrettiera? (operetta, 3), Rome, Adriano, 16 Oct 1919

Edipo re (grand op, 1, G. Forzano, after Sophocles), Chicago, Opera, 13 Dec 1920, completed by G. Pennacchio
Il primo bacio (operetta, 1, L. Bonelli), Montecatini, Salone di Cura, 29 April 1923
La maschera nuda (operetta, 3, L. Bonelli and F. Paolieri), Naples, Politeama, 26 June 1925, completed by S. Allegra
Prometeo, unperf., unpubd
Tormenta (3, Belvederi), not completed

Librettos for other composers: *Mario Wetter*, A. Machado, 1898; *Redenzione*, G. Pennacchio, 1920

*

R. Giani and A. Engelfried: '"I Medici"', *RMI*, i (1894), 86–116
E. Hanslick: 'Der Bajazzo von Leoncavallo', *Der modernen Oper*, vii: *Fünf Jahre Musik (1891–1895): Kritiken* (Berlin, 1896, 3/1911), 96–104
——: '"Die Bohème"', *Der modernen Oper*, viii: *Am Ende des Jahrhunderts (1895–1899): musikalische Kritiken und Schilderungen* (Berlin, 1899, 3/1911), 123–32
N. Tabanelli: 'La causa Ricordi–Leoncavallo', *RMI*, vi (1899), 833–54
W. Pastor: 'Leoncavallos "Roland von Berlin": Uraufführung im Berliner Opernhaus', *Die Musik*, xiv/2 (1904–5), 45–6
J. Korngold: 'Ruggiero Leoncavallo: "Zazà", 1909', *Die romanische Oper der Gegenwart* (Vienna, 1922), 103–06
A. de Angelis: 'Il capolavoro inespresso di Leoncavallo? "Tormenta", opera di soggetto sardo', *RMI*, xxx (1923), 563–76
G. Fauré: 'Leoncavallo', *Opinions musicales* (Paris, 1930), 64–7
M. Rinaldi: *Musica e verismo* (Rome, 1932)
G. Adami: *G. Ricordi e i suoi musicisti* (Milan, 1933)
R. de Rensis: *Per Umberto Giordano e Ruggiero Leoncavallo* (Siena, 1949)
A. Holde: 'A Little-Known Letter by Berlioz and Unpublished Letters by Cherubini, Leoncavallo, and Hugo Wolf', *MQ*, xxxvii (1951), 340–53
J. W. Klein: 'Ruggero Leoncavallo (1858–1919)', *Opera*, ix (1958), 158–62, 232–6
——: 'The Other "Bohème"', *MT*, cxi (1970), 497–9
T. Lerario: 'Ruggero Leoncavallo e il soggetto dei "Pagliacci"', *Chigiana*, xxvi–xxvii (1971), 115–22
R. Mariani: *Verismo in musica* (Florence, 1976)
J. R. Nicolaisen: *Italian Opera in Transition, 1871–1893* (Ann Arbor, 1977)
L'avant-scène opéra, no.50 (1983) [*Pagliacci* issue]
D. Rubboli: *Ridi Pagliaccio: Ruggero Leoncavallo, un musicista raccontato per la prima volta* (Lucca, 1985)
A. Csampai and D. Holland, eds.: *Pietro Mascagni, Cavalleria rusticana/R. Leoncavallo, Der Bajazzo: Texte, Materialen, Kommentare* (Reinbek, 1987)
J. Maehder: 'Il libretto patriottico nell'Italia della fine del secolo e la raffigurazione dell'Antichità e del Rinascimento nel libretto prefascista italiano', *IMSCR, xiv Bologna 1987*, iii, 451–66
——: 'Paris-Bilder: zur Transformation von Henry Murgers Roman in den Bohème-Opern Puccinis und Leoncavallos', *JbO*, ii (1987), 109–76; It. trans., *NRMI*, xxiv (1990), 402–55
——: '"Questa è Mimì, gaia fioraia": zur Transformation der Gestalt Mimìs in Puccinis und Leoncavallos Bohème-Opern', *Opern und Opernfiguren: Festschrift für Joachim Herz* (Anif, 1989), 301–19
——: '"Musik über Musik": Meyerbeer, Rossini e Wagner nella "Bohème" di Ruggero Leoncavallo', *Dentro e fuori il melodramma: Venice 1989*
M. Sansone: 'The "verismo" of Ruggero Leoncavallo: a source study of "Pagliacci"', *ML*, lxx (1989), 342–62
A. M. Volpi: *'La Bohème' di Ruggero Leoncavallo* (diss., U. of Milan, 1990)
Ruggero Leoncavallo nel suo tempo: Locarno 1991

MICHELE GIRARDI

Leone, Francesco Bartolomeo de. *See* DE LEONE, FRANCESCO BARTOLOMEO.

Leonhardt, Robert (*b* Linz, 1877; *d* New York, 2 Feb 1923). Austrian baritone. After his début in Linz in 1898, he sang in Berlin from 1899, in Prague (1905–9), Brno (1909–11) and then Vienna, where his roles included the fiddler in the Viennese première of *Königskinder*. He made his Metropolitan Opera début in 1913 as Peter in *Hänsel und Gretel* and also appeared there as Alcindoro, Alberich, Klingsor and Papageno, as well as in the première of Giordano's *Madame Sans-Gêne* (1915). Bowing to anti-German sentiment, he sang under the name Robert Leonard during World War I but was nevertheless obliged to relinquish his Metropolitan contract in 1918 because of his Austrian citizenship. He returned to the company in 1920 and sang a variety of comprimario roles there until shortly before his death.   CORI ELLISON

Leoni, Franco (*b* Milan, 24 Oct 1864; *d* London, 8 Feb 1949). Italian composer. He studied at the Milan Conservatory with Dominiceti and Ponchielli. His first opera, *Raggio di Luna*, was produced at Milan in 1890. Two years later he emigrated to England, where his operas *Rip van Winkle* (1897) and *Ib and Little Christina* (Savoy Theatre, 1901) were produced. His best-known work, the one-act *L'oracolo*, was produced at Covent Garden in 1905 with Antonio Scotti as the opium dealer Chim-Fen, and conducted by André Messager. However, the piece, musically rather a long way beyond Ponchielli and Puccini, did not achieve popular success until it was produced at the Metropolitan in 1915, when Scotti proved it an apt vehicle for his vocal and dramatic abilities. He chose it for his farewell at that house in 1933, after which the work seems to have fallen out of the repertory. There were however revivals at the Curtis Institute (1949) and Philadelphia Opera (1952). A recording appeared with Tito Gobbi as Chim-Fen in 1977, when the 'Puccini-and-water' description of a contemporary critic seemed apt. His later operas were composed after he returned to Italy in 1917.

Raggio di Luna (C. Zanoni), Milan, 5 June 1890
Rip van Winkle, London, 4 Sept 1897
Ib and Little Christina (after H. C. Andersen), London, Savoy, 14 Nov 1901
L'oracolo, London, 28 June 1905
Tzigana (E. Moschini), Genoa, 3 Feb 1910
Francesca da Rimini (M. Crawford), Paris, OC (Favart), 1914
Le baruffe chiozzotte (after C. Goldoni), Milan, 2 Jan 1920
La terra del sogno (Linati), Milan, 10 Jan 1920
Falene (C. Linati), Milan, 1920
Massemarello, ? unperf.   ALAN BLYTH

Leoni, Michael [Lyon, Myer] (*b* Frankfurt, before 1760; *d* Kingston, Jamaica, 6 Nov 1796). English male alto. He was apparently brought to London to sing in the Duke's Place Synagogue and as a child had two seasons on stage from December 1760, singing in J. C. Smith's *The Enchanter* 'with great applause'. He reappeared, still as Master Leoni, in 1770 and then had a season in Dublin. In November 1774 Horace Walpole admired the 'full melancholy melody in his voice, though a *falsetta*'. The next April he was a great success as Arbaces in Arne's *Artaxerxes* and then sang regularly on the London stage until 1782, creating the role of Don Carlos in *The Duenna* (1775). With Giordani he started an English Opera Company in Dublin in 1783 but they quickly became bankrupt. He taught the young John Braham, who first appeared at Leoni's benefit in 1787. About 1790 he fled to Jamaica to escape his creditors and sang in the synagogue at Kingston.

BDA; LS
A. Pasquin [pseud. of J. Williams]: *The Children of Thespis*, ii (London, 1786, 13/1792)
C. H. Wilson: *The Myrtle and Vine* (London, 1802)
T. Gilliland: *The Dramatic Mirror*, ii (London, 1808)

R. Humphreys, ed.: *The Memoirs of J. Decastro, Comedian* (London, 1824)
R. Fiske: *English Theatre Music in the Eighteenth Century* (London, 1973)
T. J. Walsh: *Opera in Dublin 1705–1797* (Dublin, 1973)
                    OLIVE BALDWIN, THELMA WILSON

Leonora [*Leonora, ossia L'amore conjugale* ('Leonora, or Conjugal Love')]. *Dramma semiserio* in two acts by FERDINANDO PAER to a libretto *b* GIOVANNI SCHMIDT after JEAN-NICOLAS BOUILLY's libretto *Léonore, ou L'amour conjugal*; Dresden, Hoftheater, 3 October 1804.

Paer's opera is the second of four works based on Bouilly's story; the others are by Gaveaux (*Léonore, ou L'amour conjugal*, 1798), Mayr (*L'amor coniugale*, 1805) and, of course, Beethoven (*Leonore*, later *Fidelio*). In contrast to the other Italian version of this opera by Mayr and his librettist Gaetano Rossi, Paer and Schmidt's setting adheres closely to its source. Whereas Rossi would change the location, confine the action to one act, alter most of the characters and eliminate the chorus, Schmidt kept the original Spanish location and two-act format and remained relatively true to the personalities of Bouilly's characters.

Leonora (soprano), disguised as the boy Fedele, has apprenticed herself to the gaoler Rocco (*buffo* bass), hoping to free her husband Florestano (tenor), who has been unjustly imprisoned for two years by his enemy Pizzarro (tenor). Pizzarro learns that his superior, Don Fernando, who is unaware of his treachery, will arrive the next day; fearing a reprisal, Pizzarro orders Rocco to arrange for Florestano's murder by a masked man (to be Pizzarro himself) and permits Leonora to be present at the scene. Before Pizzarro can kill Florestano, Leonora intervenes, long enough for Fernando to arrive and rescue her husband. Rocco is pardoned and Pizzarro imprisoned.

Unlike Beethoven's Singspiel, Paer's *Leonora* was very successful at its première, in which the composer's wife, the noted soprano Francesca Riccardi, played the role of the heroine. Striking parallels between Paer's and Beethoven's settings – as well as the discovery of a score of Paer's opera among Beethoven's effects after his death – suggest that *Fidelio* may have been influenced by the earlier work.   SCOTT L. BALTHAZAR

Leonore [*Leonore, oder Der Triumph der ehelichen Liebe*]. Opera by Ludwig van Beethoven; see *FIDELIO*.

Leonov, Leon Ivanovich [Charpentier] (*b* St Petersburg, *c*1813; *d* Oct 1872). Russian tenor. The illegitimate son of John Field, the Irish composer and pianist, and a French mother, he appeared with his father as a child prodigy in Moscow. Having begun his career as a tenor in 1833, he was engaged in St Petersburg at the Bol'shoy Theatre, where he created Sobinin in *A Life for the Tsar* (1836) and Finn in *Ruslan and Lyudmila* (1842). Later he sang at the Mariinsky Theatre (1860–64). His repertory included the title role of *Robert le diable* and Rossini's Count Almaviva as well as many parts in Russian operas.

D. Brown: *Mikhail Glinka* (London, 1974)   ELIZABETH FORBES

Leonova, Dar'ya Mikhaylovna (*b* Vishniy Volochyok, Tver province, 9/21 March 1829; *d* St Petersburg, 25 Jan/6 Feb 1896). Russian contralto. She studied at the Imperial Opera School in St Petersburg, where she made her début in 1852 as Vanya in *A Life for the Tsar*, and sang in opera in St Petersburg and Moscow until 1874. Throughout her career she championed the cause of Russian music: she created the Princess in Dargomïzhsky's *Rusalka* (1856), the title role in Serov's *Rogneda* (1865), roles in Cui's *William Ratcliff* (1869) and Serov's *Vrazh'ya sila* ('Hostile Power', 1871), Vlasyevna in *The Maid of Pskov* (1873) and the Innkeeper in *Boris Godunov* (1874). She was also praised for her interpretations of Azucena and Ortrud. Between 1875 and 1879 she made concert tours of Russia, China, America and western Europe and published her reminiscences in *Istoricheskiy vestnik* (1891, nos.1–4). Leonova had a strong, dramatic voice with a range of two and a half octaves (*g* to *c'''*) and an engaging simplicity of expression.

A. Shteynberg: 'D. M. Leonova', *SovM* (1946), nos.2–3, p.121
V. Yakovlev: *D. M. Leonova* (Moscow, 1950)
JENNIFER SPENCER/ELIZABETH FORBES

Leontovych, Mykola Dmytrovych (*b* Selevynzi, Podillya, 1/13 Dec 1877; *d* Markivka, nr Tyl'chyn, 23 Jan 1921). Ukrainian composer. Born into the family of a priest, he received no systematic education in music, but after graduating (in 1899) he worked as a singing teacher and as an organizer of amateur choirs and orchestras. In 1904 he completed the education classes of the St Petersburg court chapel choir. From 1918 he taught at the Lysenko Music and Drama Institute, Kiev, was director of the First Ukrainian State Chapel and an inspector of the Ukrainian State SO and of cultural and educational establishments. The most brilliant of the immediate successors of Lysenko, he established with his folk music arrangements the fundamental features of the national style and decisively influenced the further assimilation of the nation's folklore by professional composers. His unfinished opera *Na Rusalchyn Velykden'* ('On Rusalka's Easter' or 'On the Mermaid's Holiday', composed 1920) surpasses in complexity and immediacy of expression all that had been achieved previously in Ukrainian music.

Yu.Yurmas, ed.: *Muzychni tvory* (Kiev, 1930)
Tvorchist' M. Leontovycha: *Zbirka statey* [Collection of Articles] (Kiev, 1977), 37-62
BOHDAN LUKANIUK

Leopold I (*b* Vienna, 9 June 1640; *d* Vienna, 5 May 1705). Holy Roman Emperor, composer and patron of music, second son of the Emperor FERDINAND III. He was trained for intellectual and spiritual pursuits rather than politics, receiving a thorough humanistic education which included music (composition, harpsichord, violin, flute) as well as Latin and Italian literature. When the first son and chosen successor to Ferdinand III died, however, Leopold fell heir to the throne. He succeeded his father as Holy Roman Emperor in 1658, and became one of the most significant patrons of Baroque opera. From Ferdinand he inherited a well-established *cappella* dominated by Italians, among them the *maestro di cappella* Antonio Bertali and his vice-*maestro*, Giovanni Felice Sances. Leopold continued this tradition through the judicious employment of Italians as *maestri di cappella*, vice-*maestri di cappella* and court composers, including Sances (who succeeded Bertali as *maestro di cappella*), Antonio Cesti, Antonio Draghi, Marc'Antonio Ziani, C. A. Badia and G. B. Bononcini. Only two native Austrian musicians are found among the leaders of the *cappella*: Johann Heinrich Schmelzer

(*c*1620–80), whose major contribution to the operatic repertory was the composition of ballets, and J. J. Fux, whose appointment as court composer in 1698 marked a peak of operatic achievement in the Viennese Baroque tradition.

These and other composers, together with the theatre architect and stage designer L. O. Burnacini and the court poets, particularly Francesco Sbarra, produced an extraordinarily large operatic repertory during Leopold's reign. The works were generally performed in connection with imperial family weddings, birthday and name-day celebrations, occasions of state, and the carnival season. Leopold's generous financial support for opera (the production of Antonio Cesti's *Il pomo d'oro* on the occasion of his first marriage cost about 100 000 florins); his own participation and that of other members of the imperial family in performances; his preference for and intimate knowledge of Italian opera; all contributed not only to the large number, but also to the high artistic quality of these productions.

His own compositional style follows the Viennese strain of the Venetian tradition as exemplified by Bertali, probably one of his teachers, and Draghi, to whose operas he often contributed single arias or scenes. It is characterized by careful attention to the text, skilful manipulation of recitative and arioso, and a preference for a simple and deeply felt melodic style rather than vocal display. His ballet music and his contributions to the developing German-language comedy, mainly short songs and arias, are light and simple and use folk music idioms; they are clearly influenced by Schmelzer.

La simpatia nell'odio overo Le amazoni amanti (opera tragicomica, 3, G. P. Monesio), Vienna, 18 Nov 1664, frag. *A-Wn*
Apollo deluso [? Act 2] (3, A. Draghi), Vienna, 13 June 1669, *Wn*, lib. (Vienna, 1669), collab. Sances
Creso (dramma per musica, N. Minato), Vienna, 6 Jan 1678
Giudizio d'amor [L'amoroso giudicio] (1), ?Vienna, *Wn*
Rimbomba mia tromba (serenata), ?Vienna, *Wn*
Del silentio profondo (serenata), ?Vienna, *Wn*

Intermezzos Orfeo y Euridice and La nobia Barbuda in P. Calderón de la Barca: *Fineza contra fineza*, Vienna, Stallburg, 11 Aug 1667, *Wn*

Recitatives and arias in works by Draghi, A. Cesti, Sances and J. H. Schmelzer; arias and instrumental music for comedies, 1680–97

L. von Köchel: *Die kaiserliche Hof-Musikkapelle in Wien von 1543 bis 1867* (Vienna, 1869)
G. Adler: 'Die Kaiser Ferdinand III., Leopold I., Joseph I. und Karl VI. als Tonsetzer und Förderer der Musik', *VMw*, viii (1892), 252
A. von Weilen: *Zur Wiener Theatergeschichte: die vom Jahre 1629 bis zum Jahre 1740 am Wiener Hofe zur Aufführung gelangten Werke theatralischen Charakters und Oratorien* (Vienna, 1901)
E. Wellesz: 'Die Opern und Oratorien in Wien, 1660–1708', *SMw*, vi (1919), 5–138
G. Tauschhuber: *Kaiser Leopold I. und das Wiener Barocktheater* (Mühldorf am Inn, 1947)
H. V. F. Somerset: 'The Habsburg Emperors as Musicians', *ML*, xxx (1949), 204
F. Hadamowsky: 'Barocktheater am Wiener Kaiserhof; mit einem Spielplan (1625–1740)', *Jb der Gesellschaft für Wiener Theaterforschung* (1951–2), 7–117; repr. separately (Vienna, 1955)
A. Bauer: *Opern und Operetten in Wien: Verzeichnis ihrer Erstaufführungen in der Zeit von 1629 bis zur Gegenwart* (Graz, 1955)
O. Wessely: 'Kaiser Leopolds I. "Vermeinte Brüder- und Schwesterliebe"', *SMw*, xxv (1962), 586
I. Bartels: *Die Instrumentalstücke in Oper und Oratorium der frühvenezianischen Zeit* (diss., U. of Vienna, 1970)
H. Seifert: 'Die Festlichkeiten zur ersten Hochzeit Kaiser Leopolds I.', *ÖMz*, xxix (1974), 6–16
G. Brosche: 'Die musikalischen Werke Kaiser Leopolds I.: ein systematisch-thematisches Verzeichnis der erhaltenen

Kompositionen', *Beiträge zur Musikdokumentation: Franz Grasberger zum 60. Geburtstag* (Tutzing, 1975), 27–82

H. Seifert: 'Die Entfaltung des Barock', *Österreichische Musikgeschichte*, ed. R. Flotzinger and G. Gruber, i (Vienna, 1977), 323–79

H. Seifert: *Die Oper am Wiener Kaiserhof im 17. Jahrhundert* (Tutzing, 1985)   RUDOLF SCHNITZLER

Leopold II [Pietro Leopoldo] (*b* Vienna, 5 May 1747; *d* Vienna, 1 March 1792). Holy Roman Emperor, patron of music, third son of Empress Maria Theresa Habsburg and Francis of Lorraine. As a patron Leopold influenced operatic life in both Tuscany, which he ruled as Grand Duke from 1765 to 1790, and Vienna. In Tuscany he hired as *virtuosi di camera* several leading opera singers, among them Giovanni Manzuoli, Giusto Ferdinando Tenducci and Tommaso Guarducci, and subsidized the performance of several innovatory operas by Traetta, including his masterpiece, *Ifigenia in Tauride* (1763, Vienna; revived in Florence in 1768). In 1790 Leopold succeeded his brother Joseph II in Vienna and brought with him a taste for Italian opera as it was cultivated in Florence. He undertook a major transformation of the Viennese court opera in 1791, dismissing some of those who had contributed much to Viennese opera during the previous decade (including Lorenzo da Ponte) and hiring singers with whom he had become familiar in Florence. His policies for comic opera are reflected in Cimarosa's *Il matrimonio segreto*, first performed in Vienna only a few weeks before Leopold's death; the effects of his re-introduction of *opera seria* and ballet to the repertory of the Burgtheater and Kärntnertortheater were felt well into the 19th century.

*

O. Michtner: *Das alte Burgtheater als Opernbühne von der Einführung des deutschen Singspiels (1778) bis zum Tod Kaiser Leopolds II. (1792)* (Vienna, 1970)

J. A. Rice: *Emperor and Impresario: Leopold II and the Transformation of Viennese Musical Theater, 1790–1792* (diss., U. of California, Berkeley, 1987)   JOHN A. RICE

Leopoldstadt [Theater in der Leopoldstadt]. Theatre in Vienna, opened in 1781 and used for Singspiel and light opera until its replacement by the Carltheater in 1847. *See* VIENNA, §3.

Le Page, François (*b* Joinville, 27 Feb 1709; *d* after 1780). French baritone (*basse-taille*). His first roles at the Paris Opéra were Don Carlos and Silvandre (*L'Europe galante*, 1736 revival), Mars (*Castor et Pollux*, 1737) and Pan (*Cadmus*, 1737 revival). His position as third *basse-taille*, after Chassé and Dun, improved during the former's absence, 1738–42. He created Ismenor and Teucer in Rameau's *Dardanus* (1739), roles that reverted to Chassé in the 1744 revival, when Le Page was relegated to Antenor. In 1740 he sang the title role in Montéclair's *Jephté* for the triumphant return of Mlle Lemaure as Iphise, and the following year appeared as Destouches' Hylas to Lemaure's Issé. Le Page sang in the first performances of Rameau's *Zaïs* (1748, Cindor) and *Naïs* (1749, Jupiter and Tiresias) and took smaller roles in *Zoroastre*, *Platée* and *Acante et Céphise*. He was married to Mlle Eremans, and retired in 1752.   PHILIP WELLER

Le Peletier [Salle Le Peletier]. Home of the Paris Opéra, 1821–73; *see* PARIS, §4(ii).

Le Picq [Le Picque, Lepic, Le Pichi, Picq, Pick, Pich, Pik], **Charles** [Carlo] (*b* Naples, 1744; *d* St Petersburg,

1806). French choreographer and dancer. As a youth he was influenced by the Noverrian form of *ballet en action*. His initial contract as *figurant* at Stuttgart from February 1760, shortly before Noverre's arrival, was extended in 1761 for six more years, with the additional clause that he be given special instruction by Noverre in 'Serieux-Tanzen'. By 1766 he was a leading dancer. After Noverre's departure in 1767 Le Picq transferred to Vienna, where in 1765 he had already come into contact with Hilverding, an early exponent of dramatic dance. He may also have appeared in Warsaw. When Noverre took over at Vienna in late 1767 Le Picq became principal dancer. In 1769 he moved to Italy and, apart from two short visits to Paris to dance under Noverre (1776, 1778), remained until early 1782. He choreographed his first work, a Noverre revival, at Padua in June 1769, thereafter alternating as director of ballets at the S Benedetto in Venice and the Regio Ducal in Milan, briefly working also at the Pergola in Florence. At Milan he staged the first ballet in Hasse's last opera, *Il Ruggiero* (1771); on 26 December 1772, in Mozart's *Lucio Silla*, he both choreographed the opera's closing *ciaccona* and, after Act 1, revived Noverre's *Les jalousies du sérail*. Mozart made souvenir sketches of its music (mainly by Joseph Starzer).

For two periods, May 1773 to January 1776 and May 1777 to November 1781, Le Picq was chief choreographer at the S Carlo in Naples. There he staged the internal dances for the revival of Gluck's *Orfeo ed Euridice* (4 November 1774). In between these two contracts he made his Parisian début, dancing under Noverre's direction at the Opéra in Gluck's *Alceste* (1776), and worked as choreographer at the S Benedetto in Venice. Afterwards at Naples he became acquainted with the young Martín y Soler, who provided the music for most of his original ballets from 1780 onwards as well as a new setting to replace Gluck's original for a revival of Angiolini's *Semiramide* (13 August 1780). Le Picq moved to London in 1782. At the King's Theatre he was first dancer, again under Noverre, and then director of ballets (December 1782 to April 1785). His initial successes there led Catherine II to instruct the Russian ambassador in May 1783 to engage him for her court ballets, but prior contracts did not permit his acceptance until 1786. He was ballet-master at St Petersburg until his retirement in 1799, collaborating on several occasions with Martín y Soler, court composer since 1790. Le Picq was instrumental in promoting an Italian translation of Noverre's *Lettres sur la danse*, but only two of the original 15 chapters were published (as *Due lettere scritte a diversi soggetti*, Naples, 1774). In a final expression of gratitude to the master who had promoted his own career, he issued a lavish edition of Noverre's works at St Petersburg in 1803–4.

*

R.-A. Mooser: *Annales de la musique et des musiciens en Russie au XVIIIe siècle*, ii (Geneva, 1951), 495–6

M. H. Winter: *The Pre-Romantic Ballet* (London, 1974)

R. Cafiero: 'Aspetti della musica coreutica fra settecento e ottocento', *Il Teatro di San Carlo 1737–1987*, ed. B. Cagli and A. Ziino, ii (Naples, 1987), 309–31

K. K. Hansell: 'Il ballo teatro e l'opera italiana', *SOI*, v (1988), 214–42   KATHLEEN KUZMICK HANSELL

L'Epine, (Francesca) Margherita [Françoise Marguérite] **de** (*b* c1680; *d* London, 8 Aug 1746). Italian soprano, perhaps of Huguenot extraction. She sang at Venice in 1698–1700, described as a virtuoso of the court of Mantua. In 1702 she went to London, probably with the composer Jakob Greber (whose mistress she was) and her sister MARIA GALLIA, also a singer. L'Epine sang at Lincoln's Inn Fields in plays and concerts in 1703, and was employed regularly at Drury Lane, from 1704 to 1708, when she moved with the rest of the opera company to the Queen's Theatre, remaining there until 1714. At first her repertory was confined to songs and cantatas, including music by Purcell, G. Bononcini and A. Scarlatti; her rivalry at this time with Catherine Tofts was notorious. The first London opera in which she is known to have appeared was Haym's adaptation of Bononcini's *Camilla* at Drury Lane in 1706. From 1707 to 1714 she sang in almost all the operas produced in London, most of them pasticcios, often playing male parts: *Thomyris* and (in a different role) *Camilla* (1707), *Love's Triumph* and A. Scarlatti's *Pirro e Demetrio*(1708), *Clotilda* (1709), *Almahide* and Mancini's *Idaspe fedele* (1710), Gasparini's *Antioco* (1711) and *Ambleto* (1712), Galliard's English opera *Calypso and Telemachus* (Calypso, 1712), *Ernelinda* (1713), and *Dorinda*, *Creso* and *Arminio* (1714). She sang Goffredo in revivals of Handel's *Rinaldo* (1712, 1713) and created Eurilla in his *Il pastor fido* (1712), Agilea in *Teseo* (1713) and probably Flavia in *Silla* (1713).

In 1715 L'Epine joined Pepusch, whom she later married, at Drury Lane, and sang in several masques by him including *Venus and Adonis*, *Myrtillo*, *Apollo and Daphne* and *The Death of Dido* (1715–16), and in English revivals of *Camilla*, *Calypso and Telemachus* and *Thomyris* (1717). In 1719 she sang in Galliard's *Circe*and retired, but appeared in three performances (including one of Handel's *Radamisto*) during the Royal Academy's first season at the King's (1720). She sang once at Drury Lane as late as 1733.

The leading female singer in the years just before and after the introduction of Italian opera to London, and the first Italian to establish a lasting reputation there, L'Epine was immensely popular. Burney was impressed by the difficulty of some of her songs: 'Indeed, her musical merit must have been very considerable to have kept her so long in favour'. The compass of the parts Handel composed for her is d' to a'', but others take her down to c' and up to bb''. She was a fine harpsichordist, much admired for her performance of pieces from the Fitzwilliam Virginal Book, then owned by Pepusch.

*

BurneyH; *HawkinsH*
E. L. Moor: 'Some Notes on the Life of Françoise Marguérite de L'Epine', *ML*, xxviii (1947), 341–6
D. F. Cook: 'Françoise Marguérite de l'Epine: the Italian Lady?', *Theatre Notebook*, xxxv (1981), 58–73, 104–13

WINTON DEAN

Leppard, Raymond (John) (*b* London, 11 Aug 1927). English conductor. He studied at Cambridge and made his London début as a conductor in 1952 in music of the 17th and 18th centuries. He was briefly music director for the Royal Court Theatre, London, and a répétiteur at Glyndebourne (1954–5), then made his Covent Garden début in Handel's *Samson* (1959). His edition of Monteverdi's *L'incoronazione di Poppea*, produced at Glyndebourne in 1962 (he conducted it there in 1964), inaugurated a series of realizations of Monteverdi and Cavalli operas that did much to introduce Baroque opera to a wider public. Leppard took a free attitude to the original texts, involving transpositions and cuts, enhanced sonorities and remodelled librettos, an approach defined in his article 'Cavalli's Operas' (*PRMA*, xciii,

1966–7, pp.67–76). Several of his editions have been published and a number of recordings made that originate from his Glyndebourne performances.

Leppard extended his activity to the USA in 1974 with *Egisto* at Santa Fe, where in 1976 he conducted *The Mother of Us All* with an added overture he composed with the composer's approval. He made his début at the Metropolitan in 1978 with *Billy Budd*, having settled in the USA. Since then he has conducted opera widely for New York City Opera, in Houston, Miami, San Francisco and elsewhere. He conducted his performing edition of Rameau's *Dardanus* at the Paris Opéra (1981), and has added to the Cavalli series *Orione* (1984) at Santa Fe and Scottish Opera. His recordings include *The Mother of Us All* (1976), as well as video recordings of the 1984 Glyndebourne production of *Poppea* (issued 1989) with Maria Ewing, and the 1973 Glyndebourne production of *Il ritorno d'Ulisse* (issued 1990) with Janet Baker. His performances are characterized by light, dance-like rhythms, polished phrasing and a keen sense of vocal and instrumental colour. He was named Commendatore of the Italian Republic in 1974 and was made CBE in 1983.

STANLEY SADIE, NOËL GOODWIN

Lerescu, Emil (*b* Piteşti, 26 Jan 1921). Romanian composer. He studied at the Bucharest Conservatory (1941–6) with Mihail Jora (harmony), Constantin Brăiloiu (folklore) and Maria Fotino (piano) and then taught in Piteşti (1946–52), Craiova (1952–4) and Bucharest (1954–81). His output ranges from songs to symphonic works, favouring dramatic genres. His writing is lyrical and uses classical forms with traditional harmony and orchestration. His considerable experience as a composer of vocal music is reflected in the melodic richness of his arias.

Ecaterina Teodoroiu, 1964, rev. 1967 (heroic op, 3 acts, 6 tableaux, N. Tăutu), Bucharest, Romanian Opera, 16 May 1971
Peneş Curcanul, 1977 (op-ballad, prol., 1, epilogue, Lerescu, after V. Alecsandri), Iaşi, Romanian Opera, 30 Dec 1981
D-ale carnavalului [Carnival Stories], 1978 (comic op, prol., 3, Lerescu, after I. L. Caragiale), Bucharest TV, 17 June 1982
Steaua fără nume [Star without a Name], 1981 (lyric op, 3, after M. Sebastian), Bucharest TV, Aug 1983

VIOREL COSMA

Lermontov, Mikhail Yur'yevich (*b* Moscow, 3/15 Oct 1814; *d* Pyatigorsk, 15/27 July 1841). Russian poet and novelist of Scottish descent. Both in his life – a brief whirlwind of aristocratic privilege, exotic military postings, windswept peaks and duels – and in his work, he epitomized the meteoric heyday of Romanticism in Russia. With their extremes of mood, their aesthetic and moral idealism on the one hand and their portrayal of social pathology on the other, and above all with their Caucasian settings, his works have been a magnet for Russian and Soviet composers. Adaptations of his plotted works for the Russian lyric stage include operas by Anton Rubinstein and B. V. Asaf'yev, while settings of his lyrics number in the high hundreds.

Khadzhi-Abrek [Hadji-Abrek] (narrative poem, 1835): Rubinstein, 1852, as Mest' [Revenge]
Tambovskaya kaznacheysha [The Wife of the Treasurer of Tambov] (narrative poem, 1838): B. V. Asaf'yev, 1937, as Kaznacheysha
Geroy nashego vremeni [A Hero of our Time] (novel, 1840): V. A. Gaigerova, 1941, as Krepost' u kamennogo broda [The Fortress at the Rocky Ford]; V. A. Dekhteryov, 1941, as Knyazhna Meri [Princess Mary]; A. N. Alexandrov, 1946, as Bela
Pesnya pro tsarya Ivana Vasil'yevicha, molodogo oprichnika i udalogo kuptsa Kalashnikova [Song of Tsar Ivan Vasil'yevich, the Young Oprichnik and the Brave Merchant Kalashnikov] (narra-

tive poem, 1840): Rubinstein, 1880, as Kupets Kalashnikov [The Merchant Kalashnikov]; S. V. Aksyuk, 1940

Boyarin Orsha [The Nobleman Orsha] (narrative poem, 1842): N. S. Krotkov, 1898; K. D. Agrenev-Slavyansky, 1910

Maskarad [A Masked Ball] (drama, pubd 1842): N. A. Kolesnikov, 1890; V. N. Denbsky, 1940; A. V. Mosolov, 1940; R. S. Bunin, 1944; B. I. Zeydman, 1945; B. P. Nersesov, comp. 1942–8; D. A. Tolstoy, 1956–; A. P. Artamonov, 1957

Beglets [The Fugitive] (narrative poem, 1846): B. K. Avetisov, 1943

Demon [The Demon] (dramatic-narrative poem, 1856): A. Rubinstein, 1875; B. A. Fitingof-Shel', 1886, as Tamara; A. S. Yur'yevich, 1891; P. Gilson, 1893; P. I. Blaramberg, 1908

Angel smerti [The Angel of Death] (narrative poem, 1857): A. N. Koreshchenko, 1893

Vadim (historical novel, 1873): G. G. Kreytner, 1952, as V groznïy god [In the Terrible Year]

*

E. Kann: *M. Yu. Lermontov i muzïka* (Moscow, 1939)
B. Glovatsky: *Lermontov i muzïka* (Leningrad, 1964)

RICHARD TARUSKIN

Le Rochois, Marie ['La Rochois'] (*b* Caen, *c*1658; *d* Paris, 8 Oct 1728). French soprano and singing teacher, commonly but incorrectly known as Marthe Le Rochois. She may have studied with Michel Lambert, who presumably brought her to the attention of his son-in-law, Lully. In 1678 she entered the Paris Opéra, where Lully chose her to create the roles of Arethusa in *Proserpine*(1680), Merope in *Persée* (1682), Arcabonne in *Amadis* (1684), Angélique in *Roland* (1685), Armide in *Armide* (1686) and Galatea in *Acis et Galatée* (1686). She also sang in Lully revivals, as Medea in *Thésée* (1688), Cybele in *Atys* (1689) and Hermione in *Cadmus et Hermione* (1690). In the post-Lully period she created Polyxena in the Lully-Collasse *Achille et Polyxène* (1687), Thetis in Collasse's *Thétis et Pélée* (1689), Lavinia in Collasse's *Enée et Lavinie* (1690), Dido in Desmarets' *Didon* (1693), and Medea in Charpentier's *Médée* (1693). Fearing the loss of her voice, Le Rochois was absent from the Opéra from 1694 to 1696, when she returned as Ariadne in Marais' *Ariane et Bacchus*. In 1697 she created the roles of Venus in Desmarets' *Vénus et Adonis* and Roxane in Campra's *L'Europe galante*. Her final role (shared with Mlle Desmatins) was Isis in Destouches' *pastorale-héroïque*, performed in December 1697. She retired in 1698.

Le Rochois was best known for her performance of Armide, the memory of which caused Le Cerf de la Viéville (*Comparaison de la musique*, 1704–6) to 'shiver' with delight. Titon du Tillet (*Le Parnasse françois*, 1732) called her the 'greatest actress and the best model for declamation to have appeared on the stage' and gave a detailed description of her performance of Armide's great recitative, 'Enfin il est en ma puissance'. Although most French observers seem to have been in general agreement with Titon's appraisal, J. E. Galliard, in his English translation (1709) of Raguenet's *Paralèle des italiens et des françois*, added: 'I saw that woman at Paris: she was a good figure enough and had a tolerable voice, but then she was a wretched actress and sang insufferably out of tune'.

Upon retirement from the Opéra, Le Rochois purchased a small country house outside Paris where she received important musicians, actors and actresses, who profited from her 'pleasant conversation, her knowledge and her good taste' (Titon du Tillet). Of strong moral character and untouched by professional jealousy, she gave singing lessons in her retirement to a new generation of opera singers, chief among whom were Mlles Journet and Antier. After a long illness, she died in an apartment on the rue St Honoré and was buried at St Eustache.

JAMES R. ANTHONY

Leroux, Xavier (Henry Napoléon) (*b* Velletri, Italy, 11 Oct 1863; *d* Paris, 2 Feb 1919). French composer. His father was a musical director in the army, his mother Italian. According to several of his contemporaries, Leroux was proud of his fiery Italian blood and would easily rise to an argument, especially when it concerned making cuts to his operas which were initially far too long. A near contemporary of Dukas and Debussy, Leroux appears in several photographs with young composers of that generation, but the path he was to follow was conservative rather than adventurous. He was strongly influenced by the traditional harmony teaching of his professors at the Conservatoire, Dubois and Massenet, and in 1885 he won the Prix de Rome with the cantata *Endymion*. He continued using a similar harmonic style well into the 20th century.

Astarté, given at the Paris Opéra under Taffanel in 1901, achieved a modest success; it was followed in 1903 by *La reine Fiamette* at the Opéra-Comique. This latter opera was staged in many countries up to World War II, as was *Le chemineau* (1907), widely considered his finest work. *1814*, a *drame lyrique* set in the Napoleonic wars, includes elaborate effects (Napoleon dreaming of a Te Deum for example) and choral representations of the voices of Joan of Arc. Eschewing harmonic and rhythmic complexity and untinged by Wagner, Leroux is at his best when using relatively simple musical devices. The pastoral naturalism of *Le chemineau* has caused some critics to place him with other French *verismo* composers but this rather ignores the more imaginative side of his work. In 1896 Leroux was appointed professor of harmony at the Conservatoire, a post he held until his death; at one time he counted André Caplet among his pupils. Neither his teaching nor his music possessed the distinctiveness to ensure him any lasting influence.

unless otherwise stated, first performed in Paris and printed works published in Paris

Evangéline (légende acadienne, 4, L. de Gramont, G. Hartmann and A. Alexandre, after H. W. Longfellow), Brussels, Monnaie, 18 Dec 1895, vs (1895)
Vénus et Adonis (scène lyrique, 2, de Gramont), Opéra, 24 Jan 1897
Astarté (4, de Gramont), Opéra, 15 Feb 1901, vs (1901)
La reine Fiamette (conte dramatique, 4, C. Mendès), OC (Favart), 23 Dec 1903, vs (*c*1910)
William Ratcliff (tragédie musicale, 4, de Gramont, after H. Heine), Nice, 22 Jan 1906, vs (1906)
Théodora (drame musical, 3, V. Sardou and P. Ferrier), Monte Carlo, 19 March 1907 (1907)
Le chemineau [The Vagrant] (J. Richepin), OC (Favart), 6 Nov 1907 (1907)
Le carillonneur (pièce lyrique, 3, Richepin, after G. Rodenbach), OC (Favart), 20 March 1913, vs (1913)
La fille de Figaro, (oc, 3, M. Hennequin and H. Delorme), Apollo, 11 March 1914
Les cadeaux de Noël (conte héroïque, 1, E. Fabre), OC (Favart), 25 Dec 1915, vs (1915)
1814 (drame lyrique, 1, L. Augé de Lassus and A. Gandrey), Monte Carlo, Casino, 6 April 1918, vs (1918)
Nausithoé (oc, 1, M. de Magre), Nice, Casino municipal, 9 April 1920
La plus forte (drame lyrique, 4, Richepin and P. de Choudens), OC (Favart), 11 Jan 1924 (1924)
L'ingénu (ob, 3, C. Méré and R. Gignoux, after Voltaire), Bordeaux, Grand, 13 Feb 1931, vs (1930)

*

A. Jullien: 'Astarté', *Le théâtre*, no.61 (1901), 3–14
H. Barbuse: 'La reine Fiamette à l'Opéra-Comique', *Musica*, no.17 (1904), 259–61

A. Sardoux: 'La reine Fiamette', *Le théâtre*, no.124 (1904), 3–24
E. Destranges: *Consonances et dissonances* (Paris, 1906)
D. C. Parker: 'Xavier Leroux', *Musical Standard*, ix (1917), 198
H. de Curzon: 'Xavier Leroux, Alexandre Georges, Henry Février', *Le théâtre lyrique en France* (Paris, 1937–9) [pubn. of Poste National/Radio-Paris], iii, 121–4
P. Landormy: *La musique française de Franck à Debussy* (Paris, 1943, 2/1948), 8, 158–9
P. Bertrand: *Le monde de la musique* (Geneva, 1947)
M. Cooper: *French Music from the Death of Berlioz to the Death of Fauré (1869–1924)* (London, 1951)
R. Dumesnil: 'Réalistes et naturalistes', *Histoire de la musique*, iv (Paris, 1958)
M. Kelkel: *Naturalisme, vérisme et réalisme dans l'opéra* (Paris, 1984)   RICHARD LANGHAM SMITH

Leschetizky, Theodor [Leszetycki, Teodor] (*b* Łańcut, Galicia, 22 June 1830; *d* Dresden, 14 Nov 1915). Polish pianist, teacher and composer. A pupil of Czerny and a friend of Anton Rubinstein, he was in great demand as a piano teacher, first in St Petersburg (1852–77), then in Vienna (from 1878). His vigorous, practical methods earned him the respect of hundreds of pupils, among them Paderewski, Artur Schnabel and Ossip Gabrilovich. Most of his 49 compositions are piano miniatures, but they also include two operas, the unperformed *Die Brüder von Marco*, and *Die erste Falte* (komische Oper, 1, S. H. Mosenthal), first given in Prague on 9 October 1867.   TADEUSZ PRZYBYLSKI

Lescot, C. François (*b* *c*1720; *d* *c*1801). French composer. He was *maître de musique* at Auch Cathedral from 1747 to 1764, and at Nantes Cathedral probably from 1764 to 1768. In 1768 he moved to Paris and joined the orchestra of the Comédie-Italienne as a violinist. Apart from a brief absence between 1785 and autumn 1787, he remained there until his retirement in 1790. Lescot's first three stage works, for which he wrote both librettos and music, were first performed at the Théâtre d'Auch, two in 1761 and the third in 1767; these and his other theatre works were suited to contemporary French taste and were well received. Many were later included in the repertories of the Parisian theatres in the late 18th century and the early 19th. His first stage work presented in Paris, *La négresse, ou Le pouvoir de la reconnaissance* (1787, Comédie-Italienne) was highly praised in the *Mercure de France*. All his Parisian stage works included vaudevilles and couplets. Lescot also composed sacred music, songs and chamber works.

L'amour et l'hymen (oc, 1, Lescot), Auch, 1761 (Auch, 1761)
La fête de Thalie (pastorale, 1, Lescot), Auch, 1761 (Auch, 1761)
La fête de Thémire (pastorale with vaudeville and ariettes, 1, Lescot), Auch, 1767
La négresse, ou Le pouvoir de la reconnaissance (comédie with vaudevilles and divertissements, 2, P.-Y. Barré and J.-B. Radet), Paris, Comédie-Italienne, 15 June 1787 (Paris, 1787)
Les solitaires de Normandie (oc with vaudevilles, 1, A.-P.-A. de Piis and Barré), Paris, Comédie-Italienne, 15 Jan 1788 (Paris, 1788)
Candide marié, ou Il faut cultiver son jardin (comédie with vaudevilles, 2, Barré and Radet), Paris, Comédie-Italienne, 20 June 1788 (Paris, 1788)

*

Mercure de France (July 1764, Sept 1764, July 1787, Jan 1788, June 1788)
Almanach des spectacles (Paris, 1769–90)
Almamach musical/Calendrier musical universel (Paris, 1782–9)
Babault: *Annales dramatiques, ou Dictionnaire général des théâtres* (Paris, 1808–12)   ETHYL L. WILL

Le Sénéchal de Kerkado, Mlle. *See* KERKADO, LE SÉNÉCHAL DE.

Lessel, Wincenty Ferdynand (*b* Jilové, nr Prague, *c*1750; *d* Puławy or Warsaw, after 1825). Polish composer of Bohemian descent. He received his musical education in Germany, where his family settled in 1762. He studied composition, the keyboard, violin and viola in Dresden under J. G. Schürer and from 1762 to about 1776 played the viola in the Dresden royal orchestra. By 1780 he was in Warsaw, and the following year he took the post of piano teacher at Prince Adam Kazimierz Czartoryski's establishment in Puławy. In 1787 he was appointed court Kapellmeister. By 1812 he was also music director of the theatre at Sieniawa (the other Czartoryski residence). In 1825 he was living at Puławy and was a singing teacher. His works show technical competence, and, like those of many of his contemporary compatriots, are characterized by elements of Polish folk music.

first performed at Puławy unless otherwise stated
Cyganie [The Gypsies] (F. D. Kniaźnin), 1787
Dwaj strzelcy i mleczarka [Two Huntsmen and the Milkmaid] (operetta, L. Anseaume, trans. J. Baudouin), 1787; rev. version (trans. A. Hoffman), 1804; duet frag., *PL-Wtm*
Matka spartanka [The Spartan Mother] (Kniaźnin), 1787
Troiste wesele [Triple Wedding] (5, Kniaźnin), 1787
Piast (melodrama, J. U. Niemcewicz), 1800; rev. version (L. A. Dmuszewski), Sieniawa, 27 Jan 1820
Pantomima, 1805
I plotka czasem się przyda [Even Gossip is sometimes Useful] (idyll, I. Tański), 1805; sequel [same title], Sieniawa, 1818
Domek na gościńcu [Little House in the High-road] (1, Dmuszewski), Sieniawa, 1818
Pielgrzym z Dobromila [The Pilgrim from Dobromil] (2, A. Kłodziński), Sieniawa, 31 March 1819
Przyjazd pożądany [Wished-for Arrival] (2, Kłodziński), Sieniawa, 31 March 1820

*

J. Prosnak: *Kultura muzyczna Warszawy XVIII wieku* (Kraków, 1955)
H. Rudnicka-Kruszewska: *Wincenty Lessel* (Kraków, 1968)
S. Durski: 'Zabawy teatralne w Sieniawie' [Theatre Amusements in Sieniawa], *Pamiętnik teatralny* (Warsaw, 1970), 28
                    ALINA NOWAK-ROMANOWICZ

Lesson on Consent. Music theatre work by Paul Hindemith; *see* LEHRSTÜCK.

Lesta, ili Dneprovskaya rusalka ('Lesta, or The Dnepr Water Nymph'). Magical comic opera in three acts by STEPAN IVANOVICH DAVÏDOV to a libretto by N. S. Krasnopol'sky after FERDINAND KAUER's Singspiel *Das Donauweibchen* (1798); St Petersburg, Bol'shoy Theatre, 25 October/6 November 1805.

When Kauer's original Singspiel was first performed in Russia in 1803, it contained six supplementary numbers by Davïdov, a staff composer for the St Petersburg theatres, added for the sake of local colour to facilitate the transplanting of the action from the Danube to the Dnepr. The production was so successful that a sequel (with additional numbers by Catterino Cavos) was given the following year. To meet the still insatiable demand, the directorate of the Imperial Theatres commissioned another sequel from Davïdov with a wholly original score, though still to Krasnopol'sky's adaptation of the original libretto by K. F. Hensler. This was *Lesta*, the first Russian Romantic opera. It held the stage until the 1850s (far outlasting yet another sequel, to a new libretto by Alexander Shakhovskoy entitled *Rusalka*, 'The Water Nymph', which Davïdov produced in 1807) and furnished the model for the dramatic poem by Pushkin that in turn provided the basis (and much of the text) for Dargomïzhsky's famous opera of 1856.

The subject of all these operas was the old legend of the mermaid or water nymph impossibly in love with a mortal man. Prince Vidostan (in the Russian adaptation) (tenor) has forsaken Lesta (soprano), the queen of the Dnepr water nymphs (who has appeared to him in the form of a beautiful girl), and married Princess Miloslava (soprano). Before long the prince, having grown cold towards his spouse, is wandering through stormy woods with an entourage of hunters in a vain search for his old love. The second act takes place on the Dnepr banks by moonlight. Hearing the hunters' horns, Lesta magically clears a path and awaits her old love, whom she has never forgotten. In the third act the two lovers have a rendezvous, but Lesta finally renounces Vidostan at an oracle's behest and he returns chastened to the bosom of his family.

Davïdov's music is notable chiefly for its evocative effects of 'supernatural' harmony and orchestration, and also for its use of melodrama (later developed by Dargomïzhsky in Act 4 of *Rusalka*). Three numbers in piano-vocal score – the opening chorus and melodramas from Act 2 – have been printed (Ginzburg 1969), and the magic music with glass harmonica from Act 1 is printed in full score (Rabinovich 1948). A recording of excerpts from *Lesta* and other works of Davïdov was issued by Melodiya to mark the composer's bicentenary in 1977.
RICHARD TARUSKIN

Le Sueur [Lesueur], Jean-François (*b* Drucat-Plessiel, nr Abbeville, 15 Feb 1760; *d* Paris, 6 Oct 1837). French composer. From a peasant family in the north of France, he cultivated his talent for music in cathedral choir schools where the education was free. He was a choirboy first in Abbeville, then in Amiens. At 17 he became a choirmaster himself, and held posts in the cathedral cities of Sées, Dijon, Tours and Le Mans. In Paris he made his mark as a composer at an early age, notably with performances of his grand motets at the Concert Spirituel, 1782–6. In 1786 he obtained the most coveted post of all, choirmaster at the cathedral of Notre Dame. He was to remain there only a year, time enough to cause a great stir by presenting what he called his 'reform of sacred music'. By introducing 'imitative' (i.e. essentially theatrical) music into church and by taking great liberties with Latin texts, including the Ordinary of the Mass, he incurred the wrath of the clergy. All his scores of this period are lost, but the young composer subsequently published several treatises that provide a good idea of his intentions.

From the end of the *ancien régime* Le Sueur had been working on an opera, *Télémaque*, and within a short time he had three works performed successively at the Théâtre Feydeau: *La caverne* (1793), *Paul et Virginie* (1794) and *Télémaque* (1796). Of these three operas, which have spoken dialogue instead of recitative in accordance with the general rule of the Théâtre Feydeau, *La caverne* is undoubtedly the most original. A modern work for its period, it breaks with the then sacrosanct principle whereby the stylistic features of different genres were kept separate: in the middle of a sombre and violent drama there are several *ariettes* in the purest *opéra comique* tradition. The work was extremely successful at the time of the Terror, and was subsequently produced in translation in several European countries. In some ways *Paul et Virginie*, and above all *Télémaque*, originally intended for the Opéra

on the eve of the Revolution, are more traditional, but they still display several characteristic features of Le Sueur's musical style: harmonic asperities, and jarring and rather harsh melodies, together with an expressive tremor and constant tension which prove his incontestable dramatic talent.

Appointed inspector of the Conservatoire when that establishment was founded in 1795, Le Sueur made a considerable contribution to the vast body of Revolutionary hymns. His contemporaries, most notably Napoleon, particularly admired his *Chant du 1er vendémiaire an IX*, performed at the Hôtel des Invalides by four orchestras and four choirs, a work in which the composer made remarkable use of the effects of acoustic spatialization. After several difficult years (1800–04) when he tried in vain to get two new works (*Ossian* and *La mort d'Adam*) produced at the Opéra, his career was furthered by Napoleon himself, who in 1804 appointed him musical director of the new Tuileries Chapel, opened in 1802, and ordered *Ossian* to be performed at the Opéra. Le Sueur became in effect the regime's official composer.

Ossian, performed at the Opéra in 1804, was a triumph. Though an uneven work certain scenes undoubtedly brought a breath of fresh air to the French musical stage, foreshadowing the birth of the Romantic sensibility. In this sense the piece, which did not long survive the Napoleonic era (it was last performed in 1817), provides an important date in the history of French opera. *La mort d'Adam*, however, failed at the Opéra in 1809 and was subsequently ignored. Inspired by Klopstock's play of the same name, this work has some weaknesses, including far too static a dramatic action. Nonetheless the opera contains several great passages of a remarkable religio-dramatic character. Among them is the finale of the third act, entirely of Le Sueur's invention, conjuring up a grand epic vision of the struggle between Satan and God for Adam's soul.

Under the Empire, Le Sueur collaborated (no doubt to a very minor degree) in two occasional works of musical drama at the Opéra in 1807, *L'inauguration du temple de la victoire* and *Le triomphe de Trajan*, most of the music being written by the composer Louis-Luc Loiseau de Persuis. The second work, wholly devoted to an apologia for the ruler and his regime and conjuring up Roman antiquity, with processions of chariots on stage, was an outstanding success and remained popular even under the restored monarchy.

In 1814 Le Sueur composed a grand opera in three acts entitled *Alexandre à Babylone*. It was never produced, despite the composer's efforts and, after his death, those of his wife. Some historians have even described it as lost. In fact Le Sueur's widow had the score engraved after his death, though only a few copies are still extant. In this last opera the composer's style broadened out; the orchestral writing is both more brilliant and more refined, and the choruses have a new musical and dramatic importance. Le Sueur was obviously influenced by Spontini's great French masterpieces, *La vestale* and in particular *Fernand Cortez*. *Alexandre à Babylone* easily bears comparison with Spontini's later work, *Olympie*.

In 1826 Le Sueur began publishing his sacred works; this project was completed, again through the efforts of his widow, only after his death. After 1830 the composer devoted himself exclusively to teaching (among his pupils at the Conservatoire was Berlioz, who mentions him with much respect in his *Mémoires*), and to writing long treatises on music that were never published. When he died he was already half forgotten.

Le Sueur occupies a prominent place in that generation of composers who, born in the century of the Enlightenment, died in the middle of the flowering of Romanticism. His work bears the marks of that experience: shot through with flashes of genius, it nonetheless remains uneven, as if the artist sometimes feared to lose himself in that unknown future territory of which, however, he had presentiments.

See also CAVERNE, LA; OSSIAN, OU LES BARDES; and PAUL ET VIRGINIE.

all first performed and published in Paris

La caverne (drame lyrique, 3, P. Dercy [Palat], after A.-R. Le Sage: *Gil Blas de Santillane*), OC (Feydeau), 16 Feb 1793, *F-Pim**, *Po**; (1794/*R*1986: FO, lxxiv)
Paul et Virginie, ou Le temple de la vertu (oc, 3, A. du Congé Dubreuil, after B. de Saint-Pierre), OC (Feydeau), 13 Jan 1794 (1796)
Télémaque (tragédie lyrique, 3, Dercy), OC (Feydeau), 10 May 1796 (*c*1796–1802)
Ossian, ou Les bardes (opéra, 5, Dercy, rev. J.-M. Deschamps), Opéra, 10 July 1804, *D-B**, *F-Po**; (*c*1804–5/*R*1979: ERO, xxxvii)
Le triomphe de Trajan (tragédie lyrique, 3, J. Esmenard), Opéra, 23 Oct 1807, *Po*, collab. L.-L. de Persuis
La mort d'Adam (tragédie lyrique religieuse, 3, N.-F. Guillard, after F. G. Klopstock), Opéra, 21 March 1809, *Po**; (1822)
Alexandre à Babylone, 1814 (opéra, 3, Baour-Lormian), unperf., *Pn*; (*c*1859–60)

*

J. Coutts: *Jean-François Le Sueur: a Study of the Composer and Five of his Operas* (diss., U. of Cardiff, 1966)
W. Dean: 'Opera under the French Revolution', *PRMA*, xciv (1967–8), 77–96
O. F. Saloman: *Aspects of 'Gluckian' Operatic Thought and Practice in France: the Musico-Dramatic Vision of Le Sueur and La Cépède (1785–1809) in Relation to Aesthetic and Critical Tradition* (diss., Columbia U., 1970)
——: 'The Orchestra in Le Sueur's Musical Aesthetics', *MQ*, lx (1974), 616–24
——: 'La Cépède's La poétique de la musique and Le Sueur', *AcM*, xlvii (1975), 144–54
E. Dent: *The Rise of Romantic Opera*, ed. W. Dean (Cambridge, 1976)
D. Charlton: 'Ossian, Le Sueur and Opera', *SMA*, xi (1977), 37–48
J. Mongrédien: *Catalogue thématique de l'oeuvre complète du compositeur Jean-François Le Sueur (1760–1837)* (New York, 1980)
——: *Jean-François Le Sueur: Contribution à l'étude d'un demi-siècle de musique française (1780–1830)* (Berne, 1980)
C. Keith: *The Operas of Jean-François Le Sueur* (diss., U. of Cincinnati, 1981)
G. Buschmeier: *Die Entwicklung von Arie und Szene in der französischen Oper von Gluck bis Spontini* (Tutzing, 1991)
JEAN MONGRÉDIEN

Lesur, Daniel. *See* DANIEL-LESUR.

Leterrier, Eugène (*b* 1843; *d* Paris, 22 Dec 1884). French librettist. After working as a clerk in the Hôtel de Ville in Paris for a short period he turned to the theatre and produced librettos in collaboration with Albert Vanloo. Leterrier and Vanloo worked together for more than a decade and a half; their relationship was highly productive and, as Vanloo records, free from stress. They wrote in the light-hearted vein of *opéra bouffe*, and among the more important composers who set their texts were Lecocq, Chabrier and Offenbach.

all written in collaboration with Albert Vanloo

Le Petit Poucet (opéra bouffe), L. de Rillé, 1868; Madeleine (oc), H. Potier, 1869; *La nuit du 15 octobre* (opérette), G. Jacob, 1869; Nabucho (opéra bouffe), A. de Villebichet, 1871; *Giroflé-Girofla* (opéra bouffe), Lecocq, 1874; *Le voyage dans la lune* (opéra féerie, with A. Mortier), Offenbach, 1875; *La petite mariée* (oc),

Lecocq, 1875; *La marjolaine* (opéra bouffe), Lecocq, 1877; *L'étoile* (opéra bouffe), Chabrier, 1877; *La Camargo* (oc), Lecocq, 1878; *La jolie Persane* (oc), Lecocq, 1879; *Le beau Nicolas* (oc), P. Lacome, 1880; *Le jour et la nuit* (opéra bouffe), Lecocq, 1881; *Le droit de l'aînesse* (opéra bouffe), F. Chassaigne, 1883; *Le roi de carreau* (oc), Lajarte, 1883; *La Béarnaise* (oc), Messager, 1885; *La gamine de Paris* (opéra bouffe), G. Serpette, 1887; *La gardeuse d'oies* (oc), Lacome, 1888
CHRISTOPHER SMITH

Let's Make an Opera. 'Entertainment for young people' by Benjamin Britten, which incorporates, as its third act, the opera THE LITTLE SWEEP.

Leuven, Adolphe de [Grenvallet; Count Adolph Ribbing] (*b* 1800; *d* Paris, 14 April 1884). French librettist and director. Of Swedish descent, de Leuven assumed his grandmother's name, and occasionally wrote under the pseudonyms Grenvallet, Granval or Adolphe. As a young man he befriended Alexandre Dumas *père* and collaborated with him for his first play, a one-act vaudeville (1825). In all he produced more than 170 plays and librettos (usually vaudevilles or *opéras comiques*), collaborating with Brunswick, Pittaud de Forges, de Planard (his father-in-law) and others. Some of his six dozen operas (with Adam, Clapisson or Thomas) were quite popular in their own era. He was named a member of the Légion d'honneur (29 April 1847) and an officer (9 August 1870).

From 20 December 1862 to 19 January 1874 de Leuven directed the Opéra-Comique, first with Ritt and from January 1870 with Du Locle. His old-fashioned tastes served to counterbalance Du Locle's adventurousness, but also created friction between them. Ludovic Halévy claimed that de Leuven resigned in 1874 due partly to his antipathy to the subject of Bizet's *Carmen*.

La marquise (oc, with J.-H. Vernoy de Saint-Georges), A. Adam, 1835; *La fermière de Bolbec* (oc, with Pittaud de Forges), A. Pilati, 1835; *Le luthier de Vienne* (oc, with Saint-Georges), Monpou, 1836; *Le postillon de Lonjumeau* (oc, with Brunswick [L. Lhérie]), Adam, 1836; *Léona, ou Le Parisien en Corse* (opéra vaudeville, with Saint-Georges), Pilati, 1836; *Un conte d'autrefois* (oc, with Brunswick), Monpou, 1838; *Thérèse* (oc, with F. de Planard), Carafa, 1838
Le brasseur de Preston (oc, with Brunswick), Adam, 1838; *La suisse à Trianon* (comédie mêlée de chant, with Saint-Georges), Grisar, 1838; *Lady Melvil, ou Le joaillier de St-James* (oc, with Saint-Georges), Grisar and Flotow, 1838; *Le panier fleuri* (oc, with Brunswick), A. Thomas, 1839; *Eva* (drame lyrique, with Brunswick), N. Girard, 1839; *Carline* (oc, with Brunswick), Thomas, 1840; *L'automate de Vaucanson* (oc, with ?Petitjean), L. Bordèse, 1840
La reine Jeanne (oc, with Brunswick), Monpou and Bordèse, 1840; *La rose de Péronne* (oc, with A. P. d'Ennery), Adam, 1840; *Les deux voleurs* (oc, with Brunswick), Girard, 1841; *La main de fer, ou Un mariage secret* (oc, with E. Scribe), Adam, 1841; *Mlle de Mérange* (oc, with Brunswick), H. Potier, 1841; *Les dix* (oc, with Brunswick), Girard, 1842; *Le roi d'Yvetot* (oc, with Brunswick), Adam, 1842; *Le puits d'amour* (oc, with Scribe and Saint-Georges), Balfe, 1843
Les quatre fils Aymon (oc, with Brunswick), Balfe, 1844; *Le caquet du couvent* (oc, with de Planard), Potier, 1846; *Gibby la cornemuse* (oc, with Brunswick), Clapisson, 1846; *Le bouquet de l'Infante* (oc, with de Planard), L. Boieldieu, 1847; *Le braconnier* (oc, with Vanderburch), G. Héquet [L. Durocher], 1847; *Il Signor Pascarello* (oc, with Brunswick), Potier, 1848; *Les deux bambins* (oc, with Brunswick), Bordèse, 1848; *Le songe d'une nuit d'été* (oc, with J. B. Rosier), Thomas, 1850; *La chanteuse voilée* (oc, with Scribe), Massé, 1850
Raymond, ou Le secret de la reine (oc, with Rosier), Thomas, 1851; *Murdock le bandit* (oc), E. Gautier, 1851; *La poupée de Nuremberg* (oc, with A. de Beauplan), Adam, 1852; *Flore et Zéphire* (oc, with Deslys), Gautier, 1852; *Choisy-le-roi* (oc, with M. Carré), Gautier, 1852; *Guillery le trompette* (oc, with A. de Beauplan), S.

Sarmiento, 1852; *Le sourd, ou L'auberge pleine* (oc, with F. Langlé, after a Desforges comédie), Adam, 1853; *Le roi des Halles* (oc, with Brunswick), Adam, 1853
Le bijou perdu (oc, with Pittaud de Forges ?and Saint-Georges), Adam, 1853; *Elisabeth, ou La fille du proscrit* (drame lyrique, with Brunswick), U. Fontana, 1853, after D. Gilardoni: *Otto mesi in due ore*; *La promise* (oc, with Brunswick), Clapisson, 1854; *Le billet de Marguerite* (oc, with Brunswick), Gevaert, 1854; *Schahabaham II* (opéra bouffe, with Carré), Gautier, 1854; *L'amant et le frère* (oc), C. van der Does, 1855; *Les charmeurs* (oc), Poise, 1855
Yvonne (oc), Prince de la Moskowa [J.-N. Ney], 1855; *Jaguarita l'Indienne* (oc, with Saint-Georges), F. Halévy, 1855; *L'inconsolable* (oc, with Saint-Georges), Alberti [Halévy], 1855; *Falstaff* (oc, with Saint-Georges, after W. Shakespeare), Adam, 1856; *La fanchonnette* (oc, with Saint-Georges), Clapisson, 1856; *Maître Pathelin* (oc, with F. Langlé), Bazin, 1856; *Les commères* (oc), A. Montuoro, 1857; *Euryanthe* (opéra, with Saint-Georges, trans. and adapted from 1823 original), C. M. von Weber, 1857; *Margot* (oc, with Saint-Georges), Clapisson, 1857
Les désespérés (oc, with J. Moinaux), Bazin, 1858; *Le moulin du roi* (oc), L. Boieldieu, 1858; *La bacchante* (oc, with A. de Beauplan), Gautier, 1858; *Les dernières armes de Richelieu* (opéra), Marquis d'Aguilar, 1858; *Programme en action* (with Lurieu, Vanderburch, Dupeuty, M. Masson, Langlois [Langlé], Dumanoir, Saint-Georges, Clairville and R. de Beauvoir), Pilati, 1859; *Don Grégorio, ou Le précepteur dans l'embarras* (oc, with T. Sauvage), N. Gabrielli, 1859
Le roman d'Elvire (oc, with Dumas père), Thomas, 1860; *Le jardinier galant* (oc, with P. Siraudin), Poise, 1861; *Maître Claude* (oc, with Saint-Georges), J. Cohen, 1861; *La poularde de Caux* (opérette, with V. Prilleux), Clapisson, Gevaert, Gautier, Poise, Bazille and S. Mangeant, 1861; *Le joaillier de St-James* (oc, with Saint-Georges), Grisar, 1862; *Le saphir* (oc, with Carré and T. Hadot, after Shakespeare: *All's Well that Ends Well*), F. David, 1865
La fleur de Harlem (opéra, with Saint-Georges, after Dumas), Flotow, 1876; *L'aumônier du régiment* (oc, arr. of comédie by Saint-Georges and de Leuven, 1835), H. Salomon, 1877; *Le trompette de Chamboran* (op, with Adenis), P.-L. Deffès, 1877; *Actéon et le centaure Chiron* (fantaisie lyrico-mythologique, after farce-mythologique by Duvert, Théaulon and de Leuven, 1836), F. Chassaigne, 1878

*
G. Vapereau: *Dictionnaire universel des contemporains* (Paris, 5/1880)
L. Gallet: *Notes d'un librettiste* (Paris, 1891)
A. Soubies and C. Malherbe: *Histoire de l'Opéra-Comique*, ii (Paris, 1892)
M. Curtiss: *Bizet and his World* (New York, 1958)
T. J. Walsh: *Second Empire Opera* (London, 1981)
LESLEY A. WRIGHT

Levadé, Charles(-Gaston) (*b* Paris, 3 Jan 1869; *d* Paris, 27 Oct 1948). French composer. A youthful admirer of the music of Wagner, Levadé became a pupil of Massenet at the Paris Conservatoire; in 1899 he won the Prix de Rome. His first operatic work, the historical fantasy *Les hérétiques*, was commissioned for the Roman theatre at Béziers and was set in this same town during the 13th century. *La rôtisserie de la Reine Pédauque* is concerned with the habitués of a restaurant. A doctor of theology researches the possibility of using the rotisserie flames to convert ordinary metals into gold. The moral of the tale is that it is better to eat and drink than to think; Lévade uses an eclectic, traditional style to respond to the narrative of the text, mostly through declamation but with occasional passages of lyrical aria. His operatic adaptation of Balzac's *La peau de chagrin* opens with one of the characters playing Hummel on an onstage piano.

L'amour d'Heliodora (salon op), Paris, 19 June 1903
Les hérétiques (3, A.-F. Hérold), Béziers, Théâtre des Arènes, 27 Aug 1905, vs (Paris, 1905)
La rôtisserie de la Reine Pédauque (comédie lyrique, 4, G. Docquois, after A. France), Paris, OC (Favart), 12 Jan 1920, vs (Paris, 1919)
La peau de chagrin (comédie lyrique, 4, P. Décourcelle and M. Carré, after H. de Balzac), Paris, OC (Favart), 24 April 1929 (Paris, 1929)

*
R. Brévannes: 'Les hérétiques à Béziers', *Musica*, no.34 (1905), 139–40
E. Héros: 'Ville de Béziers – Théâtre des Arènes: Les hérétiques', *Le théâtre*, no.162 (1905), 17–19
C. Oulmont: 'G. Hüe, les frères Hillemacher, Levadé', *Le théâtre lyrique en France* (Paris, 1937–9) [pubn of Poste National/Radio-Paris], iii, 146–8
RICHARD LANGHAM SMITH

Levasseur, Nicolas (Prosper) (*b* Bresles, 9 March 1791; *d* Paris, 7 Dec 1871). French bass. He made his début at the Opéra in 1813 in Grétry's *La caravane du Caire*, then sang for two seasons in London, making his début at the King's Theatre (1815) in Mayr's *Adelasia ed Aleramo*. In 1819 he joined the Théâtre Italien, first appearing as Almaviva. The following year he sang at La Scala in the première of Meyerbeer's *Margherita d'Anjou*. At the Théâtre Italien he sang in many Rossini operas new to Paris, notably in the title role of *Mosè in Egitto* (1822), which he repeated in the revised version for the Opéra (1827). In 1828 he rejoined the Opéra, creating virtually every important new bass role in its repertory over the next 12 years, including Bertram in *Robert le diable* (1831), Brogni in *La Juive* (1835), Marcel in *Les Huguenots* (1836) and Balthazar in *La favorite* (1840). He left in 1845, but at Meyerbeer's request returned to sing in the première of *Le prophète* (1849), finally retiring in 1853. In 1869 Levasseur was made a Chevalier of the Légion d'honneur.

For illustration *see* ROBERT LE DIABLE. PHILIP ROBINSON

Levasseur [Le Vasseur], Rosalie [Marie-Rose-(Claude-)Josephe] (*b* Valenciennes, 8 Oct 1749; *d* Neuwied am Rhein, 6 May 1826). French soprano. She made her début at the Paris Opéra in 1766 as Zäide in Campra's *L'Europe galante* and appeared there regularly until 1785. Known as Mlle Rosalie during her first ten years at the Opéra, she took only minor roles until, in 1776, she was entrusted with Eurydice and Iphigenia in revivals of Gluck's operas. She was then preferred over her rival, Sophie Arnould, to create the title role in the French *Alceste*. She became Gluck's close friend and favourite interpreter, creating the title roles in *Armide* (1777) and *Iphigénie en Tauride* (1779), and was successful in the title role of Philidor's *Ernelinde* (1777 revival), but less so in Piccinni's works, relinquishing his Angélique (*Roland*) and Sangaride (*Atys*) to other singers. She was a powerful rather than flexible singer, with a good stage presence if unattractive features.

*
ES (H. Boschot)
J. G. Prod'homme: 'Rosalie Levasseur, Ambassadress of Opera', *MQ*, ii (1916), 210–43
JULIAN RUSHTON

Leveridge, Richard (*b* ?London, 1670–71; *d* London, 22 March 1758). English bass and composer. For more than half a century he was a leading singer on the London stage and a popular composer. His solo career began in 1695, when he sang 'Ye twice ten hundred deities' as the magician Ismeron in Henry Purcell's last important stage work, *The Indian Queen*. In the next few seasons he sang in revivals of Purcell's dramatic operas and in similar works with music by Purcell's brother Daniel, Jeremiah Clarke and himself. For D'Urfey's 'New Opera' *Cinthia and Endimion* he wrote the bass aria 'Black and gloomy as the grave', which he sang as a Druid. His music and singing played a large part in the success of *The Island Princess* (1699), as the author, Peter Motteux, acknowledged in his preface: 'And the Dialogue and Enthusiastic Song, which Mr. Leveridge set, are too particularly lik'd not to engage me to thank him for gracing my words with his Composition, as much as for his celebrated singing'. On 25 December 1699 Vanbrugh wrote: 'Leveridge is in Ireland, he Owes so much money he dare not come over, so for want of him we han't had one Opera play'd this Winter'. He returned to the London stage in 1702 for a revival of *The Island Princess* and a new production of *Macbeth* with 'Vocal and Instrumental Musick, all new Compos'd by Mr. Leveridge'. He was to sing Hecate in this version for over 40 years, and his music, later attributed to Matthew Locke, remained an integral part of performances of *Macbeth* until 1875.

He continued to sing in dramatic operas, but a new element was added with the introduction of all-sung English operas in the Italian style. Between 1705 and 1707 he was the leading bass in *Arsinoe*, *Camilla*, *Rosamond* and *Thomyris*. In 1707 he made an English adaptation of Scarlatti's *La Didone delirante*, which the *Muses Mercury* for September reported 'is now learning by the Performers, and will be ready to be practis'd within three Weeks'. However, it was abandoned in favour of *Love's Triumph*, which was sung partly in Italian to accommodate the newly arrived castrato Valentini (Valentino Urbani). The operas were taken over by Italian singers and the Italian language. After a lean period Leveridge sang in Galliard's English opera *Calypso and Telemachus* (1712). He then had a season with Handel's Italian opera company, when he was in the first performances of *Il pastor fido* and *Teseo* and played Argante in a revival of *Rinaldo*. He had no roles in Handel's operas thereafter, but in 1731 was Polyphemus in the first public performance of *Acis and Galatea*. A number of Handel's Italian opera arias became popular songs with English words by Leveridge.

In 1714 he moved to the new theatre at Lincoln's Inn Fields, which was managed by John Rich, with whom he was to work until his retirement in 1751. He returned to his English repertory and a new form, the musical afterpiece. These lightweight works were often comic, and for his benefit in 1716 Leveridge produced his own afterpiece, *Pyramus and Thisbe*. It is an amusing and good-natured burlesque of Italian opera, and Leveridge wrote the music, adapted the libretto from Shakespeare and sang Pyramus to the Thisbe of the tenor George Pack. His music is lost but the libretto was published and Lampe reset it in 1745. Between 1720 and 1723 the company was in financial difficulties and Leveridge went into semi-retirement, concentrating on running his coffee shop in Tavistock Street. In 1723 Rich revived the company's fortunes with his phenomenally successful series of pantomime afterpieces starting with *Jupiter and Europa*, for which Leveridge wrote music, and *The Necromancer*, which brought him back to the stage. Leveridge remained the leading bass in these semi-operatic works until his retirement in 1751, specializing in impressive roles as gods and magicians. His voice, if no longer as flexible as when Purcell wrote for him, was still firm and powerful. His chief contribution to the other new musical form of the period, the ballad opera, was as a composer, for the tunes of his popular songs were frequently used for ballad opera airs, including two in *The Beggar's Opera*. He rarely sang in ballad operas, but he had a small role in Gay's *Achilles* (1733).

He moved with Rich's company to the newly built Covent Garden Theatre in 1732 and continued to perform regularly, his last new role being Dick Shamwell in Lampe's *The Sham Conjuror* (1741). He was finally forced to leave the stage in 1751 because of the 'infirmities incident to his great age' and in his retirement his friends organized a subscription for 'honest Dick Leveridge, the father of the English Stage'.

See also MACBETH (i).

all first performed in London

LDL – *Drury Lane*   LLF – *Lincoln's Inn Fields*

Cinthia and Endimion (dramatic op, T. D'Urfey), LDL, ?Jan 1697, collab. D. Purcell and J. Clarke, 1 song (London, 1697)

The Island Princess (dramatic op, P. Motteux, after J. Fletcher), LDL, Feb 1699, collab. Purcell and Clarke, 4 songs *GB-Lbl*(*R*1985: MLE, C3), songs (London, 1699)

Macbeth (play with musical scenes, W. Davenant, after W. Shakespeare and T. Middleton), LDL, 21 Nov 1702, *Cfm*, ed. Boyce [attrib. Locke] (London, 1770)

Britain's Happiness, a Musical Interlude (Motteux), LLF, 7 March 1704, lib. (London, 1704), 1 song (London, 1709)

The Mountebank, or The Humours of the Fair (Motteux), LDL, 18 Jan 1705 [musical interlude in Farewell Folly], 2 songs (London, 1728)

The Mountebank, or The Country Lass (comic masque), LLF, 21 Dec 1715, 2 songs (London, 1728)

Pyramus and Thisbe (comick masque, Leveridge, after Shakespeare), LLF, 11 April 1716, lib. (London, 1716/*R*1969)

Jupiter and Europa (pantomime), LLF, 23 March 1723, collab. Cobston and J. E. Galliard, songs (London, 1723)

*

BurneyH; HawkinsH

'An Account of Richard Leveridge', *European Magazine*, xxiv (1793), 243, 363

G. Hogarth: *Memoirs of the Opera* (London, 1851)

R. E. Moore: 'The Music to Macbeth', *MQ*, xlvii (1961), 22–40

R. Fiske: 'The Macbeth Music', *ML*, xlv (1964), 114–25

O. Baldwin and T. Wilson: 'Richard Leveridge, 1670–1758', *MT*, cxi (1970), 592–4, 891–3, 988–90

——: 'The Music for Durfey's Cinthia and Endimion', *Theatre Notebook*, xli (1987), 70–74

OLIVE BALDWIN, THELMA WILSON

Levi, Hermann (*b* Giessen, Upper Hesse, 7 Nov 1839; *d* Munich, 13 May 1900). German conductor. He studied with Hauptmann and Julius Rietz at the Leipzig Conservatory (1855–8). After a short stay in Paris he became music director at Saarbrücken (1859), and two years later he was made assistant Kapellmeister of the Mannheim Nationaltheater Opera, on Lachner's recommendation, and Kapellmeister at Rotterdam (1861–4). As Hofkapellmeister in Karlsruhe (1864–72), he became a friend of Clara Schumann (in nearby Baden-Baden) and Brahms, and this led him to produce Schumann's *Genoveva*; he also became interested in Wagner's operas, and in 1869 he gained Wagner's recognition with his performances of *Die Meistersinger* and *Rienzi*. From 1872 to 1896 he was Hofkapellmeister in Munich, and was made general music director of the city in 1894.

A distinguished and serious-minded artist of great personal qualities and musical gifts, Levi was universally recognized as one of the greatest conductors of his time. His modern, flowing, declamatory translations of Mozart's operas (*Le nozze di Figaro*, *Don Giovanni* and *Così fan tutte*), to which he also made alterations in the score, were great successes. But it was at Bayreuth that he made his strongest mark; he must be ranked with Richter, Mottl and Seidl as one of the greatest of the first generation of Bayreuth conductors. Cosima Wagner regarded him as 'a most excellent person, with real delicacy of feeling', and for Wagner he was 'the ideal *Parsifal* conductor'. However, Wagner had made a clumsy and unsuccessful attempt to convert Levi to Christianity, and his attitude, especially in connection with the idea of a Jew conducting *Parsifal* with its representation of the central Christian mystery, compounded by an anonymous letter complaining of this and also accusing Levi of being Cosima's lover, drove Levi to attempt to withdraw from conducting the work. Eventually Wagner, largely at King Ludwig's insistence, made peace with Levi, who conducted the première on 26 July 1882. In 1888 Cosima replaced Levi as *Parsifal* conductor with Mottl, but Levi was recalled for the performances in 1889–94. He retired in 1896 but was persuaded to conduct again in 1897; however, the effort precipitated a nervous breakdown, and he was by that time mortally ill.

The 'spiritual' quality of Levi's interpretations was widely admired, and the economy of his gestures, as well as his masterly technique, exercised an influence on a number of conductors of the following generation, especially Weingartner.

*

E. von Possart: *Erinnerungen an Hermann Levi* (Munich, 1901)

J. Kniese: *Der Kampf zweier Welten um das Bayreuther Erbe* (Leipzig, 1931)

C. Schünemann: 'Mozart in deutscher Übertragung', *JbMP 1940*, 62–9

H. Schonberg: *The Great Conductors* (New York, 1970)

P. Gay: 'Hermann Levi and the Cult of Wagner', *Times Literary Supplement* (11 April 1975)   FRIEDRICH BASER

Levi, Samuele (*b* Venice, 1813; *d* Florence, 13 March 1883). Italian composer. He studied composition with L. A. Calegari and later had some lessons from the theorist Siegfried Wilhelm Dehn (1799–1858). His many salon songs were popular, but none of his four staged operas made a great impression. His *Giuditta*, produced at the Fenice a month before the première of Verdi's *Ernani*, filled in the time until Carlo Guasco, the tenor Verdi wanted for his opera, could get to Venice and learn his part. Its predecessor in Levi's output, *Ginevra degli Almieri* (which bore the inauspicious alternative title *La peste di Firenze*), never achieved a second performance.

An old-fashioned composer for his day, Levi did not long persevere in writing for the stage. The last time his music was heard in an opera house was probably on 21 February 1867, when his hymn in honour of the King of Italy was sung at a benefit performance at the Teatro La Fenice.

Iginia d'Asti, Venice, S Benedetto, aut. 1837, ed. in IOG, ix (1978)

Ginevra degli Almieri, ossia La peste di Firenze (os), Trieste, Comunale, 17 March 1840

Giuditta (tragedia lirica, 2, G. Peruzzini), Venice, Fenice, 14 Feb 1844

La Biscaglia (os, 3, F. M. Piave), Turin, Carignano, aut. 1860

Don Marzio (ob), unperf.   WILLIAM ASHBROOK

Levine, James (*b* Cincinnati, 23 June 1943). American conductor. His early facility as a pianist brought him a concerto début with the Cincinnati SO at the age of ten. When later he studied at the Juilliard School his main energies turned more and more towards conducting, which he studied with Jean Morel, and later with Alfred Wallenstein and Fausto Cleva. Over the last six years of George Szell's life (1964–70) Levine was assistant conductor of the Cleveland Orchestra; he also built up a much-admired student orchestra at the Cleveland Institute. He conducted *Mavra* at Aspen in 1964, and in 1970 made his début with the WNO (*Aida*) and with the San Francisco Opera (*Tosca*). *Tosca* was the opera he conducted when in 1971 he made his début at the Metropolitan Opera. That led directly to his appointment in 1973 to the post of principal conductor and in 1976 music director, the key development in his career.

Since then he has conducted well over a thousand performances at the Metropolitan, taking on a high proportion of productions and, through television relays from the opera house, becoming well known to a wide audience as a bluff, ebullient personality. At the Metropolitan he has always covered the central repertory of Mozart, Verdi, Wagner, Puccini and Strauss, but among the French operas he has conducted are *Les Troyens*, *Pelléas et Mélisande* and *Carmen*, while his 20th-century repertory has included *Porgy and Bess*, *Mahagonny*, *Lulu* and Zandonai's *Francesca da Rimini*. His vigour has brought new vitality to the company, particularly since 1986 when he took on additional responsibilities as artistic director. The rigorous training he had under Szell, always applied with sharp psychological insight, has also markedly raised the opera house's orchestral standards.

In 1976 he made his Salzburg operatic début, conducting *La clemenza di Tito* in Jean-Pierre Ponnelle's spectacular production; this led to an exceptionally fruitful association with Ponnelle, who was also the stage director in 1978 when Levine conducted *Die Zauberflöte* in a production that has been revived more frequently than any other at the Salzburg Festival. Much was owed to the conductor's clearcut direction, combined with his ability, when necessary, to act as comic foil to the singers. Outstanding too was the 1987 production of *Moses und Aron*, also with Ponnelle directing.

Levine made his début at Bayreuth in 1982, conducting *Parsifal* in a sustained and spacious reading even slower than that of Toscanini half a century earlier. Levine has also made many opera recordings, starting with *Giovanna d'Arco* (1972), most of which have been made in Europe; however, his reading of the *Ring* cycle in the late 1980s allowed him at last to demonstrate on disc the quality of his own company at the Metropolitan. His strength as a conductor has always been based on meticulous, if often speedy, preparation. His readings are more remarkable for structural clarity and sustained intensity than for new insights.

EDWARD GREENFIELD

Levins Mühle ('Levin's Mill'). Opera in nine scenes by UDO ZIMMERMANN to a libretto by Ingo Zimmermann after Johannes Bobrowski's novel *Levins Mühle*; Dresden, Staatstheater, 27 March 1973.

Composed in 1970–72, Zimmermann's third opera gained him a high reputation throughout Germany. The story, set in a village in Weichsel in 1874, is based on an incident from Bobrowski's family history. Johann, a rich mill owner (baritone), rids himself of competition by attacking the mill belonging to his Polish Jewish rival, Leo Levin (baritone). Levin finds no justice in the corrupt courts but the poor people are willing to help an underdog and they oppose the attacker, forcing him to surrender.

Zimmermann (whose wife is Polish) uses Polish melodies and chant for realistic effect and employs methods of musical collage to achieve dramatic contrast in the spirit of the theatre of the absurd. The work's première, directed by Harry Kupfer and conducted by Siegfried Kurz, was followed by performances in Berlin, Leningrad, Prague and Wiesbaden. Kurt Horres conducted the first production in the West at Wuppertal and further performances have been given at Hanover, Darmstadt, Bielefeld, Kassel, Düsseldorf and Brunswick.   DETLEF GOJOWY

Lévy, Léon. See BRUNSWICK (i).

Levy, Marvin David (*b* Passaic, NJ, 2 Aug 1932). American composer. He learned to play the piano as a child, then studied composition with Philip James at New York University (BA 1954) and with Otto Luening at Columbia University (MA 1956). Drawn almost immediately to the stage, he composed (and at once withdrew) his first opera while still an undergraduate. He subsequently wrote three successful one-act operas while working as a freelance music critic, on the strength of which he was awarded several Guggenheim and Prix de Rome fellowships and a Metropolitan Opera commission (the last is particularly noteworthy, since the Metropolitan performs, and commissions, very few American operas). This was for *Mourning Becomes Electra* (1967), his best-known work. His next opera, *The Balcony*, was also commissioned by the Metropolitan, but was never performed, owing to a change of administration there. Responding to a different American opera climate, in 1989 Levy began to recast *The Balcony* as a musical, *The Grand Balcony*, a significant change of direction for him.

Levy has composed several orchestral, choral, and chamber works, but is known primarily for his operas. He has preferred librettos of a distinctly expressionist bent, and has developed a musical style appropriate to such material. However, atonality occurs only briefly in his music, usually in passing; expressionist harmonic tension is maintained through the extensive use of bitonality at dissonant intervals. Levy's vocal writing, always eminently singable, is seldom angular, and does not use extremes of range. *The Grand Balcony*, aimed at the nascent 'music theatre' audience, employs a markedly more relaxed idiom than any of his earlier works.

See also MOURNING BECOMES ELECTRA.

Riders to the Sea, 1954 (after J. M. Synge), withdrawn
The Tower, 1955 (1, T. Brewster), Santa Fe, 2 Aug 1957
Sotoba Komachi (1, S. H. Brock, after Kwanami), New York, 7 April 1957
Escorial (1, Levy and L. Abel, after M. de Ghelderode), New York, 4 May 1958, vs (New York, 1966)
Mourning Becomes Electra (3, H. Butler, after E. O'Neill: *Homecoming*; *The Hunted*; *The Haunted*), New York, Metropolitan, 17 March 1967
The Balcony, 1978 (after J. Genet), inc., withdrawn; rev. as The Grand Balcony, 1989– (musical)

*

F. S.: '"Mourning" Becomes an Opera', ON, xxxi/23 (1966–7), 15–16
J. W. Freeman: 'Drawn from Within', ibid, 24–5
                                    ANDREW STILLER

Lévy, Paul. See LHÉRIE, PAUL.

Lévy, Roland Alexis Manuel. See ROLAND-MANUEL.

Lewis, Sir Anthony (Carey) (*b* Bermuda, 2 March 1915; *d* Haslemere, 5 June 1983). English musicologist and conductor. He studied with E. J. Dent at Cambridge and later with Nadia Boulanger before joining the BBC music department in 1935. There he planned a memorable series on Handel, and as director, after the war, of all Third Programme music, was responsible for broadcasting many unfamiliar works. In 1947 he became professor of music at Birmingham University, and during his 21-year tenure he conducted with discretion but directness revivals of Handel operas, collaborating with other members of the university in preparing the musical texts and making English singing translations of the librettos. These performances are remembered not only for their considerable success but also for the high standards they established for revivals of Handel operas. During this time Lewis also made the first English gramophone recordings of Purcell's *The Fairy-Queen* and *King Arthur*, and Handel's *Semele* and *Sosarme* (for which he had conducted broadcast excerpts in 1948).

From the 1950s Lewis became increasingly involved in administrative work. His proposals to the Royal Musical Association led to the publication of Musica Britannica, of which he became general editor, and he served as president of the RMA and chairman of the Purcell Society. He published *The Language of Purcell* (Hull, 1968), as well as many articles, and collaborated on editions of Blow's *Venus and Adonis*, Handel's *Apollo e Dafne*, *Athalia* and *Semele*, and Purcell's *The Fairy-Queen*. Lewis was knighted in 1972.

                                    DAVID SCOTT

Lewis, Henry (*b* Los Angeles, 16 Oct 1932). American conductor. As a boy he learnt the double bass and the piano, and later studied at the University of California, Los Angeles. He made his conducting début with the US 7th Army SO while serving in Europe. After conducting appointments in Los Angeles and New Jersey, he became, in 1972, the first black conductor engaged at the Metropolitan (*La bohème*) and returned there regularly until 1977, his connection then being broken by disagreements with James Levine. He accompanied the Metropolitan tour to Japan in 1975. His British operatic début was with *Simon Boccanegra* for Scottish Opera in 1978, followed by *Manon* for the ENO (1985) and Covent Garden's concert performances of *Semiramide* in 1986 as well as *Il barbiere di Siviglia* for the WNO that year. Besides opera in Los Angeles, San Francisco and Canadian centres, Lewis works extensively in Europe in repertory ranging from Rossini (*La donna del lago*, *Tancredi*) to Dukas' *Ariane et Barbebleue* and Prokofiev's *The Fiery Angel*. He was for some years married to the mezzo-soprano Marilyn Horne, with whom he recorded several discs of arias and a complete performance of Meyerbeer's *Le prophète* (1989). He works sympathetically with singers, and at the same time shows concern for orchestral detail; by temperament he is thoughtful rather than fiery.

                        MICHAEL STEINBERG, NOËL GOODWIN

Lewis, Keith (Neville) (*b* Methven, 6 Oct 1950). New Zealand tenor. He studied in New Zealand, then at the London Opera Centre (1974–6) and with Richard Lewis and others. His début was as Ferrando at the St Céré Festival in France in 1977, followed that year by Don Ottavio for Glyndebourne Touring Opera and the next summer at Glyndebourne, where he returned in later seasons. He created the roles of Christ/Father in John Tavener's *Thérèse* for his Covent Garden début in 1979; other débuts include the Paris Opéra in 1983 as Aménophis in *Moïse* (Rossini), San Francisco Opera in

1984 as Don Ottavio, and the Deutsche Oper, Berlin, in 1985 as Ferrando. In 1988 he added Berlioz's Faust to his repertory at Hamburg and in 1989 Gounod's at Berlin. He has sung frequently in Australian opera productions, and in 1992 sang Pyrrhus in the British première of Rossini's *Ermione* at the Queen Elizabeth Hall. The mellifluous style of his lyric tenor is combined with smooth projection and ardently expressive character. His recordings include Don Ottavio under Haitink with the Glyndebourne company (1984).

A. Simpson and P. Downes: *Southern Voices: International Opera Singers of New Zealand* (Auckland, 1992), 260–75

NOËL GOODWIN

Lewis, Mary (*b* Hot Springs, AR, 7 Jan 1900; *d* New York, 31 Dec 1941). American soprano. She sang first in San Francisco cabarets and musical shows, then in operetta and the Ziegfeld Follies in New York. Her operatic début was in 1923 at the Vienna Volksoper as Marguerite in *Faust*. There followed guest appearances in Berlin, Monte Carlo and at the Opéra-Comique, but probably the most important and unexpected of her engagements was to sing Mary in the 1924 première of Vaughan Williams's *Hugh the Drover*, in London, conducted by Sargent. Her Metropolitan début was in 1925 as Mimì; later she sang Nedda in *Pagliacci* and Giulietta in *Les contes d'Hoffmann*. She remained at the Metropolitan till 1930, her performances being found creditable but not distinguished. She is best heard in the selection from *Hugh the Drover* recorded shortly after the première.

J. B. STEANE

Lewis, Richard [Thomas, Thomas] (*b* Manchester, 10 May 1914; *d* Eastbourne, E. Sussex, 13 Nov 1990). English tenor. He studied in Manchester with Norman Allin and made his début in 1941 with the Carl Rosa Company, singing Almaviva and Pinkerton. After World War II he resumed his studies in London. In 1947 he sang the Male Chorus (*Rape of Lucretia*) at Glyndebourne and at Covent Garden, adding Peter Grimes with the resident company the same season and later singing Tamino and Alfredo. For Glyndebourne (1948–74) he sang Don Ottavio, Ferrando, Admetus (*Alceste*), Idomeneus, Tom Rakewell (British première of *The Rake's Progress*, at Edinburgh, 1953), Bacchus, Florestan and Monteverdi's Nero and Eumaeus. He created Gwyn in Arwell Hughes's *Menna* (WNO, 1953). For Covent Garden he created Troilus in Walton's *Troilus and Cressida* (1954), Mark in *The Midsummer Marriage* (1955) and Achilles in *King Priam* (1962, Coventry) and sang Don José, Hoffmann, Hermann, Captain Vere, and Aaron in the first British staging of *Moses und Aron* (1965), which he also sang at Boston in its American stage première (1966). He made his San Francisco début in 1955 as Don José, then sang Troilus, Jeník, Grigory, Massenet's Des Grieux, the Captain (*Wozzeck*), Alwa (*Lulu*), Jason, Pinkerton, Eisenstein and Herod. At the Deutsche Oper, Berlin, he created Amphitryon in Klebe's *Alkmene* (1961). From 1968 to 1971 he taught in Philadelphia. His mellifluous, flexible voice was used with great intelligence. His Idomeneus, which he recorded, and his Hoffmann, Rakewell, Grimes and Achilles were especially memorable.

For illustration *see* KING PRIAM; MIDSUMMER MARRIAGE, THE; and TROILUS AND CRESSIDA.

H. D. Rosenthal: 'Richard Lewis', *Opera*, vi (1955), 144–8
A. Blyth: 'Richard Lewis 1914–1990', *Opera*, xlii (1991), 33–6

ALAN BLYTH

Lewis, William (*b* Tulsa, 23 Nov 1935). American tenor. He studied at Fort Worth, where he made his début in 1953 as Rinuccio, and in New York. After his Metropolitan début in 1958 as Narraboth, he sang Aegisthus, Grigory, Števa, Hermann (*The Queen of Spades*), Rodolfo (*Bohème*), Turiddu, Hoffmann, Berlioz's Aeneas, and Malatestino (*Francesca da Rimini*). He has also sung in Spoleto, San Francisco, Philadelphia, Santa Fe, Salzburg and Cologne, with Scottish Opera and Opera North, and at Covent Garden, where he made his début as Gabriele Adorno (1981). At Wexford he sang the King's Son (*Königskinder*) in 1986. His repertory includes Pollione, Radames, Riccardo, Manrico, Cavaradossi, Canio, Erik, Loge, the Emperor (*Die Frau ohne Schatten*), Guntram, Apollo (*Daphne*) and Boris (*Kát'a Kabanová*). A fine musician whose lyric voice has grown heavier, he excels in modern parts: Oedipus, the Drum Major, Alwa, Aaron, Peter Grimes, Aschenbach and the title role of Testi's *Riccardo III*, which he created at La Scala (1987). He took part in the première of Corghi's *Blimunda* at the Teatro Lirico, Milan, in 1990.

ELIZABETH FORBES

Lewiston. American town in New York State. Artpark is a state park above the Niagara River Gorge and the name of a summer festival for the visual and performing arts, during which opera productions are given in the 2300-seat Artpark Theater (built 1974), a wide structure with a raked floor and rear walls that can be opened on to a natural amphitheatre lawn for non-operatic events. With the exception of 1984 and 1989 when visits by the New York City Opera replaced Artpark's own productions, two or three operas (two to four performances of each) were presented each summer from 1976 to 1988, generally works from the standard repertory, although the American première of Philip Glass's *Satyagraha* was given in 1981. In 1985 Artpark embarked on a four year project, producing one opera from the *Ring* cycle each year. Its last productions were *Götterdämmerung* and *Tosca* in 1988, a total of six performances that drew 14000 patrons. No operas were given in 1990 or 1991.

ROBERT V. PALMER

Lhérie, Léon. *See* BRUNSWICK (i).

Lhérie [Lévy], **Paul** (*b* Paris, 8 Oct 1844; *d* Paris, 17 Oct 1937). French tenor, later baritone. He studied in Paris, making his début at the Opéra-Comique in 1866 as Ruben in Méhul's *Joseph*. At the Théâtre de la Monnaie he sang Fabrice in Flotow's *L'ombre* (1871) and Reinhild in Gevaert's *Le billet de Marguerite*. Back at the Opéra-Comique, he created Charles II in Massenet's *Don César de Bazan* (1872), Benoît in Delibes's *Le Roi l'a dit* (1873) and Don José in *Carmen* (1875). In 1882 he became a baritone and in 1884 sang Posa in the revised version of Verdi's *Don Carlos* at La Scala. At Covent Garden in 1887 he sang Zurga, Rigoletto, Germont, Luna and Alphonse (*La favorite*). In 1891 he created the Rabbi David in Mascagni's *L'amico Fritz* at the Teatro Costanzi, Rome; in 1894 he sang Gudleik in the first performance of Franck's *Hulda* at Monte Carlo and then retired.

ELIZABETH FORBES

Lhotka-Kalinski, Ivo (*b* Zagreb, 30 July 1913; *d* Zagreb, 29 Jan 1987). Croatian composer. He studied composition with his father, the composer Fran Lhotka, and solo singing at the Zagreb Academy of Music until 1937, when he went to Rome for two years of composition study with Pizzetti. After holding various teaching posts (1939–51) he became a professor of singing at the Zagreb Academy.

Lhotka-Kalinski's early works were mainly romantic and programmatic. An intense study of folksong resulted in his making more than a hundred arrangements for vocal and instrumental groups, and also influenced the melodic patterns of his own music. However, he gradually abandoned this folk style for a neo-classical idiom and even experimented with atonality and dodecaphony. An excellent singer with a well-developed dramatic sense, Lhotka-Kalinski was a natural operatic composer. He gained an enviable reputation with his four brilliant, comic one-act radio and television operas to texts by Branislav Nušić (1954–8) in the tradition of Musorgsky's *opéra dialogué*. The second, *Putovanje* ('The Journey'), was the first Croatian television opera. His later, much expanded atonal opera *Svjetleći grad* ('The Shining City') is a bitter indictment of all that is worthless in society, mirrored musically by a coarsely dissonant harmonic idiom. Among his other works are ballets and film scores.

Pomet, meštar od ženidbe [Pomet, the Marriage Maker], 1942–4 (comic op, 3, M. Fotez, after M. Držić: *Dundo Maroje*), Zagreb, 31 Oct 1944
Matija Gubec (historical musical drama, 3, Lhotka-Kalinski, Fotez and T. Prpić), Zagreb, 8 May 1948
Skup [The Miser] (melodrama, M. Kombol, after Držić), Zagreb, 13 Sept 1950
Pepeljuga [Cinderella] (melodrama, J. Kušan), Zagreb, 14 Feb 1953
Velika coprarija [The Great Sorcery] (children's op, 3, B. Chudoba), Zagreb, 1953
Analfabeta [The Illiterate] (radio op, musical burlesque, 1, Lhotka-Kalinski, after B. Nušić), Belgrade, 19 Oct 1954, vs (Zagreb, 1957)
Putovanje [The Journey] (television op, musical satire, 1, Lhotka-Kalinski, after Nušić), Zagreb television, 10 June 1957, vs (Kassel, 1958)
Dugme [The Button] (television op, musical grotesque, 1, Lhotka-Kalinski, after Nušić), Zagreb television, 21 April 1958, vs (Zagreb, 1961)
Vlast [Political Power] (television op, musical portrait, 1, Lhotka-Kalinski, after Nušić), Belgrade television, 18 Oct 1958; stage, Belgrade, 25 Oct 1959; vs (Kassel, 1961)
Svjetleći grad [The Shining City] ('a musical farce of the prisoners of the absurd', P. Šegedin), Zagreb, 26 Dec 1967, vs (Zagreb, n.d.)
Tko će svima da ugodi? [Who could Please Everybody?], 1968 (musical tale, B. Slanina), unperf.

*

I. Kirigin: 'I. Lhotka-Kalinski, *Matija Gubec*', *Muzičke novine* (1948), 7
D. Gostuški: 'Ivo Lhotka-Kalinski: "Analfabeta"', *Zvuk* (1955), no.1, pp.21–8
K. Kovačević: *Hrvatski kompozitori i njihova djela* [Croatian Composers and their Works] (Zagreb, 1960), 261–74
I. Supičić: 'Estetski pogledi u novijoj hrvatskoj muzici: pregled temeljnih gledanja četrnaestorice kompozitora' [Aesthetic Approaches in Contemporary Croatian Music: a Survey of the Basic Views of 14 Composers], *Arti musices*, i (1969), 23–61
J. Andreis: *Music in Croatia* (Zagreb, 1974)
KORALJKA KOS, NIALL O'LOUGHLIN

Libau (Ger.). LIEPĀJA.

Liberec (Ger. Reichenberg). Czech town in north Bohemia. Records mention performances in 1796 of *Die Zauberflöte*. After the opening of the Zunfttheater in 1820 opera was performed by various companies; the theatre burnt down in 1879. The Stadttheater was completed in 1883 in German Renaissance style, designed by Fellner and Helmer; the costs were covered through subscriptions. It was reconstructed in 1966 and 1974–6, with 651 seats. Until 1918 it presented German plays, operas and operettas. Friedrich Sommer (1906–7), Karl Rankl (1925–7) and Josef Trauneck (1927–8) introduced a demanding repertory: *Ariadne auf Naxos* and *The Fair at Sorochintsï*, as well as works by Wagner, Verdi, Smetana, Dvořák and Janáček. Czech operas were staged regularly by the Olomouc company, 1924–38.

A permanent Czech theatre, the Severočeské Národní Divadlo (North Czech National Theatre), was established after World War II. After many changes of name and management, in 1957 it was named the F. X. Šalda Theatre, and in 1963 its management was taken over by the Regional National Committee in Ústí nad Labem. The theatre opened in 1945 with *The Bartered Bride*. The company was progressively consolidated under a succession of musical directors culminating in Rudolf Vašata (1960–71); although the emphasis has always been on Czech opera, in 1962 a 20th-century festival was held, with works by Martinů, Iša Krejčí, Pauer, Prokofiev, Britten and Liebermann. Other landmarks have included, in 1967, *L'Africaine* and *War and Peace*.

*

Stadttheater Reichenberg (1927–8, 1928–9) [programme books]
Severočeské národní divadlo v Liberci 1945–1948 [The North Czech National Theatre in Liberec] (Liberec, 1948)
Divadlo F. X. Šaldy v Liberci 1945–1960 [The F. X. Šalda Theatre in Liberec] (Liberec, 1960)
EVA HERRMANNOVÁ

Libraries and archives. This article surveys the opera and opera-related holdings of institutional libraries and archives. It does not include private collections, broadcasting libraries or specific sound archives, although important collections of sound recordings in libraries are noted.

1. Introduction. 2. List.

1. INTRODUCTION. It may reasonably be assumed that written records of various kinds were kept from the time opera first appeared as an art form in the early 17th century. The bringing together of artists skilled in aspects of operatic creation – music, scenery, dance or, later, even administration – necessitated a higher degree of professional organization than had, for example, the assembling of a small troupe of actors and dancers to re-create, in semi-improvised fashion and often *al fresco*, legends and stories already well known to their hearers. Dramatic representations at a court where singers and players were already retained for the private entertainment of the household probably required only a small extension of musicians' duties, and the hiring of dancers and a suitable librettist, for the presentation of an operatic spectacle. However, the opening of public opera houses and theatres, beginning with the S Cassiano in Venice in 1637 and spreading rapidly to other centres such as Paris and Hamburg, led to the rise of the theatre manager and impresario who, in addition to making agreements with artists, had to negotiate with local nobility, town and city councils and ecclesiastical authorities in order to bring about a performance. It is important to take account of this distinction between public and private opera when considering the types of archival record that might be expected to have survived or when attempting to locate such records.

Unlike historians of other musical genres, who arguably give less attention to the music's public presentation than they do to the musical text itself, historians of opera have always recognized the importance of the actual operatic event and the circumstances giving rise to it, i.e. the coming together of heterogeneous elements controlled by a number of professionals in different fields whose paths cross sufficiently for each to be able to make a contribution. The larger the number of professionals involved, the greater the need for an appropriate administrative and legal framework of contracts, disbursements, licences and so on, with a concomitant increase in the number of administrative records. Thus it may be expected, other things being equal, that the quantity of records generated by a large 19th-century opera house would far exceed that generated in previous centuries, because of increasing administrative sophistication (quite apart from the tendency for more recent material to have a higher survival rate). Operatic archives that survive bear witness to the competence of those in charge of operatic enterprises in keeping accurate and comprehensive records; to the success or failure of administrators and, subsequently, of librarians and archivists in realizing the value of these materials to posterity and preserving them in an appropriate manner; and to the occasional disasters, natural or man-made, that have resulted in large- and small-scale losses of materials (theatre fires account for a considerable proportion).

The quantity of records relating to a particular opera house or theatre, or even to an individual production, is potentially vast. Almost every piece of paper, from a composer's manuscript to a humble theatre ticket, may be of value to the archivist, librarian, ephemerist or scholar, and may assist in the historical reconstruction of an institution's affairs. Levels of research and bibliographic control vary widely and in many cases may be rudimentary, especially where documents are concerned more with what goes on outside a theatre than inside it: censors' records, theatre licences, architects' plans, contracts with ticket and publicity agents, bankruptcy pleas and records of theatre fires held in municipal archives all fall within this category. The attainment of researchers in such areas depends on the organization of record offices and, to an extent, on government policies: where a regime wishes to diminish the achievements of its predecessors, records may well be destroyed. Fortunately, given the number of duplicate copies made of legal documents, even officially sanctioned destruction may not entirely succeed in effacing the written record, although it may make it more difficult to track down. Changes in political boundaries may lead to the wholesale removal of materials from one national institution to another, with an almost inevitable loss of materials.

Nor is the opera researcher's field confined to written documents: costumes and 'props', especially when associated with a famous performer, may survive in theatre museums or private collections. Many opera houses contain sound and sometimes video archives of their productions, and many libraries and museums possess collections of prints and paintings that bear witness to the importance of iconography in operatic research and to the popularity of stage spectacle at the time such images were created. Operatic and other theatrical ephemera are not difficult to come by and remain comparatively inexpensive. Control (bibliographic and financial) of such materials is therefore largely in the hands of individual collectors and dealers,

and the few ephemera journals – such as the quarterly *Ephemerist* (London, 1975–) and *Ephemera News* (Peterborough, New Hampshire, 1981–) – along with dealers' catalogues give an overview of the field. The extent and condition of ephemera collections outside Europe, Australia and North America (the few areas in which organized ephemera societies exist) can only be guessed at, but given the low commercial value attached to such items it is probably very patchy. Researchers should perhaps be grateful for the survival of any materials at all rather than bemoan a lack of systematic collecting and ordering. Few institutions with ephemera collections can afford a specialist conservator.

Present library and archive collections have come about in three ways. First, the system of legal deposit, centuries old in some European countries, has helped build substantial national collections of printed books and scores. Under this system publishers and, occasionally printers, are obliged to deposit copies of their publications with their country's national library and, usually, with a few other para-national institutions. Scores and books are regularly deposited, but opera librettos, because of their restricted circulation, may or may not fall within the terms of the legislation; systems of legal deposit of sound recordings are much less developed than those for other materials. Second, private collectors, in many cases opera enthusiasts or performers, have built important collections. Often quite substantial, these are frequently characterized by the idiosyncratic collecting habits of their owners, and may include ephemera such as tickets, programmes and correspondence in addition to music scores and librettos. A considerable number of these collections have found their way into institutional libraries and archives. In countries whose social structure has included the encouragement of music through aristocratic patronage, such as Germany and Italy, many important court collections have migrated from castle or court libraries to municipal institutions; while in others, such as Austria and Czechoslovakia, many libraries created in this way still survive (and are often open to the public) in castles and other historic buildings. Such court libraries and archives are a rich source of information on operatic life from the early 17th century to the mid-19th. Some private collections belonging or relating to individual composers have subsequently become the basis of research institutes devoted to that composer, as at Bayreuth (Wagner), the Fondazione Rossini in Pesaro, the Civico Istituto Musicale Gaetano Donizetti in Bergamo and the Puccini house in Lucca.

Third, public theatres and opera houses themselves have maintained their own collections, which may either be kept on the premises or deposited in a nearby library (which latter solution usually safeguards them from dispersal for commercial rather than artistic or bibliographic reasons). It would be difficult to overestimate the importance of such primary source materials to the researcher, for they detail the minutiae of opera and, by so doing, go some way towards humanizing the figures who played a large or small part in the fortunes of a particular house. The archives might contain variant versions of an aria written specifically for the opera house, or for a special singer. They might have details of the early career of an artist whose subsequent success is well documented, but whose early musical achievements are less well known; and they will almost certainly record the theatre's financial successes and failures from season to season. Some of the larger opera houses employ an archivist to safeguard their holdings and to set them in order, but the survival of records in the plethora of smaller theatres which (in Europe and the USA at least) occasionally ventured an opera or operetta alongside mainstream repertory theatre in the 19th and early 20th centuries is much more a matter of chance. Even where an archive is in good order, it is rare to find a published catalogue of the collection: the details of opera materials held in the French Archives Nationales and those published in the *Annals of the Metropolitan Opera* (1990) and the *Cronologia degli spettacoli 1792–1936* (1989) of the Teatro La Fenice, Venice, are important exceptions. Fortunately for the researcher, where collections formerly belonging to public theatres under the control of a local administration survive, they will rarely have strayed far from their place of origin. Making contact with the nearest municipal library or regional archive, and with the theatre itself (where it survives), is probably the most effective first step in tracing materials. Further, the holdings (especially in manuscript) of a particular regional library or archive may also reflect the importance of that region as a centre of operatic activity, and contain clues about the transmission of a given work from one centre to another. The survival of individual music manuscripts in the libraries of many European centres may attest to the wide popularity of an opera and its composer. Thus the presence in libraries from St Petersburg to Brussels and London of manuscript copies of operas by Domenico Cimarosa mirrors that composer's success in such centres. The situation regarding the transmission of music changed somewhat in the 19th century, due to such factors as the development of copyright and the increase in agreements between composers and publishers to have vocal and full scores of their works printed to coincide with premières. Some of these have continued to be held in publishers' archives, of which the only one still important is Ricordi in Milan; others have been destroyed or given or sold to national collections. The agency for transmission of music moved from manuscript to printed score and the composer's autograph gained the status both of an 'authorized version' of the work and of a legal document, able to be called in evidence should any questions involving copyright arise.

The writing of a history of opera libraries would probably be an impossible task, if by the term 'library' is meant an institution established to collect and make available written or other records, a structured policy of collection development and conservation. In this sense, many of the private opera collections now in public libraries sit uncomfortably alongside the library's other stock: most have separate catalogues and are unlikely to be augmented except where their original owner provides additional materials or lays down specific conditions for their development. After all, collections of opera materials grew up largely as a necessary adjunct to opera houses or court theatres. They were not intended as general repositories of a part of human knowledge that was considered worth keeping (at least part of the *raison d'être* of the medieval monastic libraries or of state libraries). Their own justification was purely to facilitate an operatic performance: and once that performance was over, zealous theatre managers might dispose of most of the records relating to it (or keep such materials as were necessary to bring about a revival at a later date), while their less diligent counterparts would leave them to gather dust. Historically, libraries have not paid much attention to the collection of opera

materials other than scores and librettos until the present century, either because such materials have been regarded as unimportant or because of a general acceptance that theatrical documents normally enjoy only a short life.

See also COPYRIGHT; EDITING; and PUBLISHING.

2. LIST. In the compilation of this list, emphasis has been laid on the special collections of opera and opera-related materials in the libraries and archives included. Fuller accounts of the history and general collections of particular libraries, and of matters such as national systems of legal deposit, may be found in Rita Benton's *Directory of Music Research Libraries* (Kassel, 1967–85, vol.i rev. 1983; hereafter *BentonD*) which, although out of date in some respects, is still an excellent source of general information (a new edition is planned). André Veinstein and A. S. Golding's directory *Bibliothèques et musées des arts du spectacle dans le monde/Performing Arts Libraries and Museums of the World* (Paris, 3/1984) is likewise an invaluable source of information, and includes much detail, especially on museums, which is outside the scope of this article (a fourth edition is in progress).

The list is arranged alphabetically by country and then town or city and name of institution. Names and addresses of national libraries and archives are given at the beginning of each section, along with a statement of the national legal-deposit arrangements (where appropriate) and a general bibliography. Given the widely different levels of bibliographic control of materials, access to collections through national institutions is often the best introduction to a country's bibliographical and archival heritage. Sigla assigned by the Répertoire International des Sources Musicales (RISM) are given where applicable; selective bibliographies are supplied for individual institutions where appropriate.

ARGENTINA (*ARG*)

National library: Biblioteca Nacional, México 564, 1097 Buenos Aires.
National archives: Archivo General de la Nación, Leandro N. Alem 246, 1003 Buenos Aires.

BUENOS AIRES. Biblioteca de Musica y Arte del Teatro Colón, Cerrito no.618, Buenos Aires. Founded in 1940, the library holds a complete collection of programmes for the Teatro Colón's productions from 1908, as well as programmes of the Buenos Aires Opera. The theatre's holdings of music scores are small.

AUSTRALIA (*AUS*)

National library: National Library of Australia, Parkes Place, Canberra 2600 (*CAnl*). Legal deposit since 1912.
National archives: Australian Archives, POB34, Dickson, ACT 2602.

General literature: *BentonD*, iv, 3–38

ADELAIDE. State Opera of South Australia, 20 Rowlands Place, Adelaide 5000. The company holds archives relating to its own productions, including videos. Most of the company's repertory is 19th-century, and it holds some orchestral parts from that period. Further archival materials are housed in the Performing Arts Collection of the Adelaide Festival Centre, and in other local depositories.

R. Holmes, ed.: *Through the Opera Glass: a Chronological Register of Opera Performed in South Australia, 1836–1988* (Adelaide, 1991)

MELBOURNE. Victoria State Opera, State Opera Centre, Bicentennial Boulevard, Arts City, Melbourne 3004. In addition to archives for its own productions, the centre houses the Barry Shelton Memorial Music Library, the largest specialized opera collection in Australia, with MS and printed music, librettos, playbills and programmes.

SYDNEY. Sydney Opera House, Dennis Wolanski Library and Archives of the Performing Arts, Box 4274, Sydney NSW 2001. The library was established in 1973 to conserve materials relating to performances at the Sydney Opera House, and to provide a general research collection covering the performing arts. The library does not hold archives for the Australian Opera Company (the principal user of the opera house), since the company maintains archives in its own library (569 George Street, Sydney NSW 2000). Neither does it include the archives relating to the conception and building of the opera house: these are held in the National Library in Canberra. The Wolanski collections contain playbills, photographs and press cuttings, but exclude music scores and librettos.

P. Bentley: 'Dennis Wolanski: Library of the Performing Arts and the Sydney Opera House', *Australian Special Library News*, ix (1976), 102–8; idem: 'The Dennis Wolanski Library and Archives of the Performing Arts, the Sydney Opera House', *Biblionews* (1986), March, 15–19

——. Sydney University, Fisher Library, Sydney NSW 2006 (*Sfl*). Founded in 1851, the library has enjoyed legal-deposit status for New South Wales since 1879. Its most important opera holdings are in the collection of Robert Dalley-Scarlett, which includes Handel materials.

R. Illing: 'Dalley-Scarlett Collection of Music and Books about Music', *Australian Library Journal*, xix (1970), 459–67; P. Brown: 'Introduction to Robert Dalley-Scarlett and his Collections', *Studies in Music* [Australia], v (1971), 87–9

AUSTRIA (A)

National library: Österreichische Nationalbibliothek, Josefsplatz 1, 1015 Vienna (*Wn*). For details of opera holdings see under 'Vienna'.
National archives: Österreichisches Staatsarchiv, Nottendorfergasse 2, 1030 Vienna.

General literature: *BentonD*, ii, 1–18

GRAZ. Universität, Institut für Musikwissenschaft, Mozartgasse 3, 8010 Graz (*Gmi*). Founded in 1940, the library holds some 600 music MSS and 11 000 scores.

SALZBURG. Universitätsbibliothek, Hofstallgasse 2–4, 5010 Salzburg (*Su*). The Friderica Derra de Moroda Dance Archives contain opera-related materials (Derra de Moroda worked with the Berlin Staatsoper in the 1940s).

S. Dahms and L. Roth-Woelfle: *F. Derra de Moroda: the Dance Library 1480–1980, a Catalogue* (Munich, 1982)

VIENNA. Gesellschaft der Musikfreunde, Bösendorferstrasse 12, 1010 Vienna (*Wgm*). Founded in 1812, the library holds performance materials (including MS and printed sets of parts), letters, librettos, programmes, portraits, scene designs and illustrations of theatres and opera houses, as well as MS and printed opera scores from the 17th century to the 20th.

——. Hochschule für Musik und Darstellende Kunst, Lothringerstrasse 18, 1037 Vienna. There is a small collection of MS and printed opera scores, and performance materials (fewer than 100 items in each category).

——. Österreichische Nationalbibliothek, Musik-, Porträt-, Theatersammlungen, Augustinerstrasse 1, 1010 Vienna (*Wn*). This is the most important music and theatre collection in Austria. It has an archive of several thousand volumes, including materials relating to the Theater an der Wien (approximately 1400 vols., dating from the 19th century) and the Burgtheater (662 vols. from the 19th and 20th centuries), a Kaisersammlung (from the collections of Charles VI) and a Leopoldina Collection (from Leopold I). Further items concern the Theater in der Josefstadt and the Kärntnertortheater (500 vols. from the 18th and 19th centuries). The library possesses some 10 000 MS scores, 3000 MS performance parts, 80 000 programmes and 12 000 librettos, as well as papers relating to Berg, Schreker, Leo Fall and Alexander Steinbrecher. Private collections include that of the Schloss Schwertberg (17th- and 18th-century opera and domestic music). Other local theatre materials are held in the Vienna Stadtbibliothek. In 1991 the Theatersammlung became the Theatermuseum.

F. Trojan and F. Hadamowsky: *Katalog der Alten Bibliothek des Theaters an der Wien*, Kataloge der Theatersammlung der Nationalbibliothek in Wien, i (Vienna, 1928); J. Gregor and F. Hadamowsky: *Die Handzeichnungen der Theatersammlung*, Kataloge der Theatersammlung der Nationalbibliothek in Wien, ii (Vienna, 1930); F. Hadamowsky: *Das Theater in der Wiener Leopoldstadt 1781–1860*, Kataloge der Theatersammlung der Nationalbibliothek in Wien, iii (Vienna, 1934); J. Gregor and K. Ecker: 'Die Theatersammlung', *Die Österreichische Nationalbibliothek: Festschrift herausgegeben zum 25-jährigen Dienstjubiläum des Generaldirektors Univ.-Prof. Dr. Josef Bich* (Vienna, 1948), 180–99; L. Novak: 'Die Musiksammlung', ibid, 119–38, 505–22; H. Pauer: 'Die Porträtsammlung und das Bildarchiv', ibid, 165–79; J. Stummvoll and R. Fiedler, eds.: *Geschichte der Österreichischen Nationalbibliothek* (Vienna, 1968–73); K. Zobel and F. E. Warner: 'The Old Burgtheater: a Structural History, 1741–1888', *Theatre Studies*, xix (1972–3), 19–53

BELGIUM (B)

National library: Bibliothèque Royale Albert 1er/ Koninklijke Bibliotheek Albert I, Boulevard de l'Empereur 4, 1000 Brussels (*Br*). Legal deposit since 1966. For details of opera holdings see under 'Brussels'.
National archives: Archives Générales du Royaume, rue de Ruysbroeck 2–4, 1000 Brussels.

General literature: *BentonD*, ii, 19–24; K. Cooremans: 'Music Libraries in Belgium', *FAM*, xxii (1975), 101–3

ANTWERP. Archief en Museum voor het Vlaamse Culturleven/Archives et Musée pour la Vie Culturelle Flamande, Minderbroedersstraat 22, 2000 Antwerp (*Aac*). The museum houses materials from the Koninklijke Vlaamse (Royal Flemish) Opera.

BRUSSELS. Archives de la Ville, rue des Tanneurs 965, 1000 Brussels (*Ba*). In addition to a large ballet collection, the archives house materials from the Théâtre de la Monnaie, founded in 1700. There are more than 500 opera MSS, as well as a programme collection and other materials relating to theatre in the city.

——. Bibliothèque Royale Albert 1er/Koninklijke Bibliotheek Albert I, Boulevard de l'Empereur 4, 1000

Brussels (*Br*). Holdings include the collection formerly belonging to F.-J. Fétis and opera librettos from the 17th and 18th centuries.

B. Huys: *Catalogue des imprimés musicaux des XVe, XVIe et XVII siècles* (Brussels, 1965–74); idem: 'La section de la musique', *Bibliothèque Royale: memorial 1559–1969* (Brussels, 1969), 311–33; idem: *Catalogue des imprimés musicaux du XVIIIe siècle* (Brussels, 1974)

——. Centre Belge de Documentation Musicale [CeBeDeM], rue d'Arlon 75–7, 1040 Brussels (*Bcdm*). The centre aims to stimulate the promotion and performance of works by Belgian composers since 1870; to this end, its library contains scores and parts of works by native musicians.

——. Conservatoire Royal de Musique/Koninklijke Muziekconservatorium, rue de la Régence 30, Brussels (*Bc*). The conservatory was founded in 1832. Of its many thousand librettos, a large proportion are Italian 17th-century works.

A. Wotquenne: *Catalogue de la Bibliothèque du Conservatoire royal de musique de Bruxelles* (Brussels, 1898–1912), suppl.: *Libretti d'opéras et d'oratorios italiens du XVIIe siècle* (Brussels, 1901)

——. Théâtre Royal de la Monnaie, rue Léopold 4, 1000 Brussels. The theatre holds a small amount of archival material relating to its activities, mainly from the 20th century. It includes programmes and press cuttings, but no music scores. The majority of the company's archives are in the Archives de la Ville.

GHENT. Bibliotheek van de Rijksuniversiteit te Gent, 9 Rozier, 9000 Ghent (*Gu*). The collection includes opera and ballet scores from the Grand Théâtre, Ghent, and librettos from the collection of François du Bus.

P. Bergmans: 'Une collection de livrets d'opéras italiens (1669–1710), à la Bibliothèque de l'Université de Gand', *SIMG*, xii (1910–11), 221–34

LIÈGE. Conservatoire Royal de Musique, rue Forgeur 14, 4000 Liège (*Lc*). The conservatory's holdings are small (fewer than 1000 items), but include the Grétry Collection and MS and printed opera scores and parts. The Léonard Terry Collection is concerned mainly with local musical life.

M. Barthélemy: 'Le fonds Terry de la Bibliothèque du Conservatoire royal de musique de Liège', *FAM*, xxiii (1976), 124–6; idem: *Inventaire général des manuscrits anciens du Conservatoire royal de musique de Liège* (Liège, 1977)

——. Opéra Royal de Wallonie, rue des Dominicains 1, 4000 Liège. Like the Liège Conservatory, the Opéra possesses some Grétry materials. There are also printed scores and parts used in its own productions, and a collection of programmes, publicity materials, scene designs and about 1000 librettos.

BULGARIA

National library (arts): Nacionalna Biblioteka 'Kiril i Metodij' [Cyril and Methodius National Library], boulevard Vassil Levski 11, 1504 Sofia.
National archives: (1) Central State Archives of the People's Republic of Bulgaria, Slavjanska 4, 1000 Sofia; (2) Central Historical State Archives, 3 April 5, 1000 Sofia.

CANADA (*C*)

National library: National Library of Canada/Bibliothèque Nationale de Canada, 395 Wellington Street, Ottawa, Ontario K1A 0N4 (*On*). Legal deposit since 1868.
National archives: National Archives of Canada, 395 Wellington Street, Ottawa, Ontario K1A 0N3.

General literature: *BentonD*, i, 25–46; *EMC* ('Libraries'; H. Kallmann)

HAMILTON. McMaster University Library, 1280 Main Street West, Hamilton, Ontario L8S 4L6 (*HNu*). The music collection is small, but includes extracts from English operas in a group of Georgian songs acquired by the library in 1989 (see Foley and Fletcher); composers include Arne, Dibdin and Storace. The library has materials used by Eric Walter White for his *History of English Opera*, letters from Tippett to Edward Sackville-West concerning *The Midsummer Marriage*, and the Herbert Menges Collection (correspondence, MS music and other materials concerning his work in England with the Old Vic Theatre, London). There is also a small programme collection.

B. Whiteman: 'The Herbert Menges Collection', *McMaster University Library Research News*, ix/1 (1985) [entire issue]; C. A. Stewart and C. Spadoni: 'The Research Collections at McMaster University Library', *McMaster University Library Research News*, xi (1987) [entire issue]; W. Warnken: 'A Study of Ontario's Performing Arts Resources', *Theatre History in Canada*, ix/1 (1988), 110–23; M. Foley and K. Fletcher: 'Georgian Songs, 1714–1830: a Descriptive Catalogue', *McMaster University Library Research News*, xiii (1989) [entire issue]

LONDON. University of Western Ontario, Music Library, 1151 Richmond Street North, London, Ontario N6A 3K7 (in *Lu*). The Opera Collection contains about 1500 operas, mainly in MS or printed first editions (17th–19th centuries), including works by Lully, Rameau, Handel, Hasse, Bellini, Cimarosa and Massenet. The Metastasio Collection has scores and librettos of operas produced between 1780 and 1830, including works by Meyerbeer and Cherubini. The bulk of the collection (*c*300 titles) consists of microform or photostat copies of European primary sources.

D. Neville, ed.: *Opera 1600–1750 in Contemporary Editions and Manuscripts now in the Holdings of the Music Library of the University of Western Ontario* (London, Ont., 1979); J. A. Pearce Baldwin, W. G. Guthrie and L. Smith: 'Special Collections at the Music Library of the University of Western Ontario', *FAM*, xxxiv (1987), 240–42; W. Warnken: 'A Study of Ontario's Performing Arts Resources', *Theatre History in Canada*, ix/1 (1988), 110–23

MONTREAL. Opéra de Montréal, 1157 St Catherine Street East, Montreal, Quebec H2L 2G8. The company has a small archive covering its own productions from 1980.

TORONTO. Canadian Music Centre, 20 St Joseph Street, Toronto, Ontario M4Y 1J9. The centre holds a small archive, including more than 100 opera MSS by contemporary Canadian composers. Performance parts are available, and there is a collection of programmes and press cuttings.

——. Canadian Opera Company, Joan Baillie Archives, 227 Front Street East, Toronto, Ontario M5E 1B2. The company maintains an archive not only of its own materials (1950 onwards) but also of materials from other Toronto theatre companies (some items date back to the 19th century). The collection does not include music scores.

——. Metropolitan Toronto Reference Library, 789 Yonge Street, Toronto, Ontario M4W 2G8 (incl. *Tp*). The library owns the Cara Hartwell Collection of correspondence and ephemera relating to famous 20th-century opera singers. Many items in the general collection relate to the Canadian Opera Company, and there is a picture collection (theatrical photographs: more than 800 000 items) and a collection of more than 3000 stage designs from Canadian theatre and opera companies.

H. McCallum: 'The Theatre Department of the Metropolitan Toronto Library', *Theatre and Performing Arts Collections*, ed. L. Rachow (New York, 1981), 75–86

———. University Library, Edward Johnson Building, Toronto, Ontario M5S 1A1 (*Tu*). The Edward Johnson Music Library is responsible for the Collection Théâtre Lyrique, comprising French opera scores, 1750–1900. It contains some 2200 vocal scores and 250 full scores, along with a microfilm-photostat collection of similar materials held in other locations. The Thomas Fisher Rare Book Library and the Robarts Library hold a libretto collection of some 6500 items, including some operatic works.

R. Elliott and H. M. White: 'A Collection of Oratorio Libretti, 1700–1800, in the Thomas Fisher Rare Book Library, University of Toronto', *FAM*, xxxii (1985), 102–14

CROATIA (*HV*)

National library: Nacionalna i Sveučilišna Biblioteka [National and State Library], Marulićev trg 21, Zagreb (*Zu*). Founded in the 17th century; it was the centre for legal deposit for Yugoslavia from 1919.

National archives: Arhiv Hrvatske [Archives of Croatia], Marulićev trg 21, 41000 Zagreb. Founded in 1643.

General literature: *BentonD*, v, 179–267; A. Stipčevic, ed.: *Libraries in Croatia* (Zagreb, 1975)

CZECHOSLOVAKIA (*CS*)

National library: Národní Knihovna v Praze [National Library in Prague], Klementinum 190, 110–01 Prague 1 (*Pu*). Legal-deposit status has been shared between more than 100 libraries in the former Czechoslovakia.

National archives: Státní Ústřední Archiv [Central Archives of the Czech Academy of Sciences], Karmelitska 2, 118–00 Prague 1

General literature: *BentonD*, v, 17–68; F. Horák: 'Die wissenschaftlichen Bibliotheken in der Tschechoslowakei', *Zentralblatt für Bibliothekswesen*, lxvi (1952), 9–27; J. Kouba, ed.: *Průvodce po pramenech k dějinám hudby: fondy a sbírky uložené v Čechách* [Guide to Sources of Music History: Czech Holdings and Collections] (Prague, 1969); J. Wágnerová: 'Music Libraries in Czechoslovakia', *Brio*, xxiv (1987), 26–9

BRNO. Státní Vědecká Knihovna, Universitní Knihovna [State Scientific Library, University Library], Leninova 5, Brno (*Bu*). The university has a collection of opera librettos from the 18th and 19th centuries.

ČESKÝ KRUMLOV. Pracoviště Státního Archivu Třeboň, Hudební Sbírka [State Regional Archive], Zámek, Český Krumlov (*K*). Most of the collection consists of sacred music, but there is an important opera and ballet archive containing materials from theatrical productions in 18th-century Vienna.

KUTNÁ HORA. Okresní Muzeum v Kutné Hore [Kutná Hora Regional Museum], Barborská 28, 284–80 Kutná Hora-Hrádek (*KU*). The museum possesses more than 1000 MSS from the 18th century to the 20th, including works by Scarlatti and Gluck.

PRAGUE. Konservatoř, Na rejdišti 1, 110–00 Prague (*Pk*). The MS collection of 18th- and 19th-century

works includes items by Leo and Mozart. There is a collection of MS orchestral parts from Czech theatres.

———. Muzeum České Hudby [Museum of Czech Music], Novotného lávka 1, 110–01 Prague. A state institution (affiliated with the National Museum) collecting all types of Czech music, it contains some of the archives of the Prague National Theatre (including 19th-century scores and parts, some MS), and the Lobkovic Collection of scores and parts for 18th- and 19th-century operas. There are items pertaining to Smetana and Dvořák, including autograph MSS, playbills and newspaper cuttings covering 19th- and 20th-century Czech theatre, and stage designs.

———. Národní Muzeum [National Museum], Tr. Vítezného února 74, 115–79 Prague (*Pnm*). The museum has archives from the National Theatre and related institutions. There is a costume collection, and a separate Divadelní Oddělení (Theatre Division).

O. Pulkert: 'The Musical Development of the National Museum in Prague', *FAM*, ii (1955), 112–17

DENMARK (*DK*)

National library: Kongelige Bibliotek, POB2149, 1016 Copenhagen (*Kk*). Legal deposit since 1697. For details of opera holdings see under 'Copenhagen'.

National archives: Rigsarkivet, Rigsdagsgarden 9, 1218 Copenhagen.

General literature: *BentonD*, ii, 152–8; E. Steinaa: 'Institutions for Theatre Research in Copenhagen', *Theatre Studies*, xix (1972–3), 16–18; B. Stribolt and others: *Teatersamlinger i norden: Katalog over teatermuseer, -biblioteker og -arkiver i Danmark, Finland, Norge og Sverige* (Copenhagen, 1984, 2/1986)

COPENHAGEN. Byggeriets Studiearkiv [Danish Archive for Building Documentation], Peder Skramsgade 2D, 1054 Copenhagen. Founded in 1930, the centre has a special collection on building and design, including theatre.

———. Kongelige Bibliotek, POB2149, 1016 Copenhagen (*Kk*). Besides being the national library, the Kongelige Bibliotek houses the Dan Fog Music Collection. Devoted to Danish music, it covers the period 1783–1940 and contains Danish vaudevilles (1825–1900), a libretto collection and programmes for the Kongelige Teater, Copenhagen. There are few music scores in the Fog collection: holdings are mainly documentary materials.

———. Kongelige Teaters Arkiv og Bibliotek [Royal Theatre Archive and Library], POB2195, 1017 Copenhagen. Founded in 1748, the archive includes theatre documentation from 1773, costume and stage designs from the 19th and 20th centuries, programmes, librettos and a photographic archive. The Royal Theatre Music Archive is housed in the same building.

———. Musikhistorisk Museum og Carl Claudius' Samling, Abenra 30, 1124 Copenhagen (*Km(m)*). The museum was founded in 1898, and the Claudius Collection added in 1900. Of moderate size, it contains librettos, press cuttings, programmes and some printed and MS music (fewer than 100 MSS), from the late 18th century to about 1970.

———. Teatermuseet, Christiansborg, Ridebane 10 and 18, 1218 Copenhagen. The library is part of the Danish court theatre, founded in the 18th century.

ESTONIA (*EE*)

National library: Eesti Rahvusnaamatukogu [National Library of Estonia], Kiriku plats 1, 200106 Tallinn. Founded in 1918.

TALLINN. Muzej Teatra i Muzyki Estonskoj [Estonian Theatre and Music Museum], Müürivake 12, 200001 Tallinn. The museum was founded in 1924. Although it possesses no special opera collections, it houses a general collection of composers' letters, music MSS and other documentary materials.

FINLAND (*SF*)

National library: Helsingin Yliopiston Kirjasto [Helsinki University Library], Unioninkatu 36, POB312, 00171 Helsinki (*Hy*). Legal deposit since 1707 (and for Russia, 1820–1917).
National archives: Valtionarkisko, POB258, 00171 Helsinki.

General literature: BentonD, ii, 209–12; B. Stribolt and others: *Teatersamlinger i norden: Katalog over teatermuseer, -biblioteker og -arkiver i Danmark, Finland, Norge og Sverige* (Copenhagen, 1984, 2/1986); H. Poroila, ed.: *Directory of Music Libraries in Finland/Suomalaisten musikkikirjasten hakemisto* (Helsinki, 1991)

HELSINKI. Helsingin Yliopiston Kirjasto, Unioninkatu 36, POB312, 00171 Helsinki (*Hy*). The library was founded in 1640; a separate department is given over to Finnish composers.

TURKU. Sibelius Museum, Åbo Akademi, Biskopsgatan 17, 20500 Turku (*A*). The library collects programmes from the Finnish National Opera (1865 onwards) and from some provincial Finnish companies. It holds press cuttings for the National Opera from 1876. There is a small collection of printed scores and librettos.

FRANCE (*F*)

National library: Bibliothèque Nationale, 58 rue Richelieu, 75084 Paris (*Pn*). Legal deposit for France; there is also a network of regional libraries which enjoy legal-deposit status for their areas. For details of opera holdings see under 'Paris'.
National archives: Archives Nationales, 60 rue des Francs-Bourgeois, 75141 Paris. See also under 'Paris'.

General literature: BentonD, iii, 57–135

AIX-EN-PROVENCE. Bibliothèque Municipale, 8–10 rue des Allumettes, 13098 Aix-en-Provence (*AIXm*). The collection originally belonged to the Marquis of Méjanes (*fl* 18th century). It includes the Boissy Collection of theatrical material, and some 18th-century operas.

AMIENS. Bibliothèque Municipale, 50 rue de la République, 80037 Amiens (*AM*). This is a small collection, with some 17th- and 18th-century first editions of French operas, about 120 items of archival material relating to theatre in the region from the 17th century to the 20th, and some of J.-F. Le Sueur's works in MS.

AVIGNON. Bibliothèque Municipale, Musée Clavet, 65 rue Joseph Vernet, 84000 Avignon (*A*). The library houses the collection of the French critic Castil-Blaze, with materials from the late 17th century to the 19th, including autographs by Meyerbeer; autographs by Rossini, Boieldieu and other composers are also held.

BERNAY. Bibliothèque Municipale, place Gustave Heon, 27300 Bernay (*BER*). First-edition holdings of

17th- and 18th-century French operas include Lully's *Amadis* and *Thésée*, Collasse's *Thétis et Pélée* and Marais' *Alcyone*.

BORDEAUX. Bibliothèque Municipale, 3 rue Mably, 33075 Bordeaux (*BO*). The library holds 18th- and 19th-century scores and librettos from the Grand Théâtre in Bordeaux.

CHARTRES. Bibliothèque Municipale, 35 rue S Michel, 28000 Chartres (*CHR*). The library holds some 18th-century opera MSS, the remnant of a larger collection destroyed in 1944.

DIJON. Bibliothèque Municipale, 3–7 rue de l'Ecole de Droit, 21000 Dijon (*Dm*). The library holds archives for its département (Côte d'Or) and has a few Rossini autographs.

——. Ecole Nationale de Musique et d'Art Dramatique de Dijon, 5 rue de l'Ecole de Droit, 21000 Dijon (*Dc*). Housed in the same building as the Bibliothèque Municipale, the collection includes the library of the counts of Kervéguen (more than 12 000 scores and parts), which was donated in 1895.

LILLE. Bibliothèque Municipale, 34 rue Edouard Delesalle, 59043 Lille (*Lm*). The large opera collection dates from the late 17th and 18th centuries, and includes works by Destouches, Campra and Rameau. There is a large libretto collection, as well as materials from the Théâtre Municipal.

LYONS. Bibliothèque Municipale, 30 boulevard Vivier-Merle, 69431 Lyons (*LYm*). This important library holds almost the complete collection of the Lyons Académie d'Opéra (17th and 18th centuries), including MSS of works by Cherubini, Dalayrac, Desmarets, Lully and Rameau, as well as the autograph of Rousseau's *Le devin du village*.

P. Guillot: *Catalogue des manuscrits musicaux de la Bibliothèque municipale de Lyon* (Lyons, 1985)

MÂCON. Bibliothèque Municipale, place des Carmélites, 71000 Mâcon (*MAC*). Opera holdings comprise early editions of works by Collasse, Lully, Destouches and Rameau.

MONTAUBAN. Bibliothèque Municipale, square du Général Picquart, 82000 Montauban (*MON*). Founded in 1779, the library houses a sizable collection of 18th-century operas.

NÎMES. Bibliothèque Municipale, 19 Grand-Rue, 30000 Nîmes (*NS*). The Sabatier Collection contains 18th- and 19th-century opera scores, as well as orchestral parts for 17th- and 18th-century works. There is a large collection of theatre materials.

PARIS. Archives Nationales, 60 rue des Francs-Bourgeois, 75141 Paris. Among the documents held are those in series AJ[13], relating to the Paris Opéra, 18th–20th centuries; series O[1], for the Menus-Plaisirs du Roi; series O[3], covering French theatre, 1815–1830; series F[17], part of which deals with the theatres of Paris, 1792–1821; and series F[18], which contains censors' records.

B. Labat-Poussin: *Archives du Théâtre national de l'Opéra (AJ[13], 1–1466): inventaire* (Paris, 1977); *Danseurs et ballet de l'Opéra de Paris depuis 1671* (Paris, 1988) [exhibition catalogue]

——. Bibliothèque de l'Arsenal, 1 rue de Sully, 75004 Paris (*Pa*). The theatre holdings were begun in about

1797, with part of the collection of the dukes de la Vallière. They have been built up subsequently through gifts and bequests by theatre managers, administrators and performers, including a large bequest of 50 000 items from the composer Georges Douay in 1919. The Rondel Collection (donated by Auguste Rondel, a Marseilles banker) was added in 1925. Since 1974 the Arsenal has functioned as the Département des Arts du Spectacle of the Bibliothèque Nationale. It includes materials from 18th-century marionette plays, and from the Vaudeville, Odéon, Variétés and Nations theatres.

A. Rondel: *Catalogue analytique sommaire de la collection théâtrale Rondel* (Paris, 1932); L. de la Laurencie and A. Gastoué: *Catalogue des livres de musique de la Bibliothèque de l'Arsenal* (Paris, 1936); A. Veinstein: 'La collection théâtrale Auguste Rondel', *Ohio State University Collection Bulletin*, xiv (1967), 8–11; *Trésors de la Bibliothèque de l'Arsenal* (Paris, 1980) [exhibition catalogue]

——. Bibliothèque Historique de la Ville de Paris, 24 rue Pavée, 75004 Paris. The library holds a large collection of Paris theatre plans, programmes and press cuttings. It also houses the Bibliothèque de l'Association de la Régie Théâtrale, founded in 1920, which contains some 1700 items relating to staging.

H. R. Cohen and M.-O. Gigou: *Cent ans de mise en scène lyrique en France (env. 1830–1930)/One Hundred Years of Operatic Staging in France* (New York, 1986)

——. Bibliothèque-Musée de la Comédie-Française, 98 galérie des Beaujolais, Jardins du Palais-Royal, 75001 Paris (*Pcf*). The library exists mainly to preserve documents pertaining to the Comédie-Française from the 17th century onwards and includes important archival material concerning the genesis of French opera. The majority of the musical holdings are of incidental music for stage productions. There are collections of costume designs and production photographs.

S. Chevalley: 'The Library of the Comédie-Française', *Ohio State University Collection Bulletin*, vii (1960), 5–7

——. Bibliothèque-Musée de l'Opéra, 1 place Charles Garnier, 75009 Paris (*Po*). One of the most important national opera collections in existence, the library holds scores and parts (many autograph) from the time of the foundation of the Opéra (1671). The Fonds Silvestri consists of Italian opera librettos. Dance holdings relate to operatic productions.

T. Lajarte: *Bibliothèque musicale du théâtre de l'Opéra: catalogue historique, chronologique, anecdotique* (Paris, 1878); J.-G. Prod'homme: 'État alphabétique sommaire des archives de l'Opéra', *RdM*, xiv (1933), 193–205; M. E. C. Bartlet: 'Archival Sources for the Opéra-Comique and its *registres* at the Bibliothèque de l'Opéra', *19th Century Music*, vii (1983–4), 119–29; M. Kahane: 'Archives of the Dance, (4a): the Library and Archives of the Paris Opéra, part 2', *Dance Research*, iii/1 (1984), 67–71

——. Bibliothèque Nationale, 58 rue Richelieu, 75084 Paris (*Pn*). The Cabinet des Estampes, established by Colbert in 1667, includes many prints of theatre architecture. The music collection was established in 1725 with materials donated by Sébastien de Brossard. Besides its own collections, built up by legal deposit, gifts and bequests, the library has materials from the Paris Conservatoire library and administers the library of the Opéra (see above). A portion of the Toulouse-Philidor collection, formerly at St Michael's College, Tenbury, has reverted to the library.

C. Giteau: 'Models of Scenery and Costumes in the Performing Arts Department of the Bibliothèque nationale, Paris', *Performing Arts Resources*, viii (1983), 55–8; C. Massip: 'La collection Toulouse-Philidor à la Bibliothèque nationale', *FAM*, xxx (1983), 184–207; idem: 'Les collections d'opéras italiens à la Bibliothèque nationale',

L'opera tra Venezia e Parigi, ed. M. T. Muraro (Florence, 1988), 105–17

——. Direction des Services d'Archives de Paris, 19 boulevard Sérurier, 75019 Paris. This office contains a special collection of books and archives on Paris and its environs. Materials include, for example, account books relating to theatres.

——. Musée du Louvre, quai du Louvre, 75041 Paris. The Cabinet des Dessins includes drawings from the 17th and 18th centuries; some relate to theatre.

Le théâtre et la danse en France, 17–18 siècles (Paris, 1959) [exhibition catalogue]

——. Université de Paris-Sorbonne, Bibliothèque de l'Unité de Formation et de Recherche de Musique et Musicologie (Bibliothèque Pierre Aubry), 3 rue Michelet, 75006 Paris (*Pim*). The library holds the Reinach Collection of 18th- and 19th-century editions of operas and *opéras comiques*, as well as operatic extracts. There is also a collection of vocal scores acquired from P.-M. Masson.

ROUEN. Bibliothèque Municipale, 3 rue Jacques-Villon, 76043 Rouen (*R(m)*). The Fonds Baudry contains orchestral parts for 560 operas. There is also material relating to the local Théâtre des Arts (18th- and 19th-century ballet and opera).

SALINS. Bibliothèque Municipale, place Emile Zola, 39110 Salins (*SA*). The Charles Magnin Collection includes Grétry autographs and other operatic materials from the 17th century to the 19th.

STRASBOURG. Université, Institut de Musicologie, 6 place de la République, BP1029/F, 67070 Strasbourg (*Sim*). The theatre collection contains operas from Paris, including first editions of the works of Lully, his contemporaries and successors.

TOULOUSE. Bibliothèque Municipale, 1 rue de Périgord, 31000 Toulouse (*TLm*). Founded in 1762, the library possesses 86 MS and more than 900 printed French 18th-century operas, which form part of the collection of the librettist Jean-Jacques Lefranc de Pompignan. There are 114 MS orchestral parts, and the library houses cast-lists of the Théâtre du Capitole, which mounted opera and vaudeville productions in Toulouse (*c*1826–41).

J. Laborie: 'Le fonds musical de la Bibliothèque municipale de Toulouse', *Revue internationale de la musique française*, xi (1983), 105–9

VERSAILLES. Bibliothèque Municipale, 5 rue de l'Indépendance-Américaine, 78000 Versailles (*V*). The principal opera collection is that of the *ancienne musique du roi*, dating from the 17th and 18th centuries; the library also owns operettas from 19th-century productions at the local Théâtre des Variétés.

GERMANY (*D*)

National library: Deutsche Staatsbibliothek, PF1312, Unter den Linden 8, 1086 Berlin (*Bds*). There is a network of regional libraries which have legal-deposit status for their areas. For details of opera holdings see under 'Berlin'.

There is no national archive; archives are held in regional centres, such as Bonn and Munich.

General literature: *Benton*D, ii, 41–152; R. Schaal: *Führer durch deutsche Musikbibliotheken* (Wilhelmshaven, 1971); W. Gebhardt: *Spezialbestände in deutschen Bibliotheken/Special Collections in*

German Libraries (Berlin, 1977); M. Giesing: *Theatersammlungen in der Bundesrepublik Deutschland und Berlin (West)* (Berlin, 1985)

ANSBACH. Staatliche Bibliothek, Schloss, 8800 Ansbach (*AN*). A small collection of 17th- and 18th-century works includes printed scores and librettos for operas by Lully, Charpentier and Collasse. There are a few items in MS.

AUGSBURG. Staats- und Stadtbibliothek, Schaezler-strasse 25, 8900 Augsburg (*As*). Founded in the 16th century, the library is a regional centre for Swabia. It includes programmes for Augsburg theatres from 1776, and a libretto collection of more than 300 items covering the period 1798–1953.

BERLIN. General literature: P. S. Ulrich: 'Theatre Research Resources in West Berlin', *Performing Arts Resources*, iv (1978), 55–71; H. Haas: 'Die Theaterhistorische Sammlung Walter Unruh in Berlin', *Theatersammlungen in der Bundesrepublik Deutschland und Berlin (West)*, ed. M. Giesing (Berlin, 1985), 11–24

——. Deutsche Akademie der Künste, Abteilung für Deutsche Theatergeschichte, Robert-Koch-Platz 7, 104 Berlin (*Ba*). The collection comprises materials from the 18th, 19th and 20th centuries, including stage designs. Its publications include Hugo Fetting's *Geschichte der deutschen Staatsoper* (Berlin, 1955).

——. Deutsche Staatsbibliothek, PF1312, Unter den Linden 8, 1086 Berlin (*Bds*). Founded in the 17th century, the library contains a large portrait collection, and MSS of Mozart's *Le nozze di Figaro* (Acts 1 and 2) and Weber's *Der Freischütz*. The music section was established in 1824. In 1992 it amalgamated with the Staatsbibliothek Preussischer Kulturbesitz to form the Staatsbibliothek zu Berlin, Preussischer Kulturbesitz (*Bsb*).

——. Deutsche Staatsoper, Unter den Linden 7, 1080 Berlin (*Bdso*). This is a conventional archive of prompt-books, programmes, press cuttings and so on. It includes MS performing materials, and items from the library of the royal theatre.

——. Freie Universität Berlin, Institut für Theaterwissenschaft, Garystrasse 39, 1000 Berlin 33. The institute holds a general collection relating to the history of Berlin theatres.

——. Hochschule der Künste, Abteilung Musik und Darstellende Kunst, Fasanenstrasse 1B, 1000 Berlin 12 (*Bhm*). There is a collection of more than 600 librettos (late 16th–19th centuries), most of which relate to Berlin productions.

——. Komische Oper, Unter den Linden 41, PF1311, 1086 Berlin (*Bko*). Founded in 1947, the company's archive includes numerous production books, about 5000 programmes and a large press-cuttings archive. There are no music MSS.

——. Märkisches Museum, Am Köllnischen Park 5, 1020 Berlin (*Bmm*). The Abteilung Berliner Literatur- und Theatergeschichte forms a special department of the museum, which concentrates on the history of Berlin. Most materials date from the 19th and 20th centuries: they include programmes from the Königliches Opernhaus and a collection of musicians' portraits.

——. Staatsbibliothek Preussischer Kulturbesitz, PF1407, Potsdamerstrasse 33, 1000 Berlin (*B*). Besides a large collection of composers' correspondence, the library holds 11 000 librettos. In 1992 it amalgamated

with the Deutsche Staatsbibliothek to form the Staatsbibliothek zu Berlin, Preussischer Kulturbesitz (*Bsb*).

BONN. Universitätsbibliothek, PF2460, Adenauerallee 39–41, 5300 Bonn 1 (*BNu*). The university has a special collection of German stage designs.

BRUNSWICK. Öffentliche Bücherei, Steintorwall 15, 3300 Brunswick (*BS*). The library specializes in local materials, and has a collection of some 800 librettos from the 17th century to the 20th, primarily for operas performed in Brunswick. There is no special music collection. The Braunschweig and the Friedrich Hausler programme collections date from 1710 and 1757 respectively.

F. Hamel and A. Rodemann: 'Unbekannte Musikalien im Braunschweiger Landestheater', *Festschrift für Hermann Abert* (Halle, 1928), 72–9

COBURG. Landesbibliothek, Schlossplatz 1, 8630 Coburg (*Cl*). The original castle library was founded in 1547. It holds the collection of the Coburg court theatre (mainly 19th-century items).

J. Erdmann, ed.: *Landesbibliothek Coburg* (Coburg, 1982)

COLOGNE. Universitäts- und Stadtbibliothek, Institut für Theater-, Film- und Fernsehwissenschaft, Universitätsstrasse 33, 5000 Cologne 41 (*KNu*). In addition to a portrait collection, the institute houses a theatre museum and library and holds programmes and librettos. There is a collection of items relating to theatre architecture (mainly of the 20th century).

R. Flatz and M. Giesing: 'Das Theatermuseum der Universität zu Köln', *Theatersammlungen in der Bundesrepublik Deutschland und Berlin (West)*, ed. M. Giesing (Berlin, 1985), 69–82

DARMSTADT. Hessische Landes- und Hochschulbibliothek, Schloss, 6100 Darmstadt (*DS*). The Musikabteilung has a picture archive, including items from the 1790s and some specializing in local performances. A vast proportion of holdings was lost during World War II.

F. Kaiser: 'Zur Geschichte der Darmstadter Musikaliensammlung', *Durch der Jahrhunderte Strom: Beiträge zur Geschichte der Hessischen Landes- und Hochschulbibliothek Darmstadt* (Frankfurt, 1967), 108–40; O. Bill: 'Die Theatersammlung der Hessischen Landes- und Hochschulbibliothek Darmstadt', *Theatersammlungen in der Bundesrepublik Deutschland und Berlin (West)*, ed. M. Giesing (Berlin, 1985) [incl. illustration from an opera perf., c1790]

DETMOLD. Lippische Landesbibliothek, Hornsche Strasse 41, 4930 Detmold (*DT*). The library contains music from the Fürstliche Hofkapelle, and more than 2000 librettos.

DONAUESCHINGEN. Fürstlich Fürstenbergische Hofbibliothek, Haldenstrasse 5, 7710 Donaueschingen (*DO*). 3000 MSS of 18th- and 19th-century operatic and symphonic music are held in the library.

DRESDEN. Sächsische Landesbibliothek, PF467–8, Marienallee 12, 8060 Dresden (*Dlb*). Founded in 1556, the library holds archival materials from the former Dresden Hofoper (18th and 19th centuries), the Königliche Privat-Musikaliensammlung (donated in 1896), and the Oelser Hoftheater (1790–1805); it also has plans of Dresden theatres. Local newspapers from about 1800 are held, along with a collection of Italian opera librettos. In 1955 the library took in material from the Dresden Staatstheater, including opera scores and parts.

——. Staatsoper Dresden, PF75, 8012 Dresden. The Staatsoper has an archive containing materials for its own productions and some documents from the Dresden Staatskapelle. Because of damage during World War II and subsequent neglect, the archive is in a poor state: but it includes printed and MS librettos (19th and 20th centuries), performance parts and a programme collection.

FRANKFURT AM MAIN. Stadt- und Universitäts-bibliothek, Musik- und Theaterabteilung, Bocken-heimer Landstrasse 134–8, 6000 Frankfurt 1 (*F*). This is a large collection, relating mainly to local history. The Frankfurt Opernsammlung contains performance materials for productions at the Comödienhaus, Stadttheater and the Frankfurt opera house from 1782; it includes music MSS, prompt-books (17th–20th centuries), librettos (of which *c*800 are in MS), theatre programmes and posters, and some 500 20th-century stage designs. There are also materials from the collection of Engelbert Humperdinck.

H. Schaeffer and W. Wenzel: 'Die Musik- und Theaterabteilung der Stadt- und Universitätsbibliothek Frankfurt-am-Main', *Theater-sammlungen in der Bundesrepublik Deutschland und Berlin (West)*, ed. M. Giesing (Berlin, 1985), 49–54; R. Didion and J. Schlichte: *Thematischer Katalog der Opernsammlung in der Stadt- und Uni-versitätsbibliothek Frankfurt-am-Main (Signaturgruppe Mus. Hs. Opera)* (Frankfurt, 1990)

HAMBURG. Hamburger Öffentliche Bücherhallen, Grosse Bleichen 23–7, 2000 Hamburg 36 (incl. *Hmb*). The library has some 3200 volumes of opera, operetta and Singspiel from the 18th century to the 20th.

Oper, Operette, Singspiel: ein Katalog der Hamburger Bücherei (Hamburg, 1965)

——. Staats- und Universitätsbibliothek, Von-Melle-Park 3, 2000 Hamburg 13 (*Hs*). This important local collection, which has legal-deposit status for the surrounding area, holds materials relating to the Ham-burg Opera since its foundation in 1678, as well as the archives of the Hamburg Stadt-Theater. The collection is especially strong in 18th-century opera, and the library has a separate theatre section (*Hth*).

W. Schulze: *Die Quellen der Hamburger Oper 1678–1738* (Ham-burg, 1938); *Katalog der Theatersammlung in der Staats- und Uni-versitätsbibliothek Hamburg* (Hamburg, 1962); D. Diederichsen: 'Die Theatersammlung der Freien und Hansestadt Hamburg', *Theatersammlungen in der Bundesrepublik Deutschland und Berlin (West)*, ed. M. Giesing (Berlin, 1985), 55–68

HANOVER. Niedersächsische Landesbibliothek, Waterloostrasse 8, 3000 Hanover 1 (*HVl*). The libretto collection has more than 2000 items; a number are from the period 1660–1750.

KARLSRUHE. Badische Landesbibliothek, PF1429, Erbprinzenstrasse 15, 7500 Karlsruhe 1 (*KA*). This is a small collection which includes correspondence between Wagner and Eduard Devrient, and material from the Grossherzogliches Hoftheater. There are MSS of Italian 18th-century opera arias, and a collection of some 700 librettos (mainly of the 20th century). Much of the original collection was destroyed during World War II.

KIEL. Schleswig-Holsteinische Landesbibliothek, Schloss, 2300 Kiel (*KIl*). The library houses opera librettos (including some from Denmark) from about 1750 to 1830.

K. Hortschansky: *Katalog der Kieler Musiksammlungen: die Notendrucke, Handschriften, Libretti und Bücher über Musik aus der Zeit bis 1830* (Kassel, 1963)

LEIPZIG. Musikbibliothek der Stadt, Ferdinand-Lassalle Strasse 21, 7010 Leipzig (*LEm*). Founded in 1953, the library incorporates the Musikbibliothek Peters and the former Leipzig Stadtbibliothek. It is a pre-dominantly 19th- and 20th-century collection. There are some 4500 librettos, as well as programmes and posters for Leipzig theatres from 1770. The Cichorius Collection contains pictures of opera singers associated with Leipzig, 1800–1960; further photographs are to be found in the Theodor Horand Collection.

K. H. Köhler: 'Die Musikabteilung', *Deutsche Staatsbibliothek 1661–1961* (Leipzig, 1961), 241–74; C. Krumbiegel and P. Krause, eds.: *Katalog der vor 1800 gedruckten Opernlibretti in der Musikbibliothek der Stadt Leipzig* (Leipzig, 1981–2)

——. Oper Leipzig, Karl-Marx-Platz 12, PF35, 7010 Leipzig. The company keeps an archive of materials relating to its own productions (1960 onwards). There are no music scores.

MANNHEIM. Städtisches Reiss-Museum, Zeughaus, 6800 N———m (*MHrm*). The original collection, which included opera and theatre materials (18th–20th centuries), suffered severe damage in World War II. There is a photo archive of Mannheim theatre produc-tions from the 1930s onwards, besides a press cuttings collection.

W. Hermann: 'Die Mannheimer Operntextsammlung', *Mannheim und Italien: zur Vorgeschichte der Mannheimer*, ed. R. Wurtz (Mainz, 1984), 66–77; 'Die Theatersammlung des Städtischen Reiss-Museums Mannheim', *Theatersammlungen in der Bundesrepublik Deutschland und Berlin (West)*, ed. M. Giesing (Berlin, 1985), 83–92

MUNICH. Bayerische Staatsbibliothek, PF340150, Ludwigstrasse 16, 8000 Munich 34 (*Mbs*). The library has benefited from legal-deposit status since 1661, and houses some 20000 music MSS. There is an archive of local materials, including 18th-century scores from the Munich Hofoper, materials from the Bayerische Staatsoper from about 1800, and operettas from the Theater am Gärtnerplatz (mainly 20th-century items).

——. Theatermuseum der Clara-Ziegler-Stiftung, Galeriestrasse 4a, 8000 Munich 22 (*Mth*). The library was opened in 1910. It contains some 80000 items, in-cluding a large portrait collection (especially of singers) and an important programme archive.

R. Schaal: *Die vor 1801 gedruckten Libretti des Theatermuseums München* (Kassel, 1962) [orig. in *Mf*, x–xiv (1957–61)]; G. Schöne: *Porträt-Katalog des Theatermuseums München (früher Clara-Ziegler-Stiftung)* (Wilhelmshaven, 1978–81); E. Nölle: 'Das Deutsche Theatermuseum (früher Clara-Ziegler-Stiftung) in München', *Theatersammlungen in der Bundesrepublik Deutschland und Berlin (West)*, ed. M. Giesing (Berlin, 1985), 93–100

MÜNSTER. Diözesan-Bibliothek, Überwasserkirchplatz 3, 4400 Münster (*MÜp*). Although mainly a collection of church music, the library holds the Fortunato Santini Collection (*MÜs*) of operas and operatic extracts of English, Italian and German provenance from before 1850.

NUREMBERG. Stadtbibliothek, Königstorgraben 3, 8500 Nuremberg (*Nst*). The library holds materials rela-ting to local theatres, including programmes for the Nuremberg Opernhaus from 1905, and programme books.

REGENSBURG. Fürstlich Thurn und Taxis'sche Hofbibliothek, Schloss Emmeramsplatz 5, 8400 Regens-burg (*Rtt*). The library is based on the collections of the Thurn und Taxis Hofkapelle. Most materials are from the period 1748–1806, when the musical life of the court was at its peak, although smaller collections from before and after this period are also held.

G. Haberkamp: *Die Musikhandschriften der Fürst Thurn und Taxis Hofbibliothek Regensburg*, Kataloge Bayerischer Musiksammlungen, vi (Munich, 1981)

RUDOLSTADT. Staatsarchiv, Schloss Heidecksburg, 682 Rudolstadt (*RUl*). There is a small collection of MS music from the Rudolstadt and Sondershausen Hofkapelle (18th–19th centuries), as well as a number of Singspiels.

SCHWERIN. Wissenschaftliche Allgemeinbibliothek des Bezirkes Schwerin, PF665–6, Wismarsche Strasse 144, 2751 Schwerin (*SWl*). The collection, which includes many 18th-century items, is based on those of the courts of Mecklenburg-Schwerin; there are additional items from the Grossherzogliches Hoftheater in Schwerin and the Grossherzogliches Hoftheater in Neustrelitz.

STUTTGART. Württembergische Landesbibliothek, PF105441, Konrad Adenauerstrasse 8, 7000 Stuttgart (*Sl*). Holdings include MS operas from the Hofkapelle and Hoftheater in the 18th and 19th centuries.

WEIMAR. Deutsches Nationaltheater, Theaterplatz, 5300 Weimar (*WRdn*). The theatre collection contains 18th- and 19th-century materials, including MSS.

WOLFENBÜTTEL. Herzog-August Bibliothek, PF1364, Lessingplatz 1, 3340 Wolfenbüttel (*W*). The collection includes 1743 librettos (mainly 17th-century) from Venice, Paris and Brunswick, formerly in the library of Duke Anton Ulrich.

E. Thiel and G. Rohr: *Verzeichnis der bis 1800 erschienen Textbücher* (Frankfurt, 1970)

GREAT BRITAIN (*GB*)

National library: British Library, Great Russell Street, London WC1B 3DG (*Lbl*). A form of legal deposit was in place by the beginning of the 17th century and was consolidated after the foundation of the British Museum Library in 1753. For details of opera holdings see under 'London'. The National Library of Scotland, George IV Bridge, Edinburgh EH1 1EW (*En*), has enjoyed legal-deposit status since 1709, and the National Library of Wales, Aberystwyth, Dyfed SY23 3BU (*AB*), since 1909. Legal-deposit privileges are also shared by the Bodleian Library, Oxford; Cambridge University Library; and the library of Trinity College, Dublin. Of these six, the Bodleian's privilege is the oldest.
National archives: Public Record Office, Ruskin Avenue, Kew, Richmond, Surrey TW9 4DU.

General literature: *BentonD*, ii, 161–89; R. Gilder and G. Freedley: *Theatre Collections in Libraries and Museums* (London, 1936); D. Howard: *Directory of Theatre Research and Information Sources in the United Kingdom* (London, 1980, 2/1986); J. Foster and J. Sheppard: *British Archives: a Guide to Archive Resources in the United Kingdom* (London, 1982, 2/1989)

ALDEBURGH. Britten-Pears Library, The Red House, Aldeburgh, Suffolk IP15 5PZ (*ALb*). While specializing in the life and works of Benjamin Britten, the library also houses the archives of the English Opera Group.

P. S. Wilson: 'The Britten-Pears Library', *Brio*, xxiii (1986), 12–14

BRISTOL. University of Bristol Library, Tyndal Avenue, Bristol BS8 1TJ (*BRu*). The University Theatre Collection includes records from the Bristol Old Vic,

and materials on theatre architecture and stage machinery.

G. Rowell: 'The University of Bristol Theatre Collection', *Performing Arts Resources*, iv (1978), 72–8

CAMBRIDGE. Fitzwilliam Museum, Trumpington Street, Cambridge CB2 1RB (*Cfm*). The museum holds Italian operas and operatic extracts (by Jommelli, Vinci, Hasse and others), along with items by Purcell and a Handel MS collection which includes *Vincer se stesso* (*Rinaldo*), *Rodrigo* and *Amadigi*. French items include Lully's *Alceste* (in an 18th-century MS copy) and music by Henry Desmarets.

J. A. Fuller Maitland and A. H. Mann: *Catalogue of Music in the Fitzwilliam Museum, Cambridge* (London, 1893)

CARDIFF. University of Wales College of Cardiff, Corbett Road, Cardiff CF1 3EB (*CDu*). The university holds the Mackworth Collection (formerly in the Cardiff Central Library, *CDp*), which contains MS full scores of operas by Bononcini, Porpora and Alessandro Scarlatti, as well as operatic extracts by Hasse, Vinci and Handel.

M. Boyd: 'Music Manuscripts in the Mackworth Collection at Cardiff', *ML*, liv (1973), 133–41; idem: 'The Mackworth and Aylward Collections at Cardiff', *Brio*, xxviii (1991), 35–6

EDINBURGH. National Library of Scotland, George IV Bridge, Edinburgh EH1 1EW (*En*). The library has had legal-deposit status since 1709. It includes the Balfour Collection of Handel first editions and Cecil Hopkinson's collection of Verdi material.

GLASGOW. Mitchell Library, North Street, Glasgow G3 7DN (*Gm*). Public library; it includes the Fanny Moody and Charles Manners Collection of opera scores (*c*3000 items), and opera scores from the Robert Turnbull Collection. The Kidson Collection of 18th-century popular music contains extracts from operas; and there is 18th-century material from Sadler's Wells.

——. Scottish Music Information Centre, 1 Bowmont Gardens, Glasgow G12 9LR. The centre holds an MS collection of works by Peter Maxwell Davies (1971 onwards). Most of the collection is 20th-century in scope.

——. University Library, Glasgow G12 8QE (*Gu*), incorporating the Euing Musical Library (*Ge*). The library holds the Scottish Theatre Archive and a small collection of printed vocal scores (17th–19th centuries).

Catalogue of the Musical Library of the late William Euing, Esq. (Glasgow, 1878)

GLYNDEBOURNE. Glyndebourne Festival Opera, Glyndebourne, Lewes, East Sussex BN8 5UU. The company keeps an archive of material from its foundation in the 1930s to the present, including costume and set designs, plans, programmes and playbills.

LEEDS. Opera North, Grand Theatre, 46 New Briggate, Leeds LS1 6NU. The company has an archive for its own productions (including scores) from 1978.

LIVERPOOL. Public Library, William Brown Street, Liverpool L3 8EW (*LVp*). The collections include the Carl Rosa Opera Library.

LONDON. British Library, Great Russell Street, London WC1B 3DG (*Lbl*). The library holds autograph scores by Steffani; printed holdings include zarzuelas. The Hirsch Collection includes MS operas (mainly 19th-century items); and the library has a card catalogue of illustrations of operatic scenes found in its music holdings. The Royal Music Library contains an outstanding collection of materials for the study of opera in 18th-century England (including several Handel autographs).

H. M. Nixon: 'Theatrical Holdings of the Department of Printed Books, British Museum', *Ohio State University Library Collection Bulletin*, viii (1961), 5–9; M. Turner and A. Searle: 'The Music Collections of the British Library Reference Division', *Notes*, xxxviii (1981–2), 499–549; A. Hyatt King: *A Wealth of Music in the Collections of the British Library (Reference Division) and the British Museum* (London, 1983); M. Turner: 'Card Catalogues in the BL Music Library', *Brio*, xxv (1988), 51–4

——. City of London Guildhall Library, Guildhall, Aldermansbury, London EC2P 2EJ. Mainly (but not exclusively) London orientated, the collection includes a large amount of material relating to London theatre architecture, nearly 15 000 posters and prints and drawings. The Gresham Music Library (*Lgc*) has a small collection of 18th-century operas, both printed and MS.

A. Bunch: 'Playbills and Programmes in Guildhall Library', *Theatre Notebook*, xiv/2 (1959–60), 66–7; *Gresham Music Library: a Catalogue of the Printed Books and Manuscripts* (London, 1965)

——. Finsbury Library, 245 St John Street, London EC1 4NB. The library holds 18th-century material from Sadler's Wells Theatre.

——. Public Record Office, Ruskin Avenue, Kew, Richmond, Surrey TW9 4DU (*Lpro*). The collection includes 87 volumes of records from the Lord Chamberlain's department, plus architects' plans, petitions and other documentation.

J. Milhous and R. D. Hume: 'An Annotated Guide to the Theatrical Documents in PRO LC7/1, 7/2 and 7/3', *Theatre Notebook*, xxxv (1980–81), 77–87, 122–9

——. Royal Academy of Music, Marylebone Road, London NW1 5HT (*Lam*). The collection includes MSS of 17th- and 18th-century operas from the collection of R. J. S. Stevens, an MS of Purcell's *The Fairy-Queen*, and music formerly belonging to J. C. Pepusch. A Sullivan archive has recently been established.

N. Bhimani: 'A History of Selected Manuscripts in the Royal Academy of Music Library', *FAM*, xxxv (1988), 216–24

——. Royal College of Music, Prince Consort Road, London SW7 2BS (*Lcm*). The library of the Sacred Harmonic Society came to the college in 1883. It includes MSS of operas by Anfossi, Pepusch and Salieri, and a large number of printed works from the 19th-century British repertory.

W. B. Squire: *Catalogue of Printed Music in the Library of the Royal College of Music, London* (London, 1909)

——. Royal Institute of British Architects' Library, 66 Portland Place, London W1N 4AD. The Sir Banister Fletcher Library has one of the world's most important collections for the study of architecture and includes theatre plans. There are more than 400 000 drawings and 80 000 prints.

——. Royal Opera House, Covent Garden, London WC2E 7QA. Fires in 1808 and 1856 led to losses of some of the theatre's archives. Materials include programmes from *c*1850 to the present, prints and plans of the Covent Garden theatres, a ballet collection, costume designs and press cuttings.

D. A. Day: 'An Inventory of Manuscript Sources at the Royal Opera House, Covent Garden', *Notes*, xliv (1987–8), 456–62; F. Franchi: 'Archives of the Dance, (8): Dance Material in the Archives of the Royal Opera House, Covent Garden', *Dance Research*, vi/2 (1988), 78–82

——. Theatre Museum, 1E Tavistock Street, London WC2E 7PA. The museum opened in Covent Garden in 1987, but was founded in 1924, when the collection of Gabrielle Enthoven was bequeathed to the Victoria and Albert Museum, London. Besides opera materials, items relating to ballet and music hall are included. There are programmes from more than 150 British theatres, and biographical files, prompt-books and costumes. The library also houses the London Archives of the Dance, and the Arts Council collection of designs.

J. Laver: 'The Gabrielle Enthoven Theatre Collection in the Victoria and Albert Museum', *Ohio State University Collection Bulletin*, v (1958), 3–5; J. Fowler: 'Archives of the Dance, (9): Early Dance Holdings of the Theatre Museum, London', *Dance Research*, vii/2 (1989), 81–8; S. C. Woodcock: 'Archives of the Dance, (10): Later Dance Holdings of the Theatre Museum Library', *Dance Research*, viii/1 (1990), 62–77

MANCHESTER. Central Public Library, Henry Watson Music Library, St Peter's Square, Manchester M2 5PD (*Mp*). Library holdings include the Newman Flower Collection of Aylesford Handel MSS.

OXFORD. Bodleian Library, Oxford OX1 3BG (*Ob*). The library acquired the Harding Collection of sheet music and opera vocal scores in 1974. There is further operatic material in the Tenbury Collection (*T*), previously in the possession of St Michael's College, Tenbury, and originally belonging to F. A. G. Ouseley. The John Johnson Collection of Printed Ephemera, housed in another part of the library, includes programmes and playbills, filed by theatre. The Bodleian also holds opera programmes and press cuttings, *c*1930–1985, from the collection of Harold Rosenthal, former editor of *Opera* magazine.

J. Tonkin: 'Theatre Material in the John Johnson Collection of Printed Ephemera, Bodleian Library, Oxford', *Theatre Notebook*, xxvi/2 (1971–2), 72–5; E. Selfridge-Field: 'One Hundred Venetian Arias of the Late *seicento* in the Bodleian Library', *Notes*, xl (1983–4), 503–9; W. Shaw: 'Sir Frederick Ouseley and his Collection', *Brio*, xxvii (1990), 45–7; P. Ward Jones: 'The Fate of the Music Collections of St Michael's College, Tenbury', *Brio*, xxvii (1990), 48–9

HUNGARY (*H*)

National library: Országos Széchényi Könyvtár [National Széchényi Library], Budavári Palota F-epület, 1827 Budapest (*Bn*). Legal deposit since 1802; a group of regional libraries also receive deposit copies. For details of opera holdings see under 'Budapest'.

National archives: Magyar Országos Levéltár [Hungarian National Archives], Bécsi-kapu-ter 4, 1014 Budapest. Founded in 1756.

General literature: *BentonD*, v, 71–109; I. Pethes: 'Musikbibliotheken in Ungarn', *FAM*, xv (1968), 114–18

BUDAPEST. Magyar Állami Operaház [Hungarian State Opera House], Andrássy utca 22, 1061 Budapest VI (*Bo*). The archives and museum hold materials connected with the opera house (1884 onwards) and the Hungarian National Theatre (1837–84). Music scores and parts are housed in a separate collection. The National Theatre collection consists mainly of librettos and playbills, and has some stage designs, contracts and correspondence.

——. Országos Széchényi Könyvtár, Budavári Palota F-epület, 1827 Budapest (*Bn*). Founded in 1802, the library holds part of the Esterházy archives; music and librettos from the Budapest People's Theatre

(1875–1919, including some operettas; the administrative papers are in the Budapest Municipal Archives); and a large MS opera collection. There is also a theatre collection, established in the late 19th century; it includes more than 300000 playbills, a large portrait collection, and prompt-books from Budapest theatres.

K. Berczeli: 'A Népszinház könyvtára' [The Library of the Budapest People's Theatre], Az Országos Széchényi könyvtár évkönyve [Yearbook of the National Széchényi Library] (1958), 369–78; J. Vécsey: 'Az Országos Széchényi könyvtár zenei gyűjtemenyének fej odése az elm ult tizenöt évben' [The Development of the Music Collection of the National Széchényi Library over the Past 50 Years], Az Országos Széchényi könyvtár évkönyve (1958), 80–97; D. Bartha and L. Somfai: 'Catalogue raisonné der Esterházy-Opernsammlung', Haydn als Kapellmeister: die Haydn-Dokumente der Esterházy-Opernsammlung (Budapest, 1960), 179–403; J. Pukánszky-Kádár and J. and E. Berczeli-Monori: 'Az Országos Széchényi könyvtár színháztörténeti tára' [The Theatre History Collection of the Széchényi Library], Az Országos Széchényi könyvtár évkönyve (1965–6), 241–6; G. Zechmeister: 'Das Keglevich-Archiv', Jb der Gesellschaft für Wiener Theaterforschung, xvii (1970), 81–6; D. Keresztury: 'Az önálló magyar opera és balett-szcenika kialakulása' [Development of a Hungarian National Ballet and Opera Scenery], Az Országos Széchényi könyvtár évkönyve (1972), 343–69; The National Széchényi Library (Budapest, 1972, 2/1985)

ITALY (I)

National library: Biblioteca Nazionale Centrale, piazza Cavalleggeri 1, 50122 Florence (Fn). Legal deposit since 1886; a group of regional libraries in provincial centres also receive deposit copies. For details of opera holdings see under 'Florence'.

National archives: Archivio Centrale dello Stato, piazzale degli Archivi, EUR, 00144 Rome. Italy has a network of regional archives housed in centres such as Florence, Genoa and Bologna.

General literature: BentonD, iii, 137–292

BERGAMO. Biblioteca Civica Angelo Mai, piazza Vecchia 15, 24100 Bergamo (BGc). The library houses the Mayr Collection, which contains opere serie, opere semiserie and opere buffe of J. S. Mayr and his contemporaries, from the 18th and 19th centuries. There are also administrative papers, including contracts.

BOLOGNA. Accademia Filarmonica, via Gerrazzi 13, 41025 Bologna (Baf). Founded in 1666, the library has a large libretto collection.

——. Civico Museo Bibliografico Musicale, piazza G. Rossini 2, 40126 Bologna (Bc). Based around materials owned by Padre Martini, this is a large collection, with some 11000 librettos (17th–20th centuries). Opera holdings include more than 500 MS scores and orchestral parts, and a large printed collection of scores and programmes.

G. Gaspari: Catalogo del biblioteca del Liceo musicale di Bologna (Bologna, 1890–1943) [esp. vols.iii and v]

——. Convento di S Francesco, piazza Malpighi 9, 40123 Bologna (Bsf). The library holds a collection of 18th-century librettos.

BOLZANO. Conservatorio Statale di Musica 'C. Monteverdi', piazza Domenicani 19, 39100 Bolzano. The conservatory holds the Fondo Toggenburg (BZtoggenburg), a collection based on that of Anton Melchior von Menz (fl second half of the 18th century). The opera scores are mainly works by Paisiello and Cimarosa, often with performance parts.

T. Chini and G. Tonini: La raccolta di manoscritti e stampe musicali 'Toggenburg' di Bolzano (sec. XVIII–XIX), Cataloghi di fondi musicali italiani, v (Turin, 1986)

CREMONA. Biblioteca Statale e Libreria Civica, via Ugolani Dati 4, 26100 Cremona (CR). The most important opera collections are the Fondo della Pia Istituzione Musicale (a gift of about 450 items of local provenance which include administrative papers as well as printed and MS music) and the collection of the Banda Musicale di Cremona (c900 musical items). The library has a small programme collection from local theatres.

FANO. Biblioteca Comunale Federiciana, via Castracane 1, 61032 Fano (FAN). This is a small collection which includes archival materials from the Teatro della Fortuna in Fano from 1863.

FERMO. Biblioteca Comunale, piazza del Popolo 63, Fermo (FERc). The Fondo Gigliucci was donated in 1958. It is part of a larger collection, the remainder of which is in the Accademia Musicale Chigiana in Siena. There are only 67 opera librettos, dating from the late 17th century to the 19th. Materials either have a local connection (with the Teatro dell'Aquila in Fermo) or are related to centres such as London, Milan and Genoa.

U. Gironacci: 'I libretti del fondo Gigliucci della Biblioteca comunale di Fermo', Le fonti musicali in Italia, ii (1988), 173–98 [incl. catalogue and indexes]

FLORENCE. Biblioteca Marucelliana, via Cavour 45, 50100 Florence (Fm). The principal operatic resource is the collection of about 10000 librettos (17th–19th centuries) formerly owned by the Bonamici family.

R. Lustig: 'Saggio di catalogo della collezione di melodrammi della R. Biblioteca Marucelliana', La bibliofilia, xxv (1923–4), 239–47, 305–12; xxvi (1924), 67–74 [lists librettos]

——. Biblioteca Nazionale Centrale, piazza Cavalleggeri 1, 50122 Florence (Fn). The library was founded in the 18th century and has a small collection of opera MSS.

B. Becherini: Catalogo dei manoscritti musicali della Biblioteca nazionale di Firenze (Kassel, 1959)

——. Conservatorio Statale di Musica 'Luigi Cherubini', piazzetta delle Belle Arti 2, 50121 Florence (Fc). The conservatory holds compositions and letters of Cherubini, Donizetti, Monteverdi, Rossini and others, as well as materials from the Teatro della Pergola (MS scores and parts by Cimarosa and Paisiello).

R. Gandolfi, C. Cordara and A. Bonaventura: Catalogo delle opere musicali teoriche e pratiche di diversi autori vissuti sino al primi decenni del secolo XX: Biblioteca del conservatorio di musica di Firenze, Bibliotheca musica Bononiensis, ser. 1/11 (Parma, 1929)

——. Galleria degli Uffizi, piazzale degli Uffizi, 50122 Florence. The Uffizi collection contains much material relating to Medici theatrical entertainments in the 17th century.

——. Teatro Comunale, via Solferino 15, 50123 Florence. The theatre has kept its archives since 1931. The majority of items in the music collection are printed, with very few MSS. There is an audio archive of past productions.

GENOA. Conservatorio di Musica 'Nicolò Paganini', via Albaro 38, 16145 Genoa (Gl). In addition to a general collection of opera scores and librettos, the library possesses some Galuppi autographs.

LIVORNO. Biblioteca Comunale Labronica Francesco Domenico Guerrazzi, Villa Fabbricotti, viale della Libertà 30, 57100 Livorno (LI). This is a public library with a collection of about 600 librettos, as well as music belonging to the baritone Enrico Delle Sedie (mainly vocal scores of 18th-century works). There are archival items relating to local theatres, including correspondence, but no substantial music holdings.

LUCCA. Istituto Musicale 'Luigi Boccherini', piazza S Ponziano 7, 55100 Lucca (*Li*). The Fondo Bottini consists of the library of a wealthy Lucchese family of the late 18th and early 19th centuries, and contains more than 200 MSS, including operas and operatic excerpts.

MACERATA. Biblioteca Comunale 'Mozzi-Borgetti', piazza Vittorio Veneto 2, 62100 Macerata (*MAC*). Founded in 1773, the library has 820 librettos, and theatre materials covering a number of Italian cities, from the collection of Giambattista Bruti-Liberati.

MILAN. General literature: M. Donà: *La musica nelle biblioteche milanesi: mostra di libri e documenti* (Milan, 1963)

——. Archivio Storico Civico e Biblioteca Trivulziana, Castello Sforzesco, 20121 Milan (*Mt*). A series of 123 box files contains archival material on 'spettacoli pubblici' from 1776 to 1861.

——. Biblioteca del Conservatorio di Musica 'Giuseppe Verdi', via Conservatorio 12, 20122 Milan (*Mc*). The library has legal-deposit status for the Milan area. Opera holdings include MSS of all operas written for La Scala and the Teatro Cannobiana from 1816 to 1856, along with a collection of Hasse MSS. The Fondo Noseda contains Italian opera MSS (18th and 19th centuries), and there is a collection of about 6000 librettos for operas produced in Milan from the 17th century to the 19th. Autograph MSS include works by Cimarosa, Paisiello and Cherubini.

——. Biblioteca Nazionale Braidense, via Brera 28, 20121 Milan (*Mb*). Besides some 6000 librettos, there is a ballet collection. Much material is connected with local productions, including those at La Scala.

M. Viale Ferrero: 'Costume Designs by Alessandro Sanquirico and Others for Ballets Produced at the Teatro alla Scala, Milan, 1820–24', *Dance Research*, ii/2 (1984), 24–40

——. Archivio Storico Ricordi (Casa Editrice), via Salomone 77, 20138 Milan (*Mr*). The firm's archive holds autographs and printed works by composers on its roster. The works are chiefly operatic, but include chamber, orchestral and other vocal music, as well as letters from composers, singers and musicologists. In 1888 the collection of the Milanese publisher Francesco Lucca was incorporated.

——. Biblioteca Teatrale Livia Simoni, Via Filodrammatici 2, 20121 Milan (*Ms*). Situated in La Scala's theatrical museum, the library holds *c*30000 items, mainly secondary sources but some autographs (including works by Bellini, Cilea, Donizetti, Jommelli and Mascagni) as well as 16th- and 17th-century librettos. In 1930 a collection of Verdiana was added, and in 1954 the library of Renato Simoni. Holdings also include stage designs and costumes, and La Scala posters.

S. Vittadini: *Catalogo del Museo teatrale alla Scala* (Milan, 1940, suppl. 1959); S. Vittadini: 'La biblioteca de Renato Simoni al Museo teatrale alla Scala', *Accademie e biblioteche d'Italia*, xxii (1954), 579; T. Rogledi Manni: 'La biblioteca Livia Simoni', *Il Museo teatrale alla Scala, 1931–1963* (Milan, 1964)

Catalogo (in ordine numerico) delle opere pubblicate ... di Gio. Ricordi (Milan, 1857); *Internationale Musik- und Theater-Ausstellung, Wien 1892: G. Ricordi & Co., Drucker und Verleger, Mailand* (Milan, 1892), 145–55 [list of autographs in the archive]; C. Sartori: *Casa Ricordi, 1808–1958: profilo storico* (Milan, 1958); F. Degrada and others: *Musica, musicisti, editoria: 175 anni di Casa Ricordi, 1808–1983* (Milan, 1983); P. Gossett: 'The Ricordi Numerical Catalogues: a Background', *Notes*, xlii (1985–6), 22–8

MODENA. Accademia Nazionale di Scienze, Lettere ed Arti, corso Vittorio Emanuele II 59, 41100 Modena (*MOa*). The library has a small collection of about 900 librettos, and MS operas and operettas from the 18th century to the 20th.

——. Biblioteca Estense, Largo porta S Agostino 309, 41100 Modena (*MOe*). The older part of the collection (including music materials) belonged to the dukes of Este. There are 80 MS opera scores of the late 17th and early 18th centuries, about 90 MS scores of later 18th-century works (mainly French and German, and including sets of parts) and a collection of works by Stradella.

P. Lodi: *Catalogo delle opere musicali: città di Modena, Biblioteca Estense* (Bologna, 1923)

MONTE CASSINO. Biblioteca dell'Abbazia, 03043 Monte Cassino (*MC*). The library houses the city's music archive and the Rignani bequest of 18th-century operas and oratorios.

NAPLES. Archivio di Stato, piazzetta Grande Archivio 5, 80138 Naples (*Na*). The archives include the Fondo Teatro, documenting Neapolitan opera performances.

——. Biblioteca Lucchesi-Palli, piazza del Plebescito, Palazzo Reale, 80133 Naples (*Nlp*). The Lucchesi-Palli library is a special section of the Biblioteca Nazionale 'Vittorio Emanuele III' (*Nn*) and deals with theatre, cinema and music. It holds programmes for the Teatro S Carlo from 1920 to 1972, as well as about 1800 librettos (18th and 19th centuries).

——. Conservatorio di Musica 'S Pietro a Majella', via S Pietro a Majella 35, 80100 Naples (*Nc*). The conservatory houses an important collection of librettos and 18th-century autographs, including works by Jommelli, Paisiello, Cimarosa and Piccinni.

G. Gasperini and F. Gallo: *Catalogo delle opere musicali, città di Napoli: Biblioteca del R. conservatorio di musica di S. Pietro a Majella* (Parma, 1934); F. Melisi, ed.: *Biblioteca del Conservatorio di San Pietro a Majella di Napoli: catalogo dei libretti per musica dell'ottocento (1800–1860)* (Lucca, 1990)

PADUA. Biblioteca Civica e Archivio Comunale, via Orto Botanico 5, 35123 Padua (*Pci*). The library has a large libretto collection; items date from the 17th century to the 19th.

——. Biblioteca del Conservatorio 'Cesare Pollini', via Eremitani 6, 35100 Padua (*Pl*). The library has materials from the Teatro Verdi in Padua (mid-18th–19th centuries), including *opere serie* and *opere buffe* (97 items) by Anfossi, Mayr and Rossini.

S. Durante and M. Nevilla Massaro: *Catalogo dei manoscritti musicali del Conservatorio 'Cesare Pollini' di Padova*, Cataloghi di fondi musicali italiani, i (Turin, 1982)

PARMA. Archivio Storico del Teatro Regio, via M. d'Azeglio 45, 43100 Parma (*PAt*). A historical theatre collection, the archive contains librettos for the Teatro Regio from 1829 to 1970. The Ferrarini bequest is a special collection of 596 librettos and 3500 photographs. The library holds no MS scores, but has a few sets of MS parts.

——. Biblioteca Palatina, Conservatorio di Musica 'Arrigo Boito', via Conservatorio 27, 43100 Padua (*PAc*). The library, which was founded in 1762, holds 7000 librettos as well as theatre plans and drawings.

——. Istituto Nazionale di Studi Verdiani, strada della Repubblica 56, 43100 Parma (*PAi*). Almost entirely given over to Verdi studies, the institute includes the Collezione Scalvini (18th- and 19th-century vocal scores).

PESARO. Biblioteca della Fondazione Rossini, Conservatorio di Musica 'Gioacchino Rossini', piazza Olivieri 5, 61100 Pesaro (*PESc*). The library has 270 librettos. It contains Rossini autographs from his periods in Naples and Paris, 1815–22, and works by Spontini and Meyerbeer. The foundation sponsors the *Bollettino del Centro rossiniano di studi* (published irregularly).

PIACENZA. Conservatorio di Musica G. Nicolini, via S Franca 35, 29100 Piacenza (*PCcon*). The library holds autographs by Rossini, Cimarosa, Paisiello and others.

ROME. Biblioteca Apostolica Vaticana, Vatican City, 00120 Rome (*Rvat*). Although known primarily for its rich holdings of medieval and Renaissance liturgical material, the library also possesses some operatic items. The Fondo Ferraioli, donated in 1826, includes some 200 librettos for operas performed in Rome in the 18th century; it also has play texts relating to theatres including the Valle, Torre, Argentina and Capranica. Composers represented in the collection include Anfossi, Cimarosa, Galuppi, Jommelli and Paisiello.

E. Mori: *Libretti di melodrammi e balli del secolo XVIII: fondo Ferraioli della Biblioteca Apostolica Vaticana* (Florence, 1984)

———. Biblioteca Casanatense, via S Ignazio 52, 00186 Rome (*Rc*). Founded in 1698, the library has a fine MS collection of Baroque operas. Many items are duplicates of materials in the Allacci Collection at the Vatican Library (*Rvat*). The Casanatense Library belonged originally to Cardinal Girolamo Casanate (*d* 1700); it came into state ownership in 1884.

L. Cairo and P. Quilici, eds.: *Raccolta teatrale dal '500 al '700: la raccolta della Biblioteca Casanatense* (Rome, 1981)

———. Conservatorio di Musica 'S Cecilia', via dei Greci 18, 00187 Rome (*Rsc*). The conservatory houses 17th-century operas of the Roman school, some 21 000 librettos, the Carotti Collection of a further 4000 librettos (17th–19th centuries) and much of the Silvestri collection of 6000 librettos from theatres of Milan and Monza, 1670–1885.

———. Istituto Nazionale di Archeologia e Storia dell'Arte, piazza Venezia 3, 00187 Rome (*Ria*). The institute holds the collection of Alessandro Vessella, comprising MS and printed items (18th–20th centuries); there are more than 250 MS scores, over 100 orchestral parts, and librettos.

ROVIGO. Accademia dei Concordi, piazza Vittorio Emanuele II 14, 45100 Rovigo (*RVI*). The library has a small collection, mainly noteworthy for MS librettos from the 18th century (fewer than 100 items).

TRENT. Biblioteca Comunale, via Roma 51, 38100 Trent (*TRc*). The main interest of the collection lies in local materials from the Teatro Sociale (administrative archives, 1830–1934; MS scores of works by local composers of the second half of the 19th century; and choreographic sketches).

TRIESTE. Civico Museo Teatrale di Fondazione Carlo Schmidl, piazza Verdi 1, 34121 Trieste (*TSmt*). Founded in 1924, the Schmidl Collection covers theatre in the Trieste region from the end of the 17th century. The museum houses the archives of the Teatro Verdi

(1801–1930) and materials from other local theatres. There are some 2500 librettos.

TURIN. Biblioteca Civica Musicale Andrea Della Corte, via Roma 53, 10123 Turin (*Tci*). The Valentino Carrera Collection contains ballet and opera librettos from the 17th century to the 20th.

———. Biblioteca Nazionale Universitaria, piazza Carlo Alberto 3, 10124 Turin (*Tn*). Opera holdings are mainly from the collection of Giacomo Durazzo, director of the Viennese theatres, 1754–64, and include works by Gluck, Haydn and Rameau. Stradella is also represented.

I. Fragala Data and A. Colturato: *Biblioteca nazionale universitaria di Torino*, i: *raccolta Mauro Foà; raccolta Renzo Giordano* (Rome, 1987)

———. Conservatorio Statale di Musica Giuseppe Verdi, via Mazzini 11, 10123 Turin (*Tco*). The collection includes MS parts for local opera productions of the 18th and 19th centuries.

VENICE. Biblioteca Nazionale Marciana, Palazzi della Libreria Vecchia e della Zecca, S Marco 7, 30124 Venice (*Vnm*). An important repository of Venetian sources, the library is especially rich in opera librettos for the periods 1637–1767 (the Groppo Collection), 1637–1790 (the Rossi Collection) and 1637–1750 (the Zeno Collection). The Girolamo Contarini Collection contains 112 MS *drammi per musica* of the 17th century. A number of Italian theatres, including La Fenice, regularly deposit materials in the library.

T. Wiel: *I codici contariniani del secolo 17 nella R. biblioteca di San Marco in Venezia*, Bibliotheca musica Bononiensis, ser. 1/4 (Venice, 1888); A. Alberati: 'La musica del 16 e 17 secolo nella Biblioteca nazionale Marciana', *Miscellanea Marciana*, i (1986), 178–221

———. Casa Goldoni, S Polo 2794, 30125 Venice (*Vcg*). Holdings include an exceptional libretto collection and 1500 18th-century opera scores.

———. Conservatorio di Musica 'Benedetto Marcello', Palazzo Pisani, S Marco 2809, 30124 Venice (*Vc*). The Giustiniani Collection, originating with the proprietors of the S Moisè opera house, 1792–1818, includes 672 MSS.

M. G. Miggiani: *Il fondo Giustiniani del Conservatorio Benedetto Marcello: catalogo dei manoscritti e delle stampe*, Historiae musicae cultores biblioteca, li (Florence, 1990)

———. Fondazione Giorgio Cini, Isola S Giorgio Maggiore, 30124 Venice (*Vgc*). The Ulderico Rolandi Collection contains 40 000 librettos (16th–19th centuries) and 14 000 production photographs. Cataloguing of the collection is in progress.

A. L. Bellina, B. Brizi and M. G. Pensa: 'La collezione di libretti d'opera della Fondazione "Cini" di Venezia', *Le fonti musicali in Italia*, i (1987), 218

———. Fondazione Scientifica 'Querini-Stampalia', Castello 4778, 30122 Venice (*Vqs*). The collection includes 18 volumes of MS opera arias of the late 17th century (mainly 1682–4), including works by Legrenzi, and 450 librettos from the early 18th century covering performances in Milan and Venice.

F. Rossi: *Le opere musicali della Fondazione 'Querini-Stampalia' di Venezia*, Cataloghi di fondi musicali italiani, ii (Turin, 1984)

———. Fondazione Ugo Levi, rio di S Vidal 2893, 30100 Venice (*Vlevi*). The foundation has a libretto collection, and early editions of 18th-century French operas.

——. Teatro La Fenice, campo S Fantin 1965, 30124 Venice. The theatre's archives cover its history from the 18th century to the 20th.

M. Girardi and F. Rossi: *Il teatro La Fenice: cronologia degli spettacoli 1792–1936* (Venice, 1989)

VERONA. Biblioteca Civica, via Cappello 43, 37121 Verona (*VEc*). The library houses local items only, from the Teatro Filarmonico and other Verona theatres of the 18th and 19th centuries.

LATVIA (*LV*)

National library: Latvijas Nacìonātā Bibliotēka, Krišjanis Barona iela 14, 226-011 Riga. Founded in 1919.

LITHUANIA (*LT*)

National library: Martynas Mažrydas National Library of Lithuania, Gedimino prospektas 51, 232635 Vilnius. Founded in 1919.

THE NETHERLANDS (*NL*)

National library: Koninklijke Bibliotheek, POB90407, Prins Willem-Alexanderhof 5, 2509 LK The Hague (*DHk*).

National archives: Algemeen Rijksarchief te 's-Gravenhage, Prins Willem-Alexanderhof 20, 2595 The Hague.

General literature: *BentonD*, ii, 192–8

AMSTERDAM. Nederlands Theater Instituut, Herengracht 166–8, 1016 BP Amsterdam. The institute is a centre for theatre studies in the Netherlands and holds archives for a number of Dutch opera companies including the Nederlandse Opera Stichting. It also houses the archives of the Dutch Wagner Vereeniging. There are costume designs for about 25 operas, and a video collection of recent Dutch opera productions. Holdings of programmes reaching back to the 18th century complement a small libretto collection.

THE HAGUE. Gemeentemuseum, Stadhouderslaan 41, 2517 HV The Hague (*DHgm*). The museum holds librettos (18th and 19th centuries), concert programmes (19th and 20th centuries), and materials from the Théâtre Français de la Haye. It possesses archives relating to more than 200 Dutch musicians, including opera singers such as Cornelie van Zanten.

F. W. Zwart: *Nederlandse muziekarchieven: overzicht van de collecties/Dutch Musical Archives: Survey of the Collections* (The Hague, 1987)

NEW ZEALAND (*NZ*)

National library: National Library of New Zealand, Private Bag, Wellington 1.

National archives: National Archives of New Zealand, Air New Zealand Building, 129–41 Vivian Street, Wellington 1.

General literature: *BentonD*, iv, 167–76

WELLINGTON. Alexander Turnbull Library, 40 Molesworth Street, POB12 349, Wellington (*Wt*). The Alexander Turnbull Library is a division of the National Library. Holdings include the archives of the New Zealand Opera Company (1953–72) and of the National Opera of New Zealand (1979–84), as well as the papers of Donald Munro, founder of the New Zealand Opera Company. The Rosina Buckman Collection of press cuttings covers the period 1900–48.

NORWAY (*N*)

National library: Universitetsbiblioteket i Oslo, Drammensveien 42, 0242 Oslo 2 (*Ou*). Legal deposit since 1883.

National archives: Riksarkivet, Folke Bernadottes vei 21, Oslo 8 (*Ora*).

General literature: *BentonD*, ii, 190–92; B. Stribolt and others: *Teatersamlinger i norden: Katalog over teatermuseer, -biblioteker og -arkiver i Danmark, Finland, Norge og Sverige* (Copenhagen, 1984, 2/1986)

BERGEN. Teaterarkivet, villavei 5, 5000 Bergen. The theatre archive forms part of the Bergen theatre museum, covering local and national theatre from the late 18th century; it includes some Norwegian operatic materials.

OSLO. Teatermuseet i Oslo, Nedre Slottsgate 1, 0157 Oslo 1. The museum covers Oslo theatre between 1800 and about 1950.

POLAND (*PL*)

National library: Biblioteka Narodowa, Aleja Niepodleg losci 213, 00–973 Warsaw (*Wn*).

National archives: Archiwum Główne Akt Dawnych [Central Archive of Historical Records: up to 1918], ulica Długa 7, 00–263 Warsaw; Archiwum Akt Nowych [Archive for Recent Records: from 1919], Aleja Niepodleg losci 162, 02–554 Warsaw.

General literature: *BentonD*, v, 113–75; M. Prokopowicz, ed.: *Przewodnik po bibliotekach i zbiorach muzycznych w Polsce* [Guide to Libraries and Music Collections in Poland] (Warsaw, 1982); W. Smialek: *Polish Music: a Research and Information Guide* (New York and London, 1989)

KRAKÓW. Biblioteka Czartoryskich, Muzeum Narodowe w Krakowie, ulica św. Marka 17, 31–109 Kraków (*Kc*). The library has texts of 19th-century operas, in Polish.

W. Hordyński: 'Zbiór muzyczny w Bibliotece XX. Czartoryskich' [The Music Collection of the Czartoryski Library], *Przeglad biblioteczny*, iii (1937), 184–9

——. Biblioteka Jagiellońska, Uniwersytet Jagielloński, Aleja Mickiewicza 22, 30–059 Kraków (*Kj*). This is a legal-deposit library. Opera materials are included in the massive ephemera collection (more than 100 000 items in 1964), as well as among the items formerly belonging to the Preussische Staatsbibliothek.

J. Baumgart: 'The Jagiellonian Library, Past and Present', *Libri*, xiv (1964), 264–83

WARSAW. Biblioteka Narodowa, Zakład Zbiorów Muzycznych, plac Krasínckich 3/5, Warsaw (*Wn*). The music department was founded in 1934 and re-established in 1951, following heavy damage in World War II.

M. Prokopowicz: 'Zbiory muzyczne Biblioteki narodowej' [Music Collections of the National Library], *Rocznik Biblioteki narodowej*, v (1969), 293–314; idem: 'Zbiory muzyczne', *50 lat Biblioteki narodowej, Warszawa 1928–1978* (Warsaw, 1984), 177–85

——. Biblioteka Uniwersytecka, Krakowskie Przedmieście 26–8, 00 325 Warsaw (*Wu*). Although much of the collection was damaged during World War II, the Department of Prints and Drawings still holds documents on Polish theatre.

——. Muzeum Teatralne Warszawe, ulica Moliera 3–5, w gmachu Teatru Wielkigo, Warsaw. Although this is mainly a 20th-century collection, there are some opera posters from the 19th century.

WROCŁAW [Breslau]. Biblioteka Zakładu Narodowego im Ossliński [Library of the Ossoliński Institute], ulica Szewska 37, 50–139 Wrocław (*WRzno*). Founded in 1817, the institute houses a large collection of Polish plays.

PORTUGAL (*P*)

National library: Biblioteca Nacional, campo Grande 83, 1751 Lisbon (*Ln*). Legal deposit since 1931; there is a network of regional libraries that receive deposit copies.
National archives: Arquivo Nacional da Torre do Tombo, Palácio de S Bento, 1200 Lisbon (*Lan*).

General literature: *BentonD*, iii, 295–316

LISBON. Biblioteca do Ajuda, Palácio da Ajuda, Lisbon 3 (*La*). A former royal library founded in 1756, it is strong in holdings of 18th-century opera.

——. Teatro Nacional de S Carlos, Rua Serpa Pinta 9, 1200 Lisbon (*Lt*). Although the theatre was founded at the end of the 18th century, the library was not established until 1840. The collection includes 2000 MSS, as well as stage designs and photographs.

ROMANIA (*R*)

National library: Biblioteca Naţională, strada Ion Ghica 4, Bucharest (*Bc*) [partially destroyed in 1990].
National archives: Arhivele Statului, boulevard M. Kogălniceanu 29, Bucharest.

BUCHAREST. Institutul de Istoria Artei, Calea Victoriei 196, 71104 Bucharest. Founded in 1919, the institute includes a section for theatre and music research.

RUSSIA (*RU*)

National library: Rossiyskaya Gosudarstvennaya Biblioteka [Russian State Library], Prospekt Kalinina 3, 101000 Moscow (*Mrg*). See also under 'Moscow'.

General literature: M. Levy: 'Theatre Research in Moscow and Leningrad', *Performing Arts Resources*, iv (1978), 44–54

MOSCOW. General literature: 'Moscow Music Archives', *Canon*, ix (1956), 209–10.

——. A. A. Bakhrushin Museum, ulitsa Bakhrushina 31/12, 113054 Moscow. Founded in 1894, the museum has a large music collection and holds theatre-related items such as architectural materials and 'props'.

——. Bol'shoy Theatre Museum, Prospekt Marksa 8/2, 103009 Moscow. Founded in 1920, the museum holds materials used for Bol'shoy ballet and opera productions, including correspondence with composers.

——. Gosudarstvenniy Tsentral'niy Muzey Muzïkal'noy Kul'turï imeni M. I. Glinki, Georgiyevskiy pereulok 4, Moscow K–9 (*Mcm*). Founded in 1948, the museum contains personal archives, both compositions and papers, of Tchaikovsky, Musorgsky, Prokofiev, Shostakovich and others.

——. Rossiyskaya Gosudarstvennaya Biblioteka, Prospekt Kalinina 3, 101000 Moscow (*Mrg*). In spite of its function as a national library (it has enjoyed legal-deposit status since 1862), the Russian State Library is not rich in music MSS. Holdings include materials of B. V. Asaf'yev.

——. Tsentral'niy Gosudarstvenniy Arkhiv Literaturï i Iskusstva [Central State Archive of Literature and Art], ulitsa Vïborgskaya 3/2, Moscow (*Mcl*). The library con-

tains the collections of N. G. Raysky (1876–1958), a former lecturer at the Moscow Conservatory; they include vocal scores of 19th-century Russian and foreign operas. There is also a Ricordi Collection (*c*100 vocal scores). A catalogue of the opera and operetta MSS in the library (18th–20th centuries) is in progress.

ST PETERSBURG [Leningrad]. Gosudarstvennaya Ordena Trudovogo Krasnogo Znameni Publichnaya Biblioteka imeni M. E. Saltïkova-Shchedrina [Saltïkov-Shchedrin Public Library], Sadovaya ulitsa 18, St Petersburg D-69 (*SPsc*). The library was opened in 1814, since when it has received depository copies of everything published in the country. Among its holdings are 18th-century Russian imprints and French and Italian opera collections of the 17th and 18th centuries. The MS division has papers of Borodin, Glinka, Rimsky-Korsakov and others.

L. N. Pavlova-Sil'vanskaya and A. A. Rachkova: 'Le département de la musique de la Bibliothèque publique de Leningrad', *FAM*, vii (1960), 1–7

——. Gosudarstvenniy Institut Teatra, Muzïki i Kinematografii [State Institute of Theatre, Music and Cinematography], ploshchad' Ostrovskogo 6, 191011 St Petersburg (*SPit*). St Petersburg theatres have been obliged to deposit material with the State Theatre Museum since 1950. The collections include such items as scene paintings and costume designs. The institution includes the Rimsky-Korsakov Museum and the Museum of the History of Russian Opera (in Shalyapin's former house).

——. Tsentral'naya Muzïkal'naya Biblioteka Gosudarstvennogo Akademicheskogo Teatra Operï i Baleta [Central Music Library of the State Academic Theatre of Opera and Ballet], ulitsa Zodchego Rossi 2, St Petersburg (*SPtob*). This is one of the largest collections in the world of Russian MS music. The library holds materials from the St Petersburg Imperial Theatre (formerly the Kirov, now the Mariinsky): a massive collection of scores, librettos and correspondence.

SERBIA

National library: Narodna Biblioteka Srbije [National Library of Serbia], Skerlićeva 1, Belgrade (*Bn*). Founded in 1832; legal deposit since 1928.
——. Biblioteka Matice Srpske [Serbian National Library], ulica Matice Srpske 1, 21000 Novi Sad.
National archives: Arhiv Srbije [Serbian Archive], Karnedžijeva 2, 11000 Belgrade.

General literature: *BentonD*, v, 179–267

BELGRADE. Muzej Pozorišne Umetnosti Srbije [Performing Arts Museum of the Serbian Republic], Gospodar Jevremova 19, 11000 Belgrade. The museum houses a 19th-century music and drama collection, along with books on stage design, costume and theatre architecture.

SLOVENIA [*SLN*]

National library: Narodna in Univerzitetna Knjižnica [National and University Library], Turjaška 1, Ljubljana (*Lu*). Founded in 1774; some legal deposit for local area from 1807, and for Yugoslavia from 1919. For details of opera holdings see under 'Ljubljana'.
National archives: Arhiv Republike Slovenije [Archives

of the Slovene Republic], Zvezdarska 1, 61000 Ljubljana.

General literature: *BentonD*, v, 179–267

LJUBLJANA. Narodna in Univerzitetna Knjižnica, Turjaška 1, Ljubljana (*Lu*). The library holds theatre music connected with Italian and German opera companies that visited the area.

——. Semeniska Knjižnica [Seminary Library], Dolničarjeva 4, 61000 Ljubljana. The library holds a collection of Baroque opera librettos.

M. Smolik: 'Die Seminarbibliothek in Ljubljana', *Biblos*, xxiv (1975), 293–9

SOUTH AFRICA

National library: South African Library, POB496, Queen Victoria Street, Cape Town 8000.
National archives: State Archives and Heraldic Services, Private Bag X236, Pretoria 0001.

CAPE TOWN. University of Cape Town, Private Bag, Rondebosch, Cape 7700. The South African Collection includes operas and operettas by W. H. Bell and the operas of Erik Chisholm in MS. There is a collection of programmes and press cuttings.

SPAIN (*E*)

National library: Biblioteca Nacional, paseo de Recoletos 20, 28001 Madrid (*Mn*).
National archives: Archivos Estatales, plaza del Rey 1, 28071 Madrid.

General literature: *BentonD*, iii, 1–55; *LaborD* ('Bibliotecas y archivos musicales: España')

BARCELONA. Institut del Teatre, 3–5 carrer Nou de la Rambla, 08001 Barcelona (*Bit*). The institute library includes the zarzuela collection of Don Arturo Sedó, while programmes and stage designs are housed in the Centre de Documentació, which also includes materials on theatre architecture.

J. Montaner: *La colección teatral de Don Arturo Sedó* (Barcelona, 1951) [catalogue]

MADRID. Biblioteca y Archivo Municipal, plaza Mayor 27, Madrid 12 (*Mm*). The library has works from the Teatro Príncipe and Teatro de la Cruz, and is especially strong in music for 18th-century Spanish plays by Calderón de la Barca, Lope de Vega and others.

B. Weiss: 'Music and Theatre Collections in Madrid Municipal Library', *Biblos*, xxx (1981), 296–301

——. Biblioteca Nacional, paseo de Recoletos 20, 28001 Madrid (*Mn*). Founded in 1712, the library receives copyright deposit copies of all Spanish publications. It holds works by Ruperto Chapí and other 19th-century Spanish composers, and among the private libraries incorporated is that of Francisco Asenjo Barbieri.

H. Anglès and J. Subirá: *Catálogo musical de la Biblioteca nacional de Madrid* (Barcelona, 1946–51); J. Subirá: 'Notas sobre la sección de música de la Biblioteca nacional', *Revista de archivos*, ser.4, liii (1947), 51–78, lv (1949), 309–28; N. I. Martinez, ed.: *Catálogo del Teatro lírico español en la Biblioteca nacional* (Madrid, 1986–)

——. Biblioteca del Palacio Real, Palacio Real, calle Bailen s/n, 28071 Madrid (*Mp*). The library has several thousand 18th-century opera MSS and includes works by Pergolesi and Jommelli.

J. Subirá: *El teatro del Real palacio (1849–1851)* (Madrid, 1950)

National library: Kungliga Biblioteket, Box 5039, 10241 Stockholm (*Sk*). Legal deposit since 1661; deposit copies are also sent to the university libraries of Göteborg, Lund and Uppsala.
National archives: Riksarkivet, Fryverarbacken 13–17, Box 12541, 10229 Stockholm.

General literature: *BentonD*, ii, 198–208; Å. Davidsson: 'Cultural Background to Collections of Old Music in Swedish Libraries', *FAM*, xi (1964), 21–8; B. Stribolt and others: *Teatersamlinger i norden: Katalog over teatermuseer, -biblioteker og -archiver; Danmark, Finland, Norge og Sverige* (Copenhagen, 1984, 2/1986)

STOCKHOLM. Dansemuseet, Laboratoriegatan 10, 15527 Stockholm. The museum was founded in 1950 by Rolf de Maré and holds the Archives Internationales de la Danse, which were transferred from the Paris Opéra.

——. Drottningholms Teatermuseum, 17011 Drottningholm (*Sdt*). The museum holds the Kungliga Teatrarnas Arkiv (archives of the Swedish royal theatres) from 1773 to 1940, as well as a large MS collection of plays and an international library of works on the history of scenery. More recent theatre archival materials are in the Riksarkivet (see above).

B. Stribolt: 'Eighteenth-Century Stage Settings at the Court Theatres of Drottningholm and Gripsholm', *Performing Arts Resources*, xiii (1983), 83–9

——. Kungliga Musikaliska Akademiens Bibliotek, Box 16326, 10326 Stockholm (*Skma*). The largest music collection in Sweden, it includes printed and MS opera materials from the P. A. d'Otrante Collection (French and Italian full scores, 1790–1826) and the G. G. Oxenstierna Collection (1700–1858), and the Berwald family archive. A group of scores and parts is on deposit from the Royal Swedish Opera.

A. Lönn: 'Musikaliska Akademiens Bibliothek (MAB): the Library of the Swedish Academy of Music', *FAM*, xxxiii (1986), 162–71

——. Kungliga Teaterns Bibliotek Gustav Adolfs Torg 4, 11152 Stockholm (*St*). The library of the Royal Opera (now in *Skma*) has archives dating from about 1750, including 1500 sets of MS parts, 1000 MS scores, playbills (1826–1941) and programmes (1910 onwards). Holdings include French *opéras comiques*.

——. Musikmuseet, Box 16326, 10326 Stockholm (*Sm*). Housed at the Kungliga Musikaliska Akademiens, the museum has some 10 000 librettos and 100 000 posters, along with MS opera scores. Models of scenery used at the Royal Swedish Opera are also included.

UPPSALA. Universitetsbiblioteket, Box 510, 75120 Uppsala (*Uu*). This is an important legal-deposit library (since 1692), containing the Kraus Collection (works by J. M. Kraus in *c*100 MS vols.), the Düben Collection (works by the Lully school, printed and MS, in *c*30 vols.) and the Gimo Collection (18th-century Italian instrumental music, mainly by Neapolitan composers). Much of the Gimo Collection is operatic in scope.

MGG (Å. Davidsson); C.-A. Moberg: 'Essais d'opéras en Suède, sous Charles XII', *Mélanges de musicologie offerts à M. Lionel de la Laurencie* (Paris, 1933), 123–32; Å. Davidsson: *Catalogue critique et descriptif des imprimés de musique des XVIe et XVIIe siècles conservés à la Bibliothèque de l'Université royale d'Upsala*, ii (Uppsala, 1951), 113–28; idem: *Catalogue of the Gimo Collection of Italian Manuscript Music in the University Library of Uppsala* (Uppsala, 1963)

SWITZERLAND (*CH*)

National library: Schweizerische Landesbibliothek, Hallwylstrasse 15, 3003 Berne (*BEl*). It incorporates the library of the Schweizerische Gesellschaft für Theaterforschung; there is no legal-deposit law in Switzerland.

National archives: Schweizerisches Bundesarchiv, Archivstrasse 24, 3003 Berne.

General literature: *BentonD*, ii, 25–40; R. Wyler, ed.: *Archive, Bibliotheken und Dokumentationsstellen der Schweiz* (Berne, 3/1958)

BASLE. Öffentliche Bibliothek der Universität Basel, Schönbeinstrasse 18–20, 4056 Basle (incl. *Bu*). The richest collection in Switzerland, it includes the library of the Schweizerische Musikforschende Gesellschaft.

E. Refardt: *Katalog der Musikabteilung der Öffentlichen Bibliothek der Universitätsbibliothek Basel und der in ihr erhaltenen Schweizerischen Musikbibliothek* (Basle, 1925)

GENEVA. Bibliothèque du Conservatoire, place Neuve, 1204 Geneva (*Gc*). The library is strong in works by Swiss composers, but also houses 18th-century printed and MS operas from other countries, a large collection of early 19th-century French operas (by Grétry, Boieldieu and others), and MS operatic extracts. The library holds sketches for Britten's *Rape of Lucretia*, and a programme collection for the Grand Théâtre of Geneva, 1897–1924.

——. Bibliothèque Musicale de la Ville de Genève, Maison des Arts 'Le Grütli', 16 rue Général-Dufour, 1204 Geneva. Holdings include programmes and playbills for the Grand Théâtre in Geneva (1861 onwards), and a collection of scores, parts and librettos from the late 18th century. The administrative archive of the Grand Théâtre is held in the Archives de la Ville.

NEUCHÂTEL. Bibliothèque Publique et Universitaire, 3 place Numa-Droz, 2000 Neuchâtel (*N*). The library has 18th-century opera MSS.

UKRAINE (*UA*)

National library: Tsentral'na Naukova Biblioteka, Akademii Nauk [Central Scientific Library of the Ukrainian Academy of Sciences], ulitsa Vladimirska 62, Kiev 17 (*Kan*). Founded in 1866. For details of opera holdings see under 'Kiev'.

KIEV. Tsentral'na Naukova Biblioteka, Akademii Nauk. The library includes the collections of the Counts Razumovsky, which contain some operas.

——. Ukraïns'kyy Derzhavnyy Muzey Teatral'noho Muzychnoho ta Kinematografichnoho Uystetstva [Ukrainian State Museum of Theatrical, Musical and Cinematographic Art], Yanvarskogo vosstaniya 21, Kiev. The museum specializes in Ukrainian theatre, and includes music MSS and theatre programmes.

UNION OF SOVIET SOCIALIST REPUBLICS

For the former Soviet Union see under 'Latvia', 'Lithuania', 'Russia' and 'Ukraine'.

UNITED STATES OF AMERICA (*US*)

National library: Library of Congress, Washington, DC 20540 (*Wc*). For details of opera holdings see under 'Washington, DC'.

National archives: National Archives and Records Administration, National Archives Building, 8th Street at Pennsylvania Avenue, Washington, DC 20408.

General literature: *GroveAM* (M. W. Davidson and D. W. Krummel, with D. Thompson); W. C. Young: *American Theatrical Arts: a Guide to Manuscript Sources and Special Collections in the United States and Canada* (Chicago, 1971); C. J. Bradley: *Music Collections in American Libraries: a Chronology* (Detroit, 1981); D. W. Krummel: *Resources of American Music History* (Urbana, IL, 1981); L. A. Rachow: *Theatre and Performing Arts Collections* (New York, 1981)

ALBUQUERQUE. University of New Mexico, Fine Arts Library, Fine Arts Center, Albuquerque, NM 87131. There are two important opera collections: the Helm Collection of mid-19th-century French music, consisting of about 600 items, of which many are first editions of vocal scores; and the Manuel Areu Collection, some 170 zarzuelas from the late 19th century including printed and MS scores, parts and librettos, as well as playbills.

ANN ARBOR. University of Michigan, Music Library, Ann Arbor, MI 48109 (*AA*). The library purchased the J. A. Stellfeld music library from Belgium in the mid-1950s. This highly important collection includes operas by Auber, Dalayrac, Gossec, Piccinni and Grétry, as well as MSS of Hasse works.

L. E. Cuyler, G. A. Sutherland and H. T. David: 'The University of Michigan's Purchase of the Stellfeld Music Library', *Notes*, xii (1954–5), 41–57

AUSTIN. University of Texas, Harry Ransom Humanities Research Center, P. O. Drawer 7129, Austin, TX 78713 (*AUS*). The centre houses the principal rare books library of the university. Its main strengths are in American, British and French arts. Opera holdings include: the H. P. Kraus Libretto Collection, containing 3800 Italian librettos, mainly for opera (52 items are from the 17th century, *c*400 from the 18th); the W. H. Auden-Chester Kallman Collection, including MS drafts and translations of opera librettos; the Carlton Lake Collection which, although not focussing on opera, has MSS of Ravel's *L'heure espagnole*, Chausson's *Le roi Arthus* and Roussel's *Padmâvatî* and sketches by Debussy for *Pelléas et Mélisande*, by Verdi for *Alzira*, and by Berlioz for *Benvenuto Cellini*; the Edwin Bachmann Collection, containing 100 first editions of 18th- and 19th-century works; the Theodore M. Finney Collection of MSS (17th–19th centuries), including extracts from operas by Piccinni, Gluck and Galuppi. The library also holds papers of Edouard Dujardin and Emile Vuillermoz.

The Theatre Arts Collection is rich in materials for opera and musical theatre from the 18th century to the 20th, including items from the B. J. Simmons Theatrical Costume Company and some 7000 librettos.

F. J. Hunter: *Guide to the Theatre and Drama Collections at the University of Texas* (Austin, 1967); W. H. Crain: 'The Hoblitzelle Theatre Arts Library, University of Texas at Austin', *Theatre and Performing Arts Collections*, ed. L. A. Rachow (New York, 1981), 53–64; M. Wells: 'Una biblioteca italiana nel Texas', *Biblioteca oggi*, vii (1989), 53–62

BALTIMORE. Peabody Conservatory Library, 17 East Mount Vernon Place, Baltimore, MD 21202 (*BApi*). The library, founded in 1868, merged with the Enoch Pratt Free Library in 1966. The collection concerns local history, but includes Caruso's papers and scrapbooks.

BATON ROUGE. Louisiana State University, Hill Memorial Library, Baton Rouge, LA 70803 (*BAT*). The library houses the papers of Louis Hasselmans (conductor of the Metropolitan Opera and the Paris Opéra-

Comique), some Adelina Patti letters, and materials from New Orleans, including 19th-century librettos.

BERKELEY. University of California, Music Library, 240 Morrison Hall, Berkeley, CA 94720 (*BE*). The collection includes a large number of extracts from 19th- and 20th-century operas, and some 18th-century English and French materials. Printed opera scores from the collection of Alfred Cortot are also housed, together with some 4500 scores in the Sigmund Romberg Collection. An Italian libretto collection contains some 4400 items, besides a special collection of Sicilian librettos (831 items; 17th–20th centuries). The library possesses 45 letters from Jommelli relating to opera in Lisbon, 1769–73.

V. Duckles: 'The University of California, Berkeley, Music Library', *Notes*, xxxvi (1979–80), 7–22; *Catalogs of the Opera Collections in the Music Libraries: University of California, Berkeley* (Boston, 1983); J. A. Emerson: *Catalogue of pre-1900 Vocal Manuscripts in the Music Library, University of California at Berkeley* (Berkeley and London, 1988)

BLOOMINGTON. Indiana University, School of Music Library, Bloomington, IN 47401 (*BLu*). The library's most interesting opera holdings are sound recordings, notably an archive of the Swedish tenor Jussi Björling (*c*3000 items) and the Ross Allen and Alvin M. Ehret collections of commercial recordings (3600 and 12 000 items respectively). The Robert Orchard Opera Collection includes non-commercial recordings of opera performances. The university houses rare books, including some early Handel editions from the Gerald R. Coke and W. C. Smith collections, in the Lilly Library (*BLl*).

W. R. Stump: 'Indiana University [Lilly Library] acquires New Collection of Nineteenth-Century Plays', *Theatre Notebook*, xxii (1967–8), 120–21; J. A. Falconer: 'Music in the Lilly Library: Handel, Opera and Latin Americana', *Notes*, xxix (1972–3), 5–9

BOSTON. Boston Public Library, Music Department, Copley Square, Boston, MA 02117 (*Bp*). The Allen A. Brown Collection (more than 6000 items) contains MS scores, mainly of the late 19th and 20th centuries. The Herbert Beerbohm Tree Collection includes incidental music for about 65 productions in London at the Haymarket and Her Majesty's theatres, 1897–1916, as well as autograph full scores of operas by Stanford and Mascagni, Edward German and Granville Bantock. There is a collection of costume designs for operas and ballets performed in Italian theatres between 1850 and 1937.

——. Boston University, Mugar Memorial Library, 771 Commonwealth Avenue, Boston, MA 02215 (*Bm*). The library is rich in special collections relating to opera, including papers of opera personalities such as Rudolf Bing and Alexander Kipnis. On deposit from the Boston SO are 260 MS volumes of Italian operas, comprising 171 complete operas from the first half of the 19th century including works by Verdi, Bellini and Meyerbeer; the volumes were originally connected with the Teatro Carolino in Palermo. The H. C. Robbins Landon Collection includes an MS of Paisiello's *Il barbiere di Siviglia*. The Richards Collection contains correspondence from late 19th-century French opera composers and an MS score of Weber's *Oberon*.

BUFFALO. State University of New York at Buffalo, Music Library, Baird Music Hall, Buffalo, NY 14214 (*BUu*). The library has a dozen MS copies of Lully operas and librettos, MSS and early editions of works by Clari and Paer, and early editions of 18th-century operas.

CAMBRIDGE. Harvard University, Cambridge, MA 02138 (*CA*). Among the university's several libraries, two are important for opera-related holdings. The Houghton Library houses papers of the impresario Augustin Daly and has a large portrait collection. It also holds the Harvard Theatre Collections, with drawings of London theatre interiors, a large group of Victorian costume designs, MS and printed materials of works by Charles Dibdin, items concerning Vauxhall Gardens, and an 18th-century account book for Lincoln's Inn Fields Theatre. The Evert Wendell Collection contains about 600 000 playbills and other ephemera, and the Henry M. Rogers Collection is strong in 19th- and 20th-century opera. The library also possesses autograph letters, including some of opera composers.

The Eda Kuhn Loeb Music Library owns about 1500 MS librettos of Italian operas and cantatas.

L. A. Hall: *Catalogue of Dramatic Portraits* (Cambridge, MA, 1930–34); W. Van Lennep: 'Theatre Collections at Harvard', *Harvard Library Bulletin*, vi (1952), 281–301; D. A. Wood: *Music in Harvard Libraries* (Cambridge, MA, 1980)

CHAPEL HILL. University of North Carolina, Louis Round Wilson Library, Chapel Hill, NC 27514. The Tomas Borras Collection of Spanish plays (17th–19th centuries) includes a large number of opera librettos. The Music Library, Hill Hall (*CHH*), has more than 4000 Italian librettos.

CHICAGO. Chicago Public Library, 78 East Washington Street, Chicago, IL 60602. Like the Newberry Library in Chicago, the Public Library holds archival materials relating to opera in Chicago (1910 onwards), as well as the Plitt Theatre Music Collection (1920–50).

——. Lyric Opera of Chicago, 20 North Wacker Drive, Chicago, IL 60606. The company, founded in 1954, keeps a collection of printed music, librettos and press cuttings for its own productions. Its administrative archive is held by the Chicago Historical Society (*Chs*).

——. Newberry Library, 60 West Walton Street, Chicago, IL 60610 (*Cn*). The library was founded in 1887. Besides a first edition of Peri's *Euridice* and some Wagner material, it holds large amounts of material concerning opera and theatre in Chicago and the surrounding area, including scrapbooks from the Chicago Auditorium Theatre (1889–1939) and the archives of the American Opera Society of Chicago (1932 onwards). There are programmes from other Chicago theatres (*c*1885–1930) and some opera vocal scores and parts.

CLAREMONT. Libraries of the Claremont Colleges, Honnold Library, 800 North Dartmouth Avenue, Claremont, CA 91711 (*CLAc*). The John Laurence Seymour Collection contains about 600 printed opera scores and librettos (mainly from the 19th century), while the collection of Ernestine Schumann-Heink comprises materials associated with her, including over 5000 scores.

DENTON. North Texas State University, Music Library, Denton, TX 76203 (*DN*). The library's Lloyd Hibberd Collection contains French first editions of works by Lully and others, and houses some 18th-century English materials.

DENVER. Central City Opera House Association, 910 16th Street, Denver, CO 80202. The association holds the company's records (1932 onwards).

FORT WORTH. Fort Worth Opera, 3505 West Lancaster, Fort Worth, TX 76107. The company holds a small archive relating to its own productions (1946 onwards; most materials date from 1980 onwards).

GAINESVILLE. University of Florida Library, S. Y. Belknap Collection, Gainesville, FL 32611 (G). Although the library has no significant holdings of music scores, it houses a large collection of programmes and other 19th- and 20th-century ephemera, as well as materials relating to opera in San Francisco.

L. Correll: 'The Belknap Collection of Performing Arts, University of Florida Libraries', *Performing Arts Resources*, i (1974), 56–65

ITHACA. Cornell University, Music Library, Ithaca, NY 14853 (I). The library possesses about 1000 18th- and 19th-century librettos and a microfilm collection of primary sources of Italian and French operas.

LOS ANGELES. University of California, Walter H. Rubsamen Music Library, 1102 Schoenberg Hall, Los Angeles, CA 90024 (LAu). The library contains some 1200 Venetian and Paduan librettos of the 17th and 18th centuries. It also holds German and English items of the 18th and 19th centuries, English theatre music of the late 18th century and some French opera scores. The William Andrews Clark Memorial Library (LAuc) is rich in music and librettos of English and Italian operas, masques, ballad operas and other musical plays, 1728–1810.

LOUISVILLE. University of Louisville, Dwight Anderson Music Library, 2301 South Third Street, Louisville, KY 40292 (LOu). The library has recently acquired a number of MS scores of 18th-century Italian operas, including Anfossi's *Isabella e Rodrigo*, J. S. Mayr's *L'amor coniugale* and *Ginevra di Scozia*, and Paisiello's *Barbiere di Siviglia* and *Nina*.

MADISON. State Historical Society of Wisconsin, 816 State Street, Madison, WI 53706 (MAhs). The society houses some of the Tams-Witmark Collection, notably opera parts from the period 1790–1925 (other sections of the collection are at the University of Wisconsin and at Princeton University). The society incorporates the Wisconsin Center for Theatre Research, founded in 1960; it concentrates on 20th-century American theatre and includes operatic ephemera.

B. J. Kaiser: 'Resources in the Wisconsin Center for Theatre Research', *American Archivist*, xxx (1967), 483–92

MEDFORD. Tufts University Library, Medford, MA 02155 (MED). Besides some Rameau material in the main library, the Nils Yngre Wessell Music Library holds a group of 19th-century operas from the collection of Frédéric L. Ritter.

MINNEAPOLIS. University of Minnesota, Music Library, Twin Cities Campus, Minneapolis, MN 55455 (MSu). The library holds several hundred opera scores of the 18th and 19th centuries, many of them first editions, from the collection of Donald N. Ferguson.

NEW HAVEN. Yale University, New Haven, CT 06520. The John Herrick Jackson Music Library (NH) includes the Francesco Galeazzi Collection of Italian opera MSS, some Gilbert and Sullivan materials, and iconographic sources formerly belonging to Marc Pincherle. The Beinecke Rare Book Library houses the J. R. Crawford Theatre Collection (programmes for British and American theatre, c1750–1900, including music theatre) and the Lady Emma Hamilton Collection of late 18th-century Italian operas in MS. A separate collection devoted to the American musical theatre was established by the Beinecke in the 1950s.

R. Barlow: 'A University Approach to the American Musical Theatre', *Notes*, xii (1954–5), 25–32; idem: 'The American Musical Theatre Collection', *Yale University Library Gazette*, xxxiii (1959), 126–8; D. Crawford: 'The Crawford Theatre Collection', *Yale University Library Gazette*, xli (1967), 131–5

NEW YORK. General literature: L. A. Rachow: 'Performing Arts Research Collections in New York City', *Performing Arts Resources*, i (1974), 1–16

——. Columbia University Library, New York, NY 10027. The library holds a large ephemera collection, along with the Roger Wheeler Collection of theatrical memorabilia (18th–20th centuries). The Brander Matthews Dramatic Music Collection includes theatrical correspondence, mainly from the USA, and covers the period 1732–1902. The Rare Books Library includes the Frederick C. Shang Collection of musicians' visiting cards, 1800–1977. The Music Library (NYcu) is strong in late 18th- and early 19th-century opera scores.

——. Metropolitan Opera Association Archives, c/o The Metropolitan Opera, Lincoln Center, New York, NY 10023. The collection comprises the company's archives from 1883.

M. E. Peltz: 'The Metropolitan Opera Archives', *American Archivist*, xxx (1967), 471–5; G. Fitzgerald, ed.: *Annals of the Metropolitan Opera: a Complete Chronicle of Performances and Artists* (Boston and New York, 1990)

——. New York Public Library, Lincoln Center, NY 10023 (NYp). Besides the Music Division's comprehensive holdings of printed editions of opera (17th–20th centuries), there are important special collections. Those for dance include the Cia Fornaroli Collection of music and ballet librettos (mainly 19th-century materials). The Theatre Collection houses the Robinson Locke Collection of dramatic scrapbooks (c40 000 items, 1870–1920) and the Hiram Stead Collection of posters and portraits from the British stage (1709–1932). There are also letters of Giuditta Pasta, and the Rodgers and Hammerstein Archive of Recorded Sound. The Billy Rose Theatre Collection includes stage and costume designs for the Metropolitan Opera.

G. Freedley: 'The New York Public Library Theatre Collection', *Ohio State University Collection Bulletin*, iii (1956), 4–7; *Dictionary Catalog of the Dance Collection* (Boston, 1974–); S. P. Williams: *Guide to the Research Collections of the New York Public Library* (Chicago, 1975); P. Myers: 'The New York Public Library: the Billy Rose Collection', *Theatre and Performing Arts Collections*, ed. L. A. Rachow (New York, 1981), 23–8; S. Sommer: 'The Treatment of Programs at the New York Public Library', *FAM*, xxviii (1981), 78–80; F. C. Campbell: 'How the Music Division of the New York Public Library Grew: a Memoir, Part 4', *Notes*, xxxviii (1981–2), 14–41

——. Pierpont Morgan Library, 29 East 36th Street, New York, NY 10016 (NYpm). The library's main strength is in Gilbert and Sullivan materials, from the Reginald Allen Collection and elsewhere; there are also two Wagner imprints (of *Die Meistersinger* and the *Ring*) heavily annotated by the composer. The Mary Flagler Cary Collection includes additional 19th-century operatic items (notably a collection of bel canto cadenzas for some 30 operas), and the library owns autographs of Debussy's *Pelléas et Mélisande*, Gounod's *Mireille*, Lecocq's *Le petit duc*, Massenet's *Manon* and Offenbach's *Les contes d'Hoffmann* and *La permission de dix heures*.

O. E. Albrecht: 'Musical Treasures in the Morgan Library', *Notes*, xxviii (1971–2), 643–51

PHILADELPHIA. Free Library of Philadelphia, Logan Square, Philadelphia, PA 19103 (*PHf*). The library owns many 18th- and 19th-century English theatre posters, as well as items related to Colley Cibber.

——. University of Pennsylvania Libraries, Philadelphia, PA 19104 (*PHu*). The Otto E. Albrecht Music Library is now in the Van Pelt Library. There is a collection of archival opera recordings, part of Alfred Cortot's Nachlass and a collection of some 1800 French opera scores. The Van Pelt Library also has important holdings of English materials.

PITTSBURGH. University of Pittsburgh, Hillman Library, Pittsburgh, PA 15260. The library holds archives for Pittsburgh Opera, as well as the Ford E. and Harriet R. Curtis Collection of local theatre programmes and the Oliver Paxton Merriman Collection of theatre scrapbooks.

PRINCETON. Princeton University, Harvey S. Firestone Memorial Library, Princeton, NJ 08540 (*PRu*). In addition to the William Seymour Theatre Collection, which contains several thousand prompt-books, some 70 000 programmes and a large number of press cuttings, the library owns the Richard Pleasant Dance Collection (mainly 20th-century items), the James S. Hall Handel Collection, and the Tams-Witmark Collection of scores for musical comedies, 1895–1915 (other items from this collection are held in Madison, Wisconsin).

M. A. Jensen: 'The William Seymour Theatre Collection, Princeton University', *Theatre and Performing Arts Collections*, ed. L. A. Rachow (New York, 1981), 41–52; idem: 'The William Seymour Theatre Collection: a Curator's View', *Princeton University Library Chronicle*, xlviii (1986), 6–20

ROCHESTER. University of Rochester, Eastman School of Music, Sibley Music Library, 26 Gibbs Street, Rochester, NY 14604 (*R*). The library has about 3000 items from the collection of Arthur Pougin concerning French theatre from the 17th century to the 19th, as well as collections of comic operas from late 18th-century London and Paris, and nearly 1000 additional operas (mostly French, 1880–1930).

R. Watanabe: 'Concert Programmes in the Sibley Music Library, Rochester, New York', *FAM*, xxviii (1981), 75–7; L. Goldberg and C. Lindahl: 'Gathering the Sources: a Case History', *Modern Music Librarianship: Essays in Honor of Ruth Watanabe* (Stuyvesant, NY, 1989), 3–26; I. Buff: 'Sibley Music Library Research: a Selective Bibliography', ibid, 227–34

ST LOUIS. Missouri State Historical Society, Jefferson Memorial Building, St Louis, MO 63112. The society holds opera and theatre programmes for St Louis and the surrounding area, including materials relating to the St Louis Opera.

SAN FRANCISCO. San Francisco Public Library, Archives of the Performing Arts, 3150 Sacramento Street, San Francisco, CA 94115 (*SFp*). The library collects primary source materials for opera and theatre in the San Francisco Bay area. It includes archives from the San Francisco Opera (1943 onwards) and the San Francisco SO, and possesses the largest collection in the world of materials relating to the singer Kirsten Flagstad. The Richard F. Larson Libretto Collection contains items from the 17th century to the 20th.

——. San Francisco State University, 1630 Holloway Avenue, San Francisco, CA 94132 (*SFsc*). The Frank de

Bellis Collection holds about 20 000 archival recordings of Italian singers. The library also houses full scores of operas by Paisiello, Cimarosa and others.

SAN MARINO. Henry E. Huntington Library, 1151 Oxford Road, San Marino, CA 91108 (*SM*). The collection is not primarily music-based, but includes English theatre materials such as playbills for performances at Covent Garden, 1760–1831, and at Drury Lane, 1750–82. The library also holds the diaries of James Winston (a 19th-century Drury Lane manager). Of great importance is the John Larpent Collection, consisting of English and Italian MS plays and librettos submitted to the English censor between 1737 and 1824. Larpent's wife's diaries, which deal in part with opera at Drury Lane and Covent Garden, are also held.

D. McMillan: *Catalogue of the Larpent Plays in the Huntington Library* (San Marino, 1939); E. N. Backus: *Catalogue of Music in the Huntington Library Printed before 1801* (San Marino, 1949); C. S. Bliss: 'Theatrical Collections in the Huntington Library', *Ohio State University Collection Bulletin*, ii (1956), 4–5; L. W. Conolly: 'The Censor's Wife at the Theatre: the Diary of Anna Margaretta Larpent, 1790–1800', *Huntington Library Quarterly*, xxxv (1971), 49–64

SANTA BARBARA. University of California, Arts Library, Santa Barbara, CA 93106 (*SB*). The Anthony Boucher Archival Collection of Recorded Sound contains 10 000 78 r.p.m. recordings of opera performances (mainly 1900–50). The Lotte Lehmann Collection, in the University Library, contains the singer's personal and business papers.

STANFORD. Stanford University, Music Library, Stanford, CA 94305 (*STu*). The library collects primary sources of Lully operas, mainly microform reproductions of materials from foreign institutions. The main university library owns some of Jenny Lind's papers and the autograph of *Cavalleria rusticana*, and has a general theatre collection.

A. Cohen: 'The Lully Archive at Stanford University', *Notes*, xliv (1987–8), 5–6

SYRACUSE. Syracuse University Library, Syracuse, NY 13210. The library has about 1350 19th-century Italian librettos.

URBANA. University of Illinois Library at Urbana-Champaign, Urbana, IL 61801. The library's strengths are more in the field of theatre than opera in the strict sense. The Aleyne Westall Prehn Collection contains Chicago theatre programmes (1871–1930); and the Cavagna Collection has 19th-century opera librettos. The Theodore Leavitt Theatre Print Collection includes engravings, prints and posters from British and American theatres.

J. A. Major: *Collections Acquired by the University of Illinois Library at Urbana-Champaign, 1897–1974* (Urbana, 1974)

WASHINGTON DC. Folger Shakespeare Library, Washington, DC 20003 (*Ws*). In addition to housing the largest collection of Shakespeare and Shakespeare-related materials in the world, the library has prompt-books from Drury Lane, London (1747–76), and from Covent Garden (1803–8), as well as items from Daly's Theatre. There is a large collection of playbills from London and provincial English theatres, and the correspondence collection includes letters from Mrs Cibber, George Colman and Sarah Siddons. There are theatre plans for Covent Garden and Drury Lane, and some Sullivan items.

N. H. Krivasky and L. Yeandle: 'Theatrical Holdings of the Folger Shakespeare Library', *Performing Arts Resources*, i (1974), 48–55

——. Library of Congress, Washington, DC 20540. The library holds the national music collection (*Wc*). The most important separate opera collection is probably that of Albert Schatz, who, besides amassing a libretto collection, left materials on opera of various European cities. Other collections include the Geraldine Farrar Collection (correspondence of 20th-century singers, including Emma Eames), a large sound archive, and architectural materials on American theatres and opera houses, featuring both interiors and exteriors.

O. Sonneck: *Catalogue of Opera Libretti Printed Before 1800* (Washington DC, 1914); P. Vanderbilt: *Guide to the Special Collections of Prints and Photographs in the Library of Congress* (Washington DC, 1955); E. Breitenbach: 'Picture Research at the Library of Congress', *Special Libraries*, li (1960), 281–7; C. F. Peatross: 'Architectural Collections of the Library of Congress', *Quarterly Journal of the Library of Congress*, xxxiv (1977), 249–84; A. Melville: *Special Collections in the Library of Congress: a Selective Guide* (Washington DC, 1980); W. Zvonchenko: 'Theatre Materials in the Library of Congress', *Theatre and Performing Arts Collections*, ed. L. A. Rachow (New York, 1981), 13–22; M. E. Bonds: 'The Albert Schatz Opera Collection at the Library of Congress: a Guide and Supplemental Catalogue', *Notes*, xliv (1987–8), 655–95

YUGOSLAVIA (*YU*)

For the former republic of Yugoslavia see under 'Croatia', 'Serbia' and 'Slovenia'.   JOHN WAGSTAFF

Libretto (i) (It.: 'small book'; Fr. *livret*; Ger. *Textbuch*). A printed or manuscript book giving the literary text, both sung and spoken, of an opera (or other musical work). The word has also come to mean the text itself; for discussion of the literary text, *see* LIBRETTO (ii).

1. General. 2. Italy. 3. Other main centres. 4. The 20th century.

1. GENERAL. For three centuries the principal purpose of the published libretto was to provide for those attending a performance of an opera the text and a list of the characters. In most operatic centres until late in the 19th century, and in many until early in the 20th, a new libretto was customarily printed for each production and was available before the first performance. From simple beginnings the libretto gradually developed in extent and scope to become a detailed and reliable source of information on many aspects of the performance of individual operas, and it sometimes provides the sole surviving record of the very existence of an opera.

Up to about 1900 the libretto generally gives information about the date of the production, the size and constitution of the orchestra (often with the names of the principals), the names of the composer, the poet, the singers (which enables their mobility, careers and repertories to be studied), the musical director, the impresario, the scene designers, the machinists and other stage staff, the choreographer and the dancers; sometimes it also gives details of the dances performed and, especially in Italy, full synopses of the ballets that were traditionally given on the same bill as operas. Evidence of censorship is often present, especially in Italy and France. In Italy until about 1800 (half a century later in Rome) the title pages usually carry the phrase 'Con licenza de' Superiori' or, less commonly, 'Con permesso' or 'Colla permissione'; in addition there is often an *imprimatur* at the end of the libretto. French title pages until the Revolution invariably make reference to a royal privilege, and often the whole privilege (a page or more) or a shorter 'Approbation' is

printed at the end. It is evident therefore that the libretto, as well as providing valuable testimony about textual variants between different productions of individual operas, enables the study of the repertories and histories of opera houses, local customs, censorship and many other factors relating to the mounting of particular operas and to the history of opera in general.

Although librettos are now recognized as important tools for researchers, when originally published they were intended for nothing more than immediate, practical use. Until well into the second half of the 19th century they were the basic source of information for the operagoer, who would purchase a copy inside or outside the theatre (profits being the perquisite of the librettist) together with the playbill, and would be able to follow the text during the performance, thanks to undimmed lighting and assisted if necessary by wax tapers. Librettos were usually pocket-sized, printed on cheap paper, sewn into wrappers and rife with typographical errors: ephemeral objects, quickly redundant. Especially valuable to scholars are copies that survive with contemporary annotations – noting a change of cast, a cut or, all too rarely, details of stage movement (e.g. in a prompt copy of Handel's *Radamisto* (1720), at the Theatre Museum, Victoria and Albert Museum, London; *see* PRODUCTION, fig.7); a few are still extant that show extensive manuscript alterations by a librettist or impresario for a revised version of the work to be produced some time after the original. Among the most important of all is Verdi's own copy of the libretto of *Aida* (Milan, *c*1871) in which he recorded, with intricate diagrams, numerous details of the production (Pierpont Morgan Library, New York; *see* VERDI, GIUSEPPE, fig.4).

Towards the end of the 19th century, the flexibility brought by electricity to theatre lighting, combined with the evolution of the opera programme and the standardization of the repertory, transformed the libretto into an object intended to have a more enduring function, with much of its topical content discarded – a source to be read or referred to not so much in the theatre as at home, before and after the performance.

A number of collected editions, providing permanent records of the writings of several eminent librettists, have been published, invariably in more elegant form than the original separate editions. They include the works of G. F. Busenello (Venice, 1656 – the first appearance of his librettos in print), G. A. Moniglia (Florence, 1689–90), P. Metastasio (Venice, 1733–7; Paris, 1755; Paris, 1780–82; and many more), A. Zeno (Venice, 1744, and Orléans, 1785–6), C. Goldoni (Turin, 1757, and Venice, 1788–95), C.-S. Favart (Paris, 1763–77), and E. Scribe (Paris, 1874–85); among more recent collected editions have been those devoted to A. Boito (Milan, 1942), H. von Hofmannsthal (Stockholm and Frankfurt am Main, 1946–9) and W. S. Gilbert (New York, 1958). A collected edition of 129 operas staged at the Paris Opéra between 1671 and 1737, *Recueil general des opéra représentez par l'Académie royale de musique depuis son établissement*, was published by Ballard in 16 volumes (Paris, 1703–45).

2. ITALY. The earliest librettos, published in Florence, were printed in small quarto format (about 21 cm high) and contained between 12 and 20 leaves. The first to appear was for the first opera, Peri's setting of Rinuccini's *Dafne*, performed in Carnival 1598 and

published by Giorgio Marescotti in 1600. The title page names the poet, the sponsor of the performance (Jacopo Corsi), the person in whose honour it was given, the place and date of publication and the publisher. The only other preliminary to the text is the list of characters (without the singers' names), here called 'interlocutori' – for which alternative terms include 'personaggi', 'intervenienti' and 'attori'. The libretto concludes with verses addressed to Corsi – the first tribute of a kind that was to become a common feature of 17th-century librettos. The title page of the second published libretto, Rinuccini's *Euridice* (1600), mentions the occasion for the performance; the preliminaries include a three-page dedication from Rinuccini to Maria de' Medici, an important historical note that refers to the previous performances of *Dafne*, expresses Rinuccini's approval of the suitability of the modern music for the setting of tragedies, names Peri as the composer, and justifies his own alterations to the conclusion of the fable.

These two librettos contain only brief stage directions; those for Monteverdi's *Arianna* and *Ballo delle*

1. Alessandro Scarlatti, 'La caduta de' Decemviri': first edition of the libretto by Silvio Stampiglia (Naples, 1697), showing verses in inverted commas ('versi virgolati') to indicate a passage cut in the performance

ingrate (published in *Compendio delle sontuose feste*, Mantua, 1608) are more extensive. Gradually during the first half of the century further information began to be given and librettos were more commonly printed in a smaller format (octavo, duodecimo or sextodecimo). Exceptions were sometimes made for special occasions, when a more sumptuous publication, perhaps illustrated with scene designs, might be produced; one of the earliest such examples is the libretto for Marco da Gagliano's *La Flora* (Florence, 1628), text by Andrea Salvadori, which includes illustrations of five scenes, designed by Giulio Parigi and engraved by his son Alfonso (*see* FLORENCE, fig.1).

It was usual for an 'argomento' (an outline of the plot before the action commences) to be printed. From about 1650 this was sometimes divided by the words 'che si finge' into two sections, the first having historical or documentary precedent while the second was the invention of the author. From the 1620s for about a century the *argomento* was occasionally published separately from, or instead of, the libretto. An early example is Marco da Gagliano's sacred drama *La regina Sant'Orsola* (text by A. Salvadori): the *argomento* was published in 1624 and the libretto in the following year. In 1638 an 'Argomento e scenario' was published for Manelli's *La Delia* (text by G. Strozzi): this formula was occasionally reverted to during the following half-century.

It was also customary to print an address to the reader (headed, for example, 'ai lettori' or 'l'autore a chi legge'); this was sometimes written and signed by the composer, impresario or printer but more often by the librettist. The names of the performers were seldom printed in 17th-century Italian librettos. A rare exception occurs in the publisher's informative preface to *Andromeda* (the opera that inaugurated in 1637 the first public opera house, the S Cassiano in Venice); this names and makes brief comments on the composer, singers, dancers and choreographer. One of the earliest librettos to print a formal cast list was *Alessandro vincitor di se stesso*, text by F. Sbarra, music by A. Cesti and M. Bigongiari (1654, Lucca), but it was not until about 1700 that the singers were regularly named in Italian librettos; when they were, the posts they held at court were often stated and, where relevant (particularly for castratos), their nicknames.

Librettos vary in content and appearance according to their publisher and the place of performance, but by early in the 18th century most contained not only the features already mentioned but others as well. Among these were lists of scenes and of machines and effects, a 'protesta' (an affirmation of the poet's belief in the Catholic church, despite what might be inferred from the characters and subject matter of the opera), alternative arias (usually printed as a supplement at the end) and cuts observed in the performance. The latter were often indicated (from the late 17th century) by *versi virgolati*, double commas in the margin to indicate passages which either were not set to music at all or were omitted from the performance for the sake of brevity (fig.1): this procedure allowed the poet's work to be read unabridged. Paste-over slips were also used to make changes or to correct mistakes.

During the first half of the 18th century it became customary to name the musical director and costume designer and, in the second half, the producer, copyist, orchestral principals, chorus and even (though rarely) the understudies; occasionally notices were printed

Chör und Tänze.

I.

Von denen Innwohnern, und Solda-ten von Damasco.

II.

Von Art-geistern, so sich in Nymphen, und Schäfer verwandelt haben.

III.

Von Furien, und derselben Gefolge, als da sind der Haß, die Rachgierde, die Ver-rähterey, die Grausamkeit, die Raserey, die Verzweiflung ꝛc.

IV.

Von, in beglückte Liebhabere, und Amoret-ten verwandelten Art-geistern.

Die Vorstellung ist theils in Damasco, der Haupt-stadt des Sorischen König-reichs, und dasiger Gegenden, theils aber auf der bekannten bezauberten Insul der Armide, so zugleich eine der Glücks-insuln in dem Atlantischen Meere ist.

Ar-

Armide.

Erster Auftritt.

Ein grosser Platz von Damasco mit herrlichen Triumpf-bögen, welche alldaselbsten, um die Zurückkunft der Armide aus dem Lager des Godofredus von Bouil-lon zu feyern, bevorab aber weilen selbe mit ihren künstlichen Streichen viele Feld-herrn ihres Feindes gefangen genommen, und also mit sich gebracht, auf-gerichtet worden. Auf einer Seite stehet ein präch-tiger Thron, und in der Weite sind viele Schaaren des Volkes, der Wache, und Soldaten versammelt.

Armide, Phönicia, und Argene.

Argene.

Was ist die Ursache, o Armide, daß an einem von deinen Sieges-palmen also verherrlichten Tage eine unbekannte, und düstere Trauer-wolke den Glanz deiner Augen verdunklet?

A 3   Phö-

2. Tommaso Traetta, 'Armida': German translation (as 'Armide') of the libretto by Giacomo Durazzo and G. A. Migliavacca, published at the time of the original production (Vienna, 1761), showing the list of dances and first page of text

about the precise dates of performance during the season and the availability of the music. Librettos of this period were seldom illustrated, but that for Paisiello's *I giuochi d'agrigendo*, composed for the opening of the new Fenice theatre in Venice in 1792, contained an engraved frontispiece showing the façade of the theatre and, within the text, portraits of the composer and the three leading singers. From the early years of the 19th century it became usual to name the prompter and lighting director and from the 1820s the whole orchestra was sometimes listed.

Dance was an important ingredient of opera until the mid-19th century and the libretto is one of the best sources of information about it. There are numerous references to ballets, dances, dancers and choreographers in 17th-century librettos, but it was not until the mid-18th century that synopses of full-length ballets and lists of all the participants began to be printed within the libretto, normally on a few pages at the end or, less frequently, between the acts of the opera (fig.2). This practice lasted until the 1860s, after which ballet synopses were published as separate booklets on their own, a custom that had been initiated as early as the 1770s.

During the 19th century there were many further innovations in the development of the Italian libretto. Printed wrappers, replacing plain ones, were introduced no later than 1814, and by the early 1830s the back wrappers had started to be used for announcing the ballets to be performed or for advertising publications. At about this time publishers began to print the price of the libretto, on either the wrappers or the title page, and to give typographical emphasis to star names in the cast list; and in the mid-1830s polychrome printing on both title page and wrappers was introduced. Until the 1840s the libretto was not normally printed by the publisher of the music but by a general publisher who had the concession from the theatre. Thereafter the more powerful music publishers also began to take over publication of the text. In addition to the fully detailed librettos printed for particular performances, copies of regularly performed operas were printed for general sale without any performance or production details; these could be adapted for use for a specific performance by the substitution of a newly printed title page and cast-leaf or by paste-over addenda slips. New forms of in-house control were instigated: from 1843 Ricordi included librettos within their regular system of plate numbers, from 1860 they applied blind date stamps to indicate the year and month of issue, and from 1865 both they and Lucca sometimes used printed date stamps. Until 1874 wrappers were generally printed by letterpress, often embellished by typographical ornaments, but in that year Ricordi published the first Italian libretto (Verdi, *Macbeth*, designed by Prina) whose wrappers set out to give a visual impression of the flavour of the opera, usually by depicting a scene from the work. *Macbeth* was printed in monochrome, but from 1877 chromolithographic wrappers on librettos, just as on vocal scores, were frequently used; among the artists employed were Alfredo Edel (fig.3), Adolfo Hohenstein and, especially in the 1920s and 30s, Giulio Cisari. A further innovation occurred in 1883 when Ricordi introduced wire-stitching for binding, rather than the traditional linen or cotton sewing thread – a practice that was mercifully slow to be adopted by other publishers.

3. Emilio Usiglio, 'Le nozze in prigione': first edition of the libretto by A. Zanardini (Milan, 1881), in the original wrappers designed by Alfredo Edel

3. OTHER MAIN CENTRES. The development of the libretto in Italy strongly influenced the form in which the artefact was published elsewhere. The first libretto for a German opera was for Schütz's *Dafne*, to a text by Martin Opitz after Rinuccini, published in 1627. This quarto names both the composer and the librettist and contains a dedicatory poem and a list of characters. Among the earliest Italian operas to be performed in Germany was Antonio Bertali's *L'inganno d'amore* (Regensburg, 1653): Benedetto Ferrari's libretto, printed in Italian, includes a synopsis in German and is embellished with seven engraved scene designs by

Giovanni Burnacini, the pioneer of Venetian theatrical machinery. Burnacini's earlier designs for *La Gara*, text by Alberto Vimina, had also been published in the same manner (Vienna, 1652). This was a libretto of the commemorative type, published after the performance; it included a description of each act and an account of the impression made by the spectacle. Burnacini's son, Ludovico, worked principally in Vienna, where nine librettos between 1661 and 1700 carried engravings of his scene designs, including Cesti's *Il pomo d'oro* (1668; for illustration see POMO D'ORO, IL, and STAGE DESIGN, fig.4) and Draghi's *Il fuoco eterno* (1674; for illustration see DRAGHI, ANTONIO). Viennese 17th-century librettos tended to follow the Italian models and usually named the librettist, composer and machinist but not the singers. German librettos did not always name even the librettist, and rarely the composer. That for Handel's first opera, *Almira* (published in Hamburg, 1704), gives no names at all but lists in the preliminaries the dances and scenes. The arias are in German and Italian, a German translation being provided for the latter. Later in the 18th century and early in the 19th the participants are sometimes named in both German and Viennese librettos, and translations into German often given for foreign-language texts. Three editions of Gluck's *Orfeo* (Vienna, 1762) were published at about the time of the première – one with Italian and French text, one with German and one with Italian only; all three name the singers. The first printing of *Idomeneo* (Munich, 1781) names the composer, librettist, translator and also the singers (the only libretto of one of Mozart's major operas to name them); it has an *argomento* and list of scenes, and a German translation faces the Italian text (for illustration see IDOMENEO, RE DI CRETA). The second edition, which reflects the changes made in the rehearsals for the original production (see Mozart's letters to his father in early 1781), has Italian text only. There are exceptions, but in general the German and Viennese libretto from about 1750 is sadly uninformative, usually having a list of characters ('Personen') but no other preliminaries. The 1805 Vienna libretto of *Fidelio* provides an example of this, while Weber's *Freischütz* (Berlin, c1821) names the singers but, in common with many other German librettos, contains the text of only the 'Arien und Gesänge'.

The first opera produced in France was Luigi Rossi's *Orfeo*, to a text by F. Buti; an *abrégé* in French was published but not a libretto. The first French libretto was probably Buti's text for Carlo Caproli's *Le nozze di Peleo e di Theti* (Paris, 1654); this was published with dual Italian and French texts and named the singers. In the same year an English translation, *The Nuptials of Peleus and Thetis*, was published in London – probably the earliest libretto to be published in England, though no performance was given. The librettos of the first French opera, Michel de La Guerre's *Le triomphe de l'amour*, text by C. de Beys, and that of Cambert's *Pomone*, which inaugurated the Paris Opéra, were published at the end of 1654 and in 1671 respectively. In 1672 the first of Lully's operas was given. The original editions of his librettos are quartos and many have an engraved frontispiece depicting a scene from the work. In most of them the names of the singers and dancers, and sometimes also the leading instrumentalists, are given before the prologue and first act (fig.4); further names are occasionally inserted at points within the text. For works produced at the Opéra the quarto format was maintained throughout the 18th century, after

ACTEURS
DU PROLOGUE.

 A RENOMME'E. Mademoiselle
Verdier.

Chœur de la suite de la Renommée.
Les Rumeurs , les Bruits , &c.

Cinq Trompettes. Les Sieurs Lorange, Beaupré, Bar-
beray, Chervillac, & la Plaine.

Vingt-six suivants de la Renommée chantants.

Messieurs Bony, Bernard, Rebel, Gillet, Beaumont,
Perchot, Aubert, Pouyadon, Leroy, Gaudin,
Jollain, Huart, Champenois, Lescuyer, Prevost,
Moreau, Beaupuits, Martial, Hannot, Laurent,
Liron , & Boutelou. Les Sieurs Lanneau, Paisible,
Henry, & de Lorme Pages.

NEPTVNE. Monsieur Forestier.

Suite de Neptune, Tritons , & autres Dieux de la Mer.

Six Tritons jouants de la Flûte.

Messieurs Louys, Nicolas Hotteterre, Philidor l'aisné,
Philidor cadet, Piesche, & Bonnet.

Deux Tritons chantants. Messieurs du Mesny , &
Nouveau.
* ij

4. Jean-Baptiste Lully, 'Isis': first edition of the libretto by Philippe Quinault (Paris, 1677), showing the first page of the list of singers and instrumentalists for the Prologue

which the octavo format used by the other Paris theatres was adopted. From the 1720s comic operas appeared in a new type of publication that was to become popular in England with the advent of ballad opera: the music of some or all of the airs, though usually only the melodic lines, was printed within or as a supplement to the libretto. This format was continued, principally by the publisher Duchesne, in librettos of many comic operas and parodies from the 1730s to the 1770s, especially those of C.-S. Favart. Until the late 1820s publishers had issued librettos in plain wrappers; thenceforward printed wrappers were gradually adopted and frequently carried advertisements.

In England the early librettos were usually quartos, similar to the contemporary playbooks. The libretto for the first English opera, William Davenant's *The Siege of Rhodes*, music by Matthew Locke and others, is particularly informative: it names the place of performance, the singers, the composers of each entry and of the instrumental music, and it gives precise descriptions of the scenery and includes an address from Davenant to the reader. Other pre-1700 librettos normally have a dedication or preface but do not name the singers, though publisher's advertisements are sometimes included: Henry Purcell's *King Arthur* (1691), for example, contains a list of Dryden's other published works for the stage.

From the beginning of the 18th century the normal format changed to small quarto or octavo. From this period English librettos invariably name the composer, librettist, singers and dancers and often include a preface or dedication. *Arsinoe* (1705) has a preface by the composer, Thomas Clayton, in which he defines his aims in introducing the Italian manner to the English stage, while Owen MacSwiney uses the Dedication in Giovanni Bononcini's *Camilla* (1706) for the same purpose. The libretto of Handel's first London opera, *Rinaldo* (1711), has the Dedication, Preface and Argument in English, Giacomo Rossi's address to the reader in Italian and Aaron Hill's English translation of the text facing Rossi's Italian original; the printing of dual texts became routine for most operas performed in a foreign language in London until about the end of the 19th century (fig.5). In 1728 the libretto of *The Beggar's Opera* was published in two octavo editions, the first having the melodic lines of the airs printed as a supplement, the second having them interspersed with the text, preceded by the overture in score (*see* PUBLISHING, fig.5). This remained the standard format in which the early ballad operas appeared (the tunes usually being printed from woodcuts).

Innovations later in the 18th century include the occasional provision of a frontispiece depicting a singer or a scene from the production, while an abridged form of libretto was introduced for some English-language operas, in which the text of only the vocal numbers was printed and the spoken dialogue omitted. Printed wrappers were first used in the 1820s. An early example, for *Der Freischütz* at Drury Lane in 1824 (published retrospectively in the series *Dolby's British Theatre*, 1825), includes six pages of 'critical remarks' on the music, a description of the costumes, and stage directions supplied by the editors 'from their own personal observations, during the most recent performances'. An advertisement for further titles in the series appears on the back wrapper. From the late 1840s Covent Garden librettos often include a full list of the orchestra and give the name of the conductor. In the 1850s Davidson's began a series of 'Musical Libretto-Books' in which the original and English texts were printed in double column and 'the music of the principal airs' interspersed, a practice occasionally copied by other publishers; some of Davidson's librettos have extensive prefaces commenting on the history of the opera and previous productions and giving the cast of the current production (where necessary brought up to date on a tipped-in printed slip – a practice followed in other librettos of the period). By the 1860s it is not uncommon to find advertisements for miscellaneous goods and services printed on the wrappers and on several pages at the front and back of the libretto itself.

4. THE 20TH CENTURY. During the 20th century the libretto has become associated with publishers and recording companies rather than with opera houses, although occasionally an opera programme will print the complete libretto (more often in Italy, and particularly for a concert performance, when a translation is likely to be included). Most opera publishers still issue librettos, both for new and repertory operas, printed on better paper and in thicker wrappers than formerly; their contents are generally confined to normal title-page information, copyright claims, a list of the characters and scenes, a statement of the place and date of the first performance, possibly a preface and synopsis, the text itself, and advertisements for other publications. Boxed sets of gramophone records norm-

32

Tutti. Che tuono orrendo! che mai seguì?
> [*Grida interne, quindi sbucano dagli al-*
> *beri Donne scapigliate con fanciulli.*

Don. La terra trema, s'abbuja il dì.
Oh noi perdute!—soccorso! ajuto!—
Il finimondo certo è venuto.
> [*Spariscono di nuovo fra gli alberi.*

SCENA V.

ROLLA *ed altri Masnadieri, poi* CARLO MOOR.

Mas. Morte e demonio! chi si fa presso?
L'ombra del Rolla?—per Dio, gli è
desso!
D'onde ne vieni così serrato?

Rol. [*anel.*] Io? dalla forca dritto, filato.
Dell'aquavite! non reggo più.

Mas. Bevi, e poi narra!
> [*Gli mescono un bicchier d'acquavite.*

Rol. [*ad uno della Mas.*]   Narralo tu.

Mas. I cittadini correano alla festa,
E noi, lanciate più cánape ardenti,
Gridammo: "al foco!" da quella, da
questa;
Ed ecco pressa, tumulto, lamenti—
La polveriera scoppiò con tempesta,
E la paura confuse i sergenti,
Allora il Capo fra lor s'avventò,
E il prigioniero dal laccio salvò.

Rol. Sì! m'ha tirato fuor della fossa.

Mas. Eccolo!—ha l'aria mesta e commossa!
> [CAR. *entra pensoso e contempla il sole*
> *che tramonta.*

MAS. Capitano! qual è la tua mente?

CAR. Noi partiam coll'aurora vegnente.
> [*La Mas. si perde nella selva.*

33

All. What a fearful sound! what will follow?
> [*Cries within, several ladies rush forward*
> *with dishevelled hair, and dragging*
> *on their children.*

Ladies. The earth trembles, daylight is waning.
Oh, we are lost!—help!—assistance!
All is over with us.
> [*They disperse amongst the trees.*

SCENE V.

ROLLA *and other Robbers.* *Afterwards* CARLO
MOOR.

Rob. 'Sdeath! who is this?
The shade of Rolla?—by Heavens 'tis him!
Whence come you?

ROL. [*panting*] I? Flying from death—
Some water; I am quite exhausted!

Rob. Drink, and then relate.
> [*They give a glass of water.*

ROL. [*to one of the Robbers*] Do you relate the
story.

Rob. The citizens were hastening to the feast,
And we, after throwing in many places
burning ropes,
Screamed "Fire" here and there;
And immediately arose a fearful tumult.
The powder burst with a noise like thunder,
And fear quite confused the serjeants;
Then our Captain rushed into the midst,
And rescued the prisoner, as you see.

ROL. Yes! he dragged me out of a ditch.

Rob. Here he is—he looks sad, and troubled!
> [CAR. *enters with a pensive countenance,*
> *and contemplates the setting sun.*

ROL. Captain! what are you thinking about?

CAR. We must depart at the dawn of day.
> [*The Robbers disperse among the woods.*

c 3

5. Giuseppe Verdi, 'I masnadieri': first edition of the libretto by Andrea Maffei (London, 1847), showing parallel Italian and English text

ally contain a booklet (up to 30.5 cm square) that includes the text, often in several (usually four) languages, laid out in columns; the same procedure is normally followed for the booklets (12.5 × 14.5 cm) that accompany CDs. Reprint publishers have not ignored the libretto: Garland have issued facsimiles of the first editions of Handel's and Mozart's operas (a critical facsimile of Handel librettos and their sources is also appearing from Olschki in Florence), a substantial series of English ballad opera librettos, and the librettos of the operas of which they have published manuscripts in facsimile. Facsimiles of librettos are also included in the series Music for London Entertainment, 1660–1800.

A number of private individuals and institutions have assembled significant collections of librettos. The most internationally representative is probably that formed by Albert Schatz, now in the Library of Congress, Washington; other particularly fine collections are held at the British Library, London, the Manoel de Carvalhoes Collection at the Accademia di S Cecilia, Rome, and the Ulderico Rolandi collection at the Fondazione Cini, Venice. Further extensive collections are at the Österreichische Nationalbibliothek, Vienna, the Bayerische Staatsbibliothek, Munich, the Herzog August Bibliothek, Wolfenbüttel, the Biblioteca

Marciana, Venice, the Central Library of the Mariinsky Theatre at St Petersburg, the New York Public Library, the university libraries of California (at Berkeley) and Texas (at Austin), and the conservatory libraries of Bologna, Brussels, Milan, Naples and Paris. The best-known catalogue of librettos is O. G. T. Sonneck's *Library of Congress: Catalogue of Opera Librettos printed before 1800* (Washington, DC, 1914), a monumental work, extensively annotated, in which librettos are listed by title, librettist and composer. In progress (1992) is Claudio Sartori's important and long-awaited catalogue, *I libretti italiani a stampa dalle origini al 1800* (Cuneo, 1990–), which lists all Italian and Latin libretto texts published up to and including 1800 and states the location of copies worldwide; 16 indexes are promised.

The importance of librettos not only as texts but as documentary evidence of multifarious aspects of operatic history has now come to be fully appreciated and has in recent years inspired a major bibliographical undertaking known as the U.S. RISM Libretto Project, with its seat at the University of Virginia, Charlottesville. The object is to coordinate the cataloguing in machine-readable form of all historical librettos in collections in the USA, beginning with the Schatz Collection. The records (which are entered into the Research Libraries Information Network, where they are accessible as work proceeds) include not only the standard bibliographic descriptions but the indexing of all performance and production personnel named in the source, the names of the characters and the city and theatre of production.

AllacciD; *Grove6* (E. J. Dent and P. J. Smith); *LoewenbergA*; *MGG* (A. A. Abert); *StiegerO*

A. Wotquenne: *Libretti d'opéras et d'oratorios italiens du XVIIe siècle* (Brussels, 1901–14) [suppl. to *Catalogue de la Bibliothèque du Conservatoire royal*]

G. and C. Salvioli: *Bibliografia universale del teatro drammatico italiano* (Venice, 1903), i

A. Solerti: *Le origini del melodramma* (Turin, 1903)

——: *Gli albori del melodramma* (Milan, 1904–5)

——: *Musica, ballo e drammatica alla Corte Medicea dal 1600 al 1637* (Florence, 1905)

P. Bergmans: 'Une collection de livrets d'opéras italiens 1669–1710', *SIMG*, xii (1910–11), 22–34

O. G. T. Sonneck: 'Italienische Opernlibretti des 17. Jahrhunderts in der Library of Congress', *SIMG*, xiii (1911–12), 392–9

——: *Catalogue of 19th Century Librettos* (Washington DC, 1914)

——: *Library of Congress: Catalogue of Opera Librettos printed before 1800* (Washington DC, 1914)

R. Haas: 'Zur Bibliographie der Operntexte', *Kongressbericht: Leipzig 1925*, 59–61

V. Raeli: 'Catalogazione statistica delle collezioni di libretti per musica', *Musica d'oggi*, xii (1930), 356–8

F. Biach-Schiffmann: *Giovanni und Ludovico Burnacini: Theater und Feste am Wiener Hofe* (Vienna and Berlin, 1931)

T. Searle: *Sir William Schwenck Gilbert: a Topsy-Turvy Adventure* (London, 1931)

A. Loewenberg: *Annals of Opera 1597–1940* (Geneva, 1943, 2/1955)

U. Sesini: *Catalogo della Biblioteca del Liceo musicale di Bologna*, v: *Libretti d'opera in musica* (Bologna, 1943)

A. Loewenberg: *Early Dutch Librettos and Plays with Music in the British Museum* (London, 1947)

O. Strunk: *Source Readings in Music History* (New York, 1950), 367–76

U. Rolandi: *Il libretto per musica attraverso i tempi* (Rome, 1951)

S. T. Worsthorne: *Venetian Opera in the Seventeenth Century* (Oxford, 1954)

U. Manferrari: *Dizionario universale delle opere melodrammatiche* (Florence, 1954–5)

R. Schaal: 'Die vor 1801 gedruckten Libretti des Theatermuseums München', *Mf*, x (1957), 388–96, 487–97; xi (1958), 54–69, 168–77, 321–36, 462–77; xii (1959), 60–75, 161–77, 299–306, 454–61; xiii (1960), 38–46, 164–72, 299–306, 441–8; xiv (1961), 36–43, 166–83

R. Allen, ed.: *The First Night Gilbert and Sullivan, Containing Complete Librettos of his Fourteen Operas, Exactly as Presented at their Première Performances* (New York, 1958, 2/1975)

R. Allen: *W. S. Gilbert: an Anniversary Survey and Exhibition Checklist* (Charlottesville, VA, 1963)

A. Caselli: *Catalogo delle opere liriche pubblicate in Italia* (Florence, 1969)

P. E. Gossett: *The Operas of Rossini: Problems of Textual Criticism in Nineteenth-Century Opera* (diss., Princeton U., 1970)

P. J. Smith: *The Tenth Muse: a Historical Study of the Opera Libretto* (New York, 1970)

E. Thiel and G. Rohr: *Kataloge der Herzog August-Bibliothek Wolfenbüttel*, xiv: *Libretti: Verzeichnis der bis 1800 erschienenen Textbücher* (Frankfurt, 1970)

A. C. Ramelli: *Libretti e librettisti* (Milan, 1973)

M. Chusid: *A Catalog of Verdi's Operas* (Hackensack, NJ, 1974)

R. L. and N. W. Weaver: *A Chronology of Music in the Florentine Theater 1590–1750* (Detroit, 1978)

H. F. G. Klein: *Erst- und Frühdrucke der Textbücher von Richard Wagner: Bibliographie* (Tutzing, 1979)

Studies in Music from the University of Western Ontario, iv/1–3 [*Opera 1*, ed. D. J. Neville], iv/4 [*Opera 2*, ed. R. Macnutt, M. H. Rose and L. Levetus] (London, Ont., 1979)

J. Black: *The Italian Romantic Libretto: a Study of Salvadore Cammarano* (Edinburgh, 1984)

J. J. Fuld: *The Book of World-Famous Librettos: the Musical Theater from 1598 to Today* (New York, 1984)

J. Rosselli: *The Opera Industry in Italy from Cimarosa to Verdi: the Role of the Impresario* (Cambridge, 1984)

J. Milhous and R. D. Hume: 'A Prompt Copy of Handel's "Radamisto"', *MT*, cxxvii (1986), 316–21

M. P. McClymonds and D. Parr Walker: 'U.S. RISM Libretto Project: with Guidelines for Cataloguing in the MARC Format', *Notes*, xliii (1986–7), 19–35

W. Dean and J. M. Knapp: *Handel's Operas 1704–1726* (Oxford, 1987)

F. Melisi, ed.: *Biblioteca del Conservatorio di San Pietro a Majella di Napoli: catalogo dei libretti per musica dell'ottocento (1800–1860)* (Lucca, 1990)

C. Sartori: *I libretti italiani a stampa dalle origini al 1800: catalogo analitico con 16 indici* (Cuneo, 1990–)

For further bibliography of libretto collections, anthologies etc., *see* LIBRETTO (ii), H.　　　　RICHARD MACNUTT

Libretto (ii). The verbal text of an opera. For discussion of the printed wordbook, *see* LIBRETTO (i).

I. Words for music. II. Historical survey. III. Bibliography.

I. Words for music

1. Introduction. 2. The issue of 'number opera'. 3. The libretto as literature. 4. Prima la musica? 5. Literary men and librettists. 6. A secondary art?

1. INTRODUCTION. The term 'libretto' has been extended from its literal meaning of 'small book' to denote the literary content of an opera, not merely its separate physical existence. The sung text will also appear in the musical score, though the visual layout of verse forms and poetic lineation will there vanish, and scene descriptions and stage directions will often be omitted or shortened. Score and wordbook together form a blueprint for theatrical performance, where the words will (one hopes) be heard, as song, as recitative, or in some forms of opera as speech, and the other arts prescribed or implicit in the libretto will be realized as acting, movement in space, dance, decor (including machines), lighting and costume. It is evident that 'literary content' is an insufficient description, for the libretto, unlike the play text, is only part of the blueprint. With these cautions in mind the libretto, like the play text, may be discussed as literature.

'Libretto' has also given rise to the professional term 'librettista' (librettist; Ger. *Textdichter*), though Italian usage has normally preferred *poeta* and French *poète*. The standard practice of title pages, until our own times, was to omit such descriptions, ascribing the opera (often under a genre title) to the librettist and its music to the composer, thus: '*Madama Butterfly* … Tragedia giapponese di L. Illica e G. Giacosa, musica di Giacomo Puccini'. 'Librettista' has in turn engendered 'librettistica' ('librettistics'), denoting the study of the librettist's art and of the literary contribution to the amalgam of opera. It is not yet possible, however, to write an adequate history of the libretto and librettists, although there have been valuable attempts at general studies: Istel 1914 and 1922, Rolandi 1951, Smith 1970, Cassi Ramelli 1973, Basso 1977, Fabbri 1990 (for 17th-century Italy) and dictionary articles by A. A. Abert, Cagli, Della Corte and Tagliavini. The bibliographical data are not yet near completion; in spite of the magnificent coverage of Italian printed librettos before 1800 achieved by Sartori (1973, 1990), the wider work of the *RISM Libretto Project* is badly needed. Much of the 19th century remains uncharted. There is also a lack of librettos in modern or facsimile editions for study, and of the scores that go with them; while an equal or greater problem of assessment is caused by the as yet modest repertory to be seen on the stage, for it is difficult to know how a libretto works until one has seen it in action.

It would be premature, then, to attempt even a summary history of the libretto, save as a facet of the history of publishing (*see* LIBRETTO (i)). The decades since 1950 have however witnessed an extraordinary expenditure of scholarly effort devoted to the history of opera: many scores of hitherto unpublished works have appeared, and proper editions of familiar works have offered many surprises; the bibliography of opera and the repertory of particular centres has been studied as never before, and many hundreds of articles and books have appeared, creating a new sense of order in the diffuse and often imperfect archive of operatic history. This intense effort has not been purely academic and text-orientated. It has extended to operatic aesthetics, theory and criticism, and to the connections between opera and literature and the history of ideas. Further, it has coincided with an ever-growing public appetite for the exploration of forgotten repertory and supposedly obscure conventions.

This article is therefore accompanied by a classified bibliography showing where information and examples may be found to illuminate the history of opera through its literary component. It also aims to exemplify the nature of scholarly research into opera, which ideally should mingle literary and musical skills with scientific method in equal proportions, but keeping practical considerations in the forefront of the mind, partly because composers and librettists normally did, but also with an eye to the restoration and revival of lost conventions. Finally, lists of libretto collections and catalogues, and a list of librettos anthologies and reprints, many in facsimile, will assist readers who wish to examine librettos for themselves.

2. THE ISSUE OF 'NUMBER OPERA'. One consequence of recent investigation and practical experiment, and of the publication of primary materials, is the gaining of new insights into the perennial debate between the advocates of 'number opera' and those who wish opera to pursue the more continuous development and uniform time-scale of spoken drama. Both approaches have produced great works of art and it is increasingly understood that naive arguments in favour of 'naturalism' have little place in the discussion. The procedures of Monteverdi, Gluck or Wagner depend upon sophisticated conventions, consciously or tacitly agreed between stage and audience, quite as much as those of Handel, Mozart or Verdi. What is important is not naturalism, verisimilitude or the cruder kind of likeness to life, but expressive realism, the ability to catch, encapsulate, re-create and make permanent some aspect of human experience or emotion whose artistic analogue can be made to seem true to the audience in a variety of ways.

The debate, although it may now seem artificial, has coloured a great deal of the argument over the methods and aesthetic of opera, and has affected the structure of the libretto and the theorizing of librettists. A libretto envisaged in the first place as a play will often be in prose, and the steady development of a drama will not easily accommodate opportunities for music to contribute in its own way to the heightening and unwinding of tension, to make plateaux and valleys, transitions and contrasts. Opera began as a functional, naive setting of a new kind of poetic drama, the pastoral play; this had no single root in the classical culture beloved of the Renaissance but had been created by combining the pastoral world of Ovid and Virgil and their Greek models, and the poetic dialogue of the eclogue, with the larger form of Greek drama. The latter was believed to have been sung throughout, but for early opera audiences the novelty of the music may have been secondary to the novelty of the new type of drama. Peri and Caccini set these plays almost throughout in the recently invented recitative style (which had first been used for epic, not dramatic singing), save at the very few points where Rinuccini had provided strophic verse for a festive or moralizing chorus. Musicians and audience alike came to find this almost unvaried continuum tedious, and from as early as Monteverdi and Striggio's *Orfeo* (1607) we find the welcome relief of arias, strophic variations, choral *balli* and so forth, often alternating with instrumental ritornellos and symphonies.

This trend grew, until, during the Arcadian Academy's first reform of Italian opera, from about 1690, the librettist Apostolo Zeno and his circle felt it necessary to express resentment at the large number of increasingly long solo arias demanded by singers and audience; they regarded arias as excrescences interrupting the stately flow of the true business of the drama, which was conducted in the recitative. Metastasio came to the opinion that even accompanied recitatives slowed up the drama, and advised Hasse to use them only sparingly. Reformers of the 1750s, led by Francesco Algarotti, pointed to the more fluid structure of French opera – though mainly in envy of the choral scenes, dances and visual spectacle that had largely vanished from the Italian tradition – and Calzabigi and Gluck, along with other Italian composers and poets such as Traetta, Jommelli and Verazi, began to experiment with longer units. But it took the radical innovations of Wagner from 1848 onwards to devise a method whereby a text resembling that of a play might be set without verbal repetition to continuous music; his methods were adapted by Debussy in his almost complete setting of Maeterlinck's prose drama *Pelléas et Mélisande*, and were used for the *Literaturoper* ('literary opera') of Richard Strauss, who set first a play and then specially written librettos by Hofmannsthal and later others. Berg elaborated musical frameworks of unparalleled complexity in order to sustain the weight of plays by Büchner and Wedekind. (The 'continuous drama' type of opera makes great demands on a composer's power of structural articulation: it is all too easy to hand over responsibility to the librettist.)

Alongside these achievements, however, the 'number opera' continued its italianate method of telling a dramatic story by means of two different time-scales, in speedy, naturalistic and loosely organized recitative where the action demanded, and in 'psychological time' when a state of feeling or thought required lyrical expansion and balanced phrases. In 1951 Stravinsky's masterpiece *The Rake's Progress*, with libretto perfectly calculated by W. H. Auden and Chester Kallman, triumphantly reasserted this tradition. More significantly, audiences in recent years have learnt to understand the conventions of pre-Gluckian Italianate operas, notably those of Handel: these consist almost entirely of recitative and solo arias. It is not simply a matter of the acceptability of two different musical representations of dramatic time, the Wagnerian more uniform, the Handelian sharply differentiated; there is also the question of the presentation of character, in Wagner continuous, 'in-the-round' and Shakespearean, in Handel analytical, exploring one state of feeling at a time. In the history of operatic criticism, the long dispute as to whether an opera and its libretto should proceed as a drama does has largely been a dialogue between two workable conventions, the adherents of each thinking their own approach more 'natural'.

The 'number' type of opera, at least in the more fluid form evolved by Verdi and Boito in *Otello* and above all *Falstaff*, where recitative has largely become song, has in many ways offered the more fruitful ground for development; if the units are reasonably short and apprehensible, audiences can follow them. Operas of this kind have achieved a sense of tradition and even popular success (Puccini, Britten, Stravinsky). Attempts at continuous operatic drama have very often left librettists and composers unaware of the possibilities for stylization that music offers to the playwright and drama to the composer. The result is too often a play sung in a kind of perpetual recitative, with very elaborate accompaniments. Wagner knew that from time to time musical themes must walk the stage, not be confined to the orchestra pit: yet many later composers, afraid to stylize the utterance of language beyond the obvious (but musically inert) values of 'good' recitative, have been content to set texts all at the same naturalistic *andante* tempo in melodically unmemorable speech-song, while confining thematic and motivic life and contrast of pace and colour to the pit. It is curious that one tried and successful solution to these problems, the number opera with spoken dialogue, is now almost entirely banished to the sphere of operetta and the musical.

This broad debate has to some extent drawn mainstream composers into two schools and damped down the consciousness of other traditions and possibilities of musical theatre. Experience of unfamiliar types of stylized drama from outside Europe suggest that a Western audience might in time come to understand and enjoy still more extreme conventions of musical theatre, such as those of a noh play or the puppet drama of the Malayan shadow-play. Britten and Plomer did in fact blend noh play and liturgical drama in their church parables. Other composers have experimented with yet more sophisticated techniques: Hindemith and Ferdinand Lion dissociated music and drama at one point in *Cardillac*, where a murder is committed to the accompaniment of a neo-classical sonata; Blacher, Schat and others have attempted abstract opera. Surprisingly, 20th-century electronic media seem to have had little effect in extending the conventions of opera. The most permanent new forms have come from mixing genres, as with the opera-oratorio (whether staged, as in Stravinsky and Cocteau's *Oedipus rex*, or in concert performance, as in Honegger and Claudel's *Jeanne d'Arc au bûcher*), and with music theatre.

In an age of perpetual experiment, however, it is all but impossible to build up any continuity of style and convention, shared between stage and audience, of the kind which in ages past has produced schools and traditions of opera. There is probably no answer to the problem that, where public subsidy is high, the desire to please and even simple clarity may easily be discounted. Why else should Henze and Edward Bond, an experienced opera composer and playwright respectively, have baffled the audience by presenting three scenes simultaneously in *We Come to the River* (1976)? This, surely, is stylization taken too far. The point may be that horrors come at us from all sides, too fast for comprehension; but the artistic effect is a kind of confusion that does not tempt one to consult the libretto after the show to find out what one should have been experiencing. Of course, sophisticated composers now expect us to study the words carefully before hearing the music. Dallapiccola has claimed this as the composer's right, and Boulez has written: 'You want to understand the words? Then read them'. With comments such as these, and with the invention of subtitles for film and television opera and surtitles in the opera house itself – even when the opera is not in a foreign language – we are again in the condition of an audience in 17th-century Milan: 'Dove andaré stassera? A l'opera? Havi let el librett?' ('Going to the opera tonight? have you read the libretto?': G. M. Maggi, *Consigli di Meneghino*, 1697).

3. THE LIBRETTO AS LITERATURE. Considered as a literary genre – and usually by literary men – the libretto has more often evoked contempt, or at best an amused indifference, than praise. The reasons for this are complex. The commonest cause of difficulty, overriding and compounding all others, is an inability to see (or hear) beyond the words on the printed page. Even a writer possessed of the most acute literary and dramatic sensibility will misunderstand the function and effect of the libretto unless he or she is also endowed with sufficient musicality to respond to the mysterious new compound that results from the fusion of words with music. Lodovico Muratori in the early 18th century actually described aria verses as 'parole non necessarie' (unnecessary words); but Victor Hugo, though at first angry with Piave for the liberties he took in transforming *Le roi s'amuse* into *Rigoletto*, later came to envy Verdi the power and unique resources of the operatic medium. Hugo had himself once written an opera libretto (*Esmeralda*, for Louise Bertin, 1836, on his own novel *Notre-Dame de Paris*).

In reading early criticism of opera and the libretto, it is important to remember that for the first two centuries of the genre's existence almost all the commentary comes from literary men. Only with the arrival of Berlioz and Wagner do we regularly find composers who are able to enter the public debate as educated intellectuals of high literary ability. Literary discussion is usually one-sided, rarely viewing opera as a composite art where the partners are on equal terms. The more useful texts are often modest practical treatises and observations by men of the theatre; these include the anonymous author, perhaps Rinuccini's son, of the manuscript treatise *Il corago* ('The Choragus', i.e. opera director, c1630), the practical guide to operatic versification by G. G. Salvadori (1691), and the observations of the much-travelled German librettist and translator Barthold Feind (1708).

Other more distinguished literary men have made valuable contributions to the operatic debate, and figures of the front rank have produced librettos; but until fairly recently the overwhelming impression left in the minds of interested students of the libretto, particularly if they are English speaking, is that the libretto is hardly worth writing about. The notion that the words of an Italian opera were nonsense became a catch-phrase in English criticism as early as Addison, and a predisposition to expect nonsense in a libretto leads to unthinking and destructive lapses of judgment. There are many passages in Antonio Somma's texts that deserve criticism, or at least sympathy, but (as Cassi Ramelli has pointed out) the moment when Renato 'hears the track of merciless steps' is not really one of them ('Sento l'orma dei passi spietati', *Un ballo in maschera*, Verdi, Act 2.iii). This is an example of synaesthesia, a kind of transference or compression like Milton's 'blind mouths' (*Lycidas*); Somma may well have had in mind the almost identical phrase in Manzoni's *I promessi sposi* (1828).

Some of the non-musical factors that have combined to give the libretto such a bad press need to be considered. First, however, it should be emphasized that for some two centuries of operatic history no one writing about opera would easily have been able to consult a score: operas were rarely published, and almost never complete. The critic had only the libretto to work from; nor would he normally be discussing an actual performance, for analytical reviews in the modern sense did not exist. It is not therefore surprising that the appearance of the words on the printed page should have assumed such importance in its own right. (That may explain why it was not until the 19th century that the composer's habit of repeating the words of arias is seriously discussed, for of course the repeats of the words are not shown in the libretto; this was a habit approved by Grillparzer, disliked by Tennyson, avoided by Wagner through the use of paraphrase, and brilliantly parodied by A. E. Housman.) Even today it remains hard to assert the rights of the ear over those of the eye. It is partly the look of the page, partly the false stress on the last rhyming syllable, and partly unfair modern associations that move us, still, to laughter, when we read Nahum Tate's couplet, placed in the mouth of Dido during a furious quarrel:

> Thus on the fatal Banks of *Nile*,
> Weeps the deceitful Crocodile.

In live performance this passes unnoticed. That is to some extent because of the sheer impetus of the quarrel at the opera's crisis point, but mainly because Purcell's setting (ex.1) removes the (visual) false stress and places

Ex.1 Purcell and Tate: *Dido and Aeneas*, Act 3

the dangerous word in deep shadow by his astonishing reinforcement of the word 'weeps'. He omits the comma and rides over the enjambement, so that the rhyme-word 'Nile' is not emphasized, placing 'weeps' unexpectedly on the next (weak) beat, and strengthens the trochaic stress still further with an irregularly resolved appoggiatura placed over an acrid off-beat dissonance; the disturbance is heightened by a syncopation that suppresses the third beat of the bar. An imaginative and resourceful composer has made a purely literary problem disappear.

On a more general level, a composer may add an unsuspected depth and complexity to words that seem innocuous or even jejune. At the end of Handel's *Tamerlano* (Piovene, adapted by Haym; 1724), the audience has witnessed the tragic suicide of the ex-emperor Bajazet, the intense grief of his daughter and the chastening of the tyrant Tamerlane. The libretto offers a conventional *coro* for all the survivors to sing: the lovers are to marry their appropriate partners, and Tamerlane has abandoned his anger and cruelty. The

verse is probably not intended to provide anything more than the expected *lieto fine*:

> D'atra notte già mirasi a scorno
> d'un bel giorno
> brillar lo splendor.
> Frà le tede, che Lachesi accende,
> chiara splende
> la face d'Amor.

(We now see the radiance of a fair day shining out, defying the dark night. Among the torches lit by [the Fate] Lachesis, brightly shines the lamp of Love.)

After the tragedy, the text seems to the cursory eye an inadequate response. Handel's setting of it shows the ability of a Saint-Simon to penetrate behind the ceremonial of court life to the human passions behind the masks. Tamerlane has promised to reform, but has been deeply shamed; his bride-to-be has suffered from his infidelity and witnessed his cruelty; Asteria has seen her father die, a man admired and loved by her future husband. They are still in the presence of a potentially dangerous autocrat. Handel therefore sets the *coro* not as a conventional paean of joy, such as the text seems to demand, but as a stark, penitential, sorrowing E minor ensemble that reaches down past the surface of the courtly words to the true feelings beneath (ex.2). It is

Ex.2 Handel and Haym/Piovene: *Tamerlano*, Act 3 (voices only)

unclear whether this is an early example of irony, the music supplying a contradictory setting of a glib text routinely provided by the poet. In performance, one is aware of no dissociation or jar between words and music; but one would hardly have foreseen, reading the words beforehand, what a rich complex of feeling and thought the music would add.

It is important to remember that a libretto is addressed in the first place to the composer, and that the convenience of an audience or critic is only a secondary function. The verbal text alone gives no more than a schematic indication of the way in which the librettist expects the music to be articulated ('Recitativo', 'Aria', 'Introduzione', 'Stretta' etc., or a change in the structure of the verse). It shows nothing of the musical time-scale, or of what music can do in the way of contrast and transition. In the earlier part of the 18th century, when Italian opera had adopted a rigid division between recitative in largely unrhymed *versi sciolti* of eleven or seven syllables and aria verse in other metres and always rhymed, opportunities for composers to disregard the prevailing convention were rare. Even so, the desire to establish the mood of a scene by giving a character an opening arioso had led them to invent the cavatina, a short aria 'cavata' ('extracted', 'excavated') from verse intended by the poet as recitative and originally printed as such. Handel rarely departed from the expected pattern, but when he omitted or foreshortened an expected da capo the result is accordingly all the more effective. In *Ariodante*, Antonio Salvi can hardly have intended that the king should so charmingly interrupt the da capo of the duet between his daughter and her lover (in the middle of a word, and on a dissonance too: ex.3).

Ex.3 Handel and A. Salvi: *Ariodante*, Act 1 (omitting upper strings)

When in the 1760s the formal divisions of libretto and music begin to grow less sharply defined, the role of music in articulating the progress of the drama becomes ever more important; composer and poet begin to plan as more equal partners, though this is not always evident from the words alone, and the librettist was often very likely unaware that he was beginning to lose his responsibility for organizing the business in hand. 'Che puro ciel' in *Orfeo ed Euridice* (Act 2) looks to the eye like any other recitative in *versi sciolti*. Calzabigi, the librettist, probably had no idea that Gluck would set the phrases of recitative as four meditative interventions in what is essentially an aria for oboe (derived in its turn from two earlier arias). Mozart's perfectly judged musical divisions in the long Act 2 finale of *Le nozze di Figaro* do not always fall where Da Ponte's adoption of a new metre or rhyme scheme suggests that they should, notably at the Allegro that begins when the Count is hunting in the closet for Cherubino, and at the velvety Andante when Antonio produces the papers that the page had dropped in his escape (see Carter 1987). An even more striking case is the sublime Andante when the Count asks for and receives his wife's forgiveness in the Act 4 finale. The text is:

> COUNT: (*in tono supplichevole*)
> Contessa, perdono.
>
> COUNTESS: Più docile sono,
> E dico di sì.
>
> ALL: Ah! tutti contenti
> Saremo così.

(*Pleading* Countess, pardon. I am less obstinate, and say 'Yes'. Ah! that will make us all happy.)

There is a stage direction, and later a new masculine rhyme-word ('sì'), but the Count's 'perdono' repeats the plea (and its rhyme) that everyone else has been making to him, and there is no change in the metre, *senari*, when the Count speaks. The wonderful contrast that places a halo around the principal characters and the principal message of the opera is apparently Mozart's idea. More remarkable yet is that, in order to achieve it, he has refused to interrupt the preceding Allegro assai with pauses and has denied to Da Ponte the sure-fire laughter he must have expected as the jealous Count pulls four other characters, one by one, out of the arbour where he thinks his wife is hiding. In a performance of Beaumarchais' play this scene is a riot, and the Count's increasing discomfiture may be spun out to last a good minute; but Mozart permits no pause or ritardando,

even when the Countess herself emerges from the opposite arbour (though many conductors slow up at this point). From the printed libretto, one would expect none of this.

All critical treatments of the libretto seen as literature, then, must be read with caution. That is not to say that criticism of a libretto's language is necessarily misplaced. It was recognized quite early in the 17th century that the claims of musical form, and the increased difficulty of distinguishing words and retaining them in the mind in a large theatre with the resonant acoustic necessary for music, demanded brevity and simple sentences from the librettist (Fabbri 1990). But if the literary expression of a libretto needs to be terse to the point of baldness, that is no reason for it to be threadbare or slovenly, or for the audience to be left in confusion over the plot and the motivation of the characters. In English-speaking countries, more so than in others, both critics and naive audiences have often reacted unfavourably to the conventions and language of opera librettos. That is partly because of the unusually rich and popular tradition of spoken drama (not to mention the dialogue of characters in novels, and the exceptional wealth of lyric poetry). It is easy to go to the opera house with false expectations. Fine language has its own music, with which added music may not chime, as may be noticed when straining to follow the long blank-verse lines in Britten's *A Midsummer Night's Dream* – where the lyric songs are magically effective because intended for setting. Vaughan Williams's *Sir John in Love* fares better because its source, *The Merry Wives of Windsor*, is in prose. Otherwise, it is no accident that the completely successful Shakespeare operas were composed to foreign-language librettos, in which the thought could be presented more trenchantly and clearly and in more modern language.

Much unfavourable literary criticism of the opera libretto by British writers should properly have been directed at the English translations in which operas were heard and read. Translators into English experience difficulties in finding equivalents in their basically iambic language for the normally trochaic endings of Italian verse, difficulties that may lead them into those special 'librettese' forms of verbs, the operatic future tense ('From their ambush they soon will be bursting': Dent, *Un ballo in maschera*) and the operatic reflexive ('Out we'll go then, till we find us/With the garden gate behind us': Dennis Arundell, *Il matrimonio segreto*). No wonder opera librettos enjoy such a bad reputation. (*See also* TRANSLATION.)

4. PRIMA LA MUSICA? It should not necessarily be assumed that the words always preceded and inspired the musical setting, or that, particularly in the texts of arias, the poet had an entirely free rein, as if he were writing verse for its own sake. Quite early on we find conventions governing the choice of metre and verse form thought suitable for aria verse: *decasillabi*, for example, are passionate and excitable (as in Cherubino's 'Non sò più' in *Le nozze di Figaro*, or even when he is, though absent, the subject of intense discussion in the Act 2 finale); *sdruccioli* and *bisdruccioli*, lines ending with two or three weak syllables, are fitting for comic or rustic characters; musical structure determined the verse-form of the da capo arias and rondeau. (For a fuller discussion, *see* VERSIFICATION.) The use of conventional verse types, and the tradition of depicting only one emotion at a time in an aria, allowed composers to raid their

stock of works and to re-use an old aria in a new context; one might also raid another composer's stock as well, and make whole operas, pasticcios, by stringing together arias and linking them with newly-composed recitative. The re-texting of music is only one aspect of this technique. In the French vaudeville comedy or 'play with couplets', as in Gay's *The Beggar's Opera*, new words are written to old tunes; in the dance-music of French 18th-century operas, according to the painter and librettist Mondorge (1743), the choreographer and composer agreed the steps and the music and the librettist had then to write words suitable both to the intention of the dance and the phrasing of its tune – a teasing yet humble task, akin to that of a translator, which one might have thought beneath the dignity of an independent literary artist.

These are obvious constraints on the literary freedom of the librettist, and they are found in an age when the routines of librettist and composer were by and large so clearly defined, and their intellectual stations normally so different, that often they did not even meet. It is perhaps not surprising, then, that we come across yet more interesting cases of *parodie* (or re-texting) in the 19th century, when composers began to claim a status equal to or senior to that of their librettists, and were much more highly rewarded for their contribution (Boito, passing through Verdi's farmyard at Sant' Agata, ruefully pointed out that a load of manure commanded a much higher price than a libretto). Music has its own powers of characterization, and a strong situation may remove the need for words altogether, as when Rigoletto, hunting among the courtiers for his abducted daughter, sings nothing more than 'larà larà'. A composer sensitive to questions of personality and dramatic motivation may be visited by melodic compulsions independently of any words; or his melody, taking flight from the librettist's text, may demand a different continuation; or an unused idea from some aborted work, or a borrowed tune better than anything he can contrive, may force its way into his mind, so that his librettist is required to produce verses that fit the phrasing and musical rhyme-scheme of an existing tune.

An expert librettist will not find this compromising, but he has unquestionably lost his literary independence. It is nevertheless startling to learn that a climactic aria so perfectly placed as the Flower Song in *Carmen* began life to quite different words as an aria for baritone in the unfinished *Grisélidis*; it is better known that Bizet adapted another man's tune for the Habanera, but not that he suggested most of the words for it, giving precise instructions for the metre of eight lines which the librettists had to supply. Donizetti, himself no mean comic librettist, insisted on gaining our sympathy for the otherwise rather namby-pamby Nemorino in *L'elisir d'amore* by inserting the romance 'Una furtiva lagrima', and had the music ready before Romani had agreed to its inclusion, let alone written the words. The text of Musetta's Waltz Song in *La bohème* seems to have led Puccini to a perfect characterization of its singer, but it was the melody that came first: the words interpret the characterization inherent in the tune, which was sent to Giacosa and Illica with its rhythm defined by means of the gibberish 'Cocoricò, cocoricò, bistecca'. In the case of Wagner, although he completed his librettos, read them out to admirers and published them long before he produced his first musical drafts, early verbal sketches bear marginal annotations of metre and theme which suggest that the careful arrangement of strophic

structures and metrical parallels, in passages which rise from *Sprechgesang* into balanced melody, was so conceived because he had a tune in mind from the first.

An interesting case is Bellini's relationship with Romani. Already a practised librettist, Romani sent him the following text for 'Casta diva' (*Norma*, Act 1), a strophic aria in which the priestess invokes the consolation of the moon goddess:

> Casta diva che inargenti
> Questo suol col vergin volto
> Nel tenace umor raccolto
> Spandi influsso di virtù.
>
> Sia quel balsamo alle genti
> Che le piaghe disacerbi
> Che costanti ancor le serbi
> In sì lunga servitù.

(Chaste goddess, who with your virgin countenance turn this ground to silver, wrapped in clinging mist, shed on us your strength-giving influence. Be for your people that balm which soothes our wounds, so that you may keep us faithful in such long servitude.)

These are beautiful lines, and the image evoked in Bellini's imagination is a fitting melodic correlative; but it is a tune so much greater than the words that it starts to go its own way, with wave-like phrases of invocation which demand verbal upbeats and feminine endings at the mid-line caesura that are often lacking in the verse; and it reaches a peak at the end of the third line, with repeated high b''s rising eventually to c''' (the first part of the aria was conceived in G, like the *secondo tempo*, and put down into F only later). The third line ends with the word 'raccolto', which provides a poor vowel for Bellini's climax and a literary image which has nothing to do with the main purpose of the aria: Norma is imploring the goddess not merely to sustain her enslaved people but also to forgive her own hidden guilt. The third-line climax in a four-line aria verse became a regular requirement for Verdi, but it evidently had to be explained to Romani. Bellini exemplified what he needed by suggesting alternative verses that solve some of his problems but create others:

> Casta diva che il [? 'col'] vergin volto
> Della quercia ai numi sacra
> [...] Imbianchi ...
> Spargi influssi di vertù
>
> Sia quel balsamo alle genti
> Che sollievo almeno apporti
> Che nel male ci conforti
> Della nostra servitù.

(Chaste goddess, who whiten the virgin countenance of the oak sacred to the gods, scatter your strength-giving influence. Be for your people that balm which at least brings solace, which comforts us in the evil of our servitude.)

'Imbianchi' (whiten) seems intended to produce an 'a' vowel for the top notes, but displaces 'inargenti' from line one; 'vergin volto' from line two is substituted and indeed suits the music better; 'spargi' is more open than the nasal 'spandi'. 'Della quercia ai numi sacri' makes nonsense but it provides an elision, '-cia ai' which, though it counts in metrics as one syllable, may be broken into two by a rest, giving Bellini his feminine ending at the caesura and an upbeat after it, as the music requires. He suggests a similar solution in line two of the second strophe, which has to fit an exact repeat of the music, but leaves other problems here unsolved. Once Romani had realized the musical difficulties, doubtless after further discussion and after receiving the sublime melody, he produced the following text, allowing his 'official' poetic structure to be spoilt – in the score, less so in the printed libretto – by the interpolations here bracketed. Bellini breaks the elision in line 1 at 'che in-argenti' and the mid-line elisions in lines 2 and 3; he adds a 'sì' to line 4; he accommodates strophe 2 to the music by inserting 'o diva' in line 1, replacing the truncated last syllable of 'ancora' in line 2, and interpolating 'ah' in line 3. At the climaxes, there is now an 'a' vowel ('sembiante', 'pace').

> Casta diva, che inargenti
> Queste sacre antiche piante
> A noi volgi il bel sembiante
> Senza nube [sì] e senza vel.
>
> Tempra [o diva] tu de' cori ardenti
> Tempra ancor[a] lo zelo audace
> Spargi in terra [ah] quella pace
> Che regnar tu fai nel ciel.

(Chaste goddess, who turn to silver these ancient sacred trees, direct your fair countenance on us, without cloud [yes] or veil. Restrain [o goddess], still restrain the daring zeal of our ardent hearts, scatter on earth [ah] that peace which you spread through the heavens.)

These lines have less poetic character than the originals, but they are still respectable; and they fit the music perfectly.

5. LITERARY MEN AND LIBRETTISTS. Romani was quite a distinguished literary figure outside the world of opera, yet he had the good sense and the musicality to submit to the demands of the composer. That was not common before his time, for there had been few composers of sufficient stature and authority to make such claims. From comments in his letters about various lost or aborted projects we know that Monteverdi had exacting ideas as to what was suitable for his music. Lully subjected Quinault's draft librettos to extensive revision, even after they had received the stamp of literary approval from the Académie française. Handel evidently disliked the rising rhythms so characteristic of English verse, which forced him to begin his melodies with upbeats, and cried 'Damn your iambics' when Thomas Morell presented him with 'Convey me to some peaceful shore' for the last air in *Alexander Balus* (an oratorio, but dramatic in form): Morell switched to trochaics by altering 'Convey' to 'Lead'. Voltaire, already a famous writer by 1744, when he was engaged on the libretto of *La princesse de Navarre* for Rameau, was only partly jesting when he complained that 'he orders me to put into fours everything that's in eight, and into eights everything that's in four'. Gluck, for all his public insistence on the primacy of words, sent Guillard the text of a quatrain by Metastasio that he had already set in an Italian opera and wished to re-use for 'O malheureuse Iphigénie'; he gave minute instructions about line-length and caesura, adding that 'Your last line must be sombre and solemn, if you wish it to agree with my music': the result, although the word setting is not always quite natural, was the finest aria in *Iphigénie en Tauride*.

Few of the distinguished literary men and critics who have felt moved to comment on the opera libretto have had first-hand experience of such minute marquetry or of the other limitations within which the librettist must work. When they have, they offer useful insights: Dryden, writing *King Arthur* for Purcell, knew that he must 'cramp his verses' and reduce the spoken part of the drama to a minimum so that the music would have time to expand, and that he must restrain his habitual lyric flights in writing strophes for 'the songish part'. *King Arthur* was a semi-opera, a play with musical in-

sertions, the form in which a literary writer is free to move unrestricted for much of the time in his normal medium, speech. This was the preference of Pierre Corneille, who understood the value, even in a non-musical drama, of breaking the march of his alexandrines for a lyrical, aria-like meditation (as can be seen in the 'stances' or stanzas that he employed in *Le Cid* and elsewhere). In his two plays with music, however, the music is allowed no part in the main business of the drama: it is used for masque-like, magical, allegorical or ritual purposes, for an interlude or a climactic finale, as in the English semi-operas that surely derive from his example. He knew that listeners heard words differently when they were sung, and that the qualities of a singer are not necessarily those of an actor. His 'Excuse à Ariste' (1637) may stand for the many objections to song and to sung drama that literary men have uttered. Speaking of a true poet, he says:

> Cent vers lui coûtent moins que deux mots de chanson;
> Son feu ne peut agir quand il faut qu'il s'explique
> Sur les fantasques airs d'un rêveur de musique,
> Et que, pour donner lieu de paroître à sa voix,
> De sa bizarre quinte il se fasse des lois;
> Qu'il ait sur chaque ton ses rimes ajustées,
> Sur chaque tremblement ses syllabes comptées,
> Et qu'une froide pointe à la fin d'un couplet
> En dépit de Phébus donne à l'art un soufflet:
> Enfin cette prison déplaît à son génie;
> Il ne peut rendre hommage à cette tyrannie;
> Il ne se leurre point d'animer de beaux chants,
> Et veut pour se produire avoir la clef des champs.

(A hundred lines cost him less than two words of song; his inspiration is powerless when it depends for utterance on the capricious tunes of a musical dreamer; when it must take its laws from his strange whims in order to let him show off his voice; when rhymes must be adapted to every musical inflection, syllables counted for every trill, and when a cold cadential formula at the end of every couplet flouts Apollo and gives his art a slap in the face: in the end such imprisonment offends the poet's genius; he cannot bow the knee to such tyranny; he refuses to be tempted into providing the inspiration for pretty songs and, in order to show what he can do, needs to escape into open country.)

These are irreproachable aesthetic arguments, and Corneille was perfectly justified in refusing to write any more lyrics for 'Ariste' to set to music. But many literary attacks on opera – which nearly always means on its librettos – have been motivated by reasons that had nothing to do with aesthetics or mixed in certain other important considerations. Opera is an image as well as an art. When Italian opera spread to other countries (with its Italian personnel), it was to be resisted for three reasons: as an import, as a luxury and as a threat to spoken drama. These underlie much of Addison's critique in *The Spectator*, and very probably Saint-Evremond's memorable attack on the mixed aesthetics of poetry-and-music (written in ignorance of the *tragédie en musique*, for he was banished before Lully and Quinault had invented the form). The libretto was bound to reflect the concerns of the society that paid for it, whether authoritarian, courtly and pleasure-loving or mercantile, less educated but equally pleasure-loving. Opera's concern with extremes of passion and, in the case of early French opera, its enthusiastic exhortations to free love, quite rightly drew the fire of moralists such as Bossuet, who would have banned all forms of theatre, or of Boileau and his friend the playwright Racine. All three were dependent on Louis XIV, so that Boileau was rather daring when he condemned Quinault for lending his art to the 'lubricious morality' of entertainments that celebrated the double adultery of Louis and Mme de

Montespan. Boileau's other criticisms of opera, that it cannot narrate, nor give full scope to the passions, nor accommodate sublime grandiloquence, are so obviously wide of the mark that one must suspect prejudice at work.

Another cause for proprietary dyspepsia on the part of authors was opera's almost invariable habit of taking its plots from other forms of literature. There are remarkably few librettos, at least until recent times, that are not adaptations. When the librettists turned to classical literature, history and myth, the main objections came at first from the church authorities, who feared a return to paganism and, where they could, imposed a system of censorship on published librettos (though they still had to permit the 'usual folly' of a character invoking a heathen 'dio'). But the same sources were exploited by neo-classical dramatists, and opera librettists were much more likely to pilfer from a ready-made modern play by Racine, by Pierre or Thomas Corneille or many a lesser light, than to fashion their own drama from Euripides or Tacitus. This would lead sometimes to recriminations, and certainly to unflattering literary comparisons.

Later on, with the European vogue for Richardson, librettists started to exploit the novel. The virtues of the genre naturally vanished in compression: expansive plots were curtailed so that interesting episodes vanished (though they sometimes became separate operas) and 'minor' characters – often, like Meg Merrilies, the most vividly drawn – were removed in order to concentrate on the love interest, which is often the element that least attracts the modern reader. The elaborate historical research underpinning a Waverley novel, the almost antiquarian re-creation of a former age, would survive only in the costumes and the painted canvas of the sets. The colourful demotic dialogue of the lower-class characters would be ironed out, where it survived, into standard French or Italian. No wonder that Walter Scott's expectations were low when he attended an operatic *Ivanhoe* in Paris in 1826, which was not even set to original music but was a pasticcio from Rossini. 'It was superbly got up ... but it was an opera, and, of course, the story sadly mangled, and the dialogue, in part, nonsense'. There is a regrettable weight of contempt in that 'of course'; but both Rowena and Richard the Lionheart had disappeared, while Ivanhoe was married off to Rebecca. To get everything in would have required a tetralogy on the scale of the *Ring*.

Scott had evidently come across an extreme example of arbitrary adaptation here; his resentment would have been increased by the fact that the rudimentary laws of intellectual copyright then prevailing enabled an author neither to forbid the theft of plots and ideas nor to exact payment for their use. (The situation had changed by the time Giovanni Verga sued Mascagni and his publishers over *Cavalleria rusticana*.) One wonders how Scott would have judged a more workmanlike transformation with finer music, such as Cammarano and Donizetti effected when they turned *The Bride of Lammermoor* into *Lucia di Lammermoor*. Hugo, we have noted, came to admire *Rigoletto*. Da Ponte quotes a letter from Salieri, who had given a copy of his *Le nozze di Figaro* to its progenitor, Beaumarchais, and later asked his opinion of it: '"I admired", said he, "the art of the Italian poet, in contracting so many Colpi di Scena [*coups de théâtre*] in so short a time, without the one destroying the other. Had I altered thus a comedy of

another author, I would not hesitate to call it my own work"' (1819). The aristocratic dramatist Cesare Della Valle, whose plays had been rifled, put the opposite view in 1856 when he condemned the Procrustean methods by which librettists lopped and stretched literary material in adapting it to operatic stereotypes:

Formerly people wrote dramas for music; now they write music for drama. Once, there was poetry for setting to music; now there is music to which poetry has to be fitted. Before long we shall see factories churning out pieces of theatre music, such as arias, cabalettas, romances, duets and finales, to sol-fa [syllables] – left blank, for verses to be filled in as the market requires.

6. A SECONDARY ART? Beyond these causes of authorial resentment, the question persists as to why librettists were such inveterate borrowers (of repertory operas before recent times, there is virtually none that has an entirely original plot). The use of a well-known story, whether from history or from fiction, offers great advantage to a librettist. His art is one of compression. As Andrea Maffei observed, he must construct miniature dramas which the lens of music will magnify. Narrative, local colour and historical explanations must be cut to the bone. In reducing a widely-read novel or a fashionable drama or a well-known episode from history to the dimensions of a libretto, he may be able to invoke the sense of predestination and dramatic irony familiar from the ancient Greek dramatists' use of myth. He will certainly be able to rely on the audience's bringing with them to the theatre a whole train of associations deriving from the original author's treatment of a subject, and will be spared much of the need to re-create them in time-consuming descriptions and explanations. Beaumarchais' *Le mariage de Figaro*, though banned from the stage, was nevertheless available to the Viennese public in the form of a book, notorious for its attacks on aristocratic privilege and on the injustices enshrined in French law. To make it acceptable as a court opera, Da Ponte excised all overt political comment, including the famous monologue for Figaro in his Act 4, which he turned into a bitter invective against woman's inconstancy, 'Aprite un po' quegl' occhi'. He was bold enough, all the same, to end the aria with a couplet referring the audience to the omitted material, which included mention of the Bastille and the *lettre de cachet*, from which Beaumarchais had himself suffered and which he had attacked in a number of pamphlets as famous as the play. The couplet runs:

> Il resto nol dico,
> Già ognuno lo sà.

(I won't mention the rest; everyone knows it already.)

Mozart, the greater dramatist and more interested in humanity than politics, did his best to confine the reference to the subject matter of the aria by adding a punning flourish on the horns, symbolic of cuckoldry.

A less hypothetical notion of what impressions and associations a librettist might expect his audience to bring to the opera house may be gained from Flaubert's *Madame Bovary* (1857), where the heroine attends a performance of *Lucie de Lammermoor* in provincial Rouen. Though fiction, the scene is shrewdly and realistically observed. This image of opera as an escape from the restrictions of bourgeois life into a world of strong but vague and unanchored feeling is crucially placed at the turning-point of the novel, since Emma's husband, after disgracing himself with his comically uncomprehending remarks, re-introduces her to the cause of her downfall, Léon, whom he has met in the bar.

Flaubert also gives a remarkable account of matters that emphasize how much more there is to the reception of libretto and music in a live theatre than any purely critical and textual analysis can encompass: the effect of the scenery and costumes, and of the star singer as a focus of unexpendable sexual desire. After wondering at the strangeness of the Scottish décor and costumes, Emma 'found herself once more amid her girlhood reading, *en plein Walter Scott* … her memory of the novel assisting her understanding of the libretto, she could follow the plot phrase by phrase, while thoughts kept coming back to her which she could not hold on to, for they would vanish immediately in the gusts of music'.

Not all great writers have understood opera so well. The scene recalls another, equally symbolic and equally crucially placed, which must have been written in imitation of Flaubert's, where Countess Natasha Rostova attends an unnamed and unidentifiable opera in Tolstoy's *War and Peace* (see Lowe 1990). Tolstoy hated opera for its empty luxury, believing that it stupefied the mind and feelings just as tobacco and alcohol stupefied the body. He probably also knew Carlyle's apoplectic essay on a Rossini performance, which horrified him in its waste of money and of rare talent, and in its perversion, for frivolous ends, of the God-given art of song (1852). Carlyle and his admirer Tolstoy were, as critics, social moralists, but other important writers have seen Italian opera, with its enormous output of librettos of low intrinsic artistic value, as a kind of literary immorality, pandering to popular demand and standing in the way of the development of Italian tragedy in its spoken form. This was the burden of the complaints by the tragic dramatist Scipione Maffei and other members of the Arcadian movement. It explains Alfieri's contempt for Metastasio, expressed in his satire *L'educazione*, through the mouth of a nobleman instructing a domestic tutor about the reading suitable for his daughter. She will finish up in a convent anyway, but meanwhile 'let her skim through the odd book, especially Metastasio's *ariette*, which she's dotty about, so that she'll teach herself':

> Farete leggicchiar di quando in quando;
> Metastasio … le ariette; ella n'è pazza.
> Là si va da sè stesso esercitando …

During the period of the Risorgimento, opera was to play an honourable part in raising national consciousness, but it is curious that Mazzini, who was an aesthetician and critic of music as well as a political activist, should have failed to see a new role for the chorus as symbolizing the people, so that he praised Donizetti and ignored the potential of Verdi. Laudable political intent, however, does not guarantee literary excellence, and complaints about over-production and hack-work continued through the 19th century. The literary historian Bocecardon categorized the libretto as 'la miseria della patria letteratura' ('wretchedness of our national literature', *Enciclopedia italiana*, 6/1881). Yet some who came to mock stayed on to cheer. Carducci, who wrote that libretto writing was 'a pimp's trade, to be left to street porters' ('roba da ruffiano … abbandonare ai facchini'), wished later in his life to engage in it. D'Annunzio, a man of unusual musical discrimination, said in 1887 that opera was 'a sterile, illogical and useless form', suitable only 'for those who are superannuated, out of date and unable to recover' ('forma sterile pei sorpassati, trascorsi e incapaci di risorgere e illogico e inutile'); in his youth, he would no

doubt have preferred the Wagnerian model to the Italian, but he proposed a *Rosa di Cipro* to Puccini in 1906, and from 1912 enthusiastically tailored plays into librettos, some of them for Pizzetti.

Librettists themselves were often defensive about the need to earn a living by producing works that an uneducated public would pay to see, and Rolandi (1951) and Fabbri (1990) cite many prefaces from 17th-century Venetian librettos in which such poets as Cicognini, Sbarra and even Zeno proclaim, sometimes without apology, that the market must rule. In 18th-century France, Fuzelier and others said much the same. Poets of higher ambition who produced librettos on the side sometimes disguised their identities, or disclaimed librettos as products of their true selves, by anagrammatizing their names. In the 17th century, Giulio Strozzi became 'Luigi Zorzisto' and Matteo Giannini 'Ignatio Teomagnini', while Francesco Antonio Tullio became triply anonymous as 'Col'Antuono Feralintisco', 'Tertulliano Fonsaconico' and 'Filostrato Lucano Cinneo'. Later and more famous figures disguised themselves as 'Luciano Lantino' (Antonio Villani), 'Partenio Chriter' or 'Terentio Chirrap' (Pietro Trinchera), 'Loran Glodici' (Carlo Goldoni), 'Valsini' (F. Silvani) and eventually 'Tobia Gorrio' (Arrigo Boito). In France, Truinet became 'Nuitter', and eventually the fashion spread to include the theatre historian Giovanni Salvioli ('Livio Niso Galvani', 'Luigi Lianovasani').

These were literary men who did not wish their occasional role as librettist to be confused with that of the poor professional theatre-poet, engaged by the management to provide librettos, or more often to doctor librettos written by others, subject to the contrary demands of singers, composers and impresarios, compelled also to act as stage director, stage manager and general factotum. He was paid a pittance (for Piave's duties and remuneration at La Scala, Milan, see Cassi-Ramelli 1973). It is not surprising to find Da Ponte telling us that 'poet of the opera house and idiot were at a certain time synonymous among the learned of London' (1819). The theatre poet cuts a poor figure in the many depictions of theatrical life that we find, not only in avowedly anti-operatic satirical pamphlets such as Benedetto Marcello's hugely entertaining *Il teatro alla moda* but also in a host of comic operas from Metastasio's *L'impresario delle Canarie* through Calzabigi's *L'opera seria* (1769, one of the earliest uses – ironic – of the genre title) and Bertati's *Il capriccio drammatico* (1787, whose second part is the source libretto for Da Ponte's *Don Giovanni*) to Donizetti's own libretto for *Le convenienze teatrali* (1827). But behind all the in-house jokes there is always the sense of what opera might be and should be. In Calzabigi's riotous libretto for *L'opera seria* the Poet for once stands up for himself and tries to prevent cuts which make nonsense of the plot; it is the Impresario who is satirized when he replies

> Questo che importa?
> Son già più di trenta anni che non s'usa
> di legger le parole: e se una scena
> coll'altra non si unisce
> il discreto uditorio vi supplisce.

(What does that matter? People stopped reading the words 30 years ago; and if one scene doesn't follow on from another, the audience knows how to bridge the gap.)

Such comments and others like them, particularly Marcello's, make tasty reading and tend to be repeated in popular histories of opera (mainly concerned with later periods) with a frequency that hardly reflects their true weight or significance. They certainly show a dissatisfaction with the working conditions and lack of autonomy of the less privileged type of librettist, as also do the riotous burlesques of opera in the *parodies* of the Théâtre de la Foire, of Henry Carey or Nestroy; but it would be foolish to regard them as a kind of negative aesthetic, governing whole periods and genres. Competent librettists may never have been common, though the general level of literary attainment in opera was perhaps no worse than in Grub Street at large. Lame or stilted words, however, acquire a new dimension of bathos when they are sung. An indifferent play or novel may be left unread in decent obscurity, but to hear operas by Handel, Mozart or Verdi we must accept their poets, even if we are aware that Rolli, Schikaneder or Piave were not as discriminating in their art as the composer was in his.

Such an assessment is not made on purely literary grounds; nor does it seriously affect the standing of the durable masterpieces that resulted from unequal collaborations. We are entitled, though, to measure them against more evenly balanced partnerships, some of which were long-lasting: Lully and Quinault, Gluck and Calzabigi, Mozart and Da Ponte, Bellini and Romani, Wagner and Wagner, Verdi and Boito, Stravinsky and Auden-Kallman, and many would say Strauss and Hofmannsthal. Several of these poets wrote other librettos, set by other composers, in collaborations that proved more ephemeral or at least are less highly regarded. Similarly, there have been partnerships where librettos of a high standard have not evoked imperishable music to match them: Metastasio and Hasse, Goldoni and Galuppi, Zola and Bruneau; some would add Brecht and Weill. Whatever one may say about the literary standard of a libretto or about its potential for music, the ultimate badge of quality has to be that it found a composer who knew what to do with it, whether the result was an effective minor opera or an imaginative masterpiece.

It is easy, nevertheless, to underestimate the importance of opera as seen from the world of literature. Many figures whose present international fame derives entirely from their librettos would prefer to have been remembered in some more independent, purely literary capacity. The Arcadian librettists considered themselves playwrights, not librettists, and published their *drammi per musica* in carefully collected editions from which all mention of music and opera was excised, including the 'da capo' indications in the aria verses; a friend of Zeno's even advised him to remove the arias and replace them with lengthened dialogue. Metastasio was proud that his librettos were not merely read but acted without their music, omitting the arias, which might be admired on their own (and rightly) as lyric verse. It is surprising too, considering how frequently the more distinguished writers of the 17th and 18th centuries apologized for their involvement with opera, to discover that over 60 of them were in fact pleased enough with their librettos to preserve them in collected editions – sometimes, admittedly, under a self-deprecating title such as Busenello's *Delle hore ociose* ('Idle Hours'). No doubt there was the further motive that these authentic texts might preserve something of the poet's reputation amid the multitude of single librettos issued each time his work was re-set in a version garbled by some other hand. There was

nevertheless pride at work, and a belief that the libretto offered a viable literary medium in its own right.

Librettos might be issued unset and unperformed, and not merely as exemplars in a work of criticism, like the *Iphigénie en Aulide* or the sketch for *Enea in Troia* in Algarotti's *Saggio sopra l'opera in musica*: G. G. Boccherini published at least two, and the French poet A.-L. Le Brun a whole *Théâtre lyrique* (1712), comprising six tragedies and a pastoral, intended purely for reading; Quinault's opera texts, of course, had long been read for their own sake.

Librettists who did not earn a humble living as a theatre poet or through some other direct connection with opera – impresarios, singers, dancers, theatrical agents, even copyists, and of course composers – were not normally opera specialists but literary men. As such, they supported themselves, where writing alone did not suffice, by an amazing variety of trades and professions, especially the learned professions and diplomacy, though the full range of occupations ranges from gondolier, lithographer and embroiderer, through the army and navy, banking, politics, the church (a surprising number, from friar to pope), and amateurs, from Saint-Saëns' cousin and Humperdinck's sister to dukes, kings and a tsar. Many of the more productive librettists, such as Romani, Ghislanzoni and Boito, made their income from journalism, criticism or editing. But the roster of those who produced fewer or less well-known librettos, sometimes only one, or who can be shown to have drafted librettos or offered them, includes a remarkable number of illustrious names, some important only to their time or country, but many of lasting international fame. The list is a valuable corrective to the notion that the libretto is of scant literary worth, or of no interest to literary historians.

In Italy there are Rinuccini, Chiabrera, G. Strozzi, Busenello, C. M. Maggi, C. I. Frugoni, P. A. Chiari, Baretti, Casti, Parini, A. Maffei, Pascoli, D'Annunzio and Pirandello. In France, P. Corneille, T. Corneille, Racine and Boileau (a *Phaëton*, destroyed save for part of the Prologue), Molière, La Fontaine, Fontenelle, Le Sage, Diderot, Voltaire, Marmontel, J.-J. Rousseau, Beaumarchais, T. Gautier, Hugo, C. Mendès, Dumas père, G. de Nerval, A. de Vigny, Zola, Apollinaire, Cocteau, Claudel, Colette and Valéry. In German-speaking lands: Opitz, Herder, Frederick the Great (versified by others), Wieland, Goethe, Collin, Grillparzer, E. T. A. Hoffmann, Tieck, Brentano, Nestroy, Hofmannsthal, Zweig, Kaiser and Brecht. In English-speaking lands: Ben Jonson (masques), Dryden, Congreve, Gay, Fielding, Sheridan, Dickens, Arnold Bennett, Edgar Wallace, E. M. Forster, W. H. Auden, Ezra Pound, Gertrude Stein and Thornton Wilder. Spain offers Lope de Vega and Calderón de la Barca, Denmark H. C. Andersen, and Norway Bjørnsen, while Ibsen toyed with librettos as a young man. Further east we find Čapek, Béla Balász, and in Russia Ostrovsky, Turgenev, Nemirovich-Danchenko and Chekhov (an offer to Tchaikovsky). If we extend the list to include literary men who, like many of the above, have brought unusual insights to bear in writing about opera, we must include Defoe, Chastellux, Schiller, T. L. Peacock, Sand, De Musset, Stendhal, Meredith, G. B. Shaw, Werfel and Mann.

It is perhaps to be regretted that the example of Wagner and Berlioz (hardly true poets, but effective craftsmen) led so many later composers to follow their lead and write their own librettos, partly through pride and partly because musical style grew ever more individual and idiosyncratic. There were very few composer-librettists in or before this time, though Cammarano suggested in a letter to Verdi of 1849 that it would solve many problems if the two functions were combined in a single intelligence. There are nevertheless isolated figures of some distinction, even if they do not constitute a tradition: in the 17th century, Stefano Landi, Loreto Vittori, Benedetto Ferrari and a little later A. and G. B. Draghi; in the 18th, G. M. Buini, Arne, Dittersdorf and Charles Dibdin. Donizetti and Lortzing were more recent examples.

Once Wagner had made the idea seem almost a necessity, however, the trickle became a flood: Boito, Borodin, Bruneau, Bungert, Cornelius, Cui, Dargomïzhky, d'Indy, Glinka, Goetz, Leoncavallo, Musorgsky, Ponchielli, Rimsky-Korsakov, Tchaikovsky, Siegfried Wagner, Weingartner and Zöllner (though not all would have been directly inspired by Wagner); later, Blacher, Busoni, Charpentier, Dallapiccola, Egk, Henze, Hindemith, Janáček, Krenek, A. Lualdi, Malipiero, Maxwell Davies, Menotti, Orff, Pizzetti, Prokofiev, Sauguet, Schoenberg, Schreker, Ethel Smyth, Strauss and Tippett. Some of these also wrote or worked on librettos for other composers (Leoncavallo, Egk, Menotti); some also adapted plays for their own use, most notably Debussy, Strauss and Berg. Composers might at times suggest verses which their librettists were happy to take on board (Bizet; Puccini with Liù's aria in *Turandot*).

Many of the above proved very competent; others seem decidedly to fumble. One would not go so far as to say of the composer who acts as his own librettist that, like the man who acts in court as his own lawyer, he has a fool for a client. There are plenty of examples of well-known poets letting their composers down by inexperience in the theatre, let alone the specialized medium of opera, and T. S. Eliot gave shrewd advice to Tippett when he refused a request for a libretto and told him to consider writing his own because the poets 'are going to do with the words what your music should do'. All the same, opera has gained in earlier periods from the challenge of matching new literary techniques with appropriate music, and has always been alive to new trends and sometimes unconsciously-sensed new directions in literary sensibility. But writing one's own libretto brings the danger of isolation, if not of literary naivety. Composers may be intellectuals, but the evidence seems to suggest that they are not commonly skilled creative writers; however sensitive they may be to language, their literary tastes will often have become fixed at a fairly early age, after which development is rare or slow. Berlioz's *Les Troyens* is a case in point: the music is modern for its time, but the language of the libretto is that of an earlier generation. Wagner's ability to rethink the whole basis of opera and to forge an appropriate new verbal medium from medieval *Stabreim* or 16th-century *Knittelvers* remains unique.

It was not merely a desire to evoke the world of the medieval Germanic epic, or of Hans Sachs's Nuremberg, that led Wagner to adopt modern equivalents for antique verse-forms. Nor was it simply his vision of a new kind of continuously-developing motivic texture, able to span whole scenes and acts and support a libretto more like a play than had been possible hitherto. He knew that *Sprechgesang*, speech-song, would need to rise to peaks of expressive melody at climactic points, and that he must somehow escape from the straitjacket

of his *Lohengrin* verse. He ruefully admitted that its decasyllabics had too often forced his tunes into repetitive moulds such as the one he cites (ex.4). Compare this

Ex.4

squareness with the flexible, subtle, intensely expressive phrasing of Wotan's 'Muss ich dich meiden' or 'Der Augen leuchtendes Paar', in Act 3 of *Die Walküre*. It cannot be proved that the melodic impulse in such passages did not exist in his mind before he conceived the words, but the question of priority does not affect the fact that it is the melody, not the words, that endows such moments with their immortality.

Whoever writes the libretto for an opera must acknowledge that, unless the form changes beyond recognition, melodic and musical forces must play the primary role in shaping its success. Composers must assert themselves. Rossini, a great master who never found an ideal librettist partner but was compelled to work with almost as many poets as he wrote operas, is said to have stated that 'if the composer follows the sense of the words step by step he will compose music that is inexpressive, impoverished, vulgar, made like a mosaic, inconsequent and ridiculous'. The opposite thought was expressed by a later librettist, Louis Gallet: 'A libretto is a work in verse which is entrusted to a composer to be turned into prose' – a paradox that is witty on the surface only, for in essence the reverse is true. A more balanced, if gnomic view comes from Verdi, who was much more willing to experiment with form than Rossini: 'For theatrical works it is necessary that poets and composers should have the talent to produce neither poetry, nor music'. But perhaps the last word should come from a leading poet of our own age, W. H. Auden, whose love of opera and fascination with verse technique led him to become, with his collaborator Chester Kallman, the finest librettist of modern times. There is of course more to it than his modesty suggests, but the thought is found as early as Lessing, and the author of the unrepeatable *Rake's Progress* must be heard with respect (Auden 1952; in Weisstein 1964):

The verses which the librettist writes are not addressed to the public, but are really a private letter to the composer. They have their moment of glory, the moment in which they suggest to him a certain melody: once that is over, they are as expendable as infantry to a Chinese general: they must efface themselves and cease to care what happens to them.

II. Historical survey

1. The first operas and their context. 2. Italian librettos to c1730. 3. French opera to c1760. 4. Italian reforms. 5. Italian comic opera to 1800. 6. Vernacular opera in England, Germany and Spain. 7. French popular opera. 8. The 19th century and beyond. 9. German Romantic opera and its legacy. 10. The 'number opera' and alternative paths.

1. THE FIRST OPERAS AND THEIR CONTEXT. The art of opera has complex origins, but it is no accident that the first successful attempts to find a way of setting an entire dramatic action to music should have taken place around 1600 at the grand-ducal court of Medicean Florence. The city had played a leading role in Renaissance humanism since the 14th century and still housed quasi-classical 'academies' such as the Alterati

and the societies (in which Count Bardi was a prime mover) collectively known as the 'Camerata', where humanists, poets and musicians met to debate and experiment. A principal interest of the latter was an attempt to understand the lost world of ancient Greek music: what had 'harmony', 'number' and 'metre' meant to the ancients, and what kinds of melody had resulted when different types of Greek verse were sung? Theirs was no purely 'academic' inquiry: in attempting to recover the lost ethical power of Greek music, they resolved to conduct practical experiments; elements of a theory designed for quantitative Greek verse were applied to modern Italian poetry, which relied not on quantity and the classical 'feet' but upon number and the counting of syllables. At first they turned to the epic verse of Dante, but then decided to attempt a whole play; and this was not a translated Greek tragedy, as one might have expected, but a specially written piece in the modern and non-classical form of a pastoral drama.

While allowing due weight to their antiquarian interests, it is equally important to recognize the urge of the Camerata to innovate; this places them in relation to the contemporary ferment of new scientific thought which also radiated from Florence. Galileo Galilei's father, the musician Vincenzo, had contributed early on to the Camerata's discussions, both as thinker and as composer; and Bardi himself was later to conduct experiments in physics.

The ruling house of Florence, the Medici, formed the third element necessary for the creation of opera; they provided the milieu, the personnel and the money that allowed the recherché private experiments of a tiny intellectual and musical élite to take wing as an expensive and highly professional public entertainment. The first full opera, *Euridice* (1600), formed part of the celebrations surrounding a royal wedding, so that the art took its place as another genre in the series of festive entertainments – plays, comedies with interludes, concerts, jousts, balls, ballets, even horse-ballets and tattoos – with which a ruling house commemorated its joyful occasions. Opera remained the exclusive property of princes and magnates for nearly 40 years, and even after the creation of public opera houses it was the courtly opera of France and Vienna that continued to dictate the new art's aesthetic and iconology until the last quarter of the 18th century. Whether by design or not, the creators of opera had gained entry to a citadel of unparalleled power, wealth and prestige.

No doubt this was done merely with an eye to the main chance, for the first operas are unheroic pastorals, and celebrate the virtues of patrons only briefly, in their prologues. But the creative members among the Camerata had all gained their first experience of theatrical music by participating in such sumptuous Medicean *feste* as the musical *intermedi* ending each act of Bargagli's *La pellegrina* (1589). These contain monodies, one of them sung 'with marvellous art' by the composer of *Dafne* and most of *Euridice* (as first performed), Jacopo Peri. They also contain elaborate choruses, mostly homophonic, which would have taught the first opera-makers the summative and punctuative value of placing a chorus, or indeed any unit in a more rounded and closed form, at the final climax of a scene. (The interludes had in fact no connection with the drama, but there is evidence that the courtiers were often bored with plays and tolerated them mainly for the periodic excitement of the musical interruptions.) One of the *intermedi* of 1589, represent-

ing the combat of Apollo with the Python, was to be adapted and lengthened by the poet Ottavio Rinuccini into the first opera, *Dafne* (1597), of which the music is almost entirely lost. Other members of the Camerata involved in the 1589 festivities were Emilio de' Cavalieri, composer of *La Rappresentatione di Anima, et di Corpo* (1600, Rome), a sacred and entirely allegorical work, in some ways resembling opera; and Francesco Caccini, a famous singing teacher who contributed to *Euridice* and later, like Peri, published an entire setting of his own. Though many of these men belonged, like the amateur composer Count Corsi, to the minor nobility, none was amateurish in his art: all were leaders in their professions.

The musicians may nevertheless have held a kind of subaltern status in the Camerata, as they did in other Italian academies; one of the academies' functions was simply to give concerts. The intellectual lead would mainly have been taken by the learned members, humanists such as Mei and poets such as Rinuccini and Tasso, who were abreast of the latest intellectual tendencies. Sometimes such tendencies were subversive of received ideas, which caused certain academies and their members to mask their activities by adopting strange or ridiculous names. Italian academies were important but often mysterious agents in early opera. Monteverdi's *Orfeo* was performed by the Invaghiti ('Lovestruck') of Mantua; the Incogniti ('Unknowns') of Venice, certainly a set of freethinkers in a city which had protected the heterodox Paolo Sarpi, provided most of the librettos for early operas in Venice. The adoption of classical culture, forms and norms meant the adoption of the old Greco-Roman gods and of elements of pagan philosophy, a feature of 17th- and 18th-century opera that constantly troubled the church authorities. It is interesting, though, that in the 16th century these same church authorities, whether Lutheran or counter-reformatory, had shared the humanists' preoccupation with the clear and understandable musical presentation of words (which involved the suppression or restriction of imitative counterpoint). Their motives were not entirely dissimilar: it was no longer God alone or the singers of individual voice-parts who were to hear and understand the words, but a congregation of mute listeners observing the performance from the outside, whose hearts and minds were to be moved, both individually and collectively: an audience, whether sacred or secular. It was no accident that opera and its sacred equivalent, oratorio, were born at the same time. Many later librettists, such as Zeno and Metastasio, provided texts for both, and many composers felt equally at home in opera and in dramatic oratorio (which was however presented, like the serenata, without action).

Rinuccini's audience was used to plays, but the ladies would not have been permitted to attend comedies such as Machiavelli's immodest *La mandragola*, nor the *commedia dell'arte*, which could be even cruder. Tragedies were rare, certainly as court events, for neither rulers nor the ecclesiastical authorities thought that moral matters and the behaviour of the great were fit subjects for public show and debate. (Humanist attempts to revive Greek tragedy, sometimes in translation, had not proved popular, though Andrea Gabrieli had composed the choruses for an *Oedipus tyrannus* in Vicenza in 1585.) The pastoral play had for some time been the favourite form of court entertainment. Its subject matter was usually love, innocent, virginal love set in the Golden Age among shepherd folk, with none of the true-life trappings of marriage settlements and adultery often surrounding erotic experience in a society that married for money, power or dynastic ambition. Its appeal to the ladies was real but safe; its simple morality would no doubt have consoled those who had endured or suppressed love-longings, without forcing them to confront the choice that Mme de Lafayette's more realistic heroine the Princess of Cleves would have to make. In *Dafne*, the sinful desire of Apollo for the river nymph results, not in the avenging of the assault, still less in a lawsuit, but in the magical transformation of the victim into a laurel. The problem is not solved but suspended. Apollo will continue to love without attaining Daphne, and she will remain undeflowered, but no one else shall love her now. Transmuted, she shall provide wreaths to crown heroes and poets, such as her would-be ravisher, now repentant. Rinuccini's verse, seconded by Peri's (and also Corsi's) music, has frozen the god of lyric poetry, in his too-mortal shape and behaviour, into a symbol of mortal longing for the untouchable virgin, whose fear of man and role as inspirer have also been immortalized; the generalizing power of art has gone a stage further, and the human story has become a symbol for the unsatisfied desire, and fear of desire, on which post-Renaissance poetry and music so often feed. Capturing this in a structured, finite, temporal form, transforming it into art, helps us to live with our condition.

That is the pastoral equivalent of Aristotle's description of the effect of tragedy, which he thought purged the emotions by sympathetic feelings of pity and terror. Full tragedy does not enter the pastoral world; the undeserved and accidental death of Eurydice may elicit pity, but terror does not come into play. Yet the pastoral can accommodate loss, and loss by death, among the feelings centring around love, and contemporary theorists recognized early on that it was a mixed genre, *tragicommedia* or *ilarotragedia*; it also came to accept elements of the comic as we understand the term today, and take in the more realistic and amusing aspects of lowly rustic life. But the classical pastoral had not done this, and Rinuccini and Striggio (librettist of Monteverdi's *Orfeo*) did not indulge such a taste.

The libretto of *Dafne*, short and episodic though it is, proved successful and even durable, though its first performances were experimental and simple and were not backed by the purse of a courtly festivity. The text was reset, somewhat adapted, by the Florentine Marco da Gagliano in Mantua in 1608; translated and further adapted by Martin Opitz, it became the first German opera in Schütz's setting (1627) and was set again in that form later in the century.

Two further considerations ensured that early opera revolved around divinities and the pastoral. One was symbolic: the first operatic protagonists, Apollo and Orpheus, were poet-musicians, surely selected as fitting oracles to introduce the new art of opera. Allied to that is the fact that Apollo is a god and Orpheus of divine descent, and that their stories take place among shepherds, who were believed to have invented song.

The revolutionary step in the first operas was to expect an audience to accept the entirely new convention that the whole unfolding argument of a play could be presented in accompanied song, that a dramatic character could 'recitar cantando', act while singing. A song in a play is normally what a song is in real life, and will be introduced plausibly, whatever its symbolic intent or value in characterization or the creation of atmosphere. But sung dialogue, in metres unlike those used for songs, was familiar to Peri's audiences only in forms remoter from opera than is commonly supposed, liturgical drama and the Passion (where the ritual context, however, provides a significant parallel) and the polyphonic madrigal comedy (where several singers impersonate the speech of a single character, commonly in homophonic declamation). The first theorists of opera, writing around 1640, still say that librettists should stick to personages such as celestial and infernal deities, shepherds, mages reciting incantatory spells, and so forth, who may realistically be accepted as uttering their thoughts in song. To hear a historical personage singing dialogue, 'especially one known to the audience', would evoke laughter. Once the crucial step had been taken and the new convention created, however, it was not long before any kind of character might sing on stage; the first personages taken from secular history appear in opera in the 1640s; the most famous, but not the earliest, are those in Busenello's *L'incoronazione di Poppea*. In the years around 1600, the entire audience shared the prejudice against sung drama still familiar from the naive reaction of many a modern first-time operagoer. In fact, Rinuccini's first librettos attempt to make the recitative, conducted in the seven- and eleven-syllable lines that became standard practice for centuries, resemble as closely as possible the more conventional song-like verses of the choral strophes: it is almost all rhymed in the manner of madrigal verse. Yet 'blank', unrhymed verse (*versi sciolti*) was by then familiar in the Italian theatre as a medium which, though metrical, was felt to be close to prose and well suited to the developing thought of dramatic argument: it was to hand, and he chose not to use it. Later librettists moved more and more to *versi sciolti*, and reserved rhyme in recitative for moments of particular importance, or in order to elevate the tone and claim attention at the approach to an aria, rather as Shakespeare employs a rhymed couplet to end a scene.

Later librettists, however, were working in an environment where frequent arias were expected, and the contrast between these and the surrounding recitative was to be emphasized. Rinuccini avoids such incongruity of style. Strophes are used in *Euridice* only for the prologue and the choruses. The latter, which sometimes imply dancing, are placed at the ends of scenes and mark a division of the drama into five short acts (not named as such). Playing out the action before a chorus of Thracians suggests the Greek drama; but the placing of the choruses perhaps owes more to the author's experience of *intermedi*.

What were the traditions of writing verses (stanzas, or strophes) for a repeating musical form (aria)? If the poet expects each of his strophes to be set to the same closed and rounded musical unit, then each must keep to the same number of lines with the same number of syllables in corresponding lines, and normally to the same rhyme scheme as well. The mid-line breaks (caesuras) should ideally be identical from strophe to strophe, and the sense should normally pause at the end of each line (end-stopping). These requirements have to be met if the composer wishes to set the verse to a repeating vocal melody, as the English poet Daniel pointed out in a discussion, printed in 1603, of the sung lyric: tunes were made of phrases which had to end with cadences, the musical equivalent of punctuation. If the composer wishes to set the strophes as recitative, he will write the vocal lines as free declamation over a repeating bass pattern determining the harmony: cadences will commonly fall at the same points in the course of each strophe, but the durations of the bass notes may be varied: this technique, known as strophic variation, may of course be forced on the musician if the poet has not provided strophes so contrived that all will fit the same vocal melody.

Of the strophes in *Euridice*, all save those of the final chorus employ the same seven- or eleven-syllable lines used in the recitative. Unity of tone is paramount, and the only difference lies in the regular arrangement of metre and rhyme in the strophes and in the occasional repetition of lines to provide a refrain. The privilege of aria strophes is not yet extended to the solo singers; monologues such as Orpheus's 'Funeste piaggi', or the narrative descriptions of offstage actions delivered by Daphne or Arcetro (imitating the 'Messenger scenes' of antique drama), are uttered in recitative. In short, Rinuccini has made no concessions to the composer beyond those that a Greek dramatist might have made in the provision of matching choral strophes. In other respects he has largely followed the traditions established in pastoral drama by Tasso and Guarini, together with a type of verse favoured by madrigalists; he has not even trimmed his lengthier allocutions to take account of music's tendency to stretch out the words and make it hard for the listener to follow long grammatical constructions. His principal concern has been to inaugurate an art no longer experimental by reinterpreting the most potent and appropriate of all antique myths, that of Orpheus; but he has changed its end – no longer a tragedy nor an apotheosis – to show how human faith, expressed through the combined arts, can redeem and immortalize ideal beauty (Eurydice, now the title role). He has enshrined this in language so noble that it was revisited not only by literary and musical historians, but also by librettists, for nearly two centuries (Sternfeld 1993).

What does the music add, apart from the novelty of the experiment? First of all, still greater unity of tone, modest though its contribution to the recitative undoubtedly is: we do not have to adjust our mode of listening between the choruses and the rest of the drama, as we would if the recitative were spoken. (The junction between speech and music can still jar, in *Die Zauberflöte* or *Fidelio* just as much as in a modern musical, and not only because singers rarely speak as well as actors and must often declaim in languages foreign to them; the mixture of speech and song presents aesthetic problems which the Italians, unlike other Europeans, have never been prepared to countenance.) Recitative also allows the whole proceeding to take place in an acoustic favourable to concerted vocal and instrumental music. A resonant acoustic offers difficulties for the sliding, imprecisely pitched intonations of speech. Focus the words on a monotone, or on the euphonious intervals of slow-moving triadic harmony, and the otherwise conflicting reverberations of the vowels and voiced consonants come into focus.

To underpin its own verbal music, the verse of *Euridice* demands mainly pathos, majesty and a sense of ritual from the composer and the singers, and these the modest talents of Peri and Caccini were able to supply. They provided almost nothing, compared with Monteverdi, towards the deeper organization or varied pacing of the recitative and the illustration of character and emotion. It was the literary value of Rinuccini's verse that ensured the survival of the new genre (though

new operas were infrequent until 1637); but no later poet attempting the high style in courtly opera could come near his excellence, so that audiences found recitative increasingly tedious, and non-literary values came to matter much more than at first. Further, singers were not actors (Peri himself, by all accounts, was a rather strange-looking and eccentric individual): their art lay in the singing voice, and their task was to interpret the verse in syllabic values and intonations fixed by the composer (and at a somewhat slower speed than an actor's recitation). Their powers of fascination were vocal, not histrionic, and they built on their strength: even in the non-melodious recitative of *Euridice*, as Peri's and Caccini's prefaces make clear, Vittoria Archilei was applauded for introducing ornamentation, 'long flights of the voice': vocal virtuosity, which the composers clearly regarded as expressive and dramatic, was even then asserting itself at the expense of pure prosody, and was soon – and justifiably – to demand greater scope in a form specifically devoted to it, the solo aria.

Strophic arias, often incorporating internal repeats, were common in the music of the time but found their way into opera rather slowly. Poets were used to supplying appropriate texts for the lighter forms associated with the madrigal such as the canzonetta, dance-forms such as the *balletto* (fitted for the stage, and in line with ancient Greek practice), and later the monodic madrigal. The other leading librettist of court opera, Chiabrera, was famous for developing a variety of new metrical forms of the lighter kind familiar from Monteverdi's *Scherzi*, but used them little in his stage librettos. The memorable qualities of a closed tune were evidently important to the Roman practice of oratorio, in which pleasure was used to make piety attractive, and there are many strophic constructions in Manni's libretto for *La Rappresentatione di Anima, et di Corpo* (mostly in seven-syllable verse, with some elevens). Even dialogue is conducted in this way. The example was not lost on the poets of early Roman opera, Rospigliosi, Tronsarelli and the composer-librettists Landi and Vittori, and no doubt played its part in the framing of the first opera which may be revived today without apology or explanation, Monteverdi's *Orfeo* (1607).

Its librettist, Alessandro Striggio, was a court official socially superior to Monteverdi; but his father had been a distinguished madrigalist and he was plainly willing to accommodate the desires of his composer. It would have been his own idea to invoke the shade of Dante by suddenly changing into *terza rima* at the approach to Hades (including the famous strophic variations of 'Possente spirto'); but the frequent use of repeating strophic forms for the shepherds' rejoicings (some danced) and invocations of the gods, and for Orpheus's songs – not to mention the many opportunities for instrumental symphonies and ritornellos, played by a much larger ensemble than earlier operas had employed – must surely have been Monteverdi's idea. The composer even introduces repeats of lines, to make a more rounded musical form, beyond what was envisaged in the printed libretto (in 'Vi ricorda, o bosch' ombrosi'). The recitative, however, remains the backbone of the dramatic experience. Particularly in the first three acts of the five, Monteverdi shows how verse inferior to Rinuccini's may be lifted by music so as to provide a communal theatrical experience deeper than any that a literary reading or spoken drama can normally invoke. Opera as we know it is born here.

Striggio made Orpheus the protagonist, and kept to classical authority by reintroducing the second loss of Eurydice and, at first, the tragic ending, in which Orpheus renounced love and was torn to pieces by Maenads. The music for the latter is lost (unless the Moresca formed part of it), and the revised ending is an apotheosis, also on classical lines: Apollo, Orpheus's father, takes him up to heaven, where his lyre becomes a constellation. The traditional view of the allegory, retailed by Boethius, tells us that the poet must not look back on the darkness of worldly things (Hades and its possessions, including the love of woman) but must seek the divine light. The eventual result was a story that had two endings, the human one tragic, the apotheosis triumphant.

For his second opera, *Arianna* (1608), Monteverdi had the benefit of a libretto by Rinuccini, his best. Unlike *Orfeo*, written for an academy though performed at court, *Arianna* was a wedding opera; the subject may have been selected because it was presented by Catullus (poem LXIV, lines 50–264) as a story embroidered on the coverlet of the nuptial couch of Thetis (who married the mortal Peleus, the topic of a later Mantuan libretto by Agnelli which Monteverdi refused to set). As in *Orfeo*, the desire of the collaborators was to show a drama rather than to recount it, but this time the main personages are royal. The plot is still a unity, but the leading characters are noble visitors to the island of Naxos: in place of a society of shepherd kinsfolk and acquaintances, those who witness the story of Theseus and Ariadne are a group of strangers, lowly fisherfolk, whose choruses do more than mark act divisions; they address minor characters, and even intervene in Ariadne's famous lament, with a distanced yet sympathetic commentary far more like that of a Greek chorus. (They are also able to appear as Theseus's sailors or Bacchus's followers.) The central emphasis, though, falls on Ariadne's recitative, partly organized through verbal repeats, in which an innocent protagonist protests against an undeserved injustice. Again, her suffering is recompensed by apotheosis, through marriage to a god. The single surviving fragment, Ariadne's lament, is so fine that it is easy to understand why the opera was revived in Venice. With the joint authority of Rinuccini and Monteverdi behind it, *Arianna* must have been regarded as an exemplary work. Its lament established a popular topos, and was directly imitated by the poet Salvadori in *La regina Sant'Orsola* (1624). Its prologue too set a new fashion for using two or more characters: after the customary address by a single personage, in this case Apollo, there is a scene in dialogue between Venus and Love. The libretto is still cast mainly in lines of seven and eleven syllables, with a great deal of rhyme and a considerable use of short lines, but there are now three passages in eights (trochaic *ottonari*, which were thought of as a dancing, leaping metre). Although there is no subplot, Rinuccini's use of the chorus now shows a clear understanding of the need for contrast and closed units to enhance the dialogue. With these two librettos of 1607–8, most of the essential principles for the future development of Italian serious opera were established.

2. ITALIAN LIBRETTOS TO c1730. Opera in Rome evinced much greater variety of tone and technique than that of Florence and its artistic satellite Mantua. Roman opera was still a private and princely affair, but many of the patrons were churchmen, so that opera on sacred

themes developed, sometimes with an admixture of allegorical characters of the kind who took to the stage in *La Rappresentatione di Anima, et di Corpo*. Other librettos prepared the way for historical characters in opera by exploring sacred biography or hagiography, as did Rospigliosi's *Il Sant'Alessio*, set by Landi (1631–2). Here, the Counter-Reformation desire to use the arts to the full in the service of the faith unites with the feeling of the nascent Roman Baroque for mannerist surprises and contrasts, leading the librettist to introduce a kind of comic antimasque in the shape of a pair of pages in the saint's household. Comic servants and demons, with many other low-life characters, later join with the boastful soldiers, ludicrous pedants and similar types imitated from Plautus and Terence in riotous scenes which remind us not merely of old Roman comedy but also, perhaps, of the Greek satyr-play. Wholly comic operas appear, again from Rospigliosi's pen. In all kinds of opera, frequent arias interrupt the drama and introduce a variety of new metres such as the amphibrachic *senario* and other types of verse structure which may reflect, as does the conduct of the plot, the many-metred contemporary Spanish theatre of intrigue. Rospigliosi, a gifted littérateur who eventually became Pope Clement IX, spent some years in Spain and on his return to Rome brought back with him a sacred Spanish opera or musical play, which he translated and later adapted as *La comica del cielo* (1668). Spanish theatre and the anti-Aristotelian dramatic theory of Lope de Vega were also known to early librettists of Venetian opera.

With the widening of the social range of characters portrayed goes a widening of the spectrum of diction employed. There is a notable willingness to explore beyond the antique world for subject matter. Mythological themes still appear, but the taste for variety ensures that comic scenes are inserted among the serious ones in Landi's *La morte d'Orfeo* (1619). The modern romantic epic of the *cinquecento* is raided (Tasso, in Rospigliosi's *L'Erminia sul Giordano*, set by Michelangelo Rossi in 1633; Ariosto, in his *Il palazzo incantato*, Luigi Rossi, 1642, which introduces magical scenic effects); even more up-to-date was *La catena d'Adone* (Domenico Mazzocchi, 1626), adapted by Tronsarelli from Marino's recently published *L'Adone*. Pastoral was not forgotten, but the last true specimen was Loreto Vittori's *La Galatea* (set by himself, 1639), from Ovid. Roman opera is important, too, as the type of opera first imported into France by Richelieu's successor, Cardinal Mazarin (né Mazarino, an Italian). The example of Roman comic opera did not commend itself to Venetian librettists, who preferred the mixed genre, while adopting the double intrigue of two (sometimes more) pairs of lovers familiar from Rospigliosi's *Dal male il bene* (Abbatini and Marazzoli, 1654), a romantic comedy owing much to Calderón. Wholly comic opera found an echo in local types of opera in Florence and Naples, drawing on dialect and rustic manners, as in Moniglia's *Il potestà di Colognole* (Jacopo Melani, 1657), though this shares with some of Rospigliosi's work a common ancestry in the comedies of the younger Michelangelo Buonarroti.

Opera was slow to reach Venice, but when it did – with Ferrari's *L'Andromeda* (Francesco Manelli, 1637) – it began to develop with a rapidity previously impossible. There was a two-fold inheritance: from Rome, in that several of the artists concerned, especially singers, had gained their first experience there, reaching Venice after further service in touring companies about which we know little; and from courtly opera, in that the aging Monteverdi was at hand in S Marco, a senior practitioner and authoritative teacher who could transmit his knowledge of the Florentine and Mantuan tradition. The larger environment of a city once rich and powerful, now in decline, with the decadent, often cynical atmosphere of a pleasure-house, but still free, independent of church control (save its own state religion), and willing to harbour unorthodox ideas, opened up the libretto to unusual intellectual perspectives. The city's long-established artistic taste for sensuous realism and magnificence, in contrast with Florentine intellectualism, favoured scenic spectacle, including the use of large casts and dancers and earthy and amorous subjects. But the smaller environment of the public opera-house, run by an impresario who mounted annual seasons during carnival time, needing new operas every year and new excitements to ensure packed houses, brought about a quantitative change in the supply of operas which engendered or at least speeded up qualitative change: a librettist or composer who produces one or two operas a year for a fairly stable audience soon acquires know-how (as do the members of the audience), so that practicable conventions and stereotypes become established. At the same time, there are the twin dangers of routine, art without thought or imagination, and, on the other hand, a hasty grasping after novelty, a desire to shock or to test decorum to its limits. With these mingled vices and advantages, opera took its place in Venice as a commercial entertainment, attracting spectators of all tastes and pockets, many of them visitors to Venice (especially foreign), alongside the masquerades – held in the same theatres – the gaming and the courtesans.

The first theatres were built by noblemen, and it was their junior sons and nephews, mostly ensconced in the professional class, who took the place of court poets and provided many of the earlier librettos, since they were also poets, intellectuals and prose writers. Among these were Busenello (a librettist of real distinction), Badoaro, Bisaccioni and Giulio Strozzi. These, and others such as Cicognini, were also members of the Accademia degli Incogniti, an important centre of free thought; they were intellectuals of good classical education who were not afraid to champion republicanism and oppose the tyranny of absolutist rule and the compliance of courtiers; they brought the first historical characters on to the operatic stage, and were prepared to confront, with a sense of moral realism, the implications of free love and sensuous enjoyment so mindlessly advocated by the poet Marini (and later Quinault). The best-known libretto of this kind is *L'incoronazione di Poppea*, for which Busenello turned to accounts by Tacitus and Suetonius of vice triumphant at the court of Nero; the educated members of the audience would have known, of course, that Poppaea's apparent triumph would eventually end in an ignominious death, and it may be that Busenello understood from the first the Greek sense of dramatic irony which the wider associations of a historical subject may bring into operation. His colleague Bisaccioni was the first librettist to treat the story of Boris Godunov, the usurper Tsar, in *Demetrio moscovita* (1643).

The other type of Venetian librettist, a type which all too quickly tended to displace the dilettante nobleman, earned his living almost exclusively from his trade. Some were impresarios, like Ferrari (also a composer and a theorbist); others were the first theatre poets, such as

Cavalli's partner Giovanni Faustini (whose brother was an impresario, a trade he dabbled in himself), or Melosio. Their librettos were not written in 'idle hours' like Busenello's, pondered with delight in a quest for poetic fame, but rapidly, coolly and professionally produced with an eye to the next contract: success would bring a new commission, as well as profit from the sale of librettos. That need not necessarily preclude great art and will often ensure a certain level of competence. It was always the case that 'The drama's laws the drama's patrons give / And we that live to please must please to live', as Samuel Johnson put it; but in Venice, for the first time, the operatic patron was not an educated ruler or magnate but a many-headed, anonymous, fleeting public. Failure to please was no doubt frequent; but in an age when audiences saw only new works, which did not have to compete for space with a repertory of established masterpieces as at present, failures, less shameful than now, were rapidly forgotten.

Venetian opera's subject matter rapidly widened after the first wave of mythological and pastoral subjects, with their inherited *topoi* of laments, lovers' leave-takings, echo effects, magical and supernatural scenes, oracles and prayers. Later operas add further items to the stock, such as sieges and mad scenes. Comic characters were introduced from the first, on the Roman model, servants, nurses, lascivious old men, and so forth, for whom comic metrical devices were often employed, such as the *sdrucciola* verse-ending (long-short-short).

The Incogniti librettists looked further afield for source and genre. To the romantic epic they add the classical; Greek, Roman, Middle Eastern, medieval, even recent history are explored; as well as the modern poetic romance we find the prose novel. The aria grows in importance. An early opera might have ten or 15, but by the end of the century there will be 30 or 40 or even more. A character might launch into song at any point in a scene, sometimes when the librettist had not expected it (a 'cavata'). The same character might sing two or three arias in a row; only towards the end of the century do we find a move beginning towards the idea that an aria should be placed at the end of a scene as its logical emotional climax, after which the singer should leave the stage, and that the dramaturgy of the opera should be so contrived that the various characters sing arias turn by turn. Arias were by then growing longer, as the da capo form was beginning to assert itself; the repeat of the opening section was known as a 'ritornello', and the practice of re-inserting the opening lines (which might be the composer's doing, not the librettist's) was called 'intercalare'. By then, too, the full range of classical Italian metrics had come into being with the addition first of the *quinario* (five-syllabled) and later of the *decasillabo* (ten-syllabled), whose anapaestic motion was found well suited to depict excited or passionate states of mind.

As Venetian opera moved into full flood, librettists developed the idea of a double plot, even a triple plot, to an unprecedented degree. To secure variety and accommodate the wider range of emotions that musical portraiture could now delineate, fictional characters were added to known stories, whether historical or not, and 'authentic' characters might be subjected to newly imagined experiences. To modern readers, seeking perhaps naively after historical 'truth', this seems an impertinence, but such a view is beside the point.

History then was simply 'story', and what mattered was the original writer's authority: to depart from a received 'story' was, at its best, a kind of artistic game, legitimate if successful. Librettists' prefaces and *argomenti* regularly came to distinguish their own contributions – often with some pride – from those of their sources (which in any case were often multiple and conflicting). Artistic verisimilitude was what mattered, then as later. Schiller was a notable historian who sought after truth in his historical investigations; yet, when he came to write *Don Carlos*, he was content to take material from the novelistic, largely fictionalized account of Philip II's son presented by Varillas; he makes us believe it, as also do Verdi, Méry and Du Locle. Of course, lesser artists might have failed, as 17th- and 18th-century librettists often did, to make their fictional 'accidenti naturali' seem convincing 'natural happenings'; but, to a spectator willing to suspend disbelief, the lack of success would be a failure of art, not of fidelity to historical fact.

The same goes for many other devices bequeathed by Venetian operas to later generations of librettists. Their heroic roles were sung by castratos; as in the case of boy actors taking female parts in the Elizabethan theatre, this led naturally to transsexual disguise: without pausing to consider fashionable sub-texts, we need to remember, reading a bald and compressed Venetian libretto, that the device might actually work, and work to good artistic effect, as we grant with Rosalind or Fidelio. It opened a new sphere of action and social mobility to female characters, and can even afford the opportunity for subtle playing with convention, as when Handel's Amastre, disguised in Minato's *Xerse* as a soldier, is ushered on stage with the ritornello of an *aria all'unisono*, traditionally employed for bass singers.

The leading librettists of the middle and later years of the 17th century were Sbarra, Minato (a nobleman), Aureli, Mauro and Noris, with Zeno, Stampiglia, Silvani and Pariati continuing on into the 18th. Several of them, most notably Minato, Zeno and Stampiglia, spent the climax of their careers in Vienna at the court of the Habsburg emperors, who became leading and consistent patrons of opera in the time of Cesti, long before Louis XIV adopted that role in France. The output of new operas and ballets celebrating their weddings, birthdays, name-days and other festive occasions – not to mention domestic chamber opera performed by the royal children – far exceeded contemporaneous production at Versailles, although it has until recently remained far less well known. Vienna was for long the second pole of Italian opera besides Venice, with which it maintained strong links; as a stable and durable centre of courtly opera production whose patrons could dictate rather than follow fashion, it probably outweighed Venice in aesthetic importance and intellectual prestige, as it did in providing unusually sumptuous circumstances for opera, including the use of an expensive chorus, which Venetian opera had abandoned early on. Since the example of Minato, the most honorific position that a librettist could aspire to was that of 'Caesarean poet', an office held by Zeno and Metastasio and coveted by Paolo Rolli. Other south German courts also offered more honorific employment to Italian poets than a public theatre could.

While the urge to reform the rambling plots, truly 'Baroque' structure and at times unseemly buffoonery of typically Venetian opera first began among native literati living in Italy, some of them librettists who argued in their prefaces that questions of morality in opera plots should be resolved in ways conducive to the public good, it is notable that the eyes of the reformers were increasingly looking abroad, to the two leading centres of courtly opera. Both offered majesty and dignity, but France added a remarkable expertise in décor, costume and dance, and – outside the world of opera – the example of two great neo-classical dramatists, Pierre Corneille and Jean Racine.

3. FRENCH OPERA TO c1760. Italian opera reached France – as indeed it reached Poland – in the 1640s, and Venetian-style works by Cavalli were presented at the court of Louis XIV in the 1660s. The native taste, though, was for spoken plays with musical interludes, especially involving dance, and for ballet itself, in which however singing had always played a part. Molière wrote *comédie-ballets* of a quality that invites revival today, and his leading musical collaborator, Lully (born in Florence, but an adoptive Frenchman since boyhood), provided music for some of these, evincing a truly modern wit besides a fully professional choreographic expertise. The French were moved by Italian opera, but their rationalism resisted the notion that dramatic characters, particularly historical ones, might sing in French; and for this reason, even when native opera developed, the stories were usually taken from the Golden Age pastoral world of Ovid or the magical legends of the romantic epic, as early Italian opera plots had been. French taste in serious drama was for the rolling rhetoric of the ex-barrister Corneille, in which real moral questions were powerfully and emotionally debated, and later for the ever-narrowing, neo-classical concentration of Racine.

The language of these great poets was purified to an extreme degree and employs a tiny vocabulary compared with the wealth of Shakespeare or even the Augustan Pope. The poetic form in Racine and most of Corneille operates within the confines of an unvaried sequence of alexandrines, rhyming in couplets which alternate couplets of 12-syllables (*rime rare*) and 13 (*rime riche*). The art lies in the psychology of the interactions of a few characters, and in the play of passionate rhythm and imagery within the tight constraints of the external form. The plot of Racine's most concentrated drama, *Bérénice*, may be summed up in the single Tacitean sentence 'Rex Titus reginam Berenicem dimisit invitus invitam'. Plots are taken from many sources, often the same ones favoured by early Venetian opera, though with a pronounced liking for Roman history and Greek drama, particularly Euripides. Gods do not directly intervene on stage, nor any form of magic, and although Corneille twice experimented with italianate scenic device and music, the more characteristic plays are presented without music or dance, and in simple scenery, often a single set. The so-called Aristotelean unities of time, place and action are observed, to such an extent that the playing-time of *Bérénice* parallels the time that the action would have taken in real life. Nothing could be less Baroque, or further from the world of Quinault and French opera or of contemporary mid-century Italian opera. This explains not only the dislike of Racine and his friend and critical counterpart, Boileau, for the aesthetic as well as the morality of opera, but also why a native opera was for so long thought unnecessary in France.

When it came, in the 1670s, it fed on all that neo-classical drama had avoided, and its success must mean that it answered a need for unreason and excess whose very suppression became an artistic quality in a play such as Racine's last tragedy, *Phèdre*. Its plots were pastoral, mythological or romantic; it thrived on divine intervention, magic and irrationality, on striking and sumptuous décor with frequent changes of scenery, on the deployment of chorus and dancers in masque-like *divertissements* which have little to do, usually, with the main action. The psychology – though Quinault was known as a playwright before he was drawn into opera – is, at least in the earlier operas, that of the sentimental romantic novel of de Scudéry, 'le tendre' rather than passion or real love. Elements of comedy, of which Lully was a master, regrettably disappeared quite early on. The verse for the most part lacks any kind of formal regularity, save the alternation of masculine and feminine rhymes, sometimes in couplets, sometimes not, and there is little distinction between *récit* and the infrequent arias and duets for the principals. But this is to reckon without its undeniable qualities of sweetness ('doucereux', saccharine, Boileau called it), and its aptness for the singing voice. Lully exercised a dictatorial control over every aspect of French opera, including the libretto, and he brought to the art a broader sense of architecture, seeing an entire scene as a carefully planned whole in key, rhythm and the deployment of forces and textures, of a kind impossible to achieve in the more ramshackle world of Italian opera.

The period of Quinault's operas coincided with the more adventurous and successful phase of Louis XIV's achievements in war and adultery, and his themes, stated in elaborate allegorical prologues, openly celebrate his master's interests. The *tragédie en musique* formed one of the rituals with which the Sun King simultaneously entertained his courtiers and forced them to worship his greatness, as unwilling prisoners in a court life which kept them from conspiring on their country estates. It is striking that the imagery and iconology of the operas is exactly that which the courtiers saw all around them adorning the monumentality of Versailles in paintings and statuary. The operas were repeated in Paris, where they continued in repertory and apparently suited French taste to such an extent that the whole audience might hum along with the *airs*, a phenomenon noted by many travellers, possible only because the operas, unlike Italian ones, were kept alive on stage. The essential architecture (and pastoral themes) endured to the eve of the Revolution, though the five-act structure became more apparent than real after the arrival of the *opéra-ballet*, which had separate stories for each act. In this way (in Masson's apt image) the internal architecture behind the great façades of Mansart was broken up, and the draughty halls were converted into the cosier interiors of Boffrand or De Cotte. The principal librettists of this later phase, mostly after Lully's death, were Thomas Corneille, Campistron, De La Motte, Danchet, Pellegrin, Gentil-Bernard, Cahusac, Marmontel and Voltaire.

4. ITALIAN REFORMS. The Arcadian Academy, founded in Rome in 1690 by members of a group which had formed around the illustrious ex-Queen Christina of Sweden, who had settled there, looked to the example of the French neo-classical dramatists in their quest for greater operatic dignity and decorum, but also directly back to the ancient Greek drama and Aristotelian theory. French plays were widely known in Italian translation and formed the sources for innumerable librettos. Much of the theorizing retailed expertly by

Freeman (in his perhaps unfortunately named *Opera without Drama*, 1967) was carried only patchily into practice. The Arcadians, Zeno at their head, might inveigh against too-frequent arias and the inclusion of comic characters, but Zeno proved slow to drop them for, as he ruefully said, an empty theatre is no use to anyone. When Stampiglia turned a play by Metastasio's teacher Gravina into *La caduta de' Decemviri* (1697), his inclusion of a comic subplot must have rendered Gravina, an important dramatic theorist and classical scholar, speechless with rage. Nevertheless, the reformers won, and by Metastasio's time greater dignity prevailed. Comic scenes were omitted altogether: though they might still be present, perhaps written by some other hand, in the shape of entertainment between the acts, as was Federico's *La serva padrona* (1733, set by Pergolesi). It had for some time been customary, in an 'unreformed' piece, to use them to end the first two acts of a three-act opera, where they developed a life of their own that did not need to reflect on the main plot (though that had been their principal artistic virtue). Banished from serious opera, they soon acquired an independent existence as short comic operas, at first commonly in two acts. Uniting with existing traditions of comic opera, often in dialect, in Naples, Florence and Milan, they launched the lively tradition of the *dramma giocoso*.

A less welcome development, in the main Viennese, was the notion that opera should show the exemplary behaviour of the great. Zeno attached great importance to this; though it has attracted the criticism, particularly to Metastasio, that the behaviour of the heroes and heroines of serious opera portrays impossible magnanimity and incredible triumphs of honour and virtue over temptation and vice, this was a prominent theme in contemporary literature, from Richardson's novels to Fénelon's *Télémaque*, which was actually written to instruct a crown prince. The pursuit of 'gloire', personal honour and repute, was one of Pierre Corneille's favourite themes and, more subtly expressed, concerned Racine as well. Autocracy and absolutism are today no longer dynastic, or not often so, but the modern age boasts enough examples of tyranny to enable us to imagine how important a matter it was in earlier societies. The pages of Saint-Simon reveal what dangerous tendencies lay behind the formal ritual exterior of Louis XIV's court, dangerous for his immediate family and courtiers; and whole nations came to suffer from dynastic wars such as that of the Spanish Succession. How far the great were affected by the exemplary heroes held up to them is a doubtful matter. After seeing Corneille's *Cinna*, source of many a *Clemenza di Tito*, Louis XIV is said to have thought of sparing the life of the Chevalier de Rohan (but did not); Napoleon too read it with delight, saying of its author 'How he would have understood me!' – but that failed to save the Duc d'Enghien. Corneille's descendant, Charlotte Corday, read the play rather differently before visiting Citoyen Marat.

Corneille's passionate arguments had become decidedly attenuated in the world of Metastasio, most famous of librettists; in spite of the poet's surprising beginnings as a poor lad adopted by the homosexual Gravina, and the young abate's subsequent history of amours with operatic sopranos and noble ladies, explosive passions of the Cornelian or Racinian kind are not allowed into the lovely melody of his verse. In his librettos he had attained a decorum fitting the Age of

Reason before he went to Vienna; this was not a feature dictated by the Habsburg court. There he had other crosses to bear, such as having to write operas on Chinese themes for the archduchesses to take part in, because they might not show their legs in classical costumes when taking male parts. In his letters to Hasse, who had inquired whether the characters should stand on stage in the order printed at the head of each scene, even if this breached royal etiquette, he answered evasively, but in terms of that same etiquette, not in terms of dramatic truth. (This feature of printed plays and librettos, as yet unnoticed by 'authentic' revivers of early opera, may also be demonstrated from remarks by Beaumarchais.)

Metastasio's virtues are real enough, as a clear expositor of plots placing a handful of characters, especially young ones, in slowly evolving rotations of mutual misunderstanding and doubt, which eventually come to a happy resolution in some unexpected way. The characters may now seem unreal in an age that lacks style and the virtue of understatement, but the generalized emotions they embody ring true. The flawless diction of the recitatives, the easy management of the *liaison des scènes* (the Racinian virtue of arranging the characters' entrances and exits so as to seem natural, much harder to achieve when each scene ends with an aria), the gift for telling image and pithy epigram revealed in the double quatrains of the short, highly-polished da capo arias: these are considerable virtues. He said that he never wrote an aria without also composing music for it (though it was shown to no one), and this unfailing sense of musicality and latent melody tempted generations of composers to keep on resetting his librettos and audiences to wish to hear them over and over again. In spite of his perfection of surface, however, he seems to have sensed that his type of opera, essentially a series of jewelled solo arias arranged on a golden chain of recitative, was inappropriate to the darker concerns that began increasingly to preoccupy the thinkers and writers of the latter half of the 18th century. He devoted his latter years to an interesting but unpublished discussion of Greek drama and Aristotle's theory of tragedy and an annotated translation of Horace's *Ars poetica*, with implications for operatic practice which he did not put into practical effect.

Deeper emotions and greater psychological realism come into play in the work of a less elegant poet, but a more adventurous intellectual, Raniero de' Calzabigi. He admired Metastasio enough to edit and introduce an important collected edition of his works, but concluded his laudatory remarks by hinting that a further reform of Italian opera might be effected by looking to French opera (not drama) for its mastery of spectacle and dance and its involvement of a large chorus. He probably also admired the much greater complexity of French recitative and Rameau's ability to accompany a recitative monologue with symphonically textured accompaniments. He desired a greater singleness of action, bidding farewell to the accustomed round dance of two pairs of lovers, and aimed for simplicity of plot and a deeper exploration of tragic themes. This would leave less room for arias, which in his librettos become either shorter, like the French *petit air*, or longer and more prominent, placed now at important junctures in the drama. (Metastasio had disliked accompanied recitatives, and his arias, though beautifully varied in character, tend to come out at the same length, so that the over-all rhythm of the dramaturgy becomes predictable even if not

mechanical.) Calzabigi was by no means alone in this new approach, which had been suggested and exemplified by Algarotti in his widely translated *Saggio sopra l'opera in musica* of 1755, and adumbrated by Diderot also (he too sketched a libretto). There were practical experiments in Parma, conducted by the francophile C. I. Frugoni, who had however little feel for the stage; his adaptations and librettos were set by Jommelli, who wanted more verses to vary the music of his now longer arias and was no admirer of Metastasio. A sense of real tragedy and a desire to construct longer scene complexes are also to be found in other librettists, such as Mattia Verazi, though the Milanese public did not take to his ideas. Ornamental singing, of course, and the vanity of its exponents and the admiration of their aficionados, got in the way of such reforms, but the desire for change was widespread.

It seems at first rather surprising that Calzabigi should have found his ideal collaborator in a German, half Czech, who had written some of the longest coloratura runs and roulades in the history of opera, namely Gluck. They met in Vienna, where the composer had settled after a wandering but reasonably successful career as a thoroughly italianate opera composer. Other members of their group were the court official Count Durazzo, who had translated Lully's *Armide*, and the outstanding but now neglected choreographer Angiolini, whose ideas on the dance were similar to Noverre's. After a ballet on the theme of *Don Juan*, incorporating more mime than was usual, the experimental *Orfeo ed Euridice* was staged in 1762 – not a full-length serious opera, but a short, less formal *azione teatrale*, which by its nature employed few characters.

Though of uneven quality and inconsistent in detail (Gluck was surely the clumsiest of great composers), this return to the primary myth of opera has never since been forgotten. Its sure and single action is sometimes static, but Gluck knew how to endow such scenes as the Gallic opening *tombeau* with an architectonic quality, so that the long sequence of choruses, dance and mourning aria (a *rondeau* with recitative episodes and a verbally varied refrain) is experienced as a compelling dramatic whole; the same is true of the Furies' scene, though here the command of tonality is used to portray a developing action. There is coloratura in Orpheus's pleas to the Furies, but it is relevant coloratura, used not for its own sake but as a rhetorical element progressively intensifying his prayer.

With their next opera, *Alceste* (1767), Gluck and Calzabigi carried their message to the wider world, publishing it with a challenging preface which is essentially a plea for more action (though a simpler plot) and fewer arias, particularly of the type that was framed and interrupted by formal instrumental ritornellos. Just as Angiolini wished the ballet to narrate more continuously, to a new kind of music, they felt that dramatic narrative in opera must now flow more consistently, the regular alternation of recitative and solo aria being disguised and assembled into longer sequences. *Alceste* again concentrates mainly on two characters, the queen and her husband, but this is now a full-length opera. Again, it is not an entire artistic success, particularly in its ending (as with *Orfeo*), and the lack of incident in the action can make the long sequences of accompanied recitatives, each magnificent in itself, seem rather monotonous.

Calzabigi claimed much of the credit for the new realization of ideas for reform, but it is plain from Gluck's subsequent career that the essential elements stemmed from the composer himself, since he went on developing them and imposing them on the librettists with whom he worked during his years in Paris. He did not accept the normal status of the composer as a mere purveyor of music, and insisted on taking over the theatre poet's traditional role as stage director. Wagner too was to oversee the details of movement, acting and stage production, and Gluck is an important precursor who saw opera as a whole and new works as unique and un-repeatable fusions of text, music, action, dance and decor.

From now on, the librettist's art begins to change: the composer's vision and needs become decisive factors. Gluck's attempts to reform Italian opera by importing French methods, and French opera by importing Italian, the whole reposing on a new command of classical tonality and texture, had no real successors at the time, for no other composers could deploy his individual musical abilities. But they were to be more important for Mozart's dramaturgy than is usually recognized, and formed a valuable ideal and example for later composers such as Berlioz and Wagner. Gluck's principal Parisian collaborators were Guillard and du Roullet; but their chief claim to fame is that they did what they were told. Gluck also took part in the curious revival of interest in Quinault's librettos that seized Parisian composers after Mondonville's example, and reset *Armide*. Unlike Italian composers, the French had almost never re-used old librettos: the new fashion was an attempt to revivify the failing fortunes of the serious opera by returning to first principles. Gluck, however, recognized a kindred spirit in Lully; in recomposing the finest of the librettos that Quinault had tailored to Lully's needs, he managed to produce a masterpiece of his own.

It is extraordinarily interesting to see a new order of musical intelligence at work on a libretto from a much earlier age. Quinault's fluid verse is reorganized into much larger units. Perhaps the most striking feature is the treatment of the recitative. The older French technique had been to set the verse at a surprisingly consistent pace, closely paralleling that of an actor's declamation. This had led Lully and his successors to evolve a complicated system of varied metres, so as to ensure that cadences at the end of sentences and lines fell on the main beat. Into the common time (4/4, or C) characteristic of all Italian recitative they interpolated triple-time bars, and half-bars of duple time, notated in doubled note-values but with a diminished time-signature (2/2, or barred C), so that they would be sung twice as fast.

In Rameau's operas this complexity was increased by the composer's desire to underline and dictate to the singer – by means that reach beyond minutiae of rhythm to further subtleties of melody and harmony – every slightest inflection of thought, feeling and action. The harmonic complexity, in fact, is often greater in recitative than in the clearer air of the concerted pieces. In *Armide*, as in his earlier French operas to modern librettos, Gluck gives back to the singers a greater freedom to pace and declaim the verse as they wish, by adopting Italian-style recitative in common time; this allows a much more exact control of the large orchestra now employed to accompany all the recitative, and permits the singer to deliver recitative verse much more spontaneously, according to the 'feel' of the situation on stage. Once again, the aim is to achieve the quality to

which the preface of *Alceste* chiefly aspires, 'a noble simplicity'. This famous phrase, a watchword of neo-classicism, had been popularized in the 1750s by the art historian Winckelmann, but had long been a desideratum of all critics who opposed the excessive complexity of Baroque art, such as Scheibe and Gottesched.

5. ITALIAN COMIC OPERA TO 1800. Comic opera, as we have seen, existed in the 17th century and emerged as an important genre in Venetian and international Italian opera following the removal of comic scenes from serious opera. The most vital elements in early, independent comic opera drew strength from local cultures and audiences, and many such operas, like local plays, employed dialect for the appropriate characters, who might of course comprise the entire cast. The librettists who developed this type in Florence, Naples, Milan and elsewhere were Oliva, Saddumene, Trinchera, Cerlone, Maggi and Federico. Dialect was less common in the comic scenes of Venetian 'un-reformed' opera and, apparently, in higher-class opera generally. Alessandro Scarlatti's comedy *Il trionfo dell'onore* (1718, Naples, libretto by Tullio) employs no dialect; Federico's *La serva padrona*, likewise (inter-mezzos for Pergolesi's *Il prigionier superbo*, 1733, Naples). Dialect plays and operas were restricted to theatres and audiences who could understand the proceedings and, alas, seem likely to remain so. The greatest librettist of 18th-century comic opera, Goldoni, wrote plays in Venetian dialect, but did not use it for opera librettos, which needed to be accessible to a general audience, whether in Venice or in the other cities that attracted pleasure-seeking visitors from abroad and from other Italian states (local dialects in Italy are less easily understood than most of the regional dialects of France, Germany or England).

In Goldoni's hands the comic opera libretto acquired all the Molièrean virtues of his plays; he fixed in witty yet realistic language all that he had inherited from earlier forms of comedy (save obscenity), in the process dealing the death-blow to the extemporized buffoonery of the *commedia dell'arte*. He was a literary artist, like Metastasio, and his librettos too were set over and over again by different composers. One may still read them with pleasure today. For all his well-developed sense of the ludicrous (which becomes accentuated when stylized by music), he transmits good middle-class common sense even when he involves aristocratic characters in the action. The range of social comment and of the portrayal of different classes of society sets him poles apart from Metastasio, as does his brevity and point; yet his habit of including a pair of serious young lovers in the drama – the 'parti serie', which normally require singers of real distinction as opposed to the 'buffo' or 'caricato' roles, designed for an actor who can sing tolerably, enables him to allow room for the higher emotions as well as the base, for aspiration as well as farce. His willingness to allow the composer his rights, and his realization that music can add considerable impetus to a dramatic climax, led him to develop the prototype for the Mozartian-Da Pontean comic finale. Like Molière, he enjoyed having the whole cast pile one by one on to the stage as the confusion increased towards the end of an act, and contrived verse forms allowing this to develop, in a libretto, into a suite of contrasted movements without the interruption of recitative. One needs to remember, all the same, that a similar trend was beginning to emerge in contemporary serious opera.

By the time of his leading heirs, Casti and Da Ponte, comic opera (normally called 'dramma giocoso', not 'opera buffa') had won an important position alongside serious opera as an entertainment for the upper classes; it was probably more welcome at court (notably in Vienna), and certainly in noblemen's palaces such as Eszterháza, than its serious rival, which was more costly to cast and to stage, though the latter was still the preferred genre for marking important dynastic occasions. Comic opera could accommodate material from a much wider variety of literary sources and relate more immediately to the general reading of a leisured and fashionable audience. The novel becomes a valuable source, and English influences begin to admit a more sentimental strain with such librettos as Goldoni's *La Cecchina*, first set by Duni in 1756 but more familiar under its secondary title, *La buona figliuola*, set by Piccinni in 1760. Goldoni had first dramatized Richardson's famous novel *Pamela* as a prose play, but in the libretto turned the dialogue into verse. Even in comic opera, where one might have expected greater realism to permit greater latitude, the Italians' feeling for unity of tone ensured that the recitative matched the arias and ensembles not merely in its musical but also in its metrical stylization. In Paris, on the other hand, when *La serva padrona* was performed in French, the recitative verse was translated into prose and spoken.

The comedy of manners and above all the comedy of sentiment (*comédie larmoyante*), itself owing much to Richardson, allow the importation into comic opera of matter more normally associated with serious opera. Even a recent and controversial play might form the basis for an opera, as with Beaumarchais' *Le mariage de Figaro*, in Da Ponte's almost miraculous condensation of its five acts and intricate chain of incident. With the faster pace of comic opera and the composer's increasing ability to encapsulate scenes of developing action in a balanced and coherent musical argument, the discrete ensemble grew up alongside the concerted finale. Librettists now worked more closely with composers in providing schemes of metre and rhyme to match the musical possibilities. Since comic librettists were now writing for the same educated and discriminating patrons as the poets of serious opera, Casti and Da Ponte developed an elegance of diction in their aria verse far beyond the ambitions (or the needs) of Goldoni. Of the two, Casti has the finer wit and the greater originality, even audacity, and it is to be lamented that his texts were not set by greater composers; Da Ponte, however, bears the palm as a supremely clever adapter who knew how to suit the qualities latent in a source to the qualities he discerned in a composer. Almost nothing is known about the detailed process of his discussions with Mozart, but it is fair to conclude from passages in Mozart's letters relating to the dramaturgy of *Idomeneo* and *Die Entführung aus dem Serail* that he would have played no subservient role. One tiny piece of evidence that rings true is Da Ponte's comment late in life, reported by a New York surgeon who knew him, that he had to work very hard to persuade Mozart to let him put enough humour into *Don Giovanni*.

6. VERNACULAR OPERA IN ENGLAND, GERMANY AND SPAIN. Venetian opera found ready patrons very early on in the courts of Austria and southern Germany, but the prestige of Italian music was so great – particularly, but by no means only, in the Catholic south – that the Italian language was imported along with the Italian singers, librettists and composers. Though composers of German stock might set Italian librettos and learn how the operatic art functioned, it was a very long time before Germanic rulers were prepared to put serious money behind vernacular opera and native artists. Joseph II's desire for a national theatre led to the production of Mozart's *Die Entführung* and other operas with spoken dialogue around 1780, but the experiment was short-lived; even in the early decades of the 19th century, Weber was still trying to get his colleagues to band together in an attempt to remove Italians from positions of influence. In the 17th century, in spite of attempts by leading writers such as the italianizing Opitz and Harsdörffer to produce German-language pastorals, the first consistent policy favouring opera in German (but somewhere still in Italian) grew up in the public theatre of a mercantile free city, Hamburg, towards the end of the century. Here the type was italianate, though with French dancing; the more important composers were Keiser, Mattheson and the tyro Handel, their librettists such figures as Bressand, Feustking and – an expert translator and an interesting theorist – Barthold Feind.

Opera with sung recitative, however, did not become the typical form of German 18th-century opera; this was to be what we have come to call the 'Singspiel', opera with spoken dialogue (though the term, originally meaning 'sung play', was at first used to describe any form of musical theatre, including Italian opera). The most important lessons learnt from Hamburg opera might also have been learnt from Italian oratorio: how to frame arias and recitatives and verses fit for them; the leading beneficiary of this process was a man actually forbidden, in Leipzig, to have anything to do with opera, J. S. Bach.

Before considering the Singspiel we must backtrack to the arrival of opera in England. Here (in contrast to Germany) there was a magnificent and highly sophisticated tradition of spoken poetic drama, that of Shakespeare and his contemporaries. It has sometimes been suggested that, because of this, opera was in some way felt to be unnecessary; but that did not prove to be the case in Spain, where similar circumstances obtained: we have librettos by Calderón de la Barca. More germane, perhaps, was the well-established convention of using music in the Jacobean and Caroline masque. Here, not only songs, choruses and dancing, but even recitatives were known, but the music is illustrative and does not narrate an action or depict emotion resulting from drama to any important extent; the action proper is conducted in speech. What is more, for all the resources and prestige lavished upon the masque as a courtly celebration, the audience was not a purely external body of spectators but interacted with the stage; prominent courtiers danced the noble dances, which culminated in a general dance. In fact, memories of masques and of the masquing interpolations in plays were to affect English opera much later on, after the Restoration; but the Civil War and the interregnum of the Commonwealth delayed such developments and greatly reduced the available funding. The English tradition was otherwise quite close to the French tradition of the *ballet de cour*, and – with a national treasury behind it, as in France, and with an uninterrupted period of development – might have produced a native amalgam of its own.

The type that emerged after the Restoration was the 'semi-opera' or 'dramatick opera'. This was a heroic play with musical interpolations. Sometimes they took the form of masques unrelated to the drama save by allegorical theme, as in Purcell's *The Fairy-Queen* (1692–3, adapted from Shakespeare's *A Midsummer Night's Dream*, perhaps by Betterton), or presented as a masque before the characters in the play proper; sometimes the business of the drama continued through the musical scenes, as in Dryden's *King Arthur* (1691, music again by Purcell), in which priests, supernatural characters, pastoral folk and soldiers are allowed to sing while the principal heroic characters are confined to speech.

This categorization gives only the most general idea of the manifold uses of music in the Restoration theatre, which range from the play with a song or two through music of increasing complexity right up to the extended interpolations in the true 'semi-operas', in which Purcell shows a Lullian ability to organize a long scene by means of tonality and well-judged proportioning. The English were familiar with French pastoral opera and Venetian opera (and italianate singing); a contemporary English translation of Cavalli's *Erismena* shows great practical understanding, even keeping vowel sounds intact, so that 'Vaghe stelle' becomes 'Stars resplendent'. But they did not develop a tradition of all-sung opera, in spite of one perfect example in Purcell's *Dido and Aeneas*, with its excellent libretto by Tate, a short work designed for private performance which expertly mixes the best elements of Cavallian and Lullian opera with the best of the native tradition.

The theory of the semi-opera is set out by Dryden in prefatory essays appended to various plays, especially the 'Essay on Musical Drama' appended to *Albion and Albanius* (1685, music by Grabu; this had originally been designed as the prologue to a larger piece which eventually became *King Arthur*). While showing an acute appreciation of the kind of poetry needed for song, Dryden thinks that singing is apt only for the classes of character favoured by many early Italian and French theorists of opera, and wishes 'the fable of it' – the dramatic narrative, Horace's *fabula* – to be 'all spoken and acted by the best of the comedians' (meaning simply actors).

This has the result that the resources of music, however imaginatively deployed in the masques and in supernatural, ritual, pastoral and battle scenes, are never brought to bear on the principal characters, so that true *dramma per musica* cannot develop. The same criticism might be made of the French *tragédie en musique*, in which the weightier musical forces are normally reserved for similarly episodic material. Other conventions of Restoration semi-opera, though, can seem curiously modern, as when Purcell's song 'What shall I do to show how much I love her' is performed behind the scenes to express the silent Maximinian's thoughts in *Dioclesian* (1690, adapted by Betterton from Massinger's and Fletcher's *The Prophetess*); he is to stand 'gazing on the Princess [Aurelia] all the time of the song'. Modern revival has shown, nevertheless, that *King Arthur*, *The Fairy-Queen* and *The Tempest* (Shakespeare 'made into a play' by Dryden, Davenant and perhaps Shadwell) can provide an authentic theatrical experience in their kind, although in the former the spectator must accept fustian heroics, and in the latter two considerable cuts and rearrangement of and surprising additions to the familiar text of Shakespeare.

Short all-sung operas on the Italian model continued to be produced in the early decades of the 18th century, but the arrival of Italian opera as an expensive and prestigious entertainment for fashionable London in the 1710s and 1720s threatened and annoyed the theatre folk and produced, by reaction, a more characteristic form of English musical theatre than semi-opera. This was the ballad opera, a play with songs in which new words were written for pre-existing tunes, usually well-known ones. The first was a brilliant satire on both Italian opera and contemporary politics, John Gay's *The Beggar's Opera* (1728). Its phenomenal success ensured a regular stream of imitations which created a tradition very like that of the contemporary French vaudeville comedy. Not all were satirical, though there are riotous examples by the novelist Fielding and the poet-composer Henry Carey; the former caused such alarm to a corrupt government that Sir Robert Walpole instituted the censorship of plays and librettos under the office of the Lord Chamberlain. When original songs and more ambitious music came to be composed in place of the borrowed tunes, a style of native opera came into existence, equivalent to the French *opéra comique*, capable of pathos as well as humour, with simple but melodious music never far from the rhythm and rate of delivery of speech, which dominated the English popular theatre from Bickerstaff through Sheridan and Dibdin to Gilbert and beyond.

Ballad opera shared with the semi-opera the advantage that the drama, since it was spoken, had much more space in which to unfold in its own terms and develop the psychological, intellectual and narrative matter forming its subject. There was no use of recitative and only a minimal orchestra, so that the sung words, when they came, could be easily heard, and the audience did not need to learn the sophisticated conventions of singing and musical portraiture that governed Italian opera. A company of actors, assuming that some of them could also sing, could perform such pieces in venues suitable for spoken plays, with little more instrumental support than a couple of violins and continuo. In this form ballad opera was taken on tour and even found its way abroad into Germany, where the success of Coffey's *The Devil to Pay* and other pieces evoked a succession of adaptations and imitations (Coffey was also exploited by French and Italian composers). It is likely that French plays with music similarly migrated through the Rhinelands into Germany, and also proved well fitted for the capacities of the troupes of touring players and singers who supplied the need for German popular theatre (there was then no higher class German theatre). Later on, in the 1770s, Benda was to imitate J.-J. Rousseau's invention of the *mélodrame* – speech and mime accompanied by instrumental music – using texts by Brandes and Gotter; Arne also tried his hand at melodrama in England, but no music survives.

Spoken drama with modest musical insertions became the typical German form of opera, used in Weisse's librettos and little school plays and in Reichardt's *Liederspiele* (which employed well-known songs and poems with their original words). But since composers such as Dittersdorf (also a librettist) and Mozart were at the same time composing Italian operas with recitatives, employing musical forms and methods of continuity that became ever more complex and ambitious, the proportion between music and dialogue in the so-called

Singspiel became ever more unbalanced. It is one thing when dialogue is punctuated at, say, three- or five-minute intervals by a song lasting a minute or two at the most; quite another when large and important pieces of vocal music lasting five or ten minutes are punctuated by short dialogues generally lasting for less than two or three. The contrast between the more naturalistic, linear time-scale of spoken drama and the slower, psychological, spiralling time-scale of operatic song becomes increasingly noticeable, and we are on the way to the eventual solution, all-sung vernacular opera, which Weber achieved. (The ever larger orchestra, wider pit and more resonant acoustic of a regular opera theatre also played their part in the extinction of spoken dialogue, as of course did the increasing ability of the audiences to understand and accept the conventions of sung drama.)

While early attempts were made, as in England with Arne's *Artaxerxes*, to create a German equivalent to Italian serious opera using antique or historical subjects, the librettos of such figures as Wieland, Herder and Klein met little lasting success. Wieland's *Alceste* (1773) was followed by a series of essays on opera in his periodical *Der teutsche Merkur*, but the young Goethe mercilessly ridiculed both in his farcical Lucianic dialogue *Götter Helden und Wieland*, in which the schoolmasterly German is berated by Euripides and his characters (and by Mercury) for his narrow Christian ethic and misunderstanding of Greek art. Mozart had the chance to set a libretto by Klein on a historical subject, but did not take up the offer. More successful librettos of a lighter kind were produced by Goethe, Bretzner, Stephanie the Younger, Schikaneder, Johann André and Kotzebue, among whom the informed eye will recognize the librettists of Mozart's *Die Entführung aus dem Serail* and *Die Zauberflöte*. The taste for exoticism and magical fantasy that Mozart's German operas reveal, tempered by humanity and the deeper passions, pointed the way in theme if not method to Romantic opera; while the first of them was the fruit of an initiative from the emperor, the second was written for an independent actor-manager librettist and a truly popular audience. Goethe himself sketched the scenario of a sequel on the same theme, the education suitable for a ruler and for his subjects, in which Tamino and Pamina have borne a child (and the Papagenos eggs); but in spite of much highly intelligent discussion of libretto writing, especially in his letters to the composer Kayser, Goethe's many attempts to found a German school of comic opera were never crowned by the collaboration of a great composer. His friend and fellow playwright Schiller, while he never wrote a libretto, also speculated interestingly about the ideal, unreal nature of opera, which like Grillparzer he found attractive; in 1800 he directed a stage production of Gluck's *Iphigénie en Tauride*, and later he published a pertinent essay on the function of the Greek chorus, prefaced to his tragedy *Die Braut von Messina* (1803). For the true heir to the young Schiller's revolutionary fervour, we must turn to Beethoven's much-revised *Fidelio* (1805, Sonnleithner, rev. 1814 by Treitschke); though adapted from a French libretto by Bouilly, its themes of liberty, opposition to tyranny, human endurance and female heroism are as Schillerian as its sublimity of tone.

The great dramatists of the Golden Age of Spanish theatre were certainly interested in opera, but much of the music accompanying their librettos has been lost, including that for a pastoral by Lope de Vega that was entirely sung, *La selva sin amor* (1627). We possess the scores that Hidalgo apparently composed for Juan Vélez de Guevara's *Los celos hacen estrellas* (1672), a zarzuela with spoken dialogue – the preferred Spanish type – and for Calderón de la Barca's *Celos aun del aire matan* (1660), a three-act piece with recitatives. The early zarzuela was a courtly kind of opera, not unlike the French *comédie-ballet*, and became a light form equivalent to operetta only much later on. What appears to have been a lively and interesting native tradition in Spain was however extinguished around 1700 by a fashion for imported Italian opera, favoured by the ease with which Spaniards can understand Italian. The importance of the Spanish theatre for early Italian opera was nevertheless considerable. It offered the example of a great variety of verse forms and a non-classical tragicomic dramaturgy with the theory to justify it (Lope de Vega's *Arte nueva de hacer comedias en este tiempo*, 1609: G. A. Cicognini corresponded with its author). Rospigliosi, who spent some years in Spain, adapted two Spanish comedies by Antonio Sigler de Huerta and Calderón in the 1650s and Luis Vélez de Guevara's *Baltasarina* in 1668 (for his sacred opera *La comica del cielo*).

7. FRENCH POPULAR OPERA. English ballad opera may owe more to French example than we know, for Gay visited Paris and has left us in a letter an amusing account of a visit to a *tragédie en musique*; he may well have ventured into a popular entertainment in one of the Paris Foires and encountered a subversive parody of Quinault. The amazing variety of the enormous production of the little theatres and stages of Paris in the 18th century may be studied in Isherwood (1986) – not in the first place a literary or librettistic study, but a succinct and vivid picture of the different types of play with music, of the theatres and other venues, the many attempts to license, ban and control their rebellious and often indecent activities, the theatre wars and mergers, the wide social range for which they catered and the other forms of cheap entertainment that surrounded them.

Molière's *comédie-ballets*, in which speech alternated with smaller or larger musical units, as in the immortal *Le bourgeois gentilhomme* (1670, music by Lully), might have formed the ideal foundation for comic opera in French. But Molière died in 1673, and in the previous year Lully had secured a privilege which enabled him alone to present operas in Paris. Even he, however, had not managed to suppress a small company, originally of Italian extemporizers, presenting dramas, sometimes improvised, which might include scenes and later whole plays in French, as well as dances. They were silenced from 1697 to 1715, when Gherardi, himself a leading actor, began to collect and publish their repertory. Parisian audiences had enjoyed farces, moralities and parodies since the later Middle Ages, and were not so easily to be deprived of their pleasures. The little stages in the two Foires put on plays with rudimentary music in the form of well-known songs, to which new words might be written (though the refrain might be kept); this was not unlike the English ballad opera, except that in Paris the original words of the songs, often ribald or obscene, and instantly recalled by the tune, might be used to point a satirical reference. The texts of the songs were of course in rhymed verse, the spoken portion normally in prose. Verse dialogue was also known, however, in parodies of Quinault's operas; operatic pomp and machinery had been the subject of burlesque as early as the very funny prologue to Molière's *Amphitryon* (1668).

The various attempts to regulate or ban unlicensed performances led to the adoption of an equal number of ingenious counter-measures designed to circumvent them. While these, and indeed the whole early repertory, are more properly a matter for the social or purely literary historian, it is interesting to note what a range of different styles and conventions the audiences learnt to recognize and interpret – perhaps because all classes, from dukes and duchesses downwards, enjoyed these shows, and clever writers took part in the fun. The most famous and productive of the latter was the novelist Lesage, author of *Gil Blas* (who also wrote high-class plays). In 1736 he put together a four-act burlesque, *Histoire de l'opéra comique, ou Les métamorphoses de la foire*, deploying all the anti-censorship devices in turn. Act 1 scene i is a *parade* (rudimentary slapstick in mime, largely obscene, a crude and early form of entertainment at the Foires, still useful when speech was forbidden); scene ii is a *farce*, mixing words and music to an absurd action on a fashionable oriental theme (sung words might be allowed when speech was banned). Act 2 scene i is a *monologue* (to be used when only one actor was allowed to appear at a time; two or more might take part, however, provided that each waited behind the scenery, jumping on stage when it was his turn to speak and dodging smartly off again when he had finished, while another took over); scene ii is a *pantomime*, a more expressive and athletic dumbshow in the manner of the *commedia dell'arte* (for use when speech was banned). Act 3 is a *pièce par écriteaux*, in which large placards were held up to communicate the actors' words while they mimed – a sort of mobile comic-strip cartoon (again to circumvent the ban on speech). Act 4 is a more normal allegorical piece 'in the modern taste', showing the more decorous style that the regulations – and a higher literary sophistication – now permitted.

It was a dramatist of the next generation who raised the tone more decisively: Favart. Even before his arrival in the early 1730s there had been playwrights who wished to improve the quality of the music, as when, in the 1720s, the witty Piron invited Rameau to provide songs and dances (they are now lost) for two comedies in the Foires. During Favart's long career, the desire for more ambitious music grew surprisingly, though at first only slowly. The diminutive vaudevilles or *couplets* lasting perhaps 24 bars might be replaced by original melodies more than twice as long; short popular *airs* from operas might also be fitted out with new text, and not always with burlesque intent (it had long been the practice to furnish them with sacred verses for domestic devotional consumption: Rameau's first librettist, Pellegrin, is said to have versified Thomas à Kempis's *Imitation of Christ* to operatic *airs*). A play incorporating music of higher pretensions was known as a *comédie mêlée d'ariettes*; but, although the musical interpolations are somewhat longer, and may be used to extend a lyrical moment, create atmosphere or point a moral sentiment, they still do not do much, until the 1750s and 60s, to create character or suggest psychological or dramatic development. They are more like woodcuts or engravings in a popular book, and cover a similar artistic range, from naivety to sophistication. Meanwhile, Lesage's wit and mastery of stage intrigue gave way to a tone of greater simplicity, usually relying on a city-dweller's entirely false idealization of rural peasant life.

Slapstick and extempore comic business are largely banished, as in Goldoni, but Favart lacked Goldoni's powers of wide social observation and his sense of realism. This is the escapist art of Boucher, pretty, unspiritual, at times luscious. Overt obscenity has gone; but Favart preferred to arrange his plots around the naive country girl of 15 or 16, a type of ingénue played to perfection by his wife (who also wrote plays); the ramifications of love are restricted to pleasurable sensation, and there are many opportunities for sexual innuendo and *double-entendre*. He was nevertheless complimented by Voltaire and other *philosophes* for raising popular theatre to the status of art; and his distant collaboration with Gluck, who spent some ten years from 1754 arranging and composing music for French comic operas at the Viennese court, has left behind an interesting correspondence. Besides his own texts, Favart sent Gluck librettos by such colleagues as Anseaume, Moline, Sedaine and Dancourt; Gluck's comic operas and arrangements offer a picture of the complete development of the French type from vaudeville comedy with negligible music to the wholly original, three-act *La rencontre imprévue* (1764, by Dancourt, also known as *Les pèlerins de la Mecque*) in which the weight of the music seems to overbalance the rather slight prose of the spoken dialogue.

Both cultural and institutional factors favoured the growth of the musical element in comic opera. In 1715, in an attempt to control them, all the theatre music of the Foires had been brought together into an institution called the Opéra-Comique, which has confusingly lent its title to the genre of French opera with spoken dialogue ever since, whether or not the work is funny. A year later, the Regent allowed the Italian troupe to re-establish themselves in Paris as the Comédie-Italienne. Italian intermezzos therefore came into competition with native comic opera, and French audiences slowly learnt to appreciate Italian arias and a new art, to them, of characterization through song. In 1752, a visiting Italian troupe – no doubt boasting better than usual singers – scored an outstanding success with Pergolesi's *La serva padrona* (which Paris had heard before). This happened to coincide with a growing campaign of criticism directed by Encyclopedist critics against the stale pastorals and heroics of the 'official' operas at the Académie Royale de Musique, and indeed against the equally stale world of spoken tragedy at the 'official' Comédie Française; Diderot wished to challenge the latter with the *drame bourgeois*, realistic in its detailed portrayal of domestic middle-class life and its virtues, but sentimental (*larmoyante*, weeping) in its favourite effects; the naturalism and the pathos of such plays as his *Le fils naturel* had a considerable effect on the librettos of both French and Italian opera. His attacks were supported by Baron Grimm, and also by the young J.-J. Rousseau, who proclaimed the virtue of italianate melody linked by recitative – no longer the prerogative of the heroic, upper-class *tragédie lyrique* – and provided a practical demonstration in a little rustic opera entitled *Le devin du village*. In spite of his flimsy musical attainments, it appealed to the idealized, *petit Trianon* view of rural life which had enfeebled the long tradition of pastoral, and also became a hit. (Its fame was crowned by a parody, which the boy Mozart later reset as *Bastien und Bastienne*). This conjunction of circumstances led to a critical battle royal known as the QUERELLE DES BOUFFONS, and although most of the discussion centred on the *tragédie lyrique*, the public's attention also came to focus on the possibilities that the attractive Italian style offered for the development of French opera. Though the Opéra-Comique had been well housed and well run, with properly contracted singers and quite a large orchestra, since Monnet took over its management in 1752, its finances were rickety and it was merged with the Italian company ten years later; the latter played the leading role in the new institution, and to the combined resources was added the further advantage that all unofficial musical theatre in the Foires was now banned. Italian composers such as Duni came to Paris, and French-speaking composers from Philidor and Monsigny to Grétry and beyond learnt the delights of italianate melody and methods of musical continuity. The librettists, from the mid-century onwards, were Favart (still), Vadé, Anseaume, Poinsinet, Marmontel (who also wrote *tragédies*) and – the finest, with Favart – Sedaine.

One might have expected, after all the discussion of Italian comic opera, that the French would adopt recitative for the dialogue in their comedies; but they did not, although in Grétry's hands the instrumentally accompanied recitative, half-way between speech and song, became a valuable resource in raising the tone and tension before an important aria. They did, however, realize that for certain types of subject a greater unity of tone and heightened stylization might be obtained by writing the spoken dialogue in verse. Favart did this, for example, in *Soliman II* (Gibert, 1761) and *Les moissonneurs* (Duni, 1768); Anseaume in *La clochette* (Duni, 1766, a one-acter) and Marmontel in *Le Huron* (Grétry, 1768). Poinsinet kept to prose for *Le sorcier* and *Tom Jones* (Philidor, 1764, 1765). Sedaine, a much less accomplished versifier than the rest, used prose for *Le déserteur* (Monsigny, 1769) and *Richard Coeur-de-lion* (Grétry, 1784). His example was largely followed thereafter. The naturalistic detail of Greuze, so much praised by Diderot, has supplanted the pretty artificiality of Boucher.

French comic opera had grown up in a much broader context of popular entertainments, to which the whole urban population subscribed, literate and illiterate, intellectual and pleasure-seeker, marquis and artisan. Operatic 'parodie', the writing of new verses for an old tune, was part of a larger practice which included satirical lampoons, sometimes written by skilled hands, directed against the great and carrying messages important to the social historian. Nor was the taste for obscenity and jokes about bodily functions confined to the vulgar: some of the most scabrous surviving examples were specially written by Collé, Laujon and Audinot for the private theatres of rich noblemen such as the Duke of Chartres and the Prince of Conti. Noble rakes had sought mistresses among the singers and dancers of opera companies since the time of Louis XIV (assisted by the managers, as Saint-Simon reveals). The 'filles d'opéra' were by no means restricted to the lower ranks: the liaisons of Adrienne Lecouvreur, Sophie Arnould or the dancer Camargo and many other stars were not, as one might say, *affaires de choeur*. Just as one must keep this atmosphere of sexuality in mind when reading Favart's elegant love-intrigues, whether pastoral or exotic, so one must remember the alertness of the Parisian public to political innuendo and social criticism. Operatic institutions may have been brought under firmer control, and librettos made more respectable, but Favart's very successful *Ninette à la cour* (1755) still manages to present an unflattering picture of

aristocratic misbehaviour; he had taken the plot from the sharper-eyed Goldoni, but the piece's popularity tells us that Parisian audiences had not lost their taste for subversive comment. (The borrowing reveals the growing internationalism of Franco-Italian opera; still more so the re-translation of Favart's libretto into Italian ten years later.)

The most famous play of this kind, Beaumarchais' *Le mariage de Figaro* (1778, but not staged until 1784), makes more direct and overt connections between the sexual licence of the nobility and other ways in which they might use wealth and institutions such as the law to oppress the underprivileged. It draws on a long stage history of such comment; in the same year in which it appeared (with a certain amount of music, arranged by the author), Voltaire's comedy of the 1760s, *Le droit du seigneur*, was made into an opera by J.-P.-E. Martini Schwarzendorf. The subversive message in *Figaro* is made acid by wit, but sugared with sentimentality and repressed sensuality, especially in the relationship of Chérubin and the Countess, which like the anti-aristocratic stance has a long theatrical history, going back to Rochon de Chabannes' little play *Heureusement* (itself taken from one of Marmontel's inaptly named *Contes moraux*). In reviving the play today (or the perfect Italian opera that Da Ponte and Mozart made of it only two years after its first production), in the comfortable surroundings of a modern democracy, it is hard to communicate the qualities of daring and danger that accompanied it over 200 years ago. In order to prevent it from seeming little more than an adroit but humane farce, scattered with now proverbial *bons mots*, Figaro is often portrayed as a barely disguised *sans-culotte*. In the opera, the elegant minuet 'Se vuol ballare' is usually not sung but angrily barked, yet the point is that the young Count (*contino*) has learnt what he knows of aristocratic dancing and deportment from teachers of Figaro's social class, who remain greater masters of the art than the pupil can ever be. (The ensuing fencing lesson is of course another matter, and fair game.)

A less controversial aspect of *Le mariage de Figaro* is its mastery of the art of surprise in the management of the plot. This too had recently become important in French comic opera. Favart had been a smooth and seamless narrator of stories, but the ability to create dramatic tension, to involve an audience so that they identify with characters in the drama and share in their imagined emotions and dangers, was fully achieved only later, in the work of Sedaine and his musical collaborators, especially Philidor, Monsigny and Grétry. The subject matter grows increasingly serious, and is usually a far cry from the well-known classical material of the *tragédie lyrique*, where the emphasis fell not on surprise and successive dramatic revelations but on the manner in which familiar stories were treated. In Sedaine's librettos, a character is often placed in a situation where his life is threatened by injustice or misunderstanding, as in *Le déserteur* (Monsigny); the darkness of his fate may be contrasted with the happiness and normality of those who do not know or perhaps do not care what is happening to him – but we, the audience, are made to care, and the moment of his release or salvation brings us great relief from pent-up anxiety. Music can obviously play an important role in piling up the tension and in furnishing contrasted blocks of light and shade; it may also offer moving effects in its own right, as when the imprisoned King Richard answers Blondel's voice singing his own song, so that the faithful minstrel learns that his long quest for his vanished master has succeeded (Grétry's *Richard Coeur-de-lion*). The shrewd management of dramatic sympathy and tension, culminating in a last-minute rescue, usually by a king or his agent, was a familiar feature of French opera long before the Revolution, but the wider personal experience of such dangers during the 1790s and later – not only in the Terror, but also in the repression of liberals in Austrian prisons and elsewhere (as in Pellico's *Le mie prigioni*) – turned the 'rescue' theme into an anti-tyrannical one. Bouilly exploited it several times, notably in *Les deux journées* (Cherubini, 1800, known as *The Water Carrier* from its German title), but most memorably in the libretto later adapted for Beethoven's *Fidelio*, first set by Gaveaux, *Léonore, ou L'amour conjugal* (1798). Beethoven, no republican for all his hatred of tyranny, still allowed the rescue to be effected by the agent of a just king.

As after the Soviet revolution of 1917, a new type of official and propagandist subject matter was favoured in French opera of the 1790s; its heroic tone, though not its insistence on the rights of man, was to prove valuable to Napoleon under the Empire. Like the enthusiasm for the noble peasant or non-European savage consequent on Rousseau's assertion that society corrupts human nature (Marmontel, *Le Huron*, set by Grétry, and many other examples), it had less effect on the development of opera and the libretto than did the new dramaturgy of the period before the Revolution. With the death of the old *tragédie lyrique* and the more gradual collapse of *opera seria*, important and much more highly skilled composers such as Cherubini and Beethoven found the new range of techniques of the Franco-Italian *opéra comique*, whether serious or comic, ready and serviceable for their needs.

8. THE 19TH CENTURY AND BEYOND.

The repertory of 19th-century opera is much better known, and only the main outlines and more unusual new departures in the history of the libretto call for comment. As the century progresses, it becomes harder to discern consistent patterns in the development of the libretto, beyond the polarization between Wagnerism and the number opera. In western Europe, during the first half of the century, the resources and prestige of the Parisian theatres began to attract the interest of leading composers from Italy and Germany – including Wagner, though he did not take root there – and the trend towards an international style, already noticed, continued to gather momentum. One French characteristic that endured was the preference for spoken dialogue in smaller theatres such as the Théâtre Lyrique and the Opéra-Comique, where the acoustic did not preclude it; when operas such as Gounod's *Faust* and Bizet's *Carmen* were promoted to the vaster resonance of the Opéra, they had to be kitted out with sung recitatives.

The nationalistic desire of the more easterly European countries to assert their own individual cultural identities did not produce radically different types of libretto. Glinka's springboard was Italian opera; Smetana and Dvořák favoured Germany in their dramatic thinking, as in their harmonization of folk like melody and dance. Szymanowski took off from Richard Strauss. Musorgsky's greater musical originality did not deeply affect his librettos; his liking (shared by the Russians) for concatenating disparate scenes on a loose thread of narrative in what one might call an epic-

episodic type of libretto brings nothing essentially new. In operas less imaginatively compelling than *Boris Godunov* one can sense that the genre results from happy but often amateurish experiment. Perhaps the most individual characteristic of certain national types is the new kind of musical prosody engendered by different languages; while this might lead to decidedly boring or crude naturalistic imitation of speech, it could also evoke the musically organized blend of recitative and arioso that characterizes Musorgsky's remarkable monologues, or speech-themes such as Janáček's, which may become the musical basis for a scene; also to the point is the distinctive utterance of Bartók's one opera, *A Kékszakállú herceg vára* (*Bluebeard's Castle*, 1918).

The hiving-off of popular light opera into separate, musically unambitious genres such as *opérette*, operetta, zarzuela or musical play, in which tunefulness, not musical characterization, is the primary aim, must have reduced the audience for more serious kinds of opera; certainly, real topicality (as opposed to the choice of distant exotic subjects favoured by imperial opera houses), and even comedy itself, became progressively rarer and harder to achieve for a 'serious' composer, though there were always exceptions. The other characteristic of the 19th-century scene working against a steady development of the libretto, as already noted, is that composers themselves, now increasingly well-educated and literate middle-class intellectuals, expected to play a leading part in the planning of a libretto or, increasingly, to write their own. This came at a time of sharpening differentiation between musical styles and a pursuit of originality which, while it led to remarkable achievements, is now in danger of creating a well-funded Tower of Babel. The effect, as the 19th century progressed, was that a new libretto tended increasingly to be a special solution to a special set of desiderata posited by the technique and expressive needs of the composer. In any opera worth serious discussion, the functioning of the libretto becomes so inseparably entangled with the functioning of the music that it becomes only superficially useful to discuss the work of a librettist as a whole, independently of the various composers who shaped it.

9. GERMAN ROMANTIC OPERA AND ITS LEGACY.

The surprising emergence of German opera needs to be placed in its native context. It was partly due to the gradual creation of a German theatre, in which plays and opera might run in tandem (several leading German and Austrian singers also doubled as actors). This was itself part of a growing national selfconsciousness and an awareness that French and Italian modes of thought and expression in serious and comic opera, as in literature – which German writers and composers well knew how to use – were not enough for their needs. French and Italian opera dominated the court companies, but even here there were rulers who felt that subservience to foreign-language opera was not an adequate policy. Frederick the Great might write scenarios for Tagliazucchi to translate into Italian, but Gustavus III of Sweden – to look a little further afield – wrote them to be versified and sung in Swedish, and in Russia Catherine the Great – a German – wrote librettos in Russian. The enlightened Joseph II attempted to found a national opera theatre in the late 1770s, and Duke Karl August of Weimar encouraged his prime minister, friend and former tutor Goethe to perform German operas as well as plays in the little theatre there; at first an amateur affair, it had been rebuilt and equipped with professional resources by the time Schiller came to join Goethe as playwright and producer.

Many German writers became fascinated by music's ability to suggest and communicate emotion. The great critic and playwright Lessing wrote intelligently about Favart, and noted that music, in the theatre, might act on audiences more strongly than the accompanying words, in that it could anticipate the drama (even in the overture), create moods, effect transitions; he was probably the first to see that the librettist's duty was to prompt the composer's imagination. In Germany, writers such as Hamann went beyond the English cult of sensibility to proclaim the power of passion and instinctive forces, as against the rationality of the French Enlightenment. (To be fair, the heterodox Diderot also looked into the abyss of moral and aesthetic emptiness opening up beneath French culture in *Le neveu de Rameau*, a private pamphlet in which opera is an important image; it was first published in German, translated by Goethe.) Consideration of German music led Mme de Staël to point out, in *De l'Allemagne*, that for a musically sensitive listener the potent suggestions of vocal line and harmony relegated the words of an opera text to a secondary position in the live experience of opera. Germanic composers had for long been able to master the forms and styles of Italian music and enrich them with deeper passion, wider psychological range, more energetic bass-lines, more telling harmony, greater contrapuntal density and instrumental colour, and the ability to plan large-scale formal designs. When performing flimsy comic operas by Italians at Eszterháza, Haydn regularly made them more interesting by adding wind parts, and posterity acknowledged that the three greatest masters of italianate opera of the 18th century were the 'peripheral' Handel, Gluck and Mozart. Their professionalism and advanced musical techniques, all developed for the most part within opera itself and later placed at the disposal of oratorio, mass or symphony, together with the power of Beethoven's more recent example, doubtless owed their inspiration to the darker and more complicated passions and fantastic imaginings that were stirring in German literature and drama. As public interest focussed increasingly on the theatre and on opera, musical expression inevitably converged more and more with the new ideas and feelings.

Part of the price paid for the extraordinary diversity of forms, poetic styles and source material now available in German literature and drama was a certain clumsiness and amateurism which (as later in Russia) seems necessarily to accompany experiment and exploration, though there is no doubting the excitement of Lenz's *Sturm and Drang* dramas, Goethe's Shakespearean *Götz von Berlichingen* or Schiller's revolutionary *Die Räuber*. Yet the writing of librettos is more of a craft and demands a certain modesty and a cool head, perhaps the more so when the subject-matter turns on mysterious and magical folk-legends, fantastic tales, or a most un-latinate love of wild Nature and her pagan, unseen agencies. Kind's *Der Freischütz* works, all the same, and carried Weber's fame to Paris and even to London, where his last opera, *Oberon*, was first performed. Its English librettist, however, was J. R. Planché, a writer of extravaganzas who was less at home than Weber with the Germanic associations of magic and medieval chivalric legend. In *Der Freischütz*, with its more realistic domestic scenes contrasting with those

of magic and horror, we start to become aware of three problems. First, the disparity between speech and music: in his next opera, *Euryanthe* (von Chézy, 1823), Weber maintained continuity of tone by setting the whole to music. Secondly, naturalism sits uncomfortably alongside powerful depictions of the supernatural (though Kind's device of the fallen portrait that opens Act 2 would be clumsy stagecraft by any standards). The other problem is that on occasion the scale of Weber's music has so increased that there are not enough words to support its length without undue repetition. One does not really notice the 14-fold repetition of 'Lebewohl' ('Farewell') in the Act 2 terzetto of *Die Zauberflöte*, but there are 31 Farewells in the Act 2 trio of *Der Freischütz*, after which Rudolf then sings, six times in a row (though in ensemble), 'Doch hast du auch vergeben / den Vorwurf, den Verdacht' ('But have you really forgiven me my reproach, my suspicion?'). Weber could not have made the music shorter; given the state of technique at the time, the proportions of the sections are right. Nor would it have helped to lengthen the text by paraphrasing the thought: the vocal theme identified with the words also repeats. The problem is of course not unique to Weber, and even in Stravinsky's *The Rake's Progress* one is tempted, towards the end of the Auction scene, to answer Ann Trulove's 'I go to him, I go, I go, I go, I go to him' – which rather wickedly revives this earlier convention – with a Gilbertian 'Yes, but you *don't* go!'

The solution was a quite new approach to operatic dramaturgy, that effected by Wagner. He became aware of an impasse after completing a number of works, all to his own librettos, exploring subjects familiar to German composers, from fairytale through medieval history and chivalry and Germanic legend, culminating in *Lohengrin* (1848, performed 1850). The work in which the power of the future Wagner is most strongly manifest is probably *Der fliegende Holländer* (1841, performed 1843), where the North Sea myth (taken from Heine, who was also a source for *Tannhäuser*) conjures from Wagner music reminiscent of Wotan's; but when the mythic Dutchman, whose emotions echo the pull of eternal tides and the drive of stormwinds, sings a duet with the everyday Daland – perfectly competently drawn in the manner of French comic opera – one becomes aware that Wagner is trying to mix oil and water and needs to find a method capable of sustaining the hypnotic illusion of myth throughout an opera (it turned out to be four). In Act 3 of *Tannhäuser* (1845) there is another prophecy of the future when the hero relates his pilgrimage to Rome to seek papal absolution for his sins, which is refused, so that he resolves to live for sensual love. This passage, of well over 200 bars, greatly puzzled its first hearers. Its phrases are mostly song-like ('arioso'), but it is not an aria; nor is it a recitative, though the prosody resembles stretched speech rhythms. It is not in a closed form; although there is one basic metre (with some triple time offering a triplet version of the same pulse), the tempo is flexible and the music moves from A minor to F♯ major. There are themes that repeat in the orchestral accompaniment, particularly the 'Wotanesque' figure at the beginning, which returns from time to time, another that accompanies references to Eastertide joy and salvation, and yet others, such as a memorable phrase from the Venusberg music. But the recurrence of these themes is dependent on the recurrence of images and moods in the words that Tannhäuser sings. All this again anticipates the latent *Ring*.

After *Lohengrin*, Wagner took some years to establish a theoretical basis for his new genre of 'music drama', writing the cloudy *Das Kunstwerk der Zukunft* (1849) and the well argued (though perforce prejudiced) *Oper und Drama* and *Eine Mitteilung an meine Freunde* (both 1851). He continued to produce theoretical and explanatory tracts – regrettably, we lack a critical edition of Wagner's important writings, showing successive revisions (only Kropfinger's 1984 edition of *Oper und Drama* does that). He had rethought the bases of the art of opera, from the Greek theatre onwards, and it was essential to prepare the German public and performing artists for the practical demonstrations that were to follow. He dropped medieval themes and the 'real' world for a time, and took for his subject matter the myths of pagan divinities and heroic men and women preserved in Scandinavian and early German sources; they are in fact Nordic, but he adopted them as Teuton. This was not a new idea, for the sagas had been translated into modern German and imitated – in dramatic form, too – before he came to exploit them; a criticism of Raupach's play *Der Nibelungenhort* by Hebbel, to be followed by his own dramatic trilogy on the same theme (1855–60), makes it clear that the idea was generally in the air – even the alliterative verse of the sagas had been imitated by earlier writers. It was the manner of Wagner's treatment that was so remarkable; it eclipsed, in the end, all other attempts, and has radically affected the subsequent course of opera.

With Wagner, the history of ideas comes forcefully into the history of opera. Important to his tetralogy is an allegory of wealth and power based on the ideas of early German socialism; treated with great humanity and at first naively, its later stages grew progressively darker as he came to adopt a more pessimistic view of the world deriving from Schopenhauer. He also saw himself as the saviour of German art and as something of a religious guru. His literary activities extended beyond opera and his anti-French and anti-Jewish pamphlets continue to give offence. *Das Judenthum in der Musik* (1850) occasioned a telling rebuke from Gustav Freytag (*Die Grenzbote*, 1869), who pointed out that the sensationalism and excessive emphasis on scenic effect that Wagner attacked in Jewish opera (Meyerbeer) were in fact leading characteristics of his own art. Wagner's 'philosophical' use of the theatre has been imitated by Pfitzner (*Palestrina*, 1917), Hindemith (*Mathis der Maler*, 1938; *Die Harmonie der Welt*, 1957) and Schoenberg (*Moses und Aron*, incomplete, composed 1930–32), all of whom wrote their own librettos.

To the notion of a libretto as a discrete production which is then set to music, Wagner opposes the idea of the 'Wort-Ton-Drama', in which words and notes are to be the simultaneous expression of the same underlying dramatic idea. Ideally, poet and composer must be the same man. The form that the words took in *Der Ring des Nibelungen* was appropriate to the material, but also to the music. Short, flexible two- or three-stressed lines are linked by alliteration and assonance in the medieval manner, without rhyme or fixed stanza patterns, though these devices are also medieval in origin: he could have used them but did not wish to write in closed forms or compose the periodic melody with balanced phrases that they would have elicited. *Sprechgesang*, halfway between song and recitative, might from time to time be lifted into the equivalent of an aria by arranging the short-lined verses into more regular, quasi-stanzaic patterns. The lack of continuous melody in the singers' parts, which had been the most obvious kind of continuity in earlier forms of opera, was to be replaced by the play of shorter motifs and musical images in the orchestral fabric (sometimes harmonic, colouristic or dependent upon key). The motifs' appearance, and the emotional effect of harmonic modulation, would depend on the imagery of the words and on reference to the thoughts, feelings and identities of the characters in the drama. The costumes, scenery, properties and stage movement, even in the end the design of the theatre with its sunken orchestra pit and uninterrupted view of the stage from every seat, were all to serve this single, unified conception of the matter in hand, in a 'collective work of art' (*Gesamtkunstwerk*). Wagner's use of the word 'Kunst' (Art with a capital A) is modern and reflects a change in the history of ideas during the lifetime of Goethe. The arts were no longer a series of separate crafts, each with its own rationale and technique; and the artist, usually regarded in earlier times as a person of lower class unless fame crowned a career in literature, painting or architecture, was no longer an artisan. Each art came to be seen as contributing in its individual way to a common higher end, with characteristics belonging to all. *Gesamtkunstwerk* therefore implies both a collectivity and a union of the arts, and its prophet was the highest of High Artists.

Wagner's astounding achievement, his universal competence and his single-minded energy made it very hard to follow in his path, though many lesser men tried. His methods proved, in fact, to have a wider application than he had intended: they made it possible to set a whole play, perhaps suitably shortened, to music, for audiences could now accept an opera without arias, provided that the music allowed the drama to operate in its own time-scale. With less gifted composers, of course, an excess of orchestral activity, combined with a too uniform speed of delivery of the sung text, may slow the drama down to the point of monotony or at least may impede the flexibility and rapid contrasts on which most forms of play depend. This may become a virtue, if understatement and a sense of helpless undeserved suffering, slowly struggling in a world where God has died, form the basis of the play, as in Maeterlinck's *Pelléas et Mélisande* (Debussy, 1902), where however the scenes are short and numerous, affording opportunities for contrast of colour and texture. The absence of periodic melody and aria enables a prose text to be used, which may still have poetic qualities, or free verse lacking the predictability of regular metre and rhyme; in the work of an artisan-librettist of the old kind, on the other hand, the need to match metrical patterns and find rhymes often leads to word-spinning and distortion of the thought.

The Wagnerian technique allows a libretto to be very much longer in relation to the music than earlier librettos (except the very first), and to accommodate explanatory material and fuller discussion of the issues on which the drama turns; the portrayal of character no longer needs to be analytical, arranging the character into a particular psychological pose for the extended moment of an aria devoted to a single emotion, but can become Shakespearean, showing us the whole character all of the time. This allowed for the development of the *Literaturoper*, in which the literary interest is supposed to be as great as the musical. Besides the works by Debussy, Pfitzner, Hindemith and Schoenberg already mentioned, Berg's *Wozzeck* (1914–22, performed 1925) and *Lulu* (posthumously completed and performed in 1979) are of this kind, though the musical fabric of each is contrived with unusual sophistication. Strauss moved into his partnership with Hofmannsthal (a major Austrian poet in his youth, who found the music compensating for his lost lyrical inspiration and his obsession with the inadequacy of language) after his success in setting two long one-act plays, Wilde's *Salome* (1905) and Hofmannsthal's own *Elektra* (adapted by the poet, 1909); after Hofmannsthal's death, Strauss turned to Zweig, Gregor and finally the conductor Clemens Krauss for similar librettos, and his last opera, Krauss's *Capriccio* (1942), is actually described as a 'conversation piece for music', incorporating much aesthetic discussion of the relationship between music and words.

The alternative tradition was reasserted in modern times by Stravinsky. *The Rake's Progress* (Auden and Kallman, 1951) sets out to conduct its business almost entirely in song (there are a few recitatives). Britten's operas, too, are of the older kind. Both methods are valid; but there is no doubt that the greater detail of intellectual content of the *Literaturoper* and its resemblance to a play has extended the intellectual scope of the art, brought a wide audience to value complex musical theatre and attracted a number of leading writers into the opera house, together with unusual masterpieces such as the plays of Büchner, Wedekind and Maeterlinck, works which are not often performed or read outside their countries of origin.

10. THE 'NUMBER OPERA' AND ALTERNATIVE PATHS. Wagner's theory and example were slow to attract composers in France and Italy, though they fascinated writers such as Baudelaire and D'Annunzio. The only Wagnerizing opera in France before Debussy's was Reyer's *Sigurd* (Du Locle and Blau, 1884), which was at first resisted in Paris and had its première in Brussels. Boito knew and admired Wagner, but his librettos and operas do not attempt music drama. There are elements of Wagner in the Germanic Busoni's unfinished *Doktor Faust* (posthumously performed in Germany, completed by Jarnach, 1925); but the Italian, neo-classicizing strain in Busoni's make-up ensured that he stayed in the camp of 'number opera', though he wrote his own librettos. So too did the Wagnerian Pizzetti, a friend and collaborator of D'Annunzio.

In German-speaking lands, especially (but not only) in italianate Austria and the south, a thriving school of opera had continued the Mozart–Weber line and established a repertory of well-loved non-Wagnerian operas before 1848, which continued to be repeated. Nicolai (*Die lustigen Weiber von Windsor*, after Shakespeare; Mosenthal, 1849), Marschner (with Kind and others) and Lortzing, who wrote his own librettos and like Wagner suffered for his revolutionary sympathies (*Regina*, 1848), produced interesting and highly professional operas, some with, some without spoken dialogue; among literary men, E. T. A. Hoffmann, Tieck and Brentano wrote Romantic but old-style librettos set by less able composers (or left unset). The tradition continued with all-sung operas such as Goetz's *Der Widerspänstigen Zähmung* (Widmann, with the composer, 1874); even operas by Wagnerian enthusiasts such as Cornelius (*Der Barbier von Bagdad*, his libretto, 1858) and Humperdinck (*Hänsel und Gretel*, Wette, 1893) consist in the main of recognizable closed forms linked by dialogue set to looser kinds of music. Comedy and

fairy-tale gain greatly, of course, from the point and wit of balanced vocal phrasing. Non-Wagnerian traditions are alive and well in Hindemith's neo-classical *Cardillac* (Lion, 1926, revised 1952).

Wagnerian music dramas were designed for serious, literate, middle-class pan-Germanic listeners of the kind who joined the Wagner-Vereine, helped with the early financing of Bayreuth, and were prepared to study the writings of the Master and his disciples. In the commercial theatre, very different conditions obtained, and even court opera houses, like those supported by state or civic subsidy, were now under the control of impresarios whose success depended on box-office takings and, where publishers had a stake in management, on the sale of vocal scores or piano arrangements of operas which caught on. At the same time, costs were constantly increasing. In France, which meant Paris, an unsophisticated public was to be wooed at the Opéra with ever larger musical and scenic resources, and the adulation of 'star' singers meant that their salaries rose. The investment in a grand opera by Scribe and Meyerbeer, with its massed chorus and dancers and its spectacular scenic effects mingling the supernatural with the grossly naturalistic (real armour, skating), could be amortized only by keeping the opera in the repertory year after year; there was far less space, as a result, for new works. In Italy, though impresarios and publishers came to rule the opera houses, there was a multiplicity of centres, so that the old ways continued until quite late in the century. It took longer for the repertory to start 'freezing'; success meant the repetition of the work in question in other cities, rather than its perpetuation in its original home. Grand operas had to be publicized as unique events, unique collaborations of composer and librettist, and that was also the case with Verdi (for reasons to be explored); but in Italian opera generally and to some extent in lesser French opera, the 18th-century practice, whereby several successive composers might reset an old libretto, suitably remodelled, took much longer to die.

Commercialism and the appeal to the lowest common denominator of taste have obvious dangers. Even when a work was launched with proper artistic control, there was (and still is) no copyright in a stage production, and its revivals might bring appalling indignities in train: Rossini's vast *Guillaume Tell* (De Jouy and others, 1829) remained popular, especially for its ballets, but was sometimes subjected to cuts making a nonsense of the whole. On one occasion, only Act 2 was to be given; when Rossini was informed, he said 'What? Surely not all of it?'

Commercialism, and grand opera's emphasis on externals and on spectacular rather than subtle singing, no doubt played their part in leading Rossini to withdraw from operatic composition. Perhaps, too, he had felt more than most the continuing stress of constantly having to adapt himself to new partnerships: to work twice or three times with the same librettist was a rare experience for him (and even then not always welcome), and this was at a time when the nature of such a relationship was changing. The genres of opera were also shifting: in a more democratic age the heroic, classically-orientated *opera seria* collapsed; with an infusion of pathos and greater realism from the world of comic opera, the two-act *opera semiseria* was born. Greater realism came to prevail in the casting and acting also: the long reign of the castrato hero began to wane, and such parts were transferred both to female mezzo-sopranos and contraltos and, increasingly, to tenors. Love scenes could now be played in less stylized fashion, and the old 'exemplary' stories of *gloire* and the moral gave way to a deeper and more realistic treatment of love relationships; indeed, operas are now about little else.

The need for popular success did not preclude more serious literary endeavours, particularly in cities such as Milan, which was large and important enough to boast a number of *literati*. When Romani succeeded Romanelli as theatre poet there, it was as the result of a competition deliberately aiming to improve the standard of libretto writing. His collaborations with Donizetti and Bellini produced operas that have endured. Texts that manage to combine a neo-classical purity of language with stories and settings from the misty north, such as *Norma* (1831), transmit some of the feeling of Romanticism, though not its full substance (the source-play was in fact French); *Il pirata* (1827) presents for the first time in Italian opera the figure of a social rebel, like the heroes of Goethe's *Goetz von Berlichingen* or Schiller's *Die Räuber*. The emotion is not raw, but highly stylized, both in the literary language and in the still classical artifice of ornamental singing which we have come to call 'bel canto'. Florid singing lends its verve equally to comic effect, and this was the last great age of Italian comic opera. Its librettos vary greatly in literary quality, but the existence of conventions assured that they were usually well-planned for music; at least two of Rossini's authors, Sterbini and Ferretti, can claim to rank with Casti and Da Ponte.

The fantasy, violence, horror and supernatural folk-tales of German Romanticism do not find their way into the Italian libretto of this period, which favoured the pathos and more pallid emotions of Scott's novels; but deeper feelings were stirring in the long struggle of the Risorgimento, and with the early operas of Verdi – all serious, save one 'prentice failure – the opera-theatres of Italy began to seethe with revolutionary and danger-ously communal emotions which the authorities kept trying in vain to suppress. Even in 1858, on the eve of the final victory of the Risorgimento, Somma was forced to change not merely the country and social level of the regicidal *Un ballo in maschera*, but also a third of his lines; in Piave's *Rigoletto* (1851), Hugo's immoral French king had to be demoted to become a Gonzaga Duke of Mantua – a family safely extinct. In the circum-stances of armed insurrection, heroic themes gain an authentic ring of truth; anti-tyrannical, anti-aristocratic, sometimes anti-clerical plots, often depicting an en-slaved people or valiant resistance to a foreign foe, gave rise to many an anti-Austrian demonstration. The librettist who led Verdi furthest in this direction was Solera. Verdi's first success was with Solera's *Nabucodonosor* or *Nabucco* (1842), a libretto rejected by Nicolai, perhaps because it imitated the biblical background and choral grandeur of Rossini's *Mosè* (Tottola, 1818, Naples), particularly as expanded in its Paris version of 1827 (Jouy and Balocchi). Verdi developed the form of the unison aria-for-chorus to great effect, never more movingly than in the chorus of Jews in exile, 'Va, pensiero', which was intended as, and became, a great national hymn. So did 'O Signore, dal tetto natio', in his next opera, *I Lombardi alla prima crociata* (1843), also by Solera, a passionate if rough-and-ready poet who had the sense, even this early in Verdi's career, to accept suggestions from his composer. The chorus from *I Lombardi* is mentioned in Giuseppe

Giusti's famous and often anthologized short poem *Sant'Ambrogio*: it is sung by the congregation in a Milanese church, in the presence of a body of Austrian troops who sing a sad song of their own, which makes the poet realize that they are not Austrians but wretched conscript Slavs, exiles equally oppressed by tyranny. Anyone wishing to understand the difference between the best of contemporary Italian poetry and the func-tional, operatically effective verse of Solera or Piave could not do better than to compare their efforts with Giusti. But Giusti's poem could hardly be set to music.

Verdi must sometimes have been surprised at the way in which his operas lit popular flames around Italy, often because patriotic audiences lent to the situations in his operas and to phrases that he set a sense which could hardly have been in his mind. More important for his future work was his ability to fasten on to passionate and demonic personages in these early operas and magnify them into true dynamos of dramatic energy: Abigaille, in *Nabucco*, is the first example. In his later operas he sought out such unusual and impetuous characters. His quest for them took him to the same literature that other composers were exploiting, con-temporary novels and plays on a European scale, Byron, Schiller, Hugo, the Spanish Gutiérrez and the Duke of Rivas, and Shakespeare (but not Scott, whom so many others rifled: his main characters were presumably in-sufficiently passionate). Twice he set French dramas embodying social situations prefiguring Ibsen, in *Stiffelio* (Piave, 1850), which failed, and *La traviata* (Piave, 1853, from a short novel dramatized by its author, Dumas *fils*), whose initial failure he triumphantly redeemed by revision. It was not the story but the singing that led to its poor reception: the opera pushes the baritone (Germont *père*) and at times the soprano to a dangerously high tessitura, particularly in their long and uninterrupted duet scene in Act 2 (a remarkable example of Verdi's and Piave's resourceful-ness in telling a story through continuous song). Dumas' original is considerably softened in its move from prose to lyric verse, and harsh details are omitted, such as the discussion of the courtesan's income, and even the reason why she wears camellias (white when she is avail-able, red when nature forbids). But the revisions after the opera's initial failure do not further weaken the story, and the opera stands as an example, daring for its time, of a plot outlining a common situation among the moneyed classes (note that Violetta is not a king's mis-tress and has more than one client).

The success of the opera must have been due less to its socially conscious theme than to its pathos (Violetta re-deems herself, giving up both her rich protectors and true love, and dies), a feature wonderfully emphasized by the musical setting. In *Don Carlo* (at first in French as *Don Carlos*, Méry and Du Locle, 1867, adapted and translated by Ghislanzoni, 1884), another opera rich in intellectual content, we find the librettists actually suppressing an important detail in Schiller for the sake of the pathos that feeds music. Philip II's wonderful scene at the opening of Act 4, 'Elle ne m'aime pas' ('She does not love me') – already significantly different in the Italian ('Ella giammai m'amò': 'She *never* loved me'), presumably occasioned only by the rhythm of the exist-ing music – begins with slightly different words in Schiller's drama, but the difference is crucial to Schiller's portrait of the cold, calculating, brutal king. What he says is 'Nie könnt' *ich* ihr Liebe geben' (Act 3 scene i, Schiller's italics): 'I could never love her'. He has married her for reasons of state, and his inability to love her is cited as a possible further motive for her possible adultery with his son. But there must be an aria, a vehicle for pathos; and music depends on sympathy, so the old king must have a heart to break. Verdi ensures that we do not think twice about it, and indeed the aria and its prelude offer a remarkable and convincing portrait of royal loneliness; equally remarkable is that Verdi disregarded the pattern of recitative leading to aria verse offered by his librettists and moulded the scene into a single whole, following musical and thematic procedures that break down the compartments of traditional form just as much as Wagner's did, but on the scale of a scene.

Its subject is kingly power, the isolation of the ruler, the vanity and frustration of his attempts to impose his will, the lack of human contact, the ultimate emptiness of failure and death. This is a far cry from 'exemplary' pictures of a benevolent despot of the 18th century. It is a topic that interested several composers of the 19th century, partly because the nature of monarchic rule was coming into question, partly because revolutions might place, indeed had placed, absolute power in the hands of non-royal despots. There could be no better study of the disparate approaches to the same theme in 19th-century opera than to compare the scene just examined with the monologues and situation of Wagner's Wotan or Musorgsky's Boris Godunov. Portraits of equivalent depth and truth are achieved in each case, but by totally different means. Each offers intellectual matter for serious debate, but this is much more evident during a reading of the libretto, beforehand or afterwards, than while witnessing the scene (this is possibly less true of Wotan, but the strain of trying to follow his thought against the passionate orchestral background can be more than a little exhausting). What memorable music does to an important situation or subject, especially in 19th-century opera, is to sweep one's mind up in a flood, an eddying vortex of emotion raised by and around the words; only when the flood has receded is one able to reflect upon its cause and consider the subject further. The effect is not limited to music. It is what Burke called 'the sublime', known also to the ancients, and one's reaction to great poetry or painting, even architecture, is not dissimilar; when all come together in the opera house, we realize how akin it is to religious experience, and begin to understand how and why 19th-century art, and opera in particular, aspired in its greatest manifestations to invade that part of the psyche which in previous ages had found refuge and release in sacred ritual and religious ecstasy. For that reason it is, if not impossible, largely irrelevant to treat the history of the libretto, in its essential experience, as a type of purely literary, formal or intellectual development.

There is a difference between transporting an audience into a sublime state of ecstasy – in which for the musically sensitive the principal agent is the music, operating within a clearly delineated dramatic situation – and setting out to overwhelm the spectator with a more factitious kind of excitement, employing all the available theatrical media to deliver a series of Dionysiac shocks that leave no after-savour of Apollonian reflection – though they may excite sufficient aggressiveness to spark off a revolution, as did Auber's *La muette de Portici* (Scribe, 1828, better known as *Masaniello*) in Brussels in 1830. Here we have the main substance of Wagner's criticism of the grand opera of Scribe and his assembly-line of collaborators: that the 'effects' had no causes, whether within the drama or outside it, that they did not relate to each other, that they were not poetically imagined as part of a harmonious whole. Wagner himself uses many Scribean effects, but not in Scribe's haphazard manner, in which surprising contrasts count for more than meaning. One example in Wagner is the byplay between Eva and Walther during the chorale that opens *Die Meistersinger*, and their subsequent conversation in the lee of a church ceremony. But Wagner's chorale, unlike Meyerbeer's ill-harmonized 'Ein feste Burg' and his many church scenes, informs and is informed by the whole drama; it introduces the serious-minded, conservative community of Nurembergers which the young aristocrat must learn to respect, in its marriage customs as well as its art; the art is ritualized in the chorale, which the ear recognizes as resembling and in part explaining the opening theme of the overture, a theme to be associated with the Mastersingers. (Freytag, unable to respond to music that he found simply shapeless, had not been able to understand the difference between Meyerbeer's effects and Wagner's.)

Wagner learnt a great deal from French grand opera; in exile, he made attempts to establish himself in Paris and even wrote an article admiring F. Halévy's *La reine de Chypre* of 1841. But he had been forced into exile because he had wished to change society, not least for the sake of his art; whereas Scribe's desire was merely to entertain, so that his choice of subjects which might be taken as relevant to contemporary issues – revolutions, the clash of religious creeds, heroic nationalism and empire-building – really had no social purpose or imaginative unity to shape them. Scribe himself, in his address on election to the Académie Française in 1836, had publicly denied that the theatre's purpose was to depict society, and bourgeois Paris shared his view: the record of his production (including a great number of plays which, like the opera librettos, were often collaborative ventures led by himself) runs to 76 volumes. His astonishing success as a virtual dictator of taste and fashion in the French theatre for some 30 years shows that he understood his market; he could not have achieved it without a certain mastery of dramatic exposition and clear plotting – though these gifts deserted him in the bungled ending of the one grand opera that he wrote for Verdi, *Les vêpres siciliennes* (with Duveyrier, 1855, remodelled from a *Duc d'Albe* written for Halévy, then Donizetti). He also possessed real wit and a shrewd sense of comic characterization in his comedies and comic operas; through his legion of collaborators and through his example he passed on his technical clarity to the next generation.

But Scribe was no poet, and the finest grand operas that have survived the test of time have librettos by others: *Guillaume Tell* and Berlioz's *Les Troyens*. Both are imaginative unities. The first achieves that status mainly through the consequence, in all senses, of Rossini's music. For the second, the composer, a great master of prose, wrote his own dignified, rather old-fashioned verse, modelled in part on the librettos set by his admired Gluck, and perfectly suited to his own dramatic and musical intentions; but his vast and expensive conception was thought too risky, too little in conformity with the taste of the time, for it to be performed entire, and only the last three of its five acts were staged (in 1863). It was much easier to experiment in the less costly field of *opéra comique*, and that was the route taken by the more valuable French operas of the third quarter of the century, Gounod's *Faust* (Barbier and Carré, after Goethe, 1859), Berlioz's *Béatrice et Bénédict* (his own libretto, after Shakespeare, 1862), and Bizet's *Carmen* (Meilhac and L. Halévy, 1875, after Mérimée's novella of 1845).

Mention of *Carmen* leads to *verismo*, a word that is not to be translated as 'realism' (this has to do with the inducement in the spectator of a sense of imaginative and psychological truth and reality); it means something between verisimilitude and naturalism. Historians of opera have sometimes made too much of *verismo* as a genre, and also of the 20th-century *Zeitoper* on contemporary social and political issues. If veristic operas are worth having, it is not because they are naturalistic; the literary movement of naturalism affected the choice of subject and flow of sympathy in opera, but it did not create a type. Gustave Charpentier's Parisian seamstresses in *Louise* (to his own libretto, 1900), once one has got used to the sewing-machines that replace the spinning-wheels of the conventional spinning chorus, are memorable because they delight us, not because their work in the sweatshop is boring and repetitive and their lives culturally deprived (two things which, outside the opera house, Charpentier did a great deal to combat). There is really no equivalent, even in Zola's librettos, to the full-blown naturalism of Zola's novels, or to a play like Hauptmann's *Die Weber*.

Bizet's *Carmen* is often adduced as a source of the trend towards *verismo*, but its cigarette-girls, gypsies, smugglers and bullfighters are really no more than exotic 'local colour', like the composer's use of Spanish dance rhythms and Spanish popular tunes; they are depicted vividly, but not naturalistically – amusingly, rather – because the aim is to entertain, though with a mild frisson of the unusual, and not to tell us what low life is really like. Mérimée's genuinely naturalistic detail is almost all omitted, and not only observations that might offend on stage, as when he mentions that in the heat of the cigarette factory the girls work stripped to the waist. All the historical and sociological explanations about Spain, the Basques, bullfighting, the trade with Gibraltar, gypsies, the Romany language and 'M. Borrow, missionaire anglais' have vanished. Omitted too is Mérimée's scholarly narrator, who both distances the violent narrative and makes it seem all the more extraordinary, yet authentic because he vouches for it. (The librettists did however raid Mérimée's other writings on his Spanish travels here and there, and even his translation of Pushkin's *The Gypsies* – for the character of Carmen owes a good deal, even actual verses such as 'coupe-moi, brûle-moi', to Zemfira, a Russian, not a Spanish gypsy: so much for authentic local colour.)

Realism, not naturalism, is of course what both novella and opera are concerned with, though the latter adds a large dose of sentimentality in the figure of Micaëla. She serves to throw into relief the realistically presented figure of Carmen, the beautiful, cunning, opportunistic, passionate, brave, fatalistic but rootless woman who dares to claim the same freebooting amorous privileges as a man; she need not have been a gypsy at all, save that the image underlines some of her qualities and allows her freedom of movement; perhaps as important, it permitted people to believe, wrongly, that they were unlikely to run the risk of meeting such a creature in the safety of their drawing-rooms. The glamour and heroic quality of her music nevertheless contradicts Mérimée's learned Greek epigraph, a coup-

let from Palladas which proclaims that 'woman is excrement; she has two good hours, one on her marriage bed and the other at her death'.

Verismo operas are in fact 'something to do with violence and the poor', as Auden said of Housman's poetry, and allow middle-class audiences to sublimate their suppressed feelings of violence by transference to a lower order of society, feared but unknown, where anything may happen. They have their literary origin, often, in Italian tales of peasant life such as Verga's *Cavalleria rusticana* (1884, a play that he made from one of his short stories, turned into a libretto for Mascagni by Targioni-Tozzetti and Menasci in 1890); these in turn seem to imitate some of Mérimée's other short, violent *contes* such as his Corsican tale *Mateo Falcone* (1829). The resulting operas are simple stories of high emotion, so that like their originals they are often brief, and in one act, like *Pagliacci* (Leoncavallo, his own libretto, 1892). The latter soon became half of the traditional doublebill, 'Cav and Pag'. One might have expected such a concatenation of murders to prove monotonous, but the combination succeeds because of the contrast between the simplicity, almost simple-mindedness, of Mascagni's music and dramaturgy and the sophistication of Leoncavallo's, which employs the device of a play within a play and sets out his artistic credo in a prologue; within each work there is also a succession of sharply contrasting scenes and interludes unusual in such short operas. What all *verismo* operas appear to have in common with the vocalism of much of *Carmen* – and this may in part be due to a desire to reflect the utterance of simple folk – is that they abandon the grand style of singing in favour of a more direct manner, lacking fioritura and artifice, in which brilliance, intensity and often sheer volume are what counts.

The tradition of the 'number opera' continues into and throughout our own century. Composers and librettists may make more or less effort to disguise the joins between narrative time and psychological time, but the structure is readily discernible, is found artistically satisfying, and probably notches up more successes than the Wagnerian approach. Even Strauss's *Der Rosenkavalier*, essentially a music drama, probably owes much of its popularity to its various discrete set pieces, such as the sentimental duet near the end – pure *Hänsel und Gretel* – between Sophie and Octavian. Even Wagner wrote a quintet and songs in *Die Meistersinger*; the latter are of course essential to the opera's subject, but Wagner chose the subject. But such things seem to count for little beside the power of Wagner's theory and his more normal practice; in the present lack of agreed conventions of melody, the laws of prosody rule, and deservedly popular operas such as those of Puccini or, more recently, Britten are often held to belong to a lower order of creation, or condemned as old-fashioned. There are no doubt valid criticisms to be made of both composers and their librettists, but not, surely, on such grounds as these. Brecht condemned popular opera as 'culinary', merely sensuous, and saw the quality of musical enjoyment – hitherto regarded as an innocent gratification of the senses (Burney's phrase) – as a wicked diversion from more urgent matters: those who are not for us are against us. For his own opera texts, though, he stuck to the 'number' type, choosing composers who had proved good at turning out nonsensuous music for the songs of his plays, where the important verse was sung either in a raucous and declamatory manner or like a popular song in a cabaret.

On the whole, great playwright though he was, his non-culinary operas are found indigestible, or at least predictable and a monotonous diet if repeated; but it must be admitted that Kurt Weill still has his devotees.

Although there is no sustained intellectual tradition of anti-Wagnerian theory in opera (why waste time justifying methods which remained common and worked in practice?), there have always been literary men prepared to defend the 'number opera'. Plays too, particularly poetic dramas, have lyrical islands which develop a thought or emotion, connected by more narrative material. Alfieri developed a form, no doubt on Greek models, which he thought would allow discrete musical scenes with arias and choruses a place in tragedy, writing *Abele*, a 'tramelogedia', in 1786–90. De Musset, a great poet and dramatist, chose the occasion of his election to the Académie Française to defend the fragmented structure of opera, and Claudel too published a theory and implemented it in collaboration with Milhaud. He also contrived to take operatic values into the concert hall, where D'Annunzio had been before him, with *Jeanne d'Arc au bûcher* (Honegger, 1938). Honegger had made earlier attempts at 'opera-oratorio', but the most successful examples of the genre are Stravinsky's *Oedipus rex* (Cocteau, translated into Latin by Daniélou, in order to distance the intellectual immediacy of the words, 1927) and his 'melodrama' *Perséphone* (Gide, from his existing play, 1934). Stravinsky, in precept and example, has proved to be the most enduring centre of reaction against Wagnerism. He had also to fight against a Russian tradition (exemplified in Prokofiev) which favoured naturalistic declamation. His preference for closed forms has been vindicated by lasting popular and critical acclaim, but his demotion of verbal stress (as opposed to syllabic quantity) still makes some English-speaking listeners uncomfortable. He will win in the end, for ears sensitive to the logic of melodic compulsion have long accepted without question such contradictions as Moralès's 'Il y sera Quand *la* ga*r*de montante/Remplacera *la* ga*r*de descendante' (*Carmen*, Act 1: ex.5*a*) or the way in which the melody and rhythm of a sequence dictate the separation of adjective and noun in Rodolfo's 'Me, cagion del fatale – mal che l'uccide!' (*La bohème*, Act 3: ex.5*b*).

Ex.5

(a) Bizet: *Carmen*, Act 1 scene i

['There will be, when the guard coming on duty replaces the guard going off duty, . . .']

(b) Puccini: *La bohème*, Act 3

['I am the cause of that fatal wrong that has killed her']

The present century has seen many new initiatives and technical attempts to take opera in new directions, of which the most promising, probably – because it is not tied to any one artistic credo – is the way in which small-scale opera has moved into a new environment with 'music-theatre' works; they stem ultimately from Stravinsky's experiment in writing a piece for small forces, to be performed in a concert venue, when he fell on hard times in Switzerland during World War I (*Histoire du soldat*, Ramuz, 1918). The advantage, apart from arguments of economy, is that a concert hall or ad hoc venue removes the spectator's expectation of naturalistic theatrical illusion and forces the presenters to face the necessity of appealing to the audience's imagination through stylized artifice. Unlike much 'experiment' in opera, this was in the true scientific meaning a trial, an experience that could be repeated and validated by others and enter the sum of human knowledge. Many 'experiments' do not meet with such good fortune, but die as most operas have always died, with the difference that in an age of subsidized 'experiment' they serve increasingly to fragment the language of the art. It is not surprising that extremes of complexity at one end of the operatic spectrum should have begun to produce a contrary tendency, minimalism, at the other. It may yet be, of course, that this new experience, which sophisticated old operatic hands find boring in the extreme, will enable the art to build up again from basic criteria and with a wider audience.

As the end of the technological 20th century approaches, it might have been expected that the rapid development of new media would radically change the art of opera. It has certainly offered new resources in presentation, whether in the theatre (or stadium!) or on film, television or videotape; but these have been more commonly employed in popularizing or revitalizing old repertory rather than in generating new forms and styles for our time. They have undoubtedly increased the audience, but much of that increase consists of those who do not regularly attend opera in the theatre as a living, communal experience; and the general insistence on using the original language for recordings of opera and for performances in many of the more prestigious theatres means that audiences – and potential librettists and composers – get to know the art at one remove, and find it difficult to relate it to their own experience of reading, speaking and singing.

Something has been said in section I of the difficulties and possibilities that the present scene affords. It may be that the astonishing technical means now deployed in the vast 'pop' concert, and in videotape and compact disc, which have produced a new art form for popular song, may in time offer a new context and unsuspected new directions for opera; but they have changed the venue and the nature of the experience rather than the backbone of words and music. The novelties on the 'pop' scene seem to parallel those produced by grand opera: Dionysiac effects without much cause save the making of money, sensation and escape rather than Apollonian reflection. The same is true of the musical play. If opera is to grow, it will presumably be because the now dominant partners in the words-and-music amalgam, the composers, wish it to, and find musically intelligent librettists answering their needs.

This account of the development in history of the libretto has been highly selective, partial, perhaps, in both senses of the word. There are many librettists, including good ones, and many issues left unexplored. The most important of these is the question of how to read a libretto, and, equally important, how to assess what earlier and apparently authoritative critics have had to say about librettists and their craft. This and further matters form the substance of Section III.

The following librettists and other literary figures are entered in the dictionary: ACCIAIUOLI, FILIPPO; ADAMI, GIUSEPPE; ADENIS, JULES; AESCHYLUS; ALEWIJN, ABRAHAM; ALGAROTTI, FRANCESCO; ALLACCI, LEONE; ANDERSEN, HANS CHRISTIAN; ANDERSEN, LUDWIG; ANDOLFATI, PIETRO; ANDREINI, GIOVANNI BATTISTA; ANELLI, ANGELO; ANSEAUME, LOUIS; APOLLONI, GIOVANNI FILIPPO; ARCOLEO, ANTONIO; ARIOSTO, LUDOVICO; ARISTOPHANES; ARNICHES, CARLOS; AUDEN, W. H.; AUDINOT, NICOLAS-MÉDARD; AUENBRUGGER, JOSEPH LEOPOLD; AURELI, AURELIO; AVERARA, PIETRO D'; BACHMANN, INGEBORG; BACZKO, LUDWIG VON; BADINI, CARLO FRANCESCO; BADOARO, GIACOMO; BALÁZS, BÉLA; BARBIER, AUGUSTE; BARBIER, JULES; BARBIER, MARIE-ANNE; BARDARI, GIUSEPPE; BATKA, RICHARD; BAYARD, JEAN-FRANÇOIS-ALFRED; BEATTY-KINGSTON, WILLIAM; BEAUMARCHAIS, PIERRE-AUGUSTIN; BELASCO, DAVID; BEL'SKY, VLADIMIR NIKOLAYEVICH; BENELLI, SEM; BENIGNI, DOMENICO; BEREGAN, NICOLÒ; BERNARD, PIERRE-JOSEPH; BERNARDONI, PIETRO ANTONIO; BERNAUER, RUDOLF; BERTATI, GIOVANNI; BIANCHI, ANTONIO (i); BICKERSTAFF, ISAAC; BIDERA, GIOVANNI EMANUELE; BIS, HIPPOLYTE-LOUIS-FLORENT; BLAU, EDOUARD; BOCCARDI, MICHELANGELO; BOCCHE-RINI, GIOVANNI GASTONE; BOGGIO, GIANDOMENICO; BOLOGNESE, DOMENICO; BOND, EDWARD; BONIS, NOVELLO; BONLINI, GIOVANNI CARLO; BOSTEL, LUCAS VON; BOTTARELLI, GIOVANNI GUALBERTO; BOTTURINI, MATTIA; BOUCICAULT, DION; BOUILLY, JEAN-NICOLAS; BOYER, CLAUDE; BRACCIOLI, GRAZIO; BRAMMER, JULIUS; BRANDES, JOHANN CHRISTIAN; BRECHT, BERTOLT; BRENTANO, CLEMENS; BRESSAND, FRIEDRICH CHRISTIAN; BRETZNER, CHRISTOPH FRIEDRICH; BREUNING, STEPHAN VON; BRIANI, FRANCESCO; BROD, MAX; BRUNSWICK (i); BRUYR, JOSÉ; BÜCHNER, GEORG; BULGAKOV, MIKHAIL AFANAS'YEVICH; BULWER-LYTTON, EDWARD; BUNN, ALFRED; BÜRDE, SAMUEL GOTTLIEB; BURGESS, ANTHONY; BURGOYNE, JOHN; BURNAND, F. C.; BUSENELLO, GIOVANNI FRANCESCO; BUSSANI, GIACOMO FRANCESCO; BUTI, FRANCESCO; BYRON; CAHUSAC, LOUIS DE; CAIN, HENRI; CALDERÓN DE LA BARCA, PEDRO; CALVOCORESSI, MICHEL-DIMITRI; CALZABIGI, RANIERI DE'; CAMMARANO, SALVADORE; CAMPISTRON, JEAN GALBERT DE; CANDI, GIOVANNI PIETRO; CAPECE, CARLO SIGISMONDO; ČAPEK, KAREL; CARPANI, GIUSEPPE; CARRÉ, MICHEL; CASONA, ALEJANDRO; CASORRI, FERDINANDO; CASSANI, VINCENZO; CASTI, GIOVANNI BATTISTA; ČECH, SVATOPLUK; CERLONE, FRANCESCO; CERVANTES, MIGUEL DE; ČERVINKOVÁ-RIEGROVÁ, MARIE; CHABANON, MICHEL-PAUL-GUY DE; CHEKHOV, ANTON PAVLOVICH; CHEZY, HELMINA VON; CHIABRERA, GABRIELLO; CHIARI, PIETRO; CHIVOT, HENRI CHARLES; CIALLI, RINALDO; CICOGNINI, GIACINTO ANDREA; CIGNA-SANTI, VITTORIO AMEDEO; CLAIRVILLE; COBB, JAMES; COCTEAU, JEAN; COFFEY, CHARLES; COLAUTTI, ARTURO; COLETTE; COLMAN; COLTELLINI, MARCO; COLUZZI, NICCOLÒ; CONGREVE, WILLIAM; CONTINI, DOMENICO FILIPPO; CORI, ANGELO MARIA; CORMON, EUGÈNE; CORNEILLE, PIERRE; CORNEILLE, THOMAS; CORRADI, GIULIO CESARE; CRABBE, GEORGE; CRÉBILLON, PROSPER JOLYOT DE; CRÉMIEUX, HECTOR-JONATHAN; CROZIER, ERIC; CUPEDA, DONATO; DANCHET, ANTOINE; D'ANNUNZIO, GABRIELE; DANTE ALIGHIERI; DA PONTE, LORENZO; D'AVERARA, MARCO; DAVENANT, WILLIAM; DAVID, DOMENICO; DEFRANCESCHI, CARLO PROSPERO; DE GAMERRA, GIOVANNI; DEHN, PAUL; DELAVIGNE, GERMAIN; DELESTRE-POIRSON, CHARLES-GASPARD; DELLA VALLE, PIETRO; DE ROGATIS, FRANCESCO SAVERIO; DE SANTIS, LUIGI; DE TOTIS, GIUSEPPE DOMENICO; D'HÈLE, THOMAS; DICKENS, CHARLES; DIODATI, GIUSEPPE MARIA; D'ORMEVILLE, CARLO; DOSTOYEVSKY, FYODOR MIKHAYLOVICH; DRYDEN, JOHN; DUCHÉ DE VANCY, JOSEPH-FRANÇOIS; DU LOCLE, CAMILLE; DUMAS, ALEXANDRE (i); DUMAS, ALEXANDRE (ii); DUNCAN, RONALD; DUNN, GEOFFREY; DURANDI, JACOPO; ECHEGARAY, MIGUEL; EN-VALLSSON, CARL; ERCKMANN-CHATRIAN; EURIPIDES; FARNIE, H. B.; FAUSTINI, GIOVANNI; FAVART, CHARLES-SIMON; FEDERICO, GENNARO ANTONIO; FEIND, BARTHOLD; FERNÁNDEZ SHAW, CARLOS; FERNÁNDEZ SHAW, GUILLERMO; FERRETTI, JACOPO; FEUSTKING, FRIEDRICH CHRISTIAN; FIELDING, HENRY; FITZBALL, EDWARD; FONTANA, FERDINANDO; FONTENELLE, BERNARD LE BOVIER DE; FOPPA, GIUSEPPE MARIA; FORSTER, E. M.; FORZANO, GIOVACCHINO; FRAMERY, NICOLAS ETIENNE; FRANC-NOHAIN; FRIEDRICH, W.; FRIGIMELICA ROBERTI, GIROLAMO; FRISARI, GIROLAMO; FRUGONI, CARLO INNOCENZO; FUZELIER, LOUIS; GALLET, LOUIS; GALUPPI, ANTONIO; GARCÍA GUTIÉRREZ, ANTONIO; GATTA, ANTONIO; GAY, JOHN; GENÉE, RICHARD; GERSHWIN, IRA; GHISLANZONI, ANTONIO; GIACOSA, GIUSEPPE; GIESEKE, JOHANN GEORG CARL LUDWIG; GIGLI, GEROLAMO; GILARDONI, DOMENICO; GILBERT, W. S.; GILLE, PHILIPPE; GIOTTI, COSIMO; GIOVANNINI, PIETRO; GIUSTI, GIROLAMO; GIUVO, NICOLA; GOETHE, JOHANN WOLFGANG VON; GOGOL, NIKOLAY VASIL'YEVICH; GOLDONI, CARLO; GOLISCIANI, ENRICO; GONDINET, EDMOND; GONELLA, FRANCESCO; GOTTER, FRIEDRICH WILHELM; GOZZI, CARLO; GREGOR, JOSEPH; GRILLPARZER, FRANZ; GRIMANI, VINCENZO; GRIMM; GROPPO, ANTONIO; GROSSMANN, GUSTAV FRIEDRICH WILHELM; GRÜNWALD, ALFRED; GUARINI, BATTISTA; GUASTALLA, CLAUDIO;

GUICHARD, HENRY; GUIDI, FRANCESCO; GUILLARD, NICOLAS-FRANÇOIS; HAFNER, PHILIPP; HALÉVY, LUDOVIC; HAMMERSTEIN, OSCAR, II; HARRISON, TONY; HARSDÖRFFER, GEORG PHILIPP; HARTMANN, GEORGES; HASSALL, CHRISTOPHER; HEERMANN, GOTTLOB EPHRAIM; HEINE, HEINRICH; HENSLER, KARL FRIEDRICH; HERKLOTS, CARL ALEXANDER; HILL, AARON; HINSCH, HINRICH; HOARE, PRINCE; HOË, JOHANN JOACHIM; HOFFMAN, FRANÇOIS-BENOÎT; HOFMANNSTHAL, HUGO VON; HOMER; HOOD, BASIL; HOPP, JULIUS; HUBER, FRANZ XAVER; HUEFFER, FRANCIS; HUGHES, JOHN; HUGO, VICTOR; HUXLEY, ALDOUS; IBSEN, HENRIK; ILLICA, LUIGI; IVANOVICH, CRISTOFORO; JACOBI, JOHANN GEORG; JAIME, LOUIS-ADOLPHE; JAMES, HENRY; JENBACH, BÉLA; JONSON, BEN; JOUY, ETIENNE DE; KALBECK, MAX; KALISCH, ALFRED; KALLMAN, CHESTER; KARAMZIN, NIKOLAY MIKHAYLOVICH; KELLER, GOTTFRIED; KELLGREN, JOHAN HENRIK; KIND, JOHANN FRIEDRICH; KLEIST, HEINRICH VON; KNYAZHNIN, YAKOV BORISOVICH; KOCHNO, BORIS YEVGEN'YEVICH; KÖNIG, JOHANN ULRICH VON; KÖRNER, THEODOR; KÖRNER, THOMAS; KOTZEBUE, AUGUST VON; KRÁSNOHORSKÁ, ELIŠKA; KŘILOV, VIKTOR ALEXANDROVICH; KURZ, JOSEPH FELIX VON; KVAPIL, JAROSLAV (i); LA BRUÈRE, CHARLES-ANTOINE LE CLERC DE; LACHMANN, HEDWIG; LA FONT, JOSEPH DE; LAGRANGE-CHANCEL, FRANÇOIS-JOSEPH DE; LALLI, DOMENICO; LALOY, LOUIS; LAMOTTE, ANTOINE HOUDAR DE; LANFRANCHI ROSSI, CARLO GIUSEPPE; LA SERRE, JEAN-LOUIS-IGNACE DE; LEMAIRE, FERDINAND; LEMENE, FRANCESCO DE; LENZ, JAKOB MICHAEL REINHOLD; LÉON, VICTOR; LERMONTOV, MIKHAIL YUR'YEVICH; LETERRIER, EUGÈNE; LIVIGNI, FILIPPO; LOCATELLI, GIOVANNI BATTISTA; LÖHNER, FRITZ; LONG, JOHN LUTHER; LOPE DE VEGA, FÉLIX; LORENZI, GIAMBATTISTA; LOTI, PIERRE; LUCCHINI, ANTONIO MARIA; MACFARREN, NATALIA; MACHLIS, JOSEPH; MAETERLINCK, MAURICE; MAGGI, CARLO MARIA; MANN, THOMAS; MANZONI, ALESSANDRO; MARCHI, ANTONIO; MARIANI, TOMMASO; MARMONTEL, JEAN FRANÇOIS; MARSOLLIER DES VIVETIÈRES, BENOÎT-JOSEPH; MARTENS, FREDERICK HER-MAN; MARTIN, THOMAS; MARTINELLI, GAETANO; MATTEI, SAVERIO; MAURO, ORTENSIO; MAZZOLÀ, CATERINO; MEILHAC, HENRI; MEISSNER, AUGUST GOTTLIEB; MÉLESVILLE; MELOSIO, FRANCESCO; MELTZER, CHARLES HENRY; MELVILLE, HERMAN; MENDELSON, MIRA ALEXANDROVNA; MÉRIMÉE, PROSPER; MÉRY, JOSEPH; METASTASIO, PIETRO; MICHAELIS, JOHANN BENJAMIN; MIGLIAVACCA, GIOVANNI AMBROGIO; MILILOTTI, PASQUALE; MILLER, ARTHUR; MINATO, NICOLÒ; MISTRAL, FRÉDÉRIC; MITUSOV, STEPAN; MOLIÈRE; MOLINE, PIERRE LOUIS; MONCRIF, FRANÇOIS-AUGUSTIN PARADIS DE; MONEY-COUTTS, FRANCIS BURDETT; MONIGLIA, GIOVANNI ANDREA; MOODY, JOHN; MOORE, THOMAS; MORARI, LORENZO; MORETTI, FERDINANDO; MORSELLI, ADRIANO; MOSENTHAL, SALOMON HERMANN; MOTTEUX, PETER ANTHONY; MÜLLER, GERHARD; MURGER, HENRY; NAJAC, EMILE DE; NERI, GIAMBATTISTA; NERVAL, GÉRARD DE; NESTROY, JOHANN NEPOMUK; NORIS, MATTEO; NUITTER, CHARLES-LOUIS-ETIENNE; OBEY, ANDRÉ; O'KEEFFE, JOHN; OLIVA, FRANCESCO; OLIVIERI, CESARE; O'NEILL, EU-GENE; OPITZ, MARTIN; ORDONNEAU, MAURICE; ORSINI, FLAVIO; OSTROVSKY, ALEXANDER NIKOLAYEVICH; OTTOBONI, PIETRO; OVID; OXENFORD, JOHN; PAGLIUCA, GIUSEPPE; PALAZZI, GIOVANNI; PALLAVICINI, GIOVANNI DOMENICO; PALLAVICINO, STEFANO BENEDETTO; PALOMBA, ANTONIO; PALOMBA, GIUSEPPE; PAMPHILI, BENEDETTO; PAPPENHEIM, MARIE; PARIATI, PIETRO; PASQUALIGO, BENEDETTO; PASQUINI, GIOVANNI CLAUDIO; PASSARINI, FRANCESCO; PASSARO, ANDREA; PELLEGRIN, SIMON-JOSEPH; PEPOLI, ALESSANDRO; PEPOLI, CARLO; PERINET, JOACHIM; PERRIN, PIERRE; PERUZZINI, GIOVANNI; PETROSELLINI, GIUSEPPE; PIAVE, FRANCESCO MARIA; PIAZZA, ANTONIO; PIOVENE, AGOSTIN; PIPER, MYFANWY; PIXÉRÉCOURT, RENÉ CHARLES GUILBERT DE; PIZZI, GIOACCHINO; PLANCHÉ, JAMES ROBINSON; PLOMER, WILLIAM; POE, EDGAR ALLAN; PORTA, NUNZIATO; POSTEL, CHRISTIAN HEINRICH; PRAETORIUS, JOHANN PHILIPP; PREISSOVÁ, GABRIELA; PRÉVOST, ANTOINE-FRANÇOIS; PROCHÁZKA, F. S.; PRUSLIN, STEPHEN; PUCCITELLI, VIRGILIO; PUSHKIN, ALEXANDER SERGEYEVICH; QUINAULT, PHILIPPE; RACINE, JEAN; RAIMUND, FERDINAND; RAMOS CARRIÓN, MIGUEL; RAMOS MARTÍN, JOSÉ; REICHERT, HEINZ; RIDLER, ANNE; RINUCCINI, OTTAVIO; ROCCAFORTE, GAETANO; ROLLI, PAOLO ANTONIO; ROMANELLI, LUIGI; ROMANI, FELICE; ROMERO, FEDERICO; ROSMER, ERNST; ROSPIGLIOSI, GIULIO; ROSSATO, ARTURO; ROSSI, GAETANO; ROSSI, GIACOMO; ROULLET, MARIE FRANÇOIS LOUIS GAND LEBLANC; ROUSSEAU, JEAN-BAPTISTE; ROUSSEAU, JEAN-JACQUES; ROY, PIERRE-CHARLES; ROYER, ALPHONSE; ROZEN, YEGOR FYODOROVICH; RUFFINI, GIOVANNI; SABINA, KAREL; SACCHÈRO, GIACOMO; SADDUMENE, BERNARDO; SAINT-GEORGES, JULES-HENRI VERNOY DE; SAINTONGE, LOUISE-GENEVIÈVE GILLOT; SALVI, ANTONIO; SARACINELLI, FERDINANDO; SARDOU, VICTORIEN; SBARRA, FRANCESCO; SCHIEBELER, DANIEL; SCHIKANEDER, EMANUEL; SCHIKANEDER, KARL; SCHILLER, FRIEDRICH VON; SCHMIDT, GIOVANNI; SCHNITZER, IGNAZ; SCHULZOVÁ, ANEŽKA; SCHWAN, CHRISTIAN FRIEDRICH; SCOTT, WALTER; SCRIBE, EUGÈNE; SEDAINE, MICHEL-JEAN; SERIO, LUIGI; SERNICOLA, CARLO; SERTOR, GAETANO; SEYLER, SOPHIE; SHAKESPEARE, WILLIAM; SHERIDAN, RICHARD BRINSLEY; SHILOVSKY, KON-STANTIN STEPANOVICH; SHIRLEY, JAMES; SILVANI, FRANCESCO; SIMONI,

RENATO; SLATER, MONTAGU; SMITH, HARRY B.; SOGRAFI, SIMEONE ANTONIO; SOLERA, TEMISTOCLE; SOMIGLI, DOMENICO; SOMMA, ANTONIO; SONNLEITHNER, JOSEPH VON; SOPHOCLES; SPAGNA, ARCANGELO; STAMPIGLIA, SILVIO; STANZANI, TOMMASO; STEIN, GERTRUDE; STEIN, LEO; STEPHANIE, GOTTLIEB; STERBINI, CESARE; STRIGGIO, ALESSANDRO; STRINDBERG, AUGUST; STROZZI, GIULIO; SWEERTS, CORNELIS; SYNGE, JOHN MILLINGTON; TAGLIAZUCCHI, GIAMPIETRO; TARANTINI, LEOPOLDO; TASSI, NICCOLÒ; TASSO, TORQUATO; TATE, NAHUM; TCHAIKOVSKY, MODEST IL'YICH; TIECK, LUDWIG; TOLSTOY, LEV NIKOLAYEVICH; TOTTOLA, ANDREA LEONE; TRACEY, EDMUND; TRÉFEU, ETIENNE; TREITSCHKE, GEORG FRIEDRICH; TRINCHERA, PIETRO; TRONSARELLI, OTTAVIO; TROUTBECK, JOHN; TULLIO, FRANCESCO ANTONIO; TURGENEV, IVAN SERGEYEVICH; VAËZ, GUSTAVE; VANLOO, ALBERT; VANNESCHI, FRANCESCO; VARESCO, GIOVANNI BATTISTA; VERAZI, MATTIA; VERGA, GIOVANNI; VILLANI, ANTONIO; VILLATI, LEOPOLDO DE; VILLIFRANCHI, GIOVANNI COSIMO; VIRGIL; VITTURI, BARTOLOMEO; VOLTAIRE; VRCHLICKÝ, JAROSLAV; VULPIUS, CHRISTIAN AUGUST; WEDEKIND, FRANK; WEIDMANN, JOSEF; WEIDMANN, PAUL; WEISSE, CHRISTIAN FELIX; WENZIG, JOSEF; WERFEL, FRANZ; WETTE, ADELHEID; WHEELER, HUGH CALLINGHAM; WHITE, DON; WIDMANN, JOSEPH VICTOR; WIELAND, CHRISTOPH MARTIN; WILDE, OSCAR; WILLEMETZ, ALBERT; WILLNER, A. M.; WINKLER, CARL GOTTFRIED THEODOR; WOOLF, BENJAMIN EDWARD; ZANETTI, ANTONIO MARIA; ZANGARINI, CARLO; ZANIBONI, ANTONIO; ZELL, F.; ZENO, APOSTOLO; ZHUKOVSKY, VASILIY ANDREYEVICH; ZINI, FRANCESCO SAVERIO; ZOLA, EMILE; ZÜNGEL, EMANUEL; and ZWEIG, STEFAN.

The following librettos are entered in the dictionary: ACHILLE IN SCIRO; ADRIANO IN SIRIA; ALESSANDRO NELL'INDIE; ANDROMACHE; ANTIGONO; ARTASERSE; ATTILIO REGOLO; CAIO MARIO; CALLIROE; CATONE IN UTICA; CIRO RICONOSCIUTO; CLEMENZA DI TITO, LA; CONTESSINA, LA; CRESO; DEMETRIO; DEMOFOONTE; DIDONE ABBANDONATA; ERIFILE; EROE CINESE, L'; EUMENE; EZIO; GEISTERINSEL, DIE; IMPRESARIO DELLE CANARIE, L'; IPERMESTRA; ISSIPILE; LUCIO VERO; MONDO DELLA LUNA, IL; NITTETI; OLIMPIADE, L'; ORAZIO; PESCATRICI, LE; RE PASTORE, IL; ROMOLO ED ERSILIA; RUGGIERO; SEMIRAMIDE RICONOSCIUTA; SESOSTRI, RE DI EGITTO; |SIFACE RE DI NUMIDIA;| SIROE RE DI PERSIA;| SOLIMANO; TAMERLANO; TELEMACHUS; TEMISTOCLE; TITO MANLIO; TRIONFO DI CLELIA, IL; and ZENOBIA.

The following libretto subjects are entered in the dictionary: AENEAS IN LATIUM; ALCESTIS; ANDROMEDA; ANGELICA E MEDORO; ANTIGONE; ARIADNE; ARMIDA; BELLEROPHON; CID, EL; CLEOPATRA; CONVITATO DI PIETRA, IL; DISERTORE, IL; FAUST; IDOMENEUS; IPHIGENIA IN AULIS; IPHIGENIA IN TAURIS; JULIUS CAESAR; LUCIUS PAPIRIUS; MEROPE; MITHRIDATES; ORPHEUS; PYRAMUS AND THISBE; RICIMER; VENDETTA DI NINO, LA; and VERGINE DEL SOLE, LA.

III. Bibliography

The bibliography to this article aims to outline broadly the literature pertaining to the librettos, approached from a variety of standpoints. Although it will often duplicate citations to be found in bibliographies elsewhere in the dictionary, it necessarily casts its net rather wider than most bibliographies, especially in the realm of literary history and historiography. Nevertheless, it is in no sense a 'complete' bibliography of the subject, and it needs to be read in conjunction with many others in the dictionary, particularly those attached to entries on librettists and other writers (a list of these entries is printed at the end of this article) and certain general topics, but also those for composers, cities, terms and genres. The classification of sections should be reasonably self-explanatory, but additional points are made in the paragraphs that follow.

A: *General.* The extraordinary growth in libretto studies since about 1950 should be noted.

B: *Libretto as literature.* Of this section, which considers the libretto studied in connection with literature as well as its own literary aspects, the first part is devoted to the Arcadian Academy and its branches, which were important in the reform of Italian opera from about 1690, and other Italian academies such as the freethinking Incogniti of Venice, who numbered among their members most of the librettists of early public opera. (For the Florentine pioneers of opera,

however, *see* CAMERATA and FLORENCE.) The second part lists studies that are primarily literary, not merely of opera and libretto as such but also of their reverse influence on literature, for example the effect of Wagner on Thomas Mann's thought and novelistic technique, or the interesting views of Schiller on opera, expressed in his tragedy with chorus *Die Braut von Messina* and his correspondence with Goethe. Many studies of the libretto as literature disregard or underestimate the musical requirements affecting the plan and detail of a libretto, or the effect of text when sung in a theatre.

C: *Literary sources.* See also the individual entries in the dictionary for writers whose works have been adapted for librettos, as well as those on composers and librettists. The subject is almost inexhaustible; a full bibliography would be 20 times the length of that of the general studies listed here, which should at least aid the researcher seeking the origins of opera plots in Spanish, French, medieval or ancient literature, history and myth.

D: *Comparative studies.* This section, treating adaptations, revisions and imitations of librettos, offers many instructive examples demonstrating the importance of the libretto as an indispensable element in textual scholarship and in the study of the evolving language of opera, including the early but impressive article by Wilhelm Tappert which really founded the methodology by showing that it was only through comparison with the published librettos that the confusion in the musical sources over the ending of Wagner's *Tannhäuser* could be cleared up. Further such material may be found under entries for individual composers and librettists.

Some words of caution are nevertheless needed. Librettos were published by their poets (sometimes by scene designers or choreographers), who derived income from their sale. In late 18th-century Italian opera, with the increasing use of reset librettos adapted by theatre poets in their employ, the impresarios took over this profitable sideline. With the slow development of copyright law, poets regained some control, but usually through an arrangement with the publishers of the music of an opera, who took over the function of publishing librettos as well. In preparing a new production, the word-book was used in two different forms: the composer would work from a manuscript libretto or, in the frequent case of a libretto adapted for resetting, from an exemplar printed for some earlier production, to which annotations marking cuts, changes and interpolations would have been added in manuscript. During an intensive rehearsal period of perhaps as little as two or three weeks, further alterations might be made, sometimes without the poet's knowledge or approval. There are therefore discrepancies between the words in the score and those in the printed librettos, beyond the common shortening or omission of scene descriptions and stage directions, the repetition of words in arias (which leads to altered punctuation), and the loss of the poet's lineation, indentation or italicization of his text. Librettos were normally, and necessarily, 'rush jobs', set up and published at the latest possible moment, sometimes by specialist printers; even so, they do not always take account of last-minute changes. Complications and delays might be caused by the process of censorship (in the Papal States ecclesiastical, in England political, through the Lord Chamberlain's office): the prior need for an *imprimatur* might 'freeze' a form of the text differing from the actual performance. If the poet disapproved of cuts made in his work, or if the cuts contained matter helpful for the audience's understanding of the plot, excised passages might still be printed in the libretto, but were often distinguished by placing them between inverted commas ('versi virgolati'). Finding the libretto which 'goes with' a particular production, therefore, though it is an essential step and will often sort out problems in the associated musical score, may also confront the researcher or editor with additional mysteries.

The extent to which printed librettos were expected to differ from the performing score, even as late as 1829, may be gauged from the remarkable preface that Jouy added to the libretto for Rossini's *Guillaume Tell*:

We might have offered the reader a more correct work [i.e. according to literary norms]. We need only have published it in the form in which it was originally conceived; but it would then have been necessary to replace several scenes that were suppressed, to re-establish the sequence of those which were later reordered, and to remove certain passages that were necessitated by purely musical needs. But then the printed play would have been totally different from the play as performed; and since the main need of the members of the audience is to find in their librettos [*brochure*] whatever the orchestration prevents them from hearing, we have, *perhaps for the first time* [my italics], offered to the press a text that conforms to that of the score. If for this reason the critics, on the one hand, find a larger field to operate in, the public on the other will in some measure be grateful to us for this small sacrifice of our pride, which ought to increase its enjoyment.

In spite of these fine words, there are still a great many discrepancies between score and libretto.

Literary editors of librettos have not always been aware of such complications, or have reprinted the 'sanitized' collected editions of poets such as Zeno or Metastasio; but a variorum edition of Metastasio's *Artaserse* alone would fill several volumes, even if limited to versions current in the poet's lifetime. A commendable exception to the general rule is P. Lecaldano's edition of the Da Ponte-Mozart opera texts which carefully correlates printed libretto and score (1956). The problem of providing a correct literary text for modern editions of old operas is best solved by printing the libretto, preferably in facsimile, along with the version in the score, as in the later volumes of the Hallische Händel-Ausgabe; ideally, as in the complete editions of Wagner and Schoenberg, all drafts and sketch material and variants in successive later recensions should also be included. The intelligent reader needs to see the libretto more or less in the form in which the composer saw it, and to see the arias with their differing stanza patterns distinguished typographically from the recitative, as was commonly the case from the late 17th century onwards. The garbled versions presented by record companies too often include all repeats of the words and in other ways destroy the literary format of the original libretto. A number of modern anthologies of librettos are listed below (section H); further examples of reprints, often in facsimile, may be found under entries for composers and librettists.

The resetting of the same source libretto, suitably adapted, by a series of composers has proved an illuminating subject for study, and a number of striking examples, among many excellent ones, may be found (Powers 1961–2 and 1976; Holmes 1963 and 1976). Metastasio's librettos were set over and over again (see Pavan 1917; Weichlein 1956; Hucke 1956 and 1957; Lühning 1983; and Ziino 1983). One study (Burt 1968) of three unrelated librettos casts light on the Arcadian Academy's reforming aims. Also listed are a number of different recensions of famous repertory operas and

studies of the uses to which opera texts by Goethe and plays by Schiller and other authors have been put.

Omitted here are many interesting comparative studies on subjects much favoured by opera composers. For such topics as Alcestis, Ariadne, Iphigenia, Don Juan, Faust or Orpheus, the reader is referred first to the entries on libretto topics and individual librettos in this dictionary (these are listed in full at the end of the present article; the longer of these, for example FAUST and ORPHEUS, have individual bibliographies), and then to entries on original sources (Shakespeare, Racine, Goethe etc.) and the librettists and composers of principal operas (thus the fullest bibliography on Don Juan will be found in the appropriate section of the bibliography to the Mozart entry).

E: *Words and music.* The nature, function and technical characteristics of language in the theatre, and of the complex *tertium quid* that results when words are sung or otherwise accompanied by music, is a huge topic. The expectation of a poet when faced with a musical form, or of a composer faced with a literary one, takes the discussion into questions of literary and musical structure and continuity. Information about metrics and versification for the main operatic languages will be found in the entry VERSIFICATION. Here however are included studies of the technical characteristics of opera verse and many more general discussions of the relationship between words and music. Early Italian operatic verse up to and including Salvadori (1691) is authoritatively examined, with full references to theorists, by Fabbri (1990), later Italian practice by Strohm (1976) and Lippmann (1973). It is important for the critical listener to be able to judge when a composer is using or avoiding the musical stereotype that might be expected to obtain when a poet provides a particular type of verse. When one looks at the decasyllables of 'Questa o quella' in Act 1 of Verdi's *Rigoletto* and compares the expected rhythm with the tune that Verdi actually wrote, one notices how devious and elusive the Duke really is, beneath the superficial charm of his gay and airy manner.

F: *The libretto and society.* Opera was often subversive and critical of the existing order, principally, of course, in its librettos. This is reflected in the discussions listed here of censorship, nationalism, politics and socio-economics. Other 'history of ideas' topics are treated elsewhere in the dictionary under individual headings. Aspects of humanism, for example, are considered in the bibliography to the entry CAMERATA (see the studies of Pirrotta, Hanning, and above all Palisca, who has recovered and reprinted many valuable texts; the bibliographies to such separate entries as (to cite a varied selection) ALLEGORY, CENSORSHIP, EXOTICISM, MERVEILLEUX, PASTORAL, SACRED OPERA, VERISMO and ZEITOPER, and those on such individuals as FRIEDRICH NIETZSCHE and JEAN-JACQUES ROUSSEAU, touch on wider issues pertinent to opera and the libretto. An adjunct to this section embodies a variety of studies linking opera and the librettos with a yet wider range of ideas of all kinds, from fine art to ethics, among them studies of the 'mindscape' or mental world of such composers as Debussy and Pfitzner.

G: *Dramaturgy, theory, aesthetics, criticism.* This assembles a great mass of discussion of opera, distinguishing what one might regard as primary or privileged material emanating from composers and librettists as (i) and separating out comment by others as (ii). A number of valuable anthologies which mix the above categories are appended as (iii), some of them in English translation (the linking commentary in Weisstein 1964 is of particular value). The presence of the word 'aesthetic' in a title does not necessarily guarantee that a philosophical discussion of aesthetics is involved.

H: *Catalogues, anthologies, editions.* There are many thousands of librettos in libraries all round the world, but many are not catalogued as such; they will be listed under the poet's name, if known, rarely with cross-reference to the composer. Discoveries of new caches of librettos still continue, but the location and identification of Italian librettos up to the year 1800 is now greatly facilitated by the exhaustive cataloguing of Sartori (1990–). For these and the librettos of other nations, the Répertoire International des Sources Musicales has launched the *RISM Libretto Project*, with eventual worldwide coverage.

Librettos collections in libraries have mostly grown up from a process of fortuitous accumulation. More valuable are those originally built up around the interests of a private collector (who will have made a catalogue of his own), and which later found their way into a larger library. Examples are the Schatz collection (now in the Library of Congress, Washington (Sonneck 1911, 1914, 1914), the Carvalhaes collection (Carvalhaes 1928; Rolandi 1928) and the Rolandi collection, now in the Fondazione Cini, Venice (see Raeli 1927–8; Rolandi 1930; Biscotti 1942). Other collections assembled by court and theatre libraries provide valuable material for the study of repertory in particular centres (see for example Mayer, Trojan and Hadamowsky 1928; Hárich 1941; Schaal 1957–61). Italian conservatories also formed collections. The most interesting collections of all are those of professional librettists and impresarios (see Wiel 1888 and Ferrari 1949 for Zeno's collection; Gibson 1989 for Haym's, now dispersed; and Frati 1911). There are also studies of series of librettos produced by particular printers (see Esposito 1972). Another interesting survival, now available on microfiche, is the long series of librettos and plays submitted to the Lord Chamberlain, who until recently had the duty of censoring texts offered for public performance in England: there is much manuscript material here (Macmillan 1939). MS librettos are otherwise very rare (but see Wellesz 1918), though printed librettos often contain handwritten information such as the names of singers, which may prove very useful; most valuable of all, perhaps, is the occasional survival of a printed libretto marked up by the stage manager to serve as a prompt-book, with details of where characters were to enter (i.e. which side of the stage, etc.), of numbers of extras not otherwise listed, and so forth (see Milhous and Hume 1986). A prompt copy may be relied upon to present the text exactly as given in performance.

Librettos survive in far greater numbers than musical scores for the period when the music was not normally published. It is often from them that a picture of the repertory of any individual centre of opera production may be built up. In other cases, a knowledge of the repertory for a particular theatre derived from other kinds of evidence (newspaper advertisement, contemporary lists and histories, playbills) may equally be used to date and locate librettos which lack such indications. Much has been done to identify and list the repertories of the courts and public theatres, and most theatre histories will attempt a chronological survey of works performed. Such studies will be found under entries for cities.

Anthologies of librettos associated with particular theatres or seasons are known from quite early in the history of opera, though they may lack the authority of a single libretto printed for a particular production. Modern editors have put together valuable collections of libretto texts (see Solerti 1904, 1905), but more useful still are facsimile reproductions. Modern anthologies are listed here, but many more examples may be found under entries for individual librettists and composers. Certain record companies and opera managements have in recent years begun to reproduce facsimiles of librettos (particularly where there is a contemporary English translation facing an Italian text), but sometimes these have been doctored, usually undetectably, to make the text conform with cuts in the text as recorded or performed, and in other ways.

*

A General. B Libretto as literature: (i) Academies and Arcadia (ii) Other studies. C Literary sources. D Comparative studies: Adaptations, revisions, imitations. E Words and music. F The Libretto and Society: (i) General studies (ii) Miscellaneous studies. G Dramaturgy, theory, aesthetics, criticism: (i) Comment by librettists and composers (ii) Comment by others (iii) Anthologies. H Libretto collections and their bibliography: (i) Catalogues, lists (ii) Anthologies, reprints, modern editions.

A: GENERAL

DEUMM (B. Cagli); *ES* (G. Tagliavini; 'Librettista', V. Viviani); *Grove6* (E.J. Dent and P. J. Smith); *LaMusicaE* (A. Della Corte); *MGG* (A. Abert, R. Schaal); *RicordiE* (V. Viviani); *StiegerO*, III/i–iii)

G. Rovani: 'Della poesia melodrammatica in Italia', *Delle lettere e delle arti in Italia dal secolo XVIII ai nostri giorni* (Milan, 1855–8)

P. Lohmann: *Über die dramatische Dichtung mit Musik* (Leipzig, 1861, 3/1886 as *Das Ideal der Oper*)

H. M. Schletterer: *Zur Geschichte der dramatischen Musik und Poesie in Deutschland*, i: *Das deutsche Singspiel von seinen ersten Anfängen bis auf die neueste Zeit* (Augsburg, 1863)

H. Dorn: *Gesetzgebung und Operntext (eine Schrift für Männer): Zeitmässige Betrachtungen* (Berlin, 1879)

G. Cappuccini: 'Saggio d'uno studio sul libretto musicale', *Rassegna italiana*, i (1885), 296–311

E. de Bricqueville: *Le livret d'opéra français de Lully à Gluck, 1672–1779* (Brussels, Mainz and Paris, 1887)

H. Riemann: *Opern-Handbuch: Repertorium der dramatisch-musikalischen Litteratur* (Leipzig, 1887, 2/1893; suppl. 1979)

G. Senigaglia: 'Libretti e librettisti', *La nuova musica* i/5–7 (Florence, 1896)

E. Boghan-Caniglioni: *Le origini del melodramma: studi letterari* (Rocca S Casciano, 1897)

E. Moschino: 'Fra libretti e librettisti', *Annuario dell'arte lirica e coreografica italiana* (Milan, 1899), 17–29

E. Maddalena: 'Libretti del Goldoni e di altri', *RMI*, vii (1900), 739–45

S. Di Giacomo: 'Musicisti e librettisti', *Musica e musicisti* (15 Feb 1904), 81–92

G. Monaldi: 'Libretti per musica', *Nuova antologia* [Rome] (1 Nov 1904), 317–22

M. Fehr: *Apostolo Zeno und seine Reform des Operntextes: ein Beitrag zur Geschichte des Librettos* (Zürich, 1912)

S. Fassini: *Il melodramma italiano a Londra nella prima metà del settecento* (Turin, 1914)

E. Istel: *Das Libretto: Wesen, Aufbau und Wirkung des Opernbuches, nebst einer dramatischen Analyse des Librettos von Figaros Hochzeit* (Berlin and Leipzig, 1914, 2/1915; Eng. trans., rev., as *The Art of Writing Opera Librettos: a Practical Manual* (New York, 1922)

M. Scherillo: *L'opera buffa napoletana durante il settecento, storia letteraria* (Milan, 1916)

J. G. Prod'homme: 'Gluck's French Collaborators', *MQ*, iii (1917), 249–71

H. Child: 'Some Thoughts on Opera Libretti', *ML*, ii (1921), 244–53

R. Gerber: *Der Operntypus Johann Adolf Hasses und seine textlichen Grundlagen* (Leipzig, 1925)

T. W. Werner: 'Libretto', *Reallexikon der deutschen Literaturgeschichte* (Berlin, 1926–8), ii, 205ff

H. Prunières: 'I libretti dell'opera veneziana nel secolo xvii', *RaM*, iii (1930), 441–8

A. de Ternant: 'French Opera Libretti', *ML*, xi (1930), 172–6

M. Kraussold: *Geist und Stoff der Operndichtung: eine Dramaturgie in Umrissen* (Leipzig and Vienna, 1931)

R. Guiet: *L'évolution d'un genre: le livret d'opéra en France de Gluck à la révolution 1774–1793* (Paris, 1936)

E. Closson: 'Les livrets d'opéra', *Cahiers de la musique*, i (1938), 193–7

G. Gavazzeni: 'La poesia dell'opera in musica', *RaM*, xi (1938), 137–62

H. Leichtentritt: *Music, History, and Ideas* (Cambridge, MA, 1938)

I. Porter: *Aspects of the Early English Opera Libretto* (diss., U. of Leeds, 1938)

F. Vatielli: *Letteratura poetica e drammatica* (Milan, 1938)

S. Czech: *Das Operntextbuch* (St Gall, 1939)

F. Vatielli: 'Operisti-librettisti dei secoli XVII e XVIII', *RMI*, xliii (1939), 1–16, 315–32, 605–21

J. Gregor: *Kulturgeschichte der Oper: Ihre Verbindung mit dem Leben, den Werken des Geistes und der Politik* (Vienna, 1941, 3/1950)

U. Rolandi: 'Librettistica rossiniana', *Musica*, i (1942), 40–66

O. Gatscha: *Librettist und Komponist: dargestellt an den Opern Richard Strauss'* (diss, U. of Vienna, 1947)

V. Viviani: 'Libretti e librettisti', *Cento anni del Teatro S. Carlo 1848–1948* (Naples, 1948), 29–40

D. Higham: 'Librettist and Composer', *Penguin New Writing*, xxxviii (Harmondsworth, 1949), 117–28

A. Della Corte: *La 'Poesia per musica' ed il libretto d'opera: introduzione ad una storia dell'opera* (Turin, 1950)

C. Calcaterra: 'La favola per musica e il libretto', *Poesia e canto: studi sulla poesia melica italiana e sulla favola per musica* (Bologna, 1951)

A. Della Corte: *Il libretto e il melodramma* (Turin, 1951)

U. Rolandi: *Il libretto per musica attraverso i tempi* (Rome, 1951)

L. Schrade: 'Das Libretto der modernen Oper', *Melos*, xx (1953), 312–6

A. Scherle: *Das deutsche Opernlibretto von Opitz bis Hofmannsthal* (Munich, 1954)

N. Pirrotta: 'Commedia dell'arte and Opera', *MQ*, xli (1955), 305–24; repr. in *Music and Culture in Italy from the Middle Ages to the Baroque* (Cambridge, MA, 1984)

W. Huber: *Das Textbuch der frühdeutschen Oper: Untersuchung über literarische Voraussetzung, stoffliche Grundlagen und Quellen* (diss., Munich U., 1957)

A. Della Corte: 'Introduzione', *Drammi per musica dal Rinuccini allo Zeno* (Turin, 1958), i, 9–43

——: 'Tragico e comico nell'opera veneziana della seconda parte del seicento', *RaM*, xi (1958),

J. E. Rotondi: *Literary and Musical Aspects of Roman Opera, 1600–1650* (Ann Arbor, 1959)

K. Honolka: *Kulturgeschichte des Librettos, Opern, Dichter, Operndichter* (Stuttgart, 1962)

F. Lippmann: *Studien zum Libretto, Arienform und Melodik der italienischen opera seria zu Beginn des 19. Jahrhunderts* (diss., Kiel U., 1962)

E. Ortolani: *La riforma del teatro nel settecento e altri scritti* (Florence and Venice, 1962)

W. C. Holmes: *Orontea: a Study of Change and Development in the Libretto and Music of Mid-Seventeenth-Century Italian Opera* (diss., Columbia U., 1963)

R. Longyear: 'Le livret bien fait: the Opéra Comique Librettos of Eugène Scribe', *Southern Quarterly*, i (1963), 169–92

W. Mellers: *Harmonious Meeting: a Study of Music, Poetry and Drama in England, 1600–1900* (London, 1965)

R. Müller: *Das Opernlibretto im 19. Jahrhundert* (Winterthur, 1966)

H. F. Salerno: *Scenarios of the commedia dell'arte* (New York, 1967) [Flaminio Scala's *Il Teatro delle favole rappresentative*]

Cella: *Prospettive della librettistica italiana nell'età romantica* (Milan, 1968)

R. Freeman: 'Apostolo Zeno's Reform of the Libretto', *JAMS*, xxi (1968), 321–41

M. Fubini and E. Bonora: 'L'opera per musica dopo Metastasio', *Pietro Metastasio: Opere* (Milan and Naples, 1968)

L. Bragaglia: *Storia del libretto nel teatro in musica come testo o pretesto drammatico* (Rome, 1970–77)

P. E. Gossett: *The Operas of Rossini: Problems of Textual Criticism in Nineteenth-Century Opera* (Princeton, 1970), chap. 2: 'The Nature of the Sources. A. Printed Librettos' [with list of libretto printers in Italy, 1810–36]

F. Lippmann: 'Zum Verhältnis von Libretto und Musik in der italienischen Opera seria der 1. Hälfte des 19. Jahrhunderts', *GfMKB: Bonn 1970*, 162–8

V. A. Pankratova and L. V. Polyakova: *Operniye libretto: russkaya opera i opera narodov SSSR* [Opera Librettos: Russian Opera and the Operas of the Soviet Peoples] (Moscow, 1970)

W. Schuh: 'Richard Strauss und seine Libretti', *GfMKB: Bonn 1970*, 169–78

P. J. Smith: *The Tenth Muse: a Historical Study of the Opera Libretto* (New York, 1970)

E. Surian: *A Checklist of Writings on 18th-Century French and Italian Opera (excluding Mozart)* (Hackensack, NJ, 1970)

E. Haun: *But Hark! More Harmony: the Libretti of the Restoration Opera in England* (Ypsilanti, MI, 1971)

J. D. Lindberg: 'The German Baroque Opera Libretto', *The German Baroque: Literature, Music, Art* (Austin, TX, 1972), 89–122

M. F. Robinson: *Naples and Neapolitan Opera* (Oxford, 1972), chap.2: 'Heroic Opera – the Texts'; chap.5: 'Comic Opera – the Texts'

A. Cassi Ramelli: *Libretti e librettisti* (Milan, 1973) [based on *Cinquanta librettisti dell'ottocento*, 1971]

B. Corrigan: 'All Happy Endings: Libretti of the Late Seicento', *Forum italicum*, vii (1973), 250–67

R. B. Moberly: 'Mozart and his Librettists', *ML*, liv (1973), 161–9

L. Baldacci: *Libretti d'opera e altri saggi* (Florence, 1974)

E. Fischer: *Die Texte der Oper: Studien zur Struktur einer Gattung* (Bochum, 1974)

R. Strohm: 'Händel und seine italienischen Operntexte', *HJb 1975*, 101–59; rev. Eng. version in *Essays on Handel and Italian Opera* (1985), 34–79

L. Baldacci: 'I libretti di Verdi', *Il melodramma italiano dell'ottocento: studi e ricerche per Massimo Mila* (Turin, 1977), 113–24

G. Barblan and A. Basso, eds.: *Storia dell'opera* (Turin, 1977), iii/2: *La librettistica* [essays by A. Lanfranchi, F. Cella, L. Guichard and G. Hausswald]

A. L. Bellina: 'Rassegna di studi sul libretto d'opera (1965–1975)', *Lettere italiane*, xxix (1977), 81–105

S. Alberici: 'Appunti sulla librettistica rossiniana', *Bollettino del Centro rossiniano di studi*, nos. 1–3 (1978), 45–60

R. Angermüller: 'Grundzüge des nachmetastasianischen Librettos', *Die stilistische Entwicklung der italienischen Musik zwischen 1770 und 1830: Rome 1978*, *AnMc*, no. 21 (1982), 192–235

J. Glover: *Cavalli* (London, 1978), chap. 2

D. Goldin: 'Aspetti della librettistica italiana fra 1770 e 1830', *Die stilistische Entwicklung der italienischen Musik zwischen 1770 und 1830: Rome 1978*, *AnMc*, no. 21 (1982), 128–91 [repr. in Goldin 1985]

S. Leopold: 'Das geistliche Libretto im 17. Jahrhundert: zur Gattungsgeschichte der frühen Oper', *Mf*, xxxi (1978), 245–57

C. B. Schmidt: 'The "Apothéose de Lully" or, Toward a New Lully Edition', *CMc*, no. 26 (1978), 106–11

F. W. Sternfeld: 'The First Printed Opera Libretto', *ML*, lix (1978), 121–38

R. D. Lynch: *Opera at Hamburg, 1718–1738: a Study on the Libretto and Musical Style* (diss., New York U., 1979)

C. E. Troy: *The Comic Intermezzo: a Study in the History of Eighteenth-Century Comic Opera* (Ann Arbor, 1979)

E. Rosand: 'In Defense of the Venetian Libretto', *Studi musicali*, ix (1980), 271–85

F. Portinari: *'Pari siamo! Io la lingua, egli ha il pugnale': storia del melodramma ottocentesco attraverso i suoi libretti* (Turin, 1981)

G. Muresu: *La parola cantata: studi sul melodramma italiano del settecento* (Rome, 1982)

J. Black: *The Italian Romantic Libretto: a Study of Salvadore Cammarano* (Edinburgh, 1984)

J. J. Fuld: *The Book of World-Famous Libretti: the Musical Theater from 1598 to Today* (New York, 1984)

P. Gallarati: *Musica e maschera: il libretto italiano del settecento* (Turin, 1984)

G. Morelli: 'Fare un libretto: la conquista della poetica paraletteraria', Introduction to A. Aureli and F. Lucio: *Il Medoro*, DMV, iv (1984), pp. ix–lvii

N. Pirrotta *Music and Culture in Italy from the Middle Ages to the Baroque* (Cambridge, MA, 1984)

L. Baldacci: 'I libretti di Mascagni', *NRM*, xix (1985), 395–410

M.-D. Bobin: *Les livrets d'opéras français créés au Palais Garnier entre 1919 et 1939* (diss., U. of Paris-Sorbonne, 1985)

J. M. Fischer, ed.: *Oper und Operntext* (Heidelberg, 1985)

D. Goldin: *La vera Fenice: libretti e librettisti tra sette e ottocento* (Turin, 1985)

P. Robinson: *Opera and Ideas: from Mozart to Strauss* (New York, 1985)

A. Gier, ed.: *Opera als Text: Romantische Beiträge zur Libretto-Forschung* (Heidelberg, 1986)

W. Dean and J. M. Knapp: *Handel's Operas, 1704–1726* (Oxford, 1987)

F. Della Seta: 'Il librettista', *SOI*, iv: *Il sistema produttivo e le sue competenze* (1987), 233–91

P. Getrevi: *Labbra barocche: il libretto d'opera da Busenello a Goldoni* (Verona, 1987)

H. Himmelfarb: 'Un domaine méconnu de l'empire lullyste: le Trianon de Louis XIV, ses tableaux et les livrets d'opéras (1687–1714)', *Lully: Heidelberg and St-Germain-en-Laye 1987*, 287–306

G. Loubinoux: 'L'impasse castiana: un tentativo problematico di rinnovamento del libretto', *I vicini di Mozart: Venice 1987*, 173–84

M. P. McClymonds: 'The Venetian Role in the Transformation of Italian opera seria during the 1790s', ibid, 221–40

C. H. Parsons, ed.: *Mellen Opera Reference Index*, v–vi: *Opera Librettists and their Works* (Lewiston, NY, 1987)

C. B. Schmidt: 'Livrets for Lully's Ballets and Mascarades: Notes Toward a Publishing History and Chronology (1654–1671)', *Lully: Heidelberg and St-Germain-en-Laye 1987*, 331–48

S. R. Huff: 'The Early German Libretto: Some Considerations Based on Harsdörffer's *Seelewig*', *ML*, lxix (1989), 345–55

M. Lichtfuss: *Operette im Ausverkauf: Studien zum Libretto des musikalischen Unterhaltungstheaters im Oesterreich der Zwischenkriegszeit* (Vienna, 1989)

C. Nieder: *Von der 'Zauberflöte' zum 'Lohengrin': das deutsche Opernlibretto in der ersten Hälfte des 19. Jahrhunderts* (Stuttgart, 1989)

E. Rosand: 'The Opera Scenario 1638–1655: a Preliminary Survey', *In cantu et in sermone: for Nino Pirrotta on his 80th Birthday* (Florence, 1989), 335–62

C. B. Schmidt: 'The Geographical Spread of Lully's Operas during the Late Seventeenth and Early Eighteenth Centuries: New Evidence from the Livrets', *Studies on Jean-Baptiste Lully and the Music of the French Baroque: Essays in Honor of James Anthony* (Cambridge, 1989), 183–211

P. Fabbri: *Il secolo cantante: per una storia del libretto d'opera nel seicento* (Bologna, 1990; Eng. trans. forthcoming)

G. Gronda: *La carriera di un librettista: Pietro Pariati* (Bologna, 1990)

J. Joly: *Dagli Elisi all'Inferno: il melodramma tra Italia e Francia dal 1730 al 1850* (Florence, 1990)

D. O'Grady: *The Last Troubadours: Poetic Drama in Italian Opera 1597–1887* (London and New York, 1990)

F. Sternfeld: *The Birth of Opera* (Oxford, 1993)

B: LIBRETTO AS LITERATURE

(i) Academies and Arcadia

Arcadia: atti e memorie [journal]

A. Salza: *La lirica dell'Arcadia ai nostri giorni* (Milan, n.d.)

[G. Loredano]: *Le glorie degli Incogniti overo gli huomini illustri dell'Accademia d' Signori Incogniti di Venetia* (Venice, 1647)

Historia della sacra real maestà di Cristina Allessandra Regina di Svezia (Modena, 1656)

G. Malatesta Garuffi: *L'Italia accademica* (Rimini, 1688)

G. M. Crescimbeni: *L'Arcadia* (Rome, 1708–11)

——: *Le vite degli Arcadi illustri* (Rome, 1708–29)

——: *Notizie istoriche degli Arcadi morti* (Rome, 1720–21)

A. Bertacchi: *Storia dell'Accademia lucchese* (Lucca, 1881)

I. Carini: *L'Arcadia dal 1690 al 1890: Memori istoriche*, i: *Contributo alla storia letteraria d'Italia del secolo XVII e de' principii del XVIII* (Rome, 1891)

E. Bertana: *In Arcadia* (Naples, 1909)

G. Maugain: *L'évolution intellectuelle de l'Italie de 1657 à 1750 environ* (Paris, 1909)

G. Toffanin: *La eredità del Rinascimento in Arcadia* (Bologna, 1923)

A. Sandberger: 'Beziehungen der Königin Christine von Schweden zur italienischen Oper und Musik, insbesondere zu M.A. Cesti: mit einem Anhang über Cestis Innsbrucker Aufenthalt', *Bulletin de la Société union musicologique*, v (1925), 121–73

M. Maylender: *Storia delle accademie d'Italia* (Bologna, 1926–30)

A. Cametti: 'Carlo Sigismondo Capece, Alessandro e Domenico Scarlatti e la regina di Polonia a Roma', *Musica d'oggi*, xiii/Feb (1931), 55–64

——: *Cristina di Svezia, l'arte musicale e gli spettacoli teatrali in Roma* (Rome, 1931)

A. Rosini: *Il Teatro degli Accademici Illuminati* (Città di Castello, 1935)

C. Calcaterra: *Lirici del seicento e dell'Arcadia* (Milan and Rome, 1936)

R. Russo: 'Cristina di Svezia', *Enciclopedia italiana* (Milan, 1939)

C. Calcaterra: *Il Parnasso in rivolta* (Milan, 1940)

G. Toffanin: *L'Arcadia: saggio storico* (Bologna, 1947)

M. Fubini: 'Arcadia e illuminismo', *Questioni e correnti di storia letteraria* (Milan, 1948); repr. in *Dal Muratori al Baretti* (Bari, 2/1954), 292–395

C. Calcaterra: *Il Barocco in Arcadia e altri scritti* (Bologna, 1950)

G. Spini: *Ricerca dei libertini: La teoria dell'impostura delle religioni nel seicento italiano* (Rome, 1950, 2/1983)

G. L. Moncallero: *Teorica d'Arcadia* (Florence, 1953)

N. Burt: 'Opera in Arcadia', *MQ*, xli (1955), 145–70

R. Lefèvre: 'Pippo Acciajoli: Accademico Sfaccendato', *Strenna dei romanisti*, xvii (1956), 256–61

M. Fubini, ed.: *La cultura illuministica in Italia* (Turin, 1957) [incl. chap. 'Dall'Arcadia all'illuminismo: Francesco Algarotti']

R. Lefèvre: 'Gli Sfaccendati', *Studi romani*, vii (1960), 154–65

W. Binni: *L'Arcadia e il Metastasio* (Florence, 1963)

H. J. Marx: 'Die Musik am Hofe Pietro Kardinal Ottobonis unter A. Corelli', *AnMc*, no. 5 (1968), 104–77

C. Di Biase: *Arcadia edifiante* (Naples, 1970)

A. Cipriani: 'Contributo per una storia politica dell'Arcadia settecentesca', *Arcadia: Atti e memorie*, ser. 3, v/2–3 (1971), 161–6

L. Felici: 'L'Arcadia romana tra illuminismo e neoclassicismo', ibid, 167–82

E. Povoledo: 'Una rappresentazione accademica a Venezia nel 1634', *Studi sul teatro veneto fra Rinascimento ed età barocca* (Florence, 1971), 119–69

M. Viale Ferrero: 'Antonio e Pietro Ottoboni e alcuni melodrammi da loro ideati o promossi a Roma', *Venezia e il melodramma nel settecento: Venice 1973*, i, 271–94

T. Torri: *Dalle antiche accademie dell'Ateneo* (Bergamo, 1974)

E. Strainchamps: 'New Light on the *Accademia degli Elevati* of Florence', *MQ*, lxii (1976), 507–35

A.-M. Giorgetti Vichi: *Gli Arcadi dal 1690 al 1800: Onomasticon* (Rome, 1977)

N. Merola: 'Ultimissime sull'Arcadia e su Metastasio', *Studi romani*, xxvii (1979), 361–4

——: 'Un'ipotesi sul classicismo settecentesco: l'Arcadia e Metastasio', *Il Veltro: rivista della civiltà italiana*, xxiii (1979), 644; xxiv (1980), 105

M. Talbot: 'Musical Academies in Eighteenth-Century Venice', *NA*, new ser., ii (1984), 21–65

F. Piperno: 'Crateo, Olinto, Archimede e l'Arcadia: Rime per alcuni spettacoli operistici romani (1710–11)', *Händel e gli Scarlatti a Roma: Rome 1985*, 349–65

M. Talbot and C. Timms: 'Music and the Poetry of Antonio Ottoboni (1646–1710)', ibid, 367–438

M. G. Accorsi: 'Pastori e teatro: dal melodramma al dramma ebraico', *La Colonia Renie: Profilo documentario critico dell'Arcadia bolognese* (Modena, 1988), ii, 291–7

M. L. Volpicelli: 'Il teatro del Cardinale Pietro Ottoboni al Palazzo della Cancelleria', *Il teatro a Roma nel settecento*, iii (Rome, 1989), 681–782

(ii) Other studies

F. Hirsch: *Die Oper und der Literatur-Geist: ein Wort zur Operntextreform* (Leipzig, 1868)

M. Landau: *Die italienische Literatur am österreichischen Hofe* (Vienna, 1879)

A. Bock: *Deutsche Dichter in ihren Beziehungen zur Musik* (Berlin, 1893)

G. Chiuppari: *Apostolo Zeno in relazione all'erudizione del suo tempo* (Bassano, 1900)

L. Menghi: *Lo Zeno e la critica letteraria* (Camerino, 1901) [on his scholarship]

F. Lindemann: *Die Operntexte Philippe Quinaults vom literarischen Standpunkte aus betrachtet* (diss., Leipzig U., 1904)

R. Sternfeld: *Schiller und Wagner* (Berlin, 1905)

A. Heuss: 'Das dämonische Element in Mozarts Werken', *ZIMG*, vii (1905–6), 175–86

C. Déjob: *Baretti, Goldoni et Métastase* (Toulouse, 1907)

M. Ehrenhaus: *Die Operndichtung der deutschen Romantik: ein Beitrag zur Geschichte der deutschen Oper* (Breslau, 1911–18)

J. C. Griggs: 'The Influence of Comedy upon Operatic Forms', *MQ*, iii (1917), 552–61

H. Prunières: 'Stendhal and Rossini', *MQ*, vii (1921), 133–55

A. Coeuroy: *Etude de musique et de littérature comparées* (Paris, 1923)

M. Kunath: *Die Oper als literarische Form* (diss., Leipzig U., 1925)

A. W. Bartmuss: *Die Hamburger Barockoper und ihre Bedeutung für die Entwicklung der deutschen Dichtung und der deutschen Bühne* (diss., Jena U., 1926)

E. Filippini: 'Giuseppe Parini nei suoi rapporti col teatro contemporaneo', *Rassegna*, ser. 4, xxxix (1931), 209–48

A. Maecklenburg: 'Verdi and Manzoni', *MQ*, xvii (1931), 209–18

G. Woolley: *Richard Wagner et le symbolisme français* (Paris, 1931)

K. Jäckel: *Richard Wagner in der französischen Literatur* (Breslau, 1931–2)

R. Peacock: *Das Leitmotiv bei Thomas Mann* (Berne, 1934)

P. H. Láng: *The Literary Aspects of the History of the Opera in France* (diss., Cornell U., 1935)

T. Mann: *Leiden und Grösse der Meister* (Berlin, 1935; short Eng. version of essay on Wagner in *Freud, Goethe, Wagner*, 1937)

D. West: *Italian Opera in England (1660–1740) and Some of its Relationships to English Literature* (diss., U. of Illinois, 1937)

M. Moser: *Richard Wagner in der englischen Literatur des 19. Jahrhunderts* (Berne, 1938)

H. H. Unger: *Die Beziehungen zwischen Musik und Rhetorik im 16.–18. Jahrhundert* (Würzburg, 1941)

Z. Sacks: 'Verdi and the Spanish Romantic Drama', *Hispania*, xxvii (1944), 451–65

A. A. Abert: 'Schauspiel und Opern-Libretto im italienischen Barock', *Mf*, ii (1949), 133–41

P. Meylan: *Les écrivains et la musique* (Lausanne, 1951)

O. Fries: *Richard Wagner und die deutsche Romantik: Versuch einer Einordnung* (Zürich, 1952)

T. Mann: *Altes und Neues: kleine Prosa aus sechs Jahrzehnten* (Frankfurt, 1953)

L. Guichard: *La musique et les lettres au temps du romantisme* (Paris, 1955)

G. Struck: 'Die Wende zur Literatur-Oper: zur 50. Wiederkehr der *Salome*-Uraufführung', *Musica*, ix (1955), 589–94

M. Barthélemy: 'L'opéra français et la Querelle des anciens et des modernes', *Lettres romanes*, x (1956), 379–91

C. S. Brown: 'Music in Zola's Fiction, especially Wagner's Music', *Publications of the M.L.A. of America*, lxxi (1956), 84–96; lxxii (1958), 448–52

G. Clive: 'The Demonic in Mozart', *ML*, xxxvii (1956), 1–13

H. Flobert: *Littérature française et musique* (Paris, 1957)

R. H. Ruppel: 'Die literarische Wandlung der Oper', *Melos*, xxiv (1957), 345–9

M. Gregor-Dellin: *Wagner und kein Ende: Richard Wagner im Spiegel von Thomas Manns Prosawerk: eine Studie* (Bayreuth, 1958)

M. La Morgia, ed.: *La città dannunziana di Ildebrando Pizzetti: saggi e note* (Pescara and Milan, 1958)

J. E. Rotondi: *Literary and Musical Aspects of Roman Opera, 1600–1650* (diss., U. of Pennsylvania, 1959)

K. Schumann: 'Die Emanzipation des Librettos, literarische Tendezen in der modernen Oper', *Lebt die Oper?* (Bonn, 1960)

R. E. Moore: *Henry Purcell and the Restoration Theatre* (London, 1961)

U. Weisstein: 'The Libretto as Literature', *Books Abroad*, xxxv (1961), 16–22

A. Garlington: 'Gothic Literature and Dramatic Music in England: 1781–1802', *JAMS*, xv (1962), 48–64

C. Girdlestone: 'Le Cerf de la Viéville's "Comparaison": its Non-Musical Interest', *French Studies*, xvi/3 (1962), 205–28

W. Binni: *Classicismo e neoclassicismo nella letteratura del settecento* (Florence, 1963)

E. Mann, ed.: *Thomas Mann, Wagner und unsere Zeit* (Frankfurt, 1963; Eng. trans., 1985, as *Thomas Mann: Pro and contra Wagner*)

R. H. Thomas: *Poetry and Song in the German Baroque* (Oxford, 1963)

D. I. Lindberg: *Literary Aspects of German Baroque Opera: History, Theory and Practice* (diss., U. of California, Los Angeles, 1964)

W. Mellers: *Harmonious Meeting: a Study of the Relationship between English Music, Poetry, and Theatre, c.1600–1900* (London, 1965)

J. Subirá: 'Calderón de la Barca, libretista de ópera: consideraciones literario-musicales', *AnM*, xx (1965), 59–73

R. M. Adams: 'The Operatic Novel: Joyce and D'Annunzio', *New Looks at Italian Opera: Essays in Honour of Donald J. Grout* (Ithaca, 1968), 260–81

W. Binni: 'Il settecento letterario', *Storia della letteratura italiana*, vi: *Il settecento* (Milan, 1968) [incl. Goldoni and Metastasio]

L. K. Gerhartz: *Die Auseinandersetzungen des jungen Giuseppe Verdi mit dem literarischen Drama* (Berlin, 1968)

M. Naudin: *Evolution parallèle de la poésie et la musique en France* (Paris, 1968)

——: 'Tragédie et opéra', *Cahiers de l'Association internationale des études françaises*, xxiii (1971)

A. Szweykowska: 'Qualche osservazione sulla struttura letteraria del dramma musicale del primo seicento sull'esempio delle opere di Virgilio Puccitelli: 1599–1654', *Quadrivium*, xii (1971), 77–88

C. Girdlestone: *La tragédie en musique considérée comme genre littéraire (1673–1750)* (Geneva, 1972)

A. McConnell: *The Opera Ballet: Opera as Literature* (diss., U. of Arizona, 1972)

E. Koppen: *Dekadenter Wagnerismus: Studien zur europäischen Literatur des Fin de siècle* (Berlin and New York, 1973)

P. Müller: *Alessandro Pepoli als Gegenspieler Vittorio Alfieris: ein literarischer Wettstreit im Settecento* (Munich, 1974)

J. Newsom: 'Hans Pfitzner, Thomas Mann and "The Magic Mountain"', *ML*, lv (1974), 136–50

R. S. Ridgway: *Voltaire and Sensibility* (Montreal and London, 1975)

P. Branscombe: *The Connexions between Drama and Music in the Viennese Popular Theatre* (diss., U. of London, 1976)

W. Osthoff: 'Pfitzner–Goethe–Italien: die Wurzeln des Silla-Liedchens im Palestrina', *AnMc*, no.17 (1976), 194–211

P. Conrad: *Romantic Opera and Literary Form* (Berkeley and Los Angeles, 1977)

J. Sage: 'Seventeenth-Century Spanish Music Drama and Theatre', *IMSCR, xii Berkeley 1977*, 701–5

G. Salvetti: 'La scapigliatura milanese e il teatro d'opera', *Il melodramma italiano dell'ottocento: studi e ricerche per Massimo Mila* (Turin, 1977), 566–704

J. L. DiGaetani: *Richard Wagner and the Modern British Novel* (London, 1978)

K. Ringger: 'Monteverdis Libretti und die Anfänge der italienischen Tragödie', *Arcadia*, iii/2 (1978), 146–60

M. Gregor-Dellin: 'Thomas Mann: Harmonieverschiebung und Leitmotiv', *Im Zeitalter Kafkas: Essays* (Munich, 1979), 37–47

K. Achberger: *Literatur als Libretto: das deutsche Opernbuch seit 1945* (Heidelberg, 1980)

B. Adamy: *Hans Pfitzner: Literatur, Philosophie und Zeitgeschehen in seinem Weltbild und Werk* (Tutzing, 1980)

L. E. Brown: 'Oratorical Thought and the *tragédie-lyrique*: a Consideration of Musical-Rhetorical Figures', *College Music Symposium*, xx (1980), 99–116

G. Folena: 'Cesarotti, Monti e il melodramma fra sette e ottocento', *AnMc*, no. 21 (1982), 236–62

R. Furness: *Wagner and Literature* (Manchester, 1982)

S. Martin: *Wagner to 'The Waste Land': a Study of the Relationship of Wagner to English Literature* (London, 1982)

N. Pirrotta: 'Metastasio and the Demands of his Literary Environment', *SMA*, vii (1982), 10–21

F. Sternfeld and D. Harvey: 'A Musical Magpie: Words and Music in Michael Tippett's Operas', *Parnassus: Poetry in Review*, x/2 (1982), 188–98

C. Dahlhaus: *Vom Musikdrama zur Literaturoper: Aufsätze zur neuerem Operngeschichte* (Munich and Salzburg, 1983)

S. Wiesmann: *Für und wider die Literaturoper* (Laaber, 1983)

V. Kapp: 'Das Barberini-Theater und die Bedeutung der römischen Kultur unter Urban VIII: Versuch einer literarhistorischen Einordnung des Schaffens von G. Rospigliosi', *Literaturwissenschaftliches Jb*, new ser., xxvi (1985), 75–100

X. Testot: *La Querelle des Bouffons: querelle musicale et querelle littéraire* (diss., U. of Paris-Sorbonne, 1985)

H. R. Vaget: 'Erlösung durch Liebe: Wagners "Ring" und Goethes "Faust"', *Bayreuther Festspiele 1985*, no.6: Götterdämmerung, 14–31 [programme book, with Eng. trans.]

A. Gier, ed.: *Oper als Text: Romanistische Beiträge zur Libretto-Forschung* (Heidelberg, 1986)

M. G. Accorsi: 'Teoria e pratica della "variatio" nel dramma giocoso: a proposito della "Villanella rapita" di Giovanni Bertati', *I vicini di Mozart: Venice 1987*, 139–64

C: LITERARY SOURCES

J. F. Schucht: 'Mystische und historische Sujets der Oper', *NZM*, xxviii (1882), 77–9, 89–92, 101–4

A. Albertazzi: *Romanzieri e romanzi italiani del cinquecento e del seicento* (Bologna, 1891) [lists adaptations for plays and operas]

A. Lisoni: *Gli imitatori del teatro spagnolo in Italia* (Parma, 1895)

C. Déjob: *Etudes sur la tragédie* (Paris, 1896) [French models for Italian librettos]

R. Verde: *Studi sull'imitazione spagnola nel teatro italiano del seicento*, i: *G. A. Cicognini* (Catania, 1912)

A. de Carli: *Autour de quelques traductions et imitations du théâtre français publiées à Bologne de 1690–1750* (Bologna, 1920)

——: *L'influence du théâtre français à Bologne de la fin du XVII siècle à la grande révolution* (Turin, 1925)

L. Ferrari: *Le traduzioni italiane del teatro tragico francese nei secoli XVII e XVIII: saggio bibliografico* (Paris, 1925)

G. Pianko: 'Motivi plautini nel dramma lirico', *Charisteria Gustavo Przychocki a discipulis oblata* (Warsaw, 1934)

H. Bédarida and P. Hazard: *L'influence française en Italie au dix-huitième siècle* (Paris, 1935)

G. Pianko: 'Soggetti italiani nel dramma lirico polacco', *Polonia-Italia* [Warsaw], nos. 7–8 (1938)

B. Croce: 'Appunti sui costumi e letteratura spagnuoli in Italia', *Nuovi saggi sulla letteratura italiana del seicento* (Bari, 1949), 235–9

H. Hunger: *Lexicon der griechischen und römischen Mythologie mit Hinweisen auf das Fortwirken antiker Stoffe und Motive in der bildenden Kunst, Literatur und Musik des Abendlandes bis zur Gegenwart* (Vienna, 1953)

Horn-Monval: *Répertoire bibliographique des traductions et adaptations françaises du théâtre étranger, du XVe siècle à nos jours* (Paris, 1958–61)

U. Dibelius: 'Die Gegenwart der Antike im Musiktheater', *NZM*, Jg.126 (1965), 277–81 [Orff]

T. Besterman: *Music and Drama: a Bibliography of Bibliographies* (Totowa, NJ, 1971)

R. Zinar: 'The Use of Greek Tragedy in the History of Opera', *CMc*, no.12 (1971), 80–95

M. Lütolf: 'Zur Rolle der Antike in der musikalischen Tradition der französischen Epoque Classique', *Studien zur Tradition in der Musik: Kurt von Fischer zum 60. Geburtstag* (Munich, 1973), 145–64

G. Schmidgall: *Literature as Opera* (New York, 1977)

M. Murata: 'Classical Tragedy in the History of Early Opera in Rome', *Early Music History*, iv (1984), 101–34

G. Morelli: 'Il filo di Poppea: il soggetto antico-romano nell'opera veneziana del seicento, osservazioni', *Venezia e la Roma dei papi* (Milan, 1987), 245–73

M. C. de Brito: 'The Relations between Opera and Spoken Drama in 18th-Century Portugal', *JbO*, iii (1990), 7–23

M. A. Hovland: *Musical Settings of American Poetry: a Bibliography* (in preparation)

D: COMPARATIVE STUDIES: ADAPTATIONS, REVISIONS, IMITATIONS

G. Ellinger: 'Händels *Admet* und seine Quelle', *VMw*, i (1885), 201–24 [Aureli, Mauro, Rolli]

E. Prout: 'Auber's "Le philtre" and Donizetti's "L'elisir d'amore": a Comparison', *MMR*, xxx (1900), 25–7, 49–53, 73–6

W. Tappert: 'Die drei verschiedenen Schlüsse des Tannhäuser vor der jetzigen, endgültigen Fassung', *Die Musik*, i (1901–2), 1844–50

A. Drews: 'Mozarts *Zauberflöte* und Wagners *Parsifal*: eine Parallele', *Richard Wagner-Jb*, i (1906), 326–61

G.-G. Prod'homme: 'Les deux "Benvenuto Cellini" de Berlioz', *SIMG*, xiv (1912–13), 449–60

O. Sonneck: 'Die drei Fassungen des Hasse'schen *Artaserse*', *SIMG*, xiv (1912–13), 226–42

A. Lazzari: 'Giovanni Ruffini, Gaetano Donizetti e il *Don Pasquale*', *Rassegna nazionale* (1 and 16 Oct 1915), 300–16, 410–25

G. Pavan: *Contributo alla storia del teatro musicale: il dramma più musicato, l'Artaserse del Metastasio* (Cittadella, 1917)

M. Fehr: 'Zeno, Pergolesi und Jommelli', *ZMw*, i (1918–19), 281–7 [Noris, Zeno]

H. Junker: 'Zwei "Griselda"-Opern', *Festschrift Adolf Sandberger* (Munich, 1918), 51–64

A. Sandberger: 'Léonore von Bouilly und ihre Bearbeitung für Beethoven durch Joseph Sonnleithner', *Ausgewählte Aufsätze zur Musikgeschichte* (Munich, 1924), ii, 141–53, 283–365

G. M. Gatti: 'Two *Macbeths*: Verdi-Bloch', *MQ*, xii (1926), 22–31

R. Engländer: 'Päer's *Leonora* und Beethovens *Fidelio*', *NBJb*, iv (1930), 118–32

C. B. Micca: 'Giovanni Ruffini e il libretto del Don Pasquale', *Rivista di Bergamo*, x (1931), 537–41

P. A. Merbach: 'Die Wandlungen des *Hugenotten*-Librettos', *Blätter der Staatsoper* [Berlin], xii/7 (1932), 11

E. Filippini: 'Versi melodrammatici del Parini finora ignorati', *Rassegna*, 4th ser., xliii (1935), 1–18 [adaptation of Calzabigi's *Alceste*]

W. Bollert: 'Tre opere di Galuppi, Haydn e Paisiello sul *Mondo della luna* di Goldoni', *Musica d'oggi*, xxi (1939), 265–70

A. Loewenberg: 'Paisiello's and Rossini's "Barbiere di Siviglia"', *ML*, xx (1939), 157–67

F. Walker: 'Orazio: the History of a Pasticcio', *MQ*, xxxviii (1952), 369–83

W. Hess: *Beethovens Oper 'Fidelio' und ihre drei Fassungen* (Zürich, 1953)

M. Treisch: 'Goethes Singspiele in Kompositionen seiner Zeitgenossen', *Wissenschaftliche Zeitschrift der Humboldt-Universität zu Berlin*, Gesellschafts- und sprachwissenschaftliche Reihe, iii (1953–4), 253–70

V. Ferman: 'Cherevichki (*Kuznets Vakula*) P.I. Chaykovskogo i *Noch'pered rozhdestvom* N.A. Rimskogo-Korsakova (opït sravneniya opernoy dramaturgii i muzïkal'nogo stilya)' [Tchaikovsky's *Cherevichki* and Rimsky-Korsakov's *Christmas Eve*: an Attempt at Comparison of Operatic Dramaturgy and Musical Style], *Voprosï muzikoznaniya* [Problems in Music Studies], i, ed. A. Oglovets (Moscow, 1954), 205–38

P.-M. Masson: 'Les deux versions du *Dardanus* de Rameau', *AcM*, xxvi (1954), 36–48

W. Osthoff: 'Die venezianische und neapolitanische Fassung von Monteverdis "L'incoronazione di Poppea"', *AcM*, xxvi (1954), 88–113

H. Hucke: 'La Didone abbandonata di Domenico Sarri nella stesura del 1724 e nella revisione di 1730', *Gazzetta musicale di Napoli*, ii (1956), 180–89

——: 'Die beiden Fassungen der Oper "Didone abbandonata" von Domenico Sarri', *GfMKB: Hamburg 1956*, 113–17

W. J. Weichlein: *A Comparative Study of Five Musical Settings of 'La Clemenza di Tito' (1734–1791)* (diss., U. of Michigan, 1956) [Caldara, Hasse, Gluck, Galuppi, Mozart]

F. Walker: 'The Librettist of *Don Pasquale*', *MMR*, lxxxviii (1958), 219–23

P. Berri: 'Il librettista del *Don Pasquale*: leggende, ingiustizie, plagi', *La scala*, no.110 (1959), 19–24

A. D. McCredie: 'Domenico Scarlatti and his Opera *Narciso*', *AcM*, xxxiii (1961), 19–29

H. S. Powers: 'Il Serse trasformato', *MQ*, xlvii (1961), 481–92; xlviii (1962), 73–92

S. Reiner: 'Collaboration in "Chi soffre speri"', *MR*, xxii (1961), 265–82

O. Seidlin: 'Goethe's *Magic Flute*', *Essays in German and Comparative Literature* (Chapel Hill, 1961), 45–59

H. Liebsch: 'Eine Oper – zwei Texte: textkritische Bemerkungen zu Donizettis "Don Pasquale"', *Musik und Gesellschaft*, xii (1963), 91–5

W. Osthoff: 'Die beiden "Boccanegra"-Fassungen und der Beginn von Verdis Spätwerk', *AnMc*, no.1 (1963), 70–89

J. W. Klein: 'Verdi's "Othello" and Rossini's', *ML*, xlv (1964), 130–40

H. J. Macdonald: 'The Original *Benvenuto Cellini*', *MT*, cvii (1966), 104–25

S. Kunze: 'Die Entstehung eines Buffo-Librettos: Don-Quijote-Bearbeitungen', *DJbM*, xii (1967), 75–95

G. Abraham: '*Pskovityanka*: the Original Version of Rimsky-Korsakov's First Opera', *MQ*, liv (1968), 58–73

N. Burt: 'Plus ça change: or, The Progress of Reform in Seventeenth- and Eighteenth-Century Opera as Illustrated in the Books of Three Operas', *Studies in Music History: Essays for Oliver Strunk* (Princeton, 1968), 325-40 [Apolloni, *La Dori*; Zeno, *Gli inganni felici*; Metastasio, *L'olimpiade*]

R. S. Freeman: 'The Travels of Partenope' [Stampiglia], ibid, 356–85

M. Chusid: 'Schiller Revisited: some Observations on the Revision of "Don Carlos"', *2o congresso internazionale di studi verdiani: Verona 1969*, 156–69

U. Günther: 'Le livret français de "Don Carlos": le premier acte et sa révision par Verdi', ibid, 70–140

M. Tartak: 'The Two "Barbieri"', *ML*, l (1969), 453–69

J. M. Knapp: 'Handel's *Tamerlano*: the Creation of an Opera', *MQ*, xlvi (1970), 405–30

P. Isotta: 'Da Mosè a Moïse', *Bollettino del Centro rossiniano di studi* (1971), 87–117

G. I. Ascher: *Die Zauberflöte und die Frau ohne Schatten: ein Vergleich zwischen zwei Operndichtungen der Humanität* (Berne, 1972)

L. Bianconi: 'L'Ercole in Rialto', *Venezia e il melodramma nel seicento: Venice 1972*, 259–72 [Aureli, after Moniglia]

W. C. Holmes: 'Yet another "Orontea": Further Rapport between Venice and Vienna', ibid, 199–225

D. Lawton and D. Rosen: 'Verdi's Non-Definitive Versions: the Early Operas', *3o congresso internazionale di studi verdiani: Milan 1972*, 189–237

H. S. Powers: 'Il "Mutio [Scevola]" tramutato, Part I: Sources and Libretto', *Venezia e il melodramma nel seicento: Venice 1972*, 227–58

J. Budden: 'The Two Traviatas', *PRMA*, xcix (1972–3), 43–66

M. Tartak: 'Mathilde and her Cousins', *Bollettino del Centro rossiniano di studi* (1973), no. 3, pp. 13–23 [*Mathilde di Shabran*]

C. Gianturco: '*Il Trespolo tutore* di Stradella e di Pasquini: due diverse concezioni dell'opera comica', *Venezia e il melodramma nel settecento: Venice 1973–5*, i, 185–98 [Ricciardi, Villifranchi]

D. Goldin: '*Il Barbiere di Siviglia* da Beaumarchais all'opera buffa', ibid, ii, 323–49; repr. in *La vera Fenice* (1985), 164–89 [Petrosellini, Sterbini]

M. F. Robinson: 'Three Versions of Goldoni's *Il filosofo di Campagna*', ibid, ii, 75–85

H. C. Wolff: 'Die komische Oper *La Sposa fedele* (Venedig 1767) von Pietro Guglielmi und ihre deutsche Singspielfassung als *Robert und Kalliste*', ibid, ii, 123–46

T. Antonicek: 'Die Damira-Opern der beiden Ziani', *AnMc*, no.14 (1974), 176–207

F. Cacaci: 'La cambiale di matrimonio da Federici a Rossi', *Bollettino del Centro rossiniano di studi* (1975), nos.1–2, pp. 22–60

W. Dean: 'Handel's *Sosarme*, a Puzzle Opera', *Essays on Opera and English Music in Honour of Sir Jack Westrup* (Oxford, 1975), 115–47 [Salvi, Rolli]

C. Gianturco: 'Stradella e Pasquini: due approcci al libretto comico del *Trespolo tutore*' [Villifranchi], *L'opera comica nei sei-settecenti a Venezia e in Italia* (Venice, 1975)

M. F. Messenger: 'Donizetti 1840: Three "French" Operas and their Italian Counterparts', *Journal of the Donizetti Society*, ii (1975), 99–116 [*La fille du régiment, Les martyrs, La favorite*]

E. Rosand: '"Ormindo travestito" in Erismena', *JAMS*, xxviii (1975), 268–91

L. Lindgren: 'I trionfi di Camilla', *Studi musicali*, vi (1977), 89–160

H. J. Macdonald: 'Benvenuto Cellini', *RdM*, lxiii (1977), 107–45

D. White: 'Donizetti and the "Three Gabriellas"', *Opera*, xxix (1978), 962–70

D. R. B. Kimbell: 'Verdi's first *rifacimento*: *I Lombardi* and *Jérusalem*', *ML*, lx (1979), 1–36

T. K. La May: 'A New Look at the Weimar Versions of *Benvenuto Cellini*', *MQ*, lxv (1979), 559–72

B. Brizi: 'Gli *Orlandi* di Vivaldi attraverso i libretti', *Antonio Vivaldi: teatro musicale, cultura e società: Venice 1981*, 315–30 [Braccioli]

M. Collins: 'The Literary Background of Bellini's *I Capuleti ed i Montecchi*', *JAMS*, xxxv (1982), 532–8

M. F. Robinson: 'How to Demonstrate Virtue: the Case of Porpora's Two Settings of *Mitridate*', *Studies in Music* [London, Ont.], vii (1982), 47–64

V. Scherliess: '"Il barbiere di Siviglia": Paisiello e Rossini', *AnMc*, no. 21 (1982), 100–27

H. Lühning: '"Titus" Vertonungen im 18. Jahrhundert: Un-tersuchungen zur Tradition der Opera seria von Hasse bis Mozart', *AnMc*, no. 20 (1983) [whole issue]

R. Parker: '"Un giorno di regno": from Romani's Libretto to Verdi's Opera', *Studi verdiani*, ii (1983), 38–58

M. Turnbull: 'The Metamorphosis of *Psyché*', *ML*, lxiv (1983), 12–24

R. Wiesend: 'Metastasios Revisionen eigener Dramen und die Situa-tion der Opernmusik in den 1750er Jahren', *AMw*, xl (1983), 255–75

A. Ziino and others: 'Le quattro versioni dell'*Ezio* di Niccolò Jommelli', *Musica e cultura a Napoli dal XV al XIX secolo* (Florence, 1983), 239–66

C. Abbate: *The Parisian Tannhäuser* (diss., Princeton U., 1984)

J. N. Black: 'Cammarano's Self-Borrowings: the Libretto of *Poliuto*', *Journal of the Donizetti Society*, v (1984), 89–107

T. G. Kaufman: '*Lucrezia Borgia*: Various Versions and Performance History', *Journal of the Donizetti Society*, v (1984), 37–81

A. Porter: 'Verdi and the Italian Translations of Shakespeare's *Macbeth*', *Verdi's 'Macbeth': a Sourcebook* (New York, 1984), 351–5

F. D'Accone: *The History of a Baroque Opera: Alessandro Scarlatti's 'Gli equivoci nel sembiante'* (New York, 1985)

D. Lawton: '*Le trouvère*: Verdi's Revision of *Il trovatore* for Paris', *Studi verdiani*, iii (1985), 79–119

C. Monson: '*Giulio Cesare in Egitto*: from Sartorio (1677) to Han-del (1724)', *ML*, lxvi (1985), 313–43

M. Walter: 'Zwei *Hugenotten*-Bearbeitungen des 19. Jahrhunderts', *JbO*, i (1985), 122–43

J. Maehder: 'Paris-Bilder – zur Transformation von Henry Murgers Roman in den Bohème-Opern Puccinis und Leoncavallos', *JbO*, ii (1986), 109–76

G. C. Ballola: 'Dal Termidoro all'Impero: le escursioni di Elisa', *I vicini di Mozart: Venice 1987*, i, 311–24 [St Cyr/Cherubini, Rossi/Mayr]

J. Joly: 'Riscrittura di melodrammi per Salieri e Cherubini: *Tarare/Axur e Demofoonte/Démophoon*', ibid, i, 241–72 [Beaumarchais/Da Ponte, Metastasio/Marmontel]

A. Sopart: *Giuseppe Verdis 'Simon Boccanegra' (1857 und 1881): eine musikalisch-dramaturgische Analyse*, *AnMc*, no. 26 (1988) [whole issue]

C. Questa: *Semiramide redenta: archetipi, fonti classiche, censure antropologiche nel melodramma* (Urbino, 1989)

E: WORDS AND MUSIC

G. G. Salvadori: *Poetica toscana all'uso dove con brevità, e chiarezza s'insegna il modo di comporre ogni poesia* (Naples, 1691) [rules and definitions for lyric verse]

L. Mattei: *Teorica del verso volgare e prattica di retta pronunzia* (Venice, 1695)

F.-J. de Chastellux: *Essai sur l'union de la poésie et de la musique* (The Hague, 1765)

C. Ritorni: *Ammaestramenti alla composizione di ogni poema e d'ogni opera appartenente alla musica* (Milan, 1841)

L. Köhler: *Die Melodie der Sprache in ihrer Anwendung besonders auf das Lied und die Oper* (Leipzig, 1853)

R. Gandolfi: 'Sulla relazione della poesia colla musica nel melodramma', *Atti dell'Accademia del R. Istituto musicale di Firenze*, vii (1869), 63–73

H. von Wolzogen: *Poetische Lautsymbolik: Psychische Wirkungen der Sprachlaute im Stabreim* (Leipzig, 2/1876)

——: *Die Sprache in Wagners Dichtungen* (Leipzig, 1878)

J. Gautier: *Richard Wagner et son oeuvre poétique depuis Rienzi jusqu'à Parsifal* (Paris, 1882)

P. Herrmann: *Richard Wagner und der Stabreim* (Hagen, West-phalia, 1883)

A. Ernst: *L'art de Richard Wagner: l'oeuvre poétique* (Paris, 1893)

R. Giani: 'Note sulla poesia per musica', *RMI*, i (1894), 141, 321

C. Cui: 'Vliyaniye Pushkina na nashikh kompozitorov i na ikh vokal'nïy stil', *Novosti i birzhevaya gazeta* (26 May 1899); repr. in *Izbrannïye stat'i*, ed. Yu. A. Kremlyov (Leningrad, 1952), 501–5 [effects of Pushkin's language and rhythm on Russian composers]

J. M. Baroni: 'La lirica musicale di Pietro Metastasio', *RMI*, xii (1905), 383–406

W. Golther: *Richard Wagner als Dichter* (Berlin, 1904; Eng. trans., 1905)

J. Schuler: *The Language of Richard Wagner's Ring des Nibelungen* (Lancaster, PA, 1909)

A. Wernicke: 'Gebührt Richard Wagner ein Platz in der deutschen Litteratur?', *Zeitschrift für den deutschen Unterricht*, xxiii (1909), 204, 390

R. Pelissier: *Parola e musica* (Rome, 1910)

J. Chantavoine: *Musiciens et poètes* (Paris, 1912)

G. Lote: 'La déclamation des vers français à la fin du XVIIe siècle', *Revue de phonétique*, ii (1912), 313–63

K. Grunsky: 'Reim und musikalische Form in den Meistersingern', *Richard Wagner-Jb*, v (1913), 138–87

E. von Schrenk: *Richard Wagner als Dichter* (Munich, 1913)

F. Ott: *Richard Wagners poetischer Wortschatz* (diss., U. of Giessen, 1916)

G. Vollerthun: 'Das Verhältnis von Text und Musik im Musikdrama', *AMz*, xlvi (1916), 608

A. Deditius: *Theorien über die Verbindung von Poesie und Musik* (Liegnitz, 1918)

P. Mies: 'Ueber die Behandlung der Frage in 17. und 18. Jahrhundert', *ZMw*, iv (1921–2), 286–304

H. Abert: 'Wort und Ton in der Musik des 18. Jahrhunderts', *AMw*, v (1923), 31–70; repr. in *Gesammelte Schriften und Vorträge* (1929), 173–231

H. Bellaman: 'Notes on the New Aesthetic of Poetry and Music', *MQ*, ix (1923), 260–70

R. M. Eaton: 'Music or Poetry', *MQ*, ix (1923), 443–9

A. Suarès: 'Musique et poésie', *ReM*, vi/1 (1924–5), 1–6

H. Wiesner: 'Der Stabreimvers in Richard Wagners *Ring des Nibelungen*', *Germanische Studien*, xxx (Berlin, 1924)

C. Bellaigue: *Paroles et musique* (Paris, 1925)

J. P. Dabney: 'The Relation between Music and Poetry', *MQ*, xiii (1927), 377–83

P. Epstein: 'Dichtung und Musik in Monteverdis *Lamento d'Arianna*', *ZMw*, x (1927–8), 216–22

H. Mersmann: 'Probleme der gegenwärtigen Operndichtung', *Jb der Universal-Edition* (Vienna, 1927)

A. Suarès: 'Poésie et musique', *ReM*, viii/8 (1926–7), 235–9

W. Ramann: *Der dichterischer Stil Richard Wagners in seiner Entwicklung von Rienzi bis Parsifal* (Leipzig, 1929)

H. Laue: *Die Operndichtung Lortzings*, *Mnemosyne*, viii (Bonn and Würzburg, 1932) [whole issue]

P. Bekker: 'Langage et musique', *ReM*, xv (1934–5), 83–8

I. Schreiber: *Dichtung und Musik der deutschen Opernarien 1680–1700* (Botrop, 1935; Wolfenbüttel, 1936)

A. Della Corte: *Le relazioni storiche della poesia e della musica italiana* (Turin, 1936)

E. Borelli: '"Parola" e Wort-Ton-Drama', *Leonardo* [Florence], ix, (1938), 50–53

G. Gavazzeni: 'La poesia dell'opera in musica', *RaM*, xi (1938), 137–62

E. Valentin: 'Dichtung und Oper: eine Untersuchung des Stilproblems der Oper', *AMf*, iii (1938), 138–79

C. Culcasi: *Musica e poesia: rapporti estetici e storici* (Verona and Milan, 1940)

M. E. Atkinson: *The Relation of Music and Poetry as Reflected in the Works of Tieck, Wackenroder and Brentano* (diss., U. of London, 1947)

C. Calcaterra: *Poesia e canto: studi sulla poesia melica italiana e sulla favola per musica* (Bologna, 1951)

H. Zingerle: 'Musik- und Textform in Opernarien Mozarts', *MJb* 1953, 112–15

W. Wendhausen: *Das stilistische Verhältnis von Dichtung und Musik in der Entwicklung der musikdramatischen Werke Richard Strauss'* (diss., Hamburg U., 1954)

A. Greither: *Die sieben grossen Opern Mozarts: Versuche über das Verhältnis der Dichtung und Musik* (Heidelberg, 1956)

L. Ronga: 'La nascita del melodramma dallo spirito della poesia', *Arte e gusto della musica* (Milan and Naples, 1956); repr. in *Teatro del seicento* (Milan and Naples, 1956), pp. xxxvii–liii

N. Berlanda: 'Il linguaggio del Goldoni dagli intermezzi al "Campiello"', *Atti dell'Istituto di scienze, lettere ed arti* [Venice], cxviii (1959–60)

K. Honolka: *Der Musik gehorsame Tochter* (Stuttgart, 1959)

E. Staiger: *Musik und Dichtung* (Zürich, 1959)

J. C. P. Bicknell: *Interdependence of Word and Tone in the Dramatic Music of Henry Purcell* (diss., Stanford U., 1961)

H. von Stein: *Dichtung und Musik im Werk Richard Wagners* (Berlin, 1962)

C. Varese: 'Teatro prosa poesia', *Storia della letteratura italiana*, v: *Il seicento* (Milan, 1967)

F. L. Arruga: *Incontri fra poeti e musicisti nell'opera romantica italiana* (Milan, 1968)

N. Fortune: 'Monteverdi and the *seconda prattica*', *The Monteverdi Companion* (London, 1968), 192–226 [2/1985, 183–215]

S. Reiner: '"Vi sono molt'altre mezz'arie…"', *Studies in Music History: Essays for Oliver Strunk* (Princeton, 1968), 241–58

P. Fortassier: 'Musique et paroles dans les opéras de Campra', *Centre aixois d'études et de recherches sur le XVIIIe siècle: la Régence* (1970), 31–43

P. H. Neumann: 'Einige Bemerkungen über Oper und Volkslied und die Idee der Einheit von Musik und Dichtung', *Jb der Jean-Paul-Gesellschaft*, vii (1972), 103–23

W. Osthoff: 'Oper und Opernvers: zur Funktion des Verses in der italienischen Oper', *Neue Zürcher Zeitung* (8 Oct 1972); It. version, enlarged, as 'Musica e versificazione: funzioni del verso poetico nell'opera italiana', *La drammaturgia musicale* (Bologna, 1986), 125–41

B. Brizi: 'Metrica e musica verbale nella poesia teatrale di Pietro Metastasio', *Atti dell'Istituzione veneziana di scienze, lettere ed arti*, cxxxi (1973)

F. Lippmann: 'Der italienische Vers und der musikalische Rhythmus: zum Verhältnis von Vers und Musik in der italienischen Oper des 19. Jahrhunderts, mit einem Rückblick auf die 2. Hälfte des 18. Jahrhunderts', *AnMc*, no.12 (1973), 253–369; no.14 (1974), 324–410; no.15 (1975), 298–333; It. trans. as *Versificazione italiana e ritmo musicale: i rapporti tra verso e musica nell'opera italiana dell'ottocento* (Naples, 1986)

G. Scarsi: *Rapporto poesia-musica in Arrigo Boito* (Rome, 1973)

W. Osthoff: 'Gli endecasillabi villottistici in *Don Giovanni* e *Nozze di Figaro*', *Venezia e il melodramma nel settecento: Venice 1973–5*, ii, 293–311

P. Branscombe: 'Wagner as Poet', in R. Wagner: *The Ring*, Eng. trans. by A. Porter (Folkstone, 1976), pp. xxix–xli

R. Strohm: *Italienische Opernarien des frühen Settecento: 1720–1730*, *AnMc*, no.16 (1976) [whole issue]

A. Sweykowska: 'Le due poetiche venete e le ultime opere di Claudio Monteverdi', *Quadrivium*, xviii (1977), 149–57

W. Gruhn: *Musiksprache-Sprachmusik-Textvertonung: Aspekte des Verhältnisses von Musik, Sprache und Text* (Frankfurt, 1978)

K. G. Kust: 'Richard Wagner – ein Dichter? Marginalien zum Opernlibretto des 19. Jahrhunderts', *Richard Wagner: von der Oper zur Musikdrama* (Berne and Munich, 1978), 79–84

S. Leopold: '"Quelle bazzicature poetiche, appellate ariette": Dichtungsformen in der frühen italienischen Oper (1600–1640)', *HJbMw*, iii (1978), 101–41

L. Dallapiccola: 'Words and Music in Italian Nineteenth-Century Opera', *Verdi Companion* (London, 1980) [many versions, 1965–9; definitive It. version, 'Parole e musica nel melodramma', *Appunti, Incontri, Meditazioni* (Milan, 1970), 5–28]

S. Leopold: 'Chiabrera und die Monodie: die Entwicklung der Arie', *Studi musicali*, xl (1981), 75–106

G. Tomlinson: 'Madrigal, Monody, and Monteverdi's "*via naturale alla immitatione*"', *JAMS*, xxxiv (1981), 60–108

——: 'Music and the Claims of Text', *Critical Inquiry*, viii (1982), 565–89

A. L. Bellina and T. Walker: 'Il melodramma: poesia e musica nell'esperienza teatrale', *Storia della cultura veneta: il seicento* (Vicenza, 1983), 409

G. Folena: 'Una lingua per la musica', *L'italiano in Europa: esperienze linguistiche del settecento* (Turin, 1983)

R. Mueller: 'Basso ostinato und die "imitazione del parlare" in Monteverdi's *Incoronazione di Poppea*, *AMw*, xl (1983), 1–23

P. Simonelli: 'Lingua e dialetto nel teatro musicale napoletano del '700', *Musica e cultura a Napoli dal XV al XIX secolo* (Florence, 1983), 225–38

A. Fecker: *Sprache und Musik: Phänomenologie der Deklamation in Oper und Lied des 19. Jahrhunderts* (Hamburg, 1984)

J. Vysloužil: 'Zur Bedeutung der Prosa bei Leoš Janáček', *Sborník prace filozofické fakulty brněnské univerzity*, H21 (1986), 73–84

P. Weiss: 'Ancora sulle origini dell'opera comica: il linguaggio', *Studi pergolesiani / Pergolesi Studies*, i (1986), 124–48

T. Carter: 'Verse and Music in *Le nozze di Figaro*', *W. A. Mozart: Le nozze di Figaro* (Cambridge, 1987), 75–84

S. Corse: *Opera and the Uses of Language: Mozart, Verdi and Britten* (London and Toronto, 1987)

J. Maehder: 'Studi sul rapporto testo-musica nell' "Anello del Nibelungo" di Richard Wagner', *NRMI*, xxi (1987), 43–66

H.-M. Palm: *Richard Wagners 'Lohengrin': Studien zur Sprachbehandlung* (Munich, 1987)

M. A. Cicora: 'From Metonymy to Metaphor: Wagner and Nietzsche on Language', *German Life and Letters*, xlii (1988), 16–31

P. Fabbri: 'Istituti metrici e formali', *SOI*, vi (1988), 165–233

——: 'La poetica musicale di Chiabrera', *Chiabrera e il suo tempo: Savona 1988*

——: 'Metro letterario e metro musicale nelle pagine di un critico di Chiabrera: il "Discorso delle ragioni del numero del verso italiano" di Ludovico Zuccolo (1623)', ibid

A. R. W. James: 'Berlioz the Poet?', *Hector Berlioz: Les Troyens*, ed. I. Kemp (Cambridge, 1988), 67–75

C. Abbate: 'Music and Language in *Elektra*', *Richard Strauss: Elektra*, ed. D. Puffett (Cambridge, 1989)

H. Macdonald: 'The Prose Libretto', *COJ*, i (1989), 155–66

V. Thomson: *Music with Words: a Composer's View* (New Haven, 1989)

M. Hager: 'La funzione del linguaggio poetico nelle opere comiche di Amalteo, Draghi e Minato', *L'opera italiana e Vienna prima di Metastasio*, ed. M. T. Muraro (Florence, 1990), 17–30

M. Falces Sierra: *Contribución a la recuperación de la obra vocal de Isaac Albeniz: estudio lingüístico-musical del tratamiento dado a textos literarios ingleses* (diss., U. of Granada, 1991)

F: THE LIBRETTO AND SOCIETY

(i) General Studies

M. Dietz: *Geschichte des musikalischen Dramas in Frankreich während der Revolution bis zum Directorium (1787 bis 1795) in künstlerischer, sittlicher und politischer Beziehung* (Vienna, 1886, 2/1893)

G. B. Shaw: *The Perfect Wagnerite: a Commentary on the Nibelung's Ring* (London, 1898, 4/1923)

N. Tabanelli: 'La causa Ricordi–Leoncavallo', *RIM*, vi (1899), 833–54

O. Fleischer: 'Napoleon Bonapartes Musikpolitik', *ZIMG*, iii (1901–2), 431–40

L. Neretti: *L'importanza civile della nostra opera in musica* (Florence, 1902)

M. Rouff: 'Un opéra politique de Beaumarchais', *La Révolution française*, lix (1910), 212–29, 333–58

C. Forsyth: *Music and Nationalism: a Study of English Opera* (London, 1911)

A. Livingston: *La vita veneziana nelle opere di Giovan Francesco Busenello* (Venice, 1913)

W. H. Cummings: 'The Lord Chamberlain and Opera in London, 1700 to 1741', *PMA*, xl (1913–14), 37–72

D. Hussey: 'Nationalism and Opera', *ML*, vii (1926), 3–16

H. F. Redlich: 'Heimat und Freiheit: zur Ideologie der jüngsten Werke Ernst Kreneks', *Musikblätter des Anbruch*, xii (1930), 54–8

'Sumtur vmesto muzïki; ob opere "Ledi Makbet Mtsenskogo Uyezda" D. Shostakovicha' [Muddle instead of Music; on Shostakovich's opera *Lady Macbeth of Mtsensk District*], *Pravda* (20 Jan 1936), and *SovM* (1936), no. 2, pp. 4ff

E. Monti: 'Contributo ad uno studio sui "libretti d'opera" in Lombardia e sulla censura teatrale in Milano nell'ottocento', *Archivio storico lombardo* (July–Dec 1939), 306–66

P. Viereck: *Metapolitics from the Romantics to Hitler* (New York, 1941)

K. Reiber: *Volk und Oper: das Volkstümliche in der deutschen romantischen Oper* (Würzburg, 1942)

P. H. Lang: 'Background Music for *Mein Kampf*', *Saturday Review of Literature* (20 Jan 1945)

W. H. Rubsamen: 'Political and Ideological Censorship of Opera', *PAMS* (1946), 30–42

M. Boucher: *Les idées politiques de Richard Wagner* (Paris, 1948; Eng. trans., 1950, as *The Political Concepts of Richard Wagner*)

W. L. Crosten: *French Grand Opera: an Art and a Business* (New York, 1948)

R. Monterosso: *La musica nel risorgimento* (Milan, 1948)

A. Werth: *Musical Uproar in Moscow* (London, 1949)

J. Krüger-Riebow: 'Albert Lortzing als politischer Freiheitssänger', *Musik und Gesellschaft*, i (1951), 10–15

M. Mila: 'Verdi als Politiker', *Melos*, xviii (1951), 73–8

G. G. Wiessner: *Richard Wagner, der Theater-Reformer: von Werden des deutschen Nationaltheaters im Geiste des Jahres 1848* (Emsdetten, 1951)

M. S. Selden: 'Napoleon and Cherubini', *JAMS*, viii (1955), 110–15

D. K. Gordon: *Folklore in Modern English Opera* (diss., U. of California, Los Angeles, 1959)

E. Battisti: 'Per una indagine sociologica sui librettisti napoletani buffi del settecento', *Letteratura* (Rome, 1960)

M. A. Rayner: *The Social and Literary Aspects of Sedaine's Dramatic Work* (diss., U. of London, 1960)

D. Brown: 'Balakirev, Tchaikovsky and Nationalism', *ML*, xlii (1961), 227–41

W. H. Rubsamen: 'Music and Politics in the "Risorgimento"', *Italian Quarterly*, v (1961–2), 100–20

G. Seaman: 'The National Element in Early Russian Opera, 1779–1800', *ML*, xliii (1961), 252–62

B. I. Rabinovich, ed.: *P. I. Chaykovsky i narodnaya pesnya* [Tchaikovsky and Folksong] (Moscow, 1963)

C. Di Stefano: *La censura teatrale in Italia (1600–1962)* (Bologna, 1964)

H. C. Wolff: 'Das Opernpublikum der Barockzeit', *Festschrift Hans Engel* (Kassel, 1964), 442–52

A. Perris: *French Music in the Time of Louis-Philippe: Art as a Substitute for the Heroic Experience* (diss., Northwestern U., 1967)

H. Schirming: *Das erste Auftreten des Proletariats als Klasse in der deutschen Opernliteratur des 19. Jahrhunderts: neue Aspekte für die Gewinnung eines realistischen Lortzingbildes aus der Sicht der Lortzing-Oper 'Regina'* (diss., Pädagogische Hochschule, Potsdam, 1967)

A. Ringer: 'Cherubini's *Médée* and the Spirit of French Revolu-

tionary Opera', *Essays in Musicology in Honour of Dragan Plamenac* (Pittsburgh, 1969), 281–300

R. J. Dietz: 'Marc Blitzstein and the "Agit-prop" Theatre of the 1930s', *Yearbook for Inter-American Musical Research*, vi (1970), 51–66

D. Egbert: *Social Radicalism and the Arts: Western Europe: a Cultural History from the French Revolution to 1968* (New York, 1970)

J. Ehrard, ed.: *De l'Encyclopédie à la contre-révolution: Jean-François Marmontel (1723–1799): études réunies* (Clermont-Ferrand, 1970)

R. M. Longyear: 'The Ecology of 19th-Century Opera', *GfMKB: Bonn 1970*, 497–9

S. Yevseyev: *Rimsky-Korsakov i narodnaya pesnya* [Rimsky-Korsakov and Russian Folksong] (Moscow, 1970)

P. Schmid: '*Maria Stuarda* and *Buondelmonte*', *Opera*, xxiv (1973), 1060–66

R. R. Subotnik: *Popularity and Art in Lortzing's Operas: the Effects of Social Change on a National Operatic Genre* (diss., Columbia U., 1973)

G. Bezzola: 'Aspetti del clima culturale italiano nel periodo donizettiano', *1° convegno internazionale di studi donizettiani: Bergamo 1975*, 29–42

J. Commons: 'Donizetti e la censura napoletana', ibid, 65–106

B. A. Goldgar: *Walpole and the Wits* (Lincoln, NE, 1976)

J. Commons: '*Maria Stuarda* and the Neapolitan Censorship', *Journal of the Donizetti Society*, iii (1977), 151–67

R. Angermüller: 'Die entpolitisierte Oper am Wiener und am Fürstlich Esterházyschen Hof', *HayJb*, x (1978), 5–22

S. Döhring: 'Theologische Kontroversen um die Hamburger Oper', *Die frühdeutsche Oper und ihre Beziehungen zu Italien, England und Frankreich: Hamburg 1978*

I. Fenlon: 'The Politics of Spectacle', *The New Golden Age: the Florentine Intermedi of 1589* (London, 1979)

B. R. Hanning: 'Glorious Apollo: Poetic and Political Themes in the First Opera', *Renaissance Quarterly*, xxxii (1979), 485–513

C. Maurer-Zenck: 'Unbewältigte Vergangenheit: Kreneks "Karl V" in Wien. Zur nicht bevorstehenden Wiener Erstaufführung', *Mf*, xxxii (1979), 273–88

R. W. Oldani: '*Boris Godunov* and the Censor', *19th Century Music*, ii (1978–9), 245–53

N. Tschulik: 'Die verhinderte Uraufführung von Kreneks Karl V', *ÖMz*, xxiv (1979), 122–9

C. Vitali: 'Spostamenti progressivi dell'assolutismo: il fantasma del tirannicidio nel melodramma da Domenico Gabrielli a Mozart, ovvero Antistoricità di un mito di lunga durata', *Mitologie* (Venice, 1979), 165–74

E. Voss: 'Wagners "Meistersinger" als Oper des deutschen Bürgertums', *Rororo Opernbücher: Die Meistersinger von Nürnberg* (Reinbek nr Hamburg, 1980); repr. in *Wagner*, xi (1990), 39–62

C. Ballantine: 'Social and Philosophical Outlook in Mozart's Operas', *MQ*, lxvii (1981), 507–26

J. F. Fulcher: 'Meyerbeer and the Music of Society', *MQ*, lxvii (1981), 213–29

R. M. Longyear: 'Political and Social Criticism in French Opera, 1827–1920', *Essays on the Music of J. S. Bach and Other Diverse Subjects: a Tribute to Gerhard Herz* (Louisville, KY, 1981), 245–54

R. C. Ridenour: *Nationalism, Modernism, and Personal Rivalry in Nineteenth-Century Russian Music* (Ann Arbor, 1981)

G. Tomasi: 'Der Jahrmarkt von Sorocincyi und sein Beitrag zur Suche des spezifisch Russischen in der Musik', *Modest Musorgsky: Aspekte des Opernwerks* (Hamburg, 1981), 95–110

R. Martorella: *The Sociology of Opera* (New York, 1982)

P. M. Potter: 'Strauss's *Friedenstag*: a Pacifist Attempt at Political Resistance', *MQ*, lxxix (1983), 408–24

Richard Wagner und die politischen Bewegungen seiner Zeit (Koblenz, 1983) [exhibition catalogue]

M. E. C. Bartlet: 'Politics and the Fate of *Roger et Olivier*, a Newly Recovered Opera by Grétry', *JAMS*, xxxvii (1984), 98–138

L. Bianconi and T. Walker: 'Production, Consumption and Political Function of Seventeenth-Century Opera', *Early Music History*, iv (1984), 209–96

J. Black: 'Code of Instructions for the Censorship of Theatrical Works: Naples, 1849', *Journal of the Donizetti Society*, v (1984), 147–50

J. Rosselli: *The Opera Industry in Italy from Cimarosa to Verdi: the Role of the Impresario* (Cambridge, 1984)

J. Sage: 'Music as an *Instrumentum Regni* in Spanish Seventeenth-

Century Drama', *Bulletin of Hispanic Studies* (1984)

G. Abraham: 'Satire and Symbolism in *The Golden Cockerel*', *ML*, lii (1971), 46–54; repr. in *Essays on Russian and East European Music* (Oxford, 1985), 83–92

C. Maurer-Zenck: 'The Ship Loaded with Faith and Hope: Krenek's *Karl V* and the Viennese Politics of the Thirties', *MQ*, lxxi (1985), 116–34

H. Hofer: 'Jacques Offenbach und Hector Berlioz gegen Napoléon III oder: Das Schweigen der französischen Staatsanwaltschaft anstatt eines Prozesses gegen *Orphée aux enfers*, *La belle Hélène* und *Les Troyens*', *JbO*, i (1986), 75–86

R. M. Isherwood: *Farce and Fantasy: Popular Entertainment in Eighteenth-Century Paris* (New York and Oxford, 1986)

M. Kreckel: *Richard Wagner und die französischen Frühsozialisten* (Frankfurt, 1986)

A. Spires: *French Opera during the Belle Epoque: a Study in the Social History of Ideas* (diss., U. of North Carolina, 1986)

A.-M. H. Forbes: 'Celticism in British Opera: 1878–1938', *MR*, xlvii (1986–7), 176–83

C. Colombati: '"Les deux journées" di Cherubini: dalle idee rivoluzionarie allo stile neoclassico', *I vicini di Mozart: Venice 1987*, i, 325–42

J. F. Fulcher: *The Nation's Image: French Grand Opera as Politics and Politicized Art* (Cambridge, 1987)

J. Maehder: 'Il libretto patriottico nell'Italia della fine del secolo e la raffigurazione dell'Antichità e del Rinascimento nel libretto pre-fascista italiano', *IMSCR, xiv: Bologna 1987*, iii, 451–66

L. Bianconi and G. Pestelli, eds.: 'Il sistema produttivo e le sue competenze', *SOI*, iv (1987)

C. Price: 'Political Allegory in Late Seventeenth-Century English Opera', *Music and Theatre: Essays in Honour of Winton Dean* (Cambridge, 1987), 1–29

J. Tambling: *Opera, Ideology and Film* (New York, 1987)

K. Bumpass and G. J. Kauffman: 'Nationalism and Realism in Nineteenth-Century Russian Music: "The Five" and Borodin's *Prince Igor*', *MR*, xlviii (1988), 43–51

J. Southorn: *Power and Display in the Seventeenth Century: the Arts and their Patrons in Modena and Ferrara* (Cambridge, 1988)

M. E. C. Bartlet: 'On the Freedom of the Theatre and Censorship: the *Adrien* Debate (1792)', *Musique, Histoire, Démocratie: Paris 1989*

I. D. Glikman: 'Kazn' "Ledi Makbet"' [Execution of Lady Macbeth], *Sovetskaya kul'tura* (23 Sept 1989)

M. Spada: '"Ernani" e la censura napoletana', *Studi verdiani*, v (1989), 11–34

R. L. Parker: *Studies in Early Verdi (1832–1844): New Information and Perspectives on the Milanese Musical Milieu and the Operas from Oberto to Ernani* (New York, 1989)

R. Taruskin: 'The Opera and the Dictator: the Peculiar Martyrdom of Dmitri Shostakovich', *New Republic*, cc/12 (20 March 1989), 34–40

N. Temperley: 'Musical Nationalism in English Romantic Opera', *The Lost Chord*, ed. N. Temperley (Bloomington, IN, 1989), 143–57

N. Zaslaw: 'The First Opera in Paris: a Study in the Politics of Art', *Jean-Baptiste Lully and the Music of the French Baroque: Essays in Honour of James R. Anthony* (Cambridge, 1989), 7–23

U. Bermbach: 'Wagner und Lukács: über die Ästhetisierung von Politik und die Politisierung von Ästhetik', *Bayreuther Festspiele 1990, no.2: Lohengrin*, 1–27

V. Crowther: 'A Case-Study in the Power of the Purse: the Management of the Ducal "Cappella" in Modena in the Reign of Francesco II d'Este', *JRMA*, cxv (1990), 207–19

P. Gossett: 'Becoming a Citizen: the Chorus in Risorgimento Opera', *COJ*, ii (1990), 41–64

P. Alatri: 'Metastasio nel quadro politico e culturale dell'Europa', *Musica senza aggettivi: Studi per Fedele d'Amico* (Florence, 1991), i, 145–64

P. Robinson: '*Fidelio* and the French Revolution', *COJ*, iii (1991), 23–48

(ii) Miscellaneous studies

F. Hirsch: *Die Oper und der Literaturgeist: ein Wort zu Operntextreform* (Leipzig, 1868)

L. Dauriac: 'Herbert Spencer et Meyerbeer', *ZIMG*, v (1903–4), 103–9

B. Schloezer: '"Le dit de la ville invisible de Kitej": essai de psychologie musicale', *ReM*, iv/2 (1922), 155–63

L. Vallas: *Les idées de Claude Debussy, musicien français* (Paris, 1927)

R. Majut: 'Kreneks Jonny-Dichtung im geistesgeschichtlichen

Zusammenhang des Weltschmerzes und des Rousseauismus', *Germanische-Romanische Monatsschrift*, xvi/11–12 (1928)

D. Lucchesi: *Kulturgeschichte: Betrachtung von Pietro Chiari Commedie* (Munich, 1938)

E. Cassirer: *Descartes, Corneille, Christine de Suède: Etudes de psychologie et de philosophie* (Paris, 1942)

J. Bahle: *Hans Pfitzner und der geniale Mensch: eine psychologische Kulturkritik* (Konstanz, 1949)

L. Misch: '*Fidelio* als ethisches Bekenntnis', *Beethoven-Studien* (Berlin, 1950), 143–9

W. Arlt: 'Zur Deutung der Barockoper: "Il trionfo dell'amicizia e dell'amore"' [F. Conti-Ballerini], *Musik und Geschichte: Leo Schrade zum sechzigsten Geburtstag* (Cologne, 1963), 96–145

E. Lockspeiser: *Debussy: his Life and Mind* (London, 1965–6)

H. C. Wolff: 'Der Manierismus in der barocken und romantischen Oper', *Mf*, xix (1966), 261–9

C. Merchant: 'Delacroix's Tragedy of Desdemona', *Shakespeare Survey*, xxi (1968), 79–86

E. Padmore: 'German Expressionist Opera', *PRMA*, xcv (1968–9), 41–53

H. C. Wolff: 'Manierismus in den venezianischen Opernlibretti des 17. Jahrhunderts', *Venezia e il melodramma nel seicento: Venice 1972*, 319–26

C. Dahlhaus: 'Ethos und Pathos in Glucks Iphigenie auf Tauris', *Mf*, xxviii (1974), 289–300

D. Koenigsberger: 'A New Metaphor for Mozart's *Magic Flute*', *European Studies Review*, v (1975), 229–75

M. R. Maniates: *Mannerism in Italian Music and Culture, 1530–1630* (Chapel Hill, 1979)

B. Adamy: *Hans Pfitzner: Literatur, Philosophie und Zeitgeschehen in seinem Weltbild und Werk* (Tutzing, 1980)

R. Strohm: 'Zum Verständnis der Opera seria', *Werk und Wiedergabe: Musiktheater exemplarisch interpretiert* (1981); Eng. trans., rev., in *Essays on Handel and Italian Opera* (Cambridge, 1985), 93–105

S. Mauser: *Das expressionistische Musik-Theater der Wiener Schule* (Regensburg, 1982)

P. Franklin: '*Palestrina* and the Dangerous Futurists', *MQ*, lxx (1984), 499–514; repr. in *The Idea of Music: Schoenberg and Others* (London, 1985), 117–38

A. Helbo, ed.: *Approches de l'Opéra: Royaumont 1984* [semiotics]

C. Dahlhaus: 'Idylle und Utopie: zu Beethovens *Fidelio*', *NZM*, xi (1985), 4

I. Nagel: *Autonomie und Gnade: über Mozarts Opern* (Munich, 1985)

F. Pupil: *Le style troubadour, ou La nostalgie du bon vieux temps* (Nancy, 1985)

J. Pasler: '*Pelléas* and Power: Forces behind the Reception of Debussy's Opera', *19th Century Music*, x (1986–7), 147–77

P. Howard: 'The Influence of the Précieuses on Context and Structure in Quinault's and Lully's *tragédies lyriques*', *AcM*, lxiii (1991), 57–72

G: DRAMATURGY, THEORY, AESTHETICS, CRITICISM

(i) Comment by librettists and composers

BQ – H. Becker and others: *Quellentexte* (Kassel, 1981)

WE – Eng. trans. in U. Weisstein: *Essence of Opera* (London, 1964)

G. Chiabrera: 'Geri: Dialogo della tessitura delle canzoni' (MS, c1600); ed. in *Alcune prose inedite di Gabriello Chiabrera* (Geneva, 1826) and *Opere di Gabriello Chiabrera e lirici del classicismo barocco* (Turin, 2/1974)

M. Opitz: *Buch von der deutschen Poeterey* (Breslau, 1624)

——: *Teutsche Poemata* (Breslau, 1624)

——: Dedication and preface to *Dafne* (Torgau, 1627) [repr. with prologue, signed Ovidius, *BQ*, 163–5]

G. Strozzi: *Satire, e altre raccolte per l'Accademia de gli Unisoni in casa di Giulio Strozzi* (MS, *I-Vnm*, c1630)

——: *Veglie de' Signori Unisoni* (Venice, 1638)

O. Castelli: 'Dialogo sopra La Poesia Dramatica', *La Sincerità trionfante overo L'Erculeo ardire: favola boscareccia* (Rome, 1640) [excerpt in *BQ*, 51–8]

G. Badoaro: 'Al Signor Michel'angelo Torcigliani l'Assicurato Academico Incognito' [dedicatory letter], *L'Ulisse errante Opera Musicale* (Venice, 1644), 5–18 [*BQ*, 58–63]

G. P. Harsdörffer: 'Über das Wesen der Singspiele und die Oper "Seelewig"', *Gesprechspiele, iv: Samt einer Rede von dem Worte Spiel* (Nuremberg, 1644) [excerpt in *BQ*, 165–7]

G. Strozzi: *Le glorie della Signora Anna Renzi romana* (Venice, 1644)

P. Perrin: 'Avant-propos' to *Pomone, Opera, ou Representation en Musique: Pastorale* (Paris, 1671)

T. Corneille: 'Argument', *Circé* (Paris, 1675)

F. F. Frugoni: 'Discorso critico intorno alla poesia dramatica', *L'Epulone: opera melodrammatica esposta, con le prose morali-critiche dal P. Francesco Fulvio Frugoni* (Venice, 1675), 161–99

T. Corneille: Preface to *L'inconnu* (Paris, 1676)

J. de La Fontaine: *Epîtres* (Paris, 1677–80) ['A M. de Nyert' (1677), *BQ*, 141–4; 'Le Florentin' (1680), *WE*, 27–9; 'A Madame de Thiange' (1680)]

C. Ivanovich: 'Memorie teatrali di Venezia', *Minerva al Tavolino* (Venice 1681, 2/1688), 361–453 [excerpts in *BQ*, 88–92]

L. von Bostel: 'Vorbericht', *Der Glückliche Grosz-Vezier Cara Mustapha*, i (Hamburg, 1686) [*BQ*, 173–8]

F. F. Frugoni: *Del cane di Diogene*, v (Venice, 1687) [see Calcaterra, *Poesia e canto*, 1951, 234–5]

H. Elmenhorst: *Q. D. B. V. Dramatologia Antiqvo-Hodierna, Das ist: Bericht von denen Opern-Spielen* (Hamburg, 1688) [excerpt in *BQ*, 182–6]

M. Noris: *L'animo eroe, azioni istoriche de' più famosi antichi* (Venice, 1689)

N. Boileau: *Satires*, ix–x (Paris, 1692) [Perrin and Quinault; woman and opera]; repr. in *Oeuvres complètes* (Paris, 1966)

G. Frigimelica Roberti: Prefaces to 11 librettos, 1694–1708 [in praise of himself]

L. Fuzelier: Prefaces to his operas, *Recueil général des opéra*, nos. 2, 3 (Paris, 1703–46)

[C. F. Hunold]: *Theatralische Galante und Geistliche Gedichte von Menantes* (Hamburg, 1706)

A. Spagna: 'Discorso', *Oratorii overo melodrammi sacri con un discorso dogmatico intorno l'istessa materia*, i (Rome, 1706), 8–14 [*BQ*, 64–7]

E. Neumeister, ed. C.F. Hunold: *Die allerneueste Art, zur reinen und galanten Poesie zu gelangen* (Hamburg, 1707)

B. Feind: 'Gedancken von der Opera', *Deutsche Gedichte bestehend in musikalischen Schau-Spielen, sammt einer Vorrede von dem Temperament und Gemühts-Beschaffenheit eines Poeten, und Gedancken von der Opera* (Hamburg, 1708); excerpts in L. Bianconi, *Music in the Seventeenth Century* (Cambridge, 1987)

A.-L. Le Brun: *Théâtre lyrique: avec une préface ou l'on traite du poème de l'opéra* (Paris, 1712)

P. J. Martello: *Della bellezza della tragedia antica e moderna* (Rome, 1715) [6 dialogues, no. 5 devoted to opera; Eng. trans. in P. Weiss: 'Pier Jacopo Martello on Opera [1715]: an Annotated Translation', *MQ*, lxvi (1980), 378–403]

B. Marcello: *Il teatro alla moda, o sia Metodo sicuro e facile per ben comporre, ed eseguire l'Opere Italiane in musica all'uso moderno* (Venice, c1720; Eng. trans. in R. G. Pauly: 'Benedetto Marcello's Satire on Early 18th-Century Opera', *MQ*, xxxiv (1948), 222–33, 371–403; xxxv (1949), 85–105

D. Lalli: *Rime* [with sonnet dedicated to collaborator G. Polazzi] (Venice, 1732)

C.-H. Blainville: Criticisms in *Mercure de France* (Nov 1741 March 1774); repr. in J. Peyrot: *Tribune de St. Gervais* (Dec 1911)

J. Mattheson: *Die neueste Untersuchung der Singspiele* (Hamburg, 1744) [refutes Muratori, 'De' difetti', 1706]

H. Fielding: *The True Patriot*, no.9 (London, 1745) [satirical criticism of opera]

G. Baretti: Prefaces to *Traduzioni in verso italiano delle tragedie di Corneille* (Venice, 1747)

Voltaire: Preface to *Sémiramis* (Paris, 1748) [excerpt in *WE*, 75–8]

J. Mattheson: *Mithridat, wider den Gift einer welschen Satyre, gennant: La musica* (Hamburg, 1749)

P. C. Roy: 'Lettre sur l'Opéra', *Lettres sur quelques écrits de ce tems*, ed. E. Fréron, ii (Geneva and Paris, 1749)

Voltaire: *Connaissance des beautés et des défauts de la poésie et d'éloquence dans la langue française* (Paris, 1749; part in *WE*, 79–80]

D. Diderot and J. L. D'Alembert, eds.: *Encyclopédie, ou Dictionnaire raisonné* (Paris, 1751–65) [articles by L. de Cahusac and J.-F. Marmontel, incl. 'Critique', 'Déclamation']

A. Danchet: 'Avertissement' to *Théâtre complet* (Paris, 1751)

G. Baretti: *La voix de la Discorde ou la Bataille des Violons: Histoire d'un attentat sédicieux et atroce contre la vie et les biens de cinquante chanteurs et violinistes* (London, c1753) [against Vanneschi]

——: *Projet pour avoir un opéra italien à Londres dans un gout tout nouveau* (London, 1753)

S. Maffei: *De' teatri antichi e moderni* (Verona, 1753; repr. in *Opere dei Maffei*, i, 1790) [attacks Concina]

F. Algarotti: *Saggio sopra l'opera in musica* (Livorno, 1754–5, 2/1763; Eng. trans. as *An Essay on the Opera*, 1768) [excerpt in Strunk 1950]

C.-H. Blainville: *L'esprit de l'art musical, ou réflexions sur la musique et ses différentes parties* (Geneva, 1754)

L. de Cahusac: *La danse ancienne et moderne, ou Traité historique de la danse* (The Hague, 1754)

R. de' Calzabigi: *La Lulliade, o I buffi scacciati da Parigi, poema eroicomico* (MS, 1754–89); ed. G. Muresu in *La ragione dei 'buffoni' (La Lulliade di Raniero de' Calzabigi)* (Rome, 1977) [mock-heroic satire on French opera]

——: 'Dissertazione...su le poesie drammatiche del Signor Abate Pietro Metastasio', *Poesie del Signor Abate Pietro Metastasio* (Paris, 1755–69), i, pp. xix–cciv

D. Diderot: 'Troisième entretien sur Le fils naturel', *Entretiens avec Dorval* (Paris, 1757) [discussion of Racine's *Iphigénie en Aulide* as libretto for new kind of declamatory opera]

A. H. de La Motte: 'Examen de l'opéra de *Psiché*', *Mercure de France*, (April 1757)

G. M. Ortes: *Riflessioni sopra i drammi per musica, aggiuntavi una nuova azione drammatica* (Venice, 1757)

D. Diderot: *De la poésie dramatique* (Paris, 1758)

F. Algarotti: 'Epistola in versi al Metastasio', *Epistole in versi* (Venice, 1759), 22–7

[?J.-F. Marmontel]: 'Examen des réflections de M. Dalembert sur la liberté de la musique', *Mercure de France* (July 1759)

C. Goldoni: Prefaces, in *Opere*, xi (Venice, 1761–78); repr. in G. Ortolani, ed.: *Tutte le opere di Carlo Goldoni* (Verona, 1935–56), i, 683–99

G. Baretti: Review of Metastasio's *Opere drammatiche*, *La frusta letteraria*, iii (1 Nov 1763)

J.-F. Marmontel: *Le poétique françoise* (Paris, 1763)

R. de' Calzabigi: Letter to W. Kaunitz (1767), ed. V. Helfert, 'Dosud Neznámy Dopis Ran. Calsabigino z r. 1767', *Musikologie*, i (1938), 114–22; Eng. trans. in H. Hammelmann and M. Rose, 'New Light on Calzabigi and Gluck', *MT*, cx (1969), 609–11

J. A. Hiller: *Wöchentliche Nachrichten und Anmerkungen die Musik betreffend*, no. 33 (10 Feb 1767) [report on comic opera *Lisuart und Daviolette*; on setting German to music]

G. Baretti: *An Account of the Manners and Customs in Italy* (London, 1768)

R. de' Calzabigi: *L'opera seria* [satirical libretto, 1769; repr. in P. Metastasio: *Opere*, ed. M. Fubini and E. Bonora, 1968]

C. W. von Gluck: Prefaces to *Alceste* (1769) and *Paride ed Elena* (1770); Eng. trans. in Strunk 1950, 681–3, and in H. and E. H. Mueller von Asow, ed.: *The Collected Correspondence and Papers of Christoph Willibald Gluck* (London, 1962), 22–5, 27–30

M. Verazi: Correspondence with Jommelli and Württemberg Court, 1770 (MS, *D-Sl*)

G. De Gamerra: 'Osservazioni sull'opera in musica', *Armida* (Milan, 1771), 44–8

D. Diderot: 'Lettre', 1771, ed. in *Oeuvres complètes* (Paris, 1875) [on the observations of Chastellux on the *Treatise on Melodrama*, 1771; *WE*, 95–9]

C. M. Wieland: 'Briefe an einen Freund über das deutsche Singspiel Alceste', *Der teutsche Merkur* (1773), no. 1; (1774), no. 1

——: 'Ueber einige ältere teutsche Singspiele, die den Namen Alceste führen', *Der teutsche Merkur* (1773, no.4)

J. F. Reichardt: *Ueber die deutsche comische Oper* (Hamburg, 1774)

C. M. Wieland: 'Versuch über das Teutsche Singspiel und einige dahin einschlagende Gegenstände', *Der teutsche Merkur* (1775), no. 5 [excerpts in *WE*, 114–22]

M.-F.-L. G. L. Bailli du Roullet: *Lettre sur les drames-opéras* (Paris, 1776)

A. Piazza: *Discorso all'orecchio* (?Venice, 1776) [collab. with G. Casanova, attacking Ange Goudar]

J.-F. Marmontel: *Essai sur les revolutions de la musique françoise* (Paris, 1778) [repr. with criticism in Leblond, *Mémoires* (1781); see also Marmontel's reply *Polymnie* (1820)]

A. Piazza: *Il teatro, ovvero Fatti di una veneziana che lo fanno conoscere* (Venice, 1778)

M. Verazi: Prefaces to *Europa riconosciuta* (1778) and *Troia distrutta* (1778)

G. J. Vogler: *Betrachtungen der Mannheimer Tonschule* (Mannheim, 1778–81)

A. Rubbi: *Elogi degli illustri italiani* (Venice, 1782)

P. Chiari: *Secolo corrente* (Venice, 1783) [Dialogue VII on opera]

R. de' Calzabigi: *Lettera di Ranieri de' Calzabigi al Sig. Conte Vittorio Alfieri sulle quattro sue prime tragedie*, 20 Aug 1783 (n.p., 1784) [ed. in *Tutte le opere di Vittorio Alfieri* (Asti, 1951–), xxxv (1978), 171–213]

——: Letter to the editor, *Mercure de France* (21 Aug 1784) [on his advice to Gluck about banishing secco recitative and coloratura]

Voltaire: *Del teatro italiano e specialmente dell'opera in musica* (Nice, 1785)

——: *Osservazioni sulla 'Clemenza di Tito'* (Nice, 1785)

——: *Osservazioni sulla 'Semiramide'* (Nice, 1785)

J. A. Hiller: *Ueber Metastasio und seine Werke: neben einigen Uebersetzungen aus demselben* (Leipzig, 1786)

A. Rubbi: *Dialoghi fra il Sig. Arteaga e A. Rubbi* (Venice, 1786)

——: *Il bello armonico teatrale* (Venice, 1786)

P. A. C. de Beaumarchais: 'Aux abonnés de l'opéra qui voudraient aimer l'opéra', preface to *Tarare, opéra en cinq actes* (Paris, 1787, 2/1790) [excerpt in *WE*, 140–52]

J.-F. Marmontel: 'Opéra', *Elémens de littérature*; ed in *Oeuvres complètes*, ix (Paris, 1787), 47–114

A. Rubbi: *Dialoghi in difesa della letteratura italiana* (Venice, 1787)

A.-E.-M. Grétry: *Mémoires ou essais sur la musique* (Paris, 1789); repr. in *Oeuvres complètes* (1919–22) [excerpts, as 'Reflections on Music' and 'Of the Need for Comic Opera', *WE*, 153–8]

A. Pepoli: 'Lettera ad un uomo ragionevole sul melodramma detto serio' (?Venice, 1789) [preface to unset libretto for *tragedia per musica, Meleagro*; attacks Metastasio, commends Calzabigi]

R. de' Calzabigi: *Risposta...[di] Don Santigliano alla critica ragionatissima delle poesie drammatiche del C. de' Calsabigi, fatta dal baccelliere D. Stefan Arteaga* (Venice, 1790)

A. Rubbi: *Parnasso italiano*, xlvii (Venice, 1790)

R. de' Calzabigi: *Lettera del consigliere de' Calsabigi a S. E. il sig. Conte Alessandro Pepoli ... nel trasmettergli la sua nuova tragedia intitolata Elfrida* (Naples, 1792)

G. Stephanie: *Sämmtliche Singspiele* (Liegnitz, 1792) [with prefaces informative on Viennese German comic opera conventions]

J. W. von Goethe: *Über Wahrheit und Wahrscheinlichkeit der Kunstwerke: ein Gespräch* (1798); repr. in *Sämmtliche Werke: Vollständige Ausgabe* (Stuttgart, 1863), v, 365–7

J. F. Le Sueur: *Lettre en réponse à Guillard* (Paris, 1801)

G. Lorenzi: *Opere teatrali* (Naples, 1806–20) [important preface on Neapolitan comic opera]

M.-J. Sedaine: 'Discours de réception', *Choix de discours de réception à l'Académie Française* (Paris, 1808), ii, 339ff

E. T. A. Hoffmann: 'Der Dichter und der Komponist', *AMZ*, Jg.15 (1813), cols. 793–806, 809–17 [*WE*, 167–79]

G. Carpani: *Lettere due...al Signor Bombet* [Stendhal] (Vienna, 1815)

C. M. von Weber: 'Über die Opera, Undine', *AMZ*, Jg.19 (1817), cols. 201–8 [Eng. trans. in J. Warrack, ed.: *Carl Maria von Weber: Writings on Music*, 1981, 200–05; excerpts in *WE*, 180–1]

G. Carpani: *Lettera all'anonimo autore dell'articolo sul Tancredi di Rossini* (Milan, 1818)

L. da Ponte: *An Extract from the Life of Lorenzo da Ponte* (New York, 1819)

F. Grillparzer: 'Der Freischütz, Oper von Maria Weber' (1821); repr. in *Gesammelte Werke* (Munich, 1971), ii, 601–5 [*WE*,163–6]

V. E. de Jouy: *Oeuvres complètes* (Paris, 1823–8) [*Théâtre*, xviii–xxi, has informative comment on librettos; 'Essai sur l'opéra français' (1836), xxii, 225–82, repr. in Gérard 1987]

G. Carpani: *Le Rossiniane ossia Lettere musico-teatrali* (Padua, 1824); also in *Lettera sulla musica di Rossini* (1826)

J.-T. Merle: *De l'opéra* (Paris, 1827)

[C. M. von Weber]: *Hinterlassene Schriften*, ed. C. G. T. Winkler (Dresden, 1828)

G. Ferretti: 'I libretti per musica buffa ossia il Disperato – Ottave' [1830], *Bagattelle eroicomiche in versi* (Rome, 1850), 13–19

——: *Conferenza sulla storia della poesia melodrammatica romana* (1834) [see Cametti 1896]

A. E. Scribe: *Discours prononcés dans la séance publique tenue par l'Académie Française, pour la réception de M. Scribe, le 28 Janvier 1830* (Paris, 1836)

M.-J. Sedaine: 'Quelques réflexions inédites de Sedaine sur l'opéra comique', *Théâtre choisi de G. Pixérécourt* (Paris and Nancy, 1841–3), iv, 501–16

G. F. Treitschke: 'Die Zauberflöte, Der Dorfbarbier, Fidelio', *Orpheus: Musikalisches Taschenbuch für das Jahr 1841*, ed. A.

Schmidt, 239–64 [his revision of *Fidelio* with Beethoven]

J. F. Kind: *Freischützbuch* (Leipzig, 1843)

A. E. Scribe: *Discours à l'Académie Française* (Paris, 1844; repr. in *Les prix de vertu*, ii, 1858)

H. Berlioz: *Voyage musicale en Allemagne et en Italie* (Paris, 1844)

T. Gautier: 'Notice sur Norma, drame lyrique en deux actes de Romani: Musique de Bellini', in J.B. Giraldon: *Les beautés de l'Opéra, ou chefs-d'oeuvre lyriques ... Avec un texte explicatif rédigé par T. Gautier, Jules Janin et Philarète Chasles* (Paris, 1845)

P. Beltrame: 'Come si diventa librettista', 'Della poesia lirico-musicale odierna', *Componimenti editi e inediti* (Venice, 1847), 232, 43

A. Lortzing: *Albert Lortzings komische Opera* (Leipzig, 1847)

I. S. Turgenev: 'Sovremennïye zametki', *Sovremennik*, no. 1 (1847); repr. in *Sobraniye socheneniya*, ii (Moscow, 1956), 280–90 [memories of Verdi, Rossini, Meyerbeer, Berlioz, F. David etc.]

——: 'Neskol'ko slov ob opere Meyerbera "Provok"' [A few Words on Meyerbeer's *Le prophète*], *Otechestvennïye zapiski*, lxvii (1850); repr. in *Sobraniye socheneniya*, ii (Moscow, 1956), 291–4

F. Liszt: *Lohengrin et Tannhäuser de Richard Wagner* (Leipzig, 1851)

H. Berlioz: *Les soirées de l'orchestre* (Paris, 1852; Eng. trans., 1956, as *Evenings in the Orchestra*)

J. Raff: *Die Wagnerfrage kritisch beleuchtet, i: Wagners letzte künstlerische Kundgebung in 'Lohengrin'* (Brunswick, c1854)

F. Liszt: 'Richard Wagners Rheingold', *NZM*, xliii (1855), 1–3

H. Berlioz: *Le chef d'orchestre: théorie de son art* (Paris, 1856; Eng. trans., 1917)

Castil-Blaze: *Sur l'opéra français, vérités dures mais utiles* (Paris, 1856)

T. Gautier: *Histoire de l'art dramatique en France depuis vingt-cinq ans* (Paris, 1858–9)

H. Berlioz: *Les grotesques de la musique* (Paris, 1859)

——: *A travers chants: Etudes musicales* (Paris, 1862, 2/1872; Eng. trans., 1913–18)

A. Ghislanzoni: 'Conversazioni musicali', *Gazzetta musicale di Milano* (1866), nos. 3, 4, 7, 8, 10, 21, 24, 26

——: 'La commedia vaudeville in Italia', *Gazzetta musicale di Milano* (14 April 1866)

I. S. Turgenev: 'Ob opere "Mariya Tyudor" Kashperova', *Sankt-peterburgskiye vedomosti* (8 Feb 1868)

——: 'Pervoye predstavleniye operï g-zhi Viardo v Veymare', *Sankt-peterburgskiye vedomosti* (21 April 1869); repr. in *Russkiye propilei*, iii (Moscow, 1916) [on Viardot, *Le dernier sorcier*]

A. Ghislanzoni: 'L'arte di far libretti', *Gazzetta musicale di Milano* (30 Jan 1870); repr. in *Capricci letterari* (Milan, 1870)

E. Krásnohorská [A. Pechová]: 'Cesky básník a hudební drama' [The Czech Poet and Music Drama], *Hudební listy*, i (1870), 298–301, 306–10; repr. in Z. Pešat and J. Křesálková, eds.: *Vybov z díla* [Selected Works], ii (Prague, 1956), 339–50

——: 'O české deklamaci hudební' [On Czech Musical Declamation], *Hudební listy*, ii (1871), 1–4, 9–13, 17–19

R. Wagner: *Gesammelte Schriften und Dichtung* (Leipzig, 1871–83, 2/1887; Eng. trans., 1892–9, as *Prose Works*); incl. *Oper und Drama* (1852; ed. (showing revisions) by K. Kropfinger, 1984), 'Über das Opern-Dichten und Komponieren im Besonderen' (1853) and 'Über die Anwendung der Musik auf das Drama' (1879)

F. Grillparzer: *Sämmtliche Werke* (Stuttgart, 1872, 5/1892) [writings on opera aesthetics]

H.-A. Barbier: *Etudes dramatiques: Jules-César, Benvenuto Cellini* (Paris, 1874)

A. Royer: *Histoire de l'Opéra* (Paris, 1874) [with 19th-century anecdotes]

A. Ghislanzoni: 'Mie idee sul libretto per musica', *Giornale capriccio*, xv (Aug 1877), 18ff

C. Cui: *La musique en Russie* (Paris, 1880) [articles from *Revue et Gazette musicale de Paris*, 1858–60]

F. Liszt: *Gesammelte Schriften*, iii/1–2 (Leipzig, 1880–83) [incl. 'Über Meyerbeers Hugenotten', 1837, ii/1; 'Dramaturgische Blätter', 1849–54, iii]

F. Romani: 'Alcuni cenni storici sull'arte musicale e della danza desunti dall'introduzione di F. Romani alla Cronologia degli spettacoli rappresentati al Teatro della Scala in Milano', in L. Bignami: *Cronologia di tutti gli spettacoli rappresentati nel gran teatro comunale di Bologna ... (1763–1880) e annotazioni storiche sull'arte musicale e della danza di Felice Romani* (Bologna, 1880)

E. Branca, ed.: *Felice Romani: Critica letteraria: Articoli raccolti e pubblicati a cura di sua moglie E. Branca* (Turin, 1883)

T. Gautier: 'Les beautés de l'opéra', *Souvenirs de théâtre, d'art et de critique* (Paris, 1883), 70–168 [written in 1844]

A. Ghislanzoni: 'Storia aneddotica di alcuni libretti', *Gazzetta musicale di Milano* (7 Dec 1884), 448; (14 Dec 1884), 456

C.-L.-E. Nuitter [Truinet] and E. Thoinan [A. E. Roquet]: *Les origines de l'opéra français* (Paris, 1886)

A. Bruneau: 'Le drame lyrique français', *RMI*, iv (1887), 299–304

D. Diderot: *Le neveu de Rameau: Satire publiée pour la premiére fois sur le manuscrit original autographe* (Paris, 1891)

F. Pedrell: *Por nuestra musica: Algúnas observaciones sobre la magna cuestión de una escuela lírica nacional* (Barcelona, 1891)

E. Zola: 'Le drame lyrique', *Le journal* (22 Nov 1893)

V. Krïlov: 'Kompozitor Ts. A. Kyui (otrïvok iz vospominaniy)', *Istoricheskiy vestnik*, no. 2 (1894); repr. in *Prozaicheskiye sochineniya*, ii (St Petersburg, 1908), 291–300

F. Weingartner: *Die Lehre von der Wiedergeburt des musikalischen Dramas* (Kiel and Leipzig, 1895)

A. Cametti, ed.: *Una conferenza inedita di Jacopo Ferretti sulla storia della poesia melodrammatica romana* [1834] (Pesaro, 1896)

E. Zola: 'A propos du Messidor', *Le gaulois* (23 Feb 1897)

R. Batka: *Musikalische Streifzüge* (Florence and Leipzig, 1899) [reviews]

A. Bruneau: *Musiques d'hier et de demain* (Paris, 1900)

R. Heuberger: *Im Foyer: Gesammelte Essays über das Opernrepertoire der Gegenwart* (Leipzig, 1901)

——: *Musikalische Skizzen* (Leipzig, 1901)

J. Kvapil: Introduction to libretto of *Rusalka* (Prague, 1901), 5–8

C. Saint-Saëns: 'Bayreuth und der Ring des Nibelungen', *Die Musik*, i (1901–2), 751–63, 879–84 [visits to Bayreuth]

H. Berlioz: *Les musiciens et la musique* (Paris, 1903) [articles from *Journal des débats*, 1835–63]

C. Debussy: 'L'étranger, à Bruxelles', *Gil Blas* (12 Jan 1903) [on D'Indy]

F. Weingartner: *Bayreuth (1876–1896)* (Leipzig, 1904)

P. Cornelius: *Literarische Werke*, iii: *Aufsätze über Musik und Kunst* (Leipzig, 1905)

L. Halévy: 'La millième représentation de *Carmen*', *Le théâtre* (Jan 1905) [excerpts in *WE*, 223–4]

R. Batka: *Aus der Opernwelt: Prager Kritiken und Skizzen* (Munich, 1907)

F. Busoni: *Entwurf einer neuen Ästhetik der Tonkunst* (Leipzig, 1907; Eng. trans., 1911, as *Sketch of a New Esthetic of Music*) [pubd with two librettos, incl. *Die Brautwahl*]

E. Humperdinck: 'Parsifal-Skizzen: persönliche Erinnerungen an R. Wagner und an die erste Aufführung des Bühnenweihfestspieles am 25. Juli 1882', *Die Zeit* [Vienna] (1907); repr. in *Bayreuther Festspielführer 1927*, 215–29, and separately (Siegburg, 1949)

I. Pizzetti: 'La musica per "La nave" di Gabriele d'Annunzio', *RMI*, xiv (1907), 855–62

E. Kloss: 'Richard Wagner über "Lohengrin": Aussprüche des Meisters über sein Werk', *Richard Wagner-Jb*, iii (1908), 132–88

I. Pizzetti: 'Ariane et Barbebleue', *RMI*, xv (1908), 73–111 [Dukas' principles, and his own]

C. M. von Weber: *Sämtliche Schriften*, ed. G. Kaiser (Berlin and Leipzig, 1908); Eng. trans. as *Carl Maria von Weber: Critical Writings on Music*, ed. J. Warrack (Cambridge, 1981)

R. Batka: *Allgemeine Geschichte der Musik* (Stuttgart, 1909–15)

G. Giacosa: *Conferenze e discorsi: con una prefazione di Innocenzo Cappa* (Milan, 1909)

J. Gregor: 'Die historische Dramaturgie in der Geschichte der Oper', *IMusSCR*, iii Vienna 1909, 208–10

H. Pfitzner: 'Der Boycott meiner Werke am Münchner Hoftheater', *Süddeutsche Monatshefte*, vii/8 (1909), 196

E. Kloss: *Richard Wagner über die 'Meistersinger von Nürnberg': Aussprüche des Meisters über sein Werk* (Leipzig, 1910)

H. Pfitzner: 'Die Rose vom Liebesgarten in Wien', *Gustav Mahler: ein Bild seiner Persönlichkeit in Widmungen*, ed. P. Stefan (Munich, 1910), 40–41

R. Boughton: *The Music Drama of the Future: 'Uther and Igraine', Choral Drama ... with Essays by the Collaborators* (London, 1911)

J. Kvapil: 'O vzniku "Rusalky"' [On the Genesis of *Rusalka*], *MR*, iv (1911), 428–30

N. Rimsky-Korsakov: *Muzikal'niye stat'i i zametki 1869–1907* [Articles and Observations on Music], ed. N. R. Rimskaya-Korsakova (St Petersburg, 1911)

——: '"Snegurochka" vesennyaya skazka' ['The Snow Maiden': a Spring Fairy-Tale], ibid, 181–200 [more complete as 'Razbor "Snegurochki"' [An Analysis of 'The Snow Maiden'], *Polnoye sobraniye sochineniy: literaturnïye proizvedeniya i perepiska*, iv, ed. V. Protopopov (1960), 393–426]

H. von Hofmannsthal: 'Ce que nous avons voulu en écrivant *Ariane à Naxos* et *Le Bourgeois Gentilhomme*', *Mercure musical*, viii/9–10 (1912), 1–3

R. Boughton: *The Death and Resurrection of the Musical Festival; the Decay of Triennials; the Rise of Competitions; the Reform of Competitions; the Festival of the Future* (London, 1913)

M. Ravel: 'Fervaal', *Comoedia illustré* (20 Jan 1913)

G. D'Annunzio: *La musica di Wagner e la genesi del "Parsifal"* (Florence, 1914)

E. Lindner: *Richard Wagner über 'Tannhäuser': Aussprüche des Meisters über sein Werk* (Leipzig, 1914)

H. von Wolzogen: *Richard Wagner über den 'Fliegenden Holländer': die Enstehung, Gestaltung und Darstellung des Werkes aus den Schriften und Briefen des Meisters zusammengestellt* (Leipzig, 1914)

C. Nielsen: 'Musik und Wort', *AMZ* (1 Aug 1915 and 22 Feb 1924)

H. Pfitzner: *Vom musikalischen Drama: Gesammelte Aufsätze* (Munich and Leipzig, 1915)

R. Boughton: 'A National Music Drama: the Glastonbury Festival', *PMA*, xliv (1917–8), 19–35

J. Cocteau: *Le coq et l'arlequin: notes autour de la musique* (Paris, 1918; repr. in *Le rappel à l'aurore*, 1926, and in *Oeuvres complètes*, ix, 1950) [short version as 'The Cock and the Harlequin', *WE*, 268–72; manifesto of Les Six]

C. Cui: *Muzikal'no-kriticheskiye stat'i* (Petrograd, 1918)

A. Berg: 'Die musikalische Impotenz der "neuen Ästhetik Hans Pfitzners', *Musikblätter des Anbruch*, ii (1920), 399–408 [repr. in Reich 1963]

V. d'Indy: *Emmanuel Chabrier et Paul Dukas* (Paris, 1920)

B. Kochno: *Diaghilev and the Ballets Russes* (New York, 1920)

C. Debussy: *Monsieur Croche, anti-dilettante* (Paris, 1921); ed. F. Lesure in *Claude Debussy: Monsieur Croche et autres écrits* (Paris, 1971, Eng. trans., 1977)

F. Busoni: 'Dell'Opera: Saggio d'una prefazione al "Dottor Faust"', *Il Pianoforte* (April 1922)

M. Brod: *Sternenhimmel: Musik- und Theatererlebnisse* (Prague and Munich, 1923, 2/1966 as *Prager Sternenhimmel: Musik- und Theatererlebnisse aus den zwanziger Jahren*)

F. Busoni: *Von der Einheit der Musik* (Berlin, 1923, rev. 1956, ed. J. Herrmann, as *Wesen und Einheit der Musik*; Eng. trans., 1957, as *The Essence of Music and Other Papers*)

A. Boito: 'Pensieri critici giovanili', *RMI*, xxxi (1924), 161–98

R. Boughton: 'Stories for Opera', *Sackbut*, v (1923–4), 268–70

M. Brod: *Leoš Janáček: život a dílo* [Life and Works] (Prague, 1924; Ger. orig., 1925, rev. 2/1956)

G. F. Malipiero: *I profeti di Babilonia* (Milan, 1924)

R. Strauss: Preface to *Intermezzo* (1924) [on word-setting, audibility, singing; in *WE*, 294–300]

S. Zweig: 'Richard Strauss und Wien', *Neue Freie Presse* (8 June 1924); repr. in *Richard Strauss: Dokumente seines Lebens und Schaffens*, ed. F. Trenner (Munich, 1954), 173

E. Krenek: 'Zum Problem der Oper', *Von Neuer Musik: Beiträge zur Erkenntnis der neuzeitlichen Tonkunst* (Cologne, 1925), 39–43

F. Busoni: *Über die Möglichkeiten der Oper und über die Partitur des 'Doktor Faust'* (Leipzig, 1926)

H. Pfitzner: *Gesammelte Schriften* (Augsburg, 1926–9) [incl. essays 'Zur Grundfrage der Operndichtung' (1908), 'Futuristengefahr' (1917), and 'Die neue Aesthetik der musikalischen Impotenz' (1920)]

E. Krenek: 'Von dem Operntext', *Das Theater*, viii (1927), 467–8

——: '"Jonny spielt auf" und die Ausführenden', *Literarische Beilagen* (1 Oct 1927)

——: '"Materialbestimmtheit" der Oper', *Musikblätter des Anbruch*, ix (1927), 48–52

——: 'Über Sinn und Zweck des Theaters', *Musikblätter des Anbruch*, ix (1927), 281–2

G. Adami, ed.: *Giacomo Puccini: Epistolario* (Milan, 1928; Eng. trans., 1931, rev. 2/1974)

H. von Hofmannsthal: Preface to *Die ägyptische Helena* (1928); Eng. trans., *Journal of Aesthetics and Art Criticism*, xv (1956–7), 205–14 [*WE*, 300–12]

E. Krenek: 'Meine drei Einakter', *Musikblätter des Anbruch*, x (1928), 158–61

A. Berg: 'A Word about Wozzeck', *MM*, vi/1 (1928–9), 22–4, and

MQ, xxxviii (1952), 20–21 [lecture; in Reich 1963, *WE*]

——: 'Die Stimme in der Oper', *Gesang: Jb der Universal-Edition* (Vienna, 1929) [in Reich 1963, *WE*, 313–18]

E. Krenek: 'Opernerfahrung', *Musikblätter des Anbruch*, xi (1929), 233–7

G. Antheil: 'Wanted – Opera by and for Americans', *MM*, vii/4 (1929–30), 11–16

A. Berg: *Praktische Answeisungen zur Einstudierung des 'Wozzeck'* (Vienna, 1930); repr. in W. Reich, *Alban Berg: mit Bergs eigenen Schriften* (1937), Eng. trans. in *MT*, cix (1968), 518–19

B. Brecht: 'Anmerkungen zur Oper "Aufstieg und Fall der Stadt Mahagonny"', *Versuche*, no. 2 (Berlin, 1930) [repr. in *Schriften zum Theater* (1957); Eng. trans. in Willett 1964, *Score*, no. 23 (1958), 14–20, and *WE*, 334–44]

P. Claudel: 'Le drame et la musique' (1930) and 'Richard Wagner: rêverie d'un poète français' (1934); repr. in *Oeuvres complètes* (Paris, 1950–67), xvii, 284–98; xvi, 298–324 [see D. Bancroft, 'Claudel on Wagner', *ML*, l (1969), 439–52]

——: 'Modern Drama and Music', *Yale Review*, xx (1930) [*WE*, 319–29]

V. d'Indy: *Richard Wagner et son influence sur l'art musical français* (Paris, 1930)

G. Fauré: *Opinions musicales* (Paris, 1930)

D. Shostakovich: 'Nos', *opera v 3-kh aktakh po N.V. Gogolyn: 15-ye sochineniye D. Shostovicha* (Leningrad, 1930) [articles by him and others on *The Nose*]

——: 'Nos': *Opera v 3 deystviyakh, 10 Kartinakh po N. V. Gogolyn. Musika D. Shostovicha* (Leningrad, 1930) [articles by him and Malkov, with lib.]

B. Brecht: 'Anmerkungen zur Dreigroschenoper' (1931) [repr. in *Schriften zum Theater* (1957); Eng. trans. in E. Bentley, *From the Modern Repertoire*, ser.1 (1949), and *WE*, 333–4]

I. Pizzetti: 'Music and Drama', *MQ*, xvii (1931), 419–26

R. De Rensis, ed.: *Critiche e cronache musicali di Arrigo Boito (1862–1870)* (Milan, 1931)

E. Krenek: 'Zur Situation der Oper', *Auftakt*, xii (1932), 131–7

G. Adami: *Giulio Ricordi e i suoi musicisti* (Milan, 1933, rev. 1945)

G. Antheil: 'Opera – a Way Out', *MM*, xi (1933–4), 89–94

E. Krenek: 'Problemi di stile nell' opera', *RaM*, vii (1934), 199–202

D. Shostakovich: *Katerina Izmaylova* (Moscow, 1934) [articles by him and others]

——: *Ledi Makbet Mtsenskovo uyezda* (Leningrad, 1934) [articles by him and others]

——: 'My Opera *Lady Macbeth of Mtzensk*', *MM*, xii (1934–5), 23–30 [*WE*, 345–8]

G. Adami: *Puccini* (Milan, 1935)

W. Egk: 'Meine Oper "Die Zaubergeige"', *ZfM*, Jg.103 (1935), 738–40

L. Firkušný: *Leoš Janáček kritikem brněnské opery* [Leoš Janáček as Critic of the Brno Opera] (Brno, 1935) [reviews from *Hudební listy*, 1884–8]

E. Krenek: 'The New Music and Today's Theater', *MM*, xiv (1936–7), 200–03 [*WE*, 349–53]

V. d'Indy: *Introduction à l'étude de 'Parsifal' de Wagner* (Paris, 1937)

E. Krenek: *Über neue Musik: sechs Vorlesungen zur Einführung in die theoretischen Grundlagen* (Vienna, 1937; Eng. trans., rev., as *Music Here and Now*, 1939)

J. Gregor: 'Zur Entstehung von Richard Strauss' *Daphne*', *Almanach zum 35. Jahr des Verlags R. Piper & Co., München* (Munich, 1939), 104

——: *Richard Strauss, der Meister der Oper* (Munich, 1939, 3/ 1952)

L. Dallapiccola: 'Volo di notte di L. Dallapiccola', *Scenario*, ix (1940), 176–7

G. F. Malipiero: 'Favoleggiando con Pirandello', *Scenario*, ix (1940), 521

G. Adami: 'Librettisti e poeti verdiani', *Verdi: studi e memorie* (Rome, 1941)

A. Copland: *Our New Music* (New York, 1941, 2/1968)

W. Egk: 'Columbus: Bericht und Bildnis', *NZM*, Jg.109 (1941), 639–43

J. Gregor: *Kulturgeschichte der Oper: ihre Verbindung mit dem Leben, den Werken des Geistes und der Politik* (Vienna, 1941, 3/ 1950)

G. Preissová [Sekerová]: 'Má setkání s Thalií' [My Encounters with Thalia], *Divadlo a hudba* (1941–2), no. 8, 49–51

A. Boito: *Tutti gli scritti*, ed. P. Nardi (Milan, 1942)

L. Dallapiccola: 'Per la prima rappresentazione di Volo di notte', *Letteratura*, vi/3 (1942), 10 [Eng. trans. in Shackelford 1987, 79–96]

I. Pizzetti: 'La musica delle parole', *Musica*, i (1942), 125–42

I. F. Stravinsky: *Poétique musicale sous forme de six leçons* (Cambridge, MA, 1942; Eng. trans. as *Poetics*, 1956)

E. Krenek: 'Opera between the Wars', *MM*, xx (1942–3), 102–11

G. Adami: *Il romanzo della vita di Giacomo Puccini* (Milan and Rome, 1944)

E. Crozier, ed.: *Peter Grimes* (London, 1945)

E. T. A. Hoffmann: '*Don Giovanni*: a Marvellous Adventure which Befell a Traveling Enthusiast', *MQ*, xxxi (1945), 504–16

I. Pizzetti: *Musica e dramma* (Rome, 1945) [collected articles]

I. Gundry: 'The Nature of Opera as a Composite Art', *PMA*, lxxiii (1946–7), 25–33

E. Crozier: 'Foreword to Albert Herring', *Tempo*, no. 4 (1947), 10–14 [repr. with libretto]

E. Crozier, ed.: '*The Rape of Lucretia': a Symposium* (London, 1947) [by B. Britten and others]

E. Krenek: *Selbstdarstellung* (Zürich, 1948); Eng. trans., rev., as 'Self Analysis', *University of New Mexico Quarterly*, xxiii (1953), 5–57

S. Prokofiev: 'Response to the "Resolution on Music of the Central Committee of the Communist Party of the Soviet Union (Bolsheviks)"', *SovM* (1948), no. 1, pp.66–7; Eng. trans. in N. Slominsky: *Music since 1900* (4/1971), 1373–4

R. Strauss: *Betrachtungen und Erinnerungen*, ed. W. Schuh (Zürich, 1949, 2/1957); Eng. trans. W. J. Lawrence, as *Recollections and Reflections* (London, 1953) [incl. 'Betrachtungen zu Joseph Gregors "Weltgeschichte des Theaters"']

A. Mann: 'The Artistic Testament of Richard Strauss', *MQ*, xxxvi (1950), 1–8 [Eng. trans. of essay by Strauss]

W. H. Auden: 'Some Reflections on Opera as a Medium', *Tempo*, no. 20 (1951), 6–10

——: 'Some Reflections on Music and Opera', *Partisan Review*, xix (1952), 10–17 [*WE*, 354–60]

J. Cocteau: 'La collaboration Oedipus rex', *ReM*, no. 212 (1952), 51

C. Cui: *Izbanniye stat'i* [Selected Articles] (Leningrad, 1952)

J. Gregor: 'Gradus ad "Danaem": die Entfaltung der Frauengestalten von Richard Strauss', *ÖMz*, vii (1952), 204–7

P. Hindemith: *The Composer's World: Horizons and Limitations* (Cambridge, 1952)

L. Dallapiccola: 'The Genesis of the *Canti di prigionia* and *Il prigioniero*: an Autobiographical Fragment', *MQ*, xxxix (1953), 355–72 [repr. in Shackelford 1987, 35–60]

G. von Einem: '"*Der Prozess*"' *ÖMz*, viii (1953), 198–200

M. I. Glinka: *Literaturnoye naslediye* [Literary Heritage] (Leningrad, 1952–3)

W. Plomer: 'Notes on the Libretto of "Gloriana"', *Tempo*, no. 28 (1953), 5–7

——: 'Writing *Gloriana* with Benjamin Britten', *Radio Times* (5 June 1953)

F. Poulenc: *Entretiens avec Claude Rostand* (Paris, 1954)

W. Egk: 'Irische Legende', *ÖMz*, x (1955), 125–30

H. Pfitzner: *Reden, Schriften, Briefe*, ed. W. Abendroth (Berlin-Frohnau and Neuwied, 1955)

R. Simoni: *Trent' anni di cronaca drammatica* (Turin, 1955) [on Adami, Puccini]

W. Egk: 'Oper – die zauberhafte Ungeheuerlichkeit', *NZM*, Jg. 117 (1956), 132–3

J. Gregor: 'Mein Freund Richard Strauss', *Internationale Richard Strauss Gesellschaft Mitteilungen*, x (1956), 10–17

W. Osthoff: 'Zu den Quellen von Monteverdis "Ritorno di Ulisse in Patria"', *SMw*, xxiii (1956), 73–4 [letter from Badoaro to Monteverdi in MS libretto of *Il ritorno d'Ulisse in patria*]

B. Brecht: *Schriften zum Theater* (1957) [theoretical and critical writings, also in *Gesammelte Werke* (1967), xv–xvii; incl. Ger. orig. (1935) of 'Concerning the Use of Music in an Epic Theatre', *Score*, no.23 (1958), 21–6]

W. Fortner: 'Bluthochzeit nach Federico García Lorca', *Melos*, xxiv (1957), 71–3

W. Fortner, F. Lion and H. von Cramer: 'Libretto der neuen Oper', *Akzente*, iv (1957), 121–38

G. Klebe: 'Über meine Oper "Die Räuber"', *Melos*, xxiv (1957), 73–6

F. Poulenc: 'Comment j'ai composé les *Dialogues des Carmélites*', *L'Opéra de Paris*, xxxiv (1957), 277–87

W. Egk: '"Der Revisor" als Oper', *ÖMz*, xiii (1958), 47–9

E. Krenek: *Gedanken unterwegs* (Munich, 1958)

——: *Zur Sprache gebracht: Essays über Musik* (Munich, 1958; Eng. trans. as *Exploring Music*, 1966)

M. Tippett: *Moving into Aquarius* (London, 1958, 2/1974)

——: 'Our Sense of Continuity in English Drama and Music', *Henry Purcell: Essays on his Music*, ed. I. Holst (London, 1959), 42–51

I. Bachmann: 'Entstehung eines Libretto', *Melos*, xxvii (1960), 136–8 [*Der junge Lord*]

L. Dallapiccola: 'The Birth-Pangs of Job', *Musical Events*, xv/5 (1960), 26–7

W. Egk: *Musik – Wort – Bild: Texte und Anmerkungen, Betrachtungen und Gedanken* (Munich, 1960)

H. W. Henze: 'Neue Aspekte in der Musik', *NZM*, Jg.121 (1960), 3–9

H. Lindlar, ed.: *Wolfgang Fortner, eine Monographie: Werkanalysen, Aufsätze, Reden* (Rodenkirchen, 1960)

R. Strauss: 'Parerga für Joseph Gregor', *Das Antiquariat*, ix (1960), 237–9

K. Weill: *Berthold Brechts Dreigroschenbuch* (Frankfurt, 1960) [*WE*, 330–32: incl. 'On the Composition of the Dreigroschenoper', 1929]

W. H. Auden and C. Kallman: 'Genesis of a Libretto', *Elegy for Young Lovers* (Mainz, 1961)

W. H. Auden: 'A Public Art', *Opera*, xii (1961), 12–15

H. Fähnrich: 'Richard Strauss über die Verhältnis von Dichtung und Musik (Wort und Ton) in seinem Opernschaffen', *Mf*, xiv (1961), 22–35

G. Klebe: 'Meine Oper Alkmene', *Melos*, xxviii (1961), 272–5

G. F. Malipiero: 'Luigi Pirandello, mio librettista', *Pirandelliani: Venice 1961*, 913–5

S. Shlifsteyn, ed.: *S. S. Prokof'yev: materialï, dokumentï, vospominaniya* (Moscow, 2/1961) [incl. 'Semyon Kotko', 235–8; 'Obrucheniye v monastïre (Duenya)', 241–3; 'Khudozhnik i voyna' [The Artist and War], 243–9]

M. Tippett: 'At Work on King Priam', *Score*, no. 28 (1961), 58–68

W. H. Auden: *The Dyer's Hand* (New York, 1962) [incl. 4 essays on opera]

E. Beck: 'In seinem Garten liebt Don Perlimplin Belisa', *Melos*, xxix (1962), 109–11

M. Brod: *Die verkaufte Braut: der abenteuerliche Lebensroman des Textdichters Karel Sabina* (Munich, 1962)

L. Dallapiccola: 'What is the Answer to "The Prisoner"?', *San Francisco Sunday Chronicle* (2 Dec 1962)

W. Fortner: 'Wieder ein Lorca?', *Melos*, xxix (1962), 106–8

I. F. Stravinsky: 'On Oedipus rex', *Encounter*, xviii (1962), 29–35

M. Tippett: 'King Priam: some Questions Answered', *Opera*, xiii (1962), 297–9

W. Egk: '"Die Verlobung in San Domingo"', *NZM*, Jg. 124 (1963), 440–45

W. Plomer: 'Let's Crab an Opera', *London Magazine*, iii/7 (1963), 101–4

W. Reich: *Alban Berg* (Zürich, 1963; Eng. trans., 1965) [incl. essays by Berg]

F. Schnapp, ed.: *E. T. A. Hoffmann: Schriften zur Musik: Nachlese* (Munich, 1963, 2/1978)

G. Menotti: 'I am the Savage' [*L'ultimo selvaggio*], *ON*, xxviii/13 (1963–4), 8–12

B. Britten: Note in libretto of *Curlew River* (London, 1964)

H. W. Henze: *Essays* (Mainz, 1964)

W. Plomer: Note in *Curlew River: a Parable for Church Performance* (London, 1964)

H. T. Barnwell, ed.: *Pierre Corneille: Writings on the Theatre* (Oxford, 1965) [mainly prefaces, in Fr.]

M. Brod: 'Bemerkungen zur letzten Oper Janáčeks', *Sborník prací filosofické fakulty brněnské univerzity* (1965), 39–44

E. Crozier: 'Peter Grimes, an Unpublished Article of 1946', *Opera*, xiv (1965), 412–6

L. Dallapiccola: 'Parole e musica nel melodramma', *QRaM* (1965), no. 2, 117–39; rev. in *Appunti* (1970) [Eng. trans. in *PNM*, v/1 (1966), 121–33, and in Shackelford 1987, 133–63]

K. A. Hartmann: 'Zu meinem "Simplicius Simplicissimus"', *Kleine Schriften*, ed. E. Thomas (Mainz, 1965), 49–52

M. Tippett: 'Schoenberg's Moses and Aaron', *Listener*, lxxiv (1965), 164

J. Cocteau: *L'avant-scène* (1966), nos. 365–6 [Cocteau no. with documents on *Les mariés de la tour Eiffel*]

E. Crozier: 'Composer and Librettist', *Composer* [London], no. 18 (Jan 1966), 2–5

W. Egk: *Opern, Ballette, Konzertwerke* (Mainz, 1966)

——: 'Zweimal Calderón', *Melos*, xxxiii (1966), 109–13

W. Plomer: 'The *Gloriana* Libretto', *Sadler's Wells Magazine* (aut. 1966)

——: Note in score of *The Burning Fiery Furnace: Second Parable* (London, 1966)

P. Schat: 'Labyrinth: a Kind of Opera', *Opera 66* (London, 1966), 250–58

P. Boulez: 'Sprengt die Opernhäuser in die Luft', *Der Spiegel*, no.40 (1967); Eng. trans. in *Opera*, xix (1968), 440–48

M. Brod: 'Erinnerungen an Janáček', *Beiträge 1967* (Kassel, 1967), 30–40

W. H. Auden: 'World of Opera', *Secondary Worlds* (London, 1968), 76–102

L. Dallapiccola: 'Nascita di un libretto d'opera' [*Ulisse*], *NRMI*, ii (1968), 605–24 [repr. in Dallapiccola (1970), 171–87; Eng. trans. in Shackelford 1987, 232–62]

W. Plomer: 'Britten's Church Operas', *Festival of the City of London* programme book, July 1968 [*Curlew River*]

D. Shostakovich: *The Power of Music* (New York, 1968)

V. V. Stasov: *Selected Essays* (New York, 1968)

L. Berio: 'Notre Faust', *NRMI*, iii (1969), 275–81

F. Lippmann: 'Rossinis Gedanken über die Musik', *Mf*, xxii (1969), 285–98

W. E. von Lewinski: 'Musik ist eine instabile Kunst: Boris Blacher, ein Komponist unserer Zeit – Gedanken nach einem Gespräch', *Opernjournal*, ii (1969–70), 7–9

L. Dallapiccola: *Appunti, incontri, meditazioni* (Milan, 1970) [Eng. trans. of some items in Shackelford 1987]

P. Heyworth: 'I can imagine a Future …: Conversation with Hans Werner Henze', *Observer* (23 Aug 1970)

L. Stürzbecher: 'Boris Blacher', *Werkstattgespräche mit Komponisten* (Cologne, 1971), 9–18

——: 'Hans Werner Henze', ibid, 106–20

E. Crozier: 'Writing an Opera', *Aldeburgh Anthology* (London, 1972), 199–202

W. H. Auden: *Forewords and Afterwords* (London and New York, 1973) [incl. 4 essays on opera]

F. Lippmann: 'Ein neuentdecktes Autograph Richard Wagners: Rezension der Königsberger "Norma" Aufführung von 1837', *Festschrift Karl Gustav Fellerer* (Cologne, 1973), 373–9

U. Stürzbecher: 'Werner Egk', *Werkstattgespräche mit Komponisten* (Munich, 1973), 101–11

P. Griffiths: 'The Bassarids: Hans Werner Henze talks to Paul Griffiths', *MT*, cxv (1974), 831–2

E. Krenek: *Das Musikdramatische Werk* (Vienna, 1974–82)

——: *Horizons Circled: Reflections on my Music* (Berkeley, 1974)

A. Schoenberg: *Style and Idea*, ed. L. Stein (London, 1975)

K. Weill: *Ausgewählte Schriften*, ed. D. Drew (Frankfurt, 1975)

H. Eisler: *Materialen zu einer Dialektik der Musik* (Leipzig, 1976)

A. Schoenberg: *Gesammelte Schriften*, i, ed. I. Vojtěch (Frankfurt, 1976)

E. Krenek: 'Zur Vollendung von Alban Bergs Lulu: Fragment', *Musica*, xxxi (1977), 401–3

M. Tippett: 'The Composer as Librettist', *Times Literary Supplement* (8 July 1977), 834 [conversation with P. Carnegy]

D. Herbert, ed.: *The Operas of Benjamin Britten* (London, 1979) [incl. complete librettos and essays by librettists, directors, designers etc.]

J.-J. Rousseau: *Ecrits sur la musique*, ed. C. Kintzler (Paris, 1979) [with extensive bibliography]

E. Krenek: 'Jonny erinnert sich', *ÖMz*, xxxv (1980), 187–9

——: 'Marginal Remarks to Lulu', *Alban Berg Symposium: Vienna 1980*, 8–11

A. Burgess: *This Man and Music* (London, 1982)

H. W. Henze: *Music and Politics: Collected Writings 1953–1981* (Ithaca, NY, 1982)

C. Orff: 'Antigonae: ein Trauerspiel des Sophokles von Friedrich Hölderlin', *NZM*, Jg.143 (1982), 19–22

E. Krenek: 'Aus der Mappe eines Opernkomponisten', *ÖMz*, xxxix (1984), 506–9

——: 'Studien zu meinem Bühnenwerk Karl V', *Ernst Krenek* (Munich, 1984), 20–34

T. Sokolova, ed.: *P. Chaykovsky: Muzikal'no- kriticheskiye stat'i* [Critical Articles] (Leningrad, 1986)

A. Burgess: *Little Wilson and Big God* (London, 1987)

D. Diderot: *Ecrits sur la musique*, ed. B. Durand-Sendrail (Paris, 1987)

P. Glass: *Music by Philip Glass* (New York, 1987); as *Opera on the Beach* (1988)

M. Piper: 'The Libretto', *Benjamin Britten: Death in Venice*, ed. D. Mitchell (Cambridge, 1987), 45–54

R. Shackelford, ed.: *Dallapiccola on Opera* (London, 1987)

D. Charlton, ed.: *E. T. A. Hoffmann's Musical Writings: 'Kreis-*

leriana', 'The Poet and the Composer', *Music Criticism* (Cambridge, 1989)

M. Zemanová: *Janáček's Uncollected Essays on Music* (London, 1989)

A. Burgess: *You've Had your Time* (London, 1990)

(ii) Comment by others

A. Ingegneri: *Della poesia rappresentativa et del modo di rappresentare le favole sceniche* (Ferrara, 1598) [ed. in *Storia documentaria del teatro italiano: lo spettacolo dall' Umanesimo al Manierismo: teoria e tecnica*, 1974]

J. Savaron: *Traitté contre les masques* (Paris, 1608, 3/1611)

L. de Vega Carpio: *Arte nuevo de hacer comedias en este tiempo* (Madrid, 1609)

L. Zuccolo: *Discorso delle ragioni del numero del verso italiano* (1623) [criticizes Chiabrera's metrical experiments]

Il corago o vero Alcune osservazioni per metter bene in scena le composizioni drammatiche (MS, *c*1630); ed. P. Fabbri and A. Pompilio (Florence, 1983)

A. Mareschal: *La généreuse allemande* (Paris, ?1631)

G. B. Doni: *Compendio del trattato de' generi de' modi della musica* (Rome, 1635) [see Solerti 1903, 222–8]

G. F. Loredano and M. Dandolo: 'La contesa del canto, e delle lagrime', *Bizzarrie academiche* (Venice, 1638); Eng. trans. as *Academical Discourses* (1664) [papers from the Accademia degli Unisoni]

Le Glorie della Musica celebrate dalla sorella Poesia, rappresentandosi in Bologna La Delia e L'Ulisse (Bologna, 1640)

A. Maugars: 'Response faité à un curieux sur le sentiment de la musique d'Italie, escrite à Rome le premier octobre 1639' (Paris, *c*1640); ed. in E. Thoinan: *Maugars, célèbre joueur de viole...sa biographie suivie de sa response* (Paris, 1865; Eng. trans., *Journal of the Viola da Gamba Society of America*, viii (1971), 5–17)

M. Bisaccioni: *Il cannocchiale per la finta pazza, drama dello Strozzi* (Venice, 1641)

G. B. Doni: *De praestantia musicae veteris* (Florence, 1643) [on Monteverdi's *Arianna*, p.67]

M. Bisaccioni: '"Descrittione" of Bartolini's *Venere gelosa*', *Apparati scenici per lo teatro novissimo di Venetia nell' anno 1644, d'inventione e cura di Iacomo Torelli da Fano* (Venice, 1644)

Feste theatrali per La finta pazza, dramma del Sig.r Giulio Strozzi...e da Giacomo Torelli da Fano inventore (Paris, 1645)

P. Perrin: 'Lettre écrite à Monsieur l'archevêque de Turin', *Les oeuvres de poesie de Mr Perrin* (Paris, 1661); ed. in A. Pougin: *Les vrais créateurs de l'opéra français: Perrin et Cambert* (Paris, 1881), 56–68 [*BQ*, 105–11; on *Pastorale d'Issy*, 1659]

F. Balducci: 'Per don Flavio Orsino, figliuolo di don Ferdinando', *Rime* (Venice, 1663), 169

M. de Pure: 'Des Airs de Ballet', *Idée des spectacles anciens et nouveaux*, pt. 10 (Paris, 1668) [*BQ*, 111–14]

Prince of Conti: *Traité de la comédie et des spectacles selon la tradition l'église, tirée des conciles & des saints pères* (Paris, 1669)

D. Bouhours: *Entretiens d'Ariste et d'Eugène* (Paris, 1671)

I. Voss: *De poematum cantu et viribus rythmi* (Oxford, 1673) [French language held unlyrical: opposed by Ménestrier 1681]

C. Perrault: *Critique de l'Opéra, ou Examen de la tragédie intitulée Alceste, ou le Triomphe d'Alcide* (Paris, 1674)

C.-F. Ménestrier: *Des ballets anciens et modernes selon les règles du théâtre* (Paris, 1682)

——: *Des représentations en musique anciennes et modernes* (Paris, 1682) [*BQ*, 146–9]

C. M. de Saint-Denis, Seigneur de Saint-Evremond: *Oeuvres meslées* (Paris, 1684, 2/1709; Eng. trans., 1685, as *Mixt-Essays: Tragedies, Comedies, English Comedies and Operas*); ed. in *Oeuvres en prose* (Paris, 1962–9) [incl. 'Sur les opéra, à Monsieur le duc de Bouquinquant [Buckingham]' (ii, 214–22), excerpt *BQ*, 136–40, and *WE*, 31–5; 'Les opéra, comédie' (ii, 223–92); 'A Monsieur Lulli' (iii, 106–7)]

D. Bouhours: *La manière de bien penser dans les ouvrages d'esprit* (Paris, 1687, rev. 1715)

J. de La Bruyère: 'Des ouvrages de l'esprit', *Les caractères ou Les moeurs de ce siècle* (Paris, 1688) [excerpt *WE*, 29–30]

B. Dotti: *Satire* (Amsterdam, 1690) [cites howlers from librettos]

A. Werckmeister: *Der edlen Music-Kunst Würde, Gebrauch und Missbrauch* (Frankfurt and Leipzig, 1691)

C. Perrault: *Parallèle des Anciens et des Modernes en ce qui regarde La Poésie* (Paris, 1692) [defence of Quinault; *BQ*,154–5]

J.-B. Bossuet: *Maximes et réflexions sur la comédie* (Paris, 1694; Eng. trans., 1699) [ed. of 1881 incl. extracts from F. Caffaro's

letter in Boursault: *Pièces de théâtre* (1694), supporting comedy and opera against 1694 ban, to which Bossuet was replying]

G. M. Crescimbeni: *L'Istoria della volgar poesia* (Rome, 1698, rev. 1731)

C. Sweerts: *Inleiding tot de Zang en Speelkunst* (?Amsterdam or Utrecht, 1698)

A. Perrucci: *Dell'arte rappresentativa premeditata ed all'improviso* (Naples, 1699)

G. M. Crescimbeni: *La bellezza della volgar poesia* (Rome, 1700, rev. 1730)

——: *Comentari...intorno al'"Istoria della volgar poesia italiana"*, i (Rome, 1702, rev. 1731)

F. Raguenet: *Paralèle des italiens et des françois en ce qui regarde la musique et les opéra* (Paris, 1702; Eng. trans., 1709, as *A Comparison between the French and Italian Musick and Opera's*)

G. G. Orsi: *Considerazioni sopra la maniera di ben pensare* (Bologna, 1703) [reply to Bouhours 1687]

J.-L. Le Cerf de la Viéville: *Comparison de la musique italienne et de la musique françoise* (Paris, 1704–6) [reply to Raguenet 1702]

F. Raguenet: *Défense du parallèle des italiens et des françois en ce qui regarde la musique et les opéra* (Paris, 1705) [reply to Le Cerf]

J. Dennis: *An Essay on the Opera's after the Italian Manner, which are About to be Established on the English Stage: with Some Reflections on the Damage which they may Bring to the Publick* (London, 1706)

L. A. Muratori: *Della perfetta poesia italiana, spiegata e dimostrata con varie osservazioni* (Modena, 1706) [bk 3 chap. 5 (vol. ii, 30–45) contains 'De' difetti, che possono osservarsi ne' moderni Drammi']

J. L. Le Gallois de Grimarest: *Traité du récitatif* (Paris, 1707, 2/1740)

G. Gravina: *Della ragion poetica, libri due* (Rome, 1708; repr. in *Prose*, 1819)

Critical Discourse on Operas and Music in England (London, 1709) [with Eng. trans. of Raguenet 1702]; excerpt in D. Arundell: *The Critic at the Opera* (1957), 180–92

Il giornale dei letterati d'Italia (Venice, 1710–27) [promoted Arcadian and anti-French taste; Zeno an editor]

The Spectator (London, 1711–14) [incl. discussions of opera by Addison and Steele]

Villiers: *Epître sur l'opéra et sur les autres spectacles* (Paris, 1711)

[F. Gâcon]: *L'anti-Rousseau, par le poëte sans fard* (Rotterdam, 1712) [refers to J.-B. Rousseau]

F. de S. de la Mothe-Fénelon: *Lettre sur les occupations de l'Académie* (Paris, 1714)

F. H. D'Aubignac: *La pratique du théâtre* (Amsterdam, 1715); ed. J. Carbonel (1927) [on the period *c*1650]

G. Gravina: *Della tragedia* (Naples, 1715)

Lettres historiques à M. Dxxx sur la nouvelle Comédie Italienne (Paris, 1717)

J.-B. Dubos: *Réflexions critiques sur la poésie, la peinture et la musique* (Paris, 1719, 7/1770; Eng. trans. of 5/1748, 1748)

D. Lovisa: *Il gran teatro di Venezia* (Venice, 1721)

J. P. Praetorius: *Il pregio dell'ignoranza, oder Die Bass-Geige* (Hamburg, 1724) [satirical pamphlet against Telemann and others]

G. Riva: *Advice to the Composers and Performers of Vocal Music* (London, 1727)

E. Titon du Tillet: *Le Parnasse français* (Paris, 1727–55)

J. Ralph: *The Touch-Stone: or, Historical, Critical, Political, Philosophical and Theological Essays on the Reigning Diversions of the Town...By a Person of Some Taste and Some Quality* (London, 1728; repr. as *The Taste of the Town: or, a Guide to all Publick Diversions*, 1731) [satire on Italian opera]

L. A. Riccoboni: *Lettre d'un comédien français au sujet de l'histoire du théâtre italien* (Paris, 1728)

J. C. Gottsched: *Versuch einer critischen Dichtkunst vor die Deutschen* (Leipzig, 1730, 4/1751)

P. Lebrun: *Discours sur la comédie ou Traité historique et dogmatique des jeux du théâtre* (Paris, 1731)

G. C. Becelli: *Della novella poesia cioè del vero genere e particolari bellezze della poesia italiana* (Verona, 1732)

See and Seem Blind: or, A Critical Dissertation on the Publick Diversions (London, 1732)

N. C. J. Trublet: 'Lettre sur M. H. de La Motte et ses ouvrages', *Mercure de France* (Jan 1732), 62

J. C. Walther: *Musikalisches Lexicon* (Leipzig, 1732)

A. Hill and W. Popple, eds.: *The Prompter* (London, 1734–6); ed. W. W. Appleton and K. A. Burnim (New York, 1966)

P.-F. G. Desfontaines: *Observations sur les écrits modernes* (Paris, 1735–43)

E. Edesimo [F. Rosellini]: *Considerazioni sopra Il 'Demofoonte' del Sig. Pietro Metastasio, scritte in una lettera da Evandro Edesimo ad un suo amico in Venezia* (Venice, 1735)

L. A. Riccoboni: *Réflexions historiques et critiques sur les différens théâtres de l'Europe* (Paris, 1738; Eng. trans. as *An Historical and Critical Account of the Theatres in Europe*, 1741)

J. A. Scheibe: *Der critische Musikus* (Leipzig, 1738–40)

A. Conti: 'Prefazione', *Prose e poesie*, i (Venice, 1739)

L. C. Mizler: *Neu eröffnete musikalische Bibliothek* (Leipzig, 1739–54)

Nouvelle lettre sur la comédie italienne (Paris, 1739)

F. S. Quadrio: *Della storia e della ragione d'ogni poesia* (Bologna and Milan, 1739–52)

G. B. de Mably, attrib.: *Lettres à Madame la Marquise de P...sur l'opéra* (Paris, 1740)

T. Rémond de Saintmard: *Réflexions sur l'opéra* (Paris and The Hague, 1741)

A. Gautier de Mondorge: *Réflexions d'un peintre sur l'opéra* (The Hague, 1743)

L. A. Riccoboni: *De la réformation du théâtre* (Paris, 1743)

F. S. Rovati: *Osservazioni all'"Artaserse"* (Forlì, 1744)

G. R. Carli: *Dell'Indole del teatro tragico* (Venice, 1744–5)

E. C. Fréron, ed.: *Lettres sur quelques écrits de ce temps* (Geneva and Paris, 1749–54)

G. E. Lessing: *Tarantula* (Berlin, 1749) [satire on *opera seria*]

S. Rosa: 'La musica', in J. Mattheson: *Mithridate* (Hamburg, 1749), pp. i–lvi

G. E. Lessing: *Nachricht von dem gegenwärtigen Zustand des Theaters in Berlin* (Berlin, *c*1750)

V. Martinelli: *Origini dell'opera in musica* (London, *c*1750)

——: *Ragioni del suono* (London, *c*1750)

F. Arnaud: *Lettre sur la musique à Monsieur le Comte de Caylus* (Paris, 1751)

C. G. Krause: *Abhandlung von der musikalischen Poesie* (Berlin, 1752)

Laurisio Tragiense [G. A. Bianchi]: *De vizi e de' difetti del moderno teatro e del modo di correggerli e di emendarli* (Rome, 1753)

La paix de l'opéra, une paralléle de la musique française et de la musique italienne (Paris, 1753)

F. M. von Grimm: *Le petit prophète de Boehmisch-broda* (Paris, 1753) [excerpt in Strunk 1950]

F. Arnaud: *Réflexions* (Paris, 1754)

M. de Caux de Capperal: *Apologie du goût français relativement à l'opéra: poème* (Paris, 1754)

F. W. Marpurg: *Historisch-kritische Beiträge zur Aufnahme der Musik* (Berlin, 1754–62)

De Rochemont: *Réflexions d'un patriote sur l'opéra français et l'opéra italien* (Lausanne, 1754)

A. F. Adami: 'Dissertazione sopra la poesia drammatica e musica del teatro', *Poesie del Cav.re A. F. Adami* (Florence, 1755), 1–32

S. Bettinelli: 'Discorso del teatro italiano' (1755), *Opere*, vi (Venice, 1782)

G. R. Carli: *Osservazioni sulla musica antica e moderna* (?Venice, 1756); repr. in *Opere*, iv (Milan, 1786)

Lettre sur le méchanisme de l'opéra italien: Ni Guelfe, ni Gibelin; ni Wigh, ni Thoris (Florence and Paris, 1756) [attrib. to J. de Villeneuve, also to G. Durazzo]

J. G. Gottsched: *Nöthiger Vorrath zur Geschichte der deutschen dramatischen Dichtkunst oder Verzeichniss aller deutschen Trauer- Lust- und Sing-Spiele, die im Druck erschienen von 1450 bis zur Hälfte des jetzigen Jahrhunderts. Nebst: Des nöthigen Vorraths…2. Theil* (Leipzig, 1757–65)

C. Gozzi: *La Tartana degli influssi per l'anno bissestile 1756* (Venice, 1757) [mock almanac, rejecting both Chiari and Goldoni]

M. de Marolles: *Traité des ballets* (Amsterdam, 1758)

V. Martinelli: *Lettere familiari e critiche* (London, 1758)

Trébuchet d'Auxerre: *Lettre d'un ancien officier de la reine à tous les français sur les spectacles* (Paris, 1759)

L. C. de La Baume: *Ballets, opéra et autres ouvrages lyriques* (Paris, 1760)

J.-G. Noverre: *Lettres sur la danse, et sur les ballets* (Lyons and Stuttgart, 1760, 2/1783; Eng. trans., 1783, rev. 1803)

E. Arnaldi: *Idea di un teatro nelle principali sue parti simile a' teatri antichi* (Vicenza, 1762)

J. Brown: *Dissertation on the Union and Power, the Progressions, Separations and Corruptions of Poetry and Music* (London, 1763)

J.-R. D'Alembert: 'De la liberté de la musique', *Mélanges de littérature, d'histoire et de philosophie*, iv (Amsterdam, 1763)

P. Della Valle: 'Della musica dell'età nostra', *Trattati di musica di G.B. Doni* (Florence, 1763), ii, 249–64 [ed. in Solerti 1903, 148–79]

G. B. Doni: 'Trattato della musica scenica', *De' trattati di musica*, ii (Florence, 1763) [excerpts in Solerti 1903, 195–221, and *BQ*, 41–51]

F. M. von Grimm: 'Poème lyrique', *Encyclopédie*, ed. D. Diderot, xii (1765), 822–36

F. de Chastellux: *Essai sur l'union de la poésie et de la musique* (Paris, 1765)

P. Verri: 'La musica', *Il caffè* (Milan, 1765), ii, 57–96

Le nouveau spectateur ou examen des nouvelles pièces de théâtre, ed. Le Fuel de Méricourt (Paris, 1766–78)

J.-G. Noverre: *Théorie et pratique de la danse simple et composée, de l'art des ballets, de la musique, du costume et des décorations* (MS, *PL-Wn*, 1766)

G. E. Lessing: *Hamburgische Dramaturgie* (Bremen, 1767–9; Eng. trans., 1962)

F. Albergati Capacelli: *Della commedia* (Trévoux, 1768)

Memorie galanti: Centuria prima di pensieri ed annotazioni sopra le opere dell'Abate Metastasio (Venice, 1768)

P. J. B. Nougaret: *De l'art du théâtre en général* (Paris, 1768–9)

Trattato dei giuochi e de' divertimenti permessi o proibiti ai cristiani (Rome, 1768)

J. G. Sulzer: *Allgemeine Theorie der Schönen Künste* (Leipzig, 1771–4)

L. Garcins: *Traité du mélodrame ou réflexions sur la musique dramatique* (Paris, 1772)

A. Planelli: *Trattato dell'opera in musica* (Naples, 1772)

J. Potter: *The Theatrical Review; or, New Companion to the Playhouse; Containing a Critical and Historical Account of Every Tragedy, Comedy, Opera, Farce &c Exhibited at the Theatres during the Last Season* (London, 1772)

G. Tiraboschi: *Storia della letteratura italiana* (Modena, 1772–81)

M. Torcia: *Elogio del Metastasio* (Naples, 1772)

M.-P. G. de Chabanon: 'Lettre', *Mercure de France* (Jan 1773) [on the musical properties of the French language; refers to Rousseau's letter on music]

S. Goudar: *De Venise: Remarques sur la musique et la danse ou lettres de Mr. G à Milord Pembroke* (Venice, 1773)

A. Eximeno: *Dell'origine e delle regole della musica* (Rome, 1774)

S. Mattei: *Saggio di poesie latine, ed italiane* (Naples, 1774, rev. 1785 as *Memorie per servire alla vita del Metastasio* [contains 'Elogio dello Jommelli o sia il progresso della poesia, e musica teatrale']

V. Migliacci: *Elogio del teatro musicale e del suo poeta Pietro Metastasio* (Bologna, 1774)

P. L. Moline: *Dialogue entre Lully, Rameau et Orphée dans Les Champs Elysées* (Amsterdam, 1774)

S. Bettinelli: 'Discorso sopra la poesia italiana' (1775), *Opere*, vi (Venice, 1782)

B. Farmian de Rosoy: *Dissertation sur le drame lyrique* (The Hague and Paris, 1775)

A. Goudar: *Le brigandage de la musique italienne* (Venice, 1777)

J. F. La Harpe: Polemic exchange with Gluck in *Journal de politique et de littérature* (1777); repr. with discussion in *The Collected Correspondence and Papers of Christoph Willibald Gluck*, ed. H. and E. H. Mueller von Asow (London, 1962), 99–124

P. Napoli-Signorelli: *Storia critica de'teatri antichi e moderni* (Naples, 1777)

A. M. Beloselsky: *De la musique en Italie* (The Hague, 1778)

F. Franceschi: *Apologia delle opere del Metastasio* (Lucca, 1778)

M. Sherloch: *Consigli a un giovane poeta* (Naples, 1778)

T. Iriarte: *La musica: poema* (Madrid, 1779, 2/1784)

A. Zorzi: *Tre lettere intorno a ciò che ha scritto M. Scherloch della poesia italiana, dell'Ariosto e dello Shakespeare* (Ferrara, 1779)

B. Basso: *Observations sur les poètes italiens* (London, 1780)

J. B. de La Borde: *Essai sur la musique ancienne et moderne* (Paris, 1780) [with biographical sketches of 17th- and 18th-century Italian librettists]

Rolland: *Lettres ecrites de Suisse, d'Italie, de Sicile, et de Malthe* (Amsterdam, 1780) [on French models for Italian librettos]

B. J. B. D——: 'Du mélodrame en général', *Ariane abandonnée: mélodrame imité de l'allemand* [Benda] (Paris, 1781), 3–13

G. M. Leblond: *Mémoires pour servir à l'histoire de la révolution opérée dans la musique par M. le Chevalier Gluck* (Naples and Paris, 1781) [incl. C. Beccaria, 'Dissertazione sul melodramma']

S. Mattei: 'Filosofia della musica o sia Riforma del teatro per musica', *Opere del Signor Abate Pietro Metastasio*, iii (Naples, 1781)

Lafont du Cujala: 'Réflexions sur l'état actuel de la musique dramatique en France', *Mercure de France* (Feb 1782), 38–44

G. Andres: *Delle origini, dello stato, de' progressi d'ogni letteratura* (Parma, 1783)

S. Arteaga: *Le rivoluzioni del teatro musicale italiano dalla sua origine fino al presente* (Bologna, 1783–8, 2/1785)

P. A. Metastasio: *Opere...con dissertazioni e osservazioni*, ed. D. Bonaventura (Nice, 1783–5) [with appreciations by writers, incl. Arteaga, Durandi, Eximeno, Pindemonte and Voltaire, many in *Osservazioni di vari letterati sopra i drammi dell'Abate Pietro Metastasio* (Nice, 1785)]

A. Bertola: *Osservazioni sopra il Metastasio, con alcuni versi* (Bassano, 1784)

P. Napoli-Signorelli: *Vicende della coltura nelle Due Sicilie* (Naples, 1784–6)

M. Borsa: *Del gusto presente in letteratura italiana* (Venice, 1785)

M.-P. G. de Chabanon: *Dissertation sur la musique considerée en elle-meme, et dans ses rapports avec la parole, les langues, la poésie, et le théâtre* (Paris, 1785)

B. G. E. M. de la Ville-sur-Illon Lacépède: *La poëtique de la musique* (Paris, 1785, 3/1797)

L. Adimari: 'Satira quarta: contro alcuni vizi delle donne, e particolarmente contro le cantatrici', *Satire del marchese Lodovico Adimari* (London, 1788), 183–253

S. Bettinelli: *Dialoghi sopra il teatro moderno* (Venice, 1788)

V. Manfredini: *Difesa della moderna musica e de' suoi celebri esecutori* (Bologna, 1788)

J. Brown: *Letters upon the Poetry and Music of the Italian Opera* (London, 1789, 2/1791)

Abbé Parisis: *Questions importantes sur la comédie* (Valenciennes, 1789)

G. De Gamerra: 'Osservazioni sullo spettacolo in generale...per servire allo stabilimento del novo Teatro Nazionale', *Nuovo teatro*, i (Venice, 1790)

A. Buonafede: *Novelle menipee di Luciano di Firenzuola contro una Frusta pseudoepigrafa di Aristarco Scannabue* (Naples, 1794) [i.e. Baretti]

D. Colombo: *Il dramma e la tragedia d'Italia* (Venice, 1794)

J. F. Schütze: *Hamburgische Theatergeschichte* (Hamburg, 1794)

C. G. Körner: 'Über Charakterdarstellung in der Musik', *Die Horen*, ii/5 (1795), 97–121

W. H. Wackenroder: *Herzensergiessungen eines kunstliebenden Klosterbruders* (Berlin, 1797; ed. with addns by L. Tieck as *Phantasien über die Kunst*, 1799)

F. Albergati Capacelli: *Della drammatica* (Milan, 1798)

P. Napoli-Signorelli: *Addizioni alla storia critica de' teatri antichi e moderni* (Naples, 1798)

J. C. Walker: *Historical Memoir on Italian Tragedy* (London, 1799)

M. Borsa: 'Lettera sulla musica imitativa', *Opere di Matteo Borsa*, i (Verona, 1800)

M. Cesarotti: 'Lettere e apologhi', *Opere* (Pisa, Florence, Paris, 1800–13)

P. Napoli-Signorelli: *Elementi di poesia drammatica* (Milan, 1801)

J. Perinet: *Mozart und Schikaneder: ein theatralisches Gespräch* (Vienna, 1801)

J.-B. Bonet de Treiches: *De l'Opéra en l'an XII* (Paris, 1803)

W. Heinse: *Musikalische Dialogen, oder Philosophische Unterredungen berühmter Gelehrten, Dichter und Tonkünstler über den Kunstgeschmack in der Musik* (Altenberg, 1805)

C. F. D. Schubart: *Ideen zu einer Ästhetik der Tonkunst* (Vienna, 1806)

F. W. J. von Schelling: *Die Philosophie der Kunst: Über das Verhältniss der bildenden Künste zu der Natur* (Munich, 1807; Eng. trans., 1845)

F. Pananti: *Il poeta di teatro* (London, 1808) [verse novel]

F. M. von Grimm: *Correspondance littéraire, philosophique et critique par Grimm, Diderot, Raynal, Meister, etc.* [review of 1756–90, circulated in MS] (Paris, 1812–14; uncensored edn, 1877–82) ['Lettre sur Omphale', xvi, 287–309]

J. D. Martine: *De la musique dramatique en France* (Paris, 1813)

I. F. Mosel: *Versuch einer Aesthetik des dramatischen Tonsatzes* (Vienna, 1813)

F. Pananti: 'Musica e parole', *Saggi teatrali* (London, 1813)

L. A. C. Bombet [Stendhal, pseud. of M. H. Beyle]: *Lettres écrites de Vienne en Autriche sur le célèbre compositeur Joseph Haydn: suivies d'une vie de Mozart et considérations sur Métastase* (Paris, 1814, rev. 2/1817 as *Les Vies de Haydn, de Mozart et de Métastase*, Eng. trans., 1972)

G. U. Pagani Cesa: 'Discorso...sull'opera seria in generale', *La moglie indiana* (?Venice, 1816), 3–34

Stendhal [M. H. Beyle]: *Vie de Rossini, suivi des notes d'un dilettante* (Paris, 1817; Eng. trans., 1824, as *Memoirs of Rossini*, and 1956)

V. A. Cimaglia: *Saggi di diverse rappresentazioni musicali* (Naples, 1817)

——: *Saggi teatrali analitici* (Naples, 1817)

A. Schopenhauer: *Die Welt als Wille und Vorstellung* (Leipzig, 1819; Eng. trans., 1950, as *The World as Will and Idea*)

L. Buonavoglia: *Difesa del teatro moderno in riposta alle riflessioni publicate in Livorno da Bartolomeo Guidetti* (Lucca, 1820)

G. Carpani: *Le Rossiniane ossia Lettere musico-teatrali* (Padua, 1824)

B. Guidetti: *Che cosa è il teatro?* (Livorno, 1828)

E. F——: 'Des poèmes d'opéras', *La revue musicale* (25 Nov 1830)

B. Guidetti: *Appendice all'opuscolo che cosa è il teatro?* (Rome, 1831)

J. d'Ortigue: *Le balcon de l'opéra* (Paris, 1833)

G. Polcastro: 'Osservazioni critiche ai drammi seri e giocosi offerti al concorso aperto dalla Direzione Generale di Pubblica Istruzione del cessato Regno d'Italia con programma 26 dicembre 1809', *Opere* (Padua, 1833), iii, 59–90 [commission's report, 82–90]

N. Tacchinardi: *Dell'opera in musica sul teatro italiano e de' suoi difetti* (Florence, 2/1833)

G. W. F. Hegel: *Aesthetik* (Berlin, 1835–8); repr. in *Sämtliche Werke*, xiv (1927)

L. de Montigny: 'Du style et de la poésie des opéras français', *Revue et Gazette musicale de Paris* (13 Dec 1835), 405–6

G. Mazzini: *Filosofia della musica* (Paris, 1836)

T. L. Peacock: 'Lord Mount Edgcumbe's Musical Reminiscences', *London Review*, ii (Oct 1836) [review of 4th edn and defence of It. lyric verse]; repr. in *Halliford Edition of Peacock's Works* (1924–34), ix, 1221–52, and in H. Mills, ed.: *Thomas Love Peacock: Memoirs of Shelley and other Essays and Reviews* (1970), 180–98

G. W. Fink: *Wesen und Geschichte der Oper* (Leipzig, 1838)

W. Heinse: *Sämmtliche Schriften*, ed. H. Laube (Leipzig, 1838)

A. De Musset: 'Débuts de Mademoiselle Pauline Garcia', *Revue de deux mondes* (1 Nov 1839); repr. in *Mélanges de littérature et de critique* (1887) [Shakespeare, Rossini's *Otello*]

C. F. D. Schubart: *Gesammelte Schriften und Schicksale* (Stuttgart, 1839)

The Italian Opera in 1839; its Latest Improvements and Existing Defects Impartially Considered: By the Author of The Star of La Scala, etc (London, 1840)

A. Ferrari: *Rodigino: le convenienze teatrali: analisi della condizione presente del teatro musicale italiano* (Milan, 1843)

S. Kierkegaard: 'The Immediate Stages of the Erotic or the Musical Erotic', *Either/Or, a Fragment of Life* [1843], i, trans. D. F. Swenson and L. M. Swenson (Princeton and London, 1944), 35–110

L. Lespès: *Les mystères du grand-opéra* (Paris, 1843)

G. B. Rinuccini: *Sulla musica e sulla poesia melodrammatica italiana nel secolo XIX* (Lucca, 1843)

A. Keferstein: *Herder in Beziehung auf Musik* (Weimar, 1845)

A. L. Lusson: *Projet d'un théâtre d'opéra définitif pour la ville de Paris en remplacement de l'Opéra provisoire* (Paris, 1846)

W. R. Griepenkerl: *Die Oper der Gegenwart* (Leipzig, 1847)

P. Napoli-Signorelli: 'Richerche sul sistema melodrammatico lette...ai Soci Pontaniani nel nov. e dic. del 1812', *Atti dell'Accademia Pontaniana*, iv (Naples, 1847), 1–125

F. von Biedenfeld: *Die komische Oper der Italiener, der Franzosen und der Deutschen* (Leipzig, 1848)

J. Cornet: *Die Oper in Deutschland und das Theater der Neuzeit* (Hamburg, 1849)

T. Carlyle: 'The Opera', *The Keepsake* (London, 1852); repr. in *Critical and Miscellaneous Essays* (London, 1904), iii, 509–14

E. Hanslick: *Vom Musikalisch-Schönen: ein Beitrag zur Revision der Aesthetik der Tonkunst* (Leipzig, 1854)

J. C. Lobe: *Fliegende Blätter für Musik* (Leipzig, 1855–7)

C. Della Valle, Duke of Ventignano: *Considerazione sullo stato attuale del teatro italiano* (Naples, 1856)

E. Sobolewski: *Oper, nicht Drama* (Bremen, 1857)

G. De Simone: *Della musica melodrammatica: Ragionamento* (Naples, 1859)

A. von Wolzogen: *Ueber Theater und Musik: Historisch-kritische Studien* (Breslau, 1860)

H. T. Rötscher: *Dramaturgische und ästetische Abhandlungen* (Leipzig, 1867)

H. Zopff: *Grundzüge einer Theorie der Oper* (Leipzig, 1868)

J. Carlez: *Grimm et la musique de son temps* (Caen, 1872)

F. Nietzsche: *Die Geburt der Tragödie aus dem Geiste der Musik* (Leipzig, 1872, 3/1886; Eng. trans., 1967, and ed. M. S. Silk and J. P. Stern, 1981); repr. in *Gesammelte Werke* (Munich, 1920–29), iii, and *Complete Works*, ed. O. Levy (1924)

F. Del Seppia: 'Del melodramma e della musica', *I primi studi* (Milan, 1874), 330–58

G. J. B. E. W. Legouvé: *Conférence des matinées littéraires E. Scribe* (Paris, 1874) [on *Le part du diable*]

E. Hanslick: *Die moderne Oper: Kritiken und Studien* (Berlin, 1875; part Eng. trans., *Vienna's Golden Years of Music*, 1950, 2/1963 as *Music Criticisms 1846–99*)

R. Zimmermann: *Schellings Philosophie der Kunst* (Vienna, 1875)

M. Kalbeck: *Richard Wagners Nibelungen* (Breslau, ?1876, 2/1883)

F. Nietzsche: 'Richard Wagner in Bayreuth', *Unzeitmässige Betrachtungen*, no. 4 (Leipzig, 1876; Eng. trans., 1910); *Gesammelte Werke*, iv

C. Beauquier: *La musique e le drame: Etude d'ésthétique* (Paris, 1877, 2/1884)

M. Kalbeck: *Das Bühnenfestspiel zu Bayreuth* (Breslau, 1877)

F. von Hausegger: *Richard Wagner und Schopenhauer* (Leipzig, 1878, 2/1892)

L. Meinardus: 'Johann Mattheson und seine Verdienste um die deutsche Tonkunst', *Sammlung musikalischer Vorträge* (Leipzig, 1879–98), 215–72

L. A. Villanis: 'Estetica del libretto per musica', *Gazzetta musicale di Milano*, xlvii et seq. (1882), 699–702

M. Kalbeck: *Richard Wagners Parsifal* (Breslau, 1883)

L. Morandi: *Voltaire contro Shakespeare, Baretti contro Voltaire* (Città di Castello, 1884)

F. X. Haberl: 'Johann Mattheson: Biographische Skizze', *Caecilien Kalender* (1885), 53–60

M. Kalbeck: *Wiener Opernabende* (Vienna, 1885)

F. Nietzsche: *Jenseits von Gut und Böse* (Leipzig, 1886; Eng. trans., 1966); *Gesammelte Werke*, xv

H. Bulthaupt: *Dramaturgie der Oper* (Leipzig, 1887, 3/1925)

F. Nietzsche: *Der Fall Wagner* (Leipzig, 1888; Eng. trans., 1954); *Gesammelte Werke*, xvii

M. Kalischer: *Lessing als Musikästhetiker* (Dresden, 1889)

F. Nietzsche: *Götzen-Dämmerung, oder Wie man mit dem Hammer philosophirt* (Leipzig, 1889; Eng. trans., 1954); *Gesammelte Werke*, xvii

E. Reich: *G.V. Gravina als Aesthetiker* (Vienna, 1890)

L. Spada: 'Ricetta per fare un melodramma', *Luminario del Don Chisciotte* (Rome, 1890), 34

P. Fodale: 'Sulla ricerca del vero e del nuovo nelle Arti e specialmente nel melodramma', *Atti dell'Accademia del R. istituto musicale di Firenze*, xxix (1891), 56–63

J. Combarieu: *Les rapports de la musique et de la poésie considerées au point de vue de l'expression* (Paris, 1894) [excerpt in Bujic 1988]

Atti dell'accademia del R. istituto musicale di Firenze, xxxiii: *Commemorazione della riforma melodrammatica* (1895) [with articles on Peri and Rinuccini]

H. Lion: *Les tragédies et les théories dramatiques de Voltaire* (Paris, 1895)

A. Donadoni: *Dalla Didone all'Attilio Regolo: osservazioni sulla struttura del melodramma metastasiano* (Rome, 1897)

J. Du Tillet: 'A propos du drame lyrique: une lettre de M. Camille Saint-Saëns', *Revue politique et littéraire* (3 July 1897), 27–30

H. Schmidt: *Johann Mattheson, ein Förderer der deutschen Tonkunst, im Licht seiner Werke* (Leipzig, 1897)

M. Kalbeck: *Opern-Abende* (Berlin, 1898)

A. Galli: *Estetica della musica ossia del bello nella musica sacra, teatrale, e da concerto in ordine alla sua storia* (Turin, 1899)

E. Reichel: 'Gottsched und Johann Adolph Scheibe', *SIMG*, ii (1900–01), 654–68 [Scheibe defends opera]

F. Sarcey: *Quarante ans de théâtre* (Paris, 1900)

A. Galletti: *Le teorie drammatiche e la tragedia in Italia nel secolo XVIII* (Cremona, 1901)

'Umano' [G. Meale]: *Teatro nuovo drammelodico* (Milan, 1901)

C. T. Malherbe: 'Un précurseur de Gluck: Le comte Algarotti', *RHCM*, ii (1902), 369–74, 414–23

B. Peroni: 'I melodrammi e le teorie drammatiche di Pietro Metastasio', *Rivista teatrale italiana* (1902), 305–19

H. Günther: *Herders Stellung zur Musik* (diss., Leipzig U., 1903)

K. Krapp: *Die ästhetischen Tendenzen Georg Philipp Harsdörffers* (Berlin, 1903)

H. Kretzschmar: 'Die *Correspondance littéraire* als musikgeschichtliche Quelle', *JbMP*, x (1903), 77–92; repr. in *Gesammelte Aufsätze*, ii, 210–25

M. Ténéo: 'Correspondance théâtrale du XVIIe siècle', *Mercure musical*, i (1905), 576–83, 620–27

W. Wimmerhoff: *Oper oder Drama?* (Rostock, 1905)

J. Ecorcheville: *De Lulli à Rameau, 1690–1730: L'esthétique musicale* (Paris, 1906)

P. Marsop: '"Italien" und der "Fall Salome", nebst Glossen zur Kritik und Ästhetik', *Die Musik*, vi (1906–7), 139–57 [Strauss's realism]

P. Moos: *Richard Wagner als Aesthetiker: Versuch einer kritischen Darstellung* (Berlin and Leipzig, 1906)

H. von Wolzogen: *Musikalisch-dramatische Parallelen: Beiträge zur Erkenntnis von der Musik als Ausdruck* (Leipzig, 1906)

C. Déjob: *Baretti, Goldoni et Métastase* (Toulouse, 1907)

L. Laloy: 'Les idées de Jean-Philippe Rameau sur la musique', *Mercure musical*, iii (1907), 1144–59

E. Schmidt: *Richard Strauss als Dramatiker: eine aesthetisch-kritische Studie* (Munich, 1907)

L. D'Auriac: 'Un problème d'esthétique Wagnérienne', *Mercure musical*, iv (1908), 50–5

H. Prunières: 'Lecerf de la Viéville et l'esthétique musicale classique au XVIIe siècle', *Mercure musical*, iv (1908), 619–54

P. Bekker: *Das Musikdrama der Gegenwart* (Stuttgart, 1909)

G. Dost: *Houdart de la Motte als Tragiker und dramatischer Theoretiker* (diss., Weide, Thuringia, 1909)

E. Fondi: *La vita e l'opera letteraria del musicista Benedetto Marcello* (Rome, 1909)

H. Goldschmidt: 'Die Reform der italienischen Oper des 18. Jahrhunderts und ihre Beziehungen zur musikalischen Aesthetik', *IMusSCR: Leipzig 1909*, 196–207

E. Kroll: *E. T. A. Hoffmanns musikalische Anschauungen* (Königsberg, 1909)

O. R. Hübner: *Richard Strauss und das Musikdrama: Betrachtungen über den Wert oder Unwert gewisser Opernmusiken* (Leipzig, 1910)

H. Kretzschmar: 'Allgemeines und Besonderes zur Affektenlehre', *JbMP*, xviii (1911), 63–77; xix (1912), 65–78

A. Corbellini: 'Le prime rappresentazioni della 'Scala' ed un'invettiva contro un poeta aulico settecentesco', *Archivio storico lombardo*, 4th ser., xviii (1912), 509–23 [Mattia Verazi]

G. Cucuel: 'La critique musicale dans les "revues" du XVIIIe siècle', *L'année musicale*, ii (1912), 127–303

A. von Lauppert: *Die Musikästhetik Wilhelm Heinses: Zugleich eine Quellenstudie zur Hildegard von Hohenthal* (Greifswald, 1912)

W. Altmann: 'Lortzing als dramaturgischer Lehrer', *Die Musik*, xiii (1913–14), 157–8

A. Cogo: *La farsa del dramma lirico* (Milan, 1913)

A. Lombard: *L'Abbé Du Bos* (Paris, 1913)

I. F. Treat: *Un cosmopolite italien du XVIIIème siècle: Francesco Algarotti* (Trévoux, 1913)

E. Wellesz: 'Francesco Algarotti und seine Stellung zur Musik', *SIMG*, xv (1913–14), 427–39

C. Levi: 'La critica metastasiana in Italia', *Rivista teatrale italiana*, xii–xiv (1913–15)

A. Calza: 'Wagner e D'Annunzio: il critico contro il librettista', *Harmonia* [Rome], ii/1–2 (1914), 18

E. Mollenhauer: *Saint-Evremond als Kritiker* (Thurau and Greifswald, 1914)

F. Vatielli: 'Riflessi della lotta Gluckista in Italia', *RMI*, xxi (1914), 639–72

H. Cohen: *Die dramatische Idee in Mozarts Operntexten* (Berlin, 1915)

H. Goldschmidt: *Die Musikästhetik des 18. Jahrhunderts und ihre Beziehungen zu seinem Kunstschaffen* (Zürich, 1915)

F. Hühne: *Die Oper Carmen als Typ musikalischer Poetik* (diss., U. of Greifswald, 1915)

P. Chaponnière: 'La critique et les poétiques au XVIIIe siècle', *Revue d'histoire littéraire de France*, xxiii (1916), 375–98

J. Daninger: *Sage und Märchen im Musikdrama: eine ästhetische Untersuchung an der Sagen- und Märchenoper des 19. Jahrhunderts* (Prague, 1916)

R. De Rensis: *Musica italiana in Francia: la riforma intitolata a Gluck* (Rome, 1916)

P. Gordon: 'Franz Grillparzer: Critic of Music', *MQ*, ii (1916), 552–67

H. Michel: 'Ranieri Calzabigi als Dichter von Musikdramen und als

Kritiker', *Gluck-Jb*, iv (1918), 99–171

P. Long des Clavières: 'Les *Réflexions d'un Solitaire* par A. E. M. Grétry', *RMI*, xxvi (1919), 565–614

B. Matthews: 'The Conventions of Music Drama', *MQ*, v (1919), 255–63

Alain [E.A. Chartier]: *Système des beaux-arts* (Paris, 1920, rev. 1948)

W. Mausolf: *E. T. A. Hoffmans Stellung zu Drama und Theater* (Berlin, 1920)

M. Stenhouse: *The Character of the Opera Libretto According to Quinault* (diss., Columbia U., 1920)

H. W. K. S. von Waltershausen: *Die Zauberflöte: eine operndramaturgische Studie* (Munich, 1920)

A. Della Corte: 'Appunti sull'estetica musicale di Pietro Metastasio', *RMI*, xxviii (1921), 94–119

V. Gui: 'Il Concetto del melodramma nel pensiero Leopardiano', *Musica d'oggi*, iii (1921), 301

C. Van den Borren: *Alessandro Scarlatti et l'esthétique de l'opéra napolitain* (Brussels and Paris, 1921)

A. Della Corte: 'L'estetica musicale di Pietro Metastasio', *Settecento italiano: Paisiello e Metastasio* (Turin, 1922)

W. Fröhlich: *Jean Pauls Beziehungen zur Musik* (diss., Frankfurt U., 1922)

P. Bertrand: 'Pure music and dramatic music', *MQ*, ix (1923), 545–55

G. Donati-Petténi: *D'Annunzio e Wagner* (Florence, 1923)

O. G. T. Sonneck: 'Heinrich Heine's Musical Feuilletons', *MQ*, viii (1923), 119–59, 273–95, 435–68

M. Steidel: *Oper und Drama* (Karlsruhe, 1923)

E. Bücken: *Der heroische Stil in der Oper* (Leipzig, 1924)

G. P. Dilla: 'Music Drama: an Art in Four Dimensions', *MQ*, x (1924), 492–9

M. Friedland: 'Vom Dichterreicht auf "Unwahrscheinlichkeit"', *AMz* [Berlin] (19 Nov 1924)

A. Ghislanzoni: 'Melodramma o dramma musicale?', *Rivista nazionale di musica* [Rome] (Jan 1924)

L. Gilman: *Aspects of Modern Opera* (London and New York, 1924)

R. M. Haas: 'Josse de Villeneuves Brief über den Mechanismus der italienischen Oper von 1756', *ZMw*, vii (1924–5), 129–63

E. Istel: 'For a Reversion to Opera', *MQ*, x (1924), 405–37

F. Malizia: 'La critica in parrucca – Saggi di estetica musicale del settecento', *La Prora* [Rome] (March–April 1924)

O. Strobel: *Richard Wagner über sein Schaffen: ein Beitrag zur 'Künstlerästhetik'* (Munich, 1924)

H. W. K. S. von Waltershausen: 'Zur Dramaturgie des *Fidelio*', *NBJb*, i (1924), 142–58

A. Coeuroy: 'Weber as a Writer', *MQ*, xi (1925), 482–505

G. Mazzoni: *Le odi, il giorno e poesie minori* (Florence, 1925, rev. 1947) [with ode 'La evirazione [La musica] and 'Il giorno' by G. Parini]

A. Aber: *Die Musik im Schauspiel: Geschichtliches und Aesthetisches* (Leipzig, 1926)

[A. Berg]: 'Alban Bergs "Wozzeck" und die Musikkritik', *Musikblätter des Anbruch*, viii (1926)

M. Brand: '"Mechanische" Musik und das Problem der Oper', *Musikblätter des Anbruch*, viii (1926), 356–9

K. Burdach: 'Schillers Chordrama und die Geburt des tragischen Stils aus der Musik', *Vorspiel: Gesammelte Schriften zur Geschichte des deutschen Geistes*, ii (Halle, 1926), 116–237

H. F. Peyser: 'Some Fallacies of Modern Anti-Wagnerism', *MQ*, xii (1926), 175–89

B. F. Schloezer: 'The Operatic Paradox', *MM*, iv/1 (1926), 3–8

K. Westphal: 'Das musikdramatische Prinzip bei Richard Strauss', *Die Musik*, xix (1926–7), 859–64

G. Monaldi: *Il melodramma in Italia nella critica del secolo XIX* (Rome, 1927)

W. B. Schwan: *Die opernästhetischen Theorien der deutschen klassischen Dichter* (diss., Bonn U., 1928)

I. Glebov (B. Asaf'yev): 'Die ästhetischen Anschauungen Mussorgskijs', *Die Musik*, xxi (1928–9), 561–9

C. Minuiti: *Concezioni sul melodramma* (Carletini, 1929)

A. Valente: *Musica e opera lirica* (Naples, 1929)

D. de Paoli: 'Italy's New Music of the Theatre', *MM*, viii/1 (1930), 21–9

A. Fuchs: 'Wieland et l'aesthétique de l'opéra', *Revue de littérature comparée*, x (1930), 608–33

L. D. Green: 'Schopenhauer and Music', *MQ*, xvi (1930), 199–206

F. H. Martens: 'Music Mirrors of the Second Empire', *MQ*, xvi (1930), 415–35, 563–87

A. Parente: 'Note sull'estetica musicale contemporanea in Italia', *RaM*, iii (1930), 289–310

——: *L'essenza del dramma musicale* (Turin, 1930)

L. N. Tolstoy: *What is Art? and Essays on Art* (London, 1930) [uncensored authorized version]

M. Becker: 'Der Einfluss der Philosophie Schellings auf Richard Wagner', *ZMw*, xix (1931–2), 433–47

J. W. Draper: *Eighteenth-Century English Aesthetics* (Heidelberg, 1931)

E. Istel: 'Gluck's Dramaturgy', *MQ*, xvii (1931), 227–33

G. Mazzini: *Scritti di letteratura e di arte* (Florence, 1931)

J. Müller-Blattau: *Hamann und Herder in ihren Beziehungen zur Musik* (Königsberg, 1931)

A. Parente: 'L'estetica di Fausto Torrefranca', *RaM*, iv (1931), 86–97

A. Costa: 'Schopenhauer e Wagner', *RMI*, xxxix (1932), 1–12

I. Glebov (B. Asaf'yev): 'Muzïkal'no-esteticheskiye vozzreniya Musorgskogo' [Mussorgsky's Musical and Aesthetic Approach], *M.P. Musorgskiy: K pyatidesyatiletibiyu so dnya smerti 1881–1931: stat'i i materialï* [On the 50th Anniversary of Musorgsky's Death, 1881–1931: Articles and Documents] (Moscow, 1932), 33–49 [Ger. trans. in *Die Musik*, xxi (1929), 561]

A. Parente: 'Musica ed estetica nella filosofia di Antonio Tari', *RaM*, v (1932) [see Tari 1932]

G. B. Shaw: *Music in London 1890–94* (London, 1932) [see also *The Complete Music Criticism*, ed. D. H. Lawrence, 1981]

A. Tari: 'Opera, melodramma, dramma', *Opere di A. Tari* (Bari, 1932) [see Parente 1932]

V. Tommasini: 'Del dramma lirico', *RMI*, xxxix/1–2 (1932), 73–113

H. Bédarida: 'L'opéra italien jugé par un amateur français en 1756' [?Josse de Villeneuve], *Mélanges de musicologie* (Paris, 1933), 185–200

A. Ghislanzoni: *Il problema dell'opera* (Rome, 1933)

G. Abraham: 'Weber as Novelist and Critic', *MQ*, xx (1934), 27–38

M. Rinaldi: *L'opera in musica: Saggio estetico* (Rome, 1934)

E. Schramm: 'Goethe und Diderots Dialog *Rameau's Neffe*', *ZMw*, xvi (1934), 294–307

P. Bekker: 'The Opera Walks New Paths', *MQ*, xxi (1935), 266–78

H. D. Albright: *The Theory and Staging of Musical Drama* (diss., Cornell U., 1936)

M. Armitage, ed.: *Igor Stravinsky: Articles and Critiques* (New York, 1936)

A. Corbet: *Het Muziekdrama in de XVIe en XVIIe Eeuwen in Italie gezien in het Licht van H. Wölfflins 'Kunstgeschichtliche Grundbegriffen': ein Bijdrage tot de Theorie van het Parallelisme in de Kunst* (Antwerp, 1936)

I. Knox: *The Aesthetic Theories of Kant, Hegel and Schopenhauer* (New York, 1936)

M. Pekelis: 'Dramaturgiya Pushkina i russkaya opera', *SovM*, (1937), no. 5, 45–9

L. Richebourg: *Contribution à l'histoire de la 'Querelle des Bouffons'* (Paris, 1937)

S. Zetowski: 'Teoria polskiej opery narodowej z konca XVIII i poczatku XIX wieku', *Muzyka Polska*, iv (1937), 274–80

R.G. Collingwood: *The Principles of Art* (Oxford, 1938)

H. Freund and R. Reinking: *Musikalisches Theater in Hamburg: Versuch über die Dramaturgie der Oper* (Hamburg, 1938)

H. Closson: *Musique et drame* (Brussels, 1939)

J. G. Robertson: *Lessing's Dramatic Theory* (Cambridge, 1939)

B. Brunelli: 'Grandezza e decadenza della riforma metastasiana', *Rivista italiana del dramma*, iv (1940)

A. Della Corte: 'Gli elementi drammatici nella musica operistica di Paisiello', ibid

A. Pochon: *J.-J. Rousseau musicien et la critique* (Montreux, 1940)

M. A. Barrenechea: *Historia estética de la música, con dos estudios mas sobre consideraciones historicas y tecnicas acerca del canto y la obra maestra del teatro melodramatico* (Buenos Aires, 1941)

T. M. Campbell: 'Nietzsche's "Die Geburt der Tragödie" and Richard Wagner', *Germanic Review*, xvi (1941), 185–200

J. Gaudefroy-Demombynes: *Les jugements allemands sur la musique française au XVIII siècle* (Paris, 1941)

G. Ortolani: 'Carlo Gozzi e la riforma del teatro', *Rivista italiana del dramma* (1940), no. 4, and (1941), nos. 1, 4

S. Pugliatti: 'Il dramma musicale nella poetica di Ildebrando Pizzetti', *RaM*, xiv (1941), 277

U. Rolandi: 'Il teatro alla moda di B. Marcello e le sue propaggini',

La scuola veneziana (Siena, 1941), 51–6

L. Conrad: *Mozarts Dramaturgie der Oper* (Würzburg, 1943)

J. W. Klein: 'Stendhal as Music Critic', *MQ*, xxix (1943), 18–31

E. Betz: 'The Operatic Criticism of the *Tatler* and the *Spectator*', *MQ*, xxxi (1945), 318–30

P.-M. Masson: 'La *Lettre sur Omphale* (1752)', *RdM*, xxvii (1945), 1–19

I. Pizzetti: *Musica e dramma* (Rome, 1945)

R. Giazotto: 'Apostolo Zeno, Pietro Metastasio e la critica del Settecento', *RMI*, xlviii (1946), 324–60; xlix (1947), 46–56; xl (1948), 39–65, 248–58; xli (1949), 43–66, 130–61

J. Harthan: 'Stendhal and Mozart', *ML*, xvii (1946), 174–9

W. Irvine: 'George Bernard Shaw's Musical Criticism', *MQ*, xxxii (1946), 319–32

B. C. Cannon: *Johann Mattheson: Spectator in Music* (New Haven, 1947)

A. R. Oliver: *The Encyclopaedists as Critics of Music* (New York, 1947)

R. G. Pauly: *Benedetto Marcello's 'Il teatro alla moda', a Critique of Early Settecento Opera* (diss., Columbia U., 1947)

B. M. Yarustovsky: *Opernaya dramaturgya Chaykovskogo* (Moscow and Leningrad, 1947)

E. D. Mackerness: 'Thomas Love Peacock's Musical Criticism', *The Wind and the Rain*, iv/3 (1948), 177–87

M. Doisy: *Musique et drame* (Paris and Brussels, 1949)

M. Winesanker: 'Musico-Dramatic Criticism of English Comic Opera, 1750–1800', *JAMS*, ii (1949), 87–96

A. A. Abert: 'Zum metastasianischen Reformdrama', *GfMKB: Lüneburg 1950*, 138–9

R. Allorto: 'Stefano Arteaga e *Le rivoluzioni del teatro musicale italiano*', *RMI*, lii (1950), 124–47

Tutte le opere di Vittorio Alfieri (Asti, 1951–) [incl. 'I viaggi', *Satira IV*, ii; 'Prefazione alla tramelogedia [*sic*] *Abele*'; 'Lettera al Calsabigi' (1783); *Misogallo*]

H. H. Eggebrecht: 'Der Begriff des Komischen in der Musikästhetik des 18. Jahrhunderts', *Mf*, iv (1951), 144–52

A. R. Neumann: *The Evolution of the Concept Gesamtkunstwerk in German Romanticism* (Ann Arbor, 1951)

M. Rinaldi: *Verdi critico: i suoi giudizi, la sua estetica* (Rome, 1951)

M. S. Druskin: *Voprosï muzïkal'noy dramaturgii operï* (Leningrad, 1952)

K. G. Fellerer: 'Vom "stylo theatrali" in der Musiktheorie des 18. Jahrhunderts', *Mimus und Logos: eine Festgabe für Carl Niessen* (Emsdetten, 1952), 57–61

R. Giazotto: *Poesia melodrammatica e pensiero critico nel Settecento* (Milan, 1952)

W. Hess: 'Die Meistersinger von Nürnberg": ihre dichterisch-musikalische Gesamtform', *ZfM*, Jg. 113 (1952), 394–7

Sovetskaya opera: sbornik kriticheskikh statey [Soviet Opera: Collection of Critical Essays] (Moscow, 1953)

B. M. Yarustovsky: *Dramaturgiya russkoy opernoy klassiki* (Moscow, 1953)

B. Asaf'yev: 'Muzïkal'no-dramaturgicheskaya kontseptsiya operï "Boris Godunov" Musorgskogo' (1928), *Izbrannïye trudï*, iii (Moscow, 1954)

G. Friedrich: *Die humanistische Idee der 'Zauberflöte': ein Beitrag zur Dramaturgie der Oper* (Dresden, 1954)

G. Gavazzeni: *La morte dell'opera* (Milan, 1954)

——: *La musica e il teatro* (Pisa, 1954)

A. Goléa: *Esthétique de la musique contemporaine* (Paris, 1954)

J. Marothy: *Erkel Ferenc opera-dramaturgiája* (Budapest, 1954)

J. Scherer: *La dramaturgie de Beaumarchais* (Paris, 1954)

W. Binni, ed.: *I classici italiani nella storia della critica* (Florence, 1955) [chap. on Metastasio by S. Romagnoli]

J. K. Jones: *The 'Elektra' of Strauss: the Relation of the Music to the Drama* (diss., U. of California, Berkeley, 1955)

A. Liess: *Carl Orff: Idee und Werk* (Zürich, 1955, 3/1980; Eng. trans., 1966, 2/1971)

G. Serrau: *Bertolt Brecht Dramaturge* (Paris, 1955)

T. H. Croxall: *Kierkegaard Commentary* (New York, 1956) [pp. 47–59 on music in *Either/Or*]

A. Della Corte: 'Questioni melodrammaturgiche in un saggio sul libretto', *CHM*, ii (1956), 127–34

M. Dietrich: 'Episches Theater? Beitrag zur Dramaturgie des 20. Jahrhunderts', *Maske und Kothurn*, ii (1956), 97–124, 301–34

M. Gnesin: 'O muzïkal'noy dramaturgii Rimskogo-Korsakova v opere "Kashchey bessmertnïy"' [On the Musical Dramaturgy of 'Kaschey the Deathless'], *Mïsli i vospominaniya o N. A. Rimskom-Korsakove* (Moscow, 1956), 128–60

J. Kerman: *Opera as Drama* (New York, 1956, 2/1988)

D. Mitchell: 'Prokofiev's "Three Oranges": a Note on Its Musical-Dramatic Organisation', *Tempo*, no. 41 (1956), 20–24

W. Seifert: *Christian Gottfried Körner und seine Musikästhetik im Lichte der klassischen deutschen Ästhetik* (diss., Jena U., 1956)

A. N. Dmitriyev: *Muzïkal'naya dramaturgiya orkestra M.I. Glinki* (Leningrad, 1957)

W. D. Halls: 'Les débuts du théâtre nouveau', *Annales de la Fondation Maeterlinck*, iii (1957)

C. P. Janz: 'Kierkegaard und das Musikalische, dargestellt an seiner Auffassung von Mozarts *Don Juan*', *Mf*, x (1957), 364–81

T. N. Livanova: *Stasov i russkaya klassicheskaya opera* (Moscow, 1957)

A. M. Wilson: *Diderot: the Testing Years 1713–1759* (New York, 1957)

D. Drew: 'Brecht versus Opera', *Score*, no. 23 (1958), 7–10

E. A. Lippmann: 'The Esthetic Theories of Richard Wagner', *MQ*, xliv (1958), 209–20

A. Schöne: 'Bertolt Brechts Theatertheorie und dramatische Dichtung', *Euphorion*, lii (1958), 272–96

T. Serafin and A. Toni: *Stile, tradizioni e convenzioni del melodramma italiano del settecento e dell'ottocento* (Milan, 1958)

G. Hartung: 'Zur epischen Oper Brechts und Weills', *Wissenschaftliche Zeitschrift des Martin-Luther-Universität Halle-Wittenberg*, viii (1959), 659–73

I. Lowens: 'Saint-Evremond, Dryden and the Theory of Opera', *Criticism*, i (1959), 226–48

——: 'The *Touch-stone* (1728): a Neglected View of London Opera', *MQ*, xlv (1959), 325–42

J. W. Klein: 'Nietzsche's Attitude to Bizet', *MR*, xxi (1960), 215

C. Palisca, ed.: *Girolamo Mei (1519–1594): Letters on Ancient and Modern Music to Vincenzo Galilei and Giovanni Bardi: a Study with Annotated Texts* (Rome, 1960)

J. M. Stein: *Richard Wagner and the Synthesis of the Arts* (Detroit, 1960)

A. Della Corte: 'Una "Poetica" del melodramma alla fine del seicento', *RaM*, xxxii (1962), 43–5 [Salvadori]

F. A. Gallo: 'L'estetica dell'opera buffa nel saggio sulla "Musica imitativa teatrali" di Matteo Borsa', *RaM*, xxxii (1962), 56–65

G. Petronio, ed.: *Carlo Gozzi: Opere: teatro e polemiche teatrali* (Milan, 1962)

Q. M. Hope: *Saint-Evremond: the Honnête Homme as critic* (Bloomington, 1962)

F. E. Kirby: 'Herder and Opera', *JAMS*, xv (1962), 316–29

G. R. Marek: *Opera as Theater* (New York, 1962)

J. Mittenzwei: 'Brechts Kampf gegen die kulinarische Musik', *Das Musikalische in der Literatur* (Halle, 1962), 427–62

A. Shnitke: 'Zametki o dramaturgii pervoy kartinï i o muzïkal'nom tematizme operï S. Prokof'yeva "Voyna i mir"' [Notes on the Form of the First Scene and on the Musical Thematicism of Prokofiev's Opera 'War and Peace'], *Chertï stilya S. Prokof'yeva: Sbornik teoreticheskikh statei*, ed. L. Berger (Moscow, 1962), 32–57

W. Vetter: 'Zur Stilproblematik der italienischen Oper des 17. und 18. Jahrhunderts', *SMw*, xxv (1962), 561–73

U. Weisstein: 'Cocteau, Stravinsky, Brecht, and the Birth of Epic Drama', *Modern Drama*, v (1962), 142–53

G. Barblan: 'Una donizettiana farsa di costume: "Le convenienze e le inconvenienze teatrali"', *Chigiana*, xx (1963), 217–36

R. M. Longyear: '"Le livret bien fait": the Opéra Comique Librettos of Eugène Scribe', *Southern Quarterly*, i (1963), 169–92

M. M. Raraty: *E. T. A. Hoffmann and the Theatre: a Study of the Origins, Development, and Nature of his Relationship with the Theatre* (diss., U. of Sheffield, 1963)

M. Sabinina: '*Semyon kotko*': i problemï opernoy dramaturgii Prokof'yeva' (Moscow, 1963)

G. Snyders: 'Une révolution dans le goût musical au XVIIIe siècle: l'apport de Diderot et de Jean-Jacques Rousseau', *Annales Economies Sociétés Civilisations*, xviii (1963), 20–43

A. Whittall: *La Querelle des Bouffons* (diss., U. of Cambridge, 1963)

A. Berger: *Richard Strauss als geistige Macht: Versuch eines philosophischen Verständnisses* (Gisch, 1964)

H. Kirchmeyer: 'Die deutsche Librettokritik bei Eugène Scribe und Giacomo Meyerbeer', *NZM*, Jg.125 (1964), 372–6

G. Roncaglia: 'Il Conte Francesco Algarotti e il rinnovamento del melodramma', *Chigiana*, xxi (1964), 63–75

L. Schrade: *Tragedy in the Art of Music* (Cambridge, MA, 1964)

A. Whittall: 'Rousseau and the Scope of Opera', *ML*, xlv (1964), 369–76

C. Dahlhaus: 'Wagners Begriff der "dichterisch-musikalischen Periode"', *Beiträge zur Geschichte der Musikanschauung im 19. Jahrhundert* (Regensburg, 1965), i, 179–87

A. Garlington: *The Concept of the Marvelous in French and German Opera, 1770–1840: a Chapter in the History of Opera Esthetics* (diss., U. of Illinois, 1965)

S. Přibáňová: 'Janáčkovy opery ve světle zahraničních kritik' [Janáček's Operas in the Light of Foreign Criticism], *ČMm*, 1 (1965), 231–42 [with German précis]

W. Benjamin: *Versuch über Brecht* (Frankfurt, 1966)

Y. Kremlyov: *Esteticheskiye vsglyadï S. Prokof'yeva* [Prokofiev's Aesthetic Standpoint] (Moscow, 1966)

A. Ogovolets: *Vokal'naya dramaturgiya Musorgskova* (Moscow, 1966)

H. G. Helms: 'Voraussetzungen eines neuen Musiktheaters', *Melos*, xxxiv (1967), 118–30

D. Heartz: 'From Garrick to Gluck: the Reform of Theatre and Opera in the Mid-Eighteenth Century', *PRMA*, xciv (1967–8), 111–27

R. D. Bremner: *The Operas of Reinhard Keiser in their Relationship to the Affektenlehre* (diss., Brandeis U., 1968)

C. Gallico: 'Discorso di G. B. Doni sul recitare in scena', *RIM*, iii (1968), 286–302

A. Petrella: 'Carlo Maria Maggi's Theory of Comedy', *Italian Quarterly*, xii (1968), 223–37

S. Sacaluga: 'Diderot, Rousseau, et la querelle musicale de 1752: nouvelle mise au point', *Diderot Studies*, x (1968), 134–73

E. Allroggen: 'Die Opern-Ästhetik E.T.A. Hoffmanns', *Beiträge zur Geschichte der Oper* (Regensburg, 1969), 25–33

C. Annibaldi: 'Musica gestuale e nuovo teatro: ritorno alla teatralità', *Musica moderna*, iii (1969), 145

D. Cain: *Wagner and Brecht as Major Theorists of Aesthetic Distance in the Theatre* (diss., U. of Michigan, 1969)

L. K. Gerhartz: 'Il sogno di Fontainebleau: alcuni riflessioni sulla tecnica dell'introduzione nel dramma schilleriano e nell'opera verdiana', *2° congresso internazionale di studi verdiani: Verona 1969*, 186–92

E. Pöhlmann: 'Antikenverständnis und Antikenmissverständnis in der Operntheorie der Florentiner Camerata', *Mf*, xxii (1969), 5–13

C. Rizza: 'Costanti estetiche nella critica teatrale di Théophile Gautier', *Studi francesi*, xiii (1969), 442–55

P. Rumyantsev: *Stanislavsky i opera* (Moscow, 1969; Eng. trans., 1975)

S. Stringham: 'Schiller and Verdi: Some Notes on Verdi's Dramaturgy', *2o congresso internazionale di studi verdiani: Verona 1969*, 234–40

T. Adorno: *Ästhetische Theorie* (Frankfurt, 1970; Eng. trans., 1984)

C. Frese: *Dramaturgie der grossen Opern Giacomo Meyerbeers* (Berlin, 1970)

D. M. Hsu: 'Weber on Opera: a Challenge to Eighteenth-Century Tradition', *Studies in Eighteenth-Century Music: a Tribute to Karl Geiringer on his 70th Birthday* (London, 1970), 297–309

R. G. Saisselin: *The Rule of Reason and the Ruses of the Heart: a Philosophical Dictionary of Classical French Criticism, Critics, and Aesthetic Issues* (Cleveland and London, 1970)

O. F. Saloman: *Aspects of 'Gluckian' Operatic Thought and Practice in France: the Musico-Dramatic Vision of Le Sueur and La Cépède (1785–1809) in Relation to the Aesthetic and Critical Tradition* (diss., Columbia U., 1970)

Y. Tyulin and others: 'Kizucheniyu naslediya M. P. Musorgskogo: stsena "pod Kromami" v dramaturgii "Boris Godunova" [Towards an Understanding of Musorgsky's Legacy: the Scene 'Near Kromï' in the Dramatic Plan of *Boris Godunov*], *SovM* (1970), no.3, 90–114

P. Wagner: 'Zu Bertolt Brechts Theorie des epischen Theaters', *Zeitschrift für deutsche Philologie*, lxxxix (1970), 601–15

U. Weisstein: 'Reflections on a Golden Style: W. H. Auden's Theory of Opera', *Comparative Literature*, xxii (1970), 108–24

A. Ziino, ed.: *Antologia della critica wagneriana in Italia* (Messina, 1970)

L. Alexandrovsky: 'Muzïkal'naya dramaturgiya operï S. Prokof'yeva "Povest' o nastoyashchem cheloveke"', *Iz istorii russkoy i sovetskoy muzïki*, i (Moscow, 1971), 189–206

C. Dahlhaus: *Wagners Konzeption des musikalischen Dramas* (Regensburg, 1971)

M. Aranovsky: 'Rechevaya situatsiya v dramaturgii operï "Semyon Kotko"', *S. S. Prokof'yev: Stat'i i issledovaniya* (Moscow, 1972), 59–95

B. Brizi: 'Teoria e prassi melodrammatica di G.F. Busenello e "L'incoronazione di Poppea"', *Venezia e il melodramma nel seicento: Venice 1972*, 51–74

T. Fenner: *Leigh Hunt and Opera Criticism* (Lawrence, KA, 1972)

S. Kunze: 'Richard Wagners Idee des Gesamtkunstwerks', *Beiträge zur Theorie der Künste im 19. Jahrhundert* (Frankfurt, 1972), 196–229

T. E. Lawrenson: 'Les "Noces de Pélée" et la guerre des bouffons', *Venezia e il melodramma nel seicento: Venice 1972*, 121–9

P. Petrobelli: 'Note sulla poetica di Bellini: a proposito di *I puritani*', *MZ*, viii (1972), 99–118

——: 'Per un' esegesi della struttura drammatica del *Trovatore*', *3o congresso internazionale di studi verdiani: Milan 1972*, 387–400; Eng. trans., as 'Towards an Explanation of the Dramatic Structure of *Il trovatore*', *Music Analysis*, i (1982), 129–41

G. Witzke: *Das epische Theater Wedekinds und Brechts* (diss., U. of Tübingen, 1972)

G. B. G. Cinzio: 'Discorso over lettera…intorno al comporre delle comedie e delle tragedie', *Scritti critici*, ed. C. G. Crocetti (Milan, 1973)

P. H. Lang: *The Experience of Opera* (New York, 1973)

B. Brizi: 'Le componenti del linguaggio melodrammatico nelle *Cinesi* di P. Metastasio', *Venezia e il melodramma nel settecento: Venice 1973–5*, i, 389–406

A. Bretanitskaya: 'O muzïkal'naya dramaturgii operï "Nos"' [On the Musical Dramaturgy of the Opera *The Nose*], *SovM* (1974), no. 9, 47–53

C. Casini: 'Iterazione, circolarità e metacronia nel Barbiere di Siviglia', *Bollettino del Centro rossiniano di studi* (1974), 37–100

C. Dahlhaus: 'Wagners Berlioz-Kritik und die Ästhetik des Hässlichen', *Festschrift für Arno Volk* (Copenhagen, 1974), 107–23; repr. in *Klassische und romantischer Musikästhetik* (1988)

P. Dircks: 'Musical Drama and the Artistic Whole: the Necessity for Special Criteria', *Studies in Burke and his Time*, xv (1974), 277–86

A. Fraser: 'Truth and Reality in Opera Librettos', *Opera*, xxv (1974), 9–15

P. Gossett: 'Verdi, Ghislanzoni and *Aida*: the Uses of Convention', *Critical Inquiry*, i (1974), 291–334

R. B. Moberley: 'The Influence of French Classical Drama on *La clemenza di Tito*', *ML*, lv (1974), 286–98

S. Moisson-Franckhauser: *Serge Prokofiev et les courants esthétiques de son temps* (Paris, 1974)

E. Zuckerman: 'Nietzsche and Music: "The Birth of Tragedy" and "Nietzsche contra Wagner"', *Symposium*, xxviii (1974), 17–32

K. Gräwe: 'Die "ungeordnete" Dramaturgie der "Chowanschtchina"', *Jb der Hamburgischen Staatsoper 1974–5*

F. L. Arruga: 'Appunti e prospettive sulle drammaturgia di Donizetti', *1° convegno internazionale di studi donizettiani: Bergamo 1975*, 743–73

W. Ashbrook: 'La struttura drammatica nella produzione di Donizetti dopo il 1838', *1° convegno internazionale di studi donizettiani: Bergamo 1975*, 721–41

M. A. Sheppach: *The Operas of Michael Tippett in the Light of Twentieth-Century Opera Aesthetics* (diss., U. of Rochester, 1975)

R. Angermüller: 'Reformideen von Du Roullet und Beaumarchais als Opernlibrettisten', *AcM*, xlviii (1976), 227–53

W. Müller-Seidel: 'Episches im Theater der deutschen Klassik', *Jb der deutschen Schillergesellschaft*, xx (1976), 338–86

A. Stratiyevsky: 'Nekotorïye osobennoti rechitativa operï "Igrok" Prokof'yeva' [Some Peculiarities of the Recitative in Prokofiev's Opera 'The Gambler'], *Russkaya muzïka na rubezhe XX veka* (Moscow and Leningrad, 1976)

H. Federhofer, ed.: *Peter Cornelius als Komponist, Dichter, Kritiker und Essayist* (Regensburg, 1977)

P. Gallarati: 'Dramma e ludus dall'*Italiana* al *Barbiere*', *Il melodramma italiano dell'ottocento* (Turin, 1977)

A. Garlington: 'August von Schlegel and the German Romantic Opera', *JAMS*, xxx (1977), 500–6

H. F. Garten: *Wagner the Dramatist* (London, 1977)

M. Kesting: 'Wagner/Meyerhold/Brecht oder die Erfindung des "epischen Theaters"', *Brecht-Jb* (1977), 111–30

P. Petersen: 'Die dichterisch-musikalische Periode: ein verkannter Begriff Richard Wagners', *HJbMw*, ii (1977), 105–23

F. Portinari: '"Pari siamo": sulla struttura del libretto romantico', *Il melodramma italiano dell'ottocento* (Turin, 1977)

M. Voigts: *Brechts Theaterkonzeptionen* (Munich, 1977)

W. E. McDonald: 'Words, Music and Dramatic Development in "Die Meistersinger"', *19th Century Music*, i (1977–8), 246–60

R. Strohm: 'Dramatic Time and Operatic Form in Wagner's "Tannhäuser"', *PRMA*, civ (1977–8), 1–10

G. Flaherty: *Opera in the Development of German Critical Thought* (Princeton, NJ, 1978)

O. Kolleritsch, ed.: *50 Jahre Wozzeck von Alban Berg: Vorgeschichte und Auswirkung in der Opernästhetik* (Graz, 1978)

S. Kunze: 'Über den Kunstcharakter des Wagnerischen Musikdramas', *Richard Wagner: von der Oper zum Musikdrama* (Berne and Munich, 1978), 9–24

H. E. Renk: 'Anmerkungen zur Beziehung zwischen Musiktheater und Semiotik', *Theaterarbeit an Wagners Ring* (Munich, 1978), 275–88

R. Monelle: *'Opera seria' as Drama: the Musical Dramas of Hasse and Metastasio* (diss., U. of Edinburgh, 1979)

M. Tanner: 'The Total Work of Art', *Wagner Companion* (London, 1979), 140–224

D. Borchmeyer: 'Tristan, Tasso und die Kunst des "unendlichen Details": zu Richard Wagners musikalischer Dramaturgie', *Jb der Bayerischen Staatsoper*, iii (1979–80), 23–32

P. Gallarati: 'L'estetica musicale di Raniero de' Calzabigi: il caso Metastasio', *NRMI*, xiv (1980), 497–538

I. Lavin: 'Bernini and the Theater', *Bernini and the Unity of the Visual Arts* (New York, 1980), 146–57

P. Petrobelli: 'Music in the Theatre (à propos of *Aida*, Act III)', *Themes in Drama*, iii: *Drama, Dance and Music* (Cambridge, 1980), 129–42

R. Schusky, ed.: *Das deutsche Singspiel im 18. Jahrhundert: Quellen und Zeugnisse zur Ästhetik und Rezeption* (Bonn, 1980)

W. Weber: 'Learned and General Musical Taste in Eighteenth-Century France', *Past and Present: a Journal of Historical Studies*, lxxxix (1980), 58–85

W. Kinderman: 'Dramatic Recapitulation in Wagner's "Götterdämmerung"', *19th Century Music*, iv (1980–1), 101–12

R. S. Freeman: *Opera without Drama: Currents of Change in Italian Opera, 1675–1725* (Ann Arbor, 1981)

D. Möller: *Jean Cocteau und Igor Strawinsky: Untersuchungen zur Ästhetik und zu Oedipus Rex* (Hamburg, 1981)

A. M. Morazzoni, ed.: *Musorgski: l'opera, il pensiero: Milan 1981*

F. Schnapp, ed.: *E. T. A. Hoffmann: ein Dokumentenband* (Hildesheim, 1981)

R. Strohm: 'Zum Verständnis der Opera Seria', *Werk und Wiedergabe: Musiktheater exemplarisch interpretiert* (Bayreuth, 1981); Eng. trans. as 'Towards an Understanding of the *opera seria*', *Essays on Handel and the Italian Opera* (Cambridge, 1985), 91–105

P. Weiss: 'Teorie drammatiche e "infranciosamento": motivi della "riforma" melodrammatica nel primo Settecento', *Antonio Vivaldi: teatro musicale, cultura e società: Venice 1981*, 273–96

A. Newcomb: 'The Birth of Music out of the Spirit of Drama: an Essay in Wagnerian Formal Analysis', *19th Century Music*, v (1981–2), 38–66

F. Pulcini: *Per una ricognizione italiana del teatro musicale di Leos Janáček: aspetti della drammaturgia di 'Da una casa di morti'* (diss., U. of Turin, 1981–2)

D. Borchmeyer: *Das Theater Richard Wagners: Idee, Dichtung, Wirkung* (Stuttgart, 1982; Eng. trans., 1991, as *Richard Wagner: Theory and Theatre*)

E. Fischer: *Zur Problematik der Opernstruktur: das künstlerische System und seine Krisis im 20. Jahrhundert* (Wiesbaden, 1982)

J. B. Kopp: *The 'Drame Lyrique': a Study in the Esthetics of opéra comique, 1762–1791* (diss., U. of Pennsylvania, 1982)

S. Kunze: 'Ironie des Klassizismus: Aspekte des Umbruchs in der musikalischen Komödie um 1800', *AnMc*, no. 21 (1982), 72–99

M. P. McClymonds: 'Mattia Verazi and the Opera at Mannheim, Stuttgart and Ludwigsburg', *Studies in Music from the University of Western Ontario*, vii/2 (1982), 99–136

H. Pfotenhaus: 'Richard Wagners Kunstmythologie und Friedrich Nietzsches Ästhetik', *Deutsche Literatur*, vii (1982), 345–57

H. Schneider: *Die Rezeption der Opern Lullys im Frankreich des Ancien Régime* (Tutzing, 1982)

R. Taruskin: *Opera and Drama in Russia as Preached and Practised in the 1860s* (Ann Arbor, 1982)

P. Weiss: 'Metastasio, Aristotle, and the *Opera Seria*', *JM*, i (1982), 385–94

R. Würtz: 'Anton Schweizer and Christoph Martin Wieland: the Theory of the Eighteenth-Century Singspiel', *SMA*, vii (1982), 148

J. N. Black: 'Salvadore Cammarano's Programma for "Il trovatore" and the Problems of the finale', *Studi verdiani*, ii (1983), 78–107

R. Franke: *Richard Wagners Zürcher Kunstschriften* (Hamburg, 1983)

F. W. Glass: *The Fertilizing Seed: Wagner's Concept of the Poetic Intent* (Ann Arbor, 1983)

C. Kintzler: *Jean-Philippe Rameau: splendeur et naufrage de l'esthétique du plaisir à l'âge classique* (Paris, 1983, 2/1988)

S. Kunze: *Der Kunstbegriff Richard Wagners* (Regensburg, 1983)

B. Magee: *The Philosophy of Schopenhauer* (Oxford, 1983) [with appx. on Schopenhauer and Wagner]

Y. Olkhovsky: *Vladimir Stasov and Russian National Culture* (Ann Arbor, 1983)

C. Palisca: 'A Discourse on the Performance of Tragedy by Giovanni de' Bardi (?)', *MD*, xxxvii (1983), 327–43

J. Rohr: 'Wenn Sprache und Handlung Musik werden: E. T. A. Hoffmanns Begriff der "romantischen Oper"', *Festschrift Hans Conradin* (Berne, 1983), 61–9

E. Sala di Felice: *Metastasio: ideologia, drammaturgia, spettacolo* (Milan, 1983)

H. Schulze: *E. T. A. Hoffmann als Musikschriftsteller und Komponist* (Leipzig, 1983)

A. D. Aberbach: *The Ideas of Richard Wagner* (Lanhem, ID, 1984, 2/1988)

A. L. Bellina: 'Ranieri Calzabigi: teoria e prassi melodrammatica tra Parigi e Vienna', *Lettere italiane* (1984), 25–36

——: *L'ingegnosa congiunzione: 'Melos' e immagine nella 'favola' per musica* (Florence, 1984)

G. Corapi: 'Théophile Gautier e il marmo rossiniano', *Bollettino del Centro rossiniano di studi* (1984), 21–42

S. Gozzi: 'Nuovi orientamenti della critica wagneriana', *RIM*, xix (1984), 147–77

D. R. B. Kimbell: 'Neo-classical Countercurrents in Italian Romantic Opera', *Italian Studies*, xxxix (1984), 67–78

H. Lindberger: *Opera – the Extravagant Art* (Ithaca, NY, 1984)

G. Morelli: 'Fare un libretto: la conquista della poetica paraletteraria', *A. Aureli-F. Lucio, 'Il Medoro', DMV*, iv (1984), pp.ix–lvii

P. Robinson: *Jean-Jacques Rousseau's Doctrine of the Arts* (Berne, 1984)

J. Söring: 'Wagner und Brecht: zur Bestimmung des Musiktheaters', *Richard Wagner 1883–1983* (Stuttgart, 1984), 451–73

M. Vogel: *Nietzsche und Wagner: ein deutsches Lesebuch* (Bonn, 1984)

P. Weiss: 'Baroque Opera and the Two Verisimilitudes', *Music and Civilization: Essays in Honour of Paul Henry Lang* (New York, 1984), 117–26

R. Bledsoe: 'Henry Fothergill Chorley and the Reception of Verdi's Early Operas in England', *Victorian Studies*, xxviii (1984–5), 631–55

S. L. Balthazar: *Evolving Conventions in Italian Serious Opera: Scene Structure in the Works of Rossini, Bellini, Donizetti and Verdi, 1810–1850* (diss., U. of Pennsylvania, 1985)

G. Bimberg: *Dramaturgie der Händel-Opern* (Halle, 1985)

E.-T. Forsius: *Der 'goût français' in der Darstellungen des coin du roi: Versuch zur Rekonstruktion einer 'Laienästhetik' während des Pariser Buffonistenstreites 1752–1754* (Tutzing, 1985)

M. Lécrivain: *L'esprit de réforme dans l'opéra français de 1750 à 1790* (diss., U. of Paris-Sorbonne, 1985)

T. N. McGeary: *English Opera Criticism and Aesthetics 1685–1747* (diss., U. of Illinois, 1985)

H. M. Riley: Review of critical text of Wagner's *Oper und Drama*, ed. K. Kropfinger (1984), *Colloquia Germanica*, xviii (1985), 174–7

J. Rohr: *E. T. A. Hoffmanns Theorie des musikalischen Dramas* (Baden-Baden, 1985)

L. C. Shulman: *Music Criticism of the Paris Opéra in the 1830s* (diss., Cornell U., 1985)

U. Weisstein: 'Brecht und das Musiktheater: die epische Oper als Ausdruck des europäischen Avantgardismus', *Kontroversen, alte und neue: VII. Internationales Germanisten-Kongress: Göttingen 1985*, ix, 72–85

M.-C. Benard: *Orphée de Gluck: naissance d'une esthétique* (diss., U. of Paris-Sorbonne, 1986)

C. Dahlhaus: 'Comedy with Music and Musical Comedy: on the Poetics of Comic Opera as seen in Donizetti', *NZM*, Jg.147 (1986), 24–7

W. Darcy: 'The Pessimism of the *Ring*', *OQ*, iv/2 (1986), 24–48

A. Duault: *Verdi, la musique et le drame* (Paris, 1986)

R. T. Katz: *Divining the Powers of Music: Aesthetic Theory and the*

Origins of Opera (New York, 1986)

C. Kintzler: 'De la pastorale à la tragédie lyrique: quelques éléments d'un système poétique', *RdM*, lxxii (1986), 67–96

H. O'Kelly-Watanabe: 'Barthold Feind, Gottsched and *Cato* – or Opera Reviled', *Proceedings of the English Goethe Society*, new ser., lv (1986), 107

J. A. Rice: 'Sense, Sensibility, and Opera Seria: an Epistolary Debate', *Studi musicali*, xv (1986), 101–38

D. Becker: 'La *Plática sobre la música* en toscano, y los principios del teatro musical barroco en España', *Rivista di musicologia*, x (1987), 501

A. L. Bellina: 'I gesti parlanti ovvero il recitar danzando: *Le festin de pierre* e *Sémiramis*', *La figura e l'opera di Ranieri de' Calzabigi: Livorno 1987*, 107–17

M. A. Cicora: '*Parsifal* Reception in the '*Bayreuther Blätter*' (New York, 1987)

P. Conrad: *A Song of Love and Death: the Meaning of Opera* (London, 1987)

C. Dahlhaus: 'Operndramaturgie im 19. Jahrhundert', *AcM*, lix (1987), 32–5

P. Gallarati: 'Ranieri de' Calzabigi e la teoria della "musica di declamazione"', *La figura e l'opera di Ranieri de' Calzabigi: Livorno 1987*, 5–13

A. Gerhard: 'Incantesimo o Specchio dei costumi: un'estetica dell'opera del librettista di *Guillaume Tell*' [Jouy], *Bollettino del Centro rossiniano di studi* (1987), 45–60

M. P. McClymonds: '*La morte di Semiramide ossia La vendetta di Nino* and the Restoration of Death and Tragedy to the Italian Operatic Stage in the 1780s and 90s', *IMSCR, xiv: Bologna 1987*, iii, 285–92

——: 'The Venetian Role in the Transformation of Italian Opera Seria during the 1790s', *I vicini di Mozart: Venice 1987*, i, 221–40

H. S. Powers: '"La solita forma" and "The Uses of Convention"', *AcM*, lix (1987), 65–90

T. Schacher: *Idee und Erscheinungsformen des Dramatischen bei Hector Berlioz* (Hamburg, 1987)

P. Weiss: 'Neoclassical Criticism and Opera', *Studies in the History of Music*, ii (1987), 1–30

J. Webster: 'To Understand Verdi and Wagner we must Understand Mozart', *19th Century Music*, xi (1987–8), 175–93

B. Bujic: *Music in European Thought 1851–1912* (Cambridge, 1988)

M.-H. Coudroy: *La Critique parisienne des 'grands opéras' de Meyerbeer: 'Robert le diable', 'Les Huguenots', 'Le Prophète', 'L'Africaine'* (Saarbrücken, 1988)

C. Dahlhaus: 'Drammaturgia dell'opera italiana', *SOI*, vi (1988), 79–162

E. J. Dent: Letter to Stevens on libretto for planned opera and on *Peter Grimes, Bernard Stevens and his Music: a Symposium*, ed. B. Stevens (London, 1988), 150–53

R. di Benedetto: 'Poetiche e polemiche', *SOI*, vi (1988), 3–76

S. Durante: 'Vizi privati e virtù pubbliche del polemista teatrale da Muratori a Marcello', *Benedetto Marcello: la sua opera e il suo tempo* (Florence, 1988), 415–24

P. Fabbri: 'Questioni drammaturgiche del teatro di Stradella', *Chigiana*, xxxix, new ser. no.19 (1988), 91–108

H.-V. Fuss: 'Richard Strauss in der Interpretation Adornos', *AMw*, xlv (1988), 65–71

A. Gerhard: '"Ce cinquième acte sans intérêt": Preoccupazioni di Scribe e di Verdi per la drammaturgia di "Les vêpres siciliennes"', *Studi verdiani*, iv (1988), 65–86

A. Groos and R. Parker, eds.: *Reading Opera* (Princeton, NJ, 1988)

H. C. Jacobs: *Literatur, Musik und Gesellschaft in Italien und Österreich in der Epoche Napoleons und der Restauration: Studien zu Giuseppe Carpani (1751–1825)* (Frankfurt, 1988)

P. Kivy: *Osmin's Rage: Philosophical Reflections on Opera, Drama, and Text* (Princeton, NJ, 1988)

D. Neville: 'Aesthetic Considerations in Metastasio's Dramatic Theories', *Musica Antiqua*, viii: *Bydgoszcz 1988*, 723–45

M. E. C. Bartlet: 'A Musician's View of Rameau after the Advent of Gluck: Grétry's *Les trois âges de l'opéra* and its Background', *Studies on Jean-Baptiste Lully and the Music of the French Baroque: Essays in Honor of James R. Anthony* (Cambridge, 1989), 291–318

P. Ciarlatini: 'Una testimonianza sul teatro musicale degli inizi dell'Ottocento: il saggio "Dell'Opera in Musica" di Nicola Tacchinardi', *Bollettino del Centro rossiniano di studi* (1989), 63–135

E. T. Cone: 'The World of Opera and its Inhabitants', *Music: a View*

from Delft (Chicago, 1989), 125–38

C. Dahlhaus: 'What is a Musical Drama?', *COJ*, i (1989), 95–111

S. McClary: 'Constructions of Gender in Monteverdi's Dramatic Music', *COJ*, i (1989), 202–23

M. Milosevic: 'Il contributo dei libretti e della corrispondenza di Cristoforo Ivanovich nell'evoluzione del melodramma seicentesco', *Il libro nel bacino adriatico (secc. XV–XVIII): Venice 1989*

C. Palisca: *The Florentine Camerata: Documentary Studies and Translations* (New Haven and London, 1989) [Bardi, V. Galilei, Strozzi]

M. R. Wade: 'The Poetics of the *Singspiel*', *Studies on Modern and Classical Literatures and Languages*, ii (1989), 77–85

J. C. G. Waterhouse: 'Between Opera and Music Theatre: Gian Francesco Malipiero's Rebellion against the Italian Operatic Establishment 1917–29', *ATI Journal*, no. 56 (1989), 27–38 [Association of Teachers of Italian pubn.]

I. Cavallini: 'Questioni di poetica del melodramma del seicento nelle lettere di Cristoforo Ivanovich', *Giovanni Legrenzi: Clusone 1990*

E. Haeringer: *L'esthétique de l'opéra en France au temps de Jean-Philippe Rameau* (Oxford, 1990)

U. Mazurowicz: 'Wielands Singspieltheorie und ihr Niederschlag bei zeitgenössischen Komponisten', *JbO*, iii (1990), 25–42

M. Sansone: 'Verga and Mascagni: the Critics' Response to "Cavalleria rusticana"', *ML*, lxxi (1990), 198–214

A. Whittall: '"Forceful Muting" or "Phatic Dithering"? Some Recent Writing on Opera', *ML*, lxxi (1990), 65–71

H. M. Brown: *Leitmotiv and Drama: Wagner, Brecht, and the Limits of 'Epic' Theatre* (Oxford, 1991)

P. Kivy: 'Opera Talk: a Philosophical "phantasie"', *COJ*, iii (1991), 63–77

P. Fabbri: 'Riflessioni teoriche sul teatro per musica nel seicento: "La poetica toscana all'uso" di Giuseppe Gaetano Salvadori', *Opera e libretto* (in preparation)

M. P. McClymonds: 'The Myth of Metastasian Dramaturgy', *Patrons, Politics, Music, and Art in Italy 1738–1859* (in preparation)

——: 'Verazi's Controversial *drammi in azione* as Realized in the Music of Salieri, Anfossi, Alessandri and Mortellari for the Opening of La Scala 1778–1779', *Omaggio al Claudio Sartori* (forthcoming)

O. F. Saloman: 'Chabanon and Chastellux on Music and Language, 1764–1773', *IRASM* (in preparation)

(iii) Anthologies

A. Cametti: 'Critiche e satire teatrali romane del '700', *RMI*, ix (1902), 1–35

A. Solerti, ed.: *Le origini del' melodramma: testimonianze dei contemporanei* (Milan, 1903) [prefaces and dedications by Guidotti, Rinuccini, Peri, Caccini, Gagliano, Vitali; writings etc. by Vincenzo, Bonini, Bardi, Della Valle, Doni]

L. Frati: 'Satire di musicisti', *RMI*, xxxiii (1926), 551–7

I. Kolodin, ed.: *The Critical Composer: the Musical Writings of Berlioz, Wagner, Schumann, Tchaikovsky and Others* (New York, 1940)

A. Della Corte: *Satire e grotteschi di musiche e di musicisti d'ogni tempo* (Turin, 1946)

O. Strunk: *Source Readings in Music History* (New York, 1950) [texts in Eng. trans. from Rinuccini to Wagner]

U. Rolandi: *Il libretto per musica attraverso i tempi* (Rome, 1951) [with list of references to relevant prolegomena in librettos, p.223]

'Composers' Forum: Subject Opera', *Musical America*, lxxiii (1953), repr. in Weisstein (1964), 362–6 [forum, arranged by *World Theatre*, with Blacher, Bliss, Dallapiccola, Delannoy, Egk, Malipiero, Pizzetti]

D. Arundell: *The Critic at the Opera* (London, 1957) [with critical material on opera in London]

U. Weisstein: *The Essence of Opera* (London, 1964) [Eng. trans. of selected comment, much by composers and librettists; *WE*]

D. Launay, ed.: *La Querelle des Bouffons* (Geneva, 1973) [facs. of 61 pamphlets, 1752–4]

L. E. Lindgren and C. B. Schmidt: 'A Collection of 137 Broadsides Concerning Theatre in Late Seventeenth-Century Italy: an Annotated Catalogue', *Harvard Library Bulletin*, xxviii (1980), 185–233

H. Becker, W. Osthoff, H. Schneider and H. C. Wolff, eds.: *Quellentexte zur Konzeption der europäischen Oper im 17. Jahrhundert* (Kassel, 1981) [contemporary material on 17th-century Italian, French and German opera in original language; *BQ*]

F. Lesure, ed.: *Querelle des Gluckistes et des Piccinistes: Texte des pamphlets avec introduction, commentaires et index* (Geneva, 1984) [facs.; vol.i is Leblond's *Mémoires* (1781)]

P. Weiss and R. Taruskin, ed.: *Music in the Western World: a History in Documents* (New York and London, 1984) [incl. much operatic material in Eng. trans.]

E. Selfridge-Field: *Pallade veneta: Writings on Music in Venetian Society, 1650–1750* (Venice, 1985)

Textes sur Lully et l'opéra français (Geneva, 1987) [C. Perrault, Saint-Evremond, Le Brun]

H: LIBRETTO COLLECTIONS AND THEIR BIBLIOGRAPHY

(i) Catalogues, lists

L. Allacci: *Drammaturgia ... divisa in sette indici* (Rome, 1666) [dramas and librettos, incl. unpubd. works]; (Venice, 2/1755, enlarged by G. Cendoni, A. Zeno, G. degli Apostoli and others, as *Drammaturgia accresciuta e continuata fino all'anno MDCCLV*)

Indice delle opere in musica sin'ora stampate in Bologna e si fanno vendere dalli Eredi di Giuseppe Antonio Silvani in capo al Pavaglione (Bologna, 1727)

J. A. Jullien: *Histoire du Théâtre de l'Opéra-Comique* (Paris, 1769) [list of 226 librettos]

T. de Lajarte: *Bibliothèque musicale du théâtre de l'Opéra: catalogue historique, chronologique, anecdotique* (Paris, 1878)

D. Muoni: *Libretti di melodrammi e balli autografi di musicisti e di altri artisti teatrali presentati all'esposizione musicale in Milano* (Milan, 1881)

E. Picquot: *Catalogue des livres composant la bibliothèque de feu M. le baron James de Rothschild* (Paris, 1884–1920) [livrets listed; illustrated title-pages]

T. Wiel: *I codici musicali Contariniani del secolo XVII nella R. Biblioteca di San Marco in Venezia* (Venice, 1888), xiv–xxiv [lists *I-Vnm* Codd. 1613 and 1114, Append. Classe VII degli Italiani: two collections, including Zeno's, of 213 vols. (no. 30018, 1637–1796) and 220 vols. (no. 60848 and 43 *buste*, 1791–1836)]

A. Wotquenne: *Libretti d'opéras et d'oratorios italiens du XVIIe siècle: Catalogue de la Bibliothèque du Conservatoire Royal de Musique de Bruxelles*, Annexe I (Brussels, 1901)

L. S. Olschki: 'Una visita alla collezione del comm. C. Lozzi di autografi e documenti riguardante la musica e il teatro in tutte le loro appertenenze e ogni sorta di spettacolo', *La bibliofilia*, iii (1901–2), 231–59 [with list of autographs and reproductions]

P. Bergmans: 'Une collection de livrets d'opéra italiens (1669–1710), à la Bibliothèque de l'Université de Gand', *SIMG*, xii (1910–11), 221–34

L. Frati: 'Un impresario teatrale del settecento e la sua biblioteca', *RMI*, xviii (1911), 64–84 [Count F.M. Zambeccari]

O. G. T. Sonneck: 'Italienische Opernlibretti des 17. Jahrhunderts in der Library of Congress', *SIMG*, xiii (1911–12), 392–9

Turin: Biblioteca civica, sezione teatrale (Letteratura drammatica) (Turin, 1911–12)

F. Fano and M. Ferrigni: *Il libro dei libretti* (Milan, 1912) [list of 176 librettos]

P. Lacroix: *Table de pièces de théâtre décrites dans le catalogue de la bibliothèque de M. Soleinne* (Paris, 1914)

O. G. T. Sonneck: *Catalogue of 19th-Century Librettos* [*US-Wc*] (Washington DC, 1914)

——: *Catalogue of Opera Librettos Printed before 1800* [*US-Wc*] (Washington DC, 1914)

E. Wellesz: 'Einige handschriftliche Libretti aus der Frühzeit der Wiener Oper', *ZMw*, i (1918–19), 278–81

Allen A. Brown Collection: a Catalogue of the Allen A. Brown Collection of Books Relating to the Stage (Boston, 1919) [*US-Bp*]

P. Nettl: 'Exerpzte aus der Raudnitzer Textbüchersammlung', *SMw*, vii (1920), 143–4

R. Lustig: 'Saggio di catalogo della collezione di melodrammi della R. Biblioteca Marucelliana in Firenze', *La bibliofilia*, xxv (1923), 239–47; xxvi (1924), 67–74

E. Kastner: 'Bibliografia dei libri italiani stampati in Ungheria', *Corvina: Rivista di scienze, lettere ed arti della Società Ungherese-Italiana Mattia Corvino*, 1st ser., iv/7 (1924), 125–8 [with 77 18th-century librettos]

R. Haas: 'Zur Bibliographie der Operntexte', *Deutschen Musikgesellschaft: Leipzig 1925*, 59–66

V. Raeli: 'La collezione Rolandi di libretti d'opera musicali', *Accademie e biblioteche*, i/3 (1927), and *Rivista nazionale di musica*, ix (March 1928) [collection now in *I-Vgc*]

F. Mayer, F. Trojan and F. Hadamowsky: *Kataloge der alten Bibliothek des Theaters an der Wien* (Vienna, 1928)

M. Pereira Peixoto d'Almeida Carvalhaes: *Catálogo da importante*

biblioteca que pertencen ao...erudito e bibliofilo ilustre Manuel de Carvalhaes...organisado par Augusta Sâ da Costa (Lisbon, 1928) [see U. Rolandi: 'La più ricca collezione di libretti d'opera all'Italia', *Rivista nazionale di musica*, ix (Jan 1928)]

V. Raeli: 'Catalogazione e statistica delle collezioni di libretti per musica', *Musica d'Oggi*, xii (1930), 356–8

U. Rolandi: 'Storia e vicende della Collezione Rolandi di libretti per musica', *Sardegna* (Cagliari, April 1930) [now in *I-Vgc*]

S. Färber: 'Verzeichnis der vollständigen Opern...wie auch der Operntextbücher der fürstlichen Thurn-und-Taxisschen Hofbibliothek Regensburg', *Verhandlungen des Historischen Vereins von Oberpfalz und Regensburg*, lxxxvi (Regensburg, 1936), 125–54

R. Gilder and G. Freedley: *Theatre Collections in Libraries and Museums: an International Handbook* (New York, 1936)

E. J. Luin: *Repertorio dei libri musicali di S. A. S. Francesco II d'Este nell'Archivo di Stato di Modena* (Florence, 1936)

D. Macmillan: *Catalogue of the Larpent Plays in the Huntington Library* (San Marino, CA, 1939) [MS plays and librettos on microfiche: *Three Centuries of Drama: Plays submitted to the Lord Chamberlain*]

J. Hárich: *Catalogue of the Esterházy Libretto Collection* [MS, *H-Bn*, 1941; collection destroyed 1945]

G. Biscotti: 'La Biblioteca musicale Rolandi e la sua collezione di libretti per musica', *Accademie e biblioteche d'Italia*, xvi/4 (29 April 1942) [now in *I-Vgc*]

G. Gaspari and others: *Catalogo della Biblioteca del Liceo Musicale di Bologna* v: *Libretti d'Opera in musica* (Bologna, 1943)

A. Loewenberg: 'Early Dutch Librettos and Plays with Music in the BM', *Journal of Documentation*, ii (1946–7), 210–37

L. Ferrari: 'Per una bibliografia del teatro italiano in Vienna', *Studi di bibliografia e di argomento romano: in memoriam di Luigi Gregori* (Rome, 1949), 136–50 [identifies Zeno's libretto collection]

F. Grasberger: 'Zur Bibliographie und Katalogisierung der Textbücher', *Zentralblatt für Bibliothek-Wesen* (1952), 206–19

R. Schaal: 'Die vor 1801 gedruckten Libretti des Theatermuseums München', *Mf*, x (1957), 388–96, 487–97; xi (1958), 54–69, 168–177, 321–36, 462–77; xii (1959), 60–75, 161–77, 299–306, 454–61; xiii (1960), 38–46, 164–72, 299–306, 441–48; xiv (1961), 36–43, 166–83

J. Hárich: *Esterházy-Musikgeschichte im Spiegel der zeitgenössischen Textbücher* (Eisenstadt, 1959)

M. T. Herrick: *Italian Plays 1500–1700 in the University of Illinois Library* (Urbana, 1960)

B. Corrigan: *Catalogue of the Italian Plays 1500–1700 in the Library of the University of Toronto* (Toronto, 1961)

F. Pitzu: 'Bibliografia della Collana Palatina di drammi', *Studi secenteschi*, ii (1961), 293–320

G. Favilli: 'Bibliografia della Collana Palatina di commedie', *Studi secenteschi*, iii (1962), 184–225; iv (1963), 193–223

P. Kneidl: *Teatrali Zàmecki knihovny z Radenina* (Prague, 1962–3)

R. De Bello: 'Bibliografia della Collana Palatina delle Pastorali', *Studi secenteschi* (Florence), v (1964), 161–74; vi (1965), 285–98

P. Kneidl: *Libreta italské opery v Praza v 18. stoleté*, *Stakovská krikovna*, ii (1967), 115

L. G. Clubb: *Italian Plays (1500–1700) in the Folger Library: a Bibliography with Introduction* (Florence, 1968)

A. Caselli: *Catalogo delle opere liriche pubblicate in Italia* (Florence, 1969) [librettos of first performances only]

N. Pirrotta: 'Early Venetian Libretti at Los Angeles', *Essays in Musicology in Honor of Dragan Plamenac* (Pittsburgh, 1969); repr. in *Music and Culture in Italy from the Middle Ages to the Baroque* (Cambridge, MA, 1984), 317–24

E. Thiel and G. Rohr, eds.: *Katalog der Herzog August-Bibliothek Wolfenbüttel*, xiv: *Die Libretti: Verzeichnis der bis 1800 erschienenen Textbücher* (Frankfurt, 1970)

E. Esposito: *Annali di Antonio De Rossi stampatore in Roma (1695–1755)* (Florence, 1972) [libretto publisher]

E. I. Zimmerman: *American Opera Librettos 1767–1825* (diss., U. of Tennessee, 1972)

C. Sartori: *Primo tentativo di un catalogo unico dei libretti italiani a stampa fino all'anno 1800* (MS, Milan, 1973–) [enlarged as Sartori 1990]

F. Degrada and M. T. Muraro, eds.: *Antonio Vivaldi da Venezia all'Europa* (Milan, 1978) [exhibition catalogue of 56 librettos, 1713–50]

C. Krombiegel and P. Krause: *Katalog der vor 1800 gedruckten Opernlibretti in der Musikbibliothek der Stadt Leipzig* (Leipzig, 1981–2)

A. L. Bellini, B. Brizi and A. G. Pensa: *I libretti vivaldiani: recensione e collazione dei testimoni a stampa* (Florence, 1982)

E. Mori: *Libretti di melodrammi e balli del secolo XVIII: Fondo Ferraioli della Biblioteca apostolica vaticana* (Florence, 1984)

F. Rossi: *Le opere musicali della Fondazione 'Querini- Stampalia' di Venezia* (Turin, 1984), 185–600 [573 opera librettos]

C. Timms: 'Handelian and Other Librettos in Birmingham Central Library', *ML*, lxv (1984), 141–67

F. Melisi: *Conservatorio di Musica 'S. Pietro a Majella' di Napoli: Biblioteca: Catalogo dei libretti d'opera in musica dei secoli XVII e XVIII* (Naples, 1985)

J. S. Powell: 'The Musical Sources of the Bibliothèque-Musée de la Comédie Française', *CMc*, no. 41 (1986), 7–45

M. L. Dorsi: *I libretti d'opera dal 1800 al 1825 nella Biblioteca del Conservatorio 'G. Verdi' di Milano* (Milan, 1987)

S. Franchi: *Drammaturgia romana: Repertorio bibliografico cronologico dei testi drammatici pubblicati a Roma e nel Lazio, secolo XVII* (Rome, 1988)

E. Gibson: 'Nicola F. Haym's Collection of Opera Libretti', *The Royal Academy of Music 1719–1728: the Institution and its Directors* (New York, 1989) [sale of 1730]

F. Melisi: *Conservatorio di Musica 'S. Pietro a Majella' di Napoli: Biblioteca: Catalogo dei libretti per musica dell'ottocento: 1800–1860* (Lucca, 1990)

C. Sartori: *I libretti italiani a stampa dalle origini al 1800: Catalogo analitico con 16 indici* (Cuneo, 1990–)

'RISM Libretto Project' [worldwide catalogue, in progress; components of this incl. on-line catalogue of librettos in US libraries (see *Notes*, xliii (1986–7), 19–35) and catalogue and database of pre-1801 librettos in the British Isles (see J. Smith: 'Catalogue of pre-1800 libretti in the British Isles', *FAM*, xxvii (1980), 215f., and 'Catalogue and database of pre-1801 librettos held in the British Isles', *Brio*, xxi (1984), 12–14)]

(ii) Anthologies, reprints, modern editions

F. Scala: *Il teatro delle favole rappresentative* [commedia dell'arte plots] (Venice, 1611) [ed. F. Marotti (Milan, 1976); Eng. trans. in H. F. Salerno: *Scenarios of the Commedia dell'arte* (New York, 1967)]

Recueil general des opera (Paris, 1703–45) [with interesting prefaces]

E. Gherardi, ed.: *Le théâtre italien de Gherardi* (Paris, 1717, 5/1721; rev. 1733–53 as *Le nouveau théâtre italien*)

A. R. Le Sage and d'Orneval: *Le Théâtre de la Foire ou l'Opéra Comique* (Paris, 1721–37)

Les parodies du nouveau Théâtre Italien, ou Receuil de parodies représentées sur le Théâtre de l'Hôtel de Bourgogne...avec les airs gravés (Paris, 1738)

O. Diodati, ed.: *Biblioteca teatrale italiana scelta e disposta da O. Diodati ... Con un suo capitolo in verso per ogni tomo, correlativo alle cose teatrali, per servire di trattato completo di drammaturgia* (Lucca, 1762–5)

C.-S. Favart: *Théâtre de M. [et Mme] Favart* (Paris, 1763–77)

J. A. Hiller: *Ueber Metastasio und seine Werke: Neben einigen Uebersetzungen aus demselben* (Leipzig, 1786) [some whole dramas translated]

Theatro Comico Portuguez ou Colecção das operas portuguezas que se representárão na casa do Theatro Público do Bairro Alto de Lisboa (Lisbon, 1744, also 1787–92)

J. Hoole, ed.: *Pietro Metastasio: Dramas and other Poems* (London, 1800)

G. Gherardini, ed.: *Raccolta di melodrammi seri scritti nel secolo XVIII* (Milan, 1822)

——: *Raccolta di melodrammi giocosi scritti nel secolo XVIII* (Milan, 1826)

J. Tittmann, ed.: *Ausgewählte Dichtungen von Martin Opitz* (Leipzig, 1869) [incl. *Dafne*]

A. E. Scribe: *Oeuvres complètes* (Paris, 1874–85)

E. d'Auriac: *Théâtre de la Foire: Recueil de pièces représentées aux foires St.-Germain et St.-Laurent, précedé d'un essai historique sur les spectacles forains* (Paris, 1878)

H. Morley, ed.: *Burlesque Plays and Poems* (London, 1885) [Carey's *Chrononhotonthologos*, pp.183–95]

M. Drack: *Le Théâtre de La Foire, la Comédie Italienne et l'Opéra-Comique, recueil de pièces choisies jouées de la fin du XVIIe siècle aux premières années du XIXe siècle* (Paris, 1889)

A. Solerti: *Gli albori del melodramma* (Milan, Palermo, Naples, 1904–5)

——: *Musica ballo e drammatica alla corte medicea dal 1600 al 1637* (Florence, 1905)

E. Cotarelo y Mori, ed.: *Colección de entremeses, loas, bailes,*

jácaras y mojingangas desde fines del siglo XVI á medíados del XVII (Madrid, 1911)

G. Parini: *Opere*, ed. G. Mazzoni (Florence, 1925, rev. 1947)

A. Areana, ed.: *Scipione Maffei, opere drammatiche e poesie varie* (Bari, 1928) [*La fida ninfa*, pp.226–68]

M. Fehr, ed.: *Drammi scelti* (Bari, 1929) [incl. 4 operas, 2 oratorios by Zeno]

R. Wagner: *Skizzen und Entwürfe zur Ring-Dichtung*, ed. O. Strobel (Munich, 1930)

W. Flemming: *Die Oper*, v: *Barockdrama* (Leipzig, 1933) [17th-century German librettos]

C. Calcaterra: *Lirici del seicento e dell'Arcadia* (Milan, 1936) [incl. many aria texts]

The Authentic Librettos of the Italian Operas (New York, 1939)

L. Da Ponte: *Tre libretti per Mozart*, ed. P. Lecaldano (Milan, 1956) [collates librettos and scores]

L. Fassò, ed.: *Teatro del seicento* (Milan, 1956)

A. Della Corte, ed.: *Drammi per musica dal Rinuccini allo Zeno* (Turin, 1958)

W. H. Auden and others: *The Great Operas of Mozart: Complete Librettos...English Versions by W. H. Auden etc.* (London, 1962)

J. de La Fontaine: *Oeuvres Complètes*, ed. Jean Marmier (Paris, 1965) [incl. *Daphné, Galateé, Astrée*]

V. Viviani, ed.: *I libretti di Rossini* (Milan, 1965) [4 most famous operas]

E. Zola: *Oeuvres complètes*, ed. H. Mittérand (Paris, 1966–70)

S. J. Trussler, ed.: *Burlesque Plays of the Eighteenth Century* (London, 1969) [Carey etc.]

C. Girdlestone: *La tragédie en musique (1673–1750) considérée comme genre littéraire* (Geneva and Paris, 1972) [extracts from librettos, pp.347–409]

A. Schoenberg: *Sämtliche Werke*, Abt. III, B, vii/1, *Von heute auf morgen* (Mainz and Vienna, 1972) [incl. libretto and draft]

L. J. Morrissey: *The Grub-Street Opera* (Edinburgh, 1973) [ballad opera librettos]

P. Isotta, ed.: *Gioacchino Rossini: Mosè in Egitto, Azione tragico-sacro; Moïse et Pharaon, Opéra en quatre actes; Mosè, Melodramma sacro in quattro atti* (Turin, 1974)

Journal of the Donizetti Society (1974–) [some issues incl. librettos and trans.: ii (1975), *Les martyrs*; iii (1977), *Maria Stuarda*]

W. Rubsamen, ed.: *The Ballad Opera: a Collection of 171 Original Texts of Musical Plays Printed in Photo-Facsimile* (New York, 1974)

M. Turchi, ed.: *Opere di Gabriello Chiabrera e lirici del classicismo barocco* (Turin, 2/1974) [also critical dialogues, e.g. *Geri*]

L. Baldacci: *Tutti i libretti di Verdi* (Milan, 1975)

Richard Wagner: Sämtliche Werke, ed. C. Dahlhaus, E. Voss and others (Mainz, 1970–) [*Dokumentenbände* incl. prose drafts, MS and published librettos with variants, published and MS scores and notes on further variants and versions and authorized translations]

H. M. Brown, ed.: *Italian Opera, 1640–1770: Major Unpublished Works in a Central Baroque Tradition* (New York, 1977–84) [incl. 81 facsimile librettos]

L'avant-scène opéra (Paris, 1979–) [incl. librettos]

The Works of Henry Purcell, iii: *Dido and Aeneas* (Sevenoaks, 1979) [incl. facs. of unique libretto]

D. Herbert, ed.: *The Operas of Benjamin Britten: the Complete Librettos* (London, 1979)

ENO Opera Guides, ed. N. John (London, 1980–) [incl. librettos; see esp. *The Operas of Michael Tippett* (1985) and *The Stage Works of Béla Bartók* (1991)]

P. I. Martello: *Teatro*, ed. Annibal Noce (Bari, 1980)

R. Meyer: *Die Hamburger Oper: eine Sammlung von Texten der Hamburger Oper aus der Zeit 1678–1730*, i–iii (Munich, 1980), iv (Milwood, NY, 1984)

G. Muresu: *La parola cantata: studi sul melodramma italiano del settecento* (Rome, 1982) [incl. 3 Casti librettos]

B. S. Brook, ed.: *French Opera in the Seventeenth and Eighteenth Centuries* (New York, 1983–) [incl. librettos]

G. Morelli, R. Strohm and T. Walker, eds.: *Drammaturgia musicale veneta* [DMV] (Milan, 1983–) [incl. librettos]

E. Voss: *Die Entstehung der Meistersinger von Nürnberg: Geschichten und Geschichte* (Mainz, 1983) [incl. facs. of 1862 libretto]

E. M. Ferrando: *Tutti i libretti di Puccini* (Milan, 1984)

T. Bauman, ed.: *German Opera 1770–1800* (New York, 1985) [incl. 20 facs. librettos, vols. xviii–xxii]

J. M. Roberts, ed.: *Handel Sources: Materials for the Study of Handel's Borrowing* (New York, 1986) [with 11 librettos]

E. Warburton, ed.: *Johann Christian Bach 1735–1782: the Collected Works* (New York, 1986–7) [incl. facs. of librettos]

C. Pollak, ed.: *Franz Schubert: Bühnenwerke: kritische Gesamtausgabe der Texte* (Tutzing, 1988) [incidental music, operas, oratorios]

E. T. Harris, ed.: *The Librettos of Handel's Operas: a Collection of Seventy-One Librettos Documenting Handel's Operatic Career* (New York, 1989)

F. de Lemene: *Scherzi e favole per musica*, ed. M. G. Accorsi (Modena, 1990)

B. Baselt, ed.: *Oreste*, Hallische Händel-Ausgabe (Kassel and Halle, 1991) [incl. libretto, with facs. and Ger. and Eng. trans.]

E. Warburton, ed.: *The Librettos of Mozart's Operas* (New York, 1992–) [facs., incl. pasticcios]

L. Bianconi and G. La Face Bianconi: *I libretti italiani di Georg Friedrich Händel e le loro fonti* (Florence, 1992–)

BRIAN TROWELL

Libuše. 'Festival' opera in three acts by BEDŘICH SMETANA to a libretto by JOSEF WENZIG; Prague, National Theatre, 11 June 1881.

Libuše *Princess of Bohemia*	soprano
Přemysl ze Stadic	tenor
Chrudoš od Otavy ⎱ *brothers*	bass
Šťáhlav na Radbuze ⎰	baritone
Lutobor z Dobroslavského Chlumce *their uncle*	bass
Radovan od Kamena mosta	baritone
Krasava *Lutobor's daughter*	soprano
Radmila *sister of the two brothers*	contralto
Four reapers (offstage)	soprano, soprano, contralto, tenor

Elders, chieftains and warriors, young women and girls from Libuše's court, Přemysl's retainers, people

Setting Vyšehrad ([a high castle] part of present-day Prague) and rugged countryside nearby, and Stadice, in pagan times

Smetana's fourth opera, *Libuše*, came about in the same way as his previous one, *Dalibor*. Wenzig's text, *Libušas Urtheilsspruch und Vermählung*, was ready in the spring of 1866 and was translated into Czech by Ervín Špindler, again preserving the original syllable counts and stresses of the German. Špindler completed his work by February 1868; a few additions were written directly in Czech by Wenzig. Smetana did not date his piano sketches or mention the work in correspondence or diaries, but the full score is dated 2 September 1871 (Act 1), 18 February 1872 (Act 2) and 12 November 1872 (Act 3).

Libuše was not performed for another nine years. At the time of its composition Smetana had thought it suitable for the coronation of Franz Josef as Czech king; this (and the constitutional changes it implied) did not come about so Smetana kept the work in reserve for the opening of the National Theatre, whose building continued in fits and starts during the 1870s. *Libuše* won first prize in the National Theatre competition and its première accordingly opened the theatre. Since then the opera has been held in reserve by the Czechs as a festival opera for days of special national celebration.

The overture is Smetana's grandest. It opens with ceremonial, antiphonal brass (ex.1); its main section develops a slow processional theme (ex.2) and a more rhythmic, triumphant one (ex.3).

Ex.1

Ex.2

Ex.3

ACT 1: 'Libuše's Judgment'

1.i *Libuše's chamber at Vyšehrad, with a view of the Vltava valley* Libuše, who has inherited the throne of Bohemia from her father, is about to arbitrate in a land dispute. She is seen first with her female retinue before leaving for the place of judgment, with exx.1 and 2 now clearly identified as her processional music. Radmila and Krasava remain. In a passionate outburst Krasava reveals her disturbed state, but refuses to disclose its cause.

1.ii *An open space at Vyšehrad, a lime-tree in the background* An agitated prelude suggests violent events ahead. As a counterpart to scene i, this scene begins with male voices: a chorus, and then the two brothers, whose rivalry their uncle Lutobor is unable to quell. Exx.1 and 2 announce the arrival of Libuše, and at her invitation each brother states his claim. She pronounces that they should share the land but Chrudoš (the elder) refuses to accept judgment from a woman. So Libuše asks the people to choose a husband for her. In chorus, the people insist she should choose as her heart prompts. Her choice is Přemysl (ex.3). A substantial choral ensemble (with the solo voices of Libuše and Radmila added) and Libuše's processional music conclude the act.

ACT 2: 'Libuše's Marriage'

2.i *A mountainous, wooded landscape, with a grave mound at the back* In revenge for Chrudoš's seeming indifference to her, Krasava had pretended to love his brother Šťáhlav, thereby alienating her father Lutobor and provoking the dispute between the brothers. Penitently at the grave of the brothers' father, she now restores the peace, first by placating her father, and then by confessing the truth to Chrudoš. This scene, added to the original libretto, is the most emotional part

*'Libuše' (Smetana), Act 3
scene i: design by the
studio of Carlo Brioschi,
Hermann Burghart and
Johann Kautsky for the
original production which
opened the National
Theatre, Prague, on 11
June 1881*

of the opera, with fine declamatory passages for Krasava, Lutobor and Chrudoš. Šť'áhlav and Radmila join the others in the concluding ensemble of reconciliation.

2.ii *The countryside near Stadice* A bucolic atmosphere is established by the offstage solo chorus of reapers, framing Přemysl's ruminations, a multi-tempo aria, 'Již plane slunce' ('The sun now burns'), as he contemplates the harvest and his seemingly unrequited love for Libuše. The tempo quickens with the full chorus now on stage singing a polka-like chorus to greet Přemysl and celebrate the harvest. They go off, leaving Přemysl thoughtful again in the best-known aria of the opera, an invocation to the sacred lime-trees: 'Ó vy lípy'. He is surprised by the approaching delegation, led by Radovan, to offer him a throne and a wife. Urged by the chorus, Přemysl accepts, and takes leave of his home. The act concludes with an ensemble as all set off for Vyšehrad and Libuše.

ACT 3: 'Prophecy'
    Libuše's chambers at Vyšehrad After the prelude Libuše, with her court, welcomes the union of Krasava and Chrudoš, forgives the latter and, after the ensemble of six soloists, prepares to meet her bridegroom. A substantial chorus and a long orchestral march herald Přemysl's entrance. He greets his people and his consort (a perfunctory duet of 14 bars), and after rebuking the brothers for their quarrel, concludes the peace. A full ensemble appears to bring everything to an end.

But now there is a dramatic interruption. Libuše is a prophetess and she now looks into the future of the Czech nation. A series of *tableaux vivants* follow as famous characters from Czech history appear to Libuše's commentary. The mood darkens in the fifth, depicting the last native Czech ruler. In the sixth and last (the Prague castle magically illuminated) Libuše proclaims in the best known passage of the opera that her beloved Czech nation will not die ('Můj drahý národ český neskoná'), a cry enthusiastically taken up by all on stage.

*   *   *

Thus concludes in full monumental splendour the opera that Smetana regarded as his finest (few would agree today) and the most overtly nationalist opera written by a Czech composer. Yet its credentials as a uniquely Czech work rest on shaky foundations. The libretto, originally prepared in German, is based partly on a notorious 19th-century forgery; the rest comes from a source almost as dubious, which gave rise to a series of 17th-century Italian operas and 19th-century German plays. The opera's patriotic resonance dates only from the late 19th century and is due mostly to the carefully implanted national images such as the 'Czech' lime-trees, and to its association with the opening of the National Theatre.   JOHN TYRRELL

Licence. A term with two distinct meanings in connection with early opera in London: (*a*) permission to operate a theatre, usually obtained annually from the Lord Chamberlain; and (*b*) written approval for the words of an opera, obtained from the Lord Chamberlain's office before the première of any new work.

Patent grants by Charles II in the 1660s created a theatre monopoly in London. When Sir John Vanbrugh built the Haymarket theatre as an opera house in 1704, it operated on the basis of licences granted by the Lord Chamberlain 'at pleasure'. From 1719 to 1740 opera was staged there under the 21-year patent granted to the Royal Academy of Music by George I; after its expiration, the theatre reverted to occasional licences. No other opera patent as such was ever granted in England: George III agreed to one in 1790, but it was blocked by the Lord Chancellor. The theatre-licensing procedure finally eroded during the second quarter of the 19th century.

The Licensing Act of 1737 both codified the monopoly and created a strict censorship process (*see* CENSORSHIP). Any script performed in a London theatre had to be approved by the licenser; his deletions and amendments had to be strictly observed under penalty of heavy fines and imprisonment. This censorship procedure was not finally abolished until 1968.

L. W. Conolly: *The Censorship of English Drama, 1737–1824* (San Marino, CA, 1976)

V. J. Liesenfeld: *The Licensing Act of 1737* (Madison, WI, 1984)

J. Milhous and R. D. Hume: 'The Charter for the Royal Academy of Music', *ML*, lxvii (1986), 50–58

C. Price, J. Milhous and R. D. Hume: 'A Royal Opera House in Leicester Square (1790)', *COJ*, ii (1990), 1–27

ROBERT D. HUME

Licenza (It.: 'licence'). In the 17th and 18th centuries, a passage or cadenza inserted into a piece 'at licence' by a performer. It could also signify an epilogue inserted into a stage work (opera or play) in honour of a patron's birthday or wedding, or for some other festive occasion. This could consist of a single aria, or a group of recitatives and arias; choruses might also be included. The *licenza* could be an integral part of the main work (as in *Costanza e Fortezza*, 1723) or could be written later by a different composer and librettist: in 1667 the Emperor Leopold I composed his own *licenza* for the Viennese performances of Antonio Cesti's *Le disgrazie d'amore*. Mozart included a *licenza* aria in his serenata *Il sogno di Scipione* (1772) in tribute to the Archbishop of Salzburg.

Liceo [Gran Teatro del Liceo; Gran Teatre del Liceu]. Theatre opened in 1847 in BARCELONA.

Licette, Miriam (*b* Chester, 9 Sept 1892; *d* Twyford, 11 Aug 1969). English soprano. She studied under Marchesi, Jean de Reszke and Sabbatini, making her début in Rome as Butterfly (1911). After further European appearances, she returned to England, and became one of the leading lyric sopranos, singing with the Beecham Opera Company (1916), the British National Opera Company (1922), and at Covent Garden (1919–29). Her roles included Mimì, Desdemona, Eva and Louise, and she was specially admired in Mozart. Her voice was pure and steady, with firmly placed tone and a remarkably even scale, well represented in Beecham's *Faust* recording.   J. B. STEANE

Licht ('Light'). The collective title of a projected cycle of seven operas by KARLHEINZ STOCKHAUSEN, each of which is named after a day of the week. Up to 1990 three had been completed and performed: DONNERSTAG AUS LICHT ('Thursday'), 1978–81; SAMSTAG AUS LICHT ('Saturday'), 1981–3; and MONTAG AUS LICHT ('Monday'), 1984–8. The cycle, first conceived in 1977, is scheduled for completion in 2002.

Licht, writes Stockhausen's biographer Michael Kurtz, is an 'attempt to create a cosmic World Theatre which summarizes and intensifies his lifelong concern: the unity of music and religion, allied to the vision of an essentially musical mankind'. Light is to be understood here as a symbol of both the Divinity and divine revelation. The work draws its names and symbols from a variety of religious traditions: the three main protagonists of the cycle are Eve, Lucifer and the archangel Michael.

Inevitably, comparisons have been made with Wagner's *Ring* cycle. Apart from the sheer scale of the project (the operas to date are, on average, of *Walküre* length), the most obvious points of similarity are: the cyclic nature of the operas; the musical integration of the cycle through the pervasive use of three melodic 'formulae' (extensions of serialism) for the main characters, welded together in a triple 'superformula'; the conception of opera as a medium for socio-spiritual reform; the

integration of words, music and spectacle as *Gesamtkunstwerk*. In this latter respect Stockhausen goes much further than Wagner, supplying not only words and music, but also highly detailed stage movement and choreography. Perhaps the most striking aspect of Stockhausen's conception of opera is that it removes the primacy of the voice: instrumental music, vocal music and gesture are equally privileged components.   RICHARD TOOP

Lichtenstein, Karl August, Freiherr von (*b* Lahm, Franconia, 8 Sept 1767; *d* Berlin, 10 Sept 1845). German composer and theatre manager. After spending his childhood in Gotha, where his father was a government official, and further education at Göttingen, he served for a while with the English army before entering Hanoverian service; his opera *Glück und Zufall*, to his own libretto, was performed at Hanover in 1793. In 1797 he was appointed manager of the court opera in Dessau, whose new house opened on 26 December 1798 with a performance of his opera *Bathmendi*. Apart from his administrative responsibilities and the works he wrote, he and his wife frequently performed in operas. His Singspiel *Die steinerne Braut* proved very successful in 1799; a duet from it was published in the *Allgemeine musikalische Zeitung*.

In 1800, following financial difficulties after an ambitious and artistically successful guest season at Leipzig, Lichtenstein left Dessau for Vienna, where he became Kapellmeister and artistic director under Baron von Braun, Intendant of the Hoftheater, for three years. *Bathmendi* was a failure when, newly revised, it was given on 16 April 1801. Five years later Lichtenstein gave up theatrical activities and returned to diplomacy, as minister to the Duke of Saxe-Hildburghausen, but in 1811 he went to Bamberg and in 1813 became director of the theatre. He also took up composing again, with *Die Waldburg* (1811), *Imago* (1813–14) and a considerable number of other stage works. In 1814 Lichtenstein moved from Bamberg to Strasbourg, as musical director. He returned to Bamberg in 1817, and in 1823, after a brief stay in Dresden, he settled in Berlin, where his opera *Die Edelknaben* was given. After a period of responsibility for the spoken theatre, he took up an appointment at the opera in 1825. He was pensioned in 1832 though he continued to adapt, translate and even compose stage works.

In addition to his own operas, Lichtenstein provided librettos for other composers (including a revision of *Agnes von Hohenstaufen* for Spontini in 1837), and he translated or arranged nearly 20 operas by some of the leading composers of the day.

Glück und Zufall (komische Oper, 2, Lichtenstein), Hanover, 26 April 1793

Knall und Fall, Bamberg, 1795

Bathmendi (grosse allegorisch-komische Oper, 2, E. W. Behrisch), Dessau, Hof, 26 Dec 1798; rev. version, Vienna, Hof, 16 April 1801

Die steinerne Braut (Spl, Lichtenstein), Dessau, Hof, 25 April 1799

Ende gut, alles gut (komische Oper, 1, F. X. Huber), Dessau, Hof, 26 Oct 1800

Mitgefühl (Liederspiel, 1, Troitzske), Dessau, Hof, 26 Oct 1800

Der Kaiser als [und der] Zimmermann, oder Frauenwerth (grosse komische Oper, 3, Lichtenstein, after J.-N. Bouilly), Strasbourg, 22 June 1814

Imago, die Tochter der Zwietracht, 1813–14, ?unperf.

Das Mädchen aus der Fremde (Operette, 3), Bamberg, National, 1821

Die Waldburg, 1811 (2, Lichtenstein), Dresden, 11 June 1822

Die Edelknaben, oder Zur guten Stunde (Spl, 2, Lichtenstein, after N. Dezède), Berlin, Kgl, 27 May 1823

Jerusalem (lyrisches Drama, 2, Lichtenstein), Bamberg, National, 1824

Singethee und Liedertafel (Spl, 2, Lichtenstein), Berlin, 25 March 1825

Die deutschen Herren in Nürnberg (grosse Oper, 3, Lichtenstein, after E. T. A. Hoffmann), Berlin, 14 March 1834

Der Gluthengeist, ? Darmstadt

Trübsale eines Hofbankiers (komische Oper), sent to Dessau in 1838, ? unperf.

*

ADB (R. Eitner); *SteigerO*; *WurzbachL*

G. Schilling: *Das musikalische Europa* (Speyer, 1842), 210

J. Schladebach and E. Bernsdorf: *Neues Universal-Lexikon der Tonkunst*, ii (Dresden, 1856)

C. Schäffer and C. Hartmann: *Die königlichen Theater in Berlin: statistischer Rückblick* (Berlin, 1886)

F. Leist: 'Geschichte des Theaters in Bamberg', *Bericht des historischen Vereins zu Bamberg*, iv (Bamberg, 1893)

M. von Prosky: *Das herzogliche Theater zu Dessau* (Dessau, 2/ 1894)

G. Fischer: *Musik in Hannover* (Hanover, 2/1903)

F. Schnapp, ed.: *E. T. A. Hoffmanns Briefwechsel*, iii (Munich, 1969)

——: *E. T. A. Hoffmann: Tagebücher* (Munich, 1971)

PETER BRANSCOMBE

Lickl, Johann Georg (*b* Korneuburg, Lower Austria, 11 April 1769; *d* Fünfkirchen [now Pécs], Hungary, 12 May 1843). Austrian composer. Orphaned at an early age, he studied music with the Korneuburg church organist. In 1785 he went to Vienna, teaching music and himself studying with Albrechtsberger and Haydn. He was appointed organist at the Carmelite Church in the Leopoldstadt, where Eybler was choirmaster. From about 1789 (or later) he was on the music staff of Schikaneder's Freihaus-Theater auf der Wieden, from 1793 contributing complete or partial scores to a series of popular Singspiels and plays. For the new Theater an der Wien he wrote *Der Brigitten-Kirchtag* in 1802, and in 1812 he supplied the Leopoldstadt theatre with a comic opera, *Slawina von Pommern*. Despite these successes, church music was his particular interest and in 1805 he was appointed *regens chori* at the cathedral in Fünfkirchen, where he lived and worked for nearly 40 years.

first performed in Vienna

Die verdeckten Sachen (Spl, 2, E. Schikaneder), Freihaus, 26 Sept 1789, vs *I-Fc*, songs *A-Wgm*, collab. F. X. Gerl and B. Schack [2nd 'Anton' Spl]

Der Zauberpfeil, oder Das Kabinett der Wahrheit (grosse Oper, 2, Schikaneder), Freihaus, 9 June 1793

Das Zigeunermädchen (Lustspiel mit Gesang, 3, J. A. Haselbeck), Freihaus, 10 Nov 1793

Die Haushaltung nach der Mode, oder Der 30-jährige Bernhardl (Spl, 2, Haselbeck), Freihaus, 15 March 1794

Der Bruder von Kagran (komische Oper, 2, M. Stegmayer), Freihaus, 2 June 1797

Der Kampf mit dem Fürsten der Finsternis (komische Oper, 2, J. Perinet), Freihaus, 20 April 1799 [sequel to Astaroth der Verführer, perf. Freihaus, 13 April 1799; music by Haibel and Seyfried]

Fausts Leben, Taten und Höllenfahrt (romantisches Schauspiel mit Gesang, M. Voll), Freihaus, 28 June 1799

Der vermeinte Hexenmeister (ländliche Operette, 2), Freihaus, 29 March 1800

Der Orgelspieler, oder Die Abenteuer im Gebirge (komisches Spl, 3), Freihaus, 2 Aug 1800

Der Durchmarsch (Spl, 3, Schildbach), Freihaus, 27 Dec 1800

Der Brigitten-Kirchtag (Spl, 2, J. Richter), An der Wien, 3 July 1802

Slawina von Pommern (komische Oper, 2), Leopoldstadt, 29 Feb 1812

*

ADB (R. Eitner); *GerberNL*; *WurzbachL*

A. Gross: Obituary, *Allgemeine Wiener Musik Zeitung*, no.84 (15 July 1843), 349

J. Schladebach and E. Bernsdorf: *Neues Universal-Lexikon der Tonkunst*, ii (Dresden, 1856)
PETER BRANSCOMBE

Lidón, José [Josef] (*b* Béjar, nr Salamanca, ?1746; *d* Madrid, 11 ?Feb 1827). Spanish composer. He was appointed organist at the Real Colegio in Madrid in 1768, 'maestro de estilo italiano' at the Royal College of Boy Singers there in 1771 and in 1805 became master of the royal chapel and rector of the Real Colegio. He wrote some 50 pieces for organ and numerous sacred vocal works. His *drama heroico Glaura y Cariolano* (or *Cariolán*), given at the Teatro Príncipe in Madrid in about 1791 (*E-Mn*), is an *opera seria* in Castilian in which Lidón set out to emulate 'la grande ópera italiana'. The libretto, adapted anonymously from a 16th-century epic by Ercilla, conveys a remarkable cross-cultural admiration for the noble Araucanian Indian of Chile. He also is thought to have written a zarzuela, *El barón de Illescas* (now lost).

*

J. Subirá: *Historia de la música teatral en España* (Barcelona, 1945), 123–4

A. Martín Moreno: *Historia de la música española: vol. iv: siglo XVIII* (Madrid, 1985), 58ff
JACK SAGE

Liebe der Danae, Die ('The Love of Danae'). *Heitere Mythologie* ('cheerful mythology') in three acts by RICHARD STRAUSS to a libretto by JOSEPH GREGOR; Salzburg, Festspielhaus, 14 August 1952 (on 16 August 1944 a public dress rehearsal for a performance subsequently cancelled had been given there).

Jupiter	baritone
Merkur [Mercury]	tenor
Pollux *King of Eos*	tenor
Danae *his daughter*	soprano
Xanthe *her servant*	soprano
Midas *King of Lydia*	tenor
Four Kings *nephews of Pollux*	two tenors, two basses
Semele	soprano
Europa	soprano
Alkmene [Alcmene] *their wives*	mezzo-soprano
Leda	contralto
Four Guards	basses

Chorus of creditors (tenors and basses); servants, people

Setting The island kingdom of Eos and an Eastern land; mythological times

As far back as 1920 Strauss's great collaborator Hofmannsthal had proposed Danae as the heroine of a mythological opera, though they settled instead upon Helen of Troy (*Die ägyptische Helena*). After the writer's untimely death in 1929, the composer took Stefan Zweig as librettist (*Die schweigsame Frau*), then lost him and accepted his friend Gregor as substitute: first to fill out Zweig's sketch for *1648* (to become *Friedenstag*), next to write his own *Daphne* – under Strauss's correction – and at last, in 1936, to develop the Danae idea. Gregor's version was entirely his own, but like Hofmannsthal he had the irresistible if unauthentic notion of connecting the unlucky King Midas with the maiden whom Zeus visited as a shower of gold. Strauss disliked the first draft; then Hofmannsthal's published sketch, which he had quite forgotten, came to his notice, and he pressed Gregor to adopt its story line. There was

'Die Liebe der Danae'
(Richard Strauss): the
final scene in Act 1 of the
original production at the
Festspielhaus, Salzburg,
14 August 1952, with sets
and costumes by Emil
Preetorius (Jupiter, centre,
was sung by Paul
Schöffler)

long, painful rewriting, and as usual the composer wounded his subservient partner by taking outside advice (from Zweig and Clemens Krauss again, and the director Lothar Wallerstein) and thrusting it upon him.

The unlikely brew that resulted was different from either of the original sketches. On the one hand, Strauss insisted, as often before, that he was aiming at comic-operetta style, though he wanted to take full orchestral advantage of the 'magical' points in the action; the solemn Gregor, who had no gift for lascivious farce, did his best to comply. On the other, Gregor persuaded him that Zeus must have a leading part (Hofmannsthal had left him out, and Strauss had refused to let Gregor put him into *Daphne*). Strauss's empathy with their aging, wiser-but-sadder 'Jupiter' – their choice of the Roman name remains a puzzle – elevated the role to that of Composer's Own Voice: the last of his idealized self-portraits, not farcical at all. The score was finished in June 1940.

Strauss was reluctant to see this 'oeuvre posthume' staged during his lifetime, and after the 1944 première (meant to celebrate his 80th birthday) was aborted by Goebbels, when the Allies' Second Front threatened, he never sanctioned another performance. The famous Salzburg *Generalprobe* had boasted Hotter as Jupiter, Ursuleac as Danae and Horst Taubmann as Midas, conducted by Krauss (Ursuleac's husband) and directed by Rudolf Hartmann; for the posthumous official première in 1952 – memorably if imperfectly recorded – there were new principals, Paul Schöffler, Annelies Kupper and Josef Gostic. *Die Liebe der Danae* has enjoyed no continuing life, and remains virtually unknown. It is long, and needs costly stage-effects, with orchestra and cast on the same expensive scale. Like the Isotta and Carlotta of *Die schweigsame Frau*, Xanthe, Mercury and the four queens demand highly expert singing in minor roles. Evidently Strauss imagined *Die Liebe der Danae* as his swansong, an unconstrained last testament, and faithful Gregor devised opportunities for the Master to exercise all his familiar strengths. A clever production, on a suitably outsize budget, may yet show it to be a better piece than is generally assumed.

ACT 1 *The throne room of King Pollux* After a few bars of chromatic bustle, the curtain rises on a crowd of angry creditors in the dilapidated throne room. Old King Pollux is broke, and everything on Eos is in hock. He emerges to assure them, over sceptical protests, that help is on the way: to find a rich husband for his daughter Danae, his four royal nephews have travelled far and wide bearing her portrait, and now King Midas is interested. The creditors know that Danae scorns men; frustrated, they smash up the throne and seize the pieces. This brisk tenor-and-chorus number ends with a curtain, and the orchestra begins to depict the Golden Rain – the guise in which Jupiter has secretly been visiting Danae. Amid the G♭ shimmer a Jupiter theme enters (in C, of course), and the interlude reaches an erotic peak; while it subsides, the sleeping Danae begins to be visible through a glittering shower. On waking she describes her heavenly dream to Xanthe, and their voices twine in rapturous duet, recalling *Arabella*. An offstage march (in quintuple time) signals the return of the nephews; Danae swears to accept no man who cannot bring her the joy of gold.

The march becomes an entr'acte. In a pillared yard with a sea view, the anxious court and creditors greet the triumphant travellers – the nephews, their pages and their four queens. (These last all happen to be old loves of Jupiter: he came to Semele in the guise of a cloud, to Europa as a bull, to Alcmene in her husband's likeness and to Leda as a swan.) Together they recount their journeyings, and how at last in Lydia the portrait captured King Midas's heart, and turned to gold at his touch (whereupon the music brightens into F♯). It veers into B♭ and then F when Midas's ship is seen, and everyone but Danae hurries to the harbour to welcome him. Alone and dreaming (in G♭ again), she is startled when the real Midas enters quietly (in sensible C). They find an instant rapport; but Midas pretends to be 'Chrysopher', a mere servant, for he is bound by a secret bargain. Jupiter longs to come to Danae as a man instead of a mineral; he gave a donkey-driver, Midas, the 'golden touch' so that as a king the latter could win her hand but cede the bridal bed to the god disguised as himself (as with Alcmene). Now the scene is transformed: golden minions come to dress Danae, the pillars melt away and 'Chrysopher' leads Danae towards her Lord of Dreams. The crowd at the quayside hails Jupiter-'Midas' as he alights from the ship and calls to her. Suddenly torn, Danae faints; 'Midas' stamps his foot, and thunder rolls.

ACT 2 *The nuptial chamber* A chattering prelude (in D) finds the superannuated queens carolling away while they deck the chamber. Embarrassed to learn that they all recognized him in Lydia, Jupiter begs them to keep silent for fear of Juno's wrath. Danae's coolness has whetted his appetite but raised a suspicion: he interrogates Midas about his meeting with her, warns him sternly and storms out. Danae enters in her bridal dress, escorted by the queens (who counsel her to hold to the handsome servant, not the fickle god). Alone with her, Midas confesses his true condition, demonstrating his two-edged gift by turning most of the chamber into gold. Irresistibly the scene grows into a joyful love duet, with a heroic E major unison. Imprudently, the mortal lovers embrace; darkness falls with a thunderclap, and as pale light returns Danae is seen to be a golden statue. Midas curses Jupiter, who retorts that it was Midas who broke their bargain. In vociferous competition, each pleads with Danae to accept his own terms – respectively, divine glory and destitution. (With *Daphne*, we seem to have been here before.) The voice within the statue chooses Midas. Amid thunder and lightning Danae revives and disappears into the darkness with him; Jupiter pronounces a bitter oration, lofty Db hardening into F minor at the end.

ACT 3 *A palm grove, by a dusty road* After a review of many familiar themes in a Molto allegro prelude, the curtain rises. Danae and Midas awaken in a daze (much like the Barak couple in *Die Frau ohne Schatten*). She knows now that it was the messenger she loved, not the gold, and he tells her the whole story of how he became 'Chrysopher'. They face their new, reduced situation with a naive duet, in Bb (like the one that ends *Rosenkavalier*, but no less like Tamino and Pamina after their trials), which the orchestra extends through an interlude.

A mountainous forest Jupiter is discovered deep in thought (richly spelt out in the orchestra). With a 6/8 scherzo, Mercury skips in to report malicious glee on Olympus over Danae's preferring a donkey-driver, ruin and despair on Eos – and the imminent arrival of the laughing queens. They tease and flatter Jupiter with reminiscences: they want him back. But he feels old now, and bids a dignified farewell to them all and indeed to earthly love. Suddenly Pollux, nephews and creditors burst in (echoing the first scene of the opera), demanding restitution for their lost Danae. Upon a hint from Mercury, Jupiter conjures up another Golden Rain and they follow it eagerly away, grabbing at coins. The whole scherzo ends with another Mercurial hint: may not poor Danae be susceptible now, after all?

A modest hut After an interlude of noble warmth and breadth (in C; Strauss called it 'Jupiter's resignation'), Danae is seen alone. In a limpid Bb aria (specially requested for Ursuleac), she sings of the loving peace she has found with Midas. When the god appears, disguised in a heavy burnous, Danae remembers that just such an 'old man' (Jupiter flinches) sent Midas on his dizzy career up and down. Seduction forgotten, a long, tenderly candid duologue ensues. It blossoms into a brief duet as they recall the Golden Rain; the 'Majaerzählung', Jupiter's rapt memory-vision (in A) of his early love for the spring-goddess Maia, inspires another duet. With a final Wotan-like benediction, the god departs. The music returns to Bb as the husband is heard coming home, and from Danae there is a glad cry (with a top C#): 'Midas!'

* * *

Musically, *Die Liebe der Danae* is without doubt an anthology of Strauss's familiar modes, but it offers much more than self-repetition. None of his other three post-Hofmannsthal operas had given full scope to his best strengths: in *Die schweigsame Frau* he overestimated his knack for closed-form numbers, the narrow dramatic terms of *Friedenstag* cramped him, the Freudian-pastoral *Daphne* was slightly bloodless. Gregor, like a liberal sweet-seller, gave the Great Composer everything he wanted for his *Danae* 'swansong'. If the resultant theatrical mishmash sets knotty problems for a director (not least the disproportionate length of Act 3), it allowed Strauss to weave his intricate thematic webs again, to devise vocal flights of every kind and to make his orchestra glow – in a new vein of seasoned maturity, weary but infinitely experienced and resourceful. *Capriccio*, his real operatic swansong, would be far more elegantly consistent; *Danae* is our last glimpse of the old unconfined Strauss, prodigal with importunate feeling.

DAVID MURRAY

Liebe im Narrenhause, Die ('Love in the Madhouse'). Komische Oper in two acts by CARL DITTERS VON DITTERSDORF to a libretto by GOTTLIEB STEPHANIE (the younger); Vienna, Kärntnertortheater, 12 April 1787.

Trübe (bass) has promised his daughter Constanze (soprano) to his friend Bast (bass), the supervisor of a lunatic asylum who believes himself on the brink of inheriting a considerable fortune from his brother. Constanze's lover Albert (tenor) feigns insanity in order to be admitted to the asylum, where Trübe has taken up residence in order to amuse himself with the antics of the inmates. An escape attempt by the lovers is foiled, but when Trübe learns that Bast's brother has left his fortune to none other than Albert, Trübe immediately gives them his blessing.

Stephanie's contemporaries found his story – especially its ridicule of the asylum's inmates – in very dubious taste. But Dittersdorf's music ensured the opera's popularity on nearly all German operatic stages. F. L. Schröder at Hamburg went so far as to rework a less offensive satire by Kurz-Bernardon (as *Orpheus der Zweyte*) in order to capitalize on the score.

THOMAS BAUMAN

Liebermann, Rolf (*b* Zürich, 14 Sept 1910). Swiss administrator and composer. He studied law at Zürich University and later studied conducting with Hermann Scherchen and composition with Wladimir Vogel. In 1950 he was appointed musical director of Swiss Radio and from 1957 held a similar post with North German Radio in Hamburg. From 1959 to 1973 he was director of the Staatsoper, where his administration was marked by a widening of the repertory to include many 20th-century operas, several of which he commissioned; he also attempted to reach a wider audience through televised productions. In 1973 he became general administrator of the Paris Opéra, a post he held for seven years. With Solti as musical director (1973–6) and Joan Ingpen as director of planning, Liebermann raised the standards of casting and production there to the highest international level. He commissioned the completion of Berg's *Lulu* (performed at the Opéra in 1979) and Messiaen's *Saint François d'Assise*; the latter was not however completed and performed until after

Liebermann had left Paris. From 1985, for three seasons, he was again director of the Hamburg Opera. As president of the Louis Vuitton Foundation for Opera and Music (since 1986), Liebermann has commissioned many operas.

Liebermann's own compositions include three operas to librettos by Heinrich Strobel. The first, *Leonore 40/ 45*, was produced in Basle in 1952; *Penelope*, a modern adaptation of the legend, based on an incident from World War II, was first performed at the 1954 Salzburg Festival; *Die Schule der Frauen*, first performed in English in Louisville, Kentucky (1955), had its European première in the original German at the 1957 Salzburg Festival. *La forêt* (1987), to a libretto by his wife, Hélène Vidal, deals with the constant confrontation between the bourgeoisie and the artist, and has an autobiographical element. Liebermann's musical style, always experimental and based on a sympathetic knowledge of the voice, has ranged from 12-note serialism to jazz; *La forêt* shows a return to a bel canto style, while his music-theatre work *Cosmopolitan Greetings* (1988) is scored for jazz singers and symphony orchestra.

Das neue Land (Festspiel, A. Ehrismann), Basle, 1946
Leonore 40/45 (opera semiseria, 2, H. Strobel), Basle, 26 March 1952
Penelope (opera semiseria, 2 pts, Strobel), Salzburg, 17 Aug 1954
Die Schule der Frauen (ob, 3, Strobel, after Molière), as The School for Wives, Louisville, KY, 3 Dec 1955; Ger. orig., Salzburg, 17 Aug 1957
La forêt (5, H. Vidal, after A. N. Ostrovsky), Geneva, 11 April 1987
Cosmopolitan Greetings (music theatre, A. Ginsburg), Hamburg, 1988

I. Scharberth: *Musiktheater mit Rolf Liebermann* (Hamburg, 1975)
R. Liebermann: *Actes et entractes* (Paris, 1976) [autobiography]

CHARLES PITT

Liebesverbot, Das [*Das Liebesverbot, oder Die Novize von Palermo* ('The Ban on Love, or The Novice of Palermo')]. *Grosse komische Oper* in two acts by Richard Wagner (*see* WAGNER family, (1)) to his own libretto after WILLIAM SHAKESPEARE's *Measure for Measure*; Magdeburg, Stadttheater, 29 March 1836.

Das Liebesverbot was written under the influence of the emancipatory hedonism of Wilhelm Heinse's novel *Ardinghello und die glückseeligen Inseln* (1787), of Heinrich Laube's *Das junge Europa* (1833–7) and of the Young Germans generally. A celebration of free love and a humorous attack on sexual puritanism and bourgeois morality *per se*, it transfers the action of *Measure for Measure* to sunny Palermo. Musically *Das Liebesverbot* is indebted to Italian and French models, in particular Bellini and Auber.

Wagner made his prose sketch for the work in June 1834 and started the versification two months later. The music was begun in January 1835 and completed early in 1836. The single performance in March 1836 was a fiasco: none of the singers had mastered their roles. The work was not given again in Germany until 1923 (in Munich) and not in England until 1965 (in an abridged version at University College, London).

The Regent Friedrich (bass) has outlawed all licentious behaviour – even love itself, it seems, certainly that expressed extra-maritally – on pain of death. The young nobleman Claudio (tenor) is the first to be condemned under the new law, and his sister Isabella (soprano), a novice, is persuaded with some reluctance to make a personal appeal to the Regent. It transpires that Friedrich was once married to Isabella's fellow-novice Mariana (soprano) but for the sake of ambition repudiated her; in defiance of his own decree, he now offers to set Claudio free in exchange for Isabella's favours. Isabella pretends to agree, but in fact sends Mariana – Friedrich's own wife – to the rendezvous; the fancy-dress carnival forbidden by the Regent himself. Friedrich's lubricious hypocrisy is exposed and although he is willing to accept the penalty, the people set him free and a new era of unfettered sensuality is ushered in by the return of their own king.

Das Liebesverbot is characterized by several recurring motifs foreshadowing the leitmotif principle. Chief among them is the motif associated with Friedrich's ban on love: in the overture it takes the form of a falling minor 6th followed by two rising semi-tones; on subsequent appearances the downward leap may range from a perfect 4th or 5th to a diminished 7th.

BARRY MILLINGTON

Liebhaber als Arzt, Der. Opera by Ermanno Wolf-Ferrari; *see* AMORE MEDICO, L'.

Liebling, Estelle (*b* New York, 21 April 1880; *d* New York, 25 Sept 1970). American soprano and teacher. Trained in Paris by Mathilde Marchesi and in Berlin by Selma Nicklass-Kempner, she made her début at the Dresden Hofoper in the title role of Donizetti's *Lucia di Lammermoor* at the age of 18. She then sang with the Stuttgart Opera and at the Opéra-Comique, and appeared three times at the Metropolitan Opera (1902–4), where her début role was Marguerite in *Les Huguenots*. After her 50th birthday she turned her energies to teaching and was on the faculty of the Curtis Institute from 1936 to 1938. Thereafter she settled in New York, where her pupils included Beverly Sills. She wrote an influential book on singing technique, *The Estelle Liebling Coloratura Digest* (New York, 1943).

KAREN MONSON/R

Liederspiel (Ger.: 'song-play'). A kind of dramatic entertainment developed in Germany in the early 19th century in which songs are introduced into a play. It differs from the older Singspiel principally in its inclusion of songs that as lyric poems already enjoyed some currency; the melodies (normally with simple instrumentation) were new, though some songs from such works later came to be regarded as folksongs. Ensembles and choruses were not at first admitted, and the music had an almost entirely lyrical rather than a dramatic character. The Liederspiel differs generically from the French vaudeville and the British ballad opera, in both of which the melodies were normally familiar airs specially provided with new words; normally, in the Liederspiel, the words were pre-existing and the melodies new.

The first Liederspiel was *Lieb' und Treue*, by J. F. Reichardt, staged at the Berlin Royal Opera House on 31 March 1800 with text by the composer, using poems by Goethe, Herder and Salis, as well as folksongs. The somewhat enlarged second edition of the libretto (Berlin, 1800) contains 12 songs, including the Swiss folksong 'Wenn ich ein Vöglein wär', Goethe's 'Heidenröslein' and three other poems, and two each by Herder and Salis. An afterword by the author mentions that the songs are reproduced as set for the piano, without preludes and interludes, and that the complete score (suitable also for domestic performance) could be obtained cheaply from the composer.

Reichardt was the principal theoretician and apologist for the genre as well as being its best-known author and composer. The *Allgemeine musikalische Zeitung* for 22 July 1801 contains his article about the Liederspiel, which he says was born of the desire to encourage simple, pleasant songs as opposed to brilliant and difficult operatic music. *Lieb' und Treue* was written for a domestic occasion; the idea came to Reichardt when he so often found himself invited to perform the song 'Ach was ist die Liebe' from his own Singspiel *Die Geisterinsel* (a version of *The Tempest*; 1798, Berlin). As *Lieb' und Treue* drew criticism for its sentimental tone, Reichardt followed it with a comic and gay example, *Der Jubel, oder Juchhei* (Berlin, Nationaltheater, 21 March 1800), which included military songs. In the *Allgemeine musikalische Zeitung* article, Reichardt chided Himmel for the inappropriately heavy orchestration of his Liederspiel *Frohsinn und Schwärmerey* (libretto by C. A. Herklots; 1801, Berlin), though it enjoyed considerable popularity. Eberwein, Bergt and Lindpaintner were among other successful exponents of the genre.

Mendelssohn's *Die Heimkehr aus der Fremde* and Schumann's *Spanisches Liederspiel* are examples of later works misleadingly entitled 'Liederspiel'. Schletterer (1863) is not strictly accurate in his statement that the Liederspiel led to the racy vaudeville developed in Germany and Austria by Louis Angely and others.

J. F. Reichardt: 'Etwas über das Liederspiel', *AMZ*, iii (1801), col.709
——: *Liederspiele* (Tübingen, 1804)
——: *Musik zu J. F. Reichardts Liederspielen* (Strasbourg, 1804)
H. M. Schletterer: *Das deutsche Singspiel von seinen ersten Anfängen bis auf die neueste Zeit* (Augsburg, 1863)
L. Kraus: *Das deutsche Liederspiel in den Jahren 1800–1830* (diss., U. of Halle, 1921)
PETER BRANSCOMBE

Liège [Liége] (Flem. Luik). City in southern Belgium. It was the capital of an independent principality until 1793, when it was annexed by France (until 1815) and then formed part of the Netherlands (1815–30); it became Belgian in 1830. Opera was introduced about 1740 by a travelling troupe performing *opera buffa*. In 1757 J.-N. Hamal's *Voëgge di Chôfontaine*, a comic opera in Walloon dialect, one of a series of four, was produced in concert form in the Hôtel de Ville; on 23 September 1757 it inaugurated the first Grand Théâtre. The present Grand Théâtre, or Théâtre Royal de Liège, on the rue des Dominicains opened in 1820 with *Zémire et Azor* by Grétry (a native of Liège). Its architecture was loosely based on that of the Paris Opéra. It was built to seat 1300 but now has a capacity of 1050. Because the city is in the centre of Wallonie, the French-speaking part of Belgium, operas have been given principally in French. An effort by the Belgian violinist Eugène Ysaÿe to revive the tradition of operas in Liège dialect with his *Piére li houïeu* ('Peter the Miner') in 1931 had no lasting effect. Since 1967, under the direction of Raymond Rossius, the theatre has been the home of the Opéra Royal de Wallonie and the Centre Lyrique de la Communauté Française de Belgique; its productions are taken on tour to the Palais des Beaux-Arts at Charleroi, the Grand Théâtre at Verviers and the Théâtre Royal at Mons. The company, the biggest permanent lyric troupe in the French-speaking world, employs 400, of whom 26 are principal artists singing the leading roles (with international guests). It gives some 300 performances each year; each September a large-scale production is mounted for 10 to 12 performances in the Palais des Sports de Liège (cap. 3000). The company has also toured to France, Canada, Poland, Germany, Romania and Russia.

J. Martiny: *Histoire du Théâtre de Liège depuis son origine jusqu'à nos jours* (Liège, 1887)
CHARLES PITT

Liepāja (Ger.: Libau). Latvian city on the Baltic coast. From 1784 travelling troupes performed operas. The Liepāja Latvian Theatre, established in 1907, gave its first opera, Glinka's *A Life for the Tsar*, in 1913. Between 1922 and 1934 there existed a separate theatre, Liepāja Opera, which presented opera, ballet and operetta performances; the 60 or so works presented included Tchaikovsky's *Yevgeny Onegin* and *The Queen of Spades*, Rubinstein's *Demon*, Verdi's *Aida*, *Rigoletto* and *La traviata* and Bizet's *Carmen*. The first artistic director was the conductor A. Pārups (1890–1946); conductors have included B. Ķuņķis (1877–1970), Oto Karls (1886–1944) and T. Andersons (1886–1970), and among the directors have been P. Melnikovs (1867–1940) and N. Vasiļjevs (1891–1961).

In 1934–50 and 1957–62 the opera company, under various names, was part of the drama company. The repertory was enlarged by D'Albert's *Valley*, Puccini's *Madama Butterfly*, Rossini's *Il barbiere di Siviglia* and Dargomïzhsky's *Rusalka*. Works from the Latvian repertory included J. Kalniņš's *Ugunī* ('In the Fire') and J. Ķepītis's *Minhauzena precības* ('Münchhausen's Wedding'), and from the Estonian E. Kapp's *Tasuleegid* ('Flames of Vengeance') and G. Ernesak's *Kosilased Mulgimaalt* ('Bridegroom of Mulgimaa'). Conductors have included K. Bunka (1890–1978) and J. Dreimanis (1909–63). Several members of the Liepāja Opera company have subsequently gone on to perform in the Latvian National Opera.
ARNOLDS KLOTIŅŠ

Lieto fine (It.: 'happy ending'). A term used to denote the happy conclusion of a drama or operatic libretto, a basic ingredient of the genre of opera, particularly during the first two centuries of its development. Few periodical or dictionary articles deal with the term or the concept specifically; rather, its discussion is buried in monographs on such topics as opera, libretto, finale or ensemble. To appreciate the general sway of the concept of 'lieto fine', two statistical facts applying to operas from about 1598 to about 1815 need to be kept in mind: first, that these works almost invariably deal with a pair (or several pairs) of lovers, as a rule happily united at the end; and secondly, that this general convention is confirmed by the paucity of exceptions – even tragedies (as opposed to mythological pastorals) usually have a happy conclusion attached to them, and are classified as 'tragedie di lieto fine' (Clubb 1973; Strohm 1988–9). Of Metastasio's 27 *drammi per musica*, probably the librettos set to music more frequently than any others, only three lack the *lieto fine* (*Didone*, *Catone*, *Attilio Regolo*).

For the present purposes, librettos of the 17th and 18th centuries (and beyond) may be subdivided as follows:

1. The couple of lovers are happily united at the end, regardless of the original plot or myth, as in Peri's *Euridice* and Gluck's *Orfeo*. This need not be the result of divine intervention (concerning which *see* DEUS EX MACHINA).

2. When compound (rather than simple) plots involve

several pairs of lovers (usually two), both are united at the end, as in Wagenseil's *Euridice* or Mozart's *Così fan tutte*.

3. The rather implausible and sudden way in which the *lieto fine* is sometimes reached seems to refer, ironically, to a well-known and widely used tradition with which librettist and composer assume the public to be familiar, as in Mozart's *Così fan tutte* or Cocteau's film *Orphée* (concerning the latter, *see* ORPHEUS, as indeed for all works derived from that myth).

4. The obligatory, happily united pair provides the *lieto fine*, but the lovers are not those of the exposition: e.g. in Monteverdi's *Arianna* (and Strauss's *Ariadne*) Ariadne is paired with Bacchus, not Theseus; in Sartorio's *Orfeo*, Orpheus and Eurydice do not even appear in the last three scenes, but Orpheus's rival Aristaeus is paired with Autonoe; similarly, in Rameau's *Hippolyte et Aricie*, Phaedra is not gratified with the love of Hippolytus, who remains attached to Aricia.

5. The finale consists of a *licenza* which addresses and dismisses the audience, indicating that the 'show' is over. This may be combined with the *lieto fine* for the expected couple (Fux, *Orfeo*), or other couples may draw the conclusion from the punishment of the protagonist (the survivors in Mozart's *Don Giovanni*), or the moral lesson may be articulated without any couples being happily united (Stravinsky's *The Rake's Progress*, with a clear reference to the model of *Don Giovanni*).

6. With a complete shift of emphasis, the loving couple is forgotten, and the hero (or a symbolic representation of him) is transferred to the heavens: in Monteverdi's *Orfeo* and Stravinsky's *Orpheus* the apotheosis of the protagonist (or his lyre) provides the finale.

7. Finally, there are the few exceptions to the rule, namely operas before 1815 without any *lieto fine*: for example various settings of Metastasio's *Didone*, *Catone* or *Attilio Regolo*. Such works are quite untypical of the period, and it must be remembered that, in Cavalli's *Didone*, Dido does not commit suicide but is consoled by Iarba.

Modern researchers have emphasized that one aim of the choice and construction of operatic plots was to please the taste and political aspirations of the aristocratic patrons. There is obvious truth in this, and it helps our understanding to know that Peri's *Euridice* celebrated a Medici wedding, that Lully's *tragédies lyriques* had to gratify the 'Roi Soleil', and that Gluck's *Orfeo* was connected with the name-day celebrations of a Habsburg emperor. But patronage and social considerations offer only a partial explanation for the procedure of the early librettists. The extant evidence suggests that the *lieto fine* was also aesthetically attractive to composers from Monteverdi to Mozart and Beethoven. Monteverdi complains in a letter (7 May 1627) that a text of Rinuccini suffered from 'a lack of variety, and a *fine tragico e mesto*'. Nor is there any ground to believe that a fondness of pleasure and an escapist desire for happiness is restricted to audiences of high rank. The artistic belief in a non-tragic conclusion transcends the realm of opera: Beethoven's *Fidelio* is complemented by his Ninth Symphony, the finale of which has been illuminatingly contrasted with that of Tchaikovsky's *Pathétique* (Furtwängler 1953).

On the other hand, there can be no doubt that most operas written after the Congress of Vienna project a tragic vision of life which extends from *Norma* via *Aida* and *Carmen* to *Madama Butterfly* and *Lulu*. After all,

among the works of Verdi and Wagner *Die Meistersinger* and *Falstaff* are exceptions, and so – in our century – are *Der Rosenkavalier* and *The Rake's Progress*. The predominant note sounded in opera and theatre for the last hundred years and more has been one of the futility of man's striving. A wasteland of bleak desolation stretches from Strindberg to Beckett, not unreasonably reflected in modern opera.

A good instance of different emotional stances towards happy or tragic conclusions is provided by the finale of *Don Giovanni*. The attempts of Hermann Levi and Richard Strauss (1895) to remove the 19th-century cuts and restore the original 'lieto' ending did not succeed. The customary cuts persisted even under so sensitive an interpreter as Gustav Mahler at the Vienna Opera. It was not until the 1930s, under Bruno Walter at Salzburg and Fritz Busch at Glyndebourne, that a neo-classical and neo-Baroque spirit prevailed and the opera finished not with the death of Don Giovanni but the final sextet in D major.

In its heyday, that is in the mythological operas of the 17th century, the *lieto fine* acted as an effective foil for the solo lament (prima donna or primo uomo) which so frequently preceded it. The opposition between a concertino lament and an ensemble finale is therefore related to the Baroque concertato which looms so large in the age of Gabrieli, Viadana and Monteverdi. The happy final ensemble (and it would be a mistake to visualize a chorus of 19th-century size), whether in five parts for soloists or chamber choir (as in Peri or early Monteverdi) or whether scored as a love duet (as in Venetian opera), fulfilled therefore an important role, dramatically as well as musically.

See also DEUS EX MACHINA; FINALE; LIBRETTO (ii); and ORPHEUS, for historical information and for additional bibliography.

*

H. Kretzschmar: 'Zwei Opern N. Logroscinos', *JbMP*, xv (1908), 47–68

E. J. Dent: 'Ensembles and Finales in 18th-Century Italian Opera', *SIMG*, xi (1909–10), 543–69; xii (1910–11), 112–38

M. Fehr: *Apostolo Zeno, 1668–1750, und seine Reform des Operntextes* (Zürich, 1912)

M. Fuchs: *Die Entwicklung des Finale in der italienischen opera buffa vor Mozart* (diss., U. of Vienna, 1932)

W. Furtwängler: *Concerning Music* (London, 1953)

H. Engel: 'Die Finali der Mozartschen Opern', *MJb 1954*, 113–34

D. Rossel: *The Formal Construction of Mozart's Operatic Ensembles and Finales* (diss., George Peabody College, Nashville, 1955)

H. Abert: *W. A. Mozart* (Leipzig, 7/1955–66)

K. Leich: *G. Frigimelica-Robertis Libretti (1694–1708)* (Munich, 1972)

L. G. Clubb: 'The Making of the Pastoral Play: some Italian Experiments between 1573 and 1590', *Italian Criticism and Theatre*, ed. J. A. Molinaro (Toronto, 1973), 45–72

B. Corrigan: 'All Happy Endings: Libretti of the Late Seicento', *Forum Italicum*, vii (1973), 250–67

F. W. Sternfeld: 'The Birth of Opera: Ovid, Poliziano and the *lieto fine*', *AnMc*, no. 19 (1979), 30–51

R. Strohm: *Die italienische Oper im 18. Jahrhundert* (Wilhelmshaven, 1979)

R. S. Freeman: *Opera without Drama: Currents of Change in Italian Opera 1675–1725* (Ann Arbor, 1981)

L. Bianconi and T. Walker: 'Production, Consumption and Political Function of 17th-century Italian Opera', *Early Music History*, iv (1984), 209–96

S. Henze-Döhring: 'Die *Attilio Regolo* – Vertonungen Hasses und Jommellis – ein Vergleich', *AnMc*, no. 25 (1987), 131–58

D. J. Grout and H. W. Williams: *A Short History of Opera* (New York, 3/1988)

R. Strohm: ' "Tragédie" into "Dramma per musica" ', *Informazioni e Studi Vivaldiani*, ix (1988), 14–25; x (1989), 57–102

FREDERICK W. STERNFELD

Life for the Tsar, A [*Zhizn' za tsarya*; *Ivan Susanin*]. 'Patriotic heroic-tragic opera' in five acts (or four acts with epilogue) by MIKHAIL IVANOVICH GLINKA to a libretto by Baron YEGOR FYODOROVICH ROZEN, Vladimir Sollogub, Nestor Vasil'yevich Kukol'nik and VASILIY ANDREYEVICH ZHUKOVSKY; St Petersburg, Bol'shoy Theatre, 27 November/9 December 1836 (as *Ivan Susanin*, with a new libretto by Sergey Gorodetsky, Moscow, Bol'shoy Theatre, 21 February 1939).

Ivan Susanin *a peasant from the village of*	
Domnino	bass
Antonida *his daughter*	soprano
Bogdan Sobinin *her fiancé*	tenor
Vanya *an orphan, Susanin's ward*	contralto
Head of a Polish Detachment	baritone
Head of a Russian Detachment	bass
Polish Messenger	tenor

Russian and Polish choruses; soldiers, gentry, peasants, crowd

Setting Russia and Poland, 1613

The earliest Russian opera to achieve permanent repertory status (hence the cornerstone of the Russian national repertory) and the first to be performed abroad (in Prague under Balakirev, 1866), *A Life for the Tsar* was, quite simply, the first Russian opera that was truly an opera (not a Singspiel), competitive with yet stylistically distinct from its most advanced Western European counterparts. For these reasons its historical significance is impossible to overrate: in Yury Keldïsh's memorable phrase, the opera 'marked the boundary between the past and the future of Russian music', and it was immediately so perceived (especially, at first, by literary men such as Pushkin and Gogol).

The nature of that boundary is often misunderstood. Historiographical prestige has made Glinka's music and his image sacrosanct. He is habitually viewed as a kind of demiurge through whom the (variously defined) Russian national school derives its legitimacy. As a result, he and his music are often invested with a concept of 'nationalism' that is quite foreign to his time. As regards *A Life for the Tsar*, the music has in Soviet times been divorced from its original context and made the bearer of a new libretto that replaced the notion of nationhood to which the composer subscribed with one that separates the idea of nation from the idea of a divinely sanctioned monarchy. The implicit claim is that music, being transcendent, is ideologically adaptable. But the claim is contradicted by the opera's critical reception, as witness the difficulties both Soviet and Western scholars have had in identifying and justifying the opera's national character.

A Life for the Tsar was hatched in the aristocratic literary salon of the poet Vasily Andreyevich Zhukovsky, to which Glinka became attached immediately on his return to St Petersburg from Italy in 1834. 'When I declared my ambition to undertake an opera in Russian', Glinka recalled in his memoirs, 'Zhukovsky sincerely approved of my intention and suggested the subject of Ivan Susanin'. It was a predictable choice at a time in Russian cultural history when 'national' in the context of high art inevitably connoted 'patriotic', and 'folk' inevitably connoted 'peasant'. Ivan Susanin was the quasi-legendary hero of popular resistance to Polish infiltration in the wake of the 'False Dmitry''s triumph over Boris Godunov in the early 17th century. A volunteer militia, financed by Kuz'ma Minin, a merchant from Nizhnïy-Novgorod, and commanded by Prince Dmitry Pozharsky, was challenging the Polish forces abroad in the land in the name of Mikhail Romanov, the 16-year-old scion of an old boyar family, who had been elected tsar by a popular assembly in February 1613 and who immediately went into hiding in a monastery near his family estate in Kostroma. Susanin, a local peasant, concealed from a Polish search party the whereabouts of the young tsar, the founder of the last Russian dynasty, under torture and at the eventual cost of his life. The event was first recorded in a crown charter granted the martyr's son-in-law Sobinin in 1619, and renewed in the name of Susanin's heirs by every Romanov ruler down to Nikolay I. The name entered historical literature in 1792 and was immortalized by Sergey Glinka (the composer's cousin) in his *Russian History for Purposes of Upbringing* (1817), since which time it went into all children's textbooks and became part of every Russian's patriotic consciousness.

Parallels with Susanin's deed were suggested by the activities of peasant partisans in the Patriotic War of 1812 against Napoleon; in the aftermath of that war 'Ivan Susanin' became a fixture of Russian Romantic literature (e.g. the eponymous ballad, or 'duma', by Kondraty Rïleyev) and the Russian stage, including the musical stage (e.g. Catterino Cavos's eponymous Singspiel, to a libretto by Alexander Shakhovskoy; Glinka's opera, too, was originally to have been called *Ivan Susanin*: its eventual title was conferred upon it by Tsar Nikolay I in return for the dedication). Before suggesting the subject to Glinka, Zhukovsky had tried to interest the historical novelist Mikhail Zagoskin in it. By the time of Glinka's association with Zhukovsky, moreover, ideas of national and patriotic art had been given a new context as part of the doctrine of Official Nationality associated with the reign of Nikolay I (for a discussion of the doctrine, *see* GLINKA, MIKHAIL IVANOVICH). Zhukovsky, not only a great poet but also an official of Nikolay's court and tutor to the tsarevich (the future Alexander II), was one of its most enthusiastic proponents.

Except for the epilogue, which he wrote himself (it remains a prime historical document of Nikolayan state ideology), Zhukovsky farmed out the actual task of composing the text to his court colleague Baron Rozen, the German-born secretary to the tsarevich, who, after augmenting the title character's household so far as necessary to obtain a standard operatic quartet, seems for the most part to have followed Rïleyev's treatment of the Susanin legend with its dramatic scene in the woods. Before Rozen's involvement in the project Vladimir Sollogub wrote the texts for the opening choruses and for Antonida's cavatina and rondo in Act 1. Nestor Kukol'nik, one of Glinka's closest friends, contributed the text for Vanya's scene at the monastery gates, which was composed at Peterhof in August 1837 (that is, ten months after the première) as a vehicle for Anna Vorob'yova, who had had a sensational success in the part; it was first performed on 18 October, and since then has usually replaced the heroic aria for Sobinin that originally opened Act 4. (The original Ivan was Osip Petrov; the first Sobinin was the debutant Lev Ivanovich Leonov, natural son of John Field; Mariya Stepanova sang Antonida; and Catterino Cavos conducted the première.)

A detailed scenario, modelled largely on the formal conventions of the contemporary Italian opera, was drawn up late in 1834 and guided the composer and librettist(s) as they worked independently, the music frequently outrunning the text. Glinka relied as well on an unusually complete and well thought-out musical plan that reflected not only his acquaintance with French rescue operas and an aspiration to achieve 'a single shapely whole', but also his enthusiastic commitment to the state ideology and his determination to embody it in symbolic sounds.

As the composer put it in an oft-quoted passage from his memoirs, his root conception of the drama underlying his first opera lay in the opposition of Russian music *v* Polish, a structural antithesis that has many surface manifestations. The Poles (the 'other') are at all times and places represented by stereotyped dance genres in triple metre (polonaise, mazurka) or highly syncopated duple (krakowiak); they express themselves only collectively, in impersonal choral declamation. The Russian music is at all times highly lyrical. While drawing to a small extent on existing folk melodies, it is chiefly modelled on the idiom of the contemporary sentimental urban romance, in which the Russian folk melos was put through an italianate refining process. The chief identifying traits of the *style russe* as practised by Glinka are predominance of duple (or compound-duple) time, though duple bars are often grouped very irregularly, as in Vanya's song with its seven-bar phrases; cadential terminations by (sometimes heavily embellished) falling 4ths or 5ths (what Glinka called the 'soul of Russian music'); and a very free, seemingly unstable interplay of relative major and minor keys (reflecting what ethnomusicologists call the 'mutable mode' of Russian melismatic songs). The prime examples of 'pure' (Italo-) Russian style in *A Life for the Tsar* are from Act 1: Antonida's cavatina and the first part of the concluding trio. The second act is entirely given over to Polish dances. Thereafter the rhythm of the musical contrast becomes more rapid: the Poles' approach in Act 3 is signalled by a few strategic allusions to the Act 2 polonaise; their colloquies with Susanin both in that act and in Act 4 are always couched (on both sides) in stereotyped generic terms. At the tensest moment in Act 3, where the Poles forcibly seize Susanin and he cries out 'God, save the Tsar!', Polish (triple) and Russian (duple) rhythms are briefly superimposed. The symbolic battle of styles is also played out in the overture, which (contrary to usual practice) was the first number from the opera to be composed.

Derivations from actual folklore in *A Life for the Tsar* are few. Susanin's first replique in Act 1 is based on a coachman's song Glinka had taken down from life, while a very famous song, *Vniz po matushke po Volge* ('Downstream on the Mother Volga'), reduced to a characteristic motif, accompanies the denouement in Act 4 as an ostinato. The bridesmaids' chorus in Act 3 (a brilliant adaptation of an old Russian decorative stage convention to a novel dramatic purpose, while set to an original melody, is composed in the authentic pentasyllabic hemistichs of Russian wedding songs, which Glinka was the first artist-composer to set in an actual quintuple metre instead of adapting it to a more conventional one. (The result is another form of 'Russian' compound duple, precisely as in the famous Allegro con grazia from Tchaikovsky's Sixth Symphony.) Wholly, if very skilfully, feigned are the choruses in Act 1, including the one for boatmen in which an elaborate pizzicato accompaniment in imitation of balalaika strumming cunningly pits the theme of the earlier women's chorus in counterpoint against the boatmen's tune.

Far more important than the sheer amount of folk or folklike material in the score (meagre, and therefore problematic, compared with the works either of such predecessors as Verstovsky or those of later musicians in the 'Glinka tradition') is the use to which that material is put. This was Glinka's great breakthrough, as Odoyevsky was first to discern, amounting to 'a new element in art'. What Glinka 'proved' was that 'Russian melody', as Odoyevsky put it, 'may be elevated to the level of tragedy'. In other words, he had without loss of scale integrated the national material into the stuff of his 'heroic' drama instead of relegating it, as was customary, to incidental decorative numbers. Of the dramatic crux, including Susanin's Act 4 scena in which the national style is particularly marked, Odoyevsky wrote: 'One must hear it to be convinced of the feasibility of such a union, which until now has been considered an unrealizable dream'. One reason why it had been so considered, of course, was that before Glinka Russian composers had never aspired to the tragic style at all. What made it feasible was that the main characters in Glinka's opera were all peasants, hence eligible, within the conventions of the day, to employ a folkish idiom.

But that hardly made the opera 'democratic'. The most advanced of all Glinka's musico-dramatic techniques was one that enabled him to harp from beginning to end on the opera's overriding theme of zealous submission to divinely ordained dynastic authority. The epilogue, which portrays Mikhail Romanov's triumphant entrance into Moscow, is built around a choral anthem (Glinka called it a 'hymn-march') proclaimed by massed forces, including two wind bands on stage, to the following quatrain by Zhukovsky:

> Slav'sya, slav'sya nash russkiy Tsar',
> Gospodom danniy nam Tsar'-gosudar'!
> Da budet bessmerten tvoy tsarskiy rod!
> Da im blagodenstvuyet russkiy narod!

(Glory, glory to thee our Russian Caesar, Our sovereign given us by God! May thy royal line be immortal! May the Russian people prosper through it!) (In the 1939 Gorodetsky text, this reads: 'Slav'sya, slav'sya tï, Rus' moya! Slav'sya tï, russkaya nasha zemlya! Da budet vo veki vekov sil'na Lyubimaya nasha, rodnaya strana!': 'Glory, glory to thee, my Russia! Glory to thee, our Russian land! May our beloved, our native land be strong throughout all ages!')

Glinka's setting is in a recognizable 'period' style — that of the 17th- and 18th-century *kantï*, three- or four-part polyphonic songs that were the oldest of all 'Westernized' Russian repertories (ironically, and perhaps unknown to Glinka, their ancestry was part Polish), and which in Peter the Great's time were often used for civic panegyrics (in which form they were known as 'Vivats'). The *Slav'sya* theme is related to that of the opening chorus in Act 1 (and through that relationship to the opening phrase of the overture; see ex.1).

But that only begins to describe its unifying role. As Alexander Serov was the first to point out, the *Slav'sya* theme (which in Nikolayan and Alexandrine Russia became virtually a second national anthem) is foreshadowed throughout the opera wherever the topic of dynastic legitimacy is broached. The approach is gradual, beginning in Act 1 with a minor-mode

Ex.1

(a) Epilogue, hymn-march (no. 24)

['Glory, glory to thee our Russian Caesar']

(b) Act 1, opening chorus

['In blizzard, in storm']

(c) Overture

reference to the first two bars of the theme when Susanin (seconded by the chorus) dreams of 'Tsar'! Zakonnïy tsar'!' ('A tsar! A lawful tsar!'). In Act 3, when news arrives of Mikhail's election, paving the way to Antonida's wedding, Susanin and his household bless their good fortune by falling to their knees in prayer: 'Bozhe! Bozhe lyubi Tsarya! Bozhe proslav' Tsarya!' ('Lord! Love our tsar! Make him glorious!') – and between lines the orchestral strings insinuate the same fragment of the *Slav'sya* theme, only this time in the major. When later in the same act the Poles demand to be taken to the tsar, Susanin answers defiantly to an extended if somewhat simplified snatch of the *Slav'sya* theme, disguised mainly in tempo:

> Visok i svyat nash tsarskiy dom
> I krepost' bozhiya krugom!
> Pod neyu sila Rusi tseloy,
> A na stene v odezhde beloy
> Stoyat krïlatïye vozhdi!

(Our tsar's home is a high and holy place, Surrounded with God's staunch strength! Beneath it is the power of all of Russia, and on the walls, dressed all in white, winged angels stand guard!)

Thus *A Life for the Tsar* is thematically unified in both verbal and musical dimensions by the tenets of Official Nationality – a congruence that is sundered if the libretto is replaced. The irony, of course, is that Glinka adapted the techniques by which he achieved this broadly developed musico-dramatic plan from the rescue operas of the revolutionary period and applied them to an opera where rescue is thwarted (though in Cavos's version it had been provided), and in which the political sentiment was literally counter-revolutionary.

Although the Gorodetsky libretto is the one to which the opera has been most frequently performed and recorded since 1939 (Mark Reyzen sang Ivan under Samuil Samosud at the première), the original libretto was revived – in the spirit, one gathers, of *glasnost'* – at the Bol'shoy in 1989. Performance materials are no doubt forthcoming, and one may assume that the days of the ersatz libretto are numbered. In anticipation of its restoration the following synopsis is based on the original.

ACT 1 *The village of Domnino on the river Shacha* Groups of male and female peasants enter from opposite sides, the men singing of their devotion to tsar and country, the women of the coming of spring. Antonida enters and sings of her longing for Sobinin, then of her approaching wedding day ('V pole chistoye glyazhu': 'I gaze over the broad field'). Susanin enters and quashes his daughter's happy daydreams: there can be no talk of weddings while the country's fate remains uncertain. Boatmen are heard on the river; their boat appears bringing Sobinin. He brings news of Pozharsky's resistance and (supported by the chorus) asks for permission to wed Antonida forthwith; Susanin says only when there is a lawful tsar on the throne will he permit it; Sobinin says it will not be long, for the assembly has already elected Mikhail Romanov; all rejoice at this.

ACT 2 *A ball given by the Head of the Polish detachment; guests of both sexes* Couples are dancing a polonaise. They express confidence in their victory over the Russians in a chorus. The dancing continues with a krakowiak and a Pas de quatre (waltz). A messenger rushes in with news of the election of Mikhail, who would displace the Polish prince Władysław as chief claimant to the throne. A group of soldiers immediately sets out towards Kostroma, where Mikhail is known to be hiding, so as to kidnap the tsar-elect and prevent his installation (mazurka and finale).

ACT 3 *Susanin's hut* After an entr'acte, the curtain goes up on Vanya, who is singing of his happy life in the bosom of Susanin's family. Susanin enters and tells Vanya the news of Mikhail's election. Vanya expresses his fear that the Poles might come after Mikhail; Susanin reassures him that they would never succeed in finding him, for no one would betray the tsar. Peasants stop by on their way to work to offer congratulations on Antonida's wedding. Sobinin enters, then Antonida; all four members of the family express their joyous anticipations in a quartet. Sobinin goes out to attend to final arrangements. Susanin gives thanks that he has lived to see his daughter married; he and Antonida reassure Vanya that one day he will have the same good fortune as his sister. Their musing is interrupted by the sound of approaching horses. The Poles burst in. They pose as a 'deputation' and ask to be led to the tsar. At first Susanin refuses indignantly, but after threats (and after reflecting that if he refuses another might not) he feigns agreement. He tells Vanya that he will attempt to lead the Poles astray and that Vanya must hasten to the monastery and warn the tsar's people of the imminent danger. Antonida realizes the Poles will kill her father; she begs him not to go. The Poles pull them apart and leave with Susanin. Antonida falls on a bench weeping. At this point Antonida's friends arrive for the bridal party, singing a ritual song of comfort; they break off singing when they see that Antonida is genuinely weeping. She tells them what has happened ('Ne o tom skorblyu, podruzhen'ki': 'Not for that do I grieve, dear friends'). Sobinin comes back with peasants, having heard that the Poles have been in the village; the peasants swear vengeance.

ACT 4.i *A forest glade; night* After an entr'acte, Sobinin enters with the peasants, armed. They have lost their way in the dark. Sobinin encourages them (aria, 'Brattsï, v metel'': 'Brothers, into the storm!').

4.ii *The monastery gates* Vanya arrives on foot, exhausted; he beats on the door for a long time before anyone stirs. He identifies himself, explains the situation, and bids everyone leave with him (aria, 'Bednïy

'A Life for the Tsar' (Glinka): watercolour by Grigory Gagarin showing a scene from Act 3 (in Susanin's hut) of the original production at the Bol'shoy Theatre, St Petersburg, 27 November/9 December 1836

kon' v pole pal': 'My poor horse has fallen in the field').

4.iii *A dark, snow-bound forest* The Poles curse Susanin for not finding the high road to the monastery; they decide to light a fire and rest. They fall asleep, and Susanin reflects on his fate: the Poles have begun to sense the truth; will he be able to hold them off till dawn (aria, 'Ti priydyosh', moya zarya': 'You will come, my dawn')? Susanin reminisces about his family and bids them a vicarious farewell. A storm blows up. The Poles stir. They question Susanin, who finally reveals his ruse with a taunt. The Poles fall upon Susanin and kill him, but not before he has seen the first rays of sun and knows that he has succeeded. Immediately, Sobinin and his peasants enter and fall upon the Poles.

ACT 5 (Epilogue) *Red Square, Moscow* After an entr'acte, a vast crowd is seen rejoicing at Mikhail's coronation, among them Antonida, Sobinin and Vanya. Susanin's heirs lament him passionately; soldiers tell them the tsar will not forget their father's sacrifice. Bells ring out as the tsar approaches. All are caught up in the hymn (finale, 'Slav'sya, slav'sya, nash russkiy Tsar'': 'Glory to thee our Russian Caesar').

For further illustration *see* RUSSIA.   RICHARD TARUSKIN

Ligabue, Ilva (*b* Reggio Emilia, 23 May 1932). Italian soprano. Trained at the Scuola della Scala, Milan, she made her début there in 1953 as Marina in *I quattro rusteghi*. Engagements followed elsewhere in Italy and in Germany; she achieved a major success at Glyndebourne in 1958 as Alice (*Falstaff*) and returned as Fiordiligi and Donna Elvira. In 1961 she sang Bellini's Beatrice at La Scala and made her American début with the Chicago Lyric Opera as Margherita (*Mefistofele*). She also sang Alice at Covent Garden (1963) and appeared at the Vienna Staatsoper, in Buenos Aires and elsewhere. A lyric soprano of great tonal beauty and musical sensibility, she had a dramatic stage presence.   NOËL GOODWIN

Ligendza, Catarina [Beyron, Katarina] (*b* Stockholm, 18 Oct 1937). Swedish soprano, daughter of Einar Beyron.

She studied at Würzburg and Vienna, and in Saarbrücken with Josef Greindl. She made her début at Linz in 1963 as Countess Almaviva, which was followed by engagements in Brunswick and Saarbrücken (1966–9), where she sang Elisabeth de Valois, Desdemona, Arabella and her first Brünnhilde. In 1970 she joined the Deutsche Oper, Berlin, where she remained until her retirement in 1988, singing a wide repertory that included Amelia (*Ballo*), Elsa and Ariadne as well as Isolde and Brünnhilde. She first appeared at La Scala as Arabella in 1970. That year she sang the First Norn at the Salzburg Easter Festival and in 1971 made her débuts at Bayreuth (as Brünnhilde) and the Metropolitan (as Beethoven's Leonore). In 1972 she sang Senta at Covent Garden and that autumn made her first appearances in Stockholm. Ligendza returned to Bayreuth (1972–87) as Brünnhilde and Isolde and was highly praised for her fresh, even and beautiful voice, gleaming tone and expressive acting. Although she was not at first considered a true Wagnerian dramatic soprano, her characterizations of Wagner's heroines were unusually credible.   HAROLD ROSENTHAL/R

Ligeti, György (Sándor) (*b* Diciosânmartin [now Tîrnăveni], Romania, 28 May 1923). Hungarian composer. He studied at the conservatory in Kolozsvár (now Cluj-Napoca, Romania), 1941–3, and then at the Budapest Academy (1945–9), where he later taught while establishing himself as a composer. Partly for reasons of Soviet-bloc cultural policy, partly from Ligeti's inevitable ignorance of much 20th-century music, his early works joined the Bartók tradition, though all the time he was writing other pieces of a more experimental character, not intended for public performance. In 1956 he left Hungary, and rapidly began to catch up with the western European and American avant-garde trends, though he remained an inquisitive, observant outsider, exploring unexpected areas of slow change and orchestral clustering (*Atmosphères*, 1961) or abrupt, mechanical oddity. The irony of his position became unmistakable in a group of theatrical pieces following the direction of LaMonte

Young (*Trois bagatelles* for pianist, 1961; *Poème symphonique* for 100 metronomes, 1962), and then in *Aventures* (1962) and *Nouvelles aventures* (1962–5). The stage version of these two pieces opened the way to opera, and in 1971 he began work on a comic-strip *Oedipus*, to a libretto by Göran Gentele. Gentele's death in 1972 put a stop to that project, and Ligeti used the sketches in two orchestral pieces: *Clocks and Clouds* (1972–3) and *San Francisco Polyphony* (1974). Meanwhile he had begun a new opera, *Le Grand Macabre* (1974–7). A second full-length opera, to a libretto by Geoffrey Skelton based on *The Tempest*, has been delayed by the composer's ill health, and perhaps also by the complexity of the musical world in which he has chosen to operate, full of rhythmic intricacies and unreal, impalpable veils of tonality.

See also AVENTURES; *NOUVELLES AVENTURES*; and *GRAND MACABRE, LE*.

*

O. Nordwall, ed.: *Ligeti-dokument* (Stockholm, 1968)
O. Nordwall: *György Ligeti: eine Monographie* (Mainz, 1971)
P. Griffiths: *György Ligeti* (London, 1983)   PAUL GRIFFITHS

Lighthouse, The. Chamber opera in one act with prologue by PETER MAXWELL DAVIES to his own libretto; Edinburgh, Moray House Gymnasium, 2 September 1980.

Davies's second chamber opera is based on the unexplained desertion of the Flannan Isles lighthouse in 1900. After a prologue set in an Edinburgh courtroom, in which the officers who discovered the deserted lighthouse are questioned by a solo horn at the back of the auditorium, the main act, subtitled 'The Cry of the Beast', depicts the three keepers, Blazes (baritone), Sandy (tenor) and Arthur (bass), on their final evening. They eat supper, play cards and sing songs that reveal their characters and their backgrounds: brutalized Glasgow childhood, lost teenage love, revivalist guilt. When the lighthouse is surrounded by fog, their fears of the past surface; each encounters his own ghost, and hysteria takes over. While the foghorn sounds, they mistake the lights of an approaching ship for the eyes of a devouring beast. The keepers are replaced by the three officers, who imply that they have been attacked by the deranged men and were forced to kill them. A short coda reveals that the lighthouse is now automatic, but the ghosts of the keepers are seen, still endlessly reliving their final moments.

All the roles are taken by the three singers; the accompanying ensemble consists of 12 instrumentalists. Musical and dramatic structure are more tightly interwoven in *The Lighthouse* than in Davies's previous chamber opera *The Martyrdom of St Magnus* (1977), and its range of expressive effects is more convincingly controlled and paced. The score is permeated with number-symbolism, derived from the Tower of the Tarot, which emerges in the words sung by Arthur during the card game.   ANDREW CLEMENTS

Lighting.

1. Historical overview. 2. Lighting technology since 1800. 3. Scenic projection.

1. HISTORICAL OVERVIEW. Modern assumptions – that an audience usually sits in a darkened auditorium watching a brightly lit stage – apply only since the late 19th century. Before then, the audience normally sat in a house that was dimly lit, peering at a dimly lit stage, and earlier still spectators needed individual candles in the light of which they could read their librettos (or other literature). Period prints showing brilliantly illuminated stages and auditoriums are misleading. It has been estimated that at Drury Lane Theatre in London during the 17th and 18th centuries there may have been about 88 candles in the auditorium, giving a total illumination approximately equivalent to one 75-watt lamp.

When Renaissance theatrical performances began to take place indoors, in academies and palace banquet halls in late 15th-century Italy, the illumination came from oil lamps and candles in chandeliers and sconces (and, if it was daylight outside, windows). Revived classical plays made use of the new Renaissance toy, perspective scenery. In his *Architettura* of 1545 (quoted in Nagler, 79), Sebastiano Serlio described the three standard stage settings (tragic, comic and satiric) and how to light them. His scenery was built and painted in perspective, and scenic units representing buildings had actual windows, behind which lights were placed; coloured liquid in bottles (later, coloured glass plates) could be used to colour the illumination.

Serlio seems also to describe the principle of a lens in front of a light to intensify it, and a reflector: if you 'need a great light to show more than the rest, then set a torch behind, and behind the torch a bright Bason; the brightness whereof will shew like the beames of the Sunne'. General illumination of the stage was provided by chandeliers, and 'above the candlesticks you may place some vessels with water, wherein you may put a piece of Camphir, which burning, will show a very good light, and smell well'. By 1598, when Angelo Ingegneri wrote his *Della poesia rappresentativa e del modo di rappresentare le favole sceniche*, stage lighting was already recognized as an important area of production.

Candles in chandeliers over the auditorium and stage of a theatre had to be lit, trimmed and snuffed, as was necessary with such lighting in any hall. Samuel Chappuzeau, writing in 1674 of French theatres, described what had probably been standard procedure all over Europe for over a century (Nagler, 185):

It is ... the [two] decorators' task to provide two candle snuffers if they do not wish to perform that job themselves. Whether it is they or others, they must perform the task promptly so as not to keep the audience waiting between the acts, and with skill so as not to offend the spectator with a bad odour. One does the snuffing at the front of the stage, the other at the rear, always keeping a watchful eye that the [scenery] flats do not catch fire.

Chappuzeau's description implies that the candles would not last throughout a performance. The stage chandeliers, in full view of the audience until the middle of the 18th century, even in exterior scenes, were lowered to give the snuffers access and then raised when the old candles had been trimmed or new ones installed and lit. Chappuzeau did not mention footlights, but there is pictorial evidence that they were similarly cared for (fig.1a). Chandeliers and sconces in the auditorium were presumably looked after in the same fashion by snuffers, working under the house manager.

The location of the stage chandeliers would have made some areas of the stage almost useless to performers (fig.2). Most illustrations of old theatres show two upstage-downstage rows of chandeliers, as in the print of Covent Garden during the 1763 riot (for illustration *see* ARTAXERXES); that would have provided the best illumination along the centre line of the stage and poor light to each side, under the chandeliers (though the artist who drew the Covent Garden picture made the stage look brightly lit all over). Lighting improved if a performer was well upstage, within the

1. Candle-light: (a) theatre house servant
snuffing footlights near the prompter's
box: engraving, 19th century (the use of
candles for footlights continued until
c1850 in provincial theatres); (b) a rank
of candle-holders between the side wings
at the Drottningholm court theatre, late
18th century; (c) open-ended cans used as
a dimming device; woodcut from Nicolo
Sabbatini, 'Pratica di fabricar scene e
macchine ne' teatri' (Ravenna, 1638)

(a)

(b)

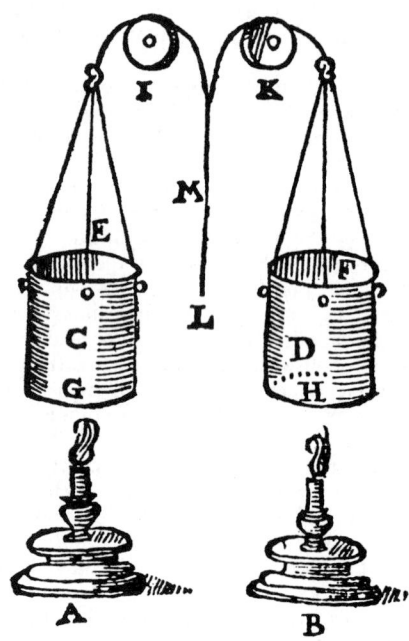

(c)

scenic area, and could benefit from lighting instruments
behind the side wings (fig.1b), or far enough downstage
to be lit by the footlights. Period prints do not always
show stage chandeliers and footlights, not because they
did not exist but because artists wished to do what
audiences did: pretend the visible lighting instruments
were not there and thus enhance the illusion.

Nicolo Sabbatini (*Pratica*, 1638) described a way to
dim stage lights, by lowering an open-ended can over a
flame (fig.1c). This would reduce the amount of light
without snuffing out the candle. The cans could be
raised and lowered by remote control (Hewitt, 112).
Certainly by the middle of the 18th century the dimming
of stage lighting behind side wings was controlled by
rotating 'blinds' (shields) to throw the light onstage or
off. Footlights were usually in a trough, which could be

raised or lowered to increase or decrease the illumination; these added to the intricacy of the system of cords
and pulleys, also used to send signals to stagehands
above and below the stage and to musicians in the pit.

Leone de' Sommi (*Dialogues*, 1565) had recognized
that reducing the illumination in the auditorium made
the stage seem brighter, so he argued for fewer lamps in
the house (Nicoll, 275). Since chandeliers could be
raised and lowered, in some theatres they were pulled up
through holes in the ceiling of the auditorium or
proscenium arch to darken the house when the
performance began. There is no need for great control
over lighting if there is not much light to begin with. Until the introduction of electric lighting in the 1880s, most
auditoriums remained at least partly lit throughout a
performance. Patrons expected to be able to follow the

action by reading the printed libretto; moreover going to the theatre was, especially for the aristocracy, a social occasion of considerable importance, and the show in the house was sometimes as entertaining as that on the stage.

Though some advances were made in the 18th century – experiments with transparencies, colouring light with silk, and the use in the 1780s of Argand lamps that provided 12 times as much light as a single candle – it was not until gas and then electricity were introduced in the 19th century that there was a real revolution in stage lighting and its control. The actual lighting fixtures on the 19th-century stage had not changed much over 300 years; the electric footlights and borderlights were identical in construction and purpose with those that had been built to accommodate candles, oil lamps or gas jets, and ranks of battens (pipes) with strip lights above the stage provided general illumination. When opera was given in repertory it saved time, effort and money to have a general lighting set-up that provided full stage illumination for virtually all productions. The new dimmer boards allowed for whatever light changes might be required. For centuries scenery had been used

in a similar way: stock stage settings – street, palace, forest, seashore, mountain etc. – could serve a great variety of productions, and audiences did not expect (nor did they often get) newly-designed scenery for a new show. In like manner, for centuries stage lighting remained much the same from one production to another, and the performing area received what amounted to a flood of light.

The change to electricity brought not only greater control over light but the ability to plunge the auditorium into real darkness and thus quieten the audience. Spectators were no longer so aware of themselves or each other during a performance; no longer were they the important part of the show that they had been for centuries. They became in time more orderly and docile, and their social activity was confined, more or less, to the intervals.

On stage, the use of electric lighting affected almost all other production areas: painted perspective now lost the illusion of three-dimensionality under the merciless bright lights, shabby costumes and wigs would no longer do, new make-up was needed. Scene designers and painters complained that the soft quality of gas lighting

2. Interior of the National Theatre, Warsaw, during a performance of Paisiello's 'Pirro', with chandeliers and sconces used to illuminate the stage and auditorium (note also the candles lighting the orchestra pit): painting (after 1791), artist unknown

(a)

(b)

(c)

3. Gas installations: (a) sliding wing ladders fitted with gas lights: engraving from the 'Scientific American' (1886), supplement 21; (b) gas floats (footlights) at Her Majesty's Theatre, London, during a rehearsal of Bellini's 'I puritani' in 1863: engraving from the 'Illustrated London News' (2 May 1863); (c) jeu d'orgue (control centre) for the gas distribution system at the Paris Opéra (Salle Garnier): from Charles Nuitter, 'Le nouvel Opéra' (Paris, 1875); for further illustration see RHEINGOLD, DAS

had been lost, and with it the effectiveness of their work, in favour of the harsh illumination provided by clear glass incandescent lamps. The larger-than-life performing style that had dominated the stage for so many years, and which in the dim lighting of the 17th and 18th centuries had probably been not only acceptable but necessary, now appeared exaggerated and unbelievable. It is significant that the introduction of electricity in theatres in the 1880s and 90s corresponded with the move towards realism in performing style (Stanislavsky) and playwriting (Ibsen and Chekhov) in the legitimate

theatre and towards *verismo* in opera (Leoncavallo, Mascagni, Puccini and Giordano).

Two designers, Adolphe Appia and Gordon Craig, pointed the way towards a new approach to staging that, though resisted at first, finally came into its own by the 1950s, especially in opera. Appia saw lighting as a way of unifying the three-dimensional performer and new three-dimensional scenery (for illustration *see* CRAIG, EDWARD GORDON and STAGE DESIGN, fig.16). In *Die Musik und die Inszenierung* (1899; trans. in Simonson) he wrote:

Light is the most important plastic medium on the stage ... Without its unifying power our eyes would be able to perceive what objects were but not what they expressed ... Light and light alone, quite apart from its subsidiary importance in illuminating a dark stage, has the greatest plastic power, for it is subject to a minimum of conventions and so is able to reveal vividly in its most expressive form the eternally fluctuating appearance of a phenomenal world.

Appia not only created designs for many of Wagner's music dramas but wrote detailed, scene-by-scene lighting plots for them; Wagner's widow, however, determined to produce the music dramas exactly as her husband had wished, adamantly refused to look at his drawings. Ironically, his designs and some by Craig anticipated the ideas of Cosima's grandson, Wieland Wagner, by decades, and the work of the Czech designer Josef Svoboda (for illustration *see* INTOLLERANZA 1960 and SVOBODA, JOSEF) in the 1960s and 70s shows a considerable debt to Appia.

The latest technology in stage lighting systems may make the task of lighting technicians simpler, but it does not guarantee an effectively lit production. An imaginative lighting designer is still needed, and not many theatres have one. Some opera houses still follow the old system of assigning the master electrician the task of designing the lighting. The Metropolitan Opera did not employ a full-time resident lighting designer until 1976. At many houses stage lighting is, technically, the most advanced production area; but lighting design in opera has only recently come into its own.

2. LIGHTING TECHNOLOGY SINCE 1800. In 1803 the Lyceum Theatre in London was piped for gas lighting. The evolution of city-wide distribution of gas in the first half of the 19th century made it possible for most theatres to adopt this new technique over a relatively short time, although each theatre had its own gas manufacturing plant before central distribution systems were built. The London Light and Heat Company was formed in 1807 to distribute gas. In 1810, Covent Garden was using 300 Argand lamps on the stage and another 300 elsewhere in the building. In 1817 the main chandelier was converted to gas. The Chesnut Street Opera House in Philadelphia was piped for gas in 1816. In 1819 Giovanni Aldini saw the gas installation at Covent Garden and went home to advocate the conversion of La Scala to gas.

The introduction of gas lighting systems permitted, for the first time, remote control of specific light sources, which could now easily be brightened or dimmed. The gas control panels (fig.3*c*; known as 'gas plates' in Britain, 'gas tables' in the USA) provided the ability to control the lights by location – footlights (fig.3*b*), borderlights, sidelights (fig.3*a*) portable lighting units, etc. – and, when the gas system was so designed, by colour 'circuits' as well. The use of coloured glass filters surrounding the gas jets became quite common. The gas lighting battens (fig.5 below) were at first ignited by a stagehand touching the jets with a flame at the end of a long pole. This procedure was not only slow but also dangerous, and within a short time pilot lights, which were left burning, were installed, and this permitted the extinguishing of a row of lights and the instant relighting of the same row. A number of 'automatic' lighting schemes were produced over the years, the last being an electric heating element to ignite the gas. Gas lights provided a steadier and brighter light, and this allowed scene painters to use darker, more saturated colours in their painting. But gas did not make it possible to darken auditoriums completely or to have blackouts on-stage; nor did it reduce the danger of fire.

While candles, oil lamps and gas-operated lighting equipment were used for general lighting, both in the auditorium and on the stage, it was not until the development in Britain of the calcium light ('limelight') in the early 19th century that directional lighting over tightly controlled areas became possible (fig.4). Originally developed for night surveying purposes by the British Army in 1825, and for lighthouse use in 1830, the high intensity of limelight now allowed designers to use optical lenses in lighting equipment and to make the earliest of the variable-focus 'spotlights'. A block of lime was heated to incandescence by an oxygen and hydrogen gas mixture; each spotlight required an operator to maintain the light output and to control the gas production and flow. The season of 1837–8 saw the introduction of this new lighting system in London theatres.

Soon after the development of limelight, the electric arc lamp was gradually introduced into theatrical productions. The Paris Opéra was using electric arcs in 1847 and the next year they were employed in Britain; the Opéra also introduced lensed spotlights with electric arc sources run from primary batteries as early as 1860. With the invention of dynamos and central power stations, however, and the establishment of electrical distribution systems, arc lighting became a cleaner, quieter and less expensive device. Both limelight and electric arc equipment reached a high level of development in the 1890s. As with limelight, each arc required an operator to advance the carbons and maintain a steady light output; and, again like limelight, these units were normally fixed in place and did not lend themselves to remote mounting or control.

The first part of the theatre where the new lighting

4. *Spotlight (using 'limelight') from the wings: drawing (1859) by William Talbin from 'The Magazine of Art' (1889)*

sources were adopted was usually the auditorium. Theatre managers were always anxious to eliminate heat, smoke, glare and smell from the chandeliers that typically lit the halls. It was not uncommon in the early 19th century to find gas chandeliers lighting the house while lamps and candles were still used on the stage. The size of the gas chandeliers could reach prodigious proportions: the Alhambra Theatre in London, after the 1883 rebuilding, installed a chandelier with 819 gas jets, producing the lighting equivalent of 12 000 standard candles.

In 1879, Edison in the USA and Swan in Great Britain introduced the first practical carbon-filament incandescent electric light bulbs. Theatres immediately began conversion to electric light. The Munich International Electro-Mechanical Exhibition in 1882 stimulated European interest (fig.5a). An experimental electrical installation was tested at the Paris Opéra as early as 1880; the theatre was completely electrified in 1882 (fig.5b and c). Four opera houses in Germany had major electrical installations by that date. In the USA, theatres in New York, Boston, Chicago and San Francisco had been electrified by 1881. Many major installations had been completed by 1885; virtually no new theatres built after 1890 installed gas systems, though many existing ones maintained their gas capability until either their own power stations, or centrally operated sources of power, became more stable and reliable.

The choice of control systems was related to the type of installation. When, in 1881, the Savoy Theatre in London was electrified, Siemens alternating-current dynamos were used; the installation was later changed to a direct-current supply from the Savoy Hotel. Curiously, the first dimming installation in this theatre was an early form of 'solid-state' remote control which could be used only with alternating current. Direct current prevailed in Europe and the USA until well after the turn of the century, and consequently resistance-type dimmers were most commonly used. In continental European practice until the 1940s, central coiled wire resistance cores were operated remotely by tracker wires; and control board technology also continued to become more sophisticated until, by World War II, mechanical presetting, motor controls, colour mastering and variable speed controls had become common.

In the USA and Britain, the introduction of the resistance plate (modular) dimmer in the 1890s produced a different line of development for the control equipment. Direct-action controls were favoured, with the dimmers in the operating panel, directly behind the operating handles and switches. The configuration of horizontal rows of colour mastering and vertical rows of outlet location was similar to European systems, but the mechanical linkages were usually direct, not operating remote dimmers. These systems were simpler to make and operate but less sophisticated than their continental counterparts.

Several electrical circuits of different colours could be easily provided and controlled. Open reflector floodlights were easier to manufacture, and with compact filament sources, lensed spotlights were developed and refined. Reflector design now became as important as the lighting source. Linear, round, square and changeable fields of light could be produced, and soft-edge and hard-edge beams could be created as the production required. Colour filters of animal gelatine as well as

glass could be fitted to the equipment. Special-effect devices were designed for mounting on the spotlights, and the incandescent scenic projection apparatus was refined (see §3).

The further evolution of the incandescent electric bulb, with drawn tungsten filaments, resulted in ever-increasing lighting efficiency and brightness, and the development of the high-wattage concentrated filament lamps early in the 20th century made it possible for the first time to make high-wattage spotlight lamps and eliminate the need for limelight and most of the electric-arc spotlights and floodlights.

The introduction of the incandescent spotlight in the second decade of the 20th century freed designers from the many physical constraints imposed by continuous rows of borderlights and footlights. Specific lighting units could now be placed exactly where they were wanted, while improved suspension systems meant that these units were more closely integrated with the scenic elements so that an operator at each unit was no longer required. This flexibility of equipment placement permitted more effective use of large-scale stage machinery. The innovatory Carl Lautenschläger (Berlin) and Max Hasait (Dresden) advocated the use of stage lifts, revolving stages, rolling stage wagons, the flying of performers etc.; this type of scenic movement was no longer obstructed by fixed lighting positions. The increased portability of equipment also permitted more extensive use of trans-illuminated drops, scrims and gauzes.

The development of soft-edged lenses (based on lighthouse designs by Fresnel) in the 1920s provided better blending of lighting areas; and the introduction in the USA in the 1930s of the ellipsoidal reflector, made possible by the availability of tubular lamps, caused a substantial improvement in performance from each spotlight.

Spotlights had begun to replace strip lights about 1913, though as late as the 1930s strip lights and their general illumination were still used in many theatres. Control boards were developed to provide lighting technicians with dimmer control over each spotlight, allowing for much greater variety in stage lighting and the possibility of designing special lighting for each production.

The improvement in bulb technology continued during the 1920s and 30s. The commercial introduction of the fluorescent lamp in the late 1930s had little impact on theatre lighting technology, but the introduction in Europe of the sealed short-arc lamp paved the way for substantial developments after World War II. The Xenon (short-arc) lamp, introduced in the 1950s for scenic projection equipment as well as in spotlights, was the first of a series of lamp types that found widespread use. In the USA the late 1950s saw the development of the tungsten-halogen cycle quartz enclosed lamp, which allowed a significant improvement in the efficiency and size of most theatrical lighting equipment. This, unlike the sealed short-arc lamp, was dimmable, could be operated at standard voltages, had longer life and incorporated an internal self-cleaning cycle that reduced blackening. In the 1970s and 80s several improved types of sealed short-arc lamps of similar operational concept were introduced.

Other types of lighting sources new in the 1980s, designed to make striking (or at times just different) effects, include sodium lamps, which emit a yellow light, mercury vapour lamps with a blue-white colour spec-

*5. Early electrical
equipment: (a) the
Munich Electro-
Mechanical Exhibition,
1882, demonstrated the
replacement of gas jets
with electric light bulbs
for overhead lights and
footlights, and the use of
the electric arc source for
spotlights (the control
panel can be seen in the
foreground, stage left):
engraving from F.
Kranich, 'Die
Bühnentechnike der
Gegenwart', ii (Munich,
1929–33)*

*5. (b) electric battens and wing lights at the Paris Opéra,
with (inset) the gas fittings which they replaced: engraving
from 'L'illustration' (18 June 1887)*

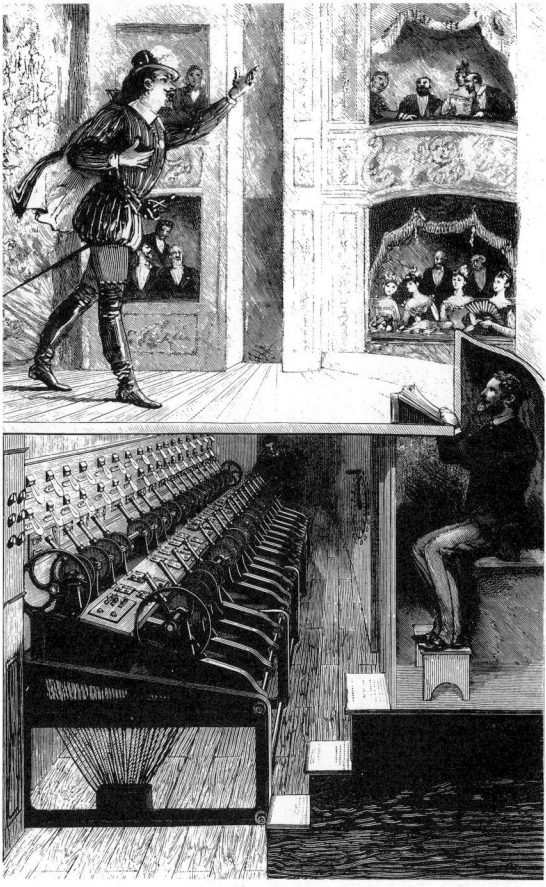

*5. (c) electric switchboard (with mechanical interlocking
controls) below the stage at the Paris Opéra (Salle Garnier)
in 1887 (note the position of the prompter in his box):
engraving from 'L'illustration' (18 June 1887)*

6. Typical backstage lighting installation, 1920s: (1) control balcony; (2) footlights; (3) borderlights; (4) scenery; (5) cyclorama footlights; (6) cyclorama floodlight bridge; (7) moving cloud projector; (8) floodlights with colour filters; (9) high-intensity spotlights; (10) incandescent and arc projectors; from P. Sonrel, 'Traité de scénographie' (Paris, 1944)

7. Part of the multi-scene presetting lighting control system at the Metropolitan Opera House, New York, 1966

trum, and other metal halide or speciality lamps (more often used for street or industrial lighting).

True remote-control equipment had been developed as early as the 1920s in the USA and Britain, using saturable core reactor dimmers operating on alternating current. For the first time electrical presetting of intensities became practical. The first large-scale installations of this type in the USA were the thyratron-controlled reactor systems in the Chicago Civic Opera House (1929), Radio City Music Hall in New York (1932) and the Metropolitan Opera House (1933). The development of sophisticated control panels for large-capacity dimmers in a remote location continued until the late 1940s. In 1947 George C. Izenour in the USA in-troduced a dimmer in which the lighting load was dimmed by the tube only, rendering obsolete the reactor dimmer; in Britain, a similar system was introduced: a three-phase rectifier producing direct current. Both systems were rapidly accepted and, with the further refinements of multi-scene presetting of lighting intensities, began to replace the direct mechanical systems (fig.7). In a simultaneous line of development, the further evolution of the reactor into the magnetic amplifier dimmer was taking place; but it was superseded when, in 1958, the silicon-controlled rectifier as a power-handling device became available, with advantages in size, cost and flexibility. This general type of power control is still in use.

8. Backstage lighting positions at Covent Garden, London, 1988, typical of the systems installed in most European opera houses until c1960

9. Computerized lighting control room at the Opéra Bastille, Paris, 1990

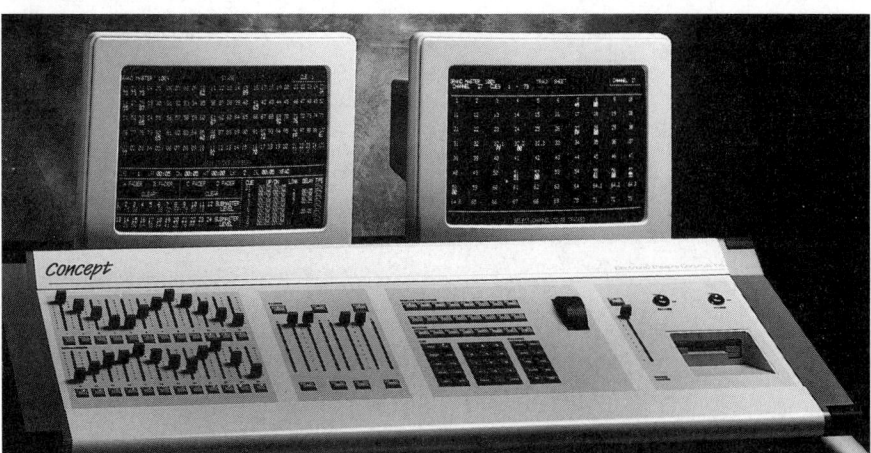

10. Computerized lighting control console, 1992

Various systems of memorizing lighting control intensities were developed. The earliest were mechanical setting devices for controls that were repeatable. Rows of control potentiometers forming 'scenes' of control were built from the 1930s. Data processing punch-cards were used in the 1960s but their mechanical complexity and slow operating speed limited their success. Magnetic tape was used for early attempts at memorizing intensity control information, but this was also slow compared with other systems. In the late 1960s the first control systems using 'computer' technology were introduced, first in television broadcasting studios and later in theatres. The first such system installed in New York was at the Vivian Beaumont Theatre in the Lincoln Center, in 1973; the first American opera-house installation was at the Chicago Civic Opera House in 1974, with later installations at San Francisco and, in 1979, at the Metropolitan Opera. These permitted the instantaneous memorization of lighting intensity information, speed of transition between lighting memories and the instant recall of any data, as well as a means of permanently recording data on tape or computer disk or in printed form. Automated lighting was employed at a Los Angeles production of *Tristan und Isolde* in 1987; each instrument had remotely adjustable pan and tilt, intensity, focus, pattern selection, iris control and colour selection (see Harvey, 38). There were technical problems in the *Tristan* production, among them the noise made by the instrument-cooling systems; such automation had previously been used only for rock concerts.

3. SCENIC PROJECTION. With the development of the Argand burner for oil lamps in the 18th century, the use of the 'magic lantern' became more important in public entertainments. It was used in 1820 by Edmund Kean for a moving colour effect in *King Lear* at Drury Lane. The first documented use as a scenic projection technique in a British theatre was in a production of the play *The Flying Dutchman* at the Adelphi Theatre, London, in 1827; the ship was the projected scenic element. The Paris Opéra, using the new electric arc source, projected a sunrise for Meyerbeer's *Le prophète* as early as 1849 (fig.11). (This was an early use of shadow projection technique, which was brought to a high degree of development by Adolf Linnebach in Germany after 1910.) In the London première of Auber's *L'enfant prodigue* (1851), hand-painted slides were projected for a supernatural vision effect.

During this period limelight was being perfected, and because of its much brighter light it became the choice of those producing the 'magic lantern' (i.e. projected slide shows) and found its way into opera productions. These units, usually fixed in location, were used both backstage and from the front of the house (fig.12). Very small units were developed as hand-held follow-spots, with the operator carrying the gas tanks

11. Electric arc used to produce a sunrise effect in the first production of Meyerbeer's 'Le prophète' at the Paris Opéra, 1849: engraving from M. J. Moynet, 'L'envers du théâtre' (Paris, 1873)

12. Design by Carl Emil Doepler for a lantern slide for the first complete 'Ring' cycle at Bayreuth, 1876 (above), with (below) back projection, using a lantern slide, for the 'Ride of the Valkyries' in Act 3 of the first Paris production of Wagner's 'Die Walküre' (Opéra, 12 May 1893): from 'L'exposition internationale des arts décoratifs et industriels modernes' (Paris, 1925)

13. Design by Günther
Schneider-Siemssen for
projected scenic effects in
the 1957 Bremen
production of
Hindemith's 'Die
Harmonie der Welt',
directed by the composer

on his back. Small hand-held arc lamps were later adapted from this technique.

The electric arc was a still brighter source, and in time displaced limelight. Today scenic projectors generally use short-arc sources encapsulated into sealed glass enclosures, and do not require a special operator; fundamentally they use the same principles as the earlier open arc.

The use of projected effects (such as falling snow, rain, sandstorms, the *aurora borealis*, moving clouds, water ripples, ocean waves, fire, sunrises and sunsets etc.) became common in popular entertainments as well as in opera. Audiences demanded ever more spectacle, realistic or otherwise. With the introduction of *verismo*-style productions there was an increased demand for realistic effects to support the more realistic staging.

From the 1890s to the 1930s the electric arc was used as a high-intensity projection source when incandescent lamps were not bright enough. The early projection techniques of Linnebach and Mariano Fortuny were designed around arc sources. Like the early spotlights, these required an attending operator. As the 20th century progressed, increasingly bright incandescent light sources became available and were used whenever possible, since they could be dimmed, were cleaner and cheaper and did not require an operator.

Fortuny, working with Linnebach in Germany at the beginning of the century, created the 'Fortuny system' of lighting and design. This used a quarter-sphere ('cyclorama') as a large sky background with built-up staging elements downstage. The cyclorama was lit from just behind the proscenium with large-scale electric arc floodlights, equipped with colour change mechanisms operated by tracker wire on what became known as the first electric bridge. This physical arrangement precluded the use of borders and flying scenery over the stage. The projection of scenic backgrounds on this sky became an obvious design option and was used extensively, creating ever more realistic effects, the most famous of which was the use of projected moving clouds. Modified forms of the cyclorama are still in use, as is the practice of using projected backgrounds. The Berlin Opera was the first to install the Fortuny system in 1910; in 1912 the Dresden Opera followed. The concept influenced several generations of designers including those of the Bayreuth productions of the 1950s and 60s.

Since the 1930s enclosed arc sources have been used. Wieland Wagner, at Bayreuth, began in 1951 to revolutionize the production of the Wagner operas by extensive use of these high-intensity sources for scenic projection equipment as well as for general and specific lighting needs. This style once again spread across Europe and to North America. With varying degrees of application, the use of built scenery combined with projected images, fixed or moving, continues as a favoured design technique.

*

A. Ingegneri: *Della poesia rappresentativa e del modo di rappresentare le favole sceniche* (Ferrara, 1598)

G. Saunders: *A Treatise on Theatres* (London, 1790)

G. Aldini: *Memoria sulla illuminazione a gas dei teatri e progetto di applicarla all'I.R. teatro della Scala in Milano* (Milan, 1820)

C. Constant and J. de Filippi: *Parallèle des principaux théâtres modernes de l'Europe et des machineries théâtrales françaises* (Paris, 1842)

M. J. Moynet: *L'envers du théâtre* (Paris, 1873; Eng. trans., enlarged, as *French Theatrical Production in the Nineteenth Century*, ed. M. A. Carlson, 1976)

G. Kobbé: 'Behind the Scenes of an Opera-House', *Scribner's Magazine*, iv (Oct 1888), 435

G. Moynet: *La machinerie théâtrale: truc et décors* (Paris, 1893)

A. Appia: *La mise-en-scène du drame wagnérien* (Paris, 1895; Eng. trans., 1982)

E. O. Sachs and E. A. E. Woodrow: *Modern Opera Houses and Theatres* (London, 1896–8)

A. Appia: *Die Musik und die Inszenierung* (Munich, 1899; Eng. trans., 1962)

T. Weil: *Die elektrische Bühnen- und Effekt-Beleuchtung: ein Überblick über die Methoden und neuesten Apparate der elektrischen Bühnenbeleuchtung* (Vienna, 1904)

C. Lautenschläger: 'Theatrical Engineering Past and Present', *Scientific American*, lx (1905), suppl.

A. von Berger: 'Beleuchtung und Erleuchtung', *Österreichische Rundschau*, xxv/1 (1910), 22–9

A. von Engel: *Bühnenbeleuchtung* (Leipzig, 1914)

F. Benford: *Studies in the Projection of Light* (Schenectady, NY, 1923)

L. B. Campbell: *Scenes and Machines on the English Stage during the Renaissance* (Cambridge, 1923)

J. M. Holeman: *The Optical Properties of Ellipsoidal Reflectors* (Schenectady, NY, 1923)

S. McCandless: *A Method of Lighting the Stage* (New York, 1923)

Moderne Bühnenbeleuchtung (Berlin, 1923) [pubn of Schwabe & Co.]

A. Nicoll: *The Development of the Theatre* (New York, 1927, 5/1966)

T. Fuchs: *Stage Lighting* (New York, 1929)

F. Kranich: *Bühnentechnik der Gegenwart* (Munich, 1929–33)

L. Hartmann: *Theatre Lighting* (New York, 1930)

L. Simonson: *The Stage is Set* (New York, 1932)

M. A. Allévy: *La mise en scène en France dans la première moitié du dix-neuvième siècle* (Paris, 1938)

P. Sonrel: *Traité de scenographie* (Paris, 1944)

F. Hansing and W. Unruh: *Hilfsbuch der Bühnentechnik* (Berlin, 1950)

A. M. Nagler, ed.: *Sources of Theatrical History* (New York, 1952)

R. Southern: *Changeable Scenery* (London, 1952)

B. Hewitt, ed.: *The Renaissance Stage: Documents of Serlio (1545), Sabbattini (1638) and Furttenbach (1628, 1640, 1663)* (Coral Gables, FL, 1958) [based on lectures given at Yale U. by A. Nicoll, 1934–6, and on transs. by Nicoll, J. H. McDowell and G. R. Kernodle of 16th- and 17th-century treatises]

H. Brunner: *The Old Residence Theatre in Munich* (Munich, 1960)

J. E. Rubin: *Technical Development of Stage Lighting Apparatus in the United States, 1900–1950* (diss., Stanford U., 1960)

B. Mello: *Trattato di scenotecnica* (Milan, 1962)

W. Unruh, ed.: *Unsere Theaterneubauten nach 1945* (Berlin, 1966)

G. Grauber: *Theaterbau – Aufgabe und Planung* (Munich, 1968)

W. R. Volbach: *Adolphe Appia, Prophet of the Modern Theatre: a Profile* (Middletown, CT, 1968)

W. Unruh: *Theatertechnik* (Berlin, 1969)

J. Burian: *The Scenography of Josef Svoboda* (Middletown, CT, 1971)

G. Loney: 'Lighting for Opera and Ballet in Repertory: an Interview with Hans Sondheimer at the New York State Theatre', *Theatre Crafts*, vii/1 (1973), 12–19, 34–8

H. de Leeuwe: 'Amsterdam, 11. Mai 1772: die Schauburg brennt!', *Bühnenformen – Bühnenräume – Bühnendekorationen*, ed. R. Badenhausen and H. Zielske (Berlin, 1974), 108–27

P. MacKay: '*A Chorus Line*: Computerized Lighting Control comes to Broadway', *Theatre Crafts*, ix/6 (1975), 6–11, 26–9

C. Molinari: *Theatre through the Ages* (New York, 1975)

D. Mack: *Der Bayreuther Inszenierungsstil (1876–1976)* (Munich, 1976)

D. Bablet: *Les révolutions scéniques du XXe siècle* (Paris, 1977)

G. M. Bergman: *Lighting in the Theatre* (Totowa, NY, 1977)

R. Hartmann, ed.: *Opera* (New York, 1977)

F. Penzel: *Theatre Lighting before Electricity* (Middletown, CT, 1978)

T. Rees: *Theatre Lighting in the Age of Gas* (London, 1978)

C. F. Baumann: *Bühnentechnik im Festspielhaus Bayreuth* (Munich, 1980)

D. C. Mullin: 'Lighting on the Eighteenth-Century London Stage: a Reconsideration', *Theatre Notebook*, xxxiv/2 (1980), 73–85

D. Bablet: *Esthétique générale du décor de théâtre* (Paris, 1983)

G. Loney: 'It's All in the Plot', *Theatre Crafts*, xvii/9 (1983), 20–23, 65–9

M. L. Bablet-Hahn, ed.: *A. Appia: Oeuvres complètes* (Lausanne, 1983–)

G. Isgrò: *Fortuny e il teatro* (Palermo, 1986)

G. Loney: 'Grand Designs at the Met', *Lighting Dimensions*, x/2 (1986), 55–70, 94

S. Pollock: 'Remote Controlled Luminaires', *Theatre Crafts*, xx/8 (1986), 30, 67–9

C. Mobley: 'Light Show: Behind the Scenes with Met Designer Gil Wechsler', *ON*, li/13 (1986–7), 14–18

D. F. Sisk: 'Computers in Theatre', *Theatre Crafts*, xxi/7 (1987), 38, 92–5

C. F. Baumann: *Licht im Theater: von der Argand-Lampe bis zum Glühlampen-Scheinwerfer* (Stuttgart, 1988)

C. Harvey, R. Pilbrow and S. Terry: 'Glimpsing the Future: Symposium Discusses Prospects for Automated Lighting on the Legitimate Stage', *Lighting Dimensions*, xii/2 (1988), 30–43

G. C. Izenour: *Theater Technology* (New York, 1988)

M. J. Kümin: 'Die erste elektrische Beleuchtungsanlage der k.u.k. Hofoper Wien', *Bühnentechnische Rundschau*, 82, 5 (1988), 36–41

M. Loeffler: 'Lighting Director for Lighting Designers: Drafting by Cursor instead of Pencil', *Theatre Crafts*, xxii/9 (1988), 94–7

R. C. Beacham, ed.: *Adolphe Appia: Essays, Scenarios and Designs* (Ann Arbor, 1989)

M. Callahan: 'Are there Standards after DMX512?', *Theatre Design & Technology*, xxv/1 (1989), 31–5, 58–61

M. S. Eddy: 'Ready or not: is CADD [Computer Aided Design and Drafting] Right for You?', *Lighting Dimensions*, xiii/3 (1989), 44–9

L. Watson: *Lighting Design Handbook* (New York, 1990)

J. Milhous: 'Lighting at the King's Theatre, Haymarket, 1780–82', *Theatre Research International*, xvi/3 (1991), 215–36

EDWARD A. LANGHANS, ROBERT BENSON

Light soprano (Fr. *soprano léger*; It. *soprano leggiero*). Typical roles for the light soprano are Despina, Susanna, Norina and Nannetta, as well as Sophie (both *Der Rosenkavalier* and *Werther*). The lightness in volume of such a voice is usually matched by a brightly produced, freely carrying tone, which in the Italian and French schools tends to be of a more sharply edged, forward quality than with the Germans or British. The term SOUBRETTE is sometimes used in connection with such roles and voices; its original meaning of 'coy' or 'shrewd' and its later use, as a noun, to denote a lady's maid suggest the character of the roles assigned to the soubrette in opera. Light sopranos admired in the 20th century have included Elisabeth Schumann and the Americans Kathleen Battle and Barbara Hendricks. Many sopranos, such as Elisabeth Schwarzkopf and Mirella Freni, have begun their career in this category and have developed into singers of the lyric or lyric-dramatic type.

See also SOPRANO. J. B. STEANE

Lille. Town in northern France, formerly the capital of Flanders. After the town was ceded to France in 1668, opera was first performed when the composer Pascal Collasse obtained a royal charter to perform at the Hôtel de Ville. This building burnt down in 1700 after a performance of M.-A. Charpentier's *Médée*. Louis XIV made a gift of 90 000 florins to enable it to be rebuilt, and it reopened in 1718. A larger auditorium (built by the local architect Lequeux) opened in 1787. It too was eventually destroyed by fire, in 1903; the Théâtre Sébastopol (cap. 1450) replaced it. When the Théâtre de l'Opéra (cap. 1500) was opened in 1919, the Sébastopol became an operetta house, and for many years the Lille public enjoyed extensive seasons at both theatres, administered jointly by Alexandre Vanderdonckt. Among premières given were Henri Büsser's *Vénus d'Ille* (1964), Bozza's *La duchesse de Langeais* (1967) and Tony Aubin's *Goya* (1974). In 1981 the Opéra du Nord was established, grouping Lille (the Grand Opéra) with Roubaix (the ballet company) and Tourcoing (the Atelier Lyrique). This structure broke down in 1985 and the Opéra de Lille was run independently for two further seasons. In 1986 it was closed by the mayor for financial reasons, and the city no longer has a company or an orchestra. Recitals and concerts are still given at the Opéra; very occasionally visiting companies give opera performances. An annual festival, which has included opera, began in 1971.

*

L. J. Brote: 'A propos du répertoire lyrique des théâtres français', *Le Théâtre lyrique français 1945–1985*, ed. D. Pistone (Paris, 1987), 51–73

CHARLES PITT

Lillo, Giuseppe (*b* Galatina, Lecce, 26 Feb 1814; *d* Naples, 4 Feb 1863). Italian composer. He was first taught by his father, the conductor Giosuè Lillo; he completed his studies at the Naples Conservatory, where his teachers included Zingarelli. He made a successful début with a mass for four voices and orchestra. In 1834 his first opera, *La moglie per 24 ore, ossia L'ammalato di buona salute*, was also a success. He then composed mainly for the theatre, winning much popularity with the Naples public; this first period culminated with *L'osteria di Andujar* (1840), his most celebrated work. Various failures followed, and he began teaching the piano. During a visit to Paris in 1847–8 he received support from Spontini. He held posts at the Naples Conservatory, including professor of harmony from 1859.

Lillo's theatrical works show him to be a faithful follower of Rossini, with a rich melodic vein in which the vocal virtuosity is always subjected to expressive aims; his piano music, which seems outdated, is of less significance.

first performed in Naples unless otherwise stated
oss – *opera semiseria*

La moglie per 24 ore, ossia L'ammalato di buona salute (opera buffa, 2, A. Passaro), Reale Collegio di Musica, carn. 1834

Il gioiello (oss, 2, L. Tarantini), Nuovo, aut. 1835

Odda di Bernaver (opera seria, 2, G. E. Bidera), S Carlo, 28 Feb 1837

Rosmunda in Ravenna (tragedia lirica, 2, L. A. Paladini), Venice, Fenice, 26 Dec 1837

Alisia di Rieux (oss, 3, G. Rossi), Rome, Argentina, spr. 1838

La modista (oss, 2), Florence, Pergola, 9 May 1839

Il conte di Chalais (opera seria, 2, S. Cammarano, after Lockroy), S Carlo, Oct 1839

Le disgrazie di un bel giovane, ossia Il zio e il nipote (opera giocosa, 2, Tarantini), Florence, Pergola, spr. 1840

L'osteria di Andujar (opera comica, 3, Tarantini), Fondo, 30 Sept 1840

Cristina di Svezia (tragedia lirica, 3, Cammarano), S Carlo, 21 Jan 1841

Lara (tragedia lirica, 2, Tarantini), S Carlo, carn. 1842

Il cavaliere di S Giorgio, ossia Il mulatto (oss, 2, J. Ferretti), Turin, Carignano, aut. 1846

Caterina Howard (opera tragica, 4, G. Giacchetti), S Carlo, 26 Sept 1849

La Delfina (oss, 2, M. d'Arienzo), Nuovo, March 1850

La gioventù di Shakespeare, ossia Il sogno d'una notte estiva (commedia lirica, 3, G. S. Giannini), Nuovo, 29 Dec 1851

Ser Babbeo (oss, 3, L. E. Bardare), Nuovo, 8 May 1853

Il figlio della schiava (dramma lirico, 3, Giannini), Fondo, 9 July 1853

ES (G. Saponaro); *FlorimoN*   FRANCESCO BUSSI

Lily of Killarney, The. Grand romantic opera in three acts by JULIUS BENEDICT to a libretto by JOHN OXENFORD and DION BOUCICAULT after Boucicault's play *The Colleen Bawn, or The Brides of Garryowen*; London, Covent Garden, 10 February 1862.

Boucicault's play (1860) was itself based on an earlier work, Gerald Griffin's novel of 1829, *The Collegians, or The Colleen Bawn*. Hardress Cregan (tenor) has secretly married Eily O'Connor (soprano), the 'Colleen Bawn' ('bawn' means 'white', used here to mean 'fair' or 'blonde'). Mrs Cregan (contralto), his widowed mother, unaware of her son's marriage, is visited by Mr Corrigan (bass), who holds a mortgage on the Cregan lands. He threatens that he will demand her hand in marriage unless Hardress redeems the debt by marrying the heiress Ann Shute (soprano). Hardress tries to induce Eily to surrender her marriage certificate to him, but Myles na Coppaleen (tenor), who also loves her, and

Father Tom (bass), the local priest, make her promise never to part with it.

In Act 2 Hardress reluctantly pays court to Ann Shute. His faithful friend, the boatman Danny Mann (baritone), offers to resolve the situation by killing Eily, and tells Hardress to send him his glove as a signal should he decide on her death. Hardress and his mother quarrel, and Danny tells Mrs Cregan that all will be well if she can persuade Hardress to send him his glove; unaware of the possible consequences, she gives it to him herself. Danny rows Eily across the lake and, on landing, demands her marriage certificate or her life. When she refuses to give him the certificate he pushes her into the water. Myles meanwhile has decided to go otter-shooting; he fires, and Danny falls, fatally wounded. Believing he has killed Eily, Danny makes a dying confession, but she has been rescued by Myles.

In Act 3 Hardress is about to marry Ann Shute when Corrigan arrives with soldiers to arrest him for plotting Eily's murder. Mrs Cregan discloses that she gave Danny the glove, and Myles and Eily promptly arrive to prove the charge of murder groundless. Overwhelmed by his love for Eily, Hardress proudly proclaims her as his wife, and Ann Shute generously rescues the Cregans from their financial predicament.

The Lily of Killarney is a work not entirely characteristic of its composer's usual style. It owes its success to its melodic strength and Irish idiom: the 'Irishness' of Myles's 'It is a charming girl I love' might be considered superficial, but the recitative which precedes it ('From Inchigela all the way') strikes a more authentic Celtic note. At one point the folktune *Cruiskeen Lawn* ('Little jug filled') is employed, with a refrain in Gaelic. There are several examples of pentatonic writing, and modulations to the flattened seventh, as in Eily's 'I'm alone', strengthen the Irish atmosphere. In the quartet 'Ah, never was seen such a beautiful star', the Act 2 finale, and the overture, Benedict handles the larger operatic forms far more convincingly than Balfe or Wallace, and his contrapuntal facility adds interest to the duet 'The moon hath raised her lamp above'. His orchestration is superb: never obtrusive, always sensitive to each instrument's obbligato qualities, yet sometimes prophetic of Elgar in its subtle blends of colour. Finest of all is Hardress's ballad 'Eily Mavourneen', in which Benedict does, perhaps, find his own unique voice: the soaring italianate vocal line, German appoggiaturas, and spacious orchestral textures momentarily combine to create an English operatic ballad of incandescent beauty.

The Lily of Killarney, Balfe's *The Bohemian Girl* and Wallace's *Maritana* were once dubbed the English 'Ring', but ironically it was the German-born Benedict who produced the trilogy's most 'Irish' work rather than the two Irishmen. The date of the première is often given as Saturday, 8 February 1862, the evening on which the season's last performance of Balfe's *Puritan's Daughter* took place; Benedict's opera followed on the Monday night. The opera was widely performed in the 19th century: in Philadelphia (1867), New York (1868), and as *Die Rose von Erin* in Brunswick, Hamburg (both 1863) and Berlin (1864). It was revived at Covent Garden (1902) and Sadler's Wells (1931).

NIGEL BURTON

Lima. Capital of Peru, founded in 1535 by Pizarro. The earliest extant New World opera, Tomás de Torrejón y Velasco's *La púrpura de la rosa*, was mounted on 19

October 1701 at the viceregal palace in Lima to celebrate Philip V's 18th birthday and the first year of Bourbon rule in Spain. It is in the tradition of Juan Hidalgo's music for the earliest extant Spanish opera, *Celos aun del aire matan* (1660); in both, repeated *coplas* (couplets) replace Italian *recitativo secco*. The plot of *La púrpura* recounts Ovid's tale of Venus and Adonis. Seven years later, on 17 September 1708, Roque Ceruti (*b* Milan, *c*1683; *d* Lima, 6 Dec 1760) inaugurated Italian opera at the palace, where he conducted his *El mejor escudo de Perseo*, a mythological spectacle with a libretto by the Peruvian viceroy himself. Bartolomé Massa (*b* Novi, *c*1721; *d* Lima, 1799), who divided his New World career between Lima and Buenos Aires, wrote the music for *Primero es la honra opera representada en el Coliceo de Lima el día 25 de Diziembre ... 1762*; his troupe included Micaela Villegas (*b* Lima, 28 Sept 1748; *d* Lima, 16 May 1819), 'La Perricholi', whose impudence Offenbach immortalized in *La Périchole*.

In 1812 Andrés Bolognesi, a native of Genoa who resided in Peru from 1810 to his death at Arequipa on 27 August 1834, conducted Cimarosa's *Il matrimonio segreto*, Pergolesi's *La serva padrona* and three of Paisiello's operas, *Il barbiere di Siviglia*, *Nina, o La pazza per amore* and *La pupilla*. After independence (1824) Lima was host to a succession of travelling opera companies. In 1840 the Compañía Lírica Pantanelli gave operas by Rossini, Bellini and Donizetti, remaining based there until 1844. Throughout the rest of the century the élite of Lima were constantly entertained by touring companies presenting current Italian operas, French *opéras-bouffes* and Spanish zarzuelas. J. J. White's *La hija del duca* had its première in Lima on 19 September 1868. Among the Italian composers who settled in Peru, Carlo Enrico Pasta, whose *La fronda* had its première in the city on 6 September 1871, was the first to compose and mount at Lima an opera on an indigenous subject: *Atahualpa*, heard in Genoa in 1875, then given at the Teatro Principal in 1877 and repeated eight times.

A new Teatro Principal seating 1400 was inaugurated on 11 December 1889 with the zarzuela *El hermano Baltasar*; this was replaced by still another theatre, now called the Municipal, authorized by the Peruvian Congress in 1901 and opened in 1904. The Politeama and Olimpo theatres were also used for opera. Napoleone Maffezzoli, a native of Bergamo residing in Peru from 1898, composed five operas at Lima, *Arte ed amore* (1901), *Francesca da Rimini* (1904), *Vanozza* (1910), *Daniela* (1917) and *Rafaello* (incomplete). The first native of Lima to compose an opera on a national subject was José María Valle-Riestra (*b* Lima, 9 Nov 1858; *d* Lima, 25 Jan 1925), who succeeded in having his *Ollanta* produced by the visiting Mario Lambardi company on 26 December 1900 at the Teatro Principal. Modified, it was successfully revived in 1920 by the Bracale company, which frequently visited Lima, in the Teatro Forero. Other Peruvians who wrote operas based on indigenous legends include Daniel Alomía Robles (*Illa Ccori*) and Ernesto López Mindreau (*Cajamarca*, *Francisco Pizarro*). For lack of a resident company in the city, Peruvian singers made their débuts abroad.

*

M. Moncloa y Covarrubias: *Diccionario teatral del Perú* (Lima, 1905)

E. Calcagnoli: *L'Italia al Peru* (Lima, 1905–6) [incl. 'Rassegna della vita e dell'opera italiana nel Peru']

C. Raygada: 'Guía musical del Perú', *Fénix*, xii (1956–7), 3–77; xiii (1963), 1–82; xiv (1964), 3–95

R. Stevenson: *Foundations of New World Opera and a Transcription of the Earliest Extant American Opera, 1701* (Lima, 1973)

ROBERT STEVENSON

Lima, Jerónimo Francisco de (*b* Lisbon, 30 Sept 1741; *d* Lisbon, 19 Feb 1822). Portuguese composer. He studied at the Seminário da Patriarcal in Lisbon, and from 1761 to 1767 at the Conservatorio di S Onofrio a Capuana in Naples, together with João de Sousa Carvalho. On his return to Lisbon he was appointed organist and *mestre* at the Seminário da Patriarcal and began to write in a variety of genres, including serenatas and *drammi per musica da cantarsi* written for court or private performance. Among them was *Le nozze d'Ercole e d'Ebe*, given in 1785 at the Spanish Ambassador's palace in Lisbon to celebrate a double wedding between the Spanish and Portuguese royal families. In 1787 he was in the service of the English writer William Beckford during the latter's stay in Sintra, near Lisbon, and his music is favourably mentioned by Beckford, who, however, was not pleased with the £200 bill that Lima presented on his departure. He was also composing much sacred music and became *mestre de capela* of Lisbon's Patriarchal Cathedral in 1798, followed by the appointment in 1800 as organist of the royal chamber until 1822. Lima's two three-act *drammi giocosi* were first performed during Carnival at the court's winter palace at Salvaterra de Magos: *Lo spirito di contradizione* (Gaetano Martinelli; in *P-La*) in 1772, and *La vera costanza* (in *La*, *VV*) in 1785. *Lo spirito di contradizione*, which was revived at the S Carlos Theatre in Lisbon in 1985, reveals in its accompanied recitatives and rich orchestration the possible influence of Jommelli, the favourite composer of the Lisbon court.

DBP

J. Mazza: *Dicionário biográfico de músicos portugueses*, ed. J. A. Alegria (Lisbon 1945); pubd in *Ocidente* 1944–5

B. Alexander, ed.: *The Journal of William Beckford in Portugal and Spain, 1787–1788* (London, 1954)

L. Pereira Leal: Introduction to PM, ser. B, xxiii (1973)

M. C. de Brito: *Opera in Portugal in the Eighteenth Century* (Cambridge, 1989)   MANUEL CARLOS DE BRITO

Lima, Luis (*b* Córdoba, Argentina, 12 Sept 1948). Argentine tenor. After studying in Buenos Aires and Madrid, he made his début in 1974 at Lisbon as Turiddu. He was then engaged at Mainz and also sang in Stuttgart, Hamburg, Munich and Berlin; in 1977 he sang Edgardo (*Lucia di Lammermoor*) at La Scala. He made his début at the Metropolitan in 1978 as Alfredo, at the Teatro Colón in 1982 as Cavaradossi and at Covent Garden in 1984 as Nemorino. He has also appeared at Verona, Rome, Paris, Geneva, Salzburg and Savonlinna, where in 1986 he sang Don Carlos. His repertory includes Don José, Hoffmann, Gounod's Romeo, Faust and Vincent, Berlioz's and Boito's Faust, Riccardo (*Ballo*) and Rodolfo (*Bohème*). A lyric tenor with an elegant style, he has sometimes taken roles that are too heavy for his voice.   ELIZABETH FORBES

Lincke, (Carl Emil) Paul (*b* Berlin, 7 Nov 1866; *d* Clausthal-Zellerfeld, 3 Sept 1946). German composer and conductor. He studied with Rudolf Kleinow in Wittenberge (1880–84) and learnt the bassoon, horn and percussion. He played in dance orchestras in Berlin and was occasional conductor and house composer at variety theatres. He enjoyed success with popular songs and from 1893 to 1897 was conductor and resident composer at the main variety theatre in Berlin, the Apollo. After a period as conductor at the Folies Bergère, Paris (1897–9), his revue-operetta *Frau Luna* made his name and also his fortune through his own publishing company, Apollo-Verlag. It was followed by further stage scores and orchestral pieces. Orchestral items such as the 'Glühwürmchen-Idyll' from *Lysistrata* (1902) achieved wide international popularity, while songs such as the march from *Berliner Luft* (1904) established him as a symbol of Berlin as Offenbach was of Paris or Johann Strauss of Vienna.

In the 1920s and 1930s *Frau Luna*, *Im Reiche des Indra* and *Lysistrata*, originally written as items on variety programmes, were revised and expanded to incorporate hit numbers from *Berliner Luft* and other shows. Particularly through *Frau Luna* in this extended form, Lincke's music retained its local popularity, in due course being exploited by the Nazis. Lincke was made a freeman of Berlin in 1941 and named professor in 1942. Though his music seeks to achieve no great dramatic characterization, it is skilfully constructed and full of lilting, often rousing melodies.

operettas, selective list: librettos by H. Bolten-Bäckers unless otherwise stated; performed in Berlin at the Apollo and published in vocal score in Berlin at time of first production
Venus auf Erden (1), 6 June 1897; Frau Luna (1), 1 May 1899, rev. version (2), Döbeln, Stadt, 1929; Im Reiche des Indra (1), 18 Dec 1899; Fräulein Loreley (1), 1 April 1900; Lysistrata (1), 1 April 1902; Nakiris Hochzeit (2), 6 Nov 1902; Berliner Luft (2), 28 April 1904; Grigri (2, with J. Chancel), Cologne, Metropol, 25 March 1911; Casanova (3, J. Glück, W. Sternberg, after Lebrun), Chemnitz, Stadt, 5 Nov 1913; Ein Liebestraum (3, A. O. Erler and Neumann), Berlin Radio, 20 July 1940, Hamburg, Reeperbahn, 1940

*

E. Nick: *Paul Lincke* (Hamburg, 1953)
O. Schneidereit: *Paul Lincke und die Entstehung der Berliner Operette* (Berlin, 1974)   ANDREW LAMB

Lincoln's Inn Fields Theatre. London theatre opened in 1661; see LONDON, §II, 2.

Lind [Lind-Goldschmidt], **Jenny** [Johanna Maria] (*b* Stockholm, 6 Oct 1820; *d* Wynds Point, Herefordshire, 2 Nov 1887). Swedish soprano. She was nicknamed 'the Swedish nightingale'. In 1830 she was enrolled at the Royal Opera School, Stockholm. She made her début in 1838 as Agathe in *Der Freischütz*; later that year she sang Pamina and Euryanthe. She appeared in *La vestale*, *Robert le diable* (1839), *Don Giovanni* (as Donna Anna), *Lucia di Lammermoor* (1840) and *La straniera*, and as Norma, which she sang for the first time in 1841. Her voice began to show signs of fatigue, the middle register being particularly worn, and she went to Paris to consult the younger Manuel García, who imposed a period of rest before taking her as a pupil. When she returned to Stockholm, appearing in *Norma* in October 1842, an improvement in her voice and technique was immediately apparent. The middle register remained veiled in tone and relatively weak for the rest of her career, but the notes from c'' to a'' had become marvellously strong and flexible, and her range extended to g'''.

Lind's new roles included Valentine (*Les Huguenots*), Ninetta (*La gazza ladra*), Countess Almaviva, and Amina (*La sonnambula*), which she sang for the first time in 1843. During the next season she added *Il turco in Italia*, Gluck's *Armide* and *Anna Bolena* to her repertory. In 1844 she went to Germany, making her début in Berlin in *Norma* and in 1845 singing Vielka in

Jenny Lind as Amina in the sleepwalking scene from Bellini's 'La sonnambula', Act 2 (Her Majesty's Theatre, London, 1847): lithograph from a contemporary sheet music cover

Meyerbeer's *Ein Feldlager in Schlesien*, written for her but created by Leopoldine Tuczek-Ehrenburg. Returning to Stockholm, she sang Marie (*La fille du régiment*) for the first time.

Lind made her Viennese début at the Theater an der Wien in April 1846 as Norma. She then toured extensively in Germany, returning in January 1847 to Vienna, where she scored an immense success as Marie. Her triumphant London début was at Her Majesty's in 1847, when she sang (in Italian) Alice in *Robert le diable* before Queen Victoria and Prince Albert, followed by *La sonnambula* and *La fille du régiment* with even greater success. She also created Amalia in *I masnadieri* (22 July) and sang Susanna. Having decided to give up the theatre, she made her operatic farewell to Stockholm after a second season at Her Majesty's in 1848, and made her last stage appearance there as Alice on 10 May 1849.

The greater part of Lind's career was in recitals and oratorio; outside Sweden, her operatic career lasted less than five years and was virtually restricted to Germany and England. While on tour in the USA (1850–52) she included selections from her operatic roles in her recitals but did not appear in opera. Her stage reputation was based largely on her interpretations of four roles, one of which (Norma) failed because of her temperamental inability to realize the character fully; thus Amina, Alice and Marie were probably her most satisfying operatic achievements (though her own preference was for Julia in *La vestale*).

For further illustration see HAMBURG, fig.3; MASNADIERI, I; and NEW YORK, fig.1.

*

B. Lumley: *Reminiscences of the Opera* (London, 1864)
H. S. Holland and W. S. Rockstro: *Memoir of Madame Jenny Lind-Goldschmidt: her Early Art-Life and Dramatic Career* (London, 1891)   ELIZABETH FORBES

Linda di Chamounix ('Linda of Chamonix'). *Melodramma semiserio* in three acts by GAETANO DONIZETTI to a libretto by GAETANO ROSSI after Adolphe-Philippe d'Ennery and Gustave Lemoine's play *La grâce de Dieu* (1841, Paris); Vienna, Kärntnertortheater, 19 May 1842.

The full-scale overture is taken from the first movement of a string quartet that Donizetti had written in 1836. The action opens in a farm courtyard in Haute Savoie, about 1760. Linda's parents, Antonio Loustolot (baritone) and Maddalena (soprano), are concerned that they may have to leave their native place because of the Marquis's unwelcome attentions to their only child. Antonio expresses his nostalgia for the valley where they were born (Moderato, 'Ambo nati in questa valle'). The Marquis (*buffo* bass) appears, hoping to begin a flirtation with Linda, but she does not come out of her room. Only when everyone has gone does Linda (soprano) appear (aria, 'O luce di quest'anima': her *sortita*, a one-movement aria but in two-verse cabaletta form, was not in the original Viennese version, when the role was sung by Eugenia Tadolini, but was added by Donizetti – writing the words himself – for the Paris première with Fanny Tacchinardi-Persiani).

Linda loves Carlo (tenor), whom she believes to be an itinerant painter but who in reality is the Viscount de Sirval, the Marquis's nephew. Some of the young people assemble, as each autumn they form a group that leaves Chamonix to try to earn their sustenance in Paris. Pierotto (mezzo-soprano *en travesti*) entertains them with a sad ballad ('Per sua madre') about a girl who forgot her mother's wise advice; the melody of this D minor aria becomes an important reminiscence theme later. Linda and Carlo meet, pledging their love (duet, 'A consolarmi affrettisi') – the theme to that phrase will also serve an important function in the last act. The Prefect (bass), a Calvinist clergyman, tells Antonio that he was shocked to learn that the Marquis is willing to exchange the mortgage on Antonio's fields and dairy for Linda's favours; he recommends that Antonio send his daughters, consigned to Pierotto's protection, with the group going to Paris. Linda's only regret is that she is to be separated from Carlo. The Prefect leads the populace in a prayer before the leave-taking ('O tu che regoli'). This expansive prayer is a variant of that in the last scene of *Maria Stuarda*, a work Donizetti seems to have abandoned some time after the problems associated with its première at La Scala; here it forms the basis of the single-tempo first finale. (This is another example of Donizetti's anticipation of a practice that Verdi would later adopt: the omission of the conventional stretta at this point.)

Some months later (Act 2), Linda, still innocent, is installed in a grand apartment in Paris furnished by Carlo, who has followed her and revealed not only his true identity but his plan to persuade his mother to allow him to marry her. Linda hears Pierotto playing his hurdy-gurdy as he passes in the street outside and calls him in. Their florid duet ('Al bel destin'), a single-tempo Larghetto, is a late, nostalgic echo of the *rossinianismo* of Donizetti's earliest operas. Seeing her in luxury, Pierotto suspects the worst; Linda is able to reassure him and allays his fears but explains that the planned marriage must remain a secret. The Marquis has seen her on the balcony and mistaken her for some nobleman's mistress, and he offers to take her on; his proposition is expressed with a debonair worldliness showing the typical charm of Donizetti's *buffo* idiom. Linda

however is outraged, orders him away, and retires.

Carlo's mother has discovered his intentions towards Linda; in an expressive *romanza* ('Se tanto in ira agl'uomini') he reveals how loath he would be to betray her, although his mother is making speedy arrangements for his wedding to a noblewoman. Linda returns and they declare their love; but when Carlo begs for even a chaste embrace, the sound of Pierotto's tune on his hurdy-gurdy from outside reminds Linda of her mother. She sends Carlo away. A beggar appears; Linda is horrified to recognize him as her father and tries to hide her agitation as she gives him a purse ('Ah! che il ciel vi benedica'; with its harmonic shifts and its structure left incomplete for dramatic reasons, this duet contains much of the raw material of the idiom we associate with Verdi's Gilda and Rigoletto). When Linda identifies herself, Antonio is so stunned to see his daughter amid such luxury that he curses her; he storms out, leaving Linda shaken, and her equilibrium is further shattered by the arrival of Pierotto, with news of the preparations for Carlo's wedding. Linda, unable to believe she has been betrayed, lapses into a pathetic state. Her mad scene ('No! non è ver … mentirono'), unlike its counterpart in *Lucia*, is a single movement in two-verse cabaletta form, and so functions as a true pendant to the father-daughter duet. (In the works of Donizetti's final years such redistributions – and occasional omissions – of the sections of the conventional four-movement structure are increasingly common.)

In Act 3 the young people have returned from Paris to their valley. Carlo searches anxiously for Linda; his mother has now relented and he is free to marry her. When the Prefect relates that she was seduced and abandoned, Carlo admits that he is inadvertently responsible. The Marquis arrives, bubbling over with wedding plans, but refuses to identify the bride (he sings an engaging aria, 'Ell'è un giglio', typical of Donizetti's mature, refined mastery of the *buffo* style). When everyone has left, Pierotto gently leads in the deranged Linda to the tune of his ballad played on his hurdy-gurdy; only this way can she be persuaded to come home. Carlo learns of Linda's plight and renews his pledge of love ('A consolarmi affrettisi'); the music of their first-act duet helps restore her reason. Everyone joyfully looks forward to their wedding.

* * *

The score of *Linda* is a monument to Donizetti's unfailing good taste, from the finely crafted overture to the final ensemble. A particularly effective moment is the brief unaccompanied prayer for five solo voices in Act 3. *Linda*, although a fixture on the Italian stage for its first 50 years, deserves to be better known: it makes clear much about the musical environment in which Verdi developed. Although its naive, *demi-caractère* plot strains the credulity, the score is vocally so grateful and possesses so much cohesiveness that it largely overcomes this liability.

WILLIAM ASHBROOK

Lindberg, Armas. *See* LAUNIS, ARMAS.

Lindelheim, Joanna Maria ['The Baroness'] (*fl* 1703–17; *d* London, Dec 1724). German or Flemish soprano. According to Burney she was trained in Italy and sang at many German courts before appearing in London concerts in 1703. She was a pupil of Haym, with whom she lived for some 20 years. She sang at the Queen's Theatre, Haymarket, in Jakob Greber's *Gli amori d'Ergasto* in 1705, and in 1706 at Drury Lane in

1281

Haym's arrangement of Giovanni Bononcini's *Camilla* as 'Mrs Joanna Maria'. Called 'The Baroness' in the *Camilla* score, she appeared under that title subsequently, in a Drury Lane revival of *Camilla* in 1707, and the pasticcios *Love's Triumph* and *Tomiri* and Haym's arrangement of Alessandro Scarlatti's *Pirro e Demetrio*, all at the Queen's Theatre in 1708. She became a singing teacher but continued to appear in concerts at least up to 1717.

BurneyH
L. Lindgren: 'The Accomplishments of the Learned and Ingenious Nicola Francesco Haym (1678–1729)', *Studi musicali*, xiv (1987), 247–380   WINTON DEAN

Lindenstrand, Sylvia (*b* Stockholm, 24 June 1942). Swedish mezzo-soprano. She studied in Stockholm, making her début there in 1962 as Olga. In 1964 she appeared as a flowermaiden at Bayreuth. She has sung in Edinburgh, Drottningholm, Paris, Geneva, Amsterdam, Bonn and Aix-en-Provence and at Glyndebourne, where she was heard as Dorabella (1975) and Amaranta (*La fedeltà premiata*, 1979). Her repertory includes Paris (Gluck's *Paride ed Elena*), Clori (Cavalli's *Egisto*), Cenerentola, Rosina, Brangäne, Fricka, Octavian, Marina and the title role of Tchaikovsky's *The Maid of Orleans*. A stylish singer who has excelled in Mozart, notably as Idamantes, Cherubino, Countess Almaviva, Zerlina, Donna Elvira and Sextus, she has taken on heavier roles such as Kundry in the 1990s.

ELIZABETH FORBES

Lindholm, Berit (*b* Stockholm, 18 Oct 1934). Swedish soprano. She studied at the Stockholm Opera School (1961–3), and in 1963 made her début as Mozart's Countess Almaviva at the Royal Opera, Stockholm; there she went on to sing Elisabeth, Aida, and, in 1965, opposite Birgit Nilsson's Electra, the Chrysothemis that brought her international attention (in this role she made her Covent Garden début, in April 1966). After her first *Walküre*, Brünnhilde in Munich (1967), she became a leading exponent of the role, which she sang for her Metropolitan début in 1975. Her first London *Walküre* (October 1974) revealed a large, steel-tipped, slightly unsteady soprano, without the smooth schooling or vocal abundance of great Wagnerians in former years, but warmed by lively dramatic intelligence. An important recorded role was Cassandra in the first complete *Les Troyens* (1970); in the later stages of her career she sang in new and less familiar operas, creating Divana in Alexander Goehr's *Behold the Sun* (1985).

MAX LOPPERT

Lindpaintner, Peter Joseph von (*b* Koblenz, 9 Dec 1791; *d* Nonnenhorn, Lake Constance, 21 Aug 1856). As a small child, Lindpaintner, whose father was a tenor at the court of the Bishop-Elector of Trier, accompanied the court into exile in Augsburg after the French secularization of Trier. In 1806 the elector arranged for him to study composition with Peter Winter in Munich. Though Winter was an ineffective teacher, Lindpaintner made progress in composition, and his first opera, *Demophoon*, was successfully performed in Munich in 1811. The following year he became music director at the Isartortheater, and for the next six years produced a steady stream of stage works. Schilling relates that he became complacent about his abilities during this period

but that, having been convinced by an old friend that he had much more to learn, he resumed the study of composition, with the contrapuntist Joseph Graetz.

In 1819 Lindpaintner took up the post of Kapellmeister at Stuttgart, where he remained for the rest of his life. Here he established his reputation as one of the finest German conductors and continued to compose assiduously for the stage. A number of his operas were enthusiastically received, though few held the stage for long. Schilling observed: 'Unfortunately their texts are mostly of too little dramatic worth to allow his operas to obtain the recognition by the wider musical public that their musical worth deserves'. Lindpaintner's achievements were acknowledged by the bestowal of the aristocratic 'von' in 1844, but in his later years his reputation as a composer declined. In 1854 Hans von Bülow castigated 'the supreme impropriety of the pretensions with which Kapellmeister Lindpaintner now represents himself as the old master of the departing epoch, forgetting that Spohr alone can bear this honour'.

See also VAMPYR, DER (ii).

Demophoon (os, 3, I. F. Castelli, after P. Metastasio), Munich, 29 Jan 1811 (Munich, 1811); rev. as Timantes (F. K. Heimer), Stuttgart, Hof, 22 Jan 1820
Die Pflegekinder (Spl, 2, K. Thienemann), Munich, Isartor, 1812 or 19 Nov 1814, vs (Leipzig, 1830)
Der blinde Gärtner, oder Die blühende Aloe (Spl, 1, A. von Kotzebue), Munich, Isartor, 10 July 1813 or 21 Nov 1815
Die Prinzessin von Cacambo (komische Oper, 2, Kotzebue), Munich, Isartor, 1814 or 2 March 1815
Die Sternkönigin (romantische komische Volksmärchen, J. A. Voss, after L. Huber), Munich, Isartor, 13 July or Sept 1815; also perf. as Das Sternenmädchen
Das Christusbild, oder Kunstsinn und Liebe (Spl, 2, Zahlhaus), ?Stuttgart, May 1816
Hans Max Giesbrecht von der Humpenburg, oder Die neue Ritterzeit (Spl, 1, Kotzebue), Munich, Isartor, May or 6 June 1816
Pervonte, oder Die Wünsche (komische Oper, 3, Lindpaintner, after C. M. Wieland), Munich, Isartor, June or 14 Aug 1816
Die Rosenmädchen (Spl, 3, Lindpaintner and Kotzebue, after M. Théaulon: *Les rosières*), Vienna, an der Wien, 3 June 1818
Sulmona (Oper, 3, Lindpaintner and Heimer, after C. F. Bretzner: *Der Irrwisch*), Stuttgart, Hof, 11 April 1823
Der Bergkönig (romantische Oper, 3, K. Hanisch), Stuttgart, Hof, 30 Jan 1825
Der Vampyr (romantische Oper, 3, C. M. Heigel, after J. W. Polidori: *The Vampyre*), Stuttgart, Hof, 21 Sept 1828, vs (Leipzig, 1829); rev. 1850
Die Amazone, oder Der Frauen und der Liebe Sieg (Oper, 3, L. Robert), Stuttgart, Hof, 28 Sept 1831
Die Bürgschaft (grosse Oper, 3, F. L. K. Biedenfeld), Stuttgart, Hof, 28 Sept 1834
Die Macht des Liedes (komische Oper, 3, Castelli), Stuttgart, Hof, 13 March 1836, vs (Leipzig, 1837)
Die Genueserin (grosse romantische Oper, 2, C. P. Berger), Vienna, Kärntnertor, 8 Feb 1839, vs (Vienna, 1839)
Die sicilianische Vesper (grosse romantische Oper, 4, H. Rau), Stuttgart, 6 or 10 May 1843, vs (Mainz, 1844)
Lichtenstein (grosse Oper, 5, F. Dingelstedt), Stuttgart, 26 Aug 1846, vs (Hamburg, 1845)
Giulia, oder Die Corsen (Oper, 3, A. Lewald), Stuttgart, 20 Nov 1853
Libella, 1855 (Oper, 2, Heigel)

*
StiegerO
'Lindpaintner, Peter Joseph von', *Encyclopädie der gesammten musikalischen Wissenschaften*, ed. G. Schilling (Stuttgart, 1837)
W. Neumann: *Peter von Lindpaintner* (Kassel, 1856)
R. Kraus: *Das Stuttgarter Hoftheater von den ältesten Zeiten bis zur Gegenwart* (Stuttgart, 1908)
R. Hänsler: *Peter Lindpaintner als Opernkomponist* (diss., U. of Munich, 1928)
H. Truscott: 'Wagner: the Growth of an Art', *The Listener* (16 May 1963)

Model of a set designed by Tom Lingwood for Prokofiev's 'War and Peace' (Part I scene 6; a room in Mariya Akhrosimova's house, Moscow), performed by the Australian Opera at the official opening of the Sydney Opera House, 28 September 1973

S. Johns: *Das szenische Liederspiel zwischen 1800 und 1830* (Frankfurt, 1988)

CLIVE BROWN

Lindroos, Peter (*b* Pohja, 26 Feb 1944). Finnish tenor. He studied in Helsinki, Rome and Treviso, making his début in 1968 at Helsinki as Rodolfo (*Bohème*). After two seasons at Göteborg, in 1971 he was engaged at Copenhagen and in 1974 at Stuttgart. He has also sung in Oslo, Munich, Vienna, Berlin, Cologne, Paris, Savonlinna and San Francisco; he first appeared at Covent Garden in 1975 as the Duke (*Rigoletto*), returning in 1976 as Bacchus (*Ariadne auf Naxos*). Among his other roles are Parsifal, Manrico, Gabriele Adorno, Verdi's Otello, Cavaradossi, Vladimir (*Prince Igor*), Grigory (*Boris Godunov*), Laca (*Jenůfa*), Hermann (*The Queen of Spades*), Don José, Sergey (*Lady Macbeth of the Mtsensk District*), Apollo (*Daphne*) and David (Nielsen's *Saul og David*). He created Johann von Gobyn in Rautavaara's *Thomas* at Joensuu (1985) and the title role in Cerha's *Der Rattenfänger* at Graz (1987). An excellent actor, he has a powerful voice that is heard to best advantage in Russian and Slav music.

ELIZABETH FORBES

Lindsey [Lindsy, Linsey], **Mary** (*fl* 1697–1712). English contralto. She was in Daniel Purcell and Jeremiah Clarke's play *The World in the Moon* (summer 1697) and then appeared regularly on the London stage, singing between the acts of plays and in *The Island Princess* and Daniel Purcell's *The Grove*. She may have played Orpheus in *Orpheus and Euridice*, a masque with music by Goodson and Weldon, at a girls' boarding school near Oxford in October 1697; she certainly sang in Weldon's *The Judgment of Paris*. Her comic gifts were exploited in a series of older-woman parts in the English operas in the Italian style from Clayton's *Arsinoe* (1705) to the pasticcio *Almahide* (1710). She disappears from the records with the triumph of opera in Italian.

BDA; LS

O. Baldwin and T. Wilson: 'Richard Leveridge, 1670–1758: the Italian Opera', *MT*, cxi (1970), 891–3

N. Zaslaw: 'An English *Orpheus and Euridice* of 1697', *MT*, cxviii (1977), 805–8

J. Milhous and R. D. Hume: *Vice Chamberlain Coke's Theatrical Papers 1706–1715* (Carbondale, IL, 1982)

OLIVE BALDWIN, THELMA WILSON

Lingwood, Tom [Thomas] (*b* Guildford, Surrey, 15 Sept 1927). Australian stage designer and director of English birth. He was educated at Guildford Grammar School, the Guildford School of Art and St Martin's School of Art, London (and expelled from all of them). He was resident designer and scenic artist for the Donald Wolfit company, London (1953–4), and senior designer for Associated Television (1955–64). The first operas he designed were Martín y Soler's *Una cosa rara* (1965, London, Jeannetta Cochrane Theatre), Britten's *The Turn of the Screw* (1967, Ledlanet Festival, Scotland) and *Manon Lescaut* for Covent Garden (1968).

For Australian Opera in 1970 Lingwood designed *La bohème*, which has been revived many times and won an international Emmy Award in 1989. After working on the company's *La forza del destino* (1970) and *Nabucco* (1971) he became its resident designer, 1972–8. In 1973 he designed Prokofiev's *War and Peace*, which officially opened the Sydney Opera House (see illustration); later he designed and co-directed *Aida*, the first production staged in the Sydney Opera House Concert Hall (1975). He has also designed and directed *Salome* (1976) and *Don Pasquale* (1978).

Lingwood has been one of the most influential designers in Australia and has taught at the New South Wales Conservatorium of Music and the National Institute of Dramatic Art. His technical use of colour and false perspective is unmatched, and he is highly regarded as a scene painter. His desire to direct as well as design, while welcomed by singers, was not always appreciated by management.

DAVID J. HOUGH

Linley, George (*b* Leeds, 1798; *d* London, 10 Sept 1865). English author and composer. As a young man he wrote satirical literature directed against the magnates of Leeds. Moving to London, he did literary work of various kinds and wrote the words or the music – frequently both – of some of the most popular songs of his day, including *Ever of thee, I cannot mind my wheel, mother* and *Thou art gone from my gaze*. His operas include *Francesca Doria* (1849), *The Toymaker* (1861, an adaptation of Adam's *La poupée de Nuremberg*) and *Law versus Love* (1862). He also wrote the librettos of several operas including Balfe's *Catherine Grey* (the first 19th-century English opera without spoken dialogue) and, with R. B. Peake, Benedict's *The Gypsy's Warning*. In *Musical Cynics of London*

(London, 1862) he attacked the London music critics, chiefly H. F. Chorley.

Linley, Thomas (i)

Linley, Thomas (i) (*b* Badminton, Gloucs., 17 Jan 1733; *d* London, 19 Nov 1795). English composer. He showed a marked gift for music when young and studied with Thomas Chilcot, the organist of Bath Abbey. Later he studied with Boyce, and probably Paradies, in London. Linley's capacities as a singing teacher were amply proved by the extraordinary abilities of his own children, three of whom (Elizabeth, Mary and Maria) were precocious soloists. He also worked as a harpsichordist and concert director.

Away from Bath, Linley's first success in London was with the opera *The Royal Merchant* in 1767, and his growing reputation led in 1774 to his appointment as joint director of Drury Lane theatre. He collaborated with his son-in-law, Richard Brinsley Sheridan (husband of Elizabeth), and his son Thomas Linley (ii) in *The Duenna* at Drury Lane in 1775, and made his permanent home in London in 1776, becoming joint manager of Drury Lane with Sheridan. Between that date and his death Linley arranged and composed music for some 20 plays, pantomimes, operas and other entertainments. Sometimes this consisted of only a song or two, while at other times the musical contributions were more extensive and elaborate. Many of the songs from the shows became favourites in the concert rooms of the times. Among his other works was a setting of Sheridan's *Verses to the Memory of Garrick*, performed at Drury Lane on 21 March 1779.

Linley's eldest daughter, Elizabeth Ann (*b* Bath, 5 Sept 1754; *d* Bristol, 28 June 1792), became a famous soprano. She made her London début at Covent Garden in 1767 in Thomas Hull's masque *The Fairy Favour*, as Goss'mour (with her brother Thomas as Puck), and then made regular appearances in the London oratorio seasons and at the Three Choirs Festival until 1773, the year of her marriage to Sheridan. Her brother William (*b* Bath, Feb 1771; *d* London, 6 May 1835), Linley's youngest son, produced two operas that failed, *The Honey Moon* (Drury Lane, 7 January 1797) and *The Pavilion* (Drury Lane, 16 November 1799; revived as *The Ring*, January 1800). His music for the pantomime *Harlequin Captive* (Drury Lane, 18 January 1796) does not survive.

See also DUENNA, THE.

LCG – *London, Covent Garden* LDL – *London, Drury Lane*

The Royal Merchant (op, T. Hull, after F. Beaumont and J. Fletcher: *The Beggar's Bush*), LCG, 14 Dec 1767
The Duenna, or The Double Elopement (comic op, 3, R. B. Sheridan), LCG, 21 Nov 1775, *GB-Lbl*; songs, vs (London, 1775); collab. T. Linley (ii)
Selima and Azor (comic op, G. Collier, after J. F. Marmontel), LDL, 5 Dec 1776
The Beggar's Opera (ballad op, J. Gay), LDL, 29 Jan 1777
The Camp (musical entertainment, Sheridan and R. Tickell), LDL, 15 Oct 1778; incl. music from The Royal Merchant
Zoraida (tragedy, W. Hodson), LDL, 13 Dec 1779
The Generous Imposter (comedy, T. L. O'Beirne, after P. N. Destouches: *Le dissipateur*), LDL, 22 Nov 1780
The Gentle Shepherd (pastoral, Tickell, after A. Ramsay), LDL, 29 Oct 1781; 3rd movt of ov. adapted from a vn concerto by T. Linley (ii)
The Carnival of Venice (comic op, Tickell), LDL, 13 Dec 1781
The Spanish Rivals (musical farce, M. Lonsdale), LDL, 4 Nov 1784
The Strangers at Home (comic op, J. Cobb), LDL, 8 Dec 1785
Love in the East, or Adventures of Twelve Hours (comic op, Cobb), LDL, 25 Feb 1788

LoewenbergA; *LS*
London Chronicle (21–3 Nov 1775) [incl. detailed synopsis of *The Duenna*]
Morning Chronicle (22 Nov 1775)
T. Davies: *Memoirs of the Life of David Garrick Esq* (London, 1780)
W. Hazlitt: *Lectures on the English Comic Writers* (London, 1819)
T. Moore: *Memoirs of the Life of the Right Honourable R-d B-y Sheridan* (London, 1825)
M. Kelly: *Reminiscences of the King's Theatre* (London, 1826, 2/1826); ed. R. Fiske (London, 1975)
T. Philipps: *The Duenna* (London, 1835)
W. F. Rae: *Sheridan's Plays* (London, 1902)
W. S. Sichel: *Sheridan* (London, 1909)
C. Black: *The Linleys of Bath* (London, 1911, enlarged 3/1971)
E. Gagey: *Ballad Opera* (New York, 1937)
R. Fiske: 'A Score for "The Duenna"', *ML*, xlii (1961), 132–41
M. Bor and L. Clelland: *Still the Lark: a Biography of Elizabeth Linley* (London, 1962)
D. M. Little and G. M. Kahrl, eds.: *The Letters of David Garrick* (London, 1963)
R. Fiske: *English Theatre Music in the Eighteenth Century* (London, 1973, 2/1986)
C. Price, ed.: *The Dramatic Works of Richard Brinsley Sheridan* (London, 1973)
——:'The Duenna', *MT*, cxvii (1976), 217–19
L. Troost: 'The Characterizing Power of Song in Sheridan's *The Duenna*', *Eighteenth-Century Studies*, xx (1986–7), 153–72
GWILYM BEECHEY

Linley, Thomas (ii)

Linley, Thomas (ii) (*b* Bath, 5 May 1756; *d* Grimsthorpe, Lincs., 5 Aug 1778). English composer, son of Thomas Linley (i). He was one of the most precocious composers and performers that have been known in England. A superb violinist, he first played a concerto at a concert in Bristol on 29 July 1763. He studied with Boyce from 1763 to 1768, and on 29 January 1767 at Covent Garden made his theatrical début as Puck in Thomas Hull's *The Fairy Favour*, with music by J. C. Bach. (His sister Elizabeth also made her début then, as Goss'mour). After study with Nardini in Florence (*c*1768–71) Linley returned to Bath to assist his father in various musical enterprises there and in London, where he also pursued further studies with Boyce.

The music that Linley composed after 1771 was of an astonishingly high quality, but only a fairly small proportion of it survives. Very little was published in his lifetime, and none of his large-scale works in full score. For the theatre he collaborated with R. B. Sheridan and his father in 1775 in the three-act comic opera *The Duenna, or The Double Elopement* (London, Covent Garden, 21 November 1775; *GB-Lbl*), writing the overture and a large share of the songs and ensembles himself, especially for Act 3, for which his autograph full score survives (*Lgc*). A further collaboration with Sheridan in a production of Shakespeare's *The Tempest* (London, Drury Lane, 4 January 1777) gave Linley the chance to compose a storm chorus and airs, for some of which Sheridan wrote the texts (score *Lbl*). His final work for the theatre was the comic opera *The Cady of Bagdad* (A. Portal; Drury Lane, 19 February 1778; *Lbl*), which was based on the same tale that Gluck and Monsigny had used in their operas *Le cadi dupé*. Linley's work was a failure owing to a poor libretto, although one or two of the airs show his genial inventiveness. During the 1770s a number of vocal works by him were also performed in the London theatres, notably his *Ode on the Spirits of Shakespeare* (F. Laurence; Drury Lane, 20 March 1776; ed. in MB, xxx, 1970, 2/1985).

Linley's tragic early death in a boating accident while on holiday with his family at Grimsthorpe Castle was one of the greatest losses that English music has suffered.

Gainsborough painted portraits of both Thomas Linleys and of other members of the family. He made three portraits of the younger Thomas Linley (1768, *c*1773, *c*1777), the first of them with his sister Elizabeth.

See also DUENNA, THE.

[T. Hull]: *The Fairy Favour: a Masque* (London, 1766)

W. Linley: *The Dramatic Songs of Shakespeare* (London, 1816)

C. Camden: 'Songs and Chorusses in The Tempest', *Philological Quarterly*, lxi (1962), 114–22

G. E. Beechey: *Thomas Linley, Junior: his Life, Work and Times* (diss., U. of Cambridge, 1964)

——: 'Thomas Linley, 1756–1778, and his Vocal Music', *MT*, cxix (1978), 669–71

For further bibliography *see* LINLEY, THOMAS (i).

GWILYM BEECHEY

Linz. Austrian city on the Danube. In 1501 a 'Humanistendrama mit Musik' was performed for Maximilian I, and from 1608 Latin school dramas, many with music, were given at the theatre of the Jesuit school. The town's first opera production, Antonio Draghi's *Hercole acquistatore dell'immortalità*, took place on 7 January 1677 in the presence of Leopold I. Over the next hundred years such performances remained isolated events, associated with great occasions at the court; regular opera performances began in the 1760s. The Neue Ständische Theater was built in 1803 after a fire had destroyed its predecessor in 1800. Following the model of Schikaneder's Theater an der Wien, it mounted the most popular operas of the period, especially Mozart's, and in the later 19th century laid emphasis on new works. In 1863 Bruckner attended a performance of *Tannhäuser*, which left a lasting impression on him. Promising young singers often began their careers in Linz before moving to the Vienna Opera.

The theatre has been rebuilt twice, and since about 1920 it has been known as the Landestheater. In 1958 Clemens Holzmeister designed a new theatre complex comprising a small Kammerspiele (cap. 421) as well as the new Landestheater (cap. 756). This has, however, proved too small and acoustically problematic; a new building is under discussion. Performances take place all the year round and as well as operetta and musicals each season normally includes two modern operas. The Landestheater also maintains a tradition of premières, in particular of works by Upper Austrian composers. These have included Helmut Eder's *Der Aufstand* (1976) and *George Dandin, oder Der betrogene Ehemann* (1978), Baldwin Sulzer's *In seinem Garten liebt Don Perlimplin Belisa* (1984), and Heinrich Gattermeyer's *Kirbisch* (1986). The theatre is owned and operated by Upper Austria, with subsidies from the federal government and the city of Linz.

G. Gugitz: 'Beiträge zur älteren Geschichte des Theaters in Linz in den Jahren 1722 bis 1802', *Heimatgaue*, viii (1927), 37

E. Haller: 'Zur älteren Linzer Theatergeschichte', *Jb des Oberösterreichischen Musealvereins*, lxxxii (1928), 143

O. Wessely: 'Die ersten Linzer Opernaufführungen', *Oberösterreichische Heimatblätter*, iii (1949), 64–6

H. Wimmer: 'Das Linzer Landestheater 1945–51: eine theaterstatische und theatersoziologische Untersuchung', *Oberösterreichische Heimatblätter*, vi (1952), 189–207

——: *Das Linzer Landestheater 1803–1958* (Linz, 1958)

O. Wessely: 'Musik und Theater in Linz zu Bruckners Zeit', *Anton Bruckner und Linz: Ausstellung im Steinernen Saal des Landhauses zu Linz* (Linz, 1964), 35

HARALD GOERTZ, OTHMAR WESSELY

Lionel and Clarissa [*Lionel and Clarissa, or A School for Fathers*]. Comic opera in three acts by CHARLES DIBDIN to a libretto by ISAAC BICKERSTAFF; London, Covent Garden, 25 February 1768.

This was the last full-length opera to a text by Bickerstaff to be produced in London before he fled the country in 1772. After the recent disaster of his *Love in the City* (also set by Dibdin) Bickerstaff reverted to more conventional country gentry for the characters in this work. Apparently not based on earlier sources, the story carries the moral that fathers should allow their daughters to choose their own husbands – hence the subtitle of the work.

Colonel Oldboy (tenor) has arranged for his son, Mr Jessamy (tenor), to marry Sir John Flowerdale's daughter Clarissa (soprano). She, however, is in love with Lionel (tenor). A visitor, Harman (tenor), runs off with Colonel Oldboy's daughter, Diana (soprano). But neither daughter wants to offend her father, and finally both men accept their daughters' wishes.

Dibdin originally composed about half of the music for the opera, and the remainder was taken from operas by composers such as Scolari and Vento. Despite the quality of Dibdin's music, the opera was not very successful at Covent Garden, probably because of inadequate rehearsal time. The work was revised, and brought out under its subtitle, *A School for Fathers*, at Drury Lane two years later (8 February 1770). Changes to the prose were minimal, and had mostly been made when the opera was running at Covent Garden (they were already evident in the fourth edition of the libretto, published in 1768). However, important alterations were made to the songs. Naturally, Dibdin wanted to increase his own contribution, but he was also compelled to rewrite many of the songs because of the different vocal ranges of the new cast. In particular, he was instructed to compose rather more demanding songs for Mrs Wrighten, Garrick's latest new soprano. The casts of the first performances were (Covent Garden/Drury Lane): Colonel Oldboy: Shuter/Parsons; Mr Jessamy: Dyer/Dodd; Lionel: Mattocks/Vernon; Harman: Mahon/Fawcett; Jenkins (bass): Dunstall/Bannister; Diana: Mrs Baker/Mrs Wrighten; Clarissa: Miss Macklin/Mrs Baddeley; Jenny: Mrs Mattocks/Miss Radley. The opera had little more success at Drury Lane than at Covent Garden. However, it fared significantly better outside London. One notable early success was at the Capel Street theatre in Dublin where, after its première on 2 April 1770, it ran for 26 nights.

IRENA CHOLIJ

Lipkowska [Lipkovskaya, née Marschner], **Lydia (Yakovlevna)** (*b* Babino, 25 May/6 June 1882; *d* Beirut, 22 March 1958). Russian soprano. She studied at the St Petersburg Conservatory, and sang in St Petersburg at the Imperial Opera (1906–8 and 1911–13) and in private opera companies (1913–15). In 1909 she sang in Paris and then in the USA, appearing with the companies of Boston (1909) and Chicago (1910), and singing with the Metropolitan Opera (1909–11). She made her Covent Garden début as Mimì in 1911, later appearing as Wolf-Ferrari's Susanna, Gilda and Violetta. At Monte Carlo in 1914 she took part in the first performances of Ponchielli's *I Mori di Valenza* with Georgy Baklanov and Giovanni Martinelli. After emigrating to France in 1919, she appeared with different émigré opera troupes in western Europe, toured the USSR (1928–9) and later lived and taught in Romania;

among her students was the soprano Virginia Zeani. Lipkowska returned to Paris in 1945 before settling in Lebanon. Her repertory included Lakmé, Lucia, Rimsky-Korsakov's Marfa (*The Tsar's Bride*), the Snow Maiden and Olga (*Ivan the Terrible*), and Tchaikovsky's Tatyana and Iolanta. According to contemporary critics she was a good actress with an attractive presence and a pure voice capable of expressing uncomplicated emotions. She made 29 recordings between 1911 and 1914.

S. Yu. Levik: *Zapiski opernogo pevtsa* [Notes of an Opera Singer] (Moscow, 1955, enlarged 2/1962)   HAROLD BARNES

Lipovšek, Marjana (*b* Ljubljana, 3 Dec 1946). Slovene mezzo-soprano. She studied in Graz and in Vienna, joining the Staatsoper there in 1979 and then singing in Berlin, Hamburg, Frankfurt, Munich, Madrid and at La Scala. Her repertory includes Dorabella, Carmen, Ulrica (*Un ballo in maschera*), Azucena, Amneris, Magdalene, Marina (*Boris Godunov*), the Composer, Octavian and Delilah (which she sang at Bregenz). In 1986 she created Rosa Sacchi in *Die schwarze Maske* at Salzburg, and in 1990 she made her Covent Garden début as Clytemnestra and her Metropolitan début as Fricka. A fine actress, she has a vibrant voice particularly strong in the lower register.   ELIZABETH FORBES

Lipp, Wilma (*b* Vienna, 26 April 1925). Austrian soprano. She studied in Vienna, making her début there in 1943 as Rosina and joining the Staatsoper two years later. In 1948 she sang the Queen of Night, a role she repeated at Salzburg (1949), La Scala (1950) and the Paris Opéra (1953). In 1951 she sang the Woodbird at Bayreuth and made her Covent Garden début as Gilda, returning in 1955 as Violetta. In 1957 she sang Konstanze at Glyndebourne and in 1962 made her American début as Nannetta at San Francisco. Her roles included Blonde, Servilia (*La clemenza di Tito*), Adèle, Sophie and the Italian Singer (*Capriccio*); later she took on lyrical roles such as Ilia, Pamina, Donna Elvira, Countess Almaviva, Eva, and Alice Ford. She sang Marianne (*Der Rosenkavalier*) at Salzburg (1983) and Turin (1986). The pure tone of her voice and her accurate coloratura are displayed in her recordings of the Queen of Night for Karajan and Böhm.
          ALAN BLYTH

Lippmann, Friedrich (*b* Dresden, 25 July 1932). German musicologist. He studied in Berlin and Kiel, where his professors included A. A. Abert, Blume and Wiora; he took the doctorate in 1962 with a dissertation on the structure of early 19th-century Italian *opera seria* (published in *AnMc*, 1969, as *Vincenzo Bellini und die Italienische Opera seria seiner Zeit*). After working at the Joseph Haydn-Institut in Cologne (1962–4) he moved to Rome as director of the music history section of the Deutsches Historisches Institut; he became editor of *Analecta musicologica* in 1966. His research has been concerned with 18th- and 19th-century Italian opera, centring on Bellini, and the relationship between libretto and music. He has published extensively in German and Italian periodicals and collective works.

Liprandi, Nicolo. *See* ANELLI, ANGELO.

Lipton, Martha (*b* New York, 6 April 1916). American mezzo-soprano. She studied with Paul Reimers at the Juilliard School and made her début with the New Opera Company, New York, in 1941, as Pauline in *The Queen of Spades*. At the Metropolitan she gave almost 300 performances between 1941 and 1961, notably as Cherubino, Siébel (Gounod's *Faust*), Amneris and Hänsel. She appeared in the Netherlands (1952–3) and Chicago (Herodias in *Salome*, 1956), and at the Carnegie Hall in 1959 she sang in the American première of Wolf's *Der Corregidor*.   DAVID CUMMINGS

Lirico (It.). The term, meaning 'lyric', is used in English writing generally to describe a singer whose voice is lighter than that required for more dramatic roles and which suits a smooth, melodic style rather than a more declamatory form of utterance. In Italy, the *tenore lirico* is distinguished from the *tenore leggiero* on the one hand and the *tenore spinto* on the other, though their roles may overlap (the term 'lirico spinto' describes an intermediate type). A similar gradation exists for the soprano, whose roles appropriate for the lyric voice include Mimì and Manon Lescaut, Eva and Elsa, Micaëla in *Carmen* and Tatyana in *Yevgeny Onegin*.

          J. B. STEANE

Lirico Internazionale. Theatre in MILAN, formerly the Teatro della Cannobiana.

Lisbon (Port. Lisboa). Capital of Portugal. During the first quarter of the 18th century several zarzuelas and other Spanish semi-operatic works were performed at the Lisbon court and at the houses of the nobility, and from 1731 onwards attempts were also made to promote public performances of opera. It was only in December 1735, however, that an Italian court violinist, Alessandro Paghetti, opened the first Italian opera house, the Academia da Trindade. During the next eight years Metastasian *opere serie* by Leo, Rinaldo di Capua, Schiassi and others were performed there and at the Teatro Novo da Rua dos Condes, which replaced it in 1738. To the latter belonged the singers Annibale Pio Fabri and Maria Caterina Negri and the set designer Roberto Clerici, who had been members of Handel's company in London.

From 1733 the Teatro do Bairro Alto competed with the Italians, presenting puppet operas with spoken dialogues. The enthusiasm of the Portuguese aristocracy for opera, which led some of its members to try to involve themselves in the opera business or promote private opera productions, does not seem to have been shared by João V (ruled 1707–50), who created difficulties over the opening of the Italian opera house. During his reign only half a dozen operas, all of them comic, were performed at court during Carnival, notably by F. A. de Almeida, who had been a royal scholar in Rome. In his last eight years illness led João V to forbid every kind of entertainment, including opera.

However, soon after José I's accession a handsome theatre, the Casa da Opera, now known as the Opera do Tejo (cap. 600), was built near the royal palace and the river Tagus by Giovanni Carlo Sicinivale Galli-Bibiena, and was inaugurated on 31 March 1755 with *Alessandro nell'Indie* by David Perez, who had moved to Portugal from Italy (fig.1). This theatre was, however, destroyed in the earthquake of 1 November 1755 (fig.2). Court performances were resumed only eight years later at the Ajuda and Salvaterra theatres, both also built by Galli-Bibiena. The former (cap. *c*130) was near the wooden palace in the suburbs of the Ajuda, where the court took up residence after the earthquake; the latter

1. 'Alessandro nell'Indie' (David Perez), Act 1 scene xi: design by Giovanni Carlo Sicinivale Galli-Bibiena for the original production which inaugurated the Casa de Opera, Lisbon, on 31 March 1755

(cap. 500) was near the country palace at Salvaterra de Magos, some 65 km north of Lisbon, where the royal family spent the carnival season (both theatres were demolished in the 19th century). There were also occasional performances at the small temporary theatres built during the summer at the Palácio de Queluz near Lisbon. All these spectacles were now produced on a more modest scale, the all-male casts, including several castratos, being in the service of both the court theatres and the royal chapel. Besides Perez's operas, works by other leading Italian composers of the day were performed, including many by Jommelli. There was also now a growing interest in *opera buffa*.

The public theatres of the Bairro Alto and the Rua dos Condes were rebuilt after the earthquake and in 1763 again began presenting operas, sung by visiting Italian companies. The interest in opera led to the creation in 1771 of a Sociedade para a Subsistência dos Teatros Públicos, organized by a group of Lisbon businessmen, but the excessive expenditure on singers and dancers led to its dissolution in 1774 or 1775, occasioning a further 15-year gap in the operatic activity of the public theatres. Only between 1790 and 1792 was there a brief revival of Italian opera at the Rua dos Condes theatre, conducted – apparently for the first time in a public theatre – by a Portuguese composer, António Leal Moreira. By then female singers and dancers had been banned from the public stage in Lisbon.

The opening of the Teatro de S Carlos in Lisbon in 1793 and of the Teatro de S João in Oporto in 1798

2. Ruins of the Casa de Opera after the earthquake of 1 November 1755: engraving (1757) by J. P. le Bas after Paris and Pedegache

signalled both the end of court opera and the establishment of bourgeois opera houses presenting the Italian repertory. The former was built by business enterprise, the latter by public subscription. Both operated on a system similar to that of their Italian counterparts: they were rented to an impresario who mounted the whole season and directed the companies, consisting almost exclusively of Italian singers, a system that prevailed for most of the 19th century. The repertory of both theatres generally followed contemporary Italian trends closely, the most popular composers being Rossini, Donizetti and Verdi. In particular Verdi's operas were generally heard soon after their Italian premières. But Meyerbeer and Wagner, and Gounod and Massenet in the later part of the century, were also performed. Portuguese operas were rarely staged.

In 1825 the Count of Farrobo, the impresario of the Teatro de S Carlos, built a private opera house on his farm, the Laranjeiras, in what is now the Zoological Garden; only the outer walls remain, following a fire in 1862. Many serious and comic operas were performed there by casts of both professional and amateur singers. During the first half of the century operas were also occasionally produced elsewhere, for example at the Academia Filarmónica, also presided over by the Count of Farrobo.

In the second half of the 19th century the Rua dos Condes, Ginásio (1846), Don Fernando (1849) and Trindade (1867) theatres specialized in a mixed repertory which included *opéras comiques*, burlettas, burlesque operas, operettas, vaudevilles and Spanish zarzuelas, many of them written in, or translated into, Portuguese and thus marking a fundamental difference from the repertory of the Teatro de S Carlos. In the last quarter of the century three other theatres opened which also specialized in comic operas and zarzuelas: the Recreios Wyttoyne (1875), the Real Coliseu de Lisboa (1887) and the Avenida (1888).

After 1940 the repertory of the S Carlos was enlarged to include regular productions of French and German operas, sung in the original language by foreign companies who also performed at the Coliseu dos Recreios, in an attempt to reach a wider audience. Operas were also performed irregularly at the S Luís and Politeama theatres. When, after 1974, efforts were made to create a national opera company, it was established first at the Teatro da Trindade and later at the S Carlos. More recently the S Carlos has mounted productions of operas by contemporary Portuguese composers.

*

DBP
F. da Fonseca Benevides: *O Real Theatro de S. Carlos de Lisboa desde a sua fundação em 1793 até á actualidade* (Lisbon, 1883–1902)
A. Sousa Bastos: *Diccionário do theatro portuguez* (Lisbon, 1908)
G. de Matos Sequeira: *Teatro de outros tempos* (Lisbon, 1933)
T. Borba and F. Lopes Graça: *Dicionário de musica (ilustrado)* (Lisbon, 1956)
M. V. de Carvalho: 'Denken ist Sterben', oder Das Opernhaus von Lissabon (São Carlos-Theater) im Wandel sozial-kommunikativer Systeme vom ausgehenden 18. Jahrhundert bis zu unserer Zeit (diss., Humboldt U., Berlin, 1984)
M. C. de Brito: *Opera in Portugal in the Eighteenth Century* (Cambridge, 1989)
M. C. de Brito and D. Cranmer: *Crónicas da vida musical portuguesa na primeira metade do século XIX* (Lisbon, 1990)
M. C. de Brito: 'La penisola iberica', *SOI*, ii (forthcoming) [18th century only]   MANUEL CARLOS DE BRITO

Lïsenko, Nikolay Vital'yevich. *See* LYSENKO, MYKOLA VITALIYOVYCH.

Lisinski, Vatroslav [Fuchs, Ignacije] (*b* Zagreb, bap. 8 July 1819; *d* Zagreb, 31 May 1854). Croatian composer. He studied music privately, graduated in arts and law, and began work as an unpaid clerk. His first compositions were enthusiastically received, and he rapidly progressed from small-scale works to an opera, *Ljubav i zloba* ('Love and Malice'; 2, D. Demeter, Zagreb, 28 March 1846; ed. L. Županović, Zagreb, 1969). This was the first opera of modern Croatian and South Slavonic music, and its performance was recognized as a significant event by the *Wiener allgemeine Theaterzeitung* (8 May 1846). Lisinski now decided to concentrate wholly on music and left for Prague to study at the conservatory, but finding that he was over the age limit, he was obliged to take private lessons with J. B. Kittl and K. F. Pitsch. The music of this period, solo songs, an overture, *Bellona*, and parts of his second opera, *Porin* (1848–51; 5, Zagreb, 2 Oct 1897; ed. L. Županović, Zagreb, 1969), testifies to his rapid development.

With his return to Zagreb, the most difficult phase of his life began. Having legalized his name as Vatroslav Lisinski, he endeavoured, in the exceptionally hard circumstances of the years after 1848, to make his way as a professional musician, working as a teacher, composer and conductor. He failed to make a living, however, and was forced by 1853 to abandon music; disillusioned, he accepted a post as a clerk. He died from dropsy.

Lisinski was the leading early Romantic composer in Croatia. Born at the time of national revival during the years before 1848, he expertly reflected the enthusiasm and dynamism of those days as well as the renewal of interest in vocal music. Between 1841 and 1852 he wrote 145 works, drawing on Czech and Croatian folk melody in some of them – he was the first to do so. Parts of *Porin*, a chivalric opera in the grand-opera tradition, also show that he tried to make use of broader Slavonic characteristics (as in Sveslav's Act 4 aria 'Strogi oče na nebesi': 'Our father', which suggests an acquaintance with the music of Glinka). In his use of leitmotif for Porin himself, and in the masterly ensembles, he revealed a true gift for operatic writing.

*

V. Klaić: *V. Lisinski i prve dvije hrvatske opere* [Lisinski and the First Two Croatian Operas] (Zagreb, 1919)
L. Županović: *Vatroslav Lisinski (1819–1854): život – djelo – značenje* [Lisinski: his Life, Work and Significance] (Zagreb, 1969)
Zvuk, nos.96–7 (1969) [Lisinski issue]
J. Bezić and K. Kos: 'Prilog problematici folklornog i nacionalnog u opusu Vatroslava Lisinskog', *Arti musices*, ii (1971), 121–30
J. Andreis: *Music in Croatia* (Zagreb, 1974)
                                        LOVRO ŽUPANOVIĆ

Lisitsyan, Pavel [Pogos] **Gerasim** (*b* Vladikavkaz, 24 Oct/6 Nov 1911). Armenian baritone. He studied in Leningrad, and made his début there in 1935. He first sang with the Bol'shoy Opera in 1940 and was for many years the company's leading baritone. He appeared at the Metropolitan as Amonasro in 1960, when he made a concert tour of the USA. He was a notable Yevgeny Onegin, Yeletsky, Escamillo and Janusz (*Halka*), and also sang in the standard Italian and Russian repertories. Lisitsyan had one of the century's most beautiful baritone voices allied to considerable artistry, as can be heard on many of his records; he was also a fine actor.   ALAN BLYTH

List [Fleissig], **Emanuel** (*b* Vienna, 22 March 1888; *d* Vienna, 21 June 1967). Austrian bass, later naturalized American. He was a chorister at the Theater an der Wien, then emigrated to the USA, where he studied with Josiah Zuro. Returning to Vienna in 1920, he made his début at the Volksoper in 1922 as Méphistophélès. The next year he went to the Berlin Städtische Oper, and from 1925 to 1933 was a member of the Staatsoper. He made his Covent Garden début in 1925 as Pogner and returned (1934–6) as Hunding, Hagen, King Mark, Ramfis and Ochs, his most famous role. He sang at the Metropolitan (where he made his début as the Landgrave in *Tannhäuser*) from 1933 to 1950 and at San Francisco, Chicago and Buenos Aires. At Salzburg between 1931 and 1935 he sang Osmin, the Commendatore, Rocco and King Mark, and at the 1933 Bayreuth Festival, Fafner, Hunding and Hagen. Forced to leave Germany, he did not return to Berlin until 1950. List had a deep, rich bass which, with his imposing presence, admirably fitted him for the Wagner villains he so tellingly portrayed.   HAROLD ROSENTHAL/R

Lisuart und Dariolette [*Lisuart und Dariolette, oder Die Frage und die Antwort* ('Lisuart and Dariolette, or the Question and the Answer')]. *Romantisch-comische Oper* in two acts by JOHANN ADAM HILLER to a libretto by DANIEL SCHIEBELER after CHARLES-SIMON FAVART's *La fée Urgèle* (based on Geoffrey Chaucer's *The Wife of Bath's Tale*); Leipzig, Theater am Rannstädter Thore, 25 November 1766 (revised version in three acts, 7 January 1767).

Queen Ginevra of England (soprano) has sent the knight Lisuart (tenor) with his squire Derwin (bass) to find her beautiful daughter Dariolette (soprano), missing for a year. Lisuart fails in his mission and stands to forfeit his life unless he can answer the question, 'What pleases women most?'. An old lady gives him the answer ('supremacy'), on condition that he marry her. She turns out to be Dariolette, put under a spell by a wicked fairy.

In *Lisuart*, first given by the Koch company, Hiller experimented with serious elements, including da capo arias. This attempt to infuse German opera with italianate vocal ideals remained an isolated deviation from his successful portrayal of popular and comic manners in his other operas of the period.

THOMAS BAUMAN

Liszt, Franz [Ferenc] (*b* Raiding, nr Sopron, 22 Oct 1811; *d* Bayreuth, 31 July 1886). Hungarian composer, pianist and conductor. His importance to opera was threefold: through his conducting, his operatic transcriptions for piano, and his essays and other pioneering work on behalf of contemporary opera composers. Although he had ambitions to be an opera composer until the early 1850s, he completed only a single, youthful one-act work, *Don Sanche, ou Le château d'amour*.

After studies in Vienna with Salieri (composition) and Czerny (piano), Liszt toured widely but was based mainly in Paris from 1823 until 1835. His teachers in his first years there were Paer and Reicha, and the former may well have had a hand in the orchestration of *Don Sanche*. The overture was heard in Manchester in 1825, during a visit by Liszt, and the complete opera was given at the Académie Royale later that year just before the composer's 14th birthday. The libretto by Mme Théaulon and de Rancé was based on a tale by Claris de

Florian. Adolphe Nourrit sang the title role, and the conductor was Rodolphe Kreutzer. Only three further performances were given and the score was subsequently lost. The 1825 performance parts were rediscovered in 1903 and *Don Sanche* has been revived occasionally in modern times as a tuneful youthful curiosity (vocal score, ed. G. Woolfenden, 1977).

Liszt was greatly influenced by the melodic styles of Rossini, Bellini and Donizetti; in Paris he also admired Auber, Halévy and Meyerbeer. His large corpus of piano works based on opera (*fantaisies, variations, réminiscences, illustrations, paraphrases* etc.) began to appear in 1824, with an *Impromptu brillant* on themes from Rossini and Spontini, and continued throughout his career. His last opera transcription (1882) was based on the revised Verdi-Boito *Simon Boccanegra*. The contemporary impact of these works (especially when played by himself or by pupils such as Hans von Bülow or Karl Tausig) was enormous. At their finest they rank as piano compositions of intrinsic originality, both technically and in terms of form, harmony and tonality. Either they encapsulate the dramatic essence of an entire work (as in the *Réminiscences* of Bellini's *Norma* and the fantasy on *Don Giovanni*, both of which also exist in two-piano versions) or they reproduce a specific section or number from an opera (as in the famous *Rigoletto* paraphrase of the Act 3 quartet, in which Liszt characteristically adds several felicitous harmonic touches of his own). Successful composers such as Donizetti and Meyerbeer recorded their admiration and gratitude for Liszt's efforts; for others, his arrangements provided a kind of propaganda, as in the case of Wagner, from whose operas Liszt made 14 arrangements, from the *Tannhäuser* overture (1848) to the 'Feierlicher Marsch zum heiligen Gral' from *Parsifal* (1882).

After a period of travel in Switzerland and Italy, Liszt's most remarkable period of virtuoso tours throughout Europe occupied him from 1839–47, during which his operatic transcriptions were prominent in his repertory. But his ambitions as composer and conductor grew in those years and he first conducted an opera, *Die Zauberflöte*, in Breslau, in 1843. The previous year he had been appointed honorary Kapellmeister to the Grand Ducal Court at Weimar, an appointment he took up fully in 1848; the first opera he conducted there was *Martha*. His own numerous operatic plans came to nothing but included *Sardanapale*, after Byron (1845–51; 111 pages of sketches exist), and operas based on *Faust* and the *Divina Commedia*. (These last subjects bore fruit in other ways, notably in the *Faust* and *Dante* symphonies.)

His major achievements at the Weimar Hofoper were *Tannhäuser* (1849), the first production since the Dresden première, and the premières of *Lohengrin* (1850), Schubert's *Alfonso ed Estrella* (1854), the revised version of *Benvenuto Cellini* (1852) and Cornelius's *Der Barbier von Bagdad* (1858), a new production of Schumann's *Genoveva*, four operas by Gluck, Rubinstein's *Sibirskiye okhotniki* ('The Siberian Hunters', as *Die sibirischen Jäger*), Raff's *König Alfred* and others. For Wagner, an exile from Germany, Weimar was a vital flagship for his music; the *Ring* cycle was even considered for performance there and Liszt helped Wagner with his purse and his pen, through arrangements and articles on the operas from *Der fliegende Holländer* to *Das Rheingold*. For Berlioz, so rarely performed in France, Weimar was a huge encouragement; Liszt's mistress and mentor, Princess Carolyne von Sayn-Wittgenstein, was the moving force behind his greatest opera, *Les Troyens*.

In addition to those on Berlioz and Wagner, Liszt wrote essays on Gluck, Beethoven, Weber, Schubert, Meyerbeer, Bellini, Auber, Boieldieu and Donizetti; on the art of performance, and on singers, such as his pupil and friend Pauline Viardot.

As a conductor he was renowned for his flexibility of beat and innovatory use of gestures and facial expression to achieve the desired phrasing and shaping. His philosophy of conducting was summed up in his oft-quoted phrase, 'We are steersmen, not oarsmen', and Cornelius considered his rehearsals as the finest musical education. He belongs to the founding fathers of modern operatic conducting, along with Wagner, and Liszt's own disciples, von Bülow, Nikisch and Weingartner.

Although he resigned his Weimar post in 1858, Liszt continued his association with the town. Thanks to him Saint-Saëns' *Samson et Dalila* received its première there; and through colleagues such as Alexander Ritter, his influence on the course of German opera extended to Richard Strauss. Liszt's second daughter, Cosima, married first von Bülow (conductor of the first *Tristan und Isolde* and *Die Meistersinger*) and secondly, Wagner himself, and Liszt himself was a prominent figure at the rehearsals and premières of the *Ring* and *Parsifal* at Bayreuth. He died there while on a visit to attend the première of Cosima's production of *Tristan*.

One other work of Liszt's has been performed as an opera: *Die Legende von der heiligen Elisabeth* (1857–62), an oratorio to a libretto by Otto Roquette; it was staged at Weimar in 1881 (without the composer's approval) and notably at the Metropolitan Opera, during the American engagement in World War I, when Wagner's music was proscribed.

TRANSCRIPTIONS, ARRANGEMENTS AND COMPOSITIONS BASED ON OPERA THEMES

s – Searle numbers

for piano two hands

Auber: La fiancée (Grande fantaisie sur la tyrolienne s385, 1829; Tyrolean Melody s385a, pubd 1856); Auber: La muette de Portici (Tarantelle di bravura s386, 1846; 2 pieces s387, unpubd); Bellini: Norma (Réminiscences s394, 1841); Bellini: I puritani (Réminiscences, s390, 1836; Hexaméron [variations] s392, 1837; Introduction et polonaise s391, 1840); Bellini: La sonnambula (Fantasie s393, 1839); Berlioz: Benvenuto Cellini (Bénédiction et serment s396, 1852); Donizetti: Dom Sébastien (Marche funèbre s402, 1844); Donizetti: Lucia di Lammermoor (Réminiscences s397, 1839; Marche et cavatine s398, 1839; Valse à capriccio sur deux motifs de Lucia et Parisina [2 versions] s401, 1842, ?1850); Donizetti: Lucrezia Borgia (Réminiscences s400, pubd 1841–2)

Erkel: Hunyadi László (Schwanengesang and march s405, 1847); Glinka: Ruslan i Lyudmila (Tscherkessen-Marsch s406, 1843); Gounod: Faust (Valse s407, pubd 1861); Gounod: La reine de Saba (Les sabéennes [berceuse] s408, pubd 1865); Gounod: Roméo et Juliette (Les adieux [rêverie] s409, 1867): Halévy: La Juive (Réminiscences s409a, 1835); Méhul: Joseph (Variationen über Romanze, 1834); Mercadante: Il giuramento (Réminiscences de La Scala, 1838); Meyerbeer: L'Africaine (Illustrations s415, 1865); Meyerbeer: Les Huguenots (Grande fantaisie s412, 1836); Meyerbeer: Le prophète (Illustrations s414, 1849–50); Meyerbeer: Robert le diable (Réminiscences s413, 1841); Mosonyi: Szép Ilonka (Fantaisie s417, 1867); Mozart: Don Juan (Réminiscences s418, 1841); Mozart: Le nozze di Figaro and Don Juan (double fantasia s697, 1842)

Pacini: Niobe (Divertissement sur la cavatine 'I tuoi frequenti palpiti' s419, 1835–6); Raff: König Alfred (Andante finale and march s421, 1853); Rossini: Ermione (Sept variations brillants s149, 1824); Rossini: La donna del lago (Impromptu brillant s150, 1824); Rossini: Le siège de Corinthe (Variations sur une

marche ['Questo nome qui suono vittoria'] s421a, 1830); Rossini: Otello (Canzonetta in Venezia e Napoli s162, ?1859); Tchaikovsky: Yevgeny Onegin (Polonaise s429, 1879); Verdi: Aida (Danza sacra e duetto final s436, pubd 1879); Verdi: Don Carlos (Coro di festa e marcia funebre s435, 1867–8); Verdi: Ernani (Concert paraphrase [2 versions] s432, 1847, before 1859); Verdi: I Lombardi (Salve Maria de Jérusalem s431, 1848); Verdi: Rigoletto (Paraphrase de concert s434, 1859); Verdi: Simon Boccanegra (Réminiscences s438, 1882); Verdi: Il trovatore (Miserere s433, 1859)

Wagner: Der fliegende Holländer (Spinning Chorus s440, 1860; Ballad s441, 1872); Wagner: (2 pieces from Lohengrin s446, 1854; 2 pieces from Lohengrin and Tännhauser s445, 1852); Wagner: Die Meistersinger (Am stillen Herd s448, 1871); Wagner: Parsifal (Feierlicher Marsch zum heiligen Gral s450, 1882); Wagner: Rienzi (Phantasiestück s439, 1859); Wagner: Der Ring des Nibelungen (Walhall s449, ?1876); Wagner: Tannhäuser (ov. s442, 1848; O du mein holder Abendstern s444, 1849; Pilgrims' Chorus s443, 1861); Wagner: Tristan und Isolde (Liebestod s447, 1867); Weber: Der Freischütz (Fantasia s451, 1840); Weber: La preciosa ('Einsam bin ich nicht allein' s453, 1848)

for piano four hands

Bellini: La sonnambula (Fantasia s627, c1852); Berlioz: Benvenuto Cellini (Bénédiction et serment s628, pubd 1854); Donizetti: Lucia di Lammermoor (Marche et cavatine s628a, ?1839); Raff: König Alfred (Andante finale and march s631, ?1853); Mozart: Die Zauberflöte (Adagio ['Der welcher diese Strasse'] s634a, 1875–81)

for two pianos

Bellini: Norma (Réminiscences s655, after 1841); Bellini: I puritani (Hexaméron [variations] s654, after 1837); Mozart: Don Giovanni (Réminiscences s656, after 1841)

for miscellaneous instruments

Cornelius: Der Barbier von Bagdad (ov. s352, 1877) orchestra; Wagner: Tannhäuser (O du mein holder Abendstern s444, 1852), vn, pf; Tannhäuser (Pilgrims' Chorus s676, 1860), organ

piano scores

Berlioz: Les francs-juges (Ouverture, 1833); L. Bertin: Esmeralda (complete opera, 1837; Air chanté par Massol, 1837; 3 pieces, 1837); Rossini: Guillaume Tell (Ouverture, 1838); Weber: Oberon (ov., 1843); Weber: Der Freischütz (ov., 1843)

*

Grove5 (H. Searle)

K. Hamilton: *The Operatic Transcriptions of Franz Liszt* (diss., U. of Cambridge, 1989)

DEREK WATSON

Literaturoper (Ger.: 'literature-opera'). A term of recent origin used to denote an opera in which the composer sets an already existing literary text, however abbreviated (as opposed to a specially written libretto). Examples include Debussy's *Pelléas et Mélisande* (text by Maeterlinck; 1902), Mascagni's *Guglielmo Ratcliff* (Heine, trans. A. Maffei; 1895), Zandonai's *Francesca da Rimini* (D'Annunzio; 1914), Dargomïzhky's *The Stone Guest* (Pushkin; 1872), Rimsky-Korsakov's *Mozart and Salieri* (Pushkin; 1898), Vaughan Williams's *Riders to the Sea* (Synge; 1937), Boughton's *Alkestis* (Euripides, trans. Gilbert Murray; 1922), Searle's *Hamlet* (Shakespeare; 1968) and Henze's *Ein Landarzt* (Kafka; 1951).

JULIAN BUDDEN

Literes, Antonio de (*b* Artá, Majorca, ? 18 June 1673; *d* Madrid, 18 Jan 1747). Spanish composer. He began his formal musical training in 1686 in the choir school of the Spanish royal chapel and studied the *violón* with Manuel de Soba. In 1693 he was acknowledged by the patriarch of the chapel to be a skilled player of the viol, violin and *violón*, and competent as a composer. Upon examination he was awarded the position of *violón* in the chapel and interim instructor of the choirboys. Later he became principal *violón* in the royal chapel and esteemed as a composer for both his sacred and his secular works.

By 1697, in addition to his duties with the royal chapel, Literes was increasingly called upon to perform in the royal theatrical orchestra and probably participated in revivals with music by Juan Hidalgo and productions of new works with music by Sebastián Durón and Juan de Navas. This exposure evidently bore fruit: he succeeded the exiled Durón as leading theatrical composer for a limited period, composing seven zarzuelas (four with texts by José de Cañizares) and one short opera, *Los elementos*, described as an 'ópera armónica al estilo italiano'. Four of the zarzuela scores survive in addition to the score of *Los elementos*. Literes's importance as a theatrical composer extended beyond the court to the commercial public theatres of Madrid, as the first court composer to benefit fully from the flexible patronage of the newly installed Bourbon monarchy. According to the surviving accounts of the Cruz and Príncipe theatres, revivals of zarzuelas with music by Literes were heard with consistent success season after season as late as 1734, although they were originally composed before 1715. The most striking example is *Acis y Galatea*. Following its court première in 1708, it became the most acclaimed work of the first half of the century in the public theatres, enjoying popular support for two decades.

Although he continued to compose for the royal chapel, Literes's ascendancy at court was eclipsed by the newly-arrived Italian composers favoured by the queen, in spite of the fact that Literes clearly belonged to the small group of Spanish court composers who deliberately adopted the foreign style early in the century. Some of his pieces in Spanish forms preserve a traditionally Spanish approach to the text and to affective expression, with controlled treatment of dissonance. At the same time, his scores contain many set pieces written in an italianate or pan-European style: da capo arias with highly melismatic vocal lines, fragmentation of the poetic text, rapid figurations in the instrumental parts and italianate expressive devices. Although Literes was indeed a leader in an epoch of stylistic plurality, contemporaries who condemned stylistic importations and innovations judged his music as preserving truly Spanish qualities of 'sweetness' and 'elegance'.

See also ACIS Y GALATEA.

Júpiter y Danae (zar, 3), Madrid, Alcázar or Buen Retiro, 6 Jan 1700, *E-Mn*

Los elementos (ópera, 1), *Mn*

Acis y Galatea (zar, 2, J. de Cañizares), Madrid, Alcázar or Buen Retiro, 19 Dec 1708, *Mn*, *P-EVp*, 1 tonada (Madrid, ?1708)

Hasta lo insensible adora (zar, 2, Cañizares), Madrid, Cruz, 16 May 1713, *EVp*

El estrago en la fineza (zar, 2, Cañizares), Madrid, Cruz, 9 May 1718, *EVp*

*

E. Cotarelo y Mori: *Historia de la zarzuela* (Madrid, 1934), 76ff

A. Martín Moreno: 'El compositor mallorquín Antonio Literes (1673–1747)', *Tesoro sacro musical*, xi/1 (1978), 24–6

W. M. Bussey: *French and Italian Influence on the Zarzuela 1700–1770* (Ann Arbor, 1982)

A. Martín Moreno: *Historia de la música española 4: siglo XVIII* (Madrid, 1985), 45–7, 386–8   LOUISE K. STEIN

Lithuania. The earliest opera performances in Lithuania took place in Vilnius in 1634, but for social and historical reasons no national opera developed until the 20th century. *Birutė* by Mikas Petrauskas (1873–1937), produced in Vilnius in 1906, is usually considered the first Lithuanian national opera, but in fact is a play with incidental music; it did however pave the way for the composer's more mature opera *Eglė žalčių karalienė* ('Eglė, Queen of the Grass-Snakes'), based on a popular folktale and completed in 1920. Only two operas had firmly entered the national repertory during the years of Lithuanian independence (1919–40) when most operatic activity shifted to the then capital, Kaunas. The first was the historical-heroic *Gražina* (1933) by Jurgis Karnavičius (1884–1941), the second the fantasy *Trys talismanai* ('The Three Talismans', 1936) by Antanas Račiūnas (1905–84). *Gražina*, based on Adam Mickiewicz's heroic poem, depicts the Lithuanians' struggle with the Knights of the Cross and speaks of patriotism, self-sacrifice and heroism; the music is sincere, simple and appealing, drawing on folk melodies, and won the opera considerable popularity. In *The Three Talismans* Račiūnas, a pupil of Nadia Boulanger, combined simple means of expression with a slightly modern idiom, in a depiction of the struggle between good and evil. Also historically significant are Karnavičius's second opera, *Radvila Perkūnas* (1937), and *Pagirėnai* (1941) by Stasys Šimkus (1887–1943).

From 1953 onwards the Vilnius, Kaunas and Klaipėda theatres gave the premières of about 40 operas of Lithuanian composers, works of uneven merit. The doctrine of 'socialist realism' hung over composers' heads like the sword of Damocles, demanding ideological 'purity', adherence to party principles, representation of the revolutionary spirit, etc. As a rule, works written in spite of these doctrines were the more impressive. Historical themes dominate in the operas of Klova, of which *Pilėnai* is especially successful, in *Dalia* (1957, produced in Vilnius in 1959 and televised in 1985) by Balys Dvarionas (1904–72) and in *Sukilėliai* ('The Rebels', 1957, staged in 1977) by Julius Juzeliūnas (b 1916). The tragedy of a village girl is depicted in *Paskenduolė* ('The Drowned Maiden', 1957) by Vitolis Baumilas (1928–91). Račiūnas's *Saulės miestas* ('The City of the Sun', 1965), after the book by Tommaso Campanella, tells of Kazimieras Liščinskis (in Polish, Łyszczyński), a prominent representative of free thought in 17th-century Lithuania. Characteristic of these and later Lithuanian operas are the use of classical European and Russian operatic forms and of leitmotifs, as well as folkmusic traits in the melodies and vivid choral scenes. But there are also unconvincing plots, weak librettos and uncertain musical dramaturgy.

Composers who have provided the impulse for the further development of Lithuanian opera include Eduardas Balsys (1919–84), Vytautas Paltanavičius (b 1924), Vytautas Laurušas (b 1930), Vytautas Barkauskas (b 1931) and Bronius Kutavičius (b 1932). Paltanavičius's *Kryžkelėje* ('At the Crossroads', 1967), about a Lithuanian professor who perishes in a Nazi concentration camp, Laurušas's *Paklydę paukščiai* ('The Strayed Birds', 1967), depicting the life of Lithuanian émigrés, and Balsys's *Kelionė į Tilžę* (1980), after Hermann Sudermann's short story *Die Reise nach Tilsit*, combine dramaturgical novelties and symphonic development with psychological insight. Opera and oratorio features are mixed in *Šviesos baladė* ('The Ballad of Light', 1970) by Antanas Rekašius (b 1928) and *Kristijonas* (1983) by Algimantas Bražinskas (b 1937), the latter treating the life of the 18th-century poet Kristijonas Donelaitis. Kutavičius, in his *Strazdas: žalias paukštis* ('The Thrush is a Green Bird', 1981), recalls the life and works of another Lithuanian poet, Antanas Strazdas (1760–1833), in highly poetical terms. Among operas on non-Lithuanian subjects mention should be made of Klova's *Amerikoniškoji tragedija* (1968), after Theodor Dreiser's novel, Barkauskas's *Legenda apie meilę* ('A Legend about Love', 1975), after the Turkish writer Nâzim Hikmet's play, and *Ten viduje* (1977) by Giedrius Kuprevičius (*b* 1944) after Maeterlinck's play *L'intérieur*. Children's operas have been written by Viktoras Kuprevičius (1901–92), Antanas Belazaras (1913–76), Jurgis Gaižauskas (*b* 1922), Kutavičius and Vytautas Juozapaitis (*b* 1942), some of them for radio or television. Works by Lithuanian composers who settled in the USA include *Jūratė ir Kastytis* (1955), based on a folk legend, by Kazimieras Viktoras Banaitis (1896–1963), *Dana* and *Gintaro šaly* ('In the Land of Amber') by Julius Gaidelis (1909–83), *Juodasis laivas* ('The Black Ship') by Jeronimas Kačinskas (*b* 1907), and *Maras* ('The Plague'), *Lokis* ('The Bear', after Mérimée) and *Dux Magnus* by Darius Lapinskas (*b* 1934). The means of expression used by these composers is slightly more advanced and 'international' than those of their colleagues in the native country. Several Lithuanian operas have been left unfinished, *Vaidilutė* ('The Vestal Virgin') by Vytautas Bacevičius (1905–70) among them. Important works recently staged include *Žaidimas* ('The Play') by Juzeliūnas, after Dürrenmatt's *Die Panne*, and *Dievo avinėlis* ('The Lamb of God') by Feliksas Bajoras (*b* 1934), both in 1991.

For further information on operatic life in the country's principal centres *see* KAUNAS and VILNIUS.

*
A. Miller: *Teatr i muzyka na Litwie 1745–1865* (Vilnius, 1935)
S. Yla, ed.: *Lietuvių nacionalinė opera* (Vilnius, 1960)
A. Tauragis: *Lithuanian Music: Past and Present* (Vilnius, 1971)
J. Bagdanskis: *The Lithuanian Musical Scene* (Vilnius, 1974)
V. Nakas: 'Gražina: the First Lithuanian National Opera', *Lituanus*, xxi/1 (Chicago, 1975), 45–7
V. Venckus: 'Musïkal'nïy teatr: operï i operettï', *Iz istoriy litovskoy mizïki*, iii (Leningrad, 1978), 19–44   ADEODATAS TAURAGIS

Litolff, Henry (Charles) (*b* London, 7 Aug 1818; *d* Bois-Colombes, 5 Aug 1891). French composer. His life can be divided compositionally into two periods: up to 1860 he composed and performed his own piano compositions, and from 1860 until his death he was known for his conducting and for his composition of a dozen operas (although three of them are known to have been composed before that date). Berlioz consulted him about *Benvenuto Cellini* and both composers co-operated in a concert in Paris on 2 May 1858. This event was apparently a turning point in Litolff's career; he settled in Paris in 1860. His operatic activity was limited but some of his works were popular, and his influence on operatic matters is attested by the letters of Georges Bizet. Since Litolff was the Kapellmeister at Coburg, his operas became the focus of the festivals there. Most of the operas reflect compositional styles current at the time, from German Romantic opera to French operetta modelled on Offenbach.

printed works published in Paris unless otherwise stated

Catherine Howard, Brussels, Conservatoire, April 1847
Die Braut von Kynast (grosse romantische Oper, 3, F. Fischer), Brunswick, 3 Oct 1847, vs (Brunswick, *c*1847)
Rodrigo von Toledo, *c*1848
Le chevalier Nahal, ou La gageure du diable (oc, 3, E. Plouvier), Baden-Baden, 10 Aug 1866

La boîte de Pandore (3, T. Barrière), Paris, Folies-Dramatiques, Oct 1871, vs (1871)
Héloïse et Abélard (3, L. F. Clairville and W. Busnach), Paris, Folies-Dramatiques, 17 Oct 1872, *F-Po*, vs (*c*1872)
La belle au bois dormant (opéra féerie, 3, Busnach and Clairville), Paris, Châtelet, 4 April 1874
La fiancée du roi de Garbe (4, A. Dennery and Chabrillat), Paris, Folies-Dramatiques, 29 Oct 1874, vs (1874)
La mandragore (oc, 3, J. Brésil, after A. Dumas *père: Mémoires d'un médecin*), Brussels, Fantaisies Parisiennes, 29 Jan 1876
Les templiers (5, J. Adenis, A. Silvestre and L. Bonnemère), Brussels, Monnaie, 25 Jan 1886, vs and full ballet score (1886)
L'escadron volant de la reine (3, Dennery and Brésil), Paris, 14 Dec 1888, vs (1888)
Le roi Lear [König Lear] (3, J. Adenis and E. Adenis, after W. Shakespeare and R. Holinshed), *Po*, ov. (Brunswick, 1890)
                                                               TED M. BLAIR

Little(-Augustithis), Vera (Pearl) (*b* Memphis, 10 Dec 1928). American mezzo-soprano. Trained in Alabama and in Europe, she made her début in 1958 as Carmen at the Städtische (later the Deutsche) Oper, Berlin, where she continued to sing for 30 years. She created Begonia in Henze's *Der junge Lord* in Berlin (1965) and Beroe in his *The Bassarids* at Salzburg (1966). Her repertory included Monteverdi's Octavia, Erda, Delilah, Clytemnestra, Gaea (*Daphne*) and many Verdi roles, to which her vibrant, rich-toned voice was well suited. She also sang modern parts, such as Baba the Turk, Jocasta, Circe and Melanto (Dallapiccola's *Ulisse*), with great proficiency.
                                                          ELIZABETH FORBES

Little Rock. American city, capital of Arkansas. The first successful professional opera company in the state was the Arkansas Opera Theatre in Little Rock, founded in 1973 by Ann Chotard, who continues to serve as general director and artistic director. All performances are in English and leading roles are generally taken by singers from outside the area. The Arkansas Symphony, under a variety of conductors, provides orchestral support. The company has commissioned and given first performances of two full-length operas: Libby Larsen's *Clair de lune* (22 February 1985) and Raymond Pannell's *As Long as a Child Remembers* (10 April 1986).

The company has the fourth largest school touring programme among American opera companies, and under its auspices a one-act children's opera by the Arkansas composer William Underwood, *Jorinda and Joringle*, was commissioned and given its première in 1977. The company's productions have also included operetta and musicals, and until 1989 a typical season featured four productions (three performances each) at the Arkansas Arts Center in MacArthur Park (seating 389; built in 1962).

In November 1989 the company was renamed Opera Theatre at Wildwood, and its headquarters moved to a 105-acre plot in west Little Rock, where construction began on Wildwood Park for the Performing Arts. With the move came a reorganization of the company's focus, the major operatic activity being concentrated in a two-week festival in late spring, with three to four performances each of several operas in the Studio Theatre at Wildwood (seating 315); the 1991 season included *La traviata*, *Don Giovanni* and *Don Pasquale*. A new Wildwood Theatre (seating 700) will replace the Studio Theatre as the main performance site and an outdoor amphitheatre seating 10 000 is also planned.

The University of Arkansas at Little Rock had an opera workshop from the 1950s until 1973, when Blanche Thebom was asked to create an opera theatre programme for students and professionals; that programme was dissolved in 1979. In 1989 the university's theatre and music departments combined for the première on 1 April of the one-act comic opera *Bowl, Cat and Broomstick* by Robert Boury, a composer based at the university.

DERRICK HENRY

Little Shoes [*Little Slippers*], **The**. Opera by P. I. Tchaikovsky; *see* CHEREVICHKI.

Little Sweep, The. 'An entertainment for young people' by BENJAMIN BRITTEN to a libretto by ERIC CROZIER; Aldeburgh, Jubilee Hall, 14 June 1949.

This is the third and final act of *Let's Make an Opera* op.45, a work first heard at the second Aldeburgh Festival (1949) and intended to strengthen the involvement of local young people and adult amateurs in the new enterprise. In the first two acts a group of contemporary children plan their performance and the four audience songs are rehearsed. The 45-minute entertainment itself (set in 1810, in the nursery of Iken Hall, Suffolk) alternates mainly strophic numbers with spoken dialogue. It begins with the first of the audience songs. Black Bob (bass), the sweep master, and Clem (tenor), his assistant, drag in their reluctant apprentice, Sam (treble), and eventually dispatch him up the chimney. The family children and visiting friends are playing hide-and-seek when they hear Sam calling for help. They free him and, when he pleads not to be sent back up the chimney, hide him in the toy cupboard. Black Bob, Clem and Mrs Baggott (contralto), the housekeeper, are furious at Sam's disappearance, but once they have gone to search for him elsewhere the children, led by Rowan (soprano), the nursery maid, let him out of the cupboard and give him a good bath (to the second audience song).

Sam tells the children his sad story, and they decide to help him escape, but the housekeeper's precipitate reappearance means he must return to the toy cupboard. Only a feigned collapse by one of the children, Juliet (soprano), prevents Mrs Baggott from finding him there, but when she leaves Sam is safe for the night. A nocturnal interlude, the third audience song, precedes the final scene, which takes place the following morning. Sam is given breakfast and some money, and hidden in the top of a trunk which is to accompany the visiting children as they return home. Two servants attempt to take the trunk downstairs, but only when the children help can it be moved. A final audience song, typical of the unpretentious yet lively music of *The Little Sweep*, describes the departure of the coach carrying the trunk, and Sam, to freedom.

ARNOLD WHITTALL

Little Theatre in the Haymarket. London theatre built in 1720 on the east side of the Haymarket, opposite the King's Theatre; *see* LONDON, §II, 2.

Lituani, I ('The Lithuanians'). *Dramma lirico* in a prologue and three acts by AMILCARE PONCHIELLI to a libretto by ANTONIO GHISLANZONI after Adam Mickiewicz's ballad *Konrad Wallenrod*; Milan, Teatro alla Scala, 7 March 1874.

The action is set in Marienburg during the Middle Ages. Lithuania is attempting to repel the invasion of the Teutonic knights, but the Lithuanian cause is betrayed by Vitoldo (bass). Walter (tenor), the Lithuanian captain, resolves to infiltrate the enemy ranks accompanied by his old retainer Albano (bass). He leaves his wife Aldona (soprano) to the care of her brother Arnoldo (baritone). Ten years pass. Under the name of Conrad Wallenrod, Walter has led the German army to numerous victories, for which he is now invested as Grand Master of the Teutonic Order. He commands the release of a number of prisoners; among them is Arnoldo, later joined by Aldona in the guise of a pilgrim. Both are invited by Albano to a feast in Walter's honour. Surfeited with wine and dancing, Walter calls for a heroic ballad. Arnoldo steps forward dressed as a bard. He declares himself a Lithuanian and sings of a lost leader who left his wife and dear ones ten years ago. Realizing that his secret has been discovered, Walter orders Arnoldo's arrest, whereupon Aldona cries out that Arnoldo is her brother. Walter recognizes his wife's voice beneath her disguise and entrusts her and Arnoldo to the custody of Albano. In the insurrection that follows, the Germans are defeated. Walter is once more united with Aldona, but their happiness is cut short by the distant voices of the Vehmgericht under Vitoldo, who condemn Walter to death. Walter takes poison to avoid falling into their hands, and as freedom is proclaimed throughout the land he dies in Aldona's arms, surrounded by his countrymen, while an unseen chorus of Willis (ghosts of betrothed girls who died before their marriage) sing the hero to his eternal rest.

I lituani is Ponchielli's most ambitious opera, making the fewest concessions to popular taste. Each act, and the Prologue, contains massive ensembles in which all the resources of elaborate part-writing are brought into play. There is a full-length overture in orthodox sonata form preceded by a lyrical introduction. Of the two *allegro* themes the first is taken from the battle at the start of Act 3, the second from the orchestral peroration of the finale ultimo. The opera's only motivic label, a graphic orchestral gesture connoting the defeated Lithuanians, is confined to the Prologue and Act 1; but in general the themes are deployed on a large scale. Arnoldo's ballad in Act 2 is followed by fragments of the previously heard exotic dance; and the sequel to Walter's brindisi ('Dal letargo vi destate') forms the basis of the act's concluding stretta. Especially effective is the unison writing for the chorus of the Vehmgericht. The melodies are plain yet richly harmonized, the pace measured and the rhythmic cut one of varied regularity. The final, cabaletta-like section of the duet for hero and heroine in Act 3 ('Noi torneremo alla romita valle') shows a skill in handling 11-syllable verse worthy of Verdi. The opera is coloured by an abundance of minor tonality, which, however appropriate to the subject, was not calculated to endear it to an Italian public. Nonetheless the score bears abiding witness to Ponchielli's prowess as a musician.

JULIAN BUDDEN

Litvinne, Félia (**Vasil'yevna**) [Schütz, Françoise Jeanne] (*b* St Petersburg, ? 11 Oct 1860; *d* Paris, 12 Oct 1936). Russian soprano of German and Canadian descent. She studied with Pauline Viardot and Victor Maurel in Paris, making her début with the Théâtre Italien troupe as Amelia (*Simon Boccanegra*) in 1883. She then sang throughout Europe, in New York, at La Monnaie as Brünnhilde in the first French *Die Walküre* (1887), the Opéra, La Scala, and in Rome and Venice. From 1890 she appeared in the imperial theatres in Moscow and St Petersburg. She made her Metropolitan début in 1896 as Valentine (*Les Huguenots*) and sang, among other roles,

1293

Aida, Donna Anna, Brünnhilde (*Siegfried*) and Sélika (*L'Africaine*). In 1899 she appeared at Covent Garden, as Isolde, returning periodically until 1910; in her last season she sang Brünnhilde in *Götterdämmerung*. She sang in several Russian *Ring* cycles, 1899–1914, and, with Charles Dalmorès, in a series of French performances of *Götterdämmerung* and *Tristan* under Cortot in 1902. An excellent musician and linguist, she had a large, flexible voice and great stage presence.

GV (R. Celletti; R. Vegeto)

F. Litvinne: *Ma vie et mon art* (Paris, 1933; Russ. trans., abridged, 1967)

H. M. Barnes and V. Girard: 'Félia Litvinne', *Record Collector*, viii (1953), 125–32, 143, 235; xx (1971–2), 147–56 [discography by L. C. Witten], 283

S. Yu. Levik: *Zapiski opernogo pevtsa* [Notes of an Opera Singer] (Moscow, 1955, enlarged 2/1962)   HAROLD BARNES

Liverati, Giovanni (*b* Bologna, 27 March 1772; *d* Florence, 18 Feb 1846). Italian composer, conductor and singer. He had his first training as a singer from Giuseppe and Ferdinando Tibaldi. From the age of 14 he was taught singing by Lorenzo Gibelli and composition by Stanislao Mattei. He began as an opera composer in Bologna in 1790 with *Il divertimento in campagna* and from 1792 was first tenor at the Italian theatres in Barcelona and Madrid. In 1796 he went to Potsdam as Kapellmeister of the Italian Opera and in 1799 to Prague as Kapellmeister to the Estates Theatre. He taught singing in Vienna (1805–14), where he knew Haydn, Beethoven and Salieri, as well as the singers J. M. Vogel and Giuseppe Siboni.

In 1815 Liverati succeeded Vincenzo Pucitta as composer and music director at the King's Theatre in London. In 1822 he was listed as a professor on the original staff of the Royal Academy of Music. He apparently spent his last years in Florence, where he was a professor at the Accademia di Belle Arti and also a member of the Bologna Accademia Filarmonica. His sacred drama *David* (1813) was performed in Florence in 1844.

Liverati's best-known opera was *La prova generale* (1799), written in the *buffo* manner, and performed in various capitals besides Vienna. The late Neapolitan style of his *opere serie* and cantatas resembles that of Salieri and Spontini, while his skilfully written ensembles are in the tradition of G. B. Martini. In Vienna it was just these stylistic idiosyncrasies and the occasionally arbitrary instrumental accompaniments of his arias (as in the use of obbligato bassoon and trombone or waldhorn in *David*) that excited the indignation of Weber and other representatives of Romantic German opera.

Il divertimento in campagna (1), Bologna, 1790
Enea in Cartagine, ?Potsdam, 1796; excerpts pubd
La prova generale al teatro (1, G. Rossi), ?Vienna, 1799, *A-Wgm, I-Fc*, excerpts pubd
Il convito degli dei, Vienna, *c*1800
La presa d'Egea, Vienna, Burg, 1809
Il tempio d'eternità (after P. Metastasio), Vienna, 1810
David, oder Goliaths Tod (op biblica, 2, de Antoni), Vienna, Kärntnertor, 8 April 1813, *A-Wgm, Wn, I-Fc*, vs (Vienna, n.d.)
I selvaggi (2), London, King's, 27 June 1815, *Fc*, excerpts pubd
Gli amanti fanatici, London, 1816
Gastone e Bajardo (S. Vestris), London, 26 Feb 1820, excerpts pubd
The Nymph of the Grotto (W. Dimond), London, CG, 1829, collab. A. Lee
Amore e Psiche (S. E. Petronj), London, Royal, 1831, excerpts pubd

C. Ricci: *I teatri di Bologna nei secoli XVII e XVIII: storia aneddotica* (Bologna, 1888), 517   HELENE WESSELY

Liverpool. City in north-west England on the Mersey estuary. It is chiefly notable in opera as the claimed setting for Donizetti's *Emilia di Liverpool* (1824), but as the libretto describes it as 'a beautiful city in an Alpine landscape not many leagues from London', his Liverpool must be taken as imaginary. In the 18th and 19th centuries much opera was given in the city's many theatres, especially the Theatre Royal, Williamson Square (demolished in the 1960s), and the 4000-seat Royal Amphitheatre, rebuilt in the 20th century as the Royal Court and for a time owned by Carl Rosa. The British National Opera Company gave three-week seasons at the Olympia Theatre (including a complete *Ring* cycle in 1923), on some occasions longer than their London seasons. Liverpool was almost a second home for the Carl Rosa Opera Company, who gave there the English première of Massenet's *Manon* (17 January 1885). In the 20th century the Empire Theatre and Royal Court have accommodated touring opera as well as a dwindling number of amateur companies, some supported by commerce such as Martin's (later Barclays) Bank Operatic Society, the Liverpool Opera Company and the Liverpool Grand Opera Company. In the 1930s John Tobin founded and conducted the semi-professional Liverpool Repertory Opera, which gave the première of Holst's *The Wandering Scholar* on 31 January 1934 under J. E. Wallace, in the David Lewis Theatre (demolished 1970s). In the 1920s and 30s the Sandon Studios Society organized amateur but pioneering performances of chamber operas directed by A. K. Holland (1892–1980), music critic of the *Liverpool Daily Post*; these included productions of Holst's *The Perfect Fool* and Purcell's *Dido and Aeneas*.

R. J. Broadbent: *The Annals of the Liverpool Stage* (Liverpool, 1908)   FRITZ SPIEGL

Livietta e Tracollo [*La contadina astuta*] ('Livietta and Tracollo' [The Astute Peasant Woman']). *Intermezzo in musica* in two parts by GIOVANNI BATTISTA PERGOLESI to a libretto by TOMMASO MARIANI; Naples, Teatro S Bartolomeo, 25 October 1734.

In the first intermezzo a peasant woman, Livietta (soprano), and her friend, Fulvia (silent), attempt to ambush the thief and rascal Tracollo (bass). Livietta is disguised as a French country boy and Fulvia as a rich woman adorned with fake necklaces and jewellery. Tracollo, disguised as a pregnant Polish woman and accompanied by his servant, Faccenda (silent), disguised as an old beggar, approaches the two women who pretend to be asleep. Not recognizing them, Tracollo attempts to steal Fulvia's jewellery, only to be caught by Livietta. In keeping with their respective foreign disguises, she and Tracollo converse in broken Italian. Finally, she reveals her identity and calls on a group of peasants for help to have Tracollo imprisoned. Despite his attempts to arouse her pity, and his last-minute offer to marry her, the furious Livietta rejects him in her aria 'Sarebbe bella questa'.

The second intermezzo opens with Tracollo's attempting to soften Livietta's heart by another strategy – he disguises himself as an astrologer. Feigning madness in his accompanied recitative 'Misero, a chi mi volgero?', he talks to the stars and pretends to be Tracollo's ghost, who has come to take Livietta to the underworld. She pretends to faint, and Tracollo wonders if she is really frightened. When they both realize that each is concerned about the other's welfare, they decide to stop their pretences and pledge faithfulness to each other.

The work is full of slapstick elements such as the use of multiple disguises, dialogue in broken Italian and fainting fits. In contrast with Pergolesi's *La serva padrona* (1733), the imagery and language in *Livietta e Tracollo* are frequently crude. Tracollo calls Faccenda a 'beetle-brained, cowardly numbskull', and when his disguise is restored Tracollo shouts: 'Do not allow my virginity to be contaminated by the hands of these indiscreet peasants, for I am yet a maiden'.

Livietta e Tracollo was first performed between the acts of Pergolesi's *Adriano in Siria*. The two works employed different casts of singers and had no musical or textual connection. More popular than *Adriano*, in the course of two decades *Livietta e Tracollo* was performed in most major European theatres. Each time it was coupled with a different *opera seria*, and over the years was revised and performed under a number of different titles, including *Il ladro finto pazzo* (1739, Milan), *Il Tracollo* (1744, Venice), *Livietta* (1746, Venice) and *La finta Polacca* (1748, Rome). Two reworkings of the text and music were undertaken by Goldoni and Pietro Chiarini, as *Il finto pazzo* (1741, Venice) and *Amor fa l'uomo cieco* (1742, Venice).

GORDANA LAZAREVICH

Livigni, Filippo (*fl* Venice, 1773–86). Italian librettist. He wrote comic opera librettos for Venetian theatres between 1773 and 1786 and one work, *La cameriera per amore*, for Turin in 1774. Although half of his librettos received no revivals or additional settings, many of the rest were celebrated works. *La frascatana*, set by Paisiello, was the composer's most frequently performed work, as were *Giannina e Bernardone* (Cimarosa) and *La finta principessa* (Alessandri). Gazzaniga counted his setting of *La moglie capricciosa* among his most successful, as did Anfossi his *I viaggiatori felici*. The latter, as well as Anfossi's *Le gelosie fortunate*, were selected for revivals at Eszterháza. Livigni's works, typical of *drammi giocosi* of the time, were sophisticated pieces dealing with gentry and their servants – ordinary people – in amorous imbroglios and intrigues. *I viaggiatori felice* introduces an Englishman and a Spaniard into the action, while *L'innocente fortunata* involves Spaniards and Bretons; *Il convito* is a spoof on opera.

Livigni's librettos of the 1770s each have three acts, but of the later ones all but *Lo sposo di tre* have only two. Each work consists of a succession of recitatives and arias, with an action ensemble introducing Act 1 and long, multi-sectional, action ensemble finales to Acts 1 and 2, extending over several scenes; these involve the *parti serie* or *di mezzo carattere* as well as the *buffo* characters. *Buffo* duets and arias with interjections by a second character (*pertichino*), usually for men, can also be found within acts, as can one additional ensemble or more (duets, trios, quartets and even quintets); often one of the duets or trios involves dancing. Interior ensembles occur most frequently, and begin to include action, in the works of the 1780s.

all drammi giocosi
L'innocente fortunata, ossia La semplice fortunata, Paisiello, 1773; La serva per amore, Galuppi, 1773; La cameriera per amore, Alessandri, 1774; La frascatana, Paisiello, 1774; Il marchese carbonaro, Salari, 1776; La molinara, Fischietti, 1778; I viaggiatori felici, Anfossi, 1780; Giannina e Bernardone [Il villano geloso], Cimarosa, 1781 (Dittersdorf, 1788, as Das rote Käppchen); Il convito, Cimarosa, 1781; La finta principessa [I due fratelli Papamosca], Alessandri, 1782 (Cherubini, 1785; Marinelli, 1796; Paer, 1797, as Il principe di Taranto; G. Nicolini, 1798, as I fratelli ridicoli)
I puntigli gelosi, Alessandri, 1783 (V. Fabrizi, 1786, as Chi la fà l'aspetti, ossi I puntigli di gelosia); Lo sposo di tre e marito di nessuna, Cherubini, 1783; I due castellani burlati [I due rivali in amore], Giovanni Valentini, 1785 (Fabrizi, 1785); La moglie capricciosa [Chi la fà l'aspetti], Gazzaniga, 1785; Le gelosie fortunate, Anfossi, 1786; Le rivali in puntiglio, L. Caruso, 1786

MARITA P. McCLYMONDS

Liviyets. Opera by M. P. Musorgsky; *see* SALAMMBÔ (i).

Livorno (Eng. Leghorn). Italian city on the west coast of Tuscany. The first recorded operatic performance – of *Giasone* (probably Cavalli's), given by the Fedeli company – is datable to Carnival 1656–7. From then until the beginning of the 20th century, operatic activity was sponsored first by the Medici, then by the Lorena family and private individuals; at first it was confined to the carnival season and the autumn. Later it was extended to the whole year, in several theatres that often staged performances concurrently. At the Teatro Nuovo (also known as 'delle Commedie' or 'da S Sebastiano', *c*1658–1782), Gasparini made his début as an opera composer in 1686. The Nuovo was replaced by the Teatro dagli Armeni (or Avvalorati, 1782–1944; a cinema from 1920), which was inaugurated with the first performance of Cherubini's *Adriano in Siria*, on 16 April 1782. The Teatro Carlo Lodovico (also known as the Floridi or S Marco, 1806–1944) was the most important theatre in the 19th century, followed by the Teatro Rossini (also known as the Fulgidi, 1842–1944), Teatro Leopoldo (also known as the Caporali or Goldoni, 1847–1984) and the Teatro Politeama (1878–1968; a cinema after World War II). In the 19th century performances were also given in private theatres (Pellettier, Vecchio Giardinetto or Gherardi del Testa or Strozzi), arenas (Labronica, Alfieri, Garibaldi) and in the outdoor Teatro della Fiera. Between 1821 and 1848 the impresario Alessandro Lanari was active in the city; after 1890 Mascagni's operas dominated the repertory. More recently performances have taken place in the cinema-theatre La Gran Guardia (1952) and in the Villa Mimbelli outdoor theatre. The composers Cambini, Campana and Mascagni, the librettists Calzabigi, De Gamerra and Giovanni Schmidt, the singers Celeste Coltellini, Nicola Tacchinardi, Enrico Delle Sedie, Mario Ancona and Galliano Masini and the conductor Auguste Vianesi were all natives of Livorno.

*

ES (A. Guerrieri)
G. Vivoli: *Annali di Livorno* (Livorno, 1842–6)
G. Piombanti: *Guida storica e artistica della città* (Livorno, 1873, 2/1907)
F. Mazzei: 'Il primo teatro sorto in Livorno', *Miscellanea livornese di storia e di erudizione*, i (1894), 100–02
A. Taddei: 'Musica e musicisti', *Livorno nell'ottocento*, ed. P. Vigo and others (Livorno, 1900), 177–212
A. Bonaventura: 'La vita musicale in Toscana', *La Toscana alla fine del Granducato*, ed. O. Bacci and others (Florence, 1909), 275–311
G. Orsini: *Il teatro di musica nella medicea Livorno (1644–1703)* (Livorno, 1913)
F. Guerri: 'Il teatro S Marco', *Liburni civitas*, i (1928), 93–108
E. Grassi: *Le accademie di Livorno* (diss., U. of Pisa, 1937)
M. Conti: *I vecchi teatri di Livorno* (diss., U. of Pisa, 1979)
C. Venturi: *Il Teatro delle Commedie in Livorno* (Livorno, 1980)

G. Fontanelli: 'La città e il teatro – il caso Livorno', *Studi livornesi*, ii (1987), 137–49

D. Filippi, ed.: *La fabbrica del Goldoni: architettura e cultura teatrale a Livorno (1658–1847)* (Venice, 1989)   ROSSANA CHITI

Lizzie Borden. A 'family portrait' in three acts by JACK BEESON to a libretto by Kenward Elmslie based on a scenario by Richard Plant; New York, City Center of Music and Drama, 25 March 1965.

The plot is derived from an actual crime, which took place in Fall River, Massachusetts, in 1892: Lizzie Borden, daughter of a wealthy banker, was accused of killing her father and stepmother by hacking them to death with an axe. Lizzie was brought to trial, but was acquitted and lived out the rest of her life on her share of her father's fortune.

Act 1 shows the family at home: Andrew Borden (bass-baritone), his daughters, Lizzie (mezzo-soprano) and Margret (soprano), and second wife Abigail (soprano). Borden is mean and disagreeable, refusing a church donation to the Rev. Harrington (tenor) and money to his daughters.

In Act 2, Captain Jason MacFarlane (baritone) asks for Margret's hand, interrupting a family quarrel about Abigail's increasing ascendancy over Borden at his daughters' expense. Borden tries to turn Lizzie out of the house, and the balance of her mind is shown to be upset. Margret's elopement in Act 3 precipitates the murders of Borden and Abigail, the action taking place offstage. At the end, children are heard chanting:

> Lizzie Borden took an axe
> And gave her mother forty whacks.
> When she saw what she had done,
> She gave her father forty-one.

The musical style of the opera ranges from affectionate likenesses of 19th-century American hymnody and parlour song to the musical idioms of 20th-century expressionism. Identifiable arias and ensembles coexist with continuous through-composed sections. After its first performance by the New York City Opera *Lizzie Borden* was presented on television by NET Opera in 1966–7.   HOWARD SHANET

Ljubljana (Ger. Laibach). Capital of Slovenia. Even in the 17th century, and especially in the 18th and 19th centuries, opera performances in Ljubljana, the capital of the former duchy of Krain, were entirely in the hands of foreign theatre companies (Italian until 1780, Italian and German thereafter) whose repertories were not essentially different from those of the larger cultural centres of the Habsburg empire. Theatrical companies performed first at the court of Prince Auersperg and after 1765 in the new Ständische Theater. Renamed the Landestheater in 1862, it was the city's most important musical institution. In contrast to the present day, the repertory consisted almost entirely of contemporary drama.

The first Slovene opera was Jakob Zupan's *Belin*, composed between 1780 and 1782. J. B. Novak's incidental music for A. T. Linhart's play, which he renamed *Figaro* (based on Beaumarchais' play), was first performed in 1790. But native opera did not flourish until after the mid-19th century, when it was stimulated in particular by the Slovene Dramatično Društvo (Dramatic Society), which was able to provide adequate singing forces for operatic performances towards the end of the 1880s. Mahler was appointed Kapellmeister for the 1881–2 season. The German Landestheater burnt down

in 1887, and in 1892 a new theatre was built by J. V. Hrasky and A. J. Hruby; it was the home of the Slovensko Deželno Gledališče (Slovene Provincial Theatre; cap. 700), which produced both opera and drama and enjoyed the same privileges as the German theatre. In 1918, as it was now within the new Yugoslav state, the company was renamed the Opera of the Slovene National Theatre. Besides international works of classic and modern drama, the theatre staged the first performances of many operas by Slovene composers, including Anton Foerster, Victor Parma, Risto Savin, Marij Kogoj, Slavko Osterc, Matija Bravničar, Danilo Švara, Marjan Kozina, Mirko Polič, Pavel Šivic and Darijan Božič. The conductors Vaclav Talich, Fritz Reiner and Lovro von Matačić, and the singers Anton Dermota, Beniamino Gigli and Josip Gostič, have appeared with native performers. The opera company has often toured abroad, to Austria, Germany, Switzerland, Italy, the Netherlands and the former USSR. Its greatest success was a production of Prokofiev's *The Love for Three Oranges* at the 1956 Holland Festival which was repeated at the Paris Opéra. Since 1980 operas have also been performed in the Cankar Hall.

A. Dimitz: *Hundert Jahre der Laibacher Bühne* (Laibach, 1865)

P. P. von Radics: *Die Entwicklung des deutschen Bühnenwesens in Laibach* (Laibach, 1912)

D. Cvetko: *Histoire de la musique slovène* (Maribor, 1967)

J. Sivec: *Opera v Stanovskem gledališču v Ljubljani od leta 1790 – 1861* [Opera in the Estates Theatre in Ljubljana from 1790 to 1861] (Ljubljana, 1971)

S. Skerlj: *Italijansko gledalisce v Ljubljana v preteklih dobah* [Italian Theatre at Ljubljana in Past Centuries] (Ljubljana, 1973)

D. Cvetko: *Slovenska glasba v evropskem prostoru* [Slovene Music within the European Context] (Ljubljana, 1991)

MANICA ŠPENDAL

Ljungberg, Göta (*b* Sundsvall, 4 Oct 1893; *d* Lidingö, nr Stockholm, 30 June 1955). Swedish soprano. She studied in Stockholm with Gillis Brand, then in Milan and Berlin, making her début in 1917 as Gutrune with the Stockholm Opera, where she was engaged until 1926. She then joined the Berlin Staatsoper. She made her Covent Garden début in 1924 as Sieglinde, later singing Salome, Kundry, Tosca, Elisabeth (*Tannhäuser*) and the title role of Goossens's *Judith*, which she created (1929). At the Metropolitan (1932–5), she sang Salome and Wagner heroines, and created Lady Marigold Sandys in Hanson's *Merry Mount* (1934). Visually and vocally ideal as Salome, she lost the clear, cool quality of her voice by singing heavier roles such as Brünnhilde and Isolde. She retired in 1935.

LEO RIEMENS, ELIZABETH FORBES

Lleó (y Balbastre), Vicente (*b* Torrent, Valencia, 19 Nov 1870; *d* Madrid, 27 or 28 Nov 1922). Spanish composer. When he was five his family moved to Valencia, where he became a choirboy at the college church of Corpus Christi, for whose choir he composed a six-part motet in 1883. He became interested in the zarzuela, and from 1885 his works in that genre were performed in Valencia. In 1890 he moved to Barcelona, where he was a theatre conductor for some years before moving to Madrid in 1896. His first major success there came in 1899 with *Los presupuestos de Villapierde*, and in 1910 he had a huge success with the biblical zarzuela *La corte de faraón*. He also had success adapting foreign works for Spain, among them Giuseppe Mazza's *La prova d'un opera seria* (1845) as the one-act zarzuela *El maestro Campanone* (1903) and Viennese operettas such as Lehár's *Der Graf von Luxemburg* (with a baritone lead). His output of more than 100 works includes revues as well as operas and zarzuelas.

selective list, mainly of operas and zarzuelas: most in one act

Duo con la sultana, Valencia; De Valencia al Grao, Valencia, ?1885–7; Las traviatas, Valencia; El tenor de Baberillos, Valencia; Un casament del dimone, Valencia; Las once mil, Valencia; Las de Farandul (E. López Marín), Madrid, Maravillas, 10 Aug 1898; Los cenceros (Ramirez), Madrid, Romea, 11 Feb 1899; Variétés (E. Montesinos and L. P. Frutos), Madrid, Nuevo, April 1899, collab. Zavala; El traje de boda (G. Perrín and M. de Palacios), Madrid, 7 April 1899, collab. A. Rubio

Los gladiatores (Pazos and Gijon), Madrid, Zarzuela, 5 June 1899, collab. Chalons; El estado de sitio (Sorinao and Falcado), Madrid, Maravillas, 20 June 1899, collab. Calleja; Los presupuestos de Villapierde (opereta-revista, S. M. Granés, E. García Alvarez and A. Paso), Madrid, Maravillas, 15 July 1899 (rev. 1900), collab. Calleja; Cambios naturales (V. de la Vega), Madrid, Maravillas, 19 Aug 1899, collab. Rubio; La tiple mimada (J. E. Prieto), Madrid, Martin, 17 Oct 1899

Venus Salón (revista, F. Limendoux and López Marín), Madrid, Romea, 14 Dec 1899 (rev. 31 Oct 1906 as Venus Kursaal), collab. Calleja; La maestra (E. Navarro Gonzalvo and J. López Silva), Madrid, Eslava, 19 Jan 1901, collab. T. Barrera and Calleja; El jilguero chico (J. C. de Luna), Madrid, Cómico, Oct 1901, collab. Calleja; El dios Apolo (Limendoux), Madrid, Apolo, 19 Oct 1901, collab. Calleja; Gubasta nacional (fantasia-lirica, Navarro Gonzalvo), Madrid, Apolo, Jan 1902, collab. Calleja

El respetable publica (revista, Paso, Gabaldon and Canevas), Madrid, Eslava, Oct 1902, collab. Calleja; Inés de Castro, ó Reinar después de morir (op, 3, Paris and J. J. Cadenas), Madrid, Lírico, 1903, collab. Calleja; El mozo crúo (Prieto), Madrid, Sept 1903, collab. Calleja; Copito de nieve, Madrid, 1903, collab. Calleja; El pícaro mundo, 1903/4, collab. Caballero; Gloria pura (Paso and Cruselles), Madrid, Zarzuela, 24 May 1904, collab. Calleja; Hulé (intermedio, Arias and Arroyo), Madrid, Zarzuela, 14 June 1904, collab. Calleja

Music-Hall (revista), Madrid, 18 Feb 1905, collab. Calleja; ¿Quo vadis, Montero?, Madrid, 8 July 1905, collab. Calleja; Las piedras preciosas, Madrid, Oct 1905; La taza de te (J. Abati), Madrid, Cómico, March 1906; La guedeja rubia (F. Irayzoz), Madrid, Cómico, 7 Dec 1906; La loba (Paso), Madrid, Eslava, 23 Feb 1907; Tupinamba, Madrid, Cómico, 8 May 1907; La golfa del Manzanares (Soler and Eustachio), Madrid, 1908, collab. Calleja; Pepe Botella (M. Ramos Carrión), Madrid, Zarzuela, 17 March 1908, collab. A. Vives

Episodios nacionales (M. Thous and E. Cerdá), Madrid, Zarzuela, 30 April 1908, collab. Vives; Mayo florido (López Silva), Madrid, Cómico, June 1908; La vuelta del presidio (López Silva), Madrid, Cómico, June 1908; El quinto pelao, Madrid, Eslava, 1908; La república del amor (Paso and G. Martínez Sierra), Madrid, Eslava, Oct 1908; La balsa de aceite (S. Delgado), Madrid, Eslava, Oct 1908; Si las mujeres mantasa (Frutos and M. Fernández de Puente), Madrid, Eslava, Dec 1908, collab. L. Foglietti

Las molineras (Thous and Cerdá), Madrid, Gran, Dec 1908; La moral en peligro, Madrid, Eslava, Oct 1909; Ninfas y satiros, Madrid, 1909; La corte de Faraón (Perrín and Palacios, after Fr. operetta Madame Putiphar by E. Diet), Madrid, Eslava, 21 Jan 1910; La partina de la porra, Madrid, Jan 1911; Livio entre espinas, Madrid, 1911; El método Górritz (C. Arniches and García Alvarez), Madrid, ?1911/12; El barrio latino (Cadenas and R. Asensio Más), Madrid, Eslava, Sept 1912

La tirena (Martínez Sierra), Madrid, Eslava, April 1913; El rey del valor, Madrid, Cómico, Aug 1914, collab. Calleja; La pandereta, Madrid, Apolo, 3 April 1915, collab. J. Giménez; Sierra Morena (Paso and Abati), Madrid, El Paraiso, Aug 1915; Ave César (T. Borrás and J. González Pastor), Madrid, Apolo, Dec 1922

Other works: La alegre trompetería (Paso); Apaga y vámonos; La capa encantada (J. Benavente); La carne flaca; La guedeja rubia; Los tres maridos burlados

Revisions of G. Mazza: La prova d'un opera seria, as El maestro Campanone, 1903; Lehár: Der Graf von Luxemburg, 1911, and other Viennese operettas

*

StiegerO

Enciclopedia ilustrada europeo-americana (Barcelona, 1907–30), xxxi, 1038; appx vi (1931), 1350

R. Alier and others: *El libro de la zarzuela* (Barcelona, 1982, rev. as *Diccionario de la zarzuela*, 1986)   ANDREW LAMB

Lloveras, Juan (*b* Villanueva y Geltrú, nr Barcelona, 6 April 1934). Spanish tenor. He studied singing at the Conservatorio del Liceo, Barcelona, and made his début in 1966 as Rodolfo in Tel-Aviv. From 1973 he was based at the Hamburg Staatsoper, where he sang some 200 performances of leading roles in the Italian repertory. He made his American début as Manrico in *Il trovatore* with the San Francisco Opera in 1975, and at the Metropolitan as Turiddu (*Cavalleria rusticana*) in 1979, following it with the Duke (*Rigoletto*) and Manrico. He has also sung leading roles at Berlin, Munich, Vienna, Paris, Prague and other European centres, as a lyric tenor of style and ardent vocal character.   NOËL GOODWIN

Lloyd, David (*b* Minneapolis, 29 Feb 1920). American tenor. He studied in Philadelphia and in 1950 joined New York City Opera with which he sang for some years. He also appeared with other American and Canadian companies. He sang Idamantes at Athens (1955) and Tamino and Bacchus (*Ariadne auf Naxos*) at Glyndebourne (1957). His roles included Belmonte, Ferrando, Don Ramiro, Jaquino, the Duke, Pinkerton, Rodolfo, Gonzalve (*L'heure espagnole*), Flamand, Albert Herring and Tom Rakewell. His lyric voice was heard to best advantage in Mozart and the lighter side of his repertory. As Bacchus he was overparted.   CHARLES JAHANT, ELIZABETH FORBES

Lloyd, George (*b* St Ives, Cornwall, 28 June 1913). English composer. He studied the violin and composition in London with Albert Sammons and Harry Farjeon and enjoyed early success with his first three symphonies and his first opera, to a libretto by his father, produced in Penzance when Frank Howes was on holiday nearby (1934). Howes's review helped achieve a London run the following year, prompting Beecham to include Lloyd's second opera, *The Serf*, in his 1938 London season. Lloyd suffered injury and shellshock as a marine during World War II and another breakdown after writing *John Socman*, whereupon he abandoned music for market gardening, resuming full-time composition only in 1973. Since then he has been active in symphonic writing and conducting but has not so far returned to opera. This is regrettable, for his music abounds in operatic virtues: within a colourful style which is a personable digest of the tonal tradition, he enjoys an uninhibited propensity for melody and rhythmic characterization which has been compared with the bel canto aesthetic of Verdi or, closer to home, Balfe.

See also JOHN SOCMAN.

MSS with the composer

Iernin (3, W. Lloyd), Penzance, 6 Nov 1934

The Serf (3, W. Lloyd), London, CG, 20 Oct 1938, vs (London, 1948)

John Socman (3, W. Lloyd), Bristol, Hippodrome, 15 May 1951, vs (London, 1951)

*

Grove5 (F. Howes)

F. Howes: 'A Celtic Opera', *MT*, lxxv (1934), 1133

W. McNaught: 'The Serf', *MT*, lxxix (1938), 859–60

H. D. Rosenthal: 'John Socman', *Opera*, ii (1951), 421–3

L. Foreman: 'British Opera comes of Age: 1916–61', *British Opera in Retrospect* (n.p., 1986) [pubn of the British Music Society], 113–14

——: *From Parry to Britten: British Music in Letters 1900–1945* (London, 1987), 187–8   STEPHEN BANFIELD

Lloyd, Robert (*b* Southend-on-Sea, 2 March 1940). English bass. He studied in London with Otakar Kraus, making his début there in 1969 at the Collegiate Theatre as Don Fernando in *Leonora*. Later he sang with Sadler's Wells Opera, then in 1972 joined the Royal Opera, Covent Garden. He has also sung with Scottish Opera, at Glyndebourne and La Scala and in Aix-en-Provence, Amsterdam, Munich, Vienna and San Francisco. His repertory includes Osmin, Sarastro, Don Giovanni, Don Basilio, the Landgrave, King Henry, Daland, Fasolt, Gurnemanz, Arkel, Fiesco, Banquo, Ashby (*La fanciulla del West*) and Rossini's Walter Furst; his resonant voice and acting ability are well displayed in the title role of *Boris Godunov*, which he sang at Covent Garden (1983), and with the Kirov Opera in Leningrad (1990), broadcast live on BBC television.

R. Milnes: 'Robert Lloyd', *Opera*, xxxiv (1983), 368–74
                                     ELIZABETH FORBES

Lloyd-Jones, David (**Mathias**) (*b* London, 19 Nov 1934). English conductor, editor and translator. He studied at Oxford University and privately with Iain Hamilton. As a Russian-language specialist, his first professional engagement was to coach *Boris Godunov* in Russian at Covent Garden in 1959. He became assistant conductor and chorus master for the New Opera Company in 1960, and in 1967 conducted Scottish Opera in his own translation of *Boris Godunov*. He gave the first British performances of Fauré's *Pénélope* (1970, RAM) and Haydn's *La fedeltà premiata* (1971, Camden Festival). He was engaged by the WNO and the Wexford Festival and made his Covent Garden début in 1971 with *Boris*, of which he prepared a new critical edition (London, 1975) from Musorgsky's originals; it has been used widely abroad, including Russia.

Lloyd-Jones joined Sadler's Wells Opera in 1972 as assistant to the music director and conducted, with conspicuous success, the first British stage production of Prokofiev's *War and Peace* that year. He was appointed music director of ENO North on its foundation in Leeds (1977) and when it became independent of the ENO in 1981 he was artistic director from 1981 to 1990. During the company's first ten years he conducted 44 operas, including the première of Wilfred Josephs's *Rebecca* (1983), and the first British stage productions of Krenek's *Jonny spielt auf* (1984) and Strauss's *Daphne* (1987). He took the company to Dortmund (*Boris*) and the Edinburgh Festival (*The Love for Three Oranges*) in 1989, and was responsible for establishing a sound musical basis in chorus and orchestra and for an enterprising level and variety of productions that helped to build strong regular audiences in Leeds and other northern centres.

He continued to enjoy working with young people, notably in opera productions at the GSM, where he was appointed artistic director of the opera course in 1989. He has also worked elsewhere in Europe, including Amsterdam, Paris and Karlsruhe, and in Britain has conducted much opera for television. Besides *Boris*, his translations include *The Love for Three Oranges*, *Yevgeny Onegin* and Rakhmaninov's *Francesca da Rimini*. His edition of *The Gondoliers* (1984) was the first critical edition of any of the Sullivan operettas to be published in full (miniature) score. Lloyd-Jones's recordings include Massenet's *Hérodiade* from a live French radio performance in 1974. His versatility and authority in performance are combined with stylistic feeling and scholarship, and a belief in opera's lyrical qualities and verbal clarity.

N. Payne: 'Tutto nel mondo è burla: Ten Years of Opera North', *Opera*, xxxix (1988), 1040–48 [includes checklist of new productions]   ARTHUR JACOBS, NOËL GOODWIN

Lloyd Webber, Sir **Andrew** (*b* London, 22 March 1948). English composer. He was born into a musical family: his father was director of the London College of Music and his brother Julian is a cellist. He studied for a while at the RCM, but for the most part avoided an orthodox musical education. In 1965 he met Tim Rice, with whom he began to write popular songs, and in 1968 they collaborated on the stage cantata *Joseph and the Amazing Technicolor Dreamcoat*, originally written as a 15-minute piece for Colet Court School pupils. It was later extended into a full-length stage show, mixing bright modern melodies and much parody of other musical styles in a colloquial retelling of the biblical story. With their second piece, the more substantial *Jesus Christ Superstar* (1971), which they subtitled a rock opera, the pair developed on a larger scale the style initiated in *Joseph*. At first an unprecedented success as a double-disc recording, most particularly in the USA, the show was initially staged there in a deliberately outrageous style which attracted both controversy and attention. In its less flamboyant London production it established a record as the longest-running musical in West End history. *Evita* (1978) dealt with another controversial subject, the life and work of the Argentine popular heroine Eva Perón. In this work Lloyd Webber's musical style was further developed in line with the dramatic content the subject imposed. Again issued as a recording and subsequently transferred to the stage, *Evita* showed, even more strongly than *Jesus Christ Superstar* had, the composer's ability to weld the elements of an effective and dramatic stage score with those of popular success (songs from both musicals did well on the popular music charts). During the three collaborations with Rice, Lloyd Webber stepped aside to work with the playwright Alan Ayckbourn on *Jeeves*, a piece based on P. G. Wodehouse's tales of the famous butler. An uneven show, it proved a failure, but the score of light 1920s- and 30s-flavoured melodies showed that the composer was capable of writing in styles other than the richly theatrical.

This was again proved when he took a turn into a mostly lighter vein with his setting of the Old Possum poems of T. S. Eliot in the song-and-dance spectacular *Cats* (1981), a theatrical sensation which outran even its record-breaking predecessors and like *Jesus Christ Superstar* and *Evita* produced a hit-parade song, 'Memory'. He then essayed in yet another direction with the consciously youth- and pop-orientated *Starlight Express* (1984), a railway fable performed on roller skates, which was another London hit. The staged pairing of his solo song cycle 'Tell Me on a Sunday' and a choreographed set of variations for cello on a Paganini theme as *Song and Dance* (1982) proved a further major success. His next stage work, the full-blown musical melodrama *The Phantom of the Opera* (1986), used a mélange of opera pastiche and lush soprano-baritone love songs ('All I ask of you', 'The Phantom of the

Opera', 'Music of the night') and, for the first time, some highly developed ensembles; these features contributed largely to the work's international success. In the manner which has come to characterize his ventures, Lloyd Webber changed styles and followed this most romantic of pieces with a comparatively intimate and unshowy adaptation of David Garnett's novel *Aspects of Love* (1989), illustrating the tale of gentle love with a score of delicate warmth which put aside the ensembles and vocal exploration of the *Phantom of the Opera* score in favour of a less expansive style and which produced one of his most successful popular songs, 'Love changes everything'.

His works also include film scores and television material, but Lloyd Webber remains above all a theatre composer. Especially in his collaboration with the lyricist Tim Rice, he was responsible for the development of a new style of musical show which replaced the old song-and-scene variety of musical comedy long popular on English-language stages. Not only did the pair reintroduce the all-sung formula, not successfully used in the light musical theatre since Gilbert and Sullivan's *Trial by Jury*, but Lloyd Webber introduced a novel blend of classical and modern popular musical styles which set the style for the musical theatre of the later years of the 20th century. Hugely effective as theatrical music, his scores have yet contained songs, and musical sections which cannot strictly be called songs, which have regularly become both top-ten hit parade material and world-wide concert standards.

Joseph and the Amazing Technicolor Dreamcoat (musical, 1, T. Rice), London, Colet Court School, 1 March 1968; rev. in 2 acts, Edinburgh, Haymarket Ice Rink, 21 Aug 1972
Jesus Christ Superstar (rock op, 2, Rice), New York, Mark Hellinger, 12 Oct 1971
Jeeves (musical, 2, A. Ayckbourn, after P. G. Wodehouse), Bristol, Hippodrome, 20 March 1975
Evita (op, 2, Rice), London, Prince Edward, 21 June 1978
Cats (musical, 2, T. S. Eliot, add lyrics by T. Nunn, after Eliot: *Old Possum's Book of Practical Cats*), London, New London, 11 May 1981
Song and Dance (concert for the theatre, 2, D. Black), London, Palace, 26 March 1982
Starlight Express (musical, 2, R. Stilgoe), London, Apollo Victoria, 19 March 1984
The Phantom of the Opera (musical, prol., 2, A. Lloyd Webber and Stilgoe, after G. Leroux; lyrics C. Hart), London, Her Majesty's, 9 Oct 1986
Aspects of Love (musical, 2, Black and Hart, after D. Garnett), London, Prince of Wales, 12 April 1989

*

GänzlBMT
N. Rorem: 'Jesus Christ Superstar', *Harper's*, no.1453/June (1971), 22–4; repr. in *Pure Contraption* (New York, 1974)
K. Gänzl: *The Music of Andrew Lloyd Webber* (London, 1989)
J. Mantle: *Fanfare: the Unauthorized Biography of Andrew Lloyd Webber* (London, 1989)
J. P. Swain: *The Broadway Musical: a Critical and Musical Surrey* (New York, 1990), 293–307   KURT GÄNZL

Lobanov, Vasily (*b* Moscow, 2 Jan 1947). Russian composer. Known as both a pianist and a minimalist composer, he has written instrumental works and song cycles. His opera *Antigone* (begun in 1984 and staged at the Yekaterinburg Opera and Ballet Theatre on 28 December 1989) is to a libretto by Alexey Parin, after Sophocles' tragedy. Fundamental changes made to the original text include prominence given to the conflict between Antigone (soprano) and the Elders as representing blind hatred of the masses; Creon (bass), here seen as a noble and just ruler, is sympathetic to Antigone, but he is a hostage to the people and forced to obey their laws. Various aesthetic, musical and dramatic principles are united in the opera: reliance on classical traditions, including a structure based on separate numbers, exists alongside extended scenes in the style of a montage, elements of the Passion alongside features of epic theatre, lampoon alongside magical scenes of ballet with vocal and instrumental accompaniment. The colourful disparity of the episodes is counterbalanced by the tight structure of the libretto; leitmotifs and consistent tonal and harmonic principles preserve the unity of the whole.
                                          MARINA NEST'YEVA

Lobe, Johann Christian (*b* Weimar, 30 May 1797; *d* Leipzig, 27 July 1881). German composer. He received his earliest musical training from his father, a keen amateur musician. His precocious abilities on the flute attracted the patronage of Grand Duchess Maria Paulowna, who sponsored his musical education. At the age of 13 he left school to join the Weimar Hofkapelle as a violinist. Over the next few years he cultivated his talents as a flautist and furthered his knowledge of composition. His first publicly performed opera, *Wittekind, Herzog von Sachsen*, was described as showing his 'fine talent, good knowledge of composition and great industriousness' (*AMZ*, xxiv, 1822, col. 574), but it survived only two performances. His next opera, *Die Flibustier* (1829), was given a much more enthusiastic reception and shortly afterwards appeared in vocal score. *Die Fürstin von Granada*, given its première in 1833, created a sensation and was soon mounted in other major theatres. It held a place in the repertory for many years. In the wake of this success, Schilling's *Encyclopädie* described Lobe in 1837 as 'among the most outstanding German opera composers of recent times'. His last two operas were politely received but made no lasting impression. After becoming editor of the *Allgemeine musikalische Zeitung* in 1846 he forsook composition almost entirely and became principally a writer on music.

See also FÜRSTIN VON GRANADA, DIE.

all first produced at Weimar, Hoftheater
Der Käfig [La Cage], ? before 1820 (1, A. von Kotzebue), lost
Wittekind, Herzog von Sachsen [Wittekinds Bekehrung], ?1819 (grosse Oper, 2, J. C. Lobe), 1821
Die Flibustier (Oper, 3, E. Gehe), 5 Sept 1829, vs (Leipzig, 1831)
Die Fürstin von Granada, oder Der Zauberblick (grosse Zauberoper, 5, Lobe and P. C. C. Sondershausen), 28 Sept 1833, full score, pts, vs (Paris, Mainz and Antwerp, [1833])
Der rote Domino, ?1835 (komische Oper, 3, Theophania [P. M. J. Brachowskal]), 22 April 1837
König und Pächter (komische Oper, 3, F. L. C. von Biedenfeld, after *Carl XII auf Rügen*), 1844

*

Reviews of *Die Fürstin von Granada*, *AMZ*, xxv (1833), cols. 709–11, 810–18
K. Stein: 'Lobe, Johann Christian', *Encyclopädie der gesammten musikalischen Wissenschaften*, ed. G. Schilling, iv (Stuttgart, 1837)
W. Bode: *Goethes Schauspieler und Musiker* (Berlin, 1912) [incl. biographical recollections by Lobe]   CLIVE BROWN

Lobetanz. Singspiel in three acts, op.10, by LUDWIG THUILLE to a libretto by Otto Julius Bierbaum; Karlsruhe, 6 February 1898.

A young minstrel, Lobetanz (tenor), wins the heart of a lovesick Princess (soprano) through song and masterful violin playing, but is thereby accused of black magic and imprisoned in a dungeon. Love and happiness triumph however as the minstrel, vindicated in the end, marries the princess. The opera, for the most part, is lightly textured and lyrical, with occasional set numbers: these provide a striking contrast with the sinister but impressive dungeon scene. In the New York performance (1911), recitatives, arranged by Walter Courvoisier, replaced the original dialogue.

EDWARD F. KRAVITT

Lobkowitz [Lobkowicz, Lobkovic]. Bohemian noble family, notable for its patronage of the arts, particularly music. The family was founded in the early 15th century and by the mid-17th had begun to influence music history. Ferdinand August Lobkowitz (1655–1715) was an amateur lutenist and guitarist. His sons (1) Philipp Hyacinth Lobkowitz and Johann Georg Christian (Jan Jiří Kristián) Lobkowitz (1686–1755) both played important roles in Gluck's early development; the latter, as Austrian governor of Milan, received the dedications of his *Arsace* (1743), *La Sofonisba* (1744) and *Ippolito* (1745).

(1) **Philipp Hyacinth** [Filipp Hyacint] **Lobkowitz** (*b* Neustadt an der Waldnab, 25 Feb 1680; *d* Vienna, 21 Dec 1734). Lutenist and composer. In 1727 Gluck's father became his head forester at Eisenberg (now Jezeří), and about 1735–6 Gluck started his career at private concerts in the Lobkowitz-Althan family's palace in Vienna, where Philipp Hyacinth lived from 1729. A suite by him survives in the Nationalbibliothek, Vienna.

(2) **Ferdinand Philipp Joseph** [Ferdinand Filipp Josef] **Lobkowitz** (*b* Prague, 27 April 1724; *d* Vienna, 11 Jan 1784). Composer, son of (1) P. H. Lobkowitz. He was the ruling prince at Vienna from 1743. In 1745 he took Gluck to London, where he attended performances of the latter's works. His compositions, which were highly appreciated by Burney in Vienna in 1772, are apparently lost.

(3) **Joseph Franz Maximilian** [Josef František Maximilián] **Lobkowitz** (*b* Roudnice nad Labem, 7 Dec 1772; *d* Třeboň, 15 Dec 1816). Son of (2) F. P. J. Lobkowitz, he was the first Duke of Roudnice. He was a bass singer, performing in Handel's *Alexander's Feast* at Vienna (3 December 1812), and played the violin and the cello. A member of the association of noblemen responsible for the direction of the Vienna court theatres from January 1807, he later had the sole direction of the opera for several years and led the Hoftheater-Musik-Verlag; he resigned from the direction of the court theatres in 1814. He was one of the founders of the Gesellschaft der Musikfreunde in Vienna and of the association which began the Prague Conservatory in 1810–11. As a patron he supported principally Beethoven and Haydn. His private orchestra played in Vienna as well as at the family's country seats at Roudnice, Eisenberg and Bílina. In opera and concert performances outstanding soloists from Vienna and abroad took part, as well as Czech musicians. Goethe attended the opera at Eisenberg in 1810.

(4) **Ferdinand Joseph Johann** [Ferdinand Josef Jan] **Lobkowitz** (*b* Oberhollabrunn, Lower Austria, 13 April 1797; *d* Vienna, 18 Dec 1868). Son of (3) J. F. M. Lobkowitz. He maintained a private orchestra and had a special hunting band. He was a patron of Adalbert Gyrowetz.

BurneyH; *MGG* (R. Schaal)

G. J. Dlabacż: *Allgemeines historisches Künstler-Lexikon*, ii (Prague, 1815), cols. 121, 214–16, 538
A. W. Thayer: 'The Lobkowitz Family', *Musical World*, lvii (1879), 307, 325–6, 335
K. Fiala: *Z hudební minulosti severočeského kraje* [From the Musical Past of North Bohemia] (Liberec, 1969), 7–39
MILAN POŠTOLKA

Lôbo, Elías Alvares (*b* Itu, São Paulo, 9 Aug 1834; *d* São Paulo, 15 Dec 1901). Brazilian composer. He was orphaned at an early age and educated by a local priest, although in music he was mostly self-taught. He studied the violin and early in his career wrote salon pieces in the *modinha* and *lundu* genres. In 1858, his *Missa a São Pedro de Alcântara*, dedicated to Emperor Pedro II, was sung in the imperial chapel at Rio de Janeiro. He became nationally known after the première of his opera *A noite de São João*, which took place on 14 December 1860 under the direction of Carlos Gomes. Produced at the Teatro São Pedro de Alcântara, this was the first opera dealing with a regional subject written by a Brazilian composer and a Brazilian librettist, the latter being the well-known Indianist novelist José de Alencar. In two acts, the opera is of comic character and tells of the love affair of two cousins in the town of Brás (São Paulo); after much intrigue they get married on St John's night (a reference to the association of fertility with that festival). A second opera, *A louca* (1861), on a libretto by Antônio Aquiles de Miranda Varejão, was never performed. Most of Lôbo's later life was spent composing and conducting church music in São Paulo. In 1890 he was appointed a music professor at the São Paulo Escola Normal.

L. H. C. de Azevedo: *Relação das óperas de autores brasileiros* (Rio de Janeiro, 1938)
——: *150 anos de música no Brasil (1800–1950)* (Rio de Janeiro, 1956)
A. de Andrade: *Francisco Manuel da Silva e seu tempo, 1808–1865* (Rio de Janeiro, 1967)
GERARD BÉHAGUE

Locanda, La ('The Inn'). *Dramma giocoso* in three acts by GIUSEPPE GAZZANIGA to a libretto by GIOVANNI BERTATI; Venice, Teatro S Moisè, 1771.

Arsenio (tenor), the avaricious older brother of Guerina (soprano), has brought her to an inn as part of a plan to make a financially advantageous marriage for her. They are followed there by Guerina's beloved, Riccardo (tenor). Another couple, Valerio (bass) and Rosaura (soprano), is at the inn; through a series of misunderstandings Valerio thinks Rosaura has fallen for Riccardo. Riccardo finally wins Arsenio's permission to marry Guerina by disguising himself as the King of Calcutta, complete with the attendant glitter and foreign babble. The cast also includes an innkeeper, Marinetta (soprano). Gazzaniga's music is alternately lively and touching; later versions (notably from Vienna and Eszterháza) have substitutions by Gassmann, Salieri and others. A relatively early work by Gazzaniga, *La locanda* was popular in Italy and in central European cities until the early 1780s. It was given a production in Copenhagen in 1775, probably arranged by Giuseppe Sarti.

MARY HUNTER

Locatelli, Giovanni Battista (*b* Milan or Venice, 7 Jan 1713; *d* after 1790). Italian impresario and librettist, active in central Europe and Russia. He was a member of Pietro Mingotti's opera troupe and wrote the librettos for Filippo Finazzi's intermezzo *Il matrimonio sconcertato, per forza del Bacco* (Prague, Carnival

1744), and a three-act opera *Diana nelle selve* (Prague, 23 November 1745; score in *CS-Pnm*). From 1748 to 1757 he rented the city theatre, Prague. He founded his own opera company and engaged good singers – notably Rosa Costa, Catarina Fumagalli, and his wife Giovanna della Stella, who also sang at the Bonn court and at Dresden from 1745 to 1749. For several seasons at Prague his Kapellmeister was Gluck, who directed the premières of his own *Ezio* (1750) and *Issipile* (1752), and a revival of *Ipermestra* (1750).

Locatelli's concern to employ excellent singers and mount impressive productions was largely responsible for the growing financial difficulties under which his company operated. Leaving large debts, he moved to Russia after the outbreak of the Seven Years War, and became head of the tsarina's opera in St Petersburg (1757–62); its first performance under his leadership was a pasticcio on his own text *Il retiro degli dei* (3 December 1757). With Italian singers and conductors (Francesco Zoppis and G. M. Rutini), he introduced *opere buffe* by Galuppi, Fischietti and others to Russia. He was also engaged to take his own troupe to Moscow; it opened there on 9 February 1759 with Galuppi's *La calamità de' cuori*, but in 1761 its performances ceased through lack of public interest. As a reward for *Il consiglio delle muse*, a birthday serenata for Catherine II (1763), Locatelli gained permission to open a place of entertainment called Krasnïy Kabak ('The Pretty Tavern'). In later years he occasionally wrote cantata texts. After a gala benefit in St Petersburg (1783) he left public life.

M. Fürstenau: *Zur Geschichte der Musik und des Theaters am Hofe zu Dresden* (Dresden, 1861–2)

O. Teuber: *Geschichte des Prager Theaters*, i (Prague, 1883)

R. Haas: 'Beitrag zur Geschichte der Oper in Prag und Dresden', *Neues Archiv für sächsische Geschichte und Altertumskunde*, xxxvii (1916), 68–96

H. Kindermann: *Theatergeschichte Europas*, v (Salzburg, 1962), 569–73, 615–17

R. Brockpähler: *Handbuch zur Geschichte der Barockoper in Deutschland* (Emsdetten, 1964)

P. Kneidl: 'Libreta italské opery v Praze v 18. století', *Strahovská knihovna*, ii (1967), 115–86   TOMISLAV VOLEK

Locke, Matthew (*b* Devon, *c*1622; *d* London, Aug 1677). English composer. A chorister at Exeter Cathedral from 1638 to 1641, he spent part of the Interregnum in the Netherlands, perhaps in the service of the exiled Charles II. Locke went to London before the Restoration and was appointed composer for the King's Violins in 1660. He was closely associated with the court and Chapel Royal for the rest of his life and a prolific writer of consort music; his primary interest nevertheless lay in the professional theatre, and he may rightly be called 'the father of English opera'.

In 1656 Locke was among the composers who wrote the music for Sir William Davenant's *The Siege of Rhodes*, the first all-sung English opera: the first and fifth entries (acts) were composed by Henry Lawes, the second and third by Captain Henry Cooke and the fourth by Locke; additional instrumental music was furnished by Charles Coleman and George Hudson. Locke himself sang the role of the Admiral of Rhodes, while the part of Ianthe was taken by Mrs Edward Coleman, one of the first women ever to appear on the public stage in London. Performed on a small, makeshift stage erected in Rutland House, Charterhouse Yard, London, the work seems to have been set 'in *Recitative* Musick'. Davenant was staking a claim on a royal theatre patent

well in advance of the anticipated Restoration. None of the music survives, and when the opera was revived a few years later (Davenant having been duly rewarded with a royal patent), it was altered into a play with music.

In 1659 Locke revised and expanded Christopher Gibbons's score for James Shirley's masque *Cupid and Death*, which had first been performed in London before the Portuguese ambassador on 26 March 1653; whether Locke had also contributed to the original version is unknown. Aesop's fable about the confusion wrought when Cupid and Death exchange arrows is told with a mixture of spoken dialogue, declamatory song and dance. In the second version (autograph in *GB-Lbl*) Locke, by converting most of the spoken dialogue into recitative, transformed the fifth entry – in which Mercury descends to appease Mother Nature – into a virtual opera.

After the Restoration Locke was in effect composer-in-residence at the Duke's Theatre in Lincoln's Inn Fields (later Dorset Garden), providing overtures, act tunes and longer musical interludes for a series of plays, the most important of which was Elkanah Settle's heroic drama *The Empress of Morocco* (1673). The fourth-act masque of Orpheus and Eurydice is an opera in miniature, with four-square 'English' recitative, brief triple-metre arias in the Venetian manner and a final chorus.

Locke's most important achievement in the theatre was his role in the invention of SEMI-OPERA, the earliest examples of which were the musically enriched revival of Davenant's adaptation of *Macbeth* (1673; only fragments of the music survive) and a revival of the Davenant-Dryden version of *The Tempest* (1674). The latter was a spectacular production with music by several composers; Locke was primarily responsible for the instrumental music, which includes the remarkable storm overture replete with appropriate tempo and dynamic markings ('lowder by degrees', 'violent' etc.). This was published in full score in *The English Opera* (1675), which also includes most of the music for Locke's last major stage work, Thomas Shadwell's semi-opera *Psyche* (1675). Though based on the *tragédie-ballet* of Lully, Molière, Corneille and Quinault, this is a remarkably innovative work that comes closer to true *dramma per musica* than any of the semi-operas, Purcell's included. There is still spoken dialogue, but one of the main characters, Venus, expresses herself in speech, recitative and airs. Though grand and richly scored for diverse instruments, the music is disappointing in comparison with Locke's earlier efforts for the stage.

While he was irascible in his advocacy of an English alternative to French and Italian opera, Locke's dramatic music (though not his anthems and chamber music) is rather primitive, especially in the awkwardness of its melodic lines. But he exerted a great influence on Blow and Purcell by creating a style of recitative that forms the life-blood of both *Venus and Adonis* and *Dido and Aeneas* and in providing a structural model for Purcell's semi-operas.

See also CUPID AND DEATH and PSYCHE.

W. B. Squire: 'The Music of Shadwell's Tempest', *MQ*, vii (1921), 565–78

E. J. Dent: *Foundations of English Opera* (Cambridge, 1928)

J. M. Buttrey: *The Evolution of English Opera between 1656 and 1695* (diss., U. of Cambridge, 1967)

R. E. M. Harding: *A Thematic Catalogue of the Works of Matthew Locke* (Oxford, 1971)

M. Lefkowitz: 'Shadwell and Locke's *Psyche*: the French Connection', *PRMA*, cvi (1979–80), 42–55

E. T. Harris: *Handel and the Pastoral Tradition* (London, 1980)

J. McDonald: 'Matthew Locke's *The English Opera*, and the Theatre Music of Purcell', *SMA*, xv (1981), 62–76

E. W. White: *A History of English Opera* (London, 1983)

C. Price: *Henry Purcell and the London Stage* (Cambridge, 1984)

M. Tilmouth, ed.: *M. Locke: Dramatic Music*, MB, li (1986)

CURTIS PRICE

Lockhart, James (Lawrence) (*b* Edinburgh, 16 Oct 1930). Scottish conductor. He studied at Edinburgh University and the RCM, and worked as a répétiteur successively at Münster, Munich, Glyndebourne and Covent Garden, as well as directing the opera workshop of the University of Texas at Austin (1957–9). He made his début with Sadler's Wells Opera in 1960 (*Figaro*), and after two seasons there became resident conductor at Covent Garden (1962–8), notably of Mozart, Puccini and Verdi. He conducted the première of Walton's *The Bear* for the English Opera Group at the Aldeburgh Festival (1967), which he also recorded. He was music director of the WNO (1968–73), where his wide repertory included the first production of Berg's *Lulu* by a British opera company (1971), and his qualities as a trainer and his overall skill decisively strengthened the company's musical standards.

Having already worked frequently in German centres he became West Germany's first British musician to be appointed Generalmusikdirektor at Kassel (1972–81), where his activities ranged from the *Ring* cycle to the first German production of Gilbert and Sullivan's *The Yeomen of the Guard* (as *Der Gaukler von London*) in 1972. He moved to Koblenz (1981), where he introduced several Britten works to the repertory and a Janáček cycle. In the USA he made his Metropolitan début (1984) conducting the ENO in *War and Peace*, and conducted *Peter Grimes* at San Diego. In 1986 he became director of opera at the RCM, where his productions have included the première of Paul Max Edlin's *The Fisherman* (1989) in association with London International Opera Festival. His experience as an accompanist (notably with the soprano Margaret Price) gives him a special sensitivity to singers, and his performances with student as well as professional musicians generally combine stringent working policies with sensitive imagination.

ARTHUR JACOBS, NOËL GOODWIN

Lockwood, Normand (*b* New York, 19 March 1906). American composer. After attending the University of Michigan he studied composition with Respighi in Rome (1924–5), with Boulanger in Paris (1925–8) and as a fellow of the American Academy in Rome (1929–32). He then taught at various American institutions, finally becoming professor of composition and composer-in-residence at the University of Denver (1961–75). Among the many honours he has received are two successive Guggenheim fellowships (1943, 1944), a commission from the Alice M. Ditson fund for his chamber opera *The Scarecrow* (1945), and one from the National Opera Association for *Requiem for a Rich Young Man*.

Lockwood is a prolific composer who has worked in almost every genre. His music is usually logical and concise, unified by such devices as germinal chords, repeated rhythmic and melodic fragments, and quoted

tunes; it is nonetheless accessible and at times romantic. He has been especially original and expressive in his numerous vocal works.

The Scarecrow (chamber op, 3, D. Lockwood, after P. McKaye), New York, Columbia U., 19 May 1945

Early Dawn (3, R. Porter), Denver, 7 Aug 1961

The Wizards of Balizar (children's op, 2, Porter), Denver, 1 Aug 1962

The Inevitable Hour (3, Porter), Denver, March 1964; also perf. as The Hanging Judge

Requiem for a Rich Young Man (1, D. Sutherland), Denver, 24 Nov 1964

EwenD

SUSAN L. PORTER

Loder, Edward (James) (*b* Bath, 1813; *d* London, 5 April 1865). English composer. His father was an eminent violinist. In 1826 Loder was sent to Frankfurt to study with Ferdinand Ries, who was a family friend. After visiting England in 1828, he returned to Germany the following year to study medicine but soon abandoned this idea and once again placed himself under Ries's tuition.

On his final return to England Loder was commissioned by S. J. Arnold to compose the music for *Nourjahad*, an old play by Arnold who had decided to convert it into an opera for the first season at his newly opened English Opera House (the rebuilt Lyceum Theatre). After a week of established operas, *Nourjahad* was given on 21 July 1834, and although its success was partially overshadowed by Barnett's *The Mountain Sylph* (given at the same theatre on 25 August), it was later recognized by Macfarren as 'the inaugural work of the institution of modern English operas'.

At about this time Loder, for financial reasons, entered into a contract with D'Almaine & Co. to supply them with a new composition weekly. Under this arrangement, which continued for some years, he produced a vast number of songs and partsongs, mostly of inferior quality. To the end of his life he faced the dilemma that the public preferred the compositions which he knew to be hack-work to those that represented his highest artistic endeavours. The opera *Francis the First* (1838, Drury Lane) is in reality a collation of his D'Almaine songs; its most famous number, 'The Old House at Home', was probably Loder's most popular composition during his lifetime, but now appears to have been little more than second-hand Bishop.

In 1846 Loder became musical director at the Princess's Theatre, an incentive which spurred him to the production of his second significant opera, *The Night Dancers*. Based on a subject made familiar by Adolphe Adam's ballet *Giselle*, this enjoyed greater success, and by 1847 had reached New York and Sydney; it was revived at Covent Garden in 1860. In 1851 Loder was appointed musical director at the Theatre Royal, Manchester, but here apparently, as in London, 'his unbusinesslike habits and want of punctuality told against him' (Robert Sharp). After several delays, in 1855 he produced the work now generally regarded as his masterpiece, the four-act romantic opera *Raymond and Agnes*. The music seems to have been too difficult for the provincial singers and above the heads of the local audience; reduced to three acts, it was performed in London in 1859. By 1856, however, Loder had developed a brain disease which forced him to give up his Manchester position and return to London. He never really recovered, and despite the efforts of his family and friends to raise subscriptions on his behalf, his last years were spent in poverty.

Loder's operatic output, like the rest of his works, is variable, and for the same reasons. His later, more ephemeral stage pieces often contain music of great charm and delicacy, however; this is particularly true of *Robin Goodfellow* (1848, Princess's Theatre) and the operetta *Never Judge by Appearances* (1859, Adelphi), probably written during his Manchester period. But it is in his three attempts at serious operatic composition that his real musical personality emerges. Nicholas Temperley, who revived *Raymond and Agnes* at Cambridge in 1966, considers that 'Loder's three serious operas show him to have been a composer of outstanding ability' (*The New Grove*), a judgment which the music emphatically vindicates. Moreover, they display a consistent and impressive stylistic development. *Nourjahad* is heavily influenced by Weber, but in the ballad 'The mariner who daring braves', Loder behaves accordingly, suddenly plunging into the flattened mediant at the words 'Forlorn in frightful solitudes'. This typical modulation is a clue to his spiritual kinship with Schubert: there is already a combination of suave and refined melodic lines with a warm and passionate lyricism. *The Night Dancers* points the way forward in two important respects: in 'The Legend', which tells of two rival suitors whose test is to spend a night in a haunted ruin, Loder creates a wonderfully eerie atmosphere, and in the Grand Scena 'Giselle's Dream' he furthers his ability to handle large musico-dramatic structures. Finally, in *Raymond and Agnes*, all these qualities reach their full maturity. Here the sense of drama and depth of musical characterization is close to Verdi, especially in the magnificent confrontation between Raymond and Inigo in Act 2, and in the quintet 'Lost! and in a dream'. In Raymond's ballad 'Farewell, the forest and the plain' Loder rivals Balfe, and in his ability to conceive whole acts at a time surpasses him. It is not exaggerated to regard Loder as the foremost composer of serious British opera in the early Victorian period, and the main signpost to Sullivan, whose music his own so often prophesies.

See also RAYMOND AND AGNES.

first performed in London unless otherwise stated; publications are vocal scores, published in London

LLY – *London, Lyceum Theatre (English Opera House)*

† – *partly adapted* †† – *wholly adapted*

†† Black-eyed Susan (play, D. Jerrold), Bath, Royal, 18 Nov 1830 [from Dibdin's airs]
Nourjahad (grand romantic op, 3, S. J. Arnold), LLY, 21 July 1834, *GB-LbL** (1835)
The Widow Queen (historical drama, T. J. Serle), LLY, 9 Oct 1834
† The Covenanters (Scottish ballad op, 2, T. J. Dibdin), LLY, 10 Aug 1835 [from Scottish airs]
The Dice of Death (romantic drama, 3, J. Oxenford), LLY, 14 Sept 1835, *Lbl**
The Foresters, or Twenty-Five Years Since (drama, 3, Serle), Covent Garden, 19 Oct 1838, 1 song (?1845)
† Francis the First (grand op, McKinlan), Drury Lane, 6 Nov 1838 (1839)
†The Deer Stalkers, or The Outlaw's Daughter (Scottish operatic melodrama, M. Lemon), LLY, 12 April 1841, 1 song (?1845) [from Scottish airs]
The Night Dancers, or The Wilis (grand romantic op, introduction, 2, G. Soane), Princess's, 28 Oct 1846, *Us-Wc** (1847)
†The Sultana (play, R. Toff), Princess's, 8 Jan 1848
†The Andalusian, or The Young Guard (operetta, Soane), Princess's, 20 Jan 1848, selections (1849)
Robin Goodfellow, or The Frolics of Puck (ballad op, Loder), Princess's, 6 Dec 1848 (1849)

Dick Whittington and his Cat (pantomime), Manchester, Royal, Dec 1852
Balcony Courtship (farce), Manchester, Royal, 6 May 1853
Raymond and Agnes (romantic op, 4, E. Fitzball), Manchester, Royal, 14 Aug 1855, *Wc**; rev. (3), St James's, 11 June 1859 (1859; ed. N. Temperley, 1966)
Never Judge by Appearances (operetta, 1, H. Drayton), Adelphi, 7 July 1859, selections (1857–8)

Unperf.: Little Red Riding Hood, 1839; Pizarro; Sir Roger de Coverley (M. D. Ryan); †† The Beggar's Opera

DNB (R. F. Sharp); Grove6 (N. Temperley); LoewenbergA; SteigerO
Monthly Supplement to the Musical Library, i, (1834), 71
Musical World, xv (1841), 251; xxiv (1849), 609; xxx (1855), 550–51; xxxi (1856), 760; xxxii (1857), 203, 345; xxxvii (1859), 120–21
The Times (29 Oct 1846)
Theatre Royal, Manchester: Playbills (1 Jan 1853–8 Sept 1855), GB-Lbl
Illustrated London News (27 Nov 1858)
H. C. Banister: George Alexander Macfarren (London, 1891), 246
J. A. Fuller Maitland: English Music in the XIXth Century (London, 1902), 41–2, 105–6
H. Davison, ed.: From Mendelssohn to Wagner (London, 1912), 67
A. W. Ganz: Berlioz in London (London, 1950), 130–32
E. Walker: A History of Music in England (Oxford, 3/1952 rev. J. A. Westrup), 308–10
I. Guest: 'Parodies of Giselle on the English Stage (1841–1871)', Theatre Notebook, viii (1953–4), 41–3
N. Temperley: 'The English Romantic Opera', Victorian Studies, ix (1965–6), 293–301
——: 'Raymond and Agnes', MT, cvii (1966), 307–10
M. Hurd: 'Opera: 1834–1865', Music in Britain: the Romantic Age, 1800–1914, ed. N. Temperley (London, 1981), 313, 321–7
E. W. White: A History of English Opera (London, 1983)
——: A Register of First Performances of English Operas and Semi-operas (London, 1983)   NIGEL BURTON

Lodoiska (i). Afterpiece dialogue opera in three acts by STEPHEN STORACE to a libretto by John Philip Kemble after J. E. B. Dejaure's libretto of the same name; London, Drury Lane, 9 June 1794.

Storace's *Lodoiska* is partly based on two operas of the same name by Rodolphe Kreutzer and Luigi Cherubini, both produced in Paris in 1791. They were to different librettos based on the same novel, *Les amours du Chevalier de Faublas* by Jean-Baptiste Louvet de Couvrai. The tenor Michael Kelly, who saw the operas, probably brought back both operas (which contain the spoken dialogue) to his colleagues John Philip Kemble and Storace at Drury Lane. Kemble followed the outline of Dejaure's libretto (written for Kreutzer), although he did not translate the dialogue literally, nor did he always position musical numbers identically. To open Act 3 he inserted a new episode, to present a situation in which Thomas Welsh, as the page, would sing 'Sweet bird that cheer'st the heavy hours' to amuse his master. The scene is dramatically extraneous but the song is the most virtuoso in the opera. *Lodoiska*, a work with spoken dialogue and normally referred to by contemporary writers as a 'musical romance', had four successful seasons at Drury Lane, followed by a series of revivals up to the 1830s.

Lodoiska is an 'escape' opera, a genre that became increasingly popular after the French Revolution. Lodoiska (soprano) is a Polish princess who had been betrothed, with the approval of her father Prince Lupanski (spoken), to Count Floreski (tenor). After the count opposed the prince in a political matter, the prince withdrew his consent and sent his daughter into hiding with Baron Lovinski (spoken). Floreski and his servant Varbel (baritone) search for Lodoiska and fall in with

Kera Khan (tenor), who with his Tartars is preparing to attack the baron's castle. Floreski and Varbel gain admittance as messengers from the prince, but their deceit is discovered because the prince himself arrives. When Lodoiska tells her father that Baron Lovinski has treated her badly, Lovinski seizes all the visitors. Kera Khan and his Tartars storm and burn the castle and free the captives. Floreski rescues Lodoiska from the flames and the lovers are united with the prince's approval.

Although Storace's *Lodoiska* was always positioned as an afterpiece at Drury Lane, it contains many of the hallmarks of a mainpiece opera. It is both serious and spectacular – including an onstage battle, a fire and a dramatic rescue – and there are large and important choruses sung by the Poles, captives, Tartars and 'the Horde'. The première apparently lasted two and a half hours and the work had to be drastically shortened. As a result, the chorus that originally began Act 1 and the quartet and chorus that ended the act were cut, and are now lost. *Lodoiska* has an unusually large amount of instrumental music for an English opera, with 'symphonies' to begin Acts 2 and 3. These short preludes and the overture were adapted from Kreutzer's music; the overture proved particularly popular in England. As well as composing original music, Storace adapted vocal numbers from both the French operas: five from Kreutzer and two from Cherubini. The vocal music includes a typical mix of the simple and complex styles, from folklike melodies to coloratura airs. The ensembles are simple in form, as befitted an afterpiece.

For illustration *see* GREENWOOD, THOMAS.   JANE GIRDHAM

Lodoiska (ii) [*La Lodoiska*]. *Dramma per musica* in three acts by SIMON MAYR to a libretto by FRANCESCO GONELLA; Venice, Teatro La Fenice, 26 January 1796 (revised version in two acts, Milan, Teatro alla Scala, 26 December 1799).

Mayr's first major success, *Lodoiska*, is a 'Polish opera' in the tradition of Cherubini's *Lodoïska* (1791) and *Faniska* (1806) and Mayr's Polish version of *Léonore* (1805). Mayr attempted to capture the *tinta* of the locale in the sinfonia of the Venetian version, which has a waltz and a polacca as two of its four movements. Both versions of the opera present essentially the same plot. Boleslao (tenor), the palatine of the castle of Ostropoli, has imprisoned Lodoiska (soprano) and is trying to force her to marry him. Her lover Lovinski (soprano), using the name Siveno, manages to gain Boleslao's confidence when he and his companion Narseno defeat a band of marauding Tartars led by the prince Giskano. At the same time he gains an ally by sparing Giskano's life and releasing him. When Boleslao decides to proceed with the wedding despite Lodoiska's resistance, Lovinski and her father, Sigeski, interrupt the ceremony and Boleslao has them arrested. Eventually they are rescued by Giskano and the Tartars, the couple are reunited and Boleslao is forgiven.

Despite their concurrence on the broad outlines of the action, the two versions present significant differences. In his Milanese revision Mayr devoted a greater proportion of its lyric numbers to the principal characters and introduced Lodoiska and Boleslao more formally, while giving relatively less weight to secondary characters. He provided numerous replacement arias and duets and expanded the finales of what had been Acts 1 and 2. He added a connecting scene to bridge the original Acts 2

and 3, while eliminating from the original Act 3 several scenes in which the rescue is plotted. He also reduced somewhat the repetitiveness of the villain's persistent efforts to seduce the heroine.

The Biblioteca Civica in Bergamo has a third, incomplete version of *Lodoiska* (without recitatives), partly in Mayr's hand, which appears to be an *opera semiseria* and which is not closely related to the other two versions.

SCOTT L. BALTHAZAR

Lodoïska. *Comédie-héroïque* in three acts by LUIGI CHERUBINI to a libretto by Claude-François Fillette-Loraux after an episode from Jean-Baptiste Louvet de Couvrai's novel *Les amours du chevalier de Faublas*; Paris, Théâtre Feydeau, 18 July 1791.

Many aspects of this opera, including the plot, have a close affinity with Beethoven's *Fidelio*. Titzikan (baritone), leader of a band of Tartar warriors who are seeking to avenge the cruelty of Baron Dourlinski (bass), meets the Polish Count Floreski (tenor) outside Dourlinski's castle in Poland. Floreski is in search of Lodoïska (soprano), whom he wishes to marry now that her father is dead. He proclaims his love for her in the famous polonaise 'Souvent près d'une belle j'osai parler d'amour'; he and his servant sing alternate couplets in contrasting melodic styles, combining in the final strophe. Dourlinski, however, has imprisoned Lodoïska until she consents to marry him. Floreski succeeds in entering the castle in disguise but is seen and captured. Dourlinski is aware of the love of Lodoïska for Floreski but is prevented from taking revenge because of an attack by Titzikan and the Tartars. The back of the castle collapses to reveal the ensuing battle and fire caused by the tumult. Floreski rescues Lodoïska from the burning tower, Dourlinski is captured by Titzikan; and Floreski and Lodoïska embrace in front of the ruined castle in a typical Cherubini ensemble-finale, the linked arias, dialogues and ensembles underlain by orchestration which characterizes each of the participants.

The work was greeted with enthusiasm, although the libretto fell short of being a masterpiece. Everything pleased, from beautiful and effective music to sensational stage devices, and *Lodoïska* ran for 200 performances. It was so popular that it was revived at the Feydeau in 1819 and was performed frequently in the Germanic countries in the early 19th century, including a production in Vienna in 1805, while Cherubini was there, for which he provided additional music. Its success was assured by its flowing vocal lines, its novel orchestration and its romantic plot, which seized the imagination of the inhabitants of revolutionary Paris by setting the righteousness of heroism, liberty and fraternity against the evil of tyranny. With *Lodoïska* Cherubini turned his back on his training as an Italian composer of *opera seria*, choosing the freer form of *opéra comique* over the more stilted and confining *tragédie lyrique* and embarking on a course of development of *opéra comique* which was to lead to the eradication of almost all differences between the two genres except for the spoken dialogue. The simple strophic *ariettes* become fully developed emotive arias, the ensemble becomes the norm rather than the exception, and the orchestration acquires symphonic proportions. With *Lodoïska* Cherubini secured the admiration of the French populace and the esteem of his fellow musicians.

STEPHEN C. WILLIS

Łódź. Town in central Poland, under Russian domination 1795–1918. From 1844 touring theatre companies, mostly from Warsaw, visited the young industrial city, performing lighter works by Polish composers (Stefani, Kurpiński, Baszny and Duniecki), as well as operas by Weber, Bellini, Donizetti, Rossini and Verdi; Moniuszko's *Halka* was given in 1875 and followed by his other works. The Victoria Theatre opened in 1877; among the companies that performed here was the successful Opera Łódzka, 1892–6. From 1901 numerous operettas were performed in the newly opened Teatr Wielki (Grand Theatre). After World War I, operatic life depended on occasional guest performances organized by the Opera Society (from 1925), just as after World War II it relied on regular visits from the Silesian Opera of Bytom (1946–54).

On 18 October 1954 the Society of the Friends of Opera, under the musical direction of Władysław Raczkowski, opened the first permanent opera house in the city, the Opera Łódzka. In 1967 the company moved to the new Teatr Wielki (the largest theatre in Poland outside Warsaw; cap. 1400). Since then it has built a reputation as the best opera company in Poland after those in Warsaw and Poznań, presenting an ambitious repertory, both classical (*Fidelio, Mefistofele, La Juive* and *Die Walküre*) and modern (works by Henryk Czyż and Romuald Twardowski), and reaching a high standard of singing and production under its music directors; in 1977 the post was filled by Sławomir Pietras. A second music theatre, the Operetka Łódzka (State Łódź Operetta), has been in use since 1946.

A. Pellowski: 'Opera w dawnej Łodzi' [Opera in Ancient Łódź], *Ruch muzyczny*, vii/20 (1963), 13

S. Dyzbardis, ed.: *Teatr Wielki w Łodzi* (Łódź, 1966)

——: *20 lat sceny operowej w Łodzi* [20 Years of the Operatic Stage in Łódź] (Łódź, 1974)   KORNEL MICHAŁOWSKI

Loeffler, Charles Martin (*b* Schöneberg bei Berlin, 30 Jan 1861; *d* Medfield, MA, 19 May 1935). German-born American composer. After an itinerant childhood spent in Germany, France, Hungary and Russia, he studied the violin and composition at the Hochschule für Musik in Berlin (1874–7) and privately in Paris. He played in the orchestras of Pasdeloup and of Baron Paul von Derwies (1879–81). In 1881 he emigrated to the USA. After a year in New York, he joined the Boston SO with which he spent 21 years as assistant leader and soloist. Upon leaving the orchestra he spent a year in Paris and then retired to his farm in Medfield, where he devoted his time principally to teaching and composing.

Loeffler was the leading proponent of French music in the USA during his lifetime. His own style, though eclectic, was primarily impressionistic, and he wrote major works for orchestra, chamber ensembles, solo strings, voice and chorus. In opera, his first work was administrative: he served on the Board of Directors of the Boston Opera Company, 1909–15, and in 1910 was a judge for the Metropolitan Opera Company's competition for an American opera.

His interest in composing opera dates from as early as 1893 when he proposed to Owen Wister a collaboration on a comic opera about François Villon. The project never materialized, and for two more decades Loeffler looked for a suitable libretto, finally setting William Sharp's *The Passion of Hilarion* in one act and two tableaux. It was completed in 1913 but never performed (a facsimile of the MS was published in 1936). He next worked on *The White Fox*, written for him by Kakuzo Okakura, but never completed it, although he maintained his rights to the libretto when Terhune and Miramor sought permission to set it in 1920. No music survives.

Loeffler later attempted writing his own librettos. He wrote *Les amants jaloux* after a poem by 'M' in 1918, and sketched some music. About 1919 he produced two nearly identical librettos, *The Peony Lantern* and *The Lantern Ghosts*, based on a narrative by Okakura, one set in Japan, one in China. Though sketches for the former survive, this project, like all his operas after *Hilarion*, was abandoned. Three other unset librettos in Loeffler's collection are *Duniascha, The Failure* and *The Tribulations of Mr Pillgarlic*. His MSS are at the Library of Congress, Washington, DC.

E. Knight: *Charles Martin Loeffler* (forthcoming)

ELLEN KNIGHT

Loesser, Frank (*b* New York, 29 June 1910; *d* New York, 26 July 1969). American composer and librettist. Although his father Henry and half-brother Arthur were both pianists, he refused piano lessons and was largely self-taught in music. He worked in journalism and as a nightclub pianist, and began to write satirical lyrics and sketches for vaudeville. In 1936 he moved to Hollywood and wrote lyrics for musical films. He began to compose during World War II when, as a member of the Army Air Forces, he wrote songs for army shows. He is best known, however, for his Broadway shows, beginning in 1948 with *Where's Charley?*; *Guys and Dolls* (1950) was even more popular, its success deriving in part from Loesser's witty lyrics and the remarkable cohesion and varied pacing of the score. He also wrote the libretto for his next show, *The Most Happy Fella* (1956); it is his most ambitious work, a quasi-opera (he referred to it as an 'extended musical comedy'), with less than 15 minutes of spoken dialogue. The libretto is an adaptation of a drama of the 1920s concerning the romance between an old Italian farmer and a young waitress; Loesser used traditional Broadway styles for the American characters and music tinged with Neapolitan melody and bel canto for the Italians. *Greenwillow* (1960), an unusual, bucolic musical, was a commercial failure, but *How to Succeed in Business without Really Trying* (1961) ran for 1416 performances. Loesser's last work, *Pleasures and Palaces* (1965), was the only one to fail to reach Broadway. At the time of his death, Loesser left in draft form a new show, *Señor Discretion*, based on a story by Budd Schulberg; the composer's widow worked with Schulberg to put the piece in shape for a workshop performance, which took place in 1985, but it has not been commercially produced.

Loesser's music and lyrics were unrivalled among his contemporaries. No other songwriter so successfully caught the flavour of colloquial speech, not only in his rhymes but also in his often witty melodies. His effective employment of such traditional forms as waltzes and college hymns was matched by the inventive use of freer, newer forms and fresh harmonies; known for his daring, he tried never to repeat the style or tone of an earlier work.

lyrics and, unless otherwise indicated, librettos by Loesser; dates are of first New York performance

Where's Charley? (G. Abbott), St James, 11 Oct 1948; Guys and Dolls (A. Burrows and J. Swerling, after D. Runyon), 46th Street, 24 Nov 1950; The Most Happy Fella (after S. Howard: *They*

Knew what they Wanted), Imperial, 3 May 1956; Greenwillow (with L. Samuels), Alvin, 8 March 1960; How to Succeed in Business without Really Trying (Burrows, J. Weinstock and W. Gilbert), 46th Street, 14 Oct 1961; Pleasures and Palaces (with S. Spewack), Detroit, 1965

A. Loesser: 'My Brother Frank', *Notes*, vii (1949–50), 217 [incl. list of songs]
S. Green: *The World of Musical Comedy* (New York, 1960, enlarged 4/1980)
D. Ewen: *Great Men of American Popular Song* (Englewood Cliffs, NJ, 1970)
M. A. Mann: *The Musicals of Frank Loesser* (diss., CUNY, 1974)
Frank Loesser Remembered (New York, 1977) [incl. list of pubd songs]
S. G. Freedman: '"New" Loesser Musical on the Boards', *New York Times* (26 Nov 1985), C17
J. Swain: *The Broadway Musical: a Critical and Musical Survey* (New York, 1990), 153–78

GERALD BORDMAN, STEVEN LEDBETTER

Loevendie, Theo (*b* Amsterdam, 17 Sept 1930). Dutch composer. He studied the clarinet and composition at the Amsterdam Conservatory, and he concentrated mainly on jazz until 1968, when he was appointed a teacher of theory and improvisation at the Rotterdam Conservatory. He was senior lecturer in composition there from 1970 and later taught at the Royal Conservatory in The Hague.

His first opera, *Naima* (3, L. de Boer), was first performed during the 1985 Holland Festival (Amsterdam, Carré, 7 June 1985), and received the 1986 Matthijs Vermeulen Prize of the City of Amsterdam. *Naima* is about the power of an institutionalized society (symbolized by the Institute and its representatives, including a choir, who sing in Latin) and the power or strength of individual freedom (symbolized by a group of improvising musicians and actors, who perform in English). In order to underline the contrast between both groups, Loevendie confronts the severe expression and strict technique of the Institution with the improvisation of the small group. The libretto and the score are packed with quotations from Cicero, Tacitus, Augustinus, Shakespeare, John Webster and Boito's versions of Shakespeare, together with Verdi's *Otello* and a French overture in the style of Lully. The style is reminiscent of Stravinsky's *Oedipus Rex*. Loevendie's one-act opera *Gassier, the Hero* (to his own libretto, based on an African folktale) was first performed at the Holland Festival (Amsterdam) in 1991.

A. van der Ven: 'Dutch Opera in Progress', *Key Notes*, xix (1984), 30–33
R. de Beer: 'The Smell of Grease-paint and Drying Scenery: Theo Loevendie's Opera Naima, a Score of Uncommon Theatrical Quality', *Key Notes*, xxii (1985), 2–5
T. Loevendie: 'The Curve-based Architecture of Naima', *Key Notes*, xxii (1985), 6–11
L. Samama: *Zeventig jaar Nederlandse muziek (1915–1985)* (Amsterdam, 1986), 276, 277, 283

LEO SAMAMA

Loewe, Carl (*b* Loebjuen, nr Halle, 30 Nov 1796; *d* Kiel, 20 April 1869). German composer. He showed an early aptitude for word-setting; his first surviving songs date from about 1810 and his setting of Friedrich Kind's *Klotar* was published in 1813. Throughout his life songs, particularly narrative ballads, formed a central part of his output. In 1816 he made an attempt at writing for the theatre with a setting of Kotzebue's *Die Alpenhütte*; individual numbers are melodically attractive but the work was apparently not staged. His first serious opera, *Rudolf der deutsche Herr*, was composed almost ten years later, when he was Musikdirektor in Stettin; it was submitted to the theatre authorities in Berlin but, although considered stageworthy by Spontini, was never put into production. *Malek-Adhel*, his next opera, was well received at a concert performance in Stettin but seems not to have been staged. His comic opera *Neckereien* was also unsuccessful. It was only with his Singspiel *Die drei Wünsche*, produced at the Berlin Schauspielhaus in 1834, that Loewe finally obtained a modest success in the theatre; it was his only opera to be published. A critic in the *Allgemeine musikalische Zeitung*, however, remarked equivocally: 'Dr Loewe is even more suited to the serious, heroic or tragic opera than to the comic Singspiel'.

During the 1830s, following the undoubted success of his oratorio *Die Zerstörung Jerusalems* in Berlin in 1832, Loewe's interest began to focus increasingly on the composition of oratorios. He treated many of these dramatically, in a style similar to that of his serious operas. In his last 35 years he made several international concert tours as a singer of his own songs and wrote some 14 oratorios but only a single opera, *Emmy*, after Sir Walter Scott's *Kenilworth*; this was completed in 1842, but seems not to have been staged. In 1864 he suffered a stroke and was obliged to resign his post in Stettin; he retired to Kiel and died soon afterwards.

Loewe's operas, like his songs, are characterized by sensitivity to the dramatic potential of the text; they show an easy command of melodic invention, harmonic colour and rich but not overpowering orchestration. However, he lacked essential experience of the theatre and was not sufficiently adept at creating dramatic effects. Moreover, because he reacted against the prevailing tendency towards extravagance, his operas, despite their many attractive qualities, proved too restrained for the taste of the day.

Edition: *Carl Loewes Werke: Gesamtausgabe der Balladen, Legenden, Lieder und Gesäng*, ed. M. Runze (Leipzig, 1899–1904) [GA]

Die Alpenhütte, 1816 (Spl, A. von Kotzebue), excerpts in GA i, 12
Rudolf der deutsche Herr, 1825 (grosse romantische Oper, 3, C. Loewe and Vocke), excerpts in GA ii, 112, 122; xvi, 121, 156, 207
Malek-Adhel, 1832 (grosse tragische Oper, 3, C. Pichler, after W. Scott: *The Talisman*), excerpt in GA xiv, 4
Neckereien, 1833 (komische Oper, 3, Mühlbach), excerpt in GA ii, 116
Die drei Wünsche (Spl, 3, E. Raupach), Berlin, Schauspielhaus, 2 Feb 1834, vs (Berlin, 1834)
Emmy, 1842 (romantische Oper, 3, Melzer and Hauser, after Scott: *Kenilworth*), excerpts in GA ii, 26, 128

*

'Die drei Wünsche', *AMZ*, xxxvi (1834), 229
C. H. Bitter, ed.: *Dr. Carl Loewe's Selbstbiographie* (Berlin, 1870)
K. König: *Karl Loewe: eine aesthetische Beurteilung* (Leipzig, 1884)
A. Wellmer: *Karl Loewe, ein deutscher Komponist* (Leipzig, 1887)
M. Runze: *Karl Loewe* (Leipzig, 1905)
H. Engel: *Carl Loewe: Überblick und Würdigung seines Schaffens* (Greifswald, 1934)

CLIVE BROWN

Loewe, Frederick (*b* Berlin, 10 June 1901; *d* Palm Springs, 14 Feb 1988). American composer. The son of Edmund Loewe, an operetta tenor, he studied the piano with Busoni and d'Albert and composition with Reznìček, and began to write songs while in his teens. He emigrated to the USA in 1924 and in the mid-1930s began to establish himself in the Broadway theatre. The first of his own shows was *Great Lady* (1938), in the outmoded Viennese operetta style, and *Salute to Spring*

(1937), some of the songs from which were re-used in *Life of the Party* (1942). Alan Jay Lerner (1918–86), who rewrote the play of this last, was the lyricist and playwright for his subsequent works. Their first Broadway shows together were *What's Up?* (1943), a short-lived musical comedy, and, two years later, *The Day Before Spring*. These contain elements from operetta as well as popular songs modelled on those of the swing era, many of which contain adventurous harmonic writing. This mixture of divergent styles was resolved in *Brigadoon* (1947), which established the team's reputation. Like the musical plays of Rodgers and Hammerstein, there is a synthesis of elements from the American musical – its quick pacing and credible book – with aspects of European operetta: the prominence of the chorus, the inclusion of ballet, the use of trained voices for the romantic and more serious roles, a plot set in the past in an exotic locale (18th-century Scotland) and a musical idiom owing little to contemporary popular song. *Paint Your Wagon* (1951) is Lerner and Loewe's only mature show set in the USA (during the California gold strikes of the 1850s).

Their most successful musical, however, was *My Fair Lady* (1956, adapted from G. B. Shaw's *Pygmalion*). Music and plot are closely integrated as, for example, in the changes in the character of Eliza, which are paralleled by the types of song she is given: a cockney number, 'Wouldn't it be loverly?'; 'Just you wait', where she seethes with indignation over her insensitive treatment by the bullying Henry Higgins; and finally 'Without you', in which she adopts Higgins's impeccably pronounced upper-class disdain. To accommodate the untrained singing voice of the leading actor, Rex Harrison, Loewe set nearly all his songs in fast, sputtering rhythms. *My Fair Lady* broke the box-office record of its day by running for 2717 performances. The film *Gigi* (1958, after Colette; adapted for the stage, 1973) is similar to *My Fair Lady* in its turn-of-the-century milieu and in having a leading character (Louis Jourdan) who 'talk-sings' his numbers; many of the songs were written in a gentle, relaxed style for the veteran Maurice Chevalier. The last of Lerner and Loewe's wholly original stage shows was *Camelot* (1960). White's novel on which it is based was possibly too long and unwieldy and *Camelot* was extensively rewritten even after its Broadway opening, with numbers excised to reduce the length and to bring the story into better focus. The authors created for Richard Burton a form of melodrama for his extensive solos at the end of each act.

Loewe's dramatic music, with its old-fashioned operetta element, bears few of the marks of a composer living in the USA in the postwar years. His style differs with the demands of each play: sufficiently Scottish-sounding for *Brigadoon* or akin to music-hall song for Eliza's boozing father without resorting to quotations or parodies. It is well written for the voice and suited to the dramatic requirements of the libretto, but there is little to stamp it indelibly as Loewe's.

first performed in New York unless otherwise stated

Salute to Spring (E. Crooker), St Louis, 12 July 1937; Great Lady (Crooker and L. Brentano), Majestic, 1 Dec 1938; Life of the Party (Lerner and Crooker), Detroit, Royal, 8 Oct 1942; What's Up? (Lerner and A. Pierson), National, 11 Nov 1943; The Day Before Spring (Lerner), National, 22 Nov 1945; Brigadoon (2, Lerner), Ziegfeld, 13 March 1947; Paint Your Wagon (Lerner), Shubert, 12 Nov 1951; My Fair Lady (2, Lerner, after G. B. Shaw: Pygmalion), Hellinger, 15 March 1956; Camelot (2, Lerner, after T. H. White: *The Once and Future King*), Majestic, 3 Dec 1960

S. Green: *The World of Musical Comedy* (New York, 1960, enlarged 4/1980)
A. Sirmay, ed.: *The Lerner and Loewe Songbook* (New York, 1962)
C. Palmer: 'A Cosmopolitan of Music: Frederick Loewe', *Crescendo International*, xii/12 (1974), 23–4
G. Bordman: *American Musical Theatre* (New York, 1978, 2/1986)
A. J. Lerner: *The Street where I Live* (New York, 1978)

WILLIAM W. DEGUIRE

Loewe, Sophie (Johanna Christina) (*b* Oldenburg, 24 May 1812; *d* Budapest, 29 Nov 1866). German soprano. She studied in Vienna and with Lamperti in Milan. In 1831 she was in Naples, where she sang Adelaide in Rossini's *Tancredi*. The following year she sang Elisabetta in Donizetti's *Otto mesi in due ore* at the Kärntnertortheater, Vienna. After an engagement at Berlin, where she sang Isabelle (*Robert le diable*) and Amina, in 1841 she sang at Her Majesty's Theatre, London, as Alaide (*La straniera*), Donna Elvira and Elena (*Marino Faliero*). The same year she created the title role of Donizetti's *Maria Padilla* at La Scala. In 1844 she sang Elvira in the first performance of *Ernani* and in 1846 she created Odabella in *Attila*, both at La Fenice. She also sang Abigaille (*Nabucco*) and Giselda (*I Lombardi*) at Parma. In 1848 she retired. A forceful singer, she excelled in roles such as Norma.

ELIZABETH FORBES

Loewenberg, Alfred (*b* Berlin, 14 May 1902; *d* London, 29 Dec 1949). British lexicographer of German birth. He studied in Berlin and Jena, and at first intended to be a lecturer in philosophy while taking a lively interest in opera. He began to accumulate voluminous data about operatic history: details of titles, composers, librettists, places and dates of production and subsequent performances. He had to leave Germany in 1935, and settled in London, where he supplemented the material through research in the British Museum; his long-planned book, *The Annals of Opera*, appeared in 1943. It remains an invaluable work of reference, a monument of accurate, painstaking research. A third edition with corrections and additions, prepared by Harold Rosenthal, appeared in 1978.

Loewenberg's remarkable capacity for organizing a complex mass of data led to his appointment, in 1947, as editor of the *British Union Catalogue of Periodicals*. He also contributed numerous articles and lists of operas to the fifth edition of *Grove's Dictionary of Music and Musicians* and wrote some important essays on operatic history.

Logar, Mihovil (*b* Rijeka, 6 Oct 1902). Serbian composer. He studied composition at the Prague Conservatory with K. B. Jirák and in Josef Suk's master-classes. From 1927 until 1972 he taught in Belgrade, as professor at the Academy of Music from 1945. His early works were rhapsodic, atonal and expressionist, but later he came to adopt a style more conventional in harmony and more direct in feeling. The first of his stage works, *Četiri scene iz Šekspira* ('Four Scenes from Shakespeare'), took fragments from *King Lear*, *The Merchant of Venice*, *Antony and Cleopatra* and *A Midsummer Night's Dream*, set in contrasted movements on the model of a symphony. His densely orchestrated opera *Pokondirena tikva* ('The Stuck-up Woman'), based on a comedy by the Serbian writer Jovan Sterija Popović, was frequently performed in Yugoslavia. The characteristic pervading Logar's works is gaiety, evoked in brisk rhythms and picturesque harmonic and orchestral colouring; burlesque and caprice often prevail over lyrical sensibility.

Četiri scene iz Šekspira [Four Scenes from Shakespeare], 1930 (stage symphony, after W. Shakespeare)
Sablazan u dolini šentflorijanskoj [Temptation in the Valley of St Florian], 1937 (comic op, 3), Sarajevo, 1968
Pokondirena tikva [The Stuck-up Woman] (3, after J. S. Popović), Belgrade, National, 20 Oct 1956
Četrdesetprva [1941], 1959 (music drama, 3), Sarajevo, 10 Feb 1961
Paštrovski vitez [The Knight of Paštrovići] (television op, after S. M. Llubiša), 1978

*

M. Kozina: '"Pokondirena tikva" Mihovila Logara', *Zvuk*, nos. 9–10 (1957), 381–3
Z. Kučukalić: 'Mihovil Logar: Četrdeset Prva', *Zvuk* nos.49–50 (1961), 471–9
R. Pejović: '"Četrdesetprva" Mihovila Logara', *Pro musica* (1966), no.19
V. Peričić: *Muzički stvaraoci u Srbiji* [Composers in Serbia] (Belgrade, 1969), 219–37 [incl. Eng. abstract]
STANA ĐURIĆ-KLAJN/DIMITRIJE STEFANOVIĆ

Logroscino, Nicola Bonifacio (*b* Bitonto, bap. 22 Oct 1698; *d* ?Palermo, 1765–7). Italian composer. In June 1714 he and his younger brother Pietro entered the conservatory of S Maria di Loreto, Naples. On 1 October 1727 the conservatory expelled them both 'for bad traits of character'. Pietro was later readmitted, but Nicola was not. In May 1728 he became organist to the Bishop of Conza (Avellino) and stayed in this post until June 1731 when he returned to Naples, marrying a local girl there in November of the same year.

Logroscino's first known composition was an oratorio, *Il mondo trionfante nella concezione di Maria sempre Virgine*, performed near Brno in 1730 at the court of Cardinal von Schrattenbach. In 1735 his first known comic opera, *Lo creduto infedele*, was given at the Teatro della Pace, Naples. In a statement written in October 1738 by one of the ministers of the King of Naples, recommending Logroscino for an opera commission for the Teatro S Carlo, the minister added that he had already 'set many comedies to music in the small theatres of the capital'. Two other comic operas reputedly by him may belong to this period: *Tanto ben che male* and *Il vecchio marito*. His first known, full-length *opera seria*, *Il Quinto Fabio* (1738), was written for the Teatro delle Dame, Rome. Thereafter he wrote, sometimes in collaboration with other composers, numerous comic operas, most of which were for the 'small' Neapolitan theatres such as the Fiorentini and Nuovo. It is on these comic operas that his reputation is chiefly built.

Confusion reigns about when Logroscino left Naples to settle in Palermo, where he spent several of his last years teaching at the Ospedale dei Figliuoli Dispersi. Some scholars (including Frank Walker) suggest that he may have begun to work at the Ospedale in the 1740s. On the other hand, Prota-Giurleo claimed to have seen documents proving that he took up his post there in September 1758. In view of the popularity of Logroscino's music in Naples throughout the 1740s and early 1750s, it seems plausible that his home was Naples till 1756 or later. Prota-Giurleo asserted that he worked at the Ospedale at least until 30 November 1764, that there is a gap in the Ospedale records between this date and 2 September 1767, and that his name no longer appears in the records for 2 September 1767 or later; this would mean that at some time between November 1764 and September 1767 he ceased to be in the Ospe-

dale's employ. His last opera, *La gelosia*, was produced in Venice in autumn 1765, and he may have travelled there to supervise the performances. Since there is no later trace of him, it is assumed that he died between the end of 1765 and September 1767.

Though Logroscino has always been considered an important composer of opera, especially comic opera, too many facts about his life and music are missing for a proper assessment to be made. It seems that his popularity as a composer of comic opera rose sharply in the years after 1738 and that he had no serious rival among composers of this genre in Naples between 1744, when Leonardo Leo died, and 1754, when Nicola Piccinni composed and presented his first comic opera to the Neapolitan public. By 1757–8 Piccinni had superseded Logroscino as the favourite composer among Neapolitan comic opera audiences. Logroscino's posthumous fame owed much to the statement of La Borde that 'he was the god of the comic genre, and has served as model for almost all composers of this type of work'. Later writers exaggerated his position in other ways. Gerber declared that he was the 'creator' of comic opera, while others, notably Florimo, said that he instigated the practice of ending the acts of comic opera with an important vocal ensemble. Although by 1900 it was clear to historians that he was not the inventor of the ensemble finale as such, Kretzschmar still gave him credit for inventing a new type of ensemble finale whose musical structure was determined solely by the action and the text. Even this view has since been exploded.

Modern opinion of Logroscino's comic operas must remain flexible until more of the music is discovered. At present this music is limited to one complete work, *Il governatore*, and the Act 1 finale to *Il Leandro*. There is no evidence here that Logroscino's finales were more advanced structurally than those of his predecessor Leo, who also composed finales with a freely evolving form to suit the words. *Il governatore* is weak melodically, but the dramatic characterization and instrumentation are strong. Other surviving music includes two heroic operas, *Giunio Bruto* and *Olimpiade*, a few arias and ensembles in manuscript, and a small amount of liturgical music including two *Stabat mater* settings modelled on Pergolesi's.

See also GOVERNATORE, IL.

three-act comic operas, performed in Naples, unless otherwise stated

Lo creduto infedele (A. Palomba), Pace, wint. 1735
Il Quinto Fabio (heroic op, 3, A. Salvi), Rome, Dame, carn. 1738
Inganno per inganno (G. A. Federico), Fiorentini, aut. 1738
L'inganno felice (T. Mariani), Nuovo, wint. 1739
La violante (Palomba), Nuovo, carn. 1741 [rev. of Auletta's L'amor costante]
Amore ed amistade, Fiorentini, spr. 1742
La Lionora (Federico), Fiorentini, wint. 1742, collab. V. Ciampi
Il Riccardo, Fiorentini, carn. 1743
Festa teatrale per la nascita del R. Infante [pt 1], Naples, July 1743 [pt 2 by G. Manna, unperf.]
Il Leandro (A. Villani), Nuovo, spr. 1744, *GB-Cfm* (frag.), modern copy *US-Wc*
Ciommetella correvata (P. Trinchera), Pace, aut. 1744; rev. as Lo cicisbeo, Nuovo, aut. 1751
Li zite (Trinchera), Pace, spr. 1745
Don Paduano (Trinchera), Pace, aut. 1745
Il governatore (D. Canicà), Nuovo, carn. 1747, *D-MÜs* (R1978: IOB, xlii)
La costanza (Palomba), Nuovo, 1747
Giunio Bruto (heroic op, 3), Rome, Argentina, Jan 1748, *MÜs*
La contessa di Belcolore (comic int, 2, N. Carulli), Florence, Intrepidi, carn. 1748
Li dispiette d'ammore [Acts 1 and 2] (Palomba), Pace, carn. 1748 [Act 3 by N. Calandra]

La finta frascatana (Federico), Nuovo, carn. 1751, rev. of Leo's Amor vuol sofferenza with addns by Logroscino and A. Ferradini

Amore figlio dei piacere (Palomba), Nuovo, aut. 1751, collab. G. Ventura

Lo finto Perziano (Trinchera), Nuovo, carn. 1752

La Griselda (Palomba), Fiorentini, aut. 1752

La pastorella scaltra (comic int, 2), Rome, Valle, carn. 1753

Elmira generosa (Trinchera), Nuovo, carn. 1753, collab. E. Bartella

Olimpiade (heroic op, 3, P. Metastasio), Rome, Argentina, carn. 1753, *US-R*

Le chiajese cantarine (Trinchera), Nuovo, carn. 1754, collab. D. Fischietti and G. Maraucci, rev. of Fischietti: L'abate Collarone, 1749

La Rosmonda [buffa music, finales] (Palomba), Nuovo, carn. 1755, collab. C. Cecere, P. Gomes and T. Traetta

Le finte magie, Fiorentini, carn. 1756

I disturbi, Nuovo, sum. 1756, collab. Traetta

La finta 'mbreana (G. Bisceglia), Nuovo, wint. 1756, collab. P. Errichelli

La fante di buon gusto (Palomba), ?1758; rev. as La furba burlata (P. de' Napoli [P. Napoli Signorelli] after Palomba), Fiorentini, aut. 1760, addns by N. Piccinni; new addns by G. Insanguine, 1762

Il natale di Achille (azione drammatica, 1), Palermo, 20 Jan 1760

Perseo (azione drammatica, G. Baldanza), Palermo, 1762

L'innamorato balordo (de' Napoli), Nuovo, carn. 1763, collab. Insanguine and G. Geremia

La viaggiatrice di bell'umore (de' Napoli), Nuovo, 1763, collab. Insanguine

Il tempo dell'onore (componimento drammatico), Palermo, 20 Jan 1765, collab. A. Sperandeo

La gelosia (unknown Bolognese writer), Venice, S Samuele, aut. 1765

Tanto ben che male, ?Naples

Il vecchio marito, ?Naples

Doubtful: Adriano (Metastasio), ?1742

*

ES (U. Prota-Giurleo); *FlorimoN*; *GerberL*; *Grove5* (F. Walker and others); *LaMusicaD*; *MGG* (A. Mondolfi)

J.-B. de La Borde: *Essai sur la musique ancienne et moderne*, iii (Paris, 1780)

P. Napoli Signorelli: *Vicende della coltura nelle due Sicilie*, v (Naples, 1786)

H. Kretzschmar: 'Zwei Opern Nicolo Logroscinos', *JbMP* (1908), 47–68

E. J. Dent: 'Ensembles and Finales in 18th century Italian Opera, pt 2', *SIMG*, xi (1909–10), 543–69; xii (1910-11), 112–38

U. Prota-Giurleo: *Nicola Logroscino 'il dio dell'opera buffa'* (Naples, 1927)

M. Bellucci La Salandra: *Triade musicale Bitontina, Brevi cenni biografici di Bonifacio Nicola Logroscino, 1698–1760* (Bitonto, 1936)

G. Tintori: *L'opera napolitana* (Milan, 1958)

G. Hardie: 'Neapolitan Comic Opera, 1707–1750: Some Addenda and Corrigenda for *The New Grove*', *JAMS*, xxxvi (1983), 124–7

MICHAEL F. ROBINSON (with DALE E. MONSON)

Lohengrin (i). *Romantische Oper* in three acts by Richard Wagner (*see* WAGNER family, (1)) to his own libretto; Weimar, Grossherzogliches Hoftheater, 28 August 1850.

Wagner's acquaintance with the Lohengrin legend dates back to the winter of 1841–2, when he encountered it in the form of a synopsis and commentary in the annual proceedings of the Königsberg Germanic Society. In the summer of 1845 he became engrossed in the legend of the Holy Grail, reading Wolfram von Eschenbach's poems *Parzivâl* and *Titurel* in editions by Simrock and San-Marte, and the anonymous epic *Lohengrin* in an edition by J. Görres.

By 3 August of that year a prose scenario had been outlined and by 27 November the versification completed. Wagner then made his first complete draft, on two staves (completed 30 July 1846), followed by the second draft with elaboration of instrumental and choral parts. Various changes were made to the poem

Heinrich der Vogler [King Henry the Fowler]	bass
Lohengrin	tenor
Elsa of Brabant	soprano
Duke Gottfried *her brother*	silent
Friedrich von Telramund *a count of Brabant*	baritone
Ortrud *his wife*	mezzo-soprano
The King's Herald	bass
Four Noblemen of Brabant	tenors, basses
Four Pages	sopranos, altos

Saxon and Thuringian counts and nobles, Brabantine counts and nobles, noblewomen, pages, vassals, ladies, serfs

Setting Antwerp; first half of the 10th century

during composition, especially in Act 3. Probably for this reason the second complete draft for Act 3 was made before those for Acts 1 and 2, but there is no evidence to suggest that the acts were originally composed in anything other than the usual order. The full score was written out between 1 January and 28 April 1848.

Wagner, by 1850 in exile in Switzerland, was unable to be present at the first performance which took place at Weimar under Liszt's direction with a cast including Rosa von Milde-Agthe, Fastlinger, Johann Beck, von Milde and Höfer. The work was received well in Germany, but Wagner was unable to hear it until 1861, when it was given in Vienna. The first performance in Bayreuth did not take place until 1894, when Mottl conducted a cast including Ernest van Dyck and Lillian Nordica. The performances at Bologna in 1871 were the first of any Wagner opera to be given in Italy. The work was first performed in Great Britain in 1875 in Italian, in 1880 in English and in 1882 in German; before World War I *Lohengrin* was by far the most popular of Wagner's operas in Britain. Notable exponents of the title role have included Niemann, De Reszke, Slezak, Melchior, Svanholm, Jess Thomas, Peter Hofmann and Domingo. Elsa has been sung by Eames, Melba, Gadski, Destinn, Jeritza, Rethberg, Lotte Lehmann, Flagstad, Varnay, Grümmer, Tomowa-Sintow and Norman.

Unlike *Holländer* and *Tannhäuser*, *Lohengrin* was not subjected to revision by Wagner, except for the excision of the second part of Lohengrin's Narration (Act 3), a cut carried out at his request at the first performance and ever since (a recording under Leinsdorf reinstating the passage bears out Wagner's conviction that it would have an anti-climactic effect). The double male-voice chorus 'In Früh'n versammelt uns der Ruf' in Act 2 is often cut in performance, despite its imaginative antiphony. A cut traditionally made after Lohengrin's Narration (from Elsa's swoon to 'Der Schwan!') is particularly regrettable in that it gives Elsa no chance to express remorse.

The prelude opens with the sounds of a body of divided strings high up in their compass, alternating with four solo violins and a chorus of flutes and oboes: a striking aural image for the shimmering of the Holy Grail. In contrast to all Wagner's earlier overtures, it is conceived like a single breath, as a unified movement, rather than in the traditional sections, yet with references to forthcoming thematic ideas. According to Wagner, the prelude represented the descent from heaven of a host of angels bearing the Grail, and their return to heaven.

'Lohengrin' (Wagner), Act 1 scene ii (the arrival of Lohengrin) in the original production at the Grossherzogliches Hoftheater, Weimar, 28 August 1850: engraving from the 'Illustrirte Zeitung' (Leipzig, 12 April 1851)

ACT 1 *A meadow on the banks of the Scheldt near Antwerp* King Henry (the historical Henry the Fowler) has come to Antwerp to exhort the Brabantines to join him in defending Germany against the imminent invasion from the Hungarians in the east. The curtain rises on two groups of people: the king, under the Oak of Justice, surrounded by Saxon counts and nobles, and opposite them the Brabantine counts and nobles headed by Friedrich von Telramund, by whose side stands his wife Ortrud. The Herald summons the Brabantines to arms and they respond with fervour. But there is dissension in the air. Telramund, charged to give account, accuses Elsa, in a quasi-recitative, of murdering her brother Gottfried, the heir to the dukedom of Brabant; he claims the succession for himself.

The king summons Elsa and she comes forward timidly (scene ii). The subdued wind chorus, contrasting with the clashing brass of the previous scene, suggests her vulnerability. At first she is silent, but then she tells how she had prayed to God in her distress, 'Einsam in trüben Tagen', falling into a sweet sleep. The king urges her to defend herself, but her trance-like state gives way only to an exultant account of a vision of a knightly champion. The latter is prefaced by the Grail music on high strings and accompanied with extreme delicacy on wind and strings, with harp arpeggios and a magical touch on a solo trumpet. The king and bystanders are much moved, but Telramund is unimpressed. He demands judgment through combat; Elsa invokes her visionary champion.

Herald and trumpeters twice sound the call. There is no response, but when Elsa sinks to her knees in prayer, a modulation from Ab (the tonality associated with her) to A major (that associated with Lohengrin), combined with an increase in tempo and agitated tremolando strings, signifies the distant approach of the knight, in a boat drawn by a swan. The arrival is greeted by excited choral ejaculations, which at the beginning of scene iii coalesce into a hymn of welcome. Lohengrin bids farewell to the swan and, after making his obeisance to the king, offers himself as Elsa's champion. Shifting into her tonality of Ab, he makes her promise that she will never

ask his name or origin, sounding a phrase (ex.1) that will act as a motif of reminiscence. They pledge themselves to each other and Telramund, ignoring entreaties to desist, braces himself for battle.

Ex.1

Nie sollst du mich be - fra - gen
['Never may you question me']

The ground is measured out and the Herald announces the rules of combat. In a passage in triple time – the only such example in the entire work – the king invokes the blessing of heaven, 'Mein Herr und Gott'. His prayer is taken up by the chorus and built to a climax. Onstage trumpeters sound the call to battle and, after the king has struck three times with his sword on his shield, the two men fight. Lohengrin defeats Telramund but spares his life. Elsa is overcome with joy, while the crowd acclaim Lohengrin victor in a triumphant finale. Ortrud wonders who the stranger is that renders her magical powers useless. Telramund, crushed and humiliated, falls at her feet.

ACT 2 *The fortress at Antwerp* The curtain rises to reveal the palace at the back and the kemenate at the front (the dwellings of respectively the knights and the womenfolk). The minster stands to the right and on its steps are seated Telramund and Ortrud. It is night. A sustained, muted drum roll and a baleful theme given out on the cello evoke the presence of dark, malignant forces. In the 12th bar an ominous-sounding theme based on the traditionally 'supernatural' chord of the diminished 7th, and associated specifically with Ortrud (ex.2), is announced by cellos and two bassoons. The

Ex.2

motif of the 'forbidden question' (ex.1) is also heard on the english horn and bass clarinet. Telramund rouses himself, launching into a bitter tirade punctuated by an aggressively dotted string figure and a rushing, rising semiquaver scale in the bass, blaming Ortrud for his disgrace, 'Durch dich musst' ich verlieren'. The underlying eight-bar structure of this 'aria' is only slightly varied. But after a recitative exchange, in which Ortrud promises a way to undermine Lohengrin's heavenly protection, a more freely structured section begins, 'Du wilde Seherin', in which Ortrud tells Telramund that Lohengrin's power would be nullified if Elsa were to ask him about his name and origins. It is this passage in particular that has caused the scene as a whole to be regarded, with justification, as the most stylistically advanced by Wagner to date. A descending chromatic phrase (a pre-echo of the 'magic sleep' harmonies in the *Ring*) sounded at 'Du wilde Seherin' is the first of a nexus of themes (associated with Ortrud, her sorcery and the 'forbidden question') which have more than an ornamental function: they form the substance of the musical argument. Quasi-recitative and arioso here alternate and merge imperceptibly. As was to be the case in the *Ring*, motivic development acquires a form-building function when conventional phrase structure gives way to musical prose. The scene ends with a dramatically effective if stylistically regressive revenge duet for the two voices in unison over tremolando strings.

An ethereal wind chorus opens the second scene, heralding the appearance of Elsa, dressed in white, on the balcony of the kemenate. Ortrud, dismissing Telramund, calls up to Elsa (oboes and stopped horns producing a sinister sound next to Elsa's flute) and hypocritically appeals to her generous nature. As Elsa disappears to descend to ground level, Ortrud invokes the pagan gods in a powerful outburst. Affectedly prostrating herself before Elsa, Ortrud listens while the bride-to-be sings of her naive matrimonial bliss in a succession of untroubled diatonic harmonies. Gradually Ortrud instils the poison. First her diminished 7th theme (ex.2) sounds on the bassoons, then, to the accompaniment of the 'forbidden question' motif, she comments darkly on Lohengrin's mysterious origins and appearance. Elsa shudders with dread (tremolando diminished 7th chords), but recovers her composure. In a brief duet, both express their feelings, though Ortrud's vengeance is subjugated musically to the ecstasy of Elsa's line, which is also reinforced by mellifluous strings. As day breaks, Elsa and Ortrud go inside; Telramund reappears briefly, gloating over his expected triumph.

Scene iii opens with an antiphonal exchange between two trumpets blowing the reveille from the tower, answered by two in the distance. As the rest of the orchestra joins in, the palace gates open and four royal trumpeters cause a brief, dramatic plunge into C major (from and back into D major) with their onstage fanfares. The filling of the stage is matched by gathering momentum in the orchestra, leading to the double chorus for male voices 'In Früh'n versammelt uns der Ruf'. Though belonging to the grand operatic tradition soon to be abjured by Wagner, this and subsequent choruses show skill in their part-writing and can be exhilarating in performance. The Herald announces that Telramund is banished; anyone who consorts with him suffers the same fate. The stranger sent by God, he continues, wishes to take as his title not Duke, but Protector of Brabant; today he celebrates his wedding, tomorrow he will lead them into battle. These announcements are punctuated by choral acclamations, following which four disgruntled nobles, formerly liegemen of Telramund, detach themselves from the crowd and are recruited by Telramund, who has been skulking in the shadows.

The fourth scene initiates the wedding procession to the minster, but as Elsa reaches its steps, Ortrud interposes herself (on a dramatically interrupted cadence, leading to diminished 7th agitation) to claim precedence. In a regularly phrased 'aria' she goes on to taunt Elsa for her ignorance of her champion's origins, 'Wenn falsch Gericht'. Elsa's reply is forthright and confident, supported by a full wind chorus in exultant sextuplets. Ortrud's next onslaught is interrupted by the arrival of the king, Lohengrin and the Saxon nobles from the palace (scene v). Lohengrin consoles Elsa and begins to lead her to the minster once more. This time the procession is interrupted by Telramund, who vehemently accuses Lohengrin of sorcery. His demand that the knight reveal his name is brushed aside by Lohengrin. No king or prince can command him, he replies, only Elsa. But as he turns to his bride, he sees with dismay that she is agitated: the motifs of Ortrud and the 'forbidden question' tell us why. The following ensemble ironically juxtaposes Elsa's doubt, expressed to herself, with the unquestioning trust of the onlookers.

The king expresses his satisfaction and, as the nobles crowd round Lohengrin to pledge their allegiance, Telramund prevails on Elsa to allow him to expose the sorcerer by spilling just a drop of his blood. Lohengrin repulses Telramund and Ortrud, and the procession sets off once again. A climax built by sequential means brings the act to a rousing conclusion. But there is a final *coup de théâtre*. As Elsa and Lohengrin reach the top step of the minster, she looks down to see Ortrud raising her arm in a gesture of triumph. The motif of the 'forbidden question' rings out on trumpets and trombones, its F minor colouring casting a menacing shadow over the radiance of the predominating C major.

ACT 3.i–ii *The bridal chamber* The celebrated orchestral introduction to Act 3, which has become a concert piece in its own right, is notable for its metric displacements – in contradistinction to the regular common-time periods elsewhere, dictated by the conventional poetic metres adopted. The curtain rises on the bridal chamber. To the strains of the even more celebrated bridal march, 'Treulich geführt', two processions enter from behind: Elsa escorted by the ladies, and Lohengrin by the king and nobles. The couple embrace and are blessed by the king. The attendants retire to a repetition of the march.

With an enharmonic modulation from B♭ to E major an atmosphere of tender devotion is immediately established for scene ii, 'Das süsse Lied verhallt'. Muted strings provide the background for a profusion of melodic ideas, launched by first a solo clarinet then a solo oboe. Except for a few brief bars, the voices are heard in succession rather than combination. Elsa's first suggestion that Lohengrin share with her the secret of his name is deflected, but she becomes more and more insistent, despite his alternate warnings and protestations of love. Attempting to reassure her, he says that he renounced glorious and blissful delights to woo her. But Elsa is far from reassured: he may tire of her and return to the joys he left behind. The tempo quickens. Ortrud's theme (ex.2) is ubiquitous: at one point Elsa's line becomes a diatonic version of it, in E minor. Finally, as the motif of the 'forbidden question' rings out, Elsa asks outright who he is. Telramund and his henchmen break into the chamber. With Elsa's assistance, Lohengrin fells Telramund at a stroke; the henchmen kneel before Lohengrin. He orders Telramund's body to be taken to the king's judgment seat; there he will answer Elsa's question.

3.iii *The banks of the Scheldt; daybreak* Brabantines appear from all sides, stirringly heralded by trumpets in successively Eb, D, F, E and, finally, C (the king's trumpeters). Telramund's covered body is brought in. Then Elsa enters, followed by Lohengrin, who tells the king that he can no longer lead his troops into battle. He explains how he killed Telramund in self-defence and goes on to denounce Elsa for breaking her vow. Now he is forced to reveal his origins. The shimmering Grail music of the work's opening introduces Lohengrin's Narration, 'In fernem Land'. He tells how he came as a servant of the Grail; such knights are granted invincible power on condition of anonymity. Now that his secret is revealed, he must return to Monsalvat. His father is Parzival and his name is Lohengrin. The Narration begins with conventionally balanced phrases but develops into a freer structure more appropriate to narrative as the unfolding of the tale seizes the imagination of teller and listener. Elsa momentarily swoons; then to Lohengrin's remonstrations she begs forgiveness. The king and chorus add their pleas, Elsa's voice soaring above them all. But the laws of the Grail are immutable. The swan appears, drawing an empty boat. After addressing the swan, Lohengrin turns to Elsa and tells her that had they lived together for just a year, her brother Gottfried would have been restored to her. He entrusts her with his sword, horn and ring, to be given to Gottfried should he return one day. Ortrud comes forward declaring that she recognizes the swan, by the chain round its neck, as Gottfried, whom she bewitched; now he is lost to Elsa for ever. To the radiant music of the Grail, Lohengrin kneels silently in prayer. A white dove descends and hovers over the boat. Seeing it, Lohengrin loosens the chain round the swan, which sinks. In its place appears a boy in shining silver: Gottfried. Lohengrin lifts him to the bank, proclaiming him Duke of Brabant. Ortrud falls to the ground, while Gottfried advances first to the king and then to Elsa. Her joy turns to sorrow as she watches Lohengrin depart. As the Grail knight vanishes from sight, Elsa falls lifeless to the ground.

* * *

Lohengrin is the last of Wagner's works that can fairly be described as an opera rather than a music drama. It contains, however, the seeds of future developments and is a powerfully conceived, imaginatively scored work in its own right.

BARRY MILLINGTON

Lohengrin (ii). *Azione invisibile* by SALVATORE SCIARRINO to his own libretto after Jules Laforgue's *Lohengrin fils de Parsifal* (from *Moralités légendaires*); Milan, Piccola Scala, 15 January 1983.

In Laforgue Sciarrino found a kindred spirit who placed myths ancient and modern before a distorting mirror of irony and obliquity. Laforgue's version of the *Lohengrin* story transforms the Wagnerian protagonists into creatures of hopeless and hilarious immaturity. On a moonlit shore Elsa, a Vestal virgin, is accused of impurity: Lohengrin, a vainglorious adolescent, arrives on his swan to defend her. The scene shifts to the nuptial villa made available to newlyweds by the Ministry of Cults. For all her attempts at romantic intimacy, Elsa inspires little enthusiasm in Lohengrin, who prefers to embrace his white pillow. This mutates into his swan, on whose back he flies out of the window and back to the moon.

Compounding the estrangement from the familiar story, Sciarrino inverts the two halves of Laforgue's narration (so that the action proceeds from nuptial villa to seashore) and gives the roles of both Lohengrin and Elsa to a single female vocalist. These manoeuvres resolve into coherence only when, at the end, it becomes clear that the singer is an inmate in a mental hospital. The lunar/lunatic atmosphere is one to which Sciarrino's musical language is in any case native: the vocal part explores an alarmingly wide gamut of articulations, while the instruments make obsessive patterns from harmonics and other marginal sounds. A radio version of *Lohengrin* won the 1984 Italia Prize.

DAVID OSMOND-SMITH

Löhner [Löhner-Beda], **Fritz** [Löhner, Beda] (*b* Wildenschwert, Bohemia, 24 June 1883; *d* Auschwitz, Poland, 4 December 1942). Austrian librettist. A lawyer, classical scholar and officer, he gained popular success as a satirical writer under the name Beda. He was a prolific writer for cabaret, revues and popular songs before collaborating on more substantial theatrical works. As an operetta librettist he worked most notably with the Viennese gynaecologist and playwright Ludwig Herzer (the pseudonym of Ludwig Herl; 1872–1939). His librettos included four for Lehár, *Das Land des Lächelns* (1929) and *Giuditta* (1934) among them. In 1938 he was confined to Buchenwald concentration camp, where he wrote the text of a 'Buchenwaldlied'. He was later transferred to Auschwitz and sent to the gas chamber.

Operetten unless otherwise stated

Der fromme Silvanus (Spl), L. Ascher, 1910; *Die keusche Susanne* (musikalisches Lustspiel), Ascher, 1910; *Rampsenit* (groteske Operette), Ascher, 1911; *Eine fidele Nacht,* Ascher, 1911; *Das Gartenhäuschen,* B. Laszky, 1913; *Die goldene Hanna,* Ascher, 1913; *So wird's gemacht* (Operetten-Parodie, with R. Blum), R. Haller, 1913; *Frühling am Rhein* (with C. Lindau and O. Fronz), E. Eysler, 1914; *Der Weltenbummler* (with Lindau), R. Fall, 1915; *Der Sterngucker,* Lehár, 1916; *Die Dame von Welt* (Spl, with H. Kottow), R. Fall, 1917; *Das Herz* (Tanzmimodrie), A. Guttmann, 1917

Ans Marie (Spl), M. Eggar, 1917; *Muschi* (Spl), ?Stolz, ?1918 (? E. Arnold, 1920); *Zuckergoscherl* (Operette-Parodie), Guttmann, 1918; *Kikeriki* (with O. Hein), Stolz, 1920; *Der keusche Heinrich* (Operetten-Schwank, with Lindau), H. Duval-Diamant, 1921; *Der Herr der Welt* (Operetten-Revue, with K. Brettschneider and E. Wolf), K. Hajos, 1921; *Der schwarze Pierrot,* Hajos, 1922; *Die Brasilianerin* (with M. Neal), O. Jascha, 1923; *Revanche* (with F. Lunzer), Jascha, 1924; *Die Bojarenbraut* (with Kottow), W. Engel-Berger, 1925; *Die Annemarie* (Spl), F. Egger, 1927

Ich hab' mein Herz in Heidelberg verloren (Spl, with B. Hardt-Warden and E. Neubach), F. Raymond, 1927; *Friederike* (Spl, with L. Herzer), Lehár, 1928; *Das Land des Lächelns* (komische Operette, with Herzer, after V. Léon: *Die gelbe Jacke*), Lehár, 1929; *Frühling im Wienerwald* (lustiges Spl, with F. Lunzer), Ascher, 1930; *Viktoria und ihr Husar* (with A. Grünwald), P. Abraham, 1930; *Schön ist die Welt!* (with Herzer), Lehár, 1930; *Die Blume von Hawaii* (with Grünwald and E. Földes), Abraham, 1931; *Ball im Savoy* (with Grünwald), Abraham, 1932; *Rosen im Schnee* (Spl, with Hardt-Warden), Jascha, 1933

Giuditta (musikalische Komödie, with P. Knepler), Lehár, 1934; *Märchen im Grand-Hotel* (Lustspiel-Operette, with Grünwald), Abraham, 1934; *Der Prinz von Schiras* (romantische Operette, with Herzer), J. Beer, 1934; *Die verliebte Königin* (with

Grünwald), N. Brodszky, 1934; *Dschainah, das Mädchen aus dem Teehaus* (with Grünwald), Abraham, 1935; *Der gütige Antonius* (grosse Operette, with H. Wiener), J. Beneš, 1935; *Auf der grünen Wiese* (Revue-Operette, with Wiener), Beneš, 1936; *Gruss und Kuss aus der Wachau* (grosse Operette, with Wiener and Breuer), Beneš, 1938   ANDREW LAMB

Löhner, Johann (*b* Nuremberg, bap. 21 Nov 1645; *d* Nuremberg, 2 April 1705). German composer. He played the regal in Nuremberg from 1665 to 1670, then served briefly as a tenor at Bayreuth; after a journey to Vienna, Salzburg and Leipzig he again worked in churches in Nuremberg (from 1672), becoming organist of the Spitalkirche (1682) and of St Lorenz (1694).

Only Löhner and S. T. Staden are known to have written operas in Nuremberg during the 17th century. There is record of three operas by Löhner. *Die triumphirende Treue* was dedicated to Johanna Elisabeth, margravine of the Brandenburg court in Ansbach, and performed there in 1679. The long-missing tablature of this work was found in the late 20th century, enabling a modern edition of this early German opera. The libretto for the opera *Der gerechte Zaleukus* was Löhner's translation of an Italian text, as was *Theseus*, which was performed in Nuremberg in 1688 with the support of 'some admirers'. An inventory of court property in Ansbach in 1686 includes the opera *Lisylla*, which was probably *Die triumphirende Treue* (its main role is Lisylla). Löhner's opera 'arias', like those of Staden, are strophic songs in the same rather folklike style as his many sacred works in this form.

Die triumphirende Treue (C. Heuchelin and P. Keller), Ansbach, court, 1679, ed. W. Braun, DTB, new ser., vi (1984); some arias in Keusche Liebs- und Tugend-Gedancken (Nuremberg, 1680); 4 arias ed. in Sandberger, 99
Der gerechte Zaleukus (J. Löhner, trans. of G. F. Minato: *Seleuco*), 1687
Theseus (Löhner, trans. of G. F. Aureli: *Teseo fra li rivali*), Nuremberg, 1688; arias pubd in XLIV Arien aus der Opera von Theseus (Nuremberg, 1688); 8 arias ed. in Sandberger, 102

*

G. A. Will: *Nürnbergisches Gelehrten-Lexikon* (Nuremberg and Altdorf, 1755–8)
C. Sachs: 'Die Ansbacher Hofkapelle', SIMG, xi (1909–10), 105–37
A. Sandberger: 'Zur Geschichte der Oper in Nürnberg in der zweiten Hälfte des 17. und zu Anfang des 18. Jahrhunderts', *AMw*, i (1918–19), 84–107; repr. in A. Sandberger: *Ausgewählte Aufsätze zur Musikgeschichte* (Munich, 1921), 188–217
W. Braun: 'Johann Valentin Meders Opernexperiment in Revel 1680', *Beiträge zur Musikgeschichte Nordeuropas: Kurt Gudewill zum 65. Geburtstag* (Wolfenbüttel, 1978), 69–78
                                                    HAROLD E. SAMUEL

Lohse, Otto (*b* Dresden, 21 Sept 1858; *d* Baden-Baden, 5 May 1925). German conductor. After studying with Franz Wüllner he began his conducting career in Riga. In 1894 he directed the German opera season in London, then went to the Hamburg city theatre. Damrosch called him to New York in 1895 to direct the German opera season for two years and from 1897 to 1904 he was at the Strasbourg city theatre; during his last three years there he simultaneously directed the Royal Opera in London. During his subsequent seven-year directorship of the Cologne Opera he made guest appearances in Monte Carlo, Moscow, Paris, Brussels and London. His later success as the director of the Leipzig Opera was even greater. He retired to Baden-Baden in 1923 but continued to conduct there until his death.

A specialist in the works of Wagner and Strauss and other contemporary German composers, Lohse

exhibited extraordinary animation as an opera conductor. The Munich critics, however, found his style too angular, in contrast with the romantic style of Mottl.
                                                    FRIEDRICH BASER

Loini, Domenico. *See* LUINI, DOMENICO.

Lombard, Alain (*b* Paris, 4 Oct 1940). French conductor. He studied at the Paris Conservatoire. His first appointment was at the Lyons Opéra (1961–5), as assistant and then as principal conductor. At the instigation of Régine Crespin he was engaged to conduct Massenet's *Hérodiade* for the American Opera Society at New York in 1963. He won the gold medal at the 1966 Dimitri Mitropoulos competition, and made his Metropolitan Opera début with *Faust* in 1967. He held an appointment with the Miami Philharmonic (1966–74), where he conducted some opera performances, then became director of the Opéra du Rhin (1974–80), where he earned recognition for his artistic enterprise while sharing a modest budget between the three centres the company serves at Strasbourg, Colmar and Mulhouse. He was appointed music director at the Paris Opéra (1981–3), then of the Opéra-Comique (1983), extending his guest engagements to include the Hamburg Staatsoper and his South African début with *Turandot* (1985, Johannesburg). In 1988 he became musical director of the Bordeaux Opéra. His recordings include Gounod's *Roméo et Juliette* (1968) and *Faust* (1977), Delibes' *Lakmé* (1971), *Carmen* (1974), *Turandot* (1977), *Così fan tutte* (1977), *Die Zauberflöte* (1978) and Offenbach operettas. He is a brilliant technician and has a dynamic personality in performance.
                    CHRISTIANE SPIETH-WEISSENBACHER/NOËL GOODWIN

Lombardi alla prima crociata, I ('The Lombards on the First Crusade'). *Dramma lirico* in four acts by GIUSEPPE VERDI to a libretto by TEMISTOCLE SOLERA after Tommaso Grossi's poem *I Lombardi alla prima crociata*; Milan, Teatro alla Scala, 11 February 1843. (For the revised French version of 1847, *see* JÉRUSALEM.)

Arvino } *sons of Folco, Lord of Rò*		tenor
Pagano }		bass
Viclinda *Arvino's wife*		soprano
Giselda *her daughter*		soprano
Pirro *Arvino's squire*		bass
Prior of the City of Milan		tenor
Acciano *tyrant of Antioch*		bass
Oronte *his son*		tenor
Sofia *Acciano's wife, a secret Christian convert*		soprano

Nuns, priors, populace, hired ruffians, armigers in Folco's palace, ambassadors from Persia, Media, Damascus and Chaldea, harem women, knights and crusading soldiers, pilgrims, celestial virgins, Lombard women

Setting Milan, in and around Antioch, and near Jerusalem in 1096–7

As with Verdi's previous opera, *Nabucco*, there seems to be hardly any surviving information about the genesis of *I Lombardi*. No records exist of negotiations with La Scala, although popular rumour has it that, after the huge success of *Nabucco*, Merelli (the impresario there)

left to the composer's discretion the fee for the new opera, and that Verdi took advice on a proper sum from his future wife, Giuseppina Strepponi. Nor is there any surviving correspondence between Verdi and his librettist, Temistocle Solera. They were both in Milan during the period of composition (presumably the second half of 1842) and, if we are to trust Verdi's later recollections, he altered very little of Solera's initial draft. The opera was apparently frowned upon by the religious censors in Milan but eventually escaped with only a few unimportant changes. The first night was a wild public success, with a cast that included Giovanni Severi (Arvino), Prosper Dérivis (Pagano), Carlo Guasco (Oronte) and Erminia Frezzolini (Giselda). For a revival in Senigallia in July 1843, Verdi composed a new cabaletta in Act 2 for Antonio Poggi (as Oronte). His revised, French version of the opera was given as *Jérusalem* in Paris in 1847.

The prelude (the first Verdi wrote) is very short and follows the conventional strategy of attempting a kind of radical synopsis of the ensuing action.

ACT 1: 'The Vendetta'

1.i *The piazza of S Ambrogio, Milan* To a *banda* accompaniment, the opening chorus celebrates new friendship between the brothers Arvino and Pagano ('Oh nobile esempio!'); the two have been enemies ever since Pagano jealously attacked Arvino during the latter's wedding to Viclinda 18 years ago. Pagano and Arvino appear with their family and supporters to announce publicly their reconciliation. This leads to a large-scale concertato movement, 'T'assale un tremito! … padre che fia?', which is led off by Giselda, who anxiously asks why her father seems so ill at ease; as the ensemble develops, all the principals are musically differentiated. A Prior of the city announces that Arvino will lead a group to the Crusades. All join in a bellicose chorus, 'All'empio che infrange', and process off to a robust march. An offstage chorus of nuns introduces Pagano, who, in the Andante movement of a double aria, 'Sciagurata! hai tu creduto', informs us that he can never forget Viclinda. A group of supporters enters, swearing to help him against Arvino, and he finishes the scene with a fierce cabaletta of revenge, 'O speranza di vendetta'.

1.ii *A gallery in the Folco palace* Viclinda and Giselda are still uneasy. Arvino enters to inform Viclinda that his father, Folco, is in the adjoining room. Giselda offers a prayer for divine assistance, the subtly scored and harmonically bold preghiera 'Salve Maria!'. As the women go off, Pagano and his henchman Pirro appear. Pagano enters Arvino's room, to emerge a little later, bloody dagger in hand, dragging Viclinda after him. But, as flames are seen through the windows, Arvino and his followers intercept the villain. The discovery that Pagano has killed his own father precipitates the central Andante mosso, 'Mostro d'averno orribile'. Arvino demands his brother's death while Giselda counsels mercy; Pagano tries unsuccessfully to kill himself, and all join in pronouncing his banishment in a final stretta, 'Va! sul capo ti grava'.

ACT 2: 'The Man of the Cave'

2.i *A room in Acciano's palace in Antioch* Months have passed; Vielinda has died and the Crusaders are at the gates of Antioch. Acciano and his supporters remain defiant in the chorus 'È dunque vero?'. The stage empties to leave Acciano's wife Sofia

(who has converted to Christianity) and their son Oronte. Oronte has fallen in love with Giselda, who has been taken prisoner, and recalls her in an Andante ('La mia letizia infondere') remarkable for its motivic economy. With his mother's prompting, Oronte agrees to convert, celebrating his decision in the gentle cabaletta, 'Come poteva un angelo'.

2.ii *The mouth of a cave at a mountain peak* A suitably sombre orchestral prelude introduces Pagano (now called 'The Hermit'), who emphasizes his new-found faith in the minor–major *romanza* 'Ma quando un suon terribile'. Pirro enters and, failing to recognize his old accomplice, confesses his sins and seeks to atone by revealing to the Crusaders Antioch's defences. A distant *banda* march heralds the Crusaders, who appear with Arvino at their head. Arvino tells 'The Hermit' that Giselda has been captured, and Pagano swears to aid them in battle. The scene closes with a brash, warlike chorus, 'Stolto Allhà!'.

2.iii *Inside the harem at Antioch* A female chorus, complete with rather bland musical gestures towards 'eastern' local colour, introduces Giselda, who closes the act with a full-scale double aria billed as a 'Rondò-Finale'. In the first movement, 'Se vano è il pregare', she prays to her dead mother. The *tempo di mezzo* sees the stage suddenly filled with fleeing women and pursuing Crusaders: Sofia tells Giselda that Arvino has killed her husband and son, and in the closing cabaletta, 'No! … giusta causa non è d'Iddio', Giselda turns on her father for his ungodly violence.

ACT 3: 'The Conversion'

3.i *The valley of Jehoshaphat* A group of Crusaders and their followers cross the stage, singing the noble chorus, 'Gerusalem!', one of the simplest but most effective pieces in the opera. Giselda appears and is soon joined by Oronte, whom she had believed dead. The lovers' decision to run off together is played out in a traditional four-movement duet, notable for its second movement, 'Oh belle, a questa misera', in which the couple bid farewell to their homelands; and for an unusually curtailed cabaletta, 'Ah, vieni, sol morte', punctuated by offstage warlike cries from the Lombard soldiers.

3.ii *Arvino's tent* Arvino has discovered the disappearance of his daughter and calls down a curse on her. A group of Crusaders reports that Pagano has been seen nearby and in a driving aria with chorus, 'Sì! del ciel che non punisce', Arvino vows to search Pagano out and kill him.

3.iii *Inside a cave* An elaborate orchestral prelude with solo violin, divided into three contrasting sections, begins the scene. Giselda helps on Oronte, wounded by the Crusaders. Railing against God, she launches the first movement of an ensemble, 'Tu la madre mi togliesti'; but she is interrupted by Pagano (still 'The Hermit'), who brings holy water with which to bless Oronte. The solo violin is still much in evidence (a sure sign that Oronte is destined for heaven) in the second, lyrical movement, the richly melodic Andantino 'Qual voluttà trascorrere'.

ACT 4: 'The Holy Sepulchre'

4.i *A cave near Jerusalem* A brief dialogue in the original printed libretto, not set to music, explains that Giselda has been brought back to her father by 'The Hermit', and that Arvino has forgiven his daughter. The scene then opens with Giselda, overtaken in sleep by a chorus of celestial spirits. A vision of Oronte appears to

'I Lombardi alla prima crociata' (Verdi), Act 2 scene iii (inside the harem at Antioch): design by Giuseppe Bertoja for a production at the Teatro Regio, Turin, soon after the Milan première of 1843

sing the Andante 'In cielo benedetto', in which he tells his beloved that the Crusaders will find much-needed water at Siloim. When the vision vanishes, Giselda breaks into a brilliant cabaletta of joy, 'Non fu sognò!' – apparently one of the most popular numbers in the opera with contemporary audiences.

4.ii *The Lombard camp near Rachel's tomb* The Lombards, dying of thirst, conjure up visions of their distant homeland in the famous chorus 'O Signore, dal tetto natio', a number whose hymn-like slowness and predominantly unison texture suggest it was modelled on 'Va pensiero' from *Nabucco*. Giselda announces that the Lombards can find water at Siloim, and they prepare for battle with the warlike chorus 'Guerra! guerra!', first heard in Act 2 as 'Stolto Allhà!'.

4.iii *Arvino's tents* 'The Hermit', gravely wounded, is supported on by Giselda and Arvino. Pagano reveals his true identity and leads off the final ensemble, 'Un breve istante'. The tent is thrown open to reveal Jerusalem, now in the hands of the Crusaders, and the opera ends with a grand choral hymn, 'Te lodiamo, gran Dio di vittoria'.

*   *   *

I Lombardi has often been compared to *Nabucco*, the immensely successful opera that preceded it in the Verdi canon. It is easy to see how such comparisons usually find the later opera less satisfactory. *I Lombardi* has a wider-ranging action than *Nabucco*, but Verdi, at this stage of his career, was less able or willing to depict various sharply contrasting locales, and many of the opera's choral sections (which traditionally carried the weight of such depictions) are pallid and routine. The great exception is the chorus 'O Signore, dal tetto natio', which rightly stands beside 'Va pensiero' as representative of Verdi's new voice in Italian opera. The opera's musical characterization is strangely uneven: the presence of two leading tenors seems to divide attention where it might usefully have been focussed; but the leading soprano, Giselda, stamps her personality on the drama at a very early stage and succeeds in emerging with impressive effect.   ROGER PARKER

Lombardini, Antonio (*b* ?Montagnana, nr Padua; *fl* 1688–9). Italian composer. The libretto of his opera *Imperio deluso, ovvero La Dorice* (A. Schietti; composed for Palmanova in 1688), reported in Allacci, describes him as a native of Montagnana and as a parish priest at Pozzuolo del Friuli, near Udine. He also composed *Il trionfo di Amore e di Marte* (P. E. Badi) for the Teatro S Moisè, Venice, in 1689.

Lomonosov. ORANIENBAUM.